This
Holy
Bible

is presented to

_____

_____

_____

by

_____

_____

on

_____

_____

Church Record

EVENT
_____

MINISTER
_____

CHURCH _____ DATE

EVENT
_____

MINISTER
_____

CHURCH _____ DATE

EVENT
_____

MINISTER
_____

CHURCH _____ DATE

EVENT
_____

MINISTER
_____

CHURCH _____ DATE

EVENT
_____

MINISTER
_____

CHURCH _____ DATE

EVENT
_____

MINISTER
_____

CHURCH _____ DATE

Marriages

HUSBAND

WIFE

PLACE   DATE

HUSBAND

WIFE

PLACE   DATE

HUSBAND

WIFE

PLACE   DATE

HUSBAND

WIFE

PLACE   DATE

HUSBAND

WIFE

PLACE   DATE

HUSBAND

WIFE

PLACE   DATE

Wife's Family Tree

NAME

BIRTHPLACE   DATE

BROTHERS AND SISTERS

PARENTS

FATHER   MOTHER

NAME   NAME

BIRTHPLACE   DATE BIRTHPLACE   DATE

GRANDPARENTS

PATERNAL   MATERNAL

GRANDFATHER   GRANDFATHER

BIRTHPLACE   DATE BIRTHPLACE   DATE

GRANDMOTHER   GRANDMOTHER

BIRTHPLACE   DATE BIRTHPLACE   DATE

GREAT-GRANDPARENTS

PATERNAL   MATERNAL

GRANDFATHER'S FATHER   GRANDFATHER'S FATHER

BIRTHPLACE   DATE BIRTHPLACE   DATE

GRANDFATHER'S MOTHER   GRANDFATHER'S MOTHER

BIRTHPLACE   DATE BIRTHPLACE   DATE

GRANDMOTHER'S FATHER   GRANDMOTHER'S FATHER

BIRTHPLACE   DATE BIRTHPLACE   DATE

GRANDMOTHER'S MOTHER   GRANDMOTHER'S MOTHER

BIRTHPLACE   DATE BIRTHPLACE   DATE

Husband's Family Tree

NAME _____

BIRTHPLACE _____ DATE _____

BROTHERS AND SISTERS _____

_____

PARENTS

FATHER   **MOTHER**

NAME _____   NAME _____

BIRTHPLACE _____ DATE ____   BIRTHPLACE _____ DATE ____

GRANDPARENTS

PATERNAL   **MATERNAL**

GRANDFATHER _____   GRANDFATHER _____

BIRTHPLACE _____ DATE ____   BIRTHPLACE _____ DATE ____

GRANDMOTHER _____   GRANDMOTHER _____

BIRTHPLACE _____ DATE ____   BIRTHPLACE _____ DATE ____

GREAT-GRANDPARENTS

PATERNAL   **MATERNAL**

GRANDFATHER'S FATHER _____   GRANDFATHER'S FATHER _____

BIRTHPLACE _____ DATE ____   BIRTHPLACE _____ DATE ____

GRANDFATHER'S MOTHER _____   GRANDFATHER'S MOTHER _____

BIRTHPLACE _____ DATE ____   BIRTHPLACE _____ DATE ____

GRANDMOTHER'S FATHER _____   GRANDMOTHER'S FATHER _____

BIRTHPLACE _____ DATE ____   BIRTHPLACE _____ DATE ____

GRANDMOTHER'S MOTHER _____   GRANDMOTHER'S MOTHER _____

BIRTHPLACE _____ DATE ____   BIRTHPLACE _____ DATE ____

Births

NAME _____ DATE _____

BORN TO _____

NAME _____ DATE _____

BORN TO _____

NAME _____ DATE _____

BORN TO _____

NAME _____ DATE _____

BORN TO _____

NAME _____ DATE _____

BORN TO _____

NAME _____ DATE _____

BORN TO _____

NAME _____ DATE _____

BORN TO _____

NAME _____ DATE _____

BORN TO _____

NAME _____ DATE _____

BORN TO _____

Deaths

NAME

DATE

NAME

DATE

NAME

DATE

NAME

DATE

NAME

DATE

NAME

DATE

NAME

DATE

NAME

DATE

NAME

DATE

Special Events

EVENT
_____

PLACE   DATE

EVENT
_____

PLACE   DATE

EVENT
_____

PLACE   DATE

EVENT
_____

PLACE   DATE

EVENT
_____

PLACE   DATE

EVENT
_____

PLACE   DATE

NRSV
HARPER
STUDY BIBLE
EXPANDED AND UPDATED

Study helps written by
HAROLD LINDSELL, Ph.D., D.D.

Edited by
VERLYN D. VERBRUGGE, Ph.D.

ZONDERVAN™

GRAND RAPIDS, MICHIGAN 49530 USA

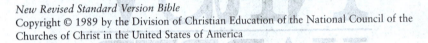

The Names And Order Of
The Books Of The Bible

The Old Testament

The New Testament

Maps and Charts

Abbreviations

The following abbreviations are used for the books of the Bible:

Old Testament

Gen	Genesis	2 Chr	2 Chronicles	Dan	Daniel
Ex	Exodus	Ezra	Ezra	Hos	Hosea
Lev	Leviticus	Neh	Nehemiah	Joel	Joel
Num	Numbers	Esth	Esther	Am	Amos
Deut	Deuteronomy	Job	Job	Ob	Obadiah
Josh	Joshua	Ps	Psalms	Jon	Jonah
Judg	Judges	Prov	Proverbs	Mic	Micah
Ruth	Ruth	Eccl	Ecclesiastes	Nah	Nahum
1 Sam	1 Samuel	Song	Song of Solomon	Hab	Habakkuk
2 Sam	2 Samuel	Isa	Isaiah	Zeph	Zephaniah
1 Kings	1 Kings	Jer	Jeremiah	Hag	Haggai
2 Kings	2 Kings	Lam	Lamentations	Zech	Zechariah
1 Chr	1 Chronicles	Ezek	Ezekiel	Mal	Malachi

New Testament

Mt	Matthew	Eph	Ephesians	Heb	Hebrews
Mk	Mark	Phil	Philippi ans	Jas	James
Lk	Luke	Col	Colossians	1 Pet	1 Peter
Jn	John	1 Thess	1 Thessalonians	2 Pet	2 Peter
Acts	Acts of the Apostles	2 Thess	2 Thessalonians	1 Jn	1 John
Rom	Romans	1 Tim	1 Timothy	2 Jn	2 John
1 Cor	1 Corinthians	2 Tim	2 Timothy	3 Jn	3 John
2 Cor	2 Corinthians	Titus	Titus	Jude	Jude
Gal	Galatians	Philem	Philemon	Rev	Revelation

Abbreviations

In the notes to the books of the Old Testament the following abbreviations are used:

Ant.	Josephus, *Antiquities of the Jews*
Aram	Aramaic
Ch, chs	Chapter, chapters
Cn	Correction; made where the text has suffered in transmission and the versions provide no satisfactory restoration but where the Standard Bible Committee agrees with the judgment of competent scholars as to the most probable reconstruction of the original text.
Gk	Septuagint, Greek version of the Old Testament
Heb	Hebrew of the consonantal Masoretic Text of the Old Testament
Josephus	Flavius Josephus (Jewish historian, about A.D. 37 to about 95)
Macc.	The book(s) of the Maccabees
Ms(s)	Manuscript(s)
MT	The Hebrew of the pointed Masoretic Text of the Old Testament
OL	Old Latin
Q Ms(s)	Manuscript(s) found at Qumran by the Dead Sea
Sam	Samaritan Hebrew text of the Old Testament
Syr	Syriac Version of the Old Testament
Syr H	Syriac Version of Origen's Hexapla
Tg	Targum
Vg	Vulgate, Latin Version of the Old Testament

FOREWORD

"The Bible can serve its function in the modern world only if it is understood." — Ira M. Price (Harper & Row). Such is the purpose of the *NRSV Harper Study Bible*.

The origin of the present work lies with the highly popular *Harper Study Bible*, a study Bible based on the Revised Standard Version of the Bible. The release of the New Revised Standard Version by the National Council of Churches in 1990 led to a decision to revise the notes in the earlier edition and to add thousands of new ones, all based upon the new translation.

The *NRSV Harper Study Bible* has been written in clear and simple language and is geared to students, clergy, and lay people who prefer the NRSV. It is not intended to be a commentary on the Bible or a Bible dictionary, nor does it deal extensively with the complex questions of text, translation, and technical scholarship. Rather, the annotations are designed to be helpful in a basic understanding of the Bible and useful for personal devotional reading, pulpit exposition, and classroom study.

The *NRSV Harper Study Bible* is made up of eight parts, each having an integral relationship to the others. You are encouraged to make a serious study of all these parts, for only a thorough knowledge of the individual segments will bring the whole Bible into sharper focus and lead to a greater appreciation of and love for the Bible as the inspired Word of God.

1. The Introductions. Prefacing each book is an extensive introduction, discussing such issues as the authorship, date of writing, and historical background of the book. This is followed by a description of the characteristics of the book, a summary of its contents, and a brief outline.
2. The Text. The text of the New Revised Standard Version appears precisely as copyrighted, together with the translators' notes. Its single column setting provides maximum ease of reading and study.
3. Internal Outline. Each book has been divided within the text of the NRSV into units that provide you with a reliable guide to the basic contents and teachings of the book. The subdivisions are non-theological and non-interpretative in nature and should enable you to grasp quickly and easily the structure of the book as a whole and the meaning of its individual parts.
4. The Marginal Cross-Reference System. In the outer margin on each page are Bible references that connect one text of the Bible with others having a similar theme. By using this system, difficult or obscure passages of the Bible are clarified by Scripture itself. The cross references for each verse are not listed in Bible book order but in the sequence of their relevance to the material of the verse.
5. The Annotations. In addition to the NRSV footnotes, the *NRSV Harper Study Bible* has thousands of interpretative notes, located at the bottom of most pages and written from the standpoint of evangelical Christian scholarship. The annotations furnish historical, archaeological, biographical, and textual information. Some discuss a given theme or subject, others set forth major doctrines of the Christian faith, and still others shed light on difficult passages. They frequently include references to other Bible passages or other notes. Thus this feature is a useful tool for church schools, Bible classes, and discussion groups, and is indispensable for students of the Word who do not have ready access to extensive Bible reference works.
6. Maps and charts. Scattered throughout the Bible are fourteen maps and charts that help to illustrate where certain events in the Bible took place or to summarize large segments of Bible history (see index of these maps and charts on p. iv). At

the very end of this book are six color maps relevant to the world of the Old and New Testaments.

7. The Index. At the end of the Bible text is an index to the annotations of the *NRSV Harper Study Bible*, directing you to any subject discussed in the footnote material. Each entry has both the Bible reference and the page number of the note for easy location.

8. The NRSV Concordance. Following the index is a concordance to the New Revised Standard Version, built around favorite Bible passages and key theological ideas in the Bible. Also included are biographical summaries of leading characters in the Bible, giving Biblical references to the main events in their lives. Careful use of the index *and* the concordance will uncover many of the riches contained in the Scriptures.

I would like to thank Bruce Ryskamp, Vice President of the Book and Bible Division of Zondervan Publishing House, for his encouragement to revise the *Harper Study Bible* to the New Revised Standard Version. I would also like to acknowledge the work of Verlyn D. Vebrugge in his editorial skills and constructive criticism of the study notes. Together we have produced a study Bible for the edification of every reader and for the glory of the Triune God, the Father, the Son, and the Holy Spirit. *Ad majorem Dei gloriam.*

–Harold Lindsell

Laguna Hills, California
January, 1991

To The Reader

This preface is addressed to you by the Committee of translators, who wish to explain, as briefly as possible, the origin and character of our work. The publication of our revision is yet another step in the long, continual process of making the Bible available in the form of the English language that is most widely current in our day. To summarize in a single sentence: the New Revised Standard Version of the Bible is an authorized revision of the Revised Standard Version, published in 1952, which was a revision of the American Standard Version, published in 1901, which, in turn, embodied earlier revisions of the King James Version, published in 1611.

In the course of time, the King James Version came to be regarded as "the Authorized Version." With good reason it has been termed "the noblest monument of English prose," and it has entered, as no other book has, into the making of the personal character and the public institutions of the English-speaking peoples. We owe to it an incalculable debt.

Yet the King James Version has serious defects. By the middle of the nineteenth century, the development of biblical studies and the discovery of many biblical manuscripts more ancient than those on which the King James Version was based made it apparent that these defects were so many as to call for revision. The task was begun, by authority of the Church of England, in 1870. The (British) Revised Version of the Bible was published in 1881-1885; and the American Standard Version, its variant embodying the preferences of the American scholars associated with the work, was published, as was mentioned above, in 1901. In 1928 the copyright of the latter was acquired by the International Council of Religious Education and thus passed into the ownership of the churches of the United States and Canada that were associated in this Council through their boards of education and publication.

The Council appointed a committee of scholars to have charge of the text of the American Standard Version and to undertake inquiry concerning the need for further revision. After studying the questions whether or not revision should be undertaken, and if so, what its nature and extent should be, in 1937 the Council authorized a revision. The scholars who served as members of the Committee worked in two sections, one dealing with the Old Testament and one with the New Testament. In 1946 the Revised Standard Version of the New Testament was published. The publication of the Revised Standard Version of the Bible, containing the Old and New Testaments, took place on September 30, 1952. A translation of the Apocryphal/Deuterocanonical Books of the Old Testament followed in 1957. In 1977 this collection was issued in an expanded edition, containing three additional texts received by Eastern Orthodox communions (3 and 4 Maccabees and Psalm 151). Thereafter the Revised Standard Version gained the distinction of being officially authorized for use by all major Christian churches: Protestant, Anglican, Roman Catholic, and Eastern Orthodox.

The Revised Standard Version Bible Committee is a continuing body, comprising about thirty members, both men and women. Ecumenical in representation, it includes scholars affiliated with various Protestant denominations, as well as several Roman Catholic members, an Eastern Orthodox member, and a Jewish member who serves in the Old Testament section. For a period of time the Committee included several members from Canada and from England.

Because no translation of the Bible is perfect or is acceptable to all groups of readers, and because discoveries of older manuscripts and further investigation of linguistic features of the text continue to become available, renderings of the Bible have proliferated. During the years following the publication of the Revised Standard Version, twenty-six other English translations and revisions of the Bible were produced by committees and by individual scholars—not to mention twenty-five other translations and revisions of the New Testament alone. One of the latter was the second edition of the RSV New Testament, issued in 1971, twenty-five years after its initial publication.

Following the publication of the RSV Old Testament in 1952, significant advances were made in the discovery and interpretation of documents in Semitic languages related to Hebrew. In addition to the information that had become available in the late 1940s from the Dead Sea texts of Isaiah and Habakkuk, subsequent acquisitions from the same area brought to light many other early copies of all the books of the Hebrew Scriptures (except Esther), though most of these copies are fragmentary. During the same period early Greek manuscript copies of books of the New Testament also became available.

In order to take these discoveries into account, along with recent studies of documents in Semitic languages related to Hebrew, in 1974 the Policies Committee of the Revised Standard Version, which is a standing committee of the National Council of the Churches of Christ in the U.S.A., authorized the preparation of a revision of the entire RSV Bible.

For the Old Testament the Committee has made use of the *Biblia Hebraica Stuttgartensia* (1977; ed. sec. emendata, 1983). This is an edition of the Hebrew and Aramaic text as current early in the Christian era and fixed by Jewish scholars (the "Masoretes") of the sixth to the ninth centuries. The vowel signs, which were added by the Masoretes, are accepted in the main, but where a more probable and convincing reading can be obtained by assuming different vowels, this has been done. No notes are given in such cases, because the vowel points are less ancient and reliable than the consonants. When an alternative reading given by the Masoretes is translated in a footnote, this is identified by the words "Another reading is."

Departures from the consonantal text of the best manuscripts have been made only where it seems clear that errors in copying had been made before the text was standardized. Most of the corrections adopted are based on the ancient versions (translations into Greek, Aramaic, Syriac, and Latin), which were made prior to the time of the work of the Masoretes and which therefore may reflect earlier forms of the Hebrew text. In such instances a footnote specifies the version or versions from which the correction has been derived and also gives a translation of the Masoretic Text. Where it was deemed appropriate to do so, information is supplied in footnotes from subsidiary Jewish traditions concerning other textual readings (the *Tiqqune Sopherim*, "emendations of the scribes"). These are identified in the footnotes as "Ancient Heb tradition."

Occasionally it is evident that the text has suffered in transmission and that none of the versions provides a satisfactory restoration. Here we can only follow the best judgment of competent scholars as to the most probable reconstruction of the original text. Such reconstructions are indicated in footnotes by the abbreviation Cn ("Correction"), and a translation of the Masoretic Text is added.

For the New Testament the Committee has based its work on the most recent edition of *The Greek New Testament*, prepared by an interconfessional and international committee and published by the United Bible Societies (1966; 3rd ed. corrected, 1983; information concerning changes to be introduced into the critical apparatus of the forthcoming 4th edition was available to the Committee). As in that edition, double brackets are used to enclose a few passages that are generally regarded to be later additions to the text, but which we have retained because of their evident antiquity and their importance in the textual tradition. Only in very rare instances have we replaced the text or the punctuation of the Bible Societies' edition by an alternative that seemed to us to be superior. Here and there in the footnotes the phrase, "Other ancient authorities read," identifies alternative readings preserved by Greek manuscripts and early versions. In both Testaments, alternative renderings of the text are indicated by the word "Or."

As for the style of English adopted for the present revision, among the mandates given to the Committee in 1980 by the Division of Education and Ministry of the National Council of Churches of Christ (which now holds the copyright of the RSV Bible) was the directive to continue in the tradition of the King-James Bible, but to introduce such changes as are warranted on the basis of accuracy, clarity, euphony, and current English usage. Within the constraints set by the original texts and by the mandates of the Division, the Committee has followed the maxim, "As literal as possible, as free as necessary." As a consequence, the New Revised Standard Version (NRSV) remains essentially a literal translation. Paraphrastic renderings have been adopted only sparingly, and then chiefly to compensate for a deficiency in the English language—the lack of a common gender third person singular pronoun.

During the almost half a century since the publication of the RSV, many in the churches have become sensitive to the danger of linguistic sexism arising from the inherent bias of the English language towards the masculine gender, a bias that in the case of the Bible has often restricted or obscured the meaning of the original text. The mandates from the Division specified that, in references to men and women, masculine-oriented language should be eliminated as far as this can be done without altering passages that reflect the historical situation of ancient patriarchal culture. As can be appreciated, more than once the Committee found that the several mandates stood in tension and even in conflict. The various concerns had to be balanced case by case in order to provide a faithful and acceptable rendering without using contrived English. Only very occasionally has the pronoun "he" or "him" been retained in passages where the reference may have been to a woman as well as to a man; for example, in several legal texts in Leviticus and Deuteronomy. In such instances of formal, legal language, the options of either putting the passage in the plural or of introducing additional nouns to avoid masculine pronouns in English seemed to the Committee to obscure the historic structure and literary character of the original. In the vast majority of cases, however, inclusiveness has been attained by simple rephrasing or by introducing plural forms when this does not distort the meaning of the passage. Of course, in narrative and in parable no attempt was made to generalize the sex of individual persons.

Another aspect of style will be detected by readers who compare the more stately English rendering of the Old Testament with the less formal rendering adopted for the New Testament. For example, the traditional distinction between *shall* and *will* in English has been retained in the Old Testament as appropriate in rendering a document that embodies what may be termed the classic form of Hebrew, while in the New Testament the abandonment of such distinctions in the usage of the future tense in English reflects the more colloquial nature of the koine Greek used by most New Testament authors except when they are quoting the Old Testament.

Careful readers will notice that here and there in the Old Testament the word LORD (or in certain cases GOD) is printed in capital letters. This represents the traditional manner in English versions of rendering the Divine Name, the "Tetragrammaton" (see the notes on Exodus 3.14, 15), following the precedent of the ancient Greek and Latin translators and the long established practice in the reading of the Hebrew Scriptures in the synagogue. While it is almost if not quite certain that the Name was originally pronounced "Yahweh," this pronunciation was not indicated when the Masoretes added vowel sounds to the consonantal Hebrew text. To the four consonants YHWH of the Name, which had come to be regarded as too sacred to be pronounced, they attached vowel signs indicating that in its place should be read the Hebrew word *Adonai* meaning "Lord" (or *Elohim* meaning "God").

Ancient Greek translators employed the word *Kyrios* ("Lord") for the Name. The Vulgate likewise used the Latin word *Dominus* ("Lord"). The form "Jehovah" is of late medieval origin; it is a combination of the consonants of the Divine Name and the vowels attached to it by the Masoretes but belonging to an entirely different word. Although the American Standard Version (1901) had used "Jehovah" to render the Tetragrammaton (the sound of Y being represented by J and the sound of W by V, as in Latin), for two reasons the Committees that produced the RSV and the NRSV returned to the more familiar usage of the King James Version. (1) The word "Jehovah" does not accurately represent any form of the Name ever used in Hebrew. (2) The use of any proper name for the one and only God, as though there were other gods from whom the true God had to be distinguished, began to be discontinued in Judaism before the Christian era and is inappropriate for the universal faith of the Christian Church.

It will be seen that in the Psalms and in other prayers addressed to God the archaic second person singular pronouns (*thee, thou, thine*) and verb forms (*art, hast, hadst*) are no longer used. Although some readers may regret this change, it should be pointed out that in the original languages neither the Old Testament nor the New makes any linguistic distinction between addressing a human being and addressing the Deity. Furthermore, in the tradition of the King James Version one will not expect to find the use of capital letters for pronouns that refer to the Deity—such capitalization is an unnecessary innovation that has only recently been introduced into a few English translations of the Bible. Finally, we have left to the discretion of the licensed publishers such matters as section headings, cross-references, and clues to the pronunciation of proper names.

This new version seeks to preserve all that is best in the English Bible as it has been known and used through the years. It is intended for use in public reading and congregational worship, as well as in private study, instruction, and meditation. We have resisted the temptation to introduce terms and phrases that merely reflect current moods, and have tried to put the message of the Scriptures in simple, enduring words and expressions that are worthy to stand in the great tradition of the King James Bible and its predecessors.

In traditional Judaism and Christianity, the Bible has been more than a historical document to be preserved or a classic of literature to be cherished and admired; it is recognized as the unique record of God's dealings with people over the ages. The Old Testament sets forth the call of a special people to enter into covenant relation with the God of justice and steadfast love and to bring God's law to the nations. The New Testament records the life and work of Jesus Christ, the one in whom "the Word became flesh," as well as describes the rise and spread of the early Christian Church. The Bible carries its full message, not to those who regard it simply as a noble literary heritage of the past or who wish to use it to enhance political purposes and advance otherwise desirable goals, but to all persons and communities who read it so that they may discern and understand what God is saying to them. That message must not be disguised in phrases that are no longer clear, or hidden under words that have changed or lost their meaning; it must be presented in language that is direct and plain and meaningful to people today. It is the hope and prayer of the translators that this version of the Bible may continue to hold a large place in congregational life and to speak to all readers, young and old alike, helping them to understand and believe and respond to its message.

For the Committee,

Bruce Metzger

THE HEBREW SCRIPTURES
commonly called

The Old Testament

New Revised Standard Version

INTRODUCTION TO
GENESIS

Authorship, Date, and Background: Genesis is the first book in the Pentateuch (the first five books in the O.T.; also known as the Law or the books of Moses). The Septuagint (the Greek translation of the Hebrew O.T., ca. 150 B.C.) translators used the name Genesis, which means "origin, beginning." The Hebrew title, *Bereshith*, is the first word in 1.1, meaning "in the beginning." Everything in Genesis predates the time of Moses, to whom the authorship of the Pentateuch has been attributed. This implies that he secured his information from extant written materials, by oral transmission, by revelation from God, or a combination of these. The source of his knowledge does not matter materially so long as we remember that in the use of the materials the Holy Spirit enabled him to record what is true.

No verse in the Pentateuch names Moses directly as the author, but there are internal evidences favoring the Mosaic authorship as well as statements in the N.T. by Jesus and others which lead to this conclusion. In the Pentateuch itself (see Ex 17.14; 24.4–7; 34.27; Num 33.1,2; Deut 32.9–11) Moses was instructed by God to write down certain information. In addition, other books in the O.T. speak of "the law of Moses" (1 Kings 2.3; 2 Kings 14.6) or "the book of Moses" (Ezra 6.18; Neh 13.1). Moreover, the N.T. refers again and again to the law of Moses in one form or another (e.g., Mt 19.8; Mk 1.44; 10.4,5; Lk 5.14; 16.31; 20.37; Acts 3.23; 13.39; 15.5ff; 26.22; Rom 10.5,19; 1 Cor 9.9; 2 Cor 3.15; Rev 15.3).

Many modern scholars have vigorously rejected the Mosaic authorship of the Pentateuch. Most of them accept the J E P D theory. But this Documentary Hypothesis of Wellhausen, the best known of these viewpoints, has been challenged by other modern scholars as well as by evangelical scholars. The latter generally hold to the Mosaic authorship of the first five books of the Bible, with certain exceptions. The account of Moses' death, for example, was probably added by a later writer. And possibly later minor name changes may have been inserted to clarify for readers what they might not otherwise have known. For example, in 14.14 the name of a city is given as Dan, whereas in Judg 18.29 it says that the city named Dan "was formerly Laish."

Characteristics and Content: The book of Genesis sets the scene for the entire Bible. Without it the reader would not know some of the most important happenings in the history of the world. Genesis tells us about the creation of the entire universe, including humankind, the beginning of sin in the human race, the provision of God for redemption, the selection of one man through whose descendants salvation would be made possible, the person and nature of God, as well as the fact of divine judgment and human responsibility. The first two chapters of Genesis speak of generation; chs. 3—11 deal with degeneration; chs. 12—50 have to do with regeneration.

Genesis is remarkably compact, encompassing long periods of time in a few sentences. It is written in a fascinating style which commands the interest of young and old alike. It is largely biographical, describing significant individuals who are essential participants in the story of redemption. From its earliest pages it points the way to salvation through the as yet unidentified descendant of Abraham, Jesus Christ, God's Son and our redeemer. In the fall of Adam, the judgment of God on sin may be seen; in the flood, the retributive justice of God; in the choice of Abraham as the man through whom Messiah shall come, God's sovereign election.

Genesis recounts how the twelve patriarchs, from whom all of Israel would someday come, were fathered by Jacob, the grandson of Abraham and the son of Isaac. Despite sin and human error, the divine will is being worked out in the events which take place. The book tells us about some of the people of God who are unselfish, heroic, and faithful. Others are guilty of trickery, deception, fraud, and unfaithfulness. The characters are pictured as they really are, not as we wish they might have been. Perhaps most important of all, Genesis reveals that God chose to make himself known to the human race. Without that self-revelation the true knowledge of God would be impossible to attain. It is the story of God reaching down to sinful people, not of sinful people reaching up to God.

Outline:

  I. The generations of the heavens and the earth (1.1—4.26)

 II. The descendants of Adam (5.1—6.8)

III. The descendants of Noah (6.9—9.29)

 IV. The descendants of the sons of Noah (10.1—11.9)

  V. The descendants of Shem (11.10—26)

 VI. The descendants of Terah (11.27—25.11)

VII. The descendants of Ishmael (25.12—18)

VIII. The descendants of Isaac (25.19—35.29)

 IX. The descendants of Esau (36.1—43)

  X. The descendants of Jacob (37.1—50.26)

GENESIS

I. *The generations of the heavens and the earth (1.1–4.26)*

A. *The seven creative days*

1. *First day: light*

1 In the beginning when God created*ᵃ* the heavens and the earth, 2 the earth was a formless void and darkness covered the face of the deep, while a wind from God*ᵇ* swept over the face of the waters. 3 Then God said, "Let there be light"; and there was light. 4 And God saw that the light was good; and God separated the light from the darkness. 5 God called the light Day, and the darkness he called Night. And there was evening and there was morning, the first day.

2. *Second day: dome*

6 And God said, "Let there be a dome in the midst of the waters, and let it separate the waters from the waters." 7 So God made the dome and separated the waters that were under the dome from the waters that were above the dome. And it was so. 8 God called the dome Sky. And there was evening and there was morning, the second day.

ᵃ Or *when God began to create* or *In the beginning God created*   *ᵇ* Or *while the spirit of God* or *while a mighty wind*

1.1
Jn 1.1, 2;
Ps 8.3;
Isa 44.24;
42.5; 45.18
1.2
1.3
Jer 4.23;
Ps 104.30
1.3
Ps 33.6, 9;
2 Cor 4.6
1.4
Isa 45.7
1.5
Ps 74.16
1.6
Jer 10.12
1.7
Prov 8.28;
Ps 148.4

1.1 Monotheism, the belief in one God, has existed from time immemorial even in the earliest religions. This view is the opposite of the modern notion that the idea of one God evolved from a primitive animism, to polytheism, to henotheism, to monotheism. Some recent scholars strongly support primitive monotheism. Polytheism and lower views of God point to retrogression, explained by the advent of sin and the spiritual decline which followed. In Rom 1.19–23 Paul summarizes the tragic devolution from monotheism.
1.2 *the earth was,* or, "the earth became . . ."; *a formless void,* or, "shapeless and void"; *the face of the deep,* or, "over the cloud of darkness," or, "over the darkness and waters," or even, "over the dark gaseous mass." There is no one "correct" way to translate these words.
1.3 The Genesis account of creation is only one of many extant records of the beginning. While there may be similarities to the biblical account, the other creation narratives are marked by polytheism, strange monsters, animal gods, impossible cosmology, and crude myths. The Babylonian and Assyrian stories are among the oldest and do no more than show that behind these accounts there was a creation. The Genesis account is unique in that it comes to us from God by revelation through the pen of the sacred writer, inspired by the Holy Spirit. The basic question is whether matter is eternal or came into being sometime in the past. The Bible makes it clear that God, who is spirit, created matter by the word of his power (Ps 33.6). He made all things, so that nothing was made without him (Jn 1.3), and in him all things hold

together (Col 1.17). Matter was created by God *ex nihilo,* i.e., "out of nothing" (cf. Heb 11.3). *God said, "Let there be light."* Before the sun and moon were created, there was light. Note that in the New Jerusalem the sun and moon are not needed: "its lamp is the Lamb" (Rev 21.23).
1.5 *And there was evening and there was morning, the first day,* i.e., evening and morning formed the first day. There are two views about the six days of creation: one holds that "days" were literal 24-hour periods, the other that each "day" consisted of an extended period of time. Both of these views have been supported strongly by evangelical Christians, though the six-day, 24-hour per day view appears to have fewer problems. Note that though the Hebrew word for day (*yom*) does not always mean a 24-hour day, generally it does. And if the seventh day was a long period of time, then 2.3, which speaks of the Sabbath —a day that can only be a 24-hour day—becomes difficult to interpret. On the other hand, in response to the claim of scientists that the earth is millions or billions of years old, some Christians assert that there is a gap between 1.1 and 1.2. In this view, the first creation was wrecked by Satan's fall; the six days were really a re-creation. Furthermore, the claim that the six days are long periods is defended by the perspective of God's scale of time as given by the apostle Peter: "with the Lord one day is like a thousand years, and a thousand years are like one day" (2 Pet 3.8).
1.8 *And there was evening and there was morning, the second day,* i.e., "this all happened on the second day." So also for 1.13 (the third day); 1.19 (the fourth day); 1.23 (the fifth day); 1.31 (the sixth day).

3. *Third day: dry land and vegetation*

1.9
Job 26.10;
Prov 8.29;
Jer 5.22;
2 Pet 3.5
1.10
Ps 33.7
1.11
Lk 6.44

9 And God said, "Let the waters under the sky be gathered together into one place, and let the dry land appear." And it was so. 10 God called the dry land Earth, and the waters that were gathered together he called Seas. And God saw that it was good. 11 Then God said, "Let the earth put forth vegetation: plants yielding seed, and fruit trees of every kind on earth that bear fruit with the seed in it." And it was so. 12 The earth brought forth vegetation: plants yielding seed of every kind, and trees of every kind bearing fruit with the seed in it. And God saw that it was good. 13 And there was evening and there was morning, the third day.

4. *Fourth day: lights*

1.14
Ps 74.16;
104.19

1.16
Ps 136.8, 9;
Job 38.7

1.18
Jer 31.35

14 And God said, "Let there be lights in the dome of the sky to separate the day from the night; and let them be for signs and for seasons and for days and years, 15 and let them be lights in the dome of the sky to give light upon the earth." And it was so. 16 God made the two great lights — the greater light to rule the day and the lesser light to rule the night — and the stars. 17 God set them in the dome of the sky to give light upon the earth, 18 to rule over the day and over the night, and to separate the light from the darkness. And God saw that it was good. 19 And there was evening and there was morning, the fourth day.

5. *Fifth day: birds and fish*

1.21
Ps 104.25, 26

1.22
Gen 8.17

20 And God said, "Let the waters bring forth swarms of living creatures, and let birds fly above the earth across the dome of the sky." 21 So God created the great sea monsters and every living creature that moves, of every kind, with which the waters swarm, and every winged bird of every kind. And God saw that it was good. 22 God blessed them, saying, "Be fruitful and multiply and fill the waters in the seas, and let birds multiply on the earth." 23 And there was evening and there was morning, the fifth day.

6. *Sixth day: animals and humankind*

1.25
Jer 27.5

1.26
Ps 100.3;
Acts 17.26,
28, 29;
Col 3.10

1.27
1 Cor 11.7;
Gen 5.2;
Mt 19.4

24 And God said, "Let the earth bring forth living creatures of every kind: cattle and creeping things and wild animals of the earth of every kind." And it was so. 25 God made the wild animals of the earth of every kind, and the cattle of every kind, and everything that creeps upon the ground of every kind. And God saw that it was good.

26 Then God said, "Let us make humankind*c* in our image, according to our likeness; and let them have dominion over the fish of the sea, and over the birds of the air, and over the cattle, and over all the wild animals of the earth,*d* and over every creeping thing that creeps upon the earth."

27 So God created humankind*c* in his image,

c Heb *adam*   *d* Syr: Heb *and over all the earth*

1.16 *two great lights,* i.e., the sun and the moon. Since the creation of plants and other vegetation preceded this fourth-day creative act, we can see that God as light would make vegetation to grow and flower.
1.22 *Be fruitful and multiply,* i.e., the fish and birds were to reproduce themselves. The creation of male and female existed before the coming of Adam and Eve. The sexes are God's order for all created things.
1.26 *Let us make humankind.* Adam means "humankind" and Eve means "(she who gives) life." Because the names have such meanings, some have concluded that the Adam and Eve story is not real history. We must note, however, that all through the Bible, names are derived from words common to the speech of the

people. Abram means "exalted ancestor" and Moses means "drawn out." Since these people were historical persons, it strengthens the case for the historicity of Adam and Eve.
1.27 The root question about the origin of the human race is: Were humans immediately created by God or did they evolve from lower forms of vertebrate life over a long period of time? Those who hold to the six literal days of creation must necessarily say that Adam was created by God in a 24-hour period. Others accept the theory of evolution — that inorganic matter became organic matter (life) and that humans were derived from the organic by progressing from lower to higher forms of life. Many scientists have long since

in the image of God he created them;*
male and female he created them.
28God blessed them, and God said to them, "Be fruitful and multiply, and
fill the earth and subdue it; and have dominion over the fish of the sea
and over the birds of the air and over every living thing that moves upon
the earth." 29God said, "See, I have given you every plant yielding seed
that is upon the face of all the earth, and every tree with seed in its fruit;
you shall have them for food. 30And to every beast of the earth, and to
every bird of the air, and to everything that creeps on the earth, everything
that has the breath of life, I have given every green plant for food." And
it was so. 31God saw everything that he had made, and indeed, it was very
good. And there was evening and there was morning, the sixth day.

7. Seventh day: the sabbath

2 Thus the heavens and the earth were finished, and all their multitude.
2And on the seventh day God finished the work that he had done,
and he rested on the seventh day from all the work that he had done. 3So
God blessed the seventh day and hallowed it, because on it God rested
from all the work that he had done in creation.

B. The creation of man

1. Man made: placed in Eden

4 These are the generations of the heavens and the earth when they
were created.
In the day that the LORD*ee* God made the earth and the heavens, 5when
no plant of the field was yet in the earth and no herb of the field had yet
sprung up—for the LORD God had not caused it to rain upon the earth,
and there was no one to till the ground; 6but a stream would rise from
the earth, and water the whole face of the ground— 7then the LORD God
formed man from the dust of the ground,*f* and breathed into his nostrils
the breath of life; and the man became a living being. 8And the LORD God
planted a garden in Eden, in the east; and there he put the man whom

e Heb *him*   *ee* Heb YHWH, as in other places where LORD is spelled with capital letters (see also
Exod 3.14–15 with notes).   *f* Or *formed a man* (Heb *adam*) *of dust from the ground* (Heb *adamah*)

Margin references:
1.28 Gen 9.1, 7; Lev 26.9
1.29 Ps 104.14, 15; 136.25
1.30 Ps 145.15; Job 38.41
1.31 Ps 104.24
2.1 Ps 33.6
2.2 Ex 20.11; Heb 4.4
2.3 Isa 58.13
2.5 Gen 1.12; Job 38.26-28
2.7 Gen 3.19; Ps 103.14; Job 33.4; Acts 17.25; 1 Cor 15.45
2.8 Isa 51.3; Gen 3.24; 4.16

abandoned organic evolution, but it remains a popular theory. Most Christians, however, see Adam and
Eve as a special creation of God. The Hebrew word
bara ("to create") is used here to describe the creation
of the heaven and the earth (1.1), the creation of life
(1.21), and the creation of human life (1.27). The
entire human race has descended from Adam and
Eve.
1.28 *have dominion.* This was part of God's plan for
the human race (sometimes called the cultural mandate). Humankind was to have charge of all creation,
which would be subject to him. This could be for
good or for evil.
2.2 *he rested on the seventh day.* The Hebrew word
used here is *shabat* ("to cease, rest"). Thus the seventh day was designated as *Shabbath,* the holy day of
rest. It later was spelled "sabbath" (from the Septuagint, Greek translation of the Old Testament). To
assume that creation occurred without a supreme and
divine being at work is ridiculous. To suppose that
accident, not design, lies behind the creation takes
greater faith to believe than the simple message of
Scripture: God was present and at work in bringing
everything into being. The complexity of living things
would require chance selection of greater magnitude
than the human mind can contemplate.
2.4 The names for God are varied in the Old Testament. Not only are single names given but there are
compound ones as well. Some contend that the use of

different names in Genesis presupposes multiple authorship. Others hold that Moses may have drawn his
material from different sources which used different
names, or he may have used different names himself.
(1) *El, Eloah,* and its plural *Elohim* (all of which are
translated "God" and imply the Mighty One, the
ruler over all the universe); (2) *Yahweh,* the covenantal name for the God of Israel (see note on Ex 3.15);
(3) *Adonai,* meaning "Lord" (emphasizing God's sovereignty as King); (4) *Elyan,* signifying "the Most
High"; and (5) *Shaddai,* "the Almighty." Here in 2.4
the compound *Yahweh Elohim* ("LORD God") is used,
indicating that the mighty Creator of ch. 1 is the one
who enters into covenant relations with humankind.
2.5 Some maintain that rain did not occur until the
time of the flood and thereafter.
2.7 *from the dust of the ground.* God fashioned Adam
"from a lump of soil" or "from a clod of clay."
2.8 No one has been able to determine the precise
location of the Garden of Eden. It seems to have been
near the Tigris and Euphrates rivers, where they were
joined by the rivers Pishon and Gihon (which have
never been identified). Tradition has it that Eden was
south of Ur at a place known as *Eridu.* Eridu was
excavated by British archeologists in 1918–1919, but
this did not guarantee the certainty of the location of
Eden. Albright holds the view that Pishon and Gihon
may be the Blue and White Nile Rivers.

2.9
Ezek 31.8;
Gen 3.22;
Rev 2.7;
22.2, 14
he had formed. 9 Out of the ground the LORD God made to grow every tree that is pleasant to the sight and good for food, the tree of life also in the midst of the garden, and the tree of the knowledge of good and evil.

10 A river flows out of Eden to water the garden, and from there it divides and becomes four branches. 11 The name of the first is Pishon; it is the one that flows around the whole land of Havilah, where there is gold;

2.12
Num 11.7
12 and the gold of that land is good; bdellium and onyx stone are there. 13 The name of the second river is Gihon; it is the one that flows around

2.14
Dan 10.4;
Hiddekel-Tigris
the whole land of Cush. 14 The name of the third river is Tigris, which flows east of Assyria. And the fourth river is the Euphrates.

2. The forbidden tree

15 The LORD God took the man and put him in the garden of Eden to till it and keep it. 16 And the LORD God commanded the man, "You

2.17
Deut 30.15,
19, 20;
Rom 6.23;
Jas 1.15
may freely eat of every tree of the garden; 17 but of the tree of the knowledge of good and evil you shall not eat, for in the day that you eat of it you shall die."

3. The creation of Eve

18 Then the LORD God said, "It is not good that the man should be

2.18
1 Cor 11.9
2.19
Gen 1.20, 24;
Ps 8.7
alone; I will make him a helper as his partner." 19 So out of the ground the LORD God formed every animal of the field and every bird of the air, and brought them to the man to see what he would call them; and whatever the man called every living creature, that was its name. 20 The man gave names to all cattle, and to the birds of the air, and to every animal of the field; but for the man[g] there was not found a helper as his

2.21
1 Sam 26.12
partner. 21 So the LORD God caused a deep sleep to fall upon the man, and he slept; then he took one of his ribs and closed up its place with flesh. 22 And the rib that the LORD God had taken from the man he made into

2.23
Eph 5.30;
1 Cor 11.8
a woman and brought her to the man. 23 Then the man said,

"This at last is bone of my bones
and flesh of my flesh;
this one shall be called Woman,[h]

2.24
Mt 19.5;
Mk 10.7, 8;
1 Cor 6.16;
Eph 5.31
2.25
Gen 3.7, 10,
11
for out of Man[i] this one was taken."

24 Therefore a man leaves his father and his mother and clings to his wife, and they become one flesh. 25 And the man and his wife were both naked, and were not ashamed.

g Or for Adam   h Heb ishshah   i Heb ish

2.11,12 *the whole land of Havilah*, located along the border of Babylonia.

2.16,17 God made a covenant of works with Adam in the Garden of Eden. God gave him the right to eat of the fruit of every tree in the garden except for the tree of the knowledge of good and evil. This single prohibition was to signal Adam's perfect obedience. God warned Adam what the consequences would be if he broke the covenant by eating the fruit. Every covenant has a seal. Here the seal was the tree of life. Adam broke the covenant when he ate the fruit of the tree of the knowledge of good and evil (3.1–7). Death came for him and for the human race, since he was its designated head (Rom 5.12,18). Moreover, Adam was separated from the tree of life, lest he eat of it and live forever. The tree of life will become available to believers in the glory of the new heaven and new earth because of Christ's redemption (cf. Rev 22.2).

2.22 *the rib . . . he made into a woman.* Well spoken are the words of an ancient interpreter: that Eve was not made out of Adam's head to rule over him, nor out of his feet to be trampled upon by him, but out

of his side to be equal with him, under his arm to be protected, and near his heart to be beloved.

2.23 Eve, like Adam, was made after the moral and spiritual image of God (1.27). Taken from Adam's side, Eve was to be a helper, complementing man. She was made for Adam (1 Cor 11.3), was subject to him (1 Cor 11.3), and was to be his glory (1 Cor 11.7). Adam and Eve deliberately disobeyed God and broke the covenant, meriting guilt and death.

2.24 God ordained and instituted marriage for the good of the human race. Woman was designed to complement man, and as partners they were to increase the human race (1.28; 2.18; 9.1). The N.T. expands our knowledge on this subject by teaching that (1) marriage is lawful and good (1 Cor 7.2,28; 1 Tim 5.14); (2) marriage must be held in honor (Heb 13.4); (3) Christians should not marry unbelievers (2 Cor 6.14–18); (4) marriage is for life, except for certain biblical reasons that permit divorce (Mt 19.6ff; Rom 7.2,3). *they become one flesh,* i.e., "the two become one person."

C. The fall of Adam

1. The temptation and sin of Adam and Eve

3 Now the serpent was more crafty than any other wild animal that the LORD God had made. He said to the woman, "Did God say, 'You shall not eat from any tree in the garden'?" ²The woman said to the serpent, "We may eat of the fruit of the trees in the garden; ³but God said, 'You shall not eat of the fruit of the tree that is in the middle of the garden, nor shall you touch it, or you shall die.'" ⁴But the serpent said to the woman, "You will not die; ⁵for God knows that when you eat of it your eyes will be opened, and you will be like God,ʲ knowing good and evil." ⁶So when the woman saw that the tree was good for food, and that it was a delight to the eyes, and that the tree was to be desired to make one wise, she took of its fruit and ate; and she also gave some to her husband, who was with her, and he ate. ⁷Then the eyes of both were opened, and they knew that they were naked; and they sewed fig leaves together and made loincloths for themselves.

2. The judgment of God

a. The sin uncovered

8 They heard the sound of the LORD God walking in the garden at the time of the evening breeze, and the man and his wife hid themselves from the presence of the LORD God among the trees of the garden. ⁹But the LORD God called to the man, and said to him, "Where are you?" ¹⁰He said, "I heard the sound of you in the garden, and I was afraid, because I was naked; and I hid myself." ¹¹He said, "Who told you that you were naked? Have you eaten from the tree of which I commanded you not to eat?" ¹²The man said, "The woman whom you gave to be with me, she gave me fruit from the tree, and I ate." ¹³Then the LORD God said to the woman, "What is this that you have done?" The woman said, "The serpent tricked me, and I ate." ¹⁴The LORD God said to the serpent,

b. The curse on the serpent

"Because you have done this,
    cursed are you among all animals
    and among all wild creatures;
upon your belly you shall go,
    and dust you shall eat
    all the days of your life.
¹⁵ I will put enmity between you and the woman,

ʲ *Or gods*

Marginal references:

3.1 2 Cor 11.3; Rev 12.9; 20.2

3.3 2 Cor 11.3

3.4 Jn 8.44

3.6 1 Tim 2.14

3.8 Job 31.33; Jer 23.24

3.10 1 Jn 3.20

3.12 Prov 28.13
3.13 2 Cor 11.3; 1 Tim 2.14
3.14 Isa 65.25; Mic 7.17

3.15 Jn 8.44; Acts 13.10; 1 Jn 3.8; Isa 7.14; Mt 1.23; Rom 16.20; Rev 12.7

3.2,3 The seal of God's covenant with Adam was that no one should eat the forbidden fruit (see note on 2.16,17).

3.6 Adam's sin consisted in disobeying God's express prohibition (3.6–12; Rom 5.12–19). Satan provided the temptation (3.1–5, Rev 12.9), but Adam acted voluntarily, by his own choice. Being tempted to sin does not, in itself, constitute guilt.

3.10 *because I was naked.* Since Adam lived in innocence, nakedness was normal and provided no problems. Following his transgression Adam had a different understanding of nakedness, for it had become associated with the fallen condition of the human race. Virtually all people cover themselves in part or in whole.

3.12 Adam blames God for giving him the woman who caused him to sin. And Eve in v. 13 pleads that she could not help herself. It was not her fault. The refusal to accept responsibility for our actions is commonplace.

3.14 Subsequent to Adam's fall, God reordered life for Adam and his descendants (3.14–19,24). (1) The serpent was cursed for his evil work. (2) The Redeemer was promised for the salvation of the human race. (3) Women could expect multiplied pain in childbirth and were placed in subjection to their husbands. (4) The ground was cursed to produce thorns and thistles. (5) Humans were to eke out a living by the sweat of their faces. (6) The human race experienced spiritual death by becoming corrupted and separated from their Creator. (7) Physical death for humankind also resulted, although this sentence was not to be carried out immediately. (8) The N.T. clearly teaches that both physical and spiritual death have been transmitted through Adam to the entire human race (Rom 5.12–14). (9) Adam and Eve were banished from the Garden of Eden.

3.15 Here God promises redemption to lost people through the coming of Jesus Christ the Redeemer. This age will witness constant warfare between the

and between your offspring and hers;
  he will strike your head,
    and you will strike his heel."

c. The curse on Eve

3.16
Isa 13.8;
Gen 4.7;
1 Cor 11.3;
Eph 5.22

16To the woman he said,
  "I will greatly increase your pangs in childbearing;
    in pain you shall bring forth children,
  yet your desire shall be for your husband,
    and he shall rule over you."

d. The curse on Adam

3.17
1 Sam 15.23;
Gen 2.17;
Rom 8.20-22

17And to the man[k] he said,
  "Because you have listened to the voice of your wife,
    and have eaten of the tree
  about which I commanded you,
    'You shall not eat of it,'
  cursed is the ground because of you;
    in toil you shall eat of it all the days of your life;

3.18
Ps 104.14

18 thorns and thistles it shall bring forth for you;
    and you shall eat the plants of the field.

3.19
Gen 2.7;
Ps 90.3;
104.29;
Eccl 12.7

19 By the sweat of your face
  you shall eat bread
  until you return to the ground,
    for out of it you were taken;
  you are dust,
    and to dust you shall return."

e. The expulsion from the garden

20 The man named his wife Eve,[l] because she was the mother of all living. 21And the Lord God made garments of skins for the man[m] and for his wife, and clothed them.

3.22
Rev 22.2

22 Then the Lord God said, "See, the man has become like one of us, knowing good and evil; and now, he might reach out his hand and take also from the tree of life, and eat, and live forever"— 23therefore the

3.23
Gen 4.2

Lord God sent him forth from the garden of Eden, to till the ground from which he was taken. 24He drove out the man; and at the east of the garden

3.24
Gen 2.8, 9

of Eden he placed the cherubim, and a sword flaming and turning to guard the way to the tree of life.

---

k Or *to Adam*   *l* In Heb *Eve* resembles the word for *living*   *m* Or *for Adam*

---

offspring of the woman and the offspring of the serpent. Christ, however, will ultimately defeat Satan and his offspring. Satan will strike the heel of the Redeemer (note Isa 53.10—that Christ is bruised by the sovereign permissive will of God the Father), while Christ will strike the head of the serpent. In the drama of redemption Satan prompted Cain to slay Abel, but God raised up Seth (4.25). Satan was foiled at the flood when God spared Noah and his family (chs. 6—9). Satan appeared to be victorious when Abraham and Sarah had no heir, but God miraculously intervened and Sarah gave birth to Isaac (21.1–8). Satan sought to have the infant Jesus slain but God prevented him from succeeding (Mt 2). Jesus resisted Satan's temptations in the wilderness. In the Garden of Gethsemane Satan was defeated again. At Calvary Jesus struck the death blow to our greatest enemy, and he sealed his victory by his glorious resurrection from the grave.
3.17 *listened to the voice of your wife.* The influence

of a wife—for good or for evil—cannot be overestimated. Later, Abraham was to listen to the voice of Sarah and take Hagar to wife. Ishmael, the son of this relationship, was to become the father of the inveterate enemies of Israel. Both Adam and Abraham leave us an example that underscores the need for discretion when others try to influence our decisions.
3.22 *the tree of life.* Only two of the trees are mentioned by name. One is the tree of life. God did not forbid Adam to eat of that tree. Why he did not eat remains a mystery. He preferred the fruit of the one forbidden tree. It appears that eating of the tree of life would have gained Adam immortality, but certainly not the forgiveness of his sin.
3.24 *he drove out the man.* Adam had no choice. God displaced him from his original inheritance. Disobedience always has temporal consequences which should be thought of prior to the act. God would restore the human race by making reconciliation possible through the death of Jesus Christ.

D. Cain and his descendants

1. The offerings of Cain and Abel

4 Now the man knew his wife Eve, and she conceived and bore Cain, saying, "I have produced[n] a man with the help of the LORD." 2 Next she bore his brother Abel. Now Abel was a keeper of sheep, and Cain a tiller of the ground. 3 In the course of time Cain brought to the LORD an offering of the fruit of the ground, 4 and Abel for his part brought of the firstlings of his flock, their fat portions. And the LORD had regard for Abel and his offering, 5 but for Cain and his offering he had no regard. So Cain was very angry, and his countenance fell. 6 The LORD said to Cain, "Why are you angry, and why has your countenance fallen? 7 If you do well, will you not be accepted? And if you do not do well, sin is lurking at the door; its desire is for you, but you must master it."

2. Cain kills Abel: God's curse

8 Cain said to his brother Abel, "Let us go out to the field."[o] And when they were in the field, Cain rose up against his brother Abel, and killed him. 9 Then the LORD said to Cain, "Where is your brother Abel?" He said, "I do not know; am I my brother's keeper?" 10 And the LORD said, "What have you done? Listen; your brother's blood is crying out to me from the ground! 11 And now you are cursed from the ground, which has opened its mouth to receive your brother's blood from your hand. 12 When you till the ground, it will no longer yield to you its strength; you will be a fugitive and a wanderer on the earth." 13 Cain said to the LORD, "My punishment is greater than I can bear! 14 Today you have driven me away from the soil, and I shall be hidden from your face; I shall be a fugitive and a wanderer on the earth, and anyone who meets me may kill me." 15 Then the LORD said to him, "Not so![p] Whoever kills Cain will suffer a sevenfold vengeance." And the LORD put a mark on Cain, so that no one who came upon him would kill him. 16 Then Cain went away from the presence of the LORD, and settled in the land of Nod,[q] east of Eden.

3. Cain's children

17 Cain knew his wife, and she conceived and bore Enoch; and he built a city, and named it Enoch after his son Enoch. 18 To Enoch was born Irad; and Irad was the father of Mehujael, and Mehujael the father of Methushael, and Methushael the father of Lamech. 19 Lamech took two wives; the name of the one was Adah, and the name of the other Zillah. 20 Adah bore Jabal; he was the ancestor of those who live in tents and have livestock. 21 His brother's name was Jubal; he was the ancestor of all those

Side references:
4.2 Lk 11.50, 51
4.3 Num 18.12
4.4 Num 18.17; Lev 3.16; Heb 11.4
4.5 Isa 3.9; Jude 11
4.8 Mt 23.35; 1 Jn 3.12
4.10 Heb 12.24; Rev 6.10
4.12 v. 14
4.14 Ps 51.11; Gen 9.6; Num 35.19, 21, 27
4.15 Ps 79.12; Ezek 9.4, 6
4.17 Ps 49.11
4.18 Gen 5.25, 28, 30

---

n The verb in Heb resembles the word for Cain   o Sam Gk Syr Compare Vg: MT lacks Let us go out to the field   p Gk Syr Vg: Heb Therefore   q That is Wandering

---

4.1 The man knew his wife, i.e., he had sexual relations with her. She conceived.

4.4,5 Cain offered the fruit of the ground while Abel offered the blood of an animal. Abel's sacrifice was accepted because it was a response of obedient faith. Heb 11.4 states specifically that "Abel offered to God a more acceptable sacrifice than Cain's." Righteous Abel was the first martyr for the faith (Mt 23.35); he is listed as a hero of the faith in Heb 11.4. Abel's death is favorably compared with Christ's death in Heb 12.24.

4.6 angry. This is the first instance of human anger recorded in the Bible. Anger is neutral: it can be good or bad, depending on the reason for the anger.

4.7 The same Hebrew word — chattah — is used for "sin" and "sin-offering." Under the old covenant, the one who offered the animal sacrifice placed his hand

on the head of the victim, thus identifying himself with his sin-offering. This act was fulfilled in Christ, who became sin for us (2 Cor 5.21) that we might become righteous through faith in him (see note on 1 Pet 2.24).

4.13 my punishment is greater than I can bear! If Cain had thought of the consequences of murder before the act, he may have restrained himself. To complain about the punishment a person deserves for a transgression, as Cain did, exposes the true depravity of an individual.

4.19 Lamech took two wives. This is the first instance of polygamy in the Scriptures. Scripture indicates that it was not God's intention for a man to have more than one wife, for it violates the "one flesh" principle (2.24; cf. Mt 19.3ff).

who play the lyre and pipe. 22 Zillah bore Tubal-cain, who made all kinds of bronze and iron tools. The sister of Tubal-cain was Naamah.

23   Lamech said to his wives:
"Adah and Zillah, hear my voice;
   you wives of Lamech, listen to what I say:
I have killed a man for wounding me,
   a young man for striking me.
24 If Cain is avenged sevenfold,
   truly Lamech seventy-sevenfold."

E. The birth of Seth

25 Adam knew his wife again, and she bore a son and named him Seth, for she said, "God has appointed[r] for me another child instead of Abel, because Cain killed him." 26 To Seth also a son was born, and he named him Enosh. At that time people began to invoke the name of the LORD.

II. The descendants of Adam (5.1–6.8)

A. Adam and Seth

5 This is the list of the descendants of Adam. When God created humankind,[s] he made them[t] in the likeness of God. 2 Male and female he created them, and he blessed them and named them "Human-kind"[s] when they were created. 3 When Adam had lived one hundred thirty years, he became the father of a son in his likeness, according to his image, and named him Seth. 4 The days of Adam after he became the father of Seth were eight hundred years; and he had other sons and daughters. 5 Thus all the days that Adam lived were nine hundred thirty years; and he died.

B. Seth and Enosh

6   When Seth had lived one hundred five years, he became the father of Enosh. 7 Seth lived after the birth of Enosh eight hundred seven years, and had other sons and daughters. 8 Thus all the days of Seth were nine hundred twelve years; and he died.

C. Enosh and Kenan

9   When Enosh had lived ninety years, he became the father of Kenan. 10 Enosh lived after the birth of Kenan eight hundred fifteen years, and had other sons and daughters. 11 Thus all the days of Enosh were nine hundred five years; and he died.

D. Kenan and Mahalalel

12   When Kenan had lived seventy years, he became the father of Mahalalel. 13 Kenan lived after the birth of Mahalalel eight hundred and

Cross references (left margin):
4.23 Ex 20.13; Lev 19.18; Deut 32.35; Lk 3.36; v. 18
4.24 v. 15
4.25 Gen 5.3; v. 8
4.26 1 Kings 18.24; Ps 116.17; Joel 2.32; Zeph 3.9; 1 Cor 1.2
5.1 Gen 1.26; Eph 4.24; Col 3.10
5.2 Gen 1.27
5.3 Gen 4.25
5.5 Gen 3.19; Heb 9.27
5.6 Gen 4.26
5.7 Lk 3.38
5.11 1 Chr 1.1
5.12 1 Chr 1.2

r The verb in Heb resembles the word for Seth   s Heb adam   t Heb him

5.1 list of the descendants of Adam, i.e., a list or catalog of those descendants of Adam who were look-ing for the coming of Jesus Christ. It is not a list of all the offspring of Adam, but only those who came from Seth.
5.3 In the seventeenth century Archbishop Ussher of England developed a scheme of Bible chronology, based on the judgment that Adam commenced his life around 4004 B.C. But the modern carbon dating tech-niques makes this chronology very suspect. Many scholars allow for gaps in the chronologies that appear in Genesis 5 and 11 (see also note on 1.27).
5.5 Adam lived for 930 years. Longevity was com-mon at that time. Human life expectancy was short-ened so that by Abraham's time it was less than 200 years. Then in Ps 90.10 we are told that "the days of our life are seventy years, or perhaps eighty . . . ."
5.7 other sons and daughters. This refrain is repeated in vv. 9,13,16,19,22,26,30. Thus the population in-creased far more rapidly than some suppose. Moses, under the Spirit's guidance, did not mention all the descendants of each person mentioned in these verses.

forty years, and had other sons and daughters. 14 Thus all the days of Kenan were nine hundred and ten years; and he died.

E. Mahalalel and Jared

15 When Mahalalel had lived sixty-five years, he became the father of Jared. 16 Mahalalel lived after the birth of Jared eight hundred thirty years, and had other sons and daughters. 17 Thus all the days of Mahalalel were eight hundred ninety-five years; and he died.

5.15
1 Chr 1.2

F. Jared and Enoch

18 When Jared had lived one hundred sixty-two years he became the father of Enoch. 19 Jared lived after the birth of Enoch eight hundred years, and had other sons and daughters. 20 Thus all the days of Jared were nine hundred sixty-two years; and he died.

5.18
Jude 14, 15

G. Enoch and Methuselah

21 When Enoch had lived sixty-five years, he became the father of Methuselah. 22 Enoch walked with God after the birth of Methuselah three hundred years, and had other sons and daughters. 23 Thus all the days of Enoch were three hundred sixty-five years. 24 Enoch walked with God; then he was no more, because God took him.

5.21
1 Chr 1.3;
Lk 3.37;
Jude 14
5.24
2 Kings 2.11;
Heb 11.5

H. Methuselah and Lamech

25 When Methuselah had lived one hundred eighty-seven years, he became the father of Lamech. 26 Methuselah lived after the birth of Lamech seven hundred eighty-two years, and had other sons and daughters. 27 Thus all the days of Methuselah were nine hundred sixty-nine years; and he died.

5.26
Lk 3.36

I. Lamech and Noah

28 When Lamech had lived one hundred eighty-two years, he became the father of a son; 29 he named him Noah, saying, "Out of the ground that the LORD has cursed this one shall bring us relief from our work and from the toil of our hands." 30 Lamech lived after the birth of Noah five hundred ninety-five years, and had other sons and daughters. 31 Thus all the days of Lamech were seven hundred seventy-seven years; and he died.

5.29
Gen 3.17-19

J. Noah and his sons

32 After Noah was five hundred years old, Noah became the father of Shem, Ham, and Japheth.

5.32
Gen 6.10;
10.21

K. The wickedness of humankind: the judgment of God

6 When people began to multiply on the face of the ground, and daughters were born to them, 2 the sons of God saw that they were

6.1
Gen 1.28
6.2
Deut 7.1-4

5.24 *he was no more*, i.e., "Enoch was taken so that he did not experience death" (Heb 11.5). This was a miracle; the Bible records only one other such event — that of Elijah (2 Kings 2.11).
5.27 According to this Scripture, Methuselah lived for 969 years. Three possible solutions have been advanced to explain such large ages. One is that physical conditions before the flood made such longevity possible. Human life span has been reduced since the flood, according to this view. The second theory is that these age spans are figurative and must be reduced proportionally. This theory does not work, however. For example, if all of the ages were divided by ten, then Methuselah lived to be almost 100; but

when the life span of his father Enoch is so reduced, we are faced with Enoch's being six and a half years old when his son Methuselah was born. The third explanation is that the age span applies not to individuals but to families. But Heb 11.5 speaks of Enoch being taken away to heaven as an individual and makes no mention of his family being involved in the incident.
6.1–4 *sons of God.* The "sons of God" may mean God's created, supernatural beings, who were no longer godly in character (6.3). Some commentators believe, however, that this expression refers to the "godly line" of Seth and that "daughters of humans" (v. 4) refer to women from the line of Cain. Most

fair; and they took wives for themselves of all that they chose. 3 Then the LORD said, "My spirit shall not abide^u in mortals forever, for they are flesh; their days shall be one hundred twenty years." 4 The Nephilim were on the earth in those days—and also afterward—when the sons of God went in to the daughters of humans, who bore children to them. These were the heroes that were of old, warriors of renown.

5   The LORD saw that the wickedness of humankind was great in the earth, and that every inclination of the thoughts of their hearts was only evil continually. 6 And the LORD was sorry that he had made humankind on the earth, and it grieved him to his heart. 7 So the LORD said, "I will blot out from the earth the human beings I have created—people together with animals and creeping things and birds of the air, for I am sorry that I have made them." 8 But Noah found favor in the sight of the LORD.

III. *The descendants of Noah (6.9–9.29)*

A. *The command to build the ark*

9   These are the descendants of Noah. Noah was a righteous man, blameless in his generation; Noah walked with God. 10 And Noah had three sons, Shem, Ham, and Japheth.

11   Now the earth was corrupt in God's sight, and the earth was filled with violence. 12 And God saw that the earth was corrupt; for all flesh had corrupted its ways upon the earth. 13 And God said to Noah, "I have determined to make an end of all flesh, for the earth is filled with violence because of them; now I am going to destroy them along with the earth. 14 Make yourself an ark of cypress^u wood; make rooms in the ark, and cover it inside and out with pitch. 15 This is how you are to make it: the length of the ark three hundred cubits, its width fifty cubits, and its height thirty cubits. 16 Make a roof^v for the ark, and finish it to a cubit above; and put the door of the ark in its side; make it with lower, second, and third decks. 17 For my part, I am going to bring a flood of waters on the earth, to destroy from under heaven all flesh in which is the breath of life; everything that is on the earth shall die. 18 But I will establish my covenant with you; and you shall come into the ark, you, your sons, your wife, and your sons' wives with you. 19 And of every living thing, of all flesh, you shall bring two of every kind into the ark, to keep them alive with you; they shall be male and female. 20 Of the birds according to their kinds, and of the animals according to their kinds, of every creeping thing of the ground according to its kind, two of every kind shall come in to you, to

^{u} Meaning of Heb uncertain ^{v} Or *window*

Cross-references (margin)

6.3 1 Pet 3.19; Ps 78.39
6.5 Gen 8.21
6.6 1 Sam 15.11, 29; 2 Sam 24.16; Mal 3.6; Jas 1.17; Isa 63.10
6.8 Gen 19.19; Ex 33.12; Lk 1.30; Acts 7.46
6.9 Gen 17.1; Ezek 14.14, 20; Heb 11.7; 2 Pet 2.5; Gen 5.22
6.10 Gen 5.32
6.11 Rom 2.13; Ezek 8.17
6.12 Ps 14.1-3
6.13 Ezek 7.2, 3; v. 17
6.14 Heb 11.7; 1 Pet 3.20
6.17 Gen 7.4, 21-23
6.18 Gen 7.1, 7, 13; 1 Pet 3.20; 2 Pet 2.5
6.19 Gen 7.8, 9, 15, 16
6.20 Gen 7.9, 15

---

likely the phrase refers to those descendants of Seth who trusted in the LORD but whose children intermarried with women descended from Cain. Those marriages were not with angels then, but between godly and ungodly human families. Angels neither marry nor are given in marriage (Mt 22.30), so that this verse hardly applies to them. On the other hand, Peter speaks of angels who sinned (2 Pet 2.4), apparently referring to the book of Enoch (20.2) where "sons of God" are interpreted as "angels." *Nephilim* are strong, violent, tyrannous men of great wickedness. It may well be that the explanation of these verses has been lost to us.
6.9   Three expressions characterize the life of Noah: he was righteous (i.e., he was redeemed and the righteousness of Christ was imputed to him); he was blameless; and he "walked with God." He is the prototype of the kind of people Christians ought to be in this generation.
6.13   *God said to Noah.* God revealed to Noah what his intentions were in advance of the happening. The Scriptures do not tell us how God did this. God used

different methods to make his will known; he was not limited to a single method of revelation.
6.14   Noah's ark was approximately 450 feet long by 75 feet wide, and was three-storied, with 15 feet between each story. It was made of cypress wood and covered with pitch. It has been estimated by some that it could have carried some seven thousand animals. The ark is representative of Christ, who is the place of refuge for sinners who wish to be saved from the wrath to come (see 1 Pet 3.20,21).
6.17   Three different views have emerged about the extent of the flood: (1) not all land was covered, and not all life died; (2) not all land was covered, but all life died; (3) all land was covered, and all life died. Though the last view is disliked especially by many modern scholars, there is a universal tradition about the flood among all peoples of the world. Recent evidence of a gigantic cataclysm in all parts of the world clearly suggests a universal flood.
6.18   God announces to Noah that he will make a covenant with him, but the details of that covenant are not made known until ch. 9.

keep them alive. 21 Also take with you every kind of food that is eaten, and store it up; and it shall serve as food for you and for them." 22 Noah did this; he did all that God commanded him.

6.22
Heb 11.7;
Gen 7.5

B. The command to fill the ark

7 Then the LORD said to Noah, "Go into the ark, you and all your household, for I have seen that you alone are righteous before me in this generation. 2 Take with you seven pairs of all clean animals, the male and its mate; and a pair of the animals that are not clean, the male and its mate; 3 and seven pairs of the birds of the air also, male and female, to keep their kind alive on the face of all the earth. 4 For in seven days I will send rain on the earth for forty days and forty nights; and every living thing that I have made I will blot out from the face of the ground." 5 And Noah did all that the LORD had commanded him.

7.1
Mt 24.38;
Lk 17.26
7.2
Lev ch. 11;
10.10;
Ezek 44.23

C. The flood

6 Noah was six hundred years old when the flood of waters came on the earth. 7 And Noah with his sons and his wife and his sons' wives went into the ark to escape the waters of the flood. 8 Of clean animals, and of animals that are not clean, and of birds, and of everything that creeps on the ground, 9 two and two, male and female, went into the ark with Noah, as God had commanded Noah. 10 And after seven days the waters of the flood came on the earth.

7.7
Gen 6.22;
v. 1

11 In the six hundredth year of Noah's life, in the second month, on the seventeenth day of the month, on that day all the fountains of the great deep burst forth, and the windows of the heavens were opened. 12 The rain fell on the earth forty days and forty nights. 13 On the very same day Noah with his sons, Shem and Ham and Japheth, and Noah's wife and the three wives of his sons entered the ark, 14 they and every wild animal of every kind, and all domestic animals of every kind, and every creeping thing that creeps on the earth, and every bird of every kind—every bird, every winged creature. 15 They went into the ark with Noah, two and two of all flesh in which there was the breath of life. 16 And those that entered, male and female of all flesh, went in as God had commanded him; and the LORD shut him in.

7.11
Gen 8.2;
Prov 8.28;
Ezek 26.19
7.12
vv. 4, 17
7.13
vv. 1, 7; 6.18

7.15
Gen 6.20
7.16
vv. 2, 3

17 The flood continued forty days on the earth; and the waters increased, and bore up the ark, and it rose high above the earth. 18 The waters swelled and increased greatly on the earth; and the ark floated on the face of the waters. 19 The waters swelled so mightily on the earth that all the high mountains under the whole heaven were covered; 20 the waters swelled above the mountains, covering them fifteen cubits deep. 21 And all flesh died that moved on the earth, birds, domestic animals, wild animals, all swarming creatures that swarm on the earth, and all human beings; 22 everything on dry land in whose nostrils was the breath of life died. 23 He blotted out every living thing that was on the face of the ground, human beings and animals and creeping things and birds of the air; they were blotted out from the earth. Only Noah was left, and those

7.17
vv. 4, 12
7.18
Ps 104.26

7.21
Gen 6.13, 17

7.22
Gen 2.7
7.23
1 Pet 3.20;
2 Pet 2.5

6.22 Noah was obedient and did precisely what God told him to do. In 7.1 we are told: "I have seen that you alone are righteous before me." His righteousness was vindicated by his walk of life, fulfilling what James writes in his epistle (see Jas 2): we are saved by faith alone, yet saving faith is never alone; it is always accompanied by good works.
7.8 *of clean animals, and of animals that are not clean.* God had not yet told people which animals were good for food and which were not. Up to this point humans may not have eaten animal flesh (cf. 9.2–4). Some Christians are vegetarians, though Scripture does not

speak clearly on this issue.
7.11 When the flood waters came, God caused windows in the dome of heaven (cf. 1.6,7) to open as rain (perhaps for the first time, cf. 2.5) and he caused water to bubble up from the ground. It is apparent that humans knew about the seasons of the year and had calendar months. There were months and days known to them.
7.23 The effect of the flood did not extend to sea life, only to what lived on land, including both birds and animals.

7.24
Gen 8.3

that were with him in the ark. 24 And the waters swelled on the earth for one hundred fifty days.

D. The subsiding of the waters

8.1
Gen 19.29;
Ex 2.24;
1 Sam 1.19;
Ex 14.21;
Job 12.15;
Ps 29.10;
Isa 44.27;
Nah 1.4
8.2
Gen 7.11;
Job 38.37
8.3
Gen 7.24
8.4
Jer 51.27
8.6
2 Pet 2.5
8.7
1 Kings 17.4, 6

8 But God remembered Noah and all the wild animals and all the domestic animals that were with him in the ark. And God made a wind blow over the earth, and the waters subsided; 2 the fountains of the deep and the windows of the heavens were closed, the rain from the heavens was restrained, 3 and the waters gradually receded from the earth. At the end of one hundred fifty days the waters had abated; 4 and in the seventh month, on the seventeenth day of the month, the ark came to rest on the mountains of Ararat. 5 The waters continued to abate until the tenth month; in the tenth month, on the first day of the month, the tops of the mountains appeared.

6 At the end of forty days Noah opened the window of the ark that he had made 7 and sent out the raven; and it went to and fro until the waters were dried up from the earth. 8 Then he sent out the dove from

8.11
Mt 10.16

him, to see if the waters had subsided from the face of the ground; 9 but the dove found no place to set its foot, and it returned to him to the ark, for the waters were still on the face of the whole earth. So he put out his hand and took it and brought it into the ark with him. 10 He waited another seven days, and again he sent out the dove from the ark; 11 and the dove came back to him in the evening, and there in its beak was a freshly plucked olive leaf; so Noah knew that the waters had subsided from the earth. 12 Then he waited another seven days, and sent out the dove; and it did not return to him any more.

E. The return to dry land

8.13
2 Pet 3.5, 6

13 In the six hundred first year, in the first month, on the first day of the month, the waters were dried up from the earth; and Noah removed the covering of the ark, and looked, and saw that the face of the ground was drying. 14 In the second month, on the twenty-seventh day of the

8.16
Gen 7.13
8.17
Gen 1.22

month, the earth was dry. 15 Then God said to Noah, 16 "Go out of the ark, you and your wife, and your sons and your sons' wives with you. 17 Bring out with you every living thing that is with you of all flesh — birds and animals and every creeping thing that creeps on the earth — so that they may abound on the earth, and be fruitful and multiply on the earth." 18 So Noah went out with his sons and his wife and his sons' wives. 19 And every animal, every creeping thing, and every bird, everything that moves on the earth, went out of the ark by families.

8.20
Gen 12.7, 8;
13.18; 22.9;
7.2; 22.2;
Ex 10.25
8.21
Lev 1.9;
2 Cor 2.15;
Gen 3.17;
6.17; 9.11,
15

F. The altar of sacrifice: God will never curse the ground again

20 Then Noah built an altar to the LORD, and took of every clean animal and of every clean bird, and offered burnt offerings on the altar. 21 And when the LORD smelled the pleasing odor, the LORD said in his heart, "I will never again curse the ground because of humankind, for the

---

8.2 *the windows of the heavens were closed.* God was sovereignly doing what he pleased. He started the rain and stopped it when his purposes had been accomplished.
8.3,4 *the mountains of Ararat* constituted a range of mountains rising to a height of almost 17,000 feet above sea level. The ark probably rested on one of the lower mountains of this range, closer to sea level. The Babylonian flood epic says that the ark came to rest on Mount Nisir, east of the Tigris River.
8.5 *in the tenth month, on the first day of the month,* i.e., three months later.

8.7 *the raven . . . went to and fro.* The raven apparently lighted from time to time upon carcasses of dead animals floating on the water. The dove, which Noah next dispatched, would not alight on such floating carrion, and this was a good indication of the water level.
8.13 *in the six hundred first year, in the first month, the first day of the month,* i.e., twenty-nine days after that.
8.20 *clean animal . . . clean bird,* i.e., ritually approved by God. *Noah . . . offered burnt offerings.* Animal sacrifices were already known as a means for obtaining atonement and forgiveness (4.4).

inclination of the human heart is evil from youth; nor will I ever again
destroy every living creature as I have done.

22 As long as the earth endures,
    seedtime and harvest, cold and heat,
    summer and winter, day and night,
    shall not cease."

8.22
Isa 54.9;
Jer 33.20, 25

G. *God allows meat but forbids blood*

9 God blessed Noah and his sons, and said to them, "Be fruitful and
multiply, and fill the earth. 2 The fear and dread of you shall rest on
every animal of the earth, and on every bird of the air, on everything that
creeps on the ground, and on all the fish of the sea; into your hand they
are delivered. 3 Every moving thing that lives shall be food for you; and
just as I gave you the green plants, I give you everything. 4 Only, you shall
not eat flesh with its life, that is, its blood. 5 For your own lifeblood I will
surely require a reckoning: from every animal I will require it and from
human beings, each one for the blood of another, I will require a reckoning for human life.

9.1
v. 7;
Gen 1.28

9.3
Deut 12.15;
Gen 1.29
9.4
Lev 17.10-16;
Deut 12.23;
1 Sam 14.33
9.5
Ex 21.28;
Gen 4.9, 10

6 Whoever sheds the blood of a human,
    by a human shall that person's blood be shed;
for in his own image
    God made humankind.

9.6
Ex 21.12, 14;
Lev 24.17;
Mt 26.52;
Gen 1.27

7 And you, be fruitful and multiply, abound on the earth and multiply in
it."

9.7
vv. 1, 19

H. *The Noahic covenant: the rainbow*

8 Then God said to Noah and to his sons with him, 9 "As for me, I
am establishing my covenant with you and your descendants after you,
10 and with every living creature that is with you, the birds, the domestic
animals, and every animal of the earth with you, as many as came out of
the ark. *w* 11 I establish my covenant with you, that never again shall all
flesh be cut off by the waters of a flood, and never again shall there be
a flood to destroy the earth." 12 God said, "This is the sign of the covenant
that I make between me and you and every living creature that is with you,
for all future generations: 13 I have set my bow in the clouds, and it shall
be a sign of the covenant between me and the earth. 14 When I bring
clouds over the earth and the bow is seen in the clouds, 15 I will remember
my covenant that is between me and you and every living creature of all
flesh; and the waters shall never again become a flood to destroy all flesh.
16 When the bow is in the clouds, I will see it and remember the everlasting
covenant between God and every living creature of all flesh that is on the

9.9
Gen 6.18;
Isa 54.9
9.10
Ps 149.9

9.11
Isa 54.9

9.12
Gen 17.11

9.13
Ezek 1.28;
Rev 4.3
9.15
Lev 26.42,
45;
Deut 7.9

9.16
Gen 17.13, 19

---

w Gk: Heb adds *every animal of the earth*

9.1 Following the flood, God made a covenant with
Noah. The agreement specified that: (1) there would
always be the seasons of the year with planting and
harvest (8.22); (2) Noah and his family would replen-
ish the earth (9.1); (3) law and government were to be
reinstituted (9.1–6); (4) meat, except for the blood,
and vegetables were to be given to humans for food
(9.3,4); and (5) there would never again be a universal
flood (9.15). God sealed the covenant with a rainbow
(9.16,17).
9.6 This verse institutes capital punishment
for murder. In Ex 21.12–17 murder and other crimes
worthy of capital punishment are spelled out by Moses. Christians everywhere cannot agree whether or
not this O.T. teaching is applicable under the doctrine of grace today.
9.13 *the covenant between me and the earth.* God made
a covenant with Noah but he also made a covenant
with the earth. God the creator is interested in his

inanimate creation as well as in the human race. He
determined to preserve the earth from the effects of
the flood. Redemption was accomplished for the cosmos as well as for people. God's people should be
careful about the way they use the earth on which they
depend for sustenance.
9.16 *covenant between God and every living creature.*
Here God speaks of his covenant with all living creatures. God is concerned about everything he created.
Birds and animals are included in this everlasting
covenant. Humans should have a concern for all life,
human and non-human, because all life comes as a gift
from the Creator.
9.16,17 God's covenants are always two-way
streets. In them God obligates himself when he makes
promises to humans. Thus the Noahic covenant included a promise from God that never again would life
be destroyed by a universal flood. The seal of this
covenant was the rainbow.

earth." 17 God said to Noah, "This is the sign of the covenant that I have established between me and all flesh that is on the earth."

9.18
Gen 10.6
9.19
Gen 5.32

18   The sons of Noah who went out of the ark were Shem, Ham, and Japheth. Ham was the father of Canaan. 19 These three were the sons of Noah; and from these the whole earth was peopled.

I. Canaan cursed; Shem blessed

20   Noah, a man of the soil, was the first to plant a vineyard. 21 He drank some of the wine and became drunk, and he lay uncovered in his tent. 22 And Ham, the father of Canaan, saw the nakedness of his father,

9.23
Ex 20.12

and told his two brothers outside. 23 Then Shem and Japheth took a garment, laid it on both their shoulders, and walked backward and covered the nakedness of their father; their faces were turned away, and they did not see their father's nakedness. 24 When Noah awoke from his wine and knew what his youngest son had done to him, 25 he said,

9.25
Deut 27.16

"Cursed be Canaan;
    lowest of slaves shall he be to his brothers."

9.26
Ps 144.15

26 He also said,

"Blessed by the LORD my God be Shem;
    and let Canaan be his slave.

9.27
Eph 2.13, 14;
3.6

27   May God make space for x Japheth,
    and let him live in the tents of Shem;
    and let Canaan be his slave."

28   After the flood Noah lived three hundred fifty years. 29 All the days of Noah were nine hundred fifty years; and he died.

IV. The descendants of the sons of Noah (10.1–11.9)

A. The sons of Japheth

10 These are the descendants of Noah's sons, Shem, Ham, and Japheth; children were born to them after the flood.

10.2
1 Chr 1.5-7

2   The descendants of Japheth: Gomer, Magog, Madai, Javan, Tubal, Meshech, and Tiras. 3 The descendants of Gomer: Ashkenaz, Riphath, and Togarmah. 4 The descendants of Javan: Elishah, Tarshish, Kittim,

10.5
Gen 5.32

and Rodanim. y 5 From these the coastland peoples spread. These are the descendants of Japheth z in their lands, with their own language, by their families, in their nations.

x Heb *yapht,* a play on *Japheth*   y Heb Mss Sam Gk See 1 Chr 1.7: MT *Dodanim*   z Compare verses 20, 31. Heb lacks *These are the descendants of Japheth*

9.25 The Canaanites came from Canaan, who was the son of Ham, against whom Noah pronounced a curse. Noah's curse was fulfilled when the Canaanites were overcome by the descendants of Shem and later by the Persians, Greeks, and Romans. Seven nations of people came from Canaan (Deut 7.1); they were idolatrous, superstitious, and abominably wicked. Abraham roamed their land, and to him was the promise made to inherit Canaan. Centuries went by before Abraham's descendants occupied the land. When they entered their inheritance God commanded them: (1) to make no agreements with the Canaanites and show no mercy toward them (Deut 7.2); (2) not to worship but to destroy their idols (Ex 23.24; Deut 7.5, 25); (3) not to follow their customs (Lev 18.26,27); (4) not to fear them (Deut 7.17,18; 31.7). When Israel sinned, God permitted a remnant to remain in Canaan for chastisement (Num 33.55; Judg 2.3,21,22; 3.1–4; 4.2).

10.1–32 After the flood, the human race descended from the children of Noah just as Noah's family had descended from Adam and Eve. In some instances the descendants must be understood by their political

rather than their racial ancestors. The Canaanites were Semites (sons of Shem) and are listed as sons of Ham (10.6), for prior to Israel's occupation of Canaan it had been under the control of the Hamites, the peoples of northeast Africa. If Lud refers to the Lydians of Asia Minor, they were racially Japhethites, not Shemites. Ancient archeological data have made probable identification fairly certain in many instances: *Madai* (10.2) are the Medes; *Javan* (10.2) are the Ionians or Greeks; *Ashkenaz* (10.3) probably refers to the Scythians; *Elishah* (10.3) is likely an ancient name for the people of Cyprus; *Tarshish* (10.3) is probably Spain or Sardinia; *Kittim* (10.3), the people of Cyprus; *Put*, Cyrenaica of North Africa; *Shinar*, Babylonia; *Caphtorim*, the Cretans; *Heth*, the Hittites; and *Sheba*, southwest Arabia, whose queen visited King Solomon.

10.5 *with their own language.* This verse does not mean that the sons of Noah spoke different languages. It looks forward, rather, to the event of the tower of Babel, which is soon to occur and out of which God will divide the human race into a variety of language groupings.

B. The sons of Ham

6 The descendants of Ham: Cush, Egypt, Put, and Canaan. 7 The descendants of Cush: Seba, Havilah, Sabtah, Raamah, and Sabteca. The descendants of Raamah: Sheba and Dedan. 8 Cush became the father of Nimrod; he was the first on earth to become a mighty warrior. 9 He was a mighty hunter before the LORD; therefore it is said, "Like Nimrod a mighty hunter before the LORD." 10 The beginning of his kingdom was Babel, Erech, and Accad, all of them in the land of Shinar. 11 From that land he went into Assyria, and built Nineveh, Rehoboth-ir, Calah, and 12 Resen between Nineveh and Calah; that is the great city. 13 Egypt became the father of Ludim, Anamim, Lehabim, Naphtuhim, 14 Pathrusim, Casluhim, and Caphtorim, from which the Philistines come.*a*

15 Canaan became the father of Sidon his firstborn, and Heth, 16 and the Jebusites, the Amorites, the Girgashites, 17 the Hivites, the Arkites, the Sinites, 18 the Arvadites, the Zemarites, and the Hamathites. Afterward the families of the Canaanites spread abroad. 19 And the territory of the Canaanites extended from Sidon, in the direction of Gerar, as far as Gaza, and in the direction of Sodom, Gomorrah, Admah, and Zeboiim, as far as Lasha. 20 These are the descendants of Ham, by their families, their languages, their lands, and their nations.

C. The sons of Shem

21 To Shem also, the father of all the children of Eber, the elder brother of Japheth, children were born. 22 The descendants of Shem: Elam, Asshur, Arpachshad, Lud, and Aram. 23 The descendants of Aram: Uz, Hul, Gether, and Mash. 24 Arpachshad became the father of Shelah; and Shelah became the father of Eber. 25 To Eber were born two sons: the name of the one was Peleg,*b* for in his days the earth was divided, and his brother's name was Joktan. 26 Joktan became the father of Almodad, Sheleph, Hazarmaveth, Jerah, 27 Hadoram, Uzal, Diklah, 28 Obal, Abimael, Sheba, 29 Ophir, Havilah, and Jobab; all these were the descendants of Joktan. 30 The territory in which they lived extended from Mesha in the direction of Sephar, the hill country of the east. 31 These are the descendants of Shem, by their families, their languages, their lands, and their nations.

32 These are the families of Noah's sons, according to their genealogies, in their nations; and from these the nations spread abroad on the earth after the flood.

D. The tower of Babel: the confusion of speech

11 Now the whole earth had one language and the same words. 2 And as they migrated from the east,*c* they came upon a plain in the land of Shinar and settled there. 3 And they said to one another, "Come, let us make bricks, and burn them thoroughly." And they had brick for stone, and bitumen for mortar. 4 Then they said, "Come, let us build

---

a Cn: Heb *Casluhim, from which the Philistines come, and Caphtorim*   *b* That is *Division*   *c* Or *migrated eastward*

Marginal references:
10.6 1 Chr 1.8-10
10.9 Mic 5.6
10.10 Mic 5.6
10.13 1 Chr 1.8, 11
10.15 1 Chr 1.13
10.18 1 Chr 1.16; 18.3
10.19 Num 34.2-12
10.22 1 Chr 1.17; Gen 14.1, 9; 2 Kings 15.29; Gen 11.10; Isa 66.19
10.23 Job 1.1
10.24 Gen 11.12; Lk 3.35
10.25 1 Chr 1.19
10.26-29 1 Chr 1.20-23
10.32 v. 1
11.2 Ex 1.11, 14; 5.7-19
11.4ff Deut 1.28

11.1 Up to this time, everyone spoke the same language. The period following the tower of Babel incident is anticipated in 10.5,20,31. When people at Babel sinned, God confused their languages; in so doing he made the advancement of wicked knowledge more difficult because of language barriers. Later, Pentecost was a sign of the reversal of the confusion (Acts 2.1–11). The time will come when language will no longer be a barrier in God's kingdom.
11.4–9 The location of the tower of Babel is unknown. Birs Minrud, approximately seven miles from ancient Babylon, has been suggested as the site. Am-

ran, which is within the city, is another. King Nebuchadnezzar spoke of the *Ziggurat Babili* ("Tower of Babylon"), which he restored after finding it in ruins. But *Bab-ili* is from the Assyrian tongue and is the native name for the Greek Babylon; it means "Gate of God" and has nothing to do with the Hebrew word *balal*, which means "to confuse." The Babel story finds its counterparts in ancient mythology, such as the Greek myth of the Titans who tried to climb to heaven. The biblical account is far older and is, of course, a historical fact which may have been influential in the formation of mythical tales elsewhere.

ourselves a city, and a tower with its top in the heavens, and let us make a name for ourselves; otherwise we shall be scattered abroad upon the face of the whole earth." 5 The LORD came down to see the city and the tower, which mortals had built. 6 And the LORD said, "Look, they are one people, and they have all one language; and this is only the beginning of what they will do; nothing that they propose to do will now be impossible for them. 7 Come, let us go down, and confuse their language there, so that they will not understand one another's speech." 8 So the LORD scattered them abroad from there over the face of all the earth, and they left off building the city. 9 Therefore it was called Babel, because there the LORD confused[d] the language of all the earth; and from there the LORD scattered them abroad over the face of all the earth.

11.5
Gen 18.21
11.6
Acts 17.26;
Gen 9.19

11.7
Gen 1.26;
42.23;
Ex 4.11;
1 Cor 14.2,
11
11.8
Lk 1.51;
Gen 10.25, 32
11.9
Gen 10.10

V. *The descendants of Shem (11.10–26)*

11.10
Gen 10.22;
1 Chr 1.17

10   These are the descendants of Shem. When Shem was one hundred years old, he became the father of Arpachshad two years after the flood; 11 and Shem lived after the birth of Arpachshad five hundred years, and had other sons and daughters.

11.12
Lk 3.36

12   When Arpachshad had lived thirty-five years, he became the father of Shelah; 13 and Arpachshad lived after the birth of Shelah four hundred three years, and had other sons and daughters.

14   When Shelah had lived thirty years, he became the father of Eber; 15 and Shelah lived after the birth of Eber four hundred three years, and had other sons and daughters.

11.16
1 Chr 1.19

16   When Eber had lived thirty-four years, he became the father of Peleg; 17 and Eber lived after the birth of Peleg four hundred thirty years, and had other sons and daughters.

18   When Peleg had lived thirty years, he became the father of Reu; 19 and Peleg lived after the birth of Reu two hundred nine years, and had other sons and daughters.

11.20
Lk 3.35

20   When Reu had lived thirty-two years, he became the father of Serug; 21 and Reu lived after the birth of Serug two hundred seven years, and had other sons and daughters.

22   When Serug had lived thirty years, he became the father of Nahor; 23 and Serug lived after the birth of Nahor two hundred years, and had other sons and daughters.

11.24
Lk 3.34

24   When Nahor had lived twenty-nine years, he became the father of Terah; 25 and Nahor lived after the birth of Terah one hundred nineteen years, and had other sons and daughters.

11.26
Josh 24.2

26   When Terah had lived seventy years, he became the father of Abram, Nahor, and Haran.

VI. *The descendants of Terah (11.27–25.11)*

A. *The genealogy of Abraham*

27   Now these are the descendants of Terah. Terah was the father of Abram, Nahor, and Haran; and Haran was the father of Lot. 28 Haran

---

d Heb *balal*, meaning *to confuse*

11.6 Language is the basis on which science feeds upon itself and grows. This was the beginning of an explosion of knowledge, nipped in the bud because of wrong motives and wrong use of the knowledge gained.
11.7 *let us.* The plural certainly suggests the triune personhood of God, who is one God in three persons — the Father, the Son, and the Holy Spirit.
11.12,13 From here on, the lifespan of humans will decline sharply. The ages when people procreate will

also be far younger than before. Noah (5.32) was five hundred years old when his wife had her three sons. In vv. 12–26 the age of the fathers ranged from twenty-nine to thirty-five — except for Terah, who was seventy.
11.28 Abram was not an uneducated, illiterate nomad. Archeological discoveries show that Ur of the Chaldees enjoyed an advanced culture, with libraries, schools, and temples. The people had textbooks on mathematics, religion, and politics, and used gram-

died before his father Terah in the land of his birth, in Ur of the Chaldeans. 29 Abram and Nahor took wives; the name of Abram's wife was Sarai, and the name of Nahor's wife was Milcah. She was the daughter of Haran the father of Milcah and Iscah. 30 Now Sarai was barren; she had no child.

31   Terah took his son Abram and his grandson Lot son of Haran, and his daughter-in-law Sarai, his son Abram's wife, and they went out together from Ur of the Chaldeans to go into the land of Canaan; but when they came to Haran, they settled there. 32 The days of Terah were two hundred five years; and Terah died in Haran.

B. The call of Abram

1. The promise to make him a blessing

12 Now the LORD said to Abram, "Go from your country and your kindred and your father's house to the land that I will show you. 2 I will make of you a great nation, and I will bless you, and make your name great, so that you will be a blessing. 3 I will bless those who bless you, and the one who curses you I will curse; and in you all the families of the earth shall be blessed."*e*

2. The promise of the land of Canaan

4   So Abram went, as the LORD had told him; and Lot went with him. Abram was seventy-five years old when he departed from Haran. 5 Abram took his wife Sarai and his brother's son Lot, and all the possessions that they had gathered, and the persons whom they had acquired in Haran; and they set forth to go to the land of Canaan. When they had come to the land of Canaan, 6 Abram passed through the land to the place at Shechem, to the oak*f* of Moreh. At that time the Canaanites were in the land. 7 Then the LORD appeared to Abram, and said, "To your offspring*g* I will give this land." So he built there an altar to the LORD, who had appeared to him. 8 From there he moved on to the hill country on the east of Bethel, and pitched his tent, with Bethel on the west and Ai on the east; and there he built an altar to the LORD and invoked the name of the LORD. 9 And Abram journeyed on by stages toward the Negeb.

e Or by you all the families of the earth shall bless themselves   f Or terebinth   g Heb seed

11.29
Gen 24.10;
17.15; 20.12;
22.20
11.30
Gen 16.1
11.31
Gen 15.7;
Neh 9.7;
Acts 7.4

12.1
Acts 7.3;
Heb 11.8
12.2
Gen 15.5;
17.4, 5;
18.18; 22.17;
28.14; 32.12;
35.11; 46.3
12.3
Gen 27.29;
Ex 23.22;
Num 24.9;
Gen 18.18;
22.18; 26.4;
Acts 3.25;
Gal 3.8
12.4
Gen 11.27, 31
12.5
Gen 14.14;
11.31
12.6
Heb 11.9;
Deut 11.30;
Gen 10.18, 19
12.7
Gen 17.1;
13.15; 17.8;
Ps 105.9;
Gen 13.4
12.8
Gen 13.4

mars, dictionaries, and encyclopedias. Egypt also had developed an advanced culture a thousand years before Abram's birth. Abram may have left written records for posterity that could have been used by Moses when he wrote the Pentateuch.
11.31 Abram's ancestors stemmed from this area because near Haran were towns called Peleg, Serug, Nahor, and Terah — all names of Abram's ancestors.
11.32 Terah died at the age of 205 years, Sarah at 127, Abraham at 175, Isaac at 180, Jacob at 147, and Joseph at 110. By the time of the monarchy David died at seventy. He was thirty when he began to reign and he reigned for forty years, according to 2 Sam 5.4. Thus lifespans declined considerably from the days of Adam and of the patriarchs.
12.1 *Abram.* His name meant "exalted ancestor." He was renamed "Abraham" when God made his covenant with him, meaning "ancestor of a multitude" (17.5). From him came Isaac, Ishmael, and the descendants of his six sons born to Keturah, his wife after the death of Sarah. He was monogamous; yet a vast progeny can be traced back to him.
12.2 *you will be a blessing,* or paraphrased, "I will make your name so famous that it will be used to pronounce blessings on others." The covenant God made with Abram is mentioned several times in Genesis (13.14–17; 15; 17; 18; 21.12; 22.16–18). God made certain promises to him based upon his obedi-

ence or trust in God. The land of Palestine was promised, as was a posterity more numerous than the grains of sand on the seashore. God guaranteed him a son and stated that, through Abram, all the nations of the earth were to be blessed. Abram believed God, and the Lord reckoned it to him as righteousness (15.6).

12.3 *in you all the families of the earth shall be blessed.* There can be no doubt that 12.1–3 represents a unique disclosure of God's plan of salvation via missionary outreach. Paul clearly states that this Scripture foresees the N.T. gospel. In Gal 3.8, he writes: "And the scripture, foreseeing that God would justify the Gentiles by faith, declared the gospel beforehand to Abraham, saying, 'All the Gentiles shall be blessed in you.'"

12.7 Abram's altar implies animal sacrifice, common to the Semite peoples. This can undoubtedly be traced back to the earliest of all animal sacrifices — that of Abel. From the beginning, humans knew that God had to be propitiated by blood sacrifice.

12.9 We now know that the Negeb was occupied during the time of Abram (2100–1880 B.C.). He followed the trade route, which had water stations, from Mamre (Hebron) to Kadesh (later known as Kadesh-barnea). Jacob and Moses were also familiar with this route.

3. *The residence in Egypt as an alien*

10 Now there was a famine in the land. So Abram went down to Egypt to reside there as an alien, for the famine was severe in the land. 11 When he was about to enter Egypt, he said to his wife Sarai, "I know well that you are a woman beautiful in appearance; 12 and when the Egyptians see you, they will say, 'This is his wife'; then they will kill me, but they will let you live. 13 Say you are my sister, so that it may go well with me because of you, and that my life may be spared on your account." 14 When Abram entered Egypt the Egyptians saw that the woman was very beautiful. 15 When the officials of Pharaoh saw her, they praised her to Pharaoh. And the woman was taken into Pharaoh's house. 16 And for her sake he dealt well with Abram; and he had sheep, oxen, male donkeys, male and female slaves, female donkeys, and camels.

17 But the LORD afflicted Pharaoh and his house with great plagues because of Sarai, Abram's wife. 18 So Pharaoh called Abram, and said, "What is this you have done to me? Why did you not tell me that she was your wife? 19 Why did you say, 'She is my sister,' so that I took her for my wife? Now then, here is your wife, take her, and be gone." 20 And Pharaoh gave his men orders concerning him; and they set him on the way, with his wife and all that he had.

13 So Abram went up from Egypt, he and his wife, and all that he had, and Lot with him, into the Negeb.

C. *The separation of Abram and Lot*

1. *The strife between the herders of Lot and Abram*

2 Now Abram was very rich in livestock, in silver, and in gold. 3 He journeyed on by stages from the Negeb as far as Bethel, to the place where his tent had been at the beginning, between Bethel and Ai, 4 to the place where he had made an altar at the first; and there Abram called on the name of the LORD. 5 Now Lot, who went with Abram, also had flocks and herds and tents, 6 so that the land could not support both of them living together; for their possessions were so great that they could not live together, 7 and there was strife between the herders of Abram's livestock and the herders of Lot's livestock. At that time the Canaanites and the Perizzites lived in the land.

2. *Lot chooses Sodom*

8 Then Abram said to Lot, "Let there be no strife between you and me, and between your herders and my herders; for we are kindred. 9 Is not the whole land before you? Separate yourself from me. If you take the left hand, then I will go to the right; or if you take the right hand, then I will go to the left." 10 Lot looked about him, and saw that the plain of

Cross references (left margin):
- 12.12 — Gen 20.11
- 12.13 — Gen 20.5, 13
- 12.15 — Gen 20.2
- 12.16 — Gen 20.14
- 12.17 — Gen 20.18; 1 Chr 16.21; Ps 105.14
- 12.18 — Gen 20.9, 10
- 12.20 — Prov 21.1
- 13.1 — Gen 12.9
- 13.3 — Gen 12.8, 9
- 13.4 — Gen 12.7, 8
- 13.7 — Gen 26.20
- 13.8 — Prov 15.18; 20.3
- 13.10 — Gen 19.17-29; Deut 34.3; Gen 2.8; 47.6; 14.8

12.10 In times of famine it was customary, according to Egyptian records, for peoples of Palestine and Syria to seek refuge in Egypt.

12.11–13 Abram faltered in his trust in God when he told Sarai to say she was his sister. By failing to tell the full truth, namely, that she was also his wife, he was walking by sight and not by faith. Abram was a man of faith, yet he was not perfect. The consequences demonstrate that deceitfulness is never justified. Also, the end does not justify the means and situational ethics are not acceptable to God. God's will must be done God's way.

13.2 *Abram . . . rich . . . in silver, and in gold.* From the earliest times humans have prized silver and gold as precious. The record does not say how Abraham was able to gather so much wealth. Probably he traded cattle for silver and gold. In the O.T. there is

a definite relationship between fidelity to God and material benefits. God blessed the patriarch exceedingly and the surrounding people knew that God was his mentor.

13.7 The strife between the herdsmen of Abram and Lot represents the first threat to the promise of God that Abram would possess the land. He lived above this threat in faith, and his gracious attitude toward Lot was rewarded by another confirmation of the promise by God (see vv. 14–17 and ch. 15).

13.9 Abram depended on God. He manifested this truth when he arranged for Lot to choose where he would go. Lot chose what was, humanly speaking, the more attractive place for his cattle. But with every rose there is a thorn; Lot's choice brought disaster to him and to his family.

the Jordan was well watered everywhere like the garden of the Lord, like the land of Egypt, in the direction of Zoar; this was before the Lord had destroyed Sodom and Gomorrah. 11 So Lot chose for himself all the plain of the Jordan, and Lot journeyed eastward; thus they separated from each other. 12 Abram settled in the land of Canaan, while Lot settled among the cities of the Plain and moved his tent as far as Sodom. 13 Now the people of Sodom were wicked, great sinners against the Lord.

3. Abram chooses Hebron

14 The Lord said to Abram, after Lot had separated from him, "Raise your eyes now, and look from the place where you are, northward and southward and eastward and westward; 15 for all the land that you see I will give to you and to your offspringʰ forever. 16 I will make your offspring like the dust of the earth; so that if one can count the dust of the earth, your offspring also can be counted. 17 Rise up, walk through the length and the breadth of the land, for I will give it to you." 18 So Abram moved his tent, and came and settled by the oaksⁱ of Mamre, which are at Hebron; and there he built an altar to the Lord.

D. Abram delivers Lot

1. The war of the kings

14 In the days of King Amraphel of Shinar, King Arioch of Ellasar, King Chedorlaomer of Elam, and King Tidal of Goiim, 2 these kings made war with King Bera of Sodom, King Birsha of Gomorrah, King Shinab of Admah, King Shemeber of Zeboiim, and the king of Bela (that is, Zoar). 3 All these joined forces in the Valley of Siddim (that is, the Dead Sea).ʲ 4 Twelve years they had served Chedorlaomer, but in the thirteenth year they rebelled. 5 In the fourteenth year Chedorlaomer and the kings who were with him came and subdued the Rephaim in Ashteroth-karnaim, the Zuzim in Ham, the Emim in Shaveh-kiriathaim, 6 and the Horites in the hill country of Seir as far as El-paran on the edge of the wilderness; 7 then they turned back and came to En-mishpat (that is, Kadesh), and subdued all the country of the Amalekites, and also the Amorites who lived in Hazazon-tamar. 8 Then the king of Sodom, the king of Gomorrah, the king of Admah, the king of Zeboiim, and the king of Bela (that is, Zoar) went out, and they joined battle in the Valley of Siddim 9 with King Chedorlaomer of Elam, King Tidal of Goiim, King Amraphel of Shinar, and King Arioch of Ellasar, four kings against five. 10 Now the Valley of Siddim was full of bitumen pits; and as the kings of Sodom and Gomorrah fled, some fell into them, and the rest fled to the hill country. 11 So the enemy took all the goods of Sodom and Gomorrah, and all their provisions, and went their way; 12 they also took Lot, the son of Abram's brother, who lived in Sodom, and his goods, and departed.

13 Then one who had escaped came and told Abram the Hebrew, who was living by the oaksⁱ of Mamre the Amorite, brother of Eshcol and of Aner; these were allies of Abram. 14 When Abram heard that his nephew

ʰ Heb *seed*   ⁱ Or *terebinths*   ʲ Heb *Salt Sea*

13.12
Gen 19.29
13.13
Gen 18.20;
2 Pet 2.7, 8

13.14
Gen 28.14;
Deut 3.27
13.15
Gen 12.7;
17.8;
Deut 34.3;
Acts 7.5;
2 Chr 20.7
13.16
Gen 16.10;
28.14
13.17
Num 13.17-24
13.18
Gen 14.13;
35.27

14.1
Isa 11.11;
Dan 8.2
14.2
Gen 10.19;
Deut 29.23;
Gen 13.10
14.3
Num 34.12;
Deut 3.17;
Josh 3.16
14.5
Gen 15.20;
Deut 2.20
14.6
Deut 2.12, 22
14.7
2 Chr 20.2

14.11
vv. 16, 21
14.12
Gen 12.5;
13.12
14.13
Gen 13.18;
v. 24
14.14
Gen 13.8;
15.3

13.13 Lot could not have been unaware of the fact that the people of Sodom were wicked. The text literally reads that they were "wicked and sinners exceedingly". It is hard to understand why any follower of God would choose to reside among people like that. **14.7** Archaeology has found that these kings so devastated the area from Transjordan down to Kadesh-barnea that sedentary culture stopped ca. the 20th century B.C. **14.12** Lot's decision to settle in Sodom and Gomorrah was unwise. The Scriptures consistently warn

about fraternization with unbelieving people. The apostle Peter says that Lot was "a righteous man . . . tormented . . . by their lawless deeds" (2 Pet 2.7,8). Why he did not remove himself and his family from that rotten environment is not known. He smarted for his sin, was taken captive, was delivered by Abram, and was at last delivered from Sodom and Gomorrah when God destroyed them. Here we see the kindness and mercy of God displayed to a saved but backslidden Lot and his family. *the son of Abram's brother*, i.e., "his nephew."

had been taken captive, he led forth his trained men, born in his house, three hundred eighteen of them, and went in pursuit as far as Dan. 15 He divided his forces against them by night, he and his servants, and routed them and pursued them to Hobah, north of Damascus. 16 Then he brought back all the goods, and also brought back his nephew Lot with his goods, and the women and the people.

14.16
vv. 11, 12

2. Melchizedek and Abram's tithe

17 After his return from the defeat of Chedorlaomer and the kings who were with him, the king of Sodom went out to meet him at the Valley of Shaveh (that is, the King's Valley). 18 And King Melchizedek of Salem brought out bread and wine; he was priest of God Most High.^k 19 He blessed him and said,

14.17
1 Sam 18.6, 18
14.18
Heb 7.1;
Ps 110.4;
Heb 5.6, 10
14.19
v. 22;
Mt 11.25
14.20
Gen 24.27;
Heb 7.4

"Blessed be Abram by God Most High,^k
    maker of heaven and earth;
20 and blessed be God Most High,^k
    who has delivered your enemies into your hand!"

3. Abram's refusal to take spoil

And Abram gave him one-tenth of everything. 21 Then the king of Sodom said to Abram, "Give me the persons, but take the goods for yourself." 22 But Abram said to the king of Sodom, "I have sworn to the LORD, God Most High,^k maker of heaven and earth, 23 that I would not take a thread or a sandal-thong or anything that is yours, so that you might not say, 'I have made Abram rich.' 24 I will take nothing but what the young men have eaten, and the share of the men who went with me — Aner, Eshcol, and Mamre. Let them take their share."

14.22
Dan 12.7;
v. 19
14.23
2 Kings 5.16

E. The Abramic covenant

1. The promise of an heir

15 After these things the word of the LORD came to Abram in a vision, "Do not be afraid, Abram, I am your shield; your reward shall be very great." 2 But Abram said, "O Lord GOD, what will you give me, for I continue childless, and the heir of my house is Eliezer of Damascus?"^l 3 And Abram said, "You have given me no offspring, and so a slave born

15.1
Dan 10.1;
Gen 21.17;
26.24;
Deut 33.29;
Prov 11.8
15.2f
Acts 7.5
15.3
Gen 14.14

^k Heb El Elyon ^l Meaning of Heb uncertain

14.14 Abraham was not only wealthy; he had a large retinue of servants attached to him as well. They must have been instructed in the skills of warfare, for when Abram delivered Lot from captivity, it was accomplished by force. These military personnel were born in Abram's house.
14.18 Melchizedek, whose name means "king of righteousness," was the king of Salem and a priest of God. The author of Hebrews presents him as a representation of Christ and speaks of Christ's priesthood as springing from Melchizedek. In other words, Christ's priesthood preceded the priesthood of Aaron, was superior to it, and is eternal (see Heb 5.6–10; 7.1–28).
14.20 Tithing has a long history. This is the first instance in the O.T. of a practice that is widely taught and practiced today. Abram paid tithes to Melchizedek, priest of God Most High. That is, in addition to Abram and his family, there were other true believers who worshiped and served the living God. Abram's tithing practice was carried on by Jacob, who at Bethel promised to tithe (28.22).
14.22 I have sworn, i.e., "I have solemnly promised." Oaths, covenants, or promises have been employed from earliest time. God himself used oaths

(e.g., to show his immutability, see 22.16; Num 14.28; Heb 6.16,17). Oaths were used in the O.T. (1) to confirm covenants (26.28ff; 31.44,53); (2) to resolve controversies in courts of law (Ex 22.11; Num 5.19); and (3) to guarantee the carrying out of promised acts (50.25). Followers of God have been forbidden to take oaths in the name of idols and created things (Josh 23.7; Mt 5.34–36; Jas 5.12). Jesus taught that believers should do what they promise without making oaths; their pledged word should be all that is needed (Mt 5.34–37).
15.1 God appeared to Abram in a vision and spoke to him. Visions were not frequent, but there is no reason to suppose that God cannot visit people in visions today, even though the revelation of God is complete in the Bible. If there should be any visions, they would not include further revelation, because nothing can be added to the Bible (see note on Ps 89.19).
15.2,3 The Nuzu tablets indicate that childless couples often adopted a slave who would care for them, give them a proper burial, then inherit their estate, unless a son was born after the slave's adoption. In that event, the slave heir was usually disinherited.

in my house is to be my heir." 4 But the word of the LORD came to him, "This man shall not be your heir; no one but your very own issue shall be your heir." 5 He brought him outside and said, "Look toward heaven and count the stars, if you are able to count them." Then he said to him, "So shall your descendants be." 6 And he believed the LORD; and the LORD *m* reckoned it to him as righteousness.

15.4
Gal 4.28
15.5
Ps 147.4;
Jer 33.22;
Gen 22.17;
Rom 4.18;
Heb 11.12

2. The sacrifice offered

7 Then he said to him, "I am the LORD who brought you from Ur of the Chaldeans, to give you this land to possess." 8 But he said, "O Lord GOD, how am I to know that I shall possess it?" 9 He said to him, "Bring me a heifer three years old, a female goat three years old, a ram three years old, a turtledove, and a young pigeon." 10 He brought him all these and cut them in two, laying each half over against the other; but he did not cut the birds in two. 11 And when birds of prey came down on the carcasses, Abram drove them away.

15.7
Gen 11.31;
13.15, 17
15.8
Lk 1.18
15.10
Jer 34.18;
Lev 1.17

12 As the sun was going down, a deep sleep fell upon Abram, and a deep and terrifying darkness descended upon him. 13 Then the LORD *m* said to Abram, "Know this for certain, that your offspring shall be aliens in a land that is not theirs, and shall be slaves there, and they shall be oppressed for four hundred years; 14 but I will bring judgment on the nation that they serve, and afterward they shall come out with great possessions. 15 As for yourself, you shall go to your ancestors in peace; you shall be buried in a good old age. 16 And they shall come back here in the fourth generation; for the iniquity of the Amorites is not yet complete."

15.12
Gen 2.21
15.13
Acts 7.6;
Ex 12.40
15.14
Ex 12.36
15.15
Gen 25.8
15.16
1 Kings 21.26

3. The promise of a land

17 When the sun had gone down and it was dark, a smoking fire pot and a flaming torch passed between these pieces. 18 On that day the LORD made a covenant with Abram, saying, "To your descendants I give this land, from the river of Egypt to the great river, the river Euphrates, 19 the land of the Kenites, the Kenizzites, the Kadmonites, 20 the Hittites, the Perizzites, the Rephaim, 21 the Amorites, the Canaanites, the Girgashites, and the Jebusites."

15.17
Jer 34.18, 19
15.18
Gen 24.7;
12.7;
Ex 23.31;
Num 34.3;
Deut 11.24;
Josh 1.4

F. The birth of Ishmael

1. Sarai gives Hagar to Abram

16 Now Sarai, Abram's wife, bore him no children. She had an Egyptian slave-girl whose name was Hagar, 2 and Sarai said to

16.1
Gen 11.30;
21.9;
Gal 4.24
16.2
Gen 30.3, 4,
9, 10

m Heb *he*

15.6 In the covenant of the O.T., salvation was by grace through faith, just as it is in the new covenant. Abram was saved the same way every believer is saved today. Indeed, Paul uses Abram as a prime illustration of one who was justified by his faith, a new birth which occurred before his circumcision. Circumcision, then, was a seal that followed, not preceded, faith.
15.8ff Abram heard the voice of God and his promise. He wanted to be sure that he was not mistaken, so he asked for outward corroboratory evidence to certify the promise to him. The smoking furnace and the burning lamp (v. 17) supplied him with that evidence. What Abram asked for is similar to the request of Gideon in Judg 6.36ff.
15.10 *cut them in two.* In 15.18 the Hebrew reads that God "cut a covenant" with Abram. Cutting animals in half is related to that phrase. Data found at Qatna and Mari indicate that covenants were sealed by a ritual involving the cutting up of asses.

15.13 God revealed some of his descendants' future history to Abram. The bondage in Egypt is set forth and its length (400 years) specified. This bondage was part of the divine plan for the numerical growth of the Hebrew race.
15.16 *fourth generation.* At that time a generation was a hundred years. Later on, with the decline in longevity, it became less. *the iniquity of the Amorites is not yet complete,* i.e., punishment will come when their wickedness has come to full flower.
15.18 *river of Egypt,* i.e., "Wadi-el-Arish," at the southern border of Judah.
16.2,3 Abram was seventy-five years old when he left Haran and received God's covenantal promise (12.4). Inherent in the covenant was the promise of offspring. Now at eighty-five years, it appeared quite impossible of fulfillment. *Sarai, Abram's wife, took Hagar . . . and gave her to her husband Abram as a wife.* Archaeological evidence of Nuzu customs indicates that in some marriage contracts a childless wife was

Abram, "You see that the Lord has prevented me from bearing children; go in to my slave-girl; it may be that I shall obtain children by her." And Abram listened to the voice of Sarai. ³So, after Abram had lived ten years in the land of Canaan, Sarai, Abram's wife, took Hagar the Egyptian, her slave-girl, and gave her to her husband Abram as a wife. ⁴He went in to Hagar, and she conceived; and when she saw that she had conceived, she looked with contempt on her mistress. ⁵Then Sarai said to Abram, "May the wrong done to me be on you! I gave my slave-girl to your embrace, and when she saw that she had conceived, she looked on me with contempt. May the Lord judge between you and me!" ⁶But Abram said to Sarai, "Your slave-girl is in your power; do to her as you please." Then Sarai dealt harshly with her, and she ran away from her.

16.3
Gen 12.5

16.5
Gen 31.53

2. God's promise to Hagar

7 The angel of the Lord found her by a spring of water in the wilderness, the spring on the way to Shur. ⁸And he said, "Hagar, slave-girl of Sarai, where have you come from and where are you going?" She said, "I am running away from my mistress Sarai." ⁹The angel of the Lord said to her, "Return to your mistress, and submit to her." ¹⁰The angel of the Lord also said to her, "I will so greatly multiply your offspring that they cannot be counted for multitude." ¹¹And the angel of the Lord said to her,

"Now you have conceived and shall bear a son;
   you shall call him Ishmael,ⁿ
for the Lord has given heed to your affliction.

12 He shall be a wild ass of a man,
   with his hand against everyone,
      and everyone's hand against him;
   and he shall live at odds with all his kin."

¹³So she named the Lord who spoke to her, "You are El-roi";ᵒ for she said, "Have I really seen God and remained alive after seeing him?"ᵖ ¹⁴Therefore the well was called Beer-lahai-roi;�q it lies between Kadesh and Bered.

16.7
Gen 21.17,
18; 22.11;
15; 31.11;
20.1

16.10
Gen 17.20

16.11
Ex 3.7, 9

16.12
Gen 25.18

16.13
Gen 32.30

3. The birth of the baby

15 Hagar bore Abram a son; and Abram named his son, whom Hagar bore, Ishmael. ¹⁶Abram was eighty-six years old when Hagar bore himʳ Ishmael.

16.15
Gal 4.22

ⁿ That is *God hears*   ᵒ Perhaps *God of seeing* or *God who sees*   ᵖ Meaning of Heb uncertain   q That is *the Well of the Living One who sees me*   ʳ Heb *Abram*

required to furnish a substitute for her husband. In oriental eyes, childlessness was the greatest of tragedies. Nuzu custom stipulated further that the slave wife and her children could not be sent away. Thus the action of Sarai and Abram was undoubtedly consonant with the customs of that day. When Abram was eighty-six years of age Hagar gave birth to Ishmael (16.16). This incident reveals how two genuine believers may seek to fulfill God's will by culturally acceptable methods but spiritually carnal ones. The promise of God was not to Hagar but to Sarai. Sarai suggested the use of Hagar, and Abram consented to the arrangement. Both were guilty. The birth of Ishamel introduced a people (the nucleus of the later Muslims) who have been a challenge both to the Jews and the Christian Church. It was not until Abram was a hundred years old that Isaac was born (21.5). From the length of time between the promise and the fulfillment we learn that God's ways are not our ways and

his thoughts are higher than our thoughts (Isa 55.8, 9).
16.5 Sarai experiences the contempt of Hagar who has borne a son for Abram. Had she trusted God in the first place, this would not have happened. Implicitly, she seems to place the blame on Abraham rather than herself.
16.7 *angel of the Lord.* See note on Ex 3.2.
16.14 The well of Beer-lahai-roi, located near Kadesh (called Kadesh-barnea in Num 32.8 and 34.4, as well as in Deuteronomy and Joshua), denotes how far Hagar had wandered in the wilderness. Isaac dwelt in this region (24.62; 25.11).
16.15 *Ishmael* means "God (is) hearing." God promised that Ishmael would beget twelve princes (17.20), so Abram was the ancestor of the twelve tribes of Ishmael and the twelve tribes of Israel, who have been enemies. Isaac and Ishmael met again at the funeral of their common father (25.9).

G. The circumcision of Abraham

1. The covenant restated

17 When Abram was ninety-nine years old, the LORD appeared to Abram, and said to him, "I am God Almighty;*s* walk before me, and be blameless. 2 And I will make my covenant between me and you, and will make you exceedingly numerous." 3 Then Abram fell on his face; and God said to him, 4 "As for me, this is my covenant with you: You shall be the ancestor of a multitude of nations. 5 No longer shall your name be Abram,*t* but your name shall be Abraham;*u* for I have made you the ancestor of a multitude of nations. 6 I will make you exceedingly fruitful; and I will make nations of you, and kings shall come from you. 7 I will establish my covenant between me and you, and your offspring after you throughout their generations, for an everlasting covenant, to be God to you and to your offspring*v* after you. 8 And I will give to you, and to your offspring after you, the land where you are now an alien, all the land of Canaan, for a perpetual holding; and I will be their God."

2. The sign of the covenant

9 God said to Abraham, "As for you, you shall keep my covenant, you and your offspring after you throughout their generations. 10 This is my covenant, which you shall keep, between me and you and your offspring after you: Every male among you shall be circumcised. 11 You shall circumcise the flesh of your foreskins, and it shall be a sign of the covenant between me and you. 12 Throughout your generations every male among you shall be circumcised when he is eight days old, including the slave born in your house and the one bought with your money from any foreigner who is not of your offspring. 13 Both the slave born in your house and the one bought with your money must be circumcised. So shall my covenant be in your flesh an everlasting covenant. 14 Any uncircumcised male who is not circumcised in the flesh of his foreskin shall be cut off from his people; he has broken my covenant."

3. The promise of Isaac

15 God said to Abraham, "As for Sarai your wife, you shall not call her Sarai, but Sarah shall be her name. 16 I will bless her, and moreover I will give you a son by her. I will bless her, and she shall give rise to nations; kings of peoples shall come from her." 17 Then Abraham fell on

s Traditional rendering of Heb *El Shaddai*   *t* That is *exalted ancestor*   *u* Here taken to mean *ancestor of a multitude*   *v* Heb *seed*

17.1
Gen 28.3;
Ex 6.3;
Deut 18.13
17.2
Gen 15.18
17.4
Gen 35.11;
48.19
17.5
Neh 9.7;
Rom 4.17
17.6
Gen 35.11;
Mt 1.6
17.7
Gal 3.17;
Gen 26.24;
28.13;
Rom 9.8
17.8
Gen 12.7;
Ps 105.9, 11;
Gen 23.4;
28.4;
Ex 6.7;
Lev 26.12
17.10
Acts 7.8
17.11
Ex 12.48;
Deut 10.16;
Rom 4.11
17.12
Lev 12.3;
Lk 2.21
17.14
Ex 4.24
17.16
Gen 18.10;
35.11;
Gal 4.31
17.17
Gen 18.12;
21.6

17.1 *God Almighty (El Shaddai)* comes from the Hebrew root word *shadad*, meaning "violent," or "irresistibly strong." Another interpretation has it as "God of the mountain," because God appeared to Abram on the mountain. Thus no nature worship or animism was implied. Abram was ninety-nine years old when God appeared to him as *El Shaddai*, at a time when the birth of a son by Sarai seemed impossible; a year later Isaac was born. The Almighty stepped in and did the impossible. This Almighty God is also (1) eternal (1.1); (2) infinite and omnipresent (Ps 139.7–10); (3) immutable (Mal 3.6; Ps 102.26, 27; Jas 1.17); (4) omniscient (Ps 147.5; Acts 15.18; Ps 139.1–6; Prov 5.21); (5) holy (Isa 6.3; Ps 99.9); (6) just (Deut 32.4; Rev 15.3,4); (7) love (1 Jn 4.8,16). At Calvary, "steadfast love and faithfulness will meet; righteousness and peace will kiss other" (Ps 85.10).
17.9,10 God changed Abram's name to Abraham (meaning "ancestor of a multitude," cf. NRSV footnote) and instituted circumcision as the seal or sign of the covenant he had made with him (17.11). Any

failure to keep the seal meant that the individual was to be cut off from the people of Israel. Moses reiterated the law of circumcision (Lev 12; Jn 7.22,23). Circumcision as a seal was abolished in the N.T. (Eph 2.11–15; Col 3.11); to insist on it was to become a legalist (see Acts 15.1ff). Circumcision now is of the heart and not of the flesh (Deut 30.6; Jer 4.4; Rom 2.28,29), but even under the Abrahamic covenant it was useless unless accompanied by saving faith. Abraham himself was justified by faith (Gen 15.6; Rom 2.25; 3.30; 1 Cor 7.19; Gal 5.6).
17.15 The promise to Abraham that Sarai would have a child was ratified by a change in her name, even as Abram became Abraham. Sarai meant "my princess," which limited her honor to one family. But in Isaac Abraham's seed was to have greater significance. So God changed Sarai's name to Sarah ("princess"). Verse 16 says that she "shall (i.e., in addition to being Isaac's mother) give rise to nations; kings of peoples shall come from her." Through her offspring the Messiah-king would come.

his face and laughed, and said to himself, "Can a child be born to a man who is a hundred years old? Can Sarah, who is ninety years old, bear a child?" 18 And Abraham said to God, "O that Ishmael might live in your sight!" 19 God said, "No, but your wife Sarah shall bear you a son, and you shall name him Isaac.*w* I will establish my covenant with him as an everlasting covenant for his offspring after him. 20 As for Ishmael, I have heard you; I will bless him and make him fruitful and exceedingly numerous; he shall be the father of twelve princes, and I will make him a great nation. 21 But my covenant I will establish with Isaac, whom Sarah shall bear to you at this season next year." 22 And when he had finished talking with him, God went up from Abraham.

4. The circumcisions performed

23 Then Abraham took his son Ishmael and all the slaves born in his house or bought with his money, every male among the men of Abraham's house, and he circumcised the flesh of their foreskins that very day, as God had said to him. 24 Abraham was ninety-nine years old when he was circumcised in the flesh of his foreskin. 25 And his son Ishmael was thirteen years old when he was circumcised in the flesh of his foreskin. 26 That very day Abraham and his son Ishmael were circumcised; 27 and all the men of his house, slaves born in the house and those bought with money from a foreigner, were circumcised with him.

H. Sodom and Gomorrah destroyed

1. Abraham entertains heavenly visitors

18 The LORD appeared to Abraham*x* by the oaks*y* of Mamre, as he sat at the entrance of his tent in the heat of the day. 2 He looked up and saw three men standing near him. When he saw them, he ran from the tent entrance to meet them, and bowed down to the ground. 3 He said, "My lord, if I find favor with you, do not pass by your servant. 4 Let a little water be brought, and wash your feet, and rest yourselves under the tree. 5 Let me bring a little bread, that you may refresh yourselves, and after that you may pass on — since you have come to your servant." So they said, "Do as you have said." 6 And Abraham hastened into the tent to Sarah, and said, "Make ready quickly three measures*z* of choice flour, knead it, and make cakes." 7 Abraham ran to the herd, and took a calf, tender and good, and gave it to the servant, who hastened to prepare it. 8 Then he took curds and milk and the calf that he had prepared, and set it before them; and he stood by them under the tree while they ate.

2. Sarah laughs

9 They said to him, "Where is your wife Sarah?" And he said, "There, in the tent." 10 Then one said, "I will surely return to you in due season, and your wife Sarah shall have a son." And Sarah was listening at the tent entrance behind him. 11 Now Abraham and Sarah were old, advanced in

Cross-references (left and center margin)

17.19 Gen 18.10; 21.2; 26.2-5
17.20 Gen 16.10; 25.12, 16
17.23 Gen 14.14
17.24 Rom 4.11
18.1 Gen 13.18; 14.13
18.2 vv. 16, 22; Gen 32.24; Josh 5.13; Judg 13.6-11
18.4 Gen 19.2; 43.24
18.5 Judg 6.18, 19; 13.15, 16
18.8 Gen 19.3
18.10 Rom 9.9
18.11 Gen 17.17; Rom 4.19

w That is *he laughs*   *x* Heb *him*   *y* Or *terebinths*   *z* Heb *seahs*

17.17 After twenty-four years of impatient waiting, the words of God seem an idle fancy to Abraham. All of the outward circumstances were against him. The biological facts of life stood over against the promise of God. Sight and sense told him the promise was impossible of fulfillment. Yet Abraham was a man of faith who had moments of doubts. How much we can learn from his laugh of disbelief here.
17.18 Abraham still hoped that Ishmael would be recognized, but this plea and God's answer in v. 19 show that man's answers and ways can never be substituted for God's.

17.22–27 Abraham's faith triumphed over his doubts. He responded to the covenant by circumcising himself and all his males. Thus he passed another crucial stage in his walk and experience with the covenant-keeping God.
18.2 *three men.* Apparently one was Yahweh (God), accompanied by two angels. Abraham said, "my lord" (v. 3; cf. "LORD" in vv. 13,26), not "my lords," suggesting that he knew there was a difference between the Lord and the two angels. In 19.1 the two angels go to Sodom to destroy the city, while the Lord stays behind.

age; it had ceased to be with Sarah after the manner of women. 12 So Sarah laughed to herself, saying, "After I have grown old, and my husband is old, shall I have pleasure?" 13 The LORD said to Abraham, "Why did Sarah laugh, and say, 'Shall I indeed bear a child, now that I am old?' 14 Is anything too wonderful for the LORD? At the set time I will return to you, in due season, and Sarah shall have a son." 15 But Sarah denied, saying, "I did not laugh"; for she was afraid. He said, "Oh yes, you did laugh."

18.12ff
1 Pet 3.6

18.14
Jer 32.17, 27;
Zech 8.6;
Mt 3.9;
Lk 1.37

3. God informs Abraham of the end of Sodom and Gomorrah

16 Then the men set out from there, and they looked toward Sodom; and Abraham went with them to set them on their way. 17 The LORD said, "Shall I hide from Abraham what I am about to do, 18 seeing that Abraham shall become a great and mighty nation, and all the nations of the earth shall be blessed in him?ᵃ 19 No, for I have chosenᵇ him, that he may charge his children and his household after him to keep the way of the LORD by doing righteousness and justice; so that the LORD may bring about for Abraham what he has promised him." 20 Then the LORD said, "How great is the outcry against Sodom and Gomorrah and how very grave their sin! 21 I must go down and see whether they have done altogether according to the outcry that has come to me; and if not, I will know."

18.18
Gal 3.8

18.19
Deut 4.9, 10;
6.7;
Josh 24.15;
Eph 6.4
18.20
Gen 19.13;
Ezek 16.49,
50
18.21
Gen 11.5

4. Abraham intercedes for Sodom

22 So the men turned from there, and went toward Sodom, while Abraham remained standing before the LORD.ᶜ 23 Then Abraham came near and said, "Will you indeed sweep away the righteous with the wicked? 24 Suppose there are fifty righteous within the city; will you then sweep away the place and not forgive it for the fifty righteous who are in it? 25 Far be it from you to do such a thing, to slay the righteous with the wicked, so that the righteous fare as the wicked! Far be that from you! Shall not the Judge of all the earth do what is just?" 26 And the LORD said, "If I find at Sodom fifty righteous in the city, I will forgive the whole place for their sake." 27 Abraham answered, "Let me take it upon myself to speak to the Lord, I who am but dust and ashes. 28 Suppose five of the fifty righteous are lacking. Will you destroy the whole city for lack of five?" And he said, "I will not destroy it if I find forty-five there." 29 Again he spoke to him, "Suppose forty are found there." He answered, "For the sake of forty I will not do it." 30 Then he said, "Oh do not let the Lord be angry if I speak. Suppose thirty are found there." He answered, "I will not do it, if I find thirty there." 31 He said, "Let me take it upon myself to speak to the Lord. Suppose twenty are found there." He answered, "For the sake of twenty I will not destroy it." 32 Then he said, "Oh do

18.22
Gen 19.1
18.23
Heb 10.22;
Num 16.22
18.24
Jer 5.1

18.25
Job 8.20;
Isa 3.10, 11;
Rom 3.6

18.27
Gen 3.19;
Job 4.19;
30.19; 42.6;
2 Cor 5.1

18.32
Judg 6.39;
Jas 5.16

ᵃ Or and all the nations of the earth shall bless themselves by him   ᵇ Heb known   ᶜ Another ancient tradition reads while the LORD remained standing before Abraham

18.12–15 Sarah, like us, went through periods of doubt and disbelief. Sarah's laughter in her heart explains why God said to Abraham, "Is anything too wonderful for the LORD? At the set time . . . Sarah shall have a son." Here God's purpose was not annulled at the disbelief of Sarah.
18.17–19 These verses convey God's intention to let Abraham know what he would do and his reason for doing it. This was a soliloquy in which God was speaking his inner thoughts, intentions, and reasonings. It was given through the Holy Spirit's revelation to Moses, the author of the book.
18.25 God is love (1 Jn 4.8) but he is also just (Ps 89.14; 145.17). The judgments of God are: (1) according to truth (Rev 19.2); (2) universal and certain (Rom 2.6); (3) impartial (Rom 2.11); (4) based on the

state of our hearts as well as our outward acts (Rom 2.16; Lk 12.2,3). Three major judgments of God are mentioned in Scripture: (1) the judgment of believers' sins, which were taken care of at Calvary (Jn 5.24; Rom 8.1); (2) the believers' judgment for rewards (Rom 14.10; 1 Cor 3.10–15; 2 Cor 5.10); and (3) the judgment of unbelievers at the great white throne (Rev 20.11–15).
18.32 Abraham offered six petitions for Sodom. God said "yes" six times. He did not stop answering until Abraham stopped asking. This incident should encourage every Christian to expect God to answer prayer. In Sodom's case it is clear that the city's spiritual state was so awful that it did not contain even ten righteous people.

not let the Lord be angry if I speak just once more. Suppose ten are found there." He answered, "For the sake of ten I will not destroy it." 33 And the Lord went his way, when he had finished speaking to Abraham; and Abraham returned to his place.

5. Lot entertains two angels

19 The two angels came to Sodom in the evening, and Lot was sitting in the gateway of Sodom. When Lot saw them, he rose to meet them, and bowed down with his face to the ground. 2 He said, "Please, my lords, turn aside to your servant's house and spend the night, and wash your feet; then you can rise early and go on your way." They said, "No; we will spend the night in the square." 3 But he urged them strongly; so they turned aside to him and entered his house; and he made them a feast, and baked unleavened bread, and they ate. 4 But before they lay down, the men of the city, the men of Sodom, both young and old, all the people to the last man, surrounded the house; 5 and they called to Lot, "Where are the men who came to you tonight? Bring them out to us, so that we may know them." 6 Lot went out of the door to the men, shut the door after him, 7 and said, "I beg you, my brothers, do not act so wickedly. 8 Look, I have two daughters who have not known a man; let me bring them out to you, and do to them as you please; only do nothing to these men, for they have come under the shelter of my roof." 9 But they replied, "Stand back!" And they said, "This fellow came here as an alien, and he would play the judge! Now we will deal worse with you than with them." Then they pressed hard against the man Lot, and came near the door to break it down. 10 But the men inside reached out their hands and brought Lot into the house with them, and shut the door. 11 And they struck with blindness the men who were at the door of the house, both small and great, so that they were unable to find the door.

6. Lot informed of the imminent destruction

12 Then the men said to Lot, "Have you anyone else here? Sons-in-law, sons, daughters, or anyone you have in the city — bring them out of the place. 13 For we are about to destroy this place, because the outcry against its people has become great before the Lord, and the Lord has sent us to destroy it." 14 So Lot went out and said to his sons-in-law, who were to marry his daughters, "Up, get out of this place; for the Lord is about to destroy the city." But he seemed to his sons-in-law to be jesting.

7. The departure of the family of Lot

15 When morning dawned, the angels urged Lot, saying, "Get up, take your wife and your two daughters who are here, or else you will be consumed in the punishment of the city." 16 But he lingered; so the men seized him and his wife and his two daughters by the hand, the Lord being merciful to him, and they brought him out and left him outside the city.

Cross references (left margin):

19.1
Gen 18.22;
18.1ff
19.2
Heb 13.2;
Gen 18.4

19.3
Gen 18.8

19.5
Isa 3.9;
Judg 19.22;
Rom 1.24
19.6
Judg 19.23
19.8
see
Judg 19.24
19.9
2 Pet 2.7, 8;
Ex 2.14

19.11
see
2 Kings 6.18;
Acts 13.11

19.12
Gen 7.1;
2 Pet 2.7, 9
19.13
Gen 18.20;
1 Chr 21.15
19.14
Num 16.21;
Ex 9.21;
Lk 17.28

19.15
Num 16.24,
26;
Rev 18.4
19.16
Lk 18.13;
Ps 34.22

19.1 Abraham and Lot were both righteous men (15.6; 2 Pet 2.7,8), yet their world and life views differed greatly. Abraham had his eyes fixed on "the . . . city whose architect and builder is God" (Heb 11.10). Lot looked toward the secular city of humanity, his thoughts centering on the "here and now" without regard for eternity. He chose Sodom (13.5ff) and ended up bankrupt.

19.5 that we may know them. The Sodomites wanted to have homosexual relations with these male strangers. It is reinforced by the fact that Lot offered his two daughters who "have not known a man" — which could only have reference to sexual relations between a male and a female. The fact that he was willing to sacrifice his daughters indicates how seriously the people of those days took their responsibility of caring for the strangers who lodged in their homes as guests.

19.13 the Lord has sent us to destroy it. The incident tells us something about the power of angels, who exist to do the bidding of God. That same angelic power is available to the saints of God, for God has given his angels charge over us as ministering spirits (Heb 1.14).

19.14 Lot was a true believer but suffered from severe family difficulties. His two daughters apparently were to marry unbelievers who thought Lot was joking when he forecast the destruction of their city. These two men died as a consequence of their unbelief.

17 When they had brought them outside, they[d] said, "Flee for your life; do not look back or stop anywhere in the Plain; flee to the hills, or else you will be consumed." 18 And Lot said to them, "Oh, no, my lords; 19 your servant has found favor with you, and you have shown me great kindness in saving my life; but I cannot flee to the hills, for fear the disaster will overtake me and I die. 20 Look, that city is near enough to flee to, and it is a little one. Let me escape there — is it not a little one? — and my life will be saved!" 21 He said to him, "Very well, I grant you this favor too, and will not overthrow the city of which you have spoken. 22 Hurry, escape there, for I can do nothing until you arrive there." Therefore the city was called Zoar.[e] 23 The sun had risen on the earth when Lot came to Zoar.

8. Sodom and Gomorrah destroyed

24 Then the LORD rained on Sodom and Gomorrah sulfur and fire from the LORD out of heaven; 25 and he overthrew those cities, and all the Plain, and all the inhabitants of the cities, and what grew on the ground. 26 But Lot's wife, behind him, looked back, and she became a pillar of salt.

27 Abraham went early in the morning to the place where he had stood before the LORD; 28 and he looked down toward Sodom and Gomorrah and toward all the land of the Plain and saw the smoke of the land going up like the smoke of a furnace.

29 So it was that, when God destroyed the cities of the Plain, God remembered Abraham, and sent Lot out of the midst of the overthrow, when he overthrew the cities in which Lot had settled.

9. The sin of Lot's daughters:
the origins of the Moabites and Ammonites

30 Now Lot went up out of Zoar and settled in the hills with his two daughters, for he was afraid to stay in Zoar; so he lived in a cave with his two daughters. 31 And the firstborn said to the younger, "Our father is old, and there is not a man on earth to come in to us after the manner of all the world. 32 Come, let us make our father drink wine, and we will lie with him, so that we may preserve offspring through our father." 33 So they made their father drink wine that night; and the firstborn went in, and lay with her father; he did not know when she lay down or when she rose. 34 On the next day, the firstborn said to the younger, "Look, I lay last night with my father; let us make him drink wine tonight also; then you go in and lie with him, so that we may preserve offspring through our father." 35 So they made their father drink wine that night also; and the younger rose, and lay with him; and he did not know when she lay down or when she rose. 36 Thus both the daughters of Lot became pregnant by

d Gk Syr Vg: Heb *he*   *e* That is *Little*

Marginal references:

19.17 1 Kings 19.3; Jer 48.6; v. 26

19.21 Job 42.8, 9; Ps 145.9

19.24 Deut 29.23; Isa 13.19; Lk 17.29; Jude 7

19.25 Ps 107.34

19.26 Lk 17.32

19.27 Gen 18.22

19.28 Rev 9.2; 18.9

19.29 2 Pet 2.7

19.31 Gen 38.8, 9; Deut 25.5

19.32 Mk 12.19

19.17 *do not look back .* Scripture admonishes us to forget those things which are behind, not to look back, but rather to go forward (Phil 3.13). Though we cannot change the past, we need not carry it with us into the future.

19.22 *Zoar.* Its exact location is now unknown, yet it must have been within walking distance of Sodom and Gomorrah.

19.24 Sodom and Gomorrah were located in the Valley of Siddim (or the Valley of the Dead Sea). The area was filled with bitumen pits (14.3,10) and God probably sent an earthquake or lightning to destroy the two cities.

19.26 *Lot's wife . . . looked back, and she became a pillar of salt.* This appeared to be a small sin, but it was a great one because Lot's wife had been expressly

told not to look back. Lot's wife either disbelieved the angels, who warned them not to look back, or she was defiantly disobedient (v.26). Scripture everywhere declares that disbelief and defiance have their own rewards. The punishment tells us something about the gravity of the sin, for the Scriptures say that the worse the sin is, the greater the penalty. Jesus specifically refers to Lot's wife in Lk 17.32 and cautions his hearers to remember her.

19.30 Lot lost everything in the destruction of Sodom and Gomorrah. At the time he left Abraham, he had much wealth; now he is seen living in a cave. His last estate was due to his mistaken decision to identify himself with the people of Sodom.

19.36 Moab and Ammon were born of incest. Had Lot spurned the alcohol offered by his daughters, he

19.37
Deut 2.9
19.38
Deut 2.19

their father. 37 The firstborn bore a son, and named him Moab; he is the ancestor of the Moabites to this day. 38 The younger also bore a son and named him Ben-ammi; he is the ancestor of the Ammonites to this day.

I. Abraham and Abimelech

1. Abimelech's sin of ignorance

20.1
Gen 18.1;
16.7, 14;
26.6
20.2
v. 12;
Gen 12.13, 15
20.3
Ps 105.14;
Job 33.15;
Gen 26.11
20.5
1 Kings 9.4;
2 Kings 20.3

20 From there Abraham journeyed toward the region of the Negeb, and settled between Kadesh and Shur. While residing in Gerar as an alien, 2 Abraham said of his wife Sarah, "She is my sister." And King Abimelech of Gerar sent and took Sarah. 3 But God came to Abimelech in a dream by night, and said to him, "You are about to die because of the woman whom you have taken; for she is a married woman." 4 Now Abimelech had not approached her; so he said, "Lord, will you destroy an innocent people? 5 Did he not himself say to me, 'She is my sister'? And she herself said, 'He is my brother.' I did this in the integrity of my heart and the innocence of my hands." 6 Then God said to him in the dream, "Yes, I know that you did this in the integrity of your heart; furthermore it was I who kept you from sinning against me. Therefore I did not let

20.7
1 Sam 7.5;
Job 42.8

you touch her. 7 Now then, return the man's wife; for he is a prophet, and he will pray for you and you shall live. But if you do not restore her, know that you shall surely die, you and all that are yours."

2. Abraham's prayer for Abimelech

20.9
Gen 26.10;
Ex 32.21;
Josh 7.25;
Gen 34.7

8 So Abimelech rose early in the morning, and called all his servants and told them all these things; and the men were very much afraid. 9 Then Abimelech called Abraham, and said to him, "What have you done to us? How have I sinned against you, that you have brought such great guilt on me and my kingdom? You have done things to me that ought not to be done." 10 And Abimelech said to Abraham, "What were you thinking of, that you did this thing?" 11 Abraham said, "I did it because I thought, There is no fear of God at all in this place, and they will kill me because of my wife. 12 Besides, she is indeed my sister, the daughter of my father but not the daughter of my mother; and she became my wife. 13 And when God caused me to wander from my father's house, I said to her, 'This is the kindness you must do me: at every place to which we come, say of me, He is my brother.'" 14 Then Abimelech took sheep and oxen, and male and female slaves, and gave them to Abraham, and restored his wife Sarah to him. 15 Abimelech said, "My land is before you; settle where it pleases you." 16 To Sarah he said, "Look, I have given your brother a thousand pieces of silver; it is your exoneration before all who are with you; you are completely vindicated." 17 Then Abraham prayed to God; and God healed Abimelech, and also healed his wife and female slaves so

20.11
Ps 36.1;
Gen 12.12;
26.7

20.13
v. 5

20.14
Gen 12.16

20.15
Gen 13.9

20.17
Num 12.13;
Job 42.9

---

would not have cohabited with them. This verse marks the last we hear of Lot, and we do not know what became of him. Yet even in this case of incest, God used it to bring forth good and to glorify his name. Ruth was a Moabitess who married into the tribe of Judah and her name is listed in the genealogy of Jesus as an ancestress of the human Son of God.
19.37,38 See notes on Ezek 25.2,9 for information on the Ammonites and Moabites.
20.2 *She is my sister.* Abraham used this half-truth twice. He had not learned from his earlier experience that he could trust God in everything. So while he lied to protect himself, he opened the way for Sarah to commit adultery.
20.6 God respected the integrity of Abimelech. He kept Abimelech from sinning in ignorance when Abraham deceived him by failing to inform him that

Sarah was his wife. We too can expect God to protect us in similar situations, when our hearts are right but we lack knowledge of the true facts.
20.7 God said that Abraham was a prophet and that Abraham's prayer for Abimelech's deliverance would be answered. Why God spoke this way is not clear. Perhaps since Abraham thought there was no fear of God in that place (v. 11), he needed to learn that God is concerned for unbelievers whose intentions are not evil and that he can deliver them in cases of this sort.
20.17 *Abraham prayed to God.* Since Abraham was responsible for what had happened, it was proper that he should ask God to deliver the man and the family of the one he had wronged. The prayer would also afford him the opportunity to confess his own transgressions and find forgiveness.

that they bore children. ¹⁸For the LORD had closed fast all the wombs of the house of Abimelech because of Sarah, Abraham's wife.

J. The birth of Isaac

1. Birth and circumcision

21 The LORD dealt with Sarah as he had said, and the LORD did for Sarah as he had promised. ²Sarah conceived and bore Abraham a son in his old age, at the time of which God had spoken to him. ³Abraham gave the name Isaac to his son whom Sarah bore him. ⁴And Abraham circumcised his son Isaac when he was eight days old, as God had commanded him. ⁵Abraham was a hundred years old when his son Isaac was born to him. ⁶Now Sarah said, "God has brought laughter for me; everyone who hears will laugh with me." ⁷And she said, "Who would ever have said to Abraham that Sarah would nurse children? Yet I have borne him a son in his old age."

2. The expulsion of Ishmael

8   The child grew, and was weaned; and Abraham made a great feast on the day that Isaac was weaned. ⁹But Sarah saw the son of Hagar the Egyptian, whom she had borne to Abraham, playing with her son Isaac.ᶠ ¹⁰So she said to Abraham, "Cast out this slave woman with her son; for the son of this slave woman shall not inherit along with my son Isaac." ¹¹The matter was very distressing to Abraham on account of his son. ¹²But God said to Abraham, "Do not be distressed because of the boy and because of your slave woman; whatever Sarah says to you, do as she tells you, for it is through Isaac that offspring shall be named for you. ¹³As for the son of the slave woman, I will make a nation of him also, because he is your offspring." ¹⁴So Abraham rose early in the morning, and took bread and a skin of water, and gave it to Hagar, putting it on her shoulder, along with the child, and sent her away. And she departed, and wandered about in the wilderness of Beer-sheba.

3. The deliverance of Hagar and Ishmael

15   When the water in the skin was gone, she cast the child under one of the bushes. ¹⁶Then she went and sat down opposite him a good way off, about the distance of a bowshot; for she said, "Do not let me look on the death of the child." And as she sat opposite him, she lifted up her voice and wept. ¹⁷And God heard the voice of the boy; and the angel of God called to Hagar from heaven, and said to her, "What troubles you, Hagar? Do not be afraid; for God has heard the voice of the boy where he is. ¹⁸Come, lift up the boy and hold him fast with your hand, for I will make a great nation of him." ¹⁹Then God opened her eyes and she saw a well of water. She went, and filled the skin with water, and gave the boy a drink.

20   God was with the boy, and he grew up; he lived in the wilderness,

ᶠ Gk Vg: Heb lacks *with her son Isaac*

21.1
1 Sam 2.21;
Gen 17.16,
21;
Gal 4.23
21.2
Acts 7.8;
Gal 4.22;
Heb 11.11;
Gen 17.21
21.3
Gen 17.19
21.4
Gen 17.12;
Acts 7.8
21.5
Gen 17.17
21.6
Ps 126.2;
Isa 54.1
21.7
Gen 18.13
21.9
Gen 16.15;
Gal 4.29
21.10
Gal 4.30
21.11
Gen 17.18
21.12
Rom 9.7;
Heb 11.18
21.13
v. 18;
Gen 16.10;
17.20

21.17
Ex 3.7

21.18
v. 13
21.19
Num 22.31

21.20
Gen 28.15;
39.2, 3, 21

21.1 *the LORD dealt with Sarah as he had said.* Since Sarah was no longer fertile, God performed a miracle so she could become pregnant.
21.11   Apart from Abraham's personal hope to keep Ishmael near him, it was forbidden by the customary law of his day for a slave wife and her children to be ejected from their master's home (see 16.2,3, note). Sarah's jealousy must have been a trial for Abraham.
21.12   Sarah wanted Abraham to send Hagar and Ishmael away. God endorsed her judgment, for he intervened to command Abraham to follow her advice.

21.14   Since Ishmael was born when Abraham was eighty-six years old, he was by now a young teenager, not a baby. God protected Hagar and Ishmael and promised to make a nation out of the descendants of Ishmael.
21.20   *God was with the boy.* Abraham loved Ishmael and was sorry to send him and his mother away (21.11). God was understanding and used his divine power to protect Ishmael. Ishmael must have had some continuing contact with Abraham because he was present when Abraham was buried (25.9).

21.21
Gen 24.4

and became an expert with the bow. 21 He lived in the wilderness of Paran; and his mother got a wife for him from the land of Egypt.

4. The discord between Abraham and Abimelech

21.22
Gen 20.2;
26.26, 28

22 At that time Abimelech, with Phicol the commander of his army, said to Abraham, "God is with you in all that you do; 23 now therefore swear to me here by God that you will not deal falsely with me or with my offspring or with my posterity, but as I have dealt loyally with you, you will deal with me and with the land where you have resided as an alien." 24 And Abraham said, "I swear it."

21.25
Gen 26.15,
18, 20-22

25 When Abraham complained to Abimelech about a well of water that Abimelech's servants had seized, 26 Abimelech said, "I do not know who has done this; you did not tell me, and I have not heard of it until

21.27
Gen 26.31

today." 27 So Abraham took sheep and oxen and gave them to Abimelech, and the two men made a covenant. 28 Abraham set apart seven ewe lambs of the flock. 29 And Abimelech said to Abraham, "What is the meaning

21.30
Gen 31.48, 52

of these seven ewe lambs that you have set apart?" 30 He said, "These seven ewe lambs you shall accept from my hand, in order that you may

21.31
Gen 26.33

be a witness for me that I dug this well." 31 Therefore that place was called Beer-sheba;g because there both of them swore an oath. 32 When they had made a covenant at Beer-sheba, Abimelech, with Phicol the commander

21.33
Gen 4.26;
Deut 33.27

of his army, left and returned to the land of the Philistines. 33 Abraham h planted a tamarisk tree in Beer-sheba, and called there on the name of the LORD, the Everlasting God.i 34 And Abraham resided as an alien many days in the land of the Philistines.

K. Abraham's sacrifice of Isaac

1. God tests Abraham

22.2
Heb 11.17;
2 Chr 3.1

22 After these things God tested Abraham. He said to him, "Abraham!" And he said, "Here I am." 2 He said, "Take your son, your only son Isaac, whom you love, and go to the land of Moriah, and offer him there as a burnt offering on one of the mountains that I shall show you." 3 So Abraham rose early in the morning, saddled his donkey, and took two of his young men with him, and his son Isaac; he cut the wood for the burnt offering, and set out and went to the place in the distance that God had shown him. 4 On the third day Abraham looked up and saw the place far away. 5 Then Abraham said to his young men, "Stay here with the donkey; the boy and I will go over there; we will worship, and

22.6
Jn 19.17

then we will come back to you." 6 Abraham took the wood of the burnt offering and laid it on his son Isaac, and he himself carried the fire and the knife. So the two of them walked on together. 7 Isaac said to his father

22.7
Jn 1.29, 36;
Rev 13.8

g That is Well of seven or Well of the oath   h Heb He   i Or the LORD, El Olam

---

21.22 Abimelech was aware of how God promoted Abraham's material welfare. He sensed that God was with Abraham in all that he did. Thus he wanted to ally himself with Abraham in the interests of himself and of his family, then and for the future.
21.33 the Everlasting God (El Olem in the Hebrew) means "the God of eternity."
22.1 God tested Abraham. Abraham was an old man now. He had followed God for many years. Now that Isaac was a young man, God wanted to see whether Abraham loved Isaac more than he loved God. Abraham survived the test and left us an example. Is there anyone or anything we put in first place instead of Jesus the Lord? We too will be tested along this line.
22.2 On the basis of 2 Chr 3.1 Christian tradition has assumed that Jerusalem was the place where

Abraham offered up Isaac. Some scholars call attention to the fact that it would have been odd for Abraham to have carried wood for the offering from Beersheba to the wooded country around Jerusalem where he could easily have secured all the wood he needed. Probably the land of Moriah of this text was in the treeless ranges of Sinai down near Kadesh. Abraham knew this country well. Moreover, Isaac here may be understood to be a representation of Christ. He was an only son. He was offered up as a sacrifice. It was through Isaac that the descendants of Abraham should be named. And Abraham believed that God was able to raise Isaac from the dead, and, in a manner of speaking, did receive him back from the dead (Heb 11.17–19). Christ, like Isaac, was an only son; he was offered up as a sacrifice; he was raised from the dead.

along with Abraham's servant and his men. 60 And they blessed Rebekah and said to her,

"May you, our sister, become
thousands of myriads;
may your offspring gain possession
of the gates of their foes."

61 Then Rebekah and her maids rose up, mounted the camels, and followed the man; thus the servant took Rebekah, and went his way.

6. *Isaac and Rebekah marry*

62 Now Isaac had come from[m] Beer-lahai-roi, and was settled in the Negeb. 63 Isaac went out in the evening to walk[n] in the field; and looking up, he saw camels coming. 64 And Rebekah looked up, and when she saw Isaac, she slipped quickly from the camel, 65 and said to the servant, "Who is the man over there, walking in the field to meet us?" The servant said, "It is my master." So she took her veil and covered herself. 66 And the servant told Isaac all the things that he had done. 67 Then Isaac brought her into his mother Sarah's tent. He took Rebekah, and she became his wife; and he loved her. So Isaac was comforted after his mother's death.

N. *Abraham's children by Keturah*

25 Abraham took another wife, whose name was Keturah. 2 She bore him Zimran, Jokshan, Medan, Midian, Ishbak, and Shuah. 3 Jokshan was the father of Sheba and Dedan. The sons of Dedan were Asshurim, Letushim, and Leummim. 4 The sons of Midian were Ephah, Epher, Hanoch, Abida, and Eldaah. All these were the children of Keturah. 5 Abraham gave all he had to Isaac. 6 But to the sons of his concubines Abraham gave gifts, while he was still living, and he sent them away from his son Isaac, eastward to the east country.

O. *The death of Abraham*

7 This is the length of Abraham's life, one hundred seventy-five years. 8 Abraham breathed his last and died in a good old age, an old man and full of years, and was gathered to his people. 9 His sons Isaac and Ishmael buried him in the cave of Machpelah, in the field of Ephron son of Zohar the Hittite, east of Mamre, 10 the field that Abraham purchased from the Hittites. There Abraham was buried, with his wife Sarah. 11 After the death of Abraham God blessed his son Isaac. And Isaac settled at Beer-lahai-roi.

VII. *The descendants of Ishmael (25.12–18)*

12 These are the descendants of Ishmael, Abraham's son, whom

---

m Syr Tg: Heb *from coming to*   *n* Meaning of Heb word is uncertain

---

24.60
Gen 17.16;
22.17

24.62
Gen 16.14;
25.11; 20.1
24.63
Ps 1.2; 77.12;
119.15;
143.5; 145.5

24.67
Gen 29.18;
23.1, 2;
25.20

25.2
1 Chr 1.32,
33

25.5
Gen 24.35, 36

25.8
Gen 15.15;
35.29; 49.29,
33
25.10
Gen 23.16
25.11
Gen 24.62

25.12
Gen 16.15

24.65 *she took her veil and covered herself.* This was the custom in connection with marriages. Isaac had mourned the death of his mother and now is given a wife to fill the gap.
25.5 Abraham married Keturah and she gave birth to six children. But since Isaac was the heir, he was given the bulk of Abraham's fortune.
25.6 Hagar bore one son to Abraham; Keturah gave him six sons. Before his death Abraham distributed a portion of his wealth to these children and sent them "eastward to the east country." These descendants of Abraham were called *the people of the East*. They are mentioned in Judg 6.3,33, where they are said to be very numerous. They were enemies of the people of Israel. Today there may be multitudes of people in the Middle East who are lineal descendants of Abraham

through these two women. Especially interesting is the fact that 25.16 calls these children of Abraham through Ishmael "twelve princes according to their tribes." Thus there were the twelve tribes of Israel through Isaac and Jacob, and twelve princes through Ishmael.
25.9,10 Isaac and Ishmael buried Abraham. Abraham lived 175 years. Isaac was born when Abraham was 100 years old. Thus Isaac was 75 years old when his father died. Ishmael was fourteen years older than Isaac. Whatever may have been the friction between Isaac and Ishmael, they must have lived close to each other and they did get together to bury their father. Abraham was interred next to Sarah in the cave of Machpelah.

Hagar the Egyptian, Sarah's slave-girl, bore to Abraham. 13 These are the names of the sons of Ishmael, named in the order of their birth: Nebaioth, the firstborn of Ishmael; and Kedar, Adbeel, Mibsam, 14 Mishma, Dumah, Massa, 15 Hadad, Tema, Jetur, Naphish, and Kedemah. 16 These are the sons of Ishmael and these are their names, by their villages and by their encampments, twelve princes according to their tribes. 17 (This is the length of the life of Ishmael, one hundred thirty-seven years; he breathed his last and died, and was gathered to his people.) 18 They settled from Havilah to Shur, which is opposite Egypt in the direction of Assyria; he settled down*o* alongside of*p* all his people.

VIII. *The descendants of Isaac (25.19–35.29)*

A. *The birth of Esau and Jacob*

1. *The elder shall serve the younger*

19 These are the descendants of Isaac, Abraham's son: Abraham was the father of Isaac, 20 and Isaac was forty years old when he married Rebekah, daughter of Bethuel the Aramean of Paddan-aram, sister of Laban the Aramean. 21 Isaac prayed to the LORD for his wife, because she was barren; and the LORD granted his prayer, and his wife Rebekah conceived. 22 The children struggled together within her; and she said, "If it is to be this way, why do I live?"*q* So she went to inquire of the LORD. 23 And the LORD said to her,

"Two nations are in your womb,
    and two peoples born of you shall be divided;
the one shall be stronger than the other,
    the elder shall serve the younger."

24 When her time to give birth was at hand, there were twins in her womb. 25 The first came out red, all his body like a hairy mantle; so they named him Esau. 26 Afterward his brother came out, with his hand gripping Esau's heel; so he was named Jacob.*r* Isaac was sixty years old when she bore them.

2. *Esau sells his birthright to Jacob*

27 When the boys grew up, Esau was a skillful hunter, a man of the field, while Jacob was a quiet man, living in tents. 28 Isaac loved Esau, because he was fond of game; but Rebekah loved Jacob. 29 Once when Jacob was cooking a stew, Esau came in from the field, and he was famished. 30 Esau said to Jacob, "Let me eat some of that red stuff, for I am famished!" (Therefore he was called Edom.*s*) 31 Jacob said,

o Heb *he fell* *p* Or *down in opposition to* *q* Syr: Meaning of Heb uncertain *r* That is *He takes by the heel* or *He supplants* *s* That is *Red*

25.21 *she was barren.* Rebekah, like Sarah, was barren. Isaac, who married her when he was forty, prayed to God for a child. His prayer was answered when he was sixty years old. In the cases of both women, divine intervention was the answer to their dilemma.
25.25 Esau (whose name sounds a little like the Hebrew word for "hair") was Jacob's twin who emerged first from his mother's womb and thus was entitled to all of the rights of the firstborn, including the domestic priesthood, family headship and authority, and a double portion of the inheritance upon the death of his father. The Edomites were the descendants of Esau (*Edom* means "red"). The main points in Esau's life were: (1) the sale of the birthright for some of Jacob's stew (25.27–34), an act indicating his unconcern for the birthright; (2) the marriages Esau consummated with women unrelated to his father's family (26.34–35), except for Mahalath, whom he married to placate Isaac and Rebekah (28.6–9); (3) his failure to obtain the patriarchal blessing before Isaac died (ch. 27); and (4) the resumption of brotherly relations with Jacob and his departure from Canaan for Seir (ch. 32). Esau was careless and indifferent to spiritual things.
25.28 For some reason Isaac and his wife had different loyalties. Rebekah loved Jacob more than Esau, while Isaac had a special affection for Esau. This difference led to marital problems. Rebekah practiced deceit on her husband, which led to a family separation when Jacob had to flee for his life.
25.31 The birthright was not especially important when there was only one son. It became important when Isaac had two sons. Esau, as the firstborn, should have been the one through whom the people of God would count their descent. But he sold his

"First sell me your birthright." ³²Esau said, "I am about to die; of what use is a birthright to me?" ³³Jacob said, "Swear to me first."ᵗ So he swore to him, and sold his birthright to Jacob. ³⁴Then Jacob gave Esau bread and lentil stew, and he ate and drank, and rose and went his way. Thus Esau despised his birthright.

25.33
Heb 12.16

B. *Isaac and Abimelech*

1. *The covenant confirmed to Isaac*

26 Now there was a famine in the land, besides the former famine that had occurred in the days of Abraham. And Isaac went to Gerar, to King Abimelech of the Philistines. ²The LORD appeared to Isaacᵘ and said, "Do not go down to Egypt; settle in the land that I shall show you. ³Reside in this land as an alien, and I will be with you, and will bless you; for to you and to your descendants I will give all these lands, and I will fulfill the oath that I swore to your father Abraham. ⁴I will make your offspring as numerous as the stars of heaven, and will give to your offspring all these lands; and all the nations of the earth shall gain blessing for themselves through your offspring, ⁵because Abraham obeyed my voice and kept my charge, my commandments, my statutes, and my laws."

26.1
Gen 12.10;
20.1, 2
26.2
Gen 12.7;
17.1; 18.1;
19.1
26.3
Gen 20.1;
12.2, 7;
13.15; 15.18;
22.16-18
26.4
Gen 15.5;
22.17;
Ex 32.15;
Gen 12.3;
22.18;
Gal 3.8

2. *Isaac deceives Abimelech about Rebekah*

6 So Isaac settled in Gerar. ⁷When the men of the place asked him about his wife, he said, "She is my sister"; for he was afraid to say, "My wife," thinking, "or else the men of the place might kill me for the sake of Rebekah, because she is attractive in appearance." ⁸When Isaac had been there a long time, King Abimelech of the Philistines looked out of a window and saw him fondling his wife Rebekah. ⁹So Abimelech called for Isaac, and said, "So she is your wife! Why then did you say, 'She is my sister'?" Isaac said to him, "Because I thought I might die because of her." ¹⁰Abimelech said, "What is this you have done to us? One of the people might easily have lain with your wife, and you would have brought guilt upon us." ¹¹So Abimelech warned all the people, saying, "Whoever touches this man or his wife shall be put to death."

26.7
Gen 12.13;
20.2, 12, 13

26.10
Gen 20.9

3. *Isaac's riches*

12 Isaac sowed seed in that land, and in the same year reaped a hundredfold. The LORD blessed him, ¹³and the man became rich; he prospered more and more until he became very wealthy. ¹⁴He had possessions of flocks and herds, and a great household, so that the Philistines envied him. ¹⁵(Now the Philistines had stopped up and filled with earth all the wells that his father's servants had dug in the days of his father Abraham.) ¹⁶And Abimelech said to Isaac, "Go away from us; you have become too powerful for us."

26.12
v. 3
26.14
Gen 24.35;
37.11
26.15
Gen 21.25, 30

ᵗ Heb *today*   ᵘ Heb *him*

---

spiritual birthright for physical needs and lost it to Jacob. Jacob got the birthright and from him came the Jewish patriarchs.

26.7 *She is my sister.* Isaac does what his father had done before him: he lies about his true relationship to Rebekah to protect himself against possible enemies. This indicates a lack of faith in the protecting power of the God he professed to worship.

26.8–11 *Isaac . . . fondling his wife.* Whatever Isaac was doing was not normal for a brother and sister to do. Either he was incestuous, or Rebekah was his wife

and he was lying. Abimelech knew that if any of his people had sexual relations with her, it would have been defiling.

26.12 *The LORD blessed him.* Abraham distributed his wealth among all of his children before his death. Isaac received a fair share. Now God blesses him and he "sowed seed in that land, and in the same year reaped a hundredfold." Wealth is the gift of God; there is nothing wrong in being wealthy. The major consideration about wealth for believers is whether they use it for the glory of God.

4. *Isaac's trouble with Abimelech over the wells: their covenant*

26.18
Gen 21.31

17 So Isaac departed from there and camped in the valley of Gerar and settled there. ¹⁸Isaac dug again the wells of water that had been dug in the days of his father Abraham; for the Philistines had stopped them up after the death of Abraham; and he gave them the names that his father had given them. ¹⁹But when Isaac's servants dug in the valley and found there a well of spring water, ²⁰the herders of Gerar quarreled with Isaac's herders, saying, "The water is ours." So he called the well Esek,ᵛ because they contended with him. ²¹Then they dug another well, and they quar-

26.22
Gen 17.6

reled over that one also; so he called it Sitnah.ʷ ²²He moved from there and dug another well, and they did not quarrel over it; so he called it Rehoboth,ˣ saying, "Now the LORD has made room for us, and we shall be fruitful in the land."

26.24
Gen 17.7;
24.12;
Ex 3.6

23 From there he went up to Beer-sheba. ²⁴And that very night the LORD appeared to him and said, "I am the God of your father Abraham;

26.25
Gen 12.7, 8;
13.4, 18;
Ps 116.17

do not be afraid, for I am with you and will bless you and make your offspring numerous for my servant Abraham's sake." ²⁵So he built an altar there, called on the name of the LORD, and pitched his tent there. And there Isaac's servants dug a well.

26.26
Gen 21.22
26.27
v. 16

26 Then Abimelech went to him from Gerar, with Ahuzzath his adviser and Phicol the commander of his army. ²⁷Isaac said to them, "Why have you come to me, seeing that you hate me and have sent me

26.28
Gen 21.22, 23

away from you?" ²⁸They said, "We see plainly that the LORD has been with you; so we say, let there be an oath between you and us, and let us make a covenant with you ²⁹so that you will do us no harm, just as we have not touched you and have done to you nothing but good and have sent you away in peace. You are now the blessed of the LORD." ³⁰So he

26.31
Gen 21.31

made them a feast, and they ate and drank. ³¹In the morning they rose early and exchanged oaths; and Isaac set them on their way, and they departed from him in peace. ³²That same day Isaac's servants came and told him about the well that they had dug, and said to him, "We have

26.33
Gen 21.31

found water!" ³³He called it Shibah;ʸ therefore the name of the city is Beer-shebaᶻ to this day.

C. *Esau's marriages: Isaac's sorrow*

26.34
Gen 28.8;
36.2
26.35
Gen 27.46

34 When Esau was forty years old, he married Judith daughter of Beeri the Hittite, and Basemath daughter of Elon the Hittite; ³⁵and they made life bitter for Isaac and Rebekah.

D. *The stolen blessing*

1. *Esau hunts for game*

27.1
Gen 48.10;
1 Sam 3.2
27.2
Gen 47.29

27 When Isaac was old and his eyes were dim so that he could not see, he called his elder son Esau and said to him, "My son"; and he answered, "Here I am." ²He said, "See, I am old; I do not know the

ᵛ That is *Contention* ʷ That is *Enmity* ˣ That is *Broad places* or *Room* ʸ A word resembling the word for *oath* ᶻ That is *Well of the oath* or *Well of seven*

26.17 Gerar was located at the southern end of the territory belonging to the Canaanites, in the same region with Gaza.
26.24–25 The Lord appeared to Isaac and reconfirmed the covenant he had made with Abraham. In Isaac all the world would be blessed and his descendants would be multiplied in number. Like his father Abraham, Isaac built an altar there to celebrate the holiness of the place associated with the appearance of his God.

26.34,35 Esau foolishly married two Hittite women who were outside the family of faith. In doing this, he grieved his parents, particularly his father Isaac, who had married within the family as a result of Abraham's sending his faithful servant to Haran (ch. 24). Moveover, Esau's wives "made life bitter" for Isaac and Rebekah, with whom they lived.
27.1 Isaac's eyes were dim. Apparently he suffered either from cataracts or glaucoma, both of which are common to that area of the world today.

day of my death. ³Now then, take your weapons, your quiver and your
bow, and go out to the field, and hunt game for me. ⁴Then prepare for
me savory food, such as I like, and bring it to me to eat, so that I may
bless you before I die."

2. Rebekah schemes with Jacob

5 Now Rebekah was listening when Isaac spoke to his son Esau. So
when Esau went to the field to hunt for game and bring it, ⁶Rebekah said
to her son Jacob, "I heard your father say to your brother Esau, ⁷'Bring
me game, and prepare for me savory food to eat, that I may bless you
before the LORD before I die.' ⁸Now therefore, my son, obey my word
as I command you. ⁹Go to the flock, and get me two choice kids, so that
I may prepare from them savory food for your father, such as he likes;
¹⁰and you shall take it to your father to eat, so that he may bless you before
he dies." ¹¹But Jacob said to his mother Rebekah, "Look, my brother
Esau is a hairy man, and I am a man of smooth skin. ¹²Perhaps my father
will feel me, and I shall seem to be mocking him, and bring a curse on
myself and not a blessing." ¹³His mother said to him, "Let your curse
be on me, my son; only obey my word, and go, get them for me." ¹⁴So
he went and got them and brought them to his mother; and his mother
prepared savory food, such as his father loved. ¹⁵Then Rebekah took the
best garments of her elder son Esau, which were with her in the house,
and put them on her younger son Jacob; ¹⁶and she put the skins of the
kids on his hands and on the smooth part of his neck. ¹⁷Then she handed
the savory food, and the bread that she had prepared, to her son Jacob.

3. Jacob pretends to be Esau: he obtains the blessing

18 So he went in to his father, and said, "My father"; and he said,
"Here I am; who are you, my son?" ¹⁹Jacob said to his father, "I am Esau
your firstborn. I have done as you told me; now sit up and eat of my game,
so that you may bless me." ²⁰But Isaac said to his son, "How is it that
you have found it so quickly, my son?" He answered, "Because the LORD
your God granted me success." ²¹Then Isaac said to Jacob, "Come near,
that I may feel you, my son, to know whether you are really my son Esau
or not." ²²So Jacob went up to his father Isaac, who felt him and said,
"The voice is Jacob's voice, but the hands are the hands of Esau." ²³He
did not recognize him, because his hands were hairy like his brother
Esau's hands; so he blessed him. ²⁴He said, "Are you really my son
Esau?" He answered, "I am." ²⁵Then he said, "Bring it to me, that I may
eat of my son's game and bless you." So he brought it to him, and he ate;
and he brought him wine, and he drank. ²⁶Then his father Isaac said to
him, "Come near and kiss me, my son." ²⁷So he came near and kissed
him; and he smelled the smell of his garments, and blessed him, and said,
    "Ah, the smell of my son
      is like the smell of a field that the LORD has blessed.
28 May God give you of the dew of heaven,
      and of the fatness of the earth,
      and plenty of grain and wine.

27.3 Gen 25.27, 28 **27.4** v. 27; Gen 48.9, 15; 49.28
27.8 v. 13
27.11 Gen 25.25 **27.12** vv. 21, 22
27.13 v. 8; Mt 27.25
27.15 v. 27
27.19 v. 4
27.21 v. 12
27.23 v. 16
27.25 vv. 4, 10, 19, 31
27.27 Heb 11.20; Song 4.11
27.28 Deut 33.13, 28; Gen 45.18

27.4 *that I may bless you before I die.* It was Isaac's
intention to give Esau the blessing which belonged to
the firstborn. Whether he did not know of the stolen
birthright or disregarded what had happened earlier
we do not know. When Esau came for his blessing,
he knew that Jacob had received what he wanted,
even though he had despised it previously.
27.13 *Let your curse be on me.* Rebekah was false to
her marriage vows when she put her son Jacob before
her husband Isaac. She could have honorably reasoned with Isaac and reminded him of God's promise

that in Jacob should the offspring be called. Rather,
she planned the deceit.
27.19 In order to obtain the blessing promised by
God, Rebekah and Jacob deceived Isaac. Long before
this happened, Esau had already sold the birthright
(25.27–34) and God could and would have worked
out the solution without any deception. Two of the
consequences of Jacob's deception were his exile
and the fact that he never saw his mother again.
Only God's will done God's way brings God's
blessing.

27.29
Gen 9.25;
25.23; 49.8;
12.3;
Num 24.9;
Zeph 2.8

29 Let peoples serve you,
      and nations bow down to you.
    Be lord over your brothers,
      and may your mother's sons bow down to you.
    Cursed be everyone who curses you,
      and blessed be everyone who blesses you!"

4. Esau learns of the deception

30 As soon as Isaac had finished blessing Jacob, when Jacob had
scarcely gone out from the presence of his father Isaac, his brother Esau

27.31
v. 4
came in from his hunting. [31] He also prepared savory food, and brought
it to his father. And he said to him, "Let my father sit up and eat

27.32
v. 18
of his son's game, so that you may bless me." [32] His father Isaac said to
him, "Who are you?" He answered, "I am your firstborn son, Esau."

27.33
Gen 28.3, 4;
Rom 11.29
27.34
Heb 12.17
[33] Then Isaac trembled violently, and said, "Who was it then that hunted
game and brought it to me, and I ate it all[a] before you came, and I have
blessed him? — yes, and blessed he shall be!" [34] When Esau heard his
father's words, he cried out with an exceedingly great and bitter cry, and
said to his father, "Bless me, me also, father!" [35] But he said, "Your
brother came deceitfully, and he has taken away your blessing." [36] Esau
said, "Is he not rightly named Jacob?[b] For he has supplanted me these
two times. He took away my birthright; and look, now he has taken away
my blessing." Then he said, "Have you not reserved a blessing for me?"

27.37
vv. 28, 29
[37] Isaac answered Esau, "I have already made him your lord, and I have
given him all his brothers as servants, and with grain and wine I have

27.38
Heb 12.17
sustained him. What then can I do for you, my son?" [38] Esau said to his
father, "Have you only one blessing, father? Bless me, me also, father!"
And Esau lifted up his voice and wept.

27.39
v. 28
39 Then his father Isaac answered him:
    "See, away from[c] the fatness of the earth shall your home be,
      and away from[d] the dew of heaven on high.

27.40
Gen 25.23;
2 Kings 8.20-22
40 By your sword you shall live,
      and you shall serve your brother;
    but when you break loose,[e]
      you shall break his yoke from your neck."

5. Rebekah schemes for Jacob to visit Laban

27.41
Gen 32.3-11
41 Now Esau hated Jacob because of the blessing with which his
father had blessed him, and Esau said to himself, "The days of mourning
for my father are approaching; then I will kill my brother Jacob." [42] But
the words of her elder son Esau were told to Rebekah; so she sent and
called her younger son Jacob and said to him, "Your brother Esau is
consoling himself by planning to kill you. [43] Now therefore, my son, obey

27.43
vv. 8, 13;
Gen 24.29
my voice; flee at once to my brother Laban in Haran, [44] and stay with him
a while, until your brother's fury turns away — [45] until your brother's
anger against you turns away, and he forgets what you have done to him;
then I will send, and bring you back from there. Why should I lose both
of you in one day?"

a Cn: Heb *of all*   *b* That is *He supplants* or *He takes by the heel*   *c* Or *See, of*   *d* Or *and of*   *e* Meaning
of Heb uncertain

27.39,40 God promised Esau, through the blessing
of his father Isaac, a good living. He would have the
fatness of the earth and the dew of heaven. But he
would not have the covenant blessing, which was the
best of all; Jacob was given dominion over his
brother. God gives good earth and good weather to
many who reject his covenant of grace. This is due to
common grace, but covenant grace is much better.
27.41 Wicked Esau hated his brother Jacob who

had stolen his birthright; Esau was determined to kill
him. He hated Jacob because Isaac had blessed him
and God loved him. In his heart he committed a
murder, even as Cain had slain his brother long before. He could call Jacob "brother" and vow his
death. Possibly he intended to kill Jacob as soon as
their father died and before Jacob was married and
had a family, so that he could then have seized all of
Isaac's goods.

46 Then Rebekah said to Isaac, "I am weary of my life because of the Hittite women. If Jacob marries one of the Hittite women such as these, one of the women of the land, what good will my life be to me?"

6. *Isaac sends Jacob to Laban*

28 Then Isaac called Jacob and blessed him, and charged him, "You shall not marry one of the Canaanite women. ²Go at once to Paddan-aram to the house of Bethuel, your mother's father; and take as wife from there one of the daughters of Laban, your mother's brother. ³May God Almighty*f* bless you and make you fruitful and numerous, that you may become a company of peoples. ⁴May he give to you the blessing of Abraham, to you and to your offspring with you, so that you may take possession of the land where you now live as an alien—land that God gave to Abraham." ⁵Thus Isaac sent Jacob away; and he went to Paddan-aram, to Laban son of Bethuel the Aramean, the brother of Rebekah, Jacob's and Esau's mother.

E. *Esau's third wife*

6 Now Esau saw that Isaac had blessed Jacob and sent him away to Paddan-aram to take a wife from there, and that as he blessed him he charged him, "You shall not marry one of the Canaanite women," ⁷and that Jacob had obeyed his father and his mother and gone to Paddan-aram. ⁸So when Esau saw that the Canaanite women did not please his father Isaac, ⁹Esau went to Ishmael and took Mahalath daughter of Abraham's son Ishmael, and sister of Nebaioth, to be his wife in addition to the wives he had.

F. *Jacob's dream at Bethel*

10 Jacob left Beer-sheba and went toward Haran. ¹¹He came to a certain place and stayed there for the night, because the sun had set. Taking one of the stones of the place, he put it under his head and lay down in that place. ¹²And he dreamed that there was a ladder*g* set up on the earth, the top of it reaching to heaven; and the angels of God were ascending and descending on it. ¹³And the LORD stood beside him*h* and said, "I am the LORD, the God of Abraham your father and the God of Isaac; the land on which you lie I will give to you and to your offspring; ¹⁴and your offspring shall be like the dust of the earth, and you shall spread abroad to the west and to the east and to the north and to the south;

f Traditional rendering of Heb *El Shaddai*   *g* Or *stairway* or *ramp*   *h* Or *stood above it*

27.46
Gen 26.34, 35

28.1
Gen 24.3, 4
28.2
Gen 25.20

28.3
Gen 17.1, 6
28.4
Gen 12.2;
17.8

28.6
v. 1

28.8
Gen 24.3;
26.35
28.9
Gen 36.3

28.12
Jn 1.51

28.13
Gen 35.1;
48.3; 26.24;
13.15; 35.12
28.14
Gen 13.14-16;
22.17; 12.3;
18.18; 22.18;
26.4

27.46 Rebekah senses the danger to Jacob if he were to remain at home, and seizes on the pretext that Jacob might marry a Hittite girl. This works well with Isaac, whose other son Esau had married outside the faith. Rebekah's plea to send him to her brother Laban is accepted and Jacob departs, to see his mother no more. In any event, the decision was a good one—for Jacob would indeed marry in the faith, despite evil treatment at the hands of his uncle Laban.
28.1 Isaac had learned enough from the marriages of Esau to two of the Canaanites; he wanted Jacob to return to Rebekah's relatives and there find a wife. At the same time, unknown to him, God would make Jacob suffer under Laban in punishment for his deceitful act against his father. Jacob went from heir in his father's house to servant under Laban, who did to him what Jacob had done to his own father. Yet God included Jacob in the line of Abraham, looking toward the coming of the Messiah through Abraham's offspring. Nonetheless, Jacob's harsh experiences under Laban serve to confirm the fact that God's providences often seem to contradict his promises.

28.4 Isaac was acutely aware that the blessing promised to his father Abraham had come to him. Now he wants to assure Jacob, the supplanter who stole the birthright from Esau, that the Abrahamic promise from God would be his too—and not only his, but it would pass on to Jacob's children. The two major promises to Abraham included an innumerable posterity through whom the nations of the earth would be blessed and the inheritance of the land of promise. In v. 3 Isaac refers to the first promise and in v. 4 to the second.
28.8 Esau, now that Jacob was gone, sought to appease his father Isaac, who was displeased with his unbelieving wives. Therefore, he took Mahalath as a wife, the daughter of Ishmael (Esau's half-uncle). He sought to satisfy his father, not God, and he wanted to strengthen his own position as heir to his father's goods.
28.13,14 God certifies to Jacob what Isaac had told him in vv. 3,4: he will get the land and he will have a posterity which will bless the nations of the earth.

and all the families of the earth shall be blessed[i] in you and in your offspring. 15 Know that I am with you and will keep you wherever you go, and will bring you back to this land; for I will not leave you until I have done what I have promised you." 16 Then Jacob woke from his sleep and said, "Surely the LORD is in this place—and I did not know it!" 17 And he was afraid, and said, "How awesome is this place! This is none other than the house of God, and this is the gate of heaven."

18 So Jacob rose early in the morning, and he took the stone that he had put under his head and set it up for a pillar and poured oil on the top of it. 19 He called that place Bethel;[j] but the name of the city was Luz at the first. 20 Then Jacob made a vow, saying, "If God will be with me, and will keep me in this way that I go, and will give me bread to eat and clothing to wear, 21 so that I come again to my father's house in peace, then the LORD shall be my God, 22 and this stone, which I have set up for a pillar, shall be God's house; and of all that you give me I will surely give one-tenth to you."

G. *Jacob and Laban*

1. *Jacob meets Rachel*

29 Then Jacob went on his journey, and came to the land of the people of the east. 2 As he looked, he saw a well in the field and three flocks of sheep lying there beside it; for out of that well the flocks were watered. The stone on the well's mouth was large, 3 and when all the flocks were gathered there, the shepherds would roll the stone from the mouth of the well, and water the sheep, and put the stone back in its place on the mouth of the well.

4 Jacob said to them, "My brothers, where do you come from?" They said, "We are from Haran." 5 He said to them, "Do you know Laban son of Nahor?" They said, "We do." 6 He said to them, "Is it well with him?" "Yes," they replied, "and here is his daughter Rachel, coming with the sheep." 7 He said, "Look, it is still broad daylight; it is not time for the animals to be gathered together. Water the sheep, and go, pasture them." 8 But they said, "We cannot until all the flocks are gathered together, and the stone is rolled from the mouth of the well; then we water the sheep."

9 While he was still speaking with them, Rachel came with her father's sheep; for she kept them. 10 Now when Jacob saw Rachel, the daughter of his mother's brother Laban, and the sheep of his mother's brother Laban, Jacob went up and rolled the stone from the well's mouth, and watered the flock of his mother's brother Laban. 11 Then Jacob kissed Rachel, and wept aloud. 12 And Jacob told Rachel that he was her father's kinsman, and that he was Rebekah's son; and she ran and told her father. 13 When Laban heard the news about his sister's son Jacob, he ran

Cross references (margin)

28.15 Gen 26.3; Num 6.24; Ps 121.7, 8; Gen 48.21; Deut 31.6, 8
28.16 Ex 3.5; Josh 5.15
28.18 Gen 35.14; Lev 8.10-12
28.19 Judg 1.23, 26; Hos 4.15
28.20ff Gen 31.13; v. 15; 1 Tim 6.8
28.21 Judg 11.31; 2 Sam 19.24, 30; Deut 26.17; 2 Sam 15.8
28.22 Gen 35.7, 14; Lev 27.30
29.1 Judg 6.3, 33
29.4 Gen 28.10
29.5 Gen 24.24, 29
29.6 Gen 43.27
29.9 Ex 2.16
29.10 Ex 2.17
29.12 Gen 13.8; 14.14, 16; 24.28
29.13 Gen 24.29, 31; 33.4

---

i Or shall bless themselves j That is House of God

28.15 At this point Jacob's future was obscure. He was fleeing from Esau but had not yet come to his uncle Laban's home. God now promises that he will protect him "wherever you go" and he will return him safely to the land of promise. Jacob would have plenty of time and opportunity to remember these promises —especially as he worked for Laban and when he returned to the land of promise, fearful that Esau would execute vengeance on him because of his transgression.

28.19 *The name of the city was Luz*, meaning "almond tree"; it was renamed *Bethel* ("House of God") by Jacob after God appeared to him in a dream. Bethel became a holy place for the Israelites and was located on land given to the tribe of Benjamin. The city was about twelve miles north of Jerusalem. Jeroboam defiled this sacred place when he caused a golden calf to

be erected there (1 Kings 12.28–33). God ordered the destruction of the altar (1 Kings 13.1–5; 2 Kings 23.15–17; Am 3.14,15).

28.20–22 *If God will be with me.* Jacob was not promising to tithe in the event that God helped him. He was saying what Rom 8.31 says: "If God is for us," which allows for no doubt. He was not making a bargain with God; he vowed simply to express his profound gratitude for what God had already done, for God's undeserved favor. This became the normal way for Israelites to thank God; the intention to tithe was accompanied by a votive offering.

29.6 Once again the mystery of God's providence is manifest. Jacob unwittingly comes upon Rachel, the daughter of Laban, who is keeping her father's sheep. Such coincidences are not accidental; they are acts of God.

to meet him; he embraced him and kissed him, and brought him to his house. Jacob[k] told Laban all these things, 14 and Laban said to him, "Surely you are my bone and my flesh!" And he stayed with him a month.

29.14
Judg 9.2

2. Jacob's marriages to Leah and Rachel

15 Then Laban said to Jacob, "Because you are my kinsman, should you therefore serve me for nothing? Tell me, what shall your wages be?" 16 Now Laban had two daughters; the name of the elder was Leah, and the name of the younger was Rachel. 17 Leah's eyes were lovely,[l] and Rachel was graceful and beautiful. 18 Jacob loved Rachel; so he said, "I will serve you seven years for your younger daughter Rachel." 19 Laban said, "It is better that I give her to you than that I should give her to any other man; stay with me." 20 So Jacob served seven years for Rachel, and they seemed to him but a few days because of the love he had for her.

29.18
Hos 12.12

21 Then Jacob said to Laban, "Give me my wife that I may go in to her, for my time is completed." 22 So Laban gathered together all the people of the place, and made a feast. 23 But in the evening he took his daughter Leah and brought her to Jacob; and he went in to her. 24 (Laban gave his maid Zilpah to his daughter Leah to be her maid.) 25 When morning came, it was Leah! And Jacob said to Laban, "What is this you have done to me? Did I not serve with you for Rachel? Why then have you deceived me?" 26 Laban said, "This is not done in our country—giving the younger before the firstborn. 27 Complete the week of this one, and we will give you the other also in return for serving me another seven years." 28 Jacob did so, and completed her week; then Laban gave him his daughter Rachel as a wife. 29 (Laban gave his maid Bilhah to his daughter Rachel to be her maid.) 30 So Jacob went in to Rachel also, and he loved Rachel more than Leah. He served Laban[m] for another seven years.

29.21
Judg 15.1
29.22
Judg 14.10;
Jn 2.1, 2

29.27
Judg 14.12

29.30
vv. 17, 18

3. Jacob's children
a. Leah's four sons

31 When the LORD saw that Leah was unloved, he opened her womb; but Rachel was barren. 32 Leah conceived and bore a son, and she named him Reuben;[n] for she said, "Because the LORD has looked on my affliction; surely now my husband will love me." 33 She conceived again and bore a son, and said, "Because the LORD has heard[o] that I am hated, he has given me this son also"; and she named him Simeon. 34 Again she conceived and bore a son, and said, "Now this time my husband will be joined[p] to me, because I have borne him three sons"; therefore he was named Levi. 35 She conceived again and bore a son, and said, "This time

29.31
Ps 127.3;
Gen 30.1
29.32
Gen 16.11;
31.42
29.34
Gen 49.5

29.35
Gen 49.8;
Mt 1.2

k Heb He l Meaning of Heb uncertain m Heb him n That is See, a son o Heb shama p Heb lawah

29.21 that I may go in to her, i.e., that we may be married and I can have sexual relations with her. Even today a marriage is not consummated until the bride and groom have had sexual relations.
29.23 Laban worked under the cover of darkness, for it was evening when he brought Leah to Jacob. The bride was also covered. Jacob went to bed with Leah under the impression that it was Rachel. If he had asked the girl whether she was Rachel, he might have gotten the same response that he used when he claimed to be Esau and stole the blessing under the pretext of being his brother.
29.25 Jacob reaped as he had sown. He had cheated his brother Esau out of the birthright; now his uncle Laban practiced the same kind of deceit. Yet Jacob was under God's covenant blessing and did not ultimately become a loser. Later Jacob's own sons de-

ceived him about Joseph's abduction (37.32–36).
29.27 Complete the week . . . and we will give you the other also. The week consisted in festivities connected with the marriage. Right after that, Jacob got his second bride. He had worked for Laban for seven years before his marriage to Leah. Now he agreed to work seven more years after being married to Rachel, the one he really loved.
29.29 Since Laban was wealthy, he gave each of his daughters a servant-girl as a wedding present. Leah got Zilpah and Rachel got Bilhah. These four women bore Jacob twelve sons, who founded the twelve tribes of Israel.
29.35 Judah means "praise." Jesus was of this tribe; thus Leah, the hated wife, was in his ancestral line, not Rachel, the adored wife.

I will praise^q the LORD"; therefore she named him Judah; then she ceased bearing.

b. Bilhah's two sons

30 When Rachel saw that she bore Jacob no children, she envied her sister; and she said to Jacob, "Give me children, or I shall die!" ² Jacob became very angry with Rachel and said, "Am I in the place of God, who has withheld from you the fruit of the womb?" ³ Then she said, "Here is my maid Bilhah; go in to her, that she may bear upon my knees and that I too may have children through her." ⁴ So she gave him her maid Bilhah as a wife; and Jacob went in to her. ⁵ And Bilhah conceived and bore Jacob a son. ⁶ Then Rachel said, "God has judged me, and has also heard my voice and given me a son"; therefore she named him Dan.^r ⁷ Rachel's maid Bilhah conceived again and bore Jacob a second son. ⁸ Then Rachel said, "With mighty wrestlings I have wrestled^s with my sister, and have prevailed"; so she named him Naphtali.

c. Zilpah's two sons

9 When Leah saw that she had ceased bearing children, she took her maid Zilpah and gave her to Jacob as a wife. ¹⁰ Then Leah's maid Zilpah bore Jacob a son. ¹¹ And Leah said, "Good fortune!" so she named him Gad.^t ¹² Leah's maid Zilpah bore Jacob a second son. ¹³ And Leah said, "Happy am I! For the women will call me happy"; so she named him Asher.^u

d. Leah's last two sons; Rachel's first one

14 In the days of wheat harvest Reuben went and found mandrakes in the field, and brought them to his mother Leah. Then Rachel said to Leah, "Please give me some of your son's mandrakes." ¹⁵ But she said to her, "Is it a small matter that you have taken away my husband? Would you take away my son's mandrakes also?" Rachel said, "Then he may lie with you tonight for your son's mandrakes." ¹⁶ When Jacob came from the field in the evening, Leah went out to meet him, and said, "You must come in to me; for I have hired you with my son's mandrakes." So he lay with her that night. ¹⁷ And God heeded Leah, and she conceived and bore Jacob a fifth son. ¹⁸ Leah said, "God has given me my hire^v because I gave my maid to my husband"; so she named him Issachar. ¹⁹ And Leah conceived again, and she bore Jacob a sixth son. ²⁰ Then Leah said, "God has endowed me with a good dowry; now my husband will honor^w me, because I have borne him six sons"; so she named him Zebulun. ²¹ Afterwards she bore a daughter, and named her Dinah.

22 Then God remembered Rachel, and God heeded her and opened her womb. ²³ She conceived and bore a son, and said, "God has taken away my reproach"; ²⁴ and she named him Joseph,^x saying, "May the LORD add to me another son!"

Margin references:
30.1 — 1 Sam 1.5, 6
30.2 — Gen 20.18; 29.31
30.3 — Gen 16.2
30.4 — Gen 16.3, 4
30.6 — Lam 3.59
30.8 — Mt 4.13
30.9 — v. 4
30.13 — Prov 31.28
30.14 — Gen 25.30
30.15 — Num 16.9, 13
30.20 — Mt 4.13
30.22 — 1 Sam 1.19, 20; Gen 29.31
30.23 — Isa 4.1; Lk 1.25
30.24 — Gen 35.17

^q Heb hodah   ^r That is He judged   ^s Heb niphtal   ^t That is Fortune   ^u That is Happy   ^v Heb sakar   ^w Heb zabal   ^x That is He adds

30.1,2 Jacob's household was characterized by feuds, the result of having children by two wives and two concubines. Here Rachel, who had not yet borne any children, envied her sister and, in so doing, sinned against the God of providence. The hatred and feuding were not resolved until after the death of Rachel and the submission of Jacob's sons to Joseph in Egypt more than two decades after Joseph was sold into slavery.
30.14 Mandrakes were a leafy plant eaten by peasant women who supposed this would aid them in becoming pregnant. Rachel wanted to eat some in the hope she would have a child. She acquired some of the mandrakes from Leah by promising to allow her to go to bed with Jacob. Leah then had two more sons. Rachel, at last, did have a son, Joseph, then later died while giving birth to Benjamin.
30.22 God remembered . . . God heeded. God remembered Rachel, whom he seemed to have forgotten, and at last answered her prayers that had so long been awaiting a response.

4. Jacob's bargain with Laban

25 When Rachel had borne Joseph, Jacob said to Laban, "Send me away, that I may go to my own home and country. 26 Give me my wives and my children for whom I have served you, and let me go; for you know very well the service I have given you." 27 But Laban said to him, "If you will allow me to say so, I have learned by divination that the LORD has blessed me because of you; 28 name your wages, and I will give it." 29 Jacob said to him, "You yourself know how I have served you, and how your cattle have fared with me. 30 For you had little before I came, and it has increased abundantly; and the LORD has blessed you wherever I turned. But now when shall I provide for my own household also?" 31 He said, "What shall I give you?" Jacob said, "You shall not give me anything; if you will do this for me, I will again feed your flock and keep it: 32 let me pass through all your flock today, removing from it every speckled and spotted sheep and every black lamb, and the spotted and speckled among the goats; and such shall be my wages. 33 So my honesty will answer for me later, when you come to look into my wages with you. Every one that is not speckled and spotted among the goats and black among the lambs, if found with me, shall be counted stolen." 34 Laban said, "Good! Let it be as you have said." 35 But that day Laban removed the male goats that were striped and spotted, and all the female goats that were speckled and spotted, every one that had white on it, and every lamb that was black, and put them in charge of his sons; 36 and he set a distance of three days' journey between himself and Jacob, while Jacob was pasturing the rest of Laban's flock.

37 Then Jacob took fresh rods of poplar and almond and plane, and peeled white streaks in them, exposing the white of the rods. 38 He set the rods that he had peeled in front of the flocks in the troughs, that is, the watering places, where the flocks came to drink. And since they bred when they came to drink, 39 the flocks bred in front of the rods, and so the flocks produced young that were striped, speckled, and spotted. 40 Jacob separated the lambs, and set the faces of the flocks toward the striped and the completely black animals in the flock of Laban; and he put his own droves apart, and did not put them with Laban's flock. 41 Whenever the stronger of the flock were breeding, Jacob laid the rods in the troughs before the eyes of the flock, that they might breed among the rods, 42 but for the feebler of the flock he did not lay them there; so the feebler were Laban's, and the stronger Jacob's. 43 Thus the man grew exceedingly rich, and had large flocks, and male and female slaves, and camels and donkeys.

5. Jacob plans to return home

31 Now Jacob heard that the sons of Laban were saying, "Jacob has taken all that was our father's; he has gained all this wealth from what belonged to our father." 2 And Jacob saw that Laban did not regard him as favorably as he did before. 3 Then the LORD said to Jacob, "Return to the land of your ancestors and to your kindred, and I will be with you." 4 So Jacob sent and called Rachel and Leah into the field where his flock was, 5 and said to them, "I see that your father does not regard me as favorably as he did before. But the God of my father has been with me. 6 You know that I have served your father with all my strength; 7 yet your

Cross-references (margin):
30.25 Gen 24.54, 56
30.26 Gen 29.20, 30;
Hos 12.12
30.27 Gen 39.3, 5
30.28 Gen 29.15
30.29 Gen 31.38-40
30.30 1 Tim 5.8
30.32 Gen 31.8
30.33 Ps 37.6
30.37 Gen 31.9-12
30.43 Gen 12.16; 13.2; 24.35; 26.13, 14
31.3 Gen 28.15, 20, 21; 32.9
31.5 vv. 3, 42; Gen 48.15
31.7 v. 41; Job 19.3; Ps 37.28; 105.14

30.27 *by divination.* The same Hebrew word is used several other times and is variously translated: "divination," "soothsaying," "augury" "enchantment(s)." In any event, whether it was by personal experience or by enchantments, Laban did know that God had blessed him because of Jacob's presence and labors in their midst. Sometimes what we should know as a result of experience remains hidden and we must learn it directly from God in some other fashion. **30.31** Laban worked around the agreement with Jacob so he would benefit and Jacob would lose. In the long run it worked to Jacob's benefit, and he became a wealthy man. This only caused Laban and his sons to become envious of Jacob (31.1).

father has cheated me and changed my wages ten times, but God did not

31.8
Gen 30.32

permit him to harm me. 8 If he said, 'The speckled shall be your wages,' then all the flock bore speckled; and if he said, 'The striped shall be your wages,' then all the flock bore striped. 9 Thus God has taken away the livestock of your father, and given them to me.

10   "During the mating of the flock I once had a dream in which I looked up and saw that the male goats that leaped upon the flock were striped, speckled, and mottled. 11 Then the angel of God said to me in the

31.11
Gen 48.16

dream, 'Jacob,' and I said, 'Here I am!' 12 And he said, 'Look up and see that all the goats that leap on the flock are striped, speckled, and mottled; for I have seen all that Laban is doing to you. 13 I am the God of Bethel,*y*

31.13
Gen 28.13,
18, 20
31.14
Gen 29.15, 27

where you anointed a pillar and made a vow to me. Now leave this land at once and return to the land of your birth.' " 14 Then Rachel and Leah answered him, "Is there any portion or inheritance left to us in our father's house? 15 Are we not regarded by him as foreigners? For he has sold us, and he has been using up the money given for us. 16 All the property that God has taken away from our father belongs to us and to our children; now then, do whatever God has said to you."

6. Jacob's flight from Laban

a. Jacob steals away

17   So Jacob arose, and set his children and his wives on camels; 18 and he drove away all his livestock, all the property that he had gained, the livestock in his possession that he had acquired in Paddan-aram, to go to his father Isaac in the land of Canaan.

31.19
vv. 30, 34;
Judg 17.5;
1 Sam 19.13;
Hos 3.4
31.21
Gen 37.25

19   Now Laban had gone to shear his sheep, and Rachel stole her father's household gods. 20 And Jacob deceived Laban the Aramean, in that he did not tell him that he intended to flee. 21 So he fled with all that he had; starting out he crossed the Euphrates,*z* and set his face toward the hill country of Gilead.

b. Laban overtakes Jacob

31.23
Gen 13.8

22   On the third day Laban was told that Jacob had fled. 23 So he took his kinsfolk with him and pursued Laban for seven days until he caught up with him in the hill country of Gilead. 24 But God came to Laban the

31.24
Gen 20.3;
Job 33.15;
Gen 24.50

Aramean in a dream by night, and said to him, "Take heed that you say not a word to Jacob, either good or bad."

25   Laban overtook Jacob. Now Jacob had pitched his tent in the hill country, and Laban with his kinsfolk camped in the hill country of Gilead.

31.26
1 Sam 30.2
31.27
v. 55;
Ruth 1.9, 14;
Acts 20.37

26 Laban said to Jacob, "What have you done? You have deceived me, and carried away my daughters like captives of the sword. 27 Why did you flee secretly and deceive me and not tell me? I would have sent you away with mirth and songs, with tambourine and lyre. 28 And why did you not permit me to kiss my sons and my daughters farewell? What you have done is foolish. 29 It is in my power to do you harm; but the God of your

31.29
vv. 53, 24

father spoke to me last night, saying, 'Take heed that you speak to Jacob

31.30
v. 19

neither good nor bad.' 30 Even though you had to go because you longed greatly for your father's house, why did you steal my gods?" 31 Jacob answered Laban, "Because I was afraid, for I thought that you would take

31.32
Gen 44.9

your daughters from me by force. 32 But anyone with whom you find your

y Cn: Meaning of Heb uncertain   *z* Heb *the river*

31.11 God's time for Jacob to return to the land of his father was at hand. This was revealed to him in a dream. When Rachel and Leah heard this they were in agreement and said, "Do whatever God has said to you" (v. 16). This was at least one time when the two sisters saw eye to eye.
31.19 *Rachel stole her father's household gods.* Since

the images belonged to Laban, Rachel was a thief. Yet the real problem was whether either Laban or Rachel was truly a child of God. They were idol-worshipers, and idolatry is forbidden in the Scriptures. Since Rachel had been married to Jacob for some time, apparently he had little influence on her spiritual state.

gods shall not live. In the presence of our kinsfolk, point out what I have that is yours, and take it." Now Jacob did not know that Rachel had stolen the gods. [a]

c. Rachel and Laban's household gods

33 So Laban went into Jacob's tent, and into Leah's tent, and into the tent of the two maids, but he did not find them. And he went out of Leah's tent, and entered Rachel's. [34] Now Rachel had taken the household gods and put them in the camel's saddle, and sat on them. Laban felt all about in the tent, but did not find them. [35] And she said to her father, "Let not my lord be angry that I cannot rise before you, for the way of women is upon me." So he searched, but did not find the household gods.

36 Then Jacob became angry, and upbraided Laban. Jacob said to Laban, "What is my offense? What is my sin, that you have hotly pursued me? [37] Although you have felt about through all my goods, what have you found of all your household goods? Set it here before my kinsfolk and your kinsfolk, so that they may decide between us two. [38] These twenty years I have been with you; your ewes and your female goats have not miscarried, and I have not eaten the rams of your flocks. [39] That which was torn by wild beasts I did not bring to you; I bore the loss of it myself; of my hand you required it, whether stolen by day or stolen by night. [40] It was like this with me: by day the heat consumed me, and the cold by night, and my sleep fled from my eyes. [41] These twenty years I have been in your house; I served you fourteen years for your two daughters, and six years for your flock, and you have changed my wages ten times. [42] If the God of my father, the God of Abraham and the Fear [b] of Isaac, had not been on my side, surely now you would have sent me away empty-handed. God saw my affliction and the labor of my hands, and rebuked you last night."

d. The covenant between Jacob and Laban: Mizpah

43 Then Laban answered and said to Jacob, "The daughters are my daughters, the children are my children, the flocks are my flocks, and all that you see is mine. But what can I do today about these daughters of mine, or about their children whom they have borne? [44] Come now, let us make a covenant, you and I; and let it be a witness between you and me." [45] So Jacob took a stone, and set it up as a pillar. [46] And Jacob said to his kinsfolk, "Gather stones," and they took stones, and made a heap; and they ate there by the heap. [47] Laban called it Jegar-sahadutha; [c] but Jacob called it Galeed. [d] [48] Laban said, "This heap is a witness between you and me today." Therefore he called it Galeed, [49] and the pillar [e] Mizpah, [f] for he said, "The LORD watch between you and me, when we are absent one from the other. [50] If you ill-treat my daughters, or if you take wives in addition to my daughters, though no one else is with us, remember that God is witness between you and me."

51 Then Laban said to Jacob, "See this heap and see the pillar, which I have set between you and me. [52] This heap is a witness, and the pillar is a witness, that I will not pass beyond this heap to you, and you will not pass beyond this heap and this pillar to me, for harm. [53] May the God of Abraham and the God of Nahor"—the God of their father—"judge between us." So Jacob swore by the Fear [b] of his father Isaac, [54] and Jacob offered a sacrifice on the height and called his kinsfolk to eat bread; and they ate bread and tarried all night in the hill country.

---

a Heb *them*   b Meaning of Heb uncertain   c In Aramaic *The heap of witness*   d In Hebrew *The heap of witness*   e Compare Sam: MT lacks *the pillar*   f That is *Watchpost*

31.35 *the way of women is upon me*, i.e., "I'm having my monthly period." Either Laban did not want to disturb her during the discomfort of her period, or he recognized that whatever she sat on would be ceremonially defiled (cf. the Mosaic law in Lev 5).

31.49 *Mizpah* means "Watchpost." Jacob and Laban made God their witness, the third party in their agreement. Each expected God to enforce the covenant if either man broke it.

31.35
Ex 20.12;
Lev 19.32

31.39
Ex 22.10-13

31.41
Gen 29.27,
30; v. 7
31.42
Ps 124.1, 2;
v. 53;
Isa 8.13;
Gen 29.32;
1 Chr 12.17

31.44
Gen 21.27,
32; 26.28;
Josh 24.27
31.45
Gen 28.18
31.48
Josh 24.27
31.49
Judg 11.29;
1 Sam 7.5

31.53
Gen 16.5;
21.23; 28.13;
v. 42

31.55
Gen 18.33;
30.25

55ᵍ Early in the morning Laban rose up, and kissed his grandchildren and his daughters and blessed them; then he departed and returned home.

H. Jacob's meeting with Esau

1. The preparations

32.1
Ps 34.7;
91.11;
Heb 1.14
32.2
Ps 103.21
32.3
Gen 33.14,
16; 25.30;
36.8, 9
32.4
Prov 15.1
32.5
Gen 30.43;
33.8, 15
32.6
Gen 33.1
32.7
v. 11

32 Jacob went on his way and the angels of God met him; 2 and when Jacob saw them he said, "This is God's camp!" So he called that place Mahanaim.ʰ

3 Jacob sent messengers before him to his brother Esau in the land of Seir, the country of Edom, 4 instructing them, "Thus you shall say to my lord Esau: Thus says your servant Jacob, 'I have lived with Laban as an alien, and stayed until now; 5 and I have oxen, donkeys, flocks, male and female slaves; and I have sent to tell my lord, in order that I may find favor in your sight.'"

6 The messengers returned to Jacob, saying, "We came to your brother Esau, and he is coming to meet you, and four hundred men are with him." 7 Then Jacob was greatly afraid and distressed; and he divided the people that were with him, and the flocks and herds and camels, into two companies, 8 thinking, "If Esau comes to the one company and destroys it, then the company that is left will escape."

32.9
Gen 31.42;
28.15; 31.13
32.10
Gen 24.27;
Job 8.7
32.11
Gen 27.41,
42; 33.4
32.12
Gen 28.13-15

9 And Jacob said, "O God of my father Abraham and God of my father Isaac, O Lᴏʀᴅ who said to me, 'Return to your country and to your kindred, and I will do you good,' 10 I am not worthy of the least of all the steadfast love and all the faithfulness that you have shown to your servant, for with only my staff I crossed this Jordan; and now I have become two companies. 11 Deliver me, please, from the hand of my brother, from the hand of Esau, for I am afraid of him; he may come and kill us all, the mothers with the children. 12 Yet you have said, 'I will surely do you good, and make your offspring as the sand of the sea, which cannot be counted because of their number.'"

32.13
Gen 43.11;
Prov 18.16

13 So he spent that night there, and from what he had with him he took a present for his brother Esau, 14 two hundred female goats and twenty male goats, two hundred ewes and twenty rams, 15 thirty milch camels and their colts, forty cows and ten bulls, twenty female donkeys and ten male donkeys. 16 These he delivered into the hand of his servants, every drove by itself, and said to his servants, "Pass on ahead of me, and put a space between drove and drove." 17 He instructed the foremost, "When Esau my brother meets you, and asks you, 'To whom do you belong? Where are you going? And whose are these ahead of you?' 18 then you shall say, 'They belong to your servant Jacob; they are a present sent to my lord Esau; and moreover he is behind us.'" 19 He likewise instructed the second and the third and all who followed the droves, "You

32.20
Prov 21.14

shall say the same thing to Esau when you meet him, 20 and you shall say, 'Moreover your servant Jacob is behind us.'" For he thought, "I may appease him with the present that goes ahead of me, and afterwards I shall see his face; perhaps he will accept me." 21 So the present passed on ahead of him; and he himself spent that night in the camp.

2. Jacob becomes Israel: wrestling at the Jabbok

32.22
Deut 3.16;
Josh 12.2

22 The same night he got up and took his two wives, his two maids, and his eleven children, and crossed the ford of the Jabbok. 23 He took

ᵍ Ch 32.1 in Heb   ʰ Here taken to mean *Two camps*

32.1,2 *Jacob went on his way*, i.e., Jacob and his household. *Mahanaim*, "God's camp," or, "two camps." The angels constituted God's protecting hosts. Jacob saw them. Some commentators think there were two hosts, one in front of Jacob and the

other behind him. Thus was he fully protected.
32.20 *I may appease him*. Jacob had every reason to suppose that Esau might still hate him because of the stolen birthright and the blessing. He thought to buy him off by giving him a substantial bribe.

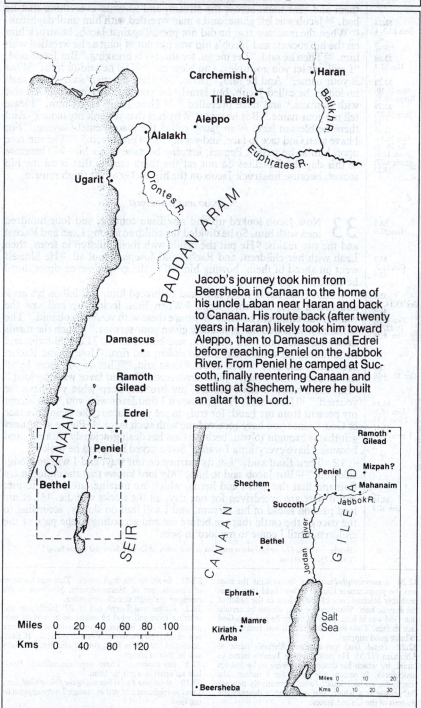

JACOB'S JOURNEYS

Jacob's journey took him from Beersheba in Canaan to the home of his uncle Laban near Haran and back to Canaan. His route back (after twenty years in Haran) likely took him toward Aleppo, then to Damascus and Edrei before reaching Peniel on the Jabbok River. From Peniel he camped at Succoth, finally reentering Canaan and settling at Shechem, where he built an altar to the Lord.

Carchemish
Haran
Balikh R.
Til Barsip
Aleppo
Alalakh
Ugarit
Orontes R.
Euphrates R.
PADDAN ARAM
Damascus
Ramoth Gilead
Edrei
CANAAN
Peniel
Bethel
SEIR

Miles 0 20 40 60 80 100
Kms 0 40 80 120

Ramoth Gilead
Mizpah?
Peniel
Mahanaim
Shechem
Jabbok R.
Succoth
GILEAD
CANAAN
Bethel
Jordan River
Ephrath
Salt Sea
Mamre
Kiriath Arba
Beersheba

Miles 0 10 20
Kms 0 10 20 30

them and sent them across the stream, and likewise everything that he had. 24 Jacob was left alone; and a man wrestled with him until daybreak. 25 When the man saw that he did not prevail against Jacob, he struck him on the hip socket; and Jacob's hip was put out of joint as he wrestled with him. 26 Then he said, "Let me go, for the day is breaking." But Jacob said, "I will not let you go, unless you bless me." 27 So he said to him, "What is your name?" And he said, "Jacob." 28 Then the man[i] said, "You shall no longer be called Jacob, but Israel,[j] for you have striven with God and with humans,[k] and have prevailed." 29 Then Jacob asked him, "Please tell me your name." But he said, "Why is it that you ask my name?" And there he blessed him. 30 So Jacob called the place Peniel,[l] saying, "For I have seen God face to face, and yet my life is preserved." 31 The sun rose upon him as he passed Penuel, limping because of his hip. 32 Therefore to this day the Israelites do not eat the thigh muscle that is on the hip socket, because he struck Jacob on the hip socket at the thigh muscle.

3. Jacob and Esau meet

33 Now Jacob looked up and saw Esau coming, and four hundred men with him. So he divided the children among Leah and Rachel and the two maids. 2 He put the maids with their children in front, then Leah with her children, and Rachel and Joseph last of all. 3 He himself went on ahead of them, bowing himself to the ground seven times, until he came near his brother.

4 But Esau ran to meet him, and embraced him, and fell on his neck and kissed him, and they wept. 5 When Esau looked up and saw the women and children, he said, "Who are these with you?" Jacob said, "The children whom God has graciously given your servant." 6 Then the maids drew near, they and their children, and bowed down; 7 Leah likewise and her children drew near and bowed down; and finally Joseph and Rachel drew near, and they bowed down. 8 Esau said, "What do you mean by all this company that I met?" Jacob answered, "To find favor with my lord." 9 But Esau said, "I have enough, my brother; keep what you have for yourself." 10 Jacob said, "No, please; if I find favor with you, then accept my present from my hand; for truly to see your face is like seeing the face of God — since you have received me with such favor. 11 Please accept my gift that is brought to you, because God has dealt graciously with me, and because I have everything I want." So he urged him, and he took it.

12 Then Esau said, "Let us journey on our way, and I will go alongside you." 13 But Jacob said to him, "My lord knows that the children are frail and that the flocks and herds, which are nursing, are a care to me; and if they are overdriven for one day, all the flocks will die. 14 Let my lord pass on ahead of his servant, and I will lead on slowly, according to the pace of the cattle that are before me and according to the pace of the children, until I come to my lord in Seir."

i Heb *he*   *j* That is *The one who strives with God* or *God strives*   *k* Or *with divine and human beings*
l That is *The face of God*

32.24 *a man wrestled with him.* Some think the man was the preincarnate Christ. Others hold that it was probably Michael, one of the highest in the order of the angelic host. Whichever it was, we can be certain that God was in him. Jacob thought he had seen God face to face. Thus the notion that it was Jesus seems to have good support.
32.28 *Israel.* God had changed Abram's name to Abraham (17.5). He now changes Jacob's name to Israel, by which his descendants were to be known henceforth. It became the name for a nation, not simply for an individual. *Israel* normatively denotes the people as a whole, just as America denotes the citizens of the United States.

32.32 *do not eat the thigh muscle.* This was a matter of custom, not of commandment. Nowhere is the eating of the thigh muscle forbidden.
33.2 *Rachel and Joseph last of all.* Jacob was not trusting Esau and what he might do by way of vengeance. He kept Rachel, whom he loved, and their one child, Joseph, as far away as possible. If Esau destroyed the others first, Rachel and Joseph might still be able to escape.
33.8 *this company.* These were the animals Jacob had set apart as a gift for Esau.
33.10 *to see your face is like seeing the face of God,* i.e., I was so frightened of you as though I were approaching God!

4. Jacob journeys to Shechem

15 So Esau said, "Let me leave with you some of the people who are with me." But he said, "Why should my lord be so kind to me?" 16 So Esau returned that day on his way to Seir. 17 But Jacob journeyed to Succoth,^{m} and built himself a house, and made booths for his cattle; therefore the place is called Succoth.

18 Jacob came safely to the city of Shechem, which is in the land of Canaan, on his way from Paddan-aram; and he camped before the city. 19 And from the sons of Hamor, Shechem's father, he bought for one hundred pieces of money^n the plot of land on which he had pitched his tent. 20 There he erected an altar and called it El-Elohe-Israel.^{o}

I. Jacob's later life

1. The rape of Dinah

34 Now Dinah the daughter of Leah, whom she had borne to Jacob, went out to visit the women of the region. 2 When Shechem son of Hamor the Hivite, prince of the region, saw her, he seized her and lay with her by force. 3 And his soul was drawn to Dinah daughter of Jacob; he loved the girl, and spoke tenderly to her. 4 So Shechem spoke to his father Hamor, saying, "Get me this girl to be my wife."

5 Now Jacob heard that Shechem^p had defiled his daughter Dinah; but his sons were with his cattle in the field, so Jacob held his peace until they came. 6 And Hamor the father of Shechem went out to Jacob to speak with him, 7 just as the sons of Jacob came in from the field. When they heard of it, the men were indignant and very angry, because he had committed an outrage in Israel by lying with Jacob's daughter, for such a thing ought not to be done.

8 But Hamor spoke with them, saying, "The heart of my son Shechem longs for your daughter; please give her to him in marriage. 9 Make marriages with us; give your daughters to us, and take our daughters for yourselves. 10 You shall live with us; and the land shall be open to you; live and trade in it, and get property in it." 11 Shechem also said to her father and to her brothers, "Let me find favor with you, and whatever you say to me I will give. 12 Put the marriage present and gift as high as you like, and I will give whatever you ask me; only give me the girl to be my wife."

13 The sons of Jacob answered Shechem and his father Hamor deceitfully, because he had defiled their sister Dinah. 14 They said to them, "We cannot do this thing, to give our sister to one who is uncircumcised, for that would be a disgrace to us. 15 Only on this condition will we consent to you: that you will become as we are and every male among you be circumcised. 16 Then we will give our daughters to you, and we will take your daughters for ourselves, and we will live among you and become one people. 17 But if you will not listen to us and be circumcised, then we will take our daughter and be gone."

^{m} That is *Booths* ^{n} Heb *one hundred qesitah* ^{o} That is *God, the God of Israel* ^{p} Heb *he*

33.15 Gen 34.11; 47.25; Ruth 2.13
33.17 Judg 8.5, 14
33.18 Josh 24.1; Judg 9.1; Gen 25.20; 28.2
33.19 Josh 24.32; Jn 4.5
34.1 Gen 30.21
34.4 Judg 14.2
34.7 Deut 22.21; Josh 7.15; Judg 20.6; 2 Sam 13.12
34.10 Gen 13.9; 20.15
34.12 Ex 22.16; Deut 22.29; 1 Sam 18.25
34.14 Gen 17.14

33.17 *Succoth.* Rather than travel south to see his father (living close to where Esau lived), Jacob, probably still afraid of Esau, traveled west to Succoth and then northwest to Shechem. It was probably several years before he finally returned to the area of his birth (cf. 31.13).

34.2 Dinah had left the security of her home to go abroad among the Hivites. The passage does not say specifically whether she was raped or was guilty of fornication. Shechem sought to marry her because he loved her. The results were disastrous for all.

34.14 *to one who is uncircumcised.* Jacob's sons used this religious ceremony as a ploy to render the men of the town incapable of defending themselves. Then they slew them in revenge for humbling their sister. Whether all the sons of Jacob were involved in some episodes in connection with the story, the Scriptures do not say. In v. 25 only Simeon and Levi are mentioned, whereas in v. 13 the phrase "the sons of Jacob" is used.

math, Ishmael's daughter, sister of Nebaioth. 4 Adah bore Eliphaz to Esau; Basemath bore Reuel; 5 and Oholibamah bore Jeush, Jalam, and Korah. These are the sons of Esau who were born to him in the land of Canaan.

6 Then Esau took his wives, his sons, his daughters, and all the members of his household, his cattle, all his livestock, and all the property he had acquired in the land of Canaan; and he moved to a land some distance from his brother Jacob. 7 For their possessions were too great for them to live together; the land where they were staying could not support them because of their livestock. 8 So Esau settled in the hill country of Seir; Esau is Edom.

9 These are the descendants of Esau, ancestor of the Edomites, in the hill country of Seir. 10 These are the names of Esau's sons: Eliphaz son of Adah the wife of Esau; Reuel, the son of Esau's wife Basemath. 11 The sons of Eliphaz were Teman, Omar, Zepho, Gatam, and Kenaz. 12 (Timna was a concubine of Eliphaz, Esau's son; she bore Amalek to Eliphaz.) These were the sons of Adah, Esau's wife. 13 These were the sons of Reuel: Nahath, Zerah, Shammah, and Mizzah. These were the sons of Esau's wife, Basemath. 14 These were the sons of Esau's wife Oholibamah, daughter of Anah son[w] of Zibeon: she bore to Esau Jeush, Jalam, and Korah.

15 These are the clans[x] of the sons of Esau. The sons of Eliphaz the firstborn of Esau: the clans[x] Teman, Omar, Zepho, Kenaz, 16 Korah, Gatam, and Amalek; these are the clans[x] of Eliphaz in the land of Edom; they are the sons of Adah. 17 These are the sons of Esau's son Reuel: the clans[x] Nahath, Zerah, Shammah, and Mizzah; these are the clans[x] of Reuel in the land of Edom; they are the sons of Esau's wife Basemath. 18 These are the sons of Esau's wife Oholibamah: the clans[x] Jeush, Jalam, and Korah; these are the clans[x] born of Esau's wife Oholibamah, the daughter of Anah. 19 These are the sons of Esau (that is, Edom), and these are their clans.[x]

20 These are the sons of Seir the Horite, the inhabitants of the land: Lotan, Shobal, Zibeon, Anah, 21 Dishon, Ezer, and Dishan; these are the clans[x] of the Horites, the sons of Seir in the land of Edom. 22 The sons of Lotan were Hori and Heman; and Lotan's sister was Timna. 23 These are the sons of Shobal: Alvan, Manahath, Ebal, Shepho, and Onam. 24 These are the sons of Zibeon: Aiah and Anah; he is the Anah who found the springs[y] in the wilderness, as he pastured the donkeys of his father Zibeon. 25 These are the children of Anah: Dishon and Oholibamah daughter of Anah. 26 These are the sons of Dishon: Hemdan, Eshban, Ithran, and Cheran. 27 These are the sons of Ezer: Bilhan, Zaavan, and Akan. 28 These are the sons of Dishan: Uz and Aran. 29 These are the clans[x] of the Horites: the clans[x] Lotan, Shobal, Zibeon, Anah, 30 Dishon, Ezer, and Dishan; these are the clans[x] of the Horites, clan by clan[z] in the land of Seir.

31 These are the kings who reigned in the land of Edom, before any king reigned over the Israelites. 32 Bela son of Beor reigned in Edom, the name of his city being Dinhabah. 33 Bela died, and Jobab son of Zerah of Bozrah succeeded him as king. 34 Jobab died, and Husham of the land of the Temanites succeeded him as king. 35 Husham died, and Hadad son of Bedad, who defeated Midian in the country of Moab, succeeded him as king, the name of his city being Avith. 36 Hadad died, and Samlah of Masrekah succeeded him as king. 37 Samlah died, and Shaul of Rehoboth

Cross-references (left margin):
36.6 Gen 12.5
36.7 Gen 13.6, 11; 17.8; 28.4
36.8 Gen 32.3
36.10 1 Chr 1.35
36.12 Ex 17.8, 14
36.15 1 Chr 1.34
36.17 1 Chr 1.35, 37
36.18 v. 25; 1 Chr 1.52
36.20 Gen 14.6; Deut 2.12, 22; 1 Chr 1.38
36.25 v. 18; 1 Chr 1.52
36.27 1 Chr 1.42
36.31 1 Chr 1.43

---

w Gk Syr: Heb *daughter*   x Or *chiefs*   y Meaning of Heb uncertain   z Or *chief by chief*

36.9 Esau was the founding father of the Edomite peoples, who lived in the hill country of Seir. They became one of Israel's deadly enemies (Ezek 35.5), though God told Israel not to hate or ravage them (Deut 2.4–6; 23.7; 2 Chr 20.10). The Edomites were unbelievers, and the prophets said they were to be the object of the wrath of God at the end of the age (Isa 11.14; 34.5,6; Ob 1.1–4; Amos 9.12).

4. Jacob journeys to Shechem

15 So Esau said, "Let me leave with you some of the people who are with me." But he said, "Why should my lord be so kind to me?" 16 So Esau returned that day on his way to Seir. 17 But Jacob journeyed to Succoth,[m] and built himself a house, and made booths for his cattle; therefore the place is called Succoth.

18 Jacob came safely to the city of Shechem, which is in the land of Canaan, on his way from Paddan-aram; and he camped before the city. 19 And from the sons of Hamor, Shechem's father, he bought for one hundred pieces of money[n] the plot of land on which he had pitched his tent. 20 There he erected an altar and called it El-Elohe-Israel.[o]

I. Jacob's later life

1. The rape of Dinah

34 Now Dinah the daughter of Leah, whom she had borne to Jacob, went out to visit the women of the region. 2 When Shechem son of Hamor the Hivite, prince of the region, saw her, he seized her and lay with her by force. 3 And his soul was drawn to Dinah the daughter of Jacob; he loved the girl, and spoke tenderly to her. 4 So Shechem spoke to his father Hamor, saying, "Get me this girl to be my wife."

5 Now Jacob heard that Shechem[p] had defiled his daughter Dinah; but his sons were with his cattle in the field, so Jacob held his peace until they came. 6 And Hamor the father of Shechem went out to Jacob to speak with him, 7 just as the sons of Jacob came in from the field. When they heard of it, the men were indignant and very angry, because he had committed an outrage in Israel by lying with Jacob's daughter, for such a thing ought not to be done.

8 But Hamor spoke with them, saying, "The heart of my son Shechem longs for your daughter; please give her to him in marriage. 9 Make marriages with us; give your daughters to us, and take our daughters for yourselves. 10 You shall live with us; and the land shall be open to you; live and trade in it, and get property in it." 11 Shechem also said to her father and to her brothers, "Let me find favor with you, and whatever you say to me I will give. 12 Put the marriage present and gift as high as you like, and I will give whatever you ask me; only give me the girl to be my wife."

13 The sons of Jacob answered Shechem and his father Hamor deceitfully, because he had defiled their sister Dinah. 14 They said to them, "We cannot do this thing, to give our sister to one who is uncircumcised, for that would be a disgrace to us. 15 Only on this condition will we consent to you: that you will become as we are and every male among you be circumcised. 16 Then we will give our daughters to you, and we will take your daughters for ourselves, and we will live among you and become one people. 17 But if you will not listen to us and be circumcised, then we will take our daughter and be gone."

33.15
Gen 34.11;
47.25;
Ruth 2.13
33.17
Judg 8.5, 14

33.18
Josh 24.1;
Judg 9.1;
Gen 25.20;
28.2
33.19
Josh 24.32;
Jn 4.5

34.1
Gen 30.21

34.4
Judg 14.2

34.7
Deut 22.21;
Josh 7.15;
Judg 20.6;
2 Sam 13.12

34.10
Gen 13.9;
20.15

34.12
Ex 22.16;
Deut 22.29;
1 Sam 18.25

34.14
Gen 17.14

---

m That is Booths   n Heb one hundred qesitah   o That is God, the God of Israel   p Heb he

---

33.17 *Succoth.* Rather than travel south to see his father (living close to where Esau lived), Jacob, probably still afraid of Esau, traveled west to Succoth and then northwest to Shechem. It was probably several years before he finally returned to the area of his birth (cf. 31.13).
34.2 Dinah had left the security of her home to go abroad among the Hivites. The passage does not say specifically whether she was raped or was guilty of fornication. Shechem sought to marry her because he

loved her. The results were disastrous for all.
34.14 *to one who is uncircumcised.* Jacob's sons used this religious ceremony as a ploy to render the men of the town incapable of defending themselves. Then they slew them in revenge for humbling their sister. Whether all the sons of Jacob were involved in some episodes in connection with the story, the Scriptures do not say. In v. 25 only Simeon and Levi are mentioned, whereas in v. 13 the phrase "the sons of Jacob" is used.

2. The revenge for the rape of Dinah

18   Their words pleased Hamor and Hamor's son Shechem. 19 And the young man did not delay to do the thing, because he was delighted with Jacob's daughter. Now he was the most honored of all his family. 20 So Hamor and his son Shechem came to the gate of their city and spoke to the men of their city, saying, 21 "These people are friendly with us; let them live in the land and trade in it, for the land is large enough for them; let us take their daughters in marriage, and let us give them our daughters. 22 Only on this condition will they agree to live among us, to become one people: that every male among us be circumcised as they are circumcised. 23 Will not their livestock, their property, and all their animals be ours? Only let us agree with them, and they will live among us." 24 And all who went out of the city gate heeded Hamor and his son Shechem; and every male was circumcised, all who went out of the gate of his city.

25   On the third day, when they were still in pain, two of the sons of Jacob, Simeon and Levi, Dinah's brothers, took their swords and came against the city unawares, and killed all the males. 26 They killed Hamor and his son Shechem with the sword, and took Dinah out of Shechem's house, and went away. 27 And the other sons of Jacob came upon the slain, and plundered the city, because their sister had been defiled. 28 They took their flocks and their herds, their donkeys, and whatever was in the city and in the field. 29 All their wealth, all their little ones and their wives, all that was in the houses, they captured and made their prey. 30 Then Jacob said to Simeon and Levi, "You have brought trouble on me by making me odious to the inhabitants of the land, the Canaanites and the Perizzites; my numbers are few, and if they gather themselves against me and attack me, I shall be destroyed, both I and my household." 31 But they said, "Should our sister be treated like a whore?"

3. Jacob returns to Bethel: God renews the covenant promises

35 God said to Jacob, "Arise, go up to Bethel, and settle there. Make an altar there to the God who appeared to you when you fled from your brother Esau." 2 So Jacob said to his household and to all who were with him, "Put away the foreign gods that are among you, and purify yourselves, and change your clothes; 3 then come, let us go up to Bethel, that I may make an altar there to the God who answered me in the day of my distress and has been with me wherever I have gone." 4 So they gave to Jacob all the foreign gods that they had, and the rings that were in their ears; and Jacob hid them under the oak that was near Shechem.

5   As they journeyed, a terror from God fell upon the cities all around them, so that no one pursued them. 6 Jacob came to Luz (that is, Bethel), which is in the land of Canaan, he and all the people who were with him, 7 and there he built an altar and called the place El-bethel,*q* because it was there that God had revealed himself to him when he fled from his brother. 8 And Deborah, Rebekah's nurse, died, and she was buried under an oak below Bethel. So it was called Allon-bacuth.*r*

9   God appeared to Jacob again when he came from Paddan-aram, and he blessed him. 10 God said to him, "Your name is Jacob; no longer shall you be called Jacob, but Israel shall be your name." So he was called

---

q That is God of Bethel   r That is Oak of weeping

34.19 1 Chr 4.9

34.24 Gen 23.10

34.25 Gen 49.5-7

34.30 Gen 49.6; Ex 5.21; Gen 36.26, 27

35.1 Gen 28.19, 13; 27.43
35.2 Gen 31.19, 30, 34; Ex 19.10, 14
35.3 Gen 32.7, 24; 28.20-22; 28.15
35.4 Hos 2.13; Josh 24.26

35.6 Gen 28.19; 48.3
35.7 Gen 28.13

35.8 Gen 24.59

35.9 Hos 12.4; Gen 32.29
35.10 Gen 32.28

34.25 *Simeon and Levi* were the second and third sons of Jacob by Leah. Dinah was also born of Leah. Reuben, Leah's first son by Jacob, is not mentioned by name in the account.
34.30 *making me odious.* Since the Canaanites and Perizzites were far more numerous than Jacob's small band, he feared they would revenge the death of their friends and exterminate Jacob and his family.

35.2 *Put away the foreign gods.* This was a sorry example of a family divided between those who worshiped the true God and those who had idols. However they had acquired these idols, Jacob commanded that they must be done away with. They were on their way to Bethel, where he was to build an altar and worship the true God with his family.

Israel. ¹¹God said to him, "I am God Almighty:^s be fruitful and multiply;
a nation and a company of nations shall come from you, and kings shall
spring from you. ¹²The land that I gave to Abraham and Isaac I will give
to you, and I will give the land to your offspring after you." ¹³Then God
went up from him at the place where he had spoken with him. ¹⁴Jacob
set up a pillar in the place where he had spoken with him, a pillar of stone;
and he poured out a drink offering on it, and poured oil on it. ¹⁵So Jacob
called the place where God had spoken with him Bethel.

4. Benjamin's birth; Rachel's death

16   Then they journeyed from Bethel; and when they were still some
distance from Ephrath, Rachel was in childbirth, and she had hard labor.
¹⁷When she was in her hard labor, the midwife said to her, "Do not be
afraid; for now you will have another son." ¹⁸As her soul was departing
(for she died), she named him Ben-oni;^t but his father called him Benjamin.^u ¹⁹So Rachel died, and she was buried on the way to Ephrath (that
is, Bethlehem), ²⁰and Jacob set up a pillar at her grave; it is the pillar of
Rachel's tomb, which is there to this day. ²¹Israel journeyed on, and
pitched his tent beyond the tower of Eder.

5. The sin of Reuben

22   While Israel lived in that land, Reuben went and lay with Bilhah
his father's concubine; and Israel heard of it.

6. The sons of Jacob

Now the sons of Jacob were twelve. ²³The sons of Leah: Reuben
(Jacob's firstborn), Simeon, Levi, Judah, Issachar, and Zebulun. ²⁴The
sons of Rachel: Joseph and Benjamin. ²⁵The sons of Bilhah, Rachel's
maid: Dan and Naphtali. ²⁶The sons of Zilpah, Leah's maid: Gad and
Asher. These were the sons of Jacob who were born to him in Paddan-
aram.

7. The death of Isaac

27   Jacob came to his father Isaac at Mamre, or Kiriath-arba (that is,
Hebron), where Abraham and Isaac had resided as aliens. ²⁸Now the days
of Isaac were one hundred eighty years. ²⁹And Isaac breathed his last; he
died and was gathered to his people, old and full of days; and his sons Esau
and Jacob buried him.

IX. The descendants of Esau (36.1–43)

36   These are the descendants of Esau (that is, Edom). ²Esau took his
wives from the Canaanites: Adah daughter of Elon the Hittite,
Oholibamah daughter of Anah son^v of Zibeon the Hivite, ³and Base-

^s Traditional rendering of Heb El Shaddai   ^t That is Son of my sorrow   ^u That is Son of the right hand
or Son of the South   ^v Sam Gk Syr: Heb daughter

Cross-references column:
35.11 Gen 17.1; 28.3; 48.4; 17.6, 16; 36.31
35.12 Gen 13.15; 26.3; 28.13
35.13 Gen 17.22
35.14 Gen 28.18
35.15 Gen 28.19
35.17 Gen 30.24
35.19 Gen 48.7; Ruth 1.2; Mic 5.2; Mt 2.6
35.20 1 Sam 10.2; 35.5; Ex 15.16; Deut 2.25; 11.25
35.22 Gen 49.2; 1 Chr 5.1; 1 Cor 5.1
35.27 Gen 18.1; 23.9
35.29 Gen 25.8; 15.15
36.1 Gen 25.30
36.2 Gen 26.34; 28.9

35.13,14 This is the first recorded instance of the drink or wine offering. In Ex 29.40 and Lev 23.13 wine offerings are specified. In Num 15.3–10 different quantities of wine are specified, depending on the kind of sacrifice offered. The Jews perverted the wine offering by using it along with sacrificial cakes offered to Ashtoreth, the Queen of Heaven (Jer 44.17–19). God censured Israel for offering wine to idols (Jer 19.13; Ezek 20.28). The wine offering symbolizes the outpoured blood of Christ on Calvary (Isa 53.12; Mt 26.28; Heb 9.11–14) and the outpouring of the Holy Spirit upon the church (Joel 2.28; Acts 2.13ff). Wine or grape juice is used at the Lord's Supper, but it is drunk, not poured out, and memorializes Christ's

death till he comes again.
35.16 *Bethel.* See note on Gen 28.19.
35.18 Benjamin was the twelfth son of Jacob and was born of Rachel, who died at his birth. He was the full brother of Joseph and half brother of the other ten sons of Jacob. He was born in Canaan and his mother's tomb may still be seen in Bethlehem. Jacob showed unusual affection for Joseph and Benjamin, who were the sons of the woman he really loved and for whom he spent seven years of hard labor with his uncle Laban. Joseph's special concern for his full brother Benjamin may be understood in light of the hatred the ten other brothers had for them.

math, Ishmael's daughter, sister of Nebaioth. [4] Adah bore Eliphaz to Esau; Basemath bore Reuel; [5] and Oholibamah bore Jeush, Jalam, and Korah. These are the sons of Esau who were born to him in the land of Canaan.

36.6
Gen 12.5

[6] Then Esau took his wives, his sons, his daughters, and all the members of his household, his cattle, all his livestock, and all the property he had acquired in the land of Canaan; and he moved to a land some distance from his brother Jacob. [7] For their possessions were too great for them to live together; the land where they were staying could not support them because of their livestock. [8] So Esau settled in the hill country of Seir; Esau is Edom.

36.7
Gen 13.6, 11;
17.8; 28.4
36.8
Gen 32.3

[9] These are the descendants of Esau, ancestor of the Edomites, in the hill country of Seir. [10] These are the names of Esau's sons: Eliphaz son of Adah the wife of Esau; Reuel, the son of Esau's wife Basemath. [11] The sons of Eliphaz were Teman, Omar, Zepho, Gatam, and Kenaz. [12] (Timna was a concubine of Eliphaz, Esau's son; she bore Amalek to Eliphaz.) These were the sons of Adah, Esau's wife. [13] These were the sons of Reuel: Nahath, Zerah, Shammah, and Mizzah. These were the sons of Esau's wife, Basemath. [14] These were the sons of Esau's wife Oholibamah, daughter of Anah son[w] of Zibeon: she bore to Esau Jeush, Jalam, and Korah.

36.10
1 Chr 1.35
36.12
Ex 17.8, 14

[15] These are the clans[x] of the sons of Esau. The sons of Eliphaz the firstborn of Esau: the clans[x] Teman, Omar, Zepho, Kenaz, [16] Korah, Gatam, and Amalek; these are the clans[x] of Eliphaz in the land of Edom; they are the sons of Adah. [17] These are the sons of Esau's son Reuel: the clans[x] Nahath, Zerah, Shammah, and Mizzah; these are the clans[x] of Reuel in the land of Edom; they are the sons of Esau's wife Basemath. [18] These are the sons of Esau's wife Oholibamah: the clans[x] Jeush, Jalam, and Korah; these are the clans[x] born of Esau's wife Oholibamah, the daughter of Anah. [19] These are the sons of Esau (that is, Edom), and these are their clans.[x]

36.15
1 Chr 1.34
36.17
1 Chr 1.35,
37
36.18
v. 25;
1 Chr 1.52

[20] These are the sons of Seir the Horite, the inhabitants of the land: Lotan, Shobal, Zibeon, Anah, [21] Dishon, Ezer, and Dishan; these are the clans[x] of the Horites, the sons of Seir in the land of Edom. [22] The sons of Lotan were Hori and Heman; and Lotan's sister was Timna. [23] These are the sons of Shobal: Alvan, Manahath, Ebal, Shepho, and Onam. [24] These are the sons of Zibeon: Aiah and Anah; he is the Anah who found the springs[y] in the wilderness, as he pastured the donkeys of his father Zibeon. [25] These are the children of Anah: Dishon and Oholibamah daughter of Anah. [26] These are the sons of Dishon: Hemdan, Eshban, Ithran, and Cheran. [27] These are the sons of Ezer: Bilhan, Zaavan, and Akan. [28] These are the sons of Dishan: Uz and Aran. [29] These are the clans[x] of the Horites: the clans[x] Lotan, Shobal, Zibeon, Anah, [30] Dishon, Ezer, and Dishan; these are the clans[x] of the Horites, clan by clan[z] in the land of Seir.

36.20
Gen 14.6;
Deut 2.12,
22;
1 Chr 1.38

36.25
v. 18;
1 Chr 1.52
36.27
1 Chr 1.42

[31] These are the kings who reigned in the land of Edom, before any king reigned over the Israelites. [32] Bela son of Beor reigned in Edom, the name of his city being Dinhabah. [33] Bela died, and Jobab son of Zerah of Bozrah succeeded him as king. [34] Jobab died, and Husham of the land of the Temanites succeeded him as king. [35] Husham died, and Hadad son of Bedad, who defeated Midian in the country of Moab, succeeded him as king, the name of his city being Avith. [36] Hadad died, and Samlah of Masrekah succeeded him as king. [37] Samlah died, and Shaul of Rehoboth

36.31
1 Chr 1.43

---

w Gk Syr: Heb *daughter*   *x* Or *chiefs*   *y* Meaning of Heb uncertain   *z* Or *chief by chief*

36.9 Esau was the founding father of the Edomite peoples, who lived in the hill country of Seir. They became one of Israel's deadly enemies (Ezek 35.5), though God told Israel not to hate or ravage them (Deut 2.4–6; 23.7; 2 Chr 20.10). The Edomites were unbelievers, and the prophets said they were to be the object of the wrath of God at the end of the age (Isa 11.14; 34.5,6; Ob 1.1–4; Amos 9.12).

on the Euphrates succeeded him as king. ³⁸Shaul died, and Baal-hanan
son of Achbor succeeded him as king. ³⁹Baal-hanan son of Achbor died,
and Hadar succeeded him as king, the name of his city being Pau; his
wife's name was Mehetabel, the daughter of Matred, daughter of Me-
zahab.

40   These are the names of the clans*ᵃ* of Esau, according to their
families and their localities by their names: the clans*ᵃ* Timna, Alvah,
Jetheth, ⁴¹Oholibamah, Elah, Pinon, ⁴²Kenaz, Teman, Mibzar, ⁴³Mag-
diel, and Iram; these are the clans*ᵃ* of Edom (that is, Esau, the father of
Edom), according to their settlements in the land that they held.

X. The descendants of Jacob (37.1–50.26)

A. Joseph sold into slavery

1. *Joseph's dream: his brothers' hatred*

37 Jacob settled in the land where his father had lived as an alien, the
land of Canaan. ²This is the story of the family of Jacob.
Joseph, being seventeen years old, was shepherding the flock with his
brothers; he was a helper to the sons of Bilhah and Zilpah, his father's
wives; and Joseph brought a bad report of them to their father. ³Now
Israel loved Joseph more than any other of his children, because he was
the son of his old age; and he had made him a long robe with sleeves.*ᵇ*
⁴But when his brothers saw that their father loved him more than all his
brothers, they hated him, and could not speak peaceably to him.

5   Once Joseph had a dream, and when he told it to his brothers, they
hated him even more. ⁶He said to them, "Listen to this dream that I
dreamed. ⁷There we were, binding sheaves in the field. Suddenly my
sheaf rose and stood upright; then your sheaves gathered around it, and
bowed down to my sheaf." ⁸His brothers said to him, "Are you indeed
to reign over us? Are you indeed to have dominion over us?" So they hated
him even more because of his dreams and his words.

9   He had another dream, and told it to his brothers, saying, "Look,
I have had another dream: the sun, the moon, and eleven stars were
bowing down to me." ¹⁰But when he told it to his father and to his
brothers, his father rebuked him, and said to him, "What kind of dream
is this that you have had? Shall we indeed come, I and your mother and
your brothers, and bow to the ground before you?" ¹¹So his brothers were
jealous of him, but his father kept the matter in mind.

2. *The conspiracy to kill Joseph*

12   Now his brothers went to pasture their father's flock near Shechem. ¹³And Israel said to Joseph, "Are not your brothers pasturing the
flock at Shechem? Come, I will send you to them." He answered, "Here
I am." ¹⁴So he said to him, "Go now, see if it is well with your brothers
and with the flock; and bring word back to me." So he sent him from the
valley of Hebron.
He came to Shechem, ¹⁵and a man found him wandering in the fields;
the man asked him, "What are you seeking?" ¹⁶"I am seeking my brothers," he said; "tell me, please, where they are pasturing the flock." ¹⁷The

ᵃ Or *chiefs*   *ᵇ* Traditional rendering (compare Gk): *a coat of many colors*; meaning of Heb uncertain

37.5 It was unwise for Joseph to tell his brothers
about his dream. They understood the implications,
and this was the cause for their hatred of him. No
doubt he told of the dream in a fit of youthful
enthusiasm—he was not yet tempered by age and
discretion.

37.17 *Dothan*, is mentioned only three times in the
Old Testament. It has been excavated by Joseph Free
and others. The results show that the site was occupied in Jacob's time. It was located near Mt. Gilboa
and was later occupied by the tribe of Mannaseh.

man said, "They have gone away, for I heard them say, 'Let us go to Dothan.'" So Joseph went after his brothers, and found them at Dothan. 18 They saw him from a distance, and before he came near to them, they conspired to kill him. 19 They said to one another, "Here comes this dreamer. 20 Come now, let us kill him and throw him into one of the pits; then we shall say that a wild animal has devoured him, and we shall see what will become of his dreams." 21 But when Reuben heard it, he delivered him out of their hands, saying, "Let us not take his life." 22 Reuben said to them, "Shed no blood; throw him into this pit here in the wilderness, but lay no hand on him" — that he might rescue him out of their hand and restore him to his father. 23 So when Joseph came to his brothers, they stripped him of his robe, the long robe with sleeves*c* that he wore; 24 and they took him and threw him into a pit. The pit was empty; there was no water in it.

3. *Joseph sold to traders*

25 Then they sat down to eat; and looking up they saw a caravan of Ishmaelites coming from Gilead, with their camels carrying gum, balm, and resin, on their way to carry it down to Egypt. 26 Then Judah said to his brothers, "What profit is it if we kill our brother and conceal his blood? 27 Come, let us sell him to the Ishmaelites, and not lay our hands on him, for he is our brother, our own flesh." And his brothers agreed. 28 When some Midianite traders passed by, they drew Joseph up, lifting him out of the pit, and sold him to the Ishmaelites for twenty pieces of silver. And they took Joseph to Egypt.

4. *Reuben's distress and Jacob's grief*

29 When Reuben returned to the pit and saw that Joseph was not in the pit, he tore his clothes. 30 He returned to his brothers, and said, "The boy is gone; and I, where can I turn?" 31 Then they took Joseph's robe, slaughtered a goat, and dipped the robe in the blood. 32 They had the long robe with sleeves*c* taken to their father, and they said, "This we have found; see now whether it is your son's robe or not." 33 He recognized it, and said, "It is my son's robe! A wild animal has devoured him; Joseph is without doubt torn to pieces." 34 Then Jacob tore his garments, and put sackcloth on his loins, and mourned for his son many days. 35 All his sons and all his daughters sought to comfort him; but he refused to be comforted, and said, "No, I shall go down to Sheol to my son, mourning." Thus his father bewailed him. 36 Meanwhile the Midianites had sold him in Egypt to Potiphar, one of Pharaoh's officials, the captain of the guard.

B. *Judah's adultery*

1. *The birth of Er and his marriage to Tamar*

38 It happened at that time that Judah went down from his brothers and settled near a certain Adullamite whose name was Hirah. 2 There Judah saw the daughter of a certain Canaanite whose name was Shua; he married her and went in to her. 3 She conceived and bore a son;

c See note on 37.3

Cross-references (left margin):

37.18
1 Sam 19.1;
Mt 27.1;
Acts 23.12

37.21
Gen 42.22

37.25
vv. 28, 36;
Gen 43.11;
Jer 8.22
37.26
v. 20;
Gen 4.10;
Job 16.18
37.27
Gen 42.21
37.28
Judg 6.3;
Gen 45.4, 5;
Acts 7.9;
Gen 39.1

37.29
Gen 44.13
37.30
Gen 42.13, 36
37.31
vv. 3, 23

37.33
v. 20;
Gen 44.28
37.34
v. 29;
2 Sam 3.31
37.35
2 Sam 12.17;
Gen 42.38;
44.29, 31
37.36
Gen 39.1

38.3
Gen 46.12;
Num 26.19

37.22 As the eldest son, Reuben wanted to save Joseph from the fate that awaited him. He intended to return to the pit (probably a cistern without water but too deep for Joseph to escape from it) and free his brother. Joseph was sold into slavery when Reuben was absent. Later (42.22) he reminded his brothers about his innocence and their guilt.
37.28 The text is not clear on what the relationship was between the Midianite traders and the Ishmaelites. The Midianites were descendants of Abraham

and Keturah; the Ishmaelites were descendants of Abraham and Hagar; 39.1 states that the Ishmaelites sold Joseph to Potiphar.
37.34 *Jacob . . . mourned.* Jacob's grief fully sustains the scriptural teaching that as a man sows, so shall he reap. He had cruelly deceived his own father; now his sons deceive him. Twenty years later, when retribution seemed likely, the sons were to experience their own anguish for their deception (see 42.21).
37.35 *Sheol.* See note on Deut 32.22.

and he named him Er. 4 Again she conceived and bore a son whom she
named Onan. 5 Yet again she bore a son, and she named him Shelah. She*d*
was in Chezib when she bore him. 6 Judah took a wife for Er his firstborn;
her name was Tamar. 7 But Er, Judah's firstborn, was wicked in the sight
of the LORD, and the LORD put him to death. 8 Then Judah said to Onan,
"Go in to your brother's wife and perform the duty of a brother-in-law
to her; raise up offspring for your brother." 9 But since Onan knew that
the offspring would not be his, he spilled his semen on the ground
whenever he went in to his brother's wife, so that he would not give
offspring to his brother. 10 What he did was displeasing in the sight of the
LORD, and he put him to death also. 11 Then Judah said to his daughter-in-
law Tamar, "Remain a widow in your father's house until my son Shelah
grows up" — for he feared that he too would die, like his brothers. So
Tamar went to live in her father's house.

2. Judah goes in to Tamar

12   In course of time the wife of Judah, Shua's daughter, died; when
Judah's time of mourning was over,*e* he went up to Timnah to his
sheepshearers, he and his friend Hirah the Adullamite. 13 When Tamar
was told, "Your father-in-law is going up to Timnah to shear his sheep,"
14 she put off her widow's garments, put on a veil, wrapped herself up,
and sat down at the entrance to Enaim, which is on the road to Timnah.
She saw that Shelah was grown up, yet she had not been given to him in
marriage. 15 When Judah saw her, he thought her to be a prostitute, for
she had covered her face. 16 He went over to her at the roadside, and said,
"Come, let me come in to you," for he did not know that she was his
daughter-in-law. She said, "What will you give me, that you may come
in to me?" 17 He answered, "I will send you a kid from the flock." And
she said, "Only if you give me a pledge, until you send it." 18 He said,
"What pledge shall I give you?" She replied, "Your signet and your cord,
and the staff that is in your hand." So he gave them to her, and went in
to her, and she conceived by him. 19 Then she got up and went away, and
taking off her veil she put on the garments of her widowhood.

20   When Judah sent the kid by his friend the Adullamite, to recover
the pledge from the woman, he could not find her. 21 He asked the
townspeople, "Where is the temple prostitute who was at Enaim by the
wayside?" But they said, "No prostitute has been here." 22 So he returned
to Judah, and said, "I have not found her; moreover the townspeople said,
'No prostitute has been here.' " 23 Judah replied, "Let her keep the things
as her own, otherwise we will be laughed at; you see, I sent this kid, and
you could not find her."

3. Tamar justified: Perez and Zerah born

24   About three months later Judah was told, "Your daughter-in-law
Tamar has played the whore; moreover she is pregnant as a result of
whoredom." And Judah said, "Bring her out, and let her be burned."
25 As she was being brought out, she sent word to her father-in-law, "It
was the owner of these who made me pregnant." And she said, "Take
note, please, whose these are, the signet and the cord and the staff."
26 Then Judah acknowledged them and said, "She is more in the right than

d Gk: Heb *He*   *e* Heb *when Judah was comforted*

38.7 1 Chr 2.3
38.8 Deut 25.5; Mt 22.24
38.9 Deut 25.6
38.11 Ruth 1.12, 13
38.12 Josh 15.10, 57
38.17 Ezek 16.33; v. 20
38.18 v. 25
38.19 v. 14
38.24 Lev 21.9; Deut 22.21
38.25 v. 18
38.26 1 Sam 24.17; v. 14

38.8 *raise up offspring for your brother.* This custom
of levirate marriage, in which the nearest relative was
to continue the family line by marriage to the widow,
is illustrated in the case of Ruth and Boaz. See note
about this custom in Deut 25.5–10.
38.15 Tamar played the role of a prostitute in order
to raise up offspring for her dead husband. Judah

refused to let Shelah his son raise up offspring by
Tamar. Judah himself was wrong not to give Shelah
to Tamar for this purpose, and he was also guilty of
fornication. He further aggravated his sins by accusing Tamar of being a prostitute without inquiring into
the circumstances surrounding her pregnancy.

I, since I did not give her to my son Shelah." And he did not lie with her again.

27 When the time of her delivery came, there were twins in her womb. 28 While she was in labor, one put out a hand; and the midwife took and bound on his hand a crimson thread, saying, "This one came out first." 29 But just then he drew back his hand, and out came his brother; and she said, "What a breach you have made for yourself!" Therefore he was named Perez.*f* 30 Afterward his brother came out with the crimson thread on his hand; and he was named Zerah.*g*

C. Joseph, man of integrity

1. His prosperity

39 Now Joseph was taken down to Egypt, and Potiphar, an officer of Pharaoh, the captain of the guard, an Egyptian, bought him from the Ishmaelites who had brought him down there. 2 The LORD was with Joseph, and he became a successful man; he was in the house of his Egyptian master. 3 His master saw that the LORD was with him, and that the LORD caused all that he did to prosper in his hands. 4 So Joseph found favor in his sight and attended him; he made him overseer of his house and put him in charge of all that he had. 5 From the time that he made him overseer in his house and over all that he had, the LORD blessed the Egyptian's house for Joseph's sake; the blessing of the LORD was on all that he had, in house and field. 6 So he left all that he had in Joseph's charge; and, with him there, he had no concern for anything but the food that he ate.

2. The solicitation to sin

Now Joseph was handsome and good-looking. 7 And after a time his master's wife cast her eyes on Joseph and said, "Lie with me." 8 But he refused and said to his master's wife, "Look, with me here, my master has no concern about anything in the house, and he has put everything that he has in my hand. 9 He is not greater in this house than I am, nor has he kept back anything from me except yourself, because you are his wife. How then could I do this great wickedness, and sin against God?" 10 And although she spoke to Joseph day after day, he would not consent to lie beside her or to be with her. 11 One day, however, when he went into the house to do his work, and while no one else was in the house, 12 she caught hold of his garment, saying, "Lie with me!" But he left his garment in her hand, and fled and ran outside. 13 When she saw that he had left his garment in her hand and had fled outside, 14 she called out to the members of her household and said to them, "See, my husband*h* has brought among us a Hebrew to insult us! He came in to me to lie with me, and I cried out with a loud voice; 15 and when he heard me raise my voice and cry out, he left his garment beside me, and fled outside." 16 Then she kept his garment by her until his master came home, 17 and she told him the same story, saying, "The Hebrew servant, whom you

f That is A breach   *g* That is Brightness; perhaps alluding to the crimson thread   *h* Heb he

---

38.29
Gen 46.12;
Num 26.20;
Mt 1.3

39.1
Gen 37.28,
36;
Ps 105.17
39.2
vv. 3, 21, 23
39.3
Gen 21.22;
26.28;
Acts 7.9
39.4
vv. 8, 22
39.5
Gen 30.27

39.7
2 Sam 13.11;
Prov 7.15-20

39.9
Gen 20.6;
42.18;
2 Sam 12.13

39.12
Prov 7.13-25

39.17
Ex 23.1;
Ps 120.3

38.29,30 Perez is listed in the genealogy of Jesus in Mt 1.3. Thus God brought forth good out of evil. The ancestors of Jesus included a number of wicked-acting people, yet the Son of God was born sinless and could be the Savior even of people like his own ancestors.
39.2 Joseph could hardly have known how God would use his brothers' evil to fulfill the divine purpose. Nor could he have known how and when his dreams were to be fulfilled. He did have faith in God, and here the Scriptures make plain that God was

watching over this young man and caring for him. In 39.21, when Joseph had been thrown in jail for a crime he never committed and when his faith must have been hard-pressed, "the LORD was with Joseph" (see also 45.7; 50.20; Ps 76.10).
39.17 This wicked woman, whose name is not given, wanted revenge against Joseph, not because of vice but because of his virtue. She lied to her husband, implying that the fault lay with him for bringing Joseph into their household.

have brought among us, came in to me to insult me; 18 but as soon as I raised my voice and cried out, he left his garment beside me, and fled outside."

3. Joseph wrongly cast into prison

19 When his master heard the words that his wife spoke to him, saying, "This is the way your servant treated me," he became enraged. 20 And Joseph's master took him and put him into the prison, the place where the king's prisoners were confined; he remained there in prison. 21 But the LORD was with Joseph and showed him steadfast love; he gave him favor in the sight of the chief jailer. 22 The chief jailer committed to Joseph's care all the prisoners who were in the prison, and whatever was done there, he was the one who did it. 23 The chief jailer paid no heed to anything that was in Joseph's care, because the LORD was with him; and whatever he did, the LORD made it prosper.

39.19
Prov 6.34, 35
39.20
Ps 105.18
39.21
v.21;
Ps 105.19;
Ex 3.21;
Dan 1.9
39.22
v. 4
39.23
vv. 2, 3, 8

D. Joseph, interpreter of dreams

1. The cupbearer and the baker

40 Some time after this, the cupbearer of the king of Egypt and his baker offended their lord the king of Egypt. 2 Pharaoh was angry with his two officers, the chief cupbearer and the chief baker, 3 and he put them in custody in the house of the captain of the guard, in the prison where Joseph was confined. 4 The captain of the guard charged Joseph with them, and he waited on them; and they continued for some time in custody. 5 One night they both dreamed — the cupbearer and the baker of the king of Egypt, who were confined in the prison — each his own dream, and each dream with its own meaning. 6 When Joseph came to them in the morning, he saw that they were troubled. 7 So he asked Pharaoh's officers, who were with him in custody in his master's house, "Why are your faces downcast today?" 8 They said to him, "We have had dreams, and there is no one to interpret them." And Joseph said to them, "Do not interpretations belong to God? Please tell them to me."

40.1
vv. 11, 13
40.3
Gen 39.20, 23

40.8
Gen 41.16;
Dan 2.27, 28

2. The cupbearer's dream and interpretation

9 So the chief cupbearer told his dream to Joseph, and said to him, "In my dream there was a vine before me, 10 and on the vine there were three branches. As soon as it budded, its blossoms came out and the clusters ripened into grapes. 11 Pharaoh's cup was in my hand; and I took the grapes and pressed them into Pharaoh's cup, and placed the cup in Pharaoh's hand." 12 Then Joseph said to him, "This is its interpretation: the three branches are three days; 13 within three days Pharaoh will lift up your head and restore you to your office; and you shall place Pharaoh's cup in his hand, just as you used to do when you were his cupbearer. 14 But remember me when it is well with you; please do me the kindness to make mention of me to Pharaoh, and so get me out of this place. 15 For in fact I was stolen out of the land of the Hebrews; and here also I have done nothing that they should have put me into the dungeon."

40.12
Gen 41.12,
25;
Dan 2.36;
4.19
40.14
Lk 23.42;
Josh 2.12
40.15
Gen 37.26-28

3. The baker's dream and interpretation

16 When the chief baker saw that the interpretation was favorable, he

---

39.21 Joseph is isolated in prison from relatives and friends. But his God is the friend of the friendless. "The LORD was with Joseph, and showed him stead-fast love." See also 39.2.
40.2 The butler and baker were important men to Pharaoh; their trustworthiness assured him he would not be poisoned either by food or by drink. Joseph

interpreted their dreams accurately. The survivor, the butler, forgot about Joseph as soon as he was freed from prison (39.23). He remembered him two years later.
40.8 Joseph gives glory to God as the interpreter of dreams. His gift of interpretation came from God.

said to Joseph, "I also had a dream: there were three cake baskets on my head, 17 and in the uppermost basket there were all sorts of baked food for Pharaoh, but the birds were eating it out of the basket on my head." 18 And Joseph answered, "This is its interpretation: the three baskets are three days; 19 within three days Pharaoh will lift up your head—from you!—and hang you on a pole; and the birds will eat the flesh from you."

4. *The fulfillment of the interpretations*

20   On the third day, which was Pharaoh's birthday, he made a feast for all his servants, and lifted up the head of the chief cupbearer and the head of the chief baker among his servants. 21 He restored the chief cupbearer to his cupbearing, and he placed the cup in Pharaoh's hand; 22 but the chief baker he hanged, just as Joseph had interpreted to them. 23 Yet the chief cupbearer did not remember Joseph, but forgot him.

E. *Joseph and Pharaoh*

1. *Pharaoh's dream*

41 After two whole years, Pharaoh dreamed that he was standing by the Nile, 2 and there came up out of the Nile seven sleek and fat cows, and they grazed in the reed grass. 3 Then seven other cows, ugly and thin, came up out of the Nile after them, and stood by the other cows on the bank of the Nile. 4 The ugly and thin cows ate up the seven sleek and fat cows. And Pharaoh awoke. 5 Then he fell asleep and dreamed a second time; seven ears of grain, plump and good, were growing on one stalk. 6 Then seven ears, thin and blighted by the east wind, sprouted after them. 7 The thin ears swallowed up the seven plump and full ears. Pharaoh awoke, and it was a dream. 8 In the morning his spirit was troubled; so he sent and called for all the magicians of Egypt and all its wise men. Pharaoh told them his dreams, but there was no one who could interpret them to Pharaoh.

2. *The cupbearer remembers Joseph*

9   Then the chief cupbearer said to Pharaoh, "I remember my faults today. 10 Once Pharaoh was angry with his servants, and put me and the chief baker in custody in the house of the captain of the guard. 11 We dreamed on the same night, he and I, each having a dream with its own meaning. 12 A young Hebrew was there with us, a servant of the captain of the guard. When we told him, he interpreted our dreams to us, giving an interpretation to each according to his dream. 13 As he interpreted to us, so it turned out; I was restored to my office, and the baker was hanged."

3. *Pharaoh tells his dream to Joseph*

14   Then Pharaoh sent for Joseph, and he was hurriedly brought out of the dungeon. When he had shaved himself and changed his clothes, he came in before Pharaoh. 15 And Pharaoh said to Joseph, "I have had a dream, and there is no one who can interpret it. I have heard it said of you that when you hear a dream you can interpret it." 16 Joseph answered Pharaoh, "It is not I; God will give Pharaoh a favorable answer." 17 Then Pharaoh said to Joseph, "In my dream I was standing on the banks of the Nile; 18 and seven cows, fat and sleek, came up out of the Nile and fed in the reed grass. 19 Then seven other cows came up after them, poor, very ugly, and thin. Never had I seen such ugly ones in all the land of Egypt.

Margin references:

40.18
v. 12
40.19
v. 13

40.20
vv. 13, 19

40.21
v. 13

40.22
v. 19

41.8
Dan 2.1, 3;
4.5, 19;
Ex 7.11, 22;
Dan 2.27; 4.7

41.10
Gen 40.2, 3
41.11
Gen 40.5
41.12
Gen 40.12ff
41.13
Gen 40.21, 22

41.14
Ps 105.20;
Dan 2.25;
Ps 113.7, 8
41.15
v. 12
41.16
Dan 2.30;
Acts 3.12;
2 Cor 3.5;
Gen 40.8

41.6 *east wind*, i.e., a "sirocco," or "a hot wind."
41.16 Joseph again disclaimed any prophetic gifts and gave the glory to God. Thus he was a missionary to a pagan ruler, bearing testimony to his faith in the true God.

20 The thin and ugly cows ate up the first seven fat cows, 21 but when they had eaten them no one would have known that they had done so, for they were still as ugly as before. Then I awoke. 22 I fell asleep a second time[i] and I saw in my dream seven ears of grain, full and good, growing on one stalk, 23 and seven ears, withered, thin, and blighted by the east wind, sprouting after them; 24 and the thin ears swallowed up the seven good ears. But when I told it to the magicians, there was no one who could explain it to me."

41.24
v. 8

4. Joseph interprets Pharaoh's dream: he proposes a solution

25 Then Joseph said to Pharaoh, "Pharaoh's dreams are one and the same; God has revealed to Pharaoh what he is about to do. 26 The seven good cows are seven years, and the seven good ears are seven years; the dreams are one. 27 The seven lean and ugly cows that came up after them are seven years, as are the seven empty ears blighted by the east wind. They are seven years of famine. 28 It is as I told Pharaoh; God has shown to Pharaoh what he is about to do. 29 There will come seven years of great plenty throughout all the land of Egypt. 30 After them there will arise seven years of famine, and all the plenty will be forgotten in the land of Egypt; the famine will consume the land. 31 The plenty will no longer be known in the land because of the famine that will follow, for it will be very grievous. 32 And the doubling of Pharaoh's dream means that the thing is fixed by God, and God will shortly bring it about. 33 Now therefore let Pharaoh select a man who is discerning and wise, and set him over the land of Egypt. 34 Let Pharaoh proceed to appoint overseers over the land, and take one-fifth of the produce of the land of Egypt during the seven plenteous years. 35 Let them gather all the food of these good years that are coming, and lay up grain under the authority of Pharaoh for food in the cities, and let them keep it. 36 That food shall be a reserve for the land against the seven years of famine that are to befall the land of Egypt, so that the land may not perish through the famine."

41.25
vv. 28, 32

41.27
2 Kings 8.1

41.28
vv. 25, 32
41.29
v. 47
41.30
vv. 54, 56;
Gen 47.13

41.32
Num 23.19;
Isa 46.10, 11

41.35
v. 48

5. Pharaoh makes Joseph a ruler

37 The proposal pleased Pharaoh and all his servants. 38 Pharaoh said to his servants, "Can we find anyone else like this—one in whom is the spirit of God?" 39 So Pharaoh said to Joseph, "Since God has shown you all this, there is no one so discerning and wise as you. 40 You shall be over my house, and all my people shall order themselves as you command; only with regard to the throne will I be greater than you." 41 And Pharaoh said to Joseph, "See, I have set you over all the land of Egypt." 42 Removing his signet ring from his hand, Pharaoh put it on Joseph's hand; he arrayed him in garments of fine linen, and put a gold chain around his neck. 43 He had him ride in the chariot of his second-in-command; and they cried out in front of him, "Bow the knee!"[j] Thus he set him over all the land of Egypt. 44 Moreover Pharaoh said to Joseph, "I am Pharaoh, and without your consent no one shall lift up hand or foot in all the land of Egypt." 45 Pharaoh gave Joseph the name Zaphenath-paneah; and he gave him

41.38
Num 27.18;
Dan 4.8, 18

41.40
Ps 105.21,
22;
Acts 7.10
41.41
Gen 42.6
41.42
Esth 3.10;
Dan 5.7, 16,
29
41.43
Esth 6.9
41.44
Ps 105.22

[i] Gk Syr Vg: Heb lacks *I fell asleep a second time*   [j] *Abrek*, apparently an Egyptian word similar in sound to the Hebrew word meaning *to kneel*

41.38 The Pharaoh bears testimony to the fact that Joseph's God is with him and in him. He saw that Joseph had the gift of wisdom, which is one of the gifts of the Holy Spirit to some of the people of God, then and now.
41.45 *Zaphnath-paaneah.* The meaning of this is uncertain. Suggestions include: "the god speaks and he lives," or "The god said: he will live," or "He has

the god-like power of life and death." *he gave him Asenath daughter of Potipherah, priest of On* [Heliopolis], *as his wife.* Heliopolis was a city in Northern Egypt noted for its chief temple of the sun, dedicated to the sun god Re. References to it may be found in Isa 19.18 and Jer 43.13. Joseph married into a family of high nobility; his father-in-law was a major priest and politician of that time.

Asenath daughter of Potiphera, priest of On, as his wife. Thus Joseph gained authority over the land of Egypt.

6. *The fulfillment of the dream*

41.46
Gen 37.2

46 Joseph was thirty years old when he entered the service of Pharaoh king of Egypt. And Joseph went out from the presence of Pharaoh, and went through all the land of Egypt. 47 During the seven plenteous years the earth produced abundantly. 48 He gathered up all the food of the seven years when there was plenty[k] in the land of Egypt, and stored up food in the cities; he stored up in every city the food from the fields around it. 49 So Joseph stored up grain in such abundance—like the sand of the sea—that he stopped measuring it; it was beyond measure.

41.50
Gen 46.20

41.52
Gen 17.6;
28.3; 49.22

50 Before the years of famine came, Joseph had two sons, whom Asenath daughter of Potiphera, priest of On, bore to him. 51 Joseph named the firstborn Manasseh,[l] "For," he said, "God has made me forget all my hardship and all my father's house." 52 The second he named Ephraim,[m] "For God has made me fruitful in the land of my misfortunes."

41.54
v. 30;
Ps 105.16;
Acts 7.11

41.56
Gen 42.6

53 The seven years of plenty that prevailed in the land of Egypt came to an end; 54 and the seven years of famine began to come, just as Joseph had said. There was famine in every country, but throughout the land of Egypt there was bread. 55 When all the land of Egypt was famished, the people cried to Pharaoh for bread. Pharaoh said to all the Egyptians, "Go to Joseph; what he says to you, do." 56 And since the famine had spread over all the land, Joseph opened all the storehouses,[n] and sold to the Egyptians, for the famine was severe in the land of Egypt. 57 Moreover, all the world came to Joseph in Egypt to buy grain, because the famine became severe throughout the world.

F. *Joseph's brothers in Egypt*

1. *Jacob sends ten sons*

42.1
Acts 7.12
42.2
Gen 43.8

42.4
Gen 35.24
42.5
Gen 41.57;
Acts 7.11

42 When Jacob learned that there was grain in Egypt, he said to his sons, "Why do you keep looking at one another? 2 I have heard," he said, "that there is grain in Egypt; go down and buy grain for us there, that we may live and not die." 3 So ten of Joseph's brothers went down to buy grain in Egypt. 4 But Jacob did not send Joseph's brother Benjamin with his brothers, for he feared that harm might come to him. 5 Thus the sons of Israel were among the other people who came to buy grain, for the famine had reached the land of Canaan.

2. *Joseph encounters his brothers*

42.6
Gen 41.41,
55; 37.7
42.7
v. 30

42.9
Gen 37.6-9

6 Now Joseph was governor over the land; it was he who sold to all the people of the land. And Joseph's brothers came and bowed themselves before him with their faces to the ground. 7 When Joseph saw his brothers, he recognized them, but he treated them like strangers and spoke harshly to them. "Where do you come from?" he said. They said, "From the land of Canaan, to buy food." 8 Although Joseph had recognized his brothers, they did not recognize him. 9 Joseph also remembered the dreams that he

---

[k] Sam Gk: MT *the seven years that were*   [l] That is *Making to forget*   [m] From a Hebrew word meaning *to be fruitful*   [n] Gk Vg Compare Syr: Heb *opened all that was in* (or, *among*) *them*

41.46 *Joseph was thirty years old.* Thirteen years had passed since Joseph dreamed his dreams. Now he has risen dramatically from being a slave of Potiphar to a position of prominence and eminence. But more years would have to pass before his most important dream could be fulfilled—the time when his brothers would bow before him. By this time Joseph spoke the Egyp-

tian tongue and had learned Egyptian manners. **42.8** *they did not recognize him.* Little did the sons of Jacob know that the man they faced was their younger brother, Joseph. However, Joseph knew them. Verse 9 makes it clear that he had a long memory and had not forgotten his dreams or their wickedness.

had dreamed about them. He said to them, "You are spies; you have come
to see the nakedness of the land!" 10 They said to him, "No, my lord; your
servants have come to buy food. 11 We are all sons of one man; we are
honest men; your servants have never been spies." 12 But he said to them,
"No, you have come to see the nakedness of the land!" 13 They said, "We,
your servants, are twelve brothers, the sons of a certain man in the land
of Canaan; the youngest, however, is now with our father, and one is no
more." 14 But Joseph said to them, "It is just as I have said to you; you
are spies! 15 Here is how you shall be tested: as Pharaoh lives, you shall
not leave this place unless your youngest brother comes here! 16 Let one
of you go and bring your brother, while the rest of you remain in prison,
in order that your words may be tested, whether there is truth in you; or
else, as Pharaoh lives, surely you are spies." 17 And he put them all
together in prison for three days.

3. Joseph gives them grain

18   On the third day Joseph said to them, "Do this and you will live,
for I fear God: 19 if you are honest men, let one of your brothers stay here
where you are imprisoned. The rest of you shall go and carry grain for
the famine of your households, 20 and bring your youngest brother to me.
Thus your words will be verified, and you shall not die." And they agreed
to do so. 21 They said to one another, "Alas, we are paying the penalty
for what we did to our brother; we saw his anguish when he pleaded with
us, but we would not listen. That is why this anguish has come upon us."
22 Then Reuben answered them, "Did I not tell you not to wrong the boy?
But you would not listen. So now there comes a reckoning for his blood."
23 They did not know that Joseph understood them, since he spoke with
them through an interpreter. 24 He turned away from them and wept; then
he returned and spoke to them. And he picked out Simeon and had him
bound before their eyes. 25 Joseph then gave orders to fill their bags with
grain, to return every man's money to his sack, and to give them provisions for their journey. This was done for them.

26   They loaded their donkeys with their grain, and departed. 27 When
one of them opened his sack to give his donkey fodder at the lodging place,
he saw his money at the top of the sack. 28 He said to his brothers, "My
money has been put back; here it is in my sack!" At this they lost heart
and turned trembling to one another, saying, "What is this that God has
done to us?"

4. The ten sons report to Jacob

29   When they came to their father Jacob in the land of Canaan, they
told him all that had happened to them, saying, 30 "The man, the lord of
the land, spoke harshly to us, and charged us with spying on the land.
31 But we said to him, 'We are honest men, we are not spies. 32 We are
twelve brothers, sons of our father; one is no more, and the youngest is
now with our father in the land of Canaan.' 33 Then the man, the lord of
the land, said to us, 'By this I shall know that you are honest men: leave
one of your brothers with me, take grain for the famine of your households, and go your way. 34 Bring your youngest brother to me, and I shall
know that you are not spies but honest men. Then I will release your
brother to you, and you may trade in the land.'"

35   As they were emptying their sacks, there in each one's sack was
his bag of money. When they and their father saw their bundles of money,

42.13
Gen 43.7;
37.30

42.18
Lev 25.43

42.20
v. 34

42.21
Hos 5.15;
Prov 21.13

42.22
Gen 37.22;
9.5, 6

42.24
Gen 43.30;
45.14, 15;
43.14, 23
42.25
Gen 44.1;
Rom 12.17,
20, 21
42.26
Gen 37.31-35

42.30
v. 7

42.31
v. 11

42.33
Gen 15.19, 20

42.35
Gen 43.12, 15

42.21 *We are paying the penalty.* The function of the
conscience is to bring to mind sins committed long
ago; in this instance it operated more than twenty
years after the crime was committed. Time neither
washes away the guilt of sin nor does it blot out the
records of conscience. In 42.22 Reuben maintains his
own innocence and the fact that he had been an advocate for Joseph. His brothers therefore sinned after
they had been admonished to do right. This furthered
their guilt.

42.36
Gen 43.14

they were dismayed. 36 And their father Jacob said to them, "I am the one you have bereaved of children: Joseph is no more, and Simeon is no more, and now you would take Benjamin. All this has happened to me!" 37 Then Reuben said to his father, "You may kill my two sons if I do not bring him back to you. Put him in my hands, and I will bring him back to you."

42.38
Gen 37.33,
35; 44.31

38 But he said, "My son shall not go down with you, for his brother is dead, and he alone is left. If harm should come to him on the journey that you are to make, you would bring down my gray hairs with sorrow to Sheol."

G. *The second trip to Egypt with Benjamin*

1. *Jacob unwillingly sends Benjamin*

43.1
Gen 41.56, 57

43 Now the famine was severe in the land. 2 And when they had eaten up the grain that they had brought from Egypt, their father said

43.3
Gen 42.20;
44.23

to them, "Go again, buy us a little more food." 3 But Judah said to him, "The man solemnly warned us, saying, 'You shall not see my face unless your brother is with you.' 4 If you will send our brother with us, we will go down and buy you food; 5 but if you will not send him, we will not go down, for the man said to us, 'You shall not see my face, unless your brother is with you.'" 6 Israel said, "Why did you treat me so badly as

43.7
v. 27;
Gen 42.13

to tell the man that you had another brother?" 7 They replied, "The man questioned us carefully about ourselves and our kindred, saying, 'Is your father still alive? Have you another brother?' What we told him was in answer to these questions. Could we in any way know that he would say, 'Bring your brother down'?" 8 Then Judah said to his father Israel, "Send the boy with me, and let us be on our way, so that we may live and not

43.9
Gen 42.37;
44.32;
Philem 18, 19

die — you and we and also our little ones. 9 I myself will be surety for him; you can hold me accountable for him. If I do not bring him back to you and set him before you, then let me bear the blame forever. 10 If we had not delayed, we would now have returned twice."

43.11
Gen 32.20;
Prov 18.16;
Gen 37.25;
Jer 8.22
43.12
Gen 42.35;
vv. 21, 22

11 Then their father Israel said to them, "If it must be so, then do this: take some of the choice fruits of the land in your bags, and carry them down as a present to the man — a little balm and a little honey, gum, resin, pistachio nuts, and almonds. 12 Take double the money with you. Carry back with you the money that was returned in the top of your sacks; perhaps it was an oversight. 13 Take your brother also, and be on your way

43.14
Gen 17.1;
28.3; 35.11;
Ps 106.46;
Gen 42.24

again to the man; 14 may God Almighty*o* grant you mercy before the man, so that he may send back your other brother and Benjamin. As for me, if I am bereaved of my children, I am bereaved." 15 So the men took the present, and they took double the money with them, as well as Benjamin. Then they went on their way down to Egypt, and stood before Joseph.

2. *Joseph dines with his brothers*

43.16
Gen 44.1

16 When Joseph saw Benjamin with them, he said to the steward of his house, "Bring the men into the house, and slaughter an animal and make ready, for the men are to dine with me at noon." 17 The man did as Joseph said, and brought the men to Joseph's house. 18 Now the men were afraid because they were brought to Joseph's house, and they said, "It is because of the money, replaced in our sacks the first time, that we

o Traditional rendering of Heb *El Shaddai*

42.36 *Simeon is no more.* Jacob bemoans the loss of both Joseph and Simeon. He is firm, at this point, that Benjamin will never be permitted to go to Egypt. Jacob did not yet know that God was working all things in his favor. Joseph kept Simeon (Jacob's second son by Leah) as a hostage. Apparently Joseph let Reuben, the firstborn by Leah, go back because he exhibited concern for Joseph and would have freed him from the pit if he had been able to do so.

43.14 Jacob finally yielded to his sons and agreed to let Benjamin go with them to Egypt. But he prayed to God for mercy and for the deliverance of Simeon and Benjamin. Here Jacob was both pious and prayerful. God not only delivered Simeon and Benjamin, he also brought Joseph back as it were from the dead.

have been brought in, so that he may have an opportunity to fall upon us, to make slaves of us and take our donkeys." ¹⁹So they went up to the steward of Joseph's house and spoke with him at the entrance to the house. ²⁰They said, "Oh, my lord, we came down the first time to buy food; ²¹and when we came to the lodging place we opened our sacks, and there was each one's money in the top of his sack, our money in full weight. So we have brought it back with us. ²²Moreover we have brought down with us additional money to buy food. We do not know who put our money in our sacks." ²³He replied, "Rest assured, do not be afraid; your God and the God of your father must have put treasure in your sacks for you; I received your money." Then he brought Simeon out to them. ²⁴When the steward^p had brought the men into Joseph's house, and given them water, and they had washed their feet, and when he had given their donkeys fodder, ²⁵they made the present ready for Joseph's coming at noon, for they had heard that they would dine there.

26 When Joseph came home, they brought him the present that they had carried into the house, and bowed to the ground before him. ²⁷He inquired about their welfare, and said, "Is your father well, the old man of whom you spoke? Is he still alive?" ²⁸They said, "Your servant our father is well; he is still alive." And they bowed their heads and did obeisance. ²⁹Then he looked up and saw his brother Benjamin, his mother's son, and said, "Is this your youngest brother, of whom you spoke to me? God be gracious to you, my son!" ³⁰With that, Joseph hurried out, because he was overcome with affection for his brother, and he was about to weep. So he went into a private room and wept there. ³¹Then he washed his face and came out; and controlling himself he said, "Serve the meal." ³²They served him by himself, and them by themselves, and the Egyptians who ate with him by themselves, because the Egyptians could not eat with the Hebrews, for that is an abomination to the Egyptians. ³³When they were seated before him, the firstborn according to his birthright and the youngest according to his youth, the men looked at one another in amazement. ³⁴Portions were taken to them from Joseph's table, but Benjamin's portion was five times as much as any of theirs. So they drank and were merry with him.

3. The seizure of Benjamin

44 Then he commanded the steward of his house, "Fill the men's sacks with food, as much as they can carry, and put each man's money in the top of his sack. ²Put my cup, the silver cup, in the top of the sack of the youngest, with his money for the grain." And he did as Joseph told him. ³As soon as the morning was light, the men were sent away with their donkeys. ⁴When they had gone only a short distance from the city, Joseph said to his steward, "Go, follow after the men; and when you overtake them, say to them, 'Why have you returned evil for good? Why have you stolen my silver cup?^q ⁵Is it not from this that my lord drinks? Does he not indeed use it for divination? You have done wrong in doing this.' "

6 When he overtook them, he repeated these words to them. ⁷They said to him, "Why does my lord speak such words as these? Far be it from your servants that they should do such a thing! ⁸Look, the money that we found at the top of our sacks, we brought back to you from the land of Canaan; why then would we steal silver or gold from your lord's house?

43.20
Gen 42.3, 10
43.21
Gen 42.35;
vv. 12, 15

43.23
Gen 42.24

43.24
Gen 18.4;
19.2; 24.32

43.26
Gen 37.7, 10
43.27
v. 7;
Gen 45.3
43.28
Gen 37.7, 10
43.29
Gen 35.17,
18; 42.13;
Num 6.25;
Ps 67.1
43.30
Gen 42.24;
45.2, 14, 15;
46.29
43.31
Gen 45.1
43.32
Gen 46.34

43.34
Gen 45.22

44.1
Gen 42.25

44.5
v. 15;
Lev 19.26;
Deut 18.10-14

44.8
Gen 43.21

_p_ Heb _the man_   _q_ Gk Compare Vg: Heb lacks _Why have you stolen my silver cup?_

43.29 _his mother's son._ Except for Benjamin, all Joseph's brothers were born of different mothers than he. He and Benjamin were the sons of Rachel, Jacob's beloved. He had not seen Benjamin for more than twenty years. This meeting was a touching reminder to him of their dead mother and of his love for his full brother.

44.9
Gen 31.32

9 Should it be found with any one of your servants, let him die; moreover the rest of us will become my lord's slaves." 10 He said, "Even so; in accordance with your words, let it be: he with whom it is found shall become my slave, but the rest of you shall go free." 11 Then each one quickly lowered his sack to the ground, and each opened his sack. 12 He searched, beginning with the eldest and ending with the youngest; and the cup was found in Benjamin's sack. 13 At this they tore their clothes. Then each one loaded his donkey, and they returned to the city.

44.13
Gen 37.29,
34;
Num 14.6

4. His brothers bow before Joseph

44.14
Gen 37.7, 10
44.15
v. 5
44.16
v. 9

14 Judah and his brothers came to Joseph's house while he was still there; and they fell to the ground before him. 15 Joseph said to them, "What deed is this that you have done? Do you not know that one such as I can practice divination?" 16 And Judah said, "What can we say to my lord? What can we speak? How can we clear ourselves? God has found out the guilt of your servants; here we are then, my lord's slaves, both we and also the one in whose possession the cup has been found." 17 But he said, "Far be it from me that I should do so! Only the one in whose possession the cup was found shall be my slave; but as for you, go up in peace to your father."

44.18
Gen 37.7, 8;
41.40-44
44.20
v. 30;
Gen 43.8;
37.33; 42.13,
38
44.23
Gen 43.3

18 Then Judah stepped up to him and said, "O my lord, let your servant please speak a word in my lord's ears, and do not be angry with your servant; for you are like Pharaoh himself. 19 My lord asked his servants, saying, 'Have you a father or a brother?' 20 And we said to my lord, 'We have a father, an old man, and a young brother, the child of his old age. His brother is dead; he alone is left of his mother's children, and his father loves him.' 21 Then you said to your servants, 'Bring him down to me, so that I may set my eyes on him.' 22 We said to my lord, 'The boy cannot leave his father, for if he should leave his father, his father would die.' 23 Then you said to your servants, 'Unless your youngest brother comes down with you, you shall see my face no more.' 24 When we went back to your servant my father we told him the words of my lord. 25 And when our father said, 'Go again, buy us a little food,' 26 we said, 'We cannot go down. Only if our youngest brother goes with us, will we go down; for we cannot see the man's face unless our youngest brother is with us.' 27 Then your servant my father said to us, 'You know that my wife bore me two sons; 28 one left me, and I said, Surely he has been torn to pieces; and I have never seen him since. 29 If you take this one also from me, and harm comes to him, you will bring down my gray hairs in sorrow to Sheol.' 30 Now therefore, when I come to your servant my father and the boy is not with us, then, as his life is bound up in the boy's life, 31 when he sees that the boy is not with us, he will die; and your servants will bring down the gray hairs of your servant our father with sorrow to Sheol. 32 For your servant became surety for the boy to my father, saying, 'If I do not bring him back to you, then I will bear the blame in the sight of my father all my life.' 33 Now therefore, please let your servant remain as a slave to my lord in place of the boy; and let the boy go back with his brothers. 34 For how can I go back to my father if the boy is not with me? I fear to see the suffering that would come upon my father."

44.28
Gen 37.31-35
44.29
Gen 42.36, 38
44.32
Gen 43.9

44.14 When Joseph's brothers "fell to the ground before him," it was the first fulfillment of the dream Joseph had had when he was seventeen years old. Here his brothers acknowledged that they were his servants or vassals. After the death of their father they fell down before him again (50.18).
44.16 Judah becomes the spokesman for his broth-

ers. Despite their sins, Judah indicates that they believe in the God of their father, and he acknowledges their guilt. In v. 32 Judah indicates that he had become surety for the return of Benjamin. He pleads for mercy and offers himself as a substitute for Benjamin. In this he is a forerunner of Christ, his offspring.

5. Joseph discloses his identity

45 Then Joseph could no longer control himself before all those who stood by him, and he cried out, "Send everyone away from me." So no one stayed with him when Joseph made himself known to his brothers. 2 And he wept so loudly that the Egyptians heard it, and the household of Pharaoh heard it. 3 Joseph said to his brothers, "I am Joseph. Is my father still alive?" But his brothers could not answer him, so dismayed were they at his presence.

4 Then Joseph said to his brothers, "Come closer to me." And they came closer. He said, "I am your brother, Joseph, whom you sold into Egypt. 5 And now do not be distressed, or angry with yourselves, because you sold me here; for God sent me before you to preserve life. 6 For the famine has been in the land these two years; and there are five more years in which there will be neither plowing nor harvest. 7 God sent me before you to preserve for you a remnant on earth, and to keep alive for you many survivors. 8 So it was not you who sent me here, but God; he has made me a father to Pharaoh, and lord of all his house and ruler over all the land of Egypt. 9 Hurry and go up to my father and say to him, 'Thus says your son Joseph, God has made me lord of all Egypt; come down to me, do not delay. 10 You shall settle in the land of Goshen, and you shall be near me, you and your children and your children's children, as well as your flocks, your herds, and all that you have. 11 I will provide for you there — since there are five more years of famine to come — so that you and your household, and all that you have, will not come to poverty.' 12 And now your eyes and the eyes of my brother Benjamin see that it is my own mouth that speaks to you. 13 You must tell my father how greatly I am honored in Egypt, and all that you have seen. Hurry and bring my father down here." 14 Then he fell upon his brother Benjamin's neck and wept, while Benjamin wept upon his neck. 15 And he kissed all his brothers and wept upon them; and after that his brothers talked with him.

6. Pharaoh invites Joseph's family to Egypt

16 When the report was heard in Pharaoh's house, "Joseph's brothers have come," Pharaoh and his servants were pleased. 17 Pharaoh said to Joseph, "Say to your brothers, 'Do this: load your animals and go back to the land of Canaan. 18 Take your father and your households and come to me, so that I may give you the best of the land of Egypt, and you may enjoy the fat of the land.' 19 You are further charged to say, 'Do this: take wagons from the land of Egypt for your little ones and for your wives, and bring your father, and come. 20 Give no thought to your possessions, for the best of all the land of Egypt is yours.' "

21 The sons of Israel did so. Joseph gave them wagons according to the instruction of Pharaoh, and he gave them provisions for the journey. 22 To each one of them he gave a set of garments; but to Benjamin he gave three hundred pieces of silver and five sets of garments. 23 To his father he sent the following: ten donkeys loaded with the good things of Egypt, and ten female donkeys loaded with grain, bread, and provision for his father on the journey. 24 Then he sent his brothers on their way, and as they were leaving he said to them, "Do not quarrel^r along the way."

---

r Or be agitated

45.1 Acts 7.13
45.2 vv. 14, 15; Gen 46.29
45.3 Gen 43.27
45.4 Gen 37.28
45.5 Isa 40.2; Gen 37.28; 44.20; 50.20
45.8 Gen 41.43
45.10 Gen 46.28, 34; 47.1
45.13 Acts 7.14
45.18 Gen 27.28; Num 18.12, 29
45.22 Gen 43.34

45.8 Joseph states that it was God who has sent him to Egypt, even though his trip was brought about by the evil acts of his own brothers. He was a firm believer in the providence of God, who knows the end from the beginning and who accomplishes all things according to his divine will. Joseph's brothers wanted to defeat his dreams by selling him into slavery. But God turned their evil into good for Joseph and, ultimately, for them as well.

45.10 *Goshen.* This is not the Goshen of Josh 10.41; rather, it is that of Egypt, located in the eastern section of the Nile Delta, which has fertile grazing land. This verse confirms 47.6, where Pharaoh told Joseph to settle his father and his brothers in Goshen.

45.24 *Do not quarrel along the way.* Joseph knew that his brothers were not wholly sanctified, so his

25 So they went up out of Egypt and came to their father Jacob in the land of Canaan. 26 And they told him, "Joseph is still alive! He is even ruler over all the land of Egypt." He was stunned; he could not believe them. 27 But when they told him all the words of Joseph that he had said to them, and when he saw the wagons that Joseph had sent to carry him, the spirit of their father Jacob revived. 28 Israel said, "Enough! My son Joseph is still alive. I must go and see him before I die."

H. *Jacob goes to Egypt*

46 When Israel set out on his journey with all that he had and came to Beer-sheba, he offered sacrifices to the God of his father Isaac. 2 God spoke to Israel in visions of the night, and said, "Jacob, Jacob." And he said, "Here I am." 3 Then he said, "I am God,ˢ the God of your father; do not be afraid to go down to Egypt, for I will make of you a great nation there. 4 I myself will go down with you to Egypt, and I will also bring you up again; and Joseph's own hand shall close your eyes."

5 Then Jacob set out from Beer-sheba; and the sons of Israel carried their father Jacob, their little ones, and their wives, in the wagons that Pharaoh had sent to carry him. 6 They also took their livestock and the goods that they had acquired in the land of Canaan, and they came into Egypt, Jacob and all his offspring with him, 7 his sons, and his sons' sons with him, his daughters, and his sons' daughters; all his offspring he brought with him into Egypt.

I. *The descendants of Jacob*

8 Now these are the names of the Israelites, Jacob and his offspring, who came to Egypt. Reuben, Jacob's firstborn, 9 and the children of Reuben: Hanoch, Pallu, Hezron, and Carmi. 10 The children of Simeon: Jemuel, Jamin, Ohad, Jachin, Zohar, and Shaul,ᵗ the son of a Canaanite woman. 11 The children of Levi: Gershon, Kohath, and Merari. 12 The children of Judah: Er, Onan, Shelah, Perez, and Zerah (but Er and Onan died in the land of Canaan); and the children of Perez were Hezron and Hamul. 13 The children of Issachar: Tola, Puvah, Jashub,ᵘ and Shimron. 14 The children of Zebulun: Sered, Elon, and Jahleel 15 (these are the sons of Leah, whom she bore to Jacob in Paddan-aram, together with his daughter Dinah; in all his sons and his daughters numbered thirty-three). 16 The children of Gad: Ziphion, Haggi, Shuni, Ezbon, Eri, Arodi, and Areli. 17 The children of Asher: Imnah, Ishvah, Ishvi, Beriah, and their sister Serah. The children of Beriah: Heber and Malchiel 18 (these are the children of Zilpah, whom Laban gave to his daughter Leah; and these she bore to Jacob — sixteen persons). 19 The children of Jacob's wife Rachel: Joseph and Benjamin. 20 To Joseph in the land of Egypt were born Manasseh and Ephraim, whom Asenath daughter of Potiphera, priest of On, bore to him. 21 The children of Benjamin: Bela, Becher, Ashbel, Gera, Naaman, Ehi, Rosh, Muppim, Huppim, and Ard 22 (these are the children of Rachel, who were born to Jacob — fourteen persons in all). 23 The children of Dan: Hashum.ᵛ 24 The children of Naphtali: Jahzeel, Guni, Jezer, and Shillem 25 (these are the children of Bilhah, whom Laban gave to his daughter Rachel, and these she bore to Jacob — seven persons in all). 26 All the persons belonging to Jacob who came into Egypt, who

46.1 Gen 28.10; 26.24; 28.13
46.2 Job 33.14, 15; Gen 22.11; 31.11
46.3 Gen 28.13; 12.2
46.4 Gen 28.15; 50.13, 24, 25; Ex 3.8; Gen 50.1
46.5 Gen 45.19, 21
46.6 Acts 7.15; Deut 26.5; Josh 24.4; Ps 105.23; Isa 52.4
46.8 Ex 1.1
46.10 Ex 6.15
46.11 1 Chr 6.1, 16
46.12 1 Chr 2.3; 4.21; 38.3, 7, 10, 29
46.17 1 Chr 7.30
46.18 Gen 30.10; 29.24
46.19 Gen 44.27
46.20 Gen 41.50
46.21 1 Chr 7.6; 8.1
46.23 1 Chr 7.12
46.24 1 Chr 7.13
46.25 Gen 30.5, 7; 29.29
46.26 Ex 1.5

ˢ Heb *the God*　ᵗ Or *Saul*　ᵘ Compare Sam Gk Num 26.24; 1 Chr 7.1: MT *Iob*　ᵛ Gk: Heb *Hushim*

admonition was fitting.
46.3,4 Some believe that Egypt always represents sin and compromise. Thus they suppose that Jacob's going to Egypt was against the directive will of God. This is not so, however, for God told Jacob to do this in order to develop a great nation which would be strong and numerous enough to conquer Canaan.

46.12 *Hezron and Hamul*, grandsons of Judah, were included to take the places of Er and Onan, who died in Canaan. They were probably born in Egypt. This is analogous to including Manasseh and Ephraim, who were born in Egypt, as among those who "came to Egypt" (see 46.7).

were his own offspring, not including the wives of his sons, were sixty-six persons in all. 27 The children of Joseph, who were born to him in Egypt, were two; all the persons of the house of Jacob who came into Egypt were seventy.

46.27
Deut 10.22;
Acts 7.14

J. The settlement in Egypt

28 Israel*w* sent Judah ahead to Joseph to lead the way before him into Goshen. When they came to the land of Goshen, 29 Joseph made ready his chariot and went up to meet his father Israel in Goshen. He presented himself to him, fell on his neck, and wept on his neck a good while. 30 Israel said to Joseph, "I can die now, having seen for myself that you are still alive." 31 Joseph said to his brothers and to his father's household, "I will go up and tell Pharaoh, and will say to him, 'My brothers and my father's household, who were in the land of Canaan, have come to me. 32 The men are shepherds, for they have been keepers of livestock; and they have brought their flocks, and their herds, and all that they have.' 33 When Pharaoh calls you, and says, 'What is your occupation?' 34 you shall say, 'Your servants have been keepers of livestock from our youth even until now, both we and our ancestors' — in order that you may settle in the land of Goshen, because all shepherds are abhorrent to the Egyptians."

46.28
Gen 47.1
46.29
Gen 45.14, 15

46.31
Gen 47.1

46.33
Gen 47.2, 3
46.34
Gen 13.7, 8;
26.20; 37.2;
45.10, 18;
Ex 8.26

47 So Joseph went and told Pharaoh, "My father and my brothers, with their flocks and herds and all that they possess, have come from the land of Canaan; they are now in the land of Goshen." 2 From among his brothers he took five men and presented them to Pharaoh. 3 Pharaoh said to his brothers, "What is your occupation?" And they said to Pharaoh, "Your servants are shepherds, as our ancestors were." 4 They said to Pharaoh, "We have come to reside as aliens in the land; for there is no pasture for your servants' flocks because the famine is severe in the land of Canaan. Now, we ask you, let your servants settle in the land of Goshen." 5 Then Pharaoh said to Joseph, "Your father and your brothers have come to you. 6 The land of Egypt is before you; settle your father and your brothers in the best part of the land; let them live in the land of Goshen; and if you know that there are capable men among them, put them in charge of my livestock."

47.1
Gen 46.31

47.3
Gen 46.33, 34
47.4
Gen 15.13;
Deut 26.5;
Gen 43.1;
46.34

47.6
v. 11;
Gen 45.10, 18

7 Then Joseph brought in his father Jacob, and presented him before Pharaoh, and Jacob blessed Pharaoh. 8 Pharaoh said to Jacob, "How many are the years of your life?" 9 Jacob said to Pharaoh, "The years of my earthly sojourn are one hundred thirty; few and hard have been the years of my life. They do not compare with the years of the life of my ancestors during their long sojourn." 10 Then Jacob blessed Pharaoh, and went out from the presence of Pharaoh. 11 Joseph settled his father and his brothers, and granted them a holding in the land of Egypt, in the best part of the land, in the land of Rameses, as Pharaoh had instructed. 12 And Joseph provided his father, his brothers, and all his father's household with food, according to the number of their dependents.

47.8
Ps 39.12;
Heb 11.9, 13;
Job 14.1;
Gen 25.7;
35.28
47.10
v. 7
47.11
Ex 1.11;
12.37; 6.27

w Heb *He*

46.27 Compare with Acts 7.14, where Jacob is said to have had seventy-five children. This number was probably taken from the Septuagint (Greek translation of the O.T.), which included five descendants of Manasseh and Ephraim, sons of Joseph. This meant there were five more people than the seventy of 46.27 of the Masoretic text (the standard Hebrew text of the O.T.).
47.9 Jacob lived seventeen years in Egypt. He died at the age of 147, which was a shorter lifespan than that of Abraham (175) and Isaac (180).
47.10 God's people are pilgrims, strangers, sojourners, and exiles, for their citizenship is in heaven (Phil

3.20). They are not of this world, although they are in it (Jn 17.16). As pilgrims, they (1) look for the coming of the heavenly city whose builder is God (Heb 11.10–16); (2) live in reverent fear of God during the days of this pilgrimage (1 Pet 1.17); and (3) constitute a heavenly commonwealth (Phil 3.20, NRSV footnote). The world will persecute God's people (Jn 17.14), but they are not to be anxious about worldly concerns (Mt 6.25). They are commanded to lay up treasures in heaven (Mt 6.19), to abstain from the passions of the flesh (1 Pet 2.11), and to shine as lights in the world (Phil 2.15).
47.11 *land of Rameses*, later known as *Goshen*.

K. *The land policies of Joseph*

47.13
Gen 41.30;
Acts 7.11
47.14
Gen 41.56
47.15
v. 19

13 Now there was no food in all the land, for the famine was very severe. The land of Egypt and the land of Canaan languished because of the famine. 14 Joseph collected all the money to be found in the land of Egypt and in the land of Canaan, in exchange for the grain that they bought; and Joseph brought the money into Pharaoh's house. 15 When the money from the land of Egypt and from the land of Canaan was spent, all the Egyptians came to Joseph, and said, "Give us food! Why should we die before your eyes? For our money is gone." 16 And Joseph answered, "Give me your livestock, and I will give you food in exchange for your livestock, if your money is gone." 17 So they brought their livestock to Joseph; and Joseph gave them food in exchange for the horses, the flocks, the herds, and the donkeys. That year he supplied them with food in exchange for all their livestock. 18 When that year was ended, they came to him the following year, and said to him, "We can not hide from my lord that our money is all spent; and the herds of cattle are my lord's. There is nothing left in the sight of my lord but our bodies and our lands. 19 Shall we die before your eyes, both we and our land? Buy us and our land in exchange for food. We with our land will become slaves to Pharaoh; just give us seed, so that we may live and not die, and that the land may not become desolate."

20 So Joseph bought all the land of Egypt for Pharaoh. All the Egyptians sold their fields, because the famine was severe upon them; and the land became Pharaoh's. 21 As for the people, he made slaves of them[x] from one end of Egypt to the other. 22 Only the land of the priests he did not buy; for the priests had a fixed allowance from Pharaoh, and lived on the allowance that Pharaoh gave them; therefore they did not sell their land. 23 Then Joseph said to the people, "Now that I have this day bought you and your land for Pharaoh, here is seed for you; sow the land. 24 And at the harvests you shall give one-fifth to Pharaoh, and four-fifths shall be your own, as seed for the field and as food for yourselves and your households, and as food for your little ones." 25 They said, "You have saved our lives; may it please my lord, we will be slaves to Pharaoh." 26 So Joseph made it a statute concerning the land of Egypt, and it stands to this day, that Pharaoh should have the fifth. The land of the priests alone did not become Pharaoh's.

47.22
Ezra 7.24
47.24
Gen 41.34
47.25
Gen 33.15
47.26
v. 22

L. *Joseph's promise to Jacob*

47.27
v. 11;
Gen 46.3;
Ex 1.7
47.29
Deut 31.14;
Gen 24.2, 49
47.30
Gen 49.29;
50.5, 13
47.31
Gen 21.23,
24; 24.3;
31.53; 50.25

27 Thus Israel settled in the land of Egypt, in the region of Goshen; and they gained possessions in it, and were fruitful and multiplied exceedingly. 28 Jacob lived in the land of Egypt seventeen years; so the days of Jacob, the years of his life, were one hundred forty-seven years.

29 When the time of Israel's death drew near, he called his son Joseph and said to him, "If I have found favor with you, put your hand under my thigh and promise to deal loyally and truly with me. Do not bury me in Egypt. 30 When I lie down with my ancestors, carry me out of Egypt and bury me in their burial place." He answered, "I will do as you have said." 31 And he said, "Swear to me"; and he swore to him. Then Israel bowed himself on the head of his bed.

x Sam Gk Compare Vg: MT *He removed them to the cities*

47.20 *bought all the land of Egypt for Pharaoh.* Before this the Egyptians owned their own land. The famine resulted in the consolidation of the land holdings in the name of Pharaoh. The landholders became tenant farmers who were allowed to keep 80 percent of their crops, while 20 percent went to the government. Verse 19 indicates their willingness to become slaves of Pharaoh in order to save their lives.

M. Jacob's last days

1. Jacob blesses Joseph's sons:
Ephraim preferred over Manasseh

48 After this Joseph was told, "Your father is ill." So he took with him his two sons, Manasseh and Ephraim. 2 When Jacob was told, "Your son Joseph has come to you," he[y] summoned his strength and sat up in bed. 3 And Jacob said to Joseph, "God Almighty[z] appeared to me at Luz in the land of Canaan, and he blessed me, 4 and said to me, 'I am going to make you fruitful and increase your numbers; I will make of you a company of peoples, and will give this land to your offspring after you for a perpetual holding.' 5 Therefore your two sons, who were born to you in the land of Egypt before I came to you in Egypt, are now mine; Ephraim and Manasseh shall be mine, just as Reuben and Simeon are. 6 As for the offspring born to you after them, they shall be yours. They shall be recorded under the names of their brothers with regard to their inheritance. 7 For when I came from Paddan, Rachel, alas, died in the land of Canaan on the way, while there was still some distance to go to Ephrath; and I buried her there on the way to Ephrath" (that is, Bethlehem).

8 When Israel saw Joseph's sons, he said, "Who are these?" 9 Joseph said to his father, "They are my sons, whom God has given me here." And he said, "Bring them to me, please, that I may bless them." 10 Now the eyes of Israel were dim with age, and he could not see well. So Joseph brought them near him; and he kissed them and embraced them. 11 Israel said to Joseph, "I did not expect to see your face; and here God has let me see your children also." 12 Then Joseph removed them from his father's knees,[a] and he bowed himself with his face to the earth. 13 Joseph took them both, Ephraim in his right hand toward Israel's left, and Manasseh in his left hand toward Israel's right, and brought them near him. 14 But Israel stretched out his right hand and laid it on the head of Ephraim, who was the younger, and his left hand on the head of Manasseh, crossing his hands, for Manasseh was the firstborn. 15 He blessed Joseph, and said,

"The God before whom my ancestors Abraham and Isaac
        walked,
the God who has been my shepherd all my life to this day,
16   the angel who has redeemed me from all harm, bless the boys;
    and in them let my name be perpetuated, and the name of my
        ancestors Abraham and Isaac;
and let them grow into a multitude on the earth."

17 When Joseph saw that his father laid his right hand on the head of Ephraim, it displeased him; so he took his father's hand, to remove it from Ephraim's head to Manasseh's head. 18 Joseph said to his father, "Not so, my father! Since this one is the firstborn, put your right hand on his head." 19 But his father refused, and said, "I know, my son, I know; he also shall become a people, and he also shall be great. Nevertheless his

48.3
Gen 35.9-12;
28.19; 35.6
48.4
Gen 18.8
48.5
Gen 46.20;
Josh 13.7;
14.4
48.7
Gen 33.18;
35.19, 20
48.9
Gen 33.5
48.10
Gen 27.1, 27
48.11
Gen 45.26
48.14
v. 19
48.15
Gen 17.1;
Heb 11.21
48.16
Gen 28.15;
31.11, 13,
24; 28.14;
46.3
48.17
v. 14
48.19
v. 14;
Num 1.33, 35

---

y Heb *Israel*   *z* Traditional rendering of Heb *El Shaddai*   *a* Heb *from his knees*

48.5 Here Jacob adopts the two sons of Joseph, and in doing so made them equal, for rights of inheritance, with all of his other sons. Joseph, through his sons, got a double portion of the inheritance, which may mean that he replaced Reuben who, technically, deserved it as the firstborn (see note on 49.4). Since the Levites did not share in the distribution of the land, there were still twelve tribes who got the land. **48.13** Jacob had deceived his father in order to obtain Esau's blessing. Now when Joseph wants his firstborn to receive the firstborn's blessing, Jacob de-

liberately crosses his hands and places his right hand on the head of Ephraim, who was the younger son. Manasseh was given second place by Jacob. **48.16** Christ is the Angel of the covenant who redeemed Jacob from all evil. As he bore this testimony, Jacob was saying good-bye to life on earth. As we approach death, it is good for us to witness to the graciousness of the God who has kept us through the long years of life. This is an encouragement to those we leave behind and a pattern for them to follow through their daily walk.

younger brother shall be greater than he, and his offspring shall become a multitude of nations." 20 So he blessed them that day, saying,

"By you[b] Israel will invoke blessings, saying,
     'God make you[b] like Ephraim and like Manasseh.' "

So he put Ephraim ahead of Manasseh. 21 Then Israel said to Joseph, "I am about to die, but God will be with you and will bring you again to the land of your ancestors. 22 I now give to you one portion[c] more than to your brothers, the portion[c] that I took from the hand of the Amorites with my sword and with my bow."

2. Jacob blesses his sons

49 Then Jacob called his sons, and said: "Gather around, that I may tell you what will happen to you in days to come.
2 Assemble and hear, O sons of Jacob;
    listen to Israel your father.

3 Reuben, you are my firstborn,
    my might and the first fruits of my vigor,
    excelling in rank and excelling in power.
4 Unstable as water, you shall no longer excel
    because you went up onto your father's bed;
    then you defiled it—you[d] went up onto my couch!

5 Simeon and Levi are brothers;
    weapons of violence are their swords.
6 May I never come into their council;
    may I not be joined to their company—
    for in their anger they killed men,
    and at their whim they hamstrung oxen.
7 Cursed be their anger, for it is fierce,
    and their wrath, for it is cruel!
I will divide them in Jacob,
    and scatter them in Israel.

8 Judah, your brothers shall praise you;
    your hand shall be on the neck of your enemies;
    your father's sons shall bow down before you.
9 Judah is a lion's whelp;
    from the prey, my son, you have gone up.
He crouches down, he stretches out like a lion,
    like a lioness—who dares rouse him up?
10 The scepter shall not depart from Judah,
    nor the ruler's staff from between his feet,
until tribute comes to him;[e]
    and the obedience of the peoples is his.

Cross references (left margin):

48.21
Gen 26.3;
28.15; 46.4;
50.24
48.22
Josh 24.32;
Jn 4.5

49.1
Num 24.14

49.3
Gen 29.32;
Deut 21.17

49.4
Gen 35.22;
Deut 27.20

49.5
Gen 34.25-30

49.6
Prov 1.15;
Eph 5.11;
Gen 34.26

49.7
Josh 19.1, 9;
21.1-42

49.8
Deut 33.7;
1 Chr 5.2

49.9
Ezek 19.5-7;
Mic 5.8

49.10
Num 24.17;
Ps 60.7;
Lk 1.32;
Isa 2.2; 11.1

---

[b] you here is singular in Heb   [c] Or mountain slope (Heb shekem, a play on the name of the town and district of Shechem)   [d] Gk Syr Tg: Heb he   [e] Or until Shiloh comes or until he comes to Shiloh or (with Syr) until he comes to whom it belongs

---

49.4 you shall no longer excel, i.e., Reuben has lost his status, along with the rights, of the firstborn. Moreover, the Moabites seized the territory the Reubenites had occupied upon entering Canaan.
49.7 I will . . . scatter them in Israel, i.e., the tribes of Simeon (cf. Josh 19.1,9) and Levi were not given land holdings, as were their brother-tribes.
49.10 until tribute comes to him means also "he to whom it belongs." The "him" and "he" here doubtless refer first to David and second to the reign of Messiah, who would come from David—even Jesus Christ. By faith, Jacob foresaw Christ's day and was

comforted. There are other prophecies from the Old Testament related to the person of Jesus and his origin. Among them are: (1) he would come from the stock of Israel, "a star from Jacob" (Num 24.17; see note on that verse); (2) he would be of the family of David and of the tribe of Judah (49.10; Isa 11.1; Lk 1.31–33); (3) he would be born in Bethlehem (Mic 5.2; Lk 2.4,6,7); (4) he would be born of a virgin (Isa 7.14; Mt 1.18,22); (5) he would come at the appointed time (Dan 9.14–26); (6) his coming would be announced by John the Baptist (Isa 40.3; Mt 3.3); and (7) he would be God (Isa 9.6; Jn 1.14).

11 Binding his foal to the vine
    and his donkey's colt to the choice vine,
he washes his garments in wine
    and his robe in the blood of grapes;
12 his eyes are darker than wine,
    and his teeth whiter than milk.

13 Zebulun shall settle at the shore of the sea;
    he shall be a haven for ships,
    and his border shall be at Sidon.

14 Issachar is a strong donkey,
    lying down between the sheepfolds;
15 he saw that a resting place was good,
    and that the land was pleasant;
so he bowed his shoulder to the burden,
    and became a slave at forced labor.

16 Dan shall judge his people
    as one of the tribes of Israel.
17 Dan shall be a snake by the roadside,
    a viper along the path,
that bites the horse's heels
    so that its rider falls backward.

18 I wait for your salvation, O LORD.

19 Gad shall be raided by raiders,
    but he shall raid at their heels.

20 Asher's*f* food shall be rich,
    and he shall provide royal delicacies.

21 Naphtali is a doe let loose
    that bears lovely fawns.*g*

22 Joseph is a fruitful bough,
    a fruitful bough by a spring;
his branches run over the wall.*h*
23 The archers fiercely attacked him;
    they shot at him and pressed him hard.
24 Yet his bow remained taut,
    and his arms*i* were made agile
by the hands of the Mighty One of Jacob,
    by the name of the Shepherd, the Rock of Israel,
25 by the God of your father, who will help you,
    by the Almighty*j* who will bless you
with blessings of heaven above,
blessings of the deep that lies beneath,
    blessings of the breasts and of the womb.
26 The blessings of your father
    are stronger than the blessings of the eternal mountains,
    the bounties*k* of the everlasting hills;
may they be on the head of Joseph,

Cross references
49.13 Deut 33.18, 19; Josh 19.10, 11
49.16 Deut 33.22; Judg 18.1, 2
49.17 Judg 18.26, 27
49.18 Ex 15.2; Ps 25.5; 119.166, 174; Isa 25.9; Mic 7.7
49.19 Deut 33.20; 1 Chr 5.18
49.20 Deut 33.24, 25;
Josh 19.24
49.21 Deut 33.23
49.22 Deut 33.13-17
49.23 Gen 37.4, 24, 28
49.24 Ps 18.34; Isa 41.10; Ps 132.2, 5; Isa 1.24; Ps 23.1; Isa 28.16; 1 Pet 2.6-8
49.25 Gen 28.3, 13; 32.9; 48.3; 27.28
49.26 Deut 33.15, 16

---

f Gk Vg Syr: Heb *From Asher* *g* Or *that gives beautiful words* *h* Meaning of Heb uncertain *i* Heb *the arms of his hands* *j* Traditional rendering of Heb *Shaddai* *k* Cn Compare Gk: Heb *of my progenitors to the boundaries*

49.16 *Dan shall judge his people.* Samson, one of the great judges of Israel, was a Danite.

on the brow of him who was set apart from his brothers.

27 Benjamin is a ravenous wolf,
   in the morning devouring the prey,
   and at evening dividing the spoil."

3. The death and burial of Jacob

28 All these are the twelve tribes of Israel, and this is what their father said to them when he blessed them, blessing each one of them with a suitable blessing.

29 Then he charged them, saying to them, "I am about to be gathered to my people. Bury me with my ancestors — in the cave in the field of Ephron the Hittite, 30 in the cave in the field at Machpelah, near Mamre, in the land of Canaan, in the field that Abraham bought from Ephron the Hittite as a burial site. 31 There Abraham and his wife Sarah were buried; there Isaac and his wife Rebekah were buried; and there I buried Leah — 32 the field and the cave that is in it were purchased from the Hittites." 33 When Jacob ended his charge to his sons, he drew up his feet into the bed, breathed his last, and was gathered to his people.

50 Then Joseph threw himself on his father's face and wept over him and kissed him. 2 Joseph commanded the physicians in his service

49.28
Gen 23.16-20

49.29
Gen 25.8;
47.30
49.30
Gen 23.16
49.31
Gen 23.19;
25.9; 35.29
49.33
Gen 25.8;
Acts 7.15;
v. 29
50.1
Gen 46.4
50.2
v. 26

THE TRIBES OF ISRAEL

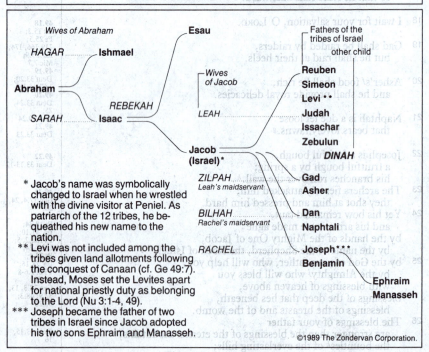

Wives of Abraham

Esau

Fathers of the tribes of Israel

HAGAR .... **Ishmael**

other child

Abraham

REBEKAH

Wives of Jacob

Reuben
Simeon
Levi **
Judah
Issachar
Zebulun

SARAH   **Isaac**

LEAH

DINAH

**Jacob
(Israel)***

* Jacob's name was symbolically changed to Israel when he wrestled with the divine visitor at Peniel. As patriarch of the 12 tribes, he bequeathed his new name to the nation.

** Levi was not included among the tribes given land allotments following the conquest of Canaan (cf. Ge 49:7). Instead, Moses set the Levites apart for national priestly duty as belonging to the Lord (Nu 3:1-4, 49).

*** Joseph became the father of two tribes in Israel since Jacob adopted his two sons Ephraim and Manasseh.

ZILPAH
Leah's maidservant

Gad
Asher

BILHAH
Rachel's maidservant

Dan
Naphtali

RACHEL

Joseph***
Benjamin

Ephraim
Manasseh

©1989 The Zondervan Corporation.

49.27 King Saul was a Benjaminite; so was the apostle Paul. Bad and good characters can come from the same family.
49.31 *there I buried Leah.* Rachel was buried in Bethlehem, where they happened to be when she died

in childbirth. Ironically Jacob was to lie next to Leah in death, while Rachel, whom Jacob loved so dearly, was to lie alone. Leah had the first sons of Jacob and now, in death, she supplanted Rachel again.
50.2 *embalmed.* This was an Egyptian custom. It

to embalm his father. So the physicians embalmed Israel; 3 they spent forty days in doing this, for that is the time required for embalming. And the Egyptians wept for him seventy days.

4 When the days of weeping for him were past, Joseph addressed the household of Pharaoh, "If now I have found favor with you, please speak to Pharaoh as follows: 5 My father made me swear an oath; he said, 'I am about to die. In the tomb that I hewed out for myself in the land of Canaan, there you shall bury me.' Now therefore let me go up, so that I may bury my father; then I will return." 6 Pharaoh answered, "Go up, and bury your father, as he made you swear to do."

7 So Joseph went up to bury his father. With him went up all the servants of Pharaoh, the elders of his household, and all the elders of the land of Egypt, 8 as well as all the household of Joseph, his brothers, and his father's household. Only their children, their flocks, and their herds were left in the land of Goshen. 9 Both chariots and charioteers went up with him. It was a very great company. 10 When they came to the threshing floor of Atad, which is beyond the Jordan, they held there a very great and sorrowful lamentation; and he observed a time of mourning for his father seven days. 11 When the Canaanite inhabitants of the land saw the mourning on the threshing floor of Atad, they said, "This is a grievous mourning on the part of the Egyptians." Therefore the place was named Abel-mizraim;*l* it is beyond the Jordan. 12 Thus his sons did for him as he had instructed them. 13 They carried him to the land of Canaan and buried him in the cave of the field at Machpelah, the field near Mamre, which Abraham bought as a burial site from Ephron the Hittite. 14 After he had buried his father, Joseph returned to Egypt with his brothers and all who had gone up with him to bury his father.

N. *Joseph's kindness to his brothers*

15 Realizing that their father was dead, Joseph's brothers said, "What if Joseph still bears a grudge against us and pays us back in full for all the wrong that we did to him?" 16 So they approached*m* Joseph, saying, "Your father gave this instruction before he died, 17 'Say to Joseph: I beg you, forgive the crime of your brothers and the wrong they did in harming you.' Now therefore please forgive the crime of the servants of the God of your father." Joseph wept when they spoke to him. 18 Then his brothers also wept,*n* fell down before him, and said, "We are here as your slaves." 19 But Joseph said to them, "Do not be afraid! Am I in the place of God? 20 Even though you intended to do harm to me, God intended it for good, in order to preserve a numerous people, as he is doing today. 21 So have no fear; I myself will provide for you and your little ones." In this way he reassured them, speaking kindly to them.

O. *The death and embalming of Joseph*

22 So Joseph remained in Egypt, he and his father's household; and Joseph lived one hundred ten years. 23 Joseph saw Ephraim's children of the third generation; the children of Machir son of Manasseh were also born on Joseph's knees.

24 Then Joseph said to his brothers, "I am about to die; but God will

l That is mourning (or meadow) *of Egypt*   *m Gk Syr: Heb they commanded*   *n Cn: Heb also came*

50.3
v. 10;
Num 20.29;
Deut 34.8

50.5
Gen 47.29-31

50.8
Ex 8.22

50.10
2 Sam 1.17;
1 Sam 31.13;
Job 2.13

50.13
Gen 49.29,
30; 23.16

50.15
Gen 37.28;
42.21, 22

50.18
Gen 37.7, 10;
41.43
50.19
Gen 45.5;
Deut 32.35;
Rom 12.19;
Heb 10.30
50.20
Gen 37.26,
27; 45.5, 7
50.21
Gen 45.11;
47.12

50.24
Gen 48.21;
Heb 11.22;
Gen 13.15,
17; 15.7, 8;
26.3; 28.13;
35.12

was used here for Jacob, whose body would have disintegrated had his children brought him back for burial beside Leah without having his body embalmed. Both the Egyptians and the Israelites believed in a life after death, but their viewpoints were quite different.
50.18 The dreams of Joseph that were given him by God are now finally and completely fulfilled, as his brothers fall before him. They somehow never did

understand Joseph because they thought he was being kind to them only while their father Jacob was alive; after his death they expected Joseph would wreak vengeance on them. Instead he acted graciously and thus demonstrated his spiritual maturity and his understanding that what had happened was in the will of God and had worked together for good.
50.24 Joseph understood and believed God's promise of a land for Abraham's descendants. Thus he

surely come to you, and bring you up out of this land to the land that he swore to Abraham, to Isaac, and to Jacob." 25 So Joseph made the Israelites swear, saying, "When God comes to you, you shall carry up my bones from here." 26 And Joseph died, being one hundred ten years old; he was embalmed and placed in a coffin in Egypt.

knew that their stay in Egypt would end, although he probably did not foresee their slavery under later Pharaohs. He made his family promise that they would take his bones with them when the exodus came.

INTRODUCTION TO

EXODUS

Authorship, Date, and Background: Exodus, like the other books of the Pentateuch, takes its name in the Hebrew Bible from the opening words of the text which mean "these are the names of." The Septuagint (Greek translation) uses the title Exodos, meaning "departure," and this title has come into our English Bibles as "Exodus." This is the second of the five books of Moses, to whom its authorship has been attributed (see the introduction to Genesis).

Exodus cannot be understood apart from Genesis, for it simply continues the story that begins in Genesis. The central character of Exodus is Moses, the great lawgiver, the leader of the people of Israel, and the founding father of Israel's religion. Genesis ends with the family of Jacob in Egypt; Exodus opens with Jacob's descendants in slavery, a situation which developed after the death of Joseph. During their four and a half centuries in Egypt, the number of the Israelites increased very substantially. Now the time had come for God to free them from slavery and deliver them from Egypt.

Scholars are divided about the date of Israel's flight from Egypt. Many evangelicals place it around 1440 B.C.; others place it around 1290 B.C. If the exodus occurred around 1440 B.C., the composition of this book by Moses can be dated in the last two decades of the fifteenth century B.C.

Characteristics and Content: The hard bondage to which the Israelites were subjected constituted a need for their liberation. God heard their prayers for help and chose Moses as their leader, through whom the liberation would take place. In preparation for that deliverance, Moses spent the first forty years of his life in the court of the Pharaoh, where he learned about politics and statecraft. He spent the second forty years in the desert, learning about God in preparation for the most important last forty years of his life. In the last part of his life Moses directed the Israelites, during which time they became a nation under God, a theocracy governed by a covenant, which was spelled out in what might be called the constitution for the people of God.

Probably the most notable event in Exodus is the crossing of the Red (Reed) Sea. This miraculous incident is referred to again and again in the O.T. and N.T. When the event took place, Israel was a conglomerate mass of undisciplined slaves who need to be welded together into a nation. Moses describes how this came to pass.

The exodus begins with the celebration of the Passover, at which time the firstborn of the Egyptians died. It was the story of redemption by blood which became the central motif of God's salvation for all people through animal sacrifices, anticipating the death and resurrection of the Lord Jesus. It had been God's intention to bring the Israelites into the promised land of Canaan shortly after their liberation from Egypt. When the people accepted the adverse report of ten of the twelve spies, God condemned them to forty years of wandering before they were fit to enter the land; indeed, all Israelites twenty years or older (Num 14.29) were slated to perish. Only Joshua and Caleb of that generation would enter Canaan. Even Moses fell short when he sinfully struck the rock in the wilderness instead of speaking to it (Num 20.1–13).

During the long wilderness journey, God gave Israel the law, including the ten

commandments, by which they were to be governed. God established a covenant
with Israel which bound the people to obey him. The tabernacle in the wilderness
was set up for the worship of God by the people and for the offering of the blood
of bulls and goats for sin. Along with the tabernacle God ordained the priesthood,
choosing Aaron and his descendants to minister at the altar. When the tabernacle was
finished and dedicated, the glory of God entered the Holy Place, which was forbidden to all except the high priest, who was to enter once a year to sprinkle blood on
the mercy seat.

God marvelously provided for his people in the wilderness. He sent the cloud for
daytime and the pillar of fire by night. He gave them manna each day. Their clothes
and their shoes never wore out. Yet they were a people who disobeyed God's law
again and again, so that one divine punishment followed another as God sought to
teach them the truth that those who obey his voice prosper while those who disobey
experience chastisement and sometimes even death.

Outline:

I. The deliverance from Egypt (1.1—15.21)

II. The journey to Sinai (15.22—18.27)

III. The covenant and the law (19.1—24.18)

IV. The tabernacle in the wilderness (25.1—40.38)

EXODUS

I. The deliverance from Egypt (1.1–15.21)

A. Introduction

1. The numerical growth of Israel

1 These are the names of the sons of Israel who came to Egypt with Jacob, each with his household: 2 Reuben, Simeon, Levi, and Judah, 3 Issachar, Zebulun, and Benjamin, 4 Dan and Naphtali, Gad and Asher. 5 The total number of people born to Jacob was seventy. Joseph was already in Egypt. 6 Then Joseph died, and all his brothers, and that whole generation. 7 But the Israelites were fruitful and prolific; they multiplied and grew exceedingly strong, so that the land was filled with them.

2. Israel as slaves

8 Now a new king arose over Egypt, who did not know Joseph. 9 He said to his people, "Look, the Israelite people are more numerous and more powerful than we. 10 Come, let us deal shrewdly with them, or they will increase and, in the event of war, join our enemies and fight against us and escape from the land." 11 Therefore they set taskmasters over them to oppress them with forced labor. They built supply cities, Pithom and Rameses, for Pharaoh. 12 But the more they were oppressed, the more they multiplied and spread, so that the Egyptians came to dread the Israelites. 13 The Egyptians became ruthless in imposing tasks on the Israelites, 14 and made their lives bitter with hard service in mortar and brick and in every kind of field labor. They were ruthless in all the tasks that they imposed on them.

3. The background for Moses

15 The king of Egypt said to the Hebrew midwives, one of whom was named Shiphrah and the other Puah, 16 "When you act as midwives to the Hebrew women, and see them on the birthstool, if it is a boy, kill him; but if it is a girl, she shall live." 17 But the midwives feared God; they did not do as the king of Egypt commanded them, but they let the boys live. 18 So the king of Egypt summoned the midwives and said to them, "Why have you done this, and allowed the boys to live?" 19 The midwives said to Pharaoh, "Because the Hebrew women are not like the Egyptian

Marginal cross-references:
1.1 Gen 46.8-27
1.5 Gen 46.27
1.6 Gen 50.26
1.7 Gen 46.3; 47.27; Acts 7.17
1.8
1.8 Acts 7.18, 19
1.9 Ps 105.24, 25
1.11 Ex 3.7; 5.6
1.14 Ps 81.6
1.16 Acts 7.19
1.17 v. 21

1.7 *land*, the land of Goshen or Rameses (see notes on Gen 45.10 and 47.11).

1.8 *a new king arose.* This incident occurred approximately 400 years after Joseph's death.

1.9 The Pharaoh feared the increasing number of Israelites, whose proliferation was part of God's plan before they entered the promised land. In Egypt the Israelites were able to build a mighty nation in spite of being made slaves, and thus they presented a threat to the military security of the Egyptian state.

1.11 *Pithom and Raamses*, cities in the Nile Delta. If this is a reference to the building operations of the nineteenth dynasty kings of Egypt, then the exodus took place shortly after 1301 B.C.

1.15 There must have been many midwives. The

two mentioned here were probably chief midwives.

1.16 *birthstool*, i.e., two stones that supported the females' thighs. The stones were separated so that the midwives could effect a delivery from beneath the mother. *kill him.* The Egyptian Pharaoh did not hesitate to practice genocide by ordering the killing of all Israelite male babies. In one form or another this type of atrocity has been the curse of many nations throughout history, including some in the twentieth century, for human nature has not changed.

1.19 If this were true there would have been no need for midwives. Apparently the midwives lied. They are to be commended for preserving the lives of male babies, even though they lied.

women; for they are vigorous and give birth before the midwife comes to them." ²⁰ So God dealt well with the midwives; and the people multiplied and became very strong. ²¹ And because the midwives feared God, he gave them families. ²² Then Pharaoh commanded all his people, "Every boy that is born to the Hebrews*a* you shall throw into the Nile, but you shall let every girl live."

B. *God's servant Moses*

1. *Moses' birth*

2 Now a man from the house of Levi went and married a Levite woman. ² The woman conceived and bore a son; and when she saw that he was a fine baby, she hid him three months. ³ When she could hide him no longer she got a papyrus basket for him, and plastered it with bitumen and pitch; she put the child in it and placed it among the reeds on the bank of the river. ⁴ His sister stood at a distance, to see what would happen to him.

5 The daughter of Pharaoh came down to bathe at the river, while her attendants walked beside the river. She saw the basket among the reeds and sent her maid to bring it. ⁶ When she opened it, she saw the child. He was crying, and she took pity on him: "This must be one of the Hebrews' children," she said. ⁷ Then his sister said to Pharaoh's daughter, "Shall I go and get you a nurse from the Hebrew women to nurse the child for you?" ⁸ Pharaoh's daughter said to her, "Yes." So the girl went and called the child's mother. ⁹ Pharaoh's daughter said to her, "Take this child and nurse it for me, and I will give you your wages." So the woman took the child and nursed it. ¹⁰ When the child grew up, she brought him to Pharaoh's daughter, and she took him as her son. She named him Moses,*b* "because," she said, "I drew him out*c* of the water."

2. *Moses' crime and flight*

11 One day, after Moses had grown up, he went out to his people and saw their forced labor. He saw an Egyptian beating a Hebrew, one of his kinsfolk. ¹² He looked this way and that, and seeing no one he killed the Egyptian and hid him in the sand. ¹³ When he went out the next day, he saw two Hebrews fighting; and he said to the one who was in the wrong, "Why do you strike your fellow Hebrew?" ¹⁴ He answered, "Who made you a ruler and judge over us? Do you mean to kill me as you killed the Egyptian?" Then Moses was afraid and thought, "Surely the thing is known." ¹⁵ When Pharaoh heard of it, he sought to kill Moses.

But Moses fled from Pharaoh. He settled in the land of Midian, and sat down by a well. ¹⁶ The priest of Midian had seven daughters. They came to draw water, and filled the troughs to water their father's flock. ¹⁷ But some shepherds came and drove them away. Moses got up and came to their defense and watered their flock. ¹⁸ When they returned to their father Reuel, he said, "How is it that you have come back so soon today?"

a Sam Gk Tg: Heb lacks *to the Hebrews*   *b* Heb *Mosheh*   *c* Heb *mashah*

1.20
v. 12;
Isa 3.10
1.21
1 Sam 2.35
1.22
Acts 7.19

2.1
Ex 6.19, 20
2.2
Acts 7.20;
Heb 11.23

2.4
Ex 15.20;
Num 26.59

2.10
Acts 7.21

2.11
Acts 7.23;
Heb 11.24-26
2.12
Acts 7.24
2.13
Acts 7.26-28
2.14
Gen 19.9;
Acts 7.27
2.15
Acts 7.29;
Gen 24.11;
29.2
2.16
Ex 3.1;
18.12;
Gen 24.13, 19
2.17
Gen 29.3, 10
2.18
Ex 3.1;
Num 10.29

2.1 We learn later that the father and mother of Moses are named Amram and Jochebed (6.20). Jochebed was the sister of Amram's father.
2.3 *bituman and pitch*. The ark basket, constructed from papyrus reeds, was made waterproof by using asphalt or bitumen to cover the reeds.
2.10 Moses ranks among the greatest of all humans who ever lived. He was born into the tribe of Levi and was well educated in Egypt; his training included literature, law, astronomy, geometry, writing, music, art, medicine, philosophy, and athletics. He could have been a politician, a writer, or a soldier. As Israel's leader he was deliverer, lawgiver, builder, mili-

tary leader, judge, author, and intermediary between Israel and God. At 40 he fled from Egypt (cf. Ex 2.15; Acts 7.23–29); at 80 he delivered Israel from Egypt; at 120 he died in fullness of strength. Moses was meek, faithful, and selfless, as well as courageous.
2.12 Moses was guilty of murder even though his intention to help a fellow Israelite was good. The end does not justify the means.
2.15 *the land of Midian* was an area east and southeast of Canaan. It was peopled by descendants of Abraham born to Keturah (see Gen 25).
2.18 Reuel, who eventually became Moses' father-in-law, was also called Jethro (3.1) and Hobab (Judg

19 They said, "An Egyptian helped us against the shepherds; he even drew water for us and watered the flock." 20 He said to his daughters, "Where is he? Why did you leave the man? Invite him to break bread." 21 Moses agreed to stay with the man, and he gave Moses his daughter Zipporah in marriage. 22 She bore a son, and he named him Gershom; for he said, "I have been an alien[d] residing in a foreign land."

3. The call of Moses at the burning bush

a. Moses' conversations with God

23 After a long time the king of Egypt died. The Israelites groaned under their slavery, and cried out. Out of the slavery their cry for help rose up to God. 24 God heard their groaning, and God remembered his covenant with Abraham, Isaac, and Jacob. 25 God looked upon the Israelites, and God took notice of them.

3 Moses was keeping the flock of his father-in-law Jethro, the priest of Midian; he led his flock beyond the wilderness, and came to Horeb, the mountain of God. 2 There the angel of the LORD appeared to him in a flame of fire out of a bush; he looked, and the bush was blazing, yet it was not consumed. 3 Then Moses said, "I must turn aside and look at this great sight, and see why the bush is not burned up." 4 When the LORD saw that he had turned aside to see, God called to him out of the bush, "Moses, Moses!" And he said, "Here I am." 5 Then he said, "Come no closer! Remove the sandals from your feet, for the place on which you are standing is holy ground." 6 He said further, "I am the God of your father, the God of Abraham, the God of Isaac, and the God of Jacob." And Moses hid his face, for he was afraid to look at God.

7 Then the LORD said, "I have observed the misery of my people who are in Egypt; I have heard their cry on account of their taskmasters. Indeed, I know their sufferings, 8 and I have come down to deliver them from the Egyptians, and to bring them up out of that land to a good and broad land, a land flowing with milk and honey, to the country of the Canaanites, the Hittites, the Amorites, the Perizzites, the Hivites, and the Jebusites. 9 The cry of the Israelites has now come to me; I have also seen how the Egyptians oppress them. 10 So come, I will send you to Pharaoh to bring my people, the Israelites, out of Egypt." 11 But Moses said to God, "Who am I that I should go to Pharaoh, and bring the Israelites out of Egypt?" 12 He said, "I will be with you; and this shall be the sign for you that it is I who sent you: when you have brought the people out of Egypt, you shall worship God on this mountain."

13 But Moses said to God, "If I come to the Israelites and say to them, 'The God of your ancestors has sent me to you,' and they ask me, 'What is his name?' what shall I say to them?" 14 God said to Moses, "I AM WHO I AM."[e] He said further, "Thus you shall say to the Israelites, 'I AM has sent me to you.'" 15 God also said to Moses, "Thus you shall say to the

2.20
Gen 31.54
2.21
Acts 7.29;
Gen 4.25;
18.2
2.22
Ex 18.3;
Heb 11.13,
14

2.23
Acts 7.30;
Deut 26.7;
Ex 3.9;
Jas 5.4
2.24
Ex 6.5;
Ps 105.8, 42;
Gen 22.16-18
2.25
Ex 4.31; 3.7;
4.27; 18.5
3.1
Ex 2.18
3.2
Deut 33.16;
Mk 12.26
3.3
Acts 7.31
3.5
Josh 5.15;
Acts 7.33
3.6
Mt 22.31,
32;
Mk 12.26;
Lk 20.37;
Acts 7.32
3.7
Ex 2.25;
Neh 9.9;
Acts 7.34
3.8
Gen 50.24,
25; v. 17;
Josh 24.11
3.9
Ex 2.23;
1.13, 14
3.10
Mic 6.4
3.12
Gen 31.3;
Josh 1.5

3.14
Ex 6.3;
Jn 8.58;
Heb 13.8
3.15
Ps 135.13;
Hos 12.5

---

[d] Heb ger   [e] Or I AM WHAT I AM or I WILL BE WHAT I WILL BE

4.11). In Num 10.29, Hobab is called the son of Reuel; this means that Reuel named one of his sons Hobab.

3.2 The phrase *the angel of the LORD* may confirm what is elsewhere certain—that the preincarnate Christ made appearances in the O.T. In Judg 2.1; 6.12–16; and 13.3–22, the texts indicate that the angel in these cases was God himself.

3.3 The burning bush that was not consumed by the fire was evidence of the supernatural, providing Moses with external, corroborating proof of the presence of God. In the history of redemption, God often gave such evidence in order that believers might know it was God who spoke.

3.7 *have heard their cry.* The Lord may delay in answering prayer but he never comes too late. The Israelites had been in slavery for four centuries. God was using Egypt to fashion a great people for himself. The time had come for him to answer their prayers for deliverance.

3.15 LORD . . . God, or, "Yahweh." Some translations (erroneously) use "Jehovah," others, "LORD." The name means "he is" (i.e., he is the covenant-keeping God to his people) or "he causes (all things) to be" (the theme of the prophets and psalmists). Instead of reading the sacred name *Yahweh*, pious Israelites substituted the word *Adonai*, "Lord."

Israelites, 'The LORD,*f* the God of your ancestors, the God of Abraham, the God of Isaac, and the God of Jacob, has sent me to you':

This is my name forever,
and this my title for all generations.

16Go and assemble the elders of Israel, and say to them, 'The LORD, the God of your ancestors, the God of Abraham, of Isaac, and of Jacob, has appeared to me, saying: I have given heed to you and to what has been done to you in Egypt. 17I declare that I will bring you up out of the misery of Egypt, to the land of the Canaanites, the Hittites, the Amorites, the Perizzites, the Hivites, and the Jebusites, a land flowing with milk and honey.' 18They will listen to your voice; and you and the elders of Israel shall go to the king of Egypt and say to him, 'The LORD, the God of the Hebrews, has met with us; let us now go a three days' journey into the wilderness, so that we may sacrifice to the LORD our God.' 19I know, however, that the king of Egypt will not let you go unless compelled by a mighty hand.*g* 20So I will stretch out my hand and strike Egypt with all my wonders that I will perform in it; after that he will let you go. 21I will bring this people into such favor with the Egyptians that, when you go, you will not go empty-handed; 22each woman shall ask her neighbor and any woman living in the neighbor's house for jewelry of silver and of gold, and clothing, and you shall put them on your sons and on your daughters; and so you shall plunder the Egyptians."

b. *God equips Moses*

4 Then Moses answered, "But suppose they do not believe me or listen to me, but say, 'The LORD did not appear to you.'" 2The LORD said to him, "What is that in your hand?" He said, "A staff." 3And he said, "Throw it on the ground." So he threw the staff on the ground, and it became a snake; and Moses drew back from it. 4Then the LORD said to Moses, "Reach out your hand, and seize it by the tail" — so he reached out his hand and grasped it, and it became a staff in his hand — 5"so that they may believe that the LORD, the God of their ancestors, the God of Abraham, the God of Isaac, and the God of Jacob, has appeared to you."

6 Again, the LORD said to him, "Put your hand inside your cloak." He put his hand into his cloak; and when he took it out, his hand was leprous,*h* as white as snow. 7Then God said, "Put your hand back into your cloak" — so he put his hand back into his cloak, and when he took it out, it was restored like the rest of his body — 8"If they will not believe you or heed the first sign, they may believe the second sign. 9If they will not believe even these two signs or heed you, you shall take some water from the Nile and pour it on the dry ground; and the water that you shall take from the Nile will become blood on the dry ground."

c. *God provides Aaron to speak*

10 But Moses said to the LORD, "O my Lord, I have never been eloquent, neither in the past nor even now that you have spoken to your servant; but I am slow of speech and slow of tongue." 11Then the LORD said to him, "Who gives speech to mortals? Who makes them mute or deaf, seeing or blind? Is it not I, the LORD? 12Now go, and I will be with your mouth and teach you what you are to speak." 13But he said, "O my

f The word "LORD" when spelled with capital letters stands for the divine name, *YHWH*, which is here connected with the verb *hayah*, "to be" *g* Gk Vg: Heb *no, not by a mighty hand* *h* A term for several skin diseases; precise meaning uncertain

---

4.2 Moses asked God to give him outward confirming evidence to present to Pharaoh which would show he was from God Almighty. He was given a staff and the leprous hand (4.6). But Pharaoh's unbelief was not moved by such signs and wonders. Scripture does show that small things in God's hands and under his control can bring about mighty results: Moses had the staff, David a sling and pebbles, and Samson the jawbone of an ass. In the case of Moses, even if the signs did not convince Pharaoh, they did convince the children of Israel that Moses was God's messenger of deliverance (4.29–31).

3.17
Gen 15.14,
16;
Josh 24.11
3.18
Ex 4.31; 5.1,
3
3.19
Ex 5.2; 6.1
3.20
Ex 6.6; 9.15;
Deut 6.22;
Neh 9.10;
Ex 12.31
3.21
Ex 11.3;
12.36
3.22
Ex 11.2, 3;
12.35, 36

4.1
Ex 3.18; 6.30
4.2
vv. 17, 20

4.6
Num 12.10;
2 Kings 5.27
4.7
Num 12.13,
14;
Deut 32.39;
2 Kings 5.14;
Mt 8.3
4.9
Ex 7.19

4.10
Ex 6.12;
Jer 1.6
4.11
Ps 94.9;
Mt 11.5
4.12
Isa 50.4;
Jer 1.9;
Mt 10.19;
Mk 13.11;
Lk 12.11,
12; 21.14, 15

Lord, please send someone else." ¹⁴ Then the anger of the LORD was
kindled against Moses and he said, "What of your brother Aaron the
Levite? I know that he can speak fluently; even now he is coming out to
meet you, and when he sees you his heart will be glad. ¹⁵ You shall speak
to him and put the words in his mouth; and I will be with your mouth
and with his mouth, and will teach you what you shall do. ¹⁶ He indeed
shall speak for you to the people; he shall serve as a mouth for you, and
you shall serve as God for him. ¹⁷ Take in your hand this staff, with which
you shall perform the signs."

d. Moses starts for Egypt

18   Moses went back to his father-in-law Jethro and said to him,
"Please let me go back to my kindred in Egypt and see whether they are
still living." And Jethro said to Moses, "Go in peace." ¹⁹ The LORD said
to Moses in Midian, "Go back to Egypt; for all those who were seeking
your life are dead." ²⁰ So Moses took his wife and his sons, put them on
a donkey, and went back to the land of Egypt; and Moses carried the staff
of God in his hand.

21   And the LORD said to Moses, "When you go back to Egypt, see
that you perform before Pharaoh all the wonders that I have put in your
power; but I will harden his heart, so that he will not let the people go.
²² Then you shall say to Pharaoh, 'Thus says the LORD: Israel is my
firstborn son. ²³ I said to you, "Let my son go that he may worship me."
But you refused to let him go; now I will kill your firstborn son.' "

24   On the way, at a place where they spent the night, the LORD met
him and tried to kill him. ²⁵ But Zipporah took a flint and cut off her son's
foreskin, and touched Moses'ⁱ feet with it, and said, "Truly you are a
bridegroom of blood to me!" ²⁶ So he let him alone. It was then she said,
"A bridegroom of blood by circumcision."

27   The LORD said to Aaron, "Go into the wilderness to meet Moses."
So he went; and he met him at the mountain of God and kissed him.
²⁸ Moses told Aaron all the words of the LORD with which he had sent him,
and all the signs with which he had charged him. ²⁹ Then Moses and
Aaron went and assembled all the elders of the Israelites. ³⁰ Aaron spoke
all the words that the LORD had spoken to Moses, and performed the signs
in the sight of the people. ³¹ The people believed; and when they heard
that the LORD had given heed to the Israelites and that he had seen their
misery, they bowed down and worshiped.

C. God's method of deliverance

1. Moses and Aaron meet with Pharaoh

a. Pharaoh refuses to let Israel go

5   Afterward Moses and Aaron went to Pharaoh and said, "Thus says
     the LORD, the God of Israel, 'Let my people go, so that they may
celebrate a festival to me in the wilderness.' " ² But Pharaoh said, "Who

ⁱ Heb his

Margin references:

4.14
v. 27

4.15
Ex 7.1, 2;
Num 23.5,
12, 16;
Deut 5.31

4.17
v.;
Ex 7.9-20

4.19
Ex 2.15, 23

4.20
Ex 17.9;
Num 20.8

4.21
Ex 7.3, 13;
9.12, 35;
10.1; 14.8;
Deut 2.30;
Jn 12.40;
Rom 19.18
4.22
Isa 63.16;
64.8;
Hos 11.1;
Rom 9.4;
Jer 31.9
4.23
Ex 5.1; 6.11;
7.16; 12.29
4.24ff
Num 22.22;
Gen 17.14
4.25
Josh 5.2, 3
4.27
v. 14;
Ex 3.1
4.28
vv. 15, 16;
8.9
4.29
Ex 3.16
4.30
v. 16
4.31
v. 8, 9;
Ex 3.18;
2.25; 3.7;
12.27

5.1
Ex 3.18;
4.23; 10.9
5.2
Job 21.15;
Ex 3.19

4.21 The Scriptures say both that God hardened
Pharaoh's heart (9.12; 10.1) and that Pharaoh hardened his own heart (8.15,32; 9.34). There is nothing
to indicate that God violated Pharaoh's choice or will.
Rather, he sent circumstances into Pharaoh's life
which hardened his heart; Pharaoh rejected God's
claims. Opposing God always results in a hardened
heart.
4.25,26 The Scriptures do not tell us why Moses
had not circumcised his son. Perhaps it was to please
his wife, who was not an Israelite. But this neglect of
the covenant cut his son off from Israel (cf. Gen
17.14), for circumcision was the seal of the covenant.

Moses could not serve as God's deliverer unless and
until he obeyed this ordinance. Zipporah performed
the rite for her husband. In the N.T., real circumcision is of the heart and not of the flesh (Rom 2.29).
4.30 Aaron related to the elders of Israel the words
Moses had spoken to him, and he performed the signs
which testified to the divine origin of the words. The
signs were done in the presence of the people, who
were convinced and who "bowed down and worshiped" (4.31).
5.2 *I do not know the LORD.* Those who refuse to
listen will not hear, and those who do not want to
know God will not know him.

is the LORD, that I should heed him and let Israel go? I do not know the
LORD, and I will not let Israel go." ³Then they said, "The God of the
Hebrews has revealed himself to us; let us go a three days' journey into
the wilderness to sacrifice to the LORD our God, or he will fall upon us
with pestilence or sword." ⁴But the king of Egypt said to them, "Moses
and Aaron, why are you taking the people away from their work? Get to
your labors!" ⁵Pharaoh continued, "Now they are more numerous than
the people of the land ʲ and yet you want them to stop working!" ⁶That
same day Pharaoh commanded the taskmasters of the people, as well as
their supervisors, ⁷"You shall no longer give the people straw to make
bricks, as before; let them go and gather straw for themselves. ⁸But you
shall require of them the same quantity of bricks as they have made
previously; do not diminish it, for they are lazy; that is why they cry, 'Let
us go and offer sacrifice to our God.' ⁹Let heavier work be laid on them;
then they will labor at it and pay no attention to deceptive words."

b. Israel's task made heavier

10 So the taskmasters and the supervisors of the people went out and
said to the people, "Thus says Pharaoh, 'I will not give you straw. ¹¹Go
and get straw yourselves, wherever you can find it; but your work will not
be lessened in the least.' " ¹²So the people scattered throughout the land
of Egypt, to gather stubble for straw. ¹³The taskmasters were urgent,
saying, "Complete your work, the same daily assignment as when you
were given straw." ¹⁴And the supervisors of the Israelites, whom Pharaoh's taskmasters had set over them, were beaten, and were asked, "Why
did you not finish the required quantity of bricks yesterday and today, as
you did before?"

15 Then the Israelite supervisors came to Pharaoh and cried, "Why
do you treat your servants like this? ¹⁶No straw is given to your servants,
yet they say to us, 'Make bricks!' Look how your servants are beaten! You
are unjust to your own people."ᵏ ¹⁷He said, "You are lazy, lazy; that is
why you say, 'Let us go and sacrifice to the LORD.' ¹⁸Go now, and work;
for no straw shall be given you, but you shall still deliver the same number
of bricks." ¹⁹The Israelite supervisors saw that they were in trouble when
they were told, "You shall not lessen your daily number of bricks." ²⁰As
they left Pharaoh, they came upon Moses and Aaron who were waiting
to meet them. ²¹They said to them, "The LORD look upon you and judge!
You have brought us into bad odor with Pharaoh and his officials, and
have put a sword in their hand to kill us."

c. God's promise of deliverance to Moses

22 Then Moses turned again to the LORD and said, "O LORD, why
have you mistreated this people? Why did you ever send me? ²³Since I
first came to Pharaoh to speak in your name, he has mistreated this people,
and you have done nothing at all to deliver your people."

ʲ Sam: Heb The people of the land are now many   ᵏ Gk Compare Syr Vg: Heb beaten, and the sin of your people

5.7 *let them go and gather straw for themselves.* Bricks with straw were stronger than bricks without straw. The Israelites' taskmasters had provided straw for them, but now they had to go some distance to the fields, gather straw for themselves, and still produce as many bricks as before. This was oppression with a vengeance (see 5.14).
5.21 Moses and Aaron were Israel's deliverers. Yet the people who had cried for deliverance unfairly reproached them for their efforts to answer those prayers.
5.22 Moses was perplexed when the situation wors-

ened; God's guarantee to deliver Israel seemed farther away than ever. Moses did not understand that miraculous deliverances may be preceded by great difficulties and times when conditions appear most unfavorable. But we walk by faith and not by sight. Believers should not allow external circumstances to daunt them when they have clear promises from God to deliver them. Note the example of Joseph: before he became prime minister of Egypt he was first a slave, then imprisoned for a crime he never committed. Strong faith is challenged, not defeated, by adverse circumstances.

6 Then the LORD said to Moses, "Now you shall see what I will do to Pharaoh: Indeed, by a mighty hand he will let them go; by a mighty hand he will drive them out of his land."

2 God also spoke to Moses and said to him: "I am the LORD. 3 I appeared to Abraham, Isaac, and Jacob as God Almighty,*l* but by my name 'The LORD'*m* I did not make myself known to them. 4 I also established my covenant with them, to give them the land of Canaan, the land in which they resided as aliens. 5 I have also heard the groaning of the Israelites whom the Egyptians are holding as slaves, and I have remembered my covenant. 6 Say therefore to the Israelites, 'I am the LORD, and I will free you from the burdens of the Egyptians and deliver you from slavery to them. I will redeem you with an outstretched arm and with mighty acts of judgment. 7 I will take you as my people, and I will be your God. You shall know that I am the LORD your God, who has freed you from the burdens of the Egyptians. 8 I will bring you into the land that I swore to give to Abraham, Isaac, and Jacob; I will give it to you for a possession. I am the LORD.' " 9 Moses told this to the Israelites; but they would not listen to Moses, because of their broken spirit and their cruel slavery.

10   Then the LORD spoke to Moses, 11 "Go and tell Pharaoh king of Egypt to let the Israelites go out of his land." 12 But Moses spoke to the LORD, "The Israelites have not listened to me; how then shall Pharaoh listen to me, poor speaker that I am?"*n* 13 Thus the LORD spoke to Moses and Aaron, and gave them orders regarding the Israelites and Pharaoh king of Egypt, charging them to free the Israelites from the land of Egypt.

d. The genealogy of Israel

14   The following are the heads of their ancestral houses: the sons of Reuben, the firstborn of Israel: Hanoch, Pallu, Hezron, and Carmi; these are the families of Reuben. 15 The sons of Simeon: Jemuel, Jamin, Ohad, Jachin, Zohar, and Shaul,*o* the son of a Canaanite woman; these are the families of Simeon. 16 The following are the names of the sons of Levi according to their genealogies: Gershon,*p* Kohath, and Merari, and the length of Levi's life was one hundred thirty-seven years. 17 The sons of Gershon:*p* Libni and Shimei, by their families. 18 The sons of Kohath: Amram, Izhar, Hebron, and Uzziel, and the length of Kohath's life was one hundred thirty-three years. 19 The sons of Merari: Mahli and Mushi. These are the families of the Levites according to their genealogies. 20 Amram married Jochebed his father's sister and she bore him Aaron and Moses, and the length of Amram's life was one hundred thirty-seven years. 21 The sons of Izhar: Korah, Nepheg, and Zichri. 22 The sons of Uzziel: Mishael, Elzaphan, and Sithri. 23 Aaron married Elisheba, daughter of Amminadab and sister of Nahshon, and she bore him Nadab, Abihu, Eleazar, and Ithamar. 24 The sons of Korah: Assir, Elkanah, and Abiasaph; these are the families of the Korahites. 25 Aaron's son Eleazar married one of the daughters of Putiel, and she bore him Phinehas. These are the heads of the ancestral houses of the Levites by their families.

26   It was this same Aaron and Moses to whom the LORD said, "Bring the Israelites out of the land of Egypt, company by company." 27 It was

6.1	Ex 3.19, 20; 7.4, 5; 12.31, 33, 39
6.3	Ps 68.4; 83.18; Isa 52.6; Jer 16.21; Ezek 37.6, 13
6.4	Gen 15.18; 28.4
6.5	Ex 2.24
6.6	Deut 26.8
6.7	Deut 4.20; 26.8; Ps 81.6; Ex 16.12; Isa 41.20
6.8	Gen 15.18
6.14	Gen 46.9; Num 26.5-11
6.15	Gen 46.10; 1 Chr 4.24
6.16	Gen 46.11; Num 3.17
6.17	1 Chr 6.17
6.18	1 Chr 6.2, 18
6.19	1 Chr 6.19
6.20	Ex 2.1, 2; Num 26.59
6.21	Num 16.1; 1 Chr 6.37, 38
6.22	Lev 10.4; Num 3.30
6.24	Num 26.11
6.25	Josh 24.33; Num 25.7-11; Ps 106.30

l Traditional rendering of Heb *El Shaddai*   *m* Heb *YHWH*; see note at 3.15   *n* Heb *me? I am uncircumcised of lips*   *o* Or *Saul*   *p* Also spelled *Gershom*; see 2.22

6.2,3 God did not reveal his name *Yahweh* to the patriarchs. Yet Gen 12.8 says that Abraham made an altar to the LORD (i.e., to Yahweh). The explanation is that while the patriarchs knew his name, they did not know him as to what the name meant, as now revealed in 6.3 — the God who performs what he has promised, perfects what he has done, and finishes his own work.

6.9 *their broken spirit and their cruel slavery.* Moses' first contest with the Pharaoh only worsened the slave conditions of the Israelites (5.6–14). When Moses brought them a message of encouragement, promising that God would deliver them from their slavery, they did not listen. Their spirit had been broken and their conditions made more cruel.

they who spoke to Pharaoh king of Egypt to bring the Israelites out of Egypt, the same Moses and Aaron.

e. *Moses commanded to speak to Pharaoh again*

28 On the day when the LORD spoke to Moses in the land of Egypt, 29 he said to him, "I am the LORD; tell Pharaoh king of Egypt all that I am speaking to you." 30 But Moses said in the LORD's presence, "Since I am a poor speaker,*q* why would Pharaoh listen to me?"

7 The LORD said to Moses, "See, I have made you like God to Pharaoh, and your brother Aaron shall be your prophet. 2 You shall speak all that I command you, and your brother Aaron shall tell Pharaoh to let the Israelites go out of his land. 3 But I will harden Pharaoh's heart, and I will multiply my signs and wonders in the land of Egypt. 4 When Pharaoh does not listen to you, I will lay my hand upon Egypt and bring my people the Israelites, company by company, out of the land of Egypt by great acts of judgment. 5 The Egyptians shall know that I am the LORD, when I stretch out my hand against Egypt and bring the Israelites out from among them." 6 Moses and Aaron did so; they did just as the LORD commanded them. 7 Moses was eighty years old and Aaron eighty-three when they spoke to Pharaoh.

2. *The miracles of Moses*

a. *The staff becomes a snake*

8 The LORD said to Moses and Aaron, 9 "When Pharaoh says to you, 'Perform a wonder,' then you shall say to Aaron, 'Take your staff and throw it down before Pharaoh, and it will become a snake.'" 10 So Moses and Aaron went to Pharaoh and did as the LORD had commanded; Aaron threw down his staff before Pharaoh and his officials, and it became a snake. 11 Then Pharaoh summoned the wise men and the sorcerers; and they also, the magicians of Egypt, did the same by their secret arts. 12 Each one threw down his staff, and they became snakes; but Aaron's staff swallowed up theirs. 13 Still Pharaoh's heart was hardened, and he would not listen to them, as the LORD had said.

b. *The water turned into blood*

14 Then the LORD said to Moses, "Pharaoh's heart is hardened; he refuses to let the people go. 15 Go to Pharaoh in the morning, as he is going out to the water; stand by at the river bank to meet him, and take in your hand the staff that was turned into a snake. 16 Say to him, 'The LORD, the God of the Hebrews, sent me to you to say, "Let my people go, so that they may worship me in the wilderness." But until now you have not listened. 17 Thus says the LORD, "By this you shall know that I am the LORD." See, with the staff that is in my hand I will strike the water that is in the Nile, and it shall be turned to blood. 18 The fish in the river shall die, the river itself shall stink, and the Egyptians shall be unable to drink water from the Nile.'" 19 The LORD said to Moses, "Say to Aaron, 'Take your staff and stretch out your hand over the waters of Egypt—over its rivers, its canals, and its ponds, and all its pools of water—so that they may become blood; and there shall be blood throughout the whole land of Egypt, even in vessels of wood and in vessels of stone.'"

20 Moses and Aaron did just as the LORD commanded. In the sight

q Heb *am uncircumcised of lips; see 6.12*

Cross references (left margin)
6.29
v. 11;
Ex 7.2
6.30
v. 12;
Ex 4.10
7.1
Ex 4.16
7.2
Ex 4.15
7.3
Ex 4.21; 11.9
7.4
Ex 3.19, 20;
10.1; 11.9;
12.51; 13.3,
9; 6.6
7.5
v. 17;
Ex 8.19; 3.20
7.6
v. 2
7.7
Deut 34.7;
Acts 7.23, 30

7.9
Isa 7.11;
Jn 2.18;
Ex 4.2, 17
7.10
v. 9;
Ex 4.3
7.11
Gen 41.8;
v. 22;
Ex 8.7, 18
7.13
v. 4;
Ex 4.21

7.14
Ex 8.15;
10.1, 20, 27
7.15
v. 10;
Ex 4.2, 3
7.16
Ex 3.12, 18;
5.1, 3
7.17
v. 5;
Ex 5.2; 4.9;
Rev 11.6;
16.4, 6
7.18
vv. 21, 24
7.19
Ex 8.5, 6, 16;
9.22; 10.12,
21; 14.21, 26

7.20
Ps 78.44;
105.29

7.1 Aaron was eighty-three years old and Moses eighty. Some of God's servants wait a long time to be used in God's service. On the other hand, John the Baptist served and died before he was thirty-two, and Jesus the Savior died at thirty-three.
7.12 At every important juncture God provided outward evidence which bore witness to his divine work.

Aaron's rod is a case in point. Two miracles took place here: (1) The staff, in the hand of Aaron, was cast to the ground and became a serpent. The Egyptian wise men and sorcerers were able to challenge Aaron by a counter-miracle. (2) The serpents of Pharaoh's servants were swallowed by Aaron's serpent, which then again became a staff.

of Pharaoh and of his officials he lifted up the staff and struck the water in the river, and all the water in the river was turned into blood, 21 and the fish in the river died. The river stank so that the Egyptians could not drink its water, and there was blood throughout the whole land of Egypt. 22 But the magicians of Egypt did the same by their secret arts; so Pharaoh's heart remained hardened, and he would not listen to them, as the LORD had said. 23 Pharaoh turned and went into his house, and he did not take even this to heart. 24 And all the Egyptians had to dig along the Nile for water to drink, for they could not drink the water of the river.

| | 7.21 v. 18 |
| | 7.22 v. 11; Ex 8.7 |

c. The plague of frogs

25 Seven days passed after the LORD had struck the Nile.

8 [r] Then the LORD said to Moses, "Go to Pharaoh and say to him, 'Thus says the LORD: Let my people go, so that they may worship me. 2 If you refuse to let them go, I will plague your whole country with frogs. 3 The river shall swarm with frogs; they shall come up into your palace, into your bedchamber and your bed, and into the houses of your officials and of your people,[s] and into your ovens and your kneading bowls. 4 The frogs shall come up on you and on your people and on all your officials.' " 5 [t] And the LORD said to Moses, "Say to Aaron, 'Stretch out your hand with your staff over the rivers, the canals, and the pools, and make frogs come up on the land of Egypt.' " 6 So Aaron stretched out his hand over the waters of Egypt; and the frogs came up and covered the land of Egypt. 7 But the magicians did the same by their secret arts, and brought frogs up on the land of Egypt.

8 Then Pharaoh called Moses and Aaron, and said, "Pray to the LORD to take away the frogs from me and my people, and I will let the people go to sacrifice to the LORD." 9 Moses said to Pharaoh, "Kindly tell me when I am to pray for you and for your officials and for your people, that the frogs may be removed from you and your houses and be left only in the Nile." 10 And he said, "Tomorrow." Moses said, "As you say! So that you may know that there is no one like the LORD our God, 11 the frogs shall leave you and your houses and your officials and your people; they shall be left only in the Nile." 12 Then Moses and Aaron went out from Pharaoh; and Moses cried out to the LORD concerning the frogs that he had brought upon Pharaoh.[u] 13 And the LORD did as Moses requested: the frogs died in the houses, the courtyards, and the fields. 14 And they gathered them together in heaps, and the land stank. 15 But when Pharaoh saw that there was a respite, he hardened his heart, and would not listen to them, just as the LORD had said.

	8.1 Ex 3.12, 18
	8.3 Ps 105.30
	8.5 Ex 7.19
	8.6 Ps 78.45; 105.30
	8.7 Ex 7.11
	8.8 vv. 25, 28; Ex 9.27, 28; 10.17
	8.10 Ex 9.14; Deut 33.26; Ps 86.8; Isa 46.9; Jer 10.6, 7
	8.12 v. 30; Ex 9.33; 10.18
	8.15 Ex 7.4

[r] Ch 7.26 in Heb   [s] Gk: Heb *upon your people*   [t] Ch 8.1 in Heb   [u] Or *frogs, as he had agreed with Pharaoh*

7.22 Since the Nile was turned into blood by Moses, the magicians must have obtained water from newly dug wells — to turn it into blood by their arts. It was by God's permission that the magicians were able to imitate the miracle by their enchantments. If the magicians had really wanted to show their power, they should have reversed the miracle, turning the blood back into water.
8.2 *I will plague your whole country with frogs.* Moses told Aaron to use his rod, but this was the act of God, who said, "I will plague." The irony of this judgment is that the magicians made the situation worse by adding more frogs to the ones God sent. Pharaoh should have asked his magicians to reverse the act of God and make the frogs disappear!
8.7 In 7.11,22 and 8.7 the magicians of Egypt replicated the miracles of Moses and Aaron. Paul explains these kinds of phenomena when he speaks about "the

working of Satan, who uses all power, signs, lying wonders" (2 Thess 2.9). Miracles performed by Satan and his agents should not disturb us, and we should not attribute all miracles to God. Satan cannot harm the people of God, who are protected against his wiles (cf. Eph 6.11ff).
8.8 Pharaoh's magicians could replicate what Moses and Aaron were doing. But that ability could not change the situation. Pharaoh now has a glimmer of understanding, for he begs Moses and Aaron, "Pray to the LORD to take away the frogs from me and from my people."
8.12 Moses' prayer for God to remove the frogs was answered. But Moses had already told Pharaoh that the removal of the frogs would take place "so that you may know that there is no one like the LORD our God" (8.10). The gods of the Egyptians were powerless; only Yahweh could deliver Egypt from this plague.

d. The plague of gnats

16 Then the LORD said to Moses, "Say to Aaron, 'Stretch out your staff and strike the dust of the earth, so that it may become gnats throughout the whole land of Egypt.' " 17 And they did so; Aaron stretched out his hand with his staff and struck the dust of the earth, and gnats came on humans and animals alike; all the dust of the earth turned into gnats throughout the whole land of Egypt. 18 The magicians tried to produce gnats by their secret arts, but they could not. There were gnats on both humans and animals. 19 And the magicians said to Pharaoh, "This is the finger of God!" But Pharaoh's heart was hardened, and he would not listen to them, just as the LORD had said.

e. The swarms of flies

20 Then the LORD said to Moses, "Rise early in the morning and present yourself before Pharaoh, as he goes out to the water, and say to him, 'Thus says the LORD: Let my people go, so that they may worship me. 21 For if you will not let my people go, I will send swarms of flies on you, your officials, and your people, and into your houses; and the houses of the Egyptians shall be filled with swarms of flies; so also the land where they live. 22 But on that day I will set apart the land of Goshen, where my people live, so that no swarms of flies shall be there, that you may know that I the LORD am in this land. 23 Thus I will make a distinction*v* between my people and your people. This sign shall appear tomorrow.' " 24 The LORD did so, and great swarms of flies came into the house of Pharaoh and into his officials' houses; in all of Egypt the land was ruined because of the flies.

25 Then Pharaoh summoned Moses and Aaron, and said, "Go, sacrifice to your God within the land." 26 But Moses said, "It would not be right to do so; for the sacrifices that we offer to the LORD our God are offensive to the Egyptians. If we offer in the sight of the Egyptians sacrifices that are offensive to them, will they not stone us? 27 We must go a three days' journey into the wilderness and sacrifice to the LORD our God as he commands us." 28 So Pharaoh said, "I will let you go to sacrifice to the LORD your God in the wilderness, provided you do not go very far away. Pray for me." 29 Then Moses said, "As soon as I leave you, I will pray to the LORD that the swarms of flies may depart tomorrow from Pharaoh, from his officials, and from his people; only do not let Pharaoh again deal falsely by not letting the people go to sacrifice to the LORD."

30 So Moses went out from Pharaoh and prayed to the LORD. 31 And the LORD did as Moses asked: he removed the swarms of flies from Pharaoh, from his officials, and from his people; not one remained. 32 But Pharaoh hardened his heart this time also, and would not let the people go.

f. The death of the Egyptian livestock

9 Then the LORD said to Moses, "Go to Pharaoh, and say to him, 'Thus says the LORD, the God of the Hebrews: Let my people go, so that they may worship me. 2 For if you refuse to let them go and still hold them, 3 the hand of the LORD will strike with a deadly pestilence your livestock in the field: the horses, the donkeys, the camels, the herds, and the flocks. 4 But the LORD will make a distinction between the livestock of Israel and

v Gk Vg: Heb *will set redemption*

Margin references:
8.17 Ps 105.31
8.18 Ex 7.11
8.19 Ex 7.5; 10.7
8.20 Ex 9.13; 7.15; v. 1
8.22 Ex 9.4, 6, 26; 10.23; 11.6, 7
8.24 Ps 78.45; 105.31
8.27 Ex 3.18; 5.3
8.28 vv. 8, 15, 29, 32
8.29 vv. 8, 15
8.32 vv. 8, 15; Ex 4.21
9.1 Ex 8.1
9.2 Ex 8.2
9.4 Ex 8.22

8.18,19 At last Pharaoh's magicians became convinced that Moses and Aaron had gifts from God that they could not match, for they could no longer reproduce Moses' miracles. But the heart of Pharaoh remained adamant. He is a classic example of those who know the truth but still reject it in the face of all the evidences they need.

8.30 Again Moses prayed to God for the removal of a plague. By this time the Pharaoh should have been convinced that the God of Israel was greater than all the gods of Egypt.
9.4 The judgments of God on Pharaoh did not touch the Israelites, who were supernaturally preserved from the various plagues. Throughout the history of re-

the livestock of Egypt, so that nothing shall die of all that belongs to the Israelites.' " 5 The LORD set a time, saying, "Tomorrow the LORD will do this thing in the land." 6 And on the next day the LORD did so; all the livestock of the Egyptians died, but of the livestock of the Israelites not one died. 7 Pharaoh inquired and found that not one of the livestock of the Israelites was dead. But the heart of Pharaoh was hardened, and he would not let the people go.

g. *The boils on humans and animals*

8 Then the LORD said to Moses and Aaron, "Take handfuls of soot from the kiln, and let Moses throw it in the air in the sight of Pharaoh. 9 It shall become fine dust all over the land of Egypt, and shall cause festering boils on humans and animals throughout the whole land of Egypt." 10 So they took soot from the kiln, and stood before Pharaoh, and Moses threw it in the air, and it caused festering boils on humans and animals. 11 The magicians could not stand before Moses because of the boils, for the boils afflicted the magicians as well as all the Egyptians. 12 But the LORD hardened the heart of Pharaoh, and he would not listen to them, just as the LORD had spoken to Moses.

h. *The hail and fire*

13 Then the LORD said to Moses, "Rise up early in the morning and present yourself before Pharaoh, and say to him, 'Thus says the LORD, the God of the Hebrews: Let my people go, so that they may worship me. 14 For this time I will send all my plagues upon you yourself, and upon your officials, and upon your people, so that you may know that there is no one like me in all the earth. 15 For by now I could have stretched out my hand and struck you and your people with pestilence, and you would have been cut off from the earth. 16 But this is why I have let you live: to show you my power, and to make my name resound through all the earth. 17 You are still exalting yourself against my people, and will not let them go. 18 Tomorrow at this time I will cause the heaviest hail to fall that has ever fallen in Egypt from the day it was founded until now. 19 Send, therefore, and have your livestock and everything that you have in the open field brought to a secure place; every human or animal that is in the open field and is not brought under shelter will die when the hail comes down upon them.' " 20 Those officials of Pharaoh who feared the word of the LORD hurried their slaves and livestock off to a secure place. 21 Those who did not regard the word of the LORD left their slaves and livestock in the open field.

22 The LORD said to Moses, "Stretch out your hand toward heaven so that hail may fall on the whole land of Egypt, on humans and animals and all the plants of the field in the land of Egypt." 23 Then Moses stretched out his staff toward heaven, and the LORD sent thunder and hail, and fire came down on the earth. And the LORD rained hail on the land of Egypt; 24 there was hail with fire flashing continually in the midst of it, such heavy hail as had never fallen in all the land of Egypt since it

9.6
Ex 11.5; v. 4

9.7
Ex 7.14; 8.32

9.9
Rev 16.2

9.12
Ex 4.21

9.13
Ex 8.20

9.14
Ex 8.10

9.15
Ex 3.20

9.16
Rom 9.17

9.18
vv. 23, 24

9.20
Prov 13.13

9.22
Rev 16.21

9.23
Gen 19.24;
Josh 10.11;
Ps 78.47;
Isa 30.30;
Ezek 38.22;
Rev 8.7

---

demption, God has intervened on behalf of his people in many instances, delivering them, preserving them, and protecting them.

9.5 *Tomorrow the LORD will do this thing.* Before this, the plagues were brought on Egypt by the use of the staff in the hands of Moses and Aaron. Here, God performed the miracle without the use of the staff; no secondary agent was involved. If this would not move Pharaoh to change his heart, what would?

9.11 *the boils afflicted the magicians.* God will not be mocked. The magicians, who had helped to harden the Pharaoh's heart by pretending to imitate the earlier plagues, now suffered from the boils. All Egypt learned that the magicians could not keep themselves

from the plague. How then could they preserve the people from them? God disarmed his enemies and made Satan look foolish.

9.18 This severe hailstorm stopped at the edge of the land of Goshen where the Israelites resided (9.26). In this catastrophe God was gracious enough to warn the Pharaoh to bring in the animals and the laborers from the fields so they would not perish (9.19).

9.20 By this time God has gotten the attention of some of the Egyptians, for they believed God, accepted the warning, and brought their slaves and livestock into the houses. Others still refused to believe; they and their animals were overtaken by a hail such as the Egyptians had never seen before.

9.25
v. 19;
Ps 78.47;
105.32, 33
9.26
Ex 8.22; 9.4,
6; 10.23;
11.7; 12.13
9.27
Ex 8.8;
10.16, 17;
2 Chr 12.6;
Ps 129.4
9.28
Ex 8.8; 10.17
9.29
1 Kings 8.22;
Ps 143.6;
19.5; 20.11;
Ps 24.1

9.35
Ex 4.21

10.1
Ex 4.21; 7.14
10.2
Ex 12.26, 27;
13.8, 14, 15;
Deut 4.9;
Ps 44.1;
Ex 7.5, 15
10.3
Jas 4.10;
1 Pet 5.6;
Ex 4.23
10.4
Rev 9.3
10.5
Ex 9.32;
Joel 1.4; 2.25
10.6
Ex 8.3, 21

10.7
Ex 7.5; 8.19;
12.33
10.8
Ex 8.8, 25

10.9
Ex 12.37, 38;
v. 26;
Ex 5.1

became a nation. 25 The hail struck down everything that was in the open field throughout all the land of Egypt, both human and animal; the hail also struck down all the plants of the field, and shattered every tree in the field. 26 Only in the land of Goshen, where the Israelites were, there was no hail.

27 Then Pharaoh summoned Moses and Aaron, and said to them, "This time I have sinned; the Lord is in the right, and I and my people are in the wrong. 28 Pray to the Lord! Enough of God's thunder and hail! I will let you go; you need stay no longer." 29 Moses said to him, "As soon as I have gone out of the city, I will stretch out my hands to the Lord; the thunder will cease, and there will be no more hail, so that you may know that the earth is the Lord's. 30 But as for you and your officials, I know that you do not yet fear the Lord God." 31 (Now the flax and the barley were ruined, for the barley was in the ear and the flax was in bud. 32 But the wheat and the spelt were not ruined, for they are late in coming up.) 33 So Moses left Pharaoh, went out of the city, and stretched out his hands to the Lord; then the thunder and the hail ceased, and the rain no longer poured down on the earth. 34 But when Pharaoh saw that the rain and the hail and the thunder had ceased, he sinned once more and hardened his heart, he and his officials. 35 So the heart of Pharaoh was hardened, and he would not let the Israelites go, just as the Lord had spoken through Moses.

i. The plague of locusts

10 Then the Lord said to Moses, "Go to Pharaoh; for I have hardened his heart and the heart of his officials, in order that I may show these signs of mine among them, 2 and that you may tell your children and grandchildren how I have made fools of the Egyptians and what signs I have done among them—so that you may know that I am the Lord."

3 So Moses and Aaron went to Pharaoh, and said to him, "Thus says the Lord, the God of the Hebrews, 'How long will you refuse to humble yourself before me? Let my people go, so that they may worship me. 4 For if you refuse to let my people go, tomorrow I will bring locusts into your country. 5 They shall cover the surface of the land, so that no one will be able to see the land. They shall devour the last remnant left you after the hail, and they shall devour every tree of yours that grows in the field. 6 They shall fill your houses, and the houses of all your officials and of all the Egyptians—something that neither your parents nor your grandparents have seen, from the day they came on earth to this day.'" Then he turned and went out from Pharaoh.

7 Pharaoh's officials said to him, "How long shall this fellow be a snare to us? Let the people go, so that they may worship the Lord their God; do you not yet understand that Egypt is ruined?" 8 So Moses and Aaron were brought back to Pharaoh, and he said to them, "Go, worship the Lord your God! But which ones are to go?" 9 Moses said, "We will go with our young and our old; we will go with our sons and daughters and with our flocks and herds, because we have the Lord's festival to cele-

---

9.27,28 The Pharaoh admitted that he was a sinner and begged Moses to pray to God for him. Convicted sinners may well repent at the moment when judgment strikes them, but shortly thereafter they lapse into their old ways. This is not genuine repentance.
9.30 Moses exhibited spiritual insight into the true estate of the Pharaoh, for he said, in effect, "You will repent of your repentance." And he did, for his heart was hardened again.
9.31 It was January and the flax and barley crops were ready for harvesting. These crops were ruined. The wheat and the spelt (spelt was a variant form of wheat—*triticum spelta*) were not ruined, for they

would ripen a month or two later.
10.2 Seven plagues had overtaken Egypt. There were three more to come—locusts, darkness, and the death of the firstborn. God told Moses that the design of these plagues and the deliverance of the Israelites from Egypt would glorify his name and himself.
10.9 The Pharaoh's officials saw the light before the king himself did, recognizing that Egypt was in danger of total ruin. With the welfare of all the people in mind, they begged the Pharaoh to release the Israelites. Moses, they agreed, was a snare to Egypt. It is unfortunate for a whole nation to be destroyed by the obstinacy of its ruler or rulers.

brate." 10He said to them, "The LORD indeed will be with you, if ever I let your little ones go with you! Plainly, you have some evil purpose in mind. 11No, never! Your men may go and worship the LORD, for that is what you are asking." And they were driven out from Pharaoh's presence.

12   Then the LORD said to Moses, "Stretch out your hand over the land of Egypt, so that the locusts may come upon it and eat every plant in the land, all that the hail has left." 13So Moses stretched out his staff over the land of Egypt, and the LORD brought an east wind upon the land all that day and all that night; when morning came, the east wind had brought the locusts. 14The locusts came upon all the land of Egypt and settled on the whole country of Egypt, such a dense swarm of locusts as had never been before, nor ever shall be again. 15They covered the surface of the whole land, so that the land was black; and they ate all the plants in the land and all the fruit of the trees that the hail had left; nothing green was left, no tree, no plant in the field, in all the land of Egypt. 16Pharaoh hurriedly summoned Moses and Aaron and said, "I have sinned against the LORD your God, and against you. 17Do forgive my sin just this once, and pray to the LORD your God that at the least he remove this deadly thing from me." 18So he went out from Pharaoh and prayed to the LORD. 19The LORD changed the wind into a very strong west wind, which lifted the locusts and drove them into the Red Sea;w not a single locust was left in all the country of Egypt. 20But the LORD hardened Pharaoh's heart, and he would not let the Israelites go.

j. The three days' darkness

21   Then the LORD said to Moses, "Stretch out your hand toward heaven so that there may be darkness over the land of Egypt, a darkness that can be felt." 22So Moses stretched out his hand toward heaven, and there was dense darkness in all the land of Egypt for three days. 23People could not see one another, and for three days they could not move from where they were; but all the Israelites had light where they lived. 24Then Pharaoh summoned Moses, and said, "Go, worship the LORD. Only your flocks and your herds shall remain behind. Even your children may go with you." 25But Moses said, "You must also let us have sacrifices and burnt offerings to sacrifice to the LORD our God. 26Our livestock also must go with us; not a hoof shall be left behind, for we must choose some of them for the worship of the LORD our God, and we will not know what to use to worship the LORD until we arrive there." 27But the LORD hardened Pharaoh's heart, and he was unwilling to let them go. 28Then Pharaoh said to him, "Get away from me! Take care that you do not see my face again, for on the day you see my face you shall die." 29Moses said, "Just as you say! I will never see your face again."

k. The death of the firstborn

(1) THE ANNOUNCEMENT BY GOD

11 The LORD said to Moses, "I will bring one more plague upon Pharaoh and upon Egypt; afterwards he will let you go from here;

w Or Sea of Reeds

10.11 v. 28
10.12 Ex 7.19; vv. 4, 5
10.14 Ps 78.46; 105.34; Joel 2.1-11
10.15 v. 5; Ps 105.35
10.16 Ex 9.27
10.17 Ex 8.8, 29
10.20 Ex 4.21; 11.10
10.21 Deut 28.29
10.22 Ps 105.28
10.24 vv. 8, 10
10.26 v. 9
10.27 v. 20
10.28 v. 11
10.29 Heb 11.27
11.1 Ex 12.31, 33, 39

10.11 The Pharaoh indicated that the men were permitted to depart from Egypt to offer their sacrifices, but not the women and children. Undoubtedly he supposed that the men would return because of their love for their families. Yet, even if they did not return, Egypt would still have the women and children as slaves. A half loaf is better than none.
10.21 God sent darkness for three days over the land of Egypt — a darkness that could be felt. "People . . . could not move from where they were" (10.23). The Egyptians had a foretaste of what hell is like — deep darkness (cf. 2 Pet 2.17; Jude 13); for God, who is

light, is absent from there.
10.23 Again and again the Israelites were exempted from the plagues sent by God on the Egyptians. This affords us assurance that at the end of the age, when great evils occur, God will protect his people even as he then protected the Israelites.
10.24 The Pharaoh tried to bargain with God again. This time he offered to let the Israelites take their little ones with them so long as they left their flocks and herds behind. Moses refused to comply. He would not compromise the divine demands of the Lord God.

11.2
Ex 3.22;
12.35, 36
11.3
Ex 3.21;
12.36;
Deut 34.10-12

11.4
Ex 12.29
11.5
Ex 12.12, 29;
Ps 78.51;
105.36;
135.8; 136.10
11.6
Ex 12.30
11.7
Ex 8.22
11.8
Ex 12.31-33

11.9
Ex 7.3, 4
11.10
Ex 4.21;
10.20, 27

indeed, when he lets you go, he will drive you away. 2 Tell the people that every man is to ask his neighbor and every woman is to ask her neighbor for objects of silver and gold." 3 The LORD gave the people favor in the sight of the Egyptians. Moreover, Moses himself was a man of great importance in the land of Egypt, in the sight of Pharaoh's officials and in the sight of the people.

4 Moses said, "Thus says the LORD: About midnight I will go out through Egypt. 5 Every firstborn in the land of Egypt shall die, from the firstborn of Pharaoh who sits on his throne to the firstborn of the female slave who is behind the handmill, and all the firstborn of the livestock. 6 Then there will be a loud cry throughout the whole land of Egypt, such as has never been or will ever be again. 7 But not a dog shall growl at any of the Israelites — not at people, not at animals — so that you may know that the LORD makes a distinction between Egypt and Israel. 8 Then all these officials of yours shall come down to me, and bow low to me, saying, 'Leave us, you and all the people who follow you.' After that I will leave." And in hot anger he left Pharaoh.

9 The LORD said to Moses, "Pharaoh will not listen to you, in order that my wonders may be multiplied in the land of Egypt." 10 Moses and Aaron performed all these wonders before Pharaoh; but the LORD hardened Pharaoh's heart, and he did not let the people of Israel go out of his land.

(2) THE INSTITUTION OF THE PASSOVER

12.2
Ex 13.4;
Deut 16.1

12.5
Lev 22.18-20

12.6
Lev 23.5;
Num 9.3;
Deut 16.1, 6

12.8
Ex 34.25;
Num 9.11,
12;
Deut 16.7
12.10
Ex 23.18;
34.25
12.11
v. 27

12.12
Ex 11.4, 5;
Num 33.4

12 The LORD said to Moses and Aaron in the land of Egypt: 2 This month shall mark for you the beginning of months; it shall be the first month of the year for you. 3 Tell the whole congregation of Israel that on the tenth of this month they are to take a lamb for each family, a lamb for each household. 4 If a household is too small for a whole lamb, it shall join its closest neighbor in obtaining one; the lamb shall be divided in proportion to the number of people who eat of it. 5 Your lamb shall be without blemish, a year-old male; you may take it from the sheep or from the goats. 6 You shall keep it until the fourteenth day of this month; then the whole assembled congregation of Israel shall slaughter it at twilight. 7 They shall take some of the blood and put it on the two doorposts and the lintel of the houses in which they eat it. 8 They shall eat the lamb that same night; they shall eat it roasted over the fire with unleavened bread and bitter herbs. 9 Do not eat any of it raw or boiled in water, but roasted over the fire, with its head, legs, and inner organs. 10 You shall let none of it remain until the morning; anything that remains until the morning you shall burn. 11 This is how you shall eat it: your loins girded, your sandals on your feet, and your staff in your hand; and you shall eat it hurriedly. It is the passover of the LORD. 12 For I will pass through the land of Egypt that night, and I will strike down every firstborn in the land of Egypt, both human beings and animals; on all the gods of Egypt I will execute judgments: I am the LORD. 13 The blood shall be a sign for you on the houses where you live: when I see the blood, I will pass over you, and no plague shall destroy you when I strike the land of Egypt.

11.2 As slaves the Israelites had received no remuneration for their labors. God now made the Egyptians willing to give them silver and gold. The oppressors must pay for their oppression one way or another. **12.2** *the first month.* God ordained that the Israelite calendar year should start with the month Nisan, which, in our calendar, is equivalent to the latter part of March and first part of April. **12.3,4** The sacrificial lamb had to be perfect, and as a substitute for the offerer, its blood was offered as an atonement for sin. So Christ, the perfect Lamb of God, offered his own blood as our substitute (cf. Jn 1.29,36). He has delivered us from the tyranny of sin,

just as God delivered the Israelites from their Egyptian oppressor. The Hebrew word translated here as "lamb" can also mean "kid" — a baby goat. **12.11-13** On the passover night the angel of death swept through all of Egypt, respecting only those houses on whose lintels and over whose doors blood had been sprinkled (v. 7). The characters and works of those inside had nothing to do with the saving efficacy of the sprinkled blood. It was the blood alone that the angel of death regarded. Christ is our perfect sacrifice. His applied blood makes the unrighteous righteous and their sins are forgiven (Rom 3.23; 1 Pet 1.18,19).

HEBREW CALENDAR AND SELECTED EVENTS

Sacred Sequence Begins	Hebrew Name	Modern Equivalent	Biblical References	Agriculture	Feasts
1	Abib; Nisan	March-April	Ex 12:2; 13:4; 23:15; 34:18; Dt 16:1; Ne 2:1; Est 3:7	Spring (later) rains; barley and flax harvest begins	Passover; Unleavened Bread; Firstfruits
2	Ziv (Iyyar)*	April-May	1 Ki 6:1,37	Barley havest; dry season begins	
3	Sivan	May-June	Est 8:9	Wheat harvest	Pentecost (Weeks)
4	(Tammuz)*	June-July		Tending vines	
5	(Ab)*	July-August		Ripening of grapes, figs and olives	
6	Elul	August-September	Ne 6:15	Processing grapes, figs and olives	
7	Ethanim (Tishri)*	September-October	1 Ki 8:2	Autumn (early) rains begin; plowing	Trumpets; Atonement; Tabernacles (Booths)
8	Bul (Marcheshvan)*	October-November	1 Ki 6:38	Sowing of wheat and barley	
9	Chislev	November-December	Ne 1:1, Zec 7:1	Winter rains begin (snow in some areas)	Hanukkah ("Dedication")
10	Tebeth	December-January	Est 2:16		
11	Shebat	January-February	Zec 1:7		
12	Adar	February-March	Ezr 6:15; Est 3:7,13; 8:12; 9:1,15,17,19,21	Almond trees bloom; citrus fruit harvest	Purim
	(Adar Sheni)* Second Adar			This intercalary month was added about every three years so the lunar calendar would correspond to the solar year.	

* Names in parentheses are not in the Bible

14 This day shall be a day of remembrance for you. You shall celebrate it as a festival to the LORD; throughout your generations you shall observe it as a perpetual ordinance. 15 Seven days you shall eat unleavened bread; on the first day you shall remove leaven from your houses, for whoever eats leavened bread from the first day until the seventh day shall be cut off from Israel. 16 On the first day you shall hold a solemn assembly, and on the seventh day a solemn assembly; no work shall be done on those days; only what everyone must eat, that alone may be prepared by you. 17 You shall observe the festival of unleavened bread, for on this very day I brought your companies out of the land of Egypt: you shall observe this day throughout your generations as a perpetual ordinance. 18 In the first month, from the evening of the fourteenth day until the evening of the twenty-first day, you shall eat unleavened bread. 19 For seven days no leaven shall be found in your houses; for whoever eats what is leavened shall be cut off from the congregation of Israel, whether an alien or a native of the land. 20 You shall eat nothing leavened; in all your settlements you shall eat unleavened bread.

21 Then Moses called all the elders of Israel and said to them, "Go, select lambs for your families, and slaughter the passover lamb. 22 Take a bunch of hyssop, dip it in the blood that is in the basin, and touch the lintel and the two doorposts with the blood in the basin. None of you shall go outside the door of your house until morning. 23 For the LORD will pass through to strike down the Egyptians; when he sees the blood on the lintel and on the two doorposts, the LORD will pass over that door and will not allow the destroyer to enter your houses to strike you down. 24 You shall observe this rite as a perpetual ordinance for you and your children. 25 When you come to the land that the LORD will give you, as he has promised, you shall keep this observance. 26 And when your children ask you, 'What do you mean by this observance?' 27 you shall say, 'It is the passover sacrifice to the LORD, for he passed over the houses of the Israelites in Egypt, when he struck down the Egyptians but spared our houses.' " And the people bowed down and worshiped.

28 The Israelites went and did just as the LORD had commanded Moses and Aaron.

(3) THE FIRSTBORN KILLED

29 At midnight the LORD struck down all the firstborn in the land of Egypt, from the firstborn of Pharaoh who sat on his throne to the firstborn of the prisoner who was in the dungeon, and all the firstborn of the livestock. 30 Pharaoh arose in the night, he and all his officials and all the Egyptians; and there was a loud cry in Egypt, for there was not a house without someone dead. 31 Then he summoned Moses and Aaron in the night, and said, "Rise up, go away from my people, both you and the Israelites! Go, worship the LORD, as you said. 32 Take your flocks and your herds, as you said, and be gone. And bring a blessing on me too!"

33 The Egyptians urged the people to hasten their departure from the land, for they said, "We shall all be dead." 34 So the people took their dough before it was leavened, with their kneading bowls wrapped up in their cloaks on their shoulders. 35 The Israelites had done as Moses told them; they had asked the Egyptians for jewelry of silver and gold, and for clothing, 36 and the LORD had given the people favor in the sight of the

---

12.14,15 *throughout your generations you shall observe it as a perpetual ordinance.* The Jews still continue to do this today, though the passover cannot be celebrated the same way as in the O.T. since the temple with its most holy place is gone; there is no mercy seat on which to sprinkle the blood of bulls and goats according to the prescribed ritual. The tradition,

however, continues among many Jews who celebrate what is called the *seder* in their homes or communities to commemorate the exodus from Egypt. For the next seven days no leaven is to be found in any home (for the festival of unleavened bread, see note on Lev 23.6–8).

12.22 *Hyssop.* See note on Ps 51.7 for explanation.

Egyptians, so that they let them have what they asked. And so they
plundered the Egyptians.

D. *The exodus begun*

1. *The unleavened cakes*

37   The Israelites journeyed from Rameses to Succoth, about six hundred thousand men on foot, besides children. 38 A mixed crowd also went
up with them, and livestock in great numbers, both flocks and herds.
39 They baked unleavened cakes of the dough that they had brought out
of Egypt; it was not leavened, because they were driven out of Egypt and
could not wait, nor had they prepared any provisions for themselves.

40   The time that the Israelites had lived in Egypt was four hundred
thirty years. 41 At the end of four hundred thirty years, on that very day,
all the companies of the LORD went out from the land of Egypt. 42 That
was for the LORD a night of vigil, to bring them out of the land of Egypt.
That same night is a vigil to be kept for the LORD by all the Israelites
throughout their generations.

2. *The law of the passover*

43   The LORD said to Moses and Aaron: This is the ordinance for the
passover: no foreigner shall eat of it, 44 but any slave who has been
purchased may eat of it after he has been circumcised; 45 no bound or hired
servant may eat of it. 46 It shall be eaten in one house; you shall not take
any of the animal outside the house, and you shall not break any of its
bones. 47 The whole congregation of Israel shall celebrate it. 48 If an alien
who resides with you wants to celebrate the passover to the LORD, all his
males shall be circumcised; then he may draw near to celebrate it; he shall
be regarded as a native of the land. But no uncircumcised person shall eat
of it; 49 there shall be one law for the native and for the alien who resides
among you.

50   All the Israelites did just as the LORD had commanded Moses and
Aaron. 51 That very day the LORD brought the Israelites out of the land
of Egypt, company by company.

13   The LORD said to Moses: 2 Consecrate to me all the firstborn;
whatever is the first to open the womb among the Israelites, of
human beings and animals, is mine.

3. *The speech of Moses*

3   Moses said to the people, "Remember this day on which you came
out of Egypt, out of the house of slavery, because the LORD brought you
out from there by strength of hand; no leavened bread shall be eaten.
4 Today, in the month of Abib, you are going out. 5 When the LORD brings
you into the land of the Canaanites, the Hittites, the Amorites, the Hivites, and the Jebusites, which he swore to your ancestors to give you, a
land flowing with milk and honey, you shall keep this observance in this
month. 6 Seven days you shall eat unleavened bread, and on the seventh
day there shall be a festival to the LORD. 7 Unleavened bread shall be eaten
for seven days; no leavened bread shall be seen in your possession, and
no leaven shall be seen among you in all your territory. 8 You shall tell your
child on that day, 'It is because of what the LORD did for me when I came

Cross-references (right margin)

12.37
Num 33.3, 4;
Ex 38.26;
Num 1.46;
11.21
12.38
Num 11.4;
Ex 17.3
12.39
vv. 31-33;
Ex 11.1
12.40
Gen 15.13;
Acts 7.6;
Gal 3.17
12.41
v. 17;
Ex 3.8, 10;
6.6
12.42
Ex 13.10;
Deut 16.1
12.43
vv. 11, 48
12.44
Gen 17.12,
13;
Lev 22.11
12.46
Num 9.12;
Jn 19.33, 36
12.47
Num 9.13, 14

12.49
Num 15.15,
16;
Gal 3.28
12.51
v. 41

13.2
vv. 12, 13,
15;
Ex 22.29;
Lk 2.23

13.3
Ex 3.20; 6.1;
12.19

13.5
Ex 3.8;
12.25, 26

13.6
Ex 12.15-20

13.8
v. 14;
Ex 10.2

12.37 The number of the Israelites probably totaled
around two million.
12.40 Various explanations are advanced for the 430
years spoken of here, depending on which date is
selected for the beginning of the period. Some state
that it was the time span between God's promise to
Abraham (when he first entered Caanan) and Israel's

departure for Canaan.
12.46 No bone of the passover lamb was to be broken. According to Jn 19.36, this scripture is prophetic
of the condition of Jesus' body after the crucifixion —
not one of his bones was broken. Thus, Jesus is the
true passover Lamb.
13.4 *in the month of Abib*, i.e., at the end of March.

13.9
v. 16;
Ex 12.14;
Deut 6.8;
11.18
13.10
Ex 12.24, 25

13.12
v. 2;
Ex 22.29;
34.19
13.13
Ex 34.20;
Num 18.15,
16
13.14
Ex 12.26, 27;
Deut 6.20;
vv. 3, 9
13.15
Ex 12.29

13.16
v. 9

out of Egypt.' 9 It shall serve for you as a sign on your hand and as a reminder on your forehead, so that the teaching of the LORD may be on your lips; for with a strong hand the LORD brought you out of Egypt. 10 You shall keep this ordinance at its proper time from year to year.

11 "When the LORD has brought you into the land of the Canaanites, as he swore to you and your ancestors, and has given it to you, 12 you shall set apart to the LORD all that first opens the womb. All the firstborn of your livestock that are males shall be the LORD's. 13 But every firstborn donkey you shall redeem with a sheep; if you do not redeem it, you must break its neck. Every firstborn male among your children you shall redeem. 14 When in the future your child asks you, 'What does this mean?' you shall answer, 'By strength of hand the LORD brought us out of Egypt, from the house of slavery. 15 When Pharaoh stubbornly refused to let us go, the LORD killed all the firstborn in the land of Egypt, from human firstborn to the firstborn of animals. Therefore I sacrifice to the LORD every male that first opens the womb, but every firstborn of my sons I redeem.' 16 It shall serve as a sign on your hand and as an emblem^x on your forehead that by strength of hand the LORD brought us out of Egypt."

4. The pillars of cloud and of fire

13.17
Ex 14.11, 12;
Num 14.1-4;
Deut 17.16

17 When Pharaoh let the people go, God did not lead them by way of the land of the Philistines, although that was nearer; for God thought, "If the people face war, they may change their minds and return to Egypt." 18 So God led the people by the roundabout way of the wilderness toward the Red Sea.^y The Israelites went up out of the land of Egypt

13.19
Gen 50.25,
26;
Josh 24.32;
Acts 7.16
13.20
Num 33.6-8
13.21f
Ex 14.19, 24;
33.9, 10;
Ps 78.14;
105.39;
1 Cor 10.1

prepared for battle. 19 And Moses took with him the bones of Joseph who had required a solemn oath of the Israelites, saying, "God will surely take notice of you, and then you must carry my bones with you from here." 20 They set out from Succoth, and camped at Etham, on the edge of the wilderness. 21 The LORD went in front of them in a pillar of cloud by day, to lead them along the way, and in a pillar of fire by night, to give them light, so that they might travel by day and by night. 22 Neither the pillar of cloud by day nor the pillar of fire by night left its place in front of the people.

5. Crossing the Red Sea

14.2
Num 33.7, 8

14 Then the LORD said to Moses: 2 Tell the Israelites to turn back and camp in front of Pi-hahiroth, between Migdol and the sea, in front of Baal-zephon; you shall camp opposite it, by the sea. 3 Pharaoh will say of the Israelites, "They are wandering aimlessly in the land; the wilderness has closed in on them." 4 I will harden Pharaoh's heart, and he will pursue

14.4
v. 17;
Ex 4.21; 7.5

them, so that I will gain glory for myself over Pharaoh and all his army; and the Egyptians shall know that I am the LORD. And they did so.

---

^x Or *as a frontlet*; meaning of Heb uncertain   ^y Or *Sea of Reeds*

13.9 See note on Mt 23.5 on phylacteries and fringes.
13.18 Exactly where Israel crossed the Red Sea (literally, "Sea of Reeds") is not known. Those who suppose that it was marshy land and less than knee-deep are incorrect, for it was deep enough to allow for the drowning of the Egyptians who pursued them into that sea. The passage point was probably south of the present city of Suez.
13.21 *a pillar of cloud*, later known as the *Shekinah* ("abiding" or "dwelling"), was called by various names in the O.T.: *my glory (kapod)* (29.43); *cloud* and *pillar of cloud* (33.9,10; 34.5); *the cloud of the LORD* (Num 10.34); and *my presence will go with you* (33.14,15). The *Shekinah* guided Israel (13.21; Neh

9.19); controlled Israel's movements in the wilderness (40.36,37); and defended Israel (14.19; Ps 105.39). In the N.T. the cloud appeared at Jesus' transfiguration (Mt 17.5) and at his ascension (Acts 1.9). When Christ comes again it will be "in a cloud with power and great glory" (Lk 21.27).
14.2 Directing the Israelites out of Egypt, God ordered them along a route that would keep them from having to face the armies of Egypt. The pillar of cloud by day and the pillar of fire by night would move as God determined, assuring Israel's safety. God hardened Pharaoh's heart, who tracked them down until he and his army fell into God's trap. God would be glorified in disposing of the Egyptians.

5 When the king of Egypt was told that the people had fled, the minds of Pharaoh and his officials were changed toward the people, and they said, "What have we done, letting Israel leave our service?" 6 So he had his chariot made ready, and took his army with him; 7 he took six hundred picked chariots and all the other chariots of Egypt with officers over all of them. 8 The LORD hardened the heart of Pharaoh king of Egypt and he pursued the Israelites, who were going out boldly. 9 The Egyptians pursued them, all Pharaoh's horses and chariots, his chariot drivers and his army; they overtook them camped by the sea, by Pi-hahiroth, in front of Baal-zephon.

10 As Pharaoh drew near, the Israelites looked back, and there were the Egyptians advancing on them. In great fear the Israelites cried out to the LORD. 11 They said to Moses, "Was it because there were no graves in Egypt that you have taken us away to die in the wilderness? What have you done to us, bringing us out of Egypt? 12 Is this not the very thing we told you in Egypt, 'Let us alone and let us serve the Egyptians'? For it would have been better for us to serve the Egyptians than to die in the wilderness." 13 But Moses said to the people, "Do not be afraid, stand firm, and see the deliverance that the LORD will accomplish for you today; for the Egyptians whom you see today you shall never see again. 14 The LORD will fight for you, and you have only to keep still."

15 Then the LORD said to Moses, "Why do you cry out to me? Tell the Israelites to go forward. 16 But you lift up your staff, and stretch out your hand over the sea and divide it, that the Israelites may go into the sea on dry ground. 17 Then I will harden the hearts of the Egyptians so that they will go in after them; and so I will gain glory for myself over Pharaoh and all his army, his chariots, and his chariot drivers. 18 And the Egyptians shall know that I am the LORD, when I have gained glory for myself over Pharaoh, his chariots, and his chariot drivers."

19 The angel of God who was going before the Israelite army moved and went behind them; and the pillar of cloud moved from in front of them and took its place behind them. 20 It came between the army of Egypt and the army of Israel. And so the cloud was there with the darkness, and it lit up the night; one did not come near the other all night.

21 Then Moses stretched out his hand over the sea. The LORD drove the sea back by a strong east wind all night, and turned the sea into dry land; and the waters were divided. 22 The Israelites went into the sea on dry ground, the waters forming a wall for them on their right and on their left. 23 The Egyptians pursued, and went into the sea after them, all of Pharaoh's horses, chariots, and chariot drivers. 24 At the morning watch the LORD in the pillar of fire and cloud looked down upon the Egyptian army, and threw the Egyptian army into panic. 25 He clogged[z] their chariot wheels so that they turned with difficulty. The Egyptians said, "Let us flee from the Israelites, for the LORD is fighting for them against Egypt."

14.8
v. 4;
Num 33.3;
Acts 13.17
14.9
Ex 15.9

14.10
Neh 9.9

14.11
Ps 106.7, 8

14.13
Gen 15.1;
v. 30;
Ex 15.2
14.14
Ex 15.3;
Deut 1.30;
3.22;
Isa 30.15
14.16
Ex 4.17;
Num 20.8, 9, 11;
Isa 10.26
14.17
v. 4
14.18
v. 25
14.19
Ex 13.21, 22

14.21
v. 16;
Ps 106.9;
114.3, 5;
Isa 63.12, 13
14.22
Ex 15.19;
Neh 9.11;
Heb 11.29
14.24
Ex 13.21
14.25
vv. 4, 18

---

z Sam Gk Syr: MT *removed*

14.9 The fortress towns named indicate that the Israelites crossed the waters to the north of the Red Sea proper (a more accurate translation is "Sea of Reeds"; cf. NRSV footnote). The waters were deep enough for the forces of Pharaoh to drown in when they attempted to follow and recapture the Israelites.
14.11–13 Almost from the beginning of the exodus, the Israelites manifested a complaining spirit. They allowed circumstances to move them. It is true that the Red Sea was before them and the Pharaoh and his soldiers behind them, but they forgot their God, who was above them. Moses displayed his great faith in the delivering power of God, but even he failed to see how that power would operate. He told Israel to stand still

and watch God intervene on their behalf. Then God told them to move forward in faith, against the waters of the sea.
14.19 *the angel of God.* See note on Ex 3.2. Sometimes this term designates Jesus Christ and sometimes an angel who helps the people of God (Heb 1.14). The triune God — the Father, the Son, and the Holy Spirit — are seen at work again and again in the O.T. In the Red Sea story the Father and the Son are active.
14.21 *by a strong east wind all night.* This enabled the Israelites to move forward on dry ground. God promises to lead his people forward against apparently impassable barriers, opening doors previously shut.

26 Then the LORD said to Moses, "Stretch out your hand over the sea, so that the water may come back upon the Egyptians, upon their chariots and chariot drivers." 27 So Moses stretched out his hand over the sea, and at dawn the sea returned to its normal depth. As the Egyptians fled before it, the LORD tossed the Egyptians into the sea. 28 The waters returned and covered the chariots and the chariot drivers, the entire army of Pharaoh that had followed them into the sea; not one of them remained. 29 But the Israelites walked on dry ground through the sea, the waters forming a wall for them on their right and on their left.

30 Thus the LORD saved Israel that day from the Egyptians; and Israel saw the Egyptians dead on the seashore. 31 Israel saw the great work that the LORD did against the Egyptians. So the people feared the LORD and believed in the LORD and in his servant Moses.

14.27
Ex 15.1, 7

14.28
Ps 78.53;
106.11
14.29
Ex 15.19;
Neh 9.11;
Heb 11.29

14.30
Ps 106.8
14.31
Ps 106.12

6. The song of Moses

15.1
Ps 106.12;
Rev 15.3

15.2
Ps 59.17;
Ex 3.15, 16

15.3
Ps 24.8;
83.18

15.4
Ex 14.6, 7,
17, 28
15.5
v. 10;
Neh 9.11
15.6
Ps 118.15

15.7
Ex 14.27;
Ps 78.49, 50

15.8
Ex 14.22, 29;
Ps 78.13

15.9
Ex 14.5

15.10
Ex 14.28
15.11
Ex 8.10;
Deut 3.24;
Isa 6.3;
Rev 4.8;
Ps 22.23;
72.18

15 Then Moses and the Israelites sang this song to the LORD:
　"I will sing to the LORD, for he has triumphed gloriously;
　　horse and rider he has thrown into the sea.
2 The LORD is my strength and my might,[a]
　　and he has become my salvation;
　this is my God, and I will praise him,
　　my father's God, and I will exalt him.
3 The LORD is a warrior;
　　the LORD is his name.

4 "Pharaoh's chariots and his army he cast into the sea;
　　his picked officers were sunk in the Red Sea.[b]
5 The floods covered them;
　　they went down into the depths like a stone.
6 Your right hand, O LORD, glorious in power—
　　your right hand, O LORD, shattered the enemy.
7 In the greatness of your majesty you overthrew your
　　adversaries;
　　you sent out your fury, it consumed them like stubble.
8 At the blast of your nostrils the waters piled up,
　　the floods stood up in a heap;
　　the deeps congealed in the heart of the sea.
9 The enemy said, 'I will pursue, I will overtake,
　　I will divide the spoil, my desire shall have its fill of them.
　I will draw my sword, my hand shall destroy them.'
10 You blew with your wind, the sea covered them;
　　they sank like lead in the mighty waters.

11 "Who is like you, O LORD, among the gods?
　　Who is like you, majestic in holiness,

---

a Or song　b Or Sea of Reeds

15.1 *Then Moses . . . sang this song.* This song of Moses and the people of Israel is the first mention of singing in the Bible and is part of the hymnody of the Christian faith. One of the most glorious contributions of the faith has been the hymnody composed by multitudes across the centuries. Words and music put together to be sung to God for his glory are inexpressibly beautiful. According to Job 38.7, "the morning stars sang together" at the time of creation. In Rev 15.3 angels sing "the song of Moses . . . and the song of the Lamb." The apostle Paul encourages the Ephesians to "sing psalms and hymns and spiritual songs among yourselves, singing and making melody to the Lord in your hearts" (Eph 5.19).

15.3 *The LORD is a warrior.* This is like the depiction of Jesus Christ who comes with a sword in his mouth to wage the final war against Satan and to put away evil forever (Rev 19.15).

15.11 Among the chief attributes of God is his holiness. Whatever he does is right, true, and good. He cannot sin, nor is there any impurity in him. No one else's holiness can compare to that of God (1 Sam 2.2). It is manifested in his name ("the high and lofty one who inhabits eternity," Isa 57.15), in his words ("because of his holy words" Jer 23.9), and in his character ("you are holy," Ps 22.3). His people are to imitate his holiness (Lev 11.44; 1 Pet 1.15,16) and offer "thanks to his holy name" (Ps 30.4).

awesome in splendor, doing wonders?
12   You stretched out your right hand,
        the earth swallowed them.

13   "In your steadfast love you led the people whom you redeemed;
        you guided them by your strength to your holy abode.
14   The peoples heard, they trembled;
        pangs seized the inhabitants of Philistia.
15   Then the chiefs of Edom were dismayed;
        trembling seized the leaders of Moab;
        all the inhabitants of Canaan melted away.
16   Terror and dread fell upon them;
        by the might of your arm, they became still as a stone
        until your people, O LORD, passed by,
        until the people whom you acquired passed by.
17   You brought them in and planted them on the mountain of
        your own possession,
        the place, O LORD, that you made your abode,
        the sanctuary, O LORD, that your hands have established.
18   The LORD will reign forever and ever."

7. The song of Miriam

19   When the horses of Pharaoh with his chariots and his chariot
drivers went into the sea, the LORD brought back the waters of the sea
upon them; but the Israelites walked through the sea on dry ground.
20   Then the prophet Miriam, Aaron's sister, took a tambourine in her
hand; and all the women went out after her with tambourines and with
dancing. 21 And Miriam sang to them:
"Sing to the LORD, for he has triumphed gloriously;
    horse and rider he has thrown into the sea."

II. The journey to Sinai (15.22–18.27)

A. The bitter waters of Marah made sweet

22   Then Moses ordered Israel to set out from the Red Sea,c and they
went into the wilderness of Shur. They went three days in the wilderness
and found no water. 23 When they came to Marah, they could not drink
the water of Marah because it was bitter. That is why it was called
Marah.d 24 And the people complained against Moses, saying, "What
shall we drink?" 25 He cried out to the LORD; and the LORD showed him
a piece of wood;e he threw it into the water, and the water became sweet.
There the LORDf made for them a statute and an ordinance and there
he put them to the test. 26 He said, "If you will listen carefully to the voice
of the LORD your God, and do what is right in his sight, and give heed
to his commandments and keep all his statutes, I will not bring upon you
any of the diseases that I brought upon the Egyptians; for I am the LORD
who heals you."

c Or Sea of Reeds   d That is Bitterness   e Or a tree   f Heb he

Cross references (right column):
15.13 Neh 9.12; Ps 77.15; 78.54
15.14 Deut 2.25; Hab 3.7
15.15 Gen 36.15; Num 22.3; Josh 5.1
15.16 Ex 23.27; 1 Sam 25.37; Ps 74.2
15.17 Ps 44.2; 78.54
15.18 Ps 10.16
15.19 Ex 14.23, 28
15.20 Judg 4.4; Num 26.59; 1 Sam 18.6; Ps 30.11; 150.4
15.21 v. 1
15.22 Ps 77.20; Num 33.8
15.23 Num 33.8
15.24 Ex 14.11; Ps 106.13
15.25 Ex 14.10; Ps 50.15
15.26 Deut 7.12; 28.27

15.20 Miriam (Mary) was a prophetess, that is, a female preacher. God was no respecter of sex. The Scriptures mention that Deborah, Huldah, Noadiah, and Anna were all prophetesses. No one should underplay the role of women in God's scheme of redemption. The prophet Micah reports God as having said to him: "I sent before you Moses, Aaron, and Miriam" (Mic 6.4). If God identified Miriam along with Moses and Aaron as having been sent by him for the deliverance of Israel, she must have been an im-

portant figure in the divine plan.
15.23 Marah ("bitter") provides a source of assurance for believers. The Israelites, following God, came into difficulties not of their choosing, nor because of their transgressions. Without drinkable water they were in serious trouble. Their difficulty was God's opportunity. He made the bitter water sweet so they could drink of it. God does place his children in difficult situations so that his deliverances will strengthen their faith.

15.27
Num 33.9, 10

27 Then they came to Elim, where there were twelve springs of water and seventy palm trees; and they camped there by the water.

B. The manna and the quails

1. The complaint of the Israelites

16.1
Num 33.11, 12

16 The whole congregation of the Israelites set out from Elim; and Israel came to the wilderness of Sin, which is between Elim and Sinai, on the fifteenth day of the second month after they had departed

16.2
Ex 14.11;
1 Cor 10.10

from the land of Egypt. 2 The whole congregation of the Israelites complained against Moses and Aaron in the wilderness. 3 The Israelites said

16.3
Ex 17.3;
Num 11.4, 5

to them, "If only we had died by the hand of the LORD in the land of Egypt, when we sat by the fleshpots and ate our fill of bread; for you have brought us out into this wilderness to kill this whole assembly with hunger."

2. God promises bread and meat

16.4
Jn 6.31;
1 Cor 10.3;
Deut 8.2, 16

4 Then the LORD said to Moses, "I am going to rain bread from heaven for you, and each day the people shall go out and gather enough for that day. In that way I will test them, whether they will follow my instruction

16.5
v. 22

or not. 5 On the sixth day, when they prepare what they bring in, it will be twice as much as they gather on other days." 6 So Moses and Aaron said to all the Israelites, "In the evening you shall know that it was the

16.7
v. 12;
Num 14.27;
16.11

LORD who brought you out of the land of Egypt, 7 and in the morning you shall see the glory of the LORD, because he has heard your complaining against the LORD. For what are we, that you complain against us?" 8 And Moses said, "When the LORD gives you meat to eat in the evening and your fill of bread in the morning, because the LORD has heard the complaining that you utter against him — what are we? Your complaining is not against us but against the LORD.

16.9
Num 16.16

9 Then Moses said to Aaron, "Say to the whole congregation of the Israelites, 'Draw near to the LORD, for he has heard your complaining.'"

16.10
v. 7;
Num 16.19

10 And as Aaron spoke to the whole congregation of the Israelites, they looked toward the wilderness, and the glory of the LORD appeared in the cloud. 11 The LORD spoke to Moses and said, 12 "I have heard the complaining of the Israelites; say to them, 'At twilight you shall eat meat, and in the morning you shall have your fill of bread; then you shall know that I am the LORD your God.'"

3. God sends quails and gives bread

16.13
Num 11.31;
Ps 78.27, 28;
105.40
16.14
Num 11.7-9;
v. 31
16.15
v. 4

13 In the evening quails came up and covered the camp; and in the morning there was a layer of dew around the camp. 14 When the layer of dew lifted, there on the surface of the wilderness was a fine flaky substance, as fine as frost on the ground. 15 When the Israelites saw it, they

---

16.2 The Israelites were already beginning to complain; they feared they would die from hunger. God told Moses to inform them that they would be given meat for the evening meal and bread the following morning. After this first meal of meat God did not plan to give them any more until they entered Canaan, when the manna ceased.
16.3,4 *fleshpots . . . ate our fill of bread.* The Israelites harked back to the food they had in Egypt and complained at what they now had. They magnified the past and vilified the present with no regard for truth or reason. Instead of raining fire and sulphur on them for their complaints, however, God graciously rained down bread and continued this for forty years.

16.10 *the glory of the LORD appeared in the cloud.* Once more God condescended to the Israelites' incipient unbelief and manifested himself in a new and unmistakable manner so that they knew that God was with them. Although they had the cloud of the Lord, they had grown accustomed to it. Familiarity breeds contempt. Believers today do not have such manifestations. Rather, they have the full revelation of God in Jesus Christ and can walk by faith without sight.
16.15 The manna (bread) supplied by God was a free gift, sufficient for Israel's needs from day to day. It sustained life and was in plentiful supply. Christ is the bread of life and is the fulfillment of this type, although in a far greater way (see Jn 6.30–41).

said to one another, "What is it?"[g] For they did not know what it was.
Moses said to them, "It is the bread that the LORD has given you to eat.
[16] This is what the LORD has commanded: 'Gather as much of it as each
of you needs, an omer to a person according to the number of persons,
all providing for those in their own tents.' " [17] The Israelites did so, some
gathering more, some less. [18] But when they measured it with an omer,
those who gathered much had nothing over, and those who gathered little
had no shortage; they gathered as much as each of them needed. [19] And
Moses said to them, "Let no one leave any of it over until morning." [20] But
they did not listen to Moses; some left part of it until morning, and it bred
worms and became foul. And Moses was angry with them. [21] Morning by
morning they gathered it, as much as each needed; but when the sun grew
hot, it melted.

4. The sabbath commandment

[22] On the sixth day they gathered twice as much food, two omers
apiece. When all the leaders of the congregation came and told Moses,
[23] he said to them, "This is what the LORD has commanded: 'Tomorrow
is a day of solemn rest, a holy sabbath to the LORD; bake what you want
to bake and boil what you want to boil, and all that is left over put aside
to be kept until morning.' " [24] So they put it aside until morning, as Moses
commanded them; and it did not become foul, and there were no worms
in it. [25] Moses said, "Eat it today, for today is a sabbath to the LORD; today
you will not find it in the field. [26] Six days you shall gather it; but on the
seventh day, which is a sabbath, there will be none."
[27] On the seventh day some of the people went out to gather, and they
found none. [28] The LORD said to Moses, "How long will you refuse to keep
my commandments and instructions? [29] See! The LORD has given you the
sabbath, therefore on the sixth day he gives you food for two days; each
of you stay where you are; do not leave your place on the seventh day."
[30] So the people rested on the seventh day.

5. An omer of manna kept for a memorial

[31] The house of Israel called it manna; it was like coriander seed,
white, and the taste of it was like wafers made with honey. [32] Moses said,
"This is what the LORD has commanded: 'Let an omer of it be kept
throughout your generations, in order that they may see the food with
which I fed you in the wilderness, when I brought you out of the land of
Egypt.' " [33] And Moses said to Aaron, "Take a jar, and put an omer of
manna in it, and place it before the LORD, to be kept throughout your
generations." [34] As the LORD commanded Moses, so Aaron placed it
before the covenant,[h] for safekeeping. [35] The Israelites ate manna forty
years, until they came to a habitable land; they ate manna, until they came
to the border of the land of Canaan. [36] An omer is a tenth of an ephah.

C. Water from the smitten rock at Rephidim

17 From the wilderness of Sin the whole congregation of the Israelites
journeyed by stages, as the LORD commanded. They camped at
Rephidim, but there was no water for the people to drink. [2] The people
quarreled with Moses, and said, "Give us water to drink." Moses said to

g Or "It is manna" (Heb man hu, see verse 31)   h Or treaty or testimony; Heb eduth

Margin references:
16.18 — 2 Cor 8.15
16.19 — v. 23; Ex 12.10; 23.18
16.22 — v. 5; Ex 34.31
16.23ff — Ex 20.8; 23.12
16.24 — v. 20
16.28 — Ps 78.10
16.31 — Num 11.6-9
16.33 — Heb 9.4
16.34 — Ex 25.16, 21
16.35 — Josh 5.12; Neh 9.20, 21
17.1 — Ex 16.1
17.2 — Num 20.3; Deut 6.16; 1 Cor 10.9

16.16 *an omer.* This word is used only in connection
with the story about the manna in the wilderness. In
Exodus an *omer* is said to be equal to one tenth of an
ephah. Thus an *omer* would be equal to 2.087 dry
quarts (2.299 liters). An *ephah* measured somewhere
between three-eighths and two-thirds of a bushel.
These measures were employed for such things as

grain, flour, and meal. Liquids were measured by a
unit called the *bath*, which has been estimated to be
between five and six gallons.
16.23–26 Obviously the Sabbath existed before the
commandment was given in Ex 20.8–11, and it was
kept before the law was formally given.

17.3
Ex 16.2, 3

17.4
Ex 14.15;
Num 14.10;
1 Sam 30.6
17.5
Ex 3.16, 18;
7.20
17.6
Num 20.10;
Ps 114.8;
1 Cor 10.4
17.7
Ps 81.7

them, "Why do you quarrel with me? Why do you test the LORD?" 3 But the people thirsted there for water; and the people complained against Moses and said, "Why did you bring us out of Egypt, to kill us and our children and livestock with thirst?" 4 So Moses cried out to the LORD, "What shall I do with this people? They are almost ready to stone me." 5 The LORD said to Moses, "Go on ahead of the people, and take some of the elders of Israel with you; take in your hand the staff with which you struck the Nile, and go. 6 I will be standing there in front of you on the rock at Horeb. Strike the rock, and water will come out of it, so that the people may drink." Moses did so, in the sight of the elders of Israel. 7 He called the place Massah[i] and Meribah,[j] because the Israelites quarreled and tested the LORD, saying, "Is the LORD among us or not?"

D. The defeat of Amalek

17.8
Num 24.20;
Deut 25.17-19
17.9
Ex 4.20

8   Then Amalek came and fought with Israel at Rephidim. 9 Moses said to Joshua, "Choose some men for us and go out, fight with Amalek. Tomorrow I will stand on the top of the hill with the staff of God in my hand." 10 So Joshua did as Moses told him, and fought with Amalek, while Moses, Aaron, and Hur went up to the top of the hill. 11 Whenever Moses held up his hand, Israel prevailed; and whenever he lowered his hand, Amalek prevailed. 12 But Moses' hands grew weary; so they took a stone and put it under him, and he sat on it. Aaron and Hur held up his hands, one on one side, and the other on the other side; so his hands were steady until the sun set. 13 And Joshua defeated Amalek and his people with the sword.

17.14
Ex 34.27;
Num 24.20;
Deut 29.19

14   Then the LORD said to Moses, "Write this as a reminder in a book and recite it in the hearing of Joshua: I will utterly blot out the remembrance of Amalek from under heaven." 15 And Moses built an altar and called it, The LORD is my banner. 16 He said, "A hand upon the banner of the LORD [k] The LORD will have war with Amalek from generation to generation."

E. The visit of Jethro, Moses' father-in-law

1. Jethro's coming: the burnt offering and eating of bread

18.1
Ex 2.16; 3.1

18.2
Ex 4.25
18.3
Acts 7.29;
Ex 2.22

18 Jethro, the priest of Midian, Moses' father-in-law, heard of all that God had done for Moses and for his people Israel, how the LORD had brought Israel out of Egypt. 2 After Moses had sent away his wife Zipporah, his father-in-law Jethro took her back, 3 along with her two sons. The name of the one was Gershom (for he said, "I have been an

i That is Test   j That is Quarrel   k Cn: Meaning of Heb uncertain

---

17.3 The Israelites took every opportunity to complain and to find fault with Moses. Since God had given them manna, shouldn't they have realized that he would also provide water for them? Instead of exercising faith and praying to God for water, however, they once again contrasted their lack of water with what they thought was a better situation when they were slaves in Egypt. Sometimes God allows his people to lack necessities in order for them to be tested and to manifest whether their confidence is in him (cf. Deut 8.2,3).
17.6 *Strike the rock,* "with your staff," implied. The rock which Moses struck and from which water flowed is symbolic of Christ (see 1 Cor 10.4). He is our rock; from him flow the waters of everlasting life. As water satisfies physical thirst, so Christ satisfies spiritual thirst.
17.8 *Amalek,* a nomadic people who inhabited the Sinai Peninsula and the Negeb. Amalek considered

the Israelites intruders.
17.9 *Joshua.* This is the first mention of Joshua—a military leader, one of the twelve spies, and Moses' successor.
17.10 *Hur,* a man of Judah, of the family of Hezron, house of Caleb (1 Chron 2.18,19). He was the grandfather of Bezalel (31.1,2).
17.15 *"Jehovah-nissi"* in the Hebrew, i.e., "the LORD (Yahweh) is my banner."
18.1 *Jethro, the priest of Midian.* Here is a priest who was a true believer, offering sacrifices to God as well as blessing him (vv. 10,12). In v. 17ff he offers Moses excellent counsel on administrative matters.
18.3,4 Moses had two sons by Zipporah: Gershom and Eliezer. Neither son became a leader in Israel after their father. Gershom had a descendant, Shebuel, who was "chief officer in charge of the treasuries" under King David (1 Chr 26.24).

alien[l] in a foreign land"), [4]and the name of the other, Eliezer[m] (for he said, "The God of my father was my help, and delivered me from the sword of Pharaoh"). [5]Jethro, Moses' father-in-law, came into the wilderness where Moses was encamped at the mountain of God, bringing Moses' sons and wife to him. [6]He sent word to Moses, "I, your father-in-law Jethro, am coming to you, with your wife and her two sons." [7]Moses went out to meet his father-in-law; he bowed down and kissed him; each asked after the other's welfare, and they went into the tent. [8]Then Moses told his father-in-law all that the LORD had done to Pharaoh and to the Egyptians for Israel's sake, all the hardship that had beset them on the way, and how the LORD had delivered them. [9]Jethro rejoiced for all the good that the LORD had done to Israel, in delivering them from the Egyptians.

10 Jethro said, "Blessed be the LORD, who has delivered you from the Egyptians and from Pharaoh. [11]Now I know that the LORD is greater than all gods, because he delivered the people from the Egyptians,[n] when they dealt arrogantly with them." [12]And Jethro, Moses' father-in-law, brought a burnt offering and sacrifices to God; and Aaron came with all the elders of Israel to eat bread with Moses' father-in-law in the presence of God.

2. The selection of judges; the departure of Jethro

13 The next day Moses sat as judge for the people, while the people stood around him from morning until evening. [14]When Moses' father-in-law saw all that he was doing for the people, he said, "What is this that you are doing for the people? Why do you sit alone, while all the people stand around you from morning until evening?" [15]Moses said to his father-in-law, "Because the people come to me to inquire of God. [16]When they have a dispute, they come to me and I decide between one person and another, and I make known to them the statutes and instructions of God." [17]Moses' father-in-law said to him, "What you are doing is not good. [18]You will surely wear yourself out, both you and these people with you. For the task is too heavy for you; you cannot do it alone. [19]Now listen to me. I will give you counsel, and God be with you! You should represent the people before God, and you should bring their cases before God; [20]teach them the statutes and instructions and make known to them the way they are to go and the things they are to do. [21]You should also look for able men among all the people, men who fear God, are trustworthy, and hate dishonest gain; set such men over them as officers over thousands, hundreds, fifties, and tens. [22]Let them sit as judges for the people at all times; let them bring every important case to you, but decide every minor case themselves. So it will be easier for you, and they will bear the burden with you. [23]If you do this, and God so commands you, then you will be able to endure, and all these people will go to their home in peace."

24 So Moses listened to his father-in-law and did all that he had said. [25]Moses chose able men from all Israel and appointed them as heads over the people, as officers over thousands, hundreds, fifties, and tens. [26]And they judged the people at all times; hard cases they brought to Moses, but

18.5
Ex 3.1, 12

18.7
Gen 43.26-28;
Ex 4.27
18.8
Ps 81.7

18.10
Ps 68.19, 20
18.11
Ex 12.12;
15.11;
1 Sam 2.3

18.15
Num 9.8;
Deut 17.8-13

18.18
Num 11.14,
17
18.19
Ex 3.12;
Num 27.5
18.20
Deut 1.18
18.21ff
v. 25;
Deut 1.13, 15

18.22
Deut 1.17,
18;
Num 11.17

18.25
Deut 1.15
18.26
v. 22

---

[l] Heb ger   [m] Heb Eli, my God; ezer, help   [n] The clause because . . . Egyptians has been transposed from verse 10

18.5 at the mountain of God, i.e., Mt. Sinai, or, Mt. Horeb.

18.19,20 The Scriptures consistently insist on the necessity for justice to prevail. Justice has to do with what is right or righteous. Thus, God declares that the position of people in society, particularly if they are poor, shall not militate against them. Judgments must be decided on the basis of what is right. On occasion, however, the rich use their wealth to pervert justice, even as the poor can envy the rich and, by false claims, seek a share of that wealth. The idea of "social justice" as a policy that seeks the redistribution of

wealth by taking from the rich and giving to the poor is not found in the Scriptures. That term comes from the Enlightenment.

18.21ff Jethro, Moses' father-in-law, seeing that Moses was overworked, advised him to employ others to assist him. God called for a meeting with the seventy elders whom Moses had chosen, then had them take over some of Moses' duties. In the N.T. times, in imitation of the seventy elders, the number of members of the Sanhedrin was set at seventy. In the early church, the overworked apostles established the office of deacon (Acts 6).

18.27
Num 10.29,
30

any minor case they decided themselves. 27 Then Moses let his father-in-law depart, and he went off to his own country.

III. *The covenant and the law (19.1–24.18)*

A. *The covenant made*

1. *The people at Sinai*

19.2
Ex 17.1; 18.5

19.3
Ex 20;21;
Acts 7.38
19.4
Deut 29.2;
Isa 63.9
19.5ff
Deut 5.2;
7.6; 10.14
19.6
1 Pet 2.5;
Rev 1.6;
5.10;
Deut 14.21;
26.19
19.8
Ex 24.3, 7
19.9
v. 16;
Ex 24.15

19 On the third new moon after the Israelites had gone out of the land of Egypt, on that very day, they came into the wilderness of Sinai. 2 They had journeyed from Rephidim, entered the wilderness of Sinai, and camped in the wilderness; Israel camped there in front of the mountain. 3 Then Moses went up to God; the LORD called to him from the mountain, saying, "Thus you shall say to the house of Jacob, and tell the Israelites: 4 You have seen what I did to the Egyptians, and how I bore you on eagles' wings and brought you to myself. 5 Now therefore, if you obey my voice and keep my covenant, you shall be my treasured possession out of all the peoples. Indeed, the whole earth is mine, 6 but you shall be for me a priestly kingdom and a holy nation. These are the words that you shall speak to the Israelites."

7 So Moses came, summoned the elders of the people, and set before them all these words that the LORD had commanded him. 8 The people all answered as one: "Everything that the LORD has spoken we will do." Moses reported the words of the people to the LORD. 9 Then the LORD said to Moses, "I am going to come to you in a dense cloud, in order that the people may hear when I speak with you and so trust you ever after."

2. *The consecration of the people*

19.10
Lev 11.44,
45;
Heb 10.22;
Gen 35.2;
Num 8.7;
19.19
19.11
v. 16
19.12
Heb 12.20
19.13
v. 17

When Moses had told the words of the people to the LORD, 10 the LORD said to Moses: "Go to the people and consecrate them today and tomorrow. Have them wash their clothes 11 and prepare for the third day, because on the third day the LORD will come down upon Mount Sinai in the sight of all the people. 12 You shall set limits for the people all around, saying, 'Be careful not to go up the mountain or to touch the edge of it. Any who touch the mountain shall be put to death. 13 No hand shall touch them, but they shall be stoned or shot with arrows;*o* whether animal or human being, they shall not live.' When the trumpet sounds a long blast, they may go up on the mountain." 14 So Moses went down from the mountain to the people. He consecrated the people, and they washed their clothes. 15 And he said to the people, "Prepare for the third day; do not go near a woman."

3. *Moses meets God on Mount Sinai*

19.16
Heb 12.18,
19;
Ex 40.34

16 On the morning of the third day there was thunder and lightning, as well as a thick cloud on the mountain, and a blast of a trumpet so loud that all the people who were in the camp trembled. 17 Moses brought the people out of the camp to meet God. They took their stand at the foot of

o Heb lacks *with arrows*

19.4–6 Israel was a theocracy — it was governed directly by God. God told Israel when to move (40.36,37), when to battle (Num 31.1,2), who were to be appointed leaders (Num 27.18,20), and how the land of Canaan was to be divided among the twelve tribes (Josh 13.1–7). Moses and Joshua governed Israel on behalf of God, as did the judges and kings. When the first king Saul proved unworthy, God chose David to serve as his theocratic king. This appointment was conditioned on David's obedience to the covenant; God promised him an everlasting successor

in the person of God's Son, Jesus Christ.
19.7,8 Israel accepted God's contract, an agreement in which he was recognized as their Lord. It was a conditional arrangement based upon their promise to believe God and to obey him. Only unbelief and disobedience could break the terms of the contract and lose the blessing God promised.
19.9 *the people may . . . trust you ever after.* God had given Moses clear proofs that he was God's true representative. Despite this, Israel doubted and disbelieved Moses time and again.

the mountain. 18 Now Mount Sinai was wrapped in smoke, because the
LORD had descended upon it in fire; the smoke went up like the smoke
of a kiln, while the whole mountain shook violently. 19 As the blast of the
trumpet grew louder and louder, Moses would speak and God would
answer him in thunder. 20 When the LORD descended upon Mount Sinai,
to the top of the mountain, the LORD summoned Moses to the top of the
mountain, and Moses went up. 21 Then the LORD said to Moses, "Go
down and warn the people not to break through to the LORD to look;
otherwise many of them will perish. 22 Even the priests who approach the
LORD must consecrate themselves or the LORD will break out against
them." 23 Moses said to the LORD, "The people are not permitted to come
up to Mount Sinai; for you yourself warned us, saying, 'Set limits around
the mountain and keep it holy.'" 24 The LORD said to him, "Go down,
and come up bringing Aaron with you; but do not let either the priests
or the people break through to come up to the LORD; otherwise he will
break out against them." 25 So Moses went down to the people and told
them.

B. *The law given*

20 Then God spoke all these words:
2 I am the LORD your God, who brought you out of the land of
Egypt, out of the house of slavery; 3 you shall have no other gods before*p*
me.

4 You shall not make for yourself an idol, whether in the form of
anything that is in heaven above, or that is on the earth beneath, or that
is in the water under the earth. 5 You shall not bow down to them or
worship them; for I the LORD your God am a jealous God, punishing
children for the iniquity of parents, to the third and the fourth generation
of those who reject me, 6 but showing steadfast love to the thousandth
generation*q* of those who love me and keep my commandments.

7 You shall not make wrongful use of the name of the LORD your God,
for the LORD will not acquit anyone who misuses his name.

8 Remember the sabbath day, and keep it holy. 9 Six days you shall
labor and do all your work. 10 But the seventh day is a sabbath to the LORD
your God; you shall not do any work—you, your son or your daughter,
your male or female slave, your livestock, or the alien resident in your
towns. 11 For in six days the LORD made heaven and earth, the sea, and
all that is in them, but rested the seventh day; therefore the LORD blessed
the sabbath day and consecrated it.

p Or *besides*   *q* Or *to thousands*

19.18
Ps 104.32;
Heb 12.18;
Gen 19.28;
Ps 68.7, 8
19.19
Heb 12.21;
Ps 81.7
19.21
Ex 3.5
19.22
Lev 10.3;
2 Sam 6.7
19.23
v. 12

20.1
Deut 5.22
20.2
Deut 5.6; 7.8
20.3
Jer 35.15
20.4
Lev 26.1;
Deut 4.15-19;
Ps 97.7
20.5
Isa 44.15,
19;
Deut 4.24;
Jer 32.18
20.6
Deut 7.9
20.7
Lev 19.12;
Mt 5.33
20.8
Ex 23.12;
31.15
20.9
Ex 34.21;
Lk 13.14
20.11
Gen 2.2, 3

19.18 *the* LORD [Yahweh] *had descended upon it in
fire.* Fire symbolizes the holiness of God and is mentioned often in the Scriptures in connection with God
(3.2; 2 Kings 2.11; 2 Thess 1.7,8).
20.1 Beginning with the ten commandments, God
reveals his law to his people. Many of his laws have
to do with moral issues, with what is called *ethics.*
Ethics embody basic principles of good and bad and
are concerned with moral duties and obligations.
Specifically regarding the ten commandments, spoken and written by God himself (32.16; Deut 4.13;
5.4,22; 10.4), we hear what would be true even if they
had never been given to Moses. They serve a threefold
purpose: (1) they are a disciplinarian to bring people
to Christ (see Gal 3.23–25), for they point out human
guilt and make clear that no one ever keeps the law
of God completely; (2) they also help Christians to
know what their duties are toward God and others,
and to realize how they can please God and carry out
his will; (3) they serve to influence all humankind, so

that a government of law is made possible. The commandments were summed up by Christ in two injunctions: people must love God with their whole hearts
and their neighbors as themselves (Mt 22.35–40).
The law is both external and internal: some commandments pertain to overt acts while the last commandment ("You shall not covet," v. 17) deals with
the heart. Heart sin precedes overt acts of commission; overt acts depict the condition of the heart (cf.
Mk 7.17–23).
20.3 Idolatry is expressly forbidden in the Scriptures. It can take a number of forms, including:
(1) bowing before or worshiping images, whether of
God, humans, or animals (20.5; Isa 44.17; Dan 10.15;
Rom 1.22,23); (2) offering sacrifices to other gods or
images (22.20; Ps 106.38; Acts 7.41); (3) the worship
of angels (Col 2.18); (4) covetousness (Eph 5.5); and
(5) sensuality (Phil 3.19). As a general rule, anything
that takes first place away from God as the object of
our love and obedience is idolatrous.

20.12
Lev 19.3;
Mt 15.4;
Mk 7.10;
Eph 6.2
20.13
Rom 13.9
20.14
Mt 19.18
20.15
Mt 19.18
20.16
Ex 23.1;
Mt 19.18
20.17
Rom 7.7;
13.9
20.18
Heb 12.18;
Ex 19.18
20.19
Deut 5.23-27
20.20
Ex 14.13;
15.25;
Deut 4.10
20.21
Deut 5.22

12 Honor your father and your mother, so that your days may be long in the land that the LORD your God is giving you.

13 You shall not murder.^r

14 You shall not commit adultery.

15 You shall not steal.

16 You shall not bear false witness against your neighbor.

17 You shall not covet your neighbor's house; you shall not covet your neighbor's wife, or male or female slave, or ox, or donkey, or anything that belongs to your neighbor.

C. The people afraid

18 When all the people witnessed the thunder and lightning, the sound of the trumpet, and the mountain smoking, they were afraid^s and trembled and stood at a distance, 19 and said to Moses, "You speak to us, and we will listen; but do not let God speak to us, or we will die." 20 Moses said to the people, "Do not be afraid; for God has come only to test you and to put the fear of him upon you so that you do not sin." 21 Then the people stood at a distance, while Moses drew near to the thick darkness where God was.

D. The laws of the covenant

1. The law of the altar

20.22
Neh 9.13
20.23
v. 3;
Ex 32.1, 2, 4
20.24
Lev 1.2;
Deut 12.5;
Gen 12.2
20.25
Deut 27.5, 6

22 The LORD said to Moses: Thus you shall say to the Israelites: "You have seen for yourselves that I spoke with you from heaven. 23 You shall not make gods of silver alongside me, nor shall you make for yourselves gods of gold. 24 You need make for me only an altar of earth and sacrifice on it your burnt offerings and your offerings of well-being, your sheep and your oxen; in every place where I cause my name to be remembered I will come to you and bless you. 25 But if you make for me an altar of stone, do not build it of hewn stones; for if you use a chisel upon it you profane it. 26 You shall not go up by steps to my altar, so that your nakedness may not be exposed on it."

2. Laws concerning slaves

21.1
Deut 4.14
21.2
Lev 25.39-41;
Deut 15.12-18

21 These are the ordinances that you shall set before them:
2 When you buy a male Hebrew slave, he shall serve six years, but in the seventh he shall go out a free person, without debt. 3 If he comes in single, he shall go out single; if he comes in married, then his wife shall go out with him. 4 If his master gives him a wife and she bears him sons or daughters, the wife and her children shall be her master's and he shall go out alone. 5 But if the slave declares, "I love my master, my wife, and my children; I will not go out a free person," 6 then his master shall bring him before God.^t He shall be brought to the door or the doorpost; and his master shall pierce his ear with an awl; and he shall serve him for life.

21.6
Ex 22.8, 9,
28
21.7
Neh 5.5;
vv. 2, 3

7 When a man sells his daughter as a slave, she shall not go out as the

^r Or kill   ^s Sam Gk Syr Vg: MT they saw   ^t Or to the judges

20.17 In contrast to the other commandments, the command against coveting concerns human thoughts and attitudes. God wants us not only to speak and act according to his law; he wants our thoughts to be pure as well.

21.1 God gave Israel its system of civil law under which society was to be governed. These laws were, in some instances, similar to those of Sumer and Babylonia, which predated Moses. Natural revelation presupposes that even pagan nations will know and use the laws of nature, for they apply to all people. The "you shall not" phraseology, however, is peculiar

to the laws of Israel. Even though many of the laws enacted in Moses' day are not applicable to our world today, the underlying principles of justice, equality, and fairness are foundational to any system of jurisprudence.

21.2 When you buy a male Hebrew slave. Slavery was not forbidden in the O.T. But God revealed limits and governing principles to slavery and wrote them into his legislation for his people.

21.7 When a man sells his daughter. Who would suppose that a father would sell a daughter? God, the author of these injunctions, knew what evils his own

male slaves do. 8 If she does not please her master, who designated her for himself, then he shall let her be redeemed; he shall have no right to sell her to a foreign people, since he has dealt unfairly with her. 9 If he designates her for his son, he shall deal with her as with a daughter. 10 If he takes another wife to himself, he shall not diminish the food, clothing, or marital rights of the first wife. *u* 11 And if he does not do these three things for her, she shall go out without debt, without payment of money.

3. Laws relating to murder

12 Whoever strikes a person mortally shall be put to death. 13 If it was not premeditated, but came about by an act of God, then I will appoint for you a place to which the killer may flee. 14 But if someone willfully attacks and kills another by treachery, you shall take the killer from my altar for execution.

15 Whoever strikes father or mother shall be put to death.

16 Whoever kidnaps a person, whether that person has been sold or is still held in possession, shall be put to death.

17 Whoever curses father or mother shall be put to death.

4. Laws relating to noncapital offenses

18 When individuals quarrel and one strikes the other with a stone or fist so that the injured party, though not dead, is confined to bed, 19 but recovers and walks around outside with the help of a staff, then the assailant shall be free of liability, except to pay for the loss of time, and to arrange for full recovery.

20 When a slaveowner strikes a male or female slave with a rod and the slave dies immediately, the owner shall be punished. 21 But if the slave survives a day or two, there is no punishment; for the slave is the owner's property.

22 When people who are fighting injure a pregnant woman so that there is a miscarriage, and yet no further harm follows, the one responsible shall be fined what the woman's husband demands, paying as much as the judges determine. 23 If any harm follows, then you shall give life for life, 24 eye for eye, tooth for tooth, hand for hand, foot for foot, 25 burn for burn, wound for wound, stripe for stripe.

26 When a slaveowner strikes the eye of a male or female slave, destroying it, the owner shall let the slave go, a free person, to compensate for the eye. 27 If the owner knocks out a tooth of a male or female slave, the slave shall be let go, a free person, to compensate for the tooth.

28 When an ox gores a man or a woman to death, the ox shall be stoned, and its flesh shall not be eaten; but the owner of the ox shall not be liable. 29 If the ox has been accustomed to gore in the past, and its owner has been warned but has not restrained it, and it kills a man or a woman, the ox shall be stoned, and its owner also shall be put to death. 30 If a ransom is imposed on the owner, then the owner shall pay whatever is imposed for the redemption of the victim's life. 31 If it gores a boy or a girl, the owner shall be dealt with according to this same rule. 32 If the

u Heb *of her*

21.10
1 Cor 7.3, 5

21.12
Gen 9.6;
Lev 24.17
21.13
Num 35.22;
Deut 19.4, 5
21.14
Deut 19.11,
12;
Heb 10.26;
1 Kings 2.28-34
21.16
Deut 24.7
21.17
Lev 20.9;
Mt 15.4;
Mk 7.10

21.21
Lev 25.45, 46

21.23ff
Lev 24.19
21.24
Mt 5.38

21.28
Gen 9.5

21.30
v. 22
21.32
see
Zech 11.12,
13;
Mt 26.15

people were capable of and set up these regulations *before* they did these things.
21.12–15 The law about murder distinguishes between deaths which are premeditated and spring from the heart, and those caused by so-called accidents. The penalty for homicide was death. For those who killed innocently, a place of refuge was provided to which they might flee (see Deut 19.1–13). The phrase "came about by an act of God" indicates that nothing

happens by chance, even accidental death. Contemporary laws still guarantee the freedom of those who kill accidentally.
21.24,25 The idea that the punishment should be equal to the crime was a great advance over the law of revenge. The N.T. elevates both concepts with its principle of forgiveness. We must forgive those who hurt us even if they do it often, for thus we have been forgiven by God for our sins.

ox gores a male or female slave, the owner shall pay to the slaveowner thirty shekels of silver, and the ox shall be stoned.

5. *Laws relating to property rights*

21.33
Lk 14.5

33   If someone leaves a pit open, or digs a pit and does not cover it, and an ox or a donkey falls into it, 34 the owner of the pit shall make restitution, giving money to its owner, but keeping the dead animal.

35   If someone's ox hurts the ox of another, so that it dies, then they shall sell the live ox and divide the price of it; and the dead animal they shall also divide. 36 But if it was known that the ox was accustomed to gore in the past, and its owner has not restrained it, the owner shall restore ox for ox, but keep the dead animal.

22.1
2 Sam 12.6

22 *v* When someone steals an ox or a sheep, and slaughters it or sells it, the thief shall pay five oxen for an ox, and four sheep for a sheep. *w* The thief shall make restitution, but if unable to do so, shall be sold for the theft. 4 When the animal, whether ox or donkey or sheep, is found alive in the thief's possession, the thief shall pay double.

22.2
Mt 24.43;
Num 35.27
22.3
Ex 21.2

2 *x* If a thief is found breaking in, and is beaten to death, no bloodguilt is incurred; 3 but if it happens after sunrise, bloodguilt is incurred.

5   When someone causes a field or vineyard to be grazed over, or lets livestock loose to graze in someone else's field, restitution shall be made from the best in the owner's field or vineyard.

6   When fire breaks out and catches in thorns so that the stacked grain or the standing grain or the field is consumed, the one who started the fire shall make full restitution.

22.7
v. 4

7   When someone delivers to a neighbor money or goods for safekeeping, and they are stolen from the neighbor's house, then the thief, if caught, shall pay double. 8 If the thief is not caught, the owner of the house shall be brought before God, *y* to determine whether or not the owner had laid hands on the neighbor's goods.

22.8
v. 28;
Ex 21.6;
Deut 17.8, 9;
19.17
22.9
vv. 8, 28

9   In any case of disputed ownership involving ox, donkey, sheep, clothing, or any other loss, of which one party says, "This is mine," the case of both parties shall come before God; *y* the one whom God condemns *z* shall pay double to the other.

22.11
Heb 6.16

10   When someone delivers to another a donkey, ox, sheep, or any other animal for safekeeping, and it dies or is injured or is carried off, without anyone seeing it, 11 an oath before the LORD shall decide between the two of them that the one has not laid hands on the property of the other; the owner shall accept the oath, and no restitution shall be made.

22.12
Gen 31.39

12 But if it was stolen, restitution shall be made to its owner. 13 If it was mangled by beasts, let it be brought as evidence; restitution shall not be made for the mangled remains.

14   When someone borrows an animal from another and it is injured or dies, the owner not being present, full restitution shall be made. 15 If the owner was present, there shall be no restitution; if it was hired, only the hiring fee is due.

22.16
Deut 22.28,
29
22.17
Deut 22.29

16   When a man seduces a virgin who is not engaged to be married, and lies with her, he shall give the bride-price for her and make her his wife. 17 But if her father refuses to give her to him, he shall pay an amount equal to the bride-price for virgins.

---

v Ch 21.37 in Heb   *w* Verses 2, 3, and 4 rearranged thus: 3b, 4, 2, 3a   *x* Ch 22.1 in Heb   *y* Or *before the judges*   *z* Or *the judges condemn*

21.33ff God guarantees property rights as well as human life (cf. the eighth commandment). The right to property is inalienable, i.e., no one has a right to take it from the owner; and if a loss is sustained through an accident, the one who caused the accident is liable for damages.

22.13 *mangled by beasts.* Acts of God do not require payment to those whose property has been lost or damaged. Earthquakes, fires, severe weather, and volcanic eruptions may be considered acts of God.

6. Other laws

a. Crimes punishable by death

18   You shall not permit a female sorcerer to live.
19   Whoever lies with an animal shall be put to death.
20   Whoever sacrifices to any god, other than the LORD alone, shall be devoted to destruction.

b. Various duties

21   You shall not wrong or oppress a resident alien, for you were aliens in the land of Egypt. 22 You shall not abuse any widow or orphan. 23 If you do abuse them, when they cry out to me, I will surely heed their cry; 24 my wrath will burn, and I will kill you with the sword, and your wives shall become widows and your children orphans.

25   If you lend money to my people, to the poor among you, you shall not deal with them as a creditor; you shall not exact interest from them. 26 If you take your neighbor's cloak in pawn, you shall restore it before the sun goes down; 27 for it may be your neighbor's only clothing to use as cover; in what else shall that person sleep? And if your neighbor cries out to me, I will listen, for I am compassionate.

28   You shall not revile God, or curse a leader of your people.

29   You shall not delay to make offerings from the fullness of your harvest and from the outflow of your presses. a
The firstborn of your sons you shall give to me. 30 You shall do the same with your oxen and with your sheep: seven days it shall remain with its mother; on the eighth day you shall give it to me.

31   You shall be people consecrated to me; therefore you shall not eat any meat that is mangled by beasts in the field; you shall throw it to the dogs.

c. Ethical instructions

23   You shall not spread a false report. You shall not join hands with the wicked to act as a malicious witness. 2 You shall not follow a majority in wrongdoing; when you bear witness in a lawsuit, you shall not side with the majority so as to pervert justice; 3 nor shall you be partial to the poor in a lawsuit.

4   When you come upon your enemy's ox or donkey going astray, you shall bring it back.

5   When you see the donkey of one who hates you lying under its burden and you would hold back from setting it free, you must help to set it free. a

6   You shall not pervert the justice due to your poor in their lawsuits.
7 Keep far from a false charge, and do not kill the innocent and those in the right, for I will not acquit the guilty. 8 You shall take no bribe, for

a Meaning of Heb uncertain

Cross references column:

22.18 Lev 20.27; Deut 18.10
22.19 Lev 18.23; Deut 27.21
22.20 Deut 17.2, 3, 5
22.21 Lev 19.33; Deut 10.19
22.22 Deut 24.17, 18
22.23 Deut 15.9; Lk 18.7; Ps 18.6
22.24 Ps 69.24; 109.9
22.25 Lev 25.35-37; Deut 23.19, 20
22.28 Lev 24.15, 16; Acts 23.5
22.29 Ex 23.16; 13.2, 12
22.30 Deut 15.19; Lev 22.27
22.31 Lev 19.6; 22.8
23.1 Ex 20.16; Ps 35.11
23.2 Deut 16.19
23.4 Deut 22.1
23.5 Deut 22.4
23.6 vv. 2, 3
23.7 Rom 1.18
23.8 Deut 10.17; 16.19

22.25 Interest charges were forbidden when an Israelite lent money or goods to another Israelite. But a loan to a non-Israelite with interest charges was not forbidden. Usury is inordinate interest and runs counter to neighborly love.
22.27 *I am compassionate.* Grace, kindness, and compassion constitute one of God's attributes. God said he would be gracious and merciful to whomever he wanted (33.19). Grace may be defined as God's "unmerited favor" which he manifests to sinful humans, i.e., to those who deserve the exact opposite. Concerning the grace or the kindness of God, the Scriptures teach that: (1) salvation is by God's grace or kindness (Eph 1.7,8); (2) justification (i.e., being declared "not guilty") is by God's grace or kindness

(Rom 3.24; Titus 3.7); (3) God's election (i.e., being chosen by God) is of God's kindness or grace (Rom 11.5,6); (4) faith itself is a gift of God's kindness or grace (Eph 2.8,9); (5) the call to a Christian life and testimony is all of grace or kindness (Gal 1.15,16); (6) comfort, hope, and strength spring from grace (2 Thess 2.16,17).
23.1 The sin of slander is sternly forbidden in Scripture. It includes such sins as whispering, backbiting, gossiping, defaming, giving false testimony, and raising false reports (Prov 6.16, 19; Eph 4.31; Jas 4.11). The route to victory over slander is to walk in the Spirit so we can love our neighbors as we love ourselves.

a bribe blinds the officials, and subverts the cause of those who are in the right.

23.9
Ex 22.21

9 You shall not oppress a resident alien; you know the heart of an alien, for you were aliens in the land of Egypt.

7. Laws of festivals and holidays

23.10
Lev 25.3

10 For six years you shall sow your land and gather in its yield; 11 but the seventh year you shall let it rest and lie fallow, so that the poor of your people may eat; and what they leave the wild animals may eat. You shall do the same with your vineyard, and with your olive orchard.

23.12
Ex 20.8-11

12 Six days you shall do your work, but on the seventh day you shall rest, so that your ox and your donkey may have relief, and your homeborn slave and the resident alien may be refreshed. 13 Be attentive to all that I have said to you. Do not invoke the names of other gods; do not let them be heard on your lips.

23.13
Ps 39.1;
Eph 5.15

23.14
Ex 34.23
23.15
Ex 12.15;
34.20

14 Three times in the year you shall hold a festival for me. 15 You shall observe the festival of unleavened bread; as I commanded you, you shall eat unleavened bread for seven days at the appointed time in the month of Abib, for in it you came out of Egypt.

No one shall appear before me empty-handed.

23.16
Ex 34.22;
Deut 16.13

16 You shall observe the festival of harvest, of the first fruits of your labor, of what you sow in the field. You shall observe the festival of ingathering at the end of the year, when you gather in from the field the fruit of your labor. 17 Three times in the year all your males shall appear before the Lord GOD.

23.17
Deut 16.16

23.18
Ex 34.25

18 You shall not offer the blood of my sacrifice with anything leavened, or let the fat of my festival remain until the morning.

23.19
Ex 22.29;
Deut 14.21

19 The choicest of the first fruits of your ground you shall bring into the house of the LORD your God.

You shall not boil a kid in its mother's milk.

8. God's final commands

23.20
Ex 32.34;
15.16, 17
23.21
Num 14.11;
Ps 78.40, 56;
Num 14.35
23.22
Gen 12.2
23.23
Josh 24.8, 11
23.24
Ex 20.5;
Lev 18.3;
Ex 34.13
23.25
Deut 6.13;
Mt 4.10;
Deut 28.5;
Ex 15.26

20 I am going to send an angel in front of you, to guard you on the way and to bring you to the place that I have prepared. 21 Be attentive to him and listen to his voice; do not rebel against him, for he will not pardon your transgression; for my name is in him.

22 But if you listen attentively to his voice and do all that I say, then I will be an enemy to your enemies and a foe to your foes.

23 When my angel goes in front of you, and brings you to the Amorites, the Hittites, the Perizzites, the Canaanites, the Hivites, and the Jebusites, and I blot them out, 24 you shall not bow down to their gods, or worship them, or follow their practices, but you shall utterly demolish them and break their pillars in pieces. 25 You shall worship the LORD your

---

23.11 The festival of the sabbatical year was kept every seventh year. For six years the land was to be cultivated; the seventh year it was to lie fallow (Lev 25.2). God promised there would be an adequate harvest on the sixth year (Lev 25.21) so the people could live until the land was cultivated in the eighth year. Farming was to cease, the fruits of the earth became common property, debts were canceled, Hebrew slaves were set free, and the law was read publicly (see Lev 25.4ff; Deut 15.1–3,12; 31.10–13; Neh 10.31). These arrangements did not necessarily apply to non-Israelites (Deut 15.3). The later captivity by Babylonia was partially a consequence of Israel's failure to observe the sabbatical year (2 Chr 36.20,21).

23.14 All adult male Israelites were required to attend three yearly festivals at the tabernacle: the festival of unleavened bread (23.15), the festival of the

harvest (23.16), and the festival of ingathering (23.16). They are often known as the festivals of passover, Pentecost, and booths (see notes on 12.11; Lev 23.15,16; Mk 14.1).

23.16 The festival of ingathering is later called the festival of booths (Lev 23.34). It started on the fifteenth day of *Tishri*, the seventh month (Lev 23.34, 39). Coming at the end of the harvest, it lasted for eight days. The first and last days were celebrated by holy convocations (Lev 23.35,39; Num 29.12,35). The people camped out in booths for this festival, family by family (Lev 23.42), to commemorate Israel's redemption out of Egypt. It was celebrated with thanksgiving (Lev 23.41; Deut 16.14,15). Zechariah prophesied that it would become a memorial festival for all nations (Zech 14.16–21).

God, and I[b] will bless your bread and your water; and I will take sickness away from among you. 26 No one shall miscarry or be barren in your land; I will fulfill the number of your days. 27 I will send my terror in front of you, and will throw into confusion all the people against whom you shall come, and I will make all your enemies turn their backs to you. 28 And I will send the pestilence[c] in front of you, which shall drive out the Hivites, the Canaanites, and the Hittites from before you. 29 I will not drive them out from before you in one year, or the land would become desolate and the wild animals would multiply against you. 30 Little by little I will drive them out from before you, until you have increased and possess the land. 31 I will set your borders from the Red Sea[d] to the sea of the Philistines, and from the wilderness to the Euphrates; for I will hand over to you the inhabitants of the land, and you shall drive them out before you. 32 You shall make no covenant with them and their gods. 33 They shall not live in your land, or they will make you sin against me; for if you worship their gods, it will surely be a snare to you.

23.26 Deut 7.14; Mal 3.11; Job 5.26
23.27 Ex 15.14, 16; Deut 7.23
23.28 Deut 7.20; Josh 24.12
23.29 Deut 7.22
23.31 Gen 15.18; Josh 21.44; 24.12, 18
23.32 Deut 7.2; vv. 13, 24
23.33 Deut 7.1-5, 16

9. Israel's acceptance of the covenant

a. The covenant sealed by blood

24 Then he said to Moses, "Come up to the LORD, you and Aaron, Nadab, and Abihu, and seventy of the elders of Israel, and worship at a distance. 2 Moses alone shall come near the LORD; but the others shall not come near, and the people shall not come up with him."

3 Moses came and told the people all the words of the LORD and all the ordinances; and all the people answered with one voice, and said, "All the words that the LORD has spoken we will do." 4 And Moses wrote down all the words of the LORD. He rose early in the morning, and built an altar at the foot of the mountain, and set up twelve pillars, corresponding to the twelve tribes of Israel. 5 He sent young men of the people of Israel, who offered burnt offerings and sacrificed oxen as offerings of well-being to the LORD. 6 Moses took half of the blood and put it in basins, and half of the blood he dashed against the altar. 7 Then he took the book of the covenant, and read it in the hearing of the people; and they said, "All that the LORD has spoken we will do, and we will be obedient." 8 Moses took the blood and dashed it on the people, and said, "See the blood of the covenant that the LORD has made with you in accordance with all these words."

9 Then Moses and Aaron, Nadab, and Abihu, and seventy of the elders of Israel went up, 10 and they saw the God of Israel. Under his feet

24.1 Lev 10.1, 2; Num 11.16
24.3 v. 7; Ex 19.8
24.4 Deut 31.9; Gen 28.18
24.6 Heb 9.18
24.7 Heb 9.19; v. 3
24.8 Heb 9.20; 1 Pet 1.2
24.9 v. 1
24.10 Ezek 1.26; Rev 4.3; Mt 17.2

b Gk Vg: Heb *he*   *c* Or *hornets*: Meaning of Heb uncertain   *d* Or *Sea of Reeds*

23.30 The expulsion of the inhabitants from the promised land and the granting of the land to Israel were the fixed purpose of God. But the execution of that purpose was conditioned by life's realities. Thus the inhabitants were not to be driven out immediately; in the interests of preserving the productivity of the land and of keeping it from being overrun by desolation, God told Israel that the divine strategy was to accomplish this intention over a period of time. This distinction between settled principle and the carrying out of that principle is applicable to international situations today. Not every decision can be implemented immediately.

24.3 The ordinances or commandments relating to community life are here said to have been given to Moses directly by God. Thus civil law derives from God himself, not from the whims and fancies of mortals.

24.7 *the book of the covenant* constituted all the words of the Lord God spoken to Moses (24.4). When this book had been read to the people of Israel, they

were called upon to accept and ratify what it contained. The people promised to do all God had said, and they swore obedience. Then Moses sprinkled blood over the people (24.8), saying this symbolic act represented the blood of the covenant. It was the blood of bulls and goats which, in turn, were symbols of the blood of Christ shed on Calvary (Heb 9.13,14), which made up "the eternal covenant" of Heb 13.20.

24.10 A theophany is a visible appearance of God to humans. Such appearances differed greatly. Among them were: (1) the appearance of God (in what may have been a vision) to Moses, Aaron, Nadab, Abihu, and the seventy elders, in which his glory was manifested (24.10); (2) the time when God spoke to Moses face to face (33.11); (3) appearances to Isaiah (Isa 6), Ezekiel (Ezek 1), and Daniel (Dan 7), when God was seen in a vision or a dream; (4) the appearance of the angel of the Lord to Hagar (Gen 16.7—although the angel of the Lord does not always mean the appearance of God or Christ); (5) the appearance of God in the pillar of cloud (14.19); (6) the time when God

there was something like a pavement of sapphire stone, like the very heaven for clearness. 11 God[e] did not lay his hand on the chief men of the people of Israel; also they beheld God, and they ate and drank.

b. Moses on the mountain for forty days

12 The LORD said to Moses, "Come up to me on the mountain, and wait there; and I will give you the tablets of stone, with the law and the commandment, which I have written for their instruction." 13 So Moses set out with his assistant Joshua, and Moses went up into the mountain of God. 14 To the elders he had said, "Wait here for us, until we come to you again; for Aaron and Hur are with you; whoever has a dispute may go to them."

15 Then Moses went up on the mountain, and the cloud covered the mountain. 16 The glory of the LORD settled on Mount Sinai, and the cloud covered it for six days; on the seventh day he called to Moses out of the cloud. 17 Now the appearance of the glory of the LORD was like a devouring fire on the top of the mountain in the sight of the people of Israel. 18 Moses entered the cloud, and went up on the mountain. Moses was on the mountain for forty days and forty nights.

IV. *The tabernacle in the wilderness (25.1–40.38)*

A. *The offering for the tabernacle*

25 The LORD said to Moses: 2 Tell the Israelites to take for me an offering; from all whose hearts prompt them to give you shall receive the offering for me. 3 This is the offering that you shall receive from them: gold, silver, and bronze, 4 blue, purple, and crimson yarns and fine linen, goats' hair, 5 tanned rams' skins, fine leather,[f] acacia wood, 6 oil for the lamps, spices for the anointing oil and for the fragrant incense, 7 onyx stones and gems to be set in the ephod and for the breastpiece. 8 And have them make me a sanctuary, so that I may dwell among them. 9 In accordance with all that I show you concerning the pattern of the tabernacle and of all its furniture, so you shall make it.

B. *The ark*

10 They shall make an ark of acacia wood; it shall be two and a half cubits long, a cubit and a half wide, and a cubit and a half high. 11 You shall overlay it with pure gold, inside and outside you shall overlay it, and you shall make a molding of gold upon it all around. 12 You shall cast four rings of gold for it and put them on its four feet, two rings on the one side of it, and two rings on the other side. 13 You shall make poles of acacia wood, and overlay them with gold. 14 And you shall put the poles into the rings on the sides of the ark, by which to carry the ark. 15 The poles shall

Marginal cross-references

24.11 Ex 19.21; Gen 32.30; 31.54
24.12 vv. 2, 15; Ex 32.15, 16
24.13 Ex 17.9-14; 3.1
24.15 Ex 19.9
24.16 Ex 16.10
24.17 Ex 3.2; Deut 4.36; Heb 12.18, 29
24.18 Ex 34.28; Deut 9.9
25.2 Ex 35.5, 21; 2 Cor 8.12; 9.7
25.6 Ex 27.20; 30.23, 34
25.7 Ex 28.4, 6, 15
25.8 Ex 36.1, 3, 4; Heb 9.1, 2; Ex 29.45; Rev 21.3
25.9 v. 40; Acts 7.44; Heb 8.2, 5
25.10 Ex 37.1-9

e Heb *He*   f Meaning of Heb uncertain

---

showed the people of Israel his greatness and glory (Deut 5.24); and (7) the appearance of God in the incarnation of Jesus Christ, when God's Son became a human being and "lived among us" (Jn 1.14).
24.13 *his assistant Joshua.* Joshua served under Moses as a subordinate. Thus he had time to learn all he needed to know about the administration of justice and the supervision of Israel. After the death of Moses, he led the people of Israel into the land of promise. As God's choice, not Israel's, he was a well-trained replacement for Moses.
25.9 God commanded Moses to build the tabernacle. It was to be a removable sanctuary because of the unsettled life of Israel (2 Sam 7.6,7). God appointed the Levites to have charge of it (Num 1.50; 18.2-4)

and assured Israel his presence would fill the holy place (25.22; Lev 16.2; Num 7.89). During the forty years in the wilderness, the glory of God rested over the tent by day and by night (Num 9.15,16). When the *shekinah* cloud moved, the people of Israel moved too (40.36–38).
25.10 The ark was a chest made of acacia wood overlaid with gold. Reckoning the cubit at 18 inches, this chest was 3.75 feet long, 2.25 feet wide, and 2.25 feet deep (see also notes to v. 17; 26.33). Inside it were: (1) the golden urn holding manna from the wilderness journey (16.33); (2) Aaron's rod (Num 17.10); and (3) the copy of the Law (Deut 31.26; 2 Kings 22.8).

remain in the rings of the ark; they shall not be taken from it. [16] You shall put into the ark the covenant [g] that I shall give you.

17 Then you shall make a mercy seat [h] of pure gold; two cubits and a half shall be its length, and a cubit and a half its width. [18] You shall make two cherubim of gold; you shall make them of hammered work, at the two ends of the mercy seat. [i] [19] Make one cherub at the one end, and one cherub at the other; of one piece with the mercy seat [i] you shall make the cherubim at its two ends. [20] The cherubim shall spread out their wings above, overshadowing the mercy seat [i] with their wings. They shall face one to another; the faces of the cherubim shall be turned toward the mercy seat. [i] [21] You shall put the mercy seat [i] on the top of the ark; and in the ark you shall put the covenant [g] that I shall give you. [22] There I will meet with you, and from above the mercy seat, [i] from between the two cherubim that are on the ark of the covenant, [g] I will deliver to you all my commands for the Israelites.

C. The table

23 You shall make a table of acacia wood, two cubits long, one cubit wide, and a cubit and a half high. [24] You shall overlay it with pure gold, and make a molding of gold around it. [25] You shall make around it a rim a handbreadth wide, and a molding of gold around the rim. [26] You shall make for it four rings of gold, and fasten the rings to the four corners at its four legs. [27] The rings that hold the poles used for carrying the table shall be close to the rim. [28] You shall make the poles of acacia wood, and overlay them with gold, and the table shall be carried with these. [29] You shall make its plates and dishes for incense, and its flagons and bowls with which to pour drink offerings; you shall make them of pure gold. [30] And you shall set the bread of the Presence on the table before me always.

D. The lampstand

31 You shall make a lampstand of pure gold. The base and the shaft of the lampstand shall be made of hammered work; its cups, its calyxes, and its petals shall be of one piece with it; [32] and there shall be six branches going out of its sides, three branches of the lampstand out of one side of it and three branches of the lampstand out of the other side of it; [33] three cups shaped like almond blossoms, each with calyx and petals, on one branch, and three cups shaped like almond blossoms, each with calyx and petals, on the other branch—so for the six branches going out of the lampstand. [34] On the lampstand itself there shall be four cups shaped like almond blossoms, each with its calyxes and petals. [35] There shall be a calyx

Cross references (right margin):
25.16 Deut 31.26; Heb 9.4
25.17 Ex 37.6; Rom 3.25; Heb 9.5
25.20 1 Kings 8.7; Heb 9.5
25.21 Ex 26.34; v. 16
25.22 Ex 29.42, 43; 30.6, 36; Num 7.89; Ps 80.1
25.23 Ex 37.10-16; Heb 9.2
25.29 Ex 37.16; Num 4.7
25.30 Lev 24.5-9
25.31 Ex 37.17; Heb 9.2; Rev 1.12
25.32 Ex 38.18
25.34 Ex 37.20

---

[g] Or treaty, or testimony; Heb eduth   [h] Or a cover   [i] Or the cover

25.17 The mercy seat, made of pure gold, was the lid of the ark, beaten out into the form of two cherubim (winged lions with human heads) facing each other. The wings of the cherubim were outspread, and the cherubim looked down at the mercy seat. The tables of the law were inside the ark. Thus grace covered the law by God's mercy. The Hebrew term for "mercy seat" means "propitiatory" and derives from the verb kippēr ("to atone"). The high priest entered the most holy place once a year with blood to make atonement. Christ, the perfect sacrifice, met the full demands of the law, making divine mercy possible. He entered the Holy of Holies in the heavenly sanctuary once for our sins (Heb 9), and his work was finished by that one act. Now all believers have immediate access to the mercy seat through Christ, our high priest (Rom 3.25; Heb 4.14–16).
25.22 the two cherubim. The concept of the Lord of hosts being enthroned on the cherubim is noted explicitly in 1 Sam 4.4; 2 Sam 6.2; 2 Kings 29.15; 1 Chr

13.6; Isa 37.16.
25.30 the bread of Presence on the table. The twelve loaves, representing the twelve tribes of Israel, were set in two rows of six loaves each. These loaves acknowledged God's goodness to his people and served as a token of their uninterrupted communion with him. The bread is a symbol of God's spiritual provision for the church in the gospel age. Best of all, God's people shall ever eat and drink with the Savior at his table in his kingdom (Lk 22.30).
25.31 The "lampstand" provided the only light in the tabernacle, for there were no windows in it. This foreshadows that when Jesus, the sun of righteousness, would come, the relative darkness of the old dispensation would be dissipated. We now have the entire word of God, "a lamp shining in a dark place." The darkness of our minds and hearts can be regenerated by the Holy Spirit and given the light of the knowledge of God.

of one piece with it under the first pair of branches, a calyx of one piece with it under the next pair of branches, and a calyx of one piece with it under the last pair of branches—so for the six branches that go out of the lampstand. 36 Their calyxes and their branches shall be of one piece with it, the whole of it one hammered piece of pure gold. 37 You shall make the seven lamps for it; and the lamps shall be set up so as to give light on the space in front of it. 38 Its snuffers and trays shall be of pure gold. 39 It, and all these utensils, shall be made from a talent of pure gold. 40 And see that you make them according to the pattern for them, which is being shown you on the mountain.

E. *The tabernacle*

26 Moreover you shall make the tabernacle with ten curtains of fine twisted linen, and blue, purple, and crimson yarns; you shall make them with cherubim skillfully worked into them. 2 The length of each curtain shall be twenty-eight cubits, and the width of each curtain four cubits; all the curtains shall be of the same size. 3 Five curtains shall be joined to one another; and the other five curtains shall be joined to one another. 4 You shall make loops of blue on the edge of the outermost curtain in the first set; and likewise you shall make loops on the edge of the outermost curtain in the second set. 5 You shall make fifty loops on the one curtain, and you shall make fifty loops on the edge of the curtain that is in the second set; the loops shall be opposite one another. 6 You shall make fifty clasps of gold, and join the curtains to one another with the clasps, so that the tabernacle may be one whole.

7 You shall also make curtains of goats' hair for a tent over the tabernacle; you shall make eleven curtains. 8 The length of each curtain shall be thirty cubits, and the width of each curtain four cubits; the eleven curtains shall be of the same size. 9 You shall join five curtains by themselves, and six curtains by themselves, and the sixth curtain you shall double over at the front of the tent. 10 You shall make fifty loops on the edge of the curtain that is outermost in one set, and fifty loops on the edge of the curtain that is outermost in the second set.

11 You shall make fifty clasps of bronze, and put the clasps into the loops, and join the tent together, so that it may be one whole. 12 The part that remains of the curtains of the tent, the half curtain that remains, shall hang over the back of the tabernacle. 13 The cubit on the one side, and the cubit on the other side, of what remains in the length of the curtains of the tent, shall hang over the sides of the tabernacle, on this side and that side, to cover it. 14 You shall make for the tent a covering of tanned rams' skins and an outer covering of fine leather.*j*

15 You shall make upright frames of acacia wood for the tabernacle. 16 Ten cubits shall be the length of a frame, and a cubit and a half the width of each frame. 17 There shall be two pegs in each frame to fit the frames together; you shall make these for all the frames of the tabernacle. 18 You shall make the frames for the tabernacle: twenty frames for the south side; 19 and you shall make forty bases of silver under the twenty frames, two bases under the first frame for its two pegs, and two bases under the next frame for its two pegs; 20 and for the second side of the tabernacle, on the north side twenty frames, 21 and their forty bases of silver, two bases under the first frame, and two bases under the next frame; 22 and for the rear of the tabernacle westward you shall make six frames. 23 You shall make two frames for corners of the tabernacle in the rear; 24 they shall be

25.37
Ex 27.21;
Lev 24.3, 4

25.40
Ex 26.30;
Acts 7.44;
Heb 8.5

26.1
Ex 36.8

26.3
Ex 36.10

26.5
Ex 36.12

26.7
Ex 36.14

26.11
Ex 36.18

26.14
Ex 36.19

26.15
Ex 36.20

26.20
Ex 36.23

j Meaning of Heb uncertain

26.2 In antiquity, units of measure were determined by the use of the limbs of the human body. A cubit was the length of the forearm to the tip of the middle finger. Thus the people of that time had no absolute standard of measurement, for forearms differ in length. The cubit generally measured between seventeen and eighteen inches.

separate beneath, but joined at the top, at the first ring; it shall be the same with both of them; they shall form the two corners. 25 And so there shall be eight frames, with their bases of silver, sixteen bases; two bases under the first frame, and two bases under the next frame.

26 You shall make bars of acacia wood, five for the frames of the one side of the tabernacle, 27 and five bars for the frames of the other side of the tabernacle, and five bars for the frames of the side of the tabernacle at the rear westward. 28 The middle bar, halfway up the frames, shall pass through from end to end. 29 You shall overlay the frames with gold, and shall make their rings of gold to hold the bars; and you shall overlay the bars with gold. 30 Then you shall erect the tabernacle according to the plan for it that you were shown on the mountain.

F. *The curtain*

31 You shall make a curtain of blue, purple, and crimson yarns, and of fine twisted linen; it shall be made with cherubim skillfully worked into it. 32 You shall hang it on four pillars of acacia overlaid with gold, which have hooks of gold and rest on four bases of silver. 33 You shall hang the curtain under the clasps, and bring the ark of the covenant k in there, within the curtain; and the curtain shall separate for you the holy place from the most holy. 34 You shall put the mercy seat l on the ark of the covenant k in the most holy place. 35 You shall set the table outside the curtain, and the lampstand on the south side of the tabernacle opposite the table; and you shall put the table on the north side.

36 You shall make a screen for the entrance of the tent, of blue, purple, and crimson yarns, and of fine twisted linen, embroidered with needlework. 37 You shall make for the screen five pillars of acacia, and overlay them with gold; their hooks shall be of gold, and you shall cast five bases of bronze for them.

G. *The altar*

27 You shall make the altar of acacia wood, five cubits long and five cubits wide; the altar shall be square, and it shall be three cubits high. 2 You shall make horns for it on its four corners; its horns shall be of one piece with it, and you shall overlay it with bronze. 3 You shall make pots for it to receive its ashes, and shovels and basins and forks and firepans; you shall make all its utensils of bronze. 4 You shall also make for it a grating, a network of bronze; and on the net you shall make four bronze rings at its four corners. 5 You shall set it under the ledge of the altar so that the net shall extend halfway down the altar. 6 You shall make poles for the altar, poles of acacia wood, and overlay them with bronze; 7 the poles shall be put through the rings, so that the poles shall be on the two sides of the altar when it is carried. 8 You shall make it hollow, with boards. They shall be made just as you were shown on the mountain.

k Or *treaty*, or *testimony*; Heb *eduth*   l Or *the cover*

26.31 *a curtain of blue.* The curtain inside the tabernacle separated the most holy place from all people except for the high priest, who entered it only once a year on the day of atonement. When he did so, he would always sprinkle blood on the mercy seat. Sin separated mortals from God, and God would be satisfied only by the offering of blood through the priesthood.
26.33 The most holy place was the innermost chamber of the tent (and of the later temple). It was shielded by a veil through which no one but the high priest ever entered. It contained the ark (see notes on 25.10,17) and was the place where the glory of God rested. The altar of incense was just outside the veil, so that its smoke came through to cover the mercy seat. The most holy place typifies the sanctuary in heaven, which Christ entered once and for all to offer his own blood for the sins of mortals (Heb 9.23–26; note that the most holy place is called the Holy of Holies in Heb 9.3). When Christ hung on the cross, the veil of the temple was rent in two (Heb 10.20), showing that the gateway to heaven is now open for everyone through Christ's eternal priesthood.
27.1 Though only the priests were allowed to enter the tabernacle, a bronze altar was set up in the court before the tent. The people came to it with their sacrifices and gifts. This altar represents Christ; through his death on Calvary, atonement was made for our transgressions.

Margin refs: 26.25 Ex 36.30; 26.30 Ex 25.9, 40; 27.8; Acts 7.44; Heb 8.5; 26.31 Ex 36.35; Mt 27.51; Heb 9.3; 26.33 Ex 25.16; 40.21; Lev 16.2; Heb 9.2, 3; 26.34 Ex 25.21; 40.20; Heb 9.5; 26.35 Ex 40.22, 24; Heb 9.2; 26.36 Ex 36.37; 26.37 Ex 36.38; 27.1 Ex 38.1; Ezek 43.13; 27.3 Num 4.14; 27.8 Ex 25.40; 26.30

H. The court of the tabernacle

27.9
Ex 38.9

27.10
Ex 38.17

9 You shall make the court of the tabernacle. On the south side the court shall have hangings of fine twisted linen one hundred cubits long for that side; 10 its twenty pillars and their twenty bases shall be of bronze, but the hooks of the pillars and their bands shall be of silver. 11 Likewise for its length on the north side there shall be hangings one hundred cubits long, their pillars twenty and their bases twenty, of bronze, but the hooks of the pillars and their bands shall be of silver. 12 For the width of the court on the west side there shall be fifty cubits of hangings, with ten pillars and ten bases. 13 The width of the court on the front to the east shall be fifty

27.14
Ex 38.15

27.16
Ex 36.37

cubits. 14 There shall be fifteen cubits of hangings on the one side, with three pillars and three bases. 15 There shall be fifteen cubits of hangings on the other side, with three pillars and three bases. 16 For the gate of the court there shall be a screen twenty cubits long, of blue, purple, and crimson yarns, and of fine twisted linen, embroidered with needlework; it shall have four pillars and with them four bases. 17 All the pillars around the court shall be banded with silver; their hooks shall be of silver, and their bases of bronze. 18 The length of the court shall be one hundred cubits, the width fifty, and the height five cubits, with hangings of fine twisted linen and bases of bronze. 19 All the utensils of the tabernacle for every use, and all its pegs and all the pegs of the court, shall be of bronze.

I. The service and ritual

1. Oil for the lamp

27.20
Lev 24.2

27.21
Ex 26.31, 33;
30.8; 28.43;
Lev 3.17;
16.34

20 You shall further command the Israelites to bring you pure oil of beaten olives for the light, so that a lamp may be set up to burn regularly. 21 In the tent of meeting, outside the curtain that is before the covenant,[m] Aaron and his sons shall tend it from evening to morning before the LORD. It shall be a perpetual ordinance to be observed throughout their generations by the Israelites.

2. The vestments for the priesthood

28.1
Num 18.7;
Heb 5.1, 4
28.2
Ex 29.5, 29;
31.10
28.3
Ex 31.3, 6

28.4
see vv. 6, 15,
31, 39

28 Then bring near to you your brother Aaron, and his sons with him, from among the Israelites, to serve me as priests—Aaron and Aaron's sons, Nadab and Abihu, Eleazar and Ithamar. 2 You shall make sacred vestments for the glorious adornment of your brother Aaron. 3 And you shall speak to all who have ability, whom I have endowed with skill, that they make Aaron's vestments to consecrate him for my priesthood. 4 These are the vestments that they shall make: a breastpiece, an ephod, a robe, a checkered tunic, a turban, and a sash. When they make these sacred vestments for your brother Aaron and his sons to serve me as

m Or *treaty*, or *testimony*; Heb *eduth*

27.9 *the court of the tabernacle.* This court was one hundred cubits by fifty cubits. This was as far as the Israelites could enter; only the priests were allowed beyond it into the tabernacle itself. Not even kings could enter the tabernacle. David wrote glowingly of his love for the courts of God: "A day in your courts is better than a thousand elsewhere" (Ps 84.2,10). Only a few people could enter this court at one time. Since the coming of the gospel, people can pray everywhere and do not need to enter this sacred place. That is, the temporary, earthly court has given way to the eternal, heavenly court and is forever accessible to God's people by prayer.
27.20 A lamp without oil is like a well without water or clouds without rain. The priests were responsible to keep the lamp in the tabernacle lit and burning. So

it is the responsibility of the Christian ministers, by the preaching and exposition of the word of God, to bring light to believers and the knowledge of salvation to unbelievers, and to do so until Christ returns.
27.21 *tent of meeting,* clearly another designation for the tabernacle, the meeting place between God and his people.
28.1 Aaron, Israel's high priest, was symbolic of Christ, our high priest. See Heb 5.6–10; 7.1–28 for the relationship of Christ's priesthood according to the order of Melchizedek with that of Aaron.
28.3 *whom I have endowed with skill,* which is a gift from the Holy Spirit. Those filled with the Spirit of wisdom were skilled to make the vestments for the priests, so that even the robes would bring glory to God.

priests, 5 they shall use gold, blue, purple, and crimson yarns, and fine
linen.

6 They shall make the ephod of gold, of blue, purple, and crimson
yarns, and of fine twisted linen, skillfully worked. 7 It shall have two
shoulder-pieces attached to its two edges, so that it may be joined together.
8 The decorated band on it shall be of the same workmanship and materials, of gold, of blue, purple, and crimson yarns, and of fine twisted linen.
9 You shall take two onyx stones, and engrave on them the names of the
sons of Israel, 10 six of their names on the one stone, and the names of the
remaining six on the other stone, in the order of their birth. 11 As a
gem-cutter engraves signets, so you shall engrave the two stones with the
names of the sons of Israel; you shall mount them in settings of gold
filigree. 12 You shall set the two stones on the shoulder-pieces of the
ephod, as stones of remembrance for the sons of Israel; and Aaron shall
bear their names before the LORD on his two shoulders for remembrance.
13 You shall make settings of gold filigree, 14 and two chains of pure gold,
twisted like cords; and you shall attach the corded chains to the settings.

15 You shall make a breastpiece of judgment, in skilled work; you
shall make it in the style of the ephod; of gold, of blue and purple and
crimson yarns, and of fine twisted linen you shall make it. 16 It shall be
square and doubled, a span in length and a span in width. 17 You shall
set in it four rows of stones. A row of carnelian,ⁿ chrysolite, and emerald
shall be the first row; 18 and the second row a turquoise, a sapphire,ᵒ and
a moonstone; 19 and the third row a jacinth, an agate, and an amethyst;
20 and the fourth row a beryl, an onyx, and a jasper; they shall be set in
gold filigree. 21 There shall be twelve stones with names corresponding to
the names of the sons of Israel; they shall be like signets, each engraved
with its name, for the twelve tribes. 22 You shall make for the breastpiece
chains of pure gold, twisted like cords; 23 and you shall make for the
breastpiece two rings of gold, and put the two rings on the two edges of
the breastpiece. 24 You shall put the two cords of gold in the two rings at
the edges of the breastpiece; 25 the two ends of the two cords you shall
attach to the two settings, and so attach it in front to the shoulder-pieces
of the ephod. 26 You shall make two rings of gold, and put them at the
two ends of the breastpiece, on its inside edge next to the ephod. 27 You
shall make two rings of gold, and attach them in front to the lower part
of the two shoulder-pieces of the ephod, at its joining above the decorated
band of the ephod. 28 The breastpiece shall be bound by its rings to the
rings of the ephod with a blue cord, so that it may lie on the decorated
band of the ephod, and so that the breastpiece shall not come loose from
the ephod. 29 So Aaron shall bear the names of the sons of Israel in the
breastpiece of judgment on his heart when he goes into the holy place, for
a continual remembrance before the LORD. 30 In the breastpiece of judgment you shall put the Urim and the Thummim, and they shall be on
Aaron's heart when he goes in before the LORD; thus Aaron shall bear the
judgment of the Israelites on his heart before the LORD continually.

31 You shall make the robe of the ephod all of blue. 32 It shall have

28.6
Ex 39.2

28.9
1 Cor 9.22

28.12
v. 29;
Ex 39.7

28.15
Ex 39.8

28.17
Ex 39.10ff

28.21
Ex 39.14

28.24
Ex 39.17

28.26
Ex 39.17

28.29
v. 12

28.30
Lev 8.8;
Num 27.21

28.31
Ex 39.22

ⁿ The identity of several of these stones is uncertain   ᵒ Or lapis lazuli

28.6 The ephod, a priestly garment, was a close-
fitting outer vest, extending down to the hips. It was
adorned with onyx stones and a lovely woven girdle.
28.15 A breastpiece of judgment, a square piece of
richly wrought cloth, was folded and attached to the
ephod with twisted chains of gold. Only the high
priestly garment was so adorned.
28.30 Urim and Thummim signify "lights" and
"perfections." What they looked like is not known;
perhaps they were two gemstones located in the
breastplate of the high priest. They were specially

marked so that when cast to the ground, their mark-
ings and positions could be interpreted; by such deci-
pherment, the high priest could know God's answers
to questions involving national interest. In 1 Sam 14
Urim and Thummim were used by Saul to uncover
Jonathan's guilt. No mention is made of the use of the
Urim and Thummim subsequent to the kingship of
David. Ezra 2.63 and Neh 7.65 indicate that, after the
Babylonian exile, Israel had no priest with Urim and
Thummim.

an opening for the head in the middle of it, with a woven binding around the opening, like the opening in a coat of mail,^{p} so that it may not be torn. ^{33}On its lower hem you shall make pomegranates of blue, purple, and crimson yarns, all around the lower hem, with bells of gold between them all around—^{34}a golden bell and a pomegranate alternating all around the lower hem of the robe. ^{35}Aaron shall wear it when he ministers, and its sound shall be heard when he goes into the holy place before the Lord, and when he comes out, so that he may not die.

28.36
Ex 39.30, 31

28.38
v. 43;
Lev 10.17;
Num 18.1;
Heb 9.28;
1 Pet 2.24

^{36} You shall make a rosette of pure gold, and engrave on it, like the engraving of a signet, "Holy to the Lord." ^{37}You shall fasten it on the turban with a blue cord; it shall be on the front of the turban. ^{38}It shall be on Aaron's forehead, and Aaron shall take on himself any guilt incurred in the holy offering that the Israelites consecrate as their sacred donations; it shall always be on his forehead, in order that they may find favor before the Lord.

^{39} You shall make the checkered tunic of fine linen, and you shall make a turban of fine linen, and you shall make a sash embroidered with needlework.

28.40
v. 4;
Ex 39.27-29
28.41
Ex 29.7-9;
30.30;
Lev ch. 8;
Heb 7.28
28.42
Ex 39.28
28.43
Ex 20.26;
Lev 20.19,
20;
Ex 27.21;
Lev 17.7

^{40} For Aaron's sons you shall make tunics and sashes and headdresses; you shall make them for their glorious adornment. ^{41}You shall put them on your brother Aaron, and on his sons with him, and shall anoint them and ordain them and consecrate them, so that they may serve me as priests. ^{42}You shall make for them linen undergarments to cover their naked flesh; they shall reach from the hips to the thighs; ^{43}Aaron and his sons shall wear them when they go into the tent of meeting, or when they come near the altar to minister in the holy place; or they will bring guilt on themselves and die. This shall be a perpetual ordinance for him and for his descendants after him.

3. The ordination of the priests

a. The ordination ritual

29.1
Lev 8.2

29.2
Lev 6.19-23

29.4
Ex 40.12;
Heb 10.22
29.5
Ex 28.2, 8

29.6
Lev 8.9
29.7
Lev 8.12
29.8
Lev 8.13
29.9
Num 18.7;
Ex 28.41

29 Now this is what you shall do to them to consecrate them, so that they may serve me as priests. Take one young bull and two rams without blemish, ^{2}and unleavened bread, unleavened cakes mixed with oil, and unleavened wafers spread with oil. You shall make them of choice wheat flour. ^{3}You shall put them in one basket and bring them in the basket, and bring the bull and the two rams. ^{4}You shall bring Aaron and his sons to the entrance of the tent of meeting, and wash them with water. ^{5}Then you shall take the vestments, and put on Aaron the tunic and the robe of the ephod, and the ephod, and the breastpiece, and gird him with the decorated band of the ephod; ^{6}and you shall set the turban on his head, and put the holy diadem on the turban. ^{7}You shall take the anointing oil, and pour it on his head and anoint him. ^{8}Then you shall bring his sons, and put tunics on them, ^{9}and you shall gird them with sashes^q and tie headdresses on them; and the priesthood shall be theirs by a perpetual ordinance. You shall then ordain Aaron and his sons.

^{p} Meaning of Heb uncertain ^{q} Gk: Heb *sashes, Aaron and his sons*

28.34 *a golden bell.* The bells served notice to worshipers that the high priest Aaron was about God's business in the tent, where he could not be seen by the people. They could then offer their prayers outside while he was offering his inside. If Aaron attempted to minister without wearing the required vestments, death would overtake him.
28.36 *"Holy to the Lord."* By this sign Aaron must ever remember that God is holy and his priests must be holy in their minds and hearts. Aaron as high priest must "take on himself any guilt . . . in order that they

may find favor before the Lord" (v. 38). Aaron represents Christ—our mediator between God and sinners. Through him the demands of the law are met; those who trust in him are accepted by God. Having such a high priest, we can "approach the throne of grace with boldness, so that we may receive mercy and find grace to help in time of need" (Heb 4.16).
29.1ff This chapter contains the details about the ordination service for the priests, the sin and burnt offerings which were to be presented at the time of ordination, and various other matters.

b. The sin offering

10 You shall bring the bull in front of the tent of meeting. Aaron and his sons shall lay their hands on the head of the bull, 11 and you shall slaughter the bull before the LORD, at the entrance of the tent of meeting, 12 and shall take some of the blood of the bull and put it on the horns of the altar with your finger, and all the rest of the blood you shall pour out at the base of the altar. 13 You shall take all the fat that covers the entrails, and the appendage of the liver, and the two kidneys with the fat that is on them, and turn them into smoke on the altar. 14 But the flesh of the bull, and its skin, and its dung, you shall burn with fire outside the camp; it is a sin offering.

c. The burnt offering

15 Then you shall take one of the rams, and Aaron and his sons shall lay their hands on the head of the ram, 16 and you shall slaughter the ram, and shall take its blood and dash it against all sides of the altar. 17 Then you shall cut the ram into its parts, and wash its entrails and its legs, and put them with its parts and its head, 18 and turn the whole ram into smoke on the altar; it is a burnt offering to the LORD; it is a pleasing odor, an offering by fire to the LORD.

d. The sacrifice on ordination

19 You shall take the other ram; and Aaron and his sons shall lay their hands on the head of the ram, 20 and you shall slaughter the ram, and take some of its blood and put it on the lobe of Aaron's right ear and on the lobes of the right ears of his sons, and on the thumbs of their right hands, and on the big toes of their right feet, and dash the rest of the blood against all sides of the altar. 21 Then you shall take some of the blood that is on the altar, and some of the anointing oil, and sprinkle it on Aaron and his vestments and on his sons and his sons' vestments with him; then he and his vestments shall be holy, as well as his sons and his sons' vestments.

22 You shall also take the fat of the ram, the fat tail, the fat that covers the entrails, the appendage of the liver, the two kidneys with the fat that is on them, and the right thigh (for it is a ram of ordination), 23 and one loaf of bread, one cake of bread made with oil, and one wafer, out of the basket of unleavened bread that is before the LORD; 24 and you shall place all these on the palms of Aaron and on the palms of his sons, and raise them as an elevation offering before the LORD. 25 Then you shall take them from their hands, and turn them into smoke on the altar on top of the burnt offering of pleasing odor before the LORD; it is an offering by fire to the LORD.

26 You shall take the breast of the ram of Aaron's ordination and raise it as an elevation offering before the LORD; and it shall be your portion. 27 You shall consecrate the breast that was raised as an elevation offering and the thigh that was raised as an elevation offering from the ram of ordination, from that which belonged to Aaron and his sons. 28 These things shall be a perpetual ordinance for Aaron and his sons from the Israelites, for this is an offering; and it shall be an offering by the Israelites from their sacrifice of offerings of well-being, their offering to the LORD.

29 The sacred vestments of Aaron shall be passed on to his sons after him; they shall be anointed in them and ordained in them. 30 The son who is priest in his place shall wear them seven days, when he comes into the tent of meeting to minister in the holy place.

31 You shall take the ram of ordination, and boil its flesh in a holy place; 32 and Aaron and his sons shall eat the flesh of the ram and the bread that is in the basket, at the entrance of the tent of meeting. 33 They

29.10
Lev 1.4; 8.14

29.12
Lev 8.15;
Ex 27.2
29.13
Lev 3.3
29.14
Lev 4.11, 12,
21

29.18
Gen 8.21

29.21
Ex 30.25, 31;
v. 1;
Heb 9.22

29.23
Lev 8.26
29.24
Lev 7.30
29.25
Lev 8.28

29.26
Lev 8.29
29.27
Lev 7.31, 34;
Deut 18.3
29.28
Lev 10.15
29.29
Num 20.26,
28; 18.8
29.30
Num 20.28;
Lev 8.35;
9.1, 8
29.31
Lev 8.31
29.32
Mt 12.4
29.33
Lev 10.14,
15, 17; 22.10

29.14 *it is a sin offering.* See note on Gen 4.7.   29.18 *a burnt offering.* See note on Lev 1.3.

anointing of the body, and you shall make no other like it in composition; it is holy, and it shall be holy to you. 33 Whoever compounds any like it or whoever puts any of it on an unqualified person shall be cut off from the people."

8. *The incense*

34 The LORD said to Moses: Take sweet spices, stacte, and onycha, and galbanum, sweet spices with pure frankincense (an equal part of each), 35 and make an incense blended as by the perfumer, seasoned with salt, pure and holy; 36 and you shall beat some of it into powder, and put part of it before the covenant[v] in the tent of meeting where I shall meet with you; it shall be for you most holy. 37 When you make incense according to this composition, you shall not make it for yourselves; it shall be regarded by you as holy to the LORD. 38 Whoever makes any like it to use as perfume shall be cut off from the people.

J. *The appointment of the workers*

31 The LORD spoke to Moses: 2 See, I have called by name Bezalel son of Uri son of Hur, of the tribe of Judah: 3 and I have filled him with divine spirit,[w] with ability, intelligence, and knowledge in every kind of craft, 4 to devise artistic designs, to work in gold, silver, and bronze, 5 in cutting stones for setting, and in carving wood, in every kind of craft. 6 Moreover, I have appointed with him Oholiab son of Ahisamach, of the tribe of Dan; and I have given skill to all the skillful, so that they may make all that I have commanded you: 7 the tent of meeting, and the ark of the covenant,[v] and the mercy seat[x] that is on it, and all the furnishings of the tent, 8 the table and its utensils, and the pure lampstand with all its utensils, and the altar of incense, 9 and the altar of burnt offering with all its utensils, and the basin with its stand, 10 and the finely worked vestments, the holy vestments for the priest Aaron and the vestments of his sons, for their service as priests, 11 and the anointing oil and the fragrant incense for the holy place. They shall do just as I have commanded you.

K. *The observance of the sabbath*

12 The LORD said to Moses: 13 You yourself are to speak to the Israelites: "You shall keep my sabbaths, for this is a sign between me and you throughout your generations, given in order that you may know that I, the LORD, sanctify you. 14 You shall keep the sabbath, because it is holy for you; everyone who profanes it shall be put to death; whoever does any work on it shall be cut off from among the people. 15 Six days shall work be done, but the seventh day is a sabbath of solemn rest, holy to the LORD; whoever does any work on the sabbath day shall be put to death. 16 Therefore the Israelites shall keep the sabbath, observing the sabbath throughout their generations, as a perpetual covenant. 17 It is a sign forever between me and the people of Israel that in six days the LORD made heaven and earth, and on the seventh day he rested, and was refreshed."

v Or treaty, or testimony; Heb eduth   w Or with the spirit of God   x Or the cover

Marginal references

30.33 v. 38; Ex 12.15

30.35 v. 25
30.36 Ex 29.42; Lev 16.2; v. 32; Ex 29.37; Lev 2.3

31.2 Ex 35.30-36.1

31.6 Ex 35.34

31.7 Ex 36.8; 37.1, 6
31.8 Ex 37.10, 17

31.11 Ex 30.25, 31; 37.29; 30.34

31.13 Lev 19.3, 30; Ezek 20.12, 20

31.14 Ex 35.2; Num 15.32, 35
31.15 Ex 16.23; 20.9, 10

31.17 v. 13; Gen 2.2, 3

30.32 The holy oil was to be used only for the purposes ordained by God. No one else was ever to make it or use it in a common fashion, for its use was designed in perpetuity.

31.1ff. Again and again in the O.T. we see examples of saints of God who were filled with the Spirit of God. The Spirit of God filled Bezalel, giving him the gift of craftsmanship in order to construct the tabernacle, the residence of God among his people. According to v. 6, Aholiab and others were given the gift

of wisdom, so that they could make all that God had commanded in connection with this task.

31.13–17 The sabbath was established by God as a sign between himself and the people of Israel. The seventh day was set apart as a holy day for the worship of God when no work was to be performed except works of necessity and mercy. Sabbath-breaking was a capital offense. The sign of the sabbath related to the six days of creation followed by the seventh day when God rested.

priests, [5] they shall use gold, blue, purple, and crimson yarns, and fine linen.

6 They shall make the ephod of gold, of blue, purple, and crimson yarns, and of fine twisted linen, skillfully worked. [7] It shall have two shoulder-pieces attached to its two edges, so that it may be joined together. [8] The decorated band on it shall be of the same workmanship and materials, of gold, of blue, purple, and crimson yarns, and of fine twisted linen. [9] You shall take two onyx stones, and engrave on them the names of the sons of Israel, [10] six of their names on the one stone, and the names of the remaining six on the other stone, in the order of their birth. [11] As a gem-cutter engraves signets, so you shall engrave the two stones with the names of the sons of Israel; you shall mount them in settings of gold filigree. [12] You shall set the two stones on the shoulder-pieces of the ephod, as stones of remembrance for the sons of Israel; and Aaron shall bear their names before the LORD on his two shoulders for remembrance. [13] You shall make settings of gold filigree, [14] and two chains of pure gold, twisted like cords; and you shall attach the corded chains to the settings.

15 You shall make a breastpiece of judgment, in skilled work; you shall make it in the style of the ephod; of gold, of blue and purple and crimson yarns, and of fine twisted linen you shall make it. [16] It shall be square and doubled, a span in length and a span in width. [17] You shall set in it four rows of stones. A row of carnelian, [n] chrysolite, and emerald shall be the first row; [18] and the second row a turquoise, a sapphire, [o] and a moonstone; [19] and the third row a jacinth, an agate, and an amethyst; [20] and the fourth row a beryl, an onyx, and a jasper; they shall be set in gold filigree. [21] There shall be twelve stones with names corresponding to the names of the sons of Israel; they shall be like signets, each engraved with its name, for the twelve tribes. [22] You shall make for the breastpiece chains of pure gold, twisted like cords; [23] and you shall make for the breastpiece two rings of gold, and put the two rings on the two edges of the breastpiece. [24] You shall put the two cords of gold in the two rings at the edges of the breastpiece; [25] the two ends of the two cords you shall attach to the two settings, and so attach it in front to the shoulder-pieces of the ephod. [26] You shall make two rings of gold, and put them at the two ends of the breastpiece, on its inside edge next to the ephod. [27] You shall make two rings of gold, and attach them in front to the lower part of the two shoulder-pieces of the ephod, at its joining above the decorated band of the ephod. [28] The breastpiece shall be bound by its rings to the rings of the ephod with a blue cord, so that it may lie on the decorated band of the ephod, and so that the breastpiece shall not come loose from the ephod. [29] So Aaron shall bear the names of the sons of Israel in the breastpiece of judgment on his heart when he goes into the holy place, for a continual remembrance before the LORD. [30] In the breastpiece of judgment you shall put the Urim and the Thummim, and they shall be on Aaron's heart when he goes in before the LORD; thus Aaron shall bear the judgment of the Israelites on his heart before the LORD continually.

31 You shall make the robe of the ephod all of blue. [32] It shall have

Cross-references (right column):

28.6
Ex 39.2

28.9
1 Cor 9.22

28.12
v. 29;
Ex 39.7

28.15
Ex 39.8

28.17
Ex 39.10ff

28.21
Ex 39.14

28.24
Ex 39.17

28.26
Ex 39.17

28.29
v. 12

28.30
Lev 8.8;
Num 27.21

28.31
Ex 39.22

---

[n] The identity of several of these stones is uncertain   [o] Or *lapis lazuli*

28.6 The ephod, a priestly garment, was a close-fitting outer vest, extending down to the hips. It was adorned with onyx stones and a lovely woven girdle.
28.15 *A breastpiece of judgment*, a square piece of richly wrought cloth, was folded and attached to the ephod with twisted chains of gold. Only the high priestly garment was so adorned.
28.30 Urim and Thummim signify "lights" and "perfections." What they looked like is not known; perhaps they were two gemstones located in the breastplate of the high priest. They were specially marked so that when cast to the ground, their markings and positions could be interpreted; by such decipherment, the high priest could know God's answers to questions involving national interest. In 1 Sam 14 Urim and Thummim were used by Saul to uncover Jonathan's guilt. No mention is made of the use of the Urim and Thummim subsequent to the kingship of David. Ezra 2.63 and Neh 7.65 indicate that, after the Babylonian exile, Israel had no priest with Urim and Thummim.

an opening for the head in the middle of it, with a woven binding around the opening, like the opening in a coat of mail,*p* so that it may not be torn. 33 On its lower hem you shall make pomegranates of blue, purple, and crimson yarns, all around the lower hem, with bells of gold between them all around — 34 a golden bell and a pomegranate alternating all around the lower hem of the robe. 35 Aaron shall wear it when he ministers, and its sound shall be heard when he goes into the holy place before the LORD, and when he comes out, so that he may not die.

36 You shall make a rosette of pure gold, and engrave on it, like the engraving of a signet, "Holy to the LORD." 37 You shall fasten it on the turban with a blue cord; it shall be on the front of the turban. 38 It shall be on Aaron's forehead, and Aaron shall take on himself any guilt incurred in the holy offering that the Israelites consecrate as their sacred donations; it shall always be on his forehead, in order that they may find favor before the LORD.

39 You shall make the checkered tunic of fine linen, and you shall make a turban of fine linen, and you shall make a sash embroidered with needlework.

40 For Aaron's sons you shall make tunics and sashes and headdresses; you shall make them for their glorious adornment. 41 You shall put them on your brother Aaron, and on his sons with him, and shall anoint them and ordain them and consecrate them, so that they may serve me as priests. 42 You shall make for them linen undergarments to cover their naked flesh; they shall reach from the hips to the thighs; 43 Aaron and his sons shall wear them when they go into the tent of meeting, or when they come near the altar to minister in the holy place; or they will bring guilt on themselves and die. This shall be a perpetual ordinance for him and for his descendants after him.

3. The ordination of the priests

a. The ordination ritual

29 Now this is what you shall do to them to consecrate them, so that they may serve me as priests. Take one young bull and two rams without blemish, 2 and unleavened bread, unleavened cakes mixed with oil, and unleavened wafers spread with oil. You shall make them of choice wheat flour. 3 You shall put them in one basket and bring them in the basket, and bring the bull and the two rams. 4 You shall bring Aaron and his sons to the entrance of the tent of meeting, and wash them with water. 5 Then you shall take the vestments, and put on Aaron the tunic and the robe of the ephod, and the ephod, and the breastpiece, and gird him with the decorated band of the ephod; 6 and you shall set the turban on his head, and put the holy diadem on the turban. 7 You shall take the anointing oil, and pour it on his head and anoint him. 8 Then you shall bring his sons, and put tunics on them, 9 and you shall gird them with sashes*q* and tie headdresses on them; and the priesthood shall be theirs by a perpetual ordinance. You shall then ordain Aaron and his sons.

p Meaning of Heb uncertain   q Gk: Heb sashes, Aaron and his sons

Cross-references (margin):

28.36 Ex 39.30, 31
28.38 v. 43; Lev 10.17; Num 18.1; Heb 9.28; 1 Pet 2.24
28.40 v. 4; Ex 39.27-29
28.41 Ex 29.7-9; 30.30; Lev ch. 8; Heb 7.28
28.42 Ex 39.28
28.43 Ex 20.26; Lev 20.19, 20; Ex 27.21; Lev 17.7
29.1 Lev 8.2
29.2 Lev 6.19-23
29.4 Ex 40.12; Heb 10.22
29.5 Ex 28.2, 8
29.6 Lev 8.9
29.7 Lev 8.12
29.8 Lev 8.13
29.9 Num 18.7; Ex 28.41

28.34 *a golden bell.* The bells served notice to worshipers that the high priest Aaron was about God's business in the tent, where he could not be seen by the people. They could then offer their prayers outside while he was offering his inside. If Aaron attempted to minister without wearing the required vestments, death would overtake him.
28.36 *"Holy to the LORD."* By this sign Aaron must ever remember that God is holy and his priests must be holy in their minds and hearts. Aaron as high priest must "take on himself any guilt . . . in order that they

may find favor before the LORD" (v. 38). Aaron represents Christ — our mediator between God and sinners. Through him the demands of the law are met; those who trust in him are accepted by God. Having such a high priest, we can "approach the throne of grace with boldness, so that we may receive mercy and find grace to help in time of need" (Heb 4.16).
29.1ff This chapter contains the details about the ordination service for the priests, the sin and burnt offerings which were to be presented at the time of ordination, and various other matters.

b. The sin offering

10 You shall bring the bull in front of the tent of meeting. Aaron and his sons shall lay their hands on the head of the bull, 11 and you shall slaughter the bull before the Lord, at the entrance of the tent of meeting, 12 and shall take some of the blood of the bull and put it on the horns of the altar with your finger, and all the rest of the blood you shall pour out at the base of the altar. 13 You shall take all the fat that covers the entrails, and the appendage of the liver, and the two kidneys with the fat that is on them, and turn them into smoke on the altar. 14 But the flesh of the bull, and its skin, and its dung, you shall burn with fire outside the camp; it is a sin offering.

c. The burnt offering

15 Then you shall take one of the rams, and Aaron and his sons shall lay their hands on the head of the ram, 16 and you shall slaughter the ram, and shall take its blood and dash it against all sides of the altar. 17 Then you shall cut the ram into its parts, and wash its entrails and its legs, and put them with its parts and its head, 18 and turn the whole ram into smoke on the altar; it is a burnt offering to the Lord; it is a pleasing odor, an offering by fire to the Lord.

d. The sacrifice on ordination

19 You shall take the other ram; and Aaron and his sons shall lay their hands on the head of the ram, 20 and you shall slaughter the ram, and take some of its blood and put it on the lobe of Aaron's right ear and on the lobes of the right ears of his sons, and on the thumbs of their right hands, and on the big toes of their right feet, and dash the rest of the blood against all sides of the altar. 21 Then you shall take some of the blood that is on the altar, and some of the anointing oil, and sprinkle it on Aaron and his vestments and on his sons and his sons' vestments with him; then he and his vestments shall be holy, as well as his sons and his sons' vestments.

22 You shall also take the fat of the ram, the fat tail, the fat that covers the entrails, the appendage of the liver, the two kidneys with the fat that is on them, and the right thigh (for it is a ram of ordination), 23 and one loaf of bread, one cake of bread made with oil, and one wafer, out of the basket of unleavened bread that is before the Lord; 24 and you shall place all these on the palms of Aaron and on the palms of his sons, and raise them as an elevation offering before the Lord. 25 Then you shall take them from their hands, and turn them into smoke on the altar on top of the burnt offering of pleasing odor before the Lord; it is an offering by fire to the Lord.

26 You shall take the breast of the ram of Aaron's ordination and raise it as an elevation offering before the Lord; and it shall be your portion. 27 You shall consecrate the breast that was raised as an elevation offering and the thigh that was raised as an elevation offering from the ram of ordination, from that which belonged to Aaron and his sons. 28 These things shall be a perpetual ordinance for Aaron and his sons from the Israelites, for this is an offering; and it shall be an offering by the Israelites from their sacrifice of offerings of well-being, their offering to the Lord.

29 The sacred vestments of Aaron shall be passed on to his sons after him; they shall be anointed in them and ordained in them. 30 The son who is priest in his place shall wear them seven days, when he comes into the tent of meeting to minister in the holy place.

31 You shall take the ram of ordination, and boil its flesh in a holy place; 32 and Aaron and his sons shall eat the flesh of the ram and the bread that is in the basket, at the entrance of the tent of meeting. 33 They

---

29.14 *it is a sin offering.* See note on Gen 4.7.   29.18 *a burnt offering.* See note on Lev 1.3.

themselves shall eat the food by which atonement is made, to ordain and consecrate them, but no one else shall eat of them, because they are holy. 34 If any of the flesh for the ordination, or of the bread, remains until the morning, then you shall burn the remainder with fire; it shall not be eaten, because it is holy.

35 Thus you shall do to Aaron and to his sons, just as I have commanded you; through seven days you shall ordain them. 36 Also every day you shall offer a bull as a sin offering for atonement. Also you shall offer a sin offering for the altar, when you make atonement for it, and shall anoint it, to consecrate it. 37 Seven days you shall make atonement for the altar, and consecrate it, and the altar shall be most holy; whatever touches the altar shall become holy.

e. The altar of burnt offering

38 Now this is what you shall offer on the altar: two lambs a year old regularly each day. 39 One lamb you shall offer in the morning, and the other lamb you shall offer in the evening; 40 and with the first lamb one-tenth of a measure of choice flour mixed with one-fourth of a hin of beaten oil, and one-fourth of a hin of wine for a drink offering. 41 And the other lamb you shall offer in the evening, and shall offer with it a grain offering and its drink offering, as in the morning, for a pleasing odor, an offering by fire to the LORD. 42 It shall be a regular burnt offering throughout your generations at the entrance of the tent of meeting before the LORD, where I will meet with you, to speak to you there. 43 I will meet with the Israelites there, and it shall be sanctified by my glory; 44 I will consecrate the tent of meeting and the altar; Aaron also and his sons I will consecrate, to serve me as priests. 45 I will dwell among the Israelites, and I will be their God. 46 And they shall know that I am the LORD their God, who brought them out of the land of Egypt that I might dwell among them; I am the LORD their God.

4. The altar of incense

30 You shall make an altar on which to offer incense; you shall make it of acacia wood. 2 It shall be one cubit long, and one cubit wide; it shall be square, and shall be two cubits high; its horns shall be of one piece with it. 3 You shall overlay it with pure gold, its top, and its sides all around and its horns; and you shall make for it a molding of gold all around. 4 And you shall make two golden rings for it; under its molding on two opposite sides of it you shall make them, and they shall hold the poles with which to carry it. 5 You shall make the poles of acacia wood, and overlay them with gold. 6 You shall place it in front of the curtain that is above the ark of the covenant,ʳ in front of the mercy seatˢ that is over

Marginal references:
29.34 Lev 8.32
29.35 Lev 8.33
29.36 Heb 10.11; Ex 40.10
29.37 Ex 40.10; Mt 23.19
29.38 Num 28.3
29.42 Ex 30.8
29.43 1 Kings 8.11
29.44 Lev 21.15
29.45 Ex 25.8; Lev 26.12; Rev 21.3
29.46 Ex 20.2
30.1 Ex 37.25
30.6 Ex 25.21, 22

ʳ Or treaty, or testimony; Heb eduth   ˢ Or the cover

29.37 atonement for the altar. So holy is God that even the altar made by the hands of sinful people had to be first cleansed from defilement by an atonement. The altar and those who served were unfit to be employed by God until this was done. The altar was also sanctified (i.e., set apart for holy use) and was made so holy that the gifts placed on the altar would also be sanctified (see Mt 23.19). Jesus Christ is our altar; he sanctified himself for our sake so that we, in turn, might be sanctified by him and be made acceptable to God the Father.

29.44 God sanctified the altar, the tent, and the priesthood; he took possession of those things which were sanctified to him. When this was accomplished, a holy God said: "I will dwell among the Israelites, and I will be their God" (v. 45). Through all of this, God gave to the Israelites the outward evidences by which they would know that he would remain their God.

29.45 I will dwell among the Israelites. This promise was fulfilled when the shekinah glory of God filled the tent that had been sanctified so that it could be occupied by a holy God. So also should our bodies, which are indwelt by God the Spirit (1 Cor 6.19–20), be sanctified and kept in holiness.

30.1 The holy incense used on this altar was made of frankincense, salt, and equal parts of galbanum, stacte, and onycha; it was not to be used for nonreligious purposes. The burning of the incense was to honor God and represented prayer. In Rev 5.8 and 8.3,4 the burning incense or perfume is said to represent the prayers of the saints. In Lk 1.10 we read that it was at the hour of prayer and incense that the angel appeared to Zacharias to tell him that his prayer had been heard and that John would be conceived in the womb of his elderly wife, Elizabeth.

the covenant,[t] where I will meet with you. 7 Aaron shall offer fragrant incense on it; every morning when he dresses the lamps he shall offer it, 8 and when Aaron sets up the lamps in the evening, he shall offer it, a regular incense offering before the LORD throughout your generations. 9 You shall not offer unholy incense on it, or a burnt offering, or a grain offering; and you shall not pour a drink offering on it. 10 Once a year Aaron shall perform the rite of atonement on its horns. Throughout your generations he shall perform the atonement for it once a year with the blood of the atoning sin offering. It is most holy to the LORD.

5. The offerings for the tabernacle

11 The LORD spoke to Moses: 12 When you take a census of the Israelites to register them, at registration all of them shall give a ransom for their lives to the LORD, so that no plague may come upon them for being registered. 13 This is what each one who is registered shall give: half a shekel according to the shekel of the sanctuary (the shekel is twenty gerahs), half a shekel as an offering to the LORD. 14 Each one who is registered, from twenty years old and upward, shall give the LORD's offering. 15 The rich shall not give more, and the poor shall not give less, than the half shekel, when you bring this offering to the LORD to make atonement for your lives. 16 You shall take the atonement money from the Israelites and shall designate it for the service of the tent of meeting; before the LORD it will be a reminder to the Israelites of the ransom given for your lives.

6. The bronze basin

17 The LORD spoke to Moses: 18 You shall make a bronze basin with a bronze stand for washing. You shall put it between the tent of meeting and the altar, and you shall put water in it; 19 with the water[u] Aaron and his sons shall wash their hands and their feet. 20 When they go into the tent of meeting, or when they come near the altar to minister, to make an offering by fire to the LORD, they shall wash with water, so that they may not die. 21 They shall wash their hands and their feet, so that they may not die: it shall be a perpetual ordinance for them, for him and for his descendants throughout their generations.

7. The anointing oil

22 The LORD spoke to Moses: 23 Take the finest spices: of liquid myrrh five hundred shekels, and of sweet-smelling cinnamon half as much, that is, two hundred fifty, and two hundred fifty of aromatic cane, 24 and five hundred of cassia—measured by the sanctuary shekel—and a hin of olive oil; 25 and you shall make of these a sacred anointing oil blended as by the perfumer; it shall be a holy anointing oil. 26 With it you shall anoint the tent of meeting and the ark of the covenant,[t] 27 and the table and all its utensils, and the lampstand and its utensils, and the altar of incense, 28 and the altar of burnt offering with all its utensils, and the basin with its stand; 29 you shall consecrate them, so that they may be most holy; whatever touches them will become holy. 30 You shall anoint Aaron and his sons, and consecrate them, in order that they may serve me as priests. 31 You shall say to the Israelites, "This shall be my holy anointing oil throughout your generations. 32 It shall not be used in any ordinary

[t] Or treaty, or testimony; Heb eduth   [u] Heb it

Cross references: 30.7 vv. 34, 35; Ex 27.21. 30.9 Lev 10.1. 30.10 Lev 16.18. 30.12 Num 1.2, 5; 31.50; Mt 20.28; 2 Sam 24.15. 30.13 Mt 17.24. 30.15 Prov 22.2. 30.16 Ex 38.25; Num 16.40. 30.18 Ex 38.8; 40.7, 30. 30.19 Ex 40.31, 32. 30.21 Ex 28.43. 30.25 Ex 37.29; 40.9. 30.26 Lev 8.10. 30.29 Ex 29.37. 30.30 Lev 8.12, 30. 30.32 vv. 25, 37.

30.12 a ransom for their lives. See the note on 1 Pet 1.18.
30.18 The priests washed their hands and feet in the bronze basin before they entered the tent. Death by God was the penalty for failure to wash—this statute was imposed forever. When the Solomonic temple was built, a great molten sea replaced this basin. The ceremonial washing typifies that we need clean hands and a pure heart in order to come before the Lord God. Since we are all priests to the living God, we must take care to cleanse ourselves from all impurity before coming into his presence.

anointing of the body, and you shall make no other like it in composition; it is holy, and it shall be holy to you. 33 Whoever compounds any like it or whoever puts any of it on an unqualified person shall be cut off from the people."

8. The incense

34 The LORD said to Moses: Take sweet spices, stacte, and onycha, and galbanum, sweet spices with pure frankincense (an equal part of each), 35 and make an incense blended as by the perfumer, seasoned with salt, pure and holy; 36 and you shall beat some of it into powder, and put part of it before the covenant^v in the tent of meeting where I shall meet with you; it shall be for you most holy. 37 When you make incense according to this composition, you shall not make it for yourselves; it shall be regarded by you as holy to the LORD. 38 Whoever makes any like it to use as perfume shall be cut off from the people.

J. The appointment of the workers

31 The LORD spoke to Moses: 2 See, I have called by name Bezalel son of Uri son of Hur, of the tribe of Judah: 3 and I have filled him with divine spirit,^{w} with ability, intelligence, and knowledge in every kind of craft, 4 to devise artistic designs, to work in gold, silver, and bronze, 5 in cutting stones for setting, and in carving wood, in every kind of craft. 6 Moreover, I have appointed with him Oholiab son of Ahisamach, of the tribe of Dan; and I have given skill to all the skillful, so that they may make all that I have commanded you: 7 the tent of meeting, and the ark of the covenant,^{v} and the mercy seat^x that is on it, and all the furnishings of the tent, 8 the table and its utensils, and the pure lampstand with all its utensils, and the altar of incense, 9 and the altar of burnt offering with all its utensils, and the basin with its stand, 10 and the finely worked vestments, the holy vestments for the priest Aaron and the vestments of his sons, for their service as priests, 11 and the anointing oil and the fragrant incense for the holy place. They shall do just as I have commanded you.

K. The observance of the sabbath

12 The LORD said to Moses: 13 You yourself are to speak to the Israelites: "You shall keep my sabbaths, for this is a sign between me and you throughout your generations, given in order that you may know that I, the LORD, sanctify you. 14 You shall keep the sabbath, because it is holy for you; everyone who profanes it shall be put to death; whoever does any work on it shall be cut off from among the people. 15 Six days shall work be done, but the seventh day is a sabbath of solemn rest, holy to the LORD; whoever does any work on the sabbath day shall be put to death. 16 Therefore the Israelites shall keep the sabbath, observing the sabbath throughout their generations, as a perpetual covenant. 17 It is a sign forever between me and the people of Israel that in six days the LORD made heaven and earth, and on the seventh day he rested, and was refreshed."

v Or treaty, or testimony; Heb eduth w Or with the spirit of God x Or the cover

30.32 The holy oil was to be used only for the purposes ordained by God. No one else was ever to make it or use it in a common fashion, for its use was designed in perpetuity.
31.1ff. Again and again in the O.T. we see examples of saints of God who were filled with the Spirit of God. The Spirit of God filled Bezalel, giving him the gift of craftsmanship in order to construct the tabernacle, the residence of God among his people. According to v. 6, Aholiab and others were given the gift

of wisdom, so that they could make all that God had commanded in connection with this task.
31.13–17 The sabbath was established by God as a sign between himself and the people of Israel. The seventh day was set apart as a holy day for the worship of God when no work was to be performed except works of necessity and mercy. Sabbath-breaking was a capital offense. The sign of the sabbath related to the six days of creation followed by the seventh day when God rested.

18 When God[y] finished speaking with Moses on Mount Sinai, he gave him the two tablets of the covenant,[z] tablets of stone, written with the finger of God.

31.18
Ex 24.12;
32.15, 16;
34.1, 28

L. Israel breaks the covenant by idolatry

1. Aaron makes a golden calf

32 When the people saw that Moses delayed to come down from the mountain, the people gathered around Aaron, and said to him, "Come, make gods for us, who shall go before us; as for this Moses, the man who brought us up out of the land of Egypt, we do not know what has become of him." 2 Aaron said to them, "Take off the gold rings that are on the ears of your wives, your sons, and your daughters, and bring them to me." 3 So all the people took off the gold rings from their ears, and brought them to Aaron. 4 He took the gold from them, formed it in a mold,[a] and cast an image of a calf; and they said, "These are your gods, O Israel, who brought you up out of the land of Egypt!" 5 When Aaron saw this, he built an altar before it; and Aaron made proclamation and said, "Tomorrow shall be a festival to the LORD." 6 They rose early the next day, and offered burnt offerings and brought sacrifices of well-being; and the people sat down to eat and drink, and rose up to revel.

32.1
Ex 24.18;
Deut 9.9;
Acts 7.40;
Ex 13.21
32.2
Ex 35.22
32.4
Deut 9.16;
Acts 7.41
32.6
1 Cor 10.7

2. Moses intercedes for sinful Israel

7 The LORD said to Moses, "Go down at once! Your people, whom you brought up out of the land of Egypt, have acted perversely; 8 they have been quick to turn aside from the way that I commanded them; they have cast for themselves an image of a calf, and have worshiped it and sacrificed to it, and said, 'These are your gods, O Israel, who brought you up out of the land of Egypt!' " 9 The LORD said to Moses, "I have seen this people, how stiff-necked they are. 10 Now let me alone, so that my wrath may burn hot against them and I may consume them; and of you I will make a great nation."

11 But Moses implored the LORD his God, and said, "O LORD, why does your wrath burn hot against your people, whom you brought out of the land of Egypt with great power and with a mighty hand? 12 Why should the Egyptians say, 'It was with evil intent that he brought them out to kill them in the mountains, and to consume them from the face of the earth'? Turn from your fierce wrath; change your mind and do not bring disaster on your people. 13 Remember Abraham, Isaac, and Israel, your servants, how you swore to them by your own self, saying to them,

32.7
Deut 9.12;
Dan 9.24;
Gen 6.11, 12
32.8
Ex 20.3, 4,
23;
1 Kings 12.28
32.9
Num 14.11-20;
Ex 33.3, 5;
34.9;
Acts 7.31
32.10
Deut 9.14;
Num 14.12
32.11
Deut 9.18
32.12
Num 14.13;
Deut 9.28;
v. 14
32.13
Gen 22.16;
Heb 6.13;
Gen 12.7;
13.15;
Ex 13.5

y Heb he   z Or treaty, or testimony; Heb eduth   a Or fashioned it with a graving tool; Meaning of Heb uncertain

---

32.4 Aaron and the people of Israel were guilty of gross idolatry when they made the golden calf. God had worked many miracles on their behalf, yet at this moment they turned away from him. What they did was called a great sin (32.21,30,31), disobedience (Deut 9.12,16), and a forgetting of their Savior (Ps 106.21). The golden calf was intended to be a representation of God (or of the pedestal upon which God invisibly stood). Then Aaron announced a festival to the Lord which included gross immorality. God's anger resulted, for he had forbidden the use of any graven images. Any pictorial representation of God was and is included in the prohibition of the second commandment. This commandment also forbade bowing before any image of angel, person, bird, animal, or saint dwelling in heaven above. The Israelites knew this and were severely punished for their iniquity.
32.10 Israel's idolatry angered God. He threatened

to destroy all of them, then rebuild a great nation through Moses, the only survivor. Surely there must have been some among the Israelites who did not engage in this idolatry. Babies and young children, for example, would have known nothing about the evil deed and would have had no part in the creation of the golden calf. Yet sin and its consequences often have a national character, and the judgment of God overtakes even those who appear to be innocent. Moses could easily have assented to what God said; it would simply have lengthened the time span God needed to raise a nation to bring it into the land of promise. But Moses intervened in prayer for the guilty people and God repented of what he had intended to do. There would, however, come a time when the iniquity of Israel reached the point of no return, and the dispersion of the people to the ends of the earth would occur by way of divine judgment.

'I will multiply your descendants like the stars of heaven, and all this land that I have promised I will give to your descendants, and they shall inherit it forever.' " ¹⁴ And the Lord changed his mind about the disaster that he planned to bring on his people.

3. Moses destroys the calf and breaks the tablets of the law

15 Then Moses turned and went down from the mountain, carrying the two tablets of the covenant^b in his hands, tablets that were written on both sides, written on the front and on the back. ¹⁶ The tablets were the work of God, and the writing was the writing of God, engraved upon the tablets. ¹⁷ When Joshua heard the noise of the people as they shouted, he said to Moses, "There is a noise of war in the camp." ¹⁸ But he said,

"It is not the sound made by victors,
or the sound made by losers;
it is the sound of revelers that I hear."

¹⁹ As soon as he came near the camp and saw the calf and the dancing, Moses' anger burned hot, and he threw the tablets from his hands and broke them at the foot of the mountain. ²⁰ He took the calf that they had made, burned it with fire, ground it to powder, scattered it on the water, and made the Israelites drink it.

21 Moses said to Aaron, "What did this people do to you that you have brought so great a sin upon them?" ²² And Aaron said, "Do not let the anger of my lord burn hot; you know the people, that they are bent on evil. ²³ They said to me, 'Make us gods, who shall go before us; as for this Moses, the man who brought us up out of the land of Egypt, we do not know what has become of him.' ²⁴ So I said to them, 'Whoever has gold, take it off'; so they gave it to me, and I threw it into the fire, and out came this calf!"

4. The slaughter by the Levites

25 When Moses saw that the people were running wild (for Aaron had let them run wild, to the derision of their enemies), ²⁶ then Moses stood in the gate of the camp, and said, "Who is on the Lord's side? Come to me!" And all the sons of Levi gathered around him. ²⁷ He said to them, "Thus says the Lord, the God of Israel, 'Put your sword on your side, each of you! Go back and forth from gate to gate throughout the camp, and each of you kill your brother, your friend, and your neighbor.' " ²⁸ The sons of Levi did as Moses commanded, and about three thousand of the people fell on that day. ²⁹ Moses said, "Today you have ordained yourselves^c for the service of the Lord, each one at the cost of a son or a brother, and so have brought a blessing on yourselves this day."

5. The second intercession of Moses

30 On the next day Moses said to the people, "You have sinned a great sin. But now I will go up to the Lord; perhaps I can make atonement for your sin." ³¹ So Moses returned to the Lord and said, "Alas, this people

---

Cross-references (left margin):
32.14 — Ps 106.45
32.15 — Deut 9.15
32.16 — Ex 31.18
32.19 — Deut 9.16, 17
32.20 — Deut 9.21
32.21 — Gen 26.10
32.22 — Deut 9.24
32.23 — v. 1
32.24 — v. 4
32.27 — Num 25.7-13; Deut 33.9
32.30 — 1 Sam 12.20, 23; 2 Sam 16.12; Num 25.13
32.31 — Deut 9.18; Ex 20.23

---

b Or *treaty*, or *testimony*; Heb *eduth*   *c* Gk Vg Compare Tg: Heb *Today ordain yourselves*

32.22–24 There is overwhelming evidence that Aaron was responsible for the creation of the golden calf. He was the high priest and had been Moses' closest ally in the deliverance from Egypt. Now he blames the people for what happened and speciously declares that when they threw the gold in the fire, it spontaneously emerged as a golden calf. Aaron's high position did not keep him from compromise nor did he do anything significant to keep Israel from its idolatry.

32.31 Moses interceded for the people in connection with the construction and worship of the golden calf. God forgave them on behalf of their intercessor, but sin often has consequences which cause sinners pain long after they have been forgiven. Guilt and penalty will be set aside upon repentance and confession, but the temporal consequences may remain, as evidenced in Moses' own life. He smote the rock twice (Num 20.11) when told to speak to it. He was purged from his sin, but, as a temporal consequence of that sinful

has sinned a great sin; they have made for themselves gods of gold. 32 But now, if you will only forgive their sin — but if not, blot me out of the book that you have written." 33 But the LORD said to Moses, "Whoever has sinned against me I will blot out of my book. 34 But now go, lead the people to the place about which I have spoken to you; see, my angel shall go in front of you. Nevertheless, when the day comes for punishment, I will punish them for their sin."

35 Then the LORD sent a plague on the people, because they made the calf — the one that Aaron made.

6. The renewal of the covenant

a. God's command to leave

33 The LORD said to Moses, "Go, leave this place, you and the people whom you have brought up out of the land of Egypt, and go to the land of which I swore to Abraham, Isaac, and Jacob, saying, 'To your descendants I will give it.' 2 I will send an angel before you, and I will drive out the Canaanites, the Amorites, the Hittites, the Perizzites, the Hivites, and the Jebusites. 3 Go up to a land flowing with milk and honey; but I will not go up among you, or I would consume you on the way, for you are a stiff-necked people."

4 When the people heard these harsh words, they mourned, and no one put on ornaments. 5 For the LORD had said to Moses, "Say to the Israelites, 'You are a stiff-necked people; if for a single moment I should go up among you, I would consume you. So now take off your ornaments, and I will decide what to do to you.'" 6 Therefore the Israelites stripped themselves of their ornaments, from Mount Horeb onward.

b. The tent of meeting

7 Now Moses used to take the tent and pitch it outside the camp, far off from the camp; he called it the tent of meeting. And everyone who sought the LORD would go out to the tent of meeting, which was outside the camp. 8 Whenever Moses went out to the tent, all the people would rise and stand, each of them, at the entrance of their tents and watch Moses until he had gone into the tent. 9 When Moses entered the tent, the pillar of cloud would descend and stand at the entrance of the tent, and the LORD would speak with Moses. 10 When all the people saw the pillar of cloud standing at the entrance of the tent, all the people would rise and bow down, all of them, at the entrance of their tent. 11 Thus the LORD used to speak to Moses face to face, as one speaks to a friend. Then he would return to the camp; but his young assistant, Joshua son of Nun, would not leave the tent.

---

act, he was forbidden to enter the promised land.
33.3 *a stiff-necked people*, i.e., a stubborn people who have resisted the commandments of their God. Nothing in children is more offensive to their parents and teachers than stubbornness. This hardness of heart against God is repeated by the Israelites in the N.T. age, especially at the time when Stephen was stoned to death. In his sermon before his death he said, "You stiff-necked people, uncircumcised in heart and ears, you are forever opposing the Holy Spirit, just as your ancestors used to do" (Acts 7.51). Both in the O.T and N.T. Israel sinned against the Holy Spirit who had been wooing them and opening the door of salvation to them.
33.7 *the tent of meeting*. When Moses entered the tent, a cloudy pillar appeared, indicating the presence of God in communion with Moses. Inside the tent, Moses got his instructions directly from God. This was direct revelation, no longer necessary since, in the Bible, we have the completed revelation of God.
33.11 God spoke to Moses *face to face, as one speaks*

to a friend. This implies that God revealed himself to Moses more clearly than to others, manifesting a greater degree of his light to him. He talked, not as a king to a subject, but as a friend to a friend whom he loves and with whom he has sweet counsel. Whenever Moses went into the tent of meeting, he took Joshua with him. Sometimes Moses allowed Joshua to remain in the tent while he came out to address Israel. Joshua was of the tribe of Ephraim, whereas Moses was a Levite. When Joshua succeeded Moses, it clearly meant that, to God, one's gifts were more important than the tribe from which he came. *tent.* The tabernacle had not yet been constructed (see Ex 40). This tent was one set up by Moses to which he and Joshua came to meet with God and receive instructions. Thus there were two tents: the tabernacle, and a pre-tabernacle, in which God met and talked with the key leaders of Israel, Moses and Joshua. Joshua, who came from the tribe of Ephraim, did not ever enter *the* tent. Moses did, for he was commissioned by God to build it and to sanctify it.

32.32 Ps 69.28; Rom 9.3; Dan 12.1; Rev 3.5; 13.8; 17.8; 21.27
32.33 Deut 29.20; Ps 9.5
32.34 Ex 3.17; 23.20; Ps 99.8
32.35 vv. 4, 24, 28
33.1 Ex 32.7, 13; Gen 12.7
33.2 Ex 32.34; 23.27-31
33.3 Ex 3.8, 17; 32.9, 10
33.4 Num 14.1, 39
33.5 v. 3
33.7 Ex 29.42, 43; Deut 4.29
33.8 Num 16.27
33.9 Ex 25.22; 31.18; Ps 99.7
33.11 Num 12.8; Deut 34.10; Ex 24.13

c. The promise of God's presence

33.12
Ex 32.34;
v. 17;
Jer 1.5;
Jn 10.14, 15;
2 Tim 2.19
33.13
Ex 34.9;
Ps 25.4;
Deut 9.26, 29
33.14
Isa 63.9;
Josh 22.4
33.16
Num 14.14;
Ex 34.10

12 Moses said to the LORD, "See, you have said to me, 'Bring up this people'; but you have not let me know whom you will send with me. Yet you have said, 'I know you by name, and you have also found favor in my sight.' 13 Now if I have found favor in your sight, show me your ways, so that I may know you and find favor in your sight. Consider too that this nation is your people." 14 He said, "My presence will go with you, and I will give you rest." 15 And he said to him, "If your presence will not go, do not carry us up from here. 16 For how shall it be known that I have found favor in your sight, I and your people, unless you go with us? In this way, we shall be distinct, I and your people, from every people on the face of the earth."

d. Moses sees God's glory

33.17
v. 12
33.18
vv. 20, 23
33.19
Rom 9.15,
16, 18
33.20
Gen 32.20;
Isa 6.5

33.23
Jn 1.18

17 The LORD said to Moses, "I will do the very thing that you have asked; for you have found favor in my sight, and I know you by name." 18 Moses said, "Show me your glory, I pray." 19 And he said, "I will make all my goodness pass before you, and will proclaim before you the name, 'The LORD'; d and I will be gracious to whom I will be gracious, and will show mercy on whom I will show mercy. 20 But," he said, "you cannot see my face; for no one shall see me and live." 21 And the LORD continued, "See, there is a place by me where you shall stand on the rock; 22 and while my glory passes by I will put you in a cleft of the rock, and I will cover you with my hand until I have passed by; 23 then I will take away my hand, and you shall see my back; but my face shall not be seen."

e. The second tablets of stone: the covenant promise repeated

34.1
Ex 32.16, 19;
v. 28
34.2
Ex 19.20

34.3
Ex 19.12, 13,
21

34.5
Ex 33.19
34.6
Num 14.18;
Neh 9.17;
Ps 86.15;
103.8

34 The LORD said to Moses, "Cut two tablets of stone like the former ones, and I will write on the tablets the words that were on the former tablets, which you broke. 2 Be ready in the morning, and come up in the morning to Mount Sinai and present yourself there to me, on the top of the mountain. 3 No one shall come up with you, and do not let anyone be seen throughout all the mountain; and do not let flocks or herds graze in front of that mountain." 4 So Moses cut two tablets of stone like the former ones; and he rose early in the morning and went up on Mount Sinai, as the LORD had commanded him, and took in his hand the two tablets of stone. 5 The LORD descended in the cloud and stood with him there, and proclaimed the name, "The LORD." d 6 The LORD passed before him, and proclaimed,

"The LORD, the LORD,
a God merciful and gracious,
slow to anger,
and abounding in steadfast love and faithfulness,

34.7
Ex 20.6, 7;
Ps 103.3;
Dan 9.9;
Eph 4.32

7 keeping steadfast love for the thousandth generation, e
forgiving iniquity and transgression and sin,

d Heb YHWH; see note at 3.15   e Or for thousands

33.15 Moses was a great and gifted mortal. Yet he knew that it was the presence of God in his life that made the difference between victory and defeat. Thus he did not wish to proceed unless he had the assurance of the presence of God. To move forward without the presence of God can only lead to disappointment, difficulty, and even disaster.

33.18ff This account is given in human terms, for God is a spirit and is thus immaterial. The language is thus anthropomorphic when it speaks about "face," "hand," and "back." No human being can look on God in his glory and live. Moses was a redeemed sinner who had not yet been glorified. He could not behold God in his full plenitude. But all of the redeemed will see God in all of his glory in eternity,

when they will have been perfected.

33.19 *I . . . will proclaim before you the name, 'The LORD,'* i.e., "I will announce to you the meaning of my name." His name, "LORD," or "Yahweh," means, "I AM WHO I AM" (Ex 3.15; see note).

34.1 The ten commandments were engraved on the stone tablets by God himself. Ex 32.16 says, "the writing was the writing of God"; here, when the second set of the commandments was made, Moses quotes God as saying: "I will write on the tablets the words that were on the former tablets." This constitutes a miracle from the human perspective but something hardly extraordinary from the divine vantage point.

yet by no means clearing the guilty,
but visiting the iniquity of the parents
upon the children
and the children's children,
to the third and the fourth generation."
8 And Moses quickly bowed his head toward the earth, and worshiped.
9 He said, "If now I have found favor in your sight, O Lord, I pray, let
the Lord go with us. Although this is a stiff-necked people, pardon our
iniquity and our sin, and take us for your inheritance."
10   He said: I hereby make a covenant. Before all your people I will
perform marvels, such as have not been performed in all the earth or in
any nation; and all the people among whom you live shall see the work
of the LORD; for it is an awesome thing that I will do with you.

34.8	
Ex 4.31	
34.9	
Ex 33.3, 15, 16	
34.10	
Deut 5.2; 4.32	

f. Warning against heathen idolatry

11   Observe what I command you today. See, I will drive out before
you the Amorites, the Canaanites, the Hittites, the Perizzites, the Hivites,
and the Jebusites. 12 Take care not to make a covenant with the inhabitants of the land to which you are going, or it will become a snare among
you. 13 You shall tear down their altars, break their pillars, and cut down
their sacred poles.f 14 (for you shall worship no other god, because the
LORD, whose name is Jealous, is a jealous God). 15 You shall not make a
covenant with the inhabitants of the land, for when they prostitute themselves to their gods and sacrifice to their gods, someone among them will
invite you, and you will eat of the sacrifice. 16 And you will take wives
from among their daughters for your sons, and their daughters who
prostitute themselves to their gods will make your sons also prostitute
themselves to their gods.

34.11	
Deut 6.3; Ex 33.2	
34.12	
Ex 23.32, 33	
34.13	
Ex 23.24; 2 Kings 18.4	
34.14	
Ex 20.3, 5; Deut 4.24	
34.15	
Judg 2.17; Num 25.2; 1 Cor 8.4, 7, 10	
34.16	
Deut 7.3; Num 25.1	

g. Various commands

17   You shall not make cast idols.
18   You shall keep the festival of unleavened bread. Seven days you
shall eat unleavened bread, as I commanded you, at the time appointed
in the month of Abib; for in the month of Abib you came out from Egypt.
19   All that first opens the womb is mine, all your maleg livestock,
the firstborn of cow and sheep. 20 The firstborn of a donkey you shall
redeem with a lamb, or if you will not redeem it you shall break its neck.
All the firstborn of your sons you shall redeem.
No one shall appear before me empty-handed.
21   Six days you shall work, but on the seventh day you shall rest; even
in plowing time and in harvest time you shall rest. 22 You shall observe
the festival of weeks, the first fruits of wheat harvest, and the festival of
ingathering at the turn of the year. 23 Three times in the year all your males
shall appear before the LORD God, the God of Israel. 24 For I will cast out
nations before you, and enlarge your borders; no one shall covet your land
when you go up to appear before the LORD your God three times in the
year.
25   You shall not offer the blood of my sacrifice with leaven, and the
sacrifice of the festival of the passover shall not be left until the morning.

34.17	
Ex 32.8	
34.18	
Ex 12.2, 15-17; 13.4	
34.19	
Ex 13.2; 22.29	
34.20	
Ex 13.13; 23.15	
34.21	
Ex 20.9; Lk 13.14	
34.22	
Ex 23.16	
34.23	
Ex 23.14-17	
34.25	
Ex 23.18; 12.10	

f Heb Asherim   g Gk Theodotion Vg Tg: Meaning of Heb uncertain

34.13 their sacred poles. These were symbols of Asherim, the Canaanite mother-goddess, objects carved in
wood as statues of male and female genital organs.
They could be cut down, burned, or broken in pieces
(Ex 34.13; Deut 16.21; 2 Chr 34.4; Mic 5.14).
34.14 a jealous God. Here and in 20.5 God is called
jealous. "Jealous" can be understood two ways:
(1) envious, resentful, suspicious, or distrustful;
(2) careful in maintaining or guarding something pre-

cious, scrupulous, or alert. It is in the second sense
that God is jealous. He will maintain himself in his
holiness, justice, and integrity and will not allow anyone to malign or denigrate the divine person.
34.15 when they prostitute themselves, i.e., when they
commit adultery against me by worshiping other
gods. Idolatry is often referred to in the Bible as
spiritual adultery.

34.26
Ex 23.19

26 The best of the first fruits of your ground you shall bring to the house of the LORD your God.

You shall not boil a kid in its mother's milk.

34.27
Ex 17.14;
24.4
34.28
Ex 24.18;
31.18; 34.1;
Deut 4.13;
10.4

27 The LORD said to Moses: Write these words; in accordance with these words I have made a covenant with you and with Israel. 28 He was there with the LORD forty days and forty nights; he neither ate bread nor drank water. And he wrote on the tablets the words of the covenant, the ten commandments. [h]

h. Moses' shining face: the veil

34.29
Ex 32.15;
Mt 17.2;
2 Cor 3.7, 13

29 Moses came down from Mount Sinai. As he came down from the mountain with the two tablets of the covenant[i] in his hand, Moses did not know that the skin of his face shone because he had been talking with God. 30 When Aaron and all the Israelites saw Moses, the skin of his face was shining, and they were afraid to come near him. 31 But Moses called to them; and Aaron and all the leaders of the congregation returned to him, and Moses spoke with them. 32 Afterward all the Israelites came near, and he gave them in commandment all that the LORD had spoken with him on Mount Sinai. 33 When Moses had finished speaking with them, he put a veil on his face; 34 but whenever Moses went in before the LORD to speak with him, he would take the veil off, until he came out; and when he came out, and told the Israelites what he had been commanded, 35 the Israelites would see the face of Moses, that the skin of his face was shining; and Moses would put the veil on his face again, until he went in to speak with him.

34.32
Ex 24.3
34.33
2 Cor 3.13
34.34
2 Cor 3.16

M. The building of the tabernacle

1. The gathering of the materials

35.1
Ex 34.32

35 Moses assembled all the congregation of the Israelites and said to them: These are the things that the LORD has commanded you to do:

35.2
Ex 31.15

2 Six days shall work be done, but on the seventh day you shall have a holy sabbath of solemn rest to the LORD; whoever does any work on it

35.3
Ex 16.23

shall be put to death. 3 You shall kindle no fire in all your dwellings on the sabbath day.

35.4
Ex 25.1-9

4 Moses said to all the congregation of the Israelites: This is the thing that the LORD has commanded: 5 Take from among you an offering to the LORD; let whoever is of a generous heart bring the LORD's offering: gold, silver, and bronze; 6 blue, purple, and crimson yarns, and fine linen; goats' hair, 7 tanned rams' skins, and fine leather;[j] acacia wood, 8 oil for the light, spices for the anointing oil and for the fragrant incense, 9 and onyx stones and gems to be set in the ephod and the breastpiece.

35.10
Ex 31.6
35.11
Ex 26.1ff
35.13
Ex 25.23, 30;
Lev 24.5, 6
35.15
Ex 30.1

10 All who are skillful among you shall come and make all that the LORD has commanded: the tabernacle, 11 its tent and its covering, its clasps and its frames, its bars, its pillars, and its bases; 12 the ark with its poles, the mercy seat,[k] and the curtain for the screen; 13 the table with its poles and all its utensils, and the bread of the Presence; 14 the lampstand also for the light, with its utensils and its lamps, and the oil for the light; 15 and the altar of incense, with its poles, and the anointing oil and the fragrant incense, and the screen for the entrance, the entrance of the tabernacle; 16 the altar of burnt offering, with its grating of bronze, its

h Heb words i Or treaty, or testimony; Heb eduth j Meaning of Heb uncertain k Or the cover

34.27 *Write these words*, i.e., the preceding laws in 34.12–26.
34.33 The glory of God was reflected on the face of Moses whenever he left the tent of meeting. Israel then beheld Moses' face and knew he had been with God. But now, when he had finished speaking to the

people under God's authority, he put a veil over his face, removing it only when he re-entered the tent of meeting. The veil indicated his humility and modesty. In a real sense, the glory of God should always be manifested in the faces of God's people (see 2 Cor 3.18).

poles, and all its utensils, the basin with its stand; 17 the hangings of the
court, its pillars and its bases, and the screen for the gate of the court;
18 the pegs of the tabernacle and the pegs of the court, and their cords;
19 the finely worked vestments for ministering in the holy place, the holy
vestments for the priest Aaron, and the vestments of his sons, for their
service as priests.

20 Then all the congregation of the Israelites withdrew from the
presence of Moses. 21 And they came, everyone whose heart was stirred,
and everyone whose spirit was willing, and brought the LORD's offering
to be used for the tent of meeting, and for all its service, and for the sacred
vestments. 22 So they came, both men and women; all who were of a
willing heart brought brooches and earrings and signet rings and pendants, all sorts of gold objects, everyone bringing an offering of gold to
the LORD. 23 And everyone who possessed blue or purple or crimson yarn
or fine linen or goats' hair or tanned rams' skins or fine leather,*l* brought
them. 24 Everyone who could make an offering of silver or bronze brought
it as the LORD's offering; and everyone who possessed acacia wood of any
use in the work, brought it. 25 All the skillful women spun with their
hands, and brought what they had spun in blue and purple and crimson
yarns and fine linen; 26 all the women whose hearts moved them to use
their skill spun the goats' hair. 27 And the leaders brought onyx stones and
gems to be set in the ephod and the breastpiece, 28 and spices and oil for
the light, and for the anointing oil, and for the fragrant incense. 29 All the
Israelite men and women whose hearts made them willing to bring anything for the work that the LORD had commanded by Moses to be done,
brought it as a freewill offering to the LORD.

2. The workers gathered

30 Then Moses said to the Israelites: See, the LORD has called by name
Bezalel son of Uri son of Hur, of the tribe of Judah; 31 he has filled him
with divine spirit,*m* with skill, intelligence, and knowledge in every kind
of craft, 32 to devise artistic designs, to work in gold, silver, and bronze,
33 in cutting stones for setting, and in carving wood, in every kind of craft.
34 And he has inspired him to teach, both him and Oholiab son of Ahisamach, of the tribe of Dan. 35 He has filled them with skill to do every kind
of work done by an artisan or by a designer or by an embroiderer in blue,
purple, and crimson yarns, and in fine linen, or by a weaver — by any sort
of artisan or skilled designer.

36 Bezalel and Oholiab and every skillful one to whom the LORD has
given skill and understanding to know how to do any work in the
construction of the sanctuary shall work in accordance with all that the
LORD has commanded.

2 Moses then called Bezalel and Oholiab and every skillful one to
whom the LORD had given skill, everyone whose heart was stirred to come
to do the work; 3 and they received from Moses all the freewill offerings
that the Israelites had brought for doing the work on the sanctuary. They
still kept bringing him freewill offerings every morning, 4 so that all the
artisans who were doing every sort of task on the sanctuary came, each
from the task being performed, 5 and said to Moses, "The people are

l Meaning of Heb uncertain   *m* Or *the spirit of God*

35.19
Ex 31.10

35.21
Ex 25.2

35.23
1 Chr 29.8

35.25
Ex 28.3

35.27
1 Chr 29.6;
Ezra 2.68
35.28
Ex 30.23
35.29
v. 21

35.30
Ex 31.1-6

35.35
v. 31

36.1
Ex 25.8

36.2
Ex 35.21, 26;
1 Chr 29.5
36.3
Ex 35.27

36.5
2 Chr 24.14;
31.6-10;
2 Cor 8.23

35.29 *a freewill offering.* God wants our offerings to
come from the heart and be given freely and generously. He could have laid a tax on the Israelites for the
cost of constructing the tabernacle. Instead, they were
asked to give as they chose, out of glad hearts. The
work of the church today should not depend on bazaars, stipends for services performed, or other such
material devices. God's people should be glad to give
to the church, in accord with the principle of the tithe

in a non-legalistic sense.
35.31 The Spirit of God filled Bezalel and gave him
certain gifts which enabled him to construct the tabernacle for God's glory. Those gifts included wisdom,
understanding, knowledge, and the ability to construct the tent. He used these gifts in the religious
work of making the tent. For more on the Spirit's
gifts, see note on Rom 12.6.

bringing much more than enough for doing the work that the LORD has commanded us to do." 6 So Moses gave command, and word was proclaimed throughout the camp: "No man or woman is to make anything else as an offering for the sanctuary." So the people were restrained from bringing; 7 for what they had already brought was more than enough to do all the work.

3. The curtain and coverings made

36.8
Ex 26.1-14

8 All those with skill among the workers made the tabernacle with ten curtains; they were made of fine twisted linen, and blue, purple, and crimson yarns, with cherubim skillfully worked into them. 9 The length of each curtain was twenty-eight cubits, and the width of each curtain four cubits; all the curtains were of the same size.

10 He joined five curtains to one another, and the other five curtains he joined to one another. 11 He made loops of blue on the edge of the outermost curtain of the first set; likewise he made them on the edge of

36.12
Ex 26.5

the outermost curtain of the second set; 12 he made fifty loops on the one curtain, and he made fifty loops on the edge of the curtain that was in the second set; the loops were opposite one another. 13 And he made fifty clasps of gold, and joined the curtains one to the other with clasps; so the tabernacle was one whole.

36.14
Ex 26.7

14 He also made curtains of goats' hair for a tent over the tabernacle; he made eleven curtains. 15 The length of each curtain was thirty cubits, and the width of each curtain four cubits; the eleven curtains were of the same size. 16 He joined five curtains by themselves, and six curtains by themselves. 17 He made fifty loops on the edge of the outermost curtain of the one set, and fifty loops on the edge of the other connecting curtain.

36.19
Ex 26.14

18 He made fifty clasps of bronze to join the tent together so that it might be one whole. 19 And he made for the tent a covering of tanned rams' skins and an outer covering of fine leather.ⁿ

4. The framework of the tabernacle constructed

36.20
Ex 26.15-29

20 Then he made the upright frames for the tabernacle of acacia wood. 21 Ten cubits was the length of a frame, and a cubit and a half the width of each frame. 22 Each frame had two pegs for fitting together; he did this for all the frames of the tabernacle. 23 The frames for the tabernacle he

36.24
Ex 26.21

made in this way: twenty frames for the south side; 24 and he made forty bases of silver under the twenty frames, two bases under the first frame for its two pegs, and two bases under the next frame for its two pegs. 25 For the second side of the tabernacle, on the north side, he made twenty frames 26 and their forty bases of silver, two under the first frame

36.27
Ex 26.22

and two bases under the next frame. 27 For the rear of the tabernacle westward he made six frames. 28 He made two frames for corners of the tabernacle in the rear. 29 They were separate beneath, but joined at the top, at the first ring; he made two of them in this way, for the two corners. 30 There were eight frames with their bases of silver: sixteen bases, under every frame two bases.

36.31
Ex 26.26

31 He made bars of acacia wood, five for the frames of the one side of the tabernacle, 32 and five bars for the frames of the other side of the tabernacle, and five bars for the frames of the tabernacle at the rear westward. 33 He made the middle bar to pass through from end to end

---

ⁿ Meaning of Heb uncertain

36.6 *the people were restrained from bringing.* When Moses had received all that was needed for the construction of the tent, he stopped asking for or receiving additional monies. Had he been a materialist, he might have kept on taking more, storing them for future needs or using them for his own personal desires. Moses' pattern here calls into question the propriety of establishing endowments as a means of ensuring church monies.

halfway up the frames. 34 And he overlaid the frames with gold, and made
rings of gold for them to hold the bars, and overlaid the bars with gold.

5. *The making of the curtain*

35   He made the curtain of blue, purple, and crimson yarns, and fine
twisted linen, with cherubim skillfully worked into it. 36 For it he made
four pillars of acacia, and overlaid them with gold; their hooks were of
gold, and he cast for them four bases of silver. 37 He also made a screen
for the entrance to the tent, of blue, purple, and crimson yarns, and fine
twisted linen, embroidered with needlework; 38 and its five pillars with
their hooks. He overlaid their capitals and their bases with gold, but their
five bases were of bronze.

36.35
Ex 26.31-37

6. *The construction of the ark*

37 Bezalel made the ark of acacia wood; it was two and a half cubits
long, a cubit and a half wide, and a cubit and a half high. 2 He
overlaid it with pure gold inside and outside, and made a molding of gold
around it. 3 He cast for it four rings of gold for its four feet, two rings on
its one side and two rings on its other side. 4 He made poles of acacia wood,
and overlaid them with gold, 5 and put the poles into the rings on the sides
of the ark, to carry the ark. 6 He made a mercy seat*o* of pure gold; two
cubits and a half was its length, and a cubit and a half its width. 7 He made
two cherubim of hammered gold; at the two ends of the mercy seat*p* he
made them, 8 one cherub at the one end, and one cherub at the other end;
of one piece with the mercy seat*p* he made the cherubim at its two ends.
9 The cherubim spread out their wings above, overshadowing the mercy
seat*p* with their wings. They faced one another; the faces of the cherubim
were turned toward the mercy seat.*p*

37.1
Ex 25.10-20

37.3
Ex 25.12

37.6
Ex 25.17

7. *The building of the table*

10   He also made the table of acacia wood, two cubits long, one cubit
wide, and a cubit and a half high. 11 He overlaid it with pure gold, and
made a molding of gold around it. 12 He made around it a rim a handbreadth wide, and made a molding of gold around the rim. 13 He cast for
it four rings of gold, and fastened the rings to the four corners at its four
legs. 14 The rings that held the poles used for carrying the table were close
to the rim. 15 He made the poles of acacia wood to carry the table, and
overlaid them with gold. 16 And he made the vessels of pure gold that were
to be on the table, its plates and dishes for incense, and its bowls and
flagons with which to pour drink offerings.

37.16
Ex 25.29

8. *The making of the lampstand*

17   He also made the lampstand of pure gold. The base and the shaft
of the lampstand were made of hammered work; its cups, its calyxes, and
its petals were of one piece with it. 18 There were six branches going out
of its sides, three branches of the lampstand out of one side of it and three
branches of the lampstand out of the other side of it; 19 three cups shaped
like almond blossoms, each with calyx and petals, on one branch, and
three cups shaped like almond blossoms, each with calyx and petals, on
the other branch — so for the six branches going out of the lampstand.
20 On the lampstand itself there were four cups shaped like almond blossoms, each with its calyxes and petals. 21 There was a calyx of one piece
with it under the first pair of branches, a calyx of one piece with it under
the next pair of branches, and a calyx of one piece with it under the last

37.17
Ex 25.31-39

37.19
Ex 25.33

37.21
Ex 25.35

o Or *a cover*   *p* Or *the cover*

36.35 *curtain,* i.e., the inner curtain.   **37.7** *cherubim.* See note on Ezek 10.1.

pair of branches. 22 Their calyxes and their branches were of one piece with it, the whole of it one hammered piece of pure gold. 23 He made its seven lamps and its snuffers and its trays of pure gold. 24 He made it and all its utensils of a talent of pure gold.

9. The construction of the altar of incense

37.25
Ex 30.1-5

25 He made the altar of incense of acacia wood, one cubit long, and one cubit wide; it was square, and was two cubits high; its horns were of one piece with it. 26 He overlaid it with pure gold, its top, and its sides all around, and its horns; and he made for it a molding of gold all around, 27 and made two golden rings for it under its molding, on two opposite sides of it, to hold the poles with which to carry it. 28 And he made the poles of acacia wood, and overlaid them with gold.

10. The oil and incense

37.29
Ex 30.23, 34

29 He made the holy anointing oil also, and the pure fragrant incense, blended as by the perfumer.

11. The making of the altar of burnt offering

38.1
Ex 27.1-8

38 He made the altar of burnt offering also of acacia wood; it was five cubits long, and five cubits wide; it was square, and three cubits high. 2 He made horns for it on its four corners; its horns were of one piece with it, and he overlaid it with bronze. 3 He made all the utensils of the altar, the pots, the shovels, the basins, the forks, and the firepans: all its utensils he made of bronze. 4 He made for the altar a grating, a network of bronze, under its ledge, extending halfway down. 5 He cast four rings on the four corners of the bronze grating to hold the poles; 6 he made the poles of acacia wood, and overlaid them with bronze. 7 And he put the poles through the rings on the sides of the altar, to carry it with them; he made it hollow, with boards.

38.8
Ex 30.18

8 He made the basin of bronze with its stand of bronze, from the mirrors of the women who served at the entrance to the tent of meeting.

12. The construction of the court

38.9
Ex 27.9-19

9 He made the court; for the south side the hangings of the court were of fine twisted linen, one hundred cubits long; 10 its twenty pillars and their twenty bases were of bronze, but the hooks of the pillars and their bands were of silver. 11 For the north side there were hangings one hundred cubits long; its twenty pillars and their twenty bases were of bronze, but the hooks of the pillars and their bands were of silver. 12 For the west side there were hangings fifty cubits long, with ten pillars and ten bases; the hooks of the pillars and their bands were of silver. 13 And for the front to the east, fifty cubits. 14 The hangings for one side of the gate were fifteen cubits, with three pillars and three bases. 15 And so for the other side; on each side of the gate of the court were hangings of fifteen cubits, with three pillars and three bases. 16 All the hangings around the court were of fine twisted linen. 17 The bases for the pillars were of bronze, but the hooks of the pillars and their bands were of silver; the overlaying of their capitals was also of silver, and all the pillars of the court were banded with silver. 18 The screen for the entrance to the court was embroidered with needlework in blue, purple, and crimson yarns and fine twisted linen. It was twenty cubits long and, along the width of it, five cubits high, corresponding to the hangings of the court. 19 There were four pillars; their four bases were of bronze, their hooks of silver, and the overlaying of their capitals and their bands of silver. 20 All the pegs for the tabernacle and for the court all around were of bronze.

38.11
Ex 27.11

38.14
Ex 27.14

38.18
Ex 27.16

13. *The sum of the metals used*

21 These are the records of the tabernacle, the tabernacle of the covenant,*q* which were drawn up at the commandment of Moses, the work of the Levites being under the direction of Ithamar son of the priest Aaron. 22 Bezalel son of Uri son of Hur, of the tribe of Judah, made all that the LORD commanded Moses; 23 and with him was Oholiab son of Ahisamach, of the tribe of Dan, engraver, designer, and embroiderer in blue, purple, and crimson yarns, and in fine linen.

24 All the gold that was used for the work, in all the construction of the sanctuary, the gold from the offering, was twenty-nine talents and seven hundred thirty shekels, measured by the sanctuary shekel. 25 The silver from those of the congregation who were counted was one hundred talents and one thousand seven hundred seventy-five shekels, measured by the sanctuary shekel; 26 a beka a head (that is, half a shekel, measured by the sanctuary shekel), for everyone who was counted in the census, from twenty years old and upward, for six hundred three thousand, five hundred fifty men. 27 The hundred talents of silver were for casting the bases of the sanctuary, and the bases of the curtain; one hundred bases for the hundred talents, a talent for a base. 28 Of the thousand seven hundred seventy-five shekels he made hooks for the pillars, and overlaid their capitals and made bands for them. 29 The bronze that was contributed was seventy talents, and two thousand four hundred shekels; 30 with it he made the bases for the entrance of the tent of meeting, the bronze altar and the bronze grating for it and all the utensils of the altar, 31 the bases all around the court, and the bases of the gate of the court, all the pegs of the tabernacle, and all the pegs around the court.

14. *The making of the vestments of the priesthood*

a. *The materials*

39 Of the blue, purple, and crimson yarns they made finely worked vestments, for ministering in the holy place; they made the sacred vestments for Aaron; as the LORD had commanded Moses.

b. *The making of the ephod*

2 He made the ephod of gold, of blue, purple, and crimson yarns, and of fine twisted linen. 3 Gold leaf was hammered out and cut into threads to work into the blue, purple, and crimson yarns and into the fine twisted linen, in skilled design. 4 They made for the ephod shoulder-pieces, joined to it at its two edges. 5 The decorated band on it was of the same materials and workmanship, of gold, of blue, purple, and crimson yarns, and of fine twisted linen; as the LORD had commanded Moses.

6 The onyx stones were prepared, enclosed in settings of gold filigree and engraved like the engravings of a signet, according to the names of the sons of Israel. 7 He set them on the shoulder-pieces of the ephod, to be stones of remembrance for the sons of Israel; as the LORD had commanded Moses.

c. *The making of the breastpiece*

8 He made the breastpiece, in skilled work, like the work of the ephod, of gold, of blue, purple, and crimson yarns, and of fine twisted linen. 9 It was square; the breastpiece was made double, a span in length and a span in width when doubled. 10 They set in it four rows of stones. A row of carnelian,*r* chrysolite, and emerald was the first row; 11 and the

q Or *treaty,* or *testimony;* Heb *eduth*   *r* The identification of several of these stones is uncertain

38.21 Num 4.28, 33
38.22 Ex 31.2, 6
38.24 Ex 30.13
38.25 Ex 30.11-16
38.26 Ex 30.13, 15; Num 1.46
38.27 Ex 26.19, 21, 25, 32
39.1 Ex 35.23; 28.4
39.2 Ex 28.6-12
39.6 Ex 28.9
39.7 Ex 28.12
39.8 Ex 28.15-28
39.11 Ex 28.18

38.24 The value of the gold given by God's people was worth approximately ten million dollars, according to today's currency.

38.25 The value of the silver probably was worth in excess of one million dollars, according to today's currency.

second row, a turquoise, a sapphire,ˢ and a moonstone; 12 and the third row, a jacinth, an agate, and an amethyst; 13 and the fourth row, a beryl, an onyx, and a jasper; they were enclosed in settings of gold filigree.

39.14
Ex 28.21
14 There were twelve stones with names corresponding to the names of the sons of Israel; they were like signets, each engraved with its name, for the twelve tribes. 15 They made on the breastpiece chains of pure gold, twisted

39.16
Ex 28.24
like cords; 16 and they made two settings of gold filigree and two gold rings, and put the two rings on the two edges of the breastpiece; 17 and they put the two cords of gold in the two rings at the edges of the breastpiece. 18 Two ends of the two cords they had attached to the two settings of filigree; in this way they attached it in front to the shoulder-

39.19
Ex 28.26
pieces of the ephod. 19 Then they made two rings of gold, and put them at the two ends of the breastpiece, on its inside edge next to the ephod. 20 They made two rings of gold, and attached them in front to the lower part of the two shoulder-pieces of the ephod, at its joining above the decorated band of the ephod. 21 They bound the breastpiece by its rings to the rings of the ephod with a blue cord, so that it should lie on the decorated band of the ephod, and that the breastpiece should not come loose from the ephod; as the Lᴏʀᴅ had commanded Moses.

d. The robe of the ephod

39.22
Ex 28.31-34
22 He also made the robe of the ephod woven all of blue yarn; 23 and the opening of the robe in the middle of it was like the opening in a coat of mail,ᵗ with a binding around the opening, so that it might not be torn. 24 On the lower hem of the robe they made pomegranates of blue, purple, and crimson yarns, and of fine twisted linen. 25 They also made bells of pure gold, and put the bells between the pomegranates on the lower hem of the robe all around, between the pomegranates; 26 a bell and a pomegranate, a bell and a pomegranate all around on the lower hem of the robe for ministering; as the Lᴏʀᴅ had commanded Moses.

e. The remainder of the vestments

39.27
Ex 28.39, 40,
42
27 They also made the tunics, woven of fine linen, for Aaron and his sons, 28 and the turban of fine linen, and the headdresses of fine linen, and the linen undergarments of fine twisted linen, 29 and the sash of fine twisted linen, and of blue, purple, and crimson yarns, embroidered with needlework; as the Lᴏʀᴅ had commanded Moses.

39.30
Ex 28.36, 37
30 They made the rosette of the holy diadem of pure gold, and wrote on it an inscription, like the engraving of a signet, "Holy to the Lᴏʀᴅ." 31 They tied to it a blue cord, to fasten it on the turban above; as the Lᴏʀᴅ had commanded Moses.

15. Moses inspects and blesses the completed work

39.32
vv. 42, 43;
Ex 25.40
32 In this way all the work of the tabernacle of the tent of meeting was finished; the Israelites had done everything just as the Lᴏʀᴅ had commanded Moses. 33 Then they brought the tabernacle to Moses, the tent and all its utensils, its hooks, its frames, its bars, its pillars, and its bases; 34 the covering of tanned rams' skins and the covering of fine

39.35
Ex 25.16;
30.6
leather,ᵗ and the curtain for the screen; 35 the ark of the covenantᵘ with its poles and the mercy seat;ᵛ 36 the table with all its utensils, and the bread of the Presence; 37 the pure lampstand with its lamps set on it and all its utensils, and the oil for the light; 38 the golden altar, the anointing oil and the fragrant incense, and the screen for the entrance of the tent; 39 the bronze altar, and its grating of bronze, its poles, and all its utensils; the basin with its stand; 40 the hangings of the court, its pillars, and its bases, and the screen for the gate of the court, its cords, and its pegs; and all the utensils for the service of the tabernacle, for the tent of meeting;

ˢ Or lapis lazuli   ᵗ Meaning of Heb uncertain   ᵘ Or treaty, or testimony; Heb eduth   ᵛ Or the cover

41 the finely worked vestments for ministering in the holy place, the sacred vestments for the priest Aaron, and the vestments of his sons to serve as priests. 42 The Israelites had done all of the work just as the LORD had commanded Moses. 43 When Moses saw that they had done all the work just as the LORD had commanded, he blessed them.

16. The setting up and consecration of the tabernacle

a. The command of God to assemble the tabernacle

40 The LORD spoke to Moses: 2 On the first day of the first month you shall set up the tabernacle of the tent of meeting. 3 You shall put in it the ark of the covenant, *w* and you shall screen the ark with the curtain. 4 You shall bring in the table, and arrange its setting; and you shall bring in the lampstand, and set up its lamps. 5 You shall put the golden altar for incense before the ark of the covenant, *w* and set up the screen for the entrance of the tabernacle. 6 You shall set the altar of burnt offering before the entrance of the tabernacle of the tent of meeting, 7 and place the basin between the tent of meeting and the altar, and put water in it. 8 You shall set up the court all around, and hang up the screen for the gate of the court. 9 Then you shall take the anointing oil, and anoint the tabernacle and all that is in it, and consecrate it and all its furniture, so that it shall become holy. 10 You shall also anoint the altar of burnt offering and all its utensils, and consecrate the altar, so that the altar shall be most holy. 11 You shall also anoint the basin with its stand, and consecrate it. 12 Then you shall bring Aaron and his sons to the entrance of the tent of meeting, and shall wash them with water, 13 and put on Aaron the sacred vestments, and you shall anoint him and consecrate him, so that he may serve me as priest. 14 You shall bring his sons also and put tunics on them, 15 and anoint them, as you anointed their father, that they may serve me as priests: and their anointing shall admit them to a perpetual priesthood throughout all generations to come.

b. The obedience of Moses

16 Moses did everything just as the LORD had commanded him. 17 In the first month in the second year, on the first day of the month, the tabernacle was set up. 18 Moses set up the tabernacle; he laid its bases, and set up its frames, and put in its poles, and raised up its pillars; 19 and he spread the tent over the tabernacle, and put the covering of the tent over it; as the LORD had commanded Moses. 20 He took the covenant *w* and put it into the ark, and put the poles on the ark, and set the mercy seat *x* above the ark; 21 and he brought the ark into the tabernacle, and set up the curtain for screening, and screened the ark of the covenant; *w* as the LORD had commanded Moses. 22 He put the table in the tent of meeting, on the north side of the tabernacle, outside the curtain, 23 and set the bread in order on it before the LORD; as the LORD had commanded Moses. 24 He put the lampstand in the tent of meeting, opposite the table on the south side of the tabernacle, 25 and set up the lamps before the LORD; as the LORD had commanded Moses. 26 He put the golden altar in the tent of meeting before the curtain, 27 and offered fragrant incense on it; as the LORD had commanded Moses. 28 He also put in place the screen for the entrance of the tabernacle. 29 He set the altar of burnt offering at the

w Or *treaty*, or *testimony*; Heb *eduth*   *x* Or *the cover*

39.41	Ex 26.33
39.43	Lev 9.22, 23
40.2	Ex 12.2; 13.4; v. 17
40.3	vv. 21-30
40.9	Ex 30.26
40.10	Ex 29.36, 37
40.12	Lev 8.1-13
40.13	Ex 28.41
40.15	Num 25.13
40.20	Ex 25.16
40.21	Ex 26.33; 35.12
40.22	Ex 26.35
40.23	v. 4
40.25	Ex 25.37
40.26	v. 5
40.28	Ex 26.36

39.43 God had given Moses the pattern for the tabernacle. Although he did not construct it, it was done according to what had been revealed to him. He inspected the finished product, placing his stamp of approval on it, and blessed those who had done the work.

40.9 The completed tabernacle was not yet God's possession until it was sanctified by the special anointing oil. When this was done, the tabernacle became holy and the glory of God filled that residence made for him.

entrance of the tabernacle of the tent of meeting, and offered on it the
burnt offering and the grain offering as the LORD had commanded Moses.
40.30 ³⁰ He set the basin between the tent of meeting and the altar, and put water
v. 7   in it for washing, ³¹ with which Moses and Aaron and his sons washed
40.32 their hands and their feet. ³² When they went into the tent of meeting,
Ex 30.19, 20 and when they approached the altar, they washed; as the LORD had
commanded Moses. ³³ He set up the court around the tabernacle and the
altar, and put up the screen at the gate of the court. So Moses finished
the work.

c. *The glory of the LORD fills the tabernacle*

40.34 34 Then the cloud covered the tent of meeting, and the glory of the
Num 9.15-23 LORD filled the tabernacle. ³⁵ Moses was not able to enter the tent of
meeting because the cloud settled upon it, and the glory of the LORD filled
40.36 the tabernacle. ³⁶ Whenever the cloud was taken up from the tabernacle,
Num 9.17; the Israelites would set out on each stage of their journey; ³⁷ but if the
10.11;
Neh 9.19 cloud was not taken up, then they did not set out until the day that it was
40.38 taken up. ³⁸ For the cloud of the LORD was on the tabernacle by day, and
Ex 13.21; fire was in the cloud*ʸ* by night, before the eyes of all the house of Israel
Num 9.15 at each stage of their journey.

ʸ Heb *it*

40.33 Seven times in less than fourteen verses we
read that Moses was commanded to do certain things
by God. Then comes the grand finale: "So Moses
finished the work." His obedience in this task was
ended, and the finished product given to God.
40.34 See note on 13.21. Here the cloud covered the
tent and the glory of the Lord filled it, as occurred
later when the temple was dedicated (2 Chr 5.13,14).
At the time of Zedekiah's apostasy the glory left the

temple (cf. Ezek 43.1–4) and never came back, even
when the temple was rebuilt in 516 B.C. The Scriptures promised that the second temple would surpass
the first one in glory. This occurred centuries later
when Jesus came to cleanse the temple and to teach
in it. Following his rejection and crucifixion, the spiritual glory departed from the temple forever and the
building was destroyed in A.D. 70. God's temple today
is the N.T. church (cf. 1 Cor 3.16,17; 2 Cor 6.16).

INTRODUCTION TO

LEVITICUS

Authorship, Date, and Background: Leviticus is the third book of Moses and, like the other four books of the Pentateuch, was probably composed during the last two decades of the fifteenth century B.C. (depending on the date of the exodus; see introduction to Exodus). The Hebrew title for the book comes from the opening phrase of the text, meaning "and he called." The title used in the Septuagint, Leviticus, means "pertaining to the Levites." Since the Israelite priests were Levites, the title is appropriate, for the book discusses their ministry in some detail.

The key verse of Leviticus is 11.45: "You shall be holy, for I am holy." God chose Israel to be his holy people; they were a nation peculiarly set apart for God and his purposes. God, as this book constantly reiterates, gave his laws and regulations through Moses, who either wrote them down or had them written down under his supervision (4.1; 6.1; 8.1; 11.1; 12.1; 13.1, etc.). Israel was commanded to keep God's injunctions, not in order to become acceptable in his sight by their works, but rather because the keeping of God's laws would be an outward manifestation of hearts in tune with God and an expression of their love for him.

Leviticus also lays down the rules for the proper presentation of sacrifices and clearly states what is clean and unclean.

Characteristics and Content: Law and grace kiss each other in this book. Superficially it appears to be the most legalistic book in the O.T., for God demands his people conform their conduct to his rules and regulations. Yet the gospel is truly to be found here, for the obedience God requires is a response to his grace and mercy which his people must first receive as a gift. This underlying truth is fully revealed and developed in the N.T. in the writings of Paul, who champions the doctrine of God's free grace in Jesus Christ, and through James, who emphasizes the necessity of the believer's response to God's grace through works.

The pages of Leviticus contain the laws of sacrifices, the rules for the consecration of the priesthood, and the regulations for the separation of God's people from defilement with respect to foods, childbirth, diseases like leprosy, and also bodily secretions. Great emphasis is laid on the day of atonement, the place of sacrifice, and the necessity to shed blood for the remission of sins. Then follow the laws for practical holiness, a summary of the duties of the priesthood, and a list of the holy festivals together with their meanings and requirements.

Economic regulations are laid down. The people of Israel were given title to their lands in perpetuity. Mortgaged properties had to be returned to their owners in the year of jubilee. Stipulations governed the cost of using the mortgaged lands, depending on how long they would be lost to the owners until the jubilee. The sabbatical year for the land was set for every seventh year. The book comes to a close with the promise of God for blessings to be bestowed on the obedient and curses which accrue to the disobedient. The last chapter gives directions about vows and tithes.

Outline:

I. The way of approach to a holy God (1.1—16.34)

II. The maintaining of fellowship with a holy God (17.1—27.34)

LEVITICUS

I. The way of approach to a holy God (1.1–16.34)

A. The laws and rituals of worship

1. The law of burnt offering

1 The LORD summoned Moses and spoke to him from the tent of meeting, saying: 2 Speak to the people of Israel and say to them: When any of you bring an offering of livestock to the LORD, you shall bring your offering from the herd or from the flock.

3 If the offering is a burnt offering from the herd, you shall offer a male without blemish; you shall bring it to the entrance of the tent of meeting, for acceptance in your behalf before the LORD. 4 You shall lay your hand on the head of the burnt offering, and it shall be acceptable in your behalf as atonement for you. 5 The bull shall be slaughtered before the LORD; and Aaron's sons the priests shall offer the blood, dashing the blood against all sides of the altar that is at the entrance of the tent of meeting. 6 The burnt offering shall be flayed and cut up into its parts. 7 The sons of the priest Aaron shall put fire on the altar and arrange wood on the fire. 8 Aaron's sons the priests shall arrange the parts, with the head and the suet, on the wood that is on the fire on the altar; 9 but its entrails and its legs shall be washed with water. Then the priest shall turn the whole into smoke on the altar as a burnt offering, an offering by fire of pleasing odor to the LORD.

10 If your gift for a burnt offering is from the flock, from the sheep or goats, your offering shall be a male without blemish. 11 It shall be slaughtered on the north side of the altar before the LORD, and Aaron's sons the priests shall dash its blood against all sides of the altar. 12 It shall be cut up into its parts, with its head and its suet, and the priest shall arrange them on the wood that is on the fire on the altar; 13 but the entrails and the legs shall be washed with water. Then the priest shall offer the whole and turn it into smoke on the altar; it is a burnt offering, an offering by fire of pleasing odor to the LORD.

14 If your offering to the LORD is a burnt offering of birds, you shall choose your offering from turtledoves or pigeons. 15 The priest shall bring it to the altar and wring off its head, and turn it into smoke on the altar; and its blood shall be drained out against the side of the altar. 16 He shall remove its crop with its contents*a* and throw it at the east side of the altar, in the place for ashes. 17 He shall tear it open by its wings without severing

a Meaning of Heb uncertain

1.3 The burnt offering (sacrifice) is a representation of Christ, who offered himself once for all for sin (Heb 10.10). The animal was a substitute for the sinner, even as Christ is our substitute. The offerer laid his hand on the animal (v. 4) and thus identified himself with the offering as an act of faith. In the N.T. Christ stood in the sinner's place and made atonement for him as his representative and substitute (1 Pet 1.18-20). The kind of animal offered depended on the financial condition of the offerer: it could be a healthy bull, sheep, goat, turtledove, or pigeon. The burnt offering was to be completely burned; no part of it was given to the priest or the offerer to be eaten. The O.T. declares that the life is in the blood. No atonement is possible without the sacrifice of a life, for which the blood was the visible symbol (17.11). When the blood was presented to God it was proof that the life had been given. The blood that flowed from the Savior's wounds gave evidence of the offering of his life. And the presentation of his blood at the heavenly mercy seat meant that he had died for our salvation and had won the victory.

it. Then the priest shall turn it into smoke on the altar, on the wood that is on the fire; it is a burnt offering, an offering by fire of pleasing odor to the LORD.

2. The law of the grain offerings

a. Flour, oil, and frankincense

2 When anyone presents a grain offering to the LORD, the offering shall be of choice flour; the worshiper shall pour oil on it, and put frankincense on it, ²and bring it to Aaron's sons the priests. After taking from it a handful of the choice flour and oil, with all its frankincense, the priest shall turn this token portion into smoke on the altar, an offering by fire of pleasing odor to the LORD. ³And what is left of the grain offering shall be for Aaron and his sons, a most holy part of the offerings by fire to the LORD.

4 When you present a grain offering baked in the oven, it shall be of choice flour: unleavened cakes mixed with oil, or unleavened wafers spread with oil. ⁵If your offering is grain prepared on a griddle, it shall be of choice flour mixed with oil, unleavened; ⁶break it in pieces, and pour oil on it; it is a grain offering. ⁷If your offering is grain prepared in a pan, it shall be made of choice flour in oil. ⁸You shall bring to the LORD the grain offering that is prepared in any of these ways; and when it is presented to the priest, he shall take it to the altar. ⁹The priest shall remove from the grain offering its token portion and turn this into smoke on the altar, an offering by fire of pleasing odor to the LORD. ¹⁰And what is left of the grain offering shall be for Aaron and his sons; it is a most holy part of the offerings by fire to the LORD.

b. Leaven and salt

11 No grain offering that you bring to the LORD shall be made with leaven, for you must not turn any leaven or honey into smoke as an offering by fire to the LORD. ¹²You may bring them to the LORD as an offering of choice products, but they shall not be offered on the altar for a pleasing odor. ¹³You shall not omit from your grain offerings the salt of the covenant with your God; with all your offerings you shall offer salt.

14 If you bring a grain offering of first fruits to the LORD, you shall bring as the grain offering of your first fruits coarse new grain from fresh ears, parched with fire. ¹⁵You shall add oil to it and lay frankincense on it; it is a grain offering. ¹⁶And the priest shall turn a token portion of it into smoke—some of the coarse grain and oil with all its frankincense; it is an offering by fire to the LORD.

3. The law of the offering of well-being

3 If the offering is a sacrifice of well-being, if you offer an animal of the herd, whether male or female, you shall offer one without blemish before the LORD. ²You shall lay your hand on the head of the offering and slaughter it at the entrance of the tent of meeting; and Aaron's sons the priests shall dash the blood against all sides of the altar. ³You shall offer from the sacrifice of well-being, as an offering by fire to the LORD, the fat that covers the entrails and all the fat that is around the entrails; ⁴the

2.1
Lev 6.14
2.2
vv. 9, 16;
Lev 5.12;
6.15;
Acts 10.4
2.3
Lev 6.16;
10.12, 13

2.9
v. 2;
Ex 29.18
2.10
v. 3

2.11
Lev 6.16, 17;
Ex 23.18;
34.25
2.12
Lev 7.13;
23.10, 11
2.13
Mk 9.49;
Num 18.19
2.14
Lev 23.10, 14

2.16
v. 2

3.1
Lev 7.11, 19;
22.21
3.2
Lev 1.4;
Ex 29.11, 16, 20
3.3
Ex 29.13, 22

2.1 *offering shall be of choice flour.* The grain (or cereal or meal) offering was made of choice flour and was presented with oil and incense. It was unleavened. It was offered on the altar of burnt offering, not on the altar of incense (Ex 30.9; 40.29). When offered by the priests for themselves, it was to be totally burned up (6.23); when offered by the priests for others, a handful was put in the flames and the remainder eaten by the priests (6.15,16).
2.13 *shall not omit . . . the salt.* In many of the lan-guages of the ancient Near East, the word "salt" is a homonym of the word "good." It was used symbolically for "goodness" in making covenants.
3.1 *sacrifice of well-being.* Animals used for the well-being offering (also called the peace offering) were to be eaten by the priests and the worshipers (except for the kidneys and fat, which were to be burned). It was a fellowship meal, signifying that peace existed between God and the offerer as well as among the community of Israel.

two kidneys with the fat that is on them at the loins, and the appendage of the liver, which he shall remove with the kidneys. 5 Then Aaron's sons shall turn these into smoke on the altar, with the burnt offering that is on the wood on the fire, as an offering by fire of pleasing odor to the LORD.

6 If your offering for a sacrifice of well-being to the LORD is from the flock, male or female, you shall offer one without blemish. 7 If you present a sheep as your offering, you shall bring it before the LORD 8 and lay your hand on the head of the offering. It shall be slaughtered before the tent of meeting, and Aaron's sons shall dash its blood against all sides of the altar. 9 You shall present its fat from the sacrifice of well-being, as an offering by fire to the LORD: the whole broad tail, which shall be removed close to the backbone, the fat that covers the entrails, and all the fat that is around the entrails; 10 the two kidneys with the fat that is on them at the loins, and the appendage of the liver, which you shall remove with the kidneys. 11 Then the priest shall turn these into smoke on the altar as a food offering by fire to the LORD.

12 If your offering is a goat, you shall bring it before the LORD 13 and lay your hand on its head; it shall be slaughtered before the tent of meeting; and the sons of Aaron shall dash its blood against all sides of the altar. 14 You shall present as your offering from it, as an offering by fire to the LORD, the fat that covers the entrails, and all the fat that is around the entrails; 15 the two kidneys with the fat that is on them at the loins, and the appendage of the liver, which you shall remove with the kidneys. 16 Then the priest shall turn these into smoke on the altar as a food offering by fire for a pleasing odor.

All fat is the LORD's. 17 It shall be a perpetual statute throughout your generations, in all your settlements: you must not eat any fat or any blood.

4. The law of the sin offerings

a. The offering for the priest

4 The LORD spoke to Moses, saying, 2 Speak to the people of Israel, saying: When anyone sins unintentionally in any of the LORD's commandments about things not to be done, and does any one of them:

3 If it is the anointed priest who sins, thus bringing guilt on the people, he shall offer for the sin that he has committed a bull of the herd without blemish as a sin offering to the LORD. 4 He shall bring the bull to the entrance of the tent of meeting before the LORD and lay his hand on the head of the bull; the bull shall be slaughtered before the LORD. 5 The anointed priest shall take some of the blood of the bull and bring it into the tent of meeting. 6 The priest shall dip his finger in the blood and sprinkle some of the blood seven times before the LORD in front of the curtain of the sanctuary. 7 The priest shall put some of the blood on the horns of the altar of fragrant incense that is in the tent of meeting before the LORD; and the rest of the blood of the bull he shall pour out

Marginal cross-references (left column):

3.5
Lev 7.28-34;
Ex 29.13

3.6
v. 1
3.7
Lev 17.8, 9
3.8
Lev 1.4, 5;
v. 2

3.10
v. 4

3.11
vv. 5, 16;
Lev 21.6, 8,
17

3.16
Lev 7.23-25

3.17
Gen 9.4;
Lev 17.10,
14;
Deut 12.16

4.2
Lev 5.15-18;
Ps 19.12

4.3ff
vv. 14, 23, 28

4.4
Lev 1.4

4.5
Lev 16.14

4.7
Lev 8.15;
9.9;
Lev 5.9

3.6 The sacrifice of well-being required either sheep or goats. Birds were excluded for two reasons: they did not have enough fat to warrant their use, and the meat was inconsiderable so as to make the offering of little worth for food. *without blemish.* This requirement was included because the people would tend to offer a diseased or abnormal animal rather than a perfect one. God wanted no second-rate offerings. **4.2** Sins deliberately intended to reject God's sovereignty were to be punished by execution (Num 15.30, 31). For unintentional sins or sins of ignorance, provision was made for repentance and atonement by an animal sacrifice. We all sin through ignorance and without any intention of renouncing God's sovereignty or control over our lives. But sin remains sin, and God does not accept ignorance as an valid excuse for failing to keep his commandments. Believers must study the Scriptures to learn about and keep God's commandments.
4.3ff The O.T. animal sacrifices prefigured Christ's sacrifice at Calvary. The sin offering spoken of here: (1) vindicated God's justice, i.e., it met the just demands of the law (Heb 10.10–12); (2) had to be a perfect animal (Christ was the sinless or perfect servant — Heb 7.28); (3) was a substitute for the person offering the sin offering (Christ was our substitute who bore our sins — 2 Cor 5.21; 1 Pet 2.24); and (4) took away the guilt and penalty of the sin. In contrast to the burnt offering (which signified complete surrender to God and gave a person standing in God's sight), sin offerings atoned for specific sins. Once an animal was sacrificed, the sin or sins were forgiven.

OLD TESTAMENT SACRIFICES

Sacrifice	OT References	Elements	Purpose
BURNT OFFERING	Lev 1; 6:8-13; 8:18-21; 16:24	Bull, ram or male bird (dove or young pigeon for poor); wholly consumed; no defect	Voluntary act of worship; atonement for unintentional sin in general; expression of devotion, commitment and complete surrender to God
GRAIN OFFERING	Lev 2; 6:14-23	Grain, fine flour, olive oil, incense, baked bread (cakes or wafers), salt; no yeast or honey; accompanied burnt offering and fellowship offering (along with drink offering)	Voluntary act of worship; recognition of God's goodness and provisions; devotion to God
OFFERING OF WELL-BEING	Lev 3; 7:11-34	Any animal without defect from herd or flock; variety of breads	Voluntary act of worship; thanksgiving and fellowship (it included a communal meal)
SIN OFFERING	Lev 4:1-5:13; 6:24-30; 8:14-17; 16:3-22	1. Young bull: for high priest and congregation 2. Male goat: for leader 3. Female goat or lamb: for common person 4. Dove or pigeon: for the poor 5. Tenth of an ephah of fine flour: for the very poor	Mandatory atonement for specific unintentional sin; confession of sin; forgiveness of sin; cleansing from defilement
GUILT OFFERING	Lev 5:14-6:7; 7:1-6	Ram or lamb	Mandatory atonement for unintentional sin requiring restitution; cleansing from defilement; make restitution; pay 20% fine

When more than one kind of offering was presented (as in Nu 7:16, 17), the procedure was usually as follows: (1) sin offering or guilt offering, (2) burnt offering, (3) fellowship offering and grain offering (along with a drink offering). This sequence furnishes part of the spiritual significance of the sacrificial system. First, sin had to be dealt with (sin offering or guilt offering). Second, the worshiper committed himself completely to God (burnt offering and grain offering). Third, fellowship or communion between the Lord, the priest and the worshiper (fellowship offering) was established.

at the base of the altar of burnt offering, which is at the entrance of the tent of meeting. 8 He shall remove all the fat from the bull of sin offering: the fat that covers the entrails and all the fat that is around the entrails; 9 the two kidneys with the fat that is on them at the loins; and the appendage of the liver, which he shall remove with the kidneys, 10 just as these are removed from the ox of the sacrifice of well-being. The priest shall turn them into smoke upon the altar of burnt offering. 11 But the skin of the bull and all its flesh, as well as its head, its legs, its entrails, and its dung— 12 all the rest of the bull—he shall carry out to a clean place outside the camp, to the ash heap, and shall burn it on a wood fire; at the ash heap it shall be burned.

b. The offering for the whole congregation

13 If the whole congregation of Israel errs unintentionally and the matter escapes the notice of the assembly, and they do any one of the things that by the LORD's commandments ought not to be done and incur guilt; 14 when the sin that they have committed becomes known, the assembly shall offer a bull of the herd for a sin offering and bring it before the tent of meeting. 15 The elders of the congregation shall lay their hands on the head of the bull before the LORD, and the bull shall be slaughtered before the LORD. 16 The anointed priest shall bring some of the blood of the bull into the tent of meeting, 17 and the priest shall dip his finger in the blood and sprinkle it seven times before the LORD, in front of the curtain. 18 He shall put some of the blood on the horns of the altar that is before the LORD in the tent of meeting; and the rest of the blood he shall pour out at the base of the altar of burnt offering that is at the entrance of the tent of meeting. 19 He shall remove all its fat and turn it into smoke on the altar. 20 He shall do with the bull just as is done with the bull of sin offering; he shall do the same with this. The priest shall make atonement for them, and they shall be forgiven. 21 He shall carry the bull outside the camp, and burn it as he burned the first bull; it is the sin offering for the assembly.

c. The offering for a ruler

22 When a ruler sins, doing unintentionally any one of all the things that by commandments of the LORD his God ought not to be done and incurs guilt; 23 once the sin that he has committed is made known to him, he shall bring as his offering a male goat without blemish. 24 He shall lay his hand on the head of the goat; it shall be slaughtered at the spot where the burnt offering is slaughtered before the LORD; it is a sin offering. 25 The priest shall take some of the blood of the sin offering with his finger and put it on the horns of the altar of burnt offering, and pour out the rest of its blood at the base of the altar of burnt offering. 26 All its fat he shall turn into smoke on the altar, like the fat of the sacrifice of well-being. Thus the priest shall make atonement on his behalf for his sin, and he shall be forgiven.

d. The offering for ordinary people

27 If anyone of the ordinary people among you sins unintentionally in doing any one of the things that by the LORD's commandments ought

Marginal references:
4.8 Lev 3.3-5
4.12 Lev 6.11; Heb 13.11
4.13 Num 15.24-26; Lev 5.2-4, 17
4.14 vv. 3, 23, 28
4.15 Lev 1.4
4.17 v. 6
4.20 Rom 5.11; Heb 2.17; 10.10-12
4.22 vv. 2, 13
4.23 v. 14
4.25 vv. 7, 18, 30, 34
4.26 vv. 19, 20
4.27 v. 2

4.13 It was possible for the nation's leaders, through lack of complete understanding of the law of God, to lead the entire nation astray. Note that unwitting sin is talked of here. When the error was discovered, in order that God's wrath might not come upon the whole nation, a sin offering was to be presented before the Lord. Through it forgiveness would come for the nation.
4.22 When a ruler sinned unwittingly, the sin was not to be covered over when discovered. It was to be atoned for by a sin offering; then the sin would be forgiven and God appeased.
4.27 God is no respecter of persons. Sin is sin whether committed by a nation, a ruler, a religious leader, or a common person. Here God speaks of the atonement required on behalf of an individual who has unwittingly committed a trespass against the law of God. That person must admit the sin, confess it by the sin offering, and thus avert God's judgment.

not to be done and incurs guilt, 28 when the sin that you have committed is made known to you, you shall bring a female goat without blemish as your offering, for the sin that you have committed. 29 You shall lay your hand on the head of the sin offering; and the sin offering shall be slaughtered at the place of the burnt offering. 30 The priest shall take some of its blood with his finger and put it on the horns of the altar of burnt offering, and he shall pour out the rest of its blood at the base of the altar. 31 He shall remove all its fat, as the fat is removed from the offering of well-being, and the priest shall turn it into smoke on the altar for a pleasing odor to the LORD. Thus the priest shall make atonement on your behalf, and you shall be forgiven.

32 If the offering you bring as a sin offering is a sheep, you shall bring a female without blemish. 33 You shall lay your hand on the head of the sin offering; and it shall be slaughtered as a sin offering at the spot where the burnt offering is slaughtered. 34 The priest shall take some of the blood of the sin offering with his finger and put it on the horns of the altar of burnt offering, and pour out the rest of its blood at the base of the altar. 35 You shall remove all its fat, as the fat of the sheep is removed from the sacrifice of well-being, and the priest shall turn it into smoke on the altar, with the offerings by fire to the LORD. Thus the priest shall make atonement on your behalf for the sin that you have committed, and you shall be forgiven.

e. Actions requiring a sin offering

5 When any of you sin in that you have heard a public adjuration to testify and — though able to testify as one who has seen or learned of the matter — do not speak up, you are subject to punishment. 2 Or when any of you touch any unclean thing — whether the carcass of an unclean beast or the carcass of unclean livestock or the carcass of an unclean swarming thing — and are unaware of it, you have become unclean, and are guilty. 3 Or when you touch human uncleanness — any uncleanness by which one can become unclean — and are unaware of it, when you come to know it, you shall be guilty. 4 Or when any of you utter aloud a rash oath for a bad or a good purpose, whatever people utter in an oath, and are unaware of it, when you come to know it, you shall in any of these be guilty. 5 When you realize your guilt in any of these, you shall confess the sin that you have committed. 6 And you shall bring to the LORD, as your penalty for the sin that you have committed, a female from the flock, a sheep or a goat, as a sin offering; and the priest shall make atonement on your behalf for your sin.

f. Different sin offerings allowed for the poor

7 But if you cannot afford a sheep, you shall bring to the LORD, as your penalty for the sin that you have committed, two turtledoves or two pigeons, one for a sin offering and the other for a burnt offering. 8 You

Margin references:
4.28 v. 23
4.29 Lev 1.4, 5
4.32 v. 28
4.35 Lev 3.5; vv. 26, 31
5.1 Prov 29.24; v. 17
5.2 Lev 11.24-39; Num 19.11-16
5.5 Lev 16.21; 26.40; Num 5.7; Prov 28.13
5.7 Lev 12.8; 14.21
5.8 Lev 1.15, 17

5.1 Jewish justice differed from English common law (where people are not obligated to testify against themselves). In the Jewish judicial system, witnesses *and* the accused person were obligated to swear to tell the truth, the whole truth, and nothing but the truth. If a witness and/or the accused then lied, each "shall bear their guilt (Lev. 17.16)." In Mt 26.63, we read that when the high priest put Jesus under oath to tell the Jewish council whether he was the Messiah, the Son of God, Jesus broke his silence, answering (in effect), "Yes, I am." Thus Jesus in that instance subjected himself without reservation to the law of God and so fully kept it.
5.5 Confession of sin was essential in the Jewish legal system, and it is essential in the Christian life. God requires it of those who have sinned (cf. Hos 5.15; Jas 5.16; 1 Jn 1.9). Without repentance and

confession, forgiveness is not possible; with it comes the assurance of forgiveness and cleansing. Biblical confession includes: (1) godly sorrow (Ps 38.18; 2 Cor 7.10); (2) self-abasement (Jer 3.25); (3) prayer for forgiveness (Ps 51.1); (4) restitution where necessary (Num 5.6,7); (5) acceptance of God's punishment (Ezra 9.13; Neh 9.33); and (6) a turning away from sin (Prov 28.13). The prodigal son (Lk 15.11–24) and the tax collector (Lk 18.9–14) are two examples of people who confessed and were forgiven.
5.7 God had respect for the poor. Thus he allowed for those who were poor to substitute a turtledove or pigeon for sin and burnt offerings, in place of a lamb. When presenting Jesus at the temple, Mary and Joseph, because they were poor, used this provision of the O.T. law (Lk 2.24).

shall bring them to the priest, who shall offer first the one for the sin offering, wringing its head at the nape without severing it. 9 He shall sprinkle some of the blood of the sin offering on the side of the altar, while the rest of the blood shall be drained out at the base of the altar; it is a sin offering. 10 And the second he shall offer for a burnt offering according to the regulation. Thus the priest shall make atonement on your behalf for the sin that you have committed, and you shall be forgiven.

11 But if you cannot afford two turtledoves or two pigeons, you shall bring as your offering for the sin that you have committed one-tenth of an ephah of choice flour for a sin offering; you shall not put oil on it or lay frankincense on it, for it is a sin offering. 12 You shall bring it to the priest, and the priest shall scoop up a handful of it as its memorial portion, and turn this into smoke on the altar, with the offerings by fire to the LORD; it is a sin offering. 13 Thus the priest shall make atonement on your behalf for whichever of these sins you have committed, and you shall be forgiven. Like the grain offering, the rest shall be for the priest.

5. The law of the guilt offering

14 The LORD spoke to Moses, saying: 15 When any of you commit a trespass and sin unintentionally in any of the holy things of the LORD, you shall bring, as your guilt offering to the LORD, a ram without blemish from the flock, convertible into silver by the sanctuary shekel; it is a guilt offering. 16 And you shall make restitution for the holy thing in which you were remiss, and shall add one-fifth to it and give it to the priest. The priest shall make atonement on your behalf with the ram of the guilt offering, and you shall be forgiven.

17 If any of you sin without knowing it, doing any of the things that by the LORD's commandments ought not to be done, you have incurred guilt, and are subject to punishment. 18 You shall bring to the priest a ram without blemish from the flock, or the equivalent, as a guilt offering; and the priest shall make atonement on your behalf for the error that you committed unintentionally, and you shall be forgiven. 19 It is a guilt offering; you have incurred guilt before the LORD.

6 *b* The LORD spoke to Moses, saying: 2 When any of you sin and commit a trespass against the LORD by deceiving a neighbor in a matter of a deposit or a pledge, or by robbery, or if you have defrauded a neighbor, 3 or have found something lost and lied about it—if you swear falsely regarding any of the various things that one may do and sin thereby 4 when you have sinned and realize your guilt, and would restore what you took by robbery or by fraud or the deposit that was committed to you, or the lost thing that you found, 5 or anything else about which you have sworn falsely, you shall repay the principal amount and shall add one-fifth to it. You shall pay it to its owner when you realize your guilt. 6 And you shall bring to the priest, as your guilt offering to the LORD, a ram without blemish from the flock, or its equivalent, for a guilt offering. 7 The priest shall make atonement on your behalf before the LORD, and you shall be forgiven for any of the things that one may do and incur guilt thereby.

b Ch 5.20 in Heb

Cross-references (margin):

5.9 Lev 4.7, 18, 30, 34
5.10 Lev 1.14-17
5.11 Lev 2.1, 2
5.13 Lev 4.26; 2.3
5.14 Lev 22.14; 7.1-10; Ex 30.13
5.16 Lev 6.5; 22.14; Num 5.7, 8; Lev 4.26
5.17 v. 15; 4.2, 13, 22, 27
5.18 vv. 15-17
6.2 Num 5.6; Acts 5.4; Col 3.9; Ex 22.7, 10; Prov 24.28
6.3 Deut 22.1-3
6.5 Lev 5.16; Num 5.7, 8
6.6 Lev 5.16
6.7 Lev 4.26

5.15 The guilt offering (or trespass offering) resembled the sin offering. It differed in that the guilt offering provided for sins in which the amount of the injury could be assessed and restitution made. The principle of atonement by blood was inherent in the offering (6.7). Restitution was made to the injured party on a six-fifths basis. Bringing the offering was evidence of repentance of sin, faith in the blood of the slain sacrifice, and the certainty of forgiveness for the wrong act. In Isa 53.10 the word translated as "an

offering for sin" *(asham)* literally means "guilt (or trespass) offering."
5.17 See note on 4.2.
6.2 *by deceiving a neighbor.* Some read this as: "has deceitfully oppressed his neighbor." These verses speak of what is taken by violence or obtained by fraud. Any and all forms of oppression of one's neighbor were forbidden by God, required a trespass offering for forgiveness, and had to be restored by paying the principal plus 20 percent.

6. Instructions for the priests

a. On burnt offerings

8[c] The LORD spoke to Moses, saying: 9Command Aaron and his sons, saying: This is the ritual of the burnt offering. The burnt offering itself shall remain on the hearth upon the altar all night until the morning, while the fire on the altar shall be kept burning. 10The priest shall put on his linen vestments after putting on his linen undergarments next to his body; and he shall take up the ashes to which the fire has reduced the burnt offering on the altar, and place them beside the altar. 11Then he shall take off his vestments and put on other garments, and carry the ashes out to a clean place outside the camp. 12The fire on the altar shall be kept burning; it shall not go out. Every morning the priest shall add wood to it, lay out the burnt offering on it, and turn into smoke the fat pieces of the offerings of well-being. 13A perpetual fire shall be kept burning on the altar; it shall not go out.

6.10
Ex 28.39-41, 43; 39.27, 28

b. On grain offerings

14 This is the ritual of the grain offering: The sons of Aaron shall offer it before the LORD, in front of the altar. 15They shall take from it a handful of the choice flour and oil of the grain offering, with all the frankincense that is on the offering, and they shall turn its memorial portion into smoke on the altar as a pleasing odor to the LORD. 16Aaron and his sons shall eat what is left of it; it shall be eaten as unleavened cakes in a holy place; in the court of the tent of meeting they shall eat it. 17It shall not be baked with leaven. I have given it as their portion of my offerings by fire; it is most holy, like the sin offering and the guilt offering. 18Every male among the descendants of Aaron shall eat of it, as their perpetual due throughout your generations, from the LORD's offerings by fire; anything that touches them shall become holy.

6.14
Lev 2.1, 2

6.16
Lev 2.3

6.17
Lev 2.11;
vv. 26, 29, 30
6.18
v. 29;
Num 18.10;
v. 27

19 The LORD spoke to Moses, saying: 20This is the offering that Aaron and his sons shall offer to the LORD on the day when he is anointed: one-tenth of an ephah of choice flour as a regular offering, half of it in the morning and half in the evening. 21It shall be made with oil on a griddle; you shall bring it well soaked, as a grain offering of baked[d] pieces, and you shall present it as a pleasing odor to the LORD. 22And so the priest, anointed from among Aaron's descendants as a successor, shall prepare it; it is the LORD's—a perpetual due—to be turned entirely into smoke. 23Every grain offering of a priest shall be wholly burned; it shall not be eaten.

6.20
Ex 29.1, 2

6.21
Lev 2.5

c. On sin offerings

24 The LORD spoke to Moses, saying: 25Speak to Aaron and his sons, saying: This is the ritual of the sin offering. The sin offering shall be slaughtered before the LORD at the spot where the burnt offering is slaughtered; it is most holy. 26The priest who offers it as a sin offering shall eat of it; it shall be eaten in a holy place, in the court of the tent of meeting. 27Whatever touches its flesh shall become holy; and when any of its blood is spattered on a garment, you shall wash the bespattered part in a holy place. 28An earthen vessel in which it was boiled shall be broken; but if it is boiled in a bronze vessel, that shall be scoured and rinsed in

6.25
Lev 4.2, 24,
29, 33; 1.3,
5, 11
6.26
Lev 10.17,
18; v. 16
6.27
Ex 29.37
6.28
Ex 11.33;
15.12

c Ch 6.1 in Heb   d Meaning of Heb uncertain

6.13 The fire for the burnt offering came down from God supernaturally and was never to go out. This supernatural origin indicated, in effect, that only by the grace of God were sacrifices acceptable for atonement. Fire made by humans was forbidden. The sin of bringing such unholy fire to the altar resulted in the deaths of Nadab and Abihu (10.1,2).

6.27 The blood of the sin offering is representative of Christ. It is so precious that any garment which was stained by it had to be washed in a holy place to remove the stain. So Christ's blood may not be counted common. It is to be sprinkled on our consciences (Heb 10.22), so that we may be cleansed and forgiven.

water. 29 Every male among the priests shall eat of it; it is most holy. 30 But no sin offering shall be eaten from which any blood is brought into the tent of meeting for atonement in the holy place; it shall be burned with fire.

d. On guilt offerings

7 This is the ritual of the guilt offering. It is most holy; 2 at the spot where the burnt offering is slaughtered, they shall slaughter the guilt offering, and its blood shall be dashed against all sides of the altar. 3 All its fat shall be offered: the broad tail, the fat that covers the entrails, 4 the two kidneys with the fat that is on them at the loins, and the appendage of the liver, which shall be removed with the kidneys. 5 The priest shall turn them into smoke on the altar as an offering by fire to the LORD; it is a guilt offering. 6 Every male among the priests shall eat of it; it shall be eaten in a holy place; it is most holy.

7 The guilt offering is like the sin offering, there is the same ritual for them; the priest who makes atonement with it shall have it. 8 So, too, the priest who offers anyone's burnt offering shall keep the skin of the burnt offering that he has offered. 9 And every grain offering baked in the oven, and all that is prepared in a pan or on a griddle, shall belong to the priest who offers it. 10 But every other grain offering, mixed with oil or dry, shall belong to all the sons of Aaron equally.

e. On offerings of well-being

11 This is the ritual of the sacrifice of the offering of well-being that one may offer to the LORD. 12 If you offer it for thanksgiving, you shall offer with the thank offering unleavened cakes mixed with oil, unleavened wafers spread with oil, and cakes of choice flour well soaked in oil. 13 With your thanksgiving sacrifice of well-being you shall bring your offering with cakes of leavened bread. 14 From this you shall offer one cake from each offering, as a gift to the LORD; it shall belong to the priest who dashes the blood of the offering of well-being. 15 And the flesh of your thanksgiving sacrifice of well-being shall be eaten on the day it is offered; you shall not leave any of it until morning. 16 But if the sacrifice you offer is a votive offering or a freewill offering, it shall be eaten on the day that you offer your sacrifice, and what is left of it shall be eaten the next day; 17 but what is left of the flesh of the sacrifice shall be burned up on the third day. 18 If any of the flesh of your sacrifice of well-being is eaten on the third day, it shall not be acceptable, nor shall it be credited to the one who offers it; it shall be an abomination, and the one who eats of it shall incur guilt.

19 Flesh that touches any unclean thing shall not be eaten; it shall be burned up. As for other flesh, all who are clean may eat such flesh. 20 But those who eat flesh from the LORD's sacrifice of well-being while in a state of uncleanness shall be cut off from their kin. 21 When any one of you touches any unclean thing — human uncleanness or an unclean animal or any unclean creature — and then eats flesh from the LORD's sacrifice of well-being, you shall be cut off from your kin.

f. Forbidden portions

22 The LORD spoke to Moses, saying: 23 Speak to the people of Israel, saying: You shall eat no fat of ox or sheep or goat. 24 The fat of an animal

---

7.6 The meat of the guilt offering could be eaten only by the priests and in the holy place (cf. the contrast with the sacrifice of well-being, ch. 3). Since the guilt offering signified sorrow for sin, fasting was proper for the offerer. It was a time for holy mourning and for a resolve to abstain from sin in the future. 7.8 the priest . . . shall keep the skin. Money could be earned from selling the skin. Some think this provision goes back to Adam who may have offered an

animal-sacrifice after his sin and then received from God the skin to use for clothing for himself and for his wife (Gen 3.21). 7.23 The eating of fat was forbidden; it had to be burned. It appears, however, that this prohibition applied only to oxen, sheep, and goats — animals that were offered as sacrifices. The fat of the roebuck, the hart, and other clean animals could be eaten.

that died or was torn by wild animals may be put to any other use, but you must not eat it. 25 If any one of you eats the fat from an animal of which an offering by fire may be made to the LORD, you who eat it shall be cut off from your kin. 26 You must not eat any blood whatever, either of bird or of animal, in any of your settlements. 27 Any one of you who eats any blood shall be cut off from your kin.

7.26
Lev 17.10-14

g. The portion for the priesthood

28 The LORD spoke to Moses, saying: 29 Speak to the people of Israel, saying: Any one of you who would offer to the LORD your sacrifice of well-being must bring to the LORD your offering from your sacrifice of well-being. 30 Your own hands shall bring the LORD's offering by fire; you shall bring the fat with the breast, so that the breast may be raised as an elevation offering before the LORD. 31 The priest shall turn the fat into smoke on the altar, but the breast shall belong to Aaron and his sons. 32 And the right thigh from your sacrifices of well-being you shall give to the priest as an offering; 33 the one among the sons of Aaron who offers the blood and fat of the offering of well-being shall have the right thigh for a portion. 34 For I have taken the breast of the elevation offering, and the thigh that is offered, from the people of Israel, from their sacrifices of well-being, and have given them to Aaron the priest and to his sons, as a perpetual due from the people of Israel. 35 This is the portion allotted to Aaron and to his sons from the offerings made by fire to the LORD, once they have been brought forward to serve the LORD as priests; 36 these the LORD commanded to be given them, when he anointed them, as a perpetual due from the people of Israel throughout their generations.

7.29
Lev 3.1

7.31
v. 34

7.34
Num 18.18,
19

h. Summary

37 This is the ritual of the burnt offering, the grain offering, the sin offering, the guilt offering, the offering of ordination, and the sacrifice of well-being, 38 which the LORD commanded Moses on Mount Sinai, when he commanded the people of Israel to bring their offerings to the LORD, in the wilderness of Sinai.

7.37
Lev 6.9, 14,
20, 25; vv. 1,
11
7.38
Lev 1.1, 2

B. The priestly regulations

1. The consecration of the priesthood

a. Their anointing

8 The LORD spoke to Moses, saying: 2 Take Aaron and his sons with him, the vestments, the anointing oil, the bull of sin offering, the two rams, and the basket of unleavened bread; 3 and assemble the whole congregation at the entrance of the tent of meeting. 4 And Moses did as the LORD commanded him. When the congregation was assembled at the entrance of the tent of meeting, 5 Moses said to the congregation, "This is what the LORD has commanded to be done."

8.2
Ex 29.1-3;
28.2, 4;
30.24, 25

6 Then Moses brought Aaron and his sons forward, and washed them with water. 7 He put the tunic on him, fastened the sash around him, clothed him with the robe, and put the ephod on him. He then put the decorated band of the ephod around him, tying the ephod to him with it. 8 He placed the breastpiece on him, and in the breastpiece he put the Urim

8.6
Ex 29.4-6

8.8
Ex 28.30

7.26 *You must not eat any blood whatever.* Since blood represented the loss of life (Gen 9.4) and was to be used as an atonement and for nothing else, God commanded that it was never to be eaten or drunk. Some cultists believe that this commandment forbids blood transfusions. Transfusions, however, are not forbidden; rather, they serve as a wonderful illustration of the life-giving power of Christ's blood in atonement for us.
7.35,36 The Levites were given no land in Canaan.

Thus they had no active means by which to support themselves and their families. So God made provision for them by giving them the fruit of the altar. The priesthood was to be well-paid and well-provided for. Likewise the people of God today have an obligation to provide for the support of those who give themselves to the service of God.
8.8 *the Urim and the Thummim.* These were apparently a kind of sacred lot used to determine the Lord's will by a simple "yes" or "no" (see note on Ex. 28.30).

8.9 Ex 28.36, 37	and the Thummim. ⁹And he set the turban on his head, and on the turban, in front, he set the golden ornament, the holy crown, as the LORD commanded Moses.
8.10 v. 2	10 Then Moses took the anointing oil and anointed the tabernacle and all that was in it, and consecrated them. ¹¹He sprinkled some of it on the altar seven times, and anointed the altar and all its utensils, and the basin
8.12 Ex 30.30; Ps 133.2 **8.13** Ex 29.8, 9	and its base, to consecrate them. ¹²He poured some of the anointing oil on Aaron's head and anointed him, to consecrate him. ¹³And Moses brought forward Aaron's sons, and clothed them with tunics, and fastened sashes around them, and tied headdresses on them, as the LORD commanded Moses.

b. The sin offering

8.14 Ex 29.10; Lev 4.4 **8.15** Lev 4.7; Heb 9.22	14 He led forward the bull of sin offering; and Aaron and his sons laid their hands upon the head of the bull of sin offering, ¹⁵and it was slaughtered. Moses took the blood and with his finger put some on each of the horns of the altar, purifying the altar; then he poured out the blood at the base of the altar. Thus he consecrated it, to make atonement for it.
8.16 Lev 4.8	¹⁶Moses took all the fat that was around the entrails, and the appendage of the liver, and the two kidneys with their fat, and turned them into
8.17 Lev 4.11, 12	smoke on the altar. ¹⁷But the bull itself, its skin and flesh and its dung, he burned with fire outside the camp, as the LORD commanded Moses.

c. The burnt offering

8.18 Ex 29.15	18 Then he brought forward the ram of burnt offering. Aaron and his sons laid their hands on the head of the ram, ¹⁹and it was slaughtered. Moses dashed the blood against all sides of the altar. ²⁰The ram was cut into its parts, and Moses turned into smoke the head and the parts and
8.21 Ex 29.18	the suet. ²¹And after the entrails and the legs were washed with water, Moses turned into smoke the whole ram on the altar; it was a burnt offering for a pleasing odor, an offering by fire to the LORD, as the LORD commanded Moses.

d. The ram of ordination

8.22 Ex 29.19, 31	22 Then he brought forward the second ram, the ram of ordination. Aaron and his sons laid their hands on the head of the ram, ²³and it was slaughtered. Moses took some of its blood and put it on the lobe of Aaron's right ear and on the thumb of his right hand and on the big toe of his right foot. ²⁴After Aaron's sons were brought forward, Moses put some of the blood on the lobes of their right ears and on the thumbs of their right hands and on the big toes of their right feet; and Moses dashed the rest
8.25 Ex 29.22	of the blood against all sides of the altar. ²⁵He took the fat—the broad tail, all the fat that was around the entrails, the appendage of the liver,
8.26 Ex 29.23	and the two kidneys with their fat—and the right thigh. ²⁶From the basket of unleavened bread that was before the LORD, he took one cake of unleavened bread, one cake of bread with oil, and one wafer, and placed them on the fat and on the right thigh. ²⁷He placed all these on the palms of Aaron and on the palms of his sons, and raised them as an elevation
8.28 Ex 29.25	offering before the LORD. ²⁸Then Moses took them from their hands and turned them into smoke on the altar with the burnt offering. This was an ordination offering for a pleasing odor, an offering by fire to the LORD.
8.29 Ex 29.26	²⁹Moses took the breast and raised it as an elevation offering before the LORD; it was Moses' portion of the ram of ordination, as the LORD commanded Moses.
8.30 Ex 30.30; Num 3.3	30 Then Moses took some of the anointing oil and some of the blood that was on the altar and sprinkled them on Aaron and his vestments, and

---

8.15 Herein we see the formal institution of the Aaronic priesthood, with Moses acting as the priest. Moses inducted the priests into their office. Before they could function, blood atonement had to be made and the priests needed to be sanctified so that their service at the altar would be holy unto God.

also on his sons and their vestments. Thus he consecrated Aaron and his
vestments, and also his sons and their vestments.

e. The seven days of the ordination

31 And Moses said to Aaron and his sons, "Boil the flesh at the
entrance of the tent of meeting, and eat it there with the bread that is in
the basket of ordination offerings, as I was commanded, 'Aaron and his
sons shall eat it'; 32 and what remains of the flesh and the bread you shall
burn with fire. 33 You shall not go outside the entrance of the tent of
meeting for seven days, until the day when your period of ordination is
completed. For it will take seven days to ordain you; 34 as has been done
today, the LORD has commanded to be done to make atonement for you.
35 You shall remain at the entrance of the tent of meeting day and night
for seven days, keeping the LORD's charge so that you do not die; for so
I am commanded." 36 Aaron and his sons did all the things that the LORD
commanded through Moses.

2. The sacrifices

a. The offering for the priesthood

9 On the eighth day Moses summoned Aaron and his sons and the
elders of Israel. 2 He said to Aaron, "Take a bull calf for a sin offering
and a ram for a burnt offering, without blemish, and offer them before
the LORD. 3 And say to the people of Israel, 'Take a male goat for a sin
offering; a calf and a lamb, yearlings without blemish, for a burnt offering;
4 and an ox and a ram for an offering of well-being to sacrifice before the
LORD; and a grain offering mixed with oil. For today the LORD will appear
to you.' " 5 They brought what Moses commanded to the front of the tent
of meeting; and the whole congregation drew near and stood before the
LORD. 6 And Moses said, "This is the thing that the LORD commanded
you to do, so that the glory of the LORD may appear to you." 7 Then Moses
said to Aaron, "Draw near to the altar and sacrifice your sin offering and
your burnt offering, and make atonement for yourself and for the people;
and sacrifice the offering of the people, and make atonement for them;
as the LORD has commanded."

8 Aaron drew near to the altar, and slaughtered the calf of the sin
offering, which was for himself. 9 The sons of Aaron presented the blood
to him, and he dipped his finger in the blood and put it on the horns of
the altar; and the rest of the blood he poured out at the base of the altar.
10 But the fat, the kidneys, and the appendage of the liver from the sin
offering he turned into smoke on the altar, as the LORD commanded
Moses; 11 and the flesh and the skin he burned with fire outside the
camp.

12 Then he slaughtered the burnt offering. Aaron's sons brought him
the blood, and he dashed it against all sides of the altar. 13 And they
brought him the burnt offering piece by piece, and the head, which he
turned into smoke on the altar. 14 He washed the entrails and the legs and,
with the burnt offering, turned them into smoke on the altar.

b. The offering for the people

15 Next he presented the people's offering. He took the goat of the

Cross-references (margin):

8.31
Ex 29.31, 32

8.32
Ex 29.34
8.33
Ex 29.30, 35
8.34
Heb 7.16

9.2
Lev 8.18;
Ex 29.1
9.3
Lev 4.23

9.6
v. 23
9.7
Heb 5.1, 3

9.8
Lev 4.1-12
9.9
vv. 12, 18

9.11
Lev 4.11;
8.17

9.15
Lev 4.27-31

8.33 *seven days.* The newly installed priests were not
to go out of the entrance of the tent for seven days.
This symbolized the fact that they were giving themselves wholly to God. The seven days may well represent the creation days in Genesis, and they may indicate a new beginning. God was setting up an eternal
priesthood which would find its ultimate fulfillment
in his Son Jesus Christ.
9.4 *For today the LORD will appear to you.* Lest there

be any doubt in the minds of the newly installed
priests or in the minds of the people about the institution of the priesthood, Moses said the glory of God
would appear to them; this promise was fulfilled in v.
23. At the same time, fire came from God to consume
the sacrifice. These acts of God established the priesthood of Aaron as coming from God, not from Moses.
It was a divine institution through the human hands
of Moses.

9.16
Lev 1.3, 10
9.17
Lev 2.1, 2;
3.5

9.18
Lev 3.1-11

9.21
Lev 7.30-34

9.23
v. 6;
Num 14.10
9.24
1 Kings 18.38,
39

sin offering that was for the people, and slaughtered it, and presented it as a sin offering like the first one. 16 He presented the burnt offering, and sacrificed it according to regulation. 17 He presented the grain offering, and, taking a handful of it, he turned it into smoke on the altar, in addition to the burnt offering of the morning.

18 He slaughtered the ox and the ram as a sacrifice of well-being for the people. Aaron's sons brought him the blood, which he dashed against all sides of the altar, 19 and the fat of the ox and of the ram — the broad tail, the fat that covers the entrails, the two kidneys and the fat on them,*e* and the appendage of the liver. 20 They first laid the fat on the breasts, and the fat was turned into smoke on the altar; 21 and the breasts and the right thigh Aaron raised as an elevation offering before the LORD, as Moses had commanded.

22 Aaron lifted his hands toward the people and blessed them; and he came down after sacrificing the sin offering, the burnt offering, and the offering of well-being. 23 Moses and Aaron entered the tent of meeting, and then came out and blessed the people; and the glory of the LORD appeared to all the people. 24 Fire came out from the LORD and consumed the burnt offering and the fat on the altar; and when all the people saw it, they shouted and fell on their faces.

3. The death of Nadab and Abihu: their unholy fire

10.1
Num 3.4, 4;
Lev 16.12;
Ex 30.9
10.2
Num 3.4;
26.61
10.3
Ex 19.22;
30.30;
Lev 21.6

10 Now Aaron's sons, Nadab and Abihu, each took his censer, put fire in it, and laid incense on it; and they offered unholy fire before the LORD, such as he had not commanded them. 2 And fire came out from the presence of the LORD and consumed them, and they died before the LORD. 3 Then Moses said to Aaron, "This is what the LORD meant when he said,

'Through those who are near me
    I will show myself holy,
and before all the people
    I will be glorified.' "
And Aaron was silent.

10.4
Ex 6.18, 22;
Acts 5.6, 9,
10
10.6
Lev 21.1, 10;
Num 16.22,
46;
Josh 7;1;
22.18-20
10.7
Lev 21.12

4 Moses summoned Mishael and Elzaphan, sons of Uzziel the uncle of Aaron, and said to them, "Come forward, and carry your kinsmen away from the front of the sanctuary to a place outside the camp." 5 They came forward and carried them by their tunics out of the camp, as Moses had ordered. 6 And Moses said to Aaron and to his sons Eleazar and Ithamar, "Do not dishevel your hair, and do not tear your vestments, or you will die and wrath will strike all the congregation; but your kindred, the whole house of Israel, may mourn the burning that the LORD has sent. 7 You shall not go outside the entrance of the tent of meeting, or you will die; for the anointing oil of the LORD is on you." And they did as Moses had ordered.

e Gk: Heb the broad tail, and that which covers, and the kidneys

---

9.22 *lifted his hands . . . and blessed them.* The blessing of God was communicated to the people through the priest. His lifted hands indicated that the blessing came from God. Aaron here represents Christ who, at the time of his ascension, lifted up his hands and blessed them (Lk 24.50). Those who lift their hands to bless God's people have no power to do this on their own; they can only perform the function in the name of the Lord.
9.24 Fire has been regarded as a sacred symbol in many religions, and certainly plays a role in biblical faith. For example, here fire came from the Lord. The altar had a perpetual flame (6.13). Fire was used

by God as an instrument of vengeance (Ps 97.3; Isa 47.14; 66.16). It appeared miraculously as in the case of the blazing bush (Ex 3.2), of the plague God sent on the Egyptians (Ex 9.23,24), on Mount Sinai at the giving of the Law (Deut 4.11,36), and for the destruction of the enemies of Elijah (2 Kings 1.10,12). Christ is coming again in flaming fire (2 Thess 1.7).
10.1 *they offered unholy fire before the LORD.* Their fatal error is not clearly identified. Some commentators have suggested that the prohibition against the consumption of wine by the priests who were about to enter the tabernacle implies that Nadab and Abihu were drunk when they committed their offense.

4. *The command against wine for the performing priesthood*

8 And the LORD spoke to Aaron: 9 Drink no wine or strong drink, neither you nor your sons, when you enter the tent of meeting, that you may not die; it is a statute forever throughout your generations. 10 You are to distinguish between the holy and the common, and between the unclean and the clean; 11 and you are to teach the people of Israel all the statutes that the LORD has spoken to them through Moses.

5. *The law of the eating of holy things*

12 Moses spoke to Aaron and to his remaining sons, Eleazar and Ithamar: Take the grain offering that is left from the LORD's offerings by fire, and eat it unleavened beside the altar, for it is most holy; 13 you shall eat it in a holy place, because it is your due and your sons' due, from the offerings by fire to the LORD; for so I am commanded. 14 But the breast that is elevated and the thigh that is raised, you and your sons and daughters as well may eat in any clean place; for they have been assigned to you and your children from the sacrifices of the offerings of well-being of the people of Israel. 15 The thigh that is raised and the breast that is elevated they shall bring, together with the offerings by fire of the fat, to raise for an elevation offering before the LORD; they are to be your due and that of your children forever, as the LORD has commanded.

16 Then Moses made inquiry about the goat of the sin offering, and—it had already been burned! He was angry with Eleazar and Ithamar, Aaron's remaining sons, and said, 17 "Why did you not eat the sin offering in the sacred area? For it is most holy, and God*f* has given it to you that you may remove the guilt of the congregation, to make atonement on their behalf before the LORD. 18 Its blood was not brought into the inner part of the sanctuary. You should certainly have eaten it in the sanctuary, as I commanded." 19 And Aaron spoke to Moses, "See, today they offered their sin offering and their burnt offering before the LORD; and yet such things as these have befallen me! If I had eaten the sin offering today, would it have been agreeable to the LORD?" 20 And when Moses heard that, he agreed.

C. *The laws of purification*

1. *Clean and unclean animals*

11 The LORD spoke to Moses and Aaron, saying to them: 2 Speak to the people of Israel, saying:
From among all the land animals, these are the creatures that you may eat. 3 Any animal that has divided hoofs and is cleft-footed and chews the cud—such you may eat. 4 But among those that chew the cud or have divided hoofs, you shall not eat the following: the camel, for even though it chews the cud, it does not have divided hoofs; it is unclean for you. 5 The rock badger, for even though it chews the cud, it does not have divided

f Heb he

10.8,9 *Drink no . . . strong drink.* This must have been beer, since distilled liquors were unknown at that time.
10.10 *the unclean and the clean.* This is not a distinction between dirty things and clean things, but refers to what is ceremonially unclean, i.e., not to be used in connection with the worship of God.
10.16 *Aaron's remaining sons.* Nadab and Abihu, brothers of Eleazar and Ithamar, had lost their lives because they disobeyed God's instructions. Now Moses points out the sin of the two who are left alive and have become priests of God. They are warned not to repeat this error.

11.2,3 Under the old covenant, the dietary regulations were based on the following considerations: (1) some unclean birds and animals were forbidden because they fed on carrion or rotting foods; (2) pigs were associated with heathen worship and were offered to the gods of the nether world; and (3) some birds or animals were associated with objectionable connotations, such as "creeping things," which were serpent-like in their movements, or bats, which lived in dark caves and hated the light. The O.T. dietary laws have been made obsolete by the work of Christ (see note on v. 13ff).

10.9
Ezek 44.21

10.10
Lev 11.47;
20.25;
Ezek 22.26
10.11
Deut 24.8;
Mal 2.7

10.12
Lev 6.14-18;
21.22

10.14
Ex 29.24, 26, 27

10.15
Lev 7.29, 30, 34

10.17
Lev 6.24-30

10.19
Lev 9.8, 12

11.2
Deut 14.3-21

hoofs; it is unclean for you. 6 The hare, for even though it chews the cud, it does not have divided hoofs; it is unclean for you. 7 The pig, for even though it has divided hoofs and is cleft-footed, it does not chew the cud; it is unclean for you. 8 Of their flesh you shall not eat, and their carcasses you shall not touch; they are unclean for you.

9 These you may eat, of all that are in the waters. Everything in the waters that has fins and scales, whether in the seas or in the streams — such you may eat. 10 But anything in the seas or the streams that does not have fins and scales, of the swarming creatures in the waters and among all the other living creatures that are in the waters — they are detestable to you 11 and detestable they shall remain. Of their flesh you shall not eat, and their carcasses you shall regard as detestable. 12 Everything in the waters that does not have fins and scales is detestable to you.

13 These you shall regard as detestable among the birds. They shall not be eaten; they are an abomination: the eagle, the vulture, the osprey, 14 the buzzard, the kite of any kind; 15 every raven of any kind; 16 the ostrich, the nighthawk, the sea gull, the hawk of any kind; 17 the little owl, the cormorant, the great owl, 18 the water hen, the desert owl,g the carrion vulture, 19 the stork, the heron of any kind, the hoopoe, and the bat.h

20 All winged insects that walk upon all fours are detestable to you. 21 But among the winged insects that walk on all fours you may eat those that have jointed legs above their feet, with which to leap on the ground. 22 Of them you may eat: the locust according to its kind, the bald locust according to its kind, the cricket according to its kind, and the grasshopper according to its kind. 23 But all other winged insects that have four feet are detestable to you.

24 By these you shall become unclean; whoever touches the carcass of any of them shall be unclean until the evening, 25 and whoever carries any part of the carcass of any of them shall wash his clothes and be unclean until the evening. 26 Every animal that has divided hoofs but is not cleft-footed or does not chew the cud is unclean for you; everyone who touches one of them shall be unclean. 27 All that walk on their paws, among the animals that walk on all fours, are unclean for you; whoever touches the carcass of any of them shall be unclean until the evening, 28 and the one who carries the carcass shall wash his clothes and be unclean until the evening; they are unclean for you.

29 These are unclean for you among the creatures that swarm upon the earth: the weasel, the mouse, the great lizard according to its kind, 30 the gecko, the land crocodile, the lizard, the sand lizard, and the chameleon. 31 These are unclean for you among all that swarm; whoever touches one of them when they are dead shall be unclean until the evening. 32 And anything upon which any of them falls when they are dead shall be unclean, whether an article of wood or cloth or skin or sacking, any article that is used for any purpose; it shall be dipped into water, and it shall be unclean until the evening, and then it shall be clean. 33 And if any of them falls into any earthen vessel, all that is in it shall be unclean, and you shall break the vessel. 34 Any food that could be eaten shall be unclean if water from any such vessel comes upon it; and any liquid that could be drunk shall be unclean if it was in any such vessel. 35 Everything on which

g Or pelican   h Identification of several of the birds in verses 13-19 is uncertain

11.7 Isa 65.4; 66.3, 17
11.8 Isa 52.11; Heb 9.10
11.9 Deut 14.9
11.10 Lev 7.18; Deut 14.3
11.13 Deut 14.12
11.22 Mt 3.4; Mk 1.6
11.25 v. 40
11.29 Isa 66.17
11.32 Lev 15.12
11.33 Lev 6.28; 15.12

11.9,10 The Israelites were forbidden to eat shellfish, oysters, lobsters, crabs, and eels. Why they were considered unclean is not stated. The divine instructions were to be carried out, even though the reasons for them were not made plain.
11.13ff The regulations concerning the eating of fish, fowl, insects, and animals were not intended to remain in force forever. These ceremonial laws were superseded, according to Heb 8.1 — 10.18 and Acts 10.9ff, where God called clean what had been considered unclean under the old covenant. Peter needed this revelation in order to do what the Jewish law had forbidden.
11.24 By these you shall become unclean, i.e., ceremonially unclean, not dirty.

any part of the carcass falls shall be unclean; whether an oven or stove, it shall be broken in pieces; they are unclean, and shall remain unclean for you. 36 But a spring or a cistern holding water shall be clean, while whatever touches the carcass in it shall be unclean. 37 If any part of their carcass falls upon any seed set aside for sowing, it is clean; 38 but if water is put on the seed and any part of their carcass falls on it, it is unclean for you.

39   If an animal of which you may eat dies, anyone who touches its carcass shall be unclean until the evening. 40 Those who eat of its carcass shall wash their clothes and be unclean until the evening; and those who carry the carcass shall wash their clothes and be unclean until the evening. | **11.40** Lev 17.15; 22.8

41   All creatures that swarm upon the earth are detestable; they shall not be eaten. 42 Whatever moves on its belly, and whatever moves on all fours, or whatever has many feet, all the creatures that swarm upon the earth, you shall not eat; for they are detestable. 43 You shall not make yourselves detestable with any creature that swarms; you shall not defile yourselves with them, and so become unclean. 44 For I am the LORD your God; sanctify yourselves therefore, and be holy, for I am holy. You shall not defile yourselves with any swarming creature that moves on the earth. 45 For I am the LORD who brought you up out of the land of Egypt, to be your God; you shall be holy, for I am holy.

11.41 v. 29

11.43 Lev 20.25

11.44 Ex 6.7; 19.6; 1 Pet 1.15, 16

11.45 Ex 6.7

46   This is the law pertaining to land animal and bird and every living creature that moves through the waters and every creature that swarms upon the earth, 47 to make a distinction between the unclean and the clean, and between the living creature that may be eaten and the living creature that may not be eaten.

11.47 Lev 10.10

2. Purification of a woman after childbirth

12 The LORD spoke to Moses, saying: 2 Speak to the people of Israel, saying:
If a woman conceives and bears a male child, she shall be ceremonially unclean seven days; as at the time of her menstruation, she shall be unclean. 3 On the eighth day the flesh of his foreskin shall be circumcised. 4 Her time of blood purification shall be thirty-three days; she shall not touch any holy thing, or come into the sanctuary, until the days of her purification are completed. 5 If she bears a female child, she shall be unclean two weeks, as in her menstruation; her time of blood purification shall be sixty-six days.

12.2 Lev 15.19; 18.19

12.3 Gen 17.12

6   When the days of her purification are completed, whether for a son or for a daughter, she shall bring to the priest at the entrance of the tent of meeting a lamb in its first year for a burnt offering, and a pigeon or a turtledove for a sin offering. 7 He shall offer it before the LORD, and make atonement on her behalf; then she shall be clean from her flow of blood. This is the law for her who bears a child, male or female. 8 If she cannot afford a sheep, she shall take two turtledoves or two pigeons, one for a burnt offering and the other for a sin offering; and the priest shall make atonement on her behalf, and she shall be clean.

12.6 Lk 2.22

12.8 Lk 2.22-24; Lev 5.7; 4.26

11.41 *detestable.* Israel was to consider detestable whatever was offensive to God and his plan for living a righteous life, whether the unclean items were tabooed food, worship of idols, prostitution, or dishonesty.
11.45 These restrictions lead us to the question: Did God create creatures which he later disapproved of? The Bible says that all things were perfect and good when created (Gen 1.31). But after the fall of Adam, even as a curse was placed on the serpent (Gen 3.14), so other animal life was ceremonially contaminated in the fall.
12.2 A woman who gave birth to a male child was

strictly separated (isolated) for seven days. This was followed by circumcision on the eighth day. If a female child were born, the separation was for fourteen days. It is not clear why the period was double for the female child. A mother was required to be purified for thirty-three days after the birth of a male and for sixty-six days after the birth of a female child. During the time of purification, she could not come to the sanctuary, nor could she eat the passover or the sacrifice of well-being. If the mother were the wife of a priest, she could not eat anything that was holy to the Lord. All of this emphasizes the pollution of sin in which all of us are conceived and born.

3. The laws of skin disease

a. Diagnosis and treatment of skin diseases in humans

13 The LORD spoke to Moses and Aaron, saying: **2** When a person has on the skin of his body a swelling or an eruption or a spot, and it turns into a leprous[i] disease on the skin of his body, he shall be brought to Aaron the priest or to one of his sons the priests. **3** The priest shall examine the disease on the skin of his body, and if the hair in the diseased area has turned white and the disease appears to be deeper than the skin of his body, it is a leprous[i] disease; after the priest has examined him he shall pronounce him ceremonially unclean. **4** But if the spot is white in the skin of his body, and appears no deeper than the skin, and the hair in it has not turned white, the priest shall confine the diseased person for seven days. **5** The priest shall examine him on the seventh day, and if he sees that the disease is checked and the disease has not spread in the skin, then the priest shall confine him seven days more. **6** The priest shall examine him again on the seventh day, and if the disease has abated and the disease has not spread in the skin, the priest shall pronounce him clean; it is only an eruption; and he shall wash his clothes, and be clean. **7** But if the eruption spreads in the skin after he has shown himself to the priest for his cleansing, he shall appear again before the priest. **8** The priest shall make an examination, and if the eruption has spread in the skin, the priest shall pronounce him unclean; it is a leprous[i] disease.

9 When a person contracts a leprous[i] disease, he shall be brought to the priest. **10** The priest shall make an examination, and if there is a white swelling in the skin that has turned the hair white, and there is quick raw flesh in the swelling, **11** it is a chronic leprous[i] disease in the skin of his body. The priest shall pronounce him unclean; he shall not confine him, for he is unclean. **12** But if the disease breaks out in the skin, so that it covers all the skin of the diseased person from head to foot, so far as the priest can see, **13** then the priest shall make an examination, and if the disease has covered all his body, he shall pronounce him clean of the disease; since it has all turned white, he is clean. **14** But if raw flesh ever appears on him, he shall be unclean; **15** the priest shall examine the raw flesh and pronounce him unclean. Raw flesh is unclean, for it is a leprous[i] disease. **16** But if the raw flesh again turns white, he shall come to the priest; **17** the priest shall examine him, and if the disease has turned white, the priest shall pronounce the diseased person clean. He is clean.

18 When there is on the skin of one's body a boil that has healed, **19** and in the place of the boil there appears a white swelling or a reddish-white spot, it shall be shown to the priest. **20** The priest shall make an examination, and if it appears deeper than the skin and its hair has turned white, the priest shall pronounce him unclean; this is a leprous[i] disease, broken out in the boil. **21** But if the priest examines it and the hair on it is not white, nor is it deeper than the skin but has abated, the priest shall confine him seven days. **22** If it spreads in the skin, the priest shall pronounce him unclean; it is diseased. **23** But if the spot remains in one place and does not spread, it is the scar of the boil; the priest shall pronounce him clean.

24 Or, when the body has a burn on the skin and the raw flesh of the

Marginal references:
13.2 Deut 24.8
13.4 v. 21
13.6 Lev 11.25; 14.8
13.7 Lk 5.14
13.10 Num 12.10; 2 Kings 5.27; 2 Chr 26.20
13.12 Lk 5.12
13.15 Mt 8.3
13.18 Ex 9.9
13.19 v. 43
13.21 Num 12.14, 15

[i] A term for several skin diseases; precise meaning uncertain

13.2 *leprous disease* was a term that covered a number of skin diseases. It also included molds and defects in garments (13.47–59) and in houses (14.35–53). Some skin diseases were mistaken for leprosy.
13.9 The diagnosis and treatment of certain diseases were responsibilities given to the priests, though there is nothing in the Bible to suggest that such responsibilities belong to the bishops or elders in the churches today. The divine call to practice medicine is within the range of the gifts of the Holy Spirit, who endows believers with all sorts of occupations for the common good of people.

burn becomes a spot, reddish-white or white, 25 the priest shall examine it. If the hair in the spot has turned white and it appears deeper than the skin, it is a leprous^j disease; it has broken out in the burn, and the priest shall pronounce him unclean. This is a leprous^j disease. 26 But if the priest examines it and the hair in the spot is not white, and it is no deeper than the skin but has abated, the priest shall confine him seven days. 27 The priest shall examine him the seventh day; if it is spreading in the skin, the priest shall pronounce him unclean. This is a leprous^j disease. 28 But if the spot remains in one place and does not spread in the skin but has abated, it is a swelling from the burn, and the priest shall pronounce him clean; for it is the scar of the burn.

29   When a man or woman has a disease on the head or in the beard, 30 the priest shall examine the disease. If it appears deeper than the skin and the hair in it is yellow and thin, the priest shall pronounce him unclean; it is an itch, a leprous^j disease of the head or the beard. 31 If the priest examines the itching disease, and it appears no deeper than the skin and there is no black hair in it, the priest shall confine the person with the itching disease for seven days. 32 On the seventh day the priest shall examine the itch; if the itch has not spread, and there is no yellow hair in it, and the itch appears to be no deeper than the skin, 33 he shall shave, but the itch he shall not shave. The priest shall confine the person with the itch for seven days more. 34 On the seventh day the priest shall examine the itch; if the itch has not spread in the skin and it appears to be no deeper than the skin, the priest shall pronounce him clean. He shall wash his clothes and be clean. 35 But if the itch spreads in the skin after he was pronounced clean, 36 the priest shall examine him. If the itch has spread in the skin, the priest need not seek for the yellow hair; he is unclean. 37 But if in his eyes the itch is checked, and black hair has grown in it, the itch is healed, he is clean; and the priest shall pronounce him clean.

38   When a man or a woman has spots on the skin of the body, white spots, 39 the priest shall make an examination, and if the spots on the skin of the body are of a dull white, it is a rash that has broken out on the skin; he is clean.

40   If anyone loses the hair from his head, he is bald but he is clean. 41 If he loses the hair from his forehead and temples, he has baldness of the forehead but he is clean. 42 But if there is on the bald head or the bald forehead a reddish-white diseased spot, it is a leprous^j disease breaking out on his bald head or his bald forehead. 43 The priest shall examine him; if the diseased swelling is reddish-white on his bald head or on his bald forehead, which resembles a leprous^j disease in the skin of the body, 44 he is leprous,^j he is unclean. The priest shall pronounce him unclean; the disease is on his head.

45   The person who has the leprous^j disease shall wear torn clothes and let the hair of his head be disheveled; and he shall cover his upper lip and cry out, "Unclean, unclean." 46 He shall remain unclean as long as he has the disease; he is unclean. He shall live alone; his dwelling shall be outside the camp.

b. *Diagnosis and treatment of skin diseases in clothing*

47   Concerning clothing: when a leprous^j disease appears in it, in woolen or linen cloth, 48 in warp or woof of linen or wool, or in a skin or in anything made of skin, 49 if the disease shows greenish or reddish in the garment, whether in warp or woof or in skin or in anything made of

j A term for several skin diseases; precise meaning uncertain

13.45 Leprosy is a contagious disease and was known as such in the O.T. Provision was made for the separation of the contagious from general society, in order to prevent others from contracting the same disease.

Marginal references:
13.25 v. 15 · 13.27 v. 5 · 13.29 v. 44 · 13.32 v. 5 · 13.34 Lev 14.8 · 13.36 v. 30 · 13.40 Ezek 29.18 · 13.44 v. 29 · 13.45 Ezek 24.17, 22; Mic 3.7; Lam 4.15 · 13.46 Num 5.2; 12.14; 2 Kings 7.3; 15.5; Lk 17.12

skin, it is a leprous*k* disease and shall be shown to the priest. 50 The priest shall examine the disease, and put the diseased article aside for seven days.

13.51
Lev 14.44

13.52
Lev 14.44

13.54
v. 4

13.56
Lev 14.8

51 He shall examine the disease on the seventh day. If the disease has spread in the cloth, in warp or woof, or in the skin, whatever be the use of the skin, this is a spreading leprous*k* disease; it is unclean. 52 He shall burn the clothing, whether diseased in warp or woof, woolen or linen, or anything of skin, for it is a leprous*k* disease; it shall be burned in fire.

53 If the priest makes an examination, and the disease has not spread in the clothing, in warp or woof or in anything of skin, 54 the priest shall command them to wash the article in which the disease appears, and he shall put it aside seven days more. 55 The priest shall examine the diseased article after it has been washed. If the diseased spot has not changed color, though the disease has not spread, it is unclean; you shall burn it in fire, whether the leprous*k* spot is on the inside or on the outside.

56 If the priest makes an examination, and the disease has abated after it is washed, he shall tear the spot out of the cloth, in warp or woof, or out of skin. 57 If it appears again in the garment, in warp or woof, or in anything of skin, it is spreading; you shall burn with fire that in which the disease appears. 58 But the cloth, warp or woof, or anything of skin from which the disease disappears when you have washed it, shall then be washed a second time, and it shall be clean.

59 This is the ritual for a leprous*k* disease in a cloth of wool or linen, either in warp or woof, or in anything of skin, to decide whether it is clean or unclean.

c. The laws of purification for skin diseases

14.2
Mt 8.2, 4;
Mk 1.40, 44;
Lk 5.12, 14;
17.14

14.4
vv. 6, 49, 51,
52;
Num 19.6

14.7
2 Kings 5.10,
14
14.8
Lev 13.6;
Num 8.7

14.10
Mt 8.4;
Mk 1.44;
Lk 5.14

14 The Lord spoke to Moses, saying: 2 This shall be the ritual for the leprous*k* person at the time of his cleansing:

He shall be brought to the priest; 3 the priest shall go out of the camp, and the priest shall make an examination. If the disease is healed in the leprous*k* person, 4 the priest shall command that two living clean birds and cedarwood and crimson yarn and hyssop be brought for the one who is to be cleansed. 5 The priest shall command that one of the birds be slaughtered over fresh water in an earthen vessel. 6 He shall take the living bird with the cedarwood and the crimson yarn and the hyssop, and dip them and the living bird in the blood of the bird that was slaughtered over the fresh water. 7 He shall sprinkle it seven times upon the one who is to be cleansed of the leprous*k* disease; then he shall pronounce him clean, and he shall let the living bird go into the open field. 8 The one who is to be cleansed shall wash his clothes, and shave off all his hair, and bathe himself in water, and he shall be clean. After that he shall come into the camp, but shall live outside his tent seven days. 9 On the seventh day he shall shave all his hair: of head, beard, eyebrows; he shall shave all his hair. Then he shall wash his clothes, and bathe his body in water, and he shall be clean.

10 On the eighth day he shall take two male lambs without blemish, and one ewe lamb in its first year without blemish, and a grain offering of three-tenths of an ephah of choice flour mixed with oil, and one log*l*

k A term for several skin diseases; precise meaning uncertain   *l* A liquid measure

13.59 The larger question in all of these instructions is why God allows sickness, disease, and such things as leprosy to afflict his own redeemed people. This happens because God has not ordained specific exceptions to his law. Even as the sun shines on the just and the unjust, so are all people, including believers, subjected to the ordinary hazards of life.
14.7 The law of purification for deliverance from leprosy included the use of two birds. One was killed

and the other dipped in the blood of the killed bird and then set free. What does this mean? Some say the slain bird typifies Christ dying for our sins, and the living bird Christ rising again for our justification. Believers have been sprinkled by the blood of Christ, and they have been set free from the law of sin and of death (cf. Rom 8.1,2). They live to die no more, but in their living they glorify the one by whose blood they have been set free.

of oil. 11 The priest who cleanses shall set the person to be cleansed, along with these things, before the LORD, at the entrance of the tent of meeting. 12 The priest shall take one of the lambs, and offer it as a guilt offering, along with the log*m* of oil, and raise them as an elevation offering before the LORD. 13 He shall slaughter the lamb in the place where the sin offering and the burnt offering are slaughtered in the holy place; for the guilt offering, like the sin offering, belongs to the priest: it is most holy. 14 The priest shall take some of the blood of the guilt offering and put it on the lobe of the right ear of the one to be cleansed, and on the thumb of the right hand, and on the big toe of the right foot. 15 The priest shall take some of the log*m* of oil and pour it into the palm of his own left hand, 16 and dip his right finger in the oil that is in his left hand and sprinkle some oil with his finger seven times before the LORD. 17 Some of the oil that remains in his hand the priest shall put on the lobe of the right ear of the one to be cleansed, and on the thumb of the right hand, and on the big toe of the right foot, on top of the blood of the guilt offering. 18 The rest of the oil that is in the priest's hand he shall put on the head of the one to be cleansed. Then the priest shall make atonement on his behalf before the LORD: 19 the priest shall offer the sin offering, to make atonement for the one to be cleansed from his uncleanness. Afterward he shall slaughter the burnt offering; 20 and the priest shall offer the burnt offering and the grain offering on the altar. Thus the priest shall make atonement on his behalf and he shall be clean.

21 But if he is poor and cannot afford so much, he shall take one male lamb for a guilt offering to be elevated, to make atonement on his behalf, and one-tenth of an ephah of choice flour mixed with oil for a grain offering and a log*m* of oil; 22 also two turtledoves or two pigeons, such as he can afford, one for a sin offering and the other for a burnt offering. 23 On the eighth day he shall bring them for his cleansing to the priest, to the entrance of the tent of meeting, before the LORD; 24 and the priest shall take the lamb of the guilt offering and the log*m* of oil, and the priest shall raise them as an elevation offering before the LORD. 25 The priest shall slaughter the lamb of the guilt offering and shall take some of the blood of the guilt offering, and put it on the lobe of the right ear of the one to be cleansed, and on the thumb of the right hand, and on the big toe of the right foot. 26 The priest shall pour some of the oil into the palm of his own left hand, 27 and shall sprinkle with his right finger some of the oil that is in his left hand seven times before the LORD. 28 The priest shall put some of the oil that is in his hand on the lobe of the right ear of the one to be cleansed, and on the thumb of the right hand, and the big toe of the right foot, where the blood of the guilt offering was placed. 29 The rest of the oil that is in the priest's hand he shall put on the head of the one to be cleansed, to make atonement on his behalf before the LORD. 30 And he shall offer, of the turtledoves or pigeons such as he can afford, 31 one*n* for a sin offering and the other for a burnt offering, along with a grain offering; and the priest shall make atonement before the LORD on behalf of the one being cleansed. 32 This is the ritual for the one who has a leprous*o* disease, who cannot afford the offerings for his cleansing.

14.12	Lev 5.2, 8; 6.6, 7; Ex 29.24
14.13	Lev 1.5, 11; 6.24-30; 2.3; 7.6
14.14	Lev 8.23
14.18	Lev 4.26
14.19	v. 12
14.21	Lev 5.7, 11; 12.8; v. 22
14.22	Lev 12.8; 15.14, 15
14.23	vv. 10, 11
14.24	v. 12
14.25	v. 14
14.28	Lev 5.6
14.30	v. 22; Lev 15.15
14.31	Lev 5.7

---

m A liquid measure   *n* Gk Syr: Heb *afford, 31such as he can afford, one*   *o* A term for several skin diseases; precise meaning uncertain

---

14.18 *make atonement on his behalf before the LORD.* If an atonement was required for one who had been delivered from leprosy, how much more is an atonement needed for those who have been separated from God because of their sins and need to be restored to God's fellowship.
14.21 God made provision both for the rich and for the poor. Those who were poor needed to bring one

lamb and one-tenth of an ephah of choice flour. In place of the additional two lambs which well-to-do people brought, the poor needed only two turtledoves or two young pigeons. In the age of the gospel, God again has respect for the poor. Mercy is deep and free, so if you have nothing to bring, you need bring only yourself.

d. *Diagnosis and treatment of skin diseases in houses*

33 The LORD spoke to Moses and Aaron, saying:

34 When you come into the land of Canaan, which I give you for a possession, and I put a leprous*ᵖ* disease in a house in the land of your possession, 35 the owner of the house shall come and tell the priest, saying, "There seems to me to be some sort of disease in my house." 36 The priest shall command that they empty the house before the priest goes to examine the disease, or all that is in the house will become unclean; and afterward the priest shall go in to inspect the house. 37 He shall examine the disease; if the disease is in the walls of the house with greenish or reddish spots, and if it appears to be deeper than the surface, 38 the priest shall go outside to the door of the house and shut up the house seven days. 39 The priest shall come again on the seventh day and make an inspection; if the disease has spread in the walls of the house, 40 the priest shall command that the stones in which the disease appears be taken out and thrown into an unclean place outside the city. 41 He shall have the inside of the house scraped thoroughly, and the plaster that is scraped off shall be dumped in an unclean place outside the city. 42 They shall take other stones and put them in the place of those stones, and take other plaster and plaster the house.

43 If the disease breaks out again in the house, after he has taken out the stones and scraped the house and plastered it, 44 the priest shall go and make inspection; if the disease has spread in the house, it is a spreading leprous*ᵖ* disease in the house; it is unclean. 45 He shall have the house torn down, its stones and timber and all the plaster of the house, and taken outside the city to an unclean place. 46 All who enter the house while it is shut up shall be unclean until the evening; 47 and all who sleep in the house shall wash their clothes; and all who eat in the house shall wash their clothes.

48 If the priest comes and makes an inspection, and the disease has not spread in the house after the house was plastered, the priest shall pronounce the house clean; the disease is healed. 49 For the cleansing of the house he shall take two birds, with cedarwood and crimson yarn and hyssop, 50 and shall slaughter one of the birds over fresh water in an earthen vessel, 51 and shall take the cedarwood and the hyssop and the crimson yarn, along with the living bird, and dip them in the blood of the slaughtered bird and the fresh water, and sprinkle the house seven times. 52 Thus he shall cleanse the house with the blood of the bird, and with the fresh water, and with the living bird, and with the cedarwood and hyssop and crimson yarn; 53 and he shall let the living bird go out of the city into the open field; so he shall make atonement for the house, and it shall be clean.

54 This is the ritual for any leprous*ᵖ* disease: for an itch, 55 for leprous*ᵖ* diseases in clothing and houses, 56 and for a swelling or an eruption or a spot, 57 to determine when it is unclean and when it is clean. This is the ritual for leprous*ᵖ* diseases.

4. *Unclean discharges and cleansing*

a. *Uncleanness in man: purification*

15 The LORD spoke to Moses and Aaron, saying: 2 Speak to the people of Israel and say to them:

When any man has a discharge from his member,*q* his discharge makes

p A term for several skin diseases; precise meaning uncertain   q Heb flesh

---

Cross-references (left margin):

14.34 Gen 17.8; Num 32.22; Deut 7.1
14.35 Ps 91.10; Prov 3.33
14.38 Num 12.15
14.40 v. 45
14.44 Lev 13.51
14.49 v. 4
14.51 Ps 51.7
14.53 v. 20
14.54 Lev 13.30
14.56 Lev 13.2
15.2 Lev 22.4; Num 5.2; 2 Sam 3.29; Mt 9.20

14.53 *atonement for the house.* Deut 20.5 indicates that the houses of the Israelites were dedicated. Each one was to be kept free from ceremonial uncleanness; but when unclean, an atonement had to be made for it. Our bodies are the houses of the Holy Spirit (1 Cor 6.19,20); we must make our hearts fit for the service of the Lord by keeping them dedicated and clean.

him ceremonially unclean. 3 The uncleanness of his discharge is this: whether his member^r flows with his discharge, or his member^r is stopped from discharging, it is uncleanness for him. 4 Every bed on which the one with the discharge lies shall be unclean; and everything on which he sits shall be unclean. 5 Anyone who touches his bed shall wash his clothes, and bathe in water, and be unclean until the evening. 6 All who sit on anything on which the one with the discharge has sat shall wash their clothes, and bathe in water, and be unclean until the evening. 7 All who touch the body of the one with the discharge shall wash their clothes, and bathe in water, and be unclean until the evening. 8 If the one with the discharge spits on persons who are clean, then they shall wash their clothes, and bathe in water, and be unclean until the evening. 9 Any saddle on which the one with the discharge rides shall be unclean. 10 All who touch anything that was under him shall be unclean until the evening, and all who carry such a thing shall wash their clothes, and bathe in water, and be unclean until the evening. 11 All those whom the one with the discharge touches without his having rinsed his hands in water shall wash their clothes, and bathe in water, and be unclean until the evening. 12 Any earthen vessel that the one with the discharge touches shall be broken; and every vessel of wood shall be rinsed in water.

13   When the one with a discharge is cleansed of his discharge, he shall count seven days for his cleansing; he shall wash his clothes and bathe his body in fresh water, and he shall be clean. 14 On the eighth day he shall take two turtledoves or two pigeons and come before the LORD to the entrance of the tent of meeting and give them to the priest. 15 The priest shall offer them, one for a sin offering and the other for a burnt offering; and the priest shall make atonement on his behalf before the LORD for his discharge.

16   If a man has an emission of semen, he shall bathe his whole body in water, and be unclean until the evening. 17 Everything made of cloth or of skin on which the semen falls shall be washed with water, and be unclean until the evening. 18 If a man lies with a woman and has an emission of semen, both of them shall bathe in water, and be unclean until the evening.

b. Uncleanness in woman: purification

19   When a woman has a discharge of blood that is her regular discharge from her body, she shall be in her impurity for seven days, and whoever touches her shall be unclean until the evening. 20 Everything upon which she lies during her impurity shall be unclean; everything also upon which she sits shall be unclean. 21 Whoever touches her bed shall wash his clothes, and bathe in water, and be unclean until the evening. 22 Whoever touches anything upon which she sits shall wash his clothes, and bathe in water, and be unclean until the evening; 23 whether it is the bed or anything upon which she sits, when he touches it he shall be unclean until the evening. 24 If any man lies with her, and her impurity falls on him, he shall be unclean seven days; and every bed on which he lies shall be unclean.

25   If a woman has a discharge of blood for many days, not at the time

^r Heb flesh

15.7
Num 19.19

15.10
Num 19.10

15.12
Lev 6.28;
11.32, 33

15.13
v. 28

15.14
Lev 14.22, 23

15.15
Lev 14.30, 31

15.16
Lev 22.4;
Deut 23.10

15.18
1 Sam 21.4

15.19
Lev 12.2

15.21
v. 27

15.24
Lev 20.18

15.25
Mt 9.20;
Mk 5.25;
Lk 8.43

15.18 Those who had sexual intercourse, women who were menstruating, or men who had a natural emission of semen became ceremonially unclean; but there was no need for them to bring an offering or make atonement. Sexual intercourse performed under the proper biblical conditions is beautiful, is the will of God, and has the divine blessing. Only the wrongful use of sex is prohibited and requires a sin offering.
15.25 A woman who had a discharge of blood un-

related to her normal physical cycle was unclean. When she was healed of that condition, the usual guilt and burnt offerings were required. While a woman had such a condition, she contaminated all that she touched. Jesus met such a woman, who was healed by touching his garment (see Lk 8.43–48). We are not told, however, that our Savior became unclean or that an offering was required of him. The one who gave the law is above the law, for he is the giver and cannot be contaminated by those who breach the law. God

of her impurity, or if she has a discharge beyond the time of her impurity, all the days of the discharge she shall continue in uncleanness; as in the days of her impurity, she shall be unclean. 26 Every bed on which she lies during all the days of her discharge shall be treated as the bed of her impurity; and everything on which she sits shall be unclean, as in the uncleanness of her impurity. 27 Whoever touches these things shall be unclean, and shall wash his clothes, and bathe in water, and be unclean until the evening. 28 If she is cleansed of her discharge, she shall count seven days, and after that she shall be clean. 29 On the eighth day she shall take two turtledoves or two pigeons and bring them to the priest at the entrance of the tent of meeting. 30 The priest shall offer one for a sin offering and the other for a burnt offering; and the priest shall make atonement on her behalf before the LORD for her unclean discharge.

31 Thus you shall keep the people of Israel separate from their uncleanness, so that they do not die in their uncleanness by defiling my tabernacle that is in their midst.

32 This is the ritual for those who have a discharge: for him who has an emission of semen, becoming unclean thereby, 33 for her who is in the infirmity of her period, for anyone, male or female, who has a discharge, and for the man who lies with a woman who is unclean.

D. The day of atonement

1. The institution of the ceremony

16 The LORD spoke to Moses after the death of the two sons of Aaron, when they drew near before the LORD and died. 2 The LORD said to Moses:

Tell your brother Aaron not to come just at any time into the sanctuary inside the curtain before the mercy seat*s* that is upon the ark, or he will die; for I appear in the cloud upon the mercy seat.*s* 3 Thus shall Aaron come into the holy place: with a young bull for a sin offering and a ram for a burnt offering. 4 He shall put on the holy linen tunic, and shall have the linen undergarments next to his body, fasten the linen sash, and wear the linen turban; these are the holy vestments. He shall bathe his body in water, and then put them on. 5 He shall take from the congregation of the people of Israel two male goats for a sin offering, and one ram for a burnt offering.

6 Aaron shall offer the bull as a sin offering for himself, and shall make atonement for himself and for his house. 7 He shall take the two goats and set them before the LORD at the entrance of the tent of meeting; 8 and Aaron shall cast lots on the two goats, one lot for the LORD and the other lot for Azazel.*t* 9 Aaron shall present the goat on which the lot fell for the LORD, and offer it as a sin offering; 10 but the goat on which the lot fell

s Or *the cover*   *t* Traditionally rendered *a scapegoat*

Margin references:

15.27
v. 21

15.29
Gen 15.9

15.31
Ezek 44.23;
Num 5.3;
19.13, 20;
Ezek 5.11;
23.38
15.32
vv. 2, 16
15.33
vv. 19, 24, 25

16.1
Lev 10.1, 2
16.2
Ex 30.10;
Heb 9.7;
10.19;
Ex 25.21, 22
16.3
Heb 9.7, 12,
24, 25;
Lev 4.3
16.4
Ex 28.39, 42,
43; v. 24
16.5
Lev 4.13-21

16.6
Lev 9.7;
Heb 5.2;
7.27, 28; 9.7

---

cannot lose his sanctity because of the sins of the people.
16.1,2 Day of atonement. This event, celebrated once a year, was a high day for Israel, the only one when the high priest entered the inner sanctuary, that is, when he went behind the curtain that separated the most holy place with its mercy seat. He had to enter the inner sanctuary with blood to make atonement, first for his own sins and then for the sins of the people. This sanctuary represents the heavenly sanctuary into which Christ entered with his own blood to make atonement for us. Whereas the day of atonement was celebrated as a yearly event under the old covenant, Jesus entered only once; his is a finished work that never needs to be repeated (see Heb 9.12-28).
16.6 The Hebrew word *kippūr* ("atonement") is de-

rived from the verb *kippēr* ("to atone") and means to cover over by an expiatory sacrifice. In the O.T. animal sacrifices were substituted for the offerers, providing a covering for the people of Israel and anticipating Christ's great sacrifice at Calvary. He is the once-for-all substitute whose blood covers all our sins. The word used is "reconciliation" (*katallagē* in Greek) and means "effecting legal and moral reparation for injury done." The atonement makes forgiveness possible and restores to humans what was lost by Adam's sin.
16.10 *goat*, here refers to "Azazel" (NRSV footnote has "scapegoat"). In the Scriptures two types of goats are mentioned: the first one was slain as a sin offering; the other one was placed before the Lord and then sent out into the wilderness. The Scriptures are unclear as to the meaning of this second one. In some

for Azazel[u] shall be presented alive before the LORD to make atonement over it, that it may be sent away into the wilderness to Azazel.[u]

2. The sin offering for the high priest

11 Aaron shall present the bull as a sin offering for himself, and shall make atonement for himself and for his house; he shall slaughter the bull as a sin offering for himself. 12 He shall take a censer full of coals of fire from the altar before the LORD, and two handfuls of crushed sweet incense, and he shall bring it inside the curtain 13 and put the incense on the fire before the LORD, that the cloud of the incense may cover the mercy seat[v] that is upon the covenant,[w] or he will die. 14 He shall take some of the blood of the bull, and sprinkle it with his finger on the front of the mercy seat,[v] and before the mercy seat[v] he shall sprinkle the blood with his finger seven times.

3. The sin offering for the people

15 He shall slaughter the goat of the sin offering that is for the people and bring its blood inside the curtain, and do with its blood as he did with the blood of the bull, sprinkling it upon the mercy seat[v] and before the mercy seat.[v] 16 Thus he shall make atonement for the sanctuary, because of the uncleannesses of the people of Israel, and because of their transgressions, all their sins; and so he shall do for the tent of meeting, which remains with them in the midst of their uncleannesses. 17 No one shall be in the tent of meeting from the time he enters to make atonement in the sanctuary until he comes out and has made atonement for himself and for his house and for all the assembly of Israel. 18 Then he shall go out to the altar that is before the LORD and make atonement on its behalf, and shall take some of the blood of the bull and of the blood of the goat, and put it on each of the horns of the altar. 19 He shall sprinkle some of the blood on it with his finger seven times, and cleanse it and hallow it from the uncleannesses of the people of Israel.

4. The scapegoat

20 When he has finished atoning for the holy place and the tent of meeting and the altar, he shall present the live goat. 21 Then Aaron shall lay both his hands on the head of the live goat, and confess over it all the iniquities of the people of Israel, and all their transgressions, all their sins, putting them on the head of the goat, and sending it away into the wilderness by means of someone designated for the task.[x] 22 The goat shall bear on itself all their iniquities to a barren region; and the goat shall be set free in the wilderness.

23 Then Aaron shall enter the tent of meeting, and shall take off the linen vestments that he put on when he went into the holy place, and shall leave them there. 24 He shall bathe his body in water in a holy place, and put on his vestments; then he shall come out and offer his burnt offering and the burnt offering of the people, making atonement for himself and for the people. 25 The fat of the sin offering he shall turn into smoke on the altar. 26 The one who sets the goat free for Azazel[u] shall wash his clothes and bathe his body in water, and afterward may come into the camp. 27 The bull of the sin offering and the goat of the sin offering, whose blood was brought in to make atonement in the holy place, shall be taken

---

16.11
Heb 7.27; 9.7

16.12
Lev 10.1;
Ex 30.34
16.13
Lev 22.9

16.14
Heb 9.13, 25;
Lev 4.6, 17

16.15
Heb 9.3, 7,
12

16.16
Ex 29.36;
Heb 2.17

16.18
Lev 4.25;
Ezek 43.20,
22
16.19
v. 14

16.21
Isa 53.6

16.22
Isa 53.11, 12

16.23
v. 4;
Ezek 42.14;
44.19
16.24
vv. 3-5

16.27
Lev 4.12, 21;
6.30;
Heb 13.11

---

[u] Traditionally rendered a scapegoat   [v] Or the cover   [w] Or treaty, or testament; Heb eduth   [x] Meaning of Heb uncertain

---

manner, it points to Jesus Christ (Isa 53.6,11,12). Some have suggested that the scapegoat is a name for Satan, but this theory has little to commend it. In the noncanonical book of Enoch, "scapegoat" is the name of a fallen angel who misled the human race. Some think the word is a reduplicated root from the Hebrew word azal, meaning "depart" or "remove." The silence of the Scriptures indicates that the whole matter must be quite incidental, for if it were not, the Holy Spirit would have given us more information.

outside the camp; their skin and their flesh and their dung shall be consumed in fire. 28 The one who burns them shall wash his clothes and bathe his body in water, and afterward may come into the camp.

5. The day of atonement a statute forever

16.29
Lev 23.27;
Num 29.7

16.31
Lev 23.32;
Isa 58.3, 5
16.32
v. 4;
Num 20.26,
28
16.33
vv. 6, 16-18,
24
16.34
Heb 9.7, 25

29 This shall be a statute to you forever: In the seventh month, on the tenth day of the month, you shall deny yourselves,^{y} and shall do no work, neither the citizen nor the alien who resides among you. 30 For on this day atonement shall be made for you, to cleanse you; from all your sins you shall be clean before the LORD. 31 It is a sabbath of complete rest to you, and you shall deny yourselves;^{y} it is a statute forever. 32 The priest who is anointed and consecrated as priest in his father's place shall make atonement, wearing the linen vestments, the holy vestments. 33 He shall make atonement for the sanctuary, and he shall make atonement for the tent of meeting and for the altar, and he shall make atonement for the priests and for all the people of the assembly. 34 This shall be an everlasting statute for you, to make atonement for the people of Israel once in the year for all their sins. And Moses did as the LORD had commanded him.

II. The maintaining of fellowship with a holy God (17.1–27.34)

A. Rules for killing of animals

17.4
Deut 12.5-21;
Rom 5.13

17 The LORD spoke to Moses: 2 Speak to Aaron and his sons and to all the people of Israel and say to them: This is what the LORD has commanded. 3 If anyone of the house of Israel slaughters an ox or a lamb or a goat in the camp, or slaughters it outside the camp, 4 and does not bring it to the entrance of the tent of meeting, to present it as an offering to the LORD before the tabernacle of the LORD, he shall be held guilty of bloodshed; he has shed blood, and he shall be cut off from the people. 5 This is in order that the people of Israel may bring their sacrifices that they offer in the open field, that they may bring them to the LORD, to the priest at the entrance of the tent of meeting, and offer them as sacrifices of well-being to the LORD.

17.6
Lev 3.2;
Num 18.17
17.7
Ex 22.20;
32.8; 34.15;
Deut 32.17;
2 Chr 11.15

6 The priest shall dash the blood against the altar of the LORD at the entrance of the tent of meeting, and turn the fat into smoke as a pleasing odor to the LORD, 7 so that they may no longer offer their sacrifices for goat-demons, to whom they prostitute themselves. This shall be a statute forever to them throughout their generations.

17.9
v. 4

8 And say to them further: Anyone of the house of Israel or of the aliens who reside among them who offers a burnt offering or sacrifice, 9 and does not bring it to the entrance of the tent of meeting, to sacrifice it to the LORD, shall be cut off from the people.

^{y} Or shall fast

16.29,30 deny yourselves (NRSV footnote has "shall fast"). This common practice in the O.T. and N.T. included mourning, self-abasement, and abstaining from food (Deut 9.18; Neh 9.1; Joel 2.12). It was used in times of danger, affliction, calamities, and misfortune. Sins were confessed (1 Sam 7.6; Neh 9.3), and supplicatory prayers were prayed (Ezra 8.23; Dan 9.3). Fasting was an outward sign of an inward heart change. It could be practiced individually or nationally. Hypocrites used it to make people think they were pious (Mt 6.16–18). Examples of individuals who practiced fasting include David (2 Sam 12.16), Daniel (Dan 9.3), Cornelius (Acts 10.30), and Paul (2 Cor 11.27). Fasting was required one day a year, in

the seventh month, on the tenth day of the month (on our calendar, about the twenty-fifth day of September).

17.1ff The laws recorded in 17.1 – 26.45 were given to Moses by God at Sinai. They are often called "The Holiness Code," because they set forth how the Israelites were to act, think, and live if they were to be a holy people before the Lord.

17.3,4 All animal sacrifices were to be made at the tabernacle, not at a shrine of one's own choosing. Disobeying God's command resulted in being declared guilty of bloodshed and being banished from the nation. The right sacrifice at the wrong place was useless.

B. *The eating of blood prohibited*

10 If anyone of the house of Israel or of the aliens who reside among them eats any blood, I will set my face against that person who eats blood, and will cut that person off from the people. 11 For the life of the flesh is in the blood; and I have given it to you for making atonement for your lives on the altar; for, as life, it is the blood that makes atonement. 12 Therefore I have said to the people of Israel: No person among you shall eat blood, nor shall any alien who resides among you eat blood. 13 And anyone of the people of Israel, or of the aliens who reside among them, who hunts down an animal or bird that may be eaten shall pour out its blood and cover it with earth.

14 For the life of every creature—its blood is its life; therefore I have said to the people of Israel: You shall not eat the blood of any creature, for the life of every creature is its blood; whoever eats it shall be cut off. 15 All persons, citizens or aliens, who eat what dies of itself or what has been torn by wild animals, shall wash their clothes, and bathe themselves in water, and be unclean until the evening; then they shall be clean. 16 But if they do not wash themselves or bathe their body, they shall bear their guilt.

C. *Laws on sexual relations*

1. *Introduction*

18 The LORD spoke to Moses, saying: 2 Speak to the people of Israel and say to them: I am the LORD your God. 3 You shall not do as they do in the land of Egypt, where you lived, and you shall not do as they do in the land of Canaan, to which I am bringing you. You shall not follow their statutes. 4 My ordinances you shall observe and my statutes you shall keep, following them: I am the LORD your God. 5 You shall keep my statutes and my ordinances; by doing so one shall live: I am the LORD.

2. *Incest forbidden*

6 None of you shall approach anyone near of kin to uncover nakedness: I am the LORD. 7 You shall not uncover the nakedness of your father, which is the nakedness of your mother; she is your mother, you shall not uncover her nakedness. 8 You shall not uncover the nakedness of your father's wife; it is the nakedness of your father. 9 You shall not uncover the nakedness of your sister, your father's daughter or your mother's daughter, whether born at home or born abroad. 10 You shall not uncover the nakedness of your son's daughter or of your daughter's daughter, for their nakedness is your own nakedness. 11 You shall not uncover the nakedness of your father's wife's daughter, begotten by your father, since she is your sister. 12 You shall not uncover the nakedness of your father's sister; she is your father's flesh. 13 You shall not uncover the nakedness of your mother's sister, for she is your mother's flesh. 14 You shall not uncover the nakedness of your father's brother, that is, you shall not approach his wife; she is your aunt. 15 You shall not uncover the nakedness of your daughter-in-law: she is your son's wife; you shall not uncover her nakedness. 16 You shall not uncover the nakedness of your brother's wife; it is your brother's nakedness. 17 You shall not uncover the naked-

17.10
Lev 3.17;
Deut 12.16,
23
17.11
v. 14;
Gen 9.4;
Heb 9.22
17.13
Lev 7.26;
Deut 12.16

17.14
v. 11

17.15
Ex 22.31;
Deut 14.21

18.2
Ex 6.7;
Lev 11.44
18.3
Ezek 20.7, 8;
Ex 23.24;
Lev 20.23
18.5
Ezek 20.11;
Lk 10.28;
Rom 10.5;
Gal 3.12

18.7
Lev 20.11

18.9
Lev 20.17

18.12
Lev 20.19
18.14
Lev 20.20
18.15
Lev 20.12
18.16
Lev 20.21
18.17
Lev 20.14

18.6 *uncover nakedness,* i.e., "marry" or "have sexual intercourse with." God allowed sisters and brothers to marry in Adam's day. Later on, when the race was established, God laid down regulations forbidding intermarriage between close relatives; e.g., a man could not marry his sister, his mother's sister, or his daughter-in-law. The same prohibitions are gener-ally operative in the modern world, even in non-Christian societies.
18.16 Sexual relations with a brother's wife was forbidden so long as the brother was alive. But if he died and left no heir, then the living brother was to raise up seed by the widow (Deut 25.5,6). This was the levirate custom.

ness of a woman and her daughter, and you shall not take[z] her son's daughter or her daughter's daughter to uncover her nakedness; they are your[a] flesh; it is depravity. 18 And you shall not take[z] a woman as a rival to her sister, uncovering her nakedness while her sister is still alive.

3. Other sexual sins forbidden

19 You shall not approach a woman to uncover her nakedness while she is in her menstrual uncleanness. 20 You shall not have sexual relations with your kinsman's wife, and defile yourself with her. 21 You shall not give any of your offspring to sacrifice them[b] to Molech, and so profane the name of your God: I am the LORD. 22 You shall not lie with a male as with a woman; it is an abomination. 23 You shall not have sexual relations with any animal and defile yourself with it, nor shall any woman give herself to an animal to have sexual relations with it: it is perversion.

4. Warnings

24 Do not defile yourselves in any of these ways, for by all these practices the nations I am casting out before you have defiled themselves. 25 Thus the land became defiled; and I punished it for its iniquity, and the land vomited out its inhabitants. 26 But you shall keep my statutes and my ordinances and commit none of these abominations, either the citizen or the alien who resides among you 27 (for the inhabitants of the land, who were before you, committed all of these abominations, and the land became defiled); 28 otherwise the land will vomit you out for defiling it, as it vomited out the nation that was before you. 29 For whoever commits any of these abominations shall be cut off from their people. 30 So keep my charge not to commit any of these abominations that were done before you, and not to defile yourselves by them: I am the LORD your God.

D. Holiness and personal conduct: the law of love

19 The LORD spoke to Moses, saying: 2 Speak to all the congregation of the people of Israel and say to them: You shall be holy, for I the LORD your God am holy. 3 You shall each revere your mother and father, and you shall keep my sabbaths: I am the LORD your God. 4 Do not turn to idols or make cast images for yourselves: I am the LORD your God.

5 When you offer a sacrifice of well-being to the LORD, offer it in such a way that it is acceptable in your behalf. 6 It shall be eaten on the same day you offer it, or on the next day; and anything left over until the third day shall be consumed in fire. 7 If it is eaten at all on the third day, it is an abomination; it will not be acceptable. 8 All who eat it shall be subject to punishment, because they have profaned what is holy to the LORD; and any such person shall be cut off from the people.

9 When you reap the harvest of your land, you shall not reap to the very edges of your field, or gather the gleanings of your harvest. 10 You shall not strip your vineyard bare, or gather the fallen grapes of your

---

z Or marry   a Gk: Heb lacks your   b Heb to pass them over

Cross-references (margin)

18.19 Lev 15.24; 20.18
18.20 Lev 20.10; Ex 20.14; Prov 6.32; Mt 5.27
18.21 Lev 20.2-5; 19.12; 21.6
18.22 Lev 20.13; Rom 1.27
18.23 Ex 22.19; Lev 20.15; Deut 27.21
18.24 v. 3; Lev 20.23
18.25 Lev 20.23; Deut 9.5; 18.12; v. 28
18.30 Lev 22.9; Deut 11.1; v. 2

19.2 1 Pet 1.16
19.3 Ex 20.8, 12; Lev 11.44
19.4 Lev 26.1; Ps 96.5; Ex 20.23; 34.17

19.9 Lev 23.22; Deut 24.20-22

18.18 Marrying two sisters is here forbidden. Does this then mean that a male could have two wives as long as they were not sisters? Monogamy was God's rule from the beginning (Gen 2.24), but concubinage, while not approved, was regulated if it took place (see Ex 21.10).

18.22,23 God here condemns sexual relations between two males and with animals. Sodomy and bestiality are sins against nature and the commandment has never been abrogated (see also Rom 1.26-27).

19.10 It is clear from this and other Scriptures that there never would be a time when there were no poor. Therefore works of piety had to be accompanied by works of charity. Standing grain was to be left in a corner of the field for the poor and the alien. Harvest time was particularly the right time for charity, amidst the rejoicing of the reaping of the harvest. As God had blessed the product of the fields, so the reaper could bless the poor by sharing.

vineyard; you shall leave them for the poor and the alien: I am the LORD your God.

11 You shall not steal; you shall not deal falsely; and you shall not lie to one another. 12 And you shall not swear falsely by my name, profaning the name of your God: I am the LORD.

13 You shall not defraud your neighbor; you shall not steal; and you shall not keep for yourself the wages of a laborer until morning. 14 You shall not revile the deaf or put a stumbling block before the blind; you shall fear your God: I am the LORD.

15 You shall not render an unjust judgment; you shall not be partial to the poor or defer to the great: with justice you shall judge your neighbor. 16 You shall not go around as a slanderer*c* among your people, and you shall not profit by the blood*d* of your neighbor: I am the LORD.

17 You shall not hate in your heart anyone of your kin; you shall reprove your neighbor, or you will incur guilt yourself. 18 You shall not take vengeance or bear a grudge against any of your people, but you shall love your neighbor as yourself: I am the LORD.

19 You shall keep my statutes. You shall not let your animals breed with a different kind; you shall not sow your field with two kinds of seed; nor shall you put on a garment made of two different materials.

20 If a man has sexual relations with a woman who is a slave, designated for another man but not ransomed or given her freedom, an inquiry shall be held. They shall not be put to death, since she has not been freed; 21 but he shall bring a guilt offering for himself to the LORD, at the entrance of the tent of meeting, a ram as guilt offering. 22 And the priest shall make atonement for him with the ram of guilt offering before the LORD for his sin that he committed; and the sin he committed shall be forgiven him.

23 When you come into the land and plant all kinds of trees for food, then you shall regard their fruit as forbidden;*e* three years it shall be forbidden*f* to you, it must not be eaten. 24 In the fourth year all their fruit shall be set apart for rejoicing in the LORD. 25 But in the fifth year you may eat of their fruit, that their yield may be increased for you: I am the LORD your God.

26 You shall not eat anything with its blood. You shall not practice augury or witchcraft. 27 You shall not round off the hair on your temples or mar the edges of your beard. 28 You shall not make any gashes in your flesh for the dead or tattoo any marks upon you: I am the LORD.

29 Do not profane your daughter by making her a prostitute, that the land not become prostituted and full of depravity. 30 You shall keep my sabbaths and reverence my sanctuary: I am the LORD.

31 Do not turn to mediums or wizards; do not seek them out, to be defiled by them: I am the LORD your God.

32 You shall rise before the aged, and defer to the old; and you shall fear your God: I am the LORD.

33 When an alien resides with you in your land, you shall not oppress

19.11
Ex 20.15;
Lev 6.2;
Eph 4.25;
Col 3.9
19.12
Ex 20.7;
Lev 18.21
19.13
Ex 22.7-15;
21-27;
Deut 24.15;
Jas 5.4
19.14
Deut 27.18
19.15
Ex 23.6;
Deut 1.17
19.16
Ps 15.3;
Ezek 22.9;
Ex 23.7
19.17
1 Jn 2.9, 11;
3.15;
Lk 17.3;
Gal 6.1
19.18
Rom 12.19;
Ps 103.9;
Mt 19.19;
Mk 12.31;
Rom 13.9
19.19
Deut 22.9, 11
19.21
Lev 5.15

19.24
Deut 12.17,
18;
Prov 3.9

19.26
Lev 17.10;
Deut 18.10
19.27
Lev 21.5
19.28
Lev 21.5
19.29
Deut 23.17
19.30
v. 3;
Lev 26.2
19.31
Lev 20.6, 27;
Deut 18.10,
11
19.33
Ex 22.21

c Meaning of Heb uncertain   *d* Heb *stand against the blood*   *e* Heb *as their uncircumcision*
f Heb *uncircumcision*

19.15 Justice should not favor persons because of their station in life. Judges were to act impartially.
19.18 The two tables of the law can be reduced to two general commandments: love God and your neighbor as yourself (see Mt 19.19 and Lk 10.27, where Jesus quotes this verse; see also Rom 13.9; Gal 5.14).
19.22 The atonement for guilt was followed by the forgiveness of the sin. Sacrifices which do not relieve the sinner of his guilt would be useless. God's grace includes forgiveness when atonement is made.
19.26-28 Eating blood as the heathen did, asking

counsel of the devil through enchantment and witchcraft, cutting the edges of the beard, or defacing oneself for the dead were heathen practices inconsonant with the worship of the true God. The Hebrew community was told again and again to refrain from incorporating pagan practices and ideas into its culture.
19.29 God forbade here the practice of tent prostitution, common to the pagans' idolatrous worship. *that the land not become prostituted.* Dishonoring God in the tent would lead to dishonoring God and themselves in their daily living.

19.34
Ex 12.48, 49;
Deut 10.19
the alien. 34 The alien who resides with you shall be to you as the citizen among you; you shall love the alien as yourself, for you were aliens in the land of Egypt: I am the LORD your God.

35 You shall not cheat in measuring length, weight, or quantity. 36 You shall have honest balances, honest weights, an honest ephah, and an honest hin: I am the LORD your God, who brought you out of the land of Egypt. 37 You shall keep all my statutes and all my ordinances, and observe them: I am the LORD.

E. Penalties for sin

1. Giving children to Molech

20.2
Lev 18.21
20 The LORD spoke to Moses, saying: 2 Say further to the people of Israel:

20.3
Lev 15.31;
18.21
Any of the people of Israel, or of the aliens who reside in Israel, who give any of their offspring to Molech shall be put to death; the people of the land shall stone them to death. 3 I myself will set my face against them, and will cut them off from the people, because they have given of their offspring to Molech, defiling my sanctuary and profaning my holy name.

20.4
Deut 17.2, 3, 5
4 And if the people of the land should ever close their eyes to them, when they give of their offspring to Molech, and do not put them to death, 5 I myself will set my face against them and against their family, and will cut them off from among their people, them and all who follow them in prostituting themselves to Molech.

2. Consulting mediums and wizards

20.6
Lev 19.31
6 If any turn to mediums and wizards, prostituting themselves to them, I will set my face against them, and will cut them off from the people. 7 Consecrate yourselves therefore, and be holy; for I am the LORD

20.7
1 Pet 1.16
20.8
Lev 19.37;
Ex 31.13
20.9
Ex 21.17;
Deut 27.16
your God. 8 Keep my statutes, and observe them; I am the LORD; I sanctify you. 9 All who curse father or mother shall be put to death; having cursed father or mother, their blood is upon them.

3. Adultery

20.10
Lev 18.20;
Deut 22.22
20.11
Lev 18.7, 8
20.12
Lev 18.15
20.13
Lev 18.22
20.14
Deut 27.23
20.15
Lev 18.23
10 If a man commits adultery with the wife of[g] his neighbor, both the adulterer and the adulteress shall be put to death. 11 The man who lies with his father's wife has uncovered his father's nakedness; both of them shall be put to death; their blood is upon them. 12 If a man lies with his daughter-in-law, both of them shall be put to death; they have committed perversion, their blood is upon them. 13 If a man lies with a male as with a woman, both of them have committed an abomination; they shall be put to death; their blood is upon them. 14 If a man takes a wife and her mother also, it is depravity; they shall be burned to death, both he and they, that there may be no depravity among you. 15 If a man has sexual relations with an animal, he shall be put to death; and you shall kill the animal. 16 If a woman approaches any animal and has sexual relations with it, you shall kill the woman and the animal; they shall be put to death, their blood is upon them.

4. Other sexual sins

20.17
Lev 18.9
17 If a man takes his sister, a daughter of his father or a daughter of

g Heb repeats *if a man commits adultery with the wife of*

19.34 Neighborly love was not to be limited to relationships between Israelites alone. It was to be extended to aliens as well (cf. the parable of the good Samaritan, Lk 10.30–37).
19.35 Whoever shortchanged anyone was guilty of

stealing. Honest weights and measures should be the rule of thumb.
20.13 The death penalty for adultery was the same as the penalty for homosexual offenders (see next note).

his mother, and sees her nakedness, and she sees his nakedness, it is a disgrace, and they shall be cut off in the sight of their people; he has uncovered his sister's nakedness, he shall be subject to punishment. 18 If a man lies with a woman having her sickness and uncovers her nakedness, he has laid bare her flow and she has laid bare her flow of blood; both of them shall be cut off from their people. 19 You shall not uncover the nakedness of your mother's sister or of your father's sister, for that is to lay bare one's own flesh; they shall be subject to punishment. 20 If a man lies with his uncle's wife, he has uncovered his uncle's nakedness; they shall be subject to punishment; they shall die childless. 21 If a man takes his brother's wife, it is impurity; he has uncovered his brother's nakedness; they shall be childless.

5. Command to be holy

22 You shall keep all my statutes and all my ordinances, and observe them, so that the land to which I bring you to settle in may not vomit you out. 23 You shall not follow the practices of the nation that I am driving out before you. Because they did all these things, I abhorred them. 24 But I have said to you: You shall inherit their land, and I will give it to you to possess, a land flowing with milk and honey. I am the LORD your God; I have separated you from the peoples. 25 You shall therefore make a distinction between the clean animal and the unclean, and between the unclean bird and the clean; you shall not bring abomination on yourselves by animal or by bird or by anything with which the ground teems, which I have set apart for you to hold unclean. 26 You shall be holy to me; for I the LORD am holy, and I have separated you from the other peoples to be mine.

6. Penalty for being a medium or wizard

27 A man or a woman who is a medium or a wizard shall be put to death; they shall be stoned to death, their blood is upon them.

F. Rules for the priesthood

1. The holiness of the priesthood

21 The LORD said to Moses: Speak to the priests, the sons of Aaron, and say to them:
No one shall defile himself for a dead person among his relatives, 2 except for his nearest kin: his mother, his father, his son, his daughter, his brother; 3 likewise, for a virgin sister, close to him because she has had no husband, he may defile himself for her. 4 But he shall not defile himself as a husband among his people and so profane himself. 5 They shall not make bald spots upon their heads, or shave off the edges of their beards, or make any gashes in their flesh. 6 They shall be holy to their God, and not profane the name of their God; for they offer the LORD's offerings by fire, the food of their God; therefore they shall be holy. 7 They shall not marry a prostitute or a woman who has been defiled; neither shall they marry a woman divorced from her husband. For they are holy to their God, 8 and you shall treat them as holy, since they offer the food of your God; they shall be holy to you, for I the LORD, I who sanc-

20.18
Lev 18.19

20.19
Lev 18.12, 13

20.20
Lev 18.14

20.21
Lev 18.16

20.22
Lev 18.25, 26, 28
20.23
Lev 18.3, 24, 27, 30
20.24
Ex 13.5;
33.3, 16;
v. 26
20.25
Lev 11.1-47;
Deut 14.3-21

20.26
v. 24

20.27
Lev 19.31

21.1
Lev 19.28;
Ezek 44.25

21.5
Deut 14.1;
Ezek 44.20;
Lev 19.27
21.6
Lev 18.21;
3.11
21.7
vv. 13, 14

20.19ff Despite present-day latitude, adultery, incest, homosexuality, lesbianism, and coitus with animals are here forbidden in Scripture. They were crimes punishable by death. Such crimes against God and nature were prevalent among the heathen; they were also practiced to some extent among the Israelites.
20.24 Those who have the Lord for their God are

thereby separated from the heathen round about them. Believers should not devalue their relationship with God by walking in the way of the heathen.
20.26 God is holy; therefore, his people are to be like him. Holiness is fitting for the people of God. A holy life pleases God, makes credible a witness to the heathen, and encourages the hearts of believers who have not yet attained holiness.

tify you, am holy. 9 When the daughter of a priest profanes herself through prostitution, she profanes her father; she shall be burned to death.

10   The priest who is exalted above his fellows, on whose head the anointing oil has been poured and who has been consecrated to wear the vestments, shall not dishevel his hair, nor tear his vestments. 11 He shall not go where there is a dead body; he shall not defile himself even for his father or mother. 12 He shall not go outside the sanctuary and thus profane the sanctuary of his God; for the consecration of the anointing oil of his God is upon him: I am the LORD. 13 He shall marry only a woman who is a virgin. 14 A widow, or a divorced woman, or a woman who has been defiled, a prostitute, these he shall not marry. He shall marry a virgin of his own kin, 15 that he may not profane his offspring among his kin; for I am the LORD; I sanctify him.

16   The LORD spoke to Moses, saying: 17 Speak to Aaron and say: No one of your offspring throughout their generations who has a blemish may approach to offer the food of his God. 18 For no one who has a blemish shall draw near, one who is blind or lame, or one who has a mutilated face or a limb too long, 19 or one who has a broken foot or a broken hand, 20 or a hunchback, or a dwarf, or a man with a blemish in his eyes or an itching disease or scabs or crushed testicles. 21 No descendant of Aaron the priest who has a blemish shall come near to offer the LORD's offerings by fire; since he has a blemish, he shall not come near to offer the food of his God. 22 He may eat the food of his God, of the most holy as well as of the holy. 23 But he shall not come near the curtain or approach the altar, because he has a blemish, that he may not profane my sanctuaries; for I am the LORD; I sanctify them. 24 Thus Moses spoke to Aaron and to his sons and to all the people of Israel.

22   The LORD spoke to Moses, saying: 2 Direct Aaron and his sons to deal carefully with the sacred donations of the people of Israel, which they dedicate to me, so that they may not profane my holy name; I am the LORD. 3 Say to them: If anyone among all your offspring throughout your generations comes near the sacred donations, which the people of Israel dedicate to the LORD, while he is in a state of uncleanness, that person shall be cut off from my presence: I am the LORD. 4 No one of Aaron's offspring who has a leprous h disease or suffers a discharge may eat of the sacred donations until he is clean. Whoever touches anything made unclean by a corpse or a man who has had an emission of semen, 5 and whoever touches any swarming thing by which he may be made unclean or any human being by whom he may be made unclean — whatever his uncleanness may be — 6 the person who touches any such shall be unclean until evening and shall not eat of the sacred donations unless he has washed his body in water. 7 When the sun sets he shall be clean; and afterward he may eat of the sacred donations, for they are his food. 8 That which died or was torn by wild animals he shall not eat,

h A term for several skin diseases; precise meaning uncertain

Margin references (left column):

21.10 Lev 16.32; 10.6, 7
21.11 Lev 19.28
21.12 Lev 10.7; Ex 29.6, 7
21.13 v. 7; Ezek 44.22
21.17ff v. 6
21.18 Lev 22.23
21.20 Deut 23.1
21.21 v. 6
21.23 v. 12
22.3 Lev 7.20
22.4 Lev 14.1-32; Num 19.11, 12; 15.16, 17
22.5 Lev 11.24, 43, 44; 15.7, 19
22.8 Ex 22.31; Lev 17.15

21.11 *even for his father or his mother.* This rule applied only to the high priest, while the contrary regulations in 21.1–3 applied to ordinary priests.
21.14,15 The high priest could not marry a widow (as other priests could), much less one divorced or a prostitute. High priests foreshadowed Christ. As the church is to be presented as a chaste virgin to Christ (2 Cor 11.2), so the high priest could marry only a virgin. He also had to marry within his own tribe, lest he become the father of children of mixed blood — half priestly and half ordinary.
21.16,17ff God laid down certain qualifications which would prevent a Levite from being a priest. The physical disabilities and imperfections listed in

21.18–20 barred one from the office but not from receiving the proper share of the offerings for personal support (v. 22). Thus the priest as well as the animal offered for sacrifice had to be without blemish. So today, some things may disqualify an individual from the office of elder or deacon, but not disqualify him or her from the worship and fellowship of the church.
22.4 Food from the offerings belonged to the priests. Yet those who were lepers or had a discharge could not eat the holy things. They had to find food which was common, i.e., food consumed by the ordinary people.

becoming unclean by it: I am the LORD. 9 They shall keep my charge, so that they may not incur guilt and die in the sanctuary¹ for having profaned it: I am the LORD; I sanctify them.

10 No lay person shall eat of the sacred donations. No bound or hired servant of the priest shall eat of the sacred donations; 11 but if a priest acquires anyone by purchase, the person may eat of them; and those that are born in his house may eat of his food. 12 If a priest's daughter marries a layman, she shall not eat of the offering of the sacred donations; 13 but if a priest's daughter is widowed or divorced, without offspring, and returns to her father's house, as in her youth, she may eat of her father's food. No lay person shall eat of it. 14 If a man eats of the sacred donation unintentionally, he shall add one-fifth of its value to it, and give the sacred donation to the priest. 15 No one shall profane the sacred donations of the people of Israel, which they offer to the LORD, 16 causing them to bear guilt requiring a guilt offering, by eating their sacred donations: for I am the LORD; I sanctify them.

2. Acceptable and unacceptable offerings

17 The LORD spoke to Moses, saying: 18 Speak to Aaron and his sons and all the people of Israel and say to them: When anyone of the house of Israel or of the aliens residing in Israel presents an offering, whether in payment of a vow or as a freewill offering that is offered to the LORD as a burnt offering, 19 to be acceptable in your behalf it shall be a male without blemish, of the cattle or the sheep or the goats. 20 You shall not offer anything that has a blemish, for it will not be acceptable in your behalf.

21 When anyone offers a sacrifice of well-being to the LORD, in fulfillment of a vow or as a freewill offering, from the herd or from the flock, to be acceptable it must be perfect; there shall be no blemish in it. 22 Anything blind, or injured, or maimed, or having a discharge or an itch or scabs — these you shall not offer to the LORD or put any of them on the altar as offerings by fire to the LORD. 23 An ox or a lamb that has a limb too long or too short you may present for a freewill offering; but it will not be accepted for a vow. 24 Any animal that has its testicles bruised or crushed or torn or cut, you shall not offer to the LORD; such you shall not do within your land, 25 nor shall you accept any such animals from a foreigner to offer as food to your God; since they are mutilated, with a blemish in them, they shall not be accepted in your behalf.

26 The LORD spoke to Moses, saying: 27 When an ox or a sheep or a goat is born, it shall remain seven days with its mother, and from the eighth day on it shall be acceptable as the LORD's offering by fire. 28 But you shall not slaughter, from the herd or the flock, an animal with its young on the same day. 29 When you sacrifice a thanksgiving offering to the LORD, you shall sacrifice it so that it may be acceptable in your behalf. 30 It shall be eaten on the same day; you shall not leave any of it until morning: I am the LORD.

31 Thus you shall keep my commandments and observe them: I am the LORD. 32 You shall not profane my holy name, that I may be sanctified among the people of Israel: I am the LORD; I sanctify you, 33 I who brought you out of the land of Egypt to be your God: I am the LORD.

¹ Vg: Heb incur guilt for it and die in it

22.19 One would assume that no consecrated believer would bring a deformed or defective sacrifice (i.e., a valueless animal) as an offering to the Lord. Yet the prohibition stated here suggests either that human nature is such that this eventuality would occur or that it had already manifested itself among some of the people who professed to worship God.

G. *Laws concerning festivals*

1. *The sabbath*

23.2
vv. 4, 37, 44;
Num 29.39

23 The LORD spoke to Moses, saying: 2 Speak to the people of Israel and say to them: These are the appointed festivals of the LORD that you shall proclaim as holy convocations, my appointed festivals.

23.3
Lev 19.3;
Ex 31.13-17;
Deut 5.13

3 Six days shall work be done; but the seventh day is a sabbath of complete rest, a holy convocation; you shall do no work: it is a sabbath to the LORD throughout your settlements.

2. *The passover and unleavened bread*

23.4
v. 2
23.5
Ex 12.18, 19;
Num 28.16,
17

4 These are the appointed festivals of the LORD, the holy convocations, which you shall celebrate at the time appointed for them. 5 In the first month, on the fourteenth day of the month, at twilight,*j* there shall be a passover offering to the LORD, 6 and on the fifteenth day of the same month is the festival of unleavened bread to the LORD; seven days you shall eat unleavened bread. 7 On the first day you shall have a holy convocation; you shall not work at your occupations. 8 For seven days you shall present the LORD's offerings by fire; on the seventh day there shall be a holy convocation: you shall not work at your occupations.

23.8
vv. 8, 21, 25,
35, 36

3. *The festival of first fruits*

23.10
Ex 23.16, 19;
34.22, 26

9 The LORD spoke to Moses: 10 Speak to the people of Israel and say to them: When you enter the land that I am giving you and you reap its harvest, you shall bring the sheaf of the first fruits of your harvest to the priest. 11 He shall raise the sheaf before the LORD, that you may find acceptance; on the day after the sabbath the priest shall raise it. 12 On the day when you raise the sheaf, you shall offer a lamb a year old, without blemish, as a burnt offering to the LORD. 13 And the grain offering with it shall be two-tenths of an ephah of choice flour mixed with oil, an offering by fire of pleasing odor to the LORD; and the drink offering with it shall be of wine, one-fourth of a hin. 14 You shall eat no bread or parched grain or fresh ears until that very day, until you have brought the offering of your God: it is a statute forever throughout your generations in all your settlements.

23.13
Lev 2.14-16

4. *The festival of weeks*

23.15
Deut 16.9

15 And from the day after the sabbath, from the day on which you bring the sheaf of the elevation offering, you shall count off seven weeks; they shall be complete. 16 You shall count until the day after the seventh sabbath, fifty days; then you shall present an offering of new grain to the LORD. 17 You shall bring from your settlements two loaves of bread as an elevation offering, each made of two-tenths of an ephah; they shall be of

23.16
Num 28.26

23.17
Lev 2.12;
7.13

---

j Heb between the two evenings

23.5 *In the first month, on the fourteenth day of the month* (of the Hebrew calendar), i.e., around the first day of April.

23.6–8 *festival of unleavened bread.* This festival must be distinguished from the passover, although they are closely connected. The passover was celebrated on the fourteenth day of the first Jewish month; the festival of unleavened bread began the fifteenth day and lasted for seven days. Thus they constituted a double celebration. In Mk 14.1–12 and Lk 22.1 the passover and the festival of unleavened bread are mentioned as virtually one, doubtless because no period of time separated one from the other. The festival of unleavened bread celebrated Israel's deliverance from Egypt, during which time no un-

leavened bread was eaten.

23.15,16 The festival of weeks was also known as the festival of harvest. Its N.T. name, Pentecost, derives from the Greek word for "fiftieth," because the festival occurred fifty days after the festival of unleavened bread. It was prophetic of the coming of the Holy Spirit, who was poured out on the apostolic believers on the fiftieth day after Christ rose from the dead (Acts 2.1ff). In the O.T. the festival celebrated the first fruits of the harvest; in Acts, the 120 disciples represent the first fruits of Christ's harvest, and the coming of the Holy Spirit represents the first fruits of believers' heavenly inheritance (see Rom 8.23; 11.16; Jas 1.18).

choice flour, baked with leaven, as first fruits to the Lord. 18 You shall present with the bread seven lambs a year old without blemish, one young bull, and two rams; they shall be a burnt offering to the Lord, along with their grain offering and their drink offerings, an offering by fire of pleasing odor to the Lord. 19 You shall also offer one male goat for a sin offering, and two male lambs a year old as a sacrifice of well-being. 20 The priest shall raise them with the bread of the first fruits as an elevation offering before the Lord, together with the two lambs; they shall be holy to the Lord for the priest. 21 On that same day you shall make proclamation; you shall hold a holy convocation; you shall not work at your occupations. This is a statute forever in all your settlements throughout your generations.

22 When you reap the harvest of your land, you shall not reap to the very edges of your field, or gather the gleanings of your harvest; you shall leave them for the poor and for the alien: I am the Lord your God.

5. *The festival of trumpets*

23 The Lord spoke to Moses, saying: 24 Speak to the people of Israel, saying: In the seventh month, on the first day of the month, you shall observe a day of complete rest, a holy convocation commemorated with trumpet blasts. 25 You shall not work at your occupations; and you shall present the Lord's offering by fire.

6. *The day of atonement*

26 The Lord spoke to Moses, saying: 27 Now, the tenth day of this seventh month is the day of atonement; it shall be a holy convocation for you: you shall deny yourselves[k] and present the Lord's offering by fire; 28 and you shall do no work during that entire day; for it is a day of atonement, to make atonement on your behalf before the Lord your God. 29 For anyone who does not practice self-denial[l] during that entire day shall be cut off from the people. 30 And anyone who does any work during that entire day, such a one I will destroy from the midst of the people. 31 You shall do no work: it is a statute forever throughout your generations in all your settlements. 32 It shall be to you a sabbath of complete rest, and you shall deny yourselves;[k] on the ninth day of the month at evening, from evening to evening you shall keep your sabbath.

7. *The festival of booths*

33 The Lord spoke to Moses, saying: 34 Speak to the people of Israel, saying: On the fifteenth day of this seventh month, and lasting seven days, there shall be the festival of booths[m] to the Lord. 35 The first day shall be a holy convocation; you shall not work at your occupations. 36 Seven days you shall present the Lord's offerings by fire; on the eighth day you shall observe a holy convocation and present the Lord's offerings by fire; it is a solemn assembly; you shall not work at your occupations.

37 These are the appointed festivals of the Lord, which you shall celebrate as times of holy convocation, for presenting to the Lord offerings by fire — burnt offerings and grain offerings, sacrifices and drink offerings, each on its proper day — 38 apart from the sabbaths of the Lord,

23.19	Num 28.30; Lev 3.1
23.21	v. 7
23.22	Lev 19.9
23.24	Num 29.1; Lev 25.9
23.27	Lev 16.29, 30
23.29	Gen 17.14
23.30	Lev 20.3, 5, 6
23.34	Ex 23.16; Num 29.12; vv. 42, 43
23.36	Num 29.12-38
23.37	vv. 2, 4

k Or *shall fast* *l* Or *does not fast* *m* Or *tabernacles*: Heb *succoth*

23.23,24 The festival of trumpets came the first day of the seventh month of the Hebrew calendar (*Tishri*, i.e., mid-September). Trumpets were blown and sacrifices offered (Num 29.1–6). The day was set apart for a holy convocation, celebration, and rest. It marked the first day of the Jewish new year and is celebrated today as *Rosh Hashanah*.
23.32 *you shall deny yourselves*, i.e., fast (see note on

16.29,30). Except for children and sick people, the fast which began at sunset of the ninth day was continued until sundown of the tenth day. All worldly business was laid aside so that the people might better attend to spiritual matters on this day of atonement (referred to here as a "sabbath").
23.34 *festival of booths*. See note on Ex 23.16.

and apart from your gifts, and apart from all your votive offerings, and apart from all your freewill offerings, which you give to the LORD.

23.39
Ex 23.16;
Deut 16.13

39 Now, the fifteenth day of the seventh month, when you have gathered in the produce of the land, you shall keep the festival of the LORD, lasting seven days; a complete rest on the first day, and a complete rest on the eighth day. 40 On the first day you shall take the fruit of

23.40
Neh 8.15;
Deut 16.14,
15

majestic[n] trees, branches of palm trees, boughs of leafy trees, and willows of the brook; and you shall rejoice before the LORD your God for seven days. 41 You shall keep it as a festival to the LORD seven days in the year; you shall keep it in the seventh month as a statute forever throughout your generations. 42 You shall live in booths for seven days; all that are citizens

23.42
Neh 8.14-16

in Israel shall live in booths; 43 so that your generations may know that I made the people of Israel live in booths when I brought them out of the land of Egypt: I am the LORD your God.

23.44
vv. 2, 37

44 Thus Moses declared to the people of Israel the appointed festivals of the LORD.

H. Laws of ritual and ethics

1. The oil and the showbread

24.2
Ex 27.20, 21

24 The LORD spoke to Moses, saying: 2 Command the people of Israel to bring you pure oil of beaten olives for the lamp, that a light may be kept burning regularly. 3 Aaron shall set it up in the tent of meeting, outside the curtain of the covenant,[o] to burn from evening to morning before the LORD regularly; it shall be a statute forever throughout your

24.4
Ex 31.8;
39.37

generations. 4 He shall set up the lamps on the lampstand of pure gold[p] before the LORD regularly.

24.5
Ex 25.30
24.6
Ex 25.24;
1 Kings 7.48

5 You shall take choice flour, and bake twelve loaves of it; two-tenths of an ephah shall be in each loaf. 6 You shall place them in two rows, six in a row, on the table of pure gold.[q] 7 You shall put pure frankincense with each row, to be a token offering for the bread, as an offering by fire to the LORD. 8 Every sabbath day Aaron shall set them in order before the

24.8
Num 4.7;
1 Chr 9.32;
2 Chr 2.4

LORD regularly as a commitment of the people of Israel, as a covenant forever. 9 They shall be for Aaron and his descendants, who shall eat them

24.9
Mt 12.4;
Mk 2.26;
Lk 6.4;
Lev 8.31

in a holy place, for they are most holy portions for him from the offerings by fire to the LORD, a perpetual due.

2. Death for blasphemy

10 A man whose mother was an Israelite and whose father was an Egyptian came out among the people of Israel; and the Israelite woman's

24.11
v. 16

son and a certain Israelite began fighting in the camp. 11 The Israelite woman's son blasphemed the Name in a curse. And they brought him to

24.12
Num 15.34;
Ex 18.15, 16
24.14

Moses — now his mother's name was Shelomith, daughter of Dibri, of the tribe of Dan — 12 and they put him in custody, until the decision of the LORD should be made clear to them.

Deut 13.9;
17.7;
Lev 20.2, 27;
Deut 21.21
24.16
1 Kings 21.10,
13;
Mt 12.31;
Mk 3.28

13 The LORD said to Moses, saying: 14 Take the blasphemer outside the camp; and let all who were within hearing lay their hands on his head, and let the whole congregation stone him. 15 And speak to the people of Israel, saying: Anyone who curses God shall bear the sin. 16 One who

n Meaning of Heb uncertain   o Or treaty, or testament; Heb eduth   p Heb pure lampstand   q Heb pure table

24.15,16 To curse, scoff at, or revile God was blasphemous. Here we read that a profane Danite was a blasphemer. The sentence for this sin was death. Idolatry was also regarded as blasphemy (Isa 65.7) because it implied contempt for the divine name of the one true God. King Sennacherib was guilty of this crime (2 Kings 19.4,10,22), as was Hymenaeus in the

N.T. (1 Tim 1.20). The unregenerate are addicted to this sin (Ps 74.18). Jesus was called a blasphemer on the grounds that he made himself out to be God (Lk 22.66-71), and members of the early church were called blasphemers because they affirmed Jesus' deity (Acts 6.11-14).

blasphemes the name of the LORD shall be put to death; the whole congregation shall stone the blasphemer. Aliens as well as citizens, when they blaspheme the Name, shall be put to death. 17 Anyone who kills a human being shall be put to death. 18 Anyone who kills an animal shall make restitution for it, life for life. 19 Anyone who maims another shall suffer the same injury in return: 20 fracture for fracture, eye for eye, tooth for tooth; the injury inflicted is the injury to be suffered. 21 One who kills an animal shall make restitution for it; but one who kills a human being shall be put to death. 22 You shall have one law for the alien and for the citizen: for I am the LORD your God. 23 Moses spoke thus to the people of Israel; and they took the blasphemer outside the camp, and stoned him to death. The people of Israel did as the LORD had commanded Moses.

I. Laws for the sabbatical and jubilee years

1. The sabbatical year

25 The LORD spoke to Moses on Mount Sinai, saying: 2 Speak to the people of Israel and say to them: When you enter the land that I am giving you, the land shall observe a sabbath for the LORD. 3 Six years you shall sow your field, and six years you shall prune your vineyard, and gather in their yield; 4 but in the seventh year there shall be a sabbath of complete rest for the land, a sabbath for the LORD: you shall not sow your field or prune your vineyard. 5 You shall not reap the aftergrowth of your harvest or gather the grapes of your unpruned vine: it shall be a year of complete rest for the land. 6 You may eat what the land yields during its sabbath — you, your male and female slaves, your hired and your bound laborers who live with you; 7 for your livestock also, and for the wild animals in your land all its yield shall be for food.

2. The year of jubilee

8 You shall count off seven weeks[r] of years, seven times seven years, so that the period of seven weeks of years gives forty-nine years. 9 Then you shall have the trumpet sounded loud; on the tenth day of the seventh month — on the day of atonement — you shall have the trumpet sounded throughout all your land. 10 And you shall hallow the fiftieth year and you shall proclaim liberty throughout the land to all its inhabitants. It shall be a jubilee for you: you shall return, every one of you, to your property and every one of you to your family. 11 That fiftieth year shall be a jubilee for you: you shall not sow, or reap the aftergrowth, or harvest the unpruned vines. 12 For it is a jubilee; it shall be holy to you: you shall eat only what the field itself produces.

13 In this year of jubilee you shall return, every one of you, to your property. 14 When you make a sale to your neighbor or buy from your neighbor, you shall not cheat one another. 15 When you buy from your neighbor, you shall pay only for the number of years since the jubilee; the seller shall charge you only for the remaining crop years. 16 If the years

r Or sabbaths

Cross-references

24.17
Ex 21.12;
Num 35.30,
31;
Deut 19.11,
12
24.18
v. 21
24.20
Ex 21.23, 24;
Deut 19.21;
Mt 5.38
24.21
vv. 17, 18
24.22
Ex 12.49;
Num 15.16

25.2
Ex 23.10, 11

25.6
vv. 20, 21

25.9
Lev 23.24, 27

25.10
vv. 13, 28, 54

25.13
v. 10
25.14
Lev 19.13;
1 Sam 12.3,
4; 1 Cor 6.8
25.15
Lev 27.18, 23

25.9 *on the day of atonement,* which was the tenth day of the seventh month (of the Hebrew calendar). The year of jubilee occurred every fiftieth year, commencing on the day of atonement. It was called by different names, such as the "year of liberty" (Ezek 46.17), the "year of the Lord's favor" (Isa 61.2), and the "year for my redeeming work" (Isa 63.4). It was introduced with the blowing of trumpets. All field labor ceased for that year, nonurban property came back to the original owner, inheritances were restored, and slaves were freed. The year of the Lord's favor reaches fulfillment in the gospel (Lk 4.18,19), when people are set free from their bondage and brought into the glori-

ous freedom of the children of God through Jesus Christ (cf. Rom 8.21).
25.16 In v. 23 God says the land belongs to him, though he gave it to the Israelites in perpetuity. Therefore, they could not sell the land which belonged to them. But if economic hardship forced them to do so, they could, in effect, lease the land until the year of jubilee, when it would be returned to the rightful owner. Verse 16 specifies that the price given to the owner of the land was to be computed on the basis of the number of crops (years) remaining until the jubilee. The owner was not to demand more nor the buyer less. The guiding principle was eco-

are more, you shall increase the price, and if the years are fewer, you shall diminish the price; for it is a certain number of harvests that are being sold to you. 17 You shall not cheat one another, but you shall fear your God; for I am the LORD your God.

18 You shall observe my statutes and faithfully keep my ordinances, so that you may live on the land securely. 19 The land will yield its fruit, and you will eat your fill and live on it securely. 20 Should you ask, "What shall we eat in the seventh year, if we may not sow or gather in our crop?" 21 I will order my blessing for you in the sixth year, so that it will yield a crop for three years. 22 When you sow in the eighth year, you will be eating from the old crop; until the ninth year, when its produce comes in, you shall eat the old. 23 The land shall not be sold in perpetuity, for the land is mine; with me you are but aliens and tenants. 24 Throughout the land that you hold, you shall provide for the redemption of the land.

3. Release of property

25 If anyone of your kin falls into difficulty and sells a piece of property, then the next of kin shall come and redeem what the relative has sold. 26 If the person has no one to redeem it, but then prospers and finds sufficient means to do so, 27 the years since its sale shall be computed and the difference shall be refunded to the person to whom it was sold, and the property shall be returned. 28 But if there are not sufficient means to recover it, what was sold shall remain with the purchaser until the year of jubilee; in the jubilee it shall be released, and the property shall be returned.

29 If anyone sells a dwelling house in a walled city, it may be redeemed until a year has elapsed since its sale; the right of redemption shall be one year. 30 If it is not redeemed before a full year has elapsed, a house that is in a walled city shall pass in perpetuity to the purchaser, throughout the generations; it shall not be released in the jubilee. 31 But houses in villages that have no walls around them shall be classed as open country; they may be redeemed, and they shall be released in the jubilee. 32 As for the cities of the Levites, the Levites shall forever have the right of redemption of the houses in the cities belonging to them. 33 Such property as may be redeemed from the Levites — houses sold in a city belonging to them — shall be released in the jubilee; because the houses in the cities of the Levites are their possession among the people of Israel. 34 But the open land around their cities may not be sold; for that is their possession for all time.

4. The law of interest

35 If any of your kin fall into difficulty and become dependent on you,^{s} you shall support them; they shall live with you as though resident aliens. 36 Do not take interest in advance or otherwise make a profit from them, but fear your God; let them live with you. 37 You shall not lend them your money at interest taken in advance, or provide them food at a profit. 38 I am the LORD your God, who brought you out of the land of Egypt, to give you the land of Canaan, to be your God.

^{s} Meaning of Heb uncertain

Cross references (left margin):

25.17
v. 14;
Lev 19.14, 32
25.18
Lev 19.37;
26.4, 5
25.20
vv. 4, 5

25.22
Lev 26.10

25.23
Ex 19.5;
Gen 23.4;
1 Chr 29.15;
Ps 39.12

25.25
Ruth 2.20;
4.4, 6

25.27
vv. 50-52

25.28
v. 13

25.32
Num 35.1-8

25.35
Deut 15.7-11;
Ps 37.26;
Lk 6.35
25.36
Ex 22.25;
Deut 23.19,
20
25.38
Lev 11.45

nomic justice.
25.25 *If . . . your kin falls into difficulty*, i.e., becomes poor. All Israelite families had land which belonged to them in perpetuity. Thus there was equality of opportunity. Yet some were not successful and had to sell their land. Those who did could redeem it later, or it could be redeemed by the nearest relative. In any event, the land had to come back to the family in the year of jubilee.
25.35 Neighborly love meant that when fellow Israelites were poverty stricken, those able to help should lend them money but charge no interest. This law applied only to situations of poverty, not where money was borrowed for buying more land, trade, or other improvements. In those instances the lender should share profits with the borrower.

5. The redemption of servants

39 If any who are dependent on you become so impoverished that they sell themselves to you, you shall not make them serve as slaves. 40 They shall remain with you as hired or bound laborers. They shall serve with you until the year of the jubilee. 41 Then they and their children with them shall be free from your authority; they shall go back to their own family and return to their ancestral property. 42 For they are my servants, whom I brought out of the land of Egypt; they shall not be sold as slaves are sold. 43 You shall not rule over them with harshness, but shall fear your God. 44 As for the male and female slaves whom you may have, it is from the nations around you that you may acquire male and female slaves. 45 You may also acquire them from among the aliens residing with you, and from their families that are with you, who have been born in your land; and they may be your property. 46 You may keep them as a possession for your children after you, for them to inherit as property. These you may treat as slaves, but as for your fellow Israelites, no one shall rule over the other with harshness.

47 If resident aliens among you prosper, and if any of your kin fall into difficulty with one of them and sell themselves to an alien, or to a branch of the alien's family, 48 after they have sold themselves they shall have the right of redemption; one of their brothers may redeem them, 49 or their uncle or their uncle's son may redeem them, or anyone of their family who is of their own flesh may redeem them; or if they prosper they may redeem themselves. 50 They shall compute with the purchaser the total from the year when they sold themselves to the alien until the jubilee year; the price of the sale shall be applied to the number of years: the time they were with the owner shall be rated as the time of a hired laborer. 51 If many years remain, they shall pay for their redemption in proportion to the purchase price; 52 and if few years remain until the jubilee year, they shall compute thus: according to the years involved they shall make payment for their redemption. 53 As a laborer hired by the year they shall be under the alien's authority, who shall not, however, rule with harshness over them in your sight. 54 And if they have not been redeemed in any of these ways, they and their children with them shall go free in the jubilee year. 55 For to me the people of Israel are servants; they are my servants whom I brought out from the land of Egypt: I am the LORD your God.

J. Promises and warnings

1. The blessings for obedience

26 You shall make for yourselves no idols and erect no carved images or pillars, and you shall not place figured stones in your land, to worship at them; for I am the LORD your God. 2 You shall keep my sabbaths and reverence my sanctuary: I am the LORD.

3 If you follow my statutes and keep my commandments and observe them faithfully, 4 I will give you your rains in their season, and the land shall yield its produce, and the trees of the field shall yield their fruit. 5 Your threshing shall overtake the vintage, and the vintage shall overtake the sowing; you shall eat your bread to the full, and live securely in your land. 6 And I will grant peace in the land, and you shall lie down, and no one shall make you afraid; I will remove dangerous animals from the land,

25.39 Ex 21.2; Deut 15.12; 1 Kings 9.22
25.41 Ex 21.3; v. 28
25.43 vv. 46, 53; Ex 1.13, 14
25.45 Isa 56.3, 6
25.46 v. 43
25.48 Neh 5.5
25.49 v. 26
25.50 Job 7.1; Isa 16.14; 21.16
25.51 Jer 32.7
25.54 vv. 10, 13, 28
26.1 Ex 20.4, 5; Lev 19.4; Deut 5.8
26.2 Lev 19.30
26.3 Deut 28.1
26.5 Am 9.13; Lev 25.18, 19
26.6 Ps 29.11; 147.14; Zeph 3.13; vv. 22, 25

25.44 Among the Israelites, slavery was permitted when it involved non-Israelites. But no Israelite was to become a slave to another Israelite. The law permitted the slave owner to pass on his slaves to his descendants by way of inheritance.
25.55 All God's people are his servants. Therefore, they are subject to his sovereign rulership and must treat others the way God treats them. Since God is merciful, they also must be merciful to those in need.
26.3ff God's invariable law is that he will bless those who obey him. Paul repeats this truth: "for you reap whatever you sow" (Gal 6.7). If we sow righteousness and act in love toward our neighbors, we will reap a rich reward in this life and in the one to come.

and no sword shall go through your land. 7 You shall give chase to your enemies, and they shall fall before you by the sword. 8 Five of you shall give chase to a hundred, and a hundred of you shall give chase to ten thousand; your enemies shall fall before you by the sword. 9 I will look with favor upon you and make you fruitful and multiply you; and I will maintain my covenant with you. 10 You shall eat old grain long stored, and you shall have to clear out the old to make way for the new. 11 I will place my dwelling in your midst, and I shall not abhor you. 12 And I will walk among you, and will be your God, and you shall be my people. 13 I am the LORD your God who brought you out of the land of Egypt, to be their slaves no more; I have broken the bars of your yoke and made you walk erect.

2. The penalties for disobedience

14 But if you will not obey me, and do not observe all these commandments, 15 if you spurn my statutes, and abhor my ordinances, so that you will not observe all my commandments, and you break my covenant, 16 I in turn will do this to you: I will bring terror on you; consumption and fever that waste the eyes and cause life to pine away. You shall sow your seed in vain, for your enemies shall eat it. 17 I will set my face against you, and you shall be struck down by your enemies; your foes shall rule over you, and you shall flee though no one pursues you. 18 And if in spite of this you will not obey me, I will continue to punish you sevenfold for your sins. 19 I will break your proud glory, and I will make your sky like iron and your earth like copper. 20 Your strength shall be spent to no purpose: your land shall not yield its produce, and the trees of the land shall not yield their fruit.

21 If you continue hostile to me, and will not obey me, I will continue to plague you sevenfold for your sins. 22 I will let loose wild animals against you, and they shall bereave you of your children and destroy your livestock; they shall make you few in number, and your roads shall be deserted.

23 If in spite of these punishments you have not turned back to me, but continue hostile to me, 24 then I too will continue hostile to you: I myself will strike you sevenfold for your sins. 25 I will bring the sword against you, executing vengeance for the covenant; and if you withdraw within your cities, I will send pestilence among you, and you shall be delivered into enemy hands. 26 When I break your staff of bread, ten women shall bake your bread in a single oven, and they shall dole out your bread by weight; and though you eat, you shall not be satisfied.

27 But if, despite this, you disobey me, and continue hostile to me, 28 I will continue hostile to you in fury; I in turn will punish you myself sevenfold for your sins. 29 You shall eat the flesh of your sons, and you shall eat the flesh of your daughters. 30 I will destroy your high places and cut down your incense altars; I will heap your carcasses on the carcasses of your idols. I will abhor you. 31 I will lay your cities waste, will make your sanctuaries desolate, and I will not smell your pleasing odors. 32 I will devastate the land, so that your enemies who come to settle in it shall be appalled at it. 33 And you I will scatter among the nations, and I will unsheathe the sword against you; your land shall be a desolation, and your cities a waste.

34 Then the land shall enjoy[t] its sabbath years as long as it lies desolate, while you are in the land of your enemies; then the land shall

t Or make up for

26.8
Deut 32.30;
Josh 23.10
26.9
Gen 17.6, 7;
22.17;
Neh 9.23
26.10
Lev 25.22
26.11
Ex 25.8;
Ps 76.2
26.12
2 Cor 6.16

26.14
Deut 28.15;
Mal 2.2
26.16
Deut 28.22;
1 Sam 2.33;
Deut 28.35,
51
26.17
Lev 17.10;
Deut 28.25;
Ps 106.41;
53.5; vv. 36,
37
26.18
vv. 21, 24, 28
26.19
Isa 25.11;
Deut 28.23
26.20
Isa 17.10,
11;
Deut 11.17
26.21
vv. 18, 24,
27, 40
26.22
Deut 32.24
26.23
Jer 2.30; 5.3
26.24
vv. 21, 28, 41
26.25
Ezek 5.17;
Num 14.12
26.26
Ps 105.16;
Isa 3.1;
Mic 6.14

26.28
vv. 24, 41
26.29
Deut 28.53
26.30
2 Chr 34.3;
Ezek 6.3-6,
13
26.31
Ps 74.7;
Isa 63.18
26.32
Jer 9.11;
19.18
26.33
Deut 4.27;
Ezek 12.15
26.34
v. 43;
2 Chr 36.21

26.24 strike you sevenfold. If lesser judgments do not work, God will send greater judgments.
26.32,33 God reveals the punishment which would be exacted of his people if and when they disobeyed

him and broke the covenant. This threat is repeated in Deut 28.58-67. These punishments were first meted out in the Babylonian captivity of 587 B.C.

rest, and enjoy[u] its sabbath years. 35 As long as it lies desolate, it shall
have the rest it did not have on your sabbaths when you were living on
it. 36 And as for those of you who survive, I will send faintness into their
hearts in the lands of their enemies; the sound of a driven leaf shall put
them to flight, and they shall flee as one flees from the sword, and they
shall fall though no one pursues. 37 They shall stumble over one another,
as if to escape a sword, though no one pursues; and you shall have no
power to stand against your enemies. 38 You shall perish among the
nations, and the land of your enemies shall devour you. 39 And those of
you who survive shall languish in the land of your enemies because of their
iniquities; also they shall languish because of the iniquities of their ancestors.

40   But if they confess their iniquity and the iniquity of their ancestors,
in that they committed treachery against me and, moreover, that they
continued hostile to me — 41 so that I, in turn, continued hostile to them
and brought them into the land of their enemies; if then their uncircumcised heart is humbled and they make amends for their iniquity, 42 then
will I remember my covenant with Jacob; I will remember also my covenant with Isaac and also my covenant with Abraham, and I will remember
the land. 43 For the land shall be deserted by them, and enjoy[u] its sabbath
years by lying desolate without them, while they shall make amends for
their iniquity, because they dared to spurn my ordinances, and they
abhorred my statutes. 44 Yet for all that, when they are in the land of their
enemies, I will not spurn them, or abhor them so as to destroy them utterly
and break my covenant with them; for I am the LORD their God; 45 but
I will remember in their favor the covenant with their ancestors whom I
brought out of the land of Egypt in the sight of the nations, to be their
God: I am the LORD.

46   These are the statutes and ordinances and laws that the LORD
established between himself and the people of Israel on Mount Sinai
through Moses.

K. Appendix: the making of vows

1. Vows involving persons

27 The LORD spoke to Moses, saying: 2 Speak to the people of Israel
      and say to them: When a person makes an explicit vow to the LORD
concerning the equivalent for a human being, 3 the equivalent for a male
shall be: from twenty to sixty years of age the equivalent shall be fifty
shekels of silver by the sanctuary shekel. 4 If the person is a female, the
equivalent is thirty shekels. 5 If the age is from five to twenty years of age,
the equivalent is twenty shekels for a male and ten shekels for a female.
6 If the age is from one month to five years, the equivalent for a male is
five shekels of silver, and for a female the equivalent is three shekels of

u Or make up for

26.36
Ezek 21.7

26.37
Josh 7.12, 13

26.38
Deut 4.26
26.39
Deut 4.27;
Ezek 4.17

26.40ff
Jer 3.12-15;
Lk 15.18;
1 Jn 1.9
26.41
Ezek 44.9;
2 Chr 12.6, 7
26.42
Gen 28.13-15;
26.2-5;
22.15-18
26.43
vv. 34, 35, 15

26.44
Deut 4.31;
Rom 11.2
26.45
Ex 6.6-8;
Lev 25.38;
Gen 17.7

26.46
Lev 7.38;
27.34; 25.1

27.3
Ex 30.13

27.6
Num 18.16

26.46 The law of Moses covers the total economy in
which the people of Israel lived and moved. It can be
divided into three segments: (1) the moral law of the
ten commandments (Deut 5.22; 10.4); (2) the ceremonial law, which set forth the proper approach to
God in worship (7.37,38); (3) the civil law, under
which the people were governed (Deut 17.9–11). The
ceremonial law, having been fulfilled by Jesus Christ,
is no longer binding on people under the new covenant. The civil law was designed for the O.T. theocracy, so other nations living under other conditions
are not bound by it. The basic moral law, however,
applies to all people of all eras (see note on Ex 20.1
for its threefold purpose).
27.2 an explicit vow. While it was not required,
some pious Israelites wanted to consecrate themselves

and their families to serve in the tabernacle. This
would involve menial tasks, such as sweeping the
floor, carrying out the ashes, and running errands.
But God had made full provision for all such functions
through the Levites. Therefore, any such explicit vow
was redeemable by money, so non-Levites could accomplish the intentions of their devoted hearts without actually doing the work. The priests had a money
scale for the redemption of those who had such intentions. More was paid for a male than for a female.
Why? Apparently the value was related to the productivity of the sexes. In the Israelite community the
male was the chief producer as a farmer. Note, for
example, that provision was made for widows and
their children, but not for widowers.

silver. 7 And if the person is sixty years old or over, then the equivalent for a male is fifteen shekels, and for a female ten shekels. 8 If any cannot afford the equivalent, they shall be brought before the priest and the priest shall assess them; the priest shall assess them according to what each one making a vow can afford.

2. Vows involving animals

9 If it concerns an animal that may be brought as an offering to the LORD, any such that may be given to the LORD shall be holy. 10 Another shall not be exchanged or substituted for it, either good for bad or bad for good; and if one animal is substituted for another, both that one and its substitute shall be holy. 11 If it concerns any unclean animal that may not be brought as an offering to the LORD, the animal shall be presented before the priest. 12 The priest shall assess it: whether good or bad, according to the assessment of the priest, so it shall be. 13 But if it is to be redeemed, one-fifth must be added to the assessment.

3. Vows involving a house

14 If a person consecrates a house to the LORD, the priest shall assess it: whether good or bad, as the priest assesses it, so it shall stand. 15 And if the one who consecrates the house wishes to redeem it, one-fifth shall be added to its assessed value, and it shall revert to the original owner.

4. Vows involving land

16 If a person consecrates to the LORD any inherited landholding, its assessment shall be in accordance with its seed requirements: fifty shekels of silver to a homer of barley seed. 17 If the person consecrates the field as of the year of jubilee, that assessment shall stand; 18 but if the field is consecrated after the jubilee, the priest shall compute the price for it according to the years that remain until the year of jubilee, and the assessment shall be reduced. 19 And if the one who consecrates the field wishes to redeem it, then one-fifth shall be added to its assessed value, and it shall revert to the original owner; 20 but if the field is not redeemed, or if it has been sold to someone else, it shall no longer be redeemable. 21 But when the field is released in the jubilee, it shall be holy to the LORD as a devoted field; it becomes the priest's holding. 22 If someone consecrates to the LORD a field that has been purchased, which is not a part of the inherited landholding, 23 the priest shall compute for it the proportionate assessment up to the year of jubilee, and the assessment shall be paid as of that day, a sacred donation to the LORD. 24 In the year of jubilee the field shall return to the one from whom it was bought, whose holding the land is. 25 All assessments shall be by the sanctuary shekel: twenty gerahs shall make a shekel.

5. Vows involving firstlings

26 A firstling of animals, however, which as a firstling belongs to the LORD, cannot be consecrated by anyone; whether ox or sheep, it is the LORD's. 27 If it is an unclean animal, it shall be ransomed at its assessment, with one-fifth added; if it is not redeemed, it shall be sold at its assessment.

6. Vows involving devoted things

28 Nothing that a person owns that has been devoted to destruction for the LORD, be it human or animal, or inherited landholding, may be sold or redeemed; every devoted thing is most holy to the LORD. 29 No

27.8
v. 12

27.12
v. 8
27.13
vv. 15, 19

27.15
v. 20

27.18
Lev 25.15, 16

27.21
Lev 25.10,
28, 31;
Num 18.14

27.23
v. 18

27.24
Lev 25.28

27.25
Ex 30.13

27.26
Ex 13.2, 12

27.27
vv. 11, 12

27.28
Josh 6.17-19

27.25 *All assessments shall be by the sanctuary shekel: twenty gerahs shall make a shekel,* i.e., the valuations   of the land shall be stated in currency of the day.

human beings who have been devoted to destruction can be ransomed;
they shall be put to death.

7. Redeeming the tithe

30   All tithes from the land, whether the seed from the ground or the
fruit from the tree, are the LORD's; they are holy to the LORD. 31 If persons
wish to redeem any of their tithes, they must add one-fifth to them. 32 All
tithes of herd and flock, every tenth one that passes under the shepherd's
staff, shall be holy to the LORD. 33 Let no one inquire whether it is good
or bad, or make substitution for it; if one makes substitution for it, then
both it and the substitute shall be holy and cannot be redeemed.

34   These are the commandments that the LORD gave to Moses for the
people of Israel on Mount Sinai.

27.30
Gen 28.22;
Mal 3.8, 10
27.31
v. 13

27.33
v. 10

27.34
Lev 26.46;
Deut 4.5

27.30   The Israelites were to tithe from the crops of
their fields, from their trees, and from their cattle. If
money were substituted for any of these, a fifth was
added to the value. The tithe acknowledged God's
gracious material provision, for he prospered his people. It also was a token that they were mere tenants,
for the true title to the land belonged to God himself.

INTRODUCTION TO

NUMBERS

Authorship, Date, and Background: Numbers is the fourth book of the Pentateuch. The English title for the book derives from the Septuagint, which selected this name because of the two numberings of the Israelites in the wilderness journey (chs. 1 and 26). The Hebrew title was "in the wilderness of," taken from the fifth word of the first verse in the Hebrew text. This is the more appropriate title because the book describes the journey of the Israelites from Sinai to the plains of Moab. Moses is the chief figure in the book, which indicates that he wrote down their movements as the Lord instructed him (33.2). Thus he kept a record of their wanderings and incorporated them in the book of Numbers along with other source material which he used. For the date of this book, see the introduction to Exodus.

Most of the events recorded in Numbers occurred in the second and the fortieth years of Israel's pilgrimage from Egypt to the promised land. The years in between are passed over in virtual silence. Genesis recorded the beginnings of the nation of Israel through the patriarchs; Exodus traced the deliverance of the Israelites from Egypt, the making of the covenant between them and God, the giving of the law and the construction of the tabernacle; Leviticus set forth the religious, political, social, and economic laws which were to govern Israel; Numbers recorded how God prepared his people for both their entrance into and their conquest of the land he had promised to Abraham.

Characteristics and Content: Numbers describes how God leads, guides, disciplines, delivers, sustains, and protects his people. When they are disobedient he rewards them with judgment; when they repent he pardons and restores them. Their history is replete with backslidings. When Aaron and Miriam challenged the authority of their brother Moses, Miriam was chastened by God with leprosy, after which Moses intervened with God for her cleansing. The story of the quails, sent by God because of Israel's complaints against the manna, tells of the death of many at God's hands.

During this time Moses himself fell into sin. In an earlier event God instructed him to strike the rock to obtain water, which then flowed abundantly (Ex 17.1–7). On the second occasion God told him to speak to the rock. Instead of speaking to the rock, Moses smote it in anger, and for that transgression God forbad him entrance into the promised land.

Numbers recounts rather fully the story of Israel's encounter with the Moabites and the hiring of Balaam by Balak to curse the people of God (chs. 22–24). Instead Balaam pronounced a triple blessing and predicted Israel's ultimate triumph. In the latter section of the book, Moses recorded the preparations for entering Canaan, and apportioned the Transjordan territory to Reuben, Gad, and Manasseh.

Outline:

NUMBERS

I. The preparations leaving Sinai (1.1–10.10)

A. The census

1. Selection of the census takers

1 The LORD spoke to Moses in the wilderness of Sinai, in the tent of meeting, on the first day of the second month, in the second year after they had come out of the land of Egypt, saying: 2 Take a census of the whole congregation of Israelites, in their clans, by ancestral houses, according to the number of names, every male individually; 3 from twenty years old and upward, everyone in Israel able to go to war. You and Aaron shall enroll them, company by company. 4 A man from each tribe shall be with you, each man the head of his ancestral house. 5 These are the names of the men who shall assist you:

From Reuben, Elizur son of Shedeur.
6 From Simeon, Shelumiel son of Zurishaddai.
7 From Judah, Nahshon son of Amminadab.
8 From Issachar, Nethanel son of Zuar.
9 From Zebulun, Eliab son of Helon.
10 From the sons of Joseph:
  from Ephraim, Elishama son of Ammihud;
  from Manasseh, Gamaliel son of Pedahzur.
11 From Benjamin, Abidan son of Gideoni.
12 From Dan, Ahiezer son of Ammishaddai.
13 From Asher, Pagiel son of Ochran.
14 From Gad, Eliasaph son of Deuel.
15 From Naphtali, Ahira son of Enan.
16 These were the ones chosen from the congregation, the leaders of their ancestral tribes, the heads of the divisions of Israel.

2. The numbering of Israel

17 Moses and Aaron took these men who had been designated by name, 18 and on the first day of the second month they assembled the whole congregation together. They registered themselves in their clans, by their ancestral houses, according to the number of names from twenty years old and upward, individually, 19 as the LORD commanded Moses. So he enrolled them in the wilderness of Sinai.

20 The descendants of Reuben, Israel's firstborn, their lineage, in their clans, by their ancestral houses, according to the number of names, individually, every male from twenty years old and upward, everyone able

1.1
Ex 19.1;
40.2, 17
1.2
Ex 38.26;
Num 26.2

1.4
v. 16

1.14
Num 2.14,
euel
1.16
Num 16.2;
26.9

1.20
Num 26.5-11

1.1 *on the first day of the second month* (of the Jewish calendar), i.e., around the fifteenth day of April (see also v. 18).
1.2 God commanded Moses to number the people. The census was to be limited, however, to males twenty years old or over. It was a military census in preparation for the wars to possess Canaan. Excluded from the census were the lame, the deaf, the blind, and others who had bodily infirmities or chronic dis-

eases; only those who were "able to go to war" (v. 3) were numbered. Later, when David ordered another census, he paid dearly for so doing, since it was not commanded by God (2 Sam 24.1ff). The Levites were not included in this census (see note on vv. 47–49).
1.18 Anyone twenty years or older was eligible for military service. The tribe of Judah supplied the largest number of warriors—74,600 (1.27).

to go to war: 21 those enrolled of the tribe of Reuben were forty-six thousand five hundred.

22 The descendants of Simeon, their lineage, in their clans, by their ancestral houses, those of them that were numbered, according to the number of names, individually, every male from twenty years old and upward, everyone able to go to war: 23 those enrolled of the tribe of Simeon were fifty-nine thousand three hundred.

24 The descendants of Gad, their lineage, in their clans, by their ancestral houses, according to the number of the names, from twenty years old and upward, everyone able to go to war: 25 those enrolled of the tribe of Gad were forty-five thousand six hundred fifty.

26 The descendants of Judah, their lineage, in their clans, by their ancestral houses, according to the number of names, from twenty years old and upward, everyone able to go to war: 27 those enrolled of the tribe of Judah were seventy-four thousand six hundred.

28 The descendants of Issachar, their lineage, in their clans, by their ancestral houses, according to the number of names, from twenty years old and upward, everyone able to go to war: 29 those enrolled of the tribe of Issachar were fifty-four thousand four hundred.

30 The descendants of Zebulun, their lineage, in their clans, by their ancestral houses, according to the number of names, from twenty years old and upward, everyone able to go to war: 31 those enrolled of the tribe of Zebulun were fifty-seven thousand four hundred.

32 The descendants of Joseph, namely, the descendants of Ephraim, their lineage, in their clans, by their ancestral houses, according to the number of names, from twenty years old and upward, everyone able to go to war: 33 those enrolled of the tribe of Ephraim were forty thousand five hundred.

34 The descendants of Manasseh, their lineage, in their clans, by their ancestral houses, according to the number of names, from twenty years old and upward, everyone able to go to war: 35 those enrolled of the tribe of Manasseh were thirty-two thousand two hundred.

36 The descendants of Benjamin, their lineage, in their clans, by their ancestral houses, according to the number of names, from twenty years old and upward, everyone able to go to war: 37 those enrolled of the tribe of Benjamin were thirty-five thousand four hundred.

38 The descendants of Dan, their lineage, in their clans, by their ancestral houses, according to the number of names, from twenty years old and upward, everyone able to go to war: 39 those enrolled of the tribe of Dan were sixty-two thousand seven hundred.

40 The descendants of Asher, their lineage, in their clans, by their ancestral houses, according to the number of names, from twenty years old and upward, everyone able to go to war: 41 those enrolled of the tribe of Asher were forty-one thousand five hundred.

42 The descendants of Naphtali, their lineage, in their clans, by their ancestral houses, according to the number of names, from twenty years old and upward, everyone able to go to war: 43 those enrolled of the tribe of Naphtali were fifty-three thousand four hundred.

44 These are those who were enrolled, whom Moses and Aaron enrolled with the help of the leaders of Israel, twelve men, each representing his ancestral house. 45 So the whole number of the Israelites, by their ancestral houses, from twenty years old and upward, everyone able to go to war in Israel — 46 their whole number was six hundred three thousand five hundred fifty. 47 The Levites, however, were not numbered by their ancestral tribe along with them.

1.32 Although the Levites were exempted from going to war, there were still twelve tribes participating in the military. Joseph's two sons, Ephraim and Manasseh, were counted as two tribes along with the other sons of Jacob.
1.47–49 The Levites were not to be included with

3. The Levites not numbered: their duties

48 The LORD had said to Moses: 49 Only the tribe of Levi you shall not enroll, and you shall not take a census of them with the other Israelites. 50 Rather you shall appoint the Levites over the tabernacle of the covenant,*a* and over all its equipment, and over all that belongs to it; they are to carry the tabernacle and all its equipment, and they shall tend it, and shall camp around the tabernacle. 51 When the tabernacle is to set out, the Levites shall take it down; and when the tabernacle is to be pitched, the Levites shall set it up. And any outsider who comes near shall be put to death. 52 The other Israelites shall camp in their respective regimental camps, by companies; 53 but the Levites shall camp around the tabernacle of the covenant,*a* that there may be no wrath on the congregation of the Israelites; and the Levites shall perform the guard duty of the tabernacle of the covenant.*a* 54 The Israelites did so; they did just as the LORD commanded Moses.

B. The camps and leaders of the tribes

2 The LORD spoke to Moses and Aaron, saying: 2 The Israelites shall camp each in their respective regiments, under ensigns by their ancestral houses; they shall camp facing the tent of meeting on every side. 3 Those to camp on the east side toward the sunrise shall be of the regimental encampment of Judah by companies. The leader of the people of Judah shall be Nahshon son of Amminadab, 4 with a company as enrolled of seventy-four thousand six hundred. 5 Those to camp next to him shall be the tribe of Issachar. The leader of the Issacharites shall be Nethanel son of Zuar, 6 with a company as enrolled of fifty-four thousand four hundred. 7 Then the tribe of Zebulun: The leader of the Zebulunites shall be Eliab son of Helon, 8 with a company as enrolled of fifty-seven thousand four hundred. 9 The total enrollment of the camp of Judah, by companies, is one hundred eighty-six thousand four hundred. They shall set out first on the march.

10 On the south side shall be the regimental encampment of Reuben by companies. The leader of the Reubenites shall be Elizur son of Shedeur, 11 with a company as enrolled of forty-six thousand five hundred. 12 And those to camp next to him shall be the tribe of Simeon. The leader of the Simeonites shall be Shelumiel son of Zurishaddai, 13 with a company as enrolled of fifty-nine thousand three hundred. 14 Then the tribe of Gad: The leader of the Gadites shall be Eliasaph son of Reuel, 15 with a company as enrolled of forty-five thousand six hundred fifty. 16 The total enrollment of the camp of Reuben, by companies, is one hundred fifty-one thousand four hundred fifty. They shall set out second.

17 The tent of meeting, with the camp of the Levites, shall set out in the center of the camps; they shall set out just as they camp, each in position, by their regiments.

18 On the west side shall be the regimental encampment of Ephraim by companies. The leader of the people of Ephraim shall be Elishama son of Ammihud, 19 with a company as enrolled of forty thousand five hundred. 20 Next to him shall be the tribe of Manasseh. The leader of the people of Manasseh shall be Gamaliel son of Pedahzur, 21 with a company as enrolled of thirty-two thousand two hundred. 22 Then the tribe of Benjamin: The leader of the Benjaminites shall be Abidan son of Gideoni,

a Or *treaty,* or *testimony;* Heb *eduth*

1.50
Num 3.25-37

1.51
Num 4.1-33

1.52
Num 2.2
1.53
v. 50

2.2
Num 1.52

2.3
Num 10;14

2.5
Num 1.8

2.9
Num 10.14

2.10
Num 1.5

2.12
Num 1.6

2.14
Num 1.14,
euel

2.17
Num 1.53

2.20
Num 1.10

the eleven other tribes. But later they were numbered separately (3.15).
2.3 Each of the tribes camped together. Apparently this was designed to maintain their separate identity. It also helped to keep them from extensive intermarriage among the tribes; thus when the land of Canaan was divided, each geographical area was sharply distinguished and easily identifiable.
2.17 The tabernacle and the Levites were set up in the middle of the camp. This symbolized that the focal point of all the tribes was to be their devotion to God.

23 with a company as enrolled of thirty-five thousand four hundred. 24 The total enrollment of the camp of Ephraim, by companies, is one hundred eight thousand one hundred. They shall set out third on the march.

25   On the north side shall be the regimental encampment of Dan by companies. The leader of the Danites shall be Ahiezer son of Ammishaddai, 26 with a company as enrolled of sixty-two thousand seven hundred. 27 Those to camp next to him shall be the tribe of Asher. The leader of the Asherites shall be Pagiel son of Ochran, 28 with a company as enrolled of forty-one thousand five hundred. 29 Then the tribe of Naphtali: The leader of the Naphtalites shall be Ahira son of Enan, 30 with a company as enrolled of fifty-three thousand four hundred. 31 The total enrollment of the camp of Dan is one hundred fifty-seven thousand six hundred. They shall set out last, by companies. *b*

32   This was the enrollment of the Israelites by their ancestral houses; the total enrollment in the camps by their companies was six hundred three thousand five hundred fifty. 33 Just as the LORD had commanded Moses, the Levites were not enrolled among the other Israelites.

34   The Israelites did just as the LORD had commanded Moses: They camped by regiments, and they set out the same way, everyone by clans, according to ancestral houses.

C. The Levites

1. The sons of Aaron

3 This is the lineage of Aaron and Moses at the time when the LORD spoke with Moses on Mount Sinai. 2 These are the names of the sons of Aaron: Nadab the firstborn, and Abihu, Eleazar, and Ithamar; 3 these are the names of the sons of Aaron, the anointed priests, whom he ordained to minister as priests. 4 Nadab and Abihu died before the LORD when they offered unholy fire before the LORD in the wilderness of Sinai, and they had no children. Eleazar and Ithamar served as priests in the lifetime of their father Aaron.

2. The responsibilities of the Levites

5   Then the LORD spoke to Moses, saying: 6 Bring the tribe of Levi near, and set them before Aaron the priest, so that they may assist him. 7 They shall perform duties for him and for the whole congregation in front of the tent of meeting, doing service at the tabernacle; 8 they shall be in charge of all the furnishings of the tent of meeting, and attend to the duties for the Israelites as they do service at the tabernacle. 9 You shall give the Levites to Aaron and his descendants; they are unreservedly given to him from among the Israelites. 10 But you shall make a register of Aaron and his descendants; it is they who shall attend to the priesthood, and any outsider who comes near shall be put to death.

3. God chooses the Levites instead of every firstborn

11   Then the LORD spoke to Moses, saying: 12 I hereby accept the Levites from among the Israelites as substitutes for all the firstborn that open the womb among the Israelites. The Levites shall be mine, 13 for all the firstborn are mine; when I killed all the firstborn in the land of Egypt, I consecrated for my own all the firstborn in Israel, both human and animal; they shall be mine. I am the LORD.

---

b Compare verses 9, 16, 24: Heb *by their regiments*

3.9 From among the tribe of Levi, only the descendants of Aaron participated in the priesthood; the remainder of the Levites were given to Aaron for service in connection with the tabernacle and its func-tions. No Levite, other than those of the priesthood, was ever to trespass into the areas or functions reserved for the priesthood.

Cross references (margin)

2.24 Num 10.22
2.25 Num 1.12
2.27 Num 1.13
2.31 Num 10.25
2.32 Num 1.46; Ex 38.26
2.33 Num 1.47
3.2 Num 26.60
3.4 Num 26.61
3.6 Num 8.6-22; 18.1-7
3.9 Num 18.6
3.10 Ex 29.9; Num 1.51
3.12 v. 41; Num 8.16; 18.6
3.13 Ex 13.2, 12, 15; Num 8.17

4. *The Levites numbered: duties assigned*

14 Then the LORD spoke to Moses in the wilderness of Sinai, saying: 15 Enroll the Levites by ancestral houses and by clans. You shall enroll every male from a month old and upward. 16 So Moses enrolled them according to the word of the LORD, as he was commanded. 17 The following were the sons of Levi, by their names: Gershon, Kohath, and Merari. 18 These are the names of the sons of Gershon by their clans: Libni and Shimei. 19 The sons of Kohath by their clans: Amram, Izhar, Hebron, and Uzziel. 20 The sons of Merari by their clans: Mahli and Mushi. These are the clans of the Levites, by their ancestral houses.

21 To Gershon belonged the clan of the Libnites and the clan of the Shimeites; these were the clans of the Gershonites. 22 Their enrollment, counting all the males from a month old and upward, was seven thousand five hundred. 23 The clans of the Gershonites were to camp behind the tabernacle on the west, 24 with Eliasaph son of Lael as head of the ancestral house of the Gershonites. 25 The responsibility of the sons of Gershon in the tent of meeting was to be the tabernacle, the tent with its covering, the screen for the entrance of the tent of meeting, 26 the hangings of the court, the screen for the entrance of the court that is around the tabernacle and the altar, and its cords — all the service pertaining to these.

27 To Kohath belonged the clan of the Amramites, the clan of the Izharites, the clan of the Hebronites, and the clan of the Uzzielites; these are the clans of the Kohathites. 28 Counting all the males, from a month old and upward, there were eight thousand six hundred, attending to the duties of the sanctuary. 29 The clans of the Kohathites were to camp on the south side of the tabernacle, 30 with Elizaphan son of Uzziel as head of the ancestral house of the clans of the Kohathites. 31 Their responsibility was to be the ark, the table, the lampstand, the altars, the vessels of the sanctuary with which the priests minister, and the screen — all the service pertaining to these. 32 Eleazar son of Aaron the priest was to be chief over the leaders of the Levites, and to have oversight of those who had charge of the sanctuary.

33 To Merari belonged the clan of the Mahlites and the clan of the Mushites: these are the clans of Merari. 34 Their enrollment, counting all the males from a month old and upward, was six thousand two hundred. 35 The head of the ancestral house of the clans of Merari was Zuriel son of Abihail; they were to camp on the north side of the tabernacle. 36 The responsibility assigned to the sons of Merari was to be the frames of the tabernacle, the bars, the pillars, the bases, and all their accessories — all the service pertaining to these; 37 also the pillars of the court all around, with their bases and pegs and cords.

38 Those who were to camp in front of the tabernacle on the east — in front of the tent of meeting toward the east — were Moses and Aaron and Aaron's sons, having charge of the rites within the sanctuary, whatever had to be done for the Israelites; and any outsider who came near was to be put to death. 39 The total enrollment of the Levites whom Moses and Aaron enrolled at the commandment of the LORD, by their clans, all the males from a month old and upward, was twenty-two thousand.

3.32 Eleazar was the third of the four sons of Aaron. Nadab and Abihu were slain by God when they offered strange fire, probably when they were drunk (see Lev 10). Apparently Eleazar had precedence over Ithamar, his younger brother, for he became high priest upon his father's death. He had charge of the tabernacle and its furniture, and supervised the Kohathites, who carried the ark and the holy furniture on their shoulders. For reasons we do not know, the descendants of Ithamar supplanted Eleazar's descendants in the tent at Shiloh. Eli was a descendant of Ithamar but God rejected his line.
3.38 Death was the sentence for any Levite other than the descendants of Aaron who sought to perform any of the religious rites.
3.39 The Levites were numbered from a month and upward, not from twenty years old and upward as in the case of the other tribes. Still the number of Levites (which therefore included many more males) was the smallest of all the tribes — 22,000.

3.15
v. 39

3.17
Ex 6.16-22

3.20
Gen 46.11

3.21
Ex 6.17

3.25
Num 4.24-26;
Ex 25.9

3.27
1 Chr 26.23

3.29
Ex 6.18

3.33
Ex 6.19

3.36
Num 4.29-32

3.38
Num 18.5;
vv. 7, 8, 10

3.39
Num 26.62

5. The numbering of firstborn males

3.41
vv. 12, 45

40 Then the LORD said to Moses: Enroll all the firstborn males of the Israelites, from a month old and upward, and count their names. 41 But you shall accept the Levites for me — I am the LORD — as substitutes for all the firstborn among the Israelites, and the livestock of the Levites as substitutes for all the firstborn among the livestock of the Israelites. 42 So Moses enrolled all the firstborn among the Israelites, as the LORD commanded him.

3.43
v. 39

43 The total enrollment, all the firstborn males from a month old and upward, counting the number of names, was twenty-two thousand two hundred seventy-three.

3.45
vv. 12, 41

44 Then the LORD spoke to Moses, saying: 45 Accept the Levites as substitutes for all the firstborn among the Israelites, and the livestock of the Levites as substitutes for their livestock; and the Levites shall be mine.

3.46
Ex 13.13;
Num 18.15
3.47
Ex 30.13

I am the LORD. 46 As the price of redemption of the two hundred seventy-three of the firstborn of the Israelites, over and above the number of the Levites, 47 you shall accept five shekels apiece, reckoning by the shekel of the sanctuary, a shekel of twenty gerahs. 48 Give to Aaron and his sons the money by which the excess number of them is redeemed. 49 So Moses took the redemption money from those who were over and above those

3.50
vv. 46-48

redeemed by the Levites; 50 from the firstborn of the Israelites he took the money, one thousand three hundred sixty-five shekels, reckoned by the shekel of the sanctuary; 51 and Moses gave the redemption money to Aaron and his sons, according to the word of the LORD, as the LORD had commanded Moses.

6. Numbering and service of the Levites

a. The Kohathites

4 The LORD spoke to Moses and Aaron, saying: 2 Take a census of the Kohathites separate from the other Levites, by their clans and their ancestral houses, 3 from thirty years old up to fifty years old, all who qualify to do work relating to the tent of meeting. 4 The service of the Kohathites relating to the tent of meeting concerns the most holy things.

4.3
Num 8.24;
vv. 23, 30, 35

5 When the camp is to set out, Aaron and his sons shall go in and take down the screening curtain, and cover the ark of the covenant[c] with it; 6 then they shall put on it a covering of fine leather,[d] and spread over that a cloth all of blue, and shall put its poles in place. 7 Over the table of the bread of the Presence they shall spread a blue cloth, and put on it the plates, the dishes for incense, the bowls, and the flagons for the drink offering; the regular bread also shall be on it; 8 then they shall spread over them a crimson cloth, and cover it with a covering of fine leather,[d] and shall put its poles in place. 9 They shall take a blue cloth, and cover the lampstand for the light, with its lamps, its snuffers, its trays, and all the vessels for oil with which it is supplied; 10 and they shall put it with all its utensils in a covering of fine leather,[d] and put it on the carrying frame. 11 Over the golden altar they shall spread a blue cloth, and cover it with a covering of fine leather,[d] and shall put its poles in place; 12 and they shall take all the utensils of the service that are used in the sanctuary, and put them in a blue cloth, and cover them with a covering of fine leather,[d] and put them on the carrying frame. 13 They shall take away the ashes from the altar, and spread a purple cloth over it; 14 and they shall put on

4.6
v. 25
4.7
Ex 25.23, 29,
30;
Lev 24.5-9

4.9
Ex 25.31, 37,
38

4.11
Ex 30.1, 3

c Or treaty, or testimony; Heb eduth   d Meaning of Heb uncertain

---

3.47,48 The 273 firstborn males of the other tribes were in excess of the 22,000 Levites and had to be redeemed. The price of redemption was five shekels, and the money went to Aaron and his sons.
4.3 from thirty years old. Note in 8.24 the number twenty-five is used. They were probationers; in Da-

vid's time, when there was more work to be done, service began at twenty years of age (1 Chr 23.24; cf. Ezra 3.8). They were taught their duties for five years (in David's time, ten years). Novices were not to be used in the temple duties.

it all the utensils of the altar, which are used for the service there, the firepans, the forks, the shovels, and the basins, all the utensils of the altar; and they shall spread on it a covering of fine leather,*e* and shall put its poles in place. **15** When Aaron and his sons have finished covering the sanctuary and all the furnishings of the sanctuary, as the camp sets out, after that the Kohathites shall come to carry these, but they must not touch the holy things, or they will die. These are the things of the tent of meeting that the Kohathites are to carry.

16   Eleazar son of Aaron the priest shall have charge of the oil for the light, the fragrant incense, the regular grain offering, and the anointing oil, the oversight of all the tabernacle and all that is in it, in the sanctuary and in its utensils.

17   Then the LORD spoke to Moses and Aaron, saying: **18** You must not let the tribe of the clans of the Kohathites be destroyed from among the Levites. **19** This is how you must deal with them in order that they may live and not die when they come near to the most holy things: Aaron and his sons shall go in and assign each to a particular task or burden. **20** But the Kohathites*f* must not go in to look on the holy things even for a moment; otherwise they will die.

b. *The Gershonites*

21   Then the LORD spoke to Moses, saying: **22** Take a census of the Gershonites also, by their ancestral houses and by their clans; **23** from thirty years old up to fifty years old you shall enroll them, all who qualify to do work in the tent of meeting. **24** This is the service of the clans of the Gershonites, in serving and bearing burdens: **25** They shall carry the curtains of the tabernacle, and the tent of meeting with its covering, and the outer covering of fine leather*e* that is on top of it, and the screen for the entrance of the tent of meeting, **26** and the hangings of the court, and the screen for the entrance of the gate of the court that is around the tabernacle and the altar, and their cords, and all the equipment for their service; and they shall do all that needs to be done with regard to them. **27** All the service of the Gershonites shall be at the command of Aaron and his sons, in all that they are to carry, and in all that they have to do; and you shall assign to their charge all that they are to carry. **28** This is the service of the clans of the Gershonites relating to the tent of meeting, and their responsibilities are to be under the oversight of Ithamar son of Aaron the priest.

c. *The Merarites*

29   As for the Merarites, you shall enroll them by their clans and their ancestral houses; **30** from thirty years old up to fifty years old you shall enroll them, everyone who qualifies to do the work of the tent of meeting. **31** This is what they are charged to carry, as the whole of their service in the tent of meeting: the frames of the tabernacle, with its bars, pillars, and bases, **32** and the pillars of the court all around with their bases, pegs, and cords, with all their equipment and all their related service; and you shall assign by name the objects that they are required to carry. **33** This is the service of the clans of the Merarites, the whole of their service relating to the tent of meeting, under the hand of Ithamar son of Aaron the priest.

---

e Meaning of Heb uncertain   *f* Heb *they*

4.15 The sons of Kohath were to carry, not cart, the furnishings of the sanctuary. Aaron and his sons first covered them and placed them on carrying frames, at which time the Kohathites began their duties. They were never to touch the holy things, lest they die. **4.25** The Gershonites were responsible for trans- porting the curtains of the tabernacle and other items as specified in vv. 25,26. They were supervised by Ithamar, the son of Aaron (v. 28). **4.31,32** The parts of the tent to be carried by the sons of Merari, also under Ithamar's supervision, are itemized here.

4.15
Num 7.9;
2 Sam 6.6, 7

4.16
Lev 24.1-3;
Ex 30.34;
29.40; 30.23

4.19
vv. 4, 15

4.23
v. 3

4.25
Num 3.25, 26

4.27
Num 3.21

4.30
v. 3

4.31
Num 3.36, 37

4.33
v. 28

d. The results of the census

4.34
v. 2

34 So Moses and Aaron and the leaders of the congregation enrolled the Kohathites, by their clans and their ancestral houses, 35 from thirty years old up to fifty years old, everyone who qualified for work relating to the tent of meeting; 36 and their enrollment by clans was two thousand seven hundred fifty. 37 This was the enrollment of the clans of the Kohathites, all who served at the tent of meeting, whom Moses and Aaron enrolled according to the commandment of the LORD by Moses.

4.37
Num 3.27

4.38
Gen 46.11

38 The enrollment of the Gershonites, by their clans and their ancestral houses, 39 from thirty years old up to fifty years old, everyone who qualified for work relating to the tent of meeting — 40 their enrollment by their clans and their ancestral houses was two thousand six hundred thirty. 41 This was the enrollment of the clans of the Gershonites, all who served at the tent of meeting, whom Moses and Aaron enrolled according to the commandment of the LORD.

4.41
v. 22

42 The enrollment of the clans of the Merarites, by their clans and their ancestral houses, 43 from thirty years old up to fifty years old, everyone who qualified for work relating to the tent of meeting — 44 their enrollment by their clans was three thousand two hundred. 45 This is the enrollment of the clans of the Merarites, whom Moses and Aaron enrolled according to the commandment of the LORD by Moses.

4.45
v. 29

46 All those who were enrolled of the Levites, whom Moses and Aaron and the leaders of Israel enrolled, by their clans and their ancestral houses, 47 from thirty years old up to fifty years old, everyone who qualified to do the work of service and the work of bearing burdens relating to the tent of meeting, 48 their enrollment was eight thousand five hundred eighty. 49 According to the commandment of the LORD through Moses they were appointed to their several tasks of serving or carrying; thus they were enrolled by him, as the LORD commanded Moses.

4.47
vv. 3, 23, 30

D. Camp laws and regulations

1. The unclean to be put out of the camp

5.2ff
Lev 13.3, 46;
15.2; 19.11
5.3
Lev 26.11,
12;
2 Cor 6.16

5 The LORD spoke to Moses, saying: 2 Command the Israelites to put out of the camp everyone who is leprous,ᵍ or has a discharge, and everyone who is unclean through contact with a corpse; 3 you shall put out both male and female, putting them outside the camp; they must not defile their camp, where I dwell among them. 4 The Israelites did so, putting them outside the camp; as the LORD had spoken to Moses, so the Israelites did.

2. The law of restitution

5.6
Lev 6.2, 3

5.7
Lev 5.5;
26.40; 6.5
5.8
Lev 6.6, 7;
7.7

5 The LORD spoke to Moses, saying: 6 Speak to the Israelites: When a man or a woman wrongs another, breaking faith with the LORD, that person incurs guilt 7 and shall confess the sin that has been committed. The person shall make full restitution for the wrong, adding one-fifth to it, and giving it to the one who was wronged. 8 If the injured party has no next of kin to whom restitution may be made for the wrong, the

ᵍ A term for several skin diseases; precise meaning uncertain

---

5.2 One of the reasons for segregating lepers, those who had discharges, and those who had contact with the dead was to prevent contagion from spreading among other people. This principle of isolating people with contagious infections has a spiritual application (see note on 1 Cor 5.11).
5.6 Restitution was required from those who had done wrong to a neighbor. The sin was to be con-

fessed, an atonement made, and satisfaction rendered to the injured party. Verse 7 indicates that a fifth should be added to the wrong act. Thus the innocent person had a right to damages beyond the amount involved. This was a penalty the offender had to pay.
5.7 full restitution, i.e., make full payment for what was stolen.

restitution for wrong shall go to the LORD for the priest, in addition to the ram of atonement with which atonement is made for the guilty party. 9 Among all the sacred donations of the Israelites, every gift that they bring to the priest shall be his. 10 The sacred donations of all are their own; whatever anyone gives to the priest shall be his.

5.9
Lev 6.17, 18, 26; 7.6-14
5.10
Lev 10.13

3. *The law concerning jealousy*

11   The LORD spoke to Moses, saying: 12 Speak to the Israelites and say to them: If any man's wife goes astray and is unfaithful to him, 13 if a man has had intercourse with her but it is hidden from her husband, so that she is undetected though she has defiled herself, and there is no witness against her since she was not caught in the act; 14 if a spirit of jealousy comes on him, and he is jealous of his wife who has defiled herself; or if a spirit of jealousy comes on him, and he is jealous of his wife, though she has not defiled herself; 15 then the man shall bring his wife to the priest. And he shall bring the offering required for her, one-tenth of an ephah of barley flour. He shall pour no oil on it and put no frankincense on it, for it is a grain offering of jealousy, a grain offering of remembrance, bringing iniquity to remembrance.

5.12
Ex 20.14
5.13
Lev 18.20

5.15
Ezek 29.16

16   Then the priest shall bring her near, and set her before the LORD; 17 the priest shall take holy water in an earthen vessel, and take some of the dust that is on the floor of the tabernacle and put it into the water. 18 The priest shall set the woman before the LORD, dishevel the woman's hair, and place in her hands the grain offering of remembrance, which is the grain offering of jealousy. In his own hand the priest shall have the water of bitterness that brings the curse. 19 Then the priest shall make her take an oath, saying, "If no man has lain with you, if you have not turned aside to uncleanness while under your husband's authority, be immune to this water of bitterness that brings the curse. 20 But if you have gone astray while under your husband's authority, if you have defiled yourself and some man other than your husband has had intercourse with you," 21 — let the priest make the woman take the oath of the curse and say to the woman — "the LORD make you an execration and an oath among your people, when the LORD makes your uterus drop, your womb discharge; 22 now may this water that brings the curse enter your bowels and make your womb discharge, your uterus drop!" And the woman shall say, "Amen. Amen."

5.18
1 Cor 11.6

5.21
Josh 6.26;
1 Sam 14.24;
Neh 10.29
5.22
Deut 27.15;
Ps 109.18

23   Then the priest shall put these curses in writing, and wash them off into the water of bitterness. 24 He shall make the woman drink the water of bitterness that brings the curse, and the water that brings the curse shall enter her and cause bitter pain. 25 The priest shall take the grain offering of jealousy out of the woman's hand, and shall elevate the grain offering before the LORD and bring it to the altar; 26 and the priest shall take a handful of the grain offering, as its memorial portion, and turn it into smoke on the altar, and afterward shall make the woman drink the water. 27 When he has made her drink the water, then, if she has defiled herself and has been unfaithful to her husband, the water that brings the curse shall enter into her and cause bitter pain, and her womb shall discharge, her uterus drop, and the woman shall become an execration among her people. 28 But if the woman has not defiled herself and is clean, then she shall be immune and be able to conceive children.

5.25
Lev 8.27

5.27
Jer 29.18;
42.18;
Zech 8.13

29   This is the law in cases of jealousy, when a wife, while under her

5.29
vv. 12, 19

5.11ff The law of jealousy was instituted so that God himself could determine the guilt or innocence of a wife whose conduct was suspect but for whose guilt there was no proof. It was to the advantage of an innocent party to go through the ordeal and have her name cleared and her husband reassured. The Scrip-

tures afford no example of the use of this provision, nor was it used in postbiblical times.
5.29 The passage does not say what should be done if a wife suspected her husband of adultery but had no certainty that he had been unfaithful.

husband's authority, goes astray and defiles herself, 30 or when a spirit of jealousy comes on a man and he is jealous of his wife; then he shall set the woman before the LORD, and the priest shall apply this entire law to her. 31 The man shall be free from iniquity, but the woman shall bear her iniquity.

4. The law for a nazirite

6.2
Judg 13.5;
16.17;
Am 2.11, 12

6 The LORD spoke to Moses, saying: 2 Speak to the Israelites and say to them: When either men or women make a special vow, the vow of a nazirite,*h* to separate themselves to the LORD, 3 they shall separate themselves from wine and strong drink; they shall drink no wine vinegar or other vinegar, and shall not drink any grape juice or eat grapes, fresh or dried. 4 All their days as nazirites*i* they shall eat nothing that is produced by the grapevine, not even the seeds or the skins.

6.5
1 Sam 1.11

5 All the days of their nazirite vow no razor shall come upon the head; until the time is completed for which they separate themselves to the LORD, they shall be holy; they shall let the locks of the head grow long.

6.6
Lev 19.11-22;
21.1-3

6 All the days that they separate themselves to the LORD they shall not go near a corpse. 7 Even if their father or mother, brother or sister, should die, they may not defile themselves; because their consecration to God is upon the head. 8 All their days as nazirites*i* they are holy to the LORD.

6.10
Lev 5.7

9 If someone dies very suddenly nearby, defiling the consecrated head, then they shall shave the head on the day of their cleansing; on the seventh day they shall shave it. 10 On the eighth day they shall bring two turtledoves or two young pigeons to the priest at the entrance of the tent of meeting, 11 and the priest shall offer one as a sin offering and the other as a burnt offering, and make atonement for them, because they incurred guilt by reason of the corpse. They shall sanctify the head that same day,

6.12
Lev 5.6

12 and separate themselves to the LORD for their days as nazirites,*i* and bring a male lamb a year old as a guilt offering. The former time shall be void, because the consecrated head was defiled.

6.13
Acts 21.26

13 This is the law for the nazirites*i* when the time of their consecration has been completed: they shall be brought to the entrance of the tent of meeting, 14 and they shall offer their gift to the LORD, one male lamb a year old without blemish as a burnt offering, one ewe lamb a year old without blemish as a sin offering, one ram without blemish as an offering of well-being, 15 and a basket of unleavened bread, cakes of choice flour mixed with oil and unleavened wafers spread with oil, with their grain offering and their drink offerings. 16 The priest shall present them before the LORD and offer their sin offering and burnt offering, 17 and shall offer the ram as a sacrifice of well-being to the LORD, with the basket of unleavened bread; the priest also shall make the accompanying grain offering and drink offering. 18 Then the nazirites*i* shall shave the consecrated head at the entrance of the tent of meeting, and shall take the hair from the consecrated head and put it on the fire under the sacrifice of well-being. 19 The priest shall take the shoulder of the ram, when it is boiled, and one unleavened cake out of the basket, and one unleavened

6.14
Num 15.27;
Lev 14.10

6.15
Num 15.1-7

6.18
v. 9;
Acts 21.24

---

h That is one separated or one consecrated   i That is those separated or those consecrated

---

6.1,2 Vows (pledges) were made in both O.T. and N.T. They were not to be made lightly (Prov 20.25), and once made, they had to be kept (30.2) and discharged promptly (Deut 23.21-23). The Scriptures do not indicate that one must keep a vow which is made in good faith but which is later discovered to be wrong or sinful. Not to make vows was not sinful, but when made, certain restrictions were to be followed: (1) children needed parental consent for their vows (30.3-5); (2) wives needed the consent of their husbands (30.6-8, 10.13); (3) widows and divorced

women were bound by their vows (30.9). Jephthah (Judg 11.30,31), Hannah (1 Sam 1.11), David (Ps 132.2-5), Paul (Acts 18.18), and certain Jews (Acts 21.23-26) all made vows.
6.3 See note on Judg 13.5 for a description of a nazirite.
6.13 This general rule concerning the ending of a nazirite vow by going to the sanctuary and offering a sin and burnt offering was done by the apostle Paul in Acts 21.24. In his case it worked to his harm, for he was taken prisoner and ultimately sent to Rome.

wafer, and shall put them in the palms of the nazirites,*j* after they have shaved the consecrated head. 20 Then the priest shall elevate them as an elevation offering before the LORD; they are a holy portion for the priest, together with the breast that is elevated and the thigh that is offered. After that the nazirites*j* may drink wine.

21   This is the law for the nazirites*j* who take a vow. Their offering to the LORD must be in accordance with the nazirite*k* vow, apart from what else they can afford. In accordance with whatever vow they take, so they shall do, following the law for their consecration.

5. The priestly benediction

22   The LORD spoke to Moses, saying: 23 Speak to Aaron and his sons, saying, Thus you shall bless the Israelites: You shall say to them,
24   The LORD bless you and keep you;
25   the LORD make his face to shine upon you, and be gracious to
         you;
26   the LORD lift up his countenance upon you, and give you
         peace.
27   So they shall put my name on the Israelites, and I will bless them.

E. The offerings for the tabernacle

1. The dedication of the altar

7   On the day when Moses had finished setting up the tabernacle, and had anointed and consecrated it with all its furnishings, and had anointed and consecrated the altar with all its utensils, 2 the leaders of Israel, heads of their ancestral houses, the leaders of the tribes, who were over those who were enrolled, made offerings. 3 They brought their offerings before the LORD, six covered wagons and twelve oxen, a wagon for every two of the leaders, and for each one an ox; they presented them before the tabernacle. 4 Then the LORD said to Moses: 5 Accept these from them, that they may be used in doing the service of the tent of meeting, and give them to the Levites, to each according to his service. 6 So Moses took the wagons and the oxen, and gave them to the Levites. 7 Two wagons and four oxen he gave to the Gershonites, according to their service; 8 and four wagons and eight oxen he gave to the Merarites, according to their service, under the direction of Ithamar son of Aaron the priest. 9 But to the Kohathites he gave none, because they were charged with the care of the holy things that had to be carried on the shoulders. 10   The leaders also presented offerings for the dedication of the altar at the time when it was anointed; the leaders presented their offering before the altar. 11 The LORD said to Moses: They shall present their offerings, one leader each day, for the dedication of the altar.

2. Nahshon of Judah

12   The one who presented his offering the first day was Nahshon son of Amminadab, of the tribe of Judah; 13 his offering was one silver plate weighing one hundred thirty shekels, one silver basin weighing seventy shekels, according to the shekel of the sanctuary, both of them full of choice flour mixed with oil for a grain offering; 14 one golden dish weighing ten shekels, full of incense; 15 one young bull, one ram, one male lamb

j That is those separated or those consecrated   k That is one separated or one consecrated

6.23
1 Chr 23.13

6.24
Deut 28.3-6
6.25
Ps 80.3, 7,
19; 119.135;
Gen 43.29
6.26
Ps 4.6; 44.3;
Jn 14.27
6.27
Deut 28.10;
2 Chr 7.14

7.1
Ex 40.18

7.2
Num 1.5-16

7.7
Num 4.25

7.8
Num 4.28,
31, 33
7.9
Num 4.5-15

7.10
2 Chr 7.9

7.13
Num 3.47

7.14
Ex 30.34

6.22ff God commanded Aaron and his sons to give a threefold blessing on the people. The value of the blessing was due to God, not the priest himself, through whom God gave the blessing. Gospel ministers, like the priests, should dismiss their congregations with such a blessing. The N.T. contains a num-ber of apostolic benedictions (e.g., 2 Cor 13.13; Heb 13.20,21).

7.3–9 Covered wagons were used to carry certain parts of the tent, but the furnishings were not to be placed on carts. They were to be borne on the shoulders of the Kohathites.

7.17
Lev 3.1

a year old, for a burnt offering; 16 one male goat for a sin offering; 17 and for the sacrifice of well-being, two oxen, five rams, five male goats, and five male lambs a year old. This was the offering of Nahshon son of Amminadab.

3. Nethanel of Issachar

7.18
Num 1.8

18 On the second day Nethanel son of Zuar, the leader of Issachar, presented an offering; 19 he presented for his offering one silver plate weighing one hundred thirty shekels, one silver basin weighing seventy shekels, according to the shekel of the sanctuary, both of them full of choice flour mixed with oil for a grain offering; 20 one golden dish weigh-ing ten shekels, full of incense; 21 one young bull, one ram, one male lamb

7.23
v. 18

a year old, as a burnt offering; 22 one male goat as a sin offering; 23 and for the sacrifice of well-being, two oxen, five rams, five male goats, and five male lambs a year old. This was the offering of Nethanel son of Zuar.

4. Eliab of Zebulun

7.24
Num 1.9

24 On the third day Eliab son of Helon, the leader of the Zebulunites: 25 his offering was one silver plate weighing one hundred thirty shekels, one silver basin weighing seventy shekels, according to the shekel of the sanctuary, both of them full of choice flour mixed with oil for a grain offering; 26 one golden dish weighing ten shekels, full of incense; 27 one young bull, one ram, one male lamb a year old, for a burnt offering; 28 one

7.29
Lev 7.32

male goat for a sin offering; 29 and for the sacrifice of well-being, two oxen, five rams, five male goats, and five male lambs a year old. This was the offering of Eliab son of Helon.

5. Elizur of Reuben

7.30
Num 1.5

30 On the fourth day Elizur son of Shedeur, the leader of the Reuben-ites: 31 his offering was one silver plate weighing one hundred thirty shekels, one silver basin weighing seventy shekels, according to the shekel of the sanctuary, both of them full of choice flour mixed with oil for a grain offering; 32 one golden dish weighing ten shekels, full of incense; 33 one young bull, one ram, one male lamb a year old, for a burnt offering; 34 one

7.34
Heb 10.4

male goat for a sin offering; 35 and for the sacrifice of well-being, two oxen, five rams, five male goats, and five male lambs a year old. This was the offering of Elizur son of Shedeur.

6. Shelumiel of Simeon

7.36
Num 1.6

36 On the fifth day Shelumiel son of Zurishaddai, the leader of the Simeonites: 37 his offering was one silver plate weighing one hundred thirty shekels, one silver basin weighing seventy shekels, according to the shekel of the sanctuary, both of them full of choice flour mixed with oil for a grain offering; 38 one golden dish weighing ten shekels, full of incense; 39 one young bull, one ram, one male lamb a year old, for a burnt

7.40
v. 34

offering; 40 one male goat for a sin offering; 41 and for the sacrifice of well-being, two oxen, five rams, five male goats, and five male lambs a year old. This was the offering of Shelumiel son of Zurishaddai.

7. Eliasaph of Gad

7.42
Num 1.14
euel

42 On the sixth day Eliasaph son of Deuel, the leader of the Gadites: 43 his offering was one silver plate weighing one hundred thirty shekels, one silver basin weighing seventy shekels, according to the shekel of the sanctuary, both of them full of choice flour mixed with oil for a grain offering; 44 one golden dish weighing ten shekels, full of incense; 45 one

7.46
v. 34

young bull, one ram, one male lamb a year old, for a burnt offering; 46 one male goat for a sin offering; 47 and for the sacrifice of well-being, two oxen, five rams, five male goats, and five male lambs a year old. This was the offering of Eliasaph son of Deuel.

8. Elishama of Ephraim

48 On the seventh day Elishama son of Ammihud, the leader of the Ephraimites: 49 his offering was one silver plate weighing one hundred thirty shekels, one silver basin weighing seventy shekels, according to the shekel of the sanctuary, both of them full of choice flour mixed with oil for a grain offering; 50 one golden dish weighing ten shekels, full of incense; 51 one young bull, one ram, one male lamb a year old, for a burnt offering; 52 one male goat for a sin offering; 53 and for the sacrifice of well-being, two oxen, five rams, five male goats, and five male lambs a year old. This was the offering of Elishama son of Ammihud.

7.48
Num 1.10

7.52
Heb 10.4

9. Gamaliel of Manasseh

54 On the eighth day Gamaliel son of Pedahzur, the leader of the Manassites: 55 his offering was one silver plate weighing one hundred thirty shekels, one silver basin weighing seventy shekels, according to the shekel of the sanctuary, both of them full of choice flour mixed with oil for a grain offering; 56 one golden dish weighing ten shekels, full of incense; 57 one young bull, one ram, one male lamb a year old, for a burnt offering; 58 one male goat for a sin offering; 59 and for the sacrifice of well-being, two oxen, five rams, five male goats, and five male lambs a year old. This was the offering of Gamaliel son of Pedahzur.

7.54
Num 1.10

7.58
v. 52

10. Abidan of Benjamin

60 On the ninth day Abidan son of Gideoni, the leader of the Benjaminites: 61 his offering was one silver plate weighing one hundred thirty shekels, one silver basin weighing seventy shekels, according to the shekel of the sanctuary, both of them full of choice flour mixed with oil for a grain offering; 62 one golden dish weighing ten shekels, full of incense; 63 one young bull, one ram, one male lamb a year old, for a burnt offering; 64 one male goat for a sin offering; 65 and for the sacrifice of well-being, two oxen, five rams, five male goats, and five male lambs a year old. This was the offering of Abidan son of Gideoni.

7.60
Num 1.11

7.64
v. 52

11. Ahiezer of Dan

66 On the tenth day Ahiezer son of Ammishaddai, the leader of the Danites: 67 his offering was one silver plate weighing one hundred thirty shekels, one silver basin weighing seventy shekels, according to the shekel of the sanctuary, both of them full of choice flour mixed with oil for a grain offering; 68 one golden dish weighing ten shekels, full of incense; 69 one young bull, one ram, one male lamb a year old, for a burnt offering; 70 one male goat for a sin offering; 71 and for the sacrifice of well-being, two oxen, five rams, five male goats, and five male lambs a year old. This was the offering of Ahiezer son of Ammishaddai.

7.66
Num 1.12

7.70
Heb 10.4

12. Pagiel of Asher

72 On the eleventh day Pagiel son of Ochran, the leader of the Asherites: 73 his offering was one silver plate weighing one hundred thirty shekels, one silver basin weighing seventy shekels, according to the shekel of the sanctuary, both of them full of choice flour mixed with oil for a grain offering; 74 one golden dish weighing ten shekels, full of incense; 75 one young bull, one ram, one male lamb a year old, for a burnt offering; 76 one male goat for a sin offering; 77 and for the sacrifice of well-being, two oxen, five rams, five male goats, and five male lambs a year old. This was the offering of Pagiel son of Ochran.

7.72
Num 1.13

7.76
v. 70

13. Ahira of Naphtali

7.78
Num 1.15

78 On the twelfth day Ahira son of Enan, the leader of the Naphtalites: 79 his offering was one silver plate weighing one hundred thirty shekels, one silver basin weighing seventy shekels, according to the shekel of the sanctuary, both of them full of choice flour mixed with oil for a grain offering; 80 one golden dish weighing ten shekels, full of incense; 81 one young bull, one ram, one male lamb a year old, for a burnt offering; 82 one male goat for a sin offering; 83 and for the sacrifice of well-being, two oxen, five rams, five male goats, and five male lambs a year old. This was the offering of Ahira son of Enan.

7.82
v. 70

7.84
vv. 1, 10

84 This was the dedication offering for the altar, at the time when it was anointed, from the leaders of Israel: twelve silver plates, twelve silver basins, twelve golden dishes, 85 each silver plate weighing one hundred thirty shekels and each basin seventy, all the silver of the vessels two thousand four hundred shekels according to the shekel of the sanctuary, 86 the twelve golden dishes, full of incense, weighing ten shekels apiece according to the shekel of the sanctuary, all the gold of the dishes being one hundred twenty shekels; 87 all the livestock for the burnt offering twelve bulls, twelve rams, twelve male lambs a year old, with their grain offering; and twelve male goats for a sin offering; 88 and all the livestock for the sacrifice of well-being twenty-four bulls, the rams sixty, the male goats sixty, the male lambs a year old sixty. This was the dedication offering for the altar, after it was anointed.

7.87
Gen 8.20

14. The voice from above the mercy seat

7.89
Ex 33.9, 11;
25.21, 22

89 When Moses went into the tent of meeting to speak with the LORD,[l] he would hear the voice speaking to him from above the mercy seat[m] that was on the ark of the covenant[n] from between the two cherubim; thus it spoke to him.

F. Final details before the march

1. The lampstand

8.2
Ex 25.37;
Lev 24.2, 4

8 The LORD spoke to Moses, saying: 2 Speak to Aaron and say to him: When you set up the lamps, the seven lamps shall give light in front of the lampstand. 3 Aaron did so; he set up its lamps to give light in front of the lampstand, as the LORD had commanded Moses. 4 Now this was how the lampstand was made, out of hammered work of gold. From its base to its flowers, it was hammered work; according to the pattern that the LORD had shown Moses, so he made the lampstand.

8.4
Ex 25.31-40;
25.18

2. Cleansing of the Levites

8.7
Num 19.9,
17, 18;
Lev 14.8, 9;
v. 21
8.8
Lev 2.1
8.9
Lev 8.3

5 The LORD spoke to Moses, saying: 6 Take the Levites from among the Israelites and cleanse them. 7 Thus you shall do to them, to cleanse them: sprinkle the water of purification on them, have them shave their whole body with a razor and wash their clothes, and so cleanse themselves. 8 Then let them take a young bull and its grain offering of choice flour mixed with oil, and you shall take another young bull for a sin offering. 9 You shall bring the Levites before the tent of meeting, and assemble the whole congregation of the Israelites. 10 When you bring the Levites before the LORD, the Israelites shall lay their hands on the Levites, 11 and Aaron

l Heb him   m Or the cover   n Or treaty, or testimony; Heb eduth

---

7.89 Leaders from the various tribes had brought their offerings to God (7.12 – 88). Would God accept those offerings? He did so by speaking intimately with Moses, as a person speaks to a friend, from above the mercy seat. In so doing he spoke to all Israel.

8.11 Although the priesthood derived from the offspring of Aaron, there were many Levites not of Aaron's line. They were given over to God for other forms of religious service. In v. 19, God gave them back to Aaron. Whatever we give up to God, he will

shall present the Levites before the Lord as an elevation offering from the Israelites, that they may do the service of the Lord. 12 The Levites shall lay their hands on the heads of the bulls, and he shall offer the one for a sin offering and the other for a burnt offering to the Lord, to make atonement for the Levites. 13 Then you shall have the Levites stand before Aaron and his sons, and you shall present them as an elevation offering to the Lord.

14 Thus you shall separate the Levites from among the other Israelites, and the Levites shall be mine. 15 Thereafter the Levites may go in to do service at the tent of meeting, once you have cleansed them and presented them as an elevation offering. 16 For they are unreservedly given to me from among the Israelites; I have taken them for myself, in place of all that open the womb, the firstborn of all the Israelites. 17 For all the firstborn among the Israelites are mine, both human and animal. On the day that I struck down all the firstborn in the land of Egypt I consecrated them for myself, 18 but I have taken the Levites in place of all the firstborn among the Israelites. 19 Moreover, I have given the Levites as a gift to Aaron and his sons from among the Israelites, to do the service for the Israelites at the tent of meeting, and to make atonement for the Israelites, in order that there may be no plague among the Israelites for coming too close to the sanctuary.

20 Moses and Aaron and the whole congregation of the Israelites did with the Levites accordingly; the Israelites did with the Levites just as the Lord had commanded Moses concerning them. 21 The Levites purified themselves from sin and washed their clothes; then Aaron presented them as an elevation offering before the Lord, and Aaron made atonement for them to cleanse them. 22 Thereafter the Levites went in to do their service in the tent of meeting in attendance on Aaron and his sons. As the Lord had commanded Moses concerning the Levites, so they did with them.

3. Age of service for the Levites

23 The Lord spoke to Moses, saying: 24 This applies to the Levites: from twenty-five years old and upward they shall begin to do duty in the service of the tent of meeting; 25 and from the age of fifty years they shall retire from the duty of the service and serve no more. 26 They may assist their brothers in the tent of meeting in carrying out their duties, but they shall perform no service. Thus you shall do with the Levites in assigning their duties.

4. The passover command

9 The Lord spoke to Moses in the wilderness of Sinai, in the first month of the second year after they had come out of the land of Egypt, saying: 2 Let the Israelites keep the passover at its appointed time. 3 On the fourteenth day of this month, at twilight,ᵒ you shall keep it at its appointed time; according to all its statutes and all its regulations you shall keep it. 4 So Moses told the Israelites that they should keep the passover. 5 They kept the passover in the first month, on the fourteenth day of the month, at twilight,ᵒ in the wilderness of Sinai. Just as the Lord had commanded Moses, so the Israelites did. 6 Now there were certain people who were unclean through touching a corpse, so that they could not keep the passover on that day. They came before Moses and Aaron on that day, 7 and said to him, "Although we are unclean through touching a corpse, why must we be kept from presenting the Lord's offering at its

ᵒ Heb between the two evenings

8.12	Ex 29.10
8.14	Num 3.12, 45
8.15	vv. 11, 13
8.16	Num 3.12, 45
8.19	Num 1.53
8.21	vv. 7, 11, 12
8.24	Num 4.3
9.1	Num 1.1
9.2	Ex 12.6
9.5	Josh 5.10
9.6	Num 19.11-22

give back to us in numerous and wonderful ways.   **8.24** See note on 4.3.

9.8
Ex 18.15;
Num 27.5

9.11
Ex 12.8
9.12
Ex 12.10, 43,
46;
Jn 19.36
9.13
v. 7;
Ex 12.15
9.14
Ex 12.48, 49

9.15
Ex 40.34;
Neh 9.12, 19;
Ps 78.4;
Ex 13.21;
40.38
9.17
Num 10.11,
12;
Ex 40.36-38
9.18
1 Cor 10.1
9.19
Num 1.53;
3.8

9.22
Ex 40.36, 37

appointed time among the Israelites?" ⁸Moses spoke to them, "Wait, so that I may hear what the LORD will command concerning you."

9 The LORD spoke to Moses, saying: ¹⁰Speak to the Israelites, saying: Anyone of you or your descendants who is unclean through touching a corpse, or is away on a journey, shall still keep the passover to the LORD. ¹¹In the second month on the fourteenth day, at twilight,ᵖ they shall keep it; they shall eat it with unleavened bread and bitter herbs. ¹²They shall leave none of it until morning, nor break a bone of it; according to all the statute for the passover they shall keep it. ¹³But anyone who is clean and is not on a journey, and yet refrains from keeping the passover, shall be cut off from the people for not presenting the LORD's offering at its appointed time; such a one shall bear the consequences for the sin. ¹⁴Any alien residing among you who wishes to keep the passover to the LORD shall do so according to the statute of the passover and according to its regulation; you shall have one statute for both the resident alien and the native.

5. The cloud of guidance

15 On the day the tabernacle was set up, the cloud covered the tabernacle, the tent of the covenant;�q and from evening until morning it was over the tabernacle, having the appearance of fire. ¹⁶It was always so: the cloud covered it by dayʳ and the appearance of fire by night. ¹⁷Whenever the cloud lifted from over the tent, then the Israelites would set out; and in the place where the cloud settled down, there the Israelites would camp. ¹⁸At the command of the LORD the Israelites would set out, and at the command of the LORD they would camp. As long as the cloud rested over the tabernacle, they would remain in camp. ¹⁹Even when the cloud continued over the tabernacle many days, the Israelites would keep the charge of the LORD, and would not set out. ²⁰Sometimes the cloud would remain a few days over the tabernacle, and according to the command of the LORD they would remain in camp; then according to the command of the LORD they would set out. ²¹Sometimes the cloud would remain from evening until morning; and when the cloud lifted in the morning, they would set out, or if it continued for a day and a night, when the cloud lifted they would set out. ²²Whether it was two days, or a month, or a longer time, that the cloud continued over the tabernacle, resting upon it, the Israelites would remain in camp and would not set out; but when it lifted they would set out. ²³At the command of the LORD they would camp, and at the command of the LORD they would set out. They kept the charge of the LORD, at the command of the LORD by Moses.

ᵖ Heb *between the two evenings*   q Or *treaty*, or *testimony*; Heb *eduth*   ʳ Gk Syr Vg: Heb lacks *by day*

9.8 God commanded the Israelites to keep the passover. But the ceremonially unclean were not to appear before God until they first had met the requirements for cleansing. In other words, it seemed as if one law contradicted another. Moses did not answer the question himself. He referred it to the lawgiver, God. God replied that regardless of defilement for touching a dead body, all were to keep the passover (see also next note). Today we have the Holy Spirit to lead us into all truth (Jn 16.13). When matters of uncertainty arise we have the Scriptures and the Holy Spirit to aid us. We can rest assured that we will be assisted in arriving at the right course of action.
9.10,11 So important was the keeping of the passover that special provision was made for those who could not, for good reason, attend the celebration. Such people were permitted to observe it a month later.

9.13 Those who were ceremonially clean and not on a journey were to be cut off from the assembly of God if they failed to show up at the passover celebration. Such failure was looked upon as an affront to God, an impious act against the divine majesty and the grace of God. Few Christians consider this sort of conduct unacceptable today, and indiscriminately absent themselves from the worship of God and participation in the ordinances or sacraments. Such people should not be surprised if the blessing of God no longer attends them, for God is not to be mocked (cf. Gal 6.7).
9.15 When the tabernacle was dedicated, the cloud of God's presence came upon the sanctuary. When it rose from the tent, the people were to move with it. As long as it stayed still, they were to rest. God now had a house for himself.

6. *The two silver trumpets*

10 The LORD spoke to Moses, saying: 2 Make two silver trumpets; you shall make them of hammered work; and you shall use them for summoning the congregation, and for breaking camp. 3 When both are blown, the whole congregation shall assemble before you at the entrance of the tent of meeting. 4 But if only one is blown, then the leaders, the heads of the tribes of Israel, shall assemble before you. 5 When you blow an alarm, the camps on the east side shall set out; 6 when you blow a second alarm, the camps on the south side shall set out. An alarm is to be blown whenever they are to set out. 7 But when the assembly is to be gathered, you shall blow, but you shall not sound an alarm. 8 The sons of Aaron, the priests, shall blow the trumpets; this shall be a perpetual institution for you throughout your generations. 9 When you go to war in your land against the adversary who oppresses you, you shall sound an alarm with the trumpets, so that you may be remembered before the LORD your God and be saved from your enemies. 10 Also on your days of rejoicing, at your appointed festivals, and at the beginnings of your months, you shall blow the trumpets over your burnt offerings and over your sacrifices of well-being; they shall serve as a reminder on your behalf before the LORD your God: I am the LORD your God.

10.3
Jer 4.5

10.5
v. 14
10.6
v. 18

10.8
Num 31.6

10.9
Num 31.6;
Judg 2.18;
Ps 106.4

10.10
Num 29.1;
Lev 23.24;
Ps 81.3-5

II. *The journey from Sinai to Moab (10.11–21.35)*

A. *The departure*

1. *The order of march*

11 In the second year, in the second month, on the twentieth day of the month, the cloud lifted from over the tabernacle of the covenant.ˢ 12 Then the Israelites set out by stages from the wilderness of Sinai, and the cloud settled down in the wilderness of Paran. 13 They set out for the first time at the command of the LORD by Moses. 14 The standard of the camp of Judah set out first, company by company, and over the whole company was Nahshon son of Amminadab. 15 Over the company of the tribe of Issachar was Nethanel son of Zuar; 16 and over the company of the tribe of Zebulun was Eliab son of Helon.

10.11
Num 9.17

10.13
Deut 1.6
10.14
Num 2.3-9

17 Then the tabernacle was taken down, and the Gershonites and the Merarites, who carried the tabernacle, set out. 18 Next the standard of the camp of Reuben set out, company by company; and over the whole company was Elizur son of Shedeur. 19 Over the company of the tribe of Simeon was Shelumiel son of Zurishaddai, 20 and over the company of the tribe of Gad was Eliasaph son of Deuel.

10.17
Num 4.21-32
10.18
Num 2.10-16

21 Then the Kohathites, who carried the holy things, set out; and the tabernacle was set up before their arrival. 22 Next the standard of the Ephraimite camp set out, company by company, and over the whole company was Elishama son of Ammihud. 23 Over the company of the tribe of Manasseh was Gamaliel son of Pedahzur, 24 and over the company of the tribe of Benjamin was Abidan son of Gideoni.

10.21
Num 4.4-20
10.22
Num 2.18-24

25 Then the standard of the camp of Dan, acting as the rear guard of

10.25
Num 2.25-31;
Josh 6.9, 13

ˢ Or *treaty*, or *testimony*; Heb *eduth*

10.2 The two silver trumpets were designed either to call the people to a public assembly in the presence of God or to signal that they should break camp and move. They needed only two trumpets because only Aaron's two sons blew them. In Solomon's day 120 priests sounded the trumpets (2 Chr 5.12).
10.5–7 Different trumpet blasts distinguished between the summons to assemble and the signal to break camp and move onward.
10.10 The festival of the new moon was celebrated

on the first day of each month. Sacrifices were to be offered (28.11–15) and the trumpets blown (10.10; Ps 81.3,4). All labor stopped on that day (a practice detested by the ungodly — Am 8.5). God condemned the formal observance of this and other religious festivals when insincerity marked the occasions (Isa 1.13, 14). Under the new covenant these festivals have been abolished by the sacrifice of Jesus Christ (Gal 4.10,11; Col 2.16).

all the camps, set out, company by company, and over the whole company was Ahiezer son of Ammishaddai. 26 Over the company of the tribe of Asher was Pagiel son of Ochran, 27 and over the company of the tribe of Naphtali was Ahira son of Enan. 28 This was the order of march of the Israelites, company by company, when they set out.

2. The appeal to Hobab

10.29
Judg 4.11;
Ex 2.18;
Gen 12.7;
32.12;
Ex 3.8

29 Moses said to Hobab son of Reuel the Midianite, Moses' father-in-law, "We are setting out for the place of which the Lord said, 'I will give it to you'; come with us, and we will treat you well; for the Lord has promised good to Israel." 30 But he said to him, "I will not go, but I will go back to my own land and to my kindred." 31 He said, "Do not leave us, for you know where we should camp in the wilderness, and you will serve as eyes for us. 32 Moreover, if you go with us, whatever good the Lord does for us, the same we will do for you."

10.32
Ps 22.27-31;
Lev 19.34

3. The ark and the cloud of guidance

10.33
v. 11;
Deut 1.33;
Isa 11.10
10.34
Num 9.15-23
10.35
Ps 68.1, 2;
Deut 7.10;
32.41

33 So they set out from the mount of the Lord three days' journey with the ark of the covenant of the Lord going before them three days' journey, to seek out a resting place for them, 34 the cloud of the Lord being over them by day when they set out from the camp.

35 Whenever the ark set out, Moses would say,
"Arise, O Lord, let your enemies be scattered,
    and your foes flee before you."
36 And whenever it came to rest, he would say,
"Return, O Lord of the ten thousand thousands of Israel."*t*

B. The sins of Israel

1. Complaining at Taberah

11.1
Num 14.2;
16.11; 17.5;
16.35;
Lev 10.2
11.2
Num 21.7

11 Now when the people complained in the hearing of the Lord about their misfortunes, the Lord heard it and his anger was kindled. Then the fire of the Lord burned against them, and consumed some outlying parts of the camp. 2 But the people cried out to Moses; and Moses prayed to the Lord, and the fire abated. 3 So that place was called Taberah,*u* because the fire of the Lord burned against them.

2. The cry for meat

11.4
Ex 12.38;
Ps 78.18;
1 Cor 10.6
11.5
Ex 16.3
11.6
Lev 21.5
11.7
Ex 16.14, 31

4 The rabble among them had a strong craving; and the Israelites also wept again, and said, "If only we had meat to eat! 5 We remember the fish we used to eat in Egypt for nothing, the cucumbers, the melons, the leeks, the onions, and the garlic; 6 but now our strength is dried up, and there is nothing at all but this manna to look at."

7 Now the manna was like coriander seed, and its color was like the color of gum resin. 8 The people went around and gathered it, ground it in mills or beat it in mortars, then boiled it in pots and made cakes of it;

t Meaning of Heb uncertain   *u* That is *Burning*

10.31 *serve as eyes for us.* Hobab, Moses' brother-in-law, knew the region well and could serve as guide.
10.33 *the mount of the Lord,* i.e., Mount Sinai.
11.1 How quickly the Israelites forgot God, whose glory they had seen and whose bread they ate day by day. They were discontented, mutinous, and complaining throughout the wilderness journey. In this age of grace this sort of attitude is not unknown among believers who manifest their lack of faith when God uses them differently from the way they think he

should. Those who are Spirit-filled do not fall heir to such attitudes.
11.4 *the rabble,* i.e., the non-Israelites who came with the Israelites out of Egypt expecting almost instantaneous fulfillment of the promise of the land. When the fulfillment was delayed, they became pestilent discontents whose leaven worked its way through the whole community of God's children. The Israelites quickly copied their wretched ways.

and the taste of it was like the taste of cakes baked with oil. ⁹When the dew fell on the camp in the night, the manna would fall with it.

3. Moses' prayer for help

10 Moses heard the people weeping throughout their families, all at the entrances of their tents. Then the LORD became very angry, and Moses was displeased. ¹¹So Moses said to the LORD, "Why have you treated your servant so badly? Why have I not found favor in your sight, that you lay the burden of all this people on me? ¹²Did I conceive all this people? Did I give birth to them, that you should say to me, 'Carry them in your bosom, as a nurse carries a sucking child,' to the land that you promised on oath to their ancestors? ¹³Where am I to get meat to give to all this people? For they come weeping to me and say, 'Give us meat to eat!' ¹⁴I am not able to carry all this people alone, for they are too heavy for me. ¹⁵If this is the way you are going to treat me, put me to death at once—if I have found favor in your sight—and do not let me see my misery."

4. God's reply to Moses: the appointment of the seventy elders

16 So the LORD said to Moses, "Gather for me seventy of the elders of Israel, whom you know to be the elders of the people and officers over them; bring them to the tent of meeting, and have them take their place there with you. ¹⁷I will come down and talk with you there; and I will take some of the spirit that is on you and put it on them; and they shall bear the burden of the people along with you so that you will not bear it all by yourself. ¹⁸And say to the people: Consecrate yourselves for tomorrow, and you shall eat meat; for you have wailed in the hearing of the LORD, saying, 'If only we had meat to eat! Surely it was better for us in Egypt.' Therefore the LORD will give you meat, and you shall eat. ¹⁹You shall eat not only one day, or two days, or five days, or ten days, or twenty days, ²⁰but for a whole month—until it comes out of your nostrils and becomes loathsome to you—because you have rejected the LORD who is among you, and have wailed before him, saying, 'Why did we ever leave Egypt?'" ²¹But Moses said, "The people I am with number six hundred thousand on foot; and you say, 'I will give them meat, that they may eat for a whole month'! ²²Are there enough flocks and herds to slaughter for them? Are there enough fish in the sea to catch for them?" ²³The LORD said to Moses, "Is the LORD's power limited?ᵛ Now you shall see whether my word will come true for you or not."

24 So Moses went out and told the people the words of the LORD; and he gathered seventy elders of the people, and placed them all around the tent. ²⁵Then the LORD came down in the cloud and spoke to him, and took some of the spirit that was on him and put it on the seventy elders; and when the spirit rested upon them, they prophesied. But they did not do so again.

26 Two men remained in the camp, one named Eldad, and the other named Medad, and the spirit rested on them; they were among those

ᵛ Heb LORD's hand too short?

11.9 Ex 16.13, 14
11.10 Ps 78.21
11.12 Isa 40.11; 49.23; Gen 26.3; Ex 13.5
11.13 vv. 21, 22; Jn 6.5-9
11.14
11.15 Ex 18.18; 1 Kings 19.4; Jon 4.3
11.16 Ex 24.1, 9; Deut 16.18
11.17 v. 25; Ex 19.20; 1 Sam 10.6; 2 Kings 2.15
11.18 Ex 19.10; 16.7; v. 5; Acts 7.39
11.19 Ps 78.29; 106.15; Num 21.5
11.22 Mt 15.33
11.23 Isa 50.2; 59.1; Num 23.19
11.24 v. 16
11.25 v. 17; Num 12.5; 1 Sam 10.5, 6, 10; Acts 2.17, 18
11.26 1 Sam 10.6; 20.26

11.11 Moses, the meekest of all people, was deeply affected by the grumbling of the Israelites. He felt he was being so badly treated by the Lord God that he began his own complaint, which rose to a crescendo when he passionately asked God to kill him out of hand. It may seem strange how life made difficult by others could turn Moses into a feeble and despairing servant, even though he had been appointed and strengthened by God and filled with his Holy Spirit. Believers often manifest that they have feet of clay.

11.25 *the LORD . . . took some of the spirit that was on him and put it on the seventy elders; and when the spirit rested upon them, they prophesied.* This outward evidence confirmed that the Spirit was in them and at work in their lives. Two of the seventy were still in the camp (v. 26), but the Spirit came upon them also and they prophesied. When what happened was questioned, Moses made it plain that he wished all of God's people would have the Spirit laid upon them in power (v. 29).

registered, but they had not gone out to the tent, and so they prophesied in the camp. ²⁷And a young man ran and told Moses, "Eldad and Medad are prophesying in the camp." ²⁸And Joshua son of Nun, the assistant of Moses, one of his chosen men,ʷ said, "My lord Moses, stop them!" ²⁹But Moses said to him, "Are you jealous for my sake? Would that all the Lord's people were prophets, and that the Lord would put his spirit on them!" ³⁰And Moses and the elders of Israel returned to the camp.

5. God sends quails for meat

31   Then a wind went out from the Lord, and it brought quails from the sea and let them fall beside the camp, about a day's journey on this side and a day's journey on the other side, all around the camp, about two cubits deep on the ground. ³²So the people worked all that day and night and all the next day, gathering the quails; the least anyone gathered was ten homers; and they spread them out for themselves all around the camp. ³³But while the meat was still between their teeth, before it was consumed, the anger of the Lord was kindled against the people, and the Lord struck the people with a very great plague. ³⁴So that place was called Kibroth-hattaavah,ˣ because there they buried the people who had the craving. ³⁵From Kibroth-hattaavah the people journeyed to Hazeroth.

C. Miriam and Aaron oppose Moses

1. God vindicates Moses

12   While they were at Hazeroth, Miriam and Aaron spoke against Moses because of the Cushite woman whom he had married (for he had indeed married a Cushite woman); ²and they said, "Has the Lord spoken only through Moses? Has he not spoken through us also?" And the Lord heard it. ³Now the man Moses was very humble,ʸ more so than anyone else on the face of the earth. ⁴Suddenly the Lord said to Moses, Aaron, and Miriam, "Come out, you three, to the tent of meeting." So the three of them came out. ⁵Then the Lord came down in a pillar of cloud, and stood at the entrance of the tent, and called Aaron and Miriam; and they both came forward. ⁶And he said, "Hear my words:

When there are prophets among you,
     I the Lord make myself known to them in visions;
     I speak to them in dreams.
7   Not so with my servant Moses;
     he is entrusted with all my house.
8   With him I speak face to face—clearly, not in riddles;
     and he beholds the form of the Lord.
Why then were you not afraid to speak against my servant Moses?" ⁹And the anger of the Lord was kindled against them, and he departed.

2. Miriam becomes a leper; Moses prays for her healing

10   When the cloud went away from over the tent, Miriam had become

---

Cross references (left margin): 11.28 Mk 9.38-40; 11.29 1 Cor 14.5; 11.31 Ex 16.13; Ps 78.26-28; 105.40; 11.33 Ps 78.30, 31; 106.15; 11.34 Deut 9.22; 11.35 Num 33.17; 12.1 Ex 2.21; 12.2 Num 16.3; 12.3 Mt 11.29; 12.5 Num 11.25; 16.19; 12.6 Gen 46.2; 31.10, 11; 1 Kings 3.5; 12.7 Ps 105.26; Heb 3.2, 5; 12.8 Ex 33.11; Deut 34.10; Ex 33.19; 12.10 Deut 24.9; 2 Kings 5.27; 15.5

ʷ Or of Moses from his youth   ˣ That is Graves of craving   ʸ Or devout

---

12.1 *because of the Cushite woman whom he had married.* The Cushite woman was probably Moses' wife Zipporah, the Midianite daughter of Reuel (Ex 2.21). The land of Midian from which she came was sometimes called Cush. But other areas were also known as Cush, so perhaps this refers to a second wife of Moses. The text does not say whether their criticisms were because of her being a Gentile or (if she was a Cushite from Ethiopia) because of her color.
12.7,8 In many ways Moses represents Christ (see Heb 3.1–6). As Moses delivered Israel from slavery

in Egypt, so Jesus delivers his people from sin's bondage; Moses was a prophet and so was Jesus; Moses was a faithful servant, while Jesus is God's Servant-Savior; Moses frequently interceded for Israel before God, and Jesus now intercedes for his people, the church.
12.10 Miriam, the elder sister of Moses and Aaron, had watched over Moses when he was placed in the basket on the Nile River. She was obviously a person of importance, since her two brothers were the leaders of Israel. Yet along with Aaron, she presumed to

leprous,ᶻ as white as snow. And Aaron turned towards Miriam and saw
that she was leprous. ¹¹Then Aaron said to Moses, "Oh, my lord, do not
punish usᵃ for a sin that we have so foolishly committed. ¹²Do not let
her be like one stillborn, whose flesh is half consumed when it comes out
of its mother's womb." ¹³And Moses cried to the Lord, "O God, please
heal her." ¹⁴But the Lord said to Moses, "If her father had but spit in
her face, would she not bear her shame for seven days? Let her be shut
out of the camp for seven days, and after that she may be brought in
again." ¹⁵So Miriam was shut out of the camp for seven days; and the
people did not set out on the march until Miriam had been brought in
again. ¹⁶After that the people set out from Hazeroth, and camped in the
wilderness of Paran.

D. The twelve spies

1. The spies chosen

13 The Lord said to Moses, ²"Send men to spy out the land of
Canaan, which I am giving to the Israelites; from each of their
ancestral tribes you shall send a man, every one a leader among them."
³So Moses sent them from the wilderness of Paran, according to the
command of the Lord, all of them leading men among the Israelites.
⁴These were their names: From the tribe of Reuben, Shammua son of
Zaccur; ⁵from the tribe of Simeon, Shaphat son of Hori; ⁶from the tribe
of Judah, Caleb son of Jephunneh; ⁷from the tribe of Issachar, Igal son
of Joseph; ⁸from the tribe of Ephraim, Hoshea son of Nun; ⁹from the
tribe of Benjamin, Palti son of Raphu; ¹⁰from the tribe of Zebulun,
Gaddiel son of Sodi; ¹¹from the tribe of Joseph (that is, from the tribe
of Manasseh), Gaddi son of Susi; ¹²from the tribe of Dan, Ammiel son
of Gemalli; ¹³from the tribe of Asher, Sethur son of Michael; ¹⁴from the
tribe of Naphtali, Nahbi son of Vophsi; ¹⁵from the tribe of Gad, Geuel
son of Machi. ¹⁶These were the names of the men whom Moses sent to
spy out the land. And Moses changed the name of Hoshea son of Nun to
Joshua.

2. The spies sent out

17 Moses sent them to spy out the land of Canaan, and said to them,
"Go up there into the Negeb, and go up into the hill country, ¹⁸and see
what the land is like, and whether the people who live in it are strong or
weak, whether they are few or many, ¹⁹and whether the land they live
in is good or bad, and whether the towns that they live in are unwalled
or fortified, ²⁰and whether the land is rich or poor, and whether there are
trees in it or not. Be bold, and bring some of the fruit of the land." Now
it was the season of the first ripe grapes.

21 So they went up and spied out the land from the wilderness of Zin
to Rehob, near Lebo-hamath. ²²They went up into the Negeb, and came

---

12.11
2 Sam 19.19;
24.10

12.14
Lev 13.46;
Num 5.2, 3

13.2
Deut 1.22

13.8
v. 16

13.16
v. 8

13.17
v. 21

13.20
Deut 1.24,
25; 31.6, 23

13.22
Josh 15.13,
14; vv. 28,
33;
Ps 78.12

ᶻ A term for several skin diseases; precise meaning uncertain   ᵃ Heb *do not lay sin upon us*

---

speak against Moses. God judged Miriam by sending
leprosy, a disease that covered her body and made her
an outcast from the people of Israel. Aaron was repentant, and Moses prayed for God to heal his sister. His
request was granted. Miriam's death is recorded later
(20.1).
12.14 Here mercy and justice kiss each other. Miriam is forgiven by Moses and by God for her
transgression — that is mercy. But justice was fulfilled
in that she was shut out from the camp for seven days.
Mercy and justice kissed in our salvation. As sinners
we are forgiven — that is mercy. And justice was met
by the atoning death of Jesus Christ.
13.8 *Hoshea*, or, "Joshua" (see v. 16).

13.16 Moses changed the name of Hoshea (meaning
"salvation") to Joshua (meaning "Yahweh is salvation." "Joshua" is the same name in Hebrew as the
Greek name "Jesus."
13.17 *Negeb . . . hill country.* The direct route to
Canaan led northeast from Kadesh along some water
stations in the Negeb (meaning "parched") up to Hebron in the hill country. Abraham and Jacob probably
used this route going down to Egypt.
13.22 *Zoan* was built ca. 1700 B.C. in the Nile delta
by the Hyksos. *Hebron* was built seven years earlier
on a site known to Abraham as *Kiratha-arba* or
Mamre. Ps 78.43 refers to the plains of Zoan, i.e.,
Goshen, where the Israelites lived.

to Hebron; and Ahiman, Sheshai, and Talmai, the Anakites, were there. (Hebron was built seven years before Zoan in Egypt.) 23 And they came to the Wadi Eshcol, and cut down from there a branch with a single cluster of grapes, and they carried it on a pole between two of them. They also brought some pomegranates and figs. 24 That place was called the Wadi Eshcol,*b* because of the cluster that the Israelites cut down from there.

3. The adverse report of the majority

25   At the end of forty days they returned from spying out the land. 26 And they came to Moses and Aaron and to all the congregation of the Israelites in the wilderness of Paran, at Kadesh; they brought back word to them and to all the congregation, and showed them the fruit of the land. 27 And they told him, "We came to the land to which you sent us; it flows with milk and honey, and this is its fruit. 28 Yet the people who live in the land are strong, and the towns are fortified and very large; and besides, we saw the descendants of Anak there. 29 The Amalekites live in the land of the Negeb; the Hittites, the Jebusites, and the Amorites live in the hill country; and the Canaanites live by the sea, and along the Jordan."

30   But Caleb quieted the people before Moses, and said, "Let us go up at once and occupy it, for we are well able to overcome it." 31 Then the men who had gone up with him said, "We are not able to go up against this people, for they are stronger than we." 32 So they brought to the Israelites an unfavorable report of the land that they had spied out, saying, "The land that we have gone through as spies is a land that devours its inhabitants; and all the people that we saw in it are of great size. 33 There we saw the Nephilim (the Anakites come from the Nephilim); and to ourselves we seemed like grasshoppers, and so we seemed to them."

4. The rebellion of Israel

a. Their complaining

14 Then all the congregation raised a loud cry, and the people wept that night. 2 And all the Israelites complained against Moses and Aaron; the whole congregation said to them, "Would that we had died in the land of Egypt! Or would that we had died in this wilderness! 3 Why is the LORD bringing us into this land to fall by the sword? Our wives and our little ones will become booty; would it not be better for us to go back to Egypt?" 4 So they said to one another, "Let us choose a captain, and go back to Egypt."

b. The plea of Joshua and Caleb

5   Then Moses and Aaron fell on their faces before all the assembly of the congregation of the Israelites. 6 And Joshua son of Nun and Caleb son

---

Marginal references (left column):

13.26
v. 3;
Num 20.1,
16; 32.8

13.27
Ex 3.8;
Deut 1.25
13.28
Deut 1.28
13.29
Num 14.43

13.30
Num 14.6, 24
13.31
Deut 1.28
13.32
Num 14.36;
Ps 106.24;
Am 2.9

13.33
Deut 1.28;
9.2

14.2
Num 11.1, 5

14.5
Num 16.4, 22

---

b That is Cluster

13.26 God had led Israel from Egypt toward the promised land. All the way the people exhibited signs of discontent, unbelief, and rebellion. God was patient. Despite his many miracles, such as the opening of the Red Sea, the provision of manna, and protection against their enemies, the Israelites grumbled again and again. Hearing the negative report of the ten spies over against the positive testimony of Joshua and Caleb, the people accepted and endorsed that report, despite God's promise that he would take care of them and give them victory over the occupants of Canaan. They looked at outward circumstances rather than to the promises of God. The result of their

unbelief was forty years of wandering through the wilderness, during which time all adults who had voted to disobey would die off. A new generation, reared in freedom and aware of God's daily provision, would be prepared by God to enter Canaan along with Joshua and Caleb, the two men of faith.

13.28 *the towns are fortified.* Some of their cities had walls thirty to fifty feet high and twelve to fifteen feet thick.

14.2,3 The Israelites grumbled again, repeating their pitiful refrain that they wished they were back in Egypt. They complained against Moses and Aaron, and also against the Lord.

of Jephunneh, who were among those who had spied out the land, tore their clothes 7 and said to all the congregation of the Israelites, "The land that we went through as spies is an exceedingly good land. 8 If the LORD is pleased with us, he will bring us into this land and give it to us, a land that flows with milk and honey. 9 Only, do not rebel against the LORD; and do not fear the people of the land, for they are no more than bread for us; their protection is removed from them, and the LORD is with us; do not fear them." 10 But the whole congregation threatened to stone them.

c. The anger of God

Then the glory of the LORD appeared at the tent of meeting to all the Israelites. 11 And the LORD said to Moses, "How long will this people despise me? And how long will they refuse to believe in me, in spite of all the signs that I have done among them? 12 I will strike them with pestilence and disinherit them, and I will make of you a nation greater and mightier than they."

d. Moses intercedes for the people

13 But Moses said to the LORD, "Then the Egyptians will hear of it, for in your might you brought up this people from among them, 14 and they will tell the inhabitants of this land. They have heard that you, O LORD, are in the midst of this people; for you, O LORD, are seen face to face, and your cloud stands over them and you go in front of them, in a pillar of cloud by day and in a pillar of fire by night. 15 Now if you kill this people all at one time, then the nations who have heard about you will say, 16 'It is because the LORD was not able to bring this people into the land he swore to give them that he has slaughtered them in the wilderness.' 17 And now, therefore, let the power of the LORD be great in the way that you promised when you spoke, saying,

18   'The LORD is slow to anger,
    and abounding in steadfast love,
    forgiving iniquity and transgression,
    but by no means clearing the guilty,
    visiting the iniquity of the parents
    upon the children
    to the third and the fourth generation.'

19 Forgive the iniquity of this people according to the greatness of your steadfast love, just as you have pardoned this people, from Egypt even until now."

e. God pronounces judgment on Israel for unbelief

20 Then the LORD said, "I do forgive, just as you have asked; 21 nevertheless — as I live, and as all the earth shall be filled with the glory of the LORD — 22 none of the people who have seen my glory and the signs that I did in Egypt and in the wilderness, and yet have tested me these ten times and have not obeyed my voice, 23 shall see the land that I swore to give to their ancestors; none of those who despised me shall see it. 24 But

---

14.7
Num 13.27;
Deut 1.25
14.8
Deut 10.15;
Num 13.27
14.9
Deut 9.7, 23,
24; 7.18;
20.1, 3, 4
14.10
Ex 17.4;
16.10;
Lev 9.23

14.11
Deut 9.7, 8;
Ps 78.22;
106.24
14.12
Ex 32.10

14.13
Ps 106.23
14.14
Ex 15.14;
Josh 2.9, 10;
Ex 13.21

14.16
Deut 9.28

14.18
Ex 34.6, 7;
Ps 103.8;
Ex 20.5

14.19
Ex 34.9;
Ps 106.45;
78.38

14.20
Ps 106.23
14.21
Ps 72.19

14.24
vv. 7-9;
Num 32.12;
Josh 14.6-15

14.10 The Israelites wanted to choose another leader to replace Moses (v. 4) and were threatening to stone him, along with Aaron, Joshua, and Caleb. At this point God intervened and manifested his glorious presence in the tent of the congregation before all the children of Israel. God was ready to pronounce judgment on them and destroy them. This would not have meant the end of God's plan of redemption, however, for he would have raised up a new people. But Moses intervened and God pardoned them. Nevertheless,

they would suffer for their transgression: they would never enter the promised land. Only their children and children's children would do this.
14.11 If the Israelites had a complaint against God, God had a greater complaint against them. God was provoked because they still did not really believe, despite his sending them sign after sign and miracle after miracle. This same sort of attitude can be found today among certain believers who continue to doubt God, in spite of his many blessings.

my servant Caleb, because he has a different spirit and has followed me wholeheartedly, I will bring into the land into which he went, and his descendants shall possess it. 25 Now, since the Amalekites and the Canaanites live in the valleys, turn tomorrow and set out for the wilderness by the way to the Red Sea."*c*

26 And the LORD spoke to Moses and to Aaron, saying: 27 How long shall this wicked congregation complain against me? I have heard the complaints of the Israelites, which they complain against me. 28 Say to them, "As I live," says the LORD, "I will do to you the very things I heard you say: 29 your dead bodies shall fall in this very wilderness; and of all your number, included in the census, from twenty years old and upward, who have complained against me, 30 not one of you shall come into the land in which I swore to settle you, except Caleb son of Jephunneh and Joshua son of Nun. 31 But your little ones, who you said would become booty, I will bring in, and they shall know the land that you have despised. 32 But as for you, your dead bodies shall fall in this wilderness. 33 And your children shall be shepherds in the wilderness for forty years, and shall suffer for your faithlessness, until the last of your dead bodies lies in the wilderness. 34 According to the number of the days in which you spied out the land, forty days, for every day a year, you shall bear your iniquity, forty years, and you shall know my displeasure." 35 I the LORD have spoken; surely I will do thus to all this wicked congregation gathered together against me: in this wilderness they shall come to a full end, and there they shall die.

36 And the men whom Moses sent to spy out the land, who returned and made all the congregation complain against him by bringing a bad report about the land — 37 the men who brought an unfavorable report about the land died by a plague before the LORD. 38 But Joshua son of Nun and Caleb son of Jephunneh alone remained alive, of those men who went to spy out the land.

f. Israel's defeat by the Amalekites and Canaanites

39 When Moses told these words to all the Israelites, the people mourned greatly. 40 They rose early in the morning and went up to the heights of the hill country, saying, "Here we are. We will go up to the place that the LORD has promised, for we have sinned." 41 But Moses said, "Why do you continue to transgress the command of the LORD? That will not succeed. 42 Do not go up, for the LORD is not with you; do not let yourselves be struck down before your enemies. 43 For the Amalekites and the Canaanites will confront you there, and you shall fall by the sword; because you have turned back from following the LORD, the LORD will not be with you." 44 But they presumed to go up to the heights of the hill country, even though the ark of the covenant of the LORD, and Moses, had not left the camp. 45 Then the Amalekites and the Canaanites who lived in that hill country came down and defeated them, pursuing them as far as Hormah.

c Or Sea of Reeds

14.25
Deut 1.40

14.27
Num 11.1;
Ex 16.12
14.28
v. 21;
Deut 1.35;
see v. 2
14.29
Num 1.45;
26.64
14.30
v. 24;
Deut 1.36
14.31
Deut 1.39;
Ps 106.24
14.32
1 Cor 10.5
14.33
Num 32.13;
Ps 107.40
14.34
Num 13.25;
Ps 95.10
14.35
Num 23.19;
26.65

14.36
Num 13.4-16,
32

14.38
Josh 14.6

14.39
Ex 33.4
14.40
Deut 1.41

14.42
Deut 1.42

14.44
Deut 1.43

14.45
Deut 1.44;
Num 21.3

14.30 God passed sentence on all the Israelites twenty years of age or older. They would wander in the wilderness until the last one died. Only Caleb and Joshua would enter the land of promise. Since this was the tenth time the Israelites provoked God, it was about time that they were punished for their transgressions. The patience of God had worn thin and judgment was assessed.
14.37 God had intended for his people to enter into the land immediately. The ten spies, in bringing their evil report, hindered God's intention. For this they were punished: the sentence of death by plague.

Surely it is always better to do the will of God and inherit his blessing than to disobey and suffer judgment and punishment.
14.40 The Israelites never seemed to learn their lessons. God had just sentenced them to forty years of wandering. But now they thought they would return to the earlier promise and move forward to enter the land of promise. When they foolishly began their journey, leaving behind the ark of the covenant and Moses, they were defeated and chased away by the Amalekites and Canaanites. Nothing can end well that begins with sin.

E. *Additional laws and regulations*

1. *Grain offerings*

15 The LORD spoke to Moses, saying: 2 Speak to the Israelites and say to them: When you come into the land you are to inhabit, which I am giving you, 3 and you make an offering by fire to the LORD from the herd or from the flock — whether a burnt offering or a sacrifice, to fulfill a vow or as a freewill offering or at your appointed festivals — to make a pleasing odor for the LORD, 4 then whoever presents such an offering to the LORD shall present also a grain offering, one-tenth of an ephah of choice flour, mixed with one-fourth of a hin of oil. 5 Moreover, you shall offer one-fourth of a hin of wine as a drink offering with the burnt offering or the sacrifice, for each lamb. 6 For a ram, you shall offer a grain offering, two-tenths of an ephah of choice flour mixed with one-third of a hin of oil; 7 and as a drink offering you shall offer one-third of a hin of wine, a pleasing odor to the LORD. 8 When you offer a bull as a burnt offering or a sacrifice, to fulfill a vow or as an offering of well-being to the LORD, 9 then you shall present with the bull a grain offering, three-tenths of an ephah of choice flour, mixed with half a hin of oil, 10 and you shall present as a drink offering half a hin of wine, as an offering by fire, a pleasing odor to the LORD.

11 Thus it shall be done for each ox or ram, or for each of the male lambs or the kids. 12 According to the number that you offer, so you shall do with each and every one. 13 Every native Israelite shall do these things in this way, in presenting an offering by fire, a pleasing odor to the LORD. 14 An alien who lives with you, or who takes up permanent residence among you, and wishes to offer an offering by fire, a pleasing odor to the LORD, shall do as you do. 15 As for the assembly, there shall be for both you and the resident alien a single statute, a perpetual statute throughout your generations; you and the alien shall be alike before the LORD. 16 You and the alien who resides with you shall have the same law and the same ordinance.

2. *The donation of a batch of dough*

17 The LORD spoke to Moses, saying: 18 Speak to the Israelites and say to them: After you come into the land to which I am bringing you, 19 whenever you eat of the bread of the land, you shall present a donation to the LORD. 20 From your first batch of dough you shall present a loaf as a donation; you shall present it just as you present a donation from the threshing floor. 21 Throughout your generations you shall give to the LORD a donation from the first of your batch of dough.

3. *Offering for sins done unintentionally*

22 But if you unintentionally fail to observe all these commandments that the LORD has spoken to Moses — 23 everything that the LORD has commanded you by Moses, from the day the LORD gave commandment and thereafter, throughout your generations — 24 then if it was done unintentionally without the knowledge of the congregation, the whole congregation shall offer one young bull for a burnt offering, a pleasing odor to the LORD, together with its grain offering and its drink offering, according to the ordinance, and one male goat for a sin offering. 25 The priest shall make atonement for all the congregation of the Israelites, and they shall be forgiven; it was unintentional, and they have brought their

Cross references (margin):
15.2 v. 18
15.3 Lev 23.1-44
15.4 Lev 2.1; 6.14; Ex 29.40; Lev 23.13; 14.10; Num 28.5
15.5 Num 28.7, 14
15.6 Num 28.12, 14
15.8 Lev 7.11
15.9 Num 28.12, 14
15.15 v. 29; Num 9.14
15.18 v. 2
15.19 Josh 5.11, 12
15.20 Deut 26.2, 10; Lev 2.14
15.22 Lev 4.2
15.24 Lev 4.13; vv. 8-10
15.25 Lev 4.20

15.2 Although the Israelites had been punished by God in the forty years of wandering and their defeat at the hands of the Amalekites and Canaanites, God did reassure them that they would eventually enter the land. God always stands willing to forgive his people if they repent and accept his chastening. **15.24** See note on Lev 4.2 for sins of ignorance and the atonement prescribed.

offering, an offering by fire to the LORD, and their sin offering before the LORD, for their error. 26 All the congregation of the Israelites shall be forgiven, as well as the aliens residing among them, because the whole people was involved in the error.

27 An individual who sins unintentionally shall present a female goat a year old for a sin offering. 28 And the priest shall make atonement before the LORD for the one who commits an error, when it is unintentional, to make atonement for the person, who then shall be forgiven. 29 For both the native among the Israelites and the alien residing among them — you shall have the same law for anyone who acts in error. 30 But whoever acts high-handedly, whether a native or an alien, affronts the LORD, and shall be cut off from among the people. 31 Because of having despised the word of the LORD and broken his commandment, such a person shall be utterly cut off and bear the guilt.

4. *Stoning of sabbath breakers*

32 When the Israelites were in the wilderness, they found a man gathering sticks on the sabbath day. 33 Those who found him gathering sticks brought him to Moses, Aaron, and to the whole congregation. 34 They put him in custody, because it was not clear what should be done to him. 35 Then the LORD said to Moses, "The man shall be put to death; all the congregation shall stone him outside the camp." 36 The whole congregation brought him outside the camp and stoned him to death, just as the LORD had commanded Moses.

5. *The fringes of remembrance*

37 The LORD said to Moses: 38 Speak to the Israelites, and tell them to make fringes on the corners of their garments throughout their generations and to put a blue cord on the fringe at each corner. 39 You have the fringe so that, when you see it, you will remember all the commandments of the LORD and do them, and not follow the lust of your own heart and your own eyes. 40 So you shall remember and do all my commandments, and you shall be holy to your God. 41 I am the LORD your God, who brought you out of the land of Egypt, to be your God: I am the LORD your God.

F. *The rebellion and death of Korah, Dathan, and Abiram*

1. *Korah's revolt*

16 Now Korah son of Izhar son of Kohath son of Levi, along with Dathan and Abiram sons of Eliab, and On son of Peleth — descendants of Reuben — took 2 two hundred fifty Israelite men, leaders

Marginal references:

15.27 Lev 4.27, 28
15.28 Lev 4.35
15.29 v. 15
15.31 2 Sam 12.9; Lev 5.1; Ezek 18.20
15.32 Ex 31.14, 15; 35.2, 3
15.34 Lev 24.12
15.35 Ex 31.14, 15; Lev 24.14; Acts 7.58
15.38 Deut 22.12; Mt 23.5
15.39 Deut 4.23; Ps 73.27
15.40 Lev 11.44; Rom 12.1; Col 1.22; 1 Pet 1.15, 16
16.1 Ex 6.21; Jude 11
16.2 Num 26.9

15.30 *high-handedly.* This sin involves not believing eternal truth, disobeying God, and failing to fear or trust God's almighty power.

15.32 The gathering of sticks on the sabbath seems to be a small matter indeed. But it is presumptuous, a violation of the law, and demonstrates a tacit contempt for God, the author of that law.

15.36 The penalty for sabbath-breaking was death by stoning. This was Moses' injunction, given to him by God. It suggests the seriousness of the sin in which those who profess to love God defy the sabbath commandment and insult their Creator. In abrogating God's commandments, sinners put themselves above God. The man here was punished not for the simple act of picking up sticks, but for an attitude of heart and mind in revolt against God.

15.38 *fringes on the corners of their garments.* This verse describes what the fringe was to be. Its purpose was to remind the Israelites of their duties and to

distinguish them in their dress from the heathen. They were to be a people separated to God. Jesus himself wore those fringes (Mt 9.20). Phylacteries were different things, however; they were inventions of the Israelites, unlike the fringes which came from a divine institution.

16.1 Korah, from the tribe of Levi, challenged the authority of Moses and Aaron and was aided by Abiram and Dathan, from the tribe of Reuben. The revolt involved the assumption of priestly functions by non-Levites, something God had forbidden. Korah himself was of the priestly tribe but his plot was contrary to God's express commandment. God wiped out the entire families of Dathan and Abiram. He also killed Korah, but did not extend the punishment to his sons. The Israelites blamed Moses and Aaron for what happened (v. 41); subsequently, God sent a plague that killed 14,700 Israelites (v. 49).

of the congregation, chosen from the assembly, well-known men,[d] and they confronted Moses. 3 They assembled against Moses and against Aaron, and said to them, "You have gone too far! All the congregation are holy, every one of them, and the LORD is among them. So why then do you exalt yourselves above the assembly of the LORD?" 4 When Moses heard it, he fell on his face. 5 Then he said to Korah and all his company, "In the morning the LORD will make known who is his, and who is holy, and who will be allowed to approach him; the one whom he will choose he will allow to approach him. 6 Do this: take censers, Korah and all your[e] company, 7 and tomorrow put fire in them, and lay incense on them before the LORD; and the man whom the LORD chooses shall be the holy one. You Levites have gone too far!" 8 Then Moses said to Korah, "Hear now, you Levites! 9 Is it too little for you that the God of Israel has separated you from the congregation of Israel, to allow you to approach him in order to perform the duties of the LORD's tabernacle, and to stand before the congregation and serve them? 10 He has allowed you to approach him, and all your brother Levites with you; yet you seek the priesthood as well! 11 Therefore you and all your company have gathered together against the LORD. What is Aaron that you rail against him?"

2. The rebellion of Dathan and Abiram

12   Moses sent for Dathan and Abiram sons of Eliab; but they said, "We will not come! 13 Is it too little that you have brought us up out of a land flowing with milk and honey to kill us in the wilderness, that you must also lord it over us? 14 It is clear you have not brought us into a land flowing with milk and honey, or given us an inheritance of fields and vineyards. Would you put out the eyes of these men? We will not come!"

3. The punishment of the rebels

15   Moses was very angry and said to the LORD, "Pay no attention to their offering. I have not taken one donkey from them, and I have not harmed any one of them." 16 And Moses said to Korah, "As for you and all your company, be present tomorrow before the LORD, you and they and Aaron; 17 and let each one of you take his censer, and put incense on it, and each one of you present his censer before the LORD, two hundred fifty censers; you also, and Aaron, each his censer." 18 So each man took his censer, and they put fire in the censers and laid incense on them, and they stood at the entrance of the tent of meeting with Moses and Aaron. 19 Then Korah assembled the whole congregation against them at the entrance of the tent of meeting. And the glory of the LORD appeared to the whole congregation.

20   Then the LORD spoke to Moses and to Aaron, saying: 21 Separate yourselves from this congregation, so that I may consume them in a moment. 22 They fell on their faces, and said, "O God, the God of the spirits of all flesh, shall one person sin and you become angry with the whole congregation?"

23   And the LORD spoke to Moses, saying: 24 Say to the congregation: Get away from the dwellings of Korah, Dathan, and Abiram. 25 So Moses got up and went to Dathan and Abiram; the elders of Israel followed him. 26 He said to the congregation, "Turn away from the tents of these wicked men, and touch nothing of theirs, or you will be swept away for all their sins." 27 So they got away from the dwellings of Korah, Dathan, and

Cross references (right column):

16.3 Ps 106.16; Ex 19.6; Num 14.14
16.4 Num 14.5
16.5 Lev 10.3; Ps 65.4; Num 17.5, 8
16.9 Num 3.6, 9; 8.14; Deut 10.8
16.11 Ex 16.7, 8; 1 Cor 10.10
16.13 Num 11.4-6; Ex 2.14; Acts 7.27, 35
16.14 Lev 20.24
16.15 Gen 4.4, 5; 1 Sam 12.3
16.16 vv. 6, 7
16.19 v. 42; Num 14.10; Ex 16.7, 10; Lev 9.6, 23
16.21 v. 45; Ex 32.10, 12
16.22 v. 45; Num 14.5
16.26 Gen 19.12, 14

---

[d] Cn: Heb and they confronted Moses, and two hundred fifty men . . . well-known men   [e] Heb his

---

16.12–14 With hot heads and hardened hearts, Dathan and Abiram refused to obey the call of Moses, God's appointed leader. They were insolent, impudent, and treasonous.

16.19 Once again the glory of God appeared before Israel. This glory could be a sign of judgment (as in this case) or a sign of divine approval (as in the story of Aaron's ordination, see Lev 9.23).

Abiram; and Dathan and Abiram came out and stood at the entrance of their tents, together with their wives, their children, and their little ones. 28 And Moses said, "This is how you shall know that the LORD has sent me to do all these works; it has not been of my own accord: 29 If these people die a natural death, or if a natural fate comes on them, then the LORD has not sent me. 30 But if the LORD creates something new, and the ground opens its mouth and swallows them up, with all that belongs to them, and they go down alive into Sheol, then you shall know that these men have despised the LORD."

31 As soon as he finished speaking all these words, the ground under them was split apart. 32 The earth opened its mouth and swallowed them up, along with their households — everyone who belonged to Korah and all their goods. 33 So they with all that belonged to them went down alive into Sheol; the earth closed over them, and they perished from the midst of the assembly. 34 All Israel around them fled at their outcry, for they said, "The earth will swallow us too!" 35 And fire came out from the LORD and consumed the two hundred fifty men offering the incense.

36 f Then the LORD spoke to Moses, saying: 37 Tell Eleazar son of Aaron the priest to take the censers out of the blaze; then scatter the fire far and wide. 38 For the censers of these sinners have become holy at the cost of their lives. Make them into hammered plates as a covering for the altar, for they presented them before the LORD and they became holy. Thus they shall be a sign to the Israelites. 39 So Eleazar the priest took the bronze censers that had been presented by those who were burned; and they were hammered out as a covering for the altar — 40 a reminder to the Israelites that no outsider, who is not of the descendants of Aaron, shall approach to offer incense before the LORD, so as not to become like Korah and his company — just as the LORD had said to him through Moses.

4. The rebellion of the people: the plague

41 On the next day, however, the whole congregation of the Israelites rebelled against Moses and against Aaron, saying, "You have killed the people of the LORD." 42 And when the congregation had assembled against them, Moses and Aaron turned toward the tent of meeting; the cloud had covered it and the glory of the LORD appeared. 43 Then Moses and Aaron came to the front of the tent of meeting, 44 and the LORD spoke to Moses, saying, 45 "Get away from this congregation, so that I may consume them in a moment." And they fell on their faces. 46 Moses said to Aaron, "Take your censer, put fire on it from the altar and lay incense on it, and carry it quickly to the congregation and make atonement for them. For wrath has gone out from the LORD; the plague has begun." 47 So Aaron took it as Moses had ordered, and ran into the middle of the assembly, where the plague had already begun among the people. He put on the incense, and made atonement for the people. 48 He stood between the dead and the living; and the plague was stopped. 49 Those who died by the plague were fourteen thousand seven hundred, besides those who died in the affair of Korah. 50 When the plague was stopped, Aaron returned to Moses at the entrance of the tent of meeting.

f Ch 17.1 in Heb

Marginal references:

16.28 Ex 3.12; Jn 5.36; Num 24.13; Jn 6.38
16.30 v. 33; Ps 55.15
16.31 Num 26.10
16.32 Num 26.11
16.35 Num 11.1-3; 26.10
16.38 Prov 20.2; Num 26.10
16.40 Num 3.10; 2 Chr 26.18
16.41 v. 3
16.42 Ex 40.34; v. 19; Num 20.6
16.45 vv. 21, 24
16.46 Num 8.19; Ps 106.29
16.47 Num 25.7, 8, 13
16.48 Ps 106.30
16.49 vv. 32, 35

16.35–38 The blasphemous malcontents were consumed by the fire of God for their transgression. They had offered incense and in so doing had taken fire from the altar, a forbidden act. As soon as they had kindled their fire, the fire of God consumed them. The sacred fire placed on their censer plates then became holy. God had no respect for the abominable sacrifice of the wicked. Yet he commanded that the censer plates containing the true fire be recovered and beaten into a cover for the altar. This would remind the Israelites forever that rash actions provoke the wrath of God.

16.41 The Israelites blamed Moses for what God had done when the fire from heaven consumed two hundred and fifty Israelites and their leaders, Korah, Dathan, and Abiram. Blaming Moses was an insult to God, who stood behind his servant. Consequently, further judgment fell and 14,700 died from a plague.

5. The budding of Aaron's rod

17 [g] The LORD spoke to Moses, saying: 2 Speak to the Israelites, and get twelve staffs from them, one for each ancestral house, from all the leaders of their ancestral houses. Write each man's name on his staff, 3 and write Aaron's name on the staff of Levi. For there shall be one staff for the head of each ancestral house. 4 Place them in the tent of meeting before the covenant,[h] where I meet with you. 5 And the staff of the man whom I choose shall sprout; thus I will put a stop to the complaints of the Israelites that they continually make against you. 6 Moses spoke to the Israelites; and all their leaders gave him staffs, one for each leader, according to their ancestral houses, twelve staffs; and the staff of Aaron was among theirs. 7 So Moses placed the staffs before the LORD in the tent of the covenant. [h]

8 When Moses went into the tent of the covenant[h] on the next day, the staff of Aaron for the house of Levi had sprouted. It put forth buds, produced blossoms, and bore ripe almonds. 9 Then Moses brought out all the staffs from before the LORD to all the Israelites; and they looked, and each man took his staff. 10 And the LORD said to Moses, "Put back the staff of Aaron before the covenant,[h] to be kept as a warning to rebels, so that you may make an end of their complaints against me, or else they will die." 11 Moses did so; just as the LORD commanded him, so he did.

12 The Israelites said to Moses, "We are perishing; we are lost, all of us are lost! 13 Everyone who approaches the tabernacle of the LORD will die. Are we all to perish?"

G. The laws of the priests and Levites

1. The duties of the Levites

18 The LORD said to Aaron: You and your sons and your ancestral house with you shall bear responsibility for offenses connected with the sanctuary, while you and your sons alone shall bear responsibility for offenses connected with the priesthood. 2 So bring with you also your brothers of the tribe of Levi, your ancestral tribe, in order that they may be joined to you, and serve you while you and your sons with you are in front of the tent of the covenant. [h] 3 They shall perform duties for you and for the whole tent. But they must not approach either the utensils of the sanctuary or the altar, otherwise both they and you will die. 4 They are attached to you in order to perform the duties of the tent of meeting, for all the service of the tent; no outsider shall approach you. 5 You yourselves shall perform the duties of the sanctuary and the duties of the altar, so that wrath may never again come upon the Israelites. 6 It is I who now take your brother Levites from among the Israelites; they are now yours as a gift, dedicated to the LORD, to perform the service of the tent of meeting. 7 But you and your sons with you shall diligently perform your priestly duties in all that concerns the altar and the area behind the curtain. I give your priesthood as a gift; [i] any outsider who approaches shall be put to death.

17.4
Ex 25.22;
29.42, 43
17.5
Num 16.5, 11

17.7
Num 18.2;
Acts 7.44

17.10
Heb 9.4; v. 5

17.13
Num 1.51, 53

18.1
Ex 28.38

18.2
Num 3.5-10

18.3
Num 3.25,
31, 36; 4.15
18.4
Num 3.10

18.5
Num 16.46

18.6
Num 3.9, 12,
45

18.7
Num 3.10;
Heb 9.3, 6

---

g Ch 17.16 in Heb   h Or treaty, or testimony; Heb eduth   i Heb as a service of gift

---

17.5 *the staff . . . shall sprout.* Even this extraordinary sprouting did not cause Israel to cease grumbling.
17.8 Both Moses and Aaron had staves. In this instance the staff of Aaron was placed in the inner room of the tabernacle along with staves for the other eleven tribes. His staff alone budded and blossomed — a sign from God that Aaron and his house were the sole

priestly representatives before him. No longer were the Israelites to question Aaron's unique priestly authority. The staff was first kept in the sanctuary as a symbol and ultimately placed in the ark of the covenant (Heb 9.4).
17.10 Implied in this verse is the idea that if there were further complaints about his authority, Aaron should bring out the staff and show it to the people.

2. The offerings that belong to the priests

18.8
Lev 6.16, 18;
7.6, 32;
Ex 29.29;
40.13, 15
18.9
Lev 2.2, 3;
10.12, 13;
6.25, 26; 7.7
18.10
Lev 6.16, 26
18.11
Ex 29.27, 28;
Lev 22.1-16

18.12
Ex 23.19;
Deut 18.4;
Neh 10.35;
Ex 22.29
18.13
Ex 22.29;
23.19; 34.26
18.14
Lev 27.28
18.15
Ex 13.2;
Lev 27.26;
Ex 13.13
18.16
Lev 27.6
18.17
Lev 3.2, 5

18.19
v. 11;
2 Chr 13.5

18.20
Deut 10.9;
12.12; 14.27,
29; 18.1, 2;
Josh 13.33;
Ezek 44.28

18.21
Lev 27.30-33

18.22
Num 1.51
18.23
Num 3.7;
vv. 1, 20

18.26
Neh 10.38

8 The LORD spoke to Aaron: I have given you charge of the offerings made to me, all the holy gifts of the Israelites; I have given them to you and your sons as a priestly portion due you in perpetuity. 9 This shall be yours from the most holy things, reserved from the fire: every offering of theirs that they render to me as a most holy thing, whether grain offering, sin offering, or guilt offering, shall belong to you and your sons. 10 As a most holy thing you shall eat it; every male may eat it; it shall be holy to you. 11 This also is yours: I have given to you, together with your sons and daughters, as a perpetual due, whatever is set aside from the gifts of all the elevation offerings of the Israelites; everyone who is clean in your house may eat them. 12 All the best of the oil and all the best of the wine and of the grain, the choice produce that they give to the LORD, I have given to you. 13 The first fruits of all that is in their land, which they bring to the LORD, shall be yours; everyone who is clean in your house may eat of it. 14 Every devoted thing in Israel shall be yours. 15 The first issue of the womb of all creatures, human and animal, which is offered to the LORD, shall be yours; but the firstborn of human beings you shall redeem, and the firstborn of unclean animals you shall redeem. 16 Their redemption price, reckoned from one month of age, you shall fix at five shekels of silver, according to the shekel of the sanctuary (that is, twenty gerahs). 17 But the firstborn of a cow, or the firstborn of a sheep, or the firstborn of a goat, you shall not redeem; they are holy. You shall dash their blood on the altar, and shall turn their fat into smoke as an offering by fire for a pleasing odor to the LORD; 18 but their flesh shall be yours, just as the breast that is elevated and as the right thigh are yours. 19 All the holy offerings that the Israelites present to the LORD I have given to you, together with your sons and daughters, as a perpetual due; it is a covenant of salt forever before the LORD for you and your descendants as well. 20 Then the LORD said to Aaron: You shall have no allotment in their land, nor shall you have any share among them; I am your share and your possession among the Israelites.

3. The tithe for the Levites

21 To the Levites I have given every tithe in Israel for a possession in return for the service that they perform, the service in the tent of meeting. 22 From now on the Israelites shall no longer approach the tent of meeting, or else they will incur guilt and die. 23 But the Levites shall perform the service of the tent of meeting, and they shall bear responsibility for their own offenses; it shall be a perpetual statute throughout your generations. But among the Israelites they shall have no allotment, 24 because I have given to the Levites as their portion the tithe of the Israelites, which they set apart as an offering to the LORD. Therefore I have said of them that they shall have no allotment among the Israelites.

4. The Levites' tithe of the tithe

25 Then the LORD spoke to Moses, saying: 26 You shall speak to the Levites, saying: When you receive from the Israelites the tithe that I have

18.8 God's provision for the material needs of the priesthood did not spring from their personal worthiness nor did it mean they were above their fellows. The material gifts came for the sake of the office to which they had been anointed. **18.15** Some beasts were ceremonially unclean but still necessary, such as asses. The firstborn of clean and unclean beasts had to be redeemed. **18.21** The tithe was assessed for the Levites. The priests had the first fruits, said to be a fiftieth or sixtieth part, but the nonpriestly Levites did not share

in this. Since they received no land and therefore could not plow and sow, they needed support from the other tribes as a reward for their labors. This tithe was a form of tax on the Israelites. **18.26** *a tithe of the tithe.* The nonpriestly Levites had to tithe their tithe to support the priests. Some have said the tithe of the tithe went to the high priest alone, for no specific provision was made for the one who occupied that office and he would have greater expenses (see also note on Neh 10.38).

given you from them for your portion, you shall set apart an offering from it to the Lord, a tithe of the tithe. 27 It shall be reckoned to you as your gift, the same as the grain of the threshing floor and the fullness of the wine press. 28 Thus you also shall set apart an offering to the Lord from all the tithes that you receive from the Israelites; and from them you shall give the Lord's offering to the priest Aaron. 29 Out of all the gifts to you, you shall set apart every offering due to the Lord; the best of all of them is the part to be consecrated. 30 Say also to them: When you have set apart the best of it, then the rest shall be reckoned to the Levites as produce of the threshing floor, and as produce of the wine press. 31 You may eat it in any place, you and your households; for it is your payment for your service in the tent of meeting. 32 You shall incur no guilt by reason of it, when you have offered the best of it. But you shall not profane the holy gifts of the Israelites, on pain of death.

H. Purification of the unclean

1. The red heifer

19 The Lord spoke to Moses and Aaron, saying: 2 This is a statute of the law that the Lord has commanded: Tell the Israelites to bring you a red heifer without defect, in which there is no blemish and on which no yoke has been laid. 3 You shall give it to the priest Eleazar, and it shall be taken outside the camp and slaughtered in his presence. 4 The priest Eleazar shall take some of its blood with his finger and sprinkle it seven times towards the front of the tent of meeting. 5 Then the heifer shall be burned in his sight; its skin, its flesh, and its blood, with its dung, shall be burned. 6 The priest shall take cedarwood, hyssop, and crimson material, and throw them into the fire in which the heifer is burning. 7 Then the priest shall wash his clothes and bathe his body in water, and afterwards he may come into the camp; but the priest shall remain unclean until evening. 8 The one who burns the heifer[j] shall wash his clothes in water and bathe his body in water; he shall remain unclean until evening. 9 Then someone who is clean shall gather up the ashes of the heifer, and deposit them outside the camp in a clean place; and they shall be kept for the congregation of the Israelites for the water for cleansing. It is a purification offering. 10 The one who gathers the ashes of the heifer shall wash his clothes and be unclean until evening.

2. Purification of uncleanness with water

This shall be a perpetual statute for the Israelites and for the alien residing among them. 11 Those who touch the dead body of any human being shall be unclean seven days. 12 They shall purify themselves with the water on the third day and on the seventh day, and so be clean; but if they do not purify themselves on the third day and on the seventh day, they will not become clean. 13 All who touch a corpse, the body of a human being who has died, and do not purify themselves, defile the tabernacle of the Lord; such persons shall be cut off from Israel. Since water for cleansing was not dashed on them, they remain unclean; their uncleanness is still on them.

14 This is the law when someone dies in a tent: everyone who comes into the tent, and everyone who is in the tent, shall be unclean seven days. 15 And every open vessel with no cover fastened on it is unclean. 16 Whoever in the open field touches one who has been killed by a sword, or who

[j] Heb it

19.2 Whoever touched a corpse became unclean. The ritual of the *red heifer* provided cleansing for such uncleanness. The ashes of the burned animal were mixed with water (called "water for cleansing" or a "water for impurity"); this was sprinkled by someone who was clean on the tent of the dead person, the furnishings, and all those who had become unclean as a result of contact with the dead (see v. 18).

18.28
Ex 29.27

18.32
Lev 19.8;
22.2, 15, 16

19.2
Deut 21.3

19.3
Lev 4.12, 21;
16.27
19.4
Lev 4.6;
Heb 9.13

19.6
Lev 15.4, 6, 49
19.7
Lev 11.25;
16.26, 28;
22.6

19.9
Heb 9.13;
vv. 13, 20, 21

19.11
Num 5.2;
Lev 21.1;
Acts 21.26, 27
19.12
v. 19;
Num 31.19
19.13
v. 20;
Lev 15.31;
v. 9;
Num 8.7;
Lev 7.20;
22.3

19.16
v. 11

has died naturally,[k] or a human bone, or a grave, shall be unclean seven
days. 17 For the unclean they shall take some ashes of the burnt purification offering, and running water shall be added in a vessel; 18 then a clean
person shall take hyssop, dip it in the water, and sprinkle it on the tent,
on all the furnishings, on the persons who were there, and on whoever
touched the bone, the slain, the corpse, or the grave. 19 The clean person
shall sprinkle the unclean ones on the third day and on the seventh day,
thus purifying them on the seventh day. Then they shall wash their clothes
and bathe themselves in water, and at evening they shall be clean. 20 Any
who are unclean but do not purify themselves, those persons shall be cut
off from the assembly, for they have defiled the sanctuary of the LORD.
Since the water for cleansing has not been dashed on them, they are
unclean.

21   It shall be a perpetual statute for them. The one who sprinkles the
water for cleansing shall wash his clothes, and whoever touches the water
for cleansing shall be unclean until evening. 22 Whatever the unclean
person touches shall be unclean, and anyone who touches it shall be
unclean until evening.

I. Incidents at Kadesh

1. The death of Miriam

20 The Israelites, the whole congregation, came into the wilderness
of Zin in the first month, and the people stayed in Kadesh. Miriam
died there, and was buried there.

2. Water from the rock (Meribah)

2   Now there was no water for the congregation; so they gathered
together against Moses and against Aaron. 3 The people quarreled with
Moses and said, "Would that we had died when our kindred died before
the LORD! 4 Why have you brought the assembly of the LORD into this
wilderness for us and our livestock to die here? 5 Why have you brought
us up out of Egypt, to bring us to this wretched place? It is no place for
grain, or figs, or vines, or pomegranates; and there is no water to drink."
6 Then Moses and Aaron went away from the assembly to the entrance of
the tent of meeting; they fell on their faces, and the glory of the LORD
appeared to them. 7 The LORD spoke to Moses, saying: 8 Take the staff,
and assemble the congregation, you and your brother Aaron, and command the rock before their eyes to yield its water. Thus you shall bring
water out of the rock for them; thus you shall provide drink for the
congregation and their livestock.

3. The sin of Moses: his exclusion from Canaan

9   So Moses took the staff from before the LORD, as he had commanded
him. 10 Moses and Aaron gathered the assembly together before the rock,
and he said to them, "Listen, you rebels, shall we bring water for you out
of this rock?" 11 Then Moses lifted up his hand and struck the rock twice
with his staff; water came out abundantly, and the congregation and their
livestock drank. 12 But the LORD said to Moses and Aaron, "Because you

[k] Heb lacks naturally

Cross-references (margin)
- 19.17 v. 9
- 19.19 Ezek 36.25; Heb 10.22
- 19.20 v. 13
- 19.22 Hag 2.13, 14
- 20.1 Num 33.36
- 20.2 Ex 17.1
- 20.3 Ex 17.2; Num 14.2, 3; 16.31-35
- 20.4 Ex 17.3
- 20.6 Num 14.5, 10
- 20.8 Ex 17.5; Neh 9.15; Isa 43.20; 48.21
- 20.10 Ps 106.32, 33
- 20.11 Ps 78.16; Isa 48.21; 1 Cor 10.14
- 20.12 Num 27.14; Deut 1.37; 3.26, 27; Lev 10.3

20.1 *first month*, apparently in a year near the end of
the wilderness wandering. Thus this summary verse
covers a period of about thirty-seven years, the Israelites having arrived at Kadesh (13.26) not long after
leaving Sinai (see Deut 2.14).
20.8ff In Ex 17.6 God ordered Moses to strike the
rock. Here at *Kadesh* (later known as *Kadesh-barnea*)
he was commanded to speak to the rock. In anger and

with an air of pride, he imprudently struck the rock
twice and shouted: "Listen, you rebels! Shall we
bring water for you out of this rock?" (20.10). God
punished Moses for his disobedience and unbelief by
refusing to allow him to enter the promised land.
Leaders are not immune from obedience to the law of
God.

did not trust in me, to show my holiness before the eyes of the Israelites, therefore you shall not bring this assembly into the land that I have given them." [13] These are the waters of Meribah,[l] where the people of Israel quarreled with the LORD, and by which he showed his holiness.

20.13
Deut 33.8;
Ps 95.8

4. Israel refused passage through Edom

14 Moses sent messengers from Kadesh to the king of Edom, "Thus says your brother Israel: You know all the adversity that has befallen us: [15] how our ancestors went down to Egypt, and we lived in Egypt a long time; and the Egyptians oppressed us and our ancestors; [16] and when we cried to the LORD, he heard our voice, and sent an angel and brought us out of Egypt; and here we are in Kadesh, a town on the edge of your territory. [17] Now let us pass through your land. We will not pass through field or vineyard, or drink water from any well; we will go along the King's Highway, not turning aside to the right hand or to the left until we have passed through your territory."

20.14
Deut 2.4
20.15
Gen 46.6;
Acts 7.15, 19;
Ex 12.40;
Deut 26.6
20.16
Ex 2.23;
14.19

18 But Edom said to him, "You shall not pass through, or we will come out with the sword against you." [19] The Israelites said to him, "We will stay on the highway; and if we drink of your water, we and our livestock, then we will pay for it. It is only a small matter; just let us pass through on foot." [20] But he said, "You shall not pass through." And Edom came out against them with a large force, heavily armed. [21] Thus Edom refused to give Israel passage through their territory; so Israel turned away from them.

20.19
Deut 2.6, 28

20.21
Judg 11.17;
Deut 2.8

J. Events from Kadesh to Moab

1. The death of Aaron

22 They set out from Kadesh, and the Israelites, the whole congregation, came to Mount Hor. [23] Then the LORD said to Moses and Aaron at Mount Hor, on the border of the land of Edom, [24] "Let Aaron be gathered to his people. For he shall not enter the land that I have given to the Israelites, because you rebelled against my command at the waters of Meribah. [25] Take Aaron and his son Eleazar, and bring them up Mount Hor; [26] strip Aaron of his vestments, and put them on his son Eleazar. But Aaron shall be gathered to his people,[m] and shall die there." [27] Moses did as the LORD had commanded; they went up Mount Hor in the sight of the whole congregation. [28] Moses stripped Aaron of his vestments, and put them on his son Eleazar; and Aaron died there on the top of the mountain. Moses and Eleazar came down from the mountain. [29] When all the congregation saw that Aaron had died, all the house of Israel mourned for Aaron thirty days.

20.22
Num 33.37;
21.4
20.24
Gen 25.8;
v. 12

20.25
Num 33.38;
Deut 32.50

20.28
Num 33.38;
Deut 10.6

2. The victory over Arad at Hormah

21 When the Canaanite, the king of Arad, who lived in the Negeb, heard that Israel was coming by the way of Atharim, he fought against Israel and took some of them captive. [2] Then Israel made a vow to the LORD and said, "If you will indeed give this people into our hands, then we will utterly destroy their towns." [3] The LORD listened to the voice of Israel, and handed over the Canaanites; and they utterly destroyed them and their towns; so the place was called Hormah.[n]

21.1
Num 33.40;
Judg 1.16;
Num 13.21

[l] That is Quarrel   [m] Heb lacks to his people   [n] Heb Destruction

---

20.14 *your brother Israel.* The Edomites descended from Esau, while the people of Israel came from his brother Jacob, whose name was later changed to Israel.
20.17 *The King's Highway* was a well-traveled caravan route through that land.

20.24–28 Aaron was also involved in the incident in which Moses defiantly struck the rock for water (20.10,11). For their transgression both of them were kept from entering the promised land. Verse 28 records Aaron's death.

3. *The poisonous serpents*

21.4
Num 20.22
21.5
Ps 78.19;
Ex 16.3;
17.3;
Num 11.6
21.6
Deut 8.15;
1 Cor 10.9
21.7
Ps 78.34

21.9
2 Kings 18.4;
Jn 3.14, 15

4 From Mount Hor they set out by the way to the Red Sea,*o* to go around the land of Edom; but the people became impatient on the way. 5 The people spoke against God and against Moses, "Why have you brought us up out of Egypt to die in the wilderness? For there is no food and no water, and we detest this miserable food." 6 Then the LORD sent poisonous*p* serpents among the people, and they bit the people, so that many Israelites died. 7 The people came to Moses and said, "We have sinned by speaking against the LORD and against you; pray to the LORD to take away the serpents from us." So Moses prayed for the people. 8 And the LORD said to Moses, "Make a poisonous*q* serpent, and set it on a pole; and everyone who is bitten shall look at it and live." 9 So Moses made a serpent of bronze, and put it upon a pole; and whenever a serpent bit someone, that person would look at the serpent of bronze and live.

4. *Israel on the march*

21.10
Num 33.43
21.11
Num 33.44
21.12
Deut 2.13

21.15
v. 28;
Deut 2.18, 29

10 The Israelites set out, and camped in Oboth. 11 They set out from Oboth, and camped at Iye-abarim, in the wilderness bordering Moab toward the sunrise. 12 From there they set out, and camped in the Wadi Zered. 13 From there they set out, and camped on the other side of the Arnon, in*r* the wilderness that extends from the boundary of the Amorites; for the Arnon is the boundary of Moab, between Moab and the Amorites. 14 Wherefore it is said in the Book of the Wars of the LORD,
"Waheb in Suphah and the wadis.
The Arnon 15 and the slopes of the wadis
that extend to the seat of Ar,
and lie along the border of Moab."*s*

16 From there they continued to Beer;*t* that is the well of which the LORD said to Moses, "Gather the people together, and I will give them water." 17 Then Israel sang this song:
"Spring up, O well! — Sing to it! —
18 the well that the leaders sank,
that the nobles of the people dug,
with the scepter, with the staff."
From the wilderness to Mattanah, 19 from Mattanah to Nahaliel, from Nahaliel to Bamoth, 20 and from Bamoth to the valley lying in the region of Moab by the top of Pisgah that overlooks the wasteland.*u*

5. *Defeat of King Sihon of the Amorites*

21.21
Deut 2.26, 27
21.22
Num 20.16,
17
21.23
Num 20.21;
Deut 2.32

21 Then Israel sent messengers to King Sihon of the Amorites, saying, 22 "Let me pass through your land; we will not turn aside into field or vineyard; we will not drink the water of any well; we will go by the King's Highway until we have passed through your territory." 23 But Sihon would not allow Israel to pass through his territory. Sihon gathered

o Or *Sea of Reeds* *p* Or *fiery;* Heb *seraphim* *q* Or *fiery;* Heb *seraph* *r* Gk: Heb *which is in* *s* Meaning of Heb uncertain *t* That is *Well* *u* Or *Jeshimon*

21.5 Israel had bread enough and to spare. They now considered manna to be worthless compared to what they preferred. So they spoke out again against God and Moses, and God sent serpents to punish them.
21.9 According to Jn 3.14,15, the bronze serpent represents Christ. Those bitten by the serpent suffered death; so also those bitten by the serpent of sin suffer spiritual death. As Moses lifted up the serpent in the wilderness as a means of healing, so Christ was lifted up to bear the sins of many (Jn 12.32). As people needed only to look at Moses' serpent and live, so sinners need only look to Jesus Christ to be healed

from their transgressions. Christ saves sinners from the guilt, the penalty, and the power of sin.
21.14 *the Book of the Wars of the LORD.* This was probably a collection of songs used in war and/or a record of Israel's military victories. It is not noted as the "wars of Israel" but as the "wars of the LORD." The operation of God in Israel's history was more important than what the people said and did.
21.17 *Israel sang this song.* Throughout the Bible singing is emphasized. Singing glorifies God and encourages those who sing. Music in the church meeting is one of the most significant parts of true worship.

all his people together, and went out against Israel to the wilderness; he came to Jahaz, and fought against Israel. 24 Israel put him to the sword, and took possession of his land from the Arnon to the Jabbok, as far as to the Ammonites; for the boundary of the Ammonites was strong. 25 Israel took all these towns, and Israel settled in all the towns of the Amorites, in Heshbon, and in all its villages. 26 For Heshbon was the city of King Sihon of the Amorites, who had fought against the former king of Moab and captured all his land as far as the Arnon. 27 Therefore the ballad singers say,

"Come to Heshbon, let it be built;
    let the city of Sihon be established.
28 For fire came out from Heshbon,
    flame from the city of Sihon.
It devoured Ar of Moab,
    and swallowed up[v] the heights of the Arnon.
29 Woe to you, O Moab!
    You are undone, O people of Chemosh!
He has made his sons fugitives,
    and his daughters captives,
    to an Amorite king, Sihon.
30 So their posterity perished
    from Heshbon[w] to Dibon,
    and we laid waste until fire spread to Medeba."[x]

6. Defeat of King Og of Bashan

31 Thus Israel settled in the land of the Amorites. 32 Moses sent to spy out Jazer; and they captured its villages, and dispossessed the Amorites who were there.

33 Then they turned and went up the road to Bashan; and King Og of Bashan came out against them, he and all his people, to battle at Edrei. 34 But the LORD said to Moses, "Do not be afraid of him; for I have given him into your hand, with all his people, and all his land. You shall do to him as you did to King Sihon of the Amorites, who ruled in Heshbon." 35 So they killed him, his sons, and all his people, until there was no survivor left; and they took possession of his land.

III. Events in Moab (22.1–36.13)

A. Balak and Balaam

1. Balak sends for Balaam

22 The Israelites set out, and camped in the plains of Moab across the Jordan from Jericho. 2 Now Balak son of Zippor saw all that Israel had done to the Amorites. 3 Moab was in great dread of the people, because they were so numerous; Moab was overcome with fear of the people of Israel. 4 And Moab said to the elders of Midian, "This horde will now lick up all that is around us, as an ox licks up the grass of the field." Now Balak son of Zippor was king of Moab at that time. 5 He sent

Margin references:
21.24 Deut 2.33; Josh 12.1, 2; Ps 135.10, 11
21.28 Jer 48.45, 46; Deut 2.9, 18; Isa 15.1
21.29 Judg 11.24; 1 Kings 11.7, 33; 2 Kings 23.13; Jer 48.7, 13
21.30 Num 32.3, 34; Jer 48.18, 22
21.32 Num 32.1; Jer 48.32
21.33 Deut 3.1–7; Josh 13.12
21.34 Deut 3.2; v. 24
22.1 Num 33.48
22.3 Ex 15.15
22.4 Num 31.1–3, 8
22.5 Num 23.7; Josh 24.9; Deut 23.4

v Gk: Heb *and the lords of*   w Gk: Heb *we have shot at them; Heshbon has perished*   x Compare Sam Gk: Meaning of MT uncertain

21.24 *for the boundary of the Ammonites was strong*, i.e., the terrain was rugged. Deut 2.19 indicates that God had promised the land of the Ammonites to the descendants of Lot.
21.25 The Moabites had been given territory which Israel was forbidden by God to usurp. But land which once had belonged to Moab had been taken and settled by the Ammonites. Israel took the land from the Ammonites and kept it, for the title to it had long

since passed from Moab to the Ammonites.
22.1 Israel had now come close to the end of their wilderness journeys. They encamped in the plains of Moab, where they would remain until they passed over the Jordan under Joshua's leadership. Then they would begin to possess their inheritance.
22.5,11 The land from which Balaam came was noted for its diviners. Balaam himself started as a good and true prophet of God. But he succumbed to

messengers to Balaam son of Beor at Pethor, which is on the Euphrates, in the land of Amaw,[y] to summon him, saying, "A people has come out of Egypt; they have spread over the face of the earth, and they have settled next to me. 6 Come now, curse this people for me, since they are stronger than I; perhaps I shall be able to defeat them and drive them from the land; for I know that whomever you bless is blessed, and whomever you curse is cursed."

margin refs: 22.6 / v. 17; / Num 23.7

2. God forbids Balaam to go to Balak

7 So the elders of Moab and the elders of Midian departed with the fees for divination in their hand; and they came to Balaam, and gave him Balak's message. 8 He said to them, "Stay here tonight, and I will bring back word to you, just as the LORD speaks to me"; so the officials of Moab stayed with Balaam. 9 God came to Balaam and said, "Who are these men with you?" 10 Balaam said to God, "King Balak son of Zippor of Moab, has sent me this message: 11 'A people has come out of Egypt and has spread over the face of the earth; now come, curse them for me; perhaps I shall be able to fight against them and drive them out.' " 12 God said to Balaam, "You shall not go with them; you shall not curse the people, for they are blessed." 13 So Balaam rose in the morning, and said to the officials of Balak, "Go to your own land, for the LORD has refused to let me go with you." 14 So the officials of Moab rose and went to Balak, and said, "Balaam refuses to come with us."

margin refs: 22.7 / Num 23.23; / 24.1 / 22.8 / v. 19 / 22.12 / Num 23.20

3. God lets Balaam go

15 Once again Balak sent officials, more numerous and more distinguished than these. 16 They came to Balaam and said to him, "Thus says Balak son of Zippor: 'Do not let anything hinder you from coming to me; 17 for I will surely do you great honor, and whatever you say to me I will do; come, curse this people for me.' " 18 But Balaam replied to the servants of Balak, "Although Balak were to give me his house full of silver and gold, I could not go beyond the command of the LORD my God, to do less or more. 19 You remain here, as the others did, so that I may learn what more the LORD may say to me." 20 That night God came to Balaam and said to him, "If the men have come to summon you, get up and go with them; but do only what I tell you to do." 21 So Balaam got up in the morning, saddled his donkey, and went with the officials of Moab.

margin refs: 22.17 / v. 6 / 22.18 / Num 24.13; / 1 Kings 22.14; / 2 Chr 18.13 / 22.20 / v. 35; / Num 23.12; / 26; 24.13 / 22.21 / 2 Pet 2.15

4. Balaam's donkey: God's anger at Balaam's disobedience

22 God's anger was kindled because he was going, and the angel of the LORD took his stand in the road as his adversary. Now he was riding on the donkey, and his two servants were with him. 23 The donkey saw the angel of the LORD standing in the road, with a drawn sword in his hand; so the donkey turned off the road, and went into the field; and

margin refs: 22.23 / 2 Pet 2.16

[y] Or *land of his kinsfolk*

the lure of money and was willing to be hired. In his sovereignty, however, God ordained that Balaam would not do what King Balak wanted him to do. Each time, Balaam failed to curse Israel; thus Balak was defeated. But Balaam did assist Balak, for he cunningly suggested to Balak what would lead Israel to succumb to the sin of sexual license (cf. 31.15–16). This may well be what is called "the teaching of Balaam" (Rev 2.14).
22.19 God told Balaam that he was not to go to Balak (v. 12). Here he went against God's directive will by saying he needed further instruction about God's will. At this point God's directive will was put aside and his permissive will took over. Balaam was allowed to do what he wanted to do but what God had

forbidden. God still stipulated that Balaam should do or say nothing that would harm the people of God. The donkey had better sense than his master (vv. 21–34).
22.22,23 *the angel of the LORD.* The work of God's loyal angels includes the following: they (1) execute God's judgments and purposes (v. 22; Mt 13.41; Acts 12.23); (2) guide believers (Acts 8.26); (3) assist, protect, and strengthen God's people (1 Kings 19.5; Dan 6.22); (4) will accompany the Lord Jesus at his second advent (Mt 25.31; 2 Thess 1.7,8); and (5) carry God's children to heaven (Lk 16.22). Believers are superior to angels in at least two important regards: angels cannot preach the gospel whereas believers can, and they will judge angels (1 Cor 6.3).

Balaam struck the donkey, to turn it back onto the road. 24 Then the angel of the LORD stood in a narrow path between the vineyards, with a wall on either side. 25 When the donkey saw the angel of the LORD, it scraped against the wall, and scraped Balaam's foot against the wall; so he struck it again. 26 Then the angel of the LORD went ahead, and stood in a narrow place, where there was no way to turn either to the right or to the left. 27 When the donkey saw the angel of the LORD, it lay down under Balaam; and Balaam's anger was kindled, and he struck the donkey with his staff. 28 Then the LORD opened the mouth of the donkey, and it said to Balaam, "What have I done to you, that you have struck me these three times?" 29 Balaam said to the donkey, "Because you have made a fool of me! I wish I had a sword in my hand! I would kill you right now!" 30 But the donkey said to Balaam, "Am I not your donkey, which you have ridden all your life to this day? Have I been in the habit of treating you this way?" And he said, "No."

31   Then the LORD opened the eyes of Balaam, and he saw the angel of the LORD standing in the road, with his drawn sword in his hand; and he bowed down, falling on his face. 32 The angel of the LORD said to him, "Why have you struck your donkey these three times? I have come out as an adversary, because your way is perverse^z before me. 33 The donkey saw me, and turned away from me these three times. If it had not turned away from me, surely just now I would have killed you and let it live." 34 Then Balaam said to the angel of the LORD, "I have sinned, for I did not know that you were standing in the road to oppose me. Now therefore, if it is displeasing to you, I will return home." 35 The angel of the LORD said to Balaam, "Go with the men; but speak only what I tell you to speak." So Balaam went on with the officials of Balak.

5. Balaam visits Balak

36   When Balak heard that Balaam had come, he went out to meet him at Ir-moab, on the boundary formed by the Arnon, at the farthest point of the boundary. 37 Balak said to Balaam, "Did I not send to summon you? Why did you not come to me? Am I not able to honor you?" 38 Balaam said to Balak, "I have come to you now, but do I have power to say just anything? The word God puts in my mouth, that is what I must say." 39 Then Balaam went with Balak, and they came to Kiriath-huzoth. 40 Balak sacrificed oxen and sheep, and sent them to Balaam and to the officials who were with him.

6. Balaam's first blessing

41   On the next day Balak took Balaam and brought him up to Bamoth-baal; and from there he could see part of the people of Israel.^a
23 1 Then Balaam said to Balak, "Build me seven altars here, and prepare seven bulls and seven rams for me." 2 Balak did as Balaam had said; and Balak and Balaam offered a bull and a ram on each altar. 3 Then Balaam said to Balak, "Stay here beside your burnt offerings while I go aside. Perhaps the LORD will come to meet me. Whatever he shows me I will tell you." And he went to a bare height. 4   Then God met Balaam; and Balaam said to him, "I have arranged the seven altars, and have offered a bull and a ram on each altar." 5 The LORD put a word in Balaam's mouth, and said, "Return to Balak, and this is what you must say." 6 So he returned to Balak,^b who was standing beside his burnt offerings with all the officials of Moab. 7 Then Balaam^c uttered his oracle, saying:

z Meaning of Heb uncertain   a Heb lacks of Israel   b Heb him   c Heb he

22.24
Judg 6.12

22.28
2 Pet 2.16

22.29
Prov 12.10
22.30
2 Pet 2.16

22.31
Josh 5.13-15

22.34
Num 14.40;
1 Sam 15.24,
30;
2 Sam 12.13
22.35
v. 20

22.37
v. 17;
Num 24.11
22.38
v. 18;
Num 23.26;
24.13

22.41
Deut 12.2
23.1
v. 29
23.2
vv. 14, 30
23.3
v. 15
23.4
v. 16
23.5
v. 16;
Num 22.35;
Deut 18.18;
Jer 1.9
23.7
v. 18;
Num 24.3,
15, 23;
Job 27.1;
29.1;
Ps 78.2;
Num 22.6

22.37,38   Balak expected Balaam to curse Israel, for which he would be rewarded. But Balaam was rather noncommittal; he wanted his fee, yet he realized that God controlled the prophecy.

"Balak has brought me from Aram,
the king of Moab from the eastern mountains:
'Come, curse Jacob for me;
Come, denounce Israel!'

8 How can I curse whom God has not cursed?
How can I denounce those whom the LORD has not
denounced?

9 For from the top of the crags I see him,
from the hills I behold him.
Here is a people living alone,
and not reckoning itself among the nations!

10 Who can count the dust of Jacob,
or number the dust-cloud[d] of Israel?
Let me die the death of the upright,
and let my end be like his!"

11 Then Balak said to Balaam, "What have you done to me? I brought
you to curse my enemies, but now you have done nothing but bless them."
12 He answered, "Must I not take care to say what the LORD puts into my
mouth?"

7. Balaam's second blessing

13 So Balak said to him, "Come with me to another place from which
you may see them; you shall see only part of them, and shall not see them
all; then curse them for me from there." 14 So he took him to the field of
Zophim, to the top of Pisgah. He built seven altars, and offered a bull and
a ram on each altar. 15 Balaam said to Balak, "Stand here beside your burnt
offerings, while I meet the LORD over there." 16 The LORD met Balaam,
put a word into his mouth, and said, "Return to Balak, and this is what
you shall say." 17 When he came to him, he was standing beside his burnt
offerings, with the officials of Moab. Balak said to him, "What has the
LORD said?" 18 Then Balaam uttered his oracle, saying:

"Rise, Balak, and hear;
listen to me, O son of Zippor:

19 God is not a human being, that he should lie,
or a mortal, that he should change his mind.
Has he promised, and will he not do it?
Has he spoken, and will he not fulfill it?

20 See, I received a command to bless;
he has blessed, and I cannot revoke it.

21 He has not beheld misfortune in Jacob;
nor has he seen trouble in Israel.
The LORD their God is with them,
acclaimed as a king among them.

22 God, who brings them out of Egypt,
is like the horns of a wild ox for them.

23 Surely there is no enchantment against Jacob,
no divination against Israel;
now it shall be said of Jacob and Israel,
'See what God has done!'

Cross-references (margin):

23.8
Num 22.12

23.9
Ex 33.16;
Deut 32.8;
33.28

23.10
Gen 13.16;
Ps 116.15

23.11
Num 24.10

23.12
Num 22.20,
38

23.14
vv. 1, 2

23.16
Num 22.20

23.19
1 Sam 15.29;
Mal 3.6;
Rom 11.29;
Titus 1.2;
Jas 1.17

23.20
Isa 43.13

23.21
Ps 32.2, 5;
Rom 4.7, 8;
Isa 40.2;
Ex 29.45, 46;
Ps 89.15

23.22
Num 24.8

d Or fourth part

23.7ff Balaam recited his first speech in poetic form.
He asked the question: How can I curse whom God
has not cursed and denounce whom God has not denounced? Yet he did not bless Israel positively. Balak,
however, was keenly conscious that the words of Balaam constituted a blessing in disguise.
23.14 Balak took Balaam to a different place, where
he built seven altars and offered sacrifices on all of
them. These rites as used by pagan Babylonian divin-

ers did not have the acceptance or commendation of
God. The genuine always gives rise to counterfeits,
which outwardly resemble the real but inwardly
are useless, vile, and constitute an affront to the true
God.
23.18ff On this second effort Balaam helped Balak
no more than he had helped him on the first effort.
He predicted blessing for Israel, not the curse that
Balak had hired him to express.

24 Look, a people rising up like a lioness,
        and rousing itself like a lion!
   It does not lie down until it has eaten the prey
        and drunk the blood of the slain.”

23.24
Gen 49.9, 27

8. Balaam's third blessing

25 Then Balak said to Balaam, “Do not curse them at all, and do not
bless them at all.” 26 But Balaam answered Balak, “Did I not tell you,
‘Whatever the LORD says, that is what I must do’?”

23.26
v. 12;
Num 22.38

27 So Balak said to Balaam, “Come now, I will take you to another
place; perhaps it will please God that you may curse them for me from
there.” 28 So Balak took Balaam to the top of Peor, which overlooks the
wasteland.e 29 Balaam said to Balak, “Build me seven altars here, and
prepare seven bulls and seven rams for me.” 30 So Balak did as Balaam
had said, and offered a bull and a ram on each altar.

23.27
v. 13

23.29
v. 1

24 Now Balaam saw that it pleased the LORD to bless Israel, so he
did not go, as at other times, to look for omens, but set his face
toward the wilderness. 2 Balaam looked up and saw Israel camping tribe
by tribe. Then the spirit of God came upon him, 3 and he uttered his oracle,
saying:
    “The oracle of Balaam son of Beor,
        the oracle of the man whose eye is clear,f
4   the oracle of one who hears the words of God,
        who sees the vision of the Almighty,g
        who falls down, but with eyes uncovered:
5   how fair are your tents, O Jacob,
        your encampments, O Israel!
6   Like palm groves that stretch far away,
        like gardens beside a river,
    like aloes that the LORD has planted,
        like cedar trees beside the waters.
7   Water shall flow from his buckets,
        and his seed shall have abundant water,
    his king shall be higher than Agag,
        and his kingdom shall be exalted.
8   God who brings him out of Egypt,
        is like the horns of a wild ox for him;
    he shall devour the nations that are his foes
        and break their bones.
    He shall strike with his arrows.h
9   He crouched, he lay down like a lion,
        and like a lioness; who will rouse him up?
    Blessed is everyone who blesses you,
        and cursed is everyone who curses you.”

24.1
Num 23.3, 15

24.2
Num 11.25,
26;
1 Sam 10.10;
2 Chr 15.1

24.3
Num 23.7, 18

24.4
Num 22.20;
12.6

24.6
Ps 1.3;
104.16

24.7
v. 20;
1 Sam 15.8,
9;
2 Sam 5.12;
1 Chr 14.2

24.8
Num 23.22,
24;
Ps 2.9; 45.5;
Jer 50.9, 17

24.9
Gen 49.9;
12.3; 27.29

---

e Or overlooks Jeshimon   f Or closed or open   g Traditional rendering of Heb Shaddai   h Meaning of
Heb uncertain

23.25,26 Balak now wanted to silence Balaam,
wishing him to say nothing either way. If Balaam
could not assist and encourage Balak's forces, then at
least he did not want him to oppose or dishearten
them. Balaam had to admit that he was not free to
choose what to do; whatever God spoke, he must
speak.
24.2 *the spirit of God came upon him.* When the Spirit
of prophecy came upon Balaam, he did not speak his
own thoughts but the language which came to him by
the Spirit. In v. 4 he appears to be boasting that he
had heard the words of the Almighty and seen a vision

of God. Balaam had become an agent of God's will
even though he was filled with ambition and covetousness. God sometimes gets done what he wants
done through strange agencies, even by those who
have fallen far short of his glory.
24.4 *with eyes uncovered.* Balaam's eyes had been
shut, but now they were opened by the Spirit of God.
He saw that his intention to curse Israel was a mistake, though he was still blinded by covetousness and
wrong ambition. His eyes were open but his heart was
shut; he was enlightened but not sanctified. Balaam
blessed Israel the third time, to the dismay of Balak.

9. Balaam's fourth blessing and prophecy

10 Then Balak's anger was kindled against Balaam, and he struck his hands together. Balak said to Balaam, "I summoned you to curse my enemies, but instead you have blessed them these three times. ¹¹Now be off with you! Go home! I said, 'I will reward you richly,' but the LORD has denied you any reward." ¹²And Balaam said to Balak, "Did I not tell your messengers whom you sent to me, ¹³'If Balak should give me his house full of silver and gold, I would not be able to go beyond the word of the LORD, to do either good or bad of my own will; what the LORD says, that is what I will say'? ¹⁴So now, I am going to my people; let me advise you what this people will do to your people in days to come."

15 So he uttered his oracle, saying:
"The oracle of Balaam son of Beor,
   the oracle of the man whose eye is clear,ⁱ
16 the oracle of one who hears the words of God,
   and knows the knowledge of the Most High,^j
who sees the vision of the Almighty,^k
   who falls down, but with his eyes uncovered:
17 I see him, but not now;
   I behold him, but not near —
a star shall come out of Jacob,
   and a scepter shall rise out of Israel;
it shall crush the borderlands^l of Moab,
   and the territory^m of all the Shethites.
18 Edom will become a possession,
   Seir a possession of its enemies,ⁿ
while Israel does valiantly.
19 One out of Jacob shall rule,
   and destroy the survivors of Ir."

20 Then he looked on Amalek, and uttered his oracle, saying:
"First among the nations was Amalek,
   but its end is to perish forever."
21 Then he looked on the Kenite, and uttered his oracle, saying:
"Enduring is your dwelling place,
   and your nest is set in the rock;
22 yet Kain is destined for burning.
   How long shall Asshur take you away captive?"
23 Again he uttered his oracle, saying:
"Alas, who shall live when God does this?
24 But ships shall come from Kittim
   and shall afflict Asshur and Eber;
   and he also shall perish forever."

25 Then Balaam got up and went back to his place, and Balak also went his way.

---

i Or *closed* or *open*   *j* Or *of Elyon*   *k* Traditional rendering of Heb *Shaddai*   *l* Or *forehead*   *m* Some Mss read *skull*   *n* Heb *Seir, its enemies, a possession*

Marginal references:
24.11 Num 22.17, 37
24.13 Num 22.18, 20
24.14 Gen 49.1; Dan 2.28; Mic 6.5
24.17 Rev 1.7; Mt 2.2; Gen 49.10
24.18 2 Sam 8.14
24.19 Gen 49.10; Mic 5.2
24.20 Ex 17.8, 14, 16
24.24 Gen 10.4, 21; v. 20
24.25 Num 31.8

24.13 In effect Balaam told Balak that what he had done was not his fault. His intention was to help Balak but God had interfered; he could not help what he had done. It was all God's fault.

24.14 *what this people will do to your people.* Balak had dismissed Balaam; but before he left, he blessed Israel for the fourth time and prophesied what Israel would do to the people of Balak.

24.17 *a star . . . out of Jacob.* Balaam prophesied that Israel would overcome Moab and Edom. This was fulfilled in Israel's victories, but there was a greater fulfillment to come, of which Balaam undoubtedly did not himself understand. Jesus Christ is the star from Jacob. He holds a royal scepter with the promise that his dominion shall extend over the whole earth. In a spiritual sense, this is already true. Some believers in the millennial tradition look for the literal earthly manifestation of Christ's rule over the nations with a rod of iron, at the end of which period he will win the final victory over Satan and begin the eternal kingdom (Rev 19–20). *Shethites.* Sheth, an ancient name for Moab, has been found in nonbiblical texts.

24.22 *Kain,* meaning "smith," probably refers to the people who mined and smelted copper from Edomite mines.

B. Israel's idolatry in Shittim

1. Israelites yoked to Baal of Peor

25 While Israel was staying at Shittim, the people began to have sexual relations with the women of Moab. 2 These invited the people to the sacrifices of their gods, and the people ate and bowed down to their gods. 3 Thus Israel yoked itself to the Baal of Peor, and the LORD's anger was kindled against Israel. 4 The LORD said to Moses, "Take all the chiefs of the people, and impale them in the sun before the LORD, in order that the fierce anger of the LORD may turn away from Israel." 5 And Moses said to the judges of Israel, "Each of you shall kill any of your people who have yoked themselves to the Baal of Peor."

2. Phinehas kills the Israelite and the Midianite woman

6 Just then one of the Israelites came and brought a Midianite woman into his family, in the sight of Moses and in the sight of the whole congregation of the Israelites, while they were weeping at the entrance of the tent of meeting. 7 When Phinehas son of Eleazar, son of Aaron the priest, saw it, he got up and left the congregation. Taking a spear in his hand, 8 he went after the Israelite man into the tent, and pierced the two of them, the Israelite and the woman, through the belly. So the plague was stopped among the people of Israel. 9 Nevertheless those that died by the plague were twenty-four thousand.

10 The LORD spoke to Moses, saying: 11 "Phinehas son of Eleazar, son of Aaron the priest, has turned back my wrath from the Israelites by manifesting such zeal among them on my behalf that in my jealousy I did not consume the Israelites. 12 Therefore say, 'I hereby grant him my covenant of peace. 13 It shall be for him and for his descendants after him a covenant of perpetual priesthood, because he was zealous for his God, and made atonement for the Israelites.' "

14 The name of the slain Israelite man, who was killed with the Midianite woman, was Zimri son of Salu, head of an ancestral house belonging to the Simeonites. 15 The name of the Midianite woman who was killed was Cozbi daughter of Zur, who was the head of a clan, an ancestral house in Midian.

16 The LORD said to Moses, 17 "Harass the Midianites, and defeat them; 18 for they have harassed you by the trickery with which they deceived you in the affair of Peor, and in the affair of Cozbi, the daughter of a leader of Midian, their sister; she was killed on the day of the plague that resulted from Peor."

C. Israel's second census

1. The command to take the census

26 After the plague the LORD said to Moses and to Eleazar son of Aaron the priest, 2 "Take a census of the whole congregation of the Israelites, from twenty years old and upward, by their ancestral houses, everyone in Israel able to go to war." 3 Moses and Eleazar the

Cross references (right margin):
25.1 Mic 6.5; Num 31.16; 1 Cor 10.8; Rev 2.14
25.2 Ex 34.15; 20.5; 1 Cor 10.20
25.3 Ps 106.28, 29; Hos 9.10
25.4 Deut 4.3
25.7 Ps 106.30
25.9 Deut 4.3; 1 Cor 10.8
25.11 Ps 106.30; Ex 20.5; Deut 32.16, 21
25.12 Isa 54.10; Mal 2.4, 5
25.13 Ex 40.15; Num 16.46; Heb 2.17
25.15 Num 31.8
25.17 Num 31.2
25.18 Num 31.16
26.2 Ex 30.12; 38.25, 26; Num 1.2

25.1 The males of Israel committed prostitution with the daughters of the Moabites. It was both physical and spiritual prostitution: they fornicated with them and worshiped their gods. Not everyone participated, but enough of them did to kindle the anger of God, who sent a plague that killed 24,000.
25.9 See note on 1 Cor 10.8 for the resolution of the apparent contradiction between the 24,000 mentioned here and the 23,000 referred to in 1 Cor 10.8.
25.17 God had punished the Israelites with the plague; now he ordered Moses to punish the Midian-

ites with the sword. While the Israelites who sinned were guilty, so also were the Midianites who caused them to sin. They must reap what they had sown. Evil people should not have the liberty to tempt God's people, as though they have no responsibility for the crimes that follow.
26.2 The people were to be numbered a second time at the command of God. A comparison of the statistics with the earlier census reveals minor differences from tribe to tribe.

priest spoke with them in the plains of Moab by the Jordan opposite Jericho, saying, 4 "Take a census of the people,⁰ from twenty years old and upward," as the LORD commanded Moses. The Israelites, who came out of the land of Egypt, were:

2. The numbering of the tribes

26.5
Ex 6.14

5 Reuben, the firstborn of Israel. The descendants of Reuben: of Hanoch, the clan of the Hanochites; of Pallu, the clan of the Palluites; 6 of Hezron, the clan of the Hezronites; of Carmi, the clan of the Carmites. 7 These are the clans of the Reubenites; the number of those enrolled was forty-three thousand seven hundred thirty. 8 And the descendants of Pallu: Eliab. 9 The descendants of Eliab: Nemuel, Dathan, and Abiram. These are the same Dathan and Abiram, chosen from the congregation, who rebelled against Moses and Aaron in the company of Korah, when they rebelled against the LORD, 10 and the earth opened its mouth and swallowed them up along with Korah, when that company died, when the fire devoured two hundred fifty men; and they became a warning. 11 Notwithstanding, the sons of Korah did not die.

26.9
Num 16.1, 2

26.10
Num 16.32,
35, 38
26.11
Deut 24.16

12 The descendants of Simeon by their clans: of Nemuel, the clan of the Nemuelites; of Jamin, the clan of the Jaminites; of Jachin, the clan of the Jachinites; 13 of Zerah, the clan of the Zerahites; of Shaul, the clan of the Shaulites.ᵖ 14 These are the clans of the Simeonites, twenty-two thousand two hundred.

26.12
Ex 6.15
emuel;
1 Chr 4.24
arib
26.13
Gen 46.10
ohar
26.15
Gen 46.16
iphion
26.16
Gen 46.16
zbon
26.17
Gen 46.16
rodi
26.18
Num 1.25

15 The children of Gad by their clans: of Zephon, the clan of the Zephonites; of Haggi, the clan of the Haggites; of Shuni, the clan of the Shunites; 16 of Ozni, the clan of the Oznites; of Eri, the clan of the Erites; 17 of Arod, the clan of the Arodites; of Areli, the clan of the Arelites. 18 These are the clans of the Gadites: the number of those enrolled was forty thousand five hundred.

19 The sons of Judah: Er and Onan; Er and Onan died in the land of Canaan. 20 The descendants of Judah by their clans were: of Shelah, the clan of the Shelanites; of Perez, the clan of the Perezites; of Zerah, the clan of the Zerahites. 21 The descendants of Perez were: of Hezron, the clan of the Hezronites; of Hamul, the clan of the Hamulites. 22 These are the clans of Judah: the number of those enrolled was seventy-six thousand five hundred.

26.22
Num 1.27

23 The descendants of Issachar by their clans: of Tola, the clan of the Tolaites; of Puvah, the clan of the Punites; 24 of Jashub, the clan of the Jashubites; of Shimron, the clan of the Shimronites. 25 These are the clans of Issachar: sixty-four thousand three hundred enrolled.

26.24
Gen 46.13 ob
26.25
Num 1.29

26 The descendants of Zebulun by their clans: of Sered, the clan of the Seredites; of Elon, the clan of the Elonites; of Jahleel, the clan of the Jahleelites. 27 These are the clans of the Zebulunites; the number of those enrolled was sixty thousand five hundred.

26.27
Num 1.31

28 The sons of Joseph by their clans: Manasseh and Ephraim. 29 The descendants of Manasseh: of Machir, the clan of the Machirites; and Machir was the father of Gilead; of Gilead, the clan of the Gileadites. 30 These are the descendants of Gilead: of Iezer, the clan of the Iezerites; of Helek, the clan of the Helekites; 31 and of Asriel, the clan of the Asrielites; and of Shechem, the clan of the Shechemites; 32 and of Shemida, the clan of the Shemidaites; and of Hepher, the clan of the Hepherites. 33 Now Zelophehad son of Hepher had no sons, but daughters: and the names of the daughters of Zelophehad were Mahlah, Noah, Hoglah, Milcah, and Tirzah. 34 These are the clans of Manasseh; the number of those enrolled was fifty-two thousand seven hundred.

26.30
see Josh 17.2
biezer

35 These are the descendants of Ephraim according to their clans: of Shuthelah, the clan of the Shuthelahites; of Becher, the clan of the Becher-

26.35
1 Chr 7.20
ered

⁰ Heb lacks take a census of the people: Compare verse 2 ᵖ Or Saul . . . Saulites

ites; of Tahan, the clan of the Tahanites. 36 And these are the descendants of Shuthelah: of Eran, the clan of the Eranites. 37 These are the clans of the Ephraimites: the number of those enrolled was thirty-two thousand five hundred. These are the descendants of Joseph by their clans.

38   The descendants of Benjamin by their clans: of Bela, the clan of the Belaites; of Ashbel, the clan of the Ashbelites; of Ahiram, the clan of the Ahiramites; 39 of Shephupham, the clan of the Shuphamites; of Hupham, the clan of the Huphamites. 40 And the sons of Bela were Ard and Naaman: of Ard, the clan of the Ardites; of Naaman, the clan of the Naamites. 41 These are the descendants of Benjamin by their clans; the number of those enrolled was forty-five thousand six hundred.

42   These are the descendants of Dan by their clans: of Shuham, the clan of the Shuhamites. These are the clans of Dan by their clans. 43 All the clans of the Shuhamites: sixty-four thousand four hundred enrolled.

44   The descendants of Asher by their families: of Imnah, the clan of the Imnites; of Ishvi, the clan of the Ishvites; of Beriah, the clan of the Beriites. 45 Of the descendants of Beriah: of Heber, the clan of the Heberites; of Malchiel, the clan of the Malchielites. 46 And the name of the daughter of Asher was Serah. 47 These are the clans of the Asherites: the number of those enrolled was fifty-three thousand four hundred.

48   The descendants of Naphtali by their clans: of Jahzeel, the clan of the Jahzeelites; of Guni, the clan of the Gunites; 49 of Jezer, the clan of the Jezerites; of Shillem, the clan of the Shillemites. 50 These are the Naphtalites*q* by their clans: the number of those enrolled was forty-five thousand four hundred.

51   This was the number of the Israelites enrolled: six hundred and one thousand seven hundred thirty.

3. The division of the land

52   The LORD spoke to Moses, saying: 53 To these the land shall be apportioned for inheritance according to the number of names. 54 To a large tribe you shall give a large inheritance, and to a small tribe you shall give a small inheritance; every tribe shall be given its inheritance according to its enrollment. 55 But the land shall be apportioned by lot; according to the names of their ancestral tribes they shall inherit. 56 Their inheritance shall be apportioned according to lot between the larger and the smaller.

4. The numbering of the Levites

57   This is the enrollment of the Levites by their clans: of Gershon, the clan of the Gershonites; of Kohath, the clan of the Kohathites; of Merari, the clan of the Merarites. 58 These are the clans of Levi: the clan of the Libnites, the clan of the Hebronites, the clan of the Mahlites, the clan of the Mushites, the clan of the Korahites. Now Kohath was the father of Amram. 59 The name of Amram's wife was Jochebed daughter of Levi, who was born to Levi in Egypt; and she bore to Amram: Aaron, Moses, and their sister Miriam. 60 To Aaron were born Nadab, Abihu, Eleazar, and Ithamar. 61 But Nadab and Abihu died when they offered unholy fire before the LORD. 62 The number of those enrolled was twenty-three thousand, every male one month old and upward; for they were not enrolled among the Israelites because there was no allotment given to them among the Israelites.

q Heb *clans of Naphtali*

26.37
Num 1.33

26.38
Gen 46.21 *hi*

26.39
Gen 46.21
*uppim
Huppim*
26.40
1 Chr 8.3
ddar
26.41
Num 1.37
26.42
Gen 46.23
ushim
26.43
Num 1.39

26.47
Num 1.41

26.50
Num 1.43

26.53
Josh 11.23;
14.1
26.54
Num 33.54

26.55
Num 33.54;
34.13

26.59
Ex 6.20

26.60
Num 3.2
26.61
Lev 10.1, 2;
Num 3.4
26.62
Num 1.47;
18.20, 23, 24

26.54 The division of the land was to be based on numbers, not on tribes. Tribes with more members received more land. God intended to set up an economic system by which each family received land and thus had a productive base for its support. The land was to be held forever by the families to which it was given. It was God's land, held in trust by God's people, with the external title in the name of the family. See the note on Lev 25.9 for information on the jubilee principle.

5. Summary

63 These were those enrolled by Moses and Eleazar the priest, who enrolled the Israelites in the plains of Moab by the Jordan opposite Jericho. 64 Among these there was not one of those enrolled by Moses and Aaron the priest, who had enrolled the Israelites in the wilderness of Sinai. 65 For the LORD had said of them, "They shall die in the wilderness." Not one of them was left, except Caleb son of Jephunneh and Joshua son of Nun.

D. *The case of Zelophehad's daughters*

1. *Zelophehad's death without sons*

27 Then the daughters of Zelophehad came forward. Zelophehad was son of Hepher son of Gilead son of Machir son of Manasseh son of Joseph, a member of the Manassite clans. The names of his daughters were: Mahlah, Noah, Hoglah, Milcah, and Tirzah. 2 They stood before Moses, Eleazar the priest, the leaders, and all the congregation, at the entrance of the tent of meeting, and they said, 3 "Our father died in the wilderness; he was not among the company of those who gathered themselves together against the LORD in the company of Korah, but died for his own sin; and he had no sons. 4 Why should the name of our father be taken away from his clan because he had no son? Give to us a possession among our father's brothers."

2. *The inheritance to pass through the daughters*

5 Moses brought their case before the LORD. 6 And the LORD spoke to Moses, saying: 7 The daughters of Zelophehad are right in what they are saying; you shall indeed let them possess an inheritance among their father's brothers and pass the inheritance of their father on to them. 8 You shall also say to the Israelites, "If a man dies, and has no son, then you shall pass his inheritance on to his daughter. 9 If he has no daughter, then you shall give his inheritance to his brothers. 10 If he has no brothers, then you shall give his inheritance to his father's brothers. 11 And if his father has no brothers, then you shall give his inheritance to the nearest kinsman of his clan, and he shall possess it. It shall be for the Israelites a statute and ordinance, as the LORD commanded Moses."

E. *The selection of Joshua to succeed Moses*

12 The LORD said to Moses, "Go up this mountain of the Abarim range, and see the land that I have given to the Israelites. 13 When you have seen it, you also shall be gathered to your people, as your brother Aaron was, 14 because you rebelled against my word in the wilderness of Zin when the congregation quarreled with me.*r* You did not show my holiness before their eyes at the waters." (These are the waters of Meribath-kadesh in the wilderness of Zin.) 15 Moses spoke to the LORD, saying, 16 "Let the LORD, the God of the spirits of all flesh, appoint

r Heb lacks *with me*

Margin references:

26.64
Deut 2.14, 15

26.65
Num 14.28, 29;
1 Cor 10.5, 6;
Num 14.30

27.1ff
Num 26.33;
36.1

27.3
Num 26.64, 65; 26.33;
16.1, 2
27.4
Josh 17.4

27.5
Num 9.8
27.6
Num 36.2

27.12
Num 33.47;
Deut 32.49
27.13
Num 31.2
27.14
Num 20.12;
Ex 17.7

27.16
Num 16.22

26.64 *there was not one of those enrolled.* Forty years earlier, at the time of the first census, these males had been under twenty years of age and were not counted. All those counted who were over twenty were now dead.

27.1 The land was to be divided only among the males who had been numbered in the census; women were not numbered. Zelophehad had no sons, only daughters. He had died in the wilderness, so there was no hope for a male heir. Thus the daughters would get no inheritance. The daughters asked for an exception to the general rule; God granted it and

announced an amendment to the procedure (see 12.5–11).

27.12 *mountain of the Abarim range,* i.e., "the regions beyond" in Hebrew. This refers to the mountain ranges of Trans-Jordan, of which Mount Nebo was a part. Four thousand feet below these mountains is the Dead Sea.

27.15ff Moses asked God to appoint his successor. God's choice was Joshua (v. 18), who had served under Moses and was well acquainted with the Israelites. Joshua was a Spirit-filled man of God.

someone over the congregation 17who shall go out before them and come in before them, who shall lead them out and bring them in, so that the congregation of the LORD may not be like sheep without a shepherd." 18So the LORD said to Moses, "Take Joshua son of Nun, a man in whom is the spirit, and lay your hand upon him; 19have him stand before Eleazar the priest and all the congregation, and commission him in their sight. 20You shall give him some of your authority, so that all the congregation of the Israelites may obey. 21But he shall stand before Eleazar the priest, who shall inquire for him by the decision of the Urim before the LORD; at his word they shall go out, and at his word they shall come in, both he and all the Israelites with him, the whole congregation." 22So Moses did as the LORD commanded him. He took Joshua and had him stand before Eleazar the priest and the whole congregation; 23he laid his hands on him and commissioned him—as the LORD had directed through Moses.

F. The laws of offerings repeated and explained

1. The daily burnt offering

28 The LORD spoke to Moses, saying: 2Command the Israelites, and say to them: My offering, the food for my offerings by fire, my pleasing odor, you shall take care to offer to me at its appointed time. 3And you shall say to them, This is the offering by fire that you shall offer to the LORD: two male lambs a year old without blemish, daily, as a regular offering. 4One lamb you shall offer in the morning, and the other lamb you shall offer at twilight;ˢ 5also one-tenth of an ephah of choice flour for a grain offering, mixed with one-fourth of a hin of beaten oil. 6It is a regular burnt offering, ordained at Mount Sinai for a pleasing odor, an offering by fire to the LORD. 7Its drink offering shall be one-fourth of a hin for each lamb; in the sanctuary you shall pour out a drink offering of strong drink to the LORD. 8The other lamb you shall offer at twilightˢ with a grain offering and a drink offering like the one in the morning; you shall offer it as an offering by fire, a pleasing odor to the LORD.

2. The offering on the sabbath

9 On the sabbath day: two male lambs a year old without blemish, and two-tenths of an ephah of choice flour for a grain offering, mixed with oil, and its drink offering— 10this is the burnt offering for every sabbath, in addition to the regular burnt offering and its drink offering.

3. The offering at the beginning of a month

11 At the beginnings of your months you shall offer a burnt offering to the LORD: two young bulls, one ram, seven male lambs a year old without blemish; 12also three-tenths of an ephah of choice flour for a grain offering, mixed with oil, for each bull; and two-tenths of choice flour for a grain offering, mixed with oil, for the one ram; 13and one-tenth of choice flour mixed with oil as a grain offering for every lamb—a burnt offering of pleasing odor, an offering by fire to the LORD. 14Their drink offerings shall be half a hin of wine for a bull, one-third of a hin for a ram, and one-fourth of a hin for a lamb. This is the burnt offering of every month throughout the months of the year. 15And there shall be one male goat

ˢ Heb between the two evenings

27.17
Deut 31.2;
Mt 9.36;
Mk 6.34
27.18
Num 11.25-29;
Deut 34.9
27.19
Deut 31.3, 7,
8, 23
27.20
Josh 1.16, 17
27.21
Ex 28.30

28.2
Lev 3.11

28.3
Ex 29.38

28.7
Ex 29.42

28.10
v. 3

28.11
Num 10.10;
Ezek 45.17;
46.6
28.12
Num 15.4-12

28.15
v. 3

27.22,23 In a theocratic kingdom the religious and the secular aspects are joined together. Joshua, Moses' successor, had to be ordained for the position; this was done by his appearing before the high priest and the whole congregation of Israel. When Moses laid hands on Joshua, he passed the reins of his rule over to God's newly designated leader.
28.2ff Before entering the land, Moses repeated the divine instructions pertaining to the various offerings.
28.11 See note on 10.10 for details on the monthly offering.

for a sin offering to the LORD; it shall be offered in addition to the regular burnt offering and its drink offering.

4. The offerings at the festival of unleavened bread

16 On the fourteenth day of the first month there shall be a passover offering to the LORD. 17 And on the fifteenth day of this month is a festival; seven days shall unleavened bread be eaten. 18 On the first day there shall be a holy convocation. You shall not work at your occupations. 19 You shall offer an offering by fire, a burnt offering to the LORD: two young bulls, one ram, and seven male lambs a year old; see that they are without blemish. 20 Their grain offering shall be of choice flour mixed with oil: three-tenths of an ephah shall you offer for a bull, and two-tenths for a ram; 21 one-tenth shall you offer for each of the seven lambs; 22 also one male goat for a sin offering, to make atonement for you. 23 You shall offer these in addition to the burnt offering of the morning, which belongs to the regular burnt offering. 24 In the same way you shall offer daily, for seven days, the food of an offering by fire, a pleasing odor to the LORD; it shall be offered in addition to the regular burnt offering and its drink offering. 25 And on the seventh day you shall have a holy convocation; you shall not work at your occupations.

5. Offerings at the festival of weeks

26 On the day of the first fruits, when you offer a grain offering of new grain to the LORD at your festival of weeks, you shall have a holy convocation; you shall not work at your occupations. 27 You shall offer a burnt offering, a pleasing odor to the LORD: two young bulls, one ram, seven male lambs a year old. 28 Their grain offering shall be of choice flour mixed with oil, three-tenths of an ephah for each bull, two-tenths for one ram, 29 one-tenth for each of the seven lambs; 30 with one male goat, to make atonement for you. 31 In addition to the regular burnt offering with its grain offering, you shall offer them and their drink offering. They shall be without blemish.

6. Offerings at the festival of trumpets

29 On the first day of the seventh month you shall have a holy convocation; you shall not work at your occupations. It is a day for you to blow the trumpets, 2 and you shall offer a burnt offering, a pleasing odor to the LORD: one young bull, one ram, seven male lambs a year old without blemish. 3 Their grain offering shall be of choice flour mixed with oil, three-tenths of one ephah for the bull, two-tenths for the ram, 4 and one-tenth for each of the seven lambs; 5 with one male goat for a sin offering, to make atonement for you. 6 These are in addition to the burnt offering of the new moon and its grain offering, and the regular burnt offering and its grain offering, and their drink offerings, according to the ordinance for them, a pleasing odor, an offering by fire to the LORD.

7. The offering on the day of atonement

7 On the tenth day of this seventh month you shall have a holy convocation, and deny yourselves;*t* you shall do no work. 8 You shall offer a burnt offering to the LORD, a pleasing odor: one young bull, one

t Or and fast

Cross references (left margin):
28.16 Ex 12.6, 18; Lev 23.5; Deut 16.1
28.17 Lev 23.6
28.18 Ex 12.16; Lev 23.7
28.23 v. 3
28.25 Ex 12.16
28.26 Ex 23.16; 34.22; Lev 23.10, 15; Deut 16.10
28.31 vv. 3, 19
29.1 Ex 23.16; 34.22; Lev 23.24
29.6 Num 28.3, 11
29.7 Lev 16.29-34; 23.26-32

28.17 See note on Lev 23.6–8 for details on the festival of unleavened bread.
28.26 *day of the first fruits*, also called the harvest festival, Pentecost, and the festival of weeks. See note on Lev 23.15,16 for details on this festival.
29.1 *On the first day of the seventh month*, (of the Hebrew calendar), i.e., about the fifteenth day of September. See note on Lev 23.23,24 for details on the festival of trumpets.
29.8 See note on Lev 16.6 for details on the day of atonement offering.

ram, seven male lambs a year old. They shall be without blemish. ⁹ Their grain offering shall be of choice flour mixed with oil, three-tenths of an ephah for the bull, two-tenths for the one ram, ¹⁰ one-tenth for each of the seven lambs; ¹¹ with one male goat for a sin offering, in addition to the sin offering of atonement, and the regular burnt offering and its grain offering, and their drink offerings.

29.11
Lev 16.3, 5;
Num 28.3

8. *Offerings at the festival of booths*

12   On the fifteenth day of the seventh month you shall have a holy convocation; you shall not work at your occupations. You shall celebrate a festival to the LORD seven days. ¹³ You shall offer a burnt offering, an offering by fire, a pleasing odor to the LORD: thirteen young bulls, two rams, fourteen male lambs a year old. They shall be without blemish. ¹⁴ Their grain offering shall be of choice flour mixed with oil, three-tenths of an ephah for each of the thirteen bulls, two-tenths for each of the two rams, ¹⁵ and one-tenth for each of the fourteen lambs; ¹⁶ also one male goat for a sin offering, in addition to the regular burnt offering, its grain offering and its drink offering.

29.12
Lev 23.33-35

29.16
v. 11

17   On the second day: twelve young bulls, two rams, fourteen male lambs a year old without blemish, ¹⁸ with the grain offering and the drink offerings for the bulls, and for the rams, and for the lambs, as prescribed in accordance with their number; ¹⁹ also one male goat for a sin offering, in addition to the regular burnt offering and its grain offering, and their drink offerings.

29.18
vv. 3, 4, 9,
10;
Num 15.12;
28.7, 14

20   On the third day: eleven bulls, two rams, fourteen male lambs a year old without blemish, ²¹ with the grain offering and the drink offerings for the bulls, for the rams, and for the lambs, as prescribed in accordance with their number; ²² also one male goat for a sin offering, in addition to the regular burnt offering and its grain offering and its drink offering.

29.22
Num 28.15

23   On the fourth day: ten bulls, two rams, fourteen male lambs a year old without blemish, ²⁴ with the grain offering and the drink offerings for the bulls, for the rams, and for the lambs, as prescribed in accordance with their number; ²⁵ also one male goat for a sin offering, in addition to the regular burnt offering, its grain offering and its drink offering.

26   On the fifth day: nine bulls, two rams, fourteen male lambs a year old without blemish, ²⁷ with the grain offering and the drink offerings for the bulls, for the rams, and for the lambs, as prescribed in accordance with their number; ²⁸ also one male goat for a sin offering, in addition to the regular burnt offering and its grain offering and its drink offering.

29.28
Num 15.24

29   On the sixth day: eight bulls, two rams, fourteen male lambs a year old without blemish, ³⁰ with the grain offering and the drink offerings for the bulls, for the rams, and for the lambs, as prescribed in accordance with their number; ³¹ also one male goat for a sin offering, in addition to the regular burnt offering, its grain offering, and its drink offerings.

29.31
v. 22;
Gen 8.20

32   On the seventh day: seven bulls, two rams, fourteen male lambs a year old without blemish, ³³ with the grain offering and the drink offerings for the bulls, for the rams, and for the lambs, as prescribed in accordance with their number; ³⁴ also one male goat for a sin offering, besides the regular burnt offering, its grain offering, and its drink offering.

35   On the eighth day you shall have a solemn assembly; you shall not work at your occupations. ³⁶ You shall offer a burnt offering, an offering by fire, a pleasing odor to the LORD: one bull, one ram, seven male lambs

29.35
Lev 23.36

29.12   See note on Ex 23.16 for details on the festival of booths.

a year old without blemish, 37 and the grain offering and the drink offerings for the bull, for the ram, and for the lambs, as prescribed in accordance with their number; 38 also one male goat for a sin offering, in addition to the regular burnt offering and its grain offering and its drink offering.

39 These you shall offer to the LORD at your appointed festivals, in addition to your votive offerings and your freewill offerings, as your burnt offerings, your grain offerings, your drink offerings, and your offerings of well-being.

40ᵘ So Moses told the Israelites everything just as the LORD had commanded Moses.

G. The laws of vows

30 Then Moses said to the heads of the tribes of the Israelites: This is what the LORD has commanded. 2 When a man makes a vow to the LORD, or swears an oath to bind himself by a pledge, he shall not break his word; he shall do according to all that proceeds out of his mouth.

3 When a woman makes a vow to the LORD, or binds herself by a pledge, while within her father's house, in her youth, 4 and her father hears of her vow or her pledge by which she has bound herself, and says nothing to her; then all her vows shall stand, and any pledge by which she has bound herself shall stand. 5 But if her father expresses disapproval to her at the time that he hears of it, no vow of hers, and no pledge by which she has bound herself, shall stand; and the LORD will forgive her, because her father had expressed to her his disapproval.

6 If she marries, while obligated by her vows or any thoughtless utterance of her lips by which she has bound herself, 7 and her husband hears of it and says nothing to her at the time that he hears, then her vows shall stand, and her pledges by which she has bound herself shall stand. 8 But if, at the time that her husband hears of it, he expresses disapproval to her, then he shall nullify the vow by which she was obligated, or the thoughtless utterance of her lips, by which she bound herself; and the LORD will forgive her. 9 (But every vow of a widow or of a divorced woman, by which she has bound herself, shall be binding upon her.) 10 And if she made a vow in her husband's house, or bound herself by a pledge with an oath, 11 and her husband heard it and said nothing to her, and did not express disapproval to her, then all her vows shall stand, and any pledge by which she bound herself shall stand. 12 But if her husband nullifies them at the time that he hears them, then whatever proceeds out of her lips concerning her vows, or concerning her pledge of herself, shall not stand. Her husband has nullified them, and the LORD will forgive her. 13 Any vow or any binding oath to deny herself,ᵛ her husband may allow to stand, or her husband may nullify. 14 But if her husband says nothing to her from day to day,ʷ then he validates all her vows, or all her pledges, by which she is obligated; he has validated them, because he said nothing to her at the time that he heard of them. 15 But if he nullifies them some time after he has heard of them, then he shall bear her guilt.

16 These are the statutes that the LORD commanded Moses concerning a husband and his wife, and a father and his daughter while she is still young and in her father's house.

ᵘ Ch 30.1 in Heb   ᵛ Or to fast   ʷ Or from that day to the next

---

30.2 See note on Num 6.1,2 on the laws concerning vows.
30.16 No specific mention is made of male children making vows. Presumably they fell within the general prescription for males and did not need to have their vows approved by their fathers, as their sisters did. A woman was bound by her husband's decision but nothing is said to indicate that a married male was bound to the decision of his father-in-law.

Margin cross-references:

29.39
Lev 23.2;
1 Chr 23.31;
2 Chr 31.3;
Lev 7.11, 16

30.2
Deut 23.21;
Mt 5.23

30.5
Eccl 5.4

30.6
Ps 56.12

30.8
Gen 3.16

30.12
Eph 5.22

30.15
Col 3.18

30.16
Ex 15.26

H. The destruction of the Midianites

1. The killing of the Midianites

31 The LORD spoke to Moses, saying, 2"Avenge the Israelites on the Midianites; afterward you shall be gathered to your people." 3So Moses said to the people, "Arm some of your number for the war, so that they may go against Midian, to execute the LORD's vengeance on Midian. 4You shall send a thousand from each of the tribes of Israel to the war." 5So out of the thousands of Israel, a thousand from each tribe were conscripted, twelve thousand armed for battle. 6Moses sent them to the war, a thousand from each tribe, along with Phinehas son of Eleazar the priest,ˣ with the vessels of the sanctuary and the trumpets for sounding the alarm in his hand. 7They did battle against Midian, as the LORD had commanded Moses, and killed every male. 8They killed the kings of Midian: Evi, Rekem, Zur, Hur, and Reba, the five kings of Midian, in addition to others who were slain by them; and they also killed Balaam son of Beor with the sword. 9The Israelites took the women of Midian and their little ones captive; and they took all their cattle, their flocks, and all their goods as booty. 10All their towns where they had settled, and all their encampments, they burned, 11but they took all the spoil and all the booty, both people and animals. 12Then they brought the captives and the booty and the spoil to Moses, to Eleazar the priest, and to the congregation of the Israelites, at the camp on the plains of Moab by the Jordan at Jericho.

2. The command to exterminate: rite of purification

13 Moses, Eleazar the priest, and all the leaders of the congregation went to meet them outside the camp. 14Moses became angry with the officers of the army, the commanders of thousands and the commanders of hundreds, who had come from service in the war. 15Moses said to them, "Have you allowed all the women to live? 16These women here, on Balaam's advice, made the Israelites act treacherously against the LORD in the affair of Peor, so that the plague came among the congregation of the LORD. 17Now therefore, kill every male among the little ones, and kill every woman who has known a man by sleeping with him. 18But all the young girls who have not known a man by sleeping with him, keep alive for yourselves. 19Camp outside the camp seven days; whoever of you has killed any person or touched a corpse, purify yourselves and your captives on the third and on the seventh day. 20You shall purify every garment, every article of skin, everything made of goats' hair, and every article of wood."

21 Eleazar the priest said to the troops who had gone to battle: "This is the statute of the law that the LORD has commanded Moses: 22gold, silver, bronze, iron, tin, and lead— 23everything that can withstand fire, shall be passed through fire, and it shall be clean. Nevertheless it shall also be purified with the water for purification; and whatever cannot withstand fire, shall be passed through the water. 24You must wash your clothes on the seventh day, and you shall be clean; afterward you may come into the camp."

ˣ Gk: Heb adds *to the war*

Cross references (right margin):
31.2 Num 25.1, 16, 17; 27.13
31.6 Num 10.9
31.8 Josh 13.21, 22; v. 16
31.11 Deut 20.14
31.16 Num 25.1-9; 24.14; 2 Pet 2.15; Rev 2.14
31.17 Judg 21.11
31.19 Num 19.11-22
31.23 Num 19.9, 17
31.24 Lev 11.25

31.1,2 The Midianites were children of Abraham by Keturah (Gen 25.2), some of whom had settled east of Canaan. They had fallen into sin and used some of their women to entice the Israelites to prostitution and idolatry. They were confederates of the Moabites. In 31.2ff we see that God commanded the Israelites to execute divine judgment on them by war, in which all adults—male and female—were to be killed.

Some modern scholars insist Moses was mistaken and carried out an order God could not have given. **31.17,18** All male children were to be killed, so that the Midianite race would become extinct. The women captives would intermarry with the Israelites and be absorbed into their society. However, the Midianites were not completely destroyed, for we read of them again in the Book of Judges (6.1,2).

3. *The division of the booty*

25 The LORD spoke to Moses, saying, 26 "You and Eleazar the priest and the heads of the ancestral houses of the congregation make an inventory of the booty captured, both human and animal. 27 Divide the booty into two parts, between the warriors who went out to battle and all the congregation. 28 From the share of the warriors who went out to battle, set aside as tribute for the LORD, one item out of every five hundred, whether persons, oxen, donkeys, sheep, or goats. 29 Take it from their half and give it to Eleazar the priest as an offering to the LORD. 30 But from the Israelites' half you shall take one out of every fifty, whether persons, oxen, donkeys, sheep, or goats — all the animals — and give them to the Levites who have charge of the tabernacle of the LORD."

31 Then Moses and Eleazar the priest did as the LORD had commanded Moses:

32 The booty remaining from the spoil that the troops had taken totaled six hundred seventy-five thousand sheep, 33 seventy-two thousand oxen, 34 sixty-one thousand donkeys, 35 and thirty-two thousand persons in all, women who had not known a man by sleeping with him.

36 The half-share, the portion of those who had gone out to war, was in number three hundred thirty-seven thousand five hundred sheep and goats, 37 and the LORD's tribute of sheep and goats was six hundred seventy-five. 38 The oxen were thirty-six thousand, of which the LORD's tribute was seventy-two. 39 The donkeys were thirty thousand five hundred, of which the LORD's tribute was sixty-one. 40 The persons were sixteen thousand, of which the LORD's tribute was thirty-two persons. 41 Moses gave the tribute, the offering for the LORD, to Eleazar the priest, as the LORD had commanded Moses.

42 As for the Israelites' half, which Moses separated from that of the troops, 43 the congregation's half was three hundred thirty-seven thousand five hundred sheep and goats, 44 thirty-six thousand oxen, 45 thirty thousand five hundred donkeys, 46 and sixteen thousand persons. 47 From the Israelites' half Moses took one of every fifty, both of persons and of animals, and gave them to the Levites who had charge of the tabernacle of the LORD; as the LORD had commanded Moses.

4. *The offerings of the officers and commanders*

48 Then the officers who were over the thousands of the army, the commanders of thousands and the commanders of hundreds, approached Moses, 49 and said to Moses, "Your servants have counted the warriors who are under our command, and not one of us is missing. 50 And we have brought the LORD's offering, what each of us found, articles of gold, armlets and bracelets, signet rings, earrings, and pendants, to make atonement for ourselves before the LORD." 51 Moses and Eleazar the priest received the gold from them, all in the form of crafted articles. 52 And all the gold of the offering that they offered to the LORD, from the commanders of thousands and the commanders of hundreds, was sixteen thousand seven hundred fifty shekels. 53 (The troops had all taken plunder for themselves.) 54 So Moses and Eleazar the priest received the gold from the commanders of thousands and of hundreds, and brought it into the tent of meeting as a memorial for the Israelites before the LORD.

Margin references:
31.28
Num 18.21-30

31.30
Num 3.7, 8,
25; 18.3, 4

31.32
Gen 49.27;
Ex 15.9

31.37
vv. 38, 41

31.41
see
Num 18.8, 9

31.47
v. 30

31.50
Ex 30.12, 16

31.53
v. 32;
Deut 20.14
31.54
Ex 30.16

31.26 The booty taken was to be divided among soldiers and civilians. One out of every five hundred males and animals from the soldiers' booty were given to the high priest; one in fifty of all males and animals, to the Levites.
31.52 16,750 shekels of gold were offered to the Lord — an immense amount of money according to modern currency. There were no coins at this time, so that the gold and silver were bullion or comprised

jewelry and ornaments. The shekel was obviously a measure of weight and this fluctuated at different times in the Scriptures. What was more important was what the silver or gold would buy. At this time a ram was priced at two silver shekels (Lev 5.15). In Lev 27.16 fifty shekels would buy a homer (approximately four bushels) of barley seed. The value of silver and gold differed also.

I. The beginning of the settlements: Reuben and Gad in Gilead

1. Their desire to settle east of the Jordan

32 Now the Reubenites and the Gadites owned a very great number of cattle. When they saw that the land of Jazer and the land of Gilead was a good place for cattle, 2 the Gadites and the Reubenites came and spoke to Moses, to Eleazar the priest, and to the leaders of the congregation, saying, 3 "Ataroth, Dibon, Jazer, Nimrah, Heshbon, Elealeh, Sebam, Nebo, and Beon— 4 the land that the LORD subdued before the congregation of Israel—is a land for cattle; and your servants have cattle." 5 They continued, "If we have found favor in your sight, let this land be given to your servants for a possession; do not make us cross the Jordan."

6 But Moses said to the Gadites and to the Reubenites, "Shall your brothers go to war while you sit here? 7 Why will you discourage the hearts of the Israelites from going over into the land that the LORD has given them? 8 Your fathers did this, when I sent them from Kadesh-barnea to see the land. 9 When they went up to the Wadi Eshcol and saw the land, they discouraged the hearts of the Israelites from going into the land that the LORD had given them. 10 The LORD's anger was kindled on that day and he swore, saying, 11 'Surely none of the people who came up out of Egypt, from twenty years old and upward, shall see the land that I swore to give to Abraham, to Isaac, and to Jacob, because they have not unreservedly followed me— 12 none except Caleb son of Jephunneh the Kenizzite and Joshua son of Nun, for they have unreservedly followed the LORD.' 13 And the LORD's anger was kindled against Israel, and he made them wander in the wilderness for forty years, until all the generation that had done evil in the sight of the LORD had disappeared. 14 And now you, a brood of sinners, have risen in place of your fathers, to increase the LORD's fierce anger against Israel! 15 If you turn away from following him, he will again abandon them in the wilderness; and you will destroy all this people."

2. The agreement to help the others settle west of the Jordan

16 Then they came up to him and said, "We will build sheepfolds here for our flocks, and towns for our little ones, 17 but we will take up arms as a vanguard[y] before the Israelites, until we have brought them to their place. Meanwhile our little ones will stay in the fortified towns because of the inhabitants of the land. 18 We will not return to our homes until all the Israelites have obtained their inheritance. 19 We will not inherit with them on the other side of the Jordan and beyond, because our inheritance has come to us on this side of the Jordan to the east."

20 So Moses said to them, "If you do this—if you take up arms to go before the LORD for the war, 21 and all those of you who bear arms cross the Jordan before the LORD, until he has driven out his enemies from before him 22 and the land is subdued before the LORD—then after that you may return and be free of obligation to the LORD and to Israel, and this land shall be your possession before the LORD. 23 But if you do not do this, you have sinned against the LORD; and be sure your sin will find you out. 24 Build towns for your little ones, and folds for your flocks; but do what you have promised."

y Cn: Heb *hurrying*

Marginal references:

32.1 Ex 12.38; Num 21.32

32.3 v. 36 *ethnimrah;* v. 38 *ibmah;* v. 38 *aal-meon*

32.7 Num 13.27-14.4

32.8 Num 13.3, 26

32.10 Num 14.11, 21; Deut 1.34
32.11 Num 14.28-30; Deut 1.35
32.12 Num 14.24; Deut 1.36
32.13 Num 14.33-35; 26.64, 65

32.15 Deut 30.17, 18

32.17 Josh 4.12, 13

32.18 Josh 22.1-4
32.19 v. 33

32.20 Deut 3.18

32.22 Deut 3.12-20

32.24 vv. 16, 34

32.6 Moses insisted that the tribes of Gad and Reuben, who asked to settle on the east bank of the Jordan, had to help the other tribes face armed struggle as they sought to possess the land on the west bank of the Jordan. The Gadites and Reubenites agreed to this stipulation.

32.23 Moses said that the men of Gad and Reuben would be sinning against God if they failed to keep their promise to help the other tribes take the land of Canaan. Their sins would be found out by God, from whom nothing can be concealed. We do well to remember that characteristic of our God.

25 Then the Gadites and the Reubenites said to Moses, "Your servants will do as my lord commands. 26 Our little ones, our wives, our flocks, and all our livestock shall remain there in the towns of Gilead; 27 but your servants will cross over, everyone armed for war, to do battle for the LORD, just as my lord orders."

3. Moses' decision

28 So Moses gave command concerning them to Eleazar the priest, to Joshua son of Nun, and to the heads of the ancestral houses of the Israelite tribes. 29 And Moses said to them, "If the Gadites and the Reubenites, everyone armed for battle before the LORD, will cross over the Jordan with you and the land shall be subdued before you, then you shall give them the land of Gilead for a possession; 30 but if they will not cross over with you armed, they shall have possessions among you in the land of Canaan." 31 The Gadites and the Reubenites answered, "As the LORD has spoken to your servants, so we will do. 32 We will cross over armed before the LORD into the land of Canaan, but the possession of our inheritance shall remain with us on this side of[z] the Jordan."

4. The half-tribe of Manasseh settles in Gilead

33 Moses gave to them—to the Gadites and to the Reubenites and to the half-tribe of Manasseh son of Joseph—the kingdom of King Sihon of the Amorites and the kingdom of King Og of Bashan, the land and its towns, with the territories of the surrounding towns. 34 And the Gadites rebuilt Dibon, Ataroth, Aroer, 35 Atroth-shophan, Jazer, Jogbehah, 36 Beth-nimrah, and Beth-haran, fortified cities, and folds for sheep. 37 And the Reubenites rebuilt Heshbon, Elealeh, Kiriathaim, 38 Nebo, and Baal-meon (some names being changed), and Sibmah; and they gave names to the towns that they rebuilt. 39 The descendants of Machir son of Manasseh went to Gilead, captured it, and dispossessed the Amorites who were there; 40 so Moses gave Gilead to Machir son of Manasseh, and he settled there. 41 Jair son of Manasseh went and captured their villages, and renamed them Havvoth-jair.[a] 42 And Nobah went and captured Kenath and its villages, and renamed it Nobah after himself.

J. The stages of Israel's journey from Egypt to Canaan

33 These are the stages by which the Israelites went out of the land of Egypt in military formation under the leadership of Moses and Aaron. 2 Moses wrote down their starting points, stage by stage, by command of the LORD; and these are their stages according to their starting places. 3 They set out from Rameses in the first month, on the fifteenth day of the first month; on the day after the passover the Israelites went out boldly in the sight of all the Egyptians, 4 while the Egyptians were burying all their firstborn, whom the LORD had struck down among them. The LORD executed judgments even against their gods.

5 So the Israelites set out from Rameses, and camped at Succoth. 6 They set out from Succoth, and camped at Etham, which is on the edge of the wilderness. 7 They set out from Etham, and turned back to Pi-hahiroth, which faces Baal-zephon; and they camped before Migdol. 8 They set out from Pi-hahiroth, passed through the sea into the wilderness, went a three days' journey in the wilderness of Etham, and camped at Marah. 9 They set out from Marah and came to Elim; at Elim there were twelve springs of water and seventy palm trees, and they camped there. 10 They set out from Elim and camped by the Red Sea.[b] 11 They set out

32.26
Josh 1.14

32.27
Josh 4.12

32.28
Josh 1.13
32.29
v. 1

32.33
Deut 3.12-17;
Josh 12.1-6;
Num 21.24,
33, 35

32.41
Judg 10.4

33.1
Ps 77.20;
Mic 6.4

33.3
Ex 12.37;
14.8
33.4
Ex 12.12

33.6
Ex 13.20
33.7
Ex 14.2, 9
33.8
Ex 14.22

33.9
Ex 15.27

33.11
Ex 16.1

[z] Heb beyond   [a] That is the villages of Jair   [b] Or Sea of Reeds

33.1,2 Moses kept a record of the travels of the Israelites through the forty years of wandering in the wilderness. Ch. 33 contains that record.

from the Red Sea[c] and camped in the wilderness of Sin. 12 They set out
from the wilderness of Sin and camped at Dophkah. 13 They set out from
Dophkah and camped at Alush. 14 They set out from Alush and camped
at Rephidim, where there was no water for the people to drink. 15 They
set out from Rephidim and camped in the wilderness of Sinai. 16 They set
out from the wilderness of Sinai and camped at Kibroth-hattaavah.
17 They set out from Kibroth-hattaavah and camped at Hazeroth. 18 They
set out from Hazeroth and camped at Rithmah. 19 They set out from
Rithmah and camped at Rimmon-perez. 20 They set out from Rimmon-
perez and camped at Libnah. 21 They set out from Libnah and camped
at Rissah. 22 They set out from Rissah and camped at Kehelathah. 23 They
set out from Kehelathah and camped at Mount Shepher. 24 They set out
from Mount Shepher and camped at Haradah. 25 They set out from
Haradah and camped at Makheloth. 26 They set out from Makheloth and
camped at Tahath. 27 They set out from Tahath and camped at Terah.
28 They set out from Terah and camped at Mithkah. 29 They set out from
Mithkah and camped at Hashmonah. 30 They set out from Hashmonah
and camped at Moseroth. 31 They set out from Moseroth and camped at
Bene-jaakan. 32 They set out from Bene-jaakan and camped at Hor-
haggidgad. 33 They set out from Hor-haggidgad and camped at Jotbathah.
34 They set out from Jotbathah and camped at Abronah. 35 They set out
from Abronah and camped at Ezion-geber. 36 They set out from Ezion-
geber and camped in the wilderness of Zin (that is, Kadesh). 37 They set
out from Kadesh and camped at Mount Hor, on the edge of the land of
Edom.

38   Aaron the priest went up Mount Hor at the command of the LORD
and died there in the fortieth year after the Israelites had come out of the
land of Egypt, on the first day of the fifth month. 39 Aaron was one
hundred twenty-three years old when he died on Mount Hor.

40   The Canaanite, the king of Arad, who lived in the Negeb in the
land of Canaan, heard of the coming of the Israelites.

41   They set out from Mount Hor and camped at Zalmonah. 42 They
set out from Zalmonah and camped at Punon. 43 They set out from Punon
and camped at Oboth. 44 They set out from Oboth and camped at Iye-
abarim, in the territory of Moab. 45 They set out from Iyim and camped
at Dibon-gad. 46 They set out from Dibon-gad and camped at Almon-
diblathaim. 47 They set out from Almon-diblathaim and camped in the
mountains of Abarim, before Nebo. 48 They set out from the mountains
of Abarim and camped in the plains of Moab by the Jordan at Jericho;
49 they camped by the Jordan from Beth-jeshimoth as far as Abel-shittim
in the plains of Moab.

K. God's commands concerning Canaan

1. The command to drive out the inhabitants

50   In the plains of Moab by the Jordan at Jericho, the LORD spoke
to Moses, saying: 51 Speak to the Israelites, and say to them: When you
cross over the Jordan into the land of Canaan, 52 you shall drive out all
the inhabitants of the land from before you, destroy all their figured
stones, destroy all their cast images, and demolish all their high places.
53 You shall take possession of the land and settle in it, for I have given
you the land to possess. 54 You shall apportion the land by lot according
to your clans; to a large one you shall give a large inheritance, and to a
small one you shall give a small inheritance; the inheritance shall belong

c Or Sea of Reeds

33.39 Aaron died at the age of 123; Moses, Aaron's
younger brother, died at 120 (Deut 34.7). Miriam,
their sister, preceded them in death (Num 20.1).

Marginal references:

33.14
Ex 17.1
33.15
Ex 19.1
33.16
Num 11.34
33.17
Num 11.35

33.20
see
Josh 10.29

33.30
Deut 10.6

33.33
Deut 10.7
33.35
Deut 2.8
33.36
Num 20.1
33.37

33.38
Num 20.25,
28;
Deut 10.6

33.40
Num 21.1

33.43
Num 21.10
33.44
Num 21.11

33.47
Num 27.12
33.48
Num 22.1
33.49
Num 25.1

33.52
Ex 23.24, 33;
34.13;
Deut 7.2, 5;
12.3;
Josh 11.12
33.54
Num 26.53-55

to the person on whom the lot falls; according to your ancestral tribes you shall inherit. 55 But if you do not drive out the inhabitants of the land from before you, then those whom you let remain shall be as barbs in your eyes and thorns in your sides; they shall trouble you in the land where you are settling. 56 And I will do to you as I thought to do to them.

2. The boundaries of the land

34 The LORD spoke to Moses, saying: 2 Command the Israelites, and say to them: When you enter the land of Canaan (this is the land that shall fall to you for an inheritance, the land of Canaan, defined by its boundaries), 3 your south sector shall extend from the wilderness of Zin along the side of Edom. Your southern boundary shall begin from the end of the Dead Sea*d* on the east; 4 your boundary shall turn south of the ascent of Akrabbim, and cross to Zin, and its outer limit shall be south of Kadesh-barnea; then it shall go on to Hazar-addar, and cross to Azmon; 5 the boundary shall turn from Azmon to the Wadi of Egypt, and its termination shall be at the Sea.

6 For the western boundary, you shall have the Great Sea and its*e* coast; this shall be your western boundary.

7 This shall be your northern boundary: from the Great Sea you shall mark out your line to Mount Hor; 8 from Mount Hor you shall mark it out to Lebo-hamath, and the outer limit of the boundary shall be at Zedad; 9 then the boundary shall extend to Ziphron, and its end shall be at Hazar-enan; this shall be your northern boundary.

10 You shall mark out your eastern boundary from Hazar-enan to Shepham; 11 and the boundary shall continue down from Shepham to Riblah on the east side of Ain; and the boundary shall go down, and reach the eastern slope of the sea of Chinnereth; 12 and the boundary shall go down to the Jordan, and its end shall be at the Dead Sea.*d* This shall be your land with its boundaries all around.

13 Moses commanded the Israelites, saying: This is the land that you shall inherit by lot, which the LORD has commanded to give to the nine tribes and to the half-tribe; 14 for the tribe of the Reubenites by their ancestral houses and the tribe of the Gadites by their ancestral houses have taken their inheritance, and also the half-tribe of Manasseh; 15 the two tribes and the half-tribe have taken their inheritance beyond the Jordan at Jericho eastward, toward the sunrise.

3. The leaders chosen to divide the land

16 The LORD spoke to Moses, saying: 17 These are the names of the men who shall apportion the land to you for inheritance: the priest Eleazar and Joshua son of Nun. 18 You shall take one leader of every tribe to apportion the land for inheritance. 19 These are the names of the men: Of the tribe of Judah, Caleb son of Jephunneh. 20 Of the tribe of the Simeonites, Shemuel son of Ammihud. 21 Of the tribe of Benjamin, Elidad son of Chislon. 22 Of the tribe of the Danites a leader, Bukki son of Jogli. 23 Of the Josephites: of the tribe of the Manassites a leader, Hanniel son of Ephod, 24 and of the tribe of the Ephraimites a leader, Kemuel son of Shiphtan. 25 Of the tribe of the Zebulunites a leader, Eli-zaphan son of Parnach. 26 Of the tribe of the Issacharites a leader, Paltiel son of Azzan. 27 And of the tribe of the Asherites a leader, Ahihud son of Shelomi. 28 Of the tribe of the Naphtalites a leader, Pedahel son of Ammihud. 29 These

Cross references (left margin):

33.55
Josh 23.13;
Ps 106.34, 36

34.2
Gen 17.8;
Deut 1.7;
Ps 78.55;
Ezek 47.15
34.3
Josh 15.1-3

34.5
Gen 15.18;
Josh 15.4, 47

34.7
Ezek 47.15-17
34.8
Num 13.21

34.11
2 Kings 23.33;
Deut 3.17;
Josh 11.2

34.13
Josh 14.1, 2

34.14
Num 32.33;
Josh 14.2, 3

34.17
Josh 14.1

34.18
Num 1.4, 16

d Heb Salt Sea   e Syr: Heb lacks its

33.55 God commanded Israel to drive out all of Canaan's inhabitants so as not to be defiled by their idolatry. But this command was never completely carried out. As a result, Israel was defiled and the people contaminated; this ultimately resulted in apostasy and led to the Babylonian captivity.

34.8 *Lebo-hamath* was the ideal northern boundary of the land promised to Israel. It was not until the kingships of David, Solomon, and Jeroboam II that Israel's land extended to this point.

were the ones whom the Lord commanded to apportion the inheritance
for the Israelites in the land of Canaan.

4. The cities for the Levites

a. The forty-eight cities and pasture land

35 In the plains of Moab by the Jordan at Jericho, the Lord spoke
to Moses, saying: 2 Command the Israelites to give, from the
inheritance that they possess, towns for the Levites to live in; you shall
also give to the Levites pasture lands surrounding the towns. 3 The towns
shall be theirs to live in, and their pasture lands shall be for their cattle,
for their livestock, and for all their animals. 4 The pasture lands of the
towns, which you shall give to the Levites, shall reach from the wall of
the town outward a thousand cubits all around. 5 You shall measure,
outside the town, for the east side two thousand cubits, for the south side
two thousand cubits, for the west side two thousand cubits, and for the
north side two thousand cubits, with the town in the middle; this shall
belong to them as pasture land for their towns.

6   The towns that you give to the Levites shall include the six cities
of refuge, where you shall permit a slayer to flee, and in addition to them
you shall give forty-two towns. 7 The towns that you give to the Levites
shall total forty-eight, with their pasture lands. 8 And as for the towns that
you shall give from the possession of the Israelites, from the larger tribes
you shall take many, and from the smaller tribes you shall take few; each,
in proportion to the inheritance that it obtains, shall give of its towns to
the Levites.

b. The cities of refuge

9   The Lord spoke to Moses, saying: 10 Speak to the Israelites, and say
to them: When you cross the Jordan into the land of Canaan, 11 then you
shall select cities to be cities of refuge for you, so that a slayer who kills
a person without intent may flee there. 12 The cities shall be for you a
refuge from the avenger, so that the slayer may not die until there is a trial
before the congregation.

13   The cities that you designate shall be six cities of refuge for you:
14 you shall designate three cities beyond the Jordan, and three cities in
the land of Canaan, to be cities of refuge. 15 These six cities shall serve
as refuge for the Israelites, for the resident or transient alien among them,
so that anyone who kills a person without intent may flee there.

16   But anyone who strikes another with an iron object, and death
ensues, is a murderer; the murderer shall be put to death. 17 Or anyone
who strikes another with a stone in hand that could cause death, and death
ensues, is a murderer; the murderer shall be put to death. 18 Or anyone
who strikes another with a weapon of wood in hand that could cause death,
and death ensues, is a murderer; the murderer shall be put to death. 19 The
avenger of blood is the one who shall put the murderer to death; when
they meet, the avenger of blood shall execute the sentence. 20 Likewise,
if someone pushes another from hatred, or hurls something at another,
lying in wait, and death ensues, 21 or in enmity strikes another with the
hand, and death ensues, then the one who struck the blow shall be put

35.2
Lev 25.32-34;
Josh 14.3, 4

35.6
Josh 20.7-9;
21.3, 13, 21,
27, 32, 36,
38
35.8
Num 26.54;
Lev 25.32-34;
Josh 21.1-42

35.11
Deut 19.1-13;
Ex 21.13
35.12
Josh 20.2-6

35.15
v. 11

35.16
Ex 21.12, 14;
Lev 24.17

35.19
vv. 21, 24, 27

35.12   Moses repeated the law concerning killing.
The cities of refuge were designed to give initial protection to all killers, the innocent and the guilty. Any
who had been involved in a killing had to stand trial
before the congregation. A clear distinction was made
between accidental killing and unjustifiable homicide. Those who killed by accident and without malice stayed in the city of refuge until the death of the
high priest, after which they were free to return home
without being slain. Guilty murderers were to be slain

by a near relative of the deceased, called "the avenger
of blood" (see next note).
35.19   The avenger of blood was the executor of the
murderer. Obviously, this person was acting on behalf of the community which pronounced the murderer guilty. Whoever performed this function was
not considered to be a murderer. So today, those who
execute the guilty for the government are not guilty
of a crime.

to death; that person is a murderer; the avenger of blood shall put the murderer to death, when they meet.

35.22
v. 11;
Ex 21.13

22　But if someone pushes another suddenly without enmity, or hurls any object without lying in wait, 23 or, while handling any stone that could cause death, unintentionally*f* drops it on another and death ensues,

35.24
v. 12

though they were not enemies, and no harm was intended, 24 then the congregation shall judge between the slayer and the avenger of blood, in accordance with these ordinances; 25 and the congregation shall rescue the slayer from the avenger of blood. Then the congregation shall send the slayer back to the original city of refuge. The slayer shall live in it until the death of the high priest who was anointed with the holy oil. 26 But if the slayer shall at any time go outside the bounds of the original city of refuge, 27 and is found by the avenger of blood outside the bounds of the city of refuge, and is killed by the avenger, no bloodguilt shall be incurred. 28 For the slayer must remain in the city of refuge until the death of the high priest; but after the death of the high priest the slayer may return home.

29　These things shall be a statute and ordinance for you throughout your generations wherever you live.

35.30
v. 16;
Deut 17.6;
19.15;
Mt 18.16;
2 Cor 13.1;
Heb 10.28

30　If anyone kills another, the murderer shall be put to death on the evidence of witnesses; but no one shall be put to death on the testimony of a single witness. 31 Moreover you shall accept no ransom for the life of a murderer who is subject to the death penalty; a murderer must be put to death. 32 Nor shall you accept ransom for one who has fled to a city of refuge, enabling the fugitive to return to live in the land before the death of the high priest. 33 You shall not pollute the land in which you live; for

35.33
Ps 106.38;
Gen 9.6

f Heb *without seeing*

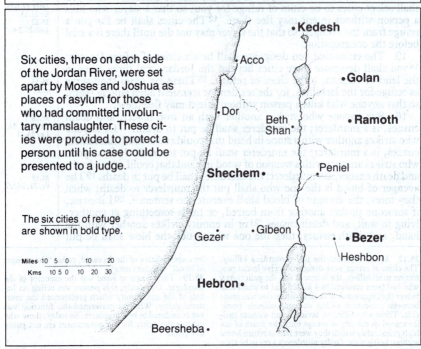

CITIES OF REFUGE

Six cities, three on each side of the Jordan River, were set apart by Moses and Joshua as places of asylum for those who had committed involuntary manslaughter. These cities were provided to protect a person until his case could be presented to a judge.

The six cities of refuge are shown in bold type.

Miles 10　5　0　　10　　20
Kms　　10 5 0　10　20　30

Kedesh

Acco

Golan

Dor

Beth
Shan

Ramoth

Shechem

Peniel

Gezer

Gibeon

Bezer

Heshbon

Hebron

Beersheba

blood pollutes the land, and no expiation can be made for the land, for the blood that is shed in it, except by the blood of the one who shed it. 34 You shall not defile the land in which you live, in which I also dwell; for I the LORD dwell among the Israelites.

35.34
Lev 18.25;
Ex 29.45, 46

5. Laws concerning the marriage of female heirs

36 The heads of the ancestral houses of the clans of the descendants of Gilead son of Machir son of Manasseh, of the Josephite clans, came forward and spoke in the presence of Moses and the leaders, the heads of the ancestral houses of the Israelites; 2 they said, "The LORD commanded my lord to give the land for inheritance by lot to the Israelites; and my lord was commanded by the LORD to give the inheritance of our brother Zelophehad to his daughters. 3 But if they are married into another Israelite tribe, then their inheritance will be taken from the inheritance of our ancestors and added to the inheritance of the tribe into which they marry; so it will be taken away from the allotted portion of our inheritance. 4 And when the jubilee of the Israelites comes, then their inheritance will be added to the inheritance of the tribe into which they have married; and their inheritance will be taken from the inheritance of our ancestral tribe."

36.1
Num 26.29;
27.1

36.2
Num 26.55;
33.54; 27.1,
7

36.4
Lev 25.10

5 Then Moses commanded the Israelites according to the word of the LORD, saying, "The descendants of the tribe of Joseph are right in what they are saying. 6 This is what the LORD commands concerning the daughters of Zelophehad, 'Let them marry whom they think best; only it must be into a clan of their father's tribe that they are married, 7 so that no inheritance of the Israelites shall be transferred from one tribe to another; for all Israelites shall retain the inheritance of their ancestral tribes. 8 Every daughter who possesses an inheritance in any tribe of the Israelites shall marry one from the clan of her father's tribe, so that all Israelites may continue to possess their ancestral inheritance. 9 No inheritance shall be transferred from one tribe to another; for each of the tribes of the Israelites shall retain its own inheritance.' "

36.6
v. 12

36.8
1 Chr 23.22

10 The daughters of Zelophehad did as the LORD had commanded Moses. 11 Mahlah, Tirzah, Hoglah, Milcah, and Noah, the daughters of Zelophehad, married sons of their father's brothers. 12 They were married into the clans of the descendants of Manasseh son of Joseph, and their inheritance remained in the tribe of their father's clan.

36.11
Num 27.1

13 These are the commandments and the ordinances that the LORD commanded through Moses to the Israelites in the plains of Moab by the Jordan at Jericho.

36.13
Num 22.1;
Lev 26.46;
27.34

36.2 *Zelophehad.* See note on 27.1 for the rule of inheritance in connection with the daughters of this person.
36.6 Moses here commanded that the daughters of families who had no son should marry within their own tribes, so that no land would pass from one tribe to another. Thus tribal identity was to be preserved

and the land inheritance was to remain indefinitely within each tribe.
36.13 The commandments that Moses spoke to the Israelites were not his own ideas but came directly from God. This was fundamental to Israel's theocracy.

INTRODUCTION TO
DEUTERONOMY

Authorship, Date, and Background: The Hebrew title for this book is simply the opening words in the text: "these are the words," or just "words." The English title derives from the Greek word *deuteronomion*, which means "second law," or "repetition of the law." The Septuagint uses this word as the title for the last book of the Pentateuch. From the earliest days, Jewish and Samaritan traditions have attributed the authorship of the book to Moses. Thus the date for its composition would depend on whether one dates the Exodus around 1440 B.C. or 1290 B.C. The early date for the Exodus is preferred by evangelicals generally.

Deuteronomy itself seems to support the Mosaic authorship by several statements such as: "Beyond the Jordan in the land of Moab, Moses undertook to expound this law" (1.5); "Then Moses wrote down this law, and gave it to the priests, the sons of Levi" (31.9); "When Moses had finished writing down in a book the words of this law to the very end, Moses commanded the Levites who carried the ark of the covenant of the LORD, saying, 'Take this book of the law and put it beside the ark of the covenant of the LORD your God; let it remain there as a witness against you'" (31.24–26). A number of scholars have claimed that Deuteronomy was written in the seventh century B.C. However this hypothesis does not seem to be in accord with the internal evidence of Deuteronomy or with the available external historical data common to the seventh century B.C. The testimony of Jesus in Mt 19.8 favors Mosaic authorship.

The background against which Deuteronomy was written presupposes the existence of the material contained in Exodus and Leviticus. At the time Moses delivered the addresses in Deuteronomy, the children of Israel were camped on the border of the promised land, which they had not yet entered. Their forty years of probation and wandering, awaiting the death of the old generation (except Joshua and Caleb) were over. But God also told Moses not to enter the land because of his sin when he struck the rock rather than speaking to it at Meribah (Num 20.11ff). God decreed that Joshua should lead Israel into the land, but Moses, prior to his own death, was to explain to the younger generation the terms and conditions of the covenant and the necessity for their obedience to it.

Characteristics and Content: Deuteronomy consists of a series of speeches which were no doubt delivered orally, and which were written down for posterity. Moses first traced the background history of Israel in the wilderness journeys. In his second speech, Moses repeated the ten commandments and expanded on their implications. Moses paid particular attention to the first commandment, which is basic to the covenant. He then discussed the ceremonial laws having to do with such matters as places of worship, idolatry, clean and unclean foods, tithes, and holy seasons. He then treated civil ordinances dealing with the appointment of judges, the election of a king, and the regulations for priests, Levites, and prophets. This is followed by criminal laws relating to murder, cities of refuge, false testimony, waging war, and crimes punishable by hanging. Miscellaneous laws on marriage, disobedient sons, unchastity, wages, remarriage, parents, children, and even weights and measures are dealt with.

Moses' third discourse outlines the nature of God's covenant with Israel. He accented the need for repentance when the covenant is violated, and called them to keep the covenant, with promises of blessing or of severest punishment depending on Israel's faithfulness or unfaithfulness. Ch. 28 contains the prediction of future judgments on Israel. Moses closed the book with his final charge, a farewell and exhortation, the intimation of his death, and the pronouncement of blessing. The account of his death was apparently added to Moses' written record by Joshua, who took over the leadership of Israel as the people prepared to enter the land.

Outline:

I. Moses' first address (1.1–4.43)

II. Moses' second address (4.44–26.19)

III. The covenant renewed (27.1–30.20)

IV. Moses' final words and death (31.1–34.12)

DEUTERONOMY

I. *Moses' first address (1.1–4.43)*

A. *The introduction*

1 These are the words that Moses spoke to all Israel beyond the Jordan — in the wilderness, on the plain opposite Suph, between Paran and Tophel, Laban, Hazeroth, and Di-zahab. 2 (By the way of Mount Seir it takes eleven days to reach Kadesh-barnea from Horeb.) 3 In the fortieth year, on the first day of the eleventh month, Moses spoke to the Israelites just as the LORD had commanded him to speak to them. 4 This was after he had defeated King Sihon of the Amorites, who reigned in Heshbon, and King Og of Bashan, who reigned in Ashtaroth and*a* in Edrei. 5 Beyond the Jordan in the land of Moab, Moses undertook to expound this law as follows:

B. *The guidance of God from Horeb to Kadesh*

1. *The command to enter the land*

6 The LORD our God spoke to us at Horeb, saying, "You have stayed long enough at this mountain. 7 Resume your journey, and go into the hill country of the Amorites as well as into the neighboring regions — the Arabah, the hill country, the Shephelah, the Negeb, and the seacoast — the land of the Canaanites and the Lebanon, as far as the great river, the river Euphrates. 8 See, I have set the land before you; go in and take possession of the land that I*b* swore to your ancestors, to Abraham, to Isaac, and to Jacob, to give to them and to their descendants after them."

2. *The choice of leaders*

9 At that time I said to you, "I am unable by myself to bear you. 10 The LORD your God has multiplied you, so that today you are as numerous as the stars of heaven. 11 May the LORD, the God of your ancestors, increase you a thousand times more and bless you, as he has promised you! 12 But how can I bear the heavy burden of your disputes all by myself? 13 Choose for each of your tribes individuals who are wise, discerning, and reputable to be your leaders." 14 You answered me, "The plan you have proposed is a good one." 15 So I took the leaders of your tribes, wise and reputable individuals, and installed them as leaders over you, commanders of thousands, commanders of hundreds, commanders of fifties, commanders of

Marginal references:

1.3 Num 33.38
1.4 Num 21.24, 33
1.6 Ex 3.1; Num 10.11-13
1.8 Gen 12.7; 15.18; 17.7, 8; 26.4; 28.13
1.9 Ex 18.18
1.10 Gen 15.5; Deut 10.22
1.11 Gen 22.17; Ex 32.13
1.13 Ex 18.21
1.15 Ex 18.25

---

a Gk Syr Vg Compare Josh 12.4: Heb lacks *and*   *b* Sam Gk: MT *the* LORD

1.1 *beyond the Jordan.* This phrase can mean one of two things. As used here, it is the equivalent of "Trans-Jordan," as used today. However, in Deut 3.20,25 the same expression clearly means Canaan. In some places, "Trans-Jordan" is referred to as "beyond the Jordan eastward" (e.g., Josh 9.10; 13.8; 18.7). Some have suggested that its use here means the writer of the introduction was in Canaan; but if Moses wrote the book it could not be so. It would then be a proleptic word from God.
1.2 *eleven days to reach Kadesh-barnea from Horeb.* This foot journey of eleven days makes vivid the fact

that it was within this area that the Israelites wandered for thirty-eight years. They were always within just a few days of Canaan, yet they were prevented from entering the land because of their sin. *Horeb* is an alternate rendering of "Sinai"; *Kadesh-barnea* was at the southern edge of the promised land.
1.5 *Moses undertook to expound this law.* Deuteronomy (meaning "second law") is an interpretation of the law, not just a repetition of it.
1.15 See note on Ex 18.1ff where Moses appointed leaders from every tribe to help him in governing Israel.

tens, and officials, throughout your tribes. 16 I charged your judges at that time: "Give the members of your community a fair hearing, and judge rightly between one person and another, whether citizen or resident alien. 17 You must not be partial in judging: hear out the small and the great alike; you shall not be intimidated by anyone, for the judgment is God's. Any case that is too hard for you, bring to me, and I will hear it." 18 So I charged you at that time with all the things that you should do.

3. The episode at Kadesh-barnea: the report of the spies

19 Then, just as the LORD our God had ordered us, we set out from Horeb and went through all that great and terrible wilderness that you saw, on the way to the hill country of the Amorites, until we reached Kadesh-barnea. 20 I said to you, "You have reached the hill country of the Amorites, which the LORD our God is giving us. 21 See, the LORD your God has given the land to you; go up, take possession, as the LORD, the God of your ancestors, has promised you; do not fear or be dismayed."

22 All of you came to me and said, "Let us send men ahead of us to explore the land for us and bring back a report to us regarding the route by which we should go up and the cities we will come to." 23 The plan seemed good to me, and I selected twelve of you, one from each tribe. 24 They set out and went up into the hill country, and when they reached the Valley of Eshcol they spied it out 25 and gathered some of the land's produce, which they brought down to us. They brought back a report to us, and said, "It is a good land that the LORD our God is giving us."

26 But you were unwilling to go up. You rebelled against the command of the LORD your God; 27 you grumbled in your tents and said, "It is because the LORD hates us that he has brought us out of the land of Egypt, to hand us over to the Amorites to destroy us. 28 Where are we headed? Our kindred have made our hearts melt by reporting, 'The people are stronger and taller than we; the cities are large and fortified up to heaven! We actually saw there the offspring of the Anakim!' " 29 I said to you, "Have no dread or fear of them. 30 The LORD your God, who goes before you, is the one who will fight for you, just as he did for you in Egypt before your very eyes, 31 and in the wilderness, where you saw how the LORD your God carried you, just as one carries a child, all the way that you traveled until you reached this place. 32 But in spite of this, you have no trust in the LORD your God, 33 who goes before you on the way to seek out a place for you to camp, in fire by night, and in the cloud by day, to show you the route you should take."

34 When the LORD heard your words, he was wrathful and swore: 35 "Not one of these — not one of this evil generation — shall see the good land that I swore to give to your ancestors, 36 except Caleb son of Jephun-

1.16 Deut 16.18; Lev 24.22

1.17 Lev 19.15; Jas 2.1; Ex 18.19-26

1.19 v. 2; Deut 8.15; Num 13.26

1.21 Josh 1.9

1.23 Num 13.1-3

1.24 Num 13.22-24 **1.25** Num 13.27

1.26 Num 14.1-4 **1.27** Deut 9.28; Ps 106.25 **1.28** Num 13.28, 31-33; Deut 9.1, 2

1.30 Ex 14.14; Deut 3.22 **1.31** Deut 32.11, 12; Acts 13.18 **1.32** Ps 106.24 **1.33** Ex 13.21; Num 10.33 **1.34** Num 14.22-30

1.22 *Let us send men ahead of us.* Moses here blames the Israelites for wanting to send the spies into Canaan. Had they entered the land by faith, not sight, God would have given them the land forty years earlier.

1.26 *You were unwilling to go up.* By this time most — if not all — of those who had been condemned by God to die before entering the land of Cannan were gone from the scene. Yet Moses was addressing the present people of Israel as though they were in some way equally responsible for what happened, thus emphasizing the unity of the Israelite nation. Those who were young when the judgment of the forty years began shared in the same penalty and are now warned by Moses not to repeat their parents' sins. The sins of the parents will be visited on their children to the third and fourth generation, and each generation should be reminded that what parents do have consequences in the lives of their children.

1.28 *the cities are . . . fortified up to heaven.* The walls of the large Canaanite cities ranged from thirty to fifty feet in height.

1.30 Moses reassured Israel that God would go before them, leading them into Canaan and delivering them from their enemies. He reminded them of what God had done for them in Egypt. God continues to promise to go before us and prepare the way; he assures us that we will be safe from all enemies and delivered from all opposition. But this protection is conditional: we must walk by faith and put our trust in God.

1.36 Caleb and Joshua were the only two of their generation who entered the promised land, commended as people who maintained complete fidelity to the Lord. They were not perfect nor sinless, but they walked blamelessly before God in obedience to his command for Israel to enter Canaan.

1.37
Num 20.12;
Deut 3.26;
Ps 106.32
1.38
Num 14.30;
Deut 3.28;
31.7
1.39
Num 14.3, 31
1.40
Num 14.25
1.41
Num 14.40

1.42
Num 14.42

1.43
Num 14.44,
45
1.44
Ps 118.12

neh. He shall see it, and to him and to his descendants I will give the land on which he set foot, because of his complete fidelity to the LORD." 37 Even with me the LORD was angry on your account, saying, "You also shall not enter there. 38 Joshua son of Nun, your assistant, shall enter there; encourage him, for he is the one who will secure Israel's possession of it. 39 And as for your little ones, who you thought would become booty, your children, who today do not yet know right from wrong, they shall enter there; to them I will give it, and they shall take possession of it. 40 But as for you, journey back into the wilderness, in the direction of the Red Sea."[c]

41 You answered me, "We have sinned against the LORD! We are ready to go up and fight, just as the LORD our God commanded us." So all of you strapped on your battle gear, and thought it easy to go up into the hill country. 42 The LORD said to me, "Say to them, 'Do not go up and do not fight, for I am not in the midst of you; otherwise you will be defeated by your enemies.' " 43 Although I told you, you would not listen. You rebelled against the command of the LORD and presumptuously went up into the hill country. 44 The Amorites who lived in that hill country then came out against you and chased you as bees do. They beat you down in Seir as far as Hormah. 45 When you returned and wept before the LORD, the LORD would neither heed your voice nor pay you any attention.

C. The years in the wilderness

1. The command to leave the Edomites alone

2.1
Num 21.4

2.4
Num 20.14

2.5
Josh 24.4

2.7
Deut 8.2-4

2.8
Judg 11.18

46 After you had stayed at Kadesh as many days as you did, 2 1 we journeyed back into the wilderness, in the direction of the Red Sea,[c] as the LORD had told me and skirted Mount Seir for many days. 2 Then the LORD said to me: 3 "You have been skirting this hill country long enough. Head north, 4 and charge the people as follows: You are about to pass through the territory of your kindred, the descendants of Esau, who live in Seir. They will be afraid of you, so, be very careful 5 not to engage in battle with them, for I will not give you even so much as a foot's length of their land, since I have given Mount Seir to Esau as a possession. 6 You shall purchase food from them for money, so that you may eat; and you shall also buy water from them for money, so that you may drink. 7 Surely the LORD your God has blessed you in all your undertakings; he knows your going through this great wilderness. These forty years the LORD your God has been with you; you have lacked nothing." 8 So we passed by our kin, the descendants of Esau who live in Seir, leaving behind the route of the Arabah, and leaving behind Elath and Ezion-geber.

2. The command to leave the Moabites alone

2.9
v. 18;
Num 21.28;
Gen 19.36, 37
2.10ff
Gen 14.5;
Num 13.22,
33

When we had headed out along the route of the wilderness of Moab, 9 the LORD said to me: "Do not harass Moab or engage them in battle, for I will not give you any of its land as a possession, since I have given Ar as a possession to the descendants of Lot." 10 (The Emim—a large and numerous people, as tall as the Anakim—had formerly inhabited it.

[c] Or Sea of Reeds

1.43 Moses again and again reminded the people that they had failed because of their lack of faith and their refusal to obey the commands of God. God wants us to learn from their mistakes so that we will not suffer the same consequences.
2.4 *the descendants of of Esau . . . will be afraid of you.* God was concerned for the children of Esau, the brother of Jacob. The Israelites were to pass through

their land but leave them alone in safety. They were to trade with them honestly in their dealings. God commanded this despite the fact that Edom earlier refused them permission to cross their territory (Num 20.21).
2.9 See note on Gen 19.36 on the Moabites, who descended from Lot. God granted protection to them and Israel was to leave them alone.

11 Like the Anakim, they are usually reckoned as Rephaim, though the Moabites call them Emim. 12 Moreover, the Horim had formerly inhabited Seir, but the descendants of Esau dispossessed them, destroying them and settling in their place, as Israel has done in the land that the LORD gave them as a possession.) 13 "Now then, proceed to cross over the Wadi Zered."

So we crossed over the Wadi Zered. 14 And the length of time we had traveled from Kadesh-barnea until we crossed the Wadi Zered was thirty-eight years, until the entire generation of warriors had perished from the camp, as the LORD had sworn concerning them. 15 Indeed, the LORD's own hand was against them, to root them out from the camp, until all had perished.

3. The command to leave the Ammonites alone

16 Just as soon as all the warriors had died off from among the people, 17 the LORD spoke to me, saying, 18 "Today you are going to cross the boundary of Moab at Ar. 19 When you approach the frontier of the Ammonites, do not harass them or engage them in battle, for I will not give the land of the Ammonites to you as a possession, because I have given it to the descendants of Lot." 20 (It also is usually reckoned as a land of Rephaim. Rephaim formerly inhabited it, though the Ammonites call them Zamzummim, 21 a strong and numerous people, as tall as the Anakim. But the LORD destroyed them from before the Ammonites so that they could dispossess them and settle in their place. 22 He did the same for the descendants of Esau, who live in Seir, by destroying the Horim before them so that they could dispossess them and settle in their place even to this day. 23 As for the Avvim, who had lived in settlements in the vicinity of Gaza, the Caphtorim, who came from Caphtor, destroyed them and settled in their place.) 24 "Proceed on your journey and cross the Wadi Arnon. See, I have handed over to you King Sihon the Amorite of Heshbon, and his land. Begin to take possession by engaging him in battle. 25 This day I will begin to put the dread and fear of you upon the peoples everywhere under heaven; when they hear report of you, they will tremble and be in anguish because of you."

D. The victories over the Amorites

1. Over King Sihon of Heshbon

26 So I sent messengers from the wilderness of Kedemoth to King Sihon of Heshbon with the following terms of peace: 27 "If you let me pass through your land, I will travel only along the road; I will turn aside neither to the right nor to the left. 28 You shall sell me food for money, so that I may eat, and supply me water for money, so that I may drink. Only allow me to pass through on foot — 29 just as the descendants of Esau who live in Seir have done for me and likewise the Moabites who live in Ar — until I cross the Jordan into the land that the LORD our God is giving us." 30 But King Sihon of Heshbon was not willing to let us pass through, for the LORD your God had hardened his spirit and made his heart defiant in order to hand him over to you, as he has now done.

31 The LORD said to me, "See, I have begun to give Sihon and his land over to you. Begin now to take possession of his land." 32 So when

2.12
v. 22

2.14
Num 13.26;
14.29-35;
26.64;
Deut 1.34, 35
2.15
Ps 106.26

2.19
v. 9

2.21
see v. 10
2.22
Gen 36.8;
v. 12
2.23
Josh 13.3;
Gen 10.14;
Am 9.7
2.24
Judg 11.18

2.25
Ex 15.14, 15;
Deut 11.25;
Josh 2.9, 10

2.26
Deut 20.10
2.27
Num 21.21,
22
2.28
Num 20.19

2.30
Num 21.23
2.31
Deut 1.8
2.32
Num 21.23,
24;
Deut 7.2;
20.16

2.19 The Ammonites, also descended from Lot, were likewise given divine protection; Israel was required to leave them alone.
2.23 Caphtor, the island of Crete.
2.25 Israel was commanded to go into the land and begin to possess it. But God also promised that, in his sovereignty, he would work among the enemies of Israel, terrifying and dispiriting them. Thus the divine power would work for Israel even though it was weaker than its enemies, and Israel would be victorious. In our battle against Satan we must look to God, not at the strongest enemy. No enemy can withstand those clothed with God's power.
2.30 the LORD your God had hardened his spirit. See note on Ex 4.21.

Sihon came out against us, he and all his people for battle at Jahaz, 33 the LORD our God gave him over to us; and we struck him down, along with his offspring and all his people. 34 At that time we captured all his towns, and in each town we utterly destroyed men, women, and children. We left not a single survivor. 35 Only the livestock we kept as spoil for ourselves, as well as the plunder of the towns that we had captured. 36 From Aroer on the edge of the Wadi Arnon (including the town that is in the wadi itself) as far as Gilead, there was no citadel too high for us. The LORD our God gave everything to us. 37 You did not encroach, however, on the land of the Ammonites, avoiding the whole upper region of the Wadi Jabbok as well as the towns of the hill country, just as*d* the LORD our God had charged.

2. Over King Og of Bashan

3 When we headed up the road to Bashan, King Og of Bashan came out against us, he and all his people, for battle at Edrei. 2 The LORD said to me, "Do not fear him, for I have handed him over to you, along with his people and his land. Do to him as you did to King Sihon of the Amorites, who reigned in Heshbon." 3 So the LORD our God also handed over to us King Og of Bashan and all his people. We struck him down until not a single survivor was left. 4 At that time we captured all his towns; there was no citadel that we did not take from them—sixty towns, the whole region of Argob, the kingdom of Og in Bashan. 5 All these were fortress towns with high walls, double gates, and bars, besides a great many villages. 6 And we utterly destroyed them, as we had done to King Sihon of Heshbon, in each city utterly destroying men, women, and children. 7 But all the livestock and the plunder of the towns we kept as spoil for ourselves.

3. The distribution of the land

8 So at that time we took from the two kings of the Amorites the land beyond the Jordan, from the Wadi Arnon to Mount Hermon 9 (the Sidonians call Hermon Sirion, while the Amorites call it Senir), 10 all the towns of the tableland, the whole of Gilead, and all of Bashan, as far as Salecah and Edrei, towns of Og's kingdom in Bashan. 11 (Now only King Og of Bashan was left of the remnant of the Rephaim. In fact his bed, an iron bed, can still be seen in Rabbah of the Ammonites. By the common cubit it is nine cubits long and four cubits wide.) 12 As for the land that we took possession of at that time, I gave to the Reubenites and Gadites the territory north of Aroer,*e* that is on the edge of the Wadi Arnon, as well as half the hill country of Gilead with its towns, 13 and I gave to the half-tribe of Manasseh the rest of Gilead and all of Bashan, Og's kingdom. (The whole region of Argob: all that portion of Bashan used to be called a land of Rephaim; 14 Jair the Manassite acquired the whole region of Argob as far as the border of the Geshurites and the Maacathites, and he named them—that is, Bashan—after himself, Havvoth-jair,*f* as it is to this day.) 15 To Machir I gave Gilead. 16 And to the Reubenites and the Gadites I gave the territory from Gilead as far as the Wadi Arnon, with the middle of the wadi as a boundary, and up to the Jabbok, the wadi being boundary of the Ammonites; 17 the Arabah also, with the Jordan and its

Marginal references (left column):

2.34
Deut 3.6

2.36
Deut 3.12;
4.48;
Ps 44.3

2.37
Num 21.24

3.1
Num 21.33-35
3.2
Num 21.34

3.3
Num 21.35

3.4
1 Kings 4.13

3.6
Deut 2.24, 34

3.9
Ps 29.6

3.11
Am 2.9;
Gen 14.5;
2 Sam 12.26;
Jer 49.2
3.12
Deut 2.36;
Num 32.32-38;
Josh 13.8-13

3.14
Num 32.41;
1 Chr 2.22

3.15
Num 32.39,
40

3.17
Num 34.11;
Josh 13.27

---

d Gk Tg: Heb *and all*   *e* Heb *territory from Aroer*   *f* That is *Settlement of Jair*

2.34 *We left not a single survivor.* This practice was called *herem* ("devoted to destruction"). Israel's enemies and their possessions were devoted to Yahweh. The males, and in some cases the females and children, were slain and the cities destroyed. The loot was divided among the victors.

3.1 Og of Bashan was a giant who may have been nine or more feet tall. He was bold and daring, yet God gave the Israelites victory over him so that the Reubenites and Gadites could have that land (v. 12).
3.17 *Chinnereth,* Lake Gennesarat, or Sea of Galilee.

banks, from Chinnereth down to the sea of the Arabah, the Dead Sea,[g] with the lower slopes of Pisgah on the east.

18 At that time, I charged you as follows: "Although the LORD your God has given you this land to occupy, all your troops shall cross over armed as the vanguard of your Israelite kin. 19 Only your wives, your children, and your livestock—I know that you have much livestock—shall stay behind in the towns that I have given to you. 20 When the LORD gives rest to your kindred, as to you, and they too have occupied the land that the LORD your God is giving them beyond the Jordan, then each of you may return to the property that I have given to you." 21 And I charged Joshua as well at that time, saying: "Your own eyes have seen everything that the LORD your God has done to these two kings; so the LORD will do to all the kingdoms into which you are about to cross. 22 Do not fear them, for it is the LORD your God who fights for you."

4. Moses forbidden to cross the Jordan

23 At that time, too, I entreated the LORD, saying: 24 "O Lord GOD, you have only begun to show your servant your greatness and your might; what god in heaven or on earth can perform deeds and mighty acts like yours! 25 Let me cross over to see the good land beyond the Jordan, that good hill country and the Lebanon." 26 But the LORD was angry with me on your account and would not heed me. The LORD said to me, "Enough from you! Never speak to me of this matter again! 27 Go up to the top of Pisgah and look around you to the west, to the north, to the south, and to the east. Look well, for you shall not cross over this Jordan. 28 But charge Joshua, and encourage and strengthen him, because it is he who shall cross over at the head of this people and who shall secure their possession of the land that you will see." 29 So we remained in the valley opposite Beth-peor.

E. The exhortation of Moses

1. The command to obedience

4 So now, Israel, give heed to the statutes and ordinances that I am teaching you to observe, so that you may live to enter and occupy the land that the LORD, the God of your ancestors, is giving you. 2 You must neither add anything to what I command you nor take away anything from it, but keep the commandments of the LORD your God with which I am charging you. 3 You have seen for yourselves what the LORD did with regard to the Baal of Peor—how the LORD your God destroyed from among you everyone who followed the Baal of Peor, 4 while those of you who held fast to the LORD your God are all alive today.

5 See, just as the LORD my God has charged me, I now teach you statutes and ordinances for you to observe in the land that you are about to enter and occupy. 6 You must observe them diligently, for this will show your wisdom and discernment to the peoples, who, when they hear all these statutes, will say, "Surely this great nation is a wise and discerning people!" 7 For what other great nation has a god so near to it as the LORD

[g] Heb Salt Sea

3.18 Num 32.20

3.20 Josh 22.4

3.22 Deut 1.30

3.24 Ex 15.11; Ps 86.8

3.26 Deut 1.37; 31.2
3.27 Num 27.12

3.28 Num 27.18, 23; Deut 31.3, 7
3.29 Deut 4.46; 34.6

4.1 Deut 5.33; 8.1; 16.20; 30.16, 19
4.2 Deut 12.32; Josh 1.7; Rev 22.18, 19
4.3 Num 25.4; Ps 106.28, 29

4.6 Deut 30.19, 20; 32.46, 47
4.7 2 Sam 7.23; Ps 46.1; Isa 55.6

3.21 Israelite victories over the two kings mentioned here should encourage the hearts of the Israelites, because God promised that he would do the same to their enemies in Canaan.
3.25 God had previously told Moses that he would not be permitted to enter the land of Canaan. In spite of that, Moses prayed that God would allow him to do so. In analogous situations Moses had prevailed with God and the circumstances had been reversed. Here, though, God told him to ask no more. Although he

was never allowed to walk in Canaan, Moses was allowed to climb the mountain and observe the land (v. 27). Thus God in judgment often remembers mercy.
4.2 Here and elsewhere we are warned against adding to or taking away from the word of God. To commit such an act is a grievous breach against the Lawgiver and represents the ever-dangerous course of judging God.
4.7,8 Moses extols the greatness of God, declaring

our God is whenever we call to him? 8 And what other great nation has statutes and ordinances as just as this entire law that I am setting before you today?

9 But take care and watch yourselves closely, so as neither to forget the things that your eyes have seen nor to let them slip from your mind all the days of your life; make them known to your children and your children's children — 10 how you once stood before the LORD your God at Horeb, when the LORD said to me, "Assemble the people for me, and I will let them hear my words, so that they may learn to fear me as long as they live on the earth, and may teach their children so"; 11 you approached and stood at the foot of the mountain while the mountain was blazing up to the very heavens, shrouded in dark clouds. 12 Then the LORD spoke to you out of the fire. You heard the sound of words but saw no form; there was only a voice. 13 He declared to you his covenant, which he charged you to observe, that is, the ten commandments;*h* and he wrote them on two stone tablets. 14 And the LORD charged me at that time to teach you statutes and ordinances for you to observe in the land that you are about to cross into and occupy.

2. Idolatry forbidden

15 Since you saw no form when the LORD spoke to you at Horeb out of the fire, take care and watch yourselves closely, 16 so that you do not act corruptly by making an idol for yourselves, in the form of any figure — the likeness of male or female, 17 the likeness of any animal that is on the earth, the likeness of any winged bird that flies in the air, 18 the likeness of anything that creeps on the ground, the likeness of any fish that is in the water under the earth. 19 And when you look up to the heavens and see the sun, the moon, and the stars, all the host of heaven, do not be led astray and bow down to them and serve them, things that the LORD your God has allotted to all the peoples everywhere under heaven. 20 But the LORD has taken you and brought you out of the iron-smelter, out of Egypt, to become a people of his very own possession, as you are now.

21 The LORD was angry with me because of you, and he vowed that I should not cross the Jordan and that I should not enter the good land that the LORD your God is giving for your possession. 22 For I am going to die in this land without crossing over the Jordan, but you are going to cross over to take possession of that good land. 23 So be careful not to forget the covenant that the LORD your God made with you, and not to make for yourselves an idol in the form of anything that the LORD your God has forbidden you. 24 For the LORD your God is a devouring fire, a jealous God.

25 When you have had children and children's children, and become complacent in the land, if you act corruptly by making an idol in the form of anything, thus doing what is evil in the sight of the LORD your God, and provoking him to anger, 26 I call heaven and earth to witness against you today that you will soon utterly perish from the land that you are crossing the Jordan to occupy; you will not live long on it, but will be utterly destroyed. 27 The LORD will scatter you among the peoples; only a few of you will be left among the nations where the LORD will lead you.

h Heb *the ten words*

4.9
Prov 4.23;
Gen 18.19;
Deut 6.7;
11.19;
Ps 78.5, 6;
Eph 6.4
4.10
Ex 19.9, 16
4.11
Ex 19.18;
Heb 12.18,
19
4.12
Deut 5.4, 22;
Ex 20.22
4.13
Deut 9.9, 11;
Ex 34.28;
24.12; 31.18

4.16
Ex 32.7;
20.4, 5;
Deut 5.8

4.19
Deut 17.3;
2 Kings 17.16;
Rom 1.25
4.20
1 Kings 8.51;
Jer 11.4;
Deut 9.29
4.21
Deut 1.37
4.22
Deut 3.25, 27
4.23
vv. 9, 16;
Ex 20.4, 5
4.24
Ex 24.17;
Deut 9.3;
Heb 12.29;
Deut 6.15
4.25
vv. 16, 23;
2 Kings 17.17
4.26
Deut 30.18,
19
4.27
Deut 28.62,
64

that none of the other nations have statutes or ordinances equal to those given to Israel by God through divine revelation. God's moral law is still part of life today and keeping or breaking it will enable a nation to survive or go down in defeat.
4.15 *you saw no form.* God is spirit and is nonmaterial.
4.20 *brought you out of the iron-smelter,* i.e., rescued you from prison (see Jer 11.4).

4.25–31 Moses warns Israel about the consequences of disobedience. God will surely judge and chastise whoever disobeys him. But if and when they repent, God will be merciful. According to v. 29, God will not seek transgressors; they must seek him. When they do so with all their heart, they will find God. In other words, the first step toward reconciliation with God must come from the offender, not the offended.

28 There you will serve other gods made by human hands, objects of wood
and stone that neither see, nor hear, nor eat, nor smell. 29 From there you
will seek the LORD your God, and you will find him if you search after
him with all your heart and soul. 30 In your distress, when all these things
have happened to you in time to come, you will return to the LORD your
God and heed him. 31 Because the LORD your God is a merciful God, he
will neither abandon you nor destroy you; he will not forget the covenant
with your ancestors that he swore to them.

3. The special relation of Israel as a chosen nation

32   For ask now about former ages, long before your own, ever since
the day that God created human beings on the earth; ask from one end
of heaven to the other: has anything so great as this ever happened or has
its like ever been heard of? 33 Has any people ever heard the voice of a
god speaking out of a fire, as you have heard, and lived? 34 Or has any
god ever attempted to go and take a nation for himself from the midst of
another nation, by trials, by signs and wonders, by war, by a mighty hand
and an outstretched arm, and by terrifying displays of power, as the LORD
your God did for you in Egypt before your very eyes? 35 To you it was
shown so that you would acknowledge that the LORD is God; there is no
other besides him. 36 From heaven he made you hear his voice to discipline
you. On earth he showed you his great fire, while you heard his words
coming out of the fire. 37 And because he loved your ancestors, he chose
their descendants after them. He brought you out of Egypt with his own
presence, by his great power, 38 driving out before you nations greater and
mightier than yourselves, to bring you in, giving you their land for a
possession, as it is still today. 39 So acknowledge today and take to heart
that the LORD is God in heaven above and on the earth beneath; there is
no other. 40 Keep his statutes and his commandments, which I am commanding you today for your own well-being and that of your descendants
after you, so that you may long remain in the land that the LORD your God
is giving you for all time.

F. The cities of refuge

41   Then Moses set apart on the east side of the Jordan three cities 42 to
which a homicide could flee, someone who unintentionally kills another
person, the two not having been at enmity before; the homicide could flee
to one of these cities and live: 43 Bezer in the wilderness on the tableland
belonging to the Reubenites, Ramoth in Gilead belonging to the Gadites,
and Golan in Bashan belonging to the Manassites.

II. Moses' second address (4.44–26.19)

A. Introduction

44   This is the law that Moses set before the Israelites. 45 These are the
decrees and the statutes and ordinances that Moses spoke to the Israelites
when they had come out of Egypt, 46 beyond the Jordan in the valley
opposite Beth-peor, in the land of King Sihon of the Amorites, who
reigned at Heshbon, whom Moses and the Israelites defeated when they
came out of Egypt. 47 They occupied his land and the land of King Og
of Bashan, the two kings of the Amorites on the eastern side of the Jordan:
48 from Aroer, which is on the edge of the Wadi Arnon, as far as Mount

4.28 Deut 28.64; 1 Sam 26.19; Ps 115.4, 5
4.29 Deut 30.1-3; 2 Chr 15.4; Isa 55.6, 7; Jer 29.12-14
4.31 2 Chr 30.9; Ps 116.5
4.32 Deut 32.7; Gen 1.27; Deut 28.64
4.33 Ex 20.22; Deut 5.24, 26
4.34 Deut 7.19; Ex 7.3; 13.3; 6.6; Deut 26.8; 34.12
4.35 Deut 32.39; 1 Sam 2.2; Isa 45.5, 18; Mk 12.29
4.36 Ex 19.9, 19; Heb 12.18
4.37 Deut 10.15; Ex 13.3, 9, 14
4.38 Deut 7.1; 9.1, 4, 5
4.39 v. 35; Josh 2.11
4.40 Lev 22.31; Deut 5.16, 29, 33; Eph 6.2, 3
4.41 Num 35.6
4.46 Deut 3.29; Num 21.21-25
4.48 Deut 2.36; 3.12

4.33,34 God performed signs and wonders for Israel
such as no other nation had experienced. By this
extrinsic evidence their faith should have been
strengthened, and they could look to the future with
expectation, knowing that God could and would show

himself strong on behalf of his people.
4.35 There is only one God who has unchanging
attributes. There is no one else like him. By acknowledging him and obeying his commandments, God's
people advance their own well-being (v. 40).

Sirion[i] (that is, Hermon), 49 together with all the Arabah on the east side of the Jordan as far as the Sea of the Arabah, under the slopes of Pisgah.

B. The covenant: the Ten Commandments

1. The commandments stated

5 Moses convened all Israel, and said to them:
Hear, O Israel, the statutes and ordinances that I am addressing to you today; you shall learn them and observe them diligently. 2 The LORD our God made a covenant with us at Horeb. 3 Not with our ancestors did the LORD make this covenant, but with us, who are all of us here alive today. 4 The LORD spoke with you face to face at the mountain, out of the fire. 5 (At that time I was standing between the LORD and you to declare to you the words[j] of the LORD; for you were afraid because of the fire and did not go up the mountain.) And he said:

6 I am the LORD your God, who brought you out of the land of Egypt, out of the house of slavery; 7 you shall have no other gods before[k] me.

8 You shall not make for yourself an idol, whether in the form of anything that is in heaven above, or that is on the earth beneath, or that is in the water under the earth. 9 You shall not bow down to them or worship them; for I the LORD your God am a jealous God, punishing children for the iniquity of parents, to the third and fourth generation of those who reject me, 10 but showing steadfast love to the thousandth generation[l] of those who love me and keep my commandments.

11 You shall not make wrongful use of the name of the LORD your God, for the LORD will not acquit anyone who misuses his name.

12 Observe the sabbath day and keep it holy, as the LORD your God commanded you. 13 Six days you shall labor and do all your work. 14 But the seventh day is a sabbath to the LORD your God; you shall not do any work — you, or your son or your daughter, or your male or female slave, or your ox or your donkey, or any of your livestock, or the resident alien in your towns, so that your male and female slave may rest as well as you. 15 Remember that you were a slave in the land of Egypt, and the LORD your God brought you out from there with a mighty hand and an outstretched arm; therefore the LORD your God commanded you to keep the sabbath day.

16 Honor your father and your mother, as the LORD your God commanded you, so that your days may be long and that it may go well with you in the land that the LORD your God is giving you.

17 You shall not murder.[m]
18 Neither shall you commit adultery.
19 Neither shall you steal.
20 Neither shall you bear false witness against your neighbor.
21 Neither shall you covet your neighbor's wife.
Neither shall you desire your neighbor's house, or field, or male or female slave, or ox, or donkey, or anything that belongs to your neighbor.

2. God and Moses at Sinai

22 These words the LORD spoke with a loud voice to your whole

Cross references (left margin):
5.2 Ex 19.5
5.4 Ex 19.9, 19; Deut 4.33, 36
5.5 Ex 20.18, 21
5.6 Ex 20.2-17
5.9 Ex 34.7
5.10 Jer 32.18
5.14 Gen 2.2; Ex 16.29, 30
5.15 Deut 15.16; 4.34, 37
5.21 Rom 7.7; 13.9
5.22 Ex 31.18; Deut 4.13

i Syr: Heb *Sion*   *j* Q Mss Sam Gk Syr Vg Tg: MT *word*   *k* Or *besides*   *l* Or *to thousands*   *m* Or *kill*

5.6 Moses reiterated for Israel the ten commandments, given years ago to the parents of the present generation (see Ex 20). They had to recall them and understand the implications. For example, Moses gave an added interpretation of the tenth commandment about coveting. He included the fields they were to inherit, such as they had not owned for centuries. 5.9,10 *a jealous God.* See note on Ex 34.14.

5.12 *Observe,* whereas Ex 20.8 says, "Remember." 5.15 In Ex 20.11 the sabbath is said to be a creation ordinance. Here Moses has added another reason for keeping the sabbath — Israel's deliverance from slavery in Egypt. 5.16 *as the LORD your God commanded you.* In slightly different ways, this significant phrase is used throughout Deuteronomy.

assembly at the mountain, out of the fire, the cloud, and the thick darkness, and he added no more. He wrote them on two stone tablets, and gave them to me. 23 When you heard the voice out of the darkness, while the mountain was burning with fire, you approached me, all the heads of your tribes and your elders; 24 and you said, "Look, the LORD our God has shown us his glory and greatness, and we have heard his voice out of the fire. Today we have seen that God may speak to someone and the person may still live. 25 So now why should we die? For this great fire will consume us; if we hear the voice of the LORD our God any longer, we shall die. 26 For who is there of all flesh that has heard the voice of the living God speaking out of fire, as we have, and remained alive? 27 Go near, you yourself, and hear all that the LORD our God will say. Then tell us everything that the LORD our God tells you, and we will listen and do it."

28   The LORD heard your words when you spoke to me, and the LORD said to me: "I have heard the words of this people, which they have spoken to you; they are right in all that they have spoken. 29 If only they had such a mind as this, to fear me and to keep all my commandments always, so that it might go well with them and with their children forever! 30 Go say to them, 'Return to your tents.' 31 But you, stand here by me, and I will tell you all the commandments, the statutes and the ordinances, that you shall teach them, so that they may do them in the land that I am giving them to possess." 32 You must therefore be careful to do as the LORD your God has commanded you; you shall not turn to the right or to the left. 33 You must follow exactly the path that the LORD your God has commanded you, so that you may live, and that it may go well with you, and that you may live long in the land that you are to possess.

3. The purpose of the law

6 Now this is the commandment — the statutes and the ordinances — that the LORD your God charged me to teach you to observe in the land that you are about to cross into and occupy, 2 so that you and your children and your children's children may fear the LORD your God all the days of your life, and keep all his decrees and his commandments that I am commanding you, so that your days may be long. 3 Hear therefore, O Israel, and observe them diligently, so that it may go well with you, and so that you may multiply greatly in a land flowing with milk and honey, as the LORD, the God of your ancestors, has promised you.

4. The law of love

4   Hear, O Israel: The LORD is our God, the LORD alone.[n] 5 You shall love the LORD your God with all your heart, and with all your soul, and with all your might. 6 Keep these words that I am commanding you today in your heart. 7 Recite them to your children and talk about them when you are at home and when you are away, when you lie down and when

[n] Or The LORD our God is one LORD, or The LORD our God, the LORD is one, or The LORD is our God, the LORD is one

Cross references (right column):

5.24
Ex 19.19

5.25
Deut 18.16

5.26
Deut 4.33

5.28
Deut 18.17

5.29
Ps 81.13;
Isa 48.18;
Deut 4.40

5.31
Ex 24.12

5.32
Deut 17.20;
28.14;
Josh 1.7; 23.6
5.33
Deut 4.40

6.2
Ex 20.20;
Deut 10.12,
13

6.3
Deut 5.33;
Gen 15.5;
Ex 3.8

6.4ff
Mk 12.29,
32;
Jn 17.3;
1 Cor 8.4, 6
6.5
Deut 10.12;
Mt 22.37;
Lk 10.27
6.7
Deut 4.9;
Eph 6.4

5.23 *while the mountain was burning with fire*, cf. 4.24, "For the LORD your God is a devouring fire," and 5.24, "we have heard his voice out of the fire." Throughout the Scriptures fire is connected with God. Here it is not clear whether there was a literal fire on the mountain or if the presence of God was an appearance of fire. In any case, the Israelites accepted the fact that "this great fire will consume us" (5.25) if God so chose.
5.33 It was highly advantageous for Israel to walk in all the ways God had commanded. Blessing attends obedience.
6.4–9 The Jews still make a practice of repeating what they call the *Shema* ("hear") twice daily. These

verses speak of the unity of the Godhead. Christians agree that God is one in essence, but insist that the Godhead subsists in three persons — the Father, the Son, and the Holy Spirit. This is a tri-unity, for God is one yet three. This is a great mystery. It has been said that those who try to understand the Trinity will lose their minds; but those who deny the Trinity will lose their souls (see also note on 2 Cor 13.13).
6.5 The first table of the law is to love God with our whole hearts. Since "heart" in the O.T. was considered the seat of the intellect, Jesus added the interpretation that we must love God with our minds (see Mk 12.30 and Lk 10.27).

6.8
Ex 13.9, 16;
Deut 11.18
6.9
Deut 11.20
6.10
Deut 9.1;
Josh 24.13
6.11
Deut 8.10

6.13
Deut 10.20

6.15
Deut 4.24

6.16
Mt 4.7;
Ex 17.2, 7
6.17
Deut 11.22
6.18
Deut 4.40

6.20
Ex 13.14

6.24
Deut 10.12
6.25
Deut 24.13

7.1
Deut 31.3;
Acts 13.19

7.2
Ex 23.32;
Deut 13.8

you rise. 8 Bind them as a sign on your hand, fix them as an emblem[o] on your forehead, 9 and write them on the doorposts of your house and on your gates.

10   When the LORD your God has brought you into the land that he swore to your ancestors, to Abraham, to Isaac, and to Jacob, to give you—a land with fine, large cities that you did not build, 11 houses filled with all sorts of goods that you did not fill, hewn cisterns that you did not hew, vineyards and olive groves that you did not plant—and when you have eaten your fill, 12 take care that you do not forget the LORD, who brought you out of the land of Egypt, out of the house of slavery. 13 The LORD your God you shall fear; him you shall serve, and by his name alone you shall swear. 14 Do not follow other gods, any of the gods of the peoples who are all around you, 15 because the LORD your God, who is present with you, is a jealous God. The anger of the LORD your God would be kindled against you and he would destroy you from the face of the earth.

16   Do not put the LORD your God to the test, as you tested him at Massah. 17 You must diligently keep the commandments of the LORD your God, and his decrees, and his statutes that he has commanded you. 18 Do what is right and good in the sight of the LORD, so that it may go well with you, and so that you may go in and occupy the good land that the LORD swore to your ancestors to give you, 19 thrusting out all your enemies from before you, as the LORD has promised.

5. Explaining the law to their children

20   When your children ask you in time to come, "What is the meaning of the decrees and the statutes and the ordinances that the LORD our God has commanded you?" 21 then you shall say to your children, "We were Pharaoh's slaves in Egypt, but the LORD brought us out of Egypt with a mighty hand. 22 The LORD displayed before our eyes great and awesome signs and wonders against Egypt, against Pharaoh and all his household. 23 He brought us out from there in order to bring us in, to give us the land that he promised on oath to our ancestors. 24 Then the LORD commanded us to observe all these statutes, to fear the LORD our God, for our lasting good, so as to keep us alive, as is now the case. 25 If we diligently observe this entire commandment before the LORD our God, as he has commanded us, we will be in the right."

6. Extermination of the Canaanites

a. The evils of idolatry

7 When the LORD your God brings you into the land that you are about to enter and occupy, and he clears away many nations before you— the Hittites, the Girgashites, the Amorites, the Canaanites, the Perizzites, the Hivites, and the Jebusites, seven nations mightier and more numerous than you— 2 and when the LORD your God gives them over to you and

o Or as a frontlet

6.13 *by his name alone you shall swear,* i.e., they must never appeal to any other person as the discerner of truth and avenger of wrong. In courts today people take an oath on the Bible to tell the truth. In so doing, they swear by God's name. Such an oath must be taken with utmost seriousness.
6.16 For Israel's testing of God at Massah, see Ex 17.1–7. There should be no circumstance or exigency which causes us to show distrust of the power, presence, or providence of God. Nor are we to quarrel with him. Simple, unquestioning faith is required of us.
7.2 God commanded the extermination of the Canaanites. Some people are horrified by this and either repudiate the God who ordered it or argue that the

Israelites erroneously believed God had commanded them to do this. How can such a command be harmonized with a God of love and mercy? The God of the O.T. and of the N.T. is the same. He is unchanging. No one can deny that God is purported to have commanded his people to slay their enemies. If the Bible is not true at this point, the door is opened to making the Bible questionable at almost any other point. And note that God has also stated that he will cast unbelievers into the lake of fire at the end of the age. If God can judge human beings at the end of the age he can also judge them before that time. He is a God of justice as well as a God of love and mercy. Life would make no sense if God did not show both his love for his own moral order and his respect for the principles

you defeat them, then you must utterly destroy them. Make no covenant with them and show them no mercy. 3 Do not intermarry with them, giving your daughters to their sons or taking their daughters for your sons, 4 for that would turn away your children from following me, to serve other gods. Then the anger of the LORD would be kindled against you, and he would destroy you quickly. 5 But this is how you must deal with them: break down their altars, smash their pillars, hew down their sacred poles,ᵖ and burn their idols with fire. 6 For you are a people holy to the LORD your God; the LORD your God has chosen you out of all the peoples on earth to be his people, his treasured possession.

b. The special status of Israel

7 It was not because you were more numerous than any other people that the LORD set his heart on you and chose you — for you were the fewest of all peoples. 8 It was because the LORD loved you and kept the oath that he swore to your ancestors, that the LORD has brought you out with a mighty hand, and redeemed you from the house of slavery, from the land of Pharaoh king of Egypt. 9 Know therefore that the LORD your God is God, the faithful God who maintains covenant loyalty with those who love him and keep his commandments, to a thousand generations, 10 and who repays in their own person those who reject him. He does not delay but repays in their own person those who reject him. 11 Therefore, observe diligently the commandment — the statutes and the ordinances — that I am commanding you today.

12 If you heed these ordinances, by diligently observing them, the LORD your God will maintain with you the covenant loyalty that he swore to your ancestors; 13 he will love you, bless you, and multiply you; he will bless the fruit of your womb and the fruit of your ground, your grain and your wine and your oil, the increase of your cattle and the issue of your flock, in the land that he swore to your ancestors to give you. 14 You shall be the most blessed of peoples, with neither sterility nor barrenness among you or your livestock. 15 The LORD will turn away from you every illness; all the dread diseases of Egypt that you experienced, he will not inflict on you, but he will lay them on all who hate you. 16 You shall devour all the peoples that the LORD your God is giving over to you, showing them no pity; you shall not serve their gods, for that would be a snare to you.

c. God is greater than the Canaanites: Israel need not fear

17 If you say to yourself, "These nations are more numerous than I; how can I dispossess them?" 18 do not be afraid of them. Just remember what the LORD your God did to Pharaoh and to all Egypt, 19 the great trials that your eyes saw, the signs and wonders, the mighty hand and the outstretched arm by which the LORD your God brought you out. The LORD your God will do the same to all the peoples of whom you are afraid.

ᵖ Heb Asherim

Cross references (right margin):

7.3 Ex 34.15, 16
7.4 Deut 6.15
7.5 Ex 23.24
7.6 Ex 19.5, 6; Deut 14.2
7.7 Deut 10.22
7.8 Deut 10.15; Ex 32.13; 13.3, 14
7.9 Deut 4.35, 39; Neh 1.5
7.12 Lev 26.3; Deut 28.1; Ps 105.8, 9
7.13 Deut 28.4
7.14 Ex 23.26
7.15 Ex 15.26
7.16 v. 2; Ex 23.33
7.18 Deut 31.6
7.19 Deut 4.34

---

of justice and retribution. God cannot love evil nor can he protect wickedness. In O.T. times the wickedness of the Canaanite nations had reached the point of no return. The long-suffering God had suffered long enough and the day of judgment was at hand for them. God used Israel as the agents of his retribution. Surely judgment in time is no worse than judgment in eternity.

7.3,5 Moses points out the unfortunate consequences of intermarriage of believers with unbelievers. Even though it is theoretically possible for an unsaved partner to become a Christian, it is also possible (and it all too often happens) that a believer leaves the faith to worship other gods or no gods at all.

7.6 *a people holy to the LORD.* Because Israel was a

holy (separated) people, chosen by God, they were to utterly destroy the peoples of Canaan (v. 2), lest they be defiled by them or be seduced to worship their idols.

7.13,14 God promises his people that his blessings will fall on them if they obey him. The earth will be blessed, their cattle bring forth young, and the people themselves not be barren. These promises belong as much to God's people today. And the condition for this blessing is unchanged — we must love God and keep his commandments (cf. vv. 9,10).

7.17 Moses warns Israel that when circumstances look bad to them, they must remember that God will deliver them, despite the apparent difficulties. However bad the circumstances, it is always too soon to quit.

7.20
Ex 23.28;
Josh 24.12
7.21
Deut 10.17
7.22
Ex 23.29, 30

7.24
v. 16

7.25
1 Chr 14.12;
Josh 7.1, 21;
Judg 8.27

20 Moreover, the LORD your God will send the pestilence[q] against them, until even the survivors and the fugitives are destroyed. 21 Have no dread of them, for the LORD your God, who is present with you, is a great and awesome God. 22 The LORD your God will clear away these nations before you little by little; you will not be able to make a quick end of them, otherwise the wild animals would become too numerous for you. 23 But the LORD your God will give them over to you, and throw them into great panic, until they are destroyed. 24 He will hand their kings over to you and you shall blot out their name from under heaven; no one will be able to stand against you, until you have destroyed them. 25 The images of their gods you shall burn with fire. Do not covet the silver or the gold that is on them and take it for yourself, because you could be ensnared by it; for it is abhorrent to the LORD your God. 26 Do not bring an abhorrent thing into your house, or you will be set apart for destruction like it. You must utterly detest and abhor it, for it is set apart for destruction.

7. Moses' reminder of God's past mercies

a. Wilderness mercies

8.1
Deut 4.1

8.2
Deut 29.5;
13.3

8.3
Ex 16.2, 3;
12, 14, 35;
Mt 4.4;
Lk 4.7
8.4
Deut 29.5
8.5
Prov 3.12;
Heb 12.5, 6
8.6
Deut 5.33
8.7
Deut 11.10-12

8.10
Deut 6.11, 12

8 This entire commandment that I command you today you must diligently observe, so that you may live and increase, and go in and occupy the land that the LORD promised on oath to your ancestors. 2 Remember the long way that the LORD your God has led you these forty years in the wilderness, in order to humble you, testing you to know what was in your heart, whether or not you would keep his commandments. 3 He humbled you by letting you hunger, then by feeding you with manna, with which neither you nor your ancestors were acquainted, in order to make you understand that one does not live by bread alone, but by every word that comes from the mouth of the LORD.[r] 4 The clothes on your back did not wear out and your feet did not swell these forty years. 5 Know then in your heart that as a parent disciplines a child so the LORD your God disciplines you. 6 Therefore keep the commandments of the LORD your God, by walking in his ways and by fearing him. 7 For the LORD your God is bringing you into a good land, a land with flowing streams, with springs and underground waters welling up in valleys and hills, 8 a land of wheat and barley, of vines and fig trees and pomegranates, a land of olive trees and honey, 9 a land where you may eat bread without scarcity, where you will lack nothing, a land whose stones are iron and from whose hills you may mine copper. 10 You shall eat your fill and bless the LORD your God for the good land that he has given you.

b. Admonition against pride

11 Take care that you do not forget the LORD your God, by failing to keep his commandments, his ordinances, and his statutes, which I am commanding you today. 12 When you have eaten your fill and have built fine houses and live in them, 13 and when your herds and flocks have

q Or hornets: Meaning of Heb uncertain   r Or by anything that the LORD decrees

7.22 Israel would need to take time to clear Canaan of the wicked nations, lest the land be overrun with animals. Even after the defeat of the enemy, the Israelites would still have much work ahead of them in the management of the land and the reestablishment of a viable economy.
7.25 Images with silver and gold content are especially dangerous because of their intrinsic value. Moses warned against them and ordered such images destroyed because they were abominable and detestable in the sight of God.
8.3 one does not live by bread alone. Even more important than physical needs are the spiritual needs of people. Jesus used this Scripture to answer Satan in

his first temptation, prefacing it with, "It is written" (Mt 4.4). For him, that settled the matter. Whatever is written is true, good, and worthy of our attention and devotion.
8.9 iron and . . . copper. This has been confirmed by archaeologists in the great rift of the Arabah, south of the Dead Sea.
8.12ff Affluence is a powerful addiction, causing people to forget the God who gave them all they have. Poverty among believers is apt to cause them to concentrate on spiritual things and to look to God for the supply of material wants. Wealth, on the other hand, tends to lead to the opposite condition — pride and a sense of autonomy from God.

multiplied, and your silver and gold is multiplied, and all that you have is multiplied, 14 then do not exalt yourself, forgetting the LORD your God, who brought you out of the land of Egypt, out of the house of slavery, 15 who led you through the great and terrible wilderness, an arid wasteland with poisonous[s] snakes and scorpions. He made water flow for you from flint rock, 16 and fed you in the wilderness with manna that your ancestors did not know, to humble you and to test you, and in the end to do you good. 17 Do not say to yourself, "My power and the might of my own hand have gotten me this wealth." 18 But remember the LORD your God, for it is he who gives you power to get wealth, so that he may confirm his covenant that he swore to your ancestors, as he is doing today. 19 If you do forget the LORD your God and follow other gods to serve and worship them, I solemnly warn you today that you shall surely perish. 20 Like the nations that the LORD is destroying before you, so shall you perish, because you would not obey the voice of the LORD your God.

c. God will give Israel the land:
not because of their righteousness

9 Hear, O Israel! You are about to cross the Jordan today, to go in and dispossess nations larger and mightier than you, great cities, fortified to the heavens, 2 a strong and tall people, the offspring of the Anakim, whom you know. You have heard it said of them, "Who can stand up to the Anakim?" 3 Know then today that the LORD your God is the one who crosses over before you as a devouring fire; he will defeat them and subdue them before you, so that you may dispossess and destroy them quickly, as the LORD has promised you.

4 When the LORD your God thrusts them out before you, do not say to yourself, "It is because of my righteousness that the LORD has brought me in to occupy this land"; it is rather because of the wickedness of these nations that the LORD is dispossessing them before you. 5 It is not because of your righteousness or the uprightness of your heart that you are going in to occupy their land; but because of the wickedness of these nations the LORD your God is dispossessing them before you, in order to fulfill the promise that the LORD made on oath to your ancestors, to Abraham, to Isaac, and to Jacob.

d. Israel's own sin: the golden calf

6 Know, then, that the LORD your God is not giving you this good land to occupy because of your righteousness; for you are a stubborn people. 7 Remember and do not forget how you provoked the LORD your God to wrath in the wilderness; you have been rebellious against the LORD from the day you came out of the land of Egypt until you came to this place.

8 Even at Horeb you provoked the LORD to wrath, and the LORD was so angry with you that he was ready to destroy you. 9 When I went up the mountain to receive the stone tablets, the tablets of the covenant that the LORD made with you, I remained on the mountain forty days and forty nights; I neither ate bread nor drank water. 10 And the LORD gave me the two stone tablets written with the finger of God; on them were all the words that the LORD had spoken to you at the mountain out of the fire on the day of the assembly. 11 At the end of forty days and forty nights

[s] Or *fiery*; Heb *seraph*

8.14
Ps 106.21

8.15
Num 21.6;
20.11;
Ps 78.15;
114.8
8.16
vv. 2, 3;
Ex 16.15
8.18
Prov 10.22;
Hos 2.8
8.19
Deut 4.26;
30.18

9.1
Deut 11.31

9.2
Num 13.22,
28, 32, 33
9.3
Deut 31.3;
4.24; 7.23,
24

9.4
Deut 8.17;
18.12;
Lev 18.24, 25
9.5
Gen 12.7

9.6
v. 13;
Ex 32.9;
Deut 31.27

9.8
Ex 32.7-10
9.9
Ex 24.12, 15,
18

9.10
Ex 31.18;
Deut 4.13

8.17,18 Moses warns Israel of the danger of supposing that they are self-sufficient. He enjoins them to remember that when they succeed, it is God "who gives you power to get wealth." The greatest danger of wealth arises when we begin to think we have made it on our own. We must always acknowledge that God is the source of everything we own.

9.4 Moses warns Israel against supposing that God is giving them the land of Palestine because of their intrinsic righteousness. He knows that God will give the land to Israel out of his grace and because of "the wickedness of these nations that the LORD is dispossessing. . . ."

the LORD gave me the two stone tablets, the tablets of the covenant. [12] Then the LORD said to me, "Get up, go down quickly from here, for your people whom you have brought from Egypt have acted corruptly. They have been quick to turn from the way that I commanded them; they have cast an image for themselves." [13] Furthermore the LORD said to me, "I have seen that this people is indeed a stubborn people. [14] Let me alone that I may destroy them and blot out their name from under heaven; and I will make of you a nation mightier and more numerous than they."

[15] So I turned and went down from the mountain, while the mountain was ablaze; the two tablets of the covenant were in my two hands. [16] Then I saw that you had indeed sinned against the LORD your God, by casting for yourselves an image of a calf; you had been quick to turn from the way that the LORD had commanded you. [17] So I took hold of the two tablets and flung them from my two hands, smashing them before your eyes. [18] Then I lay prostrate before the LORD as before, forty days and forty nights; I neither ate bread nor drank water, because of all the sin you had committed, provoking the LORD by doing what was evil in his sight. [19] For I was afraid that the anger that the LORD bore against you was so fierce that he would destroy you. But the LORD listened to me that time also. [20] The LORD was so angry with Aaron that he was ready to destroy him, but I interceded also on behalf of Aaron at that same time. [21] Then I took the sinful thing you had made, the calf, and burned it with fire and crushed it, grinding it thoroughly, until it was reduced to dust; and I threw the dust of it into the stream that runs down the mountain.

e. Israel's other sins

[22] At Taberah also, and at Massah, and at Kibroth-hattaavah, you provoked the LORD to wrath. [23] And when the LORD sent you from Kadesh-barnea, saying, "Go up and occupy the land that I have given you," you rebelled against the command of the LORD your God, neither trusting him nor obeying him. [24] You have been rebellious against the LORD as long as he has[t] known you.

f. Moses intercedes for Israel

[25] Throughout the forty days and forty nights that I lay prostrate before the LORD when the LORD intended to destroy you, [26] I prayed to the LORD and said, "Lord GOD, do not destroy the people who are your very own possession, whom you redeemed in your greatness, whom you brought out of Egypt with a mighty hand. [27] Remember your servants, Abraham, Isaac, and Jacob; pay no attention to the stubbornness of this people, their wickedness and their sin, [28] otherwise the land from which you have brought us might say, 'Because the LORD was not able to bring them into the land that he promised them, and because he hated them, he has brought them out to let them die in the wilderness.' [29] For they are the people of your very own possession, whom you brought out by your great power and by your outstretched arm."

g. The two tablets of stone

10 At that time the LORD said to me, "Carve out two tablets of stone like the former ones, and come up to me on the mountain, and make an ark of wood. [2] I will write on the tablets the words that were on

[t] Sam Gk: MT *I have*

Cross references

9.12 Ex 32.7, 8; Deut 31.29
9.13 Ex 32.9; v. 6
9.14 Ex 32.10; Deut 29.20; Num 14.12
9.15 Ex 32.15-19; 19.18
9.16 Ex 32.19
9.18 Ex 34.28
9.19 Ex 32.10-14
9.21 Ex 32.20
9.22 Num 11.3, 34; Ex 17.7
9.24 v. 7; Deut 31.27
9.25 v. 18
9.26 Ex 32.11-13
9.29 Deut 4.20, 34
10.1 Ex 34.1, 2; 25.10
10.2 Deut 4.13; Ex 25.16, 21

9.12 See note on Ex 32.4 (the golden calf incident).
9.18 God was angry with Aaron and with Israel for making and worshiping the golden calf and for committing immorality. Moses prayed for them, that the wrath of God might be stayed. He was in prayer for forty days and nights (see also v. 25). Moses diligently refused to let go. Had he faltered and stopped praying before God relented, Israel would have been destroyed.
9.25,26 Because of Moses' prayer, God refrained from slaying the Israelites. Moses wrestled with God until he answered in the affirmative and Israel was saved from destruction. We, like Moses, must persevere in prayer.

the former tablets, which you smashed, and you shall put them in the ark." ³ So I made an ark of acacia wood, cut two tablets of stone like the former ones, and went up the mountain with the two tablets in my hand. ⁴ Then he wrote on the tablets the same words as before, the ten commandments*u* that the LORD had spoken to you on the mountain out of the fire on the day of the assembly; and the LORD gave them to me. ⁵ So I turned and came down from the mountain, and put the tablets in the ark that I had made; and there they are, as the LORD commanded me.

6 (The Israelites journeyed from Beeroth-bene-jaakan*v* to Moserah. There Aaron died, and there he was buried; his son Eleazar succeeded him as priest. ⁷ From there they journeyed to Gudgodah, and from Gudgodah to Jotbathah, a land with flowing streams. ⁸ At that time the LORD set apart the tribe of Levi to carry the ark of the covenant of the LORD, to stand before the LORD to minister to him, and to bless in his name, to this day. ⁹ Therefore Levi has no allotment or inheritance with his kindred; the LORD is his inheritance, as the LORD your God promised him.)

10 I stayed on the mountain forty days and forty nights, as I had done the first time. And once again the LORD listened to me. The LORD was unwilling to destroy you. ¹¹ The LORD said to me, "Get up, go on your journey at the head of the people, that they may go in and occupy the land that I swore to their ancestors to give them."

8. God's great requirement

12 So now, O Israel, what does the LORD your God require of you? Only to fear the LORD your God, to walk in all his ways, to love him, to serve the LORD your God with all your heart and with all your soul, ¹³ and to keep the commandments of the LORD your God*w* and his decrees that I am commanding you today, for your own well-being. ¹⁴ Although heaven and the heaven of heavens belong to the LORD your God, the earth with all that is in it, ¹⁵ yet the LORD set his heart in love on your ancestors alone and chose you, their descendants after them, out of all the peoples, as it is today. ¹⁶ Circumcise, then, the foreskin of your heart, and do not be stubborn any longer. ¹⁷ For the LORD your God is God of gods and Lord of lords, the great God, mighty and awesome, who is not partial and takes no bribe, ¹⁸ who executes justice for the orphan and the widow, and who loves the strangers, providing them food and clothing. ¹⁹ You shall also love the stranger, for you were strangers in the land of Egypt. ²⁰ You shall fear the LORD your God; him alone you shall worship; to him you shall hold fast, and by his name you shall swear. ²¹ He is your praise; he is your God, who has done for you these great and awesome things that your own eyes have seen. ²² Your ancestors went down to Egypt seventy persons; and now the LORD your God has made you as numerous as the stars in heaven.

9. Moses' concluding exhortation

a. The command to love God

11 You shall love the LORD your God, therefore, and keep his charge, his decrees, his ordinances, and his commandments always. ² Re-

u Heb the ten words   *v* Or the wells of the Bene-jaakan   *w* Q Ms Gk Syr: MT lacks your God

Cross-references (margin):

10.3 Ex 37.1; 34.4
10.4 Ex 20.1
10.5 Ex 40.20
10.6 Num 33.30, 31, 38
10.7 Num 33.32-34
10.8 Num 3.6; 4.15; Deut 18.5; 21.5
10.9 Num 18.20, 24
10.10 Deut 9.18, 25; Ex 33.17
10.12 Mic 6.8; Deut 6.13; 5.33; 6.5
10.14 1 Kings 8.27; Ex 19.5
10.15 Deut 4.37
10.16 Jer 4.4; Deut 9.6
10.17 Josh 22.22; Rev 19.16; Acts 10.34
10.18 Ps 68.5
10.19 Lev 19.34
10.20 Mt 4.10; Deut 11.22; Ps 63.11
10.21 Ex 15.2; Ps 106.21, 22
10.22 Gen 46.27; Deut 1.10
11.1 Deut 10.12; Zech 3.7
11.2 Deut 8.5; 5.24

Footnotes (bottom):

10.4 Moses did not etch the ten commandments on the tables of stone; God wrote them. In other words, the commandments came directly from the Lord and were not mediated through the writing of Moses.
10.16 Circumcise, then, the foreskin of your heart, i.e., give up all your corrupt desires and inclinations, which keep you from fearing and loving God. Don't trust in the circumcision of the body, which is only an outward sign, but be circumcised in the inner person (see Rom 2.29).
10.17 God of gods, and Lord of lords. The supremacy, greatness, and uniqueness of God are here pronounced. In Rev 19.16 Jesus is called "King of kings and Lord of lords." Thus the divine titles used for God in the O.T. are applied to Jesus in the N.T. He is both God and man.
11.1 You shall love the LORD . . . and keep his charge. The idea of loving God is a common theme in Deuter-

member today that it was not your children (who have not known or seen the discipline of the LORD your God), but it is you who must acknowledge his greatness, his mighty hand and his outstretched arm, 3 his signs and his deeds that he did in Egypt to Pharaoh, the king of Egypt, and to all his land; 4 what he did to the Egyptian army, to their horses and chariots, how he made the water of the Red Sea[x] flow over them as they pursued you, so that the LORD has destroyed them to this day; 5 what he did to you in the wilderness, until you came to this place; 6 and what he did to Dathan and Abiram, sons of Eliab son of Reuben, how in the midst of all Israel the earth opened its mouth and swallowed them up, along with their households, their tents, and every living being in their company; 7 for it is your own eyes that have seen every great deed that the LORD did.

11.4
Ex 14.27, 28

11.6
Num 16.31-33

b. *The order to keep God's commandments*

8 Keep, then, this entire commandment that I am commanding you today, so that you may have strength to go in and occupy the land that you are crossing over to occupy, 9 and so that you may live long in the land that the LORD swore to your ancestors to give them and to their descendants, a land flowing with milk and honey. 10 For the land that you are about to enter to occupy is not like the land of Egypt, from which you have come, where you sow your seed and irrigate by foot like a vegetable garden. 11 But the land that you are crossing over to occupy is a land of hills and valleys, watered by rain from the sky, 12 a land that the LORD your God looks after. The eyes of the LORD your God are always on it, from the beginning of the year to the end of the year.

11.8
Josh 1.6, 7

11.9
Deut 4.40;
9.5;
Ex 3.8

11.11
Deut 8.7

c. *The consequences of obedience and disobedience*

13 If you will only heed his every commandment[y] that I am commanding you today — loving the LORD your God, and serving him with all your heart and with all your soul — 14 then he[z] will give the rain for your land in its season, the early rain and the later rain, and you will gather in your grain, your wine, and your oil; 15 and he[z] will give grass in your fields for your livestock, and you will eat your fill. 16 Take care, or you will be seduced into turning away, serving other gods and worshiping them, 17 for then the anger of the LORD will be kindled against you and he will shut up the heavens, so that there will be no rain and the land will yield no fruit; then you will perish quickly off the good land that the LORD is giving you.

11.13
v. 22;
Deut 6.17;
10.12
11.14
Deut 28.12;
Joel 2.23
11.15
Deut 6.11
11.16
Deut 29.18;
8.19
11.17
Deut 6.15;
1 Kings 8.35;
Deut 4.26

d. *The command to lay up God's law and to teach it to children*

18 You shall put these words of mine in your heart and soul, and you shall bind them as a sign on your hand, and fix them as an emblem[a] on your forehead. 19 Teach them to your children, talking about them when you are at home and when you are away, when you lie down and when you rise. 20 Write them on the doorposts of your house and on your gates,

11.18
Deut 6.6, 8

11.19
Deut 4.9, 10;
6.7
11.20
Deut 6.9

x Or *Sea of Reeds*   *y* Compare Gk: Heb *my commandments*   *z* Sam Gk Vg: MT *I*   *a* Or *as a frontlet*

---

onomy. The work of love always involves obedience, and obedience itself is acceptable to God only when it flows from a principle of love (see 1 Jn 5.3).
11.10,11 Moses compares Canaan with Egypt. Egypt lacked rain; its productive capacity depended on the overflow of the Nile River. Canaan, on the other hand, was "a land . . . watered by rain from the sky." It was ideally situated so that its fertility and productive capacity would be enhanced by rain. God controls the rain, and he promises Israel an abundant supply of water from heaven. This is a conditional promise, however, based on Israel's obedience; disobedience would close the heavens and cut off the

water (v. 17).
11.18 *emblem*, i.e., frontlet (NRSV footnote). This word appears only three times in the O.T. (here; 6.8; Ex 13.16). It is a metaphor which stresses the importance of the law in the lives of the Israelites. Jews later took the injunction quite literally. They wrote four passages of the law on small pieces of parchment, placed them in tiny boxes, then bound them on their arms and brows for use during morning prayers. Called *tephillin*, they were honored as highly as the Scriptures. Many believe the phylacteries of the Pharisees were such frontlets (cf. Mt 23.5).

21 so that your days and the days of your children may be multiplied in the land that the LORD swore to your ancestors to give them, as long as the heavens are above the earth.

22 If you will diligently observe this entire commandment that I am commanding you, loving the LORD your God, walking in all his ways, and holding fast to him, 23 then the LORD will drive out all these nations before you, and you will dispossess nations larger and mightier than yourselves. 24 Every place on which you set foot shall be yours; your territory shall extend from the wilderness to the Lebanon and from the River, the river Euphrates, to the Western Sea. 25 No one will be able to stand against you; the LORD your God will put the fear and dread of you on all the land on which you set foot, as he promised you.

e. A blessing and a curse: Israel must choose for themselves

26 See, I am setting before you today a blessing and a curse: 27 the blessing, if you obey the commandments of the LORD your God that I am commanding you today; 28 and the curse, if you do not obey the commandments of the LORD your God, but turn from the way that I am commanding you today, to follow other gods that you have not known.

29 When the LORD your God has brought you into the land that you are entering to occupy, you shall set the blessing on Mount Gerizim and the curse on Mount Ebal. 30 As you know, they are beyond the Jordan, some distance to the west, in the land of the Canaanites who live in the Arabah, opposite Gilgal, beside the oak[b] of Moreh.

31 When you cross the Jordan to go in to occupy the land that the LORD your God is giving you, and when you occupy it and live in it, 32 you must diligently observe all the statutes and ordinances that I am setting before you today.

C. Moses exposes the principal laws

1. Israel shall erect an altar: the place that the LORD will choose

12 These are the statutes and ordinances that you must diligently observe in the land that the LORD, the God of your ancestors, has given you to occupy all the days that you live on the earth.

2 You must demolish completely all the places where the nations whom you are about to dispossess served their gods, on the mountain heights, on the hills, and under every leafy tree. 3 Break down their altars, smash their pillars, burn their sacred poles[c] with fire, and hew down the idols of their gods, and thus blot out their name from their places. 4 You shall not worship the LORD your God in such ways. 5 But you shall seek the place that the LORD your God will choose out of all your tribes as his habitation to put his name there. You shall go there, 6 bringing there your burnt offerings and your sacrifices, your tithes and your donations, your votive gifts, your freewill offerings, and the firstlings of your herds and

11.22
Deut 6.17; 10.20
11.23
Deut 9.1, 5
11.24
Josh 1.3; Gen 15.18; Ex 23.31
11.25
Deut 7.24; Ex 23.27

11.26
Deut 30.1, 19
11.27
Deut 28.2
11.28
Deut 28.15

11.29
Deut 27.12; Josh 8.33
11.30
Josh 4.19; Gen 12.6

11.31
Deut 9.1; Josh 1.11

12.1
Deut 4.9, 10

12.3
Deut 7.5

12.5
v. 11

b Gk Syr: Compare Gen 12.6; Heb oaks or terebinths   c Heb Asherim

11.24 Never in the history of Israel has this divine promise been literally fulfilled. We can expect this to take place before the consummation of history and the end of the age. None of the promises of God will fall short of literal fulfillment, however impossible they may appear to be.
11.26 Moses presents two opposing options to Israel, summed up in two words: blessing and cursing. Depending on which the Israelites chose, there would be rewards or punishments. Doing the commandments of God would bring the blessing. Punishment would result from one of two sins: the sin of disobedi-

ence (by which the commandments were broken) and the sin of omission (by which the things Israel was supposed to do were simply not done).
12.3 pillars, or obelisks, large standing stones thought to have been symbols of Baal, the Canaanite fertility god. sacred poles i.e., "asherim" (see note on Ex 34.13).
12.5 the place. God would choose a place for his home. Having one central sanctuary would help to avoid idolatry. David moved the sanctuary from Shiloh to Jerusalem, which subsequently became the center for the worship of God.

12.7
Deut 14.26;
vv. 12, 18

12.10
Deut 11.31

12.11
v. 5

12.12
v. 7;
Deut 10.9

12.14
v. 11

12.15
vv. 20-23;
Deut 14.5

12.16
Lev 17.10-12

12.18
vv. 5, 7, 12

12.19
Deut 14.27

12.20
Gen 15.18

12.22
v. 15
12.23
v. 16;
Lev 17.11, 14

12.25
Deut 4.40;
13.18
12.26
v. 17

12.28
v. 25;
Deut 4.40

flocks. 7 And you shall eat there in the presence of the LORD your God, you and your households together, rejoicing in all the undertakings in which the LORD your God has blessed you.

8 You shall not act as we are acting here today, all of us according to our own desires, 9 for you have not yet come into the rest and the possession that the LORD your God is giving you. 10 When you cross over the Jordan and live in the land that the LORD your God is allotting to you, and when he gives you rest from your enemies all around so that you live in safety, 11 then you shall bring everything that I command you to the place that the LORD your God will choose as a dwelling for his name: your burnt offerings and your sacrifices, your tithes and your donations, and all your choice votive gifts that you vow to the LORD. 12 And you shall rejoice before the LORD your God, you together with your sons and your daughters, your male and female slaves, and the Levites who reside in your towns (since they have no allotment or inheritance with you).

13 Take care that you do not offer your burnt offerings at any place you happen to see. 14 But only at the place that the LORD will choose in one of your tribes—there you shall offer your burnt offerings and there you shall do everything I command you.

15 Yet whenever you desire you may slaughter and eat meat within any of your towns, according to the blessing that the LORD your God has given you; the unclean and the clean may eat of it, as they would of gazelle or deer. 16 The blood, however, you must not eat; you shall pour it out on the ground like water. 17 Nor may you eat within your towns the tithe of your grain, your wine, and your oil, the firstlings of your herds and your flocks, any of your votive gifts that you vow, your freewill offerings, or your donations; 18 these you shall eat in the presence of the LORD your God at the place that the LORD your God will choose, you together with your son and your daughter, your male and female slaves, and the Levites resident in your towns, rejoicing in the presence of the LORD your God in all your undertakings. 19 Take care that you do not neglect the Levite as long as you live in your land.

20 When the LORD your God enlarges your territory, as he has promised you, and you say, "I am going to eat some meat," because you wish to eat meat, you may eat meat whenever you have the desire. 21 If the place where the LORD your God will choose to put his name is too far from you, and you slaughter as I have commanded you any of your herd or flock that the LORD has given you, then you may eat within your towns whenever you desire. 22 Indeed, just as gazelle or deer is eaten, so you may eat it; the unclean and the clean alike may eat it. 23 Only be sure that you do not eat the blood; for the blood is the life, and you shall not eat the life with the meat. 24 Do not eat it; you shall pour it out on the ground like water. 25 Do not eat it, so that all may go well with you and your children after you, because you do what is right in the sight of the LORD. 26 But the sacred donations that are due from you, and your votive gifts, you shall bring to the place that the LORD will choose. 27 You shall present your burnt offerings, both the meat and the blood, on the altar of the LORD your God; the blood of your other sacrifices shall be poured out beside[d] the altar of the LORD your God, but the meat you may eat.

28 Be careful to obey all these words that I command you today,[e] so that it may go well with you and with your children after you forever, because you will be doing what is good and right in the sight of the LORD your God.

[d] Or on   [e] Gk Sam Syr: MT lacks today

12.20 In the wilderness Israel ate manna; in Canaan they would have all the meat to eat that they desired. The priests were commanded to eat meat, while the people generally were free to eat meat or to abstain. Vegetarianism is a choice, not a commandment.

29   When the Lord your God has cut off before you the nations whom you are about to enter to dispossess them, when you have dispossessed them and live in their land, 30 take care that you are not snared into imitating them, after they have been destroyed before you: do not inquire concerning their gods, saying, "How did these nations worship their gods? I also want to do the same." 31 You must not do the same for the Lord your God, because every abhorrent thing that the Lord hates they have done for their gods. They would even burn their sons and their daughters in the fire to their gods. 32 f You must diligently observe everything that I command you; do not add to it or take anything from it.

2. The second commandment

a. False prophets to die

13 g If prophets or those who divine by dreams appear among you and promise you omens or portents, 2 and the omens or the portents declared by them take place, and they say, "Let us follow other gods" (whom you have not known) "and let us serve them," 3 you must not heed the words of those prophets or those who divine by dreams; for the Lord your God is testing you, to know whether you indeed love the Lord your God with all your heart and soul. 4 The Lord your God you shall follow, him alone you shall fear, his commandments you shall keep, his voice you shall obey, him you shall serve, and to him you shall hold fast. 5 But those prophets or those who divine by dreams shall be put to death for having spoken treason against the Lord your God — who brought you out of the land of Egypt and redeemed you from the house of slavery — to turn you from the way in which the Lord your God commanded you to walk. So you shall purge the evil from your midst.

b. Secret idolaters to be cut off

6   If anyone secretly entices you — even if it is your brother, your father's son or h your mother's son, or your own son or daughter, or the wife you embrace, or your most intimate friend — saying, "Let us go worship other gods," whom neither you nor your ancestors have known, 7 any of the gods of the peoples that are around you, whether near you or far away from you, from one end of the earth to the other, 8 you must not yield to or heed any such persons. Show them no pity or compassion and do not shield them. 9 But you shall surely kill them; your own hand shall be first against them to execute them, and afterwards the hand of all the people. 10 Stone them to death for trying to turn you away from the Lord your God, who brought you out of the land of Egypt, out of the house of slavery. 11 Then all Israel shall hear and be afraid, and never again do any such wickedness.

f Ch 13.1 in Heb   g Ch 13.2 in Heb   h Sam Gk Compare Tg: MT lacks *your father's son or*

12.31   The heathen had sunk so low and their views of the gods they worshiped were so depraved that they burned their own children as sacrifices to their deities. The custom was barbarous and inhuman, violating the law of nature, and was a prostitution of natural parental love.
13.1   *promise you omens or portents.* Those who cause a follower of God to go after strange gods must be resisted. This is true even if false prophets perform signs and wonders, for the divine law against the worship of other gods is perpetual and unalterable. Paul expresses this same principle about the gospel: if even an angel from heaven were to give forth another gospel, it would be wrong and should be resisted (Gal 1.8,9).
13.4   The acid test of one's faith lies in obedience to God's commands. Obedience should come from the

heart (Rom 6.17); it must be done willingly (Josh 22.2,3; Isa 1.19); and it must be done at all times (Phil 2.12). Believers must obey: the law of God (11.27; Isa 42.24); the voice of God (Ex 19.5; Jer 7.23); Christ (2 Cor 10.5); the gospel (Rom 1.5; 6.17); and governing authorities (Rom 13.1). God promises blessings to those who obey and punishments for those who disobey.
13.6–9   One of Satan's trickiest devices is to entice us to sin by the mouths of those we love the most. For example, Christ was tempted by his dear friend Peter (cf. Mt 16.21–23). No matter how much we love someone, if that person tries to seduce us to give allegiance to anything or anyone other than the true God, he or she must be resisted, even if it means martyrdom.

c. Idolatrous cities to be destroyed

12 If you hear it said about one of the towns that the LORD your God is giving you to live in, **13** that scoundrels from among you have gone out and led the inhabitants of the town astray, saying, "Let us go and worship other gods," whom you have not known, **14** then you shall inquire and make a thorough investigation. If the charge is established that such an abhorrent thing has been done among you, **15** you shall put the inhabitants of that town to the sword, utterly destroying it and everything in it — even putting its livestock to the sword. **16** All of its spoil you shall gather into its public square; then burn the town and all its spoil with fire, as a whole burnt offering to the LORD your God. It shall remain a perpetual ruin, never to be rebuilt. **17** Do not let anything devoted to destruction stick to your hand, so that the LORD may turn from his fierce anger and show you compassion, and in his compassion multiply you, as he swore to your ancestors, **18** if you obey the voice of the LORD your God by keeping all his commandments that I am commanding you today, doing what is right in the sight of the LORD your God.

3. Clean and unclean animals

14 You are children of the LORD your God. You must not lacerate yourselves or shave your forelocks for the dead. **2** For you are a people holy to the LORD your God; it is you the LORD has chosen out of all the peoples on earth to be his people, his treasured possession.

3 You shall not eat any abhorrent thing. **4** These are the animals you may eat: the ox, the sheep, the goat, **5** the deer, the gazelle, the roebuck, the wild goat, the ibex, the antelope, and the mountain-sheep. **6** Any animal that divides the hoof and has the hoof cleft in two, and chews the cud, among the animals, you may eat. **7** Yet of those that chew the cud or have the hoof cleft you shall not eat these: the camel, the hare, and the rock badger, because they chew the cud but do not divide the hoof; they are unclean for you. **8** And the pig, because it divides the hoof but does not chew the cud, is unclean for you. You shall not eat their meat, and you shall not touch their carcasses.

9 Of all that live in water you may eat these: whatever has fins and scales you may eat. **10** And whatever does not have fins and scales you shall not eat; it is unclean for you.

11 You may eat any clean birds. **12** But these are the ones that you shall not eat: the eagle, the vulture, the osprey, **13** the buzzard, the kite of any kind; **14** every raven of any kind; **15** the ostrich, the nighthawk, the sea gull, the hawk of any kind; **16** the little owl and the great owl, the water hen **17** and the desert owl,*i* the carrion vulture and the cormorant, **18** the stork, the heron of any kind; the hoopoe and the bat.*j* **19** And all winged insects are unclean for you; they shall not be eaten. **20** You may eat any clean winged creature.

21 You shall not eat anything that dies of itself; you may give it to aliens residing in your towns for them to eat, or you may sell it to a foreigner. For you are a people holy to the LORD your God.

You shall not boil a kid in its mother's milk.

---

i Or *pelican*   *j* Identification of several of the birds in verses 12-18 is uncertain

---

13.15 God orders Israel to slay not only the inhabitants of the idolatrous cities of Canaan, but also the animals that have been contaminated by the pagans. So holy is our God that what may not be unclean in itself may be considered unclean by him because of its association with his enemy.

14.1,2 Three important truths are enunciated here. (1) The Israelites are the children of God. They be-

long to God by adoption, having been redeemed by blood. (2) They have been chosen by God — they are his elect, known from eternity. (3) They have been sanctified by God, for they are a holy people. As a people set apart, the Israelites are devoted to the service of God, they are governed by the law of God, and they exist for the praise of his grace.

Side references (left margin):

13.13
vv. 2, 6; see
1 Jn 2.19

13.15
Ex 22.20

13.16
Josh 6.24;
8.28

13.17
Num 25.4;
Deut 30.3;
7.13

13.18
Deut 12.28

14.1
Rom 8;16;
Lev 21.5
14.2
Deut 7.6

14.4
Lev 11.2-45;
Acts 10.14

14.8
Lev 11.26, 27

14.9
Lev 11.9

14.12
Lev 11.3

14.19
Lev 11.20

14.21
Lev 17.15;
v. 2;
Ex 29.19;
34.26

4. The tithe of produce

22   Set apart a tithe of all the yield of your seed that is brought in yearly from the field. 23 In the presence of the LORD your God, in the place that he will choose as a dwelling for his name, you shall eat the tithe of your grain, your wine, and your oil, as well as the firstlings of your herd and flock, so that you may learn to fear the LORD your God always. 24 But if, when the LORD your God has blessed you, the distance is so great that you are unable to transport it, because the place where the LORD your God will choose to set his name is too far away from you, 25 then you may turn it into money. With the money secure in hand, go to the place that the LORD your God will choose; 26 spend the money for whatever you wish—oxen, sheep, wine, strong drink, or whatever you desire. And you shall eat there in the presence of the LORD your God, you and your household rejoicing together. 27 As for the Levites resident in your towns, do not neglect them, because they have no allotment or inheritance with you.

28   Every third year you shall bring out the full tithe of your produce for that year, and store it within your towns; 29 the Levites, because they have no allotment or inheritance with you, as well as the resident aliens, the orphans, and the widows in your towns, may come and eat their fill so that the LORD your God may bless you in all the work that you undertake.

5. Laws relating to slaves and the poor

a. The year of remission

15 Every seventh year you shall grant a remission of debts. 2 And this is the manner of the remission: every creditor shall remit the claim that is held against a neighbor, not exacting it of a neighbor who is a member of the community, because the LORD's remission has been proclaimed. 3 Of a foreigner you may exact it, but you must remit your claim on whatever any member of your community owes you. 4 There will, however, be no one in need among you, because the LORD is sure to bless you in the land that the LORD your God is giving you as a possession to occupy, 5 if only you will obey the LORD your God by diligently observing this entire commandment that I command you today. 6 When the LORD your God has blessed you, as he promised you, you will lend to many nations, but you will not borrow; you will rule over many nations, but they will not rule over you.

7   If there is among you anyone in need, a member of your community in any of your towns within the land that the LORD your God is giving you, do not be hard-hearted or tight-fisted toward your needy neighbor. 8 You should rather open your hand, willingly lending enough to meet the need, whatever it may be. 9 Be careful that you do not entertain a mean

14.22ff
Lev 27.30
14.23
Deut 12.5-7;
4.10
14.24
Deut 12.5, 21

14.26
Deut 12.7, 18

14.27
Deut 12.12;
Num 18.20
14.28
Deut 26.12
14.29
Deut 26.12;
v. 27;
Deut 15.10

15.1
Deut 31.10

15.5
Deut 28.1
15.6
Deut 28.12,
13

15.7
1 Jn 3.17
15.8
Lev 25.35
15.9
v. 1;
Deut 24.15

14.22–27 The law of the tithe here differs somewhat from that described in Num 18.21–24. This law apparently superseded the earlier one.
14.26 *wine, yayin* in Hebrew, fermented juice. *strong drink, shakar* in Hebrew, beer. There were no distilled liquors in Israel. *Shakar* comes from a verb meaning "to be drunk." Scriptural warnings against drunkenness indicate that whatever they drank contained enough alcohol to make them drunk.
14.28,29 Every third year the tithe was allocated for the relief of the poor. God has a particular concern for widows and orphans. We must have a similar concern (cf. Jas 1.27). We honor God when we help the helpless and we honor ourselves when we obey God's command. What is lent to the Lord will be repaid with abundant interest.
15.3 The law which applied to the Israelites, that all debts owed each other were wiped out on the sabbatical year, did not apply to non-Israelites. God made a

distinction between his people Israel and other people. Is this not a breach of neighborly love? A similar question arose when Jesus gave the parable of the workers in the vineyard, all of whom received the same wages though some worked shorter hours than others (Mt 20.1ff). Was it fair? The reply is the same in both instances. God is free to do as he chooses. Since both Israelites and non-Israelites may be in debt, God is free to release the one and make the other pay. Favoring one debtor is a mark of grace and mercy, but it does not mean that God owes the other debtor anything.
15.9 God commanded the Israelites to relieve poverty by lending to the needy without taking into account the seven-year law for the release from debts. If there were only a short time until the sabbatical year came, a calculating mind might refuse to lend to the poor, for if not repaid by the sabbatical year, the loan would be wiped out. Spiritually speaking, this law

thought, thinking, "The seventh year, the year of remission, is near," and therefore view your needy neighbor with hostility and give nothing; your neighbor might cry to the LORD against you, and you would incur guilt. 10Give liberally and be ungrudging when you do so, for on this account the LORD your God will bless you in all your work and in all that you undertake. 11Since there will never cease to be some in need on the earth, I therefore command you, "Open your hand to the poor and needy neighbor in your land."

b. *Freedom for slaves*

12 If a member of your community, whether a Hebrew man or a Hebrew woman, is sold*k* to you and works for you six years, in the seventh year you shall set that person free. 13And when you send a male slave*l* out from you a free person, you shall not send him out empty-handed. 14Provide liberally out of your flock, your threshing floor, and your wine press, thus giving to him some of the bounty with which the LORD your God has blessed you. 15Remember that you were a slave in the land of Egypt, and the LORD your God redeemed you; for this reason I lay this command upon you today. 16But if he says to you, "I will not go out from you," because he loves you and your household, since he is well off with you, 17then you shall take an awl and thrust it through his earlobe into the door, and he shall be your slave*m* forever.

You shall do the same with regard to your female slave.*n*

18 Do not consider it a hardship when you send them out from you free persons, because for six years they have given you services worth the wages of hired laborers; and the LORD your God will bless you in all that you do.

c. *Sacrifice of firstling males*

19 Every firstling male born of your herd and flock you shall conse-crate to the LORD your God; you shall not do work with your firstling ox nor shear the firstling of your flock. 20You shall eat it, you together with your household, in the presence of the LORD your God year by year at the place that the LORD will choose. 21But if it has any defect—any serious defect, such as lameness or blindness—you shall not sacrifice it to the LORD your God; 22within your towns you may eat it, the unclean and the clean alike, as you would a gazelle or deer. 23Its blood, however, you must not eat; you shall pour it out on the ground like water.

6. *The passover*

16 Observe the month*o* of Abib by keeping the passover to the LORD your God, for in the month of Abib the LORD your God brought you out of Egypt by night. 2You shall offer the passover sacrifice to the LORD your God, from the flock and the herd, at the place that the LORD will choose as a dwelling for his name. 3You must not eat with it

---

15.10
2 Cor 9.5, 7;
Deut 24.19
15.11
Mt 26.11;
Mk 14.7;
Jn 12.8

15.12
Ex 21.2;
Lev 25.39

15.15
Deut 5.15;
16.12
15.16
Ex 21.5, 6

15.19
Ex 13.2
15.20
Deut 12.5-7,
17
15.21
Lev 22.19-25
15.22
Deut 12.15,
22
15.23
Deut 12.16,
23

16.1
Ex 12.2, 29,
42; 13.4
16.2
Deut 12.5, 26

16.3
Ex 12.8, 15

---

k Or *sells himself or herself*   *l* Heb *him*   *m* Or *bondman*   *n* Or *bondwoman*   *o* Or *new moon*

---

restrains what a wicked heart thinks. God monitors our thoughts as well as our actions. All of us need to guard against thoughts which divert us from doing our duty or discourage us from following God's law of love. When we lend to the poor in obedience to God's command, we do not trust the one who borrows from us; rather, we trust God without expecting rec-ompense in this life.

15.11 *there will never cease to be some in need on the earth.* This prophetic word recognizes a truth that cannot be denied. In a sinful world, poverty should not be unexpected—whether due to lack of diligence on the part of the poor or circumstances beyond their control. The existence of poverty is a perennial chal-lenge to the people of God to do what they can to

alleviate the poverty-stricken.

15.16,17 Israel allowed no involuntary slavery. Manumission was provided for, unless the slave him-self chose to continue as such.

16.1 See notes on Ex 12.11–13 and Mk 14.1 for information on the passover. Moses carefully reminds the Israelites that they must come to the holy place three times a year: for the passover (16.1–8), the festival of weeks or harvest (16.9–12; see note on Lev 23.15,16), and the festival of tabernacles or booths (16.13–17; see note on Ex 23.16). They were to per-form their ceremonies "at the place that the LORD will choose" (16.15). Eventually, this place became the temple in Jerusalem.

16.3 *leavened.* See note on Mt 13.33.

anything leavened. For seven days you shall eat unleavened bread with it—the bread of affliction—because you came out of the land of Egypt in great haste, so that all the days of your life you may remember the day of your departure from the land of Egypt. 4 No leaven shall be seen with you in all your territory for seven days; and none of the meat of what you slaughter on the evening of the first day shall remain until morning. 5 You are not permitted to offer the passover sacrifice within any of your towns that the LORD your God is giving you. 6 But at the place that the LORD your God will choose as a dwelling for his name, only there shall you offer the passover sacrifice, in the evening at sunset, the time of day when you departed from Egypt. 7 You shall cook it and eat it at the place that the LORD your God will choose; the next morning you may go back to your tents. 8 For six days you shall continue to eat unleavened bread, and on the seventh day there shall be a solemn assembly for the LORD your God, when you shall do no work.

7. *The festival of weeks*

9 You shall count seven weeks; begin to count the seven weeks from the time the sickle is first put to the standing grain. 10 Then you shall keep the festival of weeks to the LORD your God, contributing a freewill offering in proportion to the blessing that you have received from the LORD your God. 11 Rejoice before the LORD your God—you and your sons and your daughters, your male and female slaves, the Levites resident in your towns, as well as the strangers, the orphans, and the widows who are among you—at the place that the LORD your God will choose as a dwelling for his name. 12 Remember that you were a slave in Egypt, and diligently observe these statutes.

8. *The festival of booths*

13 You shall keep the festival of booths[p] for seven days, when you have gathered in the produce from your threshing floor and your wine press. 14 Rejoice during your festival, you and your sons and your daughters, your male and female slaves, as well as the Levites, the strangers, the orphans, and the widows resident in your towns. 15 Seven days you shall keep the festival to the LORD your God at the place that the LORD will choose; for the LORD your God will bless you in all your produce and in all your undertakings, and you shall surely celebrate.

16 Three times a year all your males shall appear before the LORD your God at the place that he will choose: at the festival of unleavened bread, at the festival of weeks, and at the festival of booths.[p] They shall not appear before the LORD empty-handed; 17 all shall give as they are able, according to the blessing of the LORD your God that he has given you.

9. *The administration of justice*

a. *Judges*

18 You shall appoint judges and officials throughout your tribes, in all your towns that the LORD your God is giving you, and they shall render just decisions for the people. 19 You must not distort justice; you must not show partiality; and you must not accept bribes, for a bribe blinds the eyes of the wise and subverts the cause of those who are in the right. 20 Justice, and only justice, you shall pursue, so that you may live and occupy the land that the LORD your God is giving you.

p Or tabernacles; Heb succoth

	16.4 Ex 13.7; 12.10
	16.6 Deut 12.5; Ex 12.6
	16.7 Ex 12.8, 9
	16.8 Ex 12.16
	16.9 Ex 23.16; 34.22; Lev 23.15; Num 28.26
	16.11 Deut 12.7, 12
	16.12 Deut 15.15
	16.13 Ex 23.16; Lev 23.34
	16.14 v. 11
	16.15 Lev 23.39
	16.16 Ex 23.14-17; 34.20, 23
	16.18 Deut 1.16
	16.19 Deut 1.17; Ex 23.8

16.20 The basic principle of the Israelite legal system was justice for all. The magistrate was to do right to everyone and to wrong no one. For comments on the modern term "social justice," see note on Ex 18.19,20.

b. Prohibitions: idolatry and defective sacrifices

16.21
Ex 34.13;
Deut 7.5

21 You shall not plant any tree as a sacred pole*q* beside the altar that you make for the Lord your God; 22 nor shall you set up a stone pillar — things that the Lord your God hates.

17.1
Deut 15.21;
Mal 1.8, 13

17 You must not sacrifice to the Lord your God an ox or a sheep that has a defect, anything seriously wrong; for that is abhorrent to the Lord your God.

17.2
Deut 13.6

2 If there is found among you, in one of your towns that the Lord your God is giving you, a man or woman who does what is evil in the sight of the Lord your God, and transgresses his covenant 3 by going to serve other gods and worshiping them — whether the sun or the moon or any

17.4
Deut 13.12,
14

of the host of heaven, which I have forbidden — 4 and if it is reported to you or you hear of it, and you make a thorough inquiry, and the charge is proved true that such an abhorrent thing has occurred in Israel, 5 then you shall bring out to your gates that man or that woman who has

17.6
Num 35.30;
Deut 19.15;
Mt 18.16

committed this crime and you shall stone the man or that woman to death. 6 On the evidence of two or three witnesses the death sentence shall be executed; a person must not be put to death on the evidence of only one

17.7
Deut 13.5, 9

witness. 7 The hands of the witnesses shall be the first raised against the person to execute the death penalty, and afterward the hands of all the people. So you shall purge the evil from your midst.

c. The court of appeal

17.8
Deut 12.5

8 If a judicial decision is too difficult for you to make between one kind of bloodshed and another, one kind of legal right and another, or one kind of assault and another — any such matters of dispute in your towns — then you shall immediately go up to the place that the Lord your God will

17.9
Deut 19.17;
Ezek 44.24

choose, 9 where you shall consult with the levitical priests and the judge who is in office in those days; they shall announce to you the decision in the case. 10 Carry out exactly the decision that they announce to you from the place that the Lord will choose, diligently observing everything they

17.11
Deut 25.1

instruct you. 11 You must carry out fully the law that they interpret for you or the ruling that they announce to you; do not turn aside from the decision that they announce to you, either to the right or to the left. 12 As for anyone who presumes to disobey the priest appointed to minister there to the Lord your God, or the judge, that person shall die. So you shall

17.13
Deut 13.11;
19.20

purge the evil from Israel. 13 All the people will hear and be afraid, and will not act presumptuously again.

10. The choice of a king

17.14
Deut 11.31;
1 Sam 8.5,
19, 20
17.15
Jer 30.21

14 When you have come into the land that the Lord your God is giving you, and have taken possession of it and settled in it, and you say, "I will set a king over me, like all the nations that are around me," 15 you

q Heb *Asherah*

16.21 Some things are wrong in themselves; others are inexpedient and may lead to sin. The pagan nations had groves of trees where images were set up. Israel is forbidden to plant a grove or even a single tree near God's altar, for it might cause the Israelites to sin. No image, statue, or pillar may be erected with the pretense that it is for the worship of the true God. God is spirit and must be worshiped as such (cf. Jn 4.21–24).
17.1 *defect*. See notes on Lev 3.6 and 22.19, that God's people may not bring blemished animals for sacrifice while keeping the perfect ones for themselves.
17.2–7 Idolatry was a capital crime and punishable by stoning. The procedure mentioned here looks toward the time when Israel was settled in the land.

Criminals were to be taken to the gates of the city, then hands were to be laid on them to transfer the guilt of the community to the offender. Two witnesses were required and they had to cast the first stones, after which the witnesses to the execution cast their stones until the victim was killed.
17.8ff Some legal cases were too difficult for local judges and courts to decide. They were referred to priests and judges at the central sanctuary. Their verdicts were binding and could not be annulled. Whoever refused to conform to the sentence of the highest court was guilty of a capital crime.
17.14 As part of God's plan, a time will come when Israel will want a king. But his rule had to be regulated by God's law (see note on v. 18).

may indeed set over you a king whom the LORD your God will choose. One of your own community you may set as king over you; you are not permitted to put a foreigner over you, who is not of your own community. 16Even so, he must not acquire many horses for himself, or return the people to Egypt in order to acquire more horses, since the LORD has said to you, "You must never return that way again." 17And he must not acquire many wives for himself, or else his heart will turn away; also silver and gold he must not acquire in great quantity for himself. 18When he has taken the throne of his kingdom, he shall have a copy of this law written for him in the presence of the levitical priests. 19It shall remain with him and he shall read in it all the days of his life, so that he may learn to fear the LORD his God, diligently observing all the words of this law and these statutes, 20neither exalting himself above other members of the community nor turning aside from the commandment, either to the right or to the left, so that he and his descendants may reign long over his kingdom in Israel.

11. The portion of the priests and Levites

18 The levitical priests, the whole tribe of Levi, shall have no allotment or inheritance within Israel. They may eat the sacrifices that are the LORD's portion[r] 2but they shall have no inheritance among the other members of the community; the LORD is their inheritance, as he promised them.

3 This shall be the priests' due from the people, from those offering a sacrifice, whether an ox or a sheep: they shall give to the priest the shoulder, the two jowls, and the stomach. 4The first fruits of your grain, your wine, and your oil, as well as the first of the fleece of your sheep, you shall give him. 5For the LORD your God has chosen Levi[s] out of all your tribes, to stand and minister in the name of the LORD, him and his sons for all time.

6 If a Levite leaves any of your towns, from wherever he has been residing in Israel, and comes to the place that the LORD will choose (and he may come whenever he wishes), 7then he may minister in the name of the LORD his God, like all his fellow-Levites who stand to minister there before the LORD. 8They shall have equal portions to eat, even though they have income from the sale of family possessions.[r]

12. The law of the prophet

a. Canaanite practices forbidden

9 When you come into the land that the LORD your God is giving you, you must not learn to imitate the abhorrent practices of those nations. 10No one shall be found among you who makes a son or daughter pass through fire, or who practices divination, or is a soothsayer, or an augur, or a sorcerer, 11or one who casts spells, or who consults ghosts or spirits, or who seeks oracles from the dead. 12For whoever does these things is abhorrent to the LORD; it is because of such abhorrent practices that the LORD your God is driving them out before you. 13You must remain

17.16ff	1 Kings 4.26; 10.26, 28; Isa 31.1; Ezek 17.15
17.17	cf. 1 Kings 11.3, 4
17.18	Deut 31.24-26
17.19	Josh 1.8
17.20	Deut 5.32
18.1	Deut 10.9; 1 Cor 9.13
18.3	Lev 7.30-34
18.4	Ex 22.29; Num 18.12
18.5	Ex 28.1; Deut 10.8
18.8	Neh 12.44, 47
18.9	Deut 12.29-31
18.10	Deut 12.31; Lev 19.26, 31
18.12	Deut 9.4

[r] Meaning of Heb uncertain   [s] Heb him

17.16–20 In the historical books we frequently read of otherwise godly people (such as David and Solomon) multiplying horses, wives, silver, and gold contrary to these regulations. In spite of violating these precepts, they still received God's blessing.
17.18 God ordained that every king of Israel was to write down for himself a copy of the law. Perhaps this refers to the five books of the Pentateuch; perhaps only to Deuteronomy. The king was to study the law daily and keep it close to him at all times (v. 19). He was also to obey the law and practice its precepts. The king was not the law, nor was he above the law. He and all the people were *under* the law of God.
18.10 The Scriptures forbid divination, augury, sorcery, witchcraft, and other heathen practices. Ancient army leaders had diviners who were quite influential in decision-making. Israel was led by the true God; thus heathen practices were inconsistent with genuine faith. Those who engaged in these practices were sentenced to death (Ex 22.18; Lev 20.27). The N.T. says that sorcerers shall not inherit the kingdom of God (Gal 5.20; Rev 22.15).

completely loyal to the LORD your God. 14 Although these nations that you are about to dispossess do give heed to soothsayers and diviners, as for you, the LORD your God does not permit you to do so.

b. The predicted coming of the prophet Messiah: the test of a false prophet

18.15ff
Jn 1.21;
Acts 3.22;
7.37
18.16
Deut 5.23-27;
Ex 20.19
18.17
Deut 5.28
18.18
v. 15;
Isa 51.16;
Jn 4.25, 26
18.19
Acts 3.23
18.20
Deut 13.1, 2,
5

18.22
Jer 28.9;
v. 20

15 The LORD your God will raise up for you a prophet[t] like me from among your own people; you shall heed such a prophet.[u] 16 This is what you requested of the LORD your God at Horeb on the day of the assembly when you said: "If I hear the voice of the LORD my God any more, or ever again see this great fire, I will die." 17 Then the LORD replied to me: "They are right in what they have said. 18 I will raise up for them a prophet[t] like you from among their own people; I will put my words in the mouth of the prophet,[v] who shall speak to them everything that I command. 19 Anyone who does not heed the words that the prophet[w] shall speak in my name, I myself will hold accountable. 20 But any prophet who speaks in the name of other gods, or who presumes to speak in my name a word that I have not commanded the prophet to speak — that prophet shall die." 21 You may say to yourself, "How can we recognize a word that the LORD has not spoken?" 22 If a prophet speaks in the name of the LORD but the thing does not take place or prove true, it is a word that the LORD has not spoken. The prophet has spoken it presumptuously; do not be frightened by it.

13. Criminal laws

a. Cities of refuge for accidental homicide

19.1
Deut 12.29

19.2
Num 35.10,
14

19.4
Num 35.15

19.6
Num 35.12

19.9
Josh 20.7, 8

19 When the LORD your God has cut off the nations whose land the LORD your God is giving you, and you have dispossessed them and settled in their towns and in their houses, 2 you shall set apart three cities in the land that the LORD your God is giving you to possess. 3 You shall calculate the distances[x] and divide into three regions the land that the LORD your God gives you as a possession, so that any homicide can flee to one of them.

4 Now this is the case of a homicide who might flee there and live, that is, someone who has killed another person unintentionally when the two had not been at enmity before: 5 Suppose someone goes into the forest with another to cut wood, and when one of them swings the ax to cut down a tree, the head slips from the handle and strikes the other person who then dies; the killer may flee to one of these cities and live. 6 But if the distance is too great, the avenger of blood in hot anger might pursue and overtake and put the killer to death, although a death sentence was not deserved, since the two had not been at enmity before. 7 Therefore I command you: You shall set apart three cities.

8 If the LORD your God enlarges your territory, as he swore to your ancestors — and he will give you all the land that he promised your ancestors to give you, 9 provided you diligently observe this entire commandment that I command you today, by loving the LORD your God and walking always in his ways — then you shall add three more cities to these

[t] Or prophets   [u] Or such prophets   [v] Or mouths of the prophets   [w] Heb he   [x] Or prepare roads to them

---

18.15–22 God would raise up a prophet like Moses. Other good prophets who spoke the true word of God were raised up after Moses, but the ultimate fulfilling of that prophecy was Jesus Christ (Acts 3.22,23; 7.37). Moses followed this up with tests on how to distinguish between true and false prophets (see next note).
18.22 The test of a false prophet is simple: what he prophesies does not come to pass. Israel need not fear such people. False prophets were subject to capital punishment. This provision would make intelligent people careful about assuming the prophetic role.
19.2–13 Six cities of refuge were to be built for the protection of those who were responsible for the accidental death of another. The first three were to be set up on the east side of the Jordan. Here Moses speaks specifically about the additional three cities to be set up on the west side of the Jordan River. For more on this, see note on Num 35.12.

three, ¹⁰ so that the blood of an innocent person may not be shed in the land that the Lord your God is giving you as an inheritance, thereby bringing bloodguilt upon you.

b. *Punishment for murderers*

11 But if someone at enmity with another lies in wait and attacks and takes the life of that person, and flees into one of these cities, ¹² then the elders of the killer's city shall send to have the culprit taken from there and handed over to the avenger of blood to be put to death. ¹³ Show no pity; you shall purge the guilt of innocent blood from Israel, so that it may go well with you.

c. *Removing boundary markers*

14 You must not move your neighbor's boundary marker, set up by former generations, on the property that will be allotted to you in the land that the Lord your God is giving you to possess.

d. *The law of witnesses*

15 A single witness shall not suffice to convict a person of any crime or wrongdoing in connection with any offense that may be committed. Only on the evidence of two or three witnesses shall a charge be sustained. ¹⁶ If a malicious witness comes forward to accuse someone of wrongdoing, ¹⁷ then both parties to the dispute shall appear before the Lord, before the priests and the judges who are in office in those days, ¹⁸ and the judges shall make a thorough inquiry. If the witness is a false witness, having testified falsely against another, ¹⁹ then you shall do to the false witness just as the false witness had meant to do to the other. So you shall purge the evil from your midst. ²⁰ The rest shall hear and be afraid, and a crime such as this shall never again be committed among you. ²¹ Show no pity: life for life, eye for eye, tooth for tooth, hand for hand, foot for foot.

14. *Laws of war*

a. *Military service*

20 When you go out to war against your enemies, and see horses and chariots, an army larger than your own, you shall not be afraid of them; for the Lord your God is with you, who brought you up from the land of Egypt. ² Before you engage in battle, the priest shall come forward and speak to the troops, ³ and shall say to them: "Hear, O Israel! Today you are drawing near to do battle against your enemies. Do not lose heart, or be afraid, or panic, or be in dread of them; ⁴ for it is the Lord your God who goes with you, to fight for you against your enemies, to give you victory." ⁵ Then the officials shall address the troops, saying, "Has anyone built a new house but not dedicated it? He should go back to his house, or he might die in the battle and another dedicate it. ⁶ Has anyone planted a vineyard but not yet enjoyed its fruit? He should go back to his house, or he might die in the battle and another be first to enjoy its fruit. ⁷ Has anyone become engaged to a woman but not yet married her? He should go back to his house, or he might die in the battle and another marry her."

Cross references (right column):

19.10 Deut 21.1-9; Num 35.33

19.13 Deut 7.2

19.14 Deut 27.17

19.15 Num 35.30; Deut 17.6; Mt 18.16; 2 Cor 13.1
19.16 Ex 23.1; Ps 27.12
19.17 Deut 17.9
19.19 Prov 19.5, 9

19.21 v. 13; Ex 21.23; Lev 24.20; Mt 5.38

20.1 Deut 31.6, 8

20.3 v. 1; Josh 23.10
20.4 Deut 1.30

20.6 1 Cor 9.7

20.7 Deut 24.5

19.14 *boundary marker.* Some Israelites would apparently be tempted to move property markers so as to steal land from their neighbors. This was prohibited.
19.15 God required that no one be declared guilty of an offense on the basis of one person's testimony. This guaranteed better justice. Whoever witnessed falsely to another's guilt would pay the same penalty that would have been exacted against the accused. The very existence of this provision is based on the presumption that some people witness falsely. This provision would keep people from doing the same thing (vv. 20–21).
19.21 *eye for eye.* No law could be any more just than that the punishment must equal the crime. A false witness must receive the penalty that would have ensued if judgment had been executed on the basis of his testimony.
20.7 The law of military service exempted a man who was engaged to marry but the marriage had not yet been consummated. He was free to remain at home for a year after the marriage — presumably so that he could raise up offspring before going to war, thus preserving the family inheritance.

20.8
Judg 7.3

8 The officials shall continue to address the troops, saying, "Is anyone afraid or disheartened? He should go back to his house, or he might cause the heart of his comrades to melt like his own." 9 When the officials have finished addressing the troops, then the commanders shall take charge of them.

b. *Sieges*

20.10ff
Lk 14.31

10   When you draw near to a town to fight against it, offer it terms of peace. 11 If it accepts your terms of peace and surrenders to you, then all the people in it shall serve you at forced labor. 12 If it does not submit to you peacefully, but makes war against you, then you shall besiege it; 13 and when the LORD your God gives it into your hand, you shall put all

20.14
Josh 8.2; 22.8

its males to the sword. 14 You may, however, take as your booty the women, the children, livestock, and everything else in the town, all its spoil. You may enjoy the spoil of your enemies, which the LORD your God has given you. 15 Thus you shall treat all the towns that are very far from

20.16
Deut 7.1, 2;
Josh 11.14

you, which are not towns of the nations here. 16 But as for the towns of these peoples that the LORD your God is giving you as an inheritance, you must not let anything that breathes remain alive. 17 You shall annihilate them — the Hittites and the Amorites, the Canaanites and the Perizzites, the Hivites and the Jebusites — just as the LORD your God has com-

20.18
Ex 23.33

manded, 18 so that they may not teach you to do all the abhorrent things that they do for their gods, and you thus sin against the LORD your God.

19   If you besiege a town for a long time, making war against it in order to take it, you must not destroy its trees by wielding an ax against them. Although you may take food from them, you must not cut them down. Are trees in the field human beings that they should come under siege from you? 20 You may destroy only the trees that you know do not produce food; you may cut them down for use in building siegeworks against the town that makes war with you, until it falls.

15. *Various laws*

a. *Sacrifice for unknown murderer's crime*

21.1
Josh 1.6

21 If, in the land that the LORD your God is giving you to possess, a body is found lying in open country, and it is not known who struck the person down, 2 then your elders and your judges shall come out to measure the distances to the towns that are near the body. 3 The elders of the town nearest the body shall take a heifer that has never been worked, one that has not pulled in the yoke; 4 the elders of that town shall bring the heifer down to a wadi with running water, which is neither plowed nor sown, and shall break the heifer's neck there in the wadi.

21.5
Deut 17.8-11

5 Then the priests, the sons of Levi, shall come forward, for the LORD your God has chosen them to minister to him and to pronounce blessings in the name of the LORD, and by their decision all cases of dispute and assault shall be settled. 6 All the elders of that town nearest the body shall wash their hands over the heifer whose neck was broken in the wadi, 7 and they shall declare: "Our hands did not shed this blood, nor were we witnesses

21.8
Jon 1.8

to it. 8 Absolve, O LORD, your people Israel, whom you redeemed; do not let the guilt of innocent blood remain in the midst of your people Israel."

21.9
Deut 19.13

Then they will be absolved of bloodguilt. 9 So you shall purge the guilt of innocent blood from your midst, because you must do what is right in the sight of the LORD.

20.10–18   See note on 2.34.
20.19,20   War, by its very nature, is destructive. So God protected humanity's best interests by forbidding the destruction of fruit trees (except for those which bore no fruit). Modern warfare, accompanied by mass bombings and the threat of nuclear destruction, suggests how far humanity has departed from

such injunctions.
21.6,7   Many crimes are committed for which the guilty cannot be identified. The community as a whole bears the responsibility and must offer the proper sacrifice, asking for divine forgiveness and professing innocence with respect to the crime.

b. Marrying a captive woman

10   When you go out to war against your enemies, and the LORD your God hands them over to you and you take them captive, 11 suppose you see among the captives a beautiful woman whom you desire and want to marry, 12 and so you bring her home to your house: she shall shave her head, pare her nails, 13 discard her captive's garb, and shall remain in your house a full month, mourning for her father and mother; after that you may go in to her and be her husband, and she shall be your wife. 14 But if you are not satisfied with her, you shall let her go free and not sell her for money. You must not treat her as a slave, since you have dishonored her.

21.12
Lev 14.8, 9;
Num 6.9

c. The law of the firstborn

15   If a man has two wives, one of them loved and the other disliked, and if both the loved and the disliked have borne him sons, the firstborn being the son of the one who is disliked, 16 then on the day when he wills his possessions to his sons, he is not permitted to treat the son of the loved as the firstborn in preference to the son of the disliked, who is the firstborn. 17 He must acknowledge as firstborn the son of the one who is disliked, giving him a double portion^y of all that he has; since he is the first issue of his virility, the right of the firstborn is his.

21.16
1 Chr 26.10

21.17
Gen 49.3

d. Stoning of a rebellious son

18   If someone has a stubborn and rebellious son who will not obey his father and mother, who does not heed them when they discipline him, 19 then his father and his mother shall take hold of him and bring him out to the elders of his town at the gate of that place. 20 They shall say to the elders of his town, "This son of ours is stubborn and rebellious. He will not obey us. He is a glutton and a drunkard." 21 Then all the men of the town shall stone him to death. So you shall purge the evil from your midst; and all Israel will hear, and be afraid.

21.18
Isa 30.1

21.21
Deut 13.5, 11

e. Burying a hanged criminal

22   When someone is convicted of a crime punishable by death and is executed, and you hang him on a tree, 23 his corpse must not remain all night upon the tree; you shall bury him that same day, for anyone hung on a tree is under God's curse. You must not defile the land that the LORD your God is giving you for possession.

21.23
Josh 8.29;
10.26, 27;
Jn 19.31;
Gal 3.13

f. The law of neighborliness

22   You shall not watch your neighbor's ox or sheep straying away and ignore them; you shall take them back to their owner. 2 If the owner does not reside near you or you do not know who the owner is, you shall bring it to your own house, and it shall remain with you until the owner claims it; then you shall return it. 3 You shall do the same with a neighbor's donkey; you shall do the same with a neighbor's garment; and

22.1
Ex 23.4

^{y} Heb two-thirds

21.11 God makes provision here for a soldier to marry a woman taken captive. She is provided protection against misuse. It was wrong for an Israelite to marry a pagan woman in the first place, but provision is made in advance in case such a marriage were to take place.

21.17 The Scriptures nowhere endorse polygamy or concubinage. But they recognize the unhappy fact that polygamy does exist. Thus, if a man had two wives and loved one more than the other, he could not transfer the rights of the firstborn son of the woman he loved less to a younger son of the woman he loved more. The double portion of the inheritance belonged to the firstborn, regardless of whether he was a child of the loved or the unloved wife.

21.20 A stubborn and rebellious son who is a glutton and a drunkard is here subjected to capital punishment. Presumably such a man was first warned not to commit such sins. Anarchy in the home is not permitted. The judgment is pronounced by the community according to its laws, not by the father as an individual.

21.22 Capital punishment normally took place by stoning. But the corpse might then be hung on a tree to warn others against committing similar crimes. However, the body was not to be left hanging overnight; it had to be buried the same day.

you shall do the same with anything else that your neighbor loses and you find. You may not withhold your help.

22.4
Ex 23.5

4 You shall not see your neighbor's donkey or ox fallen on the road and ignore it; you shall help to lift it up.

g. Incidental laws

5 A woman shall not wear a man's apparel, nor shall a man put on a woman's garment; for whoever does such things is abhorrent to the LORD your God.

22.6
Lev 22.28

6 If you come on a bird's nest, in any tree or on the ground, with fledglings or eggs, with the mother sitting on the fledglings or on the eggs, you shall not take the mother with the young. 7 Let the mother go, taking only the young for yourself, in order that it may go well with you and you may live long.

22.7
Deut 4.40

8 When you build a new house, you shall make a parapet for your roof; otherwise you might have bloodguilt on your house, if anyone should fall from it.

22.9
Lev 19.19

9 You shall not sow your vineyard with a second kind of seed, or the whole yield will have to be forfeited, both the crop that you have sown and the yield of the vineyard itself.

10 You shall not plow with an ox and a donkey yoked together.

22.11
Lev 19.19
22.12
Num 15.37-41;
Mt 23.5

11 You shall not wear clothes made of wool and linen woven together.

12 You shall make tassels on the four corners of the cloak with which you cover yourself.

h. The laws of sexual relationships

22.13
Deut 24.1

13 Suppose a man marries a woman, but after going in to her, he dislikes her 14 and makes up charges against her, slandering her by saying, "I married this woman; but when I lay with her, I did not find evidence of her virginity." 15 The father of the young woman and her mother shall then submit the evidence of the young woman's virginity to the elders of the city at the gate. 16 The father of the young woman shall say to the elders: "I gave my daughter in marriage to this man but he dislikes her; 17 now he has made up charges against her, saying, 'I did not find evidence of your daughter's virginity.' But here is the evidence of my daughter's virginity." Then they shall spread out the cloth before the elders of the town. 18 The elders of that town shall take the man and punish him; 19 they shall fine him one hundred shekels of silver (which they shall give to the young woman's father) because he has slandered a virgin of Israel. She shall remain his wife; he shall not be permitted to divorce her as long as he lives.

22.15
v. 23ff

20 If, however, this charge is true, that evidence of the young woman's virginity was not found, 21 then they shall bring the young woman out to the entrance of her father's house and the men of her town shall stone her to death, because she committed a disgraceful act in Israel by prostituting herself in her father's house. So you shall purge the evil from your midst.

22.21
Deut 23.17,
18; 13.5

22 If a man is caught lying with the wife of another man, both of them

22.22
Lev 20.10;
Jn 8.5

22.5 Since normal dress for male and female was similar, provision was made to distinguish male from female and to keep either sex from using the distinctive signs of the opposite sex.
22.12 The Israelites are told to make tassels on the four corners of their garments (see also Num 15.37, 38). This is to distinguish them from other people by showing they are not ashamed of their country or of their religion. It will also remind them of their own origins and faith. Later the Jews ceased to wear these tassels externally in order to avoid both heathen and Christian persecution. They often substituted a kind

of undergarment which covered the chest and back which had four corners to which they attached the fringes or tassels. In Jesus' day the scribes and Pharisees made the tassels long, so that observers might think more highly of their persons (see Mt 23.5).
22.13ff A woman was presumed to be a virgin at the time of her marriage. If her husband had reason to suspect that she was not a virgin, an inquiry must take place. If she was not a virgin she had to be stoned. If she was, her husband must be beaten, fined, and not allowed to put his wife away.

shall die, the man who lay with the woman as well as the woman. So you shall purge the evil from Israel.

23   If there is a young woman, a virgin already engaged to be married, and a man meets her in the town and lies with her, 24 you shall bring both of them to the gate of that town and stone them to death, the young woman because she did not cry for help in the town and the man because he violated his neighbor's wife. So you shall purge the evil from your midst.

25   But if the man meets the engaged woman in the open country, and the man seizes her and lies with her, then only the man who lay with her shall die. 26 You shall do nothing to the young woman; the young woman has not committed an offense punishable by death, because this case is like that of someone who attacks and murders a neighbor. 27 Since he found her in the open country, the engaged woman may have cried for help, but there was no one to rescue her.

28   If a man meets a virgin who is not engaged, and seizes her and lies with her, and they are caught in the act, 29 the man who lay with her shall give fifty shekels of silver to the young woman's father, and she shall become his wife. Because he violated her he shall not be permitted to divorce her as long as he lives.

30 z A man shall not marry his father's wife, thereby violating his father's rights. a

i. Those excluded from the assembly of Israel

23   No one whose testicles are crushed or whose penis is cut off shall be admitted to the assembly of the LORD.

2   Those born of an illicit union shall not be admitted to the assembly of the LORD. Even to the tenth generation, none of their descendants shall be admitted to the assembly of the LORD.

3   No Ammonite or Moabite shall be admitted to the assembly of the LORD. Even to the tenth generation, none of their descendants shall be admitted to the assembly of the LORD, 4 because they did not meet you with food and water on your journey out of Egypt, and because they hired against you Balaam son of Beor, from Pethor of Mesopotamia, to curse you. 5 (Yet the LORD your God refused to heed Balaam; the LORD your God turned the curse into a blessing for you, because the LORD your God loved you.) 6 You shall never promote their welfare or their prosperity as long as you live.

7   You shall not abhor any of the Edomites, for they are your kin. You shall not abhor any of the Egyptians, because you were an alien residing in their land. 8 The children of the third generation that are born to them may be admitted to the assembly of the LORD.

9   When you are encamped against your enemies you shall guard against any impropriety.

j. Camp sanitation in wartime

10   If one of you becomes unclean because of a nocturnal emission, then he shall go outside the camp; he must not come within the camp. 11 When evening comes, he shall wash himself with water, and when the sun has set, he may come back into the camp.

12   You shall have a designated area outside the camp to which you shall go. 13 With your utensils you shall have a trowel; when you relieve

z Ch 23.1 in Heb   a Heb uncovering his father's skirt

22.24
vv. 21, 22

22.25
Jn 8.1-11

22.28
Ex 22.16, 17

22.30
Deut 27.20

23.3
Neh 13.1, 2

23.4
Num 22.5, 6

23.7
Gen 25.24-26

23.10
Lev 15.16

22.25 If a betrothed woman were raped, the rapist would be put to death. If the rape victim were not betrothed, the rapist had to either pay a fine to her father or marry her; in the latter case, he would be forbidden to put her away.
23.3 See notes on Ezek 25.2,9 for information on the Ammonites and Moabites.

23.7 Regarding the Edomites, see note on Gen 36.9. No reason is given why Israel should not abhor an Egyptian. God orders them to forget, in effect, their slavery in Egypt and remember instead the delivering power of their God. The grandchildren of Edomites or Egyptians who turned to God could enter the assembly of Israel as members.

MAJOR SOCIAL CONCERNS IN THE COVENANT

1. PERSONHOOD
Everyone's person is to be secure (Ex 20:13; Dt 5:17; Ex 21:16-21, 26-31; Lev 19:14; Dt 24:7; 27:18).

2. FALSE ACCUSATION
Everyone is to be secure against slander and false accusation (Ex 20:16; Dt 5:20; Ex 23:1-3; Lev 19:16; Dt 19:15-21).

3. WOMAN
No woman is to be taken advantage of within her subordinate status in society (Ex 21:7-11, 20, 26-32; 22:16-17; Dt. 21:10-14; 22:13-30; 24:1-5).

4. PUNISHMENT
Punishment for wrongdoing shall not be excessive so that the culprit is dehumanized (Dt 25:1-5).

5. DIGNITY
Every Israelite's dignity and right to be God's freedman and servant are to be honored and safeguarded (Ex 21:2, 5-6; Lev 25; Dt 15:12-18).

6. INHERITANCE
Every Israelite's inheritance in the promised land is to be secure (Lev 25; Nu 27:5-7; 36:1-9; Dt 25:5-10).

7. PROPERTY
Everyone's property is to be secure (Ex 20:15; Dt 5:19; Ex 21:33-36; 22:1-15; 23:4-5; Lev 19:35-36; Dt 22:1-4; 25:13-15).

8. FRUIT OF LABOR
Everyone is to receive the fruit of his labors (Lev 19:13; Dt 24:14; 25:4).

9. FRUIT OF THE GROUND
Everyone is to share the fruit of the ground (Ex 23:10-11; Lev 19:9-10; 23:22; 25:3-55; Dt. 14:28-29; 24:19-21).

10. REST ON SABBATH
Everyone, down to the humblest servant and the resident alien, is to share in the weekly rest of God's Sabbath (Ex 20:8-11; Dt 5:12-15; Ex 23:12).

11. MARRIAGE
The marriage relationship is to be kept inviolate (Ex 20:14; Dt 5:18; see also Lev 18:6-23; 20:10-21; Dt 22:13-30).

12. EXPLOITATION
No one, however disabled, impoverished or powerless, is to be oppressed or exploited (Ex 22:21-27; Lev 19:14, 33-34; 25:35-36; Dt 23:19; 24:6, 12-15, 17; 27:18).

13. FAIR TRIAL
Everyone is to have free access to the courts and is to be afforded a fair trial (Ex 23:6,8; Lev 19:15; Dt 1:17; 10:17-18; 16:18-20; 17:8-13; 19:15-21).

14. SOCIAL ORDER
Every person's God-given place in the social order is to be honored (Ex 20:12; Dt 5:16; Ex 21:15, 17; 22:28; Lev 19:3, 32; 20:9; Dt 17:8-13; 21:15-21; 27:16).

15. LAW
No one shall be above the law, not even the king (Dt 17:18-20).

16. ANIMALS
Concern for the welfare of other creatures is to be extended to the animal world (Ex 23:5, 11; Lev 25:7, Dt 22:4, 6-7; 25:4).

yourself outside, you shall dig a hole with it and then cover up your excrement. 14 Because the LORD your God travels along with your camp, to save you and to hand over your enemies to you, therefore your camp must be holy, so that he may not see anything indecent among you and turn away from you.

23.14
Lev 26.12

k. Incidental laws

15 Slaves who have escaped to you from their owners shall not be given back to them. 16 They shall reside with you, in your midst, in any place they choose in any one of your towns, wherever they please; you shall not oppress them.

17 None of the daughters of Israel shall be a temple prostitute; none of the sons of Israel shall be a temple prostitute. 18 You shall not bring the fee of a prostitute or the wages of a male prostitute[b] into the house of the LORD your God in payment for any vow, for both of these are abhorrent to the LORD your God.

23.17
Deut 22.21

19 You shall not charge interest on loans to another Israelite, interest on money, interest on provisions, interest on anything that is lent. 20 On loans to a foreigner you may charge interest, but on loans to another Israelite you may not charge interest, so that the LORD your God may bless you in all your undertakings in the land that you are about to enter and possess.

23.19
Ex 22.25;
Lev 25.36, 37
23.20
Deut 28.12

21 If you make a vow to the LORD your God, do not postpone fulfilling it; for the LORD your God will surely require it of you, and you would incur guilt. 22 But if you refrain from vowing, you will not incur guilt. 23 Whatever your lips utter you must diligently perform, just as you have freely vowed to the LORD your God with your own mouth.

23.21
Num 30.2;
Mt 5.33

24 If you go into your neighbor's vineyard, you may eat your fill of grapes, as many as you wish, but you shall not put any in a container.

25 If you go into your neighbor's standing grain, you may pluck the ears with your hand, but you shall not put a sickle to your neighbor's standing grain.

23.25
Mt 12.1;
Mk 2.23;
Lk 6.1

l. Additional incidental laws

24 Suppose a man enters into marriage with a woman, but she does not please him because he finds something objectionable about her, and so he writes her a certificate of divorce, puts it in her hand, and sends her out of his house; she then leaves his house 2 and goes off to become another man's wife. 3 Then suppose the second man dislikes her, writes her a bill of divorce, puts it in her hand, and sends her out of his house (or the second man who married her dies); 4 her first husband, who sent her away, is not permitted to take her again to be his wife after she has been defiled; for that would be abhorrent to the LORD, and you shall

24.1
Deut 22.13-21;
Mt 5.31;
19.7;
Mk 10.4

24.4
Jer 3.1

b Heb a dog

23.15 God provides sanctuary in Israel for a slave from any neighboring nation who escapes and who, apparently, has been abused in his servitude. Similarly today, international law provides sanctuary for a citizen of one nation who flees to another, if the cause for flight is legitimate.

23.17 Canaanite worship included the use of male and female cult prostitutes. God forbade this practice for Israel.

23.24,25 Anyone was permitted to eat grapes or grain while in another's field, but no one was permitted to carry anything away with him.

24.1 Divorce was never in the will of God, but it was permitted with certain restrictions as a concession to people's waywardness and hardness of heart (cf. Mt 19.8). The provisions here were designed to protect the property rights of a woman whose husband sent

her away. He was required to surrender his claim to her dowry. Jesus forbade divorce among Christians except on the ground of adultery (Mt 5.32; 19.9). Adultery breaks the marriage bond; in the O.T. those guilty of adultery were stoned to death and the innocent parties were free to remarry. Though we do not stone people to death for adultery today, remarriage seems appropriate for a truly innocent party whose mate has committed adultery. Some say that willful desertion is also ground for remarriage, but the Scriptures do not explicitly say this. According to the Bible, any Christian who marries someone divorced for other than a biblical reason commits adultery. Others argue that there is no biblical basis for any divorce, saying marriage can be broken only by the death of a spouse.

not bring guilt on the land that the LORD your God is giving you as a possession.

5 When a man is newly married, he shall not go out with the army or be charged with any related duty. He shall be free at home one year, to be happy with the wife whom he has married.

6 No one shall take a mill or an upper millstone in pledge, for that would be taking a life in pledge.

7 If someone is caught kidnaping another Israelite, enslaving or selling the Israelite, then that kidnaper shall die. So you shall purge the evil from your midst.

8 Guard against an outbreak of a leprous*c* skin disease by being very careful; you shall carefully observe whatever the levitical priests instruct you, just as I have commanded them. 9 Remember what the LORD your God did to Miriam on your journey out of Egypt.

10 When you make your neighbor a loan of any kind, you shall not go into the house to take the pledge. 11 You shall wait outside, while the person to whom you are making the loan brings the pledge out to you. 12 If the person is poor, you shall not sleep in the garment given you as*d* the pledge. 13 You shall give the pledge back by sunset, so that your neighbor may sleep in the cloak and bless you; and it will be to your credit before the LORD your God.

14 You shall not withhold the wages of poor and needy laborers, whether other Israelites or aliens who reside in your land in one of your towns. 15 You shall pay them their wages daily before sunset, because they are poor and their livelihood depends on them; otherwise they might cry to the LORD against you, and you would incur guilt.

16 Parents shall not be put to death for their children, nor shall children be put to death for their parents; only for their own crimes may persons be put to death.

17 You shall not deprive a resident alien or an orphan of justice; you shall not take a widow's garment in pledge. 18 Remember that you were a slave in Egypt and the LORD your God redeemed you from there; therefore I command you to do this.

19 When you reap your harvest in your field and forget a sheaf in the field, you shall not go back to get it; it shall be left for the alien, the orphan, and the widow, so that the LORD your God may bless you in all your undertakings. 20 When you beat your olive trees, do not strip what is left; it shall be for the alien, the orphan, and the widow.

21 When you gather the grapes of your vineyard, do not glean what is left; it shall be for the alien, the orphan, and the widow. 22 Remember that you were a slave in the land of Egypt; therefore I am commanding you to do this.

25 Suppose two persons have a dispute and enter into litigation, and the judges decide between them, declaring one to be in the right and the other to be in the wrong. 2 If the one in the wrong deserves to be flogged, the judge shall make that person lie down and be beaten in his presence with the number of lashes proportionate to the offense. 3 Forty lashes may be given but not more; if more lashes than these are given, your neighbor will be degraded in your sight.

4 You shall not muzzle an ox while it is treading out the grain.

5 When brothers reside together, and one of them dies and has no son,

24.5
Deut 20.7

24.7
Ex 21.16

24.8
Lev 13.2;
14.2
24.9
Num 12.10

24.13
Ex 22.26;
Deut 6.25

24.14
Lev 25.35-43;
Deut 15.7-18
24.15
Lev 19.13;
Jas 5.4;
Deut 15.9

24.16
2 Kings 14.6;
2 Chr 25.4;
Jer 31.29, 30;
Ezek 18.20
24.17
Deut 1.17;
10.17; 16.19
24.18
Deut 16.12

24.19
Lev 19.9, 10;
23.22

24.20
Lev 19.10

24.22
v. 18

25.1
Deut 19.17;
1.16, 17

25.3
2 Cor 11.24
25.4
1 Cor 9.9;
1 Tim 5.18
25.5ff
Mt 22.24;
Mk 12.19;
Lk 20.28

c A term for several skin diseases; precise meaning uncertain   *d* Heb lacks *the garment given you as*

24.6 The mill for grinding grain was essential to life. Neither the mill nor one of the stones was to be taken as security for a loan. Human life always takes precedence over human property.
24.14 God is interested in those who earn their keep by working for others. Hired servants were not to be overloaded with work, unreasonably rebuked, or im-

properly cared for. This rule of thumb applied to Israelite servants and to aliens.
25.5–10 Levirate marriage was established under the Deuteronomic code. If a brother died childless, his unmarried brother was supposed to produce children by the widow. This was probably intended to protect the property rights of the deceased. The first

the wife of the deceased shall not be married outside the family to a stranger. Her husband's brother shall go in to her, taking her in marriage, and performing the duty of a husband's brother to her, 6 and the firstborn whom she bears shall succeed to the name of the deceased brother, so that his name may not be blotted out of Israel. 7 But if the man has no desire to marry his brother's widow, then his brother's widow shall go up to the elders at the gate and say, "My husband's brother refuses to perpetuate his brother's name in Israel; he will not perform the duty of a husband's brother to me." 8 Then the elders of his town shall summon him and speak to him. If he persists, saying, "I have no desire to marry her," 9 then his brother's wife shall go up to him in the presence of the elders, pull his sandal off his foot, spit in his face, and declare, "This is what is done to the man who does not build up his brother's house." 10 Throughout Israel his family shall be known as "the house of him whose sandal was pulled off."

11   If men get into a fight with one another, and the wife of one intervenes to rescue her husband from the grip of his opponent by reaching out and seizing his genitals, 12 you shall cut off her hand; show no pity.

13   You shall not have in your bag two kinds of weights, large and small. 14 You shall not have in your house two kinds of measures, large and small. 15 You shall have only a full and honest weight; you shall have only a full and honest measure, so that your days may be long in the land that the LORD your God is giving you. 16 For all who do such things, all who act dishonestly, are abhorrent to the LORD your God.

17   Remember what Amalek did to you on your journey out of Egypt, 18 how he attacked you on the way, when you were faint and weary, and struck down all who lagged behind you; he did not fear God. 19 Therefore when the LORD your God has given you rest from all your enemies on every hand, in the land that the LORD your God is giving you as an inheritance to possess, you shall blot out the remembrance of Amalek from under heaven; do not forget.

m. Offerings and thanksgiving

26 When you have come into the land that the LORD your God is giving you as an inheritance to possess, and you possess it, and settle in it, 2 you shall take some of the first of all the fruit of the ground, which you harvest from the land that the LORD your God is giving you, and you shall put it in a basket and go to the place that the LORD your God will choose as a dwelling for his name. 3 You shall go to the priest who is in office at that time, and say to him, "Today I declare to the LORD your God that I have come into the land that the LORD swore to our ancestors to give us." 4 When the priest takes the basket from your hand and sets it down before the altar of the LORD your God, 5 you shall make this response before the LORD your God: "A wandering Aramean was my ancestor; he went down into Egypt and lived there as an alien, few in number, and there he became a great nation, mighty and populous. 6 When the Egyptians treated us harshly and afflicted us, by imposing

25.6
Gen 38.9;
Ruth 4.10
25.7
Ruth 4.1, 2

25.8
Ruth 4.6
25.9f
Ruth 4.7, 11

25.13
Lev 19.35-37

25.16
Prov 11.1

25.17
Ex 17.8

25.19
1 Sam 15.2, 3

26.2
Ex 22.29;
23.16, 19;
Num 18.13

26.5
Hos 12.12;
Gen 43.1, 2;
45.7, 11;
46.27;
Deut 10.22
26.6
Ex 1.11, 14

son of the levirate marriage had the same rights he would have had if he had been fathered by his mother's dead husband. All additional children were regarded as legal heirs of the father and not of his dead brother. The custom is pre-Mosaic, being mentioned in the Nuzi tablets. Tamar (Gen 38) insisted upon this right against her father-in-law Judah, and contrived his compliance. Later this regulation was the basis of a Sadducean argument against bodily resurrection (Mt 22.23–33).
25.9,10 Compare this with the custom described in Ruth 4.7,8.

25.13 The Israelites had a common system of weights and measures. But it is obvious that some cheated by shortchanging those who did business with them. This form of stealing was prohibited, even as it is today.
25.17 Israel is reminded that the Amalekites were their enemy and that God had sworn to blot out the remembrance of them (see Ex 17.14). This judgment was deferred until Saul's time (see 1 Sam 15).
26.5 *A wandering Aramean.* This refers to Jacob, who had close ties to Paddan-aram.

26.7
Ex 2.23-25

26.8
Deut 4.34

26.9
Ex 3.8

26.11
Deut 12.7

26.12
Deut 14.28,
29;
Heb 7.5, 9,
10
26.13
Ps 119.141,
153, 176

26.14
Lev 7.20;
Hos 9.4

26.16
Deut 4.29

26.18
Deut 7.6

26.19
Deut 28.1;
Ps 148.14;
Deut 7.6

27.2
Josh 8.30-32
27.3
Deut 26.9

hard labor on us, 7 we cried to the Lord, the God of our ancestors; the Lord heard our voice and saw our affliction, our toil, and our oppression. 8 The Lord brought us out of Egypt with a mighty hand and an outstretched arm, with a terrifying display of power, and with signs and wonders; 9 and he brought us into this place and gave us this land, a land flowing with milk and honey. 10 So now I bring the first of the fruit of the ground that you, O Lord, have given me." You shall set it down before the Lord your God and bow down before the Lord your God. 11 Then you, together with the Levites and the aliens who reside among you, shall celebrate with all the bounty that the Lord your God has given to you and to your house.

12 When you have finished paying all the tithe of your produce in the third year (which is the year of the tithe), giving it to the Levites, the aliens, the orphans, and the widows, so that they may eat their fill within your towns, 13 then you shall say before the Lord your God: "I have removed the sacred portion from the house, and I have given it to the Levites, the resident aliens, the orphans, and the widows, in accordance with your entire commandment that you commanded me; I have neither transgressed nor forgotten any of your commandments: 14 I have not eaten of it while in mourning; I have not removed any of it while I was unclean; and I have not offered any of it to the dead. I have obeyed the Lord my God, doing just as you commanded me. 15 Look down from your holy habitation, from heaven, and bless your people Israel and the ground that you have given us, as you swore to our ancestors — a land flowing with milk and honey."

16. Moses' command to obey God

16 This very day the Lord your God is commanding you to observe these statutes and ordinances; so observe them diligently with all your heart and with all your soul. 17 Today you have obtained the Lord's agreement: to be your God; and for you to walk in his ways, to keep his statutes, his commandments, and his ordinances, and to obey him. 18 Today the Lord has obtained your agreement: to be his treasured people, as he promised you, and to keep his commandments; 19 for him to set you high above all nations that he has made, in praise and in fame and in honor; and for you to be a people holy to the Lord your God, as he promised.

III. The covenant renewed (27.1–30.20)

A. The altar on Mount Ebal

27 Then Moses and the elders of Israel charged all the people as follows: Keep the entire commandment that I am commanding you today. 2 On the day that you cross over the Jordan into the land that the Lord your God is giving you, you shall set up large stones and cover them with plaster. 3 You shall write on them all the words of this law when

---

26.12 See note on 14.28,29 about the third-year tithe for the poor. God left it up to the individual to follow the commandment to use the fruit of the land for the poor, the widow, and the Levites. At the end of that third year, all were required to swear before God that they had in fact used the tithe of the land for the purpose for which it was taken and that there had been no holding back or misuse of it. This oath was based on the knowledge of the potential of human sinfulness and was designed to curb coveteousness.
26.14 *not offered any of it to the dead.* Heathen people sacrificed to the spirits of the dead. This practice was forbidden in Israel; there is no indication that Israelites did this.

26.19 *High above all nations* implies that God would accept the Israelites, their friends would admire them, and their enemies would envy them. *Holy to the Lord* means they would be separated unto him, devoted to him, and rightly employed in his service. The same things may be said of the church and its people since Pentecost. God raises it above the unregenerate, and it is a holy people whose service glorifies the Redeemer.
27.1 This chapter, which speaks of Moses in the third person, is thought by some to be out of place here because it interrupts the smooth flow of Moses' address. This chapter may indeed be an interlude that was inserted in the final composition of the book.

you have crossed over, to enter the land that the LORD your God is giving you, a land flowing with milk and honey, as the LORD, the God of your ancestors, promised you. 4 So when you have crossed over the Jordan, you shall set up these stones, about which I am commanding you today, on Mount Ebal, and you shall cover them with plaster. 5 And you shall build an altar there to the LORD your God, an altar of stones on which you have not used an iron tool. 6 You must build the altar of the LORD your God of unhewn*e* stones. Then offer up burnt offerings on it to the LORD your God, 7 make sacrifices of well-being, and eat them there, rejoicing before the LORD your God. 8 You shall write on the stones all the words of this law very clearly.

9 Then Moses and the levitical priests spoke to all Israel, saying: Keep silence and hear, O Israel! This very day you have become the people of the LORD your God. 10 Therefore obey the LORD your God, observing his commandments and his statutes that I am commanding you today.

11 The same day Moses charged the people as follows: 12 When you have crossed over the Jordan, these shall stand on Mount Gerizim for the blessing of the people: Simeon, Levi, Judah, Issachar, Joseph, and Benjamin. 13 And these shall stand on Mount Ebal for the curse: Reuben, Gad, Asher, Zebulun, Dan, and Naphtali. 14 Then the Levites shall declare in a loud voice to all the Israelites:

B. *The twelve curses at Mount Ebal*

15 "Cursed be anyone who makes an idol or casts an image, anything abhorrent to the LORD, the work of an artisan, and sets it up in secret." All the people shall respond, saying, "Amen!"

16 "Cursed be anyone who dishonors father or mother." All the people shall say, "Amen!"

17 "Cursed be anyone who moves a neighbor's boundary marker." All the people shall say, "Amen!"

18 "Cursed be anyone who misleads a blind person on the road." All the people shall say, "Amen!"

19 "Cursed be anyone who deprives the alien, the orphan, and the widow of justice." All the people shall say, "Amen!"

20 "Cursed be anyone who lies with his father's wife, because he has violated his father's rights."*f* All the people shall say, "Amen!"

21 "Cursed be anyone who lies with any animal." All the people shall say, "Amen!"

22 "Cursed be anyone who lies with his sister, whether the daughter of his father or the daughter of his mother." All the people shall say, "Amen!"

23 "Cursed be anyone who lies with his mother-in-law." All the people shall say, "Amen!"

24 "Cursed be anyone who strikes down a neighbor in secret." All the people shall say, "Amen!"

25 "Cursed be anyone who takes a bribe to shed innocent blood." All the people shall say, "Amen!"

26 "Cursed be anyone who does not uphold the words of this law by observing them." All the people shall say, "Amen!"

e Heb whole f Heb uncovered his father's skirt

27.5
Ex 20.25;
Josh 8.31

27.9
Deut 26.18

27.12
Josh 8.33-35

27.15
Ex 20.4, 23;
34.17

27.16
Ex 21.17;
Lev 20.9

27.17
Lev 19.14

27.18
Lev 19.14

27.19
Deut 10.18;
24.17

27.20
Lev 18.8;
Deut 22.30

27.21
Lev 18.23

27.22
Lev 18.9;
20.17

27.23
Lev 20.14

27.24
Lev 24.17;
Num 35.31

27.25
Ex 23.7, 8

27.26
Deut 28.15;
Gal 3.10

27.11ff Once Israel entered the land, the covenant had to be publicly renewed and accepted by oral testimony. Six of the tribes were to be stationed on Mount Ebal and the other six on Mount Gerazim. The six on Mount Gerazim were children of Leah and Rachel; the other six were children of their maids. Curses were to be declared as judgments against those things that were prohibited, and the Israelites were to shout "Amen." By this, they acknowledged the equity of the curses and promised they would not do what was prohibited. Their assent would make any disobedience their own fault, and any judgment that followed would be what they deserved.

C. *The blessings for obedience*

28.1
Deut 7.12-26;
26.19

28 If you will only obey the LORD your God, by diligently observing all his commandments that I am commanding you today, the LORD your God will set you high above all the nations of the earth; 2 all these blessings shall come upon you and overtake you, if you obey the LORD your God:

28.3
Gen 39.5;
Ps 128.14

28.4
Gen 49.25;
Ps 107.38;
Prov 10.22

3 Blessed shall you be in the city, and blessed shall you be in the field.

4 Blessed shall be the fruit of your womb, the fruit of your ground, and the fruit of your livestock, both the increase of your cattle and the issue of your flock.

5 Blessed shall be your basket and your kneading bowl.

6 Blessed shall you be when you come in, and blessed shall you be when you go out.

28.7
Lev 26.7, 8

7 The LORD will cause your enemies who rise against you to be defeated before you; they shall come out against you one way, and flee before you seven ways. 8 The LORD will command the blessing upon you in your barns, and in all that you undertake; he will bless you in the land that the LORD your God is giving you.

28.9
Deut 7.6

9 The LORD will establish you as his holy people, as he has sworn to you, if you keep the commandments of the LORD your God and walk in his ways.

28.10
2 Chr 7.14

10 All the peoples of the earth shall see that you are called by the name of the LORD, and they shall be afraid of you.

28.11
Deut 30.9

11 The LORD will make you abound in prosperity, in the fruit of your womb, in the fruit of your livestock, and in the fruit of your ground in the land that the LORD swore to your ancestors to give you.

28.12
Lev 26.4;
Deut 15.6

12 The LORD will open for you his rich storehouse, the heavens, to give the rain of your land in its season and to bless all your undertakings. You will lend to many nations, but you will not borrow. 13 The LORD will make you the head, and not the tail; you shall be only at the top, and not at the bottom — if you obey the commandments of the LORD your God, which I am commanding you today, by diligently observing them, 14 and if you

28.14
Deut 5.32

do not turn aside from any of the words that I am commanding you today, either to the right or to the left, following other gods to serve them.

D. *The curses for disobedience*

28.15
Lev 26.14;
Josh 23.15;
Mal 2.2

15 But if you will not obey the LORD your God by diligently observing all his commandments and decrees, which I am commanding you today, then all these curses shall come upon you and overtake you:

16 Cursed shall you be in the city, and cursed shall you be in the field.

17 Cursed shall be your basket and your kneading bowl.

18 Cursed shall be the fruit of your womb, the fruit of your ground, the increase of your cattle and the issue of your flock.

19 Cursed shall you be when you come in, and cursed shall you be when you go out.

28.20
Deut 4.26
28.21
Lev 26.25;
Jer 24.10
28.22
Lev 26.16;
Am 4.9
28.23
Lev 26.19

20 The LORD will send upon you disaster, panic, and frustration in everything you attempt to do, until you are destroyed and perish quickly, on account of the evil of your deeds, because you have forsaken me. 21 The LORD will make the pestilence cling to you until it has consumed you off the land that you are entering to possess. 22 The LORD will afflict you with consumption, fever, inflammation, with fiery heat and drought, and with blight and mildew; they shall pursue you until you perish. 23 The sky over

---

28.2 If there are cursings for disobedience, there are also blessings for obedience. Here God makes promises to his people — for better or for worse; unfortunately, they were for the worse, resulting in the captivity and the diminution of the nation before the birth of Jesus Christ. At some later time, a repentant Israel will have the blessings restored.

28.11 *The LORD will make you abound in prosperity.*

There is nothing intrinsically wrong in having much of this world's goods, for God has promised to bless his people materially. But the more God gives them, the greater their stewardship responsibilities. Riches can be either a snare to the believer or an instrument for the glory of God and the advancement of the gospel throughout the world.

your head shall be bronze, and the earth under you iron. 24 The LORD will change the rain of your land into powder, and only dust shall come down upon you from the sky until you are destroyed.

25   The LORD will cause you to be defeated before your enemies; you shall go out against them one way and flee before them seven ways. You shall become an object of horror to all the kingdoms of the earth. 26 Your corpses shall be food for every bird of the air and animal of the earth, and there shall be no one to frighten them away. 27 The LORD will afflict you with the boils of Egypt, with ulcers, scurvy, and itch, of which you cannot be healed. 28 The LORD will afflict you with madness, blindness, and confusion of mind; 29 you shall grope about at noon as blind people grope in darkness, but you shall be unable to find your way; and you shall be continually abused and robbed, without anyone to help. 30 You shall become engaged to a woman, but another man shall lie with her. You shall build a house, but not live in it. You shall plant a vineyard, but not enjoy its fruit. 31 Your ox shall be butchered before your eyes, but you shall not eat of it. Your donkey shall be stolen in front of you, and shall not be restored to you. Your sheep shall be given to your enemies, without anyone to help you. 32 Your sons and daughters shall be given to another people, while you look on; you will strain your eyes looking for them all day but be powerless to do anything. 33 A people whom you do not know shall eat up the fruit of your ground and of all your labors; you shall be continually abused and crushed, 34 and driven mad by the sight that your eyes shall see. 35 The LORD will strike you on the knees and on the legs with grievous boils of which you cannot be healed, from the sole of your foot to the crown of your head. 36 The LORD will bring you, and the king whom you set over you, to a nation that neither you nor your ancestors have known, where you shall serve other gods, of wood and stone. 37 You shall become an object of horror, a proverb, and a byword among all the peoples where the LORD will lead you.

38   You shall carry much seed into the field but shall gather little in, for the locust shall consume it. 39 You shall plant vineyards and dress them, but you shall neither drink the wine nor gather the grapes, for the worm shall eat them. 40 You shall have olive trees throughout all your territory, but you shall not anoint yourself with the oil, for your olives shall drop off. 41 You shall have sons and daughters, but they shall not remain yours, for they shall go into captivity. 42 All your trees and the fruit of your ground the cicada shall take over. 43 Aliens residing among you shall ascend above you higher and higher, while you shall descend lower and lower. 44 They shall lend to you but you shall not lend to them; they shall be the head and you shall be the tail.

45   All these curses shall come upon you, pursuing and overtaking you until you are destroyed, because you did not obey the LORD your God, by observing the commandments and the decrees that he commanded you. 46 They shall be among you and your descendants as a sign and a portent forever.

47   Because you did not serve the LORD your God joyfully and with gladness of heart for the abundance of everything, 48 therefore you shall serve your enemies whom the LORD will send against you, in hunger and thirst, in nakedness and lack of everything. He will put an iron yoke on your neck until he has destroyed you. 49 The LORD will bring a nation from far away, from the end of the earth, to swoop down on you like an eagle, a nation whose language you do not understand, 50 a grim-faced nation showing no respect to the old or favor to the young. 51 It shall

28.25
Lev 26.17,
37;
Jer 15.4
28.26
Jer 7.33;
16.4; 34.20
28.27
vv. 60, 61

28.29
Job 5.14;
Isa 59.10
28.30
Jer 8.10;
12.13;
Am 5.11

28.32
v. 41
28.33
Jer 5.17

28.35
v. 27
28.36
2 Kings 17.4,
6; 24.12, 14;
25.7, 11;
Deut 4.28
28.37
Jer 24.9;
Ps 44.14
28.38
Mic 6.15

28.41
v. 32
28.42
v. 38
28.43
v. 13
28.44
vv. 12, 13

28.45
v. 15

28.47
Deut 32.15
28.48
Jer 28.13, 14

28.49
Jer 5.15

28.51
v. 33

28.36 This prophetic word was literally fulfilled when the ten tribes were carried captive into Assyria (2 Kings 17.6) and later when the other two tribes were taken to Babylon in the captivity of seventy years (2 Kings 24.14,15; 25.7,21).

28.49–57 Some think this judgment refers to the Babylonian captivity; others think it is the destruction of Jerusalem by the Romans in A.D. 70, as later prophesied by Jesus; still others think it refers to both judgments.

consume the fruit of your livestock and the fruit of your ground until you are destroyed, leaving you neither grain, wine, and oil, nor the increase of your cattle and the issue of your flock, until it has made you perish. 52 It shall besiege you in all your towns until your high and fortified walls, in which you trusted, come down throughout your land; it shall besiege you in all your towns throughout the land that the LORD your God has given you. 53 In the desperate straits to which the enemy siege reduces you, you will eat the fruit of your womb, the flesh of your own sons and daughters whom the LORD your God has given you. 54 Even the most refined and gentle of men among you will begrudge food to his own brother, to the wife whom he embraces, and to the last of his remaining children, 55 giving to none of them any of the flesh of his children whom he is eating, because nothing else remains to him, in the desperate straits to which the enemy siege will reduce you in all your towns. 56 She who is the most refined and gentle among you, so gentle and refined that she does not venture to set the sole of her foot on the ground, will begrudge food to the husband whom she embraces, to her own son, and to her own daughter, 57 begrudging even the afterbirth that comes out from between her thighs, and the children that she bears, because she is eating them in secret for lack of anything else, in the desperate straits to which the enemy siege will reduce you in your towns.

58 If you do not diligently observe all the words of this law that are written in this book, fearing this glorious and awesome name, the LORD your God, 59 then the LORD will overwhelm both you and your offspring with severe and lasting afflictions and grievous and lasting maladies. 60 He will bring back upon you all the diseases of Egypt, of which you were in dread, and they shall cling to you. 61 Every other malady and affliction, even though not recorded in the book of this law, the LORD will inflict on you until you are destroyed. 62 Although once you were as numerous as the stars in heaven, you shall be left few in number, because you did not obey the LORD your God. 63 And just as the LORD took delight in making you prosperous and numerous, so the LORD will take delight in bringing you to ruin and destruction; you shall be plucked off the land that you are entering to possess. 64 The LORD will scatter you among all peoples, from one end of the earth to the other; and there you shall serve other gods, of wood and stone, which neither you nor your ancestors have known. 65 Among those nations you shall find no ease, no resting place for the sole of your foot. There the LORD will give you a trembling heart, failing eyes, and a languishing spirit. 66 Your life shall hang in doubt before you; night and day you shall be in dread, with no assurance of your life. 67 In the morning you shall say, "If only it were evening!" and at evening you shall say, "If only it were morning!" — because of the dread that your heart shall feel and the sights that your eyes shall see. 68 The LORD will bring you back in ships to Egypt, by a route that I promised you would never see again; and there you shall offer yourselves for sale to your enemies as male and female slaves, but there will be no buyer.

E. The exhortation to keep the covenant

29 *g* These are the words of the covenant that the LORD commanded Moses to make with the Israelites in the land of Moab, in addition to the covenant that he had made with them at Horeb.

g Ch 28.69 in Heb

Cross references (left margin):

28.52 Jer 10.17, 18; Zeph 1.15, 16; Josh 1.4
28.53 Lev 26.29; Jer 19.9; Lam 2.20
28.56 v. 54
28.58 Ex 6.3
28.60 v. 27
28.61 Deut 4.25, 26
28.62 Deut 4.27; 10.22
28.63 Jer 12.14; 45.4
28.64 Deut 4.27, 28
28.65 Lev 26.16, 36
28.67 v. 34
29.1 Deut 5.2, 3

28.62 This prophecy concerning the Jews was fulfilled in the *diaspora* ("dispersion"), when the northern kingdom came under attack by the Assyrians in 722 B.C., when Nebuchadnezzar overcame Jerusalem in 586 B.C., and finally when Titus and Vespasian finished this work in A.D. 70 at the time Jerusalem was destroyed. The Bible has numerous prophecies concerning future events which either have been fulfilled or await fulfillment. Fulfilled prophecy attests to the truthfulness of the Word of God.

29.1 This agreement between God and Israel was made in Moab and is an extension of the Abrahamic

2 [h] Moses summoned all Israel and said to them: You have seen all that the LORD did before your eyes in the land of Egypt, to Pharaoh and to all his servants and to all his land, 3 the great trials that your eyes saw, the signs, and those great wonders. 4 But to this day the LORD has not given you a mind to understand, or eyes to see, or ears to hear. 5 I have led you forty years in the wilderness. The clothes on your back have not worn out, and the sandals on your feet have not worn out; 6 you have not eaten bread, and you have not drunk wine or strong drink — so that you may know that I am the LORD your God. 7 When you came to this place, King Sihon of Heshbon and King Og of Bashan came out against us for battle, but we defeated them. 8 We took their land and gave it as an inheritance to the Reubenites, the Gadites, and the half-tribe of Manasseh. 9 Therefore diligently observe the words of this covenant, in order that you may succeed [i] in everything that you do.

F. The punishment for forsaking the covenant

10 You stand assembled today, all of you, before the LORD your God — the leaders of your tribes, [j] your elders, and your officials, all the men of Israel, 11 your children, your women, and the aliens who are in your camp, both those who cut your wood and those who draw your water — 12 to enter into the covenant of the LORD your God, sworn by an oath, which the LORD your God is making with you today; 13 in order that he may establish you today as his people, and that he may be your God, as he promised you and as he swore to your ancestors, to Abraham, to Isaac, and to Jacob. 14 I am making this covenant, sworn by an oath, not only with you who stand here with us today before the LORD our God, 15 but also with those who are not here with us today. 16 You know how we lived in the land of Egypt, and how we came through the midst of the nations through which you passed. 17 You have seen their detestable things, the filthy idols of wood and stone, of silver and gold, that were among them. 18 It may be that there is among you a man or woman, or a family or tribe, whose heart is already turning away from the LORD our God to serve the gods of those nations. It may be that there is among you a root sprouting poisonous and bitter growth. 19 All who hear the words of this oath and bless themselves, thinking in their hearts, "We are safe even though we go our own stubborn ways" (thus bringing disaster on moist and dry alike) [k] — 20 the LORD will be unwilling to pardon them, for the LORD's anger and passion will smoke against them. All the curses written in this book will descend on them, and the LORD will blot out their names from under heaven. 21 The LORD will single them out from all the tribes of Israel for calamity, in accordance with all the curses of the covenant written in this book of the law. 22 The next generation, your children who rise up after you, as well as the foreigner who comes from a distant country, will see the devastation of that land and the afflictions with which the LORD has afflicted it — 23 all its soil burned out by sulfur and salt, nothing planted, nothing sprouting, unable to support any vegetation, like the destruction of Sodom and Gomorrah, Admah and Zeboiim, which the LORD destroyed in his fierce anger — 24 they and indeed

29.2
Ex 19.4

29.4
Isa 6.9, 10;
Acts 28.26,
27;
Eph 4.18
29.5
Deut 8.4
29.6
Deut 8.3
29.7
Num 21.21-24,
33-35;
Deut 2.32;
3.1
29.8
Num 32.33;
Deut 3.12, 13
29.9
Deut 4.6;
Josh 1.7

29.11
Josh 9.21, 23,
27

29.13
Deut 28.9;
Ex 6.7;
Gen 17.7

29.17
Deut 28.26

29.18
Deut 11.16;
Heb 12.15

29.20
Ps 74.1; 79.5;
Deut 9.14;
Ex 32.33
29.21
Mt 24.51

29.22
Jer 19.8

29.23
Gen 19.24;
Isa 34.9;
Jer 20.16

29.24
Jer 22.8, 9

---

[h] Ch 29.1 in Heb   [i] Or *deal wisely*   [j] Gk Syr: Heb *your leaders, your tribes*   [k] Meaning of Heb uncertain

---

covenant. The stipulations: (1) God will bless Israel if they obey (28.1ff); (2) God will punish Israel if they disobey (28.15ff); (3) God will disperse his people if they become apostate (28.63ff); (4) God will regather Israel after dispersion if and when they repent (30.1ff); (5) Israel will some day repossess the land (30.5); (6) Israel's enemies will be judged (30.7); and (7) God will send future prosperity (30.9).
29.10ff   This was an all-embracing covenant that included children, wives, and aliens, along with the elders, officers, and priests. The inclusion of aliens indicates God's concern for all people, demonstrated also when Peter and Paul preached the gospel to the Gentiles.
29.23   Even as Canaan would be a garden of the Lord, so it could become a barren waste like Sodom if Israel turned from God. The judgment would begin with plagues and sicknesses (v. 22) and be followed by judgment on the land itself. This came to fulfillment when Rome left Canaan desolate and barren.

all the nations will wonder, "Why has the LORD done thus to this land? What caused this great display of anger?" 25 They will conclude, "It is because they abandoned the covenant of the LORD, the God of their ancestors, which he made with them when he brought them out of the land of Egypt. 26 They turned and served other gods, worshiping them, gods whom they had not known and whom he had not allotted to them; 27 so the anger of the LORD was kindled against that land, bringing on it every curse written in this book. 28 The LORD uprooted them from their land in anger, fury, and great wrath, and cast them into another land, as is now the case." 29 The secret things belong to the LORD our God, but the revealed things belong to us and to our children forever, to observe all the words of this law.

G. Repentance to be followed by forgiveness and blessing

30 When all these things have happened to you, the blessings and the curses that I have set before you, if you call them to mind among all the nations where the LORD your God has driven you, 2 and return to the LORD your God, and you and your children obey him with all your heart and with all your soul, just as I am commanding you today, 3 then the LORD your God will restore your fortunes and have compassion on you, gathering you again from all the peoples among whom the LORD your God has scattered you. 4 Even if you are exiled to the ends of the world,[l] from there the LORD your God will gather you, and from there he will bring you back. 5 The LORD your God will bring you into the land that your ancestors possessed, and you will possess it; he will make you more prosperous and numerous than your ancestors.

6 Moreover, the LORD your God will circumcise your heart and the heart of your descendants, so that you will love the LORD your God with all your heart and with all your soul, in order that you may live. 7 The LORD your God will put all these curses on your enemies and on the adversaries who took advantage of you. 8 Then you shall again obey the LORD, observing all his commandments that I am commanding you today, 9 and the LORD your God will make you abundantly prosperous in all your undertakings, in the fruit of your body, in the fruit of your livestock, and in the fruit of your soil. For the LORD will again take delight in prospering you, just as he delighted in prospering your ancestors, 10 when you obey the LORD your God by observing his commandments and decrees that are written in this book of the law, because you turn to the LORD your God with all your heart and with all your soul.

H. Closing exhortation

1. The nearness of God's word

11 Surely, this commandment that I am commanding you today is not too hard for you, nor is it too far away. 12 It is not in heaven, that you should say, "Who will go up to heaven for us, and get it for us so that we may hear it and observe it?" 13 Neither is it beyond the sea, that you should say, "Who will cross to the other side of the sea for us, and get

---

l Heb *of heaven*

Margin references

29.28
1 Kings 14.15;
2 Chr 7.20

30.1
vv. 15, 19;
Deut 11.26;
28.64; 29.28
30.2
Deut 4.29, 30
30.3
Jer 29.14;
32.37

30.4
Neh 1.9;
Isa 43.6

30.6
Jer 32.39

30.9
Deut 28.11;
Jer 32.41

30.11
Isa 45.19
30.12
Rom 10.6-8

29.29 God has not told us everything, but he has told us all we need to know. Disobedience indicates a lack of motivation or will, not a lack of knowledge. **30.2** God promises Israel that if the nation repents after having been judged and dispersed by God, he will regather them "even if you are exiled to the ends of the world" (v. 4). This promise still awaits fulfillment, though there are different opinions as to when and how this will take place.

30.11–14 What God revealed to Israel, and through Israel to us, does not require more revelation, nor do we need to send messengers to heaven to get it. His word is forever written in the Scriptures and is available to all. The translation of the Bible into thousands of languages brings to virtually all the peoples of the world the knowledge of God and the commandments they are called upon to obey with thankful hearts.

it for us so that we may hear it and observe it?" 14No, the word is very near to you; it is in your mouth and in your heart for you to observe.

2. The choice of life versus death

15 See, I have set before you today life and prosperity, death and adversity. 16If you obey the commandments of the LORD your God[m] that I am commanding you today, by loving the LORD your God, walking in his ways, and observing his commandments, decrees, and ordinances, then you shall live and become numerous, and the LORD your God will bless you in the land that you are entering to possess. 17But if your heart turns away and you do not hear, but are led astray to bow down to other gods and serve them, 18I declare to you today that you shall perish; you shall not live long in the land that you are crossing the Jordan to enter and possess. 19I call heaven and earth to witness against you today that I have set before you life and death, blessings and curses. Choose life so that you and your descendants may live, 20loving the LORD your God, obeying him, and holding fast to him; for that means life to you and length of days, so that you may live in the land that the LORD swore to give to your ancestors, to Abraham, to Isaac, and to Jacob.

IV. Moses' final words and death (31.1–34.12)

A. Moses' final arrangements

1. The appointment of Joshua

31 When Moses had finished speaking all[n] these words to all Israel, 2he said to them: "I am now one hundred twenty years old. I am no longer able to get about, and the LORD has told me, 'You shall not cross over this Jordan.' 3The LORD your God himself will cross over before you. He will destroy these nations before you, and you shall dispossess them. Joshua also will cross over before you, as the LORD promised. 4The LORD will do to them as he did to Sihon and Og, the kings of the Amorites, and to their land, when he destroyed them. 5The LORD will give them over to you and you shall deal with them in full accord with the command that I have given to you. 6Be strong and bold; have no fear or dread of them, because it is the LORD your God who goes with you; he will not fail you or forsake you."

7 Then Moses summoned Joshua and said to him in the sight of all Israel: "Be strong and bold, for you are the one who will go with this people into the land that the LORD has sworn to their ancestors to give them; and you will put them in possession of it. 8It is the LORD who goes before you. He will be with you; he will not fail you or forsake you. Do not fear or be dismayed."

2. The teaching of the law

9 Then Moses wrote down this law, and gave it to the priests, the sons of Levi, who carried the ark of the covenant of the LORD, and to all the elders of Israel. 10Moses commanded them: "Every seventh year, in the

m Gk: Heb lacks *If you obey the commandments of the LORD your God*   *n* Q Ms Gk: MT *Moses went and spoke*

Cross-reference column

30.15
vv. 1, 19

30.18
Deut 4.26
30.19
Deut 4.26;
v. 1
30.20
Deut 6.5;
10.20;
Ps 27.1;
Jn 11.25

31.2
Deut 34.7;
3.27
31.3
Deut 9.3;
3.28

31.5
Deut 7.2
31.6
Josh 10.25;
Deut 1.29;
20.4;
Heb 13.5
31.7
Deut 1.38;
3.28
31.8
v. 6

31.9
v. 25;
Num 4.15
31.10
Deut 15.1;
Lev 23.34

31.2 *I am no longer able to get about.* Moses was not disabled by physical disability or senility of mind, for "his vigor had not abated" (34.7). Rather he was under the divine sentence that he could not go over the Jordan because of his sin. Israel was ready to enter the land. It was time, therefore, for Moses to be relieved of his responsibilities.
31.7 The appointment of Joshua was by God's com-

mand. He had been under training for a long time. God never removes a leader without raising up someone else to take his place and to carry on the work of God.
31.10–13 There were not many copies of the Pentateuch available in ancient Israel. Thus Moses appointed a time for the public reading of the law: every seventh year. Later, we know that Moses' writings

31.11
Deut 16.16;
Josh 8.34, 35
31.12
Deut 4.10

31.13
Deut 11.2;
Ps 78.6, 7

31.14
Deut 32.49,
50; v. 23

31.15
Ex 33.9

31.16
Judg 2.11,
12; 10.6, 13

31.17
Judg 2.14;
6.13;
Deut 32.20;
Num 14.42

31.20
Deut 6.10-12;
32.15-17;
v. 16

31.21
v. 17;
Hos 5.3

31.22
v. 19
31.23
v. 7;
Josh 1.6

31.25
v. 9
31.26
v. 19

31.27
Deut 9.6, 24

31.28
Deut 4.26

scheduled year of remission, during the festival of booths,[o] 11 when all Israel comes to appear before the Lord your God at the place that he will choose, you shall read this law before all Israel in their hearing. 12 Assemble the people — men, women, and children, as well as the aliens residing in your towns — so that they may hear and learn to fear the Lord your God and to observe diligently all the words of this law, 13 and so that their children, who have not known it, may hear and learn to fear the Lord your God, as long as you live in the land that you are crossing over the Jordan to possess."

3. God appears to Moses and Joshua

14 The Lord said to Moses, "Your time to die is near; call Joshua and present yourselves in the tent of meeting, so that I may commission him." So Moses and Joshua went and presented themselves in the tent of meeting, 15 and the Lord appeared at the tent in a pillar of cloud; the pillar of cloud stood at the entrance to the tent.

16 The Lord said to Moses, "Soon you will lie down with your ancestors. Then this people will begin to prostitute themselves to the foreign gods in their midst, the gods of the land into which they are going; they will forsake me, breaking my covenant that I have made with them. 17 My anger will be kindled against them in that day. I will forsake them and hide my face from them; they will become easy prey, and many terrible troubles will come upon them. In that day they will say, 'Have not these troubles come upon us because our God is not in our midst?' 18 On that day I will surely hide my face on account of all the evil they have done by turning to other gods. 19 Now therefore write this song, and teach it to the Israelites; put it in their mouths, in order that this song may be a witness for me against the Israelites. 20 For when I have brought them into the land flowing with milk and honey, which I promised on oath to their ancestors, and they have eaten their fill and grown fat, they will turn to other gods and serve them, despising me and breaking my covenant. 21 And when many terrible troubles come upon them, this song will confront them as a witness, because it will not be lost from the mouths of their descendants. For I know what they are inclined to do even now, before I have brought them into the land that I promised them on oath." 22 That very day Moses wrote this song and taught it to the Israelites.

23 Then the Lord commissioned Joshua son of Nun and said, "Be strong and bold, for you shall bring the Israelites into the land that I promised them; I will be with you."

4. Moses' counsel to the Levites

24 When Moses had finished writing down in a book the words of this law to the very end, 25 Moses commanded the Levites who carried the ark of the covenant of the Lord, saying, 26 "Take this book of the law and put it beside the ark of the covenant of the Lord your God; let it remain there as a witness against you. 27 For I know well how rebellious and stubborn you are. If you already have been so rebellious toward the Lord while I am still alive among you, how much more after my death! 28 Assemble to me all the elders of your tribes and your officials, so that I may

[o] Or *tabernacles*; Heb *succoth*

were read in Jewish synagogues every sabbath (Acts 15.21); most Jews did not have personal copies of the law. In all likelihood, the Israelites memorized the law and could probably repeat much of it from memory.
31.14,15 God now charges Moses to bring Joshua with him to the tabernacle. He is then presented to God as the new leader of Israel. This is the only time

in Deuteronomy we hear of the glory of the Lord appearing.
31.24–26 Moses completed the written word of the law of God and gave it to the priests to be deposited beside the ark of God. The two tables of the law were kept inside the ark. For the writing of Moses to be placed beside the ark indicates how wonderfully sacred that word was and ever will be.

recite these words in their hearing and call heaven and earth to witness against them. ²⁹ For I know that after my death you will surely act corruptly, turning aside from the way that I have commanded you. In time to come trouble will befall you, because you will do what is evil in the sight of the LORD, provoking him to anger through the work of your hands."

31.29
Deut 32.5;
28.15

B. *The song of Moses*

1. *Introduction*

30 Then Moses recited the words of this song, to the very end, in the hearing of the whole assembly of Israel:

32 Give ear, O heavens, and I will speak;
    let the earth hear the words of my mouth.

32.1
Isa 1.2

2 May my teaching drop like the rain,
    my speech condense like the dew;
like gentle rain on grass,
    like showers on new growth.

32.2
Isa 55.10, 11

3 For I will proclaim the name of the LORD;
    ascribe greatness to our God!

32.3
Ex 33.19;
Deut 3.24

2. *Faithfulness of God contrasted with the faithlessness of Israel*

4 The Rock, his work is perfect,
    and all his ways are just.
A faithful God, without deceit,
    just and upright is he;

32.4
vv. 15, 18,
30;
Deut 7.9;
Ps 92.15

5 yet his degenerate children have dealt falsely with him,^p
    a perverse and crooked generation.

32.5
Deut 31.29;
Lk 9.41

6 Do you thus repay the LORD,
    O foolish and senseless people?
Is not he your father, who created you,
    who made you and established you?

32.6
Deut 1.31

7 Remember the days of old,
    consider the years long past;
ask your father, and he will inform you;
    your elders, and they will tell you.

32.7
Ex 13.14

8 When the Most High^q apportioned the nations,
    when he divided humankind,
he fixed the boundaries of the peoples
    according to the number of the gods;^r

32.8
Gen 11.8;
Acts 17.26

9 the LORD's own portion was his people,
    Jacob his allotted share.

32.9
1 Kings 8.51,
53;
Jer 10.16

10 He sustained^s him in a desert land,
    in a howling wilderness waste;
he shielded him, cared for him,
    guarded him as the apple of his eye.

32.10
Jer 2.6;
Zech 2.8

11 As an eagle stirs up its nest,
    and hovers over its young;
as it spreads its wings, takes them up,
    and bears them aloft on its pinions,

32.11
Ex 19.4;
Isa 31.5

12 the LORD alone guided him;
    no foreign god was with him.

32.12
v. 39

^p Meaning of Heb uncertain   ^q Traditional rendering of Heb *Elyon*   ^r Q Ms Compare Gk Tg: MT *the Israelites*   ^s Sam Gk Compare Tg: MT *found*

32.4 *The Rock.* Outside of Deuteronomy, references to God as the Rock appear 18 times in the O.T.

32.13 Isa 58.14; Job 29.6	13 He set him atop the heights of the land, and fed him with[t] produce of the field; he nursed him with honey from the crags, with oil from flinty rock;
32.14 Ps 147.14	14 curds from the herd, and milk from the flock, with fat of lambs and rams; Bashan bulls and goats, together with the choicest wheat — you drank fine wine from the blood of grapes.
32.15 Deut 33.5, 26; Isa 1.4; vv. 6, 4	15 Jacob ate his fill;[u] Jeshurun grew fat, and kicked. You grew fat, bloated, and gorged! He abandoned God who made him, and scoffed at the Rock of his salvation.
32.16 Ps 78.58; 1 Cor 10.22	16 They made him jealous with strange gods, with abhorrent things they provoked him.
32.17 Ps 106.37; Deut 28.64; Judg 5.8	17 They sacrificed to demons, not God, to deities they had never known, to new ones recently arrived, whom your ancestors had not feared.
32.18 Isa 17.10; Ps 106.21	18 You were unmindful of the Rock that bore you;[v] you forgot the God who gave you birth.

3. Why God punished Israel

32.19 Ps 106.40; Jer 44.21-23	19 The Lord saw it, and was jealous;[w] he spurned[x] his sons and daughters.
32.20 Deut 31.17, 29; v. 5	20 He said: I will hide my face from them, I will see what their end will be; for they are a perverse generation, children in whom there is no faithfulness.
32.21 v. 16; Rom 10.19	21 They made me jealous with what is no god, provoked me with their idols. So I will make them jealous with what is no people, provoke them with a foolish nation.
32.22 Jer 15.14	22 For a fire is kindled by my anger, and burns to the depths of Sheol; it devours the earth and its increase, and sets on fire the foundations of the mountains.
32.23 Deut 29.21; Ezek 5.16	23 I will heap disasters upon them, spend my arrows against them:
32.24 Deut 28.22; Lev 26.22; v. 33	24 wasting hunger, burning consumption, bitter pestilence. The teeth of beasts I will send against them, with venom of things crawling in the dust.
32.25 Ezek 7.15; 2 Chr 36.17	25 In the street the sword shall bereave, and in the chambers terror, for young man and woman alike, nursing child and old gray head.

t Sam Gk Syr Tg: MT *he ate*   u Q Mss Sam Gk: MT lacks *Jacob ate his fill*   v Or *that begot you*
w Q Mss Gk: MT lacks *was jealous*   x Cn: Heb *he spurned because of provocation*

32.15 *Jeshurun,* i.e., Israel.
32.22 *burns to the depths of Sheol.* The Hebrew word *Sheol* means the abode of the departed spirits of the dead, both righteous and wicked. God's Spirit is there (Ps 139.8), the anger of God is felt there (Deut 32.22), and it is a gloomy place with worms (Job 17.13–15), a place where God cannot be praised (Ps 6.5; Isa 38.18). The O.T. view of Sheol is quite complex. *Sheol* is carried over into the N.T. as *hades,* the place where the wicked dead dwell. It is also associated with *gehenna* (see note on Mt 18.9). The idea that Sheol is the abode of the wicked dead developed more clearly during the intertestamental period.

26 I thought to scatter them^y
    and blot out the memory of them from humankind;
27 but I feared provocation by the enemy,
    for their adversaries might misunderstand
  and say, "Our hand is triumphant;
    it was not the Lord who did all this."

28 They are a nation void of sense;
    there is no understanding in them.
29 If they were wise, they would understand this;
    they would discern what the end would be.
30 How could one have routed a thousand,
    and two put a myriad to flight,
  unless their Rock had sold them,
    the Lord had given them up?
31 Indeed their rock is not like our Rock;
    our enemies are fools.^y
32 Their vine comes from the vinestock of Sodom,
    from the vineyards of Gomorrah;
  their grapes are grapes of poison,
    their clusters are bitter;
33 their wine is the poison of serpents,
    the cruel venom of asps.

4. God will show mercy to Israel and vengeance to her enemies

34 Is not this laid up in store with me,
    sealed up in my treasuries?
35 Vengeance is mine, and recompense,
    for the time when their foot shall slip;
  because the day of their calamity is at hand,
    their doom comes swiftly.

36 Indeed the Lord will vindicate his people,
    have compassion on his servants,
  when he sees that their power is gone,
    neither bond nor free remaining.
37 Then he will say: Where are their gods,
    the rock in which they took refuge,
38 who ate the fat of their sacrifices,
    and drank the wine of their libations?
  Let them rise up and help you,
    let them be your protection!

39 See now that I, even I, am he;
    there is no god besides me.
  I kill and I make alive;
    I wound and I heal;
  and no one can deliver from my hand.
40 For I lift up my hand to heaven,

Cross references: 32.26 Deut 4.27; Ps 34.16 | 32.27 Deut 9.26-28; Isa 10.13 | 32.29 Ps 81.13 | 32.30 Lev 26.7, 8; v. 4 | 32.31 1 Sam 2.2; 4.8 | 32.33 Ps 58.4 | 32.34 Hos 13.12 | 32.35 Rom 12.19; Heb 10.30 | 32.36 Ps 135.14; 106.45; Judg 2.18; Joel 2.14 | 32.37 Jer 2.28 | 32.39 Isa 41.4; Ps 50.22

y Gk: Meaning of Heb uncertain

32.32 *Their vine comes from the vinestock of Sodom.* The enemies of Israel fell before them because they were ripe for ruin; the measure of their iniquity was full. These heathen had come from wicked ancestors and their sins were offensive to God. *Their grapes are grapes of poison,* i.e., their deeds are poisonous.
32.39 Israel's God is the self-existent One. He is supreme; there is no other god with him or greater than he. He is absolute Sovereign who does as he pleases. No one can deliver out of his hand those who have been marked for destruction. Elsewhere Jesus states that those who are marked for everlasting life cannot be taken from his hands either (see Jn 10.28, 29).

and swear: As I live forever,

32.41
Ezek 21.9, 10

41 when I whet my flashing sword,
and my hand takes hold on judgment;
I will take vengeance on my adversaries,
and will repay those who hate me.

32.42
Jer 46.10

42 I will make my arrows drunk with blood,
and my sword shall devour flesh—
with the blood of the slain and the captives,
from the long-haired enemy.

32.43
Rom 15.10;
Rev 19.2;
Ps 85.1

43 Praise, O heavens,[z] his people,
worship him, all you gods![a]
For he will avenge the blood of his children,[b]
and take vengeance on his adversaries;
he will repay those who hate him,[a]
and cleanse the land for his people.[c]

44 Moses came and recited all the words of this song in the hearing of the people, he and Joshua[d] son of Nun. 45 When Moses had finished reciting all these words to all Israel, 46 he said to them: "Take to heart all the words that I am giving in witness against you today; give them as a command to your children, so that they may diligently observe all the words of this law. 47 This is no trifling matter for you, but rather your very life; through it you may live long in the land that you are crossing over the Jordan to possess."

32.46
Deut 6.6;
Ezek 40.4

32.47
Deut 30.20

C. *God summons Moses to die*

48 On that very day the LORD addressed Moses as follows: 49 "Ascend this mountain of the Abarim, Mount Nebo, which is in the land of Moab, across from Jericho, and view the land of Canaan, which I am giving to the Israelites for a possession; 50 you shall die there on the mountain that you ascend and shall be gathered to your kin, as your brother Aaron died on Mount Hor and was gathered to his kin; 51 because both of you broke faith with me among the Israelites at the waters of Meribath-kadesh in the wilderness of Zin, by failing to maintain my holiness among the Israelites. 52 Although you may view the land from a distance, you shall not enter it—the land that I am giving to the Israelites."

32.49
Num 27.12-14

32.51
Num 20.11-13;
27.14

32.52
Deut 34.1-3;
1.37

D. *Moses blesses the people of Israel*

33.1
Josh 14.6
33.2
Hab 3.3;
Dan 7.10;
Acts 7.53;
Gal 3.19;
Rev 5.11

33 This is the blessing with which Moses, the man of God, blessed the Israelites before his death. 2 He said:

The LORD came from Sinai,
and dawned from Seir upon us;[e]
he shone forth from Mount Paran.
With him were myriads of holy ones;[f]
at his right, a host of his own.[g]

33.3
Hos 11.1;
Deut 14.2

3 Indeed, O favorite among[h] peoples,

z Q Ms Gk: MT *nations* a Q Ms Gk: MT lacks this line b Q Ms Gk: MT *his servants* c Q Ms Sam Gk Syr: MT *his land his people* d Sam Gk Syr Vg: MT *Hoshea* e Gk Syr Vg Compare Tg: Heb *upon them* f Cn Compare Gk Sam Syr Vg: MT *He came from Ribeboth-kadesh,* g Cn Compare Gk: meaning of Heb uncertain h Or *O lover of the*

32.41,42 The God of love and grace is also the God of wrath, whose sentence cannot be escaped. He makes his "arrows drunk with blood"; i.e., when the sword of God's wrath is drawn, it will make bloody work, "as high as the horse's bridle" (Rev 14.20). **32.43** Moses now ends the song with a triumphant refrain. There is a remnant who will experience God's ultimate peace. God will avenge his servants and punish his adversaries. Atonement will be made for the

people of God and the land. God's people will rejoice everlastingly.
32.50 *die there on the mountain.* Unlike Elijah, who was taken into heaven without experiencing death, Moses was to die. The place of Moses' burial was undoubtedly to remain unknown so that his grave would not become a focal point of worship and lead to a depreciation of the true worship of God.
33.2 *holy ones,* or, holy angels.

    all his holy ones were in your charge;
    they marched at your heels,
        accepted direction from you.
4   Moses charged us with the law,
        as a possession for the assembly of Jacob.
5   There arose a king in Jeshurun,
        when the leaders of the people assembled —
        the united tribes of Israel.

6   May Reuben live, and not die out,
        even though his numbers are few.

7And this he said of Judah:
    O Lord, give heed to Judah,
        and bring him to his people;
    strengthen his hands for him,[i]
        and be a help against his adversaries.

8And of Levi he said:
    Give to Levi[j] your Thummim,
        and your Urim to your loyal one,
    whom you tested at Massah,
        with whom you contended at the waters of Meribah;
9   who said of his father and mother,
        "I regard them not";
    he ignored his kin,
        and did not acknowledge his children.
    For they observed your word,
        and kept your covenant.
10 They teach Jacob your ordinances,
        and Israel your law;
    they place incense before you,
        and whole burnt offerings on your altar.
11 Bless, O Lord, his substance,
        and accept the work of his hands;
    crush the loins of his adversaries,
        of those that hate him, so that they do not rise again.

12Of Benjamin he said:
    The beloved of the Lord rests in safety —
    the High God[k] surrounds him all day long —
        the beloved[l] rests between his shoulders.

13And of Joseph he said:
    Blessed by the Lord be his land,

Cross references (right margin):

33.4 Jn 1.17; Ps 119.111

33.7 Gen 49.8-12

33.8 Ex 28.30; 17.7

33.9 Ex 32.26-29

33.10 Deut 31.9-13; Ex 30.7, 8; Ps 51.19

33.11 2 Sam 24.23; Ps 20.3

33.13 Gen 49.25; 27.28

---

i Cn: Heb *with his hands he contended*   *j* Q Ms Gk: MT lacks *Give to Levi*   *k* Heb *above him*   *l* Heb *he*

33.5 *Jeshurun* is a poetic name for Israel (cf. 32.15), suggesting the kind of people who live righteously. The word appears three times in Deuteronomy and once in Isaiah.
33.6 Moses, the military strategist, knows that the Reubenites on the east bank of the Jordan will face the people of Moab. They especially need prayer for their survival and increase.
33.7 Simeon's name and blessing are missing. Perhaps the reason is that the tribe of Simeon lived within the borders of Judah and so was implicitly included in that tribe's blessing. Moses prays for the leadership to come from Judah, a prayer that was fulfilled in the coming of Jesus the Messiah.

33.8–11 Moses prays that God will prosper the tribe of Levi and supply their material needs, that God will accept the work of their hands in their service for him, and that God will take the side of the Levites against all of their enemies.
33.12 Benjamin, the second son of Jacob's beloved Rachel, will have divine protection. Since Mount Moriah and Jerusalem are in Benjamin's territory, that tribe is close to the heart of God, because he takes up his residence in those sacred places.
33.13 Moses' blessing for Joseph includes both Manasseh and Ephraim, Joseph's two sons. These two tribes have the choicest lands, with rich blessings and thousands of descendants.

with the choice gifts of heaven above,
and of the deep that lies beneath;
14 with the choice fruits of the sun,
and the rich yield of the months;

33.15
Gen 49.26
15 with the finest produce of the ancient mountains,
and the abundance of the everlasting hills;

33.16
Ex 3.2, 4;
Acts 7.30, 35
16 with the choice gifts of the earth and its fullness,
and the favor of the one who dwells on Sinai.*m*
Let these come on the head of Joseph,
on the brow of the prince among his brothers.

33.17
Num 23.22;
Ps 44.5
17 A firstborn*n* bull — majesty is his!
His horns are the horns of a wild ox;
with them he gores the peoples,
driving them to*o* the ends of the earth;
such are the myriads of Ephraim,
such the thousands of Manasseh.

33.18
Gen 49.13-15
18 And of Zebulun he said:
Rejoice, Zebulun, in your going out;
and Issachar, in your tents.

33.19
Isa 2.3;
Ps 4.5
19 They call peoples to the mountain;
there they offer the right sacrifices;
for they suck the affluence of the seas
and the hidden treasures of the sand.

33.20
Gen 49.19
20 And of Gad he said:
Blessed be the enlargement of Gad!
Gad lives like a lion;
he tears at arm and scalp.

33.21
Num 32.1-5,
31, 32;
Josh 4.12;
22.1-3
21 He chose the best for himself,
for there a commander's allotment was reserved;
he came at the head of the people,
he executed the justice of the LORD,
and his ordinances for Israel.

33.22
Gen 49.16
22 And of Dan he said:
Dan is a lion's whelp
that leaps forth from Bashan.

33.23
Gen 49.21
23 And of Naphtali he said:
O Naphtali, sated with favor,
full of the blessing of the LORD,
possess the west and the south.

33.24
Gen 49.20;
Job 29;6
24 And of Asher he said:
Most blessed of sons be Asher;
may he be the favorite of his brothers,
and may he dip his foot in oil.

---

m Cn: Heb *in the bush*   *n* Q Ms Gk Syr Vg: MT *His firstborn*   *o* Cn: Heb *the peoples, together*

33.18,19 The tribe of Zebulun is to be successful in business and in sea-trading, whereas the tribe of Issachar will be blessed as farmers and cattle raisers.
33.20,21 Gad will be enlarged and become a valiant, victorious tribe with great military strength against the enemy. They are commended for what they have done, especially for fulfilling their responsibilities to the other tribes of Israel.
33.22 Dan is blessed with courage and resolution to overcome the enemy. From Dan came Samson, a lion's whelp.

33.23 Naphtali is to be a happy people, loved by the other tribes and favored by God. Wealthy Bethsaida and Capernaum lay within Naphtali's borders. According to tradition, Naphtali was so fruitful that they were generally the first to bring their first fruits to the temple and so be the first to receive God's blessings.
33.24,25 Asher will be prolific. Their land will be productive because beneath its surface is vast mineral wealth. The strength of this tribe in old age will equal that of their youth.

25 Your bars are iron and bronze;
    and as your days, so is your strength.

26 There is none like God, O Jeshurun,
    who rides through the heavens to your help,
        majestic through the skies.
27 He subdues the ancient gods,[p]
        shatters[q] the forces of old;[r]
    he drove out the enemy before you,
        and said, "Destroy!"
28 So Israel lives in safety,
        untroubled is Jacob's abode[s]
    in a land of grain and wine,
        where the heavens drop down dew.
29 Happy are you, O Israel! Who is like you,
        a people saved by the LORD,
    the shield of your help,
        and the sword of your triumph!
    Your enemies shall come fawning to you,
        and you shall tread on their backs.

E. The death and burial of Moses

34 Then Moses went up from the plains of Moab to Mount Nebo, to the top of Pisgah, which is opposite Jericho, and the LORD showed him the whole land: Gilead as far as Dan, 2 all Naphtali, the land of Ephraim and Manasseh, all the land of Judah as far as the Western Sea, 3 the Negeb, and the Plain — that is, the valley of Jericho, the city of palm trees — as far as Zoar. 4 The LORD said to him, "This is the land of which I swore to Abraham, to Isaac, and to Jacob, saying, 'I will give it to your descendants'; I have let you see it with your eyes, but you shall not cross over there." 5 Then Moses, the servant of the LORD, died there in the land of Moab, at the LORD's command. 6 He was buried in a valley in the land of Moab, opposite Beth-peor, but no one knows his burial place to this day. 7 Moses was one hundred twenty years old when he died; his sight was unimpaired and his vigor had not abated. 8 The Israelites wept for Moses in the plains of Moab thirty days; then the period of mourning for Moses was ended.

9 Joshua son of Nun was full of the spirit of wisdom, because Moses had laid his hands on him; and the Israelites obeyed him, doing as the LORD had commanded Moses.

10 Never since has there arisen a prophet in Israel like Moses, whom the LORD knew face to face. 11 He was unequaled for all the signs and wonders that the LORD sent him to perform in the land of Egypt, against Pharaoh and all his servants and his entire land, 12 and for all the mighty deeds and all the terrifying displays of power that Moses performed in the sight of all Israel.

p Or The eternal God is a dwelling place   q Cn: Heb from underneath   r Or the everlasting arms
s Or fountain

Cross references: 33.25 Deut 4.40; 32.49; 33.26 Ex 15.11; Ps 68.33, 34; 33.27 Ps 90.1, 2; Josh 24.18; 33.28 Num 23.9; Gen 27.28; 33.29 Ps 144.15; 2 Sam 7.23; Ps 18.14; Deut 32.13; 34.1 Deut 32.49, 52; 34.4 Gen 12.7; 28.13; 34.5 Deut 32.50; Josh 1.1, 2; 34.7 Deut 31.2; 34.9 Isa 11.2; Num 27.18, 23; 34.10 Num 12.6, 8; 34.11 Deut 4.34

33.27 The eternal God (see NRSV footnote) is the mansion-house of all who believe. In that place they will be safe. As the Israelites settle in Canaan, they must remember that God is their dwelling place and that Canaan without him will become a wilderness and a place of darkness. God's everlasting arms will be beneath them for protection and consolation. Spiritually, all those who are right with God are at home with him; their souls will return to him and repose in him as their final resting-place.
34.1 Some hold that this story of Moses' death was added by a different writer at a later time. Others accept it as a form of predictive prophecy penned by Moses himself, who had been informed of the details of his approaching death and who told the story in advance of its actual occurrence.
34.4 I have let you see it with your eyes. God granted Moses a last look at the land promised to Israel, a land that was his by faith and by sight, though not by physical presence. His sin had cut him off from what had been his goal from the beginning — to inherit the land promised to his ancestors. God took his spirit to himself and buried his body in an unmarked grave to await the resurrection.

INTRODUCTION TO

JOSHUA

Authorship, Date, and Background: This book was named for Joshua, the chief person involved in the events described in it. Undoubtedly large sections of the book were written by Joshua himself. Many items could have been known only by Joshua. Some of the material, however, such as the decease of Joshua and a few events which took place subsequent to Joshua's death, have led scholars to conclude that the book was written after Joshua's death. Aaron's son Eleazar and grandson Phinehas have been suggested as possible writers who, under the inspiration of the Holy Spirit, completed the work.

Some modern scholars formulated the theory that the first six books of the O.T., i.e., the five books of Moses and Joshua, formed the Hexateuch (or six books) comprising materials from Moses and Joshua which were reworked or reedited as late as the seventh century B.C. At that time the anonymous compiler of Deuteronomy incorporated Joshua with the five books of Moses, forming the Hexateuch. Evangelical scholars, however, adhere to the Mosaic authorship of the first five books and maintain that Joshua was written shortly after the death of Joshua (possibly fourteenth century B.C., but not later than the twelfth century).

The children of Israel had spent forty years in the wilderness because of their refusal to enter the promised land when ten of the twelve spies reported unfavorably on the possibility of subduing its occupants. Upon the death of Moses, Joshua, their new leader, was ready to bring the people into the land which God had promised them. Thus, the book of Joshua continues the history of Israel, covering the period from the entrance into Canaan, the distribution of the land to the twelve tribes, and the pacification of the land, up to the period of the judges.

Characteristics and Content: This book tells the story of Israel's triumphant occupation of the land of promise. In it the mighty power of God was manifested over the enemies who inhabited the land. The Canaanites living in the land are pictured in all of their degeneracy, consisting of polytheism, religious prostitution, and other abominations which angered God and occasioned his command for the Israelites to exterminate the seven heathen nations. The Israelites had to be kept from contact with the Canaanites which would result in their spiritual degeneration.

The first part of Joshua tells of the conquest of the land and includes Joshua's commission by God, the miraculous crossing of the Jordan River, the capture of Jericho, the failure at Ai, and the erection of an altar at Mount Ebal where the law was solemnly read to the people. The crafty Gibeonites managed to preserve themselves in the land by deception due to the failure of Joshua to seek God's guidance before making a treaty with them. A most unusual event occurred during the conquest of southern Canaan in the battle of Gibeon when the "the sun stood still, and the moon stopped, until the nation took vengeance on their enemies" (10.13). Some commentators do not take this literally, while others do.

The latter half of Joshua describes the division of the land among the tribes. It concludes with Joshua's final charge to the Israelites, wherein he pointed out that they were a covenant people who had to trust God and who were not to permit sins of disobedience to mar their relationship to him, lest they incur God's anger and feel the lash of his judgment upon them.

Outline:

I. The conquest of Canaan (1.1—12.24)

II. The partition of the promised land (13.1—21.45)

III. The farewell addresses of Joshua (22.1—24.33)

JOSHUA

I. The conquest of Canaan (1.1–12.24)

A. Introduction: God's instructions to Joshua

1 After the death of Moses the servant of the LORD, the LORD spoke to Joshua son of Nun, Moses' assistant, saying, 2 "My servant Moses is dead. Now proceed to cross the Jordan, you and all this people, into the land that I am giving to them, to the Israelites. 3 Every place that the sole of your foot will tread upon I have given to you, as I promised to Moses. 4 From the wilderness and the Lebanon as far as the great river, the river Euphrates, all the land of the Hittites, to the Great Sea in the west shall be your territory. 5 No one shall be able to stand against you all the days of your life. As I was with Moses, so I will be with you; I will not fail you or forsake you. 6 Be strong and courageous; for you shall put this people in possession of the land that I swore to their ancestors to give them. 7 Only be strong and very courageous, being careful to act in accordance with all the law that my servant Moses commanded you; do not turn from it to the right hand or to the left, so that you may be successful wherever you go. 8 This book of the law shall not depart out of your mouth; you shall meditate on it day and night, so that you may be careful to act in accordance with all that is written in it. For then you shall make your way prosperous, and then you shall be successful. 9 I hereby command you: Be strong and courageous; do not be frightened or dismayed, for the LORD your God is with you wherever you go."

B. Preparations for crossing the Jordan

1. The order issued

10 Then Joshua commanded the officers of the people, 11 "Pass through the camp, and command the people: 'Prepare your provisions; for in three days you are to cross over the Jordan, to go in to take possession of the land that the LORD your God gives you to possess.'"

2. The reminder to Reubenites, Gadites, and the half-tribe of Manasseh

12 To the Reubenites, the Gadites, and the half-tribe of Manasseh Joshua said, 13 "Remember the word that Moses the servant of the LORD commanded you, saying, 'The LORD your God is providing you a place

1.2 Num 12.7; Deut 34.5; v. 11
1.3 Deut 11.24
1.4 Gen 15.18
1.5 Deut 7.24; 31.6-8
1.7 Deut 5.32; 28.14
1.8 Deut 17.8, 9; Ps 1.1-3
1.9 Deut 31.7, 8, 23; Jer 1.8
1.11 Joel 3.2
1.12 Num 32.20-22
1.13 Deut 3.18-20

1.1 *Joshua*, a shortened version of *Jehoshua* ("Yahweh is salvation"). Joshua had been Moses' assistant and, along with Caleb, had urged Israel to enter Canaan forty years earlier (Num 14.6–9). Moses had trained Joshua to become his successor. God chose him for this role. Joshua led Israel successfully into Canaan and was a victorious military commander. As such, he represents Christ, who is our captain, saves us, brings us to the place of rest, intercedes for us, and makes the conquest of sin possible.
1.5 God gave Joshua the same promise he made to Moses—that he would be with him all the days of his

life. Joshua had seen this fulfilled in the life of Moses and by faith believed it would be fulfilled in his life and ministry. God still promises to be with believers (cf. Heb 13.5,6).
1.8 God instructed Joshua to study the book of the law day and night and to do all that was commanded in it. The promise of success and prosperity was attached to such obedience. Churches and believers are seriously weakened today by their failure to obey what God has commanded in his word. His word is not outdated; it is normative for contemporary society and culture.

of rest, and will give you this land.' 14 Your wives, your little ones, and your livestock shall remain in the land that Moses gave you beyond the Jordan. But all the warriors among you shall cross over armed before your kindred and shall help them, 15 until the LORD gives rest to your kindred as well as to you, and they too take possession of the land that the LORD your God is giving them. Then you shall return to your own land and take possession of it, the land that Moses the servant of the LORD gave you beyond the Jordan to the east."

16   They answered Joshua: "All that you have commanded us we will do, and wherever you send us we will go. 17 Just as we obeyed Moses in all things, so we will obey you. Only may the LORD your God be with you, as he was with Moses! 18 Whoever rebels against your orders and disobeys your words, whatever you command, shall be put to death. Only be strong and courageous."

3. Two spies sent to Jericho
a. Rahab hides the spies

2 Then Joshua son of Nun sent two men secretly from Shittim as spies, saying, "Go, view the land, especially Jericho." So they went, and entered the house of a prostitute whose name was Rahab, and spent the night there. 2 The king of Jericho was told, "Some Israelites have come here tonight to search out the land." 3 Then the king of Jericho sent orders to Rahab, "Bring out the men who have come to you, who entered your house, for they have come only to search out the whole land." 4 But the woman took the two men and hid them. Then she said, "True, the men came to me, but I did not know where they came from. 5 And when it was time to close the gate at dark, the men went out. Where the men went I do not know. Pursue them quickly, for you can overtake them." 6 She had, however, brought them up to the roof and hidden them with the stalks of flax that she had laid out on the roof. 7 So the men pursued them on the way to the Jordan as far as the fords. As soon as the pursuers had gone out, the gate was shut.

b. Rahab secures a promise of safety from the spies

8   Before they went to sleep, she came up to them on the roof 9 and said to the men: "I know that the LORD has given you the land, and that dread of you has fallen on us, and that all the inhabitants of the land melt in fear before you. 10 For we have heard how the LORD dried up the water of the Red Sea[a] before you when you came out of Egypt, and what you did to the two kings of the Amorites that were beyond the Jordan, to Sihon and Og, whom you utterly destroyed. 11 As soon as we heard it, our hearts melted, and there was no courage left in any of us because of you. The LORD your God is indeed God in heaven above and on earth below. 12 Now then, since I have dealt kindly with you, swear to me by the LORD that you in turn will deal kindly with my family. Give me a sign of good faith 13 that you will spare my father and mother, my brothers and sisters, and

a Or Sea of Reeds

1.15
Josh 22.1-4

1.17
vv. 5, 9

2.1
Num 25.1;
Heb 11.31;
Jas 2.25

2.6
Jas 2.25

2.9
Ex 23.27;
Deut 2.25

2.10
Ex 14.21;
Num 21.24,
34, 35

2.11
Ex 15.14, 15;
Josh 5.1;
Deut 4.39

2.12
v. 18

1.16,17 In response to Joshua's speech the Israelites promised to obey him and prayed that God would be with him as he was with Moses. Unfortunately, the Israelites frequently disobeyed Moses and complained against him many times. Joshua was well aware of this proclivity; but his faith and confidence were not in the Israelites, but in God.

2.1 Joshua took no chances. He sent two spies, not twelve, and he sent them secretly so that if they brought back a bad report, it would not be known to Israel. He did not want to wait another forty years before entering the promised land.

2.4-6 Rahab lied in order to save the lives of the

spies. From this some have concluded that lying is sometimes permissible. But this inference is questionable. Even though the lie was told for a good purpose, it was not free from fault. In the N.T. Rahab is commended, but never for having lied (Heb 11.31; Jas 2.25). The spies would likely have been delivered by God even if Rahab had told the truth. Nowhere does Scripture say that lying is justifiable (Ex 20.16; Deut 5.20; Mt 19.19); the father of lies is Satan himself (Jn 8.44).

2.12 Rahab exacted a pledge or oath in the name of Israel's God from the two spies — that they would save her and her family when the invasion took place.

2.14
Judg 1.24

all who belong to them, and deliver our lives from death." 14 The men said to her, "Our life for yours! If you do not tell this business of ours, then we will deal kindly and faithfully with you when the LORD gives us the land."

c. *The promise of the crimson cord*

15 Then she let them down by a rope through the window, for her house was on the outer side of the city wall and she resided within the wall itself. 16 She said to them, "Go toward the hill country, so that the pursuers may not come upon you. Hide yourselves there three days, until the pursuers have returned; then afterward you may go your way." 17 The men said to her, "We will be released from this oath that you have made us swear to you 18 if we invade the land and you do not tie this crimson cord in the window through which you let us down, and you do not gather into your house your father and mother, your brothers, and all your family. 19 If any of you go out of the doors of your house into the street, they shall be responsible for their own death, and we shall be innocent; but if a hand is laid upon any who are with you in the house, we shall bear the responsibility for their death. 20 But if you tell this business of ours, then we shall be released from this oath that you made us swear to you." 21 She said, "According to your words, so be it." She sent them away and they departed. Then she tied the crimson cord in the window.

2.16
Jas 2.25

2.17
Gen 24.8

2.18
v. 12;
Josh 6.23

2.19
Ezek 33.4

d. *The return of the spies*

22 They departed and went into the hill country and stayed there three days, until the pursuers returned. The pursuers had searched all along the way and found nothing. 23 Then the two men came down again from the hill country. They crossed over, came to Joshua son of Nun, and told him all that had happened to them. 24 They said to Joshua, "Truly the LORD has given all the land into our hands; moreover all the inhabitants of the land melt in fear before us."

2.24
v. 9;
Josh 6.2

C. *Israel crossing the Jordan*

1. *The final preparations*

3.1
Josh 2.1

3.2
Josh 1.11
3.3
Deut 31.9

3 Early in the morning Joshua rose and set out from Shittim with all the Israelites, and they came to the Jordan. They camped there before crossing over. 2 At the end of three days the officers went through the camp 3 and commanded the people, "When you see the ark of the covenant of the LORD your God being carried by the levitical priests, then you shall set out from your place. Follow it, 4 so that you may know the way you should go, for you have not passed this way before. Yet there shall be a space between you and it, a distance of about two thousand cubits; do not come any nearer to it." 5 Then Joshua said to the people, "Sanctify yourselves; for tomorrow the LORD will do wonders among you." 6 To the priests Joshua said, "Take up the ark of the covenant, and pass on in front of the people." So they took up the ark of the covenant and went in front of the people.

3.5
Ex 19.10, 14;
Josh 7.13

2.15 This Canaanite city was enclosed by two walls approximately twelve to fifteen feet apart. Houses were built on timbers stretched from one wall to the other. It was easy to escape from within the city by means of windows on houses built on the outer wall. **2.18** *crimson cord.* Years before this episode, Israelite families living in Egypt had sprinkled blood on their lintels to avert the angel of death. The angel, seeing the sign of the blood, passed over their homes. Similarly, the crimson cord was a sign to all Israel that it should leave that house and its inhabitants un-

scathed. The presence of the crimson cord, not the righteousness of the people living within, made the difference. **2.24** The spies brought back an encouraging report, based on their faith that God had given them the land and on their knowledge that the inhabitants were fearful of the approaching Israelites. **3.3** The Levites preceded the people, carrying the ark of God. This guaranteed that God was going before them in victory.

2. The promise of God

7 The LORD said to Joshua, "This day I will begin to exalt you in the sight of all Israel, so that they may know that I will be with you as I was with Moses. 8 You are the one who shall command the priests who bear the ark of the covenant, 'When you come to the edge of the waters of the Jordan, you shall stand still in the Jordan.' " 9 Joshua then said to the Israelites, "Draw near and hear the words of the LORD your God." 10 Joshua said, "By this you shall know that among you is the living God who without fail will drive out from before you the Canaanites, Hittites, Hivites, Perizzites, Girgashites, Amorites, and Jebusites: 11 the ark of the covenant of the Lord of all the earth is going to pass before you into the Jordan. 12 So now select twelve men from the tribes of Israel, one from each tribe. 13 When the soles of the feet of the priests who bear the ark of the LORD, the Lord of all the earth, rest in the waters of the Jordan, the waters of the Jordan flowing from above shall be cut off; they shall stand in a single heap."

3. The crossing begun: the Jordan parted

14 When the people set out from their tents to cross over the Jordan, the priests bearing the ark of the covenant were in front of the people. 15 Now the Jordan overflows all its banks throughout the time of harvest. So when those who bore the ark had come to the Jordan, and the feet of the priests bearing the ark were dipped in the edge of the water, 16 the waters flowing from above stood still, rising up in a single heap far off at Adam, the city that is beside Zarethan, while those flowing toward the sea of the Arabah, the Dead Sea,[b] were wholly cut off. Then the people crossed over opposite Jericho. 17 While all Israel were crossing over on dry ground, the priests who bore the ark of the covenant of the LORD stood on dry ground in the middle of the Jordan, until the entire nation finished crossing over the Jordan.

4. The twelve stones of memorial

4 When the entire nation had finished crossing over the Jordan, the LORD said to Joshua: 2 "Select twelve men from the people, one from each tribe, 3 and command them, 'Take twelve stones from here out of the middle of the Jordan, from the place where the priests' feet stood, carry them over with you, and lay them down in the place where you camp tonight.' " 4 Then Joshua summoned the twelve men from the Israelites, whom he had appointed, one from each tribe. 5 Joshua said to them, "Pass on before the ark of the LORD your God into the middle of the Jordan, and each of you take up a stone on his shoulder, one for each of the tribes of the Israelites, 6 so that this may be a sign among you. When your children ask in time to come, 'What do those stones mean to you?' 7 then you shall tell them that the waters of the Jordan were cut off in front of the ark of the covenant of the LORD. When it crossed over the Jordan, the waters of the Jordan were cut off. So these stones shall be to the Israelites a memorial forever."

b Heb Salt Sea

3.7
Josh 4.7; 1.5

3.8
vv. 3, 17

3.10
Deut 7.1

3.12
Josh 4.2
3.13
Ex 15.8;
Ps 78.13

3.15
Josh 4.18

3.16
Ps 66.6;
74.15; v. 13

3.17
Ex 14.29

4.2
Josh 3.12
4.3
vv. 19, 20

4.6
v. 21;
Ex 12.26;
13.14
4.7
Josh 3.13

3.7 God planned to use signs and wonders to demonstrate that he was with Joshua and the Israelites as he had been with Moses, thereby providing them with external evidences to justify their faith.
3.15,16 The Jordan River has been blocked on occasion by a "dam" of earth caused by an earthquake which dislodges portions of cliffs overlooking the river. We do not know whether God sent such an earthquake to dam the Jordan or whether he blocked the waters as he had done when the Israelites crossed the Red Sea. Either way, it was a remarkable act of providence.

4.7 *these stones shall be . . . a memorial forever.* The memorial stones were set up for more than a commemoration. They were to bear testimony to future generations of what God had done. From then on, whenever Israel faced trouble, this memorial would cause them to look to the same God who would deliver them again. All believers should set up in their hearts "stones of remembrance" of what God has done in the past; then when trouble overtakes them, they can renew their confidence in God.

4.8
vv. 19, 20

4.9
Ex 28.21

8 The Israelites did as Joshua commanded. They took up twelve stones out of the middle of the Jordan, according to the number of the tribes of the Israelites, as the LORD told Joshua, carried them over with them to the place where they camped, and laid them down there. 9 (Joshua set up twelve stones in the middle of the Jordan, in the place where the feet of the priests bearing the ark of the covenant had stood; and they are there to this day.)

10 The priests who bore the ark remained standing in the middle of the Jordan, until everything was finished that the LORD commanded Joshua to tell the people, according to all that Moses had commanded Joshua. The people crossed over in haste. 11 As soon as all the people had finished crossing over, the ark of the LORD, and the priests, crossed over

4.12
Num 32.17

in front of the people. 12 The Reubenites, the Gadites, and the half-tribe of Manasseh crossed over armed before the Israelites, as Moses had ordered them. 13 About forty thousand armed for war crossed over before the LORD to the plains of Jericho for battle.

4.14
Josh 3.7

14 On that day the LORD exalted Joshua in the sight of all Israel; and they stood in awe of him, as they had stood in awe of Moses, all the days of his life.

5. *The crossing completed: the Jordan flows*

15 The LORD said to Joshua, 16 "Command the priests who bear the ark of the covenant,c to come up out of the Jordan." 17 Joshua therefore commanded the priests, "Come up out of the Jordan." 18 When the priests

4.18
Josh 3.15

bearing the ark of the covenant of the LORD came up from the middle of the Jordan, and the soles of the priests' feet touched dry ground, the waters of the Jordan returned to their place and overflowed all its banks, as before.

6. *The meaning of the stones*

4.19
Josh 5.9
4.20
vv. 3, 8
4.21
v. 6
4.22
Josh 3.17
4.23
Ex 14.21

19 The people came up out of the Jordan on the tenth day of the first month, and they camped in Gilgal on the east border of Jericho. 20 Those twelve stones, which they had taken out of the Jordan, Joshua set up in Gilgal, 21 saying to the Israelites, "When your children ask their parents in time to come, 'What do these stones mean?' 22 then you shall let your children know, 'Israel crossed over the Jordan here on dry ground.' 23 For the LORD your God dried up the waters of the Jordan for you until you crossed over, as the LORD your God did to the Red Sea,d which he dried up for us until we crossed over, 24 so that all the peoples of the earth may

4.24
1 Kings 8.42,
43;
Ps 89.13;
Ex 14.31
5.1
Num 13.29;
Josh 2.9-11

know that the hand of the LORD is mighty, and so that you may fear the LORD your God forever."

5 When all the kings of the Amorites beyond the Jordan to the west, and all the kings of the Canaanites by the sea, heard that the LORD had dried up the waters of the Jordan for the Israelites until they had crossed over, their hearts melted, and there was no longer any spirit in them, because of the Israelites.

D. *The encampment at Gilgal*

1. *The covenant of circumcision fulfilled*

5.2
Ex 4.25

2 At that time the LORD said to Joshua, "Make flint knives and

c Or *treaty*, or *testimony*; Heb *eduth*   d Or *Sea of Reeds*

4.9 The author of this book apparently knew that, at the time of writing, the stones in the middle of the river could be seen when the water level was low.
4.21 Later generations of Israelites would see the stones that had been set up as a memorial and would want to know what they meant. Parents then had the

opportunity to teach their children about the true faith, about God's signs and wonders, and about trusting in God, who would do great things for them, similar to what he did when their ancestors crossed the Jordan.
5.2–9 Circumcision was the seal of God's covenant

circumcise the Israelites a second time." ³So Joshua made flint knives, and circumcised the Israelites at Gibeath-haaraloth. *e* ⁴This is the reason why Joshua circumcised them: all the males of the people who came out of Egypt, all the warriors, had died during the journey through the wilderness after they had come out of Egypt. ⁵Although all the people who came out had been circumcised, yet all the people born on the journey through the wilderness after they had come out of Egypt had not been circumcised. ⁶For the Israelites traveled forty years in the wilderness, until all the nation, the warriors who came out of Egypt, perished, not having listened to the voice of the LORD. To them the LORD swore that he would not let them see the land that he had sworn to their ancestors to give us, a land flowing with milk and honey. ⁷So it was their children, whom he raised up in their place, that Joshua circumcised; for they were uncircumcised, because they had not been circumcised on the way.

8 When the circumcising of all the nation was done, they remained in their places in the camp until they were healed. ⁹The LORD said to Joshua, "Today I have rolled away from you the disgrace of Egypt." And so that place is called Gilgal *f* to this day.

2. The passover kept

10 While the Israelites were camped in Gilgal they kept the passover in the evening on the fourteenth day of the month in the plains of Jericho. ¹¹On the day after the passover, on that very day, they ate the produce of the land, unleavened cakes and parched grain. ¹²The manna ceased on the day they ate the produce of the land, and the Israelites no longer had manna; they ate the crops of the land of Canaan that year.

3. The angel of the LORD

13 Once when Joshua was by Jericho, he looked up and saw a man standing before him with a drawn sword in his hand. Joshua went to him and said to him, "Are you one of us, or one of our adversaries?" ¹⁴He replied, "Neither; but as commander of the army of the LORD I have now come." And Joshua fell on his face to the earth and worshiped, and he said to him, "What do you command your servant, my lord?" ¹⁵The commander of the army of the LORD said to Joshua, "Remove the sandals from your feet, for the place where you stand is holy." And Joshua did so.

E. The conquest of Jericho

1. The six-day march around Jericho

6 Now Jericho was shut up inside and out because of the Israelites; no one came out and no one went in. ²The LORD said to Joshua, "See,

e That is *the Hill of the Foreskins*   *f* Related to Heb *galal* to roll

Cross references:
5.4 Deut 2.16
5.6 Deut 2.7, 14; Num 14.23
5.10 Ex 12.6, 8
5.12 Ex 16.35
5.13 Gen 18.2; 32.24; Num 22.31
5.14 Gen 17.3
5.15 Ex 3.5
6.2 Josh 2.9, 24; Deut 7.24

with Abraham (see Gen 17.9,10). It had no value unless faith were present. The rite was neglected during the wilderness wandering. When Israel was about to enter Canaan, God ordered Joshua to command all males to be circumcised. By doing so, God said, "I have rolled away from you the disgrace of Egypt."
5.10–12 *The manna ceased.* God had fed the people of Israel with manna for forty years. As they began their entrance into Canaan they celebrated another passover, using the produce of Canaan. After that, the manna stopped. It was no longer necessary for God to use supernatural means to care for his people. They were now back to the normal situation where they could provide for themselves under the eye of their God.
5.14,15 This *commander of the army of the LORD* was

no mere angel. His presence was an appearance of God, of Christ in person. Joshua worshiped the commander, and his worship was accepted; he was neither rebuked nor instructed otherwise. The commander said the place was holy and Joshua removed his shoes. Just as God used the burning bush to give Moses outward, confirming evidence of his divine presence (Ex 3), so God now gave similar assurance to Joshua as he began a new phase of his life. Joshua did not need to fear, for God was on his side and victory was assured. In the same manner, Christ, as the commander of our salvation, guarantees his continuing presence among his people (Mt 28.20) with the promise of available power for every contingency.
6.1ff Jericho was not taken by military might, but by spiritual, supernatural means. This is one in a

I have handed Jericho over to you, along with its king and soldiers. 3 You shall march around the city, all the warriors circling the city once. Thus you shall do for six days, 4 with seven priests bearing seven trumpets of rams' horns before the ark. On the seventh day you shall march around the city seven times, the priests blowing the trumpets. 5 When they make a long blast with the ram's horn, as soon as you hear the sound of the trumpet, then all the people shall shout with a great shout; and the wall of the city will fall down flat, and all the people shall charge straight ahead." 6 So Joshua son of Nun summoned the priests and said to them, "Take up the ark of the covenant, and have seven priests carry seven trumpets of rams' horns in front of the ark of the Lord." 7 To the people he said, "Go forward and march around the city; have the armed men pass on before the ark of the Lord."

8 As Joshua had commanded the people, the seven priests carrying the seven trumpets of rams' horns before the Lord went forward, blowing the trumpets, with the ark of the covenant of the Lord following them. 9 And the armed men went before the priests who blew the trumpets; the rear guard came after the ark, while the trumpets blew continually. 10 To the people Joshua gave this command: "You shall not shout or let your voice be heard, nor shall you utter a word, until the day I tell you to shout. Then you shall shout." 11 So the ark of the Lord went around the city, circling it once; and they came into the camp, and spent the night in the camp.

12 Then Joshua rose early in the morning, and the priests took up the ark of the Lord. 13 The seven priests carrying the seven trumpets of rams' horns before the ark of the Lord passed on, blowing the trumpets continually. The armed men went before them, and the rear guard came after the ark of the Lord, while the trumpets blew continually. 14 On the second day they marched around the city once and then returned to the camp. They did this for six days.

2. The fall of the city

15 On the seventh day they rose early, at dawn, and marched around the city in the same manner seven times. It was only on that day that they marched around the city seven times. 16 And at the seventh time, when the priests had blown the trumpets, Joshua said to the people, "Shout! For the Lord has given you the city. 17 The city and all that is in it shall be devoted to the Lord for destruction. Only Rahab the prostitute and all who are with her in her house shall live because she hid the messengers we sent. 18 As for you, keep away from the things devoted to destruction, so as not to covet*g* and take any of the devoted things and make the camp of Israel an object for destruction, bringing trouble upon it. 19 But all silver and gold, and vessels of bronze and iron, are sacred to the Lord; they shall go into the treasury of the Lord." 20 So the people shouted, and the trumpets were blown. As soon as the people heard the sound of the trumpets, they raised a great shout, and the wall fell down flat; so the people charged straight ahead into the city and captured it. 21 Then they

Cross-references (left margin)
6.4 Num 10.8
6.5 Lev 25.9
6.7 Ex 14.15
6.9 v. 13; Isa 52.12
6.13 vv. 4, 9
6.17 Lev 27.28; Josh 2.4
6.18 Josh 7.1, 25
6.20 v. 5; Heb 11.30
6.21 Deut 7.2; 20.16

g Gk: Heb *devote to destruction* Compare 7.21

series of "foolish things" (cf. 1 Cor 1.27–29) God used to shame the wise and the mighty: e.g., the wooden stick of Moses, the slingshot of David, and the *seven trumpets of ram's horns* of Joshua (v. 4). It is not important whether the walls of Jericho collapsed because of an earthquake or because of a special miracle. God was in charge here; he always chooses his own means to accomplish his purposes.
6.9 The inhabitants of Jericho must have observed with incredulity the Israelites marching around the city day after day. No war had ever been fought like that and none has been like it since then. The Israel-

ites themselves probably thought what they were doing was strange, and they must have waited breathlessly to see what the result would be.
6.17 *The city . . . shall be devoted to the Lord.* The Hebrew word *herem* is used; see note on Deut 2.34 for explanation.
6.20 The soldiers marched around the city once a day for six days. On the seventh day they circled the city seven times, then blew their trumpets. It is absurd to think that this sound caused the walls to fall down, for it was God who miraculously caused the walls to collapse.

devoted to destruction by the edge of the sword all in the city, both men and women, young and old, oxen, sheep, and donkeys.

3. The rescue of Rahab

22 Joshua said to the two men who had spied out the land, "Go into the prostitute's house, and bring the woman out of it and all who belong to her, as you swore to her." 23 So the young men who had been spies went in and brought Rahab out, along with her father, her mother, her brothers, and all who belonged to her — they brought all her kindred out — and set them outside the camp of Israel. 24 They burned down the city, and everything in it; only the silver and gold, and the vessels of bronze and iron, they put into the treasury of the house of the LORD. 25 But Rahab the prostitute, with her family and all who belonged to her, Joshua spared. Her family[h] has lived in Israel ever since. For she hid the messengers whom Joshua sent to spy out Jericho.

4. The curse on Jericho

26 Joshua then pronounced this oath, saying,
"Cursed before the LORD be anyone who tries
to build this city — this Jericho!
At the cost of his firstborn he shall lay its foundation,
and at the cost of his youngest he shall set up its gates!"
27 So the LORD was with Joshua; and his fame was in all the land.

F. The conquest of Ai

1. Israel flees from Ai

7 But the Israelites broke faith in regard to the devoted things: Achan son of Carmi son of Zabdi son of Zerah, of the tribe of Judah, took some of the devoted things; and the anger of the LORD burned against the Israelites.

2 Joshua sent men from Jericho to Ai, which is near Beth-aven, east of Bethel, and said to them, "Go up and spy out the land." And the men went up and spied out Ai. 3 Then they returned to Joshua and said to him, "Not all the people need go up; about two or three thousand men should go up and attack Ai. Since they are so few, do not make the whole people toil up there." 4 So about three thousand of the people went up there; and they fled before the men of Ai. 5 The men of Ai killed about thirty-six of them, chasing them from outside the gate as far as Shebarim and killing them on the slope. The hearts of the people melted and turned to water.

2. Joshua's grief

6 Then Joshua tore his clothes, and fell to the ground on his face

[h] Heb She

Margin references:
6.22 Josh 2.14; Heb 11.31
6.23 Josh 2.13
6.24 v. 19
6.25 Heb 11.31
6.26 1 Kings 16.34
6.27 Josh 1.5; 9.1, 3
7.1 Josh 6.17-19
7.4 Lev 26.17; 28.25
7.6 Job 2.12; Rev 18.19

6.23 Although Rahab was a prostitute, a Canaanite, and a liar, the mercy of God worked wonders in her depraved life, for he gave her saving faith. Her works demonstrated that faith. She was an Israelite by redemption, not by birth. She married Salmon, then gave birth to Boaz, the great-grandfather of David (Ruth 4.21; Mt 1.5). Although an alien and a sinful woman, she came to stand in the promised line of the Messiah. Such is the wonderful grace of God.
6.27 The events magnified Joshua before Israel, but they also made him appear as a formidable enemy to the Canaanites, who could see that God Almighty was with him.
7.1 The sin for which Achan was punished was not the seizure of the enemy's valuable goods. Nor was it the fact that he coveted these things. His chief sin lay

in his refusal to unconditionally obey God's express command. Moreover, his sin involved corporate Israel, for no human beings live or die to themselves. Consequently, God's displeasure included Israel as a whole; the nation was not released from responsibility until Achan and his family had been dealt with.
7.6 Joshua had been promised success in warfare, but now at Ai, Israel suffered a significant defeat. He asked God why he had allowed his people to be defeated (v. 7). Joshua learned quickly that the defeat had been caused by one Israelite's sin. This apparently small transgression brought incalculable harm to all Israel. Once the situation had been rectified, Israel could continue its successful takeover of Canaan.

before the ark of the LORD until the evening, he and the elders of Israel; and they put dust on their heads. 7 Joshua said, "Ah, Lord GOD! Why have you brought this people across the Jordan at all, to hand us over to the Amorites so as to destroy us? Would that we had been content to settle beyond the Jordan! 8 O Lord, what can I say, now that Israel has turned their backs to their enemies! 9 The Canaanites and all the inhabitants of the land will hear of it, and surround us, and cut off our name from the earth. Then what will you do for your great name?"

3. God's way of uncovering sin

10 The LORD said to Joshua, "Stand up! Why have you fallen upon your face? 11 Israel has sinned; they have transgressed my covenant that I imposed on them. They have taken some of the devoted things; they have stolen, they have acted deceitfully, and they have put them among their own belongings. 12 Therefore the Israelites are unable to stand before their enemies; they turn their backs to their enemies, because they have become a thing devoted for destruction themselves. I will be with you no more, unless you destroy the devoted things from among you. 13 Proceed to sanctify the people, and say, 'Sanctify yourselves for tomorrow; for thus says the LORD, the God of Israel, "There are devoted things among you, O Israel; you will be unable to stand before your enemies until you take away the devoted things from among you." 14 In the morning therefore you shall come forward tribe by tribe. The tribe that the LORD takes shall come near by clans, the clan that the LORD takes shall come near by households, and the household that the LORD takes shall come near one by one. 15 And the one who is taken as having the devoted things shall be burned with fire, together with all that he has, for having transgressed the covenant of the LORD, and for having done an outrageous thing in Israel.' "

4. The sin of Achan uncovered

16 So Joshua rose early in the morning, and brought Israel near tribe by tribe, and the tribe of Judah was taken. 17 He brought near the clans of Judah, and the clan of the Zerahites was taken; and he brought near the clan of the Zerahites, family by family,[i] and Zabdi was taken. 18 And he brought near his household one by one, and Achan son of Carmi son of Zabdi son of Zerah, of the tribe of Judah, was taken. 19 Then Joshua said to Achan, "My son, give glory to the LORD God of Israel and make confession to him. Tell me now what you have done; do not hide it from me." 20 And Achan answered Joshua, "It is true; I am the one who sinned against the LORD God of Israel. This is what I did: 21 when I saw among the spoil a beautiful mantle from Shinar, and two hundred shekels of silver, and a bar of gold weighing fifty shekels, then I coveted them and took them. They now lie hidden in the ground inside my tent, with the silver underneath."

5. The stoning of Achan and his family

22 So Joshua sent messengers, and they ran to the tent; and there it was, hidden in his tent with the silver underneath. 23 They took them out of the tent and brought them to Joshua and all the Israelites; and they spread them out before the LORD. 24 Then Joshua and all Israel with him

i Mss Syr: MT man by man

7.7
Ex 5.22

7.9
Ex 32.12;
Deut 9.28

7.11
v. 1;
Josh 6.18, 19;
See Acts 5.1,
2

7.13
Josh 3.5; 6.18

7.15
v. 11

7.17
Num 26.20

7.19
Jer 13.16;
Jn 9.24;
Num 5.6, 7;
1 Sam 14.43
7.20
Josh 22.20;
1 Chr 2.7

7.24
Josh 15.7

7.11 *devoted things.* This refers to persons or things irrevocably given over to God, sometimes (as here) by their total destruction.
7.19 *Tell me now what you have done.* After God had pointed out the sinner, Achan could no longer hide

his deed. He had broken Israel's pledge just before crossing the Jordan to solemnly obey Joshua and God. As a result, he with his family (who were undoubtedly silent partners in his deed) suffered the penalty of death.

took Achan son of Zerah, with the silver, the mantle, and the bar of gold, with his sons and daughters, with his oxen, donkeys, and sheep, and his tent and all that he had; and they brought them up to the Valley of Achor. 25 Joshua said, "Why did you bring trouble on us? The LORD is bringing trouble on you today." And all Israel stoned him to death; they burned them with fire, cast stones on them, 26 and raised over him a great heap of stones that remains to this day. Then the LORD turned from his burning anger. Therefore that place to this day is called the Valley of Achor.*j*

7.25
Josh 6.18;
Deut 17.5
7.26
Deut 13.17;
Isa 65.10;
Hos 2.15

6. *The battle for Ai*

a. *The plan of battle*

8 Then the LORD said to Joshua, "Do not fear or be dismayed; take all the fighting men with you, and go up now to Ai. See, I have handed over to you the king of Ai with his people, his city, and his land. 2 You shall do to Ai and its king as you did to Jericho and its king; only its spoil and its livestock you may take as booty for yourselves. Set an ambush against the city, behind it."

8.1
Deut 1.21;
7.18;
Josh 1.9; 6.2
8.2
v. 27;
Deut 20.14

3 So Joshua and all the fighting men set out to go up against Ai. Joshua chose thirty thousand warriors and sent them out by night 4 with the command, "You shall lie in ambush against the city, behind it; do not go very far from the city, but all of you stay alert. 5 I and all the people who are with me will approach the city. When they come out against us, as before, we shall flee from them. 6 They will come out after us until we have drawn them away from the city; for they will say, 'They are fleeing from us, as before.' While we flee from them, 7 you shall rise up from the ambush and seize the city; for the LORD your God will give it into your hand. 8 And when you have taken the city, you shall set the city on fire, doing as the LORD has ordered; see, I have commanded you." 9 So Joshua sent them out; and they went to the place of ambush, and lay between Bethel and Ai, to the west of Ai; but Joshua spent that night in the camp.*k*

8.4
see
Judg 20.29-32

8.8
v. 2

b. *The seizure of the city*

10 In the morning Joshua rose early and mustered the people, and went up, with the elders of Israel, before the people to Ai. 11 All the fighting men who were with him went up, and drew near before the city, and camped on the north side of Ai, with a ravine between them and Ai. 12 Taking about five thousand men, he set them in ambush between Bethel and Ai, to the west of the city. 13 So they stationed the forces, the main encampment that was north of the city and its rear guard west of the city. But Joshua spent that night in the valley. 14 When the king of Ai saw this, he and all his people, the inhabitants of the city, hurried out early in the morning to the meeting place facing the Arabah to meet Israel in battle; but he did not know that there was an ambush against him behind the city. 15 And Joshua and all Israel made a pretense of being beaten before them, and fled in the direction of the wilderness. 16 So all the people who were in the city were called together to pursue them, and as they pursued Joshua they were drawn away from the city. 17 There was not a man left in Ai or Bethel who did not go out after Israel; they left the city open, and pursued Israel.

8.10
v. 33

8.14
Josh 3.16;
Judg 20.34

18 Then the LORD said to Joshua, "Stretch out the sword that is in your hand toward Ai; for I will give it into your hand." And Joshua stretched out the sword that was in his hand toward the city. 19 As soon

8.18
v. 26;
Ex 14.16;
17.9-13
8.19
v. 8

---

j That is *Trouble*   *k* Heb *among the people*

8.2 Whereas the spoil from Jericho was dedicated in its entirety to God, the Israelites were free to keep all they took at Ai.
8.12 *five thousand men.* These were evidently additional to the thirty thousand soldiers already hiding

there. Perhaps the additional five thousand were to intercept the forces expected from Bethel (v. 17).
8.13 *spent that night in the valley.* Some have suggested that he spent the night in prayer, seeking the blessing of God before the battle started the next day.

as he stretched out his hand, the troops in ambush rose quickly out of their place and rushed forward. They entered the city, took it, and at once set the city on fire. 20 So when the men of Ai looked back, the smoke of the city was rising to the sky. They had no power to flee this way or that, for the people who fled to the wilderness turned back against the pursuers. 21 When Joshua and all Israel saw that the ambush had taken the city and that the smoke of the city was rising, then they turned back and struck down the men of Ai. 22 And the others came out from the city against them; so they were surrounded by Israelites, some on one side, and some on the other; and Israel struck them down until no one was left who survived or escaped. 23 But the king of Ai was taken alive and brought to Joshua.

8.22
Deut 7.2

c. *The slaughter of the inhabitants*

24   When Israel had finished slaughtering all the inhabitants of Ai in the open wilderness where they pursued them, and when all of them to the very last had fallen by the edge of the sword, all Israel returned to Ai, and attacked it with the edge of the sword. 25 The total of those who fell that day, both men and women, was twelve thousand — all the people of Ai. 26 For Joshua did not draw back his hand, with which he stretched out the sword, until he had utterly destroyed all the inhabitants of Ai. 27 Only the livestock and the spoil of that city Israel took as their booty, according to the word of the LORD that he had issued to Joshua. 28 So Joshua burned Ai, and made it forever a heap of ruins, as it is to this day. 29 And he hanged the king of Ai on a tree until evening; and at sunset Joshua commanded, and they took his body down from the tree, threw it down at the entrance of the gate of the city, and raised over it a great heap of stones, which stands there to this day.

8.25
Deut 20.16-18
8.26
Ex 17.11, 12
8.27
v. 2;
Num 31.22
8.28
Deut 13.16
8.29
Deut 21.22,
23

7. *An altar erected on Mount Ebal*

30   Then Joshua built on Mount Ebal an altar to the LORD, the God of Israel, 31 just as Moses the servant of the LORD had commanded the Israelites, as it is written in the book of the law of Moses, "an altar of unhewn[l] stones, on which no iron tool has been used"; and they offered on it burnt offerings to the LORD, and sacrificed offerings of well-being. 32 And there, in the presence of the Israelites, Joshua[m] wrote on the stones a copy of the law of Moses, which he had written. 33 All Israel, alien as well as citizen, with their elders and officers and their judges, stood on opposite sides of the ark in front of the levitical priests who carried the ark of the covenant of the LORD, half of them in front of Mount Gerizim and half of them in front of Mount Ebal, as Moses the servant of the LORD had commanded at the first, that they should bless the people of Israel. 34 And afterward he read all the words of the law, blessings and curses, according to all that is written in the book of the law. 35 There was not a word of all that Moses commanded that Joshua did not read before all the assembly of Israel, and the women, and the little ones, and the aliens who resided among them.

8.30
Deut 27.2-8
8.31
Ex 20.24, 25;
Deut 27.5, 6
8.32
Deut 27.2, 8
8.33
Deut 31.9,
12; 27.11-14
8.34f
Deut 31.11;
Josh 1.8
8.35
Deut 31.12

l Heb *whole*   *m* Heb *he*

8.28 *Ai* (meaning "the heap" or "the ruin") was destroyed by Israel. It appears to have been located in the area near Jericho, Jerusalem, and Bethel. Ai may have been a military outpost of Bethel, which Joshua seized.
8.30 Joshua built an altar on Mount Ebal according to the instruction of Moses in Deut 27.2–8. This was more than a simple act of obedience to Moses' command. The Israelites were giving glory to God for the

victory at Ai which had first been denied them by Achan's sin. When they erected the altar, they acknowledged that they were the people of God. Joshua engraved the ten commandments on the stones of the altar (v. 32), demonstrating that they accepted God's law. Through this dedication they renewed God's covenant with them, a covenant which promised the blessing of God on an obedient people.

G. *The strategy of Gibeon*

1. *The coalition of kings*

9 Now when all the kings who were beyond the Jordan in the hill country and in the lowland all along the coast of the Great Sea toward Lebanon — the Hittites, the Amorites, the Canaanites, the Perizzites, the Hivites, and the Jebusites — heard of this, 2 they gathered together with one accord to fight Joshua and Israel.

9.1
Josh 3.10

2. *The treaty with Gibeon*

3 But when the inhabitants of Gibeon heard what Joshua had done to Jericho and to Ai, 4 they on their part acted with cunning: they went and prepared provisions,*n* and took worn-out sacks for their donkeys, and wineskins, worn-out and torn and mended, 5 with worn-out, patched sandals on their feet, and worn-out clothes; and all their provisions were dry and moldy. 6 They went to Joshua in the camp at Gilgal, and said to him and to the Israelites, "We have come from a far country; so now make a treaty with us." 7 But the Israelites said to the Hivites, "Perhaps you live among us; then how can we make a treaty with you?" 8 They said to Joshua, "We are your servants." And Joshua said to them, "Who are you? And where do you come from?" 9 They said to him, "Your servants have come from a very far country, because of the name of the LORD your God; for we have heard a report of him, of all that he did in Egypt, 10 and of all that he did to the two kings of the Amorites who were beyond the Jordan, King Sihon of Heshbon, and King Og of Bashan who lived in Ashtaroth. 11 So our elders and all the inhabitants of our country said to us, 'Take provisions in your hand for the journey; go to meet them, and say to them, "We are your servants; come now, make a treaty with us." ' 12 Here is our bread; it was still warm when we took it from our houses as our food for the journey, on the day we set out to come to you, but now, see, it is dry and moldy; 13 these wineskins were new when we filled them, and see, they are burst; and these garments and sandals of ours are worn out from the very long journey." 14 So the leaders*o* partook of their provisions, and did not ask direction from the LORD. 15 And Joshua made peace with them, guaranteeing their lives by a treaty; and the leaders of the congregation swore an oath to them.

9.3
Josh 10.2;
6.27

9.6
Josh 5.10

9.7
v. 2;
Josh 11.19;
Ex 23.32
9.8
Deut 20.11
9.9
Deut 20.15;
vv. 16, 17,
24;
Josh 2.9, 10
9.10
Num 21.24,
33

9.14
Num 27.21
9.15
Ex 23.32

3. *The punishment of the Gibeonites for their deceit*

16 But when three days had passed after they had made a treaty with them, they heard that they were their neighbors and were living among them. 17 So the Israelites set out and reached their cities on the third day. Now their cities were Gibeon, Chephirah, Beeroth, and Kiriath-jearim. 18 But the Israelites did not attack them, because the leaders of the congregation had sworn to them by the LORD, the God of Israel. Then all the congregation murmured against the leaders. 19 But all the leaders said to all the congregation, "We have sworn to them by the LORD, the God of Israel, and now we must not touch them. 20 This is what we will do to

9.17
Josh 18.25-28;
Ezra 2.25
9.18
Ps 15.4;
Eccl 5.2

---

n Cn: Meaning of Heb uncertain   *o* Gk: Heb *men*

9.2 When the inhabitants of Canaan learned about the fate of Jericho and Ai, they formed a military alliance to fight against Israel. The number of Israelites in itself presented a grave threat to these peoples, who were far fewer in number.
9.14,15 The Gibeonites deceived Israel when working out their treaty. Israel, however, was not without responsibility. *The leaders . . . did not ask direction from the LORD* makes clear that the error would have been avoided if they had sought God's advice. No matter how favorable or unfavorable external circumstances may be, believers should not rely on their own judgment when they have divine resources at hand to help them.
9.19 The leaders of Israel were constrained to keep the oath they made with the Gibeonites, for it was taken in the name of God. Even though the oath was taken as a result of the false pretensions, it had to be kept. As the psalmist says, good people "stand by their oath even to their hurt" (Ps 15.4).

them: We will let them live, so that wrath may not come upon us, because of the oath that we swore to them." 21 The leaders said to them, "Let them live." So they became hewers of wood and drawers of water for all the congregation, as the leaders had decided concerning them.

22 Joshua summoned them, and said to them, "Why did you deceive us, saying, 'We are very far from you,' while in fact you are living among us? 23 Now therefore you are cursed, and some of you shall always be slaves, hewers of wood and drawers of water for the house of my God." 24 They answered Joshua, "Because it was told to your servants for a certainty that the LORD your God had commanded his servant Moses to give you all the land, and to destroy all the inhabitants of the land before you; so we were in great fear for our lives because of you, and did this thing. 25 And now we are in your hand: do as it seems good and right in your sight to do to us." 26 This is what he did for them: he saved them from the Israelites; and they did not kill them. 27 But on that day Joshua made them hewers of wood and drawers of water for the congregation and for the altar of the LORD, to continue to this day, in the place that he should choose.

H. *The conquest of southern Canaan*

1. *The victory over the Amorites*

a. *The confederation*

10 When King Adoni-zedek of Jerusalem heard how Joshua had taken Ai, and had utterly destroyed it, doing to Ai and its king as he had done to Jericho and its king, and how the inhabitants of Gibeon had made peace with Israel and were among them, 2 he*p* became greatly frightened, because Gibeon was a large city, like one of the royal cities, and was larger than Ai, and all its men were warriors. 3 So King Adoni-zedek of Jerusalem sent a message to King Hoham of Hebron, to King Piram of Jarmuth, to King Japhia of Lachish, and to King Debir of Eglon, saying, 4 "Come up and help me, and let us attack Gibeon; for it has made peace with Joshua and with the Israelites." 5 Then the five kings of the Amorites — the king of Jerusalem, the king of Hebron, the king of Jarmuth, the king of Lachish, and the king of Eglon — gathered their forces, and went up with all their armies and camped against Gibeon, and made war against it.

b. *The battle: God sends hailstones*

6 And the Gibeonites sent to Joshua at the camp in Gilgal, saying, "Do not abandon your servants; come up to us quickly, and save us, and help us; for all the kings of the Amorites who live in the hill country are gathered against us." 7 So Joshua went up from Gilgal, he and all the fighting force with him, all the mighty warriors. 8 The LORD said to Joshua, "Do not fear them, for I have handed them over to you; not one of them shall stand before you." 9 So Joshua came upon them suddenly, having marched up all night from Gilgal. 10 And the LORD threw them into a panic before Israel, who inflicted a great slaughter on them at Gibeon, chased them by the way of the ascent of Beth-horon, and struck them down as far as Azekah and Makkedah. 11 As they fled before Israel, while

p Heb *they*

Side references (left margin)

9.21
v. 15

9.22
vv. 6, 9, 16, 17
9.23
Gen 9.25;
vv. 21, 27
9.24
Deut 7.1, 2

9.25
Gen 16.6

9.27
vv. 21, 23;
Deut 12.5

10.1
Josh 6.21;
8.22, 26, 28;
9.15

10.4
v. 1
10.5
Josh 9.2

10.8
Josh 1.5, 9;
11.6

10.10
Deut 7.23

10.11
Ps 18.13, 14;
Isa 30.30

10.1ff The Gibeonites went from the frying pan into the fire. They had made a treaty with Israel, but now five kings set up an alliance to attack Gibeon and retake it from the Israelites. The Gibeonites appealed to Joshua for help, for they had a binding treaty with Israel. Joshua had been waiting for the right time to attack the Amorites, who stood in the way of Israel's occupation of the land. Now that time had come, and

Joshua was prepared. Again God intervened and manifested himself through signs and wonders.
10.11 God providentially sent a storm in which hailstones killed more enemies than the troops of Israel had killed. God sometimes uses the weapons of nature to defend and help his people (cf. Job 38.22,23). Secular historians cannot accept a sovereign God intervening in warfare or other affairs of nations

they were going down the slope of Beth-horon, the Lord threw down huge stones from heaven on them as far as Azekah, and they died; there were more who died because of the hailstones than the Israelites killed with the sword.

c. The sun stands still

12 On the day when the Lord gave the Amorites over to the Israelites, Joshua spoke to the Lord; and he said in the sight of Israel,
    "Sun, stand still at Gibeon,
      and Moon, in the valley of Aijalon."
13 And the sun stood still, and the moon stopped,
    until the nation took vengeance on their enemies.
Is this not written in the Book of Jashar? The sun stopped in midheaven, and did not hurry to set for about a whole day. 14 There has been no day like it before or since, when the Lord heeded a human voice; for the Lord fought for Israel.

15 Then Joshua returned, and all Israel with him, to the camp at Gilgal.

d. The slaughter of the five kings

16 Meanwhile, these five kings fled and hid themselves in the cave at Makkedah. 17 And it was told Joshua, "The five kings have been found, hidden in the cave at Makkedah." 18 Joshua said, "Roll large stones against the mouth of the cave, and set men by it to guard them; 19 but do not stay there yourselves; pursue your enemies, and attack them from the rear. Do not let them enter their towns, for the Lord your God has given them into your hand." 20 When Joshua and the Israelites had finished inflicting a very great slaughter on them, until they were wiped out, and when the survivors had entered into the fortified towns, 21 all the people returned safe to Joshua in the camp at Makkedah; no one dared to speak[q] against any of the Israelites.

22 Then Joshua said, "Open the mouth of the cave, and bring those five kings out to me from the cave." 23 They did so, and brought the five kings out to him from the cave, the king of Jerusalem, the king of Hebron, the king of Jarmuth, the king of Lachish, and the king of Eglon. 24 When they brought the kings out to Joshua, Joshua summoned all the Israelites, and said to the chiefs of the warriors who had gone with him, "Come near, put your feet on the necks of these kings." Then they came near and put their feet on their necks. 25 And Joshua said to them, "Do not be afraid or dismayed; be strong and courageous; for thus the Lord will do to all the enemies against whom you fight." 26 Afterward Joshua struck them down and put them to death, and he hung them on five trees. And they hung on the trees until evening. 27 At sunset Joshua commanded, and they took them down from the trees and threw them into the cave where they had hidden themselves; they set large stones against the mouth of the cave, which remain to this very day.

2. The conquest completed

28 Joshua took Makkedah on that day, and struck it and its king with

q Heb moved his tongue

Marginal references:
10.12 Hab 3.11
10.13 2 Sam 1.18; Isa 38.8
10.14 v. 42
10.15 v. 43
10.16 v. 5
10.20 Deut 20.16
10.21 Ex 11.7
10.22 Deut 7.24
10.24 Ps 110.5; Isa 26.5, 6; Mal 4.3
10.25 v. 8
10.26 Josh 8.29
10.27 Deut 21.23; Josh 8.9
10.28 Deut 20.16; Josh 6.21

---

through such means; to them it is a matter of chance or luck.
10.13 *And the sun stood still, and the moon stopped.* The historicity of this event has been questioned even by people in the conservative tradition. They have leaned toward the notion that this is a figure of speech; the sun only *seemed* to stand still, or the day *seemed* longer than it actually was. Nevertheless, for an all-powerful God to stop the rotation of the earth for a day without the universe collapsing is no harder

than to raise the dead or create the universe.
10.24 *Put your feet on the necks of these kings.* This was customary as a symbol of victory. Egyptian and Assyrian sculptures frequently portray this custom.
10.28ff Following the slaughter of the five kings, Joshua extends his military campaign and razes city after city — Makkedah, Libnah, Lachish, Eglon, Hebron, and Debir; also the Negeb and the hill country. It was a massive assault and a complete victory, with no evidence of a contrary spirit on the part

the edge of the sword; he utterly destroyed every person in it; he left no one remaining. And he did to the king of Makkedah as he had done to the king of Jericho.

10.29
1 Chr 6.57

29 Then Joshua passed on from Makkedah, and all Israel with him, to Libnah, and fought against Libnah. 30 The LORD gave it also and its king into the hand of Israel; and he struck it with the edge of the sword, and every person in it; he left no one remaining in it; and he did to its king as he had done to the king of Jericho.

10.31
2 Kings 14.19

31 Next Joshua passed on from Libnah, and all Israel with him, to Lachish, and laid siege to it, and assaulted it. 32 The LORD gave Lachish into the hand of Israel, and he took it on the second day, and struck it with the edge of the sword, and every person in it, as he had done to Libnah.

33 Then King Horam of Gezer came up to help Lachish; and Joshua struck him and his people, leaving him no survivors.

34 From Lachish Joshua passed on with all Israel to Eglon; and they laid siege to it, and assaulted it; 35 and they took it that day, and struck it with the edge of the sword; and every person in it he utterly destroyed that day, as he had done to Lachish.

10.36
Josh 14.13;
15.13;
Judg 1.10

36 Then Joshua went up with all Israel from Eglon to Hebron; they assaulted it, 37 and took it, and struck it with the edge of the sword, and its king and its towns, and every person in it; he left no one remaining, just as he had done to Eglon, and utterly destroyed it with every person in it.

10.38
Josh 15.15;
Judg 1.11

38 Then Joshua, with all Israel, turned back to Debir and assaulted it, 39 and he took it with its king and all its towns; they struck them with the edge of the sword, and utterly destroyed every person in it; he left no one remaining; just as he had done to Hebron, and, as he had done to Libnah and its king, so he did to Debir and its king.

10.40
Deut 1.7;
7.24; 20.16,
17

40 So Joshua defeated the whole land, the hill country and the Negeb and the lowland and the slopes, and all their kings; he left no one remaining, but utterly destroyed all that breathed, as the LORD God of Israel commanded. 41 And Joshua defeated them from Kadesh-barnea to Gaza, and all the country of Goshen, as far as Gibeon. 42 Joshua took all these kings and their land at one time, because the LORD God of Israel fought for Israel. 43 Then Joshua returned, and all Israel with him, to the camp at Gilgal.

10.41
Josh 11.16;
15.51
10.42
v. 14

I. The conquest of northern Canaan

11.1
v. 10
11.2
Josh 12.3ff

11 When King Jabin of Hazor heard of this, he sent to King Jobab of Madon, to the king of Shimron, to the king of Achshaph, 2 and to the kings who were in the northern hill country, and in the Arabah south of Chinneroth, and in the lowland, and in Naphoth-dor on the west, 3 to the Canaanites in the east and the west, the Amorites, the Hittites, the Perizzites, and the Jebusites in the hill country, and the Hivites under Hermon in the land of Mizpah. 4 They came out, with all their troops, a great army, in number like the sand on the seashore, with very many horses and chariots. 5 All these kings joined their forces, and came and camped together at the waters of Merom, to fight with Israel.

11.4
Judg 7.12

of the Israelites.
10.37 *its king.* Joshua had slain the king of Hebron (10.3,26). This must have been a new king, i.e., a successor to the old king.
10.40 *defeated the whole land.* This statement pertains to most areas of Canaan, although pockets of resistance were left. According to Judg 1.27–33, a number of Canaanite cities remained uncaptured. The full conquest of the land did not come until the days of David and Solomon.

10.41 *Goshen,* not the Goshen of Egypt.
11.1 The rulers of northern Canaan formed a coalition against Joshua. They came against them in large numbers but Israel defeated the coalition. There were no supernatural signs or wonders in this campaign; God granted strength to his people to win the war without them. We need not expect God to perform miracles on every occasion, for miracles by their very nature are extraordinary. What appears to be ordinary is no less of God than the extraordinary.

6 And the LORD said to Joshua, "Do not be afraid of them, for tomorrow at this time I will hand over all of them, slain, to Israel; you shall hamstring their horses, and burn their chariots with fire." 7 So Joshua came suddenly upon them with all his fighting force, by the waters of Merom, and fell upon them. 8 And the LORD handed them over to Israel, who attacked them and chased them as far as Great Sidon and Misrephoth-maim, and eastward as far as the valley of Mizpeh. They struck them down, until they had left no one remaining. 9 And Joshua did to them as the LORD commanded him; he hamstrung their horses, and burned their chariots with fire.

10 Joshua turned back at that time, and took Hazor, and struck its king down with the sword. Before that time Hazor was the head of all those kingdoms. 11 And they put to the sword all who were in it, utterly destroying them; there was no one left who breathed, and he burned Hazor with fire. 12 And all the towns of those kings, and all their kings, Joshua took, and struck them with the edge of the sword, utterly destroying them, as Moses the servant of the LORD had commanded. 13 But Israel burned none of the towns that stood on mounds except Hazor, which Joshua did burn. 14 All the spoil of these towns, and the livestock, the Israelites took for their booty; but all the people they struck down with the edge of the sword, until they had destroyed them, and they did not leave any who breathed. 15 As the LORD had commanded his servant Moses, so Moses commanded Joshua, and so Joshua did; he left nothing undone of all that the LORD had commanded Moses.

J. Summary of the conquests

16 So Joshua took all that land: the hill country and all the Negeb and all the land of Goshen and the lowland and the Arabah and the hill country of Israel and its lowland, 17 from Mount Halak, which rises toward Seir, as far as Baal-gad in the valley of Lebanon below Mount Hermon. He took all their kings, struck them down, and put them to death. 18 Joshua made war a long time with all those kings. 19 There was not a town that made peace with the Israelites, except the Hivites, the inhabitants of Gibeon; all were taken in battle. 20 For it was the LORD's doing to harden their hearts so that they would come against Israel in battle, in order that they might be utterly destroyed, and might receive no mercy, but be exterminated, just as the LORD had commanded Moses.

21 At that time Joshua came and wiped out the Anakim from the hill country, from Hebron, from Debir, from Anab, and from all the hill country of Judah, and from all the hill country of Israel; Joshua utterly destroyed them with their towns. 22 None of the Anakim was left in the land of the Israelites; some remained only in Gaza, in Gath, and in Ashdod. 23 So Joshua took the whole land, according to all that the LORD had spoken to Moses; and Joshua gave it for an inheritance to Israel according to their tribal allotments. And the land had rest from war.

11.6
Josh 10.8;
2 Sam 8.4

11.8
Josh 13.6

11.9
v. 6

11.11
Deut 20.16,
17

11.14
Num 31.11,
12

11.15
Ex 34.11, 12;
Deut 7.2;
Josh 1.7

11.16
Josh 10.40,
41; v. 2
11.17
Josh 12.7;
Deut 7.24

11.19
Josh 9.3, 7

11.20
Deut 2.30;
Rom 9.18;
Deut 20.16,
17

11.21
Num 13.33;
Deut 9.2

11.23
Num 34.2ff

11.6 *hamstring their horses, and burn their chariots.* Israel did not need the armaments of the enemy, for they had God on their side. They were not to put their trust in horses or in chariots.

11.8 *the LORD handed them over to Israel.* God is the Lord of history. Victory is not always in the hands of those who have superior military force. God determines the outcome of the events in history and stands behind it to accomplish the divine purpose.

11.15 Joshua was obedient to the commands of Moses that had been given to his predecessor by God.

Rulers must themselves be ruled by the will of God. Joshua neither spared the idols nor the idolaters according to the commission given him. He was faithful to God.

11.20 The hearts of the enemy were hardened by God (see note on Ex 4.21) so that his immutable will against them for their idolatry and other crimes might be executed through the Israelites. These peoples were ripe for judgment, even as sinners in the end will be ripe for the judgment of God.

K. *The list of conquered kings*

1. *The kings of east Canaan*

12 Now these are the kings of the land, whom the Israelites defeated, whose land they occupied beyond the Jordan toward the east, from the Wadi Arnon to Mount Hermon, with all the Arabah eastward: 2 King Sihon of the Amorites who lived at Heshbon, and ruled from Aroer, which is on the edge of the Wadi Arnon, and from the middle of the valley as far as the river Jabbok, the boundary of the Ammonites, that is, half of Gilead, 3 and the Arabah to the Sea of Chinneroth eastward, and in the direction of Beth-jeshimoth, to the sea of the Arabah, the Dead Sea,^{r} southward to the foot of the slopes of Pisgah; 4 and King Og^s of Bashan, one of the last of the Rephaim, who lived at Ashtaroth and at Edrei 5 and ruled over Mount Hermon and Salecah and all Bashan to the boundary of the Geshurites and the Maacathites, and over half of Gilead to the boundary of King Sihon of Heshbon. 6 Moses, the servant of the Lord, and the Israelites defeated them; and Moses the servant of the Lord gave their land for a possession to the Reubenites and the Gadites and the half-tribe of Manasseh.

2. *The kings of west Canaan*

7 The following are the kings of the land whom Joshua and the Israelites defeated on the west side of the Jordan, from Baal-gad in the valley of Lebanon to Mount Halak, that rises toward Seir (and Joshua gave their land to the tribes of Israel as a possession according to their allotments, 8 in the hill country, in the lowland, in the Arabah, in the slopes, in the wilderness, and in the Negeb, the land of the Hittites, Amorites, Canaanites, Perizzites, Hivites, and Jebusites):

9	the king of Jericho	one
	the king of Ai, which is next to Bethel	one
10	the king of Jerusalem	one
	the king of Hebron	one
11	the king of Jarmuth	one
	the king of Lachish	one
12	the king of Eglon	one
	the king of Gezer	one
13	the king of Debir	one
	the king of Geder	one
14	the king of Hormah	one
	the king of Arad	one
15	the king of Libnah	one
	the king of Adullam	one
16	the king of Makkedah	one
	the king of Bethel	one
17	the king of Tappuah	one
	the king of Hepher	one
18	the king of Aphek	one
	the king of Lasharon	one
19	the king of Madon	one
	the king of Hazor	one
20	the king of Shimron-meron	one
	the king of Achshaph	one

^{r} Heb *Salt Sea* ^{s} Gk: Heb *the boundary of King Og*

Side references:
12.1 Deut 3.8, 9
12.2 Deut 2.33, 36
12.3 Josh 11.2; 13.20
12.4 Deut 3.11
12.5 Deut 3.8ff
12.6 Num 21.24, 33; 32.29, 33
12.7 Josh 11.17, 23
12.8 Josh 11.16
12.9ff Josh 6.2; 8.29
12.12 Josh 10.33
12.13 Josh 10.38

12.1 The account of the conquest of the land of Canaan is reported quickly and not in great detail. In ch. 12 a summary of the conquest is given. It starts with the victories on the east side of the Jordan and goes on from there to the west side. The abridgement reports the defeat of thirty-one kings, marking the end of the conquest for the time being and serving as a preface to the division of the land. However, pockets of resistance remained (see 13.1–7); the successors to Joshua would have to complete the conquest.

21 the king of Taanach	one
the king of Megiddo	one
22 the king of Kedesh	one
the king of Jokneam in Carmel	one
23 the king of Dor in Naphath-dor	one
the king of Goiim in Galilee,[t]	one
24 the king of Tirzah	one

thirty-one kings in all.

12.24
Deut 7.24

II. *The partition of the promised land (13.1–21.45)*

A. *The command to divide the land*

13 Now Joshua was old and advanced in years; and the LORD said to him, "You are old and advanced in years, and very much of the land still remains to be possessed. 2 This is the land that still remains: all the regions of the Philistines, and all those of the Geshurites 3 (from the Shihor, which is east of Egypt, northward to the boundary of Ekron, it is reckoned as Canaanite; there are five rulers of the Philistines, those of Gaza, Ashdod, Ashkelon, Gath, and Ekron), and those of the Avvim 4 in the south; all the land of the Canaanites, and Mearah that belongs to the Sidonians, to Aphek, to the boundary of the Amorites, 5 and the land of the Gebalites, and all Lebanon, toward the east, from Baal-gad below Mount Hermon to Lebo-hamath, 6 all the inhabitants of the hill country from Lebanon to Misrephoth-maim, even all the Sidonians. I will myself drive them out from before the Israelites; only allot the land to Israel for an inheritance, as I have commanded you. 7 Now therefore divide this land for an inheritance to the nine tribes and the half-tribe of Manasseh."

13.1
Josh 14.10

13.3
Judg 3.3;
Deut 2.23

13.6
Josh 11.8

B. *The division of east Canaan*

1. *The boundaries*

8 With the other half-tribe of Manasseh[u] the Reubenites and the Gadites received their inheritance, which Moses gave them, beyond the Jordan eastward, as Moses the servant of the LORD gave them: 9 from Aroer, which is on the edge of the Wadi Arnon, and the town that is in the middle of the valley, and all the tableland from[v] Medeba as far as Dibon; 10 and all the cities of King Sihon of the Amorites, who reigned in Heshbon, as far as the boundary of the Ammonites; 11 and Gilead, and the region of the Geshurites and Maacathites, and all Mount Hermon, and all Bashan to Salecah; 12 all the kingdom of Og in Bashan, who reigned in Ashtaroth and in Edrei (he alone was left of the survivors of the Rephaim); these Moses had defeated and driven out. 13 Yet the Israelites did not drive out the Geshurites or the Maacathites; but Geshur and Maacath live within Israel to this day.

14 To the tribe of Levi alone Moses gave no inheritance; the offerings by fire to the LORD God of Israel are their inheritance, as he said to them.

13.8
Josh 12.1-6

13.9
v. 16

13.10
Num 21.24,
25

13.12
Deut 3.11;
Num 21.24,
35

13.14
Deut 18.1, 2

---

[t] Gk: Heb *Gilgal*   [u] Cn: Heb *With it*   [v] Compare Gk: Heb lacks *from*

13.1 As Joshua was getting old and nearing death, God commanded him to divide the land according to the numbers of the families in each tribe. The division was made by lot (14.2; cf. Num 34.13). The Scriptures do not tell us precisely how lots were cast. They were used in both O.T. and N.T., especially when important decisions were required. God, who is sovereign, was behind the way the lot fell, as Prov 16.33 says: "The lot is cast into the lap; but the decision is the LORD's alone." Such a procedure avoided friction

and exempted Joshua from making decisions that might be unpopular and for which he could be blamed. Providence is better than the counsels of people.
13.8ff The Gadites, Reubenites, and half the tribe of Manasseh had already come into their possession on the east side of the Jordan. Moses gave them that land before his death. The other half of the tribe of Manasseh settled on the west side of Jordan.

2. Inheritance of the Reubenites

15 Moses gave an inheritance to the tribe of the Reubenites according to their clans. 16 Their territory was from Aroer, which is on the edge of the Wadi Arnon, and the town that is in the middle of the valley, and all the tableland by Medeba; 17 with Heshbon, and all its towns that are in the tableland; Dibon, and Bamoth-baal, and Beth-baal-meon, 18 and Jahaz, and Kedemoth, and Mephaath, 19 and Kiriathaim, and Sibmah, and Zereth-shahar on the hill of the valley, 20 and Beth-peor, and the slopes of Pisgah, and Beth-jeshimoth, 21 that is, all the towns of the tableland, and all the kingdom of King Sihon of the Amorites, who reigned in Heshbon, whom Moses defeated with the leaders of Midian, Evi and Rekem and Zur and Hur and Reba, as princes of Sihon, who lived in the land. 22 Along with the rest of those they put to death, the Israelites also put to the sword Balaam son of Beor, who practiced divination. 23 And the border of the Reubenites was the Jordan and its banks. This was the inheritance of the Reubenites according to their families, with their towns and villages.

13.16
Josh 12.2

13.21
Num 31.8

13.22
Num 31.8

3. Inheritance of the Gadites

24 Moses gave an inheritance also to the tribe of the Gadites, according to their families. 25 Their territory was Jazer, and all the towns of Gilead, and half the land of the Ammonites, to Aroer, which is east of Rabbah, 26 and from Heshbon to Ramath-mizpeh and Betonim, and from Mahanaim to the territory of Debir,^{w} 27 and in the valley Beth-haram, Beth-nimrah, Succoth, and Zaphon, the rest of the kingdom of King Sihon of Heshbon, the Jordan and its banks, as far as the lower end of the Sea of Chinnereth, eastward beyond the Jordan. 28 This is the inheritance of the Gadites according to their clans, with their towns and villages.

13.25
Num 21.32

13.27
Num 34.11

4. Inheritance of the half-tribe of Manasseh

29 Moses gave an inheritance to the half-tribe of Manasseh; it was allotted to the half-tribe of the Manassites according to their families. 30 Their territory extended from Mahanaim, through all Bashan, the whole kingdom of King Og of Bashan, and all the settlements of Jair, which are in Bashan, sixty towns, 31 and half of Gilead, and Ashtaroth, and Edrei, the towns of the kingdom of Og in Bashan; these were allotted to the people of Machir son of Manasseh according to their clans — for half the Machirites.

32 These are the inheritances that Moses distributed in the plains of Moab, beyond the Jordan east of Jericho. 33 But to the tribe of Levi Moses gave no inheritance; the LORD God of Israel is their inheritance, as he said to them.

13.30
Num 32.41

13.33
v. 14;
Num 18.20;
Deut 10.9;
18.1, 2

C. The division of west Canaan

1. Introduction

14 These are the inheritances that the Israelites received in the land of Canaan, which the priest Eleazar, and Joshua son of Nun, and the heads of the families of the tribes of the Israelites distributed to them. 2 Their inheritance was by lot, as the LORD had commanded Moses for the nine and one-half tribes. 3 For Moses had given an inheritance to the two and one-half tribes beyond the Jordan; but to the Levites he gave no inheritance among them. 4 For the people of Joseph were two tribes,

14.1
Num 34.17,
18
14.2
Num 26.55
14.3
Num 32.33;
Josh 13.14
14.4
Gen 48.5

w Gk Syr Vg: Heb Lidebir

13.33 The tribe of Levi had no land inheritance in Canaan (vv. 14,33). God provided for them by distributing them among all of the tribes to maintain the true religion and to instruct the people of God. They received their sustenance from the offerings.

Manasseh and Ephraim; and no portion was given to the Levites in the land, but only towns to live in, with their pasture lands for their flocks and herds. 5 The Israelites did as the LORD commanded Moses; they allotted the land.

2. Caleb receives Hebron

6   Then the people of Judah came to Joshua at Gilgal; and Caleb son of Jephunneh the Kenizzite said to him, "You know what the LORD said to Moses the man of God in Kadesh-barnea concerning you and me. 7 I was forty years old when Moses the servant of the LORD sent me from Kadesh-barnea to spy out the land; and I brought him an honest report. 8 But my companions who went up with me made the heart of the people melt; yet I wholeheartedly followed the LORD my God. 9 And Moses swore on that day, saying, 'Surely the land on which your foot has trodden shall be an inheritance for you and your children forever, because you have wholeheartedly followed the LORD my God.' 10 And now, as you see, the LORD has kept me alive, as he said, these forty-five years since the time that the LORD spoke this word to Moses, while Israel was journeying through the wilderness; and here I am today, eighty-five years old. 11 I am still as strong today as I was on the day that Moses sent me; my strength now is as my strength was then, for war, and for going and coming. 12 So now give me this hill country of which the LORD spoke on that day; for you heard on that day how the Anakim were there, with great fortified cities; it may be that the LORD will be with me, and I shall drive them out, as the LORD said."

13   Then Joshua blessed him, and gave Hebron to Caleb son of Jephunneh for an inheritance. 14 So Hebron became the inheritance of Caleb son of Jephunneh the Kenizzite to this day, because he wholeheartedly followed the LORD, the God of Israel. 15 Now the name of Hebron formerly was Kiriath-arba;^x this Arba was^y the greatest man among the Anakim. And the land had rest from war.

3. The inheritance of Judah

a. The boundaries of Judah

15   The lot for the tribe of the people of Judah according to their families reached southward to the boundary of Edom, to the wilderness of Zin at the farthest south. 2 And their south boundary ran from the end of the Dead Sea,^z from the bay that faces southward; 3 it goes out southward of the ascent of Akrabbim, passes along to Zin, and goes up south of Kadesh-barnea, along by Hezron, up to Addar, makes a turn to Karka, 4 passes along to Azmon, goes out by the Wadi of Egypt, and comes to its end at the sea. This shall be your south boundary. 5 And the east boundary is the Dead Sea,^z to the mouth of the Jordan. And the boundary on the north side runs from the bay of the sea at the mouth of the Jordan; 6 and the boundary goes up to Beth-hoglah, and passes along north of Beth-arabah; and the boundary goes up to the Stone of Bohan, Reuben's son; 7 and the boundary goes up to Debir from the Valley of Achor, and so northward, turning toward Gilgal, which is opposite the ascent of Adummim, which is on the south side of the valley; and the boundary passes along to the waters of En-shemesh, and ends at En-rogel; 8 then the boundary goes up by the valley of the son of Hinnom at the

Marginal references:
14.6 Num 13.6, 26, 30; 14.6, 24, 30
14.7 Num 13.6; 14.6
14.8 Num 13.31, 32; 14.24
14.9 Deut 1.36
14.10 Num 14.30
14.12 Num 13.33
14.14 Josh 22.6; vv. 8, 9
14.15 Josh 11.23
15.1 Num 34.3, 4; 33.36
15.3 Num 34.4
15.4 Num 34.5
15.6 Josh 18.17, 19
15.7 Josh 7.24
15.8 v. 63

x That is the city of Arba   y Heb lacks this Arba was   z Heb Salt Sea

14.10,11 Caleb, at eighty-five years old, was as strong and physically able as he had been when he spied out the land at forty years of age. On the other hand, Joshua apparently was feeling the infirmities of age and could not say this (13.1).
14.14 Of those who left Egypt, Caleb and Joshua were the only two male adults to enter Canaan. All the others, including Moses, died before the Jordan was crossed. The most fitting memorial for the life of Caleb is: "he wholeheartedly followed the LORD, the God of Israel."

southern slope of the Jebusites (that is, Jerusalem); and the boundary goes up to the top of the mountain that lies over against the valley of Hinnom, on the west, at the northern end of the valley of Rephaim; 9 then the boundary extends from the top of the mountain to the spring of the Waters of Nephtoah, and from there to the towns of Mount Ephron; then the boundary bends around to Baalah (that is, Kiriath-jearim); 10 and the boundary circles west of Baalah to Mount Seir, passes along to the northern slope of Mount Jearim (that is, Chesalon), and goes down to Beth-shemesh, and passes along by Timnah; 11 the boundary goes out to the slope of the hill north of Ekron, then the boundary bends around to Shikkeron, and passes along to Mount Baalah, and goes out to Jabneel; then the boundary comes to an end at the sea. 12 And the west boundary was the Mediterranean with its coast. This is the boundary surrounding the people of Judah according to their families.

b. *Caleb's inheritance*

13 According to the commandment of the LORD to Joshua, he gave to Caleb son of Jephunneh a portion among the people of Judah, Kiriath-arba,*a* that is, Hebron (Arba was the father of Anak). 14 And Caleb drove out from there the three sons of Anak: Sheshai, Ahiman, and Talmai, the descendants of Anak. 15 From there he went up against the inhabitants of Debir; now the name of Debir formerly was Kiriath-sepher. 16 And Caleb said, "Whoever attacks Kiriath-sepher and takes it, to him I will give my daughter Achsah as wife." 17 Othniel son of Kenaz, the brother of Caleb, took it; and he gave him his daughter Achsah as wife. 18 When she came to him, she urged him to ask her father for a field. As she dismounted from her donkey, Caleb said to her, "What do you wish?" 19 She said to him, "Give me a present; since you have set me in the land of the Negeb, give me springs of water as well." So Caleb gave her the upper springs and the lower springs.

c. *The towns of Judah*

20 This is the inheritance of the tribe of the people of Judah according to their families. 21 The towns belonging to the tribe of the people of Judah in the extreme south, toward the boundary of Edom, were Kabzeel, Eder, Jagur, 22 Kinah, Dimonah, Adadah, 23 Kedesh, Hazor, Ithnan, 24 Ziph, Telem, Bealoth, 25 Hazor-hadattah, Kerioth-hezron (that is, Hazor), 26 Amam, Shema, Moladah, 27 Hazar-gaddah, Heshmon, Beth-pelet, 28 Hazar-shual, Beer-sheba, Biziothiah, 29 Baalah, Iim, Ezem, 30 Eltolad, Chesil, Hormah, 31 Ziklag, Madmannah, Sansannah, 32 Lebaoth, Shilhim, Ain, and Rimmon: in all, twenty-nine towns, with their villages.

33 And in the lowland, Eshtaol, Zorah, Ashnah, 34 Zanoah, En-gannim, Tappuah, Enam, 35 Jarmuth, Adullam, Socoh, Azekah, 36 Shaaraim, Adithaim, Gederah, Gederothaim: fourteen towns with their villages.

37 Zenan, Hadashah, Migdal-gad, 38 Dilan, Mizpeh, Jokthe-el, 39 Lachish, Bozkath, Eglon, 40 Cabbon, Lahmam, Chitlish, 41 Gederoth, Beth-dagon, Naamah, and Makkedah: sixteen towns with their villages.

42 Libnah, Ether, Ashan, 43 Iphtah, Ashnah, Nezib, 44 Keilah, Achzib, and Mareshah: nine towns with their villages.

45 Ekron, with its dependencies and its villages; 46 from Ekron to the sea, all that were near Ashdod, with their villages.

47 Ashdod, its towns and its villages; Gaza, its towns and its villages; to the Wadi of Egypt, and the Great Sea with its coast.

a That is *the city of Arba*

15.17 Othniel, Caleb's younger brother, was to become one of the judges of Israel after Joshua's death (see Judg 3.7–11).
15.32 Thirty-eight towns are named, and yet said to be twenty-nine. Nine of these were afterwards transferred to the lot of Simeon. Thus those only are counted which remained to Judah.

15.9 Josh 18.15
15.10 Judg 14.1
15.12 v. 47
15.13 Jn 14.13-15
15.14 Josh 11.21, 22; Num 13.22
15.15 Josh 10.38
15.16 Judg 1.12, 13; 3.9
15.18 Judg 1.14
15.28 Gen 21.31
15.31 1 Sam 27.6
15.33 Judg 13.25; 16.31
15.35 1 Sam 22.1
15.38 2 Kings 14.7
15.39 Josh 10.3; 2 Kings 14.19
15.47 v. 4; Num 34.6

48 And in the hill country, Shamir, Jattir, Socoh, 49 Dannah, Kiriath-sannah (that is, Debir), 50 Anab, Eshtemoh, Anim, 51 Goshen, Holon, and Giloh: eleven towns with their villages.

52 Arab, Dumah, Eshan, 53 Janim, Beth-tappuah, Aphekah, 54 Humtah, Kiriath-arba (that is, Hebron), and Zior: nine towns with their villages.

55 Maon, Carmel, Ziph, Juttah, 56 Jezreel, Jokdeam, Zanoah, 57 Kain, Gibeah, and Timnah: ten towns with their villages.

58 Halhul, Beth-zur, Gedor, 59 Maarath, Beth-anoth, and Eltekon: six towns with their villages.

60 Kiriath-baal (that is, Kiriath-jearim) and Rabbah: two towns with their villages.

61 In the wilderness, Beth-arabah, Middin, Secacah, 62 Nibshan, the City of Salt, and En-gedi: six towns with their villages.

63 But the people of Judah could not drive out the Jebusites, the inhabitants of Jerusalem; so the Jebusites live with the people of Judah in Jerusalem to this day.

4. The inheritance of Joseph

a. The general boundaries

16 The allotment of the Josephites went from the Jordan by Jericho, east of the waters of Jericho, into the wilderness, going up from Jericho into the hill country to Bethel; 2 then going from Bethel to Luz, it passes along to Ataroth, the territory of the Archites; 3 then it goes down westward to the territory of the Japhletites, as far as the territory of Lower Beth-horon, then to Gezer, and it ends at the sea.

4 The Josephites—Manasseh and Ephraim—received their inheritance.

b. The territory of the Ephraimites

5 The territory of the Ephraimites by their families was as follows: the boundary of their inheritance on the east was Ataroth-addar as far as Upper Beth-horon, 6 and the boundary goes from there to the sea; on the north is Michmethath; then on the east the boundary makes a turn toward Taanath-shiloh, and passes along beyond it on the east to Janoah, 7 then it goes down from Janoah to Ataroth and to Naarah, and touches Jericho, ending at the Jordan. 8 From Tappuah the boundary goes westward to the Wadi Kanah, and ends at the sea. Such is the inheritance of the tribe of the Ephraimites by their families, 9 together with the towns that were set apart for the Ephraimites within the inheritance of the Manassites, all those towns with their villages. 10 They did not, however, drive out the Canaanites who lived in Gezer: so the Canaanites have lived within Ephraim to this day but have been made to do forced labor.

c. The allotment to the half-tribe of Manasseh

17 Then allotment was made to the tribe of Manasseh, for he was the firstborn of Joseph. To Machir the firstborn of Manasseh, the father of Gilead, were allotted Gilead and Bashan, because he was a warrior. 2 And allotments were made to the rest of the tribe of Manasseh, by their families, Abiezer, Helek, Asriel, Shechem, Hepher, and Shemida; these were the male descendants of Manasseh son of Joseph, by their families.

3 Now Zelophehad son of Hepher son of Gilead son of Machir son of Manasseh had no sons, but only daughters; and these are the names of his daughters: Mahlah, Noah, Hoglah, Milcah, and Tirzah. 4 They came

Margin references:

15.51
Josh 10.41;
11.16

15.60
Josh 18.14

15.63
Judg 1.21;
2 Sam 5.6

16.1
Josh 18.12

16.2
Josh 18.13
16.3
Josh 18.13;
2 Chr 8.5

16.5
Josh 18.13

16.6
Josh 17.7

16.7
1 Chr 7.28

16.8
Josh 17.8, 9

16.10
Judg 1.29;
1 Kings 9.16;
Josh 17.12,
13

17.1
Gen 41.41;
50.23;
Deut 3.15

17.2
Num 26.29-32

17.3
Num 26.33;
27.1-7
17.4
Num 27.5-7

15.62 *the City of Salt* may well be the ancient name for Qumran, the site where the Dead Sea Scrolls were found.

16.10 *to this day,* i.e., to the time of the writing of this book.

before the priest Eleazar and Joshua son of Nun and the leaders, and said, "The LORD commanded Moses to give us an inheritance along with our male kin." So according to the commandment of the LORD he gave them an inheritance among the kinsmen of their father. 5 Thus there fell to Manasseh ten portions, besides the land of Gilead and Bashan, which is on the other side of the Jordan, 6 because the daughters of Manasseh received an inheritance along with his sons. The land of Gilead was allotted to the rest of the Manassites.

7 The territory of Manasseh reached from Asher to Michmethath, which is east of Shechem; then the boundary goes along southward to the inhabitants of En-tappuah. 8 The land of Tappuah belonged to Manasseh, but the town of Tappuah on the boundary of Manasseh belonged to the Ephraimites. 9 Then the boundary went down to the Wadi Kanah. The towns here, to the south of the wadi, among the towns of Manasseh, belong to Ephraim. Then the boundary of Manasseh goes along the north side of the wadi and ends at the sea. 10 The land to the south is Ephraim's and that to the north is Manasseh's, with the sea forming its boundary; on the north Asher is reached, and on the east Issachar. 11 Within Issachar and Asher, Manasseh had Beth-shean and its villages, Ibleam and its villages, the inhabitants of Dor and its villages, the inhabitants of En-dor and its villages, the inhabitants of Taanach and its villages, and the inhabitants of Megiddo and its villages (the third is Naphath).b 12 Yet the Manassites could not take possession of those towns; but the Canaanites continued to live in that land. 13 But when the Israelites grew strong, they put the Canaanites to forced labor, but did not utterly drive them out.

d. The complaint of the tribe of Joseph

14 The tribe of Joseph spoke to Joshua, saying, "Why have you given me but one lot and one portion as an inheritance, since we are a numerous people, whom all along the LORD has blessed?" 15 And Joshua said to them, "If you are a numerous people, go up to the forest, and clear ground there for yourselves in the land of the Perizzites and the Rephaim, since the hill country of Ephraim is too narrow for you." 16 The tribe of Joseph said, "The hill country is not enough for us; yet all the Canaanites who live in the plain have chariots of iron, both those in Beth-shean and its villages and those in the Valley of Jezreel." 17 Then Joshua said to the house of Joseph, to Ephraim and Manasseh, "You are indeed a numerous people, and have great power; you shall not have one lot only, 18 but the hill country shall be yours; for though it is a forest, you shall clear it and possess it to its farthest borders; for you shall drive out the Canaanites, though they have chariots of iron, and though they are strong."

5. The division of the remaining land

a. The land survey: casting the lot

18 Then the whole congregation of the Israelites assembled at Shiloh, and set up the tent of meeting there. The land lay subdued before them.

2 There remained among the Israelites seven tribes whose inheritance had not yet been apportioned. 3 So Joshua said to the Israelites, "How long will you be slack about going in and taking possession of the land that the

b Meaning of Heb uncertain

Margin references:
17.6 Josh 13.30, 31
17.7 Josh 16.6
17.8 Josh 16.8
17.9 Josh 16.8, 9
17.11 1 Chr 7.29
17.12 Judg 1.27, 28
17.13 Josh 16.10
17.14 Num 26.34; 37
17.16 Judg 1.19; 4.3
18.1 Josh 19.51; Jer 7.12; Judg 18.31
18.3 Judg 18.9

17.13 *put the Canaanites to forced labor.* The children of Joseph did not destroy some of the Canaanites, but subdued them and made them pay tribute. This caused problems later.

17.16–18 In response to the complaints of Joseph's progeny that they did not have as much land as they needed, Joshua told them to clear the trees, settle the forested areas, and put away the Canaanites. The failure to exterminate all the Canaanites was contrary to God's original command — that all the inhabitants of the land were to be destroyed lest they contaminate Israel. The fact that the Canaanites had iron chariots was no problem, so long as God's people trusted in him to deliver them.

LORD, the God of your ancestors, has given you? 4 Provide three men from each tribe, and I will send them out that they may begin to go throughout the land, writing a description of it with a view to their inheritances. Then come back to me. 5 They shall divide it into seven portions, Judah continuing in its territory on the south, and the house of Joseph in their territory on the north. 6 You shall describe the land in seven divisions and bring the description here to me; and I will cast lots for you here before the LORD our God. 7 The Levites have no portion among you, for the priesthood of the LORD is their heritage; and Gad and Reuben and the half-tribe of Manasseh have received their inheritance beyond the Jordan eastward, which Moses the servant of the LORD gave them.”

8 So the men started on their way; and Joshua charged those who went to write the description of the land, saying, “Go throughout the land and write a description of it, and come back to me; and I will cast lots for you here before the LORD in Shiloh.” 9 So the men went and traversed the land and set down in a book a description of it by towns in seven divisions; then they came back to Joshua in the camp at Shiloh, 10 and Joshua cast lots for them in Shiloh before the LORD; and there Joshua apportioned the land to the Israelites, to each a portion.

b. *The inheritance of Benjamin*

11 The lot of the tribe of Benjamin according to its families came up, and the territory allotted to it fell between the tribe of Judah and the tribe of Joseph. 12 On the north side their boundary began at the Jordan; then the boundary goes up to the slope of Jericho on the north, then up through the hill country westward; and it ends at the wilderness of Beth-aven. 13 From there the boundary passes along southward in the direction of Luz, to the slope of Luz (that is, Bethel), then the boundary goes down to Ataroth-addar, on the mountain that lies south of Lower Beth-horon. 14 Then the boundary goes in another direction, turning on the western side southward from the mountain that lies to the south, opposite Beth-horon, and it ends at Kiriath-baal (that is, Kiriath-jearim), a town belonging to the tribe of Judah. This forms the western side. 15 The southern side begins at the outskirts of Kiriath-jearim; and the boundary goes from there to Ephron,c and to the spring of the Waters of Nephtoah; 16 then the boundary goes down to the border of the mountain that overlooks the valley of the son of Hinnom, which is at the north end of the valley of Rephaim; and it then goes down the valley of Hinnom, south of the slope of the Jebusites, and downward to En-rogel; 17 then it bends in a northerly direction going on to En-shemesh, and from there goes to Geliloth, which is opposite the ascent of Adummim; then it goes down to the Stone of Bohan, Reuben’s son; 18 and passing on to the north of the slope of Beth-arabahd it goes down to the Arabah; 19 then the boundary passes on to the north of the slope of Beth-hoglah; and the boundary ends at the northern bay of the Dead Sea,e at the south end of the Jordan: this is the southern border. 20 The Jordan forms its boundary on the eastern side. This is the inheritance of the tribe of Benjamin, according to its families, boundary by boundary all around.

21 Now the towns of the tribe of Benjamin according to their families were Jericho, Beth-hoglah, Emek-keziz, 22 Beth-arabah, Zemaraim, Bethel, 23 Avvim, Parah, Ophrah, 24 Chephar-ammoni, Ophni, and Geba — twelve towns with their villages: 25 Gibeon, Ramah, Beeroth, 26 Mizpeh, Chephirah, Mozah, 27 Rekem, Irpeel, Taralah, 28 Zela, Haeleph,

---

c Cn See 15.9. Heb *westward*   d Gk: Heb *to the slope over against the Arabah*   e Heb *Salt Sea*

18.6 *I will cast lots for you here before the LORD our God.* This was to be done before God in solemn assembly so that all mouths would be shut and the decision accepted without grumbling.

18.10 The land was apportioned to all families except for the Levites, for whom other arrangements were made. Each plot of land was to remain in the same family for all generations.

Marginal references:

18.5 Josh 15.1; 16.1, 4

18.7 Josh 13.33; 13.8

18.8 v. 1; Judg 18.31

18.10 Josh 19.51

18.13 Gen 28.19; Josh 16.3

18.14 Josh 15.9

18.15 Josh 15.5-9

18.16 2 Kings 23.10

18.20 Josh 21.4, 17

18.28 Josh 15.8

Jebus[f] (that is, Jerusalem), Gibeah[g] and Kiriath-jearim[h] — fourteen towns with their villages. This is the inheritance of the tribe of Benjamin according to its families.

c. The inheritance of Simeon

19.1
v. 9

19 The second lot came out for Simeon, for the tribe of Simeon, according to its families; its inheritance lay within the inheritance of the tribe of Judah. 2 It had for its inheritance Beer-sheba, Sheba,

19.5
1 Sam 30.1

Moladah, 3 Hazar-shual, Balah, Ezem, 4 Eltolad, Bethul, Hormah, 5 Ziklag, Beth-marcaboth, Hazar-susah, 6 Beth-lebaoth, and Sharuhen — thirteen towns with their villages; 7 Ain, Rimmon, Ether, and Ashan — four towns with their villages; 8 together with all the villages all around these towns as far as Baalath-beer, Ramah of the Negeb. This was the

19.9
v. 1

inheritance of the tribe of Simeon according to its families. 9 The inheritance of the tribe of Simeon formed part of the territory of Judah; because the portion of the tribe of Judah was too large for them, the tribe of Simeon obtained an inheritance within their inheritance.

d. The inheritance of Zebulun

10 The third lot came up for the tribe of Zebulun, according to its

19.11
Josh 21.34

families. The boundary of its inheritance reached as far as Sarid; 11 then its boundary goes up westward, and on to Maralah, and touches Dabbesheth, then the wadi that is east of Jokneam; 12 from Sarid it goes in the other direction eastward toward the sunrise to the boundary of Chisloth-tabor; from there it goes to Daberath, then up to Japhia; 13 from there it passes along on the east toward the sunrise to Gath-hepher, to Eth-kazin, and going on to Rimmon it bends toward Neah; 14 then on the north the boundary makes a turn to Hannathon, and it ends at the valley of Iphtah-

19.15
Mic 5.2

el; 15 and Kattath, Nahalal, Shimron, Idalah, and Bethlehem — twelve towns with their villages. 16 This is the inheritance of the tribe of Zebulun, according to its families — these towns with their villages.

e. The inheritance of Issachar

19.17
2 Sam 2.9

17 The fourth lot came out for Issachar, for the tribe of Issachar, according to its families. 18 Its territory included Jezreel, Chesulloth, Shunem, 19 Hapharaim, Shion, Anaharath, 20 Rabbith, Kishion, Ebez, 21 Remeth, En-gannim, En-haddah, Beth-pazzez; 22 the boundary also touches Tabor, Shahazumah, and Beth-shemesh, and its boundary ends at the Jordan — sixteen towns with their villages. 23 This is the inheritance of the tribe of Issachar, according to its families — the towns with their villages.

f. The inheritance of Asher

24 The fifth lot came out for the tribe of Asher according to its families. 25 Its boundary included Helkath, Hali, Beten, Achshaph, 26 Allammelech, Amad, and Mishal; on the west it touches Carmel and Shihor-libnath, 27 then it turns eastward, goes to Beth-dagon, and touches Zebulun and the valley of Iphtah-el northward to Beth-emek and Neiel; then

19.28
Josh 11.8

it continues in the north to Cabul, 28 Ebron, Rehob, Hammon, Kanah, as far as Great Sidon; 29 then the boundary turns to Ramah, reaching to the fortified city of Tyre; then the boundary turns to Hosah, and it ends

19.30
Josh 21.31

at the sea; Mahalab,[i] Achzib, 30 Ummah, Aphek, and Rehob — twenty-two towns with their villages. 31 This is the inheritance of the tribe of Asher according to its families — these towns with their villages.

---

[f] Gk Syr Vg: Heb *the Jebusite*   [g] Heb *Gibeath*   [h] Gk: Heb *Kiriath*   [i] Cn Compare Gk: Heb *Mehebel*

19.1 The territory assigned to Simeon was in the southern section of Judah's land grant. Eventually the tribe of Simeon was absorbed into the tribe of Judah and lost its tribal identity.

19.24 Asher's territory bordered on the Mediterranean. Its boundary-line went as far north as Tyre, where the Phoenicians pursued their sea-trade with vigor.

g. *The inheritance of Naphtali*

32   The sixth lot came out for the tribe of Naphtali, for the tribe of Naphtali, according to its families. 33 And its boundary ran from Heleph, from the oak in Zaanannim, and Adami-nekeb, and Jabneel, as far as Lakkum; and it ended at the Jordan; 34 then the boundary turns westward to Aznoth-tabor, and goes from there to Hukkok, touching Zebulun at the south, and Asher on the west, and Judah on the east at the Jordan. 35 The fortified towns are Ziddim, Zer, Hammath, Rakkath, Chinnereth, 36 Adamah, Ramah, Hazor, 37 Kedesh, Edrei, En-hazor, 38 Iron, Migdal-el, Horem, Beth-anath, and Beth-shemesh — nineteen towns with their villages. 39 This is the inheritance of the tribe of Naphtali according to its families — the towns with their villages.

19.34
Deut 33.23

h. *The inheritance of Dan*

40   The seventh lot came out for the tribe of Dan, according to its families. 41 The territory of its inheritance included Zorah, Eshtaol, Ir-shemesh, 42 Shaalabbin, Aijalon, Ithlah, 43 Elon, Timnah, Ekron, 44 Elte-keh, Gibbethon, Baalath, 45 Jehud, Bene-berak, Gath-rimmon, 46 Me-jarkon, and Rakkon at the border opposite Joppa. 47 When the territory of the Danites was lost to them, the Danites went up and fought against Leshem, and after capturing it and putting it to the sword, they took possession of it and settled in it, calling Leshem, Dan, after their ancestor Dan. 48 This is the inheritance of the tribe of Dan, according to their families — these towns with their villages.

19.42
Judg 1.35

19.47
Judg 18.27-31

i. *Summary*

49   When they had finished distributing the several territories of the land as inheritances, the Israelites gave an inheritance among them to Joshua son of Nun. 50 By command of the Lord they gave him the town that he asked for, Timnath-serah in the hill country of Ephraim; he rebuilt the town, and settled in it.

51   These are the inheritances that the priest Eleazar and Joshua son of Nun and the heads of the families of the tribes of the Israelites distributed by lot at Shiloh before the Lord, at the entrance of the tent of meeting. So they finished dividing the land.

19.50
Josh 24.30

19.51
Josh 14.1;
18.1, 10

6. *The six cities of refuge*

20   Then the Lord spoke to Joshua, saying, 2 "Say to the Israelites, 'Appoint the cities of refuge, of which I spoke to you through Moses, 3 so that anyone who kills a person without intent or by mistake may flee there; they shall be for you a refuge from the avenger of blood. 4 The slayer shall flee to one of these cities and shall stand at the entrance of the gate of the city, and explain the case to the elders of that city; then the fugitive shall be taken into the city, and given a place, and shall remain with them. 5 And if the avenger of blood is in pursuit, they shall not give up the slayer, because the neighbor was killed by mistake, there having been no enmity between them before. 6 The slayer shall remain in that city until there is a trial before the congregation, until the death of the one who is high priest at the time: then the slayer may return home, to the town in which the deed was done.'"

7   So they set apart Kedesh in Galilee in the hill country of Naphtali,

20.2
Num 35.6-34;
Deut 4.41;
19.2

20.4
Ruth 4.1, 2

20.5
Num 35.12

20.6
Num 35.25
20.7
Josh 21.32;
1 Chr 6.76;
Josh 21.11;
Lk 1.39

19.32   Naphtali was assigned land just east of Asher and shared a common border with that tribe.
19.49   When the land had been assigned, Joshua was given Timnath-serah by the people of Israel, a city in the hill country of Ephraim. He rebuilt and occupied it until his death.
19.51   This marks the end of the division of the land to the twelve tribes of Israel. The assignment of cities

and pasture lands for the Levites had yet to be accomplished.
20.2   In line with earlier instructions, the six cities of refuge were designated, three on the east bank and three on the west bank of the Jordan. See note on Num 35.12 for comments on these cities.
20.5   *the avenger of blood.* See note on Num 35.19.

and Shechem in the hill country of Ephraim, and Kiriath-arba (that is,
Hebron) in the hill country of Judah. 8 And beyond the Jordan east of
Jericho, they appointed Bezer in the wilderness on the tableland, from the
tribe of Reuben, and Ramoth in Gilead, from the tribe of Gad, and Golan
in Bashan, from the tribe of Manasseh. 9 These were the cities designated
for all the Israelites, and for the aliens residing among them, that anyone
who killed a person without intent could flee there, so as not to die by the
hand of the avenger of blood, until there was a trial before the congregation.

7. *The towns of the Levites*

a. *The method of distribution*

21 Then the heads of the families of the Levites came to the priest
Eleazar and to Joshua son of Nun and to the heads of the families
of the tribes of the Israelites; 2 they said to them at Shiloh in the land of
Canaan, "The LORD commanded through Moses that we be given towns
to live in, along with their pasture lands for our livestock." 3 So by
command of the LORD the Israelites gave to the Levites the following
towns and pasture lands out of their inheritance.

4 The lot came out for the families of the Kohathites. So those Levites
who were descendants of Aaron the priest received by lot thirteen towns
from the tribes of Judah, Simeon, and Benjamin.

5 The rest of the Kohathites received by lot ten towns from the
families of the tribe of Ephraim, from the tribe of Dan, and the half-tribe
of Manasseh.

6 The Gershonites received by lot thirteen towns from the families of
the tribe of Issachar, from the tribe of Asher, from the tribe of Naphtali,
and from the half-tribe of Manasseh in Bashan.

7 The Merarites according to their families received twelve towns
from the tribe of Reuben, the tribe of Gad, and the tribe of Zebulun.

b. *The assignment of the towns*

8 These towns and their pasture lands the Israelites gave by lot to the
Levites, as the LORD had commanded through Moses.

9 Out of the tribe of Judah and the tribe of Simeon they gave the
following towns mentioned by name, 10 which went to the descendants of
Aaron, one of the families of the Kohathites who belonged to the Levites,
since the lot fell to them first. 11 They gave them Kiriath-arba (Arba being
the father of Anak), that is Hebron, in the hill country of Judah, along
with the pasture lands around it. 12 But the fields of the town and its
villages had been given to Caleb son of Jephunneh as his holding.

13 To the descendants of Aaron the priest they gave Hebron, the city
of refuge for the slayer, with its pasture lands, Libnah with its pasture
lands, 14 Jattir with its pasture lands, Eshtemoa with its pasture lands,
15 Holon with its pasture lands, Debir with its pasture lands, 16 Ain with
its pasture lands, Juttah with its pasture lands, and Beth-shemesh with
its pasture lands—nine towns out of these two tribes. 17 Out of the tribe
of Benjamin: Gibeon with its pasture lands, Geba with its pasture lands,
18 Anathoth with its pasture lands, and Almon with its pasture lands—
four towns. 19 The towns of the descendants of Aaron—the priests—were
thirteen in all, with their pasture lands.

20 As to the rest of the Kohathites belonging to the Kohathite families
of the Levites, the towns allotted to them were out of the tribe of Ephraim.
21 To them were given Shechem, the city of refuge for the slayer, with its
pasture lands in the hill country of Ephraim, Gezer with its pasture lands,

20.8
Josh 21.27,
36, 38

20.9
Num 35.15;
v. 6

21.1
Num 35.1-8

21.2
Num 35.2

21.4
vv. 8, 19

21.5
v. 20ff

21.6
v. 27ff

21.7
v. 34ff

21.8
v. 3

21.11
Josh 15.13,
14;
1 Chr 6.55

21.13
Josh 15.42,
54; 1 Chr 6.57

21.15
Josh 15.49,
51;
1 Chr 6.58
21.16
Josh 15.10,
15;
1 Chr 6.59
21.18
1 Chr 6.60

21.21
Josh 20.7

21.2 The Levites were given forty-eight cities and
their pasture lands. This meant that the Levites could
exercise spiritual oversight of all Israel, since no Israelite lived more than ten miles away from a Levitical
city.

22 Kibzaim with its pasture lands, and Beth-horon with its pasture lands —
four towns. 23 Out of the tribe of Dan: Elteke with its pasture lands,
Gibbethon with its pasture lands, 24 Aijalon with its pasture lands, Gath-
rimmon with its pasture lands — four towns. 25 Out of the half-tribe of
Manasseh: Taanach with its pasture lands, and Gath-rimmon with
its pasture lands — two towns. 26 The towns of the families of the rest of the
Kohathites were ten in all, with their pasture lands.

27   To the Gershonites, one of the families of the Levites, were given
out of the half-tribe of Manasseh, Golan in Bashan with its pasture lands,
the city of refuge for the slayer, and Beeshterah with its pasture lands —
two towns. 28 Out of the tribe of Issachar: Kishion with its pasture lands,
Daberath with its pasture lands, 29 Jarmuth with its pasture lands, En-
gannim with its pasture lands — four towns. 30 Out of the tribe of Asher:
Mishal with its pasture lands, Abdon with its pasture lands, 31 Helkath
with its pasture lands, and Rehob with its pasture lands — four towns.
32 Out of the tribe of Naphtali: Kedesh in Galilee with its pasture lands,
the city of refuge for the slayer, Hammoth-dor with its pasture lands, and
Kartan with its pasture lands — three towns. 33 The towns of the several
families of the Gershonites were in all thirteen, with their pasture lands.

34   To the rest of the Levites — the Merarite families — were given out
of the tribe of Zebulun: Jokneam with its pasture lands, Kartah with its
pasture lands, 35 Dimnah with its pasture lands, Nahalal with its pasture
lands — four towns. 36 Out of the tribe of Reuben: Bezer with its pasture
lands, Jahzah with its pasture lands, 37 Kedemoth with its pasture lands,
and Mephaath with its pasture lands — four towns. 38 Out of the tribe of
Gad: Ramoth in Gilead with its pasture lands, the city of refuge for the
slayer, Mahanaim with its pasture lands, 39 Heshbon with its pasture
lands, Jazer with its pasture lands — four towns in all. 40 As for the towns
of the several Merarite families, that is, the remainder of the families of
the Levites, those allotted to them were twelve in all.

41   The towns of the Levites within the holdings of the Israelites were
in all forty-eight towns with their pasture lands. 42 Each of these towns
had its pasture lands around it; so it was with all these towns.

8. The fulfillment of the divine promise

43   Thus the LORD gave to Israel all the land that he swore to their
ancestors that he would give them; and having taken possession of it, they
settled there. 44 And the LORD gave them rest on every side just as he had
sworn to their ancestors; not one of all their enemies had withstood them,
for the LORD had given all their enemies into their hands. 45 Not one of
all the good promises that the LORD had made to the house of Israel had
failed; all came to pass.

III. The farewell addresses of Joshua (22.1–24.33)

A. The message to the two and one-half tribes

1. Joshua's blessing

22   Then Joshua summoned the Reubenites, the Gadites, and the
half-tribe of Manasseh, 2 and said to them, "You have observed
all that Moses the servant of the LORD commanded you, and have obeyed

Marginal references:

21.27 v. 6

21.32 Josh 20.7

21.34 v. 7

21.36 Josh 20.8

21.41 Num 35.7

21.43ff Gen 13.15; Deut 11.31 21.44 Josh 1.13; 11.23; Deut 7.24 21.45 Josh 23.14

22.2 Num 32.20

21.39 Heshbon was originally assigned to Reuben
(13.17), but it is mentioned here under Gad. Like the
Simeonites (see note on 19.1), the Reubenites were
absorbed and lost their special identity. The alloca-
tion of territory had been made; some of the land,
though, remained to be taken and possessed by the
individual tribes.

21.43 God's promise of giving the land to Israel had
been fulfilled for the most part. God had indicated
that the takeover would require time and the unpos-
sessed areas would be brought under the jurisdiction
of Israel bit by bit, if the people obeyed the orders of
God.

me in all that I have commanded you; ³you have not forsaken your kindred these many days, down to this day, but have been careful to keep the charge of the LORD your God. ⁴And now the LORD your God has given rest to your kindred, as he promised them; therefore turn and go to your tents in the land where your possession lies, which Moses the servant of the LORD gave you on the other side of the Jordan. ⁵Take good care to observe the commandment and instruction that Moses the servant of the LORD commanded you, to love the LORD your God, to walk in all his ways, to keep his commandments, and to hold fast to him, and to serve him with all your heart and with all your soul." ⁶So Joshua blessed them and sent them away, and they went to their tents.

7 Now to the one half of the tribe of Manasseh Moses had given a possession in Bashan; but to the other half Joshua had given a possession beside their fellow Israelites in the land west of the Jordan. And when Joshua sent them away to their tents and blessed them, ⁸he said to them, "Go back to your tents with much wealth, and with very much livestock, with silver, gold, bronze, and iron, and with a great quantity of clothing; divide the spoil of your enemies with your kindred." ⁹So the Reubenites and the Gadites and the half-tribe of Manasseh returned home, parting from the Israelites at Shiloh, which is in the land of Canaan, to go to the land of Gilead, their own land of which they had taken possession by command of the LORD through Moses.

2. The altar by the Jordan

10 When they came to the regionʲ near the Jordan that lies in the land of Canaan, the Reubenites and the Gadites and the half-tribe of Manasseh built there an altar by the Jordan, an altar of great size. ¹¹The Israelites heard that the Reubenites and the Gadites and the half-tribe of Manasseh had built an altar at the frontier of the land of Canaan, in the regionᵏ near the Jordan, on the side that belongs to the Israelites. ¹²And when the people of Israel heard of it, the whole assembly of the Israelites gathered at Shiloh, to make war against them.

13 Then the Israelites sent the priest Phinehas son of Eleazar to the Reubenites and the Gadites and the half-tribe of Manasseh, in the land of Gilead, ¹⁴and with him ten chiefs, one from each of the tribal families of Israel, every one of them the head of a family among the clans of Israel. ¹⁵They came to the Reubenites, the Gadites, and the half-tribe of Manasseh, in the land of Gilead, and they said to them, ¹⁶"Thus says the whole congregation of the LORD, 'What is this treachery that you have committed against the God of Israel in turning away today from following the LORD, by building yourselves an altar today in rebellion against the LORD? ¹⁷Have we not had enough of the sin at Peor from which even yet we have not cleansed ourselves, and for which a plague came upon the congregation of the LORD, ¹⁸that you must turn away today from following the LORD! If you rebel against the LORD today, he will be angry with the whole congregation of Israel tomorrow. ¹⁹But now, if your land is unclean, cross over into the LORD's land where the LORD's tabernacle now stands, and take for yourselves a possession among us; only do not rebel against the LORD, or rebel against usˡ by building yourselves an altar other than the altar of the LORD our God. ²⁰Did not Achan son of Zerah break faith in

Cross-references (margin):

22.4 Num 32.18; Deut 3.20
22.5 Deut 6.6, 17; 10.12
22.7 Num 32.33; Josh 17.5
22.9 Num 32.1, 26, 29
22.11 v. 19
22.12 Josh 18.1
22.13 Deut 13.14; Num 25.7
22.16 v. 11; Deut 12.13, 14
22.17 Num 25.1-9
22.19 v. 11
22.20 Josh 7.1-26

ʲ Or to Geliloth   ᵏ Or at Geliloth   ˡ Or make rebels of us

22.10ff God had specifically commanded that there be only one central place for offering sacrifices (by this time the tabernacle was at Shiloh, 18.1). Thus the other tribes protested when the Reubenites, Gadites, and half the tribe of Manasseh built a huge altar by the Jordan River. They thought this represented idolatry, until they discovered that it was intended to be a memorial which would keep the eyes of the people on the Lord God. They had no intention of offering any sacrifices; rather, the altar was a tribute to the spiritual sensitivities of those who wanted to perpetuate the name and the worship of the true God. They were willing for the judgment of God to overtake them if they were really guilty of a crime. Verses 33,34 indicate a satisfactory conclusion to this matter.

the matter of the devoted things, and wrath fell upon all the congregation of Israel? And he did not perish alone for his iniquity!' "

21   Then the Reubenites, the Gadites, and the half-tribe of Manasseh said in answer to the heads of the families of Israel, 22 "The LORD, God of gods! The LORD, God of gods! He knows; and let Israel itself know! If it was in rebellion or in breach of faith toward the LORD, do not spare us today 23 for building an altar to turn away from following the LORD; or if we did so to offer burnt offerings or grain offerings or offerings of well-being on it, may the LORD himself take vengeance. 24 No! We did it from fear that in time to come your children might say to our children, 'What have you to do with the LORD, the God of Israel? 25 For the LORD has made the Jordan a boundary between us and you, you Reubenites and Gadites; you have no portion in the LORD.' So your children might make our children cease to worship the LORD. 26 Therefore we said, 'Let us now build an altar, not for burnt offering, nor for sacrifice, 27 but to be a witness between us and you, and between the generations after us, that we do perform the service of the LORD in his presence with our burnt offerings and sacrifices and offerings of well-being; so that your children may never say to our children in time to come, "You have no portion in the LORD." ' 28 And we thought, If this should be said to us or to our descendants in time to come, we could say, 'Look at this copy of the altar of the LORD, which our ancestors made, not for burnt offerings, nor for sacrifice, but to be a witness between us and you.' 29 Far be it from us that we should rebel against the LORD, and turn away this day from following the LORD by building an altar for burnt offering, grain offering, or sacrifice, other than the altar of the LORD our God that stands before his tabernacle!"

30   When the priest Phinehas and the chiefs of the congregation, the heads of the families of Israel who were with him, heard the words that the Reubenites and the Gadites and the Manassites spoke, they were satisfied. 31 The priest Phinehas son of Eleazar said to the Reubenites and the Gadites and the Manassites, "Today we know that the LORD is among us, because you have not committed this treachery against the LORD; now you have saved the Israelites from the hand of the LORD."

32   Then the priest Phinehas son of Eleazar and the chiefs returned from the Reubenites and the Gadites in the land of Gilead to the land of Canaan, to the Israelites, and brought back word to them. 33 The report pleased the Israelites; and the Israelites blessed God and spoke no more of making war against them, to destroy the land where the Reubenites and the Gadites were settled. 34 The Reubenites and the Gadites called the altar Witness;m "For," said they, "it is a witness between us that the LORD is God."

B. Joshua's address to the nine and one-half tribes

23   A long time afterward, when the LORD had given rest to Israel from all their enemies all around, and Joshua was old and well advanced in years, 2 Joshua summoned all Israel, their elders and heads, their judges and officers, and said to them, "I am now old and well advanced in years; 3 and you have seen all that the LORD your God has done to all these nations for your sake, for it is the LORD your God who has fought for you. 4 I have allotted to you as an inheritance for your tribes those nations that remain, along with all the nations that I have already cut off, from the Jordan to the Great Sea in the west. 5 The LORD your God will push them back before you, and drive them out of your sight; and you shall possess their land, as the LORD your God promised you. 6 Therefore be very steadfast to observe and do all that is written in the book of the law of Moses, turning aside from it neither to the right nor

m Cn Compare Syr: Heb lacks Witness

23.7
Ex 23.33;
Deut 7.2, 3;
Ex 23.13;
Ps 16.4
23.8
Deut 10.20
23.9
Deut 11.23;
Josh 1.5
23.10
Lev 26.8;
v. 3;
Deut 3.22
23.12
Ex 34.15, 16;
Deut 7.3
23.13
Judg 2.3;
Ex 23.33;
Num 33.55
23.14
1 Kings 2.2;
Josh 21.45

23.15
Lev 26.16;
Deut 28.15

to the left, 7 so that you may not be mixed with these nations left here among you, or make mention of the names of their gods, or swear by them, or serve them, or bow yourselves down to them, 8 but hold fast to the LORD your God, as you have done to this day. 9 For the LORD has driven out before you great and strong nations; and as for you, no one has been able to withstand you to this day. 10 One of you puts to flight a thousand, since it is the LORD your God who fights for you, as he promised you. 11 Be very careful, therefore, to love the LORD your God. 12 For if you turn back, and join the survivors of these nations left here among you, and intermarry with them, so that you marry their women and they yours, 13 know assuredly that the LORD your God will not continue to drive out these nations before you; but they shall be a snare and a trap for you, a scourge on your sides, and thorns in your eyes, until you perish from this good land that the LORD your God has given you.

14 "And now I am about to go the way of all the earth, and you know in your hearts and souls, all of you, that not one thing has failed of all the good things that the LORD your God promised concerning you; all have come to pass for you, not one of them has failed. 15 But just as all the good things that the LORD your God promised concerning you have been fulfilled for you, so the LORD will bring upon you all the bad things, until he has destroyed you from this good land that the LORD your God has given you. 16 If you transgress the covenant of the LORD your God, which he enjoined on you, and go and serve other gods and bow down to them, then the anger of the LORD will be kindled against you, and you shall perish quickly from the good land that he has given to you."

C. Joshua's last message

1. Review of God's past dealings with Israel

24.1
Josh 23.2

24.2
Gen 11.27-32

24.3
Gen 12.1;
15.5; 21.3
24.4
Gen 25.25,
26;
Deut 2.5;
Gen 46.6, 7
24.5
Ex 3.10
24.6
Ex 12.51;
14.2-31

24.8
Num 21.21-35

24 Then Joshua gathered all the tribes of Israel to Shechem, and summoned the elders, the heads, the judges, and the officers of Israel; and they presented themselves before God. 2 And Joshua said to all the people, "Thus says the LORD, the God of Israel: Long ago your ancestors—Terah and his sons Abraham and Nahor—lived beyond the Euphrates and served other gods. 3 Then I took your father Abraham from beyond the River and led him through all the land of Canaan and made his offspring many. I gave him Isaac; 4 and to Isaac I gave Jacob and Esau. I gave Esau the hill country of Seir to possess, but Jacob and his children went down to Egypt. 5 Then I sent Moses and Aaron, and I plagued Egypt with what I did in its midst; and afterwards I brought you out. 6 When I brought your ancestors out of Egypt, you came to the sea; and the Egyptians pursued your ancestors with chariots and horsemen to the Red Sea.[n] 7 When they cried out to the LORD, he put darkness between you and the Egyptians, and made the sea come upon them and cover them; and your eyes saw what I did to Egypt. Afterwards you lived in the wilderness a long time. 8 Then I brought you to the land of the Amorites,

[n] Or Sea of Reeds

23.10 The hyperbole that one can fight a thousand is representative of the difference that God makes in any situation. Having God on one's side makes the difference between victory or defeat, regardless of the size of the opposition.

23.12,13 Joshua warned Israel against intermarriage with the heathen. Theoretically, there would have been none of this if the original mandate to slay all of the heathen peoples had been obeyed. Intermarriage between believers and unbelievers always works to the disadvantage of the true religion. As the N.T. says: "Do not be mismatched with unbelievers" (2 Cor 6.14).

23.14 Now facing death, Joshua bore testimony to the faithfulness of God in fulfilling all of the promises made to Israel. All believers should exhibit thanksgiving to God for his continued blessings, especially when on the edge of death. This is an opportune time to deposit something positive with those who are left behind.

24.3 God had sovereignly given the Israelites all they had, and he had worked his will among their enemies to accomplish his divine purposes. The God of Abraham, Isaac, and Jacob still works among the people of God today, to do the same thing for us.

who lived on the other side of the Jordan; they fought with you, and I handed them over to you, and you took possession of their land, and I destroyed them before you. 9 Then King Balak son of Zippor of Moab, set out to fight against Israel. He sent and invited Balaam son of Beor to curse you; 10 but I would not listen to Balaam; therefore he blessed you; so I rescued you out of his hand. 11 When you went over the Jordan and came to Jericho, the citizens of Jericho fought against you, and also the Amorites, the Perizzites, the Canaanites, the Hittites, the Girgashites, the Hivites, and the Jebusites; and I handed them over to you. 12 I sent the hornet*o* ahead of you, which drove out before you the two kings of the Amorites; it was not by your sword or by your bow. 13 I gave you a land on which you had not labored, and towns that you had not built, and you live in them; you eat the fruit of vineyards and oliveyards that you did not plant.

24.9
Num 22.2, 5

24.11
Josh 3.16, 17;
6.1

24.12
Ex 23.28;
Deut 7.20;
Ps 44.3, 6
24.13
Deut 6.10, 11

2. *Joshua's challenge to serve the* LORD

14 "Now therefore revere the LORD, and serve him in sincerity and in faithfulness; put away the gods that your ancestors served beyond the River and in Egypt, and serve the LORD. 15 Now if you are unwilling to serve the LORD, choose this day whom you will serve, whether the gods your ancestors served in the region beyond the River or the gods of the Amorites in whose land you are living; but as for me and my household, we will serve the LORD."

24.14
Deut 10.12;
18.13;
2 Cor 1.12
24.15
Ruth 1.15;
1 Kings 18.21;
Ezek 20.39

3. *Israel chooses the* LORD

16 Then the people answered, "Far be it from us that we should forsake the LORD to serve other gods; 17 for it is the LORD our God who brought us and our ancestors up from the land of Egypt, out of the house of slavery, and who did those great signs in our sight. He protected us along all the way that we went, and among all the peoples through whom we passed; 18 and the LORD drove out before us all the peoples, the Amorites who lived in the land. Therefore we also will serve the LORD, for he is our God."

19 But Joshua said to the people, "You cannot serve the LORD, for he is a holy God. He is a jealous God; he will not forgive your transgressions or your sins. 20 If you forsake the LORD and serve foreign gods, then he will turn and do you harm, and consume you, after having done you good." 21 And the people said to Joshua, "No, we will serve the LORD!" 22 Then Joshua said to the people, "You are witnesses against yourselves that you have chosen the LORD, to serve him." And they said, "We are witnesses." 23 He said, "Then put away the foreign gods that are among you, and incline your hearts to the LORD, the God of Israel." 24 The people said to Joshua, "The LORD our God we will serve, and him we will obey." 25 So Joshua made a covenant with the people that day, and made statutes and ordinances for them at Shechem. 26 Joshua wrote these words in the book of the law of God; and he took a large stone, and set it up there under the oak in the sanctuary of the LORD. 27 Joshua said to all the people, "See, this stone shall be a witness against us; for it has heard all the words of the LORD that he spoke to us; therefore it shall be a witness against you,

24.19
Lev 19.2;
Ex 20.5;
23.21
24.20
1 Chr 28.9;
Josh 23.15

24.23
Judg 10.16
24.24
Ex 19.8;
24.3, 7;
Deut 5.27
24.25
Ex 24.8

24.27
Josh 22.27

o Meaning of Heb uncertain

24.14 *Now therefore.* Having spoken of God's mercies toward Israel, Joshua instructed Israel to continue to fear God, accept his authority, and live in accord with the principles they have professed.
24.23 In v. 16 the Israelites told Joshua: "Far be it from us that we should forsake the LORD, to serve other gods." Joshua followed up on this affirmation by ordering them to put away their foreign gods and to serve the Lord. The command to put away the

foreign gods suggests that some of the people of Israel had already fallen into the trap of keeping images and relics secured from the heathen. This constituted idolatry, however innocent it may have appeared, and was a serious offense against the majesty and holiness of the true God. Every appearance of idolatry must be put away by those who truly love God and wish to maintain a proper relationship to him.

if you deal falsely with your God." ²⁸ So Joshua sent the people away to their inheritances.

D. *The death and burial of Joshua*

24.29
Judg 2.8
24.30
Josh 19.50

29 After these things Joshua son of Nun, the servant of the LORD, died, being one hundred ten years old. ³⁰ They buried him in his own inheritance at Timnath-serah, which is in the hill country of Ephraim, north of Mount Gaash.

24.31
Judg 2.7

31 Israel served the LORD all the days of Joshua, and all the days of the elders who outlived Joshua and had known all the work that the LORD did for Israel.

E. *The burial of Joseph*

24.32
Gen 50.24,
25;
Ex 13.19;
Gen 33.19

32 The bones of Joseph, which the Israelites had brought up from Egypt, were buried at Shechem, in the portion of ground that Jacob had bought from the children of Hamor, the father of Shechem, for one hundred pieces of money;*ᵖ* it became an inheritance of the descendants of Joseph.

F. *The death and burial of Eleazar*

24.33
Josh 22.13

33 Eleazar son of Aaron died; and they buried him at Gibeah, the town of his son Phinehas, which had been given him in the hill country of Ephraim.

ᵖ Heb *one hundred qesitah*

24.32 Joseph died in Egypt nearly four hundred years before he was buried in Canaan. He had carefully left instructions with the Israelites that he was not to be buried in that land but was to be taken away when Israel left Egypt. The coffin containing his mummy (cf. Gen 50.26) was cared for by the Israelites through the long wilderness journey and was now interred in Shechem, in the plot of ground purchased by Jacob from the sons of Hamor. His coffin must have been a constant reminder to the Israelites of their great ancestor, who believed the promise made to Abraham about Canaan.

24.33 *Eleazar* was the third son of Aaron, who succeeded his father in the high-priestly office. He supervised the Kohathites who carried the ark and the holy furniture on their shoulders in the wilderness. He played a major role in assuaging God's wrath when Korah, Dathan, and Abiram rebelled. He was the first one to prepare holy water from the ashes of the red heifer. He was also Joshua's high priest and took part in the division of the land of Canaan among the various tribes. He married an unnamed woman, a daughter of Putiel (Ex 6.25).

INTRODUCTION TO
JUDGES

Authorship, Date, and Background: The title for Judges in the Hebrew is the word *Shophetim,* which means "executive leaders" or "judges." It expresses the type of government or leadership of the people of Israel between the time of Joshua's death and the beginning of the monarchy under King Saul. The author's identity is unknown. Whoever he was, his sources included materials from northern Israel with its dialect which differed from that of the southern section of the nation.

Dating the book of Judges depends upon a number of factors. One has to do with the length of the period under discussion. Undoubtedly some of the judges overlapped each other or were contemporaneous. Adding the years of each judge consecutively yields a period of approximately 410 years. A statement in 1 Kings 6.1 ("In the four hundred eightieth year after the Israelites came out of the land of Egypt") leaves a time span of slightly less than three hundred years for the period between Eli and Othniel. Overlapping reigns account for the difference. What is more important is the date for the Exodus from Egypt. Some evangelical scholars date the Israelite conquest of Canaan at ca. 1290 B.C. Other scholars date the beginning of the Exodus from Egypt at ca. 1440 B.C. This date appears to be the better choice as a result of the Tell el-Amarna letters concerning the dating of the conquest of Canaan. The best date for the composition of Judges is the eleventh century.

Judges must be understood against the background of a recurring cycle of apostasy, repentance, and renewal. The theocracy had been set up by God through Moses, but the people slid back again and again. The period was disordered, filled with times of violence. The book of Ruth shows how the common people lived, loved, and died amidst these great difficulties. Life simply went on despite the turmoil. As part of the total history of Israel, Judges provides the indispensable connecting link between the beginning of the conquest of Canaan and the emergence of the kingship.

Characteristics and Content: Judges contains many statements such as "The Israelites did what was evil in the sight of the LORD"; and statements like "the land had rest" for *x* number of years (e.g., 3.7,12; 4.1; 6.1; 10.6; 13.1; and 3.11,30; 5.31; 8.28). With regard to the judges themselves, Othniel and Samson stand alone at the beginning and at the end of the series of the fourteen judges, while the other twelve are usually connected in pairs. Shamgar and Ehud are linked together; Barak and Deborah are paired up; Gideon and his natural son, Abimelech, are connected.

Judges clearly teaches that the people of Israel were covenant-breakers who often failed to maintain the demands of God's theocracy. They were delivered from their oppressors again and again, only to fall into sin again and repeat the mistakes of their predecessors. The key verse of the book is found in 21.25: "In those days, there was no king in Israel; all the people did what was right in their own eyes."

Judges depicts the strengths and the weaknesses of those who led Israel in times of turmoil. Deborah, Gideon, and Samson were sharply etched. The story of Gideon's fleece, by which he determined the will of God for his life, stands out boldly. The song of Deborah and Barak is a paean of praise to the wonderful victory God gives his people in their moment of distress. The tragic life of Samson is filled with pathos. His miserable departure from the faith of his fathers and his period of blindness when the Philistines took away his sight remind every Christian of the need for perseverance through all the days of this life. The closing section of Judges speaks about the strange case of the priest of Micah and the men of Dan who came to Micah's home. They took away his priest and his idols, which became a source of evil among them thereafter. The closing chapters picture the death of the unfortunate concubine and the war against the Benjaminites, whose tribal members were guilty of the atrocity. The other tribes killed so many Benjaminites that the tribe faced extinction. But the survivors were allowed to take brides from among the virgins of Shiloh, whom they kidnapped and took home as their wives.

Outline:

   I.   Introduction (1.1—2.5)

   II. The judges of Israel (2.6—16.31)

   III. The appendices (17.1—21.25)

JUDGES

I. Introduction (1.1–2.5)

A. Conquests by the people of Judah and Simeon

1 After the death of Joshua, the Israelites inquired of the LORD, "Who shall go up first for us against the Canaanites, to fight against them?" ² The LORD said, "Judah shall go up. I hereby give the land into his hand." ³ Judah said to his brother Simeon, "Come up with me into the territory allotted to me, that we may fight against the Canaanites; then I too will go with you into the territory allotted to you." So Simeon went with him. ⁴ Then Judah went up and the LORD gave the Canaanites and the Perizzites into their hand; and they defeated ten thousand of them at Bezek. ⁵ They came upon Adoni-bezek at Bezek, and fought against him, and defeated the Canaanites and the Perizzites. ⁶ Adoni-bezek fled; but they pursued him, and caught him, and cut off his thumbs and big toes. ⁷ Adoni-bezek said, "Seventy kings with their thumbs and big toes cut off used to pick up scraps under my table; as I have done, so God has paid me back." They brought him to Jerusalem, and he died there.

8 Then the people of Judah fought against Jerusalem and took it. They put it to the sword and set the city on fire. ⁹ Afterward the people of Judah went down to fight against the Canaanites who lived in the hill country, in the Negeb, and in the lowland. ¹⁰ Judah went against the Canaanites who lived in Hebron (the name of Hebron was formerly Kiriath-arba); and they defeated Sheshai and Ahiman and Talmai.

11 From there they went against the inhabitants of Debir (the name of Debir was formerly Kiriath-sepher). ¹² Then Caleb said, "Whoever attacks Kiriath-sepher and takes it, I will give him my daughter Achsah as wife." ¹³ And Othniel son of Kenaz, Caleb's younger brother, took it; and he gave him his daughter Achsah as wife. ¹⁴ When she came to him, she urged him to ask her father for a field. As she dismounted from her donkey, Caleb said to her, "What do you wish?" ¹⁵ She said to him, "Give me a present; since you have set me in the land of the Negeb, give me also Gulloth-mayim."ᵃ So Caleb gave her Upper Gulloth and Lower Gulloth.

16 The descendants of Hobabᵇ the Kenite, Moses' father-in-law, went up with the people of Judah from the city of palms into the wilderness of Judah, which lies in the Negeb near Arad. Then they went and settled with the Amalekites.ᶜ ¹⁷ Judah went with his brother Simeon, and they defeated the Canaanites who inhabited Zephath, and devoted it to destruction. So the city was called Hormah. ¹⁸ Judah took Gaza with its territory, Ashkelon with its territory, and Ekron with its territory. ¹⁹ The

Cross-references (margin):
1.1 Num 27.21
1.3 v. 17
1.4 Gen 13.7
1.8 v. 21; Josh 15.63
1.10 Josh 15.13-19
1.13 Judg 3.9
1.14 Josh 15.18, 19
1.16 Judg 4.11, 17; Deut 34.3; Judg 3.13
1.17 v. 3; Num 21.3
1.19 v. 2; Josh 17.16, 18

1.1 Joshua and Judges are complementary, not contradictory. Some have the impression that by the time of Joshua's death the land had been fully occupied by Israel, but that Judges describes the conquest as gradual and lengthy. Joshua did fight and overcome many enemies. Many Canaanites were defeated, but not all of Canaan was occupied by Israel (cf. Josh 13.1–7). Judges continues the story of the conquest; but when the book ends, the story is still incomplete. It was left to each tribe, until the time of the monarchy, to take full possession of the territory allocated to it.

1.6,7 In Josh 10.1 Adoni-bezek is identified as the king of Jerusalem (which at that time was an Amorite city called Jebus). Judah captured the city, but it later reverted to the Amorites. It was King David who took the city permanently from the Amorites and named it after himself, "The city of David" (2 Sam 5.9). "Jerusalem" means "foundation of peace."

1.19 In the hill country, where hand-to-hand battle

LORD was with Judah, and he took possession of the hill country, but could not drive out the inhabitants of the plain, because they had chariots of iron. 20 Hebron was given to Caleb, as Moses had said; and he drove out from it the three sons of Anak. 21 But the Benjaminites did not drive out the Jebusites who lived in Jerusalem; so the Jebusites have lived in Jerusalem among the Benjaminites to this day.

1.20
Josh 14.9;
15.13, 14;
v. 10
1.21
Josh 15.63

B. *The incomplete conquests of Israel*

22 The house of Joseph also went up against Bethel; and the LORD was with them. 23 The house of Joseph sent out spies to Bethel (the name of the city was formerly Luz). 24 When the spies saw a man coming out of the city, they said to him, "Show us the way into the city, and we will deal kindly with you." 25 So he showed them the way into the city; and they put the city to the sword, but they let the man and all his family go. 26 So the man went to the land of the Hittites and built a city, and named it Luz; that is its name to this day.

1.23
Gen 28.19

1.25
Josh 6.25

27 Manasseh did not drive out the inhabitants of Beth-shean and its villages, or Taanach and its villages, or the inhabitants of Dor and its villages, or the inhabitants of Ibleam and its villages, or the inhabitants of Megiddo and its villages; but the Canaanites continued to live in that land. 28 When Israel grew strong, they put the Canaanites to forced labor, but did not in fact drive them out.

1.27
Josh 17.11-13

29 And Ephraim did not drive out the Canaanites who lived in Gezer; but the Canaanites lived among them in Gezer.

1.29
Josh 16.10

30 Zebulun did not drive out the inhabitants of Kitron, or the inhabitants of Nahalol; but the Canaanites lived among them, and became subject to forced labor.

31 Asher did not drive out the inhabitants of Acco, or the inhabitants of Sidon, or of Ahlab, or of Achzib, or of Helbah, or of Aphik, or of Rehob; 32 but the Asherites lived among the Canaanites, the inhabitants of the land; for they did not drive them out.

1.31
Judg 10.6

33 Naphtali did not drive out the inhabitants of Beth-shemesh, or the inhabitants of Beth-anath, but lived among the Canaanites, the inhabitants of the land; nevertheless the inhabitants of Beth-shemesh and of Beth-anath became subject to forced labor for them.

34 The Amorites pressed the Danites back into the hill country; they did not allow them to come down to the plain. 35 The Amorites continued to live in Har-heres, in Aijalon, and in Shaalbim, but the hand of the house of Joseph rested heavily on them, and they became subject to forced labor. 36 The border of the Amorites ran from the ascent of Akrabbim, from Sela and upward.

1.34
Ex 3.17

1.36
Josh 15.3
2.1
v. 5;
Judg 6.11;
Ex 20.2;
Gen 17.7;
Deut 7.9
2.2
Ex 23.32;
34.12, 13
2.3
Josh 23.13;
Judg 3.6;
Deut 7.16;
Ps 106.36

C. *The failure of Israel to keep the covenant*

2 Now the angel of the LORD went up from Gilgal to Bochim, and said, "I brought you up from Egypt, and brought you into the land that I had promised to your ancestors. I said, 'I will never break my covenant with you. 2 For your part, do not make a covenant with the inhabitants of this land; tear down their altars.' But you have not obeyed my command. See what you have done! 3 So now I say, I will not drive them out

was important, the Israelites prevailed. In the plains they were at a disadvantage, for the enemy had chariots of iron. From the human perspective it looked bleak for the Israelites. But God is always behind history and he is not always on the side of the most powerful armies (see notes on Josh 11.6,8). In this instance, however, the superior armed might of the enemy prevailed.
1.22 *the house of Joseph,* i.e., the two tribes of

Ephraim and Manasseh.
1.27 See note on Josh 10.40.
2.1 This verse reiterates the Abrahamic covenant as renewed in Ex 34. Its seal was obedience to the voice of God. Israel failed to drive out of Canaan all of the inhabitants, thus breaking the covenant. This transgression led to disaster (see 2.2,3). *angel of the LORD.* The phrase "I brought you up" indicates this is the Lord himself (see note on Ex 3.2).

before you; but they shall become adversaries[d] to you, and their gods shall be a snare to you." 4 When the angel of the LORD spoke these words to all the Israelites, the people lifted up their voices and wept. 5 So they named that place Bochim,[e] and there they sacrificed to the LORD.

II. *The judges of Israel (2.6–16.31)*

A. *The death and burial of Joshua*

6 When Joshua dismissed the people, the Israelites all went to their own inheritances to take possession of the land. 7 The people worshiped the LORD all the days of Joshua, and all the days of the elders who outlived Joshua, who had seen all the great work that the LORD had done for Israel. 8 Joshua son of Nun, the servant of the LORD, died at the age of one hundred ten years. 9 So they buried him within the bounds of his inheritance in Timnath-heres, in the hill country of Ephraim, north of Mount Gaash. 10 Moreover, that whole generation was gathered to their ancestors, and another generation grew up after them, who did not know the LORD or the work that he had done for Israel.

B. *The unfaithfulness of Israel*

11 Then the Israelites did what was evil in the sight of the LORD and worshiped the Baals; 12 and they abandoned the LORD, the God of their ancestors, who had brought them out of the land of Egypt; they followed other gods, from among the gods of the peoples who were all around them, and bowed down to them; and they provoked the LORD to anger. 13 They abandoned the LORD, and worshiped Baal and the Astartes. 14 So the anger of the LORD was kindled against Israel, and he gave them over to plunderers who plundered them, and he sold them into the power of their enemies all around, so that they could no longer withstand their enemies. 15 Whenever they marched out, the hand of the LORD was against them to bring misfortune, as the LORD had warned them and sworn to them; and they were in great distress.

C. *Deliverance through judges and repeated unfaithfulness*

16 Then the LORD raised up judges, who delivered them out of the power of those who plundered them. 17 Yet they did not listen even to their judges; for they lusted after other gods and bowed down to them. They soon turned aside from the way in which their ancestors had walked, who had obeyed the commandments of the LORD; they did not follow their example. 18 Whenever the LORD raised up judges for them, the LORD was with the judge, and he delivered them from the hand of their enemies all the days of the judge; for the LORD would be moved to pity by their groaning because of those who persecuted and oppressed them. 19 But

---

d OL Vg Compare Gk: Heb *sides*   *e* That is *Weepers*

2.10 A new generation arose, somehow detached from its spiritual inheritance. These Israelites neither knew the Lord nor were they aware of his great works on their behalf among their ancestors. The first and principal business of parents is to raise their children in the nurture and admonition of the Lord. Some of the Israelites obviously failed to do this. But a remnant did remain that carried on the ancient traditions.
2.11–14 *Baals.* Baal was the lord of the Canaanite pantheon and a male consort of Ashtaroth, a Canaanite goddess of fertility and war. Those who do not have God as their Father often look to something or someone else to take his place. Even those who profess atheism have their own gods. Few are totally bereft of any commitment to something higher than themselves.

2.16 After the death of Joshua, Israel fell into religious apostasy. The nation experienced a recurring pattern of subjugation by neighboring peoples, followed by repentance and deliverance by God. During this period and before the appointment of prophets and kings, God raised up deliverers such as Othniel, Ehud, Deborah, and Samson. These heroes were called *judges,* a title which, in Hebrew, meant leadership in war, government, politics, and law. Israel was still a theocratic nation; God was still the ruler. None of the judges reached the stature of Moses and Joshua before them, or of Samuel and David after them. The period of the judges was marked by confusion and disorder: "the people did what was right in their own eyes" (17.6).
2.19 While living, the judges were generally able to

Marginal references:

2.6 Josh 24.28-31

2.10 1 Sam 2.12; 1 Chr 28.9; Gal 4.8

2.11 Judg 3.7, 12; 4.1; 6.1, 25; 8.33; 10.6
2.12 Deut 31.16
2.13 Judg 10.6
2.14 Judg 3.8; Ps 106.40-42; Deut 28.25

2.16 Ps 106.43-45; Acts 13.20
2.17 v. 7

2.19 Judg 3.12; 4.1; 8.33

whenever the judge died, they would relapse and behave worse than their ancestors, following other gods, worshiping them and bowing down to them. They would not drop any of their practices or their stubborn ways. 20 So the anger of the LORD was kindled against Israel; and he said, "Because this people have transgressed my covenant that I commanded their ancestors, and have not obeyed my voice, 21 I will no longer drive out before them any of the nations that Joshua left when he died." 22 In order to test Israel, whether or not they would take care to walk in the way of the LORD as their ancestors did, 23 the LORD had left those nations, not driving them out at once, and had not handed them over to Joshua.

D. *The nations left to test Israel*

3 Now these are the nations that the LORD left to test all those in Israel who had no experience of any war in Canaan 2 (it was only that successive generations of Israelites might know war, to teach those who had no experience of it before): 3 the five lords of the Philistines, and all the Canaanites, and the Sidonians, and the Hivites who lived on Mount Lebanon, from Mount Baal-hermon as far as Lebo-hamath. 4 They were for the testing of Israel, to know whether Israel would obey the commandments of the LORD, which he commanded their ancestors by Moses. 5 So the Israelites lived among the Canaanites, the Hittites, the Amorites, the Perizzites, the Hivites, and the Jebusites; 6 and they took their daughters as wives for themselves, and their own daughters they gave to their sons; and they worshiped their gods.

E. *The judgeship of Othniel*

7 The Israelites did what was evil in the sight of the LORD, forgetting the LORD their God, and worshiping the Baals and the Asherahs. 8 Therefore the anger of the LORD was kindled against Israel, and he sold them into the hand of King Cushan-rishathaim of Aram-naharaim; and the Israelites served Cushan-rishathaim eight years. 9 But when the Israelites cried out to the LORD, the LORD raised up a deliverer for the Israelites, who delivered them, Othniel son of Kenaz, Caleb's younger brother. 10 The spirit of the LORD came upon him, and he judged Israel; he went out to war, and the LORD gave King Cushan-rishathaim of Aram into his hand; and his hand prevailed over Cushan-rishathaim. 11 So the land had rest forty years. Then Othniel son of Kenaz died.

F. *The judgeship of Ehud*

1. *The sin of Israel: oppression by Moab*

12 The Israelites again did what was evil in the sight of the LORD; and

Cross references (left margin):

2.20 v. 14; Josh 23.16
2.21 Josh 23.13
2.22 Judg 3.1, 4
3.1 Judg 2.21, 22
3.3 Josh 13.3
3.4 Deut 8.2; Judg 2.22
3.6 Ex 34.16; Deut 7.3, 4
3.7 Judg 2.11, 13; Deut 4.9
3.9 v. 15; Judg 1.13
3.10 Num 11.25, 29; 24.2; Judg 6.34
3.12 Judg 2.11, 14

---

restrain their countrymen from apostasy. But when they died, the people easily departed from the true faith and behaved *worse than their ancestors*. The judges did not restrain the people through legalistic legislation, but through force of character, quality of leadership, and their own example of fidelity to God.
2.23 *handed them over to Joshua*. Joshua here is a euphemism for Israel under his leadership.
3.1 God allowed several nations to remain in Canaan after Israel occupied it, in order to keep them on their guard. Knowing that enemies surrounded them, the Israelites had to be militarily prepared at all times. This kept them from falling into a life of ease, luxury, and inefficiency.
3.8 *Aram-naharaim*, i.e., Mesopotamia (eastern Syria). Aram was located near Haran (see note on Gen 24.10).
3.10 *the spirit of the LORD came upon him*. In the O.T. we often read of the Spirit of the Lord coming upon

people. Whenever this happened, such persons received useful gifts and experienced the power of God in their work so that they could perform great exploits for God and his people Israel. Othniel enjoyed a forty-year judgeship and the Israelites under his leadership prospered spiritually and materially. Pentecost in the N.T. marked the beginning of the age of the Holy Spirit (see Acts 2). Before that great event, however, the Spirit came upon believers as he pleased, in order that they might do the will of God. He came upon some of the judges (6.34; 11.29), upon David (1 Sam 16.13), upon Zechariah (2 Chr 24.20), and upon Elizabeth (Lk 1.41). The life of Jesus likewise manifested the work of the Holy Spirit, for he was "full of the Holy Spirit" (Lk 4.1), "led by the Spirit in the wilderness" (Mt 4.1); and "through the eternal Spirit offered himself without blemish to God" (Heb 9.14). The Spirit of God was also active in creation (Gen 1.2).

the Lord strengthened King Eglon of Moab against Israel, because they had done what was evil in the sight of the Lord. 13 In alliance with the Ammonites and the Amalekites, he went and defeated Israel; and they took possession of the city of palms. 14 So the Israelites served King Eglon of Moab eighteen years.

3.13
Judg 1.16

2. Ehud murders Eglon

15 But when the Israelites cried out to the Lord, the Lord raised up for them a deliverer, Ehud son of Gera, the Benjaminite, a left-handed man. The Israelites sent tribute by him to King Eglon of Moab. 16 Ehud made for himself a sword with two edges, a cubit in length; and he fastened it on his right thigh under his clothes. 17 Then he presented the tribute to King Eglon of Moab. Now Eglon was a very fat man. 18 When Ehud had finished presenting the tribute, he sent the people who carried the tribute on their way. 19 But he himself turned back at the sculptured stones near Gilgal, and said, "I have a secret message for you, O king." So the king said,*f* "Silence!" and all his attendants went out from his presence. 20 Ehud came to him, while he was sitting alone in his cool roof chamber, and said, "I have a message from God for you." So he rose from his seat. 21 Then Ehud reached with his left hand, took the sword from his right thigh, and thrust it into Eglon's*g* belly; 22 the hilt also went in after the blade, and the fat closed over the blade, for he did not draw the sword out of his belly; and the dirt came out.*h* 23 Then Ehud went out into the vestibule,*i* and closed the doors of the roof chamber on him, and locked them.

3.15
Ps 107.13

3.17
v. 12

3. The discovery of the murder

24 After he had gone, the servants came. When they saw that the doors of the roof chamber were locked, they thought, "He must be relieving himself*j* in the cool chamber." 25 So they waited until they were embarrassed. When he still did not open the doors of the roof chamber, they took the key and opened them. There was their lord lying dead on the floor.

3.24
1 Sam 24.3

3.25
2 Kings 2.17;
8.11

4. The defeat of the Moabites

26 Ehud escaped while they delayed, and passed beyond the sculptured stones, and escaped to Seirah. 27 When he arrived, he sounded the trumpet in the hill country of Ephraim; and the Israelites went down with him from the hill country, having him at their head. 28 He said to them, "Follow after me; for the Lord has given your enemies the Moabites into your hand." So they went down after him, and seized the fords of the Jordan against the Moabites, and allowed no one to cross over. 29 At that time they killed about ten thousand of the Moabites, all strong, able-bodied men; no one escaped. 30 So Moab was subdued that day under the hand of Israel. And the land had rest eighty years.

3.28
Judg 7.9, 15,
24; 12.5

3.30
v. 11

G. Delivery by Shamgar

31 After him came Shamgar son of Anath, who killed six hundred of the Philistines with an oxgoad. He too delivered Israel.

3.31
Judg 5.6

f Heb *he said*   *g* Heb *his*   *h* With Tg Vg: Meaning of Heb uncertain   *i* Meaning of Heb uncertain
j Heb *covering his feet*

3.12–15 Subsequent to Othniel's death, Israel became apostate. After eighteen years of oppression under Eglon, Israel again sought the help of God, who heard and delivered them.
3.24 *relieving himself*, meaning, going to the toilet.
3.30 The power of the Moabites was so broken that

the land had rest for eighty years, quite an extended period of time.
3.31 *oxgoad*. The Israelites lacked real armaments. An oxgoad was a sharp stick used to prod cattle and to clean plows. It probably had a blade on one end. Shamgar used it as a spear.

H. *The judgeships of Deborah and Barak*

1. *The oppression by the Canaanites*

4.1
Judg 2.19
4.2
Josh 11.1, 10;
vv. 13, 16;
Ps 83.9
4.3
Judg 1.19

4 The Israelites again did what was evil in the sight of the LORD, after Ehud died. 2 So the LORD sold them into the hand of King Jabin of Canaan, who reigned in Hazor; the commander of his army was Sisera, who lived in Harosheth-ha-goiim. 3 Then the Israelites cried out to the LORD for help; for he had nine hundred chariots of iron, and had oppressed the Israelites cruelly twenty years.

2. *Deborah summons Barak*

4.6
Heb 11.32

4.7
Ps 83.9

4.9
v. 21

4.10
Judg 5.18;
v. 14;
Judg 5.15

4 At that time Deborah, a prophetess, wife of Lappidoth, was judging Israel. 5 She used to sit under the palm of Deborah between Ramah and Bethel in the hill country of Ephraim; and the Israelites came up to her for judgment. 6 She sent and summoned Barak son of Abinoam from Kedesh in Naphtali, and said to him, "The LORD, the God of Israel, commands you, 'Go, take position at Mount Tabor, bringing ten thousand from the tribe of Naphtali and the tribe of Zebulun. 7 I will draw out Sisera, the general of Jabin's army, to meet you by the Wadi Kishon with his chariots and his troops; and I will give him into your hand.' " 8 Barak said to her, "If you will go with me, I will go; but if you will not go with me, I will not go." 9 And she said, "I will surely go with you; nevertheless, the road on which you are going will not lead to your glory, for the LORD will sell Sisera into the hand of a woman." Then Deborah got up and went with Barak to Kedesh. 10 Barak summoned Zebulun and Naphtali to Kedesh; and ten thousand warriors went up behind him; and Deborah went up with him.

3. *The victory over the Canaanites*

4.11
Judg 1.16;
v. 6

4.13
v. 3
4.14
Deut 9.3

4.15
Josh 10.10

4.16
Ps 83.9

11 Now Heber the Kenite had separated from the other Kenites,[k] that is, the descendants of Hobab the father-in-law of Moses, and had encamped as far away as Elon-bezaanannim, which is near Kedesh. 12 When Sisera was told that Barak son of Abinoam had gone up to Mount Tabor, 13 Sisera called out all his chariots, nine hundred chariots of iron, and all the troops who were with him, from Harosheth-ha-goiim to the Wadi Kishon. 14 Then Deborah said to Barak, "Up! For this is the day on which the LORD has given Sisera into your hand. The LORD is indeed going out before you." So Barak went down from Mount Tabor with ten thousand warriors following him. 15 And the LORD threw Sisera and all his chariots and all his army into a panic[l] before Barak; Sisera got down from his chariot and fled away on foot, 16 while Barak pursued the chariots and the army to Harosheth-ha-goiim. All the army of Sisera fell by the sword; no one was left.

4. *Jael kills Sisera*

17 Now Sisera had fled away on foot to the tent of Jael wife of Heber

---

[k] Heb *from the Kain* [l] Heb adds *to the sword*; compare verse 16

4.1 For eighty years Ehud had kept a sharp eye on the people, and they did not turn away from God. But after his death they again became apostate. They feared Ehud more than God.

4.4 *Deborah, a prophetess*, is the only judge so described. As a prophetess, she conveyed to the people the word she received from the Holy Spirit. In this role she was able to foretell the future. God is not partial to men over women in principle, for the Scriptures are filled with incidents in which God employed women in his service. Prophetesses, deaconesses, and other women (such as Miriam, Rahab, Lydia, Elizabeth, and Mary) played an important role in the unfolding plan of redemption.

4.5 *the Israelites came up to her for judgment*, i.e., for her to decide their disputes.

4.11 *Heber . . . Hobab.* See note on Ex 2.18.

4.15 *the LORD threw Sisera . . . into a panic.* God likely did this by some sort of flood or great rainstorm (see 5.21). It was the Lord, not the Israelites, who made the difference in this encounter.

the Kenite; for there was peace between King Jabin of Hazor and the clan of Heber the Kenite. 18 Jael came out to meet Sisera, and said to him, "Turn aside, my lord, turn aside to me; have no fear." So he turned aside to her into the tent, and she covered him with a rug. 19 Then he said to her, "Please give me a little water to drink; for I am thirsty." So she opened a skin of milk and gave him a drink and covered him. 20 He said to her, "Stand at the entrance of the tent, and if anybody comes and asks you, 'Is anyone here?' say, 'No.'" 21 But Jael wife of Heber took a tent peg, and took a hammer in her hand, and went softly to him and drove the peg into his temple, until it went down into the ground—he was lying fast asleep from weariness—and he died. 22 Then, as Barak came in pursuit of Sisera, Jael went out to meet him, and said to him, "Come, and I will show you the man whom you are seeking." So he went into her tent; and there was Sisera lying dead, with the tent peg in his temple.

4.19
Judg 5.25

4.21
Judg 5.26

5. Jabin destroyed

23 So on that day God subdued King Jabin of Canaan before the Israelites. 24 Then the hand of the Israelites bore harder and harder on King Jabin of Canaan, until they destroyed King Jabin of Canaan.

6. The song of Deborah

5 Then Deborah and Barak son of Abinoam sang on that day, saying:
  2 "When locks are long in Israel,
    when the people offer themselves willingly—
     bless *m* the Lord!

5.1
Ex 15.1
5.2
Deut 32.41

3 "Hear, O kings; give ear, O princes;
    to the Lord I will sing,
    I will make melody to the Lord, the God of Israel.

5.3
Ps 27.6

4 "Lord, when you went out from Seir,
    when you marched from the region of Edom,
  the earth trembled,
    and the heavens poured,
     the clouds indeed poured water.

5.4
Deut 33.2;
Ps 68.7-9

5 The mountains quaked before the Lord, the One of Sinai,
    before the Lord, the God of Israel.

5.5
Ps 97.5;
Isa 64.1, 3;
Ps 68.8

6 "In the days of Shamgar son of Anath,
    in the days of Jael, caravans ceased
    and travelers kept to the byways.

5.6
Judg 3.31;
4.17

7 The peasantry prospered in Israel,
    they grew fat on plunder,
  because you arose, Deborah,
    arose as a mother in Israel.

8 When new gods were chosen,
    then war was in the gates.
  Was shield or spear to be seen
    among forty thousand in Israel?

5.8
Deut 32.17

9 My heart goes out to the commanders of Israel

m Or *You who offer yourselves willingly among the people, bless*

4.21 What Jael did did not follow the usual laws of friendship and hospitality. Normally, anyone who accepted someone into his or her tent guaranteed protection from pursuing enemies (cf. Ps 23.5). **5.1** Deborah used her gifts as a prophetess in composing the song. It is good to sing praises to God. When he gives his people victory, they should offer thanksgiving, and singing is one of the beautiful ways to do so. **5.4,5** Recalling what God had done for Israel in the exodus and desert wanderings, Deborah compares Israel's recent deliverance with those earlier events. Past mercies give God's people the hope and expectation that he will repeat them in the days to come.

who offered themselves willingly among the people.
  Bless the LORD.

10 "Tell of it, you who ride on white donkeys,
      you who sit on rich carpets[n]
      and you who walk by the way.

5.11
1 Sam 12.7;
Mic 6.5
11 To the sound of musicians[n] at the watering places,
      there they repeat the triumphs of the LORD,
      the triumphs of his peasantry in Israel.

  "Then down to the gates marched the people of the LORD.

5.12
Ps 57.8;
68.18
12 "Awake, awake, Deborah!
      Awake, awake, utter a song!
    Arise, Barak, lead away your captives,
      O son of Abinoam.

13 Then down marched the remnant of the noble;
      the people of the LORD marched down for him[o] against the
        mighty.

5.14
Judg 3.13,
27;
Num 32.39
14 From Ephraim they set out[p] into the valley,[q]
      following you, Benjamin, with your kin;
    from Machir marched down the commanders,
      and from Zebulun those who bear the marshal's staff;

5.15
Judg 4.10
15 the chiefs of Issachar came with Deborah,
      and Issachar faithful to Barak;
    into the valley they rushed out at his heels.
  Among the clans of Reuben
      there were great searchings of heart.

5.16
Num 32.1
16 Why did you tarry among the sheepfolds,
      to hear the piping for the flocks?
    Among the clans of Reuben
      there were great searchings of heart.

5.17
Josh 13.24-28;
19.29, 46
17 Gilead stayed beyond the Jordan;
      and Dan, why did he abide with the ships?
    Asher sat still at the coast of the sea,
      settling down by his landings.

5.18
Judg 4.6, 10
18 Zebulun is a people that scorned death;
      Naphtali too, on the heights of the field.

5.19ff
Josh 11.1, 2;
Judg 1.27
19 "The kings came, they fought;
      then fought the kings of Canaan,
    at Taanach, by the waters of Megiddo;
      they got no spoils of silver.

5.20
Josh 10.11-14
20 The stars fought from heaven,
      from their courses they fought against Sisera.

5.21
Judg 4.7
21 The torrent Kishon swept them away,
      the onrushing torrent, the torrent Kishon.
    March on, my soul, with might!

22 "Then loud beat the horses' hoofs
      with the galloping, galloping of his steeds.

---

[n] Meaning of Heb uncertain [o] Gk: Heb me [p] Cn: Heb From Ephraim their root [q] Gk: Heb in Amalek

---

5.10,11 Deborah calls for people of all classes — rich and poor, judges and peasants — to speak forth their praise to God for his great deliverance.
5.15-17 Some of the Israelites gave no support to those who battled Sisera. Reuben, Gilead, Asher, and Dan sat on the sidelines and contributed nothing to the victory. This was a word of reproof.

5.20 *the stars . . . fought against Sisera.* The God of heaven waged war against the enemy.
5.21,22 Kishon was ordinarily a shallow river. But a rainstorm so swelled the torrents that those who sought to cross it were drowned and their chariots mired in the mud.

23   "Curse Meroz, says the angel of the LORD,
       curse bitterly its inhabitants,
     because they did not come to the help of the LORD,
       to the help of the LORD against the mighty.

24   "Most blessed of women be Jael,
       the wife of Heber the Kenite,
       of tent-dwelling women most blessed.

5.24
Judg 4.17,
19-21

25   He asked water and she gave him milk,
       she brought him curds in a lordly bowl.

5.25
Judg 4.19

26   She put her hand to the tent peg
       and her right hand to the workmen's mallet;
     she struck Sisera a blow,
       she crushed his head,
       she shattered and pierced his temple.

5.26
Judg 4.21

27   He sank, he fell,
       he lay still at her feet;
     at her feet he sank, he fell;
       where he sank, there he fell dead.

28   "Out of the window she peered,
       the mother of Sisera gazed*r* through the lattice:
     'Why is his chariot so long in coming?
       Why tarry the hoofbeats of his chariots?'

5.28
Prov 7.6

29   Her wisest ladies make answer,
       indeed, she answers the question herself:

30   'Are they not finding and dividing the spoil? —
       A girl or two for every man;
     spoil of dyed stuffs for Sisera,
       spoil of dyed stuffs embroidered,
       two pieces of dyed work embroidered for my neck as spoil?'

5.30
Ex 15.9

31   "So perish all your enemies, O LORD!
       But may your friends be like the sun as it rises in its might."

5.31
Ps 68.2; 92.9;
19.4, 5;
Judg 3.11

And the land had rest forty years.

I. *The judgeship of Gideon*

1. *Unfaithfulness and servitude*

6 The Israelites did what was evil in the sight of the LORD, and the
LORD gave them into the hand of Midian seven years. ²The hand of
Midian prevailed over Israel; and because of Midian the Israelites provided for themselves hiding places in the mountains, caves and strongholds. ³For whenever the Israelites put in seed, the Midianites and the
Amalekites and the people of the east would come up against them. ⁴They
would encamp against them and destroy the produce of the land, as far
as the neighborhood of Gaza, and leave no sustenance in Israel, and no
sheep or ox or donkey. ⁵For they and their livestock would come up, and

6.1
Judg 2.11,
19;
Num 25.15-18;
31.1-3

6.3
Judg 3.13
6.4
Lev 26.16;
Deut 28.30,
33, 51
6.5
Judg 7.12

r Gk Compare Tg: Heb *exclaimed*

5.23 The inhabitants of Meroz did not give aid in
the battle. They were cursed, not because they were
unwilling to help their friends, but "because they did
not come to the help of the LORD."
5.24–31 Deborah rose to poetic heights as she pictured heroic Jael, the one who smote Sisera. The
king's mother would have to wait a long time for her
son to come home, for this enemy of God has per-

ished. She ended with a prayer that all the enemies of
God might perish. The upshot of the victory was that
the land was free from political turmoil for forty
years.
6.1 *Midian.* See note on Ex 2.15.
6.3 *Amalekites.* See note on Ex 17.8.
6.5 This is the first instance recorded in the Scriptures of the use of camels in warfare.

they would even bring their tents, as thick as locusts; neither they nor their camels could be counted; so they wasted the land as they came in. 6 Thus Israel was greatly impoverished because of Midian; and the Israelites cried out to the LORD for help.

6.6
Judg 3.15

2. The coming of a prophet

7 When the Israelites cried to the LORD on account of the Midianites, 8 the LORD sent a prophet to the Israelites; and he said to them, "Thus says the LORD, the God of Israel: I led you up from Egypt, and brought you out of the house of slavery; 9 and I delivered you from the hand of the Egyptians, and from the hand of all who oppressed you, and drove them out before you, and gave you their land; 10 and I said to you, 'I am the LORD your God; you shall not pay reverence to the gods of the Amorites, in whose land you live.' But you have not given heed to my voice."

6.8
Judg 2.1, 2
6.9
Ps 44.2, 3

3. Gideon called of the LORD

11 Now the angel of the LORD came and sat under the oak at Ophrah, which belonged to Joash the Abiezrite, as his son Gideon was beating out wheat in the wine press, to hide it from the Midianites. 12 The angel of the LORD appeared to him and said to him, "The LORD is with you, you mighty warrior." 13 Gideon answered him, "But sir, if the LORD is with us, why then has all this happened to us? And where are all his wonderful deeds that our ancestors recounted to us, saying, 'Did not the LORD bring us up from Egypt?' But now the LORD has cast us off, and given us into the hand of Midian." 14 Then the LORD turned to him and said, "Go in this might of yours and deliver Israel from the hand of Midian; I hereby commission you." 15 He responded, "But sir, how can I deliver Israel? My clan is the weakest in Manasseh, and I am the least in my family." 16 The LORD said to him, "But I will be with you, and you shall strike down the Midianites, every one of them." 17 Then he said to him, "If now I have found favor with you, then show me a sign that it is you who speak with me. 18 Do not depart from here until I come to you, and bring out my present, and set it before you." And he said, "I will stay until you return."

19 So Gideon went into his house and prepared a kid, and unleavened cakes from an ephah of flour; the meat he put in a basket, and the broth he put in a pot, and brought them to him under the oak and presented them. 20 The angel of God said to him, "Take the meat and the unleavened cakes, and put them on this rock, and pour out the broth." And he did so. 21 Then the angel of the LORD reached out the tip of the staff that was in his hand, and touched the meat and the unleavened cakes; and fire sprang up from the rock and consumed the meat and the unleavened cakes; and the angel of the LORD vanished from his sight. 22 Then Gideon perceived that it was the angel of the LORD; and Gideon said, "Help me, Lord GOD! For I have seen the angel of the LORD face to face." 23 But the LORD said to him, "Peace be to you; do not fear, you shall not die."

6.11
Josh 17.2
6.12
Josh 1.5
6.13
Ps 44.1;
2 Chr 15.2
6.14
Heb 11.32,
34;
Judg 4.6
6.15
Ex 3.11;
1 Sam 9.21
6.16
Ex 3.12;
Josh 1.5
6.17
vv. 36, 37;
Isa 38.7, 8
6.19
Gen 18.6-8
6.20
Judg 13.19
6.21
Lev 9.24
6.22
Judg 13.21

6.8 God sent an unnamed prophet to speak to Israel on his behalf. His sole duty was to call Israel back to faithfulness to the God they had deserted in favor of the gods of the Amorites. Eternity alone will reveal the many people who served God faithfully but whose names have been lost to history.

6.11ff the angel of the LORD. This was evidently an appearance of Christ, the Lord. Note v. 14: "the LORD turned to him"; the Hebrew word for this use of LORD is Yahweh. The angel called Gideon to the office of judge, promising that he would be with him. When Gideon asked for some outward sign that he was indeed called of God, the angel destroyed the meat and unleavened cakes with supernatural fire.

Gideon later laid out the fleece, and on the strength of that providential sign, he led the people of Israel to victory over the oppressive Midianites.

6.16 I will be with you, i.e., "I Am will be with you." The name "I Am" is also used in Ex 3.14. Thus was saying that the same one who appeared to Moses and saved Israel from Egypt (see v. 13) would now deliver Israel from Midian.

6.17-21 show me a sign. Gideon wanted some assurance that this person was God speaking to him, so he begged for a sign. In v. 21 "fire sprang up from the rock and consumed the meat and the unleavened cakes." Then Gideon knew that the call was from God.

24 Then Gideon built an altar there to the LORD, and called it, The LORD is peace. To this day it still stands at Ophrah, which belongs to the Abiezrites.

4. *Gideon destroys the altar to Baal*

25   That night the LORD said to him, "Take your father's bull, the second bull seven years old, and pull down the altar of Baal that belongs to your father, and cut down the sacred pole[s] that is beside it; 26 and build an altar to the LORD your God on the top of the stronghold here, in proper order; then take the second bull, and offer it as a burnt offering with the wood of the sacred pole[s] that you shall cut down." 27 So Gideon took ten of his servants, and did as the LORD had told him; but because he was too afraid of his family and the townspeople to do it by day, he did it by night.

28   When the townspeople rose early in the morning, the altar of Baal was broken down, and the sacred pole[s] beside it was cut down, and the second bull was offered on the altar that had been built. 29 So they said to one another, "Who has done this?" After searching and inquiring, they were told, "Gideon son of Joash did it." 30 Then the townspeople said to Joash, "Bring out your son, so that he may die, for he has pulled down the altar of Baal and cut down the sacred pole[s] beside it." 31 But Joash said to all who were arrayed against him, "Will you contend for Baal? Or will you defend his cause? Whoever contends for him shall be put to death by morning. If he is a god, let him contend for himself, because his altar has been pulled down." 32 Therefore on that day Gideon[t] was called Jerubbaal, that is to say, "Let Baal contend against him," because he pulled down his altar.

33   Then all the Midianites and the Amalekites and the people of the east came together, and crossing the Jordan they encamped in the Valley of Jezreel. 34 But the spirit of the LORD took possession of Gideon; and he sounded the trumpet, and the Abiezrites were called out to follow him. 35 He sent messengers throughout all Manasseh, and they too were called out to follow him. He also sent messengers to Asher, Zebulun, and Naphtali, and they went up to meet them.

5. *Gideon puts out the fleece*

36   Then Gideon said to God, "In order to see whether you will deliver Israel by my hand, as you have said, 37 I am going to lay a fleece of wool on the threshing floor; if there is dew on the fleece alone, and it is dry on all the ground, then I shall know that you will deliver Israel by my hand, as you have said." 38 And it was so. When they rose early next morning and squeezed the fleece, he wrung enough dew from the fleece to fill a bowl with water. 39 Then Gideon said to God, "Do not let your anger burn against me, let me speak one more time; let me, please, make trial with the fleece just once more; let it be dry only on the fleece, and on all the

6.25
Ex 34.13;
Deut 7.5

6.28
1 Kings 16.32

6.32
Judg 7.1;
1 Sam 12.11

6.33
v. 3;
Josh 17.16
6.34
Judg 3.10,
27;
1 Chr 12.18;
2 Chr 24.20

6.37
see Ex 4.3-7

6.39
Gen 18.32

---

[s] Heb *Asherah*   [t] Heb *he*

6.24 *The LORD is peace.* In Jer 33.16 the Lord is said to be our righteousness; here we learn that he is also our peace (see Eph 2.14).
6.31 Joash, Gideon's father, asked the right question: Is it not folly to pray to Baal and to solicit his help when he cannot avenge himself on the person who has pulled down his statue down? And we might well ask: If our God were so weak that he could not help himself, could we expect him to be able to help us? In fact, however, he is Almighty God; he can defend himself and protect us.
6.34 *the spirit of the LORD took possession of Gideon.* See note on 3.10. Gideon was empowered by the

Spirit of God so that he could not fail. But see also next note.
6.37 Gideon wanted to be sure that the Spirit of God was with him and that he knew the will of God. Therefore he used the fleece to obtain an outward sign from God. Once he was certain, he led the campaign against the Midianites and won a spectacular victory. Often in Scripture, God provided external evidence by which his people could know he was at work. The Pharaoh saw what the rods of Aaron and Moses could do. At Carmel, God sent fire from heaven. At Pentecost, he sent the wind, the fire, and the gift of tongues.

ground let there be dew." 40 And God did so that night. It was dry on the fleece only, and on all the ground there was dew.

6. *The defeat of the Midianites*

a. *The selection of the three hundred*

7.1
Judg 6.32

7 Then Jerubbaal (that is, Gideon) and all the troops that were with him rose early and encamped beside the spring of Harod; and the camp of Midian was north of them, below*u* the hill of Moreh, in the valley.

7.2
Deut 8.17;
Isa 10.13;
2 Cor 4.7
7.3
Deut 20.8

2 The Lord said to Gideon, "The troops with you are too many for me to give the Midianites into their hand. Israel would only take the credit away from me, saying, 'My own hand has delivered me.' 3 Now therefore proclaim this in the hearing of the troops, 'Whoever is fearful and trembling, let him return home.' " Thus Gideon sifted them out;*v* twenty-two thousand returned, and ten thousand remained.

7.4
1 Sam 14.6

4 Then the Lord said to Gideon, "The troops are still too many; take them down to the water and I will sift them out for you there. When I say, 'This one shall go with you,' he shall go with you; and when I say, 'This one shall not go with you,' he shall not go." 5 So he brought the troops down to the water; and the Lord said to Gideon, "All those who lap the water with their tongues, as a dog laps, you shall put to one side; all those who kneel down to drink, putting their hands to their mouths,*w* you shall put to the other side." 6 The number of those that lapped was three hundred; but all the rest of the troops knelt down to drink water.

7.7
1 Sam 14.6

7 Then the Lord said to Gideon, "With the three hundred that lapped I will deliver you, and give the Midianites into your hand. Let all the others go to their homes." 8 So he took the jars of the troops from their hands,*x* and their trumpets; and he sent all the rest of Israel back to their own tents, but retained the three hundred. The camp of Midian was below him in the valley.

b. *The prophecy against Midian*

7.9
Josh 2.24;
10.8; 11.6
7.11
vv. 13-15

9 That same night the Lord said to him, "Get up, attack the camp; for I have given it into your hand. 10 But if you fear to attack, go down to the camp with your servant Purah; 11 and you shall hear what they say, and afterward your hands shall be strengthened to attack the camp." Then he went down with his servant Purah to the outposts of the armed men that were in the camp. 12 The Midianites and the Amalekites and all the people of the east lay along the valley as thick as locusts; and their camels were without number, countless as the sand on the seashore. 13 When Gideon arrived, there was a man telling a dream to his comrade; and he said, "I had a dream, and in it a cake of barley bread tumbled into the camp of Midian, and came to the tent, and struck it so that it fell; it turned upside down, and the tent collapsed." 14 And his comrade answered,

7.12
Judg 6.5;
8.10;
Josh 11.4

7.14
v. 20

u Heb *from*   *v* Cn: Heb *home, and depart from Mount Gilead' "*   *w* Heb places the words *putting their hands to their mouths* after the word *lapped* in verse 6   *x* Cn: Heb *So the people took provisions in their hands*

7.2,3 The army consisted of 32,000 soldiers. Gideon thought the number too few. God told him he had more than he needed. Ten thousand went home almost immediately, fearful of the coming battle.
7.7 When the number God wanted was reduced to three hundred, everyone else went home; God promised to deliver Israel with this tiny number. God chose to glorify himself by making certain that Gideon and his band could not, by themselves, win the victory. When the fight was over they would have to give God the glory. And this would diminish the stature of Baal, in whom they had sinfully placed their trust.
7.9 No intelligent commander in his right mind

would attack the vast army of the enemy with three hundred soldiers. Yet when Gideon was told to go ahead, he had no choice but to do so. God gave him further evidence to strengthen his faith (7.13,14); consequently, he raised an altar and worshiped God. He assured his troops that God had "given it into your hand." All they needed to do was obey orders.
7.12 The vast numbers of the enemy were pitted against Gideon with a mere three hundred followers armed with trumpets, jars, and torches. From the human perspective, who would suppose that Gideon would emerge victorious? But God can deliver his people at any time, regardless of the size of the enemy.

"This is no other than the sword of Gideon son of Joash, a man of Israel; into his hand God has given Midian and all the army."

c. Battle orders

15 When Gideon heard the telling of the dream and its interpretation, he worshiped; and he returned to the camp of Israel, and said, "Get up; for the LORD has given the army of Midian into your hand." 16 After he divided the three hundred men into three companies, and put trumpets into the hands of all of them, and empty jars, with torches inside the jars, 17 he said to them, "Look at me, and do the same; when I come to the outskirts of the camp, do as I do. 18 When I blow the trumpet, I and all who are with me, then you also blow the trumpets around the whole camp, and shout, 'For the LORD and for Gideon!' "

d. The flight of the Midianites

19 So Gideon and the hundred who were with him came to the outskirts of the camp at the beginning of the middle watch, when they had just set the watch; and they blew the trumpets and smashed the jars that were in their hands. 20 So the three companies blew the trumpets and broke the jars, holding in their left hands the torches, and in their right hands the trumpets to blow; and they cried, "A sword for the LORD and for Gideon!" 21 Every man stood in his place all around the camp, and all the men in camp ran; they cried out and fled. 22 When they blew the three hundred trumpets, the LORD set every man's sword against his fellow and against all the army; and the army fled as far as Beth-shittah toward Zererah,y as far as the border of Abel-meholah, by Tabbath. 23 And the men of Israel were called out from Naphtali and from Asher and from all Manasseh, and they pursued after the Midianites.

24 Then Gideon sent messengers throughout all the hill country of Ephraim, saying, "Come down against the Midianites and seize the waters against them, as far as Beth-barah, and also the Jordan." So all the men of Ephraim were called out, and they seized the waters as far as Beth-barah, and also the Jordan. 25 They captured the two captains of Midian, Oreb and Zeeb; they killed Oreb at the rock of Oreb, and Zeeb they killed at the wine press of Zeeb, as they pursued the Midianites. They brought the heads of Oreb and Zeeb to Gideon beyond the Jordan.

e. Gideon's trouble with Ephraim

8 Then the Ephraimites said to him, "What have you done to us, not to call us when you went to fight against the Midianites?" And they upbraided him violently. 2 So he said to them, "What have I done now in comparison with you? Is not the gleaning of the grapes of Ephraim better than the vintage of Abiezer? 3 God has given into your hands the captains of Midian, Oreb and Zeeb; what have I been able to do in comparison with you?" When he said this, their anger against him subsided.

f. Succoth and Penuel refuse Gideon supplies

4 Then Gideon came to the Jordan and crossed over, he and the three hundred who were with him, exhausted and famished.z 5 So he said to

y Another reading is Zeredah   z Gk: Heb pursuing

7.15
1 Sam 15.31

7.18
vv. 14, 20

7.20
v. 14

7.21
2 Kings 7.7
7.22
Josh 6.4;
16.20;
1 Sam 14.20
7.23
Judg 6.35

7.24
Judg 3.27, 28

7.25
Judg 8.3, 4;
Ps 83.11;
Isa 10.26

8.1
Judg 12.1

8.3
Judg 7.24, 25

8.5
Gen 33.17

7.22 In the darkness of the night the trumpets and lights frightened the enemies out of their wits. Then God confused them so that they fought against each other and killed each other. God can still make the enemies of the church destroy one another.
8.1 Gideon was from the tribe of Manasseh, descendants of Joseph's older son. The Ephraimites, who also claimed Joseph as their ancestor, peevishly picked a quarrel with Gideon as to why he had not

called on them when he went after the Midianites. Gideon used a soft answer to turn away their anger. He suggested that they had done far more than he, for the fleeing princes of Midian had fallen into their hands. Compared to what you have done, he suggested, I have not done as much. The Ephraimites were satisfied.
8.5 When Gideon crossed the Jordan, chasing the two kings of Midian, Zebah and Zalmunna, he re-

the people of Succoth, "Please give some loaves of bread to my followers, for they are exhausted, and I am pursuing Zebah and Zalmunna, the kings of Midian." 6 But the officials of Succoth said, "Do you already have in your possession the hands of Zebah and Zalmunna, that we should give bread to your army?" 7 Gideon replied, "Well then, when the LORD has given Zebah and Zalmunna into my hand, I will trample your flesh on the thorns of the wilderness and on briers." 8 From there he went up to Penuel, and made the same request of them; and the people of Penuel answered him as the people of Succoth had answered. 9 So he said to the people of Penuel, "When I come back victorious, I will break down this tower."

g. The capture of Zebah and Zalmunna

10 Now Zebah and Zalmunna were in Karkor with their army, about fifteen thousand men, all who were left of all the army of the people of the east; for one hundred twenty thousand men bearing arms had fallen. 11 So Gideon went up by the caravan route east of Nobah and Jogbehah, and attacked the army; for the army was off its guard. 12 Zebah and Zalmunna fled; and he pursued them and took the two kings of Midian, Zebah and Zalmunna, and threw all the army into a panic.

h. The punishment of Succoth and Penuel

13 When Gideon son of Joash returned from the battle by the ascent of Heres, 14 he caught a young man, one of the people of Succoth, and questioned him; and he listed for him the officials and elders of Succoth, seventy-seven people. 15 Then he came to the people of Succoth, and said, "Here are Zebah and Zalmunna, about whom you taunted me, saying, 'Do you already have in your possession the hands of Zebah and Zalmunna, that we should give bread to your troops who are exhausted?' " 16 So he took the elders of the city and he took thorns of the wilderness and briers and with them he trampled* the people of Succoth. 17 He also broke down the tower of Penuel, and killed the men of the city.

i. The death of Zebah and Zalmunna

18 Then he said to Zebah and Zalmunna, "What about the men whom you killed at Tabor?" They answered, "As you are, so were they, every one of them; they resembled the sons of a king." 19 And he replied, "They were my brothers, the sons of my mother; as the LORD lives, if you had saved them alive, I would not kill you." 20 So he said to Jether his firstborn, "Go kill them!" But the boy did not draw his sword, for he was afraid, because he was still a boy. 21 Then Zebah and Zalmunna said, "You come and kill us; for as the man is, so is his strength." So Gideon proceeded to kill Zebah and Zalmunna; and he took the crescents that were on the necks of their camels.

7. Gideon refuses the kingship and makes an ephod

22 Then the Israelites said to Gideon, "Rule over us, you and your

a With verse 7, Compare Gk: Heb he taught

Marginal references:
8.6 v. 15
8.7 Judg 7.15
8.8 Gen 32.30, 31
8.9 v. 18
8.12 Ps 83.11
8.15 v. 6
8.16 v. 7
8.17 v. 9
8.18 Judg 4.6
8.21 Ps 83.11; v. 26

---

quested bread from the people of Succoth, who refused to give it to him. They feared that the Midianite princes he was pursuing might escape, come back, and hurt them for helping Gideon. The people of Penuel responded the same way. He promised Succoth and Penuel that he would repay them for their enmity when he had finished his job.
8.16,17 Gideon returned to pay off his debt to Succoth and Penuel. After showing them the captured Midianite kings, Zebah and Zalmunna, he disciplined the people of Succoth severely with thorns and briers, tore down the tower of Penuel, and killed the men of

that city.
8.20 Jether, Gideon's firstborn, was asked by his father to slay the two kings, but his youth and a sense of fear led him to decline what was obviously both a honor to him and an indignity to the kings (i.e., to be slain by a youth). So Gideon slew them himself.
8.22 Since Israel still lived under a theocracy, they should never have proposed to make Gideon ruler over them. We do not know whether it was modesty or a spiritual sense of discernment that kept him from doing so. Either way, his decision was wise.

son and your grandson also; for you have delivered us out of the hand of Midian." 23 Gideon said to them, "I will not rule over you, and my son will not rule over you; the LORD will rule over you." 24 Then Gideon said to them, "Let me make a request of you; each of you give me an earring he has taken as booty." (For the enemy[b] had golden earrings, because they were Ishmaelites.) 25 "We will willingly give them," they answered. So they spread a garment, and each threw into it an earring he had taken as booty. 26 The weight of the golden earrings that he requested was one thousand seven hundred shekels of gold (apart from the crescents and the pendants and the purple garments worn by the kings of Midian, and the collars that were on the necks of their camels). 27 Gideon made an ephod of it and put it in his town, in Ophrah, and all Israel prostituted themselves to it there, and it became a snare to Gideon and to his family. 28 So Midian was subdued before the Israelites, and they lifted up their heads no more. So the land had rest forty years in the days of Gideon.

8. Gideon's death

29 Jerubbaal son of Joash went to live in his own house. 30 Now Gideon had seventy sons, his own offspring, for he had many wives. 31 His concubine who was in Shechem also bore him a son, and he named him Abimelech. 32 Then Gideon son of Joash died at a good old age, and was buried in the tomb of his father Joash at Ophrah of the Abiezrites.

9. Israel's unfaithfulness after Gideon's death

33 As soon as Gideon died, the Israelites relapsed and prostituted themselves with the Baals, making Baal-berith their god. 34 The Israelites did not remember the LORD their God, who had rescued them from the hand of all their enemies on every side; 35 and they did not exhibit loyalty to the house of Jerubbaal (that is, Gideon) in return for all the good that he had done to Israel.

J. Abimelech son of Gideon

1. He murders seventy of his brothers and becomes king of Shechem

9 Now Abimelech son of Jerubbaal went to Shechem to his mother's kinsfolk and said to them and to the whole clan of his mother's family, 2 "Say in the hearing of all the lords of Shechem, 'Which is better for you, that all seventy of the sons of Jerubbaal rule over you, or that one rule over you?' Remember also that I am your bone and your flesh." 3 So his mother's kinsfolk spoke all these words on his behalf in the hearing of all the lords of Shechem; and their hearts inclined to follow Abimelech, for they said, "He is our brother." 4 They gave him seventy pieces of silver out of the temple of Baal-berith with which Abimelech hired worthless and reckless fellows, who followed him. 5 He went to his father's house at Ophrah, and killed his brothers the sons of Jerubbaal, seventy men, on one stone; but Jotham, the youngest son of Jerubbaal, survived, for he hid himself. 6 Then all the lords of Shechem and all Beth-millo came

[b] Heb they

Margin references

8.23 1 Sam 8.7; 10.19; 12.12

8.27 Judg 17.5; Ps 106.39; Deut 7.16
8.28 Judg 5.31

8.29 Judg 7.1
8.30 Judg 9.2, 5
8.31 Judg 9.1

8.33 Judg 2.17, 19; 9.4, 46
8.34 Judg 3.7; Deut 4.9

9.1 Judg 8.31

9.2 Judg 8.30; Gen 29.14

9.4 Judg 8.33

9.5 v. 2

8.27 *Ephod* usually referred to the priestly garment of white linen worn upon the high priest's chest. Here, however, it seems to refer to some kind of image or idol set up in the city. It became an object of idolatrous worship.
8.33 *Baal-berith*, or, "Baal (Lord) of the Covenant." Baal-berith was the god worshiped by the Canaanites at Shechem and elsewhere. In 9.46 he is called El-berith, "God of the Covenant." Arche-

ologists have found the ruins of a temple to this god.
9.1 Abimelech was Gideon's son by a concubine. Whereas his father had refused to start a monarchy, his son had no qualms about seeking kingly status. He slew his seventy brothers, except for Jotham (who escaped), and was made king (v. 6).
9.6 In naming Abimelech king, the Israelites did not consult God or any of his representatives. Thus

together, and they went and made Abimelech king, by the oak of the pillar[c] at Shechem.

2. *Jotham's parable of the bramble*

9.7
Deut 11.29;
27.12;
Jn 4.20

7 When it was told to Jotham, he went and stood on the top of Mount Gerizim, and cried aloud and said to them, "Listen to me, you lords of Shechem, so that God may listen to you.

8 The trees once went out
    to anoint a king over themselves.
So they said to the olive tree,
    'Reign over us.'
9 The olive tree answered them,
    'Shall I stop producing my rich oil
      by which gods and mortals are honored,
      and go to sway over the trees?'
10 Then the trees said to the fig tree,
    'You come and reign over us.'
11 But the fig tree answered them,
    'Shall I stop producing my sweetness
      and my delicious fruit,
      and go to sway over the trees?'
12 Then the trees said to the vine,
    'You come and reign over us.'
13 But the vine said to them,
    'Shall I stop producing my wine
      that cheers gods and mortals,
      and go to sway over the trees?'
14 So all the trees said to the bramble,
    'You come and reign over us.'
15 And the bramble said to the trees,

9.15
Isa 30.2;
v. 20

    'If in good faith you are anointing me king over you,
      then come and take refuge in my shade;
    but if not, let fire come out of the bramble
      and devour the cedars of Lebanon.'

3. *The application of the parable*

9.16
Judg 8.35

16 "Now therefore, if you acted in good faith and honor when you made Abimelech king, and if you have dealt well with Jerubbaal and his house, and have done to him as his actions deserved— 17for my father fought for you, and risked his life, and rescued you from the hand of

9.18
vv. 5, 6;
Judg 8.31

Midian; 18but you have risen up against my father's house this day, and have killed his sons, seventy men on one stone, and have made Abimelech, the son of his slave woman, king over the lords of Shechem, because he

9.19
Judg 8.35

is your kinsman— 19if, I say, you have acted in good faith and honor with Jerubbaal and with his house this day, then rejoice in Abimelech, and let him also rejoice in you; 20but if not, let fire come out from Abimelech, and devour the lords of Shechem, and Beth-millo; and let fire come out from the lords of Shechem, and from Beth-millo, and devour Abimelech." 21Then Jotham ran away and fled, going to Beer, where he remained for fear of his brother Abimelech.

4. *Discord between Abimelech and Shechem*

9.23
1 Sam 16.14;
18.9, 10

22 Abimelech ruled over Israel three years. 23But God sent an evil spirit between Abimelech and the lords of Shechem; and the lords of

[c] Cn: Meaning of Heb uncertain

the action was doomed to failure. Later, a woman dropped a millstone on Abimelech's head, fracturing his skull (v. 53). Then, upon Abimelech's insistence, his armor-bearer finished the job (v. 54).

Shechem dealt treacherously with Abimelech. 24 This happened so that the violence done to the seventy sons of Jerubbaal might be avenged[d] and their blood be laid on their brother Abimelech, who killed them, and on the lords of Shechem, who strengthened his hands to kill his brothers. 25 So, out of hostility to him, the lords of Shechem set ambushes on the mountain tops. They robbed all who passed by them along that way; and it was reported to Abimelech.

5. *The revolt of Gaal*

26 When Gaal son of Ebed moved into Shechem with his kinsfolk, the lords of Shechem put confidence in him. 27 They went out into the field and gathered the grapes from their vineyards, trod them, and celebrated. Then they went into the temple of their god, ate and drank, and ridiculed Abimelech. 28 Gaal son of Ebed said, "Who is Abimelech, and who are we of Shechem, that we should serve him? Did not the son of Jerubbaal and Zebul his officer serve the men of Hamor father of Shechem? Why then should we serve him? 29 If only this people were under my command! Then I would remove Abimelech; I would say[e] to him, 'Increase your army, and come out.' "

6. *Abimelech informed of Gaal's treachery*

30 When Zebul the ruler of the city heard the words of Gaal son of Ebed, his anger was kindled. 31 He sent messengers to Abimelech at Arumah,[f] saying, "Look, Gaal son of Ebed and his kinsfolk have come to Shechem, and they are stirring up[g] the city against you. 32 Now therefore, go by night, you and the troops that are with you, and lie in wait in the fields. 33 Then early in the morning, as soon as the sun rises, get up and rush on the city; and when he and the troops that are with him come out against you, you may deal with them as best you can."

7. *Abimelech quells Gaal's revolt*

34 So Abimelech and all the troops with him got up by night and lay in wait against Shechem in four companies. 35 When Gaal son of Ebed went out and stood in the entrance of the gate of the city, Abimelech and the troops with him rose from the ambush. 36 And when Gaal saw them, he said to Zebul, "Look, people are coming down from the mountain tops!" And Zebul said to him, "The shadows on the mountains look like people to you." 37 Gaal spoke again and said, "Look, people are coming down from Tabbur-erez, and one company is coming from the direction of Elon-meonenim."[h] 38 Then Zebul said to him, "Where is your boast[i] now, you who said, 'Who is Abimelech, that we should serve him?' Are not these the troops you made light of? Go out now and fight with them." 39 So Gaal went out at the head of the lords of Shechem, and fought with Abimelech. 40 Abimelech chased him, and he fled before him. Many fell wounded, up to the entrance of the gate. 41 So Abimelech resided at Arumah; and Zebul drove out Gaal and his kinsfolk, so that they could not live on at Shechem.

8. *Abimelech razes Shechem*

42 On the following day the people went out into the fields. When

9.24
vv. 56, 57;
Deut 27.25;
Num 35.33

9.27
Judg 8.33

9.28
Gen 34.2, 6

9.29
2 Sam 15.4

9.33
1 Sam 10.7

9.37
Ezek 38.12

9.38
vv. 28, 29

9.39
Gen 35.4

d Heb *might come*   *e* Gk: Heb *and he said*   *f* Cn See 9.41. Heb *Tormah*   *g* Cn: Heb *are besieging*   *h* That is *Diviners' Oak*   *i* Heb *mouth*

9.34ff Abimelech came down on Shechem to do battle with Gaal. Zebul taunted him and challenged him to go out and fight Abimelech. He did so and was defeated; therefore, he and his kinsmen could no longer live in Shechem.

9.42ff Little did Zebul know that what he had done would lead to the razing of Shechem. Following the defeat of Gaal, Abimelech came to Shechem, slew the inhabitants, razed the city, and sowed it with salt. The people of Shechem, who had made Abimelech

Abimelech was told, 43 he took his troops and divided them into three companies, and lay in wait in the fields. When he looked and saw the people coming out of the city, he rose against them and killed them. 44 Abimelech and the company that was[j] with him rushed forward and stood at the entrance of the gate of the city, while the two companies rushed on all who were in the fields and killed them. 45 Abimelech fought against the city all that day; he took the city, and killed the people that were in it; and he razed the city and sowed it with salt.

9. The Tower of Shechem burned

46 When all the lords of the Tower of Shechem heard of it, they entered the stronghold of the temple of El-berith. 47 Abimelech was told that all the lords of the Tower of Shechem were gathered together. 48 So Abimelech went up to Mount Zalmon, he and all the troops that were with him. Abimelech took an ax in his hand, cut down a bundle of brushwood, and took it up and laid it on his shoulder. Then he said to the troops with him, "What you have seen me do, do quickly, as I have done." 49 So every one of the troops cut down a bundle and following Abimelech put it against the stronghold, and they set the stronghold on fire over them, so that all the people of the Tower of Shechem also died, about a thousand men and women.

10. Abimelech's death

50 Then Abimelech went to Thebez, and encamped against Thebez, and took it. 51 But there was a strong tower within the city, and all the men and women and all the lords of the city fled to it and shut themselves in; and they went to the roof of the tower. 52 Abimelech came to the tower, and fought against it, and came near to the entrance of the tower to burn it with fire. 53 But a certain woman threw an upper millstone on Abimelech's head, and crushed his skull. 54 Immediately he called to the young man who carried his armor and said to him, "Draw your sword and kill me, so people will not say about me, 'A woman killed him.' " So the young man thrust him through, and he died. 55 When the Israelites saw that Abimelech was dead, they all went home. 56 Thus God repaid Abimelech for the crime he committed against his father in killing his seventy brothers; 57 and God also made all the wickedness of the people of Shechem fall back on their heads, and on them came the curse of Jotham son of Jerubbaal.

K. The judgeship of Tola

10 After Abimelech, Tola son of Puah son of Dodo, a man of Issachar, who lived at Shamir in the hill country of Ephraim, rose to deliver Israel. 2 He judged Israel twenty-three years. Then he died, and was buried at Shamir.

L. The judgeship of Jair

3 After him came Jair the Gileadite, who judged Israel twenty-two years. 4 He had thirty sons who rode on thirty donkeys; and they had thirty towns, which are in the land of Gilead, and are called Havvoth-jair to this day. 5 Jair died, and was buried in Kamon.

j Vg and some Gk Mss: Heb companies that were

Margin references:
9.45 v. 20; Deut 29.23
9.46 Judg 8.33
9.48 Ps 68.14
9.50 2 Sam 11.21
9.53 v. 50
9.56 v. 24; Ps 94.23
9.57 v. 20
10.1 Judg 2.16
10.4 Num 32.41

ruler, had now paid for their transgressions.
9.50ff This section records Abimelech's gruesome death at the hands of a woman and his armor-bearer. Verse 56 sums up the matter: "Thus God repaid Abimelech for the crime he committed against his father in killing his seventy brothers." God is known and glorified by the judgments he executes.

M. *The judgeship of Jephthah*

1. *The unfaithfulness and oppression*

6 The Israelites again did what was evil in the sight of the LORD, worshiping the Baals and the Astartes, the gods of Aram, the gods of Sidon, the gods of Moab, the gods of the Ammonites, and the gods of the Philistines. Thus they abandoned the LORD, and did not worship him. 7 So the anger of the LORD was kindled against Israel, and he sold them into the hand of the Philistines and into the hand of the Ammonites, 8 and they crushed and oppressed the Israelites that year. For eighteen years they oppressed all the Israelites that were beyond the Jordan in the land of the Amorites, which is in Gilead. 9 The Ammonites also crossed the Jordan to fight against Judah and against Benjamin and against the house of Ephraim; so that Israel was greatly distressed.

2. *Israel cries to the LORD for deliverance*

10 So the Israelites cried to the LORD, saying, "We have sinned against you, because we have abandoned our God and have worshiped the Baals." 11 And the LORD said to the Israelites, "Did I not deliver you[k] from the Egyptians and from the Amorites, from the Ammonites and from the Philistines? 12 The Sidonians also, and the Amalekites, and the Maonites, oppressed you; and you cried to me, and I delivered you out of their hand. 13 Yet you have abandoned me and worshiped other gods; therefore I will deliver you no more. 14 Go and cry to the gods whom you have chosen; let them deliver you in the time of your distress." 15 And the Israelites said to the LORD, "We have sinned; do to us whatever seems good to you; but deliver us this day!" 16 So they put away the foreign gods from among them and worshiped the LORD; and he could no longer bear to see Israel suffer.

17 Then the Ammonites were called to arms, and they encamped in Gilead; and the Israelites came together, and they encamped at Mizpah. 18 The commanders of the people of Gilead said to one another, "Who will begin the fight against the Ammonites? He shall be head over all the inhabitants of Gilead."

3. *Jephthah's background*

11 Now Jephthah the Gileadite, the son of a prostitute, was a mighty warrior. Gilead was the father of Jephthah. 2 Gilead's wife also bore him sons; and when his wife's sons grew up, they drove Jephthah away, saying to him, "You shall not inherit anything in our father's house; for you are the son of another woman." 3 Then Jephthah fled from his brothers and lived in the land of Tob. Outlaws collected around Jephthah and went raiding with him.

---

[k] Heb lacks *Did I not deliver you*

Margin references:

10.6 Judg 2.11-13; Deut 31.16, 17; 32.15
10.7 Judg 2.14
10.10 1 Sam 12.10
10.11 Ex 14.30; Num 21.21; 24.25; Judg 3.12, 13, 31
10.12 Judg 5.19; Ps 106.42, 43
10.14 Deut 32.37
10.15 1 Sam 3.18
10.16 Josh 24.23; Jer 18.7, 8; Deut 32.36; Ps 106.44, 45
10.17 Judg 11.29
10.18 Judg 11.8, 11
11.1 Heb 11.32
11.3 2 Sam 10.6, 8

10.6 Once again Israel falls into apostasy. This time they serve a number of gods from the surrounding nations, totally abandoning the true God. The Israelites on the east bank of Jordan were the first to be oppressed. The oppression spread, and the tribes on the west bank began to feel the weight of their enemies as well. Ironically, Israel found that worshiping other gods did not improve their condition; it only made it worse.
10.14 The Israelites found themselves in great distress, so they turned to the true God. He rebuked them by suggesting that if the gods they were serving were as great as they thought they were, then those gods should deliver them from their distress.

Through this rebuke they came to realize how weak those false gods really were.
10.16 Israel repented and turned to the true God. God responded to their repentance, for he grieved over their suffering. Once again God sent someone to deliver them—a judge named Jephthah.
11.1 God sometimes used strange instruments to accomplish his purposes. Jephthah was a son of a prostitute, not a wife or even a concubine. He was thrust out of his father's house, suffering indignity for something he had no control over. He became a mighty warrior and led a band of rabble in raids. When the Gileadites were attacked by the Ammonites, they appealed to Jephthah for help.

4. *Israel appeals to Jephthah for deliverance*

11.4
Judg 10.9, 17
4 After a time the Ammonites made war against Israel. 5 And when the Ammonites made war against Israel, the elders of Gilead went to bring Jephthah from the land of Tob. 6 They said to Jephthah, "Come and be our commander, so that we may fight with the Ammonites." 7 But Jephthah said to the elders of Gilead, "Are you not the very ones who rejected me and drove me out of my father's house? So why do you come to me now when you are in trouble?"
11.8
Judg 10.18
8 The elders of Gilead said to Jephthah, "Nevertheless, we have now turned back to you, so that you may go with us and fight with the Ammonites, and become head over us, over all the inhabitants of Gilead." 9 Jephthah said to the elders of Gilead, "If you bring me home again to fight with the Ammonites, and the LORD gives them over to me, I will be your head."
11.10
Jer 42.5
10 And the elders of Gilead said to Jephthah, "The LORD will be witness between us; we will surely do as you say." 11 So Jephthah went with the elders of Gilead, and the people
11.11
v. 8;
Judg 10.17
made him head and commander over them; and Jephthah spoke all his words before the LORD at Mizpah.

5. *The Ammonites want East Canaan*

12 Then Jephthah sent messengers to the king of the Ammonites and said, "What is there between you and me, that you have come to me to fight against my land?" 13 The king of the Ammonites answered the
11.13
Num 21.24-26
messengers of Jephthah, "Because Israel, on coming from Egypt, took away my land from the Arnon to the Jabbok and to the Jordan; now therefore restore it peaceably." 14 Once again Jephthah sent messengers to the king of the Ammonites 15 and said to him: "Thus says Jephthah:
11.15
Deut 2.9, 19
Israel did not take away the land of Moab or the land of the Ammonites, 16 but when they came up from Egypt, Israel went through the wilderness
11.16
Num 14.25;
20.1, 14-21
to the Red Sea*l* and came to Kadesh. 17 Israel then sent messengers to the king of Edom, saying, 'Let us pass through your land'; but the king of Edom would not listen. They also sent to the king of Moab, but he would not consent. So Israel remained at Kadesh. 18 Then they journeyed
11.18
Num 21.4;
Deut 2.1-9,
18, 19
through the wilderness, went around the land of Edom and the land of Moab, arrived on the east side of the land of Moab, and camped on the other side of the Arnon. They did not enter the territory of Moab, for the Arnon was the boundary of Moab. 19 Israel then sent messengers to King
11.19
Num 21.21,
22;
Deut 2.26, 27
Sihon of the Amorites, king of Heshbon; and Israel said to him, 'Let us pass through your land to our country.' 20 But Sihon did not trust Israel
11.20
Num 21.23;
Deut 2.32
to pass through his territory; so Sihon gathered all his people together, and encamped at Jahaz, and fought with Israel. 21 Then the LORD, the
11.21
Num 21.24,
25;
Deut 2.33, 34
God of Israel, gave Sihon and all his people into the hand of Israel, and they defeated them; so Israel occupied all the land of the Amorites, who
11.22
Deut 2.36
inhabited that country. 22 They occupied all the territory of the Amorites from the Arnon to the Jabbok and from the wilderness to the Jordan. 23 So now the LORD, the God of Israel, has conquered the Amorites for the
11.24
Num 21.29;
1 Kings 11.7;
Josh 3.10
benefit of his people Israel. Do you intend to take their place? 24 Should you not possess what your god Chemosh gives you to possess? And should we not be the ones to possess everything that the LORD our God has
11.25
Num 22.2;
Josh 24.9
conquered for our benefit? 25 Now are you any better than King Balak son of Zippor of Moab? Did he ever enter into conflict with Israel, or did he
11.26
Num 21.25;
Deut 2.36
ever go to war with them? 26 While Israel lived in Heshbon and its villages,

l Or *Sea of Reeds*

11.14ff Jephthah first tried to settle the matter by peaceful negotiations. He indicated that the Ammonite claims to some of Israel's territory was based on a false premise. Israel had taken the land from the Amorites, not the Ammonites, and therefore the Ammonites had no cause for complaint. He attributed the

success of Israel in taking the land from the Amorites to God (v. 23). His conclusion (v. 24) is that they would keep whatever God conquered for their benefit.

11.26 *three hundred years.* This is probably a round figure; it may be that some of the judges ruled concur-

and in Aroer and its villages, and in all the towns that are along the Arnon, three hundred years, why did you not recover them within that time? 27 It is not I who have sinned against you, but you are the one who does me wrong by making war on me. Let the LORD, who is judge, decide today for the Israelites or for the Ammonites." 28 But the king of the Ammonites did not heed the message that Jephthah sent him.

11.27
Gen 16.5;
18.25; 31.53;
1 Sam 24.12,
15

6. Jephthah's vow: defeat of the Ammonites

29 Then the spirit of the LORD came upon Jephthah, and he passed through Gilead and Manasseh. He passed on to Mizpah of Gilead, and from Mizpah of Gilead he passed on to the Ammonites. 30 And Jephthah made a vow to the LORD, and said, "If you will give the Ammonites into my hand, 31 then whoever comes out of the doors of my house to meet me, when I return victorious from the Ammonites, shall be the LORD's, to be offered up by me as a burnt offering." 32 So Jephthah crossed over to the Ammonites to fight against them; and the LORD gave them into his hand. 33 He inflicted a massive defeat on them from Aroer to the neighborhood of Minnith, twenty towns, and as far as Abel-keramim. So the Ammonites were subdued before the people of Israel.

11.29
Judg 3.10

11.33
Ezek 27.17

7. Jephthah fulfills his vow

34 Then Jephthah came to his home at Mizpah; and there was his daughter coming out to meet him with timbrels and with dancing. She was his only child; he had no son or daughter except her. 35 When he saw her, he tore his clothes, and said, "Alas, my daughter! You have brought me very low; you have become the cause of great trouble to me. For I have opened my mouth to the LORD, and I cannot take back my vow." 36 She said to him, "My father, if you have opened your mouth to the LORD, do to me according to what has gone out of your mouth, now that the LORD has given you vengeance against your enemies, the Ammonites." 37 And she said to her father, "Let this thing be done for me: Grant me two months, so that I may go and wander*m* on the mountains, and bewail my virginity, my companions and I." 38 "Go," he said and sent her away for two months. So she departed, she and her companions, and bewailed her virginity on the mountains. 39 At the end of two months, she returned to her father, who did with her according to the vow he had made. She had never slept with a man. So there arose an Israelite custom that 40 for four days every year the daughters of Israel would go out to lament the daughter of Jephthah the Gileadite.

11.34
Judg 10.17;
Ex 15.20;
1 Sam 18.6;
Jer 31.4
11.35
Num 30.2;
Eccl 5.2, 4, 5
11.36
Num 30.2;
2 Sam 18.19,
31;
Lk 1.38

8. Jephthah's quarrel with Ephraim: Shibboleth or Sibboleth

12 The men of Ephraim were called to arms, and they crossed to Zaphon and said to Jephthah, "Why did you cross over to fight against the Ammonites, and did not call us to go with you? We will burn

12.1
Judg 8.1

m Cn: Heb go down

---

rently. If taken seriously, this figure establishes that the exodus took place during the fifteenth century B.C. (this is accepted by many evangelicals). This runs counter to the opinion of other scholars that it occurred during the thirteenth century.
11.29 As with some of the other judges, the Spirit of God descended on Jephthah, endowing him with the gifts and power needed to deliver Israel (see note on 3.10).
11.30ff Jephthah vowed to offer up a sacrifice if God gave him victory over the Ammonites. Scholars differ as to whether Jephthah actually offered a human sacrifice. The Hebrew term used here, 'olah, means "whole burnt offering," which required the death of

the object offered. He may well have killed his daughter, but the Scriptures do not imply that he was right in making such a vow or in executing it. His background may account for his lack of understanding (cf vv. 1–3).
11.40 The annual four-day period of lamentation became a custom in Israel (v. 39), but it is never mentioned again. Evidently, it was observed only in Gilead and never became part of the whole community's customs.
12.1 The Ephraimites complained that they should have been told of the upcoming war, for they would have joined forces with Jephthah. They threatened to use force against him because of this.

your house down over you!" 2 Jephthah said to them, "My people and I were engaged in conflict with the Ammonites who oppressed us[n] severely. But when I called you, you did not deliver me from their hand. 3 When I saw that you would not deliver me, I took my life in my hand, and crossed over against the Ammonites, and the LORD gave them into my hand. Why then have you come up to me this day, to fight against me?" 4 Then Jephthah gathered all the men of Gilead and fought with Ephraim; and the men of Gilead defeated Ephraim, because they said, "You are fugitives from Ephraim, you Gileadites—in the heart of Ephraim and Manasseh."[o] 5 Then the Gileadites took the fords of the Jordan against the Ephraimites. Whenever one of the fugitives of Ephraim said, "Let me go over," the men of Gilead would say to him, "Are you an Ephraimite?" When he said, "No," 6 they said to him, "Then say Shibboleth," and he said, "Sibboleth," for he could not pronounce it right. Then they seized him and killed him at the fords of the Jordan. Forty-two thousand of the Ephraimites fell at that time.

7 Jephthah judged Israel six years. Then Jephthah the Gileadite died, and was buried in his town in Gilead.[p]

N. The judgeship of Ibzan

8 After him Ibzan of Bethlehem judged Israel. 9 He had thirty sons. He gave his thirty daughters in marriage outside his clan and brought in thirty young women from outside for his sons. He judged Israel seven years. 10 Then Ibzan died, and was buried at Bethlehem.

O. The judgeship of Elon

11 After him Elon the Zebulunite judged Israel; and he judged Israel ten years. 12 Then Elon the Zebulunite died, and was buried at Aijalon in the land of Zebulun.

P. The judgeship of Abdon

13 After him Abdon son of Hillel the Pirathonite judged Israel. 14 He had forty sons and thirty grandsons, who rode on seventy donkeys; he judged Israel eight years. 15 Then Abdon son of Hillel the Pirathonite died, and was buried at Pirathon in the land of Ephraim, in the hill country of the Amalekites.

Q. The judgeship of Samson

1. Israel's unfaithfulness and servitude

13 The Israelites again did what was evil in the sight of the LORD, and the LORD gave them into the hand of the Philistines forty years.

---

n Gk OL, Syr H: Heb lacks *who oppressed us*   *o* Meaning of Heb uncertain: Gk omits *because . . .*
Manasseh   *p* Gk: Heb *in the towns of Gilead*

12.5–7 Jephthah controlled the fords over the Jordan River; when the Ephraimites sought to cross over, a linguistic test was employed. Although they all spoke the same language, there were regional differences in dialect. The Ephraimites said "Sibboleth" instead of "Shibboleth"; those who failed the test were slain, a total of 42,000. Jephthah's judgeship lasted only six years.
12.8–15 The judgeships of Ibzan, Elon, and Abdon are passed over swiftly. They ruled for twenty-five years, a period in which there was peace. A strange fact during all of these judgeships is that no mention

is made of Israel's high priest, or any other priest, or even the Levites. No explanation is given for this absence of Israel's spiritual leaders who were so prominent in the wilderness and in the original conquest of the land.
13.1 According to Deut 2.23, Amos 9.7, and Jer 47.4, the Philistines came from Caphtor, the island of Crete. They settled along the coast of Canaan and lodged in the foothills of the territory assigned to Dan and Judah. Samson's deliverance of Israel from the Philistines was not permanent, for the Philistines plagued Israel until David's time (see note on 14.4).

Margin cross-references:

12.3 1 Sam 19.5; 28.21; Job 13.14
12.4 Judg 3.28; 7.24
12.5 Judg 3.28; 7.24; Josh 22.11
12.7 Heb 11.32
12.14 Judg 5.10; 10.4
13.1 Judg 2.11; 1 Sam 12.9

2. The background of Samson

a. The promise to Manoah and his wife

2   There was a certain man of Zorah, of the tribe of the Danites, whose name was Manoah. His wife was barren, having borne no children. 3 And the angel of the LORD appeared to the woman and said to her, "Although you are barren, having borne no children, you shall conceive and bear a son. 4 Now be careful not to drink wine or strong drink, or to eat anything unclean, 5 for you shall conceive and bear a son. No razor is to come on his head, for the boy shall be a naziriteq to God from birth. It is he who shall begin to deliver Israel from the hand of the Philistines." 6 Then the woman came and told her husband, "A man of God came to me, and his appearance was like that of an angelr of God, most awe-inspiring; I did not ask him where he came from, and he did not tell me his name; 7 but he said to me, 'You shall conceive and bear a son. So then drink no wine or strong drink, and eat nothing unclean, for the boy shall be a naziriteq to God from birth to the day of his death.' "

b. Manoah and the angel of the LORD

8   Then Manoah entreated the LORD, and said, "O LORD, I pray, let the man of God whom you sent come to us again and teach us what we are to do concerning the boy who will be born." 9 God listened to Manoah, and the angel of God came again to the woman as she sat in the field; but her husband Manoah was not with her. 10 So the woman ran quickly and told her husband, "The man who came to me the other day has appeared to me." 11 Manoah got up and followed his wife, and came to the man and said to him, "Are you the man who spoke to this woman?" And he said, "I am." 12 Then Manoah said, "Now when your words come true, what is to be the boy's rule of life; what is he to do?" 13 The angel of the LORD said to Manoah, "Let the woman give heed to all that I said to her. 14 She may not eat of anything that comes from the vine. She is not to drink wine or strong drink, or eat any unclean thing. She is to observe everything that I commanded her."

15   Manoah said to the angel of the LORD, "Allow us to detain you, and prepare a kid for you." 16 The angel of the LORD said to Manoah, "If you detain me, I will not eat your food; but if you want to prepare a burnt offering, then offer it to the LORD." (For Manoah did not know that he was the angel of the LORD.) 17 Then Manoah said to the angel of the LORD, "What is your name, so that we may honor you when your words come true?" 18 But the angel of the LORD said to him, "Why do you ask my name? It is too wonderful."

19   So Manoah took the kid with the grain offering, and offered it on the rock to the LORD, to him who workss wonders.t 20 When the flame went up toward heaven from the altar, the angel of the LORD ascended in the flame of the altar while Manoah and his wife looked on; and they

Side references:
13.2 Josh 19.41
13.3 vv. 6, 8, 10; Judg 6.12
13.4 v. 14; Num 6.2, 3
13.5 Lk 1.15; Num 6.2, 5
13.6 1 Sam 2.27; Mt 28.3; vv. 17, 18
13.8 vv. 3, 7
13.13 vv. 4, 11
13.14 Num 6.4
13.15 v. 3
13.16 Judg 6.20
13.17 Gen 32.29
13.18 Isa 9.6
13.19 Judg 6.20, 21
13.20 Lev 9.24

q That is one separated or one consecrated   r Or the angel   s Gk Vg: Heb and working   t Heb wonders, while Manoah and his wife looked on

13.5 A nazirite was a man or a woman consecrated to God by a special vow. Samson and John the Baptist were nazirites from their mothers' wombs, i.e., committed to God before they were born (13.5; Lk 1.15). Nazirites (1) used neither wine nor strong drink (Num 6.3; Lk 1.15); (2) had no contact with grapes or any product of the vine (Num 6.3,4; Judg 13.14); (3) avoided contact with the dead (Num 6.6,7); and (4) did not shave their heads (Num 6.5; Judg 13.5; 16.17). These prohibitions continued as long as the vow was in effect. When the vow was ended, the nazirite was brought to the door of the tabernacle, the head was shaved, sacrifices were offered, and the left shoulder of a ram, along with an unleavened cake,

were presented by the priest as an offering (Num 6.13–20; Acts 18.18).
13.8 Manoah believed what his wife told him. Having confidence that they would have a son, he prayed and humbly asked that the angel might appear to him also, to instruct him as to what they should do with the boy. God heard and answered that prayer (vv. 9–14).
13.18 wonderful, or, "beyond knowledge" (see Ps 139.6).
13.20 As God had done many times before, he performed supernatural acts to confirm to Manoah and his wife the words the angel spoke. From what happened Manoah knew that it was an angel.

fell on their faces to the ground. 21 The angel of the LORD did not appear again to Manoah and his wife. Then Manoah realized that it was the angel of the LORD. 22 And Manoah said to his wife, "We shall surely die, for we have seen God." 23 But his wife said to him, "If the LORD had meant to kill us, he would not have accepted a burnt offering and a grain offering at our hands, or shown us all these things, or now announced to us such things as these."

c. *The birth of Samson*

24 The woman bore a son, and named him Samson. The boy grew, and the LORD blessed him. 25 The spirit of the LORD began to stir him in Mahaneh-dan, between Zorah and Eshtaol.

3. *Samson's marriage to the woman of Timnah*

a. *Samson falls in love*

14 Once Samson went down to Timnah, and at Timnah he saw a Philistine woman. 2 Then he came up, and told his father and mother, "I saw a Philistine woman at Timnah; now get her for me as my wife." 3 But his father and mother said to him, "Is there not a woman among your kin, or among all our^u people, that you must go to take a wife from the uncircumcised Philistines?" But Samson said to his father, "Get her for me, because she pleases me." 4 His father and mother did not know that this was from the LORD; for he was seeking a pretext to act against the Philistines. At that time the Philistines had dominion over Israel.

b. *The killing of the lion*

5 Then Samson went down with his father and mother to Timnah. When he came to the vineyards of Timnah, suddenly a young lion roared at him. 6 The spirit of the LORD rushed on him, and he tore the lion apart barehanded as one might tear apart a kid. But he did not tell his father or his mother what he had done. 7 Then he went down and talked with the woman, and she pleased Samson. 8 After a while he returned to marry her, and he turned aside to see the carcass of the lion, and there was a swarm of bees in the body of the lion, and honey. 9 He scraped it out into his hands, and went on, eating as he went. When he came to his father and mother, he gave some to them, and they ate it. But he did not tell them that he had taken the honey from the carcass of the lion.

c. *Samson's riddle at the wedding feast*

10 His father went down to the woman, and Samson made a feast there as the young men were accustomed to do. 11 When the people saw him, they brought thirty companions to be with him. 12 Samson said to them, "Let me now put a riddle to you. If you can explain it to me within the seven days of the feast, and find it out, then I will give you thirty linen garments and thirty festal garments. 13 But if you cannot explain it to me, then you shall give me thirty linen garments and thirty festal garments." So they said to him, "Ask your riddle; let us hear it." 14 He said to them,
"Out of the eater came something to eat.
Out of the strong came something sweet."

^u Cn: Heb *my*

13.24 As a nazirite, Samson was separated unto God from birth. But he started off better than he finished. He was a backslider whose fleshly nature overtook him. One small sin led to larger and more grievous ones.
13.25 The Spirit of the Lord came on Samson in mighty power, and by that power he did mighty exploits for God.

14.4 Samson married a heathen woman. This was against the will of God (see note on Deut 7.3,5). Yet God used his transgression to accomplish the divine purpose of delivering Israel from its slavery to the Philistines. Nevertheless, God's higher purpose in no way excused Samson for his sinful decisions to marry an unbeliever, visit a prostitute, or ally himself with Delilah.

Margin references:

13.21 v. 16
13.22 Judg 6.22; Deut 5.26
13.24 Heb 11.32; 1 Sam 3.19
13.25 Judg 3.10; 18.11
14.2 Gen 21.21; 34.4
14.4 Josh 11.20; Judg 13.1
14.6 Judg 3.10; 13.25
14.7 v. 3
14.12 1 Kings 10.2; Ezek 17.2; Gen 29.27

But for three days they could not explain the riddle.

d. *The solution of the riddle: the treachery of Samson's wife*

15 On the fourth[v] day they said to Samson's wife, "Coax your husband to explain the riddle to us, or we will burn you and your father's house with fire. Have you invited us here to impoverish us?" 16 So Samson's wife wept before him, saying, "You hate me; you do not really love me. You have asked a riddle of my people, but you have not explained it to me." He said to her, "Look, I have not told my father or my mother. Why should I tell you?" 17 She wept before him the seven days that their feast lasted; and because she nagged him, on the seventh day he told her. Then she explained the riddle to her people. 18 The men of the town said to him on the seventh day before the sun went down,

"What is sweeter than honey?
What is stronger than a lion?"

And he said to them,

"If you had not plowed with my heifer,
you would not have found out my riddle."

19 Then the spirit of the LORD rushed on him, and he went down to Ashkelon. He killed thirty men of the town, took their spoil, and gave the festal garments to those who had explained the riddle. In hot anger he went back to his father's house. 20 And Samson's wife was given to his companion, who had been his best man.

4. *The Philistines kill Samson's wife and father-in-law*

15 After a while, at the time of the wheat harvest, Samson went to visit his wife, bringing along a kid. He said, "I want to go into my wife's room." But her father would not allow him to go in. 2 Her father said, "I was sure that you had rejected her; so I gave her to your companion. Is not her younger sister prettier than she? Why not take her instead?" 3 Samson said to them, "This time, when I do mischief to the Philistines, I will be without blame." 4 So Samson went and caught three hundred foxes, and took some torches; and he turned the foxes[w] tail to tail, and put a torch between each pair of tails. 5 When he had set fire to the torches, he let the foxes go into the standing grain of the Philistines, and burned up the shocks and the standing grain, as well as the vineyards and[x] olive groves. 6 Then the Philistines asked, "Who has done this?" And they said, "Samson, the son-in-law of the Timnite, because he has taken Samson's wife and given her to his companion." So the Philistines came up, and burned her and her father. 7 Samson said to them, "If this is what you do, I swear I will not stop until I have taken revenge on you." 8 He struck them down hip and thigh with great slaughter; and he went down and stayed in the cleft of the rock of Etam.

5. *Samson in the hands of the Philistines*

a. *Judah delivers him*

9 Then the Philistines came up and encamped in Judah, and made a raid on Lehi. 10 The men of Judah said, "Why have you come up against us?" They said, "We have come up to bind Samson, to do to him as he did to us." 11 Then three thousand men of Judah went down to the cleft of the rock of Etam, and they said to Samson, "Do you not know that the

_v_ Gk Syr: Heb *seventh*   _w_ Heb *them*   _x_ Gk Tg Vg: Heb lacks *and*

14.18 After the Philistines had, through threats, forced Samson's wife to betray him, he disrespectfully said, "If you had not plowed with my heifer. . . ." In so doing he exhibited his distaste for the infidelity of his bride to whom he had been married for only a few days. What a way to begin a honeymoon!

15.5 Samson single-handedly avenged himself on the Philistines for their trick and for the loss of his mate, who had been given by her father to another man. The life of Samson was unique, for he was the only judge who operated by himself, without having recourse to servants or soldiers to assist him.

14.15
Judg 16.5;
15.6

14.18
v. 14

14.19
Judg 3.10

14.20
Judg 15.2;
Jn 3.29

15.2
Judg 14.20

15.6
Judg 14.15

15.9
v. 19

15.11
Judg 13.1;
14.4

Philistines are rulers over us? What then have you done to us?" He replied, "As they did to me, so I have done to them." 12 They said to him, "We have come down to bind you, so that we may give you into the hands of the Philistines." Samson answered them, "Swear to me that you yourselves will not attack me." 13 They said to him, "No, we will only bind you and give you into their hands; we will not kill you." So they bound him with two new ropes, and brought him up from the rock.

b. Samson's vengeance on the Philistines

15.14
Judg 14.19;
1 Sam 11.6

15.15
Lev 26.8;
Josh 23.10;
Judg 3.31

14 When he came to Lehi, the Philistines came shouting to meet him; and the spirit of the LORD rushed on him, and the ropes that were on his arms became like flax that had caught fire, and his bonds melted off his hands. 15 Then he found a fresh jawbone of a donkey, reached down and took it, and with it he killed a thousand men. 16 And Samson said,

"With the jawbone of a donkey,
  heaps upon heaps,
with the jawbone of a donkey
I have slain a thousand men."

17 When he had finished speaking, he threw away the jawbone; and that place was called Ramath-lehi.y

15.18
Judg 16.28

15.19
Gen 45.27;
Isa 40.29

15.20
Heb 11.32;
Judg 13.1;
16.31

18 By then he was very thirsty, and he called on the LORD, saying, "You have granted this great victory by the hand of your servant. Am I now to die of thirst, and fall into the hands of the uncircumcised?" 19 So God split open the hollow place that is at Lehi, and water came from it. When he drank, his spirit returned, and he revived. Therefore it was named En-hakkore,z which is at Lehi to this day. 20 And he judged Israel in the days of the Philistines twenty years.

6. Samson and the prostitute at Gaza

16.2
Ps 118.10-12

16 Once Samson went to Gaza, where he saw a prostitute and went in to her. 2 The Gazites were told,a "Samson has come here." So they circled around and lay in wait for him all night at the city gate. They kept quiet all night, thinking, "Let us wait until the light of the morning; then we will kill him." 3 But Samson lay only until midnight. Then at midnight he rose up, took hold of the doors of the city gate and the two posts, pulled them up, bar and all, put them on his shoulders, and carried them to the top of the hill that is in front of Hebron.

7. Samson and Delilah

a. Delilah seeks the source of Samson's strength

16.5
Judg 14.15

4 After this he fell in love with a woman in the valley of Sorek, whose name was Delilah. 5 The lords of the Philistines came to her and said to her, "Coax him, and find out what makes his strength so great, and how we may overpower him, so that we may bind him in order to subdue him; and we will each give you eleven hundred pieces of silver." 6 So Delilah said to Samson, "Please tell me what makes your strength so great, and

y That is The Hill of the Jawbone   z That is The Spring of the One who Called   a Gk: Heb lacks were told

---

15.12,13 Samson, instead of resisting the Judeans, tamely allowed them to bind him with ropes, securing from them the promise that they would not hurt him. By being delivered over to the Philistines, he would have an opportunity to slay many of them and thus begin the delivery of Israel from their slavery.
15.15 Samson's strength did not come from his nazirite vow, from his spurning of strong drink, or from his long hair. It lay in his relationship with God, of which these other things were only symbols. Samson himself acknowledged that God was the author of his

power (v. 18).
16.1 Once again Samson was on the downward path. If it was wrong to marry a pagan, it was worse to fornicate with a prostitute. His sin began with his eyes, and when lust had its way, he went in to her and broke one of the ten commandments.
16.4 Samson continued his evil pattern of life, now living in sin with someone he had not married. For money, she uncovered the true source of his power and sold her paramour into the hands of the enemy.

how you could be bound, so that one could subdue you." 7 Samson said to her, "If they bind me with seven fresh bowstrings that are not dried out, then I shall become weak, and be like anyone else." 8 Then the lords of the Philistines brought her seven fresh bowstrings that had not dried out, and she bound him with them. 9 While men were lying in wait in an inner chamber, she said to him, "The Philistines are upon you, Samson!" But he snapped the bowstrings, as a strand of fiber snaps when it touches the fire. So the secret of his strength was not known.

b. Delilah's second attempt

10 Then Delilah said to Samson, "You have mocked me and told me lies; please tell me how you could be bound." 11 He said to her, "If they bind me with new ropes that have not been used, then I shall become weak, and be like anyone else." 12 So Delilah took new ropes and bound him with them, and said to him, "The Philistines are upon you, Samson!" (The men lying in wait were in an inner chamber.) But he snapped the ropes off his arms like a thread.

16.10
vv. 13, 15

c. Delilah's third attempt

13 Then Delilah said to Samson, "Until now you have mocked me and told me lies; tell me how you could be bound." He said to her, "If you weave the seven locks of my head with the web and make it tight with the pin, then I shall become weak, and be like anyone else." 14 So while he slept, Delilah took the seven locks of his head and wove them into the web,[b] and made them tight with the pin. Then she said to him, "The Philistines are upon you, Samson!" But he awoke from his sleep, and pulled away the pin, the loom, and the web.

16.13
vv. 10, 15

d. Samson succumbs to Delilah's wiles

15 Then she said to him, "How can you say, 'I love you,' when your heart is not with me? You have mocked me three times now and have not told me what makes your strength so great." 16 Finally, after she had nagged him with her words day after day, and pestered him, he was tired to death. 17 So he told her his whole secret, and said to her, "A razor has never come upon my head; for I have been a nazirite[c] to God from my mother's womb. If my head were shaved, then my strength would leave me; I would become weak, and be like anyone else."

16.15
Judg 14.16

16.17
Mic 7.5;
Num 6.5;
Judg 13.5

e. The Philistines seize Samson

18 When Delilah realized that he had told her his whole secret, she sent and called the lords of the Philistines, saying, "This time come up, for he has told his whole secret to me." Then the lords of the Philistines came up to her, and brought the money in their hands. 19 She let him fall asleep on her lap; and she called a man, and had him shave off the seven locks of his head. He began to weaken,[d] and his strength left him. 20 Then she said, "The Philistines are upon you, Samson!" When he awoke from his sleep, he thought, "I will go out as at other times, and shake myself free." But he did not know that the LORD had left him. 21 So the Philistines seized him and gouged out his eyes. They brought him down to Gaza and bound him with bronze shackles; and he ground at the mill in the

16.19
Prov 7.26, 27

16.20
Josh 7.12;
1 Sam 16.14;
18.12

---

b Compare Gk: in verses 13-14, Heb lacks and make it tight . . . into the web   c That is one separated or one consecrated   d Gk: Heb She began to torment him

---

16.20 Samson was a Spirit-filled nazirite who performed great deeds of valor (see 14.6,19; 15.14). This verse contains the saddest words about him: he disclosed the source of his strength to Delilah. When she woke him up as the Philistines came after him, once more he thought he still had the power of the Spirit in his life. But it was gone, and "he did not know that

the LORD had left him." He had slept in the lap of his lust and awoke a prisoner of his enemies, who blinded him. He *did* repent before death, however, and was subsequently numbered among the heroes of the faith (Heb 11.32). He was justified by his faith, not by any of his deeds.

prison. 22 But the hair of his head began to grow again after it had been shaved.

f. Samson's final revenge and death

16.23
1 Sam 5.2

16.24
Dan 5.4

16.25
Judg 9.27

16.27
Deut 22.8

16.28
Judg 15.18;
Jer 15.15

16.31
Judg 15.20

23 Now the lords of the Philistines gathered to offer a great sacrifice to their god Dagon, and to rejoice; for they said, "Our god has given Samson our enemy into our hand." 24 When the people saw him, they praised their god; for they said, "Our god has given our enemy into our hand, the ravager of our country, who has killed many of us." 25 And when their hearts were merry, they said, "Call Samson, and let him entertain us." So they called Samson out of the prison, and he performed for them. They made him stand between the pillars; 26 and Samson said to the attendant who held him by the hand, "Let me feel the pillars on which the house rests, so that I may lean against them." 27 Now the house was full of men and women; all the lords of the Philistines were there, and on the roof there were about three thousand men and women, who looked on while Samson performed.

28 Then Samson called to the LORD and said, "Lord GOD, remember me and strengthen me only this once, O God, so that with this one act of revenge I may pay back the Philistines for my two eyes."e 29 And Samson grasped the two middle pillars on which the house rested, and he leaned his weight against them, his right hand on the one and his left hand on the other. 30 Then Samson said, "Let me die with the Philistines." He strained with all his might; and the house fell on the lords and all the people who were in it. So those he killed at his death were more than those he had killed during his life. 31 Then his brothers and all his family came down and took him and brought him up and buried him between Zorah and Eshtaol in the tomb of his father Manoah. He had judged Israel twenty years.

III. The appendices (17.1–21.25)

A. Micah the Ephraimite and his priest

1. Micah makes his own idols

17.3
Ex 20.4, 23;
34.17;
Lev 19.4

17 There was a man in the hill country of Ephraim whose name was Micah. 2 He said to his mother, "The eleven hundred pieces of silver that were taken from you, about which you uttered a curse, and even spoke it in my hearing,—that silver is in my possession; I took it; but now I will return it to you."f And his mother said, "May my son be blessed by the LORD!" 3 Then he returned the eleven hundred pieces of silver to his mother; and his mother said, "I consecrate the silver to the LORD from my hand for my son, to make an idol of cast metal." 4 So when he returned the money to his mother, his mother took two hundred pieces of silver, and gave it to the silversmith, who made it into an idol of cast metal; and

e Or so that I may be avenged upon the Philistines for one of my two eyes   f The words but now I will return it to you are transposed from the end of verse 3 in Heb

16.28 *remember me and strengthen me.* Samson had repented; his hair had grown and his blinded eyes turned again to the God he had sinned against and sought his help. He asked for the power he once had, and God graciously heard him. He slew more Philistines in death than he had slain in life. But he died in this incident, leaving behind for all ages a reminder of what it means to be without the presence of God in one's life.
17.1 From this point on, we read nothing more about the judges; this section of the book constitutes an appendix. The priesthood, absent in the stories connected with the judges, appears again.

17.3 This is the sad story of Micah and his mother. Micah stole eleven hundred shekels of silver. When he returned the money after she had cursed the thief, she dedicated the silver to the Lord. She then used two hundred shekels to make the graven image, breaking the second commandment. Her son was left with an idolatrous shrine and hired a Levite to be his priest. The judgment of God overtook him and the Danites took his gods away from him. These people then began to engage in idolatry. Whoever has a god or gods that can be taken away, has no real god. No one can take God from his people.

it was in the house of Micah. 5 This man Micah had a shrine, and he made an ephod and teraphim, and installed one of his sons, who became his priest. 6 In those days there was no king in Israel; all the people did what was right in their own eyes.

2. Micah hires a Levite as priest

7 Now there was a young man of Bethlehem in Judah, of the clan of Judah. He was a Levite residing there. 8 This man left the town of Bethlehem in Judah, to live wherever he could find a place. He came to the house of Micah in the hill country of Ephraim to carry on his work.g 9 Micah said to him, "From where do you come?" He replied, "I am a Levite of Bethlehem in Judah, and I am going to live wherever I can find a place." 10 Then Micah said to him, "Stay with me, and be to me a father and a priest, and I will give you ten pieces of silver a year, a set of clothes, and your living."h 11 The Levite agreed to stay with the man; and the young man became to him like one of his sons. 12 So Micah installed the Levite, and the young man became his priest, and was in the house of Micah. 13 Then Micah said, "Now I know that the LORD will prosper me, because the Levite has become my priest."

3. The Danite spies: their report

18 In those days there was no king in Israel. And in those days the tribe of the Danites was seeking for itself a territory to live in; for until then no territory among the tribes of Israel had been allotted to them. 2 So the Danites sent five valiant men from the whole number of their clan, from Zorah and from Eshtaol, to spy out the land and to explore it; and they said to them, "Go, explore the land." When they came to the hill country of Ephraim, to the house of Micah, they stayed there. 3 While they were at Micah's house, they recognized the voice of the young Levite; so they went over and asked him, "Who brought you here? What are you doing in this place? What is your business here?" 4 He said to them, "Micah did such and such for me, and he hired me, and I have become his priest." 5 Then they said to them, "Inquire of God that we may know whether the mission we are undertaking will succeed." 6 The priest replied, "Go in peace. The mission you are on is under the eye of the LORD."

7 The five men went on, and when they came to Laish, they observed the people who were there living securely, after the manner of the Sidonians, quiet and unsuspecting, lackingi nothing on earth, and possessing wealth.j Furthermore, they were far from the Sidonians and had no dealings with Aram.k 8 When they came to their kinsfolk at Zorah and Eshtaol, they said to them, "What do you report?" 9 They said, "Come, let us go up against them; for we have seen the land, and it is very good. Will you do nothing? Do not be slow to go, but enter in and possess the land. 10 When you go, you will come to an unsuspecting people. The land

g Or *Ephraim, continuing his journey*   h Heb *living, and the Levite went*   i Cn Compare 18.10: Meaning of Heb uncertain   j Meaning of Heb uncertain   k Symmachus: Heb *with anyone*

Cross references:
17.5 — Judg 18.24; 8.27; 18.14; Gen 31.19
17.6 — Judg 18.1; 19.1; Deut 12.8
17.7 — Judg 19.1; Ruth 1.1, 2; Mic 5.2; Mt 2.1
17.10 — Judg 18.19
17.12 — v. 5; Judg 13.25
18.1 — Judg 17.6; 19.1; Josh 19.47
18.2 — Judg 13.25; Josh 2.1; Judg 17.1
18.4 — Judg 17.10, 12
18.5 — 1 Kings 22.5
18.6 — 1 Kings 22.6
18.7 — vv. 27, 28; Josh 19.47
18.8 — v. 2
18.9 — Num 13.30; 1 Kings 22.3
18.10 — vv. 7, 27; Deut 8.9

17.6 *There was no king in Israel.* This statement (repeated in 18.1; 19.1; 21.25) indicates that Judges itself was written sometime during the days of the monarchy (see the introduction to Judges).

17.13 Sin against God always results in muddled thinking. Micah thought God would bless his idolatrous lifestyle because he had a Levite as his priest. But no priest or minister can shield a guilty sinner from the judgment and anger of God. Micah's priest was a counterfeit, for he allowed himself to become attached to false gods and departed from the true faith.

18.1 The *Danites* still had much land to be taken from the enemy. They had occupied the highlands. Now they wanted the fertile lowlands, but the Amorites who occupied them had iron chariots. The Danites lacked the faith they needed to secure the land God had given them.

18.5 The five spies came to Micah's home and inquired of his priest whether their effort would succeed. After consulting his idols, the priest told them to go ahead. When the spies returned home, they reported the existence of these idols in Micah's house.

is broad—God has indeed given it into your hands—a place where there is no lack of anything on earth."

11 Six hundred men of the Danite clan, armed with weapons of war, set out from Zorah and Eshtaol, 12 and went up and encamped at Kiriath-jearim in Judah. On this account that place is called Mahaneh-dan[l] to this day; it is west of Kiriath-jearim. 13 From there they passed on to the hill country of Ephraim, and came to the house of Micah.

4. The Danites take Micah's idols and priest

14 Then the five men who had gone to spy out the land (that is, Laish) said to their comrades, "Do you know that in these buildings there are an ephod, teraphim, and an idol of cast metal? Now therefore consider what you will do." 15 So they turned in that direction and came to the house of the young Levite, at the home of Micah, and greeted him. 16 While the six hundred men of the Danites, armed with their weapons of war, stood by the entrance of the gate, 17 the five men who had gone to spy out the land proceeded to enter and take the idol of cast metal, the ephod, and the teraphim.[m] The priest was standing by the entrance of the gate with the six hundred men armed with weapons of war. 18 When the men went into Micah's house and took the idol of cast metal, the ephod, and the teraphim, the priest said to them, "What are you doing?" 19 They said to him, "Keep quiet! Put your hand over your mouth, and come with us, and be to us a father and a priest. Is it better for you to be priest to the house of one person, or to be priest to a tribe and clan in Israel?" 20 Then the priest accepted the offer. He took the ephod, the teraphim, and the idol, and went along with the people.

5. Micah's failure to recover his idols

21 So they resumed their journey, putting the little ones, the livestock, and the goods in front of them. 22 When they were some distance from the home of Micah, the men who were in the houses near Micah's house were called out, and they overtook the Danites. 23 They shouted to the Danites, who turned around and said to Micah, "What is the matter that you come with such a company?" 24 He replied, "You take my gods that I made, and the priest, and go away, and what have I left? How then can you ask me, 'What is the matter?'" 25 And the Danites said to him, "You had better not let your voice be heard among us or else hot-tempered fellows will attack you, and you will lose your life and the lives of your household." 26 Then the Danites went their way. When Micah saw that they were too strong for him, he turned and went back to his home.

6. The Danites burn Laish and rebuild it

27 The Danites, having taken what Micah had made, and the priest who belonged to him, came to Laish, to a people quiet and unsuspecting, put them to the sword, and burned down the city. 28 There was no deliverer, because it was far from Sidon and they had no dealings with Aram.[n] It was in the valley that belongs to Beth-rehob. They rebuilt the city, and lived in it. 29 They named the city Dan, after their ancestor Dan,

Cross references (margin)

18.12 Judg 13.25
18.13 v. 2
18.14 Judg 17.5
18.16 v. 11
18.17 vv. 2, 14
18.19 Job 21.5; Judg 17.10
18.24 Judg 17.5
18.27 vv. 7, 10; Josh 19.47
18.28 v. 7; 2 Sam 10.6
18.29 Josh 19.47

---

l That is *Camp of Dan*   *m* Compare 17.4, 5; 18.14: Heb *teraphim and the cast metal*   *n* Cn Compare verse 7: Heb *with anyone*

18.17 Six hundred armed Danites stood by as the five spies returned to seize the idol of cast metal, the ephod, and the teraphim. The priest took the idols and went with them. Instead of serving a single household he would now have an enlarged ministry and profit more from it. Coveteousness is not limited to the laity; people in God's special service are also tempted.

18.24 The irony of Micah's situation is revealed here. He had lost his gods and his priest and had nothing left. While he had them, he thought he had everything; he had not realized he was poor, wretched, and blind. Bereft of all he had depended on, he might then have turned to the living God, but nothing in the Scriptures says he did.
18.29 *Laish*, called "Leshem" in Josh 19.47.

who was born to Israel; but the name of the city was formerly Laish.
30 Then the Danites set up the idol for themselves. Jonathan son of
Gershom, son of Moses,*o* and his sons were priests to the tribe of the
Danites until the time the land went into captivity. 31 So they maintained
as their own Micah's idol that he had made, as long as the house of God
was at Shiloh.

B. *The Levite and his concubine*

1. *The Levite recovers his concubine*

19 In those days, when there was no king in Israel, a certain Levite,
residing in the remote parts of the hill country of Ephraim, took
to himself a concubine from Bethlehem in Judah. 2 But his concubine
became angry with*p* him, and she went away from him to her father's
house at Bethlehem in Judah, and was there some four months. 3 Then
her husband set out after her, to speak tenderly to her and bring her back.
He had with him his servant and a couple of donkeys. When he reached*q*
her father's house, the girl's father saw him and came with joy to meet
him. 4 His father-in-law, the girl's father, made him stay, and he remained
with him three days; so they ate and drank, and he*r* stayed there. 5 On
the fourth day they got up early in the morning, and he prepared to go;
but the girl's father said to his son-in-law, "Fortify yourself with a bit of
food, and after that you may go." 6 So the two men sat and ate and drank
together; and the girl's father said to the man, "Why not spend the night
and enjoy yourself?" 7 When the man got up to go, his father-in-law kept
urging him until he spent the night there again. 8 On the fifth day he got
up early in the morning to leave; and the girl's father said, "Fortify
yourself." So they lingered*s* until the day declined, and the two of them
ate and drank.*t* 9 When the man with his concubine and his servant got
up to leave, his father-in-law, the girl's father, said to him, "Look, the
day has worn on until it is almost evening. Spend the night. See, the day
has drawn to a close. Spend the night here and enjoy yourself. Tomorrow
you can get up early in the morning for your journey, and go home."

2. *They spend the night at Gibeah*

10 But the man would not spend the night; he got up and departed,
and arrived opposite Jebus (that is, Jerusalem). He had with him a couple
of saddled donkeys, and his concubine was with him. 11 When they were
near Jebus, the day was far spent, and the servant said to his master,
"Come now, let us turn aside to this city of the Jebusites, and spend the
night in it." 12 But his master said to him, "We will not turn aside into
a city of foreigners, who do not belong to the people of Israel; but we
will continue on to Gibeah." 13 Then he said to his servant, "Come, let
us try to reach one of these places, and spend the night at Gibeah or at
Ramah." 14 So they passed on and went their way; and the sun went
down on them near Gibeah, which belongs to Benjamin. 15 They turned

18.30
Judg 17.3, 5;
Ex 2.22
18.31
Josh 18.1

19.1
Judg 18.1

19.3
Gen 34.3;
50.21

19.5
v. 8;
Gen 18.5
19.6
vv. 9, 22

19.10
1 Chr 11.4, 5
19.11
Judg 1.21

19.12
Heb 11.13

19.15
Heb 13.2

---

o Another reading is *son of Manasseh*   *p* Gk OL: Heb *prostituted herself against*   *q* Gk: Heb *she brought
him to*   *r* Compare verse 7 and Gk: Heb *they*   *s* Cn: Heb *Linger*   *t* Gk: Heb lacks *and drank*

18.30 *until the time the land went into captivity.* Some
scholars believe this refers to the captivity of the ark
under Eli. Others believe this refers to the captivity
of the northern kingdom by the Assyrians under
Tiglath-pileser in the eighth century. If the latter is
correct, the date for the composition of Judges would
obviously be at or after that time. Verse 31, however,
must have been written around 1050 B.C., when the
Philistines took the ark, confirming the theory that
Judges was written in the early days of the monarchy.

19.2 A Levite's mate became a prostitute and left
her husband for another man. He did not press his
case against her. Instead, he tried to get her back from
his father-in-law's home, where she was staying. He
started back with her, arriving in Gibeah with no
place to stay.
19.15 In those days there were no inns or hotels.
Unless the inhabitants of a town opened their homes
to travelers and strangers, they had no place to go.

aside there, to go in and spend the night at Gibeah. He went in and sat down in the open square of the city, but no one took them in to spend the night.

3. *The Ephraimite's hospitality*

19.16
Ps 104.23;
v. 14

16 Then at evening there was an old man coming from his work in the field. The man was from the hill country of Ephraim, and he was residing in Gibeah. (The people of the place were Benjaminites.) 17 When the old man looked up and saw the wayfarer in the open square of the city,

19.18
Judg 18.31;
20.18

he said, "Where are you going and where do you come from?" 18 He answered him, "We are passing from Bethlehem in Judah to the remote parts of the hill country of Ephraim, from which I come. I went to Bethlehem in Judah; and I am going to my home.*u* Nobody has offered to take me in. 19 We your servants have straw and fodder for our donkeys, with bread and wine for me and the woman and the young man along with us. We need nothing more." 20 The old man said, "Peace be to you. I will

19.21
Gen 24.32, 33

care for all your wants; only do not spend the night in the square." 21 So he brought him into his house, and fed the donkeys; they washed their feet, and ate and drank.

4. *The abuse of the concubine*

19.22
Gen 19.4;
Deut 13.13;
Rom 1.26, 27

22 While they were enjoying themselves, the men of the city, a perverse lot, surrounded the house, and started pounding on the door. They said to the old man, the master of the house, "Bring out the man who came into your house, so that we may have intercourse with him." 23 And the

19.23
Gen 34.7;
Deut 22.21;
2 Sam 13.12

man, the master of the house, went out to them and said to them, "No, my brothers, do not act so wickedly. Since this man is my guest, do not

19.24
Gen 19.8;
Deut 21.14

do this vile thing. 24 Here are my virgin daughter and his concubine; let me bring them out now. Ravish them and do whatever you want to them; but against this man do not do such a vile thing." 25 But the men would not listen to him. So the man seized his concubine, and put her out to them. They wantonly raped her, and abused her all through the night until the morning. And as the dawn began to break, they let her go. 26 As morning appeared, the woman came and fell down at the door of the man's house where her master was, until it was light.

5. *The Levite's anger*

27 In the morning her master got up, opened the doors of the house, and when he went out to go on his way, there was his concubine lying at

19.28
Judg 20.5

the door of the house, with her hands on the threshold. 28 "Get up," he said to her, "we are going." But there was no answer. Then he put her

19.29
1 Sam 11.7

on the donkey; and the man set out for his home. 29 When he had entered his house, he took a knife, and grasping his concubine he cut her into twelve pieces, limb by limb, and sent her throughout all the territory of

19.30
Judg 20.7

Israel. 30 Then he commanded the men whom he sent, saying, "Thus shall you say to all the Israelites, 'Has such a thing ever happened*v* since the day that the Israelites came up from the land of Egypt until this day? Consider it, take counsel, and speak out.' "

u Gk Compare 19.29. Heb *to the house of the Lord*   *v* Compare Gk: Heb 30*And all who saw it said,* "Such a thing has not happened or been seen

19.27 The moral of this episode is ambiguous. Why did the Levite fail to protect the concubine with his own life? Why did he wait until morning to open the door and see her dead? Would not the second table of the law have required him to act differently, even if it meant the loss of his own life? Would a believer today not have a moral obligation to preserve the integrity of a mate, even if it meant resorting to the use of violence in such a contingency? This story certainly shows the effect of no central moral leadership—a society in which all people do as they please.

6. War between Israel and Benjamin

a. Israel gathers at Mizpah: the Levite tells his tale

20 Then all the Israelites came out, from Dan to Beer-sheba, including the land of Gilead, and the congregation assembled in one body before the LORD at Mizpah. 2 The chiefs of all the people, of all the tribes of Israel, presented themselves in the assembly of the people of God, four hundred thousand foot-soldiers bearing arms. 3 (Now the Benjaminites heard that the people of Israel had gone up to Mizpah.) And the Israelites said, "Tell us, how did this criminal act come about?" 4 The Levite, the husband of the woman who was murdered, answered, "I came to Gibeah that belongs to Benjamin, I and my concubine, to spend the night. 5 The lords of Gibeah rose up against me, and surrounded the house at night. They intended to kill me, and they raped my concubine until she died. 6 Then I took my concubine and cut her into pieces, and sent her throughout the whole extent of Israel's territory; for they have committed a vile outrage in Israel. 7 So now, you Israelites, all of you, give your advice and counsel here."

8 All the people got up as one, saying, "We will not any of us go to our tents, nor will any of us return to our houses. 9 But now this is what we will do to Gibeah: we will go up*w* against it by lot. 10 We will take ten men of a hundred throughout all the tribes of Israel, and a hundred of a thousand, and a thousand of ten thousand, to bring provisions for the troops, who are going to repay*x* Gibeah of Benjamin for all the disgrace that they have done in Israel." 11 So all the men of Israel gathered against the city, united as one.

b. The Benjaminites refuse to repent

12 The tribes of Israel sent men through all the tribe of Benjamin, saying, "What crime is this that has been committed among you? 13 Now then, hand over those scoundrels in Gibeah, so that we may put them to death, and purge the evil from Israel." But the Benjaminites would not listen to their kinsfolk, the Israelites. 14 The Benjaminites came together out of the towns to Gibeah, to go out to battle against the Israelites. 15 On that day the Benjaminites mustered twenty-six thousand armed men from their towns, besides the inhabitants of Gibeah. 16 Of all this force, there were seven hundred picked men who were left-handed; every one could sling a stone at a hair, and not miss. 17 And the Israelites, apart from Benjamin, mustered four hundred thousand armed men, all of them warriors.

c. Israel seeks the will of God

18 The Israelites proceeded to go up to Bethel, where they inquired of God, "Which of us shall go up first to battle against the Benjaminites?" And the LORD answered, "Judah shall go up first."

d. The initial victory of Benjamin

19 Then the Israelites got up in the morning, and encamped against Gibeah. 20 The Israelites went out to battle against Benjamin; and the Israelites drew up the battle line against them at Gibeah. 21 The Benjaminites came out of Gibeah, and struck down on that day twenty-two thousand of the Israelites. 23*y* The Israelites went up and wept before the

20.1 Judg 21.5; 1 Sam 7.5

20.4 Judg 19.15

20.5 Judg 19.22, 25, 26
20.6 Judg 19.29; Josh 7.15
20.7 Judg 19.30

20.12 Deut 13.14, 15
20.13 Judg 19.22

20.16 Judg 3.15; 1 Chr 12.2

20.18 vv. 23, 26, 27; Num 27.21

20.21 v. 25

20.23 v. 18

---

w Gk: Heb lacks *we will go up*   *x* Compare Gk: Meaning of Heb uncertain   *y* Verses 22 and 23 are transposed

---

20.13 Before the battle took place, Israel presented a solution which would have made war unnecessary: they wanted the guilty scoundrels surrendered to them, judged, and executed for their crime.
20.18 Before the first and the second battles, Israel asked counsel from God as to what they should do and

how they should do it. Benjamin won the first two battles and Israel went back to God, to fast and to offer burnt offerings and sacrifices of well-being (v. 26). They were told to start the third battle, and Israel won the day (vv. 35,36).

LORD until the evening; and they inquired of the LORD, "Shall we again draw near to battle against our kinsfolk the Benjaminites?" And the LORD said, "Go up against them." 22 The Israelites took courage, and again formed the battle line in the same place where they had formed it on the first day.

e. Benjamin's second victory

24 So the Israelites advanced against the Benjaminites the second day. 25 Benjamin moved out against them from Gibeah the second day, and struck down eighteen thousand of the Israelites, all of them armed men. 26 Then all the Israelites, the whole army, went back to Bethel and wept, sitting there before the LORD; they fasted that day until evening. Then they offered burnt offerings and sacrifices of well-being before the LORD. 27 And the Israelites inquired of the LORD (for the ark of the covenant of God was there in those days, 28 and Phinehas son of Eleazar, son of Aaron, ministered before it in those days), saying, "Shall we go out once more to battle against our kinsfolk the Benjaminites, or shall we desist?" The LORD answered, "Go up, for tomorrow I will give them into your hand."

f. The rout of Benjamin

29 So Israel stationed men in ambush around Gibeah. 30 Then the Israelites went up against the Benjaminites on the third day, and set themselves in array against Gibeah, as before. 31 When the Benjaminites went out against the army, they were drawn away from the city. As before they began to inflict casualties on the troops, along the main roads, one of which goes up to Bethel and the other to Gibeah, as well as in the open country, killing about thirty men of Israel. 32 The Benjaminites thought, "They are being routed before us, as previously." But the Israelites said, "Let us retreat and draw them away from the city toward the roads." 33 The main body of the Israelites drew back its battle line to Baal-tamar, while those Israelites who were in ambush rushed out of their place west[z] of Geba. 34 There came against Gibeah ten thousand picked men out of all Israel, and the battle was fierce. But the Benjaminites did not realize that disaster was close upon them.

35 The LORD defeated Benjamin before Israel; and the Israelites destroyed twenty-five thousand one hundred men of Benjamin that day, all of them armed.

36 Then the Benjaminites saw that they were defeated.[a]

The Israelites gave ground to Benjamin, because they trusted to the troops in ambush that they had stationed against Gibeah. 37 The troops in ambush rushed quickly upon Gibeah. Then they put the whole city to the sword. 38 Now the agreement between the main body of Israel and the men in ambush was that when they sent up a cloud of smoke out of the city 39 the main body of Israel should turn in battle. But Benjamin had begun to inflict casualties on the Israelites, killing about thirty of them; so they thought, "Surely they are defeated before us, as in the first battle." 40 But when the cloud, a column of smoke, began to rise out of the city, the Benjaminites looked behind them — and there was the whole city going up in smoke toward the sky! 41 Then the main body of Israel turned, and the Benjaminites were dismayed, for they saw that disaster was close upon them. 42 Therefore they turned away from the Israelites in the direction of the wilderness; but the battle overtook them, and those who came out

Margin references (left column):

20.25
v. 21

20.26
v. 23;
Judg 21.2

20.27
Josh 18.1
20.28
Josh 24.33;
Deut 18.5;
Judg 7.9

20.29
Josh 8.4

20.31
Josh 8.16

20.33
Josh 8.19

20.34
Josh 8.14

20.36
Josh 8.15

20.37
Josh 8.19

20.38
Josh 8.20

20.39
v. 32

20.40
Josh 8.20

z Gk Vg: Heb *in the plain*   *a* This sentence is continued by verse 45.

20.27 *the ark of the covenant of God.* Throughout the wilderness journeys the ark rested in the tent of meeting. During the period of the judges a house of God was built for the ark at Shiloh (see 18.31); the young Samuel slept in this house (1 Sam 3.3). We do not know what happened to the tent of meeting. The ark, however, was preserved for centuries until the time of Nebuchadnezzar. Presumably, it was destroyed when he burned the temple in 586 B.C. 20.35–39 Archeologists have uncovered evidences of the destruction of Gibeah.

of the city[b] were slaughtering them in between.[c] 43 Cutting down[d] the Benjaminites, they pursued them from Nohah[e] and trod them down as far as a place east of Gibeah. 44 Eighteen thousand Benjaminites fell, all of them courageous fighters. 45 When they turned and fled toward the wilderness to the rock of Rimmon, five thousand of them were cut down on the main roads, and they were pursued as far as Gidom, and two thousand of them were slain. 46 So all who fell that day of Benjamin were twenty-five thousand arms-bearing men, all of them courageous fighters. 47 But six hundred turned and fled toward the wilderness to the rock of Rimmon, and remained at the rock of Rimmon for four months. 48 Meanwhile, the Israelites turned back against the Benjaminites, and put them to the sword — the city, the people, the animals, and all that remained. Also the remaining towns they set on fire.

20.45
Judg 21.13

20.47
Judg 21.13

7. *The preservation of the tribe of Benjamin*

a. *Israel weeps for Benjamin*

21 Now the Israelites had sworn at Mizpah, "No one of us shall give his daughter in marriage to Benjamin." 2 And the people came to Bethel, and sat there until evening before God, and they lifted up their voices and wept bitterly. 3 They said, "O LORD, the God of Israel, why has it come to pass that today there should be one tribe lacking in Israel?" 4 On the next day, the people got up early, and built an altar there, and offered burnt offerings and sacrifices of well-being. 5 Then the Israelites said, "Which of all the tribes of Israel did not come up in the assembly to the LORD?" For a solemn oath had been taken concerning whoever did not come up to the LORD to Mizpah, saying, "That one shall be put to death." 6 But the Israelites had compassion for Benjamin their kin, and said, "One tribe is cut off from Israel this day. 7 What shall we do for wives for those who are left, since we have sworn by the LORD that we will not give them any of our daughters as wives?"

21.1
vv. 7, 18
21.2
Judg 20.18, 26

21.4
2 Sam 24.25

21.7
v. 1

b. *Wives for the Benjaminites*

(1) THE VIRGINS OF JABESH-GILEAD

8 Then they said, "Is there anyone from the tribes of Israel who did not come up to the LORD to Mizpah?" It turned out that no one from Jabesh-gilead had come to the camp, to the assembly. 9 For when the roll was called among the people, not one of the inhabitants of Jabesh-gilead was there. 10 So the congregation sent twelve thousand soldiers there and commanded them, "Go, put the inhabitants of Jabesh-gilead to the sword, including the women and the little ones. 11 This is what you shall do; every male and every woman that has lain with a male you shall devote to destruction." 12 And they found among the inhabitants of Jabesh-gilead four hundred young virgins who had never slept with a man and brought them to the camp at Shiloh, which is in the land of Canaan.

21.11
Num 31.17

13 Then the whole congregation sent word to the Benjaminites who were at the rock of Rimmon, and proclaimed peace to them. 14 Benjamin returned at that time; and they gave them the women whom they had

21.13
Judg 20.47;
Deut 20.10

---

b Compare Vg and some Gk Mss: Heb cities   c Compare Syr: Meaning of Heb uncertain   d Gk: Heb Surrounding   e Gk: Heb pursued them at their resting place

---

21.1ff The destruction of the Benjaminites, including their women, left only a few alive. The tribe of Benjamin was faced with extinction because the other tribes of Israel made a solemn pact that none of their daughters would be given in marriage to a Benjamite. The Israelites sought for a resolution to the problem without breaking its own vow.
21.8,9 Evidently the earlier marriage ties between

the Gileadites and the people of Benjamin explain why no one from Jabesh-gilead came to fight against the Benjamites.
21.12 When the people of Jabesh-gilead were slain, four hundred virgins were saved from the slaughter. They were sent to the camp at Shiloh — there to await their disposition. This solved the lack of mates available for the few people of Benjamin who were left alive.

saved alive of the women of Jabesh-gilead; but they did not suffice for them.

(2) THE DAUGHTERS OF SHILOH

21.15
v. 6

15 The people had compassion on Benjamin because the LORD had made a breach in the tribes of Israel. 16 So the elders of the congregation said, "What shall we do for wives for those who are left, since there are no women left in Benjamin?" 17 And they said, "There must be heirs for the survivors of Benjamin, in order that a tribe may not be blotted out from Israel. 18 Yet we cannot give any of our daughters to them as wives."

21.18
v. 18

21.19
Judg 18.31;
1 Sam 1.3

For the Israelites had sworn, "Cursed be anyone who gives a wife to Benjamin." 19 So they said, "Look, the yearly festival of the LORD is taking place at Shiloh, which is north of Bethel, on the east of the highway that goes up from Bethel to Shechem, and south of Lebonah." 20 And they instructed the Benjaminites, saying, "Go and lie in wait in the vineyards,

21.21
Ex 15.20;
Judg 11.34

21 and watch; when the young women of Shiloh come out to dance in the dances, then come out of the vineyards and each of you carry off a wife for himself from the young women of Shiloh, and go to the land of Benjamin.

21.22
vv. 1, 18

22 Then if their fathers or their brothers come to complain to us, we will say to them, 'Be generous and allow us to have them; because we did not capture in battle a wife for each man. But neither did you incur guilt by giving your daughters to them.' " 23 The Benjaminites did so; they

21.23
Judg 20.48

took wives for each of them from the dancers whom they abducted. Then they went and returned to their territory, and rebuilt the towns, and lived in them. 24 So the Israelites departed from there at that time by tribes and families, and they went out from there to their own territories.

8. *Summary of the age of the judges*

21.25
Judg 17.6;
18.1; 19.1

25 In those days there was no king in Israel; all the people did what was right in their own eyes.

21.23 Amidst the festivities, the Benjaminites took for themselves the virgins and went home to repopulate the tribe decimated from the battles with Israel. Thus, the tribe of Benjamin was not wiped out completely.

21.25 As Judges closes, anarchy was the order of the day. All the people did as they pleased. This prepares the way for the more centralized form of government described in the books of Samuel and Kings.

INTRODUCTION TO

RUTH

Authorship, Date, and Background: Jewish tradition attributes this book to Samuel, but the reference to David (4.17,21) suggests a later period. The story was most likely transmitted orally around Bethlehem until the reign of David when it came into prominence. The book names Boaz as the great-grandfather of David; thus it took place around 1100 B.C. This beautiful story shines brilliantly against the dark background of the anarchy pictured in Judg 17—21. In the Hebrew Bible, however, the book of Ruth is placed in its third, and last, division (*kethubim*, i.e., "writings"), following Psalms, Job, and Proverbs; it is a part of the Megilloth (see introduction to Esther). The order in the English Bible stems from the Septuagint.

Ruth was a Moabitess, and apparently in her day marriages among the people of Moab and Isreal were contracted (see Deut 23.3–6). In spite of being a non-Israelite, she became an ancestress of Jesus, the greater David, who came to break down the dividing wall of hostility between Jews and Gentiles (see Eph 2.11ff). The author of Ruth is unknown and the date it was written cannot be determined conclusively.

Relating a story from the period of Judges which was characterized by savagery, lust, strife, and lawlessness, the book of Ruth presents a strange contrast. Instead of war, bloodshed, cruelty, and intrigue, there is love and marriage, simple faith, and the tilling of the land—the common customs of ordinary people as they lived and died amid the turbulance of their age.

Characteristics and Content: Told in simple language, Ruth records tragedy and love in the lives of average people. In it we see the fortunes of Elimelech of Bethlehem, who, with his wife Naomi and his two sons, went to Moab in time of famine. He and his sons died there. Naomi yearned for her homeland and returned, accompanied by Ruth, a young Moabite woman who had been married to her deceased son. The attractiveness of the story derives from the suspense factor as faithful Ruth, still young and marriageable, was rewarded for her faithfulness when she met and married Boaz, a close relative of Naomi. Boaz's preliminary reaction to his role as her relative and the refusal of a closer relative to marry Ruth add further suspense to the story. It has a happy ending, and the sequel marks David as a descendant of Ruth and Boaz; these add luster to the narrative.

Outline:

RUTH

I. *Ruth returns with Naomi (1.1–22)*

A. *Naomi's troubles*

INTRODUCTION TO
RUTH

1.1
Judg 2.16

1.2
Gen 35.19;
Judg 3.30

1 In the days when the judges ruled, there was a famine in the land, and a certain man of Bethlehem in Judah went to live in the country of Moab, he and his wife and two sons. 2 The name of the man was Elimelech and the name of his wife Naomi, and the names of his two sons were Mahlon and Chilion; they were Ephrathites from Bethlehem in Judah. They went into the country of Moab and remained there. 3 But Elimelech, the husband of Naomi, died, and she was left with her two sons. 4 These took Moabite wives; the name of the one was Orpah and the name of the other Ruth. When they had lived there about ten years, 5 both Mahlon and Chilion also died, so that the woman was left without her two sons and her husband.

B. *Naomi decides to return to Bethlehem*

1.6
Ex 4.31

1.8
v. 5;
Ruth 2.20

1.9
Ruth 3.1

1.11
Deut 25.5

1.13
Judg 2.15;
Ps 32.4

6 Then she started to return with her daughters-in-law from the country of Moab, for she had heard in the country of Moab that the LORD had considered his people and given them food. 7 So she set out from the place where she had been living, she and her two daughters-in-law, and they went on their way to go back to the land of Judah. 8 But Naomi said to her two daughters-in-law, "Go back each of you to your mother's house. May the LORD deal kindly with you, as you have dealt with the dead and with me. 9 The LORD grant that you may find security, each of you in the house of your husband." Then she kissed them, and they wept aloud. 10 They said to her, "No, we will return with you to your people." 11 But Naomi said, "Turn back, my daughters, why will you go with me? Do I still have sons in my womb that they may become your husbands? 12 Turn back, my daughters, go your way, for I am too old to have a husband. Even if I thought there was hope for me, even if I should have a husband tonight and bear sons, 13 would you then wait until they were grown? Would you then refrain from marrying? No, my daughters, it has been far more bitter for me than for you, because the hand of the LORD has turned against me." 14 Then they wept aloud again. Orpah kissed her mother-in-law, but Ruth clung to her.

1.1 *when the judges ruled.* The earlier account of the days of the judges is noticeably different from the story of the times in which Ruth lived. There was no king in Israel—all people did what was right in their own eyes. The days were dark and gloomy, for Israel went through a series of highs and lows marked by apostasy, captivity, repentance, and restoration.
1.3 The death of Elimelech was only the beginning of Naomi's sorrows. She would soon lose both sons and neither one of them would leave her any grandchildren. Her attitude was negative: her laments were woeful and her complaints restated again and again. She apparently had not forgiven God for what happened to her. But in the end her consolation would be greater than all her afflictions.
1.4 The people of Moab descended from Lot through incest with his daughter (Gen 19.36,37). Ruth, a Moabite, became an ancestor of Jesus (Mt 1.3–6).
1.13 *the hand of the LORD has turned against me.* As Naomi tried to send her daughters-in-law back to their homes she said, in effect, that God's quarrel was with her. Affliction is not necessarily a sign that God is against the one afflicted. If it does come because of disobedience, it is deserved and should be accepted gladly; if it comes for no apparent reason, God should still be praised (cf. 1 Thess 5.18), even before deliverance appears.

C. *Ruth refuses to leave Naomi*

15 So she said, "See, your sister-in-law has gone back to her people and to her gods; return after your sister-in-law." 16 But Ruth said,

"Do not press me to leave you
  or to turn back from following you!
Where you go, I will go;
  where you lodge, I will lodge;
your people shall be my people,
  and your God my God.
17 Where you die, I will die —
  there will I be buried.
May the LORD do thus and so to me,
  and more as well,
if even death parts me from you!"

18 When Naomi saw that she was determined to go with her, she said no more to her.

D. *Ruth and Naomi return together*

19 So the two of them went on until they came to Bethlehem. When they came to Bethlehem, the whole town was stirred because of them; and the women said, "Is this Naomi?" 20 She said to them,

"Call me no longer Naomi,*f*
  call me Mara,*g*
for the Almighty*h* has dealt bitterly with me.
21 I went away full,
  but the LORD has brought me back empty;
why call me Naomi
  when the LORD has dealt harshly with*i* me,
  and the Almighty*h* has brought calamity upon me?"

22 So Naomi returned together with Ruth the Moabite, her daughter-in-law, who came back with her from the country of Moab. They came to Bethlehem at the beginning of the barley harvest.

II. *Ruth meets Boaz (2.1–23)*

A. *Ruth gleans in Boaz's field*

2 Now Naomi had a kinsman on her husband's side, a prominent rich man, of the family of Elimelech, whose name was Boaz. 2 And Ruth the Moabite said to Naomi, "Let me go to the field and glean among the ears of grain, behind someone in whose sight I may find favor." She said to her, "Go, my daughter." 3 So she went. She came and gleaned in the field behind the reapers. As it happened, she came to the part of the field belonging to Boaz, who was of the family of Elimelech. 4 Just then Boaz came from Bethlehem. He said to the reapers, "The LORD be with you." They answered, "The LORD bless you." 5 Then Boaz said to his servant who was in charge of the reapers, "To whom does this young woman belong?" 6 The servant who was in charge of the reapers answered, "She is the Moabite who came back with Naomi from the country of Moab. 7 She said, 'Please, let me glean and gather among the

f That is Pleasant   g That is Bitter   h Traditional rendering of Heb Shaddai   i Or has testified against

Cross references (margin):

1.16 2 Kings 2.2, 4, 6; Ruth 2.11, 12

1.18 Acts 21.14

1.20 Ex 6.3; Job 6.4

1.21 Job 1.21

1.22 Ex 9.31, 32; Ruth 2.23

2.1 Ruth 1.2; 3.2, 12

2.2 v. 7; Lev 19.9; Deut 24.19

2.4 Ps 129.7, 8; Lk 1.28

2.6 Ruth 1.22

1.16 Many brides today use this passage as part of their wedding ceremonies. But no bride should make her husband's God her God unless her husband's God is the true God; her decision should be rooted in her own faith and commitment to Jesus Christ.
2.1 *Boaz.* In Mt 1.5 we are told that Boaz was the son of Salmon by Rahab (see note on Josh 6.23).
2.3 Ruth was humble enough to glean, industrious enough to work, and utterly dependent on the God of grace whom she had embraced as her Redeemer. It was no accident that she gleaned in the field belonging to Boaz. God in his providence directed her steps to this particular field.
2.7 Some of the grain or grapes were left for gleaning by the poor. The law allowed anyone to glean in the fields, but Ruth did not assert her rights. She

sheaves behind the reapers.' So she came, and she has been on her feet from early this morning until now, without resting even for a moment."[j]

B. *Boaz commends faithful Ruth*

8 Then Boaz said to Ruth, "Now listen, my daughter, do not go to glean in another field or leave this one, but keep close to my young women. [9] Keep your eyes on the field that is being reaped, and follow behind them. I have ordered the young men not to bother you. If you get thirsty, go to the vessels and drink from what the young men have drawn." [10] Then she fell prostrate, with her face to the ground, and said to him, "Why have I found favor in your sight, that you should take notice of me, when I am a foreigner?" [11] But Boaz answered her, "All that you have done for your mother-in-law since the death of your husband has been fully told me, and how you left your father and mother and your native land and came to a people that you did not know before. [12] May the LORD reward you for your deeds, and may you have a full reward from the LORD, the God of Israel, under whose wings you have come for refuge!" [13] Then she said, "May I continue to find favor in your sight, my lord, for you have comforted me and spoken kindly to your servant, even though I am not one of your servants."

14 At mealtime Boaz said to her, "Come here, and eat some of this bread, and dip your morsel in the sour wine." So she sat beside the reapers, and he heaped up for her some parched grain. She ate until she was satisfied, and she had some left over. [15] When she got up to glean, Boaz instructed his young men, "Let her glean even among the standing sheaves, and do not reproach her. [16] You must also pull out some handfuls for her from the bundles, and leave them for her to glean, and do not rebuke her."

C. *Ruth confides in Naomi*

17 So she gleaned in the field until evening. Then she beat out what she had gleaned, and it was about an ephah of barley. [18] She picked it up and came into the town, and her mother-in-law saw how much she had gleaned. Then she took out and gave her what was left over after she herself had been satisfied. [19] Her mother-in-law said to her, "Where did you glean today? And where have you worked? Blessed be the man who took notice of you." So she told her mother-in-law with whom she had worked, and said, "The name of the man with whom I worked today is Boaz." [20] Then Naomi said to her daughter-in-law, "Blessed be he by the LORD, whose kindness has not forsaken the living or the dead!" Naomi also said to her, "The man is a relative of ours, one of our nearest kin."[k] [21] Then Ruth the Moabite said, "He even said to me, 'Stay close by my servants, until they have finished all my harvest.'" [22] Naomi said to Ruth, her daughter-in-law, "It is better, my daughter, that you go out with his young women, otherwise you might be bothered in another field." [23] So she stayed close to the young women of Boaz, gleaning until the end of the barley and wheat harvests; and she lived with her mother-in-law.

Marginal references:

2.10 1 Sam 25.23

2.11 Ruth 1.14, 16, 17

2.12 1 Sam 24.19; Ps 17.8; Ruth 1.16

2.14 v. 18

2.18 v. 14

2.19 v. 10

2.20 Ruth 3.10; Prov 17.17; Ruth 3.9; 4.6

2.23 Deut 16.9

---

j Compare Gk Vg: Meaning of Heb uncertain   *k Or one with the right to redeem*

---

asked for permission, demonstrating her humility and concern to do only the right thing.
2.12 *under whose wings you have come for refuge!* Boaz knew that Ruth was a convert to the true faith. Her confidence was in his God, who had become her God. He was impressed by her.

2.16 Boaz was so moved that he saw to it that Ruth would get more than a gleaner would normally get. His heart went out to this widow in distress.
2.22 *bothered in another field.* Apparently it was not uncommon for a female gleaner to be taken advantage of, particularly if she was a stranger.

III. *Boaz decides (3.1–18)*

A. *Naomi counsels Ruth*

3 Naomi her mother-in-law said to her, "My daughter, I need to seek some security for you, so that it may be well with you. 2 Now here is our kinsman Boaz, with whose young women you have been working. See, he is winnowing barley tonight at the threshing floor. 3 Now wash and anoint yourself, and put on your best clothes and go down to the threshing floor; but do not make yourself known to the man until he has finished eating and drinking. 4 When he lies down, observe the place where he lies; then, go and uncover his feet and lie down; and he will tell you what to do." 5 She said to her, "All that you tell me I will do."

B. *Ruth follows Naomi's advice: Boaz determines to act*

6 So she went down to the threshing floor and did just as her mother-in-law had instructed her. 7 When Boaz had eaten and drunk, and he was in a contented mood, he went to lie down at the end of the heap of grain. Then she came stealthily and uncovered his feet, and lay down. 8 At midnight the man was startled, and turned over, and there, lying at his feet, was a woman! 9 He said, "Who are you?" And she answered, "I am Ruth, your servant; spread your cloak over your servant, for you are next-of-kin."[l] 10 He said, "May you be blessed by the LORD, my daughter; this last instance of your loyalty is better than the first; you have not gone after young men, whether poor or rich. 11 And now, my daughter, do not be afraid, I will do for you all that you ask, for all the assembly of my people know that you are a worthy woman. 12 But now, though it is true that I am a near kinsman, there is another kinsman more closely related than I. 13 Remain this night, and in the morning, if he will act as next-of-kin[l] for you, good; let him do it. If he is not willing to act as next-of-kin[l] for you, then, as the LORD lives, I will act as next-of-kin[l] for you. Lie down until the morning."

C. *Ruth returns to Naomi*

14 So she lay at his feet until morning, but got up before one person could recognize another; for he said, "It must not be known that the woman came to the threshing floor." 15 Then he said, "Bring the cloak you are wearing and hold it out." So she held it, and he measured out six measures of barley, and put it on her back; then he went into the city. 16 She came to her mother-in-law, who said, "How did things go with you,[m] my daughter?" Then she told her all that the man had done for her, 17 saying, "He gave me these six measures of barley, for he said, 'Do not go back to your mother-in-law empty-handed.' " 18 She replied, "Wait, my daughter, until you learn how the matter turns out, for the man will not rest, but will settle the matter today."

3.1 Ruth 1.9
3.2 Deut 25.5-10; Ruth 2.8
3.3 2 Sam 14.2

3.7 Judg 19.6, 9, 22; 2 Sam 13.28

3.9 v. 12; Ruth 2.20

3.11 Prov 12.4

3.12 v. 9; Ruth 4.1
3.13 Ruth 4.5

3.18 Ps 37.3-5

---

l Or *one with the right to redeem*   *m* Or *"Who are you,*

3.1 Naomi referred to the Israelite custom of levirate marriage (see Deut 25.5–10 and notes).
3.2 The grain was winnowed and then guarded overnight. Boaz remained there to oversee the harvesting activities; the grain might have been stolen if not watched over.
3.9 Ruth's invitation to Boaz to perform the role of nearest kin (cf. Deut 25.5–10) was not immoral. It was part of the social customs of the day.

3.10 Boaz was impressed by the fact that Ruth had not sought out a younger and perhaps more vigorous relative to play the role of kinsman. Boaz happened to be rich, but a younger woman might be more interested in having children than in wealth.
3.18 When Naomi heard Ruth's report of what had happened, she knew Boaz well enough that he meant business and would not rest until he had taken care of the situation.

IV. *Boaz and Ruth marry (4.1–22)*

A. *Boaz seeks out the next-of-kin, who declines*

4.1
Ruth 3.12

4 No sooner had Boaz gone up to the gate and sat down there than the next-of-kin,[n] of whom Boaz had spoken, came passing by. So Boaz said, "Come over, friend; sit down here." And he went over and sat down. 2 Then Boaz took ten men of the elders of the city, and said, "Sit down here"; so they sat down. 3 He then said to the next-of-kin,[n] "Naomi, who has come back from the country of Moab, is selling the parcel of land that belonged to our kinsman Elimelech. 4 So I thought I would tell you of it, and say: Buy it in the presence of those sitting here, and in the presence of the elders of my people. If you will redeem it, redeem it; but if you will not, tell me, so that I may know; for there is no one prior to you to redeem it, and I come after you." So he said, "I will redeem it." 5 Then Boaz said, "The day you acquire the field from the hand of Naomi, you are also acquiring Ruth[o] the Moabite, the widow of the dead man, to maintain the dead man's name on his inheritance." 6 At this, the next-of-kin[n] said, "I cannot redeem it for myself without damaging my own inheritance. Take my right of redemption yourself, for I cannot redeem it."

4.3
Lev 25.25

4.4
Jer 32.7, 8;
Lev 25.25

4.5ff
Deut 25.5, 6

4.6
Ruth 3.12, 13

B. *Boaz fulfills the legal requirements*

4.7
Deut 25.7, 9

7 Now this was the custom in former times in Israel concerning redeeming and exchanging: to confirm a transaction, the one took off a sandal and gave it to the other; this was the manner of attesting in Israel. 8 So when the next-of-kin[n] said to Boaz, "Acquire it for yourself," he took off his sandal. 9 Then Boaz said to the elders and all the people, "Today you are witnesses that I have acquired from the hand of Naomi all that belonged to Elimelech and all that belonged to Chilion and Mahlon. 10 I have also acquired Ruth the Moabite, the wife of Mahlon, to be my wife, to maintain the dead man's name on his inheritance, in order that the name of the dead may not be cut off from his kindred and from the gate of his native place; today you are witnesses." 11 Then all the people who were at the gate, along with the elders, said, "We are witnesses. May the LORD make the woman who is coming into your house like Rachel and Leah, who together built up the house of Israel. May you produce children in Ephrathah and bestow a name in Bethlehem; 12 and, through the children that the LORD will give you by this young woman, may your house be like the house of Perez, whom Tamar bore to Judah."

4.10
Deut 25.6

4.11
Ps 127.3

4.12
v. 18;
Gen 38.29

C. *Boaz and Ruth marry: Obed is born*

4.13
Ruth 3.11;
Gen 29.31;
33.5

13 So Boaz took Ruth and she became his wife. When they came together, the LORD made her conceive, and she bore a son. 14 Then the women said to Naomi, "Blessed be the LORD, who has not left you this day without next-of-kin;[n] and may his name be renowned in Israel! 15 He shall be to you a restorer of life and a nourisher of your old age; for your daughter-in-law who loves you, who is more to you than seven sons, has

4.14
Lk 1.58
4.15
Ruth 1.16,
17; 2.11, 12

[n] Or *one with the right to redeem*   [o] OL Vg: Heb *from the hand of Naomi and from Ruth*

4.5 Boaz made certain that the purchaser of the land was also ready to marry Ruth (see Deut 25.5,6). He probably knew that the nearer relative would decline to purchase the land under those circumstances. Not all of the details of the arrangement accord with the stipulations of Deut 25, for while Boaz was a near relative, he was not the brother of Mahlon.
4.7 The handing over of the sandal was a token that the right of redemption was transmitted to "the next of kin." Boaz now had the right to raise up offspring for the dead son of Naomi, so that the family property would remain in the same hands to which it had been

originally given.
4.12 See note on Gen 38.15 for comments on Tamar.
4.13 When Ruth became the wife of Boaz, the purpose for which she had returned with Naomi to Canaan was fulfilled. "The LORD made her conceive," and she gave birth to a son who would be in the lineage of the Messiah. And Naomi, who had complained so much, was blessed far beyond her wildest dreams by becoming the grandmother and nurse of the lovely little baby.

borne him." **16** Then Naomi took the child and laid him in her bosom, and became his nurse. **17** The women of the neighborhood gave him a name, saying, "A son has been born to Naomi." They named him Obed; he became the father of Jesse, the father of David.

D. Ruth enters the Davidic line

18 Now these are the descendants of Perez: Perez became the father of Hezron, **19** Hezron of Ram, Ram of Amminadab, **20** Amminadab of Nahshon, Nahshon of Salmon, **21** Salmon of Boaz, Boaz of Obed, **22** Obed of Jesse, and Jesse of David.

4.18
Mt 1.3-6

4.18–22 The genealogy of David and thus of Jesus is traced from Perez, the child of Tamar by Judah in a situation marred by duplicity, to Obed, whose birth came by a levirate marriage consummated without any moral taint.

INTRODUCTION TO
1 SAMUEL

Authorship, Date, and Background: 1 and 2 Samuel (like 1 and 2 Kings, and 1 and 2 Chronicles), were originally one book. In the Greek Septuagint the two larger books of Samuel and Kings were divided into four books which were called "Books of the Kingdoms," since they dealt with the history of the kingdoms of Israel and Judah. In the Latin Vulgate Bible, Jerome followed the Septuagint translators except that he called the four books the "Books of Kings." Thus, what is called today 1 and 2 Samuel and 1 and 2 Kings were known as "The First, Second, Third, and Fourth Books of the Kings."

The date and authorship of the books of Samuel cannot be determined with certainty. From the evidence contained in them, it appears that the writer lived after the events occurred. He made use of extant material such as the Chronicles of Samuel, Nathan, and Gad. A late Jewish tradition attributing the authorship of these two books to Samuel indicates the degree of respect with which he was held by the Jews. He was certainly important as a prophet, priest, and judge. He started the schools of the prophets. He was the link between the period of the judges and the beginning of the monarchy. And he trained David, who was to become Israel's shepherd-king. Evangelical scholars have usually set the date for the composition of the books of Samuel somewhere between the death of Solomon in 930 B.C. and the end of the northern kingdom in 722 B.C.

Characteristics and Content: 1 Samuel recounts the history of Israel from the end of the judges to the death of Saul by telling the stories of the leading characters—Eli, Samuel, Saul, David, and Jonathan. The book begins with the birth of Samuel, the son of Elkanah who lived in Ramathaim. Elkanah may well have been a Levite, since they were distributed among the various tribes including the tribe of Ephraim, among whose people he resided. Little Samuel lived with Eli, whose sons were wicked. When Eli died, Samuel, now grown up, succeeded him and served Israel as judge, prophet, and priest.

When Israel insisted on having a king like the surrounding nations, God disclosed to Samuel that Saul was his choice. At the same time he foretold what the king would be like. Saul got off to a good start by winning military victories. But he became proud and disobeyed the commands of Samuel. Samuel pronounced God's judgment on him, saying that God delighted more in obedience than in burnt offerings. Young David entered the picture when he killed Goliath, made friends with Jonathan, and eventually served King Saul at the royal court. Saul persecuted David, who was forced to flee. He maintained his friendship with Jonathan despite Saul's objections. God revealed to Samuel that David was his choice to replace Saul as king. David had a number of opportunities to slay Saul but refused to smite the Lord's anointed.

Saul eventually became demented. At last he consulted the witch at Endor because the Spirit of God had left him. Meanwhile, David fled to the Philistines. Finally Saul died in a battle against the Philistines, as did his sons Jonathan, Abinadab, and Malchishua. A new day was about to dawn for Israel with David coming into prominence as king.

Outline:

I. The judgeship of Samuel (1.1—7.17)

II. The reign of Saul (8.1—31.13)

1 SAMUEL

I. The judgeship of Samuel (1.1–7.17)

A. Samuel's birth, growth, and background

1. Samuel born in answer to prayer

1.1
Josh 17.17,
18;
1 Chr 6.27
1.2
Deut 21.15-17;
Lk 2.36

1 There was a certain man of Ramathaim, a Zuphite[p] from the hill country of Ephraim, whose name was Elkanah son of Jeroham son of Elihu son of Tohu son of Zuph, an Ephraimite. 2 He had two wives; the name of the one was Hannah, and the name of the other Peninnah. Peninnah had children, but Hannah had no children.

1.3
Ex 34.23;
Deut 12.5;
Josh 18.1
1.4
Deut 12.17
1.5
Gen 16.1;
30.2
1.6
Job 24.21

3 Now this man used to go up year by year from his town to worship and to sacrifice to the LORD of hosts at Shiloh, where the two sons of Eli, Hophni and Phinehas, were priests of the LORD. 4 On the day when Elkanah sacrificed, he would give portions to his wife Peninnah and to all her sons and daughters; 5 but to Hannah he gave a double portion,[q] because he loved her, though the LORD had closed her womb. 6 Her rival used to provoke her severely, to irritate her, because the LORD had closed her womb. 7 So it went on year by year; as often as she went up to the house of the LORD, she used to provoke her. Therefore Hannah wept and would not eat.

1.8
Ruth 4.15

8 Her husband Elkanah said to her, "Hannah, why do you weep? Why do you not eat? Why is your heart sad? Am I not more to you than ten sons?"

1.9
1 Sam 3.3

9 After they had eaten and drunk at Shiloh, Hannah rose and presented herself before the LORD.[r] Now Eli the priest was sitting on the seat beside the doorpost of the temple of the LORD. 10 She was deeply distressed and prayed to the LORD, and wept bitterly. 11 She made this

1.11
Gen 28.20;
29.32;
Num 6.5;
Judg 13.5

vow: "O LORD of hosts, if only you will look on the misery of your servant, and remember me, and not forget your servant, but will give to your servant a male child, then I will set him before you as a nazirite[s] until the day of his death. He shall drink neither wine nor intoxicants,[t] and no razor shall touch his head."

1.13
Gen 24.42-45

12 As she continued praying before the LORD, Eli observed her mouth. 13 Hannah was praying silently; only her lips moved, but her voice

*p Compare Gk and 1 Chr 6.35-36: Heb Ramathaim-zophim   q Syr: Meaning of Heb uncertain
r Gk: Heb lacks and presented herself before the LORD   s That is one separated or one consecrated
t Cn Compare Gk Q Ms 1.22: MT then I will give him to the LORD all the days of his life*

1.1 Samuel's father was *Elkanah*. He was a Levite of the family of the Kohathites, who moved his family to Mount Ephraim. Elkanah lived in *Ramathaim,* meaning "the double Ramah." Ramah and Ramathaim are the same towns.
1.2 In a childless marriage, a man was permitted to take a second wife; she with her children would protect the land rights of the family. But in the case of the Levites the land problem was not important, for they were dispersed among all of the tribes and did not own any ancestral land.
1.6 Elkanah had two wives, Hannah and Peninnah. He loved Hannah, but Peninnah was the one who bore his children. As in Jacob's household (see Gen 29.15–35), Elkanah's family was in a state of turmoil.

Peninnah made fun of Hannah and bragged about her children. Polygamy often created more problems than it solved and never enjoyed the full approval of God.
1.10 Hannah's prayer was effective because (1) she was a true believer; (2) she fervently desired what she prayed for; (3) she asked God for what she wanted; (4) she had faith to believe God was able and willing to answer her prayer; and (5) she received the promise by faith even before the answer actually came. When the child was born, Hannah acknowledged what God had done by naming him Samuel, meaning either "His name is God," or "Asked of God."
1.11 *no razor shall touch his head.* This was the usual custom for nazirites, i.e., those wholly dedicated to God (see note on Judg 13.5).

was not heard; therefore Eli thought she was drunk. 14 So Eli said to her, "How long will you make a drunken spectacle of yourself? Put away your wine." 15 But Hannah answered, "No, my lord, I am a woman deeply troubled; I have drunk neither wine nor strong drink, but I have been pouring out my soul before the LORD. 16 Do not regard your servant as a worthless woman, for I have been speaking out of my great anxiety and vexation all this time." 17 Then Eli answered, "Go in peace; the God of Israel grant the petition you have made to him." 18 And she said, "Let your servant find favor in your sight." Then the woman went to her quarters,^{u} ate and drank with her husband,^{v} and her countenance was sad no longer.^{w}

19 They rose early in the morning and worshiped before the LORD; then they went back to their house at Ramah. Elkanah knew his wife Hannah, and the LORD remembered her. 20 In due time Hannah conceived and bore a son. She named him Samuel, for she said, "I have asked him of the LORD."

2. Samuel dedicated

21 The man Elkanah and all his household went up to offer to the LORD the yearly sacrifice, and to pay his vow. 22 But Hannah did not go up, for she said to her husband, "As soon as the child is weaned, I will bring him, that he may appear in the presence of the LORD, and remain there forever; I will offer him as a nazirite^x for all time."^{y} 23 Her husband Elkanah said to her, "Do what seems best to you, wait until you have weaned him; only—may the LORD establish his word."^{z} So the woman remained and nursed her son, until she weaned him. 24 When she had weaned him, she took him up with her, along with a three-year-old bull,^{a} an ephah of flour, and a skin of wine. She brought him to the house of the LORD at Shiloh; and the child was young. 25 Then they slaughtered the bull, and they brought the child to Eli. 26 And she said, "Oh, my lord! As you live, my lord, I am the woman who was standing here in your presence, praying to the LORD. 27 For this child I prayed; and the LORD has granted me the petition that I made to him. 28 Therefore I have lent him to the LORD; as long as he lives, he is given to the LORD."

She left him there for^b the LORD.

3. Hannah's song of praise

2 Hannah prayed and said,
"My heart exults in the LORD;
    my strength is exalted in my God.^{c}
My mouth derides my enemies,
    because I rejoice in my^d victory.

2 "There is no Holy One like the LORD,
    no one besides you;

^{u} Gk: Heb went her way ^{v} Gk: Heb lacks and drank with her husband ^{w} Gk: Meaning of Heb uncertain ^{x} That is one separated or one consecrated ^{y} Cn Compare Q Ms: MT lacks I will offer him as a nazirite for all time ^{z} MT: Q Ms Gk Compare Syr that which goes out of your mouth ^{a} Q Ms Gk Syr: MT three bulls ^{b} Gk (Compare Q Ms) and Gk at 2.11: MT And he (that is, Elkanah) worshiped there before ^{c} Gk: Heb the LORD ^{d} Q Ms: MT your

---

Cross-references (right margin):

1.14 Acts 2.4, 13
1.15 Ps 62.8
1.17 Judg 18.6; 1 Sam 25.35; Mk 5.34
1.18 Ruth 2.13; Eccl 9.7
1.19 Gen 4.1; 30.22
1.20 Gen 41.51, 52; Ex 2.10, 22
1.21 v. 3
1.22 Lk 2.22; 1 Sam 2.11, 18
1.23 Num 30.7; v. 17
1.24 Deut 12.5; Josh 18.1
1.25 Lev 1.5; Lk 2.22
1.26 2 Kings 2.2
1.27 vv. 11-13
1.28 vv. 11, 22
2.1 Lk 1.46-55; Ps 89.17; Isa 12.2, 3
2.2 Lev 19.2; 2 Sam 22.32; Deut 32.30, 31

1.19 Elkanah and Hannah maintained a righteous relationship with God. Before returning home, they rose early to worship God. When Hannah conceived the baby for which she had longed, the family tensions were somewhat abated. The phrase "the LORD remembered her" clearly indicates that the baby was conceived as a direct result of God's intervention as the author of life.
1.25 they, i.e., Elkanah and Hannah. They went

home from Shiloh to Ramah after Hannah's prayer (2.11).
2.1 Hannah offered a prayer of thanksgiving to God. She acknowledged that God was the author of life in the womb and thanked him for his mercies. Hannah's prayer is a foretaste of that offered later by the virgin Mary upon her conception (Lk 1.46–55).
2.2 there is . . . no one besides you. There may be other Samuels but there is no other God. His perfection is unparalleled and his being peerless.

there is no Rock like our God.

2.3
Prov 8.13;
1 Sam 16.7;
1 Kings 8.39;
Prov 16.2;
24.12

3 Talk no more so very proudly,
   let not arrogance come from your mouth;
   for the LORD is a God of knowledge,
    and by him actions are weighed.

2.4
Ps 76.3

4 The bows of the mighty are broken,
   but the feeble gird on strength.

2.5
Ps 113.9;
Jer 15.9

5 Those who were full have hired themselves out for bread,
   but those who were hungry are fat with spoil.
The barren has borne seven,
   but she who has many children is forlorn.

2.6
Deut 32.39;
Isa 26.19
2.7
Deut 8.17,
18;
Job 5.11;
Ps 75.6, 7
2.8
Ps 113.7, 8;
Job 36.7;
38.4, 5

6 The LORD kills and brings to life;
   he brings down to Sheol and raises up.
7 The LORD makes poor and makes rich;
   he brings low, he also exalts.
8 He raises up the poor from the dust;
   he lifts the needy from the ash heap,
to make them sit with princes
   and inherit a seat of honor. *e*
For the pillars of the earth are the LORD's,
   and on them he has set the world.

2.9
Ps 91.11, 12;
Mt 8.12;
Ps 33.16, 17
2.10
Ps 2.9; 18.13;
96.13; 21.1,
7; 89.24

9 "He will guard the feet of his faithful ones,
   but the wicked shall be cut off in darkness;
   for not by might does one prevail.
10 The LORD! His adversaries shall be shattered;
   the Most High*f* will thunder in heaven.
The LORD will judge the ends of the earth;
   he will give strength to his king,
   and exalt the power of his anointed."

4. Samuel ministers before the LORD

2.11
1 Sam 3.1

11 Then Elkanah went home to Ramah, while the boy remained to minister to the LORD, in the presence of the priest Eli.

2.12
Jer 2.8; 9.3,
6
2.13
Lev 7.29-34

12 Now the sons of Eli were scoundrels; they had no regard for the LORD 13 or for the duties of the priests to the people. When anyone offered sacrifice, the priest's servant would come, while the meat was boiling, with a three-pronged fork in his hand, 14 and he would thrust it into the pan, or kettle, or caldron, or pot; all that the fork brought up the priest would take for himself.*g* This is what they did at Shiloh to all the Israelites who came there. 15 Moreover, before the fat was burned, the priest's servant would come and say to the one who was sacrificing, "Give meat for the priest to roast; for he will not accept boiled meat from you, but only raw." 16 And if the man said to him, "Let them burn the fat first, and then take whatever you wish," he would say, "No, you must give it now; if not, I will take it by force." 17 Thus the sin of the young men was

2.15
Lev 3.3, 4

2.17
Mal 2.7-9

---

e Gk (Compare Q Ms) adds *He grants the vow of the one who vows, and blesses the years of the just*
f Cn Heb *against him he*   *g* Gk Syr Vg: Heb *with it*

2.3 *a God of knowledge.* His wisdom is unsearchable (Rom 11.33). He gives knowledge and understanding to whoever seeks him in faith.
2.4 *The bows of the mighty are broken.* However mighty people may be, all God needs to do is speak and they are disarmed, disabled, and beaten in battle.
2.6 *kills and brings to life.* God is the sovereign Lord of both death and life. He is the one who holds in his hand the keys of death and the grave (cf. Rev 1.18).
2.7,8 Promotion does not come by chance. God lifts up and pulls down whom he pleases, and whatever we have has come from the hand of the Lord.

2.9,10 God promises that he will care for and keep safely those whom he has chosen. Those who oppose him are adversaries, who will be cut off and judged. *He will give strength to his king* has messianic implications.
2.11ff A contrast is drawn between the good character of Elkanah's family and the bad character of Eli's family. Later, however, the children of Samuel turned out no better than the children of Eli (8.1–3). Grace does not run through the bloodline.
2.12 See note on 3.13 concerning the judgment of the sons of Eli.

very great in the sight of the Lord; for they treated the offerings of the Lord with contempt.

18 Samuel was ministering before the Lord, a boy wearing a linen ephod. 19 His mother used to make for him a little robe and take it to him each year, when she went up with her husband to offer the yearly sacrifice. 20 Then Eli would bless Elkanah and his wife, and say, "May the Lord repay[h] you with children by this woman for the gift that she made to[i] the Lord"; and then they would return to their home.

21 And[j] the Lord took note of Hannah; she conceived and bore three sons and two daughters. And the boy Samuel grew up in the presence of the Lord.

22 Now Eli was very old. He heard all that his sons were doing to all Israel, and how they lay with the women who served at the entrance to the tent of meeting. 23 He said to them, "Why do you do such things? For I hear of your evil dealings from all these people. 24 No, my sons; it is not a good report that I hear the people of the Lord spreading abroad. 25 If one person sins against another, someone can intercede for the sinner with the Lord;[k] but if someone sins against the Lord, who can make intercession?" But they would not listen to the voice of their father; for it was the will of the Lord to kill them.

26 Now the boy Samuel continued to grow both in stature and in favor with the Lord and with the people.

5. The prophet announces the doom of Eli's house

27 A man of God came to Eli and said to him, "Thus the Lord has said, 'I revealed[l] myself to the family of your ancestor in Egypt when they were slaves[m] to the house of Pharaoh. 28 I chose him out of all the tribes of Israel to be my priest, to go up to my altar, to offer incense, to wear an ephod before me; and I gave to the family of your ancestor all my offerings by fire from the people of Israel. 29 Why then look with greedy eye[n] at my sacrifices and my offerings that I commanded, and honor your sons more than me by fattening yourselves on the choicest parts of every offering of my people Israel?' 30 Therefore the Lord the God of Israel declares: 'I promised that your family and the family of your ancestor should go in and out before me forever'; but now the Lord declares: 'Far be it from me; for those who honor me I will honor, and those who despise me shall be treated with contempt. 31 See, a time is coming when I will cut off your strength and the strength of your ancestor's family, so that no one in your family will live to old age. 32 Then in distress you will look with greedy eye[o] on all the prosperity that shall be bestowed upon Israel; and no one in your family shall ever live to old age. 33 The only one of you whom I shall not cut off from my altar shall be spared to weep out his[p] eyes and grieve his[q] heart; all the members of your household shall die by the sword.[r] 34 The fate of your two sons, Hophni and Phinehas, shall be the sign to you—both of them shall die on the same day. 35 I will raise up for myself a faithful priest, who shall do according to what is in my heart and in my mind. I will build him a sure house, and he shall go in and out before my anointed one forever. 36 Everyone who is left in your

2.18 vv. 11, 28; 1 Sam 3.1
2.19 1 Sam 1.3
2.20 Lk 2.34; 1 Sam 1.11, 27, 28
2.21 Gen 21.1; v. 26; 1 Sam 3.19; Lk 2.40
2.22 Ex 38.8
2.24 1 Kings 15.26
2.25 Deut 1.17; Num 15.30; Josh 11.20
2.26 v. 21; Lk 2.52
2.27 1 Kings 13.1; Ex 4.14-16
2.28 Ex 28.1-4; Lev 8.7, 8
2.29 vv. 13-17; Deut 12.5; Mt 10.37
2.30 Ex 29.9; Ps 91.14; Mal 2.9
2.31 1 Sam 4.11-18; 22.17-20
2.32 1 Kings 2.26, 27; Zech 8.4
2.34 1 Kings 13.3; 1 Sam 4.11
2.35 1 Kings 2.35; 2 Sam 7.11, 27; 1 Kings 11.38; 1 Sam 12.3; 16.13
2.36 1 Kings 2.27

[h] Q Ms Gk: MT *give* [i] Q Ms Gk: MT *for the petition that she asked of* [j] Q Ms Gk: MT *When* [k] Gk Compare Q Ms: MT *another, God will mediate for him* [l] Gk Tg Syr: Heb *Did I reveal* [m] Q Ms Gk: MT lacks *slaves* [n] Q Ms Gk: MT *then kick* [o] Q Ms Gk: MT *will kick* [p] Q Ms Gk: MT *your* [q] Q Ms Gk: Heb *your* [r] Q Ms See Gk: MT *die like mortals*

2.27 *A man of God,* i.e., a prophet. The Scriptures do not identify this man of God. God has always had unidentified servants who carried out the divine will and served as preachers of the prophetic word, even when it was unwelcome. God sharply rebuked Eli for failing to discipline his children. By his failure to take action against them, he encouraged them in

their wickedness. In fact, Eli may himself have profited from the unscrupulous actions of his sons (v. 29).
2.35 *I will raise up for myself a faithful priest.* This promise and prediction was fulfilled when Solomon appointed Zadok to replace Abiathar, Eli's great-grandson (1 Kings 2.27,35).

family shall come to implore him for a piece of silver or a loaf of bread, and shall say, Please put me in one of the priest's places, that I may eat a morsel of bread.'"

6. Samuel announces the doom of Eli's house

a. Samuel before the LORD

3 Now the boy Samuel was ministering to the LORD under Eli. The word of the LORD was rare in those days; visions were not widespread.

b. The call of God to Samuel

2 At that time Eli, whose eyesight had begun to grow dim so that he could not see, was lying down in his room; 3 the lamp of God had not yet gone out, and Samuel was lying down in the temple of the LORD, where the ark of God was. 4 Then the LORD called, "Samuel! Samuel!"[s] and he said, "Here I am!" 5 and ran to Eli, and said, "Here I am, for you called me." But he said, "I did not call; lie down again." So he went and lay down. 6 The LORD called again, "Samuel!" Samuel got up and went to Eli, and said, "Here I am, for you called me." But he said, "I did not call, my son; lie down again." 7 Now Samuel did not yet know the LORD, and the word of the LORD had not yet been revealed to him. 8 The LORD called Samuel again, a third time. And he got up and went to Eli, and said, "Here I am, for you called me." Then Eli perceived that the LORD was calling the boy. 9 Therefore Eli said to Samuel, "Go, lie down; and if he calls you, you shall say, 'Speak, LORD, for your servant is listening.'" So Samuel went and lay down in his place.

c. God pronounces judgment of Eli's house

10 Now the LORD came and stood there, calling as before, "Samuel! Samuel!" And Samuel said, "Speak, for your servant is listening." 11 Then the LORD said to Samuel, "See, I am about to do something in Israel that will make both ears of anyone who hears of it tingle. 12 On that day I will fulfill against Eli all that I have spoken concerning his house, from beginning to end. 13 For I have told him that I am about to punish his house forever, for the iniquity that he knew, because his sons were blaspheming God,[t] and he did not restrain them. 14 Therefore I swear to the house of Eli that the iniquity of Eli's house shall not be expiated by sacrifice or offering forever."

d. Samuel tells Eli of the judgment of God

15 Samuel lay there until morning; then he opened the doors of the house of the LORD. Samuel was afraid to tell the vision to Eli. 16 But Eli called Samuel and said, "Samuel, my son." He said, "Here I am." 17 Eli said, "What was it that he told you? Do not hide it from me. May God do so to you and more also, if you hide anything from me of all that he told you." 18 So Samuel told him everything and hid nothing from him. Then he said, "It is the LORD; let him do what seems good to him."

[s] Q Ms Gk See 3.10: MT *the LORD called Samuel*   [t] Another reading is *for themselves*

Marginal references (left column):

3.1 / 1 Sam 2.11, 18; / Ps 74.9; / Am 8.11

3.2 / 1 Sam 4.15 / 3.3 / Lev 24.2-4 / 3.4 / Isa 6.8

3.7 / Acts 19.2

3.11 / 2 Kings 21.12; / Jer 19.3 / 3.12 / 1 Sam 2.30-36

3.13 / 1 Sam 2.12, 17, 22, 29-31 / 3.14 / Lev 15.30, 31; / Isa 22.14

3.17 / Ruth 1.17; / 2 Sam 3.35

3.18 / Job 2.10; / Isa 39.8

3.1 *visions were not widespread.* The silence of God prevailed. No one was known (publicly) to have received visions from God in those days.
3.3 This verse marks the beginning of God's open dealing with Samuel, who would soon be called to replace Eli.
3.11 God's first message to Samuel was one of judgment on the children of Eli for blasphemy (v. 13) and on Eli himself for his failure to restrain them in their evil. Samuel had to reveal this sentence to Eli.
3.13 Eli the priest favored his children above his God. In 2.12 we are told that the "sons of Eli were

scoundrels; they had no regard for the LORD." They were adulterers, and they abused their privilege as priests by breaking ceremonial arrangements (2.12–17), treating the offering of the Lord with contempt (see 2.17). Even after Eli discovered their transgressions, he did nothing to correct the situation. He failed to restrain his children and thus was guilty of being an accessory to their crimes against God. God pronounced his judgment, ending the priestly succession through Eli. When he died, he was replaced by Samuel.

e. Samuel established as a prophet

19 As Samuel grew up, the LORD was with him and let none of his
words fall to the ground. 20And all Israel from Dan to Beer-sheba knew
that Samuel was a trustworthy prophet of the LORD. 21The LORD continued to appear at Shiloh, for the LORD revealed himself to Samuel at Shiloh
4 by the word of the LORD. 1And the word of Samuel came to all Israel.

B. Samuel welds the theocracy together

1. The defeat of Israel; the capture of the ark

In those days the Philistines mustered for war against Israel,ᵘ and
Israel went out to battle against them;ᵛ they encamped at Ebenezer, and
the Philistines encamped at Aphek. 2The Philistines drew up in line
against Israel, and when the battle was joined,ʷ Israel was defeated by
the Philistines, who killed about four thousand men on the field of battle.
3When the troops came to the camp, the elders of Israel said, "Why has
the LORD put us to rout today before the Philistines? Let us bring the ark
of the covenant of the LORD here from Shiloh, so that he may come among
us and save us from the power of our enemies." 4So the people sent to
Shiloh, and brought from there the ark of the covenant of the LORD of
hosts, who is enthroned on the cherubim. The two sons of Eli, Hophni
and Phinehas, were there with the ark of the covenant of God.

5 When the ark of the covenant of the LORD came into the camp, all
Israel gave a mighty shout, so that the earth resounded. 6When the
Philistines heard the noise of the shouting, they said, "What does this
great shouting in the camp of the Hebrews mean?" When they learned that
the ark of the LORD had come to the camp, 7the Philistines were afraid;
for they said, "Gods haveˣ come into the camp." They also said, "Woe
to us! For nothing like this has happened before. 8Woe to us! Who can
deliver us from the power of these mighty gods? These are the gods who
struck the Egyptians with every sort of plague in the wilderness. 9Take
courage, and be men, O Philistines, in order not to become slaves to the
Hebrews as they have been to you; be men and fight."

10 So the Philistines fought; Israel was defeated, and they fled, everyone to his home. There was a very great slaughter, for there fell of Israel
thirty thousand foot soldiers. 11The ark of God was captured; and the two
sons of Eli, Hophni and Phinehas, died.

2. The death of Eli

a. His accident

12 A man of Benjamin ran from the battle line, and came to Shiloh
the same day, with his clothes torn and with earth upon his head. 13When
he arrived, Eli was sitting upon his seat by the road watching, for his heart
trembled for the ark of God. When the man came into the city and told

ᵘ Gk: Heb lacks *In those days the Philistines mustered for war against Israel* ᵛ Gk: Heb *against the
Philistines* ʷ Meaning of Heb uncertain ˣ Or *A god has*

3.19
1 Sam 2.21;
Gen 21.22;
39.2;
1 Sam 9.6
3.20
Judg 20.1
3.21
v. 10
4.1
1 Sam 7.12

4.3
Josh 7.7, 8;
Num 10.35

4.4
2 Sam 6.2;
Ex 25.18, 22

4.5
Josh 6.5, 20
4.6
Ex 15.14

4.9
1 Cor 16.13;
Judg 13.1

4.10
v. 2;
Deut 28.25;
2 Sam 18.17;
2 Kings 14.12
4.11
1 Sam 2.34;
Ps 78.56-64

4.12
Josh 7.6;
2 Sam 1.2;
Neh 9.1
4.13
v. 18;
1 Sam 1.9

3.19 *let none of his words fall to the ground.* Every
word that Samuel spoke as a prophet proved true.
4.1 *Philistines.* See note on Judg 13.1 for background information on these people.
4.2 *Israel was defeated,* i.e., they lost the battle
against a well-armed and aggressive foe. The Israelites
thought the absence of the ark was the reason for their
defeat (v. 3).
4.3 Israel superstitiously believed that bringing the
ark to the battle would enable them to defeat the
Philistines. But this was useless, for they were disobeying God by regarding it as an idol or an item of
magic.

4.4 *cherubim.* See note on Ex 25.22.
4.8 The Philistines regarded the ark as deity. Their
attitude is understandable because they had no
knowledge of the true God.
4.11 The presence of Hophni and Phinehas with the
ark was a sure guarantee of defeat. These children of
Eli were apostates, who denied the true faith and
sinned against God. They died for their transgressions.
4.12 *Shiloh.* This verse does not mention the destruction of Shiloh, but archaeological findings confirm what is reported in Jer 7.12; 26.6.

the news, all the city cried out. 14 When Eli heard the sound of the outcry, he said, "What is this uproar?" Then the man came quickly and told Eli.

4.15
1 Sam 3.2
4.16
2Sa 1.4

15 Now Eli was ninety-eight years old and his eyes were set, so that he could not see. 16 The man said to Eli, "I have just come from the battle; I fled from the battle today." He said, "How did it go, my son?" 17 The messenger replied, "Israel has fled before the Philistines, and there has also been a great slaughter among the troops; your two sons also, Hophni and Phinehas, are dead, and the ark of God has been captured." 18 When

4.18
v. 13

he mentioned the ark of God, Eli^y fell over backward from his seat by the side of the gate; and his neck was broken and he died, for he was an old man, and heavy. He had judged Israel forty years.

b. The birth of Ichabod

19 Now his daughter-in-law, the wife of Phinehas, was pregnant, about to give birth. When she heard the news that the ark of God was captured, and that her father-in-law and her husband were dead, she

4.20
Gen 35.16-19

bowed and gave birth; for her labor pains overwhelmed her. 20 As she was about to die, the women attending her said to her, "Do not be afraid, for you have borne a son." But she did not answer or give heed. 21 She named the child Ichabod, meaning, "The glory has departed from Israel," because the ark of God had been captured and because of her father-in-law

4.22
Jer 2.11;
v. 11

and her husband. 22 She said, "The glory has departed from Israel, for the ark of God has been captured."

3. The ark in the hands of the Philistines

a. The ark at Ashdod in the house of Dagon

5.1
1 Sam 4.1;
7.12
5.2
Judg 16.23
5.3
Isa 19.1;
46.1, 2, 7
5.4
Ezek 6.4, 6

5 When the Philistines captured the ark of God, they brought it from Ebenezer to Ashdod; 2 then the Philistines took the ark of God and brought it into the house of Dagon and placed it beside Dagon. 3 When the people of Ashdod rose early the next day, there was Dagon, fallen on his face to the ground before the ark of the LORD. So they took Dagon and put him back in his place. 4 But when they rose early on the next morning, Dagon had fallen on his face to the ground before the ark of the LORD, and the head of Dagon and both his hands were lying cut off upon the threshold; only the trunk of^z Dagon was left to him. 5 This is why the priests of Dagon and all who enter the house of Dagon do not step on the threshold of Dagon in Ashdod to this day.

b. The ark at Gath and Ekron

5.6
vv. 7, 11;
Ex 9.3;
1 Sam 6.5;
Deut 28.27;
Ps 78.66
5.8
v. 11

6 The hand of the LORD was heavy upon the people of Ashdod, and he terrified and struck them with tumors, both in Ashdod and in its territory. 7 And when the inhabitants of Ashdod saw how things were, they said, "The ark of the God of Israel must not remain with us; for his hand is heavy on us and on our god Dagon." 8 So they sent and gathered together all the lords of the Philistines, and said, "What shall we do with the ark of the God of Israel?" The inhabitants of Gath replied, "Let the ark of God be moved on to us."^a So they moved the ark of the God of

---

y Heb he   z Heb lacks the trunk of   a Gk Compare Q Ms: MT They answered, "Let the ark of the God of Israel be brought around to Gath."

4.18 To the credit of Eli, it may be said that it was the loss of the ark, not the death of his children, that caused his death. Note that Eli served both as judge and as priest.

4.19 Phinehas' wife appears to have been a devout believer who was concerned about the ark and the glory of God. She died giving birth to the child she named Ichabod, whose name means "without glory."

5.2 Dagon was the chief god of the Philistines. Temples were erected in his honor in Ashdod, Gaza, Beth-

shan, and Ugarit. He was a fertility god (or grain god) in Philistia, a land which produced much grain.

5.3 This marks the story of a pagan god against the true God. Dagon fell on its face before the ark of God. God will not be mocked. Nothing, living or dead, stone or human, can stand before the majesty of the Most High God.

5.8ff The Philistines carried the sacred ark of God to another city. They paid a high price for their error. God sent sickness so grievous that they began to panic and wanted to rid themselves of the ark.

Israel to Gath.*b* 9 But after they had brought it to Gath,*c* the hand of the LORD was against the city, causing a very great panic; he struck the inhabitants of the city, both young and old, so that tumors broke out on them. 10 So they sent the ark of the God of Israel*d* to Ekron. But when the ark of God came to Ekron, the people of Ekron cried out, "Why*e* have they brought around to us*f* the ark of the God of Israel to kill us*f* and our*g* people?" 11 They sent therefore and gathered together all the lords of the Philistines, and said, "Send away the ark of the God of Israel, and let it return to its own place, that it may not kill us and our people." For there was a deathly panic*h* throughout the whole city. The hand of God was very heavy there; 12 those who did not die were stricken with tumors, and the cry of the city went up to heaven.

4. The return of the ark

a. The ark sent away with sacrifices

6 The ark of the LORD was in the country of the Philistines seven months. 2 Then the Philistines called for the priests and the diviners and said, "What shall we do with the ark of the LORD? Tell us what we should send with it to its place." 3 They said, "If you send away the ark of the God of Israel, do not send it empty, but by all means return him a guilt offering. Then you will be healed and will be ransomed;*i* will not his hand then turn from you?" 4 And they said, "What is the guilt offering that we shall return to him?" They answered, "Five gold tumors and five gold mice, according to the number of the lords of the Philistines; for the same plague was upon all of you and upon your lords. 5 So you must make images of your tumors and images of your mice that ravage the land, and give glory to the God of Israel; perhaps he will lighten his hand on you and your gods and your land. 6 Why should you harden your hearts as the Egyptians and Pharaoh hardened their hearts? After he had made fools of them, did they not let the people go, and they departed? 7 Now then, get ready a new cart and two milch cows that have never borne a yoke, and yoke the cows to the cart, but take their calves home, away from them. 8 Take the ark of the LORD and place it on the cart, and put in a box at its side the figures of gold, which you are returning to him as a guilt offering. Then send it off, and let it go its way. 9 And watch; if it goes up on the way to its own land, to Beth-shemesh, then it is he who has done us this great harm; but if not, then we shall know that it is not his hand that struck us; it happened to us by chance."

10 The men did so; they took two milch cows and yoked them to the cart, and shut up their calves at home. 11 They put the ark of the LORD on the cart, and the box with the gold mice and the images of their tumors. 12 The cows went straight in the direction of Beth-shemesh along one highway, lowing as they went; they turned neither to the right nor to the left, and the lords of the Philistines went after them as far as the border of Beth-shemesh.

13 Now the people of Beth-shemesh were reaping their wheat harvest in the valley. When they looked up and saw the ark, they went with rejoicing to meet it.*j* 14 The cart came into the field of Joshua of Beth-

5.9
vv. 6, 11;
1 Sam 7.13;
Ps 78.66

5.11
vv. 6, 8, 9

6.2
Gen 41.8;
Ex 7.11;
Isa 2.6
6.3
Ex 23.15;
Deut 16.16;
Lev 5.15, 16
6.4
vv. 17, 18;
Josh 13.3;
Judg 3.3
6.5
1 Sam 5.3-11;
Josh 7.19;
Isa 42.12
6.6
Ex 8.15;
9.34; 12.31
6.7
2 Sam 6.3;
Num 19.2

6.8
vv. 3-5

6.9
Josh 15.10;
v. 3

6.12
v. 9;
Num 20.19

6.14
2 Sam 24.22;
1 Kings 19.21

b Gk: Heb lacks *to Gath*   *c* Ms: MT lacks *to Gath*   *d* Q Ms Gk: MT lacks *of Israel*   *e* Q Ms Gk: MT lacks *Why*   *f* Heb *me*   *g* Heb *my*   *h* Q Ms reads *a panic from the LORD*   *i* Q Ms Gk: MT *and it will be known to you*   *j* Gk: Heb *rejoiced to see it*

5.11 *let it return to its own place.* It took dire sickness for the Philistines to decide to return the ark to the place from whence it came. Apparently they had enough sense to know when they were defeated and what they needed to do about it.
6.4 The Philistines knew that they had violated the God of Israel and they decided to make a sacrifice, to arrest the sickness which had spread through their

ranks.
6.12 God can use animals to do his will (cf. Num 22.22–35). Sometimes they demonstrate more good sense than the humans who own them. The cows headed straight for Beth-shemesh without missing a turn. They shamed the faithlessness of the Israelites, who had made no effort to bring the ark to its home.

shemesh, and stopped there. A large stone was there; so they split up the wood of the cart and offered the cows as a burnt offering to the Lord. 15 The Levites took down the ark of the Lord and the box that was beside it, in which were the gold objects, and set them upon the large stone. Then the people of Beth-shemesh offered burnt offerings and presented sacrifices on that day to the Lord. 16 When the five lords of the Philistines saw it, they returned that day to Ekron.

6.16
Josh 13.3

b. The ark sent from Beth-shemesh to Kiriath-jearim

6.17
v. 4
6.18
vv. 14, 15

17 These are the gold tumors, which the Philistines returned as a guilt offering to the Lord: one for Ashdod, one for Gaza, one for Ashkelon, one for Gath, one for Ekron; 18 also the gold mice, according to the number of all the cities of the Philistines belonging to the five lords, both fortified cities and unwalled villages. The great stone, beside which they set down the ark of the Lord, is a witness to this day in the field of Joshua of Beth-shemesh.

6.19
Num 4.5, 15,
20; 2 Sam 6.7
6.20
Lev 11.44,
45; 2 Sam 6.9
6.21
Josh 9.17;
15.9, 60
7.1
2 Sam 6.3, 4

19 The descendants of Jeconiah did not rejoice with the people of Beth-shemesh when they greeted[k] the ark of the Lord; and he killed seventy men of them.[l] The people mourned because the Lord had made a great slaughter among the people. 20 Then the people of Beth-shemesh said, "Who is able to stand before the Lord, this holy God? To whom shall he go so that we may be rid of him?" 21 So they sent messengers to the inhabitants of Kiriath-jearim, saying, "The Philistines have returned the ark of the Lord. Come down and take it up to you." 1 And the people of Kiriath-jearim came and took up the ark of the Lord, and brought it to the house of Abinadab on the hill. They consecrated his son, Eleazar, to have charge of the ark of the Lord.

2 From the day that the ark was lodged at Kiriath-jearim, a long time passed, some twenty years, and all the house of Israel lamented[m] after the Lord.

5. Samuel overcomes the Philistines

a. The call to repentance

7.3
Joel 2.2;
Josh 24.14;
Judg 2.13;
Deut 6.13;
Mt 4.10

3 Then Samuel said to all the house of Israel, "If you are returning to the Lord with all your heart, then put away the foreign gods and the Astartes from among you. Direct your heart to the Lord, and serve him only, and he will deliver you out of the hand of the Philistines." 4 So Israel put away the Baals and the Astartes, and they served the Lord only.

b. The defeat of the Philistines

7.6
Ps 62.8;
Neh 9.1;
Judg 10.10

5 Then Samuel said, "Gather all Israel at Mizpah, and I will pray to the Lord for you." 6 So they gathered at Mizpah, and drew water and poured it out before the Lord. They fasted that day, and said, "We have sinned against the Lord." And Samuel judged the people of Israel at Mizpah.

7.7
1 Sam 17.11
7.8
Isa 37.4

7 When the Philistines heard that the people of Israel had gathered at Mizpah, the lords of the Philistines went up against Israel. And when the people of Israel heard of it they were afraid of the Philistines. 8 The

k Gk: Heb And he killed some of the people of Beth-shemesh, because they looked into l Heb killed seventy men, fifty thousand men m Meaning of Heb uncertain

6.19 The ark of the Lord had originally been placed within the most holy place, into which only the high priest could enter once a year. When the ark was returned to Israel from the Philistines, the tent of meeting was no longer set up. Thus the ark was exposed to everyone. Some of the Israelites wanted to look into it, perhaps to see the two tables of the law. When they invaded God's privacy, judgment fell on them and many died at the hands of an angry God.

7.3,4 Israel may have had a high regard for the ark, but they also had been worshiping other gods. Samuel called them to repent and return to the worship of the one true God. Revival took place and Israel served only the Lord.
7.6 As evidence of the sincerity of their revival, the Israelites prayed, fasted, repented, and poured out water before the Lord.

people of Israel said to Samuel, "Do not cease to cry out to the LORD our God for us, and pray that he may save us from the hand of the Philistines." 9 So Samuel took a sucking lamb and offered it as a whole burnt offering to the LORD; Samuel cried out to the LORD for Israel, and the LORD answered him. 10 As Samuel was offering up the burnt offering, the Philistines drew near to attack Israel; but the LORD thundered with a mighty voice that day against the Philistines and threw them into confusion; and they were routed before Israel. 11 And the men of Israel went out of Mizpah and pursued the Philistines, and struck them down as far as beyond Beth-car.

c. The Ebenezer

12 Then Samuel took a stone and set it up between Mizpah and Jeshanah,[n] and named it Ebenezer;[o] for he said, "Thus far the LORD has helped us." 13 So the Philistines were subdued and did not again enter the territory of Israel; the hand of the LORD was against the Philistines all the days of Samuel. 14 The towns that the Philistines had taken from Israel were restored to Israel, from Ekron to Gath; and Israel recovered their territory from the hand of the Philistines. There was peace also between Israel and the Amorites.

d. Samuel's circuit

15 Samuel judged Israel all the days of his life. 16 He went on a circuit year by year to Bethel, Gilgal, and Mizpah; and he judged Israel in all these places. 17 Then he would come back to Ramah, for his home was there; he administered justice there to Israel, and built there an altar to the LORD.

II. The reign of Saul (8.1–31.13)

A. The appointment of Saul as king

1. Israel demands a king

8 When Samuel became old, he made his sons judges over Israel. 2 The name of his firstborn son was Joel, and the name of his second, Abijah; they were judges in Beer-sheba. 3 Yet his sons did not follow in his ways, but turned aside after gain; they took bribes and perverted justice.

4   Then all the elders of Israel gathered together and came to Samuel

n Gk Syr: Heb Shen   o That is Stone of Help

Cross references (right margin):
7.9 Ps 99.6; Jer 15.1
7.10 Josh 10.10; 1 Sam 2.10; 2 Sam 22.14, 15
7.12 Gen 35.14; Josh 4.9
7.13 Judg 13.1; 1 Sam 13.5
7.15 v. 6; 1 Sam 12.11
7.17 1 Sam 1.19; 7.5; Judg 20.1; 1 Sam 8.6
8.1 Deut 16.18, 19
8.3 Ex 23.6, 8; Deut 16.19; Ps 15.5
8.4 1 Sam 7.17

7.9 Samuel was a praying prophet and priest. His prayers were heard and answered by God almost instantaneously, for thunder and lightning overtook the Philistines, who retreated. Once again God answered by a providential act.

7.12 named it Ebenezer. This incident represented the great victory the Lord God had given the Israelites over the Philistines. The stone was intended to be a memorial for future generations, so that their faith in God might be strengthened and that they might experience the same delivering power of their ancestors' God. Believers today should also raise "Ebenezers" in their souls, in order to remember the mighty deliverances of which God was, and is, capable.

7.13 Samuel, by means of prayer and the work of reformation among the Israelites, brought them peace from the threat of the Philistines all the days of his ministry. God now helped Israel and raised his hand against the Philistines. If God is on our side, who can be against us (cf. Rom 8.31)?

7.17 he would come back to Ramah. Ramah was Samuel's home town (see note on 1.1). Since Shiloh was in ruins, Samuel found it convenient to make his headquarters in Ramah.

8.1ff Samuel should have learned something from the experience of Eli, his predecessor. But he did not. Like Eli, he appointed his children as judges over Israel, even though they did not follow in his footsteps. They were guilty of taking bribes and perverting judgment. This situation prompted the elders of Israel to ask for a king; they were tired of being ruled by scoundrels. Samuel was displeased, but God ordered him to anoint the one he had chosen to be king over Israel.

8.2 It is surely ironic that the children of Samuel were no better than Eli's children, whom God slew. Since Samuel witnessed the experience of Eli and noted the conduct of Eli's children, one would have expected something better of Samuel's own children. This does indicate that good people can have problem children. Grace does not run through the blood of the family; it comes from God.

8.5ff
Deut 17.14,
15
8.6
1 Sam 15.11
8.7
1 Sam 10.19;
Ex 16.8

at Ramah, 5 and said to him, "You are old and your sons do not follow in your ways; appoint for us, then, a king to govern us, like other nations." 6 But the thing displeased Samuel when they said, "Give us a king to govern us." Samuel prayed to the LORD, 7 and the LORD said to Samuel, "Listen to the voice of the people in all that they say to you; for they have not rejected you, but they have rejected me from being king over them. 8 Just as they have done to me,*p* from the day I brought them up out of Egypt to this day, forsaking me and serving other gods, so also they are

8.9
v. 11

doing to you. 9 Now then, listen to their voice; only — you shall solemnly warn them, and show them the ways of the king who shall reign over them."

8.11
1 Sam 14.52;
2 Sam 5.1
8.12
1 Sam 22.7

10   So Samuel reported all the words of the LORD to the people who were asking him for a king. 11 He said, "These will be the ways of the king who will reign over you: he will take your sons and appoint them to his chariots and to be his horsemen, and to run before his chariots; 12 and he will appoint for himself commanders of thousands and commanders of fifties, and some to plow his ground and to reap his harvest, and to make his implements of war and the equipment of his chariots. 13 He will take

8.14
1 Kings 21.7;
Ezek 46.18

your daughters to be perfumers and cooks and bakers. 14 He will take the best of your fields and vineyards and olive orchards and give them to his courtiers. 15 He will take one-tenth of your grain and of your vineyards and give it to his officers and his courtiers. 16 He will take your male and female slaves, and the best of your cattle*q* and donkeys, and put them to his work. 17 He will take one-tenth of your flocks, and you shall be his

8.18
Prov 1.25-28;
Mic 3.4

slaves. 18 And in that day you will cry out because of your king, whom you have chosen for yourselves; but the LORD will not answer you in that day."

8.20
v. 5

19   But the people refused to listen to the voice of Samuel; they said, "No! but we are determined to have a king over us, 20 so that we also may be like other nations, and that our king may govern us and go out before us and fight our battles." 21 When Samuel had heard all the words of the

8.22
v. 7

people, he repeated them in the ears of the LORD. 22 The LORD said to Samuel, "Listen to their voice and set a king over them." Samuel then said to the people of Israel, "Each of you return home."

2. God selects Saul

a. The family of Saul

9.1
1 Sam 14.51;
1 Chr 9.36-39
9.2
1 Sam 10.23,
24

9 There was a man of Benjamin whose name was Kish son of Abiel son of Zeror son of Becorath son of Aphiah, a Benjaminite, a man of wealth. 2 He had a son whose name was Saul, a handsome young man. There was not a man among the people of Israel more handsome than he; he stood head and shoulders above everyone else.

b. The search for his father's donkeys

3   Now the donkeys of Kish, Saul's father, had strayed. So Kish said

p Gk: Heb lacks *to me*   *q* Gk: Heb *young men*

8.5ff   From the exodus on, God had ruled Israel through his servant Moses. The rule of a divinely appointed servant continued through the days of Joshua and the judges, including Samuel. When his children sinned, the people asked for a king. Samuel was unhappy but consented to the request because God commanded him to do so. Note that God had earlier outlined for his people rules for establishing Israel as a kingship (Deut 17.14-20). Samuel told the people what was in store for them (vv. 11-18), but they failed to heed the warning. They probably thought that serving *any* king would be better than serving the wicked sons of Samuel. God predicted that the kingship would prove to be disastrous, and

this prophecy was fulfilled with the rule of the ungodly kings of Judah and of Israel. At the consummation of the present age, the theocracy will be restored. God will reign over his people through Jesus Christ, whose kingdom shall endure forever (Lk 1.32; 1 Tim 1.17; 6.14-16).

8.19-22   The stubbornness of Israel strongly manifested itself. They refused to heed the counsel of Samuel and insisted on having a king. God ordered Samuel to give them what they craved.

9.2   From the human vantage point Saul was everything Israel could want in a king, i.e., in outward appearance. He was tall, handsome, and wealthy, and came from the tribe of Benjamin.

to his son Saul, "Take one of the boys with you; go and look for the donkeys." ⁴He passed through the hill country of Ephraim and passed through the land of Shalishah, but they did not find them. And they passed through the land of Shaalim, but they were not there. Then he passed through the land of Benjamin, but they did not find them.

5   When they came to the land of Zuph, Saul said to the boy who was with him, "Let us turn back, or my father will stop worrying about the donkeys and worry about us." ⁶But he said to him, "There is a man of God in this town; he is a man held in honor. Whatever he says always comes true. Let us go there now; perhaps he will tell us about the journey on which we have set out." ⁷Then Saul replied to the boy, "But if we go, what can we bring the man? For the bread in our sacks is gone, and there is no present to bring to the man of God. What have we?" ⁸The boy answered Saul again, "Here, I have with me a quarter shekel of silver; I will give it to the man of God, to tell us our way." ⁹(Formerly in Israel, anyone who went to inquire of God would say, "Come, let us go to the seer"; for the one who is now called a prophet was formerly called a seer.) ¹⁰Saul said to the boy, "Good; come, let us go." So they went to the town where the man of God was.

c. God reveals his choice to Samuel:
he and Saul talk and eat together

11   As they went up the hill to the town, they met some girls coming out to draw water, and said to them, "Is the seer here?" ¹²They answered, "Yes, there he is just ahead of you. Hurry; he has come just now to the town, because the people have a sacrifice today at the shrine. ¹³As soon as you enter the town, you will find him, before he goes up to the shrine to eat. For the people will not eat until he comes, since he must bless the sacrifice; afterward those eat who are invited. Now go up, for you will meet him immediately." ¹⁴So they went up to the town. As they were entering the town, they saw Samuel coming out toward them on his way up to the shrine.

15   Now the day before Saul came, the LORD had revealed to Samuel: ¹⁶"Tomorrow about this time I will send to you a man from the land of Benjamin, and you shall anoint him to be ruler over my people Israel. He shall save my people from the hand of the Philistines; for I have seen the suffering of[r] my people, because their outcry has come to me." ¹⁷When Samuel saw Saul, the LORD told him, "Here is the man of whom I spoke to you. It is who shall rule over my people." ¹⁸Then Saul approached Samuel inside the gate, and said, "Tell me, please, where is the house of the seer?" ¹⁹Samuel answered Saul, "I am the seer; go up before me to the shrine, for today you shall eat with me, and in the morning I will let

r Gk: Heb lacks the suffering of

Cross references (margin):
9.4 Josh 24.33; 2 Kings 4.42; Josh 19.42
9.5 1 Sam 10.2
9.6 Deut 33.1; 1 Sam 3.19
9.7 1 Kings 14.3; 2 Kings 8.8
9.9 2 Sam 24.11; 1 Chr 26.28; Isa 30.10
9.11 Gen 24.15
9.12 Num 28.11-15; 1 Sam 7.17; 10.5
9.16 1 Sam 10.1; Ex 3.7, 9
9.17 1 Sam 16.12

9.5 Providence in the search for the lost asses brought Saul to Zuph, where Samuel awaited God's choice for the kingship. God had not yet told Samuel who it would be.
9.6 *in this town,* apparently Ramah, where Samuel now had his headquarters. *Whatever he says always comes true.* This was the supreme test of a true prophet, as set forth in Deut 18.21,22.
9.9 Saul's servant suggested that they visit Samuel, who is here called a *seer* (which meant that he could see things others did not see). They planned to give him a piece of silver out of respect for his office and with the expectation that he would tell them what they needed to know.
9.12 *at the shrine.* Now that Shiloh was in ruins, Samuel had built an altar on a hill in Ramah. This became the central place for worship (see 7.17).
9.15,16 The LORD *had revealed to Samuel.* God

spoke to Samuel in a familiar and secret way so that his will was made known to the prophet. Amos says, "The LORD God does nothing, without revealing his secret to his servants the prophets" (Am 3.7). Whether this was done through prayer or through the Holy Spirit or directly by God the Father is of no account. It was a private revelation from the triune God to the listening ear of the prophet. Today God speaks to us by the Spirit through his word.
9.18–21 Evidently Samuel wore no distinctive clothing and presented no special appearance. Saul asked him for directions as to where Samuel could be found. He got more than he expected, for Samuel told him about his asses even before they were mentioned, and he ordered Saul to eat with him. When he uttered the prophetic statement, "And on whom is all Israel's desire fixed, if not on you. . . ?" Saul showed a spirit of humility and deference (v. 21).

9.20
v. 3;
1 Sam 8.5;
12.13
9.21
1 Sam 15.17;
Judg 20.46,
48

9.24
Lev 7.32, 33;
Num 18.18

9.25
Deut 22.8;
Acts 10.9

10.1
1 Sam 16.13;
2 Kings 9.3,
6;
Ps 2.12;
Deut 32.9;
Ps 78.71
10.2
Gen 35.19,
20;
1 Sam 9.3-5

10.3
Gen 28.22;
35.1, 3, 7, 8

10.5
1 Sam 13.3;
9.12; 19.20;
2 Kings 3.15

10.6
Num 11.25,
29; v. 10;
1 Sam 19.23,
24
10.7
Josh 1.5;
Judg 6.12

you go and will tell you all that is on your mind. 20 As for your donkeys that were lost three days ago, give no further thought to them, for they have been found. And on whom is all Israel's desire fixed, if not on you and on all your ancestral house?" 21 Saul answered, "I am only a Benjaminite, from the least of the tribes of Israel, and my family is the humblest of all the families of the tribe of Benjamin. Why then have you spoken to me in this way?"

22 Then Samuel took Saul and his servant-boy and brought them into the hall, and gave them a place at the head of those who had been invited, of whom there were about thirty. 23 And Samuel said to the cook, "Bring the portion I gave you, the one I asked you to put aside." 24 The cook took up the thigh and what went with it*s* and set them before Saul. Samuel said, "See, what was kept is set before you. Eat; for it is set*t* before you at the appointed time, so that you might eat with the guests."*u*

So Saul ate with Samuel that day. 25 When they came down from the shrine into the town, a bed was spread for Saul*v* on the roof, and he lay down to sleep.*w* 26 Then at the break of dawn*x* Samuel called to Saul upon the roof, "Get up, so that I may send you on your way." Saul got up, and both he and Samuel went out into the street.

3. Saul's coronation

a. Saul anointed by Samuel; his father's donkeys found

27 As they were going down to the outskirts of the town, Samuel said to Saul, "Tell the boy to go on before us, and when he has passed on, stop here yourself for a while, that I may make known to you the word of God."

10 1 Samuel took a vial of oil and poured it on his head, and kissed him; he said, "The Lord has anointed you ruler over his people Israel. You shall reign over the people of the Lord and you will save them from the hand of their enemies all around. Now this shall be the sign to you that the Lord has anointed you ruler*y* over his heritage: 2 When you depart from me today you will meet two men by Rachel's tomb in the territory of Benjamin at Zelzah; they will say to you, 'The donkeys that you went to seek are found, and now your father has stopped worrying about them and is worrying about you, saying: What shall I do about my son?' 3 Then you shall go on from there further and come to the oak of Tabor; three men going up to God at Bethel will meet you there, one carrying three kids, another carrying three loaves of bread, and another carrying a skin of wine. 4 They will greet you and give you two loaves of bread, which you shall accept from them. 5 After that you shall come to Gibeath-elohim,*z* at the place where the Philistine garrison is; there, as you come to the town, you will meet a band of prophets coming down from the shrine with harp, tambourine, flute, and lyre playing in front of them; they will be in a prophetic frenzy. 6 Then the spirit of the Lord will possess you, and you will be in a prophetic frenzy along with them and be turned into a different person. 7 Now when these signs meet you, do

---

s Meaning of Heb uncertain   *t* Q Ms Gk: MT *it was kept*   *u* Cn: Heb *it was kept for you, saying, I have invited the people*   *v* Gk: Heb *and he spoke with Saul*   *w* Gk: Heb lacks *and he lay down to sleep*   *x* Gk: Heb *and they arose early and at break of dawn*   *y* Gk: Heb lacks *over his people Israel. You shall . . . anointed you ruler*   *z* Or *the Hill of God*

9.24 Giving Saul the thigh of the meat was a symbol of honor, which placed him above all the other guests.
9.27 Undoubtedly here Samuel informed Saul what God had told him about the kingship and his appointment by God to that office. It must have come as a great surprise to Saul.
10.1 *The Lord has anointed you.* God assured Saul that he was God's choice by three external signs: two men would inform him that the asses had been found, he would receive two loaves of bread from three other

men, and he would prophesy with a band of prophets (see next note).
10.6 Samuel prophesied that the Spirit of the Lord would come mightily upon Saul and that he would prophesy. Throughout the first part of his kingship, the Spirit regularly empowered Saul, enabling him to put down Israel's enemies. When he sinned, however, the Spirit of God left Saul and rendered him incapable of doing God's will and of performing great feats (see note on 16.13).

whatever you see fit to do, for God is with you. 8 And you shall go down to Gilgal ahead of me; then I will come down to you to present burnt offerings and offer sacrifices of well-being. Seven days you shall wait, until I come to you and show you what you shall do."

9 As he turned away to leave Samuel, God gave him another heart; and all these signs were fulfilled that day. 10 When they were going from there*a* to Gibeah,*b* a band of prophets met him; and the spirit of God possessed him, and he fell into a prophetic frenzy along with them. 11 When all who knew him before saw how he prophesied with the prophets, the people said to one another, "What has come over the son of Kish? Is Saul also among the prophets?" 12 A man of the place answered, "And who is their father?" Therefore it became a proverb, "Is Saul also among the prophets?" 13 When his prophetic frenzy had ended, he went home.*c*

14 Saul's uncle said to him and to the boy, "Where did you go?" And he replied, "To seek the donkeys; and when we saw they were not to be found, we went to Samuel." 15 Saul's uncle said, "Tell me what Samuel said to you." 16 Saul said to his uncle, "He told us that the donkeys had been found." But about the matter of the kingship, of which Samuel had spoken, he did not tell him anything.

b. *Saul accepted and crowned by Israel*

17 Samuel summoned the people to the LORD at Mizpah 18 and said to them,*d* "Thus says the LORD, the God of Israel, 'I brought up Israel out of Egypt, and I rescued you from the hand of the Egyptians and from the hand of all the kingdoms that were oppressing you.' 19 But today you have rejected your God, who saves you from all your calamities and your distresses; and you have said, 'No! but set a king over us.' Now therefore present yourselves before the LORD by your tribes and by your clans."

20 Then Samuel brought all the tribes of Israel near, and the tribe of Benjamin was taken by lot. 21 He brought the tribe of Benjamin near by its families, and the family of the Matrites was taken by lot. Finally he brought the family of the Matrites near man by man,*e* and Saul the son of Kish was taken by lot. But when they sought him, he could not be found. 22 So they inquired again of the LORD, "Did the man come here?"*f* and the LORD said, "See, he has hidden himself among the baggage." 23 Then they ran and brought him from there. When he took his stand among the people, he was head and shoulders taller than any of them. 24 Samuel said to all the people, "Do you see the one whom the LORD has chosen? There is no one like him among all the people." And all the people shouted, "Long live the king!"

25 Samuel told the people the rights and duties of the kingship; and he wrote them in a book and laid it up before the LORD. Then Samuel sent all the people back to their homes. 26 Saul also went to his home at Gibeah, and with him went warriors whose hearts God had touched.

---

a Gk: Heb *they came there*   *b* Or *the hill*   *c* Cn: Heb *he came to the shrine*   *d* Heb *to the people of Israel*
e Gk: Heb lacks *Finally . . . man by man*   *f* Gk: Heb *Is there yet a man to come here?*

Cross-references

10.8 1 Sam 11.15; 13.8
10.9 v. 6
10.10 vv. 5, 6; 1 Sam 19.20
10.11 1 Sam 19.24; Mt 13.54, 55; Jn 7.15
10.16 1 Sam 9.20
10.17 1 Sam 7.5, 6
10.18 Judg 6.8, 9
10.19 1 Sam 8.6, 7; Josh 24.1
10.20 Josh 7.14, 16, 17
10.22 1 Sam 23.2, 4, 9-11
10.23 1 Sam 9.2
10.24 2 Sam 21.6; 1 Kings 1.25, 39
10.25 1 Sam 8.11-18; Deut 17.14-20
10.26 1 Sam 11.4

10.12 *Is Saul also among the prophets?* This was an expression of surprise; Saul's friends were incredulous that he had become so religious.
10.20ff God's will that Saul become king was manifested by the use of the lot. This outward sign was for Israel's benefit, for God had already chosen him as king. Samuel presented Saul fittingly by saying there was none like him in all Israel. And for the first time in Israel's history the shout rang out: "Long live the king!" (v. 24).
10.24 The choice of Saul for the kingship is somewhat of an enigma; Saul came from the tribe of Benjamin, whereas Jacob's blessing gave the kingship to Judah (Gen 49.10). Why did God choose Saul to be king? We can surmise two reasons. (1) Just as God had used Samson and the other judges to lead his people until a king could be chosen, so also he used Saul until David was full-grown and ready for the kingship. (2) Saul prepared the way for David's later conquests of the entire territory promised by God to Abraham (Gen 15.18), making it possible for David to consolidate the kingdom on a permanent basis.
10.25 No king serving under God was autonomous. God, after all, had appointed him to the kingship. Thus Samuel wrote down "the rights and duties of the kingship." This document was "laid . . . up before the LORD," signifying that it was binding and stood over the king.

10.27
1 Kings 10.25;
2 Chr 17.5

27 But some worthless fellows said, "How can this man save us?" They despised him and brought him no present. But he held his peace.

Now Nahash, king of the Ammonites, had been grievously oppressing the Gadites and the Reubenites. He would gouge out the right eye of each of them and would not grant Israel a deliverer. No one was left of the Israelites across the Jordan whose right eye Nahash, king of the Ammonites, had not gouged out. But there were seven thousand men who had escaped from the Ammonites and had entered Jabesh-gilead. *g*

B. The early kingship of Saul

1. The Ammonites defeated

11 About a month later,*h* Nahash the Ammonite went up and besieged Jabesh-gilead; and all the men of Jabesh said to Nahash, "Make a treaty with us, and we will serve you." 2 But Nahash the Ammonite said to them, "On this condition I will make a treaty with you, namely that I gouge out everyone's right eye, and thus put disgrace upon all Israel." 3 The elders of Jabesh said to him, "Give us seven days' respite that we may send messengers through all the territory of Israel. Then, if there is no one to save us, we will give ourselves up to you." 4 When the messengers came to Gibeah of Saul, they reported the matter in the hearing of the people; and all the people wept aloud.

5 Now Saul was coming from the field behind the oxen; and Saul said, "What is the matter with the people, that they are weeping?" So they told him the message from the inhabitants of Jabesh. 6 And the spirit of God came upon Saul in power when he heard these words, and his anger was greatly kindled. 7 He took a yoke of oxen, and cut them in pieces and sent them throughout all the territory of Israel by messengers, saying, "Whoever does not come out after Saul and Samuel, so shall it be done to his oxen!" Then the dread of the LORD fell upon the people, and they came out as one. 8 When he mustered them at Bezek, those from Israel were three hundred thousand, and those from Judah seventy*i* thousand. 9 They said to the messengers who had come, "Thus shall you say to the inhabitants of Jabesh-gilead: 'Tomorrow, by the time the sun is hot, you shall have deliverance.' " When the messengers came and told the inhabitants of Jabesh, they rejoiced. 10 So the inhabitants of Jabesh said, "Tomorrow we will give ourselves up to you, and you may do to us whatever seems good to you." 11 The next day Saul put the people in three companies. At the morning watch they came into the camp and cut down the Ammonites until the heat of the day; and those who survived were scattered, so that no two of them were left together.

12 The people said to Samuel, "Who is it that said, 'Shall Saul reign over us?' Give them to us so that we may put them to death." 13 But Saul said, "No one shall be put to death this day, for today the LORD has brought deliverance to Israel."

14 Samuel said to the people, "Come, let us go to Gilgal and there renew the kingship." 15 So all the people went to Gilgal, and there they made Saul king before the LORD in Gilgal. There they sacrificed offerings

11.1
1 Sam 12.12;
Judg 21.8;
1 Kings 20.34;
Ezek 17.13
11.2
Num 16.14;
1 Sam 17.26
11.4
1 Sam 10.26;
15.34; 30.4;
Judg 2.4
11.6
Judg 3.10;
6.34; 13.25;
14.6;
1 Sam 10.10;
16.13
11.7
Judg 19.29;
21.5, 8, 10
11.8
Judg 1.5;
20.2
11.10
v. 3
11.11
Judg 7.16
11.12
1 Sam 10.27;
Lk 19.27
11.13
2 Sam 19.22;
Ex 14.13;
1 Sam 19.5
11.14
1 Sam 10.8,
25
11.15
1 Sam 10.8,
17

g Q Ms Compare Josephus, *Antiquities* VI.v.1 (68-71): MT lacks *Now Nahash . . . entered Jabesh-gilead.*
h Q Ms Gk: MT lacks *About a month later* *i* Q Ms Gk: MT *thirty*

10.27 *Now Nahash.* From this point on to the end of ch. 10 is material contained in a manuscript of 1 Samuel found in the Dead Sea Scrolls. It helps explain 11.1ff.
11.1 Despite the lot that showed Israel what God's choice was for the kingship, some in Israel did not like or want to accept that verdict. That opposition had to be overcome, and Saul had to show himself as a leader with strength, wisdom, and confidence.

11.6 Note that the Spirit of God came on Saul in mighty power. In the N.T. we learn that all of God's people are indwelt by the Spirit (Rom 8.9–11) and that all should be filled with the Spirit (Eph 5.18).
11.15 *they made Saul king.* Samuel had announced God's choice of Saul in 10.24. Saul became king in the fullest sense only after his victory over the Ammonites and Samuel's summoning of the people to Gilgal.

of well-being before the LORD, and there Saul and all the Israelites rejoiced
greatly.

2. *Samuel lays down his office as judge*

12 Samuel said to all Israel, "I have listened to you in all that you have
said to me, and have set a king over you. 2 See, it is the king who
leads you now; I am old and gray, but my sons are with you. I have led
you from my youth until this day. 3 Here I am; testify against me before
the LORD and before his anointed. Whose ox have I taken? Or whose
donkey have I taken? Or whom have I defrauded? Whom have I oppressed? Or from whose hand have I taken a bribe to blind my eyes with
it? Testify against me[j] and I will restore it to you." 4 They said, "You
have not defrauded us or oppressed us or taken anything from the hand
of anyone." 5 He said to them, "The LORD is witness against you, and his
anointed is witness this day, that you have not found anything in my
hand." And they said, "He is witness."
6 Samuel said to the people, "The LORD is witness, who[k] appointed
Moses and Aaron and brought your ancestors up out of the land of Egypt.
7 Now therefore take your stand, so that I may enter into judgment with
you before the LORD, and I will declare to you[l] all the saving deeds of
the LORD that he performed for you and for your ancestors. 8 When Jacob
went into Egypt and the Egyptians oppressed them,[m] then your ancestors
cried to the LORD and the LORD sent Moses and Aaron, who brought forth
your ancestors out of Egypt, and settled them in this place. 9 But they
forgot the LORD their God; and he sold them into the hand of Sisera,
commander of the army of King Jabin of[n] Hazor, and into the hand of
the Philistines, and into the hand of the king of Moab; and they fought
against them. 10 Then they cried to the LORD, and said, 'We have sinned,
because we have forsaken the LORD, and have served the Baals and the
Astartes; but now rescue us out of the hand of our enemies, and we will
serve you.' 11 And the LORD sent Jerubbaal and Barak,[o] and Jephthah,
and Samson,[p] and rescued you out of the hand of your enemies on every
side; and you lived in safety. 12 But when you saw that King Nahash of
the Ammonites came against you, you said to me, 'No, but a king shall
reign over us,' though the LORD your God was your king. 13 See, here is
the king whom you have chosen, for whom you have asked; see, the LORD
has set a king over you. 14 If you will fear the LORD and serve him and
heed his voice and not rebel against the commandment of the LORD, and
if both you and the king who reigns over you will follow the LORD your
God, it will be well; 15 but if you will not heed the voice of the LORD, but
rebel against the commandment of the LORD, then the hand of the LORD
will be against you and your king.[q] 16 Now therefore take your stand and

12.1 1 Sam 8.7, 9, 22; 10.24; 11.14, 15
12.2 1 Sam 8.1, 5, 20
12.3 1 Sam 10.1; 24.6; 2 Sam 1.14; Num 16.15; Acts 20.33; Deut 16.19
12.5 Acts 23.9; 24.20; Ex 22.4
12.6 Ex 6.26
12.7 Isa 1.18; Mic 6.1-5
12.8 Ex 2.23; 3.10; 4.16
12.9 Judg 3.7; 4.2; 10.7; 13.1; 3.12
12.10 Judg 10.10; 2.13; 10.15
12.11 Judg 6.14, 32; 4.6; 11.1
12.12 1 Sam 11.1; 8.6, 19; Judg 8.23
12.13 1 Sam 10.24; 8.5; Hos 13.11
12.14 Josh 24.14
12.15 Josh 24.20
12.16 Ex 14.13, 31

[j] Gk: Heb lacks *Testify against me* [k] Gk: Heb lacks *is witness, who* [l] Gk: Heb lacks *and I will declare to you* [m] Gk: Heb lacks *and the Egyptians oppressed them* [n] Gk: Heb lacks *King Jabin of* [o] Gk Syr: Heb *Bedan* [p] Gk: Heb *Samuel* [q] Gk: Heb *and your ancestors*

12.1 Now that Saul had been elevated to the kingship, he would be Israel's judge and thus there was no longer any need for Samuel to act as judge. He did continue as priest and had the privilege of anointing David as king over Israel following Saul's downfall for disobedience. Samuel's death is mentioned in 25.1.
12.3 Samuel himself may have rendered fair and just judgment, but his hands were not wholly clean. He favored his children over the God he served, for he knew and approved (at least by his failure to put them out of office) of what they did (cf. 8.1–3). Yet God was gracious enough to allow him to serve out his judgeship over Israel until Saul was in place as king.
12.6ff Samuel reminded Israel of its history and God's saving deeds among them. He traced events from Jacob's trip to Egypt through the exodus, the entry into the land, and the period of the judges. He spoke of Israel's ups and downs and God's continuing grace.
12.14 God accepted the kingship on condition that the king and the people alike would follow the commandments of God, the real king. As Moses had done on the border of the promised land and as Joshua had done shortly before he died, so here Samuel reminded the Israelites of the covenant promises and responsibilities.
12.16 *this great thing that the LORD will do before your eyes.* Once again God planned to give his people confirming evidence of his presence and power. In v. 17 Samuel asked God to send thunder and rain as a token of his power and approval—at wheat-harvest time, when rain and thunder were unexpected. God re-

see this great thing that the LORD will do before your eyes. [17] Is it not the wheat harvest today? I will call upon the LORD, that he may send thunder and rain; and you shall know and see that the wickedness that you have done in the sight of the LORD is great in demanding a king for yourselves."

[18] So Samuel called upon the LORD, and the LORD sent thunder and rain that day; and all the people greatly feared the LORD and Samuel.

19   All the people said to Samuel, "Pray to the LORD your God for your servants, so that we may not die; for we have added to all our sins the evil of demanding a king for ourselves." [20] And Samuel said to the people, "Do not be afraid; you have done all this evil, yet do not turn aside from following the LORD, but serve the LORD with all your heart; [21] and do not

turn aside after useless things that cannot profit or save, for they are useless. [22] For the LORD will not cast away his people, for his great name's

sake, because it has pleased the LORD to make you a people for himself. [23] Moreover as for me, far be it from me that I should sin against the LORD by ceasing to pray for you; and I will instruct you in the good and the right

way. [24] Only fear the LORD, and serve him faithfully with all your heart; for consider what great things he has done for you. [25] But if you still do

wickedly, you shall be swept away, both you and your king."

3. *Saul's war against the Philistines*

a. *Opening battles against the Philistines*

13   Saul was . . . [r] years old when he began to reign; and he reigned . . . and two [s] years over Israel.

2   Saul chose three thousand out of Israel; two thousand were with Saul in Michmash and the hill country of Bethel, and a thousand were with Jonathan in Gibeah of Benjamin; the rest of the people he sent home to

their tents. [3] Jonathan defeated the garrison of the Philistines that was at Geba; and the Philistines heard of it. And Saul blew the trumpet throughout all the land, saying, "Let the Hebrews hear!" [4] When all Israel heard that Saul had defeated the garrison of the Philistines, and also that Israel had become odious to the Philistines, the people were called out to join Saul at Gilgal.

5   The Philistines mustered to fight with Israel, thirty thousand chariots, and six thousand horsemen, and troops like the sand on the seashore in multitude; they came up and encamped at Michmash, to the east of

Beth-aven. [6] When the Israelites saw that they were in distress (for the troops were hard pressed), the people hid themselves in caves and in holes and in rocks and in tombs and in cisterns. [7] Some Hebrews crossed the Jordan to the land of Gad and Gilead. Saul was still at Gilgal, and all the people followed him trembling.

b. *Saul intrudes into the priest's office*

8   He waited seven days, the time appointed by Samuel; but Samuel did not come to Gilgal, and the people began to slip away from Saul. [t]

[9] So Saul said, "Bring the burnt offering here to me, and the offerings of well-being." And he offered the burnt offering. [10] As soon as he had

---

[r] The number is lacking in the Heb text (the verse is lacking in the Septuagint).   [s] *Two* is not the entire number; something has dropped out.   [t] Heb *him*

---

sponded to Samuel's prayer, and the rain and thunder came. The people "greatly feared the LORD and Samuel" (v. 18).

12.24,25   Samuel concluded his admonitions to Israel with an exhortation to fear God — this is the first principle of a righteous life — and to serve him with all their hearts. Profession and practice belong together. Samuel's speech ended with a prophetic word: If Israel and the king ever failed to heed the warning, God would consume them.

13.3,4   After subjugating Israel, the Philistines had set up military garrisons throughout the land.

13.9   Saul intruded into the office reserved for the Levitical priesthood. As a Benjamite, he was ineligible for these duties. Despite the apparent need for a burnt offering, Saul should never have disobeyed God. This brought condemnation upon him. Samuel announced that Saul's kingship would be terminated and someone else would be appointed in his place (vv. 13,14).

finished offering the burnt offering, Samuel arrived; and Saul went out to meet him and salute him. 11 Samuel said, "What have you done?" Saul replied, "When I saw that the people were slipping away from me, and that you did not come within the days appointed, and that the Philistines were mustering at Michmash, 12 I said, 'Now the Philistines will come down upon me at Gilgal, and I have not entreated the favor of the Lord'; so I forced myself, and offered the burnt offering." 13 Samuel said to Saul, "You have done foolishly; you have not kept the commandment of the Lord your God, which he commanded you. The Lord would have established your kingdom over Israel forever, 14 but now your kingdom will not continue; the Lord has sought out a man after his own heart; and the Lord has appointed him to be ruler over his people, because you have not kept what the Lord commanded you." 15 And Samuel left and went on his way from Gilgal. *u* The rest of the people followed Saul to join the army; they went up from Gilgal toward Gibeah of Benjamin. *v*

c. Saul's nondescript army

Saul counted the people who were present with him, about six hundred men. 16 Saul, his son Jonathan, and the people who were present with them stayed in Geba of Benjamin; but the Philistines encamped at Michmash. 17 And raiders came out of the camp of the Philistines in three companies; one company turned toward Ophrah, to the land of Shual, 18 another company turned toward Beth-horon, and another company turned toward the mountain *w* that looks down upon the valley of Zeboim toward the wilderness.

19 Now there was no smith to be found throughout all the land of Israel; for the Philistines said, "The Hebrews must not make swords or spears for themselves"; 20 so all the Israelites went down to the Philistines to sharpen their plowshares, mattocks, axes, or sickles; *x* 21 The charge was two-thirds of a shekel *y* for the plowshares and for the mattocks, and one-third of a shekel for sharpening the axes and for setting the goads. *z* 22 So on the day of the battle neither sword nor spear was to be found in the possession of any of the people with Saul and Jonathan; but Saul and his son Jonathan had them.

d. Jonathan's exploit at Michmash

(1) JONATHAN ATTACKS

23 Now a garrison of the Philistines had gone out to the pass of Michmash. 1 One day Jonathan son of Saul said to the young man who carried his armor, "Come, let us go over to the Philistine garrison on the other side." But he did not tell his father. 2 Saul was staying in the outskirts of Gibeah under the pomegranate tree that is at Migron; the troops that were with him were about six hundred men, 3 along with Ahijah son of Ahitub, Ichabod's brother, son of Phinehas son of Eli, the priest of the Lord in Shiloh, carrying an ephod. Now the people did not know that Jonathan had gone. 4 In the pass, *a* by which Jonathan tried to go over to the Philistine garrison, there was a rocky crag on one side and a rocky crag on the other; the name of the one was Bozez, and

13.11
vv. 2, 5, 16, 23

13.13
2 Chr 16.9;
1 Sam 15.11,
22

13.14
1 Sam 15.28;
Acts 13.22

13.15
1 Sam 14.2

13.17
1 Sam 14.15

13.18
Josh 18.13,
14;
Neh 11.34

13.19
2 Kings 24.14

13.22
Judg 5.8

14.2
1 Sam 13.15

14.3
1 Sam 22.9-12,
20; 4.21;
2.28
14.4
1 Sam 13.23

---

u Gk: Heb *went up from Gilgal to Gibeah of Benjamin*   *v* Gk: Heb lacks *The rest . . . of Benjamin*
w Cn Compare Gk: Heb *toward the border*   *x* Gk: Heb *plowshare*   *y* Heb *was a pim*   *z* Cn: Meaning of Heb uncertain   *a* Heb *Between the passes*

13.19 *smith,* i.e., blacksmith. The Philistines over-powered Israel with their superior weaponry. Without blacksmiths Israel had no armaments.
14.1 Jonathan was Saul's firstborn and his heir apparent. He was a person of sterling character who loved God with his whole heart. He remained faithful to his father even as he tried to bridge the gap which separated his father Saul from David, God's anointed

choice to succeed Saul.
14.3 *carrying an ephod.* Saul sent for a priest from Shiloh, and Ahijah came wearing an ephod. This was used to ask God's advice in times of trouble. Presumably the Urim and Thummim were in the ephod and the stones determined either a yes or a no to the questions asked.

the name of the other Seneh. 5 One crag rose on the north in front of Michmash, and the other on the south in front of Geba.

14.6
Judg 7.4, 7;
1 Sam 17.46,
47

6 Jonathan said to the young man who carried his armor, "Come, let us go over to the garrison of these uncircumcised; it may be that the LORD will act for us; for nothing can hinder the LORD from saving by many or by few." 7 His armor-bearer said to him, "Do all that your mind inclines to.*b* I am with you; as your mind is, so is mine."*c* 8 Then Jonathan said, "Now we will cross over to those men and will show ourselves to them.

14.10
Gen 24.14;
Judg 6.36, 37
14.11
1 Sam 13.6

9 If they say to us, 'Wait until we come to you,' then we will stand still in our place, and we will not go up to them. 10 But if they say, 'Come up to us,' then we will go up; for the LORD has given them into our hand. That will be the sign for us." 11 So both of them showed themselves to the garrison of the Philistines; and the Philistines said, "Look, Hebrews

14.12
1 Sam 17.43,
44;
2 Sam 5.24

are coming out of the holes where they have hidden themselves." 12 The men of the garrison hailed Jonathan and his armor-bearer, saying, "Come up to us, and we will show you something." Jonathan said to his armor-bearer, "Come up after me; for the LORD has given them into the hand of Israel." 13 Then Jonathan climbed up on his hands and feet, with his armor-bearer following after him. The Philistines*d* fell before Jonathan, and his armor-bearer, coming after him, killed them. 14 In that first slaughter Jonathan and his armor-bearer killed about twenty men within

14.15
2 Kings 7.6,
7;
1 Sam 13.17

an area about half a furrow long in an acre*e* of land. 15 There was a panic in the camp, in the field, and among all the people; the garrison and even the raiders trembled; the earth quaked; and it became a very great panic.

(2) THE PHILISTINES FLEE

14.16
2 Sam 18.24

16 Saul's lookouts in Gibeah of Benjamin were watching as the multitude was surging back and forth.*f* 17 Then Saul said to the troops that were with him, "Call the roll and see who has gone from us." When they had called the roll, Jonathan and his armor-bearer were not there. 18 Saul said to Ahijah, "Bring the ark*g* of God here." For at that time the ark*g*

14.19
Num 27.21

of God went with the Israelites. 19 While Saul was talking to the priest, the tumult in the camp of the Philistines increased more and more; and Saul said to the priest, "Withdraw your hand." 20 Then Saul and all the

14.20
Judg 7.22;
2 Chr 20.23

people who were with him rallied and went into the battle; and every sword was against the other, so that there was very great confusion. 21 Now the Hebrews who previously had been with the Philistines and had gone up with them into the camp turned and joined the Israelites who were

14.22
1 Sam 13.6

with Saul and Jonathan. 22 Likewise, when all the Israelites who had gone into hiding in the hill country of Ephraim heard that the Philistines were fleeing, they too followed closely after them in the battle. 23 So the LORD

14.23
Ex 14.30;
Ps 44.6, 7;
1 Sam 13.5

gave Israel the victory that day.

The battle passed beyond Beth-aven, and the troops with Saul numbered altogether about ten thousand men. The battle spread out over the hill country of Ephraim.

(3) JONATHAN UNWITTINGLY TRANSGRESSES SAUL'S OATH

14.24
Josh 6.26

24 Now Saul committed a very rash act on that day.*h* He had laid an

b Gk: Heb *Do all that is in your mind. Turn*   *c* Gk: Heb lacks *so is mine*   *d* Heb *They*   *e* Heb *yoke*
f Gk: Heb *they went and there*   *g* Gk *the ephod*   *h* Gk: Heb *The Israelites were distressed that day*

14.8 Jonathan determined to follow providence, believing that God would guide him. He laid out a fleece before God (cf. Judg 6.36–40); when God gave him the sign he expected, he answered the signal.
14.15 At the opportune moment in the battle, God sent an earthquake, causing the Philistines to tremble and become panic-stricken. The Philistines were soundly defeated, despite their superior military strength.
14.18 The ark was stationed at Kiriath-jearim at this

time. Probably it was borrowed for a short time and brought to the battlefield as a symbol of their faith in God. Note the contrast of this occasion with 4.1–11.
14.24 Saul foolishly forbade his troops from touching any food until the evening. He enforced the command by cursing any who would disobey. But Saul's curse fell upon his own son, who, in ignorance of the command, had eaten some honey. Saul decided to execute Jonathan. The people, however, protested the action against Jonathan, whom they loved; they

oath on the troops, saying, "Cursed be anyone who eats food before it is evening and I have been avenged on my enemies." So none of the troops tasted food. 25 All the troops[i] came upon a honeycomb; and there was honey on the ground. 26 When the troops came upon the honeycomb, the honey was dripping out; but they did not put their hands to their mouths, for they feared the oath. 27 But Jonathan had not heard his father charge the troops with the oath; so he extended the staff that was in his hand, and dipped the tip of it in the honeycomb, and put his hand to his mouth; and his eyes brightened. 28 Then one of the soldiers said, "Your father strictly charged the troops with an oath, saying, 'Cursed be anyone who eats food this day.' And so the troops are faint." 29 Then Jonathan said, "My father has troubled the land; see how my eyes have brightened because I tasted a little of this honey. 30 How much better if today the troops had eaten freely of the spoil taken from their enemies; for now the slaughter among the Philistines has not been great."

31 After they had struck down the Philistines that day from Michmash to Aijalon, the troops were very faint; 32 so the troops flew upon the spoil, and took sheep and oxen and calves, and slaughtered them on the ground; and the troops ate them with the blood. 33 Then it was reported to Saul, "Look, the troops are sinning against the LORD by eating with the blood." And he said, "You have dealt treacherously; roll a large stone before me here."[j] 34 Saul said, "Disperse yourselves among the troops, and say to them, 'Let all bring their oxen or their sheep, and slaughter them here, and eat; and do not sin against the LORD by eating with the blood.' " So all of the troops brought their oxen with them that night, and slaughtered them there. 35 And Saul built an altar to the LORD; it was the first altar that he built to the LORD.

(4) JONATHAN'S GUILT DISCOVERED

36 Then Saul said, "Let us go down after the Philistines by night and despoil them until the morning light; let us not leave one of them." They said, "Do whatever seems good to you." But the priest said, "Let us draw near to God here." 37 So Saul inquired of God, "Shall I go down after the Philistines? Will you give them into the hand of Israel?" But he did not answer him that day. 38 Saul said, "Come here, all you leaders of the people; and let us find out how this sin has arisen today. 39 For as the LORD lives who saves Israel, even if it is in my son Jonathan, he shall surely die!" But there was no one among all the people who answered him. 40 He said to all Israel, "You shall be on one side, and I and my son Jonathan will be on the other side." The people said to Saul, "Do what seems good to you." 41 Then Saul said, "O LORD God of Israel, why have you not answered your servant today? If this guilt is in me or in my son Jonathan, O LORD God of Israel, give Urim; but if this guilt is in your people Israel,[k] give Thummim." And Jonathan and Saul were indicated by the lot, but the people were cleared. 42 Then Saul said, "Cast the lot between me and my son Jonathan." And Jonathan was taken.

(5) JONATHAN SAVED BY THE PEOPLE

43 Then Saul said to Jonathan, "Tell me what you have done." Jonathan told him, "I tasted a little honey with the tip of the staff that was in my hand; here I am, I will die." 44 Saul said, "God do so to me and more

14.27
1 Sam 30.12

14.29
1 Kings 18.18

14.32
1 Sam 15.19;
Lev 17.10-14

14.35
1 Sam 7.17

14.37
1 Sam 10.22;
28.6
14.38
Josh 7.14;
1 Sam 10.19
14.39
2 Sam 12.5

14.41
Prov 16.33;
Acts 1.24

14.43
Josh 7.19;
v. 23
14.44
Ruth 1.17;
v. 39

---

i Heb *land*　　*j* Gk: Heb *me this day*　　*k* Vg Compare Gk: Heb *41 Saul said to the LORD, the God of Israel*

---

subsequently ransomed him from his guilt (v. 45). In Ps 109.17,18, when David wrote of the foolishness of cursing, he may have been referring to this incident. **14.32** Although it was forbidden to eat blood (see Lev 7.26,27; 17.12), because of the extreme conditions the soldiers did what was forbidden. Saul had enough good sense to reprove them for that act and

ordered it to be stopped. He then built an altar to sacrifice the animals instead, and so kept the people from eating blood. Saul personally supervised the sacrifices.
14.41 *by the lot,* i.e., by Urim and Thummim (see note on Ex 28.30).
14.44,45 Jonathan was guilty of disobeying his fa-

14.45
2 Sam 14.11;
1 Kings 1.52;
Acts 27.34

also; you shall surely die, Jonathan!" 45 Then the people said to Saul, "Shall Jonathan die, who has accomplished this great victory in Israel? Far from it! As the LORD lives, not one hair of his head shall fall to the ground; for he has worked with God today." So the people ransomed Jonathan, and he did not die. 46 Then Saul withdrew from pursuing the Philistines; and the Philistines went to their own place.

e. Saul wars against other nations

14.47
1 Sam 11.1-13;
2 Sam 10.6;
v. 52
14.48
1 Sam 15.3, 7

47 When Saul had taken the kingship over Israel, he fought against all his enemies on every side—against Moab, against the Ammonites, against Edom, against the kings of Zobah, and against the Philistines; wherever he turned he routed them. 48 He did valiantly, and struck down the Amalekites, and rescued Israel out of the hands of those who plundered them.

f. Saul's family and army

14.49
1 Sam 31.2;
1 Chr 8.33;
1 Sam 18.17-20
14.50
2 Sam 2.8
14.51
1 Sam 9.1

49 Now the sons of Saul were Jonathan, Ishvi, and Malchishua; and the names of his two daughters were these: the name of the firstborn was Merab, and the name of the younger, Michal. 50 The name of Saul's wife was Ahinoam daughter of Ahimaaz. And the name of the commander of his army was Abner son of Ner, Saul's uncle; 51 Kish was the father of Saul, and Ner the father of Abner was the son of Abiel.

14.52
1 Sam 8.11

52 There was hard fighting against the Philistines all the days of Saul; and when Saul saw any strong or valiant warrior, he took him into his service.

C. God rejects Saul

1. The war with the Amalekites

a. God's command to destroy

15.1
1 Sam 9.16

15 Samuel said to Saul, "The LORD sent me to anoint you king over his people Israel; now therefore listen to the words of the LORD.

15.2
Ex 17.8-14;
Num 24.20;
Deut 25.17-19
15.3
Num 24.20;
Deut 20.16-18;
1 Sam 22.19

2 Thus says the LORD of hosts, 'I will punish the Amalekites for what they did in opposing the Israelites when they came up out of Egypt. 3 Now go and attack Amalek, and utterly destroy all that they have; do not spare them, but kill both man and woman, child and infant, ox and sheep, camel and donkey.'"

b. Saul's disobedience

15.6
Judg 1.16;
4.11;
Ex 18.10, 19;
Num 10.29-32
15.7
1 Sam 14.48;
Gen 16.7;
25.17, 18;
Ex 15.22
15.8
1 Kings 20.34ff;
1 Sam 30.1
15.9
vv. 3, 15

4 So Saul summoned the people, and numbered them in Telaim, two hundred thousand foot soldiers, and ten thousand soldiers of Judah. 5 Saul came to the city of the Amalekites and lay in wait in the valley. 6 Saul said to the Kenites, "Go! Leave! Withdraw from among the Amalekites, or I will destroy you with them; for you showed kindness to all the people of Israel when they came up out of Egypt." So the Kenites withdrew from the Amalekites. 7 Saul defeated the Amalekites, from Havilah as far as Shur, which is east of Egypt. 8 He took King Agag of the Amalekites alive, but utterly destroyed all the people with the edge of the sword. 9 Saul and

---

ther's order, and Saul was ready to slay him. The soldiers thought the judgment was unfair and therefore rescued Jonathan. They did it by reason and resolution, not by violence.

14.47 In a few words the writer summarizes how Saul extended his control over surrounding nations by successful warfare. In vv. 49–52 a short account of the kingly family and its members is given, ending with the statement that Saul drafted the strongest people into his service. Samuel had prophesied the king would do that when he began to reign (see 8.11).

15.1–3 God through Samuel ordered Saul to smite

Amalek for its opposition to Israel on the wilderness journey.

15.3 *utterly destroy.* The condition of the Amalekites was irremediable; God had given them sufficient time to repent. The hour of judgment had arrived for them (see note on Deut 2.34).

15.8 Evidently not all the Amalekites were slain, for a strong enclave existed in David's day (27.8; 30.1,18; 2 Sam 1.1). Apparently some of the Amalekites were elsewhere at the time. See also note on Esth 3.1 for information on the Amalekites.

15.9 Saul and the Israelites saved Agag and some of

the people spared Agag, and the best of the sheep and of the cattle and of the fatlings, and the lambs, and all that was valuable, and would not utterly destroy them; all that was despised and worthless they utterly destroyed.

c. Samuel delivers God's sentence

10 The word of the LORD came to Samuel: **11** "I regret that I made Saul king, for he has turned back from following me, and has not carried out my commands." Samuel was angry; and he cried out to the LORD all night. **12** Samuel rose early in the morning to meet Saul, and Samuel was told, "Saul went to Carmel, where he set up a monument for himself, and on returning he passed on down to Gilgal." **13** When Samuel came to Saul, Saul said to him, "May you be blessed by the LORD; I have carried out the command of the LORD." **14** But Samuel said, "What then is this bleating of sheep in my ears, and the lowing of cattle that I hear?" **15** Saul said, "They have brought them from the Amalekites; for the people spared the best of the sheep and the cattle, to sacrifice to the LORD your God; but the rest we have utterly destroyed." **16** Then Samuel said to Saul, "Stop! I will tell you what the LORD said to me last night." He replied, "Speak."

17 Samuel said, "Though you are little in your own eyes, are you not the head of the tribes of Israel? The LORD anointed you king over Israel. **18** And the LORD sent you on a mission, and said, 'Go, utterly destroy the sinners, the Amalekites, and fight against them until they are consumed.' **19** Why then did you not obey the voice of the LORD? Why did you swoop down on the spoil, and do what was evil in the sight of the LORD?" **20** Saul said to Samuel, "I have obeyed the voice of the LORD, I have gone on the mission on which the LORD sent me, I have brought Agag the king of Amalek, and I have utterly destroyed the Amalekites. **21** But from the spoil the people took sheep and cattle, the best of the things devoted to destruction, to sacrifice to the LORD your God in Gilgal." **22** And Samuel said,

"Has the LORD as great delight in burnt offerings and
    sacrifices,
  as in obedience to the voice of the LORD?
Surely, to obey is better than sacrifice,
  and to heed than the fat of rams.
23 For rebellion is no less a sin than divination,
  and stubbornness is like iniquity and idolatry.
Because you have rejected the word of the LORD,
  he has also rejected you from being king."

d. Saul appears penitent

24 Saul said to Samuel, "I have sinned; for I have transgressed the commandment of the LORD and your words, because I feared the people and obeyed their voice. **25** Now therefore, I pray, pardon my sin, and return with me, so that I may worship the LORD." **26** Samuel said to Saul, "I will not return with you; for you have rejected the word of the LORD,

15.11
Gen 6.6, 7;
2 Sam 24.16;
1 Kings 9.6, 7; 1 Sam 16.1
15.12
Josh 15.55
15.13
Gen 14.19;
Judg 17.2
15.15
vv. 9, 21;
Gen 3.12

15.17
1 Sam 9.21
15.18
v. 3
15.19
1 Sam 14.32
15.20
v. 13

15.21
v. 15
15.22
Isa 1.11-13;
Mic 6.6-8;
Heb 10.6-9;
Hos 6.6;
Mk 12.33

15.23
1 Sam 13.14

15.24
2 Sam 12.13;
Prov 29.25;
Isa 51.12, 13
15.26
1 Sam 13.14

the sheep, oxen, and lambs. They destroyed only the useless and worthless animals, despite God's command to slay all human and animal life.
15.13   Saul piously told Samuel he had followed the commandment of God, but the bleating of the sheep and the lowing of the cattle told a different tale. Samuel already knew of Saul's disobedience and had to proclaim the judgment of God to this impenitent sinner.
15.21   *the people took sheep and cattle.* Saul attempted to excuse his disobedience by blaming the people. But he too was guilty of covetousness. Note how earlier, Aaron the high priest was guilty of blaming the people

for a sin of which he too was guilty (Ex 32.22–24).
15.22   Saul's next excuse was that he had saved some of the sheep and oxen in order to sacrifice them to God. This incident was the final step in his downfall. Samuel pronounced divine judgment on Saul and Saul was rejected by God, for he had "rejected the word of the LORD" (v. 26). In his words, Samuel enunciated a vital truth: obedience is better than sacrifice. Nothing offends God more than setting up our wills in competition with his. It is always possible for a disobedient person to offer a ritual sacrifice. But when obedience rules the heart, sacrifices will inevitably be made.

15.27
1 Kings 11.30,
31
15.28
1 Sam 28.17

15.29
1 Chr 29.11;
Num 23.19;
Ezek 24.14
15.30
Jn 12.43;
Isa 29.13

and the LORD has rejected you from being king over Israel." 27 As Samuel turned to go away, Saul caught hold of the hem of his robe, and it tore. 28 And Samuel said to him, "The LORD has torn the kingdom of Israel from you this very day, and has given it to a neighbor of yours, who is better than you. 29 Moreover the Glory of Israel will not recant[l] or change his mind; for he is not a mortal, that he should change his mind." 30 Then Saul[m] said, "I have sinned; yet honor me now before the elders of my people and before Israel, and return with me, so that I may worship the LORD your God." 31 So Samuel turned back after Saul; and Saul worshiped the LORD.

e. Samuel kills Agag and sees Saul no more

15.33
Gen 9.6;
Judg 1.7

32 Then Samuel said, "Bring Agag king of the Amalekites here to me." And Agag came to him haltingly.[n] Agag said, "Surely this is the bitterness of death."[o] 33 But Samuel said,

"As your sword has made women childless,
  so your mother shall be childless among women."
And Samuel hewed Agag in pieces before the LORD in Gilgal.

15.34
1 Sam 7.17;
11.4
15.35
1 Sam 19.24;
16.1

34 Then Samuel went to Ramah; and Saul went up to his house in Gibeah of Saul. 35 Samuel did not see Saul again until the day of his death, but Samuel grieved over Saul. And the LORD was sorry that he had made Saul king over Israel.

2. David chosen to be king

a. God sends Samuel to Jesse's house

16.1
1 Sam 15.23,
35; 9.16;
2 Kings 9.1;
Ps 78.70;
Acts 13.22
16.2
1 Sam 20.29
16.3
Ex 4.15;
1 Sam 9.16
16.4
Lk 2.4;
1 Kings 2.13;
2 Kings 9.22
16.5
Ex 19.10

16 The LORD said to Samuel, "How long will you grieve over Saul? I have rejected him from being king over Israel. Fill your horn with oil and set out; I will send you to Jesse the Bethlehemite, for I have provided for myself a king among his sons." 2 Samuel said, "How can I go? If Saul hears of it, he will kill me." And the LORD said, "Take a heifer with you, and say, 'I have come to sacrifice to the LORD.' 3 Invite Jesse to the sacrifice, and I will show you what you shall do; and you shall anoint for me the one whom I name to you." 4 Samuel did what the LORD commanded, and came to Bethlehem. The elders of the city came to meet him trembling, and said, "Do you come peaceably?" 5 He said, "Peaceably; I have come to sacrifice to the LORD; sanctify yourselves and come with me to the sacrifice." And he sanctified Jesse and his sons and invited them to the sacrifice.

b. David selected and anointed king

16.6
1 Sam 17.13
16.7
Isa 55.8;
1 Kings 8.39;
1 Chr 28.9

6 When they came, he looked on Eliab and thought, "Surely the LORD's anointed is now before the LORD."[p] 7 But the LORD said to Samuel, "Do not look on his appearance or on the height of his stature,

[l] Q Ms Gk: MT deceive [m] Heb he [n] Cn Compare Gk: Meaning of Heb uncertain [o] Q Ms Gk: MT Surely the bitterness of death is past [p] Heb him

---

15.33 We do not know why Saul did not slay Agag immediately. Samuel then performed this deed.
15.34,35 Samuel went to Ramah, never to see Saul again while he was living. Both Samuel and God grieved over what had happened to Saul. He got off to a promising start but fell into sin.
16.1 God announced to Samuel that he had selected Saul's successor from the children of Jesse, but he did not tell Samuel which one. The remainder of 1 Samuel depicts the struggle between Saul and David and ends with the death of Saul.
16.2,3 Samuel feared that Saul might kill him if he anointed a new king. God told him to go to Bethlehem in order to offer an animal sacrifice. During that stay he was to anoint David as the new king. There was no deception on the part of God.

16.4 When Samuel came to Bethlehem, the elders of the town thought he might be coming to pronounce some adverse judgment of God against them. Samuel reassured them that this was not the case. Little did they know that the tribe of Judah, their tribe, would produce the next king and that he would start a line that would last eternally.
16.5 In order to attend the sacrifice it was first necessary to go through the ritual of ceremonial washings and purification. Jesse and the family did this.
16.6 Starting with the eldest, Samuel looked at each son of Jesse and was told by God that none of them was the divine choice. Finally David, the youngest, who had been tending the sheep, was sent for; and when he appeared, God said, "Rise and anoint him; for this is the one" (v. 12).

because I have rejected him; for the LORD does not see as mortals see; they look on the outward appearance, but the LORD looks on the heart." 8 Then Jesse called Abinadab, and made him pass before Samuel. He said, "Neither has the LORD chosen this one." 9 Then Jesse made Shammah pass by. And he said, "Neither has the LORD chosen this one." 10 Jesse made seven of his sons pass before Samuel, and Samuel said to Jesse, "The LORD has not chosen any of these." 11 Samuel said to Jesse, "Are all your sons here?" And he said, "There remains yet the youngest, but he is keeping the sheep." And Samuel said to Jesse, "Send and bring him; for we will not sit down until he comes here." 12 He sent and brought him in. Now he was ruddy, and had beautiful eyes, and was handsome. The LORD said, "Rise and anoint him; for this is the one." 13 Then Samuel took the horn of oil, and anointed him in the presence of his brothers; and the spirit of the LORD came mightily upon David from that day forward. Samuel then set out and went to Ramah.

3. Saul overtaken by an evil spirit; David joins his court

14 Now the spirit of the LORD departed from Saul, and an evil spirit from the LORD tormented him. 15 And Saul's servants said to him, "See now, an evil spirit from God is tormenting you. 16 Let our lord now command the servants who attend you to look for someone who is skillful in playing the lyre; and when the evil spirit from God is upon you, he will play it, and you will feel better." 17 So Saul said to his servants, "Provide for me someone who can play well, and bring him to me." 18 One of the young men answered, "I have seen a son of Jesse the Bethlehemite who is skillful in playing, a man of valor, a warrior, prudent in speech, and a man of good presence; and the LORD is with him." 19 So Saul sent messengers to Jesse, and said, "Send me your son David who is with the sheep." 20 Jesse took a donkey loaded with bread, a skin of wine, and a kid, and sent them by his son David to Saul. 21 And David came to Saul, and entered his service. Saul loved him greatly, and he became his armor-bearer. 22 Saul sent to Jesse, saying, "Let David remain in my service, for he has found favor in my sight." 23 And whenever the evil spirit from God came upon Saul, David took the lyre and played it with his hand, and Saul would be relieved and feel better, and the evil spirit would depart from him.

D. The rise of David and his persecutions by Saul

1. Goliath the Philistine

17 Now the Philistines gathered their armies for battle; they were gathered at Socoh, which belongs to Judah, and encamped between Socoh and Azekah, in Ephes-dammim. 2 Saul and the Israelites gathered and encamped in the valley of Elah, and formed ranks against the Philistines. 3 The Philistines stood on the mountain on the one side, and Israel stood on the mountain on the other side, with a valley between them. 4 And there came out from the camp of the Philistines a champion named Goliath, of Gath, whose height was six*q* cubits and a span. 5 He

q MT: Q Ms Gk four

16.8
1 Sam 17.13
16.9
1 Sam 17.13

16.11
1 Sam 17.12

16.12
1 Sam 17.42;
9.17
16.13
1 Sam 10.1,
6, 9, 10;
Judg 11.29

16.14
Judg 16.20;
1 Sam 18.10
16.16
v. 23;
1 Sam 18.10;
19.9;
2 Kings 3.15

16.18
1 Sam 17.32-36;
3.19

16.20
1 Sam 10.27;
Prov 18.16
16.21f
Gen 41.46;
Prov 22.29
16.23
vv. 14-16

17.1
1 Sam 13.5;
2 Chr 28.18
17.2
1 Sam 21.9

17.4
2 Sam 21.19;
Josh 11.21,
22

16.12 David, the shepherd-king, is a symbol of Christ. David left the sheep to become king of Israel. Christ came as the good shepherd to give his life for the sheep (Jn 10.11). He rose from the dead, ascended into glory, and is now King of kings, sitting upon the heavenly throne as David's greatest son (Lk 1.32; Acts 2.30).

16.13 *The spirit of the LORD came mightily upon David from that day forward.* The Spirit came upon believers in the O.T. as he pleased. When David was anointed to be king, the Spirit of God filled him. At the same time, the Spirit of God departed from Saul (v. 14). For more on the Spirit in the O.T., see notes on Ex 31.1ff; 35.31; Judg 3.10; 16.20.

16.23 David filled the role of physician to Saul, helping him against the worst of all diseases — affliction from an evil spirit. David refreshed the king, and the evil spirit left him for a time.

17.4–7 Goliath was approximately ten feet tall and his armor weighed more than a hundred pounds.

DAVID'S FAMILY TREE

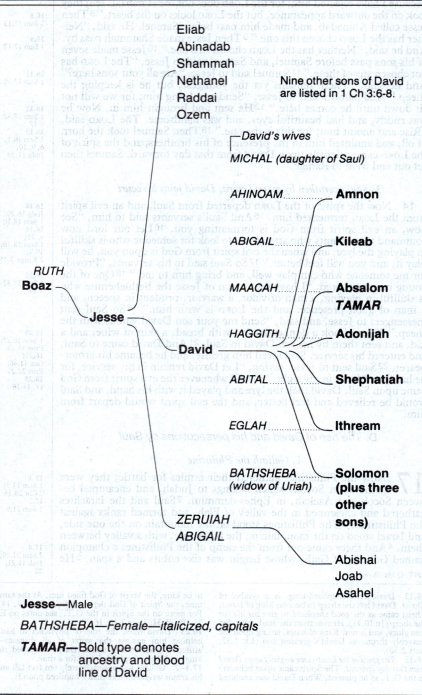

Eliab
Abinadab
Shammah
Nethanel
Raddai
Ozem

Nine other sons of David
are listed in 1 Ch 3:6-8.

David's wives
MICHAL (daughter of Saul)

RUTH
Boaz

Jesse

AHINOAM   **Amnon**

ABIGAIL   **Kileab**

MAACAH   **Absalom**
          TAMAR

David

HAGGITH   **Adonijah**

ABITAL   **Shephatiah**

EGLAH   **Ithream**

BATHSHEBA
(widow of Uriah)   **Solomon
(plus three
other
sons)**

ZERUIAH
ABIGAIL

Abishai
Joab
Asahel

Jesse—Male

BATHSHEBA—Female—italicized, capitals

TAMAR—Bold type denotes
ancestry and blood
line of David

had a helmet of bronze on his head, and he was armed with a coat of mail; the weight of the coat was five thousand shekels of bronze. 6 He had greaves of bronze on his legs and a javelin of bronze slung between his shoulders. 7 The shaft of his spear was like a weaver's beam, and his spear's head weighed six hundred shekels of iron; and his shield-bearer went before him. 8 He stood and shouted to the ranks of Israel, "Why have you come out to draw up for battle? Am I not a Philistine, and are you not servants of Saul? Choose a man for yourselves, and let him come down to me. 9 If he is able to fight with me and kill me, then we will be your servants; but if I prevail against him and kill him, then you shall be our servants and serve us." 10 And the Philistine said, "Today I defy the ranks of Israel! Give me a man, that we may fight together." 11 When Saul and all Israel heard these words of the Philistine, they were dismayed and greatly afraid.

2. David kills Goliath

12   Now David was the son of an Ephrathite of Bethlehem in Judah, named Jesse, who had eight sons. In the days of Saul the man was already old and advanced in years.ʳ 13 The three eldest sons of Jesse had followed Saul to the battle; the names of his three sons who went to the battle were Eliab the firstborn, and next to him Abinadab, and the third Shammah. 14 David was the youngest; the three eldest followed Saul, 15 but David went back and forth from Saul to feed his father's sheep at Bethlehem. 16 For forty days the Philistine came forward and took his stand, morning and evening.

17   Jesse said to his son David, "Take for your brothers an ephah of this parched grain and these ten loaves, and carry them quickly to the camp to your brothers; 18 also take these ten cheeses to the commander of their thousand. See how your brothers fare, and bring some token from them."

19   Now Saul, and they, and all the men of Israel, were in the valley of Elah, fighting with the Philistines. 20 David rose early in the morning, left the sheep with a keeper, took the provisions, and went as Jesse had commanded him. He came to the encampment as the army was going forth to the battle line, shouting the war cry. 21 Israel and the Philistines drew up for battle, army against army. 22 David left the things in charge of the keeper of the baggage, ran to the ranks, and went and greeted his brothers. 23 As he talked with them, the champion, the Philistine of Gath, Goliath by name, came up out of the ranks of the Philistines, and spoke the same words as before. And David heard him.

24   All the Israelites, when they saw the man, fled from him and were very much afraid. 25 The Israelites said, "Have you seen this man who has come up? Surely he has come up to defy Israel. The king will greatly enrich the man who kills him, and will give him his daughter and make his family free in Israel." 26 David said to the men who stood by him, "What shall be done for the man who kills this Philistine, and takes away the reproach from Israel? For who is this uncircumcised Philistine that he should defy the armies of the living God?" 27 The people answered him in the same way, "So shall it be done for the man who kills him."

28   His eldest brother Eliab heard him talking to the men; and Eliab's

ʳ Gk Syr: Heb *among men*

Cross-references (right margin)

17.6
v. 45
17.7
2 Sam 21.19;
v. 41
17.8
1 Sam 8.17

17.10
vv. 26, 36, 45

17.12
Ruth 4.22;
1 Sam 16.18;
Gen 35.19;
1 Sam 16.10,
11;
1 Chr 2.13-15
17.13
1 Sam 16.6,
8,9
17.15
1 Sam 16.19

17.18
Gen 37.14

17.23
vv. 8-10

17.25
Josh 15.16

17.26
1 Sam 11.2;
14.6; v. 10;
Deut 5.26
17.27
v. 25

17.28
Gen 37.4ff

Footnotes

17.9 Goliath challenged Israel to a two-man fight, winner take all. Israel had no one who wished to take up the challenge, until David showed up.
17.26 David spoke the language of faith when he asked, "Who is this uncircumcised Philistine that he should defy the armies of the living God?" His confidence was not in himself but in the living God, and

he lived in the mighty power of the Spirit of the Lord (cf. 16.13).
17.28 Eliab, David's oldest brother, suspected that David wanted to take on Goliath. He browbeat David by using abusive language. He would not accept the challenge himself; but for this youngster to do so would make him lose face.

anger was kindled against David. He said, "Why have you come down? With whom have you left those few sheep in the wilderness? I know your presumption and the evil of your heart; for you have come down just to see the battle." 29 David said, "What have I done now? It was only a question." 30 He turned away from him toward another and spoke in the same way; and the people answered him again as before.

31 When the words that David spoke were heard, they repeated them before Saul; and he sent for him. 32 David said to Saul, "Let no one's heart fail because of him; your servant will go and fight with this Philistine." 33 Saul said to David, "You are not able to go against this Philistine to fight with him; for you are just a boy, and he has been a warrior from his youth." 34 But David said to Saul, "Your servant used to keep sheep for his father; and whenever a lion or a bear came, and took a lamb from the flock, 35 I went after it and struck it down, rescuing the lamb from its mouth; and if it turned against me, I would catch it by the jaw, strike it down, and kill it. 36 Your servant has killed both lions and bears; and this uncircumcised Philistine shall be like one of them, since he has defied the armies of the living God." 37 David said, "The LORD, who saved me from the paw of the lion and from the paw of the bear, will save me from the hand of this Philistine." So Saul said to David, "Go, and may the LORD be with you!"

38 Saul clothed David with his armor; he put a bronze helmet on his head and clothed him with a coat of mail. 39 David strapped Saul's sword over the armor, and he tried in vain to walk, for he was not used to them. Then David said to Saul, "I cannot walk with these; for I am not used to them." So David removed them. 40 Then he took his staff in his hand, and chose five smooth stones from the wadi, and put them in his shepherd's bag, in the pouch; his sling was in his hand, and he drew near to the Philistine.

41 The Philistine came on and drew near to David, with his shield-bearer in front of him. 42 When the Philistine looked and saw David, he disdained him, for he was only a youth, ruddy and handsome in appearance. 43 The Philistine said to David, "Am I a dog, that you come to me with sticks?" And the Philistine cursed David by his gods. 44 The Philistine said to David, "Come to me, and I will give your flesh to the birds of the air and to the wild animals of the field." 45 But David said to the Philistine, "You come to me with sword and spear and javelin; but I come to you in the name of the LORD of hosts, the God of the armies of Israel, whom you have defied. 46 This very day the LORD will deliver you into my hand, and I will strike you down and cut off your head; and I will give the dead bodies of the Philistine army this very day to the birds of the air and to the wild animals of the earth, so that all the earth may know that there is a God in Israel, 47 and that all this assembly may know that the LORD does not save by sword and spear; for the battle is the LORD's and he will give you into our hand."

48 When the Philistine drew nearer to meet David, David ran quickly toward the battle line to meet the Philistine. 49 David put his hand in his bag, took out a stone, slung it, and struck the Philistine on his forehead; the stone sank into his forehead, and he fell face down on the ground. 50 So David prevailed over the Philistine with a sling and a stone,

Cross references (margin)

17.29
v. 17
17.30
vv. 26, 27

17.32
Deut 20.1-4;
1 Sam 16.18

17.37
2 Tim 4.17;
1 Sam 20.13;
1 Chr 22.11,
16

17.42
Prov 16.18;
Ps 123.3, 4;
1 Sam 16.12
17.43
1 Sam 24.14;
2 Sam 3.8
17.44
1 Kings 20.10
17.45
2 Chr 32.8;
Ps 124.8;
Heb 11.34
17.46
1 Kings 18.36;
2 Kings 19.19;
Isa 52.10

17.47
1 Sam 14.6;
2 Chr 14.11;
Ps 44.6, 7

17.33 Saul sought to dissuade David from tackling Goliath. David insisted that if he could slay a lion and a bear, he could slay Goliath.

17.43 When Goliath saw this shorter, younger, and ill-armed contender stand before him, he was disdainful and contemptuous. In effect he said, "Do you think you can beat me as easily as you would a shepherd dog?" He cursed David by his gods and thus cursed the God of David.

17.45 From the perspective of the unbeliever, David's eagerness to confront Goliath appears to be based on adolescent naiveté. Yet David knew that his God was the God of the armies of the Israelites; he was certain that God would deliver Goliath into his hand before the end of the battle (v. 46). Who can withstand even the weakest, seemingly most unprepared of God's servants, who comes as the chosen of God for a particular task?

striking down the Philistine and killing him; there was no sword in David's hand. 51 Then David ran and stood over the Philistine; he grasped his sword, drew it out of its sheath, and killed him; then he cut off his head with it.

When the Philistines saw that their champion was dead, they fled. 52 The troops of Israel and Judah rose up with a shout and pursued the Philistines as far as Gath^s and the gates of Ekron, so that the wounded Philistines fell on the way from Shaaraim as far as Gath and Ekron. 53 The Israelites came back from chasing the Philistines, and they plundered their camp. 54 David took the head of the Philistine and brought it to Jerusalem; but he put his armor in his tent.

55 When Saul saw David go out against the Philistine, he said to Abner, the commander of the army, "Abner, whose son is this young man?" Abner said, "As your soul lives, O king, I do not know." 56 The king said, "Inquire whose son the stripling is." 57 On David's return from killing the Philistine, Abner took him and brought him before Saul, with the head of the Philistine in his hand. 58 Saul said to him, "Whose son are you, young man?" And David answered, "I am the son of your servant Jesse the Bethlehemite."

3. The friendship of David and Jonathan

18 When David^t had finished speaking to Saul, the soul of Jonathan was bound to the soul of David, and Jonathan loved him as his own soul. 2 Saul took him that day and would not let him return to his father's house. 3 Then Jonathan made a covenant with David, because he loved him as his own soul. 4 Jonathan stripped himself of the robe that he was wearing, and gave it to David, and his armor, and even his sword and his bow and his belt. 5 David went out and was successful wherever Saul sent him; as a result, Saul set him over the army. And all the people, even the servants of Saul, approved.

4. The hatred of Saul

6 As they were coming home, when David returned from killing the Philistine, the women came out of all the towns of Israel, singing and dancing, to meet King Saul, with tambourines, with songs of joy, and with musical instruments.^{u} 7 And the women sang to one another as they made merry,

"Saul has killed his thousands,
   and David his ten thousands."

8 Saul was very angry, for this saying displeased him. He said, "They have ascribed to David ten thousands, and to me they have ascribed thousands;

Cross-references (right column):

17.51
1 Sam 21.9;
Heb 11.34

17.52
Josh 15.36

17.55
1 Sam 16.21,
22

17.57
v. 54

17.58
v. 12

18.1
Gen 44.30;
Deut 13.6;
1 Sam 20.17;
2 Sam 1.26
18.2
1 Sam 17.15

18.6
Ex 15.20;
Judg 11.34;
Ps 68.25

18.7
Ex 15.21;
1 Sam 21.11

18.8
1 Sam 15.8

---

^{s} Gk Syr: Heb *Gai* ^{t} Heb *he* ^{u} Or *triangles*, or *three-stringed instruments*

17.55 Neither Saul nor Abner could remember the name of David's father. Saul was indebted to that family for what David had done, and in order to reward them he needed to know who headed up the family. David himself answered the question in v. 58.
18.1 Jonathan and David became fast friends and stuck with each other through thick and thin. The friendship of Jonathan and David has never been surpassed by any friendship. Jonathan had nothing to gain and everything to lose, but he never breached his friendship with David. Jonathan wrote David's finest epitaph when he said of him and Saul: "in life and in death they were not divided" (2 Sam 1.23). Saul, however, cursed his son for what he considered to be his infidelity toward himself (1 Sam 20.30–33).
18.5 David rose rapidly to a place of standing and

honor and was well thought of by the people. Even the servants of Saul were partial toward him.
18.9 Saul became envious of David and began plotting his death. He threw his spear at David, but he escaped. He promised to give David his eldest daughter Merab in marriage, and urged him to fight against the Philistines to win her, hoping he would be slain. Then he broke his word and gave Merab to someone else (vv. 17–19). When Saul learned that another of his daughters, Michal, was in love with David, he planned to use her to entrap David. His servants told David that the king wanted a hundred foreskins of the Philistines from the one who would marry Michal. To secure these, David endangered his life, but produced the foreskins, won Michal, and frustrated Saul (vv. 20–27).

what more can he have but the kingdom?" 9 So Saul eyed David from that day on.

18.10
1 Sam 16.14,
23; 19.9, 23,
24
18.11
1 Sam 19.10;
20.33
18.12
vv. 15, 29;
1 Sam 16.13,
14, 18
18.13
v. 16;
2 Sam 5.2
18.14
1 Sam 16.18;
Gen 39.2, 3,
23
18.16
v. 5

10   The next day an evil spirit from God rushed upon Saul, and he raved within his house, while David was playing the lyre, as he did day by day. Saul had his spear in his hand; 11 and Saul threw the spear, for he thought, "I will pin David to the wall." But David eluded him twice.

12   Saul was afraid of David, because the LORD was with him but had departed from Saul. 13 So Saul removed him from his presence, and made him a commander of a thousand; and David marched out and came in, leading the army. 14 David had success in all his undertakings; for the LORD was with him. 15 When Saul saw that he had great success, he stood in awe of him. 16 But all Israel and Judah loved David; for it was he who marched out and came in leading them.

5. David loses Merab but marries Michal

18.17
1 Sam 17.25;
25.28; vv. 21,
25
18.18
v. 23;
1 Sam 9.21;
2 Sam 7.18
18.19
2 Sam 21.8;
Judg 7.22
18.20
v. 28
18.21
vv. 17, 26

17   Then Saul said to David, "Here is my elder daughter Merab; I will give her to you as a wife; only be valiant for me and fight the LORD's battles." For Saul thought, "I will not raise a hand against him; let the Philistines deal with him." 18 David said to Saul, "Who am I and who are my kinsfolk, my father's family in Israel, that I should be son-in-law to the king?" 19 But at the time when Saul's daughter Merab should have been given to David, she was given to Adriel the Meholathite as a wife.

20   Now Saul's daughter Michal loved David. Saul was told, and the thing pleased him. 21 Saul thought, "Let me give her to him that she may be a snare for him and that the hand of the Philistines may be against him." Therefore Saul said to David a second time,[v] "You shall now be my son-in-law." 22 Saul commanded his servants, "Speak to David in private and say, 'See, the king is delighted with you, and all his servants love you; now then, become the king's son-in-law.'" 23 So Saul's servants reported these words to David in private. And David said, "Does it seem to you a little thing to become the king's son-in-law, seeing that I am a poor man and of no repute?" 24 The servants of Saul told him, "This is what David said." 25 Then Saul said, "Thus shall you say to David, 'The king desires no marriage present except a hundred foreskins of the Philistines, that he may be avenged on the king's enemies.'" Now Saul planned to make David fall by the hand of the Philistines. 26 When his servants told David these words, David was well pleased to be the king's son-in-law. Before the time had expired, 27 David rose and went, along with his men, and killed one hundred[w] of the Philistines; and David brought their foreskins, which were given in full number to the king, that he might become the king's son-in-law. Saul gave him his daughter Michal as a wife. 28 But when Saul realized that the LORD was with David, and that Saul's daughter Michal loved him, 29 Saul was still more afraid of David. So Saul was David's enemy from that time forward.

18.25
Ex 22.17;
1 Sam 14.24;
v. 17
18.26
v. 21
18.27
v. 13;
2 Sam 3.14

18.30
v. 5

30   Then the commanders of the Philistines came out to battle; and as often as they came out, David had more success than all the servants of Saul, so that his fame became very great.

[v] Heb by two   [w] Gk Compare 2 Sam 3.14: Heb two hundred

18.10   Saul, jealous and malicious, gave place to the devil who came upon him. He became "afraid of David, because the LORD was with him but had departed from Saul" (v. 12). David, however, was given the wisdom and grace to avoid a premature death on two occasions as Saul sought to pin him to the wall with his javelin.

18.25   *a hundred foreskins of the Philistines.* David

may have brought two hundred foreskins to the king (v. 27; see NRSV footnote). In 2 Sam 3.14 the number is said to be one hundred. Two possibilities may explain this apparent discrepancy. (1) A scribe miscopied the original text at v. 27. (2) David did bring back twice as many as was required of him. But when he later said what he had done, he stated the original price demanded by Saul.

6. Saul seeks to kill David

a. Jonathan's effort to placate Saul

19 Saul spoke with his son Jonathan and with all his servants about killing David. But Saul's son Jonathan took great delight in David. [2] Jonathan told David, "My father Saul is trying to kill you; therefore be on guard tomorrow morning; stay in a secret place and hide yourself. [3] I will go out and stand beside my father in the field where you are, and I will speak to my father about you; if I learn anything I will tell you." [4] Jonathan spoke well of David to his father Saul, saying to him, "The king should not sin against his servant David, because he has not sinned against you, and because his deeds have been of good service to you; [5] for he took his life in his hand when he attacked the Philistine, and the LORD brought about a great victory for all Israel. You saw it, and rejoiced; why then will you sin against an innocent person by killing David without cause?" [6] Saul heeded the voice of Jonathan; Saul swore, "As the LORD lives, he shall not be put to death." [7] So Jonathan called David and related all these things to him. Jonathan then brought David to Saul, and he was in his presence as before.

b. Saul tries to kill David

[8] Again there was war, and David went out to fight the Philistines. He launched a heavy attack on them, so that they fled before him. [9] Then an evil spirit from the LORD came upon Saul, as he sat in his house with his spear in his hand, while David was playing music. [10] Saul sought to pin David to the wall with the spear; but he eluded Saul, so that he struck the spear into the wall. David fled and escaped that night.

c. Michal helps David escape

[11] Saul sent messengers to David's house to keep watch over him, planning to kill him in the morning. David's wife Michal told him, "If you do not save your life tonight, tomorrow you will be killed." [12] So Michal let David down through the window; he fled away and escaped. [13] Michal took an idol[x] and laid it on the bed; she put a net[y] of goats' hair on its head, and covered it with the clothes. [14] When Saul sent messengers to take David, she said, "He is sick." [15] Then Saul sent the messengers to see David for themselves. He said, "Bring him up to me in the bed, that I may kill him." [16] When the messengers came in, the idol[z] was in the bed, with the covering[y] of goats' hair on its head. [17] Saul said to Michal, "Why have you deceived me like this, and let my enemy go, so that he has escaped?" Michal answered Saul, "He said to me, 'Let me go; why should I kill you?' "

d. Saul goes to Naioth and prophesies

[18] Now David fled and escaped; he came to Samuel at Ramah, and told him all that Saul had done to him. He and Samuel went and settled at Naioth. [19] Saul was told, "David is at Naioth in Ramah." [20] Then Saul

---

x Heb *took the teraphim*   y Meaning of Heb uncertain   z Heb *the teraphim*

19.1 1 Sam 18.1-3, 8, 9
19.3 1 Sam 20.9, 13
19.4 1 Sam 20.32; Gen 42.22
19.5 1 Sam 17.49, 50; 11.13; 20.32
19.7 1 Sam 16.21; 18.2, 13
19.9 1 Sam 16.14; 18.10, 11
19.10 1 Sam 18.11
19.12 Josh 2.15; Acts 9.24, 25
19.14 Josh 2.5
19.18 1 Sam 7.17
19.20 vv. 11, 14; 1 Sam 10.5, 6; Num 11.25

19.1 Saul went one step further. He told Jonathan and all his servants to murder David. Saul knew of Jonathan's friendship with David but supposed that since he was heir to the throne, he would be happy to dispose of a rival contender. Saul gauged his son's intentions by his own. But Jonathan was made of different stuff and remained loyal to his friendship with David.

19.2 Jonathan warned David against his father, proving that blood is not always thicker than water. He spoke to Saul and secured a pledge from him (v. 6) that David would not be murdered.

19.9 When the evil spirit overtook Saul, he promptly forgot his pledge not to murder David. He sent soldiers to take David at home, but Michal his daughter was faithful to her husband and arranged for his escape.

19.19 *Naioth in Ramah* was the site of the school of the prophets. Samuel and David went there. When Saul heard of it, he sent messengers to take David. These men were themselves seized by the Spirit of God and joined the prophets in worshiping God and prophesying. This happened three times. Then Saul went there himself. He too was seized by the Spirit (v. 23), prophesied, stripped off his clothes, and went naked all night. The question was asked: "Is Saul also

sent messengers to take David. When they saw the company of the prophets in a frenzy, with Samuel standing in charge of[a] them, the spirit of God came upon the messengers of Saul, and they also fell into a prophetic frenzy. 21 When Saul was told, he sent other messengers, and they also fell into a frenzy. Saul sent messengers again the third time, and they also fell into a frenzy. 22 Then he himself went to Ramah. He came to the great well that is in Secu;[b] he asked, "Where are Samuel and David?" And someone said, "They are at Naioth in Ramah." 23 He went there, toward Naioth in Ramah; and the spirit of God came upon him. As he was going, he fell into a prophetic frenzy, until he came to Naioth in Ramah. 24 He too stripped off his clothes, and he too fell into a frenzy before Samuel. He lay naked all that day and all that night. Therefore it is said, "Is Saul also among the prophets?"

7. Jonathan delivers David

a. The discussion of the problem

20 David fled from Naioth in Ramah. He came before Jonathan and said, "What have I done? What is my guilt? And what is my sin against your father that he is trying to take my life?" 2 He said to him, "Far from it! You shall not die. My father does nothing either great or small without disclosing it to me; and why should my father hide this from me? Never!" 3 But David also swore, "Your father knows well that you like me; and he thinks, 'Do not let Jonathan know this, or he will be grieved.' But truly, as the LORD lives and as you yourself live, there is but a step between me and death." 4 Then Jonathan said to David, "Whatever you say, I will do for you." 5 David said to Jonathan, "Tomorrow is the new moon, and I should not fail to sit with the king at the meal; but let me go, so that I may hide in the field until the third evening. 6 If your father misses me at all, then say, 'David earnestly asked leave of me to run to Bethlehem his city; for there is a yearly sacrifice there for all the family.' 7 If he says, 'Good!' it will be well with your servant; but if he is angry, then know that evil has been determined by him. 8 Therefore deal kindly with your servant, for you have brought your servant into a sacred covenant[c] with you. But if there is guilt in me, kill me yourself; why should you bring me to your father?" 9 Jonathan said, "Far be it from you! If I knew that it was decided by my father that evil should come upon you, would I not tell you?" 10 Then David said to Jonathan, "Who will tell me if your father answers you harshly?" 11 Jonathan replied to David, "Come, let us go out into the field." So they both went out into the field.

b. The covenant of David and Jonathan

12 Jonathan said to David, "By the LORD, the God of Israel! When I have sounded out my father, about this time tomorrow, or on the third day, if he is well disposed toward David, shall I not then send and disclose it to you? 13 But if my father intends to do you harm, the LORD do so to Jonathan, and more also, if I do not disclose it to you, and send you away, so that you may go in safety. May the LORD be with you, as he has been with my father. 14 If I am still alive, show me the faithful love of the LORD; but if I die,[a] 15 never cut off your faithful love from my house, even if

a Meaning of Heb uncertain   *b* Gk reads *to the well of the threshing floor on the bare height*   *c* Heb *a covenant of the LORD*

Cross-references (margin)

19.23
Isa 20.2;
1 Sam 10.10-12

20.1
1 Sam 24.9

20.5
Num 10.10;
28.11;
1 Sam 19.2
20.6
1 Sam 17.58;
Deut 12.5

20.8
1 Sam 18.3;
23.18;
2 Sam 14.32

20.13
1 Sam 3.17;
Ruth 1.17;
1 Sam 17.37

20.15
2 Sam 9.1

Study notes

among the prophets?" (v. 24; cf. 10.12). The Spirit does sometimes overtake evil men and uses them to accomplish the divine will. In the N.T. Jesus spoke of those who in his name prophesied, cast out devils, and did mighty works (Mt 7.21,22). But even though they did these things, Jesus disowned them and said they worked iniquity. They were using good things for wrong purposes.

20.3ff David shared his inner thoughts with Jonathan, presenting the facts to show that he should not be regarded as an enemy of Saul.
20.9   Jonathan assured David of his own integrity in David's moment of distress. He swore allegiance to David, whatever the cost and whatever the outcome.
20.15   See notes on 2 Sam 9 for David's fulfillment of this promise.

the LORD were to cut off every one of the enemies of David from the face of the earth." 16 Thus Jonathan made a covenant with the house of David, saying, "May the LORD seek out the enemies of David." 17 Jonathan made David swear again by his love for him; for he loved him as he loved his own life.

c. The signal arranged

18   Jonathan said to him, "Tomorrow is the new moon; you will be missed, because your place will be empty. 19 On the day after tomorrow, you shall go a long way down; go to the place where you hid yourself earlier, and remain beside the stone there.*d* 20 I will shoot three arrows to the side of it, as though I shot at a mark. 21 Then I will send the boy, saying, 'Go, find the arrows.' If I say to the boy, 'Look, the arrows are on this side of you, collect them,' then you are to come, for, as the LORD lives, it is safe for you and there is no danger. 22 But if I say to the young man, 'Look, the arrows are beyond you,' then go; for the LORD has sent you away. 23 As for the matter about which you and I have spoken, the LORD is witness*e* between you and me forever."

d. Jonathan's plea to Saul for David

24   So David hid himself in the field. When the new moon came, the king sat at the feast to eat. 25 The king sat upon his seat, as at other times, upon the seat by the wall. Jonathan stood, while Abner sat by Saul's side; but David's place was empty.

26   Saul did not say anything that day; for he thought, "Something has befallen him; he is not clean, surely he is not clean." 27 But on the second day, the day after the new moon, David's place was empty. And Saul said to his son Jonathan, "Why has the son of Jesse not come to the feast, either yesterday or today?" 28 Jonathan answered Saul, "David earnestly asked leave of me to go to Bethlehem; 29 he said, 'Let me go; for our family is holding a sacrifice in the city, and my brother has commanded me to be there. So now, if I have found favor in your sight, let me get away, and see my brothers.' For this reason he has not come to the king's table."

e. Saul's anger at Jonathan

30   Then Saul's anger was kindled against Jonathan. He said to him, "You son of a perverse, rebellious woman! Do I not know that you have chosen the son of Jesse to your own shame, and to the shame of your mother's nakedness? 31 For as long as the son of Jesse lives upon the earth, neither you nor your kingdom shall be established. Now send and bring him to me, for he shall surely die." 32 Then Jonathan answered his father Saul, "Why should he be put to death? What has he done?" 33 But Saul threw his spear at him to strike him; so Jonathan knew that it was the decision of his father to put David to death. 34 Jonathan rose from the table in fierce anger and ate no food on the second day of the month, for he was grieved for David, and because his father had disgraced him.

f. Jonathan warns David

35   In the morning Jonathan went out into the field to the appointment with David, and with him was a little boy. 36 He said to the boy, "Run and find the arrows that I shoot." As the boy ran, he shot an arrow beyond him. 37 When the boy came to the place where Jonathan's arrow had

---

d Meaning of Heb uncertain   *e* Gk: Heb lacks *witness*

20.20 Jonathan arranged the signal by which he would tell David of his father's intentions. If he should shoot his arrow beyond the person who was assigned to recover the arrows, David would know that his life was in danger and would flee.
20.30 *son of a perverse, rebellious woman!* At this point, Saul appears to have reached a point of no

return. He accused his son Jonathan of being a traitor by his support of David. When Jonathan withstood his father, asking what David had done that made him worthy of death, Saul attempted to kill Jonathan (20.32,33). This was the last straw. Jonathan knew then that his father was irrevocably committed to slaying David.

Marginal references:

20.17
1 Sam 18.1

20.18
vv. 5, 25
20.19
1 Sam 19.2

20.22
v. 37
20.23
vv. 14, 15;
Gen 31.49, 53

20.25
v. 18

20.26
1 Sam 16.5;
Lev 7.20, 21

20.28
v. 6

20.30
Deut 21.20

20.32
1 Sam 19.5;
Mt 27.23;
Lk 23.22
20.33
v. 7

20.36
vv. 20, 21
20.37
v. 22

fallen, Jonathan called after the boy and said, "Is the arrow not beyond you?" 38 Jonathan called after the boy, "Hurry, be quick, do not linger." So Jonathan's boy gathered up the arrows and came to his master. 39 But the boy knew nothing; only Jonathan and David knew the arrangement. 40 Jonathan gave his weapons to the boy and said to him, "Go and carry them to the city." 41 As soon as the boy had gone, David rose from beside the stone heap*f* and prostrated himself with his face to the ground. He bowed three times, and they kissed each other, and wept with each other; David wept the more.*g* 42 Then Jonathan said to David, "Go in peace, since both of us have sworn in the name of the Lord, saying, 'The Lord shall be between me and you, and between my descendants and your descendants, forever.' " He got up and left; and Jonathan went into the city.*h*

20.42
1 Sam 1.17;
v. 22

8. David's flight from Saul

a. Ahimelech the priest and the holy bread

21.1
1 Sam 22.19;
14.3; 16.4

21 *i* David came to Nob to the priest Ahimelech. Ahimelech came trembling to meet David, and said to him, "Why are you alone, and no one with you?" 2 David said to the priest Ahimelech, "The king has charged me with a matter, and said to me, 'No one must know anything of the matter about which I send you, and with which I have charged you.' I have made an appointment*j* with the young men for such and such a place. 3 Now then, what have you at hand? Give me five loaves of bread, or whatever is here." 4 The priest answered David, "I have no ordinary bread at hand, only holy bread—provided that the young men have kept themselves from women." 5 David answered the priest, "Indeed women have been kept from us as always when I go on an expedition; the vessels of the young men are holy even when it is a common journey; how much more today will their vessels be holy?" 6 So the priest gave him the holy bread; for there was no bread there except the bread of the Presence, which is removed from before the Lord, to be replaced by hot bread on the day it is taken away.

21.4
Lev 24.5-9;
Mt 12.4
21.5
Ex 19.14, 15

21.6
Mt 12.3, 4;
Mk 2.25, 26;
Lev 24.8, 9

7 Now a certain man of the servants of Saul was there that day, detained before the Lord; his name was Doeg the Edomite, the chief of Saul's shepherds.

21.7
1 Sam 22.9

b. David takes Goliath's sword

8 David said to Ahimelech, "Is there no spear or sword here with you? I did not bring my sword or my weapons with me, because the king's business required haste." 9 The priest said, "The sword of Goliath the Philistine, whom you killed in the valley of Elah, is here wrapped in a cloth behind the ephod; if you will take that, take it, for there is none here except that one." David said, "There is none like it; give it to me."

21.9
1 Sam 17.2,
51

f Gk: Heb *from beside the south*   *g* Vg: Meaning of Heb uncertain   *h* This sentence is 21.1 in Heb
i Ch 21.2 in Heb   *j* Q Ms Vg Compare Gk: Meaning of MT uncertain

---

20.37ff Jonathan shot the arrow beyond his servant boy and thus warned David that Saul meant to kill him. The servant went off with the arrows, and David and Jonathan had a farewell meeting. David fell to the ground and bowed three times to Jonathan (v. 41), thus acknowledging the good services done him by his friend. In a touching scene they took leave of each other with tears and sorrow, as Jonathan said words to this effect: "We have both sworn in the name of the Lord, for ourselves and our heirs, that we and they will be faithful and kind to each other from generation to generation."

21.1 David came to Ahimelech the priest for two things: food and a weapon. David asked for five loaves of bread. But Ahimelech had no common bread, only holy bread, which normally stood for a week on the golden table and, when replaced by fresh bread, was to be eaten by the priest and his family. David pointed out how carefully he and his men had been keeping the law of God, and implied that he saw no reason why they could not have the week-old bread. Later Jesus supported this argument, saying that ritual observances must give way to moral duties and that, in emergencies, what normally was forbidden could be done (see Mt 12.3–8). Ahimelech consented to give him the bread; he also gave him the sword of Goliath.

21.2 Here David lied to Ahimelech, for he had no orders from Saul. This lie eventually brought about the death of many people (22.9–19).

c. David goes to King Achish of Gath

10 David rose and fled that day from Saul; he went to King Achish of Gath. **11** The servants of Achish said to him, "Is this not David the king of the land? Did they not sing to one another of him in dances,

'Saul has killed his thousands,
    and David his ten thousands'?"

12 David took these words to heart and was very much afraid of King Achish of Gath. **13** So he changed his behavior before them; he pretended to be mad when in their presence.[k] He scratched marks on the doors of the gate, and let his spittle run down his beard. **14** Achish said to his servants, "Look, you see the man is mad; why then have you brought him to me? **15** Do I lack madmen, that you have brought this fellow to play the madman in my presence? Shall this fellow come into my house?"

d. David in the cave of Adullam

22 David left there and escaped to the cave of Adullam; when his brothers and all his father's house heard of it, they went down there to him. **2** Everyone who was in distress, and everyone who was in debt, and everyone who was discontented gathered to him; and he became captain over them. Those who were with him numbered about four hundred.

e. David flees to Mizpah in Moab

3 David went from there to Mizpeh of Moab. He said to the king of Moab, "Please let my father and mother come[l] to you, until I know what God will do for me." **4** He left them with the king of Moab, and they stayed with him all the time that David was in the stronghold. **5** Then the prophet Gad said to David, "Do not remain in the stronghold; leave, and go into the land of Judah." So David left, and went into the forest of Hereth.

f. Doeg the Edomite betrays Ahimelech to Saul

6 Saul heard that David and those who were with him had been located. Saul was sitting at Gibeah, under the tamarisk tree on the height, with his spear in his hand, and all his servants were standing around him. **7** Saul said to his servants who stood around him, "Hear now, you Benjaminites; will the son of Jesse give every one of you fields and vineyards, will he make you all commanders of thousands and commanders of hundreds? **8** Is that why all of you have conspired against me? No one discloses to me when my son makes a league with the son of Jesse, none of you is sorry for me or discloses to me that my son has stirred up my servant against me, to lie in wait, as he is doing today." **9** Doeg the Edomite, who was in charge of Saul's servants, answered, "I saw the son of Jesse coming to Nob, to Ahimelech son of Ahitub; **10** he inquired of the LORD for him, gave him provisions, and gave him the sword of Goliath the Philistine."

g. Saul slays Ahimelech and the priests

11 The king sent for the priest Ahimelech son of Ahitub and for all his father's house, the priests who were at Nob; and all of them came to the king. **12** Saul said, "Listen now, son of Ahitub." He answered, "Here I am, my lord." **13** Saul said to him, "Why have you conspired against me, you and the son of Jesse, by giving him bread and a sword, and by

21.11
1 Sam 18.7;
29.5

21.12
1 Sam 2.19

22.1
2 Sam 23.13

22.2
1 Sam 23.13;
25.13

22.5
2 Sam 24.11;
1 Chr 29.29;
2 Chr 29.25

22.7
1 Sam 8.14

22.8
1 Sam 18.3;
20.16

22.9
1 Sam 21.1;
14.3

22.10
1 Sam 10.22;
21.6, 9

---

k Heb *in their hands*   l Syr Vg: Heb *come out*

21.10 On two occasions David took refuge in Gath, which was ruled over by a Philistine king. He saved his life on this occasion by pretending to be mad (cf. Ps 56.1). The second time he sought refuge with his wives and six hundred followers (27.1 – 28.2).
22.3 David was so afraid — not only for himself but also for his family — that he sought political asylum for his aged parents beyond the Dead Sea in the coun-

try of Moab.
22.7,8 Saul spread the fictitious story that David and his son Jonathan had made a pact to kill him. David and Jonathan were friends, but they were not enemies of the king. Saul was now so beside himself that he became obsessed with trying to find David and to slay him.

inquiring of God for him, so that he has risen against me, to lie in wait, as he is doing today?"

22.14
1 Sam 19.4, 5

14   Then Ahimelech answered the king, "Who among all your servants is so faithful as David? He is the king's son-in-law, and is quick*m* to do your bidding, and is honored in your house. 15 Is today the first time that I have inquired of God for him? By no means! Do not let the king impute anything to his servant or to any member of my father's house; for your servant has known nothing of all this, much or little." 16 The king said,

22.17
Ex 1.17

"You shall surely die, Ahimelech, you and all your father's house." 17 The king said to the guard who stood around him, "Turn and kill the priests of the LORD, because their hand also is with David; they knew that he fled, and did not disclose it to me." But the servants of the king would not raise

22.18
1 Sam 2.18, 31

their hand to attack the priests of the LORD. 18 Then the king said to Doeg, "You, Doeg, turn and attack the priests." Doeg the Edomite turned and attacked the priests; on that day he killed eighty-five who wore the linen ephod. 19 Nob, the city of the priests, he put to the sword; men and women, children and infants, oxen, donkeys, and sheep, he put to the sword.

h. Abiathar escapes to David

22.20
1 Sam 23.6, 9; 2.33
22.22
1 Sam 21.7

20   But one of the sons of Ahimelech son of Ahitub, named Abiathar, escaped and fled after David. 21 Abiathar told David that Saul had killed the priests of the LORD. 22 David said to Abiathar, "I knew on that day, when Doeg the Edomite was there, that he would surely tell Saul. I am responsible*n* for the lives of all your father's house. 23 Stay with me, and

22.23
1 Kings 2.26

do not be afraid; for the one who seeks my life seeks your life; you will be safe with me."

i. David at Keilah

23.1
Josh 15.44
23.2
vv. 4, 6, 9;
2 Sam 5.19, 23

23 Now they told David, "The Philistines are fighting against Keilah, and are robbing the threshing floors." 2 David inquired of the LORD, "Shall I go and attack these Philistines?" The LORD said to David, "Go and attack the Philistines and save Keilah." 3 But David's men said to him, "Look, we are afraid here in Judah; how much more then if we go to Keilah against the armies of the Philistines?" 4 Then David inquired

23.4
Josh 8.7;
Judg 7.7

of the LORD again. The LORD answered him, "Yes, go down to Keilah; for I will give the Philistines into your hand." 5 So David and his men went to Keilah, fought with the Philistines, brought away their livestock, and dealt them a heavy defeat. Thus David rescued the inhabitants of Keilah.

23.6
1 Sam 22.20

6   When Abiathar son of Ahimelech fled to David at Keilah, he came down with an ephod in his hand. 7 Now it was told Saul that David had come to Keilah. And Saul said, "God has given*o* him into my hand; for he has shut himself in by entering a town that has gates and bars." 8 Saul

m Heb *and turns aside*   *n* Gk Vg: Meaning of Heb uncertain   *o* Gk Tg: Heb *made a stranger of*

22.16   Saul decided to kill Ahimelech for helping David. Then he went even further, condemning Ahimelech's whole house. Saul was now assuming to himself an authority above the office of king. He did not appeal to any judge or prophet; he did not seek advice from a privy council or a council of war. It was the act of a dictator. His own soldiers refused to execute the priest and his family. Saul finally ordered Doeg, an unbelieving Edomite, to proceed with the slaughter; when he was finished, eighty-five priests lay dead (v. 18). Then he totally wiped out the priestly town of Nob.
22.22   David assumed full responsibility for the death of the priests and their loved ones. His lie produced dreadful consequences, especially since he had intuitively known that Doeg the Edomite would report his presence to Saul. Later David wrote Psalm 52 about all of this.
23.1   Keilah was in Judah but bordered on land occupied by the Philistines, who would seize the grain after it had been reaped and threshed. David was told by God to go up against the Philistines in order to stop the pillaging.
23.7   Saul erroneously assumed that God had providentially delivered David into his hands. God, however, was with David as his chosen king and frustrated the plans of Saul. The human plans cannot annul God's sovereign purposes (cf. 2 Sam 17.14; Neh 4.15; Job 5.12).

summoned all the people to war, to go down to Keilah, to besiege David and his men. 9 When David learned that Saul was plotting evil against him, he said to the priest Abiathar, "Bring the ephod here." 10 David said, "O LORD, the God of Israel, your servant has heard that Saul seeks to come down to Keilah, to destroy the city on my account. 11 And now, will*p* Saul come down as your servant has heard? O LORD, the God of Israel, I beseech you, tell your servant." The LORD said, "He will come down." 12 Then David said, "Will the men of Keilah surrender me and my men into the hand of Saul?" The LORD said, "They will surrender you." 13 Then David and his men, who were about six hundred, set out and left Keilah; they wandered wherever they could go. When Saul was told that David had escaped from Keilah, he gave up the expedition. 14 David remained in the strongholds in the wilderness, in the hill country of the Wilderness of Ziph. Saul sought him every day, but the LORD*q* did not give him into his hand.

j. The treachery of the Ziphites

15   David was in the Wilderness of Ziph at Horesh when he learned that*r* Saul had come out to seek his life. 16 Saul's son Jonathan set out and came to David at Horesh; there he strengthened his hand through the LORD.*s* 17 He said to him, "Do not be afraid; for the hand of my father Saul shall not find you; you shall be king over Israel, and I shall be second to you; my father Saul also knows that this is so." 18 Then the two of them made a covenant before the LORD; David remained at Horesh, and Jonathan went home.

19   Then some Ziphites went up to Saul at Gibeah and said, "David is hiding among us in the strongholds of Horesh, on the hill of Hachilah, which is south of Jeshimon. 20 Now, O king, whenever you wish to come down, do so; and our part will be to surrender him into the king's hand." 21 Saul said, "May you be blessed by the LORD for showing me compassion! 22 Go and make sure once more; find out exactly where he is, and who has seen him there; for I am told that he is very cunning. 23 Look around and learn all the hiding places where he lurks, and come back to me with sure information. Then I will go with you; and if he is in the land, I will search him out among all the thousands of Judah." 24 So they set out and went to Ziph ahead of Saul.

David and his men were in the wilderness of Maon, in the Arabah to the south of Jeshimon. 25 Saul and his men went to search for him. When David was told, he went down to the rock and stayed in the wilderness of Maon. When Saul heard that, he pursued David into the wilderness of Maon. 26 Saul went on one side of the mountain, and David and his men on the other side of the mountain. David was hurrying to get away from Saul, while Saul and his men were closing in on David and his men to capture them. 27 Then a messenger came to Saul, saying, "Hurry and come; for the Philistines have made a raid on the land." 28 So Saul stopped pursuing David, and went against the Philistines; therefore that place was called the Rock of Escape.*t* 29*u* David then went up from there, and lived in the strongholds of En-gedi.

23.9
v. 6;
1 Sam 30.7

23.12
v. 20

23.13
1 Sam 22.2;
25.13
23.14
Josh 15.15;
Ps 54.3, 4

23.16
1 Sam 30.6

23.17
1 Sam 20.31;
24.20
23.18
1 Sam 18.3;
20.16, 42;
2 Sam 9.1;
21.7
23.19
1 Sam 26.1

23.20
v. 12

23.21
1 Sam 22.8

23.24
Josh 15.55;
1 Sam 25.2

23.26
Ps 17.9

23.29
2 Chr 20.2

---

p Q Ms Compare Gk: MT *Will the men of Keilah surrender me into his hand? Will*   *q* Q Ms Gk: MT *God*
r Or *saw that*   *s* Compare Q Ms Gk: MT *God*   *t* Or *Rock of Division*; meaning of Heb uncertain
u Ch 24.1 in Heb

23.9   David asked directions from God through Abiathar, a son of Ahimelech who apparently had taken the ephod with him when he escaped the massacre of the priests at Nob. When God informed him that the people of Keilah (whom David had helped) would turn him over to Saul, he fled.
23.15   Saul was now in hot pursuit of David. He had many more troops than David and the situation

looked grim. The Ziphites regularly reported his movements to Saul (v. 19). In this particular episode David was on one side of the mountain in the wilderness of Maon, and Saul was on the other. Saul's troops were closing in on David (v. 26) when God intervened to rescue him; the Philistines started raids, and Saul had to stop his search for David to fend off the Philistines. David was saved for the moment.

k. David cuts off Saul's cloak at En-gedi

24 When Saul returned from following the Philistines, he was told, "David is in the wilderness of En-gedi." ²Then Saul took three thousand chosen men out of all Israel, and went to look for David and his men in the direction of the Rocks of the Wild Goats. ³He came to the sheepfolds beside the road, where there was a cave; and Saul went in to relieve himself.ᵛ Now David and his men were sitting in the innermost parts of the cave. ⁴The men of David said to him, "Here is the day of which the Lord said to you, 'I will give your enemy into your hand, and you shall do to him as it seems good to you.'" Then David went and stealthily cut off a corner of Saul's cloak. ⁵Afterward David was stricken to the heart because he had cut off a corner of Saul's cloak. ⁶He said to his men, "The Lord forbid that I should do this thing to my lord, the Lord's anointed, to raise my hand against him; for he is the Lord's anointed." ⁷So David scolded his men severely and did not permit them to attack Saul. Then Saul got up and left the cave, and went on his way.

l. David rebukes Saul

8 Afterwards David also rose up and went out of the cave and called after Saul, "My lord the king!" When Saul looked behind him, David bowed with his face to the ground, and did obeisance. ⁹David said to Saul, "Why do you listen to the words of those who say, 'David seeks to do you harm'? ¹⁰This very day your eyes have seen how the Lord gave you into my hand in the cave; and some urged me to kill you, but I sparedʷ you. I said, 'I will not raise my hand against my lord; for he is the Lord's anointed.' ¹¹See, my father, see the corner of your cloak in my hand; for by the fact that I cut off the corner of your cloak, and did not kill you, you may know for certain that there is no wrong or treason in my hands. I have not sinned against you, though you are hunting me to take my life. ¹²May the Lord judge between me and you! May the Lord avenge me on you; but my hand shall not be against you. ¹³As the ancient proverb says, 'Out of the wicked comes forth wickedness'; but my hand shall not be against you. ¹⁴Against whom has the king of Israel come out? Whom do you pursue? A dead dog? A single flea? ¹⁵May the Lord therefore be judge, and give sentence between me and you. May he see to it, and plead my cause, and vindicate me against you."

m. Saul's apparent repentance

16 When David had finished speaking these words to Saul, Saul said, "Is this your voice, my son David?" Saul lifted up his voice and wept. ¹⁷He said to David, "You are more righteous than I; for you have repaid me good, whereas I have repaid you evil. ¹⁸Today you have explained how you have dealt well with me, in that you did not kill me when the Lord put me into your hands. ¹⁹For who has ever found an enemy, and sent the enemy safely away? So may the Lord reward you with good for what you have done to me this day. ²⁰Now I know that you shall surely be king, and that the kingdom of Israel shall be established in your hand. ²¹Swear to me therefore by the Lord that you will not cut off my descendants after

ᵛ Heb *to cover his feet* ʷ Gk Syr Tg Vg: Heb *it (my eye)* spared

24.4 David, on several occasions, could have killed Saul and seized the throne. But he refused to do so, on the ground that Saul was God's anointed king (v. 6). He was willing to let God work out his will. The end would not justify the means, for good ends must be secured through good means. Only God's will done God's way results in God's blessing.
24.8 After David had taken Saul's cloak, he addressed the king from a distance and pleaded his case. He could have murdered Saul but refused to do so. Why then should Saul wish to kill him? He quoted an

old proverb that wickedness proceeds from the wicked. If his heart had been wicked, his deeds would have been wicked and he would have slain Saul (v. 13). By implication, Saul could see by this statement his own wicked condition.
24.16 Saul was moved to tears by David's words. Superficially, he appeared to be penitent. David responded to Saul's petition by swearing that he would not cut down Saul's descendants; Saul was already sensing that his days were numbered and that David would succeed him in the kingship.

Margin refs: 24.1 1 Sam 23.28,29; 24.2 1 Sam 26.2; 24.3 Judg 3.24; 24.4 1 Sam 23.17; 25.28-30; 24.5 2 Sam 24.10; 24.6 1 Sam 26.11; 24.8 1 Sam 25.23,24; 24.11 Ps 7.3; 35.7; 1 Sam 23.14,23; 26.20; 24.12 Gen 31.53; Judg 11.27; 1 Sam 26.10; Job 5.8; 24.13 Mt 7.16-20; 24.14 1 Sam 17.43; 26.20; 24.15 v. 12; Ps 35.1; Mic 7.9; 24.16 1 Sam 26.17; 24.17 1 Sam 26.21; Mt 5.44; 24.18 1 Sam 26.23; 24.20 1 Sam 23.17; 24.21 Gen 21.23; 2 Sam 21.6-8

me, and that you will not wipe out my name from my father's house."
22 So David swore this to Saul. Then Saul went home; but David and his
men went up to the stronghold.

n. David and Abigail

(1) NABAL'S REFUSAL OF HELP

25 Now Samuel died; and all Israel assembled and mourned for him.
They buried him at his home in Ramah.

Then David got up and went down to the wilderness of Paran.

2 There was a man in Maon, whose property was in Carmel. The man
was very rich; he had three thousand sheep and a thousand goats. He was
shearing his sheep in Carmel. 3 Now the name of the man was Nabal, and
the name of his wife Abigail. The woman was clever and beautiful, but
the man was surly and mean; he was a Calebite. 4 David heard in the
wilderness that Nabal was shearing his sheep. 5 So David sent ten young
men; and David said to the young men, "Go up to Carmel, and go to
Nabal, and greet him in my name. 6 Thus you shall salute him: 'Peace be
to you, and peace be to your house, and peace be to all that you have. 7 I
hear that you have shearers; now your shepherds have been with us, and
we did them no harm, and they missed nothing, all the time they were
in Carmel. 8 Ask your young men, and they will tell you. Therefore let
my young men find favor in your sight; for we have come on a feast day.
Please give whatever you have at hand to your servants and to your son
David.'"

9 When David's young men came, they said all this to Nabal in the
name of David; and then they waited. 10 But Nabal answered David's
servants, "Who is David? Who is the son of Jesse? There are many
servants today who are breaking away from their masters. 11 Shall I take
my bread and my water and the meat that I have butchered for my
shearers, and give it to men who come from I do not know where?" 12 So
David's young men turned away, and came back and told him all this.
13 David said to his men, "Every man strap on his sword!" And every one
of them strapped on his sword; David also strapped on his sword; and
about four hundred men went up after David, while two hundred remained with the baggage.

(2) ABIGAIL PLACATES DAVID

14 But one of the young men told Abigail, Nabal's wife, "David sent
messengers out of the wilderness to salute our master; and he shouted
insults at them. 15 Yet the men were very good to us, and we suffered no
harm, and we never missed anything when we were in the fields, as long
as we were with them; 16 they were a wall to us both by night and by day,
all the while we were with them keeping the sheep. 17 Now therefore know
this and consider what you should do; for evil has been decided against
our master and against all his house; he is so ill-natured that no one can
speak to him."

18 Then Abigail hurried and took two hundred loaves, two skins of

24.22
1 Sam 23.29

25.1
1 Sam 28.3;
Deut 34.8;
2 Chr 33.20;
Gen 21.21
25.2
1 Sam 23.24;
Josh 15.55

25.6
1 Chr 12.18
25.7
2 Sam 13.23,
24; vv. 15, 21
25.8
Neh 8.10-12

25.10
Judg 9.28

25.13
1 Sam 23.13;
30.24

25.15
v. 7
25.16
Ex 14.22

25.18
2 Sam 16.1;
1 Chr 12.40

24.22 *Saul went home,* temporarily convinced but
not converted. He was still envious of David, as subsequent chapters show.
25.1 Samuel the prophet died and was buried. He
had been a good friend of David and had had the
pleasure of anointing him to the kingship on the command of God. But he did not live to see David ascend
the throne.
25.2 Perhaps David went to the wilderness of Paran
after Samuel's death to mourn the prophet's death (v.
1) — but more likely to stay away from Saul. David
understandably still did not trust him. The incident
with Nabal resulted from this journey.
25.3 Nabal (meaning "fool") was a fitting name.

With his wife Abigail he lived in Maon, but they had
sheep and pasture in Carmel (not to be confused with
Mount Carmel). David and his followers protected
Nabal's workers and animals from predators. But
when David asked for Nabal's help, he so churlishly
refused that David decided to seize by force what he
had asked for.
25.11 Nabal's servants had solicited David's help
and now their master refused to recognize what good
David and his followers had done. He pretended to
be unaware of the agreement made on his behalf and
turned David's messengers away in scorn.
25.18 Nabal's wife Abigail had more good sense
than her husband. She gathered food and personally

wine, five sheep ready dressed, five measures of parched grain, one hundred clusters of raisins, and two hundred cakes of figs. She loaded them on donkeys 19 and said to her young men, "Go on ahead of me; I am coming after you." But she did not tell her husband Nabal. 20 As she rode on the donkey and came down under cover of the mountain, David and his men came down toward her; and she met them. 21 Now David had said, "Surely it was in vain that I protected all that this fellow has in the wilderness, so that nothing was missed of all that belonged to him; but he has returned me evil for good. 22 God do so to David[x] and more also, if by morning I leave so much as one male of all who belong to him."

23 When Abigail saw David, she hurried and alighted from the donkey, and fell before David on her face, bowing to the ground. 24 She fell at his feet and said, "Upon me alone, my lord, be the guilt; please let your servant speak in your ears, and hear the words of your servant. 25 My lord, do not take seriously this ill-natured fellow, Nabal; for as his name is, so is he; Nabal[y] is his name, and folly is with him; but I, your servant, did not see the young men of my lord, whom you sent.

26 "Now then, my lord, as the LORD lives, and as you yourself live, since the LORD has restrained you from bloodguilt and from taking vengeance with your own hand, now let your enemies and those who seek to do evil to my lord be like Nabal. 27 And now let this present that your servant has brought to my lord be given to the young men who follow my lord. 28 Please forgive the trespass of your servant; for the LORD will certainly make my lord a sure house, because my lord is fighting the battles of the LORD; and evil shall not be found in you so long as you live. 29 If anyone should rise up to pursue you and to seek your life, the life of my lord shall be bound in the bundle of the living under the care of the LORD your God; but the lives of your enemies he shall sling out as from the hollow of a sling. 30 When the LORD has done to my lord according to all the good that he has spoken concerning you, and has appointed you prince over Israel, 31 my lord shall have no cause of grief, or pangs of conscience, for having shed blood without cause or for having saved himself. And when the LORD has dealt well with my lord, then remember your servant."

32 David said to Abigail, "Blessed be the LORD, the God of Israel, who sent you to meet me today! 33 Blessed be your good sense, and blessed be you, who have kept me today from bloodguilt and from avenging myself by my own hand! 34 For as surely as the LORD the God of Israel lives, who has restrained me from hurting you, unless you had hurried and come to meet me, truly by morning there would not have been left to Nabal so much as one male." 35 Then David received from her hand what she had brought him; he said to her, "Go up to your house in peace; see, I have heeded your voice, and I have granted your petition."

(3) NABAL'S DEATH

36 Abigail came to Nabal; he was holding a feast in his house, like the feast of a king. Nabal's heart was merry within him, for he was very drunk; so she told him nothing at all until the morning light. 37 In the morning, when the wine had gone out of Nabal, his wife told him these things, and his heart died within him; he became like a stone. 38 About ten days later the LORD struck Nabal, and he died.

39 When David heard that Nabal was dead, he said, "Blessed be the

Cross references (left margin):
25.19 Gen 32.16, 20
25.21 Ps 109.5
25.22 1 Sam 3.17; 20.13; 1 Kings 14.10
25.23 1 Sam 20.41
25.26 Heb 10.30; 2 Sam 18.32
25.27 Gen 33.11; 1 Sam 30.26
25.28 2 Sam 7.11, 27; 18.17; 24.11
25.29 Jer 10.18
25.30 1 Sam 13.14
25.32 Ex 18.10
25.33 v. 26
25.34 v. 26
25.35 1 Sam 20.42; 2 Kings 5.19; Gen 19.21
25.36 2 Sam 13.23
25.39 1 Sam 24.15; vv. 26, 34; 1 Kings 2.44

x Gk Compare Syr: Heb *the enemies of David*   y That is *Fool*

visited David to seek deliverance from the impending attack. She manifested a true faith in her conversation with David. David complied with her request; she could go home in peace, assured that all was well. **25.38** Whatever may have been the human causes which lay behind the death of Nabal, the Scriptures state that it was God who smote him. Whoever lives without grace may die without comfort. **25.39,40** David rejoiced that God had kept him from killing Nabal and that his death had come by God's hand in a natural way. He began courting Abigail and found her to be wise as well as gracious. The

LORD who has judged the case of Nabal's insult to me, and has kept back his servant from evil; the LORD has returned the evildoing of Nabal upon his own head." Then David sent and wooed Abigail, to make her his wife. 40 When David's servants came to Abigail at Carmel, they said to her, "David has sent us to you to take you to him as his wife." 41 She rose and bowed down, with her face to the ground, and said, "Your servant is a slave to wash the feet of the servants of my lord." 42 Abigail got up hurriedly and rode away on a donkey; her five maids attended her. She went after the messengers of David and became his wife.

43 David also married Ahinoam of Jezreel; both of them became his wives. 44 Saul had given his daughter Michal, David's wife, to Palti son of Laish, who was from Gallim.

o. David spares Saul again

26 Then the Ziphites came to Saul at Gibeah, saying, "David is in hiding on the hill of Hachilah, which is opposite Jeshimon."z 2 So Saul rose and went down to the Wilderness of Ziph, with three thousand chosen men of Israel, to seek David in the Wilderness of Ziph. 3 Saul encamped on the hill of Hachilah, which is opposite Jeshimonz beside the road. But David remained in the wilderness. When he learned that Saul had come after him into the wilderness, 4 David sent out spies, and learned that Saul had indeed arrived. 5 Then David set out and came to the place where Saul had encamped; and David saw the place where Saul lay, with Abner son of Ner, the commander of his army. Saul was lying within the encampment, while the army was encamped around him.

6 Then David said to Ahimelech the Hittite, and to Joab's brother Abishai son of Zeruiah, "Who will go down with me into the camp to Saul?" Abishai said, "I will go down with you." 7 So David and Abishai went to the army by night; there Saul lay sleeping within the encampment, with his spear stuck in the ground at his head; and Abner and the army lay around him. 8 Abishai said to David, "God has given your enemy into your hand today; now therefore let me pin him to the ground with one stroke of the spear; I will not strike him twice." 9 But David said to Abishai, "Do not destroy him; for who can raise his hand against the LORD's anointed, and be guiltless?" 10 David said, "As the LORD lives, the LORD will strike him down; or his day will come to die; or he will go down into battle and perish. 11 The LORD forbid that I should raise my hand against the LORD's anointed; but now take the spear that is at his head, and the water jar, and let us go." 12 So David took the spear that was at Saul's head and the water jar, and they went away. No one saw it, or knew it, nor did anyone awake; for they were all asleep, because a deep sleep from the LORD had fallen upon them.

13 Then David went over to the other side, and stood on top of a hill far away, with a great distance between them. 14 David called to the army and to Abner son of Ner, saying, "Abner! Will you not answer?" Then Abner replied, "Who are you that calls to the king?" 15 David said to Abner, "Are you not a man? Who is like you in Israel? Why then have you not kept watch over your lord the king? For one of the people came

z Or opposite the wasteland

Cross references

25.41 Ruth 2.10, 13; Mk 1.7
25.42 Gen 24.61-67
25.43 Josh 15.56; 1 Sam 27.3
25.44 2 Sam 3.14; Isa 10.30

26.1 1 Sam 23.19
26.2 1 Sam 13.2; 24.2

26.5 1 Sam 14.50; 17.55

26.6 1 Chr 2.16; Judg 7.10, 11

26.9 1 Sam 24.6, 7; 2 Sam 1.16
26.10 1 Sam 25.38; Deut 31.14; 1 Sam 31.6
26.11 1 Sam 24.6, 12
26.12 Gen 2.21; 16.12

---

courtship was by proxy, in that his servants put David's proposal of marriage before Abigail. Without hesitation she accepted, followed after the messengers, and became David's wife.
26.2 When the Ziphites again reported to Saul the presence of David among them, the king hastened with troops to track him down and kill him. This would be the last time David and Saul saw each other. Once again David refused to take advantage of what seemed to be a God-given opportunity for revenge.
26.8 David now had another opportunity to kill

Saul. Abishai was quite willing to commit the murder. But David restrained him, continuing to trust that God would deliver him and make him king when the right time came. David did, however, take advantage of this opportunity to remove the spear and the jar of water from Saul's side as he slept. Then he announced what he had done and proved again that he had chosen not to be Saul's enemy.
26.12 God's providence was at work again. So sound was the sleep of Saul and his troops that David could do his work unheard and unseen.

in to destroy your lord the king. 16 This thing that you have done is not good. As the LORD lives, you deserve to die, because you have not kept watch over your lord, the LORD's anointed. See now, where is the king's spear, or the water jar that was at his head?"

26.17
1 Sam 24.16
26.18
1 Sam 24.9,
11-14
26.19
2 Sam 16.11

17 Saul recognized David's voice, and said, "Is this your voice, my son David?" David said, "It is my voice, my lord, O king." 18 And he added, "Why does my lord pursue his servant? For what have I done? What guilt is on my hands? 19 Now therefore let my lord the king hear the words of his servant. If it is the LORD who has stirred you up against me, may he accept an offering; but if it is mortals, may they be cursed before the LORD, for they have driven me out today from my share in the heritage of the LORD, saying, 'Go, serve other gods.' 20 Now therefore, do not let my blood fall to the ground, away from the presence of the LORD; for the king of Israel has come out to seek a single flea, like one who hunts a partridge in the mountains."

26.20
1 Sam 24.14

26.21
1 Sam 15.24;
24.17
26.22
1 Sam 24.12,
19

21 Then Saul said, "I have done wrong; come back, my son David, for I will never harm you again, because my life was precious in your sight today; I have been a fool, and have made a great mistake." 22 David replied, "Here is the spear, O king! Let one of the young men come over and get it. 23 The LORD rewards everyone for his righteousness and his faithfulness; for the LORD gave you into my hand today, but I would not raise my hand against the LORD's anointed. 24 As your life was precious today in my sight, so may my life be precious in the sight of the LORD, and may he rescue me from all tribulation." 25 Then Saul said to David, "Blessed be you, my son David! You will do many things and will succeed in them." So David went his way, and Saul returned to his place.

26.24
Ps 54.7

E. Saul's death in the Philistine war

1. David's flight to the Philistines

a. David joins Achish

27 David said in his heart, "I shall now perish one day by the hand of Saul; there is nothing better for me than to escape to the land of the Philistines; then Saul will despair of seeking me any longer within the borders of Israel, and I shall escape out of his hand." 2 So David set out and went over, he and the six hundred men who were with him, to King Achish son of Maoch of Gath. 3 David stayed with Achish at Gath, he and his troops, every man with his household, and David with his two wives, Ahinoam of Jezreel, and Abigail of Carmel, Nabal's widow. 4 When Saul was told that David had fled to Gath, he no longer sought for him.

27.2
1 Sam 25.13;
21.10
27.3
1 Sam 30.3;
25.42, 43

b. Achish gives David Ziklag

5 Then David said to Achish, "If I have found favor in your sight, let a place be given me in one of the country towns, so that I may live there; for why should your servant live in the royal city with you?" 6 So that day Achish gave him Ziklag; therefore Ziklag has belonged to the kings of

27.6
Josh 15.31;
19.5

26.17 David bantered with Saul's military leader, Abner, accusing him of leaving his king open to assault (v. 15). Then he talked again (for the last time) to Saul in order to plead his innocence (vv. 18–20). Once again Saul was touched, although this time he did not weep. He admitted, "I have done wrong" (v. 21). He wanted David to return to him, but David (wisely) refused.

26.25 David was around fifteen years of age when Samuel anointed him as Israel's next king. He was not made king until he was thirty. In other words, he waited for approximately fifteen years before the promise of God to him was fulfilled. These fifteen years were filled with incredible difficulties. They

teach us a lesson. It takes time for God to do his work; while we wait for his will to be fulfilled, we are exposed to difficulties and testings in which we come to know what God can do. David's discovery that God could meet his needs in the years before he became king prepared him to believe that God would help once he became king.

27.5 David was a well-known soldier who had been successful in his military ventures. Achish the Philistine knew this and was willing to give David the town of Ziklag. He wanted to build a political alliance with David to use him against Israel and especially against Saul.

Judah to this day. 7 The length of time that David lived in the country of the Philistines was one year and four months.

2. *David's raids*

8 Now David and his men went up and made raids on the Geshurites, the Girzites, and the Amalekites; for these were the landed settlements from Telam[a] on the way to Shur and on to the land of Egypt. 9 David struck the land, leaving neither man nor woman alive, but took away the sheep, the oxen, the donkeys, the camels, and the clothing, and came back to Achish. 10 When Achish asked, "Against whom[b] have you made a raid today?" David would say, "Against the Negeb of Judah," or "Against the Negeb of the Jerahmeelites," or, "Against the Negeb of the Kenites." 11 David left neither man nor woman alive to be brought back to Gath, thinking, "They might tell about us, and say, 'David has done so and so.'" Such was his practice all the time he lived in the country of the Philistines. 12 Achish trusted David, thinking, "He has made himself utterly abhorrent to his people Israel; therefore he shall always be my servant."

3. *The Philistine plan to battle Israel*

28 In those days the Philistines gathered their forces for war, to fight against Israel. Achish said to David, "You know, of course, that you and your men are to go out with me in the army." 2 David said to Achish, "Very well, then you shall know what your servant can do." Achish said to David, "Very well, I will make you my bodyguard for life."

4. *Saul and the medium at Endor*

a. *God does not answer Saul*

3 Now Samuel had died, and all Israel had mourned for him and buried him in Ramah, his own city. Saul had expelled the mediums and the wizards from the land. 4 The Philistines assembled, and came and encamped at Shunem. Saul gathered all Israel, and they encamped at Gilboa. 5 When Saul saw the army of the Philistines, he was afraid, and his heart trembled greatly. 6 When Saul inquired of the LORD, the LORD did not answer him, not by dreams, or by Urim, or by prophets. 7 Then Saul said to his servants, "Seek out for me a woman who is a medium, so that I may go to her and inquire of her." His servants said to him, "There is a medium at Endor."

b. *Saul visits the medium*

8 So Saul disguised himself and put on other clothes and went there, he and two men with him. They came to the woman by night. And he said, "Consult a spirit for me, and bring up for me the one whom I name to you." 9 The woman said to him, "Surely you know what Saul has done, how he has cut off the mediums and the wizards from the land. Why then

---

a Compare Gk 15.4: Heb *from of old*   b Q Ms Gk Vg: MT lacks *whom*

Cross-references (margin):

27.7 / 1 Sam 29.3
27.8 / Josh 13.2, 13; Ex 17.8;
1 Sam 15.7, 8;
Ex 15.22
27.9 / 1 Sam 15.3
27.10 / 1 Chr 2.9, 25;
Judg 1.16
28.1f / 1 Sam 29.1
28.3 / 1 Sam 25.1;
7.17; 15.23;
Lev 19.31;
Deut 18.10, 11
28.4 / 2 Kings 4.8;
1 Sam 31.1
28.6 / 1 Chr 10.13, 14;
Prov 1.28;
Ex 28.30
28.7 / Acts 16.16;
Josh 17.11
28.8 / Isa 8.19;
Deut 18.10, 11
28.9 / v. 3

27.8ff David conducted raids against the Geshurites, the Girzites, and the Amalekites. He slew them all and reported back to Achish that he had been conducting raids, but led him to think they were against his own people. It is difficult to justify these lies of David, especially since they inspired Achish's fidelity to him and confidence in him.

28.1,2 When David had first gone to Achish, he concluded that the circumstances were unfavorable, so he pretended to be mad (21.10–15). But now Achish had learned to trust David and invited him to join his forces in the upcoming battle. David agreed to this. See ch. 29 for the conclusion of this agreement.

28.6 *or by Urim.* See note on Ex 28.30.

28.7,8 God had prohibited divination and witchcraft in his law. He alone was guiding his people by his word and Spirit. But Saul, after God's Spirit had left him, sought help from the medium at Endor, in order to find the will of God. He hoped Samuel might help him if only he could speak with him. We do not know whether the medium actually brought Samuel into contact with Saul, though the king evidently thought so. In any event, this incident provides no justification for seances, witchcraft, or the like.

are you laying a snare for my life to bring about my death?" 10 But Saul swore to her by the LORD, "As the LORD lives, no punishment shall come upon you for this thing." 11 Then the woman said, "Whom shall I bring up for you?" He answered, "Bring up Samuel for me." 12 When the woman saw Samuel, she cried out with a loud voice; and the woman said to Saul, "Why have you deceived me? You are Saul!" 13 The king said to her, "Have no fear; what do you see?" The woman said to Saul, "I see a divine being^c coming up out of the ground." 14 He said to her, "What is his appearance?" She said, "An old man is coming up; he is wrapped in a robe." So Saul knew that it was Samuel, and he bowed with his face to the ground, and did obeisance.

c. *The medium calls up Samuel*

15 Then Samuel said to Saul, "Why have you disturbed me by bringing me up?" Saul answered, "I am in great distress, for the Philistines are warring against me, and God has turned away from me and answers me no more, either by prophets or by dreams; so I have summoned you to tell me what I should do." 16 Samuel said, "Why then do you ask me, since the LORD has turned from you and become your enemy? 17 The LORD has done to you just as he spoke by me; for the LORD has torn the kingdom out of your hand, and given it to your neighbor, David. 18 Because you did not obey the voice of the LORD, and did not carry out his fierce wrath against Amalek, therefore the LORD has done this thing to you today. 19 Moreover the LORD will give Israel along with you into the hands of the Philistines; and tomorrow you and your sons shall be with me; the LORD will also give the army of Israel into the hands of the Philistines."

d. *The medium feeds Saul*

20 Immediately Saul fell full length on the ground, filled with fear because of the words of Samuel; and there was no strength in him, for he had eaten nothing all day and all night. 21 The woman came to Saul, and when she saw that he was terrified, she said to him, "Your servant has listened to you; I have taken my life in my hand, and have listened to what you have said to me. 22 Now therefore, you also listen to your servant; let me set a morsel of bread before you. Eat, that you may have strength when you go on your way." 23 He refused, and said, "I will not eat." But his servants, together with the woman, urged him; and he listened to their words. So he got up from the ground and sat on the bed. 24 Now the woman had a fatted calf in the house. She quickly slaughtered it, and she took flour, kneaded it, and baked unleavened cakes. 25 She put them before Saul and his servants, and they ate. Then they rose and went away that night.

5. *The Philistines dismiss David*

a. *The question raised*

29 Now the Philistines gathered all their forces at Aphek, while the Israelites were encamped by the fountain that is in Jezreel. 2 As the lords of the Philistines were passing on by hundreds and by thousands, and David and his men were passing on in the rear with Achish, 3 the

^c Or *a god*; or *gods*

Cross-references (left margin):
28.14 — 1 Sam 15.27; 24.8
28.15 — 1 Sam 18.12; v. 6
28.17 — 1 Sam 15.28
28.18 — 1 Sam 15.9, 20, 26
28.19 — 1 Sam 31.2
28.21 — 1 Sam 19.5; Judg 12.3
28.23 — 2 Kings 5.13
29.1 — 1 Sam 28.1; 4.1; Josh 12.18
29.2 — 1 Sam 28.1, 2
29.3 — 1 Sam 27.7; Dan 6.5

28.15 Saul believed that he was talking to Samuel and received from him the unwelcome message that God would now take the kingdom from him and give the throne to David. Saul and his sons would be with Samuel the next day (v. 19). Apparently, in spite of his disobedience, Saul was still a saved man who, with his sons, would join Samuel in paradise.
29.3–5 Achish wanted David to be part of his army when the battle with the Israelites started. David's

forces were placed behind those of Achish, but he would still be fighting against his own people. The leaders of the Philistines, however, strenuously objected, thinking that in the thick of battle David might prove to be a turncoat and fight against them. Thus Achish was forced to withdraw his offer (in spite of David's objections, v. 8), and David was spared from the reproach of warring against his own people.

commanders of the Philistines said, "What are these Hebrews doing here?" Achish said to the commanders of the Philistines, "Is this not David, the servant of King Saul of Israel, who has been with me now for days and years? Since he deserted to me I have found no fault in him to this day." ⁴But the commanders of the Philistines were angry with him; and the commanders of the Philistines said to him, "Send the man back, so that he may return to the place that you have assigned to him; he shall not go down with us to battle, or else he may become an adversary to us in the battle. For how could this fellow reconcile himself to his lord? Would it not be with the heads of the men here? ⁵Is this not David, of whom they sing to one another in dances,

 'Saul has killed his thousands,
  and David his ten thousands'?"

b. Achish sends David away

6 Then Achish called David and said to him, "As the LORD lives, you have been honest, and to me it seems right that you should march out and in with me in the campaign; for I have found nothing wrong in you from the day of your coming to me until today. Nevertheless the lords do not approve of you. ⁷So go back now; and go peaceably; do nothing to displease the lords of the Philistines." ⁸David said to Achish, "But what have I done? What have you found in your servant from the day I entered your service until now, that I should not go and fight against the enemies of my lord the king?" ⁹Achish replied to David, "I know that you are as blameless in my sight as an angel of God; nevertheless, the commanders of the Philistines have said, 'He shall not go up with us to the battle.' ¹⁰Now then rise early in the morning, you and the servants of your lord who came with you, and go to the place that I appointed for you. As for the evil report, do not take it to heart, for you have done well before me. *d* Start early in the morning, and leave as soon as you have light." ¹¹So David set out with his men early in the morning, to return to the land of the Philistines. But the Philistines went up to Jezreel.

6. David destroys Amalek

a. Amalekites raid Ziklag

30 Now when David and his men came to Ziklag on the third day, the Amalekites had made a raid on the Negeb and on Ziklag. They had attacked Ziklag, burned it down, ²and taken captive the women and all*e* who were in it, both small and great; they killed none of them, but carried them off, and went their way. ³When David and his men came to the city, they found it burned down, and their wives and sons and daughters taken captive. ⁴Then David and the people who were with him raised their voices and wept, until they had no more strength to weep. ⁵David's two wives also had been taken captive, Ahinoam of Jezreel, and Abigail the widow of Nabal of Carmel. ⁶David was in great danger; for the people spoke of stoning him, because all the people were bitter in spirit for their sons and daughters. But David strengthened himself in the LORD his God.

b. God orders David to pursue the Amalekites

7 David said to the priest Abiathar son of Ahimelech, "Bring me the

---

d Gk: Heb lacks *and go to the place . . . done well before me* *e* Gk: Heb lacks *and all*

Marginal references:

29.4 1 Chr 12.19; 1 Sam 14.21

29.5 1 Sam 18.7; 21.11

29.6 v. 3

29.9 2 Sam 14.17, 20; 19.27; v. 4

29.10 1 Chr 12.19, 22

30.1 1 Sam 29.4, 11; 15.7; 27.8

30.5 1 Sam 25.42, 43

30.6 Ex 17.4; Ps 27.14; 56.3, 4, 11

30.7 1 Sam 23.9

29.11 In addition to being spared from fighting against God's people, David was unaware that he was needed at Ziklag to rescue his loved ones (see next chapter). God was working behind the scenes to make sure that David went where the Lord wanted him to go.
30.1 Strangely but providentially the Amalekites

captured all of David's people without killing any of them. They burned the town and kept its treasures. Apparently they planned to make the captured people their slaves.
30.7 David called for Abiathar and requested that he bring the ephod so that he could consult God. Clearly Abiathar must have been with David and his

30.8 1 Sam 23.2, 4; v. 18 **30.9** 1 Sam 27.2	ephod." So Abiathar brought the ephod to David. ⁸ David inquired of the LORD, "Shall I pursue this band? Shall I overtake them?" He answered him, "Pursue; for you shall surely overtake and shall surely rescue." ⁹ So David set out, he and the six hundred men who were with him. They came
30.10 vv. 9, 21	to the Wadi Besor, where those stayed who were left behind. ¹⁰ But David went on with the pursuit, he and four hundred men; two hundred stayed behind, too exhausted to cross the Wadi Besor.

c. *An Egyptian leads David to the Amalekites*

11 In the open country they found an Egyptian, and brought him to David. They gave him bread and he ate; they gave him water to drink; ¹² they also gave him a piece of fig cake and two clusters of raisins. When he had eaten, his spirit revived; for he had not eaten bread or drunk water for three days and three nights. ¹³ Then David said to him, "To whom do you belong? Where are you from?" He said, "I am a young man of Egypt, servant to an Amalekite. My master left me behind because I fell sick three days ago. ¹⁴ We had made a raid on the Negeb of the Cherethites and on that which belongs to Judah and on the Negeb of Caleb; and we burned Ziklag down." ¹⁵ David said to him, "Will you take me down to this raiding party?" He said, "Swear to me by God that you will not kill me, or hand me over to my master, and I will take you down to them."

30.12
Judg 15.19

30.14
vv. 1, 16;
2 Sam 8.18;
Ezek 25.16;
Josh 14.13

d. *David smites the Amalekites*

16 When he had taken him down, they were spread out all over the ground, eating and drinking and dancing, because of the great amount of spoil they had taken from the land of the Philistines and from the land of Judah. ¹⁷ David attacked them from twilight until the evening of the next day. Not one of them escaped, except four hundred young men, who mounted camels and fled. ¹⁸ David recovered all that the Amalekites had taken; and David rescued his two wives. ¹⁹ Nothing was missing, whether small or great, sons or daughters, spoil or anything that had been taken; David brought back everything. ²⁰ David also captured all the flocks and herds, which were driven ahead of the other cattle; people said, "This is David's spoil."

30.16
v. 14

30.17
1 Sam 15.3

30.19
v. 8

30.20
vv. 26-31

e. *David divides the spoil*

21 Then David came to the two hundred men who had been too exhausted to follow David, and who had been left at the Wadi Besor. They went out to meet David and to meet the people who were with him. When David drew near to the people he saluted them. ²² Then all the corrupt and worthless fellows among the men who had gone with David said, "Because they did not go with us, we will not give them any of the spoil that we have recovered, except that each man may take his wife and children, and leave." ²³ But David said, "You shall not do so, my brothers, with what the LORD has given us; he has preserved us and handed over to us the raiding party that attacked us. ²⁴ Who is there to listen to you in this matter? For the share of the one who goes down into the battle shall be the same as the share of the one who stays by the baggage; they shall

30.21
v. 10

30.24
Num 31.27;
Josh 22.8

---

troops. This leaves us wondering why David had not consulted God while he was still with Achish. At least here he did the right thing. The seriousness of the hour caused him to put his trust in his God, especially when his own men talked of stoning him on account of the tragedy (v. 6).
30.11 Again providence intervened on behalf of David: the abandoned Egyptian slave of the Amalekites agreed to lead David and his men to the place where they would find the Amalekites, their prisoners, and the booty. David promised to protect the Egyptian (v. 15).

30.22 Not all those on David's side were honest and compassionate people. After the battle was over and the spoils were being distributed, some of those who had fought argued that those who merely stood by the baggage without fighting were unworthy of receiving any of the spoils of war. They could take their wives and children, but nothing else. David rightly ruled that *all* who were involved, including those who stood by the baggage while the others fought, were entitled to an equal share of the booty. This became a standing arrangement for Israel.

share alike." 25 From that day forward he made it a statute and an ordinance for Israel; it continues to the present day.

f. David sends spoil to Judah

26 When David came to Ziklag, he sent part of the spoil to his friends, the elders of Judah, saying, "Here is a present for you from the spoil of the enemies of the Lord"; 27 it was for those in Bethel, in Ramoth of the Negeb, in Jattir, 28 in Aroer, in Siphmoth, in Eshtemoa, 29 in Racal, in the towns of the Jerahmeelites, in the towns of the Kenites, 30 in Hormah, in Bor-ashan, in Athach, 31 in Hebron, all the places where David and his men had roamed.

7. The death of Saul

31 Now the Philistines fought against Israel; and the men of Israel fled before the Philistines, and many fell[f] on Mount Gilboa. 2 The Philistines overtook Saul and his sons; and the Philistines killed Jonathan and Abinadab and Malchishua, the sons of Saul. 3 The battle pressed hard upon Saul; the archers found him, and he was badly wounded by them. 4 Then Saul said to his armor-bearer, "Draw your sword and thrust me through with it, so that these uncircumcised may not come and thrust me through, and make sport of me." But his armor-bearer was unwilling; for he was terrified. So Saul took his own sword and fell upon it. 5 When his armor-bearer saw that Saul was dead, he also fell upon his sword and died with him. 6 So Saul and his three sons and his armor-bearer and all his men died together on the same day. 7 When the men of Israel who were on the other side of the valley and those beyond the Jordan saw that the men of Israel had fled and that Saul and his sons were dead, they forsook their towns and fled; and the Philistines came and occupied them.

8. Saul decapitated

8 The next day, when the Philistines came to strip the dead, they found Saul and his three sons fallen on Mount Gilboa. 9 They cut off his head, stripped off his armor, and sent messengers throughout the land of the Philistines to carry the good news to the houses of their idols and to the people. 10 They put his armor in the temple of Astarte;[g] and they fastened his body to the wall of Beth-shan. 11 But when the inhabitants of Jabesh-gilead heard what the Philistines had done to Saul, 12 all the valiant men set out, traveled all night long, and took the body of Saul and the bodies of his sons from the wall of Beth-shan. They came to Jabesh and burned them there. 13 Then they took their bones and buried them under the tamarisk tree in Jabesh, and fasted seven days.

f Heb and they fell slain   g Heb plural

30.27 Josh 15.30; 19.8; 15.48 **30.28** Josh 13.16; 15.50 **30.29** 1 Sam 27.10; 15.16 **30.30** Judg 1.17 **30.31** Josh 14.13 **31.1** 1 Chr 10.1-12; 1 Sam 28.4 **31.3** 2 Sam 1.6 **31.4** Judg 9.54; 2 Sam 1.6, 10 **31.9** 2 Sam 1.20 **31.10** 1 Sam 7.3; Judg 2.13; 2 Sam 21.12; Josh 17.11 **31.11** 1 Sam 11.3, 9, 11 **31.12** 2 Sam 2.4-7; 2 Chr 16.14 **31.13** 2 Sam 21.12-14; 1 Sam 22.6; 2 Sam 1.12

30.26 David generously sent some of the booty to the elders of Judah as an expression of gratitude toward those who had helped him while he was roaming the desert. He said the gifts were spoils from the enemies of God. These gifts served the further purpose of gaining their affection and support, for he knew that Saul's reign would terminate shortly and his own would begin.
31.2 Saul and his three sons were gathered in the battle against the Philistines. The sons, including David's close friend Jonathan, were slain; Saul fell wounded to the ground and then killed himself with his sword.
31.4 *Saul took his own sword and fell upon it.* Compare this account with 2 Sam 1.9,10, where an Amalekite lied to David about Saul's death.

31.9 God used the Philistines to end Saul's regime, thus freeing David from any necessity to dispose of Saul. The Philistines displayed their victory and understood it to mean that their gods had helped them (cf. also 1 Chr 10.10). Their victory turned out to be of no consequence, however, for David would conquer the Philistines and put them to flight.
31.13 1 Samuel began with the birth of Samuel and ended with the burial of Saul. It marks the transition from the period of the judges to the beginning of the monarchy. The house of Saul had now given way to the Davidic throne. From David would come that one who is the Messiah and the Savior of the world. God's program of redemption was being formulated, despite the attacks of Satan to hinder that plan and to thwart the divine will.

INTRODUCTION TO

2 SAMUEL

Authorship, Date, and Background: See introduction to 1 Samuel.

Characteristics and Content: 1 Samuel ended with the death of King Saul. 2 Samuel records the story of David's kingship and ends before his death, which is recounted in 1 Kings. David expressed his anguish over the deaths of Saul and Jonathan. He was anointed king over Judah and civil war began with Israel. Abner made Ish-bosheth, a son of Saul, king of Israel. Joab, David's nephew and commander of his army, killed Abner. David grieved over this act. Ish-bosheth himself was slain by Rechab and Baanah, who reported their deed to David, who in turn executed them for their sin. David then became king over all Israel.

David consolidated his kingship, took the city of Jerusalem, which became the national capital, and brought back the ark to the city. He wished to build the temple but was forbidden by God; the task was left for his son. David won many victories over the surrounding nations. In the midst of these successes he fell into sin with Bathsheba, the wife of Uriah; he then had him killed to cover his adultery. Nathan arrived to pronounce God's judgment on David, and although he was forgiven when he repented, God ordained that he would smart for his sins. This was fulfilled at a later time when his own son led a revolt against him. He faced many trials, but the worst of them involved Absalom, who tried to overthrow his father. David fled from Jerusalem and a civil war began, ending in the death of Absalom and David's poignant cry, "O my son Absalom, my son, my son Absalom! Would I had died instead of you, O Absalom, my son, my son!" (18.33).

Following restoration to his kingship after the death of Absalom, David had to face one emergency after another. A famine came, due to the bloodguilt on Saul for putting the Gibeonites to death. Seven of Saul's relatives were hanged to stop the famine. In his later years, David sinned by numbering the people. He chose the punishment of pestilence in the land. The angel of the Lord was about to destroy Jerusalem, when God ordered the angel to stay his hand. David built an altar on the threshing floor of Araunah at God's command, and his burnt offering was accepted by God. The story of David's death is related in 1 Kings, the next book.

Outline:

I. The beginning of David's kingship (1.1—4.12)

II. The consolidation of David's kingship (5.1—10.19)

III. The sin of David (11.1—12.31)

IV. David's troubles (13.1—18.33)

V. David restored to his kingdom (19.1—20.26)

VI. The later years of David's kingdom (21.1—24.25)

2 SAMUEL

I. David enters into his kingship (1.1–4.12)

A. The news of Saul's death

1 After the death of Saul, when David had returned from defeating the Amalekites, David remained two days in Ziklag. 2 On the third day, a man came from Saul's camp, with his clothes torn and dirt on his head. When he came to David, he fell to the ground and did obeisance. 3 David said to him, "Where have you come from?" He said to him, "I have escaped from the camp of Israel." 4 David said to him, "How did things go? Tell me!" He answered, "The army fled from the battle, but also many of the army fell and died; and Saul and his son Jonathan also died." 5 Then David asked the young man who was reporting to him, "How do you know that Saul and his son Jonathan died?" 6 The young man reporting to him said, "I happened to be on Mount Gilboa; and there was Saul leaning on his spear, while the chariots and the horsemen drew close to him. 7 When he looked behind him, he saw me, and called to me. I answered, 'Here sir.' 8 And he said to me, 'Who are you?' I answered him, 'I am an Amalekite.' 9 He said to me, 'Come, stand over me and kill me; for convulsions have seized me, and yet my life still lingers.' 10 So I stood over him, and killed him, for I knew that he could not live after he had fallen. I took the crown that was on his head and the armlet that was on his arm, and I have brought them here to my lord."

11 Then David took hold of his clothes and tore them; and all the men who were with him did the same. 12 They mourned and wept, and fasted until evening for Saul and for his son Jonathan, and for the army of the Lord and for the house of Israel, because they had fallen by the sword. 13 David said to the young man who had reported to him, "Where do you come from?" He answered, "I am the son of a resident alien, an Amalekite." 14 David said to him, "Were you not afraid to lift your hand to destroy the Lord's anointed?" 15 Then David called one of the young men and said, "Come here and strike him down." So he struck him down and he died. 16 David said to him, "Your blood be on your head; for your own mouth has testified against you, saying, 'I have killed the Lord's anointed.' "

B. David's lamentation over Saul and Jonathan

17 David intoned this lamentation over Saul and his son Jonathan.

1.1
1 Sam 31.6;
30.17, 26
1.2
1 Sam 4.10,
12
1.6
1 Sam 31.2-4
1.8
1 Sam 15.3
1.10
Judg 9.54
1.11
2 Sam 3.31;
13.31
1.12
2 Sam 3.35
1.13
v. 8
1.14
1 Sam 24.6;
26.9
1.15
2 Sam 4.10,
12
1.16
2 Sam 3.28,
29; v. 10
1.17
2 Chr 35.25

1.1 Saul was dead and David was back in Ziklag with his family. 2 Samuel covers the life of David from the beginning of his kingship until almost the end of it. He reigned for forty years, during which time some of the lands occupied by non-Israelites were conquered and added to David's kingdom.
1.8–10 The Amalekite was evidently lying (see 1 Sam 31.3 for the true account). He probably saw Saul's dead body and supposed David would reward him for killing his great rival.

1.17 David had refused to kill Saul. Now, on the event of Saul's death, he rent his clothes, mourned, wept, and fasted (customary patterns of that time). It is significant that no mention is made of any of the sons of Saul except for Jonathan, with whom David had the closest friendship. Perhaps David's mourning was more a sign of his love for Jonathan than his sorrow over Saul. He must have been somewhat relieved that the long battle with Saul for the kingship was over.

18(He ordered that The Song of the Bow[h] be taught to the people of Judah; it is written in the Book of Jashar.) He said:
19   Your glory, O Israel, lies slain upon your high places!
         How the mighty have fallen!

20   Tell it not in Gath,
         proclaim it not in the streets of Ashkelon;
     or the daughters of the Philistines will rejoice,
         the daughters of the uncircumcised will exult.

21   You mountains of Gilboa,
         let there be no dew or rain upon you,
         nor bounteous fields![i]
     For there the shield of the mighty was defiled,
         the shield of Saul, anointed with oil no more.

22   From the blood of the slain,
         from the fat of the mighty,
     the bow of Jonathan did not turn back,
         nor the sword of Saul return empty.

23   Saul and Jonathan, beloved and lovely!
         In life and in death they were not divided;
     they were swifter than eagles,
         they were stronger than lions.

24   O daughters of Israel, weep over Saul,
         who clothed you with crimson, in luxury,
         who put ornaments of gold on your apparel.

25   How the mighty have fallen
         in the midst of the battle!

     Jonathan lies slain upon your high places.

26   I am distressed for you, my brother Jonathan;
     greatly beloved were you to me;
         your love to me was wonderful,
         passing the love of women.

27   How the mighty have fallen,
         and the weapons of war perished!

C. David anointed king over Judah

2 After this David inquired of the LORD, "Shall I go up into any of the cities of Judah?" The LORD said to him, "Go up." David said, "To which shall I go up?" He said, "To Hebron." 2So David went up there, along with his two wives, Ahinoam of Jezreel, and Abigail the widow of Nabal of Carmel. 3David brought up the men who were with him, every one with his household; and they settled in the towns of Hebron. 4Then

[h] Heb that The Bow   [i] Meaning of Heb uncertain

1.18   the Book of Jashar, an extrabiblical collection of poems and other literary material. Parts of it are also quoted in Josh 10.12 and Judg 5.
1.19   In this elegy David is generous in his praise of Saul, recalling some of the good things he had done for Israel. Everyone has good as well as bad things to be considered. Three times he speaks of "the mighty" who have fallen (1.19,25,27), and he does so in sorrow rather than judgment.
1.20   He did not want the uncircumcised and their

daughters to rejoice over what was a temporary defeat of Israel, a defeat that would be reversed as soon as possible by David himself.
2.1   Shall I go up into any of the cities of Judah? David sought guidance from God as to how he should proceed, having earlier been secretly anointed king (1 Sam 16.1-13).
2.4   The people of Judah were the first to anoint David as their king. They were not speaking for the rest of Israel. His kingdom would be set up piece by

the people of Judah came, and there they anointed David king over the house of Judah.

When they told David, "It was the people of Jabesh-gilead who buried Saul," 5 David sent messengers to the people of Jabesh-gilead, and said to them, "May you be blessed by the LORD, because you showed this loyalty to Saul your lord, and buried him! 6 Now may the LORD show steadfast love and faithfulness to you! And I too will reward you because you have done this thing. 7 Therefore let your hands be strong, and be valiant; for Saul your lord is dead, and the house of Judah has anointed me king over them."

D. The civil war with Israel

1. Abner makes Ishbaal king of Israel

8 But Abner son of Ner, commander of Saul's army, had taken Ishbaal[j] son of Saul, and brought him over to Mahanaim. 9 He made him king over Gilead, the Ashurites, Jezreel, Ephraim, Benjamin, and over all Israel. 10 Ishbaal,[j] Saul's son, was forty years old when he began to reign over Israel, and he reigned two years. But the house of Judah followed David. 11 The time that David was king in Hebron over the house of Judah was seven years and six months.

2. Abner defeated

12 Abner son of Ner, and the servants of Ishbaal[j] son of Saul, went out from Mahanaim to Gibeon. 13 Joab son of Zeruiah, and the servants of David, went out and met them at the pool of Gibeon. One group sat on one side of the pool, while the other sat on the other side of the pool. 14 Abner said to Joab, "Let the young men come forward and have a contest before us." Joab said, "Let them come forward." 15 So they came forward and were counted as they passed by, twelve for Benjamin and Ishbaal[j] son of Saul, and twelve of the servants of David. 16 Each grasped his opponent by the head, and thrust his sword in his opponent's side; so they fell down together. Therefore that place was called Helkath-hazzurim,[k] which is at Gibeon. 17 The battle was very fierce that day; and Abner and the men of Israel were beaten by the servants of David.

3. Abner kills Asahel

18 The three sons of Zeruiah were there, Joab, Abishai, and Asahel. Now Asahel was as swift of foot as a wild gazelle. 19 Asahel pursued Abner, turning neither to the right nor to the left as he followed him. 20 Then Abner looked back and said, "Is it you, Asahel?" He answered, "Yes, it

Cross-references:
2.5 / 1 Sam 23.21
2.8 / 2 Sam 14.50
2.9 / Judg 1.32; 1 Sam 29.1
2.11 / 2 Sam 5.5
2.12 / Josh 18.25
2.13 / 1 Chr 2.16
2.17 / 2 Sam 3.1
2.18 / 1 Chr 2.16; 12.8

---

j Gk Compare 1 Chr 8.33; 9.39: Heb *Ish-bosheth*, "man of shame"　　*k* That is *Field of Sword-edges*

---

piece until all Israel would acknowledge him as God's choice for them.

2.5 David began a policy of conciliation by sending a word of appreciation to the people of Jabesh-gilead for their kindness to Saul after his death. He wished to honor the memory of Saul against whom he would not speak an evil word, and to indicate that he was not seeking the kingship from pride or ambition but only because it had been pressed on him by the command of God. He carefully revealed that only Judah had anointed him king.

2.8 *Ishbaal.* The Hebrew here is "Ish-bosheth"; elsewhere his name was *Eshbaal* (1 Chr 8.33), meaning "Man of Baal." Since the Israelites detested the use of Baal in a proper name, someone may have substituted *bosheth* ("shame") in place of *baal*. Ishbaal was the youngest son of Saul and had not fought with his father in his last battle; thus he was not killed as his three brothers had been. Abner, Saul's military

commander, installed him as king over the remainder of Israel. He was the one who kept Ishbaal in power as king, though he eventually defected to David to help him gain the support of all Israel (ch. 3).

2.12 This event was not in its beginning a major battle between two opposing dynasties. It was simply a skirmish involving two small groups of men. It was Abner who engineered the scenario and David who quietly played it. Twelve men from both sides engaged in the conflict and all of the contestants were killed. Then the full forces of both sides engaged in battle and Abner's forces were turned back.

2.18ff Asahel was the son of Zeruiah, who was either David's sister or half-sister. Asahel was one of David's Thirty Mighty Men (23.24). In the battle of Gibeon he foolishly pursued Abner, a stronger warrior than he, and was brutally slain. Later Joab, the brother of Asahel, slew Abner in an act of vengeance.

is." 21 Abner said to him, "Turn to your right or to your left, and seize one of the young men, and take his spoil." But Asahel would not turn away from following him. 22 Abner said again to Asahel, "Turn away from following me; why should I strike you to the ground? How then could I show my face to your brother Joab?" 23 But he refused to turn away. So Abner struck him in the stomach with the butt of his spear, so that the spear came out at his back. He fell there, and died where he lay. And all those who came to the place where Asahel had fallen and died, stood still.

4. Abner and Joab declare a truce

24 But Joab and Abishai pursued Abner. As the sun was going down they came to the hill of Ammah, which lies before Giah on the way to the wilderness of Gibeon. 25 The Benjaminites rallied around Abner and formed a single band; they took their stand on the top of a hill. 26 Then Abner called to Joab, "Is the sword to keep devouring forever? Do you not know that the end will be bitter? How long will it be before you order your people to turn from the pursuit of their kinsmen?" 27 Joab said, "As God lives, if you had not spoken, the people would have continued to pursue their kinsmen, not stopping until morning." 28 Joab sounded the trumpet and all the people stopped; they no longer pursued Israel or engaged in battle any further.

29 Abner and his men traveled all that night through the Arabah; they crossed the Jordan, and, marching the whole forenoon,[l] they came to Mahanaim. 30 Joab returned from the pursuit of Abner; and when he had gathered all the people together, there were missing of David's servants nineteen men besides Asahel. 31 But the servants of David had killed of Benjamin three hundred sixty of Abner's men. 32 They took up Asahel and buried him in the tomb of his father, which was at Bethlehem. Joab and his men marched all night, and the day broke upon them at Hebron.

5. Abner and Ishbaal quarrel

3 There was a long war between the house of Saul and the house of David; David grew stronger and stronger, while the house of Saul became weaker and weaker.

2 Sons were born to David at Hebron: his firstborn was Amnon, of Ahinoam of Jezreel; 3 his second, Chileab, of Abigail the widow of Nabal of Carmel; the third, Absalom son of Maacah, daughter of King Talmai of Geshur; 4 the fourth, Adonijah son of Haggith; the fifth, Shephatiah son of Abital; 5 and the sixth, Ithream, of David's wife Eglah. These were born to David in Hebron.

6 While there was war between the house of Saul and the house of David, Abner was making himself strong in the house of Saul. 7 Now Saul had a concubine whose name was Rizpah daughter of Aiah. And Ishbaal[m] said to Abner, "Why have you gone in to my father's concubine?" 8 The

l Meaning of Heb uncertain   m Heb And he

Cross-references (left margin):
- 2.22 — 2 Sam 3.27
- 2.23 — 2 Sam 3.27; 4.6; 20.10
- 2.24 — Josh 10.41
- 2.27 — v. 14
- 2.29 — v. 8
- 3.2 — 1 Chr 3.1-3; 1 Sam 25.42, 43
- 3.3 — 1 Sam 27.8; 2 Sam 13.37
- 3.4 — 1 Kings 1.5
- 3.7 — 2 Sam 21.8-11; 16.21
- 3.8 — 1 Sam 24.14; 2 Sam 9.8

2.24 Joab and his forces had defeated Abner and now were in hot pursuit of those who remained. Abner realized that he was in danger of extermination and used all possible strategems to extricate himself. He spoke of the evil of a civil war among brethren and begged Joab to sound the retreat and leave things as they were. Joab placed the blame squarely where it belonged. If Abner had not started the fracas by unsheathing the sword, there would have been no need for him to plead for mercy after the defeat.

3.1 God's earlier actions in the life of David had prepared him for further delays in the fulfillment of God's promise of the kingship. The war between the two dynasties was prolonged; David's faith and patience were tested still further. But during that time

David grew stronger, while the forces of Abner and Ishbaal grew weaker. At the same time God was silently arranging for a debacle between Abner and Ishbaal.

3.2ff David's first six sons were born of different mothers. Not one of them inherited the throne. Rather, Solomon, born of Bathsheba, succeeded his father. Adonijah, David's fourth son, did aspire to become king as his father lay dying, but he failed, and Solomon had him put to death (1 Kings 1–2).

3.6,7 Abner proved to be a self-seeking aspirant for the throne occupied by Ishbaal. As a clear sign of his intentions, he apparently went to bed with Saul's concubine, Rizpah. This act of treason led to a severe dispute between Abner and Ishbaal.

words of Ishbaal[n] made Abner very angry; he said, "Am I a dog's head for Judah? Today I keep showing loyalty to the house of your father Saul, to his brothers, and to his friends, and have not given you into the hand of David; and yet you charge me now with a crime concerning this woman. 9 So may God do to Abner and so may he add to it! For just what the Lord has sworn to David, that will I accomplish for him, 10 to transfer the kingdom from the house of Saul, and set up the throne of David over Israel and over Judah, from Dan to Beer-sheba." 11 And Ishbaal[o] could not answer Abner another word, because he feared him.

12   Abner sent messengers to David at Hebron,[p] saying, "To whom does the land belong? Make your covenant with me, and I will give you my support to bring all Israel over to you." 13 He said, "Good; I will make a covenant with you. But one thing I require of you: you shall never appear in my presence unless you bring Saul's daughter Michal when you come to see me." 14 Then David sent messengers to Saul's son Ishbaal,[q] saying, "Give me my wife Michal, to whom I became engaged at the price of one hundred foreskins of the Philistines." 15 Ishbaal[q] sent and took her from her husband Paltiel the son of Laish. 16 But her husband went with her, weeping as he walked behind her all the way to Bahurim. Then Abner said to him, "Go back home!" So he went back.

6. Joab murders Abner

a. Abner visits David

17   Abner sent word to the elders of Israel, saying, "For some time past you have been seeking David as king over you. 18 Now then bring it about; for the Lord has promised David: Through my servant David I will save my people Israel from the hand of the Philistines, and from all their enemies." 19 Abner also spoke directly to the Benjaminites; then Abner went to tell David at Hebron all that Israel and the whole house of Benjamin were ready to do.

20   When Abner came with twenty men to David at Hebron, David made a feast for Abner and the men who were with him. 21 Abner said to David, "Let me go and rally all Israel to my lord the king, in order that they may make a covenant with you, and that you may reign over all that your heart desires." So David dismissed Abner, and he went away in peace.

b. Joab learns of Abner's visit

22   Just then the servants of David arrived with Joab from a raid, bringing much spoil with them. But Abner was not with David at Hebron, for David[r] had dismissed him, and he had gone away in peace. 23 When Joab and all the army that was with him came, it was told Joab, "Abner son of Ner came to the king, and he has dismissed him, and he has gone

Margin references:

3.9
1 Kings 19.2;
1 Sam 15.8
3.10
Judg 20.1;
1 Sam 3.20

3.13
Gen 43.3;
1 Sam 18.20
3.14
1 Sam 18.25, 27
3.15
see
1 Sam 25.44
3.16
2 Sam 16.5

3.18
1 Sam 9.16;
15.28
3.19
1 Sam 10.20, 21

3.21
vv. 10, 12;
1 Kings 11.37

3.22
1 Sam 27.8

---

n Gk Compare 1 Chr 8.33; 9.39: Heb Ish-bosheth, "man of shame"   o Heb And he   p Gk: Heb where he was   q Heb Ish-bosheth   r Heb he

---

3.8   We do not know whether Ishbaal's charge was in fact true, but the failure of Abner to deny it makes it appear to be true. Abner arrogantly and insolently told Ishbaal that he raised him to the kingship and he could now take it away from him and he would do so. Ishbaal (v. 11) was weak-kneed and afraid of Abner, so he remained silent.
3.12–14   Abner sent a message to David in which he acknowledged David's right to the throne and offered to bring about a reunion of the twelve tribes under David. He wanted David to make a covenant with him, one which was designed to benefit him as well as David. David agreed with one condition: Michal must be returned to him (likely to strengthen David's

claim to the throne as a son-in-law of Saul). Abner consented.
3.17–21   Abner worked out the details for the ten tribes of Israel to reunite with Judah. There was no indication that he talked with Ishbaal or that the king had any part in the decision. David received Abner and made a feast to celebrate the agreement between them that would unite the nation.
3.22   Joab had little use for Abner because he had slain his brother Asahel. When he learned that David had made a covenant with Abner and sent him away in peace, he was angry. He accused the king of being deceived by Abner and implied that David was a fool for having trusted him.

away in peace." 24 Then Joab went to the king and said, "What have you done? Abner came to you; why did you dismiss him, so that he got away? 25 You know that Abner son of Ner came to deceive you, and to learn your comings and goings and to learn all that you are doing."

c. The stabbing of Abner

26   When Joab came out from David's presence, he sent messengers after Abner, and they brought him back from the cistern of Sirah; but David did not know about it. 27 When Abner returned to Hebron, Joab took him aside in the gateway to speak with him privately, and there he stabbed him in the stomach. So he died for shedding[s] the blood of Asahel, Joab's[t] brother. 28 Afterward, when David heard of it, he said, "I and my kingdom are forever guiltless before the LORD for the blood of Abner son of Ner. 29 May the guilt[u] fall on the head of Joab, and on all his father's house; and may the house of Joab never be without one who has a discharge, or who is leprous,[v] or who holds a spindle, or who falls by the sword, or who lacks food!" 30 So Joab and his brother Abishai murdered Abner because he had killed their brother Asahel in the battle at Gibeon.

d. David's grief over Abner's death

31   Then David said to Joab and to all the people who were with him, "Tear your clothes, and put on sackcloth, and mourn over Abner." And King David followed the bier. 32 They buried Abner at Hebron. The king lifted up his voice and wept at the grave of Abner, and all the people wept. 33 The king lamented for Abner, saying,

"Should Abner die as a fool dies?
34   Your hands were not bound,
        your feet were not fettered;
as one falls before the wicked
        you have fallen."

And all the people wept over him again. 35 Then all the people came to persuade David to eat something while it was still day; but David swore, saying, "So may God do to me, and more, if I taste bread or anything else before the sun goes down!" 36 All the people took notice of it, and it pleased them; just as everything the king did pleased all the people. 37 So all the people and all Israel understood that day that the king had no part in the killing of Abner son of Ner. 38 And the king said to his servants, "Do you not know that a prince and a great man has fallen this day in Israel? 39 Today I am powerless, even though anointed king; these men, the sons of Zeruiah, are too violent for me. The LORD pay back the one who does wickedly in accordance with his wickedness!"

7. The murder of Ishbaal

4   When Saul's son Ishbaal[w] heard that Abner had died at Hebron, his courage failed, and all Israel was dismayed. 2 Saul's son had two captains of raiding bands; the name of the one was Baanah, and the name

Side references:
3.25 — 1 Sam 29.6; Isa 37.28
3.27 — 2 Sam 2.23; 4.6; 20.9, 10; 1 Kings 2.5
3.29 — 1 Kings 2.32, 33; Lev 15.2
3.30 — 2 Sam 2.23
3.31 — Gen 37.34; 2 Sam 1.2, 11
3.33 — 2 Sam 1.17
3.35 — 2 Sam 12.17; 1 Sam 3.17; 2 Sam 1.12
3.39 — 2 Sam 19.5-7; 1 Kings 2.5, 6, 33, 34
4.1 — 2 Sam 3.27; Ezra 4.4
4.2 — Josh 18.25

[s] Heb lacks shedding   [t] Heb his   [u] Heb May it   [v] A term for several skin diseases; precise meaning uncertain   [w] Heb lacks Ishbaal

3.26 Joab acted with presumption and without authority from David, when he secretly planned the murder of Abner. He succeeded, much to the dismay of David, who expressed his unbounded anger and placed a curse on the head of Joab and his posterity. **3.28–39** After Joab's assassination of Abner, King David disclaimed all knowledge of the treacherous act. He gave Abner a great funeral and placed a curse on the house of Joab. He eulogized Abner by saying: "Do you not know that a prince and a great man has fallen this day in Israel?" (v. 38).

3.33ff The untimely death of Abner did not destroy the delicate covenant worked out between him and David. The people of Israel exempted David from any guilt, for they saw he had no part in the treacherous act of Joab. **4.1** Baanah and Rechab, captains of raiding bands under Ishbaal's sovereignty, formed a plot against their master (vv. 5–7). Having slain their king, they took the head to David, expecting to be accorded high honors for having disposed of his chief competitor for the allegiance of Israel.

of the other Rechab. They were sons of Rimmon a Benjaminite from
Beeroth—for Beeroth is considered to belong to Benjamin. 3(Now the
people of Beeroth had fled to Gittaim and are there as resident aliens to
this day).

4 Saul's son Jonathan had a son who was crippled in his feet. He was
five years old when the news about Saul and Jonathan came from Jezreel.
His nurse picked him up and fled; and, in her haste to flee, it happened
that he fell and became lame. His name was Mephibosheth. x

5 Now the sons of Rimmon the Beerothite, Rechab and Baanah, set
out, and about the heat of the day they came to the house of Ishbaal,y
while he was taking his noonday rest. 6They came inside the house as
though to take wheat, and they struck him in the stomach; then Rechab
and his brother Baanah escaped. z 7Now they had come into the house
while he was lying on his bedchamber; they attacked him,
killed him, and beheaded him. Then they took his head and traveled by
way of the Arabah all night long. 8They brought the head of Ishbaaly to
David at Hebron and said to the king, "Here is the head of Ishbaal,y son
of Saul, your enemy, who sought your life; the LORD has avenged my lord
the king this day on Saul and on his offspring."

9 David answered Rechab and his brother Baanah, the sons of Rimmon the Beerothite, "As the LORD lives, who has redeemed my life out
of every adversity, 10when the one who told me, 'See, Saul is dead,'
thought he was bringing good news, I seized him and killed him at
Ziklag—this was the reward I gave him for his news. 11How much more
then, when wicked men have killed a righteous man on his bed in his own
house! And now shall I not require his blood at your hand, and destroy
you from the earth?" 12So David commanded the young men, and they
killed them; they cut off their hands and feet, and hung their bodies beside
the pool at Hebron. But the head of Ishbaaly they took and buried in the
tomb of Abner at Hebron.

II. *The consolidation of David's kingship (5.1–10.19)*

A. *David made king over all Israel*

5 Then all the tribes of Israel came to David at Hebron, and said,
   "Look, we are your bone and flesh. 2For some time, while Saul was
king over us, it was you who led out Israel and brought it in. The LORD
said to you: It is you who shall be shepherd of my people Israel, you who
shall be ruler over Israel." 3So all the elders of Israel came to the king at
Hebron; and King David made a covenant with them at Hebron before
the LORD, and they anointed David king over Israel. 4David was thirty
years old when he began to reign, and he reigned forty years. 5At Hebron
he reigned over Judah seven years and six months; and at Jerusalem he
reigned over all Israel and Judah thirty-three years.

x In 1 Chr 8.34 and 9.40, *Merib-baal*   y Heb *Ish-bosheth*   z Meaning of Heb of verse 6 uncertain

4.3	Neh 11.33
4.4	2 Sam 9.3, 6; 1 Sam 31.1-4
4.5	2 Sam 2.8
4.6	2 Sam 2.23
4.8	1 Sam 23.15; 25.29
4.9	1 Kings 1.29
4.10	2 Sam 1.2, 4, 15
4.11	Gen 9.5, 6
4.12	2 Sam 1.15; 3.32
5.1	1 Chr 11.1; 2 Sam 19.13
5.2	1 Sam 18.13; 16.1, 12; 25.30
5.3	1 Chr 11.3; 2 Sam 3.21;
2.4	
5.4	Num 4.3; Lk 3.23; 1 Chr 26.31
5.5	2 Sam 2.11

4.4 *Mephibosheth* was also called "Merib-baal"
(1 Chr 8.34). That name, meaning "my Lord is
Baal," was offensive to Israelites because of its idolatrous connections; consequently they called him Mephibosheth (cf. note on 2.8). This son of Jonathan
was, technically speaking, heir to the throne, for his
father was older than Ishbaal. But he was so crippled
that he had little chance of inheriting the throne,
especially when his uncle was vigorous and had the
support of Abner.
4.11 David executed vengeance on Baanah and Rechab for murdering Ishbaal, whom he considered to
be innocent of any crime warranting such action. He
had their hands and feet cut off and their bodies hung
(whole bodies were not hung, for that was contrary to
the law) in public as a symbol of justice and to frighten
others from committing such heinous crimes.
5.1 The event for which David had been waiting for
many years (cf. 1 Sam 16) finally came. The ten tribes
asked him to become their king, for he was one of
them and had a great record of splendid service. The
nation of Israel was once again united under one ruler.
5.3 At Hebron a covenant was made between David
and the ten tribes, and he was anointed as their king.
At thirty years of age he had reached the pinnacle of
his career.

B. *The capture of Jerusalem*

5.6
Josh 15.63;
Judg 1.8, 21

6 The king and his men marched to Jerusalem against the Jebusites, the inhabitants of the land, who said to David, "You will not come in here, even the blind and the lame will turn you back"—thinking, "David cannot come in here." 7 Nevertheless David took the stronghold of Zion,

5.8
v. 9;
2 Sam 6.12,
16;
1 Kings 2.10
5.9
v. 7

which is now the city of David. 8 David had said on that day, "Whoever would strike down the Jebusites, let him get up the water shaft to attack the lame and the blind, those whom David hates."*a* Therefore it is said, "The blind and the lame shall not come into the house." 9 David occupied the stronghold, and named it the city of David. David built the city all around from the Millo inward. 10 And David became greater and greater,

5.10
2 Sam 3.1

for the Lord, the God of hosts, was with him.

5.11
1 Chr 14.1

11 King Hiram of Tyre sent messengers to David, along with cedar trees, and carpenters and masons who built David a house. 12 David then perceived that the Lord had established him king over Israel, and that he had exalted his kingdom for the sake of his people Israel.

5.13
Deut 17.17;
1 Chr 3.9
5.14
1 Chr 3.5-8

13 In Jerusalem, after he came from Hebron, David took more concubines and wives; and more sons and daughters were born to David. 14 These are the names of those who were born to him in Jerusalem: Shammua, Shobab, Nathan, Solomon, 15 Ibhar, Elishua, Nepheg, Japhia, 16 Elishama, Eliada, and Eliphelet.

C. *David defeats the Philistines*

5.17
2 Sam 23.14

17 When the Philistines heard that David had been anointed king over Israel, all the Philistines went up in search of David; but David heard about it and went down to the stronghold. 18 Now the Philistines had come

5.18
Josh 15.18;
17.15; 18.16
5.19
1 Sam 23.2;
2 Sam 2.1
5.20
Isa 28.21

and spread out in the valley of Rephaim. 19 David inquired of the Lord, "Shall I go up against the Philistines? Will you give them into my hand?" The Lord said to David, "Go up; for I will certainly give the Philistines into your hand." 20 So David came to Baal-perazim, and David defeated them there. He said, "The Lord has burst forth against*b* my enemies before me, like a bursting flood." Therefore that place is called Baal-

5.21
1 Chr 14.12

perazim.*c* 21 The Philistines abandoned their idols there, and David and his men carried them away.

5.22
v. 18
5.23
v. 19
5.24
2 Kings 7.6;
Judg 4.14

22 Once again the Philistines came up, and were spread out in the valley of Rephaim. 23 When David inquired of the Lord, he said, "You shall not go up; go around to their rear, and come upon them opposite the balsam trees. 24 When you hear the sound of marching in the tops of

---

a Another reading is *those who hate David*   *b* Heb *paraz*   *c* That is *Lord of Bursting Forth*

5.6 The first exploit of David after he became king of all Israel was to seize Jerusalem, which lay in the territory assigned to Benjamin. The Jebusites had not been driven out by the Benjamintes (Judg 1.21), and they felt confident that the walls of their great city would protect them from David's intentions. But David attacked the city, took it, and dwelt in it. It was to become, under him and his son Solomon, the center of the nation and the site of the magnificent temple.

5.9 *the Millo*, or, "the filling." While we cannot be certain, Millo was apparently a fortification or citadel near Jerusalem. Solomon added to the Millo's existing defense works (see 1 Kings 9.15; 11.27; 1 Chr 11.8; 2 Chr 32.5).

5.10 The reason for the increasing greatness of David is stated in clear terms: "The Lord, the God of hosts, was with him." Through God's gifts and help, all of God's people can rise to heights which they could not otherwise attain.

5.13 It was the prerogative of kings to have many concubines. But nowhere has God placed his stamp of

approval on this practice. It was to David's shame that he did not seek the counsel of God about this. We cannot praise, justify, or excuse David. The Bible records several conflicts among the half-siblings within David's family.

5.17 The Philistines, as soon as they knew David was king, sought to undo him and crush him before he had time to establish himself firmly in Israel. David sought the counsel of God, and the Lord told him to attack them, assuring him of victory. When the battle was over David gave God the glory: "The Lord has burst forth aginst my enemies" (v. 20).

5.22 The Philistines tried the second time to defeat David and again God intervened, saying that he would go before David to smite the army of the Philistines.

5.24 God reveals his will to the believer in three ways: (1) directly and indirectly through the Word of God (e.g., Ex 20); (2) through circumstances (e.g., 5.24); and (3) through the inward persuasion of the Holy Spirit, which is subsequently confirmed by circumstances (e.g., Jer 32.6–8).

the balsam trees, then be on the alert; for then the LORD has gone out before you to strike down the army of the Philistines." 25 David did just as the LORD had commanded him; and he struck down the Philistines from Geba all the way to Gezer.

5.25
Josh 12.12;
see
1 Chr 14.16

D. Bringing the ark to Jerusalem

1. *The journey begun*

6 David again gathered all the chosen men of Israel, thirty thousand. 2 David and all the people with him set out and went from Baale-judah, to bring up from there the ark of God, which is called by the name of the LORD of hosts who is enthroned on the cherubim. 3 They carried the ark of God on a new cart, and brought it out of the house of Abinadab, which was on the hill. Uzzah and Ahio,*d* the sons of Abinadab, were driving the new cart 4 with the ark of God;*e* and Ahio*d* went in front of the ark. 5 David and all the house of Israel were dancing before the LORD with all their might, with songs*f* and lyres and harps and tambourines and castanets and cymbals.

6.2
1 Chr 13.5, 6;
Lev 24.16;
1 Sam 4.4
6.3
1 Sam 6.7

6.4
1 Sam 7.1
6.5
1 Sam 18.6,
7; 1 Chr 13.8

2. *The sin of Uzzah*

6 When they came to the threshing floor of Nacon, Uzzah reached out his hand to the ark of God and took hold of it, for the oxen shook it. 7 The anger of the LORD was kindled against Uzzah; and God struck him there because he reached out his hand to the ark;*g* and he died there beside the ark of God. 8 David was angry because the LORD had burst forth with an outburst upon Uzzah; so that place is called Perez-uzzah,*h* to this day. 9 David was afraid of the LORD that day; he said, "How can the ark of the LORD come into my care?" 10 So David was unwilling to take the ark of the LORD into his care in the city of David; instead David took it to the house of Obed-edom the Gittite. 11 The ark of the LORD remained in the house of Obed-edom the Gittite three months; and the LORD blessed Obed-edom and all his household.

6.6
1 Chr 13.9;
Num 4.15,
19, 20
6.7
1 Sam 6.19

6.10
1 Chr 13.13

6.11
1 Chr 13.14

3. *The ark brought to Jerusalem*

12 It was told King David, "The LORD has blessed the household of Obed-edom and all that belongs to him, because of the ark of God." So David went and brought up the ark of God from the house of Obed-edom to the city of David with rejoicing; 13 and when those who bore the ark of the LORD had gone six paces, he sacrificed an ox and a fatling. 14 David danced before the LORD with all his might; David was girded with a linen ephod. 15 So David and all the house of Israel brought up the ark of the LORD with shouting, and with the sound of the trumpet.
16 As the ark of the LORD came into the city of David, Michal

6.12
1 Chr 15.25;
1 Kings 8.1

6.14
Ex 15.20;
1 Sam 2.18
6.15
1 Chr 15.28
6.16
1 Chr 15.29

d Or *and his brother*   *e* Compare Gk: Heb *and brought it out of the house of Abinadab, which was on the hill with the ark of God*   *f* Q Ms Gk 1 Chr 13.8: Heb *fir trees*   *g* 1 Chr 13.10 Compare Q Ms: Meaning of Heb uncertain   *h* That is *Bursting Out Against Uzzah*

6.3 The instructions by God for transporting the ark were simple. It was to be carried by four priests, with the ark resting on two carrying poles suspended on the shoulders of the priests (see Num 3.27–32; 4.1–20). David disregarded these instructions, however pious his intention, disaster followed his disobedience.

6.6 Only those who were priests could touch the ark. The punishment for anyone else doing this was death. Why then did Uzzah, a Levite, do so? Perhaps he remembered that when the Philistines had handled the ark, nothing had happened to them. He may have taken this to mean that he was equally free to do so. He was mistaken and God judged him immediately,

so that he died there and then. David refers to this error and acknowledged his guilt in 1 Chr 15.13.
6.12 When David learned how the Lord had prospered Obed-edom, he decided to bring the ark in the proper fashion to Jerusalem (1 Chr 15.1–15). He laid aside his purple robe as a sign of his humility and danced all the way to show his joy.
6.16 Unknown to David, his wife Michal watched him dance before the Lord as the ark was being carried to Jerusalem. She despised her husband and soon told him so (v. 20). Possibly she was looking for reason to criticize David for having recovered her from her husband, who apparently loved her greatly (3.12–16). Or she thought it unbecoming for a great

daughter of Saul looked out of the window, and saw King David leaping and dancing before the LORD; and she despised him in her heart.

6.17
1 Chr 15.1;
16.1;
1 Kings 8.62-65
6.18
1 Kings 8.14,
15

17 They brought in the ark of the LORD, and set it in its place, inside the tent that David had pitched for it; and David offered burnt offerings and offerings of well-being before the LORD. 18 When David had finished offering the burnt offerings and the offerings of well-being, he blessed the people in the name of the LORD of hosts, 19 and distributed food among all the people, the whole multitude of Israel, both men and women, to each a cake of bread, a portion of meat,*i* and a cake of raisins. Then all the people went back to their homes.

4. *Michal's sin*

6.20
vv. 14, 16;
1 Sam 19.24

6.21
1 Sam 13.14;
15.28

20 David returned to bless his household. But Michal the daughter of Saul came out to meet David, and said, "How the king of Israel honored himself today, uncovering himself today before the eyes of his servants' maids, as any vulgar fellow might shamelessly uncover himself!" 21 David said to Michal, "It was before the LORD, who chose me in place of your father and all his household, to appoint me as prince over Israel, the people of the LORD, that I have danced before the LORD. 22 I will make myself yet more contemptible than this, and I will be abased in my own eyes; but by the maids of whom you have spoken, by them I shall be held in honor." 23 And Michal the daughter of Saul had no child to the day of her death.

E. *David's desire to build the temple*

1. *Nathan's approval*

7.1
1 Chr 17.1ff
7.2
2 Sam 5.11;
Acts 7.46;
Ex 26.1
7.3
1 Kings 8.17,
18

7 Now when the king was settled in his house, and the LORD had given him rest from all his enemies around him, 2 the king said to the prophet Nathan, "See now, I am living in a house of cedar, but the ark of God stays in a tent." 3 Nathan said to the king, "Go, do all that you have in mind; for the LORD is with you."

2. *God's intervention and disapproval*

7.5
1 Kings 5.3,
4; 8.19
7.6
1 Kings 8.16;
Ex 40.18, 34
7.7
Lev 26.11,
12;
Deut 23.14;
2 Sam 5.2
7.8
1 Sam 16.11,
12;
Ps 78.70;
2 Sam 6.21

4 But that same night the word of the LORD came to Nathan: 5 Go and tell my servant David: Thus says the LORD: Are you the one to build me a house to live in? 6 I have not lived in a house since the day I brought up the people of Israel from Egypt to this day, but I have been moving about in a tent and a tabernacle. 7 Wherever I have moved about among all the people of Israel, did I ever speak a word with any of the tribal leaders*j* of Israel, whom I commanded to shepherd my people Israel, saying, "Why have you not built me a house of cedar?" 8 Now therefore thus you shall say to my servant David: Thus says the LORD of hosts: I

i Vg: Meaning of Heb uncertain   *j* Or *any of the tribes*

---

soldier, statesman, and monarch to act in this manner. Either way she missed the true intention of David, which was to glorify God. God was not pleased with her condemnation of David, and judged her by keeping her barren (v. 23).

7.1 David was now at peace and had time to think. He surmised that a permanent building to house the ark of God was now a necessity. Such a building had been impossible during the wilderness journeys. But now Israel was in the land, while the ark was still housed in a tent. David discussed the issue with Nathan the prophet, who endorsed the idea, even though at this time there was no word from God on the matter (v. 3).

7.8ff God now entered into a specific covenant relationship with David, a covenant built upon the

Abrahamic covenant. It was both conditional and unconditional. God promised punishment for the breaking of the covenant, but he also promised that even if there were disobedience, the covenant itself would not be abrogated. The covenant contained four promises: (1) the promise of a dynasty; (2) the promise of a kingdom to rule over; (3) the promise of a land and people; and (4) the promise that the house of David would endure forever. This agreement anticipates the kingly rule of Jesus Christ. The angel Gabriel announced the fulfillment of this covenant to Jesus' mother Mary (Lk 1.31ff). The ultimate spiritual fulfillment of the covenant is the fact that Christ, since his resurrection, has been exalted to the right hand of God as the supreme and eternal ruler over the kingdom of God (see Acts 2.25ff).

took you from the pasture, from following the sheep to be prince over my people Israel; 9 and I have been with you wherever you went, and have cut off all your enemies from before you; and I will make for you a great name, like the name of the great ones of the earth. 10 And I will appoint a place for my people Israel and will plant them, so that they may live in their own place, and be disturbed no more; and evildoers shall afflict them no more, as formerly, 11 from the time that I appointed judges over my people Israel; and I will give you rest from all your enemies. Moreover the Lord declares to you that the Lord will make you a house. 12 When your days are fulfilled and you lie down with your ancestors, I will raise up your offspring after you, who shall come forth from your body, and I will establish his kingdom. 13 He shall build a house for my name, and I will establish the throne of his kingdom forever. 14 I will be a father to him, and he shall be a son to me. When he commits iniquity, I will punish him with a rod such as mortals use, with blows inflicted by human beings. 15 But I will not take[k] my steadfast love from him, as I took it from Saul, whom I put away from before you. 16 Your house and your kingdom shall be made sure forever before me;[l] your throne shall be established forever. 17 In accordance with all these words and with all this vision, Nathan spoke to David.

3. David's prayer of submission

18   Then King David went in and sat before the Lord, and said, "Who am I, O Lord God, and what is my house, that you have brought me thus far? 19 And yet this was a small thing in your eyes, O Lord God; you have spoken also of your servant's house for a great while to come. May this be instruction for the people,[m] O Lord God! 20 And what more can David say to you? For you know your servant, O Lord God! 21 Because of your promise, and according to your own heart, you have wrought all this greatness, so that your servant may know it. 22 Therefore you are great, O Lord God; for there is no one like you, and there is no God besides you, according to all that we have heard with our ears. 23 Who is like your people, like Israel? Is there another[n] nation on earth whose God went to redeem it as a people, and to make a name for himself, doing great and awesome things for them,[o] by driving out[p] before his people nations and their gods?[q] 24 And you established your people Israel for yourself to be your people forever; and you, O Lord, became their God. 25 And now, O Lord God, as for the word that you have spoken concerning your servant and concerning his house, confirm it forever; do as you have promised. 26 Thus your name will be magnified forever in the saying, 'The Lord of hosts is God over Israel'; and the house of your servant David will be established before you. 27 For you, O Lord of hosts, the God of Israel, have made this revelation to your servant, saying, 'I will build you a house'; therefore your servant has found courage to pray this

---

7.9
1 Sam 18.14;
2 Sam 5.10;
Ps 18.37-42
7.10
Ex 15.17;
Isa 5.2, 7;
Ps 89.22;
Isa 60.18
7.11
Judg 2.16;
1 Sam 12.9-11;
vv. 1, 27;
1 Sam 25.28
7.12
1 Kings 2.1
7.13
1 Kings 5.5;
Ps 89.4, 29;
36.37;
Isa 9.7
7.14
Ps 89.26, 27;
Heb 1.5;
Ps 89.30-33
7.15
1 Sam 15.23, 28
7.16
Ps 89.36, 37

7.18
Ex 3.11;
1 Sam 18.18
7.19
Isa 55.8

7.20
1 Sam 16.7;
Jn 21.17

7.22
Ps 48.1;
86.10;
Ex 15.11;
Deut 3.24;
Ps 44.1
7.23
Deut 4.7,
32-38; 10.21;
15.15; 9.26
7.24
Deut 26.18;
Ps 48.14

7.26
Ps 72.18, 19
7.27
v. 13

---

k Gk Syr Vg 1 Chr 17.13: Heb *shall not depart*   *l* Gk Heb Mss: MT *before you*; Compare 2 Sam 7.26, 29
m Meaning of Heb uncertain   *n* Gk: Heb *one*   *o* Heb *you*   *p* Gk 1 Chr 17.21: Heb *for your land*
q Cn: Heb *before your people, whom you redeemed for yourself from Egypt, nations and its gods*

7.11–13 David wanted to build a house for God, but he was forbidden to do so. Yet God was pleased with David's intention. He told David that he would build a house for him, i.e., a posterity to sit upon the throne of David. And from that posterity God would raise up someone who would build the temple David had in mind.
7.17 When Nathan first encouraged David to build the temple, he had not yet received a word from God. Now, after having received a vision from God, Nathan reported God's ultimate approval of the temple project.
7.18ff Nathan had brought God's message to Da-

vid. Now David went to God himself without any intermediary. He offered his prayer in humility and solemnity to his great God. He began by acknowledging his own nothingness in comparison to God. He expressed gratitude for the undeserved favors God had given him. All that God had done came from his free grace (v. 21), and David adored the greatness and glory of his God (v. 22). He praised God that he had brought Israel into being and had blessed this people. He closed with petitions for God to bless him and his posterity, and he magnified the fact that God's words are true (v. 28).

7.28
Jn 17.17
7.29
Num 6.24-26

prayer to you. 28 And now, O Lord GOD, you are God, and your words are true, and you have promised this good thing to your servant; 29 now therefore may it please you to bless the house of your servant, so that it may continue forever before you; for you, O Lord GOD, have spoken, and with your blessing shall the house of your servant be blessed forever."

F. David's military victories: Philistines, Moabites, Zobah, Arameans, Edomites, and Ammonites

8 Some time afterward, David attacked the Philistines and subdued them; David took Metheg-ammah out of the hand of the Philistines.

8.2
Num 24.17

2 He also defeated the Moabites and, making them lie down on the ground, measured them off with a cord; he measured two lengths of cord for those who were to be put to death, and one length^r for those who were to be spared. And the Moabites became servants to David and brought tribute.

8.3
2 Sam 10.15-19
8.4
Josh 11.6, 9

3 David also struck down King Hadadezer son of Rehob of Zobah, as he went to restore his monument^s at the river Euphrates. 4 David took from him one thousand seven hundred horsemen, and twenty thousand foot soldiers. David hamstrung all the chariot horses, but left enough for

8.5
1 Kings 11.23-25
8.6
v. 14;
2 Sam 7.9
8.7
1 Kings 10.16

a hundred chariots. 5 When the Arameans of Damascus came to help King Hadadezer of Zobah, David killed twenty-two thousand men of the Arameans. 6 Then David put garrisons among the Arameans of Damascus; and the Arameans became servants to David and brought tribute. The LORD gave victory to David wherever he went. 7 David took the gold shields that were carried by the servants of Hadadezer, and brought them to Jerusalem. 8 From Betah and from Berothai, towns of Hadadezer, King David took a great amount of bronze.

8.10
1 Chr 18.10

9 When King Toi of Hamath heard that David had defeated the whole army of Hadadezer, 10 Toi sent his son Joram to King David, to greet him and to congratulate him because he had fought against Hadadezer and defeated him. Now Hadadezer had often been at war with Toi. Joram brought with him articles of silver, gold, and bronze; 11 these also King David dedicated to the LORD, together with the silver and gold that he dedicated from all the nations he subdued, 12 from Edom, Moab, the Ammonites, the Philistines, Amalek, and from the spoil of King Hadadezer son of Rehob of Zobah.

8.11
1 Kings 7.51;
1 Chr 18.11;
26.25

8.13
2 Ki 14.7
8.14
Gen 27.29,
37, 40;
Num 24.17,
18; v. 6

13 David won a name for himself. When he returned, he killed eighteen thousand Edomites^t in the Valley of Salt. 14 He put garrisons in Edom; throughout all Edom he put garrisons, and all the Edomites became David's servants. And the LORD gave victory to David wherever he went.

^{r} Heb one full length ^{s} Compare 1 Sam 15.12 and 2 Sam 18.18 ^{t} Gk: Heb returned from striking down eighteen thousand Arameans

---

8.3 Ironically, David's defeat of Hadadezer helped make possible the rise of Assyria, which would eventually be the enemy of Israel and Judah.

8.4 Compare with 1 Chr 18.4, where the numbers are somewhat different. The Hebrew text is unclear at this point; some words have been dropped out. Because of the way numbers were written, it was easy for copyists to misread the text, particularly when it was well worn.

8.6 *The LORD gave victory to David wherever he went.* Under God's divine protection, David was kept from harm (see also v. 14; 1 Chr 18.6,13). This was part of the covenant God made with David. The same promise belongs to God's people who are under the Lordship of Christ, their preserver, by his Holy Spirit.

8.13 *Edomites.* Note NRSV footnote here; see also 1 Chr 18.12, which names the Edomites. The difference between the Hebrew spelling of "Edom" and of "Aram" (i.e., Syria) consists of but one letter — a letter *d*, which greatly resembles the Hebrew *r*); hence the reading here "Edomites" rather than "Arameans" seems well founded. Since the Valley of Salt was located at the southern extremity of the Dead Sea, it is more likely that the Edomites were the enemies fought there rather than the Syrians who dwelt to the north of Israel. 1 Chr 18.12 contributes the detail that Abishai was in immediate command of the victorious Israelite army, although of course, acting under David's authority. The heading of Ps 60 indicates that Joab, as chief of staff, masterminded the campaign and therefore deserved credit for the victory.

15 So David reigned over all Israel; and David administered justice and equity to all his people. [16] Joab son of Zeruiah was over the army; Jehoshaphat son of Ahilud was recorder; [17] Zadok son of Ahitub and Ahimelech son of Abiathar were priests; Seraiah was secretary; [18] Benaiah son of Jehoiada was over[u] the Cherethites and the Pelethites; and David's sons were priests.

8.16
2 Sam 19.13;
1 Kings 4.3;
2 Kings 18.18,
37
8.17
1 Chr 24.3
8.18
1 Sam 30.14

G. David's kindness to Mephibosheth

9 David asked, "Is there still anyone left of the house of Saul to whom I may show kindness for Jonathan's sake?" [2] Now there was a servant of the house of Saul whose name was Ziba, and he was summoned to David. The king said to him, "Are you Ziba?" And he said, "At your service!" [3] The king said, "Is there anyone remaining of the house of Saul to whom I may show the kindness of God?" Ziba said to the king, "There remains a son of Jonathan; he is crippled in his feet." [4] The king said to him, "Where is he?" Ziba said to the king, "He is in the house of Machir son of Ammiel, at Lo-debar." [5] Then King David sent and brought him from the house of Machir son of Ammiel, at Lo-debar. [6] Mephibosheth[v] son of Jonathan son of Saul came to David, and fell on his face and did obeisance. David said, "Mephibosheth!"[v] He answered, "I am your servant." [7] David said to him, "Do not be afraid, for I will show you kindness for the sake of your father Jonathan; I will restore to you all the land of your grandfather Saul, and you yourself shall eat at my table always." [8] He did obeisance and said, "What is your servant, that you should look upon a dead dog such as I?"

9 Then the king summoned Saul's servant Ziba, and said to him, "All that belonged to Saul and to all his house I have given to your master's grandson. [10] You and your sons and your servants shall till the land for him, and shall bring in the produce, so that your master's grandson may have food to eat; but your master's grandson Mephibosheth[v] shall always eat at my table." Now Ziba had fifteen sons and twenty servants. [11] Then Ziba said to the king, "According to all that my lord the king commands his servant, so your servant will do." Mephibosheth[v] ate at David's[w] table, like one of the king's sons. [12] Mephibosheth[v] had a young son whose name was Mica. And all who lived in Ziba's house became Mephibosheth's[x] servants. [13] Mephibosheth[v] lived in Jerusalem, for he always ate at the king's table. Now he was lame in both his feet.

9.1
1 Sam 20.14-17,
42
9.2
2 Sam 16.1-4;
19.17, 29
9.3
1 Sam 20.14;
2 Sam 4.4
9.4
2 Sam 17.27

9.6
2 Sam 16.4;
19.24-30

9.7
vv. 1, 3;
2 Sam 12.8;
19.28
9.8
2 Sam 16.9

9.9
2 Sam 16.4;
19.29
9.10
vv. 7, 11, 13;
2 Sam 19.28

9.12
1 Chr 8.34
9.13
vv. 3, 7, 10

[u] Syr Tg Vg 20.23; 1 Chr 18.17: Heb lacks *was over*   [v] Or *Merib-baal*: See 4.4 note   [w] Gk: Heb *my*
[x] Or *Merib-baal's*: See 4.4 note

8.17 *Zadok* is mentioned here for the first time. After this time the recognized priesthood descended from him (1 Kings 2.35). According to 1 Chr 6.8 he was in the priestly line of Aaron, Eleazar, and Phinehas. Aside from this genealogical data, the Bible says nothing about where his father, Ahitub, and his other ancestors served as priests. *secretary*. Secretaries were people who numbered or who wrote. They usually were men of great wisdom and learning (1 Chr 27,32), well versed in the law (Ezra 7.6), and competent and able writers (Ps 45.1) — at a time when many Hebrews could not write. In the O.T. many of these people apparently came from the tribe of Levi. They served as secretaries to kings (20.25; 2 Kings 12.10), notaries (Jer 32.11,12), keepers of state records (1 Chr 24.6), secretaries to prophets (Jer 36.4,26), and military secretaries who kept the rolls of the armies (2 Chr 26.11; Jer 52.25).
8.18 *David's sons were priests.* If David's non-

Levitical sons actually served as priests, there is no other passage to confirm this. There is reason to question the text here because 20.26 has: "Ira the Jairite was also David's priest," while 1 Chr 18:17 reads: "David's sons were the chief officials in the service of the king."
9.1 *for Jonathan's sake.* David did not forget his covenant with Jonathan (cf. 1 Sam 20:14–17).
9.7 Technically Mephibosheth should have succeeded Saul as king; but his uncle Ishbaal, who was younger than his father Jonathan, had seized the throne (see notes on 2.8; 4.4). David welcomed this only son of Jonathan and provided for him to eat at his table. He restored Saul's lands to him. Ziba, Saul's servant, was part of this scene. Later, he would besmirch the memory of Mephibosheth by accusing him of treachery and of having a desire to take the throne from David (16.1–4).

H. *David's victory over the Ammonites*

1. *The mistreatment of David's envoys*

10.1
1 Chr 19.1ff

10 Some time afterward, the king of the Ammonites died, and his son Hanun succeeded him. 2 David said, "I will deal loyally with Hanun son of Nahash, just as his father dealt loyally with me." So David sent envoys to console him concerning his father. When David's envoys came into the land of the Ammonites, 3 the princes of the Ammonites said to their lord Hanun, "Do you really think that David is honoring your father just because he has sent messengers with condolences to you? Has not David sent his envoys to you to search the city, to spy it out, and to overthrow it?" 4 So Hanun seized David's envoys, shaved off half the beard of each, cut off their garments in the middle at their hips, and sent them away. 5 When David was told, he sent to meet them, for the men were greatly ashamed. The king said, "Remain at Jericho until your beards have grown, and then return."

10.4
Isa 15.2;
20.4

2. *The flight of the Arameans and the Ammonites*

10.6
Gen 34.30;
2 Sam 8.3, 5;
Judg 18.28

6 When the Ammonites saw that they had become odious to David, the Ammonites sent and hired the Arameans of Beth-rehob and the Arameans of Zobah, twenty thousand foot soldiers, as well as the king of Maacah, one thousand men, and the men of Tob, twelve thousand men. 7 When David heard of it, he sent Joab and all the army with the warriors. 8 The Ammonites came out and drew up in battle array at the entrance of the gate; but the Arameans of Zobah and of Rehob, and the men of Tob and Maacah, were by themselves in the open country.

10.8
1 Chr 19.9;
Judg 11.3, 5

9 When Joab saw that the battle was set against him both in front and in the rear, he chose some of the picked men of Israel, and arrayed them against the Arameans; 10 the rest of his men he put in the charge of his brother Abishai, and he arrayed them against the Ammonites. 11 He said, "If the Arameans are too strong for me, then you shall help me; but if the Ammonites are too strong for you, then I will come and help you. 12 Be strong, and let us be courageous for the sake of our people, and for the cities of our God; and may the LORD do what seems good to him." 13 So Joab and the people who were with him moved forward into battle against the Arameans; and they fled before him. 14 When the Ammonites saw that the Arameans fled, they likewise fled before Abishai, and entered the city. Then Joab returned from fighting against the Ammonites, and came to Jerusalem.

10.12
Deut 31.6;
1 Cor 16.13;
1 Sam 3.18
10.13
1 Kings 20.13-
21

3. *The defeat of the Ammonites and Arameans at Helam*

10.16
2 Sam 8.3;
1 Chr 19.16

15 But when the Arameans saw that they had been defeated by Israel, they gathered themselves together. 16 Hadadezer sent and brought out the Arameans who were beyond the Euphrates; and they came to Helam, with Shobach the commander of the army of Hadadezer at their head. 17 When it was told David, he gathered all Israel together, and crossed the Jordan, and came to Helam. The Arameans arrayed themselves against David and fought with him. 18 The Arameans fled before Israel; and David killed of

10.18
1 Chr 19.18;
2 Sam 8.6

10.2 Nahash, an enemy of Israel, had nonetheless shown kindness to David. Upon his death David sent messengers to console the new king Hanun and to express David's kind intentions towards them. The king decided, on the advice of his princes, to degrade the messengers by shaving off half of each beard and cutting their garments to the waist. This, of course, was meant as an insult to David.

10.6 The Ammonites hired the Arameans to help them in a military engagement with Israel. Joab led David's army and skillfully managed the campaign,

which resulted in a defeat for the enemy. The Arameans fled first and then the soldiers of the Ammonites. Joab came home to Jerusalem the victor.

10.15 The Ammonites and Syrians (Arameans) gathered still larger forces to fight against David. The enemy soldiers came from as far away as the region beyond the Euphrates. They congregated on the east bank of Jordan, at Helam, where the battle took place. In this instance David himself headed up his forces and won a great victory.

10.18 *seven hundred chariot teams.* This number is

the Arameans seven hundred chariot teams, and forty thousand horse-men,^{y} and wounded Shobach the commander of their army, so that he died there. 19 When all the kings who were servants of Hadadezer saw that they had been defeated by Israel, they made peace with Israel, and became subject to them. So the Arameans were afraid to help the Ammonites any more.

III. The sin of David (11.1–12.31)

A. David commits adultery with Bathsheba

11 In the spring of the year, the time when kings go out to battle, David sent Joab with his officers and all Israel with him; they ravaged the Ammonites, and besieged Rabbah. But David remained at Jerusalem.

2 It happened, late one afternoon, when David rose from his couch and was walking about on the roof of the king's house, that he saw from the roof a woman bathing; the woman was very beautiful. 3 David sent someone to inquire about the woman. It was reported, "This is Bathsheba daughter of Eliam, the wife of Uriah the Hittite." 4 So David sent messengers to get her, and she came to him, and he lay with her. (Now she was purifying herself after her period.) Then she returned to her house. 5 The woman conceived; and she sent and told David, "I am pregnant."

B. David sends for Uriah; his plan fails

6 So David sent word to Joab, "Send me Uriah the Hittite." And Joab sent Uriah to David. 7 When Uriah came to him, David asked how Joab and the people fared, and how the war was going. 8 Then David said to Uriah, "Go down to your house, and wash your feet." Uriah went out of the king's house, and there followed him a present from the king. 9 But Uriah slept at the entrance of the king's house with all the servants of his lord, and did not go down to his house. 10 When they told David, "Uriah did not go down to his house," David said to Uriah, "You have just come from a journey. Why did you not go down to your house?" 11 Uriah said to David, "The ark and Israel and Judah remain in booths;^{z} and my lord Joab and the servants of my lord are camping in the open field; shall I then go to my house, to eat and to drink, and to lie with my wife? As you live, and as your soul lives, I will not do such a thing." 12 Then David said to Uriah, "Remain here today also, and tomorrow I will send you back." So Uriah remained in Jerusalem that day. On the next day, 13 David invited him to eat and drink in his presence and made him drunk; and in the evening he went out to lie on his couch with the servants of his lord, but he did not go down to his house.

^{y} 1 Chr 19.18 and some Gk Mss read *foot soldiers* ^{z} Or *at Succoth*

11.1
1 Chr 20.1;
1 Kings 20.22,
26;
2 Sam 12.26-28

11.2
Deut 22.8;
Mt 5.28
11.3
2 Sam 23.39
11.4
Lev 15.19,
28; 18.19
11.5
Lev 20.10

11.8
Gen 43.24;
Lk 7.44

11.10
2 Sam 7.2, 6;
20.6

11.13
v. 9

recorded as seven thousand in 1 Chr 19.18, but the smaller figure seems more accurate. The scribal error probably derived from confusion over one of the digits of the decimal system used for computation. Also, this verse mentions *forty thousand horsemen*, whereas 1 Chr 19.18 reads "forty thousand foot soldiers" (see NRSV footnote). Most copyists' errors occurred either because the manuscripts from which they worked were worn or torn, or because of human carelessness and weariness (see also note on 8.4).
11.1   David should have been with his soldiers battling for the Lord. Instead he remained at ease at home and promptly fell into sin. It seems strange that a man who had many wives and concubines found that he did not have as many as he would like and so defiled a neighbor's wife. The nature of sin is that no

matter how much a person has, he or she always wants more.
11.4   The story of David's adultery with Bathsheba enlightens us on the anatomy of sin. When he saw her from a distance, all he needed to do was to go down from the roof and forget about it. Instead, he sent for Bathsheba. She then made her decision. She knew that the king was not asking her to come for mere innocent conversation. But she was a married woman; all she needed to do was decline the invitation, even though it had been made by the king. What happened when they met was a foregone conclusion. The adultery was not committed in a moment of passion brought on by accidental circumstances; it was a deliberate act. He paid a price for his transgression for the rest of his life, even though he was forgiven when he repented (see notes on 12.7; 13.1ff).

C. David has Uriah killed

11.14
1 Kings 21.8-10
11.15
2 Sam 12.9

14 In the morning David wrote a letter to Joab, and sent it by the hand of Uriah. 15 In the letter he wrote, "Set Uriah in the forefront of the hardest fighting, and then draw back from him, so that he may be struck down and die." 16 As Joab was besieging the city, he assigned Uriah to the place where he knew there were valiant warriors. 17 The men of the city came out and fought with Joab; and some of the servants of David among the people fell. Uriah the Hittite was killed as well. 18 Then Joab sent and told David all the news about the fighting; 19 and he instructed the messenger, "When you have finished telling the king all the news about the fighting, 20 then, if the king's anger rises, and if he says to you, 'Why did you go so near the city to fight? Did you not know that they would shoot from the wall? 21 Who killed Abimelech son of Jerubbaal?[a] Did not a woman throw an upper millstone on him from the wall, so that he died at Thebez? Why did you go so near the wall?' then you shall say, 'Your servant Uriah the Hittite is dead too.' "

11.17
v. 21

11.21
Judg 9.50-54

22 So the messenger went, and came and told David all that Joab had sent him to tell. 23 The messenger said to David, "The men gained an advantage over us, and came out against us in the field; but we drove them back to the entrance of the gate. 24 Then the archers shot at your servants from the wall; some of the king's servants are dead; and your servant Uriah the Hittite is dead also." 25 David said to the messenger, "Thus you shall say to Joab, 'Do not let this matter trouble you, for the sword devours now one and now another; press your attack on the city, and overthrow it.' And encourage him."

D. David marries Bathsheba

11.26
Deut 34.8;
1 Sam 31.13
11.27
2 Sam 12.9;
Ps 51.4, 5

26 When the wife of Uriah heard that her husband was dead, she made lamentation for him. 27 When the mourning was over, David sent and brought her to his house, and she became his wife, and bore him a son.

E. Nathan and David

1. Nathan's parable

12.1
2 Sam 14.4-7;
1 Kings 20.35-
40

12 But the thing that David had done displeased the LORD, 1 and the LORD sent Nathan to David. He came to him, and said to him, "There were two men in a certain city, the one rich and the other poor. 2 The rich man had very many flocks and herds; 3 but the poor man had nothing but one little ewe lamb, which he had bought. He brought it up, and it grew up with him and with his children; it used to eat of his meager fare, and drink from his cup, and lie in his bosom, and it was like a daughter to him. 4 Now there came a traveler to the rich man, and he was loath to take one of his own flock or herd to prepare for the wayfarer who had come to him, but he took the poor man's lamb, and prepared that for

_a_ Gk Syr Judg 7.1: Heb _Jerubbesheth_

11.15 David sought to cover up his sinful deed with Bathsheba. He planned to have Uriah the Hittite come home and sleep with his wife. Then the baby would be thought to be his. When Uriah refused to go home the first night, David got him drunk the second night; that too failed. Consequently, David gave orders to have Uriah killed in battle. One sin often leads to another; one transgression requires a second and a third to cover it. David became both an adulterer and a murderer, and the second crime was worse than the first. It was committed in cold blood and with malicious forethought against an innocent military man who was more righteous than the king. **11.27** Sin will be found out. Even though David

covered and glossed it over, it was known to God, who searches the heart and whose anger would not be satisfied until the matter was settled.
12.1 God was angry with David and sent Nathan the prophet to him. The prophet spoke a parable about injustice, designed to trap David into making a condemning statement about someone else. Nathan finally pointed the finger at David and said: "You are the man!" Great was the courage of this prophet. Apart from the preserving power of God, he could have expected the same kind of treatment accorded to Uriah. Fortunately, David came under deep conviction of sin, repented, and asked for divine forgiveness (see note on v. 7).

the guest who had come to him." 5 Then David's anger was greatly kindled against the man. He said to Nathan, "As the LORD lives, the man who has done this deserves to die; 6 he shall restore the lamb fourfold, because he did this thing, and because he had no pity."

2. *The parable applied to David who repents*

7   Nathan said to David, "You are the man! Thus says the LORD, the God of Israel: I anointed you king over Israel, and I rescued you from the hand of Saul; 8 I gave you your master's house, and your master's wives into your bosom, and gave you the house of Israel and of Judah; and if that had been too little, I would have added as much more. 9 Why have you despised the word of the LORD, to do what is evil in his sight? You have struck down Uriah the Hittite with the sword, and have taken his wife to be your wife, and have killed him with the sword of the Ammonites. 10 Now therefore the sword shall never depart from your house, for you have despised me, and have taken the wife of Uriah the Hittite to be your wife. 11 Thus says the LORD: I will raise up trouble against you from within your own house; and I will take your wives before your eyes, and give them to your neighbor, and he shall lie with your wives in the sight of this very sun. 12 For you did it secretly; but I will do this thing before all Israel, and before the sun." 13 David said to Nathan, "I have sinned against the LORD." Nathan said to David, "Now the LORD has put away your sin; you shall not die. 14 Nevertheless, because by this deed you have utterly scorned the LORD,[b] the child that is born to you shall die." 15 Then Nathan went to his house.

3. *The death of the child*

The LORD struck the child that Uriah's wife bore to David, and it became very ill. 16 David therefore pleaded with God for the child; David fasted, and went in and lay all night on the ground. 17 The elders of his house stood beside him, urging him to rise from the ground; but he would not, nor did he eat food with them. 18 On the seventh day the child died. And the servants of David were afraid to tell him that the child was dead; for they said, "While the child was still alive, we spoke to him, and he did not listen to us; how then can we tell him the child is dead? He may do himself some harm." 19 But when David saw that his servants were whispering together, he perceived that the child was dead; and David said to his servants, "Is the child dead?" They said, "He is dead."

20   Then David rose from the ground, washed, anointed himself, and changed his clothes. He went into the house of the LORD, and worshiped; he then went to his own house; and when he asked, they set food before him and he ate. 21 Then his servants said to him, "What is this thing that

---

b Ancient scribal tradition: Compare 1 Sam 25.22 note: Heb scorned the enemies of the LORD

Cross references (right margin):

12.5
1 Kings 20.39, 41
12.6
Ex 22.1;
Lk 19.8

12.7
1 Kings 20.42;
1 Sam 16.13

12.9
1 Sam 15.19;
2 Sam 11.15-17, 27

12.10
2 Sam 13.28;
18.14;
1 Kings 2.25
12.11
Deut 28.30;
2 Sam 16.22
12.12
2 Sam 11.4-15;
16.22
12.13
1 Sam 15.24;
2 Sam 24.10;
Prov 28.13;
Mic 7.18
12.14
Isa 52.5;
Rom 2.24
12.15
1 Sam 25.38

12.16
2 Sam 13.31

12.20
Job 1.20

12.5,6 Little did David know at this point that the judgment he had mete out to the man who had committed a far lesser crime would be used against him. He would be charged with guilt by his own words. Those who judge must themselves be free from the same or worse sins.
12.7 Since David had not repented on his own, Nathan pointed the finger at him directly and accused him of the two crimes he had committed. From vv. 14–15 it appears that David had gone at least nine months with guilt hanging over him, for the child had already been born. God gave him plenty of time to repent on his own; but when he did not, God sent Nathan to convict David of his sin, to tell him that God was angry, and to pronounce the penalty which God would exact for his transgression. Since he had killed Uriah with the sword, the sword would not depart from his own house all the days of his life. And

as he had sinned publicly, so would others have sexual relations with David's own wives in broad daylight.
12.13 *I have sinned.* Ps 51 records the lament of David as he repented of his sins of adultery and murder. In it he warns people of all ages about the awfulness of sinning against God.
12.15 The child conceived in sin was struck by God with a grave illness that would lead to its death. The sins of the parents are sometimes visited upon their children, so that the innocent suffer along with the guilty.
12.16 David fasted and prayed for seven days and nights before the child died, hoping that God would have mercy and permit the baby to live. But God declined to do so. When David learned of the death, he stopped praying and began to eat. He was solaced by the knowledge that he had done all he could to repair the damage.

you have done? You fasted and wept for the child while it was alive; but when the child died, you rose and ate food." 22 He said, "While the child was still alive, I fasted and wept; for I said, 'Who knows? The LORD may be gracious to me, and the child may live.' 23 But now he is dead; why should I fast? Can I bring him back again? I shall go to him, but he will not return to me."

4. The birth of Solomon

24 Then David consoled his wife Bathsheba, and went to her, and lay with her; and she bore a son, and he named him Solomon. The LORD loved him, 25 and sent a message by the prophet Nathan; so he named him Jedidiah,c because of the LORD.

5. The victory over the Ammonites

26 Now Joab fought against Rabbah of the Ammonites, and took the royal city. 27 Joab sent messengers to David, and said, "I have fought against Rabbah; moreover, I have taken the water city. 28 Now, then, gather the rest of the people together, and encamp against the city, and take it; or I myself will take the city, and it will be called by my name." 29 So David gathered all the people together and went to Rabbah, and fought against it and took it. 30 He took the crown of Milcomd from his head; the weight of it was a talent of gold, and in it was a precious stone; and it was placed on David's head. He also brought forth the spoil of the city, a very great amount. 31 He brought out the people who were in it, and set them to work with saws and iron picks and iron axes, or sent them to the brickworks. Thus he did to all the cities of the Ammonites. Then David and all the people returned to Jerusalem.

IV. David's troubles (13.1–18.33)

A. Amnon and Tamar

1. The incest of Amnon

13 Some time passed. David's son Absalom had a beautiful sister whose name was Tamar; and David's son Amnon fell in love with her. 2 Amnon was so tormented that he made himself ill because of his sister Tamar, for she was a virgin and it seemed impossible to Amnon to do anything to her. 3 But Amnon had a friend whose name was Jonadab, the son of David's brother Shimeah; and Jonadab was a very crafty man. 4 He said to him, "O son of the king, why are you so haggard morning after morning? Will you not tell me?" Amnon said to him, "I love Tamar, my brother Absalom's sister." 5 Jonadab said to him, "Lie down on your bed, and pretend to be ill; and when your father comes to see you, say to him, 'Let my sister Tamar come and give me something to eat, and

c That is Beloved of the LORD   d Gk See 1 Kings 11.5, 33; Heb their kings

---

Cross-references (left margin):

12.22 Isa 38.1, 5; Jon 3.9
12.23 Gen 37.35; Job 7.8-10
12.24 Mt 1.6; 1 Chr 22.9
12.26 1 Chr 20.1-3
12.30 1 Chr 20.2
13.1 2 Sam 3.2, 3; 1 Chr 3.9
13.3 1 Sam 16.9

12.23 *I shall go to him, but he will not return to me.* David was a firm believer in the great truth of life after death.

12.24,25 David and Bathsheba were blessed by the gift of Solomon. Nathan was sent by God to tell David that this child would succeed David to the throne. Note that God's choice to take David's place was by no means his oldest son.

12.26ff It is not clear when this struggle with the Ammonites took place. It may well have occurred between the time of Uriah's death and the birth of the baby to Bathsheba and David. The Ammonites were defeated and their capital city seized.

13.1ff Subsequent to the birth of Solomon the trou-

bles of David from within his own household began to mount. They were part of the judgment of God on David for his sin. Absalom's beautiful sister, Tamar, was coveted by Amnon, her half-brother, who raped her. From that moment on he expressed hatred for the girl he had abused. She told her story to Absalom, who worked out a plan to kill Amnon in revenge. Two years went by before Absalom's plan bore its evil fruit. As a result of the murder, Absalom fled from Jerusalem, to the sorrow of his father who loved him.

13.2 *for she was a virgin and it seemed impossible to Amnon to do anything to her.* In that day and age, the sexes were kept strictly apart.

prepare the food in my sight, so that I may see it and eat it from her hand.' " 6 So Amnon lay down, and pretended to be ill; and when the king came to see him, Amnon said to the king, "Please let my sister Tamar come and make a couple of cakes in my sight, so that I may eat from her hand."

7 Then David sent home to Tamar, saying, "Go to your brother Amnon's house, and prepare food for him." 8 So Tamar went to her brother Amnon's house, where he was lying down. She took dough, kneaded it, made cakes in his sight, and baked the cakes. 9 Then she took the pan and set them *e* out before him, but he refused to eat. Amnon said, "Send out everyone from me." So everyone went out from him. 10 Then Amnon said to Tamar, "Bring the food into the chamber, so that I may eat from your hand." So Tamar took the cakes she had made, and brought them into the chamber to Amnon her brother. 11 But when she brought them near him to eat, he took hold of her, and said to her, "Come, lie with me, my sister." 12 She answered him, "No, my brother, do not force me; for such a thing is not done in Israel; do not do anything so vile! 13 As for me, where could I carry my shame? And as for you, you would be as one of the scoundrels in Israel. Now therefore, I beg you, speak to the king; for he will not withhold me from you." 14 But he would not listen to her; and being stronger than she, he forced her and lay with her.

15 Then Amnon was seized with a very great loathing for her; indeed, his loathing was even greater than the lust he had felt for her. Amnon said to her, "Get out!" 16 But she said to him, "No, my brother; *f* for this wrong in sending me away is greater than the other that you did to me." But he would not listen to her. 17 He called the young man who served him and said, "Put this woman out of my presence, and bolt the door after her." 18 (Now she was wearing a long robe with sleeves; for this is how the virgin daughters of the king were clothed in earlier times. *g*) So his servant put her out, and bolted the door after her. 19 But Tamar put ashes on her head, and tore the long robe that she was wearing; she put her hand on her head, and went away, crying aloud as she went.

2. Absalom murders Amnon

20 Her brother Absalom said to her, "Has Amnon your brother been with you? Be quiet for now, my sister; he is your brother; do not take this to heart." So Tamar remained, a desolate woman, in her brother Absalom's house. 21 When King David heard of all these things, he became very angry, but he would not punish his son Amnon, because he loved him, for he was his firstborn. *h* 22 But Absalom spoke to Amnon neither good nor bad; for Absalom hated Amnon, because he had raped his sister Tamar.

23 After two full years Absalom had sheepshearers at Baal-hazor, which is near Ephraim, and Absalom invited all the king's sons. 24 Absalom came to the king, and said, "Your servant has sheepshearers; will the king and his servants please go with your servant?" 25 But the king said

13.6
Gen 18.6

13.9
Gen 45.1

13.11
Gen 39.12
13.12
Lev 20.17;
Judg 19.23;
20.6
13.13
Gen 20.12;
Lev 18.9, 11
13.14
Deut 22.25

13.18
Gen 37.3;
Judg 5.30
13.19
1 Sam 4.12;
2 Sam 1.2;
Jer 2.37

13.20
2 Sam 14.24

13.22
Gen 31.24;
Lev 19.17, 18

---

e Heb *and poured*   *f* Cn Compare Gk Vg: Meaning of Heb uncertain   *g* Cn: Heb *were clothed in robes*
h Q Ms Gk: MT lacks *but he would not punish . . . firstborn*

13.12   *for such a thing is not done in Israel; do not do anything so vile!* i.e., you know that fornication is a capital crime in Israel (see Deut 22.25–27).
13.21   David was rightfully angry with Amnon for his sin. He should have punished Amnon, for as father and king he had the right and the power to do so. But he failed to take any concrete action. Eventually Amnon was slain by Absalom, who acted as judge of his brother.
13.23   Two years elapsed before Absalom's plan to slay Amnon matured. It may be that Absalom had more in mind than to avenge the rape of his sister.

Amnon was David's firstborn and technically the one most likely to inherit the throne. Absalom later indicated his own desire to become king.
13.25   King David undoubtedly saw in his son, in plotting the death of Amnon, the very defects he had exhibited in his own life. What Absalom did was the fulfillment of what God had promised because of David's adultery with Bathsheba. God had forgiven David's sin, but he did not take away the temporal consequences. He used wicked Absalom as an instrument for the chastisement of David.

to Absalom, "No, my son, let us not all go, or else we will be burdensome to you." He pressed him, but he would not go but gave him his blessing. 26 Then Absalom said, "If not, please let my brother Amnon go with us." The king said to him, "Why should he go with you?" 27 But Absalom pressed him until he let Amnon and all the king's sons go with him. Absalom made a feast like a king's feast.*i* 28 Then Absalom commanded his servants, "Watch when Amnon's heart is merry with wine, and when I say to you, 'Strike Amnon,' then kill him. Do not be afraid; have I not myself commanded you? Be courageous and valiant." 29 So the servants of Absalom did to Amnon as Absalom had commanded. Then all the king's sons rose, and each mounted his mule and fled.

30 While they were on the way, the report came to David that Absalom had killed all the king's sons, and not one of them was left. 31 The king rose, tore his garments, and lay on the ground; and all his servants who were standing by tore their garments. 32 But Jonadab, the son of David's brother Shimeah, said, "Let not my lord suppose that they have killed all the young men the king's sons; Amnon alone is dead. This has been determined by Absalom from the day Amnon*j* raped his sister Tamar. 33 Now therefore, do not let my lord the king take it to heart, as if all the king's sons were dead; for Amnon alone is dead."

3. Absalom flees to Geshur

34 But Absalom fled. When the young man who kept watch looked up, he saw many people coming from the Horonaim road*k* by the side of the mountain. 35 Jonadab said to the king, "See, the king's sons have come; as your servant said, so it has come about." 36 As soon as he had finished speaking, the king's sons arrived, and raised their voices and wept; and the king and all his servants also wept very bitterly.

37 But Absalom fled, and went to Talmai son of Ammihud, king of Geshur. David mourned for his son day after day. 38 Absalom, having fled to Geshur, stayed there three years. 39 And the heart of*l* the king went out, yearning for Absalom; for he was now consoled over the death of Amnon.

B. Joab secures Absalom's return

1. The woman of Tekoa

14 Now Joab son of Zeruiah perceived that the king's mind was on Absalom. 2 Joab sent to Tekoa and brought from there a wise woman. He said to her, "Pretend to be a mourner; put on mourning

Cross references (left margin):
13.28 — Judg 19.6, 9, 22; 1 Sam 25.36
13.29 — 2 Sam 18.9; 1 Kings 1.33, 38
13.31 — 2 Sam 1.11; 12.16
13.32 — v. 3
13.33 — 2 Sam 19.19
13.34 — vv. 37, 38; 2 Sam 18.24
13.37 — v. 34; 2 Sam 3.3; 14.23, 32
13.39 — 2 Sam 12.19-23
14.1 — 2 Sam 13.39
14.2 — 2 Chr 11.6; 1 Kings 20.35-43; 2 Sam 12.20

i Gk Compare Q Ms: MT lacks *Absalom made a feast like a king's feast*   *j* Heb *he*   *k* Cn Compare Gk: Heb *the road behind him*   *l* Q Ms Gk: MT *And David*

13.31 When David heard it rumored that all his sons had been slain, he tore his garments and lay on the ground, grief-stricken. Jonadab brought the good news that only Amnon was slain. This nephew of David's was a despicable character. He acknowledged that he knew of Absalom's plan to kill Amnon two years before it ever took place. Yet he never warned the king. In other words, Jonadab became an accessory to the crime.

13.34 Absalom fled and went to Geshur for three years. He did not flee to an Israelite city of refuge, for they offered no refuge to a willful murderer. David came short of proper conduct, for instead of loathing Absalom for his murder and executing justice on behalf of the dead Amnon, he yearned for Absalom. Eventually David would bring him home and restore his fortunes, little knowing that Absalom would turn against him and force him to flee from Jerusalem.

14.1 Crafty Joab perceived that David really wanted

to pardon Absalom, bring him home, and reverse his standing. He was aware, too, that the Israelites accepted Absalom as their darling; and he may have feared that if David died while Absalom was far away, a civil war might erupt for the succession. He wanted to have Absalom in Jerusalem as a provision against such a contingency. So he planned a stratagem which would commend him both to David and to Absalom if it succeeded.

14.2–11 Joab solicited the services of an unnamed woman from Tekoa, who came to David with her sad story. She posed as a widow whose one son had been killed by his brother. If sentence were to be executed on the only remaining son she had, the family would become extinct and she would have lost both sons. She pleaded on his behalf for a royal pardon. In v. 11 David rendered a verdict: No avenger of blood should touch the son. She was free to go home and rejoice.

garments, do not anoint yourself with oil, but behave like a woman who has been mourning many days for the dead. 3 Go to the king and speak to him as follows." And Joab put the words into her mouth.

4   When the woman of Tekoa came to the king, she fell on her face to the ground and did obeisance, and said, "Help, O king!" 5 The king asked her, "What is your trouble?" She answered, "Alas, I am a widow; my husband is dead. 6 Your servant had two sons, and they fought with one another in the field; there was no one to part them, and one struck the other and killed him. 7 Now the whole family has risen against your servant. They say, 'Give up the man who struck his brother, so that we may kill him for the life of his brother whom he murdered, even if we destroy the heir as well.' Thus they would quench my one remaining ember, and leave to my husband neither name nor remnant on the face of the earth."

8   Then the king said to the woman, "Go to your house, and I will give orders concerning you." 9 The woman of Tekoa said to the king, "On me be the guilt, my lord the king, and on my father's house; let the king and his throne be guiltless." 10 The king said, "If anyone says anything to you, bring him to me, and he shall never touch you again." 11 Then she said, "Please, may the king keep the LORD your God in mind, so that the avenger of blood may kill no more, and my son not be destroyed." He said, "As the LORD lives, not one hair of your son shall fall to the ground."

2. The plea for Absalom

12   Then the woman said, "Please let your servant speak a word to my lord the king." He said, "Speak." 13 The woman said, "Why then have you planned such a thing against the people of God? For in giving this decision the king convicts himself, inasmuch as the king does not bring his banished one home again. 14 We must all die; we are like water spilled on the ground, which cannot be gathered up. But God will not take away a life; he will devise plans so as not to keep an outcast banished forever from his presence.m 15 Now I have come to say this to my lord the king because the people have made me afraid; your servant thought, 'I will speak to the king; it may be that the king will perform the request of his servant. 16 For the king will hear, and deliver his servant from the hand of the man who would cut both me and my son off from the heritage of God.' 17 Your servant thought, 'The word of my lord the king will set me at rest'; for my lord the king is like the angel of God, discerning good and evil. The LORD your God be with you!"

3. David implicates Joab

18   Then the king answered the woman, "Do not withhold from me anything I ask you." The woman said, "Let my lord the king speak." 19 The king said, "Is the hand of Joab with you in all this?" The woman answered and said, "As surely as you live, my lord the king, one cannot turn right or left from anything that my lord the king has said. For it was your servant Joab who commanded me; it was he who put all these words into the mouth of your servant. 20 In order to change the course of affairs your servant Joab did this. But my lord has wisdom like the wisdom of the angel of God to know all things that are on the earth."

m Meaning of Heb uncertain

14.3
v. 19

14.4
2 Sam 1.2;
2 Kings 6.26-28
14.5
2 Sam 12.1-7

14.7
Num 35.19;
Deut 19.12;
Mt 21.38

14.9
1 Sam 25.24;
Mt 27.25;
1 Kings 2.33
14.11
Num 35.19;
1 Sam 14.45

14.13
2 Sam 12.7;
1 Kings 20.40-42;
2 Sam 13.37,
38
14.14
Job 34.15;
Heb 9.27;
Num 35.15,
25, 28

14.17
v. 20;
2 Sam 19.27

14.19
v. 3

14.20
v. 17;
2 Sam 19.27

14.12   The woman from Tekoa now applied her fictional case to David and Absalom. She asked whether the king who had just rendered a verdict ought not apply the same principle and the same grace to his son Absalom. David smelled a rat and deftly got her to admit that she was acting as an agent for Joab (vv. 19,20).

4. *David brings Absalom back*

21 Then the king said to Joab, "Very well, I grant this; go, bring back
the young man Absalom." 22 Joab prostrated himself with his face to the
ground and did obeisance, and blessed the king; and Joab said, "Today
your servant knows that I have found favor in your sight, my lord the king,
in that the king has granted the request of his servant." 23 So Joab set off,
went to Geshur, and brought Absalom to Jerusalem. 24 The king said,
"Let him go to his own house; he is not to come into my presence." So
Absalom went to his own house, and did not come into the king's presence.

C. *Absalom's revolt*

1. *Absalom's beauty; his children*

25 Now in all Israel there was no one to be praised so much for his
beauty as Absalom; from the sole of his foot to the crown of his head there
was no blemish in him. 26 When he cut the hair of his head (for at the end
of every year he used to cut it; when it was heavy on him, he cut it), he
weighed the hair of his head, two hundred shekels by the king's weight.
27 There were born to Absalom three sons, and one daughter whose name
was Tamar; she was a beautiful woman.

2. *Absalom's pride*

28 So Absalom lived two full years in Jerusalem, without coming into
the king's presence. 29 Then Absalom sent for Joab to send him to the
king; but Joab would not come to him. He sent a second time, but Joab
would not come. 30 Then he said to his servants, "Look, Joab's field is
next to mine, and he has barley there; go and set it on fire." So Absalom's
servants set the field on fire. 31 Then Joab rose and went to Absalom at
his house, and said to him, "Why have your servants set my field on fire?"
32 Absalom answered Joab, "Look, I sent word to you: Come here, that
I may send you to the king with the question, 'Why have I come from
Geshur? It would be better for me to be there still.' Now let me go into
the king's presence; if there is guilt in me, let him kill me!" 33 Then Joab
went to the king and told him; and he summoned Absalom. So he came
to the king and prostrated himself with his face to the ground before the
king; and the king kissed Absalom.

3. *Absalom's revolt*

15 After this Absalom got himself a chariot and horses, and fifty men
to run ahead of him. 2 Absalom used to rise early and stand beside
the road into the gate; and when anyone brought a suit before the king
for judgment, Absalom would call out and say, "From what city are you?"
When the person said, "Your servant is of such and such a tribe in Israel,"
3 Absalom would say, "See, your claims are good and right; but there is

---

14.21 David ordered Joab to bring Absalom back to Jerusalem, with the understanding that he would not lay eyes on Absalom and that his son would live in his own house. This interdict against coming to the king's court was a punishment — showing that David could not countenance so great a criminal or forgive him too easily.
14.27 *three sons.* In 18.18 Absalom says, "I have no son. . . ." One of two possibilities supplies the answer to this apparent discrepancy. Either the monument in 18.18 was set up before any of Absalom's sons were born, or the event occurred after the death of all three sons. In any case, Absalom was left without any male

heirs, and none is mentioned in any of the genealogies.
14.32 Insolent and imperious Absalom demanded to stand before his father and to challenge him to kill him. He well knew that David loved him too much to do that. His conduct was unbecoming of either a son or a subject. But by being reconciled with his father, Absalom felt free to begin executing his secret plans to unseat his father and become king of Israel in his stead.
15.1 Absalom was now fully engaged in his plot to unseat David and seize the throne for himself. A civil war was in the making, with unexpected results for all parties involved.

no one deputed by the king to hear you." [4] Absalom said moreover, "If only I were judge in the land! Then all who had a suit or cause might come to me, and I would give them justice." [5] Whenever people came near to do obeisance to him, he would put out his hand and take hold of them, and kiss them. [6] Thus Absalom did to every Israelite who came to the king for judgment; so Absalom stole the hearts of the people of Israel.

[7] At the end of four[n] years Absalom said to the king, "Please let me go to Hebron and pay the vow that I have made to the LORD. [8] For your servant made a vow while I lived at Geshur in Aram: If the LORD will indeed bring me back to Jerusalem, then I will worship the LORD in Hebron."[o] [9] The king said to him, "Go in peace." So he got up, and went to Hebron. [10] But Absalom sent secret messengers throughout all the tribes of Israel, saying, "As soon as you hear the sound of the trumpet, then shout: Absalom has become king at Hebron!" [11] Two hundred men from Jerusalem went with Absalom; they were invited guests, and they went in their innocence, knowing nothing of the matter. [12] While Absalom was offering the sacrifices, he sent for[p] Ahithophel the Gilonite, David's counselor, from his city Giloh. The conspiracy grew in strength, and the people with Absalom kept increasing.

4. The flight of David

[13] A messenger came to David, saying, "The hearts of the Israelites have gone after Absalom." [14] Then David said to all his officials who were with him at Jerusalem, "Get up! Let us flee, or there will be no escape for us from Absalom. Hurry, or he will soon overtake us, and bring disaster down upon us, and attack the city with the edge of the sword." [15] The king's officials said to the king, "Your servants are ready to do whatever our lord the king decides." [16] So the king left, followed by all his household, except ten concubines whom he left behind to look after the house. [17] The king left, followed by all the people; and they stopped at the last house. [18] All his officials passed by him; and all the Cherethites, and all the Pelethites, and all the six hundred Gittites who had followed him from Gath, passed on before the king.

5. The faithfulness of Ittai the Gittite

[19] Then the king said to Ittai the Gittite, "Why are you also coming with us? Go back, and stay with the king; for you are a foreigner, and also an exile from your home. [20] You came only yesterday, and shall I today make you wander about with us, while I go wherever I can? Go back, and take your kinsfolk with you; and may the LORD show[q] steadfast love and faithfulness to you." [21] But Ittai answered the king, "As the LORD lives, and as my lord the king lives, wherever my lord the king may be, whether for death or for life, there also your servant will be." [22] David said to Ittai, "Go then, march on." So Ittai the Gittite marched on, with all his men and all the little ones who were with him. [23] The whole country wept aloud

n Gk Syr: Heb forty   o Gk Mss: Heb lacks in Hebron   p Or he sent   q Gk Compare 2.6: Heb lacks may the LORD show

Cross-references
15.4 Judg 9.29
15.6 Rom 16.18
15.7ff 2 Sam 3.2, 3
15.8 2 Sam 13.37, 38; Gen 28.20, 21
15.11 1 Sam 9.13; 22.15
15.12 v. 31; Josh 15.51; Ps 3.1
15.13 v. 6; Judg 9.3
15.14 2 Sam 12.11; 19.9
15.16 2 Sam 16.21, 22
15.18 2 Sam 8.18
15.19 2 Sam 18.2
15.20 1 Sam 23.13
15.21 Ruth 1.16, 17

15.7–9 David continued to love Absalom, even though he had used deceit and treachery in influencing the hearts of the people to turn against David.

15.9 *He got up, and went to Hebron.* Hebron was King David's first capital. It was also Absalom's hometown; its people doubtless were very proud of him.

15.13 David learned that Absalom had rebelled against him and, even worse, that the people of Israel were in league with his son. David had loved his son and been indulgent with him, not repaying him for the killing of Amnon. David had to flee from Absalom.

15.19 Ittai the Gittite fled with David, who urged him to return to Jerusalem. Ittai was an alien, an exile, and a new convert. He was made of sterner stuff, however, and refused the suggestion of David. He resolved that whether it be for life or for death, he would remain faithful to the king he served and loved. He is a good model for believers who belong to Jesus, for we should cling to the Savior whether it means life or death. Jesus has given us his promise that nothing will ever cause him to leave us.

as all the people passed by; the king crossed the Wadi Kidron, and all the people moved on toward the wilderness.

6. *The return of the ark*

24 Abiathar came up, and Zadok also, with all the Levites, carrying the ark of the covenant of God. They set down the ark of God, until the people had all passed out of the city. 25 Then the king said to Zadok, "Carry the ark of God back into the city. If I find favor in the eyes of the LORD, he will bring me back and let me see both it and the place where it stays. 26 But if he says, 'I take no pleasure in you,' here I am, let him do to me what seems good to him." 27 The king also said to the priest Zadok, "Look,*r* go back to the city in peace, you and Abiathar,*s* with your two sons, Ahimaaz your son, and Jonathan son of Abiathar. 28 See, I will wait at the fords of the wilderness until word comes from you to inform me." 29 So Zadok and Abiathar carried the ark of God back to Jerusalem, and they remained there.

7. *The treachery of Ahithophel*

30 But David went up the ascent of the Mount of Olives, weeping as he went, with his head covered and walking barefoot; and all the people who were with him covered their heads and went up, weeping as they went. 31 David was told that Ahithophel was among the conspirators with Absalom. And David said, "O LORD, I pray you, turn the counsel of Ahithophel into foolishness."

8. *Hushai returns to Jerusalem*

32 When David came to the summit, where God was worshiped, Hushai the Archite came to meet him with his coat torn and earth on his head. 33 David said to him, "If you go on with me, you will be a burden to me. 34 But if you return to the city and say to Absalom, 'I will be your servant, O king; as I have been your father's servant in time past, so now I will be your servant,' then you will defeat for me the counsel of Ahithophel. 35 The priests Zadok and Abiathar will be with you there. So whatever you hear from the king's house, tell it to the priests Zadok and Abiathar. 36 Their two sons are with them there, Zadok's son Ahimaaz and Abiathar's son Jonathan; and by them you shall report to me everything you hear." 37 So Hushai, David's friend, came into the city, just as Absalom was entering Jerusalem.

9. *Ziba's lie against Mephibosheth*

16 When David had passed a little beyond the summit, Ziba the servant of Mephibosheth*t* met him, with a couple of donkeys saddled, carrying two hundred loaves of bread, one hundred bunches of raisins, one hundred of summer fruits, and one skin of wine. 2 The king

r Gk: Heb *Are you a seer* or *Do you see?*   *s* Cn: Heb lacks *and Abiathar*   *t* Or *Merib-baal*: See 4.4 note

Cross-references (margin)

15.24 2 Sam 8.17; Num 4.15; 1 Sam 22.20
15.25 Ps 43.3; Jer 25.30
15.26 2 Sam 22.20; 1 Kings 10.9; 1 Sam 3.18
15.27 1 Sam 9.6-9; 2 Sam 17.17
15.28 2 Sam 17.16
15.30 Esth 6.12; 2 Sam 19.4; Isa 20.2-4; Ps 126.6
15.31 v. 12; 2 Sam 16.23; 17.14, 23
15.32 Josh 16.2; 2 Sam 1.2
15.33 2 Sam 19.35
15.34 2 Sam 16.19
15.35 2 Sam 17.15, 16
15.36 v. 27; 2 Sam 17.17
15.37 2 Sam 16.16, 17; 1 Chr 27.33
16.1 2 Sam 15.32; 9.2-13
16.2 2 Sam 17.29

15.26 Here is David at his spiritual best. He prayed that God would deliver him from his present plight, in which his own son had seized the throne and precipitated civil war. But he accepted that whatever God did would be good. He waited patiently for either deliverance or the end of his kingship, according to the good pleasure of God. As a servant expecting orders he cried out: "Here I am."
15.30 David wept, went barefoot, and had his head covered. These were expressions of humiliation and sadness over the revolt of a beloved son. Even for the righteous there are moments in life when the face of God seems hidden and his will seems obscure.
15.31ff Tense moments in life bring out the good in some and the bad in others. Ahithophel was a traitor who gave allegiance to Absalom. In the strains and stresses of life, we find out who our friends and enemies are.
16.1 Ziba had been the manager of the estate of Mephibosheth, David's table-guest for years. Ziba was a mean and calculating person who wanted to own, not manage, his master's estate. So he craftily bore false witness by saying that his master had plans to take David's throne. David accepted his statement at face value and gave him the possessions of his master (v. 4). Unfortunately, David did not get Mephibosheth's side of the story before making his decision.

said to Ziba, "Why have you brought these?" Ziba answered, "The donkeys are for the king's household to ride, the bread and summer fruit for the young men to eat, and the wine is for those to drink who faint in the wilderness." 3 The king said, "And where is your master's son?" Ziba said to the king, "He remains in Jerusalem; for he said, 'Today the house of Israel will give me back my grandfather's kingdom.' " 4 Then the king said to Ziba, "All that belonged to Mephibosheth*u* is now yours." Ziba said, "I do obeisance; let me find favor in your sight, my lord the king."

10. Shimei curses David

5 When King David came to Bahurim, a man of the family of the house of Saul came out whose name was Shimei son of Gera; he came out cursing. 6 He threw stones at David and at all the servants of King David; now all the people and all the warriors were on his right and on his left. 7 Shimei shouted while he cursed, "Out! Out! Murderer! Scoundrel! 8 The LORD has avenged on all of you the blood of the house of Saul, in whose place you have reigned; and the LORD has given the kingdom into the hand of your son Absalom. See, disaster has overtaken you; for you are a man of blood."

9 Then Abishai son of Zeruiah said to the king, "Why should this dead dog curse my lord the king? Let me go over and take off his head." 10 But the king said, "What have I to do with you, you sons of Zeruiah? If he is cursing because the LORD has said to him, 'Curse David,' who then shall say, 'Why have you done so?' " 11 David said to Abishai and to all his servants, "My own son seeks my life; how much more now may this Benjaminite! Let him alone, and let him curse; for the LORD has bidden him. 12 It may be that the LORD will look on my distress,*v* and the LORD will repay me with good for this cursing of me today." 13 So David and his men went on the road, while Shimei went along on the hillside opposite him and cursed as he went, throwing stones and flinging dust at him. 14 The king and all the people who were with him arrived weary at the Jordan;*w* and there he refreshed himself.

11. The rule of Absalom in Jerusalem

a. Hushai pretends to serve Absalom

15 Now Absalom and all the Israelites*x* came to Jerusalem; Ahithophel was with him. 16 When Hushai the Archite, David's friend, came to Absalom, Hushai said to Absalom, "Long live the king! Long live the king!" 17 Absalom said to Hushai, "Is this your loyalty to your friend? Why did you not go with your friend?" 18 Hushai said to Absalom, "No; but the one whom the LORD and this people and all the Israelites have chosen, his I will be, and with him I will remain. 19 Moreover, whom should I serve? Should it not be his son? Just as I have served your father, so I will serve you."

b. Ahithophel's counsel about the concubines

20 Then Absalom said to Ahithophel, "Give us your counsel; what shall we do?" 21 Ahithophel said to Absalom, "Go in to your father's

u Or *Merib-baal*: See 4.4 note *v* Gk Vg: Heb *iniquity* *w* Gk: Heb lacks *at the Jordan* *x* Gk: Heb *all the people, the men of Israel*

Cross-references (right column):

16.3 — 2 Sam 9.9, 10; 19.26, 27
16.5 — 2 Sam 3.16-18; 19.16-23; 1 Kings 2.8
16.7 — 2 Sam 12.9
16.8 — 2 Sam 21.1-9
16.9 — 2 Sam 19.21; 9.8; Ex 22.28
16.10 — 2 Sam 19.22; 1 Pet 2.23; 2 Kings 18.25; Rom 9.20
16.11 — 2 Sam 12.11; Gen 45.5
16.12 — Rom 8.28
16.15 — 2 Sam 15.37
16.16 — 2 Sam 15.37
16.17 — 2 Sam 19.25
16.19 — 2 Sam 15.34
16.21 — 2 Sam 15.16; 1 Sam 13.4; 2 Sam 2.7

16.5 Shimei, a descendant of Saul, cursed David, pelted him with stones, and pronounced curses on him. David refused to let his soldiers kill Shimei, humbly accepting the possibility that God was using him for his divine purposes. He prayed that God would have mercy on him and bless him because of the curses he had received that day (v. 12).
16.16 Hushai, an Archite, was King David's friend (1 Chr 27.33). The same verse reports that Ahitho-phel was the king's counselor. The latter, however, was not the king's friend, for he had defected to Absalom. But when David was fleeing, Hushai came out to be with him and support him. David had sent him back to Jerusalem in order to offset the advice of Ahithophel (15.32–37). See notes on 17.1,5 for the rest of the story. Meanwhile, Hushai advised David to escape across the Jordan River (17.15–22).

concubines, the ones he has left to look after the house; and all Israel will hear that you have made yourself odious to your father, and the hands of all who are with you will be strengthened." 22 So they pitched a tent for Absalom upon the roof; and Absalom went in to his father's concubines in the sight of all Israel. 23 Now in those days the counsel that Ahithophel gave was as if one consulted the oracle*y* of God; so all the counsel of Ahithophel was esteemed, both by David and by Absalom.

c. *Ahithophel's counsel to pursue David*

17 Moreover Ahithophel said to Absalom, "Let me choose twelve thousand men, and I will set out and pursue David tonight. 2 I will come upon him while he is weary and discouraged, and throw him into a panic; and all the people who are with him will flee. I will strike down only the king, 3 and I will bring all the people back to you as a bride comes home to her husband. You seek the life of only one man,*z* and all the people will be at peace." 4 The advice pleased Absalom and all the elders of Israel.

d. *Hushai's counsel contrary to Ahithophel's*

5 Then Absalom said, "Call Hushai the Archite also, and let us hear too what he has to say." 6 When Hushai came to Absalom, Absalom said to him, "This is what Ahithophel has said; shall we do as he advises? If not, you tell us." 7 Then Hushai said to Absalom, "This time the counsel that Ahithophel has given is not good." 8 Hushai continued, "You know that your father and his men are warriors, and that they are enraged, like a bear robbed of her cubs in the field. Besides, your father is expert in war; he will not spend the night with the troops. 9 Even now he has hidden himself in one of the pits, or in some other place. And when some of our troops*a* fall at the first attack, whoever hears it will say, 'There has been a slaughter among the troops who follow Absalom.' 10 Then even the valiant warrior, whose heart is like the heart of a lion, will utterly melt with fear; for all Israel knows that your father is a warrior, and that those who are with him are valiant warriors. 11 But my counsel is that all Israel be gathered to you, from Dan to Beer-sheba, like the sand by the sea for multitude, and that you go to battle in person. 12 So we shall come upon him in whatever place he may be found, and we shall light on him as the dew falls on the ground; and he will not survive, nor will any of those with him. 13 If he withdraws into a city, then all Israel will bring ropes to that city, and we shall drag it into the valley, until not even a pebble is to be found there." 14 Absalom and all the men of Israel said, "The counsel of Hushai the Archite is better than the counsel of Ahithophel." For the LORD had ordained to defeat the good counsel of Ahithophel, so that the LORD might bring ruin on Absalom.

y Heb *word*   *z* Gk: Heb *like the return of the whole (is) the man whom you seek*   *a* Gk Mss: Heb *some of them*

Cross references (left margin)

16.22
2 Sam 12.11, 12
16.23
2 Sam 15.12

17.2
2 Sam 16.14; 1 Kings 22.31

17.5
2 Sam 15.32-34

17.8
Hos 13.8; 1 Sam 16.18

17.10
Josh 2.11

17.14
2 Sam 15.31, 34

16.22 This incident of Absalom fulfilled God's promise to David that someone would have sexual relations with his concubines, just as he had had sexual relations with Bathsheba, the wife of his servant Uriah (12.11). Ahithophel suggested that Absalom defile his father's concubines for all Israel to hear about it. But wicked Absalom went farther than that; he wanted all Israel to see, as well as to hear, of his defilement.

17.1 Ahithophel counseled Absalom to pursue David. Since David was on the run and had had no time to gather his own army, it would be simple for Ahithophel and his men to capture and kill David without causing numerous deaths. The people then would transfer their loyalties to Absalom and peace would reign. For some unexplained reason, undoubtedly the providence of God, Absalom wanted to hear also what

Hushai, a strong but secret supporter of David, had to say.

17.5 Hushai cautioned Absalom against haste. He favored gathering a large army to pursue David and urged that Absalom lead those forces in one great battle to settle the issue permanently. (The delay would enable David to gather his own army.) His argument was so cogent that there was unanimous agreement by Absalom and his counselors that Ahithophel's judgment was faulty. They accepted the recommendation of Hushai.

17.14 *the LORD had ordained.* God was at work behind the scenes, preparing the defeat of Absalom. He defeated the counsel of Ahithophel by working in the hearts of Absalom and his counselors to unconsciously go along with the divine will. God is behind all the events of the history of the world.

e. Hushai reports to David

15 Then Hushai said to the priests Zadok and Abiathar, "Thus and so did Ahithophel counsel Absalom and the elders of Israel; and thus and so I have counseled. 16 Therefore send quickly and tell David, 'Do not lodge tonight at the fords of the wilderness, but by all means cross over; otherwise the king and all the people who are with him will be swallowed up.'" 17 Jonathan and Ahimaaz were waiting at En-rogel; a servant-girl used to go and tell them, and they would go and tell King David; for they could not risk being seen entering the city. 18 But a boy saw them, and told Absalom; so both of them went away quickly, and came to the house of a man at Bahurim, who had a well in his courtyard; and they went down into it. 19 The man's wife took a covering, stretched it over the well's mouth, and spread out grain on it; and nothing was known of it. 20 When Absalom's servants came to the woman at the house, they said, "Where are Ahimaaz and Jonathan?" The woman said to them, "They have crossed over the brook[b] of water." And when they had searched and could not find them, they returned to Jerusalem.

21 After they had gone, the men came up out of the well, and went and told King David. They said to David, "Go and cross the water quickly; for thus and so has Ahithophel counseled against you." 22 So David and all the people who were with him set out and crossed the Jordan; by daybreak not one was left who had not crossed the Jordan.

f. Ahithophel commits suicide

23 When Ahithophel saw that his counsel was not followed, he saddled his donkey and went off home to his own city. He set his house in order, and hanged himself; he died and was buried in the tomb of his father.

D. The war between David and Absalom

1. The background

24 Then David came to Mahanaim, while Absalom crossed the Jordan with all the men of Israel. 25 Now Absalom had set Amasa over the army in the place of Joab. Amasa was the son of a man named Ithra the Ishmaelite,[c] who had married Abigal daughter of Nahash, sister of Zeruiah, Joab's mother. 26 The Israelites and Absalom encamped in the land of Gilead.

27 When David came to Mahanaim, Shobi son of Nahash from Rabbah of the Ammonites, and Machir son of Ammiel from Lo-debar, and Barzillai the Gileadite from Rogelim, 28 brought beds, basins, and earthen vessels, wheat, barley, meal, parched grain, beans and lentils,[d] 29 honey and curds, sheep, and cheese from the herd, for David and the people with him to eat; for they said, "The troops are hungry and weary and thirsty in the wilderness."

Marginal cross-references:

17.15 2 Sam 15.35
17.16 2 Sam 15.28
17.17 2 Sam 15.27, 36; Josh 15.7; 18.16
17.18 2 Sam 16.5
17.19 Josh 2.4-6
17.20 Josh 2.3-5; 1 Sam 19.12-17
17.21 vv. 15, 16
17.23 2 Sam 15.12; 2 Kings 20.1; Mt 27.5
17.24 Gen 32.2; 2 Sam 2.8
17.25 2 Sam 19.13; 20.9-12
17.27 2 Sam 10.1, 2; 12.26, 29; 19.31, 32; 1 Kings 2.7
17.29 2 Sam 16.2

---

b Meaning of Heb uncertain   c 1 Chr 2.17: Heb Israelite   d Heb and lentils and parched grain

---

17.15 Hushai recounted to Zadok and Abiathar the priests what he had told Absalom. They were to send the report to David, though Hushai warned that he was not sure Absalom would follow his counsel. The young priests ran into difficulty when a boy reported their presence to Absalom, who sent soldiers to capture them. An unnamed woman assisted them by putting them in a dry well, covering it over with a cloth, and scattering grain around it. She then lied to Absalom's servants, when they demanded to know where Ahimaaz and Jonathan were. When the news

was brought to David, he crossed the Jordan and was safe for the moment.

17.23 Suicide violates the commandment, "You shall not murder" (Ex 20.13). This presupposes a rational and premeditated decision. Mentally imbalanced people who commit suicide are not technically guilty of murder.

17.27 With Absalom now in full pursuit of David, the king met friendly people who supplied him with utensils and food as an act of affection.

2. The battle in the forest of Ephraim

18.1
Ex 18.25;
1 Sam 22.7
18.2
1 Sam 11.11;
2 Sam 15.19

18.3
2 Sam 21.17

18.4
v. 24
18.5
v. 12

18.6
Josh 17.15,
18

18.9
2 Sam 14.26

18.12
v. 5

18.14
2 Sam 14.30

18.16
2 Sam 2.28;
20.22
18.17
Josh 7.26;
8.29;
2 Sam 19.8
18.18
1 Sam 15.12;
Gen 14.17;
2 Sam 14.27

18 Then David mustered the men who were with him, and set over them commanders of thousands and commanders of hundreds. 2 And David divided the army into three groups:*e* one third under the command of Joab, one third under the command of Abishai son of Zeruiah, Joab's brother, and one third under the command of Ittai the Gittite. The king said to the men, "I myself will also go out with you." 3 But the men said, "You shall not go out. For if we flee, they will not care about us. If half of us die, they will not care about us. But you are worth ten thousand of us;*f* therefore it is better that you send us help from the city." 4 The king said to them, "Whatever seems best to you I will do." So the king stood at the side of the gate, while all the army marched out by hundreds and by thousands. 5 The king ordered Joab and Abishai and Ittai, saying, "Deal gently for my sake with the young man Absalom." And all the people heard when the king gave orders to all the commanders concerning Absalom.

6 So the army went out into the field against Israel; and the battle was fought in the forest of Ephraim. 7 The men of Israel were defeated there by the servants of David, and the slaughter there was great on that day, twenty thousand men. 8 The battle spread over the face of all the country; and the forest claimed more victims that day than the sword.

3. Absalom killed by Joab

9 Absalom happened to meet the servants of David. Absalom was riding on his mule, and the mule went under the thick branches of a great oak. His head caught fast in the oak, and he was left hanging*g* between heaven and earth, while the mule that was under him went on. 10 A man saw it, and told Joab, "I saw Absalom hanging in an oak." 11 Joab said to the man who told him, "What, you saw him! Why then did you not strike him there to the ground? I would have been glad to give you ten pieces of silver and a belt." 12 But the man said to Joab, "Even if I felt in my hand the weight of a thousand pieces of silver, I would not raise my hand against the king's son; for in our hearing the king commanded you and Abishai and Ittai, saying: For my sake protect the young man Absalom! 13 On the other hand, if I had dealt treacherously against his life*h* (and there is nothing hidden from the king), then you yourself would have stood aloof." 14 Joab said, "I will not waste time like this with you." He took three spears in his hand, and thrust them into the heart of Absalom, while he was still alive in the oak. 15 And ten young men, Joab's armor-bearers, surrounded Absalom and struck him, and killed him.

16 Then Joab sounded the trumpet, and the troops came back from pursuing Israel, for Joab restrained the troops. 17 They took Absalom, threw him into a great pit in the forest, and raised over him a very great heap of stones. Meanwhile all the Israelites fled to their homes. 18 Now

e Gk: Heb *sent forth the army*   *f* Gk Vg Symmachus: Heb *for now there are ten thousand such as we*   *g* Gk Syr Tg: Heb *was put*   *h* Another reading is *at the risk of my life*

18.1 David assembled his own army under the leadership of three skilled warriors — Joab, Abishai, and Ittai the Gittite. He wished to go with them to battle but they urged him to remain on the sideline. He gave them one warning: "Deal gently for my sake with the young man Absalom" (v. 5).
18.6 The climactic battle in the forest of Ephraim (i.e., in the territory of Gad in the Transjordan) was shaping up — the battle that would end the civil war. In the ensuing battle, Absalom accidentally got caught in the limb of an oak tree and was left hanging, helpless. Joab learned of it and slew Absalom after one of the bystanders refused to do so (vv. 14,15).
18.11 *ten pieces of silver and a belt,* i.e., "I would

have made you an officer." The belt was probably worn by a commissioned officer.
18.14 Joab wasted no time in disposing of Absalom, even though it was an act of disobedience against his commander's orders. Doubtless, David would not have permitted this to happen had he been in the battle himself. Joab performed a good service for the nation, however, for king and country would still have been endangered had he let him live.
18.16 Once Absalom was dead, there was no longer any reason for the war to continue. Joab blew the trumpet and the fighting ceased. David needed only return to Jerusalem and regain the enthusiastic support of those who had favored Absalom.

Absalom in his lifetime had taken and set up for himself a pillar that is in the King's Valley, for he said, "I have no son to keep my name in remembrance"; he called the pillar by his own name. It is called Absalom's Monument to this day.

4. Ahimaaz brings the news to David

19 Then Ahimaaz son of Zadok said, "Let me run, and carry tidings to the king that the Lord has delivered him from the power of his enemies." 20 Joab said to him, "You are not to carry tidings today; you may carry tidings another day, but today you shall not do so, because the king's son is dead." 21 Then Joab said to a Cushite, "Go, tell the king what you have seen." The Cushite bowed before Joab, and ran. 22 Then Ahimaaz son of Zadok said again to Joab, "Come what may, let me also run after the Cushite." And Joab said, "Why will you run, my son, seeing that you have no reward[i] for the tidings?" 23 "Come what may," he said, "I will run." So he said to him, "Run." Then Ahimaaz ran by the way of the Plain, and outran the Cushite.

24 Now David was sitting between the two gates. The sentinel went up to the roof of the gate by the wall, and when he looked up, he saw a man running alone. 25 The sentinel shouted and told the king. The king said, "If he is alone, there are tidings in his mouth." He kept coming, and drew near. 26 Then the sentinel saw another man running; and the sentinel called to the gatekeeper and said, "See, another man running alone!" The king said, "He also is bringing tidings." 27 The sentinel said, "I think the running of the first one is like the running of Ahimaaz son of Zadok." The king said, "He is a good man, and comes with good tidings."

28 Then Ahimaaz cried out to the king, "All is well!" He prostrated himself before the king with his face to the ground, and said, "Blessed be the Lord your God, who has delivered up the men who raised their hand against my lord the king." 29 The king said, "Is it well with the young man Absalom?" Ahimaaz answered, "When Joab sent your servant,[j] I saw a great tumult, but I do not know what it was." 30 The king said, "Turn aside, and stand here." So he turned aside, and stood still.

31 Then the Cushite came; and the Cushite said, "Good tidings for my lord the king! For the Lord has vindicated you this day, delivering you from the power of all who rose up against you." 32 The king said to the Cushite, "Is it well with the young man Absalom?" The Cushite answered, "May the enemies of my lord the king, and all who rise up to do you harm, be like that young man."

33[k] The king was deeply moved, and went up to the chamber over the gate, and wept; and as he went, he said, "O my son Absalom, my son, my son Absalom! Would I had died instead of you, O Absalom, my son, my son!"

18.19
2 Sam 15.36;
v. 31

18.24
2 Sam 19.8;
13.34;
2 Kings 9.17

18.28
2 Sam 14.4;
1 Sam 25.23;
17.46
18.29
v. 22

18.31
v. 19;
Judg 5.31
18.32
1 Sam 25.26

18.33
2 Sam 19.4;
Ex 32.32;
Rom 9.3

---

i Meaning of Heb uncertain　　*j* Heb *the king's servant, your servant*　　*k* Ch 19.1 in Heb

---

18.18 See note on 14.27.
18.19 Ahimaaz, the young priest who had brought David the news of Absalom's intentions, wanted to run to tell David the good news. Joab knew what David's reaction would be and did not want this priest to suffer any consequences (cf. 1.1–15; 4.5–12). So he sent a Cushite to carry the tidings to David.
18.23 Ahimaaz outran the Cushite and arrived first to tell David the results of the civil war. David was expecting good news.
18.29 *I do not know what it was,* i.e., "I don't know what was happening." Ahimaaz apparently was afraid to tell the king what actually had happened (see note on v. 19).

18.32 Ahimaaz wisely deferred to the Cushite to tell David the unhappy fact that Absalom was dead. Since the Cushite had been charged by Joab to do this, David would not take offense at a messenger who was not even an Israelite.
18.33 The death of Absalom brought David to the depths of despair. The king displayed here his humanness and his weaknesses, showing a preference for a graceless son who, although he was witty and handsome, had been abandoned by God and the people. Part of David's grief probably resulted from his awareness that he was responsible for what happened, since it came as God's judgment for his own adultery (12.11,12).

V. *David restored to his kingdom (19.1–20.26)*

A. *Joab rebukes David*

19.1
2 Sam 18.33

19 It was told Joab, "The king is weeping and mourning for Absalom." 2 So the victory that day was turned into mourning for all the troops; for the troops heard that day, "The king is grieving for his son." 3 The troops stole into the city that day as soldiers steal in who are ashamed when they flee in battle. 4 The king covered his face, and the king cried with a loud voice, "O my son Absalom, O Absalom, my son, my son!" 5 Then Joab came into the house to the king, and said, "Today you have covered with shame the faces of all your officers who have saved your life today, and the lives of your sons and your daughters, and the lives of your wives and your concubines, 6 for love of those who hate you and for hatred of those who love you. You have made it clear today that commanders and officers are nothing to you; for I perceive that if Absalom were alive and all of us were dead today, then you would be pleased. 7 So go out at once and speak kindly to your servants; for I swear by the LORD, if you do not go, not a man will stay with you this night; and this will be worse for you than any disaster that has come upon you from your youth until now." 8 Then the king got up and took his seat in the gate. The troops were all told, "See, the king is sitting in the gate"; and all the troops came before the king.

19.4
2 Sam 15.30;
18.33

19.6
Mt 5.46

19.8
2 Sam 15.2;
18.4

B. *David's return to Jerusalem*

1. *The elders invite David back*

19.9
2 Sam 8.1-14;
5.20; 15.14

Meanwhile, all the Israelites had fled to their homes. 9 All the people were disputing throughout all the tribes of Israel, saying, "The king delivered us from the hand of our enemies, and saved us from the hand of the Philistines; and now he has fled out of the land because of Absalom. 10 But Absalom, whom we anointed over us, is dead in battle. Now therefore why do you say nothing about bringing the king back?"

19.12
2 Sam 5.1

11 King David sent this message to the priests Zadok and Abiathar, "Say to the elders of Judah, 'Why should you be the last to bring the king back to his house? The talk of all Israel has come to the king.¹ 12 You are my kin, you are my bone and my flesh; why then should you be the last to bring back the king?' 13 And say to Amasa, 'Are you not my bone and my flesh? So may God do to me, and more, if you are not the commander of my army from now on, in place of Joab.'" 14 Amasa*m* swayed the hearts of all the people of Judah as one, and they sent word to the king, "Return, both you and all your servants." 15 So the king came

19.13
2 Sam 17.25;
1 Kings 19.2;
8.16; vv. 5-7
19.14
Judg 20.1
19.15
Josh 5.9

¹ Gk: Heb *to the king, to his house*   *m* Heb *He*

19.1,2 David was more concerned about the death of Absalom than he was about the nation, the army that won the battle, or the deaths of those who perished to save David and his kingship. This news spread through the army and great dissatisfaction arose. By his actions David was threatening himself and Israel more than Absalom had done by his revolution.

19.5–7 Joab courageously faced King David, pointing out to him the implications of his conduct with regard to the death of Absalom. David's soldiers had saved the kingdom from Absalom. They were worthy of commendation and rightly were offended at being slighted. Joab warned David that unless his attitude changed, he would lose the affection of his people and bring about the very state of affairs which would have come had the revolt of Absalom succeeded. David heeded Joab's rebuke and changed his attitude.

19.9 The ten tribes of Israel were disenchanted and angry that David had not promptly returned to Jerusalem to resume his kingship. David had apparently been waiting for the people of Judah and Israel to call for his return. The ten tribes, who had anointed Absalom to be king over them, now asked why nothing was being done to promote the return of David.

19.11 David sent word to Abiathar and Zadok, asking why the people of Judah had not sent for him to come home to Jerusalem, whereas the ten tribes expressed a desire that he do so. He wanted a vote of confidence from his own tribe of Judah.

19.13 Joab faithfully served King David. But he did not carry out David's request to protect Absalom, for he knew the whole kingdom was at stake. David, probably angry at Joab for this single act of disobedience (see note on 20.4), rashly promised to make Amasa, the leader of Absalom's army, the commander of his army instead of Joab.

back to the Jordan; and Judah came to Gilgal to meet the king and to bring him over the Jordan.

2. *The repentance and forgiveness of Shimei*

16   Shimei son of Gera, the Benjaminite, from Bahurim, hurried to come down with the people of Judah to meet King David; 17 with him were a thousand people from Benjamin. And Ziba, the servant of the house of Saul, with his fifteen sons and his twenty servants, rushed down to the Jordan ahead of the king, 18 while the crossing was taking place,ⁿ to bring over the king's household, and to do his pleasure.

Shimei son of Gera fell down before the king, as he was about to cross the Jordan, 19 and said to the king, "May my lord not hold me guilty or remember how your servant did wrong on the day my lord the king left Jerusalem; may the king not bear it in mind. 20 For your servant knows that I have sinned; therefore, see, I have come this day, the first of all the house of Joseph to come down to meet my lord the king." 21 Abishai son of Zeruiah answered, "Shall not Shimei be put to death for this, because he cursed the LORD's anointed?" 22 But David said, "What have I to do with you, you sons of Zeruiah, that you should today become an adversary to me? Shall anyone be put to death in Israel this day? For do I not know that I am this day king over Israel?" 23 The king said to Shimei, "You shall not die." And the king gave him his oath.

3. *The explanation of Mephibosheth*

24   Mephibosheth° grandson of Saul came down to meet the king; he had not taken care of his feet, or trimmed his beard, or washed his clothes, from the day the king left until the day he came back in safety. 25 When he came from Jerusalem to meet the king, the king said to him, "Why did you not go with me, Mephibosheth?"° 26 He answered, "My lord, O king, my servant deceived me; for your servant said to him, 'Saddle a donkey for me,ᵖ so that I may ride on it and go with the king.' For your servant is lame. 27 He has slandered your servant to my lord the king. But my lord the king is like the angel of God; do therefore what seems good to you. 28 For all my father's house were doomed to death before my lord the king; but you set your servant among those who eat at your table. What further right have I, then, to appeal to the king?" 29 The king said to him, "Why speak any more of your affairs? I have decided: you and Ziba shall divide the land." 30 Mephibosheth° said to the king, "Let him take it all, since my lord the king has arrived home safely."

4. *The blessing by Barzillai*

31   Now Barzillai the Gileadite had come down from Rogelim; he went

ⁿ Cn: Heb *the ford crossed*   ° Or *Merib-baal*: See 4.4 note   ᵖ Gk Syr Vg: Heb *said, 'I will saddle a donkey for myself*

19.18 Crafty Shimei, who had cursed David when he was fleeing from Absalom, now fell at the feet of the king, confessed his sin, and begged for pardon. Abishai wanted to know why Shimei should not be executed for his treason and his gall. But David forgave Shimei and assured him he would not die. We who have cursed God and his Son are also forgiven when we fall at the feet of the Savior and ask for forgiveness. This is what grace is all about, and David displayed that on this occasion.
19.24–30 Being lame, Mephibosheth was unable to join David's army and fight for his king. So he did the next best thing: being melancholy over David's plight and forsaking the amenities of life, he spent his time in mourning as he waited for the return of David. He insisted on David's innocence of the crime attributed to

him by Ziba (see 16.1–4) and received back part of his estate, which he promptly refused in his delight that the king had come back safely. David apparently forgave Ziba either because he feared him or he loved him so much that the penalty was not laid on him according to what the law required (see Deut 19.18,19).
19.31 Faithful Barzillai had helped David when he was in great need by supplying him with provisions (17.27,28) and thus supported him against Absalom and the revolution. He escorted David across the Jordan on his return to Jerusalem. David wanted to reward him by inviting him to be his guest in royal splendor at the court. Barzillai, who was eighty years old, quietly and tactfully declined the honor so that he could return to his own home in quiet-

Cross references (margin):
19.16 — 2 Sam 16.5; 1 Kings 2.8
19.17 — 2 Sam 16.1, 2
19.19 — 1 Sam 22.15; 2 Sam 16.6–8; 13.33
19.20 — 2 Sam 16.5
19.21 — 2 Sam 16.7, 8; Ex 22.28
19.22 — 2 Sam 16.10; 1 Sam 11.13
19.23 — 1 Kings 2.8
19.24 — 2 Sam 9.6-10
19.25 — 2 Sam 16.17
19.26 — 2 Sam 9.3
19.27 — 2 Sam 16.3; 14.17, 20
19.28 — 2 Sam 21.6-9; 9.7, 10, 13
19.31 — 1 Kings 2.7

19.32
1 Sam 17.27

on with the king to the Jordan, to escort him over the Jordan. 32 Barzillai was a very aged man, eighty years old. He had provided the king with food while he stayed at Mahanaim, for he was a very wealthy man. 33 The king said to Barzillai, "Come over with me, and I will provide for you in Jerusalem at my side." 34 But Barzillai said to the king, "How many years have I still to live, that I should go up with the king to Jerusalem? 35 Today

19.35
Ps 90.10;
Isa 5.11, 12

I am eighty years old; can I discern what is pleasant and what is not? Can your servant taste what he eats or what he drinks? Can I still listen to the voice of singing men and singing women? Why then should your servant be an added burden to my lord the king? 36 Your servant will go a little way over the Jordan with the king. Why should the king recompense me

19.37
v. 40;
1 Kings 2.7;
Jer 41.17

with such a reward? 37 Please let your servant return, so that I may die in my own town, near the graves of my father and my mother. But here is your servant Chimham; let him go over with my lord the king; and do for him whatever seems good to you." 38 The king answered, "Chimham shall go over with me, and I will do for him whatever seems good to you; and all that you desire of me I will do for you." 39 Then all the people

19.39
Gen 31.55

crossed over the Jordan, and the king crossed over; the king kissed Barzillai and blessed him, and he returned to his own home. 40 The king went on to Gilgal, and Chimham went on with him; all the people of Judah, and also half the people of Israel, brought the king on his way.

5. Israel's jealousy

19.41
v. 15

41 Then all the people of Israel came to the king, and said to him, "Why have our kindred the people of Judah stolen you away, and brought the king and his household over the Jordan, and all David's men with

19.42
v. 12

him?" 42 All the people of Judah answered the people of Israel, "Because the king is near of kin to us. Why then are you angry over this matter? Have we eaten at all at the king's expense? Or has he given us any gift?"

19.43
1 Kings 11.30,
31

43 But the people of Israel answered the people of Judah, "We have ten shares in the king, and in David also we have more than you. Why then did you despise us? Were we not the first to speak of bringing back our king?" But the words of the people of Judah were fiercer than the words of the people of Israel.

C. Sheba's revolt

1. Sheba calls for rebellion

20.1
2 Sam 19.43;
1 Kings 12.16;
2 Chr 10.16

20 Now a scoundrel named Sheba son of Bichri, a Benjaminite, happened to be there. He sounded the trumpet and cried out, "We have no portion in David,
   no share in the son of Jesse!
   Everyone to your tents, O Israel!"
2 So all the people of Israel withdrew from David and followed Sheba son of Bichri; but the people of Judah followed their king steadfastly from the Jordan to Jerusalem.

20.3
2 Sam 15.16;
16.21, 22

3 David came to his house at Jerusalem; and the king took the ten concubines whom he had left to look after the house, and put them in a

---

ness and peace.
19.37 *Chimham.* Chimham was likely Barzillai's son.
19.41ff David returned home to a divided people. The ten tribes had been overlooked as the people of Judah brought David home. They were angry for not having been invited to participate and said so with some vehemence. Explanations were offered to the effect that David came from the tribe of Judah and was their own kin. The last line is clear enough: "The words of the people of Judah were fiercer than the

words of the people of Israel." The Judeans lacked humility, trusted in force, and won the shouting match.
20.1 Sheba used the disaffection between the north and the south (19.41–43) to gain the support of the northerners against David and Judah.
20.3 David's ten concubines, who had been left behind when he fled, were rendered unclean by their defilement by Absalom. Those whom Absalom had sinfully taken for pleasure and politics now had to be put away for life.

house under guard, and provided for them, but did not go in to them. So they were shut up until the day of their death, living as if in widowhood.

2. Amasa slain by Joab

4 Then the king said to Amasa, "Call the men of Judah together to me within three days, and be here yourself." 5 So Amasa went to summon Judah; but he delayed beyond the set time that had been appointed him. 6 David said to Abishai, "Now Sheba son of Bichri will do us more harm than Absalom; take your lord's servants and pursue him, or he will find fortified cities for himself, and escape from us." 7 Joab's men went out after him, along with the Cherethites, the Pelethites, and all the warriors; they went out from Jerusalem to pursue Sheba son of Bichri. 8 When they were at the large stone that is in Gibeon, Amasa came to meet them. Now Joab was wearing a soldier's garment and over it was a belt with a sword in its sheath fastened at his waist; as he went forward it fell out. 9 Joab said to Amasa, "Is it well with you, my brother?" And Joab took Amasa by the beard with his right hand to kiss him. 10 But Amasa did not notice the sword in Joab's hand; Joab struck him in the belly so that his entrails poured out on the ground, and he died. He did not strike a second blow.

3. Joab pursues Sheba

Then Joab and his brother Abishai pursued Sheba son of Bichri. 11 And one of Joab's men took his stand by Amasa, and said, "Whoever favors Joab, and whoever is for David, let him follow Joab." 12 Amasa lay wallowing in his blood on the highway, and the man saw that all the people were stopping. Since he saw that all who came by him were stopping, he carried Amasa from the highway into a field, and threw a garment over him. 13 Once he was removed from the highway, all the people went on after Joab to pursue Sheba son of Bichri.

4. The killing of Sheba

14 Sheba[q] passed through all the tribes of Israel to Abel of Beth-maacah;[s] and all the Bichrites[r] assembled, and followed him inside. 15 Joab's forces[t] came and besieged him in Abel of Beth-maacah; they threw up a siege ramp against the city, and it stood against the rampart. Joab's forces were battering the wall to break it down. 16 Then a wise woman called from the city, "Listen! Listen! Tell Joab, 'Come here, I want to speak to you.'" 17 He came near her; and the woman said, "Are you Joab?" He answered, "I am." Then she said to him, "Listen to the words of your servant." He answered, "I am listening." 18 Then she said, "They used to say in the old days, 'Let them inquire at Abel'; and so they would settle a matter. 19 I am one of those who are peaceable and faithful in Israel; you seek to destroy a city that is a mother in Israel; why will you swallow up the heritage of the Lord?" 20 Joab answered, "Far be it from

Cross references (right margin):

20.4
2 Sam 19.13

20.6
2 Sam 11.11;
1 Kings 1.33
20.7
2 Sam 8.18;
1 Kings 1.38;
2 Sam 15.18

20.9
Mt 26.49

20.10
2 Sam 2.23;
3.27;
1 Kings 2.5

20.15
1 Kings 15.20;
2 Kings 19.32
20.16
2 Sam 14.2

20.19
1 Sam 26.19;
2 Sam 21.3

q Heb *He*   r Compare 20.15: Heb *and Beth-maacah*   s Compare Gk Vg: Heb *Berites*   t Heb *They*

20.4 Amasa, the commander of Absalom's army, was Joab's cousin. Following the defeat of Absalom, King David pardoned Amasa, then appointed him as captain of his army instead of Joab. Some have suggested that Joab had lost favor with the king when he deliberately disobeyed David's instructions to deal gently with Absalom. When Sheba revolted, David commanded Amasa to call up the army in three days. When he failed to fulfill the deadline, Abishai was called upon to suppress the revolt. At Gibeon, Amasa's army joined that of Abishai. Joab slew Amasa (v. 10) and then led the combined forces to victory over Sheba.
20.14 *Abel of Beth-maacah*. Abel was located in the most northern part of the country, an area populated

by the tribe of Naphtali.
20.16 Joab and his army laid siege to Abel of Beth-maacah and were trying to batter down the wall. Apparently the people of the city were either afraid of Sheba or unconcerned for the safety of their community, for they did nothing. An unnamed, discreet, and wise woman played the role of mediator by going to Joab and pleading for the city. When Joab declared that his only interest was to capture Sheba, she agreed to throw the head of the rebel over the wall of the city if Joab would leave the city and its inhabitants free from war. He consented. Thereupon Sheba was slain and his head dropped over the wall. The revolt ended and Joab, who had slain Amasa, was once again in full control of the military.

20.21
v. 2

me, far be it, that I should swallow up or destroy! 21 That is not the case! But a man of the hill country of Ephraim, called Sheba son of Bichri, has lifted up his hand against King David; give him up alone, and I will withdraw from the city." The woman said to Joab, "His head shall be

20.22
Eccl 9.13-16;
v. 1

thrown over the wall to you." 22 Then the woman went to all the people with her wise plan. And they cut off the head of Sheba son of Bichri, and threw it out to Joab. So he blew the trumpet, and they dispersed from the city, and all went to their homes, while Joab returned to Jerusalem to the king.

20.23
2 Sam 8.16-18

23 Now Joab was in command of all the army of Israel;[u] Benaiah son of Jehoiada was in command of the Cherethites and the Pelethites; 24 Adoram was in charge of the forced labor; Jehoshaphat son of Ahilud was the

20.25
2 Sam 8.17
20.26
2 Sam 23.38

recorder; 25 Sheva was secretary; Zadok and Abiathar were priests; 26 and Ira the Jairite was also David's priest.

VI. The later years of David's kingdom (21.1–24.25)

A. The famine

1. The bloodguilt of Saul

21.2
Josh 9.3,
15-17

21 Now there was a famine in the days of David for three years, year after year; and David inquired of the LORD. The LORD said, "There is bloodguilt on Saul and on his house, because he put the Gibeonites to death." 2 So the king called the Gibeonites and spoke to them. (Now the Gibeonites were not of the people of Israel, but of the remnant of the Amorites; although the people of Israel had sworn to spare them, Saul had tried to wipe them out in his zeal for the people of Israel and Judah.)

21.3
2 Sam 20.19
21.4
Num 35.31,
32

3 David said to the Gibeonites, "What shall I do for you? How shall I make expiation, that you may bless the heritage of the LORD?" 4 The Gibeonites said to him, "It is not a matter of silver or gold between us and Saul or his house; neither is it for us to put anyone to death in Israel." He said,

21.5
1 Sam 10.24,
26

"What do you say that I should do for you?" 5 They said to the king, "The man who consumed us and planned to destroy us, so that we should have no place in all the territory of Israel— 6 let seven of his sons be handed over to us, and we will impale them before the LORD at Gibeon on the mountain of the LORD."[v] The king said, "I will hand them over."

2. The hanging of seven of Saul's sons

21.7
2 Sam 4.4;
9.10;
1 Sam 18.3;
20.8, 15;
23.18
21.8
2 Sam 3.7

7 But the king spared Mephibosheth,[w] the son of Saul's son Jonathan, because of the oath of the LORD that was between them, between David and Jonathan son of Saul. 8 The king took the two sons of Rizpah daughter of Aiah, whom she bore to Saul, Armoni and Mephibosheth;[w] and the five sons of Merab[x] daughter of Saul, whom she bore to Adriel son of Barzillai the Meholathite; 9 he gave them into the hands of the Gibeonites, and they impaled them on the mountain before the LORD. The seven of

---

[u] Cn: Heb *Joab to all the army, Israel*   [v] Cn Compare Gk and 21.9: Heb *at Gibeah of Saul, the chosen of the LORD*   [w] Or *Merib-baal*: See 4.4 note   [x] Two Heb Mss Syr Compare Gk: MT *Michal*

20.23 *the Cherethites and the Pelethites*, i.e., the king's bodyguard.
21.1 God had promised Israel plentiful harvests and adequate rain. Yet here drought and famine occurred for three consecutive years. We wonder why David did not ask God about the reason for the famine until the end of the third year. When he finally did so, God told him that Saul had violated the agreement with the Gibeonites, and even though the consequences were delayed, they arrived at last. When the proper steps were taken, the famine ceased. Famines are sometimes sent by God because of transgressions. We

should never presume that famines are accidental until we have sought God to discover the reason for them and vowed to correct the problem if there is one.
21.7ff David saved the life of Mephibosheth so that while he avenged the breaking of the oath to the Gibeonites, he would not break his oath to Jonathan and his son. He turned over seven descendants of Saul, who were hung by the Gibeonites before the Lord God. Hanging was the symbol of being cursed by God. Through this the guilt of the house of Saul was expiated for the breach of the oath with the Gibeonites.

them perished together. They were put to death in the first days of harvest, at the beginning of barley harvest.

3. David's burial of Saul and Jonathan and the seven sons

10   Then Rizpah the daughter of Aiah took sackcloth, and spread it on a rock for herself, from the beginning of harvest until rain fell on them from the heavens; she did not allow the birds of the air to come on the bodies[y] by day, or the wild animals by night. 11 When David was told what Rizpah daughter of Aiah, the concubine of Saul, had done, 12 David went and took the bones of Saul and the bones of his son Jonathan from the people of Jabesh-gilead, who had stolen them from the public square of Beth-shan, where the Philistines had hung them up, on the day the Philistines killed Saul on Gilboa. 13 He brought up from there the bones of Saul and the bones of his son Jonathan; and they gathered the bones of those who had been impaled. 14 They buried the bones of Saul and of his son Jonathan in the land of Benjamin in Zela, in the tomb of his father Kish; they did all that the king commanded. After that, God heeded supplications for the land.

B. Victories over the Philistines

15   The Philistines went to war again with Israel, and David went down together with his servants. They fought against the Philistines, and David grew weary. 16 Ishbi-benob, one of the descendants of the giants, whose spear weighed three hundred shekels of bronze, and who was fitted out with new weapons,[z] said he would kill David. 17 But Abishai son of Zeruiah came to his aid, and attacked the Philistine and killed him. Then David's men swore to him, "You shall not go out with us to battle any longer, so that you do not quench the lamp of Israel."

18   After this a battle took place with the Philistines, at Gob; then Sibbecai the Hushathite killed Saph, who was one of the descendants of the giants. 19 Then there was another battle with the Philistines at Gob; and Elhanan son of Jaare-oregim, the Bethlehemite, killed Goliath the Gittite, the shaft of whose spear was like a weaver's beam. 20 There was again war at Gath, where there was a man of great size, who had six fingers on each hand, and six toes on each foot, twenty-four in number; he too was descended from the giants. 21 When he taunted Israel, Jonathan son of David's brother Shimei, killed him. 22 These four were descended from the giants in Gath; they fell by the hands of David and his servants.

C. David's psalm of praise

22   David spoke to the LORD the words of this song on the day when the LORD delivered him from the hand of all his enemies, and from the hand of Saul. 2 He said:
>   The LORD is my rock, my fortress, and my deliverer,
> 3   my God, my rock, in whom I take refuge,
>   my shield and the horn of my salvation,
>   my stronghold and my refuge,
>   my savior; you save me from violence.
> 4 I call upon the LORD, who is worthy to be praised,
>   and I am saved from my enemies.

y Heb *them*   z Heb *was belted anew*

21.10
v. 8;
Deut 21.23;
1 Sam 17.44,
46

21.12
1 Sam 31.10-13

21.14
Josh 18.28;
7.26;
2 Sam 24.25

21.17
2 Sam 18.3;
6.17

21.18
1 Chr 20.4;
11.29
21.19
1 Chr 20.5
21.20
1 Chr 20.6

21.21
see
1 Sam 16.9
21.22
1 Chr 20.8

22.1
Ex 15.1;
Judg 5.1;
Ps 18.2-50
22.2
Deut 32.4;
Ps 31.3; 71.3;
91.2; 144.2
22.3
Heb 2.13;
Gen 15.1;
Lk 1.69;
Ps 9.9; 14.6;
Jer 16.19
22.4
Ps 48.1

22.1 David sang this glorious song *on the day when the LORD delivered him.* He did not wait until long after the deliverance to praise God. He expressed what he declared in Ps 34.19. "Many are the afflictions of the righteous; but the LORD rescues them from them all."

This powerful praise psalm is replete with phrases that speak of God's protection of his people, in phrases such as "my fortress," "my rock," "my shield," and "the horn of my salvation." This psalm is also recorded as Ps 18.

22.5
Ps 93.4;
Jon 2.3;
Ps 69.14, 15
22.6
Ps 116.3

22.7
Ps 116.4;
120.1; 34.6,
15

22.8
Judg 5.4;
Ps 77.18;
Job 26.11
22.9
Ps 97.3;
Heb 12.29
22.10
Ex 19.16;
1 Kings 8.12;
Ps 97.2
22.11
Ps 104.3
22.12
Ps 97.2
22.13
v. 9
22.14
1 Sam 2.10

22.16
Hab 3.11

22.17
Ps 144.7;
32.6

22.19
Ps 23.4
22.20
Ps 31.8; 22.8

22.21
1 Kings 8.32;
Ps 24.4
22.22
Gen 18.19;
Ps 128.1
22.23
Deut 6.6-9

5 For the waves of death encompassed me,
 the torrents of perdition assailed me;
6 the cords of Sheol entangled me,
 the snares of death confronted me.

7 In my distress I called upon the LORD;
 to my God I called.
 From his temple he heard my voice,
 and my cry came to his ears.

8 Then the earth reeled and rocked;
 the foundations of the heavens trembled
 and quaked, because he was angry.
9 Smoke went up from his nostrils,
 and devouring fire from his mouth;
 glowing coals flamed forth from him.
10 He bowed the heavens, and came down;
 thick darkness was under his feet.
11 He rode on a cherub, and flew;
 he was seen upon the wings of the wind.
12 He made darkness around him a canopy,
 thick clouds, a gathering of water.
13 Out of the brightness before him
 coals of fire flamed forth.
14 The LORD thundered from heaven;
 the Most High uttered his voice.
15 He sent out arrows, and scattered them
 —lightning, and routed them.
16 Then the channels of the sea were seen,
 the foundations of the world were laid bare
 at the rebuke of the LORD,
 at the blast of the breath of his nostrils.

17 He reached from on high, he took me,
 he drew me out of mighty waters.
18 He delivered me from my strong enemy,
 from those who hated me;
 for they were too mighty for me.
19 They came upon me in the day of my calamity,
 but the LORD was my stay.
20 He brought me out into a broad place;
 he delivered me, because he delighted in me.

21 The LORD rewarded me according to my righteousness;
 according to the cleanness of my hands he recompensed me.
22 For I have kept the ways of the LORD,
 and have not wickedly departed from my God.
23 For all his ordinances were before me,
 and from his statutes I did not turn aside.

22.7 David's deliverance was an answer to prayer. Distress is always an occasion for us to seek the face of God and plead for help.
22.8ff In response to David's prayers, God manifested himself and his power in great and unusual ways. God always stands ready to help and protect those who know him and love him. No one can stand up against God when he is angry on behalf of his people.
22.20 God's favor and deliverance for David did not come from a general concept of his providence.

Rather, it sprang from his covenant love, which guarantees the promise of God to deliver all those who trust in him.
22.22–25 David insisted he has followed the commandments of God and thus stood righteous in his sight. He did not, in fact, always keep those commandments. But he did repent of and confess his sin, and he was cleansed from his iniquity. We, like David, do sin, and like him we can repent, confess, and be cleansed so that our relationship may remain unimpaired.

24 I was blameless before him,
    and I kept myself from guilt.
25 Therefore the LORD has recompensed me according to my
       righteousness,
    according to my cleanness in his sight.

26 With the loyal you show yourself loyal;
    with the blameless you show yourself blameless;
27 with the pure you show yourself pure,
    and with the crooked you show yourself perverse.
28 You deliver a humble people,
    but your eyes are upon the haughty to bring them down.
29 Indeed, you are my lamp, O LORD,
    the LORD lightens my darkness.
30 By you I can crush a troop,
    and by my God I can leap over a wall.
31 This God — his way is perfect;
    the promise of the LORD proves true;
    he is a shield for all who take refuge in him.

32 For who is God, but the LORD?
    And who is a rock, except our God?
33 The God who has girded me with strength*a*
    has opened wide my path.*b*
34 He made my*c* feet like the feet of deer,
    and set me secure on the heights.
35 He trains my hands for war,
    so that my arms can bend a bow of bronze.
36 You have given me the shield of your salvation,
    and your help*d* has made me great.
37 You have made me stride freely,
    and my feet do not slip;
38 I pursued my enemies and destroyed them,
    and did not turn back until they were consumed.
39 I consumed them; I struck them down, so that they did not
       rise;
    they fell under my feet.
40 For you girded me with strength for the battle;
    you made my assailants sink under me.
41 You made my enemies turn their backs to me,
    those who hated me, and I destroyed them.
42 They looked, but there was no one to save them;
    they cried to the LORD, but he did not answer them.
43 I beat them fine like the dust of the earth,
    I crushed them and stamped them down like the mire of the
       streets.

44 You delivered me from strife with the peoples;*e*
    you kept me as the head of the nations;
    people whom I had not known served me.
45 Foreigners came cringing to me;
    as soon as they heard of me, they obeyed me.

Cross references (right column):

22.24 Gen 7.1; 17.1;
22.25 Eph 1.4; v. 21
22.26 Mt 5.7
22.27 Lev 26.23
22.28 Ps 72.12; Isa 2.11, 12, 17
22.29 Ps 27.1
22.31 Deut 32.4; Mt 5.48; Ps 12.6; v. 3
22.32 1 Sam 2.2; v. 2
22.33 Ps 27.1; Ps 101.2, 6
22.34 Hab 3.19; Deut 32.13
22.35 Ps 144.1
22.37 Prov 4.12
22.39 Mal 4.3
22.40 Ps 44.5
22.41 Ex 23.27; Josh 10.24
22.42 Ps 50.22; 1 Sam 28.6
22.43 Ps 18.42; Isa 10;6
22.44 2 Sam 3.1; Deut 28.13; Isa 55.5
22.45 Ps 66.3

---

a Q Ms Gk Syr Vg Compare Ps 18.32: MT *God is my strong refuge*   *b* Meaning of Heb uncertain
c Another reading is *his*   *d* Q Ms: MT *your answering*   *e* Gk: Heb *from strife with my people*

22.30 With God's help David could do anything that he needed to do. With the strength of Christ, we can too (Phil 4.13).
22.32 There is no God beside our God; he is a rock or foundation that cannot be shaken. Those who find their rest on that foundation may quake on the rock but the rock will never quake under them.

22.46 Mic 7.17	46 Foreigners lost heart, and came trembling out of their strongholds.
22.47 Ps 89.26	47 The LORD lives! Blessed be my rock, and exalted be my God, the rock of my salvation,
22.48 Ps 94.1; 144.2 **22.49** Ps 44.5; 140.1	48 the God who gave me vengeance and brought down peoples under me, 49 who brought me out from my enemies; you exalted me above my adversaries, you delivered me from the violent.
22.50 Rom 15.9	50 For this I will extol you, O LORD, among the nations, and sing praises to your name.
22.51 Ps 144.10; 89.20, 29; 2 Sam 7.12-16	51 He is a tower of salvation for his king, and shows steadfast love to his anointed, to David and his descendants forever.

D. David's testament

23.1 2 Sam 7.8, 9; Ps 78.70; 89.27; 1 Sam 16.12, 13; Ps 89.20	23 Now these are the last words of David: The oracle of David, son of Jesse, the oracle of the man whom God exalted,^{f} the anointed of the God of Jacob, the favorite of the Strong One of Israel:
23.2 2 Pet 1.21	2 The spirit of the LORD speaks through me, his word is upon my tongue.
23.3 Deut 32.4; 2 Sam 22.2, 32; Ex 18.21; 2 Chr 19.7, 9 **23.4** Judg 5.31; Ps 89.36	3 The God of Israel has spoken, the Rock of Israel has said to me: One who rules over people justly, ruling in the fear of God, 4 is like the light of morning, like the sun rising on a cloudless morning, gleaming from the rain on the grassy land.
23.5 Ps 89.29; Isa 55.3	5 Is not my house like this with God? For he has made with me an everlasting covenant, ordered in all things and secure. Will he not cause to prosper all my help and my desire?
23.6 Mt 13.42	6 But the godless are^g all like thorns that are thrown away; for they cannot be picked up with the hand; 7 to touch them one uses an iron bar or the shaft of a spear. And they are entirely consumed in fire on the spot. ^{h}

E. The deeds of David's mighty men

8 These are the names of the warriors whom David had: Josheb-

^{f} Q Ms: MT *who was raised on high* ^{g} Heb *But worthlessness* ^{h} Heb *in sitting*

22.51 The promise of God is to David and to his offspring forever. This has messianic implications, pointing to Jesus Christ, whose throne and kingdom will continue to the end. By the eye of faith, David sees this. Thus, all his joys and all his hopes find their fulfillment, as ours should, in our great Redeemer.
23.1–3 *The God of Israel has spoken.* The phrase "Thus says the LORD" or its equivalent occurs more than two thousand times in the O.T. Thus the proph-

ets attest that what they speak is the word of God. David identified the Spirit as speaking through him and said, *his word is upon my tongue.* He also claimed that *the Rock of Israel has said to me*, and then stated what God did say.
23.8 *Josheb-basshebeth* is said to have slain eight hundred enemies at one time. In 1 Chr 11.11 Jashobeam (the same person with a different name) is said to have slain three hundred. In Hebrew, the first

basshebeth a Tahchemonite; he was chief of the Three;[i] he wielded his spear[j] against eight hundred whom he killed at one time.

9 Next to him among the three warriors was Eleazar son of Dodo son of Ahohi. He was with David when they defied the Philistines who were gathered there for battle. The Israelites withdrew, 10 but he stood his ground. He struck down the Philistines until his arm grew weary, though his hand clung to the sword. The LORD brought about a great victory that day. Then the people came back to him — but only to strip the dead.

11 Next to him was Shammah son of Agee, the Hararite. The Philistines gathered together at Lehi, where there was a plot of ground full of lentils; and the army fled from the Philistines. 12 But he took his stand in the middle of the plot, defended it, and killed the Philistines; and the LORD brought about a great victory.

13 Towards the beginning of harvest three of the thirty[k] chiefs went down to join David at the cave of Adullam, while a band of Philistines was encamped in the valley of Rephaim. 14 David was then in the stronghold; and the garrison of the Philistines was then at Bethlehem. 15 David said longingly, "O that someone would give me water to drink from the well of Bethlehem that is by the gate!" 16 Then the three warriors broke through the camp of the Philistines, drew water from the well of Bethlehem that was by the gate, and brought it to David. But he would not drink of it; he poured it out to the LORD, 17 for he said, "The LORD forbid that I should do this. Can I drink the blood of the men who went at the risk of their lives?" Therefore he would not drink it. The three warriors did these things.

18 Now Abishai son of Zeruiah, the brother of Joab, was chief of the Thirty.[l] With his spear he fought against three hundred men and killed them, and won a name beside the Three. 19 He was the most renowned of the Thirty,[m] and became their commander; but he did not attain to the Three.

20 Benaiah son of Jehoiada was a valiant warrior[n] from Kabzeel, a doer of great deeds; he struck down two sons of Ariel[o] of Moab. He also went down and killed a lion in a pit on a day when snow had fallen. 21 And he killed an Egyptian, a handsome man. The Egyptian had a spear in his hand; but Benaiah went against him with a staff, snatched the spear out of the Egyptian's hand, and killed him with his own spear. 22 Such were the things Benaiah son of Jehoiada did, and won a name beside the three warriors. 23 He was renowned among the Thirty, but he did not attain to the Three. And David put him in charge of his bodyguard.

24 Among the Thirty were Asahel brother of Joab; Elhanan son of Dodo of Bethlehem; 25 Shammah of Harod; Elika of Harod; 26 Helez the Paltite; Ira son of Ikkesh of Tekoa; 27 Abiezer of Anathoth; Mebunnai the

Marginal references:
23.9 1 Chr 27.4
23.10 1 Chr 11.12-14
23.11 1 Chr 11.27
23.13 1 Sam 22.1; 2 Sam 5.18
23.14 1 Sam 22.4, 5
23.17 Lev 17.10
23.18 2 Sam 10.10, 14; 1 Chr 11.20
23.20 2 Sam 8.18; 20.33; Josh 15.21
23.23 2 Sam 8.18; 20.23
23.24 2 Sam 2.18
23.25 1 Chr 11.27

i Gk Vg Compare 1 Chr 11.11: Meaning of Heb uncertain   j 1 Chr 11.11: Meaning of Heb uncertain   k Heb adds head   l Two Heb Mss Syr: MT Three   m Syr Compare 1 Chr 11.25: Heb Was he the most renowned of the Three?   n Another reading is the son of Ish-hai   o Gk: Heb lacks sons of

---

letter of the words for three and eight is the same. This, then, is a copyist's error.
23.9–12 Eleazar and Shammah along with Josheb-basshebeth are said to have been the three mightiest of David's soldiers. Only here and in 1 Chr 11 are these men mentioned and singled out as great warriors. God has not chosen to give us a detailed account of all the glories of David's reign, nor has he told us a great deal about some of its greatest heroes. In eternity we will discover that multitudes of unnamed saints through the ages have done exploits in God's name that remain unknown for now.
23.13–17 Of the three mentioned for their devotion to David when he was in flight and who risked their lives to bring him water, only two are named in the Scriptures: Abishai and Benaiah. Their exceptional bravery for labor beyond the call of duty serves as an example for us to perform works above what we are commanded to do.
23.18–23 Abishai and Benaiah are here mentioned for other acts of bravery by which they distinguished themselves. There are degrees of greatness, and while these two did not match the first three mighty men, they were worthy of acclaim. We cannot all be Luthers or Calvins, but we can all do notable works for God.
23.24–39 The remainder of the Thirty great soldiers are listed here. Perhaps the one of special interest is Uriah the Hittite, who was indirectly murdered by David (see ch. 11). The number thirty-seven indicates that the "Thirty" comprised an elite group to which successors were added for those who died.

Hushathite; 28 Zalmon the Ahohite; Maharai of Netophah; 29 Heleb son of Baanah of Netophah; Ittai son of Ribai of Gibeah of the Benjaminites; 30 Benaiah of Pirathon; Hiddai of the torrents of Gaash; 31 Abi-albon the Arbathite; Azmaveth of Bahurim; 32 Eliahba of Shaalbon; the sons of Jashen: Jonathan 33 son of *p* Shammah the Hararite; Ahiam son of Sharar the Hararite; 34 Eliphelet son of Ahasbai of Maacah; Eliam son of Ahithophel the Gilonite; 35 Hezro *q* of Carmel; Paarai the Arbite; 36 Igal son of Nathan of Zobah; Bani the Gadite; 37 Zelek the Ammonite; Naharai of Beeroth, the armor-bearer of Joab son of Zeruiah; 38 Ira the Ithrite; Gareb the Ithrite; 39 Uriah the Hittite — thirty-seven in all.

F. David's census and punishment

1. The numbering of the people

24 Again the anger of the LORD was kindled against Israel, and he incited David against them, saying, "Go, count the people of Israel and Judah." 2 So the king said to Joab and the commanders of the army,*r* who were with him, "Go through all the tribes of Israel, from Dan to Beer-sheba, and take a census of the people, so that I may know how many there are." 3 But Joab said to the king, "May the LORD your God increase the number of the people a hundredfold, while the eyes of my lord the king can still see it! But why does my lord the king want to do this?" 4 But the king's word prevailed against Joab and the commanders of the army. So Joab and the commanders of the army went out from the presence of the king to take a census of the people of Israel. 5 They crossed the Jordan, and began from *s* Aroer and from the city that is in the middle of the valley, toward Gad and on to Jazer. 6 Then they came to Gilead, and to Kadesh in the land of the Hittites; *t* and they came to Dan, and from Dan *u* they went around to Sidon, 7 and came to the fortress of Tyre and to all the cities of the Hivites and Canaanites; and they went out to the Negeb of Judah at Beer-sheba. 8 So when they had gone through all the land, they came back to Jerusalem at the end of nine months and twenty days. 9 Joab reported to the king the number of those who had been recorded: in Israel there were eight hundred thousand soldiers able to draw the sword, and those of Judah were five hundred thousand.

2. David's choice of punishment

10 But afterward, David was stricken to the heart because he had numbered the people. David said to the LORD, "I have sinned greatly in what I have done. But now, O LORD, I pray you, take away the guilt of your servant; for I have done very foolishly." 11 When David rose in the morning, the word of the LORD came to the prophet Gad, David's seer,

p Gk: Heb lacks *son of*   *q* Another reading is *Hezrai*   *r* 1 Chr 21.2 Gk: Heb *to Joab the commander of the army*   *s* Gk Mss: Heb *encamped in Aroer south of*   *t* Gk: Heb *to the land of Tahtim-hodshi*   *u* Cn Compare Gk: Heb *they came to Dan-jaan and*

24.1 This text says that *God* incited David against the Israelites. 1 Chr 21.1 says that *Satan* incited David take his census. Both are true: God was the ultimate cause, Satan the proximate one. We do not know why God was angry with David and allowed Satan as the secondary agent to cause David to number the people. David did not consult with God before he gave the order nor was there any pressing need to count heads. Yet good was to come out of this evil, for the land David bought from Araunah was later to become the site on which the temple was built.
24.3 At this point Joab seems to have had more wisdom than David. He pointed out to the king that there was no good reason for taking a census. There is nothing in the Scriptures which forbade the taking

of a census. But since the previous ones were mandated by God, it appears that David would have been well advised to consult God before he ordered this census. This he failed to do. When believers move forward on their own without consulting God, they often make mistakes that could have been averted.
24.10 The census took nine months, and it was not until the job was finished that David came under conviction of sin. His penitent reflection came before the prophet Gad, who arrived by God's order to pronounce judgment on his act. He was given a choice from three options, any one of which would serve as a proper penalty for his transgression. David did not wish to fall under any human hand, and so he chose pestilence from the hand of God.

Margin cross-references:

23.38
2 Sam 20.26
23.39
2 Sam 11.3, 6

24.1
2 Sam 20.1,
2;
1 Chr 27.23,
24
24.2
2 Sam 3.10;
Judg 20.1

24.5
Deut 2.36;
Josh 13.9, 16;
Num 32.1, 3
24.6
Josh 19.28
24.7
Josh 11.3;
Gen 21.22-33

24.9
1 Chr 21.5

24.10
1 Sam 24.5;
2 Sam 12.13;
1 Sam 13.13
24.11
1 Sam 22.5;
9.9;
1 Chr 29.29

saying, 12"Go and say to David: Thus says the LORD: Three things I offer[v] you; choose one of them, and I will do it to you." 13So Gad came to David and told him; he asked him, "Shall three[w] years of famine come to you on your land? Or will you flee three months before your foes while they pursue you? Or shall there be three days' pestilence in your land? Now consider, and decide what answer I shall return to the one who sent me." 14Then David said to Gad, "I am in great distress; let us fall into the hand of the LORD, for his mercy is great; but let me not fall into human hands."

3. *The pestilence*

15   So the LORD sent a pestilence on Israel from that morning until the appointed time; and seventy thousand of the people died, from Dan to Beer-sheba. 16But when the angel stretched out his hand toward Jerusalem to destroy it, the LORD relented concerning the evil, and said to the angel who was bringing destruction among the people, "It is enough; now stay your hand." The angel of the LORD was then by the threshing floor of Araunah the Jebusite. 17When David saw the angel who was destroying the people, he said to the LORD, "I alone have sinned, and I alone have done wickedly; but these sheep, what have they done? Let your hand, I pray, be against me and against my father's house."

4. *The altar on the threshing floor of Araunah*

18   That day Gad came to David and said to him, "Go up and erect an altar to the LORD on the threshing floor of Araunah the Jebusite." 19Following Gad's instructions, David went up, as the LORD had commanded. 20When Araunah looked down, he saw the king and his servants coming toward him; and Araunah went out and prostrated himself before the king with his face to the ground. 21Araunah said, "Why has my lord the king come to his servant?" David said, "To buy the threshing floor from you in order to build an altar to the LORD, so that the plague may be averted from the people." 22Then Araunah said to David, "Let my lord the king take and offer up what seems good to him; here are the oxen for the burnt offering, and the threshing sledges and the yokes of the oxen for the wood. 23All this, O king, Araunah gives to the king." And Araunah said to the king, "May the LORD your God respond favorably to you."

24   But the king said to Araunah, "No, but I will buy them from you for a price; I will not offer burnt offerings to the LORD my God that cost me nothing." So David bought the threshing floor and the oxen for fifty shekels of silver. 25David built there an altar to the LORD, and offered burnt offerings and offerings of well-being. So the LORD answered his supplication for the land, and the plague was averted from Israel.

v Or *hold over*   *w* 1 Chr 21.12 Gk: Heb *seven*

24.12
1 Chr 21.12

24.14
Ps 103.8, 13, 14

24.15
1 Chr 21.14; 27.24
24.16
Ex 12.23; Gen 6.6; 1 Sam 15.11

24.17
v. 10; 1 Chr 21.17

24.18
1 Chr 21.18ff

24.21
Num 16.48, 50

24.22
1 Kings 19.21

24.23
Ezek 20.40, 41
24.24
1 Chr 21.24, 25

24.25
2 Sam 21.14; v. 21

24.22 Araunah was willing to donate the ground on which the offering was to be made, while David was determined to buy it from him. The king had already sinned; he was not about to offer a sacrifice to God on land which cost him nothing. Sometimes believers wish to profess their faith and obey God at the least possible cost to themselves and with a minimum of effort. If God is all he claims to be, then the best is none too good to offer him. After all, he gave us his best when his Son died on Calvary's cross.
24.25 *David built there an altar.* On this altar, David sacrificed to the Lord, and God in mercy removed the plague. This points forward to Christ as our altar, our sacrifice. Through him alone we find favor with God, and God removes the punishment of sin from us.

INTRODUCTION TO
1 KINGS

Authorship, Date, and Background: In the Hebrew canon 1 and 2 Kings were accounted as one book (see also the introduction to 1 Samuel). The title *The Kings* is appropriate since the two books comprised a history of the Israelite people from the death of David and the accession of Solomon to the defeat of Judah before the armies of Nebuchadnezzar in 586 B.C. In the Septuagint, which divided the books of Samuel and Kings into the Books of Kingdoms, 1 and 2 Kings were the Third and Fourth Books of Kingdoms.

The period of these two books ranged from the accession of Solomon in 971 B.C. to Jehoiachin in 562 B.C.—more than four centuries. A composite authorship of the book is obvious, for nothing in the text attributes the composition to a single person. It was a compilation of writings which undoubtedly were composed by different prophets across the years who were intent on preserving the religious history of the Jewish people. Prior written documents were used when 1 and 2 Kings was finally put together. The book itself mentions the use of the Book of the Acts of Solomon (1 Kings 11.41), the Book of the Annals of the Kings of Judah (e.g., 1 Kings 14.29), and the Book of the Annals of the Kings of Israel (e.g., 1 Kings 14.19). In addition, large sections of Isaiah 36—39 are found in 2 Kings 18—20. These segments were probably copied from Isaiah and not vice versa.

Talmudic tradition associated Jeremiah the prophet with the book of Kings except for the final chapter. Since the book was written from a prophetic standpoint, either he or a number of prophets like him wrote the accounts from which the compiler produced the final product and the last chapter. A sixth century B.C. date for the final composition is likely, although much of the material used by the writer existed earlier.

Characteristics and Content: 1 and 2 Kings are characterized by consistent methodology of handling the reigns of the various monarchs. In general, the accounts report the length of each reign for Judah and Israel. In the case of Judah, the reader is told the name of the monarch's mother and the age of the king at the time of his accession. For the kings who were assassinated, the formula is not used. Each king is appraised in his relationship to God and the covenant (something a court historian would likely not do). The kings of Israel beginning with Jeroboam were all idolaters who broke the first commandment and were unfaithful to God's covenant with his people. Persistent apostasy marked the northern kingdom once the division took place after Solomon's reign. The story of the judgment of God against Israel and its dissolution in 722 B.C. with the fall of Samaria into the hands of Sennacherib is recounted in all of its tragic dimensions.

Prior to the division of the kingdom, 1 Kings depicts the golden age of Solomon. He erected his own palace and built the temple. His ventures in commerce and his international relations marked the highest tide in the fortunes of the Israelites. Despite his gift of wisdom, Solomon in his later years was unfaithful to God, largely through the influence of his many foreign wives and concubines who led him into idolatry. Solomon gave recognition to Astarte the goddess of the Sidonians, Molech the god of the Ammonites, and Chemosh the god of the Moabites, for whom he built shrines east of Jerusalem and within sight of the temple. This remained a source of spiritual temptation for more than three and a half centuries before it was done away with during the reign of Josiah (2 Kings 23.13).

1 and 2 Kings constantly reinforce the notion that Jerusalem was the only true place for worship. Whoever constructed other shrines or engaged in idolatrous worship was looked upon with a critical eye. Kings endorsed every reform movement in which idolatry was stamped out and when the covenant between God and his people was renewed or took on new force. The kingdom of Judah differed from that of Israel (Samaria) in that it experienced periodic revival under good kings such as Asa, Jehoshaphat, Uzziah, Hezekiah, and Josiah. Hezekiah and Josiah were the only kings of Judah the book of 2 Kings approves wholeheartedly. Jehoram, Ahaz, and Manasseh receive the harshest denunciations for their iniquitous conduct.

1 and 2 Kings also tell the story of the two greatest prophets of Israelite history after the death of David: Elijah and his successor, Elisha. 1 Kings recounts the miracles and ministry of Elijah; 2 Kings picks up the story of Elisha. Four clusters of miracles mark the progress of God's scheme of redemption. The first series came during Moses' day; the second cluster of miracles occurred under the ministries of Elijah and Elisha; the third cluster came in the life of Jesus; and the fourth cluster appeared in the ministry of the apostles in the early church. Other miraculous events are scattered through the Bible, of course, but they do not come in marked numbers.

The red thread running through 1 and 2 Kings consistently is the spiritual decline of God's people and their loss of affection for God's covenants and his commandments. During this period, as during the forty years in the wilderness, the people of God turned away from him and finally ended up in captivity.

Outline:

I. The end of David's reign (1.1—2.46)

II. The Solomonic reign (3.1—11.43)

III. The divided kingdom (12.1—22.53)

1 KINGS

I. The end of David's reign (1.1–2.46)

A. The struggle for the succession

1. David's declining strength

1 King David was old and advanced in years; and although they covered him with clothes, he could not get warm. 2 So his servants said to him, "Let a young virgin be sought for my lord the king, and let her wait on the king, and be his attendant; let her lie in your bosom, so that my lord the king may be warm." 3 So they searched for a beautiful girl throughout all the territory of Israel, and found Abishag the Shunammite, and brought her to the king. 4 The girl was very beautiful. She became the king's attendant and served him, but the king did not know her sexually.

2. Adonijah seeks to be king

5 Now Adonijah son of Haggith exalted himself, saying, "I will be king"; he prepared for himself chariots and horsemen, and fifty men to run before him. 6 His father had never at any time displeased him by asking, "Why have you done thus and so?" He was also a very handsome man, and he was born next after Absalom. 7 He conferred with Joab son of Zeruiah and with the priest Abiathar, and they supported Adonijah. 8 But the priest Zadok, and Benaiah son of Jehoiada, and the prophet Nathan, and Shimei, and Rei, and David's own warriors did not side with Adonijah.

9 Adonijah sacrificed sheep, oxen, and fatted cattle by the stone Zoheleth, which is beside En-rogel, and he invited all his brothers, the king's sons, and all the royal officials of Judah, 10 but he did not invite the prophet Nathan or Benaiah or the warriors or his brother Solomon.

3. Nathan advises Bathsheba

11 Then Nathan said to Bathsheba, Solomon's mother, "Have you not heard that Adonijah son of Haggith has become king and our lord David does not know it? 12 Now therefore come, let me give you advice, so that you may save your own life and the life of your son Solomon. 13 Go in at once to King David, and say to him, 'Did you not, my lord the king, swear to your servant, saying: Your son Solomon shall succeed me as king, and he shall sit on my throne? Why then is Adonijah king?' 14 Then while you

---

1.3
Josh 19.18

1.5
2 Sam 3.4;
15.1
1.6
2 Sam 3.3, 4

1.7
1 Chr 11.6;
2 Sam 20.25;
1 Kings 2.22, 28
1.8
2 Sam 20.25;
8.18; 12.1;
23.8
1.9
2 Sam 17.17
1.10
2 Sam 12.24

1.11
2 Sam 3.4

1.13
v. 30;
1 Chr 22.9-13

1.1 David was now seventy years old; his virility and vigor had waned. David's youthful lusts had given way to old age and infirmity. He was given Abishag to keep him warm but not for sexual fulfillment (see v. 4).
1.5 *Adonijah* was King David's eldest son after the death of Absalom. He normally would have expected to become king upon his father's death. David did not, however, inform Adonijah that the custom was to be bypassed in preference to Solomon. Thus Ado-

nijah was not totally at fault when he made preparations for assuming the throne (see 2.15).
1.13 David apparently had sworn to Bathsheba that Solomon would be his successor. But he certainly had not made that fact public, otherwise perhaps Adonijah would have acted differently. Verse 6 leaves the impression that David's relationship to Adonijah in no way indicated that the throne would not be his. But Nathan knew what God's will was in this matter, and he planned to bring it to pass.

are still there speaking with the king, I will come in after you and confirm your words."

4. *Bathsheba talks to David*

15 So Bathsheba went to the king in his room. The king was very old; Abishag the Shunammite was attending the king. 16 Bathsheba bowed and did obeisance to the king, and the king said, "What do you wish?" 17 She said to him, "My lord, you swore to your servant by the LORD your God, saying: Your son Solomon shall succeed me as king, and he shall sit on my throne. 18 But now suddenly Adonijah has become king, though you, my lord the king, do not know it. 19 He has sacrificed oxen, fatted cattle, and sheep in abundance, and has invited all the children of the king, the priest Abiathar, and Joab the commander of the army; but your servant Solomon he has not invited. 20 But you, my lord the king—the eyes of all Israel are on you to tell them who shall sit on the throne of my lord the king after him. 21 Otherwise it will come to pass, when my lord the king sleeps with his ancestors, that my son Solomon and I will be counted offenders."

5. *Nathan speaks for Solomon*

22 While she was still speaking with the king, the prophet Nathan came in. 23 The king was told, "Here is the prophet Nathan." When he came in before the king, he did obeisance to the king, with his face to the ground. 24 Nathan said, "My lord the king, have you said, 'Adonijah shall succeed me as king, and he shall sit on my throne'? 25 For today he has gone down and has sacrificed oxen, fatted cattle, and sheep in abundance, and has invited all the king's children, Joab the commander^x of the army, and the priest Abiathar, who are now eating and drinking before him, and saying, 'Long live King Adonijah!' 26 But he did not invite me, your servant, and the priest Zadok, and Benaiah son of Jehoiada, and your servant Solomon. 27 Has this thing been brought about by my lord the king and you have not let your servants know who should sit on the throne of my lord the king after him?"

6. *David decides for Solomon*

a. *Bathsheba informed*

28 King David answered, "Summon Bathsheba to me." So she came into the king's presence, and stood before the king. 29 The king swore, saying, "As the LORD lives, who has saved my life from every adversity, 30 as I swore to you by the LORD, the God of Israel, 'Your son Solomon shall succeed me as king, and he shall sit on my throne in my place,' so will I do this day." 31 Then Bathsheba bowed with her face to the ground, and did obeisance to the king, and said, "May my lord King David live forever!"

x Gk: Heb *the commanders*

1.15
v. 1

1.17
vv. 13, 30

1.19
v. 9

1.21
Deut 31.16;
1 Kings 2.10

1.25
v. 9;
1 Sam 10.24

1.26
vv. 8, 10

1.29
2 Sam 4.9

1.30
vv. 13, 17

1.31
Neh 2.3;
Dan 2.4

1.16–19 Bathsheba informed David that Adonijah was acting as though he was to inherit the throne. She was asking him to keep his vow and make clear to the nation that Solomon would be king. Why David had not made Solomon co-regent with him at an earlier date and worked him into the high position is not explained.
1.24 Nathan skillfully reinforced the words of Bathsheba by asking a question, not stating a conclusion: "Is Adonijah to be your successor?" And he added that people were already shouting, "Long live King Adonijah" (v. 25). That was the prompting David

needed.
1.25 Plots and counterplots for kingships were quite common in those days and Israel was no exception. Adonijah employed all the devices he could to obtain the kingship when his father David died. Here, for example, Adonijah got Abiathar and Joab (i.e., the chief priest and the commander of the armed forces) to support him. Nathan the prophet was not a supporter of Adonijah, and Zadok, an influential priest, stood with Nathan. Adonijah had carefully excluded Nathan, Zadok, Benaiah, and Solomon from the festivities.

b. *Zadok and Nathan instructed*

32 King David said, "Summon to me the priest Zadok, the prophet Nathan, and Benaiah son of Jehoiada." When they came before the king, ³³ the king said to them, "Take with you the servants of your lord, and have my son Solomon ride on my own mule, and bring him down to Gihon. ³⁴ There let the priest Zadok and the prophet Nathan anoint him king over Israel; then blow the trumpet, and say, 'Long live King Solomon!' ³⁵ You shall go up following him. Let him enter and sit on my throne; he shall be king in my place; for I have appointed him to be ruler over Israel and over Judah." ³⁶ Benaiah son of Jehoiada answered the king, "Amen! May the Lord, the God of my lord the king, so ordain. ³⁷ As the Lord has been with my lord the king, so may he be with Solomon, and make his throne greater than the throne of my lord King David."

c. *Solomon anointed*

38 So the priest Zadok, the prophet Nathan, and Benaiah son of Jehoiada, and the Cherethites and the Pelethites, went down and had Solomon ride on King David's mule, and led him to Gihon. ³⁹ There the priest Zadok took the horn of oil from the tent and anointed Solomon. Then they blew the trumpet, and all the people said, "Long live King Solomon!" ⁴⁰ And all the people went up following him, playing on pipes and rejoicing with great joy, so that the earth quaked at their noise.

7. *The submission of Adonijah*

41 Adonijah and all the guests who were with him heard it as they finished feasting. When Joab heard the sound of the trumpet, he said, "Why is the city in an uproar?" ⁴² While he was still speaking, Jonathan son of the priest Abiathar arrived. Adonijah said, "Come in, for you are a worthy man and surely you bring good news." ⁴³ Jonathan answered Adonijah, "No, for our lord King David has made Solomon king; ⁴⁴ the king has sent with him the priest Zadok, the prophet Nathan, and Benaiah son of Jehoiada, and the Cherethites and the Pelethites; and they had him ride on the king's mule; ⁴⁵ the priest Zadok and the prophet Nathan have anointed him king at Gihon; and they have gone up from there rejoicing, so that the city is in an uproar. This is the noise that you heard. ⁴⁶ Solomon now sits on the royal throne. ⁴⁷ Moreover the king's servants came to congratulate our lord King David, saying, 'May God make the name of Solomon more famous than yours, and make his throne greater than your throne.' The king bowed in worship on the bed ⁴⁸ and went on to pray thus, 'Blessed be the Lord, the God of Israel, who today has granted one of my offspring^y to sit on my throne and permitted me to witness it.'"

49 Then all the guests of Adonijah got up trembling and went their own ways. ⁵⁰ Adonijah, fearing Solomon, got up and went to grasp the horns of the altar. ⁵¹ Solomon was informed, "Adonijah is afraid of King Solomon; see, he has laid hold of the horns of the altar, saying, 'Let King Solomon swear to me first that he will not kill his servant with the sword.'" ⁵² So Solomon responded, "If he proves to be a worthy man, not one of his hairs shall fall to the ground; but if wickedness is found in him, he shall die." ⁵³ Then King Solomon sent to have him brought down from

y Gk: Heb *one*

Marginal references (left column):

1.33 — 2 Sam 20.6, 7
1.34 — 1 Sam 10.1; 16.3, 12; 2 Sam 15.10; v. 25
1.37 — Josh 1.5, 17; 1 Sam 20.13; v. 47
1.38 — vv. 8, 33; 2 Sam 8.18
1.39 — Ex 30.23-32; Ps 89.20; 1 Chr 29.22; v. 34
1.42 — 2 Sam 15.27, 36; 18.27
1.45 — v. 40
1.46 — 1 Chr 29.23
1.47 — v. 37; Gen 47.31
1.48 — 1 Kings 3.6; 2 Sam 7.12
1.50 — 1 Kings 2.28
1.52 — 1 Sam 14.45; 2 Sam 14.11

1.32ff Once the issue of the succession had been raised, David promptly took steps to ensure that Solomon would succeed him. The details of the decision made clear to all that only another civil war could alter the king's arrangements. His actions were carried out while Adonijah was still feasting with his friends. When Adonijah and his friends found out that Solomon had ridden on his father's mule, that he had been anointed, and that the people had shouted, "Long live King Solomon," they feared for their lives.

1.50 *laid hold of the horns of the altar.* This constituted an appeal for sanctuary until his case could be heard in court.

1.53 Solomon told Adonijah to go to his house and retire there. All he had lost was the kingship. Since Adonijah bowed before Solomon, the issue was closed — unless and until Adonijah reopened the matter later (see 2.13–25).

the altar. He came to do obeisance to King Solomon; and Solomon said to him, "Go home."

B. David's last words and death

1. The charge to Solomon

2 When David's time to die drew near, he charged his son Solomon, saying: 2"I am about to go the way of all the earth. Be strong, be courageous, 3and keep the charge of the LORD your God, walking in his ways and keeping his statutes, his commandments, his ordinances, and his testimonies, as it is written in the law of Moses, so that you may prosper in all that you do and wherever you turn. 4Then the LORD will establish his word that he spoke concerning me: 'If your heirs take heed to their way, to walk before me in faithfulness with all their heart and with all their soul, there shall not fail you a successor on the throne of Israel.'

2. David's last orders

5 "Moreover you know also what Joab son of Zeruiah did to me, how he dealt with the two commanders of the armies of Israel, Abner son of Ner, and Amasa son of Jether, whom he murdered, retaliating in time of peace for blood that had been shed in war, and putting the blood of war on the belt around his waist, and on the sandals on his feet. 6Act therefore according to your wisdom, but do not let his gray head go down to Sheol in peace. 7Deal loyally, however, with the sons of Barzillai the Gileadite, and let them be among those who eat at your table; for with such loyalty they met me when I fled from your brother Absalom. 8There is also with you Shimei son of Gera, the Benjaminite from Bahurim, who cursed me with a terrible curse on the day when I went to Mahanaim; but when he came down to meet me at the Jordan, I swore to him by the LORD, 'I will not put you to death with the sword.' 9Therefore do not hold him guiltless, for you are a wise man; you will know what you ought to do to him, and you must bring his gray head down with blood to Sheol."

3. David's death

10 Then David slept with his ancestors, and was buried in the city of David. 11The time that David reigned over Israel was forty years; he reigned seven years in Hebron, and thirty-three years in Jerusalem. 12So Solomon sat on the throne of his father David; and his kingdom was firmly established.

C. Solomon executes David's orders

1. Adonijah put to death

13 Then Adonijah son of Haggith came to Bathsheba, Solomon's mother. She asked, "Do you come peaceably?" He said, "Peaceably." 14Then she said, "May I have a word with you?" She said, "Go on." 15He said, "You know that the kingdom was mine, and that all Israel expected me to reign; however, the kingdom has turned about and become my brother's, for it was his from the LORD. 16And now I have one request

---

2.1
Gen 47.29;
Deut 31.14
2.2
Josh 23.14;
Deut 31.7,
23;
Josh 1.6, 7
2.3
Josh 1.7;
1 Chr 22.12,
13
2.4
2 Sam 7.25;
Ps 132.12;
2 Kings 20.3;
2 Sam 7.12,
13
2.5
2 Sam 18.5,
12, 14; 3.27;
20.10
2.6
v. 6
2.7
2 Sam 19.31,
38; 9.7, 10;
17.27
2.8
2 Sam 16.5-8;
19.18-23
2.9
v. 6
2.10
Acts 2.29;
2 Sam 5.7
2.11
2 Sam 5.4;
1 Chr 29.26,
27
2.12
1 Chr 29.23;
2 Chr 1.1
2.13
1 Sam 16.4
2.15
1 Kings 1.5;
1 Chr 22.9,
10; 28.5-7

2.3 David charged Solomon to keep the law of God, convinced that this was the way to prosper in all things. He bore witness to the fact that the law of Moses was written and available to the future king. Thus David was implicitly ordering Solomon to study the law diligently and do what it commanded.
2.5–9 David entrusted to Solomon the duty of executing judgment against Joab, who was responsible for the deaths of Abner and Amasa. The bloodguilt

would be removed only after Joab himself was executed.
2.8 Shimei had cursed David when he fled from Absalom (2 Sam 16.5–8). When the civil war was over, David swore that he would not put him to death. But David's successor was not bound to his oath. On his deathbed, David instructed Solomon to execute Shimei who cursed David *with a terrible curse.*

to make of you; do not refuse me." She said to him, "Go on." 17 He said, "Please ask King Solomon—he will not refuse you—to give me Abishag the Shunammite as my wife." 18 Bathsheba said, "Very well; I will speak to the king on your behalf."

19 So Bathsheba went to King Solomon, to speak to him on behalf of Adonijah. The king rose to meet her, and bowed down to her; then he sat on his throne, and had a throne brought for the king's mother, and she sat on his right.
20 Then she said, "I have one small request to make of you; do not refuse me." And the king said to her, "Make your request, my mother; for I will not refuse you."
21 She said, "Let Abishag the Shunammite be given to your brother Adonijah as his wife."
22 King Solomon answered his mother, "And why do you ask Abishag the Shunammite for Adonijah? Ask for him the kingdom as well! For he is my elder brother; ask not only for him but also for the priest Abiathar and for Joab son of Zeruiah!"
23 Then King Solomon swore by the LORD, "So may God do to me, and more also, for Adonijah has devised this scheme at the risk of his life!
24 Now therefore as the LORD lives, who has established me and placed me on the throne of my father David, and who has made me a house as he promised, today Adonijah shall be put to death." 25 So King Solomon sent Benaiah son of Jehoiada; he struck him down, and he died.

2. Abiathar banished

2.26
Josh 21.18;
1 Sam 23.6;
2 Sam 15.24-29;
1 Sam 22.20-23
2.27
1 Sam 2.31-35
26 The king said to the priest Abiathar, "Go to Anathoth, to your estate; for you deserve death. But I will not at this time put you to death, because you carried the ark of the Lord GOD before my father David, and because you shared in all the hardships my father endured." 27 So Solomon banished Abiathar from being priest to the LORD, thus fulfilling the word of the LORD that he had spoken concerning the house of Eli in Shiloh.

3. Joab slain

28 When the news came to Joab—for Joab had supported Adonijah though he had not supported Absalom—Joab fled to the tent of the LORD and grasped the horns of the altar. 29 When it was told King Solomon, "Joab has fled to the tent of the LORD and now is beside the altar," Solomon sent Benaiah son of Jehoiada, saying, "Go, strike him down." 30 So Benaiah came to the tent of the LORD and said to him, "The king commands, 'Come out.' " But he said, "No, I will die here." Then Benaiah brought the king word again, saying, "Thus said Joab, and thus he answered me."
31 The king replied to him, "Do as he has said, strike him down and bury him; and thus take away from me and from my father's house the guilt for the blood that Joab shed without cause. 2.32
Judg 9.24,
57;
Ps 7.16;
2 Chr 21.13;
2 Sam 3.27;
20.10 32 The LORD will bring back his bloody deeds on his own head, because, without the knowledge of my father David, he attacked and killed with the sword two men more righteous and better than himself, Abner son of Ner, commander of the army of Israel, and Amasa son of Jether, commander of the army of Judah.
33 So shall their blood come back on the head of Joab and on the head of his descendants forever; but to David, and to his descendants, and to his house, and to his throne, there shall be peace from the LORD forevermore." 34 Then Benaiah son of Jehoiada went up and struck

---

2.21 Adonijah used Bathsheba to get her son Solomon to give her Abishag as his wife. Since Abishag was the last wife of David, Adonijah might claim the throne for himself. Realizing Adonijah's treasonous intentions, Solomon refused the request and had Adonijah executed.
2.27 God foretold the end of the line of Eli the

priest. Abiathar was Eli's great-grandson. Following King David's death and Solomon's accession, Adonijah revolted and was supported by Abiathar. When King Solomon put down the revolt, he expelled Abiathar to Anathoth, marking the end of Eli's line. Jeremiah the prophet was a descendant of the priests from Anathoth (Jer 1.1).

him down and killed him; and he was buried at his own house near the wilderness. 35 The king put Benaiah son of Jehoiada over the army in his place, and the king put the priest Zadok in the place of Abiathar.

4. *Shimei's broken oath and death*

36 Then the king sent and summoned Shimei, and said to him, "Build yourself a house in Jerusalem, and live there, and do not go out from there to any place whatever. 37 For on the day you go out, and cross the Wadi Kidron, know for certain that you shall die; your blood shall be on your own head." 38 And Shimei said to the king, "The sentence is fair; as my lord the king has said, so will your servant do." So Shimei lived in Jerusalem many days.

39 But it happened at the end of three years that two of Shimei's slaves ran away to King Achish son of Maacah of Gath. When it was told Shimei, "Your slaves are in Gath," 40 Shimei arose and saddled a donkey, and went to Achish in Gath, to search for his slaves; Shimei went and brought his slaves from Gath. 41 When Solomon was told that Shimei had gone from Jerusalem to Gath and returned, 42 the king sent and summoned Shimei, and said to him, "Did I not make you swear by the LORD, and solemnly adjure you, saying, 'Know for certain that on the day you go out and go to any place whatever, you shall die'? And you said to me, 'The sentence is fair; I accept.' 43 Why then have you not kept your oath to the LORD and the commandment with which I charged you?" 44 The king also said to Shimei, "You know in your own heart all the evil that you did to my father David; so the LORD will bring back your evil on your own head. 45 But King Solomon shall be blessed, and the throne of David shall be established before the LORD forever." 46 Then the king commanded Benaiah son of Jehoiada; and he went out and struck him down, and he died. So the kingdom was established in the hand of Solomon.

II. *The Solomonic reign (3.1–11.43)*

A. *Solomon's early years: marriage to Pharaoh's daughter*

3 Solomon made a marriage alliance with Pharaoh king of Egypt; he took Pharaoh's daughter and brought her into the city of David, until he had finished building his own house and the house of the LORD and the wall around Jerusalem. 2 The people were sacrificing at the high places, however, because no house had yet been built for the name of the LORD.

B. *Prayer for wisdom granted*

3 Solomon loved the LORD, walking in the statutes of his father David; only, he sacrificed and offered incense at the high places. 4 The king went to Gibeon to sacrifice there, for that was the principal high place; Solomon used to offer a thousand burnt offerings on that altar. 5 At Gibeon the

2.35
1 Kings 4.4;
1 Chr 29.22;
v. 27

2.36
v. 8

2.37
2 Sam 15.23;
Lev 20.9;
2 Sam 1.16

2.39
1 Sam 27.2

2.40
2 Sam 19.16-23

2.44
2 Sam 16.5-13;
1 Sam 25.39;
Ezek 17.19

2.45
2 Sam 7.13
2.46
vv. 12, 25,
34; 2 Chr 1.1

3.1
1 Kings 7.8;
9.24;
2 Sam 5.7;
1 Kings 7.1;
ch. 6; 9.15,
19
3.2
Lev 17.3-5;
Deut 12.2, 4,
5
3.3f
Deut 6.5;
Ps 31.23;
1 Kings 2.3;
9.4; 11.4, 6,
38
3.4
2 Chr 1.3;
1 Chr 16.39
3.5
1 Kings 9.2;
2 Chr 1.7;
Num 12.6;
Mt 1.20

2.35 Zadok replaced Abiathar so that his descendants constituted the priestly line.
2.36,37 Solomon did not execute Shimei immediately. Instead, he ordered Shimei to remain forever in Jerusalem, apparently to keep him well within his purview. In what might have appeared to be excusable circumstances, Shimei crossed the brook Kidron in a search for two of his slaves who had run away. But it was a breach of his agreement with Solomon, who then had him executed.
3.1 Some of Solomon's many marriages were political, designed to protect his kingdom. Peace with Egypt by marriage to the princess of that realm was one of those instances.
3.3,4 Contrary to Deut 12.13,14, Solomon main-

tained *high places* outside of Jerusalem. Evidently he did not think of Jerusalem as the unique, central shrine (see also note on 12.31).
3.5 In a dream God offered to give Solomon whatever he asked for. Solomon knew that the task before him was great and that to replace David was no easy job. So he asked for wisdom or discernment rather than a long life, great riches, or even a great reputation. God was pleased to give him what he asked for. Whatever gifts we have come from God, who gives them to us through the Holy Spirit. We may ask God for any gift or gifts we think we need for his service. The mystery here, however, is why Solomon lacked wisdom about marriage and took so many wives and concubines.

3.6
2 Chr 1.8ff;
1 Kings 2.4;
9.4; 1.48

3.7
1 Chr 2.9-13;
29.1;
Num 27.17
3.8
Deut 7.6;
Gen 13.16;
15.5
3.9
2 Chr 1.10;
Prov 2.3-9;
Jas 1.5;
Ps 72.1, 2
3.11
Jas 4.3

3.12
1 Jn 5.14,
15;
1 Kings 4.29-31
3.13
Mt 6.33;
1 Kings 4.21-
24
3.14
v. 6

3.15
Gen 41.7;
1 Kings 8.65;
Esth 1.3;
Dan 5.1;
Mk 6.21

3.17
Num 27.2

3.20
Ruth 4.16

3.26
Gen 43.30;
Isa 49.15;
Jer 31.20

3.28
vv. 9, 11, 12

LORD appeared to Solomon in a dream by night; and God said, "Ask what I should give you." 6 And Solomon said, "You have shown great and steadfast love to your servant my father David, because he walked before you in faithfulness, in righteousness, and in uprightness of heart toward you; and you have kept for him this great and steadfast love, and have given him a son to sit on his throne today. 7 And now, O LORD my God, you have made your servant king in place of my father David, although I am only a little child; I do not know how to go out or come in. 8 And your servant is in the midst of the people whom you have chosen, a great people, so numerous they cannot be numbered or counted. 9 Give your servant therefore an understanding mind to govern your people, able to discern between good and evil; for who can govern this your great people?"

10   It pleased the Lord that Solomon had asked this. 11 God said to him, "Because you have asked this, and have not asked for yourself long life or riches, or for the life of your enemies, but have asked for yourself understanding to discern what is right, 12 I now do according to your word. Indeed I give you a wise and discerning mind; no one like you has been before you and no one like you shall arise after you. 13 I give you also what you have not asked, both riches and honor all your life; no other king shall compare with you. 14 If you will walk in my ways, keeping my statutes and my commandments, as your father David walked, then I will lengthen your life."

15   Then Solomon awoke; it had been a dream. He came to Jerusalem where he stood before the ark of the covenant of the LORD. He offered up burnt offerings and offerings of well-being, and provided a feast for all his servants.

C. Solomon's wise decision

16   Later, two women who were prostitutes came to the king and stood before him. 17 The one woman said, "Please, my lord, this woman and I live in the same house; and I gave birth while she was in the house. 18 Then on the third day after I gave birth, this woman also gave birth. We were together; there was no one else with us in the house, only the two of us were in the house. 19 Then this woman's son died in the night, because she lay on him. 20 She got up in the middle of the night and took my son from beside me while your servant slept. She laid him at her breast, and laid her dead son at my breast. 21 When I rose in the morning to nurse my son, I saw that he was dead; but when I looked at him closely in the morning, clearly it was not the son I had borne." 22 But the other woman said, "No, the living son is mine, and the dead son is yours." The first said, "No, the dead son is yours, and the living son is mine." So they argued before the king.

23   Then the king said, "The one says, 'This is my son that is alive, and your son is dead'; while the other says, 'Not so! Your son is dead, and my son is the living one.'" 24 So the king said, "Bring me a sword," and they brought a sword before the king. 25 The king said, "Divide the living boy in two; then give half to the one, and half to the other." 26 But the woman whose son was alive said to the king—because compassion for her son burned within her—"Please, my lord, give her the living boy; certainly do not kill him!" The other said, "It shall be neither mine nor yours; divide it." 27 Then the king responded: "Give the first woman the living boy; do not kill him. She is his mother." 28 All Israel heard of the judgment that the king had rendered; and they stood in awe of the king,

---

3.15 This text records the first application of wisdom. Before this, Solomon had offered sacrifices at Gibeon. Now he came to Jerusalem where the ark was and offered the proper sacrifices before the ark.

3.16 The case of the two prostitutes fighting over the possession of the live baby served to satisfy the people everywhere that their king indeed had the gift of wisdom.

because they perceived that the wisdom of God was in him, to execute justice.

D. *The appointment of court officials*

4 King Solomon was king over all Israel, ²and these were his high officials: Azariah son of Zadok was the priest; ³Elihoreph and Ahijah sons of Shisha were secretaries; Jehoshaphat son of Ahilud was recorder; ⁴Benaiah son of Jehoiada was in command of the army; Zadok and Abiathar were priests; ⁵Azariah son of Nathan was over the officials; Zabud son of Nathan was priest and king's friend; ⁶Ahishar was in charge of the palace; and Adoniram son of Abda was in charge of the forced labor.

7　Solomon had twelve officials over all Israel, who provided food for the king and his household; each one had to make provision for one month in the year. ⁸These were their names: Ben-hur, in the hill country of Ephraim; ⁹Ben-deker, in Makaz, Shaalbim, Beth-shemesh, and Elon-beth-hanan; ¹⁰Ben-hesed, in Arubboth (to him belonged Socoh and all the land of Hepher); ¹¹Ben-abinadab, in all Naphath-dor (he had Taphath, Solomon's daughter, as his wife); ¹²Baana son of Ahilud, in Taanach, Megiddo, and all Beth-shean, which is beside Zarethan below Jezreel, and from Beth-shean to Abel-meholah, as far as the other side of Jokmeam; ¹³Ben-geber, in Ramoth-gilead (he had the villages of Jair son of Manasseh, which are in Gilead, and he had the region of Argob, which is in Bashan, sixty great cities with walls and bronze bars); ¹⁴Ahinadab son of Iddo, in Mahanaim; ¹⁵Ahimaaz, in Naphtali (he had taken Basemath, Solomon's daughter, as his wife); ¹⁶Baana son of Hushai, in Asher and Bealoth; ¹⁷Jehoshaphat son of Paruah, in Issachar; ¹⁸Shimei son of Ela, in Benjamin; ¹⁹Geber son of Uri, in the land of Gilead, the country of King Sihon of the Amorites and of King Og of Bashan. And there was one official in the land of Judah.

E. *The household provisions*

20　Judah and Israel were as numerous as the sand by the sea; they ate and drank and were happy. ²¹ᶻSolomon was sovereign over all the kingdoms from the Euphrates to the land of the Philistines, even to the border of Egypt; they brought tribute and served Solomon all the days of his life.

22　Solomon's provision for one day was thirty cors of choice flour, and sixty cors of meal, ²³ten fat oxen, and twenty pasture-fed cattle, one hundred sheep, besides deer, gazelles, roebucks, and fatted fowl. ²⁴For he had dominion over all the region west of the Euphrates from Tiphsah to Gaza, over all the kings west of the Euphrates; and he had peace on all sides. ²⁵During Solomon's lifetime Judah and Israel lived in safety, from Dan even to Beer-sheba, all of them under their vines and fig trees. ²⁶Solomon also had forty thousand stalls of horses for his chariots, and twelve thousand horsemen. ²⁷Those officials supplied provisions for King Solomon and for all who came to King Solomon's table, each one in his month; they let nothing be lacking. ²⁸They also brought to the required

ᶻ Ch 5.1 in Heb

4.5
v. 7

4.8
Josh 24.33
4.9
Josh 1.35;
21.16
4.10
Josh 15.35;
12.17
4.11
Josh 11.1, 2
4.12
Josh 5.19;
17.11; 3.16;
1 Kings 19.16;
1 Chr 6.68
4.13
Num 32.41;
Deut 3.4
4.14
Josh 13.26
4.15
2 Sam 15.27
4.16
2 Sam 15.32
4.18
1 Kings 1.8
4.19
Deut 3.8-10
4.20
Gen 32.12;
1 Kings 3.8
4.21
2 Chr 9.26;
Gen 15.18;
Ps 68.29;
72.10, 11

4.24
Ps 72.11;
1 Chr 22.9

4.25
Jer 23.6;
Mic 4.4;
Zech 3.10;
Judg 20.1
4.26
1 Kings 10.26;
2 Chr 1.14
4.27
v. 7

4.7　Apparently Solomon divided the kingdom into twelve segments and appointed twelve officials over them in order to provide the means to support his extensive building and military ventures.
4.20　The contentment here expressed turned to discontent when Solomon began to lay a heavy yoke on the people, as may be inferred from 12.10.
4.25　Solomon had reached the height of his splendor. The twelve tribes lived in peace and were provided for by God. God had fulfilled his promises and his people could expect him to help them maintain

that state of affairs. However, as time went on, it became apparent that contentment would continue only as long as the people and the king remained faithful to God.
4.26　Here again is a variance between this verse and 2 Chr 9.25, because of a copyist misreading the Hebrew "four" for "forty." The lower number is probably correct, especially since the number of chariots is stated to be 1,400 in 10.26. Archaeologists have found some of the stalls in Megiddo.

place barley and straw for the horses and swift steeds, each according to his charge.

F. *Solomon's great wisdom*

4.29
1 Kings 3.12
4.30
Gen 25.6;
Acts 7.22
4.31
1 Kings 3.12;
1 Chr 15.19;
2.6; 6.33
4.32
Prov 1.1;
Eccl 12.9;
Song 1.1
4.34
1 Kings 10.1;
2 Chr 9.23

29   God gave Solomon very great wisdom, discernment, and breadth of understanding as vast as the sand on the seashore, 30 so that Solomon's wisdom surpassed the wisdom of all the people of the east, and all the wisdom of Egypt. 31 He was wiser than anyone else, wiser than Ethan the Ezrahite, and Heman, Calcol, and Darda, children of Mahol; his fame spread throughout all the surrounding nations. 32 He composed three thousand proverbs, and his songs numbered a thousand and five. 33 He would speak of trees, from the cedar that is in the Lebanon to the hyssop that grows in the wall; he would speak of animals, and birds, and reptiles, and fish. 34 People came from all the nations to hear the wisdom of Solomon; they came from all the kings of the earth who had heard of his wisdom.

G. *The building of the temple*

1. *Preparations for building*

5.1
vv. 10, 18;
2 Chr 2.3;
2 Sam 5.11;
1 Chr 14.1
5.3
1 Chr 22.8;
28.3
5.4
1 Kings 4.24;
1 Chr 22.9
5.5
2 Sam 7.12,
13;
1 Chr 17.12;
22.10
5.9
2 Chr 2.16;
Ezra 3.7;
Ezek 27.17;
Acts 12.20
5.11
cf. 2 Chr 2.10
5.12
1 Kings 3.12

5 *a* Now King Hiram of Tyre sent his servants to Solomon, when he heard that they had anointed him king in place of his father; for Hiram had always been a friend to David. 2 Solomon sent word to Hiram, saying, 3 "You know that my father David could not build a house for the name of the LORD his God because of the warfare with which his enemies surrounded him, until the LORD put them under the soles of his feet.*b* 4 But now the LORD my God has given me rest on every side; there is neither adversary nor misfortune. 5 So I intend to build a house for the name of the LORD my God, as the LORD said to my father David, 'Your son, whom I will set on your throne in your place, shall build the house for my name.' 6 Therefore command that cedars from the Lebanon be cut for me. My servants will join your servants, and I will give you whatever wages you set for your servants; for you know that there is no one among us who knows how to cut timber like the Sidonians."

7   When Hiram heard the words of Solomon, he rejoiced greatly, and said, "Blessed be the LORD today, who has given to David a wise son to be over this great people." 8 Hiram sent word to Solomon, "I have heard the message that you have sent to me; I will fulfill all your needs in the matter of cedar and cypress timber. 9 My servants shall bring it down to the sea from the Lebanon; I will make it into rafts to go by sea to the place you indicate. I will have them broken up there for you to take away. And you shall meet my needs by providing food for my household." 10 So Hiram supplied Solomon's every need for timber of cedar and cypress. 11 Solomon in turn gave Hiram twenty thousand cors of wheat as food for his household, and twenty cors of fine oil. Solomon gave this to Hiram year by year. 12 So the LORD gave Solomon wisdom, as he promised him. There was peace between Hiram and Solomon; and the two of them made a treaty.

13   King Solomon conscripted forced labor out of all Israel; the levy

---

a Ch 5.15 in Heb   *b* Gk Tg Vg: Heb *my feet* or *his feet*

4.29,30 The gift of wisdom was God's gift to Solomon (cf. Prov 2.6), and he is said to have possessed far greater wisdom than the finest scholars of all the nations. Yet wisdom, when it is not accompanied by right actions, loses much of its value. Wisdom did not keep him from loving and marrying heathen women from the surrounding nations; these women helped to turn his heart away from God.
5.1 Hiram had been David's friend. His people

built David a house (2 Sam 5.11), and we can be sure it was magnificent.
5.5–12 Solomon asked Hiram for help in the construction of the temple, which God had forbidden David to erect. It was to be a joint effort of the Israelites and the people of Hiram. Solomon indicated his willingness to reimburse Hiram for his troubles. They signed a treaty to seal the bargain.
5.13 Solomon conscripted thirty thousand Israelites

numbered thirty thousand men. 14 He sent them to the Lebanon, ten thousand a month in shifts; they would be a month in the Lebanon and two months at home; Adoniram was in charge of the forced labor. 15 Solomon also had seventy thousand laborers and eighty thousand stonecutters in the hill country, 16 besides Solomon's three thousand three hundred supervisors who were over the work, having charge of the people who did the work. 17 At the king's command, they quarried out great, costly stones in order to lay the foundation of the house with dressed stones. 18 So Solomon's builders and Hiram's builders and the Gebalites did the stonecutting and prepared the timber and the stone to build the house.

5.14	1 Kings 4.6
5.15	1 Kings 9.20-22; 2 Chr 2.17, 18
5.17	1 Chr 22.2

2. The description of the temple

6 In the four hundred eightieth year after the Israelites came out of the land of Egypt, in the fourth year of Solomon's reign over Israel, in the month of Ziv, which is the second month, he began to build the house of the LORD. 2 The house that King Solomon built for the LORD was sixty cubits long, twenty cubits wide, and thirty cubits high. 3 The vestibule in front of the nave of the house was twenty cubits wide, across the width of the house. Its depth was ten cubits in front of the house. 4 For the house he made windows with recessed frames.^c 5 He also built a structure against the wall of the house, running around the walls of the house, both the nave and the inner sanctuary; and he made side chambers all around. 6 The lowest story^d was five cubits wide, the middle one was six cubits wide, and the third was seven cubits wide; for around the outside of the house he made offsets on the wall in order that the supporting beams should not be inserted into the walls of the house.

7 The house was built with stone finished at the quarry, so that neither hammer nor ax nor any tool of iron was heard in the temple while it was being built.

8 The entrance for the middle story was on the south side of the house: one went up by winding stairs to the middle story, and from the middle story to the third. 9 So he built the house, and finished it; he roofed the house with beams and planks of cedar. 10 He built the structure against the whole house, each story^e five cubits high, and it was joined to the house with timbers of cedar.

11 Now the word of the LORD came to Solomon, 12 "Concerning this house that you are building, if you will walk in my statutes, obey my ordinances, and keep all my commandments by walking in them, then I will establish my promise with you, which I made to your father David. 13 I will dwell among the children of Israel, and will not forsake my people Israel."

14 So Solomon built the house, and finished it. 15 He lined the walls of the house on the inside with boards of cedar; from the floor of the house to the rafters of the ceiling, he covered them on the inside with wood; and he covered the floor of the house with boards of cypress. 16 He built twenty

6.1	2 Chr 3.1, 2; Acts 7.47
6.2	cf. Ezek 41.1ff
6.4	Ezek 40.16; 41.16
6.5	Ezek 41.6; vv. 16, 19-21, 31
6.7	Deut 27.5, 6
6.9	vv. 14, 38
6.12	1 Kings 2.4; 9.4
6.13	Ex 25.8; Deut 31.6
6.14	vv. 9, 38
6.16	Ex 26.33; Lev 16.2; 1 Kings 8.6; 2 Chr 3.8

^c Gk: Meaning of Heb uncertain   ^d Gk: Heb *structure*   ^e Heb lacks *each story*

---

to build the temple. Ten thousand worked for a month and then had two months off to tend their own affairs. Additional workers came from tributary peoples who did not share the same time-off advantages. The labor engaged in the enterprise was enormous.

6.1 *four hundred eightieth year after . . . Egypt.* This implies that the exodus occurred around 1440 B.C. Some scholars have argued at length for this date, while others argue for a later date in the middle of the thirteenth century B.C.

6.3 Solomon's temple was erected some four centuries after the tabernacle (tent) was constructed. It took seven years to finish it. The materials were secured and prepared elsewhere and simply assembled on the site of the building.

6.13 God promised Solomon that he would dwell among the people of Israel in the temple and would not forsake them. But this was a conditional promise — they had to keep God's commandments. When the temple was finally dedicated, the glory of God entered the sanctuary (2 Chr 7.2).

6.16,17 One-third of the temple comprised the most holy place, the other two-thirds the remaining interior of the temple. In the N.T. the veil between the most holy place and the other part of the temple was torn apart at the death of Christ, signifying his entrance into the holy place to obtain eternal redemption (see note on Ex 25.17).

cubits of the rear of the house with boards of cedar from the floor to the rafters, and he built this within as an inner sanctuary, as the most holy place. 17 The house, that is, the nave in front of the inner sanctuary, was forty cubits long. 18 The cedar within the house had carvings of gourds and open flowers; all was cedar, no stone was seen. 19 The inner sanctuary he prepared in the innermost part of the house, to set there the ark of the covenant of the LORD. 20 The interior of the inner sanctuary was twenty cubits long, twenty cubits wide, and twenty cubits high; he overlaid it with pure gold. He also overlaid the altar with cedar.*f* 21 Solomon overlaid the inside of the house with pure gold, then he drew chains of gold across, in front of the inner sanctuary, and overlaid it with gold. 22 Next he overlaid the whole house with gold, in order that the whole house might be perfect; even the whole altar that belonged to the inner sanctuary he overlaid with gold.

23   In the inner sanctuary he made two cherubim of olivewood, each ten cubits high. 24 Five cubits was the length of one wing of the cherub, and five cubits the length of the other wing of the cherub; it was ten cubits from the tip of one wing to the tip of the other. 25 The other cherub also measured ten cubits; both cherubim had the same measure and the same form. 26 The height of one cherub was ten cubits, and so was that of the other cherub. 27 He put the cherubim in the innermost part of the house; the wings of the cherubim were spread out so that a wing of one was touching the one wall, and a wing of the other cherub was touching the other wall; their other wings toward the center of the house were touching wing to wing. 28 He also overlaid the cherubim with gold.

29   He carved the walls of the house all around about with carved engravings of cherubim, palm trees, and open flowers, in the inner and outer rooms. 30 The floor of the house he overlaid with gold, in the inner and outer rooms.

31   For the entrance to the inner sanctuary he made doors of olivewood; the lintel and the doorposts were five-sided.*f* 32 He covered the two doors of olivewood with carvings of cherubim, palm trees, and open flowers; he overlaid them with gold, and spread gold on the cherubim and on the palm trees.

33   So also he made for the entrance to the nave doorposts of olivewood, four-sided each, 34 and two doors of cypress wood; the two leaves of the one door were folding, and the two leaves of the other door were folding. 35 He carved cherubim, palm trees, and open flowers, overlaying them with gold evenly applied upon the carved work. 36 He built the inner court with three courses of dressed stone to one course of cedar beams.

37   In the fourth year the foundation of the house of the LORD was laid, in the month of Ziv. 38 In the eleventh year, in the month of Bul, which is the eighth month, the house was finished in all its parts, and according to all its specifications. He was seven years in building it.

3. *The description of the palace buildings*

7 Solomon was building his own house thirteen years, and he finished his entire house.

f Meaning of Heb uncertain

Margin references:
6.18 — 1 Kings 7.24
6.22 — Ex 30.1, 3, 6
6.23 — 2 Chr 3.10-12
6.27 — Ex 25.20; 37.9; 1 Kings 8.7; 2 Chr 5.8
6.34 — Ezek 41.23-25
6.36 — 1 Kings 7.12
6.37 — v. 1
7.1 — 1 Kings 9.10; 2 Chr 8.1

6.22 The immense amount of gold used in the construction of the temple would make it a special attraction to foreign powers when they converged on Jerusalem.
6.23 *made two cherubim.* Some think these resembled winged lions with human heads. God was thought of as invisibly enthroned on the cherubim (see Ex 25.22). This led people to incorrectly suppose that God would never allow the temple to be destroyed (see Jer 7.4).

6.29 The Israelites had been cured of their desire for idols. Despite their later departures from the true faith, they rarely stooped to erect figures to represent their God. The art of Israel compared to that of pagan nations (like Egypt, Greece, and Rome) was remarkably lacking in statues.
7.1 Solomon apparently took six more years to build his own palace (cf. 6.37,38) because he was less anxious to build his house than the temple; thus, greater effort and less time were spent on God's house than

2 He built the House of the Forest of the Lebanon one hundred cubits long, fifty cubits wide, and thirty cubits high, built on four rows of cedar pillars, with cedar beams on the pillars. ³ It was roofed with cedar on the forty-five rafters, fifteen in each row, which were on the pillars. ⁴ There were window frames in the three rows, facing each other in the three rows. ⁵ All the doorways and doorposts had four-sided frames, opposite, facing each other in the three rows.

6 He made the Hall of Pillars fifty cubits long and thirty cubits wide. There was a porch in front with pillars, and a canopy in front of them.

7 He made the Hall of the Throne where he was to pronounce judgment, the Hall of Justice, covered with cedar from floor to floor.

8 His own house where he would reside, in the other court back of the hall, was of the same construction. Solomon also made a house like this hall for Pharaoh's daughter, whom he had taken in marriage.

9 All these were made of costly stones, cut according to measure, sawed with saws, back and front, from the foundation to the coping, and from outside to the great court. ¹⁰ The foundation was of costly stones, huge stones, stones of eight and ten cubits. ¹¹ There were costly stones above, cut to measure, and cedarwood. ¹² The great court had three courses of dressed stone to one layer of cedar beams all around; so had the inner court of the house of the LORD, and the vestibule of the house.

4. *The employment of Hiram*

13 Now King Solomon invited and received Hiram from Tyre. ¹⁴ He was the son of a widow of the tribe of Naphtali, whose father, a man of Tyre, had been an artisan in bronze; he was full of skill, intelligence, and knowledge in working bronze. He came to King Solomon, and did all his work.

5. *The casting of the bronze pillars*

15 He cast two pillars of bronze. Eighteen cubits was the height of the one, and a cord of twelve cubits would encircle it; the second pillar was the same.ᵍ ¹⁶ He also made two capitals of molten bronze, to set on the tops of the pillars; the height of the one capital was five cubits, and the height of the other capital was five cubits. ¹⁷ There were nets of checker work with wreaths of chain work for the capitals on the tops of the pillars; sevenʰ for the one capital, and sevenʰ for the other capital. ¹⁸ He made the columns with two rows around each latticework to cover the capitals that were above the pomegranates; he did the same with the other capital. ¹⁹ Now the capitals that were on the tops of the pillars in the vestibule were of lily-work, four cubits high. ²⁰ The capitals were on the two pillars and also above the rounded projection that was beside the latticework; there were two hundred pomegranates in rows all around; and so with the other capital. ²¹ He set up the pillars at the vestibule of the temple; he set up the pillar on the south and called it Jachin; and he set up the pillar on the north and called it Boaz. ²² On the tops of the pillars was lily-work. Thus the work of the pillars was finished.

g Cn: Heb *and a cord of twelve cubits encircled the second pillar*; Compare Jer 52.21   *h* Heb: Gk *a net*

7.2
1 Kings 10.17,
21

7.7
1 Kings 6.15,
16
7.8
1 Kings 3.1;
2 Chr 8.11

7.12
1 Kings 6.36;
v. 6

7.13
2 Chr 4.11
7.14
2 Chr 2.14;
4.16;
Ex 31.3-5;
35.31

7.15
2 Kings 25.17;
2 Chr 3.15

7.20
2 Chr 3.16;
4.13;
Jer 52.23
7.21
2 Chr 3.17;
1 Kings 6.3

on his own. The splendor of Solomon's own buildings was not to be compared with the temple.
7.2 *The House of the Forest of the Lebanon* was a country dwelling near Jerusalem. Some think it was a retreat in the forest of Lebanon itself. Apparently Solomon's throne was not there but in Jerusalem, called "the Hall of the Throne" and "the Hall of Justice" (v. 7).

7.8 Pharaoh's daughter, one of Solomon's wives, had her own home built by Solomon. This was a political marriage. Solomon's successor, Rehoboam, was born of Naamah, an Ammonitess.
7.13 The Hiram mentioned here is not the king spoken of in 5.1; rather, he was the chief craftsman and architect for King Solomon.
7.21 *Jachin*, i.e., "to establish." *Boaz*, i.e., "strength."

6. The molten sea

7.23
2 Kings 25.13;
2 Chr 4.2;
Jer 52.17
7.24
1 Kings 6.18;
2 Chr 4.3
7.25
2 Chr 4.4, 5;
Jer 52.20

23   Then he made the molten sea; it was round, ten cubits from brim to brim, and five cubits high. A line of thirty cubits would encircle it completely. 24 Under its brim were panels all around it, each of ten cubits, surrounding the sea; there were two rows of panels, cast when it was cast. 25 It stood on twelve oxen, three facing north, three facing west, three facing south, and three facing east; the sea was set on them. The hindquarters of each were toward the inside. 26 Its thickness was a handbreadth; its brim was made like the brim of a cup, like the flower of a lily; it held two thousand baths. [i]

7. The ten bronze basins

7.27
v. 38;
2 Chr 4.14

27   He also made the ten stands of bronze; each stand was four cubits long, four cubits wide, and three cubits high. 28 This was the construction of the stands: they had borders; the borders were within the frames; 29 on the borders that were set in the frames were lions, oxen, and cherubim. On the frames, both above and below the lions and oxen, there were wreaths of beveled work. 30 Each stand had four bronze wheels and axles of bronze; at the four corners were supports for a basin. The supports were cast with wreaths at the side of each. 31 Its opening was within the crown whose height was one cubit; its opening was round, as a pedestal is made; it was a cubit and a half wide. At its opening were carvings; its borders were four-sided, not round. 32 The four wheels were underneath the borders; the axles of the wheels were in the stands; and the height of a wheel was a cubit and a half. 33 The wheels were made like a chariot wheel; their axles, their rims, their spokes, and their hubs were all cast. 34 There were four supports at the four corners of each stand; the supports were of one piece with the stands. 35 On the top of the stand there was a round band half a cubit high; on the top of the stand, its stays and its borders were of one piece with it. 36 On the surfaces of its stays and on its borders he carved cherubim, lions, and palm trees, where each had space, with wreaths all around. 37 In this way he made the ten stands; all of them were cast alike, with the same size and the same form.

7.30
2 Kings 16.17;
25.13, 16

7.37
2 Chr 4.14

7.38
2 Chr 4.6

38   He made ten basins of bronze; each basin held forty baths; [i] each basin measured four cubits; there was a basin for each of the ten stands. 39 He set five of the stands on the south side of the house, and five on the north side of the house; he set the sea on the southeast corner of the house.

8. Other castings

7.41
vv. 17, 18

7.42
v. 20

7.44
vv. 23, 25

7.45
2 Chr 4.16

40   Hiram also made the pots, the shovels, and the basins. So Hiram finished all the work that he did for King Solomon on the house of the LORD: 41 the two pillars, the two bowls of the capitals that were on the tops of the pillars, the two latticeworks to cover the two bowls of the capitals that were on the tops of the pillars; 42 the four hundred pomegranates for the two latticeworks, two rows of pomegranates for each latticework, to cover the two bowls of the capitals that were on the pillars; 43 the ten stands, the ten basins on the stands; 44 the one sea, and the twelve oxen underneath the sea.

45   The pots, the shovels, and the basins, all these vessels that Hiram made for King Solomon for the house of the LORD were of burnished

[i] A Heb measure of volume

7.23 *the molten sea* was filled with water by the Gibeonites or Nethinim, who supplied all of the water for the house of God.
7.26 *two thousand baths*, i.e., approximately twelve thousand gallons; 2 Chr 4.5 states three thousand baths. Different Hebrew verbs were used; the bronze

tank probably normally contained two thousand baths, but when filled to the brim it would contain three thousand.
7.27   The ten brass basins for washing were set on wheels (v. 32) so they could be moved when desired. The molten sea was stationary.

bronze. 46 In the plain of the Jordan the king cast them, in the clay ground between Succoth and Zarethan. 47 Solomon left all the vessels unweighed, because there were so many of them; the weight of the bronze was not determined.

7.46
2 Chr 4.17;
Josh 13.27;
3.16

9. The golden vessels

48 So Solomon made all the vessels that were in the house of the Lord: the golden altar, the golden table for the bread of the Presence, 49 the lampstands of pure gold, five on the south side and five on the north, in front of the inner sanctuary; the flowers, the lamps, and the tongs, of gold; 50 the cups, snuffers, basins, dishes for incense, and firepans, of pure gold; the sockets for the doors of the innermost part of the house, the most holy place, and for the doors of the nave of the temple, of gold.

7.48
Ex 37.10ff
7.49
Ex 31-38

51 Thus all the work that King Solomon did on the house of the Lord was finished. Solomon brought in the things that his father David had dedicated, the silver, the gold, and the vessels, and stored them in the treasuries of the house of the Lord.

7.51
2 Sam 8.11;
2 Chr 5.1

H. The dedication of the temple

1. The ark brought to the temple

8 Then Solomon assembled the elders of Israel and all the heads of the tribes, the leaders of the ancestral houses of the Israelites, before King Solomon in Jerusalem, to bring up the ark of the covenant of the Lord out of the city of David, which is Zion. 2 All the people of Israel assembled to King Solomon at the festival in the month Ethanim, which is the seventh month. 3 And all the elders of Israel came, and the priests carried the ark. 4 So they brought up the ark of the Lord, the tent of meeting, and all the holy vessels that were in the tent; the priests and the Levites brought them up. 5 King Solomon and all the congregation of Israel, who had assembled before him, were with him before the ark, sacrificing so many sheep and oxen that they could not be counted or numbered. 6 Then the priests brought the ark of the covenant of the Lord to its place, in the inner sanctuary of the house, in the most holy place, underneath the wings of the cherubim. 7 For the cherubim spread out their wings over the place of the ark, so that the cherubim made a covering above the ark and its poles. 8 The poles were so long that the ends of the poles were seen from the holy place in front of the inner sanctuary; but they could not be seen from outside; they are there to this day. 9 There was nothing in the ark except the two tablets of stone that Moses had placed there at Horeb, where the Lord made a covenant with the Israelites, when they came out of the land of Egypt. 10 And when the priests came out of the holy place, a cloud filled the house of the Lord, 11 so that the priests could not stand to minister because of the cloud; for the glory of the Lord filled the house of the Lord.

12 Then Solomon said,
"The Lord has said that he would dwell in thick darkness.

8.1
2 Chr 5.2;
2 Sam 6.17;
5.7, 9
8.2
Lev 23.34;
2 Chr 7.8
8.3
Num 7.9
8.4
1 Kings 3.4;
2 Chr 1.3
8.5
2 Sam 6.13

8.6
2 Sam 6.17;
1 Kings 6.19,
27

8.8
Ex 25.14

8.9
Ex 25.21;
Deut 10.2-5;
Heb 9.4;
Ex 24.7, 8
8.10
Ex 40.34, 35;
2 Chr 7.1, 2

8.12
2 Chr 6.1;
Ps 97.2

8.10 a cloud filled the house of the Lord. The cloud signified both the presence (the shekinah) and the blessing of God in the temple.
8.11 The glory of the Solomonic temple was not its size, beauty, or cost. Its glory came from the divine presence which came after the ark was carried into the holy place by the priests and which filled the edifice. From that time forward, only the high priest could enter the most holy place once a year to make atonement for the sins of the people.
8.12 Solomon spoke to the priests and encouraged their hearts about the mystery they had experienced and the darkness they had encountered. He told them

that the Lord had said that he would dwell in thick darkness. He is the God who hides himself so that the holy faith may be exercised and holy fear increased. The dark cloud of the presence certified God's acceptance of the temple Solomon had built. But the dark cloud also signified the darkness of the old dispensation when compared with the light of the gospel, which would come with the advent of the Messiah, the Lord Jesus (cf 2 Cor 3.7–18). In heaven, the divine glory will be completely unveiled and all darkness will be replaced by the light of God (Rev 21.22–25).

8.13
2 Sam 7.13;
Ps 132.14

13   I have built you an exalted house,
        a place for you to dwell in forever.”

2. Solomon's speech

8.14
2 Sam 6.18
8.15
1 Chr 29.10,
20;
Neh 9.5;
2 Sam 7.12,
13
8.16
2 Sam 7.4-6;
Deut 12.11;
1 Sam 16.1;
2 Sam 7.8
8.17
2 Sam 7.2;
1 Chr 17.1
8.19
2 Sam 7.5;
12.13;
1 Kings 5.3,
5
8.20
1 Chr 28.5, 6
8.21
v. 9

14   Then the king turned around and blessed all the assembly of Israel, while all the assembly of Israel stood. 15 He said, “Blessed be the LORD, the God of Israel, who with his hand has fulfilled what he promised with his mouth to my father David, saying, 16 ‘Since the day that I brought my people Israel out of Egypt, I have not chosen a city from any of the tribes of Israel in which to build a house, that my name might be there; but I chose David to be over my people Israel.’ 17 My father David had it in mind to build a house for the name of the LORD, the God of Israel. 18 But the LORD said to my father David, ‘You did well to consider building a house for my name; 19 nevertheless you shall not build the house, but your son who shall be born to you shall build the house for my name.’ 20 Now the LORD has upheld the promise that he made; for I have risen in the place of my father David; I sit on the throne of Israel, as the LORD promised, and have built the house for the name of the LORD, the God of Israel. 21 There I have provided a place for the ark, in which is the covenant of the LORD that he made with our ancestors when he brought them out of the land of Egypt.”

3. Solomon's prayer

8.22
2 Chr 6.12ff;
Ex 9.33;
Ezra 9.5
8.23
1 Sam 2.2;
2 Sam 7.22;
Deut 7.9;
Neh 1.5, 9,
32
8.25
2 Sam 7.12,
16;
1 Kings 2.4
8.26
2 Sam 7.25

22   Then Solomon stood before the altar of the LORD in the presence of all the assembly of Israel, and spread out his hands to heaven. 23 He said, “O LORD, God of Israel, there is no God like you in heaven above or on earth beneath, keeping covenant and steadfast love for your servants who walk before you with all their heart, 24 the covenant that you kept for your servant my father David as you declared to him; you promised with your mouth and have this day fulfilled with your hand. 25 Therefore, O LORD, God of Israel, keep for your servant my father David that which you promised him, saying, ‘There shall never fail you a successor before me to sit on the throne of Israel, if only your children look to their way, to walk before me as you have walked before me.’ 26 Therefore, O God of Israel, let your word be confirmed, which you promised to your servant my father David.

8.27
2 Chr 2.6;
Isa 66.1;
Jer 23.24;
Acts 7.49
8.29
Deut 12.11;
Dan 6.10
8.30
Neh 1.6

27   “But will God indeed dwell on the earth? Even heaven and the highest heaven cannot contain you, much less this house that I have built! 28 Regard your servant's prayer and his plea, O LORD my God, heeding the cry and the prayer that your servant prays to you today; 29 that your eyes may be open night and day toward this house, the place of which you said, ‘My name shall be there,’ that you may heed the prayer that your servant prays toward this place. 30 Hear the plea of your servant and of your people Israel when they pray toward this place; O hear in heaven your dwelling place; heed and forgive.

8.31
Ex 22.11
8.32
Deut 25.1

31   “If someone sins against a neighbor and is given an oath to swear, and comes and swears before your altar in this house, 32 then hear in heaven, and act, and judge your servants, condemning the guilty by bringing their conduct on their own head, and vindicating the righteous by rewarding them according to their righteousness.

8.33
Lev 26.17;
Deut 28.25;
Lev 26.39

33   “When your people Israel, having sinned against you, are defeated before an enemy but turn again to you, confess your name, pray and plead with you in this house, 34 then hear in heaven, forgive the sin of your

---

8.22   It is good for a nation when its ruler so loves God that he can offer public prayer before the people and for them. When God is so honored, the nation will be blessed and honored in turn by God. Furthermore, this prayer has a larger frame of reference —

that the God of the temple is the God of all nations and the ruler over all peoples (cf. Isaiah's proclamation that the temple should be a “house of prayer for all peoples” (Isa 56.7).

people Israel, and bring them again to the land that you gave to their ancestors.

35 "When heaven is shut up and there is no rain because they have sinned against you, and then they pray toward this place, confess your name, and turn from their sin, because you punish[j] them, 36 then hear in heaven, and forgive the sin of your servants, your people Israel, when you teach them the good way in which they should walk; and grant rain on your land, which you have given to your people as an inheritance.

37 "If there is famine in the land, if there is plague, blight, mildew, locust, or caterpillar; if their enemy besieges them in any[k] of their cities; whatever plague, whatever sickness there is; 38 whatever prayer, whatever plea there is from any individual or from all your people Israel, all knowing the afflictions of their own hearts so that they stretch out their hands toward this house; 39 then hear in heaven your dwelling place, forgive, act, and render to all whose hearts you know — according to all their ways, for only you know what is in every human heart — 40 so that they may fear you all the days that they live in the land that you gave to our ancestors.

41 "Likewise when a foreigner, who is not of your people Israel, comes from a distant land because of your name 42 — for they shall hear of your great name, your mighty hand, and your outstretched arm — when a foreigner comes and prays toward this house, 43 then hear in heaven your dwelling place, and do according to all that the foreigner calls to you, so that all the peoples of the earth may know your name and fear you, as do your people Israel, and so that they may know that your name has been invoked on this house that I have built.

44 "If your people go out to battle against their enemy, by whatever way you shall send them, and they pray to the LORD toward the city that you have chosen and the house that I have built for your name, 45 then hear in heaven their prayer and their plea, and maintain their cause.

46 "If they sin against you — for there is no one who does not sin — and you are angry with them and give them to an enemy, so that they are carried away captive to the land of the enemy, far off or near; 47 yet if they come to their senses in the land to which they have been taken captive, and repent, and plead with you in the land of their captors, saying, 'We have sinned, and have done wrong; we have acted wickedly'; 48 if they repent with all their heart and soul in the land of their enemies, who took them captive, and pray to you toward their land, which you gave to their ancestors, the city that you have chosen, and the house that I have built for your name; 49 then hear in heaven your dwelling place their prayer and their plea, maintain their cause 50 and forgive your people who have sinned against you, and all their transgressions that they have committed against you; and grant them compassion in the sight of their captors, so that they may have compassion on them 51 (for they are your people and heritage, which you brought out of Egypt, from the midst of the iron-smelter). 52 Let your eyes be open to the plea of your servant, and to the plea of your people Israel, listening to them whenever they call to you. 53 For you have separated them from among all the peoples of the earth, to be your heritage, just as you promised through Moses, your servant, when you brought our ancestors out of Egypt, O Lord GOD."

4. Solomon's benediction

54 Now when Solomon finished offering all this prayer and this plea to the LORD, he arose from facing the altar of the LORD, where he had knelt with hands outstretched toward heaven; 55 he stood and blessed all the assembly of Israel with a loud voice:

56 "Blessed be the LORD, who has given rest to his people Israel according to all that he promised; not one word has failed of all his good

j Or when you answer   _k Gk Syr: Heb in the land_

Cross-references (margin):

8.35 Lev 26.19; Deut 28.23
8.36 1 Sam 12.23; Ps 27.11; 94.12
8.37 Lev 26.16, 25, 26; Deut 28.21-23, 38-42
8.39 1 Sam 16.7; 1 Chr 28.9; Ps 11.4; Jer 17.10
8.40 Ps 130.4
8.42 Deut 3.24
8.43 1 Sam 17.46; 2 Kings 19.19; Ps 102.15
8.46 2 Chr 6.36; Prov 20.9; 1 Jn 1.8-10; Lev 26.34-39; Deut 28.36, 64
8.47 Lev 26.40; Neh 1.6; Ps 106.6; Dan 9.5
8.48 Jer 29.12-14; Dan 6.10
8.50 2 Chr 30.9; Ps 106.46
8.51 Deut 9.29; Neh 1.10; Deut 4.20; Jer 11.4
8.53 Ex 19.5; Deut 9.26-29
8.55 v. 14
8.56 Josh 21.45; 23.14

8.57
Josh 1.5;
Rom 8.28;
Heb 13.5
8.58
Ps 119.36

promise, which he spoke through his servant Moses. 57 The LORD our God be with us, as he was with our ancestors; may he not leave us or abandon us, 58 but incline our hearts to him, to walk in all his ways, and to keep his commandments, his statutes, and his ordinances, which he commanded our ancestors. 59 Let these words of mine, with which I pleaded before the LORD, be near to the LORD our God day and night, and may he maintain the cause of his servant and the cause of his people Israel, as each day requires; 60 so that all the peoples of the earth may know that the LORD is God; there is no other. 61 Therefore devote yourselves completely to the LORD our God, walking in his statutes and keeping his commandments, as at this day."

8.60
1 Kings 18.39;
Jer 10.10-12
8.61
1 Kings 11.4;
15.3, 14;
2 Kings 20.3

5. The offerings and festival

8.62
2 Chr 7.4ff

62   Then the king, and all Israel with him, offered sacrifice before the LORD. 63 Solomon offered as sacrifices of well-being to the LORD twenty-two thousand oxen and one hundred twenty thousand sheep. So the king and all the people of Israel dedicated the house of the LORD. 64 The same day the king consecrated the middle of the court that was in front of the house of the LORD; for there he offered the burnt offerings and the grain offerings and the fat pieces of the sacrifices of well-being, because the bronze altar that was before the LORD was too small to receive the burnt offerings and the grain offerings and the fat pieces of the sacrifices of well-being.

8.64
2 Chr 7.7; 4.1

8.65
v. 2;
Lev 23.34;
Num 34.8;
Josh 13.5;
Gen 15.18;
2 Chr 7.8

65   So Solomon held the festival at that time, and all Israel with him — a great assembly, people from Lebo-hamath to the Wadi of Egypt — before the LORD our God, seven days.[l] 66 On the eighth day he sent the people away; and they blessed the king, and went to their tents, joyful and in good spirits because of all the goodness that the LORD had shown to his servant David and to his people Israel.

l. God's conditional covenant with Solomon

9.1
2 Chr 7.11ff;
1 Kings 7.1;
2 Chr 8.6
9.2
1 Kings 3.5
9.3
2 Kings 20.5;
1 Kings 8.29;
Deut 11.12
9.4
Gen 17.1;
1 Kings 15.5
9.5
2 Sam 7.12,
16;
1 Kings 2.4;
1 Chr 22.10
9.6
2 Sam 7.14;
2 Chr 7.19,
20

9 When Solomon had finished building the house of the LORD and the king's house and all that Solomon desired to build, 2 the LORD appeared to Solomon a second time, as he had appeared to him at Gibeon. 3 The LORD said to him, "I have heard your prayer and your plea, which you made before me; I have consecrated this house that you have built, and put my name there forever; my eyes and my heart will be there for all time. 4 As for you, if you will walk before me, as David your father walked, with integrity of heart and uprightness, doing according to all that I have commanded you, and keeping my statutes and my ordinances, 5 then I will establish your royal throne over Israel forever, as I promised your father David, saying, 'There shall not fail you a successor on the throne of Israel.'

6   "If you turn aside from following me, you or your children, and do

---

[l] Compare Gk: Heb seven days and seven days, fourteen days

8.60   Solomon's blessing over Israel had in it a missionary perspective. He did not want all nations to be subject to his rulership. Rather, he expressed the wish that the people of all nations might know the true God and acknowledge that there is nothing above him.

8.61   The ideal standard for the believer's daily walk is characterized by obedience that is total and complete, continuing all the days of one's life.

8.63   Some have questioned whether this number of animals could have been sacrificed in such a short period. Verse 64 explains that some animals were offered a short distance away from the middle court of the temple.

9.2   Since God's second appearance to Solomon

came in the same manner as the first one at Gibeon, it can only mean that it was a dream (3.5). Solomon had dedicated the temple to God, but only God could consecrate it by the presence of his glory in the midst of the temple.

9.6   The word "if" consistently appears in God's conversations with the leaders and the people of Israel. The promised blessings of God were conditional, i.e., they would come only if God's people obeyed his commandments and walked before him with a whole heart. If they did not, evil consequences would flow from their disobedience and the blessings would turn to curses and disaster. The promises to Solomon are of special note, since his latter days were marked by a turning away from the deep-seated convictions ex-not keep my commandments and my statutes that I have set before you, but go and serve other gods and worship them, 7 then I will cut Israel off from the land that I have given them; and the house that I have consecrated for my name I will cast out of my sight; and Israel will become a proverb and a taunt among all peoples. 8 This house will become a heap of ruins;*m* everyone passing by it will be astonished, and will hiss; and they will say, 'Why has the LORD done such a thing to this land and to this house?' 9 Then they will say, 'Because they have forsaken the LORD their God, who brought their ancestors out of the land of Egypt, and embraced other gods, worshiping them and serving them; therefore the LORD has brought this disaster upon them.' "

J. Incidental details about Solomon

10 At the end of twenty years, in which Solomon had built the two houses, the house of the LORD and the king's house, 11 King Hiram of Tyre having supplied Solomon with cedar and cypress timber and gold, as much as he desired, King Solomon gave to Hiram twenty cities in the land of Galilee. 12 But when Hiram came from Tyre to see the cities that Solomon had given him, they did not please him. 13 Therefore he said, "What kind of cities are these that you have given me, my brother?" So they are called the land of Cabul*n* to this day. 14 But Hiram had sent to the king one hundred twenty talents of gold.

15 This is the account of the forced labor that King Solomon conscripted to build the house of the LORD and his own house, the Millo and the wall of Jerusalem, Hazor, Megiddo, Gezer 16 (Pharaoh king of Egypt had gone up and captured Gezer and burned it down, had killed the Canaanites who lived in the city, and had given it as dowry to his daughter, Solomon's wife; 17 so Solomon rebuilt Gezer), Lower Beth-horon, 18 Baalath, Tamar in the wilderness, within the land, 19 as well as all of Solomon's storage cities, the cities for his chariots, the cities for his cavalry, and whatever Solomon desired to build, in Jerusalem, in Lebanon, and in all the land of his dominion. 20 All the people who were left of the Amorites, the Hittites, the Perizzites, the Hivites, and the Jebusites, who were not of the people of Israel — 21 their descendants who were still left in the land, whom the Israelites were unable to destroy completely — these Solomon conscripted for slave labor, and so they are to this day. 22 But of the Israelites Solomon made no slaves; they were the soldiers, they were his officials, his commanders, his captains, and the commanders of his chariotry and cavalry.

23 These were the chief officers who were over Solomon's work: five hundred fifty, who had charge of the people who carried on the work.

24 But Pharaoh's daughter went up from the city of David to her own house that Solomon had built for her; then he built the Millo.

25 Three times a year Solomon used to offer up burnt offerings and sacrifices of well-being on the altar that he built for the LORD, offering incense*o* before the LORD. So he completed the house.

26 King Solomon built a fleet of ships at Ezion-geber, which is near Eloth on the shore of the Red Sea,*p* in the land of Edom. 27 Hiram sent his servants with the fleet, sailors who were familiar with the sea, together with the servants of Solomon. 28 They went to Ophir, and imported from

m Syr Old Latin: Heb *will become high*   *n* Perhaps meaning *a land good for nothing*   *o* Gk: Heb *offering incense with it that was*   *p* Or *Sea of Reeds*

9.7
2 Kings 17.23;
25.21;
Jer 7.14;
Deut 28.37;
Ps 44.14
9.8
2 Chr 7.21;
Deut 29.24-26;
Jer 22.8, 9

9.10
1 Kings 6.37,
38; 7.1;
2 Chr 8.1
9.11
2 Chr 8.2

9.13
Josh 19.27

9.15
1 Kings 5.13;
v. 24;
2 Sam 5.9;
Josh 19.36;
17.11; 16.10
9.16
Josh 16.10
9.17
Josh 16.3;
2 Chr 8.5
9.19
1 Kings 4.26;
v. 1
9.20
2 Chr 8.7
9.21
Judg 1.21,
27, 29;
Josh 15.63;
17.12;
Judg 1.21;
Gen 9.25, 26;
Ezra 2.55, 58
9.22
Lev 25.39
9.23
2 Chr 8.10
9.24
1 Kings 3.1;
7.8; 11.27;
2 Chr 32.5
9.25
2 Chr 8.12,
13, 16
9.26
2 Chr 8.17,
18;
Num 33.35;
Deut 2.8;
1 Kings 22.48
9.27
1 Kings 10.11
9.28
1 Chr 29.4

pressed at the time of the dedication of the house of God.
9.8 If the temple of God were ever destroyed and people asked why God permitted it to happen, the answer is plain: God was first abandoned by his people before he abandoned them.

9.15 *Hazor, Megiddo, Gezer.* Remains from Solomon's time have been found by archaeologists in these Canaanite cities.
9.28 *Ophir*, thought by some to be located in southern Arabia. Others place it along the African coast in the area of what is now Somaliland.

there four hundred twenty talents of gold, which they delivered to King Solomon.

K. *The visit of the queen of Sheba*

10 When the queen of Sheba heard of the fame of Solomon (fame due to*q* the name of the LORD), she came to test him with hard questions. 2 She came to Jerusalem with a very great retinue, with camels bearing spices, and very much gold, and precious stones; and when she came to Solomon, she told him all that was on her mind. 3 Solomon answered all her questions; there was nothing hidden from the king that he could not explain to her. 4 When the queen of Sheba had observed all the wisdom of Solomon, the house that he had built, 5 the food of his table, the seating of his officials, and the attendance of his servants, their clothing, his valets, and his burnt offerings that he offered at the house of the LORD, there was no more spirit in her.

6 So she said to the king, "The report was true that I heard in my own land of your accomplishments and of your wisdom, 7 but I did not believe the reports until I came and my own eyes had seen it. Not even half had been told me; your wisdom and prosperity far surpass the report that I had heard. 8 Happy are your wives!*r* Happy are these your servants, who continually attend you and hear your wisdom! 9 Blessed be the LORD your God, who has delighted in you and set you on the throne of Israel! Because the LORD loved Israel forever, he has made you king to execute justice and righteousness." 10 Then she gave the king one hundred twenty talents of gold, a great quantity of spices, and precious stones; never again did spices come in such quantity as that which the queen of Sheba gave to King Solomon.

11 Moreover, the fleet of Hiram, which carried gold from Ophir, brought from Ophir a great quantity of almug wood and precious stones. 12 From the almug wood the king made supports for the house of the LORD, and for the king's house, lyres also and harps for the singers; no such almug wood has come or been seen to this day.

13 Meanwhile King Solomon gave to the queen of Sheba every desire that she expressed, as well as what he gave her out of Solomon's royal bounty. Then she returned to her own land, with her servants.

L. *The material splendor of Solomon*

14 The weight of gold that came to Solomon in one year was six hundred sixty-six talents of gold, 15 besides that which came from the traders and from the business of the merchants, and from all the kings of Arabia and the governors of the land. 16 King Solomon made two hundred large shields of beaten gold; six hundred shekels of gold went into each large shield. 17 He made three hundred shields of beaten gold; three minas of gold went into each shield; and the king put them in the House of the Forest of Lebanon. 18 The king also made a great ivory throne, and overlaid it with the finest gold. 19 The throne had six steps. The top of the throne was rounded in the back, and on each side of the seat were arm rests and two lions standing beside the arm rests, 20 while twelve lions were standing, one on each end of a step on the six steps. Nothing like it was ever made in any kingdom. 21 All King Solomon's drinking vessels

q Meaning of Heb uncertain   r Gk Syr: Heb men

Cross references (margin):
10.1 2 Chr 9.1ff; Mt 12.42; Judg 14.12
10.5 1 Chr 26.16
10.9 1 Kings 5.7; 2 Sam 8.15
10.10 v. 2
10.11 1 Kings 9.27, 28
10.12 2 Chr 9.10, 11
10.14 2 Chr 9.13-28
10.16 1 Kings 14.26-28
10.17 1 Kings 7.2
10.18 2 Chr 9.17ff

10.1 *Sheba*, the land of the Sabeans in southwestern Arabia, now part of modern Yemen. It controlled the caravan routes through which incense and spice were brought from Arabia to Palestine.
10.7 The queen of Sheba marvelled at Solomon's great wisdom. This wisdom points foward to the wisdom of Jesus, which is greater than that of Solomon

(Mt 12.42).
10.14 The 666 talents would make approximately 800,000 ounces of gold. Modern gold prices would put its value at hundreds of million of dollars.
10.21 So plentiful was gold that silver "was not considered as anything in the days of Solomon." Even the cups were made of gold.

were of gold, and all the vessels of the House of the Forest of Lebanon were of pure gold; none were of silver — it was not considered as anything in the days of Solomon. 22 For the king had a fleet of ships of Tarshish at sea with the fleet of Hiram. Once every three years the fleet of ships of Tarshish used to come bringing gold, silver, ivory, apes, and peacocks.ˢ

23 Thus King Solomon excelled all the kings of the earth in riches and in wisdom. 24 The whole earth sought the presence of Solomon to hear his wisdom, which God had put into his mind. 25 Every one of them brought a present, objects of silver and gold, garments, weaponry, spices, horses, and mules, so much year by year.

26 Solomon gathered together chariots and horses; he had fourteen hundred chariots and twelve thousand horses, which he stationed in the chariot cities and with the king in Jerusalem. 27 The king made silver as common in Jerusalem as stones, and he made cedars as numerous as the sycamores of the Shephelah. 28 Solomon's import of horses was from Egypt and Kue, and the king's traders received them from Kue at a price. 29 A chariot could be imported from Egypt for six hundred shekels of silver, and a horse for one hundred fifty; so through the king's traders they were exported to all the kings of the Hittites and the kings of Aram.

M. Solomon breaks God's covenant

1. He takes foreign wives

11 King Solomon loved many foreign women along with the daughter of Pharaoh: Moabite, Ammonite, Edomite, Sidonian, and Hittite women, 2 from the nations concerning which the LORD had said to the Israelites, "You shall not enter into marriage with them, neither shall they with you; for they will surely incline your heart to follow their gods"; Solomon clung to these in love. 3 Among his wives were seven hundred princesses and three hundred concubines; and his wives turned away his heart. 4 For when Solomon was old, his wives turned away his heart after other gods; and his heart was not true to the LORD his God, as was the heart of his father David. 5 For Solomon followed Astarte the goddess of the Sidonians, and Milcom the abomination of the Ammonites. 6 So Solomon did what was evil in the sight of the LORD, and did not completely follow the LORD, as his father David had done. 7 Then Solomon built a high place for Chemosh the abomination of Moab, and for Molech the abomination of the Ammonites, on the mountain east of Jerusalem. 8 He did the same for all his foreign wives, who offered incense and sacrificed to their gods.

2. God warns Solomon

9 Then the LORD was angry with Solomon, because his heart had

ˢ Or *baboons*

10.22
1 Kings 9.26-28;
22.48;
2 Chr 20.36

10.23
1 Kings 3.12,
13; 4.30
10.24
1 Kings 3.9,
12, 28

10.26
1 Kings 4.26;
2 Chr 1.14;
9.25;
1 Kings 9.19

10.28
2 Chr 1.16;
9.28
10.29
2 Kings 7.6,
7

11.1
Neh 13.26;
Deut 17.17
11.2
Ex 34.16;
Deut 7.3, 4

11.4
1 Kings 8.61;
9.4
11.5
v. 33;
Judg 2.13;
2 Kings 23.13
11.7
Num 21.29;
Judg 11.24;
2 Kings 23.13

11.9
vv. 2, 3;
1 Kings 3.5;
9.2

10.22 *ships of Tarshish.* These were probably large vessels trading with Tarshish (likely Sardinia or southern Spain).
10.23 Solomon had asked God for wisdom. He got both wisdom and riches. None was greater than he. Yet Solomon spoke of the vanity of all worldly concerns, their insufficiency to produce happiness, and the foolishness of setting our hearts upon them (see the book of Ecclesiastes).
11.3 Solomon's acquisition of wives, horses, silver, and gold constituted a violation of Deut 17.16,17.
11.4 Solomon's many wives turned her heart away from God, eventually leading to his downfall. His wisdom failed him at this point. This pattern occurred again and again; rather than Israel influencing

the pagan nations for good, they influenced Israel for evil. This serves as a warning for both nations and individual believers today: we should influence unbelievers for Christ rather than lose our faith through identifying ourselves with the world.
11.5 *Astarte*, a Canaanite goddess of fertility. *Milcom* was another name for Molech, the god to whom children were sacrificed (Lev 20.1–5) (see note on Zeph 1.5).
11.9,10 When one turns away from God and leaves one's first love, fellowship with God is broken. Such backsliding can occur in a variety of ways. It may be: a breach of the moral law, such as David's adultery and murder (2 Sam 11); a verbal denial of Jesus, as done by Peter (Mt 26.70–74); disobedience to an

turned away from the LORD, the God of Israel, who had appeared to him twice, 10 and had commanded him concerning this matter, that he should not follow other gods; but he did not observe what the LORD commanded. 11 Therefore the LORD said to Solomon, "Since this has been your mind and you have not kept my covenant and my statutes that I have commanded you, I will surely tear the kingdom from you and give it to your servant. 12 Yet for the sake of your father David I will not do it in your lifetime; I will tear it out of the hand of your son. 13 I will not, however, tear away the entire kingdom; I will give one tribe to your son, for the sake of my servant David and for the sake of Jerusalem, which I have chosen."

3. God raises up adversaries against Solomon

a. Hadad

14 Then the LORD raised up an adversary against Solomon, Hadad the Edomite; he was of the royal house in Edom. 15 For when David was in Edom, and Joab the commander of the army went up to bury the dead, he killed every male in Edom 16 (for Joab and all Israel remained there six months, until he had eliminated every male in Edom); 17 but Hadad fled to Egypt with some Edomites who were servants of his father. He was a young boy at that time. 18 They set out from Midian and came to Paran; they took people with them from Paran and came to Egypt, to Pharaoh king of Egypt, who gave him a house, assigned him an allowance of food, and gave him land. 19 Hadad found great favor in the sight of Pharaoh, so that he gave him his sister-in-law for a wife, the sister of Queen Tahpenes. 20 The sister of Tahpenes gave birth by him to his son Genubath, whom Tahpenes weaned in Pharaoh's house; Genubath was in Pharaoh's house among the children of Pharaoh. 21 When Hadad heard in Egypt that David slept with his ancestors and that Joab the commander of the army was dead, Hadad said to Pharaoh, "Let me depart, that I may go to my own country." 22 But Pharaoh said to him, "What do you lack with me that you now seek to go to your own country?" And he said, "No, do let me go."

b. Rezon

23 God raised up another adversary against Solomon,[t] Rezon son of Eliada, who had fled from his master, King Hadadezer of Zobah. 24 He gathered followers around him and became leader of a marauding band, after the slaughter by David; they went to Damascus, settled there, and made him king in Damascus. 25 He was an adversary of Israel all the days of Solomon, making trouble as Hadad did; he despised Israel and reigned over Aram.

c. Jeroboam

26 Jeroboam son of Nebat, an Ephraimite of Zeredah, a servant of Solomon, whose mother's name was Zeruah, a widow, rebelled against the king. 27 The following was the reason he rebelled against the king. Solo-

Marginal references:

11.10 1 Kings 6.12; 9.6, 7
11.11 v. 31; 1 Kings 12.15, 16
11.13 2 Sam 7.15; 1 Kings 12.20; Deut 12.11
11.15 2 Sam 8.14; 1 Chr 18.12, 13
11.21 1 Kings 2.10
11.23 v. 14; 2 Sam 8.3
11.24 2 Sam 8.3; 10.8, 18
11.26 1 Kings 12.2; 2 Chr 13.6; 2 Sam 20.21
11.27 1 Kings 9.24

---

t Heb *him*

---

express command of God, as done by Saul (1 Sam 15.11). Backsliding is not incurable, however, for a person can repent, confess, and return to the Lord, as did Samson (Judg 16.28), David (2 Sam 12.13), and Peter (cf. Acts 2.14ff).
11.11–13 God informed Solomon that he was angry with him because of his backsliding. How he did this we are not told, for no prophet or vision is mentioned. God gave Solomon all a king could desire and still he chose not to remain faithful. The judgment would result in the division of Solomon's kingdom, with the

loss of the ten tribes to another monarch. For the sake of David's memory, this would be delayed until after the death of Solomon.
11.14 God raised up three enemies to act as his agents in judgment upon Solomon. The first was Hadad the Edomite (vv. 14–22). Then came Rezon, who reigned over Syria and hated Israel fervently (vv. 23–25). The third was Jeroboam, who came from the tribe of Ephraim and eventually became king of Israel (vv. 26–40).

mon built the Millo, and closed up the gap in the wall^u of the city of his father David. 28 The man Jeroboam was very able, and when Solomon saw that the young man was industrious he gave him charge over all the forced labor of the house of Joseph. 29 About that time, when Jeroboam was leaving Jerusalem, the prophet Ahijah the Shilonite found him on the road. Ahijah had clothed himself with a new garment. The two of them were alone in the open country 30 when Ahijah laid hold of the new garment he was wearing and tore it into twelve pieces. 31 He then said to Jeroboam: Take for yourself ten pieces; for thus says the Lord, the God of Israel, "See, I am about to tear the kingdom from the hand of Solomon, and will give you ten tribes. 32 One tribe will remain his, for the sake of my servant David and for the sake of Jerusalem, the city that I have chosen out of all the tribes of Israel. 33 This is because he has^v forsaken me, worshiped Astarte the goddess of the Sidonians, Chemosh the god of Moab, and Milcom the god of the Ammonites, and has^v not walked in my ways, doing what is right in my sight and keeping my statutes and my ordinances, as his father David did. 34 Nevertheless I will not take the whole kingdom away from him but will make him ruler all the days of his life, for the sake of my servant David whom I chose and who did keep my commandments and my statutes; 35 but I will take the kingdom away from his son and give it to you—that is, the ten tribes. 36 Yet to his son I will give one tribe, so that my servant David may always have a lamp before me in Jerusalem, the city where I have chosen to put my name. 37 I will take you, and you shall reign over all that your soul desires; you shall be king over Israel. 38 If you will listen to all that I command you, walk in my ways, and do what is right in my sight by keeping my statutes and my commandments, as David my servant did, I will be with you, and will build you an enduring house, as I built for David, and I will give Israel to you. 39 For this reason I will punish the descendants of David, but not forever." 40 Solomon sought therefore to kill Jeroboam; but Jeroboam promptly fled to Egypt, to King Shishak of Egypt, and remained in Egypt until the death of Solomon.

N. *The death of Solomon*

41 Now the rest of the acts of Solomon, all that he did as well as his wisdom, are they not written in the Book of the Acts of Solomon? 42 The time that Solomon reigned in Jerusalem over all Israel was forty years. 43 Solomon slept with his ancestors and was buried in the city of his father David; and his son Rehoboam succeeded him.

III. *The divided kingdom (12.1–22.53)*

A. *The division of the kingdom*

1. *The revolt of the ten tribes*

12 Rehoboam went to Shechem, for all Israel had come to Shechem to make him king. 2 When Jeroboam son of Nebat heard of it (for

^u Heb lacks *in the wall*   ^v Gk Syr Vg: Heb *they have*

Margin references:
11.29 1 Kings 14.2
11.30 1 Sam 15.27, 28
11.31 vv. 11-13
11.33 vv. 5-7
11.35 1 Kings 12.16, 17
11.36 v. 13; 1 Kings 15.4; 2 Kings 8.19
11.38 Josh 1.5; 2 Sam 7.11, 27
11.41 2 Chr 9.29
11.42 2Ch 9.30
11.43 2 Chr 9.31; 1 Kings 14.21
12.1 2 Chr 10.1ff
12.2 1 Kings 11.26, 40

11.32 *One tribe will remain his.* Of the twelve tribes, Judah and Benjamin would be left to Solomon's son. Benjamin had already been assimilated by Judah, the more numerous and powerful neighbor, and both were often called "Judah."
11.40 Jeroboam was an industrious worker, "very able" (v. 28). Ahijah the prophet told him that God would give him ten tribes, for Solomon's kingdom was to be divided into two parts because of his sins. Solomon knew of this coming judgment from God, but his spiritual state was such that he refused to

accept the consequences for his transgressions. In rebellion against the word from God, he tried to slay Jeroboam, forcing him to flee to Egypt for his life; he remained there until the death of Solomon.
12.1ff Solomon's heavy taxation policies and use of forced labor had alienated the Israelites from the north. Led by Jeroboam who had returned from Egypt, they assembled at Shechem to formally make Rehoboam king as Solomon's successor. Before his investiture, though, they asked him to lighten the heavy yoke placed on them by Solomon. He inad-

he was still in Egypt, where he had fled from King Solomon), then Jeroboam returned from[w] Egypt. 3 And they sent and called him; and Jeroboam and all the assembly of Israel came and said to Rehoboam, 4 "Your father made our yoke heavy. Now therefore lighten the hard service of your father and his heavy yoke that he placed on us, and we will serve you." 5 He said to them, "Go away for three days, then come again to me." So the people went away.

6   Then King Rehoboam took counsel with the older men who had attended his father Solomon while he was still alive, saying, "How do you advise me to answer this people?" 7 They answered him, "If you will be a servant to this people today and serve them, and speak good words to them when you answer them, then they will be your servants forever." 8 But he disregarded the advice that the older men gave him, and consulted with the young men who had grown up with him and now attended him. 9 He said to them, "What do you advise that we answer this people who have said to me, 'Lighten the yoke that your father put on us'?" 10 The young men who had grown up with him said to him, "Thus you should say to this people who spoke to you, 'Your father made our yoke heavy, but you must lighten it for us'; thus you should say to them, 'My little finger is thicker than my father's loins. 11 Now, whereas my father laid on you a heavy yoke, I will add to your yoke. My father disciplined you with whips, but I will discipline you with scorpions.' "

12   So Jeroboam and all the people came to Rehoboam the third day, as the king had said, "Come to me again the third day." 13 The king answered the people harshly. He disregarded the advice that the older men had given him 14 and spoke to them according to the advice of the young men, "My father made your yoke heavy, but I will add to your yoke; my father disciplined you with whips, but I will discipline you with scorpions." 15 So the king did not listen to the people, because it was a turn of affairs brought about by the LORD that he might fulfill his word, which the LORD had spoken by Ahijah the Shilonite to Jeroboam son of Nebat.

16   When all Israel saw that the king would not listen to them, the people answered the king,

"What share do we have in David?
    We have no inheritance in the son of Jesse.
To your tents, O Israel!
    Look now to your own house, O David."

So Israel went away to their tents. 17 But Rehoboam reigned over the Israelites who were living in the towns of Judah. 18 When King Rehoboam sent Adoram, who was taskmaster over the forced labor, all Israel stoned him to death. King Rehoboam then hurriedly mounted his chariot to flee to Jerusalem. 19 So Israel has been in rebellion against the house of David to this day.

20   When all Israel heard that Jeroboam had returned, they sent and called him to the assembly and made him king over all Israel. There was no one who followed the house of David, except the tribe of Judah alone.

[w] Gk Vg Compare 2 Chr 10.2: Heb *lived in*

---

visedly responded with great rigor, "I will add to your yoke; my father disciplined you with whips, but I will discipline you with scorpions" (v. 14). Thereupon the northern tribes defected from the Davidic monarchy and set up Jeroboam as their king. Thus began the history of the two kingdoms of Israel and Judah.
12.13 Unlike his grandfather David, Rehoboam looked to his old and young political advisors instead of seeking God for his will. He was the son of Solomon the wisest of people, but he did not have his wisdom. Neither wisdom nor grace runs in the blood. If at forty years old Rehoboam did not have wisdom, he was not likely to have it thereafter.
12.15 Behind all this political maneuvering, the writer of 1 Kings makes it plain that the God of providence had brought about the decision of Rehoboam. God was fulfilling the divine prophecy uttered by Ahijah the Shilonite, who said the kingdom would be divided and Solomon's heir left with only Judah for his lot.
12.20 *the tribe of Judah alone.* Judah and Benjamin were sometimes (as in this instance) counted together as one tribe.

12.4
1 Sam 8.11-18;
1 Kings 4.7
12.5
v. 12

12.7
2 Chr 10.7

12.8
Lev 19.32

12.12
v. 5

12.14
Ex 1.13, 14;
5.5-9, 16-18
12.15
v. 24;
Judg 14.4;
2 Chr 10.15;
22.7; 25.20;
1 Kings 11.11,
31
12.16
2 Sam 20.1

12.17
1 Kings 11.13,
36
12.18
1 Kings 4.6;
5.14
12.19
2 Kings 17.21

12.20
1 Kings 11.13,
32

2. God forbids Rehoboam to fight against Jeroboam

21 When Rehoboam came to Jerusalem, he assembled all the house
of Judah and the tribe of Benjamin, one hundred eighty thousand chosen
troops to fight against the house of Israel, to restore the kingdom to
Rehoboam son of Solomon. 22 But the word of God came to Shemaiah the
man of God: 23 Say to King Rehoboam of Judah, son of Solomon, and to
all the house of Judah and Benjamin, and to the rest of the people,
24 "Thus says the LORD, You shall not go up or fight against your kindred
the people of Israel. Let everyone go home, for this thing is from me."
So they heeded the word of the LORD and went home again, according to
the word of the LORD.

12.21
2 Chr 11.1ff

12.24
v. 15

3. The institution of calf worship at Bethel and Dan

25 Then Jeroboam built Shechem in the hill country of Ephraim, and
resided there; he went out from there and built Penuel. 26 Then Jeroboam
said to himself, "Now the kingdom may well revert to the house of David.
27 If this people continues to go up to offer sacrifices in the house of the
LORD at Jerusalem, the heart of this people will turn again to their master,
King Rehoboam of Judah; they will kill me and return to King Rehoboam
of Judah." 28 So the king took counsel, and made two calves of gold. He
said to the people, x "You have gone up to Jerusalem long enough. Here
are your gods, O Israel, who brought you up out of the land of Egypt."
29 He set one in Bethel, and the other he put in Dan. 30 And this thing
became a sin, for the people went to worship before the one at Bethel and
before the other as far as Dan. y 31 He also made houses z on high places,
and appointed priests from among all the people, who were not Levites.
32 Jeroboam appointed a festival on the fifteenth day of the eighth month
like the festival that was in Judah, and he offered sacrifices on the altar;
so he did in Bethel, sacrificing to the calves that he had made. And he
placed in Bethel the priests of the high places that he had made. 33 He went
up to the altar that he had made in Bethel on the fifteenth day in the eighth
month, in the month that he alone had devised; he appointed a festival
for the people of Israel, and he went up to the altar to offer incense.

12.25
Judg 9.45;
8.17

12.27
Deut 12.5, 6

12.28
2 Kings 10.29;
17.16;
Ex 32.4, 8

12.29
Gen 28.19;
Judg 18.29
12.30
1 Kings 13.34;
2 Kings 17.21
12.31
1 Kings 13.32,
33;
Num 3.10;
2 Kings 17.32
12.32
Lev 23.33,
34;
Num 29.12;
Am 7.13
12.33
1 Kings 13.1

B. A man of God from Judah

1. The prophecy about Josiah

13 While Jeroboam was standing by the altar to offer incense, a man
      of God came out of Judah by the word of the LORD to Bethel 2 and
proclaimed against the altar by the word of the LORD, and said, "O altar,

13.1
2 Kings 23.17;
1 Kings 12.32,
33
13.2
2 Kings 23.15,
16

x Gk: Heb to them   y Compare Gk: Heb went to the one as far as Dan   z Gk Vg Compare 13.32:
Heb a house

12.21–24 Rehoboam's desire to conquer Israel by
force and reestablish his father's undivided kingdom
was forbidden him by God, who sent Shemaiah the
prophet to tell him so. God had visited Solomon by
direct communication but made no such visitation to
Rehoboam. To Rehoboam's credit, he and his troops
did obey the word of the Lord that came through
Shemaiah.
12.28 When the kingdom of Solomon was divided,
Jeroboam, king of the northern kingdom, did not
want his people to go to Jerusalem for religious services. So he set up two calves for their worship, one
in Bethel, not far from Jerusalem, and the other in
Dan in the far north. Jeroboam's statement "Here are
your gods" was taken from Ex 32.4, implying that his
images were similar to the golden calf of Aaron. Some
think Jeroboam only intended the calves to be pedes-
tals, much like the cherubim, over which the invisible

God was enthroned. Later, the people worshiped the
visible objects, incurred the wrath of God, and
brought about the end of the ten tribes in 722 B.C.
12.31 Generally, *high places* were places of worship
located on a hill or mountain and associated with false
religions. Before the end of the northern kingdom and
the destruction of Jerusalem by Nebuchadnezzar, the
Israelites built many such shrines and engaged in
pagan worship ceremonies.
12.32 *on the fifteenth day of the eighth month* (of
the Hebrew calendar), i.e., around the first of November.
13.1ff Jeroboam turned out to be an idolatrous
king. He revived the bull worship of Mesopotamian
origin, established high places for worship, and appointed non-Levites as priests. He even changed the
date of the festival of tabernacles. He reigned for
twenty-two years.

altar, thus says the Lord: 'A son shall be born to the house of David, Josiah by name; and he shall sacrifice on you the priests of the high places who offer incense on you, and human bones shall be burned on you.'"

13.3
Isa 7.14;
Judg 6.17
3 He gave a sign the same day, saying, "This is the sign that the Lord has spoken: 'The altar shall be torn down, and the ashes that are on it shall be poured out.'" 4 When the king heard what the man of God cried out against the altar at Bethel, Jeroboam stretched out his hand from the altar, saying, "Seize him!" But the hand that he stretched out against him withered so that he could not draw it back to himself. 5 The altar also was torn down, and the ashes poured out from the altar, according to the sign that the man of God had given by the word of the Lord. 6 The king said
13.6
Ex 8.8; 9.28;
Acts 8.24;
Lk 6.27, 28
to the man of God, "Entreat now the favor of the Lord your God, and pray for me, so that my hand may be restored to me." So the man of God entreated the Lord; and the king's hand was restored to him, and became
13.7
1 Sam 9.7, 8;
2 Kings 5.15
13.8
vv. 16, 17;
Num 22.18;
24.13
as it was before. 7 Then the king said to the man of God, "Come home with me and dine, and I will give you a gift." 8 But the man of God said to the king, "If you give me half your kingdom, I will not go in with you; nor will I eat food or drink water in this place. 9 For thus I was commanded by the word of the Lord: You shall not eat food, or drink water, or return by the way that you came." 10 So he went another way, and did not return by the way that he had come to Bethel.

2. The lying prophet

13.11
v. 25
11 Now there lived an old prophet in Bethel. One of his sons came and told him all that the man of God had done that day in Bethel; the words also that he had spoken to the king, they told to their father. 12 Their father said to them, "Which way did he go?" And his sons showed him the way that the man of God who came from Judah had gone. 13 Then he said to his sons, "Saddle a donkey for me." So they saddled a donkey for him, and he mounted it. 14 He went after the man of God, and found him sitting under an oak tree. He said to him, "Are you the man of God who came from Judah?" He answered, "I am." 15 Then he said to him,
13.16
vv. 8, 9
"Come home with me and eat some food." 16 But he said, "I cannot return with you, or go in with you; nor will I eat food or drink water with you
13.17
1 Kings 20.35
in this place; 17 for it was said to me by the word of the Lord: You shall not eat food or drink water there, or return by the way that you came." 18 Then the other^a said to him, "I also am a prophet as you are, and an angel spoke to me by the word of the Lord: Bring him back with you into your house so that he may eat food and drink water." But he was deceiving him. 19 Then the man of God^a went back with him, and ate food and drank water in his house.

3. The man of God killed by a lion for disobedience

13.21
1 Sam 15.26
20 As they were sitting at the table, the word of the Lord came to the prophet who had brought him back; 21 and he proclaimed to the man of

^{a} Heb he

13.4 Jeroboam was about to offer sacrifices to God on a strange altar. How could God be pleased with a sacrifice offered on an altar that was an abomination? God's anger and the prophetic word of the man of God were confirmed by signs: Jeroboam's arm was dried up so that he could not move it, and the altar was rent and the ashes poured out from it. But none of this moved Jeroboam to repentance. He invited the prophet to go home with him.
13.11 God had told the unnamed prophet not to eat or drink until he had returned home. He had already refused to be honored by Jeroboam, but now he received an invitation to visit and eat with an unnamed old prophet, who pretended to have received a con-

trary word from God through an angel. God's good prophet believed the lie, ate and drank with the false one, and was punished with death. Compare this with Paul's injunction that even if an angel from heaven preached any other gospel than the one he had received, he was to be disbelieved (Gal 1.8,9) — for the gospel does not change, nor does any word from God.
13.20 God gave a true word to the lying prophet and through him pronounced judgment on the one who ate and drank contrary to God's specific command. No one is ever excused for disobedience by the sanctity of one's profession, the dignity of office, or nearness to God.

God who came from Judah, "Thus says the LORD: Because you have disobeyed the word of the LORD, and have not kept the commandment that the LORD your God commanded you, 22 but have come back and have eaten food and drunk water in the place of which he said to you, 'Eat no food, and drink no water,' your body shall not come to your ancestral tomb." 23 After the man of God*b* had eaten food and had drunk, they saddled for him a donkey belonging to the prophet who had brought him back. 24 Then as he went away, a lion met him on the road and killed him. His body was thrown in the road, and the donkey stood beside it; the lion also stood beside the body. 25 People passed by and saw the body thrown in the road, with the lion standing by the body. And they came and told it in the town where the old prophet lived.

26 When the prophet who had brought him back from the way heard of it, he said, "It is the man of God who disobeyed the word of the LORD; therefore the LORD has given him to the lion, which has torn him and killed him according to the word that the LORD spoke to him." 27 Then he said to his sons, "Saddle a donkey for me." So they saddled one, 28 and he went and found the body thrown in the road, with the donkey and the lion standing beside the body. The lion had not eaten the body or attacked the donkey. 29 The prophet took up the body of the man of God, laid it on the donkey, and brought it back to the city,*c* to mourn and to bury him. 30 He laid the body in his own grave; and they mourned over him, saying, "Alas, my brother!" 31 After he had buried him, he said to his sons, "When I die, bury me in the grave in which the man of God is buried; lay my bones beside his bones. 32 For the saying that he proclaimed by the word of the LORD against the altar in Bethel, and against all the houses of the high places that are in the cities of Samaria, shall surely come to pass."

4. The continuing unfaithfulness of Jeroboam

33 Even after this event Jeroboam did not turn from his evil way, but made priests for the high places again from among all the people; any who wanted to be priests he consecrated for the high places. 34 This matter became sin to the house of Jeroboam, so as to cut it off and to destroy it from the face of the earth.

C. The house of Jeroboam

1. Ahijah prophesies the death of Jeroboam's son

14 At that time Abijah son of Jeroboam fell sick. 2 Jeroboam said to his wife, "Go, disguise yourself, so that it will not be known that you are the wife of Jeroboam, and go to Shiloh; for the prophet Ahijah is there, who said of me that I should be king over this people. 3 Take with you ten loaves, some cakes, and a jar of honey, and go to him; he will tell you what shall happen to the child."

4 Jeroboam's wife did so; she set out and went to Shiloh, and came

b Heb *he*   *c* Gk: Heb *he came to the town of the old prophet*

13.24	1 Kings 20.36
13.25	v. 11
13.26	v. 21
13.30	Jer 22.18
13.31	2 Kings 23.17, 18
13.32	v. 2; 2 Kings 23.16, 17, 19; see 1 Kings 16.24
13.33	1 Kings 12.31, 32; 2 Chr 11.15; 13.9
13.34	1 Kings 12.30; 14.10
14.2	1 Sam 28.8; 2 Sam 14.2; 1 Kings 11.29-31
14.3	1 Sam 9.7, 8
14.4	1 Kings 11.29; 1 Sam 3.2; 4.15

13.26 The lying prophet concluded that the death of the true prophet was the result of disobeying the command of God, and wished to be buried in the same grave with the dead prophet. See 2 Kings 23.15ff for the sequel of this event.
13.33 Jeroboam spurned the evidences God sent to convince him of his own iniquity. The pagan altar had been rent, the ashes poured out, his arm withered, and the true prophet was lying in his grave. What more could God have done to make a case against this wicked king?
14.1 The sickness of Jeroboam's son caused the king to seek the counsel of Ahijah the prophet, the same prophet who had predicted his kingship over Israel (11.29–39). Perhaps he thought that Ahijah would give him good news a second time. Jeroboam sent his wife in disguise as another woman, but God told Ahijah that Jeroboam's wife was on the way. Before she could enter into his presence he identified her and gave forth a prophetic word: the child would die, all the descendants of Jeroboam would perish, and their bodies would be disposed of in an ignominious way. God, who had given Israel to Jeroboam, was angry because he disobeyed his law and was guilty of dreadful sin.

14.5
2 Sam 14.2

14.7
1 Kings 11.28-
31;
16.2
14.8
1 Kings 11.31ff

14.9
1 Kings 12.28;
2 Chr 11.15;
Ps 50.17;
Ex 34.17;
Ezek 23.35
14.10
1 Kings 15.29;
21.21;
2 Kings 9.8;
Deut 32.36
2 Kings 14.26
14.11
1 Kings 16.4;
21.24
14.12
v. 17
14.13
2 Chr 12.12
14.14
1 Kings 15.27-
29

14.15
2 Kings 17.6;
Josh 23.15,
16;
2 Kings 15.29;
Ex 34.13;
Deut 12.3, 4
14.16
1 Kings 12.30;
13.34; 15.30,
34

14.17
1 Kings 16.6-9
14.18
v. 13

14.19
2 Chr 13.2-20

to the house of Ahijah. Now Ahijah could not see, for his eyes were dim because of his age. 5 But the LORD said to Ahijah, "The wife of Jeroboam is coming to inquire of you concerning her son; for he is sick. Thus and thus you shall say to her."

When she came, she pretended to be another woman. 6 But when Ahijah heard the sound of her feet, as she came in at the door, he said, "Come in, wife of Jeroboam; why do you pretend to be another? For I am charged with heavy tidings for you. 7 Go, tell Jeroboam, 'Thus says the LORD, the God of Israel: Because I exalted you from among the people, made you leader over my people Israel, 8 and tore the kingdom away from the house of David to give it to you; yet you have not been like my servant David, who kept my commandments and followed me with all his heart, doing only that which was right in my sight, 9 but you have done evil above all those who were before you and have gone and made for yourself other gods, and cast images, provoking me to anger, and have thrust me behind your back; 10 therefore, I will bring evil upon the house of Jeroboam. I will cut off from Jeroboam every male, both bond and free in Israel, and will consume the house of Jeroboam, just as one burns up dung until it is all gone. 11 Anyone belonging to Jeroboam who dies in the city, the dogs shall eat; and anyone who dies in the open country, the birds of the air shall eat; for the LORD has spoken.' 12 Therefore set out, go to your house. When your feet enter the city, the child shall die. 13 All Israel shall mourn for him and bury him; for he alone of Jeroboam's family shall come to the grave, because in him there is found something pleasing to the LORD, the God of Israel, in the house of Jeroboam. 14 Moreover the LORD will raise up for himself a king over Israel, who shall cut off the house of Jeroboam today, even right now! d

15 "The LORD will strike Israel, as a reed is shaken in the water; he will root up Israel out of this good land that he gave to their ancestors, and scatter them beyond the Euphrates, because they have made their sacred poles, e provoking the LORD to anger. 16 He will give Israel up because of the sins of Jeroboam, which he sinned and which he caused Israel to commit."

2. The death of Jeroboam

17 Then Jeroboam's wife got up and went away, and she came to Tirzah. As she came to the threshold of the house, the child died. 18 All Israel buried him and mourned for him, according to the word of the LORD, which he spoke by his servant the prophet Ahijah.

19 Now the rest of the acts of Jeroboam, how he warred and how he reigned, are written in the Book of the Annals of the Kings of Israel. 20 The time that Jeroboam reigned was twenty-two years; then he slept with his ancestors, and his son Nadab succeeded him.

D. The kingdom of Judah

1. Rehoboam son of Solomon

a. Judah's unfaithfulness

14.21
2 Chr 12.13;
1 Kings 11.32,
36; v. 31

14.22
2 Chr 12.1;
Deut 32.21

21 Now Rehoboam son of Solomon reigned in Judah. Rehoboam was forty-one years old when he began to reign, and he reigned seventeen years in Jerusalem, the city that the LORD had chosen out of all the tribes of Israel, to put his name there. His mother's name was Naamah the Ammonite. 22 Judah did what was evil in the sight of the LORD; they provoked

---

d Meaning of Heb uncertain   e Heb Asherim

14.17 *Tirzah* (meaning "a delight"), the first capital of northern Israel, was formerly a Canaanite city. **14.19** *The Book of the Annals of the Kings of Israel.*

These and the Annals of Kings of Judah (14.29) were the official court records. They served in part as the basis for the books of Kings and Chronicles.

him to jealousy with their sins that they committed, more than all that their ancestors had done. 23 For they also built for themselves high places, pillars, and sacred poles*f* on every high hill and under every green tree; 24 there were also male temple prostitutes in the land. They committed all the abominations of the nations that the LORD drove out before the people of Israel.

	14.23
	Deut 12.2;
	Ezek 16.24,
	25;
	2 Kings 17.9,
	10;
	Isa 57.5
	14.24
	Deut 23.17;
	1 Kings 15.12;
	2 Kings 23.7

b. Defeat by Shishak of Egypt

25 In the fifth year of King Rehoboam, King Shishak of Egypt came up against Jerusalem; 26 he took away the treasures of the house of the LORD and the treasures of the king's house; he took everything. He also took away all the shields of gold that Solomon had made; 27 so King Rehoboam made shields of bronze instead, and committed them to the hands of the officers of the guard, who kept the door of the king's house. 28 As often as the king went into the house of the LORD, the guard carried them and brought them back to the guardroom.

	14.25
	1 Kings 11.40;
	2 Chr 12.2,
	9-11
	14.26
	1 Kings 15.18;
	10.17

c. Death of Rehoboam

29 Now the rest of the acts of Rehoboam, and all that he did, are they not written in the Book of the Annals of the Kings of Judah? 30 There was war between Rehoboam and Jeroboam continually. 31 Rehoboam slept with his ancestors and was buried with his ancestors in the city of David. His mother's name was Naamah the Ammonite. His son Abijam succeeded him.

	14.29
	2 Chr 12.15
	14.30
	1 Kings 12.21-24;
	15.6
	14.31
	2 Chr 12.16;
	v. 21

2. King Abijam of Judah

15 Now in the eighteenth year of King Jeroboam son of Nebat, Abijam began to reign over Judah. 2 He reigned for three years in Jerusalem. His mother's name was Maacah daughter of Abishalom. 3 He committed all the sins that his father did before him; his heart was not true to the LORD his God, like the heart of his father David. 4 Nevertheless for David's sake the LORD his God gave him a lamp in Jerusalem, setting up his son after him, and establishing Jerusalem; 5 because David did what was right in the sight of the LORD, and did not turn aside from anything that he commanded him all the days of his life, except in the matter of Uriah the Hittite. 6 The war begun between Rehoboam and Jeroboam continued all the days of his life. 7 The rest of the acts of Abijam, and all that he did, are they not written in the Book of the Annals of the Kings of Judah? There was war between Abijam and Jeroboam. 8 Abijam slept with his ancestors, and they buried him in the city of David. Then his son Asa succeeded him.

	15.1
	2 Chr 13.1, 2
	15.3
	1 Kings 11.4
	15.4
	1 Kings 11.36;
	2 Chr 21.7
	15.5
	1 Kings 14.8;
	2 Sam 11.4,
	15-17; 12.9
	15.6
	1 Kings 14.30
	15.7
	2 Chr 13.2, 3,
	22
	15.8
	2 Chr 14.1

f Heb Asherim

14.22 Both Jeroboam and Rehoboam were wicked kings, and the people of both nations followed the bad example of their rulers. They did evil in the sight of God so that like the husband of an adulterous wife, God was offended by the breaking of the covenant relationship.
14.25,26 God sent Shishak king of Egypt to afflict Judah and to remove the treasures of both the house of God and the house of the king. This was the beginning of the diminishing of the Davidic throne. When Judah had a good king, the throne would temporarily shine again, but it did not come to its full glory until Jesus the Christ was born (cf. Lk 1.32,33).
14.30 When Rehoboam died, there had been continual warfare between him and Jeroboam. He went

regularly into the house of the Lord (v. 28), but those visits seem to have had no good effect on him or on his kingdom. Outward performances of devotion cannot hide a heart that is not right with God.
15.1 Abijam. In 2 Chr 13.1, this king has the name "Abijah," meaning "My father is the LORD." According to that passage, he called upon God for help, was heard, and was given a great victory against Jeroboam; the chronicler lays no wickedness to his charge. The writer of Kings, however, charges him with his faults. Consequently, it seems, "Jah," the name of God, was removed from his name as a disgrace and he was called "Abijam," meaning "father of light."
15.6 between Rehoboam and Jeroboam, i.e., between Judah and Israel.

3. King Asa of Judah

a. The reforms of Asa

9 In the twentieth year of King Jeroboam of Israel, Asa began to reign over Judah; 10 he reigned forty-one years in Jerusalem. His mother's name was Maacah daughter of Abishalom. 11 Asa did what was right in the sight of the LORD, as his father David had done. 12 He put away the male temple prostitutes out of the land, and removed all the idols that his ancestors had made. 13 He also removed his mother Maacah from being queen mother, because she had made an abominable image for Asherah; Asa cut down her image and burned it at the Wadi Kidron. 14 But the high places were not taken away. Nevertheless the heart of Asa was true to the LORD all his days. 15 He brought into the house of the LORD the votive gifts of his father and his own votive gifts — silver, gold, and utensils.

b. War between Asa and Baasha; death of Asa

16 There was war between Asa and King Baasha of Israel all their days. 17 King Baasha of Israel went up against Judah, and built Ramah, to prevent anyone from going out or coming in to King Asa of Judah. 18 Then Asa took all the silver and the gold that were left in the treasures of the house of the LORD and the treasures of the king's house, and gave them into the hands of his servants. King Asa sent them to King Ben-hadad son of Tabrimmon son of Hezion of Aram, who resided in Damascus, saying, 19 "Let there be an alliance between me and you, like that between my father and your father: I am sending you a present of silver and gold; go, break your alliance with King Baasha of Israel, so that he may withdraw from me." 20 Ben-hadad listened to King Asa, and sent the commanders of his armies against the cities of Israel. He conquered Ijon, Dan, Abel-beth-maacah, and all Chinneroth, with all the land of Naphtali. 21 When Baasha heard of it, he stopped building Ramah and lived in Tirzah. 22 Then King Asa made a proclamation to all Judah, none was exempt: they carried away the stones of Ramah and its timber, with which Baasha had been building; with them King Asa built Geba of Benjamin and Mizpah. 23 Now the rest of all the acts of Asa, all his power, all that he did, and the cities that he built, are they not written in the Book of the Annals of the Kings of Judah? But in his old age he was diseased in his feet. 24 Then Asa slept with his ancestors, and was buried with his ancestors in the city of his father David; his son Jehoshaphat succeeded him.

E. The immediate successors to Jeroboam in the northern kingdom

1. Nadab

25 Nadab son of Jeroboam began to reign over Israel in the second

Side references (left margin):

15.10
v. 2
15.11
2 Chr 14.2
15.12
1 Kings 14.24;
22.46
15.13
2 Chr 15.16-18;
Ex 32.20
15.14
1 Kings 22.43;
2 Chr 15.17,
18; v. 3
15.15
1 Kings 7.51

15.16
v. 32
15.17
2 Chr 16.1ff;
Josh 18.25;
1 Kings 12.27
15.18
v. 15;
2 Chr 16.2;
1 Kings 11.23,
24

15.20
2 Kings 15.29;
Judg 18.29;
2 Sam 20.14

15.22
2 Chr 16.6;
Josh 21.17

15.23
2 Chr 16.11-14

15.24
2 Chr 17.1

15.25
1 Kings 14.20

15.9 Asa's reign is compressed in this account in 1 Kings. 2 Chr 14–16 enlarges on it considerably, and it was significantly better than those of Rehoboam and Abijam. He began a reform movement and had a heart that followed God (v. 14). Still, he did not do as much as was needed to offset the reigns of his two predecessors.
15.18 The O.T. mentions three Ben-hadads of Damascus. The first one is mentioned here. His son, Ben-hadad II, was the king who warred against Ahab and besieged Samaria unsuccessfully. Ahab defeated him at Aphek and he was smothered by Hazael, who seized the crown (see 1 Kings 20; 2 Kings 7–8). The third Ben-hadad was the son of Hazael (see 2 Kings 13.24). He lost the territories his father had taken from the Israelites.

15.24 Asa, for the most part, prospered. Yet there were wars fought between Judah and Israel that afflicted and weakened each of them. This civil war aided the external enemies of God's people. Toward the end of his life Asa suffered from what probably was gout (2 Chr 16.12).
15.25 In the second year of Asa's reign, Jeroboam died. From that time until the reign of Ahab (who came to the throne at the end of Asa's reign), Israel was in turmoil. From the end of Jeroboam's reign to the beginning of Ahab's kingship there were six monarchs: Nadab, Baasha, Elah, Zimri, Tibni, and Omri. Nadab son of Jeroboam lasted two years. He was slain by Baasha, who promptly killed off all of the house of Jeroboam (v. 29), thus fulfilling the prophecy of Ahijah the Shilonite (see 14.10,11).

year of King Asa of Judah; he reigned over Israel two years. 26 He did what was evil in the sight of the LORD, walking in the way of his ancestor and in the sin that he caused Israel to commit.

27   Baasha son of Ahijah, of the house of Issachar, conspired against him; and Baasha struck him down at Gibbethon, which belonged to the Philistines; for Nadab and all Israel were laying siege to Gibbethon. 28 So Baasha killed Nadab[g] in the third year of King Asa of Judah, and succeeded him. 29 As soon as he was king, he killed all the house of Jeroboam; he left to the house of Jeroboam not one that breathed, until he had destroyed it, according to the word of the LORD that he spoke by his servant Ahijah the Shilonite — 30 because of the sins of Jeroboam that he committed and that he caused Israel to commit, and because of the anger to which he provoked the LORD, the God of Israel.

31   Now the rest of the acts of Nadab, and all that he did, are they not written in the Book of the Annals of the Kings of Israel? 32 There was war between Asa and King Baasha of Israel all their days.

2. Baasha

33   In the third year of King Asa of Judah, Baasha son of Ahijah began to reign over all Israel at Tirzah; he reigned twenty-four years. 34 He did what was evil in the sight of the LORD, walking in the way of Jeroboam and in the sin that he caused Israel to commit.

16 The word of the LORD came to Jehu son of Hanani against Baasha, saying, 2 "Since I exalted you out of the dust and made you leader over my people Israel, and you have walked in the way of Jeroboam, and have caused my people Israel to sin, provoking me to anger with their sins, 3 therefore, I will consume Baasha and his house, and I will make your house like the house of Jeroboam son of Nebat. 4 Anyone belonging to Baasha who dies in the city the dogs shall eat; and anyone of his who dies in the field the birds of the air shall eat."

5   Now the rest of the acts of Baasha, what he did, and his power, are they not written in the Book of the Annals of the Kings of Israel? 6 Baasha slept with his ancestors, and was buried at Tirzah; and his son Elah succeeded him. 7 Moreover the word of the LORD came by the prophet Jehu son of Hanani against Baasha and his house, both because of all the evil that he did in the sight of the LORD, provoking him to anger with the work of his hands, in being like the house of Jeroboam, and also because he destroyed it.

3. Elah

8   In the twenty-sixth year of King Asa of Judah, Elah son of Baasha began to reign over Israel in Tirzah; he reigned two years. 9 But his servant Zimri, commander of half his chariots, conspired against him. When he was at Tirzah, drinking himself drunk in the house of Arza, who was in charge of the palace at Tirzah, 10 Zimri came in and struck him down and

g Heb him

Cross-references (margin)

15.26
1 Kings 12.30;
14.16

15.27
1 Kings 14.14;
Josh 19.44;
21.23

15.29
1 Kings 14.10,
14

15.30
1 Kings 14.9,
16

15.31
v. 16

15.34
1 Kings 12.28,
29; 13.33;
14.16

16.1
v. 7;
2 Chr 19.2;
20.34

16.2
1 Kings 14.7;
15.34

16.3
v. 11;
1 Kings 14.10;
15.29

16.4
1 Kings 14.11

16.5
1 Kings 14.19;
15.31

16.6
1 Kings 14.17;
15.21

16.7
v. 1;
1 Kings 15.27,
29

16.9
2 Kings 9.30-33

15.29 After eliminating all possible aspirants to the throne of Israel, Baasha set up a new dynasty. The history of the northern kingdom is filled with the rise and fall of one dynasty after another. The descendants of David, however, sat on the throne of Judah without interruption until the kingship of Zedekiah, at which time the kingdom practically ceased. The northern kingdom of Israel did not have a single God-fearing king. Judah, on the other hand, had some good kings and some bad ones.
15.33 Baasha lasted twenty-four years. He was a wicked king who led his people into sin. God gave a word to Jehu son of Hanani against Baasha (16.1–4),

in which the divine judgment was mandated that the whole house of Baasha should be wiped out. When Baasha died, his son Elah became king (16.6).
16.8–11 Elah reigned for two years. He was murdered by one of his own soldiers, Zimri, who replaced him. Whereas Nadab died more honorably (on the field of battle), Elah was killed in a drunken stupor in his servant's house. Zimri proceeded to wipe out the entire family of Elah, as Baasha had wiped out that of Jeroboam. Zimri's vengeance went so far as to slay Elah's friends, so that no one was left to act as avenger for the death of Elah.

killed him, in the twenty-seventh year of King Asa of Judah, and succeeded him.

4. Zimri

16.12
v. 3;
2 Chr 19.2;
20.34
16.13
Deut 32.21;
1 Sam 12.21;
Isa 41.29
16.14
v. 5
11 When he began to reign, as soon as he had seated himself on his throne, he killed all the house of Baasha; he did not leave him a single male of his kindred or his friends. 12 Thus Zimri destroyed all the house of Baasha, according to the word of the LORD, which he spoke against Baasha by the prophet Jehu — 13 because of all the sins of Baasha and the sins of his son Elah that they committed, and that they caused Israel to commit, provoking the LORD God of Israel to anger with their idols. 14 Now the rest of the acts of Elah, and all that he did, are they not written in the Book of the Annals of the Kings of Israel?

16.15
1 Kings 15.27
15 In the twenty-seventh year of King Asa of Judah, Zimri reigned seven days in Tirzah. Now the troops were encamped against Gibbethon, which belonged to the Philistines, 16 and the troops who were encamped heard it said, "Zimri has conspired, and he has killed the king"; therefore all Israel made Omri, the commander of the army, king over Israel that day in the camp. 17 So Omri went up from Gibbethon, and all Israel with

16.18
1 Sam 31.4,
5;
2 Sam 17.23
16.19
1 Kings 12.28;
15.26, 34
16.20
vv. 5, 14, 27
him, and they besieged Tirzah. 18 When Zimri saw that the city was taken, he went into the citadel of the king's house; he burned down the king's house over himself with fire, and died — 19 because of the sins that he committed, doing evil in the sight of the LORD, walking in the way of Jeroboam, and for the sin that he committed, causing Israel to sin. 20 Now the rest of the acts of Zimri, and the conspiracy that he made, are they not written in the Book of the Annals of the Kings of Israel?

5. Omri

16.23
1 Kings 15.21
21 Then the people of Israel were divided into two parts; half of the people followed Tibni son of Ginath, to make him king, and half followed Omri. 22 But the people who followed Omri overcame the people who followed Tibni son of Ginath; so Tibni died, and Omri became king. 23 In the thirty-first year of King Asa of Judah, Omri began to reign over Israel; he reigned for twelve years, six of them in Tirzah.

16.24
1 Kings 13.32;
Jn 4.4
24 He bought the hill of Samaria from Shemer for two talents of silver; he fortified the hill, and called the city that he built, Samaria, after the name of Shemer, the owner of the hill.

16.26
Mic 6.16;
v. 19
25 Omri did what was evil in the sight of the LORD; he did more evil than all who were before him. 26 For he walked in all the way of Jeroboam son of Nebat, and in the sins that he caused Israel to commit, provoking the LORD, the God of Israel, to anger by their idols. 27 Now the rest of the acts of Omri that he did, and the power that he showed, are they not written in the Book of the Annals of the Kings of Israel? 28 Omri slept with his ancestors, and was buried in Samaria; his son Ahab succeeded him.

16.15–19 Zimri had a very short reign (seven days). While he was killing off the relatives and friends of Elah, the army of Israel was busy at Gibbethon. When it was learned that Zimri had slain Elah, Omri was made king of Israel in the field. Now Israel had two kings. Omri and the army went to Tirzah, where Zimri was, and took the city. Rather than being killed by Omri and his body being given to the birds and beasts of the field, Zimri set his house on fire and perished in the flames.
16.21,22 Omri became king only to find that Tibni was a rival claimant to the throne. Half of the people

of Israel followed Tibni. The contest lasted for some years before Tibni died and Omri reigned alone. Omri was a wicked king, known for his idolatry. It was his son Ahab, however, whose name is associated with Israel's greatest period of wickedness.
16.24 *Samaria.* Omri originated the scheme to build Samaria, which became the capital of the northern kingdom. He did more evil than all the kings who preceded him (see Mic 6.16 for Omri's importance relative to official Baal worship). But he was an important secular figure. For almost one hundred years the Assyrians called Israel "the house of Omri."

F. *Ahab of Israel and Elijah the prophet*

1. *Ahab of Israel and Jezebel his wife*

29 In the thirty-eighth year of King Asa of Judah, Ahab son of Omri began to reign over Israel; Ahab son of Omri reigned over Israel in Samaria twenty-two years. 30 Ahab son of Omri did evil in the sight of the LORD more than all who were before him.

31 And as if it had been a light thing for him to walk in the sins of Jeroboam son of Nebat, he took as his wife Jezebel daughter of King Ethbaal of the Sidonians, and went and served Baal, and worshiped him. 32 He erected an altar for Baal in the house of Baal, which he built in Samaria. 33 Ahab also made a sacred pole. *h* Ahab did more to provoke the anger of the LORD, the God of Israel, than had all the kings of Israel who were before him. 34 In his days Hiel of Bethel built Jericho; he laid its foundation at the cost of Abiram his firstborn, and set up its gates at the cost of his youngest son Segub, according to the word of the LORD, which he spoke by Joshua son of Nun.

16.30
v. 25;
1 Kings 14.9
16.31
Deut 7.3;
2 Kings 10.18;
17.16
16.32
2 Kings 10.21,
26, 27
16.33
2 Kings 13.6;
vv. 29, 30
16.34
Josh 6.26

2. *Elijah fed*

a. *The ravens at Cherith*

17 Now Elijah the Tishbite, of Tishbe*i* in Gilead, said to Ahab, "As the LORD the God of Israel lives, before whom I stand, there shall be neither dew nor rain these years, except by my word." 2 The word of the LORD came to him, saying, 3 "Go from here and turn eastward, and hide yourself by the Wadi Cherith, which is east of the Jordan. 4 You shall drink from the wadi, and I have commanded the ravens to feed you there." 5 So he went and did according to the word of the LORD; he went and lived by the Wadi Cherith, which is east of the Jordan. 6 The ravens brought him bread and meat in the morning, and bread and meat in the evening; and he drank from the wadi. 7 But after a while the wadi dried up, because there was no rain in the land.

17.1
2 Kings 3.14;
Deut 10.8;
1 Kings 18.1;
Jas 5.17;
Lk 4.25

b. *The widow at Zarephath*

8 Then the word of the LORD came to him, saying, 9 "Go now to Zarephath, which belongs to Sidon, and live there; for I have commanded a widow there to feed you." 10 So he set out and went to Zarephath. When he came to the gate of the town, a widow was there gathering sticks; he called to her and said, "Bring me a little water in a vessel, so that I may drink." 11 As she was going to bring it, he called to her and said, "Bring me a morsel of bread in your hand." 12 But she said, "As the LORD your God lives, I have nothing baked, only a handful of meal in a jar, and a

17.9
Ob 20;
Lk 4.26

17.12
v. 1;
2 Kings 4.2-7

h Heb *Asherah*   *i* Gk: Heb *of the settlers*

16.30 Ahab had the distinction of being the worst of all the kings of Israel. His wife Jezebel was equally wicked and brought in the vilest practices of the Baal cult. Their daughter Athaliah married Jehoram king of Judah, and brought with her all the evils she had learned from her mother.
17.1 Elijah springs to our attention out of nowhere. We know nothing about his family background; the names of his mother and father are never mentioned. God called him for a difficult work against a determined scoundrel, king Ahab. Since the priests and Levites had long since left Israel and gone to Judah, God raised up prophets to speak to Israel. Elijah stood before Ahab and prophesied a great famine that would last until he announced its end. As the famine got worse, Ahab began to search desperately to locate the prophet of the bad news (see 18.7–15), possibly

hoping he could twist his arm and force him to announce the end to the famine.
17.3 Elijah, following the express direction of God, fled from Ahab to the brook Cherith. There he was fed by ravens and drank from the brook. When the brook dried up, he could have gone to the Jordan, where there was water. But God directed him elsewhere.
17.9 Jezebel, the wife of wicked Ahab, was a Sidonian. God sent Elijah to the very place from which she came and protected him from Ahab among these Gentiles. Zarephath was on the Mediterranean seacoast between Sidon and Tyre. The home to which he was sent was impoverished. The widow and her son expected to die, but God performed a miracle so that the jug of oil and the jar of meal remained filled. Elijah, the widow, and her son were fed despite the famine.

little oil in a jug; I am now gathering a couple of sticks, so that I may go home and prepare it for myself and my son, that we may eat it, and die." 13 Elijah said to her, "Do not be afraid; go and do as you have said; but first make me a little cake of it and bring it to me, and afterwards make something for yourself and your son. 14 For thus says the LORD the God of Israel: The jar of meal will not be emptied and the jug of oil will not fail until the day that the LORD sends rain on the earth." 15 She went and did as Elijah said, so that she as well as he and her household ate for many days. 16 The jar of meal was not emptied, neither did the jug of oil fail, according to the word of the LORD that he spoke by Elijah.

17.14
Lk 4.25, 26

c. *The widow's dead son brought to life*

17 After this the son of the woman, the mistress of the house, became ill; his illness was so severe that there was no breath left in him. 18 She then said to Elijah, "What have you against me, O man of God? You have come to me to bring my sin to remembrance, and to cause the death of my son!" 19 But he said to her, "Give me your son." He took him from her bosom, carried him up into the upper chamber where he was lodging, and laid him on his own bed. 20 He cried out to the LORD, "O LORD my God, have you brought calamity even upon the widow with whom I am staying, by killing her son?" 21 Then he stretched himself upon the child three times, and cried out to the LORD, "O LORD my God, let this child's life come into him again." 22 The LORD listened to the voice of Elijah; the life of the child came into him again, and he revived. 23 Elijah took the child, brought him down from the upper chamber into the house, and gave him to his mother; then Elijah said, "See, your son is alive." 24 So the woman said to Elijah, "Now I know that you are a man of God, and that the word of the LORD in your mouth is truth."

17.18
2 Kings 3.13

17.21
2 Kings 4.34,
35; see
Acts 20.10
17.22
Heb 11.25

17.24
Jn 3.2; 16.30

3. *Elijah at Mount Carmel*

a. *Obadiah seeks water*

18 After many days the word of the LORD came to Elijah, in the third year of the drought,*j* saying, "Go, present yourself to Ahab; I will send rain on the earth." 2 So Elijah went to present himself to Ahab. The famine was severe in Samaria. 3 Ahab summoned Obadiah, who was in charge of the palace. (Now Obadiah revered the LORD greatly; 4 when Jezebel was killing off the prophets of the LORD, Obadiah took a hundred prophets, hid them fifty to a cave, and provided them with bread and water.) 5 Then Ahab said to Obadiah, "Go through the land to all the

18.1
1 Kings 17.1;
Lk 4.25;
Jas 5.17

18.4
v. 13

j Heb lacks *of the drought*

17.16 Elijah and Elisha together performed more miracles than any other two people since Israel had entered the land of Canaan. According to the Bible, Elijah performed five miracles and Elisha no fewer than twelve. Of course, they may have performed more than those recorded. From creation to the opening of the N.T., the number of miracles was few, and those that were performed came in clusters at times of national crisis: (1) the time of Israel's deliverance from Egypt and their entrance into the promised land; (2) the middle of the ninth century before the kingdom of Israel was finally obliterated; and (3) during the Babylonian exile, when the question of Judah's return to the land and its viability were in doubt (e.g., Dan 3; 6).
17.17 The widow's son died suddenly, to the surprise of his mother, who was living well and taking care of a prophet who performed miracles. When this sharp affliction came, she spoke as though Elijah were the cause of all her trouble, thinking God had sent Elijah to remind her of her past sins. Through Elijah's

earnest prayer to God, the dead son came back to life.
17.24 This woman knew that Elijah was a prophet of God when the jug and the jar remained filled. But at the death of her son she began to doubt. When her son came back to life she believed that Elijah had both the power and the goodness of a prophet of God. God used this miracle to confirm her faith in Israel's God. Miracles have often served that purpose (cf. Jn 20.30,31).
18.1 God's time to end the drought and to show Ahab the error of his ways had come.
18.3,4 Obadiah was a true believer who feared God and was not corrupted by the king. Because he was honest, industrious, and ingenious, he was useful to the wicked king. God used Obadiah to protect the prophets, who otherwise might have been murdered (v. 4). Sometimes some of God's people have no choice but to live in a land from which there is no escape; yet they do not succumb to evil nor do they transfer their allegiance from their God to other gods.

springs of water and to all the wadis; perhaps we may find grass to keep the horses and mules alive, and not lose some of the animals." 6 So they divided the land between them to pass through it; Ahab went in one direction by himself, and Obadiah went in another direction by himself.

b. Elijah and Obadiah meet

7 As Obadiah was on the way, Elijah met him; Obadiah recognized him, fell on his face, and said, "Is it you, my lord Elijah?" 8 He answered him, "It is I. Go, tell your lord that Elijah is here." 9 And he said, "How have I sinned, that you would hand your servant over to Ahab, to kill me? 10 As the LORD your God lives, there is no nation or kingdom to which my lord has not sent to seek you; and when they would say, 'He is not here,' he would require an oath of the kingdom or nation, that they had not found you. 11 But now you say, 'Go, tell your lord that Elijah is here.' 12 As soon as I have gone from you, the spirit of the LORD will carry you I know not where; so, when I come and tell Ahab and he cannot find you, he will kill me, although I your servant have revered the LORD from my youth. 13 Has it not been told my lord what I did when Jezebel killed the prophets of the LORD, how I hid a hundred of the LORD's prophets fifty to a cave, and provided them with bread and water? 14 Yet now you say, 'Go, tell your lord that Elijah is here'; he will surely kill me." 15 Elijah said, "As the LORD of hosts lives, before whom I stand, I will surely show myself to him today." 16 So Obadiah went to meet Ahab, and told him; and Ahab went to meet Elijah.

c. Ahab and Elijah meet

17 When Ahab saw Elijah, Ahab said to him, "Is it you, you troubler of Israel?" 18 He answered, "I have not troubled Israel; but you have, and your father's house, because you have forsaken the commandments of the LORD and followed the Baals. 19 Now therefore have all Israel assemble for me at Mount Carmel, with the four hundred fifty prophets of Baal and the four hundred prophets of Asherah, who eat at Jezebel's table."

d. The priests of Baal fail

20 So Ahab sent to all the Israelites, and assembled the prophets at Mount Carmel. 21 Elijah then came near to all the people, and said, "How long will you go limping with two different opinions? If the LORD is God, follow him; but if Baal, then follow him." The people did not answer him a word. 22 Then Elijah said to the people, "I, even I only, am left a prophet of the LORD; but Baal's prophets number four hundred fifty. 23 Let two bulls be given to us; let them choose one bull for themselves, cut it in pieces, and lay it on the wood, but put no fire to it; I will prepare the other bull and lay it on the wood, but put no fire to it. 24 Then you call on the

18.7
2 Kings 1.6-8

18.10
1 Kings 17.1

18.12
2 Kings 2.16;
Ezek 3.12,
14;
Acts 8.39
18.13
v. 4

18.15
1 Kings 17.1

18.17
1 Kings 21.20;
Josh 7.25;
Acts 16.20
18.18
2 Chr 15.2;
1 Kings 16.31;
21.25, 26
18.19
Josh 19.26;
1 Kings 16.33

18.21
2 Kings 17.41;
Mt 6.24;
Josh 24.15
18.22
1 Kings 19.10,
14; v. 19
18.24
v. 38; see
1 Chr 21.26;
Acts 20.10

18.8–12 Elijah told Obadiah to inform Ahab that Elijah was on his way to meet the king face to face. Obadiah was frightened, for he thought Ahab would blame him for not seizing Elijah and bringing him back captive. He thought the Spirit of God might carry him away. In order to quell Obadiah's fears, Elijah swore by the Lord to confront Ahab that very day.

18.17 As bad a king as there ever was once again stood face to face with as good a prophet as Israel ever knew. Ahab rudely accused Elijah of being the source of all his troubles. Elijah fearlessly pointed his finger right back at the wicked king and proclaimed that it was Ahab who had followed the Baals and forsaken the commandments of God. Elijah majestically commanded Ahab to meet him at Mount Carmel, bringing with him the 450 prophets of Baal and the 400 prophets of Asherah, who were identified with Jezebel. This would become the climactic moment of the

prophet's life.

18.20 Presumably Ahab and Israel expected that Elijah would now lift the judgment and bless the people. But Elijah had more important work to do first. Israel must be reproved for its idolatry and the name of the true God must, by word and miracle, be lifted above Baal.

18.24 Elijah knew that the people would not heed his words. They needed external corroborating evidence that the Lord was the true God. He made them a proposition based on the coming of supernatural fire from heaven. This would be an excellent test, for Baal was considered to be the god of thunder and lightning. If Baal succeeded, Elijah told them, they ought to worship him. But if Baal could not send fire and the God of Israel could, then they should worship him. Furthermore, the God who gave fire should also be able to send rain. The people agreed and the pageant began.

name of your god and I will call on the name of the LORD; the god who answers by fire is indeed God." All the people answered, "Well spoken!" 25 Then Elijah said to the prophets of Baal, "Choose for yourselves one bull and prepare it first, for you are many; then call on the name of your god, but put no fire to it." 26 So they took the bull that was given them, prepared it, and called on the name of Baal from morning until noon, crying, "O Baal, answer us!" But there was no voice, and no answer. They limped about the altar that they had made. 27 At noon Elijah mocked them, saying, "Cry aloud! Surely he is a god; either he is meditating, or he has wandered away, or he is on a journey, or perhaps he is asleep and must be awakened." 28 Then they cried aloud and, as was their custom, they cut themselves with swords and lances until the blood gushed out over them. 29 As midday passed, they raved on until the time of the offering of the oblation, but there was no voice, no answer, and no response.

e. Elijah's sacrifice burns: fire from heaven

30 Then Elijah said to all the people, "Come closer to me"; and all the people came closer to him. First he repaired the altar of the LORD that had been thrown down; 31 Elijah took twelve stones, according to the number of the tribes of the sons of Jacob, to whom the word of the LORD came, saying, "Israel shall be your name"; 32 with the stones he built an altar in the name of the LORD. Then he made a trench around the altar, large enough to contain two measures of seed. 33 Next he put the wood in order, cut the bull in pieces, and laid it on the wood. He said, "Fill four jars with water and pour it on the burnt offering and on the wood." 34 Then he said, "Do it a second time"; and they did it a second time. Again he said, "Do it a third time"; and they did it a third time, 35 so that the water ran all around the altar, and filled the trench also with water.

36 At the time of the offering of the oblation, the prophet Elijah came near and said, "O LORD, God of Abraham, Isaac, and Israel, let it be known this day that you are God in Israel, that I am your servant, and that I have done all these things at your bidding. 37 Answer me, O LORD, answer me, so that this people may know that you, O LORD, are God, and that you have turned their hearts back." 38 Then the fire of the LORD fell and consumed the burnt offering, the wood, the stones, and the dust, and even licked up the water that was in the trench. 39 When all the people saw it, they fell on their faces and said, "The LORD indeed is God; the LORD indeed is God." 40 Elijah said to them, "Seize the prophets of Baal; do not let one of them escape." Then they seized them; and Elijah brought them down to the Wadi Kishon, and killed them there.

f. The coming of the rain

41 Elijah said to Ahab, "Go up, eat and drink; for there is a sound of rushing rain." 42 So Ahab went up to eat and to drink. Elijah went up to the top of Carmel; there he bowed himself down upon the earth and put his face between his knees. 43 He said to his servant, "Go up now, look toward the sea." He went up and looked, and said, "There is nothing." Then he said, "Go again seven times." 44 At the seventh time he said,

---

18.26 Ps 115.5; Jer 10.5; 1 Cor 8.4; 12.2
18.28 Lev 19.28; Deut 14.1
18.29 v. 26
18.30 1 Kings 19.10, 14
18.31 Gen 32.28; 35.10; 2 Kings 17.34
18.32 Col 3.17
18.33 Gen 22.9; Lev 1.6-8
18.36 Ex 3.6; 1 Kings 8.43; 2 Kings 19.19; Num 16.28
18.38 Lev 9.24; 1 Chr 21.26; 2 Chr 7.1
18.39 vv. 21, 24
18.40 Deut 13.5; 18.20; 2 Kings 10.24, 25
18.42 vv. 19, 20; Jas 5.17, 18

18.29 Elijah did not interrupt the priests of Baal from cavorting around their sacrifice while they invoked Baal to send the fire. Their idols, however, were powerless. "The ruler of the power of the air" (Eph 2.2), if God had permitted him, could have made "fire come down from heaven to earth" (Rev 13.13), and gladly would have done so for the support of Baal. But God would not allow the devil to do it now.
18.38 *the fire of the LORD fell.* Unlike the gods of Ahab and Jezebel, God was not sleeping nor did he need to be persuaded by the cutting of the flesh.

Before Elijah finished speaking, the Lord was already answering. The holy fire consumed the sacrifice, sucked up the water, and burned up the stones of the altar and even the dust itself. It was so mighty a miracle that the Israelites fell on their faces to acknowledge the Lord (Yahweh) as the God who won the contest (compare v. 39 with v. 24).
18.40 Baal's prophets were seized. They were condemned and executed according to the law of God (see Deut 13.1–11).
18.44 The prayer of Elijah, which was according to the will of God (cf. v. 1), was not answered when it

"Look, a little cloud no bigger than a person's hand is rising out of the sea." Then he said, "Go say to Ahab, 'Harness your chariot and go down before the rain stops you.' " ⁴⁵ In a little while the heavens grew black with clouds and wind; there was a heavy rain. Ahab rode off and went to Jezreel. ⁴⁶ But the hand of the LORD was on Elijah; he girded up his loins and ran in front of Ahab to the entrance of Jezreel.

18.46
2 Kings 3.15;
4.29

4. Elijah goes to Horeb

a. Jezebel's intention

19 Ahab told Jezebel all that Elijah had done, and how he had killed all the prophets with the sword. ² Then Jezebel sent a messenger to Elijah, saying, "So may the gods do to me, and more also, if I do not make your life like the life of one of them by this time tomorrow." ³ Then he was afraid; he got up and fled for his life, and came to Beer-sheba, which belongs to Judah; he left his servant there.

19.1
1 Kings 18.40
19.2
1 Kings 20.10;
2 Kings 6.31

b. Elijah's flight

4 But he himself went a day's journey into the wilderness, and came and sat down under a solitary broom tree. He asked that he might die: "It is enough; now, O LORD, take away my life, for I am no better than my ancestors." ⁵ Then he lay down under the broom tree and fell asleep. Suddenly an angel touched him and said to him, "Get up and eat." ⁶ He looked, and there at his head was a cake baked on hot stones, and a jar of water. He ate and drank, and lay down again. ⁷ The angel of the LORD came a second time, touched him, and said, "Get up and eat, otherwise the journey will be too much for you." ⁸ He got up, and ate and drank; then he went in the strength of that food forty days and forty nights to Horeb the mount of God. ⁹ At that place he came to a cave, and spent the night there.

19.4
Num 11.15;
Jon 4.3, 8

19.8
Ex 34.28;
Deut 9.9-11,
18;
Mt 4.2;
Ex 3.1

c. God meets with Elijah

Then the word of the LORD came to him, saying, "What are you doing here, Elijah?" ¹⁰ He answered, "I have been very zealous for the LORD, the God of hosts; for the Israelites have forsaken your covenant, thrown down your altars, and killed your prophets with the sword. I alone am left, and they are seeking my life, to take it away."

19.10
Rom 11.3;
1 Kings 18.4,
22

11 He said, "Go out and stand on the mountain before the LORD, for the LORD is about to pass by." Now there was a great wind, so strong that it was splitting mountains and breaking rocks in pieces before the LORD, but the LORD was not in the wind; and after the wind an earthquake, but the LORD was not in the earthquake; ¹² and after the earthquake a fire, but the LORD was not in the fire; and after the fire a sound of sheer silence. ¹³ When Elijah heard it, he wrapped his face in his mantle and went out and stood at the entrance of the cave. Then there came a voice to him that said, "What are you doing here, Elijah?" ¹⁴ He answered, "I have been very zealous for the LORD, the God of hosts; for the Israelites have

19.11
Ex 24.12;
Ezek 1.4;
37.7

19.13
Ex 3.6; v. 9

19.14
v. 10

---

was first offered. Seven times the servant rose to look for the cloud in the sky. Petitions delayed are not petitions denied. We must persevere in prayer until the answer comes.
18.46 *ran in front of Ahab.* Ahab rode in his chariot in ease and comfort. God gave Elijah the ability to outrun the chariot and arrive before Ahab did.
19.1-3 Ahab recounted to Jezebel what Elijah had done. He gave credit to Elijah, thereby insulting the God of Elijah who was directly responsible for the fire. His heart remained unchanged. The report excited the hatred of his wife, who was angry that Ahab had not killed Elijah and that Elijah had killed her prophets. She planned to retaliate, so Elijah fled for his life.

19.8 *Horeb,* i.e., Mount Sinai, where Moses had gone. Elijah hoped in his despondency to be renewed by God.
19.9 Elijah here displayed his humanity and thus disclosed his own weakness in the flesh. Great faith may be less great on some occasions. Afraid Jezebel would kill him, he ran from that death to seek another death at the hand of God. He pleaded that he had had enough and asked God to kill him. But God still had something for Elijah to do. He gave him special food to nourish his tired body. He sent him to anoint Jehu to be king of Israel and to anoint Elisha to be his own successor. God answered the real, though unexpressed, needs of the prophet.

19.15
2 Kings 8.12,
13
19.16
2 Kings 9.1-3;
vv. 19-21;
2 Kings 2.9,
15
19.17
2 Kings 8.12;
9.14ff; 13.3,
22
19.18
Rom 11.4;
Hos 13.2
19.19
2 Kings 2.8,
13
19.20
Mt 8.21, 22;
Lk 9.61, 62
19.21
2 Sam 24.22

forsaken your covenant, thrown down your altars, and killed your prophets with the sword. I alone am left, and they are seeking my life, to take it away." 15 Then the LORD said to him, "Go, return on your way to the wilderness of Damascus; when you arrive, you shall anoint Hazael as king over Aram. 16 Also you shall anoint Jehu son of Nimshi as king over Israel; and you shall anoint Elisha son of Shaphat of Abel-meholah as prophet in your place. 17 Whoever escapes from the sword of Hazael, Jehu shall kill; and whoever escapes from the sword of Jehu, Elisha shall kill. 18 Yet I will leave seven thousand in Israel, all the knees that have not bowed to Baal, and every mouth that has not kissed him."

d. Elijah casts his mantle on Elisha

19 So he set out from there, and found Elisha son of Shaphat, who was plowing. There were twelve yoke of oxen ahead of him, and he was with the twelfth. Elijah passed by him and threw his mantle over him. 20 He left the oxen, ran after Elijah, and said, "Let me kiss my father and my mother, and then I will follow you." Then Elijah[k] said to him, "Go back again; for what have I done to you?" 21 He returned from following him, took the yoke of oxen, and slaughtered them; using the equipment from the oxen, he boiled their flesh, and gave it to the people, and they ate. Then he set out and followed Elijah, and became his servant.

5. Ahab's first Aramean campaign
a. Ben-hadad's demands

20.1
1 Kings 15.18,
20;
2 Kings 6.24;
1 Kings 22.31;
2 Kings 6.24-29

20 King Ben-hadad of Aram gathered all his army together; thirty-two kings were with him, along with horses and chariots. He marched against Samaria, laid siege to it, and attacked it. 2 Then he sent messengers into the city to King Ahab of Israel, and said to him: "Thus says Ben-hadad: 3 Your silver and gold are mine; your fairest wives and children also are mine." 4 The king of Israel answered, "As you say, my lord, O king, I am yours, and all that I have." 5 The messengers came again and said: "Thus says Ben-hadad: I sent to you, saying, 'Deliver to me your silver and gold, your wives and children'; 6 nevertheless I will send my servants to you tomorrow about this time, and they shall search your house and the houses of your servants, and lay hands on whatever pleases them,[l] and take it away."

b. Ahab's reply

20.7
2 Kings 5.7

7 Then the king of Israel called all the elders of the land, and said, "Look now! See how this man is seeking trouble; for he sent to me for my wives, my children, my silver, and my gold; and I did not refuse him." 8 Then all the elders and all the people said to him, "Do not listen or consent." 9 So he said to the messengers of Ben-hadad, "Tell my lord the king: All that you first demanded of your servant I will do; but this thing

[k] Heb he   [l] Gk Syr Vg: Heb you

19.16 God announced to Elijah that the dynasty of Ahab was to end. Jehu was to be the successor. Elijah's ministry also was fast coming to its close. Therefore, he had to anoint Elisha to be prophet in his place. Though Elijah was to see Ahab again face to face (21.17ff), God employed an unnamed prophet to speak God's word of judgment to this wicked king (see 20.35–42).
19.18 Despite Elijah's pessimism, 7,000 people were still faithful to the Lord. God always has his remnant (cf. Rom 11.1–5).
19.19 Elisha was plowing when the call of God came to him to take over Elijah's mantle and become God's prophet. It was the sovereign God who had chosen and called Elisha. He did not choose his office himself; he merely accepted the divine will.

20.1ff Ahab was confronted by Ben-hadad, the king of Aram, who imperiously made demands on him personally. Ahab meekly accepted (v. 4). Having lost confidence in God, he was without a defender, for Baal was of no help. Then Ben-hadad sent a more ominous note. He wished to search every house and take anything he wanted. Ahab talked with his elders and they got him to refuse to submit. Ben-hadad then intended to destroy Samaria, but God intervened. He sent a prophet to tell Ahab that he would win the battle as a sign that God was the Lord (v. 13). Ahab was successful and the Arameans went home defeated, though the prophet prophesied that they would return to battle against Ahab the next spring (v. 22). Even so, Ahab did not turn to the Lord.

I cannot do." The messengers left and brought him word again. ¹⁰Ben-hadad sent to him and said, "The gods do so to me, and more also, if the dust of Samaria will provide a handful for each of the people who follow me." ¹¹The king of Israel answered, "Tell him: One who puts on armor should not brag like one who takes it off." ¹²When Ben-hadad heard this message — now he had been drinking with the kings in the booths — he said to his men, "Take your positions!" And they took their positions against the city.

20.10
1 Kings 19.2

20.11
Prov 27.1
20.12
v. 16

c. God's promise of victory

13   Then a certain prophet came up to King Ahab of Israel and said, "Thus says the LORD, Have you seen all this great multitude? Look, I will give it into your hand today; and you shall know that I am the LORD." ¹⁴Ahab said, "By whom?" He said, "Thus says the LORD, By the young men who serve the district governors." Then he said, "Who shall begin the battle?" He answered, "You." ¹⁵Then he mustered the young men who served the district governors, two hundred thirty-two; after them he mustered all the people of Israel, seven thousand.

20.13
v. 28

d. Ahab's victory

16   They went out at noon, while Ben-hadad was drinking himself drunk in the booths, he and the thirty-two kings allied with him. ¹⁷The young men who serve the district governors went out first. Ben-hadad had sent out scouts,ᵐ and they reported to him, "Men have come out from Samaria." ¹⁸He said, "If they have come out for peace, take them alive; if they have come out for war, take them alive."

19   But these had already come out of the city: the young men who serve the district governors, and the army that followed them. ²⁰Each killed his man; the Arameans fled and Israel pursued them, but King Ben-hadad of Aram escaped on a horse with the cavalry. ²¹The king of Israel went out, attacked the horses and chariots, and defeated the Arameans with a great slaughter.

20.16
v. 12

20.18
2 Kings 14.8-12

e. A second invasion prophesied

22   Then the prophet approached the king of Israel and said to him, "Come, strengthen yourself, and consider well what you have to do; for in the spring the king of Aram will come up against you."

20.22
vv. 13, 26;
2 Sam 11.1

6. Ahab's second Aramean campaign

a. Ben-hadad defeated

23   The servants of the king of Aram said to him, "Their gods are gods of the hills, and so they were stronger than we; but let us fight against them in the plain, and surely we shall be stronger than they. ²⁴Also do this: remove the kings, each from his post, and put commanders in place of them; ²⁵and muster an army like the army that you have lost, horse for horse, and chariot for chariot; then we will fight against them in the plain, and surely we shall be stronger than they." He heeded their voice, and did so.

20.23
1 Kings 14.23

26   In the spring Ben-hadad mustered the Arameans and went up to Aphek to fight against Israel. ²⁷After the Israelites had been mustered and provisioned, they went out to engage them; the people of Israel encamped opposite them like two little flocks of goats, while the Arameans filled the country. ²⁸A man of God approached and said to the king of Israel, "Thus

20.26
v. 22;
2 Kings 13.7

20.28
v. 13

ᵐ Heb lacks scouts

20.23 The Arameans prepared for the second phase of the war against Israel. With little knowledge of the God of Israel they supposed that they lost the first battle because Israel's gods were "gods of the hills."

This time they planned to fight on the plains where the "gods of the hills" would have no power.
20.28 Ahab did not consult with the prophet of God. Instead, God sent a prophet to speak to Ahab.

says the Lord: Because the Arameans have said, 'The Lord is a god of the hills but he is not a god of the valleys,' therefore I will give all this great multitude into your hand, and you shall know that I am the Lord." 29 They encamped opposite one another seven days. Then on the seventh day the battle began; the Israelites killed one hundred thousand Aramean foot soldiers in one day. 30 The rest fled into the city of Aphek; and the wall fell on twenty-seven thousand men that were left.

b. Ahab spares Ben-hadad

Ben-hadad also fled, and entered the city to hide. 31 His servants said to him, "Look, we have heard that the kings of the house of Israel are merciful kings; let us put sackcloth around our waists and ropes on our heads, and go out to the king of Israel; perhaps he will spare your life." 32 So they tied sackcloth around their waists, put ropes on their heads, went to the king of Israel, and said, "Your servant Ben-hadad says, 'Please let me live.'" And he said, "Is he still alive? He is my brother." 33 Now the men were watching for an omen; they quickly took it up from him and said, "Yes, Ben-hadad is your brother." Then he said, "Go and bring him." So Ben-hadad came out to him; and he had him come up into the chariot. 34 Ben-hadad[n] said to him, "I will restore the towns that my father took from your father; and you may establish bazaars for yourself in Damascus, as my father did in Samaria." The king of Israel responded,[o] "I will let you go on those terms." So he made a treaty with him and let him go.

c. The judgment of God against Ahab for sparing Ben-hadad

35 At the command of the Lord a certain member of a company of prophets[p] said to another, "Strike me!" But the man refused to strike him. 36 Then he said to him, "Because you have not obeyed the voice of the Lord, as soon as you have left me, a lion will kill you." And when he had left him, a lion met him and killed him. 37 Then he found another man and said, "Strike me!" So the man hit him, striking and wounding him. 38 Then the prophet departed, and waited for the king along the road, disguising himself with a bandage over his eyes. 39 As the king passed by, he cried to the king and said, "Your servant went out into the thick of the battle; then a soldier turned and brought a man to me, and said, 'Guard this man; if he is missing, your life shall be given for his life, or else you shall pay a talent of silver.' 40 While your servant was busy here and there, he was gone." The king of Israel said to him, "So shall your judgment be; you yourself have decided it." 41 Then he quickly took the bandage away from his eyes. The king of Israel recognized him as one of the prophets. 42 Then he said to him, "Thus says the Lord, 'Because you have let the man go whom I had devoted to destruction, therefore your life shall be for his life, and your people for his people.'" 43 The king of Israel set out toward home, resentful and sullen, and came to Samaria.

n Heb He   o Heb lacks The king of Israel responded   p Heb of the sons of the prophets

Cross-reference column (left margin):

20.30 v. 26; 1 Kings 22.25; 2 Chr 18.24

20.31 Gen 37.34

20.32 vv. 3-6

20.34 1 Kings 15.20

20.35 2 Kings 2.3-7; 1 Kings 13.17, 18

20.36 1 Kings 13.24

20.39 2 Kings 10.24

20.42 v. 39; 1 Kings 22.31-37

20.43 1 Kings 21.4

He said that God would enable Ahab to defeat the Arameans and would do this solely because they had insulted the Lord. In this war both parties were defective: Ahab neither praised God nor prayed to him; the Arameans blasphemed God. God would preserve the honor of his name by giving Ahab the victory.

20.29 Aram's army was far greater in size than that of Israel, yet God allowed the lesser to destroy the greater.

20.32–34 Ben-hadad lost the battle and tamely pleaded for his life by ingratiating himself with Ahab. A treaty was made between the two leaders and Ben-hadad was set free, contrary to the instructions of God

(see vv. 35–43).

20.35 Once again God came to Ahab through a prophet. God would have no direct dealings with Ahab, who had ignored him; he dealt with him only through an intermediary.

20.42 King Ahab had disobeyed God when he spared Ben-hadad. His excuse had been that he was busy (v. 40). Busyness is never an excuse when it interferes with the plan and will of God. True believers put God and his will first and busyness second (cf. Deut 28.1ff; Mt 6.10; Rom 1.10; 15.32; Acts 21.14; Jas 4.15).

7. *Naboth's vineyard*

a. *Ahab covets the vineyard*

21 Later the following events took place: Naboth the Jezreelite had a vineyard in Jezreel, beside the palace of King Ahab of Samaria. ²And Ahab said to Naboth, "Give me your vineyard, so that I may have it for a vegetable garden, because it is near my house; I will give you a better vineyard for it; or, if it seems good to you, I will give you its value in money." ³But Naboth said to Ahab, "The LORD forbid that I should give you my ancestral inheritance." ⁴Ahab went home resentful and sullen because of what Naboth the Jezreelite had said to him; for he had said, "I will not give you my ancestral inheritance." He lay down on his bed, turned away his face, and would not eat.

b. *Jezebel seizes the vineyard*

5 His wife Jezebel came to him and said, "Why are you so depressed that you will not eat?" ⁶He said to her, "Because I spoke to Naboth the Jezreelite and said to him, 'Give me your vineyard for money; or else, if you prefer, I will give you another vineyard for it'; but he answered, 'I will not give you my vineyard.' " ⁷His wife Jezebel said to him, "Do you now govern Israel? Get up, eat some food, and be cheerful; I will give you the vineyard of Naboth the Jezreelite."

8 So she wrote letters in Ahab's name and sealed them with his seal; she sent the letters to the elders and the nobles who lived with Naboth in his city. ⁹She wrote in the letters, "Proclaim a fast, and seat Naboth at the head of the assembly; ¹⁰seat two scoundrels opposite him, and have them bring a charge against him, saying, 'You have cursed God and the king.' Then take him out, and stone him to death." ¹¹The men of his city, the elders and the nobles who lived in his city, did as Jezebel had sent word to them. Just as it was written in the letters that she had sent to them, ¹²they proclaimed a fast and seated Naboth at the head of the assembly. ¹³The two scoundrels came in and sat opposite him; and the scoundrels brought a charge against Naboth, in the presence of the people, saying, "Naboth cursed God and the king." So they took him outside the city, and stoned him to death. ¹⁴Then they sent to Jezebel, saying, "Naboth has been stoned; he is dead."

15 As soon as Jezebel heard that Naboth had been stoned and was dead, Jezebel said to Ahab, "Go, take possession of the vineyard of Naboth the Jezreelite, which he refused to give you for money; for Naboth is not alive, but dead." ¹⁶As soon as Ahab heard that Naboth was dead, Ahab set out to go down to the vineyard of Naboth the Jezreelite, to take possession of it.

c. *Elijah pronounces doom on Ahab and Jezebel*

17 Then the word of the LORD came to Elijah the Tishbite, saying: ¹⁸Go down to meet King Ahab of Israel, who rules*q* in Samaria; he is now in the vineyard of Naboth, where he has gone to take possession. ¹⁹You shall say to him, "Thus says the LORD: Have you killed, and also taken possession?" You shall say to him, "Thus says the LORD: In the place where dogs licked up the blood of Naboth, dogs will also lick up your blood."

q Heb *who is*

21.1
1 Kings 18.45, 46
21.2
1 Sam 8.14

21.3
Lev 25.23;
Num 36.7;
Ezek 46.18
21.4
1 Kings 20.43

21.7
1 Sam 8.14

21.8
Esth 3.12;
8.8, 10

21.10
Ex 22.28;
Lev 24.15,
16;
Acts 6.11

21.13
2 Kings 9.26

21.17
Ps 9.12
21.18
1 Kings 16.29
21.19
1 Kings 22.38;
2 Kings 9.8

21.1ff Ahab coveted the field that belonged to Naboth and offered to buy it, thinking that no one would deny the king such a small request. Naboth, however, had sufficient knowledge of the word of God that he refused to sell what was his by right. It belonged to God, and God forbade the sale of one's patrimony. Ahab became angry and sullen. But Jezebel would not let her husband be denied that which he coveted. So, by her evil actions, she brought about the death of Naboth and the seizure of his land. This led to Elijah's final confrontation with the king, in which he announced the end of his dynasty and promised that "the dogs shall eat Jezebel within the bounds of Jezreel" (v. 23).

20 Ahab said to Elijah, "Have you found me, O my enemy?" He answered, "I have found you. Because you have sold yourself to do what is evil in the sight of the LORD, 21 I will bring disaster on you; I will consume you, and will cut off from Ahab every male, bond or free, in Israel; 22 and I will make your house like the house of Jeroboam son of Nebat, and like the house of Baasha son of Ahijah, because you have provoked me to anger and have caused Israel to sin. 23 Also concerning Jezebel the LORD said, 'The dogs shall eat Jezebel within the bounds of Jezreel.' 24 Anyone belonging to Ahab who dies in the city the dogs shall eat; and anyone of his who dies in the open country the birds of the air shall eat."

25 (Indeed, there was no one like Ahab, who sold himself to do what was evil in the sight of the LORD, urged on by his wife Jezebel. 26 He acted most abominably in going after idols, as the Amorites had done, whom the LORD drove out before the Israelites.)

d. Ahab's repentance

27 When Ahab heard those words, he tore his clothes and put sackcloth over his bare flesh; he fasted, lay in the sackcloth, and went about dejectedly. 28 Then the word of the LORD came to Elijah the Tishbite: 29 "Have you seen how Ahab has humbled himself before me? Because he has humbled himself before me, I will not bring the disaster in his days; but in his son's days I will bring the disaster on his house."

8. Ahab's third Aramean campaign

a. Ahab's agreement with Jehoshaphat of Judah

22 For three years Aram and Israel continued without war. 2 But in the third year King Jehoshaphat of Judah came down to the king of Israel. 3 The king of Israel said to his servants, "Do you know that Ramoth-gilead belongs to us, yet we are doing nothing to take it out of the hand of Aram?" 4 He said to Jehoshaphat, "Will you go with me to battle at Ramoth-gilead?" Jehoshaphat replied to the king of Israel, "I am as you are; my people are your people, my horses are your horses."

b. The lying prophets prophesy victory

5 But Jehoshaphat also said to the king of Israel, "Inquire first for the word of the LORD." 6 Then the king of Israel gathered the prophets together, about four hundred of them, and said to them, "Shall I go to battle against Ramoth-gilead, or shall I refrain?" They said, "Go up; for the LORD will give it into the hand of the king." 7 But Jehoshaphat said, "Is there no other prophet of the LORD here of whom we may inquire?" 8 The king of Israel said to Jehoshaphat, "There is still one other by whom we may inquire of the LORD, Micaiah son of Imlah; but I hate him, for he never prophesies anything favorable about me, but only disaster." Jehoshaphat said, "Let the king not say such a thing." 9 Then the king of Israel summoned an officer and said, "Bring quickly Micaiah son of

---

21.21,22 Elijah had never brought Ahab good news, so the king expected the worst from his enemy. And that's what he got. What had happened to the houses of Jeroboam and Baasha would happen to him.
21.27 The message Elijah had been preaching so long finally got through to Ahab. He donned sackcloth and fasted. Even at this late stage, God was merciful and suspended his judgment against Ahab; it would fall on his house after his death.
22.4 Little did Ahab know that he would be the cause of his own death. He wanted to retake Ramoth-gilead from the Arameans. Jehoshaphat, the king of Judah, visited him and they arranged to fight together

against the Arameans. Jehoshaphat had enough good sense to seek the counsel of God about this. Ahab gathered a band of four hundred false prophets, and they gave him the message he wanted — Aram would be defeated and God would give the enemy into their hands. Jehoshaphat had spiritual insight; he wanted a word from a true prophet of God. He consulted Micaiah.
22.6 *the king of Israel gathered the prophets together, about four hundred of them.* These were either the four hundred Asherah prophets left alive by Elijah at Carmel, or four hundred new prophets to replace the slain prophets of Baal (see 18.19,40).

Imlah." 10 Now the king of Israel and King Jehoshaphat of Judah were sitting on their thrones, arrayed in their robes, at the threshing floor at the entrance of the gate of Samaria; and all the prophets were prophesying before them. 11 Zedekiah son of Chenaanah made for himself horns of iron, and he said, "Thus says the LORD: With these you shall gore the Arameans until they are destroyed." 12 All the prophets were prophesying the same and saying, "Go up to Ramoth-gilead and triumph; the LORD will give it into the hand of the king."

c. Micaiah's true prophecy

13 The messenger who had gone to summon Micaiah said to him, "Look, the words of the prophets with one accord are favorable to the king; let your word be like the word of one of them, and speak favorably." 14 But Micaiah said, "As the LORD lives, whatever the LORD says to me, that I will speak."

15 When he had come to the king, the king said to him, "Micaiah, shall we go to Ramoth-gilead to battle, or shall we refrain?" He answered him, "Go up and triumph; the LORD will give it into the hand of the king." 16 But the king said to him, "How many times must I make you swear to tell me nothing but the truth in the name of the LORD?" 17 Then Micaiah[r] said, "I saw all Israel scattered on the mountains, like sheep that have no shepherd; and the LORD said, 'These have no master; let each one go home in peace.' " 18 The king of Israel said to Jehoshaphat, "Did I not tell you that he would not prophesy anything favorable about me, but only disaster?"

19 Then Micaiah[r] said, "Therefore hear the word of the LORD: I saw the LORD sitting on his throne, with all the host of heaven standing beside him to the right and to the left of him. 20 And the LORD said, 'Who will entice Ahab, so that he may go up and fall at Ramoth-gilead?' Then one said one thing, and another said another. 21 until a spirit came forward and stood before the LORD, saying, 'I will entice him.' 22 'How?' the LORD asked him. He replied, 'I will go out and be a lying spirit in the mouth of all his prophets.' Then the LORD[r] said, 'You are to entice him, and you shall succeed; go out and do it.' 23 So you see, the LORD has put a lying spirit in the mouth of all these your prophets; the LORD has decreed disaster for you."

24 Then Zedekiah son of Chenaanah came up to Micaiah, slapped him on the cheek, and said, "Which way did the spirit of the LORD pass from me to speak to you?" 25 Micaiah replied, "You will find out on that day when you go in to hide in an inner chamber." 26 The king of Israel then ordered, "Take Micaiah, and return him to Amon the governor of the city and to Joash the king's son, 27 and say, 'Thus says the king: Put this fellow in prison, and feed him on reduced rations of bread and water until I come in peace.' " 28 Micaiah said, "If you return in peace, the LORD has not spoken by me." And he said, "Hear, you peoples, all of you!"

[r] Heb he

22.10	v. 6
22.11	Zech 1.18-21; Deut 33.17
22.14	1 Kings 18.10, 15; Num 22.18; 24.13
22.15	v. 12
22.17	vv. 34-36
22.18	v. 8
22.19	Isa 6.1; Dan 7.9, 10
22.22	Judg 9.23; 1 Sam 16.14; 18.10; 19.9; 2 Thess 2.11
22.23	Ezek 14.9
22.24	2 Chr 18.23
22.25	1 Kings 20.30
22.27	2 Chr 18.25-27
22.28	Deut 18.22

22.13 Ahab's messenger found Micaiah and warned him that the false prophets had promised victory for Ahab. He expected Micaiah to join the chorus and do the same. Being a true prophet, his reply was, "Whatever the LORD says to me, that I will speak." He could do no other.
22.15–17 Ahab asked Micaiah whether or not they should go. Ironically and with derision he said, "Go up and triumph." Ahab perceived Micaiah's mockery and adjured him to tell the truth. Micaiah then prophesied that Aram would win the battle. One would suppose that Ahab would have heeded the word of a true prophet of God. Instead he made light of Micaiah and said to Jehoshaphat that his message was to be expected from one like him. Micaiah then went so far as to assert that God had put a lying spirit in the mouth of all of Ahab's false prophets. It is hard to understand why Jehoshaphat, who had some spiritual insight, did not then and there divorce himself from Ahab and go home without joining the fray.
22.27 The role of prophet sometimes led to imprisonment and suffering, as happened to Micaiah, who had faithfully proclaimed the true word of God. On the other hand, Zedekiah, the false prophet, assured Ahab of victory. Ahab imprisoned Micaiah, ordering that he was to be fed reduced rations of bread and water. Ahab never doubted that he would return from the battle as victor, at which time he would slay Micaiah as a false prophet.

d. *Ahab's defeat and death*

29 So the king of Israel and King Jehoshaphat of Judah went up to Ramoth-gilead. 30 The king of Israel said to Jehoshaphat, "I will disguise myself and go into battle, but you wear your robes." So the king of Israel disguised himself and went into battle. 31 Now the king of Aram had commanded the thirty-two captains of his chariots, "Fight with no one small or great, but only with the king of Israel." 32 When the captains of the chariots saw Jehoshaphat, they said, "It is surely the king of Israel." So they turned to fight against him; and Jehoshaphat cried out. 33 When the captains of the chariots saw that it was not the king of Israel, they turned back from pursuing him. 34 But a certain man drew his bow and unknowingly struck the king of Israel between the scale armor and the breastplate; so he said to the driver of his chariot, "Turn around, and carry me out of the battle, for I am wounded." 35 The battle grew hot that day, and the king was propped up in his chariot facing the Arameans, until at evening he died; the blood from the wound had flowed into the bottom of the chariot. 36 Then about sunset a shout went through the army, "Every man to his city, and every man to his country!"

37 So the king died, and was brought to Samaria; they buried the king in Samaria. 38 They washed the chariot by the pool of Samaria; the dogs licked up his blood, and the prostitutes washed themselves in it,[s] according to the word of the LORD that he had spoken. 39 Now the rest of the acts of Ahab, and all that he did, and the ivory house that he built, and all the cities that he built, are they not written in the Book of the Annals of the Kings of Israel? 40 So Ahab slept with his ancestors; and his son Ahaziah succeeded him.

9. *Judah under Jehoshaphat*

41 Jehoshaphat son of Asa began to reign over Judah in the fourth year of King Ahab of Israel. 42 Jehoshaphat was thirty-five years old when he began to reign, and he reigned twenty-five years in Jerusalem. His mother's name was Azubah daughter of Shilhi. 43 He walked in all the way of his father Asa; he did not turn aside from it, doing what was right in the sight of the LORD; yet the high places were not taken away, and the people still sacrificed and offered incense on the high places. 44 Jehoshaphat also made peace with the king of Israel.

45 Now the rest of the acts of Jehoshaphat, and his power that he showed, and how he waged war, are they not written in the Book of the Annals of the Kings of Judah? 46 The remnant of the male temple prostitutes who were still in the land in the days of his father Asa, he exterminated.

47 There was no king in Edom; a deputy was king. 48 Jehoshaphat made ships of the Tarshish type to go to Ophir for gold; but they did not go, for the ships were wrecked at Ezion-geber. 49 Then Ahaziah son of Ahab said to Jehoshaphat, "Let my servants go with your servants in the ships," but Jehoshaphat was not willing. 50 Jehoshaphat slept with his ancestors and was buried with his ancestors in the city of his father David; his son Jehoram succeeded him.

---

[s] Heb lacks *in it*

22.29
vv. 3, 4
22.30
2 Chr 25.32
22.31
2 Chr 18.30
22.32
2 Chr 18.31

22.38
1 Kings 21.19
22.39
Am 3.15

22.41
2 Chr 20.31
22.43
2 Chr 17.3;
1 Kings 15.14;
2 Kings 12.3
22.44
2 Chr 19.2
22.45
2 Chr 20.34
22.46
1 Kings 14.24;
15.12
22.47
2 Sam 8.14;
2 Kings 3.9
22.48
2 Chr 20.35ff;
1 Kings 10.22
22.50
2 Chr 21.1

22.34 *drew his bow.* Ahab, wearing the uniform of a common soldier, was shot in the abdomen by an Aramean soldier who simply shot an arrow into the air at no particular target. God directed the arrow to its proper target. Sinners cannot finally hide themselves from the judgment of God. What appears to be accidental often comes directly from the hand of God. 22.38 God's prophetic word must always be fulfilled. The bloody chariot and bloody armor of Ahab were washed in the pool of Samaria and the dogs licked up his blood.
22.41ff A short account of Jehoshaphat's reign is given here. The longer account is found in 2 Chr 17–20. Jehoshaphat may have learned a lesson from his cooperation with wicked Ahab, for he was unwilling to assist Ahaziah, the son of Ahab, in one of his ventures (v. 49).

10. *The northern kingdom under Ahaziah*

51   Ahaziah son of Ahab began to reign over Israel in Samaria in the
seventeenth year of King Jehoshaphat of Judah; he reigned two years over
Israel. 52 He did what was evil in the sight of the LORD, and walked in
the way of his father and mother, and in the way of Jeroboam son of
Nebat, who caused Israel to sin. 53 He served Baal and worshiped him;
he provoked the LORD, the God of Israel, to anger, just as his father had
done.

22.51
v. 40

22.52
1 Kings 15.26;
21.25
22.53
1 Kings 16.30-32

INTRODUCTION TO

2 KINGS

Authorship, Date, and Background: See introduction to 1 Kings.

Characteristics and Content: See introduction to 1 Kings.

Outline:

2 KINGS

III. The divided kingdom continued (1.1–17.41)

G. The ending of Elijah's ministry

1. Ahaziah's (Israel) embassy to Baal-zebub

1 After the death of Ahab, Moab rebelled against Israel. 2 Ahaziah had fallen through the lattice in his upper chamber in Samaria, and lay injured; so he sent messengers, telling them, "Go, inquire of Baal-zebub, the god of Ekron, whether I shall recover from this injury." 3 But the angel of the LORD said to Elijah the Tishbite, "Get up, go to meet the messengers of the king of Samaria, and say to them, 'Is it because there is no God in Israel that you are going to inquire of Baal-zebub, the god of Ekron?' 4 Now therefore thus says the LORD, 'You shall not leave the bed to which you have gone, but you shall surely die.'" So Elijah went.

5 The messengers returned to the king, who said to them, "Why have you returned?" 6 They answered him, "There came a man to meet us, who said to us, 'Go back to the king who sent you, and say to him: Thus says the LORD: Is it because there is no God in Israel that you are sending to inquire of Baal-zebub, the god of Ekron? Therefore you shall not leave the bed to which you have gone, but shall surely die.'" 7 He said to them, "What sort of man was he who came to meet you and told you these things?" 8 They answered him, "A hairy man, with a leather belt around his waist." He said, "It is Elijah the Tishbite."

2. The attempts to seize Elijah

9 Then the king sent to him a captain of fifty with his fifty men. He went up to Elijah, who was sitting on the top of a hill, and said to him, "O man of God, the king says, 'Come down.'" 10 But Elijah answered the captain of fifty, "If I am a man of God, let fire come down from heaven and consume you and your fifty." Then fire came down from heaven, and consumed him and his fifty.

11 Again the king sent to him another captain of fifty with his fifty. He went up[t] and said to him, "O man of God, this is the king's order: Come down quickly!" 12 But Elijah answered them, "If I am a man of God,

---

t Gk Compare verses 9, 13: Heb *He answered*

1.1	2 Sam 8.2; 2 Kings 3.5
1.2	vv. 3, 6; Mt 10.25; see 2 Kings 8.7-10
1.4	vv. 6, 16
1.8	Zech 13.4; Mt 3.4
1.10	1 Kings 18.36-38; Lk 9.54

1.2 *Baal-zebub*, the "Lord of flies," was the Philistine god Ahaziah spoke to after he had fallen from his upper room in Samaria. There has been much speculation over this god's strange name. Some think the god protected his devotees from flies, or that the god sent messages as swiftly as the fly's flight, or that the seeming omnipresence of flies represents an all-seeing god. The name appears in the N.T. as "Beelzebul, the ruler of the demons" (Mt 12.24). This is in line with one of the Canaanite titles for Baal, which was "Prince (Zabul), Lord of the Earth."
1.3 Ahaziah had learned nothing from the mistakes of his father Ahab. Instead of consulting God, he turned to idols. God sent Elijah to inquire why he had not sought the true God. The prophet pronounced judgment: Ahaziah will die.
1.10 The public ministry of Elijah came to its close with two amazing miracles. When wicked Ahaziah sent soldiers to capture the prophet, they and their leader were consumed by fire. The second military company suffered the same fate. But this did not deter Ahaziah from persisting in an effort which had already shown itself to be imprudent. The leader of the third group of soldiers begged for their lives. God's angel then told Elijah to go with the fifty servants of Ahaziah. When Elijah faced Ahaziah, he brought the bad news to the king that he would not rise from his bed of sickness. After reigning for less than two years, Ahaziah died.

let fire come down from heaven and consume you and your fifty." Then the fire of God came down from heaven and consumed him and his fifty.

13 Again the king sent the captain of a third fifty with his fifty. So the third captain of fifty went up, and came and fell on his knees before Elijah, and entreated him, "O man of God, please let my life, and the life of these fifty servants of yours, be precious in your sight. 14 Look, fire came down from heaven and consumed the two former captains of fifty men with their fifties; but now let my life be precious in your sight." 15 Then the angel of the LORD said to Elijah, "Go down with him; do not be afraid of him." So he set out and went down with him to the king, 16 and said to him, "Thus says the LORD: Because you have sent messengers to inquire of Baal-zebub, the god of Ekron, — is it because there is no God in Israel to inquire of his word? — therefore you shall not leave the bed to which you have gone, but you shall surely die."

3. Jehoram, successor to Ahaziah

17 So he died according to the word of the LORD that Elijah had spoken. His brother,ᵘ Jehoram succeeded him as king in the second year of King Jehoram son of Jehoshaphat of Judah, because Ahaziah had no son. 18 Now the rest of the acts of Ahaziah that he did, are they not written in the Book of the Annals of the Kings of Israel?

H. *The reign of King Jehoram of Israel*

1. *Elijah's ascension*

2 Now when the LORD was about to take Elijah up to heaven by a whirlwind, Elijah and Elisha were on their way from Gilgal. 2 Elijah said to Elisha, "Stay here; for the LORD has sent me as far as Bethel." But Elisha said, "As the LORD lives, and as you yourself live, I will not leave you." So they went down to Bethel. 3 The company of prophetsᵛ who were in Bethel came out to Elisha, and said to him, "Do you know that today the LORD will take your master away from you?" And he said, "Yes, I know; keep silent."

4 Elijah said to him, "Elisha, stay here; for the LORD has sent me to Jericho." But he said, "As the LORD lives, and as you yourself live, I will not leave you." So they came to Jericho. 5 The company of prophetsᵛ who were at Jericho drew near to Elisha, and said to him, "Do you know that today the LORD will take your master away from you?" And he answered, "Yes, I know; be silent."

6 Then Elijah said to him, "Stay here; for the LORD has sent me to the Jordan." But he said, "As the LORD lives, and as you yourself live, I will not leave you." So the two of them went on. 7 Fifty men of the company of prophetsᵛ also went, and stood at some distance from them, as they both were standing by the Jordan. 8 Then Elijah took his mantle and rolled it up, and struck the water; the water was parted to the one side and to the other, until the two of them crossed on dry ground.

9 When they had crossed, Elijah said to Elisha, "Tell me what I may do for you, before I am taken from you." Elisha said, "Please let me inherit a double share of your spirit." 10 He responded, "You have asked a hard thing; yet, if you see me as I am being taken from you, it will be granted you; if not, it will not." 11 As they continued walking and talking, a chariot

ᵘ Gk Syr: Heb lacks *His brother*   ᵛ Heb *sons of the prophets*

Margin references:

1.13
1 Sam 26.21;
Ps 72.14

1.15
v. 3
1.16
v. 3

1.17
2 Kings 3.1;
8.16

2.1
Gen 5.24;
Heb 11.5;
1 Kings 19.21
2.2
Ruth 1.15,
16; vv. 4, 6;
1 Sam 1.26;
2 Kings 4.30
2.3
vv. 5, 7, 15;
2 Kings 4.1,
38
2.4
v. 2;
Josh 6.26
2.5
v. 3

2.6
v. 3;
Josh 3.8,
15-17
2.7
vv. 15, 16
2.8
1 Kings 19.13,
19; v. 14;
Ex 14.21, 22

2.11
2 Kings 6.17;
Ps 104.4

1.17 Since Ahaziah left no children, his brother Jehoram ascended the throne. Ahab had reigned twenty-two years; Ahaziah less than two.
2.1 *Gilgal.* The precise location of this city is not known; perhaps it refers to a city located in southwest Samaria.

2.9 *a double share.* Elisha was not asking to be greater than Elijah, since a double share was always given to the heir apparent or firstborn son. Elisha was in effect asking to be Elijah's spiritual heir.
2.11 *a chariot of fire and horses of fire.* The chariot and horses appeared like fire so that his ascension

of fire and horses of fire separated the two of them, and Elijah ascended in a whirlwind into heaven. [12] Elisha kept watching and crying out, "Father, father! The chariots of Israel and its horsemen!" But when he could no longer see him, he grasped his own clothes and tore them in two pieces.

2. The beginning of Elisha's ministry

13   He picked up the mantle of Elijah that had fallen from him, and went back and stood on the bank of the Jordan. [14] He took the mantle of Elijah that had fallen from him, and struck the water, saying, "Where is the Lord, the God of Elijah?" When he had struck the water, the water was parted to the one side and to the other, and Elisha went over.

15   When the company of prophets[w] who were at Jericho saw him at a distance, they declared, "The spirit of Elijah rests on Elisha." They came to meet him and bowed to the ground before him. [16] They said to him, "See now, we have fifty strong men among your servants; please let them go and seek your master; it may be that the spirit of the Lord has caught him up and thrown him down on some mountain or into some valley." He responded, "No, do not send them." [17] But when they urged him until he was ashamed, he said, "Send them." So they sent fifty men who searched for three days but did not find him. [18] When they came back to him (he had remained at Jericho), he said to them, "Did I not say to you, Do not go?"

19   Now the people of the city said to Elisha, "The location of this city is good, as my lord sees; but the water is bad, and the land is unfruitful." [20] He said, "Bring me a new bowl, and put salt in it." So they brought it to him. [21] Then he went to the spring of water and threw the salt into it, and said, "Thus says the Lord, I have made this water wholesome; from now on neither death nor miscarriage shall come from it." [22] So the water has been wholesome to this day, according to the word that Elisha spoke.

23   He went up from there to Bethel; and while he was going up on the way, some small boys came out of the city and jeered at him, saying, "Go away, baldhead! Go away, baldhead!" [24] When he turned around and saw them, he cursed them in the name of the Lord. Then two she-bears came out of the woods and mauled forty-two of the boys. [25] From there he went on to Mount Carmel, and then returned to Samaria.

3. Jehoram's campaign against Moab

3   In the eighteenth year of King Jehoshaphat of Judah, Jehoram son of Ahab became king over Israel in Samaria; he reigned twelve years. [2] He did what was evil in the sight of the Lord, though not like his father and mother, for he removed the pillar of Baal that his father had made. [3] Nevertheless he clung to the sin of Jeroboam son of Nebat, which he caused Israel to commit; he did not depart from it.

4   Now King Mesha of Moab was a sheep breeder, who used to deliver to the king of Israel one hundred thousand lambs, and the wool of one hundred thousand rams. [5] But when Ahab died, the king of Moab rebelled

w Heb *sons of the prophets*

2.12
2 Kings 13.14

2.14
v. 8

2.15
v. 7

2.16
1 Kings 18.12;
Acts 8.39

2.17
2 Kings 8.11

2.21
Ex 15.25;
2 Kings 4.41;
6.6

2.24
see
Neh 13.25-27
2.25
2 Kings 4.25;
1 Kings 18.19,
20

3.1
2 Kings 1.17
3.2
2 Kings 10.18,
26-28;
1 Kings 16.31,
32
3.3
1 Kings 12.28-32;
14.9, 16
3.4
2 Sam 8.2;
Isa 16.1
3.5
2 Kings 1.1

could be visible to those who watched it from afar.
2.14   Elisha began his ministry as the waters of the Jordan divided to let him through. Some within the company of prophets at Jericho had come near the Jordan; when they saw that the river was divided, they welcomed Elisha as one on whom the "spirit of Elijah" rested. They bowed down to him in acknowledgement of his office under God.
2.24   Many have wondered about the rightness of what Elisha did here. Even the curse of a prophet

would have no effect if the cause were not right, for "an undeserved curse goes nowhere" (Prov 26.2). Believers need never fear the curse of anyone, so long as they are not guilty of whatever occasioned the curse.
3.2   *not like his . . . mother.* Ahab, the father of Jehoram, was dead, but his mother, Jezebel, lived through his entire kingship.
3.4,5   Approximately one hundred years ago a missionary discovered a stone inscription (called the Moabite Stone) describing Mesha's revolt against Israel.

against the king of Israel. 6 So King Jehoram marched out of Samaria at that time and mustered all Israel. 7 As he went he sent word to King Jehoshaphat of Judah, "The king of Moab has rebelled against me; will you go with me to battle against Moab?" He answered, "I will; I am with you, my people are your people, my horses are your horses." 8 Then he asked, "By which way shall we march?" Jehoram answered, "By the way of the wilderness of Edom."

9   So the king of Israel, the king of Judah, and the king of Edom set out; and when they had made a roundabout march of seven days, there was no water for the army or for the animals that were with them. 10 Then the king of Israel said, "Alas! The LORD has summoned us, three kings, only to be handed over to Moab." 11 But Jehoshaphat said, "Is there no prophet of the LORD here, through whom we may inquire of the LORD?" Then one of the servants of the king of Israel answered, "Elisha son of Shaphat, who used to pour water on the hands of Elijah, is here." 12 Jehoshaphat said, "The word of the LORD is with him." So the king of Israel and Jehoshaphat and the king of Edom went down to him.

13   Elisha said to the king of Israel, "What have I to do with you? Go to your father's prophets or to your mother's." But the king of Israel said to him, "No; it is the LORD who has summoned us, three kings, only to be handed over to Moab." 14 Elisha said, "As the LORD of hosts lives, whom I serve, were it not that I have regard for King Jehoshaphat of Judah, I would give you neither a look nor a glance. 15 But get me a musician." And then, while the musician was playing, the power of the LORD came on him. 16 And he said, "Thus says the LORD, 'I will make this wadi full of pools.' 17 For thus says the LORD, 'You shall see neither wind nor rain, but the wadi shall be filled with water, so that you shall drink, you, your cattle, and your animals.' 18 This is only a trifle in the sight of the LORD, for he will also hand Moab over to you. 19 You shall conquer every fortified city and every choice city; every good tree you shall fell, all springs of water you shall stop up, and every good piece of land you shall ruin with stones." 20 The next day, about the time of the morning offering, suddenly water began to flow from the direction of Edom, until the country was filled with water.

21   When all the Moabites heard that the kings had come up to fight against them, all who were able to put on armor, from the youngest to the oldest, were called out and were drawn up at the frontier. 22 When they rose early in the morning, and the sun shone upon the water, the Moabites saw the water opposite them as red as blood. 23 They said, "This is blood; the kings must have fought together, and killed one another. Now then, Moab, to the spoil!" 24 But when they came to the camp of Israel, the Israelites rose up and attacked the Moabites, who fled before them; as they entered Moab they continued the attack.x 25 The cities they overturned, and on every good piece of land everyone threw a stone, until it was covered; every spring of water they stopped up, and every good tree they felled. Only at Kir-hareseth did the stone walls remain, until the slingers surrounded and attacked it. 26 When the king of Moab saw that the battle was going against him, he took with him seven hundred swordsmen to break through, opposite the king of Edom; but they could not. 27 Then

x Compare Gk Syr: Meaning of Heb uncertain

3.7 1 Kings 22.4
3.9 vv. 1, 7; 1 Kings 22.47
3.11 1 Kings 22.7; 19.21
3.13 Ezek 14.3-5; 1 Kings 18.19
3.14 1 Kings 17.1; 2 Kings 5.16
3.15 1 Sam 16.23; Ezek 1.3
3.19 v. 25
3.20 Ex 29.39, 40
3.21 Gen 19.37
3.25 v. 19; Isa 16.7, 11; Jer 48.31, 36
3.27 Am 2.1; Mic 6.7

3.9,10 Even as Jehoshaphat had joined Ahab against Aram, so now he joined himself to Jehoram against Moab. Jehoram boldly blamed God for his predicament of no water. He expected that God would deliver the kings of Judah and Edom and himself into the hands of the Moabites. God-fearing Jehoshaphat convinced Jehoram to send for a true prophet of the Lord, Elisha. **3.11–15** Both kings went to see Elisha. This prophet wanted nothing to do with Jehoram and declared, in insulting fashion, that if it were not for the presence of Jehoshaphat he would neither look at nor see Jehoram, who should consult his own pagan deities. **3.17ff** Elisha prophesied that Jehoram and his allies would miraculously get the water they needed and go on to win the war. The rest of the chapter describes the fulfillment of these prophecies.

he took his firstborn son who was to succeed him, and offered him as a burnt offering on the wall. And great wrath came upon Israel, so they withdrew from him and returned to their own land.

4. *Some of Elisha's miracles*

a. *The increase of the widow's oil*

4 Now the wife of a member of the company of prophets[y] cried to Elisha, "Your servant my husband is dead; and you know that your servant feared the Lord, but a creditor has come to take my two children as slaves." [2] Elisha said to her, "What shall I do for you? Tell me, what do you have in the house?" She answered, "Your servant has nothing in the house, except a jar of oil." [3] He said, "Go outside, borrow vessels from all your neighbors, empty vessels and not just a few. [4] Then go in, and shut the door behind you and your children, and start pouring into all these vessels; when each is full, set it aside." [5] So she left him and shut the door behind her and her children; they kept bringing vessels to her, and she kept pouring. [6] When the vessels were full, she said to her son, "Bring me another vessel." But he said to her, "There are no more." Then the oil stopped flowing. [7] She came and told the man of God, and he said, "Go sell the oil and pay your debts, and you and your children can live on the rest."

b. *The promise of a son to the Shunammite woman*

8 One day Elisha was passing through Shunem, where a wealthy woman lived, who urged him to have a meal. So whenever he passed that way, he would stop there for a meal. [9] She said to her husband, "Look, I am sure that this man who regularly passes our way is a holy man of God. [10] Let us make a small roof chamber with walls, and put there for him a bed, a table, a chair, and a lamp, so that he can stay there whenever he comes to us."

11 One day when he came there, he went up to the chamber and lay down there. [12] He said to his servant Gehazi, "Call the Shunammite woman." When he had called her, she stood before him. [13] He said to him, "Say to her, Since you have taken all this trouble for us, what may be done for you? Would you have a word spoken on your behalf to the king or to the commander of the army?" She answered, "I live among my own people." [14] He said, "What then may be done for her?" Gehazi answered, "Well, she has no son, and her husband is old." [15] He said, "Call her." When he had called her, she stood at the door. [16] He said, "At this season, in due time, you shall embrace a son." She replied, "No, my lord, O man of God; do not deceive your servant."

17 The woman conceived and bore a son at that season, in due time, as Elisha had declared to her.

c. *Elisha raises the dead son of the Shunammite*

18 When the child was older, he went out one day to his father among the reapers. [19] He complained to his father, "Oh, my head, my head!" The father said to his servant, "Carry him to his mother." [20] He carried him and brought him to his mother; the child sat on her lap until noon, and he died. [21] She went up and laid him on the bed of the man of God, closed the door on him, and left. [22] Then she called to her husband, and said,

---

[y] Heb *the sons of the prophets*

4.1
2 Kings 2.3;
Lev 25.39;
Mt 18.25

4.7
1 Kings 12.22

4.8
Josh 19.18

4.9
v. 7

4.12
vv. 29-31;
2 Kings 5.20-27;
8.4, 5

4.16
Gen 18.10,
14; v. 28

4.21
vv. 7, 32

4.3ff Elisha performed a miracle by increasing the oil supply for a poor widow in need, providing enough for her to pay her debt and to maintain her family. **4.12ff** Elisha appreciated what the Shunammite woman had done for him and his servant, and wanted to do something in return. Gehazi noted that she had no heir and her husband was aged. Elisha summoned her and said that in a year's time she would have a child. She found it hard to believe and suggested that the prophet must be teasing her. But she had received Elisha in the name of a prophet, and she had a prophet's reward. A son and heir was born to her.

"Send me one of the servants and one of the donkeys, so that I may quickly go to the man of God and come back again." 23 He said, "Why go to him today? It is neither new moon nor sabbath." She said, "It will be all right." 24 Then she saddled the donkey and said to her servant, "Urge the animal on; do not hold back for me unless I tell you." 25 So she set out, and came to the man of God at Mount Carmel.

When the man of God saw her coming, he said to Gehazi his servant, "Look, there is the Shunammite woman; 26 run at once to meet her, and say to her, Are you all right? Is your husband all right? Is the child all right?" She answered, "It is all right." 27 When she came to the man of God at the mountain, she caught hold of his feet. Gehazi approached to push her away. But the man of God said, "Let her alone, for she is in bitter distress; the LORD has hidden it from me and has not told me." 28 Then she said, "Did I ask my lord for a son? Did I not say, Do not mislead me?" 29 He said to Gehazi, "Gird up your loins, and take my staff in your hand, and go. If you meet anyone, give no greeting, and if anyone greets you, do not answer; and lay my staff on the face of the child." 30 Then the mother of the child said, "As the LORD lives, and as you yourself live, I will not leave without you." So he rose up and followed her. 31 Gehazi went on ahead and laid the staff on the face of the child, but there was no sound or sign of life. He came back to meet him and told him, "The child has not awakened."

32 When Elisha came into the house, he saw the child lying dead on his bed. 33 So he went in and closed the door on the two of them, and prayed to the LORD. 34 Then he got up on the bed[z] and lay upon the child, putting his mouth upon his mouth, his eyes upon his eyes, and his hands upon his hands; and while he lay bent over him, the flesh of the child became warm. 35 He got down, walked once to and fro in the room, then got up again and bent over him; the child sneezed seven times, and the child opened his eyes. 36 Elisha[a] summoned Gehazi and said, "Call the Shunammite woman." So he called her. When she came to him, he said, "Take your son." 37 She came and fell at his feet, bowing to the ground; then she took her son and left.

d. The poisonous stew made harmless

38 When Elisha returned to Gilgal, there was a famine in the land. As the company of prophets was[b] sitting before him, he said to his servant, "Put the large pot on, and make some stew for the company of prophets."[c] 39 One of them went out into the field to gather herbs; he found a wild vine and gathered from it a lapful of wild gourds, and came and cut them up into the pot of stew, not knowing what they were. 40 They served some for the men to eat. But while they were eating the stew, they cried out, "O man of God, there is death in the pot!" They could not eat it. 41 He said, "Then bring some flour." He threw it into the pot, and said, "Serve the people and let them eat." And there was nothing harmful in the pot.

e. The miraculous feeding of the hundred people

42 A man came from Baal-shalishah, bringing food from the first fruits to the man of God: twenty loaves of barley and fresh ears of grain

[z] Heb lacks *on the bed*   [a] Heb *he*   [b] Heb *sons of the prophets were*   [c] Heb *sons of the prophets*

4.23
Num 10.10;
28.11;
1 Chr 23.31
4.25
2 Kings 2.25

4.28
v. 16
4.29
1 Kings 18.46;
2 Kings 9.1;
Lk 10.4;
Ex 7.19;
14.16;
2 Kings 2.8,
14
4.30
2 Kings 2.2

4.33
v. 4;
Mt 6.6;
1 Kings 17.20
4.34
1 Kings 17.21;
Acts 20.10
4.35
1 Kings 17.21;
2 Kings 8.1,
5
4.37
1 Kings 17.23;
Heb 11.35

4.38
2 Kings 2.1,
3; 8.1;
Lk 10.39;
Acts 22.3

4.41
Ex 15.25;
2 Kings 2.21

4.42
1 Sam 9.4, 7

4.25ff The son of the Shunammite woman was dead. She was obviously deeply hurt and perplexed at how God was treating her. In her agony she sought out the prophet who was at Mt. Carmel. Elisha sent Gehazi ahead of him with the prophet's staff in his hand. He laid it on the body of the dead boy but nothing happened, for the power lay not in the staff but in the prophet. When Elisha arrived, he took

over, and through the power God gave him, the dead corpse came back to life.
4.38 During a famine, Elisha was teaching in the company of prophets. When word came about a poisonous plant in the stew, the prophet cast flour into the pot and the danger ceased. Those who wait upon God as they do their duty are protected and delivered by divine providence.

in his sack. Elisha said, "Give it to the people and let them eat." 43 But his servant said, "How can I set this before a hundred people?" So he repeated, "Give it to the people and let them eat, for thus says the LORD, 'They shall eat and have some left.' " 44 He set it before them, they ate, and had some left, according to the word of the LORD.

5. *Naaman the leper and Elisha*

a. *The testimony of the Israelite girl*

5 Naaman, commander of the army of the king of Aram, was a great man and in high favor with his master, because by him the LORD had given victory to Aram. The man, though a mighty warrior, suffered from leprosy.*d* 2 Now the Arameans on one of their raids had taken a young girl captive from the land of Israel, and she served Naaman's wife. 3 She said to her mistress, "If only my lord were with the prophet who is in Samaria! He would cure him of his leprosy."*d* 4 So Naaman*e* went in and told his lord just what the girl from the land of Israel had said. 5 And the king of Aram said, "Go then, and I will send along a letter to the king of Israel."

b. *The message of the Syrian king to Jehoram*

He went, taking with him ten talents of silver, six thousand shekels of gold, and ten sets of garments. 6 He brought the letter to the king of Israel, which read, "When this letter reaches you, know that I have sent to you my servant Naaman, that you may cure him of his leprosy."*d* 7 When the king of Israel read the letter, he tore his clothes and said, "Am I God, to give death or life, that this man sends word to me to cure a man of his leprosy?*d* Just look and see how he is trying to pick a quarrel with me."

c. *Elisha gives orders to Naaman, who is healed*

8 But when Elisha the man of God heard that the king of Israel had torn his clothes, he sent a message to the king, "Why have you torn your clothes? Let him come to me, that he may learn that there is a prophet in Israel." 9 So Naaman came with his horses and chariots, and halted at the entrance of Elisha's house. 10 Elisha sent a messenger to him, saying, "Go, wash in the Jordan seven times, and your flesh shall be restored and you shall be clean." 11 But Naaman became angry and went away, saying, "I thought that for me he would surely come out, and stand and call on the name of the LORD his God, and would wave his hand over the spot, and cure the leprosy!*d* 12 Are not Abana*f* and Pharpar, the rivers of Damascus, better than all the waters of Israel? Could I not wash in them, and be clean?" He turned and went away in a rage. 13 But his servants approached and said to him, "Father, if the prophet had commanded you

d A term for several skin diseases; precise meaning uncertain   *e* Heb *he*   *f* Another reading is *Amana*

Cross references (right margin):

4.44
Mt 14.16-21;
15.32-38

5.1
Lk 4.27

5.5
1 Sam 9.8;
2 Kings 8.8,
9

5.7
Gen 37.29;
30.2;
Deut 32.39;
1 Sam 2.6;
1 Kings 20.7

5.8
1 Kings 12.22

5.10
Jn 9.7

5.13
2 Kings 6.21;
8.9;
1 Sam 28.23

4.44 Elisha miraculously fed a hundred men who had only a small food supply. True, this miracle was small when compared with Jesus' miracles of the feeding of the five thousand and the four thousand, but it was still a miracle, accomplished by the hand of Israel's God.

5.1ff Surprisingly, the little maid from Israel showed more faith in the Lord and his prophets than did many leaders in Israel; she was sure Elisha could cure her master's illness. When Naaman came to Elisha for healing, he expected something personal and spectacular. He was disappointed and angry when Elisha suggested that he bathe seven times in the Jordan, a muddy river not to be compared with the mighty rivers of Damascus. He had to learn two things: (1) It was not the river or the prophet who made the difference, but it was God working through the prophet who performed the miracle. (2) Naaman

could not be cured without humility before the Lord and obedience to his word.

5.6 When Jehoram received the letter from the king of Aram asking him to cure Naaman of his leprosy, he tore his clothes inasmuch as the Aramean king was guilty of blasphemy for supposing that Jehoram had a power which belonged to God alone, and because he suspected a political trick. Jehoram, however, failed to send for God's prophet.

5.8 Elisha offered his service to the king to demonstrate that Israel's God was able to heal and that his prophet had power because he belonged to God.

5.13 Servants sometimes can show greater sense than their masters. When Naaman's servants argued that what was important was the cure, not how the cure would come about, Naaman followed their counsel and was healed.

to do something difficult, would you not have done it? How much more, when all he said to you was, 'Wash, and be clean'?" 14 So he went down and immersed himself seven times in the Jordan, according to the word of the man of God; his flesh was restored like the flesh of a young boy, and he was clean.

d. Elisha refuses a reward

15 Then he returned to the man of God, he and all his company; he came and stood before him and said, "Now I know that there is no God in all the earth except in Israel; please accept a present from your servant." 16 But he said, "As the LORD lives, whom I serve, I will accept nothing!" He urged him to accept, but he refused. 17 Then Naaman said, "If not, please let two mule-loads of earth be given to your servant; for your servant will no longer offer burnt offering or sacrifice to any god except the LORD. 18 But may the LORD pardon your servant on one count: when my master goes into the house of Rimmon to worship there, leaning on my arm, and I bow down in the house of Rimmon, when I do bow down in the house of Rimmon, may the LORD pardon your servant on this one count." 19 He said to him, "Go in peace."

e. Gehazi's greed and punishment

But when Naaman had gone from him a short distance, 20 Gehazi, the servant of Elisha the man of God, thought, "My master has let that Aramean Naaman off too lightly by not accepting from him what he offered. As the LORD lives, I will run after him and get something out of him." 21 So Gehazi went after Naaman. When Naaman saw someone running after him, he jumped down from the chariot to meet him and said, "Is everything all right?" 22 He replied, "Yes, but my master has sent me to say, 'Two members of a company of prophets^g have just come to me from the hill country of Ephraim; please give them a talent of silver and two changes of clothing.'" 23 Naaman said, "Please accept two talents." He urged him, and tied up two talents of silver in two bags, with two changes of clothing, and gave them to two of his servants, who carried them in front of Gehazi.^h 24 When he came to the citadel, he took the bagsⁱ from them, and stored them inside; he dismissed the men, and they left.

25 He went in and stood before his master; and Elisha said to him, "Where have you been, Gehazi?" He answered, "Your servant has not gone anywhere at all." 26 But he said to him, "Did I not go with you in spirit when someone left his chariot to meet you? Is this a time to accept money and to accept clothing, olive orchards and vineyards, sheep and oxen, and male and female slaves? 27 Therefore the leprosy^j of Naaman shall cling to you, and to your descendants forever." So he left his presence leprous,^j as white as snow.

6. The further ministry of Elisha

a. The recovery of the lost ax head

6 Now the company of prophets^g said to Elisha, "As you see, the place where we live under your charge is too small for us. 2 Let us go to the Jordan, and let us collect logs there, one for each of us, and build a

g Heb *sons of the prophets*   h Heb *him*   i Heb lacks *the bags*   j A term for several skin diseases; precise meaning uncertain

---

Marginal cross-references (left column):

5.14 v. 10; Job 33.25; Lk 4.27

5.15 1 Sam 15.46, 47; Dan 2.47; 3.29; 1 Sam 25.27

5.16 2 Kings 3.14; vv. 20, 26; Gen 14.22, 23

5.18 2 Kings 7.2, 17

5.20 2 Kings 4.12, 31, 36

5.22 2 Kings 4.26; Josh 24.33

5.25 v. 22

5.26 v. 16

5.27 Ex 4.6; Num 12.10; 2 Kings 15.5

6.1 2 Kings 4.38

5.17 *two mule-loads of earth.* Thus even in a foreign land Naaman could worship God on Israel's soil.
5.20 Many a servant of God has come to grief by expecting personal rewards from those he has helped through the power of God. Elisha himself had no thought of taking anything from Naaman for his services. But Gehazi was covetous, wily, and deceitful.

He got what he wanted from Naaman, but he also got from the prophet something he did not want — the sentence of leprosy upon him and his descendants.
5.26 Elisha affirmed that God had given him a supernatural gift to know what Gehazi was doing at the exact moment he sought a gift from Naaman for the services of his master.

place there for us to live." He answered, "Do so." 3 Then one of them said, "Please come with your servants." And he answered, "I will." 4 So he went with them. When they came to the Jordan, they cut down trees. 5 But as one was felling a log, his ax head fell into the water; he cried out, "Alas, master! It was borrowed." 6 Then the man of God said, "Where did it fall?" When he showed him the place, he cut off a stick, and threw it in there, and made the iron float. 7 He said, "Pick it up." So he reached out his hand and took it.

6.6
2 Kings 2.21

b. Elisha discloses Ben-hadad's plans to Jehoram

8 Once when the king of Aram was at war with Israel, he took counsel with his officers. He said, "At such and such a place shall be my camp." 9 But the man of God sent word to the king of Israel, "Take care not to pass this place, because the Arameans are going down there." 10 The king of Israel sent word to the place of which the man of God spoke. More than once or twice he warned such a place^k so that it was on the alert.

6.9
v. 12

c. Elisha strikes the Arameans blind

11 The mind of the king of Aram was greatly perturbed because of this; he called his officers and said to them, "Now tell me who among us sides with the king of Israel?" 12 Then one of his officers said, "No one, my lord king. It is Elisha, the prophet in Israel, who tells the king of Israel the words that you speak in your bedchamber." 13 He said, "Go and find where he is; I will send and seize him." He was told, "He is in Dothan." 14 So he sent horses and chariots there and a great army; they came by night, and surrounded the city.

6.13
Gen 37.17

15 When an attendant of the man of God rose early in the morning and went out, an army with horses and chariots was all around the city. His servant said, "Alas, master! What shall we do?" 16 He replied, "Do not be afraid, for there are more with us than there are with them." 17 Then Elisha prayed: "O Lord, please open his eyes that he may see." So the Lord opened the eyes of the servant, and he saw; the mountain was full of horses and chariots of fire all around Elisha. 18 When the Arameans^l came down against him, Elisha prayed to the Lord, and said, "Strike this people, please, with blindness." So he struck them with blindness as Elisha had asked. 19 Elisha said to them, "This is not the way, and this is not the city; follow me, and I will bring you to the man whom you seek." And he led them to Samaria.

6.16
2 Chr 32.7, 8;
Ps 55.18;
Rom 8.31
6.17
2 Kings 2.11;
Ps 68.17;
Zech 6.1-7
6.18
Gen 19.11

d. The blind Arameans led to Samaria

20 As soon as they entered Samaria, Elisha said, "O Lord, open the eyes of these men so that they may see." The Lord opened their eyes, and they saw that they were inside Samaria. 21 When the king of Israel saw them he said to Elisha, "Father, shall I kill them? Shall I kill them?" 22 He

6.20
v. 17
6.21
2 Kings 2.12;
5.13; 8.9
6.22
Deut 20.11-16;
Rom 12.20

^{k} Heb *warned it* ^{l} Heb *they*

6.6 With God's help, Elisha demonstrated great power. Here he made iron swim, contrary to its nature, since the God of nature is not tied to its laws. **6.10** God gave Elisha a word of knowledge on several occasions, so that he could warn the king of Israel concerning the plans and activities of Ben-hadad. The king paid attention to these warnings about danger from the Arameans, but not to Elisha's warning about his sins. Thus he would be saved from physical death but not from the ultimate judgment of God. **6.11,12** The king of Aram suspected that his plans were being communicated to the king of Israel by some treacherous servant. But a more observant servant told the king that Elisha knew every word the king spoke, even when he was in his own bedroom. Nothing is out of reach of God.

6.17 Elisha's servant was terrified at the sight of the enemy. Elisha prayed that God would *open his eyes, that he may see.* This meant, of course, the opening not of physical eyes but of the eyes of faith. The servant then saw the protection they were under — chariots of fire and horses of fire more numerous than the enemy. When our spiritual eyes are opened, our fears are silenced. God's angels are spiritual soldiers sent by God, powerful enough to defeat any and all enemies. **6.18** In response to Elisha's prayers, God struck the Arameans blind; then the prophet led them to Samaria where their eyes were opened — face to face with the king of Israel. Instead of their being slain, however, a feast was prepared for them. In response to this kindness, the Arameans temporarily stopped their assaults on the land of Israel.

answered, "No! Did you capture with your sword and your bow those whom you want to kill? Set food and water before them so that they may eat and drink; and let them go to their master." 23 So he prepared for them a great feast; after they ate and drank, he sent them on their way, and they went to their master. And the Arameans no longer came raiding into the land of Israel.

e. Elisha and the siege of Samaria

24 Some time later King Ben-hadad of Aram mustered his entire army; he marched against Samaria and laid siege to it. 25 As the siege continued, famine in Samaria became so great that a donkey's head was sold for eighty shekels of silver, and one-fourth of a kab of dove's dung for five shekels of silver. 26 Now as the king of Israel was walking on the city wall, a woman cried out to him, "Help, my lord king!" 27 He said, "No! Let the LORD help you. How can I help you? From the threshing floor or from the wine press?" 28 But then the king asked her, "What is your complaint?" She answered, "This woman said to me, 'Give up your son; we will eat him today, and we will eat my son tomorrow.' 29 So we cooked my son and ate him. The next day I said to her, 'Give up your son and we will eat him.' But she has hidden her son." 30 When the king heard the words of the woman he tore his clothes—now since he was walking on the city wall, the people could see that he had sackcloth on his body underneath— 31 and he said, "So may God do to me, and more, if the head of Elisha son of Shaphat stays on his shoulders today." 32 So he dispatched a man from his presence.

Now Elisha was sitting in his house, and the elders were sitting with him. Before the messenger arrived, Elisha said to the elders, "Are you aware that this murderer has sent someone to take off my head? When the messenger comes, see that you shut the door and hold it closed against him. Is not the sound of his master's feet behind him?" 33 While he was still speaking with them, the king[m] came down to him and said, "This trouble is from the LORD! Why should I hope in the LORD any longer?" 1 But Elisha said, "Hear the word of the LORD: thus says the LORD, Tomorrow about this time a measure of choice meal shall be sold for a shekel, and two measures of barley for a shekel, at the gate of Samaria." 2 Then the captain on whose hand the king leaned said to the man of God, "Even if the LORD were to make windows in the sky, could such a thing happen?" But he said, "You shall see it with your own eyes, but you shall not eat from it."

3 Now there were four leprous[n] men outside the city gate, who said to one another, "Why should we sit here until we die? 4 If we say, 'Let us enter the city,' the famine is in the city, and we shall die there; but if we sit here, we shall also die. Therefore, let us desert to the Aramean camp; if they spare our lives, we shall live; and if they kill us, we shall but die." 5 So they arose at twilight to go to the Aramean camp; but when they came to the edge of the Aramean camp, there was no one there at all. 6 For the Lord had caused the Aramean army to hear the sound of

---

6.23
vv. 8, 9;
2 Kings 5.2

6.24
1 Kings 20.1

6.29
Lev 26.27-29;
Deut 28.52,
53, 57
6.30
1 Kings 21.27

6.31
Ruth 1.17;
1 Kings 19.2
6.32
Ezek 8.1;
20.1;
1 Kings 18.4,
13, 14

6.33
Job 2.9

7.1
v. 18

7.2
vv. 17, 19,
20;
Mal 3.10

7.3
Lev 13.46
7.4
2 Kings 6.24

7.6
2 Sam 5.24;
19.7;
1 Kings 10.29

---

[m] See 7.2: Heb *messenger*   [n] A term for several skin diseases; precise meaning uncertain

---

6.25 Ben-hadad still wished to destroy Israel. So he besieged Samaria, which was soon left without food. So great was the famine that an unclean animal's head sold for an exorbitant price. The king was distraught, but he neither removed Israel's idols nor sought the face of God in repentance.
6.31 A woman described to the king a situation in which his people were eating human flesh. Struck by the horror of the situation, the king placed the blame upon Elisha, the prophet. Since God had intervened previously without the king repenting, he figured that Elisha was simply withholding the assistance of God

from Israel.
7.1 Elisha called the king a murderer (6.32). When the king and his captain stood face to face with Elisha, he had a good word from God: the famine would soon be over. When the captain disbelieved that word of prophecy, God through Elisha passed immediate judgment on him: he would see the food and know the crisis was past, but he would not eat of the food.
7.6ff The Arameans unexpectedly fled from the scene of the siege because of a direct visitation from God. Hearing the noise of chariots and horses, they thought relief had come to Israel from Egypt and the

chariots, and of horses, the sound of a great army, so that they said to one another, "The king of Israel has hired the kings of the Hittites and the kings of Egypt to fight against us." [7] So they fled away in the twilight and abandoned their tents, their horses, and their donkeys leaving the camp just as it was, and fled for their lives. [8] When these leprous[o] men had come to the edge of the camp, they went into a tent, ate and drank, carried off silver, gold, and clothing, and went and hid them. Then they came back, entered another tent, carried off things from it, and went and hid them.

[9] Then they said to one another, "What we are doing is wrong. This is a day of good news; if we are silent and wait until the morning light, we will be found guilty; therefore let us go and tell the king's household." [10] So they came and called to the gatekeepers of the city, and told them, "We went to the Aramean camp, but there was no one to be seen or heard there, nothing but the horses tied, the donkeys tied, and the tents as they were." [11] Then the gatekeepers called out and proclaimed it to the king's household. [12] The king got up in the night, and said to his servants, "I will tell you what the Arameans have prepared against us. They know that we are starving; so they have left the camp to hide themselves in the open country, thinking, 'When they come out of the city, we shall take them alive and get into the city.'" [13] One of his servants said, "Let some men take five of the remaining horses, since those left here will suffer the fate of the whole multitude of Israel that have perished already;[p] let us send and find out." [14] So they took two mounted men, and the king sent them after the Aramean army, saying, "Go and find out." [15] So they went after them as far as the Jordan; the whole way was littered with garments and equipment that the Arameans had thrown away in their haste. So the messengers returned, and told the king.

[16] Then the people went out, and plundered the camp of the Arameans. So a measure of choice meal was sold for a shekel, and two measures of barley for a shekel, according to the word of the LORD. [17] Now the king had appointed the captain on whose hand he leaned to have charge of the gate; the people trampled him to death in the gate, just as the man of God had said when the king came down to him. [18] For when the man of God had said to the king, "Two measures of barley shall be sold for a shekel, and a measure of choice meal for a shekel, about this time tomorrow in the gate of Samaria," [19] the captain had answered the man of God, "Even if the LORD were to make windows in the sky, could such a thing happen?" And he had answered, "You shall see it with your own eyes, but you shall not eat from it." [20] It did indeed happen to him; the people trampled him to death in the gate.

7. *The Shunammite woman comes home*

8 Now Elisha had said to the woman whose son he had restored to life, "Get up and go with your household, and settle wherever you can; for the LORD has called for a famine, and it will come on the land for seven years." [2] So the woman got up and did according to the word of the man

o A term for several skin diseases; precise meaning uncertain   *p* Compare Gk Syr Vg: Meaning of Heb uncertain

7.7
Ps 48.4-6

7.9
2 Sam 18.27

7.12
2 Kings 6.25-29

7.16
v. 1

7.17
v. 2;
2 Kings 6.32

7.18
v. 1

7.19
v. 2

8.1
2 Kings 4.35;
Ps 105.16;
Hag 1.11

Hittites. Four lepers who lived outside the camp observed what happened and found much food and wealth left behind by the Arameans. They brought the good news to the city and told the king what had happened. But the king thought it was only a military device and refused to believe that the enemy had gone.
7.17 The starving people rushed out to find food and booty. The king appointed his captain to guard the gate. The mob trampled on him and he died, fulfilling the prophetic word of Elisha.

8.1 God often sends famines to accomplish the divine purpose. In this instance it was to last seven years.
8.2 The Shunammite woman (4.12) to whom God had given a son was warned by Elisha to leave Israel and go to the land of the Philistines until a seven-year famine sent by God was over. On her return she asked the king for her land to be returned to her. Providentially, at that very moment the king was listening to Gehazi tell the story of her life, how God had raised her son back to life. He was moved by this testimony to grant her request.

of God; she went with her household and settled in the land of the Philistines seven years. 3 At the end of the seven years, when the woman returned from the land of the Philistines, she set out to appeal to the king for her house and her land. 4 Now the king was talking with Gehazi the servant of the man of God, saying, "Tell me all the great things that Elisha has done." 5 While he was telling the king how Elisha had restored a dead person to life, the woman whose son he had restored to life appealed to the king for her house and her land. Gehazi said, "My lord king, here is the woman, and here is her son whom Elisha restored to life." 6 When the king questioned the woman, she told him. So the king appointed an official for her, saying, "Restore all that was hers, together with all the revenue of the fields from the day that she left the land until now."

8. *Elisha anoints Hazael king of Aram*

7 Elisha went to Damascus while King Ben-hadad of Aram was ill. When it was told him, "The man of God has come here," 8 the king said to Hazael, "Take a present with you and go to meet the man of God. Inquire of the LORD through him, whether I shall recover from this illness." 9 So Hazael went to meet him, taking a present with him, all kinds of goods of Damascus, forty camel loads. When he entered and stood before him, he said, "Your son King Ben-hadad of Aram has sent me to you, saying, 'Shall I recover from this illness?'" 10 Elisha said to him, "Go, say to him, 'You shall certainly recover'; but the LORD has shown me that he shall certainly die." 11 He fixed his gaze and stared at him, until he was ashamed. Then the man of God wept. 12 Hazael asked, "Why does my lord weep?" He answered, "Because I know the evil that you will do to the people of Israel; you will set their fortresses on fire, you will kill their young men with the sword, dash in pieces their little ones, and rip up their pregnant women." 13 Hazael said, "What is your servant, who is a mere dog, that he should do this great thing?" Elisha answered, "The LORD has shown me that you are to be king over Aram." 14 Then he left Elisha, and went to his master Ben-hadad,*q* who said to him, "What did Elisha say to you?" And he answered, "He told me that you would certainly recover." 15 But the next day he took the bed-cover and dipped it in water and spread it over the king's face, until he died. And Hazael succeeded him.

I. *The reign of King Jehoram of Judah*

16 In the fifth year of King Joram son of Ahab of Israel,*r* Jehoram son of King Jehoshaphat of Judah began to reign. 17 He was thirty-two years old when he became king, and he reigned eight years in Jerusalem. 18 He walked in the way of the kings of Israel, as the house of Ahab had

---

Cross-references (left margin):

8.4
2 Kings 4.12;
5.20-27
8.5
2 Kings 4.35

8.7
1 Kings 11.24;
2 Kings 6.24
8.8
1 Kings 19.15;
14.3;
2 Kings 1.2

8.10
vv. 14, 15

8.12
2 Kings 10.32;
12.17; 13.3,
7; 15.16;
Hos 13.16;
Am 1.13
8.13
1 Sam 17.43;
1 Kings 19.15

8.15
v. 10

8.16
2 Kings 1.17;
3.1;
2 Chr 21.3, 4
8.17
2 Chr 21.5-10
8.18
v. 27

---

q Heb lacks *Ben-hadad*   *r* Gk Syr: Heb adds *Jehoshaphat being king of Judah,*

8.4 Even though Gehazi had become a leper Elisha did not dismiss him from his service. Here we find him speaking with the king about the great things Elisha had done. Lepers had to keep their distance from others according to the law, but they were not forbidden to talk with nonlepers.
8.8 Elisha was now in Damascus. Why he came is not stated, but 1 Kings 19.15 says Elijah was to go to Damascus to anoint Hazael. Some think Elisha was now fulfilling this command given to Elijah, who had not been able to do this before God took him to heaven. The king of Aram was ill and called for Elisha. It seems strange that a pagan king would do what the house of Ahab had often refused to do — consult God through his prophet. Ben-hadad wanted to know whether he would get well and sent Hazael to secure an answer from Elisha.
8.10–13 Elisha responded to the inquiry of Hazael

in a strange manner. He said the king would recover, but he would die. By that he meant that the illness would not kill him but Hazael would. Elisha then wept because he knew the terrible things Hazael would do to Israel when he became king. Hazael was unhappy with what the prophet said and assured him he was a decent man who would never be unfaithful. Then Elisha replied, "The LORD has shown me that you are to be king over Aram."
8.15 A wet *bed-cover* made an effective implement with which to smother someone.
8.16 *Joram*, also called Jehoram (see 2 Kings 1.17), was the brother of Ahaziah who died childless. The name Joram here distinguishes him from Jehoram son of Jehoshaphat, who began a co-regency with his father. Joram was the king of Israel and Jehoram the king of Judah.
8.18 Jehoram of Judah succeeded the good king

done, for the daughter of Ahab was his wife. He did what was evil in the sight of the Lord. 19 Yet the Lord would not destroy Judah, for the sake of his servant David, since he had promised to give a lamp to him and to his descendants forever.

20   In his days Edom revolted against the rule of Judah, and set up a king of their own. 21 Then Joram crossed over to Zair with all his chariots. He set out by night and attacked the Edomites and their chariot commanders who had surrounded him;^{s} but his army fled home. 22 So Edom has been in revolt against the rule of Judah to this day. Libnah also revolted at the same time. 23 Now the rest of the acts of Joram, and all that he did, are they not written in the Book of the Annals of the Kings of Judah? 24 So Joram slept with his ancestors, and was buried with them in the city of David; his son Ahaziah succeeded him.

J. The reign of King Ahaziah of Judah

25   In the twelfth year of King Joram son of Ahab of Israel, Ahaziah son of King Jehoram of Judah began to reign. 26 Ahaziah was twenty-two years old when he began to reign; he reigned one year in Jerusalem. His mother's name was Athaliah, a granddaughter of King Omri of Israel. 27 He also walked in the way of the house of Ahab, doing what was evil in the sight of the Lord, as the house of Ahab had done, for he was son-in-law to the house of Ahab.

28   He went with Joram son of Ahab to wage war against King Hazael of Aram at Ramoth-gilead, where the Arameans wounded Joram. 29 King Joram returned to be healed in Jezreel of the wounds that the Arameans had inflicted on him at Ramah, when he fought against King Hazael of Aram. King Ahaziah son of Jehoram of Judah went down to see Joram son of Ahab in Jezreel, because he was wounded.

K. The reign of King Jehu of Israel

1. Jehu anointed king

9 Then the prophet Elisha called a member of the company of prophets^t and said to him, "Gird up your loins; take this flask of oil in your hand, and go to Ramoth-gilead. 2 When you arrive, look there for Jehu son of Jehoshaphat, son of Nimshi; go in and get him to leave his companions, and take him into an inner chamber. 3 Then take the flask of oil, pour it on his head, and say, 'Thus says the Lord: I anoint you king over Israel.' Then open the door and flee; do not linger."

4   So the young man, the young prophet, went to Ramoth-gilead. 5 He

^{s} Meaning of Heb uncertain ^{t} Heb *sons of the prophets*

Cross references (right margin):

8.19 · 2 Sam 7.13; · 1 Kings 11.36; · 2 Chr 21.7
8.20 · 1 Kings 22.4; · 2 Kings 3.27; · 2 Chr 21.8-10
8.21 · 2 Sam 18.17; · 19.8
8.22 · 2 Chr 21.10
8.24 · 2 Chr 21.20; · 22.1
8.25 · 2 Chr 22.1-6
8.28 · v. 15; · 1 Kings 22.3, · 29
8.29 · 2 Kings 9.15; · 2 Chr 22.6, 7
9.1 · 2 Kings 2.3; · 4.29; 8.28, · 29
9.2 · vv. 5, 11
9.3 · 2 Chr 22.7

Jehoshaphat. He was a very bad king. He married the daughter of Jezebel, Athaliah, who was as wicked as her mother. Why Jehoshaphat ever permitted this to happen is a mystery, since he was fully acquainted with the house of Ahab.

8.21   The Edomites (descendants of Esau) revolted against Judah and king Jehoram (called Joram here). They had been overcome in David's day and had spent a hundred and fifty years under the yoke of Judah. This fulfilled Gen 27.40, which predicted that Esau's offspring would someday break Jacob's yoke from their neck. The Edomites became independent and remained enemies of the Jews. Judah was weak enough at this time to have been overcome by Edom, but God would not destroy Judah.

8.24   Joram king of Judah died at the age of forty, having served as king for only eight years. His "bowels came out . . . and he died in great agony," to "no one's regret" (2 Chr 21.19,20).

8.25ff   *Ahaziah* (an alternate form of the name Jeho-

ahaz) now became king of Judah. He was the son of Athaliah, who had taught him in the wicked ways of her mother Jezebel. He helped Joram son of Ahab against the king of Aram at Ramoth-gilead. Joram was wounded in the battle and went to Jezreel, located in the hill country of Judah, to recover. Ahab, Joram's father, had a royal residence in that city. Ahaziah made a visit to his relative while he still was ill.

8.26   *Athaliah,* the daughter of Jezebel and Ahab, was the queen mother and remained a powerful force of wickedness in religious matters.

9.2   Jehu had been appointed by God to be king of Israel (cf. 1 Kings 19.16,17); he was God's chosen man to bring an end to the dynasty of Ahab.

9.4–10   Elisha ordered a young prophet to anoint Jehu to become king of Israel, and told him to flee as soon as his job was done. Before the prophet left, however, he also prophesied that Jezebel would die ignominiously. Dogs would eat her body and no one would bury her.

arrived while the commanders of the army were in council, and he announced, "I have a message for you, commander." "For which one of us?"
asked Jehu. "For you, commander." 6 So Jehu*u* got up and went inside;
the young man poured the oil on his head, saying to him, "Thus says the
LORD the God of Israel: I anoint you king over the people of the LORD,
over Israel. 7 You shall strike down the house of your master Ahab, so that
I may avenge on Jezebel the blood of my servants the prophets, and the
blood of all the servants of the LORD. 8 For the whole house of Ahab shall
perish; I will cut off from Ahab every male, bond or free, in Israel. 9 I will
make the house of Ahab like the house of Jeroboam son of Nebat, and
like the house of Baasha son of Ahijah. 10 The dogs shall eat Jezebel in
the territory of Jezreel, and no one shall bury her." Then he opened the
door and fled.

11   When Jehu came back to his master's officers, they said to him,
"Is everything all right? Why did that madman come to you?" He answered them, "You know the sort and how they babble." 12 They said,
"Liar! Come on, tell us!" So he said, "This is just what he said to me:
'Thus says the LORD, I anoint you king over Israel.' " 13 Then hurriedly
they all took their cloaks and spread them for him on the bare*v* steps; and
they blew the trumpet, and proclaimed, "Jehu is king."

2. King Joram of Israel defeated and killed

14   Thus Jehu son of Jehoshaphat son of Nimshi conspired against
Joram. Joram with all Israel had been on guard at Ramoth-gilead against
King Hazael of Aram; 15 but King Joram had returned to be healed in
Jezreel of the wounds that the Arameans had inflicted on him, when he
fought against King Hazael of Aram. So Jehu said, "If this is your wish,
then let no one slip out of the city to go and tell the news in Jezreel."
16 Then Jehu mounted his chariot and went to Jezreel, where Joram was
lying ill. King Ahaziah of Judah had come down to visit Joram.

17   In Jezreel, the sentinel standing on the tower spied the company
of Jehu arriving, and said, "I see a company." Joram said, "Take a
horseman; send him to meet them, and let him say, 'Is it peace?' " 18 So
the horseman went to meet him; he said, "Thus says the king, 'Is it
peace?' " Jehu responded, "What have you to do with peace? Fall in
behind me." The sentinel reported, saying, "The messenger reached
them, but he is not coming back." 19 Then he sent out a second horseman,
who came to them and said, "Thus says the king, 'Is it peace?' " Jehu
answered, "What have you to do with peace? Fall in behind me." 20 Again
the sentinel reported, "He reached them, but he is not coming back. It
looks like the driving of Jehu son of Nimshi; for he drives like a maniac."

21   Joram said, "Get ready." And they got his chariot ready. Then
King Joram of Israel and King Ahaziah of Judah set out, each in his
chariot, and went to meet Jehu; they met him at the property of Naboth
the Jezreelite. 22 When Joram saw Jehu, he said, "Is it peace, Jehu?" He
answered, "What peace can there be, so long as the many whoredoms and
sorceries of your mother Jezebel continue?" 23 Then Joram reined about
and fled, saying to Ahaziah, "Treason, Ahaziah!" 24 Jehu drew his bow
with all his strength, and shot Joram between the shoulders, so that the
arrow pierced his heart; and he sank in his chariot. 25 Jehu said to his aide
Bidkar, "Lift him out, and throw him on the plot of ground belonging

u Heb *he*   *v* Meaning of Heb uncertain

Cross references (margin)

9.6
v. 3;
1 Kings 19.16;
2 Chr 22.7

9.7
Deut 32.35;
1 Kings 18.4;
21.15; vv. 32,
37

9.8
2 Kings 10.17;
1 Kings 21.21;
1 Sam 25.22;
Deut 32.36;
2 Kings 14.26

9.9
1 Kings 14.10;
15.29;
16.3-5, 11,
12

9.10
vv. 35, 36;
1 Kings 21.23

9.11
Jer 29.26;
Jn 10.20;
Acts 26.24

9.13
Mt 21.7;
2 Sam 15.10;
1 Kings 1.34,
39

9.14
2 Kings 8.28

9.15
2 Kings 8.29

9.16
2 Kings 8.29

9.18
vv. 19, 22

9.20
2 Sam 18.27;
1 Kings 19.17

9.21
2 Chr 22.7;
v. 26;
1 Kings 21.1-7,
15-19

9.22
1 Kings 16.30-
33;
18.19;
2 Chr 21.13

9.23
2 Kings 11.24

9.24
1 Kings 22.34

9.25
1 Kings 21.1,
19, 24-29

9.13 Jehu's fellow warriors demanded to know the
young prophet's business with Jehu. When Jehu explained his anointing, they put their garments on the
ground for him to walk over, blew trumpets, and
accepted Jehu as their new monarch. He made
haste to go to Jezreel, where the kings of Israel and
Judah were holding their own gathering. Joram king
of Israel sensed that a civil war was beginning and
prepared himself, along with Ahaziah of Judah, for
battle against Jehu. Jehu slew Joram and cast his body
into the field of Naboth the Jezreelite, from whom
Ahab had taken property (cf. 1 Kings 21.19,27–29).

to Naboth the Jezreelite; for remember, when you and I rode side by side behind his father Ahab how the LORD uttered this oracle against him: 26'For the blood of Naboth and for the blood of his children that I saw yesterday, says the LORD, I swear I will repay you on this very plot of ground.' Now therefore lift him out and throw him on the plot of ground, in accordance with the word of the LORD."

3. King Ahaziah of Judah defeated and killed

27 When King Ahaziah of Judah saw this, he fled in the direction of Beth-haggan. Jehu pursued him, saying, "Shoot him also!" And they shot him[w] in the chariot at the ascent to Gur, which is by Ibleam. Then he fled to Megiddo, and died there. 28 His officers carried him in a chariot to Jerusalem, and buried him in his tomb with his ancestors in the city of David.

29 In the eleventh year of Joram son of Ahab, Ahaziah began to reign over Judah.

4. Jehu's massacre of the house of Ahab

a. Jezebel killed

30 When Jehu came to Jezreel, Jezebel heard of it; she painted her eyes, and adorned her head, and looked out of the window. 31 As Jehu entered the gate, she said, "Is it peace, Zimri, murderer of your master?" 32 He looked up to the window and said, "Who is on my side? Who?" Two or three eunuchs looked out at him. 33 He said, "Throw her down." So they threw her down; some of her blood spattered on the wall and on the horses, which trampled on her. 34 Then he went in and ate and drank; he said, "See to that cursed woman and bury her; for she is a king's daughter." 35 But when they went to bury her, they found no more of her than the skull and the feet and the palms of her hands. 36 When they came back and told him, he said, "This is the word of the LORD, which he spoke by his servant Elijah the Tishbite, 'In the territory of Jezreel the dogs shall eat the flesh of Jezebel; 37 the corpse of Jezebel shall be like dung on the field in the territory of Jezreel, so that no one can say, This is Jezebel.'"

b. Ahab's seventy sons beheaded

10 Now Ahab had seventy sons in Samaria. So Jehu wrote letters and sent them to Samaria, to the rulers of Jezreel,[x] to the elders, and to the guardians of the sons of[y] Ahab, saying, 2 "Since your master's sons are with you and you have at your disposal chariots and horses, a fortified city, and weapons, 3 select the son of your master who is the best qualified, set him on his father's throne, and fight for your master's house." 4 But they were utterly terrified and said, "Look, two kings could not withstand him; how then can we stand?" 5 So the steward of the palace, and the governor of the city, along with the elders and the guardians, sent word to Jehu: "We are your servants; we will do anything you say. We will not make anyone king; do whatever you think right." 6 Then he wrote them a second letter, saying, "If you are on my side, and if you are ready to obey me, take the heads of your master's sons and come to me at Jezreel tomorrow at this time." Now the king's sons, seventy persons, were with the leaders of the city, who were charged with their upbringing. 7 When

Cross-references (right margin)

9.26 1 Kings 21.19

9.27 2 Chr 22.9

9.28 2 Kings 23.30

9.30 Jer 4.30; Ezek 23.40
9.31 1 Kings 16.9-20

9.34 1 Kings 21.25; 16.31

9.36 1 Kings 21.23

9.37 Jer 8.1-3

10.1 1 Kings 16.24-29

10.5 see 1 Kings 20.4, 32

10.7 1 Kings 21.21

---

[w] Syr Vg Compare Gk: Heb lacks *and they shot him*   [x] Or *of the city*; Vg Compare Gk   [y] Gk: Heb lacks *of the sons of*

9.30 Jezebel, unafraid and painted for the occasion, stood in the sight of Jehu and tried to put him on the defensive. Some of her attendants sided with Jehu and threw her over the railing to her death. The prophecy of Elijah was fulfilled (see 1 Kings 21.23). **10.1ff** Jehu was relentless, intrepid, and without

pity. He not only killed two kings; he also killed Ahab's seventy sons, the friends and supporters of the house of Ahab, the priests of Baal, and the worshipers of that god. He destroyed the temple and the pillars of Baal as well. They had been among the worst enemies God ever had among his people.

the letter reached them, they took the king's sons and killed them, seventy persons; they put their heads in baskets and sent them to him at Jezreel. **8** When the messenger came and told him, "They have brought the heads of the king's sons," he said, "Lay them in two heaps at the entrance of the gate until the morning." **9** Then in the morning when he went out, he stood and said to all the people, "You are innocent. It was I who conspired against my master and killed him; but who struck down all these? **10** Know then that there shall fall to the earth nothing of the word of the LORD, which the LORD spoke concerning the house of Ahab; for the LORD has done what he said through his servant Elijah." **11** So Jehu killed all who were left of the house of Ahab in Jezreel, all his leaders, close friends, and priests, until he left him no survivor.

c. Forty-two relatives of Ahaziah slain

12 Then he set out and went to Samaria. On the way, when he was at Beth-eked of the Shepherds, **13** Jehu met relatives of King Ahaziah of Judah and said, "Who are you?" They answered, "We are kin of Ahaziah; we have come down to visit the royal princes and the sons of the queen mother." **14** He said, "Take them alive." They took them alive, and slaughtered them at the pit of Beth-eked, forty-two in all; he spared none of them.

d. Jehonadab kills the rest of the house of Ahab

15 When he left there, he met Jehonadab son of Rechab coming to meet him; he greeted him, and said to him, "Is your heart as true to mine as mine is to yours?"[z] Jehonadab answered, "It is." Jehu said,[a] "If it is, give me your hand." So he gave him his hand. Jehu took him up with him into the chariot. **16** He said, "Come with me, and see my zeal for the LORD." So he[b] had him ride in his chariot. **17** When he came to Samaria, he killed all who were left to Ahab in Samaria, until he had wiped them out, according to the word of the LORD that he spoke to Elijah.

e. The massacre of the Baal worshipers

18 Then Jehu assembled all the people and said to them, "Ahab offered Baal small service; but Jehu will offer much more. **19** Now therefore summon to me all the prophets of Baal, all his worshipers, and all his priests; let none be missing, for I have a great sacrifice to offer to Baal; whoever is missing shall not live." But Jehu was acting with cunning in order to destroy the worshipers of Baal. **20** Jehu decreed, "Sanctify a solemn assembly for Baal." So they proclaimed it. **21** Jehu sent word throughout all Israel; all the worshipers of Baal came, so that there was no one left who did not come. They entered the temple of Baal, until the temple of Baal was filled from wall to wall. **22** He said to the keeper of the wardrobe, "Bring out the vestments for all the worshipers of Baal." So he brought out the vestments for them. **23** Then Jehu entered the temple of Baal with Jehonadab son of Rechab; he said to the worshipers of Baal, "Search and see that there is no worshiper of the LORD here among you,

Side references:
10.9 2 Kings 9.14-24; v. 6
10.10 2 Kings 9.7-10; 1 Kings 21.19-29
10.13 2 Kings 8.24, 29; 2 Chr 22.8
10.15 Jer 35.6ff; 1 Chr 2.55; Ezra 10.19
10.16 1 Kings 19.10
10.17 2 Kings 9.8; 2 Chr 22.8; v. 10
10.18 1 Kings 16.31, 32
10.19 1 Kings 22.6
10.20 Joel 1.14; Ex 32.4-6
10.21 1 Kings 16.32; 2 Kings 11.18

---

z Gk: Heb *Is it right with your heart, as my heart is with your heart?*   a Gk: Heb lacks *Jehu said*
b Gk Syr Tg: Heb *they*

10.11 *he left him no survivor,* i.e., no one close to him in any way. Apparently Jehu in his zeal exceeded the Lord's command in this bloodbath, for the prophet Hosea prophesied punishment upon him (Hos 1.4). **10.14** These people were from the house of Ahab through Athaliah (daughter of Jezebel). They were tainted with the wickedness of Ahab, and forty-two of them in high positions were slain by Jehu. **10.15** *Jehonadab,* an ascetic, is mentioned as "Jonadab" in Jer 35.6, where his descendants are tested by

Jeremiah. Jehu accepted Jehonadab at face value as honest. **10.18** The worship of Baal was so extensive that it had penetrated most of the northern kingdom. Jehu wanted to stamp out Baal worship entirely. So he pretended to be a worshiper of Baal and called all the Baal worshipers to a convocation. All true adherents of Baal were slain and the pillar of Baal demolished. The temple of Baal was made into a latrine (an unclean item). Jehu had accomplished his goal (see 10.28).

but only worshipers of Baal." 24 Then they proceeded to offer sacrifices and burnt offerings.

Now Jehu had stationed eighty men outside, saying, "Whoever allows any of those to escape whom I deliver into your hands shall forfeit his life." 25 As soon as he had finished presenting the burnt offering, Jehu said to the guards and to the officers, "Come in and kill them; let no one escape." So they put them to the sword. The guards and the officers threw them out, and then went into the citadel of the temple of Baal. 26 They brought out the pillar[c] that was in the temple of Baal, and burned it. 27 Then they demolished the pillar of Baal, and destroyed the temple of Baal, and made it a latrine to this day.

f. Resumé of Jehu's reign

28   Thus Jehu wiped out Baal from Israel. 29 But Jehu did not turn aside from the sins of Jeroboam son of Nebat, which he caused Israel to commit — the golden calves that were in Bethel and in Dan. 30 The LORD said to Jehu, "Because you have done well in carrying out what I consider right, and in accordance with all that was in my heart have dealt with the house of Ahab, your sons of the fourth generation shall sit on the throne of Israel." 31 But Jehu was not careful to follow the law of the LORD the God of Israel with all his heart; he did not turn from the sins of Jeroboam, which he caused Israel to commit.

32   In those days the LORD began to trim off parts of Israel. Hazael defeated them throughout the territory of Israel: 33 from the Jordan eastward, all the land of Gilead, the Gadites, the Reubenites, and the Manassites, from Aroer, which is by the Wadi Arnon, that is, Gilead and Bashan. 34 Now the rest of the acts of Jehu, all that he did, and all his power, are they not written in the Book of the Annals of the Kings of Israel? 35 So Jehu slept with his ancestors, and they buried him in Samaria. His son Jehoahaz succeeded him. 36 The time that Jehu reigned over Israel in Samaria was twenty-eight years.

L. The reign of Athaliah

1. Athaliah seizes control

11 Now when Athaliah, Ahaziah's mother, saw that her son was dead, she set about to destroy all the royal family. 2 But Jehosheba, King Joram's daughter, Ahaziah's sister, took Joash son of Ahaziah, and stole him away from among the king's children who were about to be killed; she put[d] him and his nurse in a bedroom. Thus she[e] hid him from Athaliah, so that he was not killed; 3 he remained with her six years, hidden in the house of the LORD, while Athaliah reigned over the land.

2. Jehoiada the priest overthrows Athaliah

4   But in the seventh year Jehoiada summoned the captains of the

Side references:
10.24
1 Kings 20.39

10.25
1 Kings 18.40

10.26
1 Kings 14.23
10.27
Ezra 6.11;
Dan 2.5; 3.29

10.29
1 Kings 12.28, 29
10.30
v. 35;
2 Kings 15.8, 12

10.31
v. 29

10.32
2 Kings 8.12

10.34
Am 1.3-5

11.1
2 Chr 22.10-12

11.4
2 Chr 23.1ff;
v. 19

c Gk Vg Syr Tg: Heb *pillars*   *d* With 2 Chr 22.11: Heb lacks *she put*   *e* Gk Syr Vg Compare 2 Chr 22.11: Heb *they*

10.28–31 Jehu was by no means a devout worshiper of the Lord, for he did not walk according to God's commandments. But he did do what God wanted done: he removed the house of Ahab and destroyed Baal worship. For this God said his line would continue for four generations. After a reign of twenty-eight years he died and was succeeded by his son Jehoahaz.
11.1 God had promised to have someone on the throne of David forever. Athaliah, Jezebel's daughter and Jehoram's wife, almost succeeded in extinguishing that line by destroying all of the royal seed (so far as she knew). This plan had begun with her husband,

Jehoram, who had killed all of the sons of Jehoshaphat to prevent anyone from usurping his kingship. The Arabs had killed all of Jehoram's sons except Ahaziah (2 Chr 22.1), and Athaliah now set about to kill all of Ahaziah's children (her grandchildren).
11.2,3 Jehosheba, the wife of the priest Jehoiada and an aunt of Joash, preserved Joash's life by hiding him in a place in the temple where bedroom equipment was stored. She did this for six years while Athaliah reigned over Judah. God was frustrating the evil purposes of one who sought to undo the divine arrangements.
11.4 In the O.T., religion and politics were inti-

Carites and of the guards and had them come to him in the house of the LORD. He made a covenant with them and put them under oath in the house of the LORD; then he showed them the king's son. 5 He commanded them, "This is what you are to do: one-third of you, those who go off duty on the sabbath and guard the king's house 6 (another third being at the gate Sur and a third at the gate behind the guards), shall guard the palace; 7 and your two divisions that come on duty in force on the sabbath and guard the house of the LORD *f* 8 shall surround the king, each with weapons in hand; and whoever approaches the ranks is to be killed. Be with the king in his comings and goings."

9 The captains did according to all that the priest Jehoiada commanded; each brought his men who were to go off duty on the sabbath, with those who were to come on duty on the sabbath, and came to the priest Jehoiada. 10 The priest delivered to the captains the spears and shields that had been King David's, which were in the house of the LORD; 11 the guards stood, every man with his weapons in his hand, from the south side of the house to the north side of the house, around the altar and the house, to guard the king on every side. 12 Then he brought out the king's son, put the crown on him, and gave him the covenant; *g* they proclaimed him king, and anointed him; they clapped their hands and shouted, "Long live the king!"

13 When Athaliah heard the noise of the guard and of the people, she went into the house of the LORD to the people; 14 when she looked, there was the king standing by the pillar, according to custom, with the captains and the trumpeters beside the king, and all the people of the land rejoicing and blowing trumpets. Athaliah tore her clothes and cried, "Treason! Treason!" 15 Then the priest Jehoiada commanded the captains who were set over the army, "Bring her out between the ranks, and kill with the sword anyone who follows her." For the priest said, "Let her not be killed in the house of the LORD." 16 So they laid hands on her; she went through the horses' entrance to the king's house, and there she was put to death.

17 Jehoiada made a covenant between the LORD and the king and people, that they should be the LORD's people; also between the king and the people. 18 Then all the people of the land went to the house of Baal, and tore it down; his altars and his images they broke in pieces, and they killed Mattan, the priest of Baal, before the altars. The priest posted guards over the house of the LORD. 19 He took the captains, the Carites, the guards, and all the people of the land; then they brought the king down from the house of the LORD, marching through the gate of the guards to the king's house. He took his seat on the throne of the kings. 20 So all the people of the land rejoiced; and the city was quiet after Athaliah had been killed with the sword at the king's house.

21 *h* Jehoash *i* was seven years old when he began to reign.

f Heb the LORD to the king   *g* Or treaty or testimony; Heb eduth   *h* Ch 12.1 in Heb   *i* Another spelling is Joash; see verse 19

Marginal references:
11.5 1 Chr 9.25
11.9 2 Chr 23.8
11.10 2 Sam 8.7; 1 Chr 18.7
11.12 1 Sam 10.24
11.13 2 Chr 23.12ff
11.14 2 Kings 23.3; 2 Chr 34.31; 1 Kings 1.39, 40; 2 Kings 9.23
11.17 2 Chr 23.16; 15.12-14; 2 Sam 5.3
11.18 2 Kings 10.26; Deut 12.3; 2 Chr 23.17ff
11.19 vv. 4, 6
11.21 2 Chr 24.1

---

mately linked together. The religious leaders here involved themselves in political affairs, with the cooperation of the military leaders. The plot was simple: they wished to elevate young Joash to the kingship and rid themselves of Athaliah, who had no right to the throne, had slain every contender known to her, and had reintroduced Baalism to Judah.

11.12 Joash was crowned king at the temple. Jehoiada the high priest had laid his plans well. Joash was given the covenant, that is, the word of God, to read and to obey. The soldiers and those assembled recognized him as the legitimate heir to his father's throne and cried out, "Long live the king!"

11.13 When Athaliah heard what was happening, she came to the temple and was amazed to see this young man of whom she had no knowledge standing

there as the king of Judah. To her it was treason, and she shouted that aloud for all to hear. They removed her from the house of the Lord and killed her.

11.16 Athaliah's death was the result of her upbringing by her mother, Jezebel, a Baal worshiper. Even as Jezebel had influenced Ahab, so Athaliah influenced her unresisting husband, the king of Judah. Her wickedness hastened spiritual decline within the kingdom of Judah.

11.17 Jehoiada, the real power behind the throne at this time, now made a covenant with God, the people, and the king that they would be the Lord's people. They destroyed the house of Baal and wiped out all the paraphernalia connected with that worship. Mattan the priest of Baal was also killed. Renewal had come to Judah.

M. *The reign of King Jehoash (Joash) of Judah*

1. *Faithful Jehoash*

12 In the seventh year of Jehu, Jehoash began to reign; he reigned forty years in Jerusalem. His mother's name was Zibiah of Beersheba. [2] Jehoash did what was right in the sight of the LORD all his days, because the priest Jehoiada instructed him. [3] Nevertheless the high places were not taken away; the people continued to sacrifice and make offerings on the high places.

2. *Jehoash repairs the temple*

4 Jehoash said to the priests, "All the money offered as sacred donations that is brought into the house of the LORD, the money for which each person is assessed — the money from the assessment of persons — and the money from the voluntary offerings brought into the house of the LORD, [5] let the priests receive from each of the donors; and let them repair the house wherever any need of repairs is discovered." [6] But by the twenty-third year of King Jehoash the priests had made no repairs on the house. [7] Therefore King Jehoash summoned the priest Jehoiada with the other priests and said to them, "Why are you not repairing the house? Now therefore do not accept any more money from your donors but hand it over for the repair of the house." [8] So the priests agreed that they would neither accept more money from the people nor repair the house.

9 Then the priest Jehoiada took a chest, made a hole in its lid, and set it beside the altar on the right side as one entered the house of the LORD; the priests who guarded the threshold put in it all the money that was brought into the house of the LORD. [10] Whenever they saw that there was a great deal of money in the chest, the king's secretary and the high priest went up, counted the money that was found in the house of the LORD, and tied it up in bags. [11] They would give the money that was weighed out into the hands of the workers who had the oversight of the house of the LORD; then they paid it out to the carpenters and the builders who worked on the house of the LORD, [12] to the masons and the stonecutters, as well as to buy timber and quarried stone for making repairs on the house of the LORD, as well as for any outlay for repairs of the house. [13] But for the house of the LORD no basins of silver, snuffers, bowls, trumpets, or any vessels of gold, or of silver, were made from the money that was brought into the house of the LORD, [14] for that was given to the workers who were repairing the house of the LORD with it. [15] They did not ask an accounting from those into whose hand they delivered the money to pay out to the workers, for they dealt honestly. [16] The money from the guilt offerings and the money from the sin offerings was not brought into the house of the LORD; it belonged to the priests.

3. *Jehoash pays off Hazael with temple money*

17 At that time King Hazael of Aram went up, fought against Gath, and took it. But when Hazael set his face to go up against Jerusalem, [18] King Jehoash of Judah took all the votive gifts that Jehoshaphat, Jeho-

12.3
2 Kings 14.4;
15.35

12.4
2 Kings 22.4;
Ex 35.5;
1 Chr 29.3-9

12.6
2 Chr 24.5

12.7
2 Chr 24.6

12.9
2 Chr 24.8;
Mk 12.41;
Lk 21.1

12.10
2 Kings 19.2

12.12
2 Kings 22.5,
6

12.13
2 Chr 24.14;
1 Kings 7.48,
50

12.15
2 Kings 22.7

12.16
Lev 5.15-18;
4.24, 29;
Num 18.9, 19

12.17
2 Kings 8.12;
2 Chr 24.23

12.18
1 Kings 15.18;
2 Kings 18.15,
16

12.1,2 Joash came to the throne at seven years of age and reigned for forty years. He was instructed by Jehoiada, who was his mentor and his faithful steward until the king reached a proper age.
12.3 In Judah, high places for worship to Judah's God had been set up, along with altars for incense and sacrifice. While they were not removed in Joash's day, efforts were made to bring the people to the temple for their religious observances. Private altars for worship were in tacit competition with the temple and were an offense to God.

12.9 The temple was in need of repairs. The efforts of the priests to repair the temple were ineffective, for in the twenty-third year of Joash's reign no repairs had been made. Now money was gathered in a public chest to be used for that purpose. The repair of the house of God began in earnest.
12.18 Joash revolted against God and became a fierce persecutor as well as an idolater. He had begun in the Spirit and ended up in the flesh. When he forsook God, he forfeited divine protection. When Hazael of Aram began to threaten him militarily, Jo-

2 Kings 12.19

530

ram, and Ahaziah, his ancestors, the kings of Judah, had dedicated, as well as his own votive gifts, all the gold that was found in the treasuries of the house of the Lord and of the king's house, and sent these to King Hazael of Aram. Then Hazael withdrew from Jerusalem.

4. *Jehoash succeeded by Amaziah*

19 Now the rest of the acts of Joash, and all that he did, are they not written in the Book of the Annals of the Kings of Judah? 20 His servants arose, devised a conspiracy, and killed Joash in the house of Millo, on the way that goes down to Silla. 21 It was Jozacar son of Shimeath and Jehozabad son of Shomer, his servants, who struck him down, so that he died. He was buried with his ancestors in the city of David; then his son Amaziah succeeded him.

N. *King Jehoahaz of Israel*

13 In the twenty-third year of King Joash son of Ahaziah of Judah, Jehoahaz son of Jehu began to reign over Israel in Samaria; he reigned seventeen years. 2 He did what was evil in the sight of the Lord, and followed the sins of Jeroboam son of Nebat, which he caused Israel to sin; he did not depart from them. 3 The anger of the Lord was kindled against Israel, so that he gave them repeatedly into the hand of King Hazael of Aram, then into the hand of Ben-hadad son of Hazael. 4 But Jehoahaz entreated the Lord, and the Lord heeded him; for he saw the oppression of Israel, how the king of Aram oppressed them. 5 Therefore the Lord gave Israel a savior, so that they escaped from the hand of the Arameans; and the people of Israel lived in their homes as formerly. 6 Nevertheless they did not depart from the sins of the house of Jeroboam, which he caused Israel to sin, but walked[j] in them; the sacred pole[k] also remained in Samaria. 7 So Jehoahaz was left with an army of not more than fifty horsemen, ten chariots and ten thousand footmen; for the king of Aram had destroyed them and made them like the dust at threshing. 8 Now the rest of the acts of Jehoahaz and all that he did, including his might, are they not written in the Book of the Annals of the Kings of Israel? 9 So Jehoahaz slept with his ancestors, and they buried him in Samaria; then his son Joash succeeded him.

O. *King Jehoash of Israel*

1. *The wickedness of Jehoash*

10 In the thirty-seventh year of King Joash of Judah, Jehoash son of Jehoahaz began to reign over Israel in Samaria; he reigned sixteen years. 11 He also did what was evil in the sight of the Lord; he did not depart from all the sins of Jeroboam son of Nebat, which he caused Israel to sin, but he walked in them. 12 Now the rest of the acts of Joash, and all that he did, as well as the might with which he fought against King Amaziah

j Gk Syr Tg Vg: Heb *he walked*   *k* Heb *Asherah*

ash paid him a great ransom to leave him alone.
12.20 Joash's own servants plotted against the king and slew him. The king had slain the son of Jehoiada, who had been his counselor as well as his friend (see 2 Chr 24.17–19). This may have been the provocation that resulted in his own death. Those who slew him were not averse to the kingship, for Amaziah was permitted to succeed his father.
13.1 Jehoahaz was the first of the four descendants of Jehu to occupy the throne in Israel. He started out very badly and only after many setbacks did he begin to seek the face and the aid of God. God heard his cry and sent him a savior, Jehoahaz's own son, who won

battles against the Arameans and recovered the cities they had taken (vv. 24,25). This son, Joash, ascended to the throne after Jehoahaz's death.
13.10 Jehoash (or Joash) was the second descendant of Jehu to rule over Israel. Idolatry continued during his reign. He was also in conflict with Amaziah, king of Judah. Jehoash was named after Joash (Jehoash), the king of Judah. Identical names between the kings of Israel and Judah occurred several times and makes it difficult to distinguish between them. Here the text usually calls Judah's king Joash and Israel's Jehoash. He was succeeded by his son Jeroboam (14.15,16).

of Judah, are they not written in the Book of the Annals of the Kings of Israel? 13 So Joash slept with his ancestors, and Jeroboam sat upon his throne; Joash was buried in Samaria with the kings of Israel.

2. *Elisha and the LORD's arrow of victory*

14 Now when Elisha had fallen sick with the illness of which he was to die, King Joash of Israel went down to him, and wept before him, crying, "My father, my father! The chariots of Israel and its horsemen!" 15 Elisha said to him, "Take a bow and arrows"; so he took a bow and arrows. 16 Then he said to the king of Israel, "Draw the bow"; and he drew it. Elisha laid his hands on the king's hands. 17 Then he said, "Open the window eastward"; and he opened it. Elisha said, "Shoot"; and he shot. Then he said, "The LORD's arrow of victory, the arrow of victory over Aram! For you shall fight the Arameans in Aphek until you have made an end of them." 18 He continued, "Take the arrows"; and he took them. He said to the king of Israel, "Strike the ground with them"; he struck three times, and stopped. 19 Then the man of God was angry with him, and said, "You should have struck five or six times; then you would have struck down Aram until you had made an end of it, but now you will strike down Aram only three times."

3. *The miracle at Elisha's tomb*

20 So Elisha died, and they buried him. Now bands of Moabites used to invade the land in the spring of the year. 21 As a man was being buried, a marauding band was seen and the man was thrown into the grave of Elisha; as soon as the man touched the bones of Elisha, he came to life and stood on his feet.

4. *The victories of Israel*

22 Now King Hazael of Aram oppressed Israel all the days of Jehoahaz. 23 But the LORD was gracious to them and had compassion on them; he turned toward them, because of his covenant with Abraham, Isaac, and Jacob, and would not destroy them; nor has he banished them from his presence until now.
24 When King Hazael of Aram died, his son Ben-hadad succeeded him. 25 Then Jehoash son of Jehoahaz took again from Ben-hadad son of Hazael the towns that he had taken from his father Jehoahaz in war. Three times Joash defeated him and recovered the towns of Israel.

P. *King Amaziah of Judah*

1. *Events of Amaziah's reign*

14 In the second year of King Joash son of Joahaz of Israel, King Amaziah son of Joash of Judah, began to reign. 2 He was twenty-five years old when he began to reign, and he reigned twenty-nine years in Jerusalem. His mother's name was Jehoaddin of Jerusalem. 3 He did what was right in the sight of the LORD, yet not like his ancestor David;

Marginal references

13.14
2 Kings 2.12

13.17
1 Kings 20.26

13.19
v. 25

13.20
see
2 Kings 3.7;
24.2

13.22
2 Kings 8.12
13.23
2 Kings 14.27;
Ex 2.24, 25;
Gen 16.16, 17

13.25
2 Kings 10.32,
33; 14.25;
vv. 18, 19

14.1
2 Kings 13.10;
2 Chr 25.1

Footnotes

13.14 Elisha had served God for about sixty years after he was called to the prophetic office. He was now near death. The Scriptures tell us nothing about his later life, a period of forty-five years subsequent to the anointing of Jehu. *The chariots of Israel and its horsemen*, i.e., you are the strength of Israel.
13.15 Elisha still had one more thing to do before he died. He ordered Jehoash king of Israel to shoot an arrow into the air and then to take arrows and smite the ground. He interpreted the meaning of the prophetic word.
13.20,21 Elisha died, but this did not end his minis-

try. He was the only prophet of God of whom it was said that when a dead man was cast into Elisha's grave, the man revived and stood on his feet. God had used Elisha in life and in death to raise the dead.
13.25 Elisha's prediction came to pass. Joash defeated the Arameans three times and recovered the cities they had taken from Israel.
14.1-7 Amaziah of Judah was a relatively good king, at least at the beginning. Yet he did not remove the high places. He killed those who had murdered his father, but he spared their children. He warred successfully against the Edomites (see 2 Chr 25.5ff)

in all things he did as his father Joash had done. 4 But the high places were not removed; the people still sacrificed and made offerings on the high places. 5 As soon as the royal power was firmly in his hand he killed his servants who had murdered his father the king. 6 But he did not put to death the children of the murderers; according to what is written in the book of the law of Moses, where the LORD commanded, "The parents shall not be put to death for the children, or the children be put to death for the parents; but all shall be put to death for their own sins."

7 He killed ten thousand Edomites in the Valley of Salt and took Sela by storm; he called it Jokthe-el, which is its name to this day.

2. Amaziah wars against Israel

8 Then Amaziah sent messengers to King Jehoash son of Jehoahaz, son of Jehu, of Israel, saying, "Come, let us look one another in the face." 9 King Jehoash of Israel sent word to King Amaziah of Judah, "A thornbush on Lebanon sent to a cedar on Lebanon, saying, 'Give your daughter to my son for a wife'; but a wild animal of Lebanon passed by and trampled down the thornbush. 10 You have indeed defeated Edom, and your heart has lifted you up. Be content with your glory, and stay at home; for why should you provoke trouble so that you fall, you and Judah with you?"

11 But Amaziah would not listen. So King Jehoash of Israel went up; he and King Amaziah of Judah faced one another in battle at Bethshemesh, which belongs to Judah. 12 Judah was defeated by Israel; everyone fled home. 13 King Jehoash of Israel captured King Amaziah of Judah son of Jehoash, son of Ahaziah, at Beth-shemesh; he came to Jerusalem, and broke down the wall of Jerusalem from the Ephraim Gate to the Corner Gate, a distance of four hundred cubits. 14 He seized all the gold and silver, and all the vessels that were found in the house of the LORD and in the treasuries of the king's house, as well as hostages; then he returned to Samaria.

3. Death of Jehoash

15 Now the rest of the acts that Jehoash did, his might, and how he fought with King Amaziah of Judah, are they not written in the Book of the Annals of the Kings of Israel? 16 Jehoash slept with his ancestors, and was buried in Samaria with the kings of Israel; then his son Jeroboam succeeded him.

4. Amaziah replaced by Azariah

17 King Amaziah son of Joash of Judah lived fifteen years after the death of King Jehoash son of Jehoahaz of Israel. 18 Now the rest of the deeds of Amaziah, are they not written in the Book of the Annals of the Kings of Judah? 19 They made a conspiracy against him in Jerusalem, and he fled to Lachish. But they sent after him to Lachish, and killed him there. 20 They brought him on horses; he was buried in Jerusalem with his ancestors in the city of David. 21 All the people of Judah took Azariah,

14.4
2 Kings 12.3;
16.4
14.5
2 Kings 12.20
14.6
Deut 24.16;
Ezek 18.4, 20

14.7
2 Chr 25.11;
2 Sam 8.13;
Josh 15.38

14.8
2 Chr 25.17-24

14.9
Judg 9.8-15

14.10
v. 7;
Deut 8.14;
2 Chr 26.16;
32.25

14.11
Josh 19.38

14.12
2 Sam 18.17
14.13
Neh 8.16;
12.39;
2 Chr 25.23
14.14
2 Kings 12.18

14.15
2 Kings 13.12

14.17
2 Chr 25.25-28

14.19
Josh 10.31;
2 Kings 18.14,
17

14.7 *Sela (Jokthe-el),* "rock," the capital of Edom. This was later known as Petra.
14.8 Amaziah had shortcomings that led to his downfall. He was proud and presumptuous, and challenged Jehoash of Israel to battle. Jehoash sent back a letter in which he compared Amaziah to a thistle that was trodden down by a wild beast and himself to a cedar of Lebanon. He conquered Amaziah and took him prisoner. He entered Jerusalem, removed all that was valuable, and broke down part of the city's walls.
14.15,16 Joash's death is reported in 13.12,13 and

again here. His son Jeroboam, who succeeded him, was the third king of the four promised to Jehu by Elisha years before.
14.17 Amaziah got off to a good start but ended badly. His insolence, the defeat at the hands of Jehoash, and the virtual sack of Jerusalem led the people of Judah to detest him. He fled to Lachish where he was concealed for some time before he was slain by his own people. He was succeeded by Azariah (Uzziah), who was sixteen years old at the time. At the end of his reign, God called Isaiah to become a prophet (Isa 6.1).

who was sixteen years old, and made him king to succeed his father Amaziah. 22 He rebuilt Elath and restored it to Judah, after King Amaziah[*l*] slept with his ancestors.

Q. Reign of King Jeroboam II of Israel

23 In the fifteenth year of King Amaziah son of Joash of Judah, King Jeroboam son of Joash of Israel began to reign in Samaria; he reigned forty-one years. 24 He did what was evil in the sight of the LORD; he did not depart from all the sins of Jeroboam son of Nebat, which he caused Israel to sin. 25 He restored the border of Israel from Lebo-hamath as far as the Sea of the Arabah, according to the word of the LORD, the God of Israel, which he spoke by his servant Jonah son of Amittai, the prophet, who was from Gath-hepher. 26 For the LORD saw that the distress of Israel was very bitter; there was no one left, bond or free, and no one to help Israel. 27 But the LORD had not said that he would blot out the name of Israel from under heaven, so he saved them by the hand of Jeroboam son of Joash.

28 Now the rest of the acts of Jeroboam, and all that he did, and his might, how he fought, and how he recovered for Israel Damascus and Hamath, which had belonged to Judah, are they not written in the Book of the Annals of the Kings of Israel? 29 Jeroboam slept with his ancestors, the kings of Israel; his son Zechariah succeeded him.

R. Judah under King Azariah (Uzziah)

15 In the twenty-seventh year of King Jeroboam of Israel King Azariah son of Amaziah of Judah began to reign. 2 He was sixteen years old when he began to reign, and he reigned fifty-two years in Jerusalem. His mother's name was Jecoliah of Jerusalem. 3 He did what was right in the sight of the LORD, just as his father Amaziah had done. 4 Nevertheless the high places were not taken away; the people still sacrificed and made offerings on the high places. 5 The LORD struck the king, so that he was leprous[*m*] to the day of his death, and lived in a separate house. Jotham the king's son was in charge of the palace, governing the people of the land. 6 Now the rest of the acts of Azariah, and all that he did, are they not written in the Book of the Annals of the Kings of Judah? 7 Azariah slept with his ancestors; they buried him with his ancestors in the city of David; his son Jotham succeeded him.

S. Reign of King Zechariah of Israel

8 In the thirty-eighth year of King Azariah of Judah, Zechariah son of Jeroboam reigned over Israel in Samaria six months. 9 He did what was evil in the sight of the LORD, as his ancestors had done. He did not depart from the sins of Jeroboam son of Nebat, which he caused Israel to sin.

---

l Heb *the king*　*m* A term for several skin diseases; precise meaning uncertain

---

14.22
2 Kings 16.6;
2 Chr 26.2

14.25
2 Kings 10.32;
1 Kings 8.65;
Deut 3.17;
Jon 1.1;
Mt 12.39,
40;
Josh 19.13
14.26
2 Kings 13.4;
Deut 32.36
14.27
2 Kings 13.5,
23
14.28
2 Sam 8.6;
1 Kings 11.24;
2 Chr 8.3
14.29
2 Kings 15.8

15.1
2 Kings 14.21;
2 Chr 26.1, 3,
4 *zziah*
15.2
2 Chr 26.3, 4

15.4
2 Kings 12.3;
14.4
15.5
2 Chr 26.19-21

15.7
2 Chr 26.23

14.23 Jeroboam of Israel was named after Jeroboam of Nebat, the first king of the northern kingdom. Thus he is called Jeroboam II and reigned longer than any other king of Israel—forty-one years. He was a wicked king. God was long-suffering with Israel, however, and helped the king. He gained back some of the territory that had been taken from Israel, for God had compassion on the people of those regions. He was succeeded by Zechariah, the fourth and last generation of Jehu to sit on Israel's throne.
15.1 This is a short report of Azariah's reign over Judah (see 2 Chr 16 for a fuller report of his life and acts). Like Amaziah, he began well and finished poorly. His fifty-two year reign was the longest of all the kings of either Israel or Judah. Jotham his son succeeded him (see vv. 32ff).

15.5 Azariah (Uzziah) became a leper, though the cause of his leprosy is not stated here. In 2 Chr 26.16–21, however, we learn that he sought to burn incense on the altar of incense, a job reserved for the Levitical priesthood. God punished his transgression by sending leprosy. Because of his disease, he was banned from entering the house of worship.
15.8 Zechariah was the fourth and last descendant of Jehu on the throne of Israel. His reign lasted six months. The best days of the kingdom of Israel were during the kingship of Jehu and his family. God's promise to Jehu of four generations of kings had been fulfilled (v. 12). A conspiracy started by Shallum the son of Jabesh led to Zechariah's death and the ascension of the revolter, Shallum, to the throne.

10 Shallum son of Jabesh conspired against him, and struck him down in public and killed him, and reigned in place of him. 11 Now the rest of the deeds of Zechariah are written in the Book of the Annals of the Kings of Israel. 12 This was the promise of the LORD that he gave to Jehu, "Your sons shall sit on the throne of Israel to the fourth generation." And so it happened.

T. Reign of King Shallum of Israel

13 Shallum son of Jabesh began to reign in the thirty-ninth year of King Uzziah of Judah; he reigned one month in Samaria. 14 Then Menahem son of Gadi came up from Tirzah and came to Samaria; he struck down Shallum son of Jabesh in Samaria and killed him; he reigned in place of him. 15 Now the rest of the deeds of Shallum, including the conspiracy that he made, are written in the Book of the Annals of the Kings of Israel.

16 At that time Menahem sacked Tiphsah, all who were in it and its territory from Tirzah on; because they did not open it to him, he sacked it. He ripped open all the pregnant women in it.

U. Reign of King Menahem of Israel

17 In the thirty-ninth year of King Azariah of Judah, Menahem son of Gadi began to reign over Israel; he reigned ten years in Samaria. 18 He did what was evil in the sight of the LORD; he did not depart all his days from any of the sins of Jeroboam son of Nebat, which he caused Israel to sin. 19 King Pul of Assyria came against the land; Menahem gave Pul a thousand talents of silver, so that he might help him confirm his hold on the royal power. 20 Menahem exacted the money from Israel, that is, from all the wealthy, fifty shekels of silver from each one, to give to the king of Assyria. So the king of Assyria turned back, and did not stay there in the land. 21 Now the rest of the deeds of Menahem, and all that he did, are they not written in the Book of the Annals of the Kings of Israel? 22 Menahem slept with his ancestors, and his son Pekahiah succeeded him.

V. Reign of King Pekahiah of Israel

23 In the fiftieth year of King Azariah of Judah, Pekahiah son of Menahem began to reign over Israel in Samaria; he reigned two years. 24 He did what was evil in the sight of the LORD; he did not turn away from the sins of Jeroboam son of Nebat, which he caused Israel to sin. 25 Pekah son of Remaliah, his captain, conspired against him with fifty of the Gileadites, and attacked him in Samaria, in the citadel of the palace along with Argob and Arieh; he killed him, and reigned in place of him. 26 Now the rest of the deeds of Pekahiah, and all that he did, are written in the Book of the Annals of the Kings of Israel.

W. Reign of King Pekah of Israel

27 In the fifty-second year of King Azariah of Judah, Pekah son of Remaliah began to reign over Israel in Samaria; he reigned twenty years. 28 He did what was evil in the sight of the LORD; he did not depart from the sins of Jeroboam son of Nebat, which he caused Israel to sin.

15.13 The four kings who followed Zechariah were a disaster. Confusion abounded for approximately thirty-three years. Shallum lasted one month before he was killed by Menahem—also a very bad king.
15.17 Menahem reigned for ten years. He had sacked Tiphsah and ripped open the pregnant women. Pul of Asssyria came down on Israel, and Menahem exacted money from the richer people to pay Pul not to attack but to help Menahem keep the throne. He was succeeded by his son Pekahiah.
15.19 *Pul*, another name for Tiglath-pileser III

(744–727 B.C.). His inscriptions record payment of tribute by Menahem.
15.23 Pekahiah lasted two years, doing evil in the sight of God. Pekah, a captain in his army, led a military coup against him, slew him, and became the new king of Israel.
15.27 The *twenty years* assigned to Pekah are made up of twelve years, when he was co-ruler with the two previous kings, Pekahiah and Menahem, and eight years, when he reigned alone.

29 In the days of King Pekah of Israel, King Tiglath-pileser of Assyria came and captured Ijon, Abel-beth-maacah, Janoah, Kedesh, Hazor, Gilead, and Galilee, all the land of Naphtali; and he carried the people captive to Assyria. 30 Then Hoshea son of Elah made a conspiracy against Pekah son of Remaliah, attacked him, and killed him; he reigned in place of him, in the twentieth year of Jotham son of Uzziah. 31 Now the rest of the acts of Pekah, and all that he did, are written in the Book of the Annals of the Kings of Israel.

X. Reign of King Jotham of Judah

32 In the second year of King Pekah son of Remaliah of Israel, King Jotham son of Uzziah of Judah began to reign. 33 He was twenty-five years old when he began to reign and reigned sixteen years in Jerusalem. His mother's name was Jerusha daughter of Zadok. 34 He did what was right in the sight of the LORD, just as his father Uzziah had done. 35 Nevertheless the high places were not removed; the people still sacrificed and made offerings on the high places. He built the upper gate of the house of the LORD. 36 Now the rest of the acts of Jotham, and all that he did, are they not written in the Book of the Annals of the Kings of Judah? 37 In those days the LORD began to send King Rezin of Aram and Pekah son of Remaliah against Judah. 38 Jotham slept with his ancestors, and was buried with his ancestors in the city of David, his ancestor; his son Ahaz succeeded him.

Y. Reign of King Ahaz of Judah

1. Description of Ahaz's reign

16 In the seventeenth year of Pekah son of Remaliah, King Ahaz son of Jotham of Judah began to reign. 2 Ahaz was twenty years old when he began to reign; he reigned sixteen years in Jerusalem. He did not do what was right in the sight of the LORD his God, as his ancestor David had done, 3 but he walked in the way of the kings of Israel. He even made his son pass through fire, according to the abominable practices of the nations whom the LORD drove out before the people of Israel. 4 He sacrificed and made offerings on the high places, on the hills, and under every green tree.

2. Ahaz delivered from Aram and Israel by Tiglath-pileser

5 Then King Rezin of Aram and King Pekah son of Remaliah of Israel came up to wage war on Jerusalem; they besieged Ahaz but could not conquer him. 6 At that time the king of Edom[n] recovered Elath for Edom,[o] and drove the Judeans from Elath; and the Edomites came to Elath, where they live to this day. 7 Ahaz sent messengers to King Tiglath-pileser of Assyria, saying, "I am your servant and your son. Come up, and

Cross-references (right margin)

15.29
v. 19;
2 Kings 17.6;
1 Chr 5.26

15.32
2 Chr 27.1ff

15.34
v. 3;
2 Chr 26.4, 5
15.35
v. 4;
2 Chr 27.3

15.37
2 Kings 16.5;
Isa 7.1; v. 27

16.1
2 Chr 28.1ff

16.3
Lev 18.21;
2 Kings 17.17;
21.6;
Deut 12.31;
2 Kings 21.2,
11
16.4
Deut 12.2;
2 Kings 14.4

16.5
2 Kings 15.37;
Isa 7.1;
2 Chr 28.5, 6
16.6
Jer 14.22;
2 Chr 26.2
16.7
2 Chr 28.16ff;
2 Kings 15.29

---

n Cn: Heb King Rezin of Aram   o Cn: Heb Aram

15.30 Again a king of Israel is slain in a military coup. Hoshea son of Elah was the murderer and successor to Pekah. He acted as he did because Pekah had failed to keep Tiglath-pileser from taking over parts of Israel. Hoshea was the nineteenth and the last king of Israel. His reign began in 732 B.C. Tiglath-pileser died in 727 B.C. Hoshea sought relief from Assyria by calling on Egypt for help. Shalmaneser led a campaign against Israel in 724 B.C. Hoshea capitulated and paid tribute. He was later imprisoned by Shalmaneser. See further details in 17.1ff.

15.32 Jotham's sixteen-year reign over Judah is covered quickly. Generally he was a good king, but the high places remained, where sacrifices and incense

ere offered instead of at the temple in Jerusalem. Ahaz succeeded him.

16.1 Ahaz, who followed two good kings, resumed the idolatrous practices of the kings of Israel. He was only twenty when he began to reign and died at thirty-six. He even burned some of his sons to pagan deities. Instead of worshiping only at the temple, he sacrificed and burned incense at the high places.

16.5 Aram and Israel conspired against Ahaz. Eventually Ahaz sent tribute money to Tiglath-pileser and asked for help. The Assyrians descended on Damascus and so kept Aram from attacking Ahaz and his country.

16.8
2 Kings 12.17,
18
16.9
2 Chr 28.21;
Am 1.3-5

rescue me from the hand of the king of Aram and from the hand of the king of Israel, who are attacking me." 8 Ahaz also took the silver and gold found in the house of the Lord and in the treasures of the king's house, and sent a present to the king of Assyria. 9 The king of Assyria listened to him; the king of Assyria marched up against Damascus, and took it, carrying its people captive to Kir; then he killed Rezin.

3. *Ahaz and the foreign altar*

16.10
2 Kings 15.29;
Isa 8.2

10   When King Ahaz went to Damascus to meet King Tiglath-pileser of Assyria, he saw the altar that was at Damascus. King Ahaz sent to the priest Uriah a model of the altar, and its pattern, exact in all its details. 11 The priest Uriah built the altar; in accordance with all that King Ahaz had sent from Damascus, just so did the priest Uriah build it, before King Ahaz arrived from Damascus. 12 When the king came from Damascus, the king viewed the altar. Then the king drew near to the altar, went up on it, 13 and offered his burnt offering and his grain offering, poured his drink offering, and dashed the blood of his offerings of well-being against the altar.

16.14
2 Chr 4.1

14 The bronze altar that was before the Lord he removed from the front of the house, from the place between his altar and the house of the Lord, and put it on the north side of his altar.

16.15
Ex 29.39-41

15 King Ahaz commanded the priest Uriah, saying, "Upon the great altar offer the morning burnt offering, and the evening grain offering, and the king's burnt offering, and his grain offering, with the burnt offering of all the people of the land, their grain offering, and their drink offering; then dash against it all the blood of the burnt offering, and all the blood of the sacrifice; but the bronze altar shall be for me to inquire by." 16 The priest Uriah did everything that King Ahaz commanded.

4. *Ahaz's death and the succession*

16.17
1 Kings 7.23-28

17   Then King Ahaz cut off the frames of the stands, and removed the laver from them; he removed the sea from the bronze oxen that were under it, and put it on a pediment of stone. 18 The covered portal for use on the sabbath that had been built inside the palace, and the outer entrance for the king he removed from*p* the house of the Lord. He did this because of the king of Assyria.

16.20
2 Chr 28.27

19 Now the rest of the acts of Ahaz that he did, are they not written in the Book of the Annals of the Kings of Judah? 20 Ahaz slept with his ancestors, and was buried with his ancestors in the city of David; his son Hezekiah succeeded him.

Z. *The end of Israel*

1. *Samaria captured by Assyria*

17.1
2 Kings 15.30

17   In the twelfth year of King Ahaz of Judah, Hoshea son of Elah began to reign in Samaria over Israel; he reigned nine years. 2 He did what was evil in the sight of the Lord, yet not like the kings of Israel who were before him.

17.3
2 Kings 18.9-12

3 King Shalmaneser of Assyria came up against him;

p Cn: Heb lacks *from*

16.11 The altar in God's temple was not good enough for Ahaz. He asked Urijah the priest to make a copy of an altar he had seen in Damascus; Urijah complied, thereby betraying his trust as the religious leader of Judah. Ahaz offered sacrifices on the new altar which had been placed near the bronze altar. He then removed God's altar to an obscure corner of the sanctuary.
16.20 Ahaz died and was succeeded by Hezekiah, who was to be as much a friend to the temple as his

father had been an enemy of it. This is one instance where a bad father had a good son.
17.1 Israel's captivity began under Hoshea's kingship. In his ninth year as king the Assyrians captured Samaria and sent the ten tribes into captivity in Assyria. One would have supposed that the end of the northern kingdom would have warned Judah about its own disobedience and caused king and people to repent in order to avoid a similar catastrophe.

Hoshea became his vassal, and paid him tribute. 4 But the king of Assyria found treachery in Hoshea; for he had sent messengers to King So of Egypt, and offered no tribute to the king of Assyria, as he had done year by year; therefore the king of Assyria confined him and imprisoned him.

5   Then the king of Assyria invaded all the land and came to Samaria; for three years he besieged it. 6 In the ninth year of Hoshea the king of Assyria captured Samaria; he carried the Israelites away to Assyria. He placed them in Halah, on the Habor, the river of Gozan, and in the cities of the Medes.

2. The sins of Israel that brought judgment

7   This occurred because the people of Israel had sinned against the LORD their God, who had brought them up out of the land of Egypt from under the hand of Pharaoh king of Egypt. They had worshiped other gods 8 and walked in the customs of the nations whom the LORD drove out before the people of Israel, and in the customs that the kings of Israel had introduced.q 9 The people of Israel secretly did things that were not right against the LORD their God. They built for themselves high places at all their towns, from watchtower to fortified city; 10 they set up for themselves pillars and sacred polesr on every high hill and under every green tree; 11 there they made offerings on all the high places, as the nations did whom the LORD carried away before them. They did wicked things, provoking the LORD to anger; 12 they served idols, of which the LORD had said to them, "You shall not do this." 13 Yet the LORD warned Israel and Judah by every prophet and every seer, saying, "Turn from your evil ways and keep my commandments and my statutes, in accordance with all the law that I commanded your ancestors and that I sent to you by my servants the prophets." 14 They would not listen but were stubborn, as their ancestors had been, who did not believe in the LORD their God. 15 They despised his statutes, and his covenant that he made with their ancestors, and the warnings that he gave them. They went after false idols and became false; they followed the nations that were around them, concerning whom the LORD had commanded them that they should not do as they did. 16 They rejected all the commandments of the LORD their God and made for themselves cast images of two calves; they made a sacred pole,s worshiped all the host of heaven, and served Baal. 17 They made their sons and their daughters pass through fire; they used divination and augury; and they sold themselves to do evil in the sight of the LORD, provoking him to anger. 18 Therefore the LORD was very angry with Israel and removed them out of his sight; none was left but the tribe of Judah alone.

19   Judah also did not keep the commandments of the LORD their God but walked in the customs that Israel had introduced. 20 The LORD rejected all the descendants of Israel; he punished them and gave them into the hand of plunderers, until he had banished them from his presence.

21   When he had torn Israel from the house of David, they made Jeroboam son of Nebat king. Jeroboam drove Israel from following the

q Meaning of Heb uncertain   r Heb Asherim   s Heb Asherah

Cross-references (right column):

17.5
Hos 13.16
17.6
Hos 13.16;
Deut 28.64;
29.27, 28;
1 Chr 5.26;
2 Kings 18.10,
11

17.7
Josh 23.16;
Ex 14.15-30;
Judg 6.10
17.8
Lev 18.3;
Deut 18.9;
2 Kings 16.3
17.9
2 Kings 18.8
17.10
Ex 34.12-14;
1 Kings 14.23;
Mic 5.14

17.12
Ex 20.3, 4
17.13
1 Sam 9.9;
Jer 18.11;
25.5; 35.15
17.14
Ex 32.9;
Deut 31.27;
Acts 7.51
17.15
Jer 8.9;
Deut 29.25;
32.21;
Deut 12.30,
31
17.16
1 Kings 12.28;
14.15, 23;
2 Kings 21.3;
1 Kings 16.31
17.17
Lev 19.26;
2 Kings 16.3;
Deut 18.10-12;
1 Kings 21.20
17.18
v. 6;
1 Kings 11.13,
32, 36
17.19
1 Kings 14.22,
23;
2 Kings 16.3
17.20
2 Kings 15.29
17.21
1 Kings 11.11,
31; 12.20,
28-33

17.6 Shalmaneser, the Assyrian king (727–722 B.C.), began the siege of Samaria, but he died before the city surrendered. Sargon II (722–705 B.C.), his successor, captured Samaria and took the people captive. The northern kingdom came to an end late in 722 B.C. or early in 721. **17.7** The captivity of the ten tribes (Israel or the northern kingdom) resulted from their national wickedness. That kingdom has never been restored. The returnees from the seventy years' captivity in Babylon were largely from the the people of Judah (although a small number of the returnees were from Israel). Hosea predicted that the northern kingdom would never be set up again (Hos 1.6,9). **17.13** In explaining why the ten tribes went into captivity, the author also points out that all the prophets and seers warned Judah as well as Israel. **17.17** *made their sons and their daughters pass through fire,* i.e., they even burned them to death on the altars of Molech.

LORD and made them commit great sin. 22 The people of Israel continued in all the sins that Jeroboam committed; they did not depart from them 23 until the LORD removed Israel out of his sight, as he had foretold through all his servants the prophets. So Israel was exiled from their own land to Assyria until this day.

3. Israel resettled: the origin of the Samaritans

24 The king of Assyria brought people from Babylon, Cuthah, Avva, Hamath, and Sepharvaim, and placed them in the cities of Samaria in place of the people of Israel; they took possession of Samaria, and settled in its cities. 25 When they first settled there, they did not worship the LORD; therefore the LORD sent lions among them, which killed some of them. 26 So the king of Assyria was told, "The nations that you have carried away and placed in the cities of Samaria do not know the law of the god of the land; therefore he has sent lions among them; they are killing them, because they do not know the law of the god of the land." 27 Then the king of Assyria commanded, "Send there one of the priests whom you carried away from there; let him[t] go and live there, and teach them the law of the god of the land." 28 So one of the priests whom they had carried away from Samaria came and lived in Bethel; he taught them how they should worship the LORD.

29 But every nation still made gods of its own and put them in the shrines of the high places that the people of Samaria had made, every nation in the cities in which they lived; 30 the people of Babylon made Succoth-benoth, the people of Cuth made Nergal, the people of Hamath made Ashima; 31 the Avvites made Nibhaz and Tartak; the Sepharvites burned their children in the fire to Adrammelech and Anammelech, the gods of Sepharvaim. 32 They also worshiped the LORD and appointed from among themselves all sorts of people as priests of the high places, who sacrificed for them in the shrines of the high places. 33 So they worshiped the LORD but also served their own gods, after the manner of the nations from among whom they had been carried away. 34 To this day they continue to practice their former customs.

They do not worship the LORD and they do not follow the statutes or the ordinances or the law or the commandment that the LORD commanded the children of Jacob, whom he named Israel. 35 The LORD had made a covenant with them and commanded them, "You shall not worship other gods or bow yourselves to them or serve them or sacrifice to them, 36 but you shall worship the LORD, who brought you out of the land of Egypt with great power and with an outstretched arm; you shall bow yourselves to him, and to him you shall sacrifice. 37 The statutes and the ordinances and the law and the commandment that he wrote for you, you shall always be careful to observe. You shall not worship other gods; 38 you shall not forget the covenant that I have made with you. You shall not worship other gods, 39 but you shall worship the LORD your God; he will deliver you out of the hand of all your enemies." 40 They would not listen, however, but they continued to practice their former custom.

41 So these nations worshiped the LORD, but also served their carved images; to this day their children and their children's children continue to do as their ancestors did.

[t] Syr Vg: Heb them

Margin references:
17.23 · vv. 6, 13
17.24 · Ezra 4.2, 10; 2 Kings 18.34
17.27 · Mic 3.11
17.30 · v. 24
17.31 · vv. 17, 24
17.32 · 1 Kings 12.31
17.33 · Zeph 1.5
17.34 · Gen 32.28; 35.10
17.35 · Judg 6.10; Ex 20.5
17.36 · Ex 6.6; Deut 10.20
17.37 · Deut 5.32
17.38 · Deut 4.23
17.41 · vv. 32, 33

17.24 The relocation of peoples was a policy carried on by a grandson of Sargon, Esar-haddon by name (681–669 B.C.). His son Ashurbanipal (699–633 B.C.), also called Osnapper, did the same thing (Ezra 4.10).

17.29 *the people of Samaria.* These people eventually became known as the Samaritans. They were a mixed-breed people, who worshiped their own gods while saying they served the Lord (see note on Jn 4.5).

IV. *The kingdom of Judah to the captivity (18.1–25.30)*

A. *The reign of King Hezekiah*

1. *Summary of the acts of Hezekiah*

18 In the third year of King Hoshea son of Elah of Israel, Hezekiah son of King Ahaz of Judah began to reign. 2 He was twenty-five years old when he began to reign; he reigned twenty-nine years in Jerusalem. His mother's name was Abi daughter of Zechariah. 3 He did what was right in the sight of the LORD just as his ancestor David had done. 4 He removed the high places, broke down the pillars, and cut down the sacred pole. ᵘ He broke in pieces the bronze serpent that Moses had made, for until those days the people of Israel had made offerings to it; it was called Nehushtan. 5 He trusted in the LORD the God of Israel; so that there was no one like him among all the kings of Judah after him, or among those who were before him. 6 For he held fast to the LORD; he did not depart from following him but kept the commandments that the LORD commanded Moses. 7 The LORD was with him; wherever he went, he prospered. He rebelled against the king of Assyria and would not serve him. 8 He attacked the Philistines as far as Gaza and its territory, from watchtower to fortified city.

2. *The end of the northern kingdom*

9 In the fourth year of King Hezekiah, which was the seventh year of King Hoshea son of Elah of Israel, King Shalmaneser of Assyria came up against Samaria, besieged it, 10 and at the end of three years, took it. In the sixth year of Hezekiah, which was the ninth year of King Hoshea of Israel, Samaria was taken. 11 The king of Assyria carried the Israelites away to Assyria, settled them in Halah, on the Habor, the river of Gozan, and in the cities of the Medes, 12 because they did not obey the voice of the LORD their God but transgressed his covenant—all that Moses the servant of the LORD had commanded; they neither listened nor obeyed.

3. *Sennacherib's invasion*

a. *Hezekiah pays tribute*

13 In the fourteenth year of King Hezekiah, King Sennacherib of Assyria came up against all the fortified cities of Judah and captured them. 14 King Hezekiah of Judah sent to the king of Assyria at Lachish, saying, "I have done wrong; withdraw from me; whatever you impose on me I will bear." The king of Assyria demanded of King Hezekiah of Judah three hundred talents of silver and thirty talents of gold. 15 Hezekiah gave him all the silver that was found in the house of the LORD and in the treasuries of the king's house. 16 At that time Hezekiah stripped the gold from the doors of the temple of the LORD, and from the doorposts that King Hezekiah of Judah had overlaid and gave it to the king of Assyria.

ᵘ Heb *Asherah*

18.1
2 Kings 17.1;
2 Chr 28.27
18.2
2 Chr 29.1, 2
18.4
2 Chr 31.1;
Num 21.8, 9
18.5
2 Kings 19.10;
23.25
18.6
Deut 10.20
18.7
Gen 39.2, 3;
1 Sam 18.14;
2 Kings 16.7
18.8
1 Chr 4.41;
Isa 14.29;
2 Kings 17.9
18.9
2 Kings 17.3
18.10
2 Kings 17.6
18.11
2 Kings 17.6
18.13
2 Chr 32.1ff;
Isa 36.1ff
18.15
2 Kings 16.8

18.1 Here and in vv. 9,10 the reigns of Hezekiah and Hoshea are synchronized. Verse 13 says that Sennacherib invaded Judah in the fourteenth year of Hezekiah's reign. This invasion occurred in 701 B.C., but Hoshea had ceased to reign in 722 B.C. The probable solution is that Hezekiah was co-regent with his father for twelve years, beginning in Hoshea's third year. **18.2** *Abi*, a shortened form of Abijah (see 2 Chr 29.1). **18.4** *the bronze serpent.* This refers to the bronze serpent that Moses had made in the wilderness and that spared any serpent-bit Israelite from an untimely death (see Num 21). It had now become an idolatrous object. Hezekiah broke it into pieces and disposed of it. All too often a legitimate object of religious significance becomes an idol—a stumbling block to believers and an offense to God. **18.14** Hezekiah meekly accepted the dictates of Sennacherib of Assyria and agreed to pay him tribute. Nowhere does the account suggest that Hezekiah in the midst of his difficulty sought God directly or asked help from Isaiah the prophet, who was available to him.

17 The king of Assyria sent the Tartan, the Rabsaris, and the Rabshakeh with a great army from Lachish to King Hezekiah at Jerusalem. They went up and came to Jerusalem. When they arrived, they came and stood by the conduit of the upper pool, which is on the highway to the Fuller's Field. 18 When they called for the king, there came out to them Eliakim son of Hilkiah, who was in charge of the palace, and Shebnah the secretary, and Joah son of Asaph, the recorder.

b. The Assyrian threats

19 The Rabshakeh said to them, "Say to Hezekiah: Thus says the great king, the king of Assyria: On what do you base this confidence of yours? 20 Do you think that mere words are strategy and power for war? On whom do you now rely, that you have rebelled against me? 21 See, you are relying now on Egypt, that broken reed of a staff, which will pierce the hand of anyone who leans on it. Such is Pharaoh king of Egypt to all who rely on him. 22 But if you say to me, 'We rely on the LORD our God,' is it not he whose high places and altars Hezekiah has removed, saying to Judah and to Jerusalem, 'You shall worship before this altar in Jerusalem'? 23 Come now, make a wager with my master the king of Assyria: I will give you two thousand horses, if you are able on your part to set riders on them. 24 How then can you repulse a single captain among the least of my master's servants, when you rely on Egypt for chariots and for horsemen? 25 Moreover, is it without the LORD that I have come up against this place to destroy it? The LORD said to me, Go up against this land, and destroy it."

26 Then Eliakim son of Hilkiah, and Shebnah, and Joah said to the Rabshakeh, "Please speak to your servants in the Aramaic language, for we understand it; do not speak to us in the language of Judah within the hearing of the people who are on the wall." 27 But the Rabshakeh said to them, "Has my master sent me to speak these words to your master and to you, and not to the people sitting on the wall, who are doomed with you to eat their own dung and to drink their own urine?"

28 Then the Rabshakeh stood and called out in a loud voice in the language of Judah, "Hear the word of the great king, the king of Assyria! 29 Thus says the king: 'Do not let Hezekiah deceive you, for he will not be able to deliver you out of my hand. 30 Do not let Hezekiah make you rely on the LORD by saying, The LORD will surely deliver us, and this city will not be given into the hand of the king of Assyria.' 31 Do not listen to Hezekiah; for thus says the king of Assyria: 'Make your peace with me and come out to me; then every one of you will eat from your own vine and your own fig tree, and drink water from your own cistern, 32 until I come and take you away to a land like your own land, a land of grain and wine, a land of bread and vineyards, a land of olive oil and honey, that you may live and not die. Do not listen to Hezekiah when he misleads you by saying, The LORD will deliver us. 33 Has any of the gods of the nations ever delivered its land out of the hand of the king of Assyria? 34 Where are the gods of Hamath and Arpad? Where are the gods of Sepharvaim, Hena, and Ivvah? Have they delivered Samaria out of my hand? 35 Who among all the gods of the countries have delivered their countries out of my hand, that the LORD should deliver Jerusalem out of my hand?' "

36 But the people were silent and answered him not a word, for the

---

18.17 *Tartan, the Rab-saris, and the Rabshakeh,* i.e., his highest ranked military people.
18.19–26 Hezekiah had to put up with the taunts of Sennacherib's leaders. Jerusalem was besieged and the enemy was telling Hezekiah that he had better capitulate, for he could not escape the might of the Assyrian army. Envoys from the king hoped to negotiate a settlement with the Assyrians, using the Aramaic language.

18.28 The Rabshakeh now made his biggest mistake: he appealed to the people of Judah in Hebrew over the head of the king and suggested they capitulate, for then they would be at peace and enjoy many good things under the Assyrians. His most potent argument was that their God was too weak to deliver them even if Hezekiah called on him. This affront to God, as well as to Hezekiah, led to the divine intervention that changed the picture quickly.

king's command was, "Do not answer him." 37 Then Eliakim son of Hilkiah, who was in charge of the palace, and Shebna the secretary, and Joah son of Asaph, the recorder, came to Hezekiah with their clothes torn and told him the words of the Rabshakeh.

c. Hezekiah sends to Isaiah for a word from God

19 When King Hezekiah heard it, he tore his clothes, covered himself with sackcloth, and went into the house of the LORD. 2 And he sent Eliakim, who was in charge of the palace, and Shebna the secretary, and the senior priests, covered with sackcloth, to the prophet Isaiah son of Amoz. 3 They said to him, "Thus says Hezekiah, This day is a day of distress, of rebuke, and of disgrace; children have come to the birth, and there is no strength to bring them forth. 4 It may be that the LORD your God heard all the words of the Rabshakeh, whom his master the king of Assyria has sent to mock the living God, and will rebuke the words that the LORD your God has heard; therefore lift up your prayer for the remnant that is left." 5 When the servants of King Hezekiah came to Isaiah, 6 Isaiah said to them, "Say to your master, 'Thus says the LORD: Do not be afraid because of the words that you have heard, with which the servants of the king of Assyria have reviled me. 7 I myself will put a spirit in him, so that he shall hear a rumor and return to his own land; I will cause him to fall by the sword in his own land.' "

8 The Rabshakeh returned, and found the king of Assyria fighting against Libnah; for he had heard that the king had left Lachish. 9 When the king*v* heard concerning King Tirhakah of Ethiopia,*w* "See, he has set out to fight against you," he sent messengers again to Hezekiah, saying, 10 "Thus shall you speak to King Hezekiah of Judah: Do not let your God on whom you rely deceive you by promising that Jerusalem will not be given into the hand of the king of Assyria. 11 See, you have heard what the kings of Assyria have done to all lands, destroying them utterly. Shall you be delivered? 12 Have the gods of the nations delivered them, the nations that my predecessors destroyed, Gozan, Haran, Rezeph, and the people of Eden who were in Telassar? 13 Where is the king of Hamath, the king of Arpad, the king of the city of Sepharvaim, the king of Hena, or the king of Ivvah?"

d. Hezekiah's prayer

14 Hezekiah received the letter from the hand of the messengers and read it; then Hezekiah went up to the house of the LORD and spread it before the LORD. 15 And Hezekiah prayed before the LORD, and said: "O LORD the God of Israel, who are enthroned above the cherubim, you are God, you alone, of all the kingdoms of the earth; you have made heaven and earth. 16 Incline your ear, O LORD, and hear; open your eyes, O LORD, and see; hear the words of Sennacherib, which he has sent to mock the living God. 17 Truly, O LORD, the kings of Assyria have laid waste the nations and their lands, 18 and have hurled their gods into the

v Heb *he* *w* Or *Nubia*; Heb *Cush*

18.37 vv. 18, 26; 2 Kings 6.30
19.1 2 Chr 32.20-22; Isa 37.1-38; 2 Kings 18.37; 1 Kings 21.27
19.2 Isa 1.1; 2.1
19.4 2 Sam 16.12; 2 Kings 18.35; 1.9
19.6 Isa 37.6ff; 2 Kings 18.17ff
19.7 vv. 35-37
19.8 Josh 10.29; 2 Kings 18.14
19.10 2 Kings 18.5, 30
19.12 2 Kings 18.33
19.13 2 Kings 18.34
19.14 Isa 37.14
19.15 1 Sam 4.4; 1 Kings 18.39
19.16 Ps 31.2; 2 Chr 6.40; v. 4
19.18 Ps 115.4; Jer 10.3

19.1 Chapter 19 is identical to Isa 37. From the dating of the book of 2 Kings, it appears that the unknown writer was familiar with the book of Isaiah and, under the aegis of the Holy Spirit, used its material here.

19.2–4 Hezekiah donned the sackcloth and went before God in the house of the Lord. He sent Eliakim to Isaiah the prophet to ask for his help in this emergency, wondering whether the Lord God of Isaiah had heard the mockery of the Rabshakeh (v. 4). He then asked Isaiah to pray to God for Judah. Apparently Hezekiah lacked confidence that God hears everything that anyone says and that he, like David and Solomon, could bring the concerns of the people to

God himself directly in prayer.

19.6 Isaiah sent back a message for Hezekiah not to fear: God would take care of him, for "the servants of the king of Assyria have reviled me." God would defend his own honor.

19.14 Hezekiah followed proper prayer principles (see note on 1 Sam 1.10). He was battling against an impossible situation from which there was no deliverance, humanly speaking. But he sought God's face, asked for divine help, and was sent a word from God by the prophet Isaiah. He believed God for the answer and waited expectantly until it came, having accepted the answer by faith before its fulfillment.

fire, though they were no gods but the work of human hands — wood and stone — and so they were destroyed. 19 So now, O LORD our God, save us, I pray you, from his hand, so that all the kingdoms of the earth may know that you, O LORD, are God alone."

e. Isaiah brings an answer to Hezekiah's prayer

20   Then Isaiah son of Amoz sent to Hezekiah, saying, "Thus says the LORD, the God of Israel: I have heard your prayer to me about King Sennacherib of Assyria. 21 This is the word that the LORD has spoken concerning him:

> She despises you, she scorns you —
>   virgin daughter Zion;
> she tosses her head — behind your back,
>   daughter Jerusalem.

22   "Whom have you mocked and reviled?
>   Against whom have you raised your voice
> and haughtily lifted your eyes?
>   Against the Holy One of Israel!

23   By your messengers you have mocked the Lord,
>   and you have said, 'With my many chariots
> I have gone up the heights of the mountains,
>   to the far recesses of Lebanon;
> I felled its tallest cedars,
>   its choicest cypresses;
> I entered its farthest retreat,
>   its densest forest.

24   I dug wells
>   and drank foreign waters,
> I dried up with the sole of my foot
>   all the streams of Egypt.'

25   "Have you not heard
>   that I determined it long ago?
> I planned from days of old
>   what now I bring to pass,
> that you should make fortified cities
>   crash into heaps of ruins,

26   while their inhabitants, shorn of strength,
>   are dismayed and confounded;
> they have become like plants of the field
>   and like tender grass,
> like grass on the housetops,
>   blighted before it is grown.

27   "But I know your rising[x] and your sitting,
>   your going out and coming in,
>   and your raging against me.

28   Because you have raged against me
>   and your arrogance has come to my ears,
> I will put my hook in your nose
>   and my bit in your mouth;
> I will turn you back on the way
>   by which you came.

---

[x] Gk Compare Isa 37.27 Q Ms: MT lacks *rising*

19.20 The word that Isaiah spoke to Hezekiah was the word he had received from God. This great God, so scorned by the Assyrians, would execute judgment on them, a judgment that had been determined even before the event happened (v. 25) — to put a hook in the king's nose and a bit in his mouth (v. 28).

29 "And this shall be the sign for you: This year you shall eat what grows of itself, and in the second year what springs from that; then in the third year sow, reap, plant vineyards, and eat their fruit. 30 The surviving remnant of the house of Judah shall again take root downward, and bear fruit upward; 31 for from Jerusalem a remnant shall go out, and from Mount Zion a band of survivors. The zeal of the LORD of hosts will do this.

32 "Therefore thus says the LORD concerning the king of Assyria: He shall not come into this city, shoot an arrow there, come before it with a shield, or cast up a siege ramp against it. 33 By the way that he came, by the same he shall return; he shall not come into this city, says the LORD. 34 For I will defend this city to save it, for my own sake and for the sake of my servant David.'"

f. The divine deliverance

35 That very night the angel of the LORD set out and struck down one hundred eighty-five thousand in the camp of the Assyrians; when morning dawned, they were all dead bodies. 36 Then King Sennacherib of Assyria left, went home, and lived at Nineveh. 37 As he was worshiping in the house of his god Nisroch, his sons Adrammelech and Sharezer killed him with the sword, and they escaped into the land of Ararat. His son Esarhaddon succeeded him.

4. The sickness of Hezekiah

a. His prayer and Isaiah's answer

20 In those days Hezekiah became sick and was at the point of death. The prophet Isaiah son of Amoz came to him, and said to him, "Thus says the LORD: Set your house in order, for you shall die; you shall not recover." 2 Then Hezekiah turned his face to the wall and prayed to the LORD; 3 "Remember now, O LORD, I implore you, how I have walked before you in faithfulness with a whole heart, and have done what is good in your sight." Hezekiah wept bitterly. 4 Before Isaiah had gone out of the middle court, the word of the LORD came to him: 5 "Turn back, and say to Hezekiah prince of my people, Thus says the LORD, the God of your ancestor David: I have heard your prayer, I have seen your tears; indeed, I will heal you; on the third day you shall go up to the house of the LORD. 6 I will add fifteen years to your life. I will deliver you and this city out of the hand of the king of Assyria; I will defend this city for my own sake and for my servant David's sake." 7 Then Isaiah said, "Bring a lump of figs. Let them take it and apply it to the boil, so that he may recover."

b. The sign of the shadow

8 Hezekiah said to Isaiah, "What shall be the sign that the LORD will heal me, and that I shall go up to the house of the LORD on the third day?" 9 Isaiah said, "This is the sign to you from the LORD, that the LORD will do the thing that he has promised: the shadow has now advanced ten

19.29
1 Sam 2.34;
2 Kings 20.8, 9;
Lk 2.12
19.30
2 Chr 32.22, 23
19.31
Isa 9.7

19.33
v. 28
19.34
2 Kings 20.6;
1 Kings 11.12, 13

19.35
2 Chr 32.21;
Isa 37.36
19.36
vv. 7, 28, 33;
Jon 1.2
19.37
2 Chr 32.21;
v. 7;
Ezra 4.2

20.1
2 Chr 32.24;
Isa 38.1; see
2 Sam 17.23

20.3
Neh 13.22;
2 Kings 18.3-6

20.5
1 Sam 9.16;
10.1;
2 Kings 19.20;
Ps 39.12

20.6
2 Kings 19.34

20.7
Isa 38.21

19.32 God promised Hezekiah that the enemy (1) would not enter the city; (2) would not shoot an arrow over the city walls; (3) would not stand before the city with their shields; and (4) would not build an embankment against the walls so that the troops could scale the walls and enter the city. The most gracious part of the promise was the assurance that this would all take place without Hezekiah and his small army having to do anything except trust in God.
19.35 We do not know how God defeated Sennacherib; the death of the soldiers may have come from a sudden plague or the angel of the Lord may have slain these troops in an exercise of the divine wrath. In any event, it was a miraculous deliverance. Writings of Sennacherib that have been found confirm that he

never took Jerusalem.
19.37 *Esar-haddon*, Sennacherib's successor, was not his eldest son. Like David, Sennacherib chose a favored son to replace him.
20.1ff When Hezekiah became ill and Isaiah the prophet told him he was about to die, he was approximately forty years old and there was no heir to the throne. He pled with God for an extension of his life and was granted fifteen more years. Manasseh was born several years later and was twelve years old when he succeeded his father (21.2). God had promised an unbroken succession for the house of David (2 Sam 7.16); therefore we can conclude that Hezekiah's prayer was in accord with the will of God.

intervals; shall it retreat ten intervals?" 10 Hezekiah answered, "It is normal for the shadow to lengthen ten intervals; rather let the shadow retreat ten intervals." 11 The prophet Isaiah cried to the LORD; and he brought the shadow back the ten intervals, by which the sun*y* had declined on the dial of Ahaz.

20.11
Josh 10.12-14

5. *Hezekiah's foolishness before Merodach-baladan*

12   At that time King Merodach-baladan son of Baladan of Babylon sent envoys with letters and a present to Hezekiah, for he had heard that Hezekiah had been sick. 13 Hezekiah welcomed them;*z* he showed them all his treasure house, the silver, the gold, the spices, the precious oil, his armory, all that was found in his storehouses; there was nothing in his house or in all his realm that Hezekiah did not show them. 14 Then the prophet Isaiah came to King Hezekiah, and said to him, "What did these men say? From where did they come to you?" Hezekiah answered, "They have come from a far country, from Babylon." 15 He said, "What have they seen in your house?" Hezekiah answered, "They have seen all that is in my house; there is nothing in my storehouses that I did not show them."

16   Then Isaiah said to Hezekiah, "Hear the word of the LORD: 17 Days are coming when all that is in your house, and that which your ancestors have stored up until this day, shall be carried to Babylon; nothing shall be left, says the LORD. 18 Some of your own sons who are born to you shall be taken away; they shall be eunuchs in the palace of the king of Babylon." 19 Then Hezekiah said to Isaiah, "The word of the LORD that you have spoken is good." For he thought, "Why not, if there will be peace and security in my days?"

20   The rest of the deeds of Hezekiah, all his power, how he made the pool and the conduit and brought water into the city, are they not written in the Book of the Annals of the Kings of Judah? 21 Hezekiah slept with his ancestors; and his son Manasseh succeeded him.

20.12
Isa 39.1ff
20.13
2 Chr 32.27

20.15
v. 13

20.17
2 Kings 24.13;
25.13;
Jer 52.17
20.18
2 Kings 24.12;
2 Chr 33.1;
Dan 1.3-7
20.19
1 Sam 3.18

20.20
2 Chr 32.32;
Neh 3.16
20.21
2 Chr 32.33

21.1
2 Chr 33.1ff
21.2
2 Kings 16.3
21.3
2 Kings 18.4;
1 Kings 16.32,
33;
2 Kings 17.16;
Deut 17.3
21.4
Jer 32.34;
2 Sam 7.13;
1 Kings 8.2
9
21.6
Lev 18.21;
2 Kings 16.3;
17.17;
Lev 19.26,
31;
Deut 18.20,
11

B. *The reign of King Manasseh*

1. *His wickedness*

21 Manasseh was twelve years old when he began to reign; he reigned fifty-five years in Jerusalem. His mother's name was Hephzibah. 2 He did what was evil in the sight of the LORD, following the abominable practices of the nations that the LORD drove out before the people of Israel. 3 For he rebuilt the high places that his father Hezekiah had destroyed; he erected altars for Baal, made a sacred pole,*a* as King Ahab of Israel had done, worshiped all the host of heaven, and served them. 4 He built altars in the house of the LORD, of which the LORD had said, "In Jerusalem I will put my name." 5 He built altars for all the host of heaven in the two courts of the house of the LORD. 6 He made his son pass through

y Syr See Isa 38.8 and Tg: Heb *it*   *z* Gk Vg Syr: Heb *When Hezekiah heard about them*   *a* Heb *Asherah*

20.11 *on the dial of Ahaz.* Egyptian sundials were made in the form of miniature staircases so that the shadow advanced or declined on the steps. Hezekiah's long day has been the subject of much debate. The account simply states that the sundial of Ahaz declined ten degrees. Hezekiah was expecting a genuine sign, and if it had been merely an optical illusion rather than the actual lengthening of a day, Hezekiah would hardly have been impressed. We must conclude that a miracle was performed here and that it occurred without disorder or harm to the celestial system. An infinite, all-powerful God who called the world into being can also stop, start, or rearrange the universe as he pleases.

20.20 This tunnel of Hezekiah was dug through solid rock by two crews starting at either end of the tunnel and meeting in the middle. An ancient inscription tells of the exciting moment when the two crews met.
21.1 Manasseh was co-regent with Hezekiah for ten years. Bible writers usually included the years of a co-regent in a king's total years of reign, complicating modern attempts to figure out the chronologies of kings.
21.2 Good fathers can have bad sons. Manasseh undid much, if not all, of the good things done by his father. He went so far as to burn his son as an offering to a pagan god.

fire; he practiced soothsaying and augury, and dealt with mediums and with wizards. He did much evil in the sight of the Lord, provoking him to anger. 7 The carved image of Asherah that he had made he set in the house of which the Lord said to David and to his son Solomon, "In this house, and in Jerusalem, which I have chosen out of all the tribes of Israel, I will put my name forever; 8 I will not cause the feet of Israel to wander any more out of the land that I gave to their ancestors, if only they will be careful to do according to all that I have commanded them, and according to all the law that my servant Moses commanded them." 9 But they did not listen; Manasseh misled them to do more evil than the nations had done that the Lord destroyed before the people of Israel.

2. The fall of Jerusalem predicted

10   The Lord said by his servants the prophets, 11 "Because King Manasseh of Judah has committed these abominations, has done things more wicked than all that the Amorites did, who were before him, and has caused Judah also to sin with his idols; 12 therefore thus says the Lord, the God of Israel, I am bringing upon Jerusalem and Judah such evil that the ears of everyone who hears of it will tingle. 13 I will stretch over Jerusalem the measuring line for Samaria, and the plummet for the house of Ahab; I will wipe Jerusalem as one wipes a dish, wiping it and turning it upside down. 14 I will cast off the remnant of my heritage, and give them into the hand of their enemies; they shall become a prey and a spoil to all their enemies, 15 because they have done what is evil in my sight and have provoked me to anger, since the day their ancestors came out of Egypt, even to this day."

3. Summary of Manasseh's reign

16   Moreover Manasseh shed very much innocent blood, until he had filled Jerusalem from one end to another, besides the sin that he caused Judah to sin so that they did what was evil in the sight of the Lord.

17   Now the rest of the acts of Manasseh, all that he did, and the sin that he committed, are they not written in the Book of the Annals of the Kings of Judah? 18 Manasseh slept with his ancestors, and was buried in the garden of his house, in the garden of Uzza. His son Amon succeeded him.

C. The reign of King Amon

19   Amon was twenty-two years old when he began to reign; he reigned two years in Jerusalem. His mother's name was Meshullemeth daughter of Haruz of Jotbah. 20 He did what was evil in the sight of the Lord, as his father Manasseh had done. 21 He walked in all the way in which his father walked, served the idols that his father served, and worshiped them; 22 he abandoned the Lord, the God of his ancestors, and did not walk in the way of the Lord. 23 The servants of Amon conspired against him, and killed the king in his house. 24 But the people of the land killed all those who had conspired against King Amon, and the people of the land made his son Josiah king in place of him. 25 Now the rest of the acts of Amon that he did, are they not written in the Book of the Annals of the Kings of Judah? 26 He was buried in his tomb in the garden of Uzza; then his son Josiah succeeded him.

21.7
1 Kings 8.29;
9.3;
2 Kings 23.27;
Jer 32.34
21.8
2 Sam 7.10

21.9
Prov 29.12

21.11
2 Kings 24.3,
4;
1 Kings 21.26;
v. 16
21.12
1 Sam 3.11;
Jer 19.3
21.13
Isa 34.11;
Am 7.7, 8

21.16
2 Kings 24.4

21.17
2 Chr 33.11-19
21.18
2 Chr 33.20

21.19
2 Chr 33.21-23
21.20
vv. 2-6, 11,
16

21.22
1 Kings 11.33
21.23
2 Chr 33.24,
25

21.26
v. 18

21.10–15 Judah had reached the point of no return. Consequently, God used his prophets to pronounce his judgment against Judah: Jerusalem would be sacked and the people would be given into the hand of the conqueror. It would not happen immediately, but it was coming and nothing could prevent it.

21.17 Manasseh was a bad ruler, but (according to

2 Chr 33.11–19) he had a change of heart near the end of his days. That is not recorded here.

21.19 The reign of Amon was inglorious and his wickedness great. He was given to idolatry in every form. He lasted for two years, at which time his servants killed him and his son Josiah became king.

D. *The reign of King Josiah*

1. *Faithful Josiah*

22 Josiah was eight years old when he began to reign; he reigned thirty-one years in Jerusalem. His mother's name was Jedidah daughter of Adaiah of Bozkath. 2 He did what was right in the sight of the LORD, and walked in all the way of his father David; he did not turn aside to the right or to the left.

22.1
2 Chr 34.1;
Josh 15.39
22.2
Deut 5.32

2. *The repair of the temple*

3 In the eighteenth year of King Josiah, the king sent Shaphan son of Azaliah, son of Meshullam, the secretary, to the house of the LORD, saying, 4 "Go up to the high priest Hilkiah, and have him count the entire sum of the money that has been brought into the house of the LORD, which the keepers of the threshold have collected from the people; 5 let it be given into the hand of the workers who have the oversight of the house of the LORD; let them give it to the workers who are at the house of the LORD, repairing the house, 6 that is, to the carpenters, to the builders, to the masons; and let them use it to buy timber and quarried stone to repair the house. 7 But no accounting shall be asked from them for the money that is delivered into their hand, for they deal honestly."

22.3
2 Chr 34.8ff
22.4
2 Kings 12.4,
9, 10
22.5
2 Kings 12.11-
14
22.7
2 Kings 12.15

3. *The finding of the book of the law*

8 The high priest Hilkiah said to Shaphan the secretary, "I have found the book of the law in the house of the LORD." When Hilkiah gave the book to Shaphan, he read it. 9 Then Shaphan the secretary came to the king, and reported to the king, "Your servants have emptied out the money that was found in the house, and have delivered it into the hand of the workers who have oversight of the house of the LORD." 10 Shaphan the secretary informed the king, "The priest Hilkiah has given me a book." Shaphan then read it aloud to the king.

22.8
Deut 31.24-26;
2 Chr 34.14,
15

4. *The reaction of Josiah*

11 When the king heard the words of the book of the law, he tore his clothes. 12 Then the king commanded the priest Hilkiah, Ahikam son of Shaphan, Achbor son of Micaiah, Shaphan the secretary, and the king's servant Asaiah, saying, 13 "Go, inquire of the LORD for me, for the people, and for all Judah, concerning the words of this book that has been found; for great is the wrath of the LORD that is kindled against us, because our ancestors did not obey the words of this book, to do according to all that is written concerning us."

22.12
2 Kings 25.22;
2 Chr 34.20
22.13
Deut 29.27

5. *The words of Huldah the prophetess*

14 So the priest Hilkiah, Ahikam, Achbor, Shaphan, and Asaiah went to the prophetess Huldah the wife of Shallum son of Tikvah, son of Harhas, keeper of the wardrobe; she resided in Jerusalem in the Second

22.14
2 Chr 34.22

22.1 Josiah was a good king, doing right in the eyes of God. When he grew up, he repaired the house of God. It had been allowed to deteriorate during the idolatrous reigns of his father and grandfather.
22.8 The scroll that Hilkiah discovered contained material from Deuteronomy (Josiah's reforms indicate this to be so), as well as some material in Jeremiah. This undermines the view held by many that Deuteronomy was a late production that did not come from the pen of Moses.
22.11 The book of the law was not known to Josiah. When it was discovered and read to him, he was

deeply moved by it. He acknowledged that their ancestors had not obeyed the commandments of the book, and for that reason judgment had come upon the nation.
22.14 Hilkiah the priest and others consulted with Huldah, a prophetess. She confirmed the word that had been spoken by the prophets who preceded her — that the judgment of God would fall on Jerusalem and all Judah. But she also had a good word. God had seen the good heart of Josiah and was deferring the time of the fall of Jerusalem until after his death.

Quarter, where they consulted her. 15 She declared to them, "Thus says the LORD, the God of Israel: Tell the man who sent you to me, 16 Thus says the LORD, I will indeed bring disaster on this place and on its inhabitants—all the words of the book that the king of Judah has read. 17 Because they have abandoned me and have made offerings to other gods, so that they have provoked me to anger with all the work of their hands, therefore my wrath will be kindled against this place, and it will not be quenched. 18 But as to the king of Judah, who sent you to inquire of the LORD, thus shall you say to him, Thus says the LORD, the God of Israel: Regarding the words that you have heard, 19 because your heart was penitent, and you humbled yourself before the LORD, when you heard how I spoke against this place, and against its inhabitants, that they should become a desolation and a curse, and because you have torn your clothes and wept before me, I also have heard you, says the LORD. 20 Therefore, I will gather you to your ancestors, and you shall be gathered to your grave in peace; your eyes shall not see all the disaster that I will bring on this place." They took the message back to the king.

6. The renewal of the covenant

23 Then the king directed that all the elders of Judah and Jerusalem should be gathered to him. 2 The king went up to the house of the LORD, and with him went all the people of Judah, all the inhabitants of Jerusalem, the priests, the prophets, and all the people, both small and great; he read in their hearing all the words of the book of the covenant that had been found in the house of the LORD. 3 The king stood by the pillar and made a covenant before the LORD, to follow the LORD, keeping his commandments, his decrees, and his statutes, with all his heart and all his soul, to perform the words of this covenant that were written in this book. All the people joined in the covenant.

7. The reforms of Josiah

4 The king commanded the high priest Hilkiah, the priests of the second order, and the guardians of the threshold, to bring out of the temple of the LORD all the vessels made for Baal, for Asherah, and for all the host of heaven; he burned them outside Jerusalem in the fields of the Kidron, and carried their ashes to Bethel. 5 He deposed the idolatrous priests whom the kings of Judah had ordained to make offerings in the high places at the cities of Judah and around Jerusalem; those also who made offerings to Baal, to the sun, the moon, the constellations, and all the host of the heavens. 6 He brought out the image of[b] Asherah from the house of the LORD, outside Jerusalem, to the Wadi Kidron, burned it at the Wadi Kidron, beat it to dust and threw the dust of it upon the graves of the common people. 7 He broke down the houses of the male temple prostitutes that were in the house of the LORD, where the women did weaving for Asherah. 8 He brought all the priests out of the towns of Judah, and defiled the high places where the priests had made offerings, from Geba to Beer-sheba; he broke down the high places of the gates that were at the entrance of the gate of Joshua the governor of the city, which were on the left at the gate of the city. 9 The priests of the high places,

22.17
Deut 29.25-27

22.19
Ps 51.17;
Isa 57.15;
1 Kings 21.29;
Lev 26.31;
Jer 26.6

23.1
2 Chr 34.29-32
23.2
Deut 31.10-13;
2 Kings 22.8

23.3
2 Kings 11.14,
17;
Deut 13.4

23.4ff
2 Kings 21.3,
7

23.7
1 Kings 14.24;
15.12;
Ezek 16.16
23.8
1 Kings 15.22

23.9
Ezek 44.10-14

b Heb lacks image of

23.1 The bad news given to Josiah did not leave him in a state of shock nor did he cultivate a spirit of lethargy. He called the elders of the people together, went to the temple, and read the word of God to the assembled crowd. He made a public covenant with God to walk according to the law of God, and the people joined him in that covenant.
23.4 So great had been the extent of idolatry that objects belonging to the worship of Baal, Asherah,

and the host of heaven were found lodging in the house of God itself. Josiah ordered these things to be taken out and burned. He expelled the priests who had been ordained by former kings to burn incense to Baal, the sun, the moon, and the constellations. He stopped the activities of the male cult prostitutes. The long list of what he did makes it clear that Judah had indeed sunk low into the pit of degradation.

however, did not come up to the altar of the LORD in Jerusalem, but ate
unleavened bread among their kindred. 10 He defiled Topheth, which is
in the valley of Ben-hinnom, so that no one would make a son or a
daughter pass through fire as an offering to Molech. 11 He removed the
horses that the kings of Judah had dedicated to the sun, at the entrance
to the house of the LORD, by the chamber of the eunuch Nathan-melech,
which was in the precincts;*c* then he burned the chariots of the sun with
fire. 12 The altars on the roof of the upper chamber of Ahaz, which the
kings of Judah had made, and the altars that Manasseh had made in the
two courts of the house of the LORD, he pulled down from there and broke
in pieces, and threw the rubble into the Wadi Kidron. 13 The king defiled
the high places that were east of Jerusalem, to the south of the Mount of
Destruction, which King Solomon of Israel had built for Astarte the
abomination of the Sidonians, for Chemosh the abomination of Moab, and
for Milcom the abomination of the Ammonites. 14 He broke the pillars in
pieces, cut down the sacred poles,*d* and covered the sites with human
bones.

8. The bones of the man of God

15 Moreover, the altar at Bethel, the high place erected by Jeroboam
son of Nebat, who caused Israel to sin — he pulled down that altar along
with the high place. He burned the high place, crushing it to dust; he also
burned the sacred pole.*e* 16 As Josiah turned, he saw the tombs there on
the mount; and he sent and took the bones out of the tombs, and burned
them on the altar, and defiled it, according to the word of the LORD that
the man of God proclaimed,*f* when Jeroboam stood by the altar at the
festival; he turned and looked up at the tomb of the man of God who had
predicted these things. 17 Then he said, "What is that monument that I
see?" The people of the city told him, "It is the tomb of the man of God
who came from Judah and predicted these things that you have done
against the altar at Bethel." 18 He said, "Let him rest; let no one move his
bones." So they let his bones alone, with the bones of the prophet who
came out of Samaria. 19 Moreover, Josiah removed all the shrines of the
high places that were in the towns of Samaria, which kings of Israel had
made, provoking the LORD to anger; he did to them just as he had done
at Bethel. 20 He slaughtered on the altars all the priests of the high places
who were there, and burned human bones on them. Then he returned to
Jerusalem.

9. The keeping of the passover

21 The king commanded all the people, "Keep the passover to the
LORD your God as prescribed in this book of the covenant." 22 No such
passover had been kept since the days of the judges who judged Israel,
or even during all the days of the kings of Israel and of the kings of Judah;
23 but in the eighteenth year of King Josiah this passover was kept to the
LORD in Jerusalem.

10. The zeal of Josiah

24 Moreover Josiah put away the mediums, wizards, teraphim,*g*
idols, and all the abominations that were seen in the land of Judah and

23.10
Isa 30.33;
Jer 7.31;
Lev 18.21;
Deut 18.10

23.12
Jer 19.13;
Zeph 1.5;
2 Kings 21.5;
vv. 4, 6
23.13
1 Kings 11.7

23.14
Ex 23.24;
Deut 7.5, 25

23.15
1 Kings 12.28-
33

23.16
1 Kings 13.2

23.17
1 Kings 13.1,
30

23.18
1 Kings 13.31

23.19
2 Chr 34.6, 7

23.20
2 Kings 10.25;
11.18;
2 Chr 34.5

23.21
2 Chr 35.1;
Ex 12.3;
Num 9.2;
Deut 16.2
23.22
2 Chr 35.18,
19

23.24
2 Kings 21.6,
11, 21;
Deut 18.10-12

c Meaning of Heb uncertain   *d* Heb *Asherim*   *e* Heb *Asherah*   *f* Gk: Heb *proclaimed, who had predicted these things*   *g* Or *household gods*

23.16   This was the altar constructed by Jeroboam
(see 1 Kings 13.2).
23.21   Josiah, reigning for thirty-one years, was the
best of all Judah's kings since the days of Rehoboam.
He kept the passover in a manner far better than any
of his predecessors as far back as the days of the

judges. He rooted out the abominable customs taken
over by Judah from the pagan world; the religion of
Yahweh flourished and the festivals were kept. He
not only caused Judah to cease to do evil; he also
taught them to do good.

in Jerusalem, so that he established the words of the law that were written in the book that the priest Hilkiah had found in the house of the LORD. 25 Before him there was no king like him, who turned to the LORD with all his heart, with all his soul, and with all his might, according to all the law of Moses; nor did any like him arise after him.

11. The continued anger of God against Judah

26 Still the LORD did not turn from the fierceness of his great wrath, by which his anger was kindled against Judah, because of all the provocations with which Manasseh had provoked him. 27 The LORD said, "I will remove Judah also out of my sight, as I have removed Israel; and I will reject this city that I have chosen, Jerusalem, and the house of which I said, My name shall be there."

12. The death of Josiah and the succession

28 Now the rest of the acts of Josiah, and all that he did, are they not written in the Book of the Annals of the Kings of Judah? 29 In his days Pharaoh Neco king of Egypt went up to the king of Assyria to the river Euphrates. King Josiah went to meet him; but when Pharaoh Neco met him at Megiddo, he killed him. 30 His servants carried him dead in a chariot from Megiddo, brought him to Jerusalem, and buried him in his own tomb. The people of the land took Jehoahaz son of Josiah, anointed him, and made him king in place of his father.

E. The reign of Jehoahaz; his captivity by Pharaoh Neco

31 Jehoahaz was twenty-three years old when he began to reign; he reigned three months in Jerusalem. His mother's name was Hamutal daughter of Jeremiah of Libnah. 32 He did what was evil in the sight of the LORD, just as his ancestors had done. 33 Pharaoh Neco confined him at Riblah in the land of Hamath, so that he might not reign in Jerusalem, and imposed tribute on the land of one hundred talents of silver and a talent of gold. 34 Pharaoh Neco made Eliakim son of Josiah king in place of his father Josiah, and changed his name to Jehoiakim. But he took Jehoahaz away; he came to Egypt, and died there. 35 Jehoiakim gave the silver and the gold to Pharaoh, but he taxed the land in order to meet Pharaoh's demand for money. He exacted the silver and the gold from the people of the land, from all according to their assessment, to give it to Pharaoh Neco.

F. The reign of King Jehoiakim: first capture of Jerusalem by Nebuchadnezzar

36 Jehoiakim was twenty-five years old when he began to reign; he reigned eleven years in Jerusalem. His mother's name was Zebidah daughter of Pedaiah of Rumah. 37 He did what was evil in the sight of the LORD, just as all his ancestors had done.

24 In his days King Nebuchadnezzar of Babylon came up; Jehoiakim became his servant for three years; then he turned and rebelled

Cross references (margin):

23.25
2 Kings 18.5

23.26
2 Kings 21.11, 12;
Jer 15.4
23.27
2 Kings 18.11;
21.13, 14

23.29
2 Chr 35.20;
Zech 12.11

23.30
2 Chr 35.24;
36.1

23.31
1 Chr 3.15;
Jer 22.11;
2 Kings 24.18
23.33
2 Kings 25.6;
Jer 52.27;
2 Chr 36.3
23.34
2 Chr 36.4;
2 Kings 24.17;
Ezek 19.3, 4
23.35
v. 33

23.36
2 Chr 36.5

24.1
2 Chr 36.6;
Jer 25.1

23.25 After Josiah, Judah sank lower and lower until the captivity came and Judah was ruined.
23.29 *Pharaoh Neco* was rushing to assist the Assyrians whose capital, Nineveh, fell under the onslaughts of the Babylonians in 612 B.C. He had no quarrel with Josiah, who foolishly insisted on this encounter. Josiah's death in 609–608 B.C. hastened the subsequent downfall of Judah.
23.30 The people chose Jehoahaz to be king, bypassing his older brother Eliakim (Jehoiakim).
23.31–33 Jehoahaz reigned for three months before

becoming a prisoner of Pharaoh Neco, who carried him to Egypt where he died shortly thereafter.
23.34 Eliakim means "God is setting up." When the Pharaoh made this older son of Josiah king in place of his brother Jehoahaz, he named him Jehoiakim, which name means "Jah sets up." This power to change a name indicated that Jehoiakim was subservient to Pharaoh Neco.
24.1 This is the first mention in the Scriptures of Nebuchadnezzar, about whom we learn a great deal in the book of Daniel. Most of Jehoiakim's eleven-

against him. 2 The LORD sent against him bands of the Chaldeans, bands of the Arameans, bands of the Moabites, and bands of the Ammonites; he sent them against Judah to destroy it, according to the word of the LORD that he spoke by his servants the prophets. 3 Surely this came upon Judah at the command of the LORD, to remove them out of his sight, for the sins of Manasseh, for all that he had committed, 4 and also for the innocent blood that he had shed; for he filled Jerusalem with innocent blood, and the LORD was not willing to pardon. 5 Now the rest of the deeds of Jehoiakim, and all that he did, are they not written in the Book of the Annals of the Kings of Judah? 6 So Jehoiakim slept with his ancestors; then his son Jehoiachin succeeded him. 7 The king of Egypt did not come again out of his land, for the king of Babylon had taken over all that belonged to the king of Egypt from the Wadi of Egypt to the River Euphrates.

G. The reign of King Jehoiachin: second capture of Jerusalem

8 Jehoiachin was eighteen years old when he began to reign; he reigned three months in Jerusalem. His mother's name was Nehushta daughter of Elnathan of Jerusalem. 9 He did what was evil in the sight of the LORD, just as his father had done.

10 At that time the servants of King Nebuchadnezzar of Babylon came up to Jerusalem, and the city was besieged. 11 King Nebuchadnezzar of Babylon came to the city, while his servants were besieging it; 12 King Jehoiachin of Judah gave himself up to the king of Babylon, himself, his mother, his servants, his officers, and his palace officials. The king of Babylon took him prisoner in the eighth year of his reign.

13 He carried off all the treasures of the house of the LORD, and the treasures of the king's house; he cut in pieces all the vessels of gold in the temple of the LORD, which King Solomon of Israel had made, all this as the LORD had foretold. 14 He carried away all Jerusalem, all the officials, all the warriors, ten thousand captives, all the artisans and the smiths; no one remained, except the poorest people of the land. 15 He carried away Jehoiachin to Babylon; the king's mother, the king's wives, his officials, and the elite of the land, he took into captivity from Jerusalem to Babylon. 16 The king of Babylon brought captive to Babylon all the men of valor, seven thousand, the artisans and the smiths, one thousand, all of them strong and fit for war. 17 The king of Babylon made Mattaniah, Jehoiachin's uncle, king in his place, and changed his name to Zedekiah.

H. The reign of King Zedekiah

1. The rebellion against Babylon

18 Zedekiah was twenty-one years old when he began to reign; he reigned eleven years in Jerusalem. His mother's name was Hamutal daughter of Jeremiah of Libnah. 19 He did what was evil in the sight of

24.2
Jer 25.9;
35.11;
2 Kings 23.27
24.3
2 Kings 18.25;
23.26
24.4
2 Kings 21.16

24.6
Jer 22.18, 19
24.7
Jer 37.5-7;
46.2

24.8
1 Chr 3.16;
2 Chr 36.9

24.10
Dan 1.1

24.12
Jer 24.1;
29.1, 2; 25.1;
2 Kings 25.27;
Jer 52.28

24.13
2 Kings 20.17;
Isa 39.6;
2 Kings 25.13-
15;
Jer 20.5
24.14
Jer 24.1;
52.28;
2 Kings 25.12;
Jer 40.7
24.15
2 Chr 36.10;
Jer 22.24-28
24.16
Jer 52.28
24.17
Jer 37.1;
1 Chr 3.15;
2 Chr 36.4,
10

24.18
2 Chr 36.11;
Jer 52.1ff;
2 Kings 23.31
24.19
2 Chr 36.12

---

year reign (608–597 B.C.) was marked by bondage to this leader of Babylon. In 606/605 B.C. Nebuchadnezzar conquered Jehoiakim and took the temple treasures and many Jews (including Daniel the prophet) to Babylon (see 2 Chr 36.6,7; Dan 1.1–3). A few years later Jehoiakim asked Egypt to come to his aid and suffered another defeat from Nebuchadnezzar (597 B.C.). Jehoiakim died at that time, and after a three-month reign by his son Jehoiachin, Nebuchadnezzar took the royal family, along with the rest of Judah's treasures and ten thousand of the princes, officers, and chief people, to Babylon (see 24.10–12).
24.2 *the Chaldeans*, i.e., the Babylonians.
24.10 The Babylonian captivity was starting. Jeremiah predicted it to last seventy years. Some compute

the seventy years from the first deportation (about 605 B.C.). Others start with 586 B.C., when the third and final deportation took place (see note on Jer 25.11). In any case, the end of the kingdom of Judah was at hand (see note on 25.6).
24.17 When Nebuchadnezzar took Jehoiachin as prisoner, he made his uncle Mattaniah (whose name means "Gift of Yahweh") king of Jerusalem and renamed him Zedekiah (see note on 23.34). The books of Jeremiah and Ezekiel provide the most information about Zedekiah and the events that transpired during his reign. Zedekiah rebelled against Nebuchadnezzar, even though he had taken a solemn oath of loyalty to him in the name of Yahweh and had been warned by Jeremiah not to revolt.

the LORD, just as Jehoiakim had done. 20 Indeed, Jerusalem and Judah so angered the LORD that he expelled them from his presence.

25

Zedekiah rebelled against the king of Babylon. 1 And in the ninth year of his reign, in the tenth month, on the tenth day of the month, King Nebuchadnezzar of Babylon came with all his army against Jerusalem, and laid siege to it; they built siegeworks against it all around. 2 So the city was besieged until the eleventh year of King Zedekiah. 3 On the ninth day of the fourth month the famine became so severe in the city that there was no food for the people of the land. 4 Then a breach was made in the city wall;*h* the king with all the soldiers fled*i* by night by the way of the gate between the two walls, by the king's garden, though the Chaldeans were all around the city. They went in the direction of the Arabah. 5 But the army of the Chaldeans pursued the king, and overtook him in the plains of Jericho; all his army was scattered, deserting him. 6 Then they captured the king and brought him up to the king of Babylon at Riblah, who passed sentence on him. 7 They slaughtered the sons of Zedekiah before his eyes, then put out the eyes of Zedekiah; they bound him in fetters and took him to Babylon.

2. The destruction of Jerusalem and the temple

8 In the fifth month, on the seventh day of the month—which was the nineteenth year of King Nebuchadnezzar, king of Babylon— Nebuzaradan, the captain of the bodyguard, a servant of the king of Babylon, came to Jerusalem. 9 He burned the house of the LORD, the king's house, and all the houses of Jerusalem; every great house he burned down. 10 All the army of the Chaldeans who were with the captain of the guard broke down the walls around Jerusalem. 11 Nebuzaradan the captain of the guard carried into exile the rest of the people who were left in the city and the deserters who had defected to the king of Babylon—all the rest of the population. 12 But the captain of the guard left some of the poorest people of the land to be vinedressers and tillers of the soil.

13 The bronze pillars that were in the house of the LORD, as well as the stands and the bronze sea that were in the house of the LORD, the Chaldeans broke in pieces, and carried the bronze to Babylon. 14 They took away the pots, the shovels, the snuffers, the dishes for incense, and all the bronze vessels used in the temple service, 15 as well as the firepans and the basins. What was made of gold the captain of the guard took away for the gold, and what was made of silver, for the silver. 16 As for the two pillars, the one sea, and the stands, which Solomon had made for the house of the LORD, the bronze of all these vessels was beyond weighing. 17 The height of the one pillar was eighteen cubits, and on it was a bronze capital; the height of the capital was three cubits; latticework and pomegranates, all of bronze, were on the capital all around. The second pillar had the same, with the latticework.

3. The killing of the leaders

18 The captain of the guard took the chief priest Seraiah, the second priest Zephaniah, and the three guardians of the threshold; 19 from the city he took an officer who had been in command of the soldiers, and five men of the king's council who were found in the city; the secretary who was the commander of the army who mustered the people of the land; and

24.20	2 Chr 36.13
25.1	2 Chr 36.13; 17-20; Jer 39.1-7; Ezek 24.1, 2
25.3	Jer 39.1, 2
25.4	Jer 39.4-7
25.6	Jer 34.21, 22; 2 Kings 23.33
25.7	Jer 39.6, 7; Ezek 12.13
25.8	Jer 52.12-14; 39.9
25.9	2 Chr 36.19; Ps 74.3-7; Am 2.5
25.10	Neh 1.3; Jer 52.14
25.11	2 Chr 36.20; Jer 39.9; 52.15
25.12	2 Kings 24.14; Jer 40.7
25.13	2 Chr 36.18
25.14	1 Kings 7.47-50
25.16	1 Kings 7.47
25.17	1 Kings 7.15-22
25.18	1 Chr 6.14; Ezra 7.1; Jer 21.1; 29.25

h Heb lacks *wall*   *i* Gk Compare Jer 39.4; 52.7: Heb lacks *the king* and lacks *fled*

25.6 This event marks the end of the Judean kingship over Jerusalem. Both Zedekiah and Jehoiachin were in Babylon. How did this affect the promise of God about the house of David? David's house became a dry root. Six hundred years would pass before the son of David, Jesus, would emerge as a root out of a

dry ground (see Isa 53.2).
25.8 The destruction of the temple and of Jerusalem occurred in 586 B.C. Before the destruction of the temple, the cloud of God had already left the sanctuary (cf. Ezek 10), signifying that God had left his people to a just judgment for their transgressions.

sixty men of the people of the land who were found in the city. 20 Nebuzar-adan the captain of the guard took them, and brought them to the king

25.21
Deut 28.64;
2 Kings 23.27

of Babylon at Riblah. 21 The king of Babylon struck them down and put them to death at Riblah in the land of Hamath. So Judah went into exile out of its land.

4. The appointment of Gedaliah as governor: his murder

25.22
Jer 40.5

22 He appointed Gedaliah son of Ahikam son of Shaphan as governor over the people who remained in the land of Judah, whom King Nebu-chadnezzar of Babylon had left. 23 Now when all the captains of the forces

25.23
Jer 40.7-9

and their men heard that the king of Babylon had appointed Gedaliah as governor, they came with their men to Gedaliah at Mizpah, namely, Ishmael son of Nethaniah, Johanan son of Kareah, Seraiah son of Tanhu-meth the Netophathite, and Jaazaniah son of the Maacathite. 24 Gedaliah swore to them and their men, saying, "Do not be afraid because of the Chaldean officials; live in the land, serve the king of Babylon, and it shall

25.25
Jer 41.1, 2

be well with you." 25 But in the seventh month, Ishmael son of Nethaniah son of Elishama, of the royal family, came with ten men; they struck down Gedaliah so that he died, along with the Judeans and Chaldeans who were

25.26
Jer 43.4-7

with him at Mizpah. 26 Then all the people, high and low,[j] and the captains of the forces set out and went to Egypt; for they were afraid of the Chaldeans.

5. Jehoiachin set free in Babylon

25.27
Jer 52.31-34;
Gen 40.13, 20

27 In the thirty-seventh year of the exile of King Jehoiachin of Judah, in the twelfth month, on the twenty-seventh day of the month, King Evil-merodach of Babylon, in the year that he began to reign, released King Jehoiachin of Judah from prison; 28 he spoke kindly to him, and gave him a seat above the other seats of the kings who were with him in

25.29
2 Sam 9.7

Babylon. 29 So Jehoiachin put aside his prison clothes. Every day of his life he dined regularly in the king's presence. 30 For his allowance, a regular allowance was given him by the king, a portion every day, as long as he lived.

j Or young and old

25.22ff Gedaliah was a political moderate, avoiding political intrigue and seeking to promote the interests of the Israelites who remained in Palestine. Ishmael assassinated him and his court — both the Jews and the Babylonians. The Jewish community virtually ceased to exist after this. Gedaliah's followers fled to Egypt and forced Jeremiah to go with them. In Jewish tradition the anniversary of Gedaliah's death is cele-brated by a fast.
25.27 Evil-merodach, Nebuchadnezzar's son, reigned from 561 to 560 B.C. His Babylonian name,

Amel-Marduk ("Man of Marduk"), was a variant form of Awel-merodach (hence, in Hebrew, Evil-merodach). This king released Jehoiachin from prison and took good care of him, for he represented to the Babylonians the legitimate king of Judah. Clay tablets found in the ruins of Babylon mention that food was supplied by his conquerors to Jehoiachin and five of his sons. Note, therefore, that the royal line of David continued to live, though they no longer had any power.

INTRODUCTION TO
1 CHRONICLES

Authorship, Date, and Background: 1 and 2 Chronicles in modern translations were one book in the Hebrew Bible. The name given to Chronicles in the Greek and Latin versions was *Paraleipomena*, which simply means the record of the things left out of Samuel and Kings. Chronicles was placed at the end of the Writings (the *kethubim,*), the third division of the Hebrew Bible.

The authorship and dating of 1 and 2 Chronicles stand together. Ezra, according to Jewish tradition, was the author. This view is held by many conservative scholars today. They have placed the composition of the book somewhere between 450 and 425 B.C. Chronicles was put together by Ezra after considerable research had been done. Nehemiah, with whom he was associated, was said to have had a large library (2 Maccabees 2.13–15). No doubt Ezra had access to it. In Chronicles there is a list of the various sources used; these included various books on the kings of Judah and Israel; the records of Samuel the seer, Nathan the prophet, Gad the seer, Ahijah the Shilonite, Iddo the seer, Shemaiah the prophet, Jehu the son of Hanani, and Isaiah the prophet were all consulted. Some passages of Chronicles parallel the books of Samuel and Kings.

The Israelites who had come back from Babylon were apparently unaware of their national heritage. A new generation had grown up who were unfamiliar with the land. Jerusalem was in shambles, the temple had been destroyed, and the religious ceremonies centering around it had not been celebrated for more than half a century. A need existed to unify the people by teaching them something about their former glory and about the work of God in their midst. The purpose was to give the returning Jews an understanding of their covenant relationship to God, of the meaning of the theocracy and the monarchy, and of the beginning of the line of David and his descendants.

Characteristics and Content: The author traced the rise of the Hebrew peoples from Adam and carried it through the exile under Nebuchadnezzar to the return to the land under Cyrus' edict. No doubt he did this to encourage the returnees to appreciate their heritage and to develop a national spirit. This history would give them a sense of belonging and also show that the God of mighty miracles had been with their ancestors despite the trials and tribulations brought upon them because of disobedience.

The first nine chapters of 1 Chronicles are genealogical tables showing that the Israelites were direct descendants of the first human pair, created by God. The writer did not describe the reign of Saul; he only recorded the fact that his reign ended ingloriously because he was unfaithful to God, did not keep God's commandments, and consulted a medium instead of the Lord. Beginning with ch. 11, 1 Chronicles recounts the life of King David, leaving out the bad items in David's pilgrimage (such as his adultery with Bathsheba, the rebellion of his own household, and family affairs, all of which are extensively covered in 2 Sam 11—20). Prominently described are David's major interests as king of the nation—his religious acts such as bringing the ark to Jerusalem, the organization of the priests and Levites, his covenantal relationship with God who promised him an eternal throne, and his gathering of the materials for the construction of the temple, which was to be the responsibility of Solomon.

The central theme which pervades both 1 and 2 Chronicles is the proposition that those who fear God and follow his commandments can expect the blessing and favor of God over all their works. Disobedience brings disaster; obedience brings blessing. This theme can also be found in the N.T. for the people of God, the church; some also see in the N.T. the promise of a future blessing for an obedient Israel, who will seek God in large numbers in the closing days of the present age.

Outline:

   I. The genealogies (1.1—9.44)

   II. The reign of David (10.1—29.30)

1 CHRONICLES

I. The genealogies (1.1–9.44)

A. The ancestral lines in the patriarchal period

1 Adam, Seth, Enosh; 2 Kenan, Mahalalel, Jared; 3 Enoch, Methuselah, Lamech; 4 Noah, Shem, Ham, and Japheth.

5 The descendants of Japheth: Gomer, Magog, Madai, Javan, Tubal, Meshech, and Tiras. 6 The descendants of Gomer: Ashkenaz, Diphath, *k* and Togarmah. 7 The descendants of Javan: Elishah, Tarshish, Kittim, and Rodanim. *l*

8 The descendants of Ham: Cush, Egypt, Put, and Canaan. 9 The descendants of Cush: Seba, Havilah, Sabta, Raama, and Sabteca. The descendants of Raamah: Sheba and Dedan. 10 Cush became the father of Nimrod; he was the first to be a mighty one on the earth.

11 Egypt became the father of Ludim, Anamim, Lehabim, Naphtuhim, 12 Pathrusim, Casluhim, and Caphtorim, from whom the Philistines come. *m*

13 Canaan became the father of Sidon his firstborn, and Heth, 14 and the Jebusites, the Amorites, the Girgashites, 15 the Hivites, the Arkites, the Sinites, 16 the Arvadites, the Zemarites, and the Hamathites.

17 The descendants of Shem: Elam, Asshur, Arpachshad, Lud, Aram, Uz, Hul, Gether, and Meshech. *n* 18 Arpachshad became the father of Shelah; and Shelah became the father of Eber. 19 To Eber were born two sons: the name of the one was Peleg (for in his days the earth was divided), and the name of his brother Joktan. 20 Joktan became the father of Almodad, Sheleph, Hazarmaveth, Jerah, 21 Hadoram, Uzal, Diklah, 22 Ebal, Abimael, Sheba, 23 Ophir, Havilah, and Jobab; all these were the descendants of Joktan.

24 Shem, Arpachshad, Shelah; 25 Eber, Peleg, Reu; 26 Serug, Nahor, Terah; 27 Abram, that is, Abraham.

28 The sons of Abraham: Isaac and Ishmael. 29 These are their genealogies: the firstborn of Ishmael, Nebaioth; and Kedar, Adbeel, Mibsam, 30 Mishma, Dumah, Massa, Hadad, Tema, 31 Jetur, Naphish, and Kedemah. These are the sons of Ishmael. 32 The sons of Keturah, Abraham's concubine: she bore Zimran, Jokshan, Medan, Midian, Ishbak, and

Cross references

1.1 Gen 4.25; 5.32
1.5 Gen 10.2-4
1.8 Gen 10.6ff
1.10 Gen 10.8, 13ff
1.17 Gen 10.22ff
1.24 Gen 11.10ff
1.29 Gen 25.13-16
1.32 Gen 25.1-4

k Gen 10.3 *Ripath*; See Gk Vg *l* Gen 10.4 *Dodanim*; See Syr Vg *m* Heb *Casluhim, from which the Philistines come, Caphtorim*; See Am 9.7, Jer 47.4 *n* Mash in Gen 10.23

1.1 The first twenty-seven verses start with *Adam* and end with *Abraham*. Despite modern denials of the historicity of Adam, all biblical writers view Adam as the first man in a literal sense, the common ancestor of the entire human race. By his breach of God's covenant, we are all sinners (Rom 5.12–18). By God's grace Abraham was the common ancestor of the faithful, and by the covenant of grace made between Abraham and God we can obtain salvation. By nature we are the offspring of Adam; by faith we are the offspring of Abraham (Rom 4.11,12; Gal 3.29) and have been grafted into the good olive tree (Rom 11.11–24).
1.3 *Enoch*, "was taken so that he did not experience death" (Heb 11.5). The line of Cain is not included in this list.

1.4 *Shem* is mentioned here and again in verse 24. The line of Shem was the line of Abraham and thus the line of Jesus Christ. Matthew carefully traced Jesus' genealogy back to Abraham, the first ancestor of Israel. Luke traced Jesus' genealogy back to Adam through Abraham. No one would have been the Messiah who could not trace his lineage very specifically to Adam through Abraham.
1.28 Abraham had many sons through Sarah, Hagar, and Keturah. But Sarah had only one son, Isaac, and through that one son God continued his covenant with Abraham, leading to the Messiah, Jesus Christ.
1.29–31 The twelve tribes of Ishmael are here named. Both Jacob and his uncle Ishmael had twelve sons, and thus the two are juxtaposed (see 2.1,2).

Shuah. The sons of Jokshan: Sheba and Dedan. 33 The sons of Midian:
Ephah, Epher, Hanoch, Abida, and Eldaah. All these were the descen-
dants of Keturah.
1.34 34 Abraham became the father of Isaac. The sons of Isaac: Esau and
Gen 21.2, 3; 25.25, 26 Israel. 35 The sons of Esau: Eliphaz, Reuel, Jeush, Jalam, and Korah.
1.35 36 The sons of Eliphaz: Teman, Omar, Zephi, Gatam, Kenaz, Timna, and
Gen 36.9, 10 Amalek. 37 The sons of Reuel: Nahath, Zerah, Shammah, and Mizzah.
1.38 38 The sons of Seir: Lotan, Shobal, Zibeon, Anah, Dishon, Ezer, and
Gen 36.20-28 Dishan. 39 The sons of Lotan: Hori and Homam; and Lotan's sister was
Timna. 40 The sons of Shobal: Alian, Manahath, Ebal, Shephi, and
Onam. The sons of Zibeon: Aiah and Anah. 41 The sons of Anah: Dishon.
The sons of Dishon: Hamran, Eshban, Ithran, and Cheran. 42 The sons
of Ezer: Bilhan, Zaavan, and Jaakan.[o] The sons of Dishan:[p] Uz and
Aran.
1.43 43 These are the kings who reigned in the land of Edom before any
Gen 36.31-43 king reigned over the Israelites: Bela son of Beor, whose city was called
Dinhabah. 44 When Bela died, Jobab son of Zerah of Bozrah succeeded
him. 45 When Jobab died, Husham of the land of the Temanites succeeded
him. 46 When Husham died, Hadad son of Bedad, who defeated Midian
in the country of Moab, succeeded him; and the name of his city was
Avith. 47 When Hadad died, Samlah of Masrekah succeeded him.
48 When Samlah died, Shaul[q] of Rehoboth on the Euphrates succeeded
him. 49 When Shaul[q] died, Baal-hanan son of Achbor succeeded him.
50 When Baal-hanan died, Hadad succeeded him; the name of his city was
Pai, and his wife's name Mehetabel daughter of Matred, daughter of
Me-zahab. 51 And Hadad died.
The clans[r] of Edom were: clans[r] Timna, Aliah,[s] Jetheth, 52 Oholibamah, Elah, Pinon, 53 Kenaz, Teman, Mibzar, 54 Magdiel, and Iram; these
are the clans[r] of Edom.

B. *The descendants of Judah to David*

2.1 **2** These are the sons of Israel: Reuben, Simeon, Levi, Judah, Issachar,
Gen 35.23-26; 46.8-25 Zebulun, 2 Dan, Joseph, Benjamin, Naphtali, Gad, and Asher. 3 The
2.2 sons of Judah: Er, Onan, and Shelah; these three the Canaanite woman
Gen 38.2-10 Bath-shua bore to him. Now Er, Judah's firstborn, was wicked in the sight
2.4 of the LORD, and he put him to death. 4 His daughter-in-law Tamar also
Gen 38.29, 30 bore him Perez and Zerah. Judah had five sons in all.
2.5 5 The sons of Perez: Hezron and Hamul. 6 The sons of Zerah: Zimri,
Gen 46.12 2.6 Ethan, Heman, Calcol, and Dara,[t] five in all. 7 The sons of Carmi: Achar,
Josh 7.1; 1 Kings 4.31 the troubler of Israel, who transgressed in the matter of the devoted thing;
2.7 8 and Ethan's son was Azariah.
Josh 6.18; 7.1 9 The sons of Hezron, who were born to him: Jerahmeel, Ram, and
2.10 Chelubai. 10 Ram became the father of Amminadab, and Amminadab
Ruth 4.19, 20; Mt 1.4

[o] Or *and Akan*; See Gen 36.27 [p] See 1.38: Heb *Dishon* [q] Or *Saul* [r] Or *chiefs* [s] Or *Alvah*; See Gen 36.40 [t] Or *Darda*; Compare Syr Tg some Gk Mss; See 1 Kings 4.31

1.34 As it was in the case of Abraham, so it was also in the case of Isaac. The latter had two sons, Esau and Jacob, but it was only through Jacob that Messiah was to come. Yet the Scriptures trace the non-Messianic line so as to guarantee who could *not* be the Messiah, even though one might be a descendant of Abraham and Isaac. It is apparent that multiplied millions of people have come from the line of Abraham, but they are not from the line of promise. In this verse Jacob is called "Israel," thereby suggesting that the people of Israel as a nation is meant.

1.35 Esau was not in the line of promise. From him and from other sons of Abraham, many nations came into being. This does not mean that those who were not in the line of promise were not and could not be sons and daughters of God. God has called out multitudes from all nations and recorded their names in the book of life. Not all of those attached to Israel will be saved and not all of those unattached to Israel by birth will be lost.

1.38 *Seir*, i.e., "Esau."

2.1 Jacob preferred Rachel over Leah, yet it was from Leah that the two most important tribes of Israel came: Judah (from whom the Messiah came) and Levi (the priestly tribe).

2.7 *Achar*, i.e., Achan, here called "the troubler of Israel." Every family tree has in it those who are illustrious and those who are a disgrace. Scripture does not hide the blemishes in the covenant line.

became the father of Nahshon, prince of the sons of Judah. [11]Nahshon became the father of Salma, Salma of Boaz, [12]Boaz of Obed, Obed of Jesse. [13]Jesse became the father of Eliab his firstborn, Abinadab the second, Shimea the third, [14]Nethanel the fourth, Raddai the fifth, [15]Ozem the sixth, David the seventh; [16]and their sisters were Zeruiah and Abigail. The sons of Zeruiah: Abishai, Joab, and Asahel, three. [17]Abigail bore Amasa, and the father of Amasa was Jether the Ishmaelite.

[18]   Caleb son of Hezron had children by his wife Azubah, and by Jerioth; these were her sons: Jesher, Shobab, and Ardon. [19]When Azubah died, Caleb married Ephrath, who bore him Hur. [20]Hur became the father of Uri, and Uri became the father of Bezalel.

[21]   Afterward Hezron went in to the daughter of Machir father of Gilead, whom he married when he was sixty years old; and she bore him Segub; [22]and Segub became the father of Jair, who had twenty-three towns in the land of Gilead. [23]But Geshur and Aram took from them Havvoth-jair, Kenath and its villages, sixty towns. All these were descendants of Machir, father of Gilead. [24]After the death of Hezron, in Caleb-ephrathah, Abijah wife of Hezron bore him Ashhur, father of Tekoa.

[25]   The sons of Jerahmeel, the firstborn of Hezron: Ram his firstborn, Bunah, Oren, Ozem, and Ahijah. [26]Jerahmeel also had another wife, whose name was Atarah; she was the mother of Onam. [27]The sons of Ram, the firstborn of Jerahmeel: Maaz, Jamin, and Eker. [28]The sons of Onam: Shammai and Jada. The sons of Shammai: Nadab and Abishur. [29]The name of Abishur's wife was Abihail, and she bore him Ahban and Molid. [30]The sons of Nadab: Seled and Appaim; and Seled died childless. [31]The son[u] of Appaim: Ishi. The son[u] of Ishi: Sheshan. The son[u] of Sheshan: Ahlai. [32]The sons of Jada, Shammai's brother: Jether and Jonathan; and Jether died childless. [33]The sons of Jonathan: Peleth and Zaza. These were the descendants of Jerahmeel. [34]Now Sheshan had no sons, only daughters; but Sheshan had an Egyptian slave, whose name was Jarha. [35]So Sheshan gave his daughter in marriage to his slave Jarha; and she bore him Attai. [36]Attai became the father of Nathan, and Nathan of Zabad. [37]Zabad became the father of Ephlal, and Ephlal of Obed. [38]Obed became the father of Jehu, and Jehu of Azariah. [39]Azariah became the father of Helez, and Helez of Eleasah. [40]Eleasah became the father of Sismai, and Sismai of Shallum. [41]Shallum became the father of Jekamiah, and Jekamiah of Elishama.

[42]   The sons of Caleb brother of Jerahmeel: Mesha[v] his firstborn, who was father of Ziph. The sons of Mareshah father of Hebron. [43]The sons of Hebron: Korah, Tappuah, Rekem, and Shema. [44]Shema became father of Raham, father of Jorkeam; and Rekem became the father of Shammai. [45]The son of Shammai: Maon; and Maon was the father of Beth-zur. [46]Ephah also, Caleb's concubine, bore Haran, Moza, and Gazez; and Haran became the father of Gazez. [47]The sons of Jahdai: Regem, Jotham, Geshan, Pelet, Ephah, and Shaaph. [48]Maacah, Caleb's concubine, bore Sheber and Tirhanah. [49]She also bore Shaaph

---

u Heb *sons*   *v* Gk reads *Mareshah*

2.13
1 Sam 16.6, 9

2.16
2 Sam 2.18
2.17
2 Sam 17.25

2.19
v. 50
2.20
Ex 31.2

2.21
Num 27.1

2.23
Num 32.41;
Deut 3.14;
Josh 13.30
2.24
1 Chr 4.5

2.31
vv. 34, 35

2.36
1 Chr 11.41

2.42
see
1 Chr 2.18,
19

2.15 *David the seventh.* According to 1 Sam 16.10, 11, Jesse had eight sons, of whom David was the youngest. Seven of Jesse's sons appeared before Samuel: none of them was God's choice for the kingship and all were older than David. Since 1 Chronicles was written much later than 1 Samuel, one of Jesse's sons probably died without offspring — so that the genealogy used here included only the seven sons of Jesse left.
2.16 David's three great commanders, Joab, Abishai, and Asahel, were the sons of one of his own sisters. The fourth great leader, Amasa, was the son

of his other sister. Evidently they were selected, not because of their family relationship to David, but for their excellence in military matters (cf. 11.20,26).
2.18 This *Caleb* must not be confused with the famous Caleb who was one of the twelve spies (mentioned in 4.15). Of the Caleb in this verse we know only who his ancestors and descendants were.
2.20 Bezalel was the overseer of the construction of the tabernacle, given the gift of craftsmanship by the Holy Spirit (Ex 31.2).
2.36 *Attai* must not be confused with the Gadite warrior mentioned in 12.11.

RULERS OF ISRAEL AND JUDAH

Biblical References	Kings	Years of Reign	Dates of Reign	Notes
1. 1 Ki 12:1-24 14:21-31	**Rehoboam** (J)	*17 years*	**930-913**	
2. 1 Ki 12:25–14:20	**Jeroboam I** (I)	22 years	930-909	
3. 1 Ki 15:1-8	**Abijah** (J)	*3 years*	*913-910*	
4. 1 Ki 15:9-24	**Asa** (J)	41 years	910-869	
5. 1 Ki 15:25-31	**Nadab** (I)	2 years	909-908	
6. 1 Ki 15:32–16:7	**Baasha** (I)	24 years	908-886	
7. 1 Ki 16:8-14	**Elah** (I)	2 years	886-885	
8. 1 Ki 16:15-20	**Zimri** (I)	7 days	885	
9. 1 Ki 16:21-22	**Tibni** (I)		885-880	Overlap with Omri
10. 1 Ki 16:23-28	**Omri** (I)		885	Made king by the people
			885-880	Overlap with Tibni
		12 years	885-874	Official reign = 11 actual years
11. 1 Ki 16:29–22:40	**Ahab** (I)	22 years	874-853	Official reign = 21 actual years
12. 1 Ki 22:41-50	**Jehoshaphat** (J)		872-869	*Co-regency with Asa*
		25 years	872-848	*Official reign*
			869	*Beginning of sole reign*
			853-848	*Has Jehoram as regent*
13. 1 Ki 22:51– 2 Ki 1:18	**Ahaziah** (I)	2 years	853-852	Official reign = 1 yr. actual reign
14. 2 Ki 1:17 2 Ki 3:1–8:15	**Joram** (I)	12 years	852 852-841	Official reign = 11 actual years
15. 2 Ki 8:16-24	**Jehoram** (J)	*8 years*	848 848-841	*Beginning of sole reign* *Official reign = 7 actual years*
16. 2 Ki 8:25-29 2 Ki 9:29	**Ahaziah** (J)	*1 year*	841 841	Nonaccession-year reckoning Accession-year reckoning
17. 2 Ki 9:30–10:36	**Jehu** (I)	28 years	841-814	
18. 2 Ki 11	**Athaliah** (J)	7 years	841-835	
19. 2 Ki 12	**Joash** (J)	40 years	835-796	
20. 2 Ki 13:1-9	**Jehoahaz** (I)	17 years	814-798	
21. 2 Ki 13:10-25	**Jehoash** (I)	16 years	798-782	

Biblical References	Kings	Years of Reign	Dates of Reign	Notes
22. 2 Ki 14:1-22	Amaziah (J)	29 years	796-767	
			792-767	Overlap with Azariah
23. 2 Ki 14:23-29	Jeroboam II (I)		793-782	Co-regency with Jehoash
		41 years	793-753	Total reign
24. 2 Ki 15:1-7	Azariah (J)		792-767	Overlap with Amaziah
		52 years	792-740	Total reign
			767	Beginning of sole reign
25. 2 Ki 15:8-12	Zechariah (I)	6 months	753	
26. 2 Ki 15:13-15	Shallum (I)	1 month	752	
27. 2 Ki 15:16-22	Menahem (I)	10 years	752-742	Ruled in Samaria
28. 2 Ki 15:23-26	Pekahiah (I)	2 years	742-740	
29. 2 Ki 15:27-31	Pekah (I)		752-740	In Gilead; overlapping years
		20 years	752-732	Total reign
			740	Beginning of sole reign
30. 2 Ki 15:32-38 2 Ki 15:30	Jotham (J)		750-740	Co-regency with Azariah
		16 years	750-735	Official reign
			750-732	Reign to his 20th year
			750	Beginning of co-regency
31. 2 Ki 16	Ahaz (J)		735-715	Total reign
		16 years	732-715	From 20th of Jotham
32. 2 Ki 15:30 2 Ki 17	Hoshea (I)	9 years	732 732-722	20th of Jotham
33. 2 Ki 18:1-20:21	Hezekiah (J)	29 years	715-686	
34. 2 Ki 21:1-18	Manasseh (J)		697-686	Co-regency with Hezekiah
		55 years	697-642	Total reign
35. 2 Ki 21:19-26	Amon (J)	2 years	642-640	
36. 2 Ki 22:1-23:30	Josiah (J)	31 years	640-609	
37. 2 Ki 23:31-33	Jehoahaz (J)	3 months	609	
38. 2 Ki 23:34-24:7	Jehoiakim (J)	11 years	609-598	
39. 2 Ki 24:8-17	Jehoiachin (J)	3 months	598-597	
40. 2 Ki 24:18-25:26	Zedekiah (J)	11 years	597-586	

Data and dates in order of sequence
(J) Italics denote kings of Judah. (I) non-italic type denotes kings of **Israel**.
Adapted from: *A Chronology of the Hebrew Kings* by Edwin R. Thiele.
© 1977 by The Zondervan Corporation. Used by permission.

2.50
1 Chr 4.4

father of Madmannah, Sheva father of Machbenah and father of Gibea; and the daughter of Caleb was Achsah. 50 These were the descendants of Caleb.

The sons[w] of Hur the firstborn of Ephrathah: Shobal father of Kiriath-jearim, 51 Salma father of Bethlehem, and Hareph father of Beth-gader. 52 Shobal father of Kiriath-jearim had other sons: Haroeh, half of the Menuhoth. 53 And the families of Kiriath-jearim: the Ithrites, the Puthites, the Shumathites, and the Mishraites; from these came the Zorathites and the Eshtaolites. 54 The sons of Salma: Bethlehem, the Netopha-

2.55
Judg 1.16;
Jer 35.2

thites, Atroth-beth-joab, and half of the Manahathites, the Zorites. 55 The families also of the scribes that lived at Jabez: the Tirathites, the Shimeathites, and the Sucathites. These are the Kenites who came from Hammath, father of the house of Rechab.

C. *The descendants of David*

3.1
2 Sam 3.2, 3;
Josh 15.56

3.3
2 Sam 3.5
3.4
2 Sam 2.11;
5.5
3.5
2 Sam 5.14-16;
2 Sam 12.24;
11.3
3.9
2 Sam 13.1

3 These are the sons of David who were born to him in Hebron: the firstborn Amnon, by Ahinoam the Jezreelite; the second Daniel, by Abigail the Carmelite; 2 the third Absalom, son of Maacah, daughter of King Talmai of Geshur; the fourth Adonijah, son of Haggith; 3 the fifth Shephatiah, by Abital; the sixth Ithream, by his wife Eglah; 4 six were born to him in Hebron, where he reigned for seven years and six months. And he reigned thirty-three years in Jerusalem. 5 These were born to him in Jerusalem: Shimea, Shobab, Nathan, and Solomon, four by Bathshua, daughter of Ammiel; 6 then Ibhar, Elishama, Eliphelet, 7 Nogah, Nepheg, Japhia, 8 Elishama, Eliada, and Eliphelet, nine. 9 All these were David's sons, besides the sons of the concubines; and Tamar was their sister.

3.10
1 Kings 11.43

10 The descendants of Solomon: Rehoboam, Abijah his son, Asa his son, Jehoshaphat his son, 11 Joram his son, Ahaziah his son, Joash his son, 12 Amaziah his son, Azariah his son, Jotham his son, 13 Ahaz his son, Hezekiah his son, Manasseh his son, 14 Amon his son, Josiah his son. 15 The sons of Josiah: Johanan the firstborn, the second Jehoiakim, the third Zedekiah, the fourth Shallum. 16 The descendants of Jehoiakim:

3.16
Mt 1.11

Jeconiah his son, Zedekiah his son; 17 and the sons of Jeconiah, the captive: Shealtiel his son, 18 Malchiram, Pedaiah, Shenazzar, Jekamiah, Hoshama, and Nedabiah; 19 The sons of Pedaiah: Zerubbabel and Shimei; and the sons of Zerubbabel: Meshullam and Hananiah, and Shelomith was their sister; 20 and Hashubah, Ohel, Berechiah, Hasadiah, and Jushab-hesed, five. 21 The sons of Hananiah: Pelatiah and Jeshaiah, his son[x] Rephaiah, his son[x] Arnan, his son[x] Obadiah, his son[x] Shecaniah.

3.22
Ezek 8.2

22 The son[y] of Shecaniah: Shemaiah. And the sons of Shemaiah: Hattush, Igal, Bariah, Neariah, and Shaphat, six. 23 The sons of Neariah: Elioenai, Hizkiah, and Azrikam, three. 24 The sons of Elioenai: Hodaviah, Eliashib, Pelaiah, Akkub, Johanan, Delaiah, and Anani, seven.

---

w Gk Vg: Heb *son*   *x* Gk Compare Syr Vg: Heb *sons of*   *y* Heb *sons*

2.50,51 The pedigree of several men terminated not in a person but in a place or country. Shobal is called the father of Kiriath-jearim and Salma the father of Bethlehem. These places fell to their lot in the distribution of the land.

2.55 *The scribes*, or, "the writers," were non-Levitical writers, even though some of the Levites also were called writers.

3.5 *Bath-shua*, i.e., Bathsheba.

3.9 Tamar was sexually assaulted by her half brother Amnon, who was later slain by Absalom, the full brother of Tamar (2 Sam 13). The sons of David by his concubines are mentioned only in general.

3.11,12 *Joram*, or, "Jehoram." *Azariah*, or, "Uzziah."

3.15 *Johanan*. He died young, never reigned, and is never mentioned anywhere in the historical accounts. *Shallum*, i.e., "Jehoahaz" (see Jer 22.11).

3.19 *Zerubbabel*. The man by this name who led the returnees from Babylon to Palestine was said to be "the son of Shealtiel (Ezra 3.2; Neh 12.1). Apparently Shealtiel and Pedaiah both had sons with the same name. Or Shealtiel may have died early and Pedaiah became the head of the family. In any case, the descendants listed in the second part of this verse are most likely from the Zerubbabel mentioned in Ezra.

D. *The family of Judah*

4 The sons of Judah: Perez, Hezron, Carmi, Hur, and Shobal. ² Reaiah son of Shobal became the father of Jahath, and Jahath became the father of Ahumai and Lahad. These were the families of the Zorathites. ³ These were the sons[z] of Etam: Jezreel, Ishma, and Idbash; and the name of their sister was Hazzelelponi, ⁴ and Penuel was the father of Gedor, and Ezer the father of Hushah. These were the sons of Hur, the firstborn of Ephrathah, the father of Bethlehem. ⁵ Ashhur father of Tekoa had two wives, Helah and Naarah; ⁶ Naarah bore him Ahuzzam, Hepher, Temeni, and Haahashtari.[a] These were the sons of Naarah. ⁷ The sons of Helah: Zereth, Izhar,[b] and Ethnan. ⁸ Koz became the father of Anub, Zobebah, and the families of Aharhel son of Harum. ⁹ Jabez was honored more than his brothers; and his mother named him Jabez, saying, "Because I bore him in pain." ¹⁰ Jabez called on the God of Israel, saying, "Oh that you would bless me and enlarge my border, and that your hand might be with me, and that you would keep me from hurt and harm!" And God granted what he asked. ¹¹ Chelub the brother of Shuhah became the father of Mehir, who was the father of Eshton. ¹² Eshton became the father of Beth-rapha, Paseah, and Tehinnah the father of Ir-nahash. These are the men of Recah. ¹³ The sons of Kenaz: Othniel and Seraiah; and the sons of Othniel: Hathath and Meonothai.[c] ¹⁴ Meonothai became the father of Ophrah; and Seraiah became the father of Joab father of Ge-harashim,[d] so-called because they were artisans. ¹⁵ The sons of Caleb son of Jephunneh: Iru, Elah, and Naam; and the son[e] of Elah: Kenaz. ¹⁶ The sons of Jehallelel: Ziph, Ziphah, Tiria, and Asarel. ¹⁷ The sons of Ezrah: Jether, Mered, Epher, and Jalon. These are the sons of Bithiah, daughter of Pharaoh, whom Mered married;[f] and she conceived and bore[g] Miriam, Shammai, and Ishbah father of Eshtemoa. ¹⁸ And his Judean wife bore Jered father of Gedor, Heber father of Soco, and Jekuthiel father of Zanoah. ¹⁹ The sons of the wife of Hodiah, the sister of Naham, were the fathers of Keilah the Garmite and Eshtemoa the Maacathite. ²⁰ The sons of Shimon: Amnon, Rinnah, Ben-hanan, and Tilon. The sons of Ishi: Zoheth and Ben-zoheth. ²¹ The sons of Shelah son of Judah: Er father of Lecah, Laadah father of Mareshah, and the families of the guild of linen workers at Beth-ashbea; ²² and Jokim, and the men of Cozeba, and Joash, and Saraph, who married into Moab but returned to Lehem[h] (now the records[i] are ancient). ²³ These were the potters and inhabitants of Netaim and Gederah; they lived there with the king in his service.

E. *The family of Simeon*

24 The sons of Simeon: Nemuel, Jamin, Jarib, Zerah, Shaul;[j] ²⁵ Shallum was his son, Mibsam his son, Mishma his son. ²⁶ The sons of Mishma: Hammuel his son, Zaccur his son, Shimei his son. ²⁷ Shimei had sixteen sons and six daughters; but his brothers did not have many children, nor did all their family multiply like the Judeans. ²⁸ They lived in Beer-sheba, Moladah, Hazar-shual, ²⁹ Bilhah, Ezem, Tolad, ³⁰ Bethuel, Hormah, Ziklag, ³¹ Beth-marcaboth, Hazar-susim, Beth-biri, and Shaaraim. These were their towns until David became king. ³² And their

4.1	Gen 46.12
4.4	1 Chr 2.50
4.5	1 Chr 2.24
4.9	Gen 34.19
4.13	Josh 15.17
4.14	Neh 11.35
4.21	Gen 38.1, 5
4.24	Gen 29.33
4.28	Josh 19.2
4.30	1 Chr 12.1

---

z Gk Compare Vg: Heb *the father*   a Or *Ahashtari*   b Another reading is *Zohar*   c Gk Vg: Heb lacks *and Meonothai*   d That is *Valley of artisans*   e Heb *sons*   f The clause: *These are . . . married* is transposed from verse 18   g Heb lacks *and bore*   h Vg Compare Gk: Heb *and Jashubi-lahem*   i Or *matters*   j Or *Saul*

4.10 *Jabez* must have been an unusual character whose spiritual quality of life stood out above many others. Tradition has it that he was a doctor of the law. He was a man of excellent character, whose prayer life could be emulated by Christians today. He sought the blessing of God and received what he asked for. What God did for him he can do for us today.

4.14,21 In the midst of the genealogical tables the writer takes time to express appreciation for the family of artisans and for the producers of fine linens. **4.23** *potters . . . lived there with the king in his service.* Stamped jar handles discovered in excavations by archaeologists have verified that the king did indeed have royal potters who worked for him.

villages were Etam, Ain, Rimmon, Tochen, and Ashan, five towns, 33 along with all their villages that were around these towns as far as Baal. These were their settlements. And they kept a genealogical record.

34 Meshobab, Jamlech, Joshah son of Amaziah, 35 Joel, Jehu son of Joshibiah son of Seraiah son of Asiel, 36 Elioenai, Jaakobah, Jeshohaiah, Asaiah, Adiel, Jesimiel, Benaiah, 37 Ziza son of Shiphi son of Allon son of Jedaiah son of Shimri son of Shemaiah— 38 these mentioned by name were leaders in their families, and their clans increased greatly. 39 They journeyed to the entrance of Gedor, to the east side of the valley, to seek pasture for their flocks, 40 where they found rich, good pasture, and the land was very broad, quiet, and peaceful; for the former inhabitants there belonged to Ham. 41 These, registered by name, came in the days of King Hezekiah of Judah, and attacked their tents and the Meunim who were found there, and exterminated them to this day, and settled in their place, because there was pasture there for their flocks. 42 And some of them, five hundred men of the Simeonites, went to Mount Seir, having as their leaders Pelatiah, Neariah, Rephaiah, and Uzziel, sons of Ishi; 43 they destroyed the remnant of the Amalekites that had escaped, and they have lived there to this day.

F. *The family of Reuben*

5 The sons of Reuben the firstborn of Israel. (He was the firstborn, but because he defiled his father's bed his birthright was given to the sons of Joseph son of Israel, so that he is not enrolled in the genealogy according to the birthright; 2 though Judah became prominent among his brothers and a ruler came from him, yet the birthright belonged to Joseph.) 3 The sons of Reuben, the firstborn of Israel: Hanoch, Pallu, Hezron, and Carmi. 4 The sons of Joel: Shemaiah his son, Gog his son, Shimei his son, 5 Micah his son, Reaiah his son, Baal his son, 6 Beerah his son, whom King Tilgath-pilneser of Assyria carried away into exile; he was a chieftain of the Reubenites. 7 And his kindred by their families, when the genealogy of their generations was reckoned: the chief, Jeiel, and Zechariah, 8 and Bela son of Azaz, son of Shema, son of Joel, who lived in Aroer, as far as Nebo and Baal-meon. 9 He also lived to the east as far as the beginning of the desert this side of the Euphrates, because their cattle had multiplied in the land of Gilead. 10 And in the days of Saul they made war on the Hagrites, who fell by their hand; and they lived in their tents throughout all the region east of Gilead.

G. *The family of Gad*

11 The sons of Gad lived beside them in the land of Bashan as far as Salecah: 12 Joel the chief, Shapham the second, Janai, and Shaphat in Bashan. 13 And their kindred according to their clans: Michael, Meshullam, Sheba, Jorai, Jacan, Zia, and Eber, seven. 14 These were the sons of Abihail son of Huri, son of Jaroah, son of Gilead, son of Michael, son of Jeshishai, son of Jahdo, son of Buz; 15 Ahi son of Abdiel, son of Guni, was chief in their clan; 16 and they lived in Gilead, in Bashan and in its towns, and in all the pasture lands of Sharon to their limits. 17 All of these were enrolled by genealogies in the days of King Jotham of Judah, and in the days of King Jeroboam of Israel.

18 The Reubenites, the Gadites, and the half-tribe of Manasseh had valiant warriors, who carried shield and sword, and drew the bow, expert in war, forty-four thousand seven hundred sixty, ready for service.

Cross-references (margin)

4.40 Judg 18.7-10
4.41 2 Kings 18.8
4.43 1 Sam 15.8; 30.17; 2 Sam 8.12
5.1f Gen 29.32; 35.22; 49.4; 48.15, 22
5.2 Gen 49.8, 10; Mic 5.2; Mt 2.6
5.3 Gen 46.9; Num 26.5
5.7 v. 17
5.8 Josh 13.15, 16
5.9 Josh 22.9
5.10 vv. 18-21
5.11 Josh 13.11, 24
5.16 1 Chr 27.29
5.17 2 Kings 15.5, 32; 14.16, 28

5.1,2 Although the birthright was lost to Reuben and given to the sons of Joseph, Ephraim and Manasseh, it was the tribe of Judah that became the most powerful tribe, the one that produced the royal line of David.

5.10 *Hagrites.* Whether these people descended from Hagar is uncertain. They and other Arab tribes are mentioned in an inscription of Tiglath-pileser III (745–727 B.C.).

19 They made war on the Hagrites, Jetur, Naphish, and Nodab; 20 and when they received help against them, the Hagrites and all who were with them were given into their hands, for they cried to God in the battle, and he granted their entreaty because they trusted in him. 21 They captured their livestock: fifty thousand of their camels, two hundred fifty thousand sheep, two thousand donkeys, and one hundred thousand captives. 22 Many fell slain, because the war was of God. And they lived in their territory until the exile.

H. *The half-tribe of Manasseh*

23 The members of the half-tribe of Manasseh lived in the land; they were very numerous from Bashan to Baal-hermon, Senir, and Mount Hermon. 24 These were the heads of their clans: Epher,[k] Ishi, Eliel, Azriel, Jeremiah, Hodaviah, and Jahdiel, mighty warriors, famous men, heads of their clans. 25 But they transgressed against the God of their ancestors, and prostituted themselves to the gods of the peoples of the land, whom God had destroyed before them. 26 So the God of Israel stirred up the spirit of King Pul of Assyria, the spirit of King Tilgath-pilneser of Assyria, and he carried them away, namely, the Reubenites, the Gadites, and the half-tribe of Manasseh, and brought them to Halah, Habor, Hara, and the river Gozan, to this day.

I. *The family of Levi*

6 The sons of Levi: Gershom,[m] Kohath, and Merari. 2 The sons of Kohath: Amram, Izhar, Hebron, and Uzziel. 3 The children of Amram: Aaron, Moses, and Miriam. The sons of Aaron: Nadab, Abihu, Eleazar, and Ithamar. 4 Eleazar became the father of Phinehas, Phinehas of Abishua, 5 Abishua of Bukki, Bukki of Uzzi, 6 Uzzi of Zerahiah, Zerahiah of Meraioth, 7 Meraioth of Amariah, Amariah of Ahitub, 8 Ahitub of Zadok, Zadok of Ahimaaz, 9 Ahimaaz of Azariah, Azariah of Johanan, 10 and Johanan of Azariah (it was he who served as priest in the house that Solomon built in Jerusalem). 11 Azariah became the father of Amariah, Amariah of Ahitub, 12 Ahitub of Zadok, Zadok of Shallum, 13 Shallum of Hilkiah, Hilkiah of Azariah, 14 Azariah of Seraiah, Seraiah of Jehozadak; 15 and Jehozadak went into exile when the LORD sent Judah and Jerusalem into exile by the hand of Nebuchadnezzar.

16[n] The sons of Levi: Gershom, Kohath, and Merari. 17 These are the names of the sons of Gershom: Libni and Shimei. 18 The sons of Kohath: Amram, Izhar, Hebron, and Uzziel. 19 The sons of Merari: Mahli and Mushi. These are the clans of the Levites according to their ancestry. 20 Of Gershom: Libni his son, Jahath his son, Zimmah his son, 21 Joah his son, Iddo his son, Zerah his son, Jeatherai his son. 22 The sons of Kohath: Amminadab his son, Korah his son, Assir his son, 23 Elkanah his son, Ebiasaph his son, Assir his son, 24 Tahath his son, Uriel his son, Uzziah his son, and Shaul his son. 25 The sons of Elkanah: Amasai and Ahimoth, 26 Elkanah his son, Zophai his son, Nahath his son, 27 Eliab his son,

Cross references (margin)

5.19
v. 10;
1 Chr 1.31
5.20
2 Chr 4.11-13;
Ps 22.4, 5

5.22
2 Kings 15.29;
17.6

5.25
2 Kings 17.7

5.26
2 Kings 15.19,
29; 17.6;
18.11

6.1
Ex 6.16;
Num 26.57;
1 Chr 23.6
6.3
Lev 10.1

6.8
2 Sam 8.17;
15.27

6.14
Neh 11.11
6.15
2 Kings 25.18

6.16
Ex 6.16

6.20
v. 42

6.25
vv. 35, 36
6.26
v. 34

---

k Gk Vg: Heb *and Epher*　l Ch 5.27 in Heb　m Heb *Gershon*, variant of *Gershom*; See 6.16　n Ch 6.1 in Heb

---

5.20　The chronicler attributes the victory of the Israelites on the east bank of the Jordan to their petition to God for help. However, they later "prostituted themselves to the gods of the peoples of the land" (v. 25), and this resulted in God's judgment on them in their captivity by Assyria.
5.23　*Mount Hermon* is probably a scribal explanation for *Senir*, the Amorite name for Mount Hermon (see Deut 3.9).
6.1　The tribe of Levi was especially careful to keep their genealogical tables in order. From this tribe

came the priesthood, and no one who was not in the priestly line could offer sacrifices. If anyone not of the priesthood offered sacrifices, this was an abomination punishable by death.
6.8　Zadok was the high priest during the reigns of David and Solomon.
6.15　Jehozadak was shortened to Jozadak in Ezra and Nehemiah (e.g., Ezra 3.2). He was the father of Joshua, the high priest at the time of the rebuilding of the temple after the captivity.

Jeroham his son, Elkanah his son. 28 The sons of Samuel: Joel[o] his firstborn, the second Abijah.[p] 29 The sons of Merari: Mahli, Libni his son, Shimei his son, Uzzah his son, 30 Shimea his son, Haggiah his son, and Asaiah his son.

31   These are the men whom David put in charge of the service of song in the house of the LORD, after the ark came to rest there. 32 They ministered with song before the tabernacle of the tent of meeting, until Solomon had built the house of the LORD in Jerusalem; and they performed their service in due order. 33 These are the men who served; and their sons were: Of the Kohathites: Heman, the singer, son of Joel, son of Samuel, 34 son of Elkanah, son of Jeroham, son of Eliel, son of Toah, 35 son of Zuph, son of Elkanah, son of Mahath, son of Amasai, 36 son of

Elkanah, son of Joel, son of Azariah, son of Zephaniah, 37 son of Tahath, son of Assir, son of Ebiasaph, son of Korah, 38 son of Izhar, son of Kohath, son of Levi, son of Israel; 39 and his brother Asaph, who stood on his right, namely, Asaph son of Berechiah, son of Shimea, 40 son of Michael, son of Baaseiah, son of Malchijah, 41 son of Ethni, son of Zerah,

son of Adaiah, 42 son of Ethan, son of Zimmah, son of Shimei, 43 son of Jahath, son of Gershom, son of Levi. 44 On the left were their kindred the sons of Merari: Ethan son of Kishi, son of Abdi, son of Malluch, 45 son of Hashabiah, son of Amaziah, son of Hilkiah, 46 son of Amzi, son of Bani, son of Shemer, 47 son of Mahli, son of Mushi, son of Merari, son of Levi; 48 and their kindred the Levites were appointed for all the service of the tabernacle of the house of God.

49   But Aaron and his sons made offerings on the altar of burnt offering and on the altar of incense, doing all the work of the most holy place, to make atonement for Israel, according to all that Moses the servant of God had commanded. 50 These are the sons of Aaron: Eleazar

his son, Phinehas his son, Abishua his son, 51 Bukki his son, Uzzi his son, Zerahiah his son, 52 Meraioth his son, Amariah his son, Ahitub his son, 53 Zadok his son, Ahimaaz his son.

54   These are their dwelling places according to their settlements within their borders: to the sons of Aaron of the families of Kohathites—for the lot fell to them first— 55 to them they gave Hebron in the land

of Judah and its surrounding pasture lands, 56 but the fields of the city and its villages they gave to Caleb son of Jephunneh. 57 To the sons of

Aaron they gave the cities of refuge: Hebron, Libnah with its pasture lands, Jattir, Eshtemoa with its pasture lands, 58 Hilen[q] with its pasture

lands, Debir with its pasture lands, 59 Ashan with its pasture lands, and Beth-shemesh with its pasture lands. 60 From the tribe of Benjamin, Geba with its pasture lands, Alemeth with its pasture lands, and Anathoth with its pasture lands. All their towns throughout their families were thirteen.

61   To the rest of the Kohathites were given by lot out of the family of the tribe, out of the half-tribe, the half of Manasseh, ten towns. 62 To the Gershomites according to their families were allotted thirteen towns out of the tribes of Issachar, Asher, Naphtali, and Manasseh in Bashan.

63 To the Merarites according to their families were allotted twelve towns out of the tribes of Reuben, Gad, and Zebulun. 64 So the people of Israel gave the Levites the towns with their pasture lands. 65 They also gave them by lot out of the tribes of Judah, Simeon, and Benjamin these towns that are mentioned by name.

66   And some of the families of the sons of Kohath had towns of their

---

o Gk Syr Compare verse 33 and 1 Sam 8.2: Heb lacks *Joel*   *p* Heb reads *Vashni, and Abijah* for *the second Abijah,* taking *the second* as a proper name   *q* Other readings *Hilez, Holon;* See Josh 21.15

6.31 The authority of King David in matters of temple ritual and song was equal to that of Moses in the area of law. David actively exercised his authority in these matters.

6.57 The text here makes it appear that all of the cities named were cities of refuge. Only Hebron was such a city.

territory out of the tribe of Ephraim. 67 They were given the cities of refuge: Shechem with its pasture lands in the hill country of Ephraim, Gezer with its pasture lands, 68 Jokmeam with its pasture lands, Bethhoron with its pasture lands, 69 Aijalon with its pasture lands, Gathrimmon with its pasture lands; 70 and out of the half-tribe of Manasseh, Aner with its pasture lands, and Bileam with its pasture lands, for the rest of the families of the Kohathites.

71 To the Gershomites: out of the half-tribe of Manasseh: Golan in Bashan with its pasture lands and Ashtaroth with its pasture lands; 72 and out of the tribe of Issachar: Kedesh with its pasture lands, Daberath^r with its pasture lands, 73 Ramoth with its pasture lands, and Anem with its pasture lands; 74 out of the tribe of Asher: Mashal with its pasture lands, Abdon with its pasture lands, 75 Hukok with its pasture lands, and Rehob with its pasture lands; 76 and out of the tribe of Naphtali: Kedesh in Galilee with its pasture lands, Hammon with its pasture lands, and Kiriathaim with its pasture lands. 77 To the rest of the Merarites out of the tribe of Zebulun: Rimmono with its pasture lands, Tabor with its pasture lands, 78 and across the Jordan from Jericho, on the east side of the Jordan, out of the tribe of Reuben: Bezer in the steppe with its pasture lands, Jahzah with its pasture lands, 79 Kedemoth with its pasture lands, and Mephaath with its pasture lands; 80 and out of the tribe of Gad: Ramoth in Gilead with its pasture lands, Mahanaim with its pasture lands, 81 Heshbon with its pasture lands, and Jazer with its pasture lands.

J. *The family of Issachar*

7 The sons^s of Issachar: Tola, Puah, Jashub, and Shimron, four. 2 The sons of Tola: Uzzi, Rephaiah, Jeriel, Jahmai, Ibsam, and Shemuel, heads of their ancestral houses, namely of Tola, mighty warriors of their generations, their number in the days of David being twenty-two thousand six hundred. 3 The son^t of Uzzi: Izrahiah. And the sons of Izrahiah: Michael, Obadiah, Joel, and Isshiah, five, all of them chiefs; 4 and along with them, by their generations, according to their ancestral houses, were units of the fighting force, thirty-six thousand, for they had many wives and sons. 5 Their kindred belonging to all the families of Issachar were in all eighty-seven thousand mighty warriors, enrolled by genealogy.

K. *The family of Benjamin*

6 The sons of Benjamin: Bela, Becher, and Jediael, three. 7 The sons of Bela: Ezbon, Uzzi, Uzziel, Jerimoth, and Iri, five, heads of ancestral houses, mighty warriors; and their enrollment by genealogies was twenty-two thousand thirty-four. 8 The sons of Becher: Zemirah, Joash, Eliezer, Elioenai, Omri, Jeremoth, Abijah, Anathoth, and Alemeth. All these were the sons of Becher; 9 and their enrollment by genealogies, according to their generations, as heads of their ancestral houses, mighty warriors, was twenty thousand two hundred. 10 The sons of Jediael: Bilhan. And the sons of Bilhan: Jeush, Benjamin, Ehud, Chenaanah, Zethan, Tarshish, and Ahishahar. 11 All these were the sons of Jediael according to the heads of their ancestral houses, mighty warriors, seventeen thousand two hundred, ready for service in war. 12 And Shuppim and Huppim were the sons of Ir, Hushim the son^t of Aher.

---

^r Or *Dobrath* ^s Syr Compare Vg: Heb *And to the sons* ^t Heb *sons*

6.67
Josh 21.21

6.68
see
Josh 21.22-35
where some
names are
differently
given

6.73
see
Josh 21.29;
19.21
6.76
v. 62
6.77
v. 63

7.1
Gen 46.13;
Num 26.23
7.2
2 Sam 24.1, 2

7.5
1 Chr 6.62,
72

7.6
Gen 46.21;
Num 26.38;
1 Chr 8.1-40

7.12
Num 26.39

7.6 *sons of Benjamin.* A second genealogy for Benjamin appears in 8.1–40. There is a textual question as to whether Zebulun, whose genealogy is otherwise missing, originally appeared here instead of Benjamin. The names *Zebulun* and *Benjamin* are much closer in the Hebrew than in the English.

7.12 Since the genealogy of Dan is missing, some scholars think that the text here originally read, "the sons of Dan, Hushim his one son," which is in accord with Gen 46.23 ("the sons of Dan: Hushim" — NRSV footnote). Chronicles presents a number of textual problems.

L. *The family of Naphtali*

7.13
Gen 46.24

13 The descendants of Naphtali: Jahziel, Guni, Jezer, and Shallum, the descendants of Bilhah.

M. *The family of Manasseh*

14 The sons of Manasseh: Asriel, whom his Aramean concubine bore; she bore Machir the father of Gilead. 15 And Machir took a wife for Huppim and for Shuppim. The name of his sister was Maacah. And the name of the second was Zelophehad; and Zelophehad had daughters. 16 Maacah the wife of Machir bore a son, and she named him Peresh; the name of his brother was Sheresh; and his sons were Ulam and Rekem.

7.17
1 Sam 12.11

17 The son[u] of Ulam: Bedan. These were the sons of Gilead son of Machir, son of Manasseh. 18 And his sister Hammolecheth bore Ishhod, Abiezer, and Mahlah. 19 The sons of Shemida were Ahian, Shechem, Likhi, and Aniam.

N. *The family of Ephraim*

7.20
Num 26.35

20 The sons of Ephraim: Shuthelah, and Bered his son, Tahath his son, Eleadah his son, Tahath his son, 21 Zabad his son, Shuthelah his son, and Ezer and Elead. Now the people of Gath, who were born in the land, killed them, because they came down to raid their cattle. 22 And their father Ephraim mourned many days, and his brothers came to comfort him. 23 Ephraim[v] went in to his wife, and she conceived and bore a son; and he named him Beriah, because disaster[w] had befallen his house.

7.24
Josh 16.3, 5

24 His daughter was Sheerah, who built both Lower and Upper Beth-horon, and Uzzen-sheerah. 25 Rephah was his son, Resheph his son, Telah his son, Tahan his son, 26 Ladan his son, Ammihud his son, Elishama his son, 27 Nun[x] his son, Joshua his son. 28 Their possessions and settlements were Bethel and its towns, and eastward Naaran, and westward Gezer and

7.27
Ex 17.9-14;
24.13
7.28
Josh 16.7

its towns, Shechem and its towns, as far as Ayyah and its towns; 29 also along the borders of the Manassites, Beth-shean and its towns, Taanach and its towns, Megiddo and its towns, Dor and its towns. In these lived the sons of Joseph son of Israel.

O. *The family of Asher*

7.30
Gen 46.17;
Num 26.44

30 The sons of Asher: Imnah, Ishvah, Ishvi, Beriah, and their sister Serah. 31 The sons of Beriah: Heber and Malchiel, who was the father of Birzaith. 32 Heber became the father of Japhlet, Shomer, Hotham, and their sister Shua. 33 The sons of Japhlet: Pasach, Bimhal, and Ashvath. These are the sons of Japhlet. 34 The sons of Shemer: Ahi, Rohgah, Hubbah, and Aram. 35 The sons of Helem[y] his brother: Zophah, Imna, Shelesh, and Amal. 36 The sons of Zophah: Suah, Harnepher, Shual, Beri, Imrah, 37 Bezer, Hod, Shamma, Shilshah, Ithran, and Beera. 38 The sons of Jether: Jephunneh, Pispa, and Ara. 39 The sons of Ulla: Arah, Hanniel,

7.40
v. 30

and Rizia. 40 All of these were men of Asher, heads of ancestral houses, select mighty warriors, chief of the princes. Their number enrolled by genealogies, for service in war, was twenty-six thousand men.

P. *The family of Benjamin*

8.1
Gen 46.21;
1 Chr 7.6

8 Benjamin became the father of Bela his firstborn, Ashbel the second, Aharah the third, 2 Nohah the fourth, and Rapha the fifth. 3 And Bela

---

u Heb *sons* v Heb *He* w Heb *beraah* x Here spelled *Non*; see Ex 33.11 y Or *Hotham*; see 7.32

7.15 *Zelophehad* had five daughters and no sons. In Num 27.1ff the daughters asked Moses if the female descendants could inherit the property of their father. This became standard practice. This rule was later changed (Num 36.2ff) to require female descendants

to marry within their own tribe so that their offspring would be of the same tribe, thus preventing land from going to other tribes or to strangers.
8.1 The lineage of Benjamin, which began in 7.6–12, is taken up again in this chapter. Its impor-

had sons: Addar, Gera, Abihud,[z] 4 Abishua, Naaman, Ahoah, 5 Gera, Shephuphan, and Huram. 6 These are the sons of Ehud (they were heads of ancestral houses of the inhabitants of Geba, and they were carried into exile to Manahath): 7 Naaman,[a] Ahijah, and Gera, that is, Heglam,[b] who became the father of Uzza and Ahihud. 8 And Shaharaim had sons in the country of Moab after he had sent away his wives Hushim and Baara. 9 He had sons by his wife Hodesh: Jobab, Zibia, Mesha, Malcam, 10 Jeuz, Sachia, and Mirmah. These were his sons, heads of ancestral houses. 11 He also had sons by Hushim: Abitub and Elpaal. 12 The sons of Elpaal: Eber, Misham, and Shemed, who built Ono and Lod with its towns, 13 and Beriah and Shema (they were heads of ancestral houses of the inhabitants of Aijalon, who put to flight the inhabitants of Gath); 14 and Ahio, Shashak, and Jeremoth. 15 Zebadiah, Arad, Eder, 16 Michael, Ishpah, and Joha were sons of Beriah. 17 Zebadiah, Meshullam, Hizki, Heber, 18 Ishmerai, Izliah, and Jobab were the sons of Elpaal. 19 Jakim, Zichri, Zabdi, 20 Elienai, Zillethai, Eliel, 21 Adaiah, Beraiah, and Shimrath were the sons of Shimei. 22 Ishpan, Eber, Eliel, 23 Abdon, Zichri, Hanan, 24 Hananiah, Elam, Anthothijah, 25 Iphdeiah, and Penuel were the sons of Shashak. 26 Shamsherai, Shehariah, Athaliah, 27 Jaareshiah, Elijah, and Zichri were the sons of Jeroham. 28 These were the heads of ancestral houses, according to their generations, chiefs. These lived in Jerusalem.

29 Jeiel[c] the father of Gibeon lived in Gibeon, and the name of his wife was Maacah. 30 His firstborn son: Abdon, then Zur, Kish, Baal,[d] Nadab, 31 Gedor, Ahio, Zecher, 32 and Mikloth, who became the father of Shimeah. Now these also lived opposite their kindred in Jerusalem, with their kindred. 33 Ner became the father of Kish, Kish of Saul,[e] Saul[e] of Jonathan, Malchishua, Abinadab, and Esh-baal; 34 and the son of Jonathan was Merib-baal; and Merib-baal became the father of Micah. 35 The sons of Micah: Pithon, Melech, Tarea, and Ahaz. 36 Ahaz became the father of Jehoaddah; and Jehoaddah became the father of Alemeth, Azmaveth, and Zimri; Zimri became the father of Moza. 37 Moza became the father of Binea; Raphah was his son, Eleasah his son, Azel his son. 38 Azel had six sons, and these are their names: Azrikam, Bocheru, Ishmael, Sheariah, Obadiah, and Hanan; all these were the sons of Azel. 39 The sons of his brother Eshek: Ulam his firstborn, Jeush the second, and Eliphelet the third. 40 The sons of Ulam were mighty warriors, archers, having many children and grandchildren, one hundred fifty. All these were Benjaminites.

Q. The families in Jerusalem

9 So all Israel was enrolled by genealogies; and these are written in the Book of the Kings of Israel. And Judah was taken into exile in Babylon because of their unfaithfulness. 2 Now the first to live again in their possessions in their towns were Israelites, priests, Levites, and temple servants.

3 And some of the people of Judah, Benjamin, Ephraim, and Manas-

z Or *father of Ehud*; see 8.6   a Heb *and Naaman*   b Or *he carried them into exile*   c Compare 9.35: Heb lacks *Jeiel*   d Gk Ms adds *Ner*; Compare 8.33 and 9.36   e Or *Shaul*

Margin references:
8.6 / 1 Chr 2.52
8.13 / v. 21
8.21 / v. 13
8.29 / 1 Chr 9.35
8.33 / 1 Chr 9.35-38
8.34 / 2 Sam 9.12
9.1 / 1 Chr 5.25, 26
9.2 / Neh 11.3-22; Ezra 2.43; 8.20
9.3 / Neh 11.1

---

tance springs from the fact that Saul, the first king of Israel (cf. v. 33) came from this tribe. Moreover, the people of Benjamin supported the Davidic monarchy, occupied parts of Jerusalem, were taken into the captivity with Judah, and returned from the captivity to repopulate the land.
8.33 *Esh-baal.* See note on 2 Sam 2.8.
8.34 *Merib-baal,* or, "Mephibosheth." See note on 2 Sam 4.4. The writer traces the descendants of Jonathan for about ten generations. While the other sons of Saul are named, their offspring are omitted. This may be due to David's commitment to Jonathan and

his desire to honor his friend.
9.1 The writer reminds us that Judah was taken captive to Babylon as a result of unfaithfulness and transgressions. No one should ever accuse God of injustice or suppose that his mercies have failed to protect his people. God does not hesitate to chastise believers for their sins. *the Book of the Kings of Israel* refers to court records, not to the books of 1 and 2 Kings.
9.3 Throughout the time of the divided kingdom, people from the northern kingdom who were dissatisfied with the paganism migrated to Judah and Jerusa-

seh lived in Jerusalem: 4 Uthai son of Ammihud, son of Omri, son of Imri, son of Bani, from the sons of Perez son of Judah. 5 And of the Shilonites: Asaiah the firstborn, and his sons. 6 Of the sons of Zerah: Jeuel and their kin, six hundred ninety. 7 Of the Benjaminites: Sallu son of Meshullam, son of Hodaviah, son of Hassenuah, 8 Ibneiah son of Jeroham, Elah son of Uzzi, son of Michri, and Meshullam son of Shephatiah, son of Reuel, son of Ibnijah; 9 and their kindred according to their generations, nine hundred fifty-six. All these were heads of families according to their ancestral houses.

9.10
Neh 11.10-14

10 Of the priests: Jedaiah, Jehoiarib, Jachin, 11 and Azariah son of Hilkiah, son of Meshullam, son of Zadok, son of Meraioth, son of Ahitub, the chief officer of the house of God; 12 and Adaiah son of Jeroham, son of Pashhur, son of Malchijah, and Maasai son of Adiel, son of Jahzerah, son of Meshullam, son of Meshillemith, son of Immer; 13 besides their kindred, heads of their ancestral houses, one thousand seven hundred sixty, qualified for the work of the service of the house of God.

9.14
Neh 11.15-19

14 Of the Levites: Shemaiah son of Hasshub, son of Azrikam, son of Hashabiah, of the sons of Merari; 15 and Bakbakkar, Heresh, Galal, and Mattaniah son of Mica, son of Zichri, son of Asaph; 16 and Obadiah son of Shemaiah, son of Galal, son of Jeduthun, and Berechiah son of Asa, son of Elkanah, who lived in the villages of the Netophathites.

9.18
Ezek 46.1, 2

17 The gatekeepers were: Shallum, Akkub, Talmon, Ahiman; and their kindred Shallum was the chief, 18 stationed previously in the king's gate on the east side. These were the gatekeepers of the camp of the Levites. 19 Shallum son of Kore, son of Ebiasaph, son of Korah, and his kindred of his ancestral house, the Korahites, were in charge of the work of the service, guardians of the thresholds of the tent, as their ancestors had been in charge of the camp of the LORD, guardians of the entrance.

9.20
Num 25.7-13
9.21
1 Chr 26.2,
14
9.22
1 Chr 26.1, 2;
2 Chr 31.15,
18

20 And Phinehas son of Eleazar was chief over them in former times; the LORD was with him. 21 Zechariah son of Meshelemiah was gatekeeper at the entrance of the tent of meeting. 22 All these, who were chosen as gatekeepers at the thresholds, were two hundred twelve. They were enrolled by genealogies in their villages. David and the seer Samuel established them in their office of trust. 23 So they and their descendants were in charge of the gates of the house of the LORD, that is, the house of the tent, as guards. 24 The gatekeepers were on the four sides, east, west, north, and south; 25 and their kindred who were in their villages were obliged to come in every seven days, in turn, to be with them; 26 for the four chief gatekeepers, who were Levites, were in charge of the chambers and the treasures of the house of God. 27 And they would spend the night near the house of God; for on them lay the duty of watching, and they had charge of opening it every morning.

9.25
v. 16;
2 Kings 11.5,
7; 2 Chr 23.8
9.27
1 Chr 23.30-32

28 Some of them had charge of the utensils of service, for they were required to count them when they were brought in and taken out. 29 Others of them were appointed over the furniture, and over all the holy utensils, also over the choice flour, the wine, the oil, the incense, and the spices. 30 Others, of the sons of the priests, prepared the mixing of the spices, 31 and Mattithiah, one of the Levites, the firstborn of Shallum the Korahite, was in charge of making the flat cakes. 32 Also some of their kindred of the Kohathites had charge of the rows of bread, to prepare them for each sabbath.

9.29
1 Chr 23.29
9.30
Ex 30.23-25
9.32
Lev 24.8
9.33
31 Chr 6.31;
25.1;
Ps 134.1

33 Now these are the singers, the heads of ancestral houses of the

---

lem (see 2 Chr 11.16,17; 15.9). Their descendants were eventually taken in the Babylonian captivity, and some returned to the land in the days of Ezra and Nehemiah.
9.14ff The Israelites in Babylon had learned the lesson that infidelity to God leads to punishment. As they returned to the land, they were more careful to restore the true worship of God, beginning with a tabernacle (v. 19) and moving to the rebuilt temple. The priests lodged around the house of God to be near their religious duties (v. 27), and singers were employed night and day (v. 33), praising God continually.

Levites, living in the chambers of the temple free from other service, for they were on duty day and night. 34 These were heads of ancestral houses of the Levites, according to their generations; these leaders lived in Jerusalem.

R. *The family of Saul*

35   In Gibeon lived the father of Gibeon, Jeiel, and the name of his wife was Maacah. 36 His firstborn son was Abdon, then Zur, Kish, Baal, Ner, Nadab, 37 Gedor, Ahio, Zechariah, and Mikloth; 38 and Mikloth became the father of Shimeam; and these also lived opposite their kindred in Jerusalem, with their kindred. 39 Ner became the father of Kish, Kish of Saul, Saul of Jonathan, Malchishua, Abinadab, and Esh-baal; 40 and the son of Jonathan was Merib-baal; and Merib-baal became the father of Micah. 41 The sons of Micah: Pithon, Melech, Tahrea, and Ahaz;*f* 42 and Ahaz became the father of Jarah, and Jarah of Alemeth, Azmaveth, and Zimri; and Zimri became the father of Moza. 43 Moza became the father of Binea; and Rephaiah was his son, Eleasah his son, Azel his son. 44 Azel had six sons, and these are their names: Azrikam, Bocheru, Ishmael, Sheariah, Obadiah, and Hanan; these were the sons of Azel.

9.35
1 Chr 8.29

9.39
1 Chr 8.33

9.41
1 Chr 8.35

II. *The reign of David (10.1–29.30)*

A. *Saul's closing days and death*

10 Now the Philistines fought against Israel; and the men of Israel fled before the Philistines, and fell slain on Mount Gilboa. 2 The Philistines overtook Saul and his sons; and the Philistines killed Jonathan and Abinadab and Malchishua, sons of Saul. 3 The battle pressed hard on Saul; and the archers found him, and he was wounded by the archers. 4 Then Saul said to his armor-bearer, "Draw your sword, and thrust me through with it, so that these uncircumcised may not come and make sport of me." But his armor-bearer was unwilling, for he was terrified. So Saul took his own sword and fell on it. 5 When his armor-bearer saw that Saul was dead, he also fell on his sword and died. 6 Thus Saul died; he and his three sons and all his house died together. 7 When all the men of Israel who were in the valley saw that the army*g* had fled and that Saul and his sons were dead, they abandoned their towns and fled; and the Philistines came and occupied them.

8   The next day when the Philistines came to strip the dead, they found Saul and his sons fallen on Mount Gilboa. 9 They stripped him and took his head and his armor, and sent messengers throughout the land of the Philistines to carry the good news to their idols and to the people. 10 They put his armor in the temple of their gods, and fastened his head in the temple of Dagon. 11 But when all Jabesh-gilead heard everything that the Philistines had done to Saul, 12 all the valiant warriors got up and took away the body of Saul and the bodies of his sons, and brought them to Jabesh. Then they buried their bones under the oak in Jabesh, and fasted seven days.

13   So Saul died for his unfaithfulness; he was unfaithful to the LORD in that he did not keep the command of the LORD; moreover, he had consulted a medium, seeking guidance, 14 and did not seek guidance from

10.1
1 Sam 31.1, 2

10.4
cf.
1 Sam 31.4-7

10.10
1 Sam 31.10

10.13
1 Sam 13.13;
15.23; 28.7
10.14
1 Sam 15.28;
1 Chr 12.23

---

f Compare 8.35: Heb lacks *and Ahaz*   *g* Heb *they*

9.40 *Merib-baal.* See note on 8.34.
10.1 The writer of 1 Chronicles now begins to tell the history of the nation of Judah, beginning with the kingship of Saul.
10.10 1 Sam 31.10 says the body of Saul was fastened to the wall of Beth-shan and his armor was placed in the temple of Astarte. An added detail is

given in this account: Saul's head was put in Dagon's temple (one of four Canaanite temples).
10.13 *he had consulted a medium.* See 1 Sam 28. Saul came to his tragic end, not because God had deserted him; rather, because Saul had deserted God.
10.14 God did not put Saul to death. That was done by the enemy and by Saul himself. Yet it happened

the LORD. Therefore the LORD *h* put him to death and turned the kingdom over to David son of Jesse.

B. *David made king of all Israel*

1. *The capture of Jerusalem*

11 Then all Israel gathered together to David at Hebron and said, "See, we are your bone and flesh. 2 For some time now, even while Saul was king, it was you who commanded the army of Israel. The LORD your God said to you: It is you who shall be shepherd of my people Israel, you who shall be ruler over my people Israel." 3 So all the elders of Israel came to the king at Hebron, and David made a covenant with them at Hebron before the LORD. And they anointed David king over Israel, according to the word of the LORD by Samuel.

4 David and all Israel marched to Jerusalem, that is Jebus, where the Jebusites were, the inhabitants of the land. 5 The inhabitants of Jebus said to David, "You will not come in here." Nevertheless David took the stronghold of Zion, now the city of David. 6 David had said, "Whoever attacks the Jebusites first shall be chief and commander." And Joab son of Zeruiah went up first, so he became chief. 7 David resided in the stronghold; therefore it was called the city of David. 8 He built the city all around, from the Millo in complete circuit; and Joab repaired the rest of the city. 9 And David became greater and greater, for the LORD of hosts was with him.

2. *David's mighty heroes*

10 Now these are the chiefs of David's warriors, who gave him strong support in his kingdom, together with all Israel, to make him king, according to the word of the LORD concerning Israel. 11 This is an account of David's mighty warriors: Jashobeam, son of Hachmoni, *i* was chief of the Three; *j* he wielded his spear against three hundred whom he killed at one time.

12 And next to him among the three warriors was Eleazar son of Dodo, the Ahohite. 13 He was with David at Pas-dammim when the Philistines were gathered there for battle. There was a plot of ground full of barley. Now the people had fled from the Philistines, 14 but he and David took their stand in the middle of the plot, defended it, and killed the Philistines; and the LORD saved them by a great victory.

15 Three of the thirty chiefs went down to the rock to David at the cave of Adullam, while the army of Philistines was encamped in the valley of Rephaim. 16 David was then in the stronghold; and the garrison of the Philistines was then at Bethlehem. 17 David said longingly, "O that someone would give me water to drink from the well of Bethlehem that is by the gate!" 18 Then the Three broke through the camp of the Philistines, and drew water from the well of Bethlehem that was by the gate, and they brought it to David. But David would not drink of it; he poured it out to the LORD, 19 and said, "My God forbid that I should do this. Can I drink the blood of these men? For at the risk of their lives they brought it." Therefore he would not drink it. The three warriors did these things.

20 Now Abishai, *k* the brother of Joab, was chief of the Thirty. *l*

11.1	2 Sam 5.1
11.2	2 Sam 5.2; Ps 78.71
11.3	2 Sam 5.3; 1 Sam 16.1, 12, 13
11.4	Judg 1.21; 19.10
11.6	2 Sam 8.16
11.9	2 Sam 3.1
11.10	2 Sam 23.8-39; v. 3
11.11	2 Sam 23.8
11.13	2 Sam 23.11, 12
11.15	2 Sam 23.13; 1 Chr 14.9
11.20	2 Sam 23.18

h Heb *he*   *i* Or *a Hachmonite*   *j* Compare 2 Sam 23.8: Heb *Thirty* or *captains*   *k* Gk Vg Tg Compare 2 Sam 23.18: Heb *Abshai*   *l* Syr: Heb *Three*

"according to the definite plan and foreknowledge of God" (Acts 2.23). Disobedience has fatal consequences; however great and powerful anyone may be, no one is exempted from the judgment of God. The ruin of Saul was a triumph of divine justice.
11.9 The reason David *became greater and greater*

was that God was with him. Whatever success anyone attains in this life is from God. He sets up and pulls down as he pleases. And the one who gives it can also take it away when pride, disobedience, or carelessness overtakes the one God has blessed.

mand. 33 Of Zebulun, fifty thousand seasoned troops, equipped for battle with all the weapons of war, to help David*v* with singleness of purpose. 34 Of Naphtali, a thousand commanders, with whom there were thirty-seven thousand armed with shield and spear. 35 Of the Danites, twenty-eight thousand six hundred equipped for battle. 36 Of Asher, forty thousand seasoned troops ready for battle. 37 Of the Reubenites and Gadites and the half-tribe of Manasseh from beyond the Jordan, one hundred twenty thousand armed with all the weapons of war.

38 All these, warriors arrayed in battle order, came to Hebron with full intent to make David king over all Israel; likewise all the rest of Israel were of a single mind to make David king. 39 They were there with David for three days, eating and drinking, for their kindred had provided for them. 40 And also their neighbors, from as far away as Issachar and Zebulun and Naphtali, came bringing food on donkeys, camels, mules, and oxen — abundant provisions of meal, cakes of figs, clusters of raisins, wine, oil, oxen, and sheep, for there was joy in Israel.

C. David and the ark of the covenant

1. The removal of the ark from Kiriath-jearim to Obed-edom

13 David consulted with the commanders of the thousands and of the hundreds, with every leader. 2 David said to the whole assembly of Israel, "If it seems good to you, and if it is the will of the LORD our God, let us send abroad to our kindred who remain in all the land of Israel, including the priests and Levites in the cities that have pasture lands, that they may come together to us. 3 Then let us bring again the ark of our God to us; for we did not turn to it in the days of Saul." 4 The whole assembly agreed to do so, for the thing pleased all the people.

5 So David assembled all Israel from the Shihor of Egypt to Lebo-hamath, to bring the ark of God from Kiriath-jearim. 6 And David and all Israel went up to Baalah, that is, to Kiriath-jearim, which belongs to Judah, to bring up from there the ark of God, the LORD, who is enthroned on the cherubim, which is called by his*w* name. 7 They carried the ark of God on a new cart, from the house of Abinadab, and Uzzah and Ahio*x* were driving the cart. 8 David and all Israel were dancing before God with all their might, with song and lyres and harps and tambourines and cymbals and trumpets.

9 When they came to the threshing floor of Chidon, Uzzah put out his hand to hold the ark, for the oxen shook it. 10 The anger of the LORD was kindled against Uzzah; he struck him down because he put out his hand to the ark; and he died there before God. 11 David was angry because the LORD had burst out against Uzzah; so that place is called Perez-uzzah*y* to this day. 12 David was afraid of God that day; he said, "How can I bring the ark of God into my care?" 13 So David did not take the ark into his care into the city of David; he took it instead to the house of Obed-edom the Gittite. 14 The ark of God remained with the household of Obed-edom

v Gk: Heb lacks *David*   *w* Heb lacks *his*   *x* Or *and his brother*   *y* That is *Bursting Out Against Uzzah*

12.33	Ps 12.2
12.38	2 Sam 5.1-3
12.40	1 Sam 25.18
13.2	1 Sam 31.1; Isa 37.4
13.3	1 Sam 7.1, 2
13.5	2 Sam 6.1; 1 Chr 15.3; 1 Sam 6.21; 7.1
13.6	Josh 15.9; 2 Kings 19.15
13.7	1 Sam 7.1
13.8	2 Sam 6.5
13.9	2 Sam 6.6
13.10	1 Chr 15.13, 15
13.14	1 Chr 26.4, 5

12.38 Israel was now of a single mind to make David king. Their unity for David showed their opposition to Saul, who had lost their affection. No one can rule over a people for long who has lost the confidence of the people.
13.1 This part of David's story is not to be found in the book of Samuel. David proposed to bring the ark to Jerusalem so that the royal city might be the holy city. Saul had neglected the ark and thereby showed his neglect of God. David manifested a deep respect for the ark, showing that in his government he would use God's power to advance the cause of true religion.

Those who honor God are blessed by him; those who begin with the fear of God experience the favor of God.
13.9 For comments on Uzzah's error, see note on 2 Sam 6.6.
13.13 Despite the breach made by Uzzah's act, David should have gone ahead with his plan to bring the ark to Jerusalem. God's reproof to David for this failure was shown by the blessing that attended the house of Obed-edom, into whose care the ark was committed.

in his house three months, and the Lord blessed the household of Obed-edom and all that he had.

2. *The prosperity of David*

a. *His palace and family*

14 King Hiram of Tyre sent messengers to David, along with cedar logs, and masons and carpenters to build a house for him. ²David then perceived that the Lord had established him as king over Israel, and that his kingdom was highly exalted for the sake of his people Israel.

3 David took more wives in Jerusalem, and David became the father of more sons and daughters. ⁴These are the names of the children whom he had in Jerusalem: Shammua, Shobab, and Nathan; Solomon, ⁵Ibhar, Elishua, and Elpelet; ⁶Nogah, Nepheg, and Japhia; ⁷Elishama, Beeliada, and Eliphelet.

b. *His defeats of the Philistines*

8 When the Philistines heard that David had been anointed king over all Israel, all the Philistines went up in search of David; and David heard of it and went out against them. ⁹Now the Philistines had come and made a raid in the valley of Rephaim. ¹⁰David inquired of God, "Shall I go up against the Philistines? Will you give them into my hand?" The Lord said to him, "Go up, and I will give them into your hand." ¹¹So he went up to Baal-perazim, and David defeated them there. David said, "God has burst out*ᶻ* against my enemies by my hand, like a bursting flood." Therefore that place is called Baal-perazim.*ᵃ* ¹²They abandoned their gods there, and at David's command they were burned.

13 Once again the Philistines made a raid in the valley. ¹⁴When David again inquired of God, God said to him, "You shall not go up after them; go around and come on them opposite the balsam trees. ¹⁵When you hear the sound of marching in the tops of the balsam trees, then go out to battle; for God has gone out before you to strike down the army of the Philistines." ¹⁶David did as God had commanded him, and they struck down the Philistine army from Gibeon to Gezer. ¹⁷The fame of David went out into all lands, and the Lord brought the fear of him on all nations.

3. *The bringing of the ark to Jerusalem*

a. *The preparations*

15 David*ᵇ* built houses for himself in the city of David, and he prepared a place for the ark of God and pitched a tent for it. ²Then David commanded that no one but the Levites were to carry the ark of God, for the Lord had chosen them to carry the ark of the Lord and to minister to him forever. ³David assembled all Israel in Jerusalem to bring up the ark of the Lord to its place, which he had prepared for it. ⁴Then David gathered together the descendants of Aaron and the Levites: ⁵of the sons of Kohath, Uriel the chief, with one hundred twenty of his kindred; ⁶of the sons of Merari, Asaiah the chief, with two hundred twenty of his kindred; ⁷of the sons of Gershom, Joel the chief, with one

ᶻ Heb *paraz*   *ᵃ* That is *Lord of Bursting Out*   *ᵇ* Heb *He*

Margin references:
14.1 / 2 Sam 5.11
14.4 / 1 Chr 3.5
14.8 / 2 Sam 5.17
14.9 / 1 Chr 11.15
14.13 / v. 9; / 2 Sam 5.22
14.14 / 2 Sam 5.23
14.16 / 2 Sam 5.25
14.17 / Josh 6.27; / 2 Chr 26.8; / Deut 2.25
15.1 / 1 Chr 16.1
15.2 / Num 4.15; / Deut 10.8; / 31.9
15.3 / 1 Kings 8.1; / 1 Chr 13.5

14.1 David summoned Hiram to sell him materials to build his palace. Hiram had a little kingdom; David had a large one. But David needed both the materials and the manual help Hiram could give.

14.2 David had waited a long time before the promise of Samuel that David would be king (1 Sam 16) was fulfilled. David now knew beyond a shadow of doubt that God had confirmed him in the kingship for the sake of Israel. This confirmation spurred him on to serve God with his whole heart.

14.10 David was king but he depended on God for

his instructions. Here he inquired from God as to what course of action he should take against the Philistines, who were challenging him to a war. God assured him of victory over the enemy and gave him a sign (v. 15). If God be for us, who can be against us (see Rom 8.31)?

15.1 David pitched a tent to house the ark, for as yet no temple had been constructed. The tent was probably built according to the pattern given by Moses, who obtained it from God (see also note on 16.39).

hundred thirty of his kindred; 8 of the sons of Elizaphan, Shemaiah the chief, with two hundred of his kindred; 9 of the sons of Hebron, Eliel the chief, with eighty of his kindred; 10 of the sons of Uzziel, Amminadab the chief, with one hundred twelve of his kindred.

11   David summoned the priests Zadok and Abiathar, and the Levites Uriel, Asaiah, Joel, Shemaiah, Eliel, and Amminadab. 12 He said to them, "You are the heads of families of the Levites; sanctify yourselves, you and your kindred, so that you may bring up the ark of the LORD, the God of Israel, to the place that I have prepared for it. 13 Because you did not carry it the first time,*c* the LORD our God burst out against us, because we did not give it proper care." 14 So the priests and the Levites sanctified themselves to bring up the ark of the LORD, the God of Israel. 15 And the Levites carried the ark of God on their shoulders with the poles, as Moses had commanded according to the word of the LORD.

b. *The appointment of the singers and musicians*

16   David also commanded the chiefs of the Levites to appoint their kindred as the singers to play on musical instruments, on harps and lyres and cymbals, to raise loud sounds of joy. 17 So the Levites appointed Heman son of Joel; and of his kindred Asaph son of Berechiah; and of the sons of Merari, their kindred, Ethan son of Kushaiah; 18 and with them their kindred of the second order, Zechariah, Jaaziel, Shemiramoth, Jehiel, Unni, Eliab, Benaiah, Maaseiah, Mattithiah, Eliphelehu, and Mikneiah, and the gatekeepers Obed-edom and Jeiel. 19 The singers Heman, Asaph, and Ethan were to sound bronze cymbals; 20 Zechariah, Aziel, Shemiramoth, Jehiel, Unni, Eliab, Maaseiah, and Benaiah were to play harps according to Alamoth; 21 but Mattithiah, Eliphelehu, Mikneiah, Obed-edom, Jeiel, and Azaziah were to lead with lyres according to the Sheminith. 22 Chenaniah, leader of the Levites in music, was to direct the music, for he understood it. 23 Berechiah and Elkanah were to be gatekeepers for the ark. 24 Shebaniah, Joshaphat, Nethanel, Amasai, Zechariah, Benaiah, and Eliezer, the priests, were to blow the trumpets before the ark of God. Obed-edom and Jehiah also were to be gatekeepers for the ark.

c. *David dancing before the ark*

25   So David and the elders of Israel, and the commanders of the thousands, went to bring up the ark of the covenant of the LORD from the house of Obed-edom with rejoicing. 26 And because God helped the Levites who were carrying the ark of the covenant of the LORD, they sacrificed seven bulls and seven rams. 27 David was clothed with a robe of fine linen, as also were all the Levites who were carrying the ark, and the singers, and Chenaniah the leader of the music of the singers; and David wore a linen ephod. 28 So all Israel brought up the ark of the covenant of the LORD with shouting, to the sound of the horn, trumpets, and cymbals, and made loud music on harps and lyres.

29   As the ark of the covenant of the LORD came to the city of David, Michal daughter of Saul looked out of the window, and saw King David leaping and dancing; and she despised him in her heart.

c Meaning of Heb uncertain

15.15 David now made a second effort to bring the ark to Jerusalem (see 1 Chr 13 for details about his first effort). This time the ark was carried on the shoulders of the Levites using the proper poles according to the commandment of God. When they arrived in the holy city, the ark was placed inside the tent David had pitched for it (16.1).
15.26 No doubt the Levites who carried the ark

were nervous about carrying the ark, for they remembered what had happened to Uzzah. Since they were doing the right thing, we are told that "God helped the Levites." If we are obedient to the Lord, things will go well for us.
15.29 See note on 2 Sam 6.16 on Michal's reaction to David's dancing before the Lord.

Margin references:

15.8
Ex 6.22
15.9
Ex 6.18

15.11
1 Chr 12.28;
1 Sam 22.20-23
15.12
Ex 19.14, 15;
2 Chr 35.6
15.13
2 Sam 6.3;
1 Chr 13.7,
10, 11
15.14
v. 12
15.15
Ex 25.14;
Num 4.5

15.16
1 Chr 25.1

15.17
1 Chr 6.33,
39, 44

15.24
v. 28;
1 Chr 16.6

15.25
2 Sam 6.12,
15;
1 Chr 13.13

15.28
1 Chr 13.8

15.29
2 Sam 6.16

d. *The offerings and the music*

16.1
2 Sam 6.17-19

16 They brought in the ark of God, and set it inside the tent that David had pitched for it; and they offered burnt offerings and offerings of well-being before God. 2 When David had finished offering the burnt offerings and the offerings of well-being, he blessed the people in the name of the LORD; 3 and he distributed to every person in Israel — man and woman alike — to each a loaf of bread, a portion of meat,*d* and a cake of raisins.

4 He appointed certain of the Levites as ministers before the ark of the LORD, to invoke, to thank, and to praise the LORD, the God of Israel.

16.5
Ps ch. 50; 73

5 Asaph was the chief, and second to him Zechariah, Jeiel, Shemiramoth, Jehiel, Mattithiah, Eliab, Benaiah, Obed-edom, and Jeiel, with harps and lyres; Asaph was to sound the cymbals, 6 and the priests Benaiah and Jahaziel were to blow trumpets regularly, before the ark of the covenant of God.

e. *David's psalm of gratitude*

16.7
2 Sam 23.1

7 Then on that day David first appointed the singing of praises to the LORD by Asaph and his kindred.

16.8
Ps 105.1-15

8 O give thanks to the LORD, call on his name,
    make known his deeds among the peoples.
9 Sing to him, sing praises to him,
    tell of all his wonderful works.
10 Glory in his holy name;
    let the hearts of those who seek the LORD rejoice.

16.11
Ps 24.6

11 Seek the LORD and his strength,
    seek his presence continually.

16.12
Ps 77.11;
78.43-68

12 Remember the wonderful works he has done,
    his miracles, and the judgments he uttered,
13 O offspring of his servant Israel,*e*
    children of Jacob, his chosen ones.

16.14
Isa 26.9

14 He is the LORD our God;
    his judgments are in all the earth.
15 Remember his covenant forever,
    the word that he commanded, for a thousand generations,

16.16
Gen 17.2;
26.3; 28.13;
35.11
16.17
Gen 35.11, 12

16 the covenant that he made with Abraham,
    his sworn promise to Isaac,
17 which he confirmed to Jacob as a statute,
    to Israel as an everlasting covenant,
18 saying, "To you I will give the land of Canaan
    as your portion for an inheritance."

16.19
Gen 34.30

19 When they were few in number,
    of little account, and strangers in the land,*f*
20 wandering from nation to nation,
    from one kingdom to another people,

16.21
Gen 12.17;
20.3;
Ex 7.15-18

21 he allowed no one to oppress them;
    he rebuked kings on their account,

d Compare Gk Syr Vg: Meaning of Heb uncertain   *e* Another reading is *Abraham* (compare Ps 105.6)
f Heb *in it*

16.4 Prayer consists of more than petitions and intercessions. Prayers are to be preceded by adoration of the Lord and thanksgiving for his provision and goodness.
16.8 This psalm of gratitude is found in Ps 105.1–15. Its preservation here and in Psalms assures us that repetition of praise is appropriate.

16.15 David's refrain about God's covenant is based on the assurance that God would keep his promise and do what he has said he would do. A covenant that is not intended to be kept is no covenant at all. Likewise, God expects us to keep the covenant promises we have made — to obey him in all things.

22 saying, "Do not touch my anointed ones;
        do my prophets no harm."

23 Sing to the LORD, all the earth.
        Tell of his salvation from day to day.
24 Declare his glory among the nations,
        his marvelous works among all the peoples.
25 For great is the LORD, and greatly to be praised;
        he is to be revered above all gods.
26 For all the gods of the peoples are idols,
        but the LORD made the heavens.
27 Honor and majesty are before him;
        strength and joy are in his place.

28 Ascribe to the LORD, O families of the peoples,
        ascribe to the LORD glory and strength.
29 Ascribe to the LORD the glory due his name;
        bring an offering, and come before him.
    Worship the LORD in holy splendor;
30   tremble before him, all the earth.
        The world is firmly established; it shall never be moved.
31 Let the heavens be glad, and let the earth rejoice,
        and let them say among the nations, "The LORD is king!"
32 Let the sea roar, and all that fills it;
        let the field exult, and everything in it.
33 Then shall the trees of the forest sing for joy
        before the LORD, for he comes to judge the earth.
34 O give thanks to the LORD, for he is good;
        for his steadfast love endures forever.
35 Say also:
    "Save us, O God of our salvation,
        and gather and rescue us from among the nations,
    that we may give thanks to your holy name,
        and glory in your praise.
36 Blessed be the LORD, the God of Israel,
        from everlasting to everlasting."
    Then all the people said "Amen!" and praised the LORD.

37 David left Asaph and his kinsfolk there before the ark of the
covenant of the LORD to minister regularly before the ark as each day
required, 38 and also Obed-edom and his[g] sixty-eight kinsfolk; while
Obed-edom son of Jeduthun and Hosah were to be gatekeepers. 39 And
he left the priest Zadok and his kindred the priests before the tabernacle
of the LORD in the high place that was at Gibeon, 40 to offer burnt offerings
to the LORD on the altar of burnt offering regularly, morning and evening,
according to all that is written in the law of the LORD that he commanded
Israel. 41 With them were Heman and Jeduthun, and the rest of those
chosen and expressly named to render thanks to the LORD, for his stead-

Cross-references (right margin):

16.23 Ps 96.1-13
16.25 Ps 48.1; 89.7
16.26 Ps 96.5
16.28 Ps 29.1, 2
16.31 Isa 49.13; Ps 93.1
16.32 Ps 98.7
16.34 Ps 106.1
16.35 Ps 106.47, 48
16.36 1 Kings 8.15; Deut 27.15
16.37 vv. 4, 5; 2 Chr 8.14
16.38 1 Chr 13.14; 26.10
16.39 1 Chr 15.11; 1 Kings 3.4
16.40 Ex 29.38; Num 28.3
16.41 1 Chr 6.33; 25.1-6; 2 Chr 5.13

g Gk Syr Vg: Heb their

16.25,26 *he is to be revered above all gods.* These other gods are idols; they are not real gods at all. Anything that people worship becomes a substitute for the true God. David wants all people to worship the one and only God, who is creator of all things. **16.36** Asaph and the singers had sung this song before the people in public. The people responded by saying "Amen" and by praising the Lord. The "Amen" represented their consent and concurrence. Unfortunately later events would demonstrate the transiency of their religious affections, for apostasy overtook the nation. A good start is no guarantee of perseverance. **16.39** *tabernacle . . . at Gibeon.* Apparently Israel had two sanctuaries in David's day: one was at Jerusalem with the ark (15.1; 16.1); the other was at Gibeon with the tent and its furniture (see also 21.29). One wonders why David did not consolidate worship in one place.

fast love endures forever. 42Heman and Jeduthun had with them trumpets and cymbals for the music, and instruments for sacred song. The sons of Jeduthun were appointed to the gate.

43   Then all the people departed to their homes, and David went home to bless his household.

D. *David's desire to build the temple*

1. *David's wish*

17 Now when David settled in his house, David said to the prophet Nathan, "I am living in a house of cedar, but the ark of the covenant of the LORD is under a tent." 2Nathan said to David, "Do all that you have in mind, for God is with you."

2. *God's disapproval and covenant*

3   But that same night the word of the LORD came to Nathan, saying: 4Go and tell my servant David: Thus says the LORD: You shall not build me a house to live in. 5For I have not lived in a house since the day I brought out Israel to this very day, but I have lived in a tent and a tabernacle.*h* 6Wherever I have moved about among all Israel, did I ever speak a word with any of the judges of Israel, whom I commanded to shepherd my people, saying, Why have you not built me a house of cedar? 7Now therefore thus you shall say to my servant David: Thus says the LORD of hosts: I took you from the pasture, from following the sheep, to be ruler over my people Israel; 8and I have been with you wherever you went, and have cut off all your enemies before you; and I will make for you a name, like the name of the great ones of the earth. 9I will appoint a place for my people Israel, and will plant them, so that they may live in their own place, and be disturbed no more; and evildoers shall wear them down no more, as they did formerly, 10from the time that I appointed judges over my people Israel; and I will subdue all your enemies.

Moreover I declare to you that the LORD will build you a house. 11When your days are fulfilled to go to be with your ancestors, I will raise up your offspring after you, one of your own sons, and I will establish his kingdom. 12He shall build a house for me, and I will establish his throne forever. 13I will be a father to him, and he shall be a son to me. I will not take my steadfast love from him, as I took it from him who was before you, 14but I will confirm him in my house and in my kingdom forever, and his throne shall be established forever. 15In accordance with all these words and all this vision, Nathan spoke to David.

3. *David's prayer*

16   Then King David went in and sat before the LORD, and said, "Who am I, O LORD God, and what is my house, that you have brought me thus far? 17And even this was a small thing in your sight, O God; you have also spoken of your servant's house for a great while to come. You regard

h Gk 2 Sam 7.6: Heb *but I have been from tent to tent and from tabernacle*

Cross references (margin):

17.1
2 Sam 7.1-29

17.4
1 Chr 28.2, 3
17.5
2 Sam 7.6
17.6
2 Sam 7.7

17.10
Judg 2.16

17.13
2 Sam 7.14,
15;
Heb 1.5
17.14
Lk 1.33

17.16
2 Sam 7.18

16.43   After David had carefully provided for public worship in Israel, he went home to maintain his own family worship.
17.4   David's intention to build the temple was good and God approved of that desire. But he did not wish David to be the builder nor was it to be done during his reign. When God's will was made plain to David through Nathan, he accepted the decision without complaint and began zealously to gather materials.
17.7   God reminded David that he was a mere shepherd boy who owed his power to God. God had overcome David's enemies and raised him to a high place.

He guaranteed him posterity, that from him would come kings who would forever sit on a throne. And best of all, David's son would build God a dwelling place, where the ark could rest and sacrifices be made in the divine name.
17.16   When David received God's message from the mouth of his servant Nathan, he responded in this classic prayer. He received the promises by faith and cordially embraced them. He acknowledged his unworthiness before God. He rejoiced that God was the God of Israel and magnified his name; Israel had nothing to fear with God on their side.

me as someone of high rank,[i] O LORD God! 18 And what more can David say to you for honoring your servant? You know your servant. 19 For your servant's sake, O LORD, and according to your own heart, you have done all these great deeds, making known all these great things. 20 There is no one like you, O LORD, and there is no God besides you, according to all that we have heard with our ears. 21 Who is like your people Israel, one nation on the earth whom God went to redeem to be his people, making for yourself a name for great and terrible things, in driving out nations before your people whom you redeemed from Egypt? 22 And you made your people Israel to be your people forever; and you, O LORD, became their God.

23   "And now, O LORD, as for the word that you have spoken concerning your servant and concerning his house, let it be established forever, and do as you have promised. 24 Thus your name will be established and magnified forever in the saying, 'The LORD of hosts, the God of Israel, is Israel's God'; and the house of your servant David will be established in your presence. 25 For you, my God, have revealed to your servant that you will build a house for him; therefore your servant has found it possible to pray before you. 26 And now, O LORD, you are God, and you have promised this good thing to your servant; 27 therefore may it please you to bless the house of your servant, that it may continue forever before you. For you, O LORD, have blessed and are blessed[j] forever."

E. The account of David's victories

18 Some time afterward, David attacked the Philistines and subdued them; he took Gath and its villages from the Philistines.
2   He defeated Moab, and the Moabites became subject to David and brought tribute.
3   David also struck down King Hadadezer of Zobah, toward Hamath,[i] as he went to set up a monument at the river Euphrates. 4 David took from him one thousand chariots, seven thousand cavalry, and twenty thousand foot soldiers. David hamstrung all the chariot horses, but left one hundred of them. 5 When the Arameans of Damascus came to help King Hadadezer of Zobah, David killed twenty-two thousand Arameans. 6 Then David put garrisons[k] in Aram of Damascus; and the Arameans became subject to David, and brought tribute. The LORD gave victory to David wherever he went. 7 David took the gold shields that were carried by the servants of Hadadezer, and brought them to Jerusalem. 8 From Tibhath and from Cun, cities of Hadadezer, David took a vast quantity of bronze; with it Solomon made the bronze sea and the pillars and the vessels of bronze.
9   When King Tou of Hamath heard that David had defeated the whole army of King Hadadezer of Zobah, 10 he sent his son Hadoram to King David, to greet him and to congratulate him, because he had fought against Hadadezer and defeated him. Now Hadadezer had often been at war with Tou. He sent all sorts of articles of gold, of silver, and of bronze; 11 these also King David dedicated to the LORD, together with the silver and gold that he had carried off from all the nations, from Edom, Moab, the Ammonites, the Philistines, and Amalek.
12   Abishai son of Zeruiah killed eighteen thousand Edomites in the Valley of Salt. 13 He put garrisons in Edom; and all the Edomites became subject to David. And the LORD gave victory to David wherever he went.

17.19
Isa 37.35

17.22
Ex 19.5, 6

17.24
Ps 46.7, 11

18.1
2 Sam 8.1-18

18.5
1 Chr 19.6

18.8
1 Kings 7.15, 23;
2 Chr 4.12, 15, 16

18.10
2 Sam 10.16

18.12
2 Sam 8.13

---

[i] Meaning of Heb uncertain   [j] Or *and it is blessed*   [k] Gk Vg 2 Sam 8.6 Compare Syr: Heb lacks *garrisons*

18.1   Following David's sweet fellowship with God, he rose to subdue the enemies of Israel. He succeeded against the Philistines, the Moabites, and Hadadezer. When the Arameans of Damascus intervened, they were defeated too.

18.11   The strength of David's commitment to God was demonstrated when Tou, the king of Hamath, sent him great wealth, for David set these treasures apart for God.

14 So David reigned over all Israel; and he administered justice and equity to all his people. 15 Joab son of Zeruiah was over the army; Jehoshaphat son of Ahilud was recorder; 16 Zadok son of Ahitub and Ahimelech son of Abiathar were priests; Shavsha was secretary; 17 Benaiah son of Jehoiada was over the Cherethites and the Pelethites; and David's sons were the chief officials in the service of the king.

19 Some time afterward, King Nahash of the Ammonites died, and his son succeeded him. 2 David said, "I will deal loyally with Hanun son of Nahash, for his father dealt loyally with me." So David sent messengers to console him concerning his father. When David's servants came to Hanun in the land of the Ammonites, to console him, 3 the officials of the Ammonites said to Hanun, "Do you think, because David has sent consolers to you, that he is honoring your father? Have not his servants come to you to search and to overthrow and to spy out the land?" 4 So Hanun seized David's servants, shaved them, cut off their garments in the middle at their hips, and sent them away; 5 and they departed. When David was told about the men, he sent messengers to them, for they felt greatly humiliated. The king said, "Remain at Jericho until your beards have grown, and then return."

6 When the Ammonites saw that they had made themselves odious to David, Hanun and the Ammonites sent a thousand talents of silver to hire chariots and cavalry from Mesopotamia, from Aram-maacah and from Zobah. 7 They hired thirty-two thousand chariots and the king of Maacah with his army, who came and camped before Medeba. And the Ammonites were mustered from their cities and came to battle. 8 When David heard of it, he sent Joab and all the army of the warriors. 9 The Ammonites came out and drew up in battle array at the entrance of the city, and the kings who had come were by themselves in the open country.

10 When Joab saw that the line of battle was set against him both in front and in the rear, he chose some of the picked men of Israel and arrayed them against the Arameans; 11 the rest of his troops he put in the charge of his brother Abishai, and they were arrayed against the Ammonites. 12 He said, "If the Arameans are too strong for me, then you shall help me; but if the Ammonites are too strong for you, then I will help you. 13 Be strong, and let us be courageous for our people and for the cities of our God; and may the LORD do what seems good to him." 14 So Joab and the troops who were with him advanced toward the Arameans for battle; and they fled before him. 15 When the Ammonites saw that the Arameans fled, they likewise fled before Abishai, Joab's brother, and entered the city. Then Joab came to Jerusalem.

16 But when the Arameans saw that they had been defeated by Israel, they sent messengers and brought out the Arameans who were beyond the Euphrates, with Shophach the commander of the army of Hadadezer at their head. 17 When David was informed, he gathered all Israel together, crossed the Jordan, came to them, and drew up his forces against them. When David set the battle in array against the Arameans, they fought with him. 18 The Arameans fled before Israel; and David killed seven thousand Aramean charioteers and forty thousand foot soldiers, and also killed Shophach the commander of their army. 19 When the servants of Hadadezer saw that they had been defeated by Israel, they made peace with David, and became subject to him. So the Arameans were not willing to help the Ammonites any more.

18.15
1 Chr 11.6

18.17
2 Sam 8.18

19.1
2 Sam 10.1

19.3
2 Sam 10.3

19.4
2 Sam 10.4

19.6
1 Chr 18.5, 9

19.7
Num 21.30;
Josh 13.9, 16
19.8
2 Sam 10.7

19.11
2 Sam 10.10

19.12
2 Sam 10.11

19.14
2 Sam 10.13

19.16
2 Sam 10.15

19.17
2 Sam 10.17

19.18
2 Sam 10.18

19.19
2 Sam 10.19

18.14 David was not so committed to the expansion of his kingdom that he forgot the home base. He pursued the administration of justice for his people.
19.4 David's kindness in sending messengers of comfort was interpreted as an act of aggression, as an attempt to seize Hanun's territory. They prepared to war against David. Good acts can be misunderstood and the hand of friendship can be rebuffed.
19.19 The Ammonites had hired the Arameans to help them against Israel. When David defeated the Arameans, they sought peace and paid tribute.

20 In the spring of the year, the time when kings go out to battle, Joab led out the army, ravaged the country of the Ammonites, and came and besieged Rabbah. But David remained at Jerusalem. Joab attacked Rabbah, and overthrew it. 2 David took the crown of Milcom[l] from his head; he found that it weighed a talent of gold, and in it was a precious stone; and it was placed on David's head. He also brought out the booty of the city, a very great amount. 3 He brought out the people who were in it, and set them to work[m] with saws and iron picks and axes.[n] Thus David did to all the cities of the Ammonites. Then David and all the people returned to Jerusalem.

4 After this, war broke out with the Philistines at Gezer; then Sibbecai the Hushathite killed Sippai, who was one of the descendants of the giants; and the Philistines were subdued. 5 Again there was war with the Philistines; and Elhanan son of Jair killed Lahmi the brother of Goliath the Gittite, the shaft of whose spear was like a weaver's beam. 6 Again there was war at Gath, where there was a man of great size, who had six fingers on each hand, and six toes on each foot, twenty-four in number; he also was descended from the giants. 7 When he taunted Israel, Jonathan son of Shimea, David's brother, killed him. 8 These were descended from the giants in Gath; they fell by the hand of David and his servants.

F. *David's numbering of the people*

1. *The census*

21 Satan stood up against Israel, and incited David to count the people of Israel. 2 So David said to Joab and the commanders of the army, "Go, number Israel, from Beer-sheba to Dan, and bring me a report, so that I may know their number." 3 But Joab said, "May the LORD increase the number of his people a hundredfold! Are they not, my lord the king, all of them my lord's servants? Why then should my lord require this? Why should he bring guilt on Israel?" 4 But the king's word prevailed against Joab. So Joab departed and went throughout all Israel, and came back to Jerusalem. 5 Joab gave the total count of the people to David. In all Israel there were one million one hundred thousand men who drew the sword, and in Judah four hundred seventy thousand who drew the sword. 6 But he did not include Levi and Benjamin in the numbering, for the king's command was abhorrent to Joab.

2. *The plague as a punishment*

7 But God was displeased with this thing, and he struck Israel. 8 David said to God, "I have sinned greatly in that I have done this thing. But now, I pray you, take away the guilt of your servant; for I have done very foolishly." 9 The LORD spoke to Gad, David's seer, saying, 10 "Go and say to David, 'Thus says the LORD: Three things I offer you; choose one of them, so that I may do it to you.'" 11 So Gad came to David and said to him, "Thus says the LORD, 'Take your choice: 12 either three years of famine; or three months of devastation by your foes, while the sword of

Cross-references (right column):
20.1ff 2 Sam 11.1; 12.26
20.2 2 Sam 12.30, 31
20.3 2 Sam 12.31
20.4 2 Sam 21.18
20.5 2 Sam 21.19; 1 Sam 17.7
20.6 2 Sam 21.20
21.1 2 Sam 24.1-25
21.2 1 Chr 27.23
21.3 Deut 1.11
21.5 cf. 2 Sam 24.9
21.6 1 Chr 27.24
21.8 2 Sam 24.10; 12.13
21.10 1 Chr 29.29; 1 Sam 9.9
21.12 2 Sam 24.13

---

[l] Gk Vg See 1 Kings 11.5, 33: MT *of their king*   [m] Compare 2 Sam 12.31: Heb *and he sawed*
[n] Compare 2 Sam 12.31: Heb *saws*

20.1–3 In general the chronicler follows the history of Judah as found in 2 Samuel and 1 and 2 Kings. The author features the good kings of Judah and says little about the northern kingdom except when it impinged on Judah. The author paints a positive rather than a negative picture, leaving out some material given in 2 Samuel, such as David's struggle with Saul and his seven-year stay at Hebron, David's adultery with Bathsheba, and Solomon's idolatry and punishment. He does mention David's disobedience in taking the

census and God's chastisement of him. Chronicles pays close attention to the temple, its importance, its personnel, and the rituals.
21.1 *Satan* (meaning "the adversary") is mentioned in the Bible by more than thirty different names and titles. Each one deals with some aspect about him or his work (see note on Ezek 28.12). See note on 2 Sam 24.1 on how both God and Satan were involved in David's numbering of the people.

your enemies overtakes you; or three days of the sword of the LORD, pestilence on the land, and the angel of the LORD destroying throughout all the territory of Israel.' Now decide what answer I shall return to the one who sent me." 13 Then David said to Gad, "I am in great distress; let me fall into the hand of the LORD, for his mercy is very great; but let me not fall into human hands."

14   So the LORD sent a pestilence on Israel; and seventy thousand persons fell in Israel. 15 And God sent an angel to Jerusalem to destroy it; but when he was about to destroy it, the LORD took note and relented concerning the calamity; he said to the destroying angel, "Enough! Stay your hand." The angel of the LORD was then standing by the threshing floor of Ornan the Jebusite. 16 David looked up and saw the angel of the LORD standing between earth and heaven, and in his hand a drawn sword stretched out over Jerusalem. Then David and the elders, clothed in sackcloth, fell on their faces. 17 And David said to God, "Was it not I who gave the command to count the people? It is I who have sinned and done very wickedly. But these sheep, what have they done? Let your hand, I pray, O LORD my God, be against me and against my father's house; but do not let your people be plagued!"

18   Then the angel of the LORD commanded Gad to tell David that he should go up and erect an altar to the LORD on the threshing floor of Ornan the Jebusite. 19 So David went up following Gad's instructions, which he had spoken in the name of the LORD. 20 Ornan turned and saw the angel; and while his four sons who were with him hid themselves, Ornan continued to thresh wheat. 21 As David came to Ornan, Ornan looked and saw David; he went out from the threshing floor, and did obeisance to David with his face to the ground. 22 David said to Ornan, "Give me the site of the threshing floor that I may build on it an altar to the LORD — give it to me at its full price — so that the plague may be averted from the people." 23 Then Ornan said to David, "Take it; and let my lord the king do what seems good to him; see, I present the oxen for burnt offerings, and the threshing sledges for the wood, and the wheat for a grain offering. I give it all." 24 But King David said to Ornan, "No; I will buy them for the full price. I will not take for the LORD what is yours, nor offer burnt offerings that cost me nothing." 25 So David paid Ornan six hundred shekels of gold by weight for the site. 26 David built there an altar to the LORD and presented burnt offerings and offerings of well-being. He called upon the LORD, and he answered him with fire from heaven on the altar of burnt offering. 27 Then the LORD commanded the angel, and he put his sword back into its sheath.

28   At that time, when David saw that the LORD had answered him at the threshing floor of Ornan the Jebusite, he made his sacrifices there. 29 For the tabernacle of the LORD, which Moses had made in the wilderness, and the altar of burnt offering were at that time in the high place at Gibeon; 30 but David could not go before it to inquire of God, for he

Margin references:

21.13 Ps 51.1; 130.4, 7

21.14 1 Chr 27.24
21.15 2 Sam 24.16

21.16 2 Chr 3.1

21.17 2 Sam 7.8; Ps 74.1

21.18 2 Chr 3.1

21.21 2 Chr 3.1

21.25 2 Sam 24.24
21.26 Lev 9.24; Judg 6.21

21.29 1 Chr 16.39; 1 Kings 3.4

21.13 David confessed his sin, accepted the punishment gracefully, cast himself on the mercy of God, and was greatly concerned that the people had to suffer for his transgression. He knew that the mercy of God is better than the mercilessness of humankind, should he have chosen devastation by his foes.
21.14 Punishment sometimes affects the innocent as well as the guilty. David disobediently numbered the people of Israel, and seventy thousand people perished as a result. We do not always understand God's ways.
21.25 six hundred shekels of gold by weight. Compare this with 2 Sam 24.24, where it is said David paid fifty silver shekels for a threshing floor and oxen. The difference is explained by the fact that six hundred

shekels of gold were paid for the entire property (Hebrew māqōm or "place"), with the goren ("threshing floor") priced at fifty silver shekels. David obviously bought more than the threshing floor, for the temple and other buildings were erected on the site later. All of Mount Moriah must have included considerable land. Ornan's name in 2 Sam 24.18 is given as Araunah, probably representing the earlier form of the name.
21.28 — 22.1 David knew that the altar of burnt offering which was then in Gibeon belonged with the ark of the covenant in Jerusalem. He had enough sense to realize that they belonged together and should not be separated.

22 was afraid of the sword of the angel of the LORD. [1] Then David said, "Here shall be the house of the LORD God and here the altar of burnt offering for Israel."

22.1
1 Chr 21.18-29;
2 Chr 3.1

G. Preparations for the building of the temple

1. Materials gathered

2 David gave orders to gather together the aliens who were residing in the land of Israel, and he set stonecutters to prepare dressed stones for building the house of God. [3] David also provided great stores of iron for nails for the doors of the gates and for clamps, as well as bronze in quantities beyond weighing, [4] and cedar logs without number — for the Sidonians and Tyrians brought great quantities of cedar to David. [5] For David said, "My son Solomon is young and inexperienced, and the house that is to be built for the LORD must be exceedingly magnificent, famous and glorified throughout all lands; I will therefore make preparation for it." So David provided materials in great quantity before his death.

22.2
1 Kings 9.21;
5.17, 18
22.3
1 Chr 29.2, 7;
v. 14
22.4
1 Kings 5.6
22.5
1 Chr 29.1

2. Solomon instructed

6 Then he called for his son Solomon and charged him to build a house for the LORD, the God of Israel. [7] David said to Solomon, "My son, I had planned to build a house to the name of the LORD my God. [8] But the word of the LORD came to me, saying, 'You have shed much blood and have waged great wars; you shall not build a house to my name, because you have shed so much blood in my sight on the earth. [9] See, a son shall be born to you; he shall be a man of peace. I will give him peace from all his enemies on every side; for his name shall be Solomon,*o* and I will give peace*p* and quiet to Israel in his days. [10] He shall build a house for my name. He shall be a son to me, and I will be a father to him, and I will establish his royal throne in Israel forever.' [11] Now, my son, the LORD be with you, so that you may succeed in building the house of the LORD your God, as he has spoken concerning you. [12] Only, may the LORD grant you discretion and understanding, so that when he gives you charge over Israel you may keep the law of the LORD your God. [13] Then you will prosper if you are careful to observe the statutes and the ordinances that the LORD commanded Moses for Israel. Be strong and of good courage. Do not be afraid or dismayed. [14] With great pains I have provided for the house of the LORD one hundred thousand talents of gold, one million talents of silver, and bronze and iron beyond weighing, for there is so much of it; timber and stone too I have provided. To these you must add more. [15] You have an abundance of workers: stonecutters, masons, carpenters, and all kinds of artisans without number, skilled in working [16] gold, silver, bronze, and iron. Now begin the work, and the LORD be with you.

22.7
2 Sam 7.2;
1 Chr 17.1;
Deut 12.5, 11
22.8
1 Kings 5.3;
1 Chr 28.3
22.9
1 Kings 4.20,
25;
2 Sam 12.24,
25
22.10
2 Sam 7.13;
1 Chr 17.12,
13
22.11
v. 16
22.12
1 Kings 3.9-12;
2 Chr 1.10
22.13
1 Chr 28.7;
Josh 1.6-9;
1 Chr 28.20
22.14
v. 3

22.16
v. 11

o Heb *Shelomoh*   *p* Heb *shalom*

22.6 David charged Solomon to build the temple after his decease and began gathering the building materials. Such an action should have made it obvious to David's other sons that Solomon would succeed him. Apparently this did not deter Adonijah (David's oldest son) from making an effort to supplant his brother Solomon when David appeared to be getting senile (see 1 Kings 1).
22.13 David charged Solomon to keep God's commandments and assured him that he would prosper if he did. Failure to do so would result in disaster. Even though Solomon would be king of Israel, he was still the subject of God Almighty.

22.14 *one hundred thousand talents of gold, one million talents of silver.* Some have questioned this huge amount of gold, supposing that a copyist's mistake has inflated the figure. However, we are told that the amount of gold seized by the Babylonians and carried off to Babylon was great (cf. Ezra 1.5–11), so we cannot simply dismiss the value stated here as though it were impossible for Israel to have accumulated this much of the metal. We also know that when Jerusalem was sacked in A.D. 70, so much gold was taken that the market price for that metal declined by 50 percent.

3. *The leaders charged to help*

22.17
1 Chr 28.1-6
22.18
2 Sam 7.1;
1 Chr 23.25

22.19
1 Chr 28.9;
1 Kings 8.6;
2 Chr 5.7;
v. 7

17   David also commanded all the leaders of Israel to help his son Solomon, saying, 18 "Is not the Lord your God with you? Has he not given you peace on every side? For he has delivered the inhabitants of the land into my hand; and the land is subdued before the Lord and his people. 19 Now set your mind and heart to seek the Lord your God. Go and build the sanctuary of the Lord God so that the ark of the covenant of the Lord and the holy vessels of God may be brought into a house built for the name of the Lord."

H. *The arrangements for the temple service*

1. *The Levites*

23.1
1 Kings 1.33-
39;
1 Chr 29.28;
28.5
23.3
Num 4.3-49;
v. 24
23.4
2 Chr 19.8
23.5
1 Chr 15.16

23.6
2 Chr 8.14;
29.25

23 When David was old and full of days, he made his son Solomon king over Israel. 2 David assembled all the leaders of Israel and the priests and the Levites. 3 The Levites, thirty years old and upward, were counted, and the total was thirty-eight thousand. 4 "Twenty-four thousand of these," David said, "shall have charge of the work in the house of the Lord, six thousand shall be officers and judges, 5 four thousand gatekeepers, and four thousand shall offer praises to the Lord with the instruments that I have made for praise." 6 And David organized them in divisions corresponding to the sons of Levi: Gershon,q Kohath, and Merari.

7   The sons of Gershonr were Ladan and Shimei. 8 The sons of Ladan: Jehiel the chief, Zetham, and Joel, three. 9 The sons of Shimei: Shelomoth, Haziel, and Haran, three. These were the heads of families of Ladan. 10 And the sons of Shimei: Jahath, Zina, Jeush, and Beriah. These four were the sons of Shimei. 11 Jahath was the chief, and Zizah the second; but Jeush and Beriah did not have many sons, so they were enrolled as a single family.

23.12
Ex 6.18
23.13
Ex 6.20;
28.1;
30.6-10;
Deut 21.5

23.16
1 Chr 26.24ff

12   The sons of Kohath: Amram, Izhar, Hebron, and Uzziel, four. 13 The sons of Amram: Aaron and Moses. Aaron was set apart to consecrate the most holy things, so that he and his sons forever should make offerings before the Lord, and minister to him and pronounce blessings in his name forever; 14 but as for Moses the man of God, his sons were to be reckoned among the tribe of Levi. 15 The sons of Moses: Gershom and Eliezer. 16 The sons of Gershom: Shebuel the chief. 17 The sons of Eliezer: Rehabiah the chief; Eliezer had no other sons, but the sons of Rehabiah were very numerous. 18 The sons of Izhar: Shelomith the chief. 19 The sons of Hebron: Jeriah the chief, Amariah the second, Jahaziel the third, and Jekameam the fourth. 20 The sons of Uzziel: Micah the chief and Isshiah the second.

23.21
1 Chr 24.26ff

21   The sons of Merari: Mahli and Mushi. The sons of Mahli: Eleazar and Kish. 22 Eleazar died having no sons, but only daughters; their kindred, the sons of Kish, married them. 23 The sons of Mushi: Mahli, Eder, and Jeremoth, three.

2. *Their duties*

23.24
Num 10.17,
21; v. 3

24   These were the sons of Levi by their ancestral houses, the heads

---

q Or *Gershom*; See 1 Chr 6.1, note, and 23.15   r Vg Compare Gk Syr: Heb *to the Gershonite*

22.18 Israel as a kingdom reached its greatest heights under David and Solomon. God fulfilled his word by giving Israel a land, a stable government, and a people. But the favor of God would disappear in a few short centuries because of unbelief and apostasy, and the kingdom would shrivel into nothingness.
23.1 David made Solomon king at the very end of his life. Had he made Solomon co-regent with him he

might have avoided the difficulty which arose when Adonijah tried to succeed his father (see note on 22.6). David had known for a long time that Solomon was his chosen successor.
23.24 According to Num 4.30, the Levites who served and assisted the priests began at age thirty and retired at age fifty. As the number of the Israelites had increased, so the services required of the priests in-

of families as they were enrolled according to the number of the names of the individuals from twenty years old and upward who were to do the work for the service of the house of the LORD. 25 For David said, "The LORD, the God of Israel, has given rest to his people; and he resides in Jerusalem forever. 26 And so the Levites no longer need to carry the tabernacle or any of the things for its service" — 27 for according to the last words of David these were the number of the Levites from twenty years old and upward — 28 "but their duty shall be to assist the descendants of Aaron for the service of the house of the LORD, having the care of the courts and the chambers, the cleansing of all that is holy, and any work for the service of the house of God; 29 to assist also with the rows of bread, the choice flour for the grain offering, the wafers of unleavened bread, the baked offering, the offering mixed with oil, and all measures of quantity or size. 30 And they shall stand every morning, thanking and praising the LORD, and likewise at evening, 31 and whenever burnt offerings are offered to the LORD on sabbaths, new moons, and appointed festivals, according to the number required of them, regularly before the LORD. 32 Thus they shall keep charge of the tent of meeting and the sanctuary, and shall attend the descendants of Aaron, their kindred, for the service of the house of the LORD."

3. The division of the priests

24 The divisions of the descendants of Aaron were these. The sons of Aaron: Nadab, Abihu, Eleazar, and Ithamar. 2 But Nadab and Abihu died before their father, and had no sons; so Eleazar and Ithamar became the priests. 3 Along with Zadok of the sons of Eleazar, and Ahimelech of the sons of Ithamar, David organized them according to the appointed duties in their service. 4 Since more chief men were found among the sons of Eleazar than among the sons of Ithamar, they organized them under sixteen heads of ancestral houses of the sons of Eleazar, and eight of the sons of Ithamar. 5 They organized them by lot, all alike, for there were officers of the sanctuary and officers of God among both the sons of Eleazar and the sons of Ithamar. 6 The scribe Shemaiah son of Nethanel, a Levite, recorded them in the presence of the king, and the officers, and Zadok the priest, and Ahimelech son of Abiathar, and the heads of ancestral houses of the priests and of the Levites; one ancestral house being chosen for Eleazar and one chosen for Ithamar.

7 The first lot fell to Jehoiarib, the second to Jedaiah, 8 the third to Harim, the fourth to Seorim, 9 the fifth to Malchijah, the sixth to Mijamin, 10 the seventh to Hakkoz, the eighth to Abijah, 11 the ninth to Jeshua, the tenth to Shecaniah, 12 the eleventh to Eliashib, the twelfth to Jakim, 13 the thirteenth to Huppah, the fourteenth to Jeshebeab, 14 the fifteenth to Bilgah, the sixteenth to Immer, 15 the seventeenth to Hezir, the eighteenth to Happizzez, 16 the nineteenth to Pethahiah, the twentieth to Jehezkel, 17 the twenty-first to Jachin, the twenty-second to Gamul, 18 the twenty-third to Delaiah, the twenty-fourth to Maaziah. 19 These had as their appointed duty in their service to enter the house of the LORD according to the procedure established for them by their ancestor Aaron, as the LORD God of Israel had commanded him.

Cross references (right margin):

23.25
1 Chr 22.18

23.26
Num 4.5

23.29
Lev 23.5-9;
Ex 25.30;
Lev 6.20;
2.4-7; 19.35

23.31
Isa 1.13, 14;
Lev 23.24

23.32
Num 1.53;
1 Chr 9.27;
Num 3.6

24.1
Ex 6.23
24.2
Lev 10.2;
Num 3.4

24.5
v. 31

24.10
Neh 12.4, 17;
Lk 1.5

24.19
1 Chr 9.25

---

creased. Thus the age of service was changed to start at twenty years; the retirement age remained the same.
23.26 When the temple was constructed and dedicated, there was no longer need for anyone to carry the ark, the furniture, etc. David, therefore, made a reassignment for those who had earlier performed these duties.
24.2 See notes on Lev 10.1 and 10.16 for the sin of Nadab and Abihu and God's warning to these brothers.

24.5 The lot was cast publicly and with great solemnity in the presence of the king, the priests, and the princes (see also v. 31). This was to guarantee against fraud. The lot was an appeal to God for his will. Note Prov 16.33: "The lot is cast into the lap, but the decision is the LORD's alone." In Acts 1.24,26, the lot for Matthias was made with intense prayer.
24.19 God had long ago established the duties of the priests. The casting of the lot here decided only who was to perform the duties.

20 And of the rest of the sons of Levi: of the sons of Amram, Shubael; of the sons of Shubael, Jehdeiah. 21 Of Rehabiah: of the sons of Rehabiah, Isshiah the chief. 22 Of the Izharites, Shelomoth; of the sons of Shelomoth, Jahath. 23 The sons of Hebron:ˢ Jeriah the chief,ᵗ Amariah the second, Jahaziel the third, Jekameam the fourth. 24 The sons of Uzziel, Micah; of the sons of Micah, Shamir. 25 The brother of Micah, Isshiah; of the sons of Isshiah, Zechariah. 26 The sons of Merari: Mahli and Mushi. The sons of Jaaziah: Beno.ᵘ 27 The sons of Merari: of Jaaziah, Beno,ᵘ Shoham, Zaccur, and Ibri. 28 Of Mahli: Eleazar, who had no sons. 29 Of Kish, the sons of Kish: Jerahmeel. 30 The sons of Mushi: Mahli, Eder, and Jerimoth. These were the sons of the Levites according to their ancestral houses. 31 These also cast lots corresponding to their kindred, the descendants of Aaron, in the presence of King David, Zadok, Ahimelech, and the heads of ancestral houses of the priests and of the Levites, the chief as well as the youngest brother.

4. *The arrangements for music*

25 David and the officers of the army also set apart for the service the sons of Asaph, and of Heman, and of Jeduthun, who should prophesy with lyres, harps, and cymbals. The list of those who did the work and of their duties was: 2 Of the sons of Asaph: Zaccur, Joseph, Nethaniah, and Asarelah, sons of Asaph, under the direction of Asaph, who prophesied under the direction of the king. 3 Of Jeduthun, the sons of Jeduthun: Gedaliah, Zeri, Jeshaiah, Shimei,ᵛ Hashabiah, and Mattithiah, six, under the direction of their father Jeduthun, who prophesied with the lyre in thanksgiving and praise to the Lᴏʀᴅ. 4 Of Heman, the sons of Heman: Bukkiah, Mattaniah, Uzziel, Shebuel, and Jerimoth, Hananiah, Hanani, Eliathah, Giddalti, and Romamti-ezer, Joshbekashah, Mallothi, Hothir, Mahazioth. 5 All these were the sons of Heman the king's seer, according to the promise of God to exalt him; for God had given Heman fourteen sons and three daughters. 6 They were all under the direction of their father for the music in the house of the Lᴏʀᴅ with cymbals, harps, and lyres for the service of the house of God. Asaph, Jeduthun, and Heman were under the order of the king. 7 They and their kindred, who were trained in singing to the Lᴏʀᴅ, all of whom were skillful, numbered two hundred eighty-eight. 8 And they cast lots for their duties, small and great, teacher and pupil alike.

9 The first lot fell for Asaph to Joseph; the second to Gedaliah, to him and his brothers and his sons, twelve; 10 the third to Zaccur, his sons and his brothers, twelve; 11 the fourth to Izri, his sons and his brothers, twelve; 12 the fifth to Nethaniah, his sons and his brothers, twelve; 13 the sixth to Bukkiah, his sons and his brothers, twelve; 14 the seventh to Jesarelah,ʷ his sons and his brothers, twelve; 15 the eighth to Jeshaiah, his sons and his brothers, twelve; 16 the ninth to Mattaniah, his sons and his brothers, twelve; 17 the tenth to Shimei, his sons and his brothers, twelve; 18 the eleventh to Azarel, his sons and his brothers, twelve; 19 the twelfth to Hashabiah, his sons and his brothers, twelve; 20 to the thirteenth, Shubael, his sons and his brothers, twelve; 21 to the fourteenth, Mattithiah, his sons and his brothers, twelve; 22 to the fifteenth, to Jere-

Cross references (left margin)

24.21 1 Chr 23.17
24.23 1 Chr 23.19
24.26 1 Chr 23.21
24.31 vv. 5, 6
25.1 1 Chr 6.33, 39; 15.16
25.3 1 Chr 16.41, 42
25.4 1 Chr 6.33; v. 25
25.6 1 Chr 15.16, 19
25.8 1 Chr 26.13
25.9 1 Chr 6.39
25.16 v. 4

ˢ See 23.19: Heb lacks *Hebron*   ᵗ See 23.19: Heb lacks *the chief*   ᵘ Or *his son*: Meaning of Heb uncertain   ᵛ One Ms: Gk: MT lacks *Shimei*   ʷ Or *Asarelah*; see 25.2

25.1–3 Singing praises to God is here called *prophesying*. This does not mean that all who performed this function could foretell the future or had special visions from God. Perhaps this helps define what Paul intended by prophesying in 1 Cor 11.4,24.
25.3 The purpose of singing, with the use of instruments such as harps and cymbals, was to praise God. Music here was for sacred purposes. This does not

mean that music for entertainment is wrong; but it should be free from anything that would violate the law of God.
25.7 There were 288 teachers, while the total number of singers was four thousand (23.5). The twenty-four groups (25.9–31) matched the twenty-four courses of priests (24.7–18).

moth, his sons and his brothers, twelve; 23 to the sixteenth, to Hananiah, his sons and his brothers, twelve; 24 to the seventeenth, to Joshbekashah, his sons and his brothers, twelve; 25 to the eighteenth, to Hanani, his sons and his brothers, twelve; 26 to the nineteenth, to Mallothi, his sons and his brothers, twelve; 27 to the twentieth, to Eliathah, his sons and his brothers, twelve; 28 to the twenty-first, to Hothir, his sons and his brothers, twelve; 29 to the twenty-second, to Giddalti, his sons and his brothers, twelve; 30 to the twenty-third, to Mahazioth, his sons and his brothers, twelve; 31 to the twenty-fourth, to Romamti-ezer, his sons and his brothers, twelve.

| | 25.23 v. 4 |
| | 25.25 v. 4 |

5. The arrangements for gatekeepers

26 As for the divisions of the gatekeepers: of the Korahites, Meshelemiah son of Kore, of the sons of Asaph. 2 Meshelemiah had sons: Zechariah the firstborn, Jediael the second, Zebadiah the third, Jathniel the fourth, 3 Elam the fifth, Jehohanan the sixth, Eliehoenai the seventh. 4 Obed-edom had sons: Shemaiah the firstborn, Jehozabad the second, Joah the third, Sachar the fourth, Nethanel the fifth, 5 Ammiel the sixth, Issachar the seventh, Peullethai the eighth; for God blessed him. 6 Also to his son Shemaiah sons were born who exercised authority in their ancestral houses, for they were men of great ability. 7 The sons of Shemaiah: Othni, Rephael, Obed, and Elzabad, whose brothers were able men, Elihu and Semachiah. 8 All these, sons of Obed-edom with their sons and brothers, were able men qualified for the service; sixty-two of Obed-edom. 9 Meshelemiah had sons and brothers, able men, eighteen. 10 Hosah, of the sons of Merari, had sons: Shimri the chief (for though he was not the firstborn, his father made him chief), 11 Hilkiah the second, Tebaliah the third, Zechariah the fourth: all the sons and brothers of Hosah totaled thirteen.

12 These divisions of the gatekeepers, corresponding to their leaders, had duties, just as their kindred did, ministering in the house of the LORD; 13 and they cast lots by ancestral houses, small and great alike, for their gates. 14 The lot for the east fell to Shelemiah. They cast lots also for his son Zechariah, a prudent counselor, and his lot came out for the north. 15 Obed-edom's came out for the south, and to his sons was allotted the storehouse. 16 For Shuppim and Hosah it came out for the west, at the gate of Shallecheth on the ascending road. Guard corresponded to guard. 17 On the east there were six Levites each day,ˣ on the north four each day, on the south four each day, as well as two and two at the storehouse; 18 and for the colonnadeʸ on the west there were four at the road and two at the colonnade.ʸ 19 These were the divisions of the gatekeepers among the Korahites and the sons of Merari.

	26.1 v. 19
	26.4 1 Chr 15.18
	26.10 1 Chr 16.38
	26.12 v. 1
	26.13 1 Chr 24.5, 31; 25.8

6. The arrangements for the treasuries

20 And of the Levites, Ahijah had charge of the treasuries of the house of God and the treasuries of the dedicated gifts. 21 The sons of Ladan, the

| | 26.20 1 Chr 28.12 |

x Gk: Heb lacks each day   y Heb parbar: meaning uncertain

26.1 The gatekeepers attended to certain duties pertaining to the temple. They guarded the avenues that led to it; they opened and shut the outer gates; they were charged to keep decorum among the worshipers; they turned back those who were unclean; and they guarded against thieves and any enemies.

26.6ff Some of the people named here were marked out as having special gifts and attributes. There were mighty men of valor, strong and able men, and even wise counsellors. When God calls people to special tasks, he either chooses them because they are fit or he makes them so.

26.10 Shimri was elevated above the firstborn (i.e., he was made chief) either because he enjoyed special excellence or the firstborn was not as capable. This decision did not pertain to the inheritance rights of the firstborn but only to his service for God.

26.20 The treasures of the house of God included such things as flour, wine, oil, salt, fuel, lamps, sacred vestments, utensils, and money, i.e., silver and gold. The spoils from David's wars were dedicated to the temple (v. 27). What they were is not mentioned specifically.

sons of the Gershonites belonging to Ladan, the heads of families belonging to Ladan the Gershonite: Jehieli. *z*

22 The sons of Jehieli, Zetham and his brother Joel, were in charge of the treasuries of the house of the LORD. 23 Of the Amramites, the Izharites, the Hebronites, and the Uzzielites: 24 Shebuel son of Gershom, son of Moses, was chief officer in charge of the treasuries. 25 His brothers: from Eliezer were his son Rehabiah, his son Jeshaiah, his son Joram, his son Zichri, and his son Shelomoth. 26 This Shelomoth and his brothers were in charge of all the treasuries of the dedicated gifts that King David, and the heads of families, and the officers of the thousands and the hundreds, and the commanders of the army, had dedicated. 27 From booty won in battles they dedicated gifts for the maintenance of the house of the LORD. 28 Also all that Samuel the seer, and Saul son of Kish, and Abner son of Ner, and Joab son of Zeruiah had dedicated — all dedicated gifts were in the care of Shelomoth*a* and his brothers.

7. The arrangements for officers and judges

29 Of the Izharites, Chenaniah and his sons were appointed to outside duties for Israel, as officers and judges. 30 Of the Hebronites, Hashabiah and his brothers, one thousand seven hundred men of ability, had the oversight of Israel west of the Jordan for all the work of the LORD and for the service of the king. 31 Of the Hebronites, Jerijah was chief of the Hebronites. (In the fortieth year of David's reign search was made, of whatever genealogy or family, and men of great ability among them were found at Jazer in Gilead.) 32 King David appointed him and his brothers, two thousand seven hundred men of ability, heads of families, to have the oversight of the Reubenites, the Gadites, and the half-tribe of the Manassites for everything pertaining to God and for the affairs of the king.

I. The appointment of the military and civil officials

27 This is the list of the people of Israel, the heads of families, the commanders of the thousands and the hundreds, and their officers who served the king in all matters concerning the divisions that came and went, month after month throughout the year, each division numbering twenty-four thousand:

2 Jashobeam son of Zabdiel was in charge of the first division in the first month; in his division were twenty-four thousand. 3 He was a descendant of Perez, and was chief of all the commanders of the army for the first month. 4 Dodai the Ahohite was in charge of the division of the second month; Mikloth was the chief officer of his division. In his division were twenty-four thousand. 5 The third commander, for the third month, was Benaiah son of the priest Jehoiada, as chief; in his division were twenty-four thousand. 6 This is the Benaiah who was a mighty man of the Thirty and in command of the Thirty; his son Ammizabad was in charge of his division. *b* 7 Asahel brother of Joab was fourth, for the fourth month, and his son Zebadiah after him; in his division were twenty-four thousand. 8 The fifth commander, for the fifth month, was Shamhuth, the Izrahite; in his division were twenty-four thousand. 9 Sixth, for the sixth

---

Margin references (left column):

26.24 · 1 Chr 23.16
26.25 · 1 Chr 23.18
26.26 · 2 Sam 8.11
26.28 · 1 Sam 9.9
26.29 · Neh 11.16; 1 Chr 23.4
26.30 · 1 Chr 27.17
26.31 · 1 Chr 23.19
26.32 · 2 Chr 19.11
27.2 · 2 Sam 23.8-30; 1 Chr 11.11-31
27.6 · 1 Chr 11.22ff
27.7 · 1 Chr 11.26
27.9 · 1 Chr 11.28

---

z The Hebrew text of verse 21 is confused   *a* Gk Compare 26.28: Heb *Shelomith*   *b* Gk Vg: Heb *Ammizabad was his division*

26.29 Some of the Levites were employed in the affairs of government, with no responsibilities at the temple. They were ministers of justice in the civil realm, caring for God's tithes, the king's tax money, and the affairs of the nation.
27.1 King David maintained a standing army and had control over the military operations of the nation. The military was divided into courses, as were the priests, each one led by a commander. This made their support less burdensome. The whole number of those under arms totaled 288,000.
27.7 Asahel is named as the fourth of King David's monthly chief officers. Some suppose that this is an error, for Asahel was dead before David was established as king (see 2 Sam 2.18–23). It appears that the post actually had been given to Zebadiah, Asahel's son, as a posthumous honor to Asahel.

month, was Ira son of Ikkesh the Tekoite; in his division were twenty-four thousand. [10] Seventh, for the seventh month, was Helez the Pelonite, of the Ephraimites; in his division were twenty-four thousand. [11] Eighth, for the eighth month, was Sibbecai the Hushathite, of the Zerahites; in his division were twenty-four thousand. [12] Ninth, for the ninth month, was Abiezer of Anathoth, a Benjaminite; in his division were twenty-four thousand. [13] Tenth, for the tenth month, was Maharai of Netophah, of the Zerahites; in his division were twenty-four thousand. [14] Eleventh, for the eleventh month, was Benaiah of Pirathon, of the Ephraimites; in his division were twenty-four thousand. [15] Twelfth, for the twelfth month, was Heldai the Netophathite, of Othniel; in his division were twenty-four thousand.

16   Over the tribes of Israel, for the Reubenites, Eliezer son of Zichri was chief officer; for the Simeonites, Shephatiah son of Maacah; [17] for Levi, Hashabiah son of Kemuel; for Aaron, Zadok; [18] for Judah, Elihu, one of David's brothers; for Issachar, Omri son of Michael; [19] for Zebulun, Ishmaiah son of Obadiah; for Naphtali, Jerimoth son of Azriel; [20] for the Ephraimites, Hoshea son of Azaziah; for the half-tribe of Manasseh, Joel son of Pedaiah; [21] for the half-tribe of Manasseh in Gilead, Iddo son of Zechariah; for Benjamin, Jaasiel son of Abner; [22] for Dan, Azarel son of Jeroham. These were the leaders of the tribes of Israel. [23] David did not count those below twenty years of age, for the LORD had promised to make Israel as numerous as the stars of heaven. [24] Joab son of Zeruiah began to count them, but did not finish; yet wrath came upon Israel for this, and the number was not entered into the account of the Annals of King David.

25   Over the king's treasuries was Azmaveth son of Adiel. Over the treasuries in the country, in the cities, in the villages and in the towers, was Jonathan son of Uzziah. [26] Over those who did the work of the field, tilling the soil, was Ezri son of Chelub. [27] Over the vineyards was Shimei the Ramathite. Over the produce of the vineyards for the wine cellars was Zabdi the Shiphmite. [28] Over the olive and sycamore trees in the Shephelah was Baal-hanan the Gederite. Over the stores of oil was Joash. [29] Over the herds that pastured in Sharon was Shitrai the Sharonite. Over the herds in the valleys was Shaphat son of Adlai. [30] Over the camels was Obil the Ishmaelite. Over the donkeys was Jehdeiah the Meronothite. Over the flocks was Jaziz the Hagrite. [31] All these were stewards of King David's property.

32   Jonathan, David's uncle, was a counselor, being a man of understanding and a scribe; Jehiel son of Hachmoni attended the king's sons. [33] Ahithophel was the king's counselor, and Hushai the Archite was the king's friend. [34] After Ahithophel came Jehoiada son of Benaiah, and Abiathar. Joab was commander of the king's army.

J. David's last words and death

1. The people instructed to assist Solomon

28   David assembled at Jerusalem all the officials of Israel, the officials of the tribes, the officers of the divisions that served the king, the commanders of the thousands, the commanders of the hundreds, the stewards of all the property and cattle of the king and his sons, together with the palace officials, the mighty warriors, and all the warriors. [2] Then King David rose to his feet and said: "Hear me, my brothers and my

Cross references (right margin):
27.10 / 1 Chr 11.27
27.11 / 1 Chr 11.29
27.12 / 1 Chr 11.28
27.13 / 1 Chr 11.30
27.14 / 1 Chr 11.31
27.22 / 1 Chr 28.1
27.23 / Gen 15.5
27.24 / 2 Sam 24.15; 1 Chr 21.7
27.28 / 1 Kings 10.27; 2 Chr 1.15
27.33 / 2 Sam 15.12, 32, 37
27.34 / 1 Kings 1.7; 1 Chr 11.6
28.1 / 1 Chr 27.1-31; 11.10-47
28.2 / 2 Sam 7.2; 1 Chr 17.1, 2; Ps 132.7

27.16 The chief officers were rulers or governors over the tribes of Israel. Once the monarchy was established, their role was a lesser one than when there was no king.
27.25 King David's large possessions were managed by subordinates. They were personal servants of the king himself rather than the nation.
28.1 As David approached the time of death, he gathered a large crowd of the leaders of the nation to spell out for them what the future would be upon his decease.

people. I had planned to build a house of rest for the ark of the covenant of the LORD, for the footstool of our God; and I made preparations for building. 3 But God said to me, 'You shall not build a house for my name, for you are a warrior and have shed blood.' 4 Yet the LORD God of Israel chose me from all my ancestral house to be king over Israel forever; for he chose Judah as leader, and in the house of Judah my father's house, and among my father's sons he took delight in making me king over all Israel. 5 And of all my sons, for the LORD has given me many, he has chosen my son Solomon to sit upon the throne of the kingdom of the LORD over Israel. 6 He said to me, 'It is your son Solomon who shall build my house and my courts, for I have chosen him to be a son to me, and I will be a father to him. 7 I will establish his kingdom forever if he continues resolute in keeping my commandments and my ordinances, as he is today.' 8 Now therefore in the sight of all Israel, the assembly of the LORD, and in the hearing of our God, observe and search out all the commandments of the LORD your God; that you may possess this good land, and leave it for an inheritance to your children after you forever.

2. David's instructions to Solomon

9 "And you, my son Solomon, know the God of your father, and serve him with single mind and willing heart; for the LORD searches every mind, and understands every plan and thought. If you seek him, he will be found by you; but if you forsake him, he will abandon you forever. 10 Take heed now, for the LORD has chosen you to build a house as the sanctuary; be strong, and act."

11 Then David gave his son Solomon the plan of the vestibule of the temple, and of its houses, its treasuries, its upper rooms, and its inner chambers, and of the room for the mercy seat;c 12 and the plan of all that he had in mind: for the courts of the house of the LORD, all the surrounding chambers, the treasuries of the house of God, and the treasuries for dedicated gifts; 13 for the divisions of the priests and of the Levites, and all the work of the service in the house of the LORD; for all the vessels for the service in the house of the LORD, 14 the weight of gold for all golden vessels for each service, the weight of silver vessels for each service, 15 the weight of the golden lampstands and their lamps, the weight of gold for each lampstand and its lamps, the weight of silver for a lampstand and its lamps, according to the use of each in the service, 16 the weight of gold for each table for the rows of bread, the silver for the silver tables, 17 and pure gold for the forks, the basins, and the cups; for the golden bowls and the weight of each; for the silver bowls and the weight of each; 18 for the altar of incense made of refined gold, and its weight; also his plan for the golden chariot of the cherubim that spread their wings and covered the ark of the covenant of the LORD.

19 "All this, in writing at the LORD's direction, he made clear to me — the plan of all the works."

20 David said further to his son Solomon, "Be strong and of good courage, and act. Do not be afraid or dismayed; for the LORD God, my

c Or the cover

Cross references (margin):

28.3 2 Sam 7.5, 13; 1 Chr 22.8
28.4 1 Sam 16.6-13; 1 Chr 17.23, 27; 5.2; Gen 49.8-10
28.5 1 Chr 3.1-9; 22.9, 10
28.6 2 Sam 7.13, 14; 1 Chr 22.9, 10
28.7 1 Chr 22.13
28.9 Jer 9.24; 1 Chr 29.17-19; 1 Sam 16.7; 2 Chr 15.2; Jer 29.13
28.10 1 Chr 22.13
28.11 vv. 12, 19; Ex 25.40
28.12 1 Chr 26.20
28.13 1 Chr 24.1; 23.6
28.15 Ex 25.31-39
28.18 Ex 30.1-10; 25.18-22
28.19 vv. 11, 12
28.20 Josh 1.6, 7, 9; 1 Chr 22.13; Josh 1.5

28.6 David had many sons. But it was God himself who determined who would succeed him. Solomon was David's choice because he was God's choice, a choice not based on primogeniture. It was worth, not age, that brought Solomon to the throne.

28.9,10 David publicly presented his successor to the leadership of the nation and did so by committing him to God and charging him to know God and obey him in all things. We cannot serve God rightly if we do not know him. Moreover, David commanded Solomon to build the house for God that he had hoped to erect but was forbidden to do so.

28.19 David claimed that the plans for the temple had come directly from God. As he wrote down the instructions for Solomon to follow, he was guided by God in much the same way as God supervised the giving of his own words to Moses and the prophets.

28.20 *Do not be afraid or dismayed; for the LORD God . . . is with you. He will not fail you or forsake you.* This promise can be found throughout the Scriptures, and is applicable to us today. Its fulfillment is based on the stipulation that if we obey his commandments, blessings will follow.

God, is with you. He will not fail you or forsake you, until all the work for the service of the house of the LORD is finished. 21 Here are the divisions of the priests and the Levites for all the service of the house of God; and with you in all the work will be every volunteer who has skill for any kind of service; also the officers and all the people will be wholly at your command."

3. David invites the people to give

29 King David said to the whole assembly, "My son Solomon, whom alone God has chosen, is young and inexperienced, and the work is great; for the temple[d] will not be for mortals but for the LORD God. 2 So I have provided for the house of my God, so far as I was able, the gold for the things of gold, the silver for the things of silver, and the bronze for the things of bronze, the iron for the things of iron, and wood for the things of wood, besides great quantities of onyx and stones for setting, antimony, colored stones, all sorts of precious stones, and marble in abundance. 3 Moreover, in addition to all that I have provided for the holy house, I have a treasure of my own of gold and silver, and because of my devotion to the house of my God I give it to the house of my God: 4 three thousand talents of gold, of the gold of Ophir, and seven thousand talents of refined silver, for overlaying the walls of the house, 5 and for all the work to be done by artisans, gold for the things of gold and silver for the things of silver. Who then will offer willingly, consecrating themselves today to the LORD?"

6 Then the leaders of ancestral houses made their freewill offerings, as did also the leaders of the tribes, the commanders of the thousands and of the hundreds, and the officers over the king's work. 7 They gave for the service of the house of God five thousand talents and ten thousand darics of gold, ten thousand talents of silver, eighteen thousand talents of bronze, and one hundred thousand talents of iron. 8 Whoever had precious stones gave them to the treasury of the house of the LORD, into the care of Jehiel the Gershonite. 9 Then the people rejoiced because these had given willingly, for with single mind they had offered freely to the LORD; King David also rejoiced greatly.

4. David's prayer

10 Then David blessed the LORD in the presence of all the assembly; David said: "Blessed are you, O LORD, the God of our ancestor Israel, forever and ever. 11 Yours, O LORD, are the greatness, the power, the glory, the victory, and the majesty; for all that is in the heavens and on the earth is yours; yours is the kingdom, O LORD, and you are exalted as head above all. 12 Riches and honor come from you, and you rule over all. In your hand are power and might; and it is in your hand to make great and to give strength to all. 13 And now, our God, we give thanks to you and praise your glorious name.

14 "But who am I, and what is my people, that we should be able to make this freewill offering? For all things come from you, and of your own

28.21
v. 13;
Ex 35.25-35;
36.1, 2

29.1
1 Chr 22.5;
v. 19

29.2
1 Chr 22.3-5

29.4
1 Chr 22.14;
1 Kings 9.28

29.6
1 Chr 27.1;
28.1; 27.25ff
29.7
Ezra 2.69;
Neh 7.70

29.8
1 Chr 26.21

29.9
1 Kings 8.61;
2 Cor 9.7

29.11
Mt 6.13;
1 Tim 1.17;
Rev 5.13
29.12
2 Chr 1.12;
Rom 11.36

---

d Heb *fortress*

29.1 *the temple* (NRSV footnote "fortress"). The building would be not only the temple of God but also the palace of God.
29.6–9 The temple of God was not to be built by tax money. It had to come from the hearts of God's people through freewill offerings. The freewill gifts were occasions for rejoicing by both king and people. Opportunities that we have to give should likewise be a time for rejoicing.
29.7 *ten thousand darics of gold.* A daric was a Persian coin of that day.

29.14 David knew that God was the source of all things, including his wealth and his kingship. What he gave back to God by way of gifts was God's to begin with. In other words, we are only stewards of God's possessions, which have been loaned to us and for which we will be held responsible before the judgment seat of Christ. We came into the world with nothing and we will go out with nothing (1 Tim 6.7, 8), save the treasure we have laid up in heaven (Mt 6.19–21).

have we given you. 15 For we are aliens and transients before you, as were all our ancestors; our days on the earth are like a shadow, and there is no hope. 16 O LORD our God, all this abundance that we have provided for building you a house for your holy name comes from your hand and is all your own. 17 I know, my God, that you search the heart, and take pleasure in uprightness; in the uprightness of my heart I have freely offered all these things, and now I have seen your people, who are present here, offering freely and joyously to you. 18 O LORD, the God of Abraham, Isaac, and Israel, our ancestors, keep forever such purposes and thoughts in the hearts of your people, and direct their hearts toward you. 19 Grant to my son Solomon that with single mind he may keep your commandments, your decrees, and your statutes, performing all of them, and that he may build the temple*e* for which I have made provision."

20   Then David said to the whole assembly, "Bless the LORD your God." And all the assembly blessed the LORD, the God of their ancestors, and bowed their heads and prostrated themselves before the LORD and the king. 21 On the next day they offered sacrifices and burnt offerings to the LORD, a thousand bulls, a thousand rams, and a thousand lambs, with their libations, and sacrifices in abundance for all Israel; 22 and they ate and drank before the LORD on that day with great joy.

5. Solomon made king

They made David's son Solomon king a second time; they anointed him as the LORD's prince, and Zadok as priest. 23 Then Solomon sat on the throne of the LORD, succeeding his father David as king; he prospered, and all Israel obeyed him. 24 All the leaders and the mighty warriors, and also all the sons of King David, pledged their allegiance to King Solomon. 25 The LORD highly exalted Solomon in the sight of all Israel, and bestowed upon him such royal majesty as had not been on any king before him in Israel.

6. The death of David

26   Thus David son of Jesse reigned over all Israel. 27 The period that he reigned over Israel was forty years; he reigned seven years in Hebron, and thirty-three years in Jerusalem. 28 He died in a good old age, full of days, riches, and honor; and his son Solomon succeeded him. 29 Now the acts of King David, from first to last, are written in the records of the seer Samuel, and in the records of the prophet Nathan, and in the records of the seer Gad, 30 with accounts of all his rule and his might and of the events that befell him and Israel and all the kingdoms of the earth.

e Heb *fortress*

29.22 *Solomon . . . the second time,* i.e., they installed him as co-regent with his father King David, who was not to die.
29.24 God moved the hearts of David's other sons to accept Solomon as king, giving him their oaths of allegiance. The chronicler did not mention the incident involving Adonijah and Abishag (see 1 Kings 1–2). Adonijah must have taken the oath with mental reservations.

29.29 *records of the seer Samuel* either refers to the entire material in 1 and 2 Samuel or to those parts of 1 Samuel recorded before Samuel's death. The chronicler was selective in what was reported and did not include some of the materials contained in the books of Samuel. The records of Nathan and Gad are not known, unless they formed the other parts of 1 and 2 Samuel.

INTRODUCTION TO
2 CHRONICLES

Authorship, Date, and Background: See introduction to 1 Chronicles.

Characteristics and Content: See introduction to 1 Chronicles. The first part of 2 Chronicles describes Solomon's reign; the author omits his apostasy and idolatry and stresses the good things he did, such as erecting the temple. Following the division of the Solomonic kingdom into the northern and southern kingdoms, nothing is said further about the kings of Samaria (Israel) except for those who had a direct connection with affairs involving the kingdom of Judah. The author follows the kings of Judah, one by one, devoting the greatest attention to the ones who feared God, kept his law, and promoted and taught the law to their people. He stresses over and over again those kings and their acts which contributed to the upbuilding and the preservation of the Jewish theocracy over which God was the head.

Outline:

2 CHRONICLES

III. *The reign of Solomon (1.1–9.31)*

A. *The wisdom and wealth of Solomon*

1.1
1 Kings 2.12, 46;
Gen 39.2;
1 Chr 29.25
1.2
1 Chr 28.1
1.3ff
1 Kings 3.4;
Ex 36.8
1.4
2 Sam 6.2, 17;
1 Chr 15.1
1.5
Ex 38.1, 2
1.6
1 Kings 3.4

1.7
1 Kings 3.5, 6
1.8
1 Chr 28.5
1.9
1 Kings 3.7, 8
1.10
1 Kings 3.9
1.11
1 Kings 3.11-13

1.12
1 Chr 29.25;
2 Chr 9.22

1.14ff
1 Kings 4.26;
10.26-29;
2 Chr 9.25
1.15
1 Kings 10.27;
2 Chr 9.27
1.16
1 Kings 10.28, 29;
2 Chr 9.28

1 Solomon son of David established himself in his kingdom; the LORD his God was with him and made him exceedingly great. 2 Solomon summoned all Israel, the commanders of the thousands and of the hundreds, the judges, and all the leaders of all Israel, the heads of families. 3 Then Solomon, and the whole assembly with him, went to the high place that was at Gibeon; for God's tent of meeting, which Moses the servant of the LORD had made in the wilderness, was there. 4 (But David had brought the ark of God up from Kiriath-jearim to the place that David had prepared for it; for he had pitched a tent for it in Jerusalem.) 5 Moreover the bronze altar that Bezalel son of Uri, son of Hur, had made, was there in front of the tabernacle of the LORD. And Solomon and the assembly inquired at it. 6 Solomon went up there to the bronze altar before the LORD, which was at the tent of meeting, and offered a thousand burnt offerings on it.

7 That night God appeared to Solomon, and said to him, "Ask what I should give you." 8 Solomon said to God, "You have shown great and steadfast love to my father David, and have made me succeed him as king. 9 O LORD God, let your promise to my father David now be fulfilled, for you have made me king over a people as numerous as the dust of the earth. 10 Give me now wisdom and knowledge to go out and come in before this people, for who can rule this great people of yours?" 11 God answered Solomon, "Because this was in your heart, and you have not asked for possessions, wealth, honor, or the life of those who hate you, and have not even asked for long life, but have asked for wisdom and knowledge for yourself that you may rule my people over whom I have made you king, 12 wisdom and knowledge are granted to you. I will also give you riches, possessions, and honor, such as none of the kings had who were before you, and none after you shall have the like." 13 So Solomon came from *f* the high place at Gibeon, from the tent of meeting, to Jerusalem. And he reigned over Israel.

14 Solomon gathered together chariots and horses; he had fourteen hundred chariots and twelve thousand horses, which he stationed in the chariot cities and with the king in Jerusalem. 15 The king made silver and gold as common in Jerusalem as stone, and he made cedar as plentiful as the sycamore of the Shephelah. 16 Solomon's horses were imported from Egypt and Kue; the king's traders received them from Kue at the prevailing price. 17 They imported from Egypt, and then exported, a chariot for six hundred shekels of silver, and a horse for one hundred fifty; so through them these were exported to all the kings of the Hittites and the kings of Aram.

f Gk Vg: Heb *to*

1.3–6 According to Deut 12.13,14, burnt offerings were prohibited except in Jerusalem. The chronicler explains the reason for Solomon's thousand burnt offerings at Gibeon: the tent of meeting (tabernacle) and the bronze altar were there.

1.10 Solomon's request for wisdom was granted. Wisdom is a unique gift, a gift for using knowledge correctly.
1.14–17 See note on 1 Kings 11.3 regarding Solomon's propensity for horses, silver, and gold.

B. *The building of the temple*

1. *The preparations for building*

2 [g] Solomon decided to build a temple for the name of the LORD, and a royal palace for himself. [2] [h] Solomon conscripted seventy thousand laborers and eighty thousand stonecutters in the hill country, with three thousand six hundred to oversee them.

3 Solomon sent word to King Huram of Tyre: "Once you dealt with my father David and sent him cedar to build himself a house to live in. 4 I am now about to build a house for the name of the LORD my God and dedicate it to him for offering fragrant incense before him, and for the regular offering of the rows of bread, and for burnt offerings morning and evening, on the sabbaths and the new moons and the appointed festivals of the LORD our God, as ordained forever for Israel. 5 The house that I am about to build will be great, for our God is greater than other gods. 6 But who is able to build him a house, since heaven, even highest heaven, cannot contain him? Who am I to build a house for him, except as a place to make offerings before him? 7 So now send me an artisan skilled to work in gold, silver, bronze, and iron, and in purple, crimson, and blue fabrics, trained also in engraving, to join the skilled workers who are with me in Judah and Jerusalem, whom my father David provided. 8 Send me also cedar, cypress, and algum timber from Lebanon, for I know that your servants are skilled in cutting Lebanon timber. My servants will work with your servants 9 to prepare timber for me in abundance, for the house I am about to build will be great and wonderful. 10 I will provide for your servants, those who cut the timber, twenty thousand cors of crushed wheat, twenty thousand cors of barley, twenty thousand baths[i] of wine, and twenty thousand baths of oil."

11 Then King Huram of Tyre answered in a letter that he sent to Solomon, "Because the LORD loves his people he has made you king over them." 12 Huram also said, "Blessed be the LORD God of Israel, who made heaven and earth, who has given King David a wise son, endowed with discretion and understanding, who will build a temple for the LORD, and a royal palace for himself.

13 "I have dispatched Huram-abi, a skilled artisan, endowed with understanding, 14 the son of one of the Danite women, his father a Tyrian. He is trained to work in gold, silver, bronze, iron, stone, and wood, and in purple, blue, and crimson fabrics and fine linen, and to do all sorts of engraving and execute any design that may be assigned him, with your artisans, the artisans of my lord, your father David. 15 Now, as for the wheat, barley, oil, and wine, of which my lord has spoken, let him send them to his servants. 16 We will cut whatever timber you need from Lebanon, and bring it to you as rafts by sea to Joppa; you will take it up to Jerusalem."

17 Then Solomon took a census of all the aliens who were residing in the land of Israel, after the census that his father David had taken; and there were found to be one hundred fifty-three thousand six hundred.

2.1	1 Kings 5.5
2.2	v. 18; 1 Kings 5.15, 16
2.3	1 Kings 5.2-11; 1 Chr 14.1
2.4	v. 1; Ex 30.7; 25.30; Num 28.9, 30
2.5	1 Chr 16.25; Ps 135.5
2.6	1 Kings 8.27; 2 Chr 6.18
2.7	vv. 13, 14; 1 Chr 22.15
2.8	2 Chr 9.10, 11
2.10	1 Kings 5.11
2.11	1 Kings 10.9; 2 Chr 9.8
2.12	1 Kings 5.7; Ps 33.6; 102.25
2.14	1 Kings 7.13, 14
2.15	v. 10
2.16	1 Kings 5.8, 9
2.17	1 Chr 22.2

[g] Ch 1.18 in Heb   [h] Ch 2.1 in Heb   [i] A Hebrew measure of volume

2.1 Three sanctuaries existed during Israel's long history: the first was the tent in the wilderness; the second, Solomon's temple; the third, the temple erected after the captivity (this third temple was virtually rebuilt by Herod the Great over a period of nearly fifty years; Jn 2.20). Regarding Solomon's temple, when David was forbidden by God to erect the structure, he collected the material for Solomon to do so (1 Chr 22.2–5,8,14–16; 29.2–5). Solomon spent seven years constructing it. It was called "the house of the God of Jacob" (Isa 2.3) and "Mount Zion" (Ps 74.2). At the dedication of the temple, fire came down

from heaven upon the altar and the glory of God filled it (5.13,14; 7.2,3; 1 Kings 8.10,11). The Scriptures prophesied the destruction of the first temple (Jer 26.18; Mic 3.12); this was fulfilled by the Babylonians under Nebuchadnezzar (2 Kings 25.9,13–17; 2 Chr 36.18,19).
2.4 *rows of bread*, literally, "the bread of the Presence" (cf. Ex 25.23–30).
2.13 *Huram-abi* is said to have been the son of a widow of the tribe of Naphtali (1 Kings 7.14; called *Hiram* there). He was an architect and artist.

2.18
v. 2
18 Seventy thousand of them he assigned as laborers, eighty thousand as stonecutters in the hill country, and three thousand six hundred as overseers to make the people work.

2. The construction of the temple

a. The site, dimensions, and materials

3.1
1 Kings 6.1ff;
1 Chr 21.18
3 Solomon began to build the house of the LORD in Jerusalem on Mount Moriah, where the LORD had appeared to his father David, at the place that David had designated, on the threshing floor of Ornan the Jebusite. 2 He began to build on the second day of the second month of the fourth year of his reign. 3 These are Solomon's measurements[j] for building the house of God: the length, in cubits of the old standard, was sixty cubits, and the width twenty cubits. 4 The vestibule in front of the nave of the house was twenty cubits long, across the width of the house;[k] and its height was one hundred twenty cubits. He overlaid it on the inside 3.5
1 Kings 6.17 with pure gold. 5 The nave he lined with cypress, covered it with fine gold, and made palms and chains on it. 6 He adorned the house with settings 3.7
1 Kings 6.20-
22,
29-35 of precious stones. The gold was gold from Parvaim. 7 So he lined the house with gold—its beams, its thresholds, its walls, and its doors; and he carved cherubim on the walls.

3.8
1 Kings 6.16
8 He made the most holy place; its length, corresponding to the width of the house, was twenty cubits, and its width was twenty cubits; he overlaid it with six hundred talents of fine gold. 9 The weight of the nails was fifty shekels of gold. He overlaid the upper chambers with gold.

3.10
1 Kings 6.23-28
10 In the most holy place he made two carved cherubim and overlaid[l] them with gold. 11 The wings of the cherubim together extended twenty cubits: one wing of the one, five cubits long, touched the wall of the house, and its other wing, five cubits long, touched the wing of the other cherub; 12 and of this cherub, one wing, five cubits long, touched the wall of the house, and the other wing, also five cubits long, was joined to the wing of the first cherub. 13 The wings of these cherubim extended twenty cubits; the cherubim[m] stood on their feet, facing the nave. 14 And Solo- 3.14
Ex 26.31;
Heb 9.3 mon[n] made the curtain of blue and purple and crimson fabrics and fine linen, and worked cherubim into it.

3.15
1 Kings 7.15-20
15 In front of the house he made two pillars thirty-five cubits high, with a capital of five cubits on the top of each. 16 He made encircling[o] chains and put them on the tops of the pillars; and he made one hundred pomegranates, and put them on the chains. 17 He set up the pillars in front 3.17
1 Kings 7.21 of the temple, one on the right, the other on the left; the one on the right he called Jachin, and the one on the left, Boaz.

b. The furnishings of the temple

4.1
Ex 27.1, 2;
2 Kings 16.14
4.2
1 Kings 7.23
4.3
1 Kings 7.24-26
4 He made an altar of bronze, twenty cubits long, twenty cubits wide, and ten cubits high. 2 Then he made the molten sea; it was round, ten cubits from rim to rim, and five cubits high. A line of thirty cubits would encircle it completely. 3 Under it were panels all around, each of ten cubits, surrounding the sea; there were two rows of panels, cast when it was cast. 4 It stood on twelve oxen, three facing north, three facing west,

---

j Syr: Heb *foundations*   k Compare 1 Kings 6.3: Meaning of Heb uncertain   l Heb *they overlaid*
m Heb *they*   n Heb *he*   o Cn: Heb *in the inner sanctuary*

3.1 The site for the temple had been decided by David (1 Chr 22.1). It is the place thought by many to be where Abraham offered Isaac many years before (see Gen 22.1,2).
3.3 *Cubits.* The length of the cubit differed at various times. It was the distance from the beginning of the forearm to the tip of the middle finger. Generally it was approximately 17.5 inches long.
3.6 *Parvaim.* We do not know where this was

located.
3.17 Why Solomon named the pillars Jachin and Boaz is not known. Jachin was the fourth son of Simeon; Boaz was the husband of Ruth and one of David's ancestors.
4.1 *altar of bronze.* This was the burnt offering altar (see note on Lev 1.3).
4.2 The molten sea could hold 3,000 baths of water, though normally only 2,000 baths were in it.

three facing south, and three facing east; the sea was set on them. The hindquarters of each were toward the inside. 5 Its thickness was a handbreadth; its rim was made like the rim of a cup, like the flower of a lily; it held three thousand baths.*p* 6 He also made ten basins in which to wash, and set five on the right side, and five on the left. In these they were to rinse what was used for the burnt offering. The sea was for the priests to wash in.

7 He made ten golden lampstands as prescribed, and set them in the temple, five on the south side and five on the north. 8 He also made ten tables and placed them in the temple, five on the right side and five on the left. And he made one hundred basins of gold. 9 He made the court of the priests, and the great court, and doors for the court; he overlaid their doors with bronze. 10 He set the sea at the southeast corner of the house.

11 And Huram made the pots, the shovels, and the basins. Thus Huram finished the work that he did for King Solomon on the house of God: 12 the two pillars, the bowls, and the two capitals on the top of the pillars; and the two latticeworks to cover the two bowls of the capitals that were on the top of the pillars; 13 the four hundred pomegranates for the two latticeworks, two rows of pomegranates for each latticework, to cover the two bowls of the capitals that were on the pillars. 14 He made the stands, the basins on the stands, 15 the one sea, and the twelve oxen underneath it. 16 The pots, the shovels, the forks, and all the equipment for these Huram-abi made of burnished bronze for King Solomon for the house of the Lord. 17 In the plain of the Jordan the king cast them, in the clay ground between Succoth and Zeredah. 18 Solomon made all these things in great quantities, so that the weight of the bronze was not determined.

19 So Solomon made all the things that were in the house of God: the golden altar, the tables for the bread of the Presence, 20 the lampstands and their lamps of pure gold to burn before the inner sanctuary, as prescribed; 21 the flowers, the lamps, and the tongs, of purest gold; 22 the snuffers, basins, ladles, and firepans, of pure gold. As for the entrance to the temple: the inner doors to the most holy place and the doors of the nave of the temple were of gold.

5 Thus all the work that Solomon did for the house of the Lord was finished. Solomon brought in the things that his father David had dedicated, and stored the silver, the gold, and all the vessels in the treasuries of the house of God.

C. The dedication of the temple

1. The bringing of the ark to the temple

2 Then Solomon assembled the elders of Israel and all the heads of the tribes, the leaders of the ancestral houses of the people of Israel, in Jerusalem, to bring up the ark of the covenant of the Lord out of the city of David, which is Zion. 3 And all the Israelites assembled before the king at the festival that is in the seventh month. 4 And all the elders of Israel came, and the Levites carried the ark. 5 So they brought up the ark, the tent of meeting, and all the holy vessels that were in the tent; the priests and the Levites brought them up. 6 King Solomon and all the congrega-

p A Hebrew measure of volume

4.19 *the bread of the Presence.* See note on Mk 2.25ff.
4.20 *before the inner sanctuary,* i.e., before the most holy place.
5.1 See 1 Chr 29.2–5 for the things David had dedicated to the temple.

5.2 *Zion,* another name for Jerusalem. The word is used extensively in the Psalms and in Isaiah.
5.3 *at the festival,* i.e., the festival of tabernacles (see note on Ex 23.16).

tion of Israel, who had assembled before him, were before the ark, sacrificing so many sheep and oxen that they could not be numbered or counted. 7 Then the priests brought the ark of the covenant of the LORD to its place, in the inner sanctuary of the house, in the most holy place, underneath the wings of the cherubim. 8 For the cherubim spread out their wings over the place of the ark, so that the cherubim made a covering above the ark and its poles. 9 The poles were so long that the ends of the poles were seen from the holy place in front of the inner sanctuary; but they could not be seen from outside; they are there to this day. 10 There was nothing in the ark except the two tablets that Moses put there at Horeb, where the LORD made a covenant[q] with the people of Israel after they came out of Egypt.

11   Now when the priests came out of the holy place (for all the priests who were present had sanctified themselves, without regard to their divisions), 12 all the levitical singers, Asaph, Heman, and Jeduthun, their sons and kindred, arrayed in fine linen, with cymbals, harps, and lyres, stood east of the altar with one hundred twenty priests who were trumpeters. 13 It was the duty of the trumpeters and singers to make themselves heard in unison in praise and thanksgiving to the LORD, and when the song was raised, with trumpets and cymbals and other musical instruments, in praise to the LORD,

"For he is good,
     for his steadfast love endures forever,"

the house, the house of the LORD, was filled with a cloud, 14 so that the priests could not stand to minister because of the cloud; for the glory of the LORD filled the house of God.

2. The address by Solomon

6 Then Solomon said, "The LORD has said that he would reside in thick darkness. 2 I have built you an exalted house, a place for you to reside in forever."

3   Then the king turned around and blessed all the assembly of Israel, while all the assembly of Israel stood. 4 And he said, "Blessed be the LORD, the God of Israel, who with his hand has fulfilled what he promised with his mouth to my father David, saying, 5 'Since the day that I brought my people out of the land of Egypt, I have not chosen a city from any of the tribes of Israel in which to build a house, so that my name might be there, and I chose no one as ruler over my people Israel; 6 but I have chosen Jerusalem in order that my name may be there, and I have chosen David to be over my people Israel.' 7 My father David had it in mind to build a house for the name of the LORD, the God of Israel. 8 But the LORD said to my father David, 'You did well to consider building a house for my name; 9 nevertheless you shall not build the house, but your son who shall be born to you shall build the house for my name.' 10 Now the LORD has fulfilled his promise that he made; for I have succeeded my father David, and sit on the throne of Israel, as the LORD promised, and have built the house for the name of the LORD, the God of Israel. 11 There I have set the

Cross references (left margin):

5.9
1 Kings 8.8, 9
5.10
Deut 10.2-5;
Heb 9.4

5.11
1 Chr 24.1-5
5.12
1 Chr 25.1-4;
15.24
5.13
2 Chr 7.3;
1 Chr 16.34, 42

5.14
1 Kings 8.11;
2 Chr 7.2

6.1
1 Kings 8.12-50

6.6
2 Chr 12.13;
1 Chr 28.4
6.7
1 Chr 28.2

6.11
2 Chr 5.10

q Heb lacks a covenant

5.8   cherubim. See note on Ezek 10.1.
5.10   nothing in the ark except the two tablets. Both the golden jar of manna and Aaron's rod that budded were placed in the ark (Ex 16.33,34; Num 17.10; cf. Heb 9.4). Aside from these two items the ark had in it only the two tablets of the law. However, by the time of Solomon only the two tablets of the law remained in the ark. We do not know when the other items were removed or what happened to them.
5.14   The temple became the house of God when the cloud of God's glory, the symbol of his presence,

filled it. The cloud of God indwelling the temple also indicated that God was pleased with the temple. His presence remained in the temple until Ezekiel's day, when the sins of Israel caused it to leave the temple (Ezek 10).
6.1   With no windows to give light, the temple lay in darkness. The light of the temple came from the candles, but most of all from the presence of God, who is light. God was the light of the world before he created the sun, and he will be the unique source of light for the New Jerusalem (Rev 21.23).

ark, in which is the covenant of the LORD that he made with the people of Israel."

3. Solomon's prayer of dedication

12   Then Solomon[r] stood before the altar of the LORD in the presence of the whole assembly of Israel, and spread out his hands. 13 Solomon had made a bronze platform five cubits long, five cubits wide, and three cubits high, and had set it in the court; and he stood on it. Then he knelt on his knees in the presence of the whole assembly of Israel, and spread out his hands toward heaven. 14 He said, "O LORD, God of Israel, there is no God like you, in heaven or on earth, keeping covenant in steadfast love with your servants who walk before you with all their heart — 15 you who have kept for your servant, my father David, what you promised to him. Indeed, you promised with your mouth and this day have fulfilled with your hand. 16 Therefore, O LORD, God of Israel, keep for your servant, my father David, that which you promised him, saying, 'There shall never fail you a successor before me to sit on the throne of Israel, if only your children keep to their way, to walk in my law as you have walked before me.' 17 Therefore, O LORD, God of Israel, let your word be confirmed, which you promised to your servant David.

18   "But will God indeed reside with mortals on earth? Even heaven and the highest heaven cannot contain you, how much less this house that I have built! 19 Regard your servant's prayer and his plea, O LORD my God, heeding the cry and the prayer that your servant prays to you. 20 May your eyes be open day and night toward this house, the place where you promised to set your name, and may you heed the prayer that your servant prays toward this place. 21 And hear the plea of your servant and of your people Israel, when they pray toward this place; may you hear from heaven your dwelling place; hear and forgive.

22   "If someone sins against another and is required to take an oath and comes and swears before your altar in this house, 23 may you hear from heaven, and act, and judge your servants, repaying the guilty by bringing their conduct on their own head, and vindicating those who are in the right by rewarding them in accordance with their righteousness.

24   "When your people Israel, having sinned against you, are defeated before an enemy but turn again to you, confess your name, pray and plead with you in this house, 25 may you hear from heaven, and forgive the sin of your people Israel, and bring them again to the land that you gave to them and to their ancestors.

26   "When heaven is shut up and there is no rain because they have sinned against you, and then they pray toward this place, confess your name, and turn from their sin, because you punish them, 27 may you hear in heaven, forgive the sin of your servants, your people Israel, when you teach them the good way in which they should walk; and send down rain upon your land, which you have given to your people as an inheritance.

28   "If there is famine in the land, if there is plague, blight, mildew, locust, or caterpillar; if their enemies besiege them in any of the settle-

[r] Heb he

6.12 1 Kings 8.22
6.13 1 Kings 8.54
6.14 Ex 15.11; Deut 7.9
6.15 1 Chr 22.9, 10
6.16 2 Sam 7.12, 16; 1 Kings 2.4; 2 Chr 7.18
6.18 2 Chr 2.6
6.21 Mic 7.18
6.22 Mt 5.33
6.24 2 Chr 7.14
6.26 1 Kings 17.1
6.28 2 Chr 20.9

6.12 Solomon's prayer is reiterated here (see 1 Kings 8.22ff). He stood on a bronze platform but then prayed on his knees, acknowledging the greatness and glory of God before whom all hearts must bow, as well as every knee. This looks forward to the time when every knee shall bow to Jesus Christ (Phil 2.10).
6.18 The universe itself, however large and expansive, cannot contain God. He is infinitely beyond the boundaries of the cosmos and infinitely above the worship of all human beings.
6.21 *toward this place.* Solomon prayed that God

would hear the prayers of his people if they were directed to the temple, not because the temple had worth but because it housed the glory of God. Without that presence, prayer toward the temple would lose all significance.
6.26ff All nature is subject to God's will. When natural phenomena occur and people suffer, it may be a sign of God's wrath for sins committed. Implicit in this segment of Solomon's prayer about natural catastrophes is that when people repent, God is gracious and will remove his chastisement.

ments of the lands; whatever suffering, whatever sickness there is; 29 whatever prayer, whatever plea from any individual or from all your people Israel, all knowing their own suffering and their own sorrows so that they stretch out their hands toward this house; 30 may you hear from heaven, your dwelling place, forgive, and render to all whose heart you know, according to all their ways, for only you know the human heart. 31 Thus may they fear you and walk in your ways all the days that they live in the land that you gave to our ancestors.

32 "Likewise when foreigners, who are not of your people Israel, come from a distant land because of your great name, and your mighty hand, and your outstretched arm, when they come and pray toward this house, 33 may you hear from heaven your dwelling place, and do whatever the foreigners ask of you, in order that all the peoples of the earth may know your name and fear you, as do your people Israel, and that they may know that your name has been invoked on this house that I have built.

34 "If your people go out to battle against their enemies, by whatever way you shall send them, and they pray to you toward this city that you have chosen and the house that I have built for your name, 35 then hear from heaven their prayer and their plea, and maintain their cause.

36 "If they sin against you — for there is no one who does not sin — and you are angry with them and give them to an enemy, so that they are carried away captive to a land far or near; 37 then if they come to their senses in the land to which they have been taken captive, and repent, and plead with you in the land of their captivity, saying, 'We have sinned, and have done wrong; we have acted wickedly'; 38 if they repent with all their heart and soul in the land of their captivity, to which they were taken captive, and pray toward their land, which you gave to their ancestors, the city that you have chosen, and the house that I have built for your name, 39 then hear from heaven your dwelling place their prayer and their pleas, maintain their cause and forgive your people who have sinned against you. 40 Now, O my God, let your eyes be open and your ears attentive to prayer from this place.

41 "Now rise up, O Lord God, and go to your resting place,
　　you and the ark of your might.
Let your priests, O Lord God, be clothed with salvation,
　　and let your faithful rejoice in your goodness.
42 O Lord God, do not reject your anointed one.
　　Remember your steadfast love for your servant David."

4. God's answer to Solomon's prayer

a. Fire from heaven

7 When Solomon had ended his prayer, fire came down from heaven and consumed the burnt offering and the sacrifices; and the glory of the Lord filled the temple. 2 The priests could not enter the house of the Lord, because the glory of the Lord filled the Lord's house. 3 When all the people of Israel saw the fire come down and the glory of the Lord on the temple, they bowed down on the pavement with their faces to the ground, and worshiped and gave thanks to the Lord, saying,

6.34 While the petition here concerns Israel at war against its enemies, it is equally true for believers today when they fight against the forces of darkness. Prayer will result in maintaining the cause of God's servants.
6.41 Solomon asked God to take possession of the house that had been built for him and to remain there as his resting place. Believers should ask God to come and live in their hearts as a temple for him (cf. 1 Cor 6.19).
7.1 Even as fire came down from heaven to consume

the sacrifice of Elijah on Mount Carmel, so now at the dedication of the Solomonic temple, God sent down supernatural fire to consume the burnt offerings and the sacrifices. The cloud of God's glory also filled the house. The priests had to leave the temple, for they were blinded by the cloud.
7.3 When the fire came down, the worshipers bowed their faces to the ground, indicating their dread of the divine majesty, their sense of utter unworthiness, and their willingness to submit themselves to the authority of God.

6.30 1 Sam 16.7; 1 Chr 28.9 · 6.32 Josh 12.20; Acts 8.27 · 6.33 2 Chr 7.14 · 6.36 Job 15.14-16; Jas 3.2; 1 Jn 1.8-10 · 6.37 2 Chr 7.14 · 6.40 2 Chr 7.15; Ps 17.1 · 6.41 Ps 132.8-10; 1 Chr 28.2 · 7.1 1 Kings 8.54; 18.24, 38; 2 Chr 5.13, 14 · 7.2 Deut 12.5, 11 · 7.3 2 Chr 5.13; Ps 136.1; 1 Chr 16.41

"For he is good,
    for his steadfast love endures forever."

4   Then the king and all the people offered sacrifice before the Lord.
5 King Solomon offered as a sacrifice twenty-two thousand oxen and one
hundred twenty thousand sheep. So the king and all the people dedicated
the house of God. 6 The priests stood at their posts; the Levites also, with
the instruments for music to the Lord that King David had made for
giving thanks to the Lord—for his steadfast love endures forever—
whenever David offered praises by their ministry. Opposite them the
priests sounded trumpets; and all Israel stood.

7   Solomon consecrated the middle of the court that was in front of the
house of the Lord; for there he offered the burnt offerings and the fat of
the offerings of well-being because the bronze altar Solomon had made
could not hold the burnt offering and the grain offering and the fat parts.

8   At that time Solomon held the festival for seven days, and all Israel
with him, a very great congregation, from Lebo-hamath to the Wadi of
Egypt. 9 On the eighth day they held a solemn assembly; for they had
observed the dedication of the altar seven days and the festival seven days.
10 On the twenty-third day of the seventh month he sent the people away
to their homes, joyful and in good spirits because of the goodness that the
Lord had shown to David and to Solomon and to his people Israel.

b. God's appearance and promise

11   Thus Solomon finished the house of the Lord and the king's
house; all that Solomon had planned to do in the house of the Lord and
in his own house he successfully accomplished.

12   Then the Lord appeared to Solomon in the night and said to him:
"I have heard your prayer, and have chosen this place for myself as a house
of sacrifice. 13 When I shut up the heavens so that there is no rain, or
command the locust to devour the land, or send pestilence among my
people, 14 if my people who are called by my name humble themselves,
pray, seek my face, and turn from their wicked ways, then I will hear from
heaven, and will forgive their sin and heal their land. 15 Now my eyes will
be open and my ears attentive to the prayer that is made in this place.
16 For now I have chosen and consecrated this house so that my name may
be there forever; my eyes and my heart will be there for all time. 17 As
for you, if you walk before me, as your father David walked, doing
according to all that I have commanded you and keeping my statutes and
my ordinances, 18 then I will establish your royal throne, as I made
covenant with your father David saying, 'You shall never lack a successor
to rule over Israel.'

c. God's warning against disobedience

19   "But if yous turn aside and forsake my statutes and my commandments that I have set before you, and go and serve other gods and worship
them, 20 then I will pluck yout up from the land that I have given you;t
and this house, which I have consecrated for my name, I will cast out of
my sight, and will make it a proverb and a byword among all peoples.
21 And regarding this house, now exalted, everyone passing by will be
astonished, and say, 'Why has the Lord done such a thing to this land

s The word you in this verse is plural   t Heb them

7.4	1 Kings 8.62, 63
7.6	1 Chr 15.16-21; 2 Chr 5.12
7.7	1 Kings 8.64-66
7.8	1 Kings 8.65
7.9	Lev 23.36
7.10	1 Kings 8.66
7.11	1 Kings 9.1-9
7.13	2 Chr 6.26-28
7.14	2 Chr 6.27, 30, 37-39
7.15	2 Chr 6.40
7.16	1 Kings 9.3; 2 Chr 6.6; v. 12
7.17	1 Kings 9.4ff
7.18	2 Chr 6.16
7.19	Lev 26.14, 33; Deut 28.15
7.20	Deut 29.28
7.21	Deut 29.24

7.12 1 Kings 9.2 says that God appeared to Solomon
here in the same manner as he had done at Gibeon,
i.e., in a dream (1 Kings 3.5).
7.14 This famous passage is often quoted in connection with revival and renewal. The conditions that
result in the blessing of God are national repentance,
national prayer, and national reformation. Any nation
that humbles itself and does these things in a true

spirit will be richly blessed by God (cf. Jer 18.5–11).
7.17 Solomon had asked for God's blessing. God
promised that blessing, but it was a contingent
promise—Solomon must walk in the ways of God and
keep his commandments. God knows how prone his
people are to backslide. If they turn from him, all the
sacrifices in the world will not help them unless and
until they meet the conditions stated in v. 14.

and to this house?' 22 Then they will say, 'Because they abandoned the LORD the God of their ancestors who brought them out of the land of Egypt, and they adopted other gods, and worshiped them and served them; therefore he has brought all this calamity upon them.' "

D. *Solomon's prosperity and fame*

1. *His buildings, cities, and victories*

8.1
1 Kings 9.1-28

8 At the end of twenty years, during which Solomon had built the house of the LORD and his own house, 2 Solomon rebuilt the cities that Huram had given to him, and settled the people of Israel in them.
3 Solomon went to Hamath-zobah, and captured it. 4 He built Tadmor in the wilderness and all the storage towns that he built in Hamath.

8.5
1 Chr 7.24;
2 Chr 14.7

5 He also built Upper Beth-horon and Lower Beth-horon, fortified cities, with walls, gates, and bars, 6 and Baalath, as well as all Solomon's storage towns, and all the towns for his chariots, the towns for his cavalry, and whatever Solomon desired to build, in Jerusalem, in Lebanon, and in all the land of his dominion. 7 All the people who were left of the Hittites, the Amorites, the Perizzites, the Hivites, and the Jebusites, who were not

8.8
1 Kings 4.6;
9.21

of Israel, 8 from their descendants who were still left in the land, whom the people of Israel had not destroyed — these Solomon conscripted for forced labor, as is still the case today. 9 But of the people of Israel Solomon made no slaves for his work; they were soldiers, and his officers, the commanders of his chariotry and cavalry. 10 These were the chief officers of King Solomon, two hundred fifty of them, who exercised authority over the people.

2. *The house of his Egyptian wife*

8.11
1 Kings 3.1;
7.8

11 Solomon brought Pharaoh's daughter from the city of David to the house that he had built for her, for he said, "My wife shall not live in the house of King David of Israel, for the places to which the ark of the LORD has come are holy."

3. *The offerings*

8.12
2 Chr 4.1
8.13
Ex 29.38;
Num 28.3;
Ex 23.14-17

12 Then Solomon offered up burnt offerings to the LORD on the altar of the LORD that he had built in front of the vestibule, 13 as the duty of each day required, offering according to the commandment of Moses for the sabbaths, the new moons, and the three annual festivals — the festival of unleavened bread, the festival of weeks, and the festival of booths.

8.14
1 Chr 24.1;
25.1; 26.1;
Neh 12.24,
36

14 According to the ordinance of his father David, he appointed the divisions of the priests for their service, and the Levites for their offices of praise and ministry alongside the priests as the duty of each day required, and the gatekeepers in their divisions for the several gates; for so David the man of God had commanded. 15 They did not turn away from what the king had commanded the priests and Levites regarding anything at all, or regarding the treasuries.
16 Thus all the work of Solomon was accomplished from *u* the day the foundation of the house of the LORD was laid until the house of the LORD was finished completely.

8.17
1 Kings 9.26

17 Then Solomon went to Ezion-geber and Eloth on the shore of the

u Gk Syr Vg: Heb *to*

8.4 *Tadmor*, also named Palmyra, located in the Aramean desert. It appears that some copyist confused this with Tamar (1 Kings 9.18), a caravan station in the wilderness southwest of the Dead Sea.
8.11 Solomon married the Egyptian Pharaoh's daughter for political reasons. Apparently he did not trust wholly in God for the protection of his people.

But he still had sufficient spiritual insight to build a separate palace for this wife. He had respect for the house in which his father David had lived and in which the ark of God rested for a considerable length of time. The presence of his wife would have defiled the house.

sea, in the land of Edom. 18 Huram sent him, in the care of his servants, ships and servants familiar with the sea. They went to Ophir, together with the servants of Solomon, and imported from there four hundred fifty talents of gold and brought it to King Solomon.

4. The visit of the queen of Sheba

9 When the queen of Sheba heard of the fame of Solomon, she came to Jerusalem to test him with hard questions, having a very great retinue and camels bearing spices and very much gold and precious stones. When she came to Solomon, she discussed with him all that was on her mind. 2 Solomon answered all her questions; there was nothing hidden from Solomon that he could not explain to her. 3 When the queen of Sheba had observed the wisdom of Solomon, the house that he had built, 4 the food of his table, the seating of his officials, and the attendance of his servants, and their clothing, his valets, and their clothing, and his burnt offerings*v* that he offered at the house of the LORD, there was no more spirit left in her.

5 So she said to the king, "The report was true that I heard in my own land of your accomplishments and of your wisdom, 6 but I did not believe the*w* reports until I came and my own eyes saw it. Not even half of the greatness of your wisdom had been told to me; you far surpass the report that I had heard. 7 Happy are your people! Happy are these your servants, who continually attend you and hear your wisdom! 8 Blessed be the LORD your God, who has delighted in you and set you on his throne as king for the LORD your God. Because your God loved Israel and would establish them forever, he has made you king over them, that you may execute justice and righteousness." 9 Then she gave the king one hundred twenty talents of gold, a very great quantity of spices, and precious stones: there were no spices such as those that the queen of Sheba gave to King Solomon.

10 Moreover the servants of Huram and the servants of Solomon who brought gold from Ophir brought algum wood and precious stones. 11 From the algum wood, the king made steps*x* for the house of the LORD and for the king's house, lyres also and harps for the singers; there never was seen the like of them before in the land of Judah.

12 Meanwhile King Solomon granted the queen of Sheba every desire that she expressed, well beyond what she had brought to the king. Then she returned to her own land, with her servants.

5. The wealth and wisdom of Solomon

13 The weight of gold that came to Solomon in one year was six hundred sixty-six talents of gold, 14 besides that which the traders and merchants brought; and all the kings of Arabia and the governors of the land brought gold and silver to Solomon. 15 King Solomon made two hundred large shields of beaten gold; six hundred shekels of beaten gold went into each large shield. 16 He made three hundred shields of beaten gold; three hundred shekels of gold went into each shield; and the king put them in the House of the Forest of Lebanon. 17 The king also made

v Gk Syr Vg 1 Kings 10.5: Heb *ascent*   *w* Heb *their*   *x* Gk Vg: Meaning of Heb uncertain

---

Cross references (margin):

8.18
1 Kings 9.27;
2 Chr 9.10, 13

9.1
1 Kings 10.1-13;
Mt 12.42;
Lk 11.31

9.3
1 Kings 5.12

9.5
1 Kings 10.6

9.8
1 Chr 28.5;
29.23;
2 Chr 2.11

9.9
1 Kings 10.10

9.10
2 Chr 8.18

9.13
1 Kings 10.14-28

8.18 1 Kings 9.28 speaks about 420 talents of gold; here the figure is 450 talents. This is probably a copyist's error in reading worn manuscripts, which often had illegible spots.
9.1 *Sheba*, the land of the Sabeans (see note on 1 Kings 10.1).
9.2 Solomon had greatly honored God and God honored him. The Queen of Sheba was amazed at his knowledge and understanding. But however great Solomon was, someone greater than Solomon came in

the person of Jesus (Lk 11.31).
9.8 The Queen of Sheba exhibited some wisdom herself. She knew that God set Solomon "on his throne as king for the LORD your God." All rulers should understand that they are under the rule of God and must establish true justice and execute right judgment against wickedness.
9.13ff Solomon was known for his wisdom and his wealth. Both were gifts from God. Personally, therefore, he had nothing about which to boast.

a great ivory throne, and overlaid it with pure gold. 18 The throne had six steps and a footstool of gold, which were attached to the throne, and on each side of the seat were arm rests and two lions standing beside the arm rests, 19 while twelve lions were standing, one on each end of a step on the six steps. The like of it was never made in any kingdom. 20 All King Solomon's drinking vessels were of gold, and all the vessels of the House of the Forest of Lebanon were of pure gold; silver was not considered as anything in the days of Solomon. 21 For the king's ships went to Tarshish with the servants of Huram; once every three years the ships of Tarshish used to come bringing gold, silver, ivory, apes, and peacocks.y

22   Thus King Solomon excelled all the kings of the earth in riches and in wisdom. 23 All the kings of the earth sought the presence of Solomon to hear his wisdom, which God had put into his mind. 24 Every one of them brought a present, objects of silver and gold, garments, weaponry, spices, horses, and mules, so much year by year. 25 Solomon had four thousand stalls for horses and chariots, and twelve thousand horses, which he stationed in the chariot cities and with the king in Jerusalem. 26 He ruled over all the kings from the Euphrates to the land of the Philistines, and to the border of Egypt. 27 The king made silver as common in Jerusalem as stone, and cedar as plentiful as the sycamore of the Shephelah. 28 Horses were imported for Solomon from Egypt and from all lands.

6. Solomon's death and the succession

29   Now the rest of the acts of Solomon, from first to last, are they not written in the history of the prophet Nathan, and in the prophecy of Ahijah the Shilonite, and in the visions of the seer Iddo concerning Jeroboam son of Nebat? 30 Solomon reigned in Jerusalem over all Israel forty years. 31 Solomon slept with his ancestors and was buried in the city of his father David; and his son Rehoboam succeeded him.

IV. The history of Judah from Solomon's death to the captivity (10.1–36.23)

A. The division of the kingdom

1. Rehoboam's ill-chosen words to the ten tribes

10 Rehoboam went to Shechem, for all Israel had come to Shechem to make him king. 2 When Jeroboam son of Nebat heard of it (for he was in Egypt, where he had fled from King Solomon), then Jeroboam returned from Egypt. 3 They sent and called him; and Jeroboam and all Israel came and said to Rehoboam, 4 "Your father made our yoke heavy. Now therefore lighten the hard service of your father and his heavy yoke that he placed on us, and we will serve you." 5 He said to them, "Come to me again in three days." So the people went away.

6   Then King Rehoboam took counsel with the older men who had attended his father Solomon while he was still alive, saying, "How do you advise me to answer this people?" 7 They answered him, "If you will be kind to this people and please them, and speak good words to them, then they will be your servants forever." 8 But he rejected the advice that the

Margin references (left column):

9.18 / 1 Kings 10.18
9.19 / 1 Kings 10.20
9.21 / 2 Chr 20.36, 37
9.22 / 2 Chr 1.12; 1 Kings 3.13
9.25 / 1 Kings 4.26; 10.26; 2 Chr 1.14
9.26 / 1 Kings 4.21; Ps 72.8
9.27 / 1 Kings 10.27; 2 Chr 1.15
9.28 / 1 Kings 10.28; 2 Chr 1.16
9.29 / 1 Kings 11.41; 1 Chr 29.29
9.30 / 1 Kings 11.42, 43
9.31 / 1 Kings 2.10
10.1 / 1 Kings 12.1-20
10.2 / 1 Kings 11.40
10.6 / 1 Kings 12.6

y Or baboons

9.25   four thousand stalls. See note on 1 Kings 4.26.
9.29   The chronicler omitted reference to Solomon's one thousand wives and concubines and glossed over his sins, generally limiting himself to the good points connected with Solomon's reign. Yet it was intermarriage with foreign women that brought about Solomon's spiritual decline in his latter years (see 1 Kings 11.1ff).

10.4   Now that Solomon was dead, the people expressed their unhappiness with the yoke he had laid upon them through his many marriages and his expensive lifestyle. Solomon's latter days were much worse than the earlier ones. He had given the people reason to complain.

older men gave him, and consulted the young men who had grown up with him and now attended him. 9 He said to them, "What do you advise that we answer this people who have said to me, 'Lighten the yoke that your father put on us'?" 10 The young men who had grown up with him said to him, "Thus should you speak to the people who said to you, 'Your father made our yoke heavy, but you must lighten it for us'; tell them, 'My little finger is thicker than my father's loins. 11 Now, whereas my father laid on you a heavy yoke, I will add to your yoke. My father disciplined you with whips, but I will discipline you with scorpions.' "

2. The revolt of the ten tribes

12   So Jeroboam and all the people came to Rehoboam the third day, as the king had said, "Come to me again the third day." 13 The king answered them harshly. King Rehoboam rejected the advice of the older men; 14 he spoke to them in accordance with the advice of the young men, "My father made your yoke heavy, but I will add to it; my father disciplined you with whips, but I will discipline you with scorpions." 15 So the king did not listen to the people, because it was a turn of affairs brought about by God so that the LORD might fulfill his word, which he had spoken by Ahijah the Shilonite to Jeroboam son of Nebat.

16   When all Israel saw that the king would not listen to them, the people answered the king,

"What share do we have in David?
  We have no inheritance in the son of Jesse.
Each of you to your tents, O Israel!
  Look now to your own house, O David."

So all Israel departed to their tents. 17 But Rehoboam reigned over the people of Israel who were living in the cities of Judah. 18 When King Rehoboam sent Hadoram, who was taskmaster over the forced labor, the people of Israel stoned him to death. King Rehoboam hurriedly mounted his chariot to flee to Jerusalem. 19 So Israel has been in rebellion against the house of David to this day.

3. The LORD forbids Judah to fight against Israel

11   When Rehoboam came to Jerusalem, he assembled one hundred eighty thousand chosen troops of the house of Judah and Benjamin to fight against Israel, to restore the kingdom to Rehoboam. 2 But the word of the LORD came to Shemaiah the man of God: 3 Say to King Rehoboam of Judah, son of Solomon, and to all Israel in Judah and Benjamin, 4 "Thus says the LORD: You shall not go up or fight against your kindred. Let everyone return home, for this thing is from me." So they heeded the word of the LORD and turned back from the expedition against Jeroboam.

4. Rehoboam erects fortresses

5   Rehoboam resided in Jerusalem, and he built cities for defense in

Margin references:
10.9 — 1 Kings 12.9
10.12 — v. 5
10.15 — 1 Kings 12.15, 24; 2 Chr 25.16-20; 1 Kings 11.29
10;16 — 2 Sam 20.1; v. 19
10.19 — 1 Kings 12.19
11.1 — 1 Kings 12.21-24
11.2 — 2 Chr 12.15
11.4 — 2 Chr 10.15

10.8   See note on 1 Kings 12.13.
10.14   Rough answers are likely to stir up anger and worsen any situation. Rehoboam's tactlessness and lack of love brought its own reward. The kingdom was torn in two.
10.16   After Solomon's death the kingdom was divided into two parts: Israel, the northern kingdom, led by Jeroboam, who engaged in the worship of Baal and calves; and Judah, the southern kingdom, led by Rehoboam.
10.18   Apparently Rehoboam accompanied Hadoram, and when he was stoned, the king had enough

sense to flee to Jerusalem. But even this incident did not bring him to his senses. The kingdom remained divided.
11.2   God had spoken directly to David and to Solomon. Rehoboam was beyond this sort of relationship. So God sent his prophet Shemaiah to tell Rehoboam not to fight against the revolting tribes. He obeyed the order given him by the prophet.
11.5   Rehoboam was prudent enough to defend his smaller kingdom against possible incursions by the ten revolting tribes. He fortified Jerusalem and built fortress cities surrounding Jerusalem for its protection.

Judah. 6 He built up Bethlehem, Etam, Tekoa, 7 Beth-zur, Soco, Adullam, 8 Gath, Mareshah, Ziph, 9 Adoraim, Lachish, Azekah, 10 Zorah, Aijalon, and Hebron, fortified cities that are in Judah and in Benjamin. 11 He made the fortresses strong, and put commanders in them, and stores of food, oil, and wine. 12 He also put large shields and spears in all the cities, and made them very strong. So he held Judah and Benjamin.

5. The Levites remain with Judah

13 The priests and the Levites who were in all Israel presented themselves to him from all their territories. 14 The Levites had left their common lands and their holdings and had come to Judah and Jerusalem, because Jeroboam and his sons had prevented them from serving as priests of the Lord, 15 and had appointed his own priests for the high places, and for the goat-demons, and for the calves that he had made. 16 Those who had set their hearts to seek the Lord God of Israel came after them from all the tribes of Israel to Jerusalem to sacrifice to the Lord, the God of their ancestors. 17 They strengthened the kingdom of Judah, and for three years they made Rehoboam son of Solomon secure, for they walked for three years in the way of David and Solomon.

6. The polygamy of Rehoboam

18 Rehoboam took as his wife Mahalath daughter of Jerimoth son of David, and of Abihail daughter of Eliab son of Jesse. 19 She bore him sons: Jeush, Shemariah, and Zaham. 20 After her he took Maacah daughter of Absalom, who bore him Abijah, Attai, Ziza, and Shelomith. 21 Rehoboam loved Maacah daughter of Absalom more than all his other wives and concubines (he took eighteen wives and sixty concubines, and became the father of twenty-eight sons and sixty daughters). 22 Rehoboam appointed Abijah son of Maacah as chief prince among his brothers, for he intended to make him king. 23 He dealt wisely, and distributed some of his sons through all the districts of Judah and Benjamin, in all the fortified cities; he gave them abundant provisions, and found many wives for them.

7. Shishak defeats Rehoboam

12 When the rule of Rehoboam was established and he grew strong, he abandoned the law of the Lord, he and all Israel with him. 2 In the fifth year of King Rehoboam, because they had been unfaithful to the Lord, King Shishak of Egypt came up against Jerusalem 3 with twelve hundred chariots and sixty thousand cavalry. A countless army came with him from Egypt — Libyans, Sukkiim, and Ethiopians.z 4 He took the fortified cities of Judah and came as far as Jerusalem. 5 Then the prophet Shemaiah came to Rehoboam and to the officers of Judah, who had gathered at Jerusalem because of Shishak, and said to them, "Thus says the Lord: You abandoned me, so I have abandoned you to the hand of

z Or Nubians; Heb Cushites

11.14
Num 35.2-5;
2 Chr 13.9

11.15
1 Kings 12.28-33;
13.33;
2 Chr 13.9

11.16
2 Chr 15.9

11.17
2 Chr 12.1

11.18
1 Sam 16.6

11.21
Deut 17.17

11.22
Deut 21.15-17

12.1
2 Chr 11.17;
1 Kings 14.22-24

12.2
1 Kings 14.24,
25; 11.40

12.3
2 Chr 16.8

12.5
2 Chr 11.2;
15.2;
Deut 28.15

11.13 Jeroboam had turned from God and fired the priests and Levites. They now swarmed into Jerusalem, leaving their possessions behind them. Along with them came pious believers from the ten tribes (v. 16). Their influence on Rehoboam was for good, for a short time. Thus when the northern kingdom was destroyed, there were still people from those tribes who were not involved in the captivity and destruction. Jerusalem became their haven.
11.21 Rehoboam indulged himself in pleasure, as did his father Solomon. This was a violation of God's commandments and did neither of them any good.
12.1 Rehoboam was responsible for the breakup of Solomon's kingdom because of his stupidity. He

turned against God and suffered for his folly (vv. 2–4). Nineteen kings followed after him; some were good, others evil. Judah, the southern kingdom, survived for more than three hundred years before it was destroyed by the Babylonian conquest.
12.5–9 Shishak had come down on Judah as a divine punishment for departing from the faith (v. 2). This caused God's people to turn back to Shishak and seek his help (v. 6). Thus the counsel of 7.14 was followed, and help from God stayed the hand of Shishak so that the kingdom was not destroyed. It did become a tributary to Shishak, who ransacked the royal palace and the temple. On the whole, however, "conditions were good in Judah" (v. 12).

Shishak." 6 Then the officers of Israel and the king humbled themselves and said, "The LORD is in the right." 7 When the LORD saw that they humbled themselves, the word of the LORD came to Shemaiah, saying: "They have humbled themselves; I will not destroy them, but I will grant them some deliverance, and my wrath shall not be poured out on Jerusalem by the hand of Shishak. 8 Nevertheless they shall be his servants, so that they may know the difference between serving me and serving the kingdoms of other lands."

9 So King Shishak of Egypt came up against Jerusalem; he took away the treasures of the house of the LORD and the treasures of the king's house; he took everything. He also took away the shields of gold that Solomon had made; 10 but King Rehoboam made in place of them shields of bronze, and committed them to the hands of the officers of the guard, who kept the door of the king's house. 11 Whenever the king went into the house of the LORD, the guard would come along bearing them, and would then bring them back to the guardroom. 12 Because he humbled himself the wrath of the LORD turned from him, so as not to destroy them completely; moreover, conditions were good in Judah.

8. Summary of Rehoboam's reign

13 So King Rehoboam established himself in Jerusalem and reigned. Rehoboam was forty-one years old when he began to reign; he reigned seventeen years in Jerusalem, the city that the LORD had chosen out of all the tribes of Israel to put his name there. His mother's name was Naamah the Ammonite. 14 He did evil, for he did not set his heart to seek the LORD.

15 Now the acts of Rehoboam, from first to last, are they not written in the records of the prophet Shemaiah and of the seer Iddo, recorded by genealogy? There were continual wars between Rehoboam and Jeroboam. 16 Rehoboam slept with his ancestors and was buried in the city of David; and his son Abijah succeeded him.

B. The reign of Abijah

1. War between Abijah and Jeroboam

13 In the eighteenth year of King Jeroboam, Abijah began to reign over Judah. 2 He reigned for three years in Jerusalem. His mother's name was Micaiah daughter of Uriel of Gibeah.

Now there was war between Abijah and Jeroboam. 3 Abijah engaged in battle, having an army of valiant warriors, four hundred thousand picked men; and Jeroboam drew up his line of battle against him with eight hundred thousand picked mighty warriors. 4 Then Abijah stood on the slope of Mount Zemaraim that is in the hill country of Ephraim, and said, "Listen to me, Jeroboam and all Israel! 5 Do you not know that the LORD God of Israel gave the kingship over Israel forever to David and his sons by a covenant of salt? 6 Yet Jeroboam son of Nebat, a servant of Solomon son of David, rose up and rebelled against his lord; 7 and certain worthless scoundrels gathered around him and defied Rehoboam son of Solomon, when Rehoboam was young and irresolute and could not withstand them. 8 "And now you think that you can withstand the kingdom of the

12.6
Ex 9.27;
Dan 9.14
12.7
1 Kings 21.29

12.8
Deut 28.47,
48

12.9
1 Kings 14.25,
26;
2 Chr 9.15,
16

12.12
2 Chr 19.3

12.13
1 Kings 14.21;
2 Chr 6.6

12.14
2 Chr 19.3

12.15
1 Kings 14.29,
30;
2 Chr 9.29
12.16
1 Kings 14.31;
2 Chr 11.20

13.1
1 Kings 15.1,
2
13.2
2 Chr 11.20;
1 Kings 15.7

13.4
Josh 18.22

13.5
2 Sam 7.12,
13, 16;
Num 18.19
13.6
1 Kings 11.26

13.8
1 Kings 12.28;
2 Chr 11.15

12.15 In addition to Shishak, the ten tribes that had revolted were a problem to Rehoboam, for there were wars continually between Israel and Judah. The splendor of Solomon had already departed from Israel, and the promise of blessing lost because of transgression.
13.2 God had forbidden Rehoboam to war against Jeroboam (11.4). He allowed his son Abijah to do so and gave him the victory over Jeroboam. On the sig-

nificance of the name "Abijah," see note on 1 Kings 15.1.
13.5 Abijah apprised Jereboam of an undeniable fact. God had given the kingship to David and to his posterity in a covenant of salt. Therefore Jeroboam was a rebel who had done the wrong thing. Moreover, he had taken advantage of the youthfulness of Rehoboam and his lack of tact.
13.8 Abijah's case against the northern kingdom

LORD in the hand of the sons of David, because you are a great multitude and have with you the golden calves that Jeroboam made as gods for you. 9 Have you not driven out the priests of the LORD, the descendants of Aaron, and the Levites, and made priests for yourselves like the peoples of other lands? Whoever comes to be consecrated with a young bull or seven rams becomes a priest of what are no gods. 10 But as for us, the LORD is our God, and we have not abandoned him. We have priests ministering to the LORD who are descendants of Aaron, and Levites for their service. 11 They offer to the LORD every morning and every evening burnt offerings and fragrant incense, set out the rows of bread on the table of pure gold, and care for the golden lampstand so that its lamps may burn every evening; for we keep the charge of the LORD our God, but you have abandoned him. 12 See, God is with us at our head, and his priests have their battle trumpets to sound the call to battle against you. O Israelites, do not fight against the LORD, the God of your ancestors; for you cannot succeed."

2. Defeat of Jeroboam

13 Jeroboam had sent an ambush around to come on them from behind; thus his troops[a] were in front of Judah, and the ambush was behind them. 14 When Judah turned, the battle was in front of them and behind them. They cried out to the LORD, and the priests blew the trumpets. 15 Then the people of Judah raised the battle shout. And when the people of Judah shouted, God defeated Jeroboam and all Israel before Abijah and Judah. 16 The Israelites fled before Judah, and God gave them into their hands. 17 Abijah and his army defeated them with great slaughter; five hundred thousand picked men of Israel fell slain. 18 Thus the Israelites were subdued at that time, and the people of Judah prevailed, because they relied on the LORD, the God of their ancestors. 19 Abijah pursued Jeroboam, and took cities from him: Bethel with its villages and Jeshanah with its villages and Ephron[b] with its villages. 20 Jeroboam did not recover his power in the days of Abijah; the LORD struck him down, and he died. 21 But Abijah grew strong. He took fourteen wives, and became the father of twenty-two sons and sixteen daughters. 22 The rest of the acts of Abijah, his behavior and his deeds, are written in the story of the prophet Iddo.

C. The reign of Asa

1. Faithful Asa blessed of God

14 [c] So Abijah slept with his ancestors, and they buried him in the city of David. His son Asa succeeded him. In his days the land had rest for ten years. 2[d] Asa did what was good and right in the sight of the LORD his God. 3 He took away the foreign altars and the high places, broke down the pillars, hewed down the sacred poles,[e] 4 and commanded Judah to seek the LORD, the God of their ancestors, and to keep the law and the commandment. 5 He also removed from all the cities of Judah the high

a Heb *they*   *b* Another reading is *Ephrain*   *c* Ch 13.23 in Heb   *d* Ch 14.1 in Heb   *e* Heb *Asherim*

centered around the godlessness of the ruler who made golden calves and turned Israel away from the true God. While Abijah was by no means fully obedient and under the rule of God, yet he did call on God and seek divine help against this wicked apostate.
13.13 Apparently Jeroboam was talking peace to Abijah at the same time he was preparing an ambush to take him and the soldiers of Judah by surprise. His ploy did not work.
13.14 The priests accompanied the troops of Abijah

in battle. They blew their trumpets, thus calling on the name of God. Judah prevailed, and Jeroboam never recovered from the defeat he suffered.
13.21 Abijah followed in the steps of his father and grandfather, multiplying wives to himself and becoming the father of twenty-two sons and sixteen daughters. He prospered and, fortunately for Judah, he had a good son, Asa, to succeed him.
14.2 Asa was a good king who enjoyed peace in his time. He aimed to please God, and in so doing he destroyed all items connected with idolatry.

places and the incense altars. And the kingdom had rest under him. 6 He built fortified cities in Judah while the land had rest. He had no war in those years, for the LORD gave him peace. 7 He said to Judah, "Let us build these cities, and surround them with walls and towers, gates and bars; the land is still ours because we have sought the LORD our God; we have sought him, and he has given us peace on every side." So they built and prospered. 8 Asa had an army of three hundred thousand from Judah, armed with large shields and spears, and two hundred eighty thousand troops from Benjamin who carried shields and drew bows; all these were mighty warriors.

2. Asa defeats Zerah of Ethiopia

9 Zerah the Ethiopian*f* came out against them with an army of a million men and three hundred chariots, and came as far as Mareshah. 10 Asa went out to meet him, and they drew up their lines of battle in the valley of Zephathah at Mareshah. 11 Asa cried to the LORD his God, "O LORD, there is no difference for you between helping the mighty and the weak. Help us, O LORD our God, for we rely on you, and in your name we have come against this multitude. O LORD, you are our God; let no mortal prevail against you." 12 So the LORD defeated the Ethiopians*g* before Asa and before Judah, and the Ethiopians*g* fled. 13 Asa and the army with him pursued them as far as Gerar, and the Ethiopians*g* fell until no one remained alive; for they were broken before the LORD and his army. The people of Judah*h* carried away a great quantity of booty. 14 They defeated all the cities around Gerar, for the fear of the LORD was on them. They plundered all the cities; for there was much plunder in them. 15 They also attacked the tents of those who had livestock,*i* and carried away sheep and goats in abundance, and camels. Then they returned to Jerusalem.

3. Asa's reform movement

15 The spirit of God came upon Azariah son of Oded. 2 He went out to meet Asa and said to him, "Hear me, Asa, and all Judah and Benjamin: The LORD is with you, while you are with him. If you seek him, he will be found by you, but if you abandon him, he will abandon you. 3 For a long time Israel was without the true God, and without a teaching priest, and without law; 4 but when in their distress they turned to the LORD, the God of Israel, and sought him, he was found by them. 5 In those times it was not safe for anyone to go or come, for great disturbances afflicted all the inhabitants of the lands. 6 They were broken in pieces, nation against nation and city against city, for God troubled them with every sort of distress. 7 But you, take courage! Do not let your hands be weak, for your work shall be rewarded."

8 When Asa heard these words, the prophecy of Azariah son of Oded,*j* he took courage, and put away the abominable idols from all the

f Or *Nubian;* Heb *Cushite* g Or *Nubians;* Heb *Cushites* h Heb *They* i Meaning of Heb uncertain
j Compare Syr Vg: Heb *the prophecy, the prophet Obed*

14.6,7 God was gracious to Asa and Judah and gave them peace. All who trust in God will find peace and rest as the reward of faithfulness.
14.9 *a million.* In view of the three hundred chariots, the million soldiers is probably a hyperbole or the result of misreading an illegible or worn manuscript when it was copied.
14.10 Asa enjoyed internal peace until Zerah the Ethiopian came down with a mighty army against him. Asa put his trust in God and prayed for divine help. God heard and helped.
14.12 The victory over Zerah was God's victory. Judah knew that they had not won the victory by their own strength.
15.1 The Spirit of God came on God's people in the O.T. according to his good pleasure. Here he came upon Azariah, instructing him what he should say to the king and enabling him to say it with boldness and clarity. He did not come to compliment the king for the victory; rather, he came to tell Asa what he should do as a servant of God.
15.8 Revival came to Judah after Azariah spoke to the king. Asa followed Azariah's advice by repairing the altar of God, destroying all the idols he could find in his kingdom, and calling the people to the true worship of God.

14.6
2 Chr 15.15

14.9
2 Chr 16.8;
11.8

14.11
2 Chr 13.14,
18;
1 Sam 14.6;
17.45

14.12
2 Chr 13.15
14.13
Gen 10.19

14.14
Gen 35.5;
2 Chr 17.10

15.1
Num 24.2;
2 Chr 20.14;
24.20
15.2
Jas 4.8;
vv. 4, 15;
2 Chr 24.20
15.3
Hos 3.4;
Lev 10.11;
2 Chr 17.9
15.4
Deut 4.29
15.5
Judg 5.6
15.6
Mt 24.7
15.7
Josh 1.7, 9
15.8
2 Chr 13.19

land of Judah and Benjamin and from the towns that he had taken in the hill country of Ephraim. He repaired the altar of the LORD that was in front of the vestibule of the house of the LORD. [k] 9 He gathered all Judah and Benjamin, and those from Ephraim, Manasseh, and Simeon who were residing as aliens with them, for great numbers had deserted to him from Israel when they saw that the LORD his God was with him. 10 They were gathered at Jerusalem in the third month of the fifteenth year of the reign of Asa. 11 They sacrificed to the LORD on that day, from the booty that they had brought, seven hundred oxen and seven thousand sheep. 12 They entered into a covenant to seek the LORD, the God of their ancestors, with all their heart and with all their soul. 13 Whoever would not seek the LORD, the God of Israel, should be put to death, whether young or old, man or woman. 14 They took an oath to the LORD with a loud voice, and with shouting, and with trumpets, and with horns. 15 All Judah rejoiced over the oath; for they had sworn with all their heart, and had sought him with their whole desire, and he was found by them, and the LORD gave them rest all around.

16 King Asa even removed his mother Maacah from being queen mother because she had made an abominable image for Asherah. Asa cut down her image, crushed it, and burned it at the Wadi Kidron. 17 But the high places were not taken out of Israel. Nevertheless the heart of Asa was true all his days. 18 He brought into the house of God the votive gifts of his father and his own votive gifts — silver, gold, and utensils. 19 And there was no more war until the thirty-fifth year of the reign of Asa.

4. Asa's sinful alliance with Ben-hadad

16 In the thirty-sixth year of the reign of Asa, King Baasha of Israel went up against Judah, and built Ramah, to prevent anyone from going out or coming into the territory of[l] King Asa of Judah. 2 Then Asa took silver and gold from the treasures of the house of the LORD and the king's house, and sent them to King Ben-hadad of Aram, who resided in Damascus, saying, 3 "Let there be an alliance between me and you, like that between my father and your father; I am sending to you silver and gold; go, break your alliance with King Baasha of Israel, so that he may withdraw from me." 4 Ben-hadad listened to King Asa, and sent the commanders of his armies against the cities of Israel. They conquered Ijon, Dan, Abel-maim, and all the store-cities of Naphtali. 5 When Baasha heard of it, he stopped building Ramah, and let his work cease. 6 Then King Asa brought all Judah, and they carried away the stones of Ramah and its timber, with which Baasha had been building, and with them he built up Geba and Mizpah.

5. Hanani pronounces God's judgment

7 At that time the seer Hanani came to King Asa of Judah, and said to him, "Because you relied on the king of Aram, and did not rely on the LORD your God, the army of the king of Aram has escaped you. 8 Were not the Ethiopians[m] and the Libyans a huge army with exceedingly many chariots and cavalry? Yet because you relied on the LORD, he gave them

Cross-references (left margin)

15.9
2 Chr 11.16

15.11
2 Chr 14.13-15
15.12
2 Chr 23.16;
34.31
15.13
Ex 22.20;
Deut 13.5, 9,
15
15.15
v. 2;
2 Chr 14.7

15.16
1 Kings 15.13-
15;
Ex 34.13;
2 Chr 14.2-5

16.1
1 Kings 15.17-
22

16.4
1 Kings 15.18,
20

16.7
2 Chr 19.2;
14.11; 32.7,
8
16.8
2 Chr 14.9;
12.3

---

k Heb *the vestibule of the LORD*   *l* Heb lacks *the territory of*   *m* Or *Nubians*; Heb *Cushites*

15.15 The revival led Judah, Benjamin, and the people from the northern kingdom who had come to live in Judah to take an oath before God that they would serve him faithfully. When they did this, God gave them rest.
16.2–3 *Ben-hadad.* See note on 1 Kings 15.18. Instead of trusting in God, Asa bribed Ben-hadad and worked out a military alliance with him. He was successful in repulsing Baasha, the king of Israel.
16.7–9 The prophet Hanani rebuked Asa for form-

ing an alliance with Ben-hadad instead of trusting God alone, reminding him of the great victory that God gave Judah over the Ethiopians. He pictured God as searching the farthest corners of the earth to find those who trust in him. And when he finds them he uses his might on their behalf. Those whose hearts are not upright can expect no help from God. That is, the condition for blessing and help always depends on the rightness of one's relation to God.

into your hand. 9 For the eyes of the Lord range throughout the entire earth, to strengthen those whose heart is true to him. You have done foolishly in this; for from now on you will have wars." 10 Then Asa was angry with the seer, and put him in the stocks, in prison, for he was in a rage with him because of this. And Asa inflicted cruelties on some of the people at the same time.

6. Asa's sickness and death

11 The acts of Asa, from first to last, are written in the Book of the Kings of Judah and Israel. 12 In the thirty-ninth year of his reign Asa was diseased in his feet, and his disease became severe; yet even in his disease he did not seek the Lord, but sought help from physicians. 13 Then Asa slept with his ancestors, dying in the forty-first year of his reign. 14 They buried him in the tomb that he had hewn out for himself in the city of David. They laid him on a bier that had been filled with various kinds of spices prepared by the perfumer's art; and they made a very great fire in his honor.

D. The reign of Jehoshaphat

1. Godly Jehoshaphat

17 His son Jehoshaphat succeeded him, and strengthened himself against Israel. 2 He placed forces in all the fortified cities of Judah, and set garrisons in the land of Judah, and in the cities of Ephraim that his father Asa had taken. 3 The Lord was with Jehoshaphat, because he walked in the earlier ways of his father;[n] he did not seek the Baals, 4 but sought the God of his father and walked in his commandments, and not according to the ways of Israel. 5 Therefore the Lord established the kingdom in his hand. All Judah brought tribute to Jehoshaphat, and he had great riches and honor. 6 His heart was courageous in the ways of the Lord; and furthermore he removed the high places and the sacred poles[o] from Judah.

2. The book of the law taught

7 In the third year of his reign he sent his officials, Ben-hail, Obadiah, Zechariah, Nethanel, and Micaiah, to teach in the cities of Judah. 8 With them were the Levites, Shemaiah, Nethaniah, Zebadiah, Asahel, Shemiramoth, Jehonathan, Adonijah, Tobijah, and Tob-adonijah; and with these Levites, the priests Elishama and Jehoram. 9 They taught in Judah, having the book of the law of the Lord with them; they went around through all the cities of Judah and taught among the people.

3. Jehoshaphat's prosperity

10 The fear of the Lord fell on all the kingdoms of the lands around Judah, and they did not make war against Jehoshaphat. 11 Some of the Philistines brought Jehoshaphat presents, and silver for tribute; and the Arabs also brought him seven thousand seven hundred rams and seven thousand seven hundred male goats. 12 Jehoshaphat grew steadily greater. He built fortresses and storage cities in Judah. 13 He carried out great

n Another reading is his father David   o Heb Asherim

16.9
Prov 15.3;
Zech 4.10;
1 Sam 13.13

16.11
1 Kings 15.23
16.12
Jer 17.5
16.13
1 Kings 15.24
16.14
Gen 50.2;
Jn 19.39, 40;
2 Chr 21.19;
Jer 34.5

17.1
1 Kings 15.24
17.2
2 Chr 15.8

17.4
1 Kings 12.28

17.5
2 Chr 18.1

17.6
2 Chr 15.17

17.7
2 Chr 15.3
17.8
2 Chr 19.8

17.9
Deut 6.4-9

17.10
2 Chr 14.14
17.11
2 Chr 9.14;
26.8

16.10–13 Asa angrily threw Hanani into prison and thus insulted God who sent him. After spurning the rebuke, he was afflicted with a disease. But even in that sorry condition he persistently refused to seek the face of God. The implication is plain. Had he sought God, he would have been healed, and he died for that stubborn attitude.
17.6 Evidently idol worship had still not been com-

pletely extirpated in Judah. Jehoshaphat destroyed the idolatrous high places and groves.
17.7–13 The spiritual leaders of Judah knew the word of God and taught its doctrines to the people. The devotion of the king and people to the word of God brought happiness, prosperity, and peace. Great revivals and great reforms are founded on the rediscovery of God's word.

works in the cities of Judah. He had soldiers, mighty warriors, in Jerusalem. 14 This was the muster of them by ancestral houses: Of Judah, the commanders of the thousands: Adnah the commander, with three hundred thousand mighty warriors, 15 and next to him Jehohanan the commander, with two hundred eighty thousand, 16 and next to him Amasiah son of Zichri, a volunteer for the service of the LORD, with two hundred thousand mighty warriors. 17 Of Benjamin: Eliada, a mighty warrior, with two hundred thousand armed with bow and shield, 18 and next to him Jehozabad with one hundred eighty thousand armed for war. 19 These were in the service of the king, besides those whom the king had placed in the fortified cities throughout all Judah.

4. Jehoshaphat's alliances with Ahab

a. Ahab's proposition

18 Now Jehoshaphat had great riches and honor; and he made a marriage alliance with Ahab. 2 After some years he went down to Ahab in Samaria. Ahab slaughtered an abundance of sheep and oxen for him and for the people who were with him, and induced him to go up against Ramoth-gilead. 3 King Ahab of Israel said to King Jehoshaphat of Judah, "Will you go with me to Ramoth-gilead?" He answered him, "I am with you, my people are your people. We will be with you in the war."

b. The advice of the false prophets

4 But Jehoshaphat also said to the king of Israel, "Inquire first for the word of the LORD." 5 Then the king of Israel gathered the prophets together, four hundred of them, and said to them, "Shall we go to battle against Ramoth-gilead, or shall I refrain?" They said, "Go up; for God will give it into the hand of the king." 6 But Jehoshaphat said, "Is there no other prophet of the LORD here of whom we may inquire?" 7 The king of Israel said to Jehoshaphat, "There is still one other by whom we may inquire of the LORD, Micaiah son of Imlah; but I hate him, for he never prophesies anything favorable about me, but only disaster." Jehoshaphat said, "Let the king not say such a thing." 8 Then the king of Israel summoned an officer and said, "Bring quickly Micaiah son of Imlah." 9 Now the king of Israel and King Jehoshaphat of Judah were sitting on their thrones, arrayed in their robes; and they were sitting at the threshing floor at the entrance of the gate of Samaria; and all the prophets were prophesying before them. 10 Zedekiah son of Chenaanah made for himself horns of iron, and he said, "Thus says the LORD: With these you shall gore the Arameans until they are destroyed." 11 All the prophets were prophesying the same and saying, "Go up to Ramoth-gilead and triumph; the LORD will give it into the hand of the king."

c. Micaiah's true prophecy

12 The messenger who had gone to summon Micaiah said to him, "Look, the words of the prophets with one accord are favorable to the king; let your word be like the word of one of them, and speak favorably." 13 But Micaiah said, "As the LORD lives, whatever my God says, that I will speak."

14 When he had come to the king, the king said to him, "Micaiah, shall we go to Ramoth-gilead to battle, or shall I refrain?" He answered, "Go up and triumph; they will be given into your hand." 15 But the king said to him, "How many times must I make you swear to tell me nothing

17.16
Judg 5.2, 9;
1 Chr 29.9

18.1
2 Chr 17.5
18.2
1 Kings 22.2-35

18.4
1 Sam 23.2,
4, 9;
2 Sam 2.1

18.7
1 Kings 22.8

18.9
Ruth 4.1

18.11
2 Chr 22.5

18.13
Num 22.18-20,
35

18.1 Jehoshaphat grew greater but he did not grow wiser. He foolishly made an alliance by marriage with wicked Ahab, whose daughter Athaliah became the wife of Jehoram son of Jehoshaphat. This set the stage for one of the saddest chapters in Judah's history (see chs. 21–22).

18.4–34 See the notes on 1 Kings 22 for information on these verses.

but the truth in the name of the Lord?" [16] Then Micaiah[p] said, "I saw all Israel scattered on the mountains, like sheep without a shepherd; and the Lord said, 'These have no master; let each one go home in peace.'" [17] The king of Israel said to Jehoshaphat, "Did I not tell you that he would not prophesy anything favorable about me, but only disaster?"

[18]   Then Micaiah[p] said, "Therefore hear the word of the Lord: I saw the Lord sitting on his throne, with all the host of heaven standing to the right and to the left of him. [19] And the Lord said, 'Who will entice King Ahab of Israel, so that he may go up and fall at Ramoth-gilead?' Then one said one thing, and another said another, [20] until a spirit came forward and stood before the Lord, saying, 'I will entice him.' The Lord asked him, 'How?' [21] He replied, 'I will go out and be a lying spirit in the mouth of all his prophets.' Then the Lord[p] said, 'You are to entice him, and you shall succeed; go out and do it.' [22] So you see, the Lord has put a lying spirit in the mouth of these your prophets; the Lord has decreed disaster for you."

[23]   Then Zedekiah son of Chenaanah came up to Micaiah, slapped him on the cheek, and said, "Which way did the spirit of the Lord pass from me to speak to you?" [24] Micaiah replied, "You will find out on that day when you go in to hide in an inner chamber." [25] The king of Israel then ordered, "Take Micaiah, and return him to Amon the governor of the city and to Joash the king's son; [26] and say, 'Thus says the king: Put this fellow in prison, and feed him on reduced rations of bread and water until I return in peace.'" [27] Micaiah said, "If you return in peace, the Lord has not spoken by me." And he said, "Hear, you peoples, all of you!"

d. The defeat and death of Ahab

[28]   So the king of Israel and King Jehoshaphat of Judah went up to Ramoth-gilead. [29] The king of Israel said to Jehoshaphat, "I will disguise myself and go into battle, but you wear your robes." So the king of Israel disguised himself, and they went into battle. [30] Now the king of Aram had commanded the captains of his chariots, "Fight with no one small or great, but only with the king of Israel." [31] When the captains of the chariots saw Jehoshaphat, they said, "It is the king of Israel." So they turned to fight against him; and Jehoshaphat cried out, and the Lord helped him. God drew them away from him, [32] for when the captains of the chariots saw that it was not the king of Israel, they turned back from pursuing him. [33] But a certain man drew his bow and unknowingly struck the king of Israel between the scale armor and the breastplate; so he said to the driver of his chariot, "Turn around, and carry me out of the battle, for I am wounded." [34] The battle grew hot that day, and the king of Israel propped himself up in his chariot facing the Arameans until evening; then at sunset he died.

e. Jehu reproves Jehoshaphat

19 King Jehoshaphat of Judah returned in safety to his house in Jerusalem. [2] Jehu son of Hanani the seer went out to meet him and said to King Jehoshaphat, "Should you help the wicked and love those who hate the Lord? Because of this, wrath has gone out against you from the Lord. [3] Nevertheless, some good is found in you, for you destroyed the sacred poles[q] out of the land, and have set your heart to seek God."

5. Additional reforms by Jehoshaphat

[4]   Jehoshaphat resided at Jerusalem; then he went out again among the

p Heb he   q Heb Asheroth

Side references:

18.16 Num 27.17; Ezek 34.5-8

18.20 Job 1.6

18.22 Job 12.16; Ezek 14.9

18.23 Jer 20.2; Mk 14.65; Acts 23.2

18.25 v. 8

18.26 2 Chr 16.10

18.27 Mic 1.9

18.31 2 Chr 13.14, 15

18.33 1 Kings 22.34

19.2 1 Kings 16.1; Ps 139.21; 2 Chr 32.25

19.3 2 Chr 12.12, 14; 17.6; Ezra 7.10

19.4 2 Chr 15.8-13

19.2 Jehu son of Hanani was sent by God to tell Jehoshaphat he had erred in allying himself with Ahab. The godly should never help the ungodly (cf.

2 Cor 6.14–18). God was angry but Jehoshaphat repented, so God did not cast him off.
19.4 Jehoshaphat resumed his efforts to reform the

people, from Beer-sheba to the hill country of Ephraim, and brought them back to the LORD, the God of their ancestors. 5 He appointed judges in the land in all the fortified cities of Judah, city by city, 6 and said to the judges, "Consider what you are doing, for you judge not on behalf of human beings but on the LORD's behalf; he is with you in giving judgment. 7 Now, let the fear of the LORD be upon you; take care what you do, for there is no perversion of justice with the LORD our God, or partiality, or taking of bribes."

8 Moreover in Jerusalem Jehoshaphat appointed certain Levites and priests and heads of families of Israel, to give judgment for the LORD and to decide disputed cases. They had their seat at Jerusalem. 9 He charged them: "This is how you shall act: in the fear of the LORD, in faithfulness, and with your whole heart; 10 whenever a case comes to you from your kindred who live in their cities, concerning bloodshed, law or commandment, statutes or ordinances, then you shall instruct them, so that they may not incur guilt before the LORD and wrath may not come on you and your kindred. Do so, and you will not incur guilt. 11 See, Amariah the chief priest is over you in all matters of the LORD; and Zebadiah son of Ishmael, the governor of the house of Judah, in all the king's matters; and the Levites will serve you as officers. Deal courageously, and may the LORD be with the good!"

6. *Jehoshaphat's victory over the Moabites, Ammonites, and Arameans*

a. *Jehoshaphat seeking the LORD*

20 After this the Moabites and Ammonites, and with them some of the Meunites,^{r} came against Jehoshaphat for battle. 2 Messengers^s came and told Jehoshaphat, "A great multitude is coming against you from Edom,^{t} from beyond the sea; already they are at Hazazon-tamar" (that is, En-gedi). 3 Jehoshaphat was afraid; he set himself to seek the LORD, and proclaimed a fast throughout all Judah. 4 Judah assembled to seek help from the LORD; from all the towns of Judah they came to seek the LORD.

b. *The prayer of Jehoshaphat for help*

5 Jehoshaphat stood in the assembly of Judah and Jerusalem, in the house of the LORD, before the new court, 6 and said, "O LORD, God of our ancestors, are you not God in heaven? Do you not rule over all the kingdoms of the nations? In your hand are power and might, so that no one is able to withstand you. 7 Did you not, O our God, drive out the inhabitants of this land before your people Israel, and give it forever to the descendants of your friend Abraham? 8 They have lived in it, and in it have built you a sanctuary for your name, saying, 9 'If disaster comes upon us, the sword, judgment,^{u} or pestilence, or famine, we will stand before this house, and before you, for your name is in this house, and cry to you in our distress, and you will hear and save.' 10 See now, the people of Ammon, Moab, and Mount Seir, whom you would not let Israel invade

Cross-references (left margin)
19.6 Deut 1.17
19.7 Gen 18.25; Deut 32.4; 10.17, 18; Rom 2.11; Col 3.25
19.8 2 Chr 17.8, 9
19.9 2 Sam 23.3
19.10 Deut 17.8; v. 2
19.11 v. 8; 1 Chr 28.20
20.2 Gen 14.7
20.3 2 Chr 19.3
20.6 Deut 4.39; Mt 6.9; 1 Chr 29.11, 12; Mt 6.13
20.7 Isa 41.8
20.9 1 Kings 8.33, 37; 2 Chr 6.20, 28-30
20.10 vv. 1, 22; Deut 2.4, 9, 19; Num 20.21

---

^{r} Compare 26.7: Heb *Ammonites* ^{s} Heb *They* ^{t} One Ms: MT *Aram* ^{u} Or *the sword of judgment*

---

nation. He brought the people back to the God of their fathers. God approved of this.

19.9 The king wanted justice to be done by the nation's judges. They were to judge not for people but for the Lord, fearing him alone. This meant impartiality, with no respect of persons.

19.11 Jehoshaphat made a clear separation of church and state, stating that Amariah would deal with ecclesiastical matters and Ishmael with civil matters. God exercised his will through both for his glory.

20.1 The enemies of Jehoshaphat (Ammonites, Moabites, and Meunites) organized an alliance and con-spired to ruin him and Judah. The king sensed his danger and called the nation to fast and pray.

20.6ff Jehoshaphat's prayer is a model prayer. First, he adored God and acknowledged his mighty power. Second, he reminded God of his divine promises to Israel. Third, he set forth the problem even though God knew it before he said it. Finally, he asked God specifically for help. Later, he expressed confidence that God heard his prayer and would do something about the problem (v. 20). Together with his people he thanked God for the answer before it came (vv. 21ff). See note on Mt 7.7 regarding the conditions of effectual prayer.

when they came from the land of Egypt, and whom they avoided and did not destroy — ¹¹ they reward us by coming to drive us out of your possession that you have given us to inherit. ¹² O our God, will you not execute judgment upon them? For we are powerless against this great multitude that is coming against us. We do not know what to do, but our eyes are on you."

20.11
Ps 83.12
20.12
Judg 11.27;
Ps 25.15;
121.1, 2

c. The message of deliverance by Jahaziel the prophet

13   Meanwhile all Judah stood before the LORD, with their little ones, their wives, and their children. ¹⁴ Then the spirit of the LORD came upon Jahaziel son of Zechariah, son of Benaiah, son of Jeiel, son of Mattaniah, a Levite of the sons of Asaph, in the middle of the assembly. ¹⁵ He said, "Listen, all Judah and inhabitants of Jerusalem, and King Jehoshaphat: Thus says the LORD to you: 'Do not fear or be dismayed at this great multitude; for the battle is not yours but God's. ¹⁶ Tomorrow go down against them; they will come up by the ascent of Ziz; you will find them at the end of the valley, before the wilderness of Jeruel. ¹⁷ This battle is not for you to fight; take your position, stand still, and see the victory of the LORD on your behalf, O Judah and Jerusalem.' Do not fear or be dismayed; tomorrow go out against them, and the LORD will be with you."

20.14
2 Chr 15.1;
24.20
20.15
Ex 14.13, 14;
2 Chr 32.7, 8;
1 Sam 17.47

20.17
Ex 14.13, 14;
2 Chr 15.2

18   Then Jehoshaphat bowed down with his face to the ground, and all Judah and the inhabitants of Jerusalem fell down before the LORD, worshiping the LORD. ¹⁹ And the Levites, of the Kohathites and the Korahites, stood up to praise the LORD, the God of Israel, with a very loud voice.

20.18
Ex 4.31;
2 Chr 7.3

d. God's deliverance

20   They rose early in the morning and went out into the wilderness of Tekoa; and as they went out, Jehoshaphat stood and said, "Listen to me, O Judah and inhabitants of Jerusalem! Believe in the LORD your God and you will be established; believe his prophets." ²¹ When he had taken counsel with the people, he appointed those who were to sing to the LORD and praise him in holy splendor, as they went before the army, saying,
"Give thanks to the LORD,
    for his steadfast love endures forever."

20.20
Isa 7.9

20.21
1 Chr 16.29,
34, 41;
Ps 29.2

²² As they began to sing and praise, the LORD set an ambush against the Ammonites, Moab, and Mount Seir, who had come against Judah, so that they were routed. ²³ For the Ammonites and Moab attacked the inhabitants of Mount Seir, destroying them utterly; and when they had made an end of the inhabitants of Seir, they all helped to destroy one another.

20.22
Judg 7.22;
2 Chr 13.13
20.23
1 Sam 14.20

24   When Judah came to the watchtower of the wilderness, they looked toward the multitude; they were corpses lying on the ground; no one had escaped. ²⁵ When Jehoshaphat and his people came to take the booty from them, they found livestock^v in great numbers, goods, clothing, and precious things, which they took for themselves until they could carry no more. They spent three days taking the booty, because of its abundance. ²⁶ On the fourth day they assembled in the Valley of Beracah, for there they blessed the LORD; therefore that place has been called the Valley of Beracah^w to this day. ²⁷ Then all the people of Judah and Jerusalem, with Jehoshaphat at their head, returned to Jerusalem with joy, for the LORD had enabled them to rejoice over their enemies. ²⁸ They came to Jerusalem, with harps and lyres and trumpets, to the house of the LORD. ²⁹ The fear of God came on all the kingdoms of the countries when

20.27
Neh 12.43

20.29
2 Chr 14.14;
17.10

v Gk: Heb *among them*   *w* That is *Blessing*

20.14 The Spirit of the Lord came on Jahaziel, who brought God's message to Jehoshaphat the king. The king needed to do nothing except stand still and watch God work.
20.21 As the army went out to war, nothing is said

of their swords, spears, shields, or bows. Their faith was their armor, for God told them not to fight. They believed him and that settled the matter. The battle was won without having to fight.

20.30
2 Chr 14.6, 7;
15.15

they heard that the LORD had fought against the enemies of Israel. 30 And the realm of Jehoshaphat was quiet, for his God gave him rest all around.

7. Summary of Jehoshaphat's reign

20.31
1 Kings 22.41-
43

31 So Jehoshaphat reigned over Judah. He was thirty-five years old when he began to reign; he reigned twenty-five years in Jerusalem. His mother's name was Azubah daughter of Shilhi. 32 He walked in the way of his father Asa and did not turn aside from it, doing what was right in the sight of the LORD. 33 Yet the high places were not removed; the people had not yet set their hearts upon the God of their ancestors.

20.33
2 Chr 17.6;
19.3

20.34
1 Kings 16.1,
7

34 Now the rest of the acts of Jehoshaphat, from first to last, are written in the Annals of Jehu son of Hanani, which are recorded in the Book of the Kings of Israel.

20.35
1 Kings 22.48,
49
20.37
2 Chr 9.21

35 After this King Jehoshaphat of Judah joined with King Ahaziah of Israel, who did wickedly. 36 He joined him in building ships to go to Tarshish; they built the ships in Ezion-geber. 37 Then Eliezer son of Dodavahu of Mareshah prophesied against Jehoshaphat, saying, "Because you have joined with Ahaziah, the LORD will destroy what you have made." And the ships were wrecked and were not able to go to Tarshish.

E. The reign of Jehoram

1. The wickedness of Jehoram

21.1
1 Kings 22.50

21 Jehoshaphat slept with his ancestors and was buried with his ancestors in the city of David; his son Jehoram succeeded him. 2 He had brothers, the sons of Jehoshaphat: Azariah, Jehiel, Zechariah, Azariah, Michael, and Shephatiah; all these were the sons of King Jehoshaphat of Judah. x 3 Their father gave them many gifts, of silver, gold, and valuable possessions, together with fortified cities in Judah; but he gave the kingdom to Jehoram, because he was the firstborn. 4 When Jehoram had ascended the throne of his father and was established, he put all his brothers to the sword, and also some of the officials of Israel. 5 Jehoram was thirty-two years old when he began to reign; he reigned eight years in Jerusalem. 6 He walked in the way of the kings of Israel, as the house of Ahab had done; for the daughter of Ahab was his wife. He did what was evil in the sight of the LORD. 7 Yet the LORD would not destroy the house of David because of the covenant that he had made with David, and since he had promised to give a lamp to him and to his descendants forever.

21.3
2 Chr 11.5

21.5
2 Kings 8.17-22

21.7
2 Sam 7.12,
13;
1 Kings 11.36

2. The loss of Edom and Libnah

21.8
2 Kings 8.20-24

8 In his days Edom revolted against the rule of Judah and set up a king of their own. 9 Then Jehoram crossed over with his commanders and all his chariots. He set out by night and attacked the Edomites, who had surrounded him and his chariot commanders. 10 So Edom has been in revolt against the rule of Judah to this day. At that time Libnah also

x Gk Syr: Heb *Israel*

20.33 The chronicler explains why Jehoshaphat, a godly king, did not remove the high places. The people were not yet spiritually ready for that (see 1 Kings 22.43).
20.35 Jehoshaphat appears to have forgotten Jehu the seer's prophetic message that he should not have cooperated with Ahab (see note on 19.2), for he joined with wicked Ahaziah in a commercial venture, building ships to go to Tarshish. God was displeased and the ships were wrecked. This time God came to him through the prophet Eliezer.

21.1 Good fathers do not always have good sons to succeed them. Jehoram turned out to be a wicked king. One of his first acts was to kill all of the possible aspirants to the throne. He reigned only eight years.
21.6 *the daughter of Ahab*, i.e., Athaliah, who patterned herself after her wicked mother, Jezebel.
21.8 Some of Jehoram's subjects, the Edomites, revolted against him; although he chastised them, he did not reduce their number. This should have warned him that God was not favorable to him, as God had been to his father.

revolted against his rule, because he had forsaken the LORD, the God of his ancestors.

3. *Elijah's pronouncement of judgment*

11 Moreover he made high places in the hill country of Judah, and led the inhabitants of Jerusalem into unfaithfulness, and made Judah go astray. **12** A letter came to him from the prophet Elijah, saying: "Thus says the LORD, the God of your father David: Because you have not walked in the ways of your father Jehoshaphat or in the ways of King Asa of Judah, **13** but have walked in the way of the kings of Israel, and have led Judah and the inhabitants of Jerusalem into unfaithfulness, as the house of Ahab led Israel into unfaithfulness, and because you also have killed your brothers, members of your father's house, who were better than yourself, **14** see, the LORD will bring a great plague on your people, your children, your wives, and all your possessions, **15** and you yourself will have a severe sickness with a disease of your bowels, until your bowels come out, day after day, because of the disease."

4. *The evil end of Jehoram*

16 The LORD aroused against Jehoram the anger of the Philistines and of the Arabs who are near the Ethiopians.*y* **17** They came up against Judah, invaded it, and carried away all the possessions they found that belonged to the king's house, along with his sons and his wives, so that no son was left to him except Jehoahaz, his youngest son.

18 After all this the LORD struck him in his bowels with an incurable disease. **19** In course of time, at the end of two years, his bowels came out because of the disease, and he died in great agony. His people made no fire in his honor, like the fires made for his ancestors. **20** He was thirty-two years old when he began to reign; he reigned eight years in Jerusalem. He departed with no one's regret. They buried him in the city of David, but not in the tombs of the kings.

F. *The reign of Ahaziah and Athaliah*

1. *The wickedness of Ahaziah*

22 The inhabitants of Jerusalem made his youngest son Ahaziah king as his successor; for the troops who came with the Arabs to the camp had killed all the older sons. So Ahaziah son of Jehoram reigned as king of Judah. **2** Ahaziah was forty-two years old when he began to reign; he reigned one year in Jerusalem. His mother's name was Athaliah, a granddaughter of Omri. **3** He also walked in the ways of the house of Ahab, for his mother was his counselor in doing wickedly. **4** He did what was evil in the sight of the LORD, as the house of Ahab had done; for after the death of his father they were his counselors, to his ruin. **5** He even followed their advice, and went with Jehoram son of King Ahab of Israel to make war against King Hazael of Aram at Ramoth-gilead. The Arameans wounded Joram, **6** and he returned to be healed in Jezreel of the wounds that he had received at Ramah, when he fought King Hazael of Aram. And Ahaziah son of King Jehoram of Judah went down to see Joram son of Ahab in Jezreel, because he was sick.

y Or Nubians; Heb Cushites

Cross-references (right margin):
21.11 Lev 20.5
21.12 2 Chr 17.3, 4; 14.2-5
21.13 vv. 6, 11; 1 Kings 16.31-33; v. 4
21.15 vv. 18, 19
21.16 2 Chr 33.11
21.17 2 Chr 25.23
21.18 v. 15
21.19 2 Chr 16.14
21.20 Jer 22.18, 28; 2 Chr 24.25; 28.27
22.1 2 Kings 8.24-29; 2 Chr 21.16, 17
22.2 2 Chr 21.6
22.5 2 Kings 8.28ff
22.6 2 Kings 9.15

21.17 This incident does not appear in 2 Kings. Either not all of the wives were taken or some of them were recovered, for Athaliah took charge of the realm after the death of her husband.
21.18–20 Jehoram suffered for his transgression. He was diseased and died a painful death at age forty; no one mourned his passing.
22.1 *Ahaziah,* also called Jehoahaz.
22.2 *forty-two two years old.* Compare to 2 Kings 8.26. This is a copyist's error, for the correct age is twenty-two years old.

2. Jehu murders Ahaziah

22.7
2 Chr 10.15;
2 Kings 9.6,
7, 21

7 But it was ordained by God that the downfall of Ahaziah should come about through his going to visit Joram. For when he came there he went out with Jehoram to meet Jehu son of Nimshi, whom the LORD had anointed to destroy the house of Ahab. 8 When Jehu was executing judgment on the house of Ahab, he met the officials of Judah and the sons of Ahaziah's brothers, who attended Ahaziah, and he killed them. 9 He searched for Ahaziah, who was captured while hiding in Samaria and was brought to Jehu, and put to death. They buried him, for they said, "He is the grandson of Jehoshaphat, who sought the LORD with all his heart." And the house of Ahaziah had no one able to rule the kingdom.

22.8
2 Kings 10.10-
14
22.9
2 Kings 9.27,
28;
2 Chr 17.4

3. Athaliah seizes the throne

a. The murder of the royal family except Joash

22.10
2 Kings 11.1-3

10 Now when Athaliah, Ahaziah's mother, saw that her son was dead, she set about to destroy all the royal family of the house of Judah. 11 But Jehoshabeath, the king's daughter, took Joash son of Ahaziah, and stole him away from among the king's children who were about to be killed; she put him and his nurse in a bedroom. Thus Jehoshabeath, daughter of King Jehoram and wife of the priest Jehoiada — because she was a sister of Ahaziah — hid him from Athaliah, so that she did not kill him; 12 he remained with them six years, hidden in the house of God, while Athaliah reigned over the land.

b. The revolt fostered by Jehoiada

23.1
2 Kings 11.4-20

23 But in the seventh year Jehoiada took courage, and entered into a compact with the commanders of the hundreds, Azariah son of Jeroham, Ishmael son of Jehohanan, Azariah son of Obed, Maaseiah son of Adaiah, and Elishaphat son of Zichri. 2 They went around through Judah and gathered the Levites from all the towns of Judah, and the heads of families of Israel, and they came to Jerusalem. 3 Then the whole assembly made a covenant with the king in the house of God. Jehoiada[z] said to them, "Here is the king's son! Let him reign, as the LORD promised concerning the sons of David. 4 This is what you are to do: one-third of you, priests and Levites, who come on duty on the sabbath, shall be gatekeepers, 5 one-third shall be at the king's house, and one-third at the Gate of the Foundation; and all the people shall be in the courts of the house of the LORD. 6 Do not let anyone enter the house of the LORD except the priests and ministering Levites; they may enter, for they are holy, but all the other[a] people shall observe the instructions of the LORD. 7 The Levites shall surround the king, each with his weapons in his hand; and whoever enters the house shall be killed. Stay with the king in his comings and goings."

23.3
2 Sam 7.12;
1 Kings 2.4;
2 Chr 6.16;
7.18; 21.7
23.4
1 Chr 9.25

23.7
1 Chr 23.28-32

23.8
1 Chr 24.1

8 The Levites and all Judah did according to all that the priest Jehoiada commanded; each brought his men, who were to come on duty on the sabbath, with those who were to go off duty on the sabbath; for the priest

z Heb *He*   a Heb lacks *other*

22.7 *it was ordained of God that the downfall of Ahaziah should come about.* This emphasizes the Biblical truth that God sets up on the throne and pulls down from the throne whom he pleases.
22.9 Ahaziah was given a decent burial, but only because he was "the grandson of Jehoshaphat, who sought the LORD with all his heart."
22.10 *Athaliah*, the daughter of Ahab and Jezebel, was a "wicked woman" (24.7). She married Jehoram of Judah, who became king after his father died. When her son Ahaziah died, she became queen. She was the only woman in history to usurp the Davidic

throne. After a six-year reign, Athaliah was slain and Joash (one of her grandsons) became king at seven years of age.
22.11 *Jehoshabeath, the king's daughter.* Her father was King Jehoram and her brother was King Ahaziah.
23.1 Six years of Athaliah were enough for the people of Judah. An ecclesiastical-political alliance was formed, resulting in the death of Athaliah and the accession of Joash to the throne at the tender age of seven (see notes on 2 Kings 11).

Jehoiada did not dismiss the divisions. 9 The priest Jehoiada delivered to the captains the spears and the large and small shields that had been King David's, which were in the house of God; 10 and he set all the people as a guard for the king, everyone with weapon in hand, from the south side of the house to the north side of the house, around the altar and the house. 11 Then he brought out the king's son, put the crown on him, and gave him the covenant;[b] they proclaimed him king, and Jehoiada and his sons anointed him; and they shouted, "Long live the king!"

12 When Athaliah heard the noise of the people running and praising the king, she went into the house of the Lord to the people; 13 and when she looked, there was the king standing by his pillar at the entrance, and the captains and the trumpeters beside the king, and all the people of the land rejoicing and blowing trumpets, and the singers with their musical instruments leading in the celebration. Athaliah tore her clothes, and cried, "Treason! Treason!" 14 Then the priest Jehoiada brought out the captains who were set over the army, saying to them, "Bring her out between the ranks; anyone who follows her is to be put to the sword." For the priest said, "Do not put her to death in the house of the Lord." 15 So they laid hands on her; she went into the entrance of the Horse Gate of the king's house, and there they put her to death.

16 Jehoiada made a covenant between himself and all the people and the king that they should be the Lord's people. 17 Then all the people went to the house of Baal, and tore it down; his altars and his images they broke in pieces, and they killed Mattan, the priest of Baal, in front of the altars. 18 Jehoiada assigned the care of the house of the Lord to the levitical priests whom David had organized to be in charge of the house of the Lord, to offer burnt offerings to the Lord, as it is written in the law of Moses, with rejoicing and with singing, according to the order of David. 19 He stationed the gatekeepers at the gates of the house of the Lord so that no one should enter who was in any way unclean. 20 And he took the captains, the nobles, the governors of the people, and all the people of the land, and they brought the king down from the house of the Lord, marching through the upper gate to the king's house. They set the king on the royal throne. 21 So all the people of the land rejoiced, and the city was quiet after Athaliah had been killed with the sword.

G. The reign of Joash

1. The faithfulness of Joash

24 Joash was seven years old when he began to reign; he reigned forty years in Jerusalem; his mother's name was Zibiah of Beer-sheba. 2 Joash did what was right in the sight of the Lord all the days of the priest Jehoiada. 3 Jehoiada got two wives for him, and he became the father of sons and daughters.

2. The repair of the temple

4 Some time afterward Joash decided to restore the house of the Lord. 5 He assembled the priests and the Levites and said to them, "Go out to the cities of Judah and gather money from all Israel to repair the house

b Or treaty, or testimony; Heb eduth

23.14 Athaliah's ambitions and wickedness brought about her own death by the sword. Jehoiada insisted that she not be killed in the house of the Lord, so she was removed to the entrance of the Horse Gate of the king's house for her execution.
23.16 Following the death of Athaliah the people of Judah returned to the Lord. Jehoiada sparked this renewal and advised the young king. He cleaned up

the wickedness connected with the use of the temple. The people rejoiced and peace descended for a season.
24.2 Joash got off to a good start. Under the influence of Jehoiada, he followed God, but this lasted only while he was young enough to be under the influence of his godly tutor. His end was worse than his beginning.

Side references: 23.9 v.1; 23.11 Ex 25.16; 1 Sam 10.24; 23.12 2 Kings 11.13; 23.15 Neh 3.28; Jer 31.40; 23.17 Deut 13.9; 23.18 2 Chr 5.5; 1 Chr 23.6, 30, 31; 25.1, 2, 6; 23.19 1 Chr 9.22; 23.20 2 Kings 11.19; 24.1 2 Kings 11.21; 12.1-15; 24.2 2 Chr 26.5; 24.4 v.7

of your God, year by year; and see that you act quickly." But the Levites did not act quickly. 6 So the king summoned Jehoiada the chief, and said to him, "Why have you not required the Levites to bring in from Judah and Jerusalem the tax levied by Moses, the servant of the LORD, on*c* the congregation of Israel for the tent of the covenant?"*d* 7 For the children of Athaliah, that wicked woman, had broken into the house of God, and had even used all the dedicated things of the house of the LORD for the Baals.

8   So the king gave command, and they made a chest, and set it outside the gate of the house of the LORD. 9 A proclamation was made throughout Judah and Jerusalem to bring in for the LORD the tax that Moses the servant of God laid on Israel in the wilderness. 10 All the leaders and all the people rejoiced and brought their tax and dropped it into the chest until it was full. 11 Whenever the chest was brought to the king's officers by the Levites, when they saw that there was a large amount of money in it, the king's secretary and the officer of the chief priest would come and empty the chest and take it and return it to its place. So they did day after day, and collected money in abundance. 12 The king and Jehoiada gave it to those who had charge of the work of the house of the LORD, and they hired masons and carpenters to restore the house of the LORD, and also workers in iron and bronze to repair the house of the LORD. 13 So those who were engaged in the work labored, and the repairing went forward at their hands, and they restored the house of God to its proper condition and strengthened it. 14 When they had finished, they brought the rest of the money to the king and Jehoiada, and with it were made utensils for the house of the LORD, utensils for the service and for the burnt offerings, and ladles, and vessels of gold and silver. They offered burnt offerings in the house of the LORD regularly all the days of Jehoiada.

3. The death of Jehoiada

15   But Jehoiada grew old and full of days, and died; he was one hundred thirty years old at his death. 16 And they buried him in the city of David among the kings, because he had done good in Israel, and for God and his house.

4. The unfaithfulness of Joash and Judah

17   Now after the death of Jehoiada the officials of Judah came and did obeisance to the king; then the king listened to them. 18 They abandoned the house of the LORD, the God of their ancestors, and served the sacred poles*e* and the idols. And wrath came upon Judah and Jerusalem for this guilt of theirs. 19 Yet he sent prophets among them to bring them back to the LORD; they testified against them, but they would not listen.

5. Joash kills Zechariah son of Jehoiada

20   Then the spirit of God took possession of*f* Zechariah son of the

c Compare Vg: Heb *and*   *d* Or *treaty*, or *testimony*; Heb *eduth*   *e* Heb *Asherim*   *f* Heb *clothed itself with*

Margin references:
24.6 Ex 30.12-16
24.7 2 Chr 21.17
24.9 v. 6
24.11 2 Kings 12.10
24.13 Neh 10.39
24.16 2 Chr 21.2, 20
24.18 v. 4; Ex 34.12-14; 1 Kings 14.23; Josh 22.20; 2 Chr 19.2
24.19 Jer 7.25
24.20 2 Chr 20.14; Num 14.41; 2 Chr 15.2

24.7 The house of God had been entered by Athaliah, and its treasures were used for the worship of Baal. This was an awful prostitution of things dedicated to the glory of God and an offense to him. Joash gave orders to purge the temple of anything that had been connected with idolatry.
24.17 The king and the princes had done well, but only under compulsion while Jehoiada lived. After his death they showed their true colors. They left the house of God and worshiped idols again. Apostasy was the order of the day.
24.19 God was gracious and sent not one but many prophets to warn Judah concerning its apostasy. But

the leaders and people were so wedded to their idols that warnings, reproofs, and threatenings did not move them. They were ripe for judgment.
24.20 The Spirit of God took possession of Zechariah the priest. He was given the prophetic power and used it to pronounce the verdict of God against disobedience. He lost his life as a result of his faithful preaching. God executed judgment on Joash, and the Arameans slew him. This serves as a warning to those believers who have commended themselves to God in the early years after conversion, only to backslide in later years and find themselves cut off from God.

priest Jehoiada; he stood above the people and said to them, "Thus says God: Why do you transgress the commandments of the LORD, so that you cannot prosper? Because you have forsaken the LORD, he has also forsaken you." 21 But they conspired against him, and by command of the king they stoned him to death in the court of the house of the LORD. 22 King Joash did not remember the kindness that Jehoiada, Zechariah's father, had shown him, but killed his son. As he was dying, he said, "May the LORD see and avenge!"

6. The defeat and death of Joash

23 At the end of the year the army of Aram came up against Joash. They came to Judah and Jerusalem, and destroyed all the officials of the people from among them, and sent all the booty they took to the king of Damascus. 24 Although the army of Aram had come with few men, the LORD delivered into their hand a very great army, because they had abandoned the LORD, the God of their ancestors. Thus they executed judgment on Joash. 25 When they had withdrawn, leaving him severely wounded, his servants conspired against him because of the blood of the son*g* of the priest Jehoiada, and they killed him on his bed. So he died; and they buried him in the city of David, but they did not bury him in the tombs of the kings. 26 Those who conspired against him were Zabad son of Shimeath the Ammonite, and Jehozabad son of Shimrith the Moabite. 27 Accounts of his sons, and of the many oracles against him, and of the rebuilding*h* of the house of God are written in the Commentary on the Book of the Kings. And his son Amaziah succeeded him.

H. The reign of Amaziah

1. Amaziah's early acts

25 Amaziah was twenty-five years old when he began to reign, and he reigned twenty-nine years in Jerusalem. His mother's name was Jehoaddan of Jerusalem. 2 He did what was right in the sight of the LORD, yet not with a true heart. 3 As soon as the royal power was firmly in his hand he killed his servants who had murdered his father the king. 4 But he did not put their children to death, according to what is written in the law, in the book of Moses, where the LORD commanded, "The parents shall not be put to death for the children, or the children be put to death for the parents; but all shall be put to death for their own sins."

2. The defeat of the Edomites in the Valley of Salt

5 Amaziah assembled the people of Judah, and set them by ancestral houses under commanders of the thousands and of the hundreds for all Judah and Benjamin. He mustered those twenty years old and upward, and found that they were three hundred thousand picked troops fit for war, able to handle spear and shield. 6 He also hired one hundred thousand mighty warriors from Israel for one hundred talents of silver. 7 But a man

g Gk Vg: Heb sons   *h* Heb founding

24.21 Neh 9.26; Mt 23.35; Acts 7.58, 59
24.22 Gen 9.5
24.23 2 Kings 12.17
24.24 Lev 26.25; Deut 28.25; 2 Chr 22.8; Isa 10.5
24.25 2 Kings 12.20; v. 21
24.27 2 Kings 12.18, 21
25.1 2 Kings 14.1-6
25.2 v. 14
25.4 Deut 24.16; 2 Kings 14.6
25.5 Num 1.3

24.23 Zechariah had prayed for God to avenge his death, and God did through a small band of Arameans. They made themselves masters of Jerusalem, plundered the city, slew the princes, and sent the spoil to the king of Damascus.
24.24 Ironically, those who slew Joash were children of Israelites who had married pagans. Intermarriage had been forbidden to prevent idolatry; here the children of mixed marriages caused the death of a king who had embraced idolatrous practices.
25.2 Amaziah had a long reign (twenty-nine years) and he did what was right in the sight of God. He kept the temple services going and supported the true Israelite religion. But he was not a serious and devout follower; he served God with an outward form of religion but not from the heart.
25.6 Amaziah found that his forces were too small to wage war against the Edomites, so he hired mercenaries from idolatrous Israel to assist him. When he was confronted by God's prophet, he dismissed the mercenaries at God's command, though his heart was not changed.

of God came to him and said, "O king, do not let the army of Israel go with you, for the LORD is not with Israel—all these Ephraimites. 8 Rather, go by yourself and act; be strong in battle, or God will fling you down before the enemy; for God has power to help or to overthrow." 9 Amaziah said to the man of God, "But what shall we do about the hundred talents that I have given to the army of Israel?" The man of God answered, "The LORD is able to give you much more than this." 10 Then Amaziah discharged the army that had come to him from Ephraim, letting them go home again. But they became very angry with Judah, and returned home in fierce anger.

11 Amaziah took courage, and led out his people; he went to the Valley of Salt, and struck down ten thousand men of Seir. 12 The people of Judah captured another ten thousand alive, took them to the top of Sela, and threw them down from the top of Sela, so that all of them were dashed to pieces. 13 But the men of the army whom Amaziah sent back, not letting them go with him to battle, fell on the cities of Judah from Samaria to Beth-horon; they killed three thousand people in them, and took much booty.

3. Amaziah's idolatry

14 Now after Amaziah came from the slaughter of the Edomites, he brought the gods of the people of Seir, set them up as his gods, and worshiped them, making offerings to them. 15 The LORD was angry with Amaziah and sent to him a prophet, who said to him, "Why have you resorted to a people's gods who could not deliver their own people from your hand?" 16 But as he was speaking the king[i] said to him, "Have we made you a royal counselor? Stop! Why should you be put to death?" So the prophet stopped, but said, "I know that God has determined to destroy you, because you have done this and have not listened to my advice."

4. Amaziah's defeat by Joash of Israel

17 Then King Amaziah of Judah took counsel and sent to King Joash son of Jehoahaz son of Jehu of Israel, saying, "Come, let us look one another in the face." 18 King Joash of Israel sent word to King Amaziah of Judah, "A thornbush on Lebanon sent to a cedar on Lebanon, saying, 'Give your daughter to my son for a wife'; but a wild animal of Lebanon passed by and trampled down the thornbush. 19 You say, 'See, I have defeated Edom,' and your heart has lifted you up in boastfulness. Now stay at home; why should you provoke trouble so that you fall, you and Judah with you?"

20 But Amaziah would not listen—it was God's doing, in order to hand them over, because they had sought the gods of Edom. 21 So King Joash of Israel went up; he and King Amaziah of Judah faced one another in battle at Beth-shemesh, which belongs to Judah. 22 Judah was defeated by Israel; everyone fled home. 23 King Joash of Israel captured King Amaziah of Judah, son of Joash, son of Ahaziah, at Beth-shemesh; he brought him to Jerusalem, and broke down the wall of Jerusalem from the Ephraim Gate to the Corner Gate, a distance of four hundred cubits. 24 He seized all the gold and silver, and all the vessels that were found in

i Heb he

25.8
2 Chr 14.11;
20.6

25.11
2 Kings 14.7

25.14
2 Chr 28.23;
Ex 20.3, 5
25.15
Ps 96.5;
vv. 11, 12

25.17
2 Kings 14.8-14

25.18
Judg 9.8-15

25.19
2 Chr 26.16;
32.25

25.20
1 Kings 12.15;
2 Chr 22.7

25.23
2 Chr 21.17;
22.1

25.14 The gods of the Edomites had not protected them in the battle with Amaziah. Yet Amaziah foolishly took these defeated gods, made them his own, and bowed before them in idolatrous worship. This time the rebuke of God's prophet was not effective, for the king angrily dismissed him and even threat-

ened him with death.
25.17ff For notes on Amaziah's foolish encounter with Israel, see note on 2 Kings 14.8. Amaziah lived for fifteen years after the death of Joash (v. 25), but finally had to flee to Lachish where he was slain as a result of a conspiracy against him (v. 27).

the house of God, and Obed-edom with them; he seized also the treasuries of the king's house, also hostages; then he returned to Samaria.

5. The murder of Amaziah

25 King Amaziah son of Joash of Judah, lived fifteen years after the death of King Joash son of Jehoahaz of Israel. 26 Now the rest of the deeds of Amaziah, from first to last, are they not written in the Book of the Kings of Judah and Israel? 27 From the time that Amaziah turned away from the LORD they made a conspiracy against him in Jerusalem, and he fled to Lachish. But they sent after him to Lachish, and killed him there. 28 They brought him back on horses; he was buried with his ancestors in the city of David.

25.25
2 Kings 14.17-22

I. The reign of Uzziah

1. His godly start

26 Then all the people of Judah took Uzziah, who was sixteen years old, and made him king to succeed his father Amaziah. 2 He rebuilt Eloth and restored it to Judah, after the king slept with his ancestors. 3 Uzziah was sixteen years old when he began to reign, and he reigned fifty-two years in Jerusalem. His mother's name was Jecoliah of Jerusalem. 4 He did what was right in the sight of the LORD, just as his father Amaziah had done. 5 He set himself to seek God in the days of Zechariah, who instructed him in the fear of God; and as long as he sought the LORD, God made him prosper.

26.1
2 Kings 14.21,
22; 15.2, 3

26.5
2 Chr 24.2;
Dan 1.17;
2.19;
2 Chr 15.2

2. His success

6 He went out and made war against the Philistines, and broke down the wall of Gath and the wall of Jabneh and the wall of Ashdod; he built cities in the territory of Ashdod and elsewhere among the Philistines. 7 God helped him against the Philistines, against the Arabs who lived in Gur-baal, and against the Meunites. 8 The Ammonites paid tribute to Uzziah, and his fame spread even to the border of Egypt, for he became very strong. 9 Moreover Uzziah built towers in Jerusalem at the Corner Gate, at the Valley Gate, and at the Angle, and fortified them. 10 He built towers in the wilderness and hewed out many cisterns, for he had large herds, both in the Shephelah and in the plain, and he had farmers and vinedressers in the hills and in the fertile lands, for he loved the soil. 11 Moreover Uzziah had an army of soldiers, fit for war, in divisions according to the numbers in the muster made by the secretary Jeiel and the officer Maaseiah, under the direction of Hananiah, one of the king's commanders. 12 The whole number of the heads of ancestral houses of mighty warriors was two thousand six hundred. 13 Under their command was an army of three hundred seven thousand five hundred, who could make war with mighty power, to help the king against the enemy. 14 Uzziah provided for all the army the shields, spears, helmets, coats of mail, bows, and stones for slinging. 15 In Jerusalem he set up machines, invented by skilled workers, on the towers and the corners for shooting arrows and large stones. And his fame spread far, for he was marvelously helped until he became strong.

26.6
Isa 14.29

26.7
2 Chr 21.16
26.8
2 Chr 17.11

26.9
2 Chr 25.23;
Neh 3.13

26.13
2 Chr 25.5

26.1 *Uzziah*, i.e., the Azariah mentioned in 2 Kings 15.1.
26.5 Uzziah prospered as long as he kept close to God and obeyed his voice. Later in life his pride led him to disregard the will of God; he subsequently suffered failure and loss (vv. 19–21).

26.7 *God helped him*. This follows the same pattern so familiar in Chronicles: those who trust God are helped, whereas those who turn to idols are judged and forsaken by God. Uzziah raised a large army to defend his kingdom. His fame spread, his kingdom prospered, and he became very strong.

3. His sin and punishment

26.16
Deut 32.15;
2 Chr 25.19;
2 Kings 16.12,
13
26.17
1 Chr 6.10
26.18
Num 16.39,
40;
Ex 30.7, 8

26.19
2 Kings 5.25-27

26.21
2 Kings 15.5-7;
Lev 13.46;
Num 5.2

16 But when he had become strong he grew proud, to his destruction. For he was false to the LORD his God, and entered the temple of the LORD to make offering on the altar of incense. 17 But the priest Azariah went in after him, with eighty priests of the LORD who were men of valor; 18 they withstood King Uzziah, and said to him, "It is not for you, Uzziah, to make offering to the LORD, but for the priests the descendants of Aaron, who are consecrated to make offering. Go out of the sanctuary; for you have done wrong, and it will bring you no honor from the LORD God." 19 Then Uzziah was angry. Now he had a censer in his hand to make offering, and when he became angry with the priests a leprous[j] disease broke out on his forehead, in the presence of the priests in the house of the LORD, by the altar of incense. 20 When the chief priest Azariah, and all the priests, looked at him, he was leprous[j] in his forehead. They hurried him out, and he himself hurried to get out, because the LORD had struck him. 21 King Uzziah was leprous[j] to the day of his death, and being leprous[j] lived in a separate house, for he was excluded from the house of the LORD. His son Jotham was in charge of the palace of the king, governing the people of the land.

4. His death and the succession

26.22
Isa 1.1
26.23
2 Kings 15.7;
Isa 6.1

22 Now the rest of the acts of Uzziah, from first to last, the prophet Isaiah son of Amoz wrote. 23 Uzziah slept with his ancestors; they buried him near his ancestors in the burial field that belonged to the kings, for they said, "He is leprous."[j] His son Jotham succeeded him.

J. The reign of Jotham

27.1
2 Kings 15.33-35
27.2
2 Chr 26.16
27.3
2 Chr 33.14;
Neh 3.26

27.6
2 Chr 26.5
27.7
2 Kings 15.36
27.8
v. 1

27 Jotham was twenty-five years old when he began to reign; he reigned sixteen years in Jerusalem. His mother's name was Jerushah daughter of Zadok. 2 He did what was right in the sight of the LORD just as his father Uzziah had done — only he did not invade the temple of the LORD. But the people still followed corrupt practices. 3 He built the upper gate of the house of the LORD, and did extensive building on the wall of Ophel. 4 Moreover he built cities in the hill country of Judah, and forts and towers on the wooded hills. 5 He fought with the king of the Ammonites and prevailed against them. The Ammonites gave him that year one hundred talents of silver, ten thousand cors of wheat and ten thousand of barley. The Ammonites paid him the same amount in the second and the third years. 6 So Jotham became strong because he ordered his ways before the LORD his God. 7 Now the rest of the acts of Jotham, and all his wars and his ways, are written in the Book of the Kings of Israel and Judah. 8 He was twenty-five years old when he began to reign; he reigned sixteen years in Jerusalem. 9 Jotham slept with his ancestors, and they buried him in the city of David; and his son Ahaz succeeded him.

[j] A term for several skin diseases; precise meaning uncertain

26.16–20 People often find prosperity more dangerous than poverty. Uzziah's pride led him to intrude into the house of God to burn incense on the sacred altar. This was most presumptuous, for only the Levitical priests could do this. He was angry when he was reproved by the priests. With censer in hand, he was about to do the forbidden act when leprosy broke out on his forehead. This was an act of divine judgment which took Uzziah and the priests by surprise. He died a leper.
26.22 It was in the year that Uzziah died that Isaiah

the prophet received his call to serve the Lord (see Isa 6).
27.1 Jotham succeeded Uzziah, and for sixteen years Judah prospered and was at peace. He followed his father in his devotion to God but was careful not to follow him in his folly of trying to burn incense. The people, however, did not follow their king. Their religious practices were corrupt. He died young (forty-one) but he finished his course with honor. Unfortunately, he did not have a son who would walk in his ways.

K. The reign of Ahaz

1. His evil ways

28 Ahaz was twenty years old when he began to reign; he reigned sixteen years in Jerusalem. He did not do what was right in the sight of the LORD, as his ancestor David had done, 2 but he walked in the ways of the kings of Israel. He even made cast images for the Baals; 3 and he made offerings in the valley of the son of Hinnom, and made his sons pass through fire, according to the abominable practices of the nations whom the LORD drove out before the people of Israel. 4 He sacrificed and made offerings on the high places, on the hills, and under every green tree.

2. His defeats by Aram and Israel

5 Therefore the LORD his God gave him into the hand of the king of Aram, who defeated him and took captive a great number of his people and brought them to Damascus. He was also given into the hand of the king of Israel, who defeated him with great slaughter. 6 Pekah son of Remaliah killed one hundred twenty thousand in Judah in one day, all of them valiant warriors, because they had abandoned the LORD, the God of their ancestors. 7 And Zichri, a mighty warrior of Ephraim, killed the king's son Maaseiah, Azrikam the commander of the palace, and Elkanah the next in authority to the king.

8 The people of Israel took captive two hundred thousand of their kin, women, sons, and daughters; they also took much booty from them and brought the booty to Samaria. 9 But a prophet of the LORD was there, whose name was Oded; he went out to meet the army that came to Samaria, and said to them, "Because the LORD, the God of your ancestors, was angry with Judah, he gave them into your hand, but you have killed them in a rage that has reached up to heaven. 10 Now you intend to subjugate the people of Judah and Jerusalem, male and female, as your slaves. But what have you except sins against the LORD your God? 11 Now hear me, and send back the captives whom you have taken from your kindred, for the fierce wrath of the LORD is upon you." 12 Moreover, certain chiefs of the Ephraimites, Azariah son of Johanan, Berechiah son of Meshillemoth, Jehizkiah son of Shallum, and Amasa son of Hadlai, stood up against those who were coming from the war, 13 and said to them, "You shall not bring the captives in here, for you propose to bring on us guilt against the LORD in addition to our present sins and guilt. For our guilt is already great, and there is fierce wrath against Israel." 14 So the warriors left the captives and the booty before the officials and all the assembly. 15 Then those who were mentioned by name got up and took the captives, and with the booty they clothed all that were naked among them; they clothed them, gave them sandals, provided them with food and drink, and anointed them; and carrying all the feeble among them on donkeys, they brought them to their kindred at Jericho, the city of palm trees. Then they returned to Samaria.

28.1 — 2 Kings 16.2-4
28.2 — 2 Chr 22.3; Ex 34.17
28.3 — 2 Kings 23.10; Lev 18.21; 2 Kings 16.3; 2 Chr 33.6
28.4 — v. 25
28.5 — Isa 7.1; 2 Kings 16.5, 6
28.6 — 2 Kings 15.27
28.8 — 2 Chr 11.4
28.9 — 2 Chr 25.15; Isa 10.5; 47.6; Ezra 9.6; Rev 18.5
28.10 — Lev 25.39, 42, 43, 46
28.11 — v. 8
28.15 — v. 12; 2 Kings 6.22; Prov 25.21, 22; Deut 34.3; Judg 1.16

28.1 Ahaz had everything going for him, for the kingdom was at peace and prosperous. But he chose evil instead of good, following the example of the wicked kings of Israel. He offered sacrifices and burned incense everywhere except at the house of God. He also made idols to Baal.
28.5 *Therefore,* i.e., because of his wickedness, God delivered Ahaz and his people into the hands of Aram and Israel. The blood of his people was shed and their country left desolate.

28.9 Oded the prophet had a word for Pekah king of Israel. He was about to make slaves of his blood relatives (the citizens of Judah), contrary to God's law. Oded informed him that Israel's victory over Judah was no sign that God thought Israel was good. Rather, God was punishing one wicked nation by using another to execute divine justice. He must not take the people of Judah for slavery. He accepted the word of the prophet and the people returned home.

3. *His defeats by the Edomites and Assyrians, and his death*

16   At that time King Ahaz sent to the king[k] of Assyria for help. 17 For the Edomites had again invaded and defeated Judah, and carried away captives. 18 And the Philistines had made raids on the cities in the Shephelah and the Negeb of Judah, and had taken Beth-shemesh, Aijalon, Gederoth, Soco with its villages, Timnah with its villages, and Gimzo with its villages; and they settled there. 19 For the Lord brought Judah low because of King Ahaz of Israel, for he had behaved without restraint in Judah and had been faithless to the Lord. 20 So King Tilgath-pilneser of Assyria came against him, and oppressed him instead of strengthening him. 21 For Ahaz plundered the house of the Lord and the houses of the king and of the officials, and gave tribute to the king of Assyria; but it did not help him.

22   In the time of his distress he became yet more faithless to the Lord — this same King Ahaz. 23 For he sacrificed to the gods of Damascus, which had defeated him, and said, "Because the gods of the kings of Aram helped them, I will sacrifice to them so that they may help me." But they were the ruin of him, and of all Israel. 24 Ahaz gathered together the utensils of the house of God, and cut in pieces the utensils of the house of God. He shut up the doors of the house of the Lord and made himself altars in every corner of Jerusalem. 25 In every city of Judah he made high places to make offerings to other gods, provoking to anger the Lord, the God of his ancestors. 26 Now the rest of his acts and all his ways, from first to last, are written in the Book of the Kings of Judah and Israel. 27 Ahaz slept with his ancestors, and they buried him in the city, in Jerusalem; but they did not bring him into the tombs of the kings of Israel. His son Hezekiah succeeded him.

L. *The reign of Hezekiah*

1. *The cleansing of the temple*

a. *The announcement of his intentions*

29 Hezekiah began to reign when he was twenty-five years old; he reigned twenty-nine years in Jerusalem. His mother's name was Abijah daughter of Zechariah. 2 He did what was right in the sight of the Lord, just as his ancestor David had done.

3   In the first year of his reign, in the first month, he opened the doors of the house of the Lord and repaired them. 4 He brought in the priests and the Levites and assembled them in the square on the east. 5 He said to them, "Listen to me, Levites! Sanctify yourselves, and sanctify the house of the Lord, the God of your ancestors, and carry out the filth from the holy place. 6 For our ancestors have been unfaithful and have done

Cross-references (left margin)

28.16 — 2 Kings 16.7
28.18 — Ezek 16.57
28.19 — 2 Chr 21.2
28.20 — 1 Chr 5.26; 2 Kings 16.8, 9
28.23 — 2 Chr 25.14; Jer 44.17, 18
28.24 — 2 Kings 16.17; 2 Chr 29.7; 30.14; 33.3-5
28.26 — 2 Kings 16.19, 20
28.27 — 2 Chr 24.25
29.1 — 2 Kings 18.1-3
29.2 — 2 Chr 28.1
29.3 — v. 7; 2 Chr 28.24
29.5 — vv. 15, 34; 2 Chr 35.6
29.6 — Jer 2.27; Ezek 8.16

---

[k] Gk Syr Vg Compare 2 Kings 16.7: Heb *kings*

28.16 Judah was brought so low that the Edomites and the Philistines were able to do them extensive harm. Instead of repenting and turning to God, Ahaz made an appeal to the Assyrians for military help. Ironically, King Tiglath-pileser of Assyria saw Judah's weakness and "oppressed him instead of strengthening him" (v. 20).

28.22,23 Ahaz had still not learned his lesson. His spiritual condition worsened and he "became yet more faithless to the Lord." He added the gods of the Assyrians to his collection of false gods, expecting them to help him. Tersely, the Scripture says, "they were the ruin of him."

28.24 So rash and angry had Ahaz become that he closed the temple doors to all true worship of God and set up altars in every corner of Jerusalem.

29.1 Ahaz's successor, Hezekiah, was a devout fol-

lower of God. His soul must have been vexed as he watched the antics of his father, having no power to change the situation for good. When he came to the kingship, the challenge was great and the need for reformation and a return to God a pressing necessity. He rose to the occasion and performed magnificently for God.

29.3 Hezekiah began his reforms immediately. He opened the house of God and began to repair the damage done by his father.

29.5 The house of God had been defiled. Refuse had accumulated in it, the lamps had not been lit, incense had not been burned (29.6,7), and the priests had not been carrying out their responsibilities. Judah's worship of the true God had been neglected and was in decay. Hezekiah set out to revive the true religion.

what was evil in the sight of the LORD our God; they have forsaken him, and have turned away their faces from the dwelling of the LORD, and turned their backs. 7 They also shut the doors of the vestibule and put out the lamps, and have not offered incense or made burnt offerings in the holy place to the God of Israel. 8 Therefore the wrath of the LORD came upon Judah and Jerusalem, and he has made them an object of horror, of astonishment, and of hissing, as you see with your own eyes. 9 Our fathers have fallen by the sword and our sons and our daughters and our wives are in captivity for this. 10 Now it is in my heart to make a covenant with the LORD, the God of Israel, so that his fierce anger may turn away from us. 11 My sons, do not now be negligent, for the LORD has chosen you to stand in his presence to minister to him, and to be his ministers and make offerings to him.''

29.8
2 Chr 24.18;
28.5;
Deut 28.25;
Jer 25.9, 18
29.9
2 Chr 28.5-8,
17
29.10
2 Chr 15.12;
23.16
29.11
Num 3.6;
8.14

b. The sanctifying of the Levites and
the cleansing of the temple

12   Then the Levites arose, Mahath son of Amasai, and Joel son of Azariah, of the sons of the Kohathites; and of the sons of Merari, Kish son of Abdi, and Azariah son of Jehallelel; and of the Gershonites, Joah son of Zimmah, and Eden son of Joah; 13 and of the sons of Elizaphan, Shimri and Jeuel; and of the sons of Asaph, Zechariah and Mattaniah; 14 and of the sons of Heman, Jehuel and Shimei; and of the sons of Jeduthun, Shemaiah and Uzziel. 15 They gathered their brothers, sanctified themselves, and went in as the king had commanded, by the words of the LORD, to cleanse the house of the LORD. 16 The priests went into the inner part of the house of the LORD to cleanse it, and they brought out all the unclean things that they found in the temple of the LORD into the court of the house of the LORD; and the Levites took them and carried them out to the Wadi Kidron. 17 They began to sanctify on the first day of the first month, and on the eighth day of the month they came to the vestibule of the LORD; then for eight days they sanctified the house of the LORD, and on the sixteenth day of the first month they finished. 18 Then they went inside to King Hezekiah and said, "We have cleansed all the house of the LORD, the altar of burnt offering and all its utensils, and the table for the rows of bread and all its utensils. 19 All the utensils that King Ahaz repudiated during his reign when he was faithless, we have made ready and sanctified; see, they are in front of the altar of the LORD.''

29.15
v. 5;
2 Chr 30.12;
1 Chr 23.28

29.17
v. 3

29.19
2 Chr 28.24

c. The consecraton of the temple

20   Then King Hezekiah rose early, assembled the officials of the city, and went up to the house of the LORD. 21 They brought seven bulls, seven rams, seven lambs, and seven male goats for a sin offering for the kingdom and for the sanctuary and for Judah. He commanded the priests the descendants of Aaron to offer them on the altar of the LORD. 22 So they slaughtered the bulls, and the priests received the blood and dashed it against the altar; they slaughtered the rams and their blood was dashed against the altar; they also slaughtered the lambs and their blood was dashed against the altar. 23 Then the male goats for the sin offering were brought to the king and the assembly; they laid their hands on them, 24 and the priests slaughtered them and made a sin offering with their blood at the altar, to make atonement for all Israel. For the king com-

29.21
Lev 4.3-14

29.22
Lev 4.18;
8.14

29.23
Lev 4.15

29.24
Lev 4.26

29.15ff We may well wonder why God did not remove his presence from the temple in such a state of disrepair. He was long-suffering, providing his people with every opportunity to mend their ways and follow his precepts. When the captivity finally did come, it was not from a lack of divine patience and repeated efforts to get the people to repent.

29.21–24 Blood atonement had to be made for the sins of the people. Seven of each kind of animal were brought for sacrifice. The king and others laid their hands on these animals to confess their guilt before God. The revival of the true worship of God was on the way.

manded that the burnt offering and the sin offering should be made for all Israel.

29.25
1 Chr 25.6;
2 Chr 8.14;
2 Sam 24.11;
7.2
29.26
1 Chr 23.5;
2 Chr 5.12
29.27
2 Chr 23.18

25 He stationed the Levites in the house of the LORD with cymbals, harps, and lyres, according to the commandment of David and of Gad the king's seer and of the prophet Nathan, for the commandment was from the LORD through his prophets. 26 The Levites stood with the instruments of David, and the priests with the trumpets. 27 Then Hezekiah commanded that the burnt offering be offered on the altar. When the burnt offering began, the song to the LORD began also, and the trumpets, accompanied by the instruments of King David of Israel. 28 The whole assembly worshiped, the singers sang, and the trumpeters sounded; all this continued until the burnt offering was finished. 29 When the offering

29.29
2 Chr 20.18

was finished, the king and all who were present with him bowed down and worshiped. 30 King Hezekiah and the officials commanded the Levites to sing praises to the LORD with the words of David and of the seer Asaph. They sang praises with gladness, and they bowed down and worshiped.

d. *The sacrifices at the temple*

29.31
2 Chr 13.9;
Ex 35.5, 22

31 Then Hezekiah said, "You have now consecrated yourselves to the LORD; come near, bring sacrifices and thank offerings to the house of the LORD." The assembly brought sacrifices and thank offerings; and all who were of a willing heart brought burnt offerings. 32 The number of the burnt offerings that the assembly brought was seventy bulls, one hundred rams, and two hundred lambs; all these were for a burnt offering to the LORD. 33 The consecrated offerings were six hundred bulls and three

29.34
2 Chr 35.11;
30.3

thousand sheep. 34 But the priests were too few and could not skin all the burnt offerings, so, until other priests had sanctified themselves, their kindred, the Levites, helped them until the work was finished — for the Levites were more conscientious[l] than the priests in sanctifying them-

29.35
v. 32;
Lev 3.16;
Num 15.5-10

selves. 35 Besides the great number of burnt offerings there was the fat of the offerings of well-being, and there were the drink offerings for the burnt offerings. Thus the service of the house of the LORD was restored. 36 And Hezekiah and all the people rejoiced because of what God had done for the people; for the thing had come about suddenly.

2. *The celebration of the passover*

a. *The invitation to all Israel and Judah*

30 Hezekiah sent word to all Israel and Judah, and wrote letters also to Ephraim and Manasseh, that they should come to the house of the LORD at Jerusalem, to keep the passover to the LORD the God of Israel. 2 For the king and his officials and all the assembly in Jerusalem had taken counsel to keep the passover in the second month 3 (for they could not keep it at its proper time because the priests had not sanctified themselves in sufficient number, nor had the people assembled in Jerusalem). 4 The plan seemed right to the king and all the assembly. 5 So they decreed to make a proclamation throughout all Israel, from Beer-sheba to Dan, that the people should come and keep the passover to the LORD the God of Israel, at Jerusalem; for they had not kept it in great numbers as pre-

30.2
vv. 13, 15;
Num 9.10, 11
30.3
Ex 12.6, 18;
2 Chr 29.34
30.5
Judg 20.1

---

[l] Heb *upright in heart*

29.34 Not all the Levites were priests — only the descendants of Aaron. Since there were not enough priests, other Levites, contrary to the law, were called upon to help. The legal requirements of the law were dispensed with in this case of extreme necessity.
30.1ff Hezekiah sent messengers all over Israel as well as Judah, inviting all to assemble for the celebration of the passover. The citizens of the north laughed, scorned and mocked the messengers, and refused to come to Jerusalem to celebrate. The people of Judah, on the other hand, accepted the invitation and came to Jerusalem. The people were revived and true religion prospered.
30.5 *they had not kept it in great numbers as prescribed.* By this time the northern kingdom was finished. Still, a few were interested in and willing to come to Jerusalem to celebrate the passover.

scribed. 6 So couriers went throughout all Israel and Judah with letters from the king and his officials, as the king had commanded, saying, "O people of Israel, return to the LORD, the God of Abraham, Isaac, and Israel, so that he may turn again to the remnant of you who have escaped from the hand of the kings of Assyria. 7 Do not be like your ancestors and your kindred, who were faithless to the LORD God of their ancestors, so that he made them a desolation, as you see. 8 Do not now be stiff-necked as your ancestors were, but yield yourselves to the LORD and come to his sanctuary, which he has sanctified forever, and serve the LORD your God, so that his fierce anger may turn away from you. 9 For as you return to the LORD, your kindred and your children will find compassion with their captors, and return to this land. For the LORD your God is gracious and merciful, and will not turn away his face from you, if you return to him."

10   So the couriers went from city to city through the country of Ephraim and Manasseh, and as far as Zebulun; but they laughed them to scorn, and mocked them. 11 Only a few from Asher, Manasseh, and Zebulun humbled themselves and came to Jerusalem. 12 The hand of God was also on Judah to give them one heart to do what the king and the officials commanded by the word of the LORD.

b. *The keeping of the passover*

13   Many people came together in Jerusalem to keep the festival of unleavened bread in the second month, a very large assembly. 14 They set to work and removed the altars that were in Jerusalem, and all the altars for offering incense they took away and threw into the Wadi Kidron. 15 They slaughtered the passover lamb on the fourteenth day of the second month. The priests and the Levites were ashamed, and they sanctified themselves and brought burnt offerings into the house of the LORD. 16 They took their accustomed posts according to the law of Moses the man of God; the priests dashed the blood that they received[m] from the hands of the Levites. 17 For there were many in the assembly who had not sanctified themselves; therefore the Levites had to slaughter the passover lamb for everyone who was not clean, to make it holy to the LORD. 18 For a multitude of the people, many of them from Ephraim, Manasseh, Issachar, and Zebulun, had not cleansed themselves, yet they ate the passover otherwise than as prescribed. But Hezekiah prayed for them, saying, "The good LORD pardon all 19 who set their hearts to seek God, the LORD the God of their ancestors, even though not in accordance with the sanctuary's rules of cleanness." 20 The LORD heard Hezekiah, and healed the people. 21 The people of Israel who were present at Jerusalem kept the festival of unleavened bread seven days with great gladness; and the Levites and the priests praised the LORD day by day, accompanied by loud instruments for the LORD. 22 Hezekiah spoke encouragingly to all the Levites who showed good skill in the service of the LORD. So the people ate the food of the festival for seven days, sacrificing offerings of well-being and giving thanks to the LORD the God of their ancestors.

c. *The festival continued for seven days*

23   Then the whole assembly agreed together to keep the festival for another seven days; so they kept it for another seven days with gladness. 24 For King Hezekiah of Judah gave the assembly a thousand bulls and seven thousand sheep for offerings, and the officials gave the assembly a thousand bulls and ten thousand sheep. The priests sanctified themselves in great numbers. 25 The whole assembly of Judah, the priests and the

m Heb lacks *that they received*

30.6
Esth 8.14;
Job 9.25;
Jer 51.31;
2 Chr 20.8

30.7
Ezek 20.18;
2 Chr 29.8
30.8
Ex 32.9;
2 Chr 29.10

30.9
Deut 30.2;
Ex 34.6, 7;
Mic 7.18;
Isa 55.7

30.10
2 Chr 36.16

30.11
vv. 18, 21, 25

30.13
v. 2
30.14
2 Chr 28.24

30.15
vv. 2, 3;
2 Chr 29.34

30.16
2 Chr 35.10,
15
30.17
2 Chr 29.34

30.18
vv. 11, 25;
Ex 12.43-49

30.19
2 Chr 19.3

30.21
Ex 12.15;
13.6

30.22
2 Chr 32.6;
Ezra 10.11

30.23
1 Kings 8.65

30.24
2 Chr 35.7, 8;
29.34

30.20 *healed the people.* Hezekiah prayed that God would accept those who came to worship but who had not cleansed themselves properly. The intentions of their heart were right but their performance fell short of the requirements, since few knew what they were. Thus the healing here is not physical healing from disease or sickness but forgiveness, comfort, and peace.

30.27
2 Chr 23.18;
Num 6.23;
Deut 26.15;
Ps 68.5

Levites, and the whole assembly that came out of Israel, and the resident aliens who came out of the land of Israel, and the resident aliens who lived in Judah, rejoiced. 26 There was great joy in Jerusalem, for since the time of Solomon son of King David of Israel there had been nothing like this in Jerusalem. 27 Then the priests and the Levites stood up and blessed the people, and their voice was heard; their prayer came to his holy dwelling in heaven.

3. Further reforms of Hezekiah

a. The high places destroyed

31.1
2 Kings 18.4

31 Now when all this was finished, all Israel who were present went out to the cities of Judah and broke down the pillars, hewed down the sacred poles,[n] and pulled down the high places and the altars throughout all Judah and Benjamin, and in Ephraim and Manasseh, until they had destroyed them all. Then all the people of Israel returned to their cities, all to their individual properties.

b. The levitical service reformed

31.2
1 Chr 24.1;
23.28-31

2 Hezekiah appointed the divisions of the priests and of the Levites, division by division, everyone according to his service, the priests and the Levites, for burnt offerings and offerings of well-being, to minister in the gates of the camp of the LORD and to give thanks and praise.

31.3
Num 28.29

3 The contribution of the king from his own possessions was for the burnt offerings: the burnt offerings of morning and evening, and the burnt offerings for the sabbaths, the new moons, and the appointed festivals, as it is written in the law of the LORD.

31.4
Num 18.8;
Neh 13.10
31.5
Neh 13.12

4 He commanded the people who lived in Jerusalem to give the portion due to the priests and the Levites, so that they might devote themselves to the law of the LORD. 5 As soon as the word spread, the people of Israel gave in abundance the first fruits of grain, wine, oil, honey, and of all the produce of the field; and they brought in abundantly the tithe of everything.

31.6
Lev 27.30;
Deut 14.28

6 The people of Israel and Judah who lived in the cities of Judah also brought in the tithe of cattle and sheep, and the tithe of the dedicated things that had been consecrated to the LORD their God, and laid them in heaps. 7 In the third month they began to pile up the heaps, and finished them in the seventh month. 8 When Hezekiah and the officials came and saw the heaps, they blessed the LORD and his people Israel. 9 Hezekiah questioned the priests and the Levites about the heaps.

31.10
Mal 3.10

10 The chief priest Azariah, who was of the house of Zadok, answered him, "Since they began to bring the contributions into the house of the LORD, we have had enough to eat and have plenty to spare; for the LORD has blessed his people, so that we have this great supply left over."

11 Then Hezekiah commanded them to prepare store-chambers in the house of the LORD; and they prepared them. 12 Faithfully they brought in the contributions, the tithes and the dedicated things. The chief officer in charge of them was Conaniah the Levite, with his brother Shimei as second;

31.13
2 Chr 35.9

13 while Jehiel, Azaziah, Nahath, Asahel, Jerimoth, Jozabad, Eliel, Ismachiah, Mahath, and Benaiah were overseers assisting Conaniah and his brother Shimei, by the appointment of King Hezekiah and of Azariah the chief officer of the house of God. 14 Kore son of Imnah the

---

[n] Heb Asherim

31.1 Hezekiah and his officers undoubtedly could not know of or find all of the places where monuments of idolatry existed. Thus the people themselves finished the work by destroying all those places that had escaped the king's notice. Isaiah may have had this in mind when he wrote, "On that day people will throw away . . . their idols of silver and their idols of gold, which they made for themselves to worship"

(Isa 2.20).

31.4 Apparently the people had not supported the Levites, and those who were priests had to find other ways to support themselves. Thus they neglected their duties, including the study of the word of God. Seeing the need, Hezekiah contributed to this end and urged others to do the same.

Levite, keeper of the east gate, was in charge of the freewill offerings to God, to apportion the contribution reserved for the LORD and the most holy offerings. **15** Eden, Miniamin, Jeshua, Shemaiah, Amariah, and Shecaniah were faithfully assisting him in the cities of the priests, to distribute the portions to their kindred, old and young alike, by divisions, **16** except those enrolled by genealogy, males from three years old and upwards, all who entered the house of the LORD as the duty of each day required, for their service according to their offices, by their divisions. **17** The enrollment of the priests was according to their ancestral houses; that of the Levites from twenty years old and upwards was according to their offices, by their divisions. **18** The priests were enrolled with all their little children, their wives, their sons, and their daughters, the whole multitude; for they were faithful in keeping themselves holy. **19** And for the descendants of Aaron, the priests, who were in the fields of common land belonging to their towns, town by town, the people designated by name were to distribute portions to every male among the priests and to everyone among the Levites who was enrolled.

c. The personal faithfulness of Hezekiah

20 Hezekiah did this throughout all Judah; he did what was good and right and faithful before the LORD his God. **21** And every work that he undertook in the service of the house of God, and in accordance with the law and the commandments, to seek his God, he did with all his heart; and he prospered.

4. The defeat of Sennacherib

a. The defense against Sennacherib

32 After these things and these acts of faithfulness, King Sennacherib of Assyria came and invaded Judah and encamped against the fortified cities, thinking to win them for himself. **2** When Hezekiah saw that Sennacherib had come and intended to fight against Jerusalem, **3** he planned with his officers and his warriors to stop the flow of the springs that were outside the city; and they helped him. **4** A great many people were gathered, and they stopped all the springs and the wadi that flowed through the land, saying, "Why should the Assyrian kings come and find water in abundance?" **5** Hezekiah*o* set to work resolutely and built up the entire wall that was broken down, and raised towers on it,*p* and outside it he built another wall; he also strengthened the Millo in the city of David, and made weapons and shields in abundance. **6** He appointed combat commanders over the people, and gathered them together to him in the square at the gate of the city and spoke encouragingly to them, saying, **7** "Be strong and of good courage. Do not be afraid or dismayed before the king of Assyria and all the horde that is with him; for there is one greater with us than with him. **8** With him is an arm of flesh; but with us is the LORD our God, to help us and to fight our battles." The people were encouraged by the words of King Hezekiah of Judah.

o Heb *He*   *p* Vg: Heb *and raised on the towers*

31.15
2 Chr 29.12;
Josh 21.9-19

31.16
Ezra 3.4

31.17
1 Chr 23.24

31.19
Lev 25.34;
Num 35.2;
vv. 12-15

31.20
2 Kings 20.3;
22.2

32.1
2 Kings 18.13-19;
Isa 36.1ff

32.4
2 Kings 20.20;
v. 30

32.5
2 Chr 25.23;
1 Kings 9.24

32.6
2 Chr 30.22

32.7
1 Chr 22.13;
2 Kings 6.16
32.8
Jer 17.5;
2 Chr 13.12;
20.17

31.17 It was essential for records to be kept of those who were Levites, including both those of the priesthood and those not. All Levites were supported by the rest of the people, and apportionment was made according to the numbers of the Levites. Evidently those with wives and children received more than those who were single or married with no children. **32.1** Sennacherib decided to assault Judah. Hezekiah prepared for this eventuality by gathering an army and manufacturing armaments. He reinforced the city of Jerusalem and secured its water supply.

His most important contribution was his faith in God, which he communicated to the people: "with us is the LORD our God, to help us and to fight our battles" (v. 8). Judah was soon to learn the meaning of Hezekiah's confidence when they saw the power of God displayed on their behalf. **32.2** The chronicler leaves out the fact that before this, Hezekiah meekly paid tribute to Sennacherib in order to appease him; at that time he had neither consulted God nor the prophet Isaiah (see note on 2 Kings 18.14).

b. *The message of Sennacherib*

9   After this, while King Sennacherib of Assyria was at Lachish with all his forces, he sent his servants to Jerusalem to King Hezekiah of Judah and to all the people of Judah that were in Jerusalem, saying, 10 "Thus says King Sennacherib of Assyria: On what are you relying, that you undergo the siege of Jerusalem? 11 Is not Hezekiah misleading you, handing you over to die by famine and by thirst, when he tells you, 'The LORD our God will save us from the hand of the king of Assyria'? 12 Was it not this same Hezekiah who took away his high places and his altars and commanded Judah and Jerusalem, saying, 'Before one altar you shall worship, and upon it you shall make your offerings'? 13 Do you not know what I and my ancestors have done to all the peoples of other lands? Were the gods of the nations of those lands at all able to save their lands out of my hand? 14 Who among all the gods of those nations that my ancestors utterly destroyed was able to save his people from my hand, that your God should be able to save you from my hand? 15 Now therefore do not let Hezekiah deceive you or mislead you in this fashion, and do not believe him, for no god of any nation or kingdom has been able to save his people from my hand or from the hand of my ancestors. How much less will your God save you out of my hand!"

c. *Sennacherib's blasphemy against God*

16   His servants said still more against the Lord GOD and against his servant Hezekiah. 17 He also wrote letters to throw contempt on the LORD the God of Israel and to speak against him, saying, "Just as the gods of the nations in other lands did not rescue their people from my hands, so the God of Hezekiah will not rescue his people from my hand." 18 They shouted it with a loud voice in the language of Judah to the people of Jerusalem who were on the wall, to frighten and terrify them, in order that they might take the city. 19 They spoke of the God of Jerusalem as if he were like the gods of the peoples of the earth, which are the work of human hands.

d. *Sennacherib turned back by the angel*

20   Then King Hezekiah and the prophet Isaiah son of Amoz prayed because of this and cried to heaven. 21 And the LORD sent an angel who cut off all the mighty warriors and commanders and officers in the camp of the king of Assyria. So he returned in disgrace to his own land. When he came into the house of his god, some of his own sons struck him down there with the sword. 22 So the LORD saved Hezekiah and the inhabitants of Jerusalem from the hand of King Sennacherib of Assyria and from the hand of all his enemies; he gave them rest*q* on every side. 23 Many brought gifts to the LORD in Jerusalem and precious things to King Hezekiah of Judah, so that he was exalted in the sight of all nations from that time onward.

5. *Extension of life granted to Hezekiah*

24   In those days Hezekiah became sick and was at the point of death. He prayed to the LORD, and he answered him and gave him a sign. 25 But Hezekiah did not respond according to the benefit done to him, for his heart was proud. Therefore wrath came upon him and upon Judah and

q Gk Vg: Heb *guided them*

Cross-references (margin):

32.11 2 Kings 18.30

32.12 2 Kings 18.22; 2 Chr 31.1

32.13 2 Kings 18.33-35

32.14 Isa 10.9-11

32.15 2 Kings 18.29

32.17 2 Kings 19.9, 12

32.18 2 Kings 18.26-28

32.19 2 Kings 19.18

32.20 2 Kings 19.2, 4, 15
32.21 2 Kings 19.35ff

32.23 2 Chr 17.5

32.24 2 Kings 20.1-11; Isa 38.1-8
32.25 Ps 116.12; 2 Chr 26.16; 24.18

32.20 When Jerusalem was threatened, both King Hezekiah and the prophet Isaiah laid hold of God in prayer. Not mentioned here is how the angel of God slew 185,000 Assyrians in one night (see note on 2 Kings 19.35). The victory over Sennacherib was so great that Hezekiah "was exalted in the sight of all nations from that time onward" (v. 23).

32.24 A more extended account of Hezekiah's healing is found in 2 Kings 20.1-11. The retreat of the sundial is not recorded here. Hezekiah's pride after his healing led to Isaiah's prophecy about the destruction of Judah, though this was held off until after Hezekiah's day (cf. 2 Kings 20.19).

Jerusalem. 26 Then Hezekiah humbled himself for the pride of his heart, both he and the inhabitants of Jerusalem, so that the wrath of the LORD did not come upon them in the days of Hezekiah.

6. The greatness of Hezekiah

27 Hezekiah had very great riches and honor; and he made for himself treasuries for silver, for gold, for precious stones, for spices, for shields, and for all kinds of costly objects; 28 storehouses also for the yield of grain, wine, and oil; and stalls for all kinds of cattle, and sheepfolds.r 29 He likewise provided cities for himself, and flocks and herds in abundance; for God had given him very great possessions. 30 This same Hezekiah closed the upper outlet of the waters of Gihon and directed them down to the west side of the city of David. Hezekiah prospered in all his works. 31 So also in the matter of the envoys of the officials of Babylon, who had been sent to him to inquire about the sign that had been done in the land, God left him to himself, in order to test him and to know all that was in his heart.

7. Hezekiah's death and the succession

32 Now the rest of the acts of Hezekiah, and his good deeds, are written in the vision of the prophet Isaiah son of Amoz in the Book of the Kings of Judah and Israel. 33 Hezekiah slept with his ancestors, and they buried him on the ascent to the tombs of the descendants of David; and all Judah and the inhabitants of Jerusalem did him honor at his death. His son Manasseh succeeded him.

M. The reigns of Manasseh and Amon

1. The wickedness of Manasseh

33 Manasseh was twelve years old when he began to reign; he reigned fifty-five years in Jerusalem. 2 He did what was evil in the sight of the LORD, according to the abominable practices of the nations whom the LORD drove out before the people of Israel. 3 For he rebuilt the high places that his father Hezekiah had pulled down, and erected altars to the Baals, made sacred poles,s worshiped all the host of heaven, and served them. 4 He built altars in the house of the LORD, of which the LORD had said, "In Jerusalem shall my name be forever." 5 He built altars for all the host of heaven in the two courts of the house of the LORD. 6 He made his son pass through fire in the valley of the son of Hinnom, practiced soothsaying and augury and sorcery, and dealt with mediums and with wizards. He did much evil in the sight of the LORD, provoking him to anger. 7 The carved image of the idol that he had made he set in the house of God, of which God said to David and to his son Solomon, "In this house, and in Jerusalem, which I have chosen out of all the tribes of Israel, I will put my name forever; 8 I will never again remove the feet of Israel from the land that I appointed for your ancestors, if only they will be careful to do all that I have commanded them, all the law, the statutes, and the ordinances given through Moses." 9 Manasseh misled Judah and the inhabitants of Jerusalem, so that they did more evil than the nations whom the LORD had destroyed before the people of Israel.

32.26
Jer 26.18, 19

32.29
1 Chr 29.12

32.30
2 Kings 20.20;
1 Kings 1.33

32.31
2 Kings 20.12;
Isa 39.1;
Deut 8.2, 16

32.33
2 Kings 20.21;
Prov 10.7

33.1
2 Kings 21.1-9
33.2
Deut 18.9;
2 Chr 28.3
33.3
2 Chr 31.1;
Deut 16.21;
2 Kings 23.5,
6;
Deut 17.3
33.4
2 Chr 28.24;
7.16
33.5
2 Chr 4.9
33.6
Lev 18.21;
2 Chr 28.3;
Deut 18.10,
11;
2 Kings 21.6
33.7
2 Kings 21.7;
vv. 4, 15
33.8
2 Sam 7.10

---

r Gk Vg: Heb flocks for folds   s Heb Asheroth

33.1 The first ten years of Manasseh's reign were a co-regency with his father Hezekiah.
33.3 Manasseh reversed the pattern established by his father. Judah resorted to idolatry again, the high places were rebuilt, and altars to the Baals were set up. He also committed the vilest of sins: he set up an idol in the house of God (v. 7). This was the supreme insult to Almighty God.

2. *His imprisonment and release*

10 The LORD spoke to Manasseh and to his people, but they gave no heed. [11] Therefore the LORD brought against them the commanders of the army of the king of Assyria, who took Manasseh captive in manacles, bound him with fetters, and brought him to Babylon. [12] While he was in distress he entreated the favor of the LORD his God and humbled himself greatly before the God of his ancestors. [13] He prayed to him, and God received his entreaty, heard his plea, and restored him again to Jerusalem and to his kingdom. Then Manasseh knew that the LORD indeed was God.

3. *The removal of the heathen altars*

14 Afterward he built an outer wall for the city of David west of Gihon, in the valley, reaching the entrance at the Fish Gate; he carried it around Ophel, and raised it to a very great height. He also put commanders of the army in all the fortified cities in Judah. [15] He took away the foreign gods and the idol from the house of the LORD, and all the altars that he had built on the mountain of the house of the LORD and in Jerusalem, and he threw them out of the city. [16] He also restored the altar of the LORD and offered on it sacrifices of well-being and of thanksgiving; and he commanded Judah to serve the LORD the God of Israel. [17] The people, however, still sacrificed at the high places, but only to the LORD their God.

4. *The summary of Manasseh's reign and death*

18 Now the rest of the acts of Manasseh, his prayer to his God, and the words of the seers who spoke to him in the name of the LORD God of Israel, these are in the Annals of the Kings of Israel. [19] His prayer, and how God received his entreaty, all his sin and his faithlessness, the sites on which he built high places and set up the sacred poles[t] and the images, before he humbled himself, these are written in the records of the seers.[u] [20] So Manasseh slept with his ancestors, and they buried him in his house. His son Amon succeeded him.

5. *The reign of Amon*

21 Amon was twenty-two years old when he began to reign; he reigned two years in Jerusalem. [22] He did what was evil in the sight of the LORD, as his father Manasseh had done. Amon sacrificed to all the images that his father Manasseh had made, and served them. [23] He did not humble himself before the LORD, as his father Manasseh had humbled himself, but this Amon incurred more and more guilt. [24] His servants conspired against him and killed him in his house. [25] But the people of the land killed all those who had conspired against King Amon; and the people of the land made his son Josiah king to succeed him.

N. *The reign of Josiah*

1. *His removal of the idols and high places*

34 Josiah was eight years old when he began to reign; he reigned thirty-one years in Jerusalem. [2] He did what was right in the sight of the LORD, and walked in the ways of his ancestor David; he did not

---

t Heb *Asherim*   *u* One Ms Gk: MT *of Hozai*

33.10 God had warned Manasseh. Thus, when the divine injunctions were ignored, God's judgment fell and the king was humbled.
33.13 Only after Manasseh had been taken captive and brought to Babylon in chains did he come to his senses. He pleaded with God for help and was re-

turned to Jerusalem. By then he knew the power of God and changed for the better.
33.23 Amon distinguished himself by the same wickedness that characterized most of his father's life. He was cut off when he was young.

Side column cross-references:

33.11
Deut 28.36;
Ps 107.10, 11
33.12
2 Chr 32.26;
1 Pet 5.6
33.13
1 Chr 5.20;
Ezra 8.23;
Dan 4.25, 32

33.14
1 Kings 1.33;
Neh 3.3;
2 Chr 27.3
33.15
vv. 3-7

33.17
2 Chr 32.12

33.18
vv. 10, 12, 18
33.19
vv. 3, 13

33.20
2 Kings 21.18

33.21
2 Kings 21.19-24
33.22
vv. 2-7
33.23
v. 12
33.24
see
2 Chr 25.27

34.1
2 Kings 22.1, 2

turn aside to the right or to the left. ³For in the eighth year of his reign, while he was still a boy, he began to seek the God of his ancestor David, and in the twelfth year he began to purge Judah and Jerusalem of the high places, the sacred poles,ᵛ and the carved and the cast images. ⁴In his presence they pulled down the altars of the Baals; he demolished the incense altars that stood above them. He broke down the sacred polesᵛ and the carved and the cast images; he made dust of them and scattered it over the graves of those who had sacrificed to them. ⁵He also burned the bones of the priests on their altars, and purged Judah and Jerusalem. ⁶In the towns of Manasseh, Ephraim, and Simeon, and as far as Naphtali, in their ruinsʷ all around, ⁷he broke down the altars, beat the sacred polesᵛ and the images into powder, and demolished all the incense altars throughout all the land of Israel. Then he returned to Jerusalem.

2. *His repair of the house of the LORD*

8 In the eighteenth year of his reign, when he had purged the land and the house, he sent Shaphan son of Azaliah, Maaseiah the governor of the city, and Joah son of Joahaz, the recorder, to repair the house of the LORD his God. ⁹They came to the high priest Hilkiah and delivered the money that had been brought into the house of God, which the Levites, the keepers of the threshold, had collected from Manasseh and Ephraim and from all the remnant of Israel and from all Judah and Benjamin and from the inhabitants of Jerusalem. ¹⁰They delivered it to the workers who had the oversight of the house of the LORD, and the workers who were working in the house of the LORD gave it for repairing and restoring the house. ¹¹They gave it to the carpenters and the builders to buy quarried stone, and timber for binders, and beams for the buildings that the kings of Judah had let go to ruin. ¹²The people did the work faithfully. Over them were appointed the Levites Jahath and Obadiah, of the sons of Merari, along with Zechariah and Meshullam, of the sons of the Kohathites, to have oversight. Other Levites, all skillful with instruments of music, ¹³were over the burden bearers and directed all who did work in every kind of service; and some of the Levites were scribes, and officials, and gatekeepers.

3. *The discovery of the book of the law*

14 While they were bringing out the money that had been brought into the house of the LORD, the priest Hilkiah found the book of the law of the LORD given through Moses. ¹⁵Hilkiah said to the secretary Shaphan, "I have found the book of the law in the house of the LORD"; and Hilkiah gave the book to Shaphan. ¹⁶Shaphan brought the book to the king, and further reported to the king, "All that was committed to your servants they are doing. ¹⁷They have emptied out the money that was found in the house of the LORD and have delivered it into the hand of the overseers and the workers." ¹⁸The secretary Shaphan informed the king, "The priest Hilkiah has given me a book." Shaphan then read it aloud to the king.

19 When the king heard the words of the law he tore his clothes. ²⁰Then the king commanded Hilkiah, Ahikam son of Shaphan, Abdon

ᵛ Heb *Asherim*   ʷ Meaning of Heb uncertain

34.3 2 Chr 15.2; 1 Kings 13.2; 2 Chr 33.17, 22
34.4 Lev 26.30; 2 Kings 23.4; Ex 32.20
34.5 1 Kings 13.2; 2 Kings 23.20
34.6 2 Kings 23.15, 19
34.7 2 Chr 31.1

34.8 2 Kings 22.3-20

34.9 2 Chr 35.8

34.11 2 Chr 33.4-7
34.12 1 Chr 25.1

34.13 1 Chr 23.4, 5

34.14 v. 9

34.16 v. 8

34.19 Josh 7.6

34.3 While Josiah was yet a lad (sixteen years of age) he set his heart to seek God.
34.4 When Josiah was twenty years old and firmly settled in his kingship, he destroyed the places of idolatry. He moved through the country, making a clean sweep of everything contrary to the law and will of God.
34.8 When Josiah was twenty-six, he rehabilitated the house of the Lord. Repairs were made and the

proper services of worship reinstituted.
34.14 Hilkiah the priest discovered a copy of the Pentateuch. We do not know why it had been misplaced. Evidently the priests had strayed from the book of the law or it was not sufficiently important for them to keep track of it. When Josiah heard the words of the book, he was profoundly moved by them and tore his clothes (v. 19).

son of Micah, the secretary Shaphan, and the king's servant Asaiah: 21 "Go, inquire of the LORD for me and for those who are left in Israel and in Judah, concerning the words of the book that has been found; for the wrath of the LORD that is poured out on us is great, because our ancestors did not keep the word of the LORD, to act in accordance with all that is written in this book."

22 So Hilkiah and those whom the king had sent went to the prophet Huldah, the wife of Shallum son of Tokhath son of Hasrah, keeper of the wardrobe (who lived in Jerusalem in the Second Quarter) and spoke to her to that effect. 23 She declared to them, "Thus says the LORD, the God of Israel: Tell the man who sent you to me, 24 Thus says the LORD: I will indeed bring disaster upon this place and upon its inhabitants, all the curses that are written in the book that was read before the king of Judah. 25 Because they have forsaken me and have made offerings to other gods, so that they have provoked me to anger with all the works of their hands, my wrath will be poured out on this place and will not be quenched. 26 But as to the king of Judah, who sent you to inquire of the LORD, thus shall you say to him: Thus says the LORD, the God of Israel: Regarding the words that you have heard, 27 because your heart was penitent and you humbled yourself before God when you heard his words against this place and its inhabitants, and you have humbled yourself before me, and have torn your clothes and wept before me, I also have heard you, says the LORD. 28 I will gather you to your ancestors and you shall be gathered to your grave in peace; your eyes shall not see all the disaster that I will bring on this place and its inhabitants." They took the message back to the king.

4. The reading of the Law and the renewal of the covenant

29 Then the king sent word and gathered together all the elders of Judah and Jerusalem. 30 The king went up to the house of the LORD, with all the people of Judah, the inhabitants of Jerusalem, the priests and the Levites, all the people both great and small; he read in their hearing all the words of the book of the covenant that had been found in the house of the LORD. 31 The king stood in his place and made a covenant before the LORD, to follow the LORD, keeping his commandments, his decrees, and his statutes, with all his heart and all his soul, to perform the words of the covenant that were written in this book. 32 Then he made all who were present in Jerusalem and in Benjamin pledge themselves to it. And the inhabitants of Jerusalem acted according to the covenant of God, the God of their ancestors. 33 Josiah took away all the abominations from all the territory that belonged to the people of Israel, and made all who were in Israel worship the LORD their God. All his days they did not turn away from following the LORD the God of their ancestors.

5. The keeping of the passover

35 Josiah kept a passover to the LORD in Jerusalem; they slaughtered the passover lamb on the fourteenth day of the first month. 2 He appointed the priests to their offices and encouraged them in the service of the house of the LORD. 3 He said to the Levites who taught all Israel and who were holy to the LORD, "Put the holy ark in the house that Solomon son of David, king of Israel, built; you need no longer carry it on your shoulders. Now serve the LORD your God and his people Israel.

Marginal references:

34.21
2 Chr 29.8

34.22
2 Kings 22.14

34.24
2 Chr 36.14-20;
Deut 28.15-68

34.25
2 Chr 33.3

34.27
2 Chr 12.7;
32.26

34.29
2 Kings 23.1-3
34.30
Neh 8.1-3

34.31
2 Kings 11.14;
23.3;
2 Chr 23.3,
16; 29.10

34.33
vv. 3-7;
2 Chr 33.2-7

35.1
2 Kings 23.21,
22;
Ex 12.6;
Num 9.3
35.2
2 Chr 23.18;
29.11
35.3
Deut 33.10;
2 Chr 5.7;
1 Chr 23.26

34.22 See note on 2 Kings 22.14 about Huldah the prophetess.
34.28 Josiah was so moved by the word of God that he placed himself under that word and promised to obey it. As with Hezekiah (32.26), God promised that judgment against Judah would be deferred and that Josiah would be gathered to his grave in peace.
35.1 The celebration of the passover (mentioned briefly in 2 Kings 23.21–23) is enlarged upon with many details added. The king provided numerous animals from his own flocks for the people to offer. Everyone — the king, priests, singers, gatekeepers, and people — participated in what was to be an epic event in Judah's recent history. Judah's idolatry had robbed the people of their faith and their traditions, such as the regular celebration of the passover.

4 Make preparations by your ancestral houses by your divisions, following the written directions of King David of Israel and the written directions of his son Solomon. 5 Take position in the holy place according to the groupings of the ancestral houses of your kindred the people, and let there be Levites for each division of an ancestral house.ˣ 6 Slaughter the passover lamb, sanctify yourselves, and on behalf of your kindred make preparations, acting according to the word of the LORD by Moses."

7   Then Josiah contributed to the people, as passover offerings for all that were present, lambs and kids from the flock to the number of thirty thousand, and three thousand bulls; these were from the king's possessions. 8 His officials contributed willingly to the people, to the priests, and to the Levites. Hilkiah, Zechariah, and Jehiel, the chief officers of the house of God, gave to the priests for the passover offerings two thousand six hundred lambs and kids and three hundred bulls. 9 Conaniah also, and his brothers Shemaiah and Nethanel, and Hashabiah and Jeiel and Jozabad, the chiefs of the Levites, gave to the Levites for the passover offerings five thousand lambs and kids and five hundred bulls.

10   When the service had been prepared for, the priests stood in their place, and the Levites in their divisions according to the king's command. 11 They slaughtered the passover lamb, and the priests dashed the blood that they receivedʸ from them, while the Levites did the skinning. 12 They set aside the burnt offerings so that they might distribute them according to the groupings of the ancestral houses of the people, to offer to the LORD, as it is written in the book of Moses. And they did the same with the bulls. 13 They roasted the passover lamb with fire according to the ordinance; and they boiled the holy offerings in pots, in caldrons, and in pans, and carried them quickly to all the people. 14 Afterward they made preparations for themselves and for the priests, because the priests the descendants of Aaron were occupied in offering the burnt offerings and the fat parts until night; so the Levites made preparations for themselves and for the priests, the descendants of Aaron. 15 The singers, the descendants of Asaph, were in their place according to the command of David, and Asaph, and Heman, and the king's seer Jeduthun. The gatekeepers were at each gate; they did not need to interrupt their service, for their kindred the Levites made preparations for them.

16   So all the service of the LORD was prepared that day, to keep the passover and to offer burnt offerings on the altar of the LORD, according to the command of King Josiah. 17 The people of Israel who were present kept the passover at that time, and the festival of unleavened bread seven days. 18 No passover like it had been kept in Israel since the days of the prophet Samuel; none of the kings of Israel had kept such a passover as was kept by Josiah, by the priests and the Levites, by all Judah and Israel who were present, and by the inhabitants of Jerusalem. 19 In the eighteenth year of the reign of Josiah this passover was kept.

6. Josiah's battle against Neco of Egypt and his death

20   After all this, when Josiah had set the temple in order, King Neco of Egypt went up to fight at Carchemish on the Euphrates, and Josiah went out against him. 21 But Necoᶻ sent envoys to him, saying, "What have I to do with you, king of Judah? I am not coming against you today, but against the house with which I am at war; and God has commanded me to hurry. Cease opposing God, who is with me, so that he will not destroy you." 22 But Josiah would not turn away from him, but disguised

x Meaning of Heb uncertain   y Heb lacks *that they received*   z Heb *he*

Marginal references

35.4 1 Chr 9.10-13; 2 Chr 8.14
35.5 Ps 134.1
35.6 v. 1; 2 Chr 29.5, 15; Ezra 6.20
35.7 2 Chr 30.24
35.9 2 Chr 31.12
35.10 v. 5; Ezra 6.18
35.11 vv. 1, 6; 2 Chr 29.22, 34
35.13 Ex 12.8, 9; Lev 6.25; 1 Sam 2.13-15
35.15 1 Chr 25.1; 26.12-19
35.17 Ex 12.15; 2 Chr 30.21
35.18 2 Kings 23.21-23
35.20 2 Kings 23.29, 30; Isa 10.9; Jer 46.2
35.22 2 Chr 18.29; Judg 5.19

35.18 Hezekiah's celebration of the passover had exceeded any celebration as far back as Solomon's day (30.26). But Josiah's celebration exceeded all previous ones, including Hezekiah's.

35.20 at Carchemish, i.e., against the Assyrians (see note on 2 Kings 23.29).
35.22 the plain of Megiddo. Towering above the plain is the fortress of Megiddo, named Har-megiddo

himself in order to fight with him. He did not listen to the words of Neco from the mouth of God, but joined battle in the plain of Megiddo. 23 The archers shot King Josiah; and the king said to his servants, "Take me away, for I am badly wounded." 24 So his servants took him out of the chariot and carried him in his second chariot*a* and brought him to Jerusalem. There he died, and was buried in the tombs of his ancestors. All Judah and Jerusalem mourned for Josiah. 25 Jeremiah also uttered a lament for Josiah, and all the singing men and singing women have spoken of Josiah in their laments to this day. They made these a custom in Israel; they are recorded in the Laments. 26 Now the rest of the acts of Josiah and his faithful deeds in accordance with what is written in the law of the LORD, 27 and his acts, first and last, are written in the Book of the Kings of Israel and Judah.

O. From Josiah to the captivity

1. Jehoahaz taken captive to Egypt

36 The people of the land took Jehoahaz son of Josiah and made him king to succeed his father in Jerusalem. 2 Jehoahaz was twenty-three years old when he began to reign; he reigned three months in Jerusalem. 3 Then the king of Egypt deposed him in Jerusalem and laid on the land a tribute of one hundred talents of silver and one talent of gold. 4 The king of Egypt made his brother Eliakim king over Judah and Jerusalem, and changed his name to Jehoiakim; but Neco took his brother Jehoahaz and carried him to Egypt.

2. Jehoiakim captive in Babylon

5 Jehoiakim was twenty-five years old when he began to reign; he reigned eleven years in Jerusalem. He did what was evil in the sight of the LORD his God. 6 Against him King Nebuchadnezzar of Babylon came up, and bound him with fetters to take him to Babylon. 7 Nebuchadnezzar also carried some of the vessels of the house of the LORD to Babylon and put them in his palace in Babylon. 8 Now the rest of the acts of Jehoiakim, and the abominations that he did, and what was found against him, are written in the Book of the Kings of Israel and Judah; and his son Jehoiachin succeeded him.

3. Jehoiachin captive in Babylon

9 Jehoiachin was eight years old when he began to reign; he reigned three months and ten days in Jerusalem. He did what was evil in the sight of the LORD. 10 In the spring of the year King Nebuchadnezzar sent and brought him to Babylon, along with the precious vessels of the house of the LORD, and made his brother Zedekiah king over Judah and Jerusalem.

4. Wicked Zedekiah

a. His rebellion against Nebuchadnezzar

11 Zedekiah was twenty-one years old when he began to reign; he

a Or the chariot of his deputy

Marginal references:
35.24 2 Kings 23.30; Zech 12.11
35.25 Lam 4.20; Jer 22.20
36.1 2 Kings 23.30-34; Jer 22.11
36.5 2 Kings 23.36, 37
36.6 2 Kings 24.1; 2 Chr 33.11
36.7 2 Kings 24.13
36.8 2 Kings 24.5; see 1 Chr 3.16
36.9 2 Kings 24.8-17
36.10 2 Sam 11.1; Jer 37.1
36.11 2 Kings 24.18-20; Jer 52.1

("the hill of Megiddo"). It was located in the southern part of the Jezreel (Esdralon) Valley, guarding the pass of the best north-south trade route in Canaan. Many great battles have been fought here. And here (at Harmagedon) the great climactic battle of the age will be fought, with Christ the victor (see Rev 16.16). **35.24** Josiah was still in his early thirties when he died. The next four kings reigned a total of less than twenty-three years. **36.1** 2 Kings 36.32 tells us what the chronicler does

not say here about Jehoahaz: "he did what was evil in the sight of the LORD" during his three-month reign. **36.5** Jehoiakim, whose throne name was Eliakim, was chosen king by Pharaoh Neco. He reigned in Jerusalem for eleven years. Nebuchadnezzar took him to Babylon in chains. **36.9** *eight years old.* Although some manuscripts read "eight years old," the correct age is eighteen (see 2 Kings 24.8), unless Jehoiachin had been co-regent for ten years before the death of his father.

reigned eleven years in Jerusalem. 12 He did what was evil in the sight of
the LORD his God. He did not humble himself before the prophet Jeremiah who spoke from the mouth of the LORD. 13 He also rebelled against
King Nebuchadnezzar, who had made him swear by God; he stiffened his
neck and hardened his heart against turning to the LORD, the God of
Israel. 14 All the leading priests and the people also were exceedingly
unfaithful, following all the abominations of the nations; and they polluted the house of the LORD that he had consecrated in Jerusalem.

b. *The mocking of God's messengers*

15   The LORD, the God of their ancestors, sent persistently to them by
his messengers, because he had compassion on his people and on his
dwelling place; 16 but they kept mocking the messengers of God, despising
his words, and scoffing at his prophets, until the wrath of the LORD against
his people became so great that there was no remedy.

c. *The destruction of the temple and Jerusalem: the captivity*

17   Therefore he brought up against them the king of the Chaldeans,
who killed their youths with the sword in the house of their sanctuary,
and had no compassion on young man or young woman, the aged or the
feeble; he gave them all into his hand. 18 All the vessels of the house of
God, large and small, and the treasures of the house of the LORD, and the
treasures of the king and of his officials, all these he brought to Babylon.
19 They burned the house of God, broke down the wall of Jerusalem,
burned all its palaces with fire, and destroyed all its precious vessels. 20 He
took into exile in Babylon those who had escaped from the sword, and they
became servants to him and to his sons until the establishment of the
kingdom of Persia, 21 to fulfill the word of the LORD by the mouth of
Jeremiah, until the land had made up for its sabbaths. All the days that
it lay desolate it kept sabbath, to fulfill seventy years.

5. *The return from the captivity prophesied*

22   In the first year of King Cyrus of Persia, in fulfillment of the word
of the LORD spoken by Jeremiah, the LORD stirred up the spirit of King
Cyrus of Persia so that he sent a herald throughout all his kingdom and
also declared in a written edict: 23 "Thus says King Cyrus of Persia: The
LORD, the God of heaven, has given me all the kingdoms of the earth, and
he has charged me to build him a house at Jerusalem, which is in Judah.
Whoever is among you of all his people, may the LORD his God be with
him! Let him go up."

36.12	2 Chr 33.23; Jer 21.3-7
36.13	Jer 52.3; Ezek 17.15; 2 Kings 17.14; 2 Chr 30.8
36.15	Jer 25.3, 4; 35.15; 44.4
36.16	2 Chr 30.10; Jer 5.12, 13; Prov 1.25; Ezra 5.12
36.17	2 Kings 25.1-7
36.18	2 Kings 25.13ff
36.19	2 Kings 25.9; Jer 52.13
36.20	2 Kings 25.11; Jer 27.7
36.21	Jer 29.10; Lev 26.34; 25.4
36.22	Ezra 1.1; Jer 25.12; Isa 44.28
36.23	Ezra 1.2, 3

36.11   See note on 2 Kings 24.17 for information on
Zedekiah.
36.19   *They burned the house of God.* The Jews
thought God would never let his house be destroyed,
but they were wrong. God eventually calls his people
to account for their sins.

36.21   *to fulfill seventy years.* Jeremiah spoke of the
seventy years' captivity in Jer 25.11,12; 29.10 (see
note on 2 Kings 24.10).
36.22,23   *Cyrus*, the founder of the Persian Empire,
presided over what was the largest empire the world
had ever seen up to that time.

INTRODUCTION TO

EZRA

Authorship, Date, and Background: In the Hebrew Bible, the books of Ezra and Nehemiah were considered a single book, entitled Ezra. Both must be related to the books of Chronicles and to the book of Esther. The book was part of the Writings (the *kethubim*,), the third division of the Hebrew Bible. The authorship of Ezra and Nehemiah has never been finally resolved. Ezra himself apparently wrote most of the book named after him, and Nehemiah as well. He included in the final product Nehemiah's personal memoirs, including even his form of the list of those who came back from Babylon.

Ezra returned to the land in 458 or 457 B.C. during the reign of Artaxerxes I (465–424 B.C.). Nehemiah returned twelve years later, in 445 B.C. Nehemiah's first governorship started in 445 B.C.; his second one in 433 B.C. Ezra was the son of Jozadak, whose genealogy went back to Aaron. He was a scribe of the law of Moses, who led the return of the second group of exiles, totaling approximately five thousand people. The temple had been finished years before (516 B.C.) but the walls of the city had not been rebuilt. It was to be the work of Nehemiah. Ezra, upon his return to the land, was given a blank check by the king. As a priest of the line of Zadok he was expected to teach the law. There is no record of his acting in the political office of governor as was true of Nehemiah.

Characteristics and Content: Ezra traced the return of the Jews following the edict of Cyrus, who reversed the policy of the Chaldeans. He described the preparations for the return, listed the various family groups, and noted that upon their return they went to the site of the former temple and contributed offerings of approximately five hundred thousand dollars for its rebuilding. Then follows the story of the rebuilding of the temple and the restoration of worship there. It was hampered by the malicious attacks of the Samaritans but, after a careful investigation, Darius gave order to continue the work of rebuilding. When it was completed, the festivals of the passover and unleavened bread were celebrated.

Ezra, a patriotic Jew, secured permission to return to the land himself and did so. He described the details of his return and poignantly noted that he refused to ask for armed protection, since his trust was in the Lord God. Ezra's anger knew no bounds when he discovered that the first group of returnees had intermarried with the heathen. He said, "I tore my garment and my mantle, and pulled hair from my head and beard, and sat appalled" (9.3). He prayed, lay on the ground weeping, and forcefully insisted that this evil had to be remedied. As a result, many marriages contracted by priests, Levites, singers, gatekeepers, and ordinary citizens were annulled.

Outline:

I. The first return to the land (1.1—2.70)

II. The restoration of worship and dedication of the temple (3.1—6.22)

III. The return of Ezra and the reform that followed (7.1—10.44)

C. The first return under Zerubbabel

EZRA

I. The first return to the land (1.1–2.70)

A. The edit of Cyrus

1 In the first year of King Cyrus of Persia, in order that the word of the Lord by the mouth of Jeremiah might be accomplished, the Lord stirred up the spirit of King Cyrus of Persia so that he sent a herald throughout all his kingdom, and also in a written edict declared:

2 "Thus says King Cyrus of Persia: The Lord, the God of heaven, has given me all the kingdoms of the earth, and he has charged me to build him a house at Jerusalem in Judah. ³Any of those among you who are of his people — may their God be with them! — are now permitted to go up to Jerusalem in Judah, and rebuild the house of the Lord, the God of Israel — he is the God who is in Jerusalem; ⁴and let all survivors, in whatever place they reside, be assisted by the people of their place with silver and gold, with goods and with animals, besides freewill offerings for the house of God in Jerusalem."

B. Preparation for the return

5 The heads of the families of Judah and Benjamin, and the priests and the Levites — everyone whose spirit God had stirred — got ready to go up and rebuild the house of the Lord in Jerusalem. ⁶All their neighbors aided them with silver vessels, with gold, with goods, with animals, and with valuable gifts, besides all that was freely offered. ⁷King Cyrus himself brought out the vessels of the house of the Lord that Nebuchadnezzar had carried away from Jerusalem and placed in the house of his gods. ⁸King Cyrus of Persia had them released into the charge of Mithredath the treasurer, who counted them out to Sheshbazzar the prince of Judah. ⁹And this was the inventory: gold basins, thirty; silver basins, one thousand; knives,ᵇ twenty-nine; ¹⁰gold bowls, thirty; other silver bowls, four hundred ten; other vessels, one thousand; ¹¹the total of the gold and silver

---

ᵇ Vg: Meaning of Heb uncertain

1.1ff
2 Chr 36.22, 23;
Jer 25.12; 29.10;
Ezra 5.13, 14
1.2
Isa 44.28; 45.1, 12, 13
1.3
Dan 6.26

1.5
Phil 2.13

1.7
Ezra 5.14; 6.5;
2 Kings 24.13;
2 Chr 36.7
1.8
Ezra 5.14

1.1–3 These verses are also found in 2 Chr 36.22,23. This suggests that Ezra may have written Chronicles as well as this book.

1.1 *the first year*, i.e., 539 B.C. Cyrus reigned 559–530 B.C., but his control of Babylonia began in 539. *the word of the Lord by the mouth of Jeremiah*, i.e., the prediction that the captivity in Babylon would last for seventy years (see Jer 25.12; 29.10).

1.2–4 The hearts of all rulers are in the hands of God, who turns them as he wills. Isa 45.4 says Cyrus did not know God, i.e., he did not serve him. But God knew him and used him to accomplish the divine purpose. Cyrus himself acknowledged that what he possessed had been given to him by God, and that he was ordered by God to build him a house in Jerusalem. If God can use unbelievers to do his will, how much more should believers expect God to use those who know him and who are in tune with his purposes.

1.3 *he is the God who is in Jerusalem.* Either Cyrus

was acknowledging the existence of Israel's God in order to conciliate the people, or he actually believed in that God. God alone knows his heart.

1.5 God himself moved not only Cyrus but also "the heads of the families" to return to the land. During the seventy years' captivity, the Jews had found a safe refuge in Babylon and had built their homes there. There was nothing to come back to in Jerusalem but a pile of rubble, and the task of rebuilding seemed impossible. God moved their spirits, however, giving the vision and the power to the remnant who finally went back.

1.8 Perhaps *Sheshbazzar* is the Shenazzar named in 1 Chr 3.18, although some have thought it to be the pseudonym for Zerubbabel. As a son of Jehoiachin he would have been the one entrusted with the priceless jewels of the temple. This "prince of Judah" was so highly regarded that Cyrus later appointed him to be governor over the people (see 5.14).

vessels was five thousand four hundred. All these Sheshbazzar brought up, when the exiles were brought up from Babylonia to Jerusalem.

C. *The first return under Zerubbabel*

2.1
Neh 7.6-73;
2 Kings 24.14-16;
25.11;
2 Chr 36.20

2 Now these were the people of the province who came from those captive exiles whom King Nebuchadnezzar of Babylon had carried captive to Babylonia; they returned to Jerusalem and Judah, all to their own towns. 2 They came with Zerubbabel, Jeshua, Nehemiah, Seraiah, Reelaiah, Mordecai, Bilshan, Mispar, Bigvai, Rehum, and Baanah.

The number of the Israelite people: 3 the descendants of Parosh, two thousand one hundred seventy-two. 4 Of Shephatiah, three hundred

2.5
cf. Neh 7.10
2.6
cf. Neh 7.11

seventy-two. 5 Of Arah, seven hundred seventy-five. 6 Of Pahath-moab, namely the descendants of Jeshua and Joab, two thousand eight hundred twelve. 7 Of Elam, one thousand two hundred fifty-four. 8 Of Zattu, nine hundred forty-five. 9 Of Zaccai, seven hundred sixty. 10 Of Bani, six hundred forty-two. 11 Of Bebai, six hundred twenty-three. 12 Of Azgad, one thousand two hundred twenty-two. 13 Of Adonikam, six hundred sixty-six. 14 Of Bigvai, two thousand fifty-six. 15 Of Adin, four hundred fifty-four. 16 Of Ater, namely of Hezekiah, ninety-eight. 17 Of Bezai, three

2.16
Neh 7.21
2.21
Neh 7.26

hundred twenty-three. 18 Of Jorah, one hundred twelve. 19 Of Hashum, two hundred twenty-three. 20 Of Gibbar, ninety-five. 21 Of Bethlehem, one hundred twenty-three. 22 The people of Netophah, fifty-six. 23 Of Anathoth, one hundred twenty-eight. 24 The descendants of Azmaveth, forty-two. 25 Of Kiriatharim, Chephirah, and Beeroth, seven hundred forty-three. 26 Of Ramah and Geba, six hundred twenty-one. 27 The people of Michmas, one hundred twenty-two. 28 Of Bethel and Ai, two hundred twenty-three. 29 The descendants of Nebo, fifty-two. 30 Of Mag-

2.31
see v. 7

bish, one hundred fifty-six. 31 Of the other Elam, one thousand two hundred fifty-four. 32 Of Harim, three hundred twenty. 33 Of Lod, Hadid, and Ono, seven hundred twenty-five. 34 Of Jericho, three hundred forty-five. 35 Of Senaah, three thousand six hundred thirty.

2.36
1 Chr 24.7-18
2.38
1 Chr 9.12
2.39
1 Chr 24.8

36 The priests: the descendants of Jedaiah, of the house of Jeshua, nine hundred seventy-three. 37 Of Immer, one thousand fifty-two. 38 Of Pashhur, one thousand two hundred forty-seven. 39 Of Harim, one thousand seventeen.

40 The Levites: the descendants of Jeshua and Kadmiel, of the descendants of Hodaviah, seventy-four. 41 The singers: the descendants of Asaph, one hundred twenty-eight. 42 The descendants of the gatekeepers: of Shallum, of Ater, of Talmon, of Akkub, of Hatita, and of Shobai, in all one hundred thirty-nine.

2.43
1 Chr 9.2

43 The temple servants: the descendants of Ziha, Hasupha, Tabbaoth, 44 Keros, Siaha, Padon, 45 Lebanah, Hagabah, Akkub, 46 Hagab, Shamlai, Hanan, 47 Giddel, Gahar, Reaiah, 48 Rezin, Nekoda, Gazzam,

2.48
Neh 7.50

49 Uzza, Paseah, Besai, 50 Asnah, Meunim, Nephisim, 51 Bakbuk, Haku-

---

2.2 Only two Mordecais are named in the O.T. This one is not the same Mordecai as in the book of Esther.
2.3ff Apparently the genealogical tables of the deportees to Babylon had been carefully maintained. This was for the benefit of succeeding generations, that they might know their ancestry and understand their family relationships. The names of those who returned are listed in a family sequence.
2.5 *Of Arah, seven hundred seventy-five.* Compare this figure with that given in Neh 7.10 — six hundred fifty-two. It could be a copyist's error; Jewish letters were used to represent numbers, and this often created confusion.
2.40 Generally, Judah had fewer priests than Levites. Yet only seventy-four Levites (350 if the singers

and porters are included) returned to the land, while there were 4,289 priests. No reason is given for this disparity. Perhaps the priests were spiritually discerning and wanted to reestablish proper worship according to the Mosaic pattern, whereas the other Levites were comfortable and better off financially than they had been in Jerusalem.
2.41 This is the Asaph who composed Psalms 50; 73–83. He was appointed by David as musician for the house of God; listed here are his descendants.
2.42 *the gatekeepers*, i.e., guards who kept intruders and the unclean from entering the sacred precincts of the house of God.
2.43 *The temple servants* were people assigned by David to help the Levites (see 8.20).

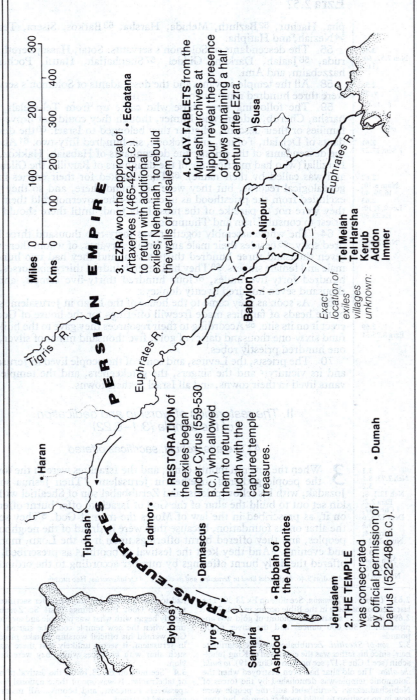

RETURN FROM EXILE

PERSIAN EMPIRE

TRANS-EUPHRATES

Miles
Kms

0   100   200   300

0   100   200   300   400

• Haran

• Ecbatana

• Susa

Tigris R.

Euphrates R.

Euphrates R.

Tiphsah

Tadmor

• Nippur

• Babylon

**Tel Melah
Tel Harsha
Kerub
Addon
Immer**

Exact
location of
exiles'
villages
unknown:

Damascus

• Dumah

Byblos

Tyre

• Rabbah of
the Ammonites

Samaria

Jerusalem

Ashdod

1. RESTORATION of
the exiles began
under Cyrus (559-530
B.C.), who allowed
them to return to
Judah with the
captured temple
treasures.

2. THE TEMPLE
was consecrated
by official permission of
Darius I (522-486 B.C.).

3. EZRA won the approval of
Artaxerxes I (465-424 B.C.)
to return with additional
exiles; Nehemiah, to rebuild
the walls of Jerusalem.

4. CLAY TABLETS from the
Murashu archives at
Nippur reveal the presence
of Jews remaining a half
century after Ezra.

©1989 The Zondervan Corporation.

pha, Harhur, [52]Bazluth, Mehida, Harsha, [53]Barkos, Sisera, Temah, [54]Neziah, and Hatipha.

2.55
Neh 7.57, 60;
11.3
55 The descendants of Solomon's servants: Sotai, Hassophereth, Peruda, [56]Jaalah, Darkon, Giddel, [57]Shephatiah, Hattil, Pochereth-hazzebaim, and Ami.

2.58
v. 55
58 All the temple servants and the descendants of Solomon's servants were three hundred ninety-two.

59 The following were those who came up from Tel-melah, Telharsha, Cherub, Addan, and Immer, though they could not prove their families or their descent, whether they belonged to Israel: [60]the descen-
2.61
2 Sam 17.27
dants of Delaiah, Tobiah, and Nekoda, six hundred fifty-two. [61]Also, of the descendants of the priests: the descendants of Habaiah, Hakkoz, and Barzillai (who had married one of the daughters of Barzillai the Gileadite, and was called by their name). [62]These looked for their entries in the
2.62
Num 3.10;
16.39, 40
2.63
Lev 2.3, 10;
Ex 28.30
genealogical records, but they were not found there, and so they were excluded from the priesthood as unclean; [63]the governor told them that they were not to partake of the most holy food, until there should be a priest to consult Urim and Thummim.

2.64
Neh 7.66ff
64 The whole assembly together was forty-two thousand three hundred sixty, [65]besides their male and female servants, of whom there were seven thousand three hundred thirty-seven; and they had two hundred male and female singers. [66]They had seven hundred thirty-six horses, two hundred forty-five mules, [67]four hundred thirty-five camels, and six thousand seven hundred twenty donkeys.

68 As soon as they came to the house of the LORD in Jerusalem, some of the heads of families made freewill offerings for the house of God, to erect it on its site. [69]According to their resources they gave to the building
2.69
Ezra 8.25-34
fund sixty-one thousand darics of gold, five thousand minas of silver, and one hundred priestly robes.

70 The priests, the Levites, and some of the people lived in Jerusalem and its vicinity;[c] and the singers, the gatekeepers, and the temple servants lived in their towns, and all Israel in their towns.

II. *The restoration of worship and dedication of the temple (3.1–6.22)*

A. *The altar rebuilt: sacrifices offered*

3.1
Neh 7.73; 8.1
3.2
Neh 12.1, 8;
Ezra 2.2;
1 Chr 3.17;
Deut 12.5, 6
3.3
Ezra 4.4;
Num 28.2-4
3.4
Neh 8.14;
Ex 23.16;
Num 29.12
3 When the seventh month came, and the Israelites were in the towns, the people gathered together in Jerusalem. [2]Then Jeshua son of Jozadak, with his fellow priests, and Zerubbabel son of Shealtiel with his kin set out to build the altar of the God of Israel, to offer burnt offerings on it, as prescribed in the law of Moses the man of God. [3]They set up the altar on its foundation, because they were in dread of the neighboring peoples, and they offered burnt offerings upon it to the LORD, morning and evening. [4]And they kept the festival of booths,[d] as prescribed, and offered the daily burnt offerings by number according to the ordinance,

---

[c] 1 Esdras 5.46: Heb lacks *lived in Jerusalem and its vicinity*   [d] Or *tabernacles*; Heb *succoth*

2.63 *Urim . . . Thummim.* See note on Ex 28.30. The last mention of these in the Bible occurs in Neh 7.65.
2.69 *darics . . . minas.* The amount of gold was approximately 300,000 ounces and the silver 6,000 pounds.
3.2 *son of Shealtiel.* Zerubbabel was the legitimate heir, since his father was the eldest son of King Jehoiachin (see 1 Chr 3.17; see note on 1 Chr 3.19). *to build the altar.* The old altar had been destroyed when the Solomonic temple was demolished by the forces of Nebuchadnezzar. Zerubbabel and the people were now in no position to build another temple, but they

had to have an altar on which to offer sacrifices and to praise God. First things first! So Zerubbabel rightly began with what was possible and awaited the time when the new temple could be started. Since God wanted his official worship to take place only in Jerusalem, it seems unlikely that there was any such altar with sacrifices while they were in Babylon.
3.4 See note on Ex 23.16 for the festival of booths or tabernacles. It was one of three national festivals (passover, Pentecost, and booths). All males were expected to attend.

as required for each day, [5]and after that the regular burnt offerings, the offerings at the new moon and at all the sacred festivals of the LORD, and the offerings of everyone who made a freewill offering to the LORD. [6]From the first day of the seventh month they began to offer burnt offerings to the LORD. But the foundation of the temple of the LORD was not yet laid. [7]So they gave money to the masons and the carpenters, and food, drink, and oil to the Sidonians and the Tyrians to bring cedar trees from Lebanon to the sea, to Joppa, according to the grant that they had from King Cyrus of Persia.

B. Rebuilding of the temple begun

[8] In the second year after their arrival at the house of God at Jerusalem, in the second month, Zerubbabel son of Shealtiel and Jeshua son of Jozadak made a beginning, together with the rest of their people, the priests and the Levites and all who had come to Jerusalem from the captivity. They appointed the Levites, from twenty years old and upward, to have the oversight of the work on the house of the LORD. [9]And Jeshua with his sons and his kin, and Kadmiel and his sons, Binnui and Hodaviah[e] along with the sons of Henadad, the Levites, their sons and kin, together took charge of the workers in the house of God.

[10] When the builders laid the foundation of the temple of the LORD, the priests in their vestments were stationed to praise the LORD with trumpets, and the Levites, the sons of Asaph, with cymbals, according to the directions of King David of Israel; [11]and they sang responsively, praising and giving thanks to the LORD,

"For he is good,
for his steadfast love endures forever toward Israel."

And all the people responded with a great shout when they praised the LORD, because the foundation of the house of the LORD was laid. [12]But many of the priests and Levites and heads of families, old people who had seen the first house on its foundations, wept with a loud voice when they saw this house, though many shouted aloud for joy, [13]so that the people could not distinguish the sound of the joyful shout from the sound of the people's weeping, for the people shouted so loudly that the sound was heard far away.

C. Opposition to the rebuilding

1. Help offered and refused

4 When the adversaries of Judah and Benjamin heard that the returned exiles were building a temple to the LORD, the God of Israel, [2]they approached Zerubbabel and the heads of families and said to them, "Let us build with you, for we worship your God as you do, and we have been sacrificing to him ever since the days of King Esar-haddon of Assyria who brought us here." [3]But Zerubbabel, Jeshua, and the rest of the heads of families in Israel said to them, "You shall have no part with us in building a house to our God; but we alone will build to the LORD, the God of Israel, as King Cyrus of Persia has commanded us."

[e] Compare 2.40; Neh 7.43; 1 Esdras 5.58: Heb *sons of Judah*

Cross-references

3.5 Num 28.3, 11, 19, 26; 29.39

3.7 2 Chr 2.10, 16; Ezra 1.2; 6.3

3.8 v. 2; Ezra 4.3; 1 Chr 23.24, 27

3.9 Ezra 2.40

3.10 1 Chr 16.5, 6, 42; 6.31; 25.1

3.11 Ex 15.21; 2 Chr 7.3; Neh 12.24; 1 Chr 16.34, 41

4.1 vv. 7-10

4.2 2 Kings 17.24, 32, 33; 19.37

4.3 Neh 2.20; Ezra 1.1-3

3.5 *the new moon.* See note on Num 10.10 for the festival of the new moon.

3.8 There was never any doubt that a new temple would be constructed. It was begun in the second year, after the celebration of the passover. The leaders, the priests, and the people were enthused for the work, and when the foundation was laid, they praised God and rejoiced together (3.10,11).

3.12 Those who had seen Solomon's temple wept because the new temple was to be smaller and far less ornate and beautiful.

4.1 *The adversaries* were those who had mixed blood, partly Jewish and partly foreign. The offer of help by a people of mixed religious sympathies would hinder, not help the project. After all, the Jews had gone into captivity because they had tried to mix the true worship of God with that of idols. Understandably, Zerubbabel and Jeshua refused this help.

4.2 *Esar-haddon.* See note on 2 Kings 17.24.

4.4
Ezra 3.3

4 Then the people of the land discouraged the people of Judah, and made them afraid to build, 5 and they bribed officials to frustrate their plan throughout the reign of King Cyrus of Persia and until the reign of King Darius of Persia.

2. The letter to Artaxerxes: the work stopped

4.6ff
Esth 1.1;
Dan 9.1
4.7
2 Kings 18.26;
Dan 2.4

6 In the reign of Ahasuerus, in his accession year, they wrote an accusation against the inhabitants of Judah and Jerusalem.

7 And in the days of Artaxerxes, Bishlam and Mithredath and Tabeel and the rest of their associates wrote to King Artaxerxes of Persia; the letter was written in Aramaic and translated.f 8 Rehum the royal deputy and Shimshai the scribe wrote a letter against Jerusalem to King Artaxerxes as follows 9 (then Rehum the royal deputy, Shimshai the scribe, and the rest of their associates, the judges, the envoys, the officials, the Persians, the people of Erech, the Babylonians, the people of Susa, that is, the Elamites, 10 and the rest of the nations whom the great and noble Osnappar deported and settled in the cities of Samaria and in the rest of the province Beyond the River wrote — and now 11 this is a copy of the letter that they sent):

4.10
v. 1

4.12
Ezra 5.3, 9

"To King Artaxerxes: Your servants, the people of the province Beyond the River, send greeting. And now 12 may it be known to the king that the Jews who came up from you to us have gone to Jerusalem. They are rebuilding that rebellious and wicked city; they are finishing the walls and repairing the foundations. 13 Now may it be known to the king that, if this city is rebuilt and the walls finished, they will not pay tribute, custom, or toll, and the royal revenue will be reduced. 14 Now because we share the salt of the palace and it is not fitting for us to witness the king's dishonor, therefore we send and inform the king, 15 so that a search may be made in the annals of your ancestors. You will discover in the annals that this is a rebellious city, hurtful to kings and provinces, and that sedition was stirred up in it from long ago. On that account this city was laid waste. 16 We make known to the king that, if this city is rebuilt and its walls finished, you will then have no possession in the province Beyond the River."

4.13
v. 20;
Ezra 7.24

17 The king sent an answer: "To Rehum the royal deputy and Shimshai the scribe and the rest of their associates who live in Samaria and in the rest of the province Beyond the River, greeting. And now 18 the letter that you sent to us has been read in translation before me. 19 So I made a decree, and someone searched and discovered that this city has risen against kings from long ago, and that rebellion and sedition have been made in it. 20 Jerusalem has had mighty kings who ruled over the whole province Beyond the River, to whom tribute, custom, and toll were paid. 21 Therefore issue an order that these people be made to cease, and that this city not be rebuilt, until I make a decree. 22 Moreover, take care not to be slack in this matter; why should damage grow to the hurt of the king?"

4.18
Neh 8.8

4.20
1 Kings 4.21;
Ps 72.8

23 Then when the copy of King Artaxerxes' letter was read before

---

f Heb adds in Aramaic, indicating that 4.8-6.18 is in Aramaic. Another interpretation is The letter was written in the Aramaic script and set forth in the Aramaic language

---

4.5 *Darius* reigned 522–486 b.c.
4.6 *Ahasuerus*, i.e., Xerxes (468–465 b.c.). Note that vv. 6–23 refer to a later opposition experienced by the Jews — the opposition to the rebuilding of the walls of the Jerusalem; chronologically they fit between chs. 6 and 7. By that time the temple had already been completed.
4.7 *Artaxerxes* reigned 465–423 b.c.
4.10 *Osnappar*, i.e., Ashurbanipal (see note on 2 Kings 17.24).

4.13ff The Samaritans wrote to Artaxerxes to stop the rebuilding of the city. They argued that (1) the Samaritans were loyal to the king and concerned for his interests; (2) the Jews were disloyal and dangerous to the kingdom; (3) their past history proved they were seditious. Their accusations were inaccurate, their fears absurd and without reason. And the claims that the Jews would not pay tribute and would lead a revolt of all the territories west of the Euphrates lacked any foundation.

Rehum and the scribe Shimshai and their associates, they hurried to the Jews in Jerusalem and by force and power made them cease. 24 At that time the work on the house of God in Jerusalem stopped and was discontinued until the second year of the reign of King Darius of Persia.

3. Rebuilding the temple under Haggai and Zechariah

a. The work begun

5 Now the prophets, Haggaiᵍ and Zechariah son of Iddo, prophesied to the Jews who were in Judah and Jerusalem, in the name of the God of Israel who was over them. 2 Then Zerubbabel son of Shealtiel and Jeshua son of Jozadak set out to rebuild the house of God in Jerusalem; and with them were the prophets of God, helping them.

5.1 Hag 1.1; Zech 1.1
5.2 Ezra 3.2

b. An investigation instituted

3 At the same time Tattenai the governor of the province Beyond the River and Shethar-bozenai and their associates came to them and spoke to them thus, "Who gave you a decree to build this house and to finish this structure?" 4 Theyʰ also asked them this, "What are the names of the men who are building this building?" 5 But the eye of their God was upon the elders of the Jews, and they did not stop them until a report reached Darius and then answer was returned by letter in reply to it.

5.3 Ezra 6.6; v. 9; Ezra 1.3
5.4 v. 10
5.5 Ezra 7.6, 28; Ps 33.18

c. Tattenai's letter to Darius

6 The copy of the letter that Tattenai the governor of the province Beyond the River and Shethar-bozenai and his associates the envoys who were in the province Beyond the River sent to King Darius; 7 they sent him a report, in which was written as follows: "To Darius the king, all peace! 8 May it be known to the king that we went to the province of Judah, to the house of the great God. It is being built of hewn stone, and timber is laid in the walls; this work is being done diligently and prospers in their hands. 9 Then we spoke to those elders and asked them, 'Who gave you a decree to build this house and to finish this structure?' 10 We also asked them their names, for your information, so that we might write down the names of the men at their head. 11 This was their reply to us: 'We are the servants of the God of heaven and earth, and we are rebuilding the house that was built many years ago, which a great king of Israel built and finished. 12 But because our ancestors had angered the God of heaven, he gave them into the hand of King Nebuchadnezzar of Babylon, the Chaldean, who destroyed this house and carried away the people to Bab-

5.6 Ezra 4.9
5.9 vv. 3, 4
5.11 1 Kings 6.1
5.12 2 Chr 36.16, 17; 2 Kings 24.2; 25.8, 9, 11

ᵍ Aram adds *the prophet*   ʰ Gk Syr: Aram *We*

4.24 The writer now returns to the subject of the temple (see note on v. 6). He admits that the work on the temple was halted for a time.
5.1 The words of Haggai and Zechariah have been recorded for us in the books that bear their names; they should be read in connection with the return to the land and the construction of the temple. Note that God still provided prophets to speak for him to the remnant.
5.2 The foundation of the temple had been laid (3.8–13) but the work was subsequently halted (4.24). The time had come for the people to stop developing their own properties and to resume the construction of the house of God, with the prophets of God providing leadership (cf. especially Hag 1.2–15). The business of God's prophets was to get God's people to do that which is good, to strengthen them, and to encourage them.
5.3 *Tattenai* was governor of the region west of the Euphrates during the reign of Darius Hystaspis. He made a report to the king of Persia about the com-

plaints of the Samaritans concerning the rebuilding of the temple.
5.5 God's eye was on the elders of the Jews, to keep them from yielding to their enemies. Whoever is employed in God's work is under God's watchful protection. This knowledge will help them to persevere and encourage them despite discouraging difficulties.
5.6 *The envoys* were from the Samaritans who signed the letter of complaint to the Persian officials against those who sought to rebuild the temple.
5.8 *Hewn stone* had to be moved on rollers because of its size and weight.
5.9 In response to the question, "Who gave you a decree to build this house. . . ?" the Jews provided the historical background for their work (5.11–15). They claimed the right to rebuild by a royal decree from King Cyrus, and they intended to continue. The enemies asked for the records to be searched to show whether their claim was fraudulent, and a decision rendered.

ylonia. 13 However, King Cyrus of Babylon, in the first year of his reign, made a decree that this house of God should be rebuilt. 14 Moreover, the gold and silver vessels of the house of God, which Nebuchadnezzar had taken out of the temple in Jerusalem and had brought into the temple of Babylon, these King Cyrus took out of the temple of Babylon, and they were delivered to a man named Sheshbazzar, whom he had made governor. 15 He said to him, "Take these vessels; go and put them in the temple in Jerusalem, and let the house of God be rebuilt on its site." 16 Then this Sheshbazzar came and laid the foundations of the house of God in Jerusalem; and from that time until now it has been under construction, and it is not yet finished.' 17 And now, if it seems good to the king, have a search made in the royal archives there in Babylon, to see whether a decree was issued by King Cyrus for the rebuilding of this house of God in Jerusalem. Let the king send us his pleasure in this matter."

d. Darius's search and reply

6 Then King Darius made a decree, and they searched the archives where the documents were stored in Babylon. 2 But it was in Ecbatana, the capital in the province of Media, that a scroll was found on which this was written: "A record. 3 In the first year of his reign, King Cyrus issued a decree: Concerning the house of God at Jerusalem, let the house be rebuilt, the place where sacrifices are offered and burnt offerings are brought;[i] its height shall be sixty cubits and its width sixty cubits, 4 with three courses of hewn stones and one course of timber; let the cost be paid from the royal treasury. 5 Moreover, let the gold and silver vessels of the house of God, which Nebuchadnezzar took out of the temple in Jerusalem and brought to Babylon, be restored and brought back to the temple in Jerusalem, each to its place; you shall put them in the house of God."

6 "Now you, Tattenai, governor of the province Beyond the River, Shethar-bozenai, and you, their associates, the envoys in the province Beyond the River, keep away; 7 let the work on this house of God alone; let the governor of the Jews and the elders of the Jews rebuild this house of God on its site. 8 Moreover I make a decree regarding what you shall do for these elders of the Jews for the rebuilding of this house of God: the cost is to be paid to these people, in full and without delay, from the royal revenue, the tribute of the province Beyond the River. 9 Whatever is needed — young bulls, rams, or sheep for burnt offerings to the God of heaven, wheat, salt, wine, or oil, as the priests in Jerusalem require — let that be given to them day by day without fail, 10 so that they may offer pleasing sacrifices to the God of heaven, and pray for the life of the king and his children. 11 Furthermore I decree that if anyone alters this edict, a beam shall be pulled out of the house of the perpetrator, who then shall be impaled on it. The house shall be made a dunghill. 12 May the God who has established his name there overthrow any king or people that shall put forth a hand to alter this, or to destroy this house of God in Jerusalem. I, Darius, make a decree; let it be done with all diligence."

---

i Meaning of Aram uncertain

6.2 *Ecbatana.* This city was located more than a mile above sea level and was a summer capital of the Parthian kings. The modern city of Hamadan has taken its place. The records kept on papyrus or leather were better preserved at a higher altitude, and it was here that the decree of Cyrus was found by Darius. Later (330 B.C.), Alexander the Great looted the palaces and pulled down the city walls.
6.3–5 The researchers discovered information in the record left by Cyrus which had added details not contained in the earlier proclamation mentioned in 1.2–4.

6.8,9 God not only ruled in the uncovering of Cyrus' decree but he also opened the heart of Darius to provide additional monies to the Jews from the tribute they paid. Thus Tattenai became a double loser: he could not stop the rebuilding, and his share of the royal revenues was cut down.
6.12 Darius pronounced a curse on kings or people who should seek to destroy the house of God. If he could not prevent this himself, he left it in the hand of the Jews' God to execute his own vengeance on any destroyers.

e. The rebuilding of the temple completed

13 Then, according to the word sent by King Darius, Tattenai, the governor of the province Beyond the River, Shethar-bozenai, and their associates did with all diligence what King Darius had ordered. **14** So the elders of the Jews built and prospered, through the prophesying of the prophet Haggai and Zechariah son of Iddo. They finished their building by command of the God of Israel and by decree of Cyrus, Darius, and King Artaxerxes of Persia; **15** and this house was finished on the third day of the month of Adar, in the sixth year of the reign of King Darius.

6.13
v. 6
6.14
Ezra 5.1, 2;
1.1; v. 12;
Ezra 7.1

f. The temple dedicated: the passover and festival of unleavened bread celebrated

16 The people of Israel, the priests and the Levites, and the rest of the returned exiles, celebrated the dedication of this house of God with joy. **17** They offered at the dedication of this house of God one hundred bulls, two hundred rams, four hundred lambs, and as a sin offering for all Israel, twelve male goats, according to the number of the tribes of Israel. **18** Then they set the priests in their divisions and the Levites in their courses for the service of God at Jerusalem, as it is written in the book of Moses.

19 On the fourteenth day of the first month the returned exiles kept the passover. **20** For both the priests and the Levites had purified themselves; all of them were clean. So they killed the passover lamb for all the returned exiles, for their fellow priests, and for themselves. **21** It was eaten by the people of Israel who had returned from exile, and also by all who had joined them and separated themselves from the pollutions of the nations of the land to worship the LORD, the God of Israel. **22** With joy they celebrated the festival of unleavened bread seven days; for the LORD had made them joyful, and had turned the heart of the king of Assyria to them, so that he aided them in the work on the house of God, the God of Israel.

6.16
1 Kings 8.63;
2 Chr 7.5
6.17
Ezra 8.35

6.18
2 Chr 35.5;
1 Chr 23.6;
Num 3.6; 8.9

6.19
Ezra 1.11;
Ex 12.6
6.20
2 Chr 29.34;
30.15; 35.11
6.21
Neh 9.2;
10.28;
Ezra 9.11
6.22
Ex 12.15;
Ezra 7.27;
1.1; 6.2

III. *The return of Ezra and the reform that followed (7.1–10.44)*

A. Ezra's genealogy and career

7 After this, in the reign of King Artaxerxes of Persia, Ezra son of Seraiah, son of Azariah, son of Hilkiah, **2** son of Shallum, son of Zadok, son of Ahitub, **3** son of Amariah, son of Azariah, son of Meraioth, **4** son of Zerahiah, son of Uzzi, son of Bukki, **5** son of Abishua, son of Phinehas, son of Eleazar, son of the chief priest Aaron— **6** this Ezra went

7.1
1 Chr 6.4-14;
vv. 12, 21;
Neh 2.1
7.6
vv. 9, 11, 12,
21, 28

6.14 This Artaxerxes was Artaxerxes I Longimanus, the son and heir of Xerxes. He reigned from 464–424 B.C. Ezra came to Jerusalem in the seventh year of this king and Nehemiah in the twentieth year of the same king.

6.16 In Ezra's references to the temple, nothing is said about a high priest or the ark of the covenant. The two tablets of the law, apparently destroyed when Solomon's temple was burned, were not in the new temple.

6.17 *this house of God.* Following the return of the remnant from Babylon, the second temple was constructed. It never attained the glory of Solomon's temple, nor was the kingship restored after the captivity. Nowhere do the Scriptures indicate that the cloud of God's glory filled the second temple as it had the first. The second temple was enlarged and spruced up by Herod the Great and his successors. It was destroyed in A.D. 70, when the Roman armies sacked Jerusalem.

6.21 Judaism always had provisions for non-Jews to participate in the worship of God. Here the Jews who had returned from the exile and all those who had sought God, separated themselves from their false religions, and stopped their idolatries and immoralities were received as fellow-citizens of the household of God. God still receives such people today.

7.1 Ezra's pedigree takes him back to Aaron, from whom he had descended. Thus he was of the priestly line. His ancestor Seraiah was high priest at the time of the deportation (see 2 Kings 25.18).

7.6 Mt 23.34, in the words of Jesus, speaks of "prophets, sages, and scribes" as people sent from God. Ezra was a scribe, a gifted scholar, and a fervent student of the word of God. Jewish tradition says he collected and collated all the copies of the law he could find and then published an accurate edition. According to this tradition, he may also have put together the

up from Babylonia. He was a scribe skilled in the law of Moses that the LORD the God of Israel had given; and the king granted him all that he asked, for the hand of the LORD his God was upon him.

7.7
Ezra 8.1-20

7 Some of the people of Israel, and some of the priests and Levites, the singers and gatekeepers, and the temple servants also went up to Jerusalem, in the seventh year of King Artaxerxes. 8 They came to Jerusalem in the fifth month, which was in the seventh year of the king. 9 On

7.9
v. 6

the first day of the first month the journey up from Babylon was begun, and on the first day of the fifth month he came to Jerusalem, for the gracious hand of his God was upon him. 10 For Ezra had set his heart to

7.10
Ps 119.45;
v. 5;
Neh 8.1-8

study the law of the LORD, and to do it, and to teach the statutes and ordinances in Israel.

B. *Ezra's commission from Artaxerxes*

11 This is a copy of the letter that King Artaxerxes gave to the priest Ezra, the scribe, a scholar of the text of the commandments of the LORD and his statutes for Israel: 12 "Artaxerxes, king of kings, to the priest Ezra,

7.12
Ezek 26.7;
Dan 2.37

the scribe of the law of the God of heaven: Peace.*j* And now 13 I decree that any of the people of Israel or their priests or Levites in my kingdom who freely offers to go to Jerusalem may go with you. 14 For you are sent

7.14
Esth 1.14

by the king and his seven counselors to make inquiries about Judah and Jerusalem according to the law of your God, which is in your hand, 15 and

7.15
2 Chr 6.2;
Ezra 6.12
7.16
Ezra 8.25;
1 Chr 29.6, 9;
Ezra 1.4, 6

also to convey the silver and gold that the king and his counselors have freely offered to the God of Israel, whose dwelling is in Jerusalem, 16 with all the silver and gold that you shall find in the whole province of Babylonia, and with the freewill offerings of the people and the priests, given willingly for the house of their God in Jerusalem. 17 With this money,

7.17
Num 15.4-13;
Deut 12.5-11

then, you shall with all diligence buy bulls, rams, and lambs, and their grain offerings and their drink offerings, and you shall offer them on the altar of the house of your God in Jerusalem. 18 Whatever seems good to you and your colleagues to do with the rest of the silver and gold, you may do, according to the will of your God. 19 The vessels that have been given you for the service of the house of your God, you shall deliver before the

7.20
Ezra 6.4

God of Jerusalem. 20 And whatever else is required for the house of your God, which you are responsible for providing, you may provide out of the king's treasury.

7.21
v. 6

21 "I, King Artaxerxes, decree to all the treasurers in the province Beyond the River: Whatever the priest Ezra, the scribe of the law of the God of heaven, requires of you, let it be done with all diligence, 22 up to one hundred talents of silver, one hundred cors of wheat, one hundred

7.23
Ezra 6.10

baths*k* of wine, one hundred baths*k* of oil, and unlimited salt. 23 Whatever is commanded by the God of heaven, let it be done with zeal for the house of the God of heaven, or wrath will come upon the realm of the king and his heirs. 24 We also notify you that it shall not be lawful to impose tribute, custom, or toll on any of the priests, the Levites, the singers, the doorkeepers, the temple servants, or other servants of this house of God.

7.25
Ex 18.21;
Deut 16.18;
v. 10

25 "And you, Ezra, according to the God-given wisdom you possess, appoint magistrates and judges who may judge all the people in the province Beyond the River who know the laws of your God; and you shall teach those who do not know them. 26 All who will not obey the law of

j Syr Vg 1 Esdras 8.9: Aram *Perfect*   *k* A Heb measure of volume

---

books which make up the canon of the O.T.
7.10 Ezra was more than a student of the word; he obeyed the commands of the Lord and taught God's word to others.
7.11–26 This segment comprises the letter from Artaxerxes to Ezra, granting him permission to settle in Jerusalem and take with him as many of his people as

he wished. He gave Ezra money ("silver and gold") and provided him with a warrant to secure further funds from the king's treasury. Ezra and all those connected with the temple did not have to pay tribute (i.e., taxes). Furthermore, he could appoint judges and magistrates for the realm.

your God and the law of the king, let judgment be strictly executed on them, whether for death or for banishment or for confiscation of their goods or for imprisonment."

C. Ezra's song of praise

27 Blessed be the LORD, the God of our ancestors, who put such a thing as this into the heart of the king to glorify the house of the LORD in Jerusalem, 28 and who extended to me steadfast love before the king and his counselors, and before all the king's mighty officers. I took courage, for the hand of the LORD my God was upon me, and I gathered leaders from Israel to go up with me.

D. The list of the returning remnant

8 These are their family heads, and this is the genealogy of those who went up with me from Babylonia, in the reign of King Artaxerxes: 2 Of the descendants of Phinehas, Gershom. Of Ithamar, Daniel. Of David, Hattush, 3 of the descendants of Shecaniah. Of Parosh, Zechariah, with whom were registered one hundred fifty males. 4 Of the descendants of Pahath-moab, Eliehoenai son of Zerahiah, and with him two hundred males. 5 Of the descendants of Zattu,[l] Shecaniah son of Jahaziel, and with him three hundred males. 6 Of the descendants of Adin, Ebed son of Jonathan, and with him fifty males. 7 Of the descendants of Elam, Jeshaiah son of Athaliah, and with him seventy males. 8 Of the descendants of Shephatiah, Zebadiah son of Michael, and with him eighty males. 9 Of the descendants of Joab, Obadiah son of Jehiel, and with him two hundred eighteen males. 10 Of the descendants of Bani,[m] Shelomith son of Josiphiah, and with him one hundred sixty males. 11 Of the descendants of Bebai, Zechariah son of Bebai, and with him twenty-eight males. 12 Of the descendants of Azgad, Johanan son of Hakkatan, and with him one hundred ten males. 13 Of the descendants of Adonikam, those who came later, their names being Eliphelet, Jeuel, and Shemaiah, and with them sixty males. 14 Of the descendants of Bigvai, Uthai and Zaccur, and with him seventy males.

E. The selection of temple servants

15 I gathered them by the river that runs to Ahava, and there we camped three days. As I reviewed the people and the priests, I found there none of the descendants of Levi. 16 Then I sent for Eliezer, Ariel, Shemaiah, Elnathan, Jarib, Elnathan, Nathan, Zechariah, and Meshullam, who were leaders, and for Joiarib and Elnathan, who were wise, 17 and sent them to Iddo, the leader at the place called Casiphia, telling them what to say to Iddo and his colleagues the temple servants at Casiphia, namely, to send us ministers for the house of our God. 18 Since the gracious hand of our God was upon us, they brought us a man of discretion, of the descendants of Mahli son of Levi son of Israel, namely Sherebiah, with his sons and kin, eighteen; 19 also Hashabiah and with him Jeshaiah of the

l Gk 1 Esdras 8.32: Heb lacks of Zattu   m Gk 1 Esdras 8.36: Heb lacks Bani

Cross references

7.27 1 Chr 29.10; Ezra 6.22
7.28 Ezra 9.9; vv. 6, 9

8.2 1 Chr 3.22
8.3 Ezra 2.3

8.15 vv. 21, 31; Ezra 7.7

8.17 Ezra 2.43

8.18 Ezra 7.6

7.27 Ezra (the author of this book) breaks out into a doxology in which he acknowledges that what the king had done was the work of God in the king's heart. He took courage from this, since he knew that God was with him (v. 28) and was thus persuaded to move forward in the work to which he had been called.

8.1–14 This list constitutes the second group of returning exiles, who left Babylon under Ezra's leadership about eighty years after the first group under Zerubbabel (chs. 1–6). The total number was 1,496, listed not individually but by families.

8.15 In the group of returning exiles led by Zerubbabel, there were a few Levites and many priests. In the second group led by Ezra, there were no Levites, only priests. The non-priestly Levites preferred to remain in Babylon (see note on 2.40).

8.16–20 Noting the absence of Levites, Ezra began a campaign to enlist some of them. He succeeded in drafting about forty of them to come with him. Among them was Sherebiah (v. 18), a man of distinction and discretion. Also two hundred twenty of those who were temple servants under David's appointment were enlisted to go back with him.

descendants of Merari, with his kin and their sons, twenty; 20 besides two hundred twenty of the temple servants, whom David and his officials had set apart to attend the Levites. These were all mentioned by name.

F. *The return to the land*

1. *A fast proclaimed*

21 Then I proclaimed a fast there, at the river Ahava, that we might deny ourselves[n] before our God, to seek from him a safe journey for ourselves, our children, and all our possessions. 22 For I was ashamed to ask the king for a band of soldiers and cavalry to protect us against the enemy on our way, since we had told the king that the hand of our God is gracious to all who seek him, but his power and his wrath are against all who forsake him. 23 So we fasted and petitioned our God for this, and he listened to our entreaty.

2. *The treasure cared for*

24 Then I set apart twelve of the leading priests: Sherebiah, Hashabiah, and ten of their kin with them. 25 And I weighed out to them the silver and the gold and the vessels, the offering for the house of our God that the king, his counselors, his lords, and all Israel there present had offered; 26 I weighed out into their hand six hundred fifty talents of silver, and one hundred silver vessels worth . . . talents,[o] and one hundred talents of gold, 27 twenty gold bowls worth a thousand darics, and two vessels of fine polished bronze as precious as gold. 28 And I said to them, "You are holy to the LORD, and the vessels are holy; and the silver and the gold are a freewill offering to the LORD, the God of your ancestors. 29 Guard them and keep them until you weigh them before the chief priests and the Levites and the heads of families in Israel at Jerusalem, within the chambers of the house of the LORD." 30 So the priests and the Levites took over the silver, the gold, and the vessels as they were weighed out, to bring them to Jerusalem, to the house of our God.

3. *The departure from Ahava and arrival at Jerusalem*

31 Then we left the river Ahava on the twelfth day of the first month, to go to Jerusalem; the hand of our God was upon us, and he delivered us from the hand of the enemy and from ambushes along the way. 32 We came to Jerusalem and remained there three days. 33 On the fourth day, within the house of our God, the silver, the gold, and the vessels were weighed into the hands of the priest Meremoth son of Uriah, and with him was Eleazar son of Phinehas, and with them were the Levites, Jozabad son of Jeshua and Noadiah son of Binnui. 34 The total was counted and weighed, and the weight of everything was recorded.

35 At that time those who had come from captivity, the returned exiles, offered burnt offerings to the God of Israel, twelve bulls for all Israel, ninety-six rams, seventy-seven lambs, and as a sin offering twelve

Cross references (left margin):
8.20 Ezra 2.43
8.21 2 Chr 20.3; Isa 58.3, 5
8.22 Ezra 7.6, 9, 28; Ps 33.18, 19; 34.16; 2 Chr 15.2
8.23 2 Chr 33.13
8.25 Ezra 7.15, 16
8.26 Ezra 1.9-11
8.28 Lev 21.6-8; 22.2, 3
8.29 vv. 33, 34
8.31 Ezra 7.6, 9, 28
8.32 Neh 2.11
8.33 vv. 26, 30
8.35 Ezra 2.1; 6.17

---

[n] Or *might fast*   [o] The number of talents is lacking

8.21,22 Ezra had boldly stated that God was his confidence. He therefore hated to ask the king for a military escort, lest it be said he did not trust God. He called for a fast and implored divine protection against all enemies on the trek. Fasting (v. 21) was designed to do two things: (1) to express their humiliation corporately before God by denying themselves food; (2) to engage in concerted and corporate prayer to God "to seek from him a safe journey for ourselves." The small band then went forward with confidence (see also note on Neh 2.8).
8.24 Ezra not only prayed; he also acted with discre-

tion. He committed the treasures into the hands of faithful men. In this instance it was the priests and Levites who could be trusted to care for the wealth (perhaps as much as 20 million dollars). And when they arrived in Jerusalem, it was to be checked carefully to see there was no loss (vv. 33,34).
8.34 When Ezra and his company arrived safely, the money was counted and found to be correct. In the church today accountability is most important, and believers do well to follow the pattern set up by Ezra so as to guarantee that none of the Lord's resources be lost.

male goats; all this was a burnt offering to the LORD. 36 They also delivered the king's commissions to the king's satraps and to the governors of the province Beyond the River; and they supported the people and the house of God.

8.36
Ezra 7.21

G. *The reformation of the people*

1. *Ezra grieves at the mixed marriages*

9 After these things had been done, the officials approached me and said, "The people of Israel, the priests, and the Levites have not separated themselves from the peoples of the lands with their abominations, from the Canaanites, the Hittites, the Perizzites, the Jebusites, the Ammonites, the Moabites, the Egyptians, and the Amorites. 2 For they have taken some of their daughters as wives for themselves and for their sons. Thus the holy seed has mixed itself with the peoples of the lands, and in this faithlessness the officials and leaders have led the way." 3 When I heard this, I tore my garment and my mantle, and pulled hair from my head and beard, and sat appalled. 4 Then all who trembled at the words of the God of Israel, because of the faithlessness of the returned exiles, gathered around me while I sat appalled until the evening sacrifice.

9.1
Ezra 6.21;
Neh 9.2;
Lev 18.24-30
9.2
Ezra 10.2,
18;
Ex 22.31;
Neh 13.3
9.3
Job 1.20;
Neh 1.4
9.4
Ezra 10.3;
Ex 29.39

2. *Ezra's prayer*

5 At the evening sacrifice I got up from my fasting, with my garments and my mantle torn, and fell on my knees, spread out my hands to the LORD my God, 6 and said,

"O my God, I am too ashamed and embarrassed to lift my face to you, my God, for our iniquities have risen higher than our heads, and our guilt has mounted up to the heavens. 7 From the days of our ancestors to this day we have been deep in guilt, and for our iniquities we, our kings, and our priests have been handed over to the kings of the lands, to the sword, to captivity, to plundering, and to utter shame, as is now the case. 8 But now for a brief moment favor has been shown by the LORD our God, who has left us a remnant, and given us a stake in his holy place, in order that he*p* may brighten our eyes and grant us a little sustenance in our slavery. 9 For we are slaves; yet our God has not forsaken us in our slavery, but has extended to us his steadfast love before the kings of Persia, to give us new life to set up the house of our God, to repair its ruins, and to give us a wall in Judea and Jerusalem.

9.5
Ex 9.29, 33
9.6
Dan 9.7, 8;
2 Chr 28.9;
Rev 18.5
9.7
Dan 9.5, 6;
Deut 28.36,
64;
Dan 9.7, 8
9.8
Isa 22.23;
Ps 13.3; 34.5
9.9
Neh 9.36;
Ezra 7.28

10 "And now, our God, what shall we say after this? For we have forsaken your commandments, 11 which you commanded by your servants the prophets, saying, 'The land that you are entering to possess is

9.11
Ezra 6.21

p Heb *our God*

9.2 Time and again in the history of Israel intermarriage with the heathen had led to grave problems — such intermarriage was forbidden by God. The returning Jews still had not learned their lesson. Ezra discovered that intermarriage with the heathen was widespread, particularly Jewish men with pagan women. Repentance and correction were called for. **9.3** Ezra's reaction to the mixed marriages indicates the seriousness with which he regarded this transgression. He tore his garment and mantle, pulled hair from his head and beard, and sat down appalled. It was made worse since priests and Levites were among the offenders. When religious leaders defect from the faith, what can be expected of their church members? **9.4** So great was the influence of Ezra that the upright believers, who took the word of God seriously, voluntarily joined Ezra for fasting and prayer to keep

the judgment of God from falling upon them all. **9.5** The prayer Ezra was about to offer came at the time of the evening sacrifice, and it was a public act before all who gathered before him. As an innocent suppliant under deep conviction about the sins of the people, he knelt and spread out his hands before the Lord God. **9.6ff** Ezra now offered a prayer of confession of sin. He identified himself with the sinners by the use of the words "I," "my," and "our." He acknowledged the greatness of the transgression, the length of time it had been practiced, and the judgments that had come as a result. His words testify to the justice and anger of a righteous God, and he knew their only hope was the mercy of God's forgiveness. This prayer, along with those in Neh 9 and Dan 9, is among the most moving of all the prayers in the Scriptures.

a land unclean with the pollutions of the peoples of the lands, with their abominations. They have filled it from end to end with their uncleanness. [12] Therefore do not give your daughters to their sons, neither take their daughters for your sons, and never seek their peace or prosperity, so that you may be strong and eat the good of the land and leave it for an inheritance to your children forever.' [13] After all that has come upon us for our evil deeds and for our great guilt, seeing that you, our God, have punished us less than our iniquities deserved and have given us such a remnant as this, [14] shall we break your commandments again and intermarry with the peoples who practice these abominations? Would you not be angry with us until you destroy us without remnant or survivor? [15] O LORD, God of Israel, you are just, but we have escaped as a remnant, as is now the case. Here we are before you in our guilt, though no one can face you because of this."

3. Ezra's reform

10 While Ezra prayed and made confession, weeping and throwing himself down before the house of God, a very great assembly of men, women, and children gathered to him out of Israel; the people also wept bitterly. [2] Shecaniah son of Jehiel, of the descendants of Elam, addressed Ezra, saying, "We have broken faith with our God and have married foreign women from the peoples of the land, but even now there is hope for Israel in spite of this. [3] So now let us make a covenant with our God to send away all these wives and their children, according to the counsel of my lord and of those who tremble at the commandment of our God; and let it be done according to the law. [4] Take action, for it is your duty, and we are with you; be strong, and do it." [5] Then Ezra stood up and made the leading priests, the Levites, and all Israel swear that they would do as had been said. So they swore.

[6] Then Ezra withdrew from before the house of God, and went to the chamber of Jehohanan son of Eliashib, where he spent the night. *q* He did not eat bread or drink water, for he was mourning over the faithlessness of the exiles. [7] They made a proclamation throughout Judah and Jerusalem to all the returned exiles that they should assemble at Jerusalem, [8] and that if any did not come within three days, by order of the officials and the elders all their property should be forfeited, and they themselves banned from the congregation of the exiles.

[9] Then all the people of Judah and Benjamin assembled at Jerusalem within the three days; it was the ninth month, on the twentieth day of the month. All the people sat in the open square before the house of God, trembling because of this matter and because of the heavy rain. [10] Then Ezra the priest stood up and said to them, "You have trespassed and married foreign women, and so increased the guilt of Israel. [11] Now make

q 1 Esdras 9.2: Heb *where he went*

Cross references (margin):

9.12 Deut 7.3; 23.6; Prov 13.22
9.13 vv. 6-8
9.14 v. 2; Neh 13.23; 27; Deut 9.8, 14
9.15 Neh 9.33; Dan 9.14; v. 6; Ps 130.3
10.1 Dan 9.4, 20; 2 Chr 20.9
10.2 Ezra 9.2; Neh 13.27
10.3 2 Chr 34.31; v. 44; Ezra 9.4; Deut 7.2, 3
10.4 1 Chr 28.10
10.5 Neh 5.12
10.6 Deut 9.18
10.9 v. 3; Ezra 9.4
10.11 Lev 26.40; v. 3

10.2 *Shechaniah*, under conviction of sin and speaking on behalf of those who had transgressed God's law, was truly repentant.
10.3 After conviction of sin came upon the congregation, the larger question remained: what remedy was to be applied to erase the wrong? In this instance, the foreign wives were to be divorced by the Jewish men who had married them. How can this be justified in the light of the N.T., where it is stated that "if any believer has a wife who is an unbeliever, and she consents to live with him, he should not divorce her" (1 Cor 7.12)? The Corinthian passage seems to apply to a marriage of two unbelievers, one of whom gets converted. Thus this teaching would not apply to the situation under Ezra. What had been sinfully gotten could not be justly kept. There had to be a separation

to cure the sin.
10.5 A revival of true religion took place on this occasion: deep conviction of sin, followed by sincere confession and a determination to correct the difficulty. The priests, the Levites, and all Israel solemnly swore they would put away their pagan spouses. The forsaking of sin often involves a strong remedy.
10.6 *Jehohanan son of Eliashib*. See note on Neh 12.22.
10.11 The marriages with pagans had initiated contact with a mass of unbelieving persons. The covenant agreement included a separation not only from the pagan partners but also "from the peoples of the land." Presumably many of the Jews who had not married pagan women nonetheless had close relationships with pagan communities.

confession to the LORD the God of your ancestors, and do his will; separate yourselves from the peoples of the land and from the foreign wives." [12] Then all the assembly answered with a loud voice, "It is so; we must do as you have said. [13] But the people are many, and it is a time of heavy rain; we cannot stand in the open. Nor is this a task for one day or for two, for many of us have transgressed in this matter. [14] Let our officials represent the whole assembly, and let all in our towns who have taken foreign wives come at appointed times, and with them the elders and judges of every town, until the fierce wrath of our God on this account is averted from us." [15] Only Jonathan son of Asahel and Jahzeiah son of Tikvah opposed this, and Meshullam and Shabbethai the Levites supported them.

10.14
2 Chr 29.10;
30.8

[16] Then the returned exiles did so. Ezra the priest selected men,[r] heads of families, according to their families, each of them designated by name. On the first day of the tenth month they sat down to examine the matter. [17] By the first day of the first month they had come to the end of all the men who had married foreign women.

10.16
Ezra 4.1

4. The list of the offending priests

[18] There were found of the descendants of the priests who had married foreign women, of the descendants of Jeshua son of Jozadak and his brothers: Maaseiah, Eliezer, Jarib, and Gedaliah. [19] They pledged themselves to send away their wives, and their guilt offering was a ram of the flock for their guilt. [20] Of the descendants of Immer: Hanani and Zebadiah. [21] Of the descendants of Harim: Maaseiah, Elijah, Shemaiah, Jehiel, and Uzziah. [22] Of the descendants of Pashhur: Elioenai, Maaseiah, Ishmael, Nethanel, Jozabad, and Elasah.

10.19
2 Kings 10.15;
2 Chr 30.8;
Lev 5.15; 6.6

[23] Of the Levites: Jozabad, Shimei, Kelaiah (that is, Kelita), Pethahiah, Judah, and Eliezer. [24] Of the singers: Eliashib. Of the gatekeepers: Shallum, Telem, and Uri.

10.23
Ex 6.25

[25] And of Israel: of the descendants of Parosh: Ramiah, Izziah, Malchijah, Mijamin, Eleazar, Hashabiah,[s] and Benaiah. [26] Of the descendants of Elam: Mattaniah, Zechariah, Jehiel, Abdi, Jeremoth, and Elijah. [27] Of the descendants of Zattu: Elioenai, Eliashib, Mattaniah, Jeremoth, Zabad, and Aziza. [28] Of the descendants of Bebai: Jehohanan, Hananiah, Zabbai, and Athlai. [29] Of the descendants of Bani: Meshullam, Malluch, Adaiah, Jashub, Sheal, and Jeremoth. [30] Of the descendants of Pahathmoab: Adna, Chelal, Benaiah, Maaseiah, Mattaniah, Bezalel, Binnui, and Manasseh. [31] Of the descendants of Harim: Eliezer, Isshijah, Malchijah, Shemaiah, Shimeon, [32] Benjamin, Malluch, and Shemariah. [33] Of the descendants of Hashum: Mattenai, Mattattah, Zabad, Eliphelet, Jeremai, Manasseh, and Shimei. [34] Of the descendants of Bani: Maadai, Amram, Uel, [35] Benaiah, Bedeiah, Cheluhi, [36] Vaniah, Meremoth, Eliashib, [37] Mattaniah, Mattenai, and Jaasu. [38] Of the descendants of Binnui:[t] Shimei, [39] Shelemiah, Nathan, Adaiah, [40] Machnadebai, Shashai, Sharai, [41] Azarel, Shelemiah, Shemariah, [42] Shallum, Amariah, and Joseph. [43] Of the descendants of Nebo: Jeiel, Mattithiah, Zabad, Zebina, Jaddai, Joel, and Benaiah. [44] All these had married foreign women, and they sent them away with their children.[u]

10.25
v. 1

10.44
v. 3

r 1 Esdras 9.16: Syr: Heb *And there were selected Ezra,*   s 1 Esdras 9.26 Gk: Heb *Malchijah*   t Gk: Heb *Bani, Binnui*   u 1 Esdras 9.36; meaning of Heb uncertain

10.15   Since four Jews opposed the plan, there was not complete unanimity. What is not clear is whether they opposed the procedure to be followed or the agreement to put away strange spouses. Meshullam opposed the plan and yet gave up a foreign spouse (v. 29). Nothing is said of the others.
10.18ff   One hundred thirteen Jews are listed as hav-

ing obeyed the agreement to put away their foreign wives. Among them were seventeen priests and ten Levites; the remainder were from other tribes. Greater was the guilt of those from the tribe of Levi, for they were responsible for religious leadership and were expected to serve as an example for the other tribes.

INTRODUCTION TO
NEHEMIAH

Authorship, Date, and Background: See the introduction to Ezra. The book of Nehemiah consists of the personal memoirs of Nehemiah, who can logically be considered the author despite objections raised by some scholars. Ezra may have had a role in its final form. This book picks up the story where the book of Ezra left off. Ezra had returned to the land in 458 or 457 B.C.; Nehemiah followed him twelve years later. The Elephantine letter No. 30, an external source, clearly shows that the book of Nehemiah cannot be dated after 400 B.C.

Nehemiah did not return to the promised land with Ezra's group. He was very successful in the land of his captivity, becoming cupbearer for Artaxerxes. It was nearly a hundred years after the first return that he became concerned about conditions there and was moved by God to go to Palestine. Discouraging reports had come via Hanani, a relative. Providentially, Artaxerxes granted him permission to return. He was an astute politician who became governor. Energetic and self-sacrificial, Nehemiah was able to cope with the plots against the Jews by the enemies who surrounded them. His account indicates the success of his efforts in the rebuilding of the walls of Jerusalem and the reassignment of Jews to strategic sections of the city to ward off possible attacks by enemy invaders.

Characteristics and Content: Nehemiah recorded his own memoirs. He recounted his sorrow over the plight of his people, the willingness of the king to allow him to return, and the supplies which were provided to ensure the rebuilding of the city walls. Upon arriving in Jerusalem, Nehemiah surveyed the situation and called for the completion of the reconstruction. Sanballat and Tobiah tried to stop him. Despite the opposition, Nehemiah persisted in his efforts to rebuild the walls. He defended the poor and stopped usury so that the work would not be interrupted. The Herculean task of finishing the rebuilding is completed in a fifty-two-day frenzy of activity. The names of the returnees and their families are listed.

The people then assembled to hear the law of Moses read to them. Ezra did the reading and expounded the meaning. The festival of booths was held and the covenant was renewed and signed. In the covenant were prohibitions against mixed marriages (something Ezra had dealt with earlier), the observance of the sabbath, and a tax to support the temple, along with pledges about tithing and food offering and first fruits.

The second reform movement of Nehemiah begins with ch. 11. Jews living outside the city of Jerusalem were relocated inside the city, the genealogies of the priests and Levites written down, the walls of the city dedicated, and collectors, singers and gatekeepers appointed. Following this, Nehemiah, who had temporarily returned to Babylon, came back and cast Tobiah out of the temple chamber provided for him by Eliashib. He concluded his memoirs by mentioning the sabbath reforms which forbad work on the holy day. He instituted marriage reforms, for the men had once again intermarried with women from Ashdod, Ammon, and Moab. He summarized his labors by saying, "Thus I cleansed them from everything foreign, and I established the duties of the priests and the Levites. . . . Remember me, O my God, for good" (13.30,31).

Outline:

NEHEMIAH

I. *The rebuilding of the walls and the first reform of Nehemiah (1.1–7.73a)*

A. *Introduction*

1. *Nehemiah's sorrow*

1.1
Neh 10.1;
2.1;
Esth 1.2;
Dan 8.2
1.3
Neh 7.6;
2.17; 2.3
1.4
Ezra 9.3;
10.1;
Neh 2.4
1.5
Neh 4.14;
9.32;
Ex 20.6
1.6
Dan 9.17;
Ezra 10.1;
Dan 9.20;
2 Chr 29.6
1.7
Dan 9.5;
Deut 28.14,
15
1.8
Lev 26.33
1.9
Deut 30.2-4;
12.5
1.10
Deut 9.29;
Dan 9.15
1.11
v. 6

1 The words of Nehemiah son of Hacaliah. In the month of Chislev, in the twentieth year, while I was in Susa the capital, 2 one of my brothers, Hanani, came with certain men from Judah; and I asked them about the Jews that survived, those who had escaped the captivity, and about Jerusalem. 3 They replied, "The survivors there in the province who escaped captivity are in great trouble and shame; the wall of Jerusalem is broken down, and its gates have been destroyed by fire."

4 When I heard these words I sat down and wept, and mourned for days, fasting and praying before the God of heaven. 5 I said, "O Lord God of heaven, the great and awesome God who keeps covenant and steadfast love with those who love him and keep his commandments; 6 let your ear be attentive and your eyes open to hear the prayer of your servant that I now pray before you day and night for your servants, the people of Israel, confessing the sins of the people of Israel, which we have sinned against you. Both I and my family have sinned. 7 We have offended you deeply, failing to keep the commandments, the statutes, and the ordinances that you commanded your servant Moses. 8 Remember the word that you commanded your servant Moses, 'If you are unfaithful, I will scatter you among the peoples; 9 but if you return to me and keep my commandments and do them, though your outcasts are under the farthest skies, I will gather them from there and bring them to the place at which I have chosen to establish my name.' 10 They are your servants and your people, whom you redeemed by your great power and your strong hand. 11 O Lord, let your ear be attentive to the prayer of your servant, and to the prayer of your servants who delight in revering your name. Give success to your servant today, and grant him mercy in the sight of this man!"

At the time, I was cupbearer to the king.

2. *Nehemiah's request to go to Jerusalem*

2.1
Neh 1.1;
Ezra 7.1;
Neh 1.11

2 In the month of Nisan, in the twentieth year of King Artaxerxes, when wine was served him, I carried the wine and gave it to the king.

1.1 *Nehemiah.* We know little about this man in relation to his ancestors. Since he offered sacrifices, it is supposed he may have been from the tribe of Levi and was a priest. This book he wrote is the last of the historical books in the O.T., just as Malachi is the last of the prophetic books. *Chislev,* i.e., early December. *In the twentieth year,* i.e., the twentieth year of the reign of King Artaxerxes (445 B.C.).
1.4 Nehemiah was a devout believer. When he heard of the sad situation in Jerusalem, he turned to prayer and fasting on behalf of the people of God for an unspecified period of time. God does not always respond to our prayers as soon as they are spoken.

God moved Nehemiah to do more than pray for the peace of Jerusalem; he commissioned him to give up his cozy job with the king and to identify himself with the suffering saints in Judah. The king responded to Nehemiah's request for a leave of absence; this called forth his statement, affirming God's providence: "the gracious hand of my God was upon me" (2.8).
1.11 *cupbearer.* Ancient monarchs were fearful of being poisoned. The cupbearer had to be a faithful and trustworthy servant of the king. Most frequently he was a eunuch, and such may have been the case with Nehemiah, especially since he was allowed in the presence of the queen (2.6).

Now, I had never been sad in his presence before. ²So the king said to me, "Why is your face sad, since you are not sick? This can only be sadness of the heart." Then I was very much afraid. ³I said to the king, "May the king live forever! Why should my face not be sad, when the city, the place of my ancestors' graves, lies waste, and its gates have been destroyed by fire?" ⁴Then the king said to me, "What do you request?" So I prayed to the God of heaven. ⁵Then I said to the king, "If it pleases the king, and if your servant has found favor with you, I ask that you send me to Judah, to the city of my ancestors' graves, so that I may rebuild it." ⁶The king said to me (the queen also was sitting beside him), "How long will you be gone, and when will you return?" So it pleased the king to send me, and I set him a date. ⁷Then I said to the king, "If it pleases the king, let letters be given me to the governors of the province Beyond the River, that they may grant me passage until I arrive in Judah; ⁸and a letter to Asaph, the keeper of the king's forest, directing him to give me timber to make beams for the gates of the temple fortress, and for the wall of the city, and for the house that I shall occupy." And the king granted me what I asked, for the gracious hand of my God was upon me.

3. Nehemiah's journey to Jerusalem: his inspection of the walls

9   Then I came to the governors of the province Beyond the River, and gave them the king's letters. Now the king had sent officers of the army and cavalry with me. ¹⁰When Sanballat the Horonite and Tobiah the Ammonite official heard this, it displeased them greatly that someone had come to seek the welfare of the people of Israel.

11   So I came to Jerusalem and was there for three days. ¹²Then I got up during the night, I and a few men with me; I told no one what my God had put into my heart to do for Jerusalem. The only animal I took was the animal I rode. ¹³I went out by night by the Valley Gate past the Dragon's Spring and to the Dung Gate, and I inspected the walls of Jerusalem that had been broken down and its gates that had been destroyed by fire. ¹⁴Then I went on to the Fountain Gate and to the King's Pool; but there was no place for the animal I was riding to continue. ¹⁵So I went up by way of the valley by night and inspected the wall. Then I turned back and entered by the Valley Gate, and so returned. ¹⁶The officials did not know where I had gone or what I was doing; I had not yet told the Jews, the priests, the nobles, the officials, and the rest that were to do the work.

2.2
Prov 15.13

2.3
Dan 2.4;
Neh 1.3

2.4
Neh 1.4

2.6
Neh 5.14;
13.6

2.7
Ezra 7.21;
8.36

2.8
Neh 7.2;
v. 18;
Ezra 7.6

2.9
v. 7;
Ezra 8.22

2.10
v. 19;
Neh 4.1

2.13
Neh 3.13;
vv. 3, 17;
Neh 1.3

2.14
Neh 3.15;
2 Kings 20.20

2.1 *Nisan*, the first month of the Jewish calendar (March/April). No one who served the king should have been sad or melancholy in his presence. When the king noticed his condition and remarked about it, Nehemiah became "very much afraid" (v. 2). Unknown to him, God was at work, using the king to make his stay in Jerusalem possible.

2.4 *So I prayed to the God of heaven.* This must have been a short inaudible prayer asking God for help as to what he should say. Compare the promise of Jesus that when we stand before people and know not what to say, it "will be given to you . . . for it is not you who speak, but the Spirit of your Father speaking through you" (Mt 10.19,20). Nehemiah received divine assistance and his prayer was answered.

2.6 *I set him a date*, i.e., when he expected to return to the king's service. What the set date was we do not know. It must have been extended, for he spent at least twelve years in Jerusalem (see 5.14).

2.8 *the gracious hand of my God was upon me.* God supplied his material needs, and letters were given him to the governors of the king who could help him. Moreover "officers of the army and cavalry" accompanied him and protected him (2.9). Note the contrast with Ezra, who had refused military help and was kept safe. Nehemiah accepted the help and was also safe. Either approach was appropriate, as far as God was concerned.

2.12 Nehemiah wisely kept his intentions to himself (cf. v. 16), for when they were discovered, persecution would begin. Those intentions had been put into his heart by God himself. All believers should find the will of God for their lives and then pursue it with vigor, perseverance, and faith.

2.13–15 Nehemiah's first job was to view the situation discreetly in order to determine what needed to be done and how he would accomplish it.

4. Nehemiah's determination to rebuild; the opposition of Sanballat and Tobiah

17 Then I said to them, "You see the trouble we are in, how Jerusalem lies in ruins with its gates burned. Come, let us rebuild the wall of Jerusalem, so that we may no longer suffer disgrace." **18** I told them that the hand of my God had been gracious upon me, and also the words that the king had spoken to me. Then they said, "Let us start building!" So they committed themselves to the common good. **19** But when Sanballat the Horonite and Tobiah the Ammonite official, and Geshem the Arab heard of it, they mocked and ridiculed us, saying, "What is this that you are doing? Are you rebelling against the king?" **20** Then I replied to them, "The God of heaven is the one who will give us success, and we his servants are going to start building; but you have no share or claim or historic right in Jerusalem."

B. The rebuilding of the walls

1. The workers and the places they worked

3 Then the high priest Eliashib set to work with his fellow priests and rebuilt the Sheep Gate. They consecrated it and set up its doors; they consecrated it as far as the Tower of the Hundred and as far as the Tower of Hananel. **2** And the men of Jericho built next to him. And next to them*v* Zaccur son of Imri built.

3 The sons of Hassenaah built the Fish Gate; they laid its beams and set up its doors, its bolts, and its bars. **4** Next to them Meremoth son of Uriah son of Hakkoz made repairs. Next to them Meshullam son of Berechiah son of Meshezabel made repairs. Next to them Zadok son of Baana made repairs. **5** Next to them the Tekoites made repairs; but their nobles would not put their shoulders to the work of their Lord.*w*

6 Joiada son of Paseah and Meshullam son of Besodeiah repaired the Old Gate; they laid its beams and set up its doors, its bolts, and its bars. **7** Next to them repairs were made by Melatiah the Gibeonite and Jadon the Meronothite — the men of Gibeon and of Mizpah — who were under the jurisdiction of*x* the governor of the province Beyond the River. **8** Next to them Uzziel son of Harhaiah, one of the goldsmiths, made repairs. Next to him Hananiah, one of the perfumers, made repairs; and they restored Jerusalem as far as the Broad Wall. **9** Next to them Rephaiah son of Hur, ruler of half the district of*y* Jerusalem, made repairs. **10** Next to them Jedaiah son of Harumaph made repairs opposite his house; and next to him Hattush son of Hashabneiah made repairs. **11** Malchijah son of Harim

v Heb him   w Or lords   x Meaning of Heb uncertain   y Or supervisor of half the portion assigned to

---

2.18 *Let us start building!* Once Nehemiah disclosed what the king had promised him, how he had surveyed the situation, and how he decided the walls of the city should be rebuilt, the people rallied behind him. He gave them the divine assurance that the hand of God was upon him and therefore upon those who would assist him. What God wants done can and will be accomplished by his servants through his power.
2.19 Whoever does the will of God will encounter opposition (cf. 2 Tim 3.12). Nehemiah was scorned, despised, and accused of rebelling against the king. This would have deterred a lesser mortal, but Nehemiah was a man of resolve; he was certain of his call and insistent on fulfilling it. He simply refused to quit or be stopped by enemies of his cause. His watchword was this: "The God of heaven . . . will give us success" (2.20).
3.1 *the Sheep Gate.* This was the gate through which the animals came that were to be sacrificed in the temple. Since the sacrifices benefited the priests, it

was to their advantage to see that this gate was reconstructed. Moreover, this route led to the temple itself. The energy of the high priest, Eliashib, who himself worked on the project, was impressive.
3.3 *The Fish Gate* was apparently so named because of the fish market nearby. Evidently those who sold fish would bring their wares through this gate.
3.5 *would not put their shoulders to the work of their Lord.* The nobles of Tekoa thought their high status exempted them from doing the manual work for God. Nothing should be below us if it will advance the interests of our God and his people.
3.6 *The Old Gate* was located on the north side of post-exilic Jerusalem. Some think the Gate of Ephraim was on its west and the Fish Gate on its east side.
3.8 *the Broad Wall,* i.e., the western wall.
3.11 *the Tower of the Ovens,* close to the Corner Gate in the northwest angle of the Jerusalem wall. There were baking ovens in the area, from which it probably

---

Margin references (left column):

2.17 — Neh 1.3
2.18 — v. 8; 2 Sam 2.7
2.19 — Ps 44.13; Neh 6.6
2.20 — v. 4
3.1 — vv. 20, 32; Neh 6.1; 7.1; 12.39; Jer 31.38
3.2 — Neh 7.36
3.3 — Neh 12.39
3.6 — Neh 12.39
3.7 — Neh 2.7
3.8 — vv. 31, 32; Neh 12.38
3.9 — vv. 12, 17
3.11 — Neh 12.38

and Hasshub son of Pahath-moab repaired another section and the Tower
of the Ovens. 12 Next to him Shallum son of Hallohesh, ruler of half the
district of*z* Jerusalem, made repairs, he and his daughters.

13   Hanun and the inhabitants of Zanoah repaired the Valley Gate;
they rebuilt it and set up its doors, its bolts, and its bars, and repaired
a thousand cubits of the wall, as far as the Dung Gate.

14   Malchijah son of Rechab, ruler of the district of*a* Beth-haccherem,
repaired the Dung Gate; he rebuilt it and set up its doors, its bolts, and
its bars.

15   And Shallum son of Col-hozeh, ruler of the district of*a* Mizpah,
repaired the Fountain Gate; he rebuilt it and covered it and set up its
doors, its bolts, and its bars; and he built the wall of the Pool of Shelah
of the king's garden, as far as the stairs that go down from the City of
David. 16 After him Nehemiah son of Azbuk, ruler of half the district of*z*
Beth-zur, repaired from a point opposite the graves of David, as far as the
artificial pool and the house of the warriors. 17 After him the Levites made
repairs: Rehum son of Bani; next to him Hashabiah, ruler of half the
district of*z* Keilah, made repairs for his district. 18 After him their kin
made repairs: Binnui,*b* son of Henadad, ruler of half the district of*z*
Keilah; 19 next to him Ezer son of Jeshua, ruler*c* of Mizpah, repaired
another section opposite the ascent to the armory at the Angle. 20 After
him Baruch son of Zabbai repaired another section from the Angle to the
door of the house of the high priest Eliashib. 21 After him Meremoth son
of Uriah son of Hakkoz repaired another section from the door of the
house of Eliashib to the end of the house of Eliashib. 22 After him the
priests, the men of the surrounding area, made repairs. 23 After them
Benjamin and Hasshub made repairs opposite their house. After them
Azariah son of Maaseiah son of Ananiah made repairs beside his own
house. 24 After him Binnui son of Henadad repaired another section, from
the house of Azariah to the Angle and to the corner. 25 Palal son of Uzai
repaired opposite the Angle and the tower projecting from the upper
house of the king at the court of the guard. After him Pedaiah son of
Parosh 26 and the temple servants living*d* on Ophel made repairs up to
a point opposite the Water Gate on the east and the projecting tower.
27 After him the Tekoites repaired another section opposite the great
projecting tower as far as the wall of Ophel.

28   Above the Horse Gate the priests made repairs, each one opposite
his own house. 29 After them Zadok son of Immer made repairs opposite
his own house. After him Shemaiah son of Shecaniah, the keeper of the
East Gate, made repairs. 30 After him Hananiah son of Shelemiah and
Hanun sixth son of Zalaph repaired another section. After him Meshullam
son of Berechiah made repairs opposite his living quarters. 31 After him
Malchijah, one of the goldsmiths, made repairs as far as the house of the
temple servants and of the merchants, opposite the Muster Gate,*e* and
to the upper room of the corner. 32 And between the upper room of the

z Or *supervisor of half the portion assigned to*   *a* Or *supervisor of the portion assigned to*   *b* Gk Syr Compare
verse 24, 10.9: Heb *Bavvai*   *c* Or *supervisor*   *d* Cn: Heb *were living*   *e* Or *Hammiphkad Gate*

3.12 v. 9	
3.13 Neh 2.13	
3.15 Neh 2.14; 2 Kings 25.4; Neh 12.37	
3.16 vv. 9, 12, 17; 2 Kings 20.20	
3.19 v. 15; 2 Chr 26.9	
3.20 v. 1; Neh 13.7	
3.22 Neh 12.28	
3.24 v. 19	
3.25 Jer 32.2	
3.26 Neh 7.46; 11.21; 8.1	
3.28 2 Kings 11.16; 2 Chr 23.15; Jer 31.40	
3.31 vv. 8, 32	
3.32 v. 1	

got its name.
3.13   *the Valley Gate,* which had had towers built by
Uzziah. It was the point from which Nehemiah
started his tour of Jerusalem before the work of reconstruction began.
3.14   *The Dung Gate* was on the south end of the city,
not far from the pool of Siloam. Refuse from the city
was carried out this gate to the Valley of Hinnom
where it was burned. "Hinnom," from the Hebrew
Ge-ben-Hinnom, became corrupted into Greek as *Gehenna,* a word used in the N.T. to designate the place
of eternal punishment.
3.15   *The Fountain Gate* was located in the southeast
section of the wall below the Pool of Siloam and along

the Kidron Valley.
3.26   *The Water Gate* was close by the Gihon spring.
There was an open square where the people assembled to hear the reading of the law by Ezra (8.1).
Booths for the festival of tabernacles were erected
there.
3.28   *The Horse Gate* was at the southeast corner of
the temple area. Athaliah had been killed there (2 Chr
23.15).
3.29   *The East Gate* is not specifically stated to have
been repaired. It was a temple gate. It may have been
the gate through which Jesus entered Jerusalem on
Palm Sunday.

corner and the Sheep Gate the goldsmiths and the merchants made repairs.

2. The opposition to the work

a. The strategies of Sanballat and Tobiah

4.1
Neh 2.10, 19
4.2
v. 10

4 *f* Now when Sanballat heard that we were building the wall, he was angry and greatly enraged, and he mocked the Jews. 2 He said in the presence of his associates and of the army of Samaria, "What are these feeble Jews doing? Will they restore things? Will they sacrifice? Will they finish it in a day? Will they revive the stones out of the heaps of rubbish — and burned ones at that?" 3 Tobiah the Ammonite was beside him, and he said, "That stone wall they are building — any fox going up on it would break it down!" 4 Hear, O our God, for we are despised; turn their taunt back on their own heads, and give them over as plunder in a land of captivity. 5 Do not cover their guilt, and do not let their sin be blotted out from your sight; for they have hurled insults in the face of the builders.

4.3
Neh 2.10, 19
4.4
Ps 123.3, 4;
79.12
4.5
Ps 69.27, 28;
Jer 18.23

6 So we rebuilt the wall, and all the wall was joined together to half its height; for the people had a mind to work.

4.7
v. 1

7 *g* But when Sanballat and Tobiah and the Arabs and the Ammonites and the Ashdodites heard that the repairing of the walls of Jerusalem was going forward and the gaps were beginning to be closed, they were very angry, 8 and all plotted together to come and fight against Jerusalem and to cause confusion in it. 9 So we prayed to our God, and set a guard as a protection against them day and night.

4.9
Ps 50.15

10 But Judah said, "The strength of the burden bearers is failing, and there is too much rubbish so that we are unable to work on the wall." 11 And our enemies said, "They will not know or see anything before we come upon them and kill them and stop the work." 12 When the Jews who lived near them came, they said to us ten times, "From all the places where they live *h* they will come up against us."*i* 13 So in the lowest parts of the space behind the wall, in open places, I stationed the people according to their families,*j* with their swords, their spears, and their bows. 14 After I looked these things over, I stood up and said to the nobles and the officials and the rest of the people, "Do not be afraid of them. Remember the Lord, who is great and awesome, and fight for your kin, your sons, your daughters, your wives, and your homes."

4.13
vv. 17, 18
4.14
Num 14.9;
Deut 1.29;
2 Sam 10.12

15 When our enemies heard that their plot was known to us, and that God had frustrated it, we all returned to the wall, each to his work. 16 From that day on, half of my servants worked on construction, and half held the spears, shields, bows, and body-armor; and the leaders posted themselves behind the whole house of Judah, 17 who were building the wall. The burden bearers carried their loads in such a way that each labored on the work with one hand and with the other held a weapon. 18 And each of the builders had his sword strapped at his side while he

4.15
2 Sam 17.14;
Job 5.12

f Ch 3.33 in Heb *g* Ch 4.1 in Heb *h* Cn: Heb *you return* *i* Compare Gk Syr: Meaning of Heb uncertain *j* Meaning of Heb uncertain

---

4.1–3 The work of God will always be opposed by the forces of evil. The Samaritans Sanballat and Tobiah indignantly protested what Nehemiah was doing. They were derogatory, scornful, and malicious. **4.4** Nehemiah's prayer was imprecatory. He called upon God to avenge himself and his servants. This is not inconsistent with Jesus' teaching to pray for our enemies, for we should pray for their salvation. But we should also pray that justice will be served and the name of God exalted. We may ask God to put down his enemies if and when they seek to do violence to his people. **4.6** Despite all of the provocations of the enemy, *the people had a mind to work*. God's people were not

disheartened by the opposition. Rather, the hardships only strengthened their determination to proceed with the work. When God's people become despondent and afraid, they become helpless and useless to themselves and to God. **4.9** Prayer and works are both mentioned. God expects work to accompany our prayers, and prayer to accompany our work. **4.10** Some of the workers lacked perseverance and allowed their difficulties to loom so large that they felt like quitting. Nehemiah had to overcome this spirit. He rejuvenated the weary and depressed and developed an "esprit-de-corps" that enabled them to finish the rebuilding of the walls.

built. The man who sounded the trumpet was beside me. 19 And I said to the nobles, the officials, and the rest of the people, "The work is great and widely spread out, and we are separated far from one another on the wall. 20 Rally to us wherever you hear the sound of the trumpet. Our God will fight for us."

21   So we labored at the work, and half of them held the spears from break of dawn until the stars came out. 22 I also said to the people at that time, "Let every man and his servant pass the night inside Jerusalem, so that they may be a guard for us by night and may labor by day." 23 So neither I nor my brothers nor my servants nor the men of the guard who followed me ever took off our clothes; each kept his weapon in his right hand.[k]

b. Disaffection among the Jews themselves

5 Now there was a great outcry of the people and of their wives against their Jewish kin. 2 For there were those who said, "With our sons and our daughters, we are many; we must get grain, so that we may eat and stay alive." 3 There were also those who said, "We are having to pledge our fields, our vineyards, and our houses in order to get grain during the famine." 4 And there were those who said, "We are having to borrow money on our fields and vineyards to pay the king's tax. 5 Now our flesh is the same as that of our kindred; our children are the same as their children; and yet we are forcing our sons and daughters to be slaves, and some of our daughters have been ravished; we are powerless, and our fields and vineyards now belong to others."

6   I was very angry when I heard their outcry and these complaints. 7 After thinking it over, I brought charges against the nobles and the officials; I said to them, "You are all taking interest from your own people." And I called a great assembly to deal with them, 8 and said to them, "As far as we were able, we have bought back our Jewish kindred who had been sold to other nations; but now you are selling your own kin, who must then be bought back by us!" They were silent, and could not find a word to say. 9 So I said, "The thing that you are doing is not good. Should you not walk in the fear of our God, to prevent the taunts of the nations our enemies? 10 Moreover I and my brothers and my servants are lending them money and grain. Let us stop this taking of interest. 11 Restore to them, this very day, their fields, their vineyards, their olive orchards, and their houses, and the interest on money, grain, wine, and oil that you have been exacting from them." 12 Then they said, "We will restore everything and demand nothing more from them. We will do as you say." And I called the priests, and made them take an oath to do as they had promised. 13 I also shook out the fold of my garment and said, "So may God shake out everyone from house and from property who does not perform this promise. Thus may they be shaken out and emptied." And all the assembly said, "Amen," and praised the LORD. And the people did as they had promised.

14   Moreover from the time that I was appointed to be their governor in the land of Judah, from the twentieth year to the thirty-second year of King Artaxerxes, twelve years, neither I nor my brothers ate the food

[k] Cn: Heb *each his weapon the water*

4.20 Ex 14.14; Deut 1.30; Josh 23.10

5.1 Lev 25.35; Deut 15.7

5.4 Ezra 4.13; 7.24
5.5 Gen 37.27; Lev 25.39

5.7 Ex 22.25; Lev 25.36
5.8 Lev 25.48

5.9 2 Sam 12.14; Neh 4.4; Rom 2.24

5.12 Ezra 10.5

5.13 Acts 18.6; Neh 8.6

5.14 Neh 13.6; Ezra 4.13, 14

5.1   The great outcry came against the rich Jews who loaned money for interest to the poor Jews. It is uncertain whether this happened while the walls were being rebuilt or after they had been finished. According to Deut 23.20, this practice is forbidden. Sometimes our greatest enemies are within the ranks rather than from the outside. Nehemiah was not slow in rebuking those who broke God's law and commanded them to restore what they had taken.

5.13   *I also shook out the fold of my garment*, i.e., he asked God to curse those who refused.
5.14   Nehemiah did the work of the governor but he did not eat the food of the governor, i.e., he did not demand what he could have had by virtue of his office. Rather, he served sacrificially, practicing self-denial and identifying himself with the sufferings of the common people. In no way would he enrich himself at the expense of others.

5.15
v. 9

5.17
1 Kings 18.19

5.18
1 Kings 4.22,
23; 2 Thess
3.8

5.19
Neh 13.14,
22, 31

6.1
Neh 2.10, 19;
4.1, 7; 3.1, 3

6.2
1 Chr 8.12

6.6
Neh 2.19

6.10
Jer 36.5

6.12
Ezek 13.22

6.13
v. 6

allowance of the governor. 15 The former governors who were before me laid heavy burdens on the people, and took food and wine from them, besides forty shekels of silver. Even their servants lorded it over the people. But I did not do so, because of the fear of God. 16 Indeed, I devoted myself to the work on this wall, and acquired no land; and all my servants were gathered there for the work. 17 Moreover there were at my table one hundred fifty people, Jews and officials, besides those who came to us from the nations around us. 18 Now that which was prepared for one day was one ox and six choice sheep; also fowls were prepared for me, and every ten days skins of wine in abundance; yet with all this I did not demand the food allowance of the governor, because of the heavy burden of labor on the people. 19 Remember for my good, O my God, all that I have done for this people.

c. The continued difficulties from Sanballat and Tobiah

6 Now when it was reported to Sanballat and Tobiah and to Geshem the Arab and to the rest of our enemies that I had built the wall and that there was no gap left in it (though up to that time I had not set up the doors in the gates), 2 Sanballat and Geshem sent to me, saying, "Come and let us meet together in one of the villages in the plain of Ono." But they intended to do me harm. 3 So I sent messengers to them, saying, "I am doing a great work and I cannot come down. Why should the work stop while I leave it to come down to you?" 4 They sent to me four times in this way, and I answered them in the same manner. 5 In the same way Sanballat for the fifth time sent his servant to me with an open letter in his hand. 6 In it was written, "It is reported among the nations—and Geshem[l] also says it—that you and the Jews intend to rebel; that is why you are building the wall; and according to this report you wish to become their king. 7 You have also set up prophets to proclaim in Jerusalem concerning you, 'There is a king in Judah!' And now it will be reported to the king according to these words. So come, therefore, and let us confer together." 8 Then I sent to him, saying, "No such things as you say have been done; you are inventing them out of your own mind" 9 — for they all wanted to frighten us, thinking, "Their hands will drop from the work, and it will not be done." But now, O God, strengthen my hands.

10 One day when I went into the house of Shemaiah son of Delaiah son of Mehetabel, who was confined to his house, he said, "Let us meet together in the house of God, within the temple, and let us close the doors of the temple, for they are coming to kill you; indeed, tonight they are coming to kill you." 11 But I said, "Should a man like me run away? Would a man like me go into the temple to save his life? I will not go in!" 12 Then I perceived and saw that God had not sent him at all, but he had pronounced the prophecy against me because Tobiah and Sanballat had hired him. 13 He was hired for this purpose, to intimidate me and make

[l] Heb Gashmu

5.19 *Remember . . . all that I have done.* Nehemiah was not boasting of what he had done. Rather, he was shaming those who had broken God's law, wanting them to follow his example and forsake greed. He himself had given up everything for God and his people, and he hoped others would do likewise. Yet his basic desire was for the approval of God, for that is worth far more than the approval of people.

6.1ff Frustrated by God's providence and Nehemiah's prudence, the enemies hatched three plots to undo the work of Nehemiah. The first was to get him away from Jerusalem for a conference, some twenty miles away in the plain of Ono (6.1,2). In his absence they might be able to assault the city or even kill Nehemiah at Ono, unaccompanied by his armed helpers. He declined their invitation four times and re-

mained in Jerusalem.
6.5 Their second stratagem was an open letter in which they accused him of wanting to be king, implying rebellion against Artaxerxes. They hoped this would frighten Nehemiah and stop the work. Nehemiah basically ignored it.
6.11 The third plot came through a messenger who informed Nehemiah that he might be assassinated. The messenger suggested that he leave his work and flee to the house of God for refuge. But Nehemiah was made of sterner stuff and saw through the plan. He refused to desert God's work and so to discredit himself before the people whom he had engaged in the work. He would rather have died while doing his duty than have lived retreating from that duty.

me sin by acting in this way, and so they could give me a bad name, in order to taunt me. [14]Remember Tobiah and Sanballat, O my God, according to these things that they did, and also the prophetess Noadiah and the rest of the prophets who wanted to make me afraid.

15   So the wall was finished on the twenty-fifth day of the month Elul, in fifty-two days. [16]And when all our enemies heard of it, all the nations around us were afraid[m] and fell greatly in their own esteem; for they perceived that this work had been accomplished with the help of our God. [17]Moreover in those days the nobles of Judah sent many letters to Tobiah, and Tobiah's letters came to them. [18]For many in Judah were bound by oath to him, because he was the son-in-law of Shecaniah son of Arah: and his son Jehohanan had married the daughter of Meshullam son of Berechiah. [19]Also they spoke of his good deeds in my presence, and reported my words to him. And Tobiah sent letters to intimidate me.

C. The new order at Jerusalem and list of returning exiles

1. The appointment of Hanani and Hananiah

7 Now when the wall had been built and I had set up the doors, and the gatekeepers, the singers, and the Levites had been appointed, [2]I gave my brother Hanani charge over Jerusalem, along with Hananiah the commander of the citadel—for he was a faithful man and feared God more than many. [3]And I said to them, "The gates of Jerusalem are not to be opened until the sun is hot; while the gatekeepers[n] are still standing guard, let them shut and bar the doors. Appoint guards from among the inhabitants of Jerusalem, some at their watch posts, and others before their own houses." [4]The city was wide and large, but the people within it were few and no houses had been built.

2. The genealogy of the returning remnant

5   Then my God put it into my mind to assemble the nobles and the officials and the people to be enrolled by genealogy. And I found the book of the genealogy of those who were the first to come back, and I found the following written in it:

6   These are the people of the province who came up out of the captivity of those exiles whom King Nebuchadnezzar of Babylon had carried into exile; they returned to Jerusalem and Judah, each to his town. [7]They came with Zerubbabel, Jeshua, Nehemiah, Azariah, Raamiah, Nahamani, Mordecai, Bilshan, Mispereth, Bigvai, Nehum, Baanah.

The number of the Israelite people: [8]the descendants of Parosh, two thousand one hundred seventy-two. [9]Of Shephatiah, three hundred seventy-two. [10]Of Arah, six hundred fifty-two. [11]Of Pahath-moab, namely the descendants of Jeshua and Joab, two thousand eight hundred

m Another reading is *saw*   *n* Heb *while they*

Cross references (right margin):

6.14 Neh 13.29; Ezek 13.17

6.16 Neh 2.10; 4.1, 7; Ex 14.25; Ps 126.2

7.1 Neh 6.1, 15
7.2 Neh 2.8

7.6 Ezra 2.1-70

7.7 Ezra 2.2

6.15 *Fifty-two days* refers to the last phase of the construction. Josephus said it took two years and four months to rebuild the walls.
6.17 Nehemiah had to face the secret treason of some nobles who exchanged communications with Tobiah, to the hurt of his cause. This secret confederacy, based partially on blood ties, became known to Nehemiah and did not succeed, even though spies reported his very words to the enemy.
7.1 Nehemiah's task was not finished when the walls were built and the gates to the doors set up; he still needed to appoint someone to administer the newly walled city of Jerusalem.
7.2 Nehemiah chose two trusted individuals to oversee the city of Jerusalem: Hanani his brother and Hananiah, a man whose reputation was impeccable.

These two consuls were charged to provide for the public peace and safety of the people, from enemies within and without. Some think Nehemiah was about to return to the Persian court and have his commission renewed; thus, he wanted to leave good people in charge in his absence.
7.3 Nehemiah wanted to be sure that the city gates were opened and shut at proper times to guarantee the safety of the city. Sentinels were to be posted to give the alarm should any contingency arise.
7.5 Nehemiah carefully preserved the genealogical records of the people. They had probably been stored carefully in the temple rooms. The records of the first returnees were examined, and, along with those of the second wave of immigrants, were updated and kept current. There follows the listing by families.

7.12
Ezra 2.7

7.17
see Ezra 2.12

7.23
Ezra 2.17

7.27
Ezra 2.23

7.34
Ezra 2.31

7.39
Ezra 2.36

7.43
Ezra 2.40

7.46
Ezra 2.43

7.57
Ezra 2.55

7.60
v. 46

7.63
Ezra 2.61

7.65
Neh 8.9; 10.1

7.70
Neh 8.9

eighteen. 12 Of Elam, one thousand two hundred fifty-four. 13 Of Zattu, eight hundred forty-five. 14 Of Zaccai, seven hundred sixty. 15 Of Binnui, six hundred forty-eight. 16 Of Bebai, six hundred twenty-eight. 17 Of Azgad, two thousand three hundred twenty-two. 18 Of Adonikam, six hundred sixty-seven. 19 Of Bigvai, two thousand sixty-seven. 20 Of Adin, six hundred fifty-five. 21 Of Ater, namely of Hezekiah, ninety-eight. 22 Of Hashum, three hundred twenty-eight. 23 Of Bezai, three hundred twenty-four. 24 Of Hariph, one hundred twelve. 25 Of Gibeon, ninety-five. 26 The people of Bethlehem and Netophah, one hundred eighty-eight. 27 Of Anathoth, one hundred twenty-eight. 28 Of Beth-azmaveth, forty-two. 29 Of Kiriath-jearim, Chephirah, and Beeroth, seven hundred forty-three. 30 Of Ramah and Geba, six hundred twenty-one. 31 Of Michmas, one hundred twenty-two. 32 Of Bethel and Ai, one hundred twenty-three. 33 Of the other Nebo, fifty-two. 34 The descendants of the other Elam, one thousand two hundred fifty-four. 35 Of Harim, three hundred twenty. 36 Of Jericho, three hundred forty-five. 37 Of Lod, Hadid, and Ono, seven hundred twenty-one. 38 Of Senaah, three thousand nine hundred thirty.

39 The priests: the descendants of Jedaiah, namely the house of Jeshua, nine hundred seventy-three. 40 Of Immer, one thousand fifty-two. 41 Of Pashhur, one thousand two hundred forty-seven. 42 Of Harim, one thousand seventeen.

43 The Levites: the descendants of Jeshua, namely of Kadmiel of the descendants of Hodevah, seventy-four. 44 The singers: the descendants of Asaph, one hundred forty-eight. 45 The gatekeepers: the descendants of Shallum, of Ater, of Talmon, of Akkub, of Hatita, of Shobai, one hundred thirty-eight.

46 The temple servants: the descendants of Ziha, of Hasupha, of Tabbaoth, 47 of Keros, of Sia, of Padon, 48 of Lebana, of Hagaba, of Shalmai, 49 of Hanan, of Giddel, of Gahar, 50 of Reaiah, of Rezin, of Nekoda, 51 of Gazzam, of Uzza, of Paseah, 52 of Besai, of Meunim, of Nephushesim, 53 of Bakbuk, of Hakupha, of Harhur, 54 of Bazlith, of Mehida, of Harsha, 55 of Barkos, of Sisera, of Temah, 56 of Neziah, of Hatipha.

57 The descendants of Solomon's servants: of Sotai, of Sophereth, of Perida, 58 of Jaala, of Darkon, of Giddel, 59 of Shephatiah, of Hattil, of Pochereth-hazzebaim, of Amon.

60 All the temple servants and the descendants of Solomon's servants were three hundred ninety-two.

61 The following were those who came up from Tel-melah, Tel-harsha, Cherub, Addon, and Immer, but they could not prove their ancestral houses or their descent, whether they belonged to Israel: 62 the descendants of Delaiah, of Tobiah, of Nekoda, six hundred forty-two. 63 Also, of the priests: the descendants of Hobaiah, of Hakkoz, of Barzillai (who had married one of the daughters of Barzillai the Gileadite and was called by their name). 64 These sought their registration among those enrolled in the genealogies, but it was not found there, so they were excluded from the priesthood as unclean; 65 the governor told them that they were not to partake of the most holy food, until a priest with Urim and Thummim should come.

66 The whole assembly together was forty-two thousand three hundred sixty, 67 besides their male and female slaves, of whom there were seven thousand three hundred thirty-seven; and they had two hundred forty-five singers, male and female. 68 They had seven hundred thirty-six horses, two hundred forty-five mules, o 69 four hundred thirty-five camels, and six thousand seven hundred twenty donkeys.

70 Now some of the heads of ancestral houses contributed to the work. The governor gave to the treasury one thousand darics of gold, fifty

o Ezra 2.66 and the margins of some Hebrew Mss: MT lacks *They had . . . forty-five mules*

basins, and five hundred thirty priestly robes. ⁷¹And some of the heads of ancestral houses gave into the building fund twenty thousand darics of gold and two thousand two hundred minas of silver. ⁷²And what the rest of the people gave was twenty thousand darics of gold, two thousand minas of silver, and sixty-seven priestly robes.

73 So the priests, the Levites, the gatekeepers, the singers, some of the people, the temple servants, and all Israel settled in their towns.

II. *The reading of the law and the renewing of the covenant (7.73b–10.39)*

A. *The law read and explained*

When the seventh month came—the people of Israel being settled in their towns—¹all the people gathered together into the square before the Water Gate. They told the scribe Ezra to bring the book of the law of Moses, which the Lord had given to Israel. ²Accordingly, the priest Ezra brought the law before the assembly, both men and women and all who could hear with understanding. This was on the first day of the seventh month. ³He read from it facing the square before the Water Gate from early morning until midday, in the presence of the men and the women and those who could understand; and the ears of all the people were attentive to the book of the law. ⁴The scribe Ezra stood on a wooden platform that had been made for the purpose; and beside him stood Mattithiah, Shema, Anaiah, Uriah, Hilkiah, and Maaseiah on his right hand; and Pedaiah, Mishael, Malchijah, Hashum, Hashbaddanah, Zechariah, and Meshullam on his left hand. ⁵And Ezra opened the book in the sight of all the people, for he was standing above all the people; and when he opened it, all the people stood up. ⁶Then Ezra blessed the Lord, the great God, and all the people answered, "Amen, Amen," lifting up their hands. Then they bowed their heads and worshiped the Lord with their faces to the ground. ⁷Also Jeshua, Bani, Sherebiah, Jamin, Akkub, Shabbethai, Hodiah, Maaseiah, Kelita, Azariah, Jozabad, Hanan, Pelaiah, the Levites,ᵖ helped the people to understand the law, while the people remained in their places. ⁸So they read from the book, from the law of God, with interpretation. They gave the sense, so that the people understood the reading.

9 And Nehemiah, who was the governor, and Ezra the priest and scribe, and the Levites who taught the people said to all the people, "This day is holy to the Lord your God; do not mourn or weep." For all the people wept when they heard the words of the law. ¹⁰Then he said to them, "Go your way, eat the fat and drink sweet wine and send portions of them to those for whom nothing is prepared, for this day is holy to our Lord; and do not be grieved, for the joy of the Lord is your strength." ¹¹So the Levites stilled all the people, saying, "Be quiet, for this day is holy; do not be grieved." ¹²And all the people went their way to eat and drink and to send portions and to make great rejoicing, because they had understood the words that were declared to them.

ᵖ 1 Esdras 9.48 Vg: Heb *and the Levites*

	7.71 Ezra 2.69
	7.73 Ezra 3.1
	8.1 Ezra 3.1; Neh 3.26; Ezra 7.6
	8.2 Deut 31.11, 12; Lev 23.24
	8.6 Neh 5.13; Gen 14.22; Ex 4.31
	8.7 2 Chr 17.7-9
	8.9 Neh 7.65, 70; 12.26; Num 29.1; Deut 16.14, 15
	8.10 Deut 26.11, 13
	8.12 vv. 10, 7, 8

8.1 This was a solemn religious assembly of people gathered to honor God and to receive edification by listening to a public reading of his law.

8.2–4 *On the first day of the seventh month,* i.e., the festival of trumpets (and thus a holy day), the people gathered together in a holy convocation. Since copies of the law were few, reading it publicly was of great importance. Ezra stood on a wooden platform to read. As he opened the scroll, the people stood, a tribute to their reverence for the word of God. This was a high moment in the lives of the returnees from Babylon.

8.8 *gave the sense.* The Hebrew language was being rapidly replaced by Aramaic; therefore, some scholars think these verses mean that Ezra's helpers gave the people a *Targum,* a translation of the Hebrew text in Aramaic, which they could understand.

8.9 The people wept when they heard the word of God. But since it was the festival of trumpets, Ezra and Nehemiah enjoined them not to weep. It was a holy day of rejoicing and the time to celebrate the completion of the task of rebuilding the walls of their sacred city.

B. *The festival of booths celebrated*

8.13
Lev 23.34, 42

13 On the second day the heads of ancestral houses of all the people, with the priests and the Levites, came together to the scribe Ezra in order to study the words of the law. 14 And they found it written in the law, which the LORD had commanded by Moses, that the people of Israel should live in booths*q* during the festival of the seventh month, 15 and

8.15
Lev 23.4;
Deut 16.16;
Lev 23.40

that they should publish and proclaim in all their towns and in Jerusalem as follows, "Go out to the hills and bring branches of olive, wild olive, myrtle, palm, and other leafy trees to make booths,*q* as it is written." 16 So the people went out and brought them, and made booths*q* for

8.16
Jer 32.29;
Neh 12.39;
2 Kings 14.13

themselves, each on the roofs of their houses, and in their courts and in the courts of the house of God, and in the square at the Water Gate and in the square at the Gate of Ephraim. 17 And all the assembly of those who

8.17
2 Chr 30.21

had returned from the captivity made booths*q* and lived in them; for from the days of Jeshua son of Nun to that day the people of Israel had not done so. And there was very great rejoicing. 18 And day by day, from the first

8.18
Deut 31.11;
Lev 23.36;
Num 29.35

day to the last day, he read from the book of the law of God. They kept the festival seven days; and on the eighth day there was a solemn assembly, according to the ordinance.

C. *The covenant renewed*

1. *Separation from foreigners*

9.1
Neh 8.2;
Ezra 8.23;
1 Sam 4.12

9 Now on the twenty-fourth day of this month the people of Israel were assembled with fasting and in sackcloth, and with earth on their heads.*r* 2 Then those of Israelite descent separated themselves from all foreigners, and stood and confessed their sins and the iniquities of their

9.2
Ezra 10.11;
Neh 13.3, 30

ancestors. 3 They stood up in their place and read from the book of the law of the LORD their God for a fourth part of the day, and for another

9.3
Neh 8.4

fourth they made confession and worshiped the LORD their God. 4 Then

9.4
Neh 8.7

Jeshua, Bani, Kadmiel, Shebaniah, Bunni, Sherebiah, Bani, and Chenani stood on the stairs of the Levites and cried out with a loud voice to the LORD their God. 5 Then the Levites, Jeshua, Kadmiel, Bani, Hashabne-

9.5
1 Chr 29.13

iah, Sherebiah, Hodiah, Shebaniah, and Pethahiah, said, "Stand up and bless the LORD your God from everlasting to everlasting. Blessed be your glorious name, which is exalted above all blessing and praise."

2. *The penitential psalm*

9.6
2 Kings 19.15;
Gen 1.1;
Ps 36.6;
Col 1.17

6 And Ezra said:*s* "You are the LORD, you alone; you have made heaven, the heaven of heavens, with all their host, the earth and all that

q Or *tabernacles*; Heb *succoth*   *r* Heb *on them*   *s* Gk: Heb lacks *And Ezra said*

8.14 From the reading and interpretation of the word of God, they learned about the tradition of dwelling in booths for the festival they were now celebrating. They proceeded to use tree branches to build booths on the rooftops of their houses, in the courts of the house of God, and in the streets. This celebration was comparable to that inaugurated in Joshua's day, when Israel first entered the land. Now they had reentered the land and this was the first time they celebrated the festival of booths.

8.18 From the first to the last day of this festival the word of God was read, expounded, and made applicable to the lives of the people.

9.1 *with fasting.* See note on Lev 16.29,30.

9.2 Revival came to the people of God. They fasted and used sackcloth. They separated themselves from unbelievers. They confessed their sins and those of their ancestors. During their six-hour service, they

spent three hours in reading, expounding, and applying the Word of God and three more in confessing sins and praying. Some commentators think they spent as many as twelve hours in these religious activities.

9.5ff The prayer offered here acknowledged (1) the majesty of God who made and preserved all things, (2) the choice of Abraham and the covenant God made with him, (3) the exodus from Egypt and Israel's wandering in the desert, (4) Israel's entrance into the land of promise and their frequent apostasies, (5) their sincere confession of sin followed by a commitment to keep the whole law of God.

9.6 The NRSV text (following the Septuagint, the Greek translation of the O.T.) attributes the prayer to Ezra but notes in a footnote that the phrase "And Ezra said" does not appear in the Hebrew. Most translations do not make it clear that it was Ezra's prayer. It is helpful to compare this prayer with the one in Ezra 9.

is on it, the seas and all that is in them. To all of them you give life, and the host of heaven worships you. 7 You are the LORD, the God who chose Abram and brought him out of Ur of the Chaldeans and gave him the name Abraham; 8 and you found his heart faithful before you, and made with him a covenant to give to his descendants the land of the Canaanite, the Hittite, the Amorite, the Perizzite, the Jebusite, and the Girgashite; and you have fulfilled your promise, for you are righteous.

9   "And you saw the distress of our ancestors in Egypt and heard their cry at the Red Sea.[t] 10 You performed signs and wonders against Pharaoh and all his servants and all the people of his land, for you knew that they acted insolently against our ancestors. You made a name for yourself, which remains to this day. 11 And you divided the sea before them, so that they passed through the sea on dry land, but you threw their pursuers into the depths, like a stone into mighty waters. 12 Moreover, you led them by day with a pillar of cloud, and by night with a pillar of fire, to give them light on the way in which they should go. 13 You came down also upon Mount Sinai, and spoke with them from heaven, and gave them right ordinances and true laws, good statutes and commandments, 14 and you made known your holy sabbath to them and gave them commandments and statutes and a law through your servant Moses. 15 For their hunger you gave them bread from heaven, and for their thirst you brought water for them out of the rock, and you told them to go in to possess the land that you swore to give them.

16   "But they and our ancestors acted presumptuously and stiffened their necks and did not obey your commandments; 17 they refused to obey, and were not mindful of the wonders that you performed among them; but they stiffened their necks and determined to return to their slavery in Egypt. But you are a God ready to forgive, gracious and merciful, slow to anger and abounding in steadfast love, and you did not forsake them. 18 Even when they had cast an image of a calf for themselves and said, 'This is your God who brought you up out of Egypt,' and had committed great blasphemies, 19 you in your great mercies did not forsake them in the wilderness; the pillar of cloud that led them in the way did not leave them by day, nor the pillar of fire by night that gave them light on the way by which they should go. 20 You gave your good spirit to instruct them, and did not withhold your manna from their mouths, and gave them water for their thirst. 21 Forty years you sustained them in the wilderness so that they lacked nothing; their clothes did not wear out and their feet did not swell. 22 And you gave them kingdoms and peoples, and allotted to them every corner,[u] so they took possession of the land of King Sihon of Heshbon and the land of King Og of Bashan. 23 You multiplied their descendants like the stars of heaven, and brought them into the land that you had told their ancestors to enter and possess. 24 So the descendants went in and possessed the land, and you subdued before them the inhabitants of the land, the Canaanites, and gave them into their hands, with their kings and the peoples of the land, to do with them as they pleased. 25 And they captured fortress cities and a rich land, and took possession of houses filled with all sorts of goods, hewn cisterns, vineyards, olive orchards, and fruit trees in abundance; so they ate, and were filled and became fat, and delighted themselves in your great goodness.

26   "Nevertheless they were disobedient and rebelled against you and cast your law behind their backs and killed your prophets, who had

9.7
Gen 11.31;
12.1; 17.5
9.8
Gen 15.6,
18-21;
Josh 21.43-45

9.9
Ex 3.7;
14.10-12
9.10
Ex 5.2; 9.16
9.11
Ex 14.21;
15.5, 10
9.12
Ex 13.21, 22

9.13
Ex 19.20;
20.1;
Ps 19.7-9
9.14
Gen 2.3;
Ex 20.8, 11
9.15
Ex 16.14;
17.6;
Num 20.7-13;
Deut 1.8
9.16
Ps 106.6;
Deut 31.27
9.17
Ps 78.11;
Num 14.4;
Ex 34.6, 7

9.18
Ex 32.4

9.19
vv. 27, 31, 12

9.20
Num 11.17;
Isa 63.11-14;
Ex 16.15;
17.6
9.21
Deut 2.7;
8.4; 29.5
9.22
Num 21.21-35
9.23
Gen 15.5
9.24
Josh 21.43;
18.1

9.25
Deut 3.9;
Num 13.27;
Deut 6.11;
32.15;
1 Kings 8.66
9.26
Judg 2.11;
1 Kings 14.9;
2 Chr 36.16;
v. 30

---

[t] Or *Sea of Reeds*   [u] Meaning of Heb uncertain

9.10   *signs and wonders.* God performed many miracles to give outward confirming evidence for those who wished to trust in him.
9.20   The Scriptures often refer to the Spirit as the divine author of the words we find therein. See, for

example, the following passages: 2 Sam 23.2; Mk 12.36; Acts 4.25; 28.25; Heb 3.7. Most notable is the passage by Peter in 2 Pet 1.21: "men and women moved by the Holy Spirit spoke from God."

warned them in order to turn them back to you, and they committed great blasphemies. 27 Therefore you gave them into the hands of their enemies, who made them suffer. Then in the time of their suffering they cried out to you and you heard them from heaven, and according to your great mercies you gave them saviors who saved them from the hands of their enemies. 28 But after they had rest, they again did evil before you, and you abandoned them to the hands of their enemies, so that they had dominion over them; yet when they turned and cried to you, you heard from heaven, and many times you rescued them according to your mercies. 29 And you warned them in order to turn them back to your law. Yet they acted presumptuously and did not obey your commandments, but sinned against your ordinances, by the observance of which a person shall live. They turned a stubborn shoulder and stiffened their neck and would not obey. 30 Many years you were patient with them, and warned them by your spirit through your prophets; yet they would not listen. Therefore you handed them over to the peoples of the lands. 31 Nevertheless, in your great mercies you did not make an end of them or forsake them, for you are a gracious and merciful God.

32 "Now therefore, our God—the great and mighty and awesome God, keeping covenant and steadfast love—do not treat lightly all the hardship that has come upon us, upon our kings, our officials, our priests, our prophets, our ancestors, and all your people, since the time of the kings of Assyria until today. 33 You have been just in all that has come upon us, for you have dealt faithfully and we have acted wickedly; 34 our kings, our officials, our priests, and our ancestors have not kept your law or heeded the commandments and the warnings that you gave them. 35 Even in their own kingdom, and in the great goodness you bestowed on them, and in the large and rich land that you set before them, they did not serve you and did not turn from their wicked works. 36 Here we are, slaves to this day—slaves in the land that you gave to our ancestors to enjoy its fruit and its good gifts. 37 Its rich yield goes to the kings whom you have set over us because of our sins; they have power also over our bodies and over our livestock at their pleasure, and we are in great distress."

38 *v* Because of all this we make a firm agreement in writing, and on that sealed document are inscribed the names of our officials, our Levites, and our priests.

3. *Those who signed the covenant*

10 *w* Upon the sealed document are the names of Nehemiah the governor, son of Hacaliah, and Zedekiah; 2 Seraiah, Azariah, Jeremiah, 3 Pashhur, Amariah, Malchijah, 4 Hattush, Shebaniah, Malluch, 5 Harim, Meremoth, Obadiah, 6 Daniel, Ginnethon, Baruch, 7 Meshullam, Abijah, Mijamin, 8 Maaziah, Bilgai, Shemaiah; these are the priests. 9 And the Levites: Jeshua son of Azaniah, Binnui of the sons of Henadad, Kadmiel; 10 and their associates, Shebaniah, Hodiah, Kelita, Pelaiah, Hanan, 11 Mica, Rehob, Hashabiah, 12 Zaccur, Sherebiah, Shebaniah, 13 Hodiah, Bani, Beninu. 14 The leaders of the people: Parosh, Pahath-moab, Elam, Zattu, Bani, 15 Bunni, Azgad, Bebai, 16 Adonijah, Bigvai, Adin, 17 Ater, Hezekiah, Azzur, 18 Hodiah, Hashum, Bezai, 19 Hariph, Anathoth, Ne-

v Ch 10.1 in Heb   *w* Ch 10.2 in Heb

Cross references (left margin):

9.27 Judg 2.14; Deut 4.29; Judg 2.16, 18

9.28 Judg 3.11; Ps 106.43

9.29 vv. 26, 30, 16; Lev 18.5; Zech 7.11

9.30 2 Kings 17.13; Acts 7.51, 52
9.31 Jer 4.27

9.32 Neh 1.5; 2 Kings 15.19; 17.3

9.33 Jer 12.1; Dan 9.5, 6, 8

9.35 Deut 28.47

9.36 Deut 28.48

9.37 Deut 28.33

9.38 2 Chr 29.10; 34.31

10.1 Neh 9.38

9.30 *warned them by your spirit through your prophets.* The Holy Spirit, then and now, brings conviction of sin. He used the prophets, who spoke what he wanted said at a time when the full revelation of God had not yet been given. Today the same Spirit speaks through the word of God and the preaching of that word by faithful servants. The Spirit and the word function together to accomplish the divine will and bring us renewal.

9.33 *you have dealt faithfully and we have acted wickedly.* Believers today must express the same thought, that they do wickedly while God has done right. Revival tarries until God's people confess their wickedness, receive forgiveness, and enjoy the fullness of the Holy Spirit.

bai, 20 Magpiash, Meshullam, Hezir, 21 Meshezabel, Zadok, Jaddua, 22 Pelatiah, Hanan, Anaiah, 23 Hoshea, Hananiah, Hasshub, 24 Hallohesh, Pilha, Shobek, 25 Rehum, Hashabnah, Maaseiah, 26 Ahiah, Hanan, Anan, 27 Malluch, Harim, and Baanah.

4. Summary of the covenant

a. Mixed marriages

28 The rest of the people, the priests, the Levites, the gatekeepers, the singers, the temple servants, and all who have separated themselves from the peoples of the lands to adhere to the law of God, their wives, their sons, their daughters, all who have knowledge and understanding, 29 join with their kin, their nobles, and enter into a curse and an oath to walk in God's law, which was given by Moses the servant of God, and to observe and do all the commandments of the LORD our Lord and his ordinances and his statutes. 30 We will not give our daughters to the peoples of the land or take their daughters for our sons; 31 and if the peoples of the land bring in merchandise or any grain on the sabbath day to sell, we will not buy it from them on the sabbath or on a holy day; and we will forego the crops of the seventh year and the exaction of every debt.

10.28
Ezra 2.36-58;
Neh 9.2

10.29
Neh 5.12;
2 Chr 34.31

10.30
Ex 34.16;
Deut 7.3
10.31
Neh 13.15-22;
Ex 23.10, 11;
Deut 15.1, 2

b. The promise to fulfill specific covenant obligations

32 We also lay on ourselves the obligation to charge ourselves yearly one-third of a shekel for the service of the house of our God: 33 for the rows of bread, the regular grain offering, the regular burnt offering, the sabbaths, the new moons, the appointed festivals, the sacred donations, and the sin offerings to make atonement for Israel, and for all the work of the house of our God. 34 We have also cast lots among the priests, the Levites, and the people, for the wood offering, to bring it into the house of our God, by ancestral houses, at appointed times, year by year, to burn on the altar of the LORD our God, as it is written in the law. 35 We obligate ourselves to bring the first fruits of our soil and the first fruits of all fruit of every tree, year by year, to the house of the LORD; 36 also to bring to the house of our God, to the priests who minister in the house of our God, the firstborn of our sons and of our livestock, as it is written in the law, and the firstlings of our herds and of our flocks; 37 and to bring the first of our dough, and our contributions, the fruit of every tree, the wine and the oil, to the priests, to the chambers of the house of our God; and to bring to the Levites the tithes from our soil, for it is the Levites who collect the tithes in all our rural towns. 38 And the priest, the descendant of Aaron, shall be with the Levites when the Levites receive the tithes; and the Levites shall bring up a tithe of the tithes to the house of our God, to the chambers of the storehouse. 39 For the people of Israel and the sons of Levi shall bring the contribution of grain, wine, and oil to the storerooms where the vessels of the sanctuary are, and where the priests that minister, and the gatekeepers and the singers are. We will not neglect the house of our God.

10.32
Ex 30.11-16

10.34
Neh 11.1;
13.31

10.35
Ex 23.19;
Deut 26.2
10.36
Ex 13.2;
Num 18.15,
16

10.37
Lev 23.17;
Neh 13.5, 9;
Lev 27.30

10.38
Num 18.26;
Neh 13.12,
13

10.39
Deut 12.6;
Neh 13.10,
11

10.28 *temple servants.* See note on Ezra 2.43.
10.30 In Ezra the chief sin had been intermarriage with the heathen. Here the Jewish men promised that they would neither take heathen women as their wives nor let Jewish women marry heathen men.
10.31,32 Though the sabbath had no meaning for non-Jews, it was a holy day for the Jews; thus they promised to refrain from commercial activities on the sabbath and on other holy days. They also promised to support the temple by paying a per capita tax of one-third of a shekel (v. 32). Ex 30.13 refers to the tax as a half shekel. Perhaps the people in Nehemiah's day were poorer.

10.34 The wood offering was designed to keep the altar fires burning for the sacrifices.
10.38 *a tithe of the tithes* (see Num 18.26). God commanded that the Levites, who constituted the priesthood and who were supported by the tithe of the other eleven tribes, were themselves required to tithe. They had to give one-tenth of the tenth they received. Thus no one was exempted from returning the tenth to God, the giver of all. God plays no favorites; even ministers of the gospel who live by the gospel have a financial obligation to God. See also Lev 27.3-33; see note on Mal 3.8.

III. *The reconstituting of Jerusalem: Nehemiah's second reform (11.1–13.31)*

A. *The repeopling of Jerusalem*

11 Now the leaders of the people lived in Jerusalem; and the rest of the people cast lots to bring one out of ten to live in the holy city Jerusalem, while nine-tenths remained in the other towns. 2 And the people blessed all those who willingly offered to live in Jerusalem.

B. *The key people in Jerusalem*

3 These are the leaders of the province who lived in Jerusalem; but in the towns of Judah all lived on their property in their towns: Israel, the priests, the Levites, the temple servants, and the descendants of Solomon's servants. 4 And in Jerusalem lived some of the Judahites and of the Benjaminites. Of the Judahites: Athaiah son of Uzziah son of Zechariah son of Amariah son of Shephatiah son of Mahalalel, of the descendants of Perez; 5 and Maaseiah son of Baruch son of Col-hozeh son of Hazaiah son of Adaiah son of Joiarib son of Zechariah son of the Shilonite. 6 All the descendants of Perez who lived in Jerusalem were four hundred sixty-eight valiant warriors.

7 And these are the Benjaminites: Sallu son of Meshullam son of Joed son of Pedaiah son of Kolaiah son of Maaseiah son of Ithiel son of Jeshaiah. 8 And his brothers[x] Gabbai, Sallai: nine hundred twenty-eight. 9 Joel son of Zichri was their overseer; and Judah son of Hassenuah was second in charge of the city.

10 Of the priests: Jedaiah son of Joiarib, Jachin, 11 Seraiah son of Hilkiah son of Meshullam son of Zadok son of Meraioth son of Ahitub, officer of the house of God, 12 and their associates who did the work of the house, eight hundred twenty-two; and Adaiah son of Jeroham son of Pelaliah son of Amzi son of Zechariah son of Pashhur son of Malchijah, 13 and his associates, heads of ancestral houses, two hundred forty-two; and Amashsai son of Azarel son of Ahzai son of Meshillemoth son of Immer, 14 and their associates, valiant warriors, one hundred twenty-eight; their overseer was Zabdiel son of Haggedolim.

15 And of the Levites: Shemaiah son of Hasshub son of Azrikam son of Hashabiah son of Bunni; 16 and Shabbethai and Jozabad, of the leaders of the Levites, who were over the outside work of the house of God; 17 and Mattaniah son of Mica son of Zabdi son of Asaph, who was the leader to begin the thanksgiving in prayer, and Bakbukiah, the second among his associates; and Abda son of Shammua son of Galal son of Jeduthun. 18 All the Levites in the holy city were two hundred eighty-four.

19 The gatekeepers, Akkub, Talmon and their associates, who kept watch at the gates, were one hundred seventy-two. 20 And the rest of Israel, and of the priests and the Levites, were in all the towns of Judah, all of them in their inheritance. 21 But the temple servants lived on Ophel; and Ziha and Gishpa were over the temple servants.

22 The overseer of the Levites in Jerusalem was Uzzi son of Bani son of Hashabiah son of Mattaniah son of Mica, of the descendants of Asaph, the singers, in charge of the work of the house of God. 23 For there was a command from the king concerning them, and a settled provision for the singers, as was required every day. 24 And Pethahiah son of Mesheza-

---

x Gk Mss: Heb *And after him*

11.1 *the holy city Jerusalem* . Due to lack of people living in the city, one-tenth of the people outside its walls were chosen by lot to dwell within the walls of the city, though there was nothing to keep people from moving into the city on their own volition. **11.3–24** The names of the families and their numbers who resided in Jerusalem are enumerated.

Marginal references:
11.1 Neh 10.34; v. 18; Isa 48.2
11.3 1 Chr 9.2, 3; v. 20; Ezra 2.43; Neh 7.57
11.4 1 Chr 9.3ff
11.7 v. 4
11.10 1 Chr 9.10
11.16 1 Chr 26.29
11.18 v. 1
11.21 Neh 3.26
11.22 vv. 9, 14
11.23 Ezra 6.8; 7.20; Neh 12.47

bel, of the descendants of Zerah son of Judah, was at the king's hand in all matters concerning the people.

C. *The villages settled outside Jerusalem*

25 And as for the villages, with their fields, some of the people of Judah lived in Kiriath-arba and its villages, and in Dibon and its villages, and in Jekabzeel and its villages, 26 and in Jeshua and in Moladah and Beth-pelet, 27 in Hazar-shual, in Beer-sheba and its villages, 28 in Ziklag, in Meconah and its villages, 29 in En-rimmon, in Zorah, in Jarmuth, 30 Zanoah, Adullam, and their villages, Lachish and its fields, and Azekah and its villages. So they camped from Beer-sheba to the valley of Hinnom. 31 The people of Benjamin also lived from Geba onward, at Michmash, Aija, Bethel and its villages, 32 Anathoth, Nob, Ananiah, 33 Hazor, Ramah, Gittaim, 34 Hadid, Zeboim, Neballat, 35 Lod, and Ono, the valley of artisans. 36 And certain divisions of the Levites in Judah were joined to Benjamin.

D. *The genealogies of the priests and Levites*

12 These are the priests and the Levites who came up with Zerubbabel son of Shealtiel, and Jeshua: Seraiah, Jeremiah, Ezra, 2 Amariah, Malluch, Hattush, 3 Shecaniah, Rehum, Meremoth, 4 Iddo, Ginnethoi, Abijah, 5 Mijamin, Maadiah, Bilgah, 6 Shemaiah, Joiarib, Jedaiah, 7 Sallu, Amok, Hilkiah, Jedaiah. These were the leaders of the priests and of their associates in the days of Jeshua.

8 And the Levites: Jeshua, Binnui, Kadmiel, Sherebiah, Judah, and Mattaniah, who with his associates was in charge of the songs of thanksgiving. 9 And Bakbukiah and Unno their associates stood opposite them in the service. 10 Jeshua was the father of Joiakim, Joiakim the father of Eliashib, Eliashib the father of Joiada, 11 Joiada the father of Jonathan, and Jonathan the father of Jaddua.

12 In the days of Joiakim the priests, heads of ancestral houses, were: of Seraiah, Meraiah; of Jeremiah, Hananiah; 13 of Ezra, Meshullam; of Amariah, Jehohanan; 14 of Malluchi, Jonathan; of Shebaniah, Joseph; 15 of Harim, Adna; of Meraioth, Helkai; 16 of Iddo, Zechariah; of Ginnethon, Meshullam; 17 of Abijah, Zichri; of Miniamin, of Moadiah, Piltai; 18 of Bilgah, Shammua; of Shemaiah, Jehonathan; 19 of Joiarib, Mattenai; of Jedaiah, Uzzi; 20 of Sallai, Kallai; of Amok, Eber; 21 of Hilkiah, Hashabiah; of Jedaiah, Nethanel.

22 As for the Levites, in the days of Eliashib, Joiada, Johanan, and Jaddua, there were recorded the heads of ancestral houses; also the priests until the reign of Darius the Persian. 23 The Levites, heads of ancestral houses, were recorded in the Book of the Annals until the days of Johanan son of Eliashib. 24 And the leaders of the Levites: Hashabiah, Sherebiah, and Jeshua son of Kadmiel, with their associates over against them, to praise and to give thanks, according to the commandment of David the man of God, section opposite to section. 25 Mattaniah, Bakbukiah, Oba-

11.25
Josh 14.15;
13.9, 17

12.1
Ezra 2.1, 2;
see
Neh 10.2-8

12.7
Ezra 3.2

12.8
Neh 11.17

12.23
1 Chr 9.14ff

12.24
Neh 11.17

12.25
1 Chr 26.15

11.25–36 The Judeans and Benjaminites living in villages outside Jerusalem are enumerated. *with their fields* probably refers to the lands outside the villages used for a variety of agricultural purposes.
12.1ff The names of priests and Levites are listed. The purpose for this is not stated here.
12.10,11 This gives a list of the succession of high priests during the Persian monarchy from Jeshua to Jaddua, the high priest at the time Alexander the Great came to Jerusalem. *Jonathan* is probably a scribal error for *Johanan* (12.22,23).
12.16 *Zechariah*. Iddo, his grandfather (v. 4), had come back from the captivity with Zerubbabel and Jeshua. Zechariah the priest was the author of the

book of Zechariah, which contains more prophecies about the Messiah than any other O.T. book except Psalms and Isaiah. Berechiah, the father of Zechariah, probably died young so that his son became the immediate successor to Iddo.
12.22 *Eliashib* was the grandson of Jeshua, the first high priest for the returned exiles. He allied himself with Tobiah, who had joined company with Sanballat and the others who opposed the work of Nehemiah. Tobiah and his son both married Jewish women. Basically Eliashib was unfaithful to his calling, for he supplied Tobiah with a guest room in the temple compound (see note on 13.4–9). *Jaddua* was a high priest during the reign of Darius the Persian.

diah, Meshullam, Talmon, and Akkub were gatekeepers standing guard at the storehouses of the gates. 26 These were in the days of Joiakim son of Jeshua son of Jozadak, and in the days of the governor Nehemiah and of the priest Ezra, the scribe.

E. Dedication of the city walls

27   Now at the dedication of the wall of Jerusalem they sought out the Levites in all their places, to bring them to Jerusalem to celebrate the dedication with rejoicing, with thanksgivings and with singing, with cymbals, harps, and lyres. 28 The companies of the singers gathered together from the circuit around Jerusalem and from the villages of the Netophathites; 29 also from Beth-gilgal and from the region of Geba and Azmaveth; for the singers had built for themselves villages around Jerusalem. 30 And the priests and the Levites purified themselves; and they purified the people and the gates and the wall.

31   Then I brought the leaders of Judah up onto the wall, and appointed two great companies that gave thanks and went in procession. One went to the right on the wall to the Dung Gate; 32 and after them went Hoshaiah and half the officials of Judah, 33 and Azariah, Ezra, Meshullam, 34 Judah, Benjamin, Shemaiah, and Jeremiah, 35 and some of the young priests with trumpets: Zechariah son of Jonathan son of Shemaiah son of Mattaniah son of Micaiah son of Zaccur son of Asaph; 36 and his kindred, Shemaiah, Azarel, Milalai, Gilalai, Maai, Nethanel, Judah, and Hanani, with the musical instruments of David the man of God; and the scribe Ezra went in front of them. 37 At the Fountain Gate, in front of them, they went straight up by the stairs of the city of David, at the ascent of the wall, above the house of David, to the Water Gate on the east.

38   The other company of those who gave thanks went to the left,^{y} and I followed them with half of the people on the wall, above the Tower of the Ovens, to the Broad Wall, 39 and above the Gate of Ephraim, and by the Old Gate, and by the Fish Gate and the Tower of Hananel and the Tower of the Hundred, to the Sheep Gate; and they came to a halt at the Gate of the Guard. 40 So both companies of those who gave thanks stood in the house of God, and I and half of the officials with me; 41 and the priests Eliakim, Maaseiah, Miniamin, Micaiah, Elioenai, Zechariah, and Hananiah, with trumpets; 42 and Maaseiah, Shemaiah, Eleazar, Uzzi, Jehohanan, Malchijah, Elam, and Ezer. And the singers sang with Jezrahiah as their leader. 43 They offered great sacrifices that day and rejoiced, for God had made them rejoice with great joy; the women and children also rejoiced. The joy of Jerusalem was heard far away.

F. The appointment of collectors, singers, and gatekeepers

44   On that day men were appointed over the chambers for the stores, the contributions, the first fruits, and the tithes, to gather into them the portions required by the law for the priests and for the Levites from the fields belonging to the towns; for Judah rejoiced over the priests and the Levites who ministered. 45 They performed the service of their God and the service of purification, as did the singers and the gatekeepers, according to the command of David and his son Solomon. 46 For in the days of

^{y} Cn: Heb *opposite*

12.26
Neh 8.9;
Ezra 7.6, 11

12.27
1 Chr 25.6

12.28
1 Chr 9.16

12.30
Neh 13.22, 30

12.31
v. 38;
Neh 2.13;
3.13

12.35
Num 10.2, 8

12.36
1 Chr 23.5

12.37
Neh 2.14;
3.15; 3.26

12.38
v. 31;
Neh 3.11; 3.8

12.39
Neh 8.16;
3.6; 3.3; 3.1;
3.25

12.44
Neh 13.5, 12, 13

12.45
1 Chr 25.1;
26.1

12.46
2 Chr 29.30

12.27 *the dedication of the wall.* The construction had been accomplished with fear and trembling. It was now time to dedicate it with a sense of joy and triumph. Probably the dedication included the entire city, which was now safely enclosed. It was God's city, possessed by him and holy unto the Lord. By this act the city was placed under divine protection. Every person and thing was purified (v. 30).
12.31 Two companies walked on the top of the walls

of the city, one group led by Ezra the priest and the other by Nehemiah the governor. They went in opposite directions and met at the place where the temple stood. Other people walked on the ground inside and outside the city walls. All joined together at the temple to rejoice and to voice their thanksgiving to God. Songs of praise, the music from instruments, and the shouts of the crowd filled the air. Sacrifices were offered as a climax to the celebration.

David and Asaph long ago there was a leader of the singers, and there were songs of praise and thanksgiving to God. ⁴⁷ In the days of Zerubbabel and in the days of Nehemiah all Israel gave the daily portions for the singers and the gatekeepers. They set apart that which was for the Levites; and the Levites set apart that which was for the descendants of Aaron.

G. Nehemiah's final reforms

1. The people separated

13 On that day they read from the book of Moses in the hearing of the people; and in it was found written that no Ammonite or Moabite should ever enter the assembly of God, ² because they did not meet the Israelites with bread and water, but hired Balaam against them to curse them — yet our God turned the curse into a blessing. ³ When the people heard the law, they separated from Israel all those of foreign descent.

2. Tobiah's furniture cast out of the temple

⁴ Now before this, the priest Eliashib, who was appointed over the chambers of the house of our God, and who was related to Tobiah, ⁵ prepared for Tobiah a large room where they had previously put the grain offering, the frankincense, the vessels, and the tithes of grain, wine, and oil, which were given by commandment to the Levites, singers, and gatekeepers, and the contributions for the priests. ⁶ While this was taking place I was not in Jerusalem, for in the thirty-second year of King Artaxerxes of Babylon I went to the king. After some time I asked leave of the king ⁷ and returned to Jerusalem. I then discovered the wrong that Eliashib had done on behalf of Tobiah, preparing a room for him in the courts of the house of God. ⁸ And I was very angry, and I threw all the household furniture of Tobiah out of the room. ⁹ Then I gave orders and they cleansed the chambers, and I brought back the vessels of the house of God, with the grain offering and the frankincense.

3. The support of the priesthood begun

¹⁰ I also found out that the portions of the Levites had not been given to them; so that the Levites and the singers, who had conducted the service, had gone back to their fields. ¹¹ So I remonstrated with the officials and said, "Why is the house of God forsaken?" And I gathered them together and set them in their stations. ¹² Then all Judah brought the tithe of the grain, wine, and oil into the storehouses. ¹³ And I appointed as treasurers over the storehouses the priest Shelemiah, the scribe Zadok, and Pedaiah of the Levites, and as their assistant Hanan son of Zaccur son of Mattaniah, for they were considered faithful; and their duty was to distribute to their associates. ¹⁴ Remember me, O my God, concerning this, and do not wipe out my good deeds that I have done for the house of my God and for his service.

Cross-references (margin)

12.47 Neh 11.23; Num 18.21
13.1 Neh 9.3; Deut 23.3-5
13.2 Num 22.3-11; 23.11
13.3 Neh 9.2; Ex 12.38
13.4 Neh 12.44; 2.10; 6.1, 17, 18
13.5 Num 18.21
13.6 Neh 5.14; Ezra 6.22
13.7 v. 5
13.9 2 Chr 29.5, 15, 16
13.10 Neh 10.37; 12.28, 29
13.11 vv. 17, 25; Neh 10.39
13.12 Neh 10.37-39; 12.44
13.13 Neh 12.44; 7.2
13.14 vv. 22, 31; Neh 5.19

13.1 They were reading Deut 23.3–5.
13.2 *hired Balaam . . . to curse them.* See Num 22.6.
13.3 Those of foreign descent comprised those of Samaritan blood, who were not counted as Jews. A separation of the non-Jews from the Jews was effected in obedience to the command of God in the Torah. This action by no means solved the problem permanently (see v. 23).
13.4–9 When Nehemiah returned to the court of King Artaxerxes for a short time, the high priest Eliashib defiled the temple by providing Tobiah (an Ammonite) a room in the temple compound. Upon his return Nehemiah saw what had been done; he acted promptly and vigorously, ejecting Tobiah and his furniture. Nehemiah had the room Tobiah occupied sprinkled with the water of purification in order to reclaim its sanctity.
13.10 Nehemiah also discovered that the Levites had been wronged, for their portions (i.e., salaries) had not been paid to them. Apparently their portions had been collected but not paid out. Nehemiah corrected this evil and appointed four reliable treasurers to oversee the payments.
13.14 See note on 5.19.

4. Sabbath reforms instituted

13.15
Ex 20.8, 10;
Neh 10.31

15 In those days I saw in Judah people treading wine presses on the sabbath, and bringing in heaps of grain and loading them on donkeys; and also wine, grapes, figs, and all kinds of burdens, which they brought into Jerusalem on the sabbath day; and I warned them at that time against selling food. 16 Tyrians also, who lived in the city, brought in fish and all kinds of merchandise and sold them on the sabbath to the people of Judah, and in Jerusalem. 17 Then I remonstrated with the nobles of Judah and said to them, "What is this evil thing that you are doing, profaning the sabbath day? 18 Did not your ancestors act in this way, and did not our God bring all this disaster on us and on this city? Yet you bring more wrath on Israel by profaning the sabbath."

13.17
vv. 11, 25
13.18
Jer 17.21-23

13.19
Lev 23.32;
Jer 17.21

19 When it began to be dark at the gates of Jerusalem before the sabbath, I commanded that the doors should be shut and gave orders that they should not be opened until after the sabbath. And I set some of my servants over the gates, to prevent any burden from being brought in on the sabbath day. 20 Then the merchants and sellers of all kinds of merchandise spent the night outside Jerusalem once or twice. 21 But I warned them and said to them, "Why do you spend the night in front of the wall? If you do so again, I will lay hands on you." From that time on they did not come on the sabbath. 22 And I commanded the Levites that they should purify themselves and come and guard the gates, to keep the sabbath day holy. Remember this also in my favor, O my God, and spare me according to the greatness of your steadfast love.

13.21
v. 15

13.22
Neh 12.30;
vv. 14, 31

5. Marriage reforms

13.23
Ezra 9.2

23 In those days also I saw Jews who had married women of Ashdod, Ammon, and Moab; 24 and half of their children spoke the language of Ashdod, and they could not speak the language of Judah, but spoke the language of various peoples. 25 And I contended with them and cursed them and beat some of them and pulled out their hair; and I made them take an oath in the name of God, saying, "You shall not give your daughters to their sons, or take their daughters for your sons or for yourselves. 26 Did not King Solomon of Israel sin on account of such women? Among the many nations there was no king like him, and he was beloved by his God, and God made him king over all Israel; nevertheless, foreign women made even him to sin. 27 Shall we then listen to you and do all this great evil and act treacherously against our God by marrying foreign women?"

13.25
vv. 11, 17;
Deut 25.2;
Ezra 10.29,
30

13.26
1 Kings 11.1;
3.13;
2 Chr 1.12;
1 Kings 11.4ff
13.27
v. 23;
Ezra 10.2

28 And one of the sons of Jehoiada, son of the high priest Eliashib, was the son-in-law of Sanballat the Horonite; I chased him away from me.

13.28
Neh 12.10;
2.10, 19

13.15 Three of the major and recurring sins of Israel were: (1) breaking the sabbath (Num 15.32–36; Neh 13.17,18; Isa 58.13,14; Ezek 20.13; 22.8); (2) contracting marriage with the heathen (Deut 7.3,4; 1 Kings 11.1,2; 13.23–25); (3) worshiping idols (1 Kings 21.26; 2 Kings 17.12; Ezek 6.1–5; Zech 13.2). These national sins could not be overlooked. They had to be dealt with if Israel was to carry out its mission.

13.19 Until this point, the gates of the city had been open on the sabbath. Because the sabbath was being desecrated, more severe action was required: the gates were to be shut from sundown Friday to sundown Saturday. Yet this did not keep faithless Jews and non-Jews from hawking their wares outside the walls of the city on the sabbath. Nehemiah threatened to lay hands on any who acted this way on the sabbath. The principles of this passage apply equally to the Christian sabbath (Sunday).

13.24 Language is a unifying force among people. When God confused the tongues of the people at Babel, his purpose was to disunify them. Here some Jews had married pagan women, who were teaching their children their own languages instead of Hebrew and thus preventing them from understanding the word of God. The ultimate solution to this problem was simply not to marry heathen women.

13.25 Nehemiah did not hesitate to use force against those who had intermarried with the heathen. He cursed them, pulled out their hair, beat them, and made them swear not to allow sons or daughters to engage in mixed marriages. Strong medicine was required to stop the contagious disease.

13.28 A grandson of the high priest had married a daughter of Sanballat, the well-known enemy of the Jews. When this young priest would not put away his wife, Nehemiah expelled him from the priesthood.

29 Remember them, O my God, because they have defiled the priesthood, the covenant of the priests and the Levites.

6. *Conclusion*

30 Thus I cleansed them from everything foreign, and I established the duties of the priests and Levites, each in his work; 31 and I provided for the wood offering, at appointed times, and for the first fruits. Remember me, O my God, for good.

13.29
Neh 6.14;
Num 25.13

13.30
Neh 10.30
13.31
Neh 10.34;
vv. 14, 22

ESTHER

Authorship, Date, and Background: Who authored the book of Esther is unknown. Tradition has accorded this role to Mordecai, Ezra, or Nehemiah. The latter two are hardly credible possibilities when any survey of the books attributed to them is compared with Esther. The name Esther is derived from a Persian word meaning "star"; her Hebrew name, Hadassah, means "myrtle." In the Hebrew Bible, the book itself is the last of the five books of the Megilloth ("Five Scrolls"), which include Ruth, Song of Solomon, Ecclesiastes, and Lamentations. Esther is thought to be the greatest of them all. The shortness of each of these five books made their public reading possible at Purim (Esther), Pentecost (Ruth), festival of booths (Ecclesiastes), the Passover (Song of Solomon), and on the ninth of Ab (Lamentations).

The writer of this book knew a great deal about Persian life and customs. The setting was the king's palace in Susa, the Persian capital. The incident occurred during the reign of Xerxes (the Greek rendering of his name) or Ahasuerus as recorded in Esther; he died in 465 B.C., so scholars have dated the composition of the book somewhere in the latter half of the fifth century. This means that the Jews involved in the incident were the ones who had not returned to Jerusalem with the first group. They had either lost their attachment to the faith of their fathers, or had been so successful that they preferred remaining in their new environment.

Mordecai, Esther's guardian, was her cousin, and he adopted her. Nothing is known about his own spiritual commitment. He was a strong nationalist and a brave man, one who kept his Jewish identity hidden for what seem to be opportunistic reasons.

Characteristics and Content: Nowhere in the book of Esther does the author mention the name of God, though fasting, which always included prayer, is part of the story. In any event, the hand of a sovereign God at work in the lives of his people is everywhere evident. The book speaks of the feast of Purim (the word Purim comes from the Assyrian term *puru,* meaning "lot"), which was instituted as a reminder of God's great deliverance of his people. Ahasuerus' wife, Vashti, refused to make a public appearance before the males of the kingdom at a drunken revelry. She was demoted from her queenship and a successor was sought for her; Esther was chosen. Later Haman, in anger over the refusal of Mordecai to bow before him, plotted the massacre of all the Jews; the king assented to his plan.

When Mordecai learned of the plot, he sought the help of Esther, asking her to intercede with the king. She willingly risked her life by entering the king's presence without being summoned. She arranged a first and second banquet with the king, herself, and Haman. Between the first and second banquet, Haman prepared the gallows on which to hang Mordecai.

As the story reaches its climax, Haman gained the king's unchanging commitment to execute all Jews. But when Haman heard his plot disclosed to Ahasuerus by Esther, he pleaded with her after the king had left the room. When the king returned, he found Haman on the couch of his queen and interpreted it as an assault upon his wife. He ordered Haman to be hung on the gallows prepared for Mordecai. Mordecai took over the vacant position of Haman. Orders were given for the Jews to defend themselves when the day of reckoning came, since the king's edict could not be annulled. The Jews successfully defended themselves. Mordecai ended up as the prime minister next to King Ahasuerus, "powerful among the Jews and popular with his many kindred, for he sought the good of his people and interceded for the welfare of all his decendants" (10.3).

Outline:

   I. Intrigues in the court at Susa (1.1—2.23)

  II. The struggle between the houses of Mordecai and Haman (3.1—9.19)

 III. The festival of Purim: observance and regulations (9.20—10.3)

ESTHER

I. Intrigues in the court at Susa (1.1–2.23)

A. The riches and splendor of Ahasuerus

1.1
Ezra 4.6;
Dan 9.1;
Esth 8.9;
9.30
1.2
Neh 1.1
1.3
Esth 2.18

1 This happened in the days of Ahasuerus, the same Ahasuerus who ruled over one hundred twenty-seven provinces from India to Ethiopia.ᶻ 2 In those days when King Ahasuerus sat on his royal throne in the citadel of Susa, 3 in the third year of his reign, he gave a banquet for all his officials and ministers. The army of Persia and Media and the nobles and governors of the provinces were present, 4 while he displayed the great wealth of his kingdom and the splendor and pomp of his majesty for many days, one hundred eighty days in all.

1.5
Esth 7.7, 8
1.6
Ezek 23.41;
Am 6.4
1.7
Esth 2.18

5 When these days were completed, the king gave for all the people present in the citadel of Susa, both great and small, a banquet lasting for seven days, in the court of the garden of the king's palace. 6 There were white cotton curtains and blue hangings tied with cords of fine linen and purple to silver ringsᵃ and marble pillars. There were couches of gold and silver on a mosaic pavement of porphyry, marble, mother-of-pearl, and colored stones. 7 Drinks were served in golden goblets, goblets of different kinds, and the royal wine was lavished according to the bounty of the king. 8 Drinking was by flagons, without restraint; for the king had given orders to all the officials of his palace to do as each one desired. 9 Furthermore, Queen Vashti gave a banquet for the women in the palace of King Ahasuerus.

B. The removal of Queen Vashti

1. Vashti's refusal

1.10
Judg 16.25;
Esth 7.9

10 On the seventh day, when the king was merry with wine, he commanded Mehuman, Biztha, Harbona, Bigtha and Abagtha, Zethar and Carkas, the seven eunuchs who attended him, 11 to bring Queen Vashti before the king, wearing the royal crown, in order to show the peoples and the officials her beauty; for she was fair to behold. 12 But

---

ᶻ Or *Nubia*; Heb *Cush*   ᵃ Or *rods*

1.1 *Ahasuerus,* another name for Xerxes (486–465 B.C.).

1.2 *Susa* was the capital of Xerxes' empire, located in Iran near the Persian Gulf. In later history it became one of Alexander's prized acquisitions. It was here that a mass marriage of royal Persian women and Greek army officers was performed. The site has been excavated by French archaeologists since the middle of the nineteenth century.

1.4 Ahasuerus had but one purpose in arranging the feast. He wanted to show the wealth of his holdings and the honor of his majesty. He arranged two feasts: one for the nobility, lasting six months, and the other for the common people "great and small," lasting a week. It was at this latter feast that the incident occurred that ultimately brought Esther to the royal throne, as wife of the monarch.

1.10ff At the end of the seventh day of the second feast, the king and his guests were drunk. He summoned his queen to appear before this multitude of drunken males whose wives were not present — for women were sequestered from appearing in public. He wanted to parade her beauty, and this could not be done unless she was unveiled. Had the king been sober he would never have done this, nor would he have endorsed such conduct by anyone else. This placed Vashti in a dilemma. She either had to lose her honor or disobey her husband. She refused repeatedly and raised the intense anger of the king, whose authority was at stake. Thus Ahasuerus summoned his royal advisors and asked the question, "What is to be done to Queen Vashti because she has not performed the command of King Ahasuerus?" (v. 15).

Queen Vashti refused to come at the king's command conveyed by the eunuchs. At this the king was enraged, and his anger burned within him.

2. Vashti's removal

13 Then the king consulted the sages who knew the laws[b] (for this was the king's procedure toward all who were versed in law and custom, [14]and those next to him were Carshena, Shethar, Admatha, Tarshish, Meres, Marsena, and Memucan, the seven officials of Persia and Media, who had access to the king, and sat first in the kingdom): [15]"According to the law, what is to be done to Queen Vashti because she has not performed the command of King Ahasuerus conveyed by the eunuchs?" [16]Then Memucan said in the presence of the king and the officials, "Not only has Queen Vashti done wrong to the king, but also to all the officials and all the peoples who are in all the provinces of King Ahasuerus. [17]For this deed of the queen will be made known to all women, causing them to look with contempt on their husbands, since they will say, 'King Ahasuerus commanded Queen Vashti to be brought before him, and she did not come.' [18]This very day the noble ladies of Persia and Media who have heard of the queen's behavior will rebel against[c] the king's officials, and there will be no end of contempt and wrath! [19]If it pleases the king, let a royal order go out from him, and let it be written among the laws of the Persians and the Medes so that it may not be altered, that Vashti is never again to come before King Ahasuerus; and let the king give her royal position to another who is better than she. [20]So when the decree made by the king is proclaimed throughout all his kingdom, vast as it is, all women will give honor to their husbands, high and low alike."

21 This advice pleased the king and the officials, and the king did as Memucan proposed; [22]he sent letters to all the royal provinces, to every province in its own script and to every people in its own language, declaring that every man should be master in his own house.[d]

C. Esther made queen

1. The search for a queen

2 After these things, when the anger of King Ahasuerus had abated, he remembered Vashti and what she had done and what had been decreed against her. [2]Then the king's servants who attended him said, "Let beautiful young virgins be sought out for the king. [3]And let the king appoint commissioners in all the provinces of his kingdom to gather all the beautiful young virgins to the harem in the citadel of Susa under custody of Hegai, the king's eunuch, who is in charge of the women; let their cosmetic treatments be given them. [4]And let the girl who pleases the king be queen instead of Vashti." This pleased the king, and he did so.

2. Esther's background

5 Now there was a Jew in the citadel of Susa whose name was Mordecai son of Jair son of Shimei son of Kish, a Benjaminite. [6]Kish[e] had been carried away from Jerusalem among the captives carried away with King

b Cn: Heb times   c Cn: Heb will tell   d Heb adds and speak according to the language of his people
e Heb a Benjaminite 6who

Cross references (margin)
1.13 Jer 10.7; Dan 2.12; 1 Chr 12.32
1.14 2 Kings 25.19
1.17 Eph 5.33
1.19 Esth 8.8; Dan 6.8
1.20 Eph 5.22; Col 3.18
1.22 Esth 8.9; Eph 5.22-24; 1 Tim 2.12
2.1 Esth 7.10; 1.19, 20
2.3 vv. 8, 15
2.5 Esth 3.2
2.6 2 Kings 24.14, 15; 24.6

1.16 In a segregated society where the females were decidedly unequal, one could expect what happened. Her act was turned into a national crisis involving male supremacy. Vashti was removed from her position as queen. Nothing is said as to what ultimately was done to her except that she was never to appear before the king again.
1.19 *it may not be altered*, a notion of immutability

expressed in 8.8 and in Dan 6.8.
2.2 The removal of Vashti required the appointment of a new queen. The servants of the king initiated a search for the most beautiful women from among whom the king would choose another queen. Esther was to be one of those chosen for consideration.
2.5 See note on Ezra 2.2.

Jeconiah of Judah, whom King Nebuchadnezzar of Babylon had carried away. 7 Mordecai[f] had brought up Hadassah, that is Esther, his cousin, for she had neither father nor mother; the girl was fair and beautiful, and when her father and her mother died, Mordecai adopted her as his own daughter. 8 So when the king's order and his edict were proclaimed, and when many young women were gathered in the citadel of Susa in custody of Hegai, Esther also was taken into the king's palace and put in custody of Hegai, who had charge of the women. 9 The girl pleased him and won his favor, and he quickly provided her with her cosmetic treatments and her portion of food, and with seven chosen maids from the king's palace, and advanced her and her maids to the best place in the harem. 10 Esther did not reveal her people or kindred, for Mordecai had charged her not to tell. 11 Every day Mordecai would walk around in front of the court of the harem, to learn how Esther was and how she fared.

2.7
v. 15

2.8
vv. 3, 15

2.9
vv. 3, 12

2.10
v. 20

3. *Ahasuerus chooses Esther*

12 The turn came for each girl to go in to King Ahasuerus, after being twelve months under the regulations for the women, since this was the regular period of their cosmetic treatment, six months with oil of myrrh and six months with perfumes and cosmetics for women. 13 When the girl went in to the king she was given whatever she asked for to take with her from the harem to the king's palace. 14 In the evening she went in; then in the morning she came back to the second harem in custody of Shaash-gaz, the king's eunuch, who was in charge of the concubines; she did not go in to the king again, unless the king delighted in her and she was summoned by name.

2.15
v. 6;
Esth 9.29

15 When the turn came for Esther daughter of Abihail the uncle of Mordecai, who had adopted her as his own daughter, to go in to the king, she asked for nothing except what Hegai the king's eunuch, who had charge of the women, advised. Now Esther was admired by all who saw her. 16 When Esther was taken to King Ahasuerus in his royal palace in the tenth month, which is the month of Tebeth, in the seventh year of his reign, 17 the king loved Esther more than all the other women; of all the virgins she won his favor and devotion, so that he set the royal crown on her head and made her queen instead of Vashti. 18 Then the king gave a great banquet to all his officials and ministers—"Esther's banquet." He also granted a holiday[g] to the provinces, and gave gifts with royal liberality.

2.17
Esth 1.11

2.18
Esth 1.3; 1.7

D. *The plot to kill Ahasuerus and its failure*

19 When the virgins were being gathered together,[h] Mordecai was sitting at the king's gate. 20 Now Esther had not revealed her kindred or her people, as Mordecai had charged her; for Esther obeyed Mordecai just as when she was brought up by him. 21 In those days, while Mordecai was sitting at the king's gate, Bigthan and Teresh, two of the king's eunuchs,

2.20
v. 10

2.21
Esth 6.2

f Heb *He*   *g* Or *an amnesty*   *h* Heb adds *a second time*

2.7 *Hadassah*, i.e., "myrtle"; her Persian name was *Esther*, meaning "star" and identical to "Ishtar" (a Babylonian goddess). Mordecai had adopted her *as his own daughter.*
2.8 Esther was selected along with many other young women and secluded in the seraglio of the king until such time as he called for her. She won the favor of Hegai, who oversaw the women and who was a eunuch, and thus no threat to the women. Mordecai told Esther not to indicate that she was a Jewess; apparently Jews were not among the people favored by the monarch. Since she was an orphan, it was easier to conceal her nationality than if her parents had been alive and were known to those who had chosen her as a candidate.

2.15 After Esther had been purified and thus prepared for the bed of the king, she was called upon to attend him. The king married every woman he took to his bed; each one became a wife of a lower rank than the queen. This custom was also practiced by the kings of Israel and even by the patriarchs (e. g., Jacob, who was married to four women). Had the king never called for Esther again, she would have remained secluded for the remainder of her life. But "the king loved Esther more than all the other women" and chose her to become his queen. Her accession to the queenship was celebrated by a great banquet.

who guarded the threshold, became angry and conspired to assassinate[i] King Ahasuerus. 22 But the matter came to the knowledge of Mordecai, and he told it to Queen Esther, and Esther told the king in the name of Mordecai. 23 When the affair was investigated and found to be so, both the men were hanged on the gallows. It was recorded in the book of the annals in the presence of the king.

2.22
Esth 6.1, 2

2.23
Esth 10.2

II. The struggle between the houses of Mordecai and Haman (3.1–9.19)

A. The promotion of Haman: the refusal of Mordecai to bow

3 After these things King Ahasuerus promoted Haman son of Hamme-datha the Agagite, and advanced him and set his seat above all the officials who were with him. 2 And all the king's servants who were at the king's gate bowed down and did obeisance to Haman; for the king had so commanded concerning him. But Mordecai did not bow down or do obeisance. 3 Then the king's servants who were at the king's gate said to Mordecai, "Why do you disobey the king's command?" 4 When they spoke to him day after day and he would not listen to them, they told Haman, in order to see whether Mordecai's words would avail; for he had told them that he was a Jew. 5 When Haman saw that Mordecai did not bow down or do obeisance to him, Haman was infuriated. 6 But he thought it beneath him to lay hands on Mordecai alone. So, having been told who Mordecai's people were, Haman plotted to destroy all the Jews, the people of Mordecai, throughout the whole kingdom of Ahasuerus.

3.1
Esth 5.11;
v. 10
3.2
Esth 2.19;
v. 5

3.3
v. 2

3.5
v. 2;
Esth 5.9
3.6
Ps 83.4

B. Haman's plot against the Jews

7 In the first month, which is the month of Nisan, in the twelfth year of King Ahasuerus, they cast Pur — which means "the lot" — before Ha-man for the day and for the month, and the lot fell on the thirteenth day[j] of the twelfth month, which is the month of Adar. 8 Then Haman said to King Ahasuerus, "There is a certain people scattered and separated among the peoples in all the provinces of your kingdom; their laws are different from those of every other people, and they do not keep the king's laws, so that it is not appropriate for the king to tolerate them. 9 If it pleases the king, let a decree be issued for their destruction, and I will pay ten thousand talents of silver into the hands of those who have charge of

3.7
Esth 9.24;
Ezra 6.15

3.8
Ezra 4.12-15;
Acts 16.20

i Heb *to lay hands on*   *j* Cn Compare Gk and verse 13 below: Heb *the twelfth month*

2.23 *hanged on the gallows,* possibly meaning that they were crucified. *recorded in the book of the annals,* i.e., court records of daily happenings. It was providential that Mordecai's action went into the book, for later it would prove to be most important to the story.
3.1 *Haman* is said to be a descendant of the line of Agag. There are two possible explanations of this ancestry. King Agag of the Amalekites is mentioned in 1 Sam 15 as the last of a tribe destroyed by King Saul (and Samuel). An ancient rabbinic tradition traces Haman to this Agag. If this is so, we see the continuing conflict between the descendants of Esau and Jacob, since Esau was an ancestor of Amalek. A more likely explanation for the use of the word Agag-ite is that a region of the Persian Empire was called Agag. Haman's father and all of Haman's sons had Persian names, which would probably not have been the case if the family had been related to Amalek.
3.2 Haman must have been a capable man to have been promoted to the position of prime minister of Persia. But he was also an ambitious and vainglorious

man, intolerant of anyone who refused to honor him.
3.4 God-fearing Jews, such as Daniel and his three friends, refused to bow down to other humans. When Haman asked why Mordecai would not bow down, he was told about this tradition of the Jews. Haman's anger did not stop with Mordecai, however. If one Jew would not bow before him, neither would any other Jew. Consequently, he determined to exterminate all Jews for this affront. Anti-Semitism is not a modern phenomenon.
3.7 *they cast Pur.* Having determined to do away with the Jews, Haman cast lots to discover what was the best time to do this evil deed. The lot fell on the twelfth month (February/March). This gave him plenty of time to work out the details of the pogrom.
3.8 The plot was simple. Haman accused the Jews of breaking the laws of the land. He offered the king a huge bribe for his royal consent, undoubtedly expecting to recover what it cost him by taking over the property of the dead Jews. He did not say who the people were, and the king did not inquire.

the king's business, so that they may put it into the king's treasuries." ¹⁰ So the king took his signet ring from his hand and gave it to Haman son of Hammedatha the Agagite, the enemy of the Jews. ¹¹ The king said to Haman, "The money is given to you, and the people as well, to do with them as it seems good to you."

12   Then the king's secretaries were summoned on the thirteenth day of the first month, and an edict, according to all that Haman commanded, was written to the king's satraps and to the governors over all the provinces and to the officials of all the peoples, to every province in its own script and every people in its own language; it was written in the name of King Ahasuerus and sealed with the king's ring. ¹³ Letters were sent by couriers to all the king's provinces, giving orders to destroy, to kill, and to annihilate all Jews, young and old, women and children, in one day, the thirteenth day of the twelfth month, which is the month of Adar, and to plunder their goods. ¹⁴ A copy of the document was to be issued as a decree in every province by proclamation, calling on all the peoples to be ready for that day. ¹⁵ The couriers went quickly by order of the king, and the decree was issued in the citadel of Susa. The king and Haman sat down to drink; but the city of Susa was thrown into confusion.

C. Mordecai appeals to Esther for help

4   When Mordecai learned all that had been done, Mordecai tore his clothes and put on sackcloth and ashes, and went through the city, wailing with a loud and bitter cry; ² he went up to the entrance of the king's gate, for no one might enter the king's gate clothed with sackcloth. ³ In every province, wherever the king's command and his decree came, there was great mourning among the Jews, with fasting and weeping and lamenting, and most of them lay in sackcloth and ashes.

4   When Esther's maids and her eunuchs came and told her, the queen was deeply distressed; she sent garments to clothe Mordecai, so that he might take off his sackcloth; but he would not accept them. ⁵ Then Esther called for Hathach, one of the king's eunuchs, who had been appointed to attend her, and ordered him to go to Mordecai to learn what was happening and why. ⁶ Hathach went out to Mordecai in the open square of the city in front of the king's gate, ⁷ and Mordecai told him all that had happened to him, and the exact sum of money that Haman had promised to pay into the king's treasuries for the destruction of the Jews. ⁸ Mordecai also gave him a copy of the written decree issued in Susa for their destruction, that he might show it to Esther, explain it to her, and charge her to go to the king to make supplication to him and entreat him for her people.

9   Hathach went and told Esther what Mordecai had said. ¹⁰ Then Esther spoke to Hathach and gave him a message for Mordecai, saying, ¹¹ "All the king's servants and the people of the king's provinces know that

Marginal cross-references (left column):

3.10 Esth 8.2; Gen 41.42; Esth 7.6

3.12 Esth 8.8-10; 1 Kings 21.8

3.13 Esth 8.10-14

3.14 Esth 8.13, 14

3.15 Esth 8.15

4.1ff Esth 3.8-10; Jon 3.5, 6; Ezek 27.30

4.3 Isa 58.5

4.7 Esth 3.9

4.8 Esth 3.14, 15

4.11 Esth 5.1; 6.4; Dan 2.9; Esth 5.2; 8.4

3.10 So great was the king's confidence in this prince of the realm that he readily assented to the scheme, even though Mordecai had done nothing to personally offend the king, and what one person did could hardly constitute sufficient reason to kill off all the others (unless it could be shown that they were in agreement with Mordecai). The king even gave his signet ring to Haman to have the decree sealed.
3.12 The orders went out to the farthest reaches of the empire: "Annihilate all Jews." By this time the king must have known that the edict was directed against the Jews, although he did not yet know that Esther was a Jewess.
4.1 *tore his clothes.* This was a traditional external sign of mourning. *sackcloth* was a garment made from goat and camel hair; it was coarse and dark-colored.

Sitting in sackcloth was another traditional sign of mourning among the Jews.
4.3 The name of God is not mentioned in the book of Esther nor is anything said about prayers to God; yet the sackcloth, fasting, and ashes told their own story. All of these things would have meant nothing and accomplished nothing without the providential care of God. Indeed the refusal of Mordecai to bow before Haman cannot be understood apart from his religious loyalty to the God of Judaism.
4.9 Esther must have told Hathach that Mordecai and the Jews were her people. She must have had confidence in him, for if he had spoken of this to the king, it would have become immediately apparent that Esther would have to die with the rest of the Jews, according to the law of the Medes and Persians.

if any man or woman goes to the king inside the inner court without being called, there is but one law — all alike are to be put to death. Only if the king holds out the golden scepter to someone, may that person live. I myself have not been called to come in to the king for thirty days." 12 When they told Mordecai what Esther had said, 13 Mordecai told them to reply to Esther, "Do not think that in the king's palace you will escape any more than all the other Jews. 14 For if you keep silence at such a time as this, relief and deliverance will rise for the Jews from another quarter, but you and your father's family will perish. Who knows? Perhaps you have come to royal dignity for just such a time as this." 15 Then Esther said in reply to Mordecai, 16 "Go, gather all the Jews to be found in Susa, and hold a fast on my behalf, and neither eat nor drink for three days, night or day. I and my maids will also fast as you do. After that I will go to the king, though it is against the law; and if I perish, I perish." 17 Mordecai then went away and did everything as Esther had ordered him.

D. Esther's intervention

1. Her appeal to Ahasuerus

5 On the third day Esther put on her royal robes and stood in the inner court of the king's palace, opposite the king's hall. The king was sitting on his royal throne inside the palace opposite the entrance to the palace. 2 As soon as the king saw Queen Esther standing in the court, she won his favor and he held out to her the golden scepter that was in his hand. Then Esther approached and touched the top of the scepter. 3 The king said to her, "What is it, Queen Esther? What is your request? It shall be given you, even to the half of my kingdom." 4 Then Esther said, "If it pleases the king, let the king and Haman come today to a banquet that I have prepared for the king." 5 Then the king said, "Bring Haman quickly, so that we may do as Esther desires." So the king and Haman came to the banquet that Esther had prepared. 6 While they were drinking wine, the king said to Esther, "What is your petition? It shall be granted you. And what is your request? Even to the half of my kingdom, it shall be fulfilled." 7 Then Esther said, "This is my petition and request: 8 If I have won the king's favor, and if it pleases the king to grant my petition and fulfill my request, let the king and Haman come tomorrow to the banquet that I will prepare for them, and then I will do as the king has said."

4.15
Esth 5.1

5.1
Esth 4.16;
4.11; 6.4

5.2
Prov 21.1;
Esth 4.11;
8.4

5.3
Esth 7.2;
Mk 6.23

5.5
Esth 6.14

5.6
Esth 7.2; v. 3

5.8
Esth 7.3; 8.5;
6.14

4.13 Mordecai clearly ordered Esther to appeal to the king against the plot of Haman to slaughter the Jews. If she did nothing she would die because she was a Jewess. If her entrance to the king's presence was denied and she suffered death, she would be no worse off than having done nothing. Her only hope was to appear before the king, come what may. In his instructions, Mordecai implied confidence that Esther's appearance would succeed; for if she refused to try, he firmly believed that deliverance would come some other way — that is, without specifically saying so, from the God of the Israelites. Mordecai believed that God had brought Esther into the kingdom for just such a time that the Jews now faced.

4.16 Fasting is a sign of confidence in the delivering power of God. It connotes a sense of need and a desire for a right relationship with God, and it constitutes an unspoken but nevertheless genuine prayer for help. Without those elements, fasting has no spiritual value.

4.17 Roles were now reversed. Mordecai had given orders to Esther. Now she gave orders to him, and he obeyed them. She would approach the king and trust

God for the outcome, but only if earnest prayer were made on her behalf. All of us ought never to hesitate to ask other believers to pray for us in a time of crisis.

5.2 No one came into the king's presence without his permission. Esther dared to violate a perceived tradition. The king held out the royal scepter to show that she might come before him. She touched the tip of the scepter; this signified that she was coming before him as a humble petitioner who sought his favor. God granted her favor with the king and preserved her in her daring. But because her actions had been preceded by prayer and fasting, she had the assurance that she was in the will of God.

5.3 The heart of the king was in the hands of God. Vashti had refused to come when sent for and lost her queenship; Esther came when she was not sent for, and God moved the king's heart to grant her request.

5.8 We can assume that Esther sensed that a second banquet would be more advantageous for her cause, and that the delay would increase the chance for success. Since Haman was the king's favorite, she wanted to present her case under the best circumstances.

2. *Haman's plan against Mordecai*

9 Haman went out that day happy and in good spirits. But when Haman saw Mordecai in the king's gate, and observed that he neither rose nor trembled before him, he was infuriated with Mordecai; 10 nevertheless Haman restrained himself and went home. Then he sent and called for his friends and his wife Zeresh, 11 and Haman recounted to them the splendor of his riches, the number of his sons, all the promotions with which the king had honored him, and how he had advanced him above the officials and the ministers of the king. 12 Haman added, "Even Queen Esther let no one but myself come with the king to the banquet that she prepared. Tomorrow also I am invited by her, together with the king. 13 Yet all this does me no good so long as I see the Jew Mordecai sitting at the king's gate." 14 Then his wife Zeresh and all his friends said to him, "Let a gallows fifty cubits high be made, and in the morning tell the king to have Mordecai hanged on it; then go with the king to the banquet in good spirits." This advice pleased Haman, and he had the gallows made.

E. *The deliverance of the Jews*

1. *Haman's plot and its failure*

6 On that night the king could not sleep, and he gave orders to bring the book of records, the annals, and they were read to the king. 2 It was found written how Mordecai had told about Bigthana and Teresh, two of the king's eunuchs, who guarded the threshold, and who had conspired to assassinate[k] King Ahasuerus. 3 Then the king said, "What honor or distinction has been bestowed on Mordecai for this?" The king's servants who attended him said, "Nothing has been done for him." 4 The king said, "Who is in the court?" Now Haman had just entered the outer court of the king's palace to speak to the king about having Mordecai hanged on the gallows that he had prepared for him. 5 So the king's servants told him, "Haman is there, standing in the court." The king said, "Let him come in." 6 So Haman came in, and the king said to him, "What shall be done for the man whom the king wishes to honor?" Haman said to himself, "Whom would the king wish to honor more than me?" 7 So Haman said to the king, "For the man whom the king wishes to honor, 8 let royal robes be brought, which the king has worn, and a horse that the king has ridden, with a royal crown on its head. 9 Let the robes and the horse be handed over to one of the king's most noble officials; let him[l] robe the man whom the king wishes to honor, and let him[l] conduct the man on horseback through the open square of the city, proclaiming before him: 'Thus shall it be done for the man whom the king wishes to honor.'" 10 Then the king said to Haman, "Quickly, take the robes and the horse, as you have said, and do so to the Jew Mordecai who sits at the king's gate. Leave out nothing that you have mentioned." 11 So Haman took the robes and the horse and robed Mordecai and led him riding through the open square of

Marginal references:

5.9 Esth 2.19; 3.5
5.10 Esth 6.13
5.11 Esth 9.7-10; 3.1
5.12 v. 8
5.13 v. 9
5.14 Esth 6.4; 7.9, 10
6.1 Dan 6.18; Esth 2.23; 10.2
6.2 Esth 2.21, 22
6.4 Esth 4.11; 5.1; 5.14
6.6 vv. 7, 9, 11
6.8 1 Kings 1.33
6.9 Gen 41.43

---

[k] Heb *to lay hands on*   [l] Heb *them*

5.9 Haman rejoiced in his good fortune, boasted of his greatness, and was more angered than ever by stubborn Mordecai's refusal to bow before him. He assumed that the private banquet would be the summit of his career.

5.14 On the advice of family and friends, Haman moved to construct the gallows on which to hang Mordecai before going to the banquet with the king and Esther. God's providence caused the hanging to be delayed by the events recorded in ch. 6.

6.1ff God works his providences in mysterious and unfathomable ways. There is no other explanation as to why the king should spend a sleepless night and ask for the very document that would call to his mind the

fact that Mordecai had saved him from assassination. The unspiritual mind would call this luck or accident, but there are no accidents in God's economy. This was part of the will and plan of God.

6.4 God, the great disposer, caused Haman to visit the king's court at the precise moment the monarch wanted advice on how to honor Haman's worst enemy, Mordecai. Ironically Haman supposed the king wished to honor him and so he selected the highest award he could think of.

6.10 Who can imagine the consternation and surprise of Haman, whose selected honor had to be conferred on his hated foe and who was charged by the king to oversee the conferring of that honor?

the city, proclaiming, "Thus shall it be done for the man whom the king wishes to honor."

12 Then Mordecai returned to the king's gate, but Haman hurried to his house, mourning and with his head covered. 13 When Haman told his wife Zeresh and all his friends everything that had happened to him, his advisers and his wife Zeresh said to him, "If Mordecai, before whom your downfall has begun, is of the Jewish people, you will not prevail against him, but will surely fall before him."

2. *The downfall of Haman*

7 14 While they were still talking with him, the king's eunuchs arrived and hurried Haman off to the banquet that Esther had prepared. 1 So the king and Haman went in to feast with Queen Esther. 2 On the second day, as they were drinking wine, the king again said to Esther, "What is your petition, Queen Esther? It shall be granted you. And what is your request? Even to the half of my kingdom, it shall be fulfilled." 3 Then Queen Esther answered, "If I have won your favor, O king, and if it pleases the king, let my life be given me — that is my petition — and the lives of my people — that is my request. 4 For we have been sold, I and my people, to be destroyed, to be killed, and to be annihilated. If we had been sold merely as slaves, men and women, I would have held my peace; but no enemy can compensate for this damage to the king."*m* 5 Then King Ahasuerus said to Queen Esther, "Who is he, and where is he, who has presumed to do this?" 6 Esther said, "A foe and enemy, this wicked Haman!" Then Haman was terrified before the king and the queen. 7 The king rose from the feast in wrath and went into the palace garden, but Haman stayed to beg his life from Queen Esther, for he saw that the king had determined to destroy him. 8 When the king returned from the palace garden to the banquet hall, Haman had thrown himself on the couch where Esther was reclining; and the king said, "Will he even assault the queen in my presence, in my own house?" As the words left the mouth of the king, they covered Haman's face. 9 Then Harbona, one of the eunuchs in attendance on the king, said, "Look, the very gallows that Haman has prepared for Mordecai, whose word saved the king, stands at Haman's house, fifty cubits high." And the king said, "Hang him on that." 10 So they hanged Haman on the gallows that he had prepared for Mordecai. Then the anger of the king abated.

3. *The promotion of Mordecai*

8 On that day King Ahasuerus gave to Queen Esther the house of Haman, the enemy of the Jews; and Mordecai came before the king, for Esther had told what he was to her. 2 Then the king took off his signet ring, which he had taken from Haman, and gave it to Mordecai. So Esther set Mordecai over the house of Haman.

m Meaning of Heb uncertain

Marginal cross-references

6.12 — 2 Sam 15.30
6.13 — Esth 5.10
6.14 — Esth 5.8
7.2 — Esth 5.6; 5.3
7.3 — Esth 5.8; 8.5
7.4 — Esth 3.9, 13
7.6 — Esth 3.10
7.8 — Esth 1.6
7.9 — Esth 1.10; 5.14; Ps 7.16; Prov 11.5, 6
8.1 — Esth 7.6; 2.7
8.2 — Esth 3.10

6.13 Friends and relatives alike now predicted the fall of Haman and the failure of his plot to hang Mordecai. Somehow they knew that because Mordecai was a Jew, Haman could not defeat him. But Haman was far too proud to repent and ask Mordecai for his forgiveness.

7.3 At the second banquet, Esther sensed the time was right to plead for her own life, thereby informing her husband that she was a Jewess. She also asked for the lives of all Jews who would be slaughtered under the royal edict. Knowing that her husband loved her (2.17), she rightly expected him to be angry at anyone who would threaten the life of his wife and the lives of her friends.

7.6 As soon as the king asked his wife who the enemy was, she pointed the accusing finger at Haman and called him "foe," "enemy," "wicked."

7.8 When the king returned to find Haman fallen on the couch or bed where his wife lay, he placed the worst possible interpretation on his act — that he was seeking to rape his wife. After all, was not his first plot to slay all the Jews so awful that an assault on the wife of the king would be small in comparison? Haman must die!

7.10 Little did Haman dream that the gallows he erected for the hanging of Mordecai would be the gallows on which he himself would be hung.

4. Esther's request and Ahasuerus's decree

3 Then Esther spoke again to the king; she fell at his feet, weeping and pleading with him to avert the evil design of Haman the Agagite and the plot that he had devised against the Jews. 4 The king held out the golden scepter to Esther, 5 and Esther rose and stood before the king. She said, "If it pleases the king, and if I have won his favor, and if the thing seems right before the king, and I have his approval, let an order be written to revoke the letters devised by Haman son of Hammedatha the Agagite, which he wrote giving orders to destroy the Jews who are in all the provinces of the king. 6 For how can I bear to see the calamity that is coming on my people? Or how can I bear to see the destruction of my kindred?" 7 Then King Ahasuerus said to Queen Esther and to the Jew Mordecai, "See, I have given Esther the house of Haman, and they have hanged him on the gallows, because he plotted to lay hands on the Jews. 8 You may write as you please with regard to the Jews, in the name of the king, and seal it with the king's ring; for an edict written in the name of the king and sealed with the king's ring cannot be revoked."

9 The king's secretaries were summoned at that time, in the third month, which is the month of Sivan, on the twenty-third day; and an edict was written, according to all that Mordecai commanded, to the Jews and to the satraps and the governors and the officials of the provinces from India to Ethiopia,[n] one hundred twenty-seven provinces, to every province in its own script and to every people in its own language, and also to the Jews in their script and their language. 10 He wrote letters in the name of King Ahasuerus, sealed them with the king's ring, and sent them by mounted couriers riding on fast steeds bred from the royal herd.[o] 11 By these letters the king allowed the Jews who were in every city to assemble and defend their lives, to destroy, to kill, and to annihilate any armed force of any people or province that might attack them, with their children and women, and to plunder their goods 12 on a single day throughout all the provinces of King Ahasuerus, on the thirteenth day of the twelfth month, which is the month of Adar. 13 A copy of the writ was to be issued as a decree in every province and published to all peoples, and the Jews were to be ready on that day to take revenge on their enemies. 14 So the couriers, mounted on their swift royal steeds, hurried out, urged by the king's command. The decree was issued in the citadel of Susa.

5. The victory of the Jews

15 Then Mordecai went out from the presence of the king, wearing royal robes of blue and white, with a great golden crown and a mantle of fine linen and purple, while the city of Susa shouted and rejoiced. 16 For the Jews there was light and gladness, joy and honor. 17 In every province and in every city, wherever the king's command and his edict came, there was gladness and joy among the Jews, a festival and a holiday. Furthermore, many of the peoples of the country professed to be Jews, because the fear of the Jews had fallen upon them.

[n] Or Nubia; Heb Cush   [o] Meaning of Heb uncertain

8.8 *cannot be revoked.* Haman's message had been sealed with the king's ring and could not be reversed, even by the king. This was part of the famed "law of the Medes and Persians." Thus the king gave Mordecai the right to fashion another decree, sealed with his ring, that would offset the first without actually cancelling it.
8.11 The king sent out another message by which the Jews were entitled to defend themselves and their property against attack. Such a decree would lessen the chances of attack against the Jews. Indeed, the fear of the Jews "had fallen upon all peoples" (9.2). The providence of God was preserving his people in their hour of adversity.
8.12 *the thirteenth day of the twelfth month,* i.e., the twenty-eighth day of February. The day authorized for the Jews to defend themselves against any attack and annihilate their enemies was the same day set by Haman for the extermination of the Jews.

9 Now in the twelfth month, which is the month of Adar, on the thirteenth day, when the king's command and edict were about to be executed, on the very day when the enemies of the Jews hoped to gain power over them, but which had been changed to a day when the Jews would gain power over their foes, 2 the Jews gathered in their cities throughout all the provinces of King Ahasuerus to lay hands on those who had sought their ruin; and no one could withstand them, because the fear of them had fallen upon all peoples. 3 All the officials of the provinces, the satraps and the governors, and the royal officials were supporting the Jews, because the fear of Mordecai had fallen upon them. 4 For Mordecai was powerful in the king's house, and his fame spread throughout all the provinces as the man Mordecai grew more and more powerful. 5 So the Jews struck down all their enemies with the sword, slaughtering, and destroying them, and did as they pleased to those who hated them. 6 In the citadel of Susa the Jews killed and destroyed five hundred people. 7 They killed Parshandatha, Dalphon, Aspatha, 8 Poratha, Adalia, Aridatha, 9 Parmashta, Arisai, Aridai, Vaizatha, 10 the ten sons of Haman son of Hammedatha, the enemy of the Jews; but they did not touch the plunder.

6. The hanging of Haman's sons

11 That very day the number of those killed in the citadel of Susa was reported to the king. 12 The king said to Queen Esther, "In the citadel of Susa the Jews have killed five hundred people and also the ten sons of Haman. What have they done in the rest of the king's provinces? Now what is your petition? It shall be granted you. And what further is your request? It shall be fulfilled." 13 Esther said, "If it pleases the king, let the Jews who are in Susa be allowed tomorrow also to do according to this day's edict, and let the ten sons of Haman be hanged on the gallows." 14 So the king commanded this to be done; a decree was issued in Susa, and the ten sons of Haman were hanged. 15 The Jews who were in Susa gathered also on the fourteenth day of the month of Adar and they killed three hundred persons in Susa; but they did not touch the plunder.

7. The festival of Purim begun

16 Now the other Jews who were in the king's provinces also gathered to defend their lives, and gained relief from their enemies, and killed seventy-five thousand of those who hated them; but they laid no hands on the plunder. 17 This was on the thirteenth day of the month of Adar, and on the fourteenth day they rested and made that a day of feasting and gladness.

18 But the Jews who were in Susa gathered on the thirteenth day and on the fourteenth, and rested on the fifteenth day, making that a day of feasting and gladness. 19 Therefore the Jews of the villages, who live in the open towns, hold the fourteenth day of the month of Adar as a day for gladness and feasting, a holiday on which they send gifts of food to one another.

9.1 Esth 8.12; v. 17; Esth 3.13

9.2 vv. 15-18; Esth 8.11; Ps 71.13, 24; Esth 8.17
9.3 Ezra 8.36

9.5 2 Sam 3.1; Prov 4.18

9.10 Esth 5.11; 8.11

9.12 Esth 7.2

9.13 Esth 8.11

9.15 v. 10

9.16 vv. 2, 10, 15

9.17 vv. 1, 21

9.18 vv. 2, 21

9.19 Deut 16.11, 14; v. 22; Neh 8.10

9.4 Mordecai rose to a place of prominence and authority. The position of the Jews was thus advanced and they were able to slay their enemies. This slaughter was done for the honor of God, however, not for material gain, for they took none of the spoil.
9.13 Esther knew that Haman's sons would be out to avenge the death of their father. Their execution would work to the advantage of the Jews, who would have nothing to fear after this.

9.17 In the outlying provinces, the Jews celebrated the fourteenth day of Adar. Those in Susa celebrated the fifteenth day, since the fourteenth day was given to further destruction of the enemy. This celebration marked the beginning of the feast of Purim, which Mordecai mandated to be remembered annually. The Jews established it as a custom to memorialize their deliverance forever (9.27,28).

III. *The festival of Purim:*
observance and regulations (9.20–10.3)

A. *The permanent establishment of Purim*

20 Mordecai recorded these things, and sent letters to all the Jews who were in all the provinces of King Ahasuerus, both near and far, 21 enjoining them that they should keep the fourteenth day of the month Adar and also the fifteenth day of the same month, year by year, 22 as the days on which the Jews gained relief from their enemies, and as the month that had been turned for them from sorrow into gladness and from mourning into a holiday; that they should make them days of feasting and gladness, days for sending gifts of food to one another and presents to the poor. 23 So the Jews adopted as a custom what they had begun to do, as Mordecai had written to them.

24 Haman son of Hammedatha the Agagite, the enemy of all the Jews, had plotted against the Jews to destroy them, and had cast Pur—that is "the lot"—to crush and destroy them; 25 but when Esther came before the king, he gave orders in writing that the wicked plot that he had devised against the Jews should come upon his own head, and that he and his sons should be hanged on the gallows. 26 Therefore these days are called Purim, from the word Pur. Thus because of all that was written in this letter, and of what they had faced in this matter, and of what had happened to them, 27 the Jews established and accepted as a custom for themselves and their descendants and all who joined them, that without fail they would continue to observe these two days every year, as it was written and at the time appointed. 28 These days should be remembered and kept throughout every generation, in every family, province, and city; and these days of Purim should never fall into disuse among the Jews, nor should the commemoration of these days cease among their descendants.

B. *The approval of Esther*

29 Queen Esther daughter of Abihail, along with the Jew Mordecai, gave full written authority, confirming this second letter about Purim. 30 Letters were sent wishing peace and security to all the Jews, to the one hundred twenty-seven provinces of the kingdom of Ahasuerus, 31 and giving orders that these days of Purim should be observed at their appointed seasons, as the Jew Mordecai and Queen Esther enjoined on the Jews, just as they had laid down for themselves and for their descendants regulations concerning their fasts and their lamentations. 32 The command of Queen Esther fixed these practices of Purim, and it was recorded in writing.

C. *The power and might of Mordecai*

10 King Ahasuerus laid tribute on the land and on the islands of the sea. 2 All the acts of his power and might, and the full account of the high honor of Mordecai, to which the king advanced him, are they not written in the annals of the kings of Media and Persia? 3 For Mordecai the Jew was next in rank to King Ahasuerus, and he was powerful among the Jews and popular with his many kindred, for he sought the good of his people and interceded for the welfare of all his descendants.

9.22
v. 19

9.24
Esth 3.6, 7
9.25
Esth 7.4-10;
3.6-15;
Ps 7.16
9.26
v. 20

9.27
Esth 8.17;
v. 20, 21

9.29
Esth 2.15;
vv. 20, 21
9.30
Esth 1.1
9.31
Esth 4.3

9.32
v. 26

10.1
Isa 24.15
10.2
Esth 8.15;
9.4; 2.23
10.3
Gen 41.40;
Neh 2.10

9.26 *Purim.* Perhaps Jn 5.1 refers to this feast. Outside of the Scriptures "Purim" is first mentioned in 2 Maccabees 15.36, where it is called "Mordecai's day."

9.29ff Mordecai and Esther together ordered that Jews established as a custom to memorialize their deliverance forever (v. 28).

fasting be observed in connection with the feast of Purim in observance of their own practice which led to victory. The thirteenth day of Adar was the date set for Esther's fast, a prelude to the two-day feast of Purim.

INTRODUCTION TO

JOB

Authorship, Date, and Background: The book of Job is listed among the five poetical books, which include Psalms, Proverbs, Ecclesiastes, and the Song of Solomon. The book of Job nowhere indicates who the author might have been. Jewish tradition has suggested writers from the time of Moses to the time of Ahasuerus. The events recorded in the book suggest a time frame early in the second millennium B.C. But this does not mean the book was authored at that time or shortly later. Scholars have placed the date anywhere from the time of Moses to the return of the Jews from the Babylonian exile. In all probability a date around the age of Solomon is preferable.

Job does not make reference to historical events, although Job himself is said to have come from the land of Uz, which may have been located in southeastern Edom. Job's three friends are spoken of as having come from the Temanites, the Shuhites, and Naamathites. Elihu is called a Buzite. The main character, Job, was a wealthy man who lived a seminomadic existence. He was a real person, and the story tells how he was suddenly caught up in a series of disasters and personal suffering. Thus the background for the book is applicable to all ages and all circumstances. The heart of the problem for Job was to find an answer to the dilemma why there is human suffering and how a loving God can allow it. It is further complicated by the inescapable fact that Job had really done nothing, humanly speaking, to deserve the disasters as a punishment for transgressions.

Characteristics and Content: The book of Job exhibits a depth of knowledge, profound thought, a superb command of language, and forceful expression and style; it is characterized by noble ideals, high ethical standards, and a love for nature. Regarded by many as one of the truly great literary works of all times, its literary style is poetry with a prose introduction and epilogue. The writer skillfully describes the contest between Job and his friends as they labored over the question of the cause of Job's plight. Job faced the inquisition after losing his children, his possessions, and his great wealth. His own body was wracked with sores and he himself reached the point where he wished he had never been born.

Neither Job nor anyone else has ever been able to solve the problem that is posed in this book. But answers to the question emerge in a somewhat different pattern. Clearly the thoughts and ways of God are beyond humankind's ability to understand them. They can only accept what God allows, believing that in the end all is for the glory of God and for the good of the sufferers. This does not answer the question, "Why me?" but it does provide a framework for acceptance of what may not always be understood. Secondly, Job teaches that God sometimes uses suffering to purify and strengthen the suffering soul. The third lesson Job teaches is that believers must love God wholly apart from whether God sends blessings or disasters into their lives.

What Job did not know was that in his case it was Satan who sought permission from God to afflict him with the expectation that he would lose his faith, curse his God, and allow Satan to win a victory over the Almighty. Job's friends never did see the rightness of Job's defense until they were rebuked by God, who allowed Job to pray for them. The final answer the life of Job brings to every believer is that God will deliver his suffering people either in this life or in that which is to come.

Outline:

JOB

I. The prologue (1.1–2.13)

A. Job and his background

1 There was once a man in the land of Uz whose name was Job. That man was blameless and upright, one who feared God and turned away from evil. 2 There were born to him seven sons and three daughters. 3 He had seven thousand sheep, three thousand camels, five hundred yoke of oxen, five hundred donkeys, and very many servants; so that this man was the greatest of all the people of the east. 4 His sons used to go and hold feasts in one another's houses in turn; and they would send and invite their three sisters to eat and drink with them. 5 And when the feast days had run their course, Job would send and sanctify them, and he would rise early in the morning and offer burnt offerings according to the number of them all; for Job said, "It may be that my children have sinned, and cursed God in their hearts." This is what Job always did.

B. The controversy of Satan with God

1. God grants Satan permission to test Job

6 One day the heavenly beings[a] came to present themselves before the LORD, and Satan[b] also came among them. 7 The LORD said to Satan,[b] "Where have you come from?" Satan[b] answered the LORD, "From going to and fro on the earth, and from walking up and down on it." 8 The LORD said to Satan,[b] "Have you considered my servant Job? There is no one like him on the earth, a blameless and upright man who fears God and turns away from evil." 9 Then Satan[b] answered the LORD, "Does Job fear God for nothing? 10 Have you not put a fence around him and his house and all that he has, on every side? You have blessed the work of his hands, and his possessions have increased in the land. 11 But stretch out your hand now, and touch all that he has, and he will curse you to your face." 12 The LORD said to Satan,[b] "Very well, all that he has is in your power; only do not stretch out your hand against him!" So Satan[b] went out from the presence of the LORD.

a Heb sons of God   b Or the Accuser; Heb ha-satan

1.1	Jer 25.20; Ezek 14.14; Jas 5.11; Gen 6.9; 17.1; Ex 18.21
1.2	Job 42.13
1.3	Job 42.12
1.5	Ex 19.10; Gen 8.20; 1 Kings 21.10, 13
1.6	Job 38.7; 1 Chr 21.1
1.7	1 Pet 5.8
1.8	Job 42.7, 8; v. 1
1.9	1 Tim 6.5
1.10	Job 29.2-6; Ps 128.1, 2; Job 31.25
1.11	Job 2.5; 19.21

1.1 *the land of Uz* was probably in Edom, east of the region occupied by Israel. *Job* , a very prosperous man, lived during the age of the patriarchs, though nothing in the book refers to Abraham, Isaac, or Jacob. God has his own people from every tribe and nation (Rev 7.9) and Job was among that multitude. He was a religious man who feared (or had a reverential trust in) God. He was a true worshiper who lived according to the will and law of God. He was not sinless but he was righteous, which means he was looking to God for salvation.
1.6 *the heavenly beings*, i.e., the angels.
1.9 *Does Job fear God for nothing?* Satan suggested that Job feared God because he gained something

from so doing. It is true that godliness is great gain, but Job certainly would have continued to fear God even if he had not gained from doing so. Satan accused Job of being a hypocrite because of his prosperity; later Job's friends said the opposite, that his afflictions proved he was a hypocrite — otherwise he would not have suffered.
1.11 Satan had no power to afflict Job without first securing God's permission. Job eventually lost his wealth (vv. 14–17), his children (vv. 18,19), and his health (2.1–8). Deprived of his most important blessings, he had good reason to turn away from God, who was allowing him to suffer so much.

2. Satan takes away Job's wealth and children

13 One day when his sons and daughters were eating and drinking wine in the eldest brother's house, 14 a messenger came to Job and said, "The oxen were plowing and the donkeys were feeding beside them, 15 and the Sabeans fell on them and carried them off, and killed the servants with the edge of the sword; I alone have escaped to tell you." 16 While he was still speaking, another came and said, "The fire of God fell from heaven and burned up the sheep and the servants, and consumed them; I alone have escaped to tell you." 17 While he was still speaking, another came and said, "The Chaldeans formed three columns, made a raid on the camels and carried them off, and killed the servants with the edge of the sword; I alone have escaped to tell you." 18 While he was still speaking, another came and said, "Your sons and daughters were eating and drinking wine in their eldest brother's house, 19 and suddenly a great wind came across the desert, struck the four corners of the house, and it fell on the young people, and they are dead; I alone have escaped to tell you."

3. Job exhibits patience

20 Then Job arose, tore his robe, shaved his head, and fell on the ground and worshiped. 21 He said, "Naked I came from my mother's womb, and naked shall I return there; the LORD gave, and the LORD has taken away; blessed be the name of the LORD."

22 In all this Job did not sin or charge God with wrongdoing.

C. Satan's second request of God

1. Satan's request granted

2 One day the heavenly beings[c] came to present themselves before the LORD, and Satan[d] also came among them to present himself before the LORD. 2 The LORD said to Satan,[d] "Where have you come from?" Satan[e] answered the LORD, "From going to and fro on the earth, and from walking up and down on it." 3 The LORD said to Satan,[d] "Have you considered my servant Job? There is no one like him on the earth, a blameless and upright man who fears God and turns away from evil. He still persists in his integrity, although you incited me against him, to destroy him for no reason." 4 Then Satan[d] answered the LORD, "Skin for skin! All that people have they will give to save their lives.[f] 5 But stretch out your hand now and touch his bone and his flesh, and he will curse you to your face." 6 The LORD said to Satan,[d] "Very well, he is in your power; only spare his life."

2. Satan afflicts Job physically

7 So Satan[d] went out from the presence of the LORD, and inflicted loathsome sores on Job from the sole of his foot to the crown of his head.

[c] Heb *sons of God* [d] Or *the Accuser;* Heb *ha-satan* [e] Or *The Accuser;* Heb *ha-satan* [f] Or *All that the man has he will give for his life*

Cross-references (margin)

1.15 Job 6.19
1.16 Gen 19.24; Lev 10.2; Num 11.1-3; 2 Kings 1.10
1.17 Gen 11.28, 31
1.18 vv. 4, 13
1.19 Jer 4.11; 13.24
1.20 Gen 37.29; 1 Pet 5.6
1.21 Eccl 5.15; 1 Tim 6.7; Job 2.10; Eph 5.20; 1 Thess 5.18
1.22 Job 2.10
2.1 Job 1.6
2.2 Job 1.7
2.3 Job 1.1, 8; 27.5, 6; 9.17
2.5 Job 1.11
2.6 Job 1.12
2.7 Job 7.5

1.14 Satan felt confident that if he stripped Job of his wealth, children, and health, he would then defect from God and curse the divine name. Job, however, continued to bless the name of the Lord (v. 21).

2.3 *He still persists in his integrity,* i.e., he is the same in adversity that he was in prosperity. Job's confidence in God was firmer and more deeply rooted than ever, in spite of his difficulties.

2.4 *Skin for skin* was probably a common expression used by traders. When Job did not sin against God in response to the loss of his possessions and loved ones,

Satan thought Job would turn away if God allowed physical affliction to come to him.

2.7 God indeed had protected Job from physical suffering. Now he permitted Satan to touch Job's body. We do not know how much Satan may have the capacity, under God's permissive hand, of striking people (and particularly the people of God) with grievous diseases, but he does have that power. Jesus said that one daughter of Abraham had been bound by Satan with illness for eighteen years before he delivered her (Lk 13.16).

⁸ Job*g* took a potsherd with which to scrape himself, and sat among the ashes.

3. *Job's continued patience*

9 Then his wife said to him, "Do you still persist in your integrity? Curse*h* God, and die." ¹⁰ But he said to her, "You speak as any foolish woman would speak. Shall we receive the good at the hand of God, and not receive the bad?" In all this Job did not sin with his lips.

D. *The friends of Job*

11 Now when Job's three friends heard of all these troubles that had come upon him, each of them set out from his home — Eliphaz the Temanite, Bildad the Shuhite, and Zophar the Naamathite. They met together to go and console and comfort him. ¹² When they saw him from a distance, they did not recognize him, and they raised their voices and wept aloud; they tore their robes and threw dust in the air upon their heads. ¹³ They sat with him on the ground seven days and seven nights, and no one spoke a word to him, for they saw that his suffering was very great.

II. *Job's discussions with his friends (3.1–31.40)*

A. *Job's lament of misery and despair*

1. *He curses the day of his birth*

3 After this Job opened his mouth and cursed the day of his birth. ² Job said:

3   "Let the day perish in which I was born,
        and the night that said,
        'A man-child is conceived.'
4   Let that day be darkness!
        May God above not seek it,
        or light shine on it.
5   Let gloom and deep darkness claim it.
        Let clouds settle upon it;
        let the blackness of the day terrify it.
6   That night — let thick darkness seize it!
        let it not rejoice among the days of the year;
        let it not come into the number of the months.
7   Yes, let that night be barren;
        let no joyful cry be heard*i* in it.
8   Let those curse it who curse the Sea,*j*
        those who are skilled to rouse up Leviathan.
9   Let the stars of its dawn be dark;
        let it hope for light, but have none;
        may it not see the eyelids of the morning —
10 because it did not shut the doors of my mother's womb,
        and hide trouble from my eyes.

g Heb *He*   *h* Heb *Bless*   *i* Heb *come*   *j* Cn: Heb *day*

2.11 *when Job's three friends heard of all these troubles,* they came to console him and to help him (though in the end their help left much to be desired). These friends came from northern Arabia. *Teman* is the name of a clan from Edom (Gen 36.11). The Shuhites were probably a brother tribe to Midian (cf. Gen 25.2; 1 Chr 1.32). Nowhere else in the Scriptures are the Naamathites mentioned.

3.2,3 Job will not curse God. But he does curse the day of his birth. He wishes he had not been born or that he had been born dead (vv. 3–19).
3.8 *those who are skilled to rouse up Leviathan.* Leviathan or the "sea monster" was thought to swallow up the sun in times of an eclipse. Job thinks that if Leviathan had been aroused and the sun eclipsed, he might never have been born!

Marginal cross-references:

2.8 Job 42.6; Ezek 27.30; Mt 11.21

2.10 Job 1.21, 22; Ps 39.1

2.11 1 Chr 1.45; Gen 25.2; Job 42.11
2.12 Josh 7.6; Lam 2.10; Ezek 27.30
2.13 Gen 50.10; Ezek 3.15

3.3 Job 10.18; Jer 20.14

3.5 Job 10.21; Ps 23.4; Jer 2.6

3.6 Job 23.17

3.8 Job 41.10

3.9 Job 41.18

2. He asks why he did not die

3.11
Job 10.18

11 "Why did I not die at birth,
   come forth from the womb and expire?

3.12
Gen 30.3;
Isa 66.12

12 Why were there knees to receive me,
   or breasts for me to suck?

13 Now I would be lying down and quiet;
   I would be asleep; then I would be at rest

3.14
Job 12.17,
18; 15.28

14 with kings and counselors of the earth
   who rebuild ruins for themselves,

15 or with princes who have gold,
   who fill their houses with silver.

3.16
Eccl 6.3

16 Or why was I not buried like a stillborn child,
   like an infant that never sees the light?

3.17
Job 17.16

17 There the wicked cease from troubling,
   and there the weary are at rest.

18 There the prisoners are at ease together;
   they do not hear the voice of the taskmaster.

19 The small and the great are there,
   and the slaves are free from their masters.

3. He cries out in his agony

3.20
1 Sam 1.10;
Prov 31.6;
Isa 38.15;
Ezek 27.31
3.21
Rev 9.6

20 "Why is light given to one in misery,
   and life to the bitter in soul,

21 who long for death, but it does not come,
   and dig for it more than for hidden treasures;

22 who rejoice exceedingly,
   and are glad when they find the grave?

3.23
Job 19.6, 8,
12;
Lam 3.7
3.24
Ps 42.3, 4

23 Why is light given to one who cannot see the way,
   whom God has fenced in?

24 For my sighing comes like[k] my bread,
   and my groanings are poured out like water.

25 Truly the thing that I fear comes upon me,
   and what I dread befalls me.

26 I am not at ease, nor am I quiet;
   I have no rest; but trouble comes."

B. The first cycle of speeches

1. The speech of Eliphaz

a. God does not punish the righteous

4 Then Eliphaz the Temanite answered:

4.2
Job 32.18-20

2 "If one ventures a word with you, will you be offended?
   But who can keep from speaking?

4.3
Isa 35.3;
Heb 12.12
4.4
Isa 35.3;
Heb 12.12

3 See, you have instructed many;
   you have strengthened the weak hands.

4 Your words have supported those who were stumbling,

[k] Heb before

3.11 Job welcomes death and curses life, regarding the grave as the best of all things.

4.1 The speeches of Eliphaz, Bildad, and Zophar are written in poetic form. The Scriptures record what they said, but this does not mean that all they said is necessarily true. God judged them defective. Nonetheless, some of their statements are true and are quoted as such in the N.T. (e.g., the statements of Eliphaz in 5.11–13 are echoed in Lk 1.52 and quoted as true in 1 Cor 3.19).

4.2ff Eliphaz claims that (1) if Job were righteous

he would trust God and not wish to die; (2) his suffering follows the rule that as one sows so shall one reap (4.8,9); (3) Job should accept God's chastening by humbly repenting, at which time he would be restored. Eliphaz's theories are inaccurate and do not apply to Job, for he is not being punished for having committed secret sins as his friends intimate. It should be pointed out, of course, that Job's friends did not have the benefit of the conversation between God and Satan as recorded in chs. 1–2.

and you have made firm the feeble knees.

5 But now it has come to you, and you are impatient;
    it touches you, and you are dismayed.

6 Is not your fear of God your confidence,
    and the integrity of your ways your hope?

7 "Think now, who that was innocent ever perished?
    Or where were the upright cut off?

8 As I have seen, those who plow iniquity
    and sow trouble reap the same.

9 By the breath of God they perish,
    and by the blast of his anger they are consumed.

10 The roar of the lion, the voice of the fierce lion,
    and the teeth of the young lions are broken.

11 The strong lion perishes for lack of prey,
    and the whelps of the lioness are scattered.

b. Sinful humans must perish

12 "Now a word came stealing to me,
    my ear received the whisper of it.

13 Amid thoughts from visions of the night,
    when deep sleep falls on mortals,

14 dread came upon me, and trembling,
    which made all my bones shake.

15 A spirit glided past my face;
    the hair of my flesh bristled.

16 It stood still,
    but I could not discern its appearance.
    A form was before my eyes;
    there was silence, then I heard a voice:

17 'Can mortals be righteous before[l] God?
    Can human beings be pure before[l] their Maker?

18 Even in his servants he puts no trust,
    and his angels he charges with error;

19 how much more those who live in houses of clay,
    whose foundation is in the dust,
    who are crushed like a moth.

20 Between morning and evening they are destroyed;
    they perish forever without any regarding it.

21 Their tent-cord is plucked up within them,
    and they die devoid of wisdom.'

c. Punishment the fruit of unrighteousness

5 "Call now; is there anyone who will answer you?
    To which of the holy ones will you turn?

2 Surely vexation kills the fool,
    and jealousy slays the simple.

[l] Or more than

Cross references (right margin):

4.5 Job 6.14; 19.21
4.6 Job 1.1
4.7 Ps 37.25
4.8 Prov 22.8; Hos 10.13; Gal 6.7, 8
4.9 Job 15.30; Isa 30.33; Ps 59.13
4.10 Ps 58.6
4.11 Ps 34.10
4.12 Job 26.14
4.14 Jer 23.9
4.17 Job 9.2; 35.10
4.18 Job 15.15
4.19 Job 10.9; 22.16
4.20 Ps 90.5, 6; Job 20.7
4.21 Job 36.12
5.1 Job 15.15
5.2 Prov 12.16

4.7 *who that was innocent ever perished?* Job's friends tell him that only the wicked suffer. Thus if he is suffering he must be wicked. Job must confess his sin, get right with God, trust in his mercy, and all will be well. Unfortunately their premise is wrong. All who suffer are not necessarily wicked, as they learn later.

4.15 Eliphaz relates the incident in which a spirit passed before him, causing his hair to stand on end. We know very little about spirits, but we do know there are both good and bad ones, and that they can interact with people. Today God sends us his message basically through the prophets who, guided by the Holy Spirit, have given us the word of God. All spirits are to be tried by testing what they say against what the Scriptures teach (cf. 1 Jn 4.1–3).

5.1 Eliphaz challenges Job to show him a single case of any saint who was reduced to the same circumstances in which Job now found himself. If God never dealt in this manner with any saint who loved his name, then it must be clear that Job is not one of them.

5.3 Ps 37.35	3 I have seen fools taking root, but suddenly I cursed their dwelling.
5.4 Am 5.12	4 Their children are far from safety, they are crushed in the gate, and there is no one to deliver them.
5.5 Job 18.8-10	5 The hungry eat their harvest, and they take it even out of the thorns;*m* and the thirsty*n* pant after their wealth.
	6 For misery does not come from the earth, nor does trouble sprout from the ground;
5.7 Job 14.1	7 but human beings are born to trouble just as sparks*o* fly upward.

d. Eliphaz implores Job to seek God

5.8 Ps 35.23	8 "As for me, I would seek God, and to God I would commit my cause.
5.9 Ps 40.5; 72.18	9 He does great things and unsearchable, marvelous things without number.
5.10 Ps 65.9	10 He gives rain on the earth and sends waters on the fields;
5.11 1 Sam 2.7; Ps 113.7	11 he sets on high those who are lowly, and those who mourn are lifted to safety.
5.12 Neh 4.15; Ps 33.10; Isa 8.10	12 He frustrates the devices of the crafty, so that their hands achieve no success.
	13 He takes the wise in their own craftiness; and the schemes of the wily are brought to a quick end.
5.14 Job 12.25; Deut 28.29	14 They meet with darkness in the daytime, and grope at noonday as in the night.
5.15 Ps 35.10	15 But he saves the needy from the sword of their mouth, from the hand of the mighty.
5.16 Ps 107.42	16 So the poor have hope, and injustice shuts its mouth.
5.17 Ps 94.12; Jas 1.12; Heb 12.5-11	17 "How happy is the one whom God reproves; therefore do not despise the discipline of the Almighty.*p*
5.18 Isa 30.26	18 For he wounds, but he binds up; he strikes, but his hands heal.
5.19 Ps 34.19; 91.10	19 He will deliver you from six troubles; in seven no harm shall touch you.
5.20 Ps 33.19; 144.10	20 In famine he will redeem you from death, and in war from the power of the sword.
5.21 Ps 31.20; 91.5, 6	21 You shall be hidden from the scourge of the tongue, and shall not fear destruction when it comes.
5.22 Ps 91.13; Ezek 34.25	22 At destruction and famine you shall laugh, and shall not fear the wild animals of the earth.
5.23 Ps 91.12; Isa 11.6-9	23 For you shall be in league with the stones of the field, and the wild animals shall be at peace with you.
5.24 Job 8.6; 21.9	24 You shall know that your tent is safe, you shall inspect your fold and miss nothing.
5.25 Ps 72.16; 112.2	25 You shall know that your descendants will be many,

m Meaning of Heb uncertain   *n* Aquila Symmachus Syr Vg: Heb *snare*   *o* Or *birds*; Heb *sons of Resheph*
p Traditional rendering of Heb *Shaddai*

5.8 *I would seek God, and to God I would commit my cause.* Eliphaz is positive that Job is suffering for his sins. Even though he is wrong in his analysis, he is right in the solution he suggests. Anyone in Job's shoes should seek God and commit his or her cause to him. God is the sinner's only refuge, and from him comes his great salvation.

5.17ff Eliphaz says that Job should receive his affliction as God's discipline and rejoice in it. He correctly states that God is the great deliverer, whether the problem be famine, war, reproach, or false accusation (vv. 18–26). Yet this does not resolve Job's problems, for they have sprung from a different situation than that envisioned by Eliphaz.

and your offspring like the grass of the earth.

26 You shall come to your grave in ripe old age,
    as a shock of grain comes up to the threshing floor in its
    season.

27 See, we have searched this out; it is true.
    Hear, and know it for yourself."

2. Job's reply to Eliphaz

a. He complains that God will not let him die

6 Then Job answered:

2 "O that my vexation were weighed,
   and all my calamity laid in the balances!

3 For then it would be heavier than the sand of the sea;
   therefore my words have been rash.

4 For the arrows of the Almighty^q are in me;
   my spirit drinks their poison;
   the terrors of God are arrayed against me.

5 Does the wild ass bray over its grass,
   or the ox low over its fodder?

6 Can that which is tasteless be eaten without salt,
   or is there any flavor in the juice of mallows?^r

7 My appetite refuses to touch them;
   they are like food that is loathsome to me.^r

8 "O that I might have my request,
   and that God would grant my desire;

9 that it would please God to crush me,
   that he would let loose his hand and cut me off!

10 This would be my consolation;
   I would even exult^r in unrelenting pain;
   for I have not denied the words of the Holy One.

11 What is my strength, that I should wait?
   And what is my end, that I should be patient?

12 Is my strength the strength of stones,
   or is my flesh bronze?

13 In truth I have no help in me,
   and any resource is driven from me.

b. Job calls his friends unfaithful

14 "Those who withhold^s kindness from a friend
   forsake the fear of the Almighty.^q

15 My companions are treacherous like a torrent-bed,
   like freshets that pass away,

16 that run dark with ice,
   turbid with melting snow.

17 In time of heat they disappear;
   when it is hot, they vanish from their place.

---

q Traditional rendering of Heb *Shaddai*   r Meaning of Heb uncertain   s Syr Vg Compare Tg: Meaning of Heb uncertain

Cross-references (right margin):

5.26 Gen 15.15; Prov 9.11

6.2 Job 31.6

6.3 Prov 27.3

6.4 Ps 38.2; Job 21.20; Ps 88.15

6.8 Job 14.13

6.9 1 Kings 19.4

6.10 Job 23.11, 12; Lev 19.2; Isa 57.15; Hos 11.9

6.11 Job 21.4

6.13 Job 26.2, 3

6.15 Ps 38.11; Jer 15.18

6.17 Job 24.19

6.1ff Job replies to Eliphaz that his troubles are far worse than those of his friends. But he insists that his sufferings are not a result of transgressions. He justifies himself and maintains that his friends have been unfaithful to him. He demands evidence to show that he has sinned, and in doing so, addresses his Maker, the only source of his deliverance.
6.8 Job passionately desires to die. Apparently he expects never to see any better days (though in this he

would be proved wrong). He thinks only death would solve his problem. Why then did he not commit suicide? Behind his words lie his knowledge that life and death come only from God. He gives and takes life (cf. 1.21); people should not die by their own hand.
6.14 Job argues that compassion is a debt owed to those who are afflicted. Eliphaz has not shown compassion, and this inhumanity is a sign of a lack of piety (fear of God). Job is deeply disappointed in his friend.

18 The caravans turn aside from their course;
    they go up into the waste, and perish.

6.19
Gen 25.15;
Isa 21.14;
1 Kings 10.1
6.20
Jer 14.3

19 The caravans of Tema look,
    the travelers of Sheba hope.
20 They are disappointed because they were confident;
    they come there and are confounded.

c. He asks for evidences of his sins

21 Such you have now become to me;*
    you see my calamity, and are afraid.
22 Have I said, 'Make me a gift'?
    Or, 'From your wealth offer a bribe for me'?
23 Or, 'Save me from an opponent's hand'?
    Or, 'Ransom me from the hand of oppressors'?

24 "Teach me, and I will be silent;
    make me understand how I have gone wrong.

6.25
Eccl 12.10,
11
6.26
Job 8.2

25 How forceful are honest words!
    But your reproof, what does it reprove?
26 Do you think that you can reprove words,
    as if the speech of the desperate were wind?

6.27
Joel 3.3;
2 Pet 3.3

27 You would even cast lots over the orphan,
    and bargain over your friend.

6.28
Job 27.4

28 "But now, be pleased to look at me;
    for I will not lie to your face.
29 Turn, I pray, let no wrong be done.
    Turn now, my vindication is at stake.

6.30
Job 27.4;
12.11

30 Is there any wrong on my tongue?
    Cannot my taste discern calamity?

d. He argues against hope

7.1
Job 10.17;
14.14;
Isa 40.2;
Job 14.6
7.2
Lev 19.13
7.3
Lam 1.7;
Ps 6.6
7.4
Deut 28.67

7 "Do not human beings have a hard service on earth,
    and are not their days like the days of a laborer?
2 Like a slave who longs for the shadow,
    and like laborers who look for their wages,
3 so I am allotted months of emptiness,
    and nights of misery are apportioned to me.
4 When I lie down I say, 'When shall I rise?'
    But the night is long,
    and I am full of tossing until dawn.
5 My flesh is clothed with worms and dirt;
    my skin hardens, then breaks out again.

7.6
Job 9.25;
13.15; 17.15,
16

6 My days are swifter than a weaver's shuttle,
    and come to their end without hope.*

e. He prays to his God

7.7
Ps 78.39;
Job 9.25
7.8
Job 20.9;
v. 21

7 "Remember that my life is a breath;
    my eye will never again see good.
8 The eye that beholds me will see me no more;

t Cn Compare Gk Syr: Meaning of Heb uncertain   *u* Or *as the thread runs out*

6.24 Job acknowledges that he and his friends do
have a difference of opinion. He insists that he is not
obstinate but is ready to change his mind if he can be
shown that his views are wrong and untrue. If they
can teach him, he will accept their perspective.
7.1,2 Job thinks he has as much reason to wish for
death as a slave who is tired of his work and looks for
the setting of the sun.

7.7 Job reflects that we must all take our leave of
temporal things. We pass this way only once and
return no more. That is, glorified saints do not return
to the cares, concerns, burdens, and sorrows of this
life, nor do damned sinners return to the gaieties and
worldly pleasures they once enjoyed. We should
never forget this in our daily pursuits.

while your eyes are upon me, I shall be gone.

9 As the cloud fades and vanishes,
    so those who go down to Sheol do not come up;
10 they return no more to their houses,
    nor do their places know them any more.

11 "Therefore I will not restrain my mouth;
    I will speak in the anguish of my spirit;
    I will complain in the bitterness of my soul.
12 Am I the Sea, or the Dragon,
    that you set a guard over me?
13 When I say, 'My bed will comfort me,
    my couch will ease my complaint,'
14 then you scare me with dreams
    and terrify me with visions,
15 so that I would choose strangling
    and death rather than this body.
16 I loathe my life; I would not live forever.
    Let me alone, for my days are a breath.
17 What are human beings, that you make so much of them,
    that you set your mind on them,
18 visit them every morning,
    test them every moment?
19 Will you not look away from me for a while,
    let me alone until I swallow my spittle?
20 If I sin, what do I do to you, you watcher of humanity?
    Why have you made me your target?
    Why have I become a burden to you?
21 Why do you not pardon my transgression
    and take away my iniquity?
For now I shall lie in the earth;
    you will seek me, but I shall not be."

3. The speech of Bildad: Bildad calls Job a hypocrite and urges repentance

8 Then Bildad the Shuhite answered:
2 "How long will you say these things,
    and the words of your mouth be a great wind?
3 Does God pervert justice?
    Or does the Almighty[v] pervert the right?
4 If your children sinned against him,
    he delivered them into the power of their transgression.
5 If you will seek God
    and make supplication to the Almighty,[v]
6 if you are pure and upright,
    surely then he will rouse himself for you
    and restore to you your rightful place.

[v] Traditional rendering of Heb *Shaddai*

Cross-references (right margin):

7.9 Job 30.15; 11.8;
7.10 2 Sam 12.23
Job 10.21; Ps 103.16
7.11 Ps 40.9; 1 Sam 1.10
7.12 Ezek 32.2, 3
7.13 Job 9.27
7.14 Job 9.34
7.15 1 Kings 19.4
7.16 Job 10.1; Eccl 7.15
7.17 Ps 8.4; 144.3; Heb 2.6
7.20 Job 35.3, 6; v. 12; Job 16.12
7.21 Job 10.14; Ps 104.29; v. 8
8.3 Gen 18.25; Deut 32.4; 2 Chr 19.7; Dan 9.14; Rom 3.5
8.4 Job 1.5, 18, 19
8.5 Job 5.8; 11.13; 9.15
8.6 Ps 7.6

7.12 Job peevishly declares that the restraints laid upon him are more than the circumstances require. He is neither so strong nor so distempered that he needs to be restrained by force to keep him from devouring all the fish of the sea!

7.21 *Why do you not pardon my transgression?* Job knows of no grievous sin he has committed. Let God forgive him, for he does not merit the awful scourging he has experienced (vv. 19,20). Job is not irreverent here. He is only seeking to reason with God as he tries to understand what, at that moment, is not under-

standable and what can at last only be made known to him by God himself.

8.1ff Bildad's argument hardly differs from that of Eliphaz: If only Job would stop rebelling against his afflictions and accept the rightness of God's dealing with him, he would shortly be restored.

8.2 Bildad hits Job hard by saying that he is a bag of wind. He accuses Job of being blustering, threatening, boisterous, and dangerous. Bildad feels he has to take God's side against his friend Job.

8.7
Job 42.12

7 Though your beginning was small,
   your latter days will be very great.

8.8
Deut 4.32;
32.7;
Job 15.18
8.9
Gen 47.9;
1 Chr 29.15;
Job 7.5

8 "For inquire now of bygone generations,
   and consider what their ancestors have found;

9 for we are but of yesterday, and we know nothing,
   for our days on earth are but a shadow.

10 Will they not teach you and tell you
   and utter words out of their understanding?

11 "Can papyrus grow where there is no marsh?
   Can reeds flourish where there is no water?

8.12
Ps 129.6;
Jer 17.6

12 While yet in flower and not cut down,
   they wither before any other plant.

8.13
Ps 9.17;
Job 11.20;
Prov 10.28
8.14
Isa 59.5, 6
8.15
Job 27.18

13 Such are the paths of all who forget God;
   the hope of the godless shall perish.

14 Their confidence is gossamer,
   a spider's house their trust.

15 If one leans against its house, it will not stand;
   if one lays hold of it, it will not endure.

8.16
Ps 37.35;
80.11

16 The wicked thrive[w] before the sun,
   and their shoots spread over the garden.

17 Their roots twine around the stoneheap;
   they live among the rocks.[x]

8.18
Job 7.10;
Ps 37.36
8.19
Job 20.5;
Eccl 1.4

18 If they are destroyed from their place,
   then it will deny them, saying, 'I have never seen you.'

19 See, these are their happy ways,[y]
   and out of the earth still others will spring.

8.20
Job 4.7;
21.30
8.21
Ps 126.2;
132.16
8.22
Ps 35.26;
109.29; v. 15

20 "See, God will not reject a blameless person,
   nor take the hand of evildoers.

21 He will yet fill your mouth with laughter,
   and your lips with shouts of joy.

22 Those who hate you will be clothed with shame,
   and the tent of the wicked will be no more."

4. Job answers Bildad

a. The doctrine and proof of God's justice

9 Then Job answered:
2 "Indeed I know that this is so;
   but how can a mortal be just before God?

9.2
Ps 143.2;
Rom 3.20

3 If one wished to contend with him,
   one could not answer him once in a thousand.

9.4
Job 36.5;
2 Chr 13.12

4 He is wise in heart, and mighty in strength
   —who has resisted him, and succeeded?—

---

w Heb *He thrives*   *x* Gk Vg: Meaning of Heb uncertain   *y* Meaning of Heb uncertain

---

8.7 Bildad expresses confidence that God can restore good things to Job. But it all is based on the notion that Job is a sinner who needs to repent, turn to God, and be forgiven. All that Bildad said is true for most of us who indeed have sinned. In Job's case, however, Bildad's primary assumption is false. Job was not guilty of the sins his friends thought he had committed.

8.8 Eliphaz had appealed to the apparition he had seen (4.12ff). Bildad appeals to past history and tradition, to scholarship rather than to mystical events. In the end, however, his perspective is the same as that of Eliphaz.

8.20 Bildad sums up his case that God's treatment of persons corresponds to their relationship with him. Since Job has fared so badly, it simply proves he is a sinner. Let him repent and his mouth would be filled with laughing and his lips with shouting.

9.1 Whoever argues with an opponent should be willing to accept any truth spoken by the opponent. Thus Job acknowledges that God does indeed bring wicked people to ruin, and that the godly are under the wings and the protection of the Almighty.

9.3 People are not an equal match against their creator, nor can they win in an argument or overcome their maker in combat.

5   he who removes mountains, and they do not know it,
     when he overturns them in his anger;

6   who shakes the earth out of its place,
     and its pillars tremble;

7   who commands the sun, and it does not rise;
     who seals up the stars;

8   who alone stretched out the heavens
     and trampled the waves of the Sea;*z*

9   who made the Bear and Orion,
     the Pleiades and the chambers of the south;

10   who does great things beyond understanding,
     and marvelous things without number.

11   Look, he passes by me, and I do not see him;
     he moves on, but I do not perceive him.

12   He snatches away; who can stop him?
     Who will say to him, 'What are you doing?'

b. Job acknowledges himself a sinner

13   "God will not turn back his anger;
     the helpers of Rahab bowed beneath him.

14   How then can I answer him,
     choosing my words with him?

15   Though I am innocent, I cannot answer him;
     I must appeal for mercy to my accuser.*a*

16   If I summoned him and he answered me,
     I do not believe that he would listen to my voice.

17   For he crushes me with a tempest,
     and multiplies my wounds without cause;

18   he will not let me get my breath,
     but fills me with bitterness.

19   If it is a contest of strength, he is the strong one!
     If it is a matter of justice, who can summon him?*b*

20   Though I am innocent, my own mouth would condemn me;
     though I am blameless, he would prove me perverse.

21   I am blameless; I do not know myself;
     I loathe my life.

22   It is all one; therefore I say,
     he destroys both the blameless and the wicked.

23   When disaster brings sudden death,
     he mocks at the calamity*c* of the innocent.

24   The earth is given into the hand of the wicked;
     he covers the eyes of its judges —
     if it is not he, who then is it?

c. Job's complaint against God

25   "My days are swifter than a runner;
     they flee away, they see no good.

Cross-references (right column):

9.5 Mic 1.4
9.6 Isa 2.19, 21; Hag 2.6; Heb 12.26; Job 26.11
9.8 Gen 1.6; Ps 104.2, 3
9.9 Gen 1.16; Job 38.31; Am 5.8
9.10 Ps 71.15
9.11 Job 23.8, 9; 35.14
9.12 Isa 45.9; Rom 9.20; Job 11.10
9.13 Job 26.12; Isa 30.7
9.14 vv. 3, 32
9.15 Job 10.15; 8.5
9.17 Job 16.12, 14; 2.3
9.18 Job 27.2
9.20 vv. 15, 29
9.21 Job 1.1; 7.16
9.22 Eccl 9.2, 3; Ezek 21.3
9.23 Ps 64.4; Heb 11.36; 1 Pet 1.7
9.24 Job 10.3; 12.6; 12.17
9.25 Job 7.6, 7

z Or *trampled the back of the sea dragon*   *a* Or *for my right*   *b* Compare Gk: Heb *me*   *c* Meaning of Heb uncertain

---

9.10 Finite people cannot understand God's counsels, apprehend his motions, or comprehend the measures he takes. They are not competent to judge his proceedings because they do not know his secret thoughts or actions.

9.22–24 Job repeats the main point of difference between him and his friends: it is not unusual for the wicked to prosper and for the righteous to be greatly afflicted. God's children must realize that they often receive problems for their honor and benefit. Furthermore, what happens in this life is not the end of the matter. Some who suffer much will be saved at last; the wicked who have flourished will at last end up in hell (cf. Ps 73).

9.25 Job now becomes more complaining, more peevish. In ch. 10 he gives vent to resentment. He refuses to impeach God but he uses violent words, making clear the bitterness of his soul. Somehow he finds it difficult to perceive that peace would come from accepting the situation.

9.26
Hab 1.8
9.27
Job 7.13
9.28
Ps 119.120;
Job 7.21
9.29
v. 20
9.30
Jer 2.22
9.32
Eccl 6.10;
Rom 9.20;
v. 3;
Ps 143.2
9.33
1 Sam 2.25
9.34
Job 13.21;
Ps 39.10
9.35
Job 13.22

26 They go by like skiffs of reed,
    like an eagle swooping on the prey.
27 If I say, 'I will forget my complaint;
    I will put off my sad countenance and be of good cheer,'
28 I become afraid of all my suffering,
    for I know you will not hold me innocent.
29 I shall be condemned;
    why then do I labor in vain?
30 If I wash myself with soap
    and cleanse my hands with lye,
31 yet you will plunge me into filth,
    and my own clothes will abhor me.
32 For he is not a mortal, as I am, that I might answer him,
    that we should come to trial together.
33 There is no umpire^d between us,
    who might lay his hand on us both.
34 If he would take his rod away from me,
    and not let dread of him terrify me,
35 then I would speak without fear of him,
    for I know I am not what I am thought to be.^e

d. Job's persistence in complaint

10.1
1 Kings 19.4;
Job 7.16;
7.11
10.2
Job 9.29;
Hos 4.1
10.3
v. 8;
Job 21.16;
22.18
10.4
1 Sam 16.7
10.5
Ps 90.4;
2 Pet 3.8
10.7
Job 9.21;
9.12
10.8
Ps 119.73
10.9
Gen 2.7;
3.19;
Isa 64.8
10.10
Ps 139.14-16
10.12
Job 33.4

10 "I loathe my life;
      I will give free utterance to my complaint;
      I will speak in the bitterness of my soul.
2 I will say to God, Do not condemn me;
    let me know why you contend against me.
3 Does it seem good to you to oppress,
    to despise the work of your hands
    and favor the schemes of the wicked?
4 Do you have eyes of flesh?
    Do you see as humans see?
5 Are your days like the days of mortals,
    or your years like human years,
6 that you seek out my iniquity
    and search for my sin,
7 although you know that I am not guilty,
    and there is no one to deliver out of your hand?

e. Job acknowledges God as creator and preserver

8 Your hands fashioned and made me;
    and now you turn and destroy me.^f
9 Remember that you fashioned me like clay;
    and will you turn me to dust again?
10 Did you not pour me out like milk
     and curdle me like cheese?
11 You clothed me with skin and flesh,
     and knit me together with bones and sinews.
12 You have granted me life and steadfast love,
     and your care has preserved my spirit.
13 Yet these things you hid in your heart;

---

d Another reading is *Would that there were an umpire*   e Cn: Heb *for I am not so in myself*
f Cn Compare Gk Syr: Heb *made me together all around, and you destroy me*

10.2 Job wants desperately to be delivered from his afflictions. He smarts under the rod of the Father, but he prays not to be cut off by the sword of the Judge. It is the comfort of all believers who are in affliction that there is no condemnation to them.
10.7 Job knows that under the grace of God he can say, "I am not guilty." He appeals to God, who knows that he is a man of integrity.
10.8 Job calls upon God to remember that he made him. Because God has made him, he submits to God and will serve him. This is his argument for mercy.

I know that this was your purpose.

f. Job again complains against God

14 If I sin, you watch me,
   and do not acquit me of my iniquity.
15 If I am wicked, woe to me!
   If I am righteous, I cannot lift up my head,
   for I am filled with disgrace
   and look upon my affliction.
16 Bold as a lion you hunt me;
   you repeat your exploits against me.
17 You renew your witnesses against me,
   and increase your vexation toward me;
   you bring fresh troops against me.[g]
18 "Why did you bring me forth from the womb?
   Would that I had died before any eye had seen me,
19 and were as though I had not been,
   carried from the womb to the grave.
20 Are not the days of my life few?[h]
   Let me alone, that I may find a little comfort[i]
21 before I go, never to return,
   to the land of gloom and deep darkness,
22 the land of gloom[j] and chaos,
   where light is like darkness."

5. The speech of Zophar

a. He accuses Job of lying and hypocrisy

11 Then Zophar the Naamathite answered:
   2 "Should a multitude of words go unanswered,
   and should one full of talk be vindicated?
3 Should your babble put others to silence,
   and when you mock, shall no one shame you?
4 For you say, 'My conduct[k] is pure,
   and I am clean in God's[l] sight.'
5 But O that God would speak,
   and open his lips to you,
6 and that he would tell you the secrets of wisdom!
   For wisdom is many-sided.[m]
   Know then that God exacts of you less than your guilt
      deserves.

b. He argues for God's sovereignty and infinity

7 "Can you find out the deep things of God?
   Can you find out the limit of the Almighty?[n]
8 It is higher than heaven[o] — what can you do?
   Deeper than Sheol — what can you know?
9 Its measure is longer than the earth,

---

g Cn Compare Gk: Heb toward me; changes and a troop are with me   h Cn Compare Gk Syr: Heb Are not
my days few? Let him cease!   i Heb that I may brighten up a little   j Heb gloom as darkness, deep darkness
k Gk: Heb teaching   l Heb your   m Meaning of Heb uncertain   n Traditional rendering of Heb Shaddai
o Heb The heights of heaven

10.18 Life to Job is a burden. He challenges God to
tell him why he gave him life in the first place. Indeed
the burden of life hinders him from glorifying God.
Therefore he welcomes death.
11.1ff Zophar simply repeats the arguments advanced by Bildad and Eliphaz. According to him, Job
is a liar and a hypocrite, and his plight is the just

recompense for his sins.
11.6 God exacts of you less than your guilt deserves.
Zophar arrogantly insists that Job is a hypocrite who
deserves more, not less, punishment. His conclusion
is based upon his own notion of right and wrong, not
on the mysticism of Eliphaz or the scholarship of
Bildad.

10.14
Job 13.27;
9.28
10.15
Isa 3.11;
Job 9.12, 15;
Ps 25.8
10.16
Isa 38.13;
Lam 3.10;
Job 5.9
10.17
Job 16.8; 7.1
10.18
Job 3.11
10.20
Job 14.1;
7.16, 19;
9.27
10.21
Ps 88.12;
23.4

11.2
Job 8.2
11.3
Jas 3.5;
Job 17.2;
21.3
11.4
Job 6.10;
10.7
11.6
Job 28.21;
Ezra 9.13

11.7
Eccl 3.11;
Rom 11.33
11.8
Job 22.12;
17.16

and broader than the sea.

11.10
Job 9.12;
Rev 3.7

10 If he passes through, and imprisons,
    and assembles for judgment, who can hinder him?

11.11
Job 34.21-25;
Ps 10.14

11 For he knows those who are worthless;
    when he sees iniquity, will he not consider it?

12 But a stupid person will get understanding,
    when a wild ass is born human. _p_

c. He assures Job of restoration upon repentance and reformation

11.13
Ps 78.8; 88.9

13 "If you direct your heart rightly,
    you will stretch out your hands toward him.

11.14
Job 22.23;
Ps 101.3

14 If iniquity is in your hand, put it far away,
    and do not let wickedness reside in your tents.

11.15
1 Jn 3.21;
Ps 27.3

15 Surely then you will lift up your face without blemish;
    you will be secure, and will not fear.

11.16
Isa 65.16;
Job 22.11

16 You will forget your misery;
    you will remember it as waters that have passed away.

11.17
Ps 37.6;
112.4;
Isa 58.8, 10

17 And your life will be brighter than the noonday;
    its darkness will be like the morning.

11.18
Ps 3.5;
Prov 3.24

18 And you will have confidence, because there is hope;
    you will be protected _q_ and take your rest in safety.

11.19
v. 18

19 You will lie down, and no one will make you afraid;
    many will entreat your favor.

11.20
Deut 28.65;
Jer 15.9

20 But the eyes of the wicked will fail;
    all way of escape will be lost to them,
    and their hope is to breathe their last."

6. Job's reply to Zophar

a. Job denies the accusations

12

Then Job answered:
2 "No doubt you are the people,
    and wisdom will die with you.

12.3
Job 13.2

3 But I have understanding as well as you;
    I am not inferior to you.
    Who does not know such things as these?

12.4
Job 6.10, 20;
21.3;
Ps 91.15;
Job 6.29

4 I am a laughingstock to my friends;
    I, who called upon God and he answered me,
    a just and blameless man, I am a laughingstock.

12.5
Ps 123.4

5 Those at ease have contempt for misfortune, _p_
    but it is ready for those whose feet are unstable.

12.6
Job 9.24;
21.9; 22.18

6 The tents of robbers are at peace,
    and those who provoke God are secure,
    who bring their god in their hands. _r_

b. He argues that God is watching over all

7 "But ask the animals, and they will teach you;

_p_ Meaning of Heb uncertain   _q_ Or _you will look around_   _r_ Or _whom God brought forth by his hand_;
Meaning of Heb uncertain

11.13ff Zophar is certain that Job is at fault. But even in error, the remedy he suggests is excellent for any who sin. He tells Job to (1) prepare his heart for a change, (2) turn his hands toward God, (3) put away his transgressions, and (4) "do not let wickedness reside in your tents" (v. 14). This last phrase charges that Job had sheltered wicked people and permitted wicked practices and that, for this, God had taken away his offspring as punishment. Zophar believed Job's home life had to be changed.

11.20 Zophar concludes his statement by saying that the eyes of the wicked shall fail. Apparently, he suspects that Job will not take his counsel. He warns him that those who persist in their wickedness are doomed.
12.2 _wisdom will die with you._ Job ironically concedes that his friends are the human embodiment of wisdom. They "know it all," so that when they perish from the earth wisdom will be gone also!
12.7 _ask the animals._ Job puts down his friends.

the birds of the air, and they will tell you;

8 ask the plants of the earth,[s] and they will teach you;
  and the fish of the sea will declare to you.

9 Who among all these does not know
    that the hand of the LORD has done this?

10 In his hand is the life of every living thing
   and the breath of every human being.

11 Does not the ear test words
   as the palate tastes food?

12 Is wisdom with the aged,
   and understanding in length of days?

c. He enlarges on God's providences

13 "With God[t] are wisdom and strength;
   he has counsel and understanding.

14 If he tears down, no one can rebuild;
   if he shuts someone in, no one can open up.

15 If he withholds the waters, they dry up;
   if he sends them out, they overwhelm the land.

16 With him are strength and wisdom;
   the deceived and the deceiver are his.

17 He leads counselors away stripped,
   and makes fools of judges.

18 He looses the sash of kings,
   and binds a waistcloth on their loins.

19 He leads priests away stripped,
   and overthrows the mighty.

20 He deprives of speech those who are trusted,
   and takes away the discernment of the elders.

21 He pours contempt on princes,
   and looses the belt of the strong.

22 He uncovers the deeps out of darkness,
   and brings deep darkness to light.

23 He makes nations great, then destroys them;
   he enlarges nations, then leads them away.

24 He strips understanding from the leaders[u] of the earth,
   and makes them wander in a pathless waste.

25 They grope in the dark without light;
   he makes them stagger like a drunkard.

d. Job's resentment of his friends

13 "Look, my eye has seen all this,
      my ear has heard and understood it.

2 What you know, I also know;
  I am not inferior to you.

3 But I would speak to the Almighty,[v]

---

[s] Or speak to the earth   [t] Heb him   [u] Heb adds of the people   [v] Traditional rendering of Heb Shaddai

Cross references:
12.9 Isa 41.20
12.10 Acts 17.28; Job 27.3; 33.4
12.11 Job 34.3
12.12 Job 32.7
12.13 Job 9.4; 11.6
12.14 Job 19.10; 37.7
12.15 1 Kings 8.35; Gen 7.11
12.16 v. 13; Job 13.7, 9
12.17 Job 3.14; 19.9; 9.24
12.18 Ps 116.16
12.20 Job 32.9
12.21 Ps 107.40; v. 18
12.22 Dan 2.22; 1 Cor 4.5; Job 3.5
12.23 Ps 107.38; Isa 9.3; Jer 25.9; Deut 12.20; Ps 78.61
12.24 v. 20; Ps 107.40
12.25 Job 5.14; Ps 107.27
13.1 Job 12.9
13.2 Job 12.3
13.3 Job 23.3, 4; v. 15

They think they have all the wisdom in the world. He suggests that animals, birds, and fish can teach them things they do not know.

12.9,10 All creatures and humans derive their being from God. They depend on him for their continuance and are used by him for his purposes. He does with them as he pleases (Ps 115.3).

12.11 The human mind has as good a faculty for discerning between truth and error as the palate has of discerning between the sweet and the sour. The wicked indeed must learn that their minds, although reprobate, will not excuse them from their responsi-

bility to discern the good from the evil.

12.13ff These verses deal with the wisdom, power, and sovereignty of God, who orders and disposes everyone's affairs according to his own will. No one can contradict or resist God. No nation is so strong that it can keep itself from falling and none is so weak that God cannot make it strong (v. 23).

13.2 Job now declares that he does not need his friends to teach him. He is not inferior to them in understanding. He vehemently says his friends "whitewash with lies" (v. 4). These are strong words in his own defense.

and I desire to argue my case with God.

13.4
Ps 119.69;
Jer 23.32

4 As for you, you whitewash with lies;
    all of you are worthless physicians.

13.5
Prov 17.28

5 If you would only keep silent,
    that would be your wisdom!

6 Hear now my reasoning,
    and listen to the pleadings of my lips.

13.7
Job 36.4

7 Will you speak falsely for God,
    and speak deceitfully for him?

8 Will you show partiality toward him,
    will you plead the case for God?

13.9
Ps 44.21;
Gal 6.7

9 Will it be well with you when he searches you out?
    Or can you deceive him, as one person deceives another?

13.10
v. 8

10 He will surely rebuke you
    if in secret you show partiality.

13.11
Job 31.23

11 Will not his majesty terrify you,
    and the dread of him fall upon you?

13.12
Job 15.3

12 Your maxims are proverbs of ashes,
    your defenses are defenses of clay.

e. Job's defense of his own integrity

13.13
v. 5

13 "Let me have silence, and I will speak,
    and let come on me what may.

13.14
1 Sam 19.5

14 I will take my flesh in my teeth,
    and put my life in my hand. *w*

13.15
Ps 23.4;
Prov 14.32;
Job 27.5

15 See, he will kill me; I have no hope; *x*
    but I will defend my ways to his face.

13.16
Ps 5.5

16 This will be my salvation,
    that the godless shall not come before him.

13.17
Job 21.2

17 Listen carefully to my words,
    and let my declaration be in your ears.

13.18
Job 23.4; 9.2

18 I have indeed prepared my case;
    I know that I shall be vindicated.

13.19
Isa 50.8;
Job 40.4

19 Who is there that will contend with me?
    For then I would be silent and die.

13.20
Job 9.34

20 Only grant two things to me,
    then I will not hide myself from your face:

13.21
Ps 39.10

21 withdraw your hand far from me,
    and do not let dread of you terrify me.

13.22
Job 14.15

22 Then call, and I will answer;
    or let me speak, and you reply to me.

*f. Job asks for the number of his sins
and complains of God's severe dealings*

13.23
1 Sam 26.18

23 How many are my iniquities and my sins?
    Make me know my transgression and my sin.

w Gk: Heb Why should I take . . . in my hand?   *x Or Though he kill me, yet I will trust in him*

13.4 Job's temper has shortened. He chastises his friends, comparing himself to them and then condemning them for their falsehoods, their willingness to act as his judge, and their deceitfulness under cover of taking God's side against him.
13.8–11 Job turns the tables on his friends, suggesting that God does not need them to conduct the divine business and that those who pass judgment on others should ask themselves whether they are righteous. He threatens them with the judgment of God for what they are doing to him. The fulfillment of this prophetic admonition took place later when Job was

called upon by God to pray for them for having judged Job unfairly (42.7–9).
13.15 Despite his low estate, Job continues to depend on God. Even if God slays him he will still trust him (cf. NRSV footnote). This is a high expression of faith. All things will work together for good for those who love God, even when everything appears to be against this (Rom 8.28).
13.23ff Job complains that he is at a loss to understand what God has against him and why his maker has treated him so rigorously.

24	Why do you hide your face, and count me as your enemy?	**13.24** Deut 32.20; Ps 13.1; Job 19.11
25	Will you frighten a windblown leaf and pursue dry chaff?	**13.25** Isa 42.3
26	For you write bitter things against me, and make me reap^y the iniquities of my youth.	**13.26** Ps 25.7

27	You put my feet in the stocks,
	    and watch all my paths;
	    you set a bound to the soles of my feet.
		13.27
		Job 33.11

28	One wastes away like a rotten thing, like a garment that is moth-eaten.	**13.28** Isa 50.9; Jas 5.2

g. Job speaks to God

14 "A mortal, born of woman, few of days and full of trouble,
2   comes up like a flower and withers,
  flees like a shadow and does not last.

		14.1 Job 5.7; Eccl 2.23 **14.2** Ps 90.5, 6; Jas 1.10; 1 Pet 1.24
3	Do you fix your eyes on such a one? Do you bring me into judgment with you?	**14.3** Ps 144.3; 143.2
4	Who can bring a clean thing out of an unclean? No one can.	**14.4** Ps 51.2, 10; Jn 3.6; Rom 5.12; Eph 2.3

5	Since their days are determined,
	    and the number of their months is known to you,
	    and you have appointed the bounds that they cannot pass,
		14.5
		Ps 139.16;
		Job 21.21;
		Acts 17.26

6	look away from them, and desist,^{z} that they may enjoy, like laborers, their days.	**14.6** Job 7.19; 7.1

7	"For there is hope for a tree,
	    if it is cut down, that it will sprout again,
	    and that its shoots will not cease.	

8	Though its root grows old in the earth, and its stump dies in the ground,	
9	yet at the scent of water it will bud and put forth branches like a young plant.	**14.9** Isa 55.10
10	But mortals die, and are laid low; humans expire, and where are they?	**14.10** Job 13.19
11	As waters fail from a lake, and a river wastes away and dries up,	**14.11** Isa 19.5

12	so mortals lie down and do not rise again;
	    until the heavens are no more, they will not awake
	    or be roused out of their sleep.
		14.12
		Ps 102.26;
		Acts 3.21;
		Rev 20.11;
		21.1

13	O that you would hide me in Sheol,
	    that you would conceal me until your wrath is past,
	    that you would appoint me a set time, and remember me!
		14.13
		Isa 26.20

14	If mortals die, will they live again?
	    All the days of my service I would wait
	    until my release should come.
		14.14
		Job 7.1

15	You would call, and I would answer you; you would long for the work of your hands.	**14.15** Job 13.22
16	For then you would not^a number my steps, you would not keep watch over my sin;	**14.16** Job 10.6; 31.4; 34.21; Prov 5.21; Jer 32.19

y Heb *inherit* z Cn: Heb *that they may desist* a Syr: Heb lacks *not*

14.1 Job reminds himself of his own frailties and mortality. Life is short, sorrowful, and sinful. He pleads for God to mitigate his miseries and deliver him from his agonies.
14.5 Our days are numbered, determined in advance by God who sets their dates; they cannot be extended or shortened by anyone (cf. Mt 6.27).
14.7 Cut down a tree and it will sprout again. Thus the fate of a tree is better than that of a human being, for such a one cannot sprout again.
14.14 *If mortals die, will they live again?* Job knows that all mortals must die. The greater question is whether they will have life beyond the grave. He answers in the affirmative. We must expect death to come; we may even desire it, as those who long to be with Christ (cf. Phil 1.23).

17 my transgression would be sealed up in a bag,
   and you would cover over my iniquity.

18 "But the mountain falls and crumbles away,
   and the rock is removed from its place;

19 the waters wear away the stones;
   the torrents wash away the soil of the earth;
   so you destroy the hope of mortals.

20 You prevail forever against them, and they pass away;
   you change their countenance, and send them away.

21 Their children come to honor, and they do not know it;
   they are brought low, and it goes unnoticed.

22 They feel only the pain of their own bodies,
   and mourn only for themselves."

C. The second cycle of speeches

1. Eliphaz's second speech

a. Job's own words condemn him

15 Then Eliphaz the Temanite answered:
2 "Should the wise answer with windy knowledge,
   and fill themselves with the east wind?

3 Should they argue in unprofitable talk,
   or in words with which they can do no good?

4 But you are doing away with the fear of God,
   and hindering meditation before God.

5 For your iniquity teaches your mouth,
   and you choose the tongue of the crafty.

6 Your own mouth condemns you, and not I;
   your own lips testify against you.

b. Job is deluding himself

7 "Are you the firstborn of the human race?
   Were you brought forth before the hills?

8 Have you listened in the council of God?
   And do you limit wisdom to yourself?

9 What do you know that we do not know?
   What do you understand that is not clear to us?

10 The gray-haired and the aged are on our side,
   those older than your father.

11 Are the consolations of God too small for you,
   or the word that deals gently with you?

c. Job is condemned before God

12 Why does your heart carry you away,
   and why do your eyes flash,[b]

---

[b] Meaning of Heb uncertain

Cross references (margin):
14.17 Deut 32.34; Hos 13.12
14.18 Job 18.4
14.19 Job 7.6
14.20 Job 34.20; Jas 1.10
14.21 Eccl 9.5; Isa 63.16
15.2 Job 6.26
15.5 Ps 36.3; Prov 16.23; Job 5.12, 13
15.6 Job 9.20; Lk 19.22
15.7 Job 38.4, 21; Ps 90.2; Prov 8.25
15.8 Rom 11.34; Job 12.2
15.9 Job 13.2
15.10 Job 32.6, 7
15.11 Job 36.15, 16; 2 Cor 1.3, 4; Zech 1.13

14.20 People are an unequal match for God. Whoever God contends against will never win the day. The divine purposes cannot be annulled or frustrated.
15.1 Eliphaz (ch. 15), Bildad (ch. 18), and Zophar (ch. 20) present striking pictures of the terrors that befall those who are wicked in this life. Job's friends are unable to answer Job's rebuttals, for experience refutes their contention that the wicked receive just retribution in this life while no injustice befalls the righteous. Later (chs. 27–28) Job acknowledges God's ultimate justice beyond this visible world. He follows this (chs. 29–31) by complaining that God deals capriciously with the world at present.
15.2 *windy knowledge*, i.e., you are a windbag. In their second speeches Job's friends are angry with him because he has refused to accept their comments. Their words now become threatening as they rebuke this tormented soul.
15.3–13 Eliphaz refuses to retreat from what he said at the beginning. Just as vehemently as before, he admonishes Job to stop justifying himself and in so doing accuses him of many evil things (all of which are unfairly inferred without adequate evidence).

13 so that you turn your spirit against God,
   and let such words go out of your mouth?

14 What are mortals, that they can be clean?
   Or those born of woman, that they can be righteous?

15 God puts no trust even in his holy ones,
   and the heavens are not clean in his sight;

16 how much less one who is abominable and corrupt,
   one who drinks iniquity like water!

d. The end of an evil person

17 "I will show you; listen to me;
   what I have seen I will declare —

18 what sages have told,
   and their ancestors have not hidden,

19 to whom alone the land was given,
   and no stranger passed among them.

20 The wicked writhe in pain all their days,
   through all the years that are laid up for the ruthless.

21 Terrifying sounds are in their ears;
   in prosperity the destroyer will come upon them.

22 They despair of returning from darkness,
   and they are destined for the sword.

23 They wander abroad for bread, saying, 'Where is it?'
   They know that a day of darkness is ready at hand;

24 distress and anguish terrify them;
   they prevail against them, like a king prepared for battle.

25 Because they stretched out their hands against God,
   and bid defiance to the Almighty,^{c}

26 running stubbornly against him
   with a thick-bossed shield;

27 because they have covered their faces with their fat,
   and gathered fat upon their loins,

28 they will live in desolate cities,
   in houses that no one should inhabit,
   houses destined to become heaps of ruins;

29 they will not be rich, and their wealth will not endure,
   nor will they strike root in the earth;^{d}

30 they will not escape from darkness;
   the flame will dry up their shoots,
   and their blossom^e will be swept away^f by the wind.

31 Let them not trust in emptiness, deceiving themselves;
   for emptiness will be their recompense.

32 It will be paid in full before their time,
   and their branch will not be green.

33 They will shake off their unripe grape, like the vine,
   and cast off their blossoms, like the olive tree.

34 For the company of the godless is barren,

^{c} Traditional rendering of Heb Shaddai ^{d} Vg: Meaning of Heb uncertain ^{e} Gk: Heb mouth
^{f} Cn: Heb will depart

Cross references (right margin):
15.13 Job 33.13
15.14 Job 14.4; Prov 20.9; Eccl 7.20; Job 25.4; Ps 51.5
15.15 Job 4.18; 25.5
15.16 Ps 14.1, 3; Job 34.7
15.18 Job 8.8
15.20 Job 27.13
15.21 Job 18.11; 20.25; 1 Thess 5.3
15.22 v. 30; Job 27.14
15.23 Ps 59.15; 109.10; Job 18.12
15.25 Job 36.9
15.27 Ps 17.10
15.29 Job 27.16, 17
15.30 Job 5.14; 22.20; 4.9
15.31 Isa 59.4
15.32 Job 22.16; Ps 55.23; Job 18.16
15.33 Hab 3.17
15.34 Job 16.7; 8.22

15.15 The heavens are not clean in the sight of God because they too have been involved in the fall of Satan and of humanity. God's redemption in Christ Jesus also provides for the restoration of the cosmos (Rom 8.18–23).
15.20 Eliphaz here speaks of "the wicked," a term in which he intends to include Job. He hopes Job will see himself from this description.
15.25–28 Eliphaz is certain that the wicked are miserable and therefore the miserable are wicked. Such people act in defiance of God's authority and power (v. 25). They fight against God and are in defiance against him (v. 26). They pamper their flesh until they become fat (v. 27). They enrich themselves by taking spoils from those about them and by delighting in driving out the inhabitants from the cities they have destroyed (v. 28). In spite of all this surface prosperity, however, they are really miserable.
15.31 The prosperity of sinners will not last. They trust in vanity and get vanity for their recompense. It yields them no satisfaction, for the guilt that cleaves to it will ruin the joy of it.

and fire consumes the tents of bribery.

35 They conceive mischief and bring forth evil
and their heart prepares deceit.''

2. Job's second reply to Eliphaz

a. He charges his friends with unkindness

16 Then Job answered:
2 "I have heard many such things;
miserable comforters are you all.

3 Have windy words no limit?
Or what provokes you that you keep on talking?

4 I also could talk as you do,
if you were in my place;
I could join words together against you,
and shake my head at you.

5 I could encourage you with my mouth,
and the solace of my lips would assuage your pain.

b. He alleges that God is angry with him

6 "If I speak, my pain is not assuaged,
and if I forbear, how much of it leaves me?

7 Surely now God has worn me out;
he has^g made desolate all my company.

8 And he has^g shriveled me up,
which is a witness against me;
my leanness has risen up against me,
and it testifies to my face.

9 He has torn me in his wrath, and hated me;
he has gnashed his teeth at me;
my adversary sharpens his eyes against me.

10 They have gaped at me with their mouths;
they have struck me insolently on the cheek;
they mass themselves together against me.

11 God gives me up to the ungodly,
and casts me into the hands of the wicked.

12 I was at ease, and he broke me in two;
he seized me by the neck and dashed me to pieces;
he set me up as his target;

13 his archers surround me.
He slashes open my kidneys, and shows no mercy;
he pours out my gall on the ground.

14 He bursts upon me again and again;
he rushes at me like a warrior.

15 I have sewed sackcloth upon my skin,
and have laid my strength in the dust.

16 My face is red with weeping,
and deep darkness is on my eyelids,

17 though there is no violence in my hands,
and my prayer is pure.

g Heb you have

16.1 In Job's reply to Eliphaz, he accuses him of endless repetition, wrong conclusions, and causeless obstinacy. Eliphaz has broken all the laws of friendship by doing to his brother what his brother would not have done to him.
16.6–22 In this passage Job states that (1) his family has been scattered; (2) he is a skeleton from his disease and pains; (3) his enemies are a terror to him; (4) he is being insolently abused; (5) instead of delivering him God has turned him over to the hands of the wicked (his so-called friends); (6) God has also afflicted him furiously; and (7) Job has stripped himself of all his honor and comfort, using sackcloth rather than silks.

c. His conscience is clear

18 "O earth, do not cover my blood;
    let my outcry find no resting place.
19 Even now, in fact, my witness is in heaven,
    and he that vouches for me is on high.
20 My friends scorn me;
    my eye pours out tears to God,
21 that he would maintain the right of a mortal with God,
    as *h* one does for a neighbor.
22 For when a few years have come,
    I shall go the way from which I shall not return.

d. Job's appeal to God against the verdict of his friends

17 My spirit is broken, my days are extinct,
    the grave is ready for me.
2 Surely there are mockers around me,
    and my eye dwells on their provocation.
3 "Lay down a pledge for me with yourself;
    who is there that will give surety for me?
4 Since you have closed their minds to understanding,
    therefore you will not let them triumph.
5 Those who denounce friends for reward—
    the eyes of their children will fail.
6 "He has made me a byword of the peoples,
    and I am one before whom people spit.
7 My eye has grown dim from grief,
    and all my members are like a shadow.
8 The upright are appalled at this,
    and the innocent stir themselves up against the godless.
9 Yet the righteous hold to their way,
    and they that have clean hands grow stronger and stronger.
10 But you, come back now, all of you,
    and I shall not find a sensible person among you.
11 My days are past, my plans are broken off,
    the desires of my heart.
12 They make night into day;
    'The light,' they say, 'is near to the darkness.'*i*
13 If I look for Sheol as my house,
    if I spread my couch in darkness,
14 if I say to the Pit, 'You are my father,'
    and to the worm, 'My mother,' or 'My sister,'
15 where then is my hope?
    Who will see my hope?
16 Will it go down to the bars of Sheol?
    Shall we descend together into the dust?"

3. Bildad's second speech

a. He reproves Job as haughty and obstinate

18 Then Bildad the Shuhite answered:
2 "How long will you hunt for words?

h Syr Vg Tg: Heb *and*   *i* Meaning of Heb uncertain

Cross references (right margin):
16.18 Isa 26.21; Ps 66.18, 19
16.19 Rom 1.9
16.20 v. 7; Lam 2.19
16.21 1 Kings 8.45; Ps 9.4
16.22 Eccl 12.5
17.1 Ps 88.3, 4
17.2 v. 6; 1 Sam 1.6, 7
17.3 Ps 119.122; Prov 6.1
17.4 Job 12.20
17.5 Lev 19.16; Job 11.20
17.6 Job 30.9, 10
17.7 Job 16.16; 16.8
17.8 Job 22.19
17.9 Prov 4.18; Job 22.30
17.10 Job 12.2
17.11 Job 7.6
17.13 Job 3.13
17.14 Ps 16.10; Job 21.26; 24.20
17.15 Job 7.6
17.16 Jon 2.6; Job 3.17-19

17.1ff Job has reached a point of no return: (1) he is a dying man (v. 1); (2) he is a despised man (v. 6); and (3) he is a man of sorrows (v. 7).
17.2–7 Job appeals to God and begs for him to appear on his behalf. He asks God to right him against these friends who have wronged him. He needs God to do this, for he does not know how to do it himself.
18.1 Bildad now strikes at Job with bitter words and

Consider, and then we shall speak.

3 Why are we counted as cattle?
   Why are we stupid in your sight?
4 You who tear yourself in your anger—
   shall the earth be forsaken because of you,
   or the rock be removed out of its place?

b. *He describes the misery and ruin of the wicked*

5 "Surely the light of the wicked is put out,
   and the flame of their fire does not shine.
6 The light is dark in their tent,
   and the lamp above them is put out.
7 Their strong steps are shortened,
   and their own schemes throw them down.
8 For they are thrust into a net by their own feet,
   and they walk into a pitfall.
9 A trap seizes them by the heel;
   a snare lays hold of them.
10 A rope is hid for them in the ground,
   a trap for them in the path.
11 Terrors frighten them on every side,
   and chase them at their heels.
12 Their strength is consumed by hunger,[j]
   and calamity is ready for their stumbling.
13 By disease their skin is consumed,[k]
   the firstborn of Death consumes their limbs.
14 They are torn from the tent in which they trusted,
   and are brought to the king of terrors.
15 In their tents nothing remains;
   sulfur is scattered upon their habitations.
16 Their roots dry up beneath,
   and their branches wither above.
17 Their memory perishes from the earth,
   and they have no name in the street.
18 They are thrust from light into darkness,
   and driven out of the world.
19 They have no offspring or descendant among their people,
   and no survivor where they used to live.
20 They of the west are appalled at their fate,
   and horror seizes those of the east.
21 Surely such are the dwellings of the ungodly,
   such is the place of those who do not know God."

4. *Job's second reply to Bildad*

a. *Job reproves his friends*

19 Then Job answered:
2 "How long will you torment me,
   and break me in pieces with words?
3 These ten times you have cast reproach upon me;

j Or Disaster is hungry for them   k Cn: Heb It consumes the limbs of his skin

Cross references (left margin):
18.3 Ps 73.22; Job 36.14
18.4 Job 13.14; 14.18
18.5 Prov 13.9; 20.20; 24.20
18.7 Prov 4.12; Job 5.13
18.8 Job 22.10; Ps 9.15; 35.8
18.9 Ps 140.5; Job 5.5
18.10 Ps 69.22
18.11 Job 15.21; Jer 6.25; 20.3
18.12 Isa 8.21
18.14 Job 8.22; 15.21
18.15 Ps 11.6
18.16 Isa 5.24; Hos 9.1-16; Am 2.9; Mal 4.1; Job 15.30, 32
18.17 Ps 34.16; Prov 2.22; 10.7
18.18 Job 5.14; 27.21-23
18.19 Isa 14.22; Jer 22.30
18.21 Jer 9.3; 1 Thess 4.5

adds to his affliction. He maintains sincerely, albeit wrongly, that Job is an obstinate, haughty sinner who refuses to repent. He goes on to describe the misery and the end of the wicked.

18.5ff Bildad acknowledges the miserable estate in which Job finds himself. He cites Job's own words that he sits in the dark, bewildered, frightened, ensnared, and on his way out of this present evil world.

Since he assumes that this is the condition of wicked people generally, he concludes that Job must be one of them.

19.1ff Job arraigns his friends for vexing his soul, breaking him in pieces, giving him a bad character, estranging themselves from him, and magnifying themselves against him. In an unkind and unjust fashion, they have impugned his integrity.

4 And even if it is true that I have erred,
  my error remains with me.

5 If indeed you magnify yourselves against me,
  and make my humiliation an argument against me,

6 know then that God has put me in the wrong,
  and closed his net around me.

7 Even when I cry out, 'Violence!' I am not answered;
  I call aloud, but there is no justice.

b. God the author of his afflictions

8 He has walled up my way so that I cannot pass,
  and he has set darkness upon my paths.

9 He has stripped my glory from me,
  and taken the crown from my head.

10 He breaks me down on every side, and I am gone,
   he has uprooted my hope like a tree.

11 He has kindled his wrath against me,
   and counts me as his adversary.

12 His troops come on together;
   they have thrown up siegeworks¹ against me,
   and encamp around my tent.

c. He is deserted by all others

13 "He has put my family far from me,
   and my acquaintances are wholly estranged from me.

14 My relatives and my close friends have failed me;

15 the guests in my house have forgotten me;
   my serving girls count me as a stranger;
   I have become an alien in their eyes.

16 I call to my servant, but he gives me no answer;
   I must myself plead with him.

17 My breath is repulsive to my wife;
   I am loathsome to my own family.

18 Even young children despise me;
   when I rise, they talk against me.

19 All my intimate friends abhor me,
   and those whom I loved have turned against me.

d. His plea for pity

20 My bones cling to my skin and to my flesh,
   and I have escaped by the skin of my teeth.

21 Have pity on me, have pity on me, O you my friends,
   for the hand of God has touched me!

22 Why do you, like God, pursue me,
   never satisfied with my flesh?

23 "O that my words were written down!
   O that they were inscribed in a book!

24 O that with an iron pen and with lead
   they were engraved on a rock forever!

e. His unshakable confidence in the living Redeemer

25 For I know that my Redeemer^m lives,

¹ Cn: Heb their way   ^m Or Vindicator

19.4	Job 6.24
19.5	Ps 35.26; 38.16
19.6	Job 27.2; 18.8-10
19.7	Job 30.20
19.8	Job 3.23; 30.26
19.9	Ps 89.44; 89.39
19.10	Job 12.14; 7.6; 24.20
19.11	Job 16.9; 13.24
19.12	Job 30.12
19.14	v. 19
19.15	Gen 14.14; Eccl 2.7
19.18	2 Kings 2.23
19.19	Ps 38.11; 55.13
19.20	Job 33.21; Ps 102.5
19.21	Job 6.14; Ps 38.2
19.22	Job 16.11
19.23	Isa 30.8
19.24	Jer 17.1
19.25	Job 16.19; Ps 78.35; Isa 43.14; Jer 50.34

19.6ff Job himself errs in thinking that what has happened to him comes from God. He does not yet know that it springs from God's conflict with Satan and from God's own confidence that Job will not wilt under the attacks.

19.25 Job cannot convince his friends of his inno-

and that at the last he[n] will stand upon the earth;[o]

19.26
Mt 5.8;
1 Cor 13.12;
1 Jn 3.2
19.27
Ps 73.26

26 and after my skin has been thus destroyed,
then in[p] my flesh I shall see God,[q]

27 whom I shall see on my side,[r]
and my eyes shall behold, and not another.
My heart faints within me!

19.28
Ps 69.26

28 If you say, 'How we will persecute him!'
and, 'The root of the matter is found in him';

19.29
Job 22.4

29 be afraid of the sword,
for wrath brings the punishment of the sword,
so that you may know there is a judgment."

5. Zophar's second discourse: the misery and ruin that await the wicked

20 Then Zophar the Naamathite answered:

2 "Pay attention! My thoughts urge me to answer,
because of the agitation within me.

20.3
Job 19.3

3 I hear censure that insults me,
and a spirit beyond my understanding answers me.

20.4
Deut 4.32

4 Do you not know this from of old,
ever since mortals were placed on earth,

20.5
Ps 37.35;
73.19
20.6
Isa 14.13,
14;
Ob 3, 4
20.7
Job 4.20;
7.10; 8.18
20.8
Ps 73.20;
90.5;
Job 18.18;
27.21-23
20.9
Job 7.8, 10
20.10
Job 5.4;
27.16, 17
20.11
Job 13.26;
21.26
20.12
Prov 20.17;
Ps 10.7

5 that the exulting of the wicked is short,
and the joy of the godless is but for a moment?

6 Even though they mount up high as the heavens,
and their head reaches to the clouds,

7 they will perish forever like their own dung;
those who have seen them will say, 'Where are they?'

8 They will fly away like a dream, and not be found;
they will be chased away like a vision of the night.

9 The eye that saw them will see them no more,
nor will their place behold them any longer.

10 Their children will seek the favor of the poor,
and their hands will give back their wealth.

11 Their bodies, once full of youth,
will lie down in the dust with them.

12 "Though wickedness is sweet in their mouth,
though they hide it under their tongues,

13 though they are loath to let it go,
and hold it in their mouths,

14 yet their food is turned in their stomachs;
it is the venom of asps within them.

15 They swallow down riches and vomit them up again;
God casts them out of their bellies.

---

[n] Or *that he the Last*   [o] Heb *dust*   [p] Or *without*   [q] Meaning of Heb of this verse uncertain   [r] Or *for myself*

---

cence. His last and only confidence is that God will vindicate him; God will be his Redeemer!
19.26 The doctrine of the resurrection appears in undeveloped form in the O.T., awaiting fuller explication in the N.T. Other O.T. references to the resurrection are Ps 16.10; 49.15; Isa 26.19; Dan 12.2; Hos 13.14. In Jesus' day the Jews looked for the resurrection of the body (Jn 11.24; Heb 6.1,2). It was denied by the Sadducees, the theological liberals of the day, whereas it was basic to Pharisee teaching (Acts 23.6–8). Jesus believed and taught the resurrection of the body (Mt 22.29–32; Lk 14.14; Jn 5.28,29). The apostles preached it constantly and consistently (Acts 4.2; 17.18; 24.15) as the central theme of the

Christian hope. This doctrine has its foundation in the resurrection of Jesus, a historical event.
20.1ff Zophar is now angry with Job, whom he charges with provocation for his failure to accept the judgment of his condemning friends. Zophar speaks about "the exulting of the wicked" and "the joy of the godless" (v. 5). According to him, Job was guilty of the lusts of the flesh (v. 11), the love of the world and its wealth (v. 15), and mistreatment of his neighbors by injustice, oppression, and violence (v. 19).
20.4–9 The prosperity of the wicked does not last for long; their ruin is certain and will come upon them shortly.

16 They will suck the poison of asps;
   the tongue of a viper will kill them.
17 They will not look on the rivers,
   the streams flowing with honey and curds.
18 They will give back the fruit of their toil,
   and will not swallow it down;
   from the profit of their trading
   they will get no enjoyment.
19 For they have crushed and abandoned the poor,
   they have seized a house that they did not build.
20 "They knew no quiet in their bellies;
   in their greed they let nothing escape.
21 There was nothing left after they had eaten;
   therefore their prosperity will not endure.
22 In full sufficiency they will be in distress;
   all the force of misery will come upon them.
23 To fill their belly to the full
   God*s* will send his fierce anger into them,
   and rain it upon them as their food.*t*
24 They will flee from an iron weapon;
   a bronze arrow will strike them through.
25 It is drawn forth and comes out of their body,
   and the glittering point comes out of their gall;
   terrors come upon them.
26 Utter darkness is laid up for their treasures;
   a fire fanned by no one will devour them;
   what is left in their tent will be consumed.
27 The heavens will reveal their iniquity,
   and the earth will rise up against them.
28 The possessions of their house will be carried away,
   dragged off in the day of God's*u* wrath.
29 This is the portion of the wicked from God,
   the heritage decreed for them by God."

6. Job's second reply to Zophar

a. He pleads to speak without interruption

21
   Then Job answered:
2 "Listen carefully to my words,
   and let this be your consolation.
3 Bear with me, and I will speak;
   then after I have spoken, mock on.
4 As for me, is my complaint addressed to mortals?
   Why should I not be impatient?
5 Look at me, and be appalled,
   and lay your hand upon your mouth.
6 When I think of it I am dismayed,
   and shuddering seizes my flesh.

b. The wicked often prosper in this life

7 Why do the wicked live on,

s Heb *he*   *t* Cn: Meaning of Heb uncertain   *u* Heb *his*

Cross references (right margin):
20.16 Deut 32.24, 33
20.17 Job 29.6; Deut 32.13, 14
20.18 vv. 10, 15
20.19 Job 24.2-4; 35.9
20.20 Eccl 5.13, 14
20.21 Job 15.29
20.23 Ps 78.30, 31
20.24 Isa 24.18; Jer 48.43; Am 5.19
20.25 Job 16.13; 18.11
20.26 Job 18.18; Ps 21.9
20.27 Deut 31.28
20.28 Deut 28.31; Job 21.30
20.29 Job 27.13
21.3 Job 16.10
21.4 Job 6.11
21.5 Judg 18.19; Job 29.9; 40.4
21.7 Job 12.6; Ps 73.3, 12; Jer 12.1

20.17–20 Job will be disappointed in his expectation of worldly wealth; he will lose his estate and his mind will have no rest.
20.22ff Job can expect wrath and vengeance against him from God. His ruin is inevitable and inescapable —a terrible ruin that will make his family suffer. It will be a righteous and just judgment.
21.7ff Job argues that, contrary to what his friends have said, the wicked sometimes prosper. They do not necessarily reap their just deserts in this life. Indirectly he is saying that those who appear to be reaping bad rewards for their wickedness may not be

reach old age, and grow mighty in power?

21.8
Ps 17.14
8 Their children are established in their presence,
  and their offspring before their eyes.

21.9
Ps 73.5
9 Their houses are safe from fear,
  and no rod of God is upon them.

21.10
Ex 23.26
10 Their bull breeds without fail;
   their cow calves and never miscarries.

11 They send out their little ones like a flock,
   and their children dance around.

21.12
Ps 81.2;
Job 30.31
12 They sing to the tambourine and the lyre,
   and rejoice to the sound of the pipe.

21.13
Job 36.11
13 They spend their days in prosperity,
   and in peace they go down to Sheol.

21.14
Job 22.17;
Prov 1.29
14 They say to God, 'Leave us alone!
   We do not desire to know your ways.

21.15
Ex 5.2;
Job 34.9;
Mal 3.14
15 What is the Almighty,^{v} that we should serve him?
   And what profit do we get if we pray to him?'

21.16
Job 22.18
16 Is not their prosperity indeed their own achievement?^{w}
   The plans of the wicked are repugnant to me.

c. A sovereign God does as he pleases with righteous and wicked alike

21.17
Job 18.5, 6,
12
17 "How often is the lamp of the wicked put out?
   How often does calamity come upon them?
   How often does God^x distribute pains in his anger?

21.18
Ps 1.4
18 How often are they like straw before the wind,
   and like chaff that the storm carries away?

21.19
Ex 20.5
19 You say, 'God stores up their iniquity for their children.'
   Let it be paid back to them, so that they may know it.

21.20
Ps 75.8;
Isa 51.17;
Jer 25.15;
Rev 14.10
20 Let their own eyes see their destruction,
   and let them drink of the wrath of the Almighty.^{v}

21.21
Job 14.5
21 For what do they care for their household after them,
   when the number of their months is cut off?

21.22
Isa 40.13,
14;
Rom 11.34
22 Will any teach God knowledge,
   seeing that he judges those that are on high?

23 One dies in full prosperity,
   being wholly at ease and secure,

24 his loins full of milk
   and the marrow of his bones moist.

25 Another dies in bitterness of soul,
   never having tasted of good.

21.26
Eccl 9.2;
Job 24.20
26 They lie down alike in the dust,
   and the worms cover them.

d. Job admits that his friends will not agree with him

27 "Oh, I know your thoughts,
   and your schemes to wrong me.

21.28
Job 12.21;
8.22
28 For you say, 'Where is the house of the prince?
   Where is the tent in which the wicked lived?'

21.30
Prov 16.4;
2 Pet 2.9;
Job 20.28;
Rom 2.5
29 Have you not asked those who travel the roads,
   and do you not accept their testimony,

30 that the wicked are spared in the day of calamity,

^{v} Traditional rendering of Heb *Shaddai* ^{w} Heb *in their hand* ^{x} Heb *he*

---

wicked, even as the prosperous may not be just.
21.17ff Job continues his argument that the wicked often end their days in pomp and prosperity. The righteous may suffer and the wicked may prosper.

But God will not let the wicked go forever unpunished or the righteous left forever in their misery. A day of judgment is coming.

and are rescued in the day of wrath?
31 Who declares their way to their face,
   and who repays them for what they have done?
32 When they are carried to the grave,
   a watch is kept over their tomb.
33 The clods of the valley are sweet to them;
   everyone will follow after,
   and those who went before are innumerable.
34 How then will you comfort me with empty nothings?
   There is nothing left of your answers but falsehood.”

D. The third cycle of speeches

1. Eliphaz's third speech

a. He charges that Job has accused God of injustice

22 Then Eliphaz the Temanite answered:
2 “Can a mortal be of use to God?
   Can even the wisest be of service to him?
3 Is it any pleasure to the Almighty^y if you are righteous,
   or is it gain to him if you make your ways blameless?
4 Is it for your piety that he reproves you,
   and enters into judgment with you?
5 Is not your wickedness great?
   There is no end to your iniquities?

b. He catalogs Job's sins

6 For you have exacted pledges from your family for no reason,
   and stripped the naked of their clothing.
7 You have given no water to the weary to drink,
   and you have withheld bread from the hungry.
8 The powerful possess the land,
   and the favored live in it.
9 You have sent widows away empty-handed,
   and the arms of the orphans you have crushed.^z
10 Therefore snares are around you,
   and sudden terror overwhelms you,
11 or darkness so that you cannot see;
   a flood of water covers you.

12 “Is not God high in the heavens?
   See the highest stars, how lofty they are!
13 Therefore you say, ‘What does God know?
   Can he judge through the deep darkness?
14 Thick clouds enwrap him, so that he does not see,
   and he walks on the dome of heaven.’

y Traditional rendering of Heb *Shaddai*   z Gk Syr Tg Vg: Heb *were crushed*

Cross references (right margin):
21.33 Job 3.22; 17.16; 3.19; 24.24
21.34 Job 16.2
22.2 Lk 17.10
22.4 Job 14.3; Ps 143.2
22.5 Job 11.6; 15.5
22.6 Ex 22.26; Deut 24.6, 17; Ezek 18.12, 16
22.7 Mt 10.42; Job 31.31
22.9 Job 24.3; Isa 10.2
22.11 Job 5.14; Ps 69.2
22.12 Job 11.7-9
22.13 Ps 10.11
22.14 Job 26.9

21.34 Job knows that his friends will disagree with him. But he concludes that because they begin with the wrong premise, they come out with the wrong conclusion. They cannot comfort him as they think they are doing when they argue that piety will be crowned by prosperity. This, he says, is an erroneous conclusion, so they cannot deliver him from his misery.
22.1ff Eliphaz makes a true statement but draws a false conclusion. He argues that Job has complained so much about his afflictions that he is accusing God of being unjust by sending them. This is true enough in itself, but inappropriate, for Job was not accusing God of injustice.
22.6 Eliphaz says in effect that they have been very lenient with Job. Now he takes off his gloves and catalogues the numerous sins he thinks Job has committed. He maintains all of Job's present troubles are the result of having committed these supposed sins. His indictment contradicts God's own appraisal of his servant (see 1.8). Job's friends are guilty of false accusations and they are sinning when they so accuse him. In retrospect, their own sin seems to be far greater than all of their accusations against Job.

c. He would awaken Job to repentance

15 Will you keep to the old way
    that the wicked have trod?

22.16
Job 15.32;
14.19;
Mt 7.26, 27

16 They were snatched away before their time;
    their foundation was washed away by a flood.

17 They said to God, 'Leave us alone,'
    and 'What can the Almighty*a* do to us?'*b*

22.18
Job 12.6;
21.16

18 Yet he filled their houses with good things—
    but the plans of the wicked are repugnant to me.

22.19
Ps 58.10;
107.42

19 The righteous see it and are glad;
    the innocent laugh them to scorn,

22.20
Ps 18.39;
Job 15.30

20 saying, 'Surely our adversaries are cut off,
    and what they left, the fire has consumed.'

d. He urges Job to repent and be restored

22.21
Jer 9.24;
Gal 4.9

21 "Agree with God,*c* and be at peace;
    in this way good will come to you.

22.22
Ps 138.4

22 Receive instruction from his mouth,
    and lay up his words in your heart.

22.23
Job 8.5;
Isa 19.22;
Acts 20.32;
Job 11.14

23 If you return to the Almighty,*a* you will be restored,
    if you remove unrighteousness from your tents,

22.24
Ps 19.10

24 if you treat gold like dust,
    and gold of Ophir like the stones of the torrent-bed,

22.25
Isa 33.6;
Mt 6.20

25 and if the Almighty*a* is your gold
    and your precious silver,

22.26
Job 27.10;
Isa 58.14

26 then you will delight yourself in the Almighty,*a*
    and lift up your face to God.

22.27
Job 33.26;
Isa 58.9;
Job 34.28;
Ps 22.25

27 You will pray to him, and he will hear you,
    and you will pay your vows.

28 You will decide on a matter, and it will be established for you,
    and light will shine on your ways.

22.28
Ps 145.19

29 When others are humiliated, you say it is pride;
    for he saves the humble.

22.29
Prov 29.23;
Mt 23.12;
1 Pet 5.5

30 He will deliver even those who are guilty;
    they will escape because of the cleanness of your hands."*d*

22.30
Job 42.7, 8;
2 Sam 22.21

2. Job's third reply to Eliphaz

a. He would find God and be tried of him

23 2 Then Job answered:
    "Today also my complaint is bitter;*e*
    his*f* hand is heavy despite my groaning.

23.2
Job 7.11; 6.2,
3

3 Oh, that I knew where I might find him,
    that I might come even to his dwelling!

23.3
Deut 4.29;
Ps 9.4

4 I would lay my case before him,
    and fill my mouth with arguments.

23.4
Job 13.18

5 I would learn what he would answer me,
    and understand what he would say to me.

a Traditional rendering of Heb *Shaddai*   *b* Gk Syr: Heb *them*   *c* Heb *him*   *d* Meaning of Heb uncertain   *e* Syr Vg Tg: Heb *rebellious*   *f* Gk Syr: Heb *my*

22.21 It may seem strange that from the same fountain both sweet and bitter water comes. Eliphaz must be given credit for seeking to get Job to repent and thus to recover his lost estate. He assures him of restoration if only he will follow what Eliphaz has laid before him. For those who are wicked, following this counsel will bring about restitution and assurance of pardon by God's grace. But for Job, this excellent counsel is built on the mistaken notion that he is wicked. If Job were to repent, he would lose his own integrity, for he is innocent of the charge his friends press against him.
23.3 Job realizes that his only refuge is God himself. His friends will not believe him, but he is confident that God will sustain his innocence. But the face of God is hidden from him. The inscrutability of the Almighty is now his problem. He wonders why God does not intervene on his behalf.

6 Would he contend with me in the greatness of his power?
       No; but he would give heed to me.
7 There an upright person could reason with him,
       and I should be acquitted forever by my judge.

8 "If I go forward, he is not there;
       or backward, I cannot perceive him;
9 on the left he hides, and I cannot behold him;
       I turn^g to the right, but I cannot see him.
10 But he knows the way that I take;
       when he has tested me, I shall come out like gold.
11 My foot has held fast to his steps;
       I have kept his way and have not turned aside.
12 I have not departed from the commandment of his lips;
       I have treasured in^h my bosom the words of his mouth.
13 But he stands alone and who can dissuade him?
       What he desires, that he does.
14 For he will complete what he appoints for me;
       and many such things are in his mind.
15 Therefore I am terrified at his presence;
       when I consider, I am in dread of him.
16 God has made my heart faint;
       the Almighty^i has terrified me;
17 If only I could vanish in darkness,
       and thick darkness would cover my face!^j

b. The punishment of the wicked is not always seen

24 "Why are times not kept by the Almighty,^i
       and why do those who know him never see his days?
2 The wicked^k remove landmarks;
       they seize flocks and pasture them.
3 They drive away the donkey of the orphan;
       they take the widow's ox for a pledge.
4 They thrust the needy off the road;
       the poor of the earth all hide themselves.
5 Like wild asses in the desert
       they go out to their toil,
   scavenging in the wasteland
       food for their young.
6 They reap in a field not their own
       and they glean in the vineyard of the wicked.
7 They lie all night naked, without clothing,
       and have no covering in the cold.
8 They are wet with the rain of the mountains,
       and cling to the rock for want of shelter.

9 "There are those who snatch the orphan child from the breast,
       and take as a pledge the infant of the poor.

Cross references (right margin):

23.6 Job 9.4
23.7 Job 13.3, 16
23.8 Job 9.11
23.10 Ps 139.1-3
23.11 Ps 44.18
23.12 Jn 4.32, 34
23.13 Job 9.12; 12.14; Ps 115.3
23.14 1 Thess 3.3
23.16 Ps 22.14; Jer 51.46
23.17 Job 10.18, 19; 19.8
24.1 Ps 31.15; Jer 46.10
24.2 Deut 19.14; 27.17; 28.31
24.3 Ex 22.26; Deut 24.6, 10, 12, 17; Job 22.6
24.4 Deut 24.14; Prov 28.28
24.5 Job 39.5-8; Ps 104.23
24.7 Ex 22.26; Job 22.6
24.8 Lam 4.5
24.9 Deut 24.17

---

g Syr Vg: Heb *he turns*   h Gk Vg: Heb *from*   i Traditional rendering of Heb *Shaddai*   j Or *But I am not destroyed by the darkness; he has concealed the thick darkness from me*   k Gk: Heb *they*

23.10 Job knows that these friends have falsely accused him with that of which he was never guilty. But his God, who knew every step he had taken, would not do so. God understands honest intentions, even though some people do not, cannot, or will not.
23.13 God's counsels cannot be changed and his power is irresistible. Mortals may desire to do things they should not do or cannot do. But the sovereign Lord, whose ways are true and pure, will do all he chooses, for all that he does is in accord with the counsel of his will.
24.1 Job once again speaks concerning the prosperity of wicked people. He argues that many who act corruptly and live in open defiance of the rules of justice and common honesty, thrive and succeed in their wrongful practices. We do not see them get their just deserts in this life.

10 They go about naked, without clothing;
   though hungry, they carry the sheaves;

11 between their terraces[l] they press out oil;
   they tread the wine presses, but suffer thirst.

24.12
Jer 51.52;
Ezek 26.15;
Job 9.23, 24

12 From the city the dying groan,
   and the throat of the wounded cries for help;
   yet God pays no attention to their prayer.

24.13
Isa 5.20;
Jn 3.19

13 "There are those who rebel against the light,
   who are not acquainted with its ways,
   and do not stay in its paths.

24.14
Mic 2.1;
Ps 10.8

14 The murderer rises at dusk
   to kill the poor and needy,
   and in the night is like a thief.

24.15
Prov 7.9;
Ps 10.11

15 The eye of the adulterer also waits for the twilight,
   saying, 'No eye will see me';
   and he disguises his face.

24.16
Ex 22.2

16 In the dark they dig through houses;
   by day they shut themselves up;
   they do not know the light.

24.17
Ps 91.5

17 For deep darkness is morning to all of them;
   for they are friends with the terrors of deep darkness.

24.18
Job 9.26;
Ps 90.5

18 "Swift are they on the face of the waters;
   their portion in the land is cursed;
   no treader turns toward their vineyards.

24.19
Job 6.16, 17;
21.13
24.20
Ps 31.12;
Prov 10.7

19 Drought and heat snatch away the snow waters;
   so does Sheol those who have sinned.

20 The womb forgets them;
   the worm finds them sweet;
   they are no longer remembered;
   so wickedness is broken like a tree.

24.21
Job 22.9

21 "They harm[m] the childless woman,
   and do no good to the widow.

24.22
Deut 28.66

22 Yet God[n] prolongs the life of the mighty by his power;
   they rise up when they despair of life.

24.23
Job 12.6;
11.11

23 He gives them security, and they are supported;
   his eyes are upon their ways.

24.24
Ps 37.10;
Job 14.21;
Isa 17.5

24 They are exalted a little while, and then are gone;
   they wither and fade like the mallow;[o]
   they are cut off like the heads of grain.

24.25
Job 6.28;
27.4

25 If it is not so, who will prove me a liar,
   and show that there is nothing in what I say?"

3. Bildad's third speech: no one is righteous before God

25 Then Bildad the Shuhite answered:
2 "Dominion and fear are with God;[p]

25.2
Job 9.4;
Rev 1.6;
Job 22.12

l Meaning of Heb uncertain   m Gk Tg: Heb *feed on* or *associate with*   n Heb *he*   o Gk: Heb *like all others*   p Heb *him*

24.13–25 Those who secretly practice villainy may go undiscovered and therefore unpunished. Experience proves that daring sinners prosper and often end their days in apparent peace. Such sinners even seem to have the protection of deity (v. 23). Job insists that they are exalted for a time, perhaps even until they die. But a day will come when they are cut off forever. Their death, even if they die in ease, will prove to be their ruin. The grave at last will consume them. Job

challenges the opposition to show him that he is wrong (v. 25).

25.1ff Bildad either knows he cannot best Job in the argument or he feels that the pursuit of the issue is no longer profitable. He is content to say that God is glorious and people are guilty and impure before him. At this point he might have profitably applied this theology to himself and joined Job in common prayer for all of them.

he makes peace in his high heaven.
3 Is there any number to his armies?
   Upon whom does his light not arise?
4 How then can a mortal be righteous before God?
   How can one born of woman be pure?
5 If even the moon is not bright
   and the stars are not pure in his sight,
6 how much less a mortal, who is a maggot,
   and a human being, who is a worm!"

4. Job's third reply to Bildad:
he knows the greatness and majesty of God

26 Then Job answered:
2 "How you have helped one who has no power!
   How you have assisted the arm that has no strength!
3 How you have counseled one who has no wisdom,
   and given much good advice!
4 With whose help have you uttered words,
   and whose spirit has come forth from you?
5 The shades below tremble,
   the waters and their inhabitants.
6 Sheol is naked before God,
   and Abaddon has no covering.
7 He stretches out Zaphon*q* over the void,
   and hangs the earth upon nothing.
8 He binds up the waters in his thick clouds,
   and the cloud is not torn open by them.
9 He covers the face of the full moon,
   and spreads over it his cloud.
10 He has described a circle on the face of the waters,
   at the boundary between light and darkness.
11 The pillars of heaven tremble,
   and are astounded at his rebuke.
12 By his power he stilled the Sea;
   by his understanding he struck down Rahab.
13 By his wind the heavens were made fair;
   his hand pierced the fleeing serpent.
14 These are indeed but the outskirts of his ways;
   and how small a whisper do we hear of him!
   But the thunder of his power who can understand?"

5. Job's last reply to his friends
a. *He vows that he speaks the truth*

27 Job again took up his discourse and said:
2 "As God lives, who has taken away my right,
   and the Almighty,*r* who has made my soul bitter,
3 as long as my breath is in me

q Or *the North*   *r* Traditional rendering of Heb *Shaddai*

Cross references:
25.3 Jas 1.17
25.4 Job 4.17; Ps 143.2; Job 14.4
25.5 Job 31.26; 15.15
25.6 Job 7.17; Ps 22.6
26.2 Ps 71.9
26.6 Ps 139.8, 11; Heb 4.13
26.7 Job 9.8
26.8 Prov 30.4
26.9 Ps 97.2
26.10 Job 38.8-11; Prov 8.29; Job 38.19, 20, 24
26.12 Ex 14.21; Isa 51.15; Jer 31.35
26.13 Job 9.8; Isa 27.1
26.14 Job 36.29
27.1 Job 13.12; 29.1
27.2 Job 34.5; 9.18
27.3 Job 32.8; 33.4

26.1ff Here Job employs irony in making light of Bildad's discourse. He goes on to praise the majesty and greatness of God, who performs deeds no one can match. Job then begins an extensive discourse that will end his argument at 31.40. Then follows the extended statement of Elihu, which leads to the intervention of God into the disputation. God puts an end to the matter; Job is delivered and his friends are dealt with in judgment.
26.7 Job gives many illustrations of the wisdom and power of God in the creation and the preservation of this planet earth. God hung the earth on nothing; he set the bounds of the waters; he created giant amphibians under the waters; he shook and even now shakes the mountains by mighty storms and tempests.
27.1 Job's goal from this point on is to back up all he has said with a solemn oath, to silence his critics, and to assume all blame if it can be shown that he is a liar.

and the spirit of God is in my nostrils,

27.4
Job 6.28

4   my lips will not speak falsehood,
      and my tongue will not utter deceit.

27.5
Job 2.9;
13.15

5   Far be it from me to say that you are right;
      until I die I will not put away my integrity from me.

27.6
Job 2.3;
13.18;
Acts 23.1

6   I hold fast my righteousness, and will not let it go;
      my heart does not reproach me for any of my days.

b. *His detestation of the wicked*

7   "May my enemy be like the wicked,
      and may my opponent be like the unrighteous.

27.8
Job 8.13;
11.20

8   For what is the hope of the godless when God cuts them off,
      when God takes away their lives?

27.9
Job 35.12;
Prov 1.28;
Isa 1.15;
Jer 14.12;
Mic 3.4

9   Will God hear their cry
      when trouble comes upon them?
10 Will they take delight in the Almighty?s
      Will they call upon God at all times?

27.10
Job 22.26, 27

11 I will teach you concerning the hand of God;
      that which is with the Almightys I will not conceal.
12 All of you have seen it yourselves;
      why then have you become altogether vain?

27.13
Job 20.29;
15.20

13 "This is the portion of the wicked with God,
      and the heritage that oppressors receive from the Almighty:s

27.14
Deut 28.41;
Hos 9.13;
Job 20.10

14 If their children are multiplied, it is for the sword;
      and their offspring have not enough to eat.

27.15
Ps 78.64

15 Those who survive them the pestilence buries,
      and their widows make no lamentation.

27.16
Zech 9.3

16 Though they heap up silver like dust,
      and pile up clothing like clay—

27.17
Prov 28.8;
Eccl 2.26

17 they may pile it up, but the just will wear it,
      and the innocent will divide the silver.
18 They build their houses like nests,
      like booths made by sentinels of the vineyard.

27.19
Ezek 29.5;
Job 7.8, 21

19 They go to bed with wealth, but will do so no more;
      they open their eyes, and it is gone.

27.20
Job 15.21;
20.8

20 Terrors overtake them like a flood;
      in the night a whirlwind carries them off.

27.21
Job 21.18;
7.10

21 The east wind lifts them up and they are gone;
      it sweeps them out of their place.

27.22
Jer 13.14;
Ezek 5.11;
Job 11.20

22 Itt hurls at them without pity;
      they flee from itsu power in headlong flight.

27.23
Lam 2.15;
Job 18.18

23 Itt claps itsu hands at them,
      and hisses at them from itsu place.

c. *How and where true wisdom is to be acquired*

28 "Surely there is a mine for silver,
      and a place for gold to be refined.

s Traditional rendering of Heb *Shaddai*   t Or *He* (that is God)   u Or *his*

27.6 Job maintains that his conscience is clear. His walk is upright and he has committed no gross sins. He has integrity and looks to the end of his days with good conscience.

27.7ff Job expresses his own hatred of the wicked, making clear that whatever prosperity, power, and adulation they attain will come to an unhappy end. Their wealth will disappear, terror will overtake them, and the wrath of God will be their portion. Their wives and offspring will participate in the ca-

lamity, for what the wicked do affects the lives of their loved ones.

28.1ff Job now declares that wisdom, not wealth and power, is everyone's greatest need. Its value is unequaled, and all other things shrink into insignificance if there is no wisdom. He concludes with a sparkling statement: "The fear of the Lord, that is wisdom; and to depart from evil is understanding" (v. 28; see note).

2 Iron is taken out of the earth,
　and copper is smelted from ore.
3 Miners put[v] an end to darkness,
　and search out to the farthest bound
　the ore in gloom and deep darkness.
4 They open shafts in a valley away from human habitation;
　they are forgotten by travelers,
　they sway suspended, remote from people.
5 As for the earth, out of it comes bread;
　but underneath it is turned up as by fire.
6 Its stones are the place of sapphires,[w]
　and its dust contains gold.

7 "That path no bird of prey knows,
　and the falcon's eye has not seen it.
8 The proud wild animals have not trodden it;
　the lion has not passed over it.

9 "They put their hand to the flinty rock,
　and overturn mountains by the roots.
10 They cut out channels in the rocks,
　and their eyes see every precious thing.
11 The sources of the rivers they probe;[x]
　hidden things they bring to light.

12 "But where shall wisdom be found?
　And where is the place of understanding?
13 Mortals do not know the way to it,[y]
　and it is not found in the land of the living.
14 The deep says, 'It is not in me,'
　and the sea says, 'It is not with me.'
15 It cannot be gotten for gold,
　and silver cannot be weighed out as its price.
16 It cannot be valued in the gold of Ophir,
　in precious onyx or sapphire.[w]
17 Gold and glass cannot equal it,
　nor can it be exchanged for jewels of fine gold.
18 No mention shall be made of coral or of crystal;
　the price of wisdom is above pearls.
19 The chrysolite of Ethiopia[z] cannot compare with it,
　nor can it be valued in pure gold.

20 "Where then does wisdom come from?
　And where is the place of understanding?
21 It is hidden from the eyes of all living,
　and concealed from the birds of the air.
22 Abaddon and Death say,
　'We have heard a rumor of it with our ears.'

23 "God understands the way to it,
　and he knows its place.
24 For he looks to the ends of the earth,
　and sees everything under the heavens.
25 When he gave to the wind its weight,
　and apportioned out the waters by measure;

Cross references (right margin):
28.2 Deut 8.9
28.5 Ps 104.14
28.9 Deut 8.15; 32.13
28.12 vv. 23, 28
28.13 Prov 3.15
28.17 Prov 8.10; 16.16
28.18 Prov 3.15; 8.11
28.19 Prov 8.19
28.20 vv. 23, 28
28.22 Job 26.6
28.23 vv. 23-28
28.24 Ps 33.13; Prov 15.3
28.25 Ps 135.7; Job 12.15

---

v Heb *He puts*　w Or *lapis lazuli*　x Gk Vg: Heb *bind*　y Gk: Heb *its price*　z Or *Nubia*; Heb *Cush*

28.12ff The price of wisdom is inestimable. Whoever has it is richer and happier than those who only have silver and gold. Wisdom can be found only in God and in true religion.

28.26
Job 37.6, 11,
12; 37.3;
38.25

26 when he made a decree for the rain,
and a way for the thunderbolt;
27 then he saw it and declared it;
he established it, and searched it out.

28.28
Deut 4.6;
Ps 111.10;
Prov 1.7;
9.10

28 And he said to humankind,
'Truly, the fear of the Lord, that is wisdom;
and to depart from evil is understanding.' "

d. *Job sums up his life*

(1) HIS EARLIER PROSPERITY

29.1
Job 13.12;
27.1

29

Job again took up his discourse and said:
2 "O that I were as in the months of old,
as in the days when God watched over me;

29.2
Jer 31.28
29.3
Job 11.17

3 when his lamp shone over my head,
and by his light I walked through darkness;

29.4
Ps 25.14

4 when I was in my prime,
when the friendship of God was upon my tent;
5 when the Almighty*a* was still with me,
when my children were around me;

29.6
Job 20.17;
Deut 32.13,
14

6 when my steps were washed with milk,
and the rock poured out for me streams of oil!
7 When I went out to the gate of the city,
when I took my seat in the square,
8 the young men saw me and withdrew,
and the aged rose up and stood;

29.9
v. 21;
Job 21.5
29.10
v. 22

9 the nobles refrained from talking,
and laid their hands on their mouths;
10 the voices of princes were hushed,
and their tongues stuck to the roof of their mouths.
11 When the ear heard, it commended me,
and when the eye saw, it approved;

29.12
Job 31.16,
17, 21
29.13
Job 31.19, 20

12 because I delivered the poor who cried,
and the orphan who had no helper.
13 The blessing of the wretched came upon me,
and I caused the widow's heart to sing for joy.

29.14
Ps 132.9;
Isa 59.17;
61.10;
Eph 6.14

14 I put on righteousness, and it clothed me;
my justice was like a robe and a turban.
15 I was eyes to the blind,
and feet to the lame.

29.16
Prov 29.7

16 I was a father to the needy,
and I championed the cause of the stranger.

29.17
Ps 3.7

17 I broke the fangs of the unrighteous,
and made them drop their prey from their teeth.

29.18
Ps 30.6

18 Then I thought, 'I shall die in my nest,
and I shall multiply my days like the phoenix;*b*

29.19
Job 18.16;
Jer 17.8
29.20
Gen 49.24;
Ps 18.34

19 my roots spread out to the waters,
with the dew all night on my branches;
20 my glory was fresh with me,
and my bow ever new in my hand.'

a Traditional rendering of Heb *Shaddai*   *b* Or *like sand*

28.28 The thought of Job may be summed up this way: to be truly religious is to be truly wise. God is the author of wisdom, and he gives it to those who fear him. No one can learn to do well who has not first ceased to do evil.
29.1ff Job rehearses the details of his life before his present catastrophe. He defends himself by a presentation of how he lived and acted, convinced that he has followed the law of love in his treatment of neighbors and was himself accepted among them as a person of honor, integrity, and wisdom.
29.2 Job describes the heights to which he had attained and the depths to which he had fallen. He had enjoyed family, wealth, and peace; he had honor and power among all people; he had done good to all he could. His prospects for the future had been bright. All of this made his present situation more calamitous and difficult to bear.

21 "They listened to me, and waited,
    and kept silence for my counsel.
22 After I spoke they did not speak again,
    and my word dropped upon them like dew.*c*
23 They waited for me as for the rain;
    they opened their mouths as for the spring rain.
24 I smiled on them when they had no confidence;
    and the light of my countenance they did not extinguish.*d*
25 I chose their way, and sat as chief,
    and I lived like a king among his troops,
    like one who comforts mourners.

        (2) HIS PRESENT SUFFERING

30 "But now they make sport of me,
    those who are younger than I,
  whose fathers I would have disdained
    to set with the dogs of my flock.
2 What could I gain from the strength of their hands?
    All their vigor is gone.
3 Through want and hard hunger
    they gnaw the dry and desolate ground,
4 they pick mallow and the leaves of bushes,
    and to warm themselves the roots of broom.
5 They are driven out from society;
    people shout after them as after a thief.
6 In the gullies of wadis they must live,
    in holes in the ground, and in the rocks.
7 Among the bushes they bray;
    under the nettles they huddle together.
8 A senseless, disreputable brood,
    they have been whipped out of the land.

9 "And now they mock me in song;
    I am a byword to them.
10 They abhor me, they keep aloof from me;
    they do not hesitate to spit at the sight of me.
11 Because God has loosed my bowstring and humbled me,
    they have cast off restraint in my presence.
12 On my right hand the rabble rise up;
    they send me sprawling,
    and build roads for my ruin.
13 They break up my path,
    they promote my calamity;
    no one restrains*e* them.
14 As through a wide breach they come;
    amid the crash they roll on.
15 Terrors are turned upon me;
    my honor is pursued as by the wind,
    and my prosperity has passed away like a cloud.

16 "And now my soul is poured out within me;
    days of affliction have taken hold of me.
17 The night racks my bones,

c Heb lacks *like dew*   *d* Meaning of Heb uncertain   *e* Cn: Heb *helps*

Cross references (right column):

29.21
v. 9

29.22
v. 10;
Job 32.2

29.25
Job 1.3;
31.37; 4.4

30.1
Job 12.4

30.9
Job 12.4;
17.6
30.10
Num 12.14;
Deut 25.9;
Isa 50.6;
Mt 26.67
30.11
Ruth 1.21;
Ps 88.7
30.12
Ps 140.4, 5;
Job 19.12

30.15
Job 3.25;
31.23;
Hos 13.3

30.16
Ps 22.14;
42.4
30.17
v. 30

30.1ff Job speaks of his great fall from prosperity, status, and acceptability to a place of suffering in which even people of low estate make light of him. They compose songs to affront him, shun him, maliciously attack him, and do all the mischief they can to him. He ends with a vivid description of his present plight and bemoans the fact that his lyre has turned to mourning (v. 31).

and the pain that gnaws me takes no rest.

18 With violence he seizes my garment;[f]
   he grasps me by[g] the collar of my tunic.

30.19
Ps 69.2, 14
19 He has cast me into the mire,
   and I have become like dust and ashes.

30.20
Ps 19.7
20 I cry to you and you do not answer me;
   I stand, and you merely look at me.

30.21
Job 10.3;
16.9, 14;
19.6, 22
21 You have turned cruel to me;
   with the might of your hand you persecute me.

30.22
Job 9.17;
27.21
22 You lift me up on the wind, you make me ride on it,
   and you toss me about in the roar of the storm.

30.23
Job 9.22;
10.8; 3.19;
17.13
23 I know that you will bring me to death,
   and to the house appointed for all living.

30.24
Job 19.7
24 "Surely one does not turn against the needy,[h]
   when in disaster they cry for help.[i]

30.25
Ps 35.13, 14;
Rom 12.15
25 Did I not weep for those whose day was hard?
   Was not my soul grieved for the poor?

30.26
Job 3.25, 26;
Jer 8.15;
Job 19.8
26 But when I looked for good, evil came;
   and when I waited for light, darkness came.

27 My inward parts are in turmoil, and are never still;
   days of affliction come to meet me.

30.28
Ps 38.6; 42.9;
43.2;
Job 19.7
28 I go about in sunless gloom;
   I stand up in the assembly and cry for help.

30.29
Mic 1.8
29 I am a brother of jackals,
   and a companion of ostriches.

30.30
Ps 119.83;
Lam 4.8;
Ps 102.3
30 My skin turns black and falls from me,
   and my bones burn with heat.

30.31
Ps 107.1, 2
31 My lyre is turned to mourning,
   and my pipe to the voice of those who weep.

(3) HIS VINDICATION OF HIMSELF

31.1
Mt 5.28
31 "I have made a covenant with my eyes;
   how then could I look upon a virgin?

31.2
Job 20.29
2 What would be my portion from God above,
   and my heritage from the Almighty[j] on high?

31.3
Job 21.30;
34.22
3 Does not calamity befall the unrighteous,
   and disaster the workers of iniquity?

31.4
2 Chr 16.9;
Prov 5.21
4 Does he not see my ways,
   and number all my steps?

31.5
Mic 2.11
5 "If I have walked with falsehood,
   and my foot has hurried to deceit—

31.6
Job 6.2, 3;
27.5, 6
6 let me be weighed in a just balance,
   and let God know my integrity!—

31.7
Job 23.11;
9.30
7 if my step has turned aside from the way,
   and my heart has followed my eyes,
   and if any spot has clung to my hands;

31.8
Lev 26.16;
Job 20.18
8 then let me sow, and another eat;
   and let what grows for me be rooted out.

31.9
Job 24.15
9 "If my heart has been enticed by a woman,

f Gk: Heb *my garment is disfigured*   g Heb *like*   h Heb *ruin*   i Cn: Meaning of Heb uncertain
j Traditional rendering of Heb *Shaddai*

30.24,25 Job consoles himself by the thought that in his own prosperity he identified with and had sympathy for those who lived in misery.
31.1ff In his final speech, Job once again maintains his integrity before God and his law. He offers to submit freely to and accept the chastisement of God if the charges against him can be proven. But within his own heart he knows that they cannot.

and I have lain in wait at my neighbor's door;
10 then let my wife grind for another,
    and let other men kneel over her.

11 For that would be a heinous crime;
    that would be a criminal offense;
12 for that would be a fire consuming down to Abaddon,
    and it would burn to the root all my harvest.

13 "If I have rejected the cause of my male or female slaves,
    when they brought a complaint against me;
14 what then shall I do when God rises up?
    When he makes inquiry, what shall I answer him?
15 Did not he who made me in the womb make them?
    And did not one fashion us in the womb?

16 "If I have withheld anything that the poor desired,
    or have caused the eyes of the widow to fail,
17 or have eaten my morsel alone,
    and the orphan has not eaten from it —
18 for from my youth I reared the orphan^k like a father,
    and from my mother's womb I guided the widow^l —
19 if I have seen anyone perish for lack of clothing,
    or a poor person without covering,
20 whose loins have not blessed me,
    and who was not warmed with the fleece of my sheep;
21 if I have raised my hand against the orphan,
    because I saw I had supporters at the gate;
22 then let my shoulder blade fall from my shoulder,
    and let my arm be broken from its socket.
23 For I was in terror of calamity from God,
    and I could not have faced his majesty.

24 "If I have made gold my trust,
    or called fine gold my confidence;
25 if I have rejoiced because my wealth was great,
    or because my hand had gotten much;
26 if I have looked at the sun^m when it shone,
    or the moon moving in splendor,
27 and my heart has been secretly enticed,
    and my mouth has kissed my hand;
28 this also would be an iniquity to be punished by the judges,
    for I should have been false to God above.

29 "If I have rejoiced at the ruin of those who hated me,
    or exulted when evil overtook them —
30 I have not let my mouth sin
    by asking for their lives with a curse —
31 if those of my tent ever said,
    'O that we might be sated with his flesh!'ⁿ —
32 the stranger has not lodged in the street;
    I have opened my doors to the traveler —
33 if I have concealed my transgressions as others do,^o
    by hiding my iniquity in my bosom,
34 because I stood in great fear of the multitude,
    and the contempt of families terrified me,
    so that I kept silence, and did not go out of doors —
35 O that I had one to hear me!

---

k Heb *him* l Heb *her* m Heb *the light* n Meaning of Heb uncertain o Or *as Adam did*

31.10
Jer 8.10
31.11
Gen 38.24;
Deut 22.22-24
31.12
Job 15.30;
26.6; 20.28
31.13
Deut 24.14,
15
31.15
Mal 2.10
31.16
Job 20.19;
22.7, 9
31.17
Job 22.7;
29.12
31.19
Job 22.6;
29.13
31.20
Deut 31.20
31.21
Job 22.9
31.22
Job 38.15
31.23
v. 3;
Job 13.11
31.24
Mk 10.24
31.25
Ps 62.10
31.26
Deut 4.19;
Ezek 8.16
31.28
v. 11
31.29
Prov 17.5
31.30
Mt 5.44
31.31
Job 22.7
31.32
Gen 19.2, 3;
Rom 12.13
31.33
Gen 3.8;
Prov 28.13
31.34
Ex 23.2
31.35
Job 19.7;
30.20, 24,
28; 35.14

(Here is my signature! Let the Almighty[p] answer me!)
O that I had the indictment written by my adversary!

36 Surely I would carry it on my shoulder;
   I would bind it on me like a crown;

37 I would give him an account of all my steps;
   like a prince I would approach him.

38 "If my land has cried out against me,
   and its furrows have wept together;

39 if I have eaten its yield without payment,
   and caused the death of its owners;

40 let thorns grow instead of wheat,
   and foul weeds instead of barley."

The words of Job are ended.

III. *The speeches of Elihu (32.1–37.24)*

A. *Elihu's anger at Job for his justification of self*

32 So these three men ceased to answer Job, because he was righteous in his own eyes. 2 Then Elihu son of Barachel the Buzite, of the family of Ram, became angry. He was angry at Job because he justified himself rather than God; 3 he was angry also at Job's three friends because they had found no answer, though they had declared Job to be in the wrong.[q] 4 Now Elihu had waited to speak to Job, because they were older than he. 5 But when Elihu saw that there was no answer in the mouths of these three men, he became angry.

6 Elihu son of Barachel the Buzite answered:
   "I am young in years,
      and you are aged;
   therefore I was timid and afraid
      to declare my opinion to you.

7 I said, 'Let days speak,
      and many years teach wisdom.'

8 But truly it is the spirit in a mortal,
      the breath of the Almighty,[p] that makes for understanding.

9 It is not the old[r] that are wise,
      nor the aged that understand what is right.

10 Therefore I say, 'Listen to me;
      let me also declare my opinion.'

11 "See, I waited for your words,
      I listened for your wise sayings,
      while you searched out what to say.

12 I gave you my attention,
      but there was in fact no one that confuted Job,
      no one among you that answered his words.

13 Yet do not say, 'We have found wisdom;
      God may vanquish him, not a human.'

p Traditional rendering of Heb *Shaddai* *q* Another ancient tradition reads *answer, and had put God in the wrong* *r* Gk Syr Vg: Heb *many*

32.2 Elihu is unhappy with Job's statement that God deals capriciously with people in this life. But he also sees that Job's three friends have lost the argument because they entertained too narrow a viewpoint. Elihu's main thesis is that God has allowed Job to suffer in order to improve him. His clearest statement on his theory of suffering is found in 36.6–15.
32.10 *Listen to me.* Elihu knew how to keep silent and listen to older and wiser minds. He also knew when and how to speak. He would betray his friends if he continued his silence. Even though his friends were superior to him, they should not be offended by being contradicted and instructed by their inferiors, for "better is a poor but wise youth than an old but foolish king" (Eccl 4.13).

Side references:
31.37
v. 4;
Job 1.3;
29.25
31.38
Gen 4.10, 11
31.39
Lev 19.13;
1 Kings 21.19;
Jas 5.4
31.40
Gen 3.18

32.1
Job 33.9
32.2
Gen 22.21;
Jer 25.23
32.3
Job 11.6;
15.16; 22.5

32.6
Job 15.10

32.8
Job 27.3;
33.4;
1 Kings 3.12;
Prov 2.6
32.9
1 Cor 1.26

32.11
Job 5.27

32.13
Jer 9.23

14 He has not directed his words against me,
    and I will not answer him with your speeches.

15 "They are dismayed, they answer no more;
    they have not a word to say.

16 And am I to wait, because they do not speak,
    because they stand there, and answer no more?

17 I also will give my answer;
    I also will declare my opinion.

18 For I am full of words;   **32.18**
    the spirit within me constrains me.   Acts 18.5

19 My heart is indeed like wine that has no vent;   **32.19**
    like new wineskins, it is ready to burst.   Acts 9.17

20 I must speak, so that I may find relief;
    I must open my lips and answer.

21 I will not show partiality to any person   **32.21**
    or use flattery toward anyone.   Lev 19.15;
                                                               Mt 22.16
22 For I do not know how to flatter —   **32.22**
    or my Maker would soon put an end to me!   1 Thess 2.5

B. *God uses pain to chasten humans*

33 "But now, hear my speech, O Job,
    and listen to all my words.

2   See, I open my mouth;
    the tongue in my mouth speaks.

3   My words declare the uprightness of my heart,   **33.3**
    and what my lips know they speak sincerely.   Job 6.28;
                                                               27.4; 36.4
4   The spirit of God has made me,   **33.4**
    and the breath of the Almighty[s] gives me life.   Gen 2.7;
                                                               Job 27.3
5   Answer me, if you can;   **33.5**
    set your words in order before me; take your stand.   v. 32;
                                                               Job 13.18
6   See, before God I am as you are;
    I too was formed from a piece of clay.

7   No fear of me need terrify you;   **33.7**
    my pressure will not be heavy on you.   Job 9.34;
                                                               13.21;
                                                               2 Cor 2.5
8   "Surely, you have spoken in my hearing,
    and I have heard the sound of your words.

9   You say, 'I am clean, without transgression;   **33.9**
    I am pure, and there is no iniquity in me.   Job 10.7;
                                                               13.23; 16.17
10 Look, he finds occasions against me,   **33.10**
                                                               Job 13.24

[s] Traditional rendering of Heb *Shaddai*

32.18 The God of providence can raise up younger people to speak when the aged have gone dry and said all they could. God can give young people things to say that will edify the church. Elihu will speak his piece with freedom and sincerity. He plans to say what is true, not what he thinks will please the listener.

33.1 Elihu does not agree with what his three companions have said. He wants to be deliberate and solemn in his speech. He will speak so he can be understood, and he is willing to listen to Job for his comments when he has finished (v. 5).

33.4 The Holy Spirit is the third person of the Trinity. He is God and has existed eternally with the Father and the Son. He is called by more than thirty different names or titles in the Scriptures. Here he is called *the spirit of God . . . and the breath of the Almighty*. Elsewhere he is called (1) "the Spirit of life" (Rom 8.2); (2) "the spirit of wisdom and understand-

ing, the spirit of counsel and might, the spirit of knowledge" (Isa 11.2); (3) "the Spirit of truth" (Jn 14.17); and (4) the "Spirit of God" (1 Cor 12.3). As God, the Holy Spirit is a person who knows, feels, and wills. He has all the attributes of deity. See also note on Gen 17.1.

33.8ff Elihu charges Job with saying things that reflect upon the justice and goodness of God. He carefully says that he is not speaking secondhand, but that he has heard Job say these things publicly. Had it been in private conversation, Elihu would not have repeated them. But since it was done in public, he would reprove Job in public.

33.9ff Elihu strikes at Job from a somewhat different perspective. He knows that Job considers himself innocent. But in so thinking, he is guilty of charging God with injustice in afflicting him. According to Elihu, this is Job's sin.

he counts me as his enemy;

33.11
Job 13.27;
14.16

11 he puts my feet in the stocks,
   and watches all my paths.'

12 "But in this you are not right. I will answer you:
   God is greater than any mortal.

33.13
Job 15.25;
Isa 45.9

13 Why do you contend against him,
   saying, 'He will answer none of my[t] words'?

33.14
Ps 62.11

14 For God speaks in one way,
   and in two, though people do not perceive it.

33.15
Num 12.6;
Job 4.13

15 In a dream, in a vision of the night,
   when deep sleep falls on mortals,
   while they slumber on their beds,

33.16
Job 36.10, 15

16 then he opens their ears,
   and terrifies them with warnings,

17 that he may turn them aside from their deeds,
   and keep them from pride,

33.18
vv. 24, 28, 30

18 to spare their souls from the Pit,
   their lives from traversing the River.

33.19
Job 30.17

19 They are also chastened with pain upon their beds,
   and with continual strife in their bones,

33.20
Ps 107.18

20 so that their lives loathe bread,
   and their appetites dainty food.

33.21
Job 16.8;
19.20
33.22
Ps 88.3

21 Their flesh is so wasted away that it cannot be seen;
   and their bones, once invisible, now stick out.

22 Their souls draw near the Pit,
   and their lives to those who bring death.

33.23
Mic 6.8

23 Then, if there should be for one of them an angel,
   a mediator, one of a thousand,
   one who declares a person upright,

33.24
Isa 38.17

24 and he is gracious to that person, and says,
   'Deliver him from going down into the Pit;
   I have found a ransom;

33.25
2 Kings 5.14

25 let his flesh become fresh with youth;
   let him return to the days of his youthful vigor';

33.26
Job 22.27;
34.28; 22.26;
Ps 51.12

26 then he prays to God, and is accepted by him,
   he comes into his presence with joy,
   and God[u] repays him for his righteousness.

33.27
Lk 15.21;
Rom 6.21

27 That person sings to others and says,
   'I sinned, and perverted what was right,
   and it was not paid back to me.

33.28
Ps 103.14;
Job 22.28

28 He has redeemed my soul from going down to the Pit,
   and my life shall see the light.'

33.29
Eph 1.11;
1 Cor 12.6;
Phil 2.13
33.30
Ps 56.13

29 "God indeed does all these things,
   twice, three times, with mortals,

30 to bring back their souls from the Pit,
   so that they may see the light of life.[v]

31 Pay heed, Job, listen to me;
   be silent, and I will speak.

32 If you have anything to say, answer me;

[t] Compare Gk: Heb *his*   [u] Heb *he*   [v] Syr: Heb *to be lighted with the light of life*

33.13ff Elihu says that God speaks in various ways to people. He first speaks through conscience. When nothing happens, he may speak through actions, including suffering. God often afflicts the body in love, with the intent of improving the soul. Sickness and suffering have their benefits.

33.32 Elihu is so confident of his analysis of the case

that he challenges Job to answer his charge. What he really wants to do is to justify Job, not simply win a debating victory over him, as his three friends sought to do. If Job has nothing to say to the charge, then Elihu has further words for him. He says: "I will teach you wisdom" (v. 33).

speak, for I desire to justify you.
33 If not, listen to me;
  be silent, and I will teach you wisdom."

C. God is not unjust

34 Then Elihu continued and said:
2 "Hear my words, you wise men,
  and give ear to me, you who know;
3 for the ear tests words
  as the palate tastes food.
4 Let us choose what is right;
  let us determine among ourselves what is good.
5 For Job has said, 'I am innocent,
  and God has taken away my right;
6 in spite of being right I am counted a liar;
  my wound is incurable, though I am without transgression.'
7 Who is there like Job,
  who drinks up scoffing like water,
8 who goes in company with evildoers
  and walks with the wicked?
9 For he has said, 'It profits one nothing
  to take delight in God.'

10 "Therefore, hear me, you who have sense,
  far be it from God that he should do wickedness,
  and from the Almighty^w that he should do wrong.
11 For according to their deeds he will repay them,
  and according to their ways he will make it befall them.
12 Of a truth, God will not do wickedly,
  and the Almighty^w will not pervert justice.
13 Who gave him charge over the earth
  and who laid on him^x the whole world?
14 If he should take back his spirit^y to himself,
  and gather to himself his breath,
15 all flesh would perish together,
  and all mortals return to dust.

16 "If you have understanding, hear this;
  listen to what I say.
17 Shall one who hates justice govern?
  Will you condemn one who is righteous and mighty,
18 who says to a king, 'You scoundrel!'
  and to princes, 'You wicked men!';
19 who shows no partiality to nobles,
  nor regards the rich more than the poor,
  for they are all the work of his hands?
20 In a moment they die;

w Traditional rendering of Heb Shaddai   x Heb lacks on him   y Heb his heart his spirit

Cross references (right margin):

33.33 Ps 34.11
34.3 Job 12.11
34.4 1 Thess 5.21
34.5 Job 33.9; 27.2
34.6 Jer 15.18; 30.12
34.7 Job 15.16
34.8 Ps 50.18
34.9 Job 21.15; 35.3
34.10 Job 8.3
34.11 Ps 62.12; Mt 16.27; Rom 2.6; 2 Cor 5.10; Rev 22.12
34.12 Job 8.3
34.13 Job 38.5, 6
34.14 Ps 104.29
34.15 Isa 40.6, 7; Gen 3.19
34.17 2 Sam 23.3
34.18 Ex 22.28
34.19 Deut 10.17; Gal 2.6; Job 31.15
34.20 Ex 12.29; Job 12.19

34.1 Elihu humbly seeks to gain the good will of his friends and get favorable attention to his arguments. Thus he addresses them as wise men who can judge what he says.
34.5ff Elihu warmly accuses Job of having complained against God's divine government. Job was wrong in charging God with injustice by maintaining his righteousness. He paints Job as one sitting in the seat of the scoffers.
34.10 Elihu asserts that, as all sensible people know, God is not unjust. Therefore, he cannot do wicked-ness, and whatever he has done to Job cannot be wicked. Moreover, no one should quarrel with God for what he does. What God does must be acknowledged and submitted to.
34.16 Elihu now addresses Job directly, saying he has no business quarreling with God for anything he chooses to do. The almighty, omniscient, just God proceeds with equity and rules over all the affairs of humankind; he does as he pleases because he is wise in all his doings.

at midnight the people are shaken and pass away,
and the mighty are taken away by no human hand.

34.21
Job 31.4

21 "For his eyes are upon the ways of mortals,
and he sees all their steps.

34.22
Ps 139.12;
Am 9.2, 3

22 There is no gloom or deep darkness
where evildoers may hide themselves.

23 For he has not appointed a time[z] for anyone
to go before God in judgment.

34.24
Dan 2.21

24 He shatters the mighty without investigation,
and sets others in their place.

34.25
vv. 11, 20

25 Thus, knowing their works,
he overturns them in the night, and they are crushed.

34.26
Job 26.12

26 He strikes them for their wickedness
while others look on,

34.27
1 Sam 15.11;
Ps 28.5;
Isa 5.12

27 because they turned aside from following him,
and had no regard for any of his ways,

34.28
Job 35.9;
Jas 5.4;
Ex 22.23

28 so that they caused the cry of the poor to come to him,
and he heard the cry of the afflicted —

34.29
1 Chr 22.9

29 When he is quiet, who can condemn?
When he hides his face, who can behold him,
whether it be a nation or an individual? —

34.30
v. 17

30 so that the godless should not reign,
or those who ensnare the people.

31 "For has anyone said to God,
'I have endured punishment; I will not offend any more;

34.32
Job 35.11;
Ps 25.4

32 teach me what I do not see;
if I have done iniquity, I will do it no more'?

33 Will he then pay back to suit you,
because you reject it?
For you must choose, and not I;
therefore declare what you know.[a]

34 Those who have sense will say to me,
and the wise who hear me will say,

34.35
Job 35.16

35 'Job speaks without knowledge,
his words are without insight.'

34.36
Job 23.10;
22.15

36 Would that Job were tried to the limit,
because his answers are those of the wicked.

37 For he adds rebellion to his sin;
he claps his hands among us,
and multiplies his words against God."

35

Elihu continued and said:

35.2
Job 32.2

2 "Do you think this to be just?
You say, 'I am in the right before God.'

35.3
Job 34.9;
9.30, 31

3 If you ask, 'What advantage have I?
How am I better off than if I had sinned?'

4 I will answer you
and your friends with you.

35.5
Job 22.12

5 Look at the heavens and see;
observe the clouds, which are higher than you.

---

[z] Cn: Heb *yet*   [a] Meaning of Heb of verses 29-33 uncertain

34.31 Elihu wants Job only to admit that he had spoken inadvisedly. Therefore, he should humble himself before God and ask him to point out his sins. Job should also promise reformation.
35.1ff Elihu reproves Job for justifying himself

more than justifying God. He also condemns Job for seeming to say that because he has suffered all of these things, there are no advantages or benefits to having faith in God.

6   If you have sinned, what do you accomplish against him?
         And if your transgressions are multiplied, what do you do to
            him?
7   If you are righteous, what do you give to him;
         or what does he receive from your hand?
8   Your wickedness affects others like you,
         and your righteousness, other human beings.

9   "Because of the multitude of oppressions people cry out;
         they call for help because of the arm of the mighty.
10   But no one says, 'Where is God my Maker,
         who gives strength in the night,
11   who teaches us more than the animals of the earth,
         and makes us wiser than the birds of the air?'
12   There they cry out, but he does not answer,
         because of the pride of evildoers.
13   Surely God does not hear an empty cry,
         nor does the Almighty[b] regard it.
14   How much less when you say that you do not see him,
         that the case is before him, and you are waiting for him!
15   And now, because his anger does not punish,
         and he does not greatly heed transgression,[c]
16   Job opens his mouth in empty talk,
         he multiplies words without knowledge."

D. *The justice of God whose ways are inscrutable*

36 Elihu continued and said:
2   "Bear with me a little, and I will show you,
         for I have yet something to say on God's behalf.
3   I will bring my knowledge from far away,
         and ascribe righteousness to my Maker.
4   For truly my words are not false;
         one who is perfect in knowledge is with you.

5   "Surely God is mighty and does not despise any;
         he is mighty in strength of understanding.
6   He does not keep the wicked alive,
         but gives the afflicted their right.
7   He does not withdraw his eyes from the righteous,
         but with kings on the throne
         he sets them forever, and they are exalted.
8   And if they are bound in fetters
         and caught in the cords of affliction,
9   then he declares to them their work
         and their transgressions, that they are behaving arrogantly.

b Traditional rendering of Heb *Shaddai*   *c* Theodotion Symmachus Compare Vg: Meaning of Heb
uncertain

Cross references (right margin):

35.6 Prov 8.36; Jer 7.19
35.7 Job 22.2, 3; Prov 9.12; Lk 17.10
35.9 Ex 2.23; Job 12.19
35.10 Job 27.10; Ps 42.8; 149.5; Acts 16.25
35.11 Ps 94.12; Lk 12.24
35.12 Prov 1.28
35.13 Job 27.9; Prov 15.29; Isa 1.15; Jer 11.11
35.14 Ps 37.5, 6
35.15 Eccl 8.11
35.16 Job 34.37, 35
36.3 Job 8.3; 37.23
36.4 Job 33.3; 37.16
36.5 Ps 22.24; Job 12.13
36.6 Job 8.22; 5.15
36.7 Ps 33.18; 113.8
36.8 Ps 107.10; vv. 15, 21
36.9 Job 15.25

35.10 Many who groan under their distresses never pay attention to what God may be saying to them. Afflictions can work to gain the attention of the sufferer. When such people turn to God, they will learn a great deal from their afflictions and bear them more patiently. God promises to give strength to those who call on him (see 2 Cor 12.7–10).
35.16 Job opens his mouth in vain because he does not rest his case with God, wait for him, and turn to him for help and sustaining grace.
36.1ff Elihu continues to build up his case as an advocate who favors God and who remains convinced

that Job is wrong. He argues that God is a God of equity who takes care of the least of his subjects, does not sustain the greatest if they are bad, avenges the poor, protects his own people, and withstands the hypocrites. He supposes that God would have delivered Job had he humbled himself under his affliction; Job must cease his argument against God, obtain right knowledge, and submit cheerfully to God's providence. Much of what he says is true, of course, but Elihu still has failed to understand God's actions in the life of Job. And only God could make that known to others.

36.10
Job 33.16;
2 Kings 17.13
36.11
Isa 1.19, 20

10 He opens their ears to instruction,
    and commands that they return from iniquity.
11 If they listen, and serve him,
    they complete their days in prosperity,
    and their years in pleasantness.

36.12
Job 15.22;
4.21

12 But if they do not listen, they shall perish by the sword,
    and die without knowledge.

36.13
Rom 2.5
36.14
Job 15.32;
22.16
36.15
Ps 119.67;
v. 10
36.16
Hos 2.14;
Ps 118.5;
23.5

13 "The godless in heart cherish anger;
    they do not cry for help when he binds them.
14 They die in their youth,
    and their life ends in shame.*d*
15 He delivers the afflicted by their affliction,
    and opens their ear by adversity.
16 He also allured you out of distress
    into a broad place where there was no constraint,
    and what was set on your table was full of fatness.

17 "But you are obsessed with the case of the wicked;
    judgment and justice seize you.

36.18
Job 34.33;
Jon 4.4, 9;
Job 33.24

18 Beware that wrath does not entice you into scoffing,
    and do not let the greatness of the ransom turn you aside.
19 Will your cry avail to keep you from distress,
    or will all the force of your strength?

36.20
Job 34.20, 25

20 Do not long for the night,
    when peoples are cut off in their place.

36.21
Ps 66.18;
Heb 11.25
36.22
Isa 40.13;
1 Cor 2.16
36.23
Job 34.13;
Job 8.3

21 Beware! Do not turn to iniquity;
    because of that you have been tried by affliction.
22 See, God is exalted in his power;
    who is a teacher like him?
23 Who has prescribed for him his way,
    or who can say, 'You have done wrong'?

36.24
2 Sam 7.26;
Ps 35.27;
59.16

24 "Remember to extol his work,
    of which mortals have sung.
25 All people have looked on it;
    everyone watches it from far away.

36.26
Ps 102.24

26 Surely God is great, and we do not know him;
    the number of his years is unsearchable.

36.27
Ps 147.8

27 For he draws up the drops of water;
    he distills*e* his mist in rain,
28 which the skies pour down
    and drop upon mortals abundantly.

36.29
Job 37.11,
16; 26.14

29 Can anyone understand the spreading of the clouds,
    the thunderings of his pavilion?
30 See, he scatters his lightning around him
    and covers the roots of the sea.

36.31
Job 37.13;
Ps 136.25
36.32
Job 37.15

31 For by these he governs peoples;
    he gives food in abundance.
32 He covers his hands with the lightning,
    and commands it to strike the mark.

36.33
Job 37.2

33 Its crashing*f* tells about him;
    he is jealous*f* with anger against iniquity.

d Heb *ends among the temple prostitutes*   *e* Cn: Heb *they distill*   *f* Meaning of Heb uncertain

36.24 The infinite and unsearchable God does nothing evil. We should behold his works and magnify his name. We know that God is, but not what he is. We know in part, but not in perfection. Therefore we must not find fault with what God does.

37

"At this also my heart trembles,
  and leaps out of its place.

2 Listen, listen to the thunder of his voice
  and the rumbling that comes from his mouth.

3 Under the whole heaven he lets it loose,
  and his lightning to the corners of the earth.

4 After it his voice roars;
  he thunders with his majestic voice
  and he does not restrain the lightnings[g] when his voice is
    heard.

5 God thunders wondrously with his voice;
  he does great things that we cannot comprehend.

6 For to the snow he says, 'Fall on the earth';
  and the shower of rain, his heavy shower of rain,

7 serves as a sign on everyone's hand,
  so that all whom he has made may know it.[h]

8 Then the animals go into their lairs
  and remain in their dens.

9 From its chamber comes the whirlwind,
  and cold from the scattering winds.

10 By the breath of God ice is given,
  and the broad waters are frozen fast.

11 He loads the thick cloud with moisture;
  the clouds scatter his lightning.

12 They turn round and round by his guidance,
  to accomplish all that he commands them
  on the face of the habitable world.

13 Whether for correction, or for his land,
  or for love, he causes it to happen.

14 "Hear this, O Job;
  stop and consider the wondrous works of God.

15 Do you know how God lays his command upon them,
  and causes the lightning of his cloud to shine?

16 Do you know the balancings of the clouds,
  the wondrous works of the one whose knowledge is perfect,

17 you whose garments are hot
  when the earth is still because of the south wind?

18 Can you, like him, spread out the skies,
  hard as a molten mirror?

19 Teach us what we shall say to him;
  we cannot draw up our case because of darkness.

20 Should he be told that I want to speak?
  Did anyone ever wish to be swallowed up?

21 Now, no one can look on the light
  when it is bright in the skies,
  when the wind has passed and cleared them.

22 Out of the north comes golden splendor;
  around God is awesome majesty.

23 The Almighty[i]—we cannot find him;
  he is great in power and justice,
  and abundant righteousness he will not violate.

24 Therefore mortals fear him;

---

g Heb *them*   h Meaning of Heb of verse 7 uncertain   i Traditional rendering of Heb *Shaddai*

37.2 God controls the thunder and the lightning. All nature is under his sway.
37.6,7 God sends snow, rain, and storms. Through his dominion over the elements God controls the actions of people.
37.24 Elihu has argued that God cannot be charged with injustice. Job's sufferings were designed to uphold the glory of God against the allegations of Satan.

37.2
Job 36.33

37.3
v. 12

37.4
Ps 29.3

37.5
Job 5.9;
36.26

37.6
Job 38.22;
36.27

37.7
Job 12.14

37.8
Ps 104.22

37.9
Job 9.9;
Ps 147.17

37.10
Job 38.29;
Ps 147.17

37.11
Job 36.27,
29; v. 15

37.12
Ps 148.8;
Isa 14.21;
27.6;
Prov 8.31

37.13
Ex 9.18;
1 Sam 12.18;
Job 38.26;
1 Kings 18.45

37.14
Ps 111.2

37.16
vv. 5, 14, 23;
Job 36.4

37.18
Job 9.8;
Ps 104.2;
Isa 44.24

37.23
1 Tim 6.16;
Job 9.4; 8.3;
Isa 63.9

37.24
Mt 10.28;
11.25;
1 Cor 1.26

he does not regard any who are wise in their own conceit."

IV. *The voice of God (38.1–42.6)*

A. *God challenges Job*

38 Then the LORD answered Job out of the whirlwind:
2 "Who is this that darkens counsel by words without knowledge?
3 Gird up your loins like a man,
  I will question you, and you shall declare to me.

B. *God's creation*

4 "Where were you when I laid the foundation of the earth?
  Tell me, if you have understanding.
5 Who determined its measurements—surely you know!
  Or who stretched the line upon it?
6 On what were its bases sunk,
  or who laid its cornerstone
7 when the morning stars sang together
  and all the heavenly beings[j] shouted for joy?

8 "Or who shut in the sea with doors
  when it burst out from the womb?—
9 when I made the clouds its garment,
  and thick darkness its swaddling band,
10 and prescribed bounds for it,
  and set bars and doors,
11 and said, 'Thus far shall you come, and no farther,
  and here shall your proud waves be stopped'?

12 "Have you commanded the morning since your days began,
  and caused the dawn to know its place,
13 so that it might take hold of the skirts of the earth,
  and the wicked be shaken out of it?
14 It is changed like clay under the seal,
  and it is dyed[k] like a garment.
15 Light is withheld from the wicked,
  and their uplifted arm is broken.

C. *Human inability to probe the mystery of God's creation*

16 "Have you entered into the springs of the sea,
  or walked in the recesses of the deep?
17 Have the gates of death been revealed to you,
  or have you seen the gates of deep darkness?
18 Have you comprehended the expanse of the earth?

j Heb *sons of God*   *k* Cn: Heb *and they stand forth*

Cross-references (left margin):
38.1 Job 40.6
38.2 Job 42.3; 35.16; 1 Tim 1.7
38.3 Job 40.7
38.4 Ps 104.5; Prov 8.29
38.6 Job 26.7
38.7 Job 1.6
38.8 Gen 1.9
38.9 Prov 30.4
38.10 Job 26.10
38.11 Ps 89.9
38.12 Ps 74.16
38.13 Ps 104.35
38.15 Job 18.5; Ps 10.15
38.16 Ps 77.19
38.17 Ps 9.13
38.18 Job 28.24

His sufferings were also the instrument by which God was perfecting his sanctification. Surely God was not unjust to allow Job to keep on suffering in order that he might be conformed to the image of God. **38.1** This is the climax of the book: God makes his appearance. God shows Job the greatness of creation compared to mortals' ignorance and finitude. Job will learn that, while he had committed no sin for which the affliction was laid on him, he erred in thinking too highly of his own ability to rationalize the actions of his creator. Soon he will kneel before his maker in humiliation and surrender. **38.2** *by words without knowledge.* They spoke in ig-norance instead of teaching what needed to be taught. **38.7** *the heavenly beings shouted for joy.* These are the angels, whom God created well before humankind. They rejoiced when the foundations of the earth were laid and when the morning stars sang together. This latter reference is probably a figure of speech indicating that even inanimate nature sings the praises of the one who made it (cf. Ps 148). **38.16** God asks Job a series of puzzling questions about nature so as to convince him of his ignorance. Job will soon come to the place where he realizes that, compared to God, he knows next to nothing.

Declare, if you know all this.

19 "Where is the way to the dwelling of light,
     and where is the place of darkness,
20 that you may take it to its territory
     and that you may discern the paths to its home?
21 Surely you know, for you were born then,
     and the number of your days is great!

22 "Have you entered the storehouses of the snow,
     or have you seen the storehouses of the hail,
23 which I have reserved for the time of trouble,
     for the day of battle and war?
24 What is the way to the place where the light is distributed,
     or where the east wind is scattered upon the earth?

25 "Who has cut a channel for the torrents of rain,
     and a way for the thunderbolt,
26 to bring rain on a land where no one lives,
     on the desert, which is empty of human life,
27 to satisfy the waste and desolate land,
     and to make the ground put forth grass?

28 "Has the rain a father,
     or who has begotten the drops of dew?
29 From whose womb did the ice come forth,
     and who has given birth to the hoarfrost of heaven?
30 The waters become hard like stone,
     and the face of the deep is frozen.

31 "Can you bind the chains of the Pleiades,
     or loose the cords of Orion?
32 Can you lead forth the Mazzaroth in their season,
     or can you guide the Bear with its children?
33 Do you know the ordinances of the heavens?
     Can you establish their rule on the earth?

34 "Can you lift up your voice to the clouds,
     so that a flood of waters may cover you?
35 Can you send forth lightnings, so that they may go
     and say to you, 'Here we are'?
36 Who has put wisdom in the inward parts,[l]
     or given understanding to the mind?[l]
37 Who has the wisdom to number the clouds?
     Or who can tilt the waterskins of the heavens,
38 when the dust runs into a mass
     and the clods cling together?

D. Human inability to probe the mysteries of animal and bird life

39 "Can you hunt the prey for the lion,

---

[l] Meaning of Heb uncertain

Cross references (right column):

38.20 Job 26.10; 24.13
38.21 Job 15.7
38.22 Job 37.6
38.23 Ex 9.18; Josh 10.11; Isa 30.30; Ezek 13.11, 13; Rev 16.21
38.24 Job 26.10; 27.21
38.25 Job 28.26
38.26 Job 36.27; Ps 107.35
38.27 Ps 104.13, 14
38.28 Ps 147.8; Jer 14.22
38.29 Ps 147.16, 17
38.31 Job 9.9; Am 5.8
38.33 Job 31.35
38.34 v. 37; Job 22.11; 36.27, 28
38.35 Job 36.32; 37.3
38.36 Job 32.8; Ps 51.6; Eccl 2.26; Job 32.8
38.39 Ps 104.21

38.28ff God makes the point that if Job cannot understand the mysteries of the universe, how is it then possible for him to understand the God of nature. The answer is plain: no one can understand unless God chooses to reveal it himself.
38.39 God now turns to things closer to humankind, but points out that there are still mysteries. For example, he asks about lions, goats, asses, oxen, ostriches, horses, and hawks. The closer God gets to things Job can see and know about, the more it is apparent that what he knows is insignificant when compared to what he does not know.

38.40
Job 38.8;
Ps 17.12
38.41
Ps 147.9;
Mt 6.26

or satisfy the appetite of the young lions,
40   when they crouch in their dens,
    or lie in wait in their covert?
41   Who provides for the raven its prey,
    when its young ones cry to God,
    and wander about for lack of food?

39 "Do you know when the mountain goats give birth?
    Do you observe the calving of the deer?
2   Can you number the months that they fulfill,
    and do you know the time when they give birth,

3   when they crouch to give birth to their offspring,
    and are delivered of their young?
4   Their young ones become strong, they grow up in the open;
    they go forth, and do not return to them.

39.5
Job 6.5;
11.12; 24.5
39.6
Job 24.5;
Jer 2.24;
Hos 8.9;
Ps 107.34

5   "Who has let the wild ass go free?
    Who has loosed the bonds of the swift ass,
6   to which I have given the steppe for its home,
    the salt land for its dwelling place?
7   It scorns the tumult of the city;
    it does not hear the shouts of the driver.
8   It ranges the mountains as its pasture,
    and it searches after every green thing.

9   "Is the wild ox willing to serve you?
    Will it spend the night at your crib?
10   Can you tie it in the furrow with ropes,
    or will it harrow the valleys after you?
11   Will you depend on it because its strength is great,
    and will you hand over your labor to it?
12   Do you have faith in it that it will return,
    and bring your grain to your threshing floor?[m]

13   "The ostrich's wings flap wildly,
    though its pinions lack plumage.[n]
14   For it leaves its eggs to the earth,
    and lets them be warmed on the ground,
15   forgetting that a foot may crush them,
    and that a wild animal may trample them.

16   It deals cruelly with its young, as if they were not its own;
    though its labor should be in vain, yet it has no fear;
17   because God has made it forget wisdom,
    and given it no share in understanding.
18   When it spreads its plumes aloft,[n]
    it laughs at the horse and its rider.

19   "Do you give the horse its might?
    Do you clothe its neck with mane?

20   Do you make it leap like the locust?
    Its majestic snorting is terrible.
21   It paws[o] violently, exults mightily;

[m] Heb *your grain and your threshing floor*   [n] Meaning of Heb uncertain   [o] Gk Syr Vg: Heb *they dig*

39.1ff Underlying God's comments here is his divine compassion toward the inferior creatures on the planet; he takes tender care of them. Therefore Job has no reason for charging God with unkindness toward him. He who cares for the lesser will be equally or more concerned for his higher beings.

39.13ff The ostrich drops her eggs anywhere on the ground and leaves them to fend for themselves. God hatches the abandoned eggs by sun and sand. By implication, God knows what has been going on with Job and has been watching over him.

22 It laughs at fear, and is not dismayed;
    it does not turn back from the sword.
23 Upon it rattle the quiver,
    the flashing spear, and the javelin.
24 With fierceness and rage it swallows the ground;
    it cannot stand still at the sound of the trumpet.
25 When the trumpet sounds, it says 'Aha!'
    From a distance it smells the battle,
    the thunder of the captains, and the shouting.

26 "Is it by your wisdom that the hawk soars,
    and spreads its wings toward the south?
27 Is it at your command that the eagle mounts up
    and makes its nest on high?
28 It lives on the rock and makes its home
    in the fastness of the rocky crag.
29 From there it spies the prey;
    its eyes see it from far away.
30 Its young ones suck up blood;
    and where the slain are, there it is."

E. *Job's penitent submission*

40 And the Lord said to Job:
  2 "Shall a faultfinder contend with the Almighty?[p]
    Anyone who argues with God must respond."

  3 Then Job answered the Lord:
4 "See, I am of small account; what shall I answer you?
    I lay my hand on my mouth.
5 I have spoken once, and I will not answer;
    twice, but will proceed no further."

F. *God's second speech*

1. *God challenges Job*

  6 Then the Lord answered Job out of the whirlwind:
7 "Gird up your loins like a man;
    I will question you, and you declare to me.
8 Will you even put me in the wrong?
    Will you condemn me that you may be justified?
9 Have you an arm like God,
    and can you thunder with a voice like his?

10 "Deck yourself with majesty and dignity;

p Traditional rendering of Heb Shaddai

Cross references:

39.24 Jer 4.19; Ezek 7.14; Am 3.6
39.25 Josh 6.5; Am 1.14; 2.2
39.27 Jer 46.16; Ob 4
39.30 Mt 24.28; Lk 17.37
40.1 Job 33.13; 13.3; 23.4; 31.35
40.4 Job 42.6; 29.9
40.5 Job 9.3, 15
40.6 Job 38.1
40.7 Job 38.3; 42.4
40.8 Isa 14.27; Rom 3.4
40.9 2 Chr 32.8; Jer 17.5; Job 37.5
40.10 Ps 93.1; 104.1

39.26ff The hawk and the eagle function by the natural power and instinct given them by God. They make their way toward food that is proper for them. Shall not humankind, the highest of God's creation, confess their own weakness and ignorance and give glory to the one who has made them?
40.2 Apparently God is reading Job's mind, disclosing what Job is thinking, for Job has not yet spoken. Indeed, God knows the thoughts of every mind; nothing is hidden from him. God demands a response from Job.
40.4 When Job's response comes, it is short and to the point. Humbled in the dust, Job now knows that he is wrong. He admits that he has spoken various times in response to the queries of his friends, but that God has now stopped his mouth and brought an end to their disputations. Job realizes that the wisdom and righteousness are all on the side of God.
40.6ff God makes clear that no one can compete with him for justice; no one can joust with him for power; no one can come close to him for beauty and majesty; and no one can overcome enemies and opposition as easily and as effectually as the living God. In v. 15 God says even the "Behemoth," the greatest of created animals, is incapable of standing up to the Creator, much less someone like Job, whose strength is as nothing when compared to this animal.

clothe yourself with glory and splendor.

40.11
Isa 42.25;
2.12;
Dan 4.37
40.12
1 Sam 2.7;
Isa 13.11;
63.3;
Job 36.20
40.14
Ps 20.6; 60.5;
108.6

11 Pour out the overflowings of your anger,
    and look on all who are proud, and abase them.
12 Look on all who are proud, and bring them low;
    tread down the wicked where they stand.
13 Hide them all in the dust together;
    bind their faces in the world below. *q*
14 Then I will also acknowledge to you
    that your own right hand can give you victory.

2. *The God who made Behemoth cannot be overcome by humans*

40.15
v. 19

15 "Look at Behemoth,
    which I made just as I made you;
    it eats grass like an ox.
16 Its strength is in its loins,
    and its power in the muscles of its belly.
17 It makes its tail stiff like a cedar;
    the sinews of its thighs are knit together.
18 Its bones are tubes of bronze,
    its limbs like bars of iron.

40.19
Job 41.33;
v. 15
40.20
Ps 104.26

19 "It is the first of the great acts of God—
    only its Maker can approach it with the sword.
20 For the mountains yield food for it
    where all the wild animals play.
21 Under the lotus plants it lies,
    in the covert of the reeds and in the marsh.

40.22
Isa 44.4

22 The lotus trees cover it for shade;
    the willows of the wadi surround it.
23 Even if the river is turbulent, it is not frightened;
    it is confident though Jordan rushes against its mouth.

40.24
Prov 1.17

24 Can one take it with hooks *r*
    or pierce its nose with a snare?

3. *The God who made Leviathan is superior to humans*

41.1
Ps 104.26;
Isa 27.1
41.2
Isa 37.29

41 *s* "Can you draw out Leviathan *t* with a fishhook,
      or press down its tongue with a cord?
2 Can you put a rope in its nose,
    or pierce its jaw with a hook?
3 Will it make many supplications to you?
    Will it speak soft words to you?
4 Will it make a covenant with you
    to be taken as your servant forever?
5 Will you play with it as with a bird,
    or will you put it on leash for your girls?
6 Will traders bargain over it?
    Will they divide it up among the merchants?
7 Can you fill its skin with harpoons,
    or its head with fishing spears?
8 Lay hands on it;
    think of the battle; you will not do it again!

q Heb *the hidden place*   *r* Cn: Heb *in his eyes*   *s* Ch 40.25 in Heb   *t* Or *the crocodile*

40.15ff The *Behemoth* is probably the hippopotamus, of whom it can be said that it is the most powerful of all God's animals. None can withstand him. God in his goodness did not make it carnivorous, for then many lives would be lost to feed it. It is aquatic and eats grass, so that other animals do not

fear it, but play about it.
41.2 God challenges Job to master the crocodile (cf. NRSV footnote), to subdue and tame it if he can. But he cannot do this. If that is so, how then can he stand before the great God who made this creature?

9^u Any hope of capturing it^v will be disappointed;
    were not even the gods^w overwhelmed at the sight of it?
10 No one is so fierce as to dare to stir it up.
    Who can stand before it?^x
11 Who can confront it^x and be safe?^y
    — under the whole heaven, who?^z
12 "I will not keep silence concerning its limbs,
    or its mighty strength, or its splendid frame.
13 Who can strip off its outer garment?
    Who can penetrate its double coat of mail?^a
14 Who can open the doors of its face?
    There is terror all around its teeth.
15 Its back^b is made of shields in rows,
    shut up closely as with a seal.
16 One is so near to another
    that no air can come between them.
17 They are joined one to another;
    they clasp each other and cannot be separated.
18 Its sneezes flash forth light,
    and its eyes are like the eyelids of the dawn.
19 From its mouth go flaming torches;
    sparks of fire leap out.
20 Out of its nostrils comes smoke,
    as from a boiling pot and burning rushes.
21 Its breath kindles coals,
    and a flame comes out of its mouth.
22 In its neck abides strength,
    and terror dances before it.
23 The folds of its flesh cling together;
    it is firmly cast and immovable.
24 Its heart is as hard as stone,
    as hard as the lower millstone.
25 When it raises itself up the gods are afraid;
    at the crashing they are beside themselves.
26 Though the sword reaches it, it does not avail,
    nor does the spear, the dart, or the javelin.
27 It counts iron as straw,
    and bronze as rotten wood.
28 The arrow cannot make it flee;
    slingstones, for it, are turned to chaff.
29 Clubs are counted as chaff;
    it laughs at the rattle of javelins.
30 Its underparts are like sharp potsherds;
    it spreads itself like a threshing sledge on the mire.
31 It makes the deep boil like a pot;
    it makes the sea like a pot of ointment.
32 It leaves a shining wake behind it;
    one would think the deep to be white-haired.
33 On earth it has no equal,
    a creature without fear.

41.10
Job 3.8

41.11
Rom 11.35;
Ex 19.5;
Deut 10.14;
Ps 24.1;
50.12;
1 Cor 10.26

41.18
Job 3.9

41.33
Job 40.19

^u Ch 41.1 in Heb ^v Heb *of it* ^w Cn Compare Symmachus Syr: Heb *one is* ^x Heb *me* ^y Gk: Heb *that
I shall repay* ^z Heb *to me* ^a Gk: Heb *bridle* ^b Cn Compare Gk Vg: Heb *pride*

41.34 God stresses the strength and power of the crocodile, who can neither be conquered nor tamed. But God limited it to the waters — not to roam the earth where it might damage other created things. However strong humans may be, the crocodile is stronger. So also God is stronger than anyone or all people together. He is king over all that are proud. And God, who controls hippopotamus and crocodile, cannot be displaced or put down by humankind. The proud shall bow down. The Lord God alone shall be

34 It surveys everything that is lofty;
   it is king over all that are proud.' "

4. *Job repentant*

42 Then Job answered the LORD:
2 "I know that you can do all things,
   and that no purpose of yours can be thwarted.
3 'Who is this that hides counsel without knowledge?'
   Therefore I have uttered what I did not understand,
      things too wonderful for me, which I did not know.
4 'Hear, and I will speak;
   I will question you, and you declare to me.'
5 I had heard of you by the hearing of the ear,
   but now my eye sees you;
6 therefore I despise myself,
   and repent in dust and ashes."

V. *Epilogue (42.7–17)*

A. *Job's prayer for his friends*

7 After the LORD had spoken these words to Job, the LORD said to Eliphaz the Temanite: "My wrath is kindled against you and against your two friends; for you have not spoken of me what is right, as my servant Job has. 8 Now therefore take seven bulls and seven rams, and go to my servant Job, and offer up for yourselves a burnt offering; and my servant Job shall pray for you, for I will accept his prayer not to deal with you according to your folly; for you have not spoken of me what is right, as my servant Job has done." 9 So Eliphaz the Temanite and Bildad the Shuhite and Zophar the Naamathite went and did what the LORD had told them; and the LORD accepted Job's prayer.

B. *The latter days of Job*

10 And the LORD restored the fortunes of Job when he had prayed for his friends; and the LORD gave Job twice as much as he had before. 11 Then there came to him all his brothers and sisters and all who had known him before, and they ate bread with him in his house; they showed him sympathy and comforted him for all the evil that the LORD had brought upon him; and each of them gave him a piece of money*c* and a gold ring. 12 The LORD blessed the latter days of Job more than his beginning; and he had fourteen thousand sheep, six thousand camels, a thousand yoke of oxen, and a thousand donkeys. 13 He also had seven sons and three daughters. 14 He named the first Jemimah, the second Keziah, and the third Keren-happuch. 15 In all the land there were no women so beautiful as Job's daughters; and their father gave them an inheritance along with their brothers. 16 After this Job lived one hundred and forty years, and saw his children, and his children's children, four generations. 17 And Job died, old and full of days.

c Heb *a qesitah*

42.2
Gen 18.14;
Mt 19.26;
Mk 10.27;
Lk 18.27;
2 Chr 20.6;
Isa 14.27
42.3
Job 38.2;
Ps 40.5;
131.1; 139.6
42.4
Job 38.3;
40.7
42.5
Job 26.14;
Judg 13.22;
Isa 6.5
42.6
Ezra 9.6;
Job 40.4

42.7
Job 32.3;
vv. 1-6;
40.3-5
42.8
Num 23.1;
Job 1.5;
Jas 5.15, 16

42.10
Ps 14.7;
126.1
42.11
Job 19.13

42.12
Job 1.10; 8.7;
1.3
42.13
Job 1.2

42.16
Job 5.26;
Prov 3.16
42.17
Gen 25.8

exalted now and forever.
42.3 Job acknowledges he has learned from his experience, even though full understanding has not come to him.
42.7,8 Job's repentance (vv. 1-6) did not mean that his friends were correct in their assessment. God says

they were wrong, they must offer sacrifices, and Job would pray for them. Thus Job forgave them their words of condemnation and God answered his prayer for his friends (v. 9).
42.10 God restored to Job twice the wealth he had when Satan began to afflict him.

THE PSALMS

Authorship, Date, and Background: The book of Psalms has followed the tradition of the Septuagint for its name. Literally, the Greek rendering *Psalmoi* means "song to the accompaniment of a stringed instrument." The Hebrew title for the book is *Tehillim*, which means "praise songs." Psalms contains 150 chapters or psalms and has been divided into five segments, each one ending with a doxology (see Outline).

The date and authorship of this book is unique in that some of the authors are known and others are not, and the dates for the composition of the various psalms range from Moses to the period of the exile and shortly thereafter, from ca. 1400 to 500 B.C. Seventy-three of them are ascribed to David, two to Solomon, one each to Ethan and Heman, one to Moses, and twenty-three to Levitical clans of Asaph, leaving forty-nine psalms whose authors cannot be ascertained. Modern scholars have challenged the Davidic authorship of a number of the psalms attributed to him and have opted for a late dating of virtually all of the psalms. Interestingly, this is inconsistent, because some of the instructions for the singing of the psalms were written in a language that had already become untranslatable in the sixth century B.C.

Characteristics and Content: The psalms vary widely in their purposes. Scholars have noted eight different categories of psalms: (1) personal psalms; (2) prayer psalms; (3) liturgical psalms; (4) historical psalms; (5) praise psalms; (6) penitential psalms; (7) Messianic psalms; (8) psalms which exalt the majesty and might of God. Some psalms fit neatly into a particular category; others fit into several categories.

The book of Psalms has always occupied a unique place in the hearts of all believers. The range of human emotions go from heavenly praises to imprecatory petitions for God to smite the enemy. Some of the sayings spoken by Christ on Calvary are found in psalms, the greatest of which is the cry: "My God, my God, why have you forsaken me?" (22.1). Nowhere in Scripture does any sinner more eloquently confess his sins and seek the mercy of God in forgiveness than does David in Ps 51, written after Nathan the prophet pointed an accusing finger at him and pronounced the judgment of God upon him for his adultery with Bathsheba and the murder of Uriah the Hittite, her husband.

The psalms not only praise the Creator; they also explore nature with respect to the universe and to its occupants. The heavens, the earth, the seas, the abyss, reptiles, sheep, pastures, deer, sparrows, and the night seasons are mentioned. In historical matters, the exodus from Egypt, the travels of Israel during their years of wandering, the covenants of God with his people, and the redeeming hand of God are referred to. Other psalms speak about human beings in all of their social relationships. The Messianic psalms tell of the humiliation and glory of David's Son, Jesus Christ—his eternity, his incarnation, his incorruption, his passion, and his priesthood and ascension; in Acts 1.20, two psalms are quoted with regard to Judas Iscariot, who betrayed him (69.25; 109.8). The shepherd's psalm (23) will remain fixed forever in the affections of God's people everywhere.

Outline:

   I. (1—41)

  II. (42—72)

 III. (73—89)

 IV. (90—106)

  V. (107—150)

THE PSALMS

BOOK I
(Psalms 1–41)

Psalm 1

I. *The happiness of the godly (1.1–3)*

1 Happy are those
  who do not follow the advice of the wicked,
or take the path that sinners tread,
  or sit in the seat of scoffers;
2 but their delight is in the law of the Lord,
  and on his law they meditate day and night.
3 They are like trees
  planted by streams of water,
which yield their fruit in its season,
  and their leaves do not wither.
In all that they do, they prosper.

II. *The misery of the wicked (1.4–6)*

4 The wicked are not so,
  but are like chaff that the wind drives away.
5 Therefore the wicked will not stand in the judgment,
  nor sinners in the congregation of the righteous;
6 for the Lord watches over the way of the righteous,
  but the way of the wicked will perish.

Psalm 2

The Messiah's psalm

A. *The Messiah rejected*

1 Why do the nations conspire,
  and the peoples plot in vain?
2 The kings of the earth set themselves,

1.1
Prov 4.14;
Job 21.16;
Ps 17.4; 26.5;
Jer 15.17

1.2
Ps 119.35;
Josh 1.8;
Ps 119.1
1.3
Jer 17.8;
Ezek 47.12;
Gen 39.3;
Ps 128.2

1.4
Job 21.18;
Isa 17.13
1.5
Ps 5.5; 9.7;
8.16; 111.1;
149.1
1.6
Ps 37.18;
2 Tim 2.19;
Ps 9.3-6
2.1ff
Acts 4.25;
Ps 21.11

2.2
Ps 48.4-6;
74.18, 23;
Jn 1.41

1.1ff This psalm instructs us concerning good and evil. The human race is divided into saints and sinners, the offspring of Eve and the offspring of the serpent. This distinction is more important than any other classifications (e.g., rich and poor, young and old), for it determines the everlasting state of all people.

2.1ff Most psalms were composed a millennium before the birth of Jesus. David is referred to in many psalms, but since he is a forerunner of the Messiah, these references often are predictive of Jesus. Among the psalms that are clearly messianic are 2; 8; 16; 22; 72; 89; 110; and 132. While Ps 2 was originally composed as a coronation song for the kings of Judah, it is messianic in focus: v. 2 speaks about *the Lord and his anointed*, and v. 6 pictures Christ, the ascended one. Christ will indeed reign over a reconstituted Zion in the future. In v. 7, *You are my Son*, while it includes human kings, also refers to the incarnation of Jesus Christ (cf. Mt 3.17; Acts 13.33; Heb 1.5). More than sixty prophecies concerning Christ were fulfilled by his earthly ministry, death, and resurrection.

2.2 This psalm was written, no doubt, against a background of a rebellion against David or some other ruler of that line. The revolt is futile, however, for God has willed that the Davidic king shall reign over all nations. Jesus, as the Messiah and the Son of David, ultimately fulfills this cosmic claim.

and the rulers take counsel together,
against the LORD and his anointed, saying,

2.3
Jer 5.5

3 "Let us burst their bonds asunder,
and cast their cords from us."

B. *The LORD's derision*

2.4
Ps 59.8;
37.13;
Prov 1.26
2.5
Ps 21.8, 9;
78.49, 50
2.6
Ps 3.4

4 He who sits in the heavens laughs;
the LORD has them in derision.
5 Then he will speak to them in his wrath,
and terrify them in his fury, saying,
6 "I have set my king on Zion, my holy hill."

C. *The Messiah triumphant*

2.7
Acts 13.33;
Heb 1.5

7 I will tell of the decree of the LORD:
He said to me, "You are my son;
today I have begotten you.

2.8
Ps 22.27

8 Ask of me, and I will make the nations your heritage,
and the ends of the earth your possession.

2.9
Ps 89.23;
Rev 2.27;
12.5

9 You shall break them with a rod of iron,
and dash them in pieces like a potter's vessel."

D. *The LORD's counsel to kings*

10 Now therefore, O kings, be wise;
be warned, O rulers of the earth.

2.11
Heb 12.28;
Ps 119.119,
120
2.12
Jn 5.23;
Rev 6.16;
Ps 34.8;
Rom 9.33

11 Serve the LORD with fear,
with trembling 12 kiss his feet,[a]
or he will be angry, and you will perish in the way;
for his wrath is quickly kindled.

Happy are all who take refuge in him.

Psalm 3

David in distress

3.1
2 Sam 15.12

A. *His complaint*

A Psalm of David, when he fled from his son Absalom.

1 O LORD, how many are my foes!
Many are rising against me;

3.2
Ps 71.11

2 many are saying to me,
"There is no help for you[b] in God."   *Selah*

B. *His confidence*

3.3
Ps 28.7; 27.6

3 But you, O LORD, are a shield around me,
my glory, and the one who lifts up my head.

3.4
Ps 34.4; 99.9

4 I cry aloud to the LORD,
and he answers me from his holy hill.   *Selah*

C. *His security*

3.5
Lev 26.6;
Ps 139.18
3.6
Ps 27.3

5 I lie down and sleep;
I wake again, for the LORD sustains me.
6 I am not afraid of ten thousands of people
who have set themselves against me all around.

a Cn: Meaning of Heb of verses 11b and 12a is uncertain   *b* Syr: Heb *him*

D. *His prayer and rejoicing*

7 Rise up, O Lord!
   Deliver me, O my God!
   For you strike all my enemies on the cheek;
   you break the teeth of the wicked.

8 Deliverance belongs to the Lord;
   may your blessing be on your people!   *Selah*

Psalm 4

Thoughts in the night

A. *Prayer for help*

To the leader: with stringed instruments. A Psalm of David.

1 Answer me when I call, O God of my right!
   You gave me room when I was in distress.
   Be gracious to me, and hear my prayer.

B. *Reproof of his enemies*

2 How long, you people, shall my honor suffer shame?
   How long will you love vain words, and seek after lies? *Selah*
3 But know that the Lord has set apart the faithful for himself;
   the Lord hears when I call to him.

C. *His enemies exhorted*

4 When you are disturbed,*c* do not sin;
   ponder it on your beds, and be silent.   *Selah*
5 Offer right sacrifices,
   and put your trust in the Lord.

D. *His confidence in God*

6 There are many who say, "O that we might see some good!
   Let the light of your face shine on us, O Lord!"
7 You have put gladness in my heart
   more than when their grain and wine abound.

8 I will both lie down and sleep in peace;
   for you alone, O Lord, make me lie down in safety.

Psalm 5

A morning prayer

A. *God hears prayer*

To the leader: for the flutes. A Psalm of David.

1 Give ear to my words, O Lord;
   give heed to my sighing.

c Or *are angry*

3.7
Ps 7.6; 6.4;
Job 16.10;
Ps 58.6

3.8
Isa 43.11;
Jer 3.23;
Num 6.23-27

4.1
Ps 27.7; 18.6;
24.5; 18.18;
25.16; 17.6

4.2
Ps 31.6, 18

4.3
Ps 31.23; 6.8,
9

4.4
Ps 33.8;
Eph 4.26;
Ps 77.6

4.5
Deut 33.19;
Ps 50.14;
37.3

4.6
Num 6.26

4.7
Acts 14.17;
Isa 9.3

4.8
Ps 3.5;
Lev 25.18

5.1
Ps 54.2;
19.14

3.8 *Deliverance belongs to the Lord.* Those who speak from human experience speak best about how God delivers and saves his people.
4.1ff Some psalms are devotional; others are doctrinal and practical. This one is of the latter category, teaching us about the nature of God in relation to his people. The psalmist finds rest and peace in his God.
5.1ff This is a prayer of David when faced with enemies who would destroy him. David assures us that God hears his people's prayers, delivers them, and acts righteously on their behalf.

2 Listen to the sound of my cry,
   my King and my God,
   for to you I pray.
5.2
Ps 3.4; 84.3

3 O Lord, in the morning you hear my voice;
   in the morning I plead my case to you, and watch.
5.3
Ps 88.13;
Hab 2.1

B. *God hates wickedness*

4 For you are not a God who delights in wickedness;
   evil will not sojourn with you.
5.4
Ps 11.5;
92.15

5 The boastful will not stand before your eyes;
   you hate all evildoers.
5.5
Ps 73.3; 1.5;
11.5

6 You destroy those who speak lies;
   the Lord abhors the bloodthirsty and deceitful.
5.6
Rev 21.8;
Ps 55.23

C. *God blesses the righteous*

7 But I, through the abundance of your steadfast love,
   will enter your house,
I will bow down toward your holy temple
   in awe of you.
5.7
Ps 69.13;
28.2

8 Lead me, O Lord, in your righteousness
   because of my enemies;
   make your way straight before me.
5.8
Ps 27.11;
31.1

9 For there is no truth in their mouths;
   their hearts are destruction;
their throats are open graves;
   they flatter with their tongues.
5.9
Deut 32.20;
Lk 11.44;
Rom 3.13;
Ps 12.2

10 Make them bear their guilt, O God;
    let them fall by their own counsels;
because of their many transgressions cast them out,
    for they have rebelled against you.
5.10
Ps 9.16;
Lam 1.5;
Ps 107.10, 11

11 But let all who take refuge in you rejoice;
    let them ever sing for joy.
Spread your protection over them,
    so that those who love your name may exult in you.
5.11
Ps 2.12;
Isa 65.13;
Zech 9.15;
Ps 69.36

12 For you bless the righteous, O Lord;
    you cover them with favor as with a shield.
5.12
Ps 112.2;
32.7, 10

Psalm 6

Prayer for mercy in time of trouble

A. *Prayer for mercy*

To the leader: with stringed instruments; according to The Sheminith.
A Psalm of David.
6.1
Ps 38.1; 2.5

1 O Lord, do not rebuke me in your anger,
   or discipline me in your wrath.

2 Be gracious to me, O Lord, for I am languishing;
   O Lord, heal me, for my bones are shaking with terror.
6.2
Ps 51.1;
102.4, 11;
41.4; 22.14

5.7 David plans to worship God publicly by attending his house. Private worship and prayer are necessary and good, but so is the gathering of God's people for worship.
5.11 *let all who take refuge in you rejoice.* All people need this refuge. We have all wandered from God's way and are lost. Without this refuge we remain alien-

ated and wander in the darkness of night.
6.1ff This is a psalm for all who are afflicted and who express their complaints to a listening, caring God. It ends with the cheerful assurance that God hears and helps, and that those who afflict the servants of God will be turned back.

3 My soul also is struck with terror,
   while you, O LORD — how long?

6.3
Jn 12.27;
Ps 90.13

4 Turn, O LORD, save my life;
   deliver me for the sake of your steadfast love.

6.4
Ps 17.13

5 For in death there is no remembrance of you;
   in Sheol who can give you praise?

6.5
Ps 30.9;
Isa 38.18

6 I am weary with my moaning;
   every night I flood my bed with tears;
   I drench my couch with my weeping.

6.6
Ps 69.3; 22.1;
42.3

7 My eyes waste away because of grief;
   they grow weak because of all my foes.

6.7
Ps 31.9

B. *Assurance of a good answer*

8 Depart from me, all you workers of evil,
   for the LORD has heard the sound of my weeping.

6.8
Ps 119.115;
Lk 13.27;
Ps 5.5; 28.6

9 The LORD has heard my supplication;
   the LORD accepts my prayer.

6.9
Ps 116.1;
66.19, 20

10 All my enemies shall be ashamed and struck with terror;
   they shall turn back, and in a moment be put to shame.

6.10
Ps 71.24;
40.14; 73.19

Psalm 7

7.1
Ps 11.1;
31.15

The prayer of a wronged individual

A. *David turns to God*

A Shiggaion of David, which he sang to the LORD concerning Cush, a
Benjaminite.

1 O LORD my God, in you I take refuge;
   save me from all my pursuers, and deliver me,
2 or like a lion they will tear me apart;
   they will drag me away, with no one to rescue.

7.2
Ps 17.12;
50.22

B. *He pleads his innocence*

3 O LORD my God, if I have done this,
   if there is wrong in my hands,

7.3
2 Sam 16.7;
1 Sam 24.11

4 if I have repaid my ally with harm
   or plundered my foe without cause,

7.4
1 Sam 24.7

5 then let the enemy pursue and overtake me,
   trample my life to the ground,
   and lay my soul in the dust.   *Selah*

C. *He cries for justice*

6 Rise up, O LORD, in your anger;
   lift yourself up against the fury of my enemies;
   awake, O my God;[d] you have appointed a judgment.

7.6
Ps 3.7; 94.2;
44.23

7 Let the assembly of the peoples be gathered around you,
   and over it take your seat[e] on high.

7.7
Ps 68.18

8 The LORD judges the peoples;

7.8
Ps 96.13;
18.20; 35.24

---

d Or *awake for me*   e Cn: Heb *return*

6.10 *they shall turn back.* This verse is either a prayer
for the conversion of David's enemies or a prediction
of their destruction.
7.1ff In this psalm David proclaims his innocence,
is convinced that God will deal with the unrighteous,

and ends by thanking and praising the Lord Most
High. As such, it encourages the hearts of those who
have been unjustly and maliciously attacked by those
who hate and despise them.

judge me, O Lᴏʀᴅ, according to my righteousness
and according to the integrity that is in me.

D. *The fate of the wicked*

7.9
Ps 34.21;
Isa 54.14;
1 Chr 28.9;
Jer 11.20;
Rev 2.23
7.10
Ps 18.2;
125.4
7.11
Ps 50.6;
Isa 34.2

9 O let the evil of the wicked come to an end,
   but establish the righteous,
you who test the minds and hearts,
   O righteous God.
10 God is my shield,
   who saves the upright in heart.
11 God is a righteous judge,
   and a God who has indignation every day.

7.12
Ezek 3.19;
33.9;
Deut 32.41;
Ps 21.12
7.13
Ps 64.7
7.14
Isa 59.4;
Jas 1.15

12 If one does not repent, God*f* will whet his sword;
   he has bent and strung his bow;
13 he has prepared his deadly weapons,
   making his arrows fiery shafts.
14 See how they conceive evil,
   and are pregnant with mischief,
   and bring forth lies.

7.15
Job 4.8;
Ps 9.15;
Eccl 10.8
7.16
Ps 140.9;
Esth 9.25

15 They make a pit, digging it out,
   and fall into the hole that they have made.
16 Their mischief returns upon their own heads,
   and on their own heads their violence descends.

E. *Praise to a righteous God*

7.17
Ps 71.15, 16;
9.2

17 I will give to the Lᴏʀᴅ the thanks due to his righteousness,
   and sing praise to the name of the Lᴏʀᴅ, the Most High.

Psalm 8

God's glory and humankind's honor

8.1
Ps 66.2;
148.13; 57.5,
11; 113.4

A. *God the great creator*

To the leader: according to The Gittith. A Psalm of David.

1 O Lᴏʀᴅ, our Sovereign,
   how majestic is your name in all the earth!

You have set your glory above the heavens.

8.2
Mt 21.16;
Ps 44.16

2   Out of the mouths of babes and infants
you have founded a bulwark because of your foes,
   to silence the enemy and the avenger.

8.3
Ps 89.11;
102.5; 136.9
8.4
Job 7.17;
Ps 144.3;
Heb 2.6

3 When I look at your heavens, the work of your fingers,
   the moon and the stars that you have established;
4 what are human beings that you are mindful of them,
   mortals*g* that you care for them?

f Heb *he*   *g* Heb *ben adam*, lit. *son of man*

7.12 Sword and bow are ready for God to execute vengeance on his enemies. However, while he is preparing his instruments of destruction, he warns all people of their danger and gives them time to repent. **7.15** There is a sense in which sinners prepare their own destruction. They are like Haman, who constructed the gallows on which he was hung, although it was intended for Mordecai (see Esth 7). So sinners dig a pit for others, only to fall into it themselves. **8.1ff** This hymn of praise exalts the glory of the Creator and speaks of the relationship of human beings to the one who has made them. Even though they are finite, God has crowned them with glory and honor. The psalm begins and ends on a note of the majesty of God our Lord.

B. *Mortals the chief agents of God*

5 Yet you have made them a little lower than God,[h]
  and crowned them with glory and honor.
6 You have given them dominion over the works of your hands;
  you have put all things under their feet,
7 all sheep and oxen,
  and also the beasts of the field,
8 the birds of the air, and the fish of the sea,
  whatever passes along the paths of the seas.

9 O LORD, our Sovereign,
  how majestic is your name in all the earth!

Psalm 9

Praise to God for deliverance

A. *Hymn of thanksgiving*

To the leader: according to Muth-labben. A Psalm of David.

1 I will give thanks to the LORD with my whole heart;
  I will tell of all your wonderful deeds.
2 I will be glad and exult in you;
  I will sing praise to your name, O Most High.

3 When my enemies turned back,
  they stumbled and perished before you.
4 For you have maintained my just cause;
  you have sat on the throne giving righteous judgment.

5 You have rebuked the nations, you have destroyed the wicked;
  you have blotted out their name forever and ever.
6 The enemies have vanished in everlasting ruins;
  their cities you have rooted out;
  the very memory of them has perished.

B. *Faith in God's righteousness*

7 But the LORD sits enthroned forever,
  he has established his throne for judgment.
8 He judges the world with righteousness;
  he judges the peoples with equity.

9 The LORD is a stronghold for the oppressed,
  a stronghold in times of trouble.
10 And those who know your name put their trust in you,
  for you, O LORD, have not forsaken those who seek you.

11 Sing praises to the LORD, who dwells in Zion.
  Declare his deeds among the peoples.
12 For he who avenges blood is mindful of them;
  he does not forget the cry of the afflicted.

[h] *Or than the divine beings or angels: Heb elohim*

8.5
Ps 103.4;
21.5;
Heb 2.9
8.6
Gen 1.26;
Heb 2.8

8.9
v. 1

9.1
Ps 86.12;
26.7

9.2
Ps 5.11;
83.18

9.3
Ps 56.9; 27.2

9.4
Ps 140.12;
47.8; 67.4;
1 Pet 2.23

9.5
Deut 9.14

9.6
Ps 40.15;
34.16

9.7
Ps 29.10;
89.14
9.8
Ps 96.13

9.9
Ps 18.2; 32.7;
37.39
9.10
Ps 91.14;
37.28

9.11
Ps 76.2;
105.1
9.12
Gen 9.5;
v. 18

8.5 *a little lower than God.* Mortals, in comparison to the cosmos, are insignificant. Yet God has "given them dominion" over everything. Jesus, the Son of God, as truly human, is sovereign over all the universe, and is in charge of everything. This is a messianic psalm (see Heb 2.5–9).

9.1ff This hymn of deliverance goes far beyond David as an individual and speaks about the nations. Implicit is the truth that nations do sin and are judged by God, rising and falling according to God's righteous judgments.

C. A prayer for help

9.13
Ps 30.10;
25.18; 38.19;
30.3

13 Be gracious to me, O LORD.
  See what I suffer from those who hate me;
  you are the one who lifts me up from the gates of death,

9.14
Ps 106.2;
87.2; 13.5

14 so that I may recount all your praises,
  and, in the gates of daughter Zion,
  rejoice in your deliverance.

D. A testimony to God's past judgments

9.15
Ps 7.15; 35.8

15 The nations have sunk in the pit that they made;
  in the net that they hid has their own foot been caught.

9.16
Isa 64.2; v. 4

16 The LORD has made himself known, he has executed judgment;
  the wicked are snared in the work of their own hands.

                                                        Higgaion. Selah

E. Assurance of, and prayer for, justice

9.17
Ps 49.14;
50.22;
Job 8.13

17 The wicked shall depart to Sheol,
  all the nations that forget God.

9.18
v. 12;
Ps 74.19

18 For the needy shall not always be forgotten,
  nor the hope of the poor perish forever.

9.19
Ps 3.7;
2 Chr 14.11;
Ps 110.6
9.20
Ps 83.15;
Isa 31.3

19 Rise up, O LORD! Do not let mortals prevail;
  let the nations be judged before you.
20 Put them in fear, O LORD;
  let the nations know that they are only human.   *Selah*

10.1
Ps 22.1; 13.1

Psalm 10

When judgment is delayed

A. The evil acts of the wicked

1 Why, O LORD, do you stand far off?
  Why do you hide yourself in times of trouble?

10.2
Ps 109.16;
7.15; 9.16

2 In arrogance the wicked persecute the poor —
  let them be caught in the schemes they have devised.

10.3
Ps 94.4;
Job 1.5, 11;
v. 13
10.4
v. 13;
Ps 14.1

3 For the wicked boast of the desires of their heart,
  those greedy for gain curse and renounce the LORD.
4 In the pride of their countenance the wicked say, "God will not
    seek it out";
  all their thoughts are, "There is no God."

5 Their ways prosper at all times;
  your judgments are on high, out of their sight;
  as for their foes, they scoff at them.

10.6
Ps 30.6;
49.11
10.7
Rom 3.14;
Ps 59.12;
73.8; 140.3

6 They think in their heart, "We shall not be moved;
  throughout all generations we shall not meet adversity."
7 Their mouths are filled with cursing and deceit and oppression;
  under their tongues are mischief and iniquity.

10.8
Prov 1.11;
Ps 94.6

8 They sit in ambush in the villages;
  in hiding places they murder the innocent.

10.1ff God is long-suffering. The wicked are not always punished right away; they continue in their evil ways with apparent impunity. The psalmist offers a prayer to God to take action against the wicked and receives assurance that justice will prevail at last and the wicked will be punished.

9   Their eyes stealthily watch for the helpless;
        they lurk in secret like a lion in its covert;
    they lurk that they may seize the poor;
        they seize the poor and drag them off in their net.

10 They stoop, they crouch,
        and the helpless fall by their might.
11 They think in their heart, "God has forgotten,
        he has hidden his face, he will never see it."

B. *A prayer for relief and confidence of an answer*

12 Rise up, O LORD; O God, lift up your hand;
        do not forget the oppressed.
13 Why do the wicked renounce God,
        and say in their hearts, "You will not call us to account"?
14 But you do see! Indeed you note trouble and grief,
        that you may take it into your hands;
    the helpless commit themselves to you;
        you have been the helper of the orphan.
15 Break the arm of the wicked and evildoers;
        seek out their wickedness until you find none.
16 The LORD is king forever and ever;
        the nations shall perish from his land.
17 O LORD, you will hear the desire of the meek;
        you will strengthen their heart, you will incline your ear
18 to do justice for the orphan and the oppressed,
        so that those from earth may strike terror no more. *i*

Psalm 11

The LORD our refuge and defender

A. *Temptation to distrust in trials*

To the leader. Of David.

1   In the LORD I take refuge; how can you say to me,
        "Flee like a bird to the mountains; *j*
2   for look, the wicked bend the bow,
        they have fitted their arrow to the string,
        to shoot in the dark at the upright in heart.
3   If the foundations are destroyed,
        what can the righteous do?"

B. *Affirmation of faith in the LORD*

4   The LORD is in his holy temple;
        the LORD's throne is in heaven.
        His eyes behold, his gaze examines humankind.
5   The LORD tests the righteous and the wicked,
        and his soul hates the lover of violence.
6   On the wicked he will rain coals of fire and sulfur;

i Meaning of Heb uncertain   *j* Gk Syr Jerome Tg: Heb *flee to your mountain, O bird*

11.1ff When in trouble we are tempted to distrust God or to quit. There is one thing the righteous can and ought to do—trust God and be assured that he will deal with the wicked, for God loves the righteous and approves of their deeds.

Cross-references (right margin):

10.9 Ps 17.12; 59.3; v. 2; 140.5

10.11 v. 4; Job 22.13; Ps 73.11

10.12 Mic 5.9; Ps 9.12
10.13 v. 3

10.14 Job 11.11; Jer 51.56; Ps 37.5; 68.5; Hos 14.3

10.15 Ps 37.17; 9.12
10.16 Ps 29.10; Deut 8.20

10.17 Ps 145.19; 1 Chr 29.18; Ps 34.15
10.18 Ps 82.3; 9.9; Isa 29.20

11.1 Ps 56.11

11.2 Ps 7.12; 64.3, 4

11.3 Ps 82.5

11.4 Ps 18.6; 103.19; 33.13; 34.15, 16
11.5 Gen 22.1; Jas 1.12; Ps 5.5
11.6 Ezek 38.22; Jer 4.11, 12; Ps 75.8

a scorching wind shall be the portion of their cup.

11.7
Ps 7.9, 11;
33.5; 17.15

7 For the LORD is righteous;
he loves righteous deeds;
the upright shall behold his face.

Psalm 12

Good thoughts for bad times

12.1
Isa 57.1

A. *Prayer for help amidst the ungodly*

To the leader: according to The Sheminith. A Psalm of David.

1 Help, O LORD, for there is no longer anyone who is godly;
the faithful have disappeared from humankind.

12.2
Ps 41.6;
55.21;
1 Chr 12.33

2 They utter lies to each other;
with flattering lips and a double heart they speak.

12.3
Ps 73.8, 9

3 May the LORD cut off all flattering lips,
the tongue that makes great boasts,
4 those who say, "With our tongues we will prevail;
our lips are our own — who is our master?"

B. *Assurance of the LORD's deliverance*

12.5
Ps 10.18; 3.7;
34.6

5 "Because the poor are despoiled, because the needy groan,
I will now rise up," says the LORD;
"I will place them in the safety for which they long."

12.6
Ps 18.30;
Prov 30.5

6 The promises of the LORD are promises that are pure,
silver refined in a furnace on the ground,
purified seven times.

12.7
Ps 37.28

7 You, O LORD, will protect us;
you will guard us from this generation forever.

12.8
Ps 55.10, 11

8 On every side the wicked prowl,
as vileness is exalted among humankind.

Psalm 13

The deserted soul

13.1
Job 13.24;
Ps 44.24;
88.14

A. *A desperate plight*

To the leader. A Psalm of David.

1 How long, O LORD? Will you forget me forever?
How long will you hide your face from me?

13.2
Ps 42.4, 9;
94.3

2 How long must I bear pain[k] in my soul,
and have sorrow in my heart all day long?
How long shall my enemy be exalted over me?

---

[k] Syr: Heb *hold counsels*

12.1ff At times people generally lack piety and honesty and integrity are in short supply. Humans on every side prowl about to destroy, but the righteous shall be refined and purified in the midst of all this evil.
12.5 This psalm contains good thoughts for bad times. God will come to the aid of his saints. Though people are false, he is faithful, his word is precious, and his promises are pure.
13.1ff This psalm is for those who experience the silence of God and feel his absence in their lives. When God is veiled and we cannot see him, we should continually call on him, for he is speaking when we do not hear him and present when he seems to be absent.

B. *A prayer for help*

3 Consider and answer me, O LORD my God!
  Give light to my eyes, or I will sleep the sleep of death,
4 and my enemy will say, "I have prevailed";
  my foes will rejoice because I am shaken.

C. *An assurance of deliverance*

5 But I trusted in your steadfast love;
  my heart shall rejoice in your salvation.
6 I will sing to the LORD,
  because he has dealt bountifully with me.

Psalm 14

The principles and practices of the wicked

To the leader. Of David.

1 Fools say in their hearts, "There is no God."
  They are corrupt, they do abominable deeds;
  there is no one who does good.

2 The LORD looks down from heaven on humankind
  to see if there are any who are wise,
  who seek after God.

3 They have all gone astray, they are all alike perverse;
  there is no one who does good,
  no, not one.

4 Have they no knowledge, all the evildoers
  who eat up my people as they eat bread,
  and do not call upon the LORD?

5 There they shall be in great terror,
  for God is with the company of the righteous.
6 You would confound the plans of the poor,
  but the LORD is their refuge.

7 O that deliverance for Israel would come from Zion!
  When the LORD restores the fortunes of his people,
  Jacob will rejoice; Israel will be glad.

Psalm 15

The happiness of the blameless

A Psalm of David.

1 O LORD, who may abide in your tent?
  Who may dwell on your holy hill?

Cross references:
13.3 Ps 5.1; Ezra 9.8; Jer 51.39
13.4 Jer 20.10; Ps 25.2
13.5 Ps 52.8; 9.14
13.6 Ps 59.16; 116.7
14.1 Ps 10.4; 53.1-6; 73.8; Rom 3.10-12
14.2 Ps 33.13; 92.6; Ezra 6.21
14.3 Ps 58.3; 2 Pet 2.7; Rev 22.11; Ps 143.2
14.4 Ps 82.5; 27.2; 79.6; Isa 64.7
14.5 Ps 73.15
14.6 Ps 9.9; 40.17
14.7 Ps 53.6; Job 42.10
15.1 Ps 24.3-5; 27.5, 6; 2.6

13.6 *he has dealt bountifully with me.* David speaks of this in the past tense, for by faith he has received the pledge of God for something which has not yet come.
14.1ff *Fools.* Here atheists are called fools. The reason is simple: no one can deny the existence of God without being omniscient, and this would make that person God. Since the doubter is not omniscient, God can exist outside the limits of any mortal's knowledge.

One *can* be an agnostic and say, "I don't know whether there is a God." But to be an atheist is irrational or simply foolish.
14.7 The wicked act corruptly, according to their principles. But there is a God who will come out of Zion and deliver his people. Israel will rejoice, as will all believers and nations whose God is the Lord.
15.1ff The way to heaven and to happiness is to be holy and honest. Christ is the way, and we must walk

15.2
Ps 24.4; 51.6;
Eph 4.25
15.3
Lev 19.16;
Ex 23.1

15.4
2 Tim 3.8;
Acts 28.10;
Judg 11.35

15.5
Ex 22.25;
23.8;
Deut 16.19;
Ps 112.6

2 Those who walk blamelessly, and do what is right,
   and speak the truth from their heart;
3 who do not slander with their tongue,
   and do no evil to their friends,
     nor take up a reproach against their neighbors;
4 in whose eyes the wicked are despised,
   but who honor those who fear the LORD;
who stand by their oath even to their hurt;
5 who do not lend money at interest,
   and do not take a bribe against the innocent.

Those who do these things shall never be moved.

Psalm 16

A Messianic prophecy

A. *Faith evidenced*

A Miktam of David.

16.1
Ps 17.8; 7.1

1 Protect me, O God, for in you I take refuge.
2 I say to the LORD, "You are my Lord;
   I have no good apart from you."[*l*]

16.2
Ps 73.25

3 As for the holy ones in the land, they are the noble,
   in whom is all my delight.

16.3
Deut 33.3;
Ps 101.6

4 Those who choose another god multiply their sorrows;[*m*]
   their drink offerings of blood I will not pour out
   or take their names upon my lips.

16.4
Ps 32.10;
106.37, 38;
Ex 23.13

B. *Calvary predicted*

5 The LORD is my chosen portion and my cup;
   you hold my lot.
6 The boundary lines have fallen for me in pleasant places;
   I have a goodly heritage.

16.5
Ps 73.26;
23.5; 125.3
16.6
Ps 78.55;
Jer 3.19

7 I bless the LORD who gives me counsel;
   in the night also my heart instructs me.
8 I keep the LORD always before me;
   because he is at my right hand, I shall not be moved.

16.7
Ps 73.24;
77.6
16.8
Ps 54.3;
73.23; 62.2

C. *The resurrection assured*

9 Therefore my heart is glad, and my soul rejoices;
   my body also rests secure.
10 For you do not give me up to Sheol,
    or let your faithful one see the Pit.

16.9
Ps 4.7; 30.12;
4.8
16.10
Acts 2.27;
13.35;
Ps 49.9

l Jerome Tg: Meaning of Heb uncertain   *m* Cn: Meaning of Heb uncertain

in his way as described in this lovely psalm. *your tent.*
God's presence by way of the cloud of glory was
manifested to his people in the tent and later on in the
temple. God's people find refuge in him not only
because they trust in him but also because that trust
is exhibited in a new life marked by distinct characteristics. **16.1ff** This psalm has much of David in it but much
more about Christ. It is messianic, closing with a

staement of confidence in the resurrection. David
may not have fully understood the message inspired
by the Spirit in this psalm (cf. Acts 2.24–33;
13.35–38). **16.8–11** These messianic verses (quoted by Peter in
Acts 2.25–28) predict the resurrection of Jesus
Christ. The Hebrew word *nephesh* (translated as
"me") refers to the whole person, not merely to the
soul as distinct from the body.

11　You show me the path of life.
　　In your presence there is fullness of joy;
　　in your right hand are pleasures forevermore.

16.11
Mt 7.14;
Ps 17.15;
36.7, 8

Psalm 17

David's desire for deliverance

17.1
Ps 9.4; 61.1;
55.1;
Isa 29.13

A. He pleads his integrity

A Prayer of David.

1　Hear a just cause, O Lᴏʀᴅ; attend to my cry;
　　give ear to my prayer from lips free of deceit.
2　From you let my vindication come;
　　let your eyes see the right.

17.2
1 Chr 29.17

3　If you try my heart, if you visit me by night,
　　if you test me, you will find no wickedness in me;
　　my mouth does not transgress.
4　As for what others do, by the word of your lips
　　I have avoided the ways of the violent.
5　My steps have held fast to your paths;
　　my feet have not slipped.

17.3
Ps 26.2;
66.10;
Job 23.10;
Jer 50.20;
Ps 39.1
17.4
Prov 1.15
17.5
Ps 44.18;
18.36

B. He prays to be preserved

6　I call upon you, for you will answer me, O God;
　　incline your ear to me, hear my words.
7　Wondrously show your steadfast love,
　　O savior of those who seek refuge
　　from their adversaries at your right hand.

17.6
Ps 86.7; 88.2
17.7
Ps 31.21;
20.6

8　Guard me as the apple of the eye;
　　hide me in the shadow of your wings,
9　from the wicked who despoil me,
　　my deadly enemies who surround me.

17.8
Deut 32.10;
Ps 36.7
17.9
Ps 31.20;
38.12; 109.3

C. He describes his enemies

10　They close their hearts to pity;
　　with their mouths they speak arrogantly.
11　They track me down;[n] now they surround me;
　　they set their eyes to cast me to the ground.
12　They are like a lion eager to tear,
　　like a young lion lurking in ambush.

17.10
Ps 73.7;
1 Sam 2.3;
Ps 31.18
17.11
Ps 88.17;
37.14
17.12
Ps 7.2; 10.9

D. He expresses his confidence in the Lᴏʀᴅ

13　Rise up, O Lᴏʀᴅ, confront them, overthrow them!
　　By your sword deliver my life from the wicked,
14　from mortals — by your hand, O Lᴏʀᴅ —
　　from mortals whose portion in life is in this world.

17.13
Ps 73.18;
22.20; 7.12
17.14
Lk 16.8;
Ps 73.3-7;
Isa 2.7;
Job 21.11

[n] One Ms Compare Syr: MT *Our steps*

17.1ff David claims the correctness of his life. He prays for God to conserve and protect him from his enemies, whose character he describes here. As a result of his confidence in God, David experienced God's comfort.

17.6 Persecution and suffering have a way of concentrating our attention on God and his mercies. People pray more when they are in trouble than when all is going well.

17.8 Whoever touches any believer touches the apple of God's eye (Zech 2.8).

May their bellies be filled with what you have stored up for
  them;
  may their children have more than enough;
  may they leave something over to their little ones.

17.15
1 Jn 3.2;
Ps 4.6, 7;
16.11

15 As for me, I shall behold your face in righteousness;
  when I awake I shall be satisfied, beholding your likeness.

18.1
Ps 27.1

Psalm 18

David's hymn of deliverance

A. *He glories in the* LORD

To the leader. A Psalm of David the servant of the LORD, who addressed
the words of this song to the LORD on the day when the LORD delivered
him from the hand of all his enemies, and from the hand of Saul. He said:

1 I love you, O LORD, my strength.
2 The LORD is my rock, my fortress, and my deliverer,
  my God, my rock in whom I take refuge,
  my shield, and the horn of my salvation, my stronghold.
3 I call upon the LORD, who is worthy to be praised,
  so I shall be saved from my enemies.

18.2
Ps 19.14;
91.2; 40.17;
11.1; 59.11;
75.10; 9.9
18.3
Ps 48.1;
Num 10.9

B. *He testifies to God's deliverances*

4 The cords of death encompassed me;
  the torrents of perdition assailed me;
5 the cords of Sheol entangled me;
  the snares of death confronted me.

18.4
Ps 116.3;
124.3, 4
18.5
Ps 116.3;
Prov 14.27

6 In my distress I called upon the LORD;
  to my God I cried for help.
  From his temple he heard my voice,
  and my cry to him reached his ears.

18.6
Ps 86.7; 11.4;
34.15

7 Then the earth reeled and rocked;
  the foundations also of the mountains trembled
  and quaked, because he was angry.

18.7
Ps 68.7, 8;
114.4, 6

8 Smoke went up from his nostrils,
  and devouring fire from his mouth;
  glowing coals flamed forth from him.

18.8
Deut 29.20;
Hab 3.5

9 He bowed the heavens, and came down;
  thick darkness was under his feet.

18.9
Ps 144.5;
Ex 20.21

10 He rode on a cherub, and flew;
  he came swiftly upon the wings of the wind.

18.10
Ps 80.1;
104.3

11 He made darkness his covering around him,
  his canopy thick clouds dark with water.

18.11
Ps 97.2
18.12
Ps 104.2;
Isa 30.30;
Ps 140.10

12 Out of the brightness before him
  there broke through his clouds
  hailstones and coals of fire.

13 The LORD also thundered in the heavens,
  and the Most High uttered his voice. *o*

18.13
Ps 29.3;
104.7
18.14
Ps 7.13;
144.6;
Ex 14.24;
Judg 4.15

14 And he sent out his arrows, and scattered them;

o Gk See 2 Sam 22.14: Heb adds *hailstones and coals of fire*

18.1ff With some alterations, this psalm is found in
2 Sam 22. David expresses thanksgiving to God for
having faithfully delivered him. As a result, David
has the assurance that this same God will deliver him
in the days which lie ahead. Such should be the attitude of all believers; Jesus and his Spirit preserve
and help us through life's journey.

15 Then the channels of the sea were seen,
   and the foundations of the world were laid bare
at your rebuke, O LORD,
   at the blast of the breath of your nostrils.

16 He reached down from on high, he took me;
   he drew me out of mighty waters.
17 He delivered me from my strong enemy,
   and from those who hated me;
   for they were too mighty for me.
18 They confronted me in the day of my calamity;
   but the LORD was my support.
19 He brought me out into a broad place;
   he delivered me, because he delighted in me.

C. *He justifies his integrity*

20 The LORD rewarded me according to my righteousness;
   according to the cleanness of my hands he recompensed me.
21 For I have kept the ways of the LORD,
   and have not wickedly departed from my God.
22 For all his ordinances were before me,
   and his statutes I did not put away from me.
23 I was blameless before him,
   and I kept myself from guilt.
24 Therefore the LORD has recompensed me according to my
      righteousness,
   according to the cleanness of my hands in his sight.

25 With the loyal you show yourself loyal;
   with the blameless you show yourself blameless;
26 with the pure you show yourself pure;
   and with the crooked you show yourself perverse.
27 For you deliver a humble people,
   but the haughty eyes you bring down.
28 It is you who light my lamp;
   the LORD, my God, lights up my darkness.
29 By you I can crush a troop,
   and by my God I can leap over a wall.
30 This God—his way is perfect;
   the promise of the LORD proves true;
   he is a shield for all who take refuge in him.

D. *He acknowledges that God has delivered him*

31 For who is God except the LORD?
   And who is a rock besides our God?—
32 the God who girded me with strength,
   and made my way safe.
33 He made my feet like the feet of a deer,
   and set me secure on the heights.
34 He trains my hands for war,
   so that my arms can bend a bow of bronze.
35 You have given me the shield of your salvation,
   and your right hand has supported me;

Cross-references:

18.15 Ps 106.9; 76.6; Ex 15.8
18.16 Ps 144.7
18.17 v. 48; Ps 35.10
18.18 Ps 59.16; Isa 10.20
18.19 Ps 31.8; 118.5; 37.23
18.20 Ps 7.8; 1 Kings 8.32; Ps 24.4
18.21 Ps 119.33; 2 Chr 34.33; Ps 119.102
18.22 Ps 119.30, 83
18.24 1 Sam 26.23
18.25 Ps 62.12; Mt 5.7
18.26 Job 25.5; Prov 3.34
18.27 Ps 72.12; Prov 6.17
18.28 Job 18.6; Ps 27.1; Job 29.3
18.29 2 Cor 12.9; Heb 11.34
18.30 Deut 32.4; Ps 12.6; 17.7
18.31 Deut 32.31, 39; Ps 86.8-10; Isa 45.5
18.32 Isa 45.5; Heb 13.21; 1 Pet 5.10
18.33 Hab 3.19; Deut 32.13
18.34 Ps 144.1; Job 20.24
18.35 Deut 33.29; Ps 119.117; 138.6

18.31 *who is a rock besides our God?* God indeed is the rock or foundation on which his people can rest secure. Likewise, his word is a rock which stands forever. Christ is our rock (cf. 1 Cor 10.4) and sure defense. No one else and nothing else can be compared to him.

18.36
Ps 31.8; 71.5

18.37
Ps 44.5;
37.20
18.38
Ps 110.6;
36.12; 47.3
18.39
vv. 32, 47

18.40
Ps 21.21;
94.23
18.41
Ps 50.22;
Prov 1.28
18.42
Ps 83.13

your help*p* has made me great.
36 You gave me a wide place for my steps under me,
   and my feet did not slip.
37 I pursued my enemies and overtook them;
   and did not turn back until they were consumed.
38 I struck them down, so that they were not able to rise;
   they fell under my feet.
39 For you girded me with strength for the battle;
   you made my assailants sink under me.
40 You made my enemies turn their backs to me,
   and those who hated me I destroyed.
41 They cried for help, but there was no one to save them;
   they cried to the LORD, but he did not answer them.
42 I beat them fine, like dust before the wind;
   I cast them out like the mire of the streets.

E. *He expresses confidence in the future*

18.43
Ps 35.1;
Isa 52.15;
55.5
18.44
Ps 66.3

43 You delivered me from strife with the peoples;*q*
   you made me head of the nations;
   people whom I had not known served me.
44 As soon as they heard of me they obeyed me;
   foreigners came cringing to me.
45 Foreigners lost heart,
   and came trembling out of their strongholds.

18.46
Ps 42.2;
51.14
18.47
Ps 94.1; 47.3
18.48
Ps 143.9;
27.6; 140.1,
4

46 The LORD lives! Blessed be my rock,
   and exalted be the God of my salvation,
47 the God who gave me vengeance
   and subdued peoples under me;
48 who delivered me from my enemies;
   indeed, you exalted me above my adversaries;
   you delivered me from the violent.

18.49
Rom 15.9;
Ps 108.1
18.50
Ps 144.10;
28.8; 89.4,
29

49 For this I will extol you, O LORD, among the nations,
   and sing praises to your name.
50 Great triumphs he gives to his king,
   and shows steadfast love to his anointed,
   to David and his descendants forever.

Psalm 19

The works and word of God

A. *The revelation of God in creation*

To the leader. A Psalm of David.

19.1
Gen 1.6;
Isa 40.22;
Rom 1.19, 20

1 The heavens are telling the glory of God;
   and the firmament*r* proclaims his handiwork.

19.2
Ps 74.16

2 Day to day pours forth speech,
   and night to night declares knowledge.
3 There is no speech, nor are there words;
   their voice is not heard;

19.4
Rom 10.18

4 yet their voice*s* goes out through all the earth,

p Or *gentleness*   *q* Gk Tg: Heb *people*   *r* Or *dome*   *s* Gk Jerome Compare Syr: Heb *line*

19.1ff God has revealed himself in two ways: (1) in nature, for the heavens show forth the divine glory and the firmament testifies to his creative power, and (2) in the written word of God, without which no one can find God. Even nature does no more than manifest the fact that God exists. Unlike the word, it does not disclose who he is or what he has done for our salvation.

and their words to the end of the world.

In the heavens[t] he has set a tent for the sun,
5   which comes out like a bridegroom from his wedding canopy,
    and like a strong man runs its course with joy.
6   Its rising is from the end of the heavens,
    and its circuit to the end of them;
    and nothing is hid from its heat.

B. *The revelation of God in the word of God*

7   The law of the LORD is perfect,
    reviving the soul;
the decrees of the LORD are sure,
    making wise the simple;
8   the precepts of the LORD are right,
    rejoicing the heart;
the commandment of the LORD is clear,
    enlightening the eyes;
9   the fear of the LORD is pure,
    enduring forever;
the ordinances of the LORD are true
    and righteous altogether.
10   More to be desired are they than gold,
    even much fine gold;
sweeter also than honey,
    and drippings of the honeycomb.

11   Moreover by them is your servant warned;
    in keeping them there is great reward.
12   But who can detect their errors?
    Clear me from hidden faults.
13   Keep back your servant also from the insolent;[u]
    do not let them have dominion over me.
Then I shall be blameless,
    and innocent of great transgression.

14   Let the words of my mouth and the meditation of my heart
    be acceptable to you,
    O LORD, my rock and my redeemer.

Psalm 20

A liturgy for the king

A. *Prayer for victory*

To the leader. A Psalm of David.

1   The LORD answer you in the day of trouble!
    The name of the God of Jacob protect you!
2   May he send you help from the sanctuary,

t Heb *In them*   *u* Or *from proud thoughts*

Cross references (right column):
19.5 Eccl 1.5
19.6 Ps 113.3; Deut 30.4
19.7 Ps 119.142; 23.3; 93.5; 111.7; 119.98-100
19.8 Ps 119.128; 12.6; 119.30
19.9 Ps 119.42
19.10 Prov 8.10; 16.24
19.11 Ps 17.4; Prov 29.18
19.12 Ps 139.6; 51.1, 2; 90.8
19.13 Ps 119.33; 32.2; 25.11
19.14 Ps 104.34; 18.2; Isa 41.14; 43.14
20.1 Ps 102.2; 91.14; 36.7, 11; 59.1
20.2 Ps 3.4; 119.28

19.14 The redemption of which the psalmist speaks begins and ends with God; it is all of grace and not of works (Job 19.25; Isa 49.26). Redemption comes from Christ (1 Cor 1.30; Gal 3.13; Eph 1.7), at the cost of his precious lifeblood (1 Pet 1.18,19); he gave his life for all humankind (1 Tim 2.6).
20.1ff God commands believers to pray for kings and those in authority (1 Tim 2.1–3); Ps 20 does this precisely. It assumes that the cause for which the nation prays is just. Beyond this, though, is the larger reference to the kingdom of God headed by Jesus Christ. We must pray for this kingdom to come and for the enthronement of Christ at his second advent.

and give you support from Zion.

20.3
Ps 51.19

3 May he remember all your offerings,
   and regard with favor your burnt sacrifices.   *Selah*

20.4
Ps 21.2;
145.19
20.5
Ps 9.14;
1 Sam 1.17

4 May he grant you your heart's desire,
   and fulfill all your plans.

5 May we shout for joy over your victory,
   and in the name of our God set up our banners.
   May the LORD fulfill all your petitions.

B. *Assurance of divine help*

20.6
Ps 41.11;
Isa 58.9;
Ps 28.8

6 Now I know that the LORD will help his anointed;
   he will answer him from his holy heaven
   with mighty victories by his right hand.

20.7
Isa 36.9;
31.1;
2 Chr 32.8
20.8
Ps 37.24

7 Some take pride in chariots, and some in horses,
   but our pride is in the name of the LORD our God.

8 They will collapse and fall,
   but we shall rise and stand upright.

20.9
Ps 3.7

9 Give victory to the king, O LORD;
   answer us when we call.*v*

21.1
Ps 59.16, 17;
9.14

Psalm 21

Praise for deliverance

A. *Thanksgiving for past victories*
To the leader. A Psalm of David.

1 In your strength the king rejoices, O LORD,
   and in your help how greatly he exults!

21.2
Ps 37.4

2 You have given him his heart's desire,
   and have not withheld the request of his lips.   *Selah*

21.3
Ps 59.10

3 For you meet him with rich blessings;
   you set a crown of fine gold on his head.

21.4
Ps 133.3;
91.16
21.5
Ps 18.50;
45.3, 4

4 He asked you for life; you gave it to him —
   length of days forever and ever.

5 His glory is great through your help;
   splendor and majesty you bestow on him.

21.6
1 Chr 17.27;
Ps 16.11
21.7
2 Kings 18.5;
Ps 16.8

6 You bestow on him blessings forever;
   you make him glad with the joy of your presence.

7 For the king trusts in the LORD,
   and through the steadfast love of the Most High he shall not
       be moved.

B. *Assurance of future victories*

21.8
Isa 10.10

8 Your hand will find out all your enemies;
   your right hand will find out those who hate you.

21.9
Mal 4.1;
Lam 2.2

9 You will make them like a fiery furnace
       when you appear.
   The LORD will swallow them up in his wrath,
       and fire will consume them.

21.10
Deut 28.18;
Ps 37.28

10 You will destroy their offspring from the earth,

v Gk: Heb *give victory, O LORD; let the King answer us when we call*

21.1ff When we pray for kings and those in authority and God answers those prayers, we must return thanks to God. This should encourage us to ask God for divine help as other emergencies arise and difficulties confront the nation. He who helped us yesterday will help us again today and tomorrow.

and their children from among humankind.

11 If they plan evil against you,
    if they devise mischief, they will not succeed.

    21.11
    Ps 2.1-3; 10.2

12 For you will put them to flight;
    you will aim at their faces with your bows.

    21.12
    Ps 18.40;
    7.12, 13

13 Be exalted, O LORD, in your strength!
    We will sing and praise your power.

    21.13
    Ps 57.5; 81.1

Psalm 22

    22.1
    Mt 27.46;
    Ps 10.1

The suffering and the glory of Messiah predicted

A. Forsaken of God

To the leader: according to The Deer of the Dawn. A Psalm of David.

1   My God, my God, why have you forsaken me?
    Why are you so far from helping me, from the words of my
        groaning?

2   O my God, I cry by day, but you do not answer;
    and by night, but find no rest.

    22.2
    Ps 42.3

3   Yet you are holy,
    enthroned on the praises of Israel.

    22.3
    Ps 99.9; 35.8

4   In you our ancestors trusted;
    they trusted, and you delivered them.

5   To you they cried, and were saved;
    in you they trusted, and were not put to shame.

    22.5
    Ps 107.6;
    25.2, 3;
    Rom 9.33

B. Scorned by humans

6   But I am a worm, and not human;
    scorned by others, and despised by the people.

    22.6
    Job 25.6;
    Isa 41.14;
    Ps 31.11;
    Isa 49.7

7   All who see me mock at me;
    they make mouths at me, they shake their heads;

    22.7
    Mt 27.39;
    Mk 15.29

8   "Commit your cause to the LORD; let him deliver —
    let him rescue the one in whom he delights!"

    22.8
    Mt 27.43;
    Mk 1.11

9   Yet it was you who took me from the womb;
    you kept me safe on my mother's breast.

    22.9
    Ps 71.6

10 On you I was cast from my birth,
    and since my mother bore me you have been my God.

    22.10
    Isa 46.3

11 Do not be far from me,
    for trouble is near
    and there is no one to help.

    22.11
    Ps 72.12

C. Encompassed by animals

12 Many bulls encircle me,
    strong bulls of Bashan surround me;

    22.12
    Ps 68.30;
    Deut 32.14

13 they open wide their mouths at me,
    like a ravening and roaring lion.

    22.13
    Ps 35.21;
    17.12

22.1ff While on the cross, Jesus quoted the beginning of this psalm (Mt 27.46; Mk 15.34). The whole psalm graphically portrays the suffering of the Messiah; it contains a specific prophecy fulfilled at the crucifixion (v. 18), that the soldiers would gamble over the seamless robe of the Savior (Mt 27.35; Lk 23.34; Jn 19.23,24). Those who performed that deed knew nothing of the prophecy. Unknown to them, they were doing what the omniscient and omnipotent God had determined long before the event.

22.6 *I am a worm.* A worm is a lowly thing, stepped on by people and regarded with contempt. David felt this way at times, but this is also prophetic of the treatment of the Son of God at his crucifixion.

22.14
Job 30.16;
Ps 31.10;
107.26
14 I am poured out like water,
    and all my bones are out of joint;
   my heart is like wax;
    it is melted within my breast;

22.15
Ps 38.10;
137.6; 104.29
15 my mouth[w] is dried up like a potsherd,
    and my tongue sticks to my jaws;
   you lay me in the dust of death.

D. *They pierce his hands; they cast lots for his raiment*

22.16
Ps 59.6;
Mt 27.35
16 For dogs are all around me;
    a company of evildoers encircles me.
   My hands and feet have shriveled;[x]
17 I can count all my bones.
   They stare and gloat over me;
18 they divide my clothes among themselves,
    and for my clothing they cast lots.

22.18
Mt 27.35

E. *His prayer for deliverance*

22.19
v. 11;
Ps 70.5
22.20
Ps 35.17
19 But you, O Lord, do not be far away!
    O my help, come quickly to my aid!
20 Deliver my soul from the sword,
    my life[y] from the power of the dog!
21 Save me from the mouth of the lion!

22.21
v. 13;
Ps 34.4

F. *Praise to the Lord*

From the horns of the wild oxen you have rescued[z] me.

22.22
Heb 2.12
22 I will tell of your name to my brothers and sisters;[a]
    in the midst of the congregation I will praise you:

22.23
Ps 135.19.
86.12; 33.8
23 You who fear the Lord, praise him!
    All you offspring of Jacob, glorify him;
    stand in awe of him, all you offspring of Israel!

22.24
Ps 102.17;
69.17;
Heb 5.7
24 For he did not despise or abhor
    the affliction of the afflicted;
   he did not hide his face from me,[b]
    but heard when I[c] cried to him.

22.25
Ps 35.18;
66.13
22.26
Ps 107.9;
40.16; 69.32
25 From you comes my praise in the great congregation;
    my vows I will pay before those who fear him.
26 The poor[d] shall eat and be satisfied;
    those who seek him shall praise the Lord.
   May your hearts live forever!

G. *Salvation offered to all*

22.27
Ps 2.8; 86.9
27 All the ends of the earth shall remember
    and turn to the Lord;
   and all the families of the nations
    shall worship before him.[e]

22.28
Ps 47.7, 8;
Mt 6.13
28 For dominion belongs to the Lord,
    and he rules over the nations.

22.29
Ps 47.7;
Isa 27.13;
Ps 95.6
29 To him,[f] indeed, shall all who sleep in[g] the earth bow down;
    before him shall bow all who go down to the dust,
    and I shall live for him.[h]

22.30
Ps 102.28;
71.18
30 Posterity will serve him;

w Cn: Heb *strength*   x Meaning of Heb uncertain   y Heb *my only one*   z Heb *answered*   a Or *kindred*
b Heb *him*   c Heb *he*   d Or *afflicted*   e Gk Syr Jerome: Heb *you*   f Cn: Heb *They have eaten and*
g Cn: Heb *all the fat ones*   h Compare Gk Syr Vg: Heb *and he who cannot keep himself alive*

future generations will be told about the Lord,
31 and[i] proclaim his deliverance to a people yet unborn,
saying that he has done it.

22.31
Ps 78.6

Psalm 23

The Lord my shepherd

A. He feeds and guides his sheep

A Psalm of David.

1 The Lord is my shepherd, I shall not want.
2   He makes me lie down in green pastures;
he leads me beside still waters;[j]
3   he restores my soul.[k]
He leads me in right paths[l]
for his name's sake.

4 Even though I walk through the darkest valley,[m]
I fear no evil;
for you are with me;
your rod and your staff—
they comfort me.

B. He is host to his people forever

5 You prepare a table before me
in the presence of my enemies;
you anoint my head with oil;
my cup overflows.
6 Surely[n] goodness and mercy[o] shall follow me
all the days of my life,
and I shall dwell in the house of the Lord
my whole life long.[p]

23.1
Isa 40.11;
Jer 23.4;
Jn 10.11;
1 Pet 2.25;
Phil 4.19

23.2
Ezek 34.14;
Rev 7.17
23.3
Ps 19.7; 5.8;
85.13; 143.11

23.4
Ps 138.7;
Job 3.5;
Ps 27.1;
Isa 43.2

23.5
Ps 78.19;
31.19; 92.10;
16.5

23.6
Ps 25.7, 10;
27.4-6

Psalm 24

Psalm to the King of glory

A. The Lord the creator

Of David. A Psalm.

1 The earth is the Lord's and all that is in it,
the world, and those who live in it;
2 for he has founded it on the seas,
and established it on the rivers.

24.1
Ex 9.29;
Job 41.11;
1 Cor 10.26;
Ps 89.11

B. The character of the Lord's people

3 Who shall ascend the hill of the Lord?
And who shall stand in his holy place?
4 Those who have clean hands and pure hearts,

24.3
Ps 15.1; 2.6;
65.4
24.4
Job 17.9;
Mt 5.8;
Ps 15.4

i Compare Gk: Heb it will be told about the Lord to the generation, 31they will come and   j Heb waters of
rest   k Or life   l Or paths of righteousness   m Or the valley of the shadow of death   n Or Only
o Or kindness   p Heb for length of days

23.1ff Of all the messianic psalms, this is the best
known and the greatest. It pictures the Lord as a
shepherd, a metaphor that is picked up in the N.T.
where Jesus is called the good shepherd (Jn 10.11),
the great shepherd (Heb 13.20), and the chief shep-

herd (1 Pet 5.4).
24.1ff This psalm has to do with the kingdom of
Jesus Christ, a kingdom which has come and is coming in its fullness when he returns in glory. It describes the character of the subjects of his kingdom.

who do not lift up their souls to what is false,
    and do not swear deceitfully.

24.5
Deut 11.26,
27;
Isa 46.13;
Ps 25.5
24.6
Ps 27.8

5 They will receive blessing from the LORD,
    and vindication from the God of their salvation.
6 Such is the company of those who seek him,
    who seek the face of the God of Jacob. *q*   *Selah*

C. *The entry of the King of glory*

24.7
Isa 26.2;
1 Cor 2.8

7 Lift up your heads, O gates!
    and be lifted up, O ancient doors!
    that the King of glory may come in.

24.8
Ps 89.13;
76.3-6

8 Who is the King of glory?
    The LORD, strong and mighty,
    the LORD, mighty in battle.

24.9
Zech 9.9;
Mt 21.5

9 Lift up your heads, O gates!
    and be lifted up, O ancient doors!
    that the King of glory may come in.
10 Who is this King of glory?
    The LORD of hosts,
    he is the King of glory.   *Selah*

25.1
Ps 86.4

Psalm 25

Prayer for guidance and protection

A. *God's way sought*

Of David.

1 To you, O LORD, I lift up my soul.

25.2
Ps 31.6;
41.11

2 O my God, in you I trust;
    do not let me be put to shame;
    do not let my enemies exult over me.

25.3
Isa 49.23;
33.1

3 Do not let those who wait for you be put to shame;
    let them be ashamed who are wantonly treacherous.

25.4
Ps 5.8; 86.11

4 Make me to know your ways, O LORD;
    teach me your paths.

25.5
Jn 16.13;
Ps 24.5; 40.1

5 Lead me in your truth, and teach me,
    for you are the God of my salvation;
    for you I wait all day long.

25.6
Ps 103.17;
Isa 63.15
25.7
Job 13.26;
Jer 3.25;
Ps 51.1

6 Be mindful of your mercy, O LORD, and of your steadfast love,
    for they have been from of old.
7 Do not remember the sins of my youth or my transgressions;
    according to your steadfast love remember me,
    for your goodness' sake, O LORD!

B. *God's way made plain*

25.8
Ps 106.1;
92.15; 32.8

8 Good and upright is the LORD;

q Gk Syr: Heb *your face, O Jacob*

24.7 The last four verses beautifully describe the "King of glory," i.e., Yahweh, Israel's God. But it also describes the Lord Jesus Christ, he who is our righteousness (1 Cor 1.30).

25.1ff David, zealously attached to God, looks for God's favor and seeks his grace. Like him, we must pray for pardon, seek God's direction for our lives, and by faith claim his deliverance from our troubles

and his protection from all our enemies, of whom Satan is the worst.

25.4 God has a perfect will for each of his children. David asks God to reveal that will to him; he exultantly declares that God will guide him in the way he should go (vv. 9,10; cf. Isa 30.20,21; Col 1.9). The only way to know and do the perfect will of God is to surrender one's life to God (Rom 12.2).

therefore he instructs sinners in the way.

9 He leads the humble in what is right,
      and teaches the humble his way.
10 All the paths of the LORD are steadfast love and faithfulness,
      for those who keep his covenant and his decrees.

11 For your name's sake, O LORD,
      pardon my guilt, for it is great.
12 Who are they that fear the LORD?
      He will teach them the way that they should choose.

13 They will abide in prosperity,
      and their children shall possess the land.
14 The friendship of the LORD is for those who fear him,
      and he makes his covenant known to them.
15 My eyes are ever toward the LORD,
      for he will pluck my feet out of the net.

C. Prayer for deliverance

16 Turn to me and be gracious to me,
      for I am lonely and afflicted.
17 Relieve the troubles of my heart,
      and bring me[r] out of my distress.
18 Consider my affliction and my trouble,
      and forgive all my sins.

19 Consider how many are my foes,
      and with what violent hatred they hate me.
20 O guard my life, and deliver me;
      do not let me be put to shame, for I take refuge in you.
21 May integrity and uprightness preserve me,
      for I wait for you.

22 Redeem Israel, O God,
      out of all its troubles.

Psalm 26

A plea for vindication

A. Prayer for divine help

Of David.

1 Vindicate me, O LORD,
      for I have walked in my integrity,
      and I have trusted in the LORD without wavering.
2 Prove me, O LORD, and try me;
      test my heart and mind.
3 For your steadfast love is before my eyes,
      and I walk in faithfulness to you.[s]

Marginal references:
25.9 Ps 23.3; 27.11
25.10 Ps 40.11; 103.18
25.11 Ps 31.1; Rom 5.20
25.13 Prov 19.23; Ps 37.11
25.14 Prov 3.32; Jn 7.17
25.15 Ps 141.8
25.16 Ps 69.16
25.17 Ps 88.3; 107.6
25.18 2 Sam 16.12
25.19 Ps 3.1; 27.12
25.20 Ps 86.2
25.21 Ps 41.12; v. 3
25.22 Ps 130.8
26.1 Ps 7.8; Prov 20.7; Ps 25.2; Heb 10.23
26.2 Ps 7.9; 66.10
26.3 2 Kings 20.3

---

r Or The troubles of my heart are enlarged; bring me   s Or in your faithfulness

---

25.21 David pleads his own integrity — not that he was sinless, but that his conscience told him that he had done his enemies no wrong. Thus he would be preserved against those who hated him.
26.1ff David apparently has suffered from slander, defamation, and false accusations. Such is often the lot of God's people (e.g., see Mt 5.11; Jn 15.20). David places his case in God's hands and looks to him for justification from the wrong judgments of his enemies.

B. *David's defense of himself*

26.4
Ps 1.1

4 I do not sit with the worthless,
  nor do I consort with hypocrites;

26.5
Ps 139.21;
1.1

5 I hate the company of evildoers,
  and will not sit with the wicked.

26.6
Ps 73.13

6 I wash my hands in innocence,
  and go around your altar, O LORD,

26.7
Ps 35.18; 9.1

7 singing aloud a song of thanksgiving,
  and telling all your wondrous deeds.

C. *His final plea for help*

26.8
Ps 27.4

8 O LORD, I love the house in which you dwell,
  and the place where your glory abides.

26.9
Ps 28.3

9 Do not sweep me away with sinners,
  nor my life with the bloodthirsty,

26.10
1 Sam 8.3

10 those in whose hands are evil devices,
  and whose right hands are full of bribes.

26.11
v. 1;
Ps 69.18

11 But as for me, I walk in my integrity;
  redeem me, and be gracious to me.

26.12
Ps 40.2;
27.11; 22.22

12 My foot stands on level ground;
  in the great congregation I will bless the LORD.

Psalm 27

27.1
Isa 60.19;
Ex 15.2;
Ps 62.2

I. *David's song of confidence (27.1–6)*

Of David.

1 The LORD is my light and my salvation;
  whom shall I fear?
The LORD is the stronghold[t] of my life;
  of whom shall I be afraid?

27.2
Ps 14.4

2 When evildoers assail me
  to devour my flesh —
my adversaries and foes —
  they shall stumble and fall.

27.3
Ps 3.6

3 Though an army encamp against me,
  my heart shall not fear;
though war rise up against me,
  yet I will be confident.

27.4
Ps 26.8;
90.17

4 One thing I asked of the LORD,
  that will I seek after:
to live in the house of the LORD
  all the days of my life,
to behold the beauty of the LORD,
  and to inquire in his temple.

t Or refuge

26.11 *in my integrity.* David purposes in his heart that no matter what anyone else may do, he will walk according to God's precepts. Divine grace will enable him to do this.
27.1ff This psalm of David manifests his courage and bravery in God, his happiness in communion with God, how he seeks the face of the Lord, and what

his expectations are of what God can and will do. It ends on a high note.
27.4 David's ardent desire was to *live in the house of the LORD.* Here he would engage in meditation as he worshiped his God, and be instructed as to his duty. Worship and teaching go hand in hand and must be followed up by obedience to God's law.

⁵ For he will hide me in his shelter
   in the day of trouble;
he will conceal me under the cover of his tent;
   he will set me high on a rock.

⁶ Now my head is lifted up
   above my enemies all around me,
and I will offer in his tent
   sacrifices with shouts of joy;
I will sing and make melody to the LORD.

II. *David's prayer for help (27.7–14)*

⁷ Hear, O LORD, when I cry aloud,
   be gracious to me and answer me!
⁸ "Come," my heart says, "seek his face!"
   Your face, LORD, do I seek.
⁹ Do not hide your face from me.

Do not turn your servant away in anger,
   you who have been my help.
Do not cast me off, do not forsake me,
   O God of my salvation!
¹⁰ If my father and mother forsake me,
   the LORD will take me up.

¹¹ Teach me your way, O LORD,
   and lead me on a level path
   because of my enemies.
¹² Do not give me up to the will of my adversaries,
   for false witnesses have risen against me,
   and they are breathing out violence.

¹³ I believe that I shall see the goodness of the LORD
   in the land of the living.
¹⁴ Wait for the LORD;
   be strong, and let your heart take courage;
   wait for the LORD!

Psalm 28

I. *The prayer for help (28.1–5)*

Of David.

¹ To you, O LORD, I call;
   my rock, do not refuse to hear me,
for if you are silent to me,
   I shall be like those who go down to the Pit.
² Hear the voice of my supplication,
   as I cry to you for help,
as I lift up my hands
   toward your most holy sanctuary.^u

³ Do not drag me away with the wicked,

^u Heb *your innermost sanctuary*

Cross-references:
27.5 Ps 31.20; 40.2
27.6 Ps 3.3
27.7 Ps 39.12; 13.3
27.8 Ps 24.6
27.9 Ps 69.17
27.10 Isa 49.15; 40.11
27.11 Ps 25.4; 86.11; 5.8
27.12 Ps 41.2; 35.11; Mt 26.60; Acts 9.1
27.13 Ps 31.19; Jer 11.19
27.14 Ps 40.1; Josh 1.6
28.1 Ps 83.1; 88.4
28.2 Ps 140.6; 5.7; 138.2
28.3 Ps 26.9; 12.2; Jer 9.8

28.1ff The first part of this psalm finds David as a saint militant, battling along in life and asking God for help. In the latter part David reflects the saint triumphant, thanking God for deliverance and knowing that God is the strength of his people.

with those who are workers of evil,
who speak peace with their neighbors,
while mischief is in their hearts.

28.4
Rev 18.6

4 Repay them according to their work,
and according to the evil of their deeds;
repay them according to the work of their hands;
render them their due reward.

28.5
Isa 5.12

5 Because they do not regard the works of the LORD,
or the work of his hands,
he will break them down and build them up no more.

II. *The assurance of an answer (28.6–9)*

28.6
Ps 116.1

6 Blessed be the LORD,
for he has heard the sound of my pleadings.

28.7
Ps 18.2; 13.5

7 The LORD is my strength and my shield;
in him my heart trusts;
so I am helped, and my heart exults,
and with my song I give thanks to him.

28.8
Ps 20.6

8 The LORD is the strength of his people;
he is the saving refuge of his anointed.

28.9
Deut 9.29;
Ezra 1.4

9 O save your people, and bless your heritage;
be their shepherd, and carry them forever.

Psalm 29

29.1
1 Chr 16.28,
29;
Ps 96.7-9

The LORD of the thunderstorm

A. *Summons to give glory to God*

A Psalm of David.

1 Ascribe to the LORD, O heavenly beings,[v]
ascribe to the LORD glory and strength.

29.2
2 Chr 20.21

2 Ascribe to the LORD the glory of his name;
worship the LORD in holy splendor.

B. *God's power in the storm*

29.3
Job 37.4, 5

3 The voice of the LORD is over the waters;
the God of glory thunders,
the LORD, over mighty waters.

29.4
Ps 68.33

4 The voice of the LORD is powerful;
the voice of the LORD is full of majesty.

29.5
Isa 2.13

5 The voice of the LORD breaks the cedars;
the LORD breaks the cedars of Lebanon.

29.6
Ps 114.4;
Deut 3.9

6 He makes Lebanon skip like a calf,
and Sirion like a young wild ox.

7 The voice of the LORD flashes forth flames of fire.

29.8
Num 13.26

8 The voice of the LORD shakes the wilderness;
the LORD shakes the wilderness of Kadesh.

v Heb *sons of gods*

28.8 All God's people should put their trust in the Lord, not in themselves, and realize that he is their only source of strength.
29.1ff David probably wrote this psalm when there

was great thunder, lightning, and rain. Despite the inclemency of nature, his heart is at rest, for God sits enthroned in the heavens and is not disturbed by the threats of nature.

9   The voice of the LORD causes the oaks to whirl,[w]
     and strips the forest bare;
     and in his temple all say, "Glory!"

29.9
Ps 26.8

C. *Prayer for the blessing of the LORD of the storm*

10   The LORD sits enthroned over the flood;
     the LORD sits enthroned as king forever.

29.10
Ps 10.16

11   May the LORD give strength to his people!
     May the LORD bless his people with peace!

29.11
Ps 28.8;
37.11

Psalm 30

30.1
Ps 28.9; 25.2

To the leader. A Psalm of David.

Song of deliverance

A. *Praise for deliverance*

A Psalm. A Song at the dedication of the temple. Of David.

1   I will extol you, O LORD, for you have drawn me up,
     and did not let my foes rejoice over me.

2   O LORD my God, I cried to you for help,
     and you have healed me.

30.2
Ps 88.13; 6.2

3   O LORD, you brought up my soul from Sheol,
     restored me to life from among those gone down to the Pit.[x]

30.3
Ps 86.13;
28.1

B. *Exhortation for others to praise the LORD*

4   Sing praises to the LORD, O you his faithful ones,
     and give thanks to his holy name.

30.4
Ps 149.1;
50.5; 97.12

5   For his anger is but for a moment;
     his favor is for a lifetime.
Weeping may linger for the night,
     but joy comes with the morning.

30.5
Ps 103.9;
63.3

6   As for me, I said in my prosperity,
     "I shall never be moved."

7   By your favor, O LORD,
     you had established me as a strong mountain;
you hid your face;
     I was dismayed.

30.7
Ps 104.29

8   To you, O LORD, I cried,
     and to the LORD I made supplication:

9   "What profit is there in my death,
     if I go down to the Pit?
Will the dust praise you?
     Will it tell of your faithfulness?

30.9
Ps 6.5

10   Hear, O LORD, and be gracious to me!
     O LORD, be my helper!"

w Or *causes the deer to calve*   *x* Or *that I should not go down to the Pit*

29.10 *The LORD sits enthroned over the flood.* The Hebrew word for flood (*mabbul*) is used only here and for the Noahic flood. God did sit on that flood in the sense that he was the judge pronouncing justice on a wicked world. This judge is enthroned as king forever. He will judge the world in righteousness at the end of the age.

30.1ff David offers praise for God's deliverance and exhorts the saints to praise God too. During a time of prosperity he was brought low. As a result of his prayers, his mourning was turned to gladness, and he promises to give thanks to God forever. Past mercies should be recalled and thanks offered to God even after a long passage of time.

30.6 David became complacent in the midst of prosperity. He was secure and overconfident that it would continue. Suddenly he fell into great trouble and distress, and then realized what he had forgotten — the help of God.

30.11
Ps 6.8;
Jer 31.4, 13;
Ps 4.7

11 You have turned my mourning into dancing;
   you have taken off my sackcloth
   and clothed me with joy,

30.12
Ps 16.9; 44.8

12 so that my soul[y] may praise you and not be silent.
   O Lord my God, I will give thanks to you forever.

Psalm 31

"My times are in your hands"

A. *Trust in God and prayer for deliverance*

To the leader. A Psalm of David.

31.1
Ps 22.5;
Isa 49.23

1 In you, O Lord, I seek refuge;
   do not let me ever be put to shame;
   in your righteousness deliver me.

31.2
Ps 71.2

2 Incline your ear to me;
   rescue me speedily.
   Be a rock of refuge for me,
   a strong fortress to save me.

31.3
Ps 18.2; 23.3

3 You are indeed my rock and my fortress;
   for your name's sake lead me and guide me,

31.4
Ps 25.15;
28.8

4 take me out of the net that is hidden for me,
   for you are my refuge.

31.5
Lk 23.46;
Acts 7.59

5 Into your hand I commit my spirit;
   you have redeemed me, O Lord, faithful God.

31.6
Jon 2.8

6 You hate[z] those who pay regard to worthless idols,
   but I trust in the Lord.

31.7
Ps 90.14;
10.14;
Jn 10.27

7 I will exult and rejoice in your steadfast love,
   because you have seen my affliction;
   you have taken heed of my adversities,

31.8
Deut 32.30;
Ps 4.1

8 and have not delivered me into the hand of the enemy;
   you have set my feet in a broad place.

B. *Complaints that require deliverance*

31.9
Ps 6.7

9 Be gracious to me, O Lord, for I am in distress;
   my eye wastes away from grief,
   my soul and body also.

31.10
Ps 13.2;
39.11; 38.3

10 For my life is spent with sorrow,
   and my years with sighing;
   my strength fails because of my misery,[a]
   and my bones waste away.

31.11
Isa 53.4;
Ps 38.11;
64.8

11 I am the scorn of all my adversaries,
   a horror[b] to my neighbors,
   an object of dread to my acquaintances;
   those who see me in the street flee from me.

31.12
Ps 88.4, 5

12 I have passed out of mind like one who is dead;
   I have become like a broken vessel.

31.13
Jer 20.10;
Lam 2.20;
Mt 27.1

13 For I hear the whispering of many—

y Heb *that glory*   *z* One Heb Ms Gk Syr Jerome: MT *I hate*   *a* Gk Syr: Heb *my iniquity*
b Cn: Heb *exceedingly*

31.1ff This is a psalm of petition, praise, and confidence in God. This triad of graces encourages our hearts to be strong and to wait for the Lord, the great deliverer. Difficulties and setbacks should afford us no occasion to lose these precious characteristics. Rather, they should be more visibly present during times of trouble.

terror all around! —
as they scheme together against me,
as they plot to take my life.

14 But I trust in you, O LORD;
   I say, "You are my God."
15 My times are in your hand;
   deliver me from the hand of my enemies and persecutors.
16 Let your face shine upon your servant;
   save me in your steadfast love.
17 Do not let me be put to shame, O LORD,
   for I call on you;
   let the wicked be put to shame;
   let them go dumbfounded to Sheol.
18 Let the lying lips be stilled
   that speak insolently against the righteous
   with pride and contempt.

C. Praise to a delivering LORD

19 O how abundant is your goodness
   that you have laid up for those who fear you,
   and accomplished for those who take refuge in you,
   in the sight of everyone!
20 In the shelter of your presence you hide them
   from human plots;
   you hold them safe under your shelter
   from contentious tongues.

21 Blessed be the LORD,
   for he has wondrously shown his steadfast love to me
   when I was beset as a city under siege.
22 I had said in my alarm,
   "I am driven far*c* from your sight."
   But you heard my supplications
   when I cried out to you for help.

23 Love the LORD, all you his saints.
   The LORD preserves the faithful,
   but abundantly repays the one who acts haughtily.
24 Be strong, and let your heart take courage,
   all you who wait for the LORD.

Psalm 32

The penitent's psalm

A. The happiness of the forgiven
Of David. A Maskil.

1 Happy are those whose transgression is forgiven,
   whose sin is covered.
2 Happy are those to whom the LORD imputes no iniquity,
   and in whose spirit there is no deceit.

c Another reading is *cut off*

31.14 Ps 140.6
31.15 Job 24.1; Ps 143.9
31.16 Num 6.25; Ps 4.6
31.17 Ps 25.2, 3
31.18 Ps 120.2; 94.4
31.19 Isa 64.4; Rom 11.22; Ps 5.11
31.20 Ps 27.5; Job 5.21
31.21 Ps 17.7; 1 Sam 23.7
31.22 Ps 116.11; Lam 3.54
31.23 Ps 34.9; 145.20; 94.2
31.24 Ps 27.14
32.1 Ps 85.2
32.2 2 Cor 5.19; Jn 1.47

31.15 *My times are in your hand.* If God has our times in his hand, he can help us; if he is our God, he will help us.
32.1ff This psalm speaks of the blessedness of righ-teousness imputed to believers, apart from good works. They are protected and guided by grace. Confessing sin, living rightly, and rejoicing in God are the attributes of the redeemed.

B. Sin confessed and forgiven

32.3
Ps 39.2, 3;
31.10; 38.8
32.4
Job 33.7

3 While I kept silence, my body wasted away
  through my groaning all day long.
4 For day and night your hand was heavy upon me;
  my strength was dried up[d] as by the heat of *Selah*
  summer.

32.5
Lev 26.40;
Job 31.33;
Prov 28.13;
Ps 103.12

5 Then I acknowledged my sin to you,
  and I did not hide my iniquity;
  I said, "I will confess my transgressions to the LORD,"
  and you forgave the guilt of my sin. *Selah*

32.6
Ps 69.13;
144.7;
Isa 43.2

6 Therefore let all who are faithful
  offer prayer to you;
  at a time of distress,[e] the rush of mighty waters
  shall not reach them.

32.7
Ps 31.20;
121.7;
Ex 15.1

7 You are a hiding place for me;
  you preserve me from trouble;
  you surround me with glad cries of deliverance. *Selah*

C. Exhortation to sinners to repent

32.8
Ps 25.8;
33.18
32.9
Jas 3.3

8 I will instruct you and teach you the way you should go;
  I will counsel you with my eye upon you.
9 Do not be like a horse or a mule, without understanding,
  whose temper must be curbed with bit and bridle,
  else it will not stay near you.

32.10
Rom 2.9;
Prov 16.20
32.11
Ps 64.10

10 Many are the torments of the wicked,
   but steadfast love surrounds those who trust in
   the LORD.
11 Be glad in the LORD and rejoice, O righteous,
   and shout for joy, all you upright in heart.

Psalm 33

33.1
Ps 32.11;
147.1

Praise to the LORD who provides and delivers

A. Exhortation to praise the LORD

1 Rejoice in the LORD, O you righteous.
  Praise befits the upright.

33.2
Ps 92.3

2 Praise the LORD with the lyre;
  make melody to him with the harp of ten strings.

33.3
Ps 96.1; 98.4

3 Sing to him a new song;
  play skillfully on the strings, with loud shouts.

---

d Meaning of Heb uncertain   *e* Cn: Heb *at a time of finding only*

33.1ff This psalm of praise, possibly written by David, takes us beyond the realm of humanity to the creative Spirit of God (called "the breath of his mouth" in v. 6). The earth is full of his goodness, for his bounty is inexhaustible. We are to praise the Lord God, who is the creator, preserver, and deliverer, and to trust in his holy name. How sad that a world so full of goodness is so empty of his praises.

33.4,5 God makes himself known to humankind through his word and his works. His word is right and any deviation from it is wrong. It is backed up by his works, performed according to justice and truth. He never has done or will do wrong to any creature. He is ready to relieve those who are wronged and delights to do so.

B. *Reasons for praising the LORD*

1. *He is the LORD the creator*

4 For the word of the LORD is upright,
   and all his work is done in faithfulness.

5 He loves righteousness and justice;
   the earth is full of the steadfast love of the LORD.

6 By the word of the LORD the heavens were made,
   and all their host by the breath of his mouth.

7 He gathered the waters of the sea as in a bottle;
   he put the deeps in storehouses.

8 Let all the earth fear the LORD;
   let all the inhabitants of the world stand in awe
    of him.

9 For he spoke, and it came to be;
   he commanded, and it stood firm.

33.4
Ps 19.8;
119.90
33.5
Ps 11.7;
119.64
33.6
Gen 11.3;
Job 23.13
33.7
Ps 78.13

33.8
Ps 67.7; 96.9

33.9
Gen 1.3;
Ps 148.5

2. *He is the LORD of providence*

10 The LORD brings the counsel of the nations to nothing;
   he frustrates the plans of the peoples.

11 The counsel of the LORD stands forever,
   the thoughts of his heart to all generations.

12 Happy is the nation whose God is the LORD,
   the people whom he has chosen as his heritage.

13 The LORD looks down from heaven;
   he sees all humankind.

14 From where he sits enthroned he watches
   all the inhabitants of the earth—

15 he who fashions the hearts of them all,
   and observes all their deeds.

16 A king is not saved by his great army;
   a warrior is not delivered by his great strength.

17 The war horse is a vain hope for victory,
   and by its great might it cannot save.

33.10
Isa 8.10;
19.3
33.11
Job 23.13;
Prov 19.21;
Ps 40.5
33.12
Ps 144.15;
Ex 19.5;
Deut 7.6
33.13
Job 28.24;
Ps 11.4

33.15
Jer 32.19

33.16
Ps 44.6

33.17
Ps 20.7;
Prov 21.31

3. *He is the deliverer of his people*

18 Truly the eye of the LORD is on those who fear him,
   on those who hope in his steadfast love,

19 to deliver their soul from death,
   and to keep them alive in famine.

20 Our soul waits for the LORD;
   he is our help and shield.

21 Our heart is glad in him,
   because we trust in his holy name.

22 Let your steadfast love, O LORD, be upon us,
   even as we hope in you.

33.18
Job 36.7;
Ps 34.15;
147.11
33.19
Ps 37.19

33.20
Ps 130.6;
115.9
33.21
Zech 10.7;
Jn 16.22

33.20 *Our soul waits for the LORD.* God does not always deliver his waiting servants as soon as they hope. They must accommodate themselves to God's providence in the dark night of the soul. While he may delay in coming he never comes too late. Therefore believers wait in faith and with assurance that deliverance will come.

Psalm 34

A psalm of praise and trust

A. Praise for God's goodness

34.1
Eph 5.20;
Ps 71.6

Of David, when he feigned madness before Abimelech, so that he drove
him out, and he went away.

1 I will bless the LORD at all times;
    his praise shall continually be in my mouth.

34.2
Jer 9.24;
Ps 119.74
34.3
Lk 1.46

2 My soul makes its boast in the LORD;
    let the humble hear and be glad.

3 O magnify the LORD with me,
    and let us exalt his name together.

34.4
Mt 7.7;
vv. 6, 17, 19
34.5
Ps 36.9; 25.3
34.6
vv. 4, 17, 19

4 I sought the LORD, and he answered me,
    and delivered me from all my fears.

5 Look to him, and be radiant;
    so your*f* faces shall never be ashamed.

6 This poor soul cried, and was heard by the LORD,
    and was saved from every trouble.

B. Exhortation to trust and seek the LORD

34.7
Dan 6.22;
2 Kings 6.17
34.8
1 Pet 2.3;
Ps 2.12
34.9
Ps 23.1

7 The angel of the LORD encamps
    around those who fear him, and delivers them.

8 O taste and see that the LORD is good;
    happy are those who take refuge in him.

9 O fear the LORD, you his holy ones,
    for those who fear him have no want.

34.10
Ps 84.11

10 The young lions suffer want and hunger,
    but those who seek the LORD lack no good thing.

C. Warning against sin

34.11
Ps 111.10

11 Come, O children, listen to me;
    I will teach you the fear of the LORD.

34.12
1 Pet 3.10

12 Which of you desires life,
    and covets many days to enjoy good?

34.13
1 Pet 2.22

13 Keep your tongue from evil,
    and your lips from speaking deceit.

34.14
Ps 37.27;
Heb 12.14

14 Depart from evil, and do good;
    seek peace, and pursue it.

D. The righteous delivered: the wicked condemned

34.15
Job 36.7;
Ps 33.18
34.16
Jer 44.11;
Prov 10.7

15 The eyes of the LORD are on the righteous,
    and his ears are open to their cry.

16 The face of the LORD is against evildoers,
    to cut off the remembrance of them from the earth.

f Gk Syr Jerome: Heb *their*

34.1ff David had feigned madness before Abimelech
(1 Sam 21.10–15). He sought the Lord, who delivered him from all his fears — especially the fear of
death. Why was David, a firm believer in the power
of God, afraid? Since no one is totally sanctified in this
life, we all have times of fear and anxiety. But God can
and does deliver his faithful ones from their fears.
34.7 God's holy angels are ministering spirits, "sent
to serve . . . those who are to inherit salvation" (Heb
1.14). They guard and protect us more than we are
aware of. We should always thank God for them.

34.11 David plans to teach children how they
should live and what sins they should avoid — to teach
them the fear of the Lord. Unfortunately he did not
succeed with some of his own children, for they
turned out to be disobedient to God and broke his
commandments. Teaching must begin at home.
34.16 *The face of the LORD is against evildoers.*
Though the wicked may bless themselves, God is
against them. As their opponent, he will ruin them by
cutting off the remembrance of them. On the other
hand, all is well for the righteous.

17 When the righteous cry for help, the LORD hears,
   and rescues them from all their troubles.
18 The LORD is near to the brokenhearted,
   and saves the crushed in spirit.

19 Many are the afflictions of the righteous,
   but the LORD rescues them from them all.
20 He keeps all their bones;
   not one of them will be broken.
21 Evil brings death to the wicked,
   and those who hate the righteous will be condemned.
22 The LORD redeems the life of his servants;
   none of those who take refuge in him will be condemned.

Psalm 35

A prayer for help

A. *From persecution*

Of David.

1 Contend, O LORD, with those who contend with me;
   fight against those who fight against me!
2 Take hold of shield and buckler,
   and rise up to help me!
3 Draw the spear and javelin
   against my pursuers;
say to my soul,
   "I am your salvation."

4 Let them be put to shame and dishonor
   who seek after my life.
Let them be turned back and confounded
   who devise evil against me.
5 Let them be like chaff before the wind,
   with the angel of the LORD driving them on.
6 Let their way be dark and slippery,
   with the angel of the LORD pursuing them.

7 For without cause they hid their net[g] for me;
   without cause they dug a pit[h] for my life.
8 Let ruin come on them unawares.
And let the net that they hid ensnare them;
   let them fall in it — to their ruin.

9 Then my soul shall rejoice in the LORD,
   exulting in his deliverance.
10 All my bones shall say,
   "O LORD, who is like you?
You deliver the weak
   from those too strong for them,

g Heb *a pit, their net*   *h* The word *pit* is transposed from the preceding line

34.17
Ps 145.19;
v. 19
34.18
Ps 145.18;
Isa 57.15
34.19
Prov 24.16;
vv. 4, 6, 17
34.20
Jn 19.36
34.21
Ps 94.23
34.22
1 Kings 1.29;
Ps 71.23
35.1
Ps 43.1

35.3
Ps 62.2

35.4
Ps 70.2, 3

35.5
Job 21.18;
Ps 1.4;
Isa 29.5
35.6
Ps 73.18;
Jer 23.12
35.7
Ps 9.15
35.8
1 Thess 5.3

35.9
Isa 61.10;
Lk 1.47
35.10
Ex 15.11;
Ps 18.17;
37.14

35.1ff Most believers can identify with this prayer offered because of indignities suffered through persecution, slander, and ill-will. The psalmist desires vindication, and he is certain that it will come. He promises to speak of God's righteousness and sing his praises all day long (v. 28).
35.4 David fervently prays not simply for deliver-

ance from his enemies but for God to bring them to shame and dishonor. Some think this is a prophetic statement rather than an imprecatory prayer. In that case it predicts what will happen to those who hate and abuse David, not a prayer asking God to do this to them.

the weak and needy from those who despoil them."

B. *From slanderers*

11 Malicious witnesses rise up;
   they ask me about things I do not know.

35.11
Ps 27.12

12 They repay me evil for good;
   my soul is forlorn.

35.12
Jn 10.32

13 But as for me, when they were sick,
   I wore sackcloth;
   I afflicted myself with fasting.
   I prayed with head bowed[i] on my bosom,
14   as though I grieved for a friend or a brother;
   I went about as one who laments for a mother,
   bowed down and in mourning.

35.13
Job 30.25;
Ps 69.10

15 But at my stumbling they gathered in glee,
   they gathered together against me;
   ruffians whom I did not know
   tore at me without ceasing;

35.15
Job 30.1, 8

16 they impiously mocked more and more,[j]
   gnashing at me with their teeth.

35.16
Lam 2.16

17 How long, O Lord, will you look on?
   Rescue me from their ravages,
   my life from the lions!

35.17
Hab 1.13;
Ps 22.20

18 Then I will thank you in the great congregation;
   in the mighty throng I will praise you.

35.18
Ps 22.22, 25

C. *From haters*

19 Do not let my treacherous enemies rejoice over me,
   or those who hate me without cause wink the eye.

35.19
Ps 13.4;
38.19;
Prov 6.13;
Ps 69.4;
Jn 15.25

20 For they do not speak peace,
   but they conceive deceitful words
   against those who are quiet in the land.

21 They open wide their mouths against me;
   they say, "Aha, Aha,
   our eyes have seen it."

35.21
Ps 22.13;
40.15

22 You have seen, O Lord; do not be silent!
   O Lord, do not be far from me!
23 Wake up! Bestir yourself for my defense,
   for my cause, my God and my Lord!

35.22
Ex 3.7;
Ps 28.1; 10.1

35.23
Ps 44.23

24 Vindicate me, O Lord, my God,
   according to your righteousness,
   and do not let them rejoice over me.

35.24
Ps 9.4; v. 19

25 Do not let them say to themselves,
   "Aha, we have our heart's desire."
   Do not let them say, "We have swallowed you[k] up."

35.25
Lam 2.16

26 Let all those who rejoice at my calamity
   be put to shame and confusion;

35.26
Ps 40.14;
38.16

---

i Or *My prayer turned back*   *j* Cn Compare Gk: Heb *like the profanest of mockers of a cake*   *k* Heb *him*

35.13 David resorts to sackcloth, fasting, and prayer — a striking example of practices that few use today.
35.19 *without cause wink the eye*, i.e., don't let my enemies rejoice. To be hated for one's evil is under-

standable; to be hated for no reason is harder to grasp. But Jesus was hated thus, and so will his people be (Jn 15.18–25). Deep is the rebellion of sinners against their maker.

let those who exalt themselves against me
   be clothed with shame and dishonor.

27 Let those who desire my vindication
    shout for joy and be glad,
  and say evermore,
  "Great is the Lord,
    who delights in the welfare of his servant."
28 Then my tongue shall tell of your righteousness
    and of your praise all day long.

35.27
Ps 32.11; 9.4;
40.16; 147.11

35.28
Ps 51.14

Psalm 36

36.1
Rom 3.18

I. The sinfulness of sin (36.1–4)

To the leader. Of David, the servant of the Lord.

1 Transgression speaks to the wicked
    deep in their hearts;
  there is no fear of God
    before their eyes.
2 For they flatter themselves in their own eyes
    that their iniquity cannot be found out and hated.
3 The words of their mouths are mischief and deceit;
    they have ceased to act wisely and do good.
4 They plot mischief while on their beds;
    they are set on a way that is not good;
    they do not reject evil.

36.3
Jer 4.22

36.4
Prov 4.16;
Mic 2.1;
Isa 65.2

II. The goodness and graciousness of God (36.5–12)

5 Your steadfast love, O Lord, extends to the heavens,
    your faithfulness to the clouds.
6 Your righteousness is like the mighty mountains,
    your judgments are like the great deep;
    you save humans and animals alike, O Lord.

36.6
Job 11.8;
Ps 77.19;
Rom 11.33

7 How precious is your steadfast love, O God!
    All people may take refuge in the shadow of your wings.
8 They feast on the abundance of your house,
    and you give them drink from the river of your delights.
9 For with you is the fountain of life;
    in your light we see light.

36.7
Ruth 2.12

36.8
Ps 65.4;
Job 20.17;
Rev 22.1
36.9
Jer 2.13;
1 Pet 2.9

10 O continue your steadfast love to those who know you,
    and your salvation to the upright of heart!
11 Do not let the foot of the arrogant tread on me,
    or the hand of the wicked drive me away.
12 There the evildoers lie prostrate;
    they are thrust down, unable to rise.

36.12
Ps 140.10

36.1ff David goes beyond his own troubles to pray for the preservation of all the saints as well as of himself (vv. 10,11). Running through the psalm is the steadfast love, faithfulness, and righteousness of God. Let God's saints take courage and let the wicked repent and turn from their evil ways.
36.9 *In your light we see light.* The divine light shines

in Scripture, the written word of God. In addition, light is seen in the face of Jesus Christ, who is the light of the world (Jn 8.12). When we see God in glory we shall see light in perfection; thus, there is no need for the sun or the moon in the new Jerusalem, for God will be its light (Rev 22.5).

Psalm 37

The wisdom of an aged person

A. *The righteous will prosper: the wicked will be cut off*

Of David.

37.1
Ps 73.3;
Prov 23.17

1 Do not fret because of the wicked;
   do not be envious of wrongdoers,

37.2
Ps 90.5, 6

2 for they will soon fade like the grass,
   and wither like the green herb.

37.3
Ps 62.8;
Deut 30.20;
Isa 40.11
37.4
Isa 58.14

3 Trust in the LORD, and do good;
   so you will live in the land, and enjoy security.
4 Take delight in the LORD,
   and he will give you the desires of your heart.

37.5
Ps 55.22;
Prov 16.3;
1 Pet 5.7
37.6
Job 11.17;
Mic 7.9

5 Commit your way to the LORD;
   trust in him, and he will act.
6 He will make your vindication shine like the light,
   and the justice of your cause like the noonday.

37.7
Ps 62.5; 40.1;
vv. 1, 8

7 Be still before the LORD, and wait patiently for him;
   do not fret over those who prosper in their way,
   over those who carry out evil devices.

37.8
Ps 73.3;
Eph 4.26
37.9
Isa 60.21

8 Refrain from anger, and forsake wrath.
   Do not fret—it leads only to evil.
9 For the wicked shall be cut off,
   but those who wait for the LORD shall inherit the land.

37.10
Job 24.24;
7.10

10 Yet a little while, and the wicked will be no more;
   though you look diligently for their place, they will not
     be there.

37.11
Mt 5.5

11 But the meek shall inherit the land,
   and delight themselves in abundant prosperity.

B. *The comparison between the wicked and the righteous*

37.12
Ps 35.16

12 The wicked plot against the righteous,
   and gnash their teeth at them;

37.13
Ps 2.4;
1 Sam 26.10

13 but the LORD laughs at the wicked,
   for he sees that their day is coming.

37.14
Ps 11.2;
35.10

14 The wicked draw the sword and bend their bows
   to bring down the poor and needy,
   to kill those who walk uprightly;

37.15
Ps 9.16

15 their sword shall enter their own heart,
   and their bows shall be broken.

37.16
Prov 15.16

16 Better is a little that the righteous person has
   than the abundance of many wicked.

37.1ff This is a teaching psalm with no prayer or praise in it. It speaks about an issue not easily answered. Since God has promised blessings to the good, why do some sinners live in prosperity and some saints experience nothing but adversity? David counsels the righteous not to be discontented by the success of the wicked. To be fretful and envious is itself wrong.

37.5 Anxiety is sin in the heart of the believer, forbidden by Jesus himself (see Mt 6.25; Lk 12.22,29; Jn 6.27). Anxiety may be overcome by putting our trust in God (Jer 17.7; Dan 3.15–18), turning our cares over to the Lord (55.22; Prov 16.3; 1 Pet 5.7), and thanking God in advance for the answers to our petitions (Phil 4.6).

17   For the arms of the wicked shall be broken,
    but the LORD upholds the righteous.

37.17
Job 38.15;
Ps 10.15

18   The LORD knows the days of the blameless,
    and their heritage will abide forever;
19   they are not put to shame in evil times,
    in the days of famine they have abundance.

37.18
Ps 1.6
37.19
Job 5.20;
Ps 33.19

20   But the wicked perish,
    and the enemies of the LORD are like the glory of the
      pastures;
    they vanish — like smoke they vanish away.

37.20
Ps 72.27;
102.3

21   The wicked borrow, and do not pay back,
    but the righteous are generous and keep giving;
22   for those blessed by the LORD shall inherit the land,
    but those cursed by him shall be cut off.

37.21
Ps 112.5, 9
37.22
Prov 3.33;
Job 5.3

C. The sure deliverance and security of the righteous

23   Our steps[l] are made firm by the LORD,
    when he delights in our[m] way;
24   though we stumble,[n] we[o] shall not fall headlong,
    for the LORD holds us[p] by the hand.

37.23
1 Sam 2.9;
Ps 147.11
37.24
Prov 24.16;
Ps 147.6

25   I have been young, and now am old,
    yet I have not seen the righteous forsaken
    or their children begging bread.
26   They are ever giving liberally and lending,
    and their children become a blessing.

37.25
Heb 13.5;
Job 15.23
37.26
v. 21;
Ps 147.13

27   Depart from evil, and do good;
    so you shall abide forever.
28   For the LORD loves justice;
    he will not forsake his faithful ones.

    The righteous shall be kept safe forever,
    but the children of the wicked shall be cut off.
29   The righteous shall inherit the land,
    and live in it forever.

37.27
Ps 34.14;
v. 18
37.28
Ps 11.7;
21.10;
Isa 14.20

37.29
vv. 9, 18

30   The mouth of the righteous utter wisdom,
    and their tongues speak justice.
31   The law of their God is in their hearts;
    their steps do not slip.

37.30
Mt 12.35
37.31
Ps 40.8;
Isa 51.7;
v. 23

32   The wicked watch for the righteous,
    and seek to kill them.
33   The LORD will not abandon them to their power,
    or let them be condemned when they are brought to trial.

37.32
Ps 10.8

37.33
2 Pet 2.9;
Ps 109.31

34   Wait for the LORD, and keep to his way,

37.34
Ps 27.14;
52.5, 6

l Heb A man's steps   m Heb his   n Heb he stumbles   o Heb he   p Heb him

---

37.25,26 Many of the more than five thousand promises found in Scripture include God's promise to provide for his people's material needs (e.g., Eph 3.20; Phil 4.19). Our estimate of our material needs may differ from God's. All believers may claim God's promises to supply them (though this should not lead to the generalization that no believer will ever be short of bread). Some interpret these verses as a promise to those who are charitable and liberal to the poor, that they will never bring themselves to poverty by their charity.

and he will exalt you to inherit the land;
you will look on the destruction of the wicked.

35 I have seen the wicked oppressing,
and towering like a cedar of Lebanon.*q*

36 Again I*r* passed by, and they were no more;
though I sought them, they could not be found.

37 Mark the blameless, and behold the upright,
for there is posterity for the peaceable.

38 But transgressors shall be altogether destroyed;
the posterity of the wicked shall be cut off.

39 The salvation of the righteous is from the LORD;
he is their refuge in the time of trouble.

40 The LORD helps them and rescues them;
he rescues them from the wicked, and saves them,
because they take refuge in him.

Psalm 38

The penitent's plea for mercy

A. The extremity of the condition

A Psalm of David, for the memorial offering.

1 O LORD, do not rebuke me in your anger,
or discipline me in your wrath.

2 For your arrows have sunk into me,
and your hand has come down on me.

3 There is no soundness in my flesh
because of your indignation;
there is no health in my bones
because of my sin.

4 For my iniquities have gone over my head;
they weigh like a burden too heavy for me.

5 My wounds grow foul and fester
because of my foolishness;

6 I am utterly bowed down and prostrate;
all day long I go around mourning.

7 For my loins are filled with burning,
and there is no soundness in my flesh.

8 I am utterly spent and crushed;
I groan because of the tumult of my heart.

B. The desire for deliverance

9 O Lord, all my longing is known to you;

q Gk: Meaning of Heb uncertain   *r* Gk Syr Jerome: Heb *he*

38.1ff In this penitential psalm, David remembers his sins and afflictions. His grief and pain remind him of what he has done; these help to keep him humble before God. He longs for deliverance, confesses his iniquities, and waits for God to help him. All believers who experience a time of great difficulty because of their own mistakes can relate to this psalm.
38.3–7 David is suffering from bodily afflictions such as those suffered by Job, though David's were caused by his own foolishness. Under the burden of these afflictions, his sense of guilt becomes a heavy burden, and he calls upon God to help him.
38.8 *because of the tumult of my heart*, or, because of the pains in my heart. In the Scriptures the word "heart" is never used for the organ of the body. It always has to do with human intelligence, emotions, and will. In other words, this disquieted heart does not refer to a physical problem but to a spiritual one.

Cross references (margin)

37.35 Job 5.3
37.36 Job 20.5
37.37 Isa 57.1, 2
37.38 Ps 1.4; vv. 9, 20, 28
37.39 Ps 3.8; 9.9
37.40 Isa 31.5; 1 Chr 5.20
38.1 Ps 6.1
38.2 Job 6.4; Ps 32.4
38.3 Isa 1.6; Ps 6.2
38.4 Ezra 9.6
38.5 Ps 69.5
38.6 Ps 35.14; 42.9
38.7 Ps 102.3; v. 3
38.8 Job 3.24; Ps 22.1
38.9 Ps 10.17; 6.6

10 My heart throbs, my strength fails me;
  as for the light of my eyes — it also has gone from me.

38.10
Ps 31.10; 6.7

11 My friends and companions stand aloof from my affliction,
  and my neighbors stand far off.

38.11
Ps 31.11;
Lk 23.49

12 Those who seek my life lay their snares;
  those who seek to hurt me speak of ruin,
  and meditate treachery all day long.

38.12
Ps 54.3;
140.5; 35.4,
20

13 But I am like the deaf, I do not hear;
  like the mute, who cannot speak.

38.13
Ps 39.2, 9

14 Truly, I am like one who does not hear,
  and in whose mouth is no retort.

C. Confidence in God

15 But it is for you, O Lord, that I wait;
  it is you, O Lord my God, who will answer.

38.15
Ps 39.7; 17.6

16 For I pray, "Only do not let them rejoice over me,
  those who boast against me when my foot slips."

38.16
Ps 13.4;
35.26

17 For I am ready to fall,
  and my pain is ever with me.

38.17
Ps 13.2

18 I confess my iniquity;
  I am sorry for my sin.

38.18
Ps 32.5;
2 Cor 7.9

19 Those who are my foes without cause[s] are mighty,
  and many are those who hate me wrongfully.

38.19
Ps 18.17;
35.19

20 Those who render me evil for good
  are my adversaries because I follow after good.

38.20
Ps 35.12;
1 Jn 3.12

21 Do not forsake me, O Lord;
  O my God, do not be far from me;

38.21
Ps 35.22

22 make haste to help me,
  O Lord, my salvation.

38.22
Ps 40.13, 17;
27.1

Psalm 39

39.1
1 Kings 2.4;
Job 2.10;
Jas 3.2

In time of trouble

A. Silence in trouble

To the leader: to Jeduthun. A Psalm of David.

1 I said, "I will guard my ways
  that I may not sin with my tongue;
  I will keep a muzzle on my mouth
  as long as the wicked are in my presence."

2 I was silent and still;
  I held my peace to no avail;
  my distress grew worse,

39.2
Ps 38.13

3   my heart became hot within me.

s Q Ms: MT *my living foes*

38.18 There can be no forgiveness without repentance. Some people preach what might be called "cheap grace" by bypassing the necessity for genuine repentance and/or leaving the impression that faith without repentance is sufficient. True faith is preceded by conviction of sin which leads to godly sorrow for the dishonor sin brings to God. Contrition is followed by confession that pleads for forgiveness. Whoever genuinely repents and seeks Christ by faith will be found of him.

39.1ff David reflects on the shortness of life and the imminent advent of death to all. He cries to be spared before death overtakes him and he is no more in this present world.

While I mused, the fire burned;
then I spoke with my tongue:

B. Desire for enlightenment

4 "LORD, let me know my end,
and what is the measure of my days;
let me know how fleeting my life is.

5 You have made my days a few handbreadths,
and my lifetime is as nothing in your sight.
Surely everyone stands as a mere breath. *Selah*

6 Surely everyone goes about like a shadow.
Surely for nothing they are in turmoil;
they heap up, and do not know who will gather.

C. Prayer for deliverance

7 "And now, O Lord, what do I wait for?
My hope is in you.

8 Deliver me from all my transgressions.
Do not make me the scorn of the fool.

9 I am silent; I do not open my mouth,
for it is you who have done it.

10 Remove your stroke from me;
I am worn down by the blows[t] of your hand.

11 "You chastise mortals
in punishment for sin,
consuming like a moth what is dear to them;
surely everyone is a mere breath. *Selah*

12 "Hear my prayer, O LORD,
and give ear to my cry;
do not hold your peace at my tears.
For I am your passing guest,
an alien, like all my forebears.

13 Turn your gaze away from me, that I may smile again,
before I depart and am no more."

Psalm 40

Delight in the will of the LORD

A. An acknowledgment of God's delivering goodness

To the leader. Of David. A Psalm.

1 I waited patiently for the LORD;
he inclined to me and heard my cry.

2 He drew me up from the desolate pit,[u]

---

[t] Heb *hostility*   [u] Cn: Heb *pit of tumult*

39.4 Death marks the end of our time of probation. People then receive recompense and retribution. For the wicked it marks the end of all joys; for the godly it marks the end of all grief. We should remember that our days on earth are few and, when compared with eternity, only a flicker of an eyelash.
39.12 All people are mere aliens on this planet, guests who come into the world with nothing and leave it the same way (cf. 1 Tim 6.7). This knowledge should wean us from a close attachment to this world. There is another country and another citizenship for those who trust in God (Phil 3.20). It is not the human city but the city of God (Heb 11.10,16), built on an everlasting foundation that can never be shaken or moved. Whoever dies without having attained citizenship in this commonwealth loses everything.
40.1ff David thanks God for divine deliverance. By the Spirit he looks forward to a greater deliverance through the work of Christ in redemption (vv. 6–10). He then prays for mercy and grace, knowing that his works will never help him. God, and God alone, is his salvation.

    out of the miry bog,
and set my feet upon a rock,
    making my steps secure.

3 He put a new song in my mouth,
    a song of praise to our God.
Many will see and fear,
    and put their trust in the LORD.

40.3
Ps 33.3

4 Happy are those who make
    the LORD their trust,
who do not turn to the proud,
    to those who go astray after false gods.

40.4
Ps 84.12

5 You have multiplied, O LORD my God,
    your wondrous deeds and your thoughts toward us;
    none can compare with you.
Were I to proclaim and tell of them,
    they would be more than can be counted.

40.5
Ps 136.4;
Isa 55.8;
Ps 139.18

B. *Grateful obedience*

6 Sacrifice and offering you do not desire,
    but you have given me an open ear.*v*
Burnt offering and sin offering
    you have not required.

40.6
1 Sam 15.22

7 Then I said, "Here I am;
    in the scroll of the book it is written of me.*w*

8 I delight to do your will, O my God;
    your law is within my heart."

40.8
Jn 4.34;
Rom 7.22;
Ps 37.31

9 I have told the glad news of deliverance
    in the great congregation;
see, I have not restrained my lips,
    as you know, O LORD.

40.9
Ps 22.22;
119.13

10 I have not hidden your saving help within my heart,
    I have spoken of your faithfulness and your salvation;
I have not concealed your steadfast love and your faithfulness
    from the great congregation.

40.10
Acts 20.20;
Ps 89.1

C. *A prayer for mercy and grace*

11 Do not, O LORD, withhold
    your mercy from me;
let your steadfast love and your faithfulness
    keep me safe forever.

40.11
Ps 43.3

12 For evils have encompassed me
    without number;
my iniquities have overtaken me,
    until I cannot see;
they are more than the hairs of my head,
    and my heart fails me.

40.12
Ps 116.3;
38.4; 69.4;
73.26

13 Be pleased, O LORD, to deliver me;
    O LORD, make haste to help me.

40.13
Ps 70.1

14 Let all those be put to shame and confusion

40.14
Ps 35.4; 63.9

---

v Heb *ears you have dug for me*   *w* Meaning of Heb uncertain

40.8 Christ applied this verse to himself (see Jn 4.34).
40.11 David is overcome by his iniquities, more in number than the hairs on his head. Yet he finds mercy

with the Lord, to whom anyone can go to find forgiveness. God is the helper and the deliverer of the worst of sinners who come to him (cf. 1 Tim 1.12–16).

who seek to snatch away my life;
let those be turned back and brought to dishonor
   who desire my hurt.

40.15
Ps 70.3

15 Let those be appalled because of their shame
   who say to me, "Aha, Aha!"

40.16
Ps 70.4;
35.27

16 But may all who seek you
   rejoice and be glad in you;
may those who love your salvation
   say continually, "Great is the LORD!"

40.17
Ps 70.5

17 As for me, I am poor and needy,
   but the Lord takes thought for me.
You are my help and my deliverer;
   do not delay, O my God.

Psalm 41

41.1
Ps 82.3, 4;
Prov 14.21

The psalm of the compassionate

A. The happiness of the compassionate

To the leader. A Psalm of David.

1 Happy are those who consider the poor;[x]
   the LORD delivers them in the day of trouble.

41.2
Ps 37.22, 28;
27.12

2 The LORD protects them and keeps them alive;
   they are called happy in the land.
You do not give them up to the will of their enemies.

41.3
Ps 6.6

3 The LORD sustains them on their sickbed;
   in their illness you heal all their infirmities.[y]

B. The malice of false friends

41.4
Ps 6.2; 51.4

4 As for me, I said, "O LORD, be gracious to me;
   heal me, for I have sinned against you."

41.5
Ps 38.12

5 My enemies wonder in malice
   when I will die, and my name perish.

41.6
Ps 12.2

6 And when they come to see me, they utter empty words,
   while their hearts gather mischief;
when they go out, they tell it abroad.

41.7
Ps 56.5

7 All who hate me whisper together about me;
   they imagine the worst for me.

41.8
Ps 71.10, 11

8 They think that a deadly thing has fastened on me,
   that I will not rise again from where I lie.

41.9
Job 19.19;
Ps 55.12;
Jn 13.18
41.10
Ps 3.3

9 Even my bosom friend in whom I trusted,
   who ate of my bread, has lifted the heel against me.

10 But you, O LORD, be gracious to me,
   and raise me up, that I may repay them.

C. Integrity vindicated

41.11
Ps 147.11;
25.2

11 By this I know that you are pleased with me;
   because my enemy has not triumphed over me.

x Or weak   y Heb you change all his bed

41.1ff As a compassionate friend, God supports and comforts his saints on their sickbeds and when faced with the troubles of life. In this psalm David's integrity is vindicated, his false friends are overcome, and he experiences help from the God who is from everlasting to everlasting.
41.9 *my bosom friend . . . has lifted the heel against me.* This verse, as Jesus himself indicated, is prophetic of his betrayal by Judas Iscariot (Jn 13.18).

12 But you have upheld me because of my integrity,
   and set me in your presence forever.

41.12
Ps 37.17;
Job 36.7

13 Blessed be the LORD, the God of Israel,
   from everlasting to everlasting.
                    Amen and Amen.

41.13
Ps 106.48

BOOK II
(Psalms 42–72)

42.1
Ps 119.131

Psalm 42

The sorrow and consolation of the godly

A. The sorrow of separation

To the leader. A Maskil of the Korahites.

1 As a deer longs for flowing streams,
   so my soul longs for you, O God.
2 My soul thirsts for God,
   for the living God.
   When shall I come and behold
   the face of God?

42.2
Ps 63.1;
Jer 10.10;
Ps 43.4

3 My tears have been my food
   day and night,
   while people say to me continually,
   "Where is your God?"

42.3
Ps 80.5;
79.10

4 These things I remember,
   as I pour out my soul:
   how I went with the throng,^{z}
   and led them in procession to the house of God,
   with glad shouts and songs of thanksgiving,
   a multitude keeping festival.

42.4
Ps 62.8;
Isa 30.29;
Ps 100.4

5 Why are you cast down, O my soul,
   and why are you disquieted within me?
   Hope in God; for I shall again praise him,
   my help 6 and my God.

42.5
Ps 38.6; 77.3;
Lam 3.24;
Ps 44.3

B. The consolation and hope of the godly

My soul is cast down within me;
   therefore I remember you
from the land of Jordan and of Hermon,
   from Mount Mizar.

7 Deep calls to deep
   at the thunder of your cataracts;
all your waves and your billows
   have gone over me.

42.7
Ps 88.7;
Jon 2.3

8 By day the LORD commands his steadfast love,
   and at night his song is with me,
   a prayer to the God of my life.

42.8
Ps 57.3;
Job 35.10;
Ps 63.6;
149.5

9 I say to God, my rock,

42.9
Ps 38.6

^{z} Meaning of Heb uncertain

42.1ff The psalmist experiences a sense of separation from God because of sin. But by turning toward God for help and depending on him, such people look with eager expectation to that moment when their disquieted souls will once more praise God, their only hope and help.

"Why have you forgotten me?
Why must I walk about mournfully
because the enemy oppresses me?"

42.10
v. 3

10 As with a deadly wound in my body,
my adversaries taunt me,
while they say to me continually,
"Where is your God?"

42.11
v. 5

11 Why are you cast down, O my soul,
and why are you disquieted within me?
Hope in God; for I shall again praise him,
my help and my God.

43.1
Ps 26.1;
1 Sam 24.15;
Ps 5.6

Psalm 43

A plea for vindication

1 Vindicate me, O God, and defend my cause
against an ungodly people;
from those who are deceitful and unjust
deliver me!

43.2
Ps 18.1; 44.9;
42.9

2 For you are the God in whom I take refuge;
why have you cast me off?
Why must I walk about mournfully
because of the oppression of the enemy?

43.3
Ps 36.9; 42.4;
84.1

3 O send out your light and your truth;
let them lead me;
let them bring me to your holy hill
and to your dwelling.

43.4
Ps 26.6; 33.2

4 Then I will go to the altar of God,
to God my exceeding joy;
and I will praise you with the harp,
O God, my God.

43.5
Ps 42.5, 11

5 Why are you cast down, O my soul,
and why are you disquieted within me?
Hope in God; for I shall again praise him,
my help and my God.

44.1
Ex 12.26;
Ps 78.3, 12

Psalm 44

A prayer for deliverance

A. Acknowledgment of past mercies

To the leader. Of the Korahites. A Maskil.

1 We have heard with our ears, O God,
our ancestors have told us,
what deeds you performed in their days,
in the days of old:

44.2
Ex 15.17;
Ps 78.55;
80.8

2 you with your own hand drove out the nations,
but them you planted;

42.9 *God, my rock.* God is a sure foundation on which to build, a rock of shelter, the rock of ages in whom is everlasting strength. By faith we have access to this rock.
43.1ff The psalmist speaks for those who take refuge in God, the one on whom they call to defend their cause. They desire to come to God's altar and to stand before him in hope.
44.1ff This psalm is applicable in many situations, for God's people suffer in all ages; they should look to their faithful God for deliverance, based on his steadfast, unchanging love.

you afflicted the peoples,
  but them you set free;

3 for not by their own sword did they win the land,
    nor did their own arm give them victory;
  but your right hand, and your arm,
    and the light of your countenance,
    for you delighted in them.

4 You are my King and my God;
    you command*a* victories for Jacob.
5 Through you we push down our foes;
    through your name we tread down our assailants.
6 For not in my bow do I trust,
    nor can my sword save me.
7 But you have saved us from our foes,
    and have put to confusion those who hate us.
8 In God we have boasted continually,
    and we will give thanks to your name forever.   *Selah*

B. Statement of present complaints

9 Yet you have rejected us and abased us,
    and have not gone out with our armies.
10 You made us turn back from the foe,
    and our enemies have gotten spoil.
11 You have made us like sheep for slaughter,
    and have scattered us among the nations.
12 You have sold your people for a trifle,
    demanding no high price for them.

13 You have made us the taunt of our neighbors,
    the derision and scorn of those around us.
14 You have made us a byword among the nations,
    a laughingstock*b* among the peoples.
15 All day long my disgrace is before me,
    and shame has covered my face
16 at the words of the taunters and revilers,
    at the sight of the enemy and the avenger.

C. Appeal to God for deliverance

17 All this has come upon us,
    yet we have not forgotten you,
    or been false to your covenant.
18 Our heart has not turned back,
    nor have our steps departed from your way,
19 yet you have broken us in the haunt of jackals,
    and covered us with deep darkness.

20 If we had forgotten the name of our God,
    or spread out our hands to a strange god,
21 would not God discover this?
    For he knows the secrets of the heart.

a Gk Syr: Heb *You are my King, O God; command*   *b* Heb *a shaking of the head*

44.3
Josh 24.12;
Ps 77.15;
Deut 4.37;
7.7, 8

44.4
Ps 74.12;
79.9
44.5
Dan 8.4;
Ps 108.13
44.6
Ps 33.16

44.7
Ps 136.24;
53.5
44.8
Ps 34.2;
30.12

44.9
Ps 60.1, 10;
74.1
44.10
Lev 26.17;
Josh 7.8;
Ps 89.41
44.11
v. 22;
Deut 4.27;
28.64;
Ps 106.27
44.12
Isa 52.3, 4;
Jer 15.13
44.13
Ps 79.4; 80.6
44.14
Jer 24.9;
Ps 109.25

44.16
Ps 74.10; 8.2

44.17
Dan 9.13;
Ps 78.7, 57

44.18
Ps 78.57;
Job 23.11
44.19
Ps 51.8;
Job 3.5

44.20
Ps 78.11;
68.31; 81.9
44.21
Ps 139.1, 2;
Jer 17.10

44.3 It was God who planted Israel in Canaan. He gave his people victory over the inhabitants of the land. However great the victories were, they could not be attributed to the Israelites but to their God. **44.9** The psalmist may have had the Babylonian captivity in mind. The God who brought them into the land and gave them victory had promised to keep them, but only if they remained faithful to him. Now God has cast them off and abased them. Again and again in the history of the two kingdoms, their kings and armies were put to shame by the enemy because they had forsaken their rock.

44.22
Rom 8.36;
Isa 53.7

22 Because of you we are being killed all day long,
and accounted as sheep for the slaughter.

44.23
Ps 7.6; 78.65;
77.7

23 Rouse yourself! Why do you sleep, O Lord?
Awake, do not cast us off forever!

44.24
Job 13.24;
Ps 42.9

24 Why do you hide your face?
Why do you forget our affliction and oppression?

44.25
Ps 119.25

25 For we sink down to the dust;
our bodies cling to the ground.

44.26
Ps 35.2;
25.22

26 Rise up, come to our help.
Redeem us for the sake of your steadfast love.

45.1
Ezra 7.6

Psalm 45

The king's marriage

A. *The king and his rule*

To the leader: according to Lilies. Of the Korahites. A Maskil. A love
song.

1 My heart overflows with a goodly theme;
I address my verses to the king;
my tongue is like the pen of a ready scribe.

45.2
Lk 4.22

2 You are the most handsome of men;
grace is poured upon your lips;
therefore God has blessed you forever.

45.3
Isa 9.6

3 Gird your sword on your thigh, O mighty one,
in your glory and majesty.

45.4
Rev 6.2

4 In your majesty ride on victoriously
for the cause of truth and to defend*c* the right;
let your right hand teach you dread deeds.

5 Your arrows are sharp
in the heart of the king's enemies;
the peoples fall under you.

45.6
Ps 93.2;
Heb 1.8, 9;
Ps 98.9
45.7
Ps 33.5;
Isa 61.1;
Ps 79.4; 21.6
45.8
Song 1.3

6 Your throne, O God,*d* endures forever and ever.
Your royal scepter is a scepter of equity;
7 you love righteousness and hate wickedness.
Therefore God, your God, has anointed you
with the oil of gladness beyond your companions;
8 your robes are all fragrant with myrrh and aloes and cassia.
From ivory palaces stringed instruments make you glad;

45.9
Song 6.8;
1 Kings 2.19

9 daughters of kings are among your ladies of honor;
at your right hand stands the queen in gold of Ophir.

B. *The bride and the wedding*

45.10
Deut 21.13

10 Hear, O daughter, consider and incline your ear;
forget your people and your father's house,

45.11
Ps 95.6;
Isa 54.5

11 and the king will desire your beauty.
Since he is your lord, bow to him;

45.12
Ps 22.29

12 the people*e* of Tyre will seek your favor with gifts,

c Cn: Heb *and the meekness of*   *d* Or *Your throne is a throne of God, it*   *e* Heb *daughter*

45.1ff This psalm celebrates the marriage of a king.
It has messianic implications, especially in v. 6, a
verse that Hebrews applies to Jesus Christ: "But of
the Son he says, 'Your throne, O God, is forever and

ever' " (Heb 1.8).
45.12 *Tyre* is pictured here as bringing gifts to a
bride (Israel). Tyre was a wealthy maritime nation
which, under Hiram, assisted David and Solomon

the richest of the people [13] with all kinds of wealth.

45.13
Isa 61.10

The princess is decked in her chamber with gold-woven
  robes;[f]
14   in many-colored robes she is led to the king;
  behind her the virgins, her companions, follow.

45.14
Song 1.4; v. 9

15 With joy and gladness they are led along
  as they enter the palace of the king.

C. The conclusion

16 In the place of ancestors you, O king,[g] shall have sons;
  you will make them princes in all the earth.
17 I will cause your name to be celebrated in all generations;
  therefore the peoples will praise you forever and ever.

45.16
1 Pet 2.9;
Rev 1.6; 20.6
45.17
Mal 1.11;
Ps 138.4

Psalm 46

46.1
Ps 14.6;
Deut 4.7;
Ps 9.9

God our refuge and strength

A. *God our refuge*

To the leader. Of the Korahites. According to Alamoth. A Song.

1 God is our refuge and strength,
  a very present[h] help in trouble.
2 Therefore we will not fear, though the earth should change,
  though the mountains shake in the heart of the sea;
3 though its waters roar and foam,
  though the mountains tremble with its tumult.   *Selah*

46.2
Ps 23.4; 82.5;
18.7
46.3
Ps 93.3, 4

B. *God our strength*

4 There is a river whose streams make glad the city of God,
  the holy habitation of the Most High.
5 God is in the midst of the city;[i] it shall not be moved;
  God will help it when the morning dawns.
6 The nations are in an uproar, the kingdoms totter;
  he utters his voice, the earth melts.
7 The LORD of hosts is with us;
  the God of Jacob is our refuge.[j]   *Selah*

46.4
Isa 8.7;
Ps 48.1, 8;
Isa 60.14
46.5
Isa 12.6;
Ps 37.40
46.6
Ps 2.1; 68.33;
Mic 1.4
46.7
2 Chr 13.12;
Ps 9.9

C. *God our victory*

8 Come, behold the works of the LORD;
  see what desolations he has brought on the earth.
9 He makes wars cease to the end of the earth;
  he breaks the bow, and shatters the spear;
  he burns the shields with fire.
10 "Be still, and know that I am God!

46.8
Ps 66.5;
Isa 61.4
46.9
Isa 2.4;
Ps 76.3;
Ezek 39.9
46.10
Ps 100.3;
Isa 2.11, 17

f Or people. [13]*All glorious is the princess within, gold embroidery is her clothing*   *g Heb lacks O king*
h Or well proved   *i Heb of it*   *j Or fortress*

in their numerous building projects (1 Chr 14.1;
2 Chr 5).
45.17 The royal bridegroom (ultimately, Christ)
will be praised forever. His Father has given him a
name that is above every name (Phil 2.9), and his
people shall extol that name by word and deed for
endless generations.
46.1ff This psalm, on which Luther based his powerful hymn "A Mighty Fortress," expresses our hope
and trust in God. It testifies to his power, providence,

and presence among his people in bad times as well
as good. We learn of what he has done for us and will
do in the future.
46.4 *There is a river,* i.e., the waters of Siloam,
which went softly by Jerusalem and served as a defense of the city in Hezekiah's day.
46.8 When God is pleased to use his sword, he can
make havoc among the nations. No power is so strong
that he cannot destroy it.
46.10 Let the enemies of God be still and know that

> I am exalted among the nations,
> I am exalted in the earth."

11 The LORD of hosts is with us;
the God of Jacob is our refuge. *k*

Selah

Psalm 47

God the king of the earth

A. The nations subdued

To the leader. Of the Korahites. A Psalm.

1 Clap your hands, all you peoples;
shout to God with loud songs of joy.
2 For the LORD, the Most High, is awesome,
a great king over all the earth.
3 He subdued peoples under us,
and nations under our feet.
4 He chose our heritage for us,
the pride of Jacob whom he loves.

Selah

B. God reigns over all the earth

5 God has gone up with a shout,
the LORD with the sound of a trumpet.
6 Sing praises to God, sing praises;
sing praises to our King, sing praises.
7 For God is the king of all the earth;
sing praises with a psalm. *l*

8 God is king over the nations;
God sits on his holy throne.
9 The princes of the peoples gather
as the people of the God of Abraham.
For the shields of the earth belong to God;
he is highly exalted.

Psalm 48

A song of Zion

A. Zion, city of our God

A Song. A Psalm of the Korahites.

1 Great is the LORD and greatly to be praised
in the city of our God.
His holy mountain, 2 beautiful in elevation,
is the joy of all the earth,

Marginal references:

47.1 Ps 98.8; Isa 55.12; Ps 106.47

47.2 Deut 7.21

47.3 Ps 18.47

47.4 1 Pet 1.4

47.5 Ps 68.33; 98.6

47.6 Ps 68.4; 89.18

47.7 1 Cor 14.15

47.8 1 Chr 16.31

47.9 Ps 72.11; Rom 4.11, 12; Ps 89.18; 97.9

48.1 Ps 96.4; Zech 8.3

48.2 Ps 50.2; Lam 2.15; Mt 5.35

k Or *fortress* *l* Heb *Maskil*

---

he is God. Let the friends of God also be still, see his deliverance, and know that he alone is able to conquer and overcome all our enemies, including that last enemy, death.
47.1ff This psalm is designed to stir up the people of God to sing his praises, for he is *king over all the earth* and *sits on his holy throne.*
47.8 The God who has created all things also reigns

over the heathen. Although they do not know him or obey him, he determines their destiny and directs their paths.
48.1ff Zion is Jerusalem, the city of the great King. In covenant with its people, he lives and reigns there and defeats its enemies. His dominion over this city is established forever. Therefore let everyone praise the God of Zion.

Mount Zion, in the far north,
   the city of the great King.
3 Within its citadels God
   has shown himself a sure defense.

B. Zion established

4 Then the kings assembled,
   they came on together.
5 As soon as they saw it, they were astounded;
   they were in panic, they took to flight;
6 trembling took hold of them there,
   pains as of a woman in labor,
7 as when an east wind shatters
   the ships of Tarshish.
8 As we have heard, so have we seen
   in the city of the LORD of hosts,
in the city of our God,
   which God establishes forever.

                                    Selah

C. Zion praising God

9 We ponder your steadfast love, O God,
   in the midst of your temple.
10 Your name, O God, like your praise,
   reaches to the ends of the earth.
Your right hand is filled with victory.
11   Let Mount Zion be glad,
let the towns[m] of Judah rejoice
   because of your judgments.

12 Walk about Zion, go all around it,
   count its towers,
13 consider well its ramparts;
   go through its citadels,
that you may tell the next generation
14   that this is God,
our God forever and ever.
   He will be our guide forever.

Psalm 49

A sermon on the foolishness of trusting in riches

A. *The summons to hear*

To the leader. Of the Korahites. A Psalm.

1 Hear this, all you peoples;
   give ear, all inhabitants of the world,

m Heb daughters

48.3	Ps 46.7
48.4	2 Sam 10.6-19
48.5	Ex 15.15
48.7	Jer 18.17
48.8	Ps 87.5
48.9	Ps 26.3
48.10	Josh 7.9; Isa 41.10
48.11	Ps 97.8
48.13	Ps 122.7; 78.5-7
48.14	Ps 23.4
49.1	Ps 78.1; 33.8

49.1ff While most psalms speak about praying and praising God, this one preaches and teaches. Its purpose is to convince worldly individuals of the folly of setting their hearts on material things that perish. They should seek a better world.

2 both low and high,
   rich and poor together.

49.3
Ps 37.30;
119.130

3 My mouth shall speak wisdom;
   the meditation of my heart shall be understanding.

49.4
Ps 78.2;
Num 12.8

4 I will incline my ear to a proverb;
   I will solve my riddle to the music of the harp.

B. The limitations of wealth

49.5
Ps 23.4

5 Why should I fear in times of trouble,
   when the iniquity of my persecutors surrounds me,

49.6
Job 31.24

6 those who trust in their wealth
   and boast of the abundance of their riches?

49.7
Mt 25.8, 9;
Job 36.18

7 Truly, no ransom avails for one's life,[n]
   there is no price one can give to God for it.

49.8
Mt 16.26

8 For the ransom of life is costly,
   and can never suffice,

49.9
Ps 22.29;
89.48

9 that one should live on forever
   and never see the grave.[o]

49.10
Eccl 2.16, 18

10 When we look at the wise, they die;
   fool and dolt perish together
   and leave their wealth to others.

49.11
Ps 64.6; 10.6;
Deut 3.14

11 Their graves[p] are their homes forever,
   their dwelling places to all generations,
   though they named lands their own.

49.12
v. 20

12 Mortals cannot abide in their pomp;
   they are like the animals that perish.

C. The fate of those who trust in wealth

49.13
Lk 12.20

13 Such is the fate of the foolhardy,
   the end of those[q] who are pleased with their lot.   *Selah*

49.14
Ps 9.17;
Dan 7.18;
Mal 4.3;
1 Cor 6.2;
Rev 2.26;
Job 24.19

14 Like sheep they are appointed for Sheol;
   Death shall be their shepherd;
  straight to the grave they descend,[r]
   and their form shall waste away;
   Sheol shall be their home.[s]

49.15
Ps 56.13;
73.24

15 But God will ransom my soul from the power of Sheol,
   for he will receive me.   *Selah*

D. The final exhortation

49.16
Ps 37.7

16 Do not be afraid when some become rich,
   when the wealth of their houses increases.

49.17
Ps 17.14

17 For when they die they will carry nothing away;
   their wealth will not go down after them.

49.18
Lk 12.19

18 Though in their lifetime they count themselves happy
  —for you are praised when you do well for yourself—

49.19
Gen 15.15;
Job 33.30

19 they[t] will go to the company of their ancestors,
   who will never again see the light.

49.20
v. 12

20 Mortals cannot abide in their pomp;
   they are like the animals that perish.

---

n Another reading is *no one can ransom a brother*   o Heb *the pit*   p Gk Syr Compare Tg: Heb *their
inward* (thought)   q Tg: Heb *after them*   r Cn: Heb *the upright shall have dominion over them in the
morning*   s Meaning of Heb uncertain   t Cn: Heb *you*

49.6 *those who trust in their wealth.* Wealth is deceptive. Those who trust in it, boast of their possessions,
and suppose they can keep it forever fail to realize its
weaknesses. It cannot keep them from dying, nor can
it affect their state after death.

Psalm 50

True and false religion

A. *God is the true judge*

A Psalm of Asaph.

1 The mighty one, God the Lord,
   speaks and summons the earth
   from the rising of the sun to its setting.
2 Out of Zion, the perfection of beauty,
   God shines forth.

3 Our God comes and does not keep silence,
   before him is a devouring fire,
   and a mighty tempest all around him.
4 He calls to the heavens above
   and to the earth, that he may judge his people:
5 "Gather to me my faithful ones,
   who made a covenant with me by sacrifice!"
6 The heavens declare his righteousness,
   for God himself is judge.   *Selah*

B. *God judges the intent, not the outward form*

7 "Hear, O my people, and I will speak,
   O Israel, I will testify against you.
   I am God, your God.
8 Not for your sacrifices do I rebuke you;
   your burnt offerings are continually before me.
9 I will not accept a bull from your house,
   or goats from your folds.
10 For every wild animal of the forest is mine,
   the cattle on a thousand hills.
11 I know all the birds of the air,[u]
   and all that moves in the field is mine.

12 "If I were hungry, I would not tell you,
   for the world and all that is in it is mine.
13 Do I eat the flesh of bulls,
   or drink the blood of goats?
14 Offer to God a sacrifice of thanksgiving,[v]
   and pay your vows to the Most High.
15 Call on me in the day of trouble;
   I will deliver you, and you shall glorify me."

C. *Hypocrisy rebuked*

16 But to the wicked God says:
   "What right have you to recite my statutes,
   or take my covenant on your lips?
17 For you hate discipline,
   and you cast my words behind you.

u Gk Syr Tg: Heb *mountains*   v Or *make thanksgiving your sacrifice to God*

50.1	Josh 22.22; Ps 113.3
50.2	Ps 48.2; Deut 33.2
50.3	Ps 96.13; 97.3; Dan 7.10
50.4	Deut 4.26; Isa 1.2
50.5	Ps 30.4; Ex 24.7; v. 8
50.6	Ps 89.5; 75.7
50.7	Ps 81.8; Ex 20.2
50.8	Ps 40.6; Hos 6.6
50.9	Ps 69.31
50.10	Ps 104.24
50.12	Ex 19.5
50.14	Heb 13.15; Deut 23.21
50.15	Ps 91.15; 81.7; 22.23
50.16	Isa 29.13
50.17	Rom 2.21, 22; Neh 9.26

50.1ff This psalm is designed to instruct, reprove, and admonish. It rebukes those who practice the externals of religion without inward faith and practical action. The threat of judgment hangs over the heads of the disobedient.
50.10 Though God commanded animal sacrifices from his people, he does not need them. The cattle on a thousand hills belong to him, and he has dominion over everything, including the animals of the forest. They wait on him and are at his disposal, so he can make any use of them that he desires.

50.18 Rom 1.32; 1 Tim 5.22	18 You make friends with a thief when you see one, and you keep company with adulterers.
50.19 Ps 10.7; 52.2	19 "You give your mouth free rein for evil, and your tongue frames deceit.
50.20 Mt 10.21	20 You sit and speak against your kin; you slander your own mother's child.
50.21 Eccl 8.11; Isa 42.14; Ps 90.8	21 These things you have done and I have been silent; you thought that I was one just like yourself. But now I rebuke you, and lay the charge before you.

D. *The conclusion stated*

50.22 Job 8.13; Ps 9.17; 7.2	22 "Mark this, then, you who forget God, or I will tear you apart, and there will be no one to deliver.
50.23 v. 14; Ps 85.13; 91.16	23 Those who bring thanksgiving as their sacrifice honor me; to those who go the right way*w* I will show the salvation of God."

Psalm 51

The penitent's psalm

A. *David's prayer for forgiveness and confession of sin*

51.1 Ps 4.1; 106.45; Isa 43.25; Acts 3.19	To the leader. A Psalm of David, when the prophet Nathan came to him, after he had gone in to Bathsheba.
	1 Have mercy on me, O God, according to your steadfast love; according to your abundant mercy blot out my transgressions.
51.2 Heb 9.14; 1 Jn 1.7	2 Wash me thoroughly from my iniquity, and cleanse me from my sin.
51.3 Isa 59.12	3 For I know my transgressions, and my sin is ever before me.
51.4 Gen 20.6; Lk 15.21; Rom 3.4	4 Against you, you alone, have I sinned, and done what is evil in your sight, so that you are justified in your sentence and blameless when you pass judgment.
51.5 Ps 58.3; Job 14.4	5 Indeed, I was born guilty, a sinner when my mother conceived me.
51.6 Ps 15.2; Prov 2.6	6 You desire truth in the inward being;*x* therefore teach me wisdom in my secret heart.
51.7 Lev 14.4; Heb 9.19; Isa 1.18	7 Purge me with hyssop, and I shall be clean; wash me, and I shall be whiter than snow.
51.8 Ps 35.10	8 Let me hear joy and gladness; let the bones that you have crushed rejoice.
51.9 Jer 16.17	9 Hide your face from my sins, and blot out all my iniquities.

w Heb *who set a way*   *x* Meaning of Heb uncertain

51.1ff This psalm, written after David's sin with Bathsheba (see 2 Sam 11–12) lays down the biblical requirements for cleansing from sin. David's repentance included a godly sorrow for his transgressions, confession of his sins, and a determination to commit these sins no more. God forgave him for his sin and restored him to fellowship with him, enabling him to rejoice and tell others of the grace of God.

51.7 *Purge me with hyssop.* Hyssop was an edible plant, whose leaves and heads were used as a spice or condiment. Its use here, however, reflects back to Ex 12.22, where the plant was dipped in the blood of an animal and then used to sprinkle the blood on the lintels and doorposts (see also Lev 14.4–8; Num 19.17,18).

B. *David's prayer and vow*

10 Create in me a clean heart, O God,
    and put a new and right[y] spirit within me.
11 Do not cast me away from your presence,
    and do not take your holy spirit from me.
12 Restore to me the joy of your salvation,
    and sustain in me a willing[z] spirit.

13 Then I will teach transgressors your ways,
    and sinners will return to you.
14 Deliver me from bloodshed, O God,
    O God of my salvation,
    and my tongue will sing aloud of your deliverance.

C. *God's acceptance of the broken and contrite heart*

15 O Lord, open my lips,
    and my mouth will declare your praise.
16 For you have no delight in sacrifice;
    if I were to give a burnt offering, you would not be pleased.
17 The sacrifice acceptable to God[a] is a broken spirit;
    a broken and contrite heart, O God, you will not despise.

D. *David's prayer for Zion*

18 Do good to Zion in your good pleasure;
    rebuild the walls of Jerusalem,
19 then you will delight in right sacrifices,
    in burnt offerings and whole burnt offerings;
    then bulls will be offered on your altar.

Psalm 52

The fate of the wicked

A. *The portrait of the wicked*

To the leader. A Maskil of David, when Doeg the Edomite came to Saul
    and said to him, "David has come to the house of Ahimelech."

1 Why do you boast, O mighty one,
   of mischief done against the godly?[b]
   All day long 2 you are plotting destruction.
   Your tongue is like a sharp razor,
   you worker of treachery.
3 You love evil more than good,
   and lying more than speaking the truth.   *Selah*
4 You love all words that devour,
   O deceitful tongue.

[y] Or *steadfast*   [z] Or *generous*   [a] Or *My sacrifice, O God,*   [b] Cn Compare Syr: Heb *the kindness of God*

51.11 The work of the Holy Spirit in the O.T. differs from that in the N.T. In the O.T., the Spirit came upon and went from people as the occasion demanded. David earnestly prays here that God will not take away the Holy Spirit who came upon him when he was chosen to be king. In this age, believers are sealed by the Spirit (Eph 1.13), who can be quenched (1 Thess 5.17) or made to sorrow (Eph 4.30), but does not leave believers once they have been converted.

52.1ff This psalm deals with the murders committed by Doeg the Edomite, who slew eighty-five priests, including Ahimelech (1 Sam 22.6–19). King Saul was behind the slaying of the priests and shared Doeg's guilt. David pictures the acts of the wicked and the judgment that falls upon them, and he offers praise for the righteous.

Cross references (right margin):

51.10 Acts 15.9; Eph 2.10; Ps 78.37
51.11 2 Kings 13.23; Eph 4.30
51.12 Ps 13.5; 2 Cor 3.17
51.13 Acts 9.21, 22; Ps 22.27
51.14 2 Sam 12.9; Ps 25.5; 35.28
51.15 Ps 9.14
51.16 1 Sam 15.22; Ps 40.6
51.17 Ps 34.18
51.18 Isa 51.3; Ps 102.16
51.19 Ps 4.5; 66.13, 15
52.1 1 Sam 22.9; Ps 94.4
52.2 Ps 50.19; 57.4; 59.7
52.3 Jer 9.4, 5
52.4 Ps 120.3

B. *The end of the wicked*

52.5
Prov 2.22;
Ps 27.13

5 But God will break you down forever;
    he will snatch and tear you from your tent;
    he will uproot you from the land of the living.   *Selah*

52.6
Job 22.19;
Ps 37.34;
40.3
52.7
Ps 49.6

6 The righteous will see, and fear,
    and will laugh at the evildoer, *c* saying,

7 "See the one who would not take
        refuge in God,
    but trusted in abundant riches,
        and sought refuge in wealth!"*d*

C. *The praise of the righteous*

52.8
Jer 11.16;
Ps 13.5

8 But I am like a green olive tree
        in the house of God.
    I trust in the steadfast love of God
        forever and ever.

52.9
Ps 30.12;
54.6

9 I will thank you forever,
        because of what you have done.
    In the presence of the faithful
        I will proclaim*e* your name, for it is good.

Psalm 53

53.1
Ps 14.1-7;
Rom 3.10

Human folly and wickedness

A. *Human depravity*

To the leader: according to Mahalath. A Maskil of David.

1 Fools say in their hearts, "There is no God."
        They are corrupt, they commit abominable acts;
        there is no one who does good.

53.2
Ps 33.13

2 God looks down from heaven on humankind
        to see if there are any who are wise,
        who seek after God.

53.3
Rom 3.12

3 They have all fallen away, they are all alike perverse;
        there is no one who does good,
        no, not one.

B. *The punishment by God*

53.4
Jer 4.22

4 Have they no knowledge, those evildoers,
        who eat up my people as they eat bread,
        and do not call upon God?

53.5
Lev 26.17,
36;
Ezek 6.5

5 There they shall be in great terror,
        in terror such as has not been.
    For God will scatter the bones of the ungodly;*f*
        they will be put to shame,*g* for God has rejected them.

---

c Heb *him*   *d* Syr Tg: Heb *in his destruction*   *e* Cn: Heb *wait for*   *f* Cn Compare Gk Syr: Heb *him who encamps against you*   *g* Gk: Heb *you have put (them) to shame*

53.1ff *Fools.* See note on 14.1ff. Some scholars think the similarities between this psalm and Ps 14 indicate that Ps 53, along with the other psalms of Book II, was used in the northern kingdom and reflects linguistic and local peculiarities.

C. The prayer for salvation

6 O that deliverance for Israel would come from Zion!
   When God restores the fortunes of his people,
   Jacob will rejoice; Israel will be glad.

53.6
Ps 14.7

Psalm 54

54.1
Ps 20.1;
2 Chr 20.6

A song for the distressed

A. Complaint and prayer for help

To the leader: with stringed instruments. A Maskil of David, when the
Ziphites went and told Saul, "David is in hiding among us."

1 Save me, O God, by your name,
   and vindicate me by your might.

2 Hear my prayer, O God;
   give ear to the words of my mouth.

54.2
Ps 55.1; 5.1

3 For the insolent have risen against me,
   the ruthless seek my life;
   they do not set God before them.   *Selah*

54.3
Ps 86.14;
40.14; 36.1

B. Assurance of God's favor and deliverance

4 But surely, God is my helper;
   the Lord is the upholder of[h] my life.

5 He will repay my enemies for their evil.
   In your faithfulness, put an end to them.

54.4
Ps 118.7;
41.12
54.5
Ps 94.23;
143.12; 89.49

6 With a freewill offering I will sacrifice to you;
   I will give thanks to your name, O LORD, for it is good.

7 For he has delivered me from every trouble,
   and my eye has looked in triumph on my enemies.

54.6
Ps 50.14;
52.9
54.7
Ps 34.6;
59.10

Psalm 55

55.1
Ps 61.1; 27.9

A song for those who have been betrayed

A. David describes his distress

To the leader: with stringed instruments. A Maskil of David.

1 Give ear to my prayer, O God;
   do not hide yourself from my supplication.

2 Attend to me, and answer me;
   I am troubled in my complaint.
I am distraught 3 by the noise of the enemy,
   because of the clamor of the wicked.
For they bring[i] trouble upon me,
   and in anger they cherish enmity against me.

55.2
Ps 66.19;
77.3;
Isa 38.14
55.3
Ps 17.9;
2 Sam 16.7,
8;
Ps 71.11

h Gk Syr Jerome: Heb *is of those who uphold* or *is with those who uphold*   i Cn Compare Gk: Heb *they
cause to totter*

54.1ff *by your name*, i.e., by your great power. This
psalm reflects on the treachery of the Ziphites, who
betrayed David to Saul on two occasions (1 Sam
23.19; 26.1). The actions of the wicked will be forever
remembered against them as a warning to others who
are tempted to follow in their evil ways.
54.5 David need not fear his enemies, for God will
judge and repay them for their wickedness. He prays,

not with malice but with faith, that God will do what
he says about sinners who refuse to repent.
55.1ff Many scholars think this psalm sprang from
the rebellion of Absalom against his father David,
when Ahithophel dealt treacherously with King David. Some liken the death of Ahithophel to the death
of Judas Iscariot; both hanged themselves (see 1 Sam
15.31 – 17.23).

4 My heart is in anguish within me,
   the terrors of death have fallen upon me.
5 Fear and trembling come upon me,
   and horror overwhelms me.
6 And I say, "O that I had wings like a dove!
   I would fly away and be at rest;
7 truly, I would flee far away;
   I would lodge in the wilderness;   *Selah*
8 I would hurry to find a shelter for myself
   from the raging wind and tempest."

B. The treachery of a friend

9 Confuse, O Lord, confound their speech;
   for I see violence and strife in the city.
10 Day and night they go around it
   on its walls,
and iniquity and trouble are within it;
11   ruin is in its midst;
oppression and fraud
   do not depart from its marketplace.

12 It is not enemies who taunt me —
   I could bear that;
it is not adversaries who deal insolently with me —
   I could hide from them.
13 But it is you, my equal,
   my companion, my familiar friend,
14 with whom I kept pleasant company;
   we walked in the house of God with the throng.
15 Let death come upon them;
   let them go down alive to Sheol;
for evil is in their homes and in their hearts.

C. David's confidence in God

16 But I call upon God,
   and the LORD will save me.
17 Evening and morning and at noon
   I utter my complaint and moan,
   and he will hear my voice.
18 He will redeem me unharmed
   from the battle that I wage,
   for many are arrayed against me.
19 God, who is enthroned from of old,   *Selah*
   will hear, and will humble them —
because they do not change,
   and do not fear God.

20 My companion laid hands on a friend
   and violated a covenant with me*j*
21 with speech smoother than butter,

j Heb lacks *with me*

55.6 David the warrior here speaks the language of a dove, which flies low, seeks shelter, and wants peace. It is the voice of an escapist who wants to flee from what life has brought, rather than face and overcome it.
55.13 David may have been thinking here of Ahithophel, who was numbered among the conspirators with Absalom. David had esteemed him as a bosom friend, but he has now deserted him and betrayed him.
55.20,21 David's enemy was a smooth talker who pretended friendship, while he was really engaged in mischief. He desired to kiss and kill David, even as Judas Iscariot did with Jesus.

but with a heart set on war;
   with words that were softer than oil,
     but in fact were drawn swords.

22 Cast your burden[k] on the LORD,
    and he will sustain you;
   he will never permit
    the righteous to be moved.

55.22
Ps 37.5;
Mt 6.25;
1 Pet 5.7;
Ps 37.24

23 But you, O God, will cast them down
    into the lowest pit;
   the bloodthirsty and treacherous
    shall not live out half their days.
But I will trust in you.

55.23
Ps 73.18; 5.6;
Job 15.32;
Prov 10.27;
Ps 25.2

Psalm 56

56.1
Ps 57.1, 3

A prayer for deliverance

A. *David's petition for help*

To the leader: according to The Dove on Far-off Terebinths. Of David. A Miktam, when the Philistines seized him in Gath.

1 Be gracious to me, O God, for people trample on me;
   all day long foes oppress me;
2 my enemies trample on me all day long,
   for many fight against me.
   O Most High, 3 when I am afraid,
    I put my trust in you.
4 In God, whose word I praise,
    in God I trust; I am not afraid;
   what can flesh do to me?

56.2
Ps 57.3; 35.1
56.3
Ps 55.4, 5;
11.1
56.4
Ps 118.6;
Heb 13.6

B. *The malice of his enemies*

5 All day long they seek to injure my cause;
   all their thoughts are against me for evil.
6 They stir up strife, they lurk,
   they watch my steps.
   As they hoped to have my life,
7 so repay[l] them for their crime;
   in wrath cast down the peoples, O God!

56.5
Ps 41.7
56.6
Ps 59.3;
140.2; 19.10,
11
56.7
Ps 36.12;
55.23

C. *His trust in God without a fear*

8 You have kept count of my tossings;
   put my tears in your bottle.
   Are they not in your record?
9 Then my enemies will retreat
   in the day when I call.
   This I know, that[m] God is for me.
10 In God, whose word I praise,
   in the LORD, whose word I praise,

56.8
Ps 139.3;
39.12;
Mal 3.16
56.9
Ps 9.3; 102.2;
Rom 8.31

---

k Or *Cast what he has given you*   *l* Cn: Heb *rescue*   *m* Or *because*

55.23 David is fully confident that in his overpowering providence, God will bring David's enemies down to the bottomless pit of destruction.
56.1ff It seems that in almost every instance of suffering and difficulty David composed psalms to reiterate the malice of those attacking him and to recount his dependence on God for deliverance. Here as elsewhere, when God answers his prayer, David expresses his thanks to God.

11 in God I trust; I am not afraid.
What can a mere mortal do to me?

D. *His gratitude for deliverance*

56.12
Ps 50.14

12 My vows to you I must perform, O God;
I will render thank offerings to you.

56.13
Ps 116.8;
Job 33.30

13 For you have delivered my soul from death,
and my feet from falling,
so that I may walk before God
in the light of life.

57.1
Ps 2.12; 17.8;
Isa 26.20

Psalm 57

David's deliverance from Saul

A. *A prayer and a complaint*

To the leader: Do Not Destroy. Of David. A Miktam, when he fled from
Saul, in the cave.

1 Be merciful to me, O God, be merciful to me,
for in you my soul takes refuge;
in the shadow of your wings I will take refuge,
until the destroying storms pass by.

57.2
Ps 138.8

2 I cry to God Most High,
to God who fulfills his purpose for me.

57.3
Ps 18.16;
56.2; 40.11

3 He will send from heaven and save me,
he will put to shame those who trample on me. *Selah*
God will send forth his steadfast love and his faithfulness.

57.4
Ps 35.17;
Prov 30.14;
Ps 55.21

4 I lie down among lions
that greedily devour[n] human prey;
their teeth are spears and arrows,
their tongues sharp swords.

57.5
Ps 108.5

5 Be exalted, O God, above the heavens.
Let your glory be over all the earth.

57.6
Ps 35.7;
145.14; 7.15;
Prov 28.10

6 They set a net for my steps;
my soul was bowed down.
They dug a pit in my path,
but they have fallen into it themselves. *Selah*

B. *Praise and thanksgiving*

57.7
Ps 108.1

7 My heart is steadfast, O God,
my heart is steadfast.
I will sing and make melody.

57.8
Ps 16.9;
30.12; 150.3

8 Awake, my soul!
Awake, O harp and lyre!
I will awake the dawn.

57.9
Ps 108.3

9 I will give thanks to you, O Lord, among the peoples;

[n] Cn: Heb *are aflame for*

57.1ff Like Ps 56, this one reflects deliverance from
trouble or temptation, followed by thanksgiving to
the God of steadfast love.
57.6 Saul was closing in on David and there seemed
to be no escape. A cave was David's only refuge. He
believed that God would let the enemy fall into the pit
they had dug for him—and they did (see 1 Sam

23.7—24.21). *Selah* appears 71 times in psalms and
twice in Habakkuk. Some think it means a lifting of
the voice in singing a benediction, others that it involves the playing of instrumental music in an interlude or postlude. The latter view has support from the
Septuagint.

I will sing praises to you among the nations.
10 For your steadfast love is as high as the heavens;
   your faithfulness extends to the clouds.

11 Be exalted, O God, above the heavens.
   Let your glory be over all the earth.

Psalm 58

The punishment of the wicked

A. Their sins

To the leader: Do Not Destroy. Of David. A Miktam.

1 Do you indeed decree what is right, you gods?*o*
   Do you judge people fairly?
2 No, in your hearts you devise wrongs;
   your hands deal out violence on earth.

3 The wicked go astray from the womb;
   they err from their birth, speaking lies.
4 They have venom like the venom of a serpent,
   like the deaf adder that stops its ear,
5 so that it does not hear the voice of charmers
   or of the cunning enchanter.

B. Their judgment

6 O God, break the teeth in their mouths;
   tear out the fangs of the young lions, O Lord!
7 Let them vanish like water that runs away;
   like grass let them be trodden down*p* and wither.
8 Let them be like the snail that dissolves into slime;
   like the untimely birth that never sees the sun.
9 Sooner than your pots can feel the heat of thorns,
   whether green or ablaze, may he sweep them away!

10 The righteous will rejoice when they see vengeance done;
   they will bathe their feet in the blood of the wicked.
11 People will say, "Surely there is a reward for the righteous;
   surely there is a God who judges on earth."

Psalm 59

David's deliverance from Saul

A. David's prayer for deliverance

To the leader: Do Not Destroy. Of David. A Miktam, when Saul ordered
his house to be watched in order to kill him.

1 Deliver me from my enemies, O my God;
   protect me from those who rise up against me.

o Or *mighty lords*   *p* Cn: Meaning of Heb uncertain

58.1ff Some have conjectured that David penned this psalm at a time preceding the effort of Saul to kill him. Saul had recourse to the law, had David condemned in his absence, and pronounced him a traitor. The elders of Israel, anxious to gain Saul's favor, agreed to do what Saul wanted. David then wrote this psalm. **59.1ff** This psalm, like some of those preceding it, registers David's complaints against those who hate and malign him. He calls upon God to defeat the enemy and ends with praise to his deliverer. This and other similar psalms reveal the intimacy of David's

Cross-refs: 57.10 Ps 36.5; 57.11 v.5; 58.1 Ps 82.2; 58.2 Mal 3.15; Ps 94.20; 58.3 Ps 51.5; Isa 48.8; 58.4 Ps 53.3; Ps 140.3; Eccl 10.11; 58.5 Ps 81.11; 58.6 Job 4.10; Ps 3.7; 58.7 Josh 7.5; Ps 112.10; 64.3; 58.8 Job 3.16; 58.9 Ps 118.12; Prov 10.25; 58.10 Ps 64.10; 91.8; 68.23; 58.11 Ps 18.20; 9.8; 59.1 Ps 143.9

59.2 Ps 28.3; 139.19	2 Deliver me from those who work evil; from the bloodthirsty save me.
59.3 Ps 56.6	3 Even now they lie in wait for my life; the mighty stir up strife against me. For no transgression or sin of mine, O Lord,
59.4 Ps 35.19, 23	4 for no fault of mine, they run and make ready.
	Rouse yourself, come to my help and see!
59.5 Ps 9.5; Jer 18.23	5 You, Lord God of hosts, are God of Israel. Awake to punish all the nations; spare none of those who treacherously plot evil. *Selah*

B. *David's trust in God*

59.6
v. 14
	6 Each evening they come back,
	   howling like dogs
	   and prowling about the city.

59.7
Ps 57.4;
10.11
	7 There they are, bellowing with their mouths,
	   with sharp words*q* on their lips —
	   for "Who," they think,*r* "will hear us?"

59.8 Ps 37.13; 2.4	8 But you laugh at them, O Lord; you hold all the nations in derision.
59.9 Ps 9.9	9 O my strength, I will watch for you; for you, O God, are my fortress.
59.10 Ps 21.3; 54.7	10 My God in his steadfast love will meet me; my God will let me look in triumph on my enemies.

C. *Prayer for defeat of the enemy*

59.11
Deut 4.9;
Ps 106.27;
84.9
	11 Do not kill them, or my people may forget;
	   make them totter by your power, and bring them down,
	   O Lord, our shield.

59.12 Prov 12.13; Zeph 3.11; Ps 10.7	12 For the sin of their mouths, the words of their lips, let them be trapped in their pride. For the cursing and lies that they utter,

59.13
Ps 104.35;
83.18
	13 consume them in wrath;
	   consume them until they are no more.
	 Then it will be known to the ends of the earth
	   that God rules over Jacob. *Selah*

59.14
v. 6
	14 Each evening they come back,
	   howling like dogs
	   and prowling about the city.

	15 They roam about for food, and growl if they do not get their fill.

D. *David's song of praise*

59.16 Ps 21.13; 101.1; 88.13; v. 9; Ps 46.1	16 But I will sing of your might; I will sing aloud of your steadfast love in the morning. For you have been a fortress for me

q Heb *with swords*   *r* Heb lacks *they think*

---

relationship to God. He always brought his problems to God, rather than trusting in himself for deliverance. God was David's first resort, not the one on whom he called in a last extremity. God should always be the first one to whom the believer turns.
59.6,7 The enemy comes howling, prowling, bel-

lowing, and snarling. Such picturesque language befits the situation.
59.16 In the midst of his distress, David sings a song of praise to God each morning, thus fitting himself for the events of that new day.

and a refuge in the day of my distress.
17 O my strength, I will sing praises to you,
        for you, O God, are my fortress,
        the God who shows me steadfast love.

59.17
vv. 9, 10

Psalm 60

60.1
Ps 44.9;
2 Sam 5.20;
Ps 79.5; 80.3

A prayer for national deliverance

A. Israel's distress

To the leader: according to the Lily of the Covenant. A Miktam of David;
    for instruction; when he struggled with Aram-naharaim and with
    Aram-zobah, and when Joab on his return killed twelve thousand
        Edomites in the Valley of Salt.

1   O God, you have rejected us, broken our defenses;
        you have been angry; now restore us!
2   You have caused the land to quake; you have torn it
            open;
        repair the cracks in it, for it is tottering.

60.2
Ps 18.7;
2 Chr 7.14

3   You have made your people suffer hard things;
        you have given us wine to drink that made us reel.

60.03
Ps 71.20;
Isa 51.17, 22

4   You have set up a banner for those who fear you,
        to rally to it out of bowshot.[s]   *Selah*

60.4
Ps 20.5

5   Give victory with your right hand, and answer us,[t]
        so that those whom you love may be rescued.

60.5
Ps 108.6;
127.2; 17.7

B. Claiming God's promise

6   God has promised in his sanctuary:[u]
        "With exultation I will divide up Shechem,
        and portion out the Vale of Succoth.

60.6
Ps 89.35;
Josh 1.6;
Gen 12.6

7   Gilead is mine, and Manasseh is mine;
        Ephraim is my helmet;
        Judah is my scepter.

60.7
Josh 13.31;
Deut 33.17;
Gen 49.10

8   Moab is my washbasin;
        on Edom I hurl my shoe;
        over Philistia I shout in triumph."

60.8
2 Sam 8.1

C. Plea for aid

9   Who will bring me to the fortified city?
        Who will lead me to Edom?
10 Have you not rejected us, O God?
        You do not go out, O God, with our armies.

60.10
v. 1;
Ps 44.9

11 O grant us help against the foe,
        for human help is worthless.

60.11
Ps 146.3

12 With God we shall do valiantly;
        it is he who will tread down our foes.

60.12
Num 24.18;
Ps 44.5

---

[s] Gk Syr Jerome: Heb *because of the truth*   [t] Another reading is *me*   [u] Or *by his holiness*

60.1ff David apparently penned this psalm when he was fighting battles with the Arameans and Edomites, asking for God's help (see 2 Sam 8.13,14). He reflects on God's promise to extend his kingdom far and wide. This is a national, not a personal, psalm.

60.12 However valiantly David and his people fight, the battle is the Lord's, not theirs. Every victory is God's gift, and their trophies shall be laid at God's feet for his glory.

Psalm 61

The prayer of the troubled heart

A. *The prayer of faith*

To the leader: with stringed instruments. Of David.

61.1
Ps 64.1; 86.6

1 Hear my cry, O God;
    listen to my prayer.

61.2
Ps 77.3; 18.2

2 From the end of the earth I call to you,
    when my heart is faint.

    Lead me to the rock
      that is higher than I;

61.3
Ps 62.7;
Prov 18.10

3 for you are my refuge,
    a strong tower against the enemy.

61.4
Ps 23.6; 91.4

4 Let me abide in your tent forever,
    find refuge under the shelter of your wings.   *Selah*

B. *The song of praise*

61.5
Ps 56.12;
86.11

5 For you, O God, have heard my vows;
    you have given me the heritage of those who fear your name.

61.6
Ps 21.4

6 Prolong the life of the king;
    may his years endure to all generations!

61.7
Ps 41.12;
40.11

7 May he be enthroned forever before God;
    appoint steadfast love and faithfulness to watch over him!

61.8
Ps 71.22;
65.1

8 So I will always sing praises to your name,
    as I pay my vows day after day.

Psalm 62

I. *The trial of faith (62.1–4)*

To the leader: according to Jeduthun. A Psalm of David.

62.1
Ps 33.20

1 For God alone my soul waits in silence;
    from him comes my salvation.

62.2
Ps 89.26; v. 6

2 He alone is my rock and my salvation,
    my fortress; I shall never be shaken.

62.3
Isa 30.13

3 How long will you assail a person,
    will you batter your victim, all of you,
    as you would a leaning wall, a tottering fence?

62.4
Ps 4.2; 28.3

4 Their only plan is to bring down a person of prominence.
    They take pleasure in falsehood;
  they bless with their mouths,
    but inwardly they curse.   *Selah*

61.1ff Like many others, this psalm begins with a troubled, crying heart but ends with songs of praise. Probably David had been in flight either from Saul or from Absalom, and this experience brought him closer to God and provided encouragement for singing songs in the night.

62.1ff Though no particular difficulty seems to underlie this psalm, it expresses David's devout faith in God in the midst of his trials. Whatever the circumstances, David always placed his hope and trust in the Lord and his power.

II. *The confidence of faith (62.5–7)*

5   For God alone my soul waits in silence,
     for my hope is from him.

6   He alone is my rock and my salvation,
     my fortress; I shall not be shaken.

7   On God rests my deliverance and my honor;
     my mighty rock, my refuge is in God.

III. *The exhortation to faith (62.8–12)*

8   Trust in him at all times, O people;
     pour out your heart before him;
  God is a refuge for us.   *Selah*

9   Those of low estate are but a breath,
     those of high estate are a delusion;
  in the balances they go up;
     they are together lighter than a breath.

10   Put no confidence in extortion,
     and set no vain hopes on robbery;
  if riches increase, do not set your heart on them.

11   Once God has spoken;
     twice have I heard this:
  that power belongs to God,

12   and steadfast love belongs to you, O Lord.
  For you repay to all
     according to their work.

Psalm 63

The thirsty soul

A. *The soul that thirsts for God*

A Psalm of David, when he was in the Wilderness of Judah.

1   O God, you are my God, I seek you,
     my soul thirsts for you;
  my flesh faints for you,
     as in a dry and weary land where there is no water.

2   So I have looked upon you in the sanctuary,
     beholding your power and glory.

3   Because your steadfast love is better than life,
     my lips will praise you.

4   So I will bless you as long as I live;
     I will lift up my hands and call on your name.

B. *The soul whose thirst is quenched by God*

5   My soul is satisfied as with a rich feast,[v]
     and my mouth praises you with joyful lips

6   when I think of you on my bed,

[v] *Heb* with fat and fatness

Cross references (right margin):

- 62.6   v. 2
- 62.7   Ps 85.9; 46.1
- 62.8   Ps 37.3; 1 Sam 1.15; Ps 42.4; Lam 2.19
- 62.9   Ps 39.5, 11; Isa 40.15, 17; Rom 3.4
- 62.10   Isa 30.12; 61.8; Job 31.25; Ps 52.7; 1 Tim 6.7
- 62.11   Job 33.14; 1 Chr 29.11
- 62.12   Job 34.11; Mt 16.27; Col 3.25
- 63.1   Ps 42.2; 84.2
- 63.2   Ps 27.4
- 63.3   Ps 69.16
- 63.4   Ps 104.33; 28.2
- 63.5   Ps 36.8; 71.23
- 63.6   Ps 42.8

63.1ff Just as Paul wrote some of his finest prose in prison, so David wrote some of his finest psalms while hiding in the wilderness. This psalm is an optimistic paean of praise from a soul that finds its refuge from the heat of the day and the wants of the wilderness under the shadow of God's wings.

63.6 We must not simply think about God; we must *meditate* on him, not occasionally but constantly. David may have been in exile and slept on the ground or in different beds every night. Regardless of where he

and meditate on you in the watches of the night;

63.7
Ps 27.9

7 for you have been my help,
and in the shadow of your wings I sing for joy.

63.8
Ps 18.35

8 My soul clings to you;
your right hand upholds me.

63.9ff
Ps 40.14;
55.15

9 But those who seek to destroy my life
shall go down into the depths of the earth;
10 they shall be given over to the power of the sword,
they shall be prey for jackals.

63.11
Ps 21.1;
Deut 6.13;
Isa 45.23

11 But the king shall rejoice in God;
all who swear by him shall exult,
for the mouths of liars will be stopped.

Psalm 64

A prayer for help against secret enemies

64.1
Ps 55.2;
140.1

A. The appeal for aid: the enemies described

To the leader. A Psalm of David.

1 Hear my voice, O God, in my complaint;
preserve my life from the dread enemy.

64.2
Ps 56.6; 59.2

2 Hide me from the secret plots of the wicked,
from the scheming of evildoers,

64.3
Ps 58.7

3 who whet their tongues like swords,
who aim bitter words like arrows,

64.4
Ps 11.2;
55.19
64.5
Ps 10.11

4 shooting from ambush at the blameless;
they shoot suddenly and without fear.
5 They hold fast to their evil purpose;
they talk of laying snares secretly,
thinking, "Who can see us?*w*

64.6
Ps 49.11

6 Who can search out our crimes?*x*
We have thought out a cunningly conceived plot."
For the human heart and mind are deep.

B. God's judgment of the wicked

7 But God will shoot his arrow at them;
they will be wounded suddenly.

64.8
Ps 9.3;
Prov 18.7;
Ps 22.7
64.9
Jer 50.28

8 Because of their tongue he will bring them to ruin;*y*
all who see them will shake with horror.
9 Then everyone will fear;
they will tell what God has brought about,
and ponder what he has done.

64.10
Ps 32.11;
25.20

10 Let the righteous rejoice in the LORD
and take refuge in him.
Let all the upright in heart glory.

w Syr: Heb *them*   *x* Cn: Heb *They search out crimes*   *y* Cn: Heb *They will bring him to ruin, their tongue being against them*

---

slept, his thoughts are centered on his God, who is with him.
64.1ff David has enemies, persecutors, and slanderers, whose darts penetrate his very soul. What occasioned the psalm is not known, but perhaps it reflects the fulfillment of divine judgment rendered against him for his sin with Bathsheba. The consequences of that transgression followed him all the days of his life.

64.6 *the human heart and mind are deep*, i.e., people spend hours making plans and thinking evil thoughts.
64.10 Again and again David ends the psalms with a note of rejoicing and praise. His undying optimism derives from his knowledge of God's grace, which justifies the worst of humankind through faith and guarantees that their end will be good.

Psalm 65

The power and goodness of God

A. *God's praise required*

To the leader. A Psalm of David. A Song.

1 Praise is due to you,
    O God, in Zion;
and to you shall vows be performed,
2   O you who answer prayer!
To you all flesh shall come.
3 When deeds of iniquity overwhelm us,
    you forgive our transgressions.
4 Happy are those whom you choose and bring near
    to live in your courts.
We shall be satisfied with the goodness of your house,
    your holy temple.

B. *God's power manifested*

5 By awesome deeds you answer us with deliverance,
    O God of our salvation;
you are the hope of all the ends of the earth
    and of the farthest seas.
6 By your*z* strength you established the mountains;
    you are girded with might.
7 You silence the roaring of the seas,
    the roaring of their waves,
    the tumult of the peoples.
8 Those who live at earth's farthest bounds are awed by your
        signs;
you make the gateways of the morning and the evening shout
        for joy.

C. *God's bounty displayed*

9 You visit the earth and water it,
    you greatly enrich it;
the river of God is full of water;
    you provide the people with grain,
    for so you have prepared it.
10 You water its furrows abundantly,
        settling its ridges,
softening it with showers,
    and blessing its growth.
11 You crown the year with your bounty;
    your wagon tracks overflow with richness.
12 The pastures of the wilderness overflow,
    the hills gird themselves with joy,
13 the meadows clothe themselves with flocks,
    the valleys deck themselves with grain,

z Gk Jerome: Heb *his*

65.1
Ps 116.18

65.2
Isa 66.23

65.3
Ps 38.4;
Heb 9.14
65.4
Ps 33.12; 4.3;
36.8

65.5
Ps 66.3; 85.4;
22.27; 107.23

65.6
Ps 93.1

65.7
Mt 8.26;
Isa 17.12

65.9
Ps 68.9, 10;
46.4; 104.14

65.12
Job 38.26,
27;
Ps 98.8
65.13
Ps 144.13;
72.16; 98.8

65.1ff The chief end of mortals is to glorify God. They accomplish this by acknowledging the power and goodness of God, manifested in nature and over all people. The years are so crowned by the divine bounty that meadows and valleys shout and sing together for joy.
65.4 Access to God is a privilege of the saints made possible by the Holy Spirit through the finished work of Christ (Eph 2.18). Believers are to come to God boldly and expect to receive mercy and help. We need no intermediaries to stand between us and God, for we have immediate and direct access to him (Rom 5.1,2).

they shout and sing together for joy.

Psalm 66

A psalm of thanksgivng

A. *For national deliverances*

To the leader. A Song. A Psalm.

66.1
Ps 100.1

1 Make a joyful noise to God, all the earth;
2   sing the glory of his name;
  give to him glorious praise.

66.2
Ps 81.1; 79.9

3 Say to God, "How awesome are your deeds!
  Because of your great power, your enemies cringe before you.

66.3
Ps 65.5;
18.44

4 All the earth worships you;
  they sing praises to you,
  sing praises to your name."   *Selah*

66.4
Ps 22.27;
67.3, 4

5 Come and see what God has done:
  he is awesome in his deeds among mortals.
6 He turned the sea into dry land;
  they passed through the river on foot.
There we rejoiced in him,
7   who rules by his might forever,
whose eyes keep watch on the nations —
  let the rebellious not exalt themselves.   *Selah*

66.5
Ps 46.8;
106.22
66.6
Ex 14.21;
Josh 3.6;
Ps 105.43
66.7
Ps 145.13;
11.4; 140.8

8 Bless our God, O peoples,
  let the sound of his praise be heard,
9 who has kept us among the living,
  and has not let our feet slip.
10 For you, O God, have tested us;
  you have tried us as silver is tried.
11 You brought us into the net;
  you laid burdens on our backs;
12 you let people ride over our heads;
  we went through fire and through water;
yet you have brought us out to a spacious place. *a*

66.8
Ps 98.4
66.9
Ps 121.3
66.10
Ps 17.3;
Isa 48.10;
Zech 13.9;
1 Pet 1.6, 7
66.11
Lam 1.13
66.12
Isa 51.23;
43.2

B. *For personal help*

13 I will come into your house with burnt offerings;
  I will pay you my vows,
14 those that my lips uttered
  and my mouth promised when I was in trouble.
15 I will offer to you burnt offerings of fatlings,
  with the smoke of the sacrifice of rams;
I will make an offering of bulls and goats.   *Selah*

66.13
Eccl 5.4
66.14
Ps 18.6
66.15
Ps 51.19;
Num 6.14

16 Come and hear, all you who fear God,
  and I will tell what he has done for me.
17 I cried aloud to him,
  and he was extolled with my tongue.
18 If I had cherished iniquity in my heart,

66.16
Ps 34.11;
71.15, 24
66.18
Job 36.21;
Isa 1.15;
Jas 4.3

a Cn Compare Gk Syr Jerome Tg: Heb *to a saturation*

66.1ff Thanksgiving is the main theme of this psalm. Let the Israelites thank God for national deliverances. Indeed let all lands and all the earth praise the divine name. Let every individual who knows God and has been helped by him bring praise to his name for what he has provided for them.
66.18 *cherished iniquity in my heart.* Unconfessed sin is one of the reasons believers do not obtain answers

19   the Lord would not have listened.
    But truly God has listened;
      he has given heed to the words of my prayer.

66.19
Ps 116.1, 2

20   Blessed be God,
      because he has not rejected my prayer
      or removed his steadfast love from me.

66.20
Ps 68.35;
22.24

Psalm 67

A missionary psalm

To the leader: with stringed instruments. A Psalm. A Song.

67.1
Num 6.25;
Ps 4.6

1   May God be gracious to us and bless us
      and make his face to shine upon us,   *Selah*
2   that your way may be known upon earth,
      your saving power among all nations.
3   Let the peoples praise you, O God;
      let all the peoples praise you.

67.2
Acts 18.25;
Titus 2.11

4   Let the nations be glad and sing for joy,
      for you judge the peoples with equity
      and guide the nations upon earth.   *Selah*
5   Let the peoples praise you, O God;
      let all the peoples praise you.

67.4
Ps 96.10;
98.9

67.5
v. 3

6   The earth has yielded its increase;
      God, our God, has blessed us.
7   May God continue to bless us;
      let all the ends of the earth revere him.

67.6
Lev 26.4;
Ps 85.12;
Ezek 34.27
67.7
Ps 33.8

Psalm 68

The God of the whole earth

A. *The God of the exodus*

To the leader. Of David. A Psalm. A Song.

68.1
Num 10.35;
Isa 33.3

1   Let God rise up, let his enemies be scattered;
      let those who hate him flee before him.
2   As smoke is driven away, so drive them away;
      as wax melts before the fire,
      let the wicked perish before God.
3   But let the righteous be joyful;
      let them exult before God;
      let them be jubilant with joy.

68.2
Isa 9.18;
Hos 13.3;
Ps 97.5;
Mic 1.4
68.3
Ps 32.11

4   Sing to God, sing praises to his name;
      lift up a song to him who rides upon the clouds[b] —
    his name is the LORD —
      be exultant before him.

68.4
Ps 66.2;
Isa 57.14;
40.3;
Ps 83.18

b Or cast up a highway for him who rides through the deserts

to their petitions.
67.1ff   This psalm witnesses to the missionary nature of biblical faith. God wishes to bless all the nations of the earth and desires that his glorious salvation be proclaimed to all people irrespective of race, color, or nationality.
68.1ff   This psalm seems based on the bringing of the ark from the house of Obed-edom to the city of

Jerusalem (2 Sam 6.12). It reflects on Israel's history, i.e., God's work of delivering his people from Egypt, his support of them in the wilderness, the conquest of Canaan, and the establishment of the kingdom with Jerusalem as its capital (where God is now established in his sanctuary). It ends with praise to the God of the whole earth.

68.5 Ps 146.9; Deut 10.18; 26.15	5 Father of orphans and protector of widows is God in his holy habitation.

68.6
Ps 113.9;
Acts 21.6;
Ps 107.34
	6 God gives the desolate a home to live in;
	    he leads out the prisoners to prosperity,
	    but the rebellious live in a parched land.

B. *The God of the wilderness*

68.7 Ex 13.21; Judg 4.14	7 O God, when you went out before your people, when you marched through the wilderness, *Selah*

68.8
Ex 19.16, 18;
Judg 5.4
	8 the earth quaked, the heavens poured down rain
	    at the presence of God, the God of Sinai,
	    at the presence of God, the God of Israel.

68.9 Deut 11.11	9 Rain in abundance, O God, you showered abroad; you restored your heritage when it languished;
68.10 Deut 26.5; Ps 74.19	10 your flock found a dwelling in it; in your goodness, O God, you provided for the needy.

C. *The God of Canaan conquest*

	11 The Lord gives the command; great is the company of those[c] who bore the tidings:
68.12 Ps 135.11; 1 Sam 30.24	12 "The kings of the armies, they flee, they flee!" The women at home divide the spoil,

68.13
Gen 49.14
	13 though they stay among the sheepfolds—
	    the wings of a dove covered with silver,
	    its pinions with green gold.

68.14 Josh 10.10	14 When the Almighty[d] scattered kings there, snow fell on Zalmon.

D. *The God of Zion*

	15 O mighty mountain, mountain of Bashan; O many-peaked mountain, mountain of Bashan!

68.16
Deut 12.5;
Ps 87.1, 2
	16 Why do you look with envy, O many-peaked mountain,
	    at the mount that God desired for his abode,
	    where the Lord will reside forever?

68.17
Deut 33.2;
Dan 7.10
	17 With mighty chariotry, twice ten thousand,
	    thousands upon thousands,
	    the Lord came from Sinai into the holy place.[e]

68.18
Acts 1.9;
Eph 4.8;
Judg 5.12;
1 Tim 1.13
	18 You ascended the high mount,
	    leading captives in your train
	    and receiving gifts from people,
	    even from those who rebel against the Lord God's abiding
	        there.

E. *The God of salvation*

68.19
Ps 55.22;
65.5
	19 Blessed be the Lord,
	    who daily bears us up;
	    God is our salvation. *Selah*

c Or *company of the women*   d Traditional rendering of Heb *Shaddai*   e Cn: Heb *The Lord among them Sinai in the holy* (place)

68.8 No people and no nation has seen the presence of the glory of God or heard the divine voice as did Israel. The earth itself shook and the mountains moved. The commandments of God dropped like rain from heaven. This glorious God was Israel's God. **68.12** *women . . . divide the spoil.* The victorious army brought back the spoils of battle which were then shared by the wives of the soldiers. **68.14** *Zalmon* is a mountain near Shechem, where God may have used a snowstorm to rout Israel's enemies (Judg 9.48). **68.18** *receiving gifts from people.* See Eph 4.8.

20 Our God is a God of salvation,
      and to GOD, the Lord, belongs escape from death.

68.20
Ps 49.15;
56.13

21 But God will shatter the heads of his enemies,
      the hairy crown of those who walk in their guilty ways.

68.21
Ps 110.6;
55.23

22 The Lord said,
      "I will bring them back from Bashan,
I will bring them back from the depths of the sea,

68.22
Num 21.33;
Ex 14.22

23 so that you may bathe*f* your feet in blood,
      so that the tongues of your dogs may have their share from
         the foe."

68.23
Ps 58.10;
1 Kings 21.19

F. The God of the sanctuary

1. The temple procession

24 Your solemn processions are seen,*g* O God,
      the processions of my God, my King, into the sanctuary—

68.24
Ps 77.13;
63.2

25 the singers in front, the musicians last,
      between them girls playing tambourines:

68.25
1 Chr 13.8;
Judg 11.34

26 "Bless God in the great congregation,
      the LORD, O you who are of Israel's fountain!"

68.26
Ps 26.12;
Deut 33.28;
Isa 48.1

27 There is Benjamin, the least of them, in the lead,
      the princes of Judah in a body,
      the princes of Zebulun, the princes of Naphtali.

68.27
1 Sam 9.21

2. The nations acknowledge him

28 Summon your might, O God;
      show your strength, O God, as you have done for us before.

29 Because of your temple at Jerusalem
      kings bear gifts to you.

68.29
Ps 72.10

30 Rebuke the wild animals that live among the reeds,
      the herd of bulls with the calves of the peoples.
      Trample*h* under foot those who lust after tribute;
      scatter the peoples who delight in war.*i*

68.30
Ps 22.12;
89.10

31 Let bronze be brought from Egypt;
      let Ethiopia*j* hasten to stretch out its hands to God.

68.31
Isa 19.19;
45.14

3. Praise to the God of the whole earth

32 Sing to God, O kingdoms of the earth;
      sing praises to the Lord,   *Selah*

33 O rider in the heavens, the ancient heavens;
      listen, he sends out his voice, his mighty voice.

68.33
Ps 18.10;
Deut 10.14;
Ps 44.6; 29.4

34 Ascribe power to God,
      whose majesty is over Israel;
      and whose power is in the skies.

68.34
Ps 29.1

35 Awesome is God in his*k* sanctuary,
      the God of Israel;
      he gives power and strength to his people.

      Blessed be God!

68.35
Ps 47.2;
29.11; 66.20

f Gk Syr Tg: Heb *shatter*   *g* Or *have been seen*   *h* Cn: Heb *Trampling*   *i* Meaning of Heb of verse 30 is uncertain   *j* Or *Nubia*; Heb *Cush*   *k* Gk: Heb *from your*

68.20 If, after the fall of Adam, God had absented himself from earth, there would have been no salvation. Only the presence of God makes eternal salvation possible. In him death too has been conquered, by the power of the resurrection (see 1 Cor 15.20–28).

68.24 Whatever the place of worship, it becomes a sanctuary for God Almighty. When we come to worship our God, we should enter its gates prayerfully and solemnly (see also Hab 2.20).

Psalm 69

A plea for deliverance: A Messianic psalm

A. *The prayer and problem of the psalmist*

To the leader: according to Lilies. Of David.

69.1
vv. 14, 15

1 Save me, O God,
    for the waters have come up to my neck.

69.2
Ps 40.2;
Jon 2.3

2 I sink in deep mire,
    where there is no foothold;
I have come into deep waters,
    and the flood sweeps over me.

69.3
Ps 6.6;
119.82;
Isa 38.14

3 I am weary with my crying;
    my throat is parched.
My eyes grow dim
    with waiting for my God.

69.4
Ps 35.19;
Jn 15.25;
Ps 38.19;
35.11

4 More in number than the hairs of my head
    are those who hate me without cause;
many are those who would destroy me,
    my enemies who accuse me falsely.
What I did not steal
    must I now restore?

69.5
Ps 38.5;
44.21

5 O God, you know my folly;
    the wrongs I have done are not hidden from you.

69.6
2 Sam 12.14

6 Do not let those who hope in you be put to shame because of
        me,
    O Lord GOD of hosts;
do not let those who seek you be dishonored because of me,
    O God of Israel.

69.7
Jer 15.15;
Ps 44.15
69.8
Ps 31.11;
Isa 53.3

7 It is for your sake that I have borne reproach,
    that shame has covered my face.
8 I have become a stranger to my kindred,
    an alien to my mother's children.

69.9
Jn 2.17;
Ps 89.50
69.10
Ps 35.13

9 It is zeal for your house that has consumed me;
    the insults of those who insult you have fallen on me.
10 When I humbled my soul with fasting,[l]
    they insulted me for doing so.

69.11
Ps 35.13;
Jer 24.9
69.12
Job 30.9

11 When I made sackcloth my clothing,
    I became a byword to them.
12 I am the subject of gossip for those who sit in the gate,
    and the drunkards make songs about me.

B. *The prayer for deliverance renewed*

69.13
Isa 49.8;
2 Cor 6.2;
Ps 51.1

13 But as for me, my prayer is to you, O LORD.
    At an acceptable time, O God,
    in the abundance of your steadfast love, answer me.

69.14
v. 2;
Ps 144.7

With your faithful help 14 rescue me
    from sinking in the mire;

---

l Gk Syr: Heb *I wept, with fasting my soul,* or *I made my soul mourn with fasting*

69.1ff The first application of this psalm has to do with some experience in the life of David. But it also has messianic reference to Jesus, for Mt 27.34,48 constitutes a literal fulfillment of v. 21. The entire psalm does not refer to Jesus, however, for David confesses his sins (v. 5).

let me be delivered from my enemies
   and from the deep waters.
15 Do not let the flood sweep over me,
   or the deep swallow me up,
   or the Pit close its mouth over me.

69.15
Ps 124.4, 5;
Num 16.33

16 Answer me, O LORD, for your steadfast love is good;
   according to your abundant mercy, turn to me.
17 Do not hide your face from your servant,
   for I am in distress — make haste to answer me.
18 Draw near to me, redeem me,
   set me free because of my enemies.

69.16
Ps 63.3; 51.1;
25.16
69.17
Ps 27.9;
66.14
69.18
Ps 49.15

19 You know the insults I receive,
   and my shame and dishonor;
   my foes are all known to you.
20 Insults have broken my heart,
   so that I am in despair.
I looked for pity, but there was none;
   and for comforters, but I found none.
21 They gave me poison for food,
   and for my thirst they gave me vinegar to drink.

69.19
Ps 22.6, 7;
Isa 53.3
69.20
Jer 23.9;
Isa 63.5;
Job 16.2
69.21
Mt 27.34;
Jn 19.29

C. *Imprecation on his enemies*

22 Let their table be a trap for them,
   a snare for their allies.
23 Let their eyes be darkened so that they cannot see,
   and make their loins tremble continually.
24 Pour out your indignation upon them,
   and let your burning anger overtake them.
25 May their camp be a desolation;
   let no one live in their tents.
26 For they persecute those whom you have struck down,
   and those whom you have wounded, they attack still more. *m*
27 Add guilt to their guilt;
   may they have no acquittal from you.
28 Let them be blotted out of the book of the living;
   let them not be enrolled among the righteous.
29 But I am lowly and in pain;
   let your salvation, O God, protect me.

69.22
Rom 11.9, 10
69.23
Isa 6.9, 10;
Dan 5.6
69.24
Ps 79.6
69.25
Mt 23.38;
Acts 1.20
69.26
Isa 53.4
69.28
Ex 32.32;
Phil 4.3;
Lk 10.20
69.29
Ps 70.5; 59.1

D. *Concluding song of praise and assurance*

30 I will praise the name of God with a song;
   I will magnify him with thanksgiving.
31 This will please the LORD more than an ox
   or a bull with horns and hoofs.
32 Let the oppressed see it and be glad;
   you who seek God, let your hearts revive.
33 For the LORD hears the needy,
   and does not despise his own that are in bonds.

69.30
Ps 28.7; 34.3;
50.14
69.31
Ps 50.13, 14
69.32
Ps 34.2;
22.26
69.33
Ps 12.9; 68.6

m Gk Syr: Heb *recount the pain of*

69.22–28 Though these verses are imprecatory, they are perhaps best seen not as a prayer of David for a curse on the enemies, but as prophetic of the destruction of the persecutors of Jesus (for this is a messianic psalm). Its larger reference has to do with the Jewish nation, which rejected the Messiah. The imprecations here were fulfilled when Jerusalem was destroyed in A.D. 70 by the forces of Rome under Titus and Vespasian.

69.34
Ps 96.11;
148.1;
Isa 44.23;
49.13

34 Let heaven and earth praise him,
    the seas and everything that moves in them.

69.35
Ps 51.18;
Isa 44.26

35 For God will save Zion
    and rebuild the cities of Judah;
    and his servants shall live[n] there and possess it;

69.36
Ps 102.28;
37.29

36 the children of his servants shall inherit it,
    and those who love his name shall live in it.

Psalm 70

70.1
Ps 40.13

Appeal for deliverance from persecutors

To the leader. Of David, for the memorial offering.

1 Be pleased, O God, to deliver me.
    O Lord, make haste to help me!

70.2
Ps 35.4, 26

2 Let those be put to shame and confusion
    who seek my life.
  Let those be turned back and brought to dishonor
    who desire to hurt me.

70.3
Ps 40.15

3 Let those who say, "Aha, Aha!"
    turn back because of their shame.

4 Let all who seek you
    rejoice and be glad in you.
  Let those who love your salvation
    say evermore, "God is great!"

70.5
Ps 40.17;
141.1

5 But I am poor and needy;
    hasten to me, O God!
  You are my help and my deliverer;
    O Lord, do not delay!

Psalm 71

71.1
Ps 25.2, 3

The prayer of an aged person for deliverance

A. The plea for help

1 In you, O Lord, I take refuge;
    let me never be put to shame.

71.2
Ps 31.1; 17.6

2 In your righteousness deliver me and rescue me;
    incline your ear to me and save me.

71.3
Ps 31.2, 3;
44.4

3 Be to me a rock of refuge,
    a strong fortress,[o] to save me,
  for you are my rock and my fortress.

71.4
Ps 140.1, 4

4 Rescue me, O my God, from the hand of the wicked,
    from the grasp of the unjust and cruel.

71.5
Jer 17.7

5 For you, O Lord, are my hope,
    my trust, O Lord, from my youth.

71.6
Ps 22.9, 10;
Isa 46.3;
Ps 34.1

6 Upon you I have leaned from my birth;
    it was you who took me from my mother's womb.
  My praise is continually of you.

n Syr: Heb *and they shall live* o Gk Compare 31.3: Heb *to come continually you have commanded*

70.1ff The language of this psalm has many links with Ps 40.13–17 and Ps 71. **71.1ff** This psalm was written toward the end of the author's life (possibly David). Afflictions attend later life as well as youth, and elderly people need the help of God the deliverer. It ends, as so many psalms do, with the assurance that God has helped in bygone days and is to be praised for past and present mercies.

7   I have been like a portent to many,
         but you are my strong refuge.   **71.7**
                                                                     1 Cor 4.9;
                                                                     Ps 61.3
8   My mouth is filled with your praise,   **71.8**
         and with your glory all day long.   Ps 35.28
9   Do not cast me off in the time of old age;   **71.9**
         do not forsake me when my strength is spent.   v. 18
10   For my enemies speak concerning me,   **71.10**
         and those who watch for my life consult together.   Ps 56.6;
                                                                     Mt 27.1
11   They say, "Pursue and seize that person   **71.11**
         whom God has forsaken,   Ps 3.2; 7.2
         for there is no one to deliver."

12   O God, do not be far from me;   **71.12**
         O my God, make haste to help me!   Ps 35.22;
                                                                     70.1
13   Let my accusers be put to shame and consumed;   **71.13**
         let those who seek to hurt me   Ps 35.4;
         be covered with scorn and disgrace.   109.29; v. 24
14   But I will hope continually,
         and will praise you yet more and more.
15   My mouth will tell of your righteous acts,   **71.15**
         of your deeds of salvation all day long,   Ps 35.28;
                                                                     40.5
         though their number is past my knowledge.
16   I will come praising the mighty deeds of the Lord God,   **71.16**
         I will praise your righteousness, yours alone.   Ps 106.2;
                                                                     51.14

17   O God, from my youth you have taught me,   **71.17**
         and I still proclaim your wondrous deeds.   Deut 4.5;
                                                                     6.7;
18   So even to old age and gray hairs,   Ps 26.7
         O God, do not forsake me,   **71.18**
     until I proclaim your might   v. 9
         to all the generations to come.[p]
     Your power [19] and your righteousness, O God,   **71.19**
         reach the high heavens.   Ps 57.10;
                                                                     35.10

     B. *Song of assurance and praise for deliverance*

     You who have done great things,
         O God, who is like you?
20   You who have made me see many troubles and calamities   **71.20**
         will revive me again;   Ps 60.3;
                                                                     Hos 6.1, 2
     from the depths of the earth
         you will bring me up again.
21   You will increase my honor,
         and comfort me once again.

22   I will also praise you with the harp   **71.22**
         for your faithfulness, O my God;   Ps 33.2;
                                                                     78.41
     I will sing praises to you with the lyre,
         O Holy One of Israel.
23   My lips will shout for joy   **71.23**
         when I sing praises to you;   Ps 5.11;
                                                                     103.4

p Gk Compare Syr: Heb *to a generation, to all that come*

71.9 Those whom God has taken from their
mother's womb (v. 6) need not fear that God will
desert them when age overtakes them and death
awaits them. Body, mind, sight, voice, and limbs
begin to fail but the God of the aged is near to help.
71.17 Those who from their youth have known and
served God still live to praise God and testify to his

saving grace. All such persons can be assured that
their prayers for the presence, power, and grace of
God will be answered. He will not leave nor forsake
them.
71.19 At the hour of death, before the saints breathe
their last, their parting words will be, "You . . . have
done great things, O God."

71.24
Ps 35.28;
v. 13

my soul also, which you have rescued.
24 All day long my tongue will talk of your righteous help,
for those who tried to do me harm
have been put to shame, and disgraced.

72.1
Ps 24.5

Psalm 72

A prayer for the king

A. *For justice*

Of Solomon.

1 Give the king your justice, O God,
and your righteousness to a king's son.

72.2
Isa 9.7;
Ps 82.3

2 May he judge your people with righteousness,
and your poor with justice.

72.3
Ps 85.10;
Isa 32.17

3 May the mountains yield prosperity for the people,
and the hills, in righteousness.

72.4
Isa 11.4

4 May he defend the cause of the poor of the people,
give deliverance to the needy,
and crush the oppressor.

B. *For length of days*

72.5
Ps 89.36

5 May he live*q* while the sun endures,
and as long as the moon, throughout all generations.

72.6
2 Sam 23.4;
Hos 6.3

6 May he be like rain that falls on the mown grass,
like showers that water the earth.

72.7
Ps 92.12

7 In his days may righteousness flourish
and peace abound, until the moon is no more.

C. *For dominion*

72.8
Ex 23.31;
Zech 9.10

8 May he have dominion from sea to sea,
and from the River to the ends of the earth.

72.9
Ps 74.14;
Isa 49.23;
Mic 7.17

9 May his foes*r* bow down before him,
and his enemies lick the dust.

72.10
2 Chr 9.21;
Ps 68.29

10 May the kings of Tarshish and of the isles
render him tribute,
may the kings of Sheba and Seba
bring gifts.

72.11
Ps 49.23

11 May all kings fall down before him,
all nations give him service.

D. *For compassion*

72.12
Job 29.12

12 For he delivers the needy when they call,
the poor and those who have no helper.

13 He has pity on the weak and the needy,
and saves the lives of the needy.

72.14
Ps 116.15

14 From oppression and violence he redeems their life;
and precious is their blood in his sight.

q Gk: Heb may they fear you   r Cn: Heb those who live in the wilderness

---

72.1ff This psalm, written with reference to Solomon and his immediate sons, is a messianic psalm that finds its ultimate fulfillment in Jesus the Messiah and in his kingdom, for many statements go far beyond any human possibility. Only the Messiah's kingdom is an eternal kingdom that extends to "the ends of the earth" (v. 8); "all nations [are to] give him service" (v. 11); "his name [shall] endure forever" (v. 17). Further-more, the psalm suggests that the King himself is eternal, all powerful, and knows all things.
72.8 We should pray that Christ will have dominion from sea to sea. In principle, this is already true, for Christ does reign at God's right hand (cf. Eph 1.20–21). At the same time, there is a future element to his kingdom. This is what we pray for when we say, "Your kingdom come" (Mt 6.10).

E. *For an enduring name*

15 Long may he live!
    May gold of Sheba be given to him.
May prayer be made for him continually,
    and blessings invoked for him all day long.
16 May there be abundance of grain in the land;
    may it wave on the tops of the mountains;
    may its fruit be like Lebanon;
and may people blossom in the cities
    like the grass of the field.
17 May his name endure forever,
    his fame continue as long as the sun.
May all nations be blessed in him;[s]
    may they pronounce him happy.

72.15
Isa 60.6

72.16
Ps 104.16;
Job 5.25

72.17
Ps 89.36;
Gen 12.3;
22.18;
Lk 1.48

F. *Benediction*

18 Blessed be the LORD, the God of Israel,
    who alone does wondrous things.
19 Blessed be his glorious name forever;
    may his glory fill the whole earth.
            Amen and Amen.

20 The prayers of David son of Jesse are ended.

72.18
Ps 41.13;
106.48; 77.14
72.19
Neh 9.5;
Zech 14.9

BOOK III

(Psalms 73–89)

Psalm 73

The end of the prosperous wicked

A. *The temptation to envy the wicked*

A Psalm of Asaph.

1 Truly God is good to the upright,[t]
    to those who are pure in heart.
2 But as for me, my feet had almost stumbled;
    my steps had nearly slipped.
3 For I was envious of the arrogant;
    I saw the prosperity of the wicked.

73.1
Ps 86.5;
51.10

73.2
Ps 94.18

73.3
Ps 37.1;
Jer 12.1

B. *The prosperity of the wicked*

4 For they have no pain;
    their bodies are sound and sleek.
5 They are not in trouble as others are;
    they are not plagued like other people.
6 Therefore pride is their necklace;

73.5
Job 21.9

73.6
Ps 109.18

---

s Or *bless themselves by him*   *t* Or *good to Israel*

72.18 The O.T. does not present us with a complete doctrine of the Trinity. But we can safely assert that when we say "Blessed be the LORD," we are praising the one God in three persons — the Father, the Son, and the Holy Spirit. Thus Christian churches sing the "Doxology" and the "Gloria Patri," both of which glorify the triune God.
73.1ff Ps 73–83 carry the name of Asaph in the titles. Asaph was appointed by David over the service of song (1 Chr 16.4–6) and by Solomon in the temple service (2 Chr 5.12). Whether these psalms are *by* Asaph or *for* Asaph we do not know. Ps 73 speaks of the conflict within the psalmist as he faced the temptation to envy the prosperity of the wicked. It ends with a note of assurance that God delivers the righteous and allows those whose hearts are far from him to perish.

violence covers them like a garment.

7 Their eyes swell out with fatness;
their hearts overflow with follies.

8 They scoff and speak with malice;
loftily they threaten oppression.

9 They set their mouths against heaven,
and their tongues range over the earth.

C. *The lament of the righteous*

10 Therefore the people turn and praise them,[u]
and find no fault in them.[v]

11 And they say, "How can God know?
Is there knowledge in the Most High?"

12 Such are the wicked;
always at ease, they increase in riches.

13 All in vain I have kept my heart clean
and washed my hands in innocence.

14 For all day long I have been plagued,
and am punished every morning.

D. *The solution to the dilemma*

15 If I had said, "I will talk on in this way,"
I would have been untrue to the circle of your children.

16 But when I thought how to understand this,
it seemed to me a wearisome task,

17 until I went into the sanctuary of God;
then I perceived their end.

18 Truly you set them in slippery places;
you make them fall to ruin.

19 How they are destroyed in a moment,
swept away utterly by terrors!

20 They are[w] like a dream when one awakes;
on awaking you despise their phantoms.

E. *The assurance that God delivers the righteous*

21 When my soul was embittered,
when I was pricked in heart,

22 I was stupid and ignorant;
I was like a brute beast toward you.

23 Nevertheless I am continually with you;
you hold my right hand.

24 You guide me with your counsel,
and afterward you will receive me with honor.[x]

25 Whom have I in heaven but you?
And there is nothing on earth that I desire other than you.

26 My flesh and my heart may fail,
but God is the strength[y] of my heart and my portion
forever.

27 Indeed, those who are far from you will perish;
you put an end to those who are false to you.

Cross-references:
73.7 Job 15.27; Ps 17.10
73.8 Ps 53.1; Jude 16
73.11 Job 22.13
73.12 Ps 49.6; Jer 49.31
73.13 Job 21.15; 34.9; 36.3; Ps 26.6
73.14 Ps 38.6; 118.18
73.16 Eccl 8.17
73.17 Ps 77.13; 37.38
73.18 Ps 35.6, 8
73.19 Num 16.21; Job 18.11
73.20 Job 20.8; Ps 78.65; 1 Sam 2.30
73.22 Ps 49.10; Job 18.3
73.24 Ps 32.8; 48.14
73.25 Phil 3.8
73.26 Ps 84.2; 16.5
73.27 Ps 37.20; 119.155

u Cn: Heb *his people return here*   v Cn: Heb *abundant waters are drained by them*   w Cn: Heb *Lord*
x Or *to glory*   y Heb *rock*

73.17 The psalmist cannot understand how to reconcile the prosperity of the wicked with the justice of God. It seems to stand in direct conflict with all that he believes about God. But when he went into God's sanctuary for meditation, instruction, the reading of the word of God, and prayer, the final end of the wicked became apparent and his soul was quieted.

28 But for me it is good to be near God;
      I have made the Lord God my refuge,
      to tell of all your works.

73.28
Heb 10.22;
Ps 71.7; 40.5

Psalm 74

74.1
Ps 44.9, 23;
Deut 29.20;
Ps 95.7

Complaint over a devastated land

A. Appeal for help against the enemy

A Maskil of Asaph.

1 O God, why do you cast us off forever?
      Why does your anger smoke against the sheep of your
          pasture?
2 Remember your congregation, which you acquired long ago,
      which you redeemed to be the tribe of your heritage.
      Remember Mount Zion, where you came to dwell.

74.2
Deut 34.6;
Ps 77.15;
68.16

3 Direct your steps to the perpetual ruins;
      the enemy has destroyed everything in the sanctuary.

74.3
Isa 61.4;
Ps 79.1

4 Your foes have roared within your holy place;
      they set up their emblems there.

74.4
Lam 2.7;
Num 2.2

5 At the upper entrance they hacked
      the wooden trellis with axes. [z]

74.5
Jer 46.22

6 And then, with hatchets and hammers,
      they smashed all its carved work.
7 They set your sanctuary on fire;
      they desecrated the dwelling place of your name,
      bringing it to the ground.

74.7
2 Kings 25.9

8 They said to themselves, "We will utterly subdue them";
      they burned all the meeting places of God in the land.

74.8
Ps 83.4

9 We do not see our emblems;
      there is no longer any prophet,
      and there is no one among us who knows how long.

74.9
Ps 78.43;
1 Sam 3.1;
Ps 79.5

10 How long, O God, is the foe to scoff?
      Is the enemy to revile your name forever?

74.10
Ps 44.16;
Lev 24.16

11 Why do you hold back your hand;
      why do you keep your hand in [a] your bosom?

74.11
Lam 2.3;
Ps 59.13

B. Assurance of a sovereign God's power

12 Yet God my King is from of old,
      working salvation in the earth.

74.12
Ps 44.4

13 You divided the sea by your might;
      you broke the heads of the dragons in the waters.

74.13
Ex 14.21;
Isa 51.9

14 You crushed the heads of Leviathan;
      you gave him as food [b] for the creatures of the wilderness.
15 You cut openings for springs and torrents;

74.15
Ex 17.5, 6;
Num 20.11;
Josh 3.13

[z] Cn Compare Gk Syr: Meaning of Heb uncertain   [a] Cn: Heb *do you consume your right hand from*
[b] Heb *food for the people*

73.28 Those who draw near to God will find that God draws near to them, but this is true because God is the divine initiator who makes it possible for us to draw near to him.

74.1ff Of the twelve psalms bearing the superscription *Asaph* (50; 73 – 83; see note on 73.1ff), this psalm and Ps 79, which describe the destruction of Jerusalem by Nebuchadnezzar, present the greatest difficulty for having been written during David's life.

Either they constitute predictive prophecy — in which event they would have been written by the same Asaph who lived in David's day — or they were written by another Asaph living at a much later time.

74.14 *You crushed the heads of Leviathan,* i.e., you crushed the sea-god's heads. *Leviathan,* or the sea-monster, is used as a symbol of evil throughout the Bible.

you dried up ever-flowing streams.

74.16
Ps 104.19

16 Yours is the day, yours also the night;
  you established the luminaries[c] and the sun.

74.17
Gen 8.22

17 You have fixed all the bounds of the earth;
  you made summer and winter.

C. *Final appeal for help*

74.18
v. 10;
Ps 39.8

18 Remember this, O LORD, how the enemy scoffs,
  and an impious people reviles your name.

74.19
Song 2.14;
Ps 9.18

19 Do not deliver the soul of your dove to the wild animals;
  do not forget the life of your poor forever.

74.20
Gen 17.7;
Ps 106.45;
88.6

20 Have regard for your[d] covenant,
  for the dark places of the land are full of the haunts of
    violence.

74.21
Ps 103.6;
35.10

21 Do not let the downtrodden be put to shame;
  let the poor and needy praise your name.

74.22
Ps 43.1; v. 18

22 Rise up, O God, plead your cause;
  remember how the impious scoff at you all day long.

74.23
v. 10;
Ps 65.7

23 Do not forget the clamor of your foes,
  the uproar of your adversaries that goes up continually.

Psalm 75

75.1
Ps 79.13;
145.18; 44.1

The justice of God

A. *Invocation*

To the leader: Do Not Destroy. A Psalm of Asaph. A Song.

1 We give thanks to you, O God;
  we give thanks; your name is near.
People tell of your wondrous deeds.

B. *Assurance of judgment*

2 At the set time that I appoint
  I will judge with equity.

75.3
Ps 46.6;
1 Sam 2.8

3 When the earth totters, with all its inhabitants,
  it is I who keep its pillars steady.   *Selah*

75.4
Zech 1.21

4 I say to the boastful, "Do not boast,"
  and to the wicked, "Do not lift up your horn;

75.5
Ps 94.4

5 do not lift up your horn on high,
  or speak with insolent neck."

C. *God is the judge*

75.6
Ps 3.3
75.7
Ps 50.6;
1 Sam 2.7;
Dan 2.21

6 For not from the east or from the west
  and not from the wilderness comes lifting up;

75.8
Job 21.20;
Ps 60.3;
Jer 26.15;
Prov 23.30;
Ps 73.10

7 but it is God who executes judgment,
  putting down one and lifting up another.

8 For in the hand of the LORD there is a cup

c Or *moon*; Heb *light*   *d* Gk Syr: Heb *the*

74.20 The psalmist begs God to have respect for the covenant he had made with Israel. He knew how the covenant was conditional: disobedience would bring dispersion; obedience would bring the eventual fulfillment of all God's promises. There were indeed many Jews who had broken faith with the covenant, but there were others, however small a minority, who had not broken the covenant and still loved God with their whole hearts. It is on their behalf that Asaph speaks.

75.1ff This psalm probably refers to the time when David, after the death of Saul, came into his kingship. Either David wrote it himself and had it delivered to Asaph his song leader, or it was crafted by Asaph, using the substance of a speech made by David.

with foaming wine, well mixed;
he will pour a draught from it,
   and all the wicked of the earth
   shall drain it down to the dregs.

D. *Praise to him*

9 But I will rejoice[e] forever;
    I will sing praises to the God of Jacob.

                                                 75.9
                                               Ps 40.10

10 All the horns of the wicked I will cut off,
    but the horns of the righteous shall be exalted.

                                               75.10
                                             Ps 89.17;
                                             148.14

Psalm 76

The victorious power of God

To the leader: with stringed instruments. A Psalm of Asaph. A Song.

                                             76.1
                                             Ps 48.3

1 In Judah God is known,
    his name is great in Israel.
2 His abode has been established in Salem,
    his dwelling place in Zion.
3 There he broke the flashing arrows,
    the shield, the sword, and the weapons of war.   *Selah*

             76.2 Ps 27.5; 9.11
             76.3 Ps 46.9

4 Glorious are you, more majestic
    than the everlasting mountains.[f]
5 The stouthearted were stripped of their spoil;
    they sank into sleep;
  none of the troops
    was able to lift a hand.
6 At your rebuke, O God of Jacob,
    both rider and horse lay stunned.

             76.5 Isa 46.12;
             Ps 13.3
             76.6 Ex 15.1, 21;
             Ps 78.53

7 But you indeed are awesome!
    Who can stand before you
    when once your anger is roused?
8 From the heavens you uttered judgment;
    the earth feared and was still
9 when God rose up to establish judgment,
    to save all the oppressed of the earth.   *Selah*

             76.7 Ps 96.4;
             Nah 1.6
             76.8 Ezek 38.20;
             2 Chr 20.29,
             30
             76.9 Ps 9.7-9; 72.4

10 Human wrath serves only to praise you,
    when you bind the last bit of your[g] wrath around you.
11 Make vows to the LORD your God, and perform them;
    let all who are around him bring gifts
    to the one who is awesome,
12 who cuts off the spirit of princes,
    who inspires fear in the kings of the earth.

             76.10 Ex 9.16;
             Rom 9.17
             76.11 Ps 50.14;
             68.29
             76.12 Ps 68.35

---

e Gk: Heb *declare* *f* Gk: Heb *the mountains of prey* *g* Heb lacks *your*

76.1ff This song features a great victory experienced by Israel (though we do not know which one). It celebrates the mighty power of God before whom no enemy of his people will be victorious.
76.11 The psalmist calls all Israelites to submit themselves to God and to become his loyal subjects. They must vow to be his and pay what they vowed. When this happens, the people of God will be fully cared for by God.

Psalm 77

Comfort in the memory of God's mighty deeds

A. The call for help

To the leader: according to Jeduthun. Of Asaph. A Psalm.

1 I cry aloud to God,
  aloud to God, that he may hear me.
2 In the day of my trouble I seek the Lord;
  in the night my hand is stretched out without wearying;
  my soul refuses to be comforted.
3 I think of God, and I moan;
  I meditate, and my spirit faints.   *Selah*

4 You keep my eyelids from closing;
  I am so troubled that I cannot speak.
5 I consider the days of old,
  and remember the years of long ago.
6 I commune[h] with my heart in the night;
  I meditate and search my spirit:[i]
7 "Will the Lord spurn forever,
  and never again be favorable?
8 Has his steadfast love ceased forever?
  Are his promises at an end for all time?
9 Has God forgotten to be gracious?
  Has he in anger shut up his compassion?"   *Selah*
10 And I say, "It is my grief
  that the right hand of the Most High has changed."

B. God's former wonders

11 I will call to mind the deeds of the LORD;
  I will remember your wonders of old.
12 I will meditate on all your work,
  and muse on your mighty deeds.
13 Your way, O God, is holy.
  What god is so great as our God?
14 You are the God who works wonders;
  you have displayed your might among the peoples.
15 With your strong arm you redeemed your people,
  the descendants of Jacob and Joseph.   *Selah*

16 When the waters saw you, O God,
  when the waters saw you, they were afraid;
  the very deep trembled.
17 The clouds poured out water;
  the skies thundered;
  your arrows flashed on every side.
18 The crash of your thunder was in the whirlwind;
  your lightnings lit up the world;
  the earth trembled and shook.

---

h Gk Syr: Heb *My music*   i Syr Jerome: Heb *my spirit searches*

77.1ff This psalm contains no hint as to the occasion for the cry for help. Believers of all ages who suffer severe testings should turn to God for solace and help. They should recall God's past mercies in the firm conviction that he who delivered Israel in its many difficulties is the same God who will help his people today when they call upon him. This is an intensely personal psalm. The word "I" is prominent: I cry; I moan; I commune; I meditate. Conversation with God has room for personal dialogue and the use of personal pronouns.

Cross references (margin):

77.1 — Ps 3.4
77.2 — Ps 50.15; Isa 26.9, 16
77.3 — Ps 142.3; 143.4
77.5 — Deut 32.7; Ps 143.5; Isa 51.9
77.6 — Ps 42.8; 4.4
77.7 — Ps 74.1; 85.1
77.8 — Ps 89.49; 2 Pet 3.9
77.9 — Isa 49.15; Ps 25.6
77.10 — Ps 31.22; 44.2, 3
77.11 — Ps 143.5
77.13 — Ps 73.17; Ex 15.11
77.15 — Ex 6.6; Deut 9.29
77.16 — Ex 14.21
77.17 — Judg 5.4; Ps 68.33; 2 Sam 22.15
77.18 — 2 Sam 22.8

19 Your way was through the sea,
    your path, through the mighty waters;
      yet your footprints were unseen.
20 You led your people like a flock
    by the hand of Moses and Aaron.

77.19
Hab 3.15;
Ex 14.28

77.20
Ex 13.21;
Isa 63.11-13;
Ex 6.26

Psalm 78

78.1
Isa 51.4

God's guidance despite his people's unfaithfulness

A. The call to hear and heed

A Maskil of Asaph.

1 Give ear, O my people, to my teaching;
    incline your ears to the words of my mouth.
2 I will open my mouth in a parable;
    I will utter dark sayings from of old,
3 things that we have heard and known,
    that our ancestors have told us.
4 We will not hide them from their children;
    we will tell to the coming generation
the glorious deeds of the LORD, and his might,
    and the wonders that he has done.

78.2
Mt 13.35

78.3
Ps 44.1

78.4
Ex 12.26;
Ps 22.30;
71.17

5 He established a decree in Jacob,
    and appointed a law in Israel,
which he commanded our ancestors
    to teach to their children;
6 that the next generation might know them,
    the children yet unborn,
and rise up and tell them to their children,
7 so that they should set their hope in God,
and not forget the works of God,
    but keep his commandments;
8 and that they should not be like their ancestors,
    a stubborn and rebellious generation,
a generation whose heart was not steadfast,
    whose spirit was not faithful to God.

78.5
Ps 147.19;
Deut 4.9

78.6
Ps 102.18

78.7
Deut 6.12;
27.1

78.8
Ezek 20.18;
Ex 32.9; v. 37

B. The sins of Israel

1. The Ephraimites' disobedience

9 The Ephraimites, armed with[j] the bow,

78.9
1 Chr 12.2;
Judg 20.39

j Heb *armed with shooting*

77.20 In Israel the shepherd never drives the flock; he always leads them, and they follow him. Christ revealed himself as our shepherd and he goes before the sheep (see Jn 10). If we follow him we will never lose our way or be separated from the flock.
78.1ff This song was meant to remind Israel of their sins and of the consequences that always followed when the judgments of God fell on them. It records the fact that God was merciful and delivered his people again and again, for they did not learn from these experiences. Those who do not learn from past history tend to repeat the mistakes of their ancestors. We should meditate on this song often, lest we fall into the

same trap as our spiritual ancestors.
78.4 When we teach our children the knowledge of God, we follow the same tradition as our parents when they instructed us.
78.8 Children should be told not to follow in the footsteps of ancestors who were not devoted to God. Good tradition, not bad tradition, is to be accepted and followed.
78.9 *The Ephraimites . . . turned back.* Probably this refers to the incident that occurred in Eli's time in which the Philistines defeated the well-armed Ephraimites and captured the ark (1 Sam 4.10,11).

turned back on the day of battle.

78.10
2 Kings 18.12;
Ps 119.1

10 They did not keep God's covenant,
   but refused to walk according to his law.

78.11
Ps 106.13
78.12
Ex 7-12;
Num 13.22;
Isa 19.11,
13;
Ezek 30.14

11 They forgot what he had done,
   and the miracles that he had shown them.

12 In the sight of their ancestors he worked marvels
   in the land of Egypt, in the fields of Zoan.

78.13
Ex 14.21;
15.8

13 He divided the sea and let them pass through it,
   and made the waters stand like a heap.

78.14
Ex 13.21

14 In the daytime he led them with a cloud,
   and all night long with a fiery light.

78.15
Num 20.11;
1 Cor 10.4

15 He split rocks open in the wilderness,
   and gave them drink abundantly as from the deep.

16 He made streams come out of the rock,
   and caused waters to flow down like rivers.

2. Craving food in the wilderness

78.17
Deut 9.22;
Heb 3.16

17 Yet they sinned still more against him,
   rebelling against the Most High in the desert.

78.18
Ex 16.2;
1 Cor 10.9

18 They tested God in their heart
   by demanding the food they craved.

78.19
Num 11.4

19 They spoke against God, saying,
   "Can God spread a table in the wilderness?

78.20
Num 20.11

20 Even though he struck the rock so that water gushed out
   and torrents overflowed,
   can he also give bread,
   or provide meat for his people?"

78.21
Num 11.1

21 Therefore, when the LORD heard, he was full of rage;
   a fire was kindled against Jacob,
   his anger mounted against Israel,

78.22
Heb 3.18

22 because they had no faith in God,
   and did not trust his saving power.

78.23
Mal 3.10

23 Yet he commanded the skies above,
   and opened the doors of heaven;

78.24
Jn 6.31

24 he rained down on them manna to eat,
   and gave them the grain of heaven.

25 Mortals ate of the bread of angels;
   he sent them food in abundance.

78.26
Num 11.31

26 He caused the east wind to blow in the heavens,
   and by his power he led out the south wind;

78.27
Ps 105.40

27 he rained flesh upon them like dust,
   winged birds like the sand of the seas;

28 he let them fall within their camp,
   all around their dwellings.

78.29
Num 11.20

29 And they ate and were well filled,
   for he gave them what they craved.

30 But before they had satisfied their craving,
   while the food was still in their mouths,

78.31
Num 11.33

31 the anger of God rose against them
   and he killed the strongest of them,

78.11 *They forgot what he had done*, i.e., they did not remember what God had done for Israel in the wilderness. His many miracles should have encouraged them and strengthened them against the Philistines. We too should remember that what God did for his people yesterday he can and will do again today.

78.24–31 God provided manna for his people in the wilderness (Ex 16). They ate it, and by it all were strengthened. But then they quarreled with God and demanded meat. He gave them quails, and they died for their disobedience (Num 11). **78.32** The judgments of God against unbelief did

and laid low the flower of Israel.

3. Israel's sinful waywardness

32 In spite of all this they still sinned;
  they did not believe in his wonders.
33 So he made their days vanish like a breath,
  and their years in terror.
34 When he killed them, they sought for him;
  they repented and sought God earnestly.
35 They remembered that God was their rock,
  the Most High God their redeemer.
36 But they flattered him with their mouths;
  they lied to him with their tongues.
37 Their heart was not steadfast toward him;
  they were not true to his covenant.
38 Yet he, being compassionate,
    forgave their iniquity,
    and did not destroy them;
  often he restrained his anger,
    and did not stir up all his wrath.
39 He remembered that they were but flesh,
  a wind that passes and does not come again.

4. Israel's forgetfulness of past mercies

40 How often they rebelled against him in the wilderness
  and grieved him in the desert!
41 They tested God again and again,
  and provoked the Holy One of Israel.
42 They did not keep in mind his power,
  or the day when he redeemed them from the foe;
43 when he displayed his signs in Egypt,
  and his miracles in the fields of Zoan.
44 He turned their rivers to blood,
  so that they could not drink of their streams.
45 He sent among them swarms of flies, which devoured
    them,
  and frogs, which destroyed them.
46 He gave their crops to the caterpillar,
  and the fruit of their labor to the locust.
47 He destroyed their vines with hail,
  and their sycamores with frost.
48 He gave over their cattle to the hail,
  and their flocks to thunderbolts.
49 He let loose on them his fierce anger,
    wrath, indignation, and distress,
  a company of destroying angels.
50 He made a path for his anger;
  he did not spare them from death,
    but gave their lives over to the plague.
51 He struck all the firstborn in Egypt,

Cross references (right margin):

78.32 Num 14, 16, 17; v. 22
78.33 Num 14.29, 35
78.34 Hos 5.15
78.35 Deut 32.4; Isa 41.14
78.36 Ezek 33.31; Ex 32.7, 8
78.38 Num 14.18; Isa 48.9; 1 Kings 21.29
78.39 Ps 103.14; Gen 6.3; Job 7.7, 16
78.40 Ps 95.8-10; Heb 3.16
78.41 Num 14.22; Ps 89.18
78.44 Ex 7.20
78.45 Ex 8.24; Ps 105.31; Ex 8.6
78.47 Ex 9.25
78.48 Ex 9.23
78.49 Ex 15.7

---

not reform the Israelites. They continued in their sinful ways and God continued his judgments. They never seemed to learn that it is best to obey God. Those who go on sinning can expect to receive trouble from God.
78.41 On at least ten occasions the Israelites tested

God (Num 14.22). Their repeated refusals to let God be God provoked him. Each time they confessed their sin and were pardoned, only to test God again. **78.43** *fields of Zoan*, i.e., Tanis, an ancient Egyptian city. In the period 1085–715 B.C. Tanis-Zoan was the capital of the Pharaohs.

78.51 Ex 12.29; Ps 106.22	the first issue of their strength in the tents of Ham.
78.52 Ps 77.20	52 Then he led out his people like sheep, and guided them in the wilderness like a flock.
78.53 Ex 14.19, 27	53 He led them in safety, so that they were not afraid; but the sea overwhelmed their enemies.
78.54 Ex 15.17; Ps 44.3	54 And he brought them to his holy hill, to the mountain that his right hand had won.
78.55 Ps 44.2; 105.11	55 He drove out nations before them; he apportioned them for a possession and settled the tribes of Israel in their tents.

5. Israel's idolatry in Canaan

78.56 vv. 18, 40	56 Yet they tested the Most High God, and rebelled against him. They did not observe his decrees,
78.57 Ezek 20.27, 28; Hos 7.16	57 but turned away and were faithless like their ancestors; they twisted like a treacherous bow.
78.58 Deut 32.16, 21; 12.2; 1 Kings 11.7	58 For they provoked him to anger with their high places; they moved him to jealousy with their idols.
	59 When God heard, he was full of wrath, and he utterly rejected Israel.
78.60 1 Sam 4.11	60 He abandoned his dwelling at Shiloh, the tent where he dwelt among mortals,
78.61 Judg 18.30	61 and delivered his power to captivity, his glory to the hand of the foe.
78.62 1 Sam 4.10	62 He gave his people to the sword, and vented his wrath on his heritage.
78.63 Jer 7.34	63 Fire devoured their young men, and their girls had no marriage song.
78.64 1 Sam 22.18; Job 27.15	64 Their priests fell by the sword, and their widows made no lamentation.
78.65 Isa 42.13	65 Then the Lord awoke as from sleep, like a warrior shouting because of wine.
78.66 1 Sam 5.6	66 He put his adversaries to rout; he put them to everlasting disgrace.

C. Judah and David chosen

	67 He rejected the tent of Joseph, he did not choose the tribe of Ephraim;
78.68 Ps 87.2	68 but he chose the tribe of Judah, Mount Zion, which he loves.
78.69 1 Sam 6.1-38	69 He built his sanctuary like the high heavens, like the earth, which he has founded forever.
78.70 1 Sam 16.11, 12	70 He chose his servant David, and took him from the sheepfolds.
78.71 2 Sam 7.8; Gen 33.13; 2 Sam 5.2; 1 Chr 11.2	71 from tending the nursing ewes he brought him to be the shepherd of his people Jacob, of Israel, his inheritance.
78.72 1 Kings 9.4	72 With upright heart he tended them, and guided them with skillful hand.

78.61 God allowed Israel's enemy to seize the ark of the covenant, the symbol of his presence, and to carry it away from Shiloh (1 Sam 4). He allowed his own glory to be disgraced by being abandoned into the hands of infidels. Israel had forsaken God; he would now forsake them.

78.70 God chose David to recover the fortunes of Israel. He was not raised as an educated or military man. He was just a shepherd boy. But from these humble beginnings, God delivered his people so that glory might come to his own name.

Psalm 79

Lament over the destruction of Jerusalem

A. *The evil described*

A Psalm of Asaph.

1 O God, the nations have come into your inheritance;
  they have defiled your holy temple;
  they have laid Jerusalem in ruins.
2 They have given the bodies of your servants
    to the birds of the air for food,
  the flesh of your faithful to the wild animals of the earth.
3 They have poured out their blood like water
    all around Jerusalem,
  and there was no one to bury them.
4 We have become a taunt to our neighbors,
  mocked and derided by those around us.

B. *The help of God sought*

5 How long, O Lord? Will you be angry forever?
  Will your jealous wrath burn like fire?
6 Pour out your anger on the nations
    that do not know you,
  and on the kingdoms
    that do not call on your name.
7 For they have devoured Jacob
  and laid waste his habitation.

8 Do not remember against us the iniquities of our
      ancestors;
  let your compassion come speedily to meet us,
  for we are brought very low.
9 Help us, O God of our salvation,
    for the glory of your name;
  deliver us, and forgive our sins,
    for your name's sake.
10 Why should the nations say,
  "Where is their God?"
  Let the avenging of the outpoured blood of your servants
    be known among the nations before our eyes.

11 Let the groans of the prisoners come before you;
  according to your great power preserve those doomed to die.
12 Return sevenfold into the bosom of our neighbors
    the taunts with which they taunted you, O Lord!
13 Then we your people, the flock of your pasture,
    will give thanks to you forever;
  from generation to generation we will recount your praise.

79.1
Ex 15.17;
Ps 74.2;
2 Kings 25.9;
Mic 3.12

79.2
Jer 7.33

79.3
Jer 14.16

79.4
Ps 44.13

79.5
Ps 74.1, 9;
Zeph 3.8
79.6
Jer 10.25;
Rev 16.1;
Isa 45.4, 5;
2 Thess 1.8

79.8
Isa 64.9

79.9
2 Chr 14.11;
Jer 14.7

79.10
Ps 42.10;
94.1, 2

79.11
Ps 102.20
79.12
Isa 65.6, 7;
Jer 32.18;
Lk 6.38;
Ps 74.18, 22
79.13
Ps 74.1; 95.7;
Isa 43.21

79.1ff Many consider this song of Asaph to be a prophetical statement concerning the ravaging of Jerusalem and the destruction of the temple by the Chaldeans under Nebuchadnezzar (see note on 74.1ff). Jer 10.25 quotes vv. 6,7.
79.5 *Will you be angry forever?* God was angry and delivered his people into the Babylonian captivity. He was angry again and delivered the temple over to complete destruction in A.D. 70 under Titus and Vespasian. Some maintain that toward the end of history, God will restore his people Israel by causing them to turn to him in repentance and confession.
79.9 *Help us . . . for the glory of your name.* Any time God gives aid to his people, his name is glorified as the omnipotent Savior. The psalmist pleads with God to once again glorify his name in this manner.

Psalm 80

Israel's prayer for deliverance from calamities

A. *The call for help*

To the leader: on Lilies, a Covenant. Of Asaph. A Psalm.

1 Give ear, O Shepherd of Israel,
   you who lead Joseph like a flock!
You who are enthroned upon the cherubim, shine forth
2   before Ephraim and Benjamin and Manasseh.
Stir up your might,
   and come to save us!

3 Restore us, O God;
   let your face shine, that we may be saved.

B. *Israel's problem*

4 O LORD God of hosts,
   how long will you be angry with your people's prayers?
5 You have fed them with the bread of tears,
   and given them tears to drink in full measure.
6 You make us the scorn[k] of our neighbors;
   our enemies laugh among themselves.

7 Restore us, O God of hosts;
   let your face shine, that we may be saved.

C. *Israel a wasted vine*

8 You brought a vine out of Egypt;
   you drove out the nations and planted it.
9 You cleared the ground for it;
   it took deep root and filled the land.
10 The mountains were covered with its shade,
   the mighty cedars with its branches;
11 it sent out its branches to the sea,
   and its shoots to the River.
12 Why then have you broken down its walls,
   so that all who pass along the way pluck its fruit?
13 The boar from the forest ravages it,
   and all that move in the field feed on it.

D. *The call for help repeated*

14 Turn again, O God of hosts;
   look down from heaven, and see;
have regard for this vine,
15   the stock that your right hand planted.[l]
16 They have burned it with fire, they have cut it down;[m]
   may they perish at the rebuke of your countenance.
17 But let your hand be upon the one at your right hand,
   the one whom you made strong for yourself.
18 Then we will never turn back from you;

k Syr: Heb *strife*   *l* Heb adds from verse 17 *and upon the one whom you made strong for yourself*
m Cn: Heb *it is cut down*

Marginal cross-references (left column):

80.1 Ps 23.1; 77.20; 99.1
80.2 Ps 35.23
80.3 Lam 5.21; Num 6.25
80.4 Ps 85.5
80.5 Ps 42.3; 102.9
80.6 Ps 44.13; 79.4
80.8 Isa 5.1, 7; Jer 2.21; Ezek 15.6; Ps 44.2
80.9 Hos 14.5
80.12 Ps 89.40; Nah 2.2
80.13 Jer 5.6
80.14 Isa 63.15
80.16 Ps 39.11; 76.6
80.17 Ps 89.21
80.18 Isa 50.5; Ps 71.20

80.1ff This psalm constitutes a prayer for divine deliverance from Israel's calamities, though the particular calamity is not spelled out. The psalmist expresses hope and confidence in the power of God to deliver Israel out of its great distress.

give us life, and we will call on your name.

19 Restore us, O Lᴏʀᴅ God of hosts;
  let your face shine, that we may be saved.

Psalm 81

The goodness of God and the stubbornness of Israel

A. *The call to praise*

To the leader: according to The Gittith. Of Asaph.

1 Sing aloud to God our strength;
  shout for joy to the God of Jacob.
2 Raise a song, sound the tambourine,
  the sweet lyre with the harp.
3 Blow the trumpet at the new moon,
  at the full moon, on our festal day.
4 For it is a statute for Israel,
  an ordinance of the God of Jacob.
5 He made it a decree in Joseph,
  when he went out over[n] the land of Egypt.

B. *The goodness of God to Israel*

I hear a voice I had not known:
6 "I relieved your[o] shoulder of the burden;
  your[o] hands were freed from the basket.
7 In distress you called, and I rescued you;
  I answered you in the secret place of thunder;
  I tested you at the waters of Meribah.   *Selah*
8 Hear, O my people, while I admonish you;
  O Israel, if you would but listen to me!
9 There shall be no strange god among you;
  you shall not bow down to a foreign god.
10 I am the Lᴏʀᴅ your God,
  who brought you up out of the land of Egypt.
  Open your mouth wide and I will fill it.

C. *God's yearning for a backslidden people*

11 "But my people did not listen to my voice;
  Israel would not submit to me.
12 So I gave them over to their stubborn hearts,
  to follow their own counsels.
13 O that my people would listen to me,
  that Israel would walk in my ways!
14 Then I would quickly subdue their enemies,
  and turn my hand against their foes.
15 Those who hate the Lᴏʀᴅ would cringe before him,
  and their doom would last forever.
16 I would feed you[p] with the finest of the wheat,
  and with honey from the rock I would satisfy you."

n Or against   o Heb his   p Cn Compare verse 16b: Heb he would feed him

81.1 Ps 59.16; 66.1

81.3 Num 10.10; Lev 23.24

81.5 Ex 11.4

81.6 Isa 9.4; 10.27
81.7 Ex 2.23; Ps 50.15; Ex 19.19; 17.6, 7
81.8 Ps 50.7
81.9 Deut 32.12; Isa 43.12
81.10 Ex 20.2; Ps 103.5

81.11 Ex 32.1
81.12 Acts 7.42; Rom 1.24
81.13 Deut 5.29; Isa 48.18; Ps 128.1
81.14 Ps 47.3; Am 1.8

81.16 Deut 32.13; Ps 147.14

81.1ff This psalm was not composed as a result of some particular historical crisis or momentous event. Rather, it was written for use on special festival occasions, such as the new moon or the festival of trumpets (see especially vv. 3–5). On special occasions,

such psalms were used either to give glory to God or to receive instructions from him.
81.7 *the secret place of thunder*, i.e., Mount Sinai.
81.9 *There shall be no strange god among you*, i.e., you shall not have an idol in your home.

Psalm 82

Unjust judgments rebuked

A Psalm of Asaph.

82.1
Isa 3.13;
Ex 21.6

1 God has taken his place in the divine council;
  in the midst of the gods he holds judgment:

82.2
Ps 58.1;
Deut 1.17;
Prov 18.5

2 "How long will you judge unjustly
  and show partiality to the wicked?   *Selah*

82.3
Deut 24.17

3 Give justice to the weak and the orphan;
  maintain the right of the lowly and the destitute.

82.4
Job 29.12

4 Rescue the weak and the needy;
  deliver them from the hand of the wicked."

82.5
Mic 3.1;
Ps 11.3

5 They have neither knowledge nor understanding,
  they walk around in darkness;
  all the foundations of the earth are shaken.

82.6
Jn 10.34;
Ps 89.26
82.7
Ps 49.12;
Ezek 31.14

6 I say, "You are gods,
  children of the Most High, all of you;
7 nevertheless, you shall die like mortals,
  and fall like any prince."*q*

82.8
Ps 12.5;
Mic 7.2, 7;
Ps 2.8;
Rev 11.15

8 Rise up, O God, judge the earth;
  for all the nations belong to you!

Psalm 83

83.1
Ps 28.1;
109.1

A prayer for God to confound the enemies

A. Prayer to judge Israel's enemies

A Song. A Psalm of Asaph.

1 O God, do not keep silence;
  do not hold your peace or be still, O God!

83.2
Ps 2.1; 81.15

2 Even now your enemies are in tumult;
  those who hate you have raised their heads.

83.3
Ps 27.5

3 They lay crafty plans against your people;
  they consult together against those you protect.

83.4
Esth 3.6

4 They say, "Come, let us wipe them out as a nation;
  let the name of Israel be remembered no more."

83.5
Ps 2.2

5 They conspire with one accord;
  against you they make a covenant —

83.6
2 Chr 20.1,
10, 11

6 the tents of Edom and the Ishmaelites,
  Moab and the Hagrites,
7 Gebal and Ammon and Amalek,
  Philistia with the inhabitants of Tyre;
8 Assyria also has joined them;
  they are the strong arm of the children of Lot.   *Selah*

q Or fall as one man, O princes

82.1ff This psalm instructs those in power (whether in church or state) how to conduct themselves with respect to the temptations of the office of the magistracy. The principles outlined here apply to all nations on earth.
83.1ff This is the last of the psalms connected with the name of Asaph. It refers by name to some of Israel's enemies and pleads with God to judge them.

The closing section (vv. 9–18) constitutes a prayer of imprecation against these enemies. Whether this practice is proper in the age instituted by Christ is the subject of much controversy — what was done in the O.T. may be forbidden to us. One thing is clear: both the O.T. and the N.T. bind God's people of all ages to the commandment that they must love their neighbors as themselves (Lev 19.18; Mt 22.39; Rom 13.9).

B. *The prayer of imprecation*

9 Do to them as you did to Midian,
   as to Sisera and Jabin at the Wadi Kishon,
10 who were destroyed at En-dor,
   who became dung for the ground.
11 Make their nobles like Oreb and Zeeb,
   all their princes like Zebah and Zalmunna,
12 who said, "Let us take the pastures of God
   for our own possession."

13 O my God, make them like whirling dust,r
   like chaff before the wind.
14 As fire consumes the forest,
   as the flame sets the mountains ablaze,
15 so pursue them with your tempest
   and terrify them with your hurricane.
16 Fill their faces with shame,
   so that they may seek your name, O Lord.
17 Let them be put to shame and dismayed forever;
   let them perish in disgrace.
18 Let them know that you alone,
   whose name is the Lord,
   are the Most High over all the earth.

83.9	Judg 4.22, 23
83.11	Judg 8.12, 21
83.12	2 Chr 20.11; Ps 132.13
83.13	Isa 17.13; Ps 35.5
83.14	Deut 32.22
83.15	Job 9.17
83.17	Ps 70.2
83.18	Ps 59.13; Ex 6.3; Ps 92.8

Psalm 84

Longing to be in the sanctuary

A. *Longing for the courts of the Lord*

To the leader: according to The Gittith. Of the Korahites. A Psalm.

1 How lovely is your dwelling place,
   O Lord of hosts!
2 My soul longs, indeed it faints
   for the courts of the Lord;
   my heart and my flesh sing for joy
   to the living God.

B. *Happiness in the Lord's house*

3 Even the sparrow finds a home,
   and the swallow a nest for herself,
   where she may lay her young,
   at your altars, O Lord of hosts,
   my King and my God.
4 Happy are those who live in your house,
   ever singing your praise.   *Selah*

C. *Happiness of this pilgrim journey*

5 Happy are those whose strength is in you,
   in whose heart are the highways to Zion.s
6 As they go through the valley of Baca

84.1	Ps 27.4
84.2	Ps 42.1, 2
84.3	Ps 43.4; 5.2
84.4	Ps 65.4
84.5	Ps 81.1
84.6	Ps 107.35

r Or *a tumbleweed*   s Heb lacks *to Zion*

84.1ff The author of this psalm is not named nor do the contents state specifically what circumstances caused it to be written. This song is well suited to the worship of God in his house, when believers gather to hear the word of God, to praise him for all his bless-ings, and to celebrate the ordinances or sacraments of the faith.

84.6 *the valley of Baca* i.e., "the valley of weeping," a normally dry valley where many balsam trees grew.

they make it a place of springs;
the early rain also covers it with pools.

84.7
Prov 4.18;
2 Cor 3.18;
Deut 16.16;
Ps 42.2

7 They go from strength to strength;
the God of gods will be seen in Zion.

D. *Expression of petition and trust*

8 O Lord God of hosts, hear my prayer;
give ear, O God of Jacob!   *Selah*

84.9
Gen 15.1;
Ps 2.2

9 Behold our shield, O God;
look on the face of your anointed.

84.10
1 Chr 23.5

10 For a day in your courts is better
than a thousand elsewhere.
I would rather be a doorkeeper in the house of my God
than live in the tents of wickedness.

84.11
Isa 60.19;
Rev 21.23;
Ps 34.10

11 For the Lord God is a sun and shield;
he bestows favor and honor.
No good thing does the Lord withhold
from those who walk uprightly.

84.12
Ps 2.12

12 O Lord of hosts,
happy is everyone who trusts in you.

Psalm 85

85.1
Ezra 1.11;
Jer 30.18;
Ezek 39.25

Prayer for mercy to Israel

A. *The Lord's past mercies*

To the leader. Of the Korahites. A Psalm.

1 Lord, you were favorable to your land;
you restored the fortunes of Jacob.

85.2
Ps 103.3;
32.1
85.3
Ps 78.38;
Deut 13.17

2 You forgave the iniquity of your people;
you pardoned all their sin.   *Selah*
3 You withdrew all your wrath;
you turned from your hot anger.

B. *The prayer for revival*

85.4
Ps 80.3, 7

4 Restore us again, O God of our salvation,
and put away your indignation toward us.

85.5
Ps 74.1; 79.5;
80.4
85.6
Hab 3.2

5 Will you be angry with us forever?
Will you prolong your anger to all generations?
6 Will you not revive us again,
so that your people may rejoice in you?

85.7
Ps 106.4

7 Show us your steadfast love, O Lord,
and grant us your salvation.

C. *The steadfast love and faithfulness of the Lord*

85.8
Hab 2.1;
Zech 9.10

8 Let me hear what God the Lord will speak,
for he will speak peace to his people,

84.9 *your anointed,* i.e., "your king."
84.11 *the Lord God is a sun.* God is the source from which we get light, life, and fruitfulness. *those who walk uprightly,* i.e., those who live the sort of life that God wants them to live, a life of obedience to his holy will.
85.1ff Some commentators think this psalm was

composed after the return of Israel to the land of promise after the Babylonian captivity. This was not an easy time, for the consequences of Israel's sins were not fully over. The psalmist depends on the faithfulness of Israel's God to turn away his anger, trusting he will find relief in God's great salvation.

to his faithful, to those who turn to him in their hearts.[t]

9   Surely his salvation is at hand for those who fear him,
        that his glory may dwell in our land.

> 85.9
> Isa 46.13;
> Zech 2.5;
> Jn 1.14

10 Steadfast love and faithfulness will meet;
        righteousness and peace will kiss each other.

> 85.10
> Ps 72.3;
> Isa 32.17;
> Lk 2.14

11 Faithfulness will spring up from the ground,
        and righteousness will look down from the sky.

12 The LORD will give what is good,
        and our land will yield its increase.

> 85.12
> Ps 84.11;
> Jas 1.17

13 Righteousness will go before him,
        and will make a path for his steps.

> 85.13
> Ps 89.14

Psalm 86

> 86.1
> Ps 17.6;
> 40.17

A prayer for deliverance from trouble

A. Appeal for help in trouble

A Prayer of David.

1   Incline your ear, O LORD, and answer me,
        for I am poor and needy.

2   Preserve my life, for I am devoted to you;
        save your servant who trusts in you.
    You are my God; 3 be gracious to me, O Lord,
        for to you do I cry all day long.

> 86.2
> Ps 25.20; 4.3;
> 31.14
> 86.3
> Ps 57.1; 88.9

4   Gladden the soul of your servant,
        for to you, O Lord, I lift up my soul.

> 86.4
> Ps 25.1;
> 143.8

5   For you, O Lord, are good and forgiving,
        abounding in steadfast love to all who call on you.

> 86.5
> Ps 130.7;
> 145.9;
> Joel 2.13

6   Give ear, O LORD, to my prayer;
        listen to my cry of supplication.

> 86.6
> Ps 55.1

7   In the day of my trouble I call on you,
        for you will answer me.

> 86.7
> Ps 50.15;
> 17.6

B. Adoration of God

8   There is none like you among the gods, O Lord,
        nor are there any works like yours.

> 86.8
> Ex 15.11;
> Ps 89.6;
> Deut 3.24

9   All the nations you have made shall come
        and bow down before you, O Lord,
        and shall glorify your name.

> 86.9
> Ps 22.31;
> Isa 43.7;
> Rev 15.4

10 For you are great and do wondrous things;
        you alone are God.

> 86.10
> Ex 15.11;
> Ps 72.18;
> Deut 6.4;
> Mk 12.29

C. Petition and thanksgiving

11 Teach me your way, O LORD,
        that I may walk in your truth;
        give me an undivided heart to revere your name.

> 86.11
> Ps 25.4

12 I give thanks to you, O Lord my God, with my whole heart,
        and I will glorify your name forever.

> 86.12
> Ps 111.1

13 For great is your steadfast love toward me;

> 86.13
> Ps 30.3

[t] Gk: Heb but let them not turn back to folly

86.1ff This seems to be a general prayer of David used in times of affliction. It continues to be useful to believers during a time of trouble, sorrow, or dismay.
86.8 *There is none like you among the gods, O LORD.* David is not acknowledging the existence of other gods, for all other so-called gods are false gods. There are, however, spiritual beings who claim to be gods. None of them is wise, mighty, and good. The God of Israel alone does great works (v. 10).

you have delivered my soul from the depths of Sheol.

D. *Assurance of God's mercy and grace*

86.14
Ps 54.3

14 O God, the insolent rise up against me;
   a band of ruffians seeks my life,
   and they do not set you before them.

86.15
Ex 34.6;
Neh 9.17;
Ps 103.8;
Joel 2.13

15 But you, O Lord, are a God merciful and gracious,
   slow to anger and abounding in steadfast love and
      faithfulness.

86.16
Ps 25.16;
68.35; 116.16

16 Turn to me and be gracious to me;
   give your strength to your servant;
   save the child of your serving girl.

86.17
Ps 112.10;
118.13

17 Show me a sign of your favor,
   so that those who hate me may see it and be put to shame,
   because you, Lord, have helped me and comforted me.

Psalm 87

The privileges of citizenship in Zion

Of the Korahites. A Psalm. A Song.

1 On the holy mount stands the city he founded;

87.2
Ps 78.67

2   the Lord loves the gates of Zion
      more than all the dwellings of Jacob.

87.3
Isa 60.1

3 Glorious things are spoken of you,
      O city of God.   *Selah*

4 Among those who know me I mention Rahab and Babylon;
      Philistia too, and Tyre, with Ethiopia[u] —
   "This one was born there," they say.

87.5
Ps 48.8

5 And of Zion it shall be said,
   "This one and that one were born in it";
   for the Most High himself will establish it.

87.6
Ezek 13.9

6 The Lord records, as he registers the peoples,
   "This one was born there."   *Selah*

87.7
Ps 36.9

7 Singers and dancers alike say,
   "All my springs are in you."

88.1
Ps 27.9;
51.14

Psalm 88

A petition to be saved from death

A. *The psalmist's petition*

A Song. A Psalm of the Korahites. To the leader: according to Mahalath
   Leannoth. A Maskil of Heman the Ezrahite.

1 O Lord, God of my salvation,
   when, at night, I cry out in your presence,

---

u Or *Nubia*; Heb *Cush*

87.1ff This short psalm praises Jerusalem, the city of
God. Some think it was written at a time when the city
lay in ruins as a means of encouraging faith and hope
for its restoration to its pristine glory. Others think it
was written when the city was flourishing, expressing
the joy of the people for its greatness.
87.4 *Rahab*, the name of a mythological monster, is

used here as a symbol for Egypt. The word means
"the haughty one" (see Isa 30.7).
88.1ff This is a penitential psalm. The writer makes
no mention of any comfort or joy but speaks only of
the dark night of the soul; he asks why God has
hidden his face from the penitent sinner. Almost every believer feels this way at one time or another.

2   let my prayer come before you;
    incline your ear to my cry.

88.2
Ps 18.6; 86.1

B. *The psalmist's troubles*

3   For my soul is full of troubles,
    and my life draws near to Sheol.

88.3
Ps 107.18, 26

4   I am counted among those who go down to the Pit;
    I am like those who have no help,

88.4
Ps 28.1

5   like those forsaken among the dead,
    like the slain that lie in the grave,
    like those whom you remember no more,
    for they are cut off from your hand.

88.5
Isa 53.8

6   You have put me in the depths of the Pit,
    in the regions dark and deep.

88.6
Ps 86.13;
143.3; 69.15

7   Your wrath lies heavy upon me,
    and you overwhelm me with all your waves.   *Selah*

88.7
Ps 42.7

8   You have caused my companions to shun me;
    you have made me a thing of horror to them.
    I am shut in so that I cannot escape;

88.8
Job 19.13;
Ps 31.11;
142.4;
Lam 3.7

9   my eye grows dim through sorrow.
    Every day I call on you, O LORD;
    I spread out my hands to you.

88.9
Ps 38.10;
86.3;
Job 11.13;
Ps 143.6

C. *The psalmist's questions*

10 Do you work wonders for the dead?
    Do the shades rise up to praise you?   *Selah*

88.10
Ps 6.5;
Isa 38.18

11 Is your steadfast love declared in the grave,
    or your faithfulness in Abaddon?

12 Are your wonders known in the darkness,
    or your saving help in the land of forgetfulness?

88.12
Job 10.21

13 But I, O LORD, cry out to you;
    in the morning my prayer comes before you.

88.13
Ps 5.3;
119.147

14 O LORD, why do you cast me off?
    Why do you hide your face from me?

88.14
Job 13.24;
Ps 13.1

D. *The psalmist's closing complaints*

15 Wretched and close to death from my youth up,
    I suffer your terrors; I am desperate. *v*

88.15
Job 6.4

16 Your wrath has swept over me;
    your dread assaults destroy me.

17 They surround me like a flood all day long;
    from all sides they close in on me.

88.17
Ps 22.16

18 You have caused friend and neighbor to shun me;
    my companions are in darkness.

88.18
Job 19.13;
Ps 31.11;
38.11

---

v Meaning of Heb uncertain

88.8,9 The psalmist feels like a prisoner under the divine wrath, sinking under sin's weight with no possibility of getting out. He weeps and prays, not grasping what the N.T. so graphically portrays — that if we confess our sins, God is faithful and just and forgives our sins (1 Jn 1.9). Mourning should then give way to rejoicing, for our sins are cast behind the back of God to be remembered against us no more (Isa 38.17; Mic 7.19).
88.18 Dolefully the psalmist's lament does not end on a cheerful note or express hope for deliverance from the difficulties. The psalm might be called an unfinished symphony.

Psalm 89

God's covenant with David and Israel's afflictions

A. The covenant with David

A Maskil of Ethan the Ezrahite.

1 I will sing of your steadfast love, O LORD,*w* forever;
  with my mouth I will proclaim your faithfulness to all
  generations.
2 I declare that your steadfast love is established forever;
  your faithfulness is as firm as the heavens.

3 You said, "I have made a covenant with my chosen one,
  I have sworn to my servant David:
4 'I will establish your descendants forever,
  and build your throne for all generations.' "   *Selah*

B. Praise to a faithful and mighty God

5 Let the heavens praise your wonders, O LORD,
  your faithfulness in the assembly of the holy ones.
6 For who in the skies can be compared to the LORD?
  Who among the heavenly beings is like the LORD,
7 a God feared in the council of the holy ones,
  great and awesome*x* above all that are around him?
8 O LORD God of hosts,
  who is as mighty as you, O LORD?
  Your faithfulness surrounds you.
9 You rule the raging of the sea;
  when its waves rise, you still them.
10 You crushed Rahab like a carcass;
  you scattered your enemies with your mighty arm.
11 The heavens are yours, the earth also is yours;
  the world and all that is in it — you have founded them.
12 The north and the south*y* — you created them;
  Tabor and Hermon joyously praise your name.
13 You have a mighty arm;
  strong is your hand, high your right hand.
14 Righteousness and justice are the foundation of your throne;
  steadfast love and faithfulness go before you.
15 Happy are the people who know the festal shout,
  who walk, O LORD, in the light of your countenance;
16 they exult in your name all day long,
  and extol*z* your righteousness.
17 For you are the glory of their strength;
  by your favor our horn is exalted.
18 For our shield belongs to the LORD,
  our king to the Holy One of Israel.

w Gk: Heb *the steadfast love of the LORD*   *x* Gk Syr: Heb *greatly awesome*   *y* Or *Zaphon and Yamin*
z Cn: Heb *are exalted in*

89.1ff This psalm deals with the Davidic covenant and the throne promised to his heirs forever. It reaffirms that his dynasty will go on forever until the end of time (v. 36). As a messianic psalm it looks forward to Jesus, the true son of David. After the fall of Jerusalem in 587 B.C., no throne existed and no king sat on a throne. This does not mean that the plan or the purpose of God changed. An unbroken line of David's male heirs continued (see Mt 1.1–17). The temporary suspension of the throne and the kingdom awaited the coming of Jesus, who now sits on the throne of his father David (Lk 1.32,33) — a throne which is gloriously heavenly but which will be manifested on earth when the Messiah comes the second time.
89.10 *Rahab*, i.e., Egypt (see note on 87.4).

89.1 Ps 101.1
89.2 Ps 103.17; 36.5
89.3 1 Kings 8.16; Ps 132.11
89.4 2 Sam 7.16; Isa 9.7; Lk 1.33
89.5 Ps 19.1; 149.1
89.6 Mic 7.18; Ps 29.1
89.7 Ps 47.2; 96.4
89.8 Ps 71.19
89.9 Ps 65.7
89.10 Ps 87.4; Isa 51.9; Ps 68.1
89.11 1 Chr 29.11; Ps 24.1, 2
89.12 Josh 19.22; 12.1
89.13 Ps 98.1
89.14 Ps 97.2; 85.13
89.15 Num 10.10
89.17 Ps 28.8; 75.10
89.18 Ps 47.9; 71.22

C. God's promises to David and his offspring

19 Then you spoke in a vision to your faithful one, and said:
      "I have set the crown[a] on one who is mighty,
      I have exalted one chosen from the people.
20 I have found my servant David;
      with my holy oil I have anointed him;
21 my hand shall always remain with him;
      my arm also shall strengthen him.
22 The enemy shall not outwit him,
      the wicked shall not humble him.
23 I will crush his foes before him
      and strike down those who hate him.
24 My faithfulness and steadfast love shall be with him;
      and in my name his horn shall be exalted.
25 I will set his hand on the sea
      and his right hand on the rivers.
26 He shall cry to me, 'You are my Father,
      my God, and the Rock of my salvation!'
27 I will make him the firstborn,
      the highest of the kings of the earth.
28 Forever I will keep my steadfast love for him,
      and my covenant with him will stand firm.
29 I will establish his line forever,
      and his throne as long as the heavens endure.
30 If his children forsake my law
      and do not walk according to my ordinances,
31 if they violate my statutes
      and do not keep my commandments,
32 then I will punish their transgression with the rod
      and their iniquity with scourges;
33 but I will not remove from him my steadfast love,
      or be false to my faithfulness.
34 I will not violate my covenant,
      or alter the word that went forth from my lips.
35 Once and for all I have sworn by my holiness;
      I will not lie to David.
36 His line shall continue forever,
      and his throne endure before me like the sun.
37 It shall be established forever like the moon,
      an enduring witness in the skies."   Selah

D. A plea for renewal of the covenant

1. The punishment of the LORD

38 But now you have spurned and rejected him;
      you are full of wrath against your anointed.
39 You have renounced the covenant with your servant;
      you have defiled his crown in the dust.
40 You have broken through all his walls;
      you have laid his strongholds in ruins.
41 All who pass by plunder him;

[a] Cn: Heb *help*

Cross references:
89.19 1 Kings 11.34
89.20 Acts 13.22; 1 Sam 16.1, 12
89.22 2 Sam 7.10
89.23 2 Sam 7.9
89.24 2 Sam 7.15
89.26 2 Sam 7.14; 22.47
89.27 Col 1.15; Num 24.7; Rev 1.5
89.28 Isa 55.3
89.29 Isa 9.7; Jer 33.17; Deut 11.21
89.30 2 Sam 7.14
89.32 2 Sam 7.14
89.33 2 Sam 7.15
89.34 Deut 7.9; Num 23.19
89.35 Am 4.2
89.36 Ps 72.5
89.38 1 Chr 28.9; Deut 32.19
89.39 Lam 5.16
89.40 Ps 80.12; Lam 2.2, 5
89.41 Ps 44.13

89.19 God often made his will known to people by visions (see Num 12.6; Acts 16.9). Some visions came at night, while others came while people were in trances. Sometimes they were not understood by the recipient. False prophets also claimed to have had visions. Among those who experienced true visions were Abraham (Gen 15.1), Moses (Ex 3.2,3), Samuel (1 Sam 3.2–15), Paul (Acts 9.3,6,12; 16.9), Peter (Acts 10.9–17), and John (Rev 1.2ff). *to your faithful one.* This apparently refers to Samuel, the one sent to anoint David as king.

he has become the scorn of his neighbors.

89.42
Ps 13.2; 80.6
42 You have exalted the right hand of his foes;
    you have made all his enemies rejoice.

89.43
Ps 44.10
43 Moreover, you have turned back the edge of his sword,
    and you have not supported him in battle.

89.44
Ezek 28.7
44 You have removed the scepter from his hand,*b*
    and hurled his throne to the ground.

89.45
Ps 102.23;
44.15
45 You have cut short the days of his youth;
    you have covered him with shame.   *Selah*

2. The prayer for renewal

89.46
Ps 79.5
46 How long, O Lord? Will you hide yourself forever?
    How long will your wrath burn like fire?

89.47
Job 7.7; 10.9;
14.1;
Ps 39.5
47 Remember how short my time is — *c*
    for what vanity you have created all mortals!

89.48
Ps 49.9;
Heb 11.5
48 Who can live and never see death?
    Who can escape the power of Sheol?   *Selah*

89.49
2 Sam 7.15;
Ps 54.5
49 Lord, where is your steadfast love of old,
    which by your faithfulness you swore to David?

89.50
Ps 69.9, 19
50 Remember, O Lord, how your servant is taunted;
    how I bear in my bosom the insults of the peoples,*d*

89.51
Ps 74.10
51 with which your enemies taunt, O Lord,
    with which they taunted the footsteps of your anointed.

89.52
Ps 41.13
52 Blessed be the Lord forever.
    Amen and Amen.

BOOK IV

(Psalms 90–106)

90.1
Deut 33.27;
Ezek 11.16

Psalm 90

God's eternity and human transitoriness

A. Eternal God and transitory humankind

A Prayer of Moses, the man of God.

1 Lord, you have been our dwelling place*e*
    in all generations.

90.2
Prov 8.25;
Ps 102.25;
93.2
2 Before the mountains were brought forth,
    or ever you had formed the earth and the world,
    from everlasting to everlasting you are God.

90.3
Gen 3.19
3 You turn us*f* back to dust,
    and say, "Turn back, you mortals."

90.4
2 Pet 3.8;
Ps 39.5
4 For a thousand years in your sight

b Cn: Heb *removed his cleanness*   *c* Meaning of Heb uncertain   *d* Cn: Heb *bosom all of many peoples*
e Another reading is *our refuge*   *f* Heb *humankind*

89.49 *your faithfulness*, i.e., your faithful pledge. The Hebrew word *emunah* ("truth") speaks of God and truth. God always keeps his word. Christ is called "the truth" (Jn 7.18; 14.6), as is the Holy Spirit — cf. the "Spirit of truth" (Jn 14.17). The word of God itself is defined as truth (Jn 17.17). God's truth should be known, believed, and practiced.
90.1ff This prayer of Moses was probably composed sometime during the wilderness journey of Israel from Egypt to Canaan. God had sentenced his people to thirty-eight years of wandering because of their unbelief, murmuring, and rebellion. This prayer may well have been used daily in their tents and in the tabernacle services. But it was also a prayer of instruction for the new generation of Israelites who would enter the land after their sinful parents had died in the wilderness. Other songs composed by Moses are found in Ex 15 (cf. Rev 15.3) and Deut 32.

are like yesterday when it is past,
or like a watch in the night.

5   You sweep them away; they are like a dream,
    like grass that is renewed in the morning;
6   in the morning it flourishes and is renewed;
    in the evening it fades and withers.

7   For we are consumed by your anger;
    by your wrath we are overwhelmed.
8   You have set our iniquities before you,
    our secret sins in the light of your countenance.

9   For all our days pass away under your wrath;
    our years come to an end[g] like a sigh.
10 The days of our life are seventy years,
    or perhaps eighty, if we are strong;
    even then their span[h] is only toil and trouble;
    they are soon gone, and we fly away.

11 Who considers the power of your anger?
    Your wrath is as great as the fear that is due you.
12 So teach us to count our days
    that we may gain a wise heart.

B. A prayer for God's favor

13 Turn, O Lord! How long?
    Have compassion on your servants!
14 Satisfy us in the morning with your steadfast love,
    so that we may rejoice and be glad all our days.
15 Make us glad as many days as you have afflicted us,
    and as many years as we have seen evil.
16 Let your work be manifest to your servants,
    and your glorious power to their children.
17 Let the favor of the Lord our God be upon us,
    and prosper for us the work of our hands —
    O prosper the work of our hands!

Psalm 91

The security of the godly

A. The promise of security

1   You who live in the shelter of the Most High,
    who abide in the shadow of the Almighty,[i]
2   will say to the Lord, "My refuge and my fortress;
    my God, in whom I trust."
3   For he will deliver you from the snare of the fowler
    and from the deadly pestilence;
4   he will cover you with his pinions,

g Syr: Heb *we bring our years to an end*   *h* Cn Compare Gk Syr Jerome Tg: Heb *pride*   *i* Traditional
rendering of Heb *Shaddai*

Cross references (right column):

90.5 Job 27.20; Ps 73.20; 103.15; Isa 40.6
90.6 Job 14.2; Ps 92.7
90.8 Ps 50.21; Jer 16.17; Ps 19.12
90.9 Ps 78.33
90.10 Eccl 12.2-7
90.11 Ps 76.7
90.12 Ps 39.4
90.13 Deut 32.26; Ps 135.14
90.14 Ps 65.4; 85.6
90.16 Hab 3.2; 1 Kings 8.11
90.17 Ps 27.4; Isa 26.12
91.1 Ps 27.5; 31.20; 17.8
91.2 Ps 142.5
91.3 Ps 124.7
91.4 Isa 51.16; Ps 57.1; 40.11; 35.2

90.12 All humans should remember that their days are few in number and that they have little time to arrange the affairs of life before the hour of death comes. While there is time, mortals should fear God and seek instruction by his Spirit so that their hearts will incline to wisdom (cf. Ps 111.10).

91.1ff The authorship of this psalm is not stated. Some think it relates to the numbering of Israel by David contrary to the will of God (cf "the pestilence that stalks in darkness" in v. 6). Its central message is the certainty that God is our deliverer from any time of danger, so that we need not fear.

and under his wings you will find refuge;
his faithfulness is a shield and buckler.

91.5
Ps 23.4;
Song 3.8;
Ps 64.4
91.6
v. 10;
Job 5.22

5 You will not fear the terror of the night,
or the arrow that flies by day,

6 or the pestilence that stalks in darkness,
or the destruction that wastes at noonday.

7 A thousand may fall at your side,
ten thousand at your right hand,
but it will not come near you.

91.8
Ps 37.34;
Mal 1.5

8 You will only look with your eyes
and see the punishment of the wicked.

B. *The witness of the psalmist*

9 Because you have made the Lord your refuge,*j*
the Most High your dwelling place,

91.10
Prov 12.21

10 no evil shall befall you,
no scourge come near your tent.

91.11
Ps 34.7;
Mt 4.6;
Lk 4.10;
Heb 1.14

11 For he will command his angels concerning you
to guard you in all your ways.

12 On their hands they will bear you up,
so that you will not dash your foot against a stone.

91.13
Lk 10.19

13 You will tread on the lion and the adder,
the young lion and the serpent you will trample under foot.

C. *The witness of the Lord*

91.14
Ps 145.20;
59.1; 9.10
91.15
Ps 50.15;
1 Sam 2.30;
Jn 12.26

14 Those who love me, I will deliver;
I will protect those who know my name.

15 When they call to me, I will answer them;
I will be with them in trouble,
I will rescue them and honor them.

91.16
Ps 21.4;
50.23

16 With long life I will satisfy them,
and show them my salvation.

Psalm 92

Praise for the Lord's goodness

A. *The command to give thanks*

A Psalm. A Song for the Sabbath Day.

92.1
Ps 157.1

1 It is good to give thanks to the Lord,
to sing praises to your name, O Most High;

92.2
Ps 89.1

2 to declare your steadfast love in the morning,
and your faithfulness by night,

92.3
1 Chr 23.5;
Ps 33.2

3 to the music of the lute and the harp,
to the melody of the lyre.

4 For you, O Lord, have made me glad by your work;
at the works of your hands I sing for joy.

j Cn: Heb *Because you, Lord, are my refuge; you have made*

91.16 Even as sin and death go hand in hand, so do life and salvation.
92.1ff This psalm was probably used on the sabbath for praising God, who blesses the righteous and judges the wicked. The psalmist lauds God's love in the morning, and when evening comes, is thankful for his faithfulness (vv. 1,2).

B. *The end of the wicked*

5 How great are your works, O Lord!
      Your thoughts are very deep!
6 The dullard cannot know,
      the stupid cannot understand this:
7 though the wicked sprout like grass
      and all evildoers flourish,
   they are doomed to destruction forever,
8   but you, O Lord, are on high forever.
9 For your enemies, O Lord,
      for your enemies shall perish;
      all evildoers shall be scattered.

10 But you have exalted my horn like that of the
            wild ox;
      you have poured over me[k] fresh oil.
11 My eyes have seen the downfall of my enemies;
      my ears have heard the doom of my evil assailants.

C. *The end of the righteous*

12 The righteous flourish like the palm tree,
      and grow like a cedar in Lebanon.
13 They are planted in the house of the Lord;
      they flourish in the courts of our God.
14 In old age they still produce fruit;
      they are always green and full of sap,
15 showing that the Lord is upright;
      he is my rock, and there is no unrighteousness
      in him.

Psalm 93

The majesty of the Lord

1 The Lord is king, he is robed in majesty;
      the Lord is robed, he is girded with strength.
   He has established the world; it shall never be moved;
2   your throne is established from of old;
      you are from everlasting.

3 The floods have lifted up, O Lord,
      the floods have lifted up their voice;
      the floods lift up their roaring.
4 More majestic than the thunders of mighty waters,
      more majestic than the waves[l] of the sea,
      majestic on high is the Lord!

5 Your decrees are very sure;
      holiness befits your house,
      O Lord, forevermore.

92.5
Ps 40.5;
Isa 28.29;
Rom 11.33
92.6
Ps 73.22
92.7
Ps 90.5; 94.3;
37.38; 93.4
92.8
Ps 83.18
92.9
Ps 68.1;
89.10

92.10
Ps 89.17;
23.5
92.11
Ps 54.7;
59.10

92.12
Ps 52.8;
Isa 65.22;
Hos 14.5, 6;
Ps 104.16
92.13
Ps 80.15;
100.4
92.14
Isa 37.31
92.15
Ps 25.8;
Deut 32.4;
Rom 9.14

93.1
Ps 96.10;
97.1; 99.1;
104.1; 65.6

93.2
Ps 45.6; 90.2

93.3
Ps 98.7, 8

93.4
Ps 65.7; 89.9

93.5
Ps 19.7;
1 Cor 3.17

---

k Syr: Meaning of Heb uncertain   *l* Cn: Heb *majestic are the waves*

93.1ff This psalm extols the majesty of the Lord, seen both in his work and in his word. The promises of God will never be broken, and all the saints may rely on his word.

Psalm 94

An appeal to avenge

A. *The cry for vengeance on the wicked*

94.1
Deut 32.35;
Nah 1.2;
Ps 50.2

1 O Lord, you God of vengeance,
   you God of vengeance, shine forth!

94.2
Ps 7.6;
Gen 18.25;
Ps 31.23
94.3
Job 20.5

2 Rise up, O judge of the earth;
   give to the proud what they deserve!
3 O Lord, how long shall the wicked,
   how long shall the wicked exult?

94.4
Ps 31.18;
10.3

4 They pour out their arrogant words;
   all the evildoers boast.
5 They crush your people, O Lord,
   and afflict your heritage.

94.6
Isa 10.2

6 They kill the widow and the stranger,
   they murder the orphan,

94.7
Ps 10.11

7 and they say, "The Lord does not see;
   the God of Jacob does not perceive."

94.8
Ps 92.6

8 Understand, O dullest of the people;
   fools, when will you be wise?

94.9
Ex 4.11;
Prov 20.12
94.10
Ps 44.2;
Job 35.11;
Isa 28.26

9 He who planted the ear, does he not hear?
   He who formed the eye, does he not see?
10 He who disciplines the nations,
   he who teaches knowledge to humankind,
   does he not chastise?

94.11
1 Cor 3.20

11 The Lord knows our thoughts,*m*
   that they are but an empty breath.

B. *The Lord will not forsake his people*

94.12
Job 5.17;
Heb 12.5
94.13
Ps 49.5; 9.15

12 Happy are those whom you discipline, O Lord,
   and whom you teach out of your law,
13 giving them respite from days of trouble,
   until a pit is dug for the wicked.

94.14
1 Sam 12.22;
Rom 11.1, 2

14 For the Lord will not forsake his people;
   he will not abandon his heritage;
15 for justice will return to the righteous,
   and all the upright in heart will follow it.

C. *The psalmist seeks the Lord*

94.16
Isa 28.21;
Ps 59.2
94.17
Ps 124.1

16 Who rises up for me against the wicked?
   Who stands up for me against evildoers?
17 If the Lord had not been my help,
   my soul would soon have lived in the land of silence.

94.18
Ps 38.16

18 When I thought, "My foot is slipping,"
   your steadfast love, O Lord, held me up.

94.19
Isa 66.13

19 When the cares of my heart are many,
   your consolations cheer my soul.

94.20
Am 6.3;
Isa 10.1

20 Can wicked rulers be allied with you,

m Heb *the thoughts of humankind*

94.1ff This psalm asks the Lord for vengeance against one's enemies. In the N.T. Jesus affirmed this notion: "Will not God grant justice to his chosen ones who cry to him day and night?" (Lk 18.7). Believers may be sure that the deeds of the wicked deserve the wrath of God and they will experience it at last. **94.12** God may use the instruments of trouble to chasten those who love him; such people are blessed whether they realize it or not. Under divine discipline they are taught, reformed, and improved.

those who contrive mischief by statute?
21 They band together against the life of the righteous,
    and condemn the innocent to death.
22 But the LORD has become my stronghold,
    and my God the rock of my refuge.
23 He will repay them for their iniquity
    and wipe them out for their wickedness;
    the LORD our God will wipe them out.

Psalm 95

A call to praise the LORD

A. The praise to be sung

1 O come, let us sing to the LORD;
    let us make a joyful noise to the rock of our salvation!
2 Let us come into his presence with thanksgiving;
    let us make a joyful noise to him with songs of praise!
3 For the LORD is a great God,
    and a great King above all gods.
4 In his hand are the depths of the earth;
    the heights of the mountains are his also.
5 The sea is his, for he made it,
    and the dry land, which his hands have formed.

6 O come, let us worship and bow down,
    let us kneel before the LORD, our Maker!
7 For he is our God,
    and we are the people of his pasture,
    and the sheep of his hand.

B. The warning to be followed

O that today you would listen to his voice!
8   Do not harden your hearts, as at Meribah,
    as on the day at Massah in the wilderness,
9 when your ancestors tested me,
    and put me to the proof, though they had seen my work.
10 For forty years I loathed that generation
    and said, "They are a people whose hearts go astray,
    and they do not regard my ways."
11 Therefore in my anger I swore,
    "They shall not enter my rest."

Psalm 96

A call to worship the LORD

A. The call to praise the LORD

1 O sing to the LORD a new song;

94.21
Ps 56.6;
Mt 27.1;
Prov 17.15
94.22
Ps 59.9; 71.7
94.23
Ps 7.16

95.1
Ps 100.1;
Deut 32.15;
2 Sam 22.47

95.2
Mic 6.6;
Ps 100.4;
81.2
95.3
Ps 96.4; 97.9;
135.5

95.5
Gen 1.9, 10

95.6
Ps 99.5, 9;
2 Chr 6.13;
Ps 100.3
95.7
Ps 79.13;
100.3;
Heb 3.7-11

95.8
Ex 17.2, 7;
Deut 6.16
95.9
Ps 78.18;
1 Cor 10.9
95.10
Heb 3.10, 17

95.11
Heb 4.3, 5

96.1
1 Chr 16.23-33

94.20,21 *contrive mischief by statute?* The wicked
have their evil intentions legalized by legislation, enabling them to convict the righteous as evildoers. The
only hope for the innocent is to turn to God.
95.1ff This psalm is divided into two parts. Only
those who have experienced God's salvation through
the gospel can make a joyful noise to God (vv. 1–7a).
The unconverted are warned not to harden their

hearts, or they will not enter God's rest (vv. 7b–11).
95.8 The elders of Israel hardened their hearts at
Massah and Meribah (Ex 17.1–7) when they quarreled with Moses and with God. Their continual re-
bellions against God eventually shut them out from
entering Canaan. The writer of Hebrews used this
psalm to warn believers (Heb 3–4).
96.1ff This psalm was delivered into the hand of

sing to the Lord, all the earth.

96.2
Ps 71.15

2 Sing to the Lord, bless his name;
tell of his salvation from day to day.

96.3
Ps 145.12

3 Declare his glory among the nations,
his marvelous works among all the peoples.

96.4
Ps 145.3;
18.3; 95.3

4 For great is the Lord, and greatly to be praised;
he is to be revered above all gods.

96.5
1 Chr 16.26;
Ps 115.15

5 For all the gods of the peoples are idols,
but the Lord made the heavens.

96.6
Ps 104.1

6 Honor and majesty are before him;
strength and beauty are in his sanctuary.

B. All the earth to praise the Lord

96.7
Ps 29.1, 2

7 Ascribe to the Lord, O families of the peoples,
ascribe to the Lord glory and strength.

96.8
Ps 79.9

8 Ascribe to the Lord the glory due his name;
bring an offering, and come into his courts.

96.9
Ps 29.2

9 Worship the Lord in holy splendor;
tremble before him, all the earth.

C. The Lord the righteous judge

96.10
Ps 93.1; 67.4

10 Say among the nations, "The Lord is king!
The world is firmly established; it shall never be moved.
He will judge the peoples with equity."

96.11
Ps 97.1; 98.7

11 Let the heavens be glad, and let the earth rejoice;
let the sea roar, and all that fills it;

12 let the field exult, and everything in it.
Then shall all the trees of the forest sing for joy

96.13
Ps 67.4;
Rev 19.11

13 before the Lord; for he is coming,
for he is coming to judge the earth.
He will judge the world with righteousness,
and the peoples with his truth.

97.1
Ps 96.10, 11

Psalm 97

The power and dominion of the Lord

A. The reign of the Lord

97.2
1 Kings 8.12;
Ps 18.11;
89.14

1 The Lord is king! Let the earth rejoice;
let the many coastlands be glad!

2 Clouds and thick darkness are all around him;
righteousness and justice are the foundation of his throne.

97.3
Ps 18.8;
Dan 7.10;
Hab 3.5;
Heb 12.29

3 Fire goes before him,
and consumes his adversaries on every side.

97.4
Ps 77.18

4 His lightnings light up the world;
the earth sees and trembles.

97.5
Mic 1.4;
Josh 3.11

5 The mountains melt like wax before the Lord,
before the Lord of all the earth.

Asaph and his kindred by David its author (1 Chr 16.7; cf. especially vv. 23–33). They sang it when the ark was brought to Jerusalem and placed in the tent David had erected to house it. The psalm has both a missionary aspect and a messianic aspect when it speaks about declaring "his glory among the nations, his marvelous works among all the peoples" (v. 3).

96.10–13 If all nature can celebrate the reign of the glorious God, everyone should follow its example and do the same.

97.1ff This psalm exalts the Lord as king, but it looks far beyond its immediate purpose. It prophetically portrays what is true concerning Jesus Christ as Lord, who will fulfill in himself everything in this psalm.

B. *The exaltation of the* Lord

6 The heavens proclaim his righteousness;
    and all the peoples behold his glory.
7 All worshipers of images are put to shame,
    those who make their boast in worthless idols;
    all gods bow down before him.
8 Zion hears and is glad,
    and the towns[n] of Judah rejoice,
    because of your judgments, O God.
9 For you, O Lord, are most high over all the earth;
    you are exalted far above all gods.

97.6
Ps 50.6
97.7
Ex 20.4;
Lev 26.1;
Heb 1.6
97.8
Ps 48.11
97.9
Ps 83.18;
Ex 18.11;
Ps 95.3

C. *The deliverance of the righteous by the* Lord

10 The Lord loves those who hate[o] evil;
    he guards the lives of his faithful;
    he rescues them from the hand of the wicked.
11 Light dawns[p] for the righteous,
    and joy for the upright in heart.
12 Rejoice in the Lord, O you righteous,
    and give thanks to his holy name!

97.10
Ps 34.14;
Am 5.15;
Prov 2.8;
Ps 37.39;
Dan 3.28
97.11
Job 22.28;
Ps 112.4
97.12
Ps 32.11;
30.4

Psalm 98

98.1
Ps 33.3; 40.5;
Ex 15.6;
Isa 52.10

A call to praise the righteous Lord

A. *The song of salvation*

A Psalm.

1 O sing to the Lord a new song,
    for he has done marvelous things.
His right hand and his holy arm
    have gotten him victory.
2 The Lord has made known his victory;
    he has revealed his vindication in the sight of the nations.
3 He has remembered his steadfast love and faithfulness
    to the house of Israel.
All the ends of the earth have seen
    the victory of our God.

98.2
Rom 3.25
98.3
Lk 1.54;
Isa 49.6

B. *The summons of humans to praise*

4 Make a joyful noise to the Lord, all the earth;
    break forth into joyous song and sing praises.
5 Sing praises to the Lord with the lyre,
    with the lyre and the sound of melody.
6 With trumpets and the sound of the horn
    make a joyful noise before the King, the Lord.

98.4
Ps 100.1

98.6
Num 10.10

C. *The summons of nature to praise*

7 Let the sea roar, and all that fills it;
    the world and those who live in it.
8 Let the floods clap their hands;
    let the hills sing together for joy

98.7
Ps 96.11;
24.1
98.8
Ps 93.3;
65.12

---

n Heb *daughters*   *o* Cn: Heb *You who love the* Lord *hate*   *p* Gk Syr Jerome: Heb *is sown*

97.9 *all gods.* See note 86.8.
98.1ff This psalm celebrates the righteous reign of the Lord God. It is also prophetic of the coming

Messiah, who will set up his kingdom and bring even the Gentiles into it. Therefore the righteous must praise their God and all nature join in the refrain.

98.9
Ps 96.10, 13

9 at the presence of the LORD, for he is coming
   to judge the earth.
He will judge the world with righteousness,
   and the peoples with equity.

Psalm 99

Praise to a holy God

99.1
Ex 25.22

A. The summons to praise

1 The LORD is king; let the peoples tremble!
   He sits enthroned upon the cherubim; let the earth quake!

99.2
Ps 97.9

2 The LORD is great in Zion;
   he is exalted over all the peoples.
3 Let them praise your great and awesome name.
   Holy is he!

99.4
Ps 11.7; 17.2;
103.6

4 Mighty King,^q lover of justice,
   you have established equity;
you have executed justice
   and righteousness in Jacob.

99.5
Ps 132.7;
Lev 19.2

5 Extol the LORD our God;
   worship at his footstool.
   Holy is he!

B. Reasons for praise

99.6
Jer 15.1;
Ex 14.15;
1 Sam 7.9

6 Moses and Aaron were among his priests,
   Samuel also was among those who called on his name.
   They cried to the LORD, and he answered them.

99.7
Ex 33.9

7 He spoke to them in the pillar of cloud;
   they kept his decrees,
   and the statutes that he gave them.

99.8
Ps 106.44;
Num 14.20;
Deut 9.20

8 O LORD our God, you answered them;
   you were a forgiving God to them,
   but an avenger of their wrongdoings.

99.9
Ps 34.3

9 Extol the LORD our God,
   and worship at his holy mountain;
   for the LORD our God is holy.

100.1
Ps 98.4

Psalm 100

Everyone exhorted to praise God

A Psalm of thanksgiving.

1 Make a joyful noise to the LORD, all the earth.
2   Worship the LORD with gladness;
   come into his presence with singing.

^q Cn: Heb And a king's strength

98.9 *he is coming to judge the earth.* This reference to the coming judgment looks to the second advent of Jesus Christ (see 2 Tim 4.1; 1 Pet 4.5; Rev 19.11). **99.1ff** Though this psalm includes the notion of the Messiah's kingdom, it is more directly related to Israelite society. God's people were to remember his rule over them in the past and the ordinances he had given them.
99.5 *Holy is he!* Holiness sums up all of God's moral

perfections. On that basis everyone should worship him.
100.1ff This psalm begins with a call for the entire human race to make *a joyful noise to the LORD.* This envisions the preaching of the gospel to all people everywhere. The psalmist urges everyone to enter God's presence, accept and thank him for his salvation, and remember that his steadfast love never ceases.

3 Know that the LORD is God.
  It is he that made us, and we are his;[r]
  we are his people, and the sheep of his pasture.

100.3
Ps 46.10;
95.6, 7

4 Enter his gates with thanksgiving,
  and his courts with praise.
  Give thanks to him, bless his name.

100.4
Ps 95.2; 96.2

5 For the LORD is good;
  his steadfast love endures forever,
  and his faithfulness to all generations.

100.5
Ps 25.8;
119.90

Psalm 101

101.1
Ps 89.1

A profession of integrity

A. David's desire for personal integrity

Of David. A Psalm.

1 I will sing of loyalty and of justice;
  to you, O LORD, I will sing.
2 I will study the way that is blameless.
  When shall I attain it?

101.2
1 Sam 18.14;
1 Kings 9.4

  I will walk with integrity of heart
  within my house;
3 I will not set before my eyes
  anything that is base.

101.3
Deut 15.9;
Ps 40.4

  I hate the work of those who fall away;
  it shall not cling to me.
4 Perverseness of heart shall be far from me;
  I will know nothing of evil.

101.4
Prov 11.20

B. David's desire for integrity in others

5 One who secretly slanders a neighbor
  I will destroy.
  A haughty look and an arrogant heart
  I will not tolerate.

101.5
Ps 50.20;
Prov 6.17

6 I will look with favor on the faithful in the land,
  so that they may live with me;
  whoever walks in the way that is blameless
  shall minister to me.

101.6
Ps 119.1

7 No one who practices deceit
  shall remain in my house;
  no one who utters lies
  shall continue in my presence.

8 Morning by morning I will destroy
  all the wicked in the land,

101.8
Ps 75.10;
118.10-12

[r] Another reading is *and not we ourselves*

101.1ff David solemnly vows to God to use his royal power for the glory of the One who gave him that power. Those who do evil can expect terror and those who do good, praise. David's attitude expressed here should still shape the mind of governments.

101.3 What we hear and see can become a great source of temptation that leads to evil. Here the eye is mentioned. Good people "shut their eyes from looking on evil" (Isa 33.15).

cutting off all evildoers
from the city of the LORD.

Psalm 102

Appeal for mercy and for Zion

A. *The sufferings of the psalmist*

A prayer of one afflicted, when faint and pleading before the LORD.

102.1
Ex 2.23;
1 Sam 9.16

1 Hear my prayer, O LORD;
    let my cry come to you.
2 Do not hide your face from me
    in the day of my distress.
  Incline your ear to me;
    answer me speedily in the day when I call.

102.2
Ps 69.17;
71.2

3 For my days pass away like smoke,
    and my bones burn like a furnace.
4 My heart is stricken and withered like grass;
    I am too wasted to eat my bread.
5 Because of my loud groaning
    my bones cling to my skin.

102.3
Jas 4.14;
Job 30.30;
Ps 31.10
102.4
Ps 37.2
102.5
Lam 4.8

6 I am like an owl of the wilderness,
    like a little owl of the waste places.
7 I lie awake;
    I am like a lonely bird on the housetop.
8 All day long my enemies taunt me;
    those who deride me use my name for a curse.
9 For I eat ashes like bread,
    and mingle tears with my drink,
10 because of your indignation and anger;
    for you have lifted me up and thrown me aside.
11 My days are like an evening shadow;
    I wither away like grass.

102.6
Isa 34.11
102.7
Ps 77.4;
38.11
102.8
Acts 26.11;
23;12
102.9
Ps 42.3
102.10
Ps 38.3;
Job 30.22
102.11
Job 14.2; v. 4

B. *The eternal God the refuge of Zion*

12 But you, O LORD, are enthroned forever;
    your name endures to all generations.
13 You will rise up and have compassion on Zion,
    for it is time to favor it;
    the appointed time has come.
14 For your servants hold its stones dear,
    and have pity on its dust.
15 The nations will fear the name of the LORD,
    and all the kings of the earth your glory.
16 For the LORD will build up Zion;
    he will appear in his glory.
17 He will regard the prayer of the destitute,
    and will not despise their prayer.

102.12
Ps 9.7;
Lam 5.19;
Ps 135.13
102.13
Isa 60.10;
Zech 1.12;
Ps 75.2
102.15
1 Kings 8.43;
Ps 138.4
102.16
Isa 60.1, 2
102.17
Neh 1.6

102.1ff The psalmist is in great affliction, but finds solace in the eternal God of comfort to whom he looks for deliverance. Since Hebrews quotes vv. 25,26 (see Heb 1.10–12), some think this psalm is primarily messianic.
102.3–5 The psalmist's body is severely emaciated — nothing but skin and bones. So bad is his condition

that he has no desire to eat.
102.12 While humans suffer pain and are mortal, God is everlasting and permanent. Those who love God can counter sorrow and death by remembering the unchangeable God who gives them blessedness forever.

18 Let this be recorded for a generation to come,
    so that a people yet unborn may praise the LORD:

19 that he looked down from his holy height,
    from heaven the LORD looked at the earth,

20 to hear the groans of the prisoners,
    to set free those who were doomed to die;

21 so that the name of the LORD may be declared in Zion,
    and his praise in Jerusalem,

22 when peoples gather together,
    and kingdoms, to worship the LORD.

C. *The assurance of deliverance*

23 He has broken my strength in midcourse;
    he has shortened my days.

24 "O my God," I say, "do not take me away
    at the midpoint of my life,
  you whose years endure
    throughout all generations."

25 Long ago you laid the foundation of the earth,
    and the heavens are the work of your hands.

26 They will perish, but you endure;
    they will all wear out like a garment.
  You change them like clothing, and they pass away;

27 but you are the same, and your years have no end.

28 The children of your servants shall live secure;
    their offspring shall be established in your presence.

Psalm 103

An exhortation to bless the LORD

A. *The exhortation to self*

Of David.

1 Bless the LORD, O my soul,
    and all that is within me,
    bless his holy name.

2 Bless the LORD, O my soul,
    and do not forget all his benefits—

3 who forgives all your iniquity,
    who heals all your diseases,

4 who redeems your life from the Pit,
    who crowns you with steadfast love and mercy,

5 who satisfies you with good as long as you live[s]
    so that your youth is renewed like the eagle's.

B. *God's mercies a reason to bless him*

6 The LORD works vindication
    and justice for all who are oppressed.

[s] Meaning of Heb uncertain

Cross-references (right margin):

102.18 Rom 15.4; Ps 22.31
102.19 Deut 26.15; Ps 33.13
102.20 Ps 79.11
102.21 Ps 22.22
102.22 Ps 86.9
102.23 Job 21.21
102.24 Isa 38.10; Ps 90.2; Hab 1.12
102.25 Gen 1.1; Heb 1.10; Ps 96.5
102.26 Isa 34.4; Mt 24.35; 2 Pet 3.7, 10; Rev 20.11
102.27 Mal 3.6; Heb 13.8; Jas 1.17
102.28 Ps 69.36; 89.4
103.1 Ps 104.1; 33.21
103.3 Ps 130.8; Isa 43.25; Ex 15.26
103.4 Ps 49.15; 5.12
103.5 Isa 40.31

102.20 All people are *doomed to die* but God sets free those who hear and believe the gospel. The groaning of the prisoners turns to shouts of praise.
103.1ff This song of praise is general in nature. The psalmist praises the God who has compassion on his children, vindicates them, and forgives their sins. His love is everlasting and his throne is forever established in the heavens. The angels, the redeemed, and all the hosts of heaven should bless the name of this great God.
103.3–5 By forgiving our sins, God restores us to his favor. All that we lost in Adam we shall regain, so that paradise itself is restored.

7 He made known his ways to Moses,
   his acts to the people of Israel.

103.8
Ex 34.6;
Neh 9.17;
Ps 145.8

8 The LORD is merciful and gracious,
   slow to anger and abounding in steadfast love.

103.9
Ps 30.5;
Isa 57.16;
Jer 3.5

9 He will not always accuse,
   nor will he keep his anger forever.

10 He does not deal with us according to our sins,
   nor repay us according to our iniquities.

103.10
Ezra 9.13

11 For as the heavens are high above the earth,
   so great is his steadfast love toward those who fear him;

103.11
Ps 36.5

103.12
2 Sam 12.13;
Isa 38.17;
Heb 9.26

12 as far as the east is from the west,
   so far he removes our transgressions from us.

103.13
Mal 3.17

13 As a father has compassion for his children,
   so the LORD has compassion for those who fear him.

103.14
Isa 29.16;
Gen 3.19

14 For he knows how we were made;
   he remembers that we are dust.

C. God's everlasting love

103.15
1 Pet 1.24;
Job 14.1, 2

15 As for mortals, their days are like grass;
   they flourish like a flower of the field;

103.16
Job 7.10

16 for the wind passes over it, and it is gone,
   and its place knows it no more.

17 But the steadfast love of the LORD is from everlasting to
   everlasting
   on those who fear him,
   and his righteousness to children's children,

103.18
Deut 7.9

18 to those who keep his covenant
   and remember to do his commandments.

D. The universal call to bless God's name

103.19
Ps 11.4; 47.2

19 The LORD has established his throne in the heavens,
   and his kingdom rules over all.

103.20
Ps 148.2;
Mt 6.10;
Heb 1.14

20 Bless the LORD, O you his angels,
   you mighty ones who do his bidding,
   obedient to his spoken word.

103.21
Ps 148.2

21 Bless the LORD, all his hosts,
   his ministers that do his will.

22 Bless the LORD, all his works,
   in all places of his dominion.
   Bless the LORD, O my soul.

104.1
Ps 103.1

Psalm 104

Praise to God the creator and sustainer

A. The beginning of creation

1 Bless the LORD, O my soul.
   O LORD my God, you are very great.
   You are clothed with honor and majesty,

104.2
Dan 7.9;
Isa 40.22

2   wrapped in light as with a garment.
   You stretch out the heavens like a tent,

103.12 God removes our transgressions so far from us that they shall never be laid to our charge nor used in judgment against us (see Rom 8.31–34).
103.20 The mighty angels are called by God to do his will and to minister to God's people (see note on Num 22.22,23).

104.1ff This psalm is noted for its poetic beauty and the splendor of its ideas. It celebrates the greatness, majesty, and sovereign control of God, manifested in his works of creation and providence. He is the God of nature as well as the God of humankind. Let them praise and rejoice in such a great God.

3   you set the beams of your[t] chambers on the waters,
    you make the clouds your[t] chariot,
        you ride on the wings of the wind,
4   you make the winds your[t] messengers,
        fire and flame your[t] ministers.

	104.3 Am 9.6; Isa 19.1; Ps 18.10

	104.4 Heb 1.7

B. *The foundations of the earth*

5   You set the earth on its foundations,
        so that it shall never be shaken.
6   You cover it with the deep as with a garment;
        the waters stood above the mountains.
7   At your rebuke they flee;
        at the sound of your thunder they take to flight.
8   They rose up to the mountains, ran down to the valleys
        to the place that you appointed for them.
9   You set a boundary that they may not pass,
        so that they might not again cover the earth.

	104.5 Job 26.7; Ps 24.2

	104.6 Gen 7.19

	104.8 Ps 33.7

	104.9 Job 38.10, 11; Jer 5.22

C. *The springs in the valleys*

10 You make springs gush forth in the valleys;
        they flow between the hills,
11 giving drink to every wild animal;
        the wild asses quench their thirst.
12 By the streams[u] the birds of the air have their habitation;
        they sing among the branches.
13 From your lofty abode you water the mountains;
        the earth is satisfied with the fruit of your work.

	104.10 Ps 107.35

	104.11 Job 39.5

	104.12 Mt 8.20

	104.13 Ps 65.9; 147.8

D. *The fruitfulness of the earth*

14 You cause the grass to grow for the cattle,
        and plants for people to use,[v]
    to bring forth food from the earth,
15   and wine to gladden the human heart,
    oil to make the face shine,
        and bread to strengthen the human heart.
16 The trees of the LORD are watered abundantly,
        the cedars of Lebanon that he planted.
17 In them the birds build their nests;
        the stork has its home in the fir trees.
18 The high mountains are for the wild goats;
        the rocks are a refuge for the coneys.

	104.14 Ps 147.8; Job 38.27; Gen 1.29; Job 28.5

	104.15 Judg 9.13; Ps 23.5

	104.18 Prov 30.26

E. *The moon and the sun*

19 You have made the moon to mark the seasons;
        the sun knows its time for setting.
20 You make darkness, and it is night,
        when all the animals of the forest come creeping out.
21 The young lions roar for their prey,
        seeking their food from God.
22 When the sun rises, they withdraw
        and lie down in their dens.

	104.19 Gen 1.14

	104.20 Isa 45.7

	104.21 Job 38.39

---

[t] Heb *his*   [u] Heb *By them*   [v] Or *to cultivate*

104.8 There is evidence of sea life on the tops of some of the highest mountains, suggesting that at one time they were submerged under the waters. God makes mountains to rise and fall according to his good pleasure.

104.14 The fruitfulness of the earth is sufficient to feed all animal and human life. Unfortunately, people have spoiled God's creation and destroyed the balance of nature.

| 104.23
Gen 3.19 | 23 | People go out to their work
and to their labor until the evening. |

F. *The creatures of the sea*

104.24 Ps 40.5; Prov 3.19; Ps 65.9	24	O LORD, how manifold are your works! In wisdom you have made them all; the earth is full of your creatures.
	25	Yonder is the sea, great and wide, creeping things innumerable are there, living things both small and great.
104.26 Ps 107.23; Job 41.1	26	There go the ships, and Leviathan that you formed to sport in it.

G. *God the sustainer of life*

104.27 Ps 136.25; 145.14	27	These all look to you to give them their food in due season;
	28	when you give to them, they gather it up; when you open your hand, they are filled with good things.
104.29 Job 34.14; Ps 146.4; Eccl 12.7	29	When you hide your face, they are dismayed; when you take away their breath, they die and return to their dust.
104.30 Isa 32.15; Ezek 37.9	30	When you send forth your spirit,^{w} they are created; and you renew the face of the ground.

H. *Concluding praise to a mighty God*

104.31 Gen 1.31	31	May the glory of the LORD endure forever; may the LORD rejoice in his works —
104.32 Ps 97.4, 5; 144.5	32	who looks on the earth and it trembles, who touches the mountains and they smoke.
104.33 Ps 63.4; 146.2	33	I will sing to the LORD as long as I live; I will sing praise to my God while I have being.
	34	May my meditation be pleasing to him, for I rejoice in the LORD.
104.35 Ps 59.13; 37.10; v. 1	35	Let sinners be consumed from the earth, and let the wicked be no more. Bless the LORD, O my soul. Praise the LORD!

Psalm 105

Praise to a covenant-keeping God

A. *The call to thanksgiving*

105.1 1 Chr 16.8; Ps 145.12	1	O give thanks to the LORD, call on his name, make known his deeds among the peoples.
105.2 Ps 77.12	2	Sing to him, sing praises to him; tell of all his wonderful works.
105.3 Ps 33.21	3	Glory in his holy name;

^{w} Or *your breath*

104.25 The seas contain food and plant life in abundance. Again, human beings have abused God's gift; they have polluted the waters and overfished the seas. People do not lack because God has not provided, but because they have failed to exercise good stewardship of those resources.
105.1ff This hymn of praise presents an overview of the God of history, who accomplished the divine purpose through his people, Israel. The psalmist tells of God's promise to Abraham, of Joseph's role in preserving a people, of their captivity in Egypt followed by Moses' divinely sent plagues, of the exodus, and, finally, of the entrance into the land of promise. The only fitting response to God's mercies, preservation, and fulfillment of his promises is for everyone to praise the Lord.

4 Seek the LORD and his strength;
    seek his presence continually.
5 Remember the wonderful works he has done,
    his miracles, and the judgments he has uttered,
6 O offspring of his servant Abraham,ˣ
    children of Jacob, his chosen ones.

B. *The Abrahamic covenant*

7 He is the LORD our God;
    his judgments are in all the earth.
8 He is mindful of his covenant forever,
    of the word that he commanded, for a thousand generations,
9 the covenant that he made with Abraham,
    his sworn promise to Isaac,
10 which he confirmed to Jacob as a statute,
    to Israel as an everlasting covenant,
11 saying, "To you I will give the land of Canaan
    as your portion for an inheritance."

12 When they were few in number,
    of little account, and strangers in it,
13 wandering from nation to nation,
    from one kingdom to another people,
14 he allowed no one to oppress them;
    he rebuked kings on their account,
15 saying, "Do not touch my anointed ones;
    do my prophets no harm."

C. *God sends Joseph to Egypt*

16 When he summoned famine against the land,
    and broke every staff of bread,
17 he had sent a man ahead of them,
    Joseph, who was sold as a slave.
18 His feet were hurt with fetters,
    his neck was put in a collar of iron;
19 until what he had said came to pass,
    the word of the LORD kept testing him.
20 The king sent and released him;
    the ruler of the peoples set him free.
21 He made him lord of his house,
    and ruler of all his possessions,
22 to instructʸ his officials at his pleasure,
    and to teach his elders wisdom.

D. *Israel in Egypt*

23 Then Israel came to Egypt;
    Jacob lived as an alien in the land of Ham.
24 And the LORD made his people very fruitful,

Cross references:
105.4 Ps 27.8
105.5 Ps 77.11
105.7 Isa 26.9
105.8 Lk 1.72
105.9 Gen 17.2; 22.16; 26.3
105.10 Gen 28.13-15
105.11 Gen 13.15; 15.18
105.12 Gen 34.30; Deut 7.7; Heb 11.9
105.14 Gen 35.5; 12.17
105.16 Gen 41.54; Lev 26.26; Isa 3.1; Ezek 4.16
105.17 Gen 45.5; 37.28, 36
105.18 Gen 39.20
105.19 Gen 40.20, 21;
Ps 66.10
105.20 Gen 41.14
105.21 Gen 41.40
105.23 Gen 46.6; Acts 13.17
105.24 Ex 1.7

x Another reading is *Israel* (compare 1 Chr 16.13) y Gk Syr Jerome: Heb *to bind*

105.9 God made a covenant with the patriarchs and passed it on to Israel from generation to generation. It was an everlasting covenant that finds its great fulfillment in Jesus Christ, who now sits forever upon the throne of his father David.
105.15 The prophets of God were precious to him; he protected them even from kings, as when he caused Jeroboam's hand to wither when it was stretched forth against God's prophet (1 Kings 13.1–5).
105.17 Joseph was sold into captivity. But God was behind the malicious act of his brothers, for he *sent a man ahead of them.* Joseph himself testified to this (Gen 45.5).

105.25
Ex 1.8, 10

25 and made them stronger than their foes,
whose hearts he then turned to hate his people,
to deal craftily with his servants.

E. Moses and the plagues

105.26
Ex 3.10;
Num 16.5

26 He sent his servant Moses,
and Aaron whom he had chosen.

105.27
Ex 7-12;
Ps 78.43

27 They performed his signs among them,
and miracles in the land of Ham.

105.28
Ex 10.22;
Ps 99.7

28 He sent darkness, and made the land dark;
they rebelled[z] against his words.

105.29
Ex 7.20

29 He turned their waters into blood,
and caused their fish to die.

105.30
Ex 8.6

30 Their land swarmed with frogs,
even in the chambers of their kings.

105.31
Ex 8.16, 21

31 He spoke, and there came swarms of flies,
and gnats throughout their country.

105.32
Ex 9.23

32 He gave them hail for rain,
and lightning that flashed through their land.

33 He struck their vines and fig trees,
and shattered the trees of their country.

105.34
Ex 10.4;
Ps 73.46

34 He spoke, and the locusts came,
and young locusts without number;

35 they devoured all the vegetation in their land,
and ate up the fruit of their ground.

105.36
Ex 12.29;
Ps 78.51

36 He struck down all the firstborn in their land,
the first issue of all their strength.

F. The exodus and the wanderings

105.37
Ex 12.35

37 Then he brought Israel[a] out with silver and gold,
and there was no one among their tribes who stumbled.

105.38
Ex 12.33

38 Egypt was glad when they departed,
for dread of them had fallen upon it.

105.39
Ex 13.21;
Neh 9.12

39 He spread a cloud for a covering,
and fire to give light by night.

105.40
Ex 16.12ff;
Ps 78.24ff

40 They asked, and he brought quails,
and gave them food from heaven in abundance.

105.41
Ex 17.6;
Ps 78.15, 16;
1 Cor 10.4

41 He opened the rock, and water gushed out;
it flowed through the desert like a river.

105.42
v. 8

42 For he remembered his holy promise,
and Abraham, his servant.

G. The settlement of Canaan

43 So he brought his people out with joy,
his chosen ones with singing.

105.44
Deut 6-10;
Josh 13.7

44 He gave them the lands of the nations,
and they took possession of the wealth of the peoples,

105.45
Deut 6.21-25

45 that they might keep his statutes
and observe his laws.
Praise the LORD!

[z] Cn Compare Gk Syr: Heb they did not rebel   [a] Heb them

105.45 The psalmist has finished recounting the
story of everything that God had done for his people

Israel. There is only one fitting response to the great
blessings they have experienced: *Praise the LORD!*

Psalm 106

Praise to God who has mercy on a sinful people

A. The prayer for mercy

1 Praise the LORD!
  O give thanks to the LORD, for he is good;
  for his steadfast love endures forever.

2 Who can utter the mighty doings of the LORD,
  or declare all his praise?

3 Happy are those who observe justice,
  who do righteousness at all times.

4 Remember me, O LORD, when you show favor to your people;
  help me when you deliver them;

5 that I may see the prosperity of your chosen ones,
  that I may rejoice in the gladness of your nation,
  that I may glory in your heritage.

B. Israel's sin at the Red Sea (cf. Exod. 14.10–12)

6 Both we and our ancestors have sinned;
  we have committed iniquity, have done wickedly.

7 Our ancestors, when they were in Egypt,
  did not consider your wonderful works;
  they did not remember the abundance of your steadfast love,
  but rebelled against the Most High[b] at the Red Sea.[c]

8 Yet he saved them for his name's sake,
  so that he might make known his mighty power.

9 He rebuked the Red Sea,[c] and it became dry;
  he led them through the deep as through a desert.

10 So he saved them from the hand of the foe,
  and delivered them from the hand of the enemy.

11 The waters covered their adversaries;
  not one of them was left.

12 Then they believed his words;
  they sang his praise.

C. Israel's sins in the wilderness (cf. Num. 11)

13 But they soon forgot his works;
  they did not wait for his counsel.

14 But they had a wanton craving in the wilderness,
  and put God to the test in the desert;

15 he gave them what they asked,
  but sent a wasting disease among them.

D. The sin of Dathan and Abiram (cf. Num. 16; Deut. 11.6)

16 They were jealous of Moses in the camp,
  and of Aaron, the holy one of the LORD.

17 The earth opened and swallowed up Dathan,
  and covered the faction of Abiram.

b Cn Compare 78.17, 56: Heb *rebelled at the sea*   *c* Or *Sea of Reeds*

106.1	Ps 105.1; 100.5; 1 Chr 16.34
106.2	Ps 145.4, 12
106.3	Ps 15.2
106.4	Ps 119.132
106.5	Ps 1.3; 118.15; 105.3
106.6	Dan 9.5
106.7	Ps 78.11, 42; Ex 14.11
106.8	Ex 9.16
106.9	Ex 14.21; Ps 18.15; 78.11, 42; Isa 63.11-14
106.10	Ex 14.30; Ps 107.2
106.11	Ex 14.28; 15.5
106.12	Ex 14.31; 15.1-21
106.13	Ex 15.24
106.14	1 Cor 10.6, 9
106.15	Num 11.31; Isa 10.16
106.16	Num 16.1-3
106.17	Deut 11.6

106.1ff This is the first of what have been called the "Hallelujah psalms." *Hallelujah* is the Hebrew word for "Praise the LORD!" (v. 1). Other "Hallelujah psalms" are 111–113; 117; 135; and 146–150 (see note on 111.1ff).
106.15 The children of Israel were unhappy in the wilderness journey when they had only manna to eat. They longed for meat and insisted on having it. God gave them what they demanded, but the consequences were disastrous; he *sent a wasting disease*. If God's people insist on their own way when he has decided differently, only disaster will result.

	18	Fire also broke out in their company;
106.18 Num 16.35		the flame burned up the wicked.

E. *The golden calf at Horeb (cf. Exod. 32; Deut. 9.8–21)*

106.19 Ex 32.14	19	They made a calf at Horeb and worshiped a cast image.
106.20 Jer 2.11; Rom 1.23	20	They exchanged the glory of God*d* for the image of an ox that eats grass.
106.21 Ps 78.11; Deut 10.21	21	They forgot God, their Savior, who had done great things in Egypt,
106.22 Ps 105.27	22	wondrous works in the land of Ham, and awesome deeds by the Red Sea.*e*
106.23 Ex 32.10; 32.11-14	23	Therefore he said he would destroy them— had not Moses, his chosen one, stood in the breach before him, to turn away his wrath from destroying them.

F. *The refusal to enter Canaan (cf. Num. 13–14)*

106.24 Deut 8.7; Heb 3.18, 19	24	Then they despised the pleasant land, having no faith in his promise.
106.25 Num 14.2	25	They grumbled in their tents, and did not obey the voice of the LORD.
106.26 Num 14.28-35; Heb 11.3	26	Therefore he raised his hand and swore to them that he would make them fall in the wilderness,
106.27 Ps 44.11	27	and would disperse*f* their descendants among the nations, scattering them over the lands.

G. *Baal of Peor (cf. Num. 25)*

106.28 Num 25.2, 3	28	Then they attached themselves to the Baal of Peor, and ate sacrifices offered to the dead;
	29	they provoked the LORD to anger with their deeds, and a plague broke out among them.
106.30 Num 25.7	30	Then Phinehas stood up and interceded, and the plague was stopped.
106.31 Num 25.11-13	31	And that has been reckoned to him as righteousness from generation to generation forever.

H. *Israel's sin at Meribah (cf. Num. 20.2–13)*

| 106.32 Num 20.3, 13; Ps 81.7 | 32 | They angered the LORD*g* at the waters of Meribah, and it went ill with Moses on their account; |
| 106.33 Num 20.10 | 33 | for they made his spirit bitter, and he spoke words that were rash. |

I. *Israel's idolatry in Canaan*

106.34 Judg 1.21; Deut 7.2, 16	34	They did not destroy the peoples, as the LORD commanded them,
106.35 Judg 3.5, 6	35	but they mingled with the nations and learned to do as they did.
106.36 Judg 2.12	36	They served their idols,

d Compare Gk Mss: Heb *exchanged their glory*   *e* Or *Sea of Reeds*   *f* Syr Compare Ezek 20.23: Heb *cause to fall*   *g* Heb *him*

106.28 *ate sacrifices offered to the dead*, i.e., ate sacrifices offered to lifeless gods. Israel offered such sacrifices again and again (e.g., see Num 25).
106.34 God's indictment against Israel was substantial. They (1) did not destroy the nations in the land as God had told them to do; (2) took over the idolatry of the heathen nations; (3) married among the heathen; and (4) offered up their children as human sacrifices. Since they would not repent, judgment had to overtake them.

which became a snare to them.

37 They sacrificed their sons
    and their daughters to the demons;
38 they poured out innocent blood,
    the blood of their sons and daughters,
    whom they sacrificed to the idols of Canaan;
    and the land was polluted with blood.
39 Thus they became unclean by their acts,
    and prostituted themselves in their doings.

J. *Israel's punishment*

40 Then the anger of the LORD was kindled against his people,
    and he abhorred his heritage;
41 he gave them into the hand of the nations,
    so that those who hated them ruled over them.
42 Their enemies oppressed them,
    and they were brought into subjection under their power.
43 Many times he delivered them,
    but they were rebellious in their purposes,
    and were brought low through their iniquity.

K. *God's mercy*

44 Nevertheless he regarded their distress
    when he heard their cry.
45 For their sake he remembered his covenant,
    and showed compassion according to the abundance of his
        steadfast love.
46 He caused them to be pitied
    by all who held them captive.

L. *Final appeal and doxology*

47 Save us, O LORD our God,
    and gather us from among the nations,
    that we may give thanks to your holy name
    and glory in your praise.

48 Blessed be the LORD, the God of Israel,
    from everlasting to everlasting.
    And let all the people say, "Amen."
    Praise the LORD!

BOOK V
(Psalms 107–150)

Psalm 107

Thanksgiving to a delivering God

A. *The call to praise*

1 O give thanks to the LORD, for he is good;

106.37
2 Kings 17.7

106.38
Ps 94.21;
Num 35.33

106.39
Ezek 20.18;
Lev 17.7;
Num 15.39

106.40
Ps 78.59

106.41
Judg 2.14;
Neh 9.27

106.43
Judg 2.16-18

106.44
Judg 3.9;
10.10

106.45
Ps 105.8;
Judg 2.18

106.46
Ezra 9.9;
Jer 42.12

106.47
1 Chr 16.35,
36;
Ps 147.2

106.48
Ps 41.13

107.1
Ps 106.1

106.44–47 Despite the punishment visited on Israel by their God, he did not forget them in their sufferings when they turned in repentance to him. The psalmist closes with a request for God to bring his people back from exile. This psalm was most likely written during or after the Babylonian captivity.

107.1ff The recurring pattern expressed in this psalm is as follows: people (1) should praise God for his goodness and mercy; (2) soon forget what they ought to remember; (3) turn from God to sin; (4) experience the judgment of God, sent to drive them to repentance; (5) sense their need for deliverance and

for his steadfast love endures forever.

107.2
Ps 106.10
2 Let the redeemed of the LORD say so,
  those he redeemed from trouble

107.3
Ps 106.47;
Isa 43.5, 6
3 and gathered in from the lands,
  from the east and from the west,
  from the north and from the south. *h*

B. *Deliverance from the desert*

107.4
Num 14.33;
32.13
4 Some wandered in desert wastes,
  finding no way to an inhabited town;
5 hungry and thirsty,
  their soul fainted within them.

107.6
Ps 50.15
6 Then they cried to the LORD in their trouble,
  and he delivered them from their distress;

107.7
Ezra 8.21
7 he led them by a straight way,
  until they reached an inhabited town.

107.8
vv. 15, 21, 31
8 Let them thank the LORD for his steadfast love,
  for his wonderful works to humankind.

107.9
Ps 22.26;
Lk 1.53
9 For he satisfies the thirsty,
  and the hungry he fills with good things.

C. *Deliverance from the prison*

107.10
Lk 1.79;
Job 36.8
10 Some sat in darkness and in gloom,
  prisoners in misery and in irons,

107.11
Ps 106.7;
2 Chr 36.16
11 for they had rebelled against the words of God,
  and spurned the counsel of the Most High.

107.12
Ps 22.11
12 Their hearts were bowed down with hard labor;
  they fell down, with no one to help.

107.13
v. 6
13 Then they cried to the LORD in their trouble,
  and he saved them from their distress;

107.14
Ps 116.16;
Lk 13.16;
Acts 12.7
14 he brought them out of darkness and gloom,
  and broke their bonds asunder.

107.15
vv. 8, 21, 31
15 Let them thank the LORD for his steadfast love,
  for his wonderful works to humankind.

107.16
Isa 45.2
16 For he shatters the doors of bronze,
  and cuts in two the bars of iron.

D. *Deliverance of the sick*

107.17
Isa 65.6, 7
17 Some were sick *i* through their sinful ways,
  and because of their iniquities endured
    affliction;

107.18
Job 33.20,
22;
Ps 9.13; 88.3
18 they loathed any kind of food,
  and they drew near to the gates of death.
19 Then they cried to the LORD in their trouble,
  and he saved them from their distress;

107.20
Mt 8.8;
Ps 30.2;
103.3
20 he sent out his word and healed them,
  and delivered them from destruction.
21 Let them thank the LORD for his steadfast love,

h Cn: Heb *sea*   *i* Cn: Heb *fools*

22 for his wonderful works to humankind.
  And let them offer thanksgiving sacrifices,
   and tell of his deeds with songs of joy.

E. *Deliverance from the sea*

23 Some went down to the sea in ships,
   doing business on the mighty waters;
24 they saw the deeds of the Lord,
   his wondrous works in the deep.
25 For he commanded and raised the stormy wind,
   which lifted up the waves of the sea.
26 They mounted up to heaven, they went down to
   the depths;
   their courage melted away in their calamity;
27 they reeled and staggered like drunkards,
   and were at their wits' end.
28 Then they cried to the Lord in their trouble,
   and he brought them out from their distress;
29 he made the storm be still,
   and the waves of the sea were hushed.
30 Then they were glad because they had quiet,
   and he brought them to their desired haven.
31 Let them thank the Lord for his steadfast love,
   for his wonderful works to humankind.
32 Let them extol him in the congregation of the people,
   and praise him in the assembly of the elders.

F. *The Lord who blesses the earth*

33 He turns rivers into a desert,
   springs of water into thirsty ground,
34 a fruitful land into a salty waste,
   because of the wickedness of its inhabitants.
35 He turns a desert into pools of water,
   a parched land into springs of water.
36 And there he lets the hungry live,
   and they establish a town to live in;
37 they sow fields, and plant vineyards,
   and get a fruitful yield.
38 By his blessing they multiply greatly,
   and he does not let their cattle decrease.

G. *The lovingkindnesses of the Lord*

39 When they are diminished and brought low
   through oppression, trouble, and sorrow,
40 he pours contempt on princes
   and makes them wander in trackless wastes;
41 but he raises up the needy out of distress,
   and makes their families like flocks.
42 The upright see it and are glad;
   and all wickedness stops its mouth.
43 Let those who are wise give heed to these things,
   and consider the steadfast love of the Lord.

Cross-references:

107.22 Lev 7.12; Ps 50.14; 9.11; 73.28; 118.17
107.25 Ps 105.31, 34; Jon 1.4; Ps 93.3, 4
107.26 Ps 22.14; 119.28
107.27 Job 12.25
107.28 vv. 6, 13, 19
107.29 Ps 89.9; Mt 8.26
107.31 vv. 8, 15, 21
107.32 Ps 22.22, 25; 35.18
107.33 Ps 74.15
107.34 Gen 13.10; 14.3; 19.25
107.35 Ps 114.8; Isa 41.18
107.37 Isa 65.21
107.38 Gen 12.2; 17.16, 20; Ex 1.7
107.39 Ezek 5.11; Ps 57.6
107.40 Job 12.21, 24
107.41 1 Sam 2.8; Ps 113.7-9
107.42 Job 22.19; Ps 52.6; Job 5.16; Ps 63.11; Rom 3.19
107.43 Ps 64.9; Jer 9.12; Hos 14.9

107.43 Experience is a great teacher. The wise will learn their lessons well from what happens to them when they sin and what happens when they turn to the Lord for salvation.

Psalm 108

A song of confidence in God

A. Thanksgiving to the LORD

A Song. A Psalm of David.

108.1
Ps 57.7

1 My heart is steadfast, O God, my heart is steadfast;^j
   I will sing and make melody.
   Awake, my soul!^k

108.2
Ps 57.8-11

2 Awake, O harp and lyre!
   I will awake the dawn.

3 I will give thanks to you, O LORD, among the
      peoples,
   and I will sing praises to you among the
      nations.

108.4
Ps 113.4

4 For your steadfast love is higher than the
      heavens,
   and your faithfulness reaches to the clouds.

5 Be exalted, O God, above the heavens,
   and let your glory be over all the earth.

B. Pleading God's promises

108.6
Ps 60.5-12

6 Give victory with your right hand, and answer me,
   so that those whom you love may be rescued.

7 God has promised in his sanctuary:^l
   "With exultation I will divide up Shechem,
   and portion out the Vale of Succoth.

108.8
Ps 60.7

8 Gilead is mine; Manasseh is mine;
   Ephraim is my helmet;
   Judah is my scepter.

9 Moab is my washbasin;
   on Edom I hurl my shoe;
   over Philistia I shout in triumph."

C. The cry for help

10 Who will bring me to the fortified city?
   Who will lead me to Edom?

108.11
Ps 44.9

11 Have you not rejected us, O God?
   You do not go out, O God, with our armies.

12 O grant us help against the foe,
   for human help is worthless.

13 With God we shall do valiantly;
   it is he who will tread down our foes.

j Heb Mss Gk Syr: MT lacks *my heart is steadfast*   k Compare 57.8: Heb *also my soul*   l Or *by his holiness*

108.1ff This is a psalm of praise and prayer. It combines parts of Ps 57 and 60 with minor variations (both of which are psalms of affliction). In this new form they can be sung in public worship or private devotions for the believer's comfort and for glorifying God.

108.9 *Moab is my washbasin; on Edom I hurl my shoe,* i.e., God despises them.

Psalm 109

A psalm of vengeance

A. The cry for help

To the leader. Of David. A Psalm.

1 Do not be silent, O God of my praise.
2 For wicked and deceitful mouths are opened against me,
   speaking against me with lying tongues.
3 They beset me with words of hate,
   and attack me without cause.
4 In return for my love they accuse me,
   even while I make prayer for them.[m]
5 So they reward me evil for good,
   and hatred for my love.

B. The imprecation

6 They say,[n] "Appoint a wicked man against him;
   let an accuser stand on his right.
7 When he is tried, let him be found guilty;
   let his prayer be counted as sin.
8 May his days be few;
   may another seize his position.
9 May his children be orphans,
   and his wife a widow.
10 May his children wander about and beg;
   may they be driven out of[o] the ruins they inhabit.
11 May the creditor seize all that he has;
   may strangers plunder the fruits of his toil.
12 May there be no one to do him a kindness,
   nor anyone to pity his orphaned children.
13 May his posterity be cut off;
   may his name be blotted out in the second generation.
14 May the iniquity of his father[p] be remembered before the
     LORD,
   and do not let the sin of his mother be blotted out.
15 Let them be before the LORD continually,
   and may his[q] memory be cut off from the earth.
16 For he did not remember to show kindness,
   but pursued the poor and needy
   and the brokenhearted to their death.
17 He loved to curse; let curses come on him.
   He did not like blessing; may it be far from him.
18 He clothed himself with cursing as his coat,
   may it soak into his body like water,
   like oil into his bones.
19 May it be like a garment that he wraps around himself,
   like a belt that he wears every day."

20 May that be the reward of my accusers from the LORD,

m Syr: Heb *I prayer*   *n* Heb lacks *They say*   *o* Gk: Heb *and seek*   *p* Cn: Heb *fathers*   *q* Gk: Heb *their*

109.1
Ps 83.1

109.2
Ps 52.4;
120.2
109.3
Ps 69.4
109.4
Ps 38.20;
69.13
109.5
Ps 35.12;
38.20

109.6
Zech 3.1
109.7
Prov 28.9
109.8
Acts 1.20
109.9
Ex 22.24

109.11
Job 5.5; 18.9
109.12
Isa 9.17
109.13
Ps 37.28;
Prov 10.7
109.14
Ex 20.5;
Neh 4.5;
Jer 18.23
109.15
Ps 34.16
109.16
Ps 37.14, 32

109.17
Prov 14.14;
Ezek 35.6
109.18
Ps 73.6;
Num 5.22

109.20
Ps 94.23;
2 Tim 4.14;
Ps 71.10

109.1ff This psalm may be sung with the conviction that the God of righteousness will some day destroy the enemies of Christ and of his church. Those who trust in God will inherit his great salvation if they keep close to him. The apostle Peter applies v. 8 to Judas Iscariot (Acts 1.20). This indicates that David, whether he realized it or not, was speaking prophetically concerning that which would take place long after his own death.
109.6–19 The imprecations here are very terrible (see note on 83.1ff). Woe to those against whom God himself says "Amen" to these imprecations.

of those who speak evil against my life.

C. *The cry for help continued*

109.21
Ps 79.9;
69.16
21 But you, O Lord my Lord,
   act on my behalf for your name's sake;
   because your steadfast love is good, deliver me.

109.22
Ps 40.17;
143.4
22 For I am poor and needy,
   and my heart is pierced within me.

109.23
Ps 102.11
23 I am gone like a shadow at evening;
   I am shaken off like a locust.

109.24
Heb 12.12
24 My knees are weak through fasting;
   my body has become gaunt.

109.25
Ps 22.6, 7;
Mt 27.39;
Mk 15.29
25 I am an object of scorn to my accusers;
   when they see me, they shake their heads.

109.26
Ps 119.86
26 Help me, O Lord my God!
   Save me according to your steadfast love.

109.27
Job 37.7
27 Let them know that this is your hand;
   you, O Lord, have done it.

109.28
2 Sam 16.11,
12;
Isa 65.14
28 Let them curse, but you will bless.
   Let my assailants be put to shame;[r] may your servant be
     glad.

109.29
Ps 35.26;
132.18
29 May my accusers be clothed with dishonor;
   may they be wrapped in their own shame as in a mantle.

109.30
Ps 35.18
30 With my mouth I will give great thanks to the Lord;
   I will praise him in the midst of the throng.

109.31
Ps 16.8;
121.5
31 For he stands at the right hand of the needy,
   to save them from those who would condemn them to death.

Psalm 110

A Messianic psalm (Messiah's dominion)

A. *Messiah the king*

Of David. A Psalm.

110.1
Mt 22.44;
Mk 12.36;
Lk 20.42;
Acts 2.34;
1 Cor 15.25
1 The Lord says to my lord,
   "Sit at my right hand
until I make your enemies your footstool."

110.2
Ps 45.6; 2.9
2 The Lord sends out from Zion
   your mighty scepter.
   Rule in the midst of your foes.

B. *Messiah the priest*

110.3
Judg 5.2;
Ps 96.9
3 Your people will offer themselves willingly
   on the day you lead your forces
   on the holy mountains.[s]
From the womb of the morning,
   like dew, your youth[t] will come to you.

---

[r] Gk: Heb *They have risen up and have been put to shame*   [s] Another reading is *in holy splendor*
[t] Cn: Heb *the dew of your youth*

109.21 So great is the pain of the psalmist that he needs God to act on his behalf. God promises to intervene for any whose heart is steadfast. Those who have God for their helper need not be afraid of what the wicked can do.
110.1ff This is a messianic psalm that was used two ways in the N.T. Jesus himself confounded his critics and made his claim to deity by using v. 1 (Mt 22.44). Heb 5.6 quotes v. 4 to endorse the eternal priesthood of Jesus. The whole psalm looks with expectation to the day in which Christ would reign over all the nations of the earth.

4 The Lord has sworn and will not change his mind,
   "You are a priest forever according to the order of
      Melchizedek."*u*

110.4
Heb 5.6, 10;
6.20; 7.11,
15, 21

5 The Lord is at your right hand;
   he will shatter kings on the day of his wrath.

110.5
Ps 16.8; 2.5,
12;
Rom 2.5;
Rev 11.18

C. *Messiah the victor*

6 He will execute judgment among the nations,
      filling them with corpses;
   he will shatter heads
      over the wide earth.

110.6
Isa 2.4;
66.24;
Ps 68.21

7 He will drink from the stream by the path;
   therefore he will lift up his head.

110.7
Ps 27.6

Psalm 111

111.1
Ps 138.1;
149.1

Praise of the Lord

A. *The call to praise*

1 Praise the Lord!
   I will give thanks to the Lord with my whole heart,
      in the company of the upright, in the congregation.

B. *The cause for praise*

2 Great are the works of the Lord,
      studied by all who delight in them.

111.2
Ps 92.5

3 Full of honor and majesty is his work,
      and his righteousness endures forever.

111.3
Ps 145.5

4 He has gained renown by his wonderful deeds;
      the Lord is gracious and merciful.

111.4
Ps 86.5;
103.8

5 He provides food for those who fear him;
      he is ever mindful of his covenant.

111.5
Mt 6.26, 33

6 He has shown his people the power of his works,
      in giving them the heritage of the nations.

7 The works of his hands are faithful and just;
      all his precepts are trustworthy.

111.7
Rev 15.3;
Ps 19.7

8 They are established forever and ever,
      to be performed with faithfulness and uprightness.

111.8
Mt 5.18;
Ps 19.9

9 He sent redemption to his people;
      he has commanded his covenant forever.
   Holy and awesome is his name.

111.9
Lk 1.68;
Ps 99.3

C. *The spirit of praise*

10 The fear of the Lord is the beginning of wisdom;
      all those who practice it*v* have a good understanding.
   His praise endures forever.

111.10
Prov 9.10;
3.4;
Ps 145.2

u Or forever, a rightful king by my edict   v Gk Syr: Heb them

111.1ff Ps 111 — 113 are songs of praise; each starts with *Praise the Lord,* i.e., "Hallelujah." The word "Hallelujah" means "Praise the Lord" and occurs exclusively in the books of Psalms and Revelation (see Rev 19.1–6, where it appears four times). Other Hebrew words for praise, *hillel* and *hallel,* appear many times in the O.T. God's people are called to sing the "Hallelujah psalms."
111.9 *Holy and awesome is his name.* The name of God is holy and worthy of all respect. No one should take his name in vain. Those who do, sin grievously against God.

Psalm 112

The excellence and reward of the pious

112.1
Ps 128.1;
119.16

1 Praise the LORD!
  Happy are those who fear the LORD,
    who greatly delight in his commandments.

112.2
Ps 25.13

2 Their descendants will be mighty in the land;
    the generation of the upright will be blessed.

112.3
Prov 3.16;
8.18

3 Wealth and riches are in their houses,
    and their righteousness endures forever.

112.4
Job 11.17;
Ps 97.11

4 They rise in the darkness as a light for the upright;
    they are gracious, merciful, and righteous.

112.5
Ps 37.26

5 It is well with those who deal generously and lend,
    who conduct their affairs with justice.

112.6
Prov 10.7

6 For the righteous will never be moved;
    they will be remembered forever.

112.7
Prov 1.33;
Ps 57.7

7 They are not afraid of evil tidings;
    their hearts are firm, secure in the LORD.

112.8
Ps 59.10;
118.7

8 Their hearts are steady, they will not be afraid;
    in the end they will look in triumph on their foes.

112.9
2 Cor 9.9;
Deut 24.13;
Ps 75.10

9 They have distributed freely, they have given to the poor;
    their righteousness endures forever;
    their horn is exalted in honor.

112.10
Ps 86.17;
37.12; 58.7,
8;
Prov 10.28;
11.7

10 The wicked see it and are angry;
    they gnash their teeth and melt away;
    the desire of the wicked comes to nothing.

Psalm 113

A hymn of praise to God

113.1
Ps 135.1

1 Praise the LORD!
  Praise, O servants of the LORD;
    praise the name of the LORD.

113.2
Dan 2.20

2 Blessed be the name of the LORD
    from this time on and forevermore.

113.3
Ps 50.1

3 From the rising of the sun to its setting
    the name of the LORD is to be praised.

113.4
Ps 97.9; 99.2;
8.1

4 The LORD is high above all nations,
    and his glory above the heavens.

113.5
Ps 89.6;
103.19

5 Who is like the LORD our God,
    who is seated on high,

113.6
Ps 11.4;
138.6;
Isa 57.15

6 who looks far down
    on the heavens and the earth?

113.7
1 Sam 2.8;
Ps 107.41

7 He raises the poor from the dust,
    and lifts the needy from the ash heap,

113.8
Job 36.7

8 to make them sit with princes,
    with the princes of his people.

113.9
1 Sam 2.5;
Ps 68.6;
Isa 54.1

9 He gives the barren woman a home,
    making her the joyous mother of children.
  Praise the LORD!

112.1ff This psalm extols the happiness of the saints. Such happiness brings glory to God, for the saints praise God for it.

113.1ff Beginning and ending with "Hallelujah," this psalm promotes the best of all works, the praise of God.

Psalm 114

In remembrance of Israel's delivering God

1 When Israel went out from Egypt,
   the house of Jacob from a people of strange language,
2 Judah became God's[w] sanctuary,
   Israel his dominion.

3 The sea looked and fled;
   Jordan turned back.
4 The mountains skipped like rams,
   the hills like lambs.

5 Why is it, O sea, that you flee?
   O Jordan, that you turn back?
6 O mountains, that you skip like rams?
   O hills, like lambs?

7 Tremble, O earth, at the presence of the LORD,
   at the presence of the God of Jacob,
8 who turns the rock into a pool of water,
   the flint into a spring of water.

Psalm 115

Give glory to God

A. *To God alone belongs glory*

1 Not to us, O LORD, not to us, but to your name give glory,
   for the sake of your steadfast love and your faithfulness.
2 Why should the nations say,
   "Where is their God?"

B. *The evil of idols*

3 Our God is in the heavens;
   he does whatever he pleases.
4 Their idols are silver and gold,
   the work of human hands.
5 They have mouths, but do not speak;
   eyes, but do not see.
6 They have ears, but do not hear;
   noses, but do not smell.
7 They have hands, but do not feel;
   feet, but do not walk;
   they make no sound in their throats.
8 Those who make them are like them;
   so are all who trust in them.

w Heb *his*

114.1	Ex 13.3
114.2	Ex 19.6; 29.45, 46
114.3	Ex 14.21; Josh 3.13, 16
114.4	Ps 29.6; Hab 3.6
114.5	Hab 3.6
114.7	Ps 96.9
114.8	Ex 17.6; Num 20.11; Ps 107.35; Deut 8.15
115.1	Isa 48.11; Ezek 36.32; Ps 96.8
115.2	Ps 42.3; 79.10
115.3	Ps 103.19; 135.6; Dan 4.35
115.4	Deut 4.28; Ps 135.15-17; Jer 10.3ff
115.5	Jer 10.5
115.8	Ps 135.18

114.1ff This psalm celebrates the deliverance of Israel from Egypt. God wanted his people to hold the exodus in everlasting remembrance, and this psalm is part of that eternal commemoration. The Israelites used this song, along with other "Hallelujah psalms," as part of their praise at the close of the passover meal.
115.1ff Though in the Hebrew this psalm is a sepa-

rate song, the Septuagint (Greek translation of the O.T.) and the Vulgate (Latin translation of the O.T.) join it to Ps 114. Its theme is similar to that of Ps 114: we must give all glory to God, not to ourselves. The song ends with *Praise the* LORD.
115.3 *he does whatever he pleases.* God is sovereign. As believers discover what God is pleased to do, they accept it and thank him for it.

C. *Israel enjoined to trust the LORD*

115.9
Ps 118.2-4;
33.20

9 O Israel, trust in the LORD!
  He is their help and their shield.

10 O house of Aaron, trust in the LORD!
   He is their help and their shield.

115.11
Ps 135.20

11 You who fear the LORD, trust in the LORD!
   He is their help and their shield.

D. *The LORD will bless Israel*

12 The LORD has been mindful of us; he will bless us;
   he will bless the house of Israel,
   he will bless the house of Aaron;

115.13
Ps 128.1, 4

13 he will bless those who fear the LORD,
   both small and great.

115.14
Deut 1.11

14 May the LORD give you increase,
   both you and your children.

115.15
Gen 14.19;
1.1;
Ps 96.5

15 May you be blessed by the LORD,
   who made heaven and earth.

115.16
Ps 89.11; 8.6

16 The heavens are the LORD's heavens,
   but the earth he has given to human beings.

115.17
Ps 6.5; 31.17

17 The dead do not praise the LORD,
   nor do any that go down into silence.

115.18
Ps 113.2

18 But we will bless the LORD
   from this time on and forevermore.
   Praise the LORD!

Psalm 116

Hymn of thanksgiving for deliverance

A. *Acknowledgment of God's deliverance*

116.1
Ps 18.1;
66.19

1 I love the LORD, because he has heard
  my voice and my supplications.

116.2
Ps 40.1

2 Because he inclined his ear to me,
  therefore I will call on him as long as I live.

116.3
Ps 18.4-6

3 The snares of death encompassed me;
  the pangs of Sheol laid hold on me;
  I suffered distress and anguish.

116.4
Ps 118.5;
22.20

4 Then I called on the name of the LORD:
  "O LORD, I pray, save my life!"

116.5
Ps 103.8;
Ezra 9.15;
Neh 9.8;
Ps 145.17;
Ex 34.6

5 Gracious is the LORD, and righteous;
  our God is merciful.

6 The LORD protects the simple;
  when I was brought low, he saved me.

116.6
Ps 19.7; 79.8
116.7
Jer 6.16;
Mt 11.29;
Ps 13.6

7 Return, O my soul, to your rest,
  for the LORD has dealt bountifully with you.

116.8
Ps 56.13
116.9
Ps 27.13

8 For you have delivered my soul from death,
  my eyes from tears,
  my feet from stumbling.

9 I walk before the LORD

116.1ff This is a psalm of thanksgiving for God's great deliverances. What occasioned it we do not know, but its content applies to believers of all times and places.

in the land of the living.
10 I kept my faith, even when I said,
    "I am greatly afflicted";
11 I said in my consternation,
    "Everyone is a liar."

B. *Resolve to pay one's vows*

12 What shall I return to the LORD
    for all his bounty to me?
13 I will lift up the cup of salvation
    and call on the name of the LORD,
14 I will pay my vows to the LORD
    in the presence of all his people.
15 Precious in the sight of the LORD
    is the death of his faithful ones.
16 O LORD, I am your servant;
    I am your servant, the child of your serving girl.
    You have loosed my bonds.
17 I will offer to you a thanksgiving sacrifice
    and call on the name of the LORD.
18 I will pay my vows to the LORD
    in the presence of all his people,
19 in the courts of the house of the LORD,
    in your midst, O Jerusalem.
    Praise the LORD!

Psalm 117

Extol God for his steadfast love

1 Praise the LORD, all you nations!
    Extol him, all you peoples!
2 For great is his steadfast love toward us,
    and the faithfulness of the LORD endures forever.
    Praise the LORD!

Psalm 118

Thanks to the LORD

A. *The LORD's mercy*

1 O give thanks to the LORD, for he is good;
    his steadfast love endures forever!

2 Let Israel say,
    "His steadfast love endures forever."
3 Let the house of Aaron say,
    "His steadfast love endures forever."
4 Let those who fear the LORD say,
    "His steadfast love endures forever."

116.10	2 Cor 4.13
116.11	Ps 31.22; Rom 3.4
116.13	Ps 16.5; 80.18
116.14	Ps 22.25; Jon 2.9
116.15	Ps 72.14
116.16	Ps 119.125; 143.12; 86.16
116.17	Ps 50.14; v. 13
116.18	v. 14
116.19	Ps 96.8; 135.2
117.1	Rom 15.11
117.2	Ps 100.5
118.1	Ps 106.1; 136.1
118.2	Ps 115.9

116.12 There is no way that we can repay God for what he has done for us. We must, of course, surrender ourselves to him and seek to glorify his name. But we can never thank him enough.
118.1ff The author, time, and circumstances of this psalm are unknown. Many attribute it to David. A segment of it has messianic implications (vv. 22,23; see Mt 21.42; Mk 12.10; Lk 20.17; Acts 4.11; Eph 2.20; 1 Pet 2.4,7). The psalm is one of thanksgiving to a mighty and wise God, who answers prayer and delivers the suppliant. It ends with a doxology.

Psalm 118.5

B. *The Lord's answer to prayer*

118.5
Ps 120.1;
18.19
118.6
Ps 27.1;
Heb 13.6;
Ps 56.4, 11
118.7
Ps 54.4;
59.10
118.8
Ps 40.4;
Jer 17.5
118.9
Ps 146.3

5 Out of my distress I called on the Lord;
  the Lord answered me and set me in a broad place.
6 With the Lord on my side I do not fear.
  What can mortals do to me?
7 The Lord is on my side to help me;
  I shall look in triumph on those who hate me.
8 It is better to take refuge in the Lord
  than to put confidence in mortals.
9 It is better to take refuge in the Lord
  than to put confidence in princes.

C. *The Lord's deliverance*

118.10
Ps 3.6; 18.40

118.12
Deut 1.44;
Ps 58.9

118.13
Ps 140.4;
86.17
118.14
Ex 15.2;
Isa 12.2

10 All nations surrounded me;
  in the name of the Lord I cut them off!
11 They surrounded me, surrounded me on every side;
  in the name of the Lord I cut them off!
12 They surrounded me like bees;
  they blazed[x] like a fire of thorns;
  in the name of the Lord I cut them off!
13 I was pushed hard,[y] so that I was falling,
  but the Lord helped me.
14 The Lord is my strength and my might;
  he has become my salvation.

D. *The Lord's mighty right hand*

118.15
Ps 68.3;
89.13
118.16
Ex 15.6
118.17
Hab 1.12;
Ps 73.28
118.18
2 Cor 6.9

118.19
Isa 26.2

15 There are glad songs of victory in the tents of the righteous:
  "The right hand of the Lord does valiantly;
16   the right hand of the Lord is exalted;
  the right hand of the Lord does valiantly."
17 I shall not die, but I shall live,
  and recount the deeds of the Lord.
18 The Lord has punished me severely,
  but he did not give me over to death.

19 Open to me the gates of righteousness,
  that I may enter through them
  and give thanks to the Lord.

118.20
Ps 24.7;
Isa 35.8;
Rev 22.14

20 This is the gate of the Lord;
  the righteous shall enter through it.

E. *The Lord's wisdom*

118.21
Ps 116.1;
v. 14
118.22
Mt 21.42;
Mk 12.10;
Lk 20.17;
Acts 4.11;
Eph 2.20;
1 Pet 2.4, 7

21 I thank you that you have answered me
  and have become my salvation.
22 The stone that the builders rejected
  has become the chief cornerstone.
23 This is the Lord's doing;
  it is marvelous in our eyes.
24 This is the day that the Lord has made;
  let us rejoice and be glad in it.[z]
25 Save us, we beseech you, O Lord!
  O Lord, we beseech you, give us success!

[x] Gk: Heb *were extinguished* [y] Gk Syr Jerome: Heb *You pushed me hard* [z] Or *in him*

118.8 Only God can be trusted absolutely. All too often, however, mortals place their confidence in those whom they can see and touch, only to regret it later.

26 Blessed is the one who comes in the name of the Lord. [a]
   We bless you from the house of the Lord.
27 The Lord is God,
   and he has given us light.
   Bind the festal procession with branches,
   up to the horns of the altar. [b]

F. *The doxology*

28 You are my God, and I will give thanks to you;
   you are my God, I will extol you.

29 O give thanks to the Lord, for he is good,
   for his steadfast love endures forever.

Psalm 119

The law of the Lord

A. *The happiness of those who keep His law*

1 Happy are those whose way is blameless,
   who walk in the law of the Lord.
2 Happy are those who keep his decrees,
   who seek him with their whole heart,
3 who also do no wrong,
   but walk in his ways.
4 You have commanded your precepts
   to be kept diligently.
5 O that my ways may be steadfast
   in keeping your statutes!
6 Then I shall not be put to shame,
   having my eyes fixed on all your commandments.
7 I will praise you with an upright heart,
   when I learn your righteous ordinances.
8 I will observe your statutes;
   do not utterly forsake me.

B. *Holiness the fruit of keeping God's law*

9 How can young people keep their way pure?
   By guarding it according to your word.
10 With my whole heart I seek you;
   do not let me stray from your commandments.
11 I treasure your word in my heart,
   so that I may not sin against you.
12 Blessed are you, O Lord;
   teach me your statutes.
13 With my lips I declare
   all the ordinances of your mouth.
14 I delight in the way of your decrees

a Or *Blessed in the name of the Lord is the one who comes*   *b* Meaning of Heb uncertain

Cross references

118.26
Mt 21.9;
Mk 11.9;
Lk 13.35;
19.38;
Jn 12.13
118.27
1 Kings 18.39;
Esth 8.16;
1 Pet 2.9

118.28
Ex 15.2;
Isa 25.1

118.29
v. 1

119.1
Ps 101.2, 6;
128.1

119.2
vv. 22, 10;
Deut 6.5
119.3
1 Jn 3.9;
5.18

119.6
v. 80
119.7
v. 62

119.9
2 Chr 6.16
119.10
2 Chr 15.15;
vv. 21, 118
119.11
Ps 37.31;
Lk 2.19, 51
119.12
vv. 26, 64,
68, 108, 124,
135, 171
119.13
Ps 40.9; v. 72

118.29 The love, mercy, and goodness of God last forever. For this the believers give thanks every day of their lives.
119.1ff This psalm is divided into twenty-two segments of eight verses each, arranged in the order of the Hebrew alphabet. Its various segments are pious declarations that stand by themselves without reference to the other parts. On the whole, the psalm exalts the law of God and sets forth the excellency and glories of divine revelation.
119.11 The kings of Israel were supposed to write out a copy of the law for their own use (Deut 17.18). To the psalmist, the law should be inscribed on the heart, for the word of God before them must be the word of God in them.

as much as in all riches.

119.15
vv. 23, 48,
78;
Ps 1.2
119.16
Ps 1.2

15 I will meditate on your precepts,
        and fix my eyes on your ways.
16 I will delight in your statutes;
        I will not forget your word.

C. *Eyes to behold the truth of God's law*

119.17
Ps 13.6

17 Deal bountifully with your servant,
        so that I may live and observe your word.
18 Open my eyes, so that I may behold
        wondrous things out of your law.

119.19
Gen 47.9;
1 Chr 29.15;
Ps 39.12;
2 Cor 5.6;
Heb 11.13
119.20
Ps 42.1, 2
119.21
vv. 10, 118
119.22
Ps 39.8
119.23
v. 15

19 I live as an alien in the land;
        do not hide your commandments from me.
20 My soul is consumed with longing
        for your ordinances at all times.
21 You rebuke the insolent, accursed ones,
        who wander from your commandments;
22 take away from me their scorn and contempt,
        for I have kept your decrees.
23 Even though princes sit plotting against me,
        your servant will meditate on your statutes.

119.24
v. 16

24 Your decrees are my delight,
        they are my counselors.

D. *Prayer to understand God's precepts*

119.25
Ps 44.25;
v. 37
119.26
v. 12

25 My soul clings to the dust;
        revive me according to your word.
26 When I told of my ways, you answered me;
        teach me your statutes.

119.27
Ps 145.5

27 Make me understand the way of your precepts,
        and I will meditate on your wondrous works.

119.28
Ps 107.26;
20.2;
1 Pet 5.10

28 My soul melts away for sorrow;
        strengthen me according to your word.
29 Put false ways far from me;
        and graciously teach me your law.
30 I have chosen the way of faithfulness;
        I set your ordinances before me.

119.31
Deut 11.22

31 I cling to your decrees, O LORD;
        let me not be put to shame.

119.32
1 Kings 4.29;
Isa 60.5;
2 Cor 6.11

32 I run the way of your commandments,
        for you enlarge my understanding.

E. *Perseverance based on God's promises*

119.33
vv. 5, 12

33 Teach me, O LORD, the way of your statutes,
        and I will observe it to the end.

119.34
v. 73;
Prov 2.6;
Jas 1.5
119.35
v. 16
119.36
1 Kings 8.58;
Lk 12.15
119.37
Isa 33.15;
Ps 71.20
119.38
2 Sam 7.25

34 Give me understanding, that I may keep your law
        and observe it with my whole heart.
35 Lead me in the path of your commandments,
        for I delight in it.
36 Turn my heart to your decrees,
        and not to selfish gain.
37 Turn my eyes from looking at vanities;
        give me life in your ways.
38 Confirm to your servant your promise,
        which is for those who fear you.

119.18 See note on v. 97.

39 Turn away the disgrace that I dread,
      for your ordinances are good.
40 See, I have longed for your precepts;
      in your righteousness give me life.

F. *Salvation through the law of the L*ORD

41 Let your steadfast love come to me, O LORD,
      your salvation according to your promise.
42 Then I shall have an answer for those who taunt me,
      for I trust in your word.
43 Do not take the word of truth utterly out of my mouth,
      for my hope is in your ordinances.
44 I will keep your law continually,
      forever and ever.
45 I shall walk at liberty,
      for I have sought your precepts.
46 I will also speak of your decrees before kings,
      and shall not be put to shame;
47 I find my delight in your commandments,
      because I love them.
48 I revere your commandments, which I love,
      and I will meditate on your statutes.

G. *The law of the L*ORD *a source of hope and comfort*

49 Remember your word to your servant,
      in which you have made me hope.
50 This is my comfort in my distress,
      that your promise gives me life.
51 The arrogant utterly deride me,
      but I do not turn away from your law.
52 When I think of your ordinances from of old,
      I take comfort, O LORD.
53 Hot indignation seizes me because of the wicked,
      those who forsake your law.
54 Your statutes have been my songs
      wherever I make my home.
55 I remember your name in the night, O LORD,
      and keep your law.
56 This blessing has fallen to me,
      for I have kept your precepts.

H. *The L*ORD *our portion*

57 The LORD is my portion;
      I promise to keep your words.
58 I implore your favor with all my heart;
      be gracious to me according to your promise.
59 When I think of your ways,
      I turn my feet to your decrees;
60 I hurry and do not delay
      to keep your commandments.
61 Though the cords of the wicked ensnare me,

119.40
vv. 20, 25

119.41
vv. 77, 116

119.42
Prov 27.11

119.46
Mt 10.18;
Acts 26.1, 2
119.47
v. 16
119.48
v. 15

119.50
Rom 15.4

119.51
Jer 20.7;
v. 157;
Job 23.11;
Ps 44.18
119.52
Ps 103.18
119.53
Ezra 9.3;
Ps 89.30

119.55
Ps 63.6

119.57
Ps 16.5;
Deut 33.9
119.58
1 Kings 13.6;
v. 41
119.59
Lk 15.17, 18

119.61
Ps 140.5;
v. 83

119.44 Unless we keep the word of God (i.e., follow it and execute its commandments), it profits us nothing.
119.49 The hope of the believer is founded on the word of God. There is no other basis for hope in life.
119.54 Wise travelers along the pathway of life sing

songs in the night with words borrowed from the Scriptures.
119.57 We should choose God as our portion, not money, fame, or any other worldly satisfaction. To do so we must think of God's ways and hasten to keep his commandments.

I do not forget your law.

119.62
Acts 16.25

62 At midnight I rise to praise you,
    because of your righteous ordinances.

119.63
Ps 101.6

63 I am a companion of all who fear you,
    of those who keep your precepts.

119.64
Ps 33.5; v. 12

64 The earth, O LORD, is full of your steadfast love;
    teach me your statutes.

I. *The law of the LORD taught by affliction*

65 You have dealt well with your servant,
    O LORD, according to your word.

66 Teach me good judgment and knowledge,
    for I believe in your commandments.

119.67
v. 71;
Jer 31.18, 19;
Heb 12.11

67 Before I was humbled I went astray,
    but now I keep your word.

119.68
Ps 106.1;
Deut 8.16;
v. 12

68 You are good and do good;
    teach me your statutes.

69 The arrogant smear me with lies,
    but with my whole heart I keep your precepts.

119.69
Job 13.4;
v. 56

70 Their hearts are fat and gross,
    but I delight in your law.

119.70
Ps 17.10;
Isa 6.10;
v. 16

71 It is good for me that I was humbled,
    so that I might learn your statutes.

119.72
v. 127;
Ps 19.10;
Prov 8.10,
11, 19

72 The law of your mouth is better to me
    than thousands of gold and silver pieces.

J. *Fellowship based upon the law of the LORD*

119.73
Job 10.8;
Ps 138.8;
v. 34

73 Your hands have made and fashioned me;
    give me understanding that I may learn your commandments.

74 Those who fear you shall see me and rejoice,
    because I have hoped in your word.

119.74
Ps 34.2; v. 43

75 I know, O LORD, that your judgments are right,
    and that in faithfulness you have humbled me.

119.75
Heb 12.10

76 Let your steadfast love become my comfort
    according to your promise to your servant.

119.77
vv. 41, 47

77 Let your mercy come to me, that I may live;
    for your law is my delight.

119.78
Jer 50.32;
vv. 86, 15

78 Let the arrogant be put to shame,
    because they have subverted me with guile;
    as for me, I will meditate on your precepts.

79 Let those who fear you turn to me,
    so that they may know your decrees.

119.80
vv. 1, 46

80 May my heart be blameless in your statutes,
    so that I may not be put to shame.

K. *A longing for peace*

119.81
Ps 84.2

81 My soul languishes for your salvation;
    I hope in your word.

119.82
Ps 69.3

82 My eyes fail with watching for your promise;
    I ask, "When will you comfort me?"

119.83
Job 30.30

83 For I have become like a wineskin in the smoke,
    yet I have not forgotten your statutes.

119.67 The psalmist can speak from experience to those who live in prosperity and peace, and then wander away from God. When they go back to God and keep his word, they recover from their wanderings.

119.73 God, the Creator, has made us by his power and intends that his creatures glorify him.
119.81,82 At times our souls faint and our eyes fail; we long for God's salvation. The hope of that salvation springs from the word of God.

84 How long must your servant endure?
    When will you judge those who persecute me?
85 The arrogant have dug pitfalls for me;
    they flout your law.
86 All your commandments are enduring;
    I am persecuted without cause; help me!
87 They have almost made an end of me on earth;
    but I have not forsaken your precepts.
88 In your steadfast love spare my life,
    so that I may keep the decrees of your mouth.

L. *The immutability of the law of the Lord*

89 The Lord exists forever;
    your word is firmly fixed in heaven.
90 Your faithfulness endures to all generations;
    you have established the earth, and it stands fast.
91 By your appointment they stand today,
    for all things are your servants.
92 If your law had not been my delight,
    I would have perished in my misery.
93 I will never forget your precepts,
    for by them you have given me life.
94 I am yours; save me,
    for I have sought your precepts.
95 The wicked lie in wait to destroy me,
    but I consider your decrees.
96 I have seen a limit to all perfection,
    but your commandment is exceedingly broad.

M. *The love of the law of the Lord*

97 Oh, how I love your law!
    It is my meditation all day long.
98 Your commandment makes me wiser than my enemies,
    for it is always with me.
99 I have more understanding than all my teachers,
    for your decrees are my meditation.
100 I understand more than the aged,
    for I keep your precepts.
101 I hold back my feet from every evil way,
    in order to keep your word.
102 I do not turn away from your ordinances,
    for you have taught me.
103 How sweet are your words to my taste,
    sweeter than honey to my mouth!
104 Through your precepts I get understanding;
    therefore I hate every false way.

Cross references (right margin):

119.84 Ps 39.4; Rev 6.10
119.85 Ps 35.7
119.86 v. 78; Ps 35.19; 109.26
119.87 Isa 58.2
119.89 Mt 24.34, 35; 1 Pet 1.25
119.90 Ps 36.5; 148.6; Eccl 1.4
119.91 Jer 33.25
119.92 vv. 16, 50
119.93 vv. 16, 25
119.94 vv. 146, 45
119.97 Ps 1.2
119.98 v. 130; Deut 4.6
119.99 v. 15
119.100 Job 32.7-9
119.101 Prov 1.15
119.103 Ps 19.10
119.104 vv. 128, 130

119.89 The word of God is eternal and unchangeable, as are all his counsels. Not one word spoken by God shall fail. Before a single letter in any single word of God can be changed or abridged, heaven and earth would first have to pass away (see Mt 5.18).
119.97 The writer of this psalm has obviously spent hours with the word of God. It is helpful for us to know various methods of Bible study: (1) book study: master one book at a time—who wrote it, what its purpose is, what its outline is, and how it relates to the remainder of the Scriptures; (2) topical study: track down words such as *love, grace, faith, prayer,* and *assurance*; (3) biographical study: look into the lives of God's saints to discover what lessons can be learned from their experiences—Moses, Abraham, Sarah, David, Mary, Paul, and, most of all, Jesus; and (4) intensive study of the great passages of Scripture (e.g., Ps 23; John 1; Rom 8; 1 Cor 13; Heb 11) or smaller segments of a book.

N. *The law of the LORD a lamp to the feet*

119.105
Prov 6.23

105 Your word is a lamp to my feet
and a light to my path.

119.106
Neh 10.29

106 I have sworn an oath and confirmed it,
to observe your righteous ordinances.

119.107
v. 25

107 I am severely afflicted;
give me life, O LORD, according to your word.

119.108
Hos 14.2;
Heb 13.15;
v. 12

108 Accept my offerings of praise, O LORD,
and teach me your ordinances.

119.109
Job 13.14;
v. 16

109 I hold my life in my hand continually,
but I do not forget your law.

119.110
Ps 140.5;
141.9; v. 10

110 The wicked have laid a snare for me,
but I do not stray from your precepts.

119.111
Deut 33.4;
vv. 14.162

111 Your decrees are my heritage forever;
they are the joy of my heart.

119.112
v. 33

112 I incline my heart to perform your statutes
forever, to the end.

O. *The law of the LORD a hiding place*

119.113
Jas 1.8; v. 47

113 I hate the double-minded,
but I love your law.

119.114
Ps 32.7; 91.1;
v. 74

114 You are my hiding place and my shield;
I hope in your word.

119.115
Ps 6.8;
139.19;
Mt 7.23

115 Go away from me, you evildoers,
that I may keep the commandments of my God.

119.116
Ps 54.4; 25.2;
Rom 5.5;
9.33

116 Uphold me according to your promise, that I may live,
and let me not be put to shame in my hope.

117 Hold me up, that I may be safe
and have regard for your statutes continually.

119.118
v. 21

118 You spurn all who go astray from your statutes;
for their cunning is in vain.

119.119
Ezek 22.18

119 All the wicked of the earth you count as dross;
therefore I love your decrees.

119.120
Hab 3.16

120 My flesh trembles for fear of you,
and I am afraid of your judgments.

P. *The psalmist has kept the law of the LORD*

121 I have done what is just and right;
do not leave me to my oppressors.

119.122
Job 17.3

122 Guarantee your servant's well-being;
do not let the godless oppress me.

119.123
vv. 81, 82

123 My eyes fail from watching for your salvation,
and for the fulfillment of your righteous promise.

119.124
v. 12

124 Deal with your servant according to your steadfast love,
and teach me your statutes.

119.125
Ps 116.16

125 I am your servant; give me understanding,
so that I may know your decrees.

126 It is time for the LORD to act,
for your law has been broken.

119.127
Ps 19.10

127 Truly I love your commandments
more than gold, more than fine gold.

119.105 The word of God is a lamp and a light. As a light it searches us out to discover whether we are blind or we see. It is also our guide for each step of our journey through life, so that we may walk the pathway of life and stay on the path, never departing from it.

119.116 Hope in God's word is the confidence that he will do what he has said he will do. Believing this, the Christian will never be disappointed that any of God's promises will not be fulfilled.
119.125 The psalmist is God's servant and prays to be taught what to do and to do it well.

128 Truly I direct my steps by all your precepts;[c]
    I hate every false way.

Q. *Prayer for grace to keep the law of the LORD*

129 Your decrees are wonderful;
    therefore my soul keeps them.
130 The unfolding of your words gives light;
    it imparts understanding to the simple.
131 With open mouth I pant,
    because I long for your commandments.
132 Turn to me and be gracious to me,
    as is your custom toward those who love your name.
133 Keep my steps steady according to your promise,
    and never let iniquity have dominion over me.
134 Redeem me from human oppression,
    that I may keep your precepts.
135 Make your face shine upon your servant,
    and teach me your statutes.
136 My eyes shed streams of tears
    because your law is not kept.

R. *The LORD and His law are righteous*

137 You are righteous, O LORD,
    and your judgments are right.
138 You have appointed your decrees in righteousness
    and in all faithfulness.
139 My zeal consumes me
    because my foes forget your words.
140 Your promise is well tried,
    and your servant loves it.
141 I am small and despised,
    yet I do not forget your precepts.
142 Your righteousness is an everlasting righteousness,
    and your law is the truth.
143 Trouble and anguish have come upon me,
    but your commandments are my delight.
144 Your decrees are righteous forever;
    give me understanding that I may live.

S. *A cry for salvation*

145 With my whole heart I cry; answer me, O LORD.
    I will keep your statutes.
146 I cry to you; save me,
    that I may observe your decrees.
147 I rise before dawn and cry for help;

c Gk Jerome: Meaning of Heb uncertain

119.128 v. 104
119.129 vv. 18, 22
119.130 Prov 6.23; Ps 19.7
119.131 Ps 42.1; v. 20
119.132 Ps 25.16
119.133 Ps 17.15; 19.13
119.134 Ps 142.6
119.135 Ps 4.6; v. 12
119.136 Jer 9.1; Ezek 9.4
119.137 Ezra 9.15; Neh 9.13; Jer 12.1
119.138 Ps 19.7-9
119.139 Ps 69.9
119.140 Ps 12.6
119.142 Ps 19.9; vv. 151, 160
119.143 vv. 24, 77
119.144 Ps 19.9; vv. 34, 73
119.145 vv. 10, 22, 55

119.140 Love for the word of God is evidence of love for the author of that word.

119.142 The Bible is the inspired and trustworthy word of God. Among the various reasons for believing the Bible to be true are the following. (1) The writers of the O.T. claimed that what they said was the word of God. "The Lord said to me" or its equivalent appears more than two thousand times (e.g., 2 Sam 23.1–3; Isa 8.1,11; Jer 1.9; 5.14; 7.27; 13.12; Ezek 3.4; Mic 5.10; Hab 2.2; etc.). (2) The apostles accepted all of the Scriptures as the infallible word of God (Gal 1.11,12; 1 Cor 14.37; 1 Thess 2.13; 2 Tim 3.16; 2 Pet 1.21). (3) Jesus Christ affirmed the word of God to be trustworthy (Mt 5.18; Jn 10.35; etc.). (4) Fulfilled prophecy shows the Bible to be true (Deut 28.37,63–65; Isa 13.19–22; Jer 46.19,20; 51.37; Ezek 29.15; 30.6; Nah 3.1,4–6; Zeph 2.13,14; Lk 21.24). (5) Archaeology confirms the truthfulness of the Scriptures. (6) Finally, the pragmatic test establishes the fact that the Bible does what it says it will do in human experience (see 34.8; Jn 7.17).

119.147,148 Before the dawning of each morning and the busyness of the day, the psalmist's heart seeks God to converse with him. When evening comes, the psalmist finds that God has been present all day long.

I put my hope in your words.

119.148
Ps 5.3

148 My eyes are awake before each watch of the night,
     that I may meditate on your promise.

119.149
vv. 40, 154

149 In your steadfast love hear my voice;
     O LORD, in your justice preserve my life.

150 Those who persecute me with evil purpose draw near;
     they are far from your law.

119.151
Ps 145.18;
v. 142
119.152
Lk 21.33

151 Yet you are near, O LORD,
     and all your commandments are true.

152 Long ago I learned from your decrees
     that you have established them forever.

T. *Keeping the law of the LORD in adversity*

119.153
v. 50;
Prov 3.1

153 Look on my misery and rescue me,
     for I do not forget your law.

119.154
1 Sam 24.15;
v. 134

154 Plead my cause and redeem me;
     give me life according to your promise.

119.155
Job 5.4

155 Salvation is far from the wicked,
     for they do not seek your statutes.

119.156
2 Sam 24.14

156 Great is your mercy, O LORD;
     give me life according to your justice.

119.157
Ps 7.1; v. 51

157 Many are my persecutors and my adversaries,
     yet I do not swerve from your decrees.

119.158
Ps 139.21

158 I look at the faithless with disgust,
     because they do not keep your commands.

119.159
vv. 47, 88

159 Consider how I love your precepts;
     preserve my life according to your steadfast love.

119.160
Ps 139.17;
v. 142

160 The sum of your word is truth;
     and every one of your righteous ordinances endures forever.

U. *Prayer for deliverance from persecution*

119.161
1 Sam 24.11

161 Princes persecute me without cause,
     but my heart stands in awe of your words.

119.162
1 Sam 30.16

162 I rejoice at your word
     like one who finds great spoil.

163 I hate and abhor falsehood,
     but I love your law.

119.164
vv. 7, 160

164 Seven times a day I praise you
     for your righteous ordinances.

119.165
Prov 3.2;
Isa 26.3;
32.17
119.166
v. 174;
Gen 49.18

165 Great peace have those who love your law;
     nothing can make them stumble.

166 I hope for your salvation, O LORD,
     and I fulfill your commandments.

167 My soul keeps your decrees;
     I love them exceedingly.

119.168
v. 22;
Prov 5.21

168 I keep your precepts and decrees,
     for all my ways are before you.

V. *The closing general petition*

119.169
Ps 18.6;
vv. 27, 65

169 Let my cry come before you, O LORD;
     give me understanding according to your word.

119.153 In the midst of affliction the believer's first resource is God.
119.164 *Seven times a day* has been taken literally by some Jewish interpreters. Rabbi Solomon said that God was to be praised in the morning twice before reading the ten commandments and once after. In the evening God was to be praised twice before reading the law and twice after.

170 Let my supplication come before you;
  deliver me according to your promise.
171 My lips will pour forth praise,
  because you teach me your statutes.
172 My tongue will sing of your promise,
  for all your commandments are right.
173 Let your hand be ready to help me,
  for I have chosen your precepts.
174 I long for your salvation, O LORD,
  and your law is my delight.
175 Let me live that I may praise you,
  and let your ordinances help me.
176 I have gone astray like a lost sheep; seek out
    your servant,
  for I do not forget your commandments.

119.170
Ps 28.2; 31.2

119.171
Ps 51.15;
94.12

119.173
Ps 37.24

119.174
vv. 166, 24

119.175
Isa 55.3

119.176
Isa 53.6;
v. 16

Psalm 120

A prayer for deliverance

A. *From lying lips*

A Song of Ascents.

1 In my distress I cry to the LORD,
  that he may answer me:
2 "Deliver me, O LORD,
  from lying lips,
  from a deceitful tongue."

3 What shall be given to you?
  And what more shall be done to you,
  you deceitful tongue?
4 A warrior's sharp arrows,
  with glowing coals of the broom tree!

B. *From haters of peace*

5 Woe is me, that I am an alien in Meshech,
  that I must live among the tents of Kedar.
6 Too long have I had my dwelling
  among those who hate peace.
7 I am for peace;
  but when I speak,
  they are for war.

120.1
Ps 102.2;
Jon 2.2

120.2
Prov 12.22;
Ps 52.4

120.4
Ps 45.5;
140.10

120.5
Gen 10.2;
Ezek 27.13;
Gen 25.13;
Jer 49.28

120.7
Ps 55.21

119.176 *like a lost sheep.* People, like sheep, go astray (cf. Isa 53.6). The loving shepherd searches and finds the lost sheep (see Mt 18.10–14; Lk 15.3–7). It is fitting that the longest psalm celebrating the word of God should end on a plea for God to rescue the lost.
120.1ff Ps 120 – 134 have been placed together under the label "Songs of Ascents." Following Ps 119, the longest of all the psalms, these fifteen are the shortest. They may have been sung together with a musical pause at the end of each. Some think they were used as the singers climbed the fifteen steps from the outward court of the temple to the inner court.

The psalms have one feature called an "ascent" or "climax." For example, in 121.1 the text reads "From where will my help come?" The next verse rises to a higher pitch, saying, "My help comes from the LORD." Some of these psalms are personal; others refer to the corporate body of believers.
120.4 *broom tree,* a big shrub with white flowers whose root makes excellent charcoal.
120.5 *Meshech . . . Kedar.* Cf. Gen 10.2; 25.13. The reference here is to two ethnic unbelieving nations in which an Israelite is either living far from home or in a place where the people have surrendered their faith in God's truth.

Psalm 121

The LORD my keeper

A Song of Ascents.

1 I lift up my eyes to the hills —
    from where will my help come?

2 My help comes from the LORD,
    who made heaven and earth.

3 He will not let your foot be moved;
    he who keeps you will not slumber.

4 He who keeps Israel
    will neither slumber nor sleep.

5 The LORD is your keeper;
    the LORD is your shade at your right hand.

6 The sun shall not strike you by day,
    nor the moon by night.

7 The LORD will keep you from all evil;
    he will keep your life.

8 The LORD will keep
    your going out and your coming in
    from this time on and forevermore.

Psalm 122

The peace of Jerusalem

A. *The house of the LORD*

A Song of Ascents. Of David.

1 I was glad when they said to me,
    "Let us go to the house of the LORD!"

2 Our feet are standing
    within your gates, O Jerusalem.

3 Jerusalem — built as a city
    that is bound firmly together.

4 To it the tribes go up,
    the tribes of the LORD,
as was decreed for Israel,
    to give thanks to the name of the LORD.

5 For there the thrones for judgment were set up,
    the thrones of the house of David.

B. *The prayer for its peace and prosperity*

6 Pray for the peace of Jerusalem:
    "May they prosper who love you.

7 Peace be within your walls,
    and security within your towers."

8 For the sake of my relatives and friends
    I will say, "Peace be within you."

Cross references (left margin)

121.2 Ps 124.8; 115.15
121.3 Ps 66.9; 127.1
121.5 Isa 25.4; Ps 16.8
121.6 Ps 91.5; Isa 49.10; Rev 7.16
121.7 Ps 91.10-12
121.8 Deut 28.6
122.1 Isa 2.3; Zech 8.21
122.3 Ps 48.13
122.4 Deut 16.16; Ex 16.34
122.5 Deut 17.8; 2 Chr 19.8
122.6 Ps 51.18

121.1ff This has been called the travelers' psalm. Those who call on their God before they leave will find that God is with them on the journey. Especially comforting is the thought that God never sleeps.

122.1ff Three times a year the people came to Jerusalem for their solemn festivals (Ex 23.14,17). Their hearts were glad when friends and neighbors would joyfully say, *Let us go to the house of the LORD!*

9   For the sake of the house of the Lord our God,
     I will seek your good.

Psalm 123

A song of confidence in God

A. *Looking to the Lord*

A Song of Ascents.

1   To you I lift up my eyes,
     O you who are enthroned in the heavens!
2   As the eyes of servants
     look to the hand of their master,
  as the eyes of a maid
     to the hand of her mistress,
  so our eyes look to the Lord our God,
     until he has mercy upon us.

B. *Prayer for mercy*

3   Have mercy upon us, O Lord, have mercy upon us,
     for we have had more than enough of contempt.
4   Our soul has had more than its fill
     of the scorn of those who are at ease,
     of the contempt of the proud.

Psalm 124

Thanksgiving for a supernatural deliverance

A. *God alone is the deliverer*

A Song of Ascents. Of David.

1   If it had not been the Lord who was on our side
     — let Israel now say —
2   if it had not been the Lord who was on our side,
     when our enemies attacked us,
3   then they would have swallowed us up alive,
     when their anger was kindled against us;
4   then the flood would have swept us away,
     the torrent would have gone over us;
5   then over us would have gone
     the raging waters.

B. *Praise to the deliverer*

6   Blessed be the Lord,
     who has not given us
     as prey to their teeth.
7   We have escaped like a bird
     from the snare of the fowlers;
  the snare is broken,
     and we have escaped.

Cross references:

122.9 Neh 2.10

123.1 Ps 121.1; 141.8; 2.4; 11.4

123.2 Prov 27.18; Ps 25.15

123.3 Ps 4.1; 51.1

123.4 Ps 79.4

124.1 Ps 94.17; 129.1

124.3 Ps 56.1; 57.3; Prov 1.12

124.5 Ps 69.2

124.6 Ps 27.2

124.7 Prov 6.5; Ps 91.3

123.1ff Some think this psalm was written when God's people were captives in Babylon. In any time of affliction it is essential to look to the Lord for his mercy.

124.1ff Without God there is no ultimate hope for deliverance from ruin or from the brink of disaster. God in his goodness makes a way of escape for his own people.

124.8
Ps 121.2;
Gen 1.1

8 Our help is in the name of the LORD,
  who made heaven and earth.

Psalm 125

The LORD the protector of his people

A Song of Ascents.

1 Those who trust in the LORD are like Mount Zion,
  which cannot be moved, but abides forever.

125.2
Zech 2.5;
Ps 121.8

2 As the mountains surround Jerusalem,
  so the LORD surrounds his people,
  from this time on and forevermore.

125.3
Prov 22.8;
Isa 14.5;
Ps 55.20

3 For the scepter of wickedness shall not rest
    on the land allotted to the righteous,
  so that the righteous might not stretch out
    their hands to do wrong.

125.4
Ps 119.68;
7.10; 94.15
125.5
Prov 2.15;
Ps 128.6

4 Do good, O LORD, to those who are good,
  and to those who are upright in their hearts.
5 But those who turn aside to their own crooked ways
  the LORD will lead away with evildoers.
  Peace be upon Israel!

Psalm 126

A song of thanks for God's deliverance

A Song of Ascents.

126.1
Ps 85.1;
Acts 12.9

1 When the LORD restored the fortunes of Zion,^{d}
  we were like those who dream.

126.2
Job 8.21;
Ps 51.14;
71.19

2 Then our mouth was filled with laughter,
  and our tongue with shouts of joy;
  then it was said among the nations,
  "The LORD has done great things for them."

126.3
Isa 25.9

3 The LORD has done great things for us,
  and we rejoiced.

126.4
Isa 35.6;
43.19
126.5
Jer 31.16;
Isa 35.10

4 Restore our fortunes, O LORD,
  like the watercourses in the Negeb.
5 May those who sow in tears
  reap with shouts of joy.
6 Those who go out weeping,
  bearing the seed for sowing,
  shall come home with shouts of joy,
  carrying their sheaves.

Psalm 127

The vanity of work without God

A Song of Ascents. Of Solomon.

127.1
Ps 78.69;
121.4

1 Unless the LORD builds the house,
  those who build it labor in vain.

---

^{d} Or *brought back those who returned to Zion*

125.1ff Of this we can be sure: it is well for the
righteous and ill for the wicked.
126.1ff This psalm may have reference to the deliverance of Israel from the captivity. When Israel's liberation came from God, the weeping of the afflicted
turned to shouts of joy.

Unless the LORD guards the city,
the guard keeps watch in vain.
2 It is in vain that you rise up early
and go late to rest,
eating the bread of anxious toil;
for he gives sleep to his beloved. *e*

3 Sons are indeed a heritage from the LORD,
the fruit of the womb a reward.
4 Like arrows in the hand of a warrior
are the sons of one's youth.
5 Happy is the man who has
his quiver full of them.
He shall not be put to shame
when he speaks with his enemies in the gate.

127.2
Gen 3.17;
Job 11.18, 19

127.3
Gen 33.5;
Josh 24.3, 4;
Deut 28.4

127.5
Job 5.4;
Prov 27.11

Psalm 128

The family that fears the LORD is happy

A. *The happiness of the individual*

A Song of Ascents.

1 Happy is everyone who fears the LORD,
who walks in his ways.
2 You shall eat the fruit of the labor of your hands;
you shall be happy, and it shall go well with you.

128.1
Ps 112.1;
119.3

128.2
Isa 3.10;
Ezek 23.29;
Eccl 8.12

B. *The happiness of the home*

3 Your wife will be like a fruitful vine
within your house;
your children will be like olive shoots
around your table.
4 Thus shall the man be blessed
who fears the LORD.

128.3
Ezek 19.10;
Ps 52.8;
144.12

C. *The happiness of the nation*

5 The LORD bless you from Zion.
May you see the prosperity of Jerusalem
all the days of your life.
6 May you see your children's children.
Peace be upon Israel!

128.5
Ps 134.3;
20.2; 122.9

128.6
Gen 50.23;
Job 42.16;
Ps 125.5

Psalm 129

A prayer for the shame of Israel's enemies

A Song of Ascents.

1 "Often have they attacked me from my youth"
—let Israel now say—
2 "often have they attacked me from my youth,

129.1
Ps 88.15;
Hos 2.15;
Ps 124.1

129.2
Mt 16.18

e Or *for he provides for his beloved during sleep*

127.1ff People seek to build a home and a family.
To do this is good in itself, but if it is done apart from
the Lord, their labors are futile.
128.1ff This psalm is thought to have been sung at
Israelite wedding ceremonies. It emphasizes marriage

and children, who are a heritage of the Lord.
129.1ff This psalm appears to have been penned
after the Babylonian captivity had begun. It emphasizes Israel's afflictions as far back as the time spent
in Egypt.

yet they have not prevailed against me.

³ The plowers plowed on my back;
   they made their furrows long."

129.4
Ps 119.137

⁴ The LORD is righteous;
   he has cut the cords of the wicked.

129.5
Mic 4.11;
Ps 71.13
129.6
Ps 37.2

⁵ May all who hate Zion
   be put to shame and turned backward.
⁶ Let them be like the grass on the housetops
   that withers before it grows up,
⁷ with which reapers do not fill their hands
   or binders of sheaves their arms,

129.8
Ruth 2.4;
Ps 118.26

⁸ while those who pass by do not say,
   "The blessing of the LORD be upon you!
   We bless you in the name of the LORD!"

Psalm 130

The soul that waits for God

A. *The cry for help*

A Song of Ascents.

130.1
Ps 42.7; 69.2

¹ Out of the depths I cry to you, O LORD.
²   Lord, hear my voice!
Let your ears be attentive
   to the voice of my supplications!

130.2
Ps 64.1;
2 Chr 6.40;
Ps 28.2

130.3
Ps 76.7

³ If you, O LORD, should mark iniquities,
   Lord, who could stand?
⁴ But there is forgiveness with you,
   so that you may be revered.

130.4
Ex 34.7;
Isa 55.7;
1 Kings 8.40;
Jer 33.8

B. *The patient waiting*

130.5
Ps 33.20;
Isa 8.17;
Ps 119.81
130.6
Ps 63.6;
119.147

⁵ I wait for the LORD, my soul waits,
   and in his word I hope;
⁶ my soul waits for the Lord
   more than those who watch for the morning,
   more than those who watch for the morning.

C. *Exhortation to hope*

130.7
Ps 131.3;
Isa 55.7

⁷ O Israel, hope in the LORD!
   For with the LORD there is steadfast love,
   and with him is great power to redeem.

130.8
Lk 1.68

⁸ It is he who will redeem Israel
   from all its iniquities.

Psalm 131

The song of a humble and a quiet heart

A Song of Ascents. Of David.

131.1
Ps 101.5;
Isa 5.15;
Rom 12.16

¹ O LORD, my heart is not lifted up,
   my eyes are not raised too high;

130.1ff People can anticipate no help apart from God, but if they call on him, he will come to their aid. Those burdened by sin and suffering should hope in God.

131.1ff The humility of David is expressed by the absence of a proud heart and of vain ambition to attain things beyond his reach. He is like a child satisfied and content at its mother's breast.

I do not occupy myself with things
   too great and too marvelous for me.
2 But I have calmed and quieted my soul,
   like a weaned child with its mother;
   my soul is like the weaned child that is with me.*f*

3 O Israel, hope in the LORD
   from this time on and forevermore.

131.2
Ps 62.1;
Mt 18.3;
1 Cor 14.20

131.3
Ps 130.7

Psalm 132

David and the ark of the LORD

A. David's vow

A Song of Ascents.

1 O LORD, remember in David's favor
   all the hardships he endured;
2 how he swore to the LORD
   and vowed to the Mighty One of Jacob,
3 "I will not enter my house
   or get into my bed;
4 I will not give sleep to my eyes
   or slumber to my eyelids,
5 until I find a place for the LORD,
   a dwelling place for the Mighty One of Jacob."

132.2
Gen 49.24

132.4
Prov 6.4

132.5
Acts 7.46

B. The fulfillment of David's vow

6 We heard of it in Ephrathah;
   we found it in the fields of Jaar.
7 "Let us go to his dwelling place;
   let us worship at his footstool."

8 Rise up, O LORD, and go to your resting place,
   you and the ark of your might.
9 Let your priests be clothed with righteousness,
   and let your faithful shout for joy.
10 For your servant David's sake
   do not turn away the face of your anointed one.

132.6
1 Sam 17.12;
7.1;
1 Chr 13.5
132.7
Ps 4.7; 99.5

132.8
Num 10.35;
2 Chr 6.41;
Ps 78.61
132.9
v. 16;
Job 29.14;
Isa 61.10

C. The promise of the LORD to David and to Zion

11 The LORD swore to David a sure oath
   from which he will not turn back:
   "One of the sons of your body
   I will set on your throne.
12 If your sons keep my covenant
   and my decrees that I shall teach them,
   their sons also, forevermore,
   shall sit on your throne."

132.11
Ps 89.3, 4;
2 Sam 7.12;
2 Chr 6.16

132.12
Lk 1.32;
Acts 2.30

f Or *my soul within me is like a weaned child*

132.1ff This psalm has been attributed by some to
Solomon and was sung at the dedication of the temple. David had vowed to God that he would build a
temple to the Lord, but the Lord informed him
through Nathan that his son would do this project
(2 Sam 7). Having done what God had commanded,
Solomon here begs God to accept his labors and occupy his dwelling place.

132.6 *Ephrathah*, meaning "fruitful land," usually
refers to Bethlehem (Gen 35.19) but here appears to
be Kiriath-jearim (i.e., "Jaar"). After having been
returned from the Philistines, the ark was first kept
in Kiriath-jearim (see 1 Sam 7.1,2), from which came
the call to worship God. David eventually brought the
ark to Jerusalem.

13 For the Lord has chosen Zion;
   he has desired it for his habitation:

14 "This is my resting place forever;
   here I will reside, for I have desired it.

15 I will abundantly bless its provisions;
   I will satisfy its poor with bread.

16 Its priests I will clothe with salvation,
   and its faithful will shout for joy.

17 There I will cause a horn to sprout up for David;
   I have prepared a lamp for my anointed one.

18 His enemies I will clothe with disgrace,
   but on him, his crown will gleam."

Psalm 133

Family unity

A Song of Ascents.

1 How very good and pleasant it is
   when kindred live together in unity!

2 It is like the precious oil on the head,
   running down upon the beard,
on the beard of Aaron,
   running down over the collar of his robes.

3 It is like the dew of Hermon,
   which falls on the mountains of Zion.
For there the Lord ordained his blessing,
   life forevermore.

Psalm 134

An exhortation for the night watch

A Song of Ascents.

1 Come, bless the Lord, all you servants of the Lord,
   who stand by night in the house of the Lord!

2 Lift up your hands to the holy place,
   and bless the Lord.

3 May the Lord, maker of heaven and earth,
   bless you from Zion.

Psalm 135

Praise to the Lord

A. The exhortation to praise

1 Praise the Lord!
   Praise the name of the Lord;
   give praise, O servants of the Lord,

2 you that stand in the house of the Lord,
   in the courts of the house of our God.

133.1ff The psalm pleads for unity among God's people. The *precious oil* (v. 2) was used for anointing the priests.
134.1ff This brief psalm appears to be a responsive reading between the worshipers of God and the Levites who kept guard over the temple at night.

135.1ff This is one of the "Hallelujah psalms" (see note on 111.1ff). It praises a sovereign God who delivers his people and shames idolatry. All categories of people among the Israelites should say "Hallelujah" to God.

3   Praise the LORD, for the LORD is good;
       sing to his name, for he is gracious.
4   For the LORD has chosen Jacob for himself,
       Israel as his own possession.

B. *The greatness of the LORD*

5   For I know that the LORD is great;
       our Lord is above all gods.
6   Whatever the LORD pleases he does,
       in heaven and on earth,
       in the seas and all deeps.
7   He it is who makes the clouds rise at the end of the earth;
       he makes lightnings for the rain
       and brings out the wind from his storehouses.

C. *The deliverances of the LORD*

8   He it was who struck down the firstborn of Egypt,
       both human beings and animals;
9   he sent signs and wonders
       into your midst, O Egypt,
       against Pharaoh and all his servants.
10 He struck down many nations
       and killed mighty kings —
11 Sihon, king of the Amorites,
       and Og, king of Bashan,
       and all the kingdoms of Canaan —
12 and gave their land as a heritage,
       a heritage to his people Israel.

D. *The vindication of the LORD*

13 Your name, O LORD, endures forever,
       your renown, O LORD, throughout all ages.
14 For the LORD will vindicate his people,
       and have compassion on his servants.

E. *The idolatry of the nations*

15 The idols of the nations are silver and gold,
       the work of human hands.
16 They have mouths, but they do not speak;
       they have eyes, but they do not see;
17 they have ears, but they do not hear,
       and there is no breath in their mouths.
18 Those who make them
       and all who trust them
       shall become like them.

F. *Concluding exhortation to praise*

19 O house of Israel, bless the LORD!
       O house of Aaron, bless the LORD!
20 O house of Levi, bless the LORD!
       You that fear the LORD, bless the LORD!
21 Blessed be the LORD from Zion,

135.3
Ps 119.68;
147.1
135.4
Deut 7.6, 7;
10.15;
Ex 19.5;
1 Pet 2.9

135.5
Ps 48.1; 97.9

135.6
Ps 115.3

135.7
Jer 10.13;
Job 28.25;
Zech 10.1;
Job 38.22

135.8
Ex 12.12;
Ps 78.51
135.9
Ps 78.43;
136.15

135.10
Num 21.24;
Ps 136.17
135.11
Num 21.21-26,
33-35;
Josh 12.7

135.12
Ps 78.55

135.13
Ex 3.15;
Ps 102.12
135.14
Deut 32.36;
Ps 106.45

135.15
Ps 115.4-8

135.19
Ps 115.9
135.20
Ps 118.4
135.21
Ps 134.3;
132.14

135.6 God is sovereign over all people and all creation. Whatever he does is good and holy.
135.15 The gods of the heathen are the products of human creation. They have no power in themselves, only what their makers give them. Thus these gods are unable either to help or to hurt anyone (see note on 14.1ff).

he who resides in Jerusalem.
Praise the LORD!

Psalm 136

Praise to the God of eternal love

A. *The exhortation to give thanks*

136.1
Ps 106.1;
107.1; 118.1;
1 Chr 16.34;
2 Chr 20.21

1 O give thanks to the LORD, for he is good,
  for his steadfast love endures forever.

136.2
Deut 10.17

2 O give thanks to the God of gods,
  for his steadfast love endures forever.

3 O give thanks to the Lord of lords,
  for his steadfast love endures forever;

B. *Praise to God the creator*

136.4
Ps 72.18

4 who alone does great wonders,
  for his steadfast love endures forever;

136.5
Gen 1.1;
Prov 3.19;
Jer 51.15

5 who by understanding made the heavens,
  for his steadfast love endures forever;

136.6
Gen 1.9;
Ps 24.2;
Jer 10.12

6 who spread out the earth on the waters,
  for his steadfast love endures forever;

136.7
Gen 1.14, 16

7 who made the great lights,
  for his steadfast love endures forever;

136.8
Gen 1.16

8 the sun to rule over the day,
  for his steadfast love endures forever;

9 the moon and stars to rule over the night,
  for his steadfast love endures forever;

C. *Praise to God the deliverer of Israel*

136.10
Ex 12.29;
Ps 135.8

10 who struck Egypt through their firstborn,
   for his steadfast love endures forever;

136.11
Ex 12.51

11 and brought Israel out from among them,
   for his steadfast love endures forever;

136.12
Ex 6.6;
Ps 44.3;
Deut 4.34

12 with a strong hand and an outstretched arm,
   for his steadfast love endures forever;

136.13
Ex 14.21;
Ps 78.13

13 who divided the Red Sea[g] in two,
   for his steadfast love endures forever;

136.14
Ex 14.22

14 and made Israel pass through the midst of it,
   for his steadfast love endures forever;

136.15
Ex 14.27;
Ps 135.9

15 but overthrew Pharaoh and his army in the Red Sea,[g]
   for his steadfast love endures forever;

136.16
Ex 13.18;
15.22;
Deut 8.15

16 who led his people through the wilderness,
   for his steadfast love endures forever;

136.17
Ps 135.10-12

17 who struck down great kings,
   for his steadfast love endures forever;

18 and killed famous kings,
   for his steadfast love endures forever;

19 Sihon, king of the Amorites,
   for his steadfast love endures forever;

20 and Og, king of Bashan,
   for his steadfast love endures forever;

g Or Sea of Reeds

136.1ff This is a most unusual psalm in that there is the constant refrain, "for his steadfast love endures forever." This repetition serves a useful purpose, calling forth a response to a particular blessing of God within the history of his people.

21 and gave their land as a heritage,
    for his steadfast love endures forever;
22 a heritage to his servant Israel,
    for his steadfast love endures forever.

D. *Praise to the God of steadfast love*

23 It is he who remembered us in our low estate,
    for his steadfast love endures forever;
24 and rescued us from our foes,
    for his steadfast love endures forever;
25 who gives food to all flesh,
    for his steadfast love endures forever.

E. *Closing thanksgiving*

26 O give thanks to the God of heaven,
    for his steadfast love endures forever.

Psalm 137

A hymn of the exiles in Babylon

A. *Their present plight*

1 By the rivers of Babylon—
    there we sat down and there we wept
    when we remembered Zion.
2 On the willows[h] there
    we hung up our harps.
3 For there our captors
    asked us for songs,
and our tormentors asked for mirth, saying,
    "Sing us one of the songs of Zion!"

B. *Their remembrance of Zion*

4 How could we sing the LORD's song
    in a foreign land?
5 If I forget you, O Jerusalem,
    let my right hand wither!
6 Let my tongue cling to the roof of my mouth,
    if I do not remember you,
if I do not set Jerusalem
    above my highest joy.

C. *Their cry for vengeance*

7 Remember, O LORD, against the Edomites
    the day of Jerusalem's fall,
how they said, "Tear it down! Tear it down!
    Down to its foundations!"
8 O daughter Babylon, you devastator![i]
    Happy shall they be who pay you back
    what you have done to us!

h Or poplars   *i Or you who are devastated*

137.1ff This mournful song commemorates the captivity of Israel in Babylon. The Septuagint indicates that the author was Jeremiah, although this is uncertain. As one of the last pieces of the O.T. to have been composed, it expresses the longing to return to Jerusalem, the golden city of David's day.

Margin references:

136.21
Josh 12.1

136.23
Ps 113.7

136.24
Ps 107.2

136.25
Ps 104.27;
145.15

137.1
Ezek 1.1, 3;
Neh 1.4

137.3
Ps 80.6

137.6
Ezek 3.26

137.7
Jer 49.7;
Lam 4.22;
Ezek 25.12;
Ob 10-14

137.8
Isa 13.1, 6;
Jer 25.12;
50.15;
Rev 18.6

137.9
2 Kings 8.12;
Isa 13.16

9 Happy shall they be who take your little ones
and dash them against the rock!

Psalm 138

The Lord the faithful God

138.1
Ps 111.1;
95.3; 96.4

A. David's acknowledgment of God's faithfulness

Of David.

1 I give you thanks, O Lord, with my whole heart;
before the gods I sing your praise;

138.2
Ps 28.2;
1 Kings 8.29,
30;
Isa 42.21

2 I bow down toward your holy temple
and give thanks to your name for your steadfast love and
your faithfulness;
for you have exalted your name and your word
above everything.[j]

138.3
Ps 118.5;
28.7; 46.1

3 On the day I called, you answered me,
you increased my strength of soul.[k]

B. All the kings shall praise the Lord

138.4
Ps 102.15

4 All the kings of the earth shall praise you, O Lord,
for they have heard the words of your mouth.
5 They shall sing of the ways of the Lord,
for great is the glory of the Lord.

138.6
Ps 113.5, 6;
Isa 57.15;
Prov 3.34;
Jas 4.6

6 For though the Lord is high, he regards the lowly;
but the haughty he perceives from far away.

C. David's confidence in God's faithfulness

138.7
Ps 23.3, 4;
71.20;
Jer 41.25;
Ps 20.6

7 Though I walk in the midst of trouble,
you preserve me against the wrath of my enemies;
you stretch out your hand,
and your right hand delivers me.

138.8
Ps 57.2;
Phil 1.6;
Ps 136.1;
27.9;
Job 10.3, 8;
14.15

8 The Lord will fulfill his purpose for me;
your steadfast love, O Lord, endures forever.
Do not forsake the work of your hands.

139.1
Ps 17.3;
Jer 12.3

Psalm 139

The prayer of a believing heart

A. The omniscient God

To the leader. Of David. A Psalm.

1 O Lord, you have searched me and known me.
2 You know when I sit down and when I rise up;
you discern my thoughts from far away.

139.2
2 Kings 19.27;
Mt 9.4;
Jn 2.24
139.3
Job 31.4

3 You search out my path and my lying down,

j Cn: Heb *you have exalted your word above all your name*   *k* Syr Compare Gk Tg: Heb *you made me arrogant in my soul with strength*

138.1ff This general psalm of remembrance was penned by David without reference to any specific incident in his life. It is a panoramic view of a lifetime filled with evidences of God's unbroken faithfulness. David had experienced many troubles, but his life had been preserved and deliverance had come time and again. The steadfast love of God does not change.
138.7,8 David believed that his sovereign God was in charge and knew what was best for him. He felt confident that God would not stop until he had done everything he intended in David's life.
139.1ff The first part of this psalm (vv. 1,2,4,6) speaks of God's omniscience (that he is all-knowing); vv. 7–13 speaks of God's omnipresence (that he is everywhere at the same time); vv. 15,16 deals with God's foreknowledge of humankind before their birth.

and are acquainted with all my ways.

4 Even before a word is on my tongue,
   O LORD, you know it completely.
                         139.4
                         Heb 4.13

5 You hem me in, behind and before,
   and lay your hand upon me.
                         139.5
                         Ps 34.7;
                         Job 9.33

6 Such knowledge is too wonderful for me;
   it is so high that I cannot attain it.
                         139.6
                         Rom 11.33;
                         Job 42.3

B. *The omnipresent God*

7 Where can I go from your spirit?
   Or where can I flee from your presence?
                         139.7
                         Jer 23.24;
                         Jon 1.3

8 If I ascend to heaven, you are there;
   if I make my bed in Sheol, you are there.
                         139.8ff
                         Am 9.2-4;
                         Job 26.6;
                         Prov 15.11

9 If I take the wings of the morning
   and settle at the farthest limits of the sea,

10 even there your hand shall lead me,
    and your right hand shall hold me fast.
                         139.10
                         Ps 23.2, 3

11 If I say, "Surely the darkness shall cover me,
    and the light around me become night,"
                         139.11
                         Job 22.13

12 even the darkness is not dark to you;
   the night is as bright as the day,
   for darkness is as light to you.
                         139.12
                         Job 34.22;
                         Dan 2.22;
                         Heb 4.13

C. *The God of creation*

13 For it was you who formed my inward parts;
   you knit me together in my mother's womb.
                         139.13ff
                         Ps 119.73;
                         Job 10.11

14 I praise you, for I am fearfully and wonderfully made.
   Wonderful are your works;
   that I know very well.
                         139.14
                         Ps 40.5

15 My frame was not hidden from you,
   when I was being made in secret,
   intricately woven in the depths of the earth.

16 Your eyes beheld my unformed substance.
   In your book were written
   all the days that were formed for me,
   when none of them as yet existed.

17 How weighty to me are your thoughts, O God!
   How vast is the sum of them!
                         139.17
                         Ps 40.5

18 I try to count them—they are more than the sand;
   I come to the end[l]—I am still with you.

D. *Concluding prayer for the wicked and for self*

19 O that you would kill the wicked, O God,
   and that the bloodthirsty would depart from me—
                         139.19
                         Isa 11.4;
                         Ps 119.115

20 those who speak of you maliciously,
   and lift themselves up against you for evil![m]
                         139.20
                         Jude 15

21 Do I not hate those who hate you, O LORD?
   And do I not loathe those who rise up against you?
                         139.21
                         Ps 119.158

22 I hate them with perfect hatred;
   I count them my enemies.

l Or *I awake* *m* Cn: Meaning of Heb uncertain

139.7ff Though God is omnipresent, he may not be identified with creation as though he were a part of it. Pantheism has no place in the Scriptures. God created the universe and he sustains it, but he is independent of it and stands above it.

139.13ff People are unique and marvelous beings,

created directly by God. The complexity of the human frame defies analysis, and what has been learned about it is as nothing compared to what is still unknown. The evolutionary hypothesis staggers the imagination with its theory that the complex human being came into being by mere chance.

23 Search me, O God, and know my heart;
   test me and know my thoughts.
24 See if there is any wicked[n] way in me,
   and lead me in the way everlasting.[o]

Psalm 140

Prayer for protection against enemies

A. Petition for deliverance from the wicked

To the leader. A Psalm of David.

1 Deliver me, O LORD, from evildoers;
   protect me from those who are violent,
2 who plan evil things in their minds
   and stir up wars continually.
3 They make their tongue sharp as a snake's,
   and under their lips is the venom of vipers.   *Selah*

4 Guard me, O LORD, from the hands of the wicked;
   protect me from the violent
   who have planned my downfall.
5 The arrogant have hidden a trap for me,
   and with cords they have spread a net,[p]
   along the road they have set snares for me.   *Selah*

B. A cry for God to hear

6 I say to the LORD, "You are my God;
   give ear, O LORD, to the voice of my supplications."
7 O LORD, my Lord, my strong deliverer,
   you have covered my head in the day of battle.
8 Do not grant, O LORD, the desires of the wicked;
   do not further their evil plot.[q]   *Selah*

C. A prayer of imprecation

9 Those who surround me lift up their heads;[r]
   let the mischief of their lips overwhelm them!
10 Let burning coals fall on them!
   Let them be flung into pits, no more to rise!
11 Do not let the slanderer be established in the land;
   let evil speedily hunt down the violent!

D. Expression of confidence in the LORD

12 I know that the LORD maintains the cause of the needy,
   and executes justice for the poor.
13 Surely the righteous shall give thanks to your name;
   the upright shall live in your presence.

n Heb *hurtful*   *o* Or *the ancient way.* Compare Jer 6.16   *p* Or *they have spread cords as a net*   *q* Heb adds *they are exalted*   *r* Cn Compare Gk: Heb *those who surround me are uplifted in head*; Heb divides verses 8 and 9 differently

140.1ff This and the next four psalms were written by David and apparently refer to his experiences when Saul was persecuting him and seeking to kill him. David sought protection and deliverance from the Lord his God.

139.23
Job 31.6;
Ps 26.2;
Jer 11.20
139.24
Prov 15.9;
Ps 5.8;
143.10

140.1
Ps 17.13;
18.48

140.2
Ps 36.4; 56.6

140.3
Ps 57.4; 68.4;
Jas 3.8

140.4
Ps 71.4

140.5
Ps 35.7; 31.4;
141.9

140.6
Ps 16.2;
143.1; 116.1
140.7
Ps 28.8;
144.10
140.8
Ps 112.10;
10.2

140.9
Ps 7.16

140.10
Ps 11.6; 21.9;
36.12
140.11
Ps 34.21

140.12
Ps 9.4; 35.10

140.13
Ps 97.12;
11.7

Psalm 141

The conduct of a good person in trouble

A. The appeal to the LORD

A Psalm of David.

1 I call upon you, O LORD; come quickly to me;
  give ear to my voice when I call to you.
2 Let my prayer be counted as incense before you,
  and the lifting up of my hands as an evening sacrifice.

B. The prayer for an upright heart

3 Set a guard over my mouth, O LORD;
  keep watch over the door of my lips.
4 Do not turn my heart to any evil,
    to busy myself with wicked deeds
  in company with those who work iniquity;
    do not let me eat of their delicacies.

C. The end of the wicked

5 Let the righteous strike me;
    let the faithful correct me.
  Never let the oil of the wicked anoint my head,ˢ
    for my prayer is continuallyᵗ against their wicked deeds.
6 When they are given over to those who shall condemn them,
    then they shall learn that my words were pleasant.
7 Like a rock that one breaks apart and shatters on the land,
    so shall their bones be strewn at the mouth of Sheol.ᵘ

D. His eyes are upon God

8 But my eyes are turned toward you, O GOD, my Lord;
    in you I seek refuge; do not leave me defenseless.
9 Keep me from the trap that they have laid for me,
    and from the snares of evildoers.
10 Let the wicked fall into their own nets,
    while I alone escape.

Psalm 142

The prisoner's prayer

A. The appeal of the prisoner

A Maskil of David. When he was in the cave. A Prayer.

1 With my voice I cry to the LORD;
    with my voice I make supplication to the LORD.
2 I pour out my complaint before him;
    I tell my trouble before him.

ˢ Gk: Meaning of Heb uncertain   ᵗ Cn: Heb *for continually and my prayer*   ᵘ Meaning of Heb of
verses 5-7 is uncertain

141.1ff In this psalm David asks to be delivered from doing anything contrary to God's will, for he knows the end of the wicked and does not wish to follow in their ways. In the conclusion he affirms that God is his refuge, who will deliver him from the snares which the enemy has set for him.

142.1ff David is trapped in a cave as a prisoner. Outside, the enemy is waiting to destroy him. He pleads with God to deliver him and save him from those persecuting him. He affirms that God alone is his refuge.

141.1
Ps 22.19;
70.5; 143.1

141.2
Rev 5.8; 8.3;
Ps 134.2;
Ex 29.39

141.4
Ps 119.36;
Prov 23.6

141.5
Prov 9.8;
Ps 23.5;
35.14

141.7
Ps 53.5

141.8
Ps 25.15;
2.12; 27.9
141.9
Ps 38.12;
140.5
141.10
Ps 35.8

142.1
Ps 77.1; 30.8

142.2
Isa 26.16

142.3
Ps 143.4;
140.5

3 When my spirit is faint,
  you know my way.

B. *The plight of the prisoner*

In the path where I walk
  they have hidden a trap for me.

142.4
Ps 31.11;
Job 11.20;
Jer 30.17

4 Look on my right hand and see—
  there is no one who takes notice of me;
no refuge remains to me;
  no one cares for me.

C. *The prayer for deliverance*

142.5
Ps 46.1; 16.5;
27.13

5 I cry to you, O Lord;
  I say, "You are my refuge,
  my portion in the land of the living."

142.6
Ps 17.1; 79.8;
116.6

6 Give heed to my cry,
  for I am brought very low.

Save me from my persecutors,
  for they are too strong for me.

142.7
Ps 146.7;
13.6

7 Bring me out of prison,
  so that I may give thanks to your name.
The righteous will surround me,
  for you will deal bountifully with me.

143.1
Ps 140.6;
89.1, 2; 71.2

Psalm 143

The prayer of a soul in distress

A. *The complaint of the psalmist*

A Psalm of David.

1 Hear my prayer, O Lord;
  give ear to my supplications in your faithfulness;
  answer me in your righteousness.

143.2
Job 14.3;
4.17;
Ps 130.3;
Eccl 7.20;
Rom 3.20

2 Do not enter into judgment with your servant,
  for no one living is righteous before you.

3 For the enemy has pursued me,
  crushing my life to the ground,
  making me sit in darkness like those long dead.

143.4
Ps 142.3;
Lam 3.11

4 Therefore my spirit faints within me;
  my heart within me is appalled.

143.5
Ps 77.5;
77.12; 105.2

5 I remember the days of old,
  I think about all your deeds,
  I meditate on the works of your hands.

143.6
Ps 88.9; 63.1

6 I stretch out my hands to you;
  my soul thirsts for you like a parched land.   *Selah*

B. *The prayer for deliverance*

143.7
Ps 69.17;
27.9; 28.1

7 Answer me quickly, O Lord;
  my spirit fails.

142.4 David is distraught that his best friends had forsaken him. This was even more true of Jesus, who was forsaken by the Father when he *alone* endured the wrath of God on the cross for our salvation. If we belong to Christ, we are never alone (cf. Mt 28.20). **143.1ff** In his affliction David cries out to God for deliverance, prays for retribution on his enemies, and expresses his confidence in God.

Do not hide your face from me,
 or I shall be like those who go down to the Pit.
8 Let me hear of your steadfast love in the morning,
 for in you I put my trust.
Teach me the way I should go,
 for to you I lift up my soul.

9 Save me, O LORD, from my enemies;
 I have fled to you for refuge.^v
10 Teach me to do your will,
 for you are my God.
Let your good spirit lead me
 on a level path.

11 For your name's sake, O LORD, preserve my life.
 In your righteousness bring me out of trouble.
12 In your steadfast love cut off my enemies,
 and destroy all my adversaries,
for I am your servant.

143.8
Ps 90.14;
25.2; 27.11;
25.1

143.9
Ps 31.15

143.10
Ps 25.4, 5;
Neh 9.20;
Ps 23.3

143.11
Ps 119.25;
31.1
143.12
Ps 54.5; 52.5;
116.16

Psalm 144

144.1
Ps 18.2, 34

The warrior's psalm

A. Praise to a great God

Of David.

1 Blessed be the LORD, my rock,
 who trains my hands for war, and my fingers for battle;
2 my rock^w and my fortress,
 my stronghold and my deliverer,
my shield, in whom I take refuge,
 who subdues the peoples^x under me.

144.2
Ps 91.2; 59.9;
84.9; 18.39

3 O LORD, what are human beings that you regard them,
 or mortals that you think of them?
4 They are like a breath;
 their days are like a passing shadow.

144.3
Ps 8.4;
Heb 2.6
144.4
Ps 39.11;
102.11

B. Prayer for help and deliverance

5 Bow your heavens, O LORD, and come down;
 touch the mountains so that they smoke.
6 Make the lightning flash and scatter them;
 send out your arrows and rout them.
7 Stretch out your hand from on high;
 set me free and rescue me from the mighty waters,
 from the hand of aliens,
8 whose mouths speak lies,
 and whose right hands are false.

144.5
Ps 18.9;
Isa 64.1;
Ps 104.32
144.6
Ps 18.13, 14;
7.13
144.7
Ps 69.1, 14;
18.44

144.8
Ps 12.2;
Isa 44.20

9 I will sing a new song to you, O God;
 upon a ten-stringed harp I will play to you,

144.9
Ps 33.2, 3

v One Heb Ms Gk: MT *to you I have hidden* *w* With 18.2 and 2 Sam 22.2: Heb *my steadfast love*
x Heb Mss Syr Aquila Jerome: MT *my people*

144.1ff A warrior sings of his victory with the help of God, his rock, fortress, shield, and deliverer. However strong he is, he must still seek God's face and pray for his help. After his victory, he promises to sing a new song to the God who rescued him (vv. 10,11). The psalm closes with an affirmation of happiness in the Lord.

144.10
Ps 18.50;
140.7

10 the one who gives victory to kings,
     who rescues his servant David.

144.11
Ps 12.2;
Isa 44.20

11 Rescue me from the cruel sword,
     and deliver me from the hand of aliens,
   whose mouths speak lies,
     and whose right hands are false.

C. *Prayer for prosperity for the people of God*

144.12
Ps 128.3

12 May our sons in their youth
     be like plants full grown,
   our daughters like corner pillars,
     cut for the building of a palace.

13 May our barns be filled,
     with produce of every kind;
   may our sheep increase by thousands,
     by tens of thousands in our fields,

14   and may our cattle be heavy with young.
   May there be no breach in the walls,*y* no exile,
     and no cry of distress in our streets.

144.15
Ps 33.12

15 Happy are the people to whom such blessings fall;
     happy are the people whose God is the LORD.

Psalm 145

145.1
Ps 30.1; 5.2;
34.1

The goodness of God

A. *The greatness of the LORD*

Praise. Of David.

1 I will extol you, my God and King,
    and bless your name forever and ever.

145.2
Ps 71.6

2 Every day I will bless you,
    and praise your name forever and ever.

145.3
Ps 96.4;
Job 5.9;
Rom 11.33

3 Great is the LORD, and greatly to be praised;
    his greatness is unsearchable.

145.4
Isa 38.19

4 One generation shall laud your works to another,
    and shall declare your mighty acts.

145.5
v. 12;
Ps 119.27

5 On the glorious splendor of your majesty,
    and on your wondrous works, I will meditate.

145.6
Ps 66.3;
Deut 32.3

6 The might of your awesome deeds shall be proclaimed,
    and I will declare your greatness.

145.7
Isa 63.7;
Ps 51.14

7 They shall celebrate the fame of your abundant goodness,
    and shall sing aloud of your righteousness.

B. *The graciousness of the LORD*

145.8
Ex 34.6;
Ps 86.5, 15

8 The LORD is gracious and merciful,
    slow to anger and abounding in steadfast love.

145.9
Ps 100.5;
Na 1.7

9 The LORD is good to all,
    and his compassion is over all that he has made.

y Heb lacks *in the walls*

145.1ff The last six psalms are songs of praise; the last five begin and end with "Hallelujah," making them "Hallelujah psalms" (see note on 111.1ff). In Ps 145 David enlarges on the subject of God's greatness, grace, mercy, and goodness. He affirms that God will destroy the wicked and preserve those who love him. All true believers, then, should praise the Lord.

10 All your works shall give thanks to you, O Lord,
    and all your faithful shall bless you.
11 They shall speak of the glory of your kingdom,
    and tell of your power,
12 to make known to all people your[z] mighty deeds,
    and the glorious splendor of your[a] kingdom.
13 Your kingdom is an everlasting kingdom,
    and your dominion endures throughout all generations.

C. The goodness of the Lord

The Lord is faithful in all his words,
    and gracious in all his deeds.[b]
14 The Lord upholds all who are falling,
    and raises up all who are bowed down.
15 The eyes of all look to you,
    and you give them their food in due season.
16 You open your hand,
    satisfying the desire of every living thing.
17 The Lord is just in all his ways,
    and kind in all his doings.
18 The Lord is near to all who call on him,
    to all who call on him in truth.
19 He fulfills the desire of all who fear him;
    he also hears their cry, and saves them.
20 The Lord watches over all who love him,
    but all the wicked he will destroy.

21 My mouth will speak the praise of the Lord,
    and all flesh will bless his holy name forever and ever.

Psalm 146

An exhortation to trust God

A. The vanity of trusting people

1 Praise the Lord!
    Praise the Lord, O my soul!
2 I will praise the Lord as long as I live;
    I will sing praises to my God all my life long.

3 Do not put your trust in princes,
    in mortals, in whom there is no help.
4 When their breath departs, they return to the earth;
    on that very day their plans perish.

B. The wisdom of trusting God

5 Happy are those whose help is the God of Jacob,
    whose hope is in the Lord their God,
6 who made heaven and earth,
    the sea, and all that is in them;
    who keeps faith forever;

Cross references (right margin):

145.10 Ps 19.1; 68.26
145.12 Ps 105.1; v. 54
145.13 Ps 146.10; 2 Pet 1.11
145.14 Ps 37.24; 146.8
145.15 Ps 104.27
145.16 Ps 124.28
145.18 Deut 4.7; Jn 4.24
145.19 Ps 37.4; Prov 15.29
145.20 Ps 31.23; 97.10; 9.5
145.21 Ps 71.8; 65.2; v. 1, 2
146.1 Ps 103.1
146.2 Ps 104.33
146.3 Ps 118.8; Isa 2.22
146.4 Ps 104.29; Eccl 12.7; Ps 33.10
146.5 Ps 144.15; 71.5
146.6 Ps 115.15; Acts 14.15; Ps 117.2

---

[z] Gk Jerome Syr: Heb *his*   [a] Heb *his*   [b] These two lines supplied by Q Ms Gk Syr

145.18 If we do not call, God will not answer. But all who do call on the Lord find that they are within reach of his help.
146.1ff Praising the Lord includes trusting him. We may not trust in mortals or princes, for they are finite.

But the Lord reigns forever; he helps all who hope in him, executing justice on their behalf, caring for the widows and orphans, opening the eyes of the blind, and setting the prisoners free.

146.7
Ps 103.6;
107.9; 68.6

7 who executes justice for the oppressed;
     who gives food to the hungry.

     The LORD sets the prisoners free;

146.8
Mt 9.30;
Jn 9.7;
Ps 145.14;
11.7

8   the LORD opens the eyes of the blind.
     The LORD lifts up those who are bowed down;
     the LORD loves the righteous.

146.9
Ex 22.21;
Deut 10.18;
Ps 68.5;
147.6

9   The LORD watches over the strangers;
     he upholds the orphan and the widow,
     but the way of the wicked he brings to ruin.

146.10
Ex 15.18;
Ps 10.16;
Rev 11.15

10 The LORD will reign forever,
     your God, O Zion, for all generations.
     Praise the LORD!

147.1
Ps 135.3;
33.1

Psalm 147

The LORD of might and grace

A. *The God of might in history*

1 Praise the LORD!
     How good it is to sing praises to our God;
     for he is gracious, and a song of praise is fitting.

147.2
Ps 102.16;
Deut 30.3

2 The LORD builds up Jerusalem;
     he gathers the outcasts of Israel.

147.3
Isa 61.1;
30.26

3 He heals the brokenhearted,
     and binds up their wounds.

147.4
Isa 40.26

4 He determines the number of the stars;
     he gives to all of them their names.

147.5
Ps 48.1;
Isa 40.28

5 Great is our Lord, and abundant in power;
     his understanding is beyond measure.

147.6
Ps 146.8, 9

6 The LORD lifts up the downtrodden;
     he casts the wicked to the ground.

B. *The God who sustains life*

147.7
Ps 33.2

7 Sing to the LORD with thanksgiving;
     make melody to our God on the lyre.

147.8
Job 38.26;
Ps 104.13

8 He covers the heavens with clouds,
     prepares rain for the earth,
     makes grass grow on the hills.

147.9
Ps 104.27;
Job 38.41

9 He gives to the animals their food,
     and to the young ravens when they cry.

147.10
Ps 33.16, 17;
1 Sam 16.7

10 His delight is not in the strength of the horse,
     nor his pleasure in the speed of a runner;*c*

147.11
Ps 102.15

11 but the LORD takes pleasure in those who fear him,
     in those who hope in his steadfast love.

---

c Heb *legs of a person*

146.10 Despite the enmity of Satan and the attacks of enemies, our God *does* reign forever. His kingdom will continue in endless glory, however strong the adversaries. Thus believers can shout "Praise the Lord!"

147.1ff This psalm supplies the believer with a number of reasons for praising the Lord. He is the God of might who has worked in history for the bene-

fit of his people Israel; he is the sustainer of life who meets the needs of his people. Let all the people of Zion join together in praise to God.

147.4 God made the stars, knows them by name, and has dominion over them. But people are more important than all the luminaries of the heavens. He intends to gather the outcasts of his people, to heal the brokenhearted, and to lift up the downtrodden.

C. *Israel exhorted to praise God*

12 Praise the Lord, O Jerusalem!
　　Praise your God, O Zion!
13 For he strengthens the bars of your gates;
　　he blesses your children within you.
14 He grants peace*d* within your borders;
　　he fills you with the finest of wheat.
15 He sends out his command to the earth;
　　his word runs swiftly.
16 He gives snow like wool;
　　he scatters frost like ashes.
17 He hurls down hail like crumbs—
　　who can stand before his cold?
18 He sends out his word, and melts them;
　　he makes his wind blow, and the waters flow.
19 He declares his word to Jacob,
　　his statutes and ordinances to Israel.
20 He has not dealt thus with any other nation;
　　they do not know his ordinances.
　　Praise the Lord!

147.13
Ps 37.26
147.14
Isa 60.17;
Ps 132.15
147.15
Job 37.12;
Ps 104.4
147.16
Job 37.6;
38.29
147.18
Ps 33.9;
107.25
147.19
Deut 33.2;
Mal 4.4
147.20
Deut 4.32

Psalm 148

Nature's praise of the Lord

A. *The heavens to praise the Lord*

1 Praise the Lord!
　Praise the Lord from the heavens;
　　praise him in the heights!
2 Praise him, all his angels;
　　praise him, all his host!

3 Praise him, sun and moon;
　　praise him, all you shining stars!
4 Praise him, you highest heavens,
　　and you waters above the heavens!

5 Let them praise the name of the Lord,
　　for he commanded and they were created.
6 He established them forever and ever;
　　he fixed their bounds, which cannot be passed.*e*

148.2
Ps 103.20, 21

148.4
1 Kings 8.27;
Gen 1.7
148.5
Gen 1.1;
Ps 33.6, 9
148.6
Ps 89.37;
Jer 33.25;
Job 38.33

B. *The earth to praise the Lord*

7 Praise the Lord from the earth,
　　you sea monsters and all deeps,
8 fire and hail, snow and frost,
　　stormy wind fulfilling his command!

148.7
Ps 74.13
148.8
Ps 147.15-18

d Or *prosperity*　　*e* Or *he set a law that cannot pass away*

147.19 The word of God was given to Israel and preserved by Israel. Though the psalmist here limits God's word to Israel, other psalms call for it to be declared by God's people among the nations (e.g., Ps 96).
148.1ff This song powerfully tells us who should sing hallelujahs to the Lord. The angelic hosts are called to praise him. So are the sun, the moon, and the myriad of stars that dot the heavens. Let the monsters of the deep, mountains and fruit trees, hail, fire, and snow sing the divine praises. Let the young and the old, the kings and all the rulers of the earth resound in song. Above all, let his people Israel sing forth in praise to their God. In sum, no one and no thing is exempt from praising God.

148.9
Isa 44.23;
49.13; 55.12

9 Mountains and all hills,
  fruit trees and all cedars!
10 Wild animals and all cattle,
  creeping things and flying birds!

11 Kings of the earth and all peoples,
  princes and all rulers of the earth!
12 Young men and women alike,
  old and young together!

148.13
Ps 8.1;
Isa 12.4;
Ps 113.4

13 Let them praise the name of the Lord,
  for his name alone is exalted;
  his glory is above earth and heaven.

148.14
Ps 75.10;
Deut 10.21;
Eph 2.17

14 He has raised up a horn for his people,
  praise for all his faithful,
  for the people of Israel who are close to him.
  Praise the Lord!

Psalm 149

The Lord's love of Israel

A. Exhortation to sing a new song

149.1
Ps 33.3;
35.18

1 Praise the Lord!
  Sing to the Lord a new song,
  his praise in the assembly of the faithful.

149.2
Ps 95.6; 47.6

2 Let Israel be glad in its Maker;
  let the children of Zion rejoice in their King.

149.3
Ps 150.4;
81.2
149.4
Ps 35.27;
132.16

3 Let them praise his name with dancing,
  making melody to him with tambourine and lyre.
4 For the Lord takes pleasure in his people;
  he adorns the humble with victory.

B. Exhortation to execute vengeance on the nations

149.5
Ps 132.16;
Job 35.10
149.6
Ps 66.17;
Heb 4.12;
Rev 1.16

5 Let the faithful exult in glory;
  let them sing for joy on their couches.
6 Let the high praises of God be in their throats
  and two-edged swords in their hands,
7 to execute vengeance on the nations
  and punishment on the peoples,
8 to bind their kings with fetters
  and their nobles with chains of iron,

149.9
Ezek 28.26;
Ps 148.14

9 to execute on them the judgment decreed.
  This is glory for all his faithful ones.
  Praise the Lord!

Psalm 150

Let everything praise the Lord

150.1
Ps 102.19;
19.1

1 Praise the Lord!

148.13 The name of our Lord is above every other name (cf. Phil 2.9–11). That name, representing his person, is the only name worthy of the praise of nature and humankind.
149.1ff Ps 148 was praise directed toward God as the Creator; this psalm is praise to God who is also the Redeemer. It looks first toward God's redeemed in

the O.T., but the theme of God as Redeemer extends to all ages, particularly to the church since the day of Pentecost.
150.1ff The Psalter closes with suggestions of how, and with what instruments, God's faithful can praise his holy name. We must praise him in the church and in the streets. We must use every instrument from the

Praise God in his sanctuary;
   praise him in his mighty firmament!*f*
2 Praise him for his mighty deeds;
   praise him according to his surpassing greatness!

	150.2
	Ps 145.5, 6;
	Deut 3.24

3 Praise him with trumpet sound;
   praise him with lute and harp!

| | 150.3 |
| | Ps 149.3 |

4 Praise him with tambourine and dance;
   praise him with strings and pipe!

	150.4
	Ex 15.20;
	Isa 38.20

5 Praise him with clanging cymbals;
   praise him with loud clashing cymbals!
6 Let everything that breathes praise the LORD!
   Praise the LORD!

	150.5
	1 Chr 13.8;
	15.16
	150.6
	Ps 145.21

f Or *dome*

trumpet and saxophone to the harp and all the stringed instruments. We must use the drums that thunder and cymbals that clang. "Let everything that breathes praise the LORD! Praise the LORD!" (v. 6).

INTRODUCTION TO

PROVERBS

Authorship, Date, and Background: Proverbs is an anthology of wise sayings. Many were written by Solomon, who was widely known for having composed three thousand proverbs and one thousand and five songs (1 Kings 4.32). The sayings of Solomon included in this book are a sample of the many he wrote. Moreover, scribes in Hezekiah's day copied down numerous other ancient sayings, most of which were Solomon's (25.1). In addition, some of the sayings in Proverbs came from other ancient sources. The last two chapters of Proverbs were written by Agur and Lemuel, about whom we have little or no knowledge. Proverbs is called "wisdom literature," a genre of writing which was common to the ancient Near East. Some have thought there is a relationship between the Egyptian "Wisdom of Amenemope" and Proverbs (especially in 22.17—24.22).

Some modern scholars hold that nothing in Proverbs can be dated earlier than 350 B.C., with later material being added in the second century. There is no solid evidence for this. Other modern scholars, however, while acknowledging that in its edited form Proverbs may date to the fifth century B.C., believe that much of its contents is considerably older. To relate the beginning of Proverbs to Solomon is certainly within reason.

Characteristics and Content: At the heart of Proverbs lies the dictum, "The fear of the LORD is the beginning of knowledge" (1.7). The book is theological, stressing the sovereignty of God, his omniscience, his creative activity, his rulership over the moral order, and the certainty that he will judge people's actions. Individual proverbs range widely over the activities of humankind, leaving virtually no area of human life untouched. Social relationships are grappled with: social evils, concern for the poor, laziness, poverty, and wealth are discussed. Family relationships are covered (e.g., that between children and parents); the importance of friendship is dealt with. The tongue, personal habits, attitudes, and the concept of life itself are examined. Wisdom is contrasted with foolishness and distinctions are drawn about simple fools, hardened fools, arrogant fools, and brutish ones.

King Lemuel ends the book with his observations about the ideal wife. It is one of the most tasteful descriptions of how such a woman conducts herself in a fitting manner. Such a wife is an example to all brides. At the heart of this wife's life and thinking lies the true reason for her greatness: "a woman who fears the LORD is to be praised" (31.30).

Outline:

I. Wisdom (1.1—9.18)

II. Proverbs of Solomon (10.1—22.16)

III. Miscellaneous sayings (22.17—24.34)

PROVERBS

I. *Wisdom (1.1–9.18)*

A. *Authorship*

1.1
1 Kings 4.32;
Eccl 12.9

1 The proverbs of Solomon son of David, king of Israel:

B. *The purpose*

2 For learning about wisdom and instruction,
  for understanding words of insight,

1.3
Prov 19.20;
2.9
1.4
Prov 8.5, 12;
2.10, 11
1.5
Prov 9.9;
14.6
1.6
Ps 78.2

3 for gaining instruction in wise dealing,
  righteousness, justice, and equity;
4 to teach shrewdness to the simple,
  knowledge and prudence to the young—
5 let the wise also hear and gain in learning,
  and the discerning acquire skill,
6 to understand a proverb and a figure,
  the words of the wise and their riddles.

C. *The major theme*

1.7
Job 28.28;
Ps 111.10;
Eccl 12.13

7 The fear of the LORD is the beginning of knowledge;
  fools despise wisdom and instruction.

D. *Warnings against violence*

1.8
Prov 4.1;
6.20
1.9
Prov 4.9;
Gen 41.42
1.10
Deut 13.8;
Eph 5.11
1.11
Prov 12.6;
v. 18
1.12
Ps 124.3;
28.1

8 Hear, my child, your father's instruction,
  and do not reject your mother's teaching;
9 for they are a fair garland for your head,
  and pendants for your neck.
10 My child, if sinners entice you,
  do not consent.
11 If they say, "Come with us, let us lie in wait for blood;
  let us wantonly ambush the innocent;
12 like Sheol let us swallow them alive
  and whole, like those who go down to the Pit.
13 We shall find all kinds of costly things;
  we shall fill our houses with booty.
14 Throw in your lot among us;
  we will all have one purse"—

1.15
Ps 1.1;
119.101
1.16
Isa 59.7

15 my child, do not walk in their way,
  keep your foot from their paths;
16 for their feet run to evil,

1.1 The major portion of this book comes from Solomon, put together several centuries after his death. Agur and Lemuel are other contributors.
1.2 *wisdom and instruction.* God gave Solomon the gift of wisdom (1 Kings 3). It was this gift that accounts for his greatness. The book of Proverbs will help us to entertain right notions of things, to distinguish between truth and falsehood, and to discern between good and evil, thus enabling us to mature in spirituality and to guard against mistakes.

1.4 The sayings were written for the least educated, to youth and the simpleminded, all of whom could understand the meaning. If the simple can understand, so can the well-educated and the learned.
1.10 *if sinners entice you, do not consent.* Sinners love to have company. Tempters do not argue or threaten; they use flattery and smooth talk. They make promises they cannot fulfill. But no one can legitimately say, "the devil made me do it," for the choice to act or not to act is individual.

and they hurry to shed blood.
17 For in vain is the net baited
        while the bird is looking on;
18 yet they lie in wait — to kill themselves!
        and set an ambush — for their own lives!
19 Such is the end[a] of all who are greedy for gain;
        it takes away the life of its possessors.

1.19
Prov 15.27

E. *Warning against the neglect of wisdom*

20 Wisdom cries out in the street;
        in the squares she raises her voice.
21 At the busiest corner she cries out;
        at the entrance of the city gates she speaks:
22 "How long, O simple ones, will you love being simple?
        How long will scoffers delight in their scoffing
        and fools hate knowledge?
23 Give heed to my reproof;
        I will pour out my thoughts to you;
        I will make my words known to you.
24 Because I have called and you refused,
        have stretched out my hand and no one heeded,
25 and because you have ignored all my counsel
        and would have none of my reproof,
26 I also will laugh at your calamity;
        I will mock when panic strikes you,
27 when panic strikes you like a storm,
        and your calamity comes like a whirlwind,
        when distress and anguish come upon you.
28 Then they will call upon me, but I will not answer;
        they will seek me diligently, but will not find me.
29 Because they hated knowledge
        and did not choose the fear of the LORD,
30 would have none of my counsel,
        and despised all my reproof,
31 therefore they shall eat the fruit of their way
        and be sated with their own devices.
32 For waywardness kills the simple,
        and the complacency of fools destroys them;
33 but those who listen to me will be secure
        and will live at ease, without dread of disaster."

1.20
Prov 8.1

1.22
vv. 4, 32;
Ps 1.1; v. 29

1.23
Joel 2.28

1.24
Isa 65.12;
Zech 7.11;
Rom 10.21
1.25
Ps 107.11;
Lk 7.30;
Prov 15.10
1.26
Ps 2.4;
Prov 6.15;
10.24

1.28
Isa 1.15;
Ezek 8.18;
Mic 3.4;
Zech 7.13

1.30
Ps 81.11

1.31
Job 4.8;
Prov 14.14;
Isa 3.11;
Jer 6.19
1.32
Jer 2.19
1.33
Ps 25.12

F. *The reward of seeking wisdom*

2   My child, if you accept my words
        and treasure up my commandments within you,

2.1
Prov 4.10

a Gk: Heb *are the ways*

1.16 Sin is a downhill run all the way. The longer sinners continue their wicked ways, the faster they hurry.
1.20 Wisdom is not silent in the midst of evil. Everyone hears its voice, so that sinners can never say, "Nobody told us," and so claim innocence.
1.24 *I have called and you refused.* To neglect wisdom is a serious fault. To ignore the counsel of wisdom results in being unable to dwell safely.
1.26 Those who have laughed at God and mocked him will discover that a time comes when God will laugh at them and mock them for their insolence and their haughty refusal to hear him and be helped by him.

1.28 The door to heaven is open now, but a time will come when it will be shut to sinners. Then when they cry, their prayers will not be heard because they did not answer when they had the opportunity.
1.31 All people's wages will be according to their works; they are choosing their own doom by those works.
2.1ff Those who are willing to be taught will obtain from God the knowledge and grace they want. Attaining this is a great advantage and will preserve them from a variety of snares that would otherwise overtake and destroy them. We are instructed how to obtain wisdom and how to use it.

2.2 Prov 3.1	2 making your ear attentive to wisdom and inclining your heart to understanding;
	3 if you indeed cry out for insight, and raise your voice for understanding;
2.4 Prov 3.14; Mt 13.44	4 if you seek it like silver, and search for it as for hidden treasures —
2.5 Prov 1.7	5 then you will understand the fear of the LORD and find the knowledge of God.

2.6
1 Kings 3.9,
12;
Jas 1.5
	6 For the LORD gives wisdom;
	  from his mouth come knowledge and
	  understanding;

2.7 Ps 84.11	7 he stores up sound wisdom for the upright; he is a shield to those who walk blamelessly,
2.8 1 Sam 2.9; Ps 66.9	8 guarding the paths of justice and preserving the way of his faithful ones.
2.9 Prov 8.20; 4.18	9 Then you will understand righteousness and justice and equity, every good path;
2.10 Prov 14.33; 22.18	10 for wisdom will come into your heart, and knowledge will be pleasant to your soul;
2.11 Prov 6.22	11 prudence will watch over you; and understanding will guard you.
	12 It will save you from the way of evil, from those who speak perversely,
2.13 Jn 3.19	13 who forsake the paths of uprightness to walk in the ways of darkness,
2.14 Prov 10.23; Jer 11.15	14 who rejoice in doing evil and delight in the perverseness of evil;
2.15 Ps 125.5	15 those whose paths are crooked, and who are devious in their ways.
2.16 Prov 6.24; 23.27	16 You will be saved from the loose*b* woman, from the adulteress with her smooth words,
2.17 Mal 2.14, 15	17 who forsakes the partner of her youth and forgets her sacred covenant;
2.18 Prov 7.27	18 for her way*c* leads down to death, and her paths to the shades;
	19 those who go to her never come back, nor do they regain the paths of life.

G. *Walking in the way of wisdom*

	20 Therefore walk in the way of the good, and keep to the paths of the just.
2.21 Ps 37.29; 28.10	21 For the upright will abide in the land, and the innocent will remain in it;
2.22 Ps 37.38; Deut 28.63	22 but the wicked will be cut off from the land, and the treacherous will be rooted out of it.

b Heb *strange*   *c* Cn: Heb *house*

2.6 *from his mouth.* God speaks by his law, his prophets, and his apostles. Inspired people have the written word of the living God, and God's ministers preach it boldly. It is not for lack of a word from God that humans are lost; it is because of the rejection of that word.
2.10 Those who give themselves over to wisdom will be possessed and preserved by it. It will enter their hearts and be pleasant to their souls.
2.16 True wisdom will save one from *the loose*

woman — that is, an adulteress, whose flattery is vile, whose sexual promiscuity violates her sacred marriage vows, and whose relation with God is defiled since she "forgets her sacred covenant" (v. 17).
2.20 No one can do well who has not first ceased to do evil. There is a way that is good, and the good person follows the example of those who have walked in the paths of righteousness. Then that life will be an example for others who come after.

H. *The blessing of wisdom*

3 My child, do not forget my teaching,
but let your heart keep my commandments;
2 for length of days and years of life
and abundant welfare they will give you.

3 Do not let loyalty and faithfulness forsake you;
bind them around your neck,
write them on the tablet of your heart.
4 So you will find favor and good repute
in the sight of God and of people.

5 Trust in the LORD with all your heart,
and do not rely on your own insight.
6 In all your ways acknowledge him,
and he will make straight your paths.
7 Do not be wise in your own eyes;
fear the LORD, and turn away from evil.
8 It will be a healing for your flesh
and a refreshment for your body.

9 Honor the LORD with your substance
and with the first fruits of all your produce;
10 then your barns will be filled with plenty,
and your vats will be bursting with wine.

11 My child, do not despise the LORD's discipline
or be weary of his reproof,
12 for the LORD reproves the one he loves,
as a father the son in whom he delights.

I. *Wisdom more precious than wealth*

13 Happy are those who find wisdom,
and those who get understanding,
14 for her income is better than silver,
and her revenue better than gold.
15 She is more precious than jewels,
and nothing you desire can compare with her.
16 Long life is in her right hand;
in her left hand are riches and honor.
17 Her ways are ways of pleasantness,
and all her paths are peace.
18 She is a tree of life to those who lay hold of her;
those who hold her fast are called happy.

19 The LORD by wisdom founded the earth;
by understanding he established the heavens;
20 by his knowledge the deeps broke open,
and the clouds drop down the dew.

3.1 Prov 4.5; Ex 20.6; Deut 30.16
3.2 Prov 4.10; Ps 119.165
3.3 2 Sam 15.20; Prov 1.9; 7.3
3.4 Prov 8.5; Ps 111.10
3.5 Ps 37.3, 5; Jer 9.23
3.6 1 Chr 28.9; Isa 45.13
3.7 Rom 12.16; Prov 16.6
3.8 Job 21.24
3.9 Isa 43.23; Ex 23.19
3.10 Deut 28.8
3.11 Heb 12.5, 6
3.12 Deut 8.5
3.13 Prov 8.32, 34
3.14 Job 28.13; Prov 8.10, 19
3.15 Job 28.18; Prov 8.11
3.16 Prov 8.18
3.17 Prov 16.7
3.18 Prov 11.30; Gen 2.9
3.19 Ps 104.24
3.20 Gen 7.11; Job 36.28

3.5 Those who have true wisdom will put their confidence in the wisdom, power, and goodness of God, trusting he will do what is best for them. By prayer they will seek divine guidance and look for heavenly advice from the author of wisdom (v. 6). When they do this, God will direct their paths amd bring them at last to their rest in the promised land.
3.9 We must honor God with our material goods as well as with our souls and bodies. The more God gives us, the more we should work to honor him.

3.13–18 Although wisdom comes from God, attaining it requires work. The true seeker will sell everything to attain that treasure and find that the result is worth far more than the effort expended. It is like the perfect tree of life that existed in Eden, and it produces happiness and long life.
3.19 God made the heavens and the earth (Gen 1.1), and they function flawlessly in orderly fashion. The sea does not overrun its banks, and all nature responds to the Creator's laws of nature.

J. The wise inherit honor

21 My child, do not let these escape from your sight:
   keep sound wisdom and prudence,

3.22
Prov 4.22;
1.9

22 and they will be life for your soul
   and adornment for your neck.

3.23
Prov 4.12

23 Then you will walk on your way securely
   and your foot will not stumble.

3.24
Ps 3.5

24 If you sit down,*d* you will not be afraid;
   when you lie down, your sleep will be sweet.

3.25
Ps 91.5;
Job 5.21

25 Do not be afraid of sudden panic,
   or of the storm that strikes the wicked;

26 for the LORD will be your confidence
   and will keep your foot from being caught.

3.27
Rom 13.7;
Gal 6.10

27 Do not withhold good from those to whom it is due,*e*
   when it is in your power to do it.

3.28
Lev 19.13

28 Do not say to your neighbor, "Go, and come again,
   tomorrow I will give it"—when you have it with you.

3.29
Prov 14.22

29 Do not plan harm against your neighbor
   who lives trustingly beside you.

3.30
Rom 12.18

30 Do not quarrel with anyone without cause,
   when no harm has been done to you.

3.31
Ps 37.1;
Prov 24.1

31 Do not envy the violent
   and do not choose any of their ways;

3.32
Prov 11.20;
Ps 25.14

32 for the perverse are an abomination to the LORD,
   but the upright are in his confidence.

3.33
Deut 11.28;
Mal 2.2;
Job 8.6

33 The LORD's curse is on the house of the wicked,
   but he blesses the abode of the righteous.

3.34
Jas 4.6;
1 Pet 5.5

34 Toward the scorners he is scornful,
   but to the humble he shows favor.

35 The wise will inherit honor,
   but stubborn fools, disgrace.

K. Admonitions of a father to his child

1. The command to obtain wisdom

4.1
Prov 1.8; 2.2

4 Listen, children, to a father's instruction,
   and be attentive, that you may gain*f* insight;

2 for I give you good precepts:
   do not forsake my teaching.

4.3
1 Chr 22.5

3 When I was a son with my father,
   tender, and my mother's favorite,

4.4
1 Chr 28.9;
Prov 7.2

4 he taught me, and said to me,
   "Let your heart hold fast my words;
   keep my commandments, and live.

4.5
v. 7;
Prov 16.16

5 Get wisdom; get insight: do not forget, nor turn away
   from the words of my mouth.

4.6
2 Thess 2.10

6 Do not forsake her, and she will keep you;
   love her, and she will guard you.

4.7
Prov 23.23

7 The beginning of wisdom is this: Get wisdom,
   and whatever else you get, get insight.

d Gk: Heb *lie down*   *e* Heb *from its owners*   *f* Heb *know*

3.28ff Wise people practice neighborly love and justice. They will not hurt their neighbors, nor will they be quarrelsome, contentious, or envious. Such people will receive honor, whereas fools will experience shame.
4.3ff Solomon was taught well by his father David,

and for much of his life continued in the things he had been taught. What puzzles us is that Solomon, the wisest king Israel ever had, forsook wisdom in his later years (especially in the number of his wives and concubines), and failed to teach it to his own successor, Rehoboam.

8   Prize her highly, and she will exalt you;
      she will honor you if you embrace her.
9   She will place on your head a fair garland;
      she will bestow on you a beautiful crown."

2. Contrast of the wise and the wicked

10 Hear, my child, and accept my words,
      that the years of your life may be many.
11 I have taught you the way of wisdom;
      I have led you in the paths of uprightness.
12 When you walk, your step will not be hampered;
      and if you run, you will not stumble.
13 Keep hold of instruction; do not let go;
      guard her, for she is your life.
14 Do not enter the path of the wicked,
      and do not walk in the way of evildoers.
15 Avoid it; do not go on it;
      turn away from it and pass on.
16 For they cannot sleep unless they have done wrong;
      they are robbed of sleep unless they have made someone
        stumble.
17 For they eat the bread of wickedness
      and drink the wine of violence.
18 But the path of the righteous is like the light of dawn,
      which shines brighter and brighter until full day.
19 The way of the wicked is like deep darkness;
      they do not know what they stumble over.

3. Positive instructions to a child

20 My child, be attentive to my words;
      incline your ear to my sayings.
21 Do not let them escape from your sight;
      keep them within your heart.
22 For they are life to those who find them,
      and healing to all their flesh.
23 Keep your heart with all vigilance,
      for from it flow the springs of life.
24 Put away from you crooked speech,
      and put devious talk far from you.
25 Let your eyes look directly forward,
      and your gaze be straight before you.
26 Keep straight the path of your feet,
      and all your ways will be sure.
27 Do not swerve to the right or to the left;
      turn your foot away from evil.

L. Instruction on marriage

1. Warning against unchastity

5   My child, be attentive to my wisdom;
      incline your ear to my understanding,
2   so that you may hold on to prudence,
      and your lips may guard knowledge.

4.14–16 The good person will shun the wicked, those who are malicious, violent, and spiteful, and who spend long hours of the night in scheming up mischief. We should stay clear of such people.

4.25 The eyes of the righteous look straight ahead to the good rather than backward to the bad. They keep their backs to the world and their faces looking up to heaven (cf. Phil 3.13,14).

4.8
1 Sam 2.30
4.9
Prov 1.9

4.10
Prov 2.1; 3.2
4.11
1 Sam 12.23
4.12
Ps 18.36;
Prov 3.23

4.14
Ps 1.1;
Prov 1.15

4.16
Ps 36.4;
Mic 2.1

4.18
Isa 26.7;
2 Sam 23.4;
Dan 12.3
4.19
Job 18.5;
Isa 59.9, 10;
Jer 23.12;
Jn 12.35

4.21
Prov 3.21;
7.1, 2
4.22
Prov 3.8;
12.18
4.23
Mt 12.34;
Mk 7.21;
Lk 6.45
4.24
Prov 6.12;
19.1

4.26
Heb 12.13;
Ps 119.5
4.27
Deut 5.32;
28.14;
Prov 1.15

5.1
Prov 4.20;
22.17
5.2
Mal 2.7

5.3
Prov 2.16;
Ps 55.21
5.4
Eccl 7.26;
Ps 57.4
5.5
Prov 7.27

5.7
Prov 7.24;
Ps 119.102
5.8
Prov 7.25;
9.14

5.12
Prov 1.29;
12.1

5.16
Prov 9.17

5.18
Eccl 9.9;
Mal 2.14
5.19
Song 2.9;
4.5; 7.3

5.20
Prov 2.16;
7.5
5.21
Job 31.4;
34.21;
Prov 15.3;
Jer 16.17;
32.19;
Hos 7.2;
Heb 4.13
5.22
Ps 9.15
5.23
Job 4.21;
36.12
6.1
Prov 11.15;
17.18; 20.16;
22.26; 27.13

3 For the lips of a loose^g woman drip honey,
    and her speech is smoother than oil;
4 but in the end she is bitter as wormwood,
    sharp as a two-edged sword.
5 Her feet go down to death;
    her steps follow the path to Sheol.
6 She does not keep straight to the path of life;
    her ways wander, and she does not know it.

7 And now, my child,^h listen to me,
    and do not depart from the words of my mouth.
8 Keep your way far from her,
    and do not go near the door of her house;
9 or you will give your honor to others,
    and your years to the merciless,
10 and strangers will take their fill of your wealth,
    and your labors will go to the house of an alien;
11 and at the end of your life you will groan,
    when your flesh and body are consumed,
12 and you say, "Oh, how I hated discipline,
    and my heart despised reproof!
13 I did not listen to the voice of my teachers
    or incline my ear to my instructors.
14 Now I am at the point of utter ruin
    in the public assembly."

2. Marital joys and responsibilities

15 Drink water from your own cistern,
    flowing water from your own well.
16 Should your springs be scattered abroad,
    streams of water in the streets?
17 Let them be for yourself alone,
    and not for sharing with strangers.
18 Let your fountain be blessed,
    and rejoice in the wife of your youth,
19 a lovely deer, a graceful doe.
    May her breasts satisfy you at all times;
    may you be intoxicated always by her love.
20 Why should you be intoxicated, my son, by another woman
    and embrace the bosom of an adulteress?
21 For human ways are under the eyes of the LORD,
    and he examines all their paths.
22 The iniquities of the wicked ensnare them,
    and they are caught in the toils of their sin.
23 They die for lack of discipline,
    and because of their great folly they are lost.

M. Warning against suretyship

6 My child, if you have given your pledge to your neighbor,
    if you have bound yourself to another,ⁱ

g Heb strange   h Gk Vg: Heb children   i Or a stranger

5.3 *of a loose woman*, i.e., of a prostitute. Herein the reader is warned to shun fornication, adultery, and all uncleanness. These sins appear attractive and the immediate satisfaction is tempting. But the end is death rather than life.
5.11 *when your flesh and body are consumed.* This possibly refers to venereal disease.

5.18 It is better to marry than burn (1 Cor 7.9). Therefore every man should have his own wife, enjoy her love, and remain faithful to her. An extramarital liaison is folly. Solomon here is endorsing monogamous marriage as the biblical ideal.
6.1 Solomon warns against co-signing a financial transaction, even for a friend. Many friendships have

2   you are snared by the utterance of your lips,[j]
        caught by the words of your mouth.
3   So do this, my child, and save yourself,
        for you have come into your neighbor's power:
        go, hurry,[k] and plead with your neighbor.
4   Give your eyes no sleep   **6.4**
        and your eyelids no slumber;   Ps 132.4
5   save yourself like a gazelle from the hunter,[l]   **6.5**
        like a bird from the hand of the fowler.   Ps 91.3

N. *Warning against idleness*

6   Go to the ant, you lazybones;   **6.6**
        consider its ways, and be wise.   Prov 30.24,
7   Without having any chief   25
        or officer or ruler,
8   it prepares its food in summer,   **6.8**
        and gathers its sustenance in harvest.   Prov 10.5
9   How long will you lie there, O lazybones?   **6.9**
        When will you rise from your sleep?   Prov 24.33
10 A little sleep, a little slumber,
        a little folding of the hands to rest,
11 and poverty will come upon you like a robber,   **6.11**
        and want, like an armed warrior.   Prov 10.4;
                                                     13.4; 20.4

O. *Warning against sowing discord*

12 A scoundrel and a villain   **6.12**
        goes around with crooked speech,   Prov 16.27;
13 winking the eyes, shuffling the feet,   10.32
        pointing the fingers,   **6.13**
14 with perverted mind devising evil,   Ps 35.19;
        continually sowing discord;   Prov 10.10
15 on such a one calamity will descend suddenly;   **6.14**
        in a moment, damage beyond repair.   Mic 2.1; v. 19
                                                     6.15
                                                     Prov 24.22;
                                                     Jer 19.11;
                                                     2 Chr 36.16

P. *Warning against seven sins*

16 There are six things that the LORD hates,
        seven that are an abomination to him:
17 haughty eyes, a lying tongue,   **6.17**
        and hands that shed innocent blood,   Ps 18.27;
18 a heart that devises wicked plans,   120.2;
        feet that hurry to run to evil,   Isa 1.15
19 a lying witness who testifies falsely,   **6.18**
        and one who sows discord in a family.   Gen 6.5;
                                                     Prov 1.16
                                                     6.19
                                                     Ps 27.12; v. 4

Q. *Warning against adultery*

20 My child, keep your father's commandment,   **6.20**
        and do not forsake your mother's teaching.   Prov 7.1; 1.8

---

j Cn Compare Gk Syr: Heb *the words of your mouth*   *k* Or *humble yourself*   *l* Cn: Heb *from the hand*

---

been ruined this way. He suggests that the arrangement be cancelled as quickly as possible.
6.6 Sluggards should watch the ant and learn a lesson from the lower life of nature that will help them
to attain a better life than they now have.
6.12 Scoundrels and villains are crafty schemers
who hide their wickedness by professing the good.
Their words sound wholesome, yet they have evil
designs in hearts and minds. The Scriptures condemn

all such connivers.
6.16–19 Solomon lists seven deadly sins here, any
one of which is enough to condemn a person. Most of
the wicked are guilty of all seven.
6.20 The commandments spoken of here constitute
the word of God. Mother and father alike are bound
by it and should teach it to their children. It is to be
remembered, thought about, and practiced when
walking, lying down, and rising up (cf. Deut 6.6–9).

6.21 Prov 3.3	21 Bind them upon your heart always; tie them around your neck.
6.22 Prov 3.23, 24	22 When you walk, they[m] will lead you; when you lie down, they[m] will watch over you; and when you awake, they[m] will talk with you.
6.23 Ps 19.8	23 For the commandment is a lamp and the teaching a light, and the reproofs of discipline are the way of life,
6.24 Prov 2.16; 5.3	24 to preserve you from the wife of another,[n] from the smooth tongue of the adulteress.
6.25 Mt 5.28	25 Do not desire her beauty in your heart, and do not let her capture you with her eyelashes;
6.26 Prov 29.3; 7.23; Ezek 13.18	26 for a prostitute's fee is only a loaf of bread,[o] but the wife of another stalks a man's very life.
	27 Can fire be carried in the bosom without burning one's clothes?
	28 Or can one walk on hot coals without scorching the feet?
6.29 Ezek 18.6; 33.26	29 So is he who sleeps with his neighbor's wife; no one who touches her will go unpunished.
	30 Thieves are not despised who steal only to satisfy their appetite when they are hungry.
6.31 Ex 22.1-4	31 Yet if they are caught, they will pay sevenfold; they will forfeit all the goods of their house.
6.32 Prov 7.7	32 But he who commits adultery has no sense; he who does it destroys himself.
	33 He will get wounds and dishonor, and his disgrace will not be wiped away.
6.34 Prov 27.4; 11.4	34 For jealousy arouses a husband's fury, and he shows no restraint when he takes revenge.
	35 He will accept no compensation, and refuses a bribe no matter how great.

R. *The folly of yielding to a prostitute*

7.1 Prov 2.1	7 My child, keep my words and store up my commandments with you;
7.2 Prov 4.4; Deut 32.10	2 keep my commandments and live, keep my teachings as the apple of your eye;
7.3 Deut 6.8; Prov 3.3	3 bind them on your fingers, write them on the tablet of your heart.
	4 Say to wisdom, "You are my sister," and call insight your intimate friend,
7.5 Prov 2.16; 5.3; 6.24	5 that they may keep you from the loose[p] woman, from the adulteress with her smooth words.
	6 For at the window of my house I looked out through my lattice,
7.7 Prov 1.22; 6.32	7 and I saw among the simple ones, I observed among the youths, a young man without sense,
7.8 vv. 12, 27	8 passing along the street near her corner,

m Heb *it*   *n* Gk: MT *the evil woman*   *o* Cn Compare Gk Syr Vg Tg: Heb *for because of a harlot to a piece of bread*   *p* Heb *strange*

6.34 Adultery is one of the most serious sins. An adulterer destroys his own soul and faces both the justice of God and the wrath of the husband whose wife has been violated. His anger is a righteous anger. Theft can be atoned for by a ransom, but a wronged husband will accept no ransom. The O.T. law de-

manded the death of persons guilty of adultery.
7.7ff Many proverbs are addressed to youths, warning them of life's pitfalls. They acknowledge that youths will be tempted, but state if they seek and find wisdom, they can avoid sin and say "no" to those who tempt them.

taking the road to her house
9   in the twilight, in the evening,
     at the time of night and darkness.

7.9
Job 24.15

10   Then a woman comes toward him,
     decked out like a prostitute, wily of heart.*q*

11   She is loud and wayward;
     her feet do not stay at home;

7.11
Prov 9.13;
1 Tim 5.13

12   now in the street, now in the squares,
     and at every corner she lies in wait.

7.12
Prov 23.28

13   She seizes him and kisses him,
     and with impudent face she says to him:

14   "I had to offer sacrifices,
     and today I have paid my vows;

7.14
Prov 7.11, 16

15   so now I have come out to meet you,
     to seek you eagerly, and I have found you!

16   I have decked my couch with coverings,
     colored spreads of Egyptian linen;

7.16
Prov 31.22;
Isa 19.9

17   I have perfumed my bed with myrrh,
     aloes, and cinnamon.

18   Come, let us take our fill of love until morning;
     let us delight ourselves with love.

19   For my husband is not at home;
     he has gone on a long journey.

20   He took a bag of money with him;
     he will not come home until full moon."

21   With much seductive speech she persuades him;
     with her smooth talk she compels him.

7.21
Prov 5.3

22   Right away he follows her,
     and goes like an ox to the slaughter,
   or bounds like a stag toward the trap*r*

23   until an arrow pierces its entrails.
   He is like a bird rushing into a snare,
     not knowing that it will cost him his life.

7.23
Eccl 9.12

24   And now, my children, listen to me,
     and be attentive to the words of my mouth.

7.24
Prov 5.7

25   Do not let your hearts turn aside to her ways;
     do not stray into her paths.

7.25
Prov 5.8

26   For many are those she has laid low,
     and numerous are her victims.

7.26
Prov 9.18

27   Her house is the way to Sheol,
     going down to the chambers of death.

7.27
Prov 2.18;
5.5; 9.18

S. Wisdom personified

1. The call of wisdom

8   Does not wisdom call,
     and does not understanding raise her voice?

8.1
Prov 1.20;
9.3

q Meaning of Heb uncertain   *r* Cn Compare Gk: Meaning of Heb uncertain

---

7.18 *let us take our fill of love.* Love here really means brutish lust; it is a pity that the word "love" should be thus abused.
7.19 This adulteress is not a common prostitute. She is a wife, who no doubt had the respect of her neighbors and the love of her husband. She engages in seduction and violates her marriage vows. Bad as she is, one must also fault her "lover," who also be-

trays the husband and is no less guilty.
8.1 God has revealed all we need to know for salvation and the conduct of life. We know these things from the works of creation, the common rules of good and evil, and the Scriptures. Wisdom everywhere calls people to a life of righteousness (vv. 8,9). Those who are wise will walk in the way of righteousness and in the paths of justice.

8.3
Job 29.7

8.5
Prov 1.4, 22,
32
8.6
Prov 22.20;
23.16
8.7
Ps 37.30

8.9
Prov 14.6;
3.13
8.10
Prov 3.14, 15
8.11
Job 28.18;
Prov 3.15
8.12
v. 5;
Prov 1.4
8.13
Prov 16.6;
16.18; 15.9;
6.12
8.14
Prov 1.25;
2.7;
Eccl 7.19
8.15
Dan 2.21;
Rom 13.1

8.17
1 Sam 2.30;
Ps 91.14;
Jn 14.21;
Jas 1.5
8.18
Prov 3.16;
Mt 6.33
8.19
Prov 3.14;
10.20

8.21
Prov 24.4

8.22
Prov 3.19

8.23
Jn 17.5

8.25
Ps 90.2

2 On the heights, beside the way,
   at the crossroads she takes her stand;
3 beside the gates in front of the town,
   at the entrance of the portals she cries out:
4 "To you, O people, I call,
   and my cry is to all that live.
5 O simple ones, learn prudence;
   acquire intelligence, you who lack it.
6 Hear, for I will speak noble things,
   and from my lips will come what is right;
7 for my mouth will utter truth;
   wickedness is an abomination to my lips.
8 All the words of my mouth are righteous;
   there is nothing twisted or crooked in them.
9 They are all straight to one who understands
   and right to those who find knowledge.
10 Take my instruction instead of silver,
   and knowledge rather than choice gold;
11 for wisdom is better than jewels,
   and all that you may desire cannot compare with her.
12 I, wisdom, live with prudence,[s]
   and I attain knowledge and discretion.
13 The fear of the LORD is hatred of evil.
   Pride and arrogance and the way of evil
   and perverted speech I hate.
14 I have good advice and sound wisdom;
   I have insight, I have strength.
15 By me kings reign,
   and rulers decree what is just;
16 by me rulers rule,
   and nobles, all who govern rightly.
17 I love those who love me,
   and those who seek me diligently find me.
18 Riches and honor are with me,
   enduring wealth and prosperity.
19 My fruit is better than gold, even fine gold,
   and my yield than choice silver.
20 I walk in the way of righteousness,
   along the paths of justice,
21 endowing with wealth those who love me,
   and filling their treasuries.

2. *The eternity of wisdom*

22 The LORD created me at the beginning[t] of his work,[u]
   the first of his acts of long ago.
23 Ages ago I was set up,
   at the first, before the beginning of the earth.
24 When there were no depths I was brought forth,
   when there were no springs abounding with water.
25 Before the mountains had been shaped,
   before the hills, I was brought forth —
26 when he had not yet made earth and fields,[s]

[s] Meaning of Heb uncertain   [t] Or *me as the beginning*   [u] Heb *way*

8.10,11 Wisdom must be accepted as well as taught. We should prefer it above silver, gold, or the brightest gem. Those who have everything else the world can offer but do not have wisdom have nothing. Those who have wisdom, have incredible wealth (vv. 18,19).

8.22 From this verse on, wisdom is personified, looked upon as a vital attribute of God. It was present already at creation. In 1 Cor 1.24 Christ is called "the wisdom of God." Many therefore see this section as prophetic of Jesus Christ (see also Jn 1.1–4).

or the world's first bits of soil.

27 When he established the heavens, I was there,
    when he drew a circle on the face of the deep,
28 when he made firm the skies above,
    when he established the fountains of the deep,
29 when he assigned to the sea its limit,
    so that the waters might not transgress his command,
    when he marked out the foundations of the earth,
30 then I was beside him, like a master worker;[v]
    and I was daily his[w] delight,
    rejoicing before him always,
31 rejoicing in his inhabited world
    and delighting in the human race.

3. The invitation to wisdom

32 "And now, my children, listen to me:
    happy are those who keep my ways.
33 Hear instruction and be wise,
    and do not neglect it.
34 Happy is the one who listens to me,
    watching daily at my gates,
    waiting beside my doors.
35 For whoever finds me finds life
    and obtains favor from the LORD;
36 but those who miss me injure themselves;
    all who hate me love death."

T. Wisdom and folly contrasted

1. The invitation of wisdom

9 Wisdom has built her house,
    she has hewn her seven pillars.
2 She has slaughtered her animals, she has mixed her wine,
    she has also set her table.
3 She has sent out her servant-girls, she calls
    from the highest places in the town,
4 "You that are simple, turn in here!"
    To those without sense she says,
5 "Come, eat of my bread
    and drink of the wine I have mixed.
6 Lay aside immaturity,[x] and live,
    and walk in the way of insight."

2. Interlude

7 Whoever corrects a scoffer wins abuse;
    whoever rebukes the wicked gets hurt.
8 A scoffer who is rebuked will only hate you;
    the wise, when rebuked, will love you.
9 Give instruction[y] to the wise, and they will become wiser still;

Cross-references (right margin):

8.27 Prov 3.19; Job 26.10
8.29 Job 38.10; Ps 104.9; Job 38.6
8.30 Jn 1.1-3
8.31 Ps 16.3
8.32 Prov 5.7; Ps 119.1, 2; Lk 11.28
8.33 Prov 4.1
8.34 Prov 3.13, 18
8.35 Prov 4.22; 12.2
8.36 Prov 20.2
9.1 Mt 16.18; Eph 2.20, 22; 1 Pet 2.5
9.2 Mt 22.4; Lk 14.16, 17
9.3 Ps 68.11; Mt 22.3; Prov 8.1, 2
9.4 Prov 8.5; 6.32
9.5 Song 5.1; Isa 55.1; Jn 6.27
9.6 Ezek 11.20; 37.24
9.7 Prov 23.9
9.8 Mt 7.6; Ps 141.5
9.9 Prov 1.5

---

v Another reading is *little child*   w Gk: Heb lacks *his*   x Or *simpleness*   y Heb lacks *instruction*

8.32 No sermon is complete without a word of exhortation. Consequently, all listeners are called to hear and diligently obey the word of wisdom. Happy are those who embrace wisdom.
8.36 The sermon ends with a final word of warning to those who reject wisdom. Whoever sins against wisdom sins against the Author of wisdom and is left to ruin and doom. In N.T terms, this is to sin against Jesus Christ, who is the wisdom of God in the flesh (Col 2.3,9). Whoever hates Christ hates wisdom, and whoever hates wisdom loves death.
9.1 Wisdom here is designated by the female gender. She is a queen who is great and generous. Those who become her disciples will sit down to a sumptuous feast.

teach the righteous and they will gain in learning.

10 The fear of the LORD is the beginning of wisdom,
   and the knowledge of the Holy One is insight.

11 For by me your days will be multiplied,
   and years will be added to your life.

12 If you are wise, you are wise for yourself;
   if you scoff, you alone will bear it.

3. The invitation of the foolish woman

13 The foolish woman is loud;
   she is ignorant and knows nothing.

14 She sits at the door of her house,
   on a seat at the high places of the town,

15 calling to those who pass by,
   who are going straight on their way,

16 "You who are simple, turn in here!"
   And to those without sense she says,

17 "Stolen water is sweet,
   and bread eaten in secret is pleasant."

18 But they do not know that the dead z are there,
   that her guests are in the depths of Sheol.

II. Proverbs of Solomon (10.1–22.16)

A. The upright and the wicked

10 The proverbs of Solomon.

A wise child makes a glad father,
   but a foolish child is a mother's grief.

2 Treasures gained by wickedness do not profit,
   but righteousness delivers from death.

3 The LORD does not let the righteous go hungry,
   but he thwarts the craving of the wicked.

4 A slack hand causes poverty,
   but the hand of the diligent makes rich.

5 A child who gathers in summer is prudent,
   but a child who sleeps in harvest brings shame.

6 Blessings are on the head of the righteous,
   but the mouth of the wicked conceals violence.

7 The memory of the righteous is a blessing,
   but the name of the wicked will rot.

8 The wise of heart will heed commandments,
   but a babbling fool will come to ruin.

9 Whoever walks in integrity walks securely,
   but whoever follows perverse ways will be found out.

10 Whoever winks the eye causes trouble,
    but the one who rebukes boldly makes peace. a

z Heb shades   a Gk: Heb but a babbling fool will come to ruin

9.10 True wisdom begins with the fear of God. It comes about when the head is filled with knowledge of God, given to us by revelation. This knowledge has come to all people through the prophets and apostles who spoke as they were moved by the Holy Spirit (2 Pet 1.20,21).
9.13–18 These verses describe the feast of folly, which begins by listening to the foolish woman's (i.e., the prostitute's) wicked lies and ends with death.
10.2 Whoever grows rich unjustly cannot profit from it in the long run. People may enjoy such wealth for a while, but it will not deliver them from death or judgment, and upon death they will leave it all behind.
10.5 Two children from the same family may live different lifestyles. One is lazy, shiftless, sleepy, and neglectful; such a one is unwise. But the other child seizes opportunities and makes provision in the fall for the coming winter. This child brings honor to his parents and is wise.

11 The mouth of the righteous is a fountain of life,
    but the mouth of the wicked conceals violence.

12 Hatred stirs up strife,
    but love covers all offenses.

13 On the lips of one who has understanding wisdom is found,
    but a rod is for the back of one who lacks sense.

14 The wise lay up knowledge,
    but the babbling of a fool brings ruin near.

15 The wealth of the rich is their fortress;
    the poverty of the poor is their ruin.

16 The wage of the righteous leads to life,
    the gain of the wicked to sin.

17 Whoever heeds instruction is on the path to life,
    but one who rejects a rebuke goes astray.

18 Lying lips conceal hatred,
    and whoever utters slander is a fool.

19 When words are many, transgression is not lacking,
    but the prudent are restrained in speech.

20 The tongue of the righteous is choice silver;
    the mind of the wicked is of little worth.

21 The lips of the righteous feed many,
    but fools die for lack of sense.

22 The blessing of the LORD makes rich,
    and he adds no sorrow with it. [b]

B. *Fear of the LORD prolongs life*

23 Doing wrong is like sport to a fool,
    but wise conduct is pleasure to a person of understanding.

24 What the wicked dread will come upon them,
    but the desire of the righteous will be granted.

25 When the tempest passes, the wicked are no more,
    but the righteous are established forever.

26 Like vinegar to the teeth, and smoke to the eyes,
    so are the lazy to their employers.

27 The fear of the LORD prolongs life,
    but the years of the wicked will be short.

28 The hope of the righteous ends in gladness,
    but the expectation of the wicked comes to nothing.

29 The way of the LORD is a stronghold for the upright,
    but destruction for evildoers.

30 The righteous will never be removed,
    but the wicked will not remain in the land.

31 The mouth of the righteous brings forth wisdom,
    but the perverse tongue will be cut off.

32 The lips of the righteous know what is acceptable,
    but the mouth of the wicked what is perverse.

C. *The godless and the upright*

11 A false balance is an abomination to the LORD,
    but an accurate weight is his delight.

b Or and toil adds nothing to it

Cross-references

10.11 Ps 37.30
10.12 1 Pet 4.8
10.13 Prov 26.3
10.14 Prov 9.9; 18.7
10.15 Job 31.24; Ps 52.7; Prov 18.11; 19.7
10.17 Prov 6.23
10.18 Prov 26.24; Ps 15.3
10.19 Prov 18.21; Eccl 5.3; Jas 3.2
10.20 Prov 8.19
10.21 v. 11; Prov 5.23
10.22 Gen 24.35; Ps 37.22
10.23 Prov 15.21
10.24 Ps 145.19; Mt 5.6; 1 Jn 5.14; 15
10.25 Prov 12.7; Ps 15.5; Mt 7.24; 16.18
10.26 Prov 26.6
10.27 Prov 9.11; Ps 55.23
10.29 Ps 28.8; Prov 21.15
10.30 Ps 37.29
10.31 Ps 37.30; Prov 17.20
11.1 Lev 19.35; Deut 25.13-16

10.12 Those who exhibit hatred stir up trouble. Those who love do not publicly flaunt or take delight in the errors of others. Love excuses every offense that springs from mistakes and is inadvertently committed. Love covers a multitude of sins (1 Pet 4.8). The love mentioned here also characterizes the love of God, who in Christ has atoned for our sins (cf. Rom 8.1–11).

11.1 When it comes to money, even Christians are tempted to engage in shady practices and to justify minor infractions of the law, for these do not constitute felonies that would land them in jail. But God desires fair and honest dealings in all things. The weight that favors the seller by half an ounce is

2 When pride comes, then comes disgrace;
   but wisdom is with the humble.
3 The integrity of the upright guides them,
   but the crookedness of the treacherous destroys them.
4 Riches do not profit in the day of wrath,
   but righteousness delivers from death.
5 The righteousness of the blameless keeps their ways straight,
   but the wicked fall by their own wickedness.
6 The righteousness of the upright saves them,
   but the treacherous are taken captive by their schemes.
7 When the wicked die, their hope perishes,
   and the expectation of the godless comes to nothing.
8 The righteous are delivered from trouble,
   and the wicked get into it instead.
9 With their mouths the godless would destroy their neighbors,
   but by knowledge the righteous are delivered.
10 When it goes well with the righteous, the city rejoices;
   and when the wicked perish, there is jubilation.
11 By the blessing of the upright a city is exalted,
   but it is overthrown by the mouth of the wicked.

D. The trustworthy and the gossiper

12 Whoever belittles another lacks sense,
   but an intelligent person remains silent.
13 A gossip goes about telling secrets,
   but one who is trustworthy in spirit keeps a confidence.
14 Where there is no guidance, a nation[c] falls,
   but in an abundance of counselors there is safety.
15 To guarantee loans for a stranger brings trouble,
   but there is safety in refusing to do so.
16 A gracious woman gets honor,
   but she who hates virtue is covered with shame.[d]
   The timid become destitute,[e]
   but the aggressive gain riches.
17 Those who are kind reward themselves,
   but the cruel do themselves harm.
18 The wicked earn no real gain,
   but those who sow righteousness get a true reward.
19 Whoever is steadfast in righteousness will live,
   but whoever pursues evil will die.
20 Crooked minds are an abomination to the LORD,
   but those of blameless ways are his delight.
21 Be assured, the wicked will not go unpunished,
   but those who are righteous will escape.
22 Like a gold ring in a pig's snout
   is a beautiful woman without good sense.
23 The desire of the righteous ends only in good;
   the expectation of the wicked in wrath.

E. The person who gives freely

24 Some give freely, yet grow all the richer;

c Or *an army* *d* Compare Gk Syr: Heb lacks *but she . . . shame* *e* Gk: Heb lacks *The timid . . . destitute*

11.12 Gossips tell their stories from house to house without checking their facts to see whether they are false or true. A good rule of thumb is: "Is it true? Is it kind? Is it necessary?" If it is not, then keep silent. 11.22 A woman whose conversation and life are not detestable to God. shaped by the Christian faith is like a pig whose snout is bedecked with a jewel of gold. Beauty without virtue is like this.
11.24,25 God blesses the giving hand and makes it a getting hand. Whoever sows liberally for the glory of God will reap liberally and experience a spiritual

others withhold what is due, and only suffer want.

25 A generous person will be enriched,
   and one who gives water will get water.

26 The people curse those who hold back grain,
   but a blessing is on the head of those who sell it.

27 Whoever diligently seeks good seeks favor,
   but evil comes to the one who searches for it.

28 Those who trust in their riches will wither,*f*
   but the righteous will flourish like green leaves.

29 Those who trouble their households will inherit wind,
   and the fool will be servant to the wise.

30 The fruit of the righteous is a tree of life,
   but violence*g* takes lives away.

31 If the righteous are repaid on earth,
   how much more the wicked and the sinner!

F. The discipline of knowledge

12 Whoever loves discipline loves knowledge,
     but those who hate to be rebuked are stupid.

2 The good obtain favor from the LORD,
   but those who devise evil he condemns.

3 No one finds security by wickedness,
   but the root of the righteous will never be moved.

4 A good wife is the crown of her husband,
   but she who brings shame is like rottenness in his bones.

5 The thoughts of the righteous are just;
   the advice of the wicked is treacherous.

6 The words of the wicked are a deadly ambush,
   but the speech of the upright delivers them.

7 The wicked are overthrown and are no more,
   but the house of the righteous will stand.

8 One is commended for good sense,
   but a perverse mind is despised.

G. Care for life and land

9 Better to be despised and have a servant,
   than to be self-important and lack food.

10 The righteous know the needs of their animals,
   but the mercy of the wicked is cruel.

11 Those who till their land will have plenty of food,
   but those who follow worthless pursuits have no sense.

12 The wicked covet the proceeds of wickedness,*h*
   but the root of the righteous bears fruit.

13 The evil are ensnared by the transgression of their lips,
   but the righteous escape from trouble.

14 From the fruit of the mouth one is filled with good things,
   and manual labor has its reward.

H. The wise and the foolish

15 Fools think their own way is right,

f Cn: Heb *fall*   *g* Cn Compare Gk Syr: Heb *a wise man*   *h* Or *covet the catch of the wicked*

11.25 2 Cor 9.6-10; Mt 5.7
11.26 Am 8.5, 6; Job 29.13
11.27 Esth 7.10; Ps 7.15; 10.2
11.28 Ps 52.7; Mk 10.24; 1 Tim 6.17; Ps 1.3; Jer 17.8
11.30 1 Cor 9.19; Jas 5.20
11.31 Prov 13.21; 2 Sam 22.21, 25
12.1 Prov 9.8; 15.10
12.2 Prov 8.35
12.3 Prov 10.25
12.4 Prov 31.23; 1 Cor 11.7; Prov 14.30
12.6 Prov 1.11; 14.3
12.7 Ps 37.36; Mt 7.24
12.10 Deut 25.4
12.11 Prov 28.19; Judg 9.4
12.13 Prov 18.7; 2 Pet 2.9
12.14 Prov 13.2; Job 34.11; Isa 3.10, 11
12.15 Prov 14.12; Lk 18.11

blessing that cannot be bought with money.
12.1 *Rebuke* by respected individuals is a discipline valued by those who seek a good education. Whoever hates it is void of common sense and lacks genuine understanding.
12.4 Picking a marriage partner is a serious matter. A good spouse is a blessing from God and will enable the other partner in the marriage to succeed. A bad spouse, however, can damage the reputation of the mate.
12.9 It is better to be content with lesser fame and have homes blessed with food and clothing, than to associate with the rich and live as though you have more than you really do.

16 Fools show their anger at once,
    but the prudent ignore an insult.
17 Whoever speaks the truth gives honest evidence,
    but a false witness speaks deceitfully.
18 Rash words are like sword thrusts,
    but the tongue of the wise brings healing.
19 Truthful lips endure forever,
    but a lying tongue lasts only a moment.
20 Deceit is in the mind of those who plan evil,
    but those who counsel peace have joy.
21 No harm happens to the righteous,
    but the wicked are filled with trouble.
22 Lying lips are an abomination to the Lord,
    but those who act faithfully are his delight.
23 One who is clever conceals knowledge,
    but the mind of a fool[i] broadcasts folly.
24 The hand of the diligent will rule,
    while the lazy will be put to forced labor.
25 Anxiety weighs down the human heart,
    but a good word cheers it up.
26 The righteous gives good advice to friends,[j]
    but the way of the wicked leads astray.
27 The lazy do not roast[k] their game,
    but the diligent obtain precious wealth.[k]
28 In the path of righteousness there is life,
    in walking its path there is no death.

I. The source of great wealth

13 A wise child loves discipline,[l]
    but a scoffer does not listen to rebuke.
2 From the fruit of their words good persons eat good things,
    but the desire of the treacherous is for wrongdoing.
3 Those who guard their mouths preserve their lives;
    those who open wide their lips come to ruin.
4 The appetite of the lazy craves, and gets nothing,
    while the appetite of the diligent is richly supplied.
5 The righteous hate falsehood,
    but the wicked act shamefully and disgracefully.
6 Righteousness guards one whose way is upright,
    but sin overthrows the wicked.
7 Some pretend to be rich, yet have nothing;
    others pretend to be poor, yet have great wealth.
8 Wealth is a ransom for a person's life,
    but the poor get no threats.
9 The light of the righteous rejoices,
    but the lamp of the wicked goes out.

Cross-references (left margin):

12.16 Prov 29.11
12.17 Prov 14.5
12.18 Ps 57.4
12.19 Ps 52.5
12.20 v. 5
12.21 Ps 91.10; 1 Pet 3.13; Prov 14.14
12.22 Prov 6.17; 11.20; Rev 22.15
12.23 Prov 13.16; 15.2
12.25 Prov 15.13; Isa 50.4
12.28 Prov 11.19
13.1 Prov 10.1; 15.12
13.2 Prov 12.14
13.3 Ps 39.1; Jas 3.2
13.4 Prov 10.4
13.6 Prov 11.3, 5
13.7 Prov 11.24; Lk 12.20, 21, 33; 2 Cor 6.10
13.9 Job 18.5; Prov 24.20

---

i Heb *the heart of fools*   j Syr: Meaning of Heb uncertain   k Meaning of Heb uncertain   l Cn: Heb *A wise child the discipline of his father*

12.16 *the prudent ignore an insult.* A person who has been insulted by a fool should not react to that insult, for though the insult will do no harm, anger and resentment will.

12.21 The surest protection against evil and temptation is a life of piety. The righteous will not be overcome by temptation, and they will work for good. On the other hand, the wicked delight in mischief, from which comes their misery and the absence of divine protection in the storms of life.

12.28 Living righteously provides immense per-sonal satisfaction. In this lifestyle, there is life and not death.

13.7 Those who have little sometimes pretend to have much and live as though they did (see note on 12.9). Others have much, but pretend that they have little. They live miserly lives and choose to bury their wealth rather than use it. Their pretense shows lack of gratitude to God and injustice to their loved ones who suffer under their stinginess. Both attitudes are wrong.

10 By insolence the heedless make strife,
       but wisdom is with those who take advice.
11 Wealth hastily gotten[m] will dwindle,
       but those who gather little by little will increase it.

J. The source of hope

12 Hope deferred makes the heart sick,
       but a desire fulfilled is a tree of life.
13 Those who despise the word bring destruction on themselves,
       but those who respect the commandment will be rewarded.
14 The teaching of the wise is a fountain of life,
       so that one may avoid the snares of death.
15 Good sense wins favor,
       but the way of the faithless is their ruin.[n]
16 The clever do all things intelligently,
       but the fool displays folly.
17 A bad messenger brings trouble,
       but a faithful envoy, healing.
18 Poverty and disgrace are for the one who ignores instruction,
       but one who heeds reproof is honored.
19 A desire realized is sweet to the soul,
       but to turn away from evil is an abomination to fools.
20 Whoever walks with the wise becomes wise,
       but the companion of fools suffers harm.
21 Misfortune pursues sinners,
       but prosperity rewards the righteous.
22 The good leave an inheritance to their children's children,
       but the sinner's wealth is laid up for the righteous.
23 The field of the poor may yield much food,
       but it is swept away through injustice.
24 Those who spare the rod hate their children,
       but those who love them are diligent to discipline them.
25 The righteous have enough to satisfy their appetite,
       but the belly of the wicked is empty.

K. The upright and the wicked

14 The wise woman[o] builds her house,
       but the foolish tears it down with her own hands.
2   Those who walk uprightly fear the LORD,
       but one who is devious in conduct despises him.
3   The talk of fools is a rod for their backs,[p]
       but the lips of the wise preserve them.
4   Where there are no oxen, there is no grain;
       abundant crops come by the strength of the ox.
5   A faithful witness does not lie,

Cross-references (right column):

13.10 Prov 11.14
13.11 Prov 10.2; 14.23
13.12 v. 19
13.13 2 Chr 36.16
13.14 Prov 10.11; Ps 18.5
13.15 Prov 3.4; 21.8
13.16 Prov 12.23; 15.2
13.17 Prov 25.13
13.18 Prov 15.5, 31, 32
13.20 Prov 15.31; 28.19
13.21 Ps 32.10
13.22 Job 27.16, 17; Prov 28.8; Eccl 2.26
13.23 Prov 12.11
13.24 Prov 19.18; 22.15; 29.15, 17
13.25 Ps 34.10; 37.3
14.1 Prov 24.3
14.2 Prov 19.1; Rom 2.4
14.3 Prov 12.6
14.5 Ex 20.16; Prov 6.19; 12.17

---

[m] Gk Vg: Heb *from vanity*   [n] Cn Compare Gk Syr Vg Tg: Heb *is enduring*   [o] Heb *Wisdom of women*
[p] Cn: Heb *a rod of pride*

13.11 The wealth of those who obtained it wickedly has a curse attached to it, and those who have secured wealth in this way are likely to spend it in equally sinful ways. It will be taken from them at last. The wealth of honest people, accumulated by industry and honesty, will increase, and such people will be blessed by God.
13.20 People are known by the company they keep. Good people do not make bad ones their intimate friends. The wise will walk with the wise and each will improve the other. To consort with evildoers is foolish.
13.24 Parents are enjoined to love their children

(Titus 2.4), bring them to Christ (Mt 19.13,14), train them up for God (22.6; Eph 1.4), instruct them in God's Word (Deut 4.9; 11.19; Isa 38.19), bless them (Gen 48.15; Heb 11.21), discipline them (13.24), provide for them (2 Cor 12.14; 1 Tim 5.8), and not treat them shabbily or provoke them (Eph 6.4; Col 3.21).
14.2 Grace and sin are here painted in their true colors. When grace reigns, there is reverence of God; when sin reigns, God is despised. Good people walk in uprightness; the wicked ones walk in perversities.
14.3 It is better to be thought wise by being silent than to open the mouth and leave no doubt about one's folly.

but a false witness breathes out lies.

14.6
Prov 24.7;
8.9; 17.24

6 A scoffer seeks wisdom in vain,
   but knowledge is easy for one who understands.

7 Leave the presence of a fool,
   for there you do not find words of knowledge.

14.8
Prov 15.21;
v. 24

8 It is the wisdom of the clever to understand where they go,
   but the folly of fools misleads.

9 Fools mock at the guilt offering,[q]
   but the upright enjoy God's favor.

10 The heart knows its own bitterness,
    and no stranger shares its joy.

14.11
Prov 3.33;
12.7; 15.25
14.12
Prov 16.25;
Rom 6.21
14.13
Prov 5.4;
Eccl 2.2
14.14
Prov 1.31;
12.14

11 The house of the wicked is destroyed,
    but the tent of the upright flourishes.

12 There is a way that seems right to a person,
    but its end is the way to death.[r]

13 Even in laughter the heart is sad,
    and the end of joy is grief.

14 The perverse get what their ways deserve,
    and the good, what their deeds deserve.[s]

15 The simple believe everything,
    but the clever consider their steps.

14.16
Prov 22.3

16 The wise are cautious and turn away from evil,
    but the fool throws off restraint and is careless.

14.17
v. 29

17 One who is quick-tempered acts foolishly,
    and the schemer is hated.

14.18
Prov 18.15

18 The simple are adorned with[t] folly,
    but the clever are crowned with knowledge.

14.19
Prov 11.29

19 The evil bow down before the good,
    the wicked at the gates of the righteous.

L. The rich and the poor

14.20
Prov 19.7

20 The poor are disliked even by their neighbors,
    but the rich have many friends.

14.21
Prov 11.12;
Ps 41.1

21 Those who despise their neighbors are sinners,
    but happy are those who are kind to the poor.

22 Do they not err that plan evil?
    Those who plan good find loyalty and faithfulness.

23 In all toil there is profit,
    but mere talk leads only to poverty.

24 The crown of the wise is their wisdom,[u]
    but folly is the garland[v] of fools.

14.25
v. 5

25 A truthful witness saves lives,
    but one who utters lies is a betrayer.

14.26
Prov 19.23;
Isa 33.6
14.27
Prov 13.14

26 In the fear of the LORD one has strong confidence,
    and one's children will have a refuge.

27 The fear of the LORD is a fountain of life,
    so that one may avoid the snares of death.

28 The glory of a king is a multitude of people;
    without people a prince is ruined.

14.29
Prov 16.32;
Jas 1.19;
Prov 29.20

29 Whoever is slow to anger has great understanding,

q Meaning of Heb uncertain   r Heb ways of death   s Cn: Heb from upon him   t Or inherit
u Cn Compare Gk: Heb riches   v Cn: Heb is the folly

14.15 It is foolish to believe all the stories that float around, however probable they may appear.

14.20 The world frowns on the poor, who are thought to be hardly worthy of respect. When God is our friend, however, he will not desert us if we are poor. Better is poverty with the friendship of God than riches without it. On the other hand, many want to be friends with the rich. Such people are governed by self-interest, expecting to get something out of that friendship. They have made the world's goods their god.

30 A tranquil mind gives life to the flesh,
    but passion makes the bones rot.
31 Those who oppress the poor insult their Maker,
    but those who are kind to the needy honor him.
32 The wicked are overthrown by their evildoing,
    but the righteous find a refuge in their integrity. [w]
33 Wisdom is at home in the mind of one who has understanding,
    but it is not [x] known in the heart of fools.
34 Righteousness exalts a nation,
    but sin is a reproach to any people.
35 A servant who deals wisely has the king's favor,
    but his wrath falls on one who acts shamefully.

M. *The tongue of the wise*

15 A soft answer turns away wrath,
    but a harsh word stirs up anger.
2 The tongue of the wise dispenses knowledge, [y]
    but the mouths of fools pour out folly.
3 The eyes of the LORD are in every place,
    keeping watch on the evil and the good.
4 A gentle tongue is a tree of life,
    but perverseness in it breaks the spirit.
5 A fool despises a parent's instruction,
    but the one who heeds admonition is prudent.
6 In the house of the righteous there is much treasure,
    but trouble befalls the income of the wicked.
7 The lips of the wise spread knowledge;
    not so the minds of fools.
8 The sacrifice of the wicked is an abomination to the LORD,
    but the prayer of the upright is his delight.
9 The way of the wicked is an abomination to the LORD,
    but he loves the one who pursues righteousness.
10 There is severe discipline for one who forsakes the way,
    but one who hates a rebuke will die.
11 Sheol and Abaddon lie open before the LORD,
    how much more human hearts!
12 Scoffers do not like to be rebuked;
    they will not go to the wise.

N. *The reward of a cheerful heart*

13 A glad heart makes a cheerful countenance,
    but by sorrow of heart the spirit is broken.
14 The mind of one who has understanding seeks knowledge,
    but the mouths of fools feed on folly.
15 All the days of the poor are hard,
    but a cheerful heart has a continual feast.
16 Better is a little with the fear of the LORD
    than great treasure and trouble with it.
17 Better is a dinner of vegetables where love is
    than a fatted ox and hatred with it.
18 Those who are hot-tempered stir up strife,

w Gk Syr: Heb *in their death*   *x* Gk Syr: Heb lacks *not*   *y* Cn: Heb *makes knowledge good*

14.30	Prov 12.4
14.31	Prov 17.5; v. 21
14.32	Job 13.15; Ps 23.4; 2 Cor 1.9; 2 Tim 4.18
14.33	Prov 2.10; 12.16
14.34	Prov 11.11
14.35	Mt 24.45
15.1	Judg 8.1-3; 1 Sam 25.10-13
15.2	Prov 12.23; 13.16
15.3	Job 34.21; Heb 4.13
15.5	Prov 13.1, 18
15.8	Isa 1.11; Jer 6.20; Mic 6.7
15.9	Prov 21.21; 1 Tim 6.11
15.10	Prov 1.29-32; 5.12
15.11	Job 26.6; Ps 139.8; 2 Chr 6.30
15.12	Prov 13.1; Am 5.10
15.13	Prov 17.22; 12.25
15.15	v. 13
15.16	Ps 37.16; Prov 16.8; 1 Tim 6.6
15.17	Prov 17.1
15.18	Prov 26.21; 29.22; 14.29

15.1 Soft and temperate speech is the mark of the sanctified heart. When people speak softly, the listener is not apt to take offense; if he or she does, it is not their fault. Upbraiding people and calling them names produces anger and offends people.

15.11 *Sheol and Abaddon. Abaddon* means destruction and is the name given to the fallen angel and king of the abyss in Rev 9.11. For *Sheol* see note on Deut 32.22.

15.18 Anger may be sinful or justifiable, depending

but those who are slow to anger calm contention.

15.19
Prov 22.5

19 The way of the lazy is overgrown with thorns,
   but the path of the upright is a level highway.

15.20
Prov 10.1;
30.17

20 A wise child makes a glad father,
   but the foolish despise their mothers.

O. Instruction in wisdom

15.21
Prov 10.23;
Eph 5.15

21 Folly is a joy to one who has no sense,
   but a person of understanding walks straight ahead.

15.22
Prov 11.14;
20.18

22 Without counsel, plans go wrong,
   but with many advisers they succeed.

15.23
Prov 25.11

23 To make an apt answer is a joy to anyone,
   and a word in season, how good it is!

15.24
Prov 4.18

24 For the wise the path of life leads upward,
   in order to avoid Sheol below.

15.25
Prov 12.7;
Ps 68.5, 6

25 The LORD tears down the house of the proud,
   but maintains the widow's boundaries.

15.26
Prov 6.16-19;
16.24

26 Evil plans are an abomination to the LORD,
   but gracious words are pure.

15.27
Prov 28.25;
1 Tim 6.10;
Isa 33.15

27 Those who are greedy for unjust gain make trouble for their
      households,
   but those who hate bribes will live.

15.28
1 Pet 3.15

28 The mind of the righteous ponders how to answer,
   but the mouth of the wicked pours out evil.

15.29
Ps 34.16;
145.18

29 The LORD is far from the wicked,
   but he hears the prayer of the righteous.

30 The light of the eyes rejoices the heart,
   and good news refreshes the body.

15.31
v. 5

31 The ear that heeds wholesome admonition
   will lodge among the wise.

15.32
Prov 1.7;
8.36; 15.5

32 Those who ignore instruction despise themselves,
   but those who heed admonition gain understanding.

15.33
Prov 1.7;
18.12

33 The fear of the LORD is instruction in wisdom,
   and humility goes before honor.

P. The LORD weighs the way of mortals

16.1
Prov 19.21

16 The plans of the mind belong to mortals,
   but the answer of the tongue is from the LORD.

16.2
Prov 21.2

2 All one's ways may be pure in one's own eyes,
   but the LORD weighs the spirit.

16.3
Ps 37.5

3 Commit your work to the LORD,
   and your plans will be established.

16.4
Isa 43.7;
Job 21.30

4 The LORD has made everything for its purpose,
   even the wicked for the day of trouble.

16.5
Prov 6.17;
11.21

5 All those who are arrogant are an abomination to the LORD;
   be assured, they will not go unpunished.

---

on the circumstances. In any event, the Scriptures say we are to be slow to anger (Prov 19.11; Jas 1.19). Sinful anger is a work of the flesh (Gal 5.20). Examples of those who displayed sinful anger include: Cain (Gen 4.5,6), Balaam (Num 22.27), Jonah (Jon 4.4), Herod (Mt 2.16), and the Jews (Lk 4.28). Those who showed justifiable anger include our Lord (Mk 3.5), Moses (Ex 11.8), and Nehemiah (Neh 5.6). In Eph 4.26 anger is validated; however, a caution is inserted — godly anger can become sinful if we nurse a grudge (Eph 4.31,32).
15.25 The proud magnify themselves and suppose they are autonomous beings. God often abases them, ordinarily using his general providence. The same

God cares for and establishes the house of the poor widow who cannot defend herself. God protects the weak among his people.
15.31 Wise persons will accept reproof and will associate with those who by their counsel enable them to see what is wrong with themselves.
16.1 People are free to think and act as they choose. They can make their plans and determine to execute them. But God is the one who makes the final decision. People cannot go ahead on their own without the blessing of God, for he can nullify their intentions and desires. For a good example of this, see the story of Balaam in Num 22—24.

6   By loyalty and faithfulness iniquity is atoned for,
      and by the fear of the LORD one avoids evil.
7   When the ways of people please the LORD,
      he causes even their enemies to be at peace with them.
8   Better is a little with righteousness
      than large income with injustice.
9   The human mind plans the way,
      but the LORD directs the steps.
10 Inspired decisions are on the lips of a king;
      his mouth does not sin in judgment.
11 Honest balances and scales are the LORD's;
      all the weights in the bag are his work.

Q. *Wisdom the fountain of life*

12 It is an abomination to kings to do evil,
      for the throne is established by righteousness.
13 Righteous lips are the delight of a king,
      and he loves those who speak what is right.
14 A king's wrath is a messenger of death,
      and whoever is wise will appease it.
15 In the light of a king's face there is life,
      and his favor is like the clouds that bring the spring rain.
16 How much better to get wisdom than gold!
      To get understanding is to be chosen rather than silver.
17 The highway of the upright avoids evil;
      those who guard their way preserve their lives.
18 Pride goes before destruction,
      and a haughty spirit before a fall.
19 It is better to be of a lowly spirit among the poor
      than to divide the spoil with the proud.
20 Those who are attentive to a matter will prosper,
      and happy are those who trust in the LORD.
21 The wise of heart is called perceptive,
      and pleasant speech increases persuasiveness.
22 Wisdom is a fountain of life to one who has it,
      but folly is the punishment of fools.
23 The mind of the wise makes their speech judicious,
      and adds persuasiveness to their lips.
24 Pleasant words are like a honeycomb,
      sweetness to the soul and health to the body.

R. *The wicked ways of humans*

25 Sometimes there is a way that seems to be right,
      but in the end it is the way to death.
26 The appetite of workers works for them;
      their hunger urges them on.
27 Scoundrels concoct evil,
      and their speech is like a scorching fire.
28 A perverse person spreads strife,
      and a whisperer separates close friends.
29 The violent entice their neighbors,
      and lead them in a way that is not good.

16.6
Dan 4.27;
Prov 14.16
16.7
2 Chr 17.10

16.9
Ps 37.23;
Prov 20.24;
Jer 10.23

16.11
Prov 11.1

16.12
Prov 25.5

16.13
Prov 14.35

16.14
Prov 19.12

16.15
Job 29.23

16.16
Prov 8.10, 19

16.18
Prov 11.2

16.20
Ps 2.12; 34.8;
Jer 17.7

16.22
Prov 13.14;
7.22
16.23
Prov 37.30

16.25
Prov 14.12

16.27
Prov 6.12,
14, 18;
Jas 3.6
16.28
Prov 15.18;
17.9
16.29
Prov 1.10

16.7 God delights in turning our enemies into our friends. He controls human hearts and works irresistibly upon them to acccomplish good for his people. It was God who made Abimelech to be Isaac's friend (Gen 26), and he moved the heart of Esau to be at peace with his brother Jacob (Gen 33).
16.9 When we make our plans for today or tomorrow, we must take into account the divine factor: "If the Lord wishes, we will live and do this or that" (Jas 4.15).

30 One who winks the eyes plans[z] perverse things;
   one who compresses the lips brings evil to pass.
31 Gray hair is a crown of glory;
   it is gained in a righteous life.
32 One who is slow to anger is better than the mighty,
   and one whose temper is controlled than one who captures a
      city.
33 The lot is cast into the lap,
   but the decision is the LORD's alone.

S. *Fine speech and false speech*

17 Better is a dry morsel with quiet
      than a house full of feasting with strife.
2 A slave who deals wisely will rule over a child who acts
      shamefully,
   and will share the inheritance as one of the family.
3 The crucible is for silver, and the furnace is for gold,
   but the LORD tests the heart.
4 An evildoer listens to wicked lips;
   and a liar gives heed to a mischievous tongue.
5 Those who mock the poor insult their Maker;
   those who are glad at calamity will not go unpunished.
6 Grandchildren are the crown of the aged,
   and the glory of children is their parents.
7 Fine speech is not becoming to a fool;
   still less is false speech to a ruler.[a]
8 A bribe is like a magic stone in the eyes of those who give it;
   wherever they turn they prosper.
9 One who forgives an affront fosters friendship,
   but one who dwells on disputes will alienate a friend.
10 A rebuke strikes deeper into a discerning person
   than a hundred blows into a fool.
11 Evil people seek only rebellion,
   but a cruel messenger will be sent against them.
12 Better to meet a she-bear robbed of its cubs
   than to confront a fool immersed in folly.

T. *The price of wisdom*

13 Evil will not depart from the house
   of one who returns evil for good.
14 The beginning of strife is like letting out water;
   so stop before the quarrel breaks out.
15 One who justifies the wicked and one who condemns the
      righteous
   are both alike an abomination to the LORD.
16 Why should fools have a price in hand

---

[z] Gk Syr Vg Tg: Heb *to plan*   [a] Or *a noble person*

Cross-references (left margin):

16.31 Prov 20.29
16.32 Prov 19.11
17.1 Prov 15.17
17.2 Prov 10.5
17.3 Prov 27.21; Ps 26.2
17.5 Prov 14.31; Job 31.29
17.6 Prov 13.22
17.8 Prov 21.14; Isa 1.23; Am 5.12
17.9 Prov 10.12; Jas 5.20; 1 Pet 4.8; Prov 16.28
17.12 Hos 13.8
17.13 Ps 109.4, 5; Jer 18.20
17.14 Prov 20.3
17.15 Ex 23.7; Isa 5.23

16.33 *The lot is cast into the lap.* As with many verses in ch. 16, the guiding factor to all of life is the providence of God. God upholds, directs, and governs all creatures, actions, and things according to his wise counsel (Eph 1.11). It is his will that ultimately takes place. Specific examples of God's providence include: preserving and providing for all creatures (Ps 104.10–30); determining the length of our days (Mt 6.25–30); power over nature such as storms, hail, snow, and frost (Ps 146.15–18); stopping the evil designs of mortals (Acts 12.3–17); and ordering even the smallest matters (Mt 10.29–31). Sometimes God's providence is dark and mysterious (Ps 73.16; 77.19; Rom 11.33).

17.11 *a cruel messenger will be sent against them,* i.e., they shall be severely punished. To render evil for evil is a sin, but to render evil for good is of the devil. Those who do so will reap as they have sown. The punishment will equal the crime, affecting not only the culprits but also their whole houses, perhaps for generations. For example, David rewarded Uriah evil for his service to the king; as a result, the sword never departed from David's house.

17 A friend loves at all times,
   and kinsfolk are born to share adversity.
18 It is senseless to give a pledge,
   to become surety for a neighbor.
19 One who loves transgression loves strife;
   one who builds a high threshold invites broken bones.
20 The crooked of mind do not prosper,
   and the perverse of tongue fall into calamity.
21 The one who begets a fool gets trouble;
   the parent of a fool has no joy.
22 A cheerful heart is a good medicine,
   but a downcast spirit dries up the bones.
23 The wicked accept a concealed bribe
   to pervert the ways of justice.
24 The discerning person looks to wisdom,
   but the eyes of a fool to the ends of the earth.
25 Foolish children are a grief to their father
   and bitterness to her who bore them.
26 To impose a fine on the innocent is not right,
   or to flog the noble for their integrity.
27 One who spares words is knowledgeable;
   one who is cool in spirit has understanding.
28 Even fools who keep silent are considered wise;
   when they close their lips, they are deemed intelligent.

U. Words of the wise and the foolish

18 The one who lives alone is self-indulgent,
   showing contempt for all who have sound judgment. *b*
2 A fool takes no pleasure in understanding,
   but only in expressing personal opinion.
3 When wickedness comes, contempt comes also;
   and with dishonor comes disgrace.
4 The words of the mouth are deep waters;
   the fountain of wisdom is a gushing stream.
5 It is not right to be partial to the guilty,
   or to subvert the innocent in judgment.
6 A fool's lips bring strife,
   and a fool's mouth invites a flogging.
7 The mouths of fools are their ruin,
   and their lips a snare to themselves.
8 The words of a whisperer are like delicious morsels,
   they go down into the inner parts of the body.
9 One who is slack in work
   is close kin to a vandal.
10 The name of the LORD is a strong tower;
   the righteous run into it and are safe.
11 The wealth of the rich is their strong city;
   in their imagination it is like a high wall.
12 Before destruction one's heart is haughty,
   but humility goes before honor.
13 If one gives answer before hearing,
   it is folly and shame.
14 The human spirit will endure sickness;

Cross references (right margin)

17.17
Ruth 1.16;
Prov 18.24
17.18
Prov 6.1
17.19
Prov 29.22;
16.18
17.20
Jas 3.8
17.21
Prov 10.1;
19.13
17.22
Prov 15.13;
Ps 22.15
17.23
Ex 23.8
17.24
Eccl 2.14
17.25
Prov 10.1
17.26
Prov 18.5
17.27
Jas 1.19
17.28
Job 13.5

18.2
Prov 12.23

18.4
Prov 20.5;
10.11
18.5
Lev 19.15;
Deut 1.17;
Prov 24.23

18.7
Prov 10.14;
Eccl 10.12
18.8
Prov 26.22
18.9
Prov 28.24
18.10
2 Sam 22.3;
Ps 18.2
18.11
Prov 10.15
18.12
Prov 11.2
18.13
Jn 7.51

---

b Meaning of Heb uncertain

18.7 One who cannot govern the tongue is a fool (cf. Jas 3). By our words we are justified or condemned (Mt 12.37). Our speech should be seasoned with salt (Col 4.6), and we should speak kind and gentle words.

but a broken spirit — who can bear?

15 An intelligent mind acquires knowledge,
   and the ear of the wise seeks knowledge.

18.16
Gen 32.20;
1 Sam 25.27

16 A gift opens doors;
   it gives access to the great.

17 The one who first states a case seems right,
   until the other comes and cross-examines.

18.18
Prov 16.33

18 Casting the lot puts an end to disputes
   and decides between powerful contenders.

19 An ally offended is stronger than a city;c
   such quarreling is like the bars of a castle.

18.20
Prov 12.14

20 From the fruit of the mouth one's stomach is satisfied;
   the yield of the lips brings satisfaction.

18.21
Mt 12.37

21 Death and life are in the power of the tongue,
   and those who love it will eat its fruits.

18.22
Prov 19.14;
8.35
18.23
Jas 2.3

22 He who finds a wife finds a good thing,
   and obtains favor from the LORD.

23 The poor use entreaties,
   but the rich answer roughly.

18.24
Prov 17.17

24 Somed friends play at friendshipe
   but a true friend sticks closer than one's nearest kin.

V. Contrasts of wealth and poverty

19.1
Prov 28.6

19 Better the poor walking in integrity
   than one perverse of speech who is a fool.

2 Desire without knowledge is not good,
   and one who moves too hurriedly misses the way.

19.3
Prov 11.3;
Ps 37.7
19.4
Prov 14.20

3 One's own folly leads to ruin,
   yet the heart rages against the LORD.

4 Wealth brings many friends,
   but the poor are left friendless.

19.5
Ex 23.1;
Prov 6.19
19.6
Prov 29.26;
17.8
19.7
v. 4;
Ps 38.11

5 A false witness will not go unpunished,
   and a liar will not escape.

6 Many seek the favor of the generous,
   and everyone is a friend to a giver of gifts.

7 If the poor are hated even by their kin,
   how much more are they shunned by their friends!
When they call after them, they are not there.f

19.8
Prov 16.20

8 To get wisdom is to love oneself;
   to keep understanding is to prosper.

19.9
v. 5

9 A false witness will not go unpunished,
   and the liar will perish.

19.10
Eccl 10.6, 7

10 It is not fitting for a fool to live in luxury,
   much less for a slave to rule over princes.

19.11
Jas 1.19;
Prov 16.32

11 Those with good sense are slow to anger,
   and it is their glory to overlook an offense.

19.12
Prov 16.14;
Hos 7.3

12 A king's anger is like the growling of a lion,
   but his favor is like dew on the grass.

19.13
Prov 10.1;
21.9
19.14
2 Cor 12.14;
Prov 18.22

13 A stupid child is ruin to a father,
   and a wife's quarreling is a continual dripping of rain.

14 House and wealth are inherited from parents,

c Gk Syr Vg Tg: Meaning of Heb uncertain   d Syr Tg: Heb A man of   e Cn Compare Syr Vg Tg:
Meaning of Heb uncertain   f Meaning of Heb uncertain

18.17 Plaintiffs in any case of law should speak only what will help the case. They can then be examined by the defendant, who presents the other side. The judge must hear both sides before pronouncing the verdict.

18.24 Sometimes a friend will be of more help to us than a brother. Traditionally, Christians have seen here a veiled reference to Jesus Christ, the sinner's best friend, who sticks closer to us than any brother.

but a prudent wife is from the LORD.

15 Laziness brings on deep sleep;
    an idle person will suffer hunger.
16 Those who keep the commandment will live;
    those who are heedless of their ways will die.
17 Whoever is kind to the poor lends to the LORD,
    and will be repaid in full.

W. Advice and instruction

18 Discipline your children while there is hope;
    do not set your heart on their destruction.
19 A violent tempered person will pay the penalty;
    if you effect a rescue, you will only have to do it again. *g*
20 Listen to advice and accept instruction,
    that you may gain wisdom for the future.
21 The human mind may devise many plans,
    but it is the purpose of the LORD that will be established.
22 What is desirable in a person is loyalty,
    and it is better to be poor than a liar.
23 The fear of the LORD is life indeed;
    filled with it one rests secure
    and suffers no harm.
24 The lazy person buries a hand in the dish,
    and will not even bring it back to the mouth.
25 Strike a scoffer, and the simple will learn prudence;
    reprove the intelligent, and they will gain knowledge.
26 Those who do violence to their father and chase away their
    mother
    are children who cause shame and bring reproach.
27 Cease straying, my child, from the words of knowledge,
    in order that you may hear instruction.
28 A worthless witness mocks at justice,
    and the mouth of the wicked devours iniquity.
29 Condemnation is ready for scoffers,
    and flogging for the backs of fools.

X. The integrity of the righteous

20 Wine is a mocker, strong drink a brawler,
    and whoever is led astray by it is not wise.
2 The dread anger of a king is like the growling of a lion;
    anyone who provokes him to anger forfeits life itself.
3 It is honorable to refrain from strife,
    but every fool is quick to quarrel.
4 The lazy person does not plow in season;

g Meaning of Heb uncertain

Cross references:
19.15 Prov 6.9; 10.4
19.16 Lk 10.28
19.17 Eccl 11.1; Mt 10.42; 2 Cor 9.6-8; Heb 6.10
19.18 Prov 13.24
19.20 Prov 8.33
19.21 Prov 16.1, 9; Ps 33.10, 11
19.23 1 Tim 4.8; Ps 25.13; Prov 12.21
19.24 Prov 26.15
19.25 Prov 21.11; 9.8
19.26 Prov 28.24; 17.2
19.28 Job 15.16
19.29 Prov 10.13; 26.3
20.1 Gen 9.21; Isa 5.22
20.2 Prov 19.12; 8.36; 1 Kings 2.23
20.3 Prov 17.14
20.4 Prov 10.4; 19.15, 24

19.15 Lazy persons are careless about their affairs. It is as if they are cast into a deep sleep, dreaming away the hours when they should be busy working. Idleness will bring people to poverty; that is why those who will not labor are not to eat (2 Thess 3.10). Nowhere are we commanded in Scripture to feed the lazy. This is no indictment, however, against someone who is industrious yet unable to find work. Provision for such people comes through the charity of those who have more of this world's goods than they need to support themselves (see Eph 4.28). See also note on 21.25,26.
19.17 This verse speaks of charity, which springs from a heart of compassion. The poor and the hungry should be objects of our care and concern. When we aid such people it is as if we have made a loan to God himself (cf. Mt 25.34–46) — and a loan with interest! Thus, charity is a wise investment that pays off well in this life and in the life to come.
19.21 The purposes of God stand sure. Whoever seeks to annul what God has intended will suffer defeat.
20.1 Everywhere the Scriptures forbid drunkenness, which destroys human relationships. Speech often becomes abusive and actions stupid. Alcohol makes fools out of people; it is a deceiver. The one sure guarantee to avoid becoming an alcoholic is never to drink, although the use of wine is not prohibited in the Scriptures.

5 harvest comes, and there is nothing to be found.
The purposes in the human mind are like deep water,
  but the intelligent will draw them out.
6 Many proclaim themselves loyal,
  but who can find one worthy of trust?
7 The righteous walk in integrity —
  happy are the children who follow them!
8 A king who sits on the throne of judgment
  winnows all evil with his eyes.
9 Who can say, "I have made my heart clean;
  I am pure from my sin"?
10 Diverse weights and diverse measures
  are both alike an abomination to the LORD.
11 Even children make themselves known by their acts,
  by whether what they do is pure and right.
12 The hearing ear and the seeing eye —
  the LORD has made them both.
13 Do not love sleep, or else you will come to poverty;
  open your eyes, and you will have plenty of bread.
14 "Bad, bad," says the buyer,
  then goes away and boasts.

Y. The hastily-gotten inheritance

15 There is gold, and abundance of costly stones;
  but the lips informed by knowledge are a precious jewel.
16 Take the garment of one who has given surety for a stranger;
  seize the pledge given as surety for foreigners.
17 Bread gained by deceit is sweet,
  but afterward the mouth will be full of gravel.
18 Plans are established by taking advice;
  wage war by following wise guidance.
19 A gossip reveals secrets;
  therefore do not associate with a babbler.
20 If you curse father or mother,
  your lamp will go out in utter darkness.
21 An estate quickly acquired in the beginning
  will not be blessed in the end.
22 Do not say, "I will repay evil";
  wait for the LORD, and he will help you.
23 Differing weights are an abomination to the LORD,
  and false scales are not good.
24 All our steps are ordered by the LORD;
  how then can we understand our own ways?
25 It is a snare for one to say rashly, "It is holy,"
  and begin to reflect only after making a vow.
26 A wise king winnows the wicked,
  and drives the wheel over them.
27 The human spirit is the lamp of the LORD,
  searching every inmost part.

20.14 The sinful nature of people can be seen in their buying and selling. Sellers overvalue their goods and buyers underestimate their value. Both drive a hard bargain. When buyers push sellers down to the lowest price, they still grumble and complain but then go home to crow about the excellent bargain they got. People, whether buyers or sellers, want as much as they can get at the lowest possible price. The principle of love for neighbor dictates a fair price for the buyers and a fair profit for the sellers.
20.22 Every believer will, at some time or other, be wrongly treated and thus have a legitimate grievance against the perpetrator. How should the believer act? Here we learn that it is wrong to recompense evil with evil; we should wait for the Lord and let him reward the evildoer (see Rom 12.17–21).
20.27 The spirit God placed in people enables them by their consciences to gauge the rightness of their thoughts and motives and by volition to make prudent decisions. The regenerated spirits of believers are indwelt by the Spirit of God, enabling them to attain the purposes for which God created them.

28 Loyalty and faithfulness preserve the king,
    and his throne is upheld by righteousness. *h*

29 The glory of youths is their strength,
    but the beauty of the aged is their gray hair.

30 Blows that wound cleanse away evil;
    beatings make clean the innermost parts.

Z. *The treasures of the wicked*

21 The king's heart is a stream of water in the hand of the LORD;
    he turns it wherever he will.

2 All deeds are right in the sight of the doer,
    but the LORD weighs the heart.

3 To do righteousness and justice
    is more acceptable to the LORD than sacrifice.

4 Haughty eyes and a proud heart —
    the lamp of the wicked — are sin.

5 The plans of the diligent lead surely to abundance,
    but everyone who is hasty comes only to want.

6 The getting of treasures by a lying tongue
    is a fleeting vapor and a snare *i* of death.

7 The violence of the wicked will sweep them away,
    because they refuse to do what is just.

8 The way of the guilty is crooked,
    but the conduct of the pure is right.

9 It is better to live in a corner of the housetop
    than in a house shared with a contentious wife.

10 The souls of the wicked desire evil;
    their neighbors find no mercy in their eyes.

11 When a scoffer is punished, the simple become wiser;
    when the wise are instructed, they increase in knowledge.

12 The Righteous One observes the house of the wicked;
    he casts the wicked down to ruin.

AA. *The treasures of the wise*

13 If you close your ear to the cry of the poor,
    you will cry out and not be heard.

14 A gift in secret averts anger;
    and a concealed bribe in the bosom, strong wrath.

15 When justice is done, it is a joy to the righteous,
    but dismay to evildoers.

16 Whoever wanders from the way of understanding
    will rest in the assembly of the dead.

17 Whoever loves pleasure will suffer want;
    whoever loves wine and oil will not be rich.

18 The wicked is a ransom for the righteous,
    and the faithless for the upright.

19 It is better to live in a desert land
    than with a contentious and fretful wife.

20 Precious treasure remains *j* in the house of the wise,

h Gk: Heb *loyalty*   *i* Gk: Heb *seekers*   *j* Gk: Heb *and oil*

Cross references (margin):

20.28 / Prov 29.14

20.29 / Prov 16.31

21.2 / Prov 16.2; 24.12; Lk 16.15
21.3 / 1 Sam 15.22; Prov 15.8; Isa 1.11-17; Hos 6.6; Mic 6.7, 8
21.4 / Prov 6.17
21.5 / Prov 10.4; 28.22
21.6 / 2 Pet 2.3
21.7 / Prov 10.25

21.9 / Prov 25.24
21.10 / Prov 2.14; 14.21
21.11 / Prov 19.25
21.12 / Prov 14.11

21.13 / Mt 18.30-34; 1 Jn 3.17; Jas 2.13
21.14 / Prov 18.16; 19.6

21.16 / Ps 49.14

21.18 / Prov 11.8
21.19 / v. 9
21.20 / Prov 22.4; Job 20.15, 18

21.4 Pride (haughtiness, conceit, arrogance) is a serious sin condemned everywhere in Scripture (6.16,17; 16.5; 1 Sam 2.3; Ps 101.5; 131.1). It is characteristic of: false teachers (1 Tim 6.3,4), the wicked (Hab 2.4,5; Rom 1.30), lovers of this world (1 Jn 2.16), and Satan himself (1 Tim 3.6). Pride produces anger, quarrelsomeness toward others, and deceiving of self (21.24; 28.25; Jer 49.16). It leads to disgrace and punishment (11.2; 29.23; Zeph 2.10–11). God resists the proud (Jas 4.6; 1 Pet 5.5) and sends judgment on them.

21.13 Some believers are lacking in charity. They show no love to the poor, refuse to give them a hearing, and turn them away from their doors. God says that such people will eventually have needs and they shall not be heard either. Just retribution comes at last.

but the fool devours it.

21 Whoever pursues righteousness and kindness
will find life[k] and honor.

22 One wise person went up against a city of warriors
and brought down the stronghold in which they trusted.

23 To watch over mouth and tongue
is to keep out of trouble.

24 The proud, haughty person, named "Scoffer,"
acts with arrogant pride.

25 The craving of the lazy person is fatal,
for lazy hands refuse to labor.

26 All day long the wicked covet,[l]
but the righteous give and do not hold back.

27 The sacrifice of the wicked is an abomination;
how much more when brought with evil intent.

28 A false witness will perish,
but a good listener will testify successfully.

29 The wicked put on a bold face,
but the upright give thought to[m] their ways.

30 No wisdom, no understanding, no counsel,
can avail against the LORD.

31 The horse is made ready for the day of battle,
but the victory belongs to the LORD.

BB. *The value of a good name*

22 A good name is to be chosen rather than great riches,
and favor is better than silver or gold.

2 The rich and the poor have this in common:
the LORD is the maker of them all.

3 The clever see danger and hide;
but the simple go on, and suffer for it.

4 The reward for humility and fear of the LORD
is riches and honor and life.

5 Thorns and snares are in the way of the perverse;
the cautious will keep far from them.

6 Train children in the right way,
and when old, they will not stray.

7 The rich rule over the poor,
and the borrower is the slave of the lender.

8 Whoever sows injustice will reap calamity,
and the rod of anger will fail.

9 Those who are generous are blessed,
for they share their bread with the poor.

10 Drive out a scoffer, and strife goes out;
quarreling and abuse will cease.

11 Those who love a pure heart and are gracious in speech
will have the king as a friend.

12 The eyes of the LORD keep watch over knowledge,
but he overthrows the words of the faithless.

13 The lazy person says, "There is a lion outside!"

Cross references (left margin)

21.21
Mt 5.6
21.22
Eccl 9.15, 16
21.23
Prov 12.13;
Jas 3.2
21.24
Ps 1.1;
Prov 1.22;
Isa 16.6;
Jer 48.29
21.25
Prov 13.4;
20.4
21.26
Ps 37.26;
Mt 5.42;
Eph 4.28
21.27
Isa 66.3;
Jer 6.20;
Am 5.22
21.28
Prov 19.5, 9
21.29
Eccl 8.1
21.30
Isa 8.9, 10;
Jer 9.23;
Acts 5.39
21.31
Isa 31.1;
Ps 3.8;
1 Cor 15.28
22.1
Eccl 7.1

22.3
Prov 14.16;
27.12

22.5
Prov 15.19

22.6
Eph 6.4

22.7
Prov 18.23;
Jas 2.6
22.8
Prov 24.16;
Ps 125.3
22.9
2 Cor 9.6

22.10
Prov 18.6;
26.20
22.11
Mt 5.8;
Prov 16.13
22.12
Prov 21.12

22.13
Prov 26.13

---

k Gk: Heb *life and righteousness*   *l* Gk: Heb *all day long one covets covetously*   *m* Another reading is *establish*

21.25,26 The lazy refuse to work even though they are able to do so. Though they refuse to work, their hearts do not cease to covet riches and pleasures. They expect everybody to do for them what they will not do for themselves. See also note on 19.15.
22.1 Wealth and position are no good to those who suffer from a bad reputation and who can find no one who genuinely cares about them.
22.6 Parents and instructors must train their children. They are to be taught, disciplined, and shown the way they should go.

I shall be killed in the streets!"
14 The mouth of a loose[n] woman is a deep pit;
    he with whom the LORD is angry falls into it.
15 Folly is bound up in the heart of a boy,
    but the rod of discipline drives it far away.
16 Oppressing the poor in order to enrich oneself,
    and giving to the rich, will lead only to loss.

III. Miscellaneous sayings (22.17–24.34)

A. Hear the words of the wise

17 The words of the wise:

Incline your ear and hear my words,[o]
    and apply your mind to my teaching;
18 for it will be pleasant if you keep them within you,
    if all of them are ready on your lips.
19 So that your trust may be in the LORD,
    I have made them known to you today—yes, to you.
20 Have I not written for you thirty sayings
    of admonition and knowledge,
21 to show you what is right and true,
    so that you may give a true answer to those who sent you?

22 Do not rob the poor because they are poor,
    or crush the afflicted at the gate;
23 for the LORD pleads their cause
    and despoils of life those who despoil them.
24 Make no friends with those given to anger,
    and do not associate with hotheads,
25 or you may learn their ways
    and entangle yourself in a snare.
26 Do not be one of those who give pledges,
    who become surety for debts.
27 If you have nothing with which to pay,
    why should your bed be taken from under you?
28 Do not remove the ancient landmark
    that your ancestors set up.
29 Do you see those who are skillful in their work?
    They will serve kings;
    they will not serve common people.

B. The desire for delicacies

23 When you sit down to eat with a ruler,
    observe carefully what[p] is before you,
2 and put a knife to your throat
    if you have a big appetite.

---

n Heb *strange*   *o* Cn Compare Gk: Heb *Incline your ear, and hear the words of the wise*   *p* Or *who*

	22.14 Prov 2.16; 5.3; 23.27; Eccl 7.26
	22.15 Prov 13.24; 23.14
	22.17 Prov 5.1; 23.12
	22.18 Prov 2.10
	22.19 Prov 3.5
	22.20 Prov 8.6, 10
	22.21 Lk 1.3, 4
	22.22 Zech 7.10; Mal 3.5
	22.23 1 Sam 25.39; Ps 12.5; 35.10; Prov 23.11
	22.26 Prov 11.15
	22.28 Prov 23.10
	22.29 Rom 12.11; 1 Kings 10.8
	23.2 v. 20

22.15 Delinquency comes naturally to young people because of original sin. Children never need to be taught how to lie, cheat, or steal. Rather, they must be taught virtue and be provided with correction and discipline.
22.16 It is sinful enough to leave the poor in their poverty. It is far worse to oppress them and take from them what little they have. Oppression that seeks to bring more wealth to the oppressor at the expense of the defenseless poor is contrary to the entire law of God. Those who oppress the poor will discover that

God is the friend of the poor and will avenge them. Such sinners will come to want, whether in this life or in the life to come.
22.22,23 See previous note.
22.28 *ancient landmark.* These were markers that set off one person's property from another's. God had assigned each family a plot of land in the promised land that was to remain with that family forever. To move the markers was to steal land from a neighbor. Apparently attempting to gain more land by this form of theft did occur among the Israelites.

3 Do not desire the ruler's*q* delicacies,
  for they are deceptive food.
4 Do not wear yourself out to get rich;
  be wise enough to desist.
5 When your eyes light upon it, it is gone;
  for suddenly it takes wings to itself,
  flying like an eagle toward heaven.
6 Do not eat the bread of the stingy;
  do not desire their delicacies;
7 for like a hair in the throat, so are they.*r*
  "Eat and drink!" they say to you;
  but they do not mean it.
8 You will vomit up the little you have eaten,
  and you will waste your pleasant words.
9 Do not speak in the hearing of a fool,
  who will only despise the wisdom of your words.
10 Do not remove an ancient landmark
  or encroach on the fields of orphans,
11 for their redeemer is strong;
  he will plead their cause against you.
12 Apply your mind to instruction
  and your ear to words of knowledge.
13 Do not withhold discipline from your children;
  if you beat them with a rod, they will not die.
14 If you beat them with the rod,
  you will save their lives from Sheol.

C. Wise words to a child

15 My child, if your heart is wise,
  my heart too will be glad.
16 My soul will rejoice
  when your lips speak what is right.
17 Do not let your heart envy sinners,
  but always continue in the fear of the LORD.
18 Surely there is a future,
  and your hope will not be cut off.

19 Hear, my child, and be wise,
  and direct your mind in the way.
20 Do not be among winebibbers,
  or among gluttonous eaters of meat;
21 for the drunkard and the glutton will come to poverty,
  and drowsiness will clothe them with rags.

22 Listen to your father who begot you,
  and do not despise your mother when she is old.
23 Buy truth, and do not sell it;
  buy wisdom, instruction, and understanding.
24 The father of the righteous will greatly rejoice;
  he who begets a wise son will be glad in him.
25 Let your father and mother be glad;
  let her who bore you rejoice.

q Heb *his*   *r* Meaning of Heb uncertain

Cross references (left margin):

23.3 v. 6; Ps 141.4
23.4 Prov 28.20; 1 Tim 6.9, 10; Rom 12.16
23.5 Prov 27.24
23.6 Ps 141.4
23.7 Prov 26.24, 25
23.9 Mt 7.6; Prov 1.7
23.10 Prov 22.28; Jer 22.3; Zech 7.10
23.11 Prov 22.23
23.12 Prov 22.17
23.13 Prov 13.24; 19.18; 22.15
23.16 vv. 24, 25; Prov 27.11
23.17 Ps 37.1; Prov 28.14
23.20 Isa 5.22; Mt 24.49; Lk 21.34; Rom 13.13; Eph 5.18
23.21 Prov 21.17; 6.10, 11
23.22 Prov 1.8; 30.17; Eph 6.1
23.23 Prov 4.5, 7; Mt 13.44
23.24 Prov 10.1; 15.20

23.13,14 There is a distinct difference between proper corporal punishment and child abuse. The latter is forever forbidden by the Scriptures; the former is appropriate when necessary. But it must always be done with a tender heart and never in a spurt of anger, in heartless revenge, or with the notion of doing physical damage to the child.
23.17,18 Believers should never envy sinners their liberty to sin, for they will someday pay for it dearly. They are to be pitied, not envied.

26 My child, give me your heart,
      and let your eyes observe[s] my ways.
27 For a prostitute is a deep pit;
      an adulteress[t] is a narrow well.
28 She lies in wait like a robber
      and increases the number of the faithless.

29 Who has woe? Who has sorrow?
      Who has strife? Who has complaining?
    Who has wounds without cause?
      Who has redness of eyes?
30 Those who linger late over wine,
      those who keep trying mixed wines.
31 Do not look at wine when it is red,
      when it sparkles in the cup
      and goes down smoothly.
32 At the last it bites like a serpent,
      and stings like an adder.
33 Your eyes will see strange things,
      and your mind utter perverse things.
34 You will be like one who lies down in the midst of the sea,
      like one who lies on the top of a mast.[u]
35 "They struck me," you will say,[v] "but I was not hurt;
      they beat me, but I did not feel it.
    When shall I awake?
      I will seek another drink."

24

1   Do not envy the wicked,
        nor desire to be with them;
2   for their minds devise violence,
      and their lips talk of mischief.

D. Wisdom weighed

3   By wisdom a house is built,
      and by understanding it is established;
4   by knowledge the rooms are filled
      with all precious and pleasant riches.
5   Wise warriors are mightier than strong ones,[w]
      and those who have knowledge than those who have strength;
6   for by wise guidance you can wage your war,
      and in abundance of counselors there is victory.
7   Wisdom is too high for fools;
      in the gate they do not open their mouths.

8   Whoever plans to do evil
      will be called a mischief-maker.
9   The devising of folly is sin,
      and the scoffer is an abomination to all.

10 If you faint in the day of adversity,
      your strength being small;
11 if you hold back from rescuing those taken away to death,

23.26
Prov 3.1; 4.4;
Ps 1.2
23.27
Prov 22.14
23.28
Prov 7.12;
Eccl 7.26
23.29
Isa 5.11, 22
23.30
Eph 5.18;
Ps 75.8
23.33
Prov 2.12
23.35
Jer 5.3
24.1
Ps 37.1; 73.3;
Prov 3.31
24.2
Jer 22.17;
Job 15.35
24.3
Prov 9.1
24.5
Prov 21.22
24.6
Lk 14.31
24.7
Ps 10.5
24.8
Prov 6.14;
Rom 1.30
24.10
Jer 51.46;
Heb 12.3
24.11
Ps 82.4;
Isa 58.6, 7

---

s Another reading is *delight in*   t Heb *an alien woman*   u Meaning of Heb uncertain   v Gk Syr Vg Tg:
Heb lacks *you will say*   w Gk Compare Syr Tg: Heb *A wise man is strength*

23.26 *give me your heart.* If the heart is right, out-ward actions will be appropriate. Those who love God with their whole hearts are free to do whatever they please; they will always seek to do what pleases God.
24.10 Days of adversity are bound to come to all.

Some become severely discouraged by adversity and experience anxiety long before it reaches them. Believers are to be of good courage, assured that God will strengthen their hearts. They need not faint in the hour of adversity (cf. Heb 12.1–13).

those who go staggering to the slaughter;

24.12
Prov 21.2;
Eccl 5.8;
Ps 121.3-8;
94.9-11;
Prov 12.14

12 if you say, "Look, we did not know this" —
    does not he who weighs the heart perceive it?
  Does not he who keeps watch over your soul know it?
    And will he not repay all according to their deeds?

E. Counsel to a child

24.13
Song 5.1

13 My child, eat honey, for it is good,
    and the drippings of the honeycomb are sweet to your taste.

24.14
Prov 2.10

14 Know that wisdom is such to your soul;
    if you find it, you will find a future,
    and your hope will not be cut off.

24.15
Ps 10.9, 10

15 Do not lie in wait like an outlaw against the home of the
      righteous;
    do no violence to the place where the righteous live;

24.16
Ps 34.19;
Mic 7.8; v. 22

16 for though they fall seven times, they will rise again;
    but the wicked are overthrown by calamity.

24.17
Job 31.29;
Ob 12

17 Do not rejoice when your enemies fall,
    and do not let your heart be glad when they stumble,
18 or else the LORD will see it and be displeased,
    and turn away his anger from them.

24.19
Ps 37.1

19 Do not fret because of evildoers.
    Do not envy the wicked;

24.20
Prov 13.9

20 for the evil have no future;
    the lamp of the wicked will go out.

24.21
Rom 13.1-7;
1 Pet 2.17

21 My child, fear the LORD and the king,
    and do not disobey either of them;ˣ
22 for disaster comes from them suddenly,
    and who knows the ruin that both can bring?

F. Sayings of the wise

24.23
Prov 1.6;
18.5;
Lev 19.15;
Deut 1.17

23 These also are sayings of the wise:

Partiality in judging is not good.

24.24
Prov 17.15

24 Whoever says to the wicked, "You are innocent,"
    will be cursed by peoples, abhorred by nations;

24.25
Prov 28.23

25 but those who rebuke the wicked will have delight,
    and a good blessing will come upon them.
26 One who gives an honest answer
    gives a kiss on the lips.

27 Prepare your work outside,
    get everything ready for you in the field;
    and after that build your house.

ˣ Gk: Heb *do not associate with those who change*

24.16 The righteous may fall many times and still rise again, because of their repentance and God's forgiveness. But the wicked who may fall only once are lost forever, because they refuse to repent.
24.19,20 Believers should not fret over the success of the wicked or envy their success and wealth. They should know that the wicked will someday receive their just deserts — on the day of judgment, if not before.

24.23,24 Those who sit in judgment are required to give their opinions and pass sentence according to the law and on the basis of the true merits of the case. Kings and judges who make decisions on the basis of what persons are rather than on what they have done pervert justice. Such officials will be abhorred by nations and cursed by the people as betrayers of their public trust.

28 Do not be a witness against your neighbor without cause,
   and do not deceive with your lips.
29 Do not say, "I will do to others as they have done to me;
   I will pay them back for what they have done."

30 I passed by the field of one who was lazy,
   by the vineyard of a stupid person;
31 and see, it was all overgrown with thorns;
   the ground was covered with nettles,
   and its stone wall was broken down.
32 Then I saw and considered it;
   I looked and received instruction.
33 A little sleep, a little slumber,
   a little folding of the hands to rest,
34 and poverty will come upon you like a robber,
   and want, like an armed warrior.

IV. *Miscellaneous sayings of Solomon (25.1–29.27)*

A. *Counsel for the king's presence*

25 These are other proverbs of Solomon that the officials of King
   Hezekiah of Judah copied.

2 It is the glory of God to conceal things,
   but the glory of kings is to search things out.
3 Like the heavens for height, like the earth for depth,
   so the mind of kings is unsearchable.
4 Take away the dross from the silver,
   and the smith has material for a vessel;
5 take away the wicked from the presence of the king,
   and his throne will be established in righteousness.
6 Do not put yourself forward in the king's presence
   or stand in the place of the great;
7 for it is better to be told, "Come up here,"
   than to be put lower in the presence of a noble.

8 What your eyes have seen
   do not hastily bring into court;
   for^y what will you do in the end,
   when your neighbor puts you to shame?
9 Argue your case with your neighbor directly,
   and do not disclose another's secret;
10 or else someone who hears you will bring shame upon you,
   and your ill repute will have no end.

11 A word fitly spoken
   is like apples of gold in a setting of silver.

y Cn: Heb *or else*

24.28	Prov 25.18; Eph 4.25
24.29	Prov 20.22; Mt 5.39; Rom 12.17
24.30	Prov 6.6-11
24.33	Prov 6.9; 20.13
25.1	Prov 1.1
25.2	Deut 29.29; Ezra 6.1
25.4	2 Tim 2.21
25.5	Prov 20.8; 16.12
25.7	Lk 14.7-11
25.8	Mt 5.25
25.9	Mt 18.15; Prov 11.13
25.11	Prov 15.23

24.29 Vengeance belongs to God, not to mortals (Rom 12.19). If righteous people seek to execute vengeance on their enemies, they are really taking the work out of God's hands. Jesus moves this proverb one step further in the Golden Rule (Mt 7.12).
25.1 *These are other proverbs of Solomon.* See 1 Kings 4.32. *Hezekiah* lived 200 years after Solomon.
25.2 God, who knows all things, has often chosen not to reveal to mortals the reasons why he acts as he does (see Rom 11.33).
25.4,5 When wicked people are removed from the nation, it is like silver that has been purified by fire. When kings or presidents abandon the wicked, it will go far in improving the morality of the nation. And the reformation of heads of state and the legislatures of the people will promote the reformation of the entire nation.
25.9 Before seeking redress at the hands of a court, try to settle the problem with your neighbor privately. This is especially true when the dispute contains a secret that should not be made public. End it privately so that it will not be disclosed to the public eye.

12 Like a gold ring or an ornament of gold
    is a wise rebuke to a listening ear.
13 Like the cold of snow in the time of harvest
    are faithful messengers to those who send them;
    they refresh the spirit of their masters.
14 Like clouds and wind without rain
    is one who boasts of a gift never given.

B. *The neighbor and the enemy*

15 With patience a ruler may be persuaded,
    and a soft tongue can break bones.
16 If you have found honey, eat only enough for you,
    or else, having too much, you will vomit it.
17 Let your foot be seldom in your neighbor's house,
    otherwise the neighbor will become weary of you and hate
    you.
18 Like a war club, a sword, or a sharp arrow
    is one who bears false witness against a neighbor.
19 Like a bad tooth or a lame foot
    is trust in a faithless person in time of trouble.
20 Like vinegar on a wound[z]
    is one who sings songs to a heavy heart.
    Like a moth in clothing or a worm in wood,
    sorrow gnaws at the human heart.[a]
21 If your enemies are hungry, give them bread to eat;
    and if they are thirsty, give them water to drink;
22 for you will heap coals of fire on their heads,
    and the LORD will reward you.
23 The north wind produces rain,
    and a backbiting tongue, angry looks.
24 It is better to live in a corner of the housetop
    than in a house shared with a contentious wife.
25 Like cold water to a thirsty soul,
    so is good news from a far country.
26 Like a muddied spring or a polluted fountain
    are the righteous who give way before the wicked.
27 It is not good to eat much honey,
    or to seek honor on top of honor.
28 Like a city breached, without walls,
    is one who lacks self-control.

C. *Fools and their folly*

26

1 Like snow in summer or rain in harvest,
    so honor is not fitting for a fool.
2 Like a sparrow in its flitting, like a swallow in its flying,
    an undeserved curse goes nowhere.
3 A whip for the horse, a bridle for the donkey,
    and a rod for the back of fools.
4 Do not answer fools according to their folly,

Cross-references (left margin):
25.12 Prov 15.31; 20.12
25.13 v. 25; Prov 13.17
25.14 Prov 20.6; Jude 12
25.15 Gen 32.4; 1 Sam 25.24; Prov 15.1; 16.14
25.16 v. 27
25.18 Ps 57.4; Prov 12.18
25.21 Ex 23.4, 5; Mt 5.44; Rom 12.20
25.22 2 Sam 16.12
25.23 Ps 101.5
25.24 Prov 21.9
25.25 v. 13; Prov 15.30
25.26 Ezek 32.2; 34.18, 19
25.27 v. 16; Prov 27.2
25.28 Prov 16.32
26.1 1 Sam 12.17
26.2 Num 23.8; Deut 23.5
26.3 Ps 32.9
26.4 Prov 23.9; 29.9

---

[z] Gk: Heb *Like one who takes off a garment on a cold day, like vinegar on lye*   [a] Gk Syr Tg: Heb lacks *Like a moth . . . human heart*

25.15 In dealing with others, two things are stressed: (1) *patience*, by which we wait for the right opportunity to make our case and then give time for consideration of it; (2) *a soft tongue*, by which we make our case without using hard words or undue passion and thus without provoking the person with whom we are dealing.
25.24 This counsel should not be understood as di-

rected only to women. It applies to both men and women. Whoever is married to a brawling and contentious spouse is likely to be better off single than married.
26.1 Often honors are given to fools, who are utterly unworthy of them and unfit for them. They do them more hurt than good and lower the value of honor for those who deserve it.

or you will be a fool yourself.

5 Answer fools according to their folly,
   or they will be wise in their own eyes.

6 It is like cutting off one's foot and drinking down violence,
   to send a message by a fool.

7 The legs of a disabled person hang limp;
   so does a proverb in the mouth of a fool.

8 It is like binding a stone in a sling
   to give honor to a fool.

9 Like a thornbush brandished by the hand of a drunkard
   is a proverb in the mouth of a fool.

10 Like an archer who wounds everybody
   is one who hires a passing fool or drunkard.[b]

11 Like a dog that returns to its vomit
   is a fool who reverts to his folly.

12 Do you see persons wise in their own eyes?
   There is more hope for fools than for them.

D. The lazy person and the lying tongue

13 The lazy person says, "There is a lion in the road!
   There is a lion in the streets!"

14 As a door turns on its hinges,
   so does a lazy person in bed.

15 The lazy person buries a hand in the dish,
   and is too tired to bring it back to the mouth.

16 The lazy person is wiser in self-esteem
   than seven who can answer discreetly.

17 Like somebody who takes a passing dog by the ears
   is one who meddles in the quarrel of another.

18 Like a maniac who shoots deadly firebrands and arrows,
19 so is one who deceives a neighbor
   and says, "I am only joking!"

20 For lack of wood the fire goes out,
   and where there is no whisperer, quarreling ceases.

21 As charcoal is to hot embers and wood to fire,
   so is a quarrelsome person for kindling strife.

22 The words of a whisperer are like delicious morsels;
   they go down into the inner parts of the body.

23 Like the glaze[c] covering an earthen vessel
   are smooth[d] lips with an evil heart.

24 An enemy dissembles in speaking
   while harboring deceit within;

25 when an enemy speaks graciously, do not believe it,
   for there are seven abominations concealed within;

26 though hatred is covered with guile,
   the enemy's wickedness will be exposed in the assembly.

27 Whoever digs a pit will fall into it,
   and a stone will come back on the one who starts it rolling.

b Meaning of Heb uncertain   *c* Cn: Heb *silver of dross*   *d* Gk: Heb *burning*

Cross-references (right margin):
26.5 Mt 16.1-4; 21.24-27
26.7 v. 9
26.8 v. 1
26.9 v. 7
26.11 2 Pet 2.22; Ex 8.15
26.12 v. 5; Prov 3.7; 29.20
26.13 Prov 22.13
26.15 Prov 19.24
26.17 Prov 3.30
26.18 Isa 50.11
26.19 Prov 24.28
26.20 Prov 16.28; 22.10
26.21 Prov 15.18
26.22 Prov 18.8
26.24 Prov 10.18; 12.20
26.25 Ps 28.3; Jer 9.8
26.26 Mt 23.28; Lk 8.17
26.27 Ps 7.15; Prov 28.10; Eccl 10.8

26.11 We should carefully listen to this striking earthy illustration. A dog will vomit and then return to eat what it has just thrown up. So are those who sin, who become aware of what they have done, and who then return to do the very things that caused them to sin in the first place. Peter applies this adage to those who have known the way of righteousness but have turned away from it (2 Pet 2.22).
26.20ff A *whisperer* is one who maliciously spreads gossip, however true the facts may be. Such individu-

als feed the fires of contention with fuel and enjoy the blaze. Those they attack with their gossip are wounded just as though they had been struck by a spear that pierced their innermost parts.
26.27 The wicked will discover that the pit they dig for others is the pit they fall into themselves. And they who start a stone rolling to the hurt of their neighbors will be crushed by the stone they first moved. For a good example of this, see Esth 5.9—7.10.

28 A lying tongue hates its victims,
    and a flattering mouth works ruin.

E. *Wisdom for today and tomorrow*

27 Do not boast about tomorrow,
    for you do not know what a day may bring.

2   Let another praise you, and not your own mouth —
    a stranger, and not your own lips.

3   A stone is heavy, and sand is weighty,
    but a fool's provocation is heavier than both.

4   Wrath is cruel, anger is overwhelming,
    but who is able to stand before jealousy?

5   Better is open rebuke
    than hidden love.

6   Well meant are the wounds a friend inflicts,
    but profuse are the kisses of an enemy.

7   The sated appetite spurns honey,
    but to a ravenous appetite even the bitter is sweet.

8   Like a bird that strays from its nest
    is one who strays from home.

9   Perfume and incense make the heart glad,
    but the soul is torn by trouble.*e*

10 Do not forsake your friend or the friend of your parent;
        do not go to the house of your kindred in the day of your
            calamity.
    Better is a neighbor who is nearby
        than kindred who are far away.

11 Be wise, my child, and make my heart glad,
    so that I may answer whoever reproaches me.

12 The clever see danger and hide;
    but the simple go on, and suffer for it.

13 Take the garment of one who has given surety for a stranger;
    seize the pledge given as surety for foreigners.*f*

14 Whoever blesses a neighbor with a loud voice,
    rising early in the morning,
    will be counted as cursing.

15 A continual dripping on a rainy day
    and a contentious wife are alike;

16 to restrain her is to restrain the wind
    or to grasp oil in the right hand.*g*

F. *Humans never satisfied*

17 Iron sharpens iron,
    and one person sharpens the wits*h* of another.

18 Anyone who tends a fig tree will eat its fruit,
    and anyone who takes care of a master will be honored.

19 Just as water reflects the face,
    so one human heart reflects another.

e Gk: Heb *the sweetness of a friend is better than one's own counsel*   *f* Vg and 20.16: Heb *for a foreign woman*   *g* Meaning of Heb uncertain   *h* Heb *face*

Cross-references
26.28 Prov 29.5
27.1 Lk 12.19, 20; Jas 4.14
27.2 Prov 25.27; 2 Cor 10.12, 18
27.3 Prov 12.16
27.5 Prov 28.23
27.7 Prov 25.16
27.10 2 Chr 10.6-8; Prov 17.17; 18.24
27.11 Prov 10.1; 23.15; Ps 119.42
27.12 Prov 22.3
27.13 Prov 20.16
27.15 Prov 19.13
27.18 1 Cor 9.7; Lk 12.42-44; 19.17

27.1 Nowhere do the Scriptures forbid us to plan for tomorrow. They do forbid us to depend upon tomorrow, for we know not what the day will bring (cf. Jas 4.13–17). As in the parable of the rich fool, we may decide to eat, drink, and be merry for many years. But before the morrow comes, God sends the angel of death to bring our souls into his presence (Lk 12.13–21).
27.6 It is better to be reproved by a friend than kissed deceitfully by an enemy (e.g., Judas Iscariot, who betrayed Jesus with a kiss).
27.8 Some people are not happy with the slot the Lord has placed them in and seek for another haven. They act like a bird that deserts its nest and wanders about, while the eggs or young ones perish.
27.10 A neighbor who helps you is better than a brother or sister far removed and disinterested in your welfare.

20 Sheol and Abaddon are never satisfied,
  and human eyes are never satisfied.
21 The crucible is for silver, and the furnace is for gold,
  so a person is tested[i] by being praised.
22 Crush a fool in a mortar with a pestle
  along with crushed grain,
  but the folly will not be driven out.

23 Know well the condition of your flocks,
  and give attention to your herds;
24 for riches do not last forever,
  nor a crown for all generations.
25 When the grass is gone, and new growth appears,
  and the herbage of the mountains is gathered,
26 the lambs will provide your clothing,
  and the goats the price of a field;
27 there will be enough goats' milk for your food,
  for the food of your household
  and nourishment for your servant-girls.

G. *The wicked and the righteous*

28   The wicked flee when no one pursues,
  but the righteous are as bold as a lion.
2 When a land rebels
  it has many rulers;
 but with an intelligent ruler
  there is lasting order.[j]
3 A ruler[k] who oppresses the poor
  is a beating rain that leaves no food.
4 Those who forsake the law praise the wicked,
  but those who keep the law struggle against them.
5 The evil do not understand justice,
  but those who seek the LORD understand it completely.
6 Better to be poor and walk in integrity
  than to be crooked in one's ways even though rich.
7 Those who keep the law are wise children,
  but companions of gluttons shame their parents.
8 One who augments wealth by exorbitant interest
  gathers it for another who is kind to the poor.
9 When one will not listen to the law,
  even one's prayers are an abomination.
10 Those who mislead the upright into evil ways
  will fall into pits of their own making,
  but the blameless will have a goodly inheritance.
11 The rich is wise in self-esteem,
  but an intelligent poor person sees through the pose.
12 When the righteous triumph, there is great glory,
  but when the wicked prevail, people go into hiding.
13 No one who conceals transgressions will prosper,

i Heb lacks *is tested*   *j* Meaning of Heb uncertain   *k* Cn: Heb *A poor person*

27.22 After gentle means, especially reason, have been tried for fools, one must then resort to more severe methods. Yet some people are so incurably bad that they resist refining in the furnace.
28.1 The wicked are secretly terrified that they may be exposed for what they really are, and thus they run away when no one is pursuing them.
28.13 It is foolish to indulge ourselves in sin. It is even worse to hide our transgressions as though they can be excused by denying them, by disguising them, or by blaming others for them. Sooner or later, our sins will be made public, for there is nothing hidden that will not be made known (Mt 10.26). When we sin, it is best to confess sin to God and reform our lives, thus receiving forgiveness by his mercy and having our consciences eased.

Cross-references (margin)

27.20 Hab 2.5; Eccl 1.8
27.21 Lk 6.26
27.22 Prov 23.35; Jer 5.3
27.24 Prov 23.5; Job 19.9
27.25 Ps 104.14
28.1 Lev 26.17; Ps 53.5
28.2 Prov 11.11
28.3 Mt 18.28
28.4 Rom 1.32; 1 Kings 18.18
28.5 Ps 92.6; Jn 7.17; 1 Cor 2.15
28.6 Prov 19.1; v. 18
28.7 Prov 23.20
28.8 Lev 25.36; Prov 13.22; 14.31
28.9 Ps 66.18; Prov 15.8
28.10 Prov 26.27; Mt 15.14; Heb 6.12
28.11 Prov 26.5, 12; 18.17
28.12 Prov 11.10; Eccl 10.5, 34
28.13 Ps 32.3, 5

but one who confesses and forsakes them will obtain mercy.

14 Happy is the one who is never without fear,
  but one who is hard-hearted will fall into calamity.
15 Like a roaring lion or a charging bear
  is a wicked ruler over a poor people.
16 A ruler who lacks understanding is a cruel oppressor;
  but one who hates unjust gain will enjoy a long life.

17 If someone is burdened with the blood of another,
  let that killer be a fugitive until death;
  let no one offer assistance.

18 One who walks in integrity will be safe,
  but whoever follows crooked ways will fall into the
    Pit.[l]

19 Anyone who tills the land will have plenty of bread,
  but one who follows worthless pursuits will have plenty
    of poverty.

20 The faithful will abound with blessings,
  but one who is in a hurry to be rich will not go
    unpunished.

21 To show partiality is not good —
  yet for a piece of bread a person may do wrong.
22 The miser is in a hurry to get rich
  and does not know that loss is sure to come.
23 Whoever rebukes a person will afterward find more
    favor
  than one who flatters with the tongue.

24 Anyone who robs father or mother
  and says, "That is no crime,"
  is partner to a thug.

25 The greedy person stirs up strife,
  but whoever trusts in the Lord will be enriched.
26 Those who trust in their own wits are fools;
  but those who walk in wisdom come through safely.
27 Whoever gives to the poor will lack nothing,
  but one who turns a blind eye will get many a curse.
28 When the wicked prevail, people go into hiding;
  but when they perish, the righteous increase.

H. *The reign of the righteous*

29 One who is often reproved, yet remains stubborn,
  will suddenly be broken beyond healing.
2 When the righteous are in authority, the people rejoice;
  but when the wicked rule, the people groan.
3 A child who loves wisdom makes a parent glad,
  but to keep company with prostitutes is to squander one's
    substance.

l Syr: Heb *fall all at once*

28.14 Sin always leads to one of two things. Either sinners turn to God for pardon and restoration or they harden their hearts. When the hardening reaches a certain point, such persons put themselves beyond the possibility of forgiveness (cf. Rom 1.24,26,28). 28.23 Though flattery may get us what we want, flatterers are liars and they hurt themselves and their own reputations. They also demean the persons flattered, because flattery supposes that they are easy victims to this vice. Those who tell their friends the truth keep their integrity, for they have done their

duty and tried to help that friend. 28.27 Those who cover their eyes to keep themselves from seeing and helping the poor will be cursed. Those who give — whether from their poverty or abundance — will not suffer for it. Rather, God will make what they had in the first place go further. 29.1 Obstinate people who reject the reproof of parents, friends, and officers of the law harden their hearts and cross the point of no return. God says such persons shall be suddenly destroyed when they are unprepared for it.

4 By justice a king gives stability to the land,
    but one who makes heavy exactions ruins it.
5 Whoever flatters a neighbor
    is spreading a net for the neighbor's feet.
6 In the transgression of the evil there is a snare,
    but the righteous sing and rejoice.
7 The righteous know the rights of the poor;
    the wicked have no such understanding.
8 Scoffers set a city aflame,
    but the wise turn away wrath.
9 If the wise go to law with fools,
    there is ranting and ridicule without relief.
10 The bloodthirsty hate the blameless,
    and they seek the life of the upright.
11 A fool gives full vent to anger,
    but the wise quietly holds it back.
12 If a ruler listens to falsehood,
    all his officials will be wicked.
13 The poor and the oppressor have this in common:
    the Lord gives light to the eyes of both.
14 If a king judges the poor with equity,
    his throne will be established forever.
15 The rod and reproof give wisdom,
    but a mother is disgraced by a neglected child.
16 When the wicked are in authority, transgression
      increases,
    but the righteous will look upon their downfall.
17 Discipline your children, and they will give you rest;
    they will give delight to your heart.
18 Where there is no prophecy, the people cast off restraint,
    but happy are those who keep the law.
19 By mere words servants are not disciplined,
    for though they understand, they will not give heed.
20 Do you see someone who is hasty in speech?
    There is more hope for a fool than for anyone like that.
21 A slave pampered from childhood
    will come to a bad end. *m*
22 One given to anger stirs up strife,
    and the hothead causes much transgression.
23 A person's pride will bring humiliation,
    but one who is lowly in spirit will obtain honor.
24 To be a partner of a thief is to hate one's own life;
    one hears the victim's curse, but discloses nothing. *n*
25 The fear of others *o* lays a snare,
    but one who trusts in the Lord is secure.
26 Many seek the favor of a ruler,
    but it is from the Lord that one gets justice.
27 The unjust are an abomination to the righteous,
    but the upright are an abomination to the wicked.

Cross references (right margin):

29.5 Ps 5.9
29.6 Prov 22.5; Ex 15.1
29.7 Job 29.16; Ps 41.1
29.8 Prov 11.11; 16.14
29.10 1 Jn 3.12
29.11 Prov 12.16; 19.11
29.13 Ps 13.3
29.14 Ps 72.4; Isa 11.4; Prov 16.12; 25.5
29.15 Prov 13.24; 10.1
29.16 Ps 37.36; 58.10; 91.8; 92.11
29.17 v. 15; Prov 10.1
29.18 1 Sam 3.1; Am 8.11, 12; Jn 13.17
29.20 Jas 1.19; Prov 26.12
29.22 Prov 15.18; 17.19
29.23 Job 22.29; Isa 66.2; Dan 4.30; Mt 23.12
29.24 Lev 5.1
29.25 Gen 12.12; Ps 91.1-16
29.26 Isa 49.4

---

m Vg: Meaning of Heb uncertain   *n* Meaning of Heb uncertain   *o* Or *human fear*

29.14 See note on 24.23,24.
29.16 When evil people rule a country, that only breeds more evil. And the more a nation sins, the closer it is to the judgment of God. The righteous should be patient, for God will bring an end to the power of the wicked.
29.18 *Where there is no prophecy*, the people are stripped of their armor and open to every evil device

and false wind of doctrine. They are destroyed because of the lack of true knowledge of God and his word.
29.26 Mortals seek to gain their own ends by currying the friendship of those who rule over them. True justice and genuine favor come from God, not from rulers. Christians should seek his favor, not human favor.

V. *The words of Agur (30.1–33)*

A. *Personal observations*

30 The words of Agur son of Jakeh. An oracle.

Thus says the man: I am weary, O God,
I am weary, O God. How can I prevail?*p*

2 Surely I am too stupid to be human;
I do not have human understanding.

3 I have not learned wisdom,
nor have I knowledge of the holy ones.*q*

4 Who has ascended to heaven and come down?
Who has gathered the wind in the hollow of the hand?
Who has wrapped up the waters in a garment?
Who has established all the ends of the earth?
What is the person's name?
And what is the name of the person's child?
Surely you know!

5 Every word of God proves true;
he is a shield to those who take refuge in him.

6 Do not add to his words,
or else he will rebuke you, and you will be found a liar.

7 Two things I ask of you;
do not deny them to me before I die:

8 Remove far from me falsehood and lying;
give me neither poverty nor riches;
feed me with the food that I need,

9 or I shall be full, and deny you,
and say, "Who is the LORD?"
or I shall be poor, and steal,
and profane the name of my God.

B. *Numerical proverbs*

10 Do not slander a servant to a master,
or the servant will curse you, and you will be held guilty.

11 There are those who curse their fathers
and do not bless their mothers.

12 There are those who are pure in their own eyes
yet are not cleansed of their filthiness.

13 There are those — how lofty are their eyes,
how high their eyelids lift! —

14 there are those whose teeth are swords,
whose teeth are knives,
to devour the poor from off the earth,
the needy from among mortals.

15 The leech*r* has two daughters;

Cross references

30.1 Prov 31.1

30.2 Ps 73.22

30.3 Prov 9.10

30.4 Jn 3.13; Ps 104.3; Isa 40.12; Job 38.8, 9; Isa 45.18

30.5 Ps 12.6; 18.30; 84.11

30.6 Deut 4.2; 12.32; Rev 22.18

30.8 Mt 6.11

30.9 Deut 8.12; Neh 9.25; Job 31.24; Hos 13.6

30.10 Eccl 7.21

30.11 Prov 20.20

30.12 Lk 18.11

30.13 Ps 131.1; Prov 6.17

30.14 Job 29.17; Ps 52.2; 14.4; Am 8.4

---

p Or *I am spent.* Meaning of Heb uncertain   *q* Or *Holy One*   *r* Meaning of Heb uncertain

---

30.5 *Every word of God proves true.* The least of the words of God have neither falsehood nor corruption in them. They are as silver purified seven times (Ps 12.6). The words of God are also sure, for they do not change and they are completely dependable; nothing can be added to them.

30.14 Here the writer portrays those who hate the poor as having teeth of iron and steel. They delight in consuming the poor. This accusation may go beyond oppression of the poor to include the condemnation of evil tongues, which slice people into pieces by slander and false reports.

"Give, give," they cry.
Three things are never satisfied;
  four never say, "Enough":
16 Sheol, the barren womb,
  the earth ever thirsty for water,
  and the fire that never says, "Enough."[s]

17 The eye that mocks a father
  and scorns to obey a mother
will be pecked out by the ravens of the valley
  and eaten by the vultures.

18 Three things are too wonderful for me;
  four I do not understand:
19 the way of an eagle in the sky,
  the way of a snake on a rock,
the way of a ship on the high seas,
  and the way of a man with a girl.

20 This is the way of an adulteress:
  she eats, and wipes her mouth,
  and says, "I have done no wrong."

21 Under three things the earth trembles;
  under four it cannot bear up:
22 a slave when he becomes king,
  and a fool when glutted with food;
23 an unloved woman when she gets a husband,
  and a maid when she succeeds her mistress.

24 Four things on earth are small,
  yet they are exceedingly wise:
25 the ants are a people without strength,
  yet they provide their food in the summer;
26 the badgers are a people without power,
  yet they make their homes in the rocks;
27 the locusts have no king,
  yet all of them march in rank;
28 the lizard[t] can be grasped in the hand,
  yet it is found in kings' palaces.

29 Three things are stately in their stride;
  four are stately in their gait:
30 the lion, which is mightiest among wild animals
  and does not turn back before any;
31 the strutting rooster,[u] the he-goat,
  and a king striding before[s] his people.

32 If you have been foolish, exalting yourself,
  or if you have been devising evil,
  put your hand on your mouth.
33 For as pressing milk produces curds,

	30.16 Prov 27.20
	30.17 Gen 9.22; Prov 23.22; Deut 28.26
	30.20 Prov 5.6
	30.22 Prov 19.10
	30.25 Prov 6.6-8
	30.26 Ps 104.18
	30.30 Judg 14.18; Mic 5.8
	30.32 Job 21.5; 40.4; Mic 7.16
	30.33 Prov 10.12; 29.22

s Meaning of Heb uncertain *t* Or *spider* *u* Gk Syr Tg Compare Vg: Meaning of Heb uncertain

30.18–20 Scripture always condemns adultery. This passage refers to a common pattern: the one who has committed adultery will use every device imaginable to conceal that treachery. So good is the cover-up that it would be easier to track the flight of an eagle than to discover that sin. What is worse, the adulterer usually feels justified in his or her actions.

and pressing the nose produces blood,
so pressing anger produces strife.

VI. *The words of Lemuel (31.1–9)*

31.1
Prov 30.1

31   The words of King Lemuel. An oracle that his mother taught him:

31.2
Isa 49.15

2   No, my son! No, son of my womb!
    No, son of my vows!

31.3
Prov 5.9;
Deut 17.17;
1 Kings 11.1;
Neh 13.26

3   Do not give your strength to women,
    your ways to those who destroy kings.

31.4
Eccl 10.17;
Prov 20.1

4   It is not for kings, O Lemuel,
    it is not for kings to drink wine,
    or for rulers to desire*v* strong drink;

31.5
Hos 4.11

5   or else they will drink and forget what has been decreed,
    and will pervert the rights of all the afflicted.

6   Give strong drink to one who is perishing,
    and wine to those in bitter distress;

7   let them drink and forget their poverty,
    and remember their misery no more.

31.8
Job 29.12-17

8   Speak out for those who cannot speak,
    for the rights of all the destitute.*w*

31.9
Lev 19.15;
Deut 1.16

9   Speak out, judge righteously,
    defend the rights of the poor and needy.

VII. *The virtuous woman (31.10–31)*

31.10
Prov 12.4;
19.14

10   A capable wife who can find?
     She is far more precious than jewels.

11   The heart of her husband trusts in her,
     and he will have no lack of gain.

12   She does him good, and not harm,
     all the days of her life.

31.13
vv. 21-24

13   She seeks wool and flax,
     and works with willing hands.

14   She is like the ships of the merchant,
     she brings her food from far away.

31.15
Rom 12.11;
Lk 12.42

15   She rises while it is still night
     and provides food for her household
     and tasks for her servant-girls.

16   She considers a field and buys it;
     with the fruit of her hands she plants a vineyard.

17   She girds herself with strength,
     and makes her arms strong.

18   She perceives that her merchandise is profitable.
     Her lamp does not go out at night.

19   She puts her hands to the distaff,
     and her hands hold the spindle.

v Cn: Heb *where*   *w* Heb *all children of passing away*

31.1 *King Lemuel. Lemuel* means "devoted to God." Nothing is known about him except what the text says. Rabbinic tradition equates Lemuel with Solomon, though modern scholars reject this.
31.2–9 Lemuel's mother counsels her beloved son to stay away from fornication and other sexual sins, to stay sober, to do good with his wealth by helping those who are poor, and to use his kingly power in the pursuit of justice.
31.10–31 This section gives us the portrait of the ideal wife. Each of the twenty-two verses begins with a letter of the Hebrew alphabet in sequence, as do some of the psalms. What is taught here is repeated in condensed form in 1 Tim 2.9,10 and 1 Pet 3.1–6. A mother has the unique opportunity of performing two invaluable services for her family: keeping true faith in the family and passing on that same faith to succeeding generations. At the same time, a godly woman may pursue her own personal interests.

20 She opens her hand to the poor,
    and reaches out her hands to the needy.
21 She is not afraid for her household when it snows,
    for all her household are clothed in crimson.
22 She makes herself coverings;
    her clothing is fine linen and purple.
23 Her husband is known in the city gates,
    taking his seat among the elders of the land.
24 She makes linen garments and sells them;
    she supplies the merchant with sashes.
25 Strength and dignity are her clothing,
    and she laughs at the time to come.
26 She opens her mouth with wisdom,
    and the teaching of kindness is on her tongue.
27 She looks well to the ways of her household,
    and does not eat the bread of idleness.
28 Her children rise up and call her happy;
    her husband too, and he praises her:
29 "Many women have done excellently,
    but you surpass them all."
30 Charm is deceitful, and beauty is vain,
    but a woman who fears the LORD is to be praised.
31 Give her a share in the fruit of her hands,
    and let her works praise her in the city gates.

31.20
Eph 4.28;
Heb 13.16
31.21
1 Sam 1.24

31.23
Ruth 4.1, 11;
Prov 12.4

31.25
v. 17
31.26
Prov 10.31

31.27
Prov 19.15

31.29
Prov 12.4

31.30
Prov 6.25;
22.4

31.26 A good mother and wife is known not only for what she does but for what she says. A mother's knee is a good place for children to hear the word of God and find Jesus Christ as their Savior.

INTRODUCTION TO
ECCLESIASTES

Authorship, Date, and Background: Ecclesiastes (meaning "The Preacher") is the title assigned to this book in the Septuagint. The Hebrew title is *Qoheleh,* which is derived from a root Hebrew word meaning "assembly, congregation." The Hebrew title is the feminine abstract noun which may have meant "the office or function of a speaker in the assembly" (hence "Teacher" in NRSV). Ecclesiastes was part of the Megilloth (see introduction to Esther). It was read publicly at the festival of tabernacles.

A number of outstanding conservative scholars think Ecclesiastes was composed in the fifth century B.C., while others assign it to the tenth century B.C. and accept Solomon as author for a variety of reasons. For example, the book itself opens with the statement, "The words of the Teacher, the son of David, king in Jerusalem." Still other scholars have assumed that the book reflects Solomonic wisdom but was written centuries after his death (ca. 430–400 B.C. or later). But the date and the authorship of this book are not vital questions relative to one's belief in the truthfulness of the word of God. The book itself settles neither the date nor the authorship.

Characteristics and Content: Ecclesiastes is not an easy book to interpret. It consists of a series of philosophical presuppositions about life and death put together in a fashion which suggests a compilation of ideas that do not form a connected whole. The vocabulary is difficult and the style is somewhat disjointed. At the same time the book is definitely marked by an unvarying theme which is treated in an amazing variety of ways. Basically the message is that life is futile when it is based upon earthly ambitions and desires. When people refuse to rise above themselves and find the meaning of life in a transcendent God, it leads to meaninglessness and frustration.

The Teacher speaks about such subjects as human wisdom, education, power, servants, wealth, pleasure, religion, temperance, and length of days. He concludes that all is in vain. None brings true satisfaction and all humans alike go down to the grave. Whoever lives for any other purpose than the glory of God is doomed to disappointment. God and his will are the highest good for any who want the best in life and desire the highest possible fulfillment.

Outline:

    I. First discourse: the vanity of human wisdom (1.1—2.26)

   II. Second discourse: the disappointing experiences of life (3.1—5.20)

 III. Third discourse: the vanity of wealth and honor (6.1—8.17)

 IV. Fourth discourse: leaving with God the injustices of this life (9.1—12.8)

  V. Conclusion: considering life in the light of eternity (12.9–14)

ECCLESIASTES

I. *First discourse: the vanity of human wisdom (1.1–2.26)*

A. *The theme advanced: the vanity of human effort and experience*

1 The words of the Teacher,ˣ the son of David, king in Jerusalem.
2 Vanity of vanities, says the Teacher,ˣ
vanity of vanities! All is vanity.
3 What do people gain from all the toil
at which they toil under the sun?

B. *The theme demonstrated*

1. *The meaningless cycle of life*

4 A generation goes, and a generation comes,
but the earth remains forever.
5 The sun rises and the sun goes down,
and hurries to the place where it rises.
6 The wind blows to the south,
and goes around to the north;
round and round goes the wind,
and on its circuits the wind returns.
7 All streams run to the sea,
but the sea is not full;
to the place where the streams flow,
there they continue to flow.
8 All thingsʸ are wearisome;
more than one can express;
the eye is not satisfied with seeing,
or the ear filled with hearing.
9 What has been is what will be,
and what has been done is what will be done;
there is nothing new under the sun.
10 Is there a thing of which it is said,
"See, this is new"?
It has already been,
in the ages before us.
11 The people of long ago are not remembered,

ˣ Heb *Qoheleth*, traditionally rendered *Preacher*   ʸ Or *words*

1.1 v. 12;
Eccl 7.27;
12.8-10
1.2 Ps 39.5, 6;
62.9; 144.4;
Eccl 12.8
1.3 Eccl 2.22; 3.9
1.4 Ps 104.5;
119.90
1.5 Ps 19.5, 6
1.6 Eccl 11.5;
Jn 3.8
1.8 Prov 27.20
1.9 Eccl 2.12;
3.15
1.11 Eccl 2.16; 9.5

1.1 *The words of the Teacher, the son of David, king in Jerusalem.* The word for "Teacher" is Qoheleth (see NRSV footnote). The word may refer to a gatherer of people or of wise sayings and proverbs. For comments on whether this "son of David" refers to Solomon, see the introduction. If the author was not Solomon, it was someone who profited from his experiences.
1.2 *All is vanity*, i.e., life is useless and empty when lived outside of fellowship with God and apart from the divine will. The final solution is found in 12.13, 14.
1.9 *there is nothing new under the sun.* Properly understood, this is correct. It is true that we know many things today which were unknown to our ancestors. They are new to us, yet not new to nature or to providence. Even in theology and philosophy there is nothing new to be said. Every so-called "new" viewpoint can usually be traced back to someone who said something similar centuries ago. There may arise new syntheses of old ideas but no new ideas.

nor will there be any remembrance
of people yet to come
by those who come after them.

2. *The vanity of human wisdom*

12 I, the Teacher,[z] when king over Israel in Jerusalem, 13 applied my
mind to seek and to search out by wisdom all that is done under heaven;
it is an unhappy business that God has given to human beings to be busy
with. 14 I saw all the deeds that are done under the sun; and see, all is
vanity and a chasing after wind.[a]
15   What is crooked cannot be made straight,
    and what is lacking cannot be counted.
16   I said to myself, "I have acquired great wisdom, surpassing all who
were over Jerusalem before me; and my mind has had great experience
of wisdom and knowledge." 17 And I applied my mind to know wisdom
and to know madness and folly. I perceived that this also is but a chasing
after wind.[a]
18   For in much wisdom is much vexation,
    and those who increase knowledge increase sorrow.

3. *The vanity of pleasure and wealth*

2 I said to myself, "Come now, I will make a test of pleasure; enjoy
    yourself." But again, this also was vanity. 2 I said of laughter, "It is
mad," and of pleasure, "What use is it?" 3 I searched with my mind how
to cheer my body with wine — my mind still guiding me with wisdom —
and how to lay hold on folly, until I might see what was good for mortals
to do under heaven during the few days of their life. 4 I made great works;
I built houses and planted vineyards for myself; 5 I made myself gardens
and parks, and planted in them all kinds of fruit trees. 6 I made myself
pools from which to water the forest of growing trees. 7 I bought male and
female slaves, and had slaves who were born in my house; I also had great
possessions of herds and flocks, more than any who had been before me
in Jerusalem. 8 I also gathered for myself silver and gold and the treasure
of kings and of the provinces; I got singers, both men and women, and
delights of the flesh, and many concubines.[b]
9   So I became great and surpassed all who were before me in Jerusalem; also my wisdom remained with me. 10 Whatever my eyes desired I
did not keep from them; I kept my heart from no pleasure, for my heart
found pleasure in all my toil, and this was my reward for all my toil.
11 Then I considered all that my hands had done and the toil I had spent

[z] Heb *Qoheleth*, traditionally rendered *Preacher*   [a] Or *a feeding on wind.* See Hos 12.1   [b] Meaning of
Heb uncertain

1.15 *What is crooked cannot be made straight.* Biblically we can say that philosophy and politics cannot
make bad people good, nor will learning restore to
people the rectitude that Adam had in the Garden of
Eden before he sinned. Even justification and regeneration will not result in the perfection of Christians
in this life. That awaits glorification, at which time
the crooked *will* become straight (cf. Isa 40.3–5).
1.18 Getting wisdom is a long and tedious task.
Remembering it is equally difficult. The more we
learn, the more we realize we do not know. Thus there
is no end to the task of learning wisdom. Wisdom
increases grief because the more we know, the more
we learn about evil and that which does not seem to
make sense.
2.1 By personal experience the author found that
pleasure does not satisfy the heart except momentarily. With Solomon, for example, before the end of
his days pleasure had caused ruin — with his many

wives and concubines and his heart turned away from
God. Overindulgence produces satiety; satiety makes
pleasure useless. We should accept this truth by the
witness of those who have tried it, rather than discov-
ering it by personal experience.
2.2ff The author tried everything: laughter, wine,
works, slaves, herds, silver, gold, singers, and concubines. Everything ended in "chasing after wind" (v.
11) (or, "vexation of spirit"). The moral is plain: only
God can fill the void in a mortal's heart and provide
lasting satisfaction and inward joy.
2.11 When God ended his six days of creation, he
saw that what he had done was good and he rested
from his work. When the author surveyed what he
had done he was far from satisfied. There was no
value either in his attempt to acquire many things or
to gratify his every desire. He had everything, only to
end up bankrupt.

in doing it, and again, all was vanity and a chasing after wind,[c] and there was nothing to be gained under the sun.

4. *Both the fool and the wise must die*

12   So I turned to consider wisdom and madness and folly; for what can the one do who comes after the king? Only what has already been done. [13] Then I saw that wisdom excels folly as light excels darkness.

14   The wise have eyes in their head,
    but fools walk in darkness.

Yet I perceived that the same fate befalls all of them. [15] Then I said to myself, "What happens to the fool will happen to me also; why then have I been so very wise?" And I said to myself that this also is vanity. [16] For there is no enduring remembrance of the wise or of fools, seeing that in the days to come all will have been long forgotten. How can the wise die just like fools? [17] So I hated life, because what is done under the sun was grievous to me; for all is vanity and a chasing after wind.[c]

5. *The futility of leaving fruit of toil to undeserving heirs*

18   I hated all my toil in which I had toiled under the sun, seeing that I must leave it to those who come after me [19] — and who knows whether they will be wise or foolish? Yet they will be master of all for which I toiled and used my wisdom under the sun. This also is vanity. [20] So I turned and gave my heart up to despair concerning all the toil of my labors under the sun, [21] because sometimes one who has toiled with wisdom and knowledge and skill must leave all to be enjoyed by another who did not toil for it. This also is vanity and a great evil. [22] What do mortals get from all the toil and strain with which they toil under the sun? [23] For all their days are full of pain, and their work is a vexation; even at night their minds do not rest. This also is vanity.

6. *The godly must be content with what God gives them*

24   There is nothing better for mortals than to eat and drink, and find enjoyment in their toil. This also, I saw, is from the hand of God; [25] for apart from him[d] who can eat or who can have enjoyment? [26] For to the one who pleases him God gives wisdom and knowledge and joy; but to the sinner he gives the work of gathering and heaping, only to give to one who pleases God. This also is vanity and a chasing after wind.[c]

II. *Second discourse: the disappointing experiences of life*
(3.1–5.20)

A. *The wise attitude toward life*

1. *A time for everything*

3   For everything there is a season, and a time for every matter under heaven:

---

[c] Or *a feeding on wind.* See Hos 12.1   [d] Gk Syr: Heb *apart from me*

Cross references (right margin):
2.12 Eccl 1.17; 7.25
2.13 Eccl 7.11, 12
2.14 Prov 17.24; Ps 49.10; Eccl 9.2, 3, 11
2.15 Eccl 6.8, 11
2.16 Eccl 1.11; 9.5; v. 14
2.17 Eccl 4.2; vv. 22, 23
2.18 v. 11; Ps 39.6; 49.10
2.20 v. 11
2.21 Eccl 4.4; v. 18
2.22 Eccl 1.3; 3.9
2.23 Job 5.7; 14.1; Eccl 1.18; Ps 127.2
2.24 Eccl 3.12, 13, 22; 5.18; 8.15
2.26 Job 32.8; 27.16, 17; Eccl 1.14
3.1 v. 17; Eccl 8.6

2.13 The author knows that it is better to have wisdom than folly, for it brings light rather than darkness. But some things happen alike to the wise and the foolish. And in the end both die, to be remembered no more. After their death, others rarely have learned enough from the wise to keep them from repeating the follies of the foolish.

2.18,19 Mortals often wait with pleasure for the advent of new rulers over them. They think things will change and conditions will get better. But who knows for sure whether the next president or prime minister will be wise or foolish? He or she will take over all the predecessor left behind and may use that legacy foolishly rather than wisely.

3.1ff The author contrasts various activities in the ebb and flow of life: birth and death, getting and losing, etc. Some changes spring from the will of God alone; others depend on the will of humans. Yet everything on earth is changeable. Only in heaven are things unchangeable. Those who have heaven for

3.2
Heb 9.27

3.4
Rom 12.15;
Ps 126.2;
Ex 15.20
3.5
1 Cor 7.5

3.7
Am 5.13

3.8
Lk 14.26

2 a time to be born, and a time to die;
   a time to plant, and a time to pluck up what is planted;
3 a time to kill, and a time to heal;
   a time to break down, and a time to build up;
4 a time to weep, and a time to laugh;
   a time to mourn, and a time to dance;
5 a time to throw away stones, and a time to gather stones
   together;
   a time to embrace, and a time to refrain from embracing;
6 a time to seek, and a time to lose;
   a time to keep, and a time to throw away;
7 a time to tear, and a time to sew;
   a time to keep silence, and a time to speak;
8 a time to love, and a time to hate;
   a time for war, and a time for peace.

2. Uselessness of human striving

3.9
Eccl 1.3
3.10
Eccl 1.13
3.11
Gen 1.31;
Eccl 8.17;
Rom 11.33
3.13
Eccl 2.24;
5.19
3.14
Jas 1.17;
Eccl 5.7; 1.3;
3.9
3.15
Eccl 1.9; 6.10

9 What gain have the workers from their toil? 10 I have seen the business that God has given to everyone to be busy with. 11 He has made everything suitable for its time; moreover he has put a sense of past and future into their minds, yet they cannot find out what God has done from the beginning to the end. 12 I know that there is nothing better for them than to be happy and enjoy themselves as long as they live; 13 moreover, it is God's gift that all should eat and drink and take pleasure in all their toil. 14 I know that whatever God does endures forever; nothing can be added to it, nor anything taken from it; God has done this, so that all should stand in awe before him. 15 That which is, already has been; that which is to be, already is; and God seeks out what has gone by. *e*

3. Humans must make the best of this present life

3.17
Mt 16.27;
Rom 2.6-8;
2 Cor 5.10;
2 Thess 1.6,
7; v. 1
3.19
Ps 73.22;
Eccl 9.12
3.20
Gen 3.19;
Eccl 12.7
3.21
Eccl 12.7
3.22
Eccl 2.24;
5.18; 6.12;
8.7; 10.14

16 Moreover I saw under the sun that in the place of justice, wickedness was there, and in the place of righteousness, wickedness was there as well. 17 I said in my heart, God will judge the righteous and the wicked, for he has appointed a time for every matter, and for every work. 18 I said in my heart with regard to human beings that God is testing them to show that they are but animals. 19 For the fate of humans and the fate of animals is the same; as one dies, so dies the other. They all have the same breath, and humans have no advantage over the animals; for all is vanity. 20 All go to one place; all are from the dust, and all turn to dust again. 21 Who knows whether the human spirit goes upward and the spirit of animals goes downward to the earth? 22 So I saw that there is nothing better than that all should enjoy their work, for that is their lot; who can bring them to see what will be after them?

B. *The disappointments of earthly life*

1. *Oppression makes life a dubious blessing*

4.1
Eccl 3.16;
5.8;
Isa 5.7;
Lam 1.9

4 Again I saw all the oppressions that are practiced under the sun. Look, the tears of the oppressed — with no one to comfort them! On

e Heb *what is pursued*

---

their hope can endure all changes, for they know that some day they will inherit the unchangeable.
3.11 God has made all things beautiful. Nature and providence work together in ways beyond people's ability to search them out. In the end, we will see everything to have been done properly and at the right time. This will be the wonder of eternity, even though we see only imperfectly now.

3.21 In v. 19 we read that beasts and humans both die. All are of dust and return to dust. Yet there is a difference. The souls of beasts die with their bodies. They go downward to the earth. The spirits of mortals go upwards to meet their Father and Maker. In the final judgment the fixed state of those spirits will be determined; some will go to everlasting blessedness and others to eternal separation from God.

the side of their oppressors there was power — with no one to comfort them. 2 And I thought the dead, who have already died, more fortunate than the living, who are still alive; 3 but better than both is the one who has not yet been, and has not seen the evil deeds that are done under the sun.

2. Life's trials better faced by partners than alone

4 Then I saw that all toil and all skill in work come from one person's envy of another. This also is vanity and a chasing after wind.*f*

5 Fools fold their hands
    and consume their own flesh.
6 Better is a handful with quiet
    than two handfuls with toil,
    and a chasing after wind.*f*

7 Again, I saw vanity under the sun: 8 the case of solitary individuals, without sons or brothers; yet there is no end to all their toil, and their eyes are never satisfied with riches. "For whom am I toiling," they ask, "and depriving myself of pleasure?" This also is vanity and an unhappy business.

9 Two are better than one, because they have a good reward for their toil. 10 For if they fall, one will lift up the other; but woe to one who is alone and falls and does not have another to help. 11 Again, if two lie together, they keep warm; but how can one keep warm alone? 12 And though one might prevail against another, two will withstand one. A threefold cord is not quickly broken.

3. Instability of political fame

13 Better is a poor but wise youth than an old but foolish king, who will no longer take advice. 14 One can indeed come out of prison to reign, even though born poor in the kingdom. 15 I saw all the living who, moving about under the sun, follow that*g* youth who replaced the king;*h* 16 there was no end to all those people whom he led. Yet those who come later will not rejoice in him. Surely this also is vanity and a chasing after wind.*f*

C. The futility of the self-seeking life

1. Warnings against certain sins

5 *i* Guard your steps when you go to the house of God; to draw near to listen is better than the sacrifice offered by fools; for they do not know how to keep from doing evil.*j* 2*k* Never be rash with your mouth, nor let your heart be quick to utter a word before God, for God is in heaven, and you upon earth; therefore let your words be few.

f Or *a feeding on wind.* See Hos 12.1 *g* Heb *the second* *h* Heb *him* *i* Ch 4.17 in Heb *j* Cn: Heb *they do not know how to do evil* *k* Ch 5.1 in Heb

---

Cross references (right margin):

4.2 Job 3.11-26; Eccl 2.17
4.3 Eccl 6.3
4.4 Eccl 2.21; 1.14
4.5 Prov 6.10; Isa 9.20
4.6 Prov 15.16, 17; 16.8
4.8 Prov 27.20; 1 Jn 2.16
4.11 1 Kings 1.1
4.13 Eccl 9.15
4.14 Gen 41.14, 41-43
4.16 Eccl 1.14
5.1 Ex 3.5; Isa 1.12; 1 Sam 15.22; Prov 15.8; 21-27; Hos 6.6
5.2 Prov 20.25; 10.19; Mt 6.7

4.1–3 The author expresses great distress over the condition of the oppressed. The oppressors have power that they use for evil purposes. The oppressed have nothing to look forward to and consider death preferable to a life of bondage.

4.7 Some people dote on themselves and think only of adding to what they have. They are people of the world who have enough to live well but whose eyes are never satisfied. Such individuals live alone and die alone. At the same time, they have barren souls and empty hearts. This is vanity.

4.9–12 The author compares the monastic life to life in fellowship with others. To live alone is no panacea, and no one truly loves God who does not also love others. The best of life is a threefold cord that cannot be broken: two humans who help each other in love and who are in fellowship with God.

4.13 Being a king himself, this son of David (1.1) knew something about the vanity of life for those in the highest places. However dignified and powerful a monarch may be, if he is a fool, he is worse off than a wise young individual who has no wealth or power. Wisdom is to be preferred above everything else, for true wisdom always leads to God and to salvation.

5.1 The Spirit of God drives us from the world so that we may rest in God. In our worship of God in his house we should behave rightly, take no false step, keep our minds fixed on him, and offer the proper sacrifices.

3 For dreams come with many cares, and a fool's voice with many words.

4 When you make a vow to God, do not delay fulfilling it; for he has no pleasure in fools. Fulfill what you vow. 5 It is better that you should not vow than that you should vow and not fulfill it. 6 Do not let your mouth lead you into sin, and do not say before the messenger that it was a mistake; why should God be angry at your words, and destroy the work of your hands?

7 With many dreams come vanities and a multitude of words;[l] but fear God.

2. The end of the oppressor and the covetous

8 If you see in a province the oppression of the poor and the violation of justice and right, do not be amazed at the matter; for the high official is watched by a higher, and there are yet higher ones over them. 9 But all things considered, this is an advantage for a land: a king for a plowed field.[l]

10 The lover of money will not be satisfied with money; nor the lover of wealth, with gain. This also is vanity.

11 When goods increase, those who eat them increase; and what gain has their owner but to see them with his eyes?

12 Sweet is the sleep of laborers, whether they eat little or much; but the surfeit of the rich will not let them sleep.

13 There is a grievous ill that I have seen under the sun: riches were kept by their owners to their hurt, 14 and those riches were lost in a bad venture; though they are parents of children, they have nothing in their hands. 15 As they came from their mother's womb, so they shall go again, naked as they came; they shall take nothing for their toil, which they may carry away with their hands. 16 This also is a grievous ill: just as they came, so shall they go; and what gain do they have from toiling for the wind? 17 Besides, all their days they eat in darkness, in much vexation and sickness and resentment.

3. Making the best of what God gives

18 This is what I have seen to be good: it is fitting to eat and drink and find enjoyment in all the toil with which one toils under the sun the few days of the life God gives us; for this is our lot. 19 Likewise all to whom God gives wealth and possessions and whom he enables to enjoy them, and to accept their lot and find enjoyment in their toil — this is the gift of God. 20 For they will scarcely brood over the days of their lives, because God keeps them occupied with the joy of their hearts.

III. Third discourse: the vanity of wealth and honor (6.1–8.17)

A. Ambition and desire frustrated

6 There is an evil that I have seen under the sun, and it lies heavy upon humankind: 2 those to whom God gives wealth, possessions, and

[l] Meaning of Heb uncertain

5.11 The more people have, the better houses they must keep, the more servants they must employ, the more guests they must entertain, the more taxes they must pay, and the more worry they have about protecting what they own. Wealth gives no guarantee for happiness.
5.12 Common laborers on a normal diet sleep better at night than overfed, overindulged rich people who

carry their worries to their beds, where they toss and turn in sleepless concern about the next day (Lk 12.17).
5.15 The more one has, the more he or she has to lose. And some lose it all, if not in this life, then at death and in the life to come. We go out of this world the way we came in — empty-handed.
6.2 Riches, wealth, and honor are gifts from God.

honor, so that they lack nothing of all that they desire, yet God does not enable them to enjoy these things, but a stranger enjoys them. This is vanity; it is a grievous ill. 3 A man may beget a hundred children, and live many years; but however many are the days of his years, if he does not enjoy life's good things, or has no burial, I say that a stillborn child is better off than he. 4 For it comes into vanity and goes into darkness, and in darkness its name is covered; 5 moreover it has not seen the sun or known anything; yet it finds rest rather than he. 6 Even though he should live a thousand years twice over, yet enjoy no good — do not all go to one place?

7   All human toil is for the mouth, yet the appetite is not satisfied. 8 For what advantage have the wise over fools? And what do the poor have who know how to conduct themselves before the living? 9 Better is the sight of the eyes than the wandering of desire; this also is vanity and a chasing after wind.[m]

10   Whatever has come to be has already been named, and it is known what human beings are, and that they are not able to dispute with those who are stronger. 11 The more words, the more vanity, so how is one the better? 12 For who knows what is good for mortals while they live the few days of their vain life, which they pass like a shadow? For who can tell them what will be after them under the sun?

B. Wise advice in a sin-corrupted world

1. Choosing the better

7 A good name is better than precious ointment,
and the day of death, than the day of birth.

2 It is better to go to the house of mourning
than to go to the house of feasting;
for this is the end of everyone,
and the living will lay it to heart.

3 Sorrow is better than laughter,
for by sadness of countenance the heart is made glad.

4 The heart of the wise is in the house of mourning;
but the heart of fools is in the house of mirth.

5 It is better to hear the rebuke of the wise
than to hear the song of fools.

6 For like the crackling of thorns under a pot,
so is the laughter of fools;
this also is vanity.

7 Surely oppression makes the wise foolish,
and a bribe corrupts the heart.

8 Better is the end of a thing than its beginning;
the patient in spirit are better than the proud in
spirit.

6.3
2 Kings 9.35;
Isa 14.19,
20;
Jer 22.19;
Eccl 4.3

6.7
Prov 16.26
6.8
Eccl 2.15
6.9
Eccl 11.9;
1.14
6.10
Eccl 1.9;
Job 9.32;
Isa 45.9;
Jer 49.19
6.12
Jas 4.14;
Ps 39.6;
Eccl 8.7

7.1
Prov 15.30;
22.1;
Eccl 4.2
7.2
Eccl 2.16;
Ps 90.12

7.3
2 Cor 7.10

7.5
Ps 141.5;
Prov 13.18;
15.31, 32
7.6
Ps 118.12;
Eccl 2.2
7.7
Ex 23.8;
Deut 16.19
7.8
v. 1;
Prov 14.29;
Gal 5.22;
Eph 4.2

---

[m] Or *a feeding on wind*. See Hos 12.1

Unlike sunshine and rain, which God has given to all people to enjoy, not everyone has received riches, wealth, and honor. In his providence God gives them to some and not to others.
6.3–6 The author asserts that a stillborn baby is better off than a wealthy person who does not enjoy the wealth and honor God has given. Though such individuals were to live a long time, they would end up in the same place as the stillborn child. In death, there is no distinction.
6.10 Our situation in life is set for us by the counsel of God. Some are born into homes of wealth, others

into homes of poverty. Some are black, some brown, some white, and others yellow. Some are born in remote areas, others in crowded cities. What cannot be altered should be accepted. It is better to reconcile ourselves to these things cheerfully and acquiesce than to quarrel with God.
7.2,3 How can a visit to a funeral home be better than going to a feast? Because the former is more apt to make us think of the ultimate issues of life, whereas a festival will bring pleasure without serious thought to life's final question: "What happens to me when I die?"

2. The value of wisdom over wealth

7.9
Prov 14.17;
Jas 1.19

9   Do not be quick to anger,
      for anger lodges in the bosom of fools.
10 Do not say, "Why were the former days better than these?"
      For it is not from wisdom that you ask this.

7.11
Prov 8.10, 11

11 Wisdom is as good as an inheritance,
      an advantage to those who see the sun.

7.12
Eccl 9.18;
Prov 3.18;
8.35

12 For the protection of wisdom is like the protection of money,
      and the advantage of knowledge is that wisdom gives life to
        the one who possesses it.

7.13
Eccl 3.11;
8.17; 1.15;
Isa 14.27

13 Consider the work of God;
      who can make straight what he has made crooked?

7.14
Eccl 3.4;
Deut 8.5

14 In the day of prosperity be joyful, and in the day of adversity
consider; God has made the one as well as the other, so that mortals may
not find out anything that will come after them.

3. Asceticism and excess contrasted

7.15
Eccl 6.12;
8.14
7.16
Rom 12.3
7.17
Job 15.32;
Ps 55.23;
Prov 10.27

15 In my vain life I have seen everything; there are righteous people
who perish in their righteousness, and there are wicked people who
prolong their life in their evildoing. 16 Do not be too righteous, and do
not act too wise; why should you destroy yourself? 17 Do not be too
wicked, and do not be a fool; why should you die before your time? 18 It
is good that you should take hold of the one, without letting go of the
other; for the one who fears God shall succeed with both.

4. The value of wisdom and wickedness of folly

7.19
Eccl 9.13-18

19 Wisdom gives strength to the wise more than ten rulers that are
in a city.

7.20
1 Kings 8.46;
2 Chr 6.36;
Prov 20.9;
Rom 3.23

20 Surely there is no one on earth so righteous as to do good without
ever sinning.
21 Do not give heed to everything that people say, or you may hear
your servant cursing you; 22 your heart knows that many times you have
yourself cursed others.

5. Wicked womanhood discussed

7.23
Rom 1.22
7.24
Job 28.12;
Rom 11.33
7.25
Eccl 1.17;
2.12
7.26
Prov 5.3, 4;
22.14
7.27
Eccl 1.1, 2

23 All this I have tested by wisdom; I said, "I will be wise," but it
was far from me. 24 That which is, is far off, and deep, very deep; who
can find it out? 25 I turned my mind to know and to search out and to seek
wisdom and the sum of things, and to know that wickedness is folly and
that foolishness is madness. 26 I found more bitter than death the woman
who is a trap, whose heart is snares and nets, whose hands are fetters; one
who pleases God escapes her, but the sinner is taken by her. 27 See, this
is what I found, says the Teacher,[n] adding one thing to another to find
the sum, 28 which my mind has sought repeatedly, but I have not found.

[n] Qoheleth, traditionally rendered Preacher

7.9 Anger is a powerful human emotion. We should
not become angry quickly nor should we remain angry long. When we do get angry, to let the anger
control us is to act like fools.
7.10 Why do people assume that yesterday was better than today? The human heart has always exhibited
wickedness, though we tend to block out the badness
of the past. Complaints about our times are really a
quarrel against God, who oversees all of life.
7.15 We may not understand but we should not be
offended when the wicked prosper, while the godly
encounter great misfortunes. The wisdom of the word
of God will help us understand how to reconcile the
calamities of life with the holiness, goodness, and
faithfulness of our God.
7.20 The righteous are not free from sin in this life.
Nevertheless, they do have the promise of forgiveness
and restoration if they confess their sins (1 Jn 1.9).
7.21 It is sometimes better to close our eyes to personal hurts, as though we did not know them. Nor
should we be overly concerned to discover what people think of us, for this knowledge will either feed our
pride or stir up our anger. If we are approved of God,
our consciences are at rest and we need not listen to
what others say about us (cf. 1 Cor 4.1–7).
7.23ff The author has left no stone unturned to find
wisdom, but he hardly scratched the surface in his
search.

One man among a thousand I found, but a woman among all these I have not found. 29 See, this alone I found, that God made human beings straightforward, but they have devised many schemes.

C. Expediency in an imperfect world

1. The acceptance of authority

8 Who is like the wise man?
   And who knows the interpretation of a thing?
Wisdom makes one's face shine,
   and the hardness of one's countenance is changed.

2 Keep[o] the king's command because of your sacred oath. 3 Do not be terrified; go from his presence, do not delay when the matter is unpleasant, for he does whatever he pleases. 4 For the word of the king is powerful, and who can say to him, "What are you doing?" 5 Whoever obeys a command will meet no harm, and the wise mind will know the time and way. 6 For every matter has its time and way, although the troubles of mortals lie heavy upon them. 7 Indeed, they do not know what is to be, for who can tell them how it will be? 8 No one has power over the wind[p] to restrain the wind,[p] or power over the day of death; there is no discharge from the battle, nor does wickedness deliver those who practice it. 9 All this I observed, applying my mind to all that is done under the sun, while one person exercises authority over another to the other's hurt.

8.2
Ezek 17.18
8.4
Job 9.12;
Dan 4.35
8.6
Eccl 3.1, 17
8.7
Prov 24.22;
Eccl 6.12;
9.12; 10.14
8.8
Ps 49.6, 7;
Deut 20.5-8;
v. 13
8.9
Eccl 4.1; 5.8

2. The judgment of the wicked

10 Then I saw the wicked buried; they used to go in and out of the holy place, and were praised in the city where they had done such things.[q] This also is vanity. 11 Because sentence against an evil deed is not executed speedily, the human heart is fully set to do evil. 12 Though sinners do evil a hundred times and prolong their lives, yet I know that it will be well with those who fear God, because they stand in fear before him, 13 but it will not be well with the wicked, neither will they prolong their days like a shadow, because they do not stand in fear before God.

8.12
Isa 65.20;
Ps 37.11, 18,
19;
Prov 1.32,
33;
Isa 3.10, 11
8.13
v. 8;
Isa 3.11;
Eccl 6.12

3. Injustices in this life

14 There is a vanity that takes place on earth, that there are righteous people who are treated according to the conduct of the wicked, and there are wicked people who are treated according to the conduct of the righteous. I said that this also is vanity. 15 So I commend enjoyment, for there is nothing better for people under the sun than to eat, and drink, and enjoy themselves, for this will go with them in their toil through the days of life that God gives them under the sun.

8.14
Ps 73.14;
Eccl 7.15;
Job 21.7;
Mal 3.15
8.15
Eccl 2.24;
3.12, 13;
5.18; 9.7

4. The ways of God are inscrutable

16 When I applied my mind to know wisdom, and to see the business that is done on earth, how one's eyes see sleep neither day nor night,

o Heb I keep   p Or breath   q Meaning of Heb uncertain

7.29 Only Adam was upright when God created him, but he became sinful and corrupt by his own choice (Gen 3). All mortals follow in the footsteps of their first parent and exhibit the same imperfection.
8.1 The wise man is a good man because he knows God, keeps his commandments, and glorifies him. Like Moses' face, the face of the good man shines, for the light of the glory of God transfigures him.
8.11 It is better to execute sentences against the guilty quickly as a deterrent rather than to let them

suppose they will never be punished. When sentences are deferred, the wicked take heart and work further evil.
8.14 The author knows that sometimes providence smiles on the wicked and allows them to become prosperous and successful, while the righteous are being laughed at and censured. He does not, however, charge God with sin, but the world with vanity.
8.16,17 Whoever seeks to discover the reasons why God acts as he does will never find the answers.

8.17
Job 5.9;
Eccl 3.11;
Rom 11.33;
Eccl 8.7;
Ps 73.16

17 then I saw all the work of God, that no one can find out what is happening under the sun. However much they may toil in seeking, they will not find it out; even though those who are wise claim to know, they cannot find it out.

IV. *Fourth discourse: leaving with God the injustices of this life (9.1–12.8)*

A. *Make the best of this life*

1. *Death inevitable for both the good and the evil*

9.1
Deut 33.3;
Job 12.10;
Ps 119.109;
v. 6;
Eccl 10.14
9.2
Job 9.22;
Eccl 6.6; 7.2
9.3
v. 2;
Eccl 8.11;
1.17

9 All this I laid to heart, examining it all, how the righteous and the wise and their deeds are in the hand of God; whether it is love or hate one does not know. Everything that confronts them 2 is vanity,*r* since the same fate comes to all, to the righteous and the wicked, to the good and the evil,*s* to the clean and the unclean, to those who sacrifice and those who do not sacrifice. As are the good, so are the sinners; those who swear are like those who shun an oath. 3 This is an evil in all that happens under the sun, that the same fate comes to everyone. Moreover, the hearts of all are full of evil; madness is in their hearts while they live, and after that they go to the dead. 4 But whoever is joined with all the living has hope, for a living dog is better than a dead lion. 5 The living know that they will die, but the dead know nothing; they have no more reward, and even the memory of them is lost. 6 Their love and their hate and their envy have already perished; never again will they have any share in all that happens under the sun.

9.5
Job 14.21;
Eccl 1.11;
2.16;
Ps 88.12;
Isa 26.14
9.6
Eccl 3.22

2. *Enjoy life while you can*

9.7
Eccl 8.15
9.8
Rev 3.4;
Ps 23.5
9.9
Eccl 6.12;
7.15
9.10
Rom 12.11;
Col 3.23;
Isa 38.10

7 Go, eat your bread with enjoyment, and drink your wine with a merry heart; for God has long ago approved what you do. 8 Let your garments always be white; do not let oil be lacking on your head. 9 Enjoy life with the wife whom you love, all the days of your vain life that are given you under the sun, because that is your portion in life and in your toil at which you toil under the sun. 10 Whatever your hand finds to do, do with your might; for there is no work or thought or knowledge or wisdom in Sheol, to which you are going.

3. *Chance operates for all*

9.11
Am 2.14, 15;
Deut 8.17,
18; 1 Sam 6.9
9.12
Eccl 8.7;
Prov 29.6;
Isa 24.18;
Lk 21.34, 35

11 Again I saw that under the sun the race is not to the swift, nor the battle to the strong, nor bread to the wise, nor riches to the intelligent, nor favor to the skillful; but time and chance happen to them all. 12 For no one can anticipate the time of disaster. Like fish taken in a cruel net, and like birds caught in a snare, so mortals are snared at a time of calamity, when it suddenly falls upon them.

r Syr Compare Gk: Heb *Everything that confronts them* 2 *is everything*   *s* Gk Syr Vg: Heb lacks *and the evil*

9.1ff Wise as he was, the author found it difficult to understand how providence made so little difference between the good and the bad as to the experiences of life. But he did grasp the truth that the good are in the tender and loving hands of God, while the wicked are sure to reap what they have sown.
9.5 *the dead know nothing.* From vv. 5,10 some have adopted the notion that the dead know nothing until the resurrection — their souls sleep. The Bible is a book of progressive revelation; God does not reveal everything at once. The O.T. does not have a fully developed doctrine of the condition of the soul upon

death. The N.T., however, is clearer on this issue. Paul, for example, teaches that it is better to die and be with Christ; this can only mean conscious fellowship. The O.T. must be interpreted in the light of the N.T., and no single part of the Bible may be interpreted without referring to the totality of God's revelation. Scripture interprets Scripture.
9.11 From the human perspective we should remember the uncertainty of the future. Who knows what the morrow will bring forth? God knows, but we do not. And our times are in his hands. Therefore, we should do with all our might what we are supposed to.

4. Wisdom is superior

13 I have also seen this example of wisdom under the sun, and it seemed great to me. 14 There was a little city with few people in it. A great king came against it and besieged it, building great siegeworks against it. 15 Now there was found in it a poor wise man, and he by his wisdom delivered the city. Yet no one remembered that poor man. 16 So I said, "Wisdom is better than might; yet the poor man's wisdom is despised, and his words are not heeded."

17 The quiet words of the wise are more to be heeded
   than the shouting of a ruler among fools.
18 Wisdom is better than weapons of war,
   but one bungler destroys much good.

B. Life is uncertain and folly harmful

1. Folly harmful; wisdom helpful

10 Dead flies make the perfumer's ointment give off a foul odor;
   so a little folly outweighs wisdom and honor.
2 The heart of the wise inclines to the right,
   but the heart of a fool to the left.
3 Even when fools walk on the road, they lack sense,
   and show to everyone that they are fools.
4 If the anger of the ruler rises against you, do not leave your post,
   for calmness will undo great offenses.

5 There is an evil that I have seen under the sun, as great an error as if it proceeded from the ruler: 6 folly is set in many high places, and the rich sit in a low place. 7 I have seen slaves on horseback, and princes walking on foot like slaves.

8 Whoever digs a pit will fall into it;
   and whoever breaks through a wall will be bitten by a snake.
9 Whoever quarries stones will be hurt by them;
   and whoever splits logs will be endangered by them.
10 If the iron is blunt, and one does not whet the edge,
   then more strength must be exerted;
   but wisdom helps one to succeed.
11 If the snake bites before it is charmed,
   there is no advantage in a charmer.

2. The folly of empty talk

12 Words spoken by the wise bring them favor,
   but the lips of fools consume them.
13 The words of their mouths begin in foolishness,
   and their talk ends in wicked madness;
14 yet fools talk on and on.
   No one knows what is to happen,
   and who can tell anyone what the future holds?
15 The toil of fools wears them out,
   for they do not even know the way to town.

9.15 Eccl 4.13; 2.16; 8.10
9.16 Prov 21.22; Eccl 7.19
9.17 Eccl 7.5; 10.12
9.18 v. 16; Josh 7.1, 11, 12

10.3 Prov 13.16; 18.2
10.4 Eccl 8.3; 1 Sam 25.24-33; Prov 25.15
10.5 Eccl 5.6
10.6 Esth 3.1
10.7 Prov 19.10; Esth 6.8
10.8 Ps 7.15; Prov 26.27

10.11 Ps 58.4, 5; Jer 8.17

10.12 Prov 10.32; Lk 4.22; Prov 10.14; 18.7
10.13 Eccl 7.25
10.14 Prov 15.2; Eccl 3.22; 6.12; 8.7

10.1 A good reputation gained over a long time may be lost in a moment with a little folly. We should abstain from all appearances of evil lest we ruin our testimony. The description here is graphic: dead flies in perfume give forth "a foul odor." **10.10** Cutting wood with an axe is always easier if we sharpen the blade first. Similarly, we will escape from harm with a little advance preparation, i.e., if we meditate before we speak and act. We will save our-

selves from having to do remedial work in the long run. **10.14** *Fools talk on and on.* The Scriptures do not forbid talking, only a foolish and unwise use of speech. Right speaking is a powerful force for good, an ally of true wisdom. The wrong use of speech is forbidden and the consequences of such use made plain.

3. Concluding maxims

10.16
Isa 3.4, 5,
12; 5.11
10.17
Prov 31.4;
Isa 5.11

10.18
Prov 24.30-34

10.19
Ps 104.15;
Eccl 7.12

10.20
Ex 22.28;
Acts 23.5;
2 Kings 6.12;
Lk 12.3

16 Alas for you, O land, when your king is a servant,[t]
   and your princes feast in the morning!
17 Happy are you, O land, when your king is a nobleman,
   and your princes feast at the proper time —
   for strength, and not for drunkenness!
18 Through sloth the roof sinks in,
   and through indolence the house leaks.
19 Feasts are made for laughter;
   wine gladdens life,
   and money meets every need.
20 Do not curse the king, even in your thoughts,
   or curse the rich, even in your bedroom;
   for a bird of the air may carry your voice,
   or some winged creature tell the matter.

C. How to invest a life

1. Works of charity

11.1
Isa 32.20;
Deut 15.10;
Prov 19.17;
Mt 10.42;
2 Cor 9.8;
Gal 6.9, 10;
Heb 6.10
11.2
Ps 112.9;
Lk 6.30;
1 Tim 6.18,
19;
Eccl 12.1

11.5
Jn 3.8;
Ps 139.14, 15

11.6
Eccl 9.10

11.7
Eccl 7.11
11.8
Eccl 9.7; 12.1

11 Send out your bread upon the waters,
   for after many days you will get it back.
2 Divide your means seven ways, or even eight,
   for you do not know what disaster may happen on earth.
3 When clouds are full,
   they empty rain on the earth;
   whether a tree falls to the south or to the north,
   in the place where the tree falls, there it will lie.
4 Whoever observes the wind will not sow;
   and whoever regards the clouds will not reap.

5 Just as you do not know how the breath comes to the bones in the mother's womb, so you do not know the work of God, who makes everything.

6 In the morning sow your seed, and at evening do not let your hands be idle; for you do not know which will prosper, this or that, or whether both alike will be good.

7 Light is sweet, and it is pleasant for the eyes to see the sun.

8 Even those who live many years should rejoice in them all; yet let them remember that the days of darkness will be many. All that comes is vanity.

2. A wasted youth brings retribution

11.9
Eccl 2.10;
Num 15.39;
Eccl 3.17;
12.14;
Rom 14.10
11.10
2 Cor 7.1;
2 Tim 2.22

9 Rejoice, young man, while you are young, and let your heart cheer you in the days of your youth. Follow the inclination of your heart and the desire of your eyes, but know that for all these things God will bring you into judgment.

10 Banish anxiety from your mind, and put away pain from your body; for youth and the dawn of life are vanity.

3. Injunction to live for God

12.1ff
Ps 63.6;
119.55;
Eccl 11.8;
2 Sam 19.35

12 Remember your creator in the days of your youth, before the days of trouble come, and the years draw near when you will say, "I

[t] Or *a child*

10.20 It is prudent to withhold saying things that may be true but are unwise to make public. What you say may be revealed at a time when you wish you had never spoken the words.
11.4 If you wait for perfect conditions, you will never get anything done.
12.1ff Here is an excellent and graphic portrayal of the changes brought on by old age — its effects on mind and body, and the gradual deterioration that overtakes us all.

have no pleasure in them"; 2 before the sun and the light and the moon and the stars are darkened and the clouds return with*u* the rain; 3 in the day when the guards of the house tremble, and the strong men are bent, and the women who grind cease working because they are few, and those who look through the windows see dimly; 4 when the doors on the street are shut, and the sound of the grinding is low, and one rises up at the sound of a bird, and all the daughters of song are brought low; 5 when one is afraid of heights, and terrors are in the road; the almond tree blossoms, the grasshopper drags itself along*v* and desire fails; because all must go to their eternal home, and the mourners will go about the streets; 6 before the silver cord is snapped,*w* and the golden bowl is broken, and the pitcher is broken at the fountain, and the wheel broken at the cistern, 7 and the dust returns to the earth as it was, and the breath*x* returns to God who gave it. 8 Vanity of vanities, says the Teacher;*y* all is vanity.

12.4
Jer 25.10;
2 Sam 19.35
12.5
Job 17.13;
Jer 9.17

12.7
Gen 3.19;
Job 34.15;
Ps 90.3;
Job 34.14;
Isa 57.16;
Zech 12.1
12.8
Eccl 1.2

V. *Conclusion: considering life in the light of eternity* (12.9–14)

A. *The Teacher's purpose*

9 Besides being wise, the Teacher*y* also taught the people knowledge, weighing and studying and arranging many proverbs. 10 The Teacher*y* sought to find pleasing words, and he wrote words of truth plainly.

12.9
1 Kings 4.32
12.10
Prov 10.32;
22.20, 21

B. *The value of the Teacher's word*

11 The sayings of the wise are like goads, and like nails firmly fixed are the collected sayings that are given by one shepherd.*z* 12 Of anything beyond these, my child, beware. Of making many books there is no end, and much study is a weariness of the flesh.

12.11
Eccl 7.5;
Acts 2.37;
Ezra 9.8;
Isa 22.23

C. *The concluding injunction*

13 The end of the matter; all has been heard. Fear God, and keep his commandments; for that is the whole duty of everyone. 14 For God will bring every deed into judgment, including*a* every secret thing, whether good or evil.

12.13
Deut 4.2;
Eccl 8.5;
Mic 6.8
12.14
Mt 10.26;
12.36;
1 Cor 4.5

u Or *after*; Heb *'ahar*   *v* Or *is a burden*   *w* Syr Vg Compare Gk: Heb *is removed*   *x* Or *the spirit*
y Qoheleth, traditionally rendered *Preacher*   *z* Meaning of Heb uncertain   *a* Or *into the judgment on*

12.10 Truth can be taught in a compelling fashion or in such a way that the listener does not profit from it. The author wants us to choose the former.
12.13 The Teacher is ready to sum up his philosophy of life. Every notion has its opposing notion and when life has been searched, no final answers are

available from that search. Worldly wisdom is not enough; we need a revelation that comes from God and not from outward observation. All of life may be comprehended in this phrase — *Fear God, and keep his commandments*. That is, "trust and obey."

INTRODUCTION TO
THE
SONG OF SOLOMON

Authorship, Date, and Background: The Song of Solomon is the first of the five Megilloth (see introduction to Esther). According to Jewish tradition, it was read publicly every year at the passover celebration. Also, because the book dealt with intimate marital details, an old rabbinical requirement forbade the reading of it until a Jew had attained the age of thirty.

Substantial differences of opinion exist even among conservative scholars about the authorship and the interpretation of the book. The opening verse of the book ascribes the authorship to Solomon, whose reign is dated 970–930 B.C. Many well-known evangelical scholars accept Solomon as the author; that dates the book as a tenth century B.C. product. The language agrees with that of Ecclesiastes and many have assumed that the same person wrote both books. The text indicates that the Davidic kingdom was still intact. The author was acquainted with the flora and fauna of the entire country. He had poetic gifts and used them to the fullest.

Characteristics and Content: Virtually all scholars agree that Solomon is involved in the story. They differ as to whether Solomon and the shepherd hero are the same person. Some think the Shulammite maiden marries Solomon and teaches him the values of monogamous love, which he gladly accepts over against the corrupt splendor of his own court; others think the shepherd hero is the one whom the Shulammite maiden loves and from whom she is separated when taken to Solomon's harem. When Solomon cannot win her love, she is permitted to return to her shepherd lover, whom she marries.

Most interpreters agree that there is more to the book than a story of love and marriage. The bridegroom is properly regarded as a representative of God, who loves Israel, his bride (cf. Isa 62.5). Many think the story typifies the N.T. revelation of Jesus Christ as the bridegroom and the church as his bride (cf. Eph 5.22ff). This interpretation receives support from the idea of the shepherd, a title Jesus gives himself in Jn 10 when he speaks of the shepherd giving his life for the sheep.

Certainly this is the most explicit book in the Bible having to do with sex and marriage. Its high and lovely view of exalted human love reminds readers of the one love that rises above all earthly and human affections—even the love of the Lord Jesus for those who are lost.

Outline:

   I. The bride and the bridegroom (1.1—2.7)

  II. The praise of her beloved (2.8—3.5)

 III. In praise of the bride (3.6—5.1)

 IV. A troubled love (5.2—7.9)

  V. The unbroken communion (7.10—8.14)

THE
SONG OF SOLOMON

I. *The bride and bridegroom (1.1–2.7)*

A. *Inscription*

1 The Song of Songs, which is Solomon's.

1.1
1 Kings 4.32

B. *The bride awaits her lover*

2 Let him kiss me with the kisses of his mouth!
　For your love is better than wine,
3 　your anointing oils are fragrant,
　your name is perfume poured out;
　　therefore the maidens love you.
4 Draw me after you, let us make haste.
　The king has brought me into his chambers.
　We will exult and rejoice in you;
　　we will extol your love more than wine;
　　rightly do they love you.

1.2
Song 4.10
1.3
Song 4.10;
Eccl 7.1
1.4
Ps 45.14, 15

5 I am black and beautiful,
　　O daughters of Jerusalem,
　like the tents of Kedar,
　like the curtains of Solomon.
6 Do not gaze at me because I am dark,
　　because the sun has gazed on me.
　My mother's sons were angry with me;
　　they made me keeper of the vineyards,
　　but my own vineyard I have not kept!
7 Tell me, you whom my soul loves,
　　where you pasture your flock,
　　where you make it lie down at noon;
　for why should I be like one who is veiled
　　beside the flocks of your companions?

1.5
Song 2.14;
4.3; 2.7; 5.8
1.6
Ps 69.8;
Song 8.11
1.7
Song 3.1-4;
2.16; 8.13

8 If you do not know,
　　O fairest among women,
　follow the tracks of the flock,
　　and pasture your kids
　　beside the shepherds' tents.

1.8
Song 5.9; 6.1

1.2 The bride desires the kisses of the bridegroom even more than wine. She waits for her lover to draw near to her. The king has drawn her into his chambers, where she awaits him. Some take this as a metaphor of Jesus Christ drawing us to himself with the bands of love. By the Spirit even those who are unwilling are made willing.
1.5 *I am black*, i.e., she had been exposed to weathering by her nomadic wanderings. The sun had tanned her; she had borne the heat of the day. Still she

was beautiful and likened herself to the sumptuous furnishings of Solomon's royal palace.
1.7 The bride loves the groom with all her heart. He is the shepherd who feeds the flock and makes them rest when the sun is hottest. So believers love the shepherd who tends his sheep. They walk through green pastures and stay beside the still waters. He gave his life for the sheep, he gives his people rest and comfort, and he watches over them with care and concern.

C. Bride and bridegroom meet

1.9
Song 2.2, 10, 13;
2 Chr 1.16
1.10
5.13

9 I compare you, my love,
      to a mare among Pharaoh's chariots.
10 Your cheeks are comely with ornaments,
      your neck with strings of jewels.
11 We will make you ornaments of gold,
      studded with silver.

12 While the king was on his couch,
      my nard gave forth its fragrance.
13 My beloved is to me a bag of myrrh
      that lies between my breasts.

1.14
Song 4.13

14 My beloved is to me a cluster of henna blossoms
      in the vineyards of En-gedi.

1.15
Song 4.1;
5.12

15 Ah, you are beautiful, my love;
      ah, you are beautiful;
      your eyes are doves.
16 Ah, you are beautiful, my beloved,
      truly lovely.
   Our couch is green;

1.17
1 Kings 6.9,
10; 2 Chr 3.5

17   the beams of our house are cedar,
      our rafters[a] are pine.

2.1
Isa 35.1, 2;
Song 5.13;
7.2

2 I am a rose[b] of Sharon,
      a lily of the valleys.

2 As a lily among brambles,
      so is my love among maidens.

2.3
Song 8.5;
4.13

3 As an apple tree among the trees of the wood,
      so is my beloved among young men.
   With great delight I sat in his shadow,
      and his fruit was sweet to my taste.

2.4
Ps 20.5

4 He brought me to the banqueting house,
      and his intention toward me was love.

2.5
Song 7.8; 5.8

5 Sustain me with raisins,
      refresh me with apples;
   for I am faint with love.

2.6
Song 8.3

6 O that his left hand were under my head,
      and that his right hand embraced me!

2.7
Song 3.5; 8.4

7 I adjure you, O daughters of Jerusalem,
      by the gazelles or the wild does:
   do not stir up or awaken love
      until it is ready!

a Meaning of Heb uncertain   *b* Heb *crocus*

1.10,13 The bride is lovely and decorated with precious jewels. Believers become beautiful as God bejewels them for his glory. As the bride here has regard for her king, so the believers reverence Christ. And as her lover lies between her breasts, so Christ's people have him close to their hearts.
1.15–17 The bride beholds the beauty of her lover, whose couch is lovely and whose house is made of sweet-smelling wood. She calls it "ours," for as husband and wife they will share all things together. There is no "mine" and "yours" where true love exists; it is always "ours."
2.1 Although the lover is probably speaking about herself, some think this verse has christological implications. Jesus, the Son of the Most High, the bright morning star, is a *rose of Sharon, a lily of the valleys.* These are beautiful pictures of the fragrant beauty and glory of the Redeemer.
2.2 The bride is *as a lily among brambles.* The groom does not think less of her because of this. The church of Jesus Christ may now lie in a sin-filled earth, but will someday be transplanted into paradise where there is no sin.
2.4 The groom has brought her *to the banqueting house,* but the food is less important than his banner over her—love. She exhibits strong and passionate love for her beloved, whose hand supports her head as he presses her to his heart.

II. *The praise of her beloved (2.8–3.5)*

A. *Her praise by day*

8 The voice of my beloved!
    Look, he comes,
leaping upon the mountains,
    bounding over the hills.

2.8
v. 17

9 My beloved is like a gazelle
    or a young stag.
Look, there he stands
    behind our wall,
gazing in at the windows,
    looking through the lattice.

2.9
v. 17

10 My beloved speaks and says to me:
    "Arise, my love, my fair one,
    and come away;

2.10
v. 13

11 for now the winter is past,
    the rain is over and gone.

12 The flowers appear on the earth;
    the time of singing has come,
and the voice of the turtledove
    is heard in our land.

2.12
Ps 74.19

13 The fig tree puts forth its figs,
    and the vines are in blossom;
    they give forth fragrance.
Arise, my love, my fair one,
    and come away.

2.13
Mt 24.32;
Song 7.12;
v. 10

14 O my dove, in the clefts of the rock,
    in the covert of the cliff,
let me see your face,
    let me hear your voice;
for your voice is sweet,
    and your face is lovely.

2.14
Song 5.2;
Jer 48.28;
Song 8.13;
1.5

15 Catch us the foxes,
    the little foxes,
that ruin the vineyards —
    for our vineyards are in blossom."

2.15
Ezek 13.4

16 My beloved is mine and I am his;
    he pastures his flock among the lilies.

2.16
Song 6.3;
7.10

17 Until the day breathes
    and the shadows flee,
turn, my beloved, be like a gazelle
    or a young stag on the cleft mountains. *c*

2.17
Song 4.6;
vv. 8, 9

B. *Her praise by night*

3 Upon my bed at night
    I sought him whom my soul loves;
I sought him, but found him not;
    I called him, but he gave no answer. *d*

3.1
Isa 26.9;
Song 1.7; 5.6

c Or *on the mountains of Bether*; meaning of Heb uncertain   *d* Gk: Heb lacks this line

---

2.8–10 The bride rejoices in the groom, who comes bounding to her like a young stag. He gazes through the windows and speaks his word of love: "arise . . . and come away."
2.16 *My beloved is mine, and I am his.* The bride has title to her beloved, for what God has joined together no one will separate. But she is also committed to him.

So also we are Christ's and Christ is ours, joined together in an unbroken and unbreakable relationship.
3.1 This is probably a song in which the bride relates a dream. Her waking and sleeping hours are always filled with thoughts of her beloved.

3.2 Jer 5.1	2	"I will rise now and go about the city, in the streets and in the squares; I will seek him whom my soul loves." I sought him, but found him not.
3.3 Song 5.7	3	The sentinels found me, as they went about in the city. "Have you seen him whom my soul loves?"

3.4
Song 8.2
	4	Scarcely had I passed them,
		    when I found him whom my soul loves.
		I held him, and would not let him go
		    until I brought him into my mother's house,
		    and into the chamber of her that conceived me.

3.5
Song 2.7; 8.4
	5	I adjure you, O daughters of Jerusalem,
		    by the gazelles or the wild does:
		do not stir up or awaken love
		    until it is ready!

III. *In praise of the bride (3.6–5.1)*

A. *The bridegroom comes*

3.6
Song 8.5;
1.13; 4.6, 14
	6	What is that coming up from the wilderness,
		    like a column of smoke,
		perfumed with myrrh and frankincense,
		    with all the fragrant powders of the merchant?

	7	Look, it is the litter of Solomon! Around it are sixty mighty men of the mighty men of Israel,

3.8
Jer 50.9;
Ps 45.3; 91.5
	8	all equipped with swords
		    and expert in war,
		each with his sword at his thigh
		    because of alarms by night.

	9	King Solomon made himself a palanquin from the wood of Lebanon.

3.10
Song 1.5
	10	He made its posts of silver,
		    its back of gold, its seat of purple;
		its interior was inlaid with love.[e]
		    Daughters of Jerusalem,

3.11
Song 3.16, 17
	11	come out.
		Look, O daughters of Zion,
		    at King Solomon,
		at the crown with which his mother crowned him
		    on the day of his wedding,
		    on the day of the gladness of his heart.

B. *His proposal accepted*

4.1 Song 1.15; 5.12; 6.5, 7	**4**	How beautiful you are, my love, how very beautiful!

[e] Meaning of Heb uncertain

3.4 She who had sought him so eagerly has now found him. She does not want to lose him, so she holds him fast. Likewise those who met Jesus after his resurrection took hold of his feet and worshiped him (Mt 28.9).
3.11 Solomon was crowned with gold by his mother on his wedding day. Jesus was crowned with thorns on his way to Golgotha, but will be crowned King of kings and Lord of lords when he comes in his kingdom. Conversion is a coronation day for sinners who become saints; it is the day when they are espoused to their Redeemer and are presented to the Father as chaste virgins (2 Cor 11.2; Rev 14.4), who have had their garments made white in the blood of the Lamb (Rev 7.13,14). It is the day of gladness, for Satan has been defeated and the angels of heaven rejoice over one sinner who repents (Lk 15.7–10).
4.1 Christ the bridegroom is engaged to his church. This church is described as beautiful. Its inner beauty is manifested in bright images and bold comparisons.

Your eyes are doves
    behind your veil.
Your hair is like a flock of goats,
    moving down the slopes of Gilead.

2 Your teeth are like a flock of shorn ewes
    that have come up from the washing,
all of which bear twins,
    and not one among them is bereaved.

3 Your lips are like a crimson thread,
    and your mouth is lovely.
Your cheeks are like halves of a pomegranate
    behind your veil.

4 Your neck is like the tower of David,
    built in courses;
on it hang a thousand bucklers,
    all of them shields of warriors.

5 Your two breasts are like two fawns,
    twins of a gazelle,
    that feed among the lilies.

6 Until the day breathes
    and the shadows flee,
I will hasten to the mountain of myrrh
    and the hill of frankincense.

7 You are altogether beautiful, my love;
    there is no flaw in you.

8 Come with me from Lebanon, my bride;
    come with me from Lebanon.
Depart*f* from the peak of Amana,
    from the peak of Senir and Hermon,
from the dens of lions,
    from the mountains of leopards.

9 You have ravished my heart, my sister, my bride,
    you have ravished my heart with a glance of your eyes,
    with one jewel of your necklace.

10 How sweet is your love, my sister, my bride!
    how much better is your love than wine,
    and the fragrance of your oils than any spice!

11 Your lips distill nectar, my bride;
    honey and milk are under your tongue;
    the scent of your garments is like the scent of Lebanon.

12 A garden locked is my sister, my bride,
    a garden locked, a fountain sealed.

13 Your channel*g* is an orchard of pomegranates
    with all choicest fruits,
    henna with nard,

14 nard and saffron, calamus and cinnamon,
    with all trees of frankincense,
myrrh and aloes,
    with all chief spices—

15 a garden fountain, a well of living water,
    and flowing streams from Lebanon.

16 Awake, O north wind,

f Or *Look*　*g* Meaning of Heb uncertain

4.16 The bride invites her beloved into her garden to enjoy the best entertainment it can afford him. She goes on to call it *his* garden, for she and all she has belong to him. So believers call nothing their own; everything belongs to Christ now and forever.

4.2
Song 6.6

4.3
Song 6.7

4.4
Song 7.4;
Neh 3.19

4.5
Song 7.3;
2.16; 6.2, 3

4.6
Song 2.17;
v. 14

4.7
Song 1.15

4.8
Song 5.1;
Deut 3.9

4.9
vv. 10, 12;
Prov 1.9;
Ezek 16.11

4.10
Song 1.2-4

4.11
Prov 5.3;
24.13;
Gen 27.27;
Hos 14.6

4.12
Prov 5.15-18;
Gen 29.3

4.13
Eccl 2.5;
Song 6.11;
7.12; v. 16;
Song 1.14

4.14
Song 1.12;
Ex 30.23;
v. 6;
Song 3.6;
Jn 19.39

4.15
Jn 4.10; 7.38

4.16
Song 5.1; 6.2

and come, O south wind!
Blow upon my garden
   that its fragrance may be wafted abroad.
Let my beloved come to his garden,
   and eat its choicest fruits.

5

5.1
Song 6.2;
4.9, 11, 14;
Lk 15.7, 10;
Jn 3.29

I come to my garden, my sister, my bride;
   I gather my myrrh with my spice,
I eat my honeycomb with my honey,
   I drink my wine with my milk.

Eat, friends, drink,
   and be drunk with love.

IV. *A troubled love (5.2–7.9)*

A. *Her disturbing dream*

5.2
Song 4.9;
6.9; v. 11

2 I slept, but my heart was awake.
Listen! my beloved is knocking.
"Open to me, my sister, my love,
   my dove, my perfect one;
for my head is wet with dew,
   my locks with the drops of the night."

5.3
Lk 11.7;
Gen 19.2

3 I had put off my garment;
   how could I put it on again?
I had bathed my feet;
   how could I soil them?

4 My beloved thrust his hand into the opening,
   and my inmost being yearned for him.

5.5
v. 13

5 I arose to open to my beloved,
   and my hands dripped with myrrh,
my fingers with liquid myrrh,
   upon the handles of the bolt.

5.6
Song 6.1;
3.1;
Prov 1.28

6 I opened to my beloved,
   but my beloved had turned and was gone.
My soul failed me when he spoke.
I sought him, but did not find him;
   I called him, but he gave no answer.

5.7
Song 3.3

7 Making their rounds in the city
   the sentinels found me;
they beat me, they wounded me,
   they took away my mantle,
   those sentinels of the walls.

5.8
Song 2.7;
3.5; 2.5

8 I adjure you, O daughters of Jerusalem,
   if you find my beloved,
tell him this:
   I am faint with love.

5.9
Song 1.8; 6.1

9 What is your beloved more than another beloved,
   O fairest among women?
What is your beloved more than another beloved,

5.2 As a symbol of the church, the bride in another dream is troubled like the churches of Revelation, which were rebuked for their weaknesses and commended for their strengths (Rev 2–3). God's people are not always what they should be. But when they waken from their slumber and renew their commitment to Christ, our Lord returns to their hearts.

5.9 Speaking of his beloved and symbolically of the church, the Spirit through the bridegroom Solomon describes the bride as the fairest among women. The church — the bride of Christ — is the wonderful society of the redeemed. The communion of saints is the finest community of people, who exhibit holiness and show forth the praise of God.

that you thus adjure us?

10 My beloved is all radiant and ruddy,
       distinguished among ten thousand.
11 His head is the finest gold;
       his locks are wavy,
         black as a raven.
12 His eyes are like doves
       beside springs of water,
     bathed in milk,
       fitly set. [h]

> 5.12
> Song 1.15;
> 4.1

13 His cheeks are like beds of spices,
       yielding fragrance.
     His lips are lilies,
       distilling liquid myrrh.

> 5.13
> Song 6.2; 2.1

14 His arms are rounded gold,
       set with jewels.
     His body is ivory work, [h]
       encrusted with sapphires. [i]
15 His legs are alabaster columns,
       set upon bases of gold.
     His appearance is like Lebanon,
       choice as the cedars.
16 His speech is most sweet,
       and he is altogether desirable.
     This is my beloved and this is my friend,
       O daughters of Jerusalem.

> 5.16
> Song 7.9;
> 2 Sam 1.23

6   Where has your beloved gone,
       O fairest among women?
     Which way has your beloved turned,
       that we may seek him with you?

> 6.1
> Song 5.6; 1.8

2   My beloved has gone down to his garden,
       to the beds of spices,
     to pasture his flock in the gardens,
       and to gather lilies.

> 6.2
> Song 4.16;
> 5.1, 13; 1.7;
> 2.1

3   I am my beloved's and my beloved is mine;
       he pastures his flock among the lilies.

> 6.3
> Song 2.16;
> 7.10

B. *The bridegroom's inner thoughts of his beloved*

4   You are beautiful as Tirzah, my love,
       comely as Jerusalem,
     terrible as an army with banners.

> 6.4
> Song 1.15;
> v. 10

5   Turn away your eyes from me,
       for they overwhelm me!
     Your hair is like a flock of goats,
       moving down the slopes of Gilead.

> 6.5
> Song 4.1

6   Your teeth are like a flock of ewes,
       that have come up from the washing;

> 6.6
> Song 4.2

h Meaning of Heb uncertain   *i* Heb *lapis lazuli*

5.16   This one whom the bride has described in vv.
10–15 is her beloved and her friend. She has committed herself to him, and on him her heart's affection is
set. So Christ loves those who love him, and to those
who once were his enemies he now is their friend.
Such are the wonders of God's grace!
6.1,2   In her dream the bride wonders where her
beloved has gone. Now she sees that he is not on the
streets of a crowded city but has gone into his garden
for privacy and retirement. It is also her garden, for
their relationship is mutual: she is his and he is hers.
6.4   *Tirzah,* the capital of the northern kingdom until Omri built Samaria (1 Kings 16.15–24). In this
verse, the beauty of Tirzah is compared to that of
Jerusalem. *You are . . . terrible as an army with banners,* i.e., "you capture my heart."

all of them bear twins,
and not one among them is bereaved.

6.7
Song 4.3

7 Your cheeks are like halves of a pomegranate
behind your veil.

6.8
1 Kings 11.3;
Song 1.3
6.9
Song 2.14;
5.2;
Gen 30.13

8 There are sixty queens and eighty concubines,
and maidens without number.
9 My dove, my perfect one, is the only one,
the darling of her mother,
flawless to her that bore her.
The maidens saw her and called her happy;
the queens and concubines also, and they praised her.

6.10
v. 4

10 "Who is this that looks forth like the dawn,
fair as the moon, bright as the sun,
terrible as an army with banners?"

6.11
Song 7.12

11 I went down to the nut orchard,
to look at the blossoms of the valley,
to see whether the vines had budded,
whether the pomegranates were in bloom.
12 Before I was aware, my fancy set me
in a chariot beside my prince.*j*

6.13
Judg 21.21;
Gen 32.2

13*k* Return, return, O Shulammite!
Return, return, that we may look upon you.

Why should you look upon the Shulammite,
as upon a dance before two armies?*l*

7.1
Ps 45.13

7 How graceful are your feet in sandals,
O queenly maiden!
Your rounded thighs are like jewels,
the work of a master hand.
2 Your navel is a rounded bowl
that never lacks mixed wine.
Your belly is a heap of wheat,
encircled with lilies.

7.3
Song 4.5

3 Your two breasts are like two fawns,
twins of a gazelle.

7.4
Song 4.4

4 Your neck is like an ivory tower.
Your eyes are pools in Heshbon,
by the gate of Bath-rabbim.
Your nose is like a tower of Lebanon,
overlooking Damascus.

7.5
Isa 35.2

5 Your head crowns you like Carmel,
and your flowing locks are like purple;
a king is held captive in the tresses.*m*

7.6
Song 1.15, 16

6 How fair and pleasant you are,
O loved one, delectable maiden!*n*
7 You are stately*o* as a palm tree,
and your breasts are like its clusters.

7.8
Song 2.5

8 I say I will climb the palm tree

j Cn: Meaning of Heb uncertain   *k* Ch 7.1 in Heb   *l* Or *dance of Mahanaim*   *m* Meaning of Heb
uncertain   *n* Syr: Heb *in delights*   *o* Heb *This your stature is*

6.13 *Shulammite*, probably came from Shulem
(likely a variant of Shunem), a town in the Plain of
Esdraelon (see 1 Sam 28.4 and 2 Kings 4.8).
7.1ff The groom describes the beauties of his spouse

in ten particulars. She has honored him and he will
now honor her. So Christ honors those who are married to him; he gives them his praise.

and lay hold of its branches.
O may your breasts be like clusters of the vine,
and the scent of your breath like apples,
9 and your kisses*p* like the best wine
that goes down*q* smoothly,
gliding over lips and teeth.*r*

V. *The unbroken communion (7.10–8.14)*

A. *The bride gives her love*

10 I am my beloved's,
and his desire is for me.
11 Come, my beloved,
let us go forth into the fields,
and lodge in the villages;
12 let us go out early to the vineyards,
and see whether the vines have budded,
whether the grape blossoms have opened
and the pomegranates are in bloom.
There I will give you my love.
13 The mandrakes give forth fragrance,
and over our doors are all choice fruits,
new as well as old,
which I have laid up for you, O my beloved.

8 O that you were like a brother to me,
who nursed at my mother's breast!
If I met you outside, I would kiss you,
and no one would despise me.
2 I would lead you and bring you
into the house of my mother,
and into the chamber of the one who bore me.*s*
I would give you spiced wine to drink,
the juice of my pomegranates.
3 O that his left hand were under my head,
and that his right hand embraced me!
4 I adjure you, O daughters of Jerusalem,
do not stir up or awaken love
until it is ready!

B. *The beauty of love*

5 Who is that coming up from the wilderness,
leaning upon her beloved?

Under the apple tree I awakened you.
There your mother was in labor with you;
there she who bore you was in labor.

6 Set me as a seal upon your heart,
as a seal upon your arm;
for love is strong as death,

7.10 Song 2.16; 6.3; Ps 45.11
7.12 Song 6.11
7.13 Gen 30.14; Song 2.3; 4.13, 16
8.2 Song 3.4
8.3 Song 2.6
8.4 Song 2.7; 3.5
8.5 Song 3.6; 2.3
8.6 Isa 49.16; Jer 22.24; Hag 2.23; Prov 6.34

p Heb *palate*   *q* Heb *down for my lover*   *r* Gk Syr Vg: Heb *lips of sleepers*   *s* Gk Syr: Heb *my mother; she* (or *you*) *will teach me*

7.10 Just as a husband's desire is toward his beloved wife, so the desire of Christ is toward his people. Between them there is a blessed communion unmarked by discord. The church needs nothing more than its bridegroom.
7.13 *Mandrakes* were supposed to produce feelings of sexual love (cf. Gen 30.14–16). They were also associated with magic.
8.1 The Shulammite bride wishes that her husband were her brother because it was considered improper in that culture for a married couple to express their love publicly, but not so for a sister and brother.

passion fierce as the grave.
Its flashes are flashes of fire,
　　a raging flame.
7 Many waters cannot quench love,
　　neither can floods drown it.
If one offered for love
　　all the wealth of one's house,
　　it would be utterly scorned.

8 We have a little sister,
　　and she has no breasts.
What shall we do for our sister,
　　on the day when she is spoken for?
9 If she is a wall,
　　we will build upon her a battlement of silver;
but if she is a door,
　　we will enclose her with boards of cedar.
10 I was a wall,
　　and my breasts were like towers;
then I was in his eyes
　　as one who brings^t peace.

11 Solomon had a vineyard at Baal-hamon;
　　he entrusted the vineyard to keepers;
　　each one was to bring for its fruit a thousand pieces of silver.
12 My vineyard, my very own, is for myself;
　　you, O Solomon, may have the thousand,
　　and the keepers of the fruit two hundred!

13 O you who dwell in the gardens,
　　my companions are listening for your voice;
　　let me hear it.

14 Make haste, my beloved,
　　and be like a gazelle
or a young stag
　　upon the mountains of spices!

^t Or finds

8.8
Ezek 16.7

8.11
Eccl 2.4;
Mt 21.33;
Song 1.6;
2.3;
Isa 7.23

8.13
Song 1.7;
2.14

8.14
Song 2.17;
4.6

8.7 True love is indestructible. It is a valiant, victorious passion. It will never desert the beloved. Water may quench a fire, but it cannot quench love. Floods will drown people and strike terror to their hearts, but they will not overwhelm love. Similarly, all the comforts of this world will never seduce the believer from his love for Christ, and Christ's love will forever hold his beloved church, both in life and in death

(Rom 8.35–39).

8.11 *Baal-hamon.* The location of this place is unknown to us today. Evidently the grapes from this vineyard were of exceptional quality. This reference may be a poetic expression. The vineyard which is so fruitful represents the church of Christ, with the members of Christ's body as the keepers of the vineyard (v. 12).

INTRODUCTION TO

ISAIAH

Authorship, Date, and Background: The author of this book was Isaiah (whose name means "Yahweh is salvation"), the son of Amoz. He lived in Jerusalem, was a student of international affairs, was well educated, and was on familiar terms with the royal court. He prophesied during the reigns of Uzziah, Jotham, Ahaz, and Hezekiah, and, according to tradition, was sawn in pieces during the kingship of Manasseh. His ministry extended over a period of more than fifty years (ca. 740–681 B.C.) and concerned itself largely with Judah, although references are made to Samaria. He lived through the days when Assyria, under either Shalmaneser V or Sargon II, conquered Samaria and brought an end to the northern kingdom.

The authorship of Isaiah has been questioned by many scholars since the late eighteenth century. These scholars have proposed that chs. 40–66 were written by someone other than Isaiah, a Deutero-Isaiah or second Isaiah. The basis of this viewpoint is the opinion that future events cannot be predicted in advance of their happening. Evangelicals have always agreed that under the aegis of the Holy Spirit the Bible does contain predictive prophecy, so that in principle the authorship of the second half of Isaiah cannot be questioned on this basis. A strong case can be made for one author on the grounds of the book's unity, style, use of words, and internal evidences for a pre-exilic date, and for its composition in Palestine rather than in Babylon. The N.T. consistently witnesses to Isaiah as the author of the entire book, the strongest affirmation being Jn 12.38–41.

Characteristics and Content: Isaiah has been and still is the most universally cherished prophetical book in the O.T. The N.T. alludes to it more than 250 times and portions of the book are quoted at least fifty times. It is perhaps the richest book of the O.T. in theological matters concerning God, creation and providence, humankind, sin, redemption, resurrection, judgment, and the coming Messiah. It is panoramic in its sweep, carrying the reader to the end of the age, when history will be consummated. The immediate message of Isaiah is to show that salvation is based upon the grace of God originating in his power as the Redeemer, not in people or their good works. God is holy and will not put up with unholiness in his covenant people. The person and work of Jesus the Messiah is detailed more fully here than in any other O.T. book. Isaiah speaks of the Messiah as the virgin-born child of God (7.14), as the suffering Messiah, who by his substitutionary atonement makes salvation possible (ch. 53), and as the eternal God who is the Prince of Peace (9.6,7).

Among the prophecies contained in the book are: the pronouncement of the doom of Samaria (the northern kingdom), the fall of Assyria (the nation that brought Samaria to its knees), and the judgment of God on the surrounding nations of Babylon, Philistia, Moab, Ethiopia, Edom, Arabia, Tyre, and Judah/Jerusalem (which would go into captivity under Nebuchadnezzar and be returned to the land under Cyrus after seventy years).

From ch. 40 to the end of the book Isaiah spoke words of comfort. He looked to the Messiah to bring Israel back to the land and to bring light to the Gentiles. God was the God of the whole earth, and salvation included Jews and Gentiles. He distinguished between true and false worship and painted a sweet picture of the restoration and peace of Zion, when the people of God would worship the Lord in the beauty of holiness and in obedience to the divine will. Many interpreters believe that Isaiah's prophecies make a distinction between national Israel and the church, and that God promises that Israel will someday be brought back as a nation again in the land of Palestine, where its people will worship the living God.

After depicting the glory of Zion, Isaiah closed his prophecy on a solemn note. Just as God saves, so God would also judge the wicked and dispense divine punishment upon them. Isaiah spoke this fateful word: "For by fire will the LORD execute judgment, and by his sword, on all flesh; and those slain by the LORD shall be many" (66.16). Those who do not now know God should be warned of their end if they do not repent and receive salvation through the blood of the Messiah, the Lamb of God.

Outline:

I. Volume of rebuke and promise (1.1—6.13)

II. Volume of Immanuel (7.1—12.6)

III. Volume of oracles upon heathen nations (13.1—23.18)

IV. First volume of general rebuke and promise (24.1—27.13)

V. Volume of woes upon the unbelievers of Israel (28.1—33.24)

VI. Second volume of general rebuke and promise (34.1—35.10)

VII. Volume of Hezekiah (36.1—39.8)

VIII. Volume of comfort and assurance (40.1—66.24)

ISAIAH

I. *Volume of rebuke and promise (1.1–6.13)*

A. *Rebellion confronted with judgment and grace*

1. *Superscription*

1 The vision of Isaiah son of Amoz, which he saw concerning Judah
and Jerusalem in the days of Uzziah, Jotham, Ahaz, and Hezekiah,
kings of Judah.

1.1
Num 12.6;
Isa 2.1;
2 Kings 15.1,
13, 32; 16.1;
18.1

2. *Judah's ingratitude*

2 Hear, O heavens, and listen, O earth;
　　for the LORD has spoken:
I reared children and brought them up,
　　but they have rebelled against me.

1.2
Deut 23.1

3 The ox knows its owner,
　　and the donkey its master's crib;
but Israel does not know,
　　my people do not understand.

1.3
Jer 8.7; 9.3,
6

4 Ah, sinful nation,
　　people laden with iniquity,
offspring who do evil,
　　children who deal corruptly,
who have forsaken the LORD,
　　who have despised the Holy One of Israel,
　　who are utterly estranged!

1.4
Isa 14.20;
v. 28;
Isa 5.24

5 Why do you seek further beatings?
　　Why do you continue to rebel?
The whole head is sick,
　　and the whole heart faint.

1.5
Isa 31.6;
33.24

6 From the sole of the foot even to the head,
　　there is no soundness in it,
but bruises and sores
　　and bleeding wounds;
they have not been drained, or bound up,
　　or softened with oil.

1.6
Job 2.7;
Ps 38.3;
Isa 30.26;
Lk 10.34

1.1 A prophet is one who has been given the gift of
foretelling future events. All of the O.T. prophets had
this gift and used it. We see O.T. prophecy fulfilled
in Israel's history as well as at the time of Christ. In
the N.T. age the prophetic gift consists mostly of
instruction in the holy faith with less emphasis on
predictive prophecy, although that is not entirely absent. At best, predictive prophecy is rare in our age
and the gift of prophecy, without which no one should
be a minister of the gospel, consists in the ability to
understand and expound the word of God.
1.2,3 Isaiah accuses Judah of ingratitude. The ox
and the donkey are wiser than Judah, for each of them
dutifully knows and serves its master. But Judah ob-

stinately chose to rebel against its master. The nation
lacked understanding, for it refused to consider its
obligations to God its creator.
1.4 Judah's rebellion was national in scope. Corruption had penetrated deep into the fabric of national
life. The people had forsaken God, and the Holy One
of Israel was now prepared to forsake them as his
people.
1.5–9 Sennacherib of Assyria attacked Judah in
701 B.C., laying waste to the countryside. Only Jerusalem was spared (2 Kings 18.13–16). Here Isaiah
describes the consequences of that invasion. Sadly,
Judah learned nothing from the experience, for the
Babylonian captivity was to come a century later.

1.7
Isa 6.11;
Jer 44.6
7   Your country lies desolate,
        your cities are burned with fire;
    in your very presence
        aliens devour your land;
        it is desolate, as overthrown by foreigners.

1.8
Job 27.18
8   And daughter Zion is left
        like a booth in a vineyard,
    like a shelter in a cucumber field,
        like a besieged city.

1.9
Rom 9.29;
Isa 10.20-22
9   If the LORD of hosts
        had not left us a few survivors,
    we would have been like Sodom,
        and become like Gomorrah.

3. God's requirement of a holy life

1.10
Isa 28.14;
3.9;
Ezek 16.46;
Rev 11.8
10 Hear the word of the LORD,
        you rulers of Sodom!
    Listen to the teaching of our God,
        you people of Gomorrah!

1.11
1 Sam 15.22;
Jer 6.20;
Mic 6.7
11 What to me is the multitude of your sacrifices?
        says the LORD;
    I have had enough of burnt offerings of rams
        and the fat of fed beasts;
    I do not delight in the blood of bulls,
        or of lambs, or of goats.

1.12
Ex 23.17
12 When you come to appear before me,[a]
        who asked this from your hand?
        Trample my courts no more;

1.13
Isa 66.3;
1 Chr 23.31;
Ex 12.16;
Jer 7.9, 10
13 bringing offerings is futile;
        incense is an abomination to me.
    New moon and sabbath and calling of convocation —
        I cannot endure solemn assemblies with iniquity.

1.14
Num 28.11;
Lev 23.2;
Isa 7.13;
43.24
14 Your new moons and your appointed festivals
        my soul hates;
    they have become a burden to me,
        I am weary of bearing them.

1.15
1 Kings 8.22;
Isa 8.17;
59.2;
Mic 3.4;
Isa 59.3
15 When you stretch out your hands,
        I will hide my eyes from you;
    even though you make many prayers,
        I will not listen;
    your hands are full of blood.

1.16
Jer 4.14;
Isa 52.11;
55.7;
Jer 25.5
16 Wash yourselves; make yourselves clean;
        remove the evil of your doings
        from before my eyes;

a Or see my face

1.9 Sodom and Gomorrah had been destroyed because not even ten righteous people could be found among the people (Gen 18.22–33). But in Judah there was still a small, faithful remnant who were not iniquitous, whom God had reserved for mercy. This tiny remnant would be preserved and kept alive from the calamity that would overtake Judah as a whole.
1.10 Having mentioned Sodom and Gomorrah, Isaiah likens the ungodly people of Judah to those two cities. They can expect the same sort of judgment for their transgressions. The prophet urges them to hear the word of God and to obey its teaching so that the upcoming judgment may be averted.
1.13 Futile offerings were sacrifices without spiri-

tual content. Judah preserved and honored religious forms and practices without real love for God.
1.15 *though you make many prayers, I will not listen.* There are times when God closes his eyes, hides his face, and refuses to listen to our prayers. This silence of God will remain until there is repentance, confession, and restoration to fellowship. God refuses to hear the prayers of the wicked even though they are accompanied by religious ceremonies and costly sacrifices. Hypocrisy is especially hated by God, who beheld the pretended zeal of Israel for the law, the temple, and the offerings, when in their hearts they were as ravenous wolves (cf. Mt 7.15).

17 cease to do evil,
        learn to do good;
    seek justice,
        rescue the oppressed,
    defend the orphan,
        plead for the widow.

4. The choice: repentance or destruction

18 Come now, let us argue it out,
        says the LORD:
    though your sins are like scarlet,
        they shall be like snow;
    though they are red like crimson,
        they shall become like wool.
19 If you are willing and obedient,
        you shall eat the good of the land;
20 but if you refuse and rebel,
        you shall be devoured by the sword;
    for the mouth of the LORD has spoken.

5. The promise to redeem Zion after judgment

21 How the faithful city
        has become a whore!
    She that was full of justice,
    righteousness lodged in her—
        but now murderers!
22 Your silver has become dross,
        your wine is mixed with water.
23 Your princes are rebels
        and companions of thieves.
    Everyone loves a bribe
        and runs after gifts.
    They do not defend the orphan,
        and the widow's cause does not come before them.

24 Therefore says the Sovereign, the LORD of hosts, the Mighty
        One of Israel:
    Ah, I will pour out my wrath on my enemies,
        and avenge myself on my foes!
25 I will turn my hand against you;
        I will smelt away your dross as with lye
        and remove all your alloy.
26 And I will restore your judges as at the first,
        and your counselors as at the beginning.
    Afterward you shall be called the city of righteousness,
        the faithful city.

27 Zion shall be redeemed by justice,
        and those in her who repent, by righteousness.
28 But rebels and sinners shall be destroyed together,

1.17 Jer 22.3; Isa 58.6; Ps 82.3
1.18 Isa 43.26; Ps 51.7; Rev 7.14
1.19 Deut 30.15, 16
1.20 Isa 3.25; 34.16
1.21 Jer 2.20; Isa 59.7
1.22 Ezek 22.18
1.23 Hos 9.15; Ex 23.8; Mic 7.3; Jer 5.28; Zech 7.10
1.24 Isa 49.26; 35.4
1.25 Mal 3.3
1.26 Jer 33.7; Zech 8.3
1.28 Isa 24.20; Ps 9.5; 2 Thess 1.8, 9

1.18 God suggests a debate with his people, saying that if they would only think straight they would see the foolishness of their ways and cleanse themselves from their defilements. Once they did this, they would be welcomed into the covenant and into communion with the true God.
1.21 Judah and Jerusalem had at one time been faithful to God. But their righteousness had disappeared and injustice flourished. Judah became a de-

bauched prostitute in whose borders murderers and thieves went unpunished.
1.26 Isaiah already had foreseen Judah's decline and God's abandonment of his people. But he also foresees a great future for God's people and God's city — a future that some see as fulfilled in the Christian church, while others see it as a future glory for the nation of Israel.
1.28 Judah's evil was so great that chastening and

and those who forsake the LORD shall be consumed.

29 For you shall be ashamed of the oaks
    in which you delighted;
    and you shall blush for the gardens
    that you have chosen.

30 For you shall be like an oak
    whose leaf withers,
    and like a garden without water.

31 The strong shall become like tinder,
    and their work*b* like a spark;
    they and their work shall burn together,
    with no one to quench them.

B. *Present judgment will lead to future glory*

1. *Promise of the triumph of God's kingdom on earth*

2 The word that Isaiah son of Amoz saw concerning Judah and Jerusalem.

2 In days to come
    the mountain of the LORD's house
  shall be established as the highest of the mountains,
    and shall be raised above the hills;
  all the nations shall stream to it.

3   Many peoples shall come and say,
  "Come, let us go up to the mountain of the LORD,
    to the house of the God of Jacob;
  that he may teach us his ways
    and that we may walk in his paths."
  For out of Zion shall go forth instruction,
    and the word of the LORD from Jerusalem.

4 He shall judge between the nations,
    and shall arbitrate for many peoples;
  they shall beat their swords into plowshares,
    and their spears into pruning hooks;
  nation shall not lift up sword against nation,
    neither shall they learn war any more.

2. *Sin to be judged before the goal is attained*

a. *The house of Jacob urged to repent*

5 O house of Jacob,
    come, let us walk
    in the light of the LORD!

6 For you have forsaken the ways of*c* your people,
    O house of Jacob.
  Indeed they are full of diviners*d* from the east
    and of soothsayers like the Philistines,
    and they clasp hands with foreigners.

7 Their land is filled with silver and gold,
    and there is no end to their treasures;

---

b Or *its makers*   *c* Heb lacks *the ways of*   *d* Cn: Heb lacks *of diviners*

correction would not avail. These transgressions had to
be destroyed and consumed.
2.1ff This passage is prophetic and looks to the day
when Christ sets up his church in the world and the
gospel will be preached to all the earth. The Christian
faith, founded on Christ Jesus, will overcome all opposition. The gates of hell will not prevail against it

(Mt 16.18). The vision goes on to foresee the day
when wars will cease and weapons will be beaten into
plowshares and pruning hooks. This will occur when
the Son of Man returns in glory and great power.
2.4 *beat their swords into plowshares, and their spears
into pruning hooks*, i.e., will convert their weapons of
war into implements of peace and constructive labor.

their land is filled with horses,
  and there is no end to their chariots.

8 Their land is filled with idols;
  they bow down to the work of their hands,
    to what their own fingers have made.

9 And so people are humbled,
  and everyone is brought low —
    do not forgive them!

10 Enter into the rock,
  and hide in the dust
from the terror of the LORD,
  and from the glory of his majesty.

11 The haughty eyes of people shall be brought low,
  and the pride of everyone shall be humbled;
and the LORD alone will be exalted on that day.

b. Human pride to be humbled in judgment

12 For the LORD of hosts has a day
  against all that is proud and lofty,
    against all that is lifted up and high;*e*

13 against all the cedars of Lebanon,
  lofty and lifted up;
    and against all the oaks of Bashan;

14 against all the high mountains,
  and against all the lofty hills;

15 against every high tower,
  and against every fortified wall;

16 against all the ships of Tarshish,
  and against all the beautiful craft.*f*

17 The haughtiness of people shall be humbled,
  and the pride of everyone shall be brought low;
and the LORD alone will be exalted on that day.

18 The idols shall utterly pass away.

19 Enter the caves of the rocks
  and the holes of the ground,
from the terror of the LORD,
  and from the glory of his majesty,
    when he rises to terrify the earth.

20 On that day people will throw away
  to the moles and to the bats
their idols of silver and their idols of gold,
  which they made for themselves to worship,

21 to enter the caverns of the rocks
  and the clefts in the crags,
from the terror of the LORD,
  and from the glory of his majesty,
    when he rises to terrify the earth.

22 Turn away from mortals,
  who have only breath in their nostrils,
    for of what account are they?

2.8	Isa 10.11; 17.8
2.9	Isa 5.15; Neh 4.5
2.10	Rev 6.15; 2 Thess 1.9
2.11	Isa 13.11; Zech 9.16
2.12	Isa 24.4, 21
2.13	Isa 10.33, 34; Zech 11.2
2.14	Isa 30.25
2.16	1 Kings 10.22
2.17	v. 11
2.18	Isa 21.9
2.19	Hos 10.8; Rev 9.6; 2 Thess 1.9; Heb 12.26
2.20	Isa 30.22
2.21	vv. 10, 19
2.22	Ps 146.3; Job 27.3; Jas 4.14

---

e Cn Compare Gk: Heb *low*   *f* Compare Gk: Meaning of Heb uncertain

---

2.10   The terror, glory, and majesty of God was such that Judeans would "enter into the rock," i.e., go into "the caves of the rocks" (v. 19) where they hoped they would not be found. They would hide in "the holes of the ground" (v. 19) where they hoped they might escape the avenging wrath of God.

2.12   *the LORD of hosts has a day.* The divine patience had been exhausted; judgment and wrath were replacing love and mercy.
2.18   Isaiah suggests that if the idols could not protect themselves against the vengeance of God, how could they deliver those who worshiped them?

c. All classes to be punished for their guilt

3 For now the Sovereign, the LORD of hosts,
 is taking away from Jerusalem and from Judah
support and staff—
 all support of bread,
 and all support of water—

3.1
Jer 37.21;
Lev 26.26

2 warrior and soldier,
 judge and prophet,
 diviner and elder,

3.2
2 Kings 24.14

3 captain of fifty
 and dignitary,
counselor and skillful magician
 and expert enchanter.

4 And I will make boys their princes,
 and babes shall rule over them.

3.4
Eccl 10.16

5 The people will be oppressed,
 everyone by another
 and everyone by a neighbor;
the youth will be insolent to the elder,
 and the base to the honorable.

3.5
Mic 7.3-6;
Isa 9.19

6 Someone will even seize a relative,
 a member of the clan, saying,
"You have a cloak;
 you shall be our leader,
and this heap of ruins
 shall be under your rule."

3.6
Isa 4.1

7 But the other will cry out on that day, saying,
"I will not be a healer;
 in my house there is neither bread nor cloak;
you shall not make me
 leader of the people."

3.7
Ezek 34.4

8 For Jerusalem has stumbled
 and Judah has fallen,
because their speech and their deeds are against the LORD,
 defying his glorious presence.

3.8
Isa 1.7; 6.11;
9.17; 65.3, 5

9 The look on their faces bears witness against them;
 they proclaim their sin like Sodom,
 they do not hide it.
Woe to them!
 For they have brought evil on themselves.

3.9
Isa 1.10;
Gen 13.13

10 Tell the innocent how fortunate they are,
 for they shall eat the fruit of their labors.

3.10
Deut 28.1-14

11 Woe to the guilty! How unfortunate they are,
 for what their hands have done shall be done to them.

3.11
Isa 65.6, 7

12 My people—children are their oppressors,
 and women rule over them.
O my people, your leaders mislead you,
 and confuse the course of your paths.

3.12
v. 4;
Isa 9.16

13 The LORD rises to argue his case;

3.13
Isa 66.16;
Mic 6.2

3.4 This is a prediction that Judah's future rulers would be youthful and inexperienced, adding to the national problems.
3.5 Basically, the nation of Judah was anarchical and had lost its moral fiber.
3.9 Like the unveiled face of a prostitute, the faces of the wicked Judeans manifested their sins. But they did not blush. Instead, they gloried in their shameless lack of virtue and refused to cease from their sins.
3.10 Those who did not share the common iniquity would not share the common calamity.

14 The LORD enters into judgment
        with the elders and princes of his people:
    It is you who have devoured the vineyard;
        the spoil of the poor is in your houses.

15 What do you mean by crushing my people,
        by grinding the face of the poor? says the Lord GOD of hosts.

16 The LORD said:
    Because the daughters of Zion are haughty
        and walk with outstretched necks,
        glancing wantonly with their eyes,
    mincing along as they go,
        tinkling with their feet;

17 the Lord will afflict with scabs
        the heads of the daughters of Zion,
        and the LORD will lay bare their secret parts.

18 In that day the Lord will take away the finery of the anklets, the headbands, and the crescents; 19 the pendants, the bracelets, and the scarfs; 20 the headdresses, the armlets, the sashes, the perfume boxes, and the amulets; 21 the signet rings and nose rings; 22 the festal robes, the mantles, the cloaks, and the handbags; 23 the garments of gauze, the linen garments, the turbans, and the veils.

24 Instead of perfume there will be a stench;
        and instead of a sash, a rope;
    and instead of well-set hair, baldness;
        and instead of a rich robe, a binding of sackcloth;
        instead of beauty, shame.[g]

25 Your men shall fall by the sword
        and your warriors in battle.

26 And her gates shall lament and mourn;
        ravaged, she shall sit upon the ground.

4 Seven women shall take hold of one man in that day, saying,
    "We will eat our own bread and wear our own clothes;
    just let us be called by your name;
        take away our disgrace."

d. Blessedness of revived Israel under Messiah

2 On that day the branch of the LORD shall be beautiful and glorious, and the fruit of the land shall be the pride and glory of the survivors of Israel. 3 Whoever is left in Zion and remains in Jerusalem will be called holy, everyone who has been recorded for life in Jerusalem, 4 once the Lord has washed away the filth of the daughters of Zion and cleansed the bloodstains of Jerusalem from its midst by a spirit of judgment and by a spirit of burning. 5 Then the LORD will create over the whole site of Mount Zion and over its places of assembly a cloud by day and smoke and the

g Q Ms: MT lacks shame

Cross references (right column):

3.14 Ezek 20.35, 36; Isa 10.1, 2; Jas 2.6
3.15 Ps 94.5
3.16 Isa 4.4
3.17 Isa 47.3
3.18 Judg 8.21
3.20 Ex 39.28
3.21 Ezek 16.12
3.24 Prov 31.24; Isa 22.12; 15.3
3.25 Isa 1.20; 65.12
3.26 Jer 14.2; Lam 2.10
4.1 Isa 13.12; 2 Thess 3.12; Isa 54.4
4.2 Isa 11.1; Zech 3.8; 6.12; Ps 72.16; Isa 10.20
4.3 Isa 28.5; 60.21; 52.1; Lk 10.20
4.4 Isa 3.16, 24; 1.15; 28.6; Mal 3.2, 3
4.5 Ex 13.21; Isa 60.1, 2

3.15 It was bad enough for some people to be poor. But they were made even poorer by oppression. Their land was seized, their persons were abused, and their faces were crushed and bleeding from their wounds.
3.16 The men of Judah were not alone in their wickedness. They were joined by the women who were haughty and wanton, lacking what Paul later enjoins in 1 Tim 2.9, that "women should dress themselves modestly . . . , not with their hair braided, or with gold, pearls, or expensive clothes."
3.18–23 The excess of finery and ornaments described in these verses would perish with the user.

The hearts of these women centered more on these outward adornments than on the worship and love of God. Whatever usurps our love to God is an idol.
4.1 The day would come when males would be few in number because of war, and women would beg for protectors for themselves.
4.2ff In the O.T., Christ is sometimes called the branch, a term referring to the Messianic king who would come from David's line. The Hebrew word tsemach means "sprout." In Jer 23.5 and 33.15 it is called a righteous Branch, and it is the personal name for the Messiah in Zech 3.8 and 6.12.

shining of a flaming fire by night. Indeed over all the glory there will be a canopy. 6 It will serve as a pavilion, a shade by day from the heat, and a refuge and a shelter from the storm and rain.

4.6
Isa 25.4

C. *Judah to be exiled for unfaithfulness*

1. *The parable of the vineyard*

5.1
Ps 80.8;
Mt 21.33;
Mk 12.1;
Lk 20.9

5 Let me sing for my beloved
   my love-song concerning his vineyard:
My beloved had a vineyard
   on a very fertile hill.

5.2
Jer 2.21;
Mt 21.19;
Mk 11.13;
Lk 13.6

2 He dug it and cleared it of stones,
   and planted it with choice vines;
he built a watchtower in the midst of it,
   and hewed out a wine vat in it;
he expected it to yield grapes,
   but it yielded wild grapes.

5.3
Mt 21.40

3 And now, inhabitants of Jerusalem
   and people of Judah,
judge between me
   and my vineyard.

5.4
Mt 23.37

4 What more was there to do for my vineyard
   that I have not done in it?
When I expected it to yield grapes,
   why did it yield wild grapes?

5.5
Ps 89.40;
Isa 6.13;
Ps 80.12;
Isa 10.6;
Lk 21.24;
Rev 11.2

5 And now I will tell you
   what I will do to my vineyard.
I will remove its hedge,
   and it shall be devoured;
I will break down its wall,
   and it shall be trampled down.

5.6
Isa 24.1, 3;
Heb 6.8;
1 Kings 8.35

6 I will make it a waste;
   it shall not be pruned or hoed,
   and it shall be overgrown with briers and thorns;
I will also command the clouds
   that they rain no rain upon it.

5.7
Ps 80.8-11;
Isa 3.14, 15

7 For the vineyard of the LORD of hosts
   is the house of Israel,
and the people of Judah
   are his pleasant planting;
he expected justice,
   but saw bloodshed;
righteousness,
   but heard a cry!

2. *Judah guilty of seven sins*

a. *Selfish greed*

5.8
Mic 2.2

8 Ah, you who join house to house,

4.6 When Messiah had come and Israel was right with the Lord, he would be a shade for them against the heat of the day and a refuge from storms and rain. God is the refuge for his people in all seasons.
5.1–7 Isaiah compares Judah to a vineyard (v. 7). God had tenderly cared for his vineyard and erected protecting fences around it, but to no avail. It had produced wild grapes — a reference to Judah's lack of gratitude and persistent disobedience. Thus judgment would come; the fences would be destroyed and the grape arbors trampled down by cattle and sheep. Jesus picks up the imagery of this passage in his parable of the wicked tenants (Mk 12.1–12).
5.8–10 Judah's greed would be repaid by God, for

who add field to field,
until there is room for no one but you,
  and you are left to live alone
    in the midst of the land!

9   The LORD of hosts has sworn in my hearing:
Surely many houses shall be desolate,
  large and beautiful houses, without inhabitant.

| | 5.9 |
| Isa 22.14; |
| 6.11, 12 |

10   For ten acres of vineyard shall yield but one bath,
  and a homer of seed shall yield a mere ephah. *h*

| 5.10 |
| Isa 7.23; |
| Ezek 45.11 |

b. *Self-indulgence*

11   Ah, you who rise early in the morning
    in pursuit of strong drink,
  who linger in the evening
    to be inflamed by wine,

| 5.11 |
| Prov 23.29, |
| 30; |
| Eccl 10.16 |

12   whose feasts consist of lyre and harp,
    tambourine and flute and wine,
  but who do not regard the deeds of the LORD,
    or see the work of his hands!

| 5.12 |
| Am 6.5, 6; |
| Job 34.27; |
| Ps 28.5 |

13   Therefore my people go into exile without knowledge;
  their nobles are dying of hunger,
    and their multitude is parched with thirst.

| 5.13 |
| Hos 4.6; |
| Isa 1.3; 3.3; |
| 9.14, 15 |

14   Therefore Sheol has enlarged its appetite
    and opened its mouth beyond measure;
  the nobility of Jerusalem*i* and her multitude go down,
    her throng and all who exult in her.

| 5.14 |
| Prov 30.16; |
| Num 16.30-34; |
| Ps 141.7 |

15   People are bowed down, everyone is brought low,
    and the eyes of the haughty are humbled.

| 5.15 |
| Isa 2.9, 11 |

16   But the LORD of hosts is exalted by justice,
    and the Holy God shows himself holy by righteousness.

| 5.16 |
| Isa 2.11, 17; |
| 8.13; 29.23 |

17   Then the lambs shall graze as in their pasture,
    fatlings and kids*j* shall feed among the ruins.

c. *Cynical materialism*

18   Ah, you who drag iniquity along with cords of falsehood,
  who drag sin along as with cart ropes,

| 5.18 |
| Isa 59.4-8 |

19   who say, "Let him make haste,
    let him speed his work
      that we may see it;
  let the plan of the Holy One of Israel hasten to fulfillment,
    that we may know it!"

| 5.19 |
| Ezek 12.22; |
| 2 Pet 3.3, 4 |

d. *Perversion of the standards of morality*

20   Ah, you who call evil good
    and good evil,
  who put darkness for light
    and light for darkness,
  who put bitter for sweet
    and sweet for bitter!

| 5.20 |
| Prov 17.15; |
| Mt 6.22, 23; |
| Lk 11.34, 35 |

h The Heb *bath*, *homer*, and *ephah* are measures of quantity   *i* Heb *her nobility*   *j* Cn Compare Gk: Heb *aliens*

its houses would go untenanted and its fields would yield little grain. The God of the whole earth would exercise retributive justice against a wicked people. **5.11** Generally people wait until the end of a day's work before they turn to alcohol and get drunk. The Judeans, however, had made drinking their major business and started to imbibe from early morning. **5.14** Sheol is personified and described as a monster licking its chops with the expectancy of devouring the inhabitants of Jerusalem.

e. Intellectual pride and self-sufficiency

5.21
Rom 12.16

21 Ah, you who are wise in your own eyes,
and shrewd in your own sight!

f. Intemperance

5.22
v. 11

22 Ah, you who are heroes in drinking wine
and valiant at mixing drink,

g. Loss of integrity

5.23
Isa 10.1, 2;
Ps 94.21

23 who acquit the guilty for a bribe,
and deprive the innocent of their rights!

3. God's judgment against Judah

5.24
Isa 9.18, 19;
Job 18.16;
Hos 5.12;
Acts 13.41

24 Therefore, as the tongue of fire devours the stubble,
and as dry grass sinks down in the flame,
so their root will become rotten,
and their blossom go up like dust;
for they have rejected the instruction of the LORD of hosts,
and have despised the word of the Holy One of Israel.

5.25
2 Kings 22.13;
Jer 4.24;
Isa 14.19;
9.12, 17, 21;
23.11

25 Therefore the anger of the LORD was kindled against his
people,
and he stretched out his hand against them and struck them;
the mountains quaked,
and their corpses were like refuse
in the streets.
For all this his anger has not turned away,
and his hand is stretched out still.

5.26
Isa 13.2, 3;
7.18;
Deut 28.49;
Isa 13.4, 5
5.27
Joel 2.7, 8;
Dan 5.6

26 He will raise a signal for a nation far away,
and whistle for a people at the ends of the earth;
Here they come, swiftly, speedily!
27 None of them is weary, none stumbles,
none slumbers or sleeps,
not a loincloth is loose,
not a sandal-thong broken;

5.28
Ps 7.12, 13;
Jer 4.13

28 their arrows are sharp,
all their bows bent,
their horses' hoofs seem like flint,
and their wheels like the whirlwind.

5.29
Jer 51.38;
Isa 10.6;
42.22

29 Their roaring is like a lion,
like young lions they roar;
they growl and seize their prey,
they carry it off, and no one can rescue.

5.30
Isa 17.12;
8.22

30 They will roar over it on that day,
like the roaring of the sea.
And if one look to the land —
only darkness and distress;
and the light grows dark with clouds.

5.24 The ruin of Judah and Jerusalem would be
just, for they had refused to submit themselves to God
and his law. They had despised and disregarded the
word of the Holy One of Israel.
5.26 God would *raise a signal* to strong pagan nations to punish his people. This was probably a reference to Assyria.

5.28–30 The nations God would use to bring judgment against Judah and Jerusalem had their weapons
ready. Their horses' hooves and the chariots' wheels
were like the whirlwind. They were like roaring lions,
eager to consume their prey. Light would give way to
darkness and distress.

D. *Isaiah cleansed and commissioned*

1. *God's holiness revealed*

6 In the year that King Uzziah died, I saw the Lord sitting on a throne, high and lofty; and the hem of his robe filled the temple. 2 Seraphs were in attendance above him; each had six wings: with two they covered their faces, and with two they covered their feet, and with two they flew. 3 And one called to another and said:

"Holy, holy, holy is the LORD of hosts;
the whole earth is full of his glory."

2. *Isaiah's repentance*

4 The pivots[k] on the thresholds shook at the voices of those who called, and the house filled with smoke. 5 And I said: "Woe is me! I am lost, for I am a man of unclean lips, and I live among a people of unclean lips; yet my eyes have seen the King, the LORD of hosts!"

3. *His cleansing and commission to preach*

6 Then one of the seraphs flew to me, holding a live coal that had been taken from the altar with a pair of tongs. 7 The seraph[l] touched my mouth with it and said: "Now that this has touched your lips, your guilt has departed and your sin is blotted out." 8 Then I heard the voice of the Lord saying, "Whom shall I send, and who will go for us?" And I said, "Here am I; send me!" 9 And he said, "Go and say to this people:

'Keep listening, but do not comprehend;
keep looking, but do not understand.'

10 Make the mind of this people dull,
    and stop their ears,
    and shut their eyes,
so that they may not look with their eyes,
    and listen with their ears,
and comprehend with their minds,
    and turn and be healed."

11 Then I said, "How long, O Lord?" And he said:
"Until cities lie waste
    without inhabitant,
and houses without people,
    and the land is utterly desolate;

12 until the LORD sends everyone far away,
    and vast is the emptiness in the midst of the land.

13 Even if a tenth part remain in it,

---

k Meaning of Heb uncertain   l Heb *He*

6.1
Isa 1.1;
2 Kings 15.7;
1 Kings 22.9
6.2
Rev 4.8;
Ezek 1.11
6.3
Rev 4.8;
Ps 72.19

6.5
Ex 33.20;
Jer 9.3-8;
51.57

6.7
Jer 1.9;
Isa 40.2;
1 Jn 1.7
6.8
Ezek 10.5;
Acts 9.4;
26.19
6.9
Ezek 3.11;
Mt 13.14,
15;
Mk 4.12;
Lk 8.10;
Jn 12.40;
Rom 11.8
6.10
Ps 119.70;
Jer 5.21

6.11
Mic 3.12

6.12
Jer 4.29
6.13
Isa 1.9;
Job 14.7;
Ezra 9.2

6.1 Isaiah here recalled the awful death of King Uzziah from leprosy, contracted when he violated the law of God by offering burnt incense in the temple (2 Chr 26.16ff). Israel's king died but Israel's God lives forever.
6.2 *Seraphs*. In the Hebrew this term means something which is burning and dazzling (see also 6.6). Isaiah applies it to angelic beings. It is used nowhere else in the Scriptures, and the Bible gives no explanation of the term. The Jews thought them to be a higher order of celestial beings, since Isaiah pictures them as worshiping and glorifying God. They acted as agents and spokespersons for God and may possibly be related to the cherubim.
6.5 Isaiah's vision of the glory of God brought terror to his heart. He was painfully aware of his own lostness and uncleanness when measured against the holiness and purity of God.

6.7 The terror of Isaiah was replaced by a sense of comfort and consolation when the angel assured him that his guilt was gone, his sins forgiven, and his standing with God made right. Renewing grace is God's response to the penitent heart.
6.8 The question, *who will go for us?*, was not addressed to Isaiah alone. It is addressed to God's people in all ages. But Isaiah had listening ears and he promptly responded; he was willing to go. The words "for us" suggest a council among the Godhead, who is triune, consisting of the Father, the Son, and the Holy Spirit.
6.10 Apparently God's patience with the people's chronic rebellion was finally exhausted.
6.13 God is frequently revealed as the God of the remnant. Here a few righteous people, left after the fall of judgment, would be the stump from which God would raise up a new nation.

it will be burned again,
like a terebinth or an oak
whose stump remains standing
when it is felled."*m*
The holy seed is its stump.

II. *Volume of Immanuel (7.1–12.6)*

A. *Immanuel rejected by the wisdom of this world*

1. *The northern coalition*

7 In the days of Ahaz son of Jotham son of Uzziah, king of Judah, King Rezin of Aram and King Pekah son of Remaliah of Israel went up to attack Jerusalem, but could not mount an attack against it. 2 When the house of David heard that Aram had allied itself with Ephraim, the heart of Ahaz*n* and the heart of his people shook as the trees of the forest shake before the wind.

2. *God's answer on behalf of his people*

3 Then the LORD said to Isaiah, Go out to meet Ahaz, you and your son Shear-jashub,*o* at the end of the conduit of the upper pool on the highway to the Fuller's Field, 4 and say to him, Take heed, be quiet, do not fear, and do not let your heart be faint because of these two smoldering stumps of firebrands, because of the fierce anger of Rezin and Aram and the son of Remaliah. 5 Because Aram—with Ephraim and the son of Remaliah—has plotted evil against you, saying, 6 Let us go up against Judah and cut off Jerusalem*p* and conquer it for ourselves and make the son of Tabeel king in it; 7 therefore thus says the Lord GOD:
It shall not stand,
and it shall not come to pass.
8 For the head of Aram is Damascus,
and the head of Damascus is Rezin.
(Within sixty-five years Ephraim will be shattered, no longer a people.)
9 The head of Ephraim is Samaria,
and the head of Samaria is the son of Remaliah.
If you do not stand firm in faith,
you shall not stand at all.

3. *The sign of Immanuel and the child who will typify him*

10 Again the LORD spoke to Ahaz, saying, 11 Ask a sign of the LORD your God; let it be deep as Sheol or high as heaven. 12 But Ahaz said, I will not ask, and I will not put the LORD to the test. 13 Then Isaiah*q* said: "Hear then, O house of David! Is it too little for you to weary mortals, that you weary my God also? 14 Therefore the Lord himself will give you

m Meaning of Heb uncertain   *n* Heb *his heart*   *o* That is *A remnant shall return*   *p* Heb *cut it off*   *q* Heb *he*

7.3 *Ahaz* would be found at the conduit, where he had gone to check the water supply. Israel and Syria had formed an alliance against Judah, and in the event of war and especially a siege, Jerusalem would need adequate water supplies.
7.6 Since Ahaz had refused to join the alliance of Israel (Ephraim) and Syria against Assyria, the two kings Pekah and Rezin decided to depose Ahaz and place their own puppet on his throne.
7.8 *Ephraim will be shattered.* Samaria, the capital of Israel, fell to the Assyrian armies in 722 B.C., in accord with this oracle. This ended the northern kingdom.

7.11 *let it be deep as Sheol or high as heaven.* Isaiah challenged Ahaz to ask for any sign he wanted, in heaven or on earth.
7.14 *the virgin is with child* (see NRSV footnote). Two Hebrew words are involved. One is *bethulah* and the other *almah*. The former means "virgin," and the latter "an unmarried female." *Almah* is used here. Its use in this context covers two cases, one in Isaiah's day and the other prophetic of Jesus (Mt 1.22–23). The wife of Isaiah was a virgin until she married and gave birth to a son (8.1–4). The virgin Mary was a virgin before the conception of Jesus, and she remained a virgin during the pregnancy, because Jo-

a sign. Look, the young woman[r] is with child and shall bear a son, and shall name him Immanuel.[s] 15 He shall eat curds and honey by the time he knows how to refuse the evil and choose the good. 16 For before the child knows how to refuse the evil and choose the good, the land before whose two kings you are in dread will be deserted. 17 The LORD will bring on you and on your people and on your ancestral house such days as have not come since the day that Ephraim departed from Judah — the king of Assyria."

18 On that day the LORD will whistle for the fly that is at the sources of the streams of Egypt, and for the bee that is in the land of Assyria. 19 And they will all come and settle in the steep ravines, and in the clefts of the rocks, and on all the thornbushes, and on all the pastures.

20 On that day the Lord will shave with a razor hired beyond the River — with the king of Assyria — the head and the hair of the feet, and it will take off the beard as well.

21 On that day one will keep alive a young cow and two sheep, 22 and will eat curds because of the abundance of milk that they give; for everyone that is left in the land shall eat curds and honey.

23 On that day every place where there used to be a thousand vines, worth a thousand shekels of silver, will become briers and thorns. 24 With bow and arrows one will go there, for all the land will be briers and thorns; 25 and as for all the hills that used to be hoed with a hoe, you will not go there for fear of briers and thorns; but they will become a place where cattle are let loose and where sheep tread.

B. *The coming war and the future deliverer*

1. *Sign of Maher-shalal-hash-baz*

8 Then the LORD said to me, Take a large tablet and write on it in common characters, "Belonging to Maher-shalal-hash-baz,"[t] 2 and have it attested[u] for me by reliable witnesses, the priest Uriah and Zechariah son of Jeberechiah. 3 And I went to the prophetess, and she conceived and bore a son. Then the LORD said to me, Name him Maher-shalal-hash-baz; 4 for before the child knows how to call "My father" or "My mother," the wealth of Damascus and the spoil of Samaria will be carried away by the king of Assyria.

2. *The river overflowing its banks*

5 The LORD spoke to me again: 6 Because this people has refused the waters of Shiloah that flow gently, and melt in fear before[v] Rezin and the son of Remaliah; 7 therefore, the Lord is bringing up against it the mighty

r Gk *the virgin*   s That is *God is with us*   t That is *The spoil speeds, the prey hastens*   u Q Ms Gk Syr:
MT *and I caused to be attested*   v Cn: Meaning of Heb uncertain

7.15
v. 22
7.16
Isa 8.4
7.17
2 Chr 28.19;
1 Kings 12.16

7.18
Isa 5.26
7.19
Isa 2.19;
Jer 16.16
7.20
Isa 24.1;
Ezek 5.1-4;
Isa 10.5, 15;
8.7

7.23
Isa 5.6

7.25
Isa 5.17

8.1
Isa 30.8;
Hab 2.2
8.2
2 Kings 16.10

8.4
Isa 7.16; 7.8,
9

8.6
Neh 3.15;
Jn 9.7;
Isa 7.1, 2, 6
8.7
Isa 17.12,
13; 7.20;
10.5, 6

...seph was not the father of Jesus; the Holy Spirit was. Stated another way, Isaiah's wife was no longer a virgin when she conceived; Mary was still a virgin *after* she conceived, for she had not yet known a male. Thus, *almah* is more appropriate than *bethulah*. Interestingly, the Septuagint translates *almah* by the use of the Greek word *parthenos* which means "virgin." And Matthew uses *parthenos* for Mary's case. In other words, the Holy Spirit carefully chose the word *almah* to cover both births involved in this prophecy: Maher-shalal-hash-baz, the son of Isaiah, had a human mother and father and his birth was a natural one; Jesus, on the other hand, had a human mother but not a human father. His birth was supernatural.
7.21ff Judah is pictured as being desolate and poverty-stricken. Its population would be greatly reduced, meat would be scarce, and curds and honey would be its food.

8.3 God had given Ahaz a sign with a double fulfillment; the first one is stated here. The prophetess, who probably was a virgin at the time 7.14 was spoken, gave birth to a son in a normal marriage relationship. His name is Maher-shalal-hash-baz (meaning "the spoil speeds, the prey hastens," NRSV footnote). Some hold that this boy represents the messianic Immanuel, who was to be fathered by the Holy Spirit and born of the virgin Mary (see note on 7.14).
8.6 *the waters of Shiloah that flow gently.* The waters of Shiloah are known as Ain Silwan and are located southwest of Mount Moriah. Here Shiloah's quiet waters are contrasted with the turbulent waters of Euphrates' mighty flood (implied in 8.7). Because God's people had rejected Shiloah (a symbol of God's rule), they would be overwhelmed by the mighty king of Assyria, who would come from beyond the Euphrates.

flood waters of the River, the king of Assyria and all his glory; it will rise above all its channels and overflow all its banks; 8it will sweep on into Judah as a flood, and, pouring over, it will reach up to the neck; and its outspread wings will fill the breadth of your land, O Immanuel.

3. The stone of stumbling

9 Band together, you peoples, and be dismayed;
    listen, all you far countries;
  gird yourselves and be dismayed;
    gird yourselves and be dismayed!
10 Take counsel together, but it shall be brought to naught;
  speak a word, but it will not stand,
    for God is with us. *w*

11 For the LORD spoke thus to me while his hand was strong upon me, and warned me not to walk in the way of this people, saying: 12Do not call conspiracy all that this people calls conspiracy, and do not fear what it fears, or be in dread. 13But the LORD of hosts, him you shall regard as holy; let him be your fear, and let him be your dread. 14He will become a sanctuary, a stone one strikes against; for both houses of Israel he will become a rock one stumbles over — a trap and a snare for the inhabitants of Jerusalem. 15And many among them shall stumble; they shall fall and be broken; they shall be snared and taken.

4. Command to trust the LORD

16 Bind up the testimony, seal the teaching among my disciples. 17I will wait for the LORD, who is hiding his face from the house of Jacob, and I will hope in him. 18See, I and the children whom the LORD has given me are signs and portents in Israel from the LORD of hosts, who dwells on Mount Zion. 19Now if people say to you, "Consult the ghosts and the familiar spirits that chirp and mutter; should not a people consult their gods, the dead on behalf of the living, 20for teaching and for instruction?" surely, those who speak like this will have no dawn! 21They will pass through the land, *x* greatly distressed and hungry; when they are hungry, they will be enraged and will curse*y* their king and their gods. They will turn their faces upward, 22or they will look to the earth, but will see only distress and darkness, the gloom of anguish; and they will be thrust into thick darkness. *z*

5. The birth of the Messianic king

9*a* But there will be no gloom for those who were in anguish. In the former time he brought into contempt the land of Zebulun and the land of Naphtali, but in the latter time he will make glorious the way of the sea, the land beyond the Jordan, Galilee of the nations.
  2*b* The people who walked in darkness
    have seen a great light;
  those who lived in a land of deep darkness —
    on them light has shined.

w Heb *immanu el* *x* Heb *it* *y* Or *curse by* *z* Meaning of Heb uncertain *a* Ch 8.23 in Heb *b* Ch 9.1 in Heb

Cross references (left margin):

8.8
Isa 10.6;
30.28; 7.14

8.10
Job 5.12;
Isa 7.7;
Rom 8.31

8.11
Ezek 3.14;
2.8
8.12
Isa 7.2;
1 Pet 3.14, 15
8.13
Isa 5.16;
29.23;
Num 20.12
8.14
Ezek 11.16;
Lk 2.34;
Rom 9.33;
1 Pet 2.8
8.15
Isa 28.13;
Mt 21.44;
Lk 20.18;
Rom 9.32
8.16
vv. 1, 2;
Dan 12.4
8.17
Isa 54.8;
Hab 2.3
8.18
Heb 2.13;
Ps 71.7;
Zech 3.8
8.19
1 Sam 28.8;
Isa 19.3;
30.2; 45.11
8.20
Lk 16.29;
Mic 3.6
8.21
Isa 9.20, 21;
Rev 16.11
8.22
Isa 5.30; 9.1
9.1
2 Kings 15.29;
2 Chr 16.4

9.2
Mt 4.15, 16

8.13,14 *let him be your fear.* The fear of the Lord cancels out all fear of mortals. His greatness eclipses all the pomp and pretense of the enemy. He becomes a sanctuary for those who trust in him.
8.16 *Bind up the testimony.* God graciously entrusted his revelation to the Jews, who had to preserve it safely for the comfort of God's faithful people as they went through the approaching times of trouble and distress.

9.1 In 2 Kings 15.29, Tiglath-pileser took Ephraim, Zebulun, and Naphtali from Israel. Isaiah looked to that day when God would revisit Israel and restore her. Three promises are made here: of a great and glorious light (v. 2), of economic plenty and universal joy (v. 3), and of glorious enlargement and freedom from the enemy (vv. 4,5). See also note on 17.12ff.

3　You have multiplied the nation,
　　　you have increased its joy;
　they rejoice before you
　　　as with joy at the harvest,
　　　as people exult when dividing plunder.

4　For the yoke of their burden,
　　　and the bar across their shoulders,
　　　the rod of their oppressor,
　　　you have broken as on the day of Midian.

5　For all the boots of the tramping warriors
　　　and all the garments rolled in blood
　　　shall be burned as fuel for the fire.

6　For a child has been born for us,
　　　a son given to us;
　authority rests upon his shoulders;
　　　and he is named
　Wonderful Counselor, Mighty God,
　　　Everlasting Father, Prince of Peace.

7　His authority shall grow continually,
　　　and there shall be endless peace
　for the throne of David and his kingdom.
　　　He will establish and uphold it
　with justice and with righteousness
　　　from this time onward and forevermore.
　The zeal of the LORD of hosts will do this.

C. The doom of boastful Samaria

1. Samaria's pride

8　The Lord sent a word against Jacob,
　　　and it fell on Israel;

9　and all the people knew it —
　　　Ephraim and the inhabitants of Samaria —
　　　but in pride and arrogance of heart they said:

10　"The bricks have fallen,
　　　but we will build with dressed stones;
　the sycamores have been cut down,
　　　but we will put cedars in their place."

11　So the LORD raised adversaries[c] against them,
　　　and stirred up their enemies,

12　the Arameans on the east and the Philistines on the west,
　　　and they devoured Israel with open mouth.
　For all this his anger has not turned away;
　　　his hand is stretched out still.

---

c Cn: Heb *the adversaries of Rezin*

9.3
Isa 26.15;
35.10;
1 Sam 30.16

9.4
Isa 10.27;
14.4; 10.26

9.5
Isa 2.4

9.6
Isa 7.14;
Lk 2.11;
Jn 3.16;
Mt 28.18;
1 Cor 15.25;
Isa 28.29;
10.21; 63.16;
Eph 2.14

9.7
Dan 2.44;
Lk 1.32, 33;
Isa 16.15;
11.4, 5;
37.32

9.9
Isa 7.8, 9;
46.12

9.11
Isa 7.1, 8

9.12
2 Kings 16.6;
2 Chr 28.18;
Ps 79.7;
Isa 5.25

9.6 *a child has been born for us.* This verse has been seen by some as a prophecy about the birth of Hezekiah. But it expresses hope for a future deliverance. The chapter began with a statement about what would happen in a more distant future (v. 1). Thus Isaiah prophesies about the birth of the Messiah King, which finds its fulfillment in Jesus Christ as the human-divine one. He is given the title *Everlasting Father* (literally, "Father of Eternity," in the sense that he made all things). Creation, of course, was the work of the Trinity: the Father, the Son, and the Holy Spirit. The title *Prince of Peace* signifies the one who brought spiritual peace to the sinful heart through regeneration. The Messiah is also called *Wonderful*

Counselor, which might also be translated "Supernatural Counselor." He came to bring us the words of everlasting life, and he will come again to rule in power and with wisdom at his second advent. He is the *Mighty God,* a title used in 10.21 for Yahweh. He has all power to do all things and to accomplish what God intended. All these names together clearly indicate the Messiah is God himself, the second person of the Trinity.

9.7 *The zeal of the LORD of hosts will do this.* The God who has all power in his hand and all people at his beck and call will preserve the throne of David until the Prince of Peace is seated on it. He will overcome all opposition.

2. Samaria's hypocrisy

13 The people did not turn to him who struck them,
    or seek the LORD of hosts.
14 So the LORD cut off from Israel head and tail,
    palm branch and reed in one day—
15 elders and dignitaries are the head,
    and prophets who teach lies are the tail;
16 for those who led this people led them astray,
    and those who were led by them were left in confusion.
17 That is why the Lord did not have pity on[d] their young
        people,
    or compassion on their orphans and widows;
for everyone was godless and an evildoer,
    and every mouth spoke folly.
For all this his anger has not turned away;
    his hand is stretched out still.

3. The self-destructiveness of sin

18 For wickedness burned like a fire,
    consuming briers and thorns;
it kindled the thickets of the forest,
    and they swirled upward in a column of smoke.
19 Through the wrath of the LORD of hosts
        the land was burned,
and the people became like fuel for the fire;
    no one spared another.
20 They gorged on the right, but still were hungry,
    and they devoured on the left, but were not satisfied;
they devoured the flesh of their own kindred;[e]
21 Manasseh devoured Ephraim, and Ephraim Manasseh,
    and together they were against Judah.
For all this his anger has not turned away;
    his hand is stretched out still.

4. The oppressors doomed to captivity

10 Ah, you who make iniquitous decrees,
    who write oppressive statutes,
2 to turn aside the needy from justice
    and to rob the poor of my people of their right,
that widows may be your spoil,
    and that you may make the orphans your prey!
3 What will you do on the day of punishment,
    in the calamity that will come from far away?
To whom will you flee for help,
    and where will you leave your wealth,
4 so as not to crouch among the prisoners
    or fall among the slain?
For all this his anger has not turned away;
    his hand is stretched out still.

d Q Ms: MT rejoice over   e Or arm

Cross-references: 9.13 Jer 5.3; Hos 7.10; Isa 31.1. 9.14 Isa 19.15; Rev 18.8. 9.15 Isa 3.2, 3; 28.15. 9.16 Isa 3.12. 9.17 Jer 18.21; Isa 27.11; 10.6; Mic 7.2; Isa 5.25. 9.18 Isa 10.17; Mal 4.1. 9.19 Isa 10.6; Joel 2.3; Isa 1.31; 24.6; Mic 7.2, 6. 9.20 Isa 8.21, 22; 49.26. 9.21 Isa 5.25. 10.1 Ps 94.20. 10.2 Isa 5.23; 1.23. 10.3 Job 31.14; Hos 9.7; Lk 19.44; Isa 5.26; 20.6. 10.4 Isa 24.22; 22.2; 5.25.

9.15 *are the tail.* The prophet who taught lies is here demoted to the lowest position. He was not the head but the tail. A dog can live without a tail but not without a head.
10.1 God's indictment against his people included the following charges: (1) they had legislated wicked laws and issued iniquitous decrees; (2) they had perverted justice; and (3) they had enriched themselves at the expense of the most unfortunate of the people—the poor, widows, and orphans. Therefore, God's anger was just and his judgment according to righteousness.

D. The false empire vanquished: a glorious empire to come

1. God's instrument of judgment shall in turn be judged

a. Assyria, the rod, to be destroyed

5 Ah, Assyria, the rod of my anger —
    the club in their hands is my fury!

6 Against a godless nation I send him,
    and against the people of my wrath I command him,
to take spoil and seize plunder,
    and to tread them down like the mire of the streets.

7 But this is not what he intends,
    nor does he have this in mind;
but it is in his heart to destroy,
    and to cut off nations not a few.

8 For he says:
    "Are not my commanders all kings?

9 Is not Calno like Carchemish?
    Is not Hamath like Arpad?
    Is not Samaria like Damascus?

10 As my hand has reached to the kingdoms of the idols
    whose images were greater than those of Jerusalem and
        Samaria,

11 shall I not do to Jerusalem and her idols
    what I have done to Samaria and her images?"

12 When the Lord has finished all his work on Mount Zion and on
Jerusalem, he*f* will punish the arrogant boasting of the king of Assyria
and his haughty pride. 13 For he says:
"By the strength of my hand I have done it,
    and by my wisdom, for I have understanding;
I have removed the boundaries of peoples,
    and have plundered their treasures;
like a bull I have brought down those who sat on thrones.

14 My hand has found, like a nest,
    the wealth of the peoples;
and as one gathers eggs that have been forsaken,
    so I have gathered all the earth;
and there was none that moved a wing,
    or opened its mouth, or chirped."

15 Shall the ax vaunt itself over the one who wields it,
    or the saw magnify itself against the one who handles it?
As if a rod should raise the one who lifts it up,
    or as if a staff should lift the one who is not wood!

16 Therefore the Sovereign, the LORD of hosts,
    will send wasting sickness among his stout warriors,
and under his glory a burning will be kindled,

f Heb I

10.5	Jer 51.20
10.6	Isa 9.17, 19; Jer 34.22; Isa 5.25, 29
10.7	Gen 50.20
10.8	2 Kings 18.24, 34; 19.10ff
10.9	Am 6.2; 2 Chr 35.20; 2 Kings 16.9
10.10	2 Kings 19.17, 18
10.12	2 Kings 19.31; Jer 50.18; Isa 37.23
10.13	Isa 37.24; Ezek 28.4; Dan 4.30
10.14	Job 31.25
10.15	Jer 51.20; Rom 9.20, 21; v. 5
10.16	Isa 17.4; Ps 106.15; v. 18

10.5 *Ah, Assyria, the rod of my anger.* God used this wicked nation to humble sinful Israel and Judah. Assyria, in turn, would be punished by a righteous God.

10.11 Proud Assyria boasted that it had conquered and overcome other nations: Calno, Carchemish, Hamath, Arpad, and Samaria. God now planned that Assyria would do to Judah and Jerusalem (and its idols) what it had done to other nations. But when Assyria had completed its work under the stern eye of God, it would be judged in turn by the God of Israel.

10.15 *the ax.* Sennacherib was the ax in the hand of God, accomplishing what God wanted done. But this profane babbler supposed that he had done it by his own might, little realizing that when God had finished using him to punish Israel, God would then destroy the destroyer. The wicked may become instruments in the hands of God and execute his righteous judgments, even when they are unaware of what they really are doing.

like the burning of fire.

10.17
Isa 30.33;
37.23; 27.4

17 The light of Israel will become a fire,
 and his Holy One a flame;
and it will burn and devour
 his thorns and briers in one day.

10.18
Jer 21.14

18 The glory of his forest and his fruitful land
 the Lord will destroy, both soul and body,
 and it will be as when an invalid wastes away.

10.19
Isa 21.17

19 The remnant of the trees of his forest will be so few
 that a child can write them down.

b. *A remnant of Israel to be saved*

10.20
2 Kings 16.7;
2 Chr 28.20;
Isa 17.7, 8
10.21
Isa 6.13; 9.6
10.22
Rom 9.27,
28;
Isa 28.22
10.23
Dan 9.27
10.24
Ps 87.5, 6;
Isa 37.6;
Ex 5.14-16
10.25
Isa 17.14;
v. 5
10.26
Isa 37.36-38;
Judg 7.25;
Ex 14.16, 27
10.27
Isa 9.4;
30.23

20 On that day the remnant of Israel and the survivors of the house of Jacob will no more lean on the one who struck them, but will lean on the Lord, the Holy One of Israel, in truth. 21 A remnant will return, the remnant of Jacob, to the mighty God. 22 For though your people Israel were like the sand of the sea, only a remnant of them will return. Destruction is decreed, overflowing with righteousness. 23 For the Lord God of hosts will make a full end, as decreed, in all the earth.*g*

24 Therefore thus says the Lord God of hosts: O my people, who live in Zion, do not be afraid of the Assyrians when they beat you with a rod and lift up their staff against you as the Egyptians did. 25 For in a very little while my indignation will come to an end, and my anger will be directed to their destruction. 26 The Lord of hosts will wield a whip against them, as when he struck Midian at the rock of Oreb; his staff will be over the sea, and he will lift it as he did in Egypt. 27 On that day his burden will be removed from your shoulder, and his yoke will be destroyed from your neck.

He has gone up from Rimmon,*h*

10.28
1 Sam 14.2;
13.2, 5;
17.22

28 he has come to Aiath;
he has passed through Migron,
 at Michmash he stores his baggage;

10.29
Josh 21.17;
18.25;
1 Sam 10.26

29 they have crossed over the pass,
 at Geba they lodge for the night;
Ramah trembles,
 Gibeah of Saul has fled.

10.30
1 Sam 25.44;
Josh 21.18

30 Cry aloud, O daughter Gallim!
 Listen, O Laishah!
 Answer her, O Anathoth!

10.31
Josh 15.31

31 Madmenah is in flight,
 the inhabitants of Gebim flee for safety.

10.32
1 Sam 21.1;
Neh 11.32;
Isa 13.2;
37.22

32 This very day he will halt at Nob,
 he will shake his fist
 at the mount of daughter Zion,
 the hill of Jerusalem.

10.33
Am 2.9

33 Look, the Sovereign, the Lord of hosts,
 will lop the boughs with terrifying power;
the tallest trees will be cut down,
 and the lofty will be brought low.

g Or land   h Cn: Heb and his yoke from your neck, and a yoke will be destroyed because of fatness

---

10.17 The God whose light shone as a beacon for those who believed in him would become a light of destroying fire against those who trifled with his word and dared to disobey him. God is not to be tampered with.

10.20ff Assyria would not be victorious over all the people of Judah, for God would save a remnant. But these verses show the inexorable march of the Assyrians toward Jerusalem. None of the cities mentioned in vv. 28ff was more than three hours away from Zion.

34 He will hack down the thickets of the forest with an ax,
    and Lebanon with its majestic trees[i] will fall.

2. The age of Messiah

a. The branch out of Jesse

11 A shoot shall come out from the stump of Jesse,
    and a branch shall grow out of his roots.

2 The spirit of the Lord shall rest on him,
    the spirit of wisdom and understanding,
    the spirit of counsel and might,
    the spirit of knowledge and the fear of the Lord.
3 His delight shall be in the fear of the Lord.

He shall not judge by what his eyes see,
    or decide by what his ears hear;
4 but with righteousness he shall judge the poor,
    and decide with equity for the meek of the earth;
he shall strike the earth with the rod of his mouth,
    and with the breath of his lips he shall kill the wicked.
5 Righteousness shall be the belt around his waist,
    and faithfulness the belt around his loins.

6 The wolf shall live with the lamb,
    the leopard shall lie down with the kid,
the calf and the lion and the fatling together,
    and a little child shall lead them.
7 The cow and the bear shall graze,
    their young shall lie down together;
    and the lion shall eat straw like the ox.
8 The nursing child shall play over the hole of the asp,
    and the weaned child shall put its hand on the adder's den.
9 They will not hurt or destroy
    on all my holy mountain;
for the earth will be full of the knowledge of the Lord
    as the waters cover the sea.

b. Messiah to restore Israel

10 On that day the root of Jesse shall stand as a signal to the peoples;
the nations shall inquire of him, and his dwelling shall be glorious.
11 On that day the Lord will extend his hand yet a second time to
recover the remnant that is left of his people, from Assyria, from Egypt,
from Pathros, from Ethiopia,[j] from Elam, from Shinar, from Hamath,
and from the coastlands of the sea.
12 He will raise a signal for the nations,

i Cn Compare Gk Vg: Heb *with a majestic one*   *j* Or *Nubia*; Heb *Cush*

Cross-references (margin):

11.1 Zech 6.12; Rev 5.5; Acts 13.23; Isa 4.2
11.2 Isa 61.1; Mt 3.16; Jn 1.32
11.3 Jn 2.25; 7.24
11.4 Isa 9.7; 3.14; 29.19; Mal 4.6; Job 4.9; 2 Thess 2.8
11.5 Eph 6.14; Isa 25.1
11.6 Isa 65.25
11.7 Isa 65.25
11.9 Job 5.23; Hab 2.14
11.10 Rom 15.12; Jn 3.14, 15; Lk 2.32; Isa 14.3
11.11 Zech 10.10; Mic 7.12; Isa 66.19
11.12 v. 10; Zech 10.6; Isa 24.16

11.1 *from the stump of Jesse . . . a branch . . . out of his roots.* Jesse, the father of David, is likened to a tree that was felled. From the stump would come a new shoot, Jesus Christ, the Messiah. So God's covenant with David would be fulfilled.

11.6 This prophetic word will be fulfilled at the end of the age, with the return of the Messiah as King of kings. The Messiah is our peace, who breaks down all the walls that separate one people from another. All enmities will be slain and lasting friendship will come between Jew and Gentile, who will be members of the one glorious flock.

11.9 This earth presently does not have the knowledge of the Lord from north to south and from east to west. But the day is coming when all that hinders or prevents the knowledge of God from sweeping over all creation will be destroyed. Then shall the fullness of God's knowledge reign from sea to sea and shore to shore.

11.12 Isaiah prophesies that a remnant of the Jews would be gathered by God from the ends of the earth. They would be united with the Gentiles, over whom the flag of God would fly. This would come about by the powerful working of the Holy Spirit in and through the word of God. A partial fulfillment of this took place in the return of the Jews from the captivity, a greater fulfillment is happening in the Christian church, but the final fulfillment awaits the future.

and will assemble the outcasts of Israel,
and gather the dispersed of Judah
    from the four corners of the earth.

11.13
Jer 3.18;
Ezek 37.16,
17, 22;
Hos 1.11

13 The jealousy of Ephraim shall depart,
    the hostility of Judah shall be cut off;
Ephraim shall not be jealous of Judah,
    and Judah shall not be hostile towards Ephraim.

11.14
Dan 11.41;
Joel 3.19;
Isa 16.14;
25.10

14 But they shall swoop down on the backs of the Philistines in
    the west,
    together they shall plunder the people of the east.
They shall put forth their hand against Edom and Moab,
    and the Ammonites shall obey them.

11.15
Isa 43.16;
19.16; 7.20;
8.7

15 And the Lord will utterly destroy
    the tongue of the sea of Egypt;
and will wave his hand over the River
    with his scorching wind;
and will split it into seven channels,
    and make a way to cross on foot;

11.16
Isa 19.23;
62.10;
Ex 14.26-29;
Isa 51.10;
63.12, 13

16 so there shall be a highway from Assyria
    for the remnant that is left of his people,
as there was for Israel
    when they came up from the land of Egypt.

3. Thanksgiving for God's salvation

12.1
Isa 26.1;
25.1; 40.1, 2

12 You will say in that day:
    I will give thanks to you, O Lord,
    for though you were angry with me,
your anger turned away,
    and you comforted me.

12.2
Isa 33.2;
26.3;
Ex 15.2;
Ps 118.14

2 Surely God is my salvation;
    I will trust, and will not be afraid,
for the Lord God *k* is my strength and my might;
    he has become my salvation.

12.3
Jn 4.10;
7.37, 38;
Isa 41.18

3 With joy you will draw water from the wells of salvation. 4 And you
will say in that day:
Give thanks to the Lord,
    call on his name;
make known his deeds among the nations;
    proclaim that his name is exalted.

12.5
Isa 24.14;
Ex 15.1;
Ps 98.1
12.6
Zeph 3.14;
Isa 49.26

5 Sing praises to the Lord, for he has done gloriously;
    let this be known *l* in all the earth.
6 Shout aloud and sing for joy, O royal *m* Zion,
    for great in your midst is the Holy One of Israel.

k Heb *for Yah, the Lord*   *l* Or *this is made known*   *m* Or *O inhabitant of*

11.15 *the sea of Egypt*, i.e., the Red Sea, particularly the Gulf of Suez. *the River*, i.e., the Euphrates. God would provide a passageway for the safe return of his people as he did during the exodus.
11.16 Even as God dried up the Red Sea for the Israelites to pass through on dry ground, so God would bring Jews and Gentiles together. He would remove all obstructions and break down every

barrier.
12.2 Since God is our salvation and guarantees that we will inherit eternal life, we can also trust him completely for all of our temporal concerns.
12.5,6 God's people are called upon to sing his praises for the glorious things he has done, for he has come into their midst and revealed himself as the Holy One of Israel.

III. *Volume of oracles upon heathen nations (13.1–23.18)*

A. *First oracle of Babylon*

1. *The doom of Babylon*

13 The oracle concerning Babylon that Isaiah son of Amoz saw.

	13.1 Jer chs. 50, 51

2 On a bare hill raise a signal,
  cry aloud to them;
 wave the hand for them to enter
  the gates of the nobles.

13.2 Jer 50.2; 51.25; Isa 10.32

3 I myself have commanded my consecrated ones,
  have summoned my warriors, my proudly exulting ones,
  to execute my anger.

13.3 Joel 3.11; Ps 149.2

4 Listen, a tumult on the mountains
  as of a great multitude!
 Listen, an uproar of kingdoms,
  of nations gathering together!
 The LORD of hosts is mustering
  an army for battle.

13.4 Isa 5.30

5 They come from a distant land,
  from the end of the heavens,
 the LORD and the weapons of his indignation,
  to destroy the whole earth.

13.5 Isa 5.26; 42.13; 10.5; 24.1

6 Wail, for the day of the LORD is near;
  it will come like destruction from the Almighty!*[n]*

13.6 Zeph 1.7; Isa 10.25; Joel 1.15

7 Therefore all hands will be feeble,
  and every human heart will melt,

13.7 Ezek 7.17; 21.7

8 and they will be dismayed.
 Pangs and agony will seize them;
  they will be in anguish like a woman in labor.
 They will look aghast at one another;
  their faces will be aflame.

13.8 Isa 21.3; 26.17

9 See, the day of the LORD comes,
  cruel, with wrath and fierce anger,
 to make the earth a desolation,
  and to destroy its sinners from it.

13.9 Isa 66.15, 16

10 For the stars of the heavens and their constellations
  will not give their light;
 the sun will be dark at its rising,
  and the moon will not shed its light.

13.10 Isa 5.30; Joel 2.10; Mt 24.29; Mk 13.24; Lk 21.25

11 I will punish the world for its evil,

13.11 Isa 26.21; 11.4; 2.11; Jer 48.29

n Traditional rendering of Heb *Shaddai*

13.1 Isaiah received God's revelation in which the doom of Babylon was predicted. Babylon would deal harshly with God's people at God's command, but God would then execute judgment on the very nation that he used to avenge himself against Judah and Jerusalem. Note that the prophecies spoken here concerning the destruction of Babylon were fulfilled about two centuries after the death of Isaiah.
13.3 God would use the Medes and the Persians under Darius and Cyrus to ruin the Babylonian monarchy. These two monarchs are called God's "consecrated ones," for they were called to this service and set apart by the providence of God to accomplish this divine purpose.
13.4,5 No mob would overthrow Babylon, but well-ordered troops from a far country. They would carry out God's mandated destruction of Babylon.
13.6 Mortals may have their day, but so will God, and it is coming soon. Those who put their own day above God's or suppose that God cannot or will not reward nations according to their works, will soon discover their error and perish in the midst of their secular splendor.
13.10 The light from the stars of heaven would not be seen because they would be clouded over. The light of the sun would be lost amid foul weather. The armies of Babylon would be like those in trouble on the sea when there is neither sun, moon, nor stars to guide them. The God of nature has the power to use nature against whomever he pleases.

and the wicked for their iniquity;
I will put an end to the pride of the arrogant,
and lay low the insolence of tyrants.

12 I will make mortals more rare than fine gold,
and humans than the gold of Ophir.

13 Therefore I will make the heavens tremble,
and the earth will be shaken out of its place,
at the wrath of the LORD of hosts
in the day of his fierce anger.

14 Like a hunted gazelle,
or like sheep with no one to gather them,
all will turn to their own people,
and all will flee to their own lands.

15 Whoever is found will be thrust through,
and whoever is caught will fall by the sword.

16 Their infants will be dashed to pieces
before their eyes;
their houses will be plundered,
and their wives ravished.

17 See, I am stirring up the Medes against them,
who have no regard for silver
and do not delight in gold.

18 Their bows will slaughter the young men;
they will have no mercy on the fruit of the womb;
their eyes will not pity children.

19 And Babylon, the glory of kingdoms,
the splendor and pride of the Chaldeans,
will be like Sodom and Gomorrah
when God overthrew them.

20 It will never be inhabited
or lived in for all generations;
Arabs will not pitch their tents there,
shepherds will not make their flocks lie down there.

21 But wild animals will lie down there,
and its houses will be full of howling creatures;
there ostriches will live,
and there goat-demons will dance.

22 Hyenas will cry in its towers,
and jackals in the pleasant palaces;
its time is close at hand,
and its days will not be prolonged.

2. Taunt against the king of Babylon

14 But the LORD will have compassion on Jacob and will again choose Israel, and will set them in their own land; and aliens will join

---

Cross references (left margin):

13.12 Isa 4.1; 6.11, 12
13.13 Isa 34.4; 51.6; Jer 10.10; Am 8.8; Hag 2.6
13.14 1 Kings 22.17; Jer 50.16; 51.9
13.15 Isa 14.19
13.16 Ps 137.9; Nah 3.10; Zech 14.2
13.17 Isa 21.2; Jer 51.11; Dan 5.28
13.18 2 Kings 8.12; Ezek 9.5, 10
13.19 Isa 21.9; Dan 4.30; Gen 19.24; Deut 29.23; Jer 49.18
13.20 Jer 51.37-43
13.21 Isa 34.11-15
13.22 Jer 51.33
14.1 Ps 102.13; Zech 1.17; 2.12; Isa 60.4, 5, 10; Eph 2.12-19

13.13 Earthquakes would shake Babylon; its armies would be fearful and run to escape from the impending judgment. Amid blood and horror the sword would destroy them utterly.
13.16 Even as the Babylonians had cruelly killed Judean infants, so would their own infants be dashed against the stones. And their houses, which had been filled with the loot gathered from Jerusalem, would be plundered and spoiled.
13.17 *The Medes* were an ancient Aryan (Iranian) people who lived southwest of the Caspian Sea. They joined forces with the Babylonians (Chaldeans) in the destruction of Nineveh (612 B.C.). Later they were incorporated into the Persian Empire which, under Cyrus, overcame and destroyed Babylon (539 B.C.).

13.20 Isaiah prophesied that Babylon would "never be inhabited." It never has been. Its ruins have been uncovered and its majesty and greatness confirmed. On the basis of this prophecy, it is proper to conclude that the Babylon of Rev 17 is not a literal Babylon. It is probably a political and ecclesiastical confederacy, of which the O.T. Babylon is a type or example.
13.21 *goat-demons*, i.e., those which in ancient mythology were part goat, part man.
14.1 God determined that he would free his people from Babylon after their captivity had reached its full course. Then it would be necessary to destroy the oppressor to free the oppressed. The yoke of repression would be broken and the prisoners set free.

them and attach themselves to the house of Jacob. 2 And the nations will take them and bring them to their place, and the house of Israel will possess the nations*o* as male and female slaves in the LORD's land; they will take captive those who were their captors, and rule over those who oppressed them.

3 When the LORD has given you rest from your pain and turmoil and the hard service with which you were made to serve, 4 you will take up this taunt against the king of Babylon:

How the oppressor has ceased!
How his insolence*p* has ceased!

5 The LORD has broken the staff of the wicked,
    the scepter of rulers,
6 that struck down the peoples in wrath
    with unceasing blows,
that ruled the nations in anger
    with unrelenting persecution.
7 The whole earth is at rest and quiet;
    they break forth into singing.
8 The cypresses exult over you,
    the cedars of Lebanon, saying,
"Since you were laid low,
    no one comes to cut us down."
9 Sheol beneath is stirred up
    to meet you when you come;
it rouses the shades to greet you,
    all who were leaders of the earth;
it raises from their thrones
    all who were kings of the nations.
10 All of them will speak
    and say to you:
"You too have become as weak as we!
    You have become like us!"
11 Your pomp is brought down to Sheol,
    and the sound of your harps;
maggots are the bed beneath you,
    and worms are your covering.

12 How you are fallen from heaven,
    O Day Star, son of Dawn!
How you are cut down to the ground,
    you who laid the nations low!
13 You said in your heart,
    "I will ascend to heaven;
I will raise my throne
    above the stars of God;
I will sit on the mount of assembly
    on the heights of Zaphon;*q*
14 I will ascend to the tops of the clouds,
    I will make myself like the Most High."

14.2 Isa 49.22; 60.9, 10; 66.20; 60.14

14.3 Isa 40.2
14.4 Isa 13.19; Hab 2.6; Rev 18.6

14.6 Isa 10.14; 47.6

14.8 Isa 55.12

14.9 Ezek 32.21

14.11 Isa 5.14; Ezek 28.13; Isa 51.8

14.12 Isa 34.4; Lk 10.18

14.13 Ezek 28.2; Dan 8.10

14.14 Isa 47.8; 2 Thess 2.4

o Heb *them* *p* Q Ms Compare Gk Syr Vg: Meaning of MT uncertain *q* Or *assembly in the far north*

14.12 Satan is called *Day Star, son of Dawn.* The phrase has two references, one to the king of Babylon (v. 4), and the other to Satan. The king of Babylon was a tool in the hands of Satan himself, who led and directed this monarch in his evildoings. The "Day Star" or "son of Dawn" (i.e., the morning star) quickly disappears from sight when the sun rises. The Babylonian king would be like that. He would shortly be removed from his place — eclipsed, as it were. Pos-sibly since the Babylonians worshiped Ishtar, an astral deity equated with Venus, the Spirit led Isaiah to use this figure of speech for the Babylonian ruler. For extended comments on Satan, see note on Ezek 28.12.
14.13 *the stars of God,* i.e., the angels. *I will sit on the mount of assembly in the far north,* (see NRSV foot-note). God would preside on the heights of Mount Zaphon, far away in the north (cf. Ps 48.2).

14.15
Mt 11.23

14.16
Jer 50.23

14.17
Joel 2.3;
Isa 45.13

14.19
Isa 22.16-18;
Jer 41.7, 9;
Isa 5.25

14.20
Job 18.19;
Ps 21.10;
37.28;
Isa 31.2

14.21
Ex 20.5;
Isa 13.16;
Mt 23.35;
Isa 27.6

14.22
Isa 26.14;
Prov 10.7;
Isa 47.9
14.23
Isa 34.11-15;
Zeph 2.14;
Isa 13.6

14.24
Isa 45.23;
55.8, 9;
Acts 4.28

14.25
Isa 10.12, 27

14.26
Isa 23.9;
Ex 15.12

14.27
2 Chr 20.6;
Isa 43.13;
Dan 4.31, 35

15 But you are brought down to Sheol,
  to the depths of the Pit.
16 Those who see you will stare at you,
  and ponder over you:
  "Is this the man who made the earth tremble,
  who shook kingdoms,
17 who made the world like a desert
  and overthrew its cities,
  who would not let his prisoners go home?"
18 All the kings of the nations lie in glory,
  each in his own tomb;
19 but you are cast out, away from your grave,
  like loathsome carrion,[r]
  clothed with the dead, those pierced by the sword,
  who go down to the stones of the Pit,
  like a corpse trampled underfoot.
20 You will not be joined with them in burial,
  because you have destroyed your land,
  you have killed your people.

  May the descendants of evildoers
  nevermore be named!
21 Prepare slaughter for his sons
  because of the guilt of their father.[s]
  Let them never rise to possess the earth
  or cover the face of the world with cities.

22 I will rise up against them, says the LORD of hosts, and will cut off from Babylon name and remnant, offspring and posterity, says the LORD. 23 And I will make it a possession of the hedgehog, and pools of water, and I will sweep it with the broom of destruction, says the LORD of hosts.

B. *The overthrow of Assyria*

24 The LORD of hosts has sworn:
  As I have designed,
  so shall it be;
  and as I have planned,
  so shall it come to pass:
25 I will break the Assyrian in my land,
  and on my mountains trample him under foot;
  his yoke shall be removed from them,
  and his burden from their shoulders.
26 This is the plan that is planned
  concerning the whole earth;
  and this is the hand that is stretched out
  over all the nations.
27 For the LORD of hosts has planned,

[r] Cn Compare Gk: Heb *like a loathed branch*   [s] Syr Compare Gk: Heb *fathers*

14.15–17 Again, the primary reference here is to the destruction of the king of Babylon. But it also refers to Satan and all the wicked, who will finally be brought down to Sheol. Sheol's inhabitants will be astonished that the one who had such great power and used it so wickedly could have such an abominable end. He who shook kingdoms and made the earth tremble will be helpless and confined.
14.23 God will destroy Babylon. His broom is a broom of destruction, not one that clears away dirt

and restores a room to its pristine state.
14.24,25 God was also planning to destroy Assyria. Because he is the sovereign ruler of the universe, his plans and purposes cannot be thwarted; what he intends to do will be done. No one and nothing can stop him.
14.27 God was determined to be the enemy of his people's enemies. He challenged all the powers of heaven and hell to change the counsel of God, knowing that they would fail in their vain attempts.

and who will annul it?
His hand is stretched out,
　　and who will turn it back?"

C. *Oracle of Philistia*

28In the year that King Ahaz died this oracle came:

29　Do not rejoice, all you Philistines,
　　　that the rod that struck you is broken,
　　for from the root of the snake will come forth an adder,
　　　and its fruit will be a flying fiery serpent.
30　The firstborn of the poor will graze,
　　　and the needy lie down in safety;
　　but I will make your root die of famine,
　　　and your remnant I*t* will kill.
31　Wail, O gate; cry, O city;
　　　melt in fear, O Philistia, all of you!
　　For smoke comes out of the north,
　　　and there is no straggler in its ranks.

32　What will one answer the messengers of the nation?
　　"The LORD has founded Zion,
　　　and the needy among his people
　　　will find refuge in her."

D. *Oracle of Moab*

1. *Scenes of her coming devastation*

15 An oracle concerning Moab.

　Because Ar is laid waste in a night,
　　　Moab is undone;
　because Kir is laid waste in a night,
　　　Moab is undone.
2　Dibon*u* has gone up to the temple,
　　　to the high places to weep;
　over Nebo and over Medeba
　　　Moab wails.
　On every head is baldness,
　　　every beard is shorn;
3　in the streets they bind on sackcloth;
　　on the housetops and in the squares
　　　everyone wails and melts in tears.
4　Heshbon and Elealeh cry out,
　　　their voices are heard as far as Jahaz;
　therefore the loins of Moab quiver;*v*
　　　his soul trembles.

t Q Ms Vg: MT *he*　*u* Cn: Heb *the house and Dibon*　*v* Cn Compare Gk Syr: Heb *the armed men of Moab cry aloud*

14.28
2 Kings 16.20

14.29
Jer 47.1-7;
2 Chr 26.6

14.30
Isa 3.14, 15;
7.21; 8.21;
Jer 25.16, 20

14.31
Isa 3.26;
v. 29;
Jer 1.14;
Isa 34.16

14.32
Isa 37.9;
Ps 87.1, 5;
Zeph 3.12;
Zech 11.11

15.1
Isa 11.14;
Jer 48;
Ezek 25.8-11;
Jer 48.41

15.2
Lev 21.5

15.3
Jon 3.6-8;
Jer 48.38;
Isa 22.4

14.29 *the rod that struck you,* i.e., Shalmaneser V of Assyria.
14.31 *smoke comes out of the north.* A perfectly trained army, led by Sargon of Assyria, was coming down against Philistia.
14.32 *The LORD has founded Zion;* therefore the Philistines must fall. Zion was a refuge for God's people, who were being afflicted but could never be removed. Thus, they did not have to be afraid of what their enemies could do.

15.1 See note on Ezek 25.9 for information about the Moabites. God said that the chief cities of Moab would be taken by surprise in one night. Evidently the people thought they dwelt securely, so they lived in luxury and indulged themselves (cf. v. 7).
15.2 City after city is named and its destruction foretold. Assyria would wreak great devastation upon all of Moab; nothing pertaining to them would be left untouched.

5 My heart cries out for Moab;
   his fugitives flee to Zoar,
   to Eglath-shelishiyah.
For at the ascent of Luhith
   they go up weeping;
on the road to Horonaim
   they raise a cry of destruction;

6 the waters of Nimrim
   are a desolation;
the grass is withered, the new growth fails,
   the verdure is no more.

7 Therefore the abundance they have gained
   and what they have laid up
they carry away
   over the Wadi of the Willows.

8 For a cry has gone
   around the land of Moab;
the wailing reaches to Eglaim,
   the wailing reaches to Beer-elim.

9 For the waters of Dibon[w] are full of blood;
   yet I will bring upon Dibon[w] even more—
a lion for those of Moab who escape,
   for the remnant of the land.

2. Moab's pride and fall

16 Send lambs
   to the ruler of the land,
from Sela, by way of the desert,
   to the mount of daughter Zion.

2 Like fluttering birds,
   like scattered nestlings,
so are the daughters of Moab
   at the fords of the Arnon.

3 "Give counsel,
   grant justice;
make your shade like night
   at the height of noon;
hide the outcasts,
   do not betray the fugitive;

4 let the outcasts of Moab
   settle among you;
be a refuge to them
   from the destroyer."

When the oppressor is no more,
   and destruction has ceased,
and marauders have vanished from the land,

5 then a throne shall be established in steadfast love
   in the tent of David,
   and on it shall sit in faithfulness
a ruler who seeks justice
   and is swift to do what is right.

[w] Q Ms Vg Compare Syr: MT *Dimon*

16.1 Refugees from Moab had escaped to Edom, which had Sela for its capital. They entreated Judah to help them so that they could resettle in that land, sending the lamb as a token of sacrifice or tribute.

16.2ff Isaiah warns the Moabites to treat the true people of God well, assuring them that God was still interested in Israel and would restore it. The throne of David would have a king who was interested in seeking justice and doing righteousness.

6 We have heard of the pride of Moab
    — how proud he is! —
of his arrogance, his pride, and his insolence;
    his boasts are false.
7 Therefore let Moab wail,
    let everyone wail for Moab.
Mourn, utterly stricken,
    for the raisin cakes of Kir-hareseth.

8 For the fields of Heshbon languish,
    and the vines of Sibmah,
whose clusters once made drunk
    the lords of the nations,
reached to Jazer
    and strayed to the desert;
their shoots once spread abroad
    and crossed over the sea.
9 Therefore I weep with the weeping of Jazer
    for the vines of Sibmah;
I drench you with my tears,
    O Heshbon and Elealeh;
for the shout over your fruit harvest
    and your grain harvest has ceased.
10 Joy and gladness are taken away
    from the fruitful field;
and in the vineyards no songs are sung,
    no shouts are raised;
no treader treads out wine in the presses;
    the vintage-shout is hushed. *x*
11 Therefore my heart throbs like a harp for Moab,
    and my very soul for Kir-heres.
12 When Moab presents himself, when he wearies himself upon the high place, when he comes to his sanctuary to pray, he will not prevail.
13 This was the word that the Lord spoke concerning Moab in the past. 14 But now the Lord says, In three years, like the years of a hired worker, the glory of Moab will be brought into contempt, in spite of all its great multitude; and those who survive will be very few and feeble.

E. *Oracle of Damascus and Samaria*

1. *The crushing of Damascus and Ephraim*

17 An oracle concerning Damascus.

See, Damascus will cease to be a city,
    and will become a heap of ruins.
2 Her towns will be deserted forever; *y*
    they will be places for flocks,
which will lie down, and no one will make them afraid.
3 The fortress will disappear from Ephraim,
    and the kingdom from Damascus;
and the remnant of Aram will be

x Gk: Heb *I have hushed*   *y* Cn Compare Gk: Heb *the cities of Aroer are deserted*

16.6 Beginning with this verse, Isaiah brings to light God's indictment of the sins of Moab. Therefore God's judgment would come upon them. It would be irreversible, for God would not hear them when they cried. The disaster would come in three years (v. 14). Moab would be brought into contempt and many would be slain.

17.1 Aram, with its capital Damascus, was in league with Ephraim (i.e., the northern kingdom of Israel) against Judah. This passage foretells the destruction of the strong cities of both nations (vv. 1–6 and vv. 9–11).

16.6
Jer 48.29, 30;
Zeph 2.8, 10

16.7
1 Chr 16.3;
2 Kings 3.25;
Jer 48.31

16.8
Isa 15.4;
Num 32.38;
Jer 48.32

16.9
Jer 48.32;
Isa 15.4;
Jer 40.10, 12

16.10
Isa 24.7, 8;
Jer 48.33;
Job 24.11

16.11
Isa 15.5;
63.15;
Jer 48.36
16.12
Jer 48.35;
1 Kings 18.29;
Isa 15.2;
2 Kings 19.12
16.14
Isa 21.16;
25.10

17.1
2 Kings 16.9;
Jer 49.23;
Am 1.3;
Zech 9.1;
Isa 8.4; 10.9
17.2
Jer 7.33

17.3
Isa 7.16; 8.4

like the glory of the children of Israel,

says the LORD of hosts.

2. Survival of an idol-hating remnant

17.4
Isa 10.3, 16

4 On that day
   the glory of Jacob will be brought low,
   and the fat of his flesh will grow lean.

17.5
Jer 51.33;
2 Sam 5.18,
22

5 And it shall be as when reapers gather standing grain
   and their arms harvest the ears,
and as when one gleans the ears of grain
   in the Valley of Rephaim.

17.6
Isa 24.13;
27.12

6 Gleanings will be left in it,
   as when an olive tree is beaten —
two or three berries
   in the top of the highest bough,
four or five
   on the branches of a fruit tree,

says the LORD God of Israel.

17.7
Isa 10.20;
Mic 7.7
17.8
Isa 27.9;
30.22; 31.7;
Ex 34.13;
Deut 7.5

7 On that day people will regard their Maker, and their eyes will look to the Holy One of Israel; 8 they will not have regard for the altars, the work of their hands, and they will not look to what their own fingers have made, either the sacred poles[z] or the altars of incense.

3. The imminent horrors of invasion

17.9
Isa 7.25

9 On that day their strong cities will be like the deserted places of the Hivites and the Amorites,[a] which they deserted because of the children of Israel, and there will be desolation.

17.10
Isa 51.13;
Ps 68.19;
Isa 26.4;
30.29

10 For you have forgotten the God of your salvation,
    and have not remembered the Rock of your refuge;
therefore, though you plant pleasant plants
    and set out slips of an alien god,

17.11
Ps 90.6;
Job 4.8

11 though you make them grow on the day that you plant them,
    and make them blossom in the morning that you sow;
yet the harvest will flee away
    in a day of grief and incurable pain.

17.12
Jer 6.23;
Ezek 43.2;
Ps 18.4

12 Ah, the thunder of many peoples,
    they thunder like the thundering of the sea!
Ah, the roar of nations,
    they roar like the roaring of mighty waters!

17.13
Isa 33.3;
Ps 9.5;
Isa 13.14;
29.5; 41.15,
16
17.14
Isa 41.12;
2 Kings 19.35

13 The nations roar like the roaring of many waters,
    but he will rebuke them, and they will flee far away,
chased like chaff on the mountains before the wind
    and whirling dust before the storm.

14 At evening time, lo, terror!
    Before morning, they are no more.
This is the fate of those who despoil us,
    and the lot of those who plunder us.

---

z Heb *Asherim*   a Cn Compare Gk: Heb *places of the wood and the highest bough*

17.7,8 The afflictions God would send on Ephraim (Israel) would cause the godly remnant to turn from their transgressions, seek the mercy of God, and destroy their idols. Any affliction God sends that separates us from our sins and makes us reject the vanity of this world is a blessing to us and an indicator of the grace of God toward repentant sinners.

17.12ff These verses foretell the failure of the Assyrian attack against Judah. At this point Judah was not yet ripe for ruin. That would come later, when Nebuchadnezzar acted as God's scourge against that nation. Chronologically, ch. 17 should be read after ch. 9, for the destruction of Damascus came to pass in the reign of Ahaz (2 Kings 16.9).

F. *Oracle of Ethiopia*

18 Ah, land of whirring wings
    beyond the rivers of Ethiopia,[b]
2 sending ambassadors by the Nile
    in vessels of papyrus on the waters!
Go, you swift messengers,
    to a nation tall and smooth,
to a people feared near and far,
    a nation mighty and conquering,
    whose land the rivers divide.

3 All you inhabitants of the world,
    you who live on the earth,
when a signal is raised on the mountains, look!
    When a trumpet is blown, listen!

4 For thus the Lord said to me:
I will quietly look from my dwelling
    like clear heat in sunshine,
    like a cloud of dew in the heat of harvest.

5 For before the harvest, when the blossom is over
    and the flower becomes a ripening grape,
he will cut off the shoots with pruning hooks,
    and the spreading branches he will hew away.

6 They shall all be left
    to the birds of prey of the mountains
    and to the animals of the earth.
And the birds of prey will summer on them,
    and all the animals of the earth will winter on them.

7 At that time gifts will be brought to the Lord of hosts from[c] a people tall and smooth, from a people feared near and far, a nation mighty and conquering, whose land the rivers divide, to Mount Zion, the place of the name of the Lord of hosts.

G. *Oracle of Egypt*

1. *The doom of Egypt*

19 An oracle concerning Egypt.

See, the Lord is riding on a swift cloud
    and comes to Egypt;
the idols of Egypt will tremble at his presence,
    and the heart of the Egyptians will melt within them.

2 I will stir up Egyptians against Egyptians,
    and they will fight, one against the other,
    neighbor against neighbor,
    city against city, kingdom against kingdom;

3 the spirit of the Egyptians within them will be emptied out,

b Or *Nubia;* Heb *Cush*   *c* Q Ms Gk Vg: MT *of*

18.1
Isa 20.3-5;
Ezek 30.4, 5,
9;
Zeph 2.12;
3.10
18.2
Ex 2.3; v. 7;
2 Chr 12.2-4

18.3
Ps 49.1;
Isa 5.26;
26.11

18.4
Isa 26.21;
2 Sam 23.4;
Isa 26.19

18.5
Ezek 17.6-10;
Isa 27.11

18.6
Isa 46.11;
56.9;
Jer 7.33

18.7
Ps 68.31;
Isa 45.14;
Zeph 3.10;
Zech 14.16,
17

19.1
Isa 13.1;
Jer 46.13-26;
Ezek chs. 29,
30;
Ps 18.10;
104.3;
Ex 12.12;
Jer 43.12
19.2
Judg 7.22;
1 Sam 14.16,
20;
2 Chr 20.23;
Mt 10.21, 36
19.3
vv. 11-14;
Isa 8.19

18.7 Sometime in the future the Ethiopians would bring their presents to Zion, to the place where the name of the Lord of hosts was enshrined. See Ps 68.31, Isa 45.14, and Zeph 3.10, which speak of the conversion of the Ethiopians and their participation in the kingdom of God at the end of the age.
19.1 *the Lord is riding on a swift cloud.* Baal, the Canaanite god, was a god of fertility, who was said to ride on the clouds. Isaiah picked up this figure of speech and used it of the Lord God, who brings fertility to the land, blesses his faithful people, and executes judgment upon the wicked.
19.2 Even as God destroyed Assyria, so he would also pass judgment against Egypt. Judah had trusted in the power of Egypt to help her in the attacks of the enemy from the north, but Egypt proved to be weak. That nation would be weakened, brought low, and made contemptible among the nations.

and I will confound their plans;
they will consult the idols and the spirits of the dead
    and the ghosts and the familiar spirits;

19.4
Isa 20.4;
Jer 46.26;
Ezek 29.19

4 I will deliver the Egyptians
    into the hand of a hard master;
a fierce king will rule over them,
    says the Sovereign, the LORD of hosts.

19.5
Jer 51.36;
Ezek 30.12
19.6
Ex 7.18;
Isa 37.25;
15.6
19.7
Isa 23.3, 10

5 The waters of the Nile will be dried up,
    and the river will be parched and dry;
6 its canals will become foul,
    and the branches of Egypt's Nile will diminish and dry up,
    reeds and rushes will rot away.
7 There will be bare places by the Nile,
    on the brink of the Nile;
and all that is sown by the Nile will dry up,
    be driven away, and be no more.

8 Those who fish will mourn;
    all who cast hooks in the Nile will lament,
    and those who spread nets on the water will languish.

19.9
Prov 7.16;
Ezek 27.7
19.10
Ps 11.3

9 The workers in flax will be in despair,
    and the carders and those at the loom will grow pale.
10 Its weavers will be dismayed,
    and all who work for wages will be grieved.

19.11
Num 13.22;
1 Kings 4.30;
Acts 7.22

11 The princes of Zoan are utterly foolish;
    the wise counselors of Pharaoh give stupid counsel.
How can you say to Pharaoh,
    "I am one of the sages,
    a descendant of ancient kings"?

19.12
1 Cor 1.20;
Isa 14.24;
Rom 9.17

12 Where now are your sages?
    Let them tell you and make known
    what the LORD of hosts has planned against Egypt.

19.13
Jer 2.16;
Ezek 30.13;
Zech 10.4

13 The princes of Zoan have become fools,
    and the princes of Memphis are deluded;
those who are the cornerstones of its tribes
    have led Egypt astray.

19.14
Isa 29.10;
Mt 17.17;
Isa 3.12;
9.16; 28.7

14 The LORD has poured into them[d]
    a spirit of confusion;
and they have made Egypt stagger in all its doings
    as a drunkard staggers around in vomit.

19.15
Isa 9.14, 15

15 Neither head nor tail, palm branch or reed,
    will be able to do anything for Egypt.

2. God's people will triumph over Egypt

19.16
Jer 51.30;
Isa 2.19;
11.15; 30.32
19.17
Isa 14.24

16 On that day the Egyptians will be like women, and tremble with fear before the hand that the LORD of hosts raises against them. 17 And the land of Judah will become a terror to the Egyptians; everyone to whom

---

[d] Gk Compare Tg: Heb *it*

19.4 Egypt would be given over to one of their own kings, who would be a cruel lord — tyrannous and oppressive. The people of Egypt would experience the same barbarous treatment the Israelites had experienced years before.
19.5ff The Nile River had been important to Egypt's defense against invaders. Now it would be dried up, the fish would die, and people who depended on fish for food would be deprived of that

staple in their diet. The loss of water would affect the production of flax and cotton, leaving the economy of the nation in shambles.
19.11 *Zoan.* See note on Num 13.22.
19.12 What God has purposed, no one can thwart. The doom of Egypt was certain. Confusion would come; Egypt would stagger and act as a vomiting drunk (v. 14,17).

it is mentioned will fear because of the plan that the LORD of hosts is planning against them.

18 On that day there will be five cities in the land of Egypt that speak the language of Canaan and swear allegiance to the LORD of hosts. One of these will be called the City of the Sun.

3. The final conversion and deliverance of Egypt

19 On that day there will be an altar to the LORD in the center of the land of Egypt, and a pillar to the LORD at its border. 20 It will be a sign and a witness to the LORD of hosts in the land of Egypt; when they cry to the LORD because of oppressors, he will send them a savior, and will defend and deliver them. 21 The LORD will make himself known to the Egyptians; and the Egyptians will know the LORD on that day, and will worship with sacrifice and burnt offering, and they will make vows to the LORD and perform them. 22 The LORD will strike Egypt, striking and healing; they will return to the LORD, and he will listen to their supplications and heal them.

23 On that day there will be a highway from Egypt to Assyria, and the Assyrian will come into Egypt, and the Egyptian into Assyria, and the Egyptians will worship with the Assyrians.

24 On that day Israel will be the third with Egypt and Assyria, a blessing in the midst of the earth, 25 whom the LORD of hosts has blessed, saying, "Blessed be Egypt my people, and Assyria the work of my hands, and Israel my heritage."

4. Egypt to be conquered by Assyria

20 In the year that the commander-in-chief, who was sent by King Sargon of Assyria, came to Ashdod and fought against it and took it — 2 at that time the LORD had spoken to Isaiah son of Amoz, saying, "Go, and loose the sackcloth from your loins and take your sandals off your feet," and he had done so, walking naked and barefoot. 3 Then the LORD said, "Just as my servant Isaiah has walked naked and barefoot for three years as a sign and a portent against Egypt and Ethiopia,ᵉ 4 so shall the king of Assyria lead away the Egyptians as captives and the Ethiopiansᶠ as exiles, both the young and the old, naked and barefoot, with buttocks uncovered, to the shame of Egypt. 5 And they shall be dismayed and confounded because of Ethiopiaᵉ their hope and of Egypt their boast. 6 In that day the inhabitants of this coastland will say, 'See, this is what has happened to those in whom we hoped and to whom we fled for help and deliverance from the king of Assyria! And we, how shall we escape?' "

H. The defeat of Babylon by Medo-Persia

21 The oracle concerning the wilderness of the sea.

As whirlwinds in the Negeb sweep on,

ᵉ Or Nubia; Heb Cush   ᶠ Or Nubians; Heb Cushites

19.18
Isa 45.23;
65.16

19.19
Isa 56.7;
Gen 28.18;
Ex 24.4;
Josh 22.10,
26, 27
19.20
Isa 43.3, 11;
49.25
19.21
Isa 11.9;
Mal 1.11;
Isa 44.5
19.22
Isa 30.26;
27.13; 45.14
19.23
Isa 11.16;
27.13

19.25
Isa 45.14;
Hos 2.23;
Eph 2.10

20.1
2 Kings 18.17;
1 Sam 5.1
20.2
Zech 13.4;
Ezek 24.17,
23;
1 Sam 19.24;
Mic 1.8
20.3
Isa 8.18;
37.9; 43.3
20.4
Isa 19.4;
3.17;
Jer 13.22, 26
20.5
2 Kings 18.21;
Isa 30.3, 5,
7;
Ezek 29.6, 7
20.6
Isa 10.3;
30.7;
Mt 13.33;
Heb 2.3
21.1
Isa 31.1;
Jer 51.42;
Zech 9.14

19.18,19 Despite the upcoming judgment God still had a spiritual concern for Egypt. Though it would become a nation without prosperity, God's blessing would bring true religion to the people. By grace he would call them to salvation. Indeed, this passage predicts a time when Egypt would call on God and worship him at an altar erected in that nation.
19.24,25 God promised that the feuds and enmities of Egyptians, Assyrians, and Israelites would end someday. These nations would be joined together in love for the Messiah and, like a three-fold cord, would not easily be broken. This united people would be a blessing and would be blessed by God. However, at

the time Isaiah wrote, Egypt was about to be conquered by Assyria (see ch. 20).
20.1 *Ashdod*, a Philistine city allied with Egypt against Assyria. The city was taken by Sargon's commander in 711 B.C., and was besieged again by Sennacherib and other attackers.
20.2 Isaiah was called by God to remove his outer clothing and go, as it were, undressed and barefoot. He would have been ridiculed for his appearance and jeered at by the young. Yet this was intended as a sign from God to Egypt, soon to be conquered by Assyria.
21.1 This prophecy refers to Babylon (see v. 9).

it comes from the desert,
from a terrible land.

^{21.2}
^{Isa 33.1;}
^{13.17;}
^{Jer 49.34}

2 A stern vision is told to me;
the betrayer betrays,
and the destroyer destroys.
Go up, O Elam,
lay siege, O Media;
all the sighing she has caused
I bring to an end.

^{21.3}
^{Isa 15.5;}
^{16.11; 13.8}

3 Therefore my loins are filled with anguish;
pangs have seized me,
like the pangs of a woman in labor;
I am bowed down so that I cannot hear,
I am dismayed so that I cannot see.

^{21.4}
^{Deut 28.67}

4 My mind reels, horror has appalled me;
the twilight I longed for
has been turned for me into trembling.

^{21.5}
^{Jer 51.39, 57;}
^{Dan 5.1-4}

5 They prepare the table,
they spread the rugs,
they eat, they drink.
Rise up, commanders,
oil the shield!

6 For thus the Lord said to me:
"Go, post a lookout,
let him announce what he sees.

^{21.7}
^{v. 9}

7 When he sees riders, horsemen in pairs,
riders on donkeys, riders on camels,
let him listen diligently,
very diligently."

^{21.8}
^{Hab 2.1}

8 Then the watcher^g called out:
"Upon a watchtower I stand, O Lord,
continually by day,
and at my post I am stationed
throughout the night.

^{21.9}
^{Jer 51.8;}
^{Rev 14.8;}
^{18.2;}
^{Isa 46.1;}
^{Jer 50.2;}
^{51.44}

9 Look, there they come, riders,
horsemen in pairs!"
Then he responded,
"Fallen, fallen is Babylon;
and all the images of her gods
lie shattered on the ground."

^{21.10}
^{Jer 51.33}

10 O my threshed and winnowed one,
what I have heard from the LORD of hosts,
the God of Israel, I announce to you.

I. Oracle of Dumah

^{21.11}
^{Gen 25.14;}
^{32.3}

11 The oracle concerning Dumah.

One is calling to me from Seir,
"Sentinel, what of the night?
Sentinel, what of the night?"
12 The sentinel says:
"Morning comes, and also the night."

^g Q Ms: MT *a lion*

21.5 This refers to the sumptuous feast that preceded Babylon's demise (see Dan 5 for the fullfilment
of this prophecy when Cyrus captured the city).
21.9 Long before Babylon actually fell, that nation
is pictured as fallen. Her day of conquest and power

has vanished irretrievably. Her idols could not protect
her; they have been ground to dust. This passage is
also prophetic of the fall of spiritual Babylon (see Rev
18).
21.11 *Dumah,* i.e., Edom.

If you will inquire, inquire;
come back again."

J. *Oracle of Arabia*

13 The oracle concerning the desert plain.

In the scrub of the desert plain you will lodge,
    O caravans of Dedanites.
14 Bring water to the thirsty,
    meet the fugitive with bread,
      O inhabitants of the land of Tema.
15 For they have fled from the swords,
    from the drawn sword,
from the bent bow,
    and from the stress of battle.

16 For thus the Lord said to me: Within a year, according to the years of a hired worker, all the glory of Kedar will come to an end; 17 and the remaining bows of Kedar's warriors will be few; for the Lord, the God of Israel, has spoken.

K. *Oracle of Jerusalem, the valley of vision*

1. *Heedless of warning, the city to fall*

22 The oracle concerning the valley of vision.

What do you mean that you have gone up,
    all of you, to the housetops,
2 you that are full of shoutings,
    tumultuous city, exultant town?
Your slain are not slain by the sword,
    nor are they dead in battle.
3 Your rulers have all fled together;
    they were captured without the use of a bow. *h*
All of you who were found were captured,
    though they had fled far away. *i*
4 Therefore I said:
Look away from me,
    let me weep bitter tears;
do not try to comfort me
    for the destruction of my beloved people.

5 For the Lord GOD of hosts has a day
    of tumult and trampling and confusion
      in the valley of vision,
a battering down of walls
    and a cry for help to the mountains.
6 Elam bore the quiver
    with chariots and cavalry, *j*
      and Kir uncovered the shield.
7 Your choicest valleys were full of chariots,
    and the cavalry took their stand at the gates.

h Or *without their bows*   *i* Gk Syr Vg: Heb *fled from far away*   *j* Meaning of Heb uncertain

Cross references (right margin):

21.13 Isa 13.1; Jer 49.28; 1 Chr 1.9, 32

21.14 Gen 25.15; Job 6.19

21.15 Isa 13.14, 15; 17.13

21.16 Isa 16.14; 17.4; Ps 120.5; Isa 60.7

21.17 Isa 10.19; Num 23.19; Zech 1.6

22.1 Isa 13.1; Joel 3.12, 14; Isa 15.3

22.2 Isa 32.13; Jer 14.18; Lam 2.20

22.3 Isa 21.15

22.4 Isa 15.3; Jer 4.19; 9.1

22.5 Isa 37.3; 63.3; Lam 1.5; 2.2; v. 1

22.6 Jer 49.35; 2 Kings 16.9

22.7 2 Chr 32.1

21.13 The *desert plain* is Arabia, a large peninsula with a landed area of approximately one million square miles. Its inhabitants are of Abrahamic extraction. The *Dedanites* were a mercantile people who traded with Tyre and Damascus.

22.1 *The valley of vision,* i.e., Jerusalem. Isaiah had

pronounced divine judgment on the nations surrounding Judah. These had either been spiteful enemies or deceitful friends to God's people. Now Judah would hear about the vision of God given to Isaiah against Judah itself.

8 He has taken away the covering of Judah.

On that day you looked to the weapons of the House of the Forest, 9 and you saw that there were many breaches in the city of David, and you collected the waters of the lower pool. 10 You counted the houses of Jerusalem, and you broke down the houses to fortify the wall. 11 You made a reservoir between the two walls for the water of the old pool. But you did not look to him who did it, or have regard for him who planned it long ago.

12 In that day the Lord God of hosts
        called to weeping and mourning,
        to baldness and putting on sackcloth;
13 but instead there was joy and festivity,
        killing oxen and slaughtering sheep,
        eating meat and drinking wine.
    "Let us eat and drink,
        for tomorrow we die."
14 The Lord of hosts has revealed himself in my ears:
    Surely this iniquity will not be forgiven you until you die,
        says the Lord God of hosts.

2. Corrupt Shebna to be replaced by Eliakim

15 Thus says the Lord God of hosts: Come, go to this steward, to Shebna, who is master of the household, and say to him: 16 What right do you have here? Who are your relatives here, that you have cut out a tomb here for yourself, cutting a tomb on the height, and carving a habitation for yourself in the rock? 17 The Lord is about to hurl you away violently, my fellow. He will seize firm hold on you, 18 whirl you round and round, and throw you like a ball into a wide land; there you shall die, and there your splendid chariots shall lie, O you disgrace to your master's house! 19 I will thrust you from your office, and you will be pulled down from your post.

20 On that day I will call my servant Eliakim son of Hilkiah, 21 and will clothe him with your robe and bind your sash on him. I will commit your authority to his hand, and he shall be a father to the inhabitants of Jerusalem and to the house of Judah. 22 I will place on his shoulder the key of the house of David; he shall open, and no one shall shut; he shall shut, and no one shall open. 23 I will fasten him like a peg in a secure place, and he will become a throne of honor to his ancestral house. 24 And they will hang on him the whole weight of his ancestral house, the offspring and issue, every small vessel, from the cups to all the flagons. 25 On that day, says the Lord of hosts, the peg that was fastened in a secure place will give way; it will be cut down and fall, and the load that was on it will perish, for the Lord has spoken.

22.8 *House of the Forest.* See 1 Kings 7.2; 10.17; 2 Chr 9.16. This was an armory or treasure house located in or near Jerusalem. Apparently weapons of war were stored there.
22.11 Judah did everything it could to defend itself against the enemy. But one thing it failed to do: look to the God who had chosen Abraham and his descendants to be his people.
22.12ff God's judgment against Judah was designed to humble the proud, bring them to repentance, and constrain them to trust in God as their only hope. Had Judah repented immediately, God would have delivered them from their enemies. But they persisted in their wrongful behavior; therefore, they had to die in their sins.
22.15 Shebna, a high official, was a crooked stick. God pronounced judgment against him, saying that he would lose his position and die. The fulfillment of this prophetic word should have warned king and people to turn to God in repentance.
22.20–25 *Eliakim.* His name means "God will establish." Eliakim was among those who stood against Shebna. He represented those who loved God and did his will. God gave him power to open and shut the house of David. He represents Christ; this prophecy is fulfilled in Christ, who has the key of David and opens and shuts (Rev 3.7).

L. *The oracle of Tyre*

1. *The fall of Tyre predicted*

23 The oracle concerning Tyre.

Wail, O ships of Tarshish,
    for your fortress is destroyed.[k]
When they came in from Cyprus
    they learned of it.

2 Be still, O inhabitants of the coast,
    O merchants of Sidon,
your messengers crossed over the sea[l]

3   and were on the mighty waters;
your revenue was the grain of Shihor,
    the harvest of the Nile;
you were the merchant of the nations.

4 Be ashamed, O Sidon, for the sea has spoken,
    the fortress of the sea, saying:
"I have neither labored nor given birth,
    I have neither reared young men
    nor brought up young women."

5 When the report comes to Egypt,
    they will be in anguish over the report about Tyre.

6 Cross over to Tarshish —
    wail, O inhabitants of the coast!

7 Is this your exultant city
    whose origin is from days of old,
whose feet carried her
    to settle far away?

8 Who has planned this
    against Tyre, the bestower of crowns,
whose merchants were princes,
    whose traders were the honored of the earth?

9 The LORD of hosts has planned it —
    to defile the pride of all glory,
    to shame all the honored of the earth.

10 Cross over to your own land,
    O ships of[m] Tarshish;
this is a harbor[n] no more.

11 He has stretched out his hand over the sea,
    he has shaken the kingdoms;
the LORD has given command concerning Canaan
    to destroy its fortresses.

12 He said:
You will exult no longer,
    O oppressed virgin daughter Sidon;
rise, cross over to Cyprus —
    even there you will have no rest.

13   Look at the land of the Chaldeans! This is the people; it was not

Cross references

23.1 Jer 25.22; 47.4; Ezek chs. 26, 27, 28; v. 12

23.2 Isa 47.5

23.3 Jer 2.18; Ezek 27.3-23

23.4 Ezek 28.21, 22

23.7 Isa 22.2; 32.13

23.9 Isa 2.11; 13.11; Job 40.11, 12; Isa 5.13; 9.15

23.11 Isa 14.26; 50.2; 25.2

23.12 Rev 18.22; Isa 47.1; v. 1

23.13 Isa 10.5, 7

---

[k] Cn Compare verse 14: Heb *for it is destroyed, without houses*   [l] Q Ms: MT *crossing over the sea, they replenished you*   [m] Cn Compare Gk: Heb *like the Nile, daughter*   [n] Cn: Heb *restraint*

23.1 *Tyre* was originally a colony of the mother-city, Sidon. *ships of Tarshish* is a term used in the O.T. for merchant ships. Tarshish probably refers to a city of Tartesus, located on the Guadalquivir River in Spain. It had been colonized by Tyrians (see note on 1 Kings 10.22).

23.8 See note on Ezek 26.2.

23.13 God would use the Chaldeans (i.e., Nebuchadnezzar) to bring about the destruction of Tyre.

Assyria. They destined Tyre for wild animals. They erected their siege towers, they tore down her palaces, they made her a ruin.*o*

23.14
v. 1

14 Wail, O ships of Tarshish,
  for your fortress is destroyed.

2. Tyre to be restored after seventy years

23.15
Jer 25.11, 22

15From that day Tyre will be forgotten for seventy years, the lifetime of one king. At the end of seventy years, it will happen to Tyre as in the song about the prostitute:

16 Take a harp,
    go about the city,
    you forgotten prostitute!
  Make sweet melody,
    sing many songs,
    that you may be remembered.

23.17
Rev 17.2

17At the end of seventy years, the LORD will visit Tyre, and she will return to her trade, and will prostitute herself with all the kingdoms of the world on the face of the earth. 18Her merchandise and her wages will be dedicated to the LORD; her profits*p* will not be stored or hoarded, but her merchandise will supply abundant food and fine clothing for those who live in the presence of the LORD.

23.18
Isa 60.5-9;
Zech 14.20

IV. *First volume of general rebuke and promise (24.1–27.13)*

A. *Sermon I: universal judgment for universal sin*

1. *Devouring judgment meted out to all classes*

24.1
vv. 19, 20;
Isa 13.13, 14

24 Now the LORD is about to lay waste the earth and make it desolate,
  and he will twist its surface and scatter its inhabitants.

24.2
Hos 4.9;
Lev 25.36,
37;
Deut 23.19,
20

2 And it shall be, as with the people, so with the priest;
    as with the slave, so with his master;
    as with the maid, so with her mistress;
  as with the buyer, so with the seller;
    as with the lender, so with the borrower;
    as with the creditor, so with the debtor.

24.3
Isa 6.11, 12

3 The earth shall be utterly laid waste and utterly despoiled;
    for the LORD has spoken this word.

24.4
Isa 33.9;
2.12

4 The earth dries up and withers,
    the world languishes and withers;
    the heavens languish together with the earth.

24.5
Gen 3.17;
Num 35.33;
Isa 59.12

5 The earth lies polluted
    under its inhabitants;
  for they have transgressed laws,

o Meaning of Heb uncertain   *p* Heb *it*

23.17   After seventy years God would allow Tyre to rise from the dust for a season. The island of Tyre itself was later destroyed under an assault by Alexander the Great, and it has remained a desolation since then. But mainland Tyre has continued to exist, in spite of numerous assaults by foreign nations. It was still there in Jesus' day, and he made reference to Tyre and Sidon several times (e.g., Mt 11.22; Lk 10.13). In Acts 21.3 Paul landed at Tyre and went up from there to Jerusalem, before going to Rome.
24.1ff   *the LORD is about to lay waste the earth.* A

change of focus takes place as Isaiah turned from prophesying about individual nations to refer to the whole earth. The use of the word *world* in v. 4 indicates that Isaiah, in apocalyptic form, foresaw a guilty world in chaos due to God's judgment.
24.5   Judah was guilty of at least three sins: (1) it had committed crimes against the laws of nature in the land; (2) it had sinned against the statutes of revealed religion, i.e., the laws of God; and (3) it had broken the contract it made with God.

    violated the statutes,
       broken the everlasting covenant.

6 Therefore a curse devours the earth,
    and its inhabitants suffer for their guilt;
  therefore the inhabitants of the earth dwindled,
    and few people are left.

7 The wine dries up,
    the vine languishes,
    all the merry-hearted sigh.

8 The mirth of the timbrels is stilled,
    the noise of the jubilant has ceased,
    the mirth of the lyre is stilled.

9 No longer do they drink wine with singing;
    strong drink is bitter to those who drink it.

10 The city of chaos is broken down,
    every house is shut up so that no one can enter.

11 There is an outcry in the streets for lack of wine;
    all joy has reached its eventide;
    the gladness of the earth is banished.

12 Desolation is left in the city,
    the gates are battered into ruins.

13 For thus it shall be on the earth
    and among the nations,
  as when an olive tree is beaten,
    as at the gleaning when the grape harvest is ended.

2. The grateful remnant praise God

14 They lift up their voices, they sing for joy;
    they shout from the west over the majesty of the Lord.

15 Therefore in the east give glory to the Lord;
    in the coastlands of the sea glorify the name of the Lord, the
      God of Israel.

3 Sure judgment and a new age

16 From the ends of the earth we hear songs of praise,
    of glory to the Righteous One.
  But I say, I pine away,
    I pine away. Woe is me!
  For the treacherous deal treacherously,
    the treacherous deal very treacherously.

17 Terror, and the pit, and the snare
    are upon you, O inhabitant of the earth!

18 Whoever flees at the sound of the terror
    shall fall into the pit;
  and whoever climbs out of the pit
    shall be caught in the snare.
  For the windows of heaven are opened,
    and the foundations of the earth tremble.

19 The earth is utterly broken,
    the earth is torn asunder,
    the earth is violently shaken.

Cross-references:

24.6 Isa 34.5; Mal 4.6; Isa 5.24; 9.19
24.7 Isa 16.8-10; Joel 1.10-12
24.8 Jer 7.34; 16.9; 25.10; Ezek 26.13; Hos 2.11; Rev 18.22
24.9 Isa 5.11, 20, 22
24.10 Isa 23.1
24.11 Jer 14.2; 46.12; Isa 16.10; 32.13
24.12 Isa 14.31; 45.2
24.13 Isa 17.5, 6
24.14 Isa 12.6; 42.10
24.15 Isa 25.3; Mal 1.11; Isa 66.19
24.16 Isa 11.12; 28.5; Jer 5.11
24.17 1 Kings 19.17
24.18 Jer 48.43, 44; Gen 7.11; Ps 18.7
24.19 v. 1; Jer 4.23

24.13,14 As in other times of judgment, a remnant would remain faithful to God. These would lift their voices in praise to God and sing for joy. Despite the catastrophic circumstances, the true people of God always find their consolation and deliverance in the God they worship.

24.15,16 In Isaiah's vision, songs of praise would be raised *to the Righteous One*, who had sent the fire that consumed the wicked but not the righteous. Fire consumes the dross and refines the gold. For the people of God, the fire purifies—so that they may be pure and spotless before him, in the glory of the new world.

<table>
<tr><td>

24.20
Isa 19.14;
66.24;
Dan 11.19;
Am 8.14

</td><td>

20 The earth staggers like a drunkard,
   it sways like a hut;
 its transgression lies heavy upon it,
   and it falls, and will not rise again.

</td></tr>
</table>

24.20
Isa 19.14;
66.24;
Dan 11.19;
Am 8.14

20 The earth staggers like a drunkard,
   it sways like a hut;
 its transgression lies heavy upon it,
   and it falls, and will not rise again.

24.21
Isa 10.12;
v. 4;
Ps 76.12

21 On that day the LORD will punish
   the host of heaven in heaven,
   and on earth the kings of the earth.

24.22
Isa 10.4;
42.22;
Ezek 38.8;
Zech 9.11, 12

22 They will be gathered together
   like prisoners in a pit;
 they will be shut up in a prison,
   and after many days they will be punished.

24.23
Isa 13.10;
60.19;
Zech 14.6, 7;
Mic 4.7;
Heb 12.22

23 Then the moon will be abashed,
   and the sun ashamed;
 for the LORD of hosts will reign
   on Mount Zion and in Jerusalem,
 and before his elders he will manifest his glory.

B. Sermon II: praise to the LORD

1. For past judgments

25.1
Ps 118.28;
98.1;
Num 23.19

25 O LORD, you are my God;
   I will exalt you, I will praise your name;
 for you have done wonderful things,
   plans formed of old, faithful and sure.

25.2
Isa 17.1;
13.22; 32.14

2 For you have made the city a heap,
   the fortified city a ruin;
 the palace of aliens is a city no more,
   it will never be rebuilt.

3 Therefore strong peoples will glorify you;
   cities of ruthless nations will fear you.

25.4
Isa 14.32;
11.4; 32.2;
49.25

4 For you have been a refuge to the poor,
   a refuge to the needy in their distress,
   a shelter from the rainstorm and a shade from the heat.
 When the blast of the ruthless was like a winter rainstorm,

25.5
Jer 51.54-56

5   the noise of aliens like heat in a dry place,
 you subdued the heat with the shade of clouds;
   the song of the ruthless was stilled.

2. For salvation yet to come

25.6
Isa 2.2-4;
Prov 9.2;
Mt 22.4;
Dan 7.14;
Mt 8.11

6 On this mountain the LORD of hosts will make for all peoples
   a feast of rich food, a feast of well-aged wines,
   of rich food filled with marrow, of well-aged wines strained
     clear.

7 And he will destroy on this mountain
   the shroud that is cast over all peoples,
   the sheet that is spread over all nations;

25.8
Hos 13.14;
1 Cor 15.54;
Rev 7.17;
21.4;
Isa 54.4

8   he will swallow up death forever.
 Then the Lord GOD will wipe away the tears from all faces,

24.20 *it falls, and will not rise again.* In place of the earth as we now know it there will be new heavens and a new earth wherein dwells nothing but righteousness (cf. 2 Pet 3.10–13). The final abode of the righteous is the New Jerusalem, which comes down from God out of heaven.
24.23 When Christ reigns in glory, the brightness of his shining will be such that the light of the moon and of the sun will appear as nothing. Some of the nations

surrounding Israel worshiped the sun and the moon. These pretended deities will be ashamed that they had ever received homage from their deluded worshipers.
25.7,8 *he will swallow up death forever.* One of the chief consequences of Christ's death on Calvary and his resurrection is the death of death (see 1 Cor 15.54). It will be abolished forever and all tears will be washed away.

and the disgrace of his people he will take away from all
    the earth,
for the Lord has spoken.

9 It will be said on that day,
    Lo, this is our God; we have waited for him, so that he
      might save us.
    This is the Lord for whom we have waited;
    let us be glad and rejoice in his salvation.

10 For the hand of the Lord will rest on this mountain.

    The Moabites shall be trodden down in their place
    as straw is trodden down in a dung-pit.

11 Though they spread out their hands in the midst of it,
    as swimmers spread out their hands to swim,
    their pride will be laid low despite the struggle*q* of
      their hands.

12 The high fortifications of his walls will be brought down,
    laid low, cast to the ground, even to the dust.

C. Sermon III: song of rejoicing

1. Praise to the Lord as Israel's defender

26 On that day this song will be sung in the land of Judah:
    We have a strong city;
he sets up victory
    like walls and bulwarks.

2 Open the gates,
    so that the righteous nation that keeps faith
    may enter in.

3 Those of steadfast mind you keep in peace —
    in peace because they trust in you.

4 Trust in the Lord forever,
    for in the Lord God*r*
    you have an everlasting rock.

5 For he has brought low
    the inhabitants of the height;
    the lofty city he lays low.
He lays it low to the ground,
    casts it to the dust.

6 The foot tramples it,
    the feet of the poor,
    the steps of the needy.

7 The way of the righteous is level;
    O Just One, you make smooth the path of the righteous.

8 In the path of your judgments,
    O Lord, we wait for you;
    your name and your renown
    are the soul's desire.

9 My soul yearns for you in the night,
    my spirit within me earnestly seeks you.

q Meaning of Heb uncertain   *r Heb in Yah, the Lord*

25.9
Isa 40.9;
30.18; 33.22;
66.10;
Ps 20.5

25.10
Isa 16.14

26.1
Isa 4.2; 12.1;
14.31; 60.18

26.2
Isa 60.11,
18; 61.3;
62.1, 2

26.4
Isa 12.2;
17.10

26.5
Isa 25.12;
Job 40.11-13

26.6
Isa 28.3;
3.14, 15

26.7
Isa 57.2;
42.16
26.8
Isa 51.4;
56.1; v. 13;
Ex 3.15

26.9
Ps 63.6;
Isa 55.6;
Hos 5.15

26.1ff *On that day.* Whoever experiences the delivering mercies of the God of grace shall sing a song. Those who sing this song are promised perfect peace, because the minds of such people remain fixed on God, in whom alone they trust. His guidance and his government constitute their strongholds, whatever the circumstances of life may be.

26.4 *you have an everlasting rock.* God indeed is the rock of ages, the only foundation upon which to build one's house. Any house built on that foundation will stand against any storm (see Mt 7.24–27).

For when your judgments are in the earth,
   the inhabitants of the world learn righteousness.

2. The doom of persistent wrongdoers

26.10
Rom 2.4;
Isa 22.12,
13;
Hos 11.7;
Jn 5.37,38

10 If favor is shown to the wicked,
   they do not learn righteousness;
in the land of uprightness they deal perversely
   and do not see the majesty of the LORD.

26.11
Isa 5.12; 9.7;
10.17; 66.15,
24

11 O LORD, your hand is lifted up,
   but they do not see it.
Let them see your zeal for your people, and be ashamed.
   Let the fire for your adversaries consume them.

26.12
v. 3;
Isa 64.8

12 O LORD, you will ordain peace for us,
   for indeed, all that we have done, you have done for us.

26.13
Isa 2.8;
10.11; 63.7

13 O LORD our God,
   other lords besides you have ruled over us,
   but we acknowledge your name alone.

26.14
Isa 8.19;
Hab 2.19;
Isa 10.3

14 The dead do not live;
   shades do not rise—
because you have punished and destroyed them,
   and wiped out all memory of them.

3. Israel's prayer for deliverance answered

26.15
Isa 9.3;
33.17

15 But you have increased the nation, O LORD,
   you have increased the nation; you are glorified;
   you have enlarged all the borders of the land.

26.16
Hos 5.15

16 O LORD, in distress they sought you,
   they poured out a prayers
   when your chastening was on them.

26.17
Isa 13.8;
Jn 16.21

17 Like a woman with child,
   who writhes and cries out in her pangs
   when she is near her time,
so were we because of you, O LORD;

26.18
Isa 33.11;
Ps 17.14

18 we were with child, we writhed,
   but we gave birth only to wind.
We have won no victories on earth,
   and no one is born to inhabit the world.

26.19
Ezek 37.1-14;
Dan 12.2

19 Your dead shall live, their corpsest shall rise.
   O dwellers in the dust, awake and sing for joy!
For your dew is a radiant dew,
   and the earth will give birth to those long dead.u

4. Appeal to take refuge in God alone

26.20
Ex 12.22, 23;
Ps 30.5;
Isa 54.7, 8;
2 Cor 4.17

20 Come, my people, enter your chambers,
   and shut your doors behind you;

s Meaning of Heb uncertain   t Cn Compare Syr Tg: Heb *my corpse*   u Heb *to the shades*

26.12 *peace.* The word "peace" is used variously in the Scriptures. The root itself (*shalom*) suggests prosperity and well-being, such as Israel enjoyed under King Solomon (1 Kings 4.20,25); it includes an earthly blessedness, wholeness, and right relations which believers will enjoy forever under Messiah's rule (Mic 4.3,4). A second meaning for the word is the absence of war. This kind of peace for the world will come only after Christ's second advent; until then, there will be wars and rumors of wars (Mt 24.6–14). For believers, the word "peace" has two further meanings: (1) "peace with God" (Rom 5.1), i.e., that

spiritual peace that comes from justification or having been made right with God through Jesus Christ; (2) "the peace of God," which surpasses all understanding" (Phil 4.7), i.e., an inner life of utter tranquility despite external trouble and difficulties.
26.19 Isaiah clearly believed in the bodily resurrection of the righteous and the wicked. Those who are "in their graves will hear his voice, and will come out—those who have done good, to the resurrection of life, and those who have done evil, to the resurrection of condemnation" (Jn 5.28,29).

hide yourselves for a little while
    until the wrath is past.
21 For the LORD comes out from his place
    to punish the inhabitants of the earth for their iniquity;
the earth will disclose the blood shed on it,
    and will no longer cover its slain.

26.21
Mic 1.3;
Jude 14;
Isa 13.11;
Job 16.18

27 On that day the LORD with his cruel and great and strong sword
will punish Leviathan the fleeing serpent, Leviathan the twisting
serpent, and he will kill the dragon that is in the sea.

27.1
Isa 34.5, 6;
Job 3.8;
Ps 74.14;
Isa 51.9

D. *Sermon IV: punishment for oppressors;*
preservation of God's people

1. *Future prosperity of Israel*

2 On that day:
A pleasant vineyard, sing about it!
3   I, the LORD, am its keeper;
      every moment I water it.
I guard it night and day
    so that no one can harm it;
4   I have no wrath.
If it gives me thorns and briers,
    I will march to battle against it.
    I will burn it up.
5 Or else let it cling to me for protection,
    let it make peace with me,
    let it make peace with me.

27.2
Ps 5.7; 80.8;
Jer 2.21
27.3
Isa 58.11;
31.5;
1 Sam 2.9
27.4
2 Sam 23.6;
Isa 33.12
27.5
Isa 25.4;
Job 22.21

6 In days to come*v* Jacob shall take root,
    Israel shall blossom and put forth shoots,
    and fill the whole world with fruit.

27.6
Isa 37.31;
Hos 14.5, 6

2. *Exile a means of purging Israel*

7 Has he struck them down as he struck down those who struck
      them?
    Or have they been killed as their killers were killed?
8 By expulsion,*w* by exile you struggled against them;
    with his fierce blast he removed them in the day of the
      east wind.
9 Therefore by this the guilt of Jacob will be expiated,
    and this will be the full fruit of the removal of his sin:
when he makes all the stones of the altars
    like chalkstones crushed to pieces,
    no sacred poles*x* or incense altars will remain standing.
10 For the fortified city is solitary,
    a habitation deserted and forsaken, like the wilderness;
the calves graze there,
    there they lie down, and strip its branches.

27.7
Isa 10.12, 17
27.8
Job 23.6;
Jer 10.23;
Ps 78.38
27.9
Isa 1.25;
Rom 11.27;
Isa 17.8
27.10
Isa 32.13,
14;
Jer 26.6, 18

v Heb *Those to come*   *w* Meaning of Heb uncertain   *x* Heb *Asherim*

27.1 *Leviathan* was a mythological monster of the
sea which, as a symbol of evil, had to be slain.
27.2–6 God contends with his people when they sin
but is reconciled to them when they repent. His anger
can be reversed only by humiliation and prayer on the
part of the transgressor. God wants his people to seek
peace and reconciliation with him for three reasons:
(1) God gives them time and space to repent — he

does not cut them off forever; (2) it is vain to think
one can win a contest with him, for no one is a match
for his omnipotence; (3) God's way is the only sure
way to reconciliation.
27.8 God had dealt out afflictions to Israel. But divine judgment and Israel's afflictions were mixed with
mercy, for his people would eventually return to him
for pardon and cleansing.

27.11
Deut 32.28;
Isa 1.3;
Jer 8.7;
Deut 32.18;
Isa 43.1, 7;
44.2, 21, 24

11 When its boughs are dry, they are broken;
   women come and make a fire of them.
For this is a people without understanding;
   therefore he that made them will not have compassion
     on them,
   he that formed them will show them no favor.

3. The future regathering of Israel

27.12
Isa 11.11;
Gen 15.18;
Deut 30.3, 4
27.13
Lev 25.9;
Mt 24.31;
Rev 11.15;
Isa 19.23-25

12 On that day the LORD will thresh from the channel of the Euphrates to the Wadi of Egypt, and you will be gathered one by one, O people of Israel. 13 And on that day a great trumpet will be blown, and those who were lost in the land of Assyria and those who were driven out to the land of Egypt will come and worship the LORD on the holy mountain at Jerusalem.

V. Volume of woes upon the unbelievers of Israel
(28.1–33.24)

A. Sermon I: God's dealing with drunkards and scoffers

1. Woe upon the drunkards of Samaria

28.1
vv. 3, 4, 7

28 Ah, the proud garland of the drunkards of Ephraim,
   and the fading flower of its glorious beauty,
  which is on the head of those bloated with rich food, of those
    overcome with wine!

28.2
Isa 40.10;
30.30;
Ezek 13.11;
Isa 29.6;
30.28
28.3
vv. 1, 18

2 See, the Lord has one who is mighty and strong;
   like a storm of hail, a destroying tempest,
like a storm of mighty, overflowing waters;
   with his hand he will hurl them down to the earth.
3 Trampled under foot will be
   the proud garland of the drunkards of Ephraim.

28.4
Hos 9.10;
Mic 7.1;
Nah 3.12

4 And the fading flower of its glorious beauty,
   which is on the head of those bloated with rich food,
will be like a first-ripe fig before the summer;
   whoever sees it, eats it up
   as soon as it comes to hand.

28.5
Isa 41.16;
62.3; 4.2
28.6
Isa 11.2;
32.15; 25.4

5 In that day the LORD of hosts will be a garland of glory,
   and a diadem of beauty, to the remnant of his people;
6 and a spirit of justice to the one who sits in judgment,
   and strength to those who turn back the battle at the gate.

28.7
Prov 20.1;
Hos 4.11;
Isa 56.10, 12

7 These also reel with wine
   and stagger with strong drink;
the priest and the prophet reel with strong drink,
   they are confused with wine,
   they stagger with strong drink;
they err in vision,
   they stumble in giving judgment.

27.12 The anger of God against his people would not last forever. When they turned to the Messiah in faith, they would be regathered from the ends of the earth to be brought back to their ancestral lands. They would then worship God with hearts that were right and deeds that corresponded to their profession. **28.1ff** The Ephraimites (residents of the northern

kingdom) are reproved here for their sins: pride, drunkenness, security, and sensuality.
28.7,8 Drunkenness was not simply the preoccupation of princes and the people; it was also common to priests and prophets. Instead of truth, righteousness, and purity there was vomit and filthiness.

8 All tables are covered with filthy vomit;
    no place is clean.

28.8
Jer 48.26

2. Scoffers to be scourged by Assyria

9 "Whom will he teach knowledge,
    and to whom will he explain the message?
  Those who are weaned from milk,
    those taken from the breast?

28.9
v. 26;
Ps 131.2;
Heb 5.12, 13

10 For it is precept upon precept, precept upon precept,
     line upon line, line upon line,
     here a little, there a little."*y*

28.10
Neh 9.30

11 Truly, with stammering lip
     and with alien tongue
   he will speak to this people,

28.11
1 Cor 14.21

12 to whom he has said,
   "This is rest;
     give rest to the weary;
   and this is repose";
     yet they would not hear.

28.12
Jer 6.16;
Mt 11.28, 29

13 Therefore the word of the LORD will be to them,
     "Precept upon precept, precept upon precept,
     line upon line, line upon line,
     here a little, there a little;"*y*
   in order that they may go, and fall backward,
     and be broken, and snared, and taken.

28.13
Mt 21.44

14 Therefore hear the word of the LORD, you scoffers
     who rule this people in Jerusalem.

28.14
v. 22;
Isa 29.20

15 Because you have said, "We have made a covenant with death,
     and with Sheol we have an agreement;
   when the overwhelming scourge passes through
     it will not come to us;
   for we have made lies our refuge,
     and in falsehood we have taken shelter";

28.15
vv. 18, 2;
Isa 59.3, 4;
29.15

16 therefore thus says the Lord GOD,
   See, I am laying in Zion a foundation stone,
     a tested stone,
   a precious cornerstone, a sure foundation:
     "One who trusts will not panic."

28.16
Ps 118.22;
Mt 21.42;
Acts 4.11;
Rom 9.33;
10.11;
Eph 2.20;
1 Pet 2.4-6
28.17
Isa 5.16; v. 2

17 And I will make justice the line,
     and righteousness the plummet;
   hail will sweep away the refuge of lies,
     and waters will overwhelm the shelter.

18 Then your covenant with death will be annulled,
     and your agreement with Sheol will not stand;
   when the overwhelming scourge passes through
     you will be beaten down by it.

28.18
v. 15

y Meaning of Heb of this verse uncertain

28.9ff Isaiah hoped to teach the people the truth, but in their wretched stupidity they were unteachable. They refused to rectify their errors, their hearts were unchanged, and their lives were unreformed. Since Samaria would not hear the comforting word of God, they would hear the dreadful roar of his rod. **28.15** *We have made a covenant with death.* Judah thought itself to be secure because of its alliance with Egypt against Assyria. But this was only a covenant with death and Sheol (i.e., the netherworld).

28.16 The *foundation stone* or *cornerstone* can only refer to Christ. As a stone he protects, delivers, and judges: (1) Christ the rock was smitten for our transgressions (Ex 17.6; Num 20.8; 1 Cor 10.4); (2) Christ is the stone that demolishes the last world power (Dan 2.34); (3) Christ's stone becomes a great mountain that will cover the whole earth (Dan 2.35); (4) Christ is the precious cornerstone (1 Pet 2.6); and (5) Christ is "a stone that will make people stumble, a rock that will make them fall" (Rom 9.32,33; 1 Pet 2.8).

19 As often as it passes through, it will take you;
   for morning by morning it will pass through,
     by day and by night;
and it will be sheer terror to understand the message.
20 For the bed is too short to stretch oneself on it,
   and the covering too narrow to wrap oneself in it.

21 For the LORD will rise up as on Mount Perazim,
   he will rage as in the valley of Gibeon
to do his deed — strange is his deed! —
   and to work his work — alien is his work!
22 Now therefore do not scoff,
   or your bonds will be made stronger;
for I have heard a decree of destruction
   from the Lord GOD of hosts upon the whole land.

3. Parable of the farmer

23 Listen, and hear my voice;
   Pay attention, and hear my speech.
24 Do those who plow for sowing plow continually?
   Do they continually open and harrow their ground?
25 When they have leveled its surface,
   do they not scatter dill, sow cummin,
and plant wheat in rows
   and barley in its proper place,
    and spelt as the border?
26 For they are well instructed;
   their God teaches them.

27 Dill is not threshed with a threshing sledge,
   nor is a cart wheel rolled over cummin;
but dill is beaten out with a stick,
   and cummin with a rod.
28 Grain is crushed for bread,
   but one does not thresh it forever;
one drives the cart wheel and horses over it,
   but does not pulverize it.

29 This also comes from the LORD of hosts;
   he is wonderful in counsel,
   and excellent in wisdom.

B. Sermon II: the doom of blind hypocrites

1. The careless Jews are to be humbled

29
Ah, Ariel, Ariel,
   the city where David encamped!
Add year to year;
   let the festivals run their round.

2 Yet I will distress Ariel,
   and there shall be moaning and lamentation,

28.20 What Samaria trusted in would never fulfill their needs or their expectations. Isaiah likens their dilemma to that of a tall man trying to sleep in a short bed. He is forced to assume a fetal position and cannot find the rest he desires. He also has a blanket that will not cover him, so he is never warm on a cold night. **28.21** God would rise up against Israel as he had risen up against the Philistines in David's time at Mt. Perazim (2 Sam 5.20) and in Joshua's time in the

valley of Gibeon (Josh 10.1ff). The destruction he worked among Israel's enemies on these occasions exemplified the destruction he would rain upon his own people. **28.23–29** As farmers use different instruments to produce their crops, so God would employ particular judgments to produce the righteousness he expected from his people. **29.1** *Ariel*, i.e., Jerusalem.

and Jerusalem^z shall be to me like an Ariel.^a

3 And like David^b I will encamp against you;
    I will besiege you with towers
    and raise siegeworks against you.

4 Then deep from the earth you shall speak,
    from low in the dust your words shall come;
your voice shall come from the ground like the voice of a ghost,
    and your speech shall whisper out of the dust.

2. Sudden destruction of Israel's foes

5 But the multitude of your foes^c shall be like small dust,
    and the multitude of tyrants like flying chaff.
And in an instant, suddenly,
6   you will be visited by the LORD of hosts
with thunder and earthquake and great noise,
    with whirlwind and tempest, and the flame of a devouring
      fire.

7 And the multitude of all the nations that fight against Ariel,
    all that fight against her and her stronghold, and who
      distress her,
    shall be like a dream, a vision of the night.

8 Just as when a hungry person dreams of eating
    and wakes up still hungry,
or a thirsty person dreams of drinking
    and wakes up faint, still thirsty,
so shall the multitude of all the nations be
    that fight against Mount Zion.

3. The folly of trying to deceive God with a sham faith

9 Stupefy yourselves and be in a stupor,
    blind yourselves and be blind!
Be drunk, but not from wine;
    stagger, but not from strong drink!

10 For the LORD has poured out upon you
    a spirit of deep sleep;
he has closed your eyes, you prophets,
    and covered your heads, you seers.

11   The vision of all this has become for you like the words of a sealed document. If it is given to those who can read, with the command, "Read this," they say, "We cannot, for it is sealed." 12 And if it is given to those who cannot read, saying, "Read this," they say, "We cannot read."

13 The Lord said:
Because these people draw near with their mouths
    and honor me with their lips,
      while their hearts are far from me,
and their worship of me is a human commandment learned
      by rote;

14 so I will again do
    amazing things with this people,

---

^z Heb *she*   ^a Probable meaning, *altar hearth*; compare Ezek 43.15   ^b Gk: Meaning of Heb uncertain
^c Cn: Heb *strangers*

Cross references (right margin):

29.3
Lk 19.43, 44

29.4
Isa 8.19;
Lev 20.6;
Deut 18.10,
11;
1 Sam 28.8,
15;
2 Chr 33.6

29.5
Isa 17.13,
14; 25.3-5;
30.13;
1 Thess 5.3
29.6
Isa 28.2;
Mt 24.7;
Mk 13.8;
Lk 21.11;
Rev 11.13,
19; 16.18
29.7
Mic 4.11, 12;
Zech 12.9;
Job 20.8;
Ps 73.20
29.8
Isa 54.17

29.9
Isa 51.17,
21, 22

29.10
Rom 11.8;
Ps 69.23;
Isa 6.9, 10;
Mic 3.6

29.11
Isa 27.7;
8.16;
Dan 12.4, 9;
Mt 13.11

29.13
Ezek 33.31;
Mt 15.8, 9;
Mk 7.6, 7

29.14
Hab 1.5;
Jer 8.9; 49.7;
1 Cor 1.19

29.11,12 God sent Isaiah to his people. He saw visions and uttered the prophecies. But this made no difference to the people of God. It was as if they had a book that was sealed and they could not read it, or as if the illiterate were given a book. Because their hearts were wrong, they could not understand what God had said in any event.

29.13 God charged his people with hypocrisy; theirs was a religion of the lip, not of the heart. They worshiped God according to their own inventions, not according to what God himself required of them in his revelation.

shocking and amazing.
The wisdom of their wise shall perish,
    and the discernment of the discerning shall be hidden.

29.15
Isa 30.1;
57.12;
Ps 94.7

15 Ha! You who hide a plan too deep for the Lord,
    whose deeds are in the dark,
    and who say, "Who sees us? Who knows us?"

29.16
Isa 45.9;
Jer 18.1-6;
Rom 9.19-21

16 You turn things upside down!
    Shall the potter be regarded as the clay?
Shall the thing made say of its maker,
    "He did not make me";
or the thing formed say of the one who formed it,
    "He has no understanding"?

4. *Future deliverance of God's people from blindness*

29.17
Isa 32.15

17 Shall not Lebanon in a very little while
    become a fruitful field,
    and the fruitful field be regarded as a forest?

29.18
Isa 35.5;
v. 11

18 On that day the deaf shall hear
    the words of a scroll,
and out of their gloom and darkness
    the eyes of the blind shall see.

29.19
Isa 61.1;
Mt 11.5;
Jas 2.5

19 The meek shall obtain fresh joy in the Lord,
    and the neediest people shall exult in the Holy One of Israel.

29.20
v. 5;
Isa 28.14;
22; 59.4

20 For the tyrant shall be no more,
    and the scoffer shall cease to be;
all those alert to do evil shall be cut off —

29.21
Am 5.10, 12;
Prov 28.21

21 those who cause a person to lose a lawsuit,
    who set a trap for the arbiter in the gate,
    and without grounds deny justice to the one in the right.

5. *Jacob's reproach rolled away*

29.22
Isa 41.8;
45.17; 54.4

22 Therefore thus says the Lord, who redeemed Abraham, concerning the house of Jacob:
No longer shall Jacob be ashamed,
    no longer shall his face grow pale.

29.23
Isa 49.20-26;
45.11; 5.16;
8.13

23 For when he sees his children,
    the work of my hands, in his midst,
    they will sanctify my name;
they will sanctify the Holy One of Jacob,
    and will stand in awe of the God of Israel.

29.24
Isa 28.7

24 And those who err in spirit will come to understanding,
    and those who grumble will accept instruction.

C. *Sermon III: trust in mortals versus trust in God*

1. *Sinful reliance upon Egypt*

30.1
v. 9;
Isa 29.15;
8.11, 12

30

Oh, rebellious children, says the Lord,
    who carry out a plan, but not mine;

30.2
Isa 31.1;
Num 27.21;
Josh 9.14;
1 Kings 22.7;
Jer 21.2

who make an alliance, but against my will,
    adding sin to sin;
2 who set out to go down to Egypt

29.18 Despite Israel's transgressions, the day would come when their ignorance would turn to intelligence, their deafness to hearing, and their blindness to sight. Those who rightly use the word of God will not be ignorant and will both hear and see as they ought.

30.2 Hezekiah was seeking a defensive alliance with Ethiopia's Egyptian dynasty against Sennacherib of Assyria. Judah sought the arm of the flesh rather than faith in God. They did not even consult God. Isaiah told them that (1) Egypt's promises were worthless (v. 7); (2) strength lay in returning and waiting on

without asking for my counsel,
to take refuge in the protection of Pharaoh,
    and to seek shelter in the shadow of Egypt;
3 Therefore the protection of Pharaoh shall become your shame,
    and the shelter in the shadow of Egypt your humiliation.
4 For though his officials are at Zoan
    and his envoys reach Hanes,
5 everyone comes to shame
    through a people that cannot profit them,
that brings neither help nor profit,
    but shame and disgrace.

2. The embassy to Egypt of no avail

6 An oracle concerning the animals of the Negeb.
Through a land of trouble and distress,
    of lioness and roaring[d] lion,
    of viper and flying serpent,
they carry their riches on the backs of donkeys,
    and their treasures on the humps of camels,
to a people that cannot profit them.
7 For Egypt's help is worthless and empty,
    therefore I have called her,
    "Rahab who sits still."[e]

3. Rebellious Judah to be crushed

8 Go now, write it before them on a tablet,
    and inscribe it in a book,
so that it may be for the time to come
    as a witness forever.
9 For they are a rebellious people,
    faithless children,
children who will not hear
    the instruction of the LORD;
10 who say to the seers, "Do not see";
    and to the prophets, "Do not prophesy to us what is right;
speak to us smooth things,
    prophesy illusions,
11 leave the way, turn aside from the path,
    let us hear no more about the Holy One of Israel."
12 Therefore thus says the Holy One of Israel:
Because you reject this word,
    and put your trust in oppression and deceit,
    and rely on them;
13 therefore this iniquity shall become for you
    like a break in a high wall, bulging out, and about to
        collapse,
    whose crash comes suddenly, in an instant;
14 its breaking is like that of a potter's vessel
    that is smashed so ruthlessly
that among its fragments not a sherd is found
    for taking fire from the hearth,
    or dipping water out of the cistern.

15 For thus said the Lord GOD, the Holy One of Israel:

d Cn: Heb *from them*   e Meaning of Heb uncertain

Cross references (right column):
30.3 Isa 20.5; Jer 37.3, 5
30.4 Isa 19.11
30.5 Jer 2.36; v. 7
30.6 Isa 46.1, 2; 8.22; 14.29; 15.7
30.7 Jer 37.7; v. 15
30.8 Isa 8.1; Hab 2.2
30.9 v. 1; Isa 28.15; 24.5
30.10 Isa 29.10; 5.20; 1 Kings 22.8, 13
30.11 Job 21.14
30.12 Isa 5.24; 59.13
30.13 Isa 26.21; Ps 62.3; Isa 29.5
30.14 Ps 2.9; Jer 19.10, 11
30.15 Isa 7.4; 28.12; 32.17

God to help them (v. 15); and (3) God was both willing and able to be gracious to his people if they would
turn to him in repentance and faith so that he could
bless them (v. 18).

In returning and rest you shall be saved;
  in quietness and in trust shall be your strength.
But you refused 16 and said,
"No! We will flee upon horses" —
  therefore you shall flee!
and, "We will ride upon swift steeds" —
  therefore your pursuers shall be swift!

17 A thousand shall flee at the threat of one,
  at the threat of five you shall flee,
until you are left
like a flagstaff on the top of a mountain,
like a signal on a hill.

4. God's promise to a repentant people

18 Therefore the LORD waits to be gracious to you;
  therefore he will rise up to show mercy to you.
For the LORD is a God of justice;
  blessed are all those who wait for him.

19 Truly, O people in Zion, inhabitants of Jerusalem, you shall weep no more. He will surely be gracious to you at the sound of your cry; when he hears it, he will answer you. 20 Though the Lord may give you the bread of adversity and the water of affliction, yet your Teacher will not hide himself any more, but your eyes shall see your Teacher. 21 And when you turn to the right or when you turn to the left, your ears shall hear a word behind you, saying, "This is the way; walk in it." 22 Then you will defile your silver-covered idols and your gold-plated images. You will scatter them like filthy rags; you will say to them, "Away with you!"

23 He will give rain for the seed with which you sow the ground, and grain, the produce of the ground, which will be rich and plenteous. On that day your cattle will graze in broad pastures; 24 and the oxen and donkeys that till the ground will eat silage, which has been winnowed with shovel and fork. 25 On every lofty mountain and every high hill there will be brooks running with water — on a day of the great slaughter, when the towers fall. 26 Moreover the light of the moon will be like the light of the sun, and the light of the sun will be sevenfold, like the light of seven days, on the day when the LORD binds up the injuries of his people, and heals the wounds inflicted by his blow.

5. Israel's enemies to be smitten

27 See, the name of the LORD comes from far away,
  burning with his anger, and in thick rising smoke;f
his lips are full of indignation,
  and his tongue is like a devouring fire;
28 his breath is like an overflowing stream
  that reaches up to the neck —
to sift the nations with the sieve of destruction,
  and to place on the jaws of the peoples a bridle that leads
    them astray.

29 You shall have a song as in the night when a holy festival is kept;

f Meaning of Heb uncertain

30.16 Isa 31.1, 3
30.17 Lev 26.8; Deut 28.25; 32.30; Josh 23.10
30.18 Isa 42.14; 33.5; 5.16; 25.9
30.19 Isa 65.9; 60.20; 61.1-3; Mt 7.7-11
30.20 1 Kings 22.27; Ps 80.5; 74.9; Am 8.11
30.21 Isa 35.8, 9; Prov 3.6; Isa 29.24
30.22 Isa 2.20; 31.7; 46.6; Mt 4.10
30.23 Ps 65.9-13; Isa 65.21, 22; 32.20
30.26 Isa 60.19; 20; Rev 21.23; 22.5; Isa 61.1; 1.6; Jer 33.6
30.27 Isa 59.19; 10.5, 13, 17; 66.15
30.28 Isa 11.4; 2 Thess 2.8; Isa 8.8; 37.29
30.29 Ps 42.4; Isa 2.3; 17.10

30.17 When sin enters our lives, it debilitates us and renders us helpless against our enemy. We become so weak that a single enemy will rout a thousand of us with ease, for the power of God departs from us (cf. Judg 16).
30.20 God waits to give his mercy to and to bless the penitent who come to him for healing. Until then, they will eat the *bread of adversity* and drink *the water of affliction*, i.e., they will survive on coarse food and drink puddle water. Retribution always has in it the possibility that the sufferer will learn from this and turn to God for deliverance. And God waits with patience for his people to repent.

and gladness of heart, as when one sets out to the sound of the flute to go to the mountain of the LORD, to the Rock of Israel. 30 And the LORD will cause his majestic voice to be heard and the descending blow of his arm to be seen, in furious anger and a flame of devouring fire, with a cloudburst and tempest and hailstones. 31 The Assyrian will be terror-stricken at the voice of the LORD, when he strikes with his rod. 32 And every stroke of the staff of punishment that the LORD lays upon him will be to the sound of timbrels and lyres; battling with brandished arm he will fight with him. 33 For his burning place*g* has long been prepared; truly it is made ready for the king,*h* its pyre made deep and wide, with fire and wood in abundance; the breath of the LORD, like a stream of sulfur, kindles it.

D. Sermon IV: Israel's deliverance by divine intervention

1. Folly of reliance on Egypt

31 Alas for those who go down to Egypt for help
　　and who rely on horses,
who trust in chariots because they are many
　　and in horsemen because they are very strong,
but do not look to the Holy One of Israel
　　or consult the LORD!
2　Yet he too is wise and brings disaster;
　　　he does not call back his words,
but will rise against the house of the evildoers,
　　and against the helpers of those who work iniquity.
3　The Egyptians are human, and not God;
　　　their horses are flesh, and not spirit.
When the LORD stretches out his hand,
　　the helper will stumble, and the one helped will fall,
　　and they will all perish together.

2. The call to trust in the LORD

4　For thus the LORD said to me,
As a lion or a young lion growls over its prey,
　　and — when a band of shepherds is called out against it —
is not terrified by their shouting
　　or daunted at their noise,
so the LORD of hosts will come down
　　to fight upon Mount Zion and upon its hill.
5　Like birds hovering overhead, so the LORD of hosts
　　will protect Jerusalem;
he will protect and deliver it,
　　he will spare and rescue it.

6　Turn back to him whom you*i* have deeply betrayed, O people of Israel. 7 For on that day all of you shall throw away your idols of silver and idols of gold, which your hands have sinfully made for you.

g Or *Topheth*　*h* Or *Molech*　*i* Heb *they*

30.30	Isa 28.2; 32.19
30.31	Isa 31.8
30.32	Isa 10.24; Jer 31.4; Ezek 32.10
30.33	Jer 7.3; 19.6; vv. 27, 28; Isa 34.9
31.1	Isa 30.2; Ezek 17.15; Isa 2.7; Ps 20.7; Dan 9.13; Isa 10.17
31.2	Isa 28.29; Rom 16.27; Isa 45.7; Num 23.19; Isa 14.20; 22.14
31.3	Ezek 28.9; Isa 36.9; 9.17; 30.5, 7
31.4	Hos 11.10; Am 3.8; Isa 42.13
31.5	Ps 91.4; Isa 17.13
31.6	Isa 44.22; 1.2, 5
31.7	Isa 2.20

31.1 It would have been proper for Israel to seek the help of Egypt and make an alliance with that nation if God had so commanded. But God forbade such an alliance and considered such action an indication of Israel's lack of confidence in the Lord God. Israel here not only sought help from Egypt; they failed to seek the help of God. This was a tragic mistake. The basic principle applies to the believer today. If we live in contempt of divine laws, i.e., if we fail to do what God has commanded us to do, then God will judge us. We must seek the face of God in everything and at all times, and do so first.

31.5 God would send a single angel to destroy the Assyrian army and save Jerusalem. Though Jerusalem deserved to be destroyed as well, the angel would draw his sword only against the besiegers. Despite this deliverance, Jerusalem would continue its wicked ways.

8 "Then the Assyrian shall fall by a sword, not of mortals;
　　and a sword, not of humans, shall devour him;
　he shall flee from the sword,
　　and his young men shall be put to forced labor.

9 His rock shall pass away in terror,
　　and his officers desert the standard in panic,"
　says the Lord, whose fire is in Zion,
　　and whose furnace is in Jerusalem.

3. *Israel's ultimate deliverance*

32 See, a king will reign in righteousness,
　　and princes will rule with justice.
2 Each will be like a hiding place from the wind,
　　a covert from the tempest,
　like streams of water in a dry place,
　　like the shade of a great rock in a weary land.

3 Then the eyes of those who have sight will not be closed,
　　and the ears of those who have hearing will listen.

4 The minds of the rash will have good judgment,
　　and the tongues of stammerers will speak readily and
　　　　distinctly.

5 A fool will no longer be called noble,
　　nor a villain said to be honorable.

6 For fools speak folly,
　　and their minds plot iniquity:
　to practice ungodliness,
　　to utter error concerning the Lord,
　to leave the craving of the hungry unsatisfied,
　　and to deprive the thirsty of drink.

7 The villainies of villains are evil;
　　they devise wicked devices
　to ruin the poor with lying words,
　　even when the plea of the needy is right.

8 But those who are noble plan noble things,
　　and by noble things they stand.

4. *After calamity, restoration*

9 Rise up, you women who are at ease, hear my voice;
　　you complacent daughters, listen to my speech.
10 In little more than a year
　　you will shudder, you complacent ones;
　for the vintage will fail,
　　the fruit harvest will not come.

11 Tremble, you women who are at ease,
　　shudder, you complacent ones;
　strip, and make yourselves bare,
　　and put sackcloth on your loins.

12 Beat your breasts for the pleasant fields,
　　for the fruitful vine,

13 for the soil of my people
　　growing up in thorns and briers;
　yes, for all the joyous houses
　　in the jubilant city.

32.1 *a king will reign in righteousness.* Despite oppression and the series of weak and unworthy monarchs, the O.T. saints looked for and prayed for a king whose chief attribute would be to rule in righteousness. So also Christians look and pray for peace, though this will never materialize until the Prince of Peace comes back to rule in righteousness.

14 For the palace will be forsaken,
  the populous city deserted;
 the hill and the watchtower
  will become dens forever,
 the joy of wild asses,
  a pasture for flocks;

15 until a spirit from on high is poured out on us,
  and the wilderness becomes a fruitful field,
  and the fruitful field is deemed a forest.

16 Then justice will dwell in the wilderness,
  and righteousness abide in the fruitful field.

17 The effect of righteousness will be peace,
  and the result of righteousness, quietness and trust forever.

18 My people will abide in a peaceful habitation,
  in secure dwellings, and in quiet resting places.

19 The forest will disappear completely,*j*
  and the city will be utterly laid low.

20 Happy will you be who sow beside every stream,
  who let the ox and the donkey range freely.

32.14 Isa 13.22; 6.11; 13.21
32.15 Isa 11.2; Ezek 39.29; Joel 2.28; Isa 29.17; 35.2
32.16 Isa 33.5
32.17 Rom 14.17; Jas 3.18; Isa 30.15
32.19 Isa 30.30; Zech 11.2
32.20 Isa 30.24

E. *Sermon V: the punishment of the treacherous and the triumph of the* LORD

1. *Treacherous Gentiles will be spoiled*

33 Ah, you destroyer,
  who yourself have not been destroyed;
 you treacherous one,
  with whom no one has dealt treacherously!
When you have ceased to destroy,
  you will be destroyed;
and when you have stopped dealing treacherously,
  you will be dealt with treacherously.

2 O LORD, be gracious to us; we wait for you.
  Be our arm every morning,
  our salvation in the time of trouble.

3 At the sound of tumult, peoples fled;
  before your majesty, nations scattered.

4 Spoil was gathered as the caterpillar gathers;
  as locusts leap, they leaped*k* upon it.

5 The LORD is exalted, he dwells on high;
  he filled Zion with justice and righteousness;

6 he will be the stability of your times,
  abundance of salvation, wisdom, and knowledge;
  the fear of the LORD is Zion's treasure.*l*

33.1 Isa 21.2; Hab 2.8; Isa 24.16; Jer 25.12-14; Mt 7.2

33.2 Isa 25.9

33.3 Isa 17.13; Jer 25.30, 31

33.5 Ps 97.9

33.6 v. 20; Isa 45.17; 11.9; Mt 6.33

j Cn: Heb *And it will hail when the forest comes down*   *k* Meaning of Heb uncertain   *l* Heb *his treasure*; meaning of Heb uncertain

---

32.15 God promised that *a spirit from on high* would be poured on them. This reached its fulfillment in the outpouring of the Holy Spirit on Pentecost (see Acts 2).

32.17 *quietness and trust forever.* Isaiah affirms the doctrine of assurance. Believers can be firmly convinced that they have been saved and will be kept by faith through the knowledge of the word of God, to which the Holy Spirit bears his witness to the believers' heart (Rom 8.15,16). The believer can be certain of salvation (12.2; Jn 3.17; Acts 16.30,31), eternal life

(1 Jn 5.13), peace with God (Rom 5.1), a glorious transformed body (Phil 3.21), an unshakable kingdom (Heb 12.28), and a crown of righteousness (2 Tim 4.7,8; James 1.12).

33.4,5 After the deaths of the Assyrian soldiers, who were slain by the angel of God (see ch. 37), Judah gathered the spoils left for them. In this "the LORD is exalted." He alone would have the praise for what happened, for Judah had nothing to do with the victory.

2. Judah's distress described

7 Listen! the valiant^m cry in the streets;
   the envoys of peace weep bitterly.
8 The highways are deserted,
   travelers have quit the road.
   The treaty is broken,
     its oaths^n are despised,
     its obligation^o is disregarded.
9 The land mourns and languishes;
   Lebanon is confounded and withers away;
   Sharon is like a desert;
   and Bashan and Carmel shake off their leaves.

3. Prediction of God's vengeance

10 "Now I will arise," says the LORD,
   "now I will lift myself up;
   now I will be exalted.
11 You conceive chaff, you bring forth stubble;
   your breath is a fire that will consume you.
12 And the peoples will be as if burned to lime,
   like thorns cut down, that are burned in the fire."

13 Hear, you who are far away, what I have done;
   and you who are near, acknowledge my might.
14 The sinners in Zion are afraid;
   trembling has seized the godless:
   "Who among us can live with the devouring fire?
   Who among us can live with everlasting flames?"
15 Those who walk righteously and speak uprightly,
   who despise the gain of oppression,
   who wave away a bribe instead of accepting it,
   who stop their ears from hearing of bloodshed
   and shut their eyes from looking on evil,
16 they will live on the heights;
   their refuge will be the fortresses of rocks;
   their food will be supplied, their water assured.

4. Promise of safety and joy under Messiah

17 Your eyes will see the king in his beauty;
   they will behold a land that stretches far away.
18 Your mind will muse on the terror:
   "Where is the one who counted?
   Where is the one who weighed the tribute?
   Where is the one who counted the towers?"
19 No longer will you see the insolent people,
   the people of an obscure speech that you cannot comprehend,
   stammering in a language that you cannot understand.
20 Look on Zion, the city of our appointed festivals!

^{m} Meaning of Heb uncertain ^{n} Q Ms: MT cities ^{o} Or everyone

33.15 Godly people speak what is true and right and do so with honest intention. Their word can be trusted, and they need not take an oath in the name of God for anyone to trust what they say. They despise ill-gotten gain, accept no bribe, refuse to hear whatever tends to bloodshed and cruelty, and keep their eyes from seeing evil.
33.17 While the phrase "the king in his beauty" refers directly to Hezekiah after the defeat of the Assyrians, it also prophesies the coming Messiah. By the eye of faith we can see the King of kings in his beauty, the beauty of holiness, a holiness that becomes ours by grace through the sacrifice of the Savior.
33.20 Isaiah was surely speaking about the deliverance of Judah from the threat presented by Sennacherib. Judah was delivered and the city and temple were safe—for a time. Eventually, however, some-

> Your eyes will see Jerusalem,
>   a quiet habitation, an immovable tent,
> whose stakes will never be pulled up,
>   and none of whose ropes will be broken.

21 But there the LORD in majesty will be for us
  a place of broad rivers and streams,
where no galley with oars can go,
  nor stately ship can pass.

22 For the LORD is our judge, the LORD is our ruler,
  the LORD is our king; he will save us.

23 Your rigging hangs loose;
  it cannot hold the mast firm in its place,
  or keep the sail spread out.

Then prey and spoil in abundance will be divided;
  even the lame will fall to plundering.
24 And no inhabitant will say, "I am sick";
  the people who live there will be forgiven their iniquity.

VI. Second volume of general rebuke and promise (34.1–35.10)

A. Sermon I: destruction of the nations who are enemies of God

1. The judgment on the nations

34 Draw near, O nations, to hear;
  O peoples, give heed!
Let the earth hear, and all that fills it;
  the world, and all that comes from it.

2 For the LORD is enraged against all the nations,
  and furious against all their hordes;
  he has doomed them, has given them over for slaughter.

3 Their slain shall be cast out,
  and the stench of their corpses shall rise;
  the mountains shall flow with their blood.

4 All the host of heaven shall rot away,
  and the skies roll up like a scroll.
All their host shall wither
  like a leaf withering on a vine,
  or fruit withering on a fig tree.

2. The example of Edom

5 When my sword has drunk its fill in the heavens,
  lo, it will descend upon Edom,
  upon the people I have doomed to judgment.

6 The LORD has a sword; it is sated with blood,
  it is gorged with fat,
  with the blood of lambs and goats,

Cross references (right margin):

33.21 Isa 41.18

33.22 Isa 2.4; Jas 4.12; v. 17; Zech 9.9; Isa 35.4
33.23 2 Kings 7.8, 16

33.24 Jer 30.17; 50.20

34.1 Ps 49.1; Deut 32.1

34.2 Isa 26.20, 21; 13.5; 30.25
34.3 Joel 2.20; Ezek 14.19

34.4 Ezek 32.7, 8; Joel 2.31; Mt 24.29; 2 Pet 3.10; Rev 6.13, 14

34.5 Jer 46.10; 49.7; Mal 1.4
34.6 Jer 49.13; Isa 63.1

---

thing far worse happened. Jerusalem and the temple were destroyed by Nebuchadnezzar; both were rebuilt only to be destroyed again in A.D. 70. While Jerusalem has more recently been brought back to a place of magnificence, the temple has never been restored. Premillennialists see a future fulfillment to this passage in a reconstructed temple. Amillennialists tend to see this as fulfilled in the Christian church, God's temple today (1 Cor 3.16,17; 6.19;

2 Cor 6.16). **34.6** Both the Old and N.T. speak of God as one who executes vengeance and whose sword drips with blood. In Revelation, John pictures Christ as having a sharp sword that comes from his mouth, which he uses to smite the nations; his robe is dipped in blood (Rev 19.11–16). God has used humans in days past to execute judgment, but the time will come when God will directly execute vengeance himself.

with the fat of the kidneys of rams.
For the LORD has a sacrifice in Bozrah,
    a great slaughter in the land of Edom.

34.7
Ps 22.21;
68.30;
Isa 29.9;
49.26

7 Wild oxen shall fall with them,
      and young steers with the mighty bulls.
   Their land shall be soaked with blood,
      and their soil made rich with fat.

34.8
Isa 63.4

8 For the LORD has a day of vengeance,
      a year of vindication by Zion's cause.*p*

34.9
Deut 29.23

9 And the streams of Edom*q* shall be turned into pitch,
      and her soil into sulfur;
   her land shall become burning pitch.

34.10
Isa 66.24;
Rev 14.11;
19.3;
Mal 1.4;
Ezek 29.11

10 Night and day it shall not be quenched;
      its smoke shall go up forever.
   From generation to generation it shall lie waste;
      no one shall pass through it forever and ever.

34.11
Isa 14.23;
Zeph 2.14;
Rev 18.2;
2 Kings 21.13;
Lam 2.8

11 But the hawk*r* and the hedgehog*r* shall possess it;
      the owl*r* and the raven shall live in it.
   He shall stretch the line of confusion over it,
      and the plummet of chaos over*s* its nobles.

12 They shall name it No Kingdom There,
      and all its princes shall be nothing.

34.13
Isa 13.22;
32.13;
Jer 9.11;
10.22

13 Thorns shall grow over its strongholds,
      nettles and thistles in its fortresses.
   It shall be the haunt of jackals,
      an abode for ostriches.

34.14
Isa 13.21

14 Wildcats shall meet with hyenas,
      goat-demons shall call to each other;
   there too Lilith shall repose,
      and find a place to rest.

34.15
Deut 14.13

15 There shall the owl nest
      and lay and hatch and brood in its shadow;
   there too the buzzards shall gather,
      each one with its mate.

34.16
Isa 30.8;
40.5

16 Seek and read from the book of the LORD:
      Not one of these shall be missing;
      none shall be without its mate.
   For the mouth of the LORD has commanded,
      and his spirit has gathered them.

34.17
Jer 13.25;
vv. 10, 11

17 He has cast the lot for them,
      his hand has portioned it out to them with the line;
   they shall possess it forever,
      from generation to generation they shall live in it.

B. *Sermon II: the return to Zion promised*

35.1f
Isa 55.12;
51.3

35 The wilderness and the dry land shall be glad,
        the desert shall rejoice and blossom;

p Or *of recompense by Zion's defender*   *q* Heb *her streams*   *r* Identification uncertain   *s* Heb lacks *over*

34.13 Edom (see v. 6) is an example of God's judgment against the nations. That land would become a habitation for poisonous dragons (cf. v. 14). The place that had been the court for princes would be occupied by jackals and ostriches. Such is the verdict of a holy God against unholy nations that spurn his grace and laugh at his laws.
34.16 *the book of the LORD.* Comparing prophecies of Scripture with the events themselves is the clearest evidence that God has foretold many things that will

happen. Everything that has been prophesied must, of necessity, take place sooner or later.
35.1,2 The previous chapter presented a dark and dreadful picture of confusion, judgment, and dismay. Now Isaiah forecasts what would happen to the wilderness and the dry land in the providence of a forgiving God. There would come (1) joy, rejoicing, and singing, (2) a blossoming desert, (3) beauty, and (4) "the glory of the LORD" and his majesty.

like the crocus 2it shall blossom abundantly,
and rejoice with joy and singing.
The glory of Lebanon shall be given to it,
the majesty of Carmel and Sharon.
They shall see the glory of the LORD,
the majesty of our God.

3 Strengthen the weak hands,
and make firm the feeble knees.
4 Say to those who are of a fearful heart,
"Be strong, do not fear!
Here is your God.
He will come with vengeance,
with terrible recompense.
He will come and save you."

5 Then the eyes of the blind shall be opened,
and the ears of the deaf unstopped;
6 then the lame shall leap like a deer,
and the tongue of the speechless sing for joy.
For waters shall break forth in the wilderness,
and streams in the desert;
7 the burning sand shall become a pool,
and the thirsty ground springs of water;
the haunt of jackals shall become a swamp,^{t}
the grass shall become reeds and rushes.

8 A highway shall be there,
and it shall be called the Holy Way;
the unclean shall not travel on it,^{u}
but it shall be for God's people;^{v}
no traveler, not even fools, shall go astray.

9 No lion shall be there,
nor shall any ravenous beast come up on it;
they shall not be found there,
but the redeemed shall walk there.
10 And the ransomed of the LORD shall return,
and come to Zion with singing;
everlasting joy shall be upon their heads;
they shall obtain joy and gladness,
and sorrow and sighing shall flee away.

35.2 Isa 32.15; v. 10; Isa 60.13; 25.9
35.3 Job 4.3, 4; Heb 12.12
35.4 Isa 1.24; 34.8; Ps 145.19
35.5 Isa 29.18; Mt 11.5; Jn 9.6, 7
35.6 Mt 15.30; Jn 5.8, 9; Acts 3.8; Mt 9.32; Isa 41.18; 43.19; Jn 7.38
35.7 Isa 49.10; 34.13
35.8 Isa 62.10; Mt 7.13, 14; Jer 14.8
35.9 Isa 30.6; 34.14; 62.12
35.10 Isa 51.11; 25.8; 65.19; Rev 7.17; 21.4

VII. *Volume of Hezekiah (36.1–39.8)*

A. *Sennacherib's challenge to the people of God*

1. *His demand for Judah to submit*

36 In the fourteenth year of King Hezekiah, King Sennacherib of
Assyria came up against all the fortified cities of Judah and cap-

36.1 2 Kings 18.13; Isa 1.1

^{t} Cn: Heb *in the haunt of jackals is her resting place* ^{u} Or *pass it by* ^{v} Cn: Heb *for them*

35.5ff These verses go far beyond what occurred in Hezekiah's flourishing kingdom after the Assyrian threat had disappeared. Isaiah foresaw a future age in which God would manifest himself through signs and wonders. The blind would see, the lame leap, and the dumb talk. Streams would flow in the desert where they were least expected. Uncleanness would disappear and holiness prevail. No wild beasts would disturb this paradise. The redeemed of God who had

been ransomed would be there. They would come to Zion with joy and gladness and their songs would redound to the Redeemer's praise. Some of these signs were fulfilled in the life and ministry of Jesus, but others still await fulfillment in the heavenly Zion, the New Jerusalem, the city of God that will not be built by human hands.
36.1 Sennacherib had taken the fortified cities of Judah but not Jerusalem. Assyria would make that

36.2
2 Kings 18.17-20;
Isa 7.3
36.3
Isa 22.15, 20

36.4
2 Kings 18.19
36.5
2 Kings 18.7
36.6
Ezek 29.6, 7;
Isa 30.3, 5, 7
36.7
2 Kings 18.4,
5

36.9
Isa 37.29;
20.5

tured them. 2 The king of Assyria sent the Rabshakeh from Lachish to King Hezekiah at Jerusalem, with a great army. He stood by the conduit of the upper pool on the highway to the Fuller's Field. 3 And there came out to him Eliakim son of Hilkiah, who was in charge of the palace, and Shebna the secretary, and Joah son of Asaph, the recorder.

4   The Rabshakeh said to them, "Say to Hezekiah: Thus says the great king, the king of Assyria: On what do you base this confidence of yours? 5 Do you think that mere words are strategy and power for war? On whom do you now rely, that you have rebelled against me? 6 See, you are relying on Egypt, that broken reed of a staff, which will pierce the hand of anyone who leans on it. Such is Pharaoh king of Egypt to all who rely on him. 7 But if you say to me, 'We rely on the LORD our God,' is it not he whose high places and altars Hezekiah has removed, saying to Judah and to Jerusalem, 'You shall worship before this altar'? 8 Come now, make a wager with my master the king of Assyria: I will give you two thousand horses, if you are able on your part to set riders on them. 9 How then can you repulse a single captain among the least of my master's servants, when you rely on Egypt for chariots and for horsemen? 10 Moreover, is it without the LORD that I have come up against this land to destroy it? The LORD said to me, Go up against this land, and destroy it."

2. Direct summons to the people to surrender

36.11
Ezra 4.7;
v. 13

11   Then Eliakim, Shebna, and Joah said to the Rabshakeh, "Please speak to your servants in Aramaic, for we understand it; do not speak to us in the language of Judah within the hearing of the people who are on the wall." 12 But the Rabshakeh said, "Has my master sent me to speak these words to your master and to you, and not to the people sitting on the wall, who are doomed with you to eat their own dung and drink their own urine?"

36.13
2 Chr 32.18

36.14
Isa 37.10
36.15
v. 18

36.16
Zech 3.10;
Prov 5.15

13   Then the Rabshakeh stood and called out in a loud voice in the language of Judah, "Hear the words of the great king, the king of Assyria! 14 Thus says the king: 'Do not let Hezekiah deceive you, for he will not be able to deliver you. 15 Do not let Hezekiah make you rely on the LORD by saying, The LORD will surely deliver us; this city will not be given into the hand of the king of Assyria.' 16 Do not listen to Hezekiah; for thus says the king of Assyria: 'Make your peace with me and come out to me; then everyone of you will eat from your own vine and your own fig tree and drink water from your own cistern, 17 until I come and take you away to a land like your own land, a land of grain and wine, a land of bread and vineyards. 18 Do not let Hezekiah mislead you by saying, The LORD will save us. Has any of the gods of the nations saved their land out of the hand of the king of Assyria? 19 Where are the gods of Hamath and Arpad? Where are the gods of Sepharvaim? Have they delivered Samaria out of my hand? 20 Who among all the gods of these countries have saved their countries out of my hand, that the LORD should save Jerusalem out of my hand?'"

36.18
v. 15

36.19
Isa 37.11-13;
2 Kings 17.6
36.20
1 Kings 20.23,
28; v. 15

---

effort, but God would intervene on behalf of Zion (see 2 Kings 18 and notes).
36.2 *Rabshakeh*, i.e., the chief officer of the Assyrian army.
36.7 Sennacherib's ambassador sought to undercut King Hezekiah by saying that his religious reforms, in which he destroyed pagan high places and practices, were an insult to the gods, a sacrilege. He implied that even Judah's God was displeased. Little did he understand true religion.
36.10 Rabshakeh claimed to have been sent by God to take Jerusalem. He was not really *for* God; he was *against* him. Many saints have been killed by those who claimed they were doing God a service. Some-

times true believers have fallen into this error and have justified actions that God never approved and the Holy Spirit never originated.
36.19,20 It was true that the gods of other nations had not been able to deliver their worshipers from the power of Assyria. What Assyria did not realize was that in this instance they were waging war against the true God who had delivered his people on numerous occasions and who could deliver them now. But Sennacherib did not fear the God of Israel. He actually challenged Israel and tried to keep him from taking the city of Jerusalem. Hezekiah's dilemma provided God the opportunity to show his mighty power.

21 But they were silent and answered him not a word, for the king's command was, "Do not answer him." 22 Then Eliakim son of Hilkiah, who was in charge of the palace, and Shebna the secretary, and Joah son of Asaph, the recorder, came to Hezekiah with their clothes torn, and told him the words of the Rabshakeh.

B. God's answer to Sennacherib

1. Hezekiah's appeal to God

37 When King Hezekiah heard it, he tore his clothes, covered himself with sackcloth, and went into the house of the LORD. 2 And he sent Eliakim, who was in charge of the palace, and Shebna the secretary, and the senior priests, covered with sackcloth, to the prophet Isaiah son of Amoz. 3 They said to him, "Thus says Hezekiah, This day is a day of distress, of rebuke, and of disgrace; children have come to the birth, and there is no strength to bring them forth. 4 It may be that the LORD your God heard the words of the Rabshakeh, whom his master the king of Assyria has sent to mock the living God, and will rebuke the words that the LORD your God has heard; therefore lift up your prayer for the remnant that is left."

2. God's first assurance of deliverance

5 When the servants of King Hezekiah came to Isaiah, 6 Isaiah said to them, "Say to your master, 'Thus says the LORD: Do not be afraid because of the words that you have heard, with which the servants of the king of Assyria have reviled me. 7 I myself will put a spirit in him, so that he shall hear a rumor, and return to his own land; I will cause him to fall by the sword in his own land.' "

3. Blasphemous challenge from Assyria

8 The Rabshakeh returned, and found the king of Assyria fighting against Libnah; for he had heard that the king had left Lachish. 9 Now the king[w] heard concerning King Tirhakah of Ethiopia,[x] "He has set out to fight against you." When he heard it, he sent messengers to Hezekiah, saying, 10 "Thus shall you speak to King Hezekiah of Judah: Do not let your God on whom you rely deceive you by promising that Jerusalem will not be given into the hand of the king of Assyria. 11 See, you have heard what the kings of Assyria have done to all lands, destroying them utterly. Shall you be delivered? 12 Have the gods of the nations delivered them, the nations that my predecessors destroyed, Gozan, Haran, Rezeph, and the people of Eden who were in Telassar? 13 Where is the king of Hamath, the king of Arpad, the king of the city of Sepharvaim, the king of Hena, or the king of Ivvah?"

4. Hezekiah's prayer to the LORD

14 Hezekiah received the letter from the hand of the messengers and read it; then Hezekiah went up to the house of the LORD and spread it before the LORD. 15 And Hezekiah prayed to the LORD, saying: 16 "O LORD of hosts, God of Israel, who are enthroned above the cherubim, you are God, you alone, of all the kingdoms of the earth; you have made heaven and earth. 17 Incline your ear, O LORD, and hear; open your eyes, O LORD, and see; hear all the words of Sennacherib, which he has sent to mock the living God. 18 Truly, O LORD, the kings of Assyria have

w Heb *he*　x Or *Nubia*; Heb *Cush*

37.1 This chapter is the same as 2 Kings 19.1–37. In all probability the account in 2 Kings was taken from the prophecy of Isaiah. See notes on that chapter.

Cross-references (right margin):

36.22
v. 3;
Isa 22.15, 20

37.1
2 Kings 19.1-37
37.2
Isa 22.15, 20
37.3
Isa 26.16-18
37.4
Isa 36.15,
18, 20

37.6
Isa 7.4; 35.4

37.7
vv. 9, 37, 38

37.9
v. 7;
Isa 18.1;
20.5
37.10
Isa 36.15
37.11
Isa 10.9-11;
36.18-20
37.12
2 Kings 17.6;
18.11;
Gen 11.31;
12.1-4;
Acts 7.2

37.16
Ex 25.22;
Deut 10.17;
Isa 42.5;
45.12
37.17
Dan 9.18;
Ps 74.22; v. 4
37.18
2 Kings 15.29;
1 Chr 5.26;
Nah 2.11, 12

37.19
Isa 2.8;
26.14
37.20
Isa 25.9;
Ps 46.10;
Ezek 36.23

laid waste all the nations and their lands, 19and have hurled their gods into the fire, though they were no gods, but the work of human hands— wood and stone—and so they were destroyed. 20So now, O LORD our God, save us from his hand, so that all the kingdoms of the earth may know that you alone are the LORD."

5. God's second answer: Sennacherib will be crushed

37.21
v. 2

21   Then Isaiah son of Amoz sent to Hezekiah, saying: "Thus says the LORD, the God of Israel: Because you have prayed to me concerning King Sennacherib of Assyria, 22this is the word that the LORD has spoken concerning him:

37.22
Jer 14.17;
Lam 2.13;
Zech 2.10;
Job 16.4

>She despises you, she scorns you—
>   virgin daughter Zion;
>she tosses her head—behind your back,
>   daughter Jerusalem.

37.23
v. 4;
Isa 2.11;
5.15, 21;
Ezek 39.7;
Hab 1.12

23   "Whom have you mocked and reviled?
>   Against whom have you raised your voice
>and haughtily lifted your eyes?
>   Against the Holy One of Israel!

37.24
Isa 8.7, 8;
10.18, 33,
34; 14.8

24   By your servants you have mocked the Lord,
>   and you have said, 'With my many chariots
>I have gone up the heights of the mountains,
>   to the far recesses of Lebanon;
>I felled its tallest cedars,
>   its choicest cypresses;
>I came to its remotest height,
>   its densest forest.

25   I dug wells
>   and drank waters,
>I dried up with the sole of my foot
>   all the streams of Egypt.'

37.26
Isa 40.21,
28;
Acts 2.23;
4.27, 28;
Isa 46.11;
10.6; 17.1

26   "Have you not heard
>   that I determined it long ago?
>I planned from days of old
>   what now I bring to pass,
>that you should make fortified cities
>   crash into heaps of ruins,

37.27
Isa 40.7;
Ps 129.6

27   while their inhabitants, shorn of strength,
>   are dismayed and confounded;
>they have become like plants of the field
>   and like tender grass,
>like grass on the housetops,
>   blighted[y] before it is grown.

37.28
Ps 139.1

28   "I know your rising up[z] and your sitting down,
>   your going out and coming in,
>   and your raging against me.

---

[y] With 2 Kings 19.26: Heb *field*   [z] Q Ms Gk: MT lacks *your rising up*

37.21 *Because you have prayed to me.* Had Hezekiah not prayed, God would not have answered. Prayer is valuable and releases tremendous power. The Scriptures are filled with illustrations of the value of prayer; we should be encouraged, for the God of Hezekiah is our God.
37.28,29 God knew Sennacherib's plans and re-

garded his arrogance as directed against himself. So God put the divine hook in his nose and a bit in his mouth. He did it so quickly that Sennacherib had no time to shoot a single arrow over the city walls, to gather his troops before its gate, or to build a mound for his soldiers to enter the city over the walls.

29 Because you have raged against me
    and your arrogance has come to my ears,
  I will put my hook in your nose
    and my bit in your mouth;
  I will turn you back on the way
    by which you came.

30 "And this shall be the sign for you: This year eat what grows of itself, and in the second year what springs from that; then in the third year sow, reap, plant vineyards, and eat their fruit. 31 The surviving remnant of the house of Judah shall again take root downward, and bear fruit upward; 32 for from Jerusalem a remnant shall go out, and from Mount Zion a band of survivors. The zeal of the LORD of hosts will do this.

33 "Therefore thus says the LORD concerning the king of Assyria: He shall not come into this city, shoot an arrow there, come before it with a shield, or cast up a siege ramp against it. 34 By the way that he came, by the same he shall return; he shall not come into this city, says the LORD. 35 For I will defend this city to save it, for my own sake and for the sake of my servant David."

6. The fulfillment of God's promise

36 Then the angel of the LORD set out and struck down one hundred eighty-five thousand in the camp of the Assyrians; when morning dawned, they were all dead bodies. 37 Then King Sennacherib of Assyria left, went home, and lived at Nineveh. 38 As he was worshiping in the house of his god Nisroch, his sons Adrammelech and Sharezer killed him with the sword, and they escaped into the land of Ararat. His son Esar-haddon succeeded him.

C. Hezekiah's sickness and recovery

1. His prayer: God's answer

38 In those days Hezekiah became sick and was at the point of death. The prophet Isaiah son of Amoz came to him, and said to him, "Thus says the LORD: Set your house in order, for you shall die; you shall not recover." 2 Then Hezekiah turned his face to the wall, and prayed to the LORD: 3 "Remember now, O LORD, I implore you, how I have walked before you in faithfulness with a whole heart, and have done what is good in your sight." And Hezekiah wept bitterly.

4 Then the word of the LORD came to Isaiah: 5 "Go and say to Hezekiah, Thus says the LORD, the God of your ancestor David: I have heard your prayer, I have seen your tears; I will add fifteen years to your life. 6 I will deliver you and this city out of the hand of the king of Assyria, and defend this city.

7 "This is the sign to you from the LORD, that the LORD will do this thing that he has promised: 8 See, I will make the shadow cast by the declining sun on the dial of Ahaz turn back ten steps." So the sun turned back on the dial the ten steps by which it had declined. a

a Meaning of Heb uncertain

37.29
Isa 10.12;
30.28;
Ezek 38.4;
v. 34

37.30
Lev 25.5, 11

37.31
v. 4;
Isa 4.2;
10.20; 27.6

37.32
v. 4;
2 Kings 19.31;
Isa 9.7;
Zech 1.14

37.33
Jer 6.6; 32.24

37.35
2 Kings 20.6;
Isa 38.6;
48.9, 11

37.36
2 Kings 19.35;
Isa 10.12,
33, 34

37.38
Jer 51.27;
Ezra 4.2

38.1
2 Kings 20.1-6,
9-11;
2 Chr 32.24;
2 Sam 17.23

38.3
Neh 13.14;
2 Kings 18.5,
6; 1 Chr 28.9;
29.19;
Deut 6.18

38.5
2 Kings 18.2,
13

38.6
Isa 37.35

38.7
Isa 7.11

38.8
2 Kings 20.9-11;
Josh 10.12-14

37.37,38 Sennacherib fled home in shame, leaving his dead troops behind him. His highest expectations had been dashed, and fear filled his heart that the angel who destroyed his army might also destroy him. But the worst was yet to come: Sennacherib's own sons, who should have been guarding their father, slew him as he worshiped before Nisroch (whose protection he sought but whose power could not keep him safe from his own children).

38.2 This chapter is found also in 2 Kings 20. See notes on that chapter.

2. His psalm of praise

9 A writing of King Hezekiah of Judah, after he had been sick and
had recovered from his sickness:

38.10
Ps 102.24;
107.18;
Job 17.11,
15; 2 Cor 1.9

10   I said: In the noontide of my days
     I must depart;
  I am consigned to the gates of Sheol
     for the rest of my years.

38.11
Ps 27.13;
116.9

11   I said, I shall not see the LORD
     in the land of the living;
  I shall look upon mortals no more
     among the inhabitants of the world.

38.12
2 Cor 5.1, 4;
Heb 1.12;
Job 7.6; 6.9;
Ps 73.14

12   My dwelling is plucked up and removed from me
     like a shepherd's tent;
  like a weaver I have rolled up my life;
     he cuts me off from the loom;
  from day to night you bring me to an end;[b]

38.13
Job 10.16;
16.12;
Ps 51.8; 32.4

13   I cry for help[c] until morning;
  like a lion he breaks all my bones;
     from day to night you bring me to an end.[b]

38.14
Isa 59.11;
Ps 119.122,
123

14   Like a swallow or a crane[b] I clamor,
     I moan like a dove.
  My eyes are weary with looking upward.
     O Lord, I am oppressed; be my security!

38.15
Ps 39.9;
1 Kings 21.27;
Job 7.11;
10.1

15   But what can I say? For he has spoken to me,
     and he himself has done it.
  All my sleep has fled[d]
     because of the bitterness of my soul.

38.16
Ps 119.71,
75; 39.13

16   O Lord, by these things people live,
     and in all these is the life of my spirit.[b]
  Oh, restore me to health and make me live!

38.17
Ps 30.3;
Isa 43.25;
Jer 31.34;
Mic 7.19

17   Surely it was for my welfare
     that I had great bitterness;
  but you have held back[e] my life
     from the pit of destruction,
  for you have cast all my sins
     behind your back.

38.18
Ps 6.5; 88.11;
115.17;
Eccl 9.10;
Ps 28.1

18   For Sheol cannot thank you,
     death cannot praise you;
  those who go down to the Pit cannot hope
     for your faithfulness.

38.19
Ps 118.17;
Deut 6.7;
Ps 78.5-7

19   The living, the living, they thank you,
     as I do this day;
  fathers make known to children
     your faithfulness.

38.20
Ps 86.5;
33.1-3;
104.33;
116.17-19

20   The LORD will save me,
     and we will sing to stringed instruments[f]
  all the days of our lives,
     at the house of the LORD.

38.21
2 Kings 20.7,
8

21   Now Isaiah had said, "Let them take a lump of figs, and apply it

---

[b] Meaning of Heb uncertain   [c] Cn: Meaning of Heb uncertain   [d] Cn Compare Syr: Heb *I will walk
slowly all my years*   [e] Cn Compare Gk Vg: Heb *loved*   [f] Heb *my stringed instruments*

38.17 When we ignore or hide our sins, God remembers them nevertheless. But when we repent
honestly and acknowledge our transgressions, God
pardons us and casts our sins behind his back and
remembers them no more.

to the boil, so that he may recover." 22 Hezekiah also had said, "What is the sign that I shall go up to the house of the Lord?"

D. Hezekiah's folly

1. His display of his wealth

39 At that time King Merodach-baladan son of Baladan of Babylon sent envoys with letters and a present to Hezekiah, for he heard that he had been sick and had recovered. 2 Hezekiah welcomed them; he showed them his treasure house, the silver, the gold, the spices, the precious oil, his whole armory, all that was found in his storehouses. There was nothing in his house or in all his realm that Hezekiah did not show them. 3 Then the prophet Isaiah came to King Hezekiah and said to him, "What did these men say? From where did they come to you?" Hezekiah answered, "They have come to me from a far country, from Babylon." 4 He said, "What have they seen in your house?" Hezekiah answered, "They have seen all that is in my house; there is nothing in my storehouses that I did not show them."

2. God's sentence of exile

5 Then Isaiah said to Hezekiah, "Hear the word of the Lord of hosts: 6 Days are coming when all that is in your house, and that which your ancestors have stored up until this day, shall be carried to Babylon; nothing shall be left, says the Lord. 7 Some of your own sons who are born to you shall be taken away; they shall be eunuchs in the palace of the king of Babylon." 8 Then Hezekiah said to Isaiah, "The word of the Lord that you have spoken is good." For he thought, "There will be peace and security in my days."

VIII. Volume of comfort and assurance (40.1–66.24)

A. Part I: the salvation of the Lord

1. The majesty of the Lord the comforter

a. The messenger of the Lord to come

40 Comfort, O comfort my people,
    says your God.
2 Speak tenderly to Jerusalem,
    and cry to her
that she has served her term,
    that her penalty is paid,
that she has received from the Lord's hand
    double for all her sins.

3 A voice cries out:

Cross references (right margin):

39.1
2 Kings 20.12-19;
2 Chr 32.31

39.2
2 Chr 32.25, 31;
2 Kings 18.15, 16

39.3
2 Sam 12.1;
2 Chr 16.7;
Jer 5.15

39.5
1 Sam 13.13, 14; 15.16

39.6
Jer 20.5

39.7
Dan 1.2-7

39.8
2 Chr 32.26;
1 Sam 3.18;
2 Chr 34.28

40.1
Isa 12.1

40.2
Isa 35.4;
41.11-13;
33.24;
Jer 16.18

40.3
Mt 3.3;
Mk 1.3;
Lk 3.4-6;
Jn 1.23;
Mal 3.1

39.1 *Merodach-baladan,* a Babylonian king who reigned from 721–710 B.C.. When Sargon II reigned in Assyria, he entered Babylon and made himself king. In 710 Sargon swept into Babylon and was not opposed by Merodach-baladan until Sargon died in 703. Then Merodach-baladan revolted again and remained king until Sennacherib defeated him and his rebels, at which time Merodach-baladan retreated to his homeland, where he died.
39.6ff God was angry with Hezekiah because of his pride. God's message through Isaiah was designed to shame the king, convince him of his foolishness, and take from him the very things he had been proud to display to the Babylonians. God graciously suspended

the fulfillment of the prophetic word until after Hezekiah's death. The king was grateful, and yet he recognized the rightness of God's judgment.
40.1 Chapters 40 — 66 were written later in Isaiah's life; they are predictive prophecy. Some scholars believe that these chapters were written by one or more prophets *after* the events took place rather than before. Since many of these prophecies relate to the end of the age, it is difficult to argue successfully for such a view.
40.3 The alarm given here by Isaiah is picked up in the N.T. and applied to John the Baptist, who was called by God to prepare the way for the Messiah. He preached repentance to all Judah and Jerusalem and

"In the wilderness prepare the way of the Lord,
    make straight in the desert a highway for our God.

4 Every valley shall be lifted up,
    and every mountain and hill be made low;
  the uneven ground shall become level,
    and the rough places a plain.

5 Then the glory of the Lord shall be revealed,
    and all people shall see it together,
  for the mouth of the Lord has spoken."

6 A voice says, "Cry out!"
    And I said, "What shall I cry?"
  All people are grass,
    their constancy is like the flower of the field.

7 The grass withers, the flower fades,
    when the breath of the Lord blows upon it;
  surely the people are grass.

8 The grass withers, the flower fades;
    but the word of our God will stand forever.

9 Get you up to a high mountain,
    O Zion, herald of good tidings;g
  lift up your voice with strength,
    O Jerusalem, herald of good tidings,h
  lift it up, do not fear;
  say to the cities of Judah,
    "Here is your God!"

10 See, the Lord God comes with might,
    and his arm rules for him;
  his reward is with him,
    and his recompense before him.

11 He will feed his flock like a shepherd;
    he will gather the lambs in his arms,
  and carry them in his bosom,
    and gently lead the mother sheep.

b. *Infinite power and wisdom of the Lord*

12 Who has measured the waters in the hollow of his hand
    and marked off the heavens with a span,
  enclosed the dust of the earth in a measure,
    and weighed the mountains in scales
    and the hills in a balance?

13 Who has directed the spirit of the Lord,
    or as his counselor has instructed him?

14 Whom did he consult for his enlightenment,
    and who taught him the path of justice?
  Who taught him knowledge,
    and showed him the way of understanding?

15 Even the nations are like a drop from a bucket,
    and are accounted as dust on the scales;
  see, he takes up the isles like fine dust.

40.4 Isa 45.2
40.5 Isa 6.3; 52.10
40.6 Job 14.2; Ps 102.11; 103.15; 1 Pet 1.24, 25
40.7 Ps 90.5, 6; v. 24
40.8 Isa 55.11; Mt 5.18; 1 Pet 1.24, 25
40.9 Isa 60.1; 52.7; Acts 10.36; Rom 10.15
40.10 Isa 59.16, 18; 62.11; Rev 22.7, 12
40.11 Ezek 34.23; Mic 5.4; Jn 10.11; Heb 13.20
40.12 Isa 48.13; Job 38.8-11; Heb 1.10-12
40.13 Rom 11.34; 1 Cor 2.16
40.14 Job 38.4; 21.22
40.15 Jer 10.10; Isa 17.13; 29.5

---

g Or *O herald of good tidings to Zion*   h Or *O herald of good tidings to Jerusalem*

---

thus made "ready a people prepared for the Lord" (Lk 1.17).
40.8 Whatever God says has eternal value and can neither be untrue nor left undone. The entire Bible is the word of God and will stand forever. This word can do for us what we cannot do for ourselves. Its perpetuity is the surest guarantee of our eternity and of our happiness.

40.11 Isaiah's description of the good shepherd is prophetic of Jesus (see also Gen 49.24; Ezek 34.23; 37.24). In the N.T., Jesus is called: (1) the good shepherd who gives his life for the sheep (Jn 10.11,14); (2) the great shepherd who completes his work in us (Heb 13.20); (3) the chief shepherd who will reward his people in glory (1 Pet 5.4).

16   Lebanon would not provide fuel enough,
            nor are its animals enough for a burnt offering.
17   All the nations are as nothing before him;
            they are accounted by him as less than nothing and
                emptiness.

c. Contrast between idols and the living God

18   To whom then will you liken God,
            or what likeness compare with him?
19   An idol? —A workman casts it,
            and a goldsmith overlays it with gold,
            and casts for it silver chains.
20   As a gift one chooses mulberry wood[i]
            —wood that will not rot—
        then seeks out a skilled artisan
            to set up an image that will not topple.

40.18
v. 25;
Isa 46.5;
Mic 7.18;
Acts 17.29
40.19
Isa 41.6, 7;
44.12;
Jer 10.3
40.20
Isa 41.7;
Jer 10.3-5

21   Have you not known? Have you not heard?
            Has it not been told you from the beginning?
            Have you not understood from the foundations of the earth?
22   It is he who sits above the circle of the earth,
            and its inhabitants are like grasshoppers;
        who stretches out the heavens like a curtain,
            and spreads them like a tent to live in;
23   who brings princes to naught,
            and makes the rulers of the earth as nothing.

40.21
Ps 19.1;
Acts 14.17;
Rom 1.19
40.22
Job 22.14;
Num 13.33;
Isa 42.5;
44.24;
Ps 104.2
40.23
Job 12.21;
Ps 107.40;
Isa 5.21

24   Scarcely are they planted, scarcely sown,
            scarcely has their stem taken root in the earth,
        when he blows upon them, and they wither,
            and the tempest carries them off like stubble.

40.24
Isa 17.10,
11; v. 7;
Isa 17.13;
41.16

25   To whom then will you compare me,
            or who is my equal? says the Holy One.
26   Lift up your eyes on high and see:
            Who created these?
        He who brings out their host and numbers them,
            calling them all by name;
        because he is great in strength,
            mighty in power,
            not one is missing.

40.25
v. 18
40.26
Isa 51.6;
42.5;
Ps 147.4;
89.11-13;
Isa 34.16

d. God's faithfulness and empowering grace

27   Why do you say, O Jacob,
            and speak, O Israel,
        "My way is hidden from the LORD,
            and my right is disregarded by my God"?
28   Have you not known? Have you not heard?

40.27
Isa 49.4, 14;
54.8;
Lk 18.7, 8;
Isa 25.1
40.28
Ps 90.2;
147.5;
Rom 11.33

i Meaning of Heb uncertain

40.21 God is the ultimate reality. All other things have been created by him. This passage implies that all people either know by nature that there is a God or they have been taught by their parents. This great God has command over all his creation. He sits above the circle of the earth (v. 22) and all animals and humans are as grasshoppers to him. The heavens do not collapse, because they are kept stretched out by him. Princes and rulers who exercise authority are controlled by God. He humbles them and makes them as nothing (vv. 23,24).

40.28 God is almighty and exists from eternity to eternity. He created the earth and his understanding is beyond the reach of finite mortals. This powerful God helps those who rely on him. He gives power to the faint and strength to the powerless (v. 29). If we wait on him, we will receive new strength to soar through life like eagles, to run through life toward heaven as the athlete who heads for the finish line.

The LORD is the everlasting God,
the Creator of the ends of the earth.
He does not faint or grow weary;
his understanding is unsearchable.

40.29
Isa 50.4;
Jer 31.25;
Isa 41.10
29 He gives power to the faint,
and strengthens the powerless.

40.30
Jer 6.11;
Isa 9.17
30 Even youths will faint and be weary,
and the young will fall exhausted;

40.31
Ps 103.5;
2 Cor 4.8-10,
16;
Deut 32.11;
2 Cor 4.1;
Heb 12.3
31 but those who wait for the LORD shall renew their strength,
they shall mount up with wings like eagles,
they shall run and not be weary,
they shall walk and not faint.

2. The God of providence challenges unbelievers

a. God's providence based on omnipotence

41.1
Zech 2.13;
Isa 40.31;
34.1; 43.26
41 Listen to me in silence, O coastlands;
let the peoples renew their strength;
let them approach, then let them speak;
let us together draw near for judgment.

41.2
Isa 45.1-3;
46.11; 42.6;
2 Chr 36.23;
Isa 29.5;
40.24
2 Who has roused a victor from the east,
summoned him to his service?
He delivers up nations to him,
and tramples kings under foot;
he makes them like dust with his sword,
like driven stubble with his bow.

3 He pursues them and passes on safely,
scarcely touching the path with his feet.

41.4
Isa 44.7;
46.10; 43.10;
44.6;
Rev 1.17;
22.13
4 Who has performed and done this,
calling the generations from the beginning?
I, the LORD, am first,
and will be with the last.

41.5
Ps 67.7
5 The coastlands have seen and are afraid,
the ends of the earth tremble;
they have drawn near and come.

41.6
Isa 40.19
6 Each one helps the other,
saying to one another, "Take courage!"

41.7
Isa 40.19, 20
7 The artisan encourages the goldsmith,
and the one who smooths with the hammer encourages the
one who strikes the anvil,
saying of the soldering, "It is good";
and they fasten it with nails so that it cannot be moved.

b. God's servant, Israel, an instrument of his providence

41.8
Isa 44.1;
2 Chr 20.7;
Jas 2.23
8 But you, Israel, my servant,
Jacob, whom I have chosen,
the offspring of Abraham, my friend;

41.9
Isa 11.11;
43.5-7; 42.1;
Ps 135.4
9 you whom I took from the ends of the earth,
and called from its farthest corners,
saying to you, "You are my servant,
I have chosen you and not cast you off";

41.4 The imagery of God as the first and the last is picked up in Revelation and applied to Jesus who, like the Father and the Spirit, is from eternity to eternity (see Rev 1.8,17; 21.6; 22.13).
41.7 Few people in the modern civilized world make graven images. Rather, they either substitute atheism, by which they deny any belief in a god, or secularism, by which they exalt humans to the

position of God as the ultimate determiner of their fate.
41.9 Israel was God's servant. Through that nation came the Messiah; to them was given the revelation of God in the O.T.; to them was entrusted the task of preserving that revelation; and to them was given the vision of taking that word to the ends of the earth for the salvation of the lost.

10   do not fear, for I am with you,
        do not be afraid, for I am your God;
     I will strengthen you, I will help you,
        I will uphold you with my victorious right hand.

| 41.10 |
| Isa 43.5; |
| Rom 8.31; |
| Isa 44.2 |

c. His chosen people will overcome their foes

11   Yes, all who are incensed against you
        shall be ashamed and disgraced;
     those who strive against you
        shall be as nothing and shall perish.

| 41.11 |
| Isa 45.24; |
| 17.13 |

12   You shall seek those who contend with you,
        but you shall not find them;
     those who war against you
        shall be as nothing at all.

| 41.12 |
| Isa 17.14; |
| 29.20 |

13   For I, the LORD your God,
        hold your right hand;
     it is I who say to you, "Do not fear,
        I will help you."

| 41.13 |
| Isa 42.6; |
| v. 10 |

14   Do not fear, you worm Jacob,
        you insect[j] Israel!
     I will help you, says the LORD;
        your Redeemer is the Holy One of Israel.

| 41.14 |
| Job 25.6; |
| Isa 43.14 |

15   Now, I will make of you a threshing sledge,
        sharp, new, and having teeth;
     you shall thresh the mountains and crush them,
        and you shall make the hills like chaff.

| 41.15 |
| Mic 4.13 |

16   You shall winnow them and the wind shall carry them away,
        and the tempest shall scatter them.
     Then you shall rejoice in the LORD;
        in the Holy One of Israel you shall glory.

| 41.16 |
| Jer 51.2; |
| Isa 45.25 |

d. God will deliver and prosper his people

17   When the poor and needy seek water,
        and there is none,
        and their tongue is parched with thirst,
     I the LORD will answer them,
        I the God of Israel will not forsake them.

| 41.17 |
| Isa 43.20; |
| 30.19; 42.16 |

18   I will open rivers on the bare heights,[k]
        and fountains in the midst of the valleys;
     I will make the wilderness a pool of water,
        and the dry land springs of water.

| 41.18 |
| Isa 35.6, 7; |
| 43.19 |

19   I will put in the wilderness the cedar,
        the acacia, the myrtle, and the olive;
     I will set in the desert the cypress,
        the plane and the pine together,

20   so that all may see and know,
        all may consider and understand,
     that the hand of the LORD has done this,
        the Holy One of Israel has created it.

| 41.20 |
| Isa 40.5; |
| Job 12.9 |

j Syr: Heb *men of*   k Or *trails*

41.11 God's people always have been surrounded by enemies. God commands his people to fight the good fight (2 Tim 4.7) and promises them victory over their foes. Until death, however, there is no relief from this warfare.
41.14 *You worm Jacob* is really a term of compassion and love. Anyone can trample the worm on the

ground. God promised to assist his helpless worm, Jacob/Israel; he promises to assist all believers who, like Jacob, need divine help.
41.17ff God can do strange and surprising things. He grants his favor and power to his needy people and assures them that nothing happens without his knowledge or control.

e. *God's omnipotence shown by foretelling the future*

41.21
v. 1;
Isa 43.15

21 Set forth your case, says the Lord;
    bring your proofs, says the King of Jacob.

41.22
Isa 45.21;
43.9

22 Let them bring them, and tell us
    what is to happen.
Tell us the former things, what they are,
    so that we may consider them,
    and that we may know their outcome;
    or declare to us the things to come.

41.23
Isa 42.9;
44.7, 8; 45.3;
Jn 13.19;
Jer 10.5

23 Tell us what is to come hereafter,
    that we may know that you are gods;
do good, or do harm,
    that we may be afraid and terrified.

41.24
Ps 115.8;
Isa 44.9;
1 Cor 8.4;
v. 29

24 You, indeed, are nothing
    and your work is nothing at all;
    whoever chooses you is an abomination.

41.25
v. 2;
Isa 10.6

25 I stirred up one from the north, and he has come,
    from the rising of the sun he was summoned by name.[l]
He shall trample[m] on rulers as on mortar,
    as the potter treads clay.

41.26
Isa 44.7;
45.21;
Hab 2.18, 19

26 Who declared it from the beginning, so that we might know,
    and beforehand, so that we might say, "He is right"?
There was no one who declared it, none who proclaimed,
    none who heard your words.

41.27
v. 4;
Isa 40.9

27 I first have declared it to Zion,[n]
    and I give to Jerusalem a herald of good tidings.

41.28
Isa 63.5;
40.13, 14;
46.7

28 But when I look there is no one;
    among these there is no counselor
    who, when I ask, gives an answer.

41.29
v. 24;
Isa 44.9;
Jer 5.13

29 No, they are all a delusion;
    their works are nothing;
    their images are empty wind.

3. *God's servant: individual and national*

a. *The mission of the servant*

42.1
Isa 43.10;
53.11;
Mt 12.18-20;
3.16, 17;
17.5;
Isa 2.4

42
Here is my servant, whom I uphold,
    my chosen, in whom my soul delights;
I have put my spirit upon him;
    he will bring forth justice to the nations.

2 He will not cry or lift up his voice,
    or make it heard in the street;

42.3
Isa 57.15;
Ps 72.2

3 a bruised reed he will not break,
    and a dimly burning wick he will not quench;
    he will faithfully bring forth justice.

42.4
Isa 40.28;
vv. 10, 12

4 He will not grow faint or be crushed
    until he has established justice in the earth;
    and the coastlands wait for his teaching.

[l] Cn Compare Q Ms Gk: MT *and he shall call on my name*   [m] Cn: Heb *come*   [n] Cn: Heb *First to Zion—Behold, behold them*

42.1 *Here is my servant.* This prophetic word has two applications. The first relates to Israel as the servant of God. The second and more important reference is to Jesus Christ as God's servant (see Mt 12.18–20, which quotes these verses). He was chosen by the Father and made his covenant of redemption with the Father. The Father had confidence in his Son that he would execute his mission on Calvary, make atonement for the sins of people, and so become our mediator. The Father gave to his Son the Holy Spirit. Christ in turn has given the Spirit to all God's people; we can live in the fullness of the Holy Spirit's power if we depend on the Lord.

b. *The servant a light to the nations*

5 Thus says God, the LORD,
   who created the heavens and stretched them out,
   who spread out the earth and what comes from it,
who gives breath to the people upon it
   and spirit to those who walk in it:

6 I am the LORD, I have called you in righteousness,
   I have taken you by the hand and kept you;
I have given you as a covenant to the people,*o*
   —a light to the nations,

7 to open the eyes that are blind,
to bring out the prisoners from the dungeon,
   from the prison those who sit in darkness.

8 I am the LORD, that is my name;
   my glory I give to no other,
   nor my praise to idols.

9 See, the former things have come to pass,
   and new things I now declare;
before they spring forth,
   I tell you of them.

c. *Song of praise to the LORD*

10 Sing to the LORD a new song,
   his praise from the end of the earth!
Let the sea roar*p* and all that fills it,
   the coastlands and their inhabitants.

11 Let the desert and its towns lift up their voice,
   the villages that Kedar inhabits;
let the inhabitants of Sela sing for joy,
   let them shout from the tops of the mountains.

12 Let them give glory to the LORD,
   and declare his praise in the coastlands.

13 The LORD goes forth like a soldier,
   like a warrior he stirs up his fury;
he cries out, he shouts aloud,
   he shows himself mighty against his foes.

d. *Idolators to be punished; backsliders restored*

14 For a long time I have held my peace,
   I have kept still and restrained myself;
now I will cry out like a woman in labor,
   I will gasp and pant.

15 I will lay waste mountains and hills,
   and dry up all their herbage;
I will turn the rivers into islands,
   and dry up the pools.

16 I will lead the blind
   by a road they do not know,
   by paths they have not known

42.5
Isa 44.24;
Zech 12.1;
Acts 17.25

42.6
Isa 43.1;
49.6, 8;
Lk 2.32;
Acts 13.47

42.7
Isa 35.5;
61.1;
Lk 4.18;
2 Tim 2.26;
Heb 2.14

42.8
Isa 48.11

42.9
Isa 48.3, 6

42.10
Isa 33.3;
40.3; 98.1;
107.23

42.12
Isa 24.15;
v. 4

42.13
Isa 9.7;
Ex 15.3;
Hos 11.10;
Isa 66.14-16

42.14
Isa 57.11

42.15
Isa 2.12-16;
44.27

42.16
Isa 29.18;
Lk 1.78, 79;
3.5;
Isa 41.17

---

o Meaning of Heb uncertain   *p* Cn Compare Ps 96.11; 98.7: Heb *Those who go down to the sea*

42.6 *I have given you as a covenant to the people.* As the Father has given us Christ, so has he also given us all of the covenantal blessings that attend the work of the mediator. This Christ is the redeemer of his people, a light to open the eyes of the Gentiles, the liberator of those who sit in darkness and under the shadow of death for their sins, and the one who brings us as prisoners from the prisonhouse into freedom and liberty.

42.12 Our chief goal in life should be to glorify the God who has redeemed us. When we do so, we enjoy life's greatest blessing.

42.16 Unconverted people are blind. God brings them sight, light, and life when he saves them. Only then are the crooked things made straight and the rough places plain.

I will guide them.
I will turn the darkness before them into light,
  the rough places into level ground.
These are the things I will do,
  and I will not forsake them.

42.17
Ps 97.7;
Isa 1.29;
44.11; 45.16

17 They shall be turned back and utterly put to shame —
  those who trust in carved images,
who say to cast images,
  "You are our gods."

e. Blindness of the servant-nation and its punishment

18 Listen, you that are deaf;
  and you that are blind, look up and see!

42.19
Isa 43.8;
Ezek 12.2

19 Who is blind but my servant,
  or deaf like my messenger whom I send?
Who is blind like my dedicated one,
  or blind like the servant of the LORD?

42.20
Jer 6.10

20 He sees many things, but does*q* not observe them;
  his ears are open, but he does not hear.

42.21
Isa 58.13

21 The LORD was pleased, for the sake of his righteousness,
  to magnify his teaching and make it glorious.

42.22
Isa 24.18,
22; 10.6

22 But this is a people robbed and plundered,
  all of them are trapped in holes
  and hidden in prisons;
they have become a prey with no one to rescue,
  a spoil with no one to say, "Restore!"

23 Who among you will give heed to this,
  who will attend and listen for the time to come?

42.24
Isa 30.15;
48.18

24 Who gave up Jacob to the spoiler,
  and Israel to the robbers?
Was it not the LORD, against whom we have sinned,
  in whose ways they would not walk,
  and whose law they would not obey?

42.25
Isa 5.25;
2 Kings 25.9;
Hos 7.9

25 So he poured upon him the heat of his anger
  and the fury of war;
it set him on fire all around, but he did not understand;
  it burned him, but he did not take it to heart.

4. Redemption by grace

a. God's love will support, redeem, and restore his people

43.1
vv. 7, 15, 21;
Isa 44.2, 6,
21

43 But now thus says the LORD,
  he who created you, O Jacob,
  he who formed you, O Israel:
Do not fear, for I have redeemed you;
  I have called you by name, you are mine.

43.2
Ps 66.12;
Deut 31.6, 8;
Dan 3.25, 27
43.3
Ex 20.2;
v. 11;
Prov 11.8;
21.18

2 When you pass through the waters, I will be with you;
  and through the rivers, they shall not overwhelm you;
when you walk through fire you shall not be burned,
  and the flame shall not consume you.
3 For I am the LORD your God,

q Heb You see many things but do

42.19 God had called Israel to be his messenger, but that select nation had become scandalously blind and deaf. They were obstinate and unbelieving, but God would not allow his purposes to be thwarted.
42.22 What happened to Israel demonstrated to the world the glory and universality of God's law, for its judgments were executed even against his chosen na-

tion when they became apostate.
43.1ff This chapter looks toward the deliverance of God's people from captivity. But it also looks beyond that to the great work of redemption by the Lord Jesus. God has gone to great lengths to provide salvation for the world of lost sinners.
43.3 *Egypt as your ransom, Ethiopia and Sheba in*

the Holy One of Israel, your Savior.
I give Egypt as your ransom,
   Ethiopia[r] and Seba in exchange for you.

4 Because you are precious in my sight,
   and honored, and I love you,
I give people in return for you,
   nations in exchange for your life.

5 Do not fear, for I am with you;
I will bring your offspring from the east,
   and from the west I will gather you;

6 I will say to the north, "Give them up,"
   and to the south, "Do not withhold;
bring my sons from far away
   and my daughters from the end of the earth —

7 everyone who is called by my name,
   whom I created for my glory,
   whom I formed and made."

b. The servant-nation a witness to the world

8 Bring forth the people who are blind, yet have eyes,
   who are deaf, yet have ears!

9 Let all the nations gather together,
   and let the peoples assemble.
Who among them declared this,
   and foretold to us the former things?
Let them bring their witnesses to justify them,
   and let them hear and say, "It is true."

10 You are my witnesses, says the Lord,
   and my servant whom I have chosen,
so that you may know and believe me
   and understand that I am he.
Before me no god was formed,
   nor shall there be any after me.

11 I, I am the Lord,
   and besides me there is no savior.

12 I declared and saved and proclaimed,
   when there was no strange god among you;
   and you are my witnesses, says the Lord.

13 I am God, and also henceforth I am He;
   there is no one who can deliver from my hand;
   I work and who can hinder it?

c. The Redeemer will restore his people from Babylon

14 Thus says the Lord,
   your Redeemer, the Holy One of Israel:

r Or *Nubia*; Heb *Cush*

43.4
Isa 63.9

43.5
Isa 41.10,
14; 44.2;
Jer 30.10, 11;
46.27, 28

43.6
Ps 107.3;
Isa 14.2

43.7
Ps 100.3;
Isa 29.23;
Eph 2.10;
v. 1

43.8
Isa 6.9;
42.19;
Ezek 12.2

43.9
Isa 41.21,
22, 26

43.10
Isa 44.8;
42.1; 41.4;
44.6

43.11
Isa 45.21

43.12
Deut 32.16;
Ps 81.9;
v. 10;
Isa 44.8

43.13
Ps 90.2;
Job 9.12;
Isa 14.27

43.14
Isa 41.14;
13.14, 15

---

exchange for you. Again Isaiah emphasizes how God is the God of all history and how all the nations are under his control. God gave these nations over to Cyrus by divine promise as consolation for the loss of the Israelites. They were conquered by Cambyses, the son of Cyrus.

43.7 God created humankind for his own glory, for his own pleasure (Rev 4.11), and for fellowship with himself. Even as humans were made to have fellowship with each other (1 Jn 1.7), so were they made to have fellowship with their Creator.

43.11 *besides me there is no savior.* The Bible claims that there is only one road to God and salvation and that the many cults which people have founded are untrue. Some maintain there are many ways to heaven. Once the uniqueness of the Christian faith is denied, syncretism takes over and the cardinal teachings of the Bible lose their force and are emptied of their content.

43.14 God through Isaiah assured his despondent people in Babylon that they would return to the land from which they had been taken and that the power of the oppressor would be broken. He reminded them of the things he had done when he brought them out of Egypt (v. 16). He who did such great things in the past could and would continue to do great things for his people. God's people can have that same confidence today.

For your sake I will send to Babylon
   and break down all the bars,
   and the shouting of the Chaldeans will be turned to
     lamentation.[s]
15 I am the Lord, your Holy One,
   the Creator of Israel, your King.

16 Thus says the Lord,
   who makes a way in the sea,
   a path in the mighty waters,
17 who brings out chariot and horse,
   army and warrior;
they lie down, they cannot rise,
   they are extinguished, quenched like a wick:
18 Do not remember the former things,
   or consider the things of old.
19 I am about to do a new thing;
   now it springs forth, do you not perceive it?
I will make a way in the wilderness
   and rivers in the desert.
20 The wild animals will honor me,
   the jackals and the ostriches;
for I give water in the wilderness,
   rivers in the desert,
to give drink to my chosen people,
21   the people whom I formed for myself
so that they might declare my praise.

d. Israel's sin was ingratitude

22 Yet you did not call upon me, O Jacob;
   but you have been weary of me, O Israel!
23 You have not brought me your sheep for burnt
     offerings,
   or honored me with your sacrifices.
I have not burdened you with offerings,
   or wearied you with frankincense.
24 You have not bought me sweet cane with money,
   or satisfied me with the fat of your sacrifices.
But you have burdened me with your sins;
   you have wearied me with your iniquities.

25 I, I am He
   who blots out your transgressions for my own
     sake,
   and I will not remember your sins.
26 Accuse me, let us go to trial;
   set forth your case, so that you may be proved
     right.
27 Your first ancestor sinned,
   and your interpreters transgressed against me.
28 Therefore I profaned the princes of the sanctuary,
   I delivered Jacob to utter destruction,
   and Israel to reviling.

[s] Meaning of Heb uncertain

43.16 Ex 14.16; Ps 77.19; Isa 51.10; Josh 3.13
43.17 Ex 14.4-9, 25
43.18 Jer 16.14
43.19 2 Cor 5.17; Rev 21.5; Ex 17.6; Num 20.11; Isa 35.6
43.20 Isa 48.21
43.21 v. 1; Ps 102.18; Lk 1.74, 75
43.22 Isa 30.9-11; Mal 1.13
43.23 Am 5.25; Mal 1.6-8
43.24 Ex 30.23; Isa 1.14; Mal 2.17
43.25 Isa 44.23; Ezek 36.22; Jer 31.34
43.26 Isa 1.18; v. 9
43.28 Isa 47.6; Lam 2.2, 6; Zech 8.13

43.22–24 Lacking gratitude for God's former mercies, God's people did not call on him for deliverance from their present plight. They had sinned against God but showed no signs of being willing to repent (cf. Ezek 8.18). Any call to God for help must be preceded by cleansing the heart from sin through repentance and confession; then will God hear and help.

e. The servant-nation shall yet be converted

44 But now hear, O Jacob my servant,
   Israel whom I have chosen!
2 Thus says the Lord who made you,
   who formed you in the womb and will help you:
Do not fear, O Jacob my servant,
   Jeshurun whom I have chosen.
3 For I will pour water on the thirsty land,
   and streams on the dry ground;
I will pour my spirit upon your descendants,
   and my blessing on your offspring.
4 They shall spring up like a green tamarisk,
   like willows by flowing streams.
5 This one will say, "I am the Lord's,"
   another will be called by the name of Jacob,
yet another will write on the hand, "The Lord's,"
   and adopt the name of Israel.

5. God's judgment upon idolaters

a. The Lord as the incomparable God

6 Thus says the Lord, the King of Israel,
   and his Redeemer, the Lord of hosts:
I am the first and I am the last;
   besides me there is no god.
7 Who is like me? Let them proclaim it,
   let them declare and set it forth before me.
Who has announced from of old the things to come?[t]
   Let them tell us[u] what is yet to be.
8 Do not fear, or be afraid;
   have I not told you from of old and declared it?
   You are my witnesses!
Is there any god besides me?
   There is no other rock; I know not one.

b. The folly of worshiping idols

9   All who make idols are nothing, and the things they delight in do not profit; their witnesses neither see nor know. And so they will be put to shame. 10 Who would fashion a god or cast an image that can do no good? 11 Look, all its devotees shall be put to shame; the artisans too are merely human. Let them all assemble, let them stand up; they shall be terrified, they shall all be put to shame.

12   The ironsmith fashions it[v] and works it over the coals, shaping it with hammers, and forging it with his strong arm; he becomes hungry and his strength fails, he drinks no water and is faint. 13 The carpenter stretches a line, marks it out with a stylus, fashions it with planes, and

---

t Cn: Heb *from my placing an eternal people and things to come*   u Tg: Heb *them*   v Cn: Heb *an ax*

44.3 *I will pour my spirit upon your descendants.* The sending of God's Spirit is like watering dry ground. The Spirit was given without measure to Jesus and was later poured out upon the followers of Jesus. Every believer is sealed and indwelt by the Spirit upon conversion. Being filled with the Spirit is God's greatest blessing; from it his people derive their power for witness and service. But not all believers have the fullness of the Spirit, for some quench its fire (1 Thes 5.19).

44.7,8 No one could foretell what would happen in the years ahead except God who, by his prophet, planned out events and announced them hundreds of years before they occurred. God challenges any who think themselves to be gods or prophets to do this. Thus Scripture itself testifies that the prophetic word offers the clearest evidence to the unbelieving mind that God is God.

44.9 Idolatry is more than making images that people worship. It can also exist in the mind and heart, when God is put out and other things are substituted in his place. Humans can worship the intellect or place material things of life above the spiritual. Whatever crowds out God is idolatry.

Cross references (right margin):

44.1 Isa 41.8; Jer 30.10; 46.27, 28
44.2 Isa 43.1, 7; Deut 32.15
44.3 Isa 35.7; Joel 2.28; Jn 7.38; Acts 2.18
44.5 Isa 19.21; Zech 8.20-22
44.6 Isa 43.1, 14; 41.4; 48.12; Rev 1.8, 17; 22.13
44.7 Isa 41.4, 22
44.8 Isa 41.22; 43.10; Deut 4.35; 1 Sam 2.2; Isa 26.4
44.9 Isa 41.24; 66.3; 43.9; 42.17
44.10 Jer 10.5; Hab 2.18
44.11 Isa 1.29; 42.17
44.12 Isa 40.19; 41.6; Jer 10.3-5
44.13 Isa 41.7; Ps 115.5-7

marks it with a compass; he makes it in human form, with human beauty, to be set up in a shrine. 14 He cuts down cedars or chooses a holm tree or an oak and lets it grow strong among the trees of the forest. He plants a cedar and the rain nourishes it. 15 Then it can be used as fuel. Part of it he takes and warms himself; he kindles a fire and bakes bread. Then he makes a god and worships it, makes it a carved image and bows down before it. 16 Half of it he burns in the fire; over this half he roasts meat, eats it and is satisfied. He also warms himself and says, "Ah, I am warm, I can feel the fire!" 17 The rest of it he makes into a god, his idol, bows down to it and worships it; he prays to it and says, "Save me, for you are my god!"

18   They do not know, nor do they comprehend; for their eyes are shut, so that they cannot see, and their minds as well, so that they cannot understand. 19 No one considers, nor is there knowledge or discernment to say, "Half of it I burned in the fire; I also baked bread on its coals, I roasted meat and have eaten. Now shall I make the rest of it an abomination? Shall I fall down before a block of wood?" 20 He feeds on ashes; a deluded mind has led him astray, and he cannot save himself or say, "Is not this thing in my right hand a fraud?"

c. *Monotheistic Israel shall be redeemed*

21   Remember these things, O Jacob,
          and Israel, for you are my servant;
      I formed you, you are my servant;
          O Israel, you will not be forgotten by me.

22   I have swept away your transgressions like a cloud,
          and your sins like mist;
      return to me, for I have redeemed you.

23   Sing, O heavens, for the LORD has done it;
          shout, O depths of the earth;
      break forth into singing, O mountains,
          O forest, and every tree in it!
      For the LORD has redeemed Jacob,
          and will be glorified in Israel.

6. *The sovereign God employing and converting the heathen*

a. *God's decree to restore Jerusalem through Cyrus*

24   Thus says the LORD, your Redeemer,
          who formed you in the womb:
      I am the LORD, who made all things,
          who alone stretched out the heavens,
          who by myself spread out the earth;

25   who frustrates the omens of liars,
          and makes fools of diviners;
      who turns back the wise,
          and makes their knowledge foolish;

26   who confirms the word of his servant,
          and fulfills the prediction of his messengers;
      who says of Jerusalem, "It shall be inhabited,"

Margin references (left column):

44.15
vv. 17, 19;
2 Chr 25.14

44.17
v. 15;
Isa 45.20;
1 Kings 18.26,
28
44.18
Isa 1.3; 6.9,
10
44.19
Isa 5.13;
45.20; 27.11;
Deut 27.15
44.20
Ps 102.9;
Job 15.31;
Isa 57.11

44.21
Isa 46.8;
vv. 1, 2;
Isa 49.15

44.22
Isa 43.25;
55.7; 43.1;
1 Pet 1.18, 19

44.23
Isa 42.10;
55.12; 43.1;
61.3

44.24
Isa 43.14;
v. 2;
Isa 40.14, 22

44.25
Isa 40.14;
29.14;
1 Cor 1.20,
27

44.26
Isa 55.11;
49.7-20;
Jer 32.15, 44

44.19 From the wood of the same tree people cook their food, warm their houses, and make an idol. They fall down before that idol, imagining they have created a god. Obviously, however, they are greater than the god they made, for they are the ones who fashioned it. Isaiah challenges the worshipers of idols to consider the ridiculousness of their religion.
44.24 No greater claims can be made than those

contained in this verse. God created all things and continues to make things at his pleasure. All being, power, life, and perfection are from God. He needed no one to advise him or assist him. The extent of his power is boundless. Every fetus is God's creation; thus, all human life comes from him and belongs to him from the moment of conception.

and of the cities of Judah, "They shall be rebuilt,
and I will raise up their ruins";

27 who says to the deep, "Be dry —
I will dry up your rivers";

28 who says of Cyrus, "He is my shepherd,
and he shall carry out all my purpose";
and who says of Jerusalem, "It shall be rebuilt,"
and of the temple, "Your foundation shall be laid."

b. Promise of victory to Cyrus

45 Thus says the LORD to his anointed, to Cyrus,
whose right hand I have grasped
to subdue nations before him
and strip kings of their robes,
to open doors before him —
and the gates shall not be closed:

2 I will go before you
and level the mountains,[w]
I will break in pieces the doors of bronze
and cut through the bars of iron,

3 I will give you the treasures of darkness
and riches hidden in secret places,
so that you may know that it is I, the LORD,
the God of Israel, who call you by your name.

4 For the sake of my servant Jacob,
and Israel my chosen,
I call you by your name,
I surname you, though you do not know me.

5 I am the LORD, and there is no other;
besides me there is no god.
I arm you, though you do not know me,

6 so that they may know, from the rising of the sun
and from the west, that there is no one besides me;
I am the LORD, and there is no other.

7 I form light and create darkness,
I make weal and create woe;
I the LORD do all these things.

8 Shower, O heavens, from above,
and let the skies rain down righteousness;
let the earth open, that salvation may spring up,[x]
and let it cause righteousness to sprout up also;
I the LORD have created it.

Cross references (right margin):

44.27
Isa 43.16;
42.15
44.28
Isa 45.1;
14.32; 45.13

45.1
Isa 44.28;
41.13;
Jer 50.3, 35;
v. 5

45.2
Isa 40.4;
Ps 107.16;
Jer 51.30

45.3
Jer 41.8;
Isa 43.1

45.4
Isa 41.8;
43.1;
Acts 17.23

45.5
v. 6;
Isa 44.6, 8;
Ps 18.39

45.6
Mal 1.11;
Isa 43.5; v. 5

45.7
Isa 42.16;
Ps 104.20;
Am 3.6

45.8
Ps 72.6;
85.11;
Isa 12.3;
60.21

---

w Q Ms Gk: MT *the swellings*   x Q Ms: MT *that they may bring forth salvation*

44.28 As Isaiah, writing before 687 B.C., prophesied here, Cyrus was God's instrument to bring about the rebuilding of the temple in Jerusalem. Cyrus' decree, given approximately 538 B.C. (Ezra 1.1,2; 6.3), was issued one hundred and fifty years prior to its fulfillment (see next note). The building became known as the second temple and was used by the Jews until Jerusalem fell in A.D. 70.
45.1 Isa 44.28 and this text refer to Cyrus II, the Great (559–530 B.C.). He founded the Achaemenid Persian Empire, which lasted for two centuries, until the time of Alexander the Great (331 B.C.). In October 539, the Medo-Persians under the command of Ug-baru captured Babylon. A few days later their king, Cyrus, entered the city and assumed the rulership.

Isaiah's prophecy is predictive, since it was written before 687. The modern liberal view of Scripture disallows predictive prophecy and thus dates the latter half of Isaiah *after* rather than *before* Cyrus' day, attributing the material to someone other than Isaiah. Those who hold to the supernatural, however, see no problem with the ability of the Holy Spirit to predict events in advance of their occurrence.
45.3 The gold and silver that Cyrus acquired became his, not because he extracted them from the earth but because he had seized the riches of those who had hidden treasures. God gave Cyrus this wealth in order to show him that God was the Lord of all, though we have no record that Cyrus ever acknowledged the God of Israel as his god.

c. The folly of striving with God

45.9
Isa 29.16;
Rom 9.20, 21

9 Woe to you who strive with your Maker,
   earthen vessels with the potter!*y*
Does the clay say to the one who fashions it, "What are you making"?
   or "Your work has no handles"?

10 Woe to anyone who says to a father, "What are you begetting?"
   or to a woman, "With what are you in labor?"

45.11
Isa 43.15;
54.5; 8.19;
Jer 31.9;
60.21

11 Thus says the LORD,
   the Holy One of Israel, and its Maker:
Will you question me*z* about my children,
   or command me concerning the work of my hands?

45.12
v. 18;
Isa 42.5;
Neh 9.6

12 I made the earth,
   and created humankind upon it;
it was my hands that stretched out the heavens,
   and I commanded all their host.

45.13
Isa 41.2;
v. 2;
Isa 44.28;
52.3

13 I have aroused Cyrus*a* in righteousness,
   and I will make all his paths straight;
he shall build my city
   and set my exiles free,
not for price or reward,
   says the LORD of hosts.

d. The future conversion of the Gentiles

45.14
Isa 14.1, 2;
Ps 149.8;
Isa 49.23;
Jer 16.19;
1 Cor 14.25;
v. 5

14 Thus says the LORD:
The wealth of Egypt and the merchandise of Ethiopia,*b*
   and the Sabeans, tall of stature,
shall come over to you and be yours,
   they shall follow you;
   they shall come over in chains and bow down to you.
They will make supplication to you, saying,
   "God is with you alone, and there is no other;
   there is no god besides him."

45.15
Isa 8.17;
43.3

15 Truly, you are a God who hides himself,
   O God of Israel, the Savior.

45.16
Isa 44.9, 11

16 All of them are put to shame and confounded,
   the makers of idols go in confusion together.

45.17
Isa 26.4;
Rom 11.26;
Isa 49.23

17 But Israel is saved by the LORD
   with everlasting salvation;
you shall not be put to shame or confounded
   to all eternity.

45.18
Isa 42.5;
v. 12;
Gen 1.2, 26;
v. 5

18 For thus says the LORD,
who created the heavens
   (he is God!),
who formed the earth and made it
   (he established it;
he did not create it a chaos,
   he formed it to be inhabited!):
I am the LORD, and there is no other.

45.19
Isa 48.16;
41.8;
Jer 29.13, 14;
Isa 63.1;
44.8

19 I did not speak in secret,
   in a land of darkness;
I did not say to the offspring of Jacob,
   "Seek me in chaos."
I the LORD speak the truth,
   I declare what is right.

---

y Cn: Heb *with the potsherds,* or *with the potters*   *z* Cn: Heb *Ask me of things to come*   *a* Heb *him*
b Or *Nubia;* Heb *Cush*

e. *The heathen invited to be saved by faith in the* LORD

20 Assemble yourselves and come together,
    draw near, you survivors of the nations!
  They have no knowledge —
    those who carry about their wooden idols,
  and keep on praying to a god
    that cannot save.

21 Declare and present your case;
    let them take counsel together!
  Who told this long ago?
    Who declared it of old?
  Was it not I, the LORD?
  There is no other god besides me,
  a righteous God and a Savior;
    there is no one besides me.

22 Turn to me and be saved,
    all the ends of the earth!
  For I am God, and there is no other.

23 By myself I have sworn,
    from my mouth has gone forth in righteousness
    a word that shall not return:
  "To me every knee shall bow,
    every tongue shall swear."

24 Only in the LORD, it shall be said of me,
    are righteousness and strength;
  all who were incensed against him
    shall come to him and be ashamed.

25 In the LORD all the offspring of Israel
    shall triumph and glory.

7. *Lessons from Babylon's fall and Israel's preservation*

a. *Babylon's helpless idols and the omnipotent God*

46 Bel bows down, Nebo stoops,
    their idols are on beasts and cattle;
  these things you carry are loaded
    as burdens on weary animals.

2 They stoop, they bow down together;
    they cannot save the burden,
    but themselves go into captivity.

3 Listen to me, O house of Jacob,
    all the remnant of the house of Israel,
  who have been borne by me from your birth,
    carried from the womb;

4 even to your old age I am he,
    even when you turn gray I will carry you.
  I have made, and I will bear;
    I will carry and will save.

5 To whom will you liken me and make me equal,
    and compare me, as though we were alike?

6 Those who lavish gold from the purse,

45.20
Isa 43.9;
44.18, 19;
Jer 10.5;
Isa 46.6, 7

45.21
Isa 41.23,
26; v. 5;
Isa 43.3, 11

45.22
Num 21.8, 9;
Isa 30.15;
49.6, 12

45.23
Isa 62.8;
Rom 14.11;
Isa 55.11;
65.16

45.24
Isa 54.17;
41.11

45.25
Isa 53.11;
60.19

46.1
Jer 50.2-4;
Isa 45.20

46.2
Jer 43.12, 13

46.3
v. 12;
Isa 45.19;
10.21, 22;
63.9

46.4
Isa 43.13;
Ps 71.18

46.5
Isa 40.18, 25
46.6
Isa 40.19;
44.15, 17

45.22 In the context of widespread idolatry (v. 20), God shows his loving concern for the human race by extending a universal call to everyone to come to him in order to be saved.

46.6,7 Is it not strange that the idols people make are fixed in their places and are immobile unless car-

and weigh out silver in the scales —
they hire a goldsmith, who makes it into a god;
then they fall down and worship!

7 They lift it to their shoulders, they carry it,
they set it in its place, and it stands there;
it cannot move from its place.
If one cries out to it, it does not answer
or save anyone from trouble.

8 Remember this and consider,*c*
recall it to mind, you transgressors,
9 remember the former things of old;
for I am God, and there is no other;
I am God, and there is no one like me,

10 declaring the end from the beginning
and from ancient times things not yet done,
saying, "My purpose shall stand,
and I will fulfill my intention,"

11 calling a bird of prey from the east,
the man for my purpose from a far country.
I have spoken, and I will bring it to pass;
I have planned, and I will do it.

12 Listen to me, you stubborn of heart,
you who are far from deliverance:
13 I bring near my deliverance, it is not far off,
and my salvation will not tarry;
I will put salvation in Zion,
for Israel my glory.

b. *Judgment against merciless Babylon*

47 Come down and sit in the dust,
virgin daughter Babylon!
Sit on the ground without a throne,
daughter Chaldea!
For you shall no more be called
tender and delicate.
2 Take the millstones and grind meal,
remove your veil,
strip off your robe, uncover your legs,
pass through the rivers.

3 Your nakedness shall be uncovered,
and your shame shall be seen.
I will take vengeance,
and I will spare no one.

4 Our Redeemer — the Lord of hosts is his name —
is the Holy One of Israel.

5 Sit in silence, and go into darkness,
daughter Chaldea!
For you shall no more be called

c Meaning of Heb uncertain

ried by their worshipers? Meanwhile, the idolaters refuse to bow before the true God, who is omnipresent and who does not need to be carried on the shoulders of those who trust in him.
46.9,10 No creature is able to to control God. He is omnipotent (all-powerful) and what he chooses to do

will be done according to his divine plan. Babylon supposed itself to have wisdom and knowledge, but still could not foresee the future. Even if its rulers had known the future, they could not have prevented the ruin to which they had been assigned by the righteous judgment of God.

the mistress of kingdoms.

6 I was angry with my people,
    I profaned my heritage;
I gave them into your hand,
    you showed them no mercy;
on the aged you made your yoke
    exceedingly heavy.

7 You said, "I shall be mistress forever,"
    so that you did not lay these things to heart
    or remember their end.

c. *Babylon's false security amid wickedness*

8 Now therefore hear this, you lover of pleasures,
    who sit securely,
who say in your heart,
    "I am, and there is no one besides me;
I shall not sit as a widow
    or know the loss of children" —
9 both these things shall come upon you
    in a moment, in one day:
the loss of children and widowhood
    shall come upon you in full measure,
in spite of your many sorceries
    and the great power of your enchantments.

10 You felt secure in your wickedness;
    you said, "No one sees me."
Your wisdom and your knowledge
    led you astray,
and you said in your heart,
    "I am, and there is no one besides me."
11 But evil shall come upon you,
    which you cannot charm away;
disaster shall fall upon you,
    which you will not be able to ward off;
and ruin shall come on you suddenly,
    of which you know nothing.

d. *Helplessness of Babylon to avert her fall*

12 Stand fast in your enchantments
    and your many sorceries,
    with which you have labored from your youth;
perhaps you may be able to succeed,
    perhaps you may inspire terror.
13 You are wearied with your many consultations;
    let those who study[d] the heavens
stand up and save you,
    those who gaze at the stars,
and at each new moon predict
    what[e] shall befall you.

14 See, they are like stubble,
    the fire consumes them;
they cannot deliver themselves

47.6
Zech 1.15;
Isa 43.28;
10.14;
Deut 28.50

47.7
v. 5;
Isa 42.25;
45.21

47.8
Isa 32.9, 11;
Zeph 2.15;
Rev 18.7

47.9
Isa 13.16,
18; 1 Thess
5.3;
Nah 3.4

47.10
Ps 52.7;
Isa 29.15;
44.20; v. 8

47.11
Isa 57.1;
1 Thess 5.3;
v. 9

47.12
v. 9

47.13
Isa 57.10;
Dan 2.2

47.14
Nah 1.10;
Mal 4.1

---

d Meaning of Heb uncertain   *e* Gk Syr Compare Vg: Heb *from what*

47.13 According to Isaiah's perspective, those who study the stars, prepare horoscopes, and foretell daily events are powerless to predict the future, nor can they give us any help in a time of need.

from the power of the flame.
No coal for warming oneself is this,
    no fire to sit before!

47.15
Rev 18.11;
Isa 43.13;
46.7

15 Such to you are those with whom you have labored,
    who have trafficked with you from your youth;
they all wander about in their own paths;
    there is no one to save you.

8. Israel punished and returned to her land

a. The prophecy of captivity fulfilled

48.1
Isa 46.12;
Num 24.7;
Ps 68.26;
Isa 45.23

48 Hear this, O house of Jacob,
    who are called by the name of Israel,
    and who came forth from the loins*f* of Judah;
who swear by the name of the LORD,
    and invoke the God of Israel,
    but not in truth or right.

48.2
Isa 52.1;
Mic 3.11;
Rom 2.17

2 For they call themselves after the holy city,
    and lean on the God of Israel;
    the LORD of hosts is his name.

48.3
Isa 41.22;
42.9; 43.9;
44.7, 8;
45.21;
Josh 21.45
48.4
Ezek 2.4;
Ex 32.9;
Deut 31.27;
Ezek 3.7-9
48.5
Ezek 2.4; 3.7

3 The former things I declared long ago,
    they went out from my mouth and I made them known;
    then suddenly I did them and they came to pass.
4 Because I know that you are obstinate,
    and your neck is an iron sinew
    and your forehead brass,
5 I declared them to you from long ago,
    before they came to pass I announced them to you,
so that you would not say, "My idol did them,
    my carved image and my cast image commanded them."

48.6
Isa 42.9;
43.19

6 You have heard; now see all this;
    and will you not declare it?
From this time forward I make you hear new things,
    hidden things that you have not known.
7 They are created now, not long ago;
    before today you have never heard of them,
    so that you could not say, "I already knew them."

48.8
Isa 42.25;
46.8;
Ps 58.3

8 You have never heard, you have never known,
    from of old your ear has not been opened.
For I knew that you would deal very treacherously,
    and that from birth you were called a rebel.

b. God's glory upheld by Israel's affliction

48.9
v. 11;
Ps 78.38;
Isa 30.18

9 For my name's sake I defer my anger,
    for the sake of my praise I restrain it for you,
    so that I may not cut you off.

48.10
Jer 9.7;
Ezek 22.18-22;
Jer 11.4
48.11
v. 9;
Deut 32.26;
Ezek 20.9;
Isa 42.8

10 See, I have refined you, but not like*g* silver;
    I have tested you in the furnace of adversity.
11 For my own sake, for my own sake, I do it,

---

f Cn: Heb *waters*   *g* Cn: Heb *with*

48.10 Silver is refined until all the impurities are gone. Similarly, sanctification is designed to make God's people purer day by day as the dross becomes less and less. Sometimes God uses adversity to achieve his goal. The refining process will not be completed until death, when we will at last be fully refined and perfected.

48.11 God would release his people from their captivity, not because they were worthy of release (for he owed them nothing) but because he did not want his name to be polluted by the triumph of heathen Babylon.

for why should my name^h be profaned?
My glory I will not give to another.

c. *God to send Cyrus against Babylon*

12 Listen to me, O Jacob,
    and Israel, whom I called:
I am He; I am the first,
    and I am the last.
13 My hand laid the foundation of the earth,
    and my right hand spread out the heavens;
when I summon them,
    they stand at attention.

14 Assemble, all of you, and hear!
    Who among them has declared these things?
The LORD loves him;
    he shall perform his purpose on Babylon,
    and his arm shall be against the Chaldeans.
15 I, even I, have spoken and called him,
    I have brought him, and he will prosper in his way.
16 Draw near to me, hear this!
    From the beginning I have not spoken in secret,
    from the time it came to be I have been there.
And now the Lord GOD has sent me and his spirit.

d. *A chastened Israel to flee from Babylon and return home*

17 Thus says the LORD,
    your Redeemer, the Holy One of Israel:
I am the LORD your God,
    who teaches you for your own good,
    who leads you in the way you should go.
18 O that you had paid attention to my commandments!
    Then your prosperity would have been like a river,
    and your success like the waves of the sea;
19 your offspring would have been like the sand,
    and your descendants like its grains;
their name would never be cut off
    or destroyed from before me.

20 Go out from Babylon, flee from Chaldea,
    declare this with a shout of joy, proclaim it,
send it forth to the end of the earth;
    say, "The LORD has redeemed his servant Jacob!"
21 They did not thirst when he led them through the deserts;
    he made water flow for them from the rock;
    he split open the rock and the water gushed out.

22 "There is no peace," says the LORD, "for the wicked."

48.12
Deut 32.39;
Isa 41.4;
Rev 1.17;
22.13

48.13
Ps 102.25;
Isa 40.26

48.14
Isa 43.9;
45.21; 46.10,
11;
Jer 50.21-29

48.15
Isa 41.2;
45.1, 2
48.16
Isa 41.1;
45.19; 43.13;
Zech 2.9, 11

48.17
Isa 43.14;
Ps 32.8

48.18
Deut 32.29;
Ps 119.165;
Isa 61.10, 11

48.19
Gen 22.17;
Jer 33.22;
Isa 56.5;
66.22

48.20
Jer 50.8;
Isa 42.10;
62.11; 43.1

48.21
Isa 41.17;
Ex 17.6;
Ps 105.41

48.22
Isa 57.21

---

h Gk Old Latin: Heb *for why should it*

48.16 The Spirit of God is here spoken of as a person, who has divine authority to send the prophets. Whomever God sends, the Spirit sends, and the words the prophets speak are the Spirit's words.

48.21 Israel should remember the providence and miracles that God performed for them in past times and be assured that he was able to do similar mighty deeds on their behalf.

B. *Part II: God's servant-king Redeemer*

1. *God's servant-king to restore Israel and bring light to the Gentiles*

a. *Messiah's call and commission; message to Israel and the heathen*

49.1
Isa 42.4;
66.19; 44.2,
24;
Isa 7.14; 9.6;
Mt 1.20;
Gal 1.15

49 Listen to me, O coastlands,
    pay attention, you peoples from far away!
The LORD called me before I was born,
    while I was in my mother's womb he named me.

49.2
Isa 11.4;
Heb 4.12;
Isa 51.16;
Hab 3.11

2 He made my mouth like a sharp sword,
    in the shadow of his hand he hid me;
he made me a polished arrow,
    in his quiver he hid me away.

49.3
Isa 42.1;
44.23

3 And he said to me, "You are my servant,
    Israel, in whom I will be glorified."

49.4
Isa 65.23

4 But I said, "I have labored in vain,
    I have spent my strength for nothing and vanity;
yet surely my cause is with the LORD,
    and my reward with my God."

49.5
Isa 44.2, 23;
27.12; 43.4;
12.2

5 And now the LORD says,
    who formed me in the womb to be his servant,
to bring Jacob back to him,
    and that Israel might be gathered to him,
for I am honored in the sight of the LORD,
    and my God has become my strength—

49.6
Isa 42.6;
Lk 2.32;
Acts 13.47;
26.23

6 he says,
"It is too light a thing that you should be my servant
    to raise up the tribes of Jacob
    and to restore the survivors of Israel;
I will give you as a light to the nations,
    that my salvation may reach to the end of the earth."

49.7
Isa 48.17;
53.3;
Ps 22.6-8;
Isa 52.15;
66.23

7 Thus says the LORD,
    the Redeemer of Israel and his Holy One,
to one deeply despised, abhorred by the nations,
    the slave of rulers,
"Kings shall see and stand up,
    princes, and they shall prostrate themselves,
because of the LORD, who is faithful,
    the Holy One of Israel, who has chosen you."

b. *God's deliverance and care of his redeemed*

49.8
Ps 69.13;
2 Cor 6.2;
Isa 42.6;
44.26

8 Thus says the LORD:
In a time of favor I have answered you,
    on a day of salvation I have helped you;
I have kept you and given you

49.1 The God who delivered Israel from captivity now addresses the Gentiles concerning the Christ whom the Father called from the day of his birth to be the Redeemer. Jesus was fitted and qualified for the office to which he was called by his Father. All people throughout the world should heed the call of God, who offers them salvation.
49.6 The servant-king, the Messiah, had a twofold work: to restore the survivors of Israel, who remained faithful to God; and to be a light to the Gentiles by providing the good news of salvation to the ends of the

earth. This is one of the key missionary verses in the O.T.
49.7 Concerning the Messiah who would eventually be received and accepted by all, Isaiah prophesies that he would be humiliated and rejected and suffer a shameful death in order to procure salvation.
49.8 The despised and rejected Son of God would be acknowledged by his Father as the one who guaranteed that the covenant of salvation and peace between God and humans would prevail.

as a covenant to the people,[i]
to establish the land,
    to apportion the desolate heritages;

9 saying to the prisoners, "Come out,"
    to those who are in darkness, "Show yourselves."
They shall feed along the ways,
    on all the bare heights[j] shall be their pasture;

10 they shall not hunger or thirst,
    neither scorching wind nor sun shall strike them down,
for he who has pity on them will lead them,
    and by springs of water will guide them.

11 And I will turn all my mountains into a road,
    and my highways shall be raised up.

12 Lo, these shall come from far away,
    and lo, these from the north and from the west,
    and these from the land of Syene.[k]

13 Sing for joy, O heavens, and exult, O earth;
    break forth, O mountains, into singing!
For the Lord has comforted his people,
    and will have compassion on his suffering ones.

c. Zion assured of God's continuing love

14 But Zion said, "The Lord has forsaken me,
    my Lord has forgotten me."

15 Can a woman forget her nursing child,
    or show no compassion for the child of her womb?
Even these may forget,
    yet I will not forget you.

16 See, I have inscribed you on the palms of my hands;
    your walls are continually before me.

17 Your builders outdo your destroyers,[l]
    and those who laid you waste go away from you.

18 Lift up your eyes all around and see;
    they all gather, they come to you.
As I live, says the Lord,
    you shall put all of them on like an ornament,
    and like a bride you shall bind them on.

19 Surely your waste and your desolate places
    and your devastated land —
surely now you will be too crowded for your inhabitants,
    and those who swallowed you up will be far away.

20 The children born in the time of your bereavement
    will yet say in your hearing:
"The place is too crowded for me;
    make room for me to settle."

21 Then you will say in your heart,
    "Who has borne me these?
I was bereaved and barren,
    exiled and put away —
    so who has reared these?
I was left all alone —
    where then have these come from?"

49.9
Isa 42.7;
Lk 4.18;
Isa 41.18

49.10
Rev 7.16;
Ps 121.6;
Isa 14.1;
40.11; 41.17

49.11
Isa 40.4;
62.10

49.12
Isa 43.5, 6

49.13
Isa 44.23;
40.1; 54.7, 8,
10;
Rev 12.12;
18.20

49.14
Isa 40.27

49.15
Isa 44.21

49.16
Song 8.6;
Isa 62.6, 7

49.17
v. 19

49.18
Isa 60.4;
43.5; 45.23;
52.1

49.19
Isa 51.3;
54.1, 2;
Zech 10.10;
Ps 56.1, 2

49.20
Isa 54.1-3

49.21
Isa 54.6, 7;
27.10; 5.13;
1.8

---

i Meaning of Heb uncertain   j Or the trails   k Q Ms: MT Sinim   l Or Your children come swiftly; your destroyers

49.14–18 The God of Zion never forsakes his people, unless they first forsake him. Those who trust in him shall never be forsaken despite external difficulties, violence against them, and even death.

d. *Glorious restoration of Israel along with converted Gentiles*

49.22
Isa 62.10;
60.4; 66.20

22 Thus says the Lord God:
　I will soon lift up my hand to the nations,
　　and raise my signal to the peoples;
　and they shall bring your sons in their bosom,
　　and your daughters shall be carried on their shoulders.

49.23
Isa 60.16;
45.14;
Ps 72.9;
Mic 7.17;
Isa 43.10;
25.9;
Ps 25.3

23 Kings shall be your foster fathers,
　　and their queens your nursing mothers.
　With their faces to the ground they shall bow down to you,
　　and lick the dust of your feet.
　Then you will know that I am the Lord;
　　those who wait for me shall not be put to shame.

24 Can the prey be taken from the mighty,
　　or the captives of a tyrant*m* be rescued?

49.25
Isa 14.1, 2;
25.9

25 But thus says the Lord:
　Even the captives of the mighty shall be taken,
　　and the prey of the tyrant shall be rescued;
　for I will contend with those who contend with you,
　　and I will save your children.

49.26
Isa 9.4, 20;
45.6; 43.3;
v. 7

26 I will make your oppressors eat their own flesh,
　　and they shall be drunk with their own blood as with wine.
　Then all flesh shall know
　　that I am the Lord your Savior,
　　and your Redeemer, the Mighty One of Jacob.

2. *Sinfulness of Israel contrasted with obedience of the servant*

a. *The Lord separated from his wife, Israel, by sin*

50.1
Deut 24.1, 3;
Jer 3.8;
Isa 54.6, 7;
Deut 32.30;
Isa 52.3;
48.8

50 Thus says the Lord:
　Where is your mother's bill of divorce
　　with which I put her away?
　Or which of my creditors is it
　　to whom I have sold you?
　No, because of your sins you were sold,
　　and for your transgressions your mother was put away.

50.2
Isa 65.12;
66.4;
Num 11.23;
Isa 59.1;
Ex 14.21;
Josh 3.16

2 Why was no one there when I came?
　　Why did no one answer when I called?
　Is my hand shortened, that it cannot redeem?
　　Or have I no power to deliver?
　By my rebuke I dry up the sea,
　　I make the rivers a desert;
　their fish stink for lack of water,
　　and die of thirst.*n*

50.3
Isa 13.10;
Rev 6.12

3 I clothe the heavens with blackness,
　　and make sackcloth their covering.

m Q Ms Syr Vg: MT *of a righteous person*　　*n* Or *die on the thirsty ground*

49.23 *those who wait for me.* God's timing is different from ours. Believers must always wait for the Lord. Thousands of years elapsed between the time of God's promise of a redeemer to Adam (Gen 3.15) and the fulfillment of that promise. A long time has elapsed since the promise of Christ's second advent. However much people may scoff because two thousand years have gone by and Jesus has not yet come, those who wait for that coming *shall not be put to shame* (cf. 2 Pet 3.3–10).
49.26 God's judgment against Babylon would show all people that although Israel had appeared defeated, they had a Redeemer. So also the church may be

assured that it too will someday be delivered from the attacks of its enemies by the omnipotent God of the whole earth.
50.1 The questions posed in this verse are rhetorical. God's people have never been divorced by God and never will be. Although they are estranged from God by their sins, God continues to reach out to them in love.
50.2 *Is my hand shortened, that it cannot redeem?* The captivity occurred, not because God was powerless to save his people, but because of their sins. The sovereign God could easily have delivered Israel.

b. Obedient response of the servant, the true Israel

4   The Lord GOD has given me
      the tongue of a teacher,[o]
    that I may know how to sustain
      the weary with a word.
    Morning by morning he wakens—
      wakens my ear
    to listen as those who are taught.

5   The Lord GOD has opened my ear,
      and I was not rebellious,
    I did not turn backward.

6   I gave my back to those who struck me,
      and my cheeks to those who pulled out the beard;
    I did not hide my face
      from insult and spitting.

7   The Lord GOD helps me;
      therefore I have not been disgraced;
    therefore I have set my face like flint,
      and I know that I shall not be put to shame;

8   he who vindicates me is near.
    Who will contend with me?
      Let us stand up together.
    Who are my adversaries?
      Let them confront me.

9   It is the Lord GOD who helps me;
      who will declare me guilty?
    All of them will wear out like a garment;
      the moth will eat them up.

c. Exhortation to trust the LORD

10 Who among you fears the LORD
      and obeys the voice of his servant,
    who walks in darkness
      and has no light,
    yet trusts in the name of the LORD
      and relies upon his God?

11 But all of you are kindlers of fire,
      lighters of firebrands.[p]
    Walk in the flame of your fire,
      and among the brands that you have kindled!
    This is what you shall have from my hand:
      you shall lie down in torment.

3. Encouragement to trust in God, not fearing humans

a. God's mercy to Abraham bestowed on his descendants

51   Listen to me, you that pursue righteousness,
       you that seek the LORD.

---

o Cn: Heb *of those who are taught*   p Syr: Heb *you gird yourselves with firebrands*

50.4 Isa 54.13; Jer 31.25; Ps 143.8	
50.5 Ps 40.6; Mt 26.39; Jn 8.29; 14.31; Phil 2.8	
50.6 Isa 53.5; Mt 26.67; Lk 22.63	
50.7 Isa 49.8; 54.4; Ezek 3.8, 9	
50.8 Rom 8.32-34	
50.9 Isa 41.10; 54.17; 5.18	
50.10 Isa 49.2, 3; 9.2; Eph 5.8; Isa 12.2	
50.11 Ps 35.8; Isa 65.13-15	
51.1 v. 7; Ps 94.15	

50.6 The servant of the Lord, the Messiah, would be smitten, scourged, have his hair pulled out, and be made the lowest in rank in the world—all for the salvation of those who come to him by faith.
50.7 Christ set his face like flint toward Jerusalem and Calvary (see Lk 9.51). He performed his work as mediator with constancy and resolution. He would not be discouraged nor did he fail to accomplish what he had set out to do.

50.10 Whoever is experiencing adversity and walking in darkness is encouraged to continue to trust God and to rely upon him for deliverance, for it will certainly come.
51.1 *you that pursue righteousness,* i.e., "you who are anxious to be both justified and sanctified." *Look to the rock from which you were hewn,* i.e., look back at such things as the stones of memorial set up after crossing the Jordan (see Josh 4), and be encouraged.

Look to the rock from which you were hewn,
and to the quarry from which you were dug.

51.2
Rom 4.16;
Heb 11.11,
12;
Gen 12.1;
24.35

2 Look to Abraham your father
and to Sarah who bore you;
for he was but one when I called him,
but I blessed him and made him many.

51.3
Isa 40.1;
52.9;
Joel 2.3;
Gen 13.10;
Isa 66.10

3 For the Lord will comfort Zion;
he will comfort all her waste places,
and will make her wilderness like Eden,
her desert like the garden of the Lord;
joy and gladness will be found in her,
thanksgiving and the voice of song.

b. *Trust in the eternal Creator, not fearing humans*

51.4
Ps 50.7;
Isa 2.3; 42.4,
6

4 Listen to me, my people,
and give heed to me, my nation;
for a teaching will go out from me,
and my justice for a light to the peoples.

51.5
Isa 46.13;
40.10; 42.4;
63.5

5 I will bring near my deliverance swiftly,
my salvation has gone out
and my arms will rule the peoples;
the coastlands wait for me,
and for my arm they hope.

51.6
Isa 40.26;
Ps 102.26;
Mt 24.35;
2 Pet 3.10;
Isa 45.17

6 Lift up your eyes to the heavens,
and look at the earth beneath;
for the heavens will vanish like smoke,
the earth will wear out like a garment,
and those who live on it will die like gnats;[q]
but my salvation will be forever,
and my deliverance will never be ended.

51.7
v. 1;
Ps 37.31;
Mt 5.11;
Acts 5.41

7 Listen to me, you who know righteousness,
you people who have my teaching in your hearts;
do not fear the reproach of others,
and do not be dismayed when they revile you.

51.8
Isa 50.9; v. 6

8 For the moth will eat them up like a garment,
and the worm will eat them like wool;
but my deliverance will be forever,
and my salvation to all generations.

c. *Prayer that God will again deliver Israel*

51.9
Isa 52.1;
Deut 4.34;
Ps 89.10;
74.13;
Ezek 29.3

9 Awake, awake, put on strength,
O arm of the Lord!
Awake, as in days of old,
the generations of long ago!
Was it not you who cut Rahab in pieces,
who pierced the dragon?

51.10
Ex 14.21;
Isa 43.16;
63.9, 16
51.11
Isa 35.10;
60.19;
Rev 7.17;
22.3

10 Was it not you who dried up the sea,
the waters of the great deep;
who made the depths of the sea a way
for the redeemed to cross over?

11 So the ransomed of the Lord shall return,

q Or in like manner

Remembering such events assures us that what God
has done in the past he can do again today.
51.11 When the redeemed Israelites would be released from their captivity, they would sing like birds
freed from their cages. This is the experience of all the
ransomed of the Lord; they will have songs in their
hearts and make melody to the Lord. Their joy is
made full when they enter the heavenly Zion upon
their death (cf. Rev 7.9–17).

and come to Zion with singing;
    everlasting joy shall be upon their heads;
      they shall obtain joy and gladness,
      and sorrow and sighing shall flee away.

d. *The Lord the Maker will faithfully deliver his people*

12 I, I am he who comforts you;
    why then are you afraid of a mere mortal who must die,
    a human being who fades like grass?
13 You have forgotten the Lord, your Maker,
    who stretched out the heavens
    and laid the foundations of the earth.
  You fear continually all day long
    because of the fury of the oppressor,
  who is bent on destruction.
  But where is the fury of the oppressor?
14 The oppressed shall speedily be released;
    they shall not die and go down to the Pit,
    nor shall they lack bread.
15 For I am the Lord your God,
    who stirs up the sea so that its waves roar —
    the Lord of hosts is his name.
16 I have put my words in your mouth,
    and hidden you in the shadow of my hand,
  stretching out*r* the heavens
    and laying the foundations of the earth,
    and saying to Zion, "You are my people."

4. *Israel summoned to awaken and return*

a. *Her cup of wrath has been drunk*

17 Rouse yourself, rouse yourself!
    Stand up, O Jerusalem,
  you who have drunk at the hand of the Lord
    the cup of his wrath,
  who have drunk to the dregs
    the bowl of staggering.
18 There is no one to guide her
    among all the children she has borne;
  there is no one to take her by the hand
    among all the children she has brought up.
19 These two things have befallen you
    — who will grieve with you? —
  devastation and destruction, famine and sword —
    who will comfort you?*s*
20 Your children have fainted,
    they lie at the head of every street
    like an antelope in a net;
  they are full of the wrath of the Lord,
    the rebuke of your God.

21 Therefore hear this, you who are wounded,*t*
    who are drunk, but not with wine:

r Syr: Heb *planting*   *s* Q Ms Gk Syr Vg: MT *how may I comfort you?*   *t* Or *humbled*

51.13 *You fear continually.* The fearful have placed themselves in bondage to Satan, for he controls them by their fear. God has not given his people a spirit of cowardice (2 Tim 1.7). In him is deliverance from all our fears, cowardice, and timidity.
51.17 Israel had drunk the cup of God's wrath. The Messiah too drank that cup, but this made it possible for God to free sinners from his wrath.

Marginal references:
51.12 v. 3; 2 Cor 1.3; Ps 118.6; Isa 40.6, 7; 1 Pet 1.24
51.13 Isa 17.10; Job 9.8; Ps 104.2; Isa 40.22; 7.4; 49.26
51.14 Isa 52.2; 38.18; 49.10
51.16 Deut 18.18; Isa 59.21; 49.2; 65.17
51.17 Isa 52.1; Job 21.20; Jer 25.15
51.18 Isa 59.21
51.19 Isa 9.20
51.20 Isa 5.25; 42.25; 66.15
51.21 Isa 54.11; 29.9

51.22
Jer 50.34;
v. 17

22 Thus says your Sovereign, the LORD,
    your God who pleads the cause of his people:
See, I have taken from your hand the cup of staggering;
you shall drink no more
    from the bowl of my wrath.

51.23
Jer 25.15-17,
26, 28;
Zech 12.2;
Josh 10.24

23 And I will put it into the hand of your tormentors,
    who have said to you,
    "Bow down, that we may walk on you";
and you have made your back like the ground
    and like the street for them to walk on.

b. *God will restore Jerusalem for his own glory*

52.1
Isa 51.9, 17;
Neh 11.1;
Mt 4.5;
Rev 21.2, 27

52 Awake, awake,
    put on your strength, O Zion!
Put on your beautiful garments,
    O Jerusalem, the holy city;
for the uncircumcised and the unclean
    shall enter you no more.

52.2
Isa 29.4; 9.4;
51.14

2 Shake yourself from the dust, rise up,
    O captive[u] Jerusalem;
loose the bonds from your neck,
    O captive daughter Zion!

52.3
Ps 44.12;
Isa 63.4;
45.13
52.4
Gen 46.6
52.5
Ezek 36.20;
Rom 2.24
52.6
Isa 49.23

3 For thus says the LORD: You were sold for nothing, and you shall be redeemed without money. 4 For thus says the Lord GOD: Long ago, my people went down into Egypt to reside there as aliens; the Assyrian, too, has oppressed them without cause. 5 Now therefore what am I doing here, says the LORD, seeing that my people are taken away without cause? Their rulers howl, says the LORD, and continually, all day long, my name is despised. 6 Therefore my people shall know my name; therefore in that day they shall know that it is I who speak; here am I.

c. *Exultant response of the captives*

52.7
Nah 1.15;
Rom 10.15;
Ps 93.1

7 How beautiful upon the mountains
    are the feet of the messenger who announces peace,
who brings good news,
    who announces salvation,
    who says to Zion, "Your God reigns."

52.8
Isa 62.6

8 Listen! Your sentinels lift up their voices,
    together they sing for joy;
for in plain sight they see
    the return of the LORD to Zion.

52.9
Isa 44.23,
26; 48.20

9 Break forth together into singing,
    you ruins of Jerusalem;
for the LORD has comforted his people,
    he has redeemed Jerusalem.

52.10
Ps 98.2, 3;
Isa 45.22;
48.20;
Lk 3.6

10 The LORD has bared his holy arm
    before the eyes of all the nations;
and all the ends of the earth shall see
    the salvation of our God.

[u] Cn: Heb *rise up, sit*

52.1 In 51.9 the people of God called upon him to awaken and put forth the divine strength. Now God calls for the saints of Zion to wake up and put on *their* strength. They must stop being sluggish and get busy doing what they were supposed to be doing. Nothing provokes God more than sleeping saints who refuse to awaken from their lethargy and to actively serve him.

52.7 God's deliverance of his people from Babylon was a figure of Jesus Christ's redemption of people. Whoever proclaims tidings of redemption does the work of God. The gospel is good news, even the best news, for the God of Zion reigns, and he forgives the sins of the repentant.

11 Depart, depart, go out from there!
    Touch no unclean thing;
go out from the midst of it, purify yourselves,
    you who carry the vessels of the Lord.
12 For you shall not go out in haste,
    and you shall not go in flight;
for the Lord will go before you,
    and the God of Israel will be your rear guard.

5. The triumph of the servant through atoning death

a. His amazing exaltation through humiliation

13 See, my servant shall prosper;
    he shall be exalted and lifted up,
    and shall be very high.
14 Just as there were many who were astonished at him[v]
    —so marred was his appearance, beyond human semblance,
    and his form beyond that of mortals—
15 so he shall startle[w] many nations;
    kings shall shut their mouths because of him;
for that which had not been told them they shall see,
    and that which they had not heard they shall contemplate.

b. The servant as seen by humans: despised and rejected

53
Who has believed what we have heard?
    And to whom has the arm of the Lord been revealed?
2 For he grew up before him like a young plant,
    and like a root out of dry ground;
he had no form or majesty that we should look at him,
    nothing in his appearance that we should desire him.
3 He was despised and rejected by others;
    a man of suffering[x] and acquainted with infirmity;
and as one from whom others hide their faces[y]
    he was despised, and we held him of no account.

c. The servant as seen by God: the Redeemer

4 Surely he has borne our infirmities
    and carried our diseases;
yet we accounted him stricken,
    struck down by God, and afflicted.
5 But he was wounded for our transgressions,
    crushed for our iniquities;
upon him was the punishment that made us whole,
    and by his bruises we are healed.
6 All we like sheep have gone astray;

---

v Syr Tg: Heb you   w Meaning of Heb uncertain   x Or a man of sorrows   y Or as one who hides his face from us

---

Cross references:

52.11 Jer 50.8; 2 Cor 6.17; 2 Tim 2.19; Isa 1.16

52.12 Ex 12.33; Isa 42.16; 58.8

52.13 Isa 42.1; Phil 2.9

52.14 Ps 22.6, 7; Isa 53.2, 3

52.15 Ezek 36.25; Rom 15.21

53.1 Jn 12.38; Rom 10.16

53.2 Isa 11.1; 52.14

53.3 Ps 22.6; v. 10; Jn 1.10, 11

53.4 Mt 8.17; Heb 9.28; 1 Pet 2.24

53.5 Rom 4.25; 1 Cor 15.3; 1 Pet 2.24

53.6 v. 11

52.12 Those who do the will of God and walk in his light will find that God goes before them to prepare the way and stands behind them to protect them from all assaults, just as he did for Israel in their wilderness journey.

52.13 *my servant.* The Servant of the Lord, as the term is used here, is the Messiah, our Lord Jesus. This passage was so interpreted by Christ himself, by the writers of the N.T. (see Mt 8.17; Lk 22.37; Jn 12.28; Acts 8.32,33; Rom 10.16; 1 Pet 2.22–25), and by orthodox Christianity ever since. Commissioned and qualified by the Father, Jesus Christ was the servant of his Father. He humbled himself that he might be exalted; every knee should bow before him

and every tongue confess his name (cf. Phil 2.5–11).

53.1ff This chapter is not looked upon by most Jews as pertaining to the Messiah. They think of it in terms of the nation Israel. The use of *he*, *his*, and *him*, however, makes it difficult to suppose that Isaiah had anyone other than the Messiah in mind. The N.T. makes this clear (see previous note).

53.5,6 These verses clearly indicate that Jesus Christ died in the place of sinners (see note on 1 Pet 2.24 regarding the doctrine of the substitutionary atonement of Jesus Christ).

53.6 Like sheep, people go astray in the paths of sin. And like sheep, lost sinners cannot find their way back home. Christ is the good shepherd who finds the

we have all turned to our own way,
and the LORD has laid on him
the iniquity of us all.

d. *His death as seen by humans: tragic failure*

7 He was oppressed, and he was afflicted,
yet he did not open his mouth;
like a lamb that is led to the slaughter,
and like a sheep that before its shearers is silent,
so he did not open his mouth.

53.7
Mt 26.63;
Acts 8.32

8 By a perversion of justice he was taken away.
Who could have imagined his future?
For he was cut off from the land of the living,
stricken for the transgression of my people.

53.8
vv. 5, 12

9 They made his grave with the wicked
and his tomb*z* with the rich,*a*
although he had done no violence,
and there was no deceit in his mouth.

53.9
Mt 27.57;
1 Pet 2.22

e. *His death as seen by God: glorious success*

10 Yet it was the will of the LORD to crush him with pain.*b*
When you make his life an offering for sin,*c*
he shall see his offspring, and shall prolong his days;
through him the will of the LORD shall prosper.

53.10
vv. 3-6;
Isa 54.3;
46.10

11 Out of his anguish he shall see light;*d*
he shall find satisfaction through his knowledge.
The righteous one,*e* my servant, shall make many righteous,
and he shall bear their iniquities.

53.11
Jn 10.14-18;
Rom 5.18,
19; vv. 5, 6

12 Therefore I will allot him a portion with the great,
and he shall divide the spoil with the strong;
because he poured out himself to death,
and was numbered with the transgressors;
yet he bore the sin of many,
and made intercession for the transgressors.

53.12
Isa 52.13;
Mt 26.38,
39, 42;
Lk 22.37;
2 Cor 5.21

6. *Israel's blessing through the servant*

a. *Captive Israel multiplied and enlarged*

54 Sing, O barren one who did not bear;
burst into song and shout,
you who have not been in labor!
For the children of the desolate woman will be more
than the children of her that is married, says the LORD.

54.1
Gal 4.27;
1 Sam 2.5;
Isa 62.4

2 Enlarge the site of your tent,
and let the curtains of your habitations be stretched out;
do not hold back; lengthen your cords
and strengthen your stakes.

54.2
Isa 49.19, 20

3 For you will spread out to the right and to the left,

54.3
Isa 43.5, 6;
49.19, 23

z Q Ms: MT *and in his death*   *a* Cn: Heb *with a rich person*   *b* Or *by disease*; meaning of Heb uncertain
c Meaning of Heb uncertain   *d* Q Mss: MT lacks *light*   *e* Or *and he shall find satisfaction. Through his knowledge, the righteous one*

lost sheep and brings them back to the fold (see Mt 18.10–14; Lk 15.3–7; Jn 10).
53.8 Isaiah foretold that Christ's death would be a perversion of justice. Among the many fulfillments connected with the death of Jesus are the following: (1) his hands and his feet would be pierced (Ps 22.14–17); (2) he would be offered poison and vinegar (Ps 69.21); (3) he would be crucified with the

wicked and transgressors (53.9,12); (4) his bones would not be broken (Ps 34.20); (5) the soldiers would cast lots for his garments (Ps 22.18); and (6) he would be buried with a rich person (53.9).
53.12 He who bore the sins of the world would win an incontestable victory and exercise a universal dominion over all things.

and your descendants will possess the nations
and will settle the desolate towns.

b. *The Lord's exiled wife restored*

4 Do not fear, for you will not be ashamed;
    do not be discouraged, for you will not suffer disgrace;
for you will forget the shame of your youth,
    and the disgrace of your widowhood you will remember no
        more.

                                               54.4
     Isa 45.17;
     Jer 31.19;
     Isa 4.1; 25.8

5 For your Maker is your husband,
    the Lord of hosts is his name;
the Holy One of Israel is your Redeemer,
    the God of the whole earth he is called.

    54.5
    Jer 3.14;
    Isa 43.14;
    48.17; 6.3

6 For the Lord has called you
    like a wife forsaken and grieved in spirit,
like the wife of a man's youth when she is cast off,
    says your God.

    54.6
    Isa 62.4

7 For a brief moment I abandoned you,
    but with great compassion I will gather you.

    54.7
    Isa 26.20;
    43.5

8 In overflowing wrath for a moment
    I hid my face from you,
but with everlasting love I will have compassion on you,
    says the Lord, your Redeemer.

    54.8
    Isa 60.10;
    v. 10;
    Isa 49.10,
    13; v. 5

c. *Promise of God's unchanging favor*

9 This is like the days of Noah to me:
    Just as I swore that the waters of Noah
      would never again go over the earth,
so I have sworn that I will not be angry with you
    and will not rebuke you.

    54.9
    Gen 9.11;
    Isa 12.1

10 For the mountains may depart
    and the hills be removed,
but my steadfast love shall not depart from you,
    and my covenant of peace shall not be removed,
    says the Lord, who has compassion on you.

    54.10
    Isa 51.6;
    Ps 89.33, 34;
    v. 8

d. *Future radiance of the new Jerusalem*

11 O afflicted one, storm-tossed, and not comforted,
    I am about to set your stones in antimony,
    and lay your foundations with sapphires.*f*

    54.11
    1 Chr 29.2;
    Rev 21.18

12 I will make your pinnacles of rubies,
    your gates of jewels,
    and all your wall of precious stones.

13 All your children shall be taught by the Lord,
    and great shall be the prosperity of your children.

    54.13
    Jer 31.34;
    Jn 6.45;
    Ps 119.165

14 In righteousness you shall be established;
    you shall be far from oppression, for you shall not fear;
    and from terror, for it shall not come near you.

    54.14
    Isa 62.1; 9.4;
    14.3; v. 4

15 If anyone stirs up strife,

    54.15
    Isa 41.11-16

f Or *lapis lazuli*

54.5 *the God of the whole earth he is called.* In the
O.T. God was known primarily as the God of Israel.
But the partition wall between Israel and the Gentiles
is being taken down (see Eph 2.11–22), for he is the
God of the whole earth.
54.10 The steadfast love and the peace of God are
greater and stronger than the strongest parts of the
visible creation. The everlasting mountains and the

perpetual hills are less secure than that love and
peace.
54.13 Isaiah prophesies here the church age.
Those born again of the Spirit would be children who
would be taught by the same Spirit. The God who
adopted them would also see that they were educated
in the things of God.

it is not from me;
whoever stirs up strife with you
   shall fall because of you.
16 See it is I who have created the smith
   who blows the fire of coals,
   and produces a weapon fit for its purpose;
I have also created the ravager to destroy.

54.17
Isa 29.8;
50.8, 9;
45.24

17 No weapon that is fashioned against you shall prosper,
   and you shall confute every tongue that rises against you in
     judgment.
This is the heritage of the servants of the LORD
   and their vindication from me, says the LORD.

7. Grace for trusting sinners

a. The repentant to be blessed

55.1
Isa 41.17;
Jn 4.14;
7.37;
Mt 13.44;
Rev 3.18

55 Ho, everyone who thirsts,
   come to the waters;
and you that have no money,
   come, buy and eat!
Come, buy wine and milk
   without money and without price.

55.2
Hos 8.7;
Isa 62.8, 9;
25.6

2 Why do you spend your money for that which is not bread,
   and your labor for that which does not satisfy?
Listen carefully to me, and eat what is good,
   and delight yourselves in rich food.

55.3
Isa 51.4;
Rom 10.5;
Isa 61.8;
Acts 13.34

3 Incline your ear, and come to me;
   listen, so that you may live.
I will make with you an everlasting covenant,
   my steadfast, sure love for David.

55.4
Jer 30.9;
Ezek 34.23,
24;
Dan 9.25
55.5
Isa 49.6, 12,
23;
Zech 8.22;
Isa 60.9

4 See, I made him a witness to the peoples,
   a leader and commander for the peoples.
5 See, you shall call nations that you do not know,
   and nations that do not know you shall run to you,
because of the LORD your God, the Holy One of Israel,
   for he has glorified you.

b. Repentant sinners commanded to seek the LORD

55.6
Ps 32.6;
Isa 49.8;
2 Cor 6.1, 2
55.7
Isa 1.16;
59.7; 31.6;
54.8, 10;
44.22

6 Seek the LORD while he may be found,
   call upon him while he is near;
7 let the wicked forsake their way,
   and the unrighteous their thoughts;
let them return to the LORD, that he may have mercy on them,
   and to our God, for he will abundantly pardon.
8 For my thoughts are not your thoughts,
   nor are your ways my ways, says the LORD.

55.9
Ps 103.11

9 For as the heavens are higher than the earth,
   so are my ways higher than your ways
   and my thoughts than your thoughts.

55.1 Whoever is thirsty is invited to come. In the larger context of Scripture, this is obviously the invitation to come to Christ (Jn 4.13,14; 7.37–39). He is the fountain opened for our sins and the rock smitten for our salvation. Whoever drinks of him finds salvation in his blood (Jn 6.53–56).
55.7 *Pardon* is a remission of the penalty for one's transgression. Only God can issue a pardon, while the assurance of the pardon may be communicated to people by the agents of God. In order to receive a pardon the guilty must acknowledge their guilt and transgression (Ps 51.3,4; Lk 15.18; 18.13); forsake their wickedness, i.e., repent (Acts 3.19; 17.30); and turn to God who alone can grant the pardon (55.6,7; Jer 33.3,8; Lk 24.47; Acts 26.20; 1 Thess 1.9).

c. The efficacy of God's word

10 For as the rain and the snow come down from heaven,
    and do not return there until they have watered the earth,
making it bring forth and sprout,
    giving seed to the sower and bread to the eater,
11 so shall my word be that goes out from my mouth;
    it shall not return to me empty,
but it shall accomplish that which I purpose,
    and succeed in the thing for which I sent it.

55.10
Isa 30.23;
2 Cor 9.10

55.11
Isa 45.23;
59.21; 46.10

d. The joyous return of the redeemed

12 For you shall go out in joy,
    and be led back in peace;
the mountains and the hills before you
    shall burst into song,
    and all the trees of the field shall clap their hands.
13 Instead of the thorn shall come up the cypress;
    instead of the brier shall come up the myrtle;
and it shall be to the LORD for a memorial,
    for an everlasting sign that shall not be cut off.

55.12
Isa 51.11;
54.10, 13;
44.23;
1 Chr 16.33

55.13
Isa 41.19;
32.13; 63.12,
14; 19.20

8. Gentiles included in Israel's blessing

a. Admonition to maintain a godly witness

56
Thus says the LORD:
    Maintain justice, and do what is right,
for soon my salvation will come,
    and my deliverance be revealed.

2 Happy is the mortal who does this,
    the one who holds it fast,
who keeps the sabbath, not profaning it,
    and refrains from doing any evil.

56.1
Isa 61.8;
46.13

56.2
Isa 58.13

b. Promised blessing to childless believers

3 Do not let the foreigner joined to the LORD say,
    "The LORD will surely separate me from his people";
and do not let the eunuch say,
    "I am just a dry tree."
4 For thus says the LORD:
To the eunuchs who keep my sabbaths,
    who choose the things that please me
    and hold fast my covenant,
5 I will give, in my house and within my walls,
    a monument and a name
    better than sons and daughters;
I will give them an everlasting name
    that shall not be cut off.

56.3
v. 6;
Acts 8.27

56.4
vv. 2, 6

56.5
v. 7;
Isa 66.20;
26.1; 62.2;
48.19

c. Believing Gentiles included in God's covenant people

6 And the foreigners who join themselves to the LORD,

56.6
Isa 60.10;
61.5; vv. 2, 4

55.11 The word that comes from the mouth of God is powerful and effective. Whatever it is sent to do, it will do. His promises of mercy and grace will not lack anything in their fulfillment. But the word is sent on different errands. To some, the word of God brings people life; to others it pronounces death. It convinces the conscience and softens the heart in some; it sears the conscience and hardens the heart in others.

56.6 We must remember the sabbath day to keep it holy (Ex 20.8–11). We should sanctify the Lord's day, not as a legalistic regulation but in the proper spirit, and so experience the acceptance and comfort of God.

to minister to him, to love the name of the LORD,
and to be his servants,
all who keep the sabbath, and do not profane it,
and hold fast my covenant —

7 these I will bring to my holy mountain,
and make them joyful in my house of prayer;
their burnt offerings and their sacrifices
will be accepted on my altar;
for my house shall be called a house of prayer
for all peoples.

8 Thus says the Lord GOD,
who gathers the outcasts of Israel,
I will gather others to them
besides those already gathered.g

9. Condemnation of the wicked rulers of Israel

a. Israel's wicked prophets

9 All you wild animals,
all you wild animals in the forest, come to devour!

10 Israel'sh sentinels are blind,
they are all without knowledge;
they are all silent dogs
that cannot bark;
dreaming, lying down,
loving to slumber.

11 The dogs have a mighty appetite;
they never have enough.
The shepherds also have no understanding;
they have all turned to their own way,
to their own gain, one and all.

12 "Come," they say, "let usi get wine;
let us fill ourselves with strong drink.
And tomorrow will be like today,
great beyond measure."

b. Heavenly reward of persecuted believers

57 The righteous perish,
and no one takes it to heart;
the devout are taken away,
while no one understands.
For the righteous are taken away from calamity,

2 and they enter into peace;
those who walk uprightly
will rest on their couches.

c. The wicked Jews sacrifice their children to idols

3 But as for you, come here,
you children of a sorceress,
you offspring of an adulterer and a whore.j

4 Whom are you mocking?
Against whom do you open your mouth wide

---

g Heb besides his gathered ones   h Heb His   i Q Ms Syr Vg Tg: MT me   j Heb an adulterer and she plays the whore

56.7 All believers are called to a life of prayer and devotion to God. God has promised to answer the prayers of his people (2 Chr 7.14; Mt 18.19).
57.1,2 God providentially takes the righteous out of this world through death. Thus they are removed from the calamities of life and enter into their eternal rest. To die in the Lord is great gain (cf. Phil 1.21).

and stick out your tongue?
Are you not children of transgression,
  the offspring of deceit—
5 you that burn with lust among the oaks,
  under every green tree;
you that slaughter your children in the valleys,
  under the clefts of the rocks?

57.5
2 Kings 16.4;
Lev 18.21;
2 Kings 16.3;
Jer 7.31

6 Among the smooth stones of the valley is your portion;
  they, they, are your lot;
to them you have poured out a drink offering,
  you have brought a grain offering.
  Shall I be appeased for these things?

57.6
Jer 3.9; 7.18;
5.9, 29

d. *Idolatrous worship on the high places*

7 Upon a high and lofty mountain
  you have set your bed,
and there you went up to offer sacrifice.

57.7
Ezek 16.16;
23.41

8 Behind the door and the doorpost
  you have set up your symbol;
for, in deserting me,*k* you have uncovered your bed,
  you have gone up to it,
  you have made it wide;
and you have made a bargain for yourself with them,
  you have loved their bed,
  you have gazed on their nakedness.*l*

57.8
Ezek 23.7,
18; 16.26, 28

9 You journeyed to Molech*m* with oil,
  and multiplied your perfumes;
you sent your envoys far away,
  and sent down even to Sheol.

57.9
Ezek 23.16,
40

10 You grew weary from your many wanderings,
  but you did not say, "It is useless."
You found your desire rekindled,
  and so you did not weaken.

57.10
Isa 47.13;
Jer 2.25

e. *Idols are helpless to deliver*

11 Whom did you dread and fear
  so that you lied,
and did not remember me
  or give me a thought?
Have I not kept silent and closed my eyes,*n*
  and so you do not fear me?

57.11
Isa 51.12;
Jer 2.32; v. 1;
Ps 50.21

12 I will concede your righteousness and your works,
  but they will not help you.

13 When you cry out, let your collection of idols deliver you!
  The wind will carry them off,
  a breath will take them away.
But whoever takes refuge in me shall possess the land
  and inherit my holy mountain.

57.13
Jer 22.20;
Isa 25.4;
60.21; 65.9

---

k Meaning of Heb uncertain   *l* Or *their phallus*; Heb *the hand*   *m* Or *the king*   *n* Gk Vg: Heb *silent even for a long time*

57.5 Those who professed to worship God but had turned to idols burned with lust and performed sexual sins. They also slew their own children as a sacrifice to idols in the valley of Hinnom and in the dark, solitary places where they thought God could not see them.

57.11–13 Because God has not immediately sen-

tenced the wicked to their just deserts, they suppose that they do not need to fear the lawgiver and that they will forever escape divine wrath. God laughs in the heavens and challenges them to find their deliverance in their idols when they are in need of help. The wind will blow their idols in every direction.

f. *Compassion for the repentant, but no peace for the wicked*

14 It shall be said,
"Build up, build up, prepare the way,
    remove every obstruction from my people's way."

15 For thus says the high and lofty one
    who inhabits eternity, whose name is Holy:
I dwell in the high and holy place,
    and also with those who are contrite and humble in spirit,
to revive the spirit of the humble,
    and to revive the heart of the contrite.

16 For I will not continually accuse,
    nor will I always be angry;
for then the spirits would grow faint before me,
    even the souls that I have made.

17 Because of their wicked covetousness I was angry;
    I struck them, I hid and was angry;
    but they kept turning back to their own ways.

18 I have seen their ways, but I will heal them;
    I will lead them and repay them with comfort,
    creating for their mourners the fruit of the lips.ᵒ

19 Peace, peace, to the far and the near, says the LORD;
    and I will heal them.

20 But the wicked are like the tossing sea
    that cannot keep still;
    its waters toss up mire and mud.

21 There is no peace, says my God, for the wicked.

C. Part III: the program of peace

1. Contrast between true and false worship

a. Right and wrong fasting

58 Shout out, do not hold back!
    Lift up your voice like a trumpet!
Announce to my people their rebellion,
    to the house of Jacob their sins.

2 Yet day after day they seek me
    and delight to know my ways,
as if they were a nation that practiced righteousness
    and did not forsake the ordinance of their God;
they ask of me righteous judgments,
    they delight to draw near to God.

3 "Why do we fast, but you do not see?
    Why humble ourselves, but you do not notice?"
Look, you serve your own interest on your fast day,
    and oppress all your workers.

4 Look, you fast only to quarrel and to fight
    and to strike with a wicked fist.
Such fasting as you do today
    will not make your voice heard on high.

5 Is such the fast that I choose,
    a day to humble oneself?
Is it to bow down the head like a bulrush,

ᵒ *Meaning of Heb uncertain*

57.14 Isa 62.10; Jer 18.15

57.15 Isa 52.13; 40.28; 66.1; Ps 34.18; 51.17; 14.2, 3; Isa 61.1

57.16 Gen 6.3; Ps 85.5; 103.9; Mic 7.18; Job 34.14; Isa 42.5

57.17 Jer 6.13; Isa 1.4

57.18 Isa 53.5; 52.12; 61.1-3

57.19 Heb 13.15; Acts 2.39; Eph 2.17

57.20 Job 18.5-14

57.21 Isa 48.22

58.1 Isa 48.8; 50.1; 59.12

58.2 Isa 1.11; 48.1; 59.13; 29.13

58.3 Mal 3.14; Isa 22.12, 13

58.4 1 Kings 21.9, 12, 13; Isa 59.2

58.5 Zech 7.5; Esth 4.3; Job 2.8

57.21 *There is no peace . . . for the wicked.* The wicked cannot be on good terms with God and will not find reconciliation with him. God asserts forthrightly that those who continue in their sins will find no rest in this life or in the life to come.
58.3 All the fasting in the world will be of no value unless the heart is right with God. Performing such ceremonies while living in sin will avail nothing.

and to lie in sackcloth and ashes?
Will you call this a fast,
　　a day acceptable to the LORD?

6　Is not this the fast that I choose:
　　　to loose the bonds of injustice,
　　　to undo the thongs of the yoke,
　　to let the oppressed go free,
　　　and to break every yoke?

58.6
Neh 5.10-12;
Jer 34.9

7　Is it not to share your bread with the hungry,
　　　and bring the homeless poor into your house;
　　when you see the naked, to cover them,
　　　and not to hide yourself from your own kin?

58.7
Ezek 18.7,
16;
Mt 25.35;
Job 31.19;
Gen 29.14;
Neh 5.5

b. Protection and blessing for the righteous

8　Then your light shall break forth like the dawn,
　　　and your healing shall spring up quickly;
　　your vindicator[p] shall go before you,
　　　the glory of the LORD shall be your rear guard.

58.8
v. 10;
Isa 30.26;
62.1;
Ex 14.19;
Isa 52.12

9　Then you shall call, and the LORD will answer;
　　　you shall cry for help, and he will say, Here I am.

　　If you remove the yoke from among you,
　　　the pointing of the finger, the speaking of evil,

58.9
Isa 55.6;
v. 6;
Ps 12.2

10　if you offer your food to the hungry
　　　and satisfy the needs of the afflicted,
　　then your light shall rise in the darkness
　　　and your gloom be like the noonday.

58.10
v. 7;
Ps 37.6

11　The LORD will guide you continually,
　　　and satisfy your needs in parched places,
　　　and make your bones strong;
　　and you shall be like a watered garden,
　　like a spring of water,
　　　whose waters never fail.

58.11
Isa 49.10;
41.17; 66.14;
Jn 4.14; 7.38

12　Your ancient ruins shall be rebuilt;
　　　you shall raise up the foundations of many generations;
　　you shall be called the repairer of the breach,
　　　the restorer of streets to live in.

58.12
Isa 49.8;
44.28; 30.13;
Am 9.11

c. The reward for keeping the sabbath

13　If you refrain from trampling the sabbath,
　　　from pursuing your own interests on my holy day;
　　if you call the sabbath a delight
　　　and the holy day of the LORD honorable;
　　if you honor it, not going your own ways,
　　　serving your own interests, or pursuing your own affairs;[q]

58.13
Isa 56.2;
Ps 84.2, 10;
Isa 55.8;
59.13

14　then you shall take delight in the LORD,
　　　and I will make you ride upon the heights of the earth;
　　I will feed you with the heritage of your ancestor Jacob,
　　　for the mouth of the LORD has spoken.

58.14
Isa 61.10;
Deut 32.13;
Isa 1.19, 20

---

p Or vindication　　q Heb or speaking words

58.9,10　The kind of fasting God wants is twofold: (1) those who fast must commit no acts of violence and fraud; (2) they must abound in acts of charity by giving freely and cheerfully for the poor and needy.
58.13　*The sabbath* was set apart for the worship of God. People were to abstain from business activities. Many Christians have abandoned these principles today. Faithfully keeping one day a week for the Lord, however, will result in the same blessings being poured out on the faithful as God promised through Isaiah (see also Neh 13.17,18).

2. Confessing national wickedness, Israel is rescued by God's grace

a. Iniquity keeps Israel from God's deliverance

59
59.1
Num 11.23;
Isa 50.2;
58.9

See, the LORD's hand is not too short to save,
nor his ear too dull to hear.

59.2
Isa 1.15;
58.4

2 Rather, your iniquities have been barriers
between you and your God,
and your sins have hidden his face from you
so that he does not hear.

59.3
Isa 1.15;
Jer 2.30;
v. 13;
Isa 28.15

3 For your hands are defiled with blood,
and your fingers with iniquity;
your lips have spoken lies,
your tongue mutters wickedness.

59.4
vv. 14, 15;
Isa 30.12;
Job 15.35;
Ps 7.14

4 No one brings suit justly,
no one goes to law honestly;
they rely on empty pleas, they speak lies,
conceiving mischief and begetting iniquity.

59.5
Isa 14.29;
Job 8.14

5 They hatch adders' eggs,
and weave the spider's web;
whoever eats their eggs dies,
and the crushed egg hatches out a viper.

59.6
Isa 28.20;
57.12; 58.4

6 Their webs cannot serve as clothing;
they cannot cover themselves with what they make.
Their works are works of iniquity,
and deeds of violence are in their hands.

59.7
Rom 3.15-17;
Isa 65.2

7 Their feet run to evil,
and they rush to shed innocent blood;
their thoughts are thoughts of iniquity,
desolation and destruction are in their highways.

59.8
vv. 9, 11;
Ps 125.5;
v. 14

8 The way of peace they do not know,
and there is no justice in their paths.
Their roads they have made crooked;
no one who walks in them knows peace.

b. Israel's confession of sins

59.9
v. 14;
Isa 5.30;
8.21, 22

9 Therefore justice is far from us,
and righteousness does not reach us;
we wait for light, and lo! there is darkness;
and for brightness, but we walk in gloom.

59.10
Deut 28.29;
Job 5.14;
Am 8.9;
Isa 8.14, 15

10 We grope like the blind along a wall,
groping like those who have no eyes;
we stumble at noon as in the twilight,
among the vigorous[r] as though we were dead.

59.11
Isa 38.14;
Ezek 7.16;
vv. 9, 14

11 We all growl like bears;
like doves we moan mournfully.
We wait for justice, but there is none;
for salvation, but it is far from us.

59.12
Isa 58.1;
Jer 14.7

12 For our transgressions before you are many,
and our sins testify against us.
Our transgressions indeed are with us,

[r] Meaning of Heb uncertain

59.1 The worshipers who had fasted and prayed to God for deliverance wanted to know why their prayers had not been answered and their fasting had gone unnoticed. Isaiah assured these inquirers that it was not because God was deaf or because he no longer had the power to deliver. Their iniquities had separated them from God and he would not listen to them nor help them. The only cure for this folly was repen-

tance and confession.
59.12ff Isaiah confessed that the people of God had broken faith with the Lord, and he had every right to contend with them for their transgressions. God who sees everything saw their iniquity immediately, and because he is pure he took immediate offense. But he also had compassion on them and provided them with the offer of the gift of righteousness (vv. 16,17).

and we know our iniquities:

13　transgressing, and denying the LORD,
　　　and turning away from following our God,
　　talking oppression and revolt,
　　　conceiving lying words and uttering them from the heart.

14　Justice is turned back,
　　　and righteousness stands at a distance;
　　for truth stumbles in the public square,
　　　and uprightness cannot enter.

15　Truth is lacking,
　　　and whoever turns from evil is despoiled.

c. God intervenes to redeem Zion

The LORD saw it, and it displeased him
　　　that there was no justice.

16　He saw that there was no one,
　　　and was appalled that there was no one to intervene;
　　so his own arm brought him victory,
　　　and his righteousness upheld him.

17　He put on righteousness like a breastplate,
　　　and a helmet of salvation on his head;
　　he put on garments of vengeance for clothing,
　　　and wrapped himself in fury as in a mantle.

18　According to their deeds, so will he repay;
　　　wrath to his adversaries, requital to his enemies;
　　to the coastlands he will render requital.

19　So those in the west shall fear the name of the LORD,
　　　and those in the east, his glory;
　　for he will come like a pent-up stream
　　　that the wind of the LORD drives on.

20　And he will come to Zion as Redeemer,
　　　to those in Jacob who turn from transgression, says the
　　　LORD.

21 And as for me, this is my covenant with them, says the LORD: my spirit
that is upon you, and my words that I have put in your mouth, shall not
depart out of your mouth, or out of the mouths of your children, or out
of the mouths of your children's children, says the LORD, from now on
and forever.

3. The future glory of Zion

a. The dawn of Zion's glory

60 Arise, shine; for your light has come,
　　　and the glory of the LORD has risen upon you.

2　For darkness shall cover the earth,
　　　and thick darkness the peoples;
　　but the LORD will arise upon you,
　　　and his glory will appear over you.

3　Nations shall come to your light,
　　　and kings to the brightness of your dawn.

Cross references (right column):

59.13 Josh 24.27; Titus 1.16; Isa 30.12; vv. 3, 4

59.14 Isa 1.21; 46.12; 48.1

59.15 Isa 5.23; 1.21-23

59.16 Isa 63.5; Ezek 22.30; Ps 98.1

59.17 Eph 6.14; 1 Thess 5.8; Isa 63.2, 3

59.18 Isa 65.6, 7; 66.6

59.19 Ps 113.3; Isa 66.12

59.20 Rom 11.26, 27; Ezek 18.30, 31; Acts 2.38, 39
59.21 Jer 31.31-34; Isa 44.3, 26; 54.10; Jer 32.40

60.1 Eph 5.14; Mal 4.2
60.2 Col 1.13; Isa 4.5

60.3 Isa 49.6, 23; v. 11

59.21 The Spirit and the word of God go together.
All the words spoken by preachers will profit no one
unless those words are empowered by the Holy Spirit.
The Spirit works through the word, and everything
we say must be tried against the written Word of
God.
60.1 Although this chapter prophesies Zion's future

glory, it also has meaning for the church. Christ the
light has come, and the glory of God in us who
are in his Son (cf. 2 Cor 3.18). People from every
nation and language should be told of Christ, the light
of the world that shines in the midst of pagan darkness. Converted Gentiles will know and worship Israel's God.

b. *Converted Gentiles to adore Israel's God*

60.4
Isa 49.18,
20-22

4 Lift up your eyes and look around;
    they all gather together, they come to you;
your sons shall come from far away,
    and your daughters shall be carried on their nurses' arms.

60.5
Ps 34.5;
Isa 23.18;
24.14; 61.6

5 Then you shall see and be radiant;
    your heart shall thrill and rejoice,ˢ
because the abundance of the sea shall be brought to you,
    the wealth of the nations shall come to you.

60.6
Gen 25.4;
Ps 72.10;
Isa 43.23;
42.10

6 A multitude of camels shall cover you,
    the young camels of Midian and Ephah;
    all those from Sheba shall come.
They shall bring gold and frankincense,
    and shall proclaim the praise of the LORD.

60.7
Gen 25.13;
Isa 56.7;
Hag 2.7, 9

7 All the flocks of Kedar shall be gathered to you,
    the rams of Nebaioth shall minister to you;
they shall be acceptable on my altar,
    and I will glorify my glorious house.

8 Who are these that fly like a cloud,
    and like doves to their windows?

60.9
Isa 66.19;
2.16; 49.22;
55.5

9 For the coastlands shall wait for me,
    the ships of Tarshish first,
to bring your children from far away,
    their silver and gold with them,
for the name of the LORD your God,
    and for the Holy One of Israel,
    because he has glorified you.

c. *Millennial peace and supremacy of God's people*

60.10
Zech 6.15;
Isa 49.23;
54.8

10 Foreigners shall build up your walls,
    and their kings shall minister to you;
for in my wrath I struck you down,
    but in my favor I have had mercy on you.

60.11
vv. 18, 5;
Ps 149.8

11 Your gates shall always be open;
    day and night they shall not be shut,
so that nations shall bring you their wealth,
    with their kings led in procession.

60.12
Zech 14.17

12 For the nation and kingdom
    that will not serve you shall perish;
    those nations shall be utterly laid waste.

60.13
Isa 35.2;
41.19;
1 Chr 28.2;
Ps 132.7

13 The glory of Lebanon shall come to you,
    the cypress, the plane, and the pine,
to beautify the place of my sanctuary;
    and I will glorify where my feet rest.

60.14
Isa 49.23;
Heb 12.22;
Rev 3.9

14 The descendants of those who oppressed you
    shall come bending low to you,
and all who despised you
    shall bow down at your feet;
they shall call you the City of the LORD,
    the Zion of the Holy One of Israel.

d. *Prosperity and peace of the Messianic kingdom*

60.15
Jer 30.17;
Isa 66.5;
33.8, 9;
65.18

15 Whereas you have been forsaken and hated,

ˢ Heb *be enlarged*

60.7 *Kedar . . . Nebaioth* were tribes of nomadic peoples descending from Ishmael.
60.15 Some see this as a prophecy that the persecu- tion and hatred of the Jews, who are still God's people and in whom he has an interest, will some day cease (see also Rom 11).

with no one passing through,
I will make you majestic forever,
    a joy from age to age.

16 You shall suck the milk of nations,
    you shall suck the breasts of kings;
and you shall know that I, the LORD, am your Savior
    and your Redeemer, the Mighty One of Jacob.

> 60.16
> Isa 49.23;
> 66.11; 63.8,
> 16

17 Instead of bronze I will bring gold,
    instead of iron I will bring silver;
instead of wood, bronze,
    instead of stones, iron.
I will appoint Peace as your overseer
    and Righteousness as your taskmaster.

18 Violence shall no more be heard in your land,
    devastation or destruction within your borders;
you shall call your walls Salvation,
    and your gates Praise.

> 60.18
> Isa 54.14;
> 51.19; 26.1;
> v. 11

19 The sun shall no longer be
    your light by day,
nor for brightness shall the moon
    give light to you by night;[t]
but the LORD will be your everlasting light,
    and your God will be your glory.

> 60.19
> Rev 21.23;
> 22.5;
> Isa 9.2;
> Zech 2.5

20 Your sun shall no more go down,
    or your moon withdraw itself;
for the LORD will be your everlasting light,
    and your days of mourning shall be ended.

> 60.20
> Isa 30.26;
> 65.19

21 Your people shall all be righteous;
    they shall possess the land forever.
They are the shoot that I planted, the work of my hands,
    so that I might be glorified.

> 60.21
> Isa 52.1;
> Ps 37.11, 22;
> Isa 29.23;
> 45.11

22 The least of them shall become a clan,
    and the smallest one a mighty nation;
I am the LORD;
    in its time I will accomplish it quickly.

> 60.22
> Isa 51.2

4. Good news of salvation

a. The commission to preach the good news

61 The spirit of the Lord GOD is upon me,
    because the LORD has anointed me;
he has sent me to bring good news to the oppressed,
    to bind up the brokenhearted,
to proclaim liberty to the captives,
    and release to the prisoners;

> 61.1f
> Isa 11.2;
> Lk 4.18;
> Ps 45.7;
> Isa 57.15;
> 42.7

2 to proclaim the year of the LORD's favor,
    and the day of vengeance of our God;
to comfort all who mourn;

> 61.2
> Isa 49.8;
> 34.8; 57.18;
> Mt 5.4

3 to provide for those who mourn in Zion —

> 61.3
> Isa 60.20;
> Ps 45.7;
> Isa 60.21

[t] Q Ms Gk Old Latin Tg: MT lacks by night

60.19 A day is coming when we will no longer need the sun and the moon, for Jesus is the light of the new Jerusalem. Just as God was the light of the world before he created the sun and the moon, so shall the triune God be the light and moon of the universe when the end of time comes (Rev 21.23–25).

61.1,2 In the synagogue at Nazareth, Jesus quoted from these verses and applied them to himself (Lk 4.18,19). However, he stopped in the middle of v. 2, after: "To proclaim the year of the LORD's favor." Why? Though Jesus stated that this passage had now been fulfilled in him, he knew that the rest of v. 2, *the day of vengeance*, was still future and unfulfilled. That day would arrive only when the Lord returned in glory at his second advent.

to give them a garland instead of ashes,
   the oil of gladness instead of mourning,
     the mantle of praise instead of a faint spirit.
They will be called oaks of righteousness,
   the planting of the LORD, to display his glory.

b. *Exaltation of Zion in the final age*

4 They shall build up the ancient ruins,
   they shall raise up the former devastations;
they shall repair the ruined cities,
   the devastations of many generations.

5 Strangers shall stand and feed your flocks,
   foreigners shall till your land and dress your vines;
6 but you shall be called priests of the LORD,
   you shall be named ministers of our God;
you shall enjoy the wealth of the nations,
   and in their riches you shall glory.
7 Because their[u] shame was double,
   and dishonor was proclaimed as their lot,
therefore they shall possess a double portion;
   everlasting joy shall be theirs.

8 For I the LORD love justice,
   I hate robbery and wrongdoing;[v]
I will faithfully give them their recompense,
   and I will make an everlasting covenant with them.
9 Their descendants shall be known among the nations,
   and their offspring among the peoples;
all who see them shall acknowledge
   that they are a people whom the LORD has blessed.

c. *Song of praise for God's redemptive love*

10 I will greatly rejoice in the LORD,
   my whole being shall exult in my God;
for he has clothed me with the garments of salvation,
   he has covered me with the robe of righteousness,
as a bridegroom decks himself with a garland,
   and as a bride adorns herself with her jewels.
11 For as the earth brings forth its shoots,
   and as a garden causes what is sown in it to spring up,
so the Lord GOD will cause righteousness and praise
   to spring up before all the nations.

5. *Zion restored and glorified*

a. *God's promise to honor Israel as a wife*

62 For Zion's sake I will not keep silent,
   and for Jerusalem's sake I will not rest,
until her vindication shines out like the dawn,
   and her salvation like a burning torch.
2 The nations shall see your vindication,
   and all the kings your glory;
and you shall be called by a new name
   that the mouth of the LORD will give.
3 You shall be a crown of beauty in the hand of the LORD,
   and a royal diadem in the hand of your God.
4 You shall no more be termed Forsaken,[w]

---

u Heb *your*   *v* Or *robbery with a burnt offering*   *w* Heb *Azubah*

Cross-references (margin):

61.4 Isa 49.8; Ezek 36.33
61.5 Isa 60.10
61.6 Isa 66.21; 60.5, 11
61.7 Isa 54.4; 40.2; Zech 9.12; Isa 60.15; Ps 16.11
61.8 Isa 30.18; 55.3
61.9 Isa 54.3; 44.3
61.10 Isa 12.1, 2; 49.4, 18; Rev 21.2
61.11 Isa 55.10; 45.23, 24; Ps 72.3; 85.11; Isa 60.18
62.1 Isa 61.11; 52.10
62.2 Isa 60.3; vv. 4, 12; Isa 65.15
62.3 Zech 9.16
62.4 Hos 1.10; Isa 54.6, 7; Jer 32.41; 3.14

and your land shall no more be termed Desolate;^x
but you shall be called My Delight Is in Her,^y
  and your land Married;^z
for the LORD delights in you,
  and your land shall be married.

5 For as a young man marries a young woman,
  so shall your builder^a marry you,
and as the bridegroom rejoices over the bride,
  so shall your God rejoice over you.

b. Zion to have rest without fear

6 Upon your walls, O Jerusalem,
  I have posted sentinels;
all day and all night
  they shall never be silent.
You who remind the LORD,
  take no rest,
7 and give him no rest
  until he establishes Jerusalem
and makes it renowned throughout the earth.
8 The LORD has sworn by his right hand
  and by his mighty arm:
I will not again give your grain
  to be food for your enemies,
and foreigners shall not drink the wine
  for which you have labored;
9 but those who garner it shall eat it
  and praise the LORD,
and those who gather it shall drink it
  in my holy courts.

c. God's favor on his holy people

10 Go through, go through the gates,
  prepare the way for the people;
build up, build up the highway,
  clear it of stones,
  lift up an ensign over the peoples.
11 The LORD has proclaimed
  to the end of the earth:
Say to daughter Zion,
  "See, your salvation comes;
his reward is with him,
  and his recompense before him."
12 They shall be called, "The Holy People,
  The Redeemed of the LORD";
and you shall be called, "Sought Out,
  A City Not Forsaken."

d. God's wrath on Zion's foes

63 "Who is this that comes from Edom,
  from Bozrah in garments stained crimson?

Cross-references (margin):
- 62.5 Isa 65.19
- 62.6 Isa 52.8; Jer 6.17; Ezek 3.17; Ps 74.2
- 62.7 Mt 15.21-28; Lk 18.1-8; Jer 33.9
- 62.8 Isa 45.23; Deut 28.31, 33; Jer 5.17
- 62.9 Isa 65.13, 21-23
- 62.10 Isa 57.14; 49.11; 11.10, 12
- 62.11 Isa 49.6; Zech 9.9; Mt 21.5; Isa 51.1; 40.10
- 62.12 Isa 4.3; 51.10; v. 4
- 63.1 Isa 34.5, 6; Am 1.12; Zeph 3.17

x Heb *Shemamah*   y Heb *Hephzibah*   z Heb *Beulah*   a Cn: Heb *your sons*

62.6 *sentinels*, i.e., intercessors.
62.12 *They shall be called, "The Holy People."* Israel, the chosen people of God, had become unholy through their transgressions. They had wandered far from God and had been dispersed throughout the earth. Isaiah prophesies their being regathered to their homeland and redeemed from their sins. By his grace, the righteous and just God would once again be able to call them "The Holy People." Contemporary Christians debate whether or not the reinstatement of the nation of Israel is a fulfillment of this prophecy.
63.1 Isaiah here predicted God's judgment on

Who is this so splendidly robed,
  marching in his great might?"

"It is I, announcing vindication,
  mighty to save."

63.2
Rev 19.13, 15

2 "Why are your robes red,
   and your garments like theirs who tread the wine press?"

63.3
Isa 22.5;
28.3;
Mic 7.10;
Rev 19.15

3 "I have trodden the wine press alone,
   and from the peoples no one was with me;
 I trod them in my anger
   and trampled them in my wrath;
 their juice spattered on my garments,
   and stained all my robes.

63.4
Isa 34.8;
61.2
63.5
Isa 59.16;
Ps 98.1;
Isa 52.10

4 For the day of vengeance was in my heart,
   and the year for my redeeming work had come.
5 I looked, but there was no helper;
   I stared, but there was no one to sustain me;
 so my own arm brought me victory,
   and my wrath sustained me.

63.6
Isa 65.12;
51.17, 21,
22; 34.3

6 I trampled down peoples in my anger,
   I crushed them in my wrath,
   and I poured out their lifeblood on the earth."

6. *Remembering past mercies, repentant Israel pleads to God for deliverance*

a. *Israel the elect of God*

63.7
Isa 54.8, 10;
1 Kings 8.66;
Ps 51.1

7 I will recount the gracious deeds of the LORD,
   the praiseworthy acts of the LORD,
 because of all that the LORD has done for us,
   and the great favor to the house of Israel
 that he has shown them according to his mercy,
   according to the abundance of his steadfast love.
8 For he said, "Surely they are my people,
   children who will not deal falsely";
 and he became their savior

63.9
Judg 10.16;
Ex 23.20-23;
Deut 7.7, 8;
Ex 19.4;
Deut 1.31

9   in all their distress.
 It was no messenger*b* or angel
   but his presence that saved them;*c*
 in his love and in his pity he redeemed them;
   he lifted them up and carried them all the days of old.

b. *God's deliverance in Moses' day*

63.10
Ps 78.40;
Acts 7.51;
Eph 4.30;
Ps 106.40

10 But they rebelled
   and grieved his holy spirit;

b Gk: Heb *anguish*   *c* Or *savior*.   *9In all their distress he was distressed; the angel of his presence saved them;*

Edom, a people who had acted treacherously against Judah at the time of its overthrow. Judah's foe would now suffer retribution. *Bozrah* was an ancient city of Edom. It was militarily strong and was practically impregnable. **63.3** *I have trodden the winepress alone.* This is a prophecy about Jesus Christ, who experienced the wrath of God for sinners alone at Calvary and thus triumphed over principalities and powers. He was deserted by everyone, including his own disciples. John foresaw a future day when an angel from heaven would put out his sickle, gather the grapes, and thrust

them into "the great wine press of the wrath of God" (Rev 14.19). **63.10** In all ages and at all times sinners are saved when they come under conviction of sin by the Holy Spirit and in faith are regenerated by him. Here we are told that Israel rebelled against the work of the Holy Spirit and by that rebellion vexed or grieved the Holy Spirit. In the N.T., believers are commanded, "Do not grieve the Holy Spirit of God, with which you were marked with a seal for the day of redemption" (Eph 4.30). In other words, it is still possible for the saints of God to grieve the Holy Spirit.

therefore he became their enemy;
    he himself fought against them.

11 Then they[d] remembered the days of old,
    of Moses his servant.[e]
Where is the one who brought them up out of the sea
    with the shepherds of his flock?
Where is the one who put within them
    his holy spirit,

12 who caused his glorious arm
    to march at the right hand of Moses,
who divided the waters before them
    to make for himself an everlasting name,

13 who led them through the depths?
Like a horse in the desert,
    they did not stumble.

14 Like cattle that go down into the valley,
    the spirit of the LORD gave them rest.
Thus you led your people,
    to make for yourself a glorious name.

c. Chastened Judah appeals to God as Father and Redeemer

15 Look down from heaven and see,
    from your holy and glorious habitation.
Where are your zeal and your might?
    The yearning of your heart and your compassion?
    They are withheld from me.

16 For you are our father,
    though Abraham does not know us
    and Israel does not acknowledge us;
you, O LORD, are our father;
    our Redeemer from of old is your name.

17 Why, O LORD, do you make us stray from your ways
    and harden our heart, so that we do not fear you?
Turn back for the sake of your servants,
    for the sake of the tribes that are your heritage.

18 Your holy people took possession for a little while;
    but now our adversaries have trampled down your sanctuary.

19 We have long been like those whom you do not rule,
    like those not called by your name.

d. God is besought for help against the heathen

64 O that you would tear open the heavens and come down,
    so that the mountains would quake at your presence —

2[f] as when fire kindles brushwood
    and the fire causes water to boil —
to make your name known to your adversaries,
    so that the nations might tremble at your presence!

3 When you did awesome deeds that we did not expect,
    you came down, the mountains quaked at your presence.

4 From ages past no one has heard,
    no ear has perceived,

d Heb *he*   *e* Cn: Heb *his people*   *f* Ch 64.1 in Heb

63.11
Ps 106.44,
45;
Ex 14.30;
Isa 51.9, 10;
Num 11.17

63.12
Ex 15.6;
14.21;
Isa 50.10, 11

63.13
Ps 106.9

63.14
Deut 32.12

63.15
Deut 26.15;
Ps 80.14;
Jer 31.20;
Hos 11.8

63.16
Isa 64.8;
51.2; 44.6;
60.16

63.17
Ezek 14.7-9;
Isa 29.13,
14;
Num 10.36

63.18
Deut 7.6;
Ps 74.3-7
63.19
Lam 3.43-45

64.1
Ps 144.5;
Judg 5.5
64.2
Jer 5.22

64.3
Ps 65.5; 66.3,
5; 106.22
64.4
1 Cor 2.9;
Isa 40.31

63.11 The Holy Spirit, the third person of the Trinity, was gloriously at work in the O.T., well before Pentecost. For example, God had put his Holy Spirit upon Moses. God gave Israel the Holy Spirit to instruct them (Neh 9.20). And the Holy Spirit gave rest to the people of Israel (v. 14).

64.4 Believers can be assured that as they wait for God, he is at work on their behalf to accomplish good for them.

no eye has seen any God besides you,
　who works for those who wait for him.

e. Confession of iniquity

64.5
Ex 20.24;
Isa 56.1;
63.7, 10

5 You meet those who gladly do right,
　those who remember you in your ways.
But you were angry, and we sinned;
　because you hid yourself we transgressed. *g*

64.6
Isa 6.5;
46.12;
Ps 90.5, 6;
Isa 50.1

6 We have all become like one who is unclean,
　and all our righteous deeds are like a filthy cloth.
We all fade like a leaf,
　and our iniquities, like the wind, take us away.

64.7
Isa 59.4;
27.5; 54.8;
9.18

7 There is no one who calls on your name,
　or attempts to take hold of you;
for you have hidden your face from us,
　and have delivered *h* us into the hand of our iniquity.

f. Appeal for pardon and restoration

64.8
Isa 63.16;
29.16; 60.21

8 Yet, O LORD, you are our Father;
　we are the clay, and you are our potter;
　we are all the work of your hand.

64.9
Isa 60.10;
43.25; 63.8

9 Do not be exceedingly angry, O LORD,
　and do not remember iniquity forever.
Now consider, we are all your people.

64.10
Isa 6.11

10 Your holy cities have become a wilderness,
　Zion has become a wilderness,
Jerusalem a desolation.

64.11
Isa 63.18;
Ps 74.5-7;
Isa 7.23

11 Our holy and beautiful house,
　where our ancestors praised you,
has been burned by fire,
　and all our pleasant places have become ruins.

64.12
Isa 42.14;
Ps 83.1

12 After all this, will you restrain yourself, O LORD?
　Will you keep silent, and punish us so severely?

7. The judgment and redemption of God's people

a. Retribution for idolatrous, hypocritical Israel

65.1
Rom 10.20;
Hos 1.10

65 I was ready to be sought out by those who did not ask,
　to be found by those who did not seek me.
I said, "Here I am, here I am,"
　to a nation that did not call on my name.

65.2
Rom 10.21;
Isa 30.1, 9;
59.7

2 I held out my hands all day long
　to a rebellious people,
who walk in a way that is not good,
　following their own devices;

65.3
Isa 3.8; 66.3,
17

3 a people who provoke me
　to my face continually,
sacrificing in gardens
　and offering incense on bricks;

65.4
Lev 11.7;
Isa 66.3, 17

4 who sit inside tombs,
　and spend the night in secret places;
who eat swine's flesh,
　with broth of abominable things in their vessels;

65.5
Mt 9.11;
Lk 18.9-12

5 who say, "Keep to yourself,

g Meaning of Heb uncertain　　*h* Gk Syr Old Latin Tg: Heb *melted*

64.8 *you are our Father.* The concept of God as our Father, i.e., the Father of believers, is found in the O.T. and expanded considerably in the N.T. God is our Father by creation, for he has made us. But he is especially our Father by covenant, for he has redeemed us, and by the death of his Son, he gave us a second birth and has restored the relationship which was broken and lost because of our sins.

do not come near me, for I am too holy for you."
These are a smoke in my nostrils,
    a fire that burns all day long.

6 See, it is written before me:
    I will not keep silent, but I will repay;
I will indeed repay into their laps

	65.6 Ps 50.3; 79.12; Jer 16.18

7   their[i] iniquities and their[i] ancestors' iniquities together,
                                     says the LORD;
because they offered incense on the mountains
    and reviled me on the hills,
I will measure into their laps
    full payment for their actions.

65.7 Isa 30.13, 14; 57.7; Ezek 20.27, 28; Jer 5.29

b. *The righteous to have an inheritance but the unfaithful to be destroyed*

8 Thus says the LORD:
As the wine is found in the cluster,
    and they say, "Do not destroy it,
    for there is a blessing in it,"
so I will do for my servants' sake,
    and not destroy them all.

9 I will bring forth descendants[j] from Jacob,
    and from Judah inheritors[k] of my mountains;
my chosen shall inherit it,
    and my servants shall settle there.

65.9f Isa 45.19, 25; 49.8; 57.13; 32.18

10 Sharon shall become a pasture for flocks,
    and the Valley of Achor a place for herds to lie down,
    for my people who have sought me.

65.10 Isa 33.9; Josh 7.24; Hos 2.15

11 But you who forsake the LORD,
    who forget my holy mountain,
who set a table for Fortune
    and fill cups of mixed wine for Destiny;

65.11 Deut 29.24, 25; Isa 56.7

12 I will destine you to the sword,
    and all of you shall bow down to the slaughter;
because, when I called, you did not answer,
    when I spoke, you did not listen,
but you did what was evil in my sight,
    and chose what I did not delight in.

65.12 Isa 34.5, 6; 63.6; 2 Chr 36.15, 16; Prov 1.24; Jer 7.13

c. *The obedient blessed; the disobedient punished*

13 Therefore thus says the Lord GOD:
My servants shall eat,
    but you shall be hungry;
my servants shall drink,
    but you shall be thirsty;
my servants shall rejoice,
    but you shall be put to shame;

65.13 Isa 1.19; 8.21; 41.17, 18; 5.13; 66.5, 14

14 my servants shall sing for gladness of heart,
    but you shall cry out for pain of heart,
    and shall wail for anguish of spirit.

65.14 Mt 8.12; Lk 13.28

15 You shall leave your name to my chosen to use as a curse,
    and the Lord GOD will put you to death;
but to his servants he will give a different name.

65.15 Zech 8.13; Isa 62.2

16 Then whoever invokes a blessing in the land
    shall bless by the God of faithfulness,
and whoever takes an oath in the land
    shall swear by the God of faithfulness;

65.16 Ps 72.17; 31.5; Isa 45.23; Jer 31.12

---

i Gk Syr: Heb *your*   j Or *a descendant*   k Or *an inheritor*

because the former troubles are forgotten
    and are hidden from my sight.

d. *Messianic bliss in the new age*

65.17
2 Pet 3.13;
Isa 43.18

17 For I am about to create new heavens
        and a new earth;
    the former things shall not be remembered
        or come to mind.

65.18
Isa 61.10

18 But be glad and rejoice forever
        in what I am creating;
    for I am about to create Jerusalem as a joy,
        and its people as a delight.

65.19
Isa 62.5;
35.10;
Rev 7.17

19 I will rejoice in Jerusalem,
        and delight in my people;
    no more shall the sound of weeping be heard in it,
        or the cry of distress.

65.20
Deut 4.40;
Eccl 8.12, 13

20 No more shall there be in it
        an infant that lives but a few days,
        or an old person who does not live out a lifetime;
    for one who dies at a hundred years will be considered a youth,
        and one who falls short of a hundred will be considered
            accursed.

65.21
Am 9.14;
Isa 37.30

21 They shall build houses and inhabit them;
        they shall plant vineyards and eat their fruit.

65.22
Isa 62.8, 9;
Ps 92.12-14;
Deut 32.46,
47

22 They shall not build and another inhabit;
        they shall not plant and another eat;
    for like the days of a tree shall the days of my people be,
        and my chosen shall long enjoy the work of their hands.

65.23
Isa 55.2;
61.9

23 They shall not labor in vain,
        or bear children for calamity;[1]
    for they shall be offspring blessed by the LORD —
        and their descendants as well.

65.24
Dan 9.27

24 Before they call I will answer,
        while they are yet speaking I will hear.

65.25
Isa 11.6, 7,
9;
Gen 3.14

25 The wolf and the lamb shall feed together,
        the lion shall eat straw like the ox;
        but the serpent — its food shall be dust!
    They shall not hurt or destroy
        on all my holy mountain,

                                                                says the LORD.

8. *The final judgments of the LORD*

a. *God's doom on the unrepentant*

66.1
1 Kings 8.27;
2 Chr 6.18;
Mt 5.34, 35;
Jer 7.4;
Acts 7.49, 50

66 Thus says the LORD:
        Heaven is my throne
        and the earth is my footstool;
    what is the house that you would build for me,
        and what is my resting place?

[1] Or *sudden terror*

65.17 This verse accords with John's great vision of the new heaven and the new earth (Rev 21.1ff).
65.24,25 How great is God! He answers the prayers of people before they have prayed them, and while they then pray, gives them what they want before they have finished their prayers. Furthermore, the utopia people dream of will come when the Messiah returns in power and glory. The wolf and the lamb will feed together. The lion will eat straw as does the ox. Peace will reign and war shall be no more. All people will live in peace with each other.

66.1 Great as the temple was, it is nothing when compared with heaven, for there rests the throne of God. Heaven is the site of his glory and of his government. The Lord sits exalted in highest dignity and dominion. From there he rules all the affairs of the cosmos, and he uses the earth as his footstool.

2 All these things my hand has made,
    and so all these things are mine, *m*
                says the LORD.
But this is the one to whom I will look,
    to the humble and contrite in spirit,
    who trembles at my word.

66.2
Isa 40.26;
57.15;
Mt 5.3, 4;
v. 5

3 Whoever slaughters an ox is like one who kills a human being;
    whoever sacrifices a lamb, like one who breaks a dog's neck;
whoever presents a grain offering, like one who offers swine's
    blood; *n*
    whoever makes a memorial offering of frankincense, like one
      who blesses an idol.
These have chosen their own ways,
    and in their abominations they take delight;

66.3
Isa 1.11, 13;
65.2, 4

4 I also will choose to mock *o* them,
    and bring upon them what they fear;
because, when I called, no one answered,
    when I spoke, they did not listen;
but they did what was evil in my sight,
    and chose what did not please me.

66.4
Prov 1.24;
Isa 65.12;
Jer 7.13

b. *The deliverance of the believing remnant*

5 Hear the word of the LORD,
    you who tremble at his word:
Your own people who hate you
    and reject you for my name's sake
have said, "Let the LORD be glorified,
    so that we may see your joy";
but it is they who shall be put to shame.

66.5
v. 2;
Isa 60.15;
Mt 5.10-12;
Lk 13.17

6 Listen, an uproar from the city!
    A voice from the temple!
The voice of the LORD,
    dealing retribution to his enemies!

66.6
Isa 6.1, 8;
65.6

7 Before she was in labor
    she gave birth;
before her pain came upon her
    she delivered a son.

66.7
Isa 37.3

8 Who has heard of such a thing?
    Who has seen such things?
Shall a land be born in one day?
    Shall a nation be delivered in one moment?
Yet as soon as Zion was in labor
    she delivered her children.

66.8
Isa 64.4

9 Shall I open the womb and not deliver?
    says the LORD;
shall I, the one who delivers, shut the womb?
    says your God.

c. *Comfort and prosperity in the Messianic age*

10 Rejoice with Jerusalem, and be glad for her,

66.10
Isa 65.18;
Ps 26.8;
137.6

m Gk Syr: Heb *these things came to be*   *n* Meaning of Heb uncertain   *o* Or *to punish*

66.5 Israel all too often refused to hear God. But in all generations there have been the few who tremble at the word of God. For them there is comfort, help, and forgiveness in the Redeemer.

66.10 Israel and the church are both objects of God's love and receive his great salvation. We must pray for the peace of Jerusalem (cf. Ps 122.6) and for the church of Christ, his bride and thus his pride and

all you who love her;
rejoice with her in joy,
all you who mourn over her —

¹¹ that you may nurse and be satisfied
from her consoling breast;
that you may drink deeply with delight
from her glorious bosom.

¹² For thus says the LORD:
I will extend prosperity to her like a river,
and the wealth of the nations like an overflowing stream;
and you shall nurse and be carried on her arm,
and dandled on her knees.

¹³ As a mother comforts her child,
so I will comfort you;
you shall be comforted in Jerusalem.

¹⁴ You shall see, and your heart shall rejoice;
your bodies^p shall flourish like the grass;
and it shall be known that the hand of the LORD is with his servants,
and his indignation is against his enemies.

d. *The wicked consigned to judgment*

¹⁵ For the LORD will come in fire,
and his chariots like the whirlwind,
to pay back his anger in fury,
and his rebuke in flames of fire.

¹⁶ For by fire will the LORD execute judgment,
and by his sword, on all flesh;
and those slain by the LORD shall be many.

¹⁷ Those who sanctify and purify themselves to go into the gardens, following the one in the center, eating the flesh of pigs, vermin, and rodents, shall come to an end together, says the LORD.

e. *God glorified in Israel and Gentile converts*

¹⁸ For I know^q their works and their thoughts, and I am^r coming to gather all nations and tongues; and they shall come and shall see my glory, ¹⁹ and I will set a sign among them. From them I will send survivors to the nations, to Tarshish, Put,^s and Lud—which draw the bow—to Tubal and Javan, to the coastlands far away that have not heard of my fame or seen my glory; and they shall declare my glory among the nations. ²⁰ They shall bring all your kindred from all the nations as an offering to the LORD, on horses, and in chariots, and in litters, and on mules, and on dromedaries, to my holy mountain Jerusalem, says the LORD, just as the Israelites bring a grain offering in a clean vessel to the house of the LORD. ²¹ And I will also take some of them as priests and as Levites, says the LORD.

Cross references (left margin):

66.11 Isa 60.16
66.12 Isa 48.18; 60.4, 5
66.13 2 Cor 1.3, 4
66.14 Isa 33.20; Zech 10.7; Isa 58.11; Ezra 7.9; Isa 34.2
66.15 Isa 31.9; 2 Thess 1.8; Ps 78.16
66.16 Isa 30.30; 65.12; 34.3
66.17 Isa 65.3, 4; Ps 37.20
66.18 Isa 59.7; 45.22-25
66.19 Isa 62.10; 42.12
66.20 Isa 60.4; 65.11, 25; 52.11
66.21 Isa 61.6; 1 Pet 2.5, 9

---

p Heb *bones*   *q* Gk Syr: Heb lacks *know*   *r* Gk Syr Vg Tg: Heb *it is*   *s* Gk: Heb *Pul*

---

joy. Israel and the church together will live forever in the new Jerusalem (cf. Rev 21.12–14), the heavenly fulfillment of what the earthly Jerusalem represented.
66.16 At the time of the final judgment, God will satisfy his wrath by fire and sword. He will cut off the impenitent, send them to the lake of fire, and judge them for their rejection of his gracious offer of eternal life.
66.18 Jewish and Gentile believers of all ages will be gathered to see the glory of God the Redeemer. This will occur at the end of the age, when all things will be delivered into the hands of the Father by Jesus Christ the Redeemer (cf. 1 Cor 15.24–28).

f. Heaven for the righteous; eternal fire for the wicked

22 For as the new heavens and the new earth,
       which I will make,
    shall remain before me, says the LORD;
    so shall your descendants and your name remain.

23 From new moon to new moon,
       and from sabbath to sabbath,
    all flesh shall come to worship before me,
    says the LORD.

24 And they shall go out and look at the dead bodies of the people who
have rebelled against me; for their worm shall not die, their fire shall not
be quenched, and they shall be an abhorrence to all flesh.

66.22
Isa 65.17;
2 Pet 3.13;
Rev 21.1;
Isa 65.22,
23; 56.5
66.23
Isa 1.13, 14;
49.7

66.24
Isa 5.25;
24.20;
Mk 9.48;
Isa 1.31;
Dan 12.2

66.22 Paradise was lost by the sin of Adam in the
garden of Eden. The whole cosmos was affected by
his transgression (cf. Rom 8.18ff). For millennia God
worked out his great plan of salvation. And now Isaiah envisions the end of the age. The work of Christ
has been fully finished. The new heavens and the new
earth have come.

INTRODUCTION TO

JEREMIAH

Authorship, Date, and Background: This book is named after the prophet Jeremiah (whose name means "Yahweh establishes"), who was born in Anathoth. His father, Hilkiah (not to be confused with Hilkiah the high priest who was associated with the discovery of the Law in the temple in 2 Kings 22—23), was a member of the priestly class. Jeremiah was undoubtedly of the line of Abiathar, not of the line of Zadok, which started under Solomon in Jerusalem. He was born ca. 652–648 B.C. and began his ministry in 627 B.C. when he was about twenty years of age, though God had planned his ministry before he was born (see 1.4–10). He was God's prophet to Judah in its last days before the captivity (627–586 B.C.). He was a reluctant prophet who suffered greatly for his bold pronouncements of coming judgment. Baruch was his faithful secretary, to whom he dictated much of the book we have.

The Septuagint version of this book differs from the Hebrew text in two important regards: the arrangement is different, and the Hebrew is approximately 2700 words longer. The text in our English Bibles comes from the Hebrew, which is not arranged chronologically. Baruch probably added details about Jeremiah's ministry, as seen in 36.32: "Then Jeremiah took another scroll and gave it to the secretary Baruch son of Neriah, who wrote on it at Jeremiah's dictation all the words of the scroll that King Jehoiakim of Judah had burned in the fire: and many similar words were added to them." Some modern scholars claim that parts of the book were not dictated by Jeremiah or written by Baruch, but were later additions. There is no adequate evidence for this assumption.

Jeremiah's ministry began when King Josiah started a reform movement that was not continued by his successors—Jehoahaz, Jehoiakim, Jehoiachin, and Zedekiah. During this time there was a triangular struggle for world supremacy by Assyria, Babylon, and Egypt. Babylon was able to crush the Assyrian army. In 605 B.C. at Carchemish, Babylon defeated the Egyptians too. Judah was caught in the middle of the warfare since it was in the pathway between Africa and the Middle East. Nebuchadnezzar laid siege to Jerusalem and eventually entered the city and burned it to the ground. He executed King Zedekiah's sons, blinded him, and led him off to Babylon. The fall of Judah and the subsequent seventy years' captivity were a direct result of Judah's apostasy and refusal to repent.

Characteristics and Content: Jeremiah is known to us as the weeping prophet. He spoke his word for God against a background of deceptive prophets (e.g., Hananiah, who was judged and killed by God); for the most part, the false prohets told the people of Judah the exact opposite of what Jeremiah said. Jeremiah wanted to remain silent and stop prophesying. But God's word was like a burning fire and he could not contain himself, in spite of being threatened by such incidents as happened to the prophet Uriah, who had fled to Egypt to escape the wrath of King Jehoiakim. There Uriah was seized and brought back to King Jehoiakim, "who struck him down with the sword and threw his dead body into the burial place of the common people" (26.20–23).

Jeremiah faithfully delivered God's word of doom and judgment to Judah. Nothing deterred him from doing this over and over again. He suffered in solitude, agonized over the gross sins of his countrymen, and felt keenly the awfulness of coming judgment. For Jeremiah personally, God promised deliverance, for when the Babylonians seized Judah and carried off the Jews, Jeremiah was allowed to remain in his homeland. Later, however, he accompanied a remnant to Egypt to continue his prophetic ministry. So far as we know, he died there among a people still unwilling to repent and turn to God.

Outline:

I. Prophecies under Josiah and Jehoiakim (1.1—20.18)

II. Prophecies under Jehoiakim and Zedekiah (21.1—39.18)

III. Prophecies after the fall of Jerusalem (40.1—45.5)

IV. Prophecies against heathen nations (46.1—51.64)

V. Historical appendix (52.1–34)

cursed over the gross sins of his countrymen, and felt keenly the swiftness of coming judgment. For Jeremiah preached promised deliverance, for when the Babylonians spread Judah was carried off the Jews, Jeremiah was allowed to remain in his homeland. Later, however, he accompanied a remnant to Egypt to continue his prophetic ministry. So far as we know, he died there among a people still unwilling to repent and turn to God.

JEREMIAH

I. *Prophecies under Josiah and Jehoiakim (1.1–20.18)*

A. *The prophet's call and commission*

1. *Superscription*

1.1
2 Chr 35.25;
1 Chr 6.60;
Isa 32.7-9

1 The words of Jeremiah son of Hilkiah, of the priests who were in Anathoth in the land of Benjamin, 2 to whom the word of the LORD came in the days of King Josiah son of Amon of Judah, in the thirteenth year of his reign. 3 It came also in the days of King Jehoiakim son of Josiah of Judah, and until the end of the eleventh year of King Zedekiah son of Josiah of Judah, until the captivity of Jerusalem in the fifth month.

1.2
1 Kings 13.2;
2 Kings 21.18,
24

1.3
Jer 25.1;
39.2; 52.12

2. *His personal call from God*

4 Now the word of the LORD came to me saying,

1.5
Ps 139.15,
16;
Isa 49.1, 5

5 "Before I formed you in the womb I knew you,
    and before you were born I consecrated you;
  I appointed you a prophet to the nations."

1.6
Ex 4.10;
Isa 6.5

6 Then I said, "Ah, Lord GOD! Truly I do not know how to speak, for I am only a boy." 7 But the LORD said to me,

"Do not say, 'I am only a boy';
  for you shall go to all to whom I send you,
  and you shall speak whatever I command you.

1.8
Ezek 2.6;
Jer 15.20

8 Do not be afraid of them,
    for I am with you to deliver you,

                                              says the LORD."

1.9
Isa 6.7;
Ex 4.11-16

9 Then the LORD put out his hand and touched my mouth; and the LORD said to me,

"Now I have put my words in your mouth.

1.10
Jer 18.7;
2 Cor 10.4, 5

10 See, today I appoint you over nations and over kingdoms,
    to pluck up and to pull down,
    to destroy and to overthrow,
    to build and to plant."

3. *Vision of the almond branch and the boiling pot*

1.11
Jer 24.3

11 The word of the LORD came to me, saying, "Jeremiah, what do you see?" And I said, "I see a branch of an almond tree."[a] 12 Then the LORD said to me, "You have seen well, for I am watching[b] over my word to

a Heb *shaqed*   *b* Heb *shoqed*

1.4 *the word of the Lord came to me.* It was not Jeremiah's word that the prophet spoke, but the word of God. Not everyone who claims to speak for God has the true message of God. There are false prophets as well as true ones. Jeremiah was to be accused of being a false prophet, but the supernatural works he performed were proof to all that he was genuine.
1.5 God's sovereign direction of Jeremiah's life tells us about how God's will operates. God had a master plan for Jeremiah even before the prophet was conceived in his mother's womb. God called Jeremiah to

the prophetic office and gave him all he needed to fulfill his ministry; thus his excuses to avoid fulfilling God's call were unworthy. Eventually Jeremiah testified he would be unable to keep from prophesying even if he decided to try to remain silent (20.9).
1.6,7 Jeremiah either lacked confidence or a willingness to become a prophet when God called him. He argued that he was only a youth (twenty years of age). A tender age is no reason to refuse to speak for God. For example, Samuel was a mere child when he conveyed God's message to Eli (1 Sam 3).

perform it." ¹³ The word of the LORD came to me a second time, saying, "What do you see?" And I said, "I see a boiling pot, tilted away from the north."

14   Then the LORD said to me: Out of the north disaster shall break out on all the inhabitants of the land. ¹⁵ For now I am calling all the tribes of the kingdoms of the north, says the LORD; and they shall come and all of them shall set their thrones at the entrance of the gates of Jerusalem, against all its surrounding walls and against all the cities of Judah. ¹⁶ And I will utter my judgments against them, for all their wickedness in forsaking me; they have made offerings to other gods, and worshiped the works of their own hands. ¹⁷ But you, gird up your loins; stand up and tell them everything that I command you. Do not break down before them, or I will break you before them. ¹⁸ And I for my part have made you today a fortified city, an iron pillar, and a bronze wall, against the whole land — against the kings of Judah, its princes, its priests, and the people of the land. ¹⁹ They will fight against you; but they shall not prevail against you, for I am with you, says the LORD, to deliver you.

B. First movement: God's summons to Judah for judgment

1. Sermon I: unfaithful Israel

a. Israel's early fidelity

2 The word of the LORD came to me, saying: ² Go and proclaim in the hearing of Jerusalem, Thus says the LORD:
I remember the devotion of your youth,
    your love as a bride,
how you followed me in the wilderness,
    in a land not sown.
³ Israel was holy to the LORD,
    the first fruits of his harvest.
All who ate of it were held guilty;
    disaster came upon them,
                        says the LORD.

b. Israel forsakes the LORD

4   Hear the word of the LORD, O house of Jacob, and all the families of the house of Israel. ⁵ Thus says the LORD:
What wrong did your ancestors find in me
    that they went far from me,
and went after worthless things, and became worthless
        themselves?
⁶ They did not say, "Where is the LORD
    who brought us up from the land of Egypt,
who led us in the wilderness,
    in a land of deserts and pits,
in a land of drought and deep darkness,
    in a land that no one passes through,
    where no one lives?"
⁷ I brought you into a plentiful land
    to eat its fruits and its good things.

1.13
Zech 4.2;
Ezek 11.3, 7;
24.3
1.14
Jer 4.6; 6.1
1.15
Isa 22.7;
Jer 9.11
1.16
Deut 28.20;
Jer 17.13;
7.9; 10.3-5
1.17
1 Kings 18.46;
Ex 3.12;
Ezek 2.6
1.18
Isa 50.7;
Jer 6.27;
15.20
1.19
Jer 11.19;
15.10, 11;
v. 8

2.1
Jer 1.2, 11
2.2
Jer 7.2; 11.6;
Ezek 16.8;
Deut 2.7

2.3
Ex 19.5, 6;
Jer 30.16;
50.7

2.5
Isa 5.4;
Mic 6.3;
Jer 8.19;
2 Kings 17.15

2.6
Ex 20.2;
Isa 63.11;
Hos 13.4;
Deut 8.15;
32.10

2.7
Num 13.27;
Lev 18.25;
Ps 78.58

1.17–19 God informed Jeremiah about his responsibilities. He was told to gird up his loins, i.e., to free himself from anything that would hinder him in his work for God, and to declare the whole counsel of God. No word from God was to be left out. He was to speak out against kings, princes, and priests; consequently, he had much to fear. But he was not to lose heart, for God would be with him. The fear of God was the best antidote against the fear of other humans. God prophesied that Jeremiah would be assaulted by those to whom he preached, but he was guaranteed that the enemy would not overcome him.
2.7 The land of Canaan was a good land, and Israel was well cared for. However, they defiled the land by their persistent idolatry and sinfulness.

But when you entered you defiled my land,
    and made my heritage an abomination.

2.8
Jer 10.21;
Mal 2.6, 7;
Rom 2.20;
Jer 23.13;
16.19

8 The priests did not say, "Where is the LORD?"
       Those who handle the law did not know me;
    the rulers[c] transgressed against me;
       the prophets prophesied by Baal,
       and went after things that do not profit.

2.9
Ezek 20.35,
36;
Mic 6.2

9 Therefore once more I accuse you,
                                                says the LORD,
    and I accuse your children's children.

2.10
Isa 23.12;
Jer 49.28

10 Cross to the coasts of Cyprus and look,
       send to Kedar and examine with care;
       see if there has ever been such a thing.

2.11
Mic 4.5;
Ps 106.20;
Rom 1.23

11 Has a nation changed its gods,
       even though they are no gods?
    But my people have changed their glory
       for something that does not profit.

12 Be appalled, O heavens, at this,
       be shocked, be utterly desolate,
                                                says the LORD,

2.13
Ps 36.9;
Jer 17.13;
Jn 4.14;
Jer 14.3

13 for my people have committed two evils:
       they have forsaken me,
    the fountain of living water,
       and dug out cisterns for themselves,
    cracked cisterns
       that can hold no water.

c. Consequences of Israel's unfaithfulness

2.14
Ex 4.22;
Jer 5.19

14 Is Israel a slave? Is he a homeborn servant?
       Why then has he become plunder?

2.15
Jer 50.17; 4.7

15 The lions have roared against him,
       they have roared loudly.
    They have made his land a waste;
       his cities are in ruins, without inhabitant.

2.16
Jer 44.1;
43.7-9; 48.45

16 Moreover, the people of Memphis and Tahpanhes
       have broken the crown of your head.

2.17
Jer 4.18;
Deut 32.10

17 Have you not brought this upon yourself
       by forsaking the LORD your God,
       while he led you in the way?

2.18
Isa 30.1, 2;
Josh 13.3;
Jer 50.17

18 What then do you gain by going to Egypt,
       to drink the waters of the Nile?
    Or what do you gain by going to Assyria,
       to drink the waters of the Euphrates?

2.19
Isa 3.9;
Hos 5.5;
11.7;
Jer 5.24;
Ps 36.1

19 Your wickedness will punish you,
       and your apostasies will convict you.
    Know and see that it is evil and bitter
       for you to forsake the LORD your God;

c Heb *shepherds*

2.8 God was against the priests who practiced their profession but did not know the God they claimed to represent. The kings had transgressed against him and the prophets were false prophets who spoke for Baal rather than for him. Through Jeremiah God prophesied against the whole political and religious establishment of Israel.
2.11 What Israel did was unique. No other nation ever changed its allegiance to its gods, yet Israel, who

knew the true God who had helped them and provided for them, changed its God. The zeal and fidelity of idol worshipers should shame God's people out of their fickleness.
2.13 Israel forsook the God of living waters and replaced him with cisterns incapable of holding water. Any idols we make, such as wealth, pleasure, or honor, are like cisterns that are useless.

the fear of me is not in you,

says the Lord GOD of hosts.

d. *Israel to be punished for her idolatry*

20 For long ago you broke your yoke
        and burst your bonds,
    and you said, "I will not serve!"
On every high hill
        and under every green tree
    you sprawled and played the whore.

21 Yet I planted you as a choice vine,
        from the purest stock.
How then did you turn degenerate
        and become a wild vine?

22 Though you wash yourself with lye
        and use much soap,
    the stain of your guilt is still before me,

says the Lord GOD.

23 How can you say, "I am not defiled,
        I have not gone after the Baals"?
Look at your way in the valley;
        know what you have done —
    a restive young camel interlacing her tracks,

24   a wild ass at home in the wilderness,
in her heat sniffing the wind!
        Who can restrain her lust?
None who seek her need weary themselves;
        in her month they will find her.

25 Keep your feet from going unshod
        and your throat from thirst.
But you said, "It is hopeless,
        for I have loved strangers,
        and after them I will go."

26 As a thief is shamed when caught,
        so the house of Israel shall be shamed —
they, their kings, their officials,
        their priests, and their prophets,

27 who say to a tree, "You are my father,"
        and to a stone, "You gave me birth."
For they have turned their backs to me,
        and not their faces.
But in the time of their trouble they say,
        "Come and save us!"

28 But where are your gods
        that you made for yourself?
Let them come, if they can save you,
        in your time of trouble;
for you have as many gods
        as you have towns, O Judah.

2.20 *On every high hill.* Israel's idolatrous worship of Baal took place at "high places," i.e., wherever there was a raised mound. Israel took over this heathen custom from their neighbors, and even in their worship of Yahweh the people adopted the idolatrous practices of Baal worship. *Sprawled and played the whore* graphically describe idol worship.
2.23 *The valley* probably refers to the Valley of Hinnom, a valley located southwest of Jerusalem where

the people of the Molech cult sacrificed children.
2.26,27 So evil had Israel become that its kings, princes, priests, and prophets worshiped wood and stone. Yet when they found no deliverance from their idols, they cried to Yahweh. God mocks them in v. 28, telling them to find help from the idols they worshiped. The realities of life overtook them as they discovered that their idol gods *could not* help them and the God whom they had deserted *would not* help them.

e. *The punishment is at hand*

2.29 Jer 5.1; 6.13	29 Why do you complain against me? You have all rebelled against me, says the LORD.
2.30 Isa 1.5; Jer 26.20-24	30 In vain I have struck down your children; they accepted no correction. Your own sword devoured your prophets like a ravening lion.
2.31 Isa 45.19; Deut 32.15	31 And you, O generation, behold the word of the LORD![d] Have I been a wilderness to Israel, or a land of thick darkness? Why then do my people say, "We are free, we will come to you no more"?
2.32 Isa 17.10; Hos 8.14	32 Can a girl forget her ornaments, or a bride her attire? Yet my people have forgotten me, days without number.
	33 How well you direct your course to seek lovers! So that even to wicked women you have taught your ways.
2.34 Jer 19.4; Ex 22.2	34 Also on your skirts is found the lifeblood of the innocent poor, though you did not catch them breaking in. Yet in spite of all these things[d]
2.35 v. 23; Jer 25.31; 1 Jn 1.8, 10	35 you say, "I am innocent; surely his anger has turned from me." Now I am bringing you to judgment for saying, "I have not sinned."
2.36 v. 23; Hos 12.1; Isa 30.3; 2 Chr 28.16, 20, 21	36 How lightly you gad about, changing your ways! You shall be put to shame by Egypt as you were put to shame by Assyria.
2.37 2 Sam 13.19; Jer 37.7-10	37 From there also you will come away with your hands on your head; for the LORD has rejected those in whom you trust, and you will not prosper through them.

f. *Let Judah repent and turn to the LORD*

3.1 Deut 24.4; Jer 2.20; Ezek 16.26, 28, 29; Zech 1.3	**3** If[e] a man divorces his wife and she goes from him and becomes another man's wife, will he return to her? Would not such a land be greatly polluted? You have played the whore with many lovers; and would you return to me? says the LORD.

[d] Meaning of Heb uncertain   [e] Q Ms Gk Syr: MT *Saying, If*

2.30 God sent prophets to warn his people of their sins. They killed God's messengers with rage, however, precisely because the prophets were faithful to their calling.
2.32 Israel had deliberately banished God from their minds and hearts so that they forgot the God who had given birth to them. They no longer remembered his former mercies. This they did for "days without number," i.e., over a long period of time covering several generations.

3.1–14 These verses contain a paradox. God knew what Judah would do and that the captivity was about to begin. Yet in his mercy, he urged the people to repent and turn to him with the promise that the imminent judgment could still be averted. At the very least, judgment would have been delayed — as was Nineveh's when they repented. However, ultimate judgment cannot be averted when disobedience has become the way of life.

2　Look up to the bare heights,*f* and see!
　　Where have you not been lain with?
　By the waysides you have sat waiting for lovers,
　　like a nomad in the wilderness.
　You have polluted the land
　　with your whoring and wickedness.

3　Therefore the showers have been withheld,
　　and the spring rain has not come;
　yet you have the forehead of a whore,
　　you refuse to be ashamed.

4　Have you not just now called to me,
　　"My Father, you are the friend of my youth —

5　will he be angry forever,
　　will he be indignant to the end?"
　This is how you have spoken,
　　but you have done all the evil that you could.

2. Sermon II: the warning example of exiled Samaria

a. The ten tribes dispersed but urged to repent

6　The LORD said to me in the days of King Josiah: Have you seen what she did, that faithless one, Israel, how she went up on every high hill and under every green tree, and played the whore there? 7 And I thought, "After she has done all this she will return to me"; but she did not return, and her false sister Judah saw it. 8 She*g* saw that for all the adulteries of that faithless one, Israel, I had sent her away with a decree of divorce; yet her false sister Judah did not fear, but she too went and played the whore. 9 Because she took her whoredom so lightly, she polluted the land, committing adultery with stone and tree. 10 Yet for all this her false sister Judah did not return to me with her whole heart, but only in pretense, says the LORD.

11　Then the LORD said to me: Faithless Israel has shown herself less guilty than false Judah. 12 Go, and proclaim these words toward the north, and say:

　Return, faithless Israel,
　　　　　　　　　　　　　　　　　says the LORD.
　I will not look on you in anger,
　　for I am merciful,
　　　　　　　　　　　　　　　　　says the LORD;
　I will not be angry forever.

13　Only acknowledge your guilt,
　　that you have rebelled against the LORD your God,
　and scattered your favors among strangers under every
　　　　　　　　green tree,
　　and have not obeyed my voice,
　　　　　　　　　　　　　　　　　says the LORD.

14　Return, O faithless children,
　　　　　　　　　　　　　　　　　says the LORD,
　for I am your master;
　I will take you, one from a city and two from a family,
　　and I will bring you to Zion.

f Or the trails   g Q Ms Gk Mss Syr: MT I

3.2
Deut 12.2;
Jer 2.20;
Prov 23.28;
Jer 2.7

3.3
Lev 26.19;
Jer 6.15;
Ezek 3.7

3.4
v. 19;
Ps 71.17
3.5
v. 12;
Isa 57.16

3.6
Jer 7.24; 17.2
3.7
Ezek 16.46,
47
3.8
2 Kings 17.6;
Isa 50.1;
Ezek 23.11
3.9
Jer 2.7, 27
3.10
Hos 7.14

3.11
Ezek 16.51;
v. 7
3.12
2 Kings 17.6;
Ps 86.15

3.13
Deut 30.1-3;
Jer 2.20, 25;
Deut 12.2

3.14
Hos 2.19;
Jer 50.4, 5

3.6 When God warns the nations, he often refers to historical incidents to illustrate what will happen if they disobey him (cf. 2 Pet 2.1–6 for a N.T. example). God warned Judah here by reminding them of what had happened to Samaria, which God had already judged. People and nations, however, learn little from history and tend to repeat the mistakes of

earlier generations.
3.11–13 God declared that faithless Israel (the northern kingdom of Samaria) was actually less guilty than Judah. Although they had already been dispersed, he sent them a message of hope — that he would have mercy on them and cease to be angry if they would repent.

3.15
Jer 23.4;
Acts 20.28
3.16
Isa 65.17
3.17
Jer 17.12;
v. 19;
Isa 60.9;
Jer 11.8
3.18
Isa 11.13;
Hos 1.11;
Jer 31.8;
Am 9.15

15 I will give you shepherds after my own heart, who will feed you with knowledge and understanding. 16 And when you have multiplied and increased in the land, in those days, says the LORD, they shall no longer say, "The ark of the covenant of the LORD." It shall not come to mind, or be remembered, or missed; nor shall another one be made. 17 At that time Jerusalem shall be called the throne of the LORD, and all nations shall gather to it, to the presence of the LORD in Jerusalem, and they shall no longer stubbornly follow their own evil will. 18 In those days the house of Judah shall join the house of Israel, and together they shall come from the land of the north to the land that I gave your ancestors for a heritage.

3.19
Dan 8.9;
Ps 16.6;
Isa 63.16

19 I thought
  how I would set you among my children,
and give you a pleasant land,
  the most beautiful heritage of all the nations.
And I thought you would call me, My Father,
  and would not turn from following me.

3.20
vv. 6, 7;
Isa 48.8

20 Instead, as a faithless wife leaves her husband,
  so you have been faithless to me, O house of Israel,
                                             says the LORD.

3.21
Isa 15.2;
Jer 2.32

21 A voice on the bare heights[h] is heard,
  the plaintive weeping of Israel's children,
because they have perverted their way,
  they have forgotten the LORD their God:

3.22
v. 14;
Hos 6.1;
14.4;
Jer 31.6

22 Return, O faithless children,
  I will heal your faithlessness.

"Here we come to you;
  for you are the LORD our God.

3.23
Ps 121.1, 2;
3.8

23 Truly the hills are[i] a delusion,
  the orgies on the mountains.
Truly in the LORD our God
  is the salvation of Israel.

3.24
Jer 8.16

24 "But from our youth the shameful thing has devoured all for which our ancestors had labored, their flocks and their herds, their sons and their daughters. 25 Let us lie down in our shame, and let our dishonor cover us; for we have sinned against the LORD our God, we and our ancestors, from our youth even to this day; and we have not obeyed the voice of the LORD our God."

3.25
Ezra 9.7;
Jer 22.21

4.1
Jer 3.1, 22;
Joel 2.12;
Jer 7.3, 7

4 If you return, O Israel,
                                             says the LORD,
  if you return to me,
if you remove your abominations from my presence,
  and do not waver,

4.2
Deut 10.20;
Gen 22.18;
Gal 3.8;
Isa 45.25;
1 Cor 1.31

2 and if you swear, "As the LORD lives!"
  in truth, in justice, and in uprightness,

h Or the trails i Gk Syr Vg: Heb Truly from the hills is

3.15 Despite the multitude and the enormity of his people's transgressions, God held out gracious promises to them if they would repent. *I will give you shepherds after my own heart*, i.e., "I will see that you have ministers and magistrates who will serve me and act justly." However greatly people sin, God still entreats them to turn from their wicked ways. Any nation will be blessed that has for its ministers and rulers those whose lives are patterned after the heart of God.

3.20 As a faithless wife deserts her husband for another mate, so had the house of Israel committed spiritual adultery by forsaking God, their husband. However bad physical adultery may be, spiritual adultery is far worse.

3.23 *Truly the hills are a delusion.* Israel could expect no help from the worship of idols on the high places, whereas they could find help and salvation in the true God of Israel.

then nations shall be blessed[j] by him,
    and by him they shall boast.

b. Judah promised a similar judgment

(1) JUDGMENT TO COME FROM THE NORTH

3 For thus says the LORD to the people of Judah and to the inhabitants
of Jerusalem:
    Break up your fallow ground,
      and do not sow among thorns.

4 Circumcise yourselves to the LORD,
    remove the foreskin of your hearts,
    O people of Judah and inhabitants of Jerusalem,
    or else my wrath will go forth like fire,
    and burn with no one to quench it,
    because of the evil of your doings.

5 Declare in Judah, and proclaim in Jerusalem, and say:
    Blow the trumpet through the land;
      shout aloud[k] and say,
    "Gather together, and let us go
      into the fortified cities!"

6 Raise a standard toward Zion,
      flee for safety, do not delay,
    for I am bringing evil from the north,
      and a great destruction.

7 A lion has gone up from its thicket,
      a destroyer of nations has set out;
    he has gone out from his place
    to make your land a waste;
      your cities will be ruins
      without inhabitant.

8 Because of this put on sackcloth,
      lament and wail:
    "The fierce anger of the LORD
      has not turned away from us."

9On that day, says the LORD, courage shall fail the king and the officials;
the priests shall be appalled and the prophets astounded. 10 Then I said,
"Ah, Lord GOD, how utterly you have deceived this people and Jerusalem,
saying, 'It shall be well with you,' even while the sword is at the throat!"

11 At that time it will be said to this people and to Jerusalem: A hot
wind comes from me out of the bare heights[l] in the desert toward my
poor people, not to winnow or cleanse — 12a wind too strong for that.
Now it is I who speak in judgment against them.

13 Look! He comes up like clouds,
    his chariots like the whirlwind;
    his horses are swifter than eagles —
      woe to us, for we are ruined!

14 O Jerusalem, wash your heart clean of wickedness
      so that you may be saved.
    How long shall your evil schemes
      lodge within you?

15 For a voice declares from Dan

Cross references (right column):

4.3 Hos 10.12; Mt 13.7, 22

4.4 Deut 10.16; 30.6; Jer 9.26; Rom 2.28, 29; Jer 21.12; Mk 9.43, 48

4.5 Jer 6.1; 8.14

4.6 Jer 1.13-15; 6.1, 22

4.7 2 Kings 24.1; Jer 5.6; Dan 7.4; Jer 25.9; Isa 1.7; Jer 2.15

4.8 Isa 22.12; Jer 6.26; 30.24

4.9 Isa 22.3-5; 29.9, 10

4.10 Ezek 14.9; 2 Thess 2.11; Jer 5.12; 14.13

4.11 Jer 51.1; Ezek 17.10; Hos 13.15

4.12 Jer 1.16

4.13 Isa 19.1; 5.28; Deut 28.49; Lam 4.19; Isa 3.8

4.14 Isa 1.16; Jas 4.8; Jer 6.19; 13.27

4.15 Jer 8.16

---

j Or shall bless themselves   k Or shout, take your weapons: Heb shout, fill (your hand)   l Or the trails

---

4.6 from the north, i.e., from Babylon.
4.7 A lion is used as a metaphor for Nebuchadnezzar
of Babylon, who later was to destroy Jerusalem.

4.15 Dan was in the far north of Palestine, and enemy invaders from the north and east began there.
They could be seen as they moved through the fertile

and proclaims disaster from Mount Ephraim.

4.16
Jer 5.6, 15;
Isa 39.3;
Ezek 21.22

16 Tell the nations, "Here they are!"
　　Proclaim against Jerusalem,
　　"Besiegers come from a distant land;
　　　they shout against the cities of Judah.

4.17
2 Kings 25.1,
4;
Jer 5.23

17 They have closed in around her like watchers of a field,
　　because she has rebelled against me,
　　　　　　　　　　　　　　　　says the Lord.

4.18
Ps 107.17;
Isa 50.1;
Jer 2.17, 19

18 Your ways and your doings
　　have brought this upon you.
　　This is your doom; how bitter it is!
　　It has reached your very heart.

4.19
Isa 15.5;
16.11; 21.3;
22.4;
Jer 9.1, 10

19 My anguish, my anguish! I writhe in pain!
　　Oh, the walls of my heart!
　　My heart is beating wildly;
　　　I cannot keep silent;
　　for I^m hear the sound of the trumpet,
　　　the alarm of war.

4.20
Ps 42.7;
Ezek 7.26;
Jer 10.20

20 Disaster overtakes disaster,
　　the whole land is laid waste.
　　Suddenly my tents are destroyed,
　　　my curtains in a moment.

21 How long must I see the standard,
　　and hear the sound of the trumpet?

4.22
Jer 10.8; 2.8;
Rom 16.19

22 "For my people are foolish,
　　they do not know me;
　　they are stupid children,
　　they have no understanding.
　　They are skilled in doing evil,
　　　but do not know how to do good."

4.23
Gen 1.2;
Isa 24.19

23 I looked on the earth, and lo, it was waste and void;
　　and to the heavens, and they had no light.

4.24
Isa 5.25;
Ezek 38.20

24 I looked on the mountains, and lo, they were quaking,
　　and all the hills moved to and fro.

4.25
Zeph 1.3

25 I looked, and lo, there was no one at all,
　　and all the birds of the air had fled.

4.26
Jer 9.10

26 I looked, and lo, the fruitful land was a desert,
　　and all its cities were laid in ruins
　　before the Lord, before his fierce anger.

4.27
Jer 12.11, 12;
5.10, 18;
30.11; 46.28

27 For thus says the Lord: The whole land shall be a desolation; yet
I will not make a full end.

4.28
Hos 4.3;
Isa 5.30;
50.3;
Num 23.19;
Jer 7.16

28 Because of this the earth shall mourn,
　　and the heavens above grow black;
　　for I have spoken, I have purposed;
　　　I have not relented nor will I turn back.

4.29
Jer 6.23;
16.16

29 At the noise of horseman and archer
　　every town takes to flight;
　　they enter thickets; they climb among rocks;

---

^m Another reading is *for you, O my soul,*

---

crescent towards the nation of Judah.
4.19 Jeremiah was not called the weeping prophet
for nothing. The prophet foresaw the ruthless advance of Nebuchadnezzar and his armies who would
destroy both Judah and Jerusalem; this knowledge
brought anguish he could hardly bear. His language
defies anyone to surpass it for vividness and horror at

the approaching doom of Judah.
4.28 God, who foreknows everything, knew that
Judah would not repent. Therefore he passed judgment on that nation and would not relent or turn
back. So certain was the destruction of Jerusalem that
not even God himself could now save it, unless he
were to break his word and annul his judgment.

all the towns are forsaken,
and no one lives in them.

30 And you, O desolate one,
what do you mean that you dress in crimson,
that you deck yourself with ornaments of gold,
that you enlarge your eyes with paint?
In vain you beautify yourself.
Your lovers despise you;
they seek your life.

4.30
Jer 13.21;
2 Kings 9.30;
Ezek 23.40;
Jer 22.20, 22

31 For I heard a cry as of a woman in labor,
anguish as of one bringing forth her first child,
the cry of daughter Zion gasping for breath,
stretching out her hands,
"Woe is me! I am fainting before killers!"

4.31
Jer 13.21;
Isa 42.14;
1.15;
Lam 1.17

(2) FUTILE SEARCH FOR AN UPRIGHT PERSON

5 Run to and fro through the streets of Jerusalem,
look around and take note!
Search its squares and see
if you can find one person
who acts justly
and seeks truth —
so that I may pardon Jerusalem.[n]

5.1
2 Chr 16.9;
Ezek 22.30;
Gen 18.23,
26, 32

2 Although they say, "As the LORD lives,"
yet they swear falsely.

5.2
Titus 1.16;
Jer 4.2; 7.9

3 O LORD, do your eyes not look for truth?
You have struck them,
but they felt no anguish;
you have consumed them,
but they refused to take correction.
They have made their faces harder than rock;
they have refused to turn back.

5.3
Isa 1.5; 9.13;
Jer 2.30;
Zeph 3.2;
Jer 7.26;
19.15

4 Then I said, "These are only the poor,
they have no sense;
for they do not know the way of the LORD,
the law of their God.

5.4
Jer 4.22; 8.7

5 Let me go to the rich[o]
and speak to them;
surely they know the way of the LORD,
the law of their God."
But they all alike had broken the yoke,
they had burst the bonds.

5.5
Mic 3.1;
Ps 2.3

6 Therefore a lion from the forest shall kill them,
a wolf from the desert shall destroy them.
A leopard is watching against their cities;
everyone who goes out of them shall be torn in pieces —
because their transgressions are many,
their apostasies are great.

5.6
Hab 1.8;
Zeph 3.3;
Hos 13.7;
Jer 30.14, 15

n Heb it   o Or the great

5.1 God was willing to suspend his judgment and recall his edict to destroy Jerusalem if just one person could be found in the streets of the city who did right. Note the change from Sodom, where God would have delivered the city if there had been as few as ten righteous people found. The melancholy answer is that there is none who could be found. Judah, therefore, is doomed.

5.6 God was angry with Judah because its *transgressions* were many, i.e., they were of many kinds and often repeated. They were committing spiritual adultery with the worship of idols, a worship due to God alone, and they were also guilty of physical adulteries. Jeremiah graphically depicted their vile affections, their scandalous conduct, and brutish lusts (vv. 7,8).

5.7
Josh 23.7;
Zeph 1.5;
Deut 32.21;
Gal 4.8;
Jer 7.9;
Num 25.1-3

7 How can I pardon you?
　　Your children have forsaken me,
　　　and have sworn by those who are no gods.
　When I fed them to the full,
　　　they committed adultery
　　　and trooped to the houses of prostitutes.

5.8
Ezek 22.11;
Jer 13.27

8 They were well-fed lusty stallions,
　　　each neighing for his neighbor's wife.

5.9
Jer 9.9; 44.22

9 Shall I not punish them for these things?
　　　　　　　　　　　　　　　　　　says the LORD;
　　and shall I not bring retribution
　　on a nation such as this?

(3) SUMMONS TO INVADE JUDAH

5.10
Jer 39.8;
v. 18;
Jer 4.27

10 Go up through her vine-rows and destroy,
　　　but do not make a full end;
　strip away her branches,
　　　for they are not the LORD's.

5.11
Jer 3.20

11 For the house of Israel and the house of Judah
　　　have been utterly faithless to me,
　　　　　　　　　　　　　　　　　says the LORD.

5.12
2 Chr 36.16;
Isa 28.15;
Jer 23.17;
14.13

12 They have spoken falsely of the LORD,
　　　and have said, "He will do nothing.
　No evil will come upon us,
　　　and we shall not see sword or famine."

5.13
Jer 14.13, 15

13 The prophets are nothing but wind,
　　　for the word is not in them.
　Thus shall it be done to them!

5.14
Jer 1.9; 23.29

14 Therefore thus says the LORD, the God of hosts:
　Because they*p* have spoken this word,
　I am now making my words in your mouth a fire,
　　　and this people wood, and the fire shall devour them.

5.15
Deut 28.49;
Isa 5.26;
Jer 1.15;
6.22; 4.16;
Isa 39.3

15 I am going to bring upon you
　　　a nation from far away, O house of Israel,
　　　　　　　　　　　　　　　　　says the LORD.
　It is an enduring nation,
　　　it is an ancient nation,
　a nation whose language you do not know,
　　　nor can you understand what they say.

5.16
Isa 5.28;
13.18

16 Their quiver is like an open tomb;
　　　all of them are mighty warriors.

5.17
Lev 26.16;
Deut 28.31,
33;
Jer 8.13;
Hos 8.14

17 They shall eat up your harvest and your food;
　　　they shall eat up your sons and your daughters;
　they shall eat up your flocks and your herds;
　　　they shall eat up your vines and your fig trees;
　they shall destroy with the sword
　　　your fortified cities in which you trust.

(4) JUDGMENT DUE TO STUBBORNNESS AND REBELLION

5.18
Jer 4.27

18 But even in those days, says the LORD, I will not make a full end

p Heb *you*

5.15 *an ancient nation.* The kingdom of Babylonia, being revived in Jeremiah's time (about 626 B.C.), had a long and illustrious history. The old Babylonian Empire lasted from about 1900 B.C. to 1550 B.C. (the days of the Hebrew patriarchs); earlier kingdoms had ruled on Babylonian soil as early as 3000 B.C.

5.18 *I will not make a full end of you.* God looked beyond the soon-to-come captivity under Nebuchadnezzar, for it would not mean the end of his people. In his compassion God indicated that the enemy would lay Judah waste but would not eliminate it completely. There was mercy in store for Judah; a

of you. ¹⁹And when your people say, "Why has the LORD our God done all these things to us?" you shall say to them, "As you have forsaken me and served foreign gods in your land, so you shall serve strangers in a land that is not yours."

5.19
Deut 29.24-26;
1 Kings 9.8,
9;
Jer 16.10-13;
Deut 28.48

20 Declare this in the house of Jacob,
 proclaim it in Judah:
21 Hear this, O foolish and senseless people,
 who have eyes, but do not see,
 who have ears, but do not hear.

5.21
v. 4;
Isa 6.9;
Ezek 12.2;
Mt 13.14;
Jer 6.10

22 Do you not fear me? says the LORD;
 Do you not tremble before me?
 I placed the sand as a boundary for the sea,
 a perpetual barrier that it cannot pass;
 though the waves toss, they cannot prevail,
 though they roar, they cannot pass over it.

5.22
Jer 2.19;
Job 26.10;
Ps 104.9

23 But this people has a stubborn and rebellious heart;
 they have turned aside and gone away.

5.23
Jer 4.17; 6.28

24 They do not say in their hearts,
 "Let us fear the LORD our God,
 who gives the rain in its season,
 the autumn rain and the spring rain,
 and keeps for us
 the weeks appointed for the harvest."

5.24
Ps 147.8;
Mt 5.45;
Joel 2.23;
Gen 8.22

25 Your iniquities have turned these away,
 and your sins have deprived you of good.

5.25
Jer 2.17; 4.18

26 For scoundrels are found among my people;
 they take over the goods of others.
 Like fowlers they set a trap;�q
 they catch human beings.

5.26
Ps 10.9;
Prov 1.11;
Hab 1.15

27 Like a cage full of birds,
 their houses are full of treachery;
 therefore they have become great and rich,

5.27
Jer 9.6; 12.1

28 they have grown fat and sleek.
 They know no limits in deeds of wickedness;
 they do not judge with justice
 the cause of the orphan, to make it prosper,
 and they do not defend the rights of the needy.

5.28
Deut 32.15;
Isa 1.23;
Zech 7.10;
Jer 2.34

29 Shall I not punish them for these things?
 says the LORD,
 and shall I not bring retribution
 on a nation such as this?

5.29
Mal 3.5

30 An appalling and horrible thing
 has happened in the land:

5.30
Hos 6.10

31 the prophets prophesy falsely,
 and the priests rule as the prophets direct;ʳ
 my people love to have it so,
 but what will you do when the end comes?

5.31
Jer 14.14;
Ezek 13.6;
Mic 2.11

(5) THE FAITHFUL ENJOINED TO FLEE BEFORE THE SIEGE

6 Flee for safety, O children of Benjamin,
 from the midst of Jerusalem!

6.1
2 Chr 11.6;
Neh 3.14;
Jer 1.14; 4.6

q Meaning of Heb uncertain   r Or *rule by their own authority*

---

return to the land left desolate would come later.
5.31 Among those who called themselves prophets, Jeremiah was one of the few true prophets. As a class, the prophets were false; though they were uninspired

and not from God, they had great influence over the people.
6.1 Jerusalem at this point seemed safe from external danger. God warned the people of Benjamin (in

Blow the trumpet in Tekoa,
　　and raise a signal on Beth-haccherem;
for evil looms out of the north,
　　and great destruction.

² I have likened daughter Zion
　　to the loveliest pasture. ^s

³ Shepherds with their flocks shall come against her.
　　They shall pitch their tents around her;
　　they shall pasture, all in their places.

⁴ "Prepare war against her;
　　up, and let us attack at noon!"
"Woe to us, for the day declines,
　　the shadows of evening lengthen!"

⁵ "Up, and let us attack by night,
　　and destroy her palaces!"

(6) THE BESIEGERS ENCOURAGED AGAINST JERUSALEM

⁶ For thus says the LORD of hosts:
Cut down her trees;
　　cast up a siege ramp against Jerusalem.
This is the city that must be punished; ^t
　　there is nothing but oppression within her.

⁷ As a well keeps its water fresh,
　　so she keeps fresh her wickedness;
violence and destruction are heard within her;
　　sickness and wounds are ever before me.

⁸ Take warning, O Jerusalem,
　　or I shall turn from you in disgust,
and make you a desolation,
　　an uninhabited land.

⁹ Thus says the LORD of hosts:
Glean ^u thoroughly as a vine
　　the remnant of Israel;
like a grape-gatherer, pass your hand again
　　over its branches.

¹⁰ To whom shall I speak and give warning,
　　that they may hear?
See, their ears are closed, ^v
　　they cannot listen.
The word of the LORD is to them an object of scorn;
　　they take no pleasure in it.

¹¹ But I am full of the wrath of the LORD;
　　I am weary of holding it in.

Pour it out on the children in the street,
　　and on the gatherings of young men as well;

---

^s Or I will destroy daughter Zion, the loveliest pasture　　^t Or the city of license　　^u Cn: Heb They shall glean
^v Heb are uncircumcised

Cross-references (left margin)

6.2 Deut 28.56; Jer 4.31
6.3 Jer 12.10; 2 Kings 25.1; Jer 4.17
6.4 Joel 3.9; Jer 15.8
6.5 Jer 52.13
6.6 Deut 20.19, 20; Jer 32.24; 22.17
6.7 Isa 57.20; Ps 55.9-11; Jer 20.8; Ezek 7.11, 23
6.8 Jer 7.28; Ezek 23.18; Hos 9.12
6.9 Jer 49.9; 8.3
6.10 Jer 7.26; Acts 7.51; Jer 20.8
6.11 Job 32.18, 19; Jer 20.9; 9.21

---

whose territory part of Jerusalem lay) to flee from the city and escape the coming tragedy. *Blow the trumpet in Tekoa.* This city was ten miles south of Jerusalem and was built on a site 2,700 feet above sea level. From there the Mount of Olives was visible. It was a good place from which warnings could be given to the inhabitants of Jerusalem. *Raise a signal on Beth-haccherem.* This city (its name means "house of the vineyard") was located on a high hill between Bethlehem and Jerusalem, also high enough above sea level for signaling Jerusalem. Thus Tekoa, ten miles away, and this city would both be signaling stations for Jerusalem in times of danger.

6.7ff Among the charges lodged against Judah and Jerusalem were oppression (v. 7), contempt for the word of God (vv. 10–12), greediness (v. 13), treachery on the part of their prophets (v. 14), no sense of shame for their sins (v. 15), and obstinacy (vv. 18,19). So God gave them up to judgment.

12 Their houses shall be turned over to others,
  their fields and wives together;
for I will stretch out my hand
  against the inhabitants of the land,

                                                  says the LORD.

6.12
Deut 28.30;
Jer 8.10; 15.6

13 For from the least to the greatest of them,
  everyone is greedy for unjust gain;
and from prophet to priest,
  everyone deals falsely.

6.13
Isa 56.11;
Jer 8.10;
22.17;
Mic 3.5, 11

14 They have treated the wound of my people carelessly,
  saying, "Peace, peace,"
when there is no peace.

6.14
Jer 8.11;
Ezek 13.10;
Jer 4.10;
23.17

15 They acted shamefully, they committed abomination;
  yet they were not ashamed,
they did not know how to blush.
Therefore they shall fall among those who fall;
  at the time that I punish them, they shall be overthrown,
                                                  says the LORD.

6.15
Jer 3.3; 8.12

(7) REFUSAL TO REPENT DESPITE IMPENDING RUIN

16 Thus says the LORD:
Stand at the crossroads, and look,
  and ask for the ancient paths,
where the good way lies; and walk in it,
  and find rest for your souls.
But they said, "We will not walk in it."

6.16
Isa 8.20;
Jer 18.15;
Mal 4.4;
Lk 16.29;
Mt 11.29

17 Also I raised up sentinels for you:
  "Give heed to the sound of the trumpet!"
But they said, "We will not give heed."

6.17
Isa 21.11;
58.1;
Jer 25.4;
Ezek 3.17;
Hab 2.1

18 Therefore hear, O nations,
  and know, O congregation, what will happen to them.

19 Hear, O earth; I am going to bring disaster on this people,
  the fruit of their schemes,
because they have not given heed to my words;
  and as for my teaching, they have rejected it.

6.19
Isa 1.2;
Jer 19.3, 15;
Prov 1.31;
Jer 8.9

20 Of what use to me is frankincense that comes from Sheba,
  or sweet cane from a distant land?
Your burnt offerings are not acceptable,
  nor are your sacrifices pleasing to me.

6.20
Isa 1.11;
Am 5.21;
Mic 6.6;
Isa 60.6;
Jer 7.21

21 Therefore thus says the LORD:
See, I am laying before this people
  stumbling blocks against which they shall stumble;
parents and children together,
  neighbor and friend shall perish.

6.21
Isa 8.14;
Jer 13.16;
9.21, 22

(8) THE INVADER WILL SUDDENLY DESTROY

22 Thus says the LORD:
See, a people is coming from the land of the north,
  a great nation is stirring from the farthest parts of the earth.

6.22
Jer 1.15;
5.15; 10.22;
50.41-43;
Neh 1.9

23 They grasp the bow and the javelin,

6.23
Jer 4.29;
50.42;
Isa 5.30

6.20 There was no lack of religious ceremonies among the people of Judah. But they were hypocrites, whose ceremonies lacked hearts in tune with God.
6.23ff The Chaldeans (the people coming from the north, see note on 4.6) were a great nation, a warlike people, a barbarous group of cut-throats who were cruel and lacking in mercy. Riding on horses and formidable with bow and spear, they frightened their enemies and their voice roared like the sea. This description should have constrained Judah to turn to God for deliverance. Instead, they hardened their hearts and became easy prey for the enemy.

they are cruel and have no mercy,
   their sound is like the roaring sea;
they ride on horses,
   equipped like a warrior for battle,
   against you, O daughter Zion!

6.24
Jer 4.31;
13.21; 49.24;
50.43
24 "We have heard news of them,
   our hands fall helpless;
anguish has taken hold of us,
   pain as of a woman in labor.

6.25
Jer 14.18;
12.12; 20.10
25 Do not go out into the field,
   or walk on the road;
for the enemy has a sword,
   terror is on every side."

6.26
Jer 4.8;
25.34;
Mic 1.10;
Zech 12.10
26 O my poor people, put on sackcloth,
   and roll in ashes;
make mourning as for an only child,
   most bitter lamentation:
for suddenly the destroyer
   will come upon us.

6.27
Jer 1.18;
15.20; 9.7
6.28
Jer 5.23; 9.4;
Ezek 22.18
27 I have made you a tester and a refiner[w] among my people
   so that you may know and test their ways.
28 They are all stubbornly rebellious,
   going about with slanders;
they are bronze and iron,
   all of them act corruptly.

6.29
Jer 15.19
29 The bellows blow fiercely,
   the lead is consumed by the fire;
in vain the refining goes on,
   for the wicked are not removed.

6.30
Jer 7.29
30 They are called "rejected silver,"
   for the LORD has rejected them.

C. Second movement: Sermon III: the great temple-sermon

1. First indictment: idolatry and immorality

7.1f
Jer 26.1, 2
7.2
Jer 17.19; 2.4
7.3
Jer 18.11;
26.13
7.4
Mic 3.11

7.5
Jer 4.1, 2;
22.3
7.6
Deut 6.14,
15; 8.19;
Jer 13.10
7 The word that came to Jeremiah from the LORD: 2 Stand in the gate of the LORD's house, and proclaim there this word, and say, Hear the word of the LORD, all you people of Judah, you that enter these gates to worship the LORD. 3 Thus says the LORD of hosts, the God of Israel: Amend your ways and your doings, and let me dwell with you[x] in this place. 4 Do not trust in these deceptive words: "This is[y] the temple of the LORD, the temple of the LORD, the temple of the LORD."

5 For if you truly amend your ways and your doings, if you truly act justly one with another, 6 if you do not oppress the alien, the orphan, and the widow, or shed innocent blood in this place, and if you do not go after other gods to your own hurt, 7 then I will dwell with you in this place, in the land that I gave of old to your ancestors forever and ever.

w Or a fortress   x Or and I will let you dwell   y Heb They are

---

6.30 God did not reject Judah without first using every proper means to reform them. They now had reached the point of no return; they were like rejected silver.
7.1–3 One way God revealed his message to his people was through the ministry of prophets, to whom God communicated what he wanted said. The phrase "Thus says the LORD" or its equivalent appears throughout the O.T. Jeremiah, for example, frequently used this phrase as a means to certify that the message was God's message and not his own. The essence of revelation is that the message comes directly from God himself.

8 Here you are, trusting in deceptive words to no avail. 9 Will you steal, murder, commit adultery, swear falsely, make offerings to Baal, and go after other gods that you have not known, 10 and then come and stand before me in this house, which is called by my name, and say, "We are safe!"—only to go on doing all these abominations? 11 Has this house, which is called by my name, become a den of robbers in your sight? You know, I too am watching, says the LORD. 12 Go now to my place that was in Shiloh, where I made my name dwell at first, and see what I did to it for the wickedness of my people Israel. 13 And now, because you have done all these things, says the LORD, and when I spoke to you persistently, you did not listen, and when I called you, you did not answer, 14 therefore I will do to the house that is called by my name, in which you trust, and to the place that I gave to you and to your ancestors, just what I did to Shiloh. 15 And I will cast you out of my sight, just as I cast out all your kinsfolk, all the offspring of Ephraim.

16 As for you, do not pray for this people, do not raise a cry or prayer on their behalf, and do not intercede with me, for I will not hear you. 17 Do you not see what they are doing in the towns of Judah and in the streets of Jerusalem? 18 The children gather wood, the fathers kindle fire, and the women knead dough, to make cakes for the queen of heaven; and they pour out drink offerings to other gods, to provoke me to anger. 19 Is it I whom they provoke? says the LORD. Is it not themselves, to their own hurt? 20 Therefore thus says the Lord GOD: My anger and my wrath shall be poured out on this place, on human beings and animals, on the trees of the field and the fruit of the ground; it will burn and not be quenched.

21 Thus says the LORD of hosts, the God of Israel: Add your burnt offerings to your sacrifices, and eat the flesh. 22 For in the day that I brought your ancestors out of the land of Egypt, I did not speak to them or command them concerning burnt offerings and sacrifices. 23 But this command I gave them, "Obey my voice, and I will be your God, and you shall be my people; and walk only in the way that I command you, so that it may be well with you." 24 Yet they did not obey or incline their ear, but, in the stubbornness of their evil will, they walked in their own counsels, and looked backward rather than forward. 25 From the day that your ancestors came out of the land of Egypt until this day, I have persistently sent all my servants the prophets to them, day after day; 26 yet they did not listen to me, or pay attention, but they stiffened their necks. They did worse than their ancestors did.

27 So you shall speak all these words to them, but they will not listen to you. You shall call to them, but they will not answer you. 28 You shall say to them: This is the nation that did not obey the voice of the LORD their God, and did not accept discipline; truth has perished; it is cut off from their lips.

29   Cut off your hair and throw it away;
     raise a lamentation on the bare heights,[z]

---

[z] Or *the trails*

7.8	Jer 13.25
7.9	Ex 20.3; Jer 11.13, 17; 19.4
7.10	Ezek 23.39; Jer 32.34; 2.23, 35
7.11	Mt 21.13
7.12	Jer 26.6; 1 Sam 4.10
7.13	2 Chr 36.15; Jer 35.17; Isa 65.12
7.14	1 Kings 9.7
7.15	Jer 15.1; 2 Kings 17.23; Ps 78.67
7.16	Ex 32.10; Jer 11.14
7.18	Jer 44.17; 19.13; 11.17
7.19	Deut 32.16
7.20	Jer 6.11, 12; 8.13; 11.16
7.21	Isa 1.11; Am 5.21; Hos 8.13
7.22	1 Sam 15.22; Ps 51.16; Hos 6.6
7.23	Ex 15.26; Lev 26.12; Isa 3.10
7.24	Ps 81.11, 12; Jer 15.6
7.25	Jer 25.4; Lk 11.49
7.26	Jer 19.15; 16.12
7.27	Ezek 2.7; Isa 50.2
7.28	Jer 6.17; 9.5
7.29	Job 1.20; Isa 15.2; Jer 16.6; Mic 1.16; Jer 3.21

7.12 *Shiloh* was the city where a sanctuary had been erected to Israel's God; it had been destroyed by the Philistines (cf. 1 Sam 4.10). Even as God had destroyed Samaria's sanctuary, so also would he destroy Jerusalem.

7.16 God forbad Jeremiah to pray for Jerusalem. It was beyond prayer, for the decree to destroy had gone forth against a people who had sinned unto death (cf. 1 Jn 5.16,17). God would not hear any prayers on their behalf.

7.18 *the queen of heaven*, a name by which Ishtar, the Mesopotamian goddess of love and war, was known. After the fall of Jerusalem the refugees who fled to Egypt continued to worship her (ch. 44). A papyrus dating from the fifth century B.C., found at Hermopo-

lis in Egypt, mentions the "queen of heaven" among the goddesses honored by the Jewish community.
7.20 Human life, animal life, and plant life would all be affected by God's judgment. This judgment would differ from the flood only in that this one would be limited.

7.24–26 Judah refused to learn anything from experience. They set their own will against God's will, spurned the law of God, walked *in their own counsels*, and *looked backward rather than forward*. In short, they said they would obey God, then did the opposite. God sent his prophets to warn them and to threaten them, but they were as deaf to the prophets as they were to the law of God. Thus God's judgment fell on them.

for the LORD has rejected and forsaken
the generation that provoked his wrath.

7.30
2 Kings 21.4;
2 Chr 33.4, 5,
7;
Jer 23.11;
Ezek 7.20;
Dan 9.27
7.31
2 Kings 23.10;
Jer 19.5;
Ps 106.38;
Deut 17.3
7.32
Jer 19.5, 7,
11;
2 Kings 23.10
7.34
Isa 24.7, 8;
Ezek 26.13;
Hos 2.11;
Rev 18.23;
Isa 1.7
8.1
Ezek 6.5
8.2
Acts 7.42;
Jer 22.19

8.3
Job 3.21;
7.15, 16;
Rev 9.6;
Jer 23.3, 8

30 For the people of Judah have done evil in my sight, says the LORD;
they have set their abominations in the house that is called by my name,
defiling it. 31 And they go on building the high place[a] of Topheth, which
is in the valley of the son of Hinnom, to burn their sons and their
daughters in the fire — which I did not command, nor did it come into my
mind. 32 Therefore, the days are surely coming, says the LORD, when it
will no more be called Topheth, or the valley of the son of Hinnom, but
the valley of Slaughter: for they will bury in Topheth until there is no more
room. 33 The corpses of this people will be food for the birds of the air,
and for the animals of the earth; and no one will frighten them away.
34 And I will bring to an end the sound of mirth and gladness, the voice
of the bride and bridegroom in the cities of Judah and in the streets of
Jerusalem; for the land shall become a waste.

8 At that time, says the LORD, the bones of the kings of Judah, the
bones of its officials, the bones of the priests, the bones of the
prophets, and the bones of the inhabitants of Jerusalem shall be brought
out of their tombs; 2 and they shall be spread before the sun and the moon
and all the host of heaven, which they have loved and served, which they
have followed, and which they have inquired of and worshiped; and they
shall not be gathered or buried; they shall be like dung on the surface of
the ground. 3 Death shall be preferred to life by all the remnant that
remains of this evil family in all the places where I have driven them, says
the LORD of hosts.

2. Second indictment: stubbornly unrepentant, they must be exiled

8.4
Prov 24.16

8.5
Jer 5.6; 7.24;
5.27; 9.6

8.6
Ps 14.2;
Ezek 22.30;
Rev 9.20;
Job 39.21-25

8.7
Isa 1.3;
Song 2.12;
Jer 5.4, 5

8.8
Jer 4.22;
Rom 2.17

4 You shall say to them, Thus says the LORD:
When people fall, do they not get up again?
If they go astray, do they not turn back?
5 Why then has this people[b] turned away
in perpetual backsliding?
They have held fast to deceit,
they have refused to return.
6 I have given heed and listened,
but they do not speak honestly;
no one repents of wickedness,
saying, "What have I done!"
All of them turn to their own course,
like a horse plunging headlong into battle.
7 Even the stork in the heavens
knows its times;
and the turtledove, swallow, and crane[c]
observe the time of their coming;
but my people do not know
the ordinance of the LORD.

8 How can you say, "We are wise,
and the law of the LORD is with us,"

a Gk Tg: Heb *high places*   *b* One Ms Gk: MT *this people, Jerusalem,*   *c* Meaning of Heb uncertain

---

7.30 Judah had defiled the temple of God, and in so
doing defiled the God of the temple.
8.1ff In this chapter Jeremiah specifies how awful
the destructive judgment of God would be for this
wicked people. But he also shows that the judgment
was righteous. The God of holiness and love is also the
God of justice and judgment for those who sin against

his holiness and spurn his love.
8.7 By instinct birds know the times and seasons —
when to fly south and when to return home in the
spring, when to mate and when to produce little ones.
But God's people had no regard for instinct or revelation, and traveled the path that led to death.

when, in fact, the false pen of the scribes
  has made it into a lie?

9 The wise shall be put to shame,
     they shall be dismayed and taken;
   since they have rejected the word of the LORD,
     what wisdom is in them?

10 Therefore I will give their wives to others
      and their fields to conquerors,
    because from the least to the greatest
      everyone is greedy for unjust gain;
    from prophet to priest
      everyone deals falsely.

11 They have treated the wound of my people carelessly,
      saying, "Peace, peace,"
      when there is no peace.

12 They acted shamefully, they committed abomination;
      yet they were not at all ashamed,
      they did not know how to blush.
    Therefore they shall fall among those who fall;
      at the time when I punish them, they shall be overthrown,
                                              says the LORD.

13 When I wanted to gather them, says the LORD,
      there are[d] no grapes on the vine,
      nor figs on the fig tree;
    even the leaves are withered,
      and what I gave them has passed away from them.[e]

14 Why do we sit still?
    Gather together, let us go into the fortified cities
      and perish there;
    for the LORD our God has doomed us to perish,
      and has given us poisoned water to drink,
      because we have sinned against the LORD.

15 We look for peace, but find no good,
      for a time of healing, but there is terror instead.

16 The snorting of their horses is heard from Dan;
      at the sound of the neighing of their stallions
      the whole land quakes.
    They come and devour the land and all that fills it,
      the city and those who live in it.

17 See, I am letting snakes loose among you,
      adders that cannot be charmed,
      and they shall bite you,
                                              says the LORD.

18 My joy is gone, grief is upon me,
      my heart is sick.

19 Hark, the cry of my poor people
      from far and wide in the land:
    "Is the LORD not in Zion?
      Is her King not in her?"

d Or I will make an end of them, says the LORD. There are   e Meaning of Heb uncertain

---

8.9
Jer 6.15, 19

8.10
Deut 28.30;
Isa 56.11

8.11
Jer 6.14;
Ezek 13.10

8.12
Jer 3.3; 6.21;
10.15

8.13
Jer 14.12;
Ezek 22.20,
21;
Isa 5.2;
Joel 1.7;
Mt 21.19

8.14
Jer 4.5;
35.11; 9.15;
Mt 27.34;
Jer 3.25;
14.20

8.15
Jer 14.19

8.16
Jer 4.15;
Judg 5.22;
Jer 3.24;
10.25

8.17
Num 21.6;
Ps 58.4, 5

8.19
Jer 4.16;
Isa 39.3;
Jer 14.9;
Deut 32.21;
Ps 31.6

8.11 False priests and prophets assured the people that all was well. Thus they aided the situation *carelessly*, failing to recognize its full seriousness.
8.16 *The snorting of their horses is heard from Dan*, i.e., the report of the invaders' presence in the far north is known by the neighing of their horses — a

sign of the immense strength of the advancing cavalry troops.
8.17 The people knew about persons who could charm poisonous snakes so they would not bite. The advancing armies could not be charmed, however, so their bite would kill off the resisting Israelites.

("Why have they provoked me to anger with their images,
  with their foreign idols?")

20 "The harvest is past, the summer is ended,
   and we are not saved."

21 For the hurt of my poor people I am hurt,
   I mourn, and dismay has taken hold of me.

22 Is there no balm in Gilead?
   Is there no physician there?
   Why then has the health of my poor people
   not been restored?

8.21
Jer 14.17;
Joel 2.6;
Nah 2.10

8.22
Gen 37.25;
Jer 14.19;
30.13

3. Third indictment: faithless and truthless, they must be scattered and killed

9 *f* O that my head were a spring of water,
      and my eyes a fountain of tears,
   so that I might weep day and night
      for the slain of my poor people!

2 *g* O that I had in the desert
      a traveler's lodging place,
   that I might leave my people
      and go away from them!
   For they are all adulterers,
      a band of traitors.

3 They bend their tongues like bows;
   they have grown strong in the land for falsehood, and not for
      truth;
   for they proceed from evil to evil,
      and they do not know me, says the Lord.

4 Beware of your neighbors,
      and put no trust in any of your kin;*h*
   for all your kin*i* are supplanters,
      and every neighbor goes around like a slanderer.

5 They all deceive their neighbors,
      and no one speaks the truth;
   they have taught their tongues to speak lies;
      they commit iniquity and are too weary to repent.*j*

6 Oppression upon oppression, deceit*k* upon deceit!
      They refuse to know me, says the Lord.

7 Therefore thus says the Lord of hosts:
   I will now refine and test them,
      for what else can I do with my sinful people?*l*

8 Their tongue is a deadly arrow;
      it speaks deceit through the mouth.
   They all speak friendly words to their neighbors,
      but inwardly are planning to lay an ambush.

9.1
Isa 22.4;
Lam 2.11;
Jer 6.26;
8.21, 22

9.2
Isa 55.6, 7;
Jer 5, 7, 8,
11; 12.1, 6

9.3
Ps 64.3;
Isa 59.4;
Jer 4.22;
1 Sam 2.12;
Hos 4.1

9.4
v. 8;
Jer 12.6;
Gen 27.35;
Jer 6.28

9.5
Mic 6.12;
Jer 12.13;
51.58, 64

9.6
Jer 5.27;
11.10;
Jn 3.19, 20

9.7
Isa 1.25;
Mal 3.3;
Hos 11.8

9.8
Ps 12.2; 28.3;
Jer 5.26

f Ch 8.23 in Heb   *g* Ch 9.1 in Heb   *h* Heb *in a brother*   *i* Heb *for every brother*   *j* Cn Compare Gk: Heb
they weary themselves with iniquity. 6*Your dwelling*   *k* Cn: Heb *Your dwelling in the midst of deceit*
l Or *my poor people*

8.22 *balm.* Gilead produced a medicinal balm noted for its curative powers. Israel's sickness, however, could not be cured by any medicine, for its problem was spiritual, not physical.
9.4 So low had the moral state of God's people be-come that no one could trust any neighbor. They were slanderers, liars, cheaters, oppressors, and deceivers. Society could not function properly and life was un-certain, disordered, and on the road to ruin.

9   Shall I not punish them for these things? says the LORD;
        and shall I not bring retribution
        on a nation such as this?

10   Take up[m] weeping and wailing for the mountains,
        and a lamentation for the pastures of the wilderness,
     because they are laid waste so that no one passes through,
        and the lowing of cattle is not heard;
     both the birds of the air and the animals
        have fled and are gone.
11   I will make Jerusalem a heap of ruins,
        a lair of jackals;
     and I will make the towns of Judah a desolation,
        without inhabitant.

12   Who is wise enough to understand this? To whom has the mouth
of the LORD spoken, so that they may declare it? Why is the land ruined
and laid waste like a wilderness, so that no one passes through? 13 And
the LORD says: Because they have forsaken my law that I set before them,
and have not obeyed my voice, or walked in accordance with it, 14 but have
stubbornly followed their own hearts and have gone after the Baals, as
their ancestors taught them. 15 Therefore thus says the LORD of hosts, the
God of Israel: I am feeding this people with wormwood, and giving them
poisonous water to drink. 16 I will scatter them among nations that neither
they nor their ancestors have known; and I will send the sword after them,
until I have consumed them.

17   Thus says the LORD of hosts:
     Consider, and call for the mourning women to come;
        send for the skilled women to come;
18   let them quickly raise a dirge over us,
        so that our eyes may run down with tears,
        and our eyelids flow with water.
19   For a sound of wailing is heard from Zion:
        "How we are ruined!
     We are utterly shamed,
     because we have left the land,
        because they have cast down our dwellings."

20   Hear, O women, the word of the LORD,
        and let your ears receive the word of his mouth;
     teach to your daughters a dirge,
        and each to her neighbor a lament.
21   "Death has come up into our windows,
        it has entered our palaces,
     to cut off the children from the streets
        and the young men from the squares."
22   Speak! Thus says the LORD:
     "Human corpses shall fall
        like dung upon the open field,
     like sheaves behind the reaper,
        and no one shall gather them."

m Gk Syr: Heb *I will take up*

9.9
Jer 5.9, 29

9.10
Jer 4.24-26;
Hos 4.3;
Ezek 14.15

9.11
Isa 25.2;
13.22; 34.13;
Jer 4.27; 26.9

9.12
Ps 107.43;
Hos 14.9;
Jer 23.10, 16
9.13
Jer 5.19;
Ps 89.30
9.14
Rom 1.21-24;
Gal 1.14;
1 Pet 1.18
9.15
Jer 8.14;
23.15
9.16
Lev 26.33;
Deut 28.64;
Jer 44.27;
Ezek 5.2
9.17
2 Chr 35.25;
Eccl 12.5;
Am 5.16
9.18
Jer 14.17

9.19
Jer 4.13;
7.15; 15.1

9.20
Isa 32.9

9.21
Jer 15.7;
18.21; 6.11

9.22
Jer 8.2; 16.4

9.14 God's people had committed a double sin.
They had left their first love, the God of Abraham.
But the vacuum created by that act led to the active
pursuit of Baalism; other gods were substituted for
Yahweh. Everyone is religious. Thus there is a ten-
dency to honor gods of human creation if the Lord is
not served. This calls forth the judgment of a righteous God.

4. *Conclusion: true wisdom is knowing the* LORD; *idolatry brings destruction*

9.23
Eccl 9.11;
Isa 10.8-12;
Ps 49.6-9
9.24
1 Cor 1.31;
2 Cor 10.17;
Gal 6.14;
Ps 36.5, 7;
Mic 7.18
9.25
Rom 2.8, 9
9.26
Jer 25.23;
Lev 26.41;
Ezek 44.7;
Rom 2.28

23   Thus says the LORD: Do not let the wise boast in their wisdom, do not let the mighty boast in their might, do not let the wealthy boast in their wealth; 24 but let those who boast boast in this, that they understand and know me, that I am the LORD; I act with steadfast love, justice, and righteousness in the earth, for in these things I delight, says the LORD.

25   The days are surely coming, says the LORD, when I will attend to all those who are circumcised only in the foreskin: 26 Egypt, Judah, Edom, the Ammonites, Moab, and all those with shaven temples who live in the desert. For all these nations are uncircumcised, and all the house of Israel is uncircumcised in heart.

10.2
Lev 18.3;
Isa 47.12-14

10   Hear the word that the LORD speaks to you, O house of Israel. 2 Thus says the LORD:
Do not learn the way of the nations,
   or be dismayed at the signs of the heavens;
   for the nations are dismayed at them.

10.3
Isa 40.19;
45.20

3   For the customs of the peoples are false:
   a tree from the forest is cut down,
      and worked with an ax by the hands of an artisan;

10.4
v. 14;
Isa 41.7

4   people deck it with silver and gold;
      they fasten it with hammer and nails
      so that it cannot move.

10.5
Ps 115.5;
1 Cor 12.2;
Isa 46.1, 7;
41.23

5   Their idols[n] are like scarecrows in a cucumber field,
      and they cannot speak;
they have to be carried,
      for they cannot walk.
Do not be afraid of them,
      for they cannot do evil,
      nor is it in them to do good.

10.6
Deut 33.26;
Isa 12.6;
Jer 32.18
10.7
Ps 22.28;
Dan 2.27, 28;
1 Cor 1.19,
20

6   There is none like you, O LORD;
      you are great, and your name is great in might.
7   Who would not fear you, O King of the nations?
      For that is your due;
among all the wise ones of the nations
      and in all their kingdoms
      there is no one like you.

10.8
v. 14;
Jer 4.22; 2.27

8   They are both stupid and foolish;
      the instruction given by idols
      is no better than wood![o]

10.9
Isa 40.19;
Ps 72.10;
Dan 10.5;
Ps 115.4

9   Beaten silver is brought from Tarshish,
      and gold from Uphaz.
They are the work of the artisan and of the hands of the
      goldsmith;

---

[n] Heb *They*   [o] Meaning of Heb uncertain

9.23 People will always glory in something. When they do not glory in the Lord, they often turn to wisdom, might, and wealth as the triad of human achievements. True glory consists in the knowledge and understanding of God, who promotes love, justice, and righteousness, a triad of qualities not to be found among this apostate people (see 1 Cor 1.31; 2 Cor 10.17).
9.25,26 *uncircumcised in heart.* Circumcision was practiced by heathen peoples as well as by Israelites. Among the heathen it was a physical matter. Among the Israelites circumcision had spiritual implications;

it was a sign of their covenant with God (see Gen 17). In Jeremiah's day, however, the people had lost the spiritual purpose behind circumcision, and thus it meant no more than circumcision meant to the heathen.
10.1 Some scholars think that this chapter was written after the first captivity, in the time of Jeconiah or Jehoiachin. Jeremiah warned the captives against embracing the astrology and idolatry of their conquerors.
10.5 Idols have no power; thus God's people should shun them in favor of the God who can speak, walk, and do what he pleases.

their clothing is blue and purple;
    they are all the product of skilled workers.

10 But the LORD is the true God;
    he is the living God and the everlasting King.
At his wrath the earth quakes,
    and the nations cannot endure his indignation.

10.10
Isa 65.16;
Jer 4.2;
50.46;
Ps 76.7

11 Thus shall you say to them: The gods who did not make the heavens and the earth shall perish from the earth and from under the heavens. *p*

10.11
Ps 96.5;
Isa 2.18;
Zeph 2.11

12 It is he who made the earth by his power,
    who established the world by his wisdom,
    and by his understanding stretched out the heavens.
13 When he utters his voice, there is a tumult of waters in the
       heavens,
    and he makes the mist rise from the ends of the earth.
He makes lightnings for the rain,
    and he brings out the wind from his storehouses.

10.12
Jer 51.15-19;
Ps 78.69;
Job 9.8;
Isa 40.22
10.13
Ps 29.3-9;
Job 36.27-29;
Ps 135.7

14 Everyone is stupid and without knowledge;
    goldsmiths are all put to shame by their idols;
for their images are false,
    and there is no breath in them.

10.14
Jer 51.17;
Isa 42.17;
Hab 2.18

15 They are worthless, a work of delusion;
    at the time of their punishment they shall perish.
16 Not like these is the LORD,*q* the portion of Jacob,
    for he is the one who formed all things,
and Israel is the tribe of his inheritance;
    the LORD of hosts is his name.

10.15
Jer 8.19;
51.18
10.16
Ps 73.26;
Jer 51.19;
Isa 45.7;
Deut 32.9;
Jer 31.35

17 Gather up your bundle from the ground,
    O you who live under siege!
18 For thus says the LORD:
I am going to sling out the inhabitants of the land
    at this time,
and I will bring distress on them,
    so that they shall feel it.

10.17
Ezek 12.3-12
10.18
1 Sam 25.29;
Ezek 6.10

19 Woe is me because of my hurt!
    My wound is severe.
But I said, "Truly this is my punishment,
    and I must bear it."
20 My tent is destroyed,
    and all my cords are broken;
my children have gone from me,
    and they are no more;
there is no one to spread my tent again,
    and to set up my curtains.
21 For the shepherds are stupid,
    and do not inquire of the LORD;
therefore they have not prospered,
    and all their flock is scattered.

10.19
Jer 4.19, 31;
14.17;
Mic 7.9

10.20
Jer 4.20;
31.15;
Isa 51.18

10.21
Jer 2.8; 23.2

---

p This verse is in Aramaic   *q* Heb lacks *the LORD*

10.14 In Jeremiah's day there were few, if any, atheists. The heathen had numerous gods and made graven images, before whom they bowed down and worshiped. The Scriptures frequently picture the difference between the gods made by the hands of sinners and the God who by his hands made mortals and the universe, and who holds all things together by divine power.
10.21 The shepherds (i.e., the rulers and priests) had no eye for God. They did not see that judgment was about to fall.

10.22
Jer 4.15;
1.14; 9.11

22 Hear, a noise! Listen, it is coming —
    a great commotion from the land of the north
  to make the cities of Judah a desolation,
    a lair of jackals.

10.23
Prov 20.24;
Isa 26.7

23 I know, O Lord, that the way of human beings is not in
        their control,
      that mortals as they walk cannot direct their steps.

10.24
Ps 6.1

24 Correct me, O Lord, but in just measure;
     not in your anger, or you will bring me to nothing.

10.25
Ps 79.6, 7;
Job 18.21;
Jer 8.16;
50.7, 17

25 Pour out your wrath on the nations that do not know you,
      and on the peoples that do not call on your name;
   for they have devoured Jacob;
      they have devoured him and consumed him,
      and have laid waste his habitation.

D. *Third movement: signs of judgments and deliverances to come*

1. *Sermon IV: the broken covenant and the ruined loincloth*

a. *Judah has broken the covenant*

11.3
Deut 27.26;
Gal 3.10
11.4
Ex 24.3-8;
Deut 4.20;
1 Kings 8.51;
Jer 7.23; 24.7
11.5
Ex 13.5;
Deut 7.12;
Jer 32.22;
28.6
11.6
Jer 3.12; v. 2;
Rom 2.13
11.7
1 Sam 8.9;
Jer 7.13, 25
11.8
Jer 7.26;
Mic 7.9;
Lev 26.14-43
11.9
Ezek 22.25;
Hos 6.9
11.10
1 Sam 15.11;
Jer 13.10;
Judg 2.11-13;
Jer 3.6-11
11.11
v. 17;
Jer 25.35;
v. 14;
Jer 14.12
11.12
Deut 32.37;
Jer 44.17
11.13
Jer 2.28;
3.24; 7.9

11 The word that came to Jeremiah from the Lord: 2 Hear the words of this covenant, and speak to the people of Judah and the inhabitants of Jerusalem. 3 You shall say to them, Thus says the Lord, the God of Israel: Cursed be anyone who does not heed the words of this covenant, 4 which I commanded your ancestors when I brought them out of the land of Egypt, from the iron-smelter, saying, Listen to my voice, and do all that I command you. So shall you be my people, and I will be your God, 5 that I may perform the oath that I swore to your ancestors, to give them a land flowing with milk and honey, as at this day. Then I answered, "So be it, Lord."

6 And the Lord said to me: Proclaim all these words in the cities of Judah, and in the streets of Jerusalem: Hear the words of this covenant and do them. 7 For I solemnly warned your ancestors when I brought them up out of the land of Egypt, warning them persistently, even to this day, saying, Obey my voice. 8 Yet they did not obey or incline their ear, but everyone walked in the stubbornness of an evil will. So I brought upon them all the words of this covenant, which I commanded them to do, but they did not.

9 And the Lord said to me: Conspiracy exists among the people of Judah and the inhabitants of Jerusalem. 10 They have turned back to the iniquities of their ancestors of old, who refused to heed my words; they have gone after other gods to serve them; the house of Israel and the house of Judah have broken the covenant that I made with their ancestors. 11 Therefore, thus says the Lord, assuredly I am going to bring disaster upon them that they cannot escape; though they cry out to me, I will not listen to them. 12 Then the cities of Judah and the inhabitants of Jerusalem will go and cry out to the gods to whom they make offerings, but they will never save them in the time of their trouble. 13 For your gods have become

---

10.23 Neither mortals nor nations can go it alone. The affairs of both are directed and determined by providence, not by their own will and wisdom. Those who look to God will be directed properly.
10.25 This is an imprecatory prayer asking God to execute his divine wrath against the enemies of Israel. Similarly, Christians have the right to ask God to pull down the strongholds of Satan and to render judg-

ment against the enemies of the true faith.
11.3–8 Israel had broken its covenant with God. Such failure could only mean judgment and dispersion, for that is what God promised when he made the covenant (see note on Deut 29.1).
11.13 Judah had as many gods as they had cities and even streets. So great was their apostasy that God in his justice had to punish them. The corruption of

as many as your towns, O Judah; and as many as the streets of Jerusalem are the altars to shame you have set up, altars to make offerings to Baal.

14 As for you, do not pray for this people, or lift up a cry or prayer on their behalf, for I will not listen when they call to me in the time of their trouble. ¹⁵What right has my beloved in my house, when she has done vile deeds? Can vows*r* and sacrificial flesh avert your doom? Can you then exult? ¹⁶The LORD once called you, "A green olive tree, fair with goodly fruit"; but with the roar of a great tempest he will set fire to it, and its branches will be consumed. ¹⁷The LORD of hosts, who planted you, has pronounced evil against you, because of the evil that the house of Israel and the house of Judah have done, provoking me to anger by making offerings to Baal.

b. *Her corruption makes doom inevitable*

18 It was the LORD who made it known to me, and I knew;
    then you showed me their evil deeds.
19 But I was like a gentle lamb
    led to the slaughter.
And I did not know it was against me
    that they devised schemes, saying,
"Let us destroy the tree with its fruit,
    let us cut him off from the land of the living,
    so that his name will no longer be remembered!"
20 But you, O LORD of hosts, who judge righteously,
    who try the heart and the mind,
let me see your retribution upon them,
    for to you I have committed my cause.

21 Therefore thus says the LORD concerning the people of Anathoth, who seek your life, and say, "You shall not prophesy in the name of the LORD, or you will die by our hand"— ²²therefore thus says the LORD of hosts: I am going to punish them; the young men shall die by the sword; their sons and their daughters shall die by famine; ²³and not even a remnant shall be left of them. For I will bring disaster upon the people of Anathoth, the year of their punishment.

12 You will be in the right, O LORD,
    when I lay charges against you;
    but let me put my case to you.
Why does the way of the guilty prosper?
    Why do all who are treacherous thrive?
2 You plant them, and they take root;
    they grow and bring forth fruit;
you are near in their mouths
    yet far from their hearts.
3 But you, O LORD, know me;
    You see me and test me—my heart is with you.
Pull them out like sheep for the slaughter,
    and set them apart for the day of slaughter.
4 How long will the land mourn,
    and the grass of every field wither?

r Gk: Heb *Can many*

Cross references (right column):

11.14 Ex 32.10; v. 11; Ps 66.18
11.15 Jer 12.7; 13.27; 4.22
11.16 Ps 52.8; 83.2; Jer 21.14
11.17 Jer 12.2; 16.10, 11; 32.27
11.18 1 Sam 23.11, 12
11.19 Isa 53.7; Jer 18.18; Ps 83.4; 52.5; 109.13
11.20 Jer 20.12; Ps 7.9
11.21 Jer 12.5, 6; Am 2.12; Jer 26.8; 38.4
11.22 Jer 21.14; 18.21
11.23 Jer 6.9; 23.12; 48.44
12.1 Jer 11.20; Job 13.3; Jer 5.27, 28; 20.5, 11
12.2 Jer 11.17; Isa 29.13; Ezek 33.31
12.3 Ps 139.1-4; Jer 11.20; 17.18
12.4 Jer 9.10; Joel 1.10-17; Hos 4.3; Jer 4.25

Judah had made its doom inevitable.
11.19 Jeremiah, God's prophet, began to experience persecution from the very people he had come to help. Judah not only laughed at his words and spurned his counsel, but the people also hurt him personally. God's prophets can expect from the wicked the same sort of treatment that Jeremiah received.
11.22 Jeremiah was warned by his enemies not to prophesy in the name of the Lord. God in turn promised that he would judge and punish those enemies. Yet God did not deliver Jeremiah from his difficulties; rather, he supported and sustained him in the midst of them.

For the wickedness of those who live in it
    the animals and the birds are swept away,
    and because people said, "He is blind to our ways."[s]

5 If you have raced with foot-runners and they have wearied you,
    how will you compete with horses?
And if in a safe land you fall down,
    how will you fare in the thickets of the Jordan?

6 For even your kinsfolk and your own family,
    even they have dealt treacherously with you;
    they are in full cry after you;
do not believe them,
    though they speak friendly words to you.

7 I have forsaken my house,
    I have abandoned my heritage;
I have given the beloved of my heart
    into the hands of her enemies.

8 My heritage has become to me
    like a lion in the forest;
she has lifted up her voice against me—
    therefore I hate her.

9 Is the hyena greedy[t] for my heritage at my command?
    Are the birds of prey all around her?
Go, assemble all the wild animals;
    bring them to devour her.

10 Many shepherds have destroyed my vineyard,
    they have trampled down my portion,
they have made my pleasant portion
    a desolate wilderness.

11 They have made it a desolation;
    desolate, it mourns to me.
The whole land is made desolate,
    but no one lays it to heart.

12 Upon all the bare heights[u] in the desert
    spoilers have come;
for the sword of the LORD devours
    from one end of the land to the other;
    no one shall be safe.

13 They have sown wheat and have reaped thorns,
    they have tired themselves out but profit nothing.
They shall be ashamed of their[v] harvests
    because of the fierce anger of the LORD.

14 Thus says the LORD concerning all my evil neighbors who touch the heritage that I have given my people Israel to inherit: I am about to pluck them up from their land, and I will pluck up the house of Judah from among them.

15 And after I have plucked them up, I will again have compassion on them, and I will bring them again to their heritage and to their land, everyone of them.

16 And then, if they will diligently learn the ways of my people, to swear by my name, "As the LORD lives," as they taught my people to swear by Baal, then they shall be built up in the midst of my people.

17 But if any nation will not listen, then I will completely uproot it and destroy it, says the LORD.

---

[s] Gk: Heb *to our future*   [t] Cn: Heb *Is the hyena, the bird of prey*   [u] Or *the trails*   [v] Heb *your*

12.5 Jeremiah's trials would become greater, not less. Instead of running against common people, he would now have to race against horses, a figure of speech signifying political and religious leaders.

c. Five warnings to Judah: the ruined loincloth in the mud

13 Thus said the LORD to me, "Go and buy yourself a linen loincloth, and put it on your loins, but do not dip it in water." ²So I bought a loincloth according to the word of the LORD, and put it on my loins. ³And the word of the LORD came to me a second time, saying, ⁴"Take the loincloth that you bought and are wearing, and go now to the Euphrates,ʷ and hide it there in a cleft of the rock." ⁵So I went, and hid it by the Euphrates,ˣ as the LORD commanded me. ⁶And after many days the LORD said to me, "Go now to the Euphrates,ʷ and take from there the loincloth that I commanded you to hide there." ⁷Then I went to the Euphrates,ʷ and dug, and I took the loincloth from the place where I had hidden it. But now the loincloth was ruined; it was good for nothing.

8 Then the word of the LORD came to me: ⁹Thus says the LORD: Just so I will ruin the pride of Judah and the great pride of Jerusalem. ¹⁰This evil people, who refuse to hear my words, who stubbornly follow their own will and have gone after other gods to serve them and worship them, shall be like this loincloth, which is good for nothing. ¹¹For as the loincloth clings to one's loins, so I made the whole house of Israel and the whole house of Judah cling to me, says the LORD, in order that they might be for me a people, a name, a praise, and a glory. But they would not listen.

12 You shall speak to them this word: Thus says the LORD, the God of Israel: Every wine-jar should be filled with wine. And they will say to you, "Do you think we do not know that every wine-jar should be filled with wine?" ¹³Then you shall say to them: Thus says the LORD: I am about to fill all the inhabitants of this land — the kings who sit on David's throne, the priests, the prophets, and all the inhabitants of Jerusalem — with drunkenness. ¹⁴And I will dash them one against another, parents and children together, says the LORD. I will not pity or spare or have compassion when I destroy them.

15 Hear and give ear; do not be haughty,
    for the LORD has spoken.
16 Give glory to the LORD your God
    before he brings darkness,
and before your feet stumble
    on the mountains at twilight;
while you look for light,
    he turns it into gloom
    and makes it deep darkness.
17 But if you will not listen,
    my soul will weep in secret for your pride;
my eyes will weep bitterly and run down with tears,
    because the LORD's flock has been taken captive.

18 Say to the king and the queen mother:
    "Take a lowly seat,
for your beautiful crown
    has come down from your head."ʸ
19 The towns of the Negeb are shut up

ʷ Or *to Parah*; Heb *perath*   ˣ Or *by Parah*; Heb *perath*   ʸ Gk Syr Vg: Meaning of Heb uncertain

Cross references:
13.1 v. 11 13.2 Isa 20.2 13.4 Jer 51.63 13.5 Ex 39.42, 43; 40.16 13.9 Lev 26.19; vv. 15-17 13.10 Jer 9.14; 11.8; 16.12 13.11 Ex 19.5, 6; Jer 7.23; 32.20; 33.9 13.13 Isa 51.17, 21; 63.6; Jer 25.27; 51.7 13.14 Jer 19.9-11; 6.21; 16.5; Isa 27.11 13.15 Prov 16.5 13.16 Ps 96.8; Isa 59.9; Jer 23.12; 2.6 13.17 Mal 2.2; Jer 9.1; 14.17; 23.1, 2 13.18 2 Chr 33.12, 19; Isa 3.20; Ezek 24.17, 23 13.19 Jer 32.44; 20.4; 52.27-30

13.1 The *linen loincloth* here is symbolic. Faithful Israel had been the linen girdle worn by God with pleasure. But the girdle had deteriorated and could no longer be worn. It had to be cast off. In other words, the degenerate people of God would be cast off, for their iniquities had separated them from their Redeemer.
13.17 The little word *if* kept rising on the lips of God. If Judah would not hear God, they had to pay the price of their failure.
13.18 *Say to the king and the queen mother*, i.e., to King Jehoiachin and his mother Nehushta.

with no one to open them;
all Judah is taken into exile,
    wholly taken into exile.

13.20
Jer 6.22;
v. 17

20 Lift up your eyes and see
    those who come from the north.
  Where is the flock that was given you,
    your beautiful flock?

13.21
Jer 5.31;
2.25; 4.31

21 What will you say when they set as head over you
    those whom you have trained
    to be your allies?
  Will not pangs take hold of you,
    like those of a woman in labor?

13.22
Deut 7.17;
Jer 5.19;
16.10

22 And if you say in your heart,
    "Why have these things come upon me?"
  it is for the greatness of your iniquity
    that your skirts are lifted up,
    and you are violated.

13.23
Prov 27.22;
Jer 4.22

23 Can Ethiopians^z change their skin
    or leopards their spots?
  Then also you can do good
    who are accustomed to do evil.

13.24
Jer 9.16;
4.11; 18.17

24 I will scatter you^a like chaff
    driven by the wind from the desert.

13.25
Ps 11.6;
Jer 2.32; 3.21

25 This is your lot,
    the portion I have measured out to you, says the Lord,
  because you have forgotten me
    and trusted in lies.

13.26
Ezek 16.37;
Hos 2.10

26 I myself will lift up your skirts over your face,
    and your shame will be seen.

13.27
Jer 5.7, 8;
11.15; 2.20;
4.14;
Hos 8.5

27 I have seen your abominations,
    your adulteries and neighings, your shameless prostitutions
    on the hills of the countryside.
  Woe to you, O Jerusalem!
    How long will it be
    before you are made clean?

2. Sermon V: the exile inevitable, yet Judah will someday be restored

a. Judah beyond deliverance: drought, sword, famine must come

14.1
Jer 17.8

14 The word of the Lord that came to Jeremiah concerning the
drought:

14.2
Isa 3.26;
Jer 8.21;
11.11; 46.12

2 Judah mourns
    and her gates languish;
  they lie in gloom on the ground,
    and the cry of Jerusalem goes up.

14.3
1 Kings 18.5;
2 Kings 18.31;
2 Sam 15.30

3 Her nobles send their servants for water;
    they come to the cisterns,
  they find no water,
    they return with their vessels empty.

^z Or *Nubians*; Heb *Cushites*   ^a Heb *them*

13.26 If the wind blows one's garment face high, the person is left exposed, naked in open view to all. God would expose his people's nakedness to public view. All the world would see their adulteries and prostitution.

14.1ff The world is always one harvest away from famine. If the earth did not give forth a harvest for a single year, many of the world's people would starve. The Scriptures plainly state that God occasionally sends drought and famine as a judgment against sinners and with the intention of motivating them to repent of their transgressions. Thus, when food is lacking, we should reflect on what God may be saying to us and look to him for help.

They are ashamed and dismayed
　　and cover their heads,
4 because the ground is cracked.
　　Because there has been no rain on the land
the farmers are dismayed;
　　they cover their heads.

5 Even the doe in the field forsakes her newborn fawn
　　because there is no grass.
6 The wild asses stand on the bare heights,[b]
　　they pant for air like jackals;
their eyes fail
　　because there is no herbage.

7 Although our iniquities testify against us,
　　act, O LORD, for your name's sake;
our apostasies indeed are many,
　　and we have sinned against you.
8 O hope of Israel,
　　its savior in time of trouble,
why should you be like a stranger in the land,
　　like a traveler turning aside for the night?
9 Why should you be like someone confused,
　　like a mighty warrior who cannot give help?
Yet you, O LORD, are in the midst of us,
　　and we are called by your name;
　　do not forsake us!

10 Thus says the LORD concerning this people:
Truly they have loved to wander,
　　they have not restrained their feet;
therefore the LORD does not accept them,
　　now he will remember their iniquity
　　and punish their sins.

11 The LORD said to me: Do not pray for the welfare of this people. 12 Although they fast, I do not hear their cry, and although they offer burnt offering and grain offering, I do not accept them; but by the sword, by famine, and by pestilence I consume them.
13 Then I said: "Ah, Lord GOD! Here are the prophets saying to them, 'You shall not see the sword, nor shall you have famine, but I will give you true peace in this place.'" 14 And the LORD said to me: The prophets are prophesying lies in my name; I did not send them, nor did I command them or speak to them. They are prophesying to you a lying vision, worthless divination, and the deceit of their own minds. 15 Therefore thus says the LORD concerning the prophets who prophesy in my name though I did not send them, and who say, "Sword and famine shall not come on this land": By sword and famine those prophets shall be consumed. 16 And the people to whom they prophesy shall be thrown out into the streets of Jerusalem, victims of famine and sword. There shall be no one to bury them—themselves, their wives, their sons, and their daughters. For I will pour out their wickedness upon them.

17 You shall say to them this word:

[b] Or the trails

14.4 Joel 1.19, 20; Jer 3.3; Joel 1.11
14.5 Isa 15.6
14.6 Jer 2.24; Joel 1.18
14.7 Isa 59.12; Jer 5.6; 8.5
14.8 Jer 17.13; Isa 43.3; 63.8; Ps 50.15
14.9 Isa 50.2; Jer 8.19; 15.16; Isa 63.19
14.10 Jer 2.25; 6.20; Hos 8.13
14.11 Ex 32.10; Jer 7.16
14.12 Isa 1.15; Jer 11.11; 6.20; 7.21; 9.16; 21.9
14.13 Jer 5.12; 23.17; 6.14
14.14 Jer 5.31; 27.15; 23.16, 26; Ezek 12.24
14.15 Jer 5.12, 13; Ezek 14.10
14.16 Isa 9.16; Jer 7.33; 8.1, 2; 13.22-25
14.17 Jer 9.1; Lam 1.15, 16; Jer 10.19; 30.14, 15

14.13 Where there are true prophets of God, there will always be false prophets as well. Here the false prophets reassured the people that the sword would not fall and the famine would disappear. But God declared that these false prophets were liars. He had not sent them, he had not spoken to them, nor was he speaking through them. These false prophets would be consumed by the sword and famine (v. 15).

Let my eyes run down with tears night and day,
 and let them not cease,
for the virgin daughter — my people — is struck down with a
  crushing blow,
 with a very grievous wound.

14.18
Jer 6.25;
Ezek 7.15;
Jer 6.13; 2.8;
5.5

18 If I go out into the field,
 look — those killed by the sword!
And if I enter the city,
 look — those sick with*c* famine!
For both prophet and priest ply their trade throughout
  the land,
 and have no knowledge.

14.19
Jer 6.30;
30.13; 8.15;
1 Thess 5.3

19 Have you completely rejected Judah?
 Does your heart loathe Zion?
Why have you struck us down
 so that there is no healing for us?
We look for peace, but find no good;
 for a time of healing, but there is terror instead.

14.20
Jer 3.25; 8.14

20 We acknowledge our wickedness, O LORD,
 the iniquity of our ancestors,
 for we have sinned against you.

14.21
v. 7;
Jer 3.17;
17.12

21 Do not spurn us, for your name's sake;
 do not dishonor your glorious throne;
 remember and do not break your covenant with us.

14.22
Isa 41.29;
Jer 10.3;
5.24;
Isa 41.4;
43.10;
Lam 3.26

22 Can any idols of the nations bring rain?
 Or can the heavens give showers?
Is it not you, O LORD our God?
 We set our hope on you,
 for it is you who do all this.

b. *Not even the intercession of Moses or Samuel*
could avert judgment

15.1
Ezek 14.14,
20;
Ex 32.11, 12;
1 Sam 7.9;
12.23;
2 Kings 17.20;
Jer 7.15;
10.20

15 Then the LORD said to me: Though Moses and Samuel stood
before me, yet my heart would not turn toward this people. Send
them out of my sight, and let them go! 2 And when they say to you,
"Where shall we go?" you shall say to them: Thus says the LORD:
 Those destined for pestilence, to pestilence,
  and those destined for the sword, to the sword;

15.2
Jer 43.11;
Ezek 5.2, 12;
Zech 11.9

 those destined for famine, to famine,
  and those destined for captivity, to captivity.

15.3
Lev 26.16;
1 Kings 21.23,
24;
Deut 28.26;
Jer 7.33

3 And I will appoint over them four kinds of destroyers, says the LORD:
the sword to kill, the dogs to drag away, and the birds of the air and the
wild animals of the earth to devour and destroy. 4 I will make them a
horror to all the kingdoms of the earth because of what King Manasseh
son of Hezekiah of Judah did in Jerusalem.

15.4
Deut 28.25;
2 Kings 21.11ff;
23.26

5 Who will have pity on you, O Jerusalem,
 or who will bemoan you?
 Who will turn aside

15.5
Ps 69.20;
Isa 51.19;
Jer 16.5

c Heb *look — the sicknesses of*

14.17,18 Jeremiah was the prophet with a broken
heart. He wept over the ruin of his country and saw
what Judah did not see — that they would perish and
that famine would come.
15.1 *Moses and Samuel* were regarded as great
prophets of God in the O.T. God had responded to
their intercession for Israel on a number of occasions,
and they were known as special favorites of God. Now

God said that even if Moses and Samuel were alive and
offered intercessory prayer for Judah, he would not
hear them or grant their petitions. Judgment
was inescapable; the verdict against the sinners was
irrevocable.
15.3 God promised to harness humans and nature
against his people. The sword, dogs, birds, and beasts
would consume the guilty.

6   You have rejected me, says the LORD,
    you are going backward;
so I have stretched out my hand against you and destroyed
    you—
    I am weary of relenting.

7   I have winnowed them with a winnowing fork
    in the gates of the land;
I have bereaved them, I have destroyed my people;
    they did not turn from their ways.

8   Their widows became more numerous
    than the sand of the seas;
I have brought against the mothers of youths
    a destroyer at noonday;
I have made anguish and terror
    fall upon her suddenly.

9   She who bore seven has languished;
    she has swooned away;
her sun went down while it was yet day;
    she has been shamed and disgraced.
And the rest of them I will give to the sword
    before their enemies,

                      says the LORD.

10   Woe is me, my mother, that you ever bore me, a man of strife and contention to the whole land! I have not lent, nor have I borrowed, yet all of them curse me. 11 The LORD said: Surely I have intervened in your life*d* for good, surely I have imposed enemies on you in a time of trouble and in a time of distress.*e* 12 Can iron and bronze break iron from the north?

13   Your wealth and your treasures I will give as plunder, without price, for all your sins, throughout all your territory. 14 I will make you serve your enemies in a land that you do not know, for in my anger a fire is kindled that shall burn forever.

c. Jeremiah encouraged to persevere

15   O LORD, you know;
    remember me and visit me,
    and bring down retribution for me on my persecutors.
In your forbearance do not take me away;
    know that on your account I suffer insult.

16   Your words were found, and I ate them,
    and your words became to me a joy
    and the delight of my heart;
for I am called by your name,
    O LORD, God of hosts.

17   I did not sit in the company of merrymakers,
    nor did I rejoice;
under the weight of your hand I sat alone,
    for you had filled me with indignation.

18   Why is my pain unceasing,
    my wound incurable,

d Heb *intervened with you*   *e* Meaning of Heb uncertain

Cross references (margin):

15.6 Jer 6.19; 7.24; 6.11, 12; 7.16

15.7 Jer 51.2; 18.21; 5.3

15.8 Isa 3.25, 26; Jer 22.7; 6.4

15.9 1 Sam 2.5; Isa 47.9; Jer 6.4; Am 8.9; Jer 50.12; 21.7

15.10 Job 3.1; Jer 20.14; Deut 23.19
15.11 Isa 41.10; Jer 39.11, 12; 40.4, 5
15.12 Jer 28.14
15.13 Ps 44.12; Jer 17.3; Isa 52.3, 5
15.14 Jer 16.13; 17.4; Deut 32.22
15.15 Jer 12.3; 20.11; Ps 69.7-9

15.16 Ezek 3.1-3; Ps 119.72; Jer 14.9

15.17 Jer 16.8; Ezek 3.24, 25

15.18 Jer 30.15; Mic 1.9; Jer 14.3

15.10ff Jeremiah now begins a lamentation or complaint. He argued his innocence before God, noting that he was being regarded as a man of strife and contention, in spite of his earnest prayers and pleas for his people.
15.13,14 God's judgment would make both those who died and those who survived aware that Jeremiah the prophet had spoken the truth, but this knowledge would be learned too late to help them.
15.15ff The prophet pleads with God for mercy and relief from the venomous persecutions, slanders, and physical abuse of his enemies.

refusing to be healed?
Truly, you are to me like a deceitful brook,
　　like waters that fail.

15.19
Jer 4.1;
Ezek 22.26

19　Therefore thus says the LORD:
If you turn back, I will take you back,
　　and you shall stand before me.
If you utter what is precious, and not what is worthless,
　　you shall serve as my mouth.
It is they who will turn to you,
　　not you who will turn to them.

15.20
Jer 1.18, 19;
20.11;
Isa 41.10

20　And I will make you to this people
　　a fortified wall of bronze;
they will fight against you,
　　but they shall not prevail over you,
for I am with you
　　to save you and deliver you,
　　　　　　　　　　　　　　　　　　says the LORD.

15.21
Jer 20.13;
31.11

21　I will deliver you out of the hand of the wicked,
　　and redeem you from the grasp of the ruthless.

3. Sermon VI: the sign of Jeremiah's unmarried state

a. Command to remain unmarried lest his children should perish

16.1
Jer 1.2, 4
16.2
1 Cor 7.26
16.3
Jer 6.11;
15.8; 6.21
16.4
Ps 83.10;
Jer 9.22;
15.3; 34.20

16 The word of the LORD came to me: 2 You shall not take a wife, nor shall you have sons or daughters in this place. 3 For thus says the LORD concerning the sons and daughters who are born in this place, and concerning the mothers who bear them and the fathers who beget them in this land: 4 They shall die of deadly diseases. They shall not be lamented, nor shall they be buried; they shall become like dung on the surface of the ground. They shall perish by the sword and by famine, and their dead bodies shall become food for the birds of the air and for the wild animals of the earth.

16.5
Ezek 24.16-23;
Jer 12.12;
13.14
16.6
Ezek 9.6;
Jer 41.5; 47.5
16.7
Ezek 24.17;
Hos 9.4
16.8
Jer 15.17
16.9
Jer 7.34;
25.10;
Hos 2.11;
Rev 18.23
16.10
Deut 29.24;
1 Kings 9.8,
9;
Jer 5.19

5　For thus says the LORD: Do not enter the house of mourning, or go to lament, or bemoan them; for I have taken away my peace from this people, says the LORD, my steadfast love and mercy. 6 Both great and small shall die in this land; they shall not be buried, and no one shall lament for them; there shall be no gashing, no shaving of the head for them. 7 No one shall break bread*f* for the mourner, to offer comfort for the dead; nor shall anyone give them the cup of consolation to drink for their fathers or their mothers. 8 You shall not go into the house of feasting to sit with them, to eat and drink. 9 For thus says the LORD of hosts, the God of Israel: I am going to banish from this place, in your days and before your eyes, the voice of mirth and the voice of gladness, the voice of the bridegroom and the voice of the bride.

10　And when you tell this people all these words, and they say to you,

f Two Mss Gk: MT *break for them*

15.19ff In Jeremiah's dark night of the soul, God spoke comfortable words to his servant. He told him to recover from his depression, to be faithful in service, and to obey what God ordered him to do. If he did this, his mind would be at rest, he would continue to be useful to God, and he would have the strength and courage to face all difficulties. God would be his protector and deliverer.
16.1ff The situation was so bad that God cautioned Jeremiah to remain celibate and not think of having a family. He must not go into either mourning or feasting. God's people had done worse than their fa-

thers (v. 12). Since Manasseh, the son of Hezekiah, had been one of the worst kings of Judah, it was almost inconceivable to suppose that those who came after could have done worse. But they did. And judgment was about to fall.
16.10 If the remnant in Babylon were to ask Jeremiah why God's judgment had happened, he was to tell them the truth, however much it hurt them. They were there because of their transgressions. If some of them were innocent, they should recognize that the innocent sometimes suffer for the sins of the guilty.

"Why has the LORD pronounced all this great evil against us? What is our iniquity? What is the sin that we have committed against the LORD our God?" 11 then you shall say to them: It is because your ancestors have forsaken me, says the LORD, and have gone after other gods and have served and worshiped them, and have forsaken me and have not kept my law; 12 and because you have behaved worse than your ancestors, for here you are, every one of you, following your stubborn evil will, refusing to listen to me. 13 Therefore I will hurl you out of this land into a land that neither you nor your ancestors have known, and there you shall serve other gods day and night, for I will show you no favor.

14   Therefore, the days are surely coming, says the LORD, when it shall no longer be said, "As the LORD lives who brought the people of Israel up out of the land of Egypt," 15 but "As the LORD lives who brought the people of Israel up out of the land of the north and out of all the lands where he had driven them." For I will bring them back to their own land that I gave to their ancestors.

16   I am now sending for many fishermen, says the LORD, and they shall catch them; and afterward I will send for many hunters, and they shall hunt them from every mountain and every hill, and out of the clefts of the rocks. 17 For my eyes are on all their ways; they are not hidden from my presence, nor is their iniquity concealed from my sight. 18 And*g* I will doubly repay their iniquity and their sin, because they have polluted my land with the carcasses of their detestable idols, and have filled my inheritance with their abominations.

19   O LORD, my strength and my stronghold,
      my refuge in the day of trouble,
  to you shall the nations come
      from the ends of the earth and say:
  Our ancestors have inherited nothing but lies,
      worthless things in which there is no profit.
20   Can mortals make for themselves gods?
      Such are no gods!

21   "Therefore I am surely going to teach them, this time I am going to teach them my power and my might, and they shall know that my name is the LORD."

b. Idolatry, Judah's sin: her only hope, the LORD

17 The sin of Judah is written with an iron pen; with a diamond point it is engraved on the tablet of their hearts, and on the horns of their altars, 2 while their children remember their altars and their sacred poles,*h* beside every green tree, and on the high hills, 3 on the mountains in the open country. Your wealth and all your treasures I will give for spoil as the price of your sin*i* throughout all your territory. 4 By your own act you shall lose the heritage that I gave you, and I will make you serve your enemies in a land that you do not know, for in my anger a fire is kindled*j* that shall burn forever.

5   Thus says the LORD:

g Gk: Heb *And first*   *h* Heb *Asherim*   *i* Cn: Heb *spoil your high places for sin*   *j* Two Mss Theodotion: *you kindled*

16.11	Jer 22.9; Ezek 11.21; 1 Pet 4.3
16.12	Jer 7.26; 13.10; Eccl 9.3
16.13	Deut 4.26-28; 28.36; Jer 15.4; 5.19
16.14	Isa 43.18; Jer 23.7, 8; Ex 20.2
16.15	Ps 106.47; Isa 11.11-16; Jer 24.6
16.16	Am 4.2; Hab 1.14, 15; Mic 7.2; Isa 2.21
16.17	Ps 90.8; 1 Cor 4.5; Heb 4.13; Jer 2.22
16.18	Rev 18.6; Ezek 11.18, 21
16.19	Jer 15.11; Ps 14.6; Hab 2.18, 19
16.20	Isa 37.19; Jer 2.11; Gal 4.8
16.21	Ps 9.16; Jer 33.2; Am 5.8
17.1	Jer 2.22; Job 19.24; Prov 3.3; 2 Cor 3.3
17.2	Jer 7.18; Ex 34.13; Jer 3.6
17.3	Jer 26.18; 15.13
17.4	Jer 12.7; 15.14; 7.20
17.5	Isa 30.1-3; 2 Chr 32.8

16.14,15   God gave his dispersed people a word of hope and encouragement. The days would come when God would bring the people back to the land from which they were taken. This would constitute one of the great wonders of their God, equal in magnitude to the exodus.
17.1   *iron pen*, i.e., an instrument used to chisel a message permanently on rock. Israel's sins were of such a nature that they could not be erased. They were indelible and had to be punished, for they had not repented.
17.5   Those who put their trust in mortals are, by that decision, rejecting God.

Cursed are those who trust in mere mortals
    and make mere flesh their strength,
    whose hearts turn away from the LORD.

6 They shall be like a shrub in the desert,
    and shall not see when relief comes.
They shall live in the parched places of the wilderness,
    in an uninhabited salt land.

7 Blessed are those who trust in the LORD,
    whose trust is the LORD.
8 They shall be like a tree planted by water,
    sending out its roots by the stream.
It shall not fear when heat comes,
    and its leaves shall stay green;
in the year of drought it is not anxious,
    and it does not cease to bear fruit.

9 The heart is devious above all else;
    it is perverse —
    who can understand it?
10 I the LORD test the mind
    and search the heart,
to give to all according to their ways,
    according to the fruit of their doings.

11 Like the partridge hatching what it did not lay,
    so are all who amass wealth unjustly;
in mid-life it will leave them,
    and at their end they will prove to be fools.

12 O glorious throne, exalted from the beginning,
    shrine of our sanctuary!
13 O hope of Israel! O LORD!
All who forsake you shall be put to shame;
those who turn away from you[k] shall be recorded in the
        underworld,[l]
    for they have forsaken the fountain of living water,
      the LORD.

14 Heal me, O LORD, and I shall be healed;
    save me, and I shall be saved;
    for you are my praise.
15 See how they say to me,
    "Where is the word of the LORD?
    Let it come!"
16 But I have not run away from being a shepherd[m] in
    your service,
    nor have I desired the fatal day.
You know what came from my lips;
    it was before your face.
17 Do not become a terror to me;

17.6
Jer 48.6;
Deut 29.23

17.7
Ps 34.8;
84.12; 40.4;
Prov 16.20
17.8
Ps 1.3;
Jer 14.1-6

17.9
Mk 7.21, 22;
Rom 7.11;
Eph 4.22
17.10
1 Sam 16.7;
Jer 11.20;
20.12;
Rom 8.27;
Jer 32.19;
Rom 2.6

17.11
Jer 6.13;
8.10; 22.13,
17

17.12
Jer 3.17;
14.21
17.13
Jer 14.8;
Ps 73.27;
Isa 1.28;
Jer 2.13, 17

17.14
Jer 30.17;
Ps 54.1;
Deut 10.21;
Ps 109.1
17.15
Isa 5.19;
Am 5.18

17.16
Jer 1.6; 12.3

17.17
Ps 88.15;
Jer 16.19

---

[k] Heb *me* [l] Or *in the earth* [m] Meaning of Heb uncertain

---

17.7,8 The contrast between trust in God and trust in human beings is the contrast between a well-watered field and an arid one. We should not rely on humans, for the unregenerate are frail, false, and deceitful, and even the regenerate are imperfect.
17.9,10 All of us have some wickedness in our hearts of which we are unaware. We think better of ourselves than we should. This often cheats us of looking for salvation, for we think that God will accept us as we are. But God knows the hearts of all and sees what we cover over or fail to detect. He is the only one who can judge; he alone truly knows what lies in our hearts.

you are my refuge in the day of disaster;

18 Let my persecutors be shamed,
      but do not let me be shamed;
    let them be dismayed,
      but do not let me be dismayed;
    bring on them the day of disaster;
      destroy them with double destruction!

4. *Sabbath observance stressed*

19 Thus said the LORD to me: Go and stand in the People's Gate, by which the kings of Judah enter and by which they go out, and in all the gates of Jerusalem, 20 and say to them: Hear the word of the LORD, you kings of Judah, and all Judah, and all the inhabitants of Jerusalem, who enter by these gates. 21 Thus says the LORD: For the sake of your lives, take care that you do not bear a burden on the sabbath day or bring it in by the gates of Jerusalem. 22 And do not carry a burden out of your houses on the sabbath or do any work, but keep the sabbath day holy, as I commanded your ancestors. 23 Yet they did not listen or incline their ear; they stiffened their necks and would not hear or receive instruction.

24 But if you listen to me, says the LORD, and bring in no burden by the gates of this city on the sabbath day, but keep the sabbath day holy and do no work on it, 25 then there shall enter by the gates of this city kings[n] who sit on the throne of David, riding in chariots and on horses, they and their officials, the people of Judah and the inhabitants of Jerusalem; and this city shall be inhabited forever. 26 And people shall come from the towns of Judah and the places around Jerusalem, from the land of Benjamin, from the Shephelah, from the hill country, and from the Negeb, bringing burnt offerings and sacrifices, grain offerings and frankincense, and bringing thank offerings to the house of the LORD. 27 But if you do not listen to me, to keep the sabbath day holy, and to carry in no burden through the gates of Jerusalem on the sabbath day, then I will kindle a fire in its gates; it shall devour the palaces of Jerusalem and shall not be quenched.

5. *Sermon VII: the sign of the potter's house and the broken vessel*

a. *First symbol: the potter and the clay*

18 The word that came to Jeremiah from the LORD: 2 "Come, go down to the potter's house, and there I will let you hear my words." 3 So I went down to the potter's house, and there he was working at his wheel. 4 The vessel he was making of clay was spoiled in the potter's hand, and he reworked it into another vessel, as seemed good to him.

5 Then the word of the LORD came to me: 6 Can I not do with you, O house of Israel, just as this potter has done? says the LORD. Just like the clay in the potter's hand, so are you in my hand, O house of Israel. 7 At one moment I may declare concerning a nation or a kingdom, that I will pluck up and break down and destroy it, 8 but if that nation,

n Cn: Heb kings and officials

17.18
Ps 35.4, 26;
35.8;
Jer 16.18

17.19
Jer 7.2; 26.2

17.20
Jer 19.3;
22.2;
Hos 5.1

17.21
Deut 4.9, 15,
23;
Num 15.32-36;
Neh 13.15-21

17.22
Ex 20.8;
23.12; 31.13;
Ezek 20.12

17.23
Jer 7.24, 26;
11.10; 19.15

17.24
Deut 11.13;
Ex 20.8-11;
Ezek 20.20

17.25
Jer 22.4;
Isa 9.7;
Lk 1.32;
Heb 12.22

17.26
Zech 7.7;
Ps 107.22

17.27
Jer 22.5;
Isa 9.18, 19;
Jer 11.16;
Am 2.5; 7.20

18.2
Jer 19.1, 2;
23.22

18.6
Isa 45.9;
Mt 20.15;
Rom 9.20, 21

18.7
Jer 1.10

18.8
Ezek 18.21;
Jer 26.3;
Jon 3.10

17.21 *do not bear a burden on the sabbath day.* Works of mercy and necessity were permitted on the sabbath, but Israel was breaking the sabbath by doing other work. The sabbath was God's gift to Israel, given for their good. People who broke the sabbath would in turn be broken.

18.4 Just as clay in the potter's hand is malleable and can be fashioned into whatever form the potter desires, so God can do the same with mortals. Paul picks up this theme and enlarges upon it in his discussion of the sovereignty of God as it relates to free will, predestination, and God's foreknowledge (see Rom

9). We will never completely understand this mystery.

18.7–12 These verses are important not only to Israel but to all nations, for the principles expounded relate to all nations in general. In his common grace God can and does bless some nations that act in accord with divine standards. He never acts capriciously, but works according to his fixed rules of equity and goodness. Any nation that turns to God can be raised up from their ruins, even as the potter can make a new vessel from the clay that was marred in his hands. The same applies to individuals.

18.9
Jer 1.10;
31.28
18.10
Jer 7.24-28;
Ezek 33.18
18.11
Jer 4.6;
2 Kings 17.13;
Isa 1.16-19;
Acts 26.20

concerning which I have spoken, turns from its evil, I will change my mind about the disaster that I intended to bring on it. 9 And at another moment I may declare concerning a nation or a kingdom that I will build and plant it, 10 but if it does evil in my sight, not listening to my voice, then I will change my mind about the good that I had intended to do to it. 11 Now, therefore, say to the people of Judah and the inhabitants of Jerusalem: Thus says the LORD: Look, I am a potter shaping evil against you and devising a plan against you. Turn now, all of you from your evil way, and amend your ways and your doings.

18.12
Jer 2.25;
7.24; 16.12

12 But they say, "It is no use! We will follow our own plans, and each of us will act according to the stubbornness of our evil will."

18.13
Jer 2.10, 11;
14.17; 5.30;
23.14

13 Therefore thus says the LORD:
    Ask among the nations:
        Who has heard the like of this?
    The virgin Israel has done
        a most horrible thing.

14 Does the snow of Lebanon leave
        the crags of Sirion?*o*
    Do the mountain*p* waters run dry,*q*
        the cold flowing streams?

18.15
Isa 65.7;
Jer 7.9; 6.16;
Isa 57.14;
62.10

15 But my people have forgotten me,
        they burn offerings to a delusion;
    they have stumbled*r* in their ways,
        in the ancient roads,
    and have gone into bypaths,
        not the highway,

18.16
Jer 25.9;
50.13; 48.27

16 making their land a horror,
        a thing to be hissed at forever.
    All who pass by it are horrified
        and shake their heads.

18.17
Job 27.21;
Jer 13.24;
2.27; 46.21

17 Like the wind from the east,
        I will scatter them before the enemy.
    I will show them my back, not my face,
        in the day of their calamity.

18.18
Jer 11.19;
Mal 2.7;
Jer 8.8; 5.13;
20.10; 43.2

18 Then they said, "Come, let us make plots against Jeremiah—for instruction shall not perish from the priest, nor counsel from the wise, nor the word from the prophet. Come, let us bring charges against him,*s* and let us not heed any of his words."

19 Give heed to me, O LORD,
        and listen to what my adversaries say!

18.20
Ps 35.7; 57.6;
106.23

20 Is evil a recompense for good?
        Yet they have dug a pit for my life.
    Remember how I stood before you
        to speak good for them,
        to turn away your wrath from them.

18.21
Ps 109.9, 10;
Isa 13.18;
Jer 15.8;
Ezek 22.25;
Jer 9.21;
11.22

21 Therefore give their children over to famine;
        hurl them out to the power of the sword,
    let their wives become childless and widowed.
        May their men meet death by pestilence,

o Cn: Heb *of the field*   *p* Cn: Heb *foreign*   *q* Cn: Heb *Are . . . plucked up?*   *r* Gk Syr Vg: Heb *they made them stumble*   *s* Heb *strike him with the tongue*

18.18 Jeremiah had faithfully proclaimed the word he received from God. Now he became the object of hatred both with respect to his person and to the word he had spoken. The enemies of God plotted to do him harm, to offset his influence, and to subtly undermine his counsel. In vv. 19–23 Jeremiah prayed earnestly that God would overrule the plans of the enemy and wreak vengeance on them. This prayer came just before the intense persecution started.

their youths be slain by the sword in battle.

22 May a cry be heard from their houses,
   when you bring the marauder suddenly upon them!
   For they have dug a pit to catch me,
   and laid snares for my feet.

23 Yet you, O LORD, know
   all their plotting to kill me.
   Do not forgive their iniquity,
   do not blot out their sin from your sight.
   Let them be tripped up before you;
   deal with them while you are angry.

b. *Second symbol: the broken jug*

19 Thus said the LORD: Go and buy a potter's earthenware jug. Take with you*t* some of the elders of the people and some of the senior priests, 2 and go out to the valley of the son of Hinnom at the entry of the Potsherd Gate, and proclaim there the words that I tell you. 3 You shall say: Hear the word of the LORD, O kings of Judah and inhabitants of Jerusalem. Thus says the LORD of hosts, the God of Israel: I am going to bring such disaster upon this place that the ears of everyone who hears of it will tingle. 4 Because the people have forsaken me, and have profaned this place by making offerings in it to other gods whom neither they nor their ancestors nor the kings of Judah have known, and because they have filled this place with the blood of the innocent, 5 and gone on building the high places of Baal to burn their children in the fire as burnt offerings to Baal, which I did not command or decree, nor did it enter my mind; 6 therefore the days are surely coming, says the LORD, when this place shall no more be called Topheth, or the valley of the son of Hinnom, but the valley of Slaughter. 7 And in this place I will make void the plans of Judah and Jerusalem, and will make them fall by the sword before their enemies, and by the hand of those who seek their life. I will give their dead bodies for food to the birds of the air and to the wild animals of the earth. 8 And I will make this city a horror, a thing to be hissed at; everyone who passes by it will be horrified and will hiss because of all its disasters. 9 And I will make them eat the flesh of their sons and the flesh of their daughters, and all shall eat the flesh of their neighbors in the siege, and in the distress with which their enemies and those who seek their life afflict them.

10   Then you shall break the jug in the sight of those who go with you, 11 and shall say to them: Thus says the LORD of hosts: So will I break this people and this city, as one breaks a potter's vessel, so that it can never be mended. In Topheth they shall bury until there is no more room to bury. 12 Thus will I do to this place, says the LORD, and to its inhabitants, making this city like Topheth. 13 And the houses of Jerusalem and the houses of the kings of Judah shall be defiled like the place of Topheth — all the houses upon whose roofs offerings have been made to the whole host of heaven, and libations have been poured out to other gods.

14   When Jeremiah came from Topheth, where the LORD had sent him to prophesy, he stood in the court of the LORD's house and said to all the people: 15 Thus says the LORD of hosts, the God of Israel: I am now bringing upon this city and upon all its towns all the disaster that I have

---

t Syr Tg Compare Gk: Heb lacks *take with you*

18.22	Jer 6.26; Ps 140.5
18.23	Ps 109.14; Isa 2.9; Jer 6.15, 21; 7.20
19.1	Jer 18.2; v. 10; Num 11.16; 2 Kings 19.2
19.2	Josh 15.8; Jer 7.31
19.3	Jer 17.20; 1 Sam 3.11; 4.18
19.4	Deut 28.20; Isa 65.11; 2 Kings 21.16; Jer 2.34
19.5	Jer 32.35; 2 Kings 17.17; Lev 18.21
19.6	Jer 7.32; Josh 15.8
19.7	Jer 15.2, 9; Ps 79.2; Jer 16.4
19.8	Jer 18.16; 49.13; 1 Kings 9.8; 2 Chr 7.21
19.9	Deut 28.53, 55; Isa 9.20; Lam 4.10
19.10	v. 1
19.11	Ps 2.9; Isa 30.14; Rev 2.27; Jer 7.32
19.13	Jer 52.13; 7.18; Ezek 20.28; Acts 7.42
19.14	Jer 26.2
19.15	Jer 7.26; 17.23; Ps 58.4

19.1ff Jeremiah asked some of the leaders of God's people to accompany him to the valley of Hinnom to hear the word of the Lord. Why they were willing to do this is uncertain. Perhaps some of them did regard him as a genuine prophet and prevailed on the others to accompany them.
19.10 Jeremiah had taken a potter's vessel with him, one that was whole and had hardened. He broke that

vessel, so that it became irrepairable and impossible to be reshaped. The message was plain: God would break Judah and Jerusalem the same way Jeremiah had broken the potter's vessel.
19.14 When Jeremiah had finished speaking at Topheth, he repeated his message to the people in the court of the Lord's house. His message was refused and he suffered abuse.

pronounced against it, because they have stiffened their necks, refusing to hear my words.

c. Jeremiah must preach despite persecution

20 Now the priest Pashhur son of Immer, who was chief officer in the house of the LORD, heard Jeremiah prophesying these things. ²Then Pashhur struck the prophet Jeremiah, and put him in the stocks that were in the upper Benjamin Gate of the house of the LORD. ³The next morning when Pashhur released Jeremiah from the stocks, Jeremiah said to him, The LORD has named you not Pashhur but "Terror-all-around." ⁴For thus says the LORD: I am making you a terror to yourself and to all your friends; and they shall fall by the sword of their enemies while you look on. And I will give all Judah into the hand of the king of Babylon; he shall carry them captive to Babylon, and shall kill them with the sword. ⁵I will give all the wealth of this city, all its gains, all its prized belongings, and all the treasures of the kings of Judah into the hand of their enemies, who shall plunder them, and seize them, and carry them to Babylon. ⁶And you, Pashhur, and all who live in your house, shall go into captivity, and to Babylon you shall go; there you shall die, and there you shall be buried, you and all your friends, to whom you have prophesied falsely.

⁷ O LORD, you have enticed me,
    and I was enticed;
you have overpowered me,
    and you have prevailed.
I have become a laughingstock all day long;
    everyone mocks me.
⁸ For whenever I speak, I must cry out,
    I must shout, "Violence and destruction!"
For the word of the LORD has become for me
    a reproach and derision all day long.
⁹ If I say, "I will not mention him,
    or speak any more in his name,"
then within me there is something like a burning fire
    shut up in my bones;
I am weary with holding it in,
    and I cannot.
¹⁰ For I hear many whispering:
    "Terror is all around!
Denounce him! Let us denounce him!"
    All my close friends
    are watching for me to stumble.
"Perhaps he can be enticed,
    and we can prevail against him,
    and take our revenge on him."
¹¹ But the LORD is with me like a dread warrior;
    therefore my persecutors will stumble,
    and they will not prevail.
They will be greatly shamed,
    for they will not succeed.
Their eternal dishonor
    will never be forgotten.

Cross references (left margin):

20.1 1 Chr 24.14; 2 Kings 25.18
20.2 Jer 1.19; Job 13.27; Jer 37.13; 38.7
20.3 v. 10
20.4 Job 18.11-21; Jer 29.21; 21.4-10; 52.27
20.5 Jer 15.13; 17.3; 2 Kings 20.17; 2 Chr 36.10; Jer 3.24
20.6 v. 1; Jer 28.15-17; 14.13-15; 29.21
20.7 Jer 1.6-8; Mic 3.8; Jer 38.19
20.8 Jer 6.7, 10; 2 Chr 36.16
20.9 1 Kings 19.3, 4; Ps 39.3; Job 32.18-20; Acts 4.20
20.10 Ps 31.13; 41.9; Lk 11.53, 54
20.11 Jer 1.8, 19; 15.20; 17.18; 23.40

20.6 Pashur was a legitimate priest but still a false prophet. Jeremiah pronounced judgment on him. Every age has priests and ministers of God who are false prophets. Each one must be tested against the Scriptures to find who are false and who are true ministers of God (1 Jn 4.1-6).
20.9 *I will not . . . speak any more in his name.* Hu-manly speaking, Jeremiah would have preferred to remain silent since his message was rejected and his person attacked. Princes, priests, and other people laughed at his warnings. Yet it was impossible for him to stop preaching, because God's word was like a fire burning in his bones and he could not contain it.

12 O Lord of hosts, you test the righteous,
     you see the heart and the mind;
let me see your retribution upon them,
     for to you I have committed my cause.

13 Sing to the Lord;
     praise the Lord!
For he has delivered the life of the needy
     from the hands of evildoers.

14 Cursed be the day
     on which I was born!
The day when my mother bore me,
     let it not be blessed!

15 Cursed be the man
     who brought the news to my father, saying,
"A child is born to you, a son,"
     making him very glad.

16 Let that man be like the cities
     that the Lord overthrew without pity;
let him hear a cry in the morning
     and an alarm at noon,

17 because he did not kill me in the womb;
     so my mother would have been my grave,
     and her womb forever great.

18 Why did I come forth from the womb
     to see toil and sorrow,
     and spend my days in shame?

II. *Prophecies under Jehoiakim and Zedekiah (21.1–39.18)*

A. *Nebuchadnezzar is God's instrument to punish Jerusalem*

1. *Sermon I: God's judgment on the wicked kings and prophets of Judah*

a. *Zedekiah's prayer for deliverance and God's negative answer*

21 This is the word that came to Jeremiah from the Lord, when King Zedekiah sent to him Pashhur son of Malchiah and the priest Zephaniah son of Maaseiah, saying, 2 "Please inquire of the Lord on our behalf, for King Nebuchadrezzar of Babylon is making war against us; perhaps the Lord will perform a wonderful deed for us, as he has often done, and will make him withdraw from us."

3 Then Jeremiah said to them: 4 Thus you shall say to Zedekiah: Thus says the Lord, the God of Israel: I am going to turn back the weapons of war that are in your hands and with which you are fighting against the king of Babylon and against the Chaldeans who are besieging you outside the walls; and I will bring them together into the center of this city. 5 I myself will fight against you with outstretched hand and mighty arm, in anger, in fury, and in great wrath. 6 And I will strike down the inhabitants of this city, both human beings and animals; they shall die of a great pestilence. 7 Afterward, says the Lord, I will give King Zedekiah of Judah, and his servants, and the people in this city — those who survive the pestilence, sword, and famine — into the hands of King Nebuchadrezzar of Babylon, into the hands of their enemies, into the hands of those

---

21.2 *perhaps the Lord will perform a wonderful deed for us, as he has often done.* King Zedekiah doubtless had in mind God's deliverances of Jerusalem from Sennacherib, king of Assyria, in the days of Hezekiah (Isa 36–37). But Zedekiah's hopes were dashed. He was Judah's last ruler before the exile of 597 B.C.

20.12 Jer 11.20; 17.10; Ps 54.7; 59.10

20.13 Jer 31.7; Ps 35.9, 10; Jer 15.21

20.14 Job 3.3; Jer 15.10

20.15 Gen 21.6, 7

20.16 Gen 19.25; Jer 18.22

20.17 Job 3.10, 11; 10.18, 19

20.18 Job 3.20; Ps 90.9; Jer 3.25

21.1 2 Kings 24.17, 18; Jer 38.1; 2 Kings 25.18; Jer 29.25; 37.3 **21.2** Jer 37.3, 7 **21.4** Zech 14.2

21.5 Isa 63.10; Jer 32.37 **21.6** Jer 7.20; 14.12 **21.7** Jer 37.17; 39.5; 52.9; 13.14

who seek their lives. He shall strike them down with the edge of the sword; he shall not pity them, or spare them, or have compassion.

8 And to this people you shall say: Thus says the LORD: See, I am setting before you the way of life and the way of death. 9 Those who stay in this city shall die by the sword, by famine, and by pestilence; but those who go out and surrender to the Chaldeans who are besieging you shall live and shall have their lives as a prize of war. 10 For I have set my face against this city for evil and not for good, says the LORD: it shall be given into the hands of the king of Babylon, and he shall burn it with fire.

11 To the house of the king of Judah say: Hear the word of the LORD, 12 O house of David! Thus says the LORD:

> Execute justice in the morning,
>   and deliver from the hand of the oppressor
>   anyone who has been robbed,
> or else my wrath will go forth like fire,
>   and burn, with no one to quench it,
>   because of your evil doings.

13 See, I am against you, O inhabitant of the valley,
>   O rock of the plain,
>   says the LORD;
> you who say, "Who can come down against us,
>   or who can enter our places of refuge?"
14 I will punish you according to the fruit of your doings,
>   says the LORD;
> I will kindle a fire in its forest,
>   and it shall devour all that is around it.

b. *Woe pronounced on the four evil kings and their dishonest prophets*

(1) THE WICKED KINGS, AND MESSIAH THE TRUE KING

22 Thus says the LORD: Go down to the house of the king of Judah, and speak there this word, 2 and say: Hear the word of the LORD, O King of Judah sitting on the throne of David—you, and your servants, and your people who enter these gates. 3 Thus says the LORD: Act with justice and righteousness, and deliver from the hand of the oppressor anyone who has been robbed. And do no wrong or violence to the alien, the orphan, and the widow, or shed innocent blood in this place. 4 For if you will indeed obey this word, then through the gates of this house shall enter kings who sit on the throne of David, riding in chariots and on horses, they, and their servants, and their people. 5 But if you will not heed these words, I swear by myself, says the LORD, that this house shall become a desolation. 6 For thus says the LORD concerning the house of the king of Judah:

> You are like Gilead to me,
>   like the summit of Lebanon;
> but I swear that I will make you a desert,
>   an uninhabited city. *u*

7 I will prepare destroyers against you,
>   all with their weapons;
> they shall cut down your choicest cedars
>   and cast them into the fire.

u Cn: Heb *uninhabited cities*

21.8 Deut 30.15, 19
21.9 Jer 38.2, 17, 18; 14.12; 39.18; 45.5
21.10 Jer 44.11, 27; 39.16; 32.28, 29; 38.18, 23; 52.13
21.11 Jer 13.18; 17.20
21.12 Isa 7.2, 13; Jer 22.3; Zech 7.9; Jer 7.20
21.13 Ezek 13.8; Jer 49.4
21.14 Isa 3.10, 11; Ezek 20.46, 48; 2 Chr 36.19; Jer 52.13

22.1 Jer 21.11; 2 Chr 25.15, 16
22.2 Jer 19.3; 29.20
22.3 Jer 21.12; Ps 72.4; Ex 22.21-24
22.4 Jer 17.25
22.5 Jer 17.27; 26.4; Heb 6.13; Jer 7.14; 26.6, 9
22.6 Jer 7.34
22.7 Isa 10.3-6; Jer 4.6, 7; Isa 10.33, 34

21.9 Judah would fall at the hands of Nebuchadnezzar. The people should surrender to Babylon; whoever refused to do so would perish. The leaders of Judah considered this message of Jeremiah treason.

22.1 God commanded Jeremiah to preach to the king again, but the king refused to acknowledge God's power over him; otherwise he would have repented and turned from his wicked ways.

8 And many nations will pass by this city, and all of them will say one to another, "Why has the LORD dealt in this way with that great city?" 9 And they will answer, "Because they abandoned the covenant of the LORD their God, and worshiped other gods and served them."

10 Do not weep for him who is dead,
    nor bemoan him;
weep rather for him who goes away,
    for he shall return no more
      to see his native land.

11 For thus says the LORD concerning Shallum son of King Josiah of Judah, who succeeded his father Josiah, and who went away from this place: He shall return here no more, 12 but in the place where they have carried him captive he shall die, and he shall never see this land again.

13 Woe to him who builds his house by unrighteousness,
    and his upper rooms by injustice;
who makes his neighbors work for nothing,
    and does not give them their wages;
14 who says, "I will build myself a spacious house
    with large upper rooms,"
and who cuts out windows for it,
    paneling it with cedar,
    and painting it with vermilion.
15 Are you a king
    because you compete in cedar?
Did not your father eat and drink
    and do justice and righteousness?
    Then it was well with him.
16 He judged the cause of the poor and needy;
    then it was well.
Is not this to know me?
    says the LORD.
17 But your eyes and heart
    are only on your dishonest gain,
for shedding innocent blood,
    and for practicing oppression and violence.

18 Therefore thus says the LORD concerning King Jehoiakim son of Josiah of Judah:
They shall not lament for him, saying,
    "Alas, my brother!" or "Alas, sister!"
They shall not lament for him, saying,
    "Alas, lord!" or "Alas, his majesty!"
19 With the burial of a donkey he shall be buried —
    dragged off and thrown out beyond the gates of Jerusalem.

20 Go up to Lebanon, and cry out,
    and lift up your voice in Bashan;
cry out from Abarim,
    for all your lovers are crushed.
21 I spoke to you in your prosperity,
    but you said, "I will not listen."
This has been your way from your youth,
    for you have not obeyed my voice.

22.8 Deut 29.24, 25; 1 Kings 9.8, 9; Jer 16.10
22.9 2 Kings 22.17; 2 Chr 34.25
22.10 2 Kings 22.20; v. 18; Jer 16.7; 44.14
22.11 2 Kings 23.30, 34
22.13 Mic 3.10; Hab 2.9; Jas 5.4
22.14 Isa 5.8, 9; 2Sa 7.2
22.15 2 Kings 23.25; Jer 7.5; 42.6
22.16 Ps 72.1-4, 12, 13; 1 Chr 28.9; Jer 9.24
22.17 Jer 6.13; 8.10; 6.6
22.18 1 Kings 13.30; Jer 34.5
22.19 Jer 36.30
22.20 Deut 32.49; Jer 2.25; 3.1
22.21 Jer 13.10; 19.15; 3.24, 25; 32.30

22 The wind shall shepherd all your shepherds,
   and your lovers shall go into captivity;
 then you will be ashamed and dismayed
   because of all your wickedness.
23 O inhabitant of Lebanon,
   nested among the cedars,
 how you will groan[v] when pangs come upon you,
   pain as of a woman in labor!

24 As I live, says the LORD, even if King Coniah son of Jehoiakim of Judah were the signet ring on my right hand, even from there I would tear you off 25 and give you into the hands of those who seek your life, into the hands of those of whom you are afraid, even into the hands of King Nebuchadrezzar of Babylon and into the hands of the Chaldeans. 26 I will hurl you and the mother who bore you into another country, where you were not born, and there you shall die. 27 But they shall not return to the land to which they long to return.
28 Is this man Coniah a despised broken pot,
   a vessel no one wants?
 Why are he and his offspring hurled out
   and cast away in a land that they do not know?
29 O land, land, land,
   hear the word of the LORD!
30 Thus says the LORD:
 Record this man as childless,
   a man who shall not succeed in his days;
 for none of his offspring shall succeed
   in sitting on the throne of David,
   and ruling again in Judah.

23 Woe to the shepherds who destroy and scatter the sheep of my pasture! says the LORD. 2 Therefore thus says the LORD, the God of Israel, concerning the shepherds who shepherd my people: It is you who have scattered my flock, and have driven them away, and have not attended to them. So I will attend to you for your evil doings, says the LORD. 3 Then I myself will gather the remnant of my flock out of all the lands where I have driven them, and I will bring them back to their fold, and they shall be fruitful and multiply. 4 I will raise up shepherds over them who will shepherd them, and they shall not fear any longer, or be dismayed, nor shall any be missing, says the LORD.

5 The days are surely coming, says the LORD, when I will raise up for David a righteous Branch, and he shall reign as king and deal wisely, and shall execute justice and righteousness in the land. 6 In his days Judah will be saved and Israel will live in safety. And this is the name by which he will be called: "The LORD is our righteousness."

7 Therefore, the days are surely coming, says the LORD, when it shall no longer be said, "As the LORD lives who brought the people of Israel up out of the land of Egypt," 8 but "As the LORD lives who brought out and led the offspring of the house of Israel out of the land of the north

---

[v] Gk Vg Syr: Heb *will be pitied*

23.3 When human shepherds fail, God is still in charge and interested in his sheep. Though they have been scattered by the failure of their shepherds, God will bring them back to the fold where they will be safe and satisfied.
23.5,6 The Messiah is here called *a righteous Branch*, a true shoot from the stock of King David. Many of David's descendants had become kings of injustice; now the people were looking for the coming of a

righteous king who would come as the Lord's anointed or Messiah. The phrase *The LORD is our righteousness* must be understood as, "Jesus is our righteousness." The word "LORD" here is "Yahweh"; in this context, it can only mean Jesus the Messiah. Thus Jesus is Yahweh, or God. And the N.T. refers to Jesus as our righteousness (cf. 1 Cor 1.30). His righteousness is imputed to us. We have no righteousness in ourselves, only his righteousness (2 Cor 5.21).

and out of all the lands where he[w] had driven them." Then they shall live in their own land.

(2) FALSE PROPHETS SHALL DIE IN MISERY AND SHAME

9 Concerning the prophets:
My heart is crushed within me,
    all my bones shake;
I have become like a drunkard,
    like one overcome by wine,
because of the LORD
    and because of his holy words.

23.9
Hab 3.16;
Jer 20.8, 9

10 For the land is full of adulterers;
    because of the curse the land mourns,
and the pastures of the wilderness are dried up.
Their course has been evil,
    and their might is not right.

23.10
Jer 5.7, 8;
Hos 4.2, 3;
Jer 9.10; 12.4

11 Both prophet and priest are ungodly;
    even in my house I have found their wickedness,
                  says the LORD.

23.11
Jer 6.13;
8.10; 7.9, 10;
32.34

12 Therefore their way shall be to them
    like slippery paths in the darkness,
    into which they shall be driven and fall;
for I will bring disaster upon them
    in the year of their punishment,
                  says the LORD.

23.12
Ps 35.6;
Jn 12.35;
Jer 11.23

13 In the prophets of Samaria
    I saw a disgusting thing:
they prophesied by Baal
    and led my people Israel astray.

23.13
Hos 9.7, 8;
Jer 2.8

14 But in the prophets of Jerusalem
    I have seen a more shocking thing:
they commit adultery and walk in lies;
    they strengthen the hands of evildoers,
    so that no one turns from wickedness;
all of them have become like Sodom to me,
    and its inhabitants like Gomorrah.

23.14
Jer 5.30;
29.23;
Ezek 13.22;
Isa 1.9, 10;
Jer 20.16

15 Therefore thus says the LORD of hosts concerning the prophets:
"I am going to make them eat wormwood,
    and give them poisoned water to drink;
for from the prophets of Jerusalem
    ungodliness has spread throughout the land."

23.15
Jer 8.14; 9.15

16 Thus says the LORD of hosts: Do not listen to the words of the prophets who prophesy to you; they are deluding you. They speak visions of their own minds, not from the mouth of the LORD. 17 They keep saying to those who despise the word of the LORD, "It shall be well with you"; and to all who stubbornly follow their own stubborn hearts, they say, "No calamity shall come upon you."

23.16
Jer 27.9, 10;
14.14; 9.12,
20
23.17
Jer 8.11;
13.10; 18.12;
5.12;
Mic 3.11

18 For who has stood in the council of the LORD

23.18
Job 15.8;
33.31

w Gk: Heb I

23.11–15 Jeremiah condemned both priests and prophets. The priests profaned the ordinances of God when their walk did not agree with their talk. They were hypocrites. The prophets claimed to prophesy in the name of God, but at the same time (11.14) they committed adultery and walked in lies. God was saying, "What you are speaks so loudly that I cannot hear what you say nor can I hear you when you pray."

23.16 The false prophets who had contradicted what Jeremiah preached and had plotted against him were an abomination to God. False prophets still exist today (cf. Mt 24.11), who undercut and malign the Christian faith and offer substitutes to the true faith. They do the work of Satan and keep many people from coming to the knowledge of Jesus Christ.

so as to see and to hear his word?
Who has given heed to his word so as to proclaim it?

19 Look, the storm of the Lord!
      Wrath has gone forth,
   a whirling tempest;
      it will burst upon the head of the wicked.

20 The anger of the Lord will not turn back
      until he has executed and accomplished
      the intents of his mind.
   In the latter days you will understand it clearly.

21 I did not send the prophets,
      yet they ran;
   I did not speak to them,
      yet they prophesied.

22 But if they had stood in my council,
      then they would have proclaimed my words to my people,
   and they would have turned them from their evil way,
      and from the evil of their doings.

23 Am I a God near by, says the Lord, and not a God far off? 24 Who can hide in secret places so that I cannot see them? says the Lord. Do I not fill heaven and earth? says the Lord. 25 I have heard what the prophets have said who prophesy lies in my name, saying, "I have dreamed, I have dreamed!" 26 How long? Will the hearts of the prophets ever turn back—those who prophesy lies, and who prophesy the deceit of their own heart? 27 They plan to make my people forget my name by their dreams that they tell one another, just as their ancestors forgot my name for Baal. 28 Let the prophet who has a dream tell the dream, but let the one who has my word speak my word faithfully. What has straw in common with wheat? says the Lord. 29 Is not my word like fire, says the Lord, and like a hammer that breaks a rock in pieces? 30 See, therefore, I am against the prophets, says the Lord, who steal my words from one another. 31 See, I am against the prophets, says the Lord, who use their own tongues and say, "Says the Lord." 32 See, I am against those who prophesy lying dreams, says the Lord, and who tell them, and who lead my people astray by their lies and their recklessness, when I did not send them or appoint them; so they do not profit this people at all, says the Lord.

33 When this people, or a prophet, or a priest asks you, "What is the burden of the Lord?" you shall say to them, "You are the burden,ˣ and I will cast you off, says the Lord." 34 And as for the prophet, priest, or the people who say, "The burden of the Lord," I will punish them and their households. 35 Thus shall you say to one another, among yourselves, "What has the Lord answered?" or "What has the Lord spoken?" 36 But "the burden of the Lord" you shall mention no more, for the burden is everyone's own word, and so you pervert the words of the living God, the Lord of hosts, our God. 37 Thus you shall ask the prophet, "What has the Lord answered you?" or "What has the Lord spoken?" 38 But if you

ˣ Gk Vg: Heb What burden

23.23 God knows everything and is present everywhere. He is transcendent and over all. At the same time, he is near us on the earth. God's power on earth is equal to his power in heaven; he rules over both in his sovereignty. No one can escape the all-seeing eye and the all-hearing ear of God.
23.33,34 True and false prophets both used the phrase *the burden of the Lord*, but it meant something different to false prophets. They saw it as something

heavy placed on them by God which they never deserved or wanted. They often used it in jest, whereas the true prophets knew it was a word of doom for those to whom they spoke God's word.
23.38 God here forbad the people to speak of his word as the "burden of the Lord." Because they failed to speak respectfully of his word, God would unburden himself of the burden by placing it on their backs in judgment. Thus, they would no longer jest

say, "the burden of the LORD," thus says the LORD: Because you have said these words, "the burden of the LORD," when I sent to you, saying, You shall not say, "the burden of the LORD," 39 therefore, I will surely lift you up[y] and cast you away from my presence, you and the city that I gave to you and your ancestors. 40 And I will bring upon you everlasting disgrace and perpetual shame, which shall not be forgotten.

23.39
Jer 7.14, 15;
Ezek 8.18
23.40
Jer 20.11

c. The sign of the good and the bad figs

24 The LORD showed me two baskets of figs placed before the temple of the LORD. This was after King Nebuchadrezzar of Babylon had taken into exile from Jerusalem King Jeconiah son of Jehoiakim of Judah, together with the officials of Judah, the artisans, and the smiths, and had brought them to Babylon. 2 One basket had very good figs, like first-ripe figs, but the other basket had very bad figs, so bad that they could not be eaten. 3 And the LORD said to me, "What do you see, Jeremiah?" I said, "Figs, the good figs very good, and the bad figs very bad, so bad that they cannot be eaten."

24.1
Am 8.1;
2 Kings 24.10-16;
2 Chr 36.10;
Jer 22.24;
29.2
24.2
Nah 3.12;
Jer 27.19
24.3
Jer 1.11, 13

4 Then the word of the LORD came to me: 5 Thus says the LORD, the God of Israel: Like these good figs, so I will regard as good the exiles from Judah, whom I have sent away from this place to the land of the Chaldeans. 6 I will set my eyes upon them for good, and I will bring them back to this land. I will build them up, and not tear them down; I will plant them, and not pluck them up. 7 I will give them a heart to know that I am the LORD; and they shall be my people and I will be their God, for they shall return to me with their whole heart.

24.5
Nah 1.7;
Zech 13.9

24.6
Jer 29.10;
Ezek 11.17;
Jer 33.7;
42.10
24.7
Jer 31.33;
32.40;
Zech 8.8;
Heb 8.10;
Jer 29.13

8 But thus says the LORD: Like the bad figs that are so bad they cannot be eaten, so will I treat King Zedekiah of Judah, his officials, the remnant of Jerusalem who remain in this land, and those who live in the land of Egypt. 9 I will make them a horror, an evil thing, to all the kingdoms of the earth—a disgrace, a byword, a taunt, and a curse in all the places where I shall drive them. 10 And I will send sword, famine, and pestilence upon them, until they are utterly destroyed from the land that I gave to them and their ancestors.

24.8
Jer 29.17;
39.5, 9;
44.26-30
24.9
Jer 15.4;
29.18; 34.17;
1 Kings 9.7;
Ps 44.13, 14;
Isa 65.15
24.10
Isa 51.19;
Jer 21.9; 27.8

2. Sermon II: the vision of the end coming upon Judah and the heathen

a. The captivity of Judah and the end of Babylon

25 The word that came to Jeremiah concerning all the people of Judah, in the fourth year of King Jehoiakim son of Josiah of Judah (that was the first year of King Nebuchadrezzar of Babylon), 2 which the prophet Jeremiah spoke to all the people of Judah and all the inhabitants of Jerusalem: 3 For twenty-three years, from the thirteenth year of King Josiah son of Amon of Judah, to this day, the word of the LORD has come to me, and I have spoken persistently to you, but you have not listened. 4 And though the LORD persistently sent you all his servants the prophets,

25.1
Jer 36.1;
2 Kings 24.1,
2
25.2
Jer 18.11
25.3
Jer 1.2;
2 Chr 34.1-3,
8;
Jer 36.2;
7.13; 22.21
25.4
Jer 7.13, 25;
26.5

y Heb Mss Gk Vg: MT *forget you*

---

of his word as a burden.
24.1 The sign of the *two baskets of figs* indicated that Judah was divided into two groups of people. Some were so evil that they would experience the avenging sword of God, the righteous judge. The others were experiencing suffering designed for their good; it was a correcting rod rather than an avenging one. God always distinguishes between the precious and the vile. The good ones would be brought back to the land and restored to their inheritance; God would "plant them, and not pluck them up" (v. 6).
25.1 *in the fourth year of Jehoiakim*, i.e., 605 B.C. Dan 1.1 says it was the third year of Jehoiakim's

reign. He was using Babylonian dating, which varied from that of Judah.
25.2,3 Jeremiah addressed this message to all the people of Judah. He had been prophesying for twenty-three years, and his warnings had been disregarded. In this sense he was an unsuccessful prophet. Other prophets' ministries led to repentance and restoration. The difference did not lie in the prophet but in the sovereignty of God. No one can blame Jeremiah for the failure of Judah to repent. Neither his message nor his preaching style was at fault; the fault lay in the hearts of the Judeans whose hearts were hardened.

25.5
Isa 55.6, 7;
Jer 4.1; 7.7
25.6
Deut 6.14;
8.19;
Jer 35.15
25.7
Deut 32.21;
2 Kings 17.17;
21.15;
Jer 7.19
25.9
Jer 1.15;
27.6; 18.16
25.10
Isa 24.7;
Ezek 26.13;
Eccl 12.4;
Isa 47.2
25.11
Jer 4.27;
12.11, 12;
Dan 9.2
25.12
Ezra 1.1;
Jer 29.10;
Isa 13.14;
13.19; 14.23
25.14
Jer 50.9;
51.27, 28;
50.41; 51.6,
24
25.15
Ps 75.8;
Isa 51.17
25.16
Jer 51.7;
Nah 3.11
25.17
v. 28;
Ezek 43.3
25.18
Isa 51.17;
Jer 24.9;
44.22
25.19
Jer 46.2-28
25.20
Job 1.1;
Jer 47.1-7;
Isa 20.1
25.21
Jer 49.1-22;
48.1-47
25.22
Jer 47.4;
49.23
25.23
Jer 49.7, 8;
9.26; 49.32
25.24
2 Chr 9.14
25.26
Jer 50.9
25.27
Hab 2.16;
Ezek 21.4, 5

you have neither listened nor inclined your ears to hear [5] when they said, "Turn now, everyone of you, from your evil way and wicked doings, and you will remain upon the land that the LORD has given to you and your ancestors from of old and forever; [6] do not go after other gods to serve and worship them, and do not provoke me to anger with the work of your hands. Then I will do you no harm." [7] Yet you did not listen to me, says the LORD, and so you have provoked me to anger with the work of your hands to your own harm.

[8] Therefore thus says the LORD of hosts: Because you have not obeyed my words, [9] I am going to send for all the tribes of the north, says the LORD, even for King Nebuchadrezzar of Babylon, my servant, and I will bring them against this land and its inhabitants, and against all these nations around; I will utterly destroy them, and make them an object of horror and of hissing, and an everlasting disgrace.[z] [10] And I will banish from them the sound of mirth and the sound of gladness, the voice of the bridegroom and the voice of the bride, the sound of the millstones and the light of the lamp. [11] This whole land shall become a ruin and a waste, and these nations shall serve the king of Babylon seventy years. [12] Then after seventy years are completed, I will punish the king of Babylon and that nation, the land of the Chaldeans, for their iniquity, says the LORD, making the land an everlasting waste. [13] I will bring upon that land all the words that I have uttered against it, everything written in this book, which Jeremiah prophesied against all the nations. [14] For many nations and great kings shall make slaves of them also; and I will repay them according to their deeds and the work of their hands.

b. *The cup of wrath visited on the nations*

[15] For thus the LORD, the God of Israel, said to me: Take from my hand this cup of the wine of wrath, and make all the nations to whom I send you drink it. [16] They shall drink and stagger and go out of their minds because of the sword that I am sending among them.

[17] So I took the cup from the LORD's hand, and made all the nations to whom the LORD sent me drink it: [18] Jerusalem and the towns of Judah, its kings and officials, to make them a desolation and a waste, an object of hissing and of cursing, as they are today; [19] Pharaoh king of Egypt, his servants, his officials, and all his people; [20] all the mixed people;[a] all the kings of the land of Uz; all the kings of the land of the Philistines—Ashkelon, Gaza, Ekron, and the remnant of Ashdod; [21] Edom, Moab, and the Ammonites; [22] all the kings of Tyre, all the kings of Sidon, and the kings of the coastland across the sea; [23] Dedan, Tema, Buz, and all who have shaven temples; [24] all the kings of Arabia and all the kings of the mixed peoples[a] that live in the desert; [25] all the kings of Zimri, all the kings of Elam, and all the kings of Media; [26] all the kings of the north, far and near, one after another, and all the kingdoms of the world that are on the face of the earth. And after them the king of Sheshach[b] shall drink.

[27] Then you shall say to them, Thus says the LORD of hosts, the God of Israel: Drink, get drunk and vomit, fall and rise no more, because of the sword that I am sending among you.

[28] And if they refuse to accept the cup from your hand to drink, then

---

[z] Gk Compare Syr: Heb *and everlasting desolations*   [a] Meaning of Heb uncertain   [b] *Sheshach* is a cryptogram for *Babel*, Babylon

---

25.11 God sentenced Judah to *seventy years* of captivity in Babylon. Some think the seventy years began in 605 B.C., when the first deportation occurred (2 Kings 24.10–15); others commence with 586 B.C., when the temple was destroyed and the last deportation took place. In the former view, the captivity terminated in 538 B.C., when Cyrus issued his decree for the return of the remnant to the land (Ezra 1.1–3). In the latter view, the terminal date would be 516 B.C., when the second temple was finished. Seventy, however, may simply be a round number (ten times seven). If so, it is unnecessary to press for the exact length of time the people of Judah spent in servitude in Babylon.

you shall say to them: Thus says the Lord of hosts: You must drink! ²⁹ See, I am beginning to bring disaster on the city that is called by my name, and how can you possibly avoid punishment? You shall not go unpunished, for I am summoning a sword against all the inhabitants of the earth, says the Lord of hosts.

c. The vengeance of the Lord

30 You, therefore, shall prophesy against them all these words, and say to them:

The Lord will roar from on high,
    and from his holy habitation utter his voice;
he will roar mightily against his fold,
    and shout, like those who tread grapes,
    against all the inhabitants of the earth.
31 The clamor will resound to the ends of the earth,
    for the Lord has an indictment against the nations;
he is entering into judgment with all flesh,
    and the guilty he will put to the sword,
                      says the Lord.

32 Thus says the Lord of hosts:
See, disaster is spreading
    from nation to nation,
and a great tempest is stirring
    from the farthest parts of the earth!
33 Those slain by the Lord on that day shall extend from one end of the earth to the other. They shall not be lamented, or gathered, or buried; they shall become dung on the surface of the ground.
34 Wail, you shepherds, and cry out;
    roll in ashes, you lords of the flock,
for the days of your slaughter have come — and your
    dispersions,^c
    and you shall fall like a choice vessel.
35 Flight shall fail the shepherds,
    and there shall be no escape for the lords of the flock.
36 Hark! the cry of the shepherds,
    and the wail of the lords of the flock!
For the Lord is despoiling their pasture,
37   and the peaceful folds are devastated,
    because of the fierce anger of the Lord.
38 Like a lion he has left his covert;
    for their land has become a waste
because of the cruel sword,
    and because of his fierce anger.

3. Four contests between Jeremiah and the false prophets

a. Jeremiah arrested and released: Uriah murdered

26 At the beginning of the reign of King Jehoiakim son of Josiah of Judah, this word came from the Lord: ² Thus says the Lord: Stand in the court of the Lord's house, and speak to all the cities of Judah that come to worship in the house of the Lord; speak to them all the words that I command you; do not hold back a word. ³ It may be that they will listen, all of them, and will turn from their evil way, that I may change

^c Meaning of Heb uncertain

26.1 This chapter paints a picture of Jeremiah's ministry in four segments: (1) he was a faithful preacher (vv. 1–6); (2) he was a persecuted preacher — by the priests and other prophets (vv. 7–11); (3) he was a brave preacher who kept speaking despite the persecution (vv. 12–15); (4) he was wonderfully protected by God through the officials and the elders (vv. 16–19).

my mind about the disaster that I intend to bring on them because of their evil doings. 4 You shall say to them: Thus says the Lord: If you will not listen to me, to walk in my law that I have set before you, 5 and to heed the words of my servants the prophets whom I send to you urgently — though you have not heeded — 6 then I will make this house like Shiloh, and I will make this city a curse for all the nations of the earth.

7 The priests and the prophets and all the people heard Jeremiah speaking these words in the house of the Lord. 8 And when Jeremiah had finished speaking all that the Lord had commanded him to speak to all the people, then the priests and the prophets and all the people laid hold of him, saying, "You shall die! 9 Why have you prophesied in the name of the Lord, saying, 'This house shall be like Shiloh, and this city shall be desolate, without inhabitant'?" And all the people gathered around Jeremiah in the house of the Lord.

10 When the officials of Judah heard these things, they came up from the king's house to the house of the Lord and took their seat in the entry of the New Gate of the house of the Lord. 11 Then the priests and the prophets said to the officials and to all the people, "This man deserves the sentence of death because he has prophesied against this city, as you have heard with your own ears."

12 Then Jeremiah spoke to all the officials and all the people, saying, "It is the Lord who sent me to prophesy against this house and this city all the words you have heard. 13 Now therefore amend your ways and your doings, and obey the voice of the Lord your God, and the Lord will change his mind about the disaster that he has pronounced against you. 14 But as for me, here I am in your hands. Do with me as seems good and right to you. 15 Only know for certain that if you put me to death, you will be bringing innocent blood upon yourselves and upon this city and its inhabitants, for in truth the Lord sent me to you to speak all these words in your ears."

16 Then the officials and all the people said to the priests and the prophets, "This man does not deserve the sentence of death, for he has spoken to us in the name of the Lord our God." 17 And some of the elders of the land arose and said to all the assembled people, 18 "Micah of Moresheth, who prophesied during the days of King Hezekiah of Judah, said to all the people of Judah: 'Thus says the Lord of hosts,

Zion shall be plowed as a field;
Jerusalem shall become a heap of ruins,
and the mountain of the house a wooded height.'

19 Did King Hezekiah of Judah and all Judah actually put him to death? Did he not fear the Lord and entreat the favor of the Lord, and did not the Lord change his mind about the disaster that he had pronounced against them? But we are about to bring great disaster on ourselves!"

20 There was another man prophesying in the name of the Lord, Uriah son of Shemaiah from Kiriath-jearim. He prophesied against this city and against this land in words exactly like those of Jeremiah. 21 And when King Jehoiakim, with all his warriors and all the officials, heard his words, the king sought to put him to death; but when Uriah heard of it, he was afraid and fled and escaped to Egypt. 22 Then King Jehoiakim

26.4
Lev 26.14;
Deut 28.15;
Jer 17.27;
32.23; 44.10,
23
26.5
2 Kings 9.7;
Jer 25.3, 4
26.6
1 Sam 4.10,
11;
Isa 65.15;
Jer 24.9
26.8
Jer 20.1, 2;
11.19; 18.23
26.9
Jer 9.11;
33.10
26.10
Jer 36.10
26.11
Jer 18.23;
Deut 18.20;
Mt 26.66;
Jer 38.4;
Acts 6.11-14
26.12
Jer 1.17, 18;
5.6; 46.16
26.13
Jer 7.3, 5;
18.11;
Joel 2.14;
Jon 3.9; 4.2
26.14
Jer 38.5
26.15
Prov 6.16,
17;
Jer 7.6
26.16
v. 11;
Acts 5.34-39;
23.9, 29;
25.25; 26.31
26.18
Mic 1.1;
Ps 79.1;
Mic 3.12;
Zech 8.3
26.19
2 Chr 29.6-11;
32.26;
2 Sam 24.16;
Acts 5.39
26.20
Josh 9.17;
1Sa 6.21; 7.2
26.21
1 Kings 19.2-4;
Mt 10.23, 28
26.22
Jer 36.12

26.9 Jeremiah cited *Shiloh* as an example of how God destroyed a sanctuary erected in his honor. God would also destroy the temple at Jerusalem even though the false prophets said the temple was inviolable.

26.11 Jeremiah had once again pronounced God's sentence against Judah. The religious leaders, i.e., the false priests and prophets, urged the princes and the people to sentence Jeremiah to death. Yet this threat did not deter the prophet from continuing to

speak the word of the Lord.

26.20ff Jeremiah escaped with his life. Here he records another righteous prophet, Uriah, who did suffer martyrdom. He fled to Egypt but Jehoiakim had him brought back, slew him, and cast his body into a common burial ground without respect of decency. God lets some of his people be martyred while others die a natural death (cf. Heb 11.32–38). We do not know the reasons, for God's ways are not our ways.

sent[d] Elnathan son of Achbor and men with him to Egypt, 23 and they took Uriah from Egypt and brought him to King Jehoiakim, who struck him down with the sword and threw his dead body into the burial place of the common people.

24　But the hand of Ahikam son of Shaphan was with Jeremiah so that he was not given over into the hands of the people to be put to death.

b. *Jeremiah testifies again that Nebuchadnezzar will conquer*

27 In the beginning of the reign of King Zedekiah[e] son of Josiah of Judah, this word came to Jeremiah from the LORD. 2 Thus the LORD said to me: Make yourself a yoke of straps and bars, and put them on your neck. 3 Send word[f] to the king of Edom, the king of Moab, the king of the Ammonites, the king of Tyre, and the king of Sidon by the hand of the envoys who have come to Jerusalem to King Zedekiah of Judah. 4 Give them this charge for their masters: Thus says the LORD of hosts, the God of Israel: This is what you shall say to your masters: 5 It is I who by my great power and my outstretched arm have made the earth, with the people and animals that are on the earth, and I give it to whomever I please. 6 Now I have given all these lands into the hand of King Nebuchadnezzar of Babylon, my servant, and I have given him even the wild animals of the field to serve him. 7 All the nations shall serve him and his son and his grandson, until the time of his own land comes; then many nations and great kings shall make him their slave.

8　But if any nation or kingdom will not serve this king, Nebuchadnezzar of Babylon, and put its neck under the yoke of the king of Babylon, then I will punish that nation with the sword, with famine, and with pestilence, says the LORD, until I have completed its[g] destruction by his hand. 9 You, therefore, must not listen to your prophets, your diviners, your dreamers,[h] your soothsayers, or your sorcerers, who are saying to you, "You shall not serve the king of Babylon." 10 For they are prophesying a lie to you, with the result that you will be removed far from your land; I will drive you out, and you will perish. 11 But any nation that will bring its neck under the yoke of the king of Babylon and serve him, I will leave on its own land, says the LORD, to till it and live there.

12　I spoke to King Zedekiah of Judah in the same way: Bring your necks under the yoke of the king of Babylon, and serve him and his people, and live. 13 Why should you and your people die by the sword, by famine, and by pestilence, as the LORD has spoken concerning any nation that will not serve the king of Babylon? 14 Do not listen to the words of the prophets who are telling you not to serve the king of Babylon, for they are prophesying a lie to you. 15 I have not sent them, says the LORD, but they are prophesying falsely in my name, with the result that I will

26.23
Jer 2.30

26.24
2 Kings 22.12-14;
Jer 39.14

27.1
Jer 26.1
27.2
Jer 28.10, 13
27.3
Jer 25.21, 22

27.5
Jer 10.12;
51.15;
Ps 115.15,
16;
Acts 17.26
27.6
Ezek 29.18-20;
Jer 25.9;
28.14
27.7
Jer 44.30;
46.13; 25.12;
Isa 14.4-6
27.8
Jer 38.17-19;
Ezek 17.19-21;
Jer 29.17, 18;
Ezek 14.21
27.9
Ex 22.18;
Deut 18.10;
Isa 8.19;
Mal 3.5
27.10
Jer 23.25;
8.19; 32.31
27.11
Jer 21.9
27.12
Jer 28.1
27.13
Ezek 18.31

27.14
Jer 14.14;
Ezek 13.22
27.15
Jer 23.21, 25;
6.13-15;
14.15, 16

---

d Heb adds *men to Egypt*　*e* Another reading is *Jehoiakim*　*f* Cn: Heb *send them*　*g* Heb *their*　*h* Gk Syr Vg: Heb *dreams*

26.24 *Ahikam* was a prominent official in the government. He was the father of Gedaliah, the man appointed governor of the land by Nebuchadnezzar following the destruction of Jerusalem. Ahikam protected Jeremiah from being put to death. *the son of Shaphan*, who was the royal secretary (see 2 Kings 22.12).
27.2 Jeremiah had pleaded with the people of Judah to repent by turning to God and keeping his commandments. When this failed, he urged Judah to give themselves over to the providence of God and submit voluntarily to the yoke of Nebuchadnezzar. Doing so would prevent the greater calamity. The land would not be laid waste by fire and sword and they would save their lives. Once again the counsel of Jeremiah

was rejected.
27.6,7 Nebuchadnezzar was an idolater, yet God in his providence gave him vast domains. Bad people may be used by God to do good things. Thus, Nebuchadnezzar is called God's *servant*, used by him to chastise the nations and God's own people of Judah. But Babylon's time would run out, and judgment would then fall on that wicked nation.
27.11,12 God declared that Babylon would rule; that was inescapable. And since it was the divine will, it would be better for Judah to give in — to bend and not break. Those who refused to bend would break, but if they did bend they would be preserved in their own lands.

drive you out and you will perish, you and the prophets who are prophesying to you.

16 Then I spoke to the priests and to all this people, saying, Thus says the LORD: Do not listen to the words of your prophets who are prophesying to you, saying, "The vessels of the LORD's house will soon be brought back from Babylon," for they are prophesying a lie to you. 17 Do not listen to them; serve the king of Babylon and live. Why should this city become a desolation? 18 If indeed they are prophets, and if the word of the LORD is with them, then let them intercede with the LORD of hosts, that the vessels left in the house of the LORD, in the house of the king of Judah, and in Jerusalem may not go to Babylon. 19 For thus says the LORD of hosts concerning the pillars, the sea, the stands, and the rest of the vessels that are left in this city, 20 which King Nebuchadnezzar of Babylon did not take away when he took into exile from Jerusalem to Babylon King Jeconiah son of Jehoiakim of Judah, and all the nobles of Judah and Jerusalem — 21 thus says the LORD of hosts, the God of Israel, concerning the vessels left in the house of the LORD, in the house of the king of Judah, and in Jerusalem: 22 They shall be carried to Babylon, and there they shall stay, until the day when I give attention to them, says the LORD. Then I will bring them up and restore them to this place.

c. Jeremiah exposes Hananiah and foretells his death

28 In that same year, at the beginning of the reign of King Zedekiah of Judah, in the fifth month of the fourth year, the prophet Hananiah son of Azzur, from Gibeon, spoke to me in the house of the LORD, in the presence of the priests and all the people, saying, 2 "Thus says the LORD of hosts, the God of Israel: I have broken the yoke of the king of Babylon. 3 Within two years I will bring back to this place all the vessels of the LORD's house, which King Nebuchadnezzar of Babylon took away from this place and carried to Babylon. 4 I will also bring back to this place King Jeconiah son of Jehoiakim of Judah, and all the exiles from Judah who went to Babylon, says the LORD, for I will break the yoke of the king of Babylon."

5 Then the prophet Jeremiah spoke to the prophet Hananiah in the presence of the priests and all the people who were standing in the house of the LORD; 6 and the prophet Jeremiah said, "Amen! May the LORD do so; may the LORD fulfill the words that you have prophesied, and bring back to this place from Babylon the vessels of the house of the LORD, and all the exiles. 7 But listen now to this word that I speak in your hearing and in the hearing of all the people. 8 The prophets who preceded you and me from ancient times prophesied war, famine, and pestilence against many countries and great kingdoms. 9 As for the prophet who prophesies peace, when the word of that prophet comes true, then it will be known that the LORD has truly sent the prophet."

Cross-references (margin)

27.16
2 Chr 36.7, 10;
Jer 28.3;
Dan 1.2;
v. 10
27.17
v. 13
27.18
1 Sam 7.8;
12.19, 23
27.19
2 Kings 25.13, 17;
Jer 52.17-23
27.20
2 Kings 24.14-16;
Jer 24.1
27.22
2 Kings 25.13;
2 Chr 36.18;
Jer 29.10;
32.5;
Ezra 1.7;
7.19
28.1
Jer 27.1, 3, 12;
Josh 9.3;
10.12
28.3
2 Kings 24.13;
2 Chr 36.10;
Jer 27.12
28.4
Jer 22.24, 26, 27; 27.8
28.5
v. 1
28.6
1 Kings 1.36;
Jer 11.5
28.7
1 Kings 22.28
28.8
1 Kings 14.15;
Isa 5.5-7;
Joel 1.20;
Am 1.2;
Nah 1.2
28.9
Deut 18.22

Study notes

27.16 Judah's false prophets forecasted that the temple vessels taken to Babylon would be brought back shortly. Jeremiah, however, knew that they would not. He prophesied that whatever was still left in Jerusalem would shortly be seized and taken to Babylon. It was customary for conquerers to seize the gods of the nations they defeated and to bring them back to their own places of worship. Since the temple in Jerusalem did not have idols, the vessels of the temple were taken back.

28.1ff *Hananiah* was a false prophet. The problem for the people was to determine which prophet was the true one and which the false one. They probably found Hananiah more to their liking than Jeremiah, who prophesied bad news. At this critical time, Jeremiah prophesied Hananiah's death. When it oc-

curred, the people should have been convinced, but they were not. Note that God may do one thing at one time in history and the opposite at another time, depending on circumstances at the time. When Sennacherib invaded the country (Isa 37.6,7), God protected Jerusalem and kept the temple unscathed. Now God said through Jeremiah that Nebuchadnezzar would triumph, the city would be captured, and the temple torn down (see 32.26–35).

28.4 *Jeconiah*, i.e., Jehoiachin.

28.9 In the final analysis, prophets are true prophets if and when their predictions are fulfilled. If they are not, they are false prophets and should be disregarded. By this test Hananiah proved to be a false prophet.

28.10 Hananiah affronted Jeremiah by removing

10 Then the prophet Hananiah took the yoke from the neck of the prophet Jeremiah, and broke it. 11 And Hananiah spoke in the presence of all the people, saying, "Thus says the LORD: This is how I will break the yoke of King Nebuchadnezzar of Babylon from the neck of all the nations within two years." At this, the prophet Jeremiah went his way.

12 Sometime after the prophet Hananiah had broken the yoke from the neck of the prophet Jeremiah, the word of the LORD came to Jeremiah: 13 Go, tell Hananiah, Thus says the LORD: You have broken wooden bars only to forge iron bars in place of them! 14 For thus says the LORD of hosts, the God of Israel: I have put an iron yoke on the neck of all these nations so that they may serve King Nebuchadnezzar of Babylon, and they shall indeed serve him; I have even given him the wild animals. 15 And the prophet Jeremiah said to the prophet Hananiah, "Listen, Hananiah, the LORD has not sent you, and you made this people trust in a lie. 16 Therefore thus says the LORD: I am going to send you off the face of the earth. Within this year you will be dead, because you have spoken rebellion against the LORD."

17 In that same year, in the seventh month, the prophet Hananiah died.

d. Jeremiah assures the captives they are safer in Babylon, for Jerusalem will be destroyed

29 These are the words of the letter that the prophet Jeremiah sent from Jerusalem to the remaining elders among the exiles, and to the priests, the prophets, and all the people, whom Nebuchadnezzar had taken into exile from Jerusalem to Babylon. 2 This was after King Jeconiah, and the queen mother, the court officials, the leaders of Judah and Jerusalem, the artisans, and the smiths had departed from Jerusalem. 3 The letter was sent by the hand of Elasah son of Shaphan and Gemariah son of Hilkiah, whom King Zedekiah of Judah sent to Babylon to King Nebuchadnezzar of Babylon. It said: 4 Thus says the LORD of hosts, the God of Israel, to all the exiles whom I have sent into exile from Jerusalem to Babylon: 5 Build houses and live in them; plant gardens and eat what they produce. 6 Take wives and have sons and daughters; take wives for your sons, and give your daughters in marriage, that they may bear sons and daughters; multiply there, and do not decrease. 7 But seek the welfare of the city where I have sent you into exile, and pray to the LORD on its behalf, for in its welfare you will find your welfare. 8 For thus says the LORD of hosts, the God of Israel: Do not let the prophets and the diviners who are among you deceive you, and do not listen to the dreams that they dream,[i] 9 for it is a lie that they are prophesying to you in my name; I did not send them, says the LORD.

10 For thus says the LORD: Only when Babylon's seventy years are completed will I visit you, and I will fulfill to you my promise and bring you back to this place. 11 For surely I know the plans I have for you, says

---

28.10
Jer 27.2
28.11
Jer 14.14;
27.10

28.12
Jer 1.2

28.13
Ps 107.16;
Isa 45.2
28.14
Deut 28.48;
Jer 27.6-8;
25.11
28.15
Jer 29.31;
Ezek 13.22
28.16
Deut 6.15;
13.5;
Jer 29.32

29.1
vv. 25, 29

29.2
2 Kings 24.12-16;
Jer 22.24-28;
24.1; 28.4

29.4ff
Isa 10.5, 6;
Jer 24.5
29.6
Jer 16.2-4
29.7
Ezra 6.10;
Dan 4.19;
1 Tim 2.2
29.8
Jer 27.9;
14.14; 23.21,
25, 27
29.9
Jer 27.15;
v. 31
29.10
2 Chr 36.21,
22;
Jer 25.12;
27.22;
Dan 9.2
29.11
Isa 40.9-11;
Jer 30.18-22;
31.17

---

i Cn: Heb *your dreams that you cause to dream*

---

the wooden yoke from his neck and breaking it. Jeremiah did not protest, revile him, or use force to prevent him from doing this. He suffered in silence. But in v. 19 the judgment of God was pronounced against this false prophet; he died that very year.
29.4ff God had Jeremiah send a letter to the prisoners in Babylon in which he countered two wrong notions. (1) False prophets had told them the captivity would be short. Jeremiah said they would be there a long time and they should build houses, marry, raise

families, and pray for the land to which they were exiled. (2) Discouragement might make them think the captivity would last forever. It would indeed be long — seventy years (v. 10) — but when the people sought God with their whole hearts (v. 13) they would find him. Sin had brought on the exile, but when sin was repented of, confessed, and forsaken, God's purpose would be realized and they would return to the land.

the LORD, plans for your welfare and not for harm, to give you a future with hope. 12 Then when you call upon me and come and pray to me, I will hear you. 13 When you search for me, you will find me; if you seek me with all your heart, 14 I will let you find me, says the LORD, and I will restore your fortunes and gather you from all the nations and all the places where I have driven you, says the LORD, and I will bring you back to the place from which I sent you into exile.

15 Because you have said, "The LORD has raised up prophets for us in Babylon,"— 16 Thus says the LORD concerning the king who sits on the throne of David, and concerning all the people who live in this city, your kinsfolk who did not go out with you into exile: 17 Thus says the LORD of hosts, I am going to let loose on them sword, famine, and pestilence, and I will make them like rotten figs that are so bad they cannot be eaten. 18 I will pursue them with the sword, with famine, and with pestilence, and will make them a horror to all the kingdoms of the earth, to be an object of cursing, and horror, and hissing, and a derision among all the nations where I have driven them, 19 because they did not heed my words, says the LORD, when I persistently sent to you my servants the prophets, but theyʲ would not listen, says the LORD. 20 But now, all you exiles whom I sent away from Jerusalem to Babylon, hear the word of the LORD: 21 Thus says the LORD of hosts, the God of Israel, concerning Ahab son of Kolaiah and Zedekiah son of Maaseiah, who are prophesying a lie to you in my name: I am going to deliver them into the hand of King Nebuchadrezzar of Babylon, and he shall kill them before your eyes. 22 And on account of them this curse shall be used by all the exiles from Judah in Babylon: "The LORD make you like Zedekiah and Ahab, whom the king of Babylon roasted in the fire," 23 because they have perpetrated outrage in Israel and have committed adultery with their neighbors' wives, and have spoken in my name lying words that I did not command them; I am the one who knows and bears witness, says the LORD.

24 To Shemaiah of Nehelam you shall say: 25 Thus says the LORD of hosts, the God of Israel: In your own name you sent a letter to all the people who are in Jerusalem, and to the priest Zephaniah son of Maaseiah, and to all the priests, saying, 26 The LORD himself has made you priest instead of the priest Jehoiada, so that there may be officers in the house of the LORD to control any madman who plays the prophet, to put him in the stocks and the collar. 27 So now why have you not rebuked Jeremiah of Anathoth who plays the prophet for you? 28 For he has actually sent to us in Babylon, saying, "It will be a long time; build houses and live in them, and plant gardens and eat what they produce."

29 The priest Zephaniah read this letter in the hearing of the prophet Jeremiah. 30 Then the word of the LORD came to Jeremiah: 31 Send to all the exiles, saying, Thus says the LORD concerning Shemaiah of Nehelam: Because Shemaiah has prophesied to you, though I did not send him, and has led you to trust in a lie, 32 therefore thus says the LORD: I am going to punish Shemaiah of Nehelam and his descendants; he shall not have anyone living among this people to seeᵏ the good that I am going to do to my people, says the LORD, for he has spoken rebellion against the LORD.

29.12 Ps 50.15; Jer 33.3; Ps 145.19
29.13 1 Chr 22.19; 2 Chr 22.9; Jer 24.7
29.14 Deut 30.1-10; Jer 30.3; Isa 43.5, 6; Jer 3.14
29.16 Jer 38.2, 3, 17-23
29.17 Jer 27.8; 32.24; 24.3, 8-10
29.18 Isa 65.15; Jer 42.18; 25.9
29.19 Jer 6.19; 25.4; 26.5
29.20 Jer 24.5
29.21 vv. 8, 9
29.22 Isa 65.15; Dan 3.6
29.23 2Sa 13.12; Prov 5.21; Jer 16.17
29.24 vv. 31, 32
29.25 vv. 1, 29; 2 Kings 25.18; Jer 21.1
29.26 Jer 20.1; 2 Kings 9.11; Acts 26.24; Jer 20.2
29.28 vv. 1, 5, 10
29.29 v. 25
29.31 vv. 20, 24; Jer 14.14, 15; 28.15
29.32 Jer 36.31; 22.30; 17.6; 28.16

_j_ Syr: Heb _you_   _k_ Gk: Heb _and he shall not see_

29.24 There was no lack of false prophets in Judah. Here *Shemaiah* opposed Jeremiah; this led to the prophecy by Jeremiah that Shemaiah and his family would perish so that not one of them would be alive to witness the return of Judah to the land after the captivity. *of Nehelam.* Nehelem was Shemaiah's home town, the name of which means "Dreamer." This seems to be another of the frequent puns in the prophetic books.

B. The glorious future of latter-day Israel and their new covenant

1. Sermon III: ultimate deliverance and blessing of the reunited kingdom

a. Israel restored; the heathen judged

30 The word that came to Jeremiah from the LORD: 2 Thus says the LORD, the God of Israel: Write in a book all the words that I have spoken to you. 3 For the days are surely coming, says the LORD, when I will restore the fortunes of my people, Israel and Judah, says the LORD, and I will bring them back to the land that I gave to their ancestors and they shall take possession of it.

4 These are the words that the LORD spoke concerning Israel and Judah:

5 Thus says the LORD:
We have heard a cry of panic,
of terror, and no peace.
6 Ask now, and see,
can a man bear a child?
Why then do I see every man
with his hands on his loins like a woman in labor?
Why has every face turned pale?
7 Alas! that day is so great
there is none like it;
it is a time of distress for Jacob;
yet he shall be rescued from it.

8 On that day, says the LORD of hosts, I will break the yoke from off his*l* neck, and I will burst his*l* bonds, and strangers shall no more make a servant of him. 9 But they shall serve the LORD their God and David their king, whom I will raise up for them.

10 But as for you, have no fear, my servant Jacob, says the LORD,
and do not be dismayed, O Israel;
for I am going to save you from far away,
and your offspring from the land of their captivity.
Jacob shall return and have quiet and ease,
and no one shall make him afraid.
11 For I am with you, says the LORD, to save you;
I will make an end of all the nations
among which I scattered you,
but of you I will not make an end.
I will chastise you in just measure,
and I will by no means leave you unpunished.

12 For thus says the LORD:
Your hurt is incurable,
your wound is grievous.
13 There is no one to uphold your cause,
no medicine for your wound,
no healing for you.

l Cn: Heb *your*

30.2
Jer 25.13;
Hab 2.2
30.3
Jer 29.10;
Ps 53.6;
Zeph 3.20;
Jer 16.15;
Ezek 20.42

30.5
Isa 5.30;
Am 5.16-18

30.6
Jer 4.31; 6.24

30.7
Isa 2.12;
Joel 2.11;
Lam 1.12;
Jer 2.27, 28;
v. 10
30.8
Isa 9.4;
Jer 27.2;
Ezek 34.27
30.9
Isa 55.3, 4;
Ezek 34.23;
37.24;
Hos 3.5;
Lk 1.69;
Acts 2.30;
13.23
30.10
Isa 43.5;
44.2;
Jer 46.27, 28;
Isa 60.4;
Jer 33.16;
Mic 4.4
30.11
Jer 46.28;
4.27; 10.24

30.12
v. 15;
Jer 15.18

30.13
Jer 14.19;
46.11

30.2,3 Jeremiah was not only a prophet of gloom and doom. Here he was ordered to put the word of God into a book, promising that God would restore his people to the land from which they had been taken. When they read the book they would know how every word of promise had been fulfilled to the letter and how great was the truth of God, which cannot be broken, annulled, or destroyed.
30.9 *David their king.* This refers to the Messiah, David's greater Son, whom God would raise up for them.

14 All your lovers have forgotten you;
  they care nothing for you;
for I have dealt you the blow of an enemy,
  the punishment of a merciless foe,
because your guilt is great,
  because your sins are so numerous.

15 Why do you cry out over your hurt?
  Your pain is incurable.
Because your guilt is great,
  because your sins are so numerous,
I have done these things to you.

16 Therefore all who devour you shall be devoured,
  and all your foes, everyone of them, shall go into captivity;
those who plunder you shall be plundered,
  and all who prey on you I will make a prey.

17 For I will restore health to you,
  and your wounds I will heal,
            says the LORD,
because they have called you an outcast:
  "It is Zion; no one cares for her!"

18 Thus says the LORD:
I am going to restore the fortunes of the tents of Jacob,
  and have compassion on his dwellings;
the city shall be rebuilt upon its mound,
  and the citadel set on its rightful site.

19 Out of them shall come thanksgiving,
  and the sound of merrymakers.
I will make them many, and they shall not be few;
  I will make them honored, and they shall not be disdained.

20 Their children shall be as of old,
  their congregation shall be established before me;
and I will punish all who oppress them.

21 Their prince shall be one of their own,
  their ruler shall come from their midst;
I will bring him near, and he shall approach me,
  for who would otherwise dare to approach me?
            says the LORD.

22 And you shall be my people,
  and I will be your God.

23 Look, the storm of the LORD!
  Wrath has gone forth,
a whirling^m tempest;
  it will burst upon the head of the wicked.

24 The fierce anger of the LORD will not turn back
  until he has executed and accomplished
  the intents of his mind.
In the latter days you will understand this.

b. *Restoration and blessing of both Ephraim and Judah*

31 At that time, says the LORD, I will be the God of all the families of Israel, and they shall be my people.

^m One Ms: Meaning of MT uncertain

31.1ff This chapter divides into three parts: (1) vv. 1–22 concern Ephraim or the northern kingdom, which was destroyed by Sennacherib in the eighth century B.C.; (2) vv. 23–26 relate to Judah or the southern kingdom, whose people were in Babylon; (3) vv. 27–40 speak about both kingdoms as one unity.

2 Thus says the LORD:
The people who survived the sword
  found grace in the wilderness;
when Israel sought for rest,

31.2
Num 14.20;
Josh 1.13;
Isa 63.14

3   the LORD appeared to him[n] from far away.[o]
I have loved you with an everlasting love;
  therefore I have continued my faithfulness to you.

31.3
Deut 7.8;
Ps 25.6;
Hos 11.4

4 Again I will build you, and you shall be built,
  O virgin Israel!
Again you shall take[p] your tambourines,
  and go forth in the dance of the merrymakers.

31.4
Jer 30.19

5 Again you shall plant vineyards
  on the mountains of Samaria;
the planters shall plant,
  and shall enjoy the fruit.

31.5
Isa 65.21;
Jer 50.19

6 For there shall be a day when sentinels will call
  in the hill country of Ephraim:
"Come, let us go up to Zion,
  to the LORD our God."

31.6
Isa 2.3;
Mic 4.2

7 For thus says the LORD:
Sing aloud with gladness for Jacob,
  and raise shouts for the chief of the nations;
proclaim, give praise, and say,
  "Save, O LORD, your people,
  the remnant of Israel."

31.7
Ps 14.7;
Deut 28.13;
Isa 61.9;
Ps 28.9;
Isa 37.31

8 See, I am going to bring them from the land of the north,
  and gather them from the farthest parts of the earth,
among them the blind and the lame,
  those with child and those in labor, together;
a great company, they shall return here.

31.8
Jer 3.18;
23.8;
Isa 43.6;
Ezek 20.34,
41;
Isa 42.16;
40.11

9 With weeping they shall come,
  and with consolations[q] I will lead them back,
I will let them walk by brooks of water,
  in a straight path in which they shall not stumble;
for I have become a father to Israel,
  and Ephraim is my firstborn.

31.9
Isa 43.19;
49.10, 11;
64.8;
Jer 3.4, 19

10 Hear the word of the LORD, O nations,
  and declare it in the coastlands far away;
say, "He who scattered Israel will gather him,
  and will keep him as a shepherd a flock."

31.10
Isa 66.19;
Jer 50.19;
Isa 40.11

11 For the LORD has ransomed Jacob,
  and has redeemed him from hands too strong for him.

31.11
Isa 44.23;
48.20;
Jer 50.34;
Isa 49.24, 25

12 They shall come and sing aloud on the height of Zion,
  and they shall be radiant over the goodness of the LORD,
over the grain, the wine, and the oil,
  and over the young of the flock and the herd;
their life shall become like a watered garden,
  and they shall never languish again.

31.12
Ezek 17.23;
Hos 3.5;
Isa 58.11;
35.10; 65.19;
Rev 21.4

13 Then shall the young women rejoice in the dance,
  and the young men and the old shall be merry.
I will turn their mourning into joy,
  I will comfort them, and give them gladness for sorrow.

31.13
Ps 30.11;
Zech 8.4, 5;
Isa 61.3;
51.11

---

n Gk: Heb me   o Or to him long ago   p Or adorn yourself with   q Gk Compare Vg Tg: Heb *supplications*

31.9 Ephraim and Manasseh were the sons of Joseph. Ephraim (the northern kingdom) was not worthy to be called a son because of his sins, but God would acknowledge him as a firstborn, as one belonging to him and never again a servant of humans.

31.14
v. 25;
Jer 50.19

14 I will give the priests their fill of fatness,
  and my people shall be satisfied with my bounty,
                                    says the LORD.

31.15
Mt 2.17, 18;
Gen 37.35;
Ps 77.2;
Jer 10.20

15 Thus says the LORD:
A voice is heard in Ramah,
  lamentation and bitter weeping.
Rachel is weeping for her children;
  she refuses to be comforted for her children,
  because they are no more.

31.16
Isa 25.8;
30.19;
Heb 6.10;
vv. 4, 5;
Jer 30.3;
Ezek 11.17

16 Thus says the LORD:
Keep your voice from weeping,
  and your eyes from tears;
for there is a reward for your work,
                                    says the LORD:
  they shall come back from the land of the enemy;

31.17
Jer 29.11

17 there is hope for your future,
                                    says the LORD:
  your children shall come back to their own country.

31.18
Job 5.17;
Ps 94.12;
Hos 4.16;
Ps 80.3, 7,
19;
Jer 17.14;
Acts 3.26
31.19
Ezek 36.31;
Zech 12.10;
Ezek 21.12;
Jer 3.25;
Ps 25.7;
Jer 22.21

18 Indeed I heard Ephraim pleading:
"You disciplined me, and I took the discipline;
  I was like a calf untrained.
Bring me back, let me come back,
  for you are the LORD my God.
19 For after I had turned away I repented;
  and after I was discovered, I struck my thigh;
I was ashamed, and I was dismayed
  because I bore the disgrace of my youth."

31.20
Hos 11.8;
Gen 43.30;
Isa 63.15;
55.7;
Hos 14.4

20 Is Ephraim my dear son?
  Is he the child I delight in?
As often as I speak against him,
  I still remember him.
Therefore I am deeply moved for him;
  I will surely have mercy on him,
                                    says the LORD.

31.21
Jer 6.16;
50.5;
Isa 48.20;
v. 4

21 Set up road markers for yourself,
  make yourself signposts;
consider well the highway,
  the road by which you went.
Return, O virgin Israel,
  return to these your cities.

31.22
Jer 2.18, 23,
36; 49.4

22 How long will you waver,
  O faithless daughter?
For the LORD has created a new thing on the earth:
  a woman encompasses[r] a man.

31.23
Jer 30.18;
32.44;
Isa 1.26;
Jer 50.7;
Zech 8.3

23 Thus says the LORD of hosts, the God of Israel: Once more they

r Meaning of Heb uncertain

31.15 *Rachel* was the mother of Joseph (and the grandmother of Ephraim and Manasseh) and Benjamin. She is pictured as weeping because her descendants had been taken into exile. The northern kingdom, many of whom were descended from Rachel, was captured and dispossessed by the Assyrians in 722 B.C. Vv. 16,17 indicate that they would return to their land later on. See also Mt 2.17, where Matthew quotes v. 15 with respect to Herod's slaughter of the innocents at the time of Christ's birth.
31.18 Ephraim (representing all of the ten tribes) repented and turned to God. The people glorified God singlemindedly and with one voice. They acknowledged God as their God and prayed for restoration, and God answered this prayer.

shall use these words in the land of Judah and in its towns when I restore their fortunes:

"The LORD bless you, O abode of righteousness,
    O holy hill!"

24 And Judah and all its towns shall live there together, and the farmers and those who wander[s] with their flocks.

25   I will satisfy the weary,
    and all who are faint I will replenish.

26   Thereupon I awoke and looked, and my sleep was pleasant to me.

27   The days are surely coming, says the LORD, when I will sow the house of Israel and the house of Judah with the seed of humans and the seed of animals. 28 And just as I have watched over them to pluck up and break down, to overthrow, destroy, and bring evil, so I will watch over them to build and to plant, says the LORD. 29 In those days they shall no longer say:

"The parents have eaten sour grapes,
    and the children's teeth are set on edge."

30 But all shall die for their own sins; the teeth of everyone who eats sour grapes shall be set on edge.

31   The days are surely coming, says the LORD, when I will make a new covenant with the house of Israel and the house of Judah. 32 It will not be like the covenant that I made with their ancestors when I took them by the hand to bring them out of the land of Egypt — a covenant that they broke, though I was their husband,[t] says the LORD. 33 But this is the covenant that I will make with the house of Israel after those days, says the LORD: I will put my law within them, and I will write it on their hearts; and I will be their God, and they shall be my people. 34 No longer shall they teach one another, or say to each other, "Know the LORD," for they shall all know me, from the least of them to the greatest, says the LORD; for I will forgive their iniquity, and remember their sin no more.

35   Thus says the LORD,
  who gives the sun for light by day
    and the fixed order of the moon and the stars for light
      by night,
  who stirs up the sea so that its waves roar —
    the LORD of hosts is his name:

36   If this fixed order were ever to cease
    from my presence, says the LORD,
  then also the offspring of Israel would cease
    to be a nation before me forever.

37   Thus says the LORD:

[s] Cn Compare Syr Vg Tg: Heb *and they shall wander*   [t] Or *master*

31.24 Jer 33.12, 13
31.25 Mt 5.6
31.27 Ezek 36.9-11; Hos 2.23
31.28 Jer 44.27; 1.10
31.29 Ezek 18.2
31.30 Deut 24.16; Ezek 18.4, 20; Gal 6.5, 7
31.31 Jer 32.40; Ezek 37.26; Heb 8.8-12
31.32 Ex 19.5; 24.6-8; Deut 1.31; Jer 11.7, 8; 3.14
31.33 Jer 32.40; 24.7; 32.38
31.34 1 Thess 4.9; Isa 54.13; Jn 6.45; Mic 7.18; Rom 11.27
31.35 Gen 1.16; Ps 19.1-6; Jer 10.16
31.36 Isa 54.9, 10; Jer 33.20; Am 9.8, 9
31.37 Jer 33.22-26

31.26 When Jeremiah perceived that both Ephraim and Judah would be brought back by God and be blessed, he was overcome with joy. His sleep was sweet because his heart's yearning would be brought to pass even though he would not live to see it.

31.29,30 *The parents have eaten sour grapes, and the children's teeth are set on edge.* This proverb was used by God's people to complain that they were suffering for the sins of their ancestors. To some extent this had been true. God was now saying that even though he would deliver nations, he would not by that act overlook an individual's sins. Children would not be held responsible for their fathers' sins; each one would bear his or her own sin.

31.31 Here Jeremiah speaks of the new contract or covenant between God and his people. The old covenant of Sinai focused on keeping the law, a document

written on stone; the new covenant would be written on human hearts. This does not mean the new covenant was totally divorced from the old contract. Rather, it gave a clearer and fuller disclosure of God's dealings with humans than was apparent in the old. It would make indisputably clear that mortals could not earn salvation by their own good works, but only by the grace of God. Both Rom 11.26–36 and Heb 8.8–12 refer to this covenant.

31.33 *on their hearts,* i.e., rather than upon tablets of stone, as were the ten commandments. Judah's sin had earlier been described as written on their hearts (17.1). This change seems to indicate an experience very much like the new birth, in which God's people would receive a new heart. God went on to promise to be their God, and they would be his people.

If the heavens above can be measured,
  and the foundations of the earth below can be explored,
then I will reject all the offspring of Israel
  because of all they have done,

says the LORD.

31.38
Neh 3.1;
Zech 14.10;
2 Kings 14.13
31.40
Jer 7.32;
2 Sam 15.23;
2 Kings 23.6;
Joel 3.17

38 The days are surely coming, says the LORD, when the city shall be rebuilt for the LORD from the tower of Hananel to the Corner Gate. 39 And the measuring line shall go out farther, straight to the hill Gareb, and shall then turn to Goah. 40 The whole valley of the dead bodies and the ashes, and all the fields as far as the Wadi Kidron, to the corner of the Horse Gate toward the east, shall be sacred to the LORD. It shall never again be uprooted or overthrown.

2. *Sermon IV: the glorious restoration of Israel after the captivity*

a. *Jeremiah's land purchase a sign of restoration to the land*

32.1
2 Kings 25.1,
2;
Jer 39.1; 25.1
32.2
Neh 3.25;
Jer 37.21;
39.14
32.3
2 Kings 6.31,
32;
Jer 26.8, 9;
34.2, 3
32.4
Jer 38.18, 23;
39.5
32.5
Jer 39.7;
27.22; 34.4,
5; 21.4
32.7
Jer 1.1;
Lev 25.25;
Ruth 4.4
32.8
vv. 2, 7, 25

32 The word that came to Jeremiah from the LORD in the tenth year of King Zedekiah of Judah, which was the eighteenth year of Nebuchadrezzar. 2 At that time the army of the king of Babylon was besieging Jerusalem, and the prophet Jeremiah was confined in the court of the guard that was in the palace of the king of Judah, 3 where King Zedekiah of Judah had confined him. Zedekiah had said, "Why do you prophesy and say: Thus says the LORD: I am going to give this city into the hand of the king of Babylon, and he shall take it; 4 King Zedekiah of Judah shall not escape out of the hands of the Chaldeans, but shall surely be given into the hands of the king of Babylon, and shall speak with him face to face and see him eye to eye; 5 and he shall take Zedekiah to Babylon, and there he shall remain until I attend to him, says the LORD; though you fight against the Chaldeans, you shall not succeed?"

6 Jeremiah said, The word of the LORD came to me: 7 Hanamel son of your uncle Shallum is going to come to you and say, "Buy my field that is at Anathoth, for the right of redemption by purchase is yours." 8 Then my cousin Hanamel came to me in the court of the guard, in accordance with the word of the LORD, and said to me, "Buy my field that is at Anathoth in the land of Benjamin, for the right of possession and redemption is yours; buy it for yourself." Then I knew that this was the word of the LORD.

32.9
Gen 23.16;
24.22;
Ex 21.32
32.10
Ruth 4.1, 9
32.11
Lk 2.27
32.12
Jer 36.4;
51.59
32.14
vv. 10-12
32.15
Jer 33.12, 13;
Zech 3.10

9 And I bought the field at Anathoth from my cousin Hanamel, and weighed out the money to him, seventeen shekels of silver. 10 I signed the deed, sealed it, got witnesses, and weighed the money on scales. 11 Then I took the sealed deed of purchase, containing the terms and conditions, and the open copy; 12 and I gave the deed of purchase to Baruch son of Neriah son of Mahseiah, in the presence of my cousin Hanamel, in the presence of the witnesses who signed the deed of purchase, and in the presence of all the Judeans who were sitting in the court of the guard. 13 In their presence I charged Baruch, saying, 14 Thus says the LORD of hosts, the God of Israel: Take these deeds, both this sealed deed of purchase and this open deed, and put them in an earthenware jar, in order that they may last for a long time. 15 For thus says the LORD of hosts, the God of Israel: Houses and fields and vineyards shall again be bought in this land.

32.6,7 We do not know how the Holy Spirit conveyed the knowledge of God's will to Jeremiah. But observe that this revelation was followed by outward, external, confirming evidence (see v. 8). So Jeremiah said: "Then I knew that this was the word of the LORD." The purpose of the purchase of land was to certify that God would restore his people to the promised land after the exile, even though Jeremiah himself would not be among the returnees.

32.14 *an earthenware jar.* This guaranteed the preservation of the deeds. The Dead Sea Scrolls, for example, were preserved for two thousand years in large jars like this.

16 After I had given the deed of purchase to Baruch son of Neriah, I prayed to the Lord, saying: 17 Ah Lord God! It is you who made the heavens and the earth by your great power and by your outstretched arm! Nothing is too hard for you. 18 You show steadfast love to the thousandth generation,*u* but repay the guilt of parents into the laps of their children after them, O great and mighty God whose name is the Lord of hosts, 19 great in counsel and mighty in deed; whose eyes are open to all the ways of mortals, rewarding all according to their ways and according to the fruit of their doings. 20 You showed signs and wonders in the land of Egypt, and to this day in Israel and among all humankind, and have made yourself a name that continues to this very day. 21 You brought your people Israel out of the land of Egypt with signs and wonders, with a strong hand and outstretched arm, and with great terror; 22 and you gave them this land, which you swore to their ancestors to give them, a land flowing with milk and honey; 23 and they entered and took possession of it. But they did not obey your voice or follow your law; of all you commanded them to do, they did nothing. Therefore you have made all these disasters come upon them. 24 See, the siege ramps have been cast up against the city to take it, and the city, faced with sword, famine, and pestilence, has been given into the hands of the Chaldeans who are fighting against it. What you spoke has happened, as you yourself can see. 25 Yet you, O Lord God, have said to me, "Buy the field for money and get witnesses" — though the city has been given into the hands of the Chaldeans.

26 The word of the Lord came to Jeremiah: 27 See, I am the Lord, the God of all flesh; is anything too hard for me? 28 Therefore, thus says the Lord: I am going to give this city into the hands of the Chaldeans and into the hand of King Nebuchadrezzar of Babylon, and he shall take it. 29 The Chaldeans who are fighting against this city shall come, set it on fire, and burn it, with the houses on whose roofs offerings have been made to Baal and libations have been poured out to other gods, to provoke me to anger. 30 For the people of Israel and the people of Judah have done nothing but evil in my sight from their youth; the people of Israel have done nothing but provoke me to anger by the work of their hands, says the Lord. 31 This city has aroused my anger and wrath, from the day it was built until this day, so that I will remove it from my sight 32 because of all the evil of the people of Israel and the people of Judah that they did to provoke me to anger — they, their kings and their officials, their priests and their prophets, the citizens of Judah and the inhabitants of Jerusalem. 33 They have turned their backs to me, not their faces; though I have taught them persistently, they would not listen and accept correction. 34 They set up their abominations in the house that bears my name, and defiled it. 35 They built the high places of Baal in the valley of the son of Hinnom, to offer up their sons and daughters to Molech, though I did not command them, nor did it enter my mind that they should do this abomination, causing Judah to sin.

36 Now therefore thus says the Lord, the God of Israel, concerning this city of which you say, "It is being given into the hand of the king of Babylon by the sword, by famine, and by pestilence": 37 See, I am going

u Or *to thousands*

Cross-references (right margin):

32.17 Jer 1.6; 4.10; 2 Kings 19.15; Isa 40.26-28
32.18 Ex 34.7; Jer 20.11; 10.16
32.19 Isa 28.29; Jer 16.17; 17.10
32.20 Ex 9.16; Dan 9.15
32.21 Ex 6.6; 1 Chr 17.21
32.22 Ex 3.8, 17; Jer 11.5
32.23 Jer 2.7; 26.4; 44.10; Neh 9.26; Jer 11.8; Dan 9.10-14
32.24 Jer 33.4; Ezek 14.21; Deut 4.26; Zech 1.6
32.25 vv. 8, 24
32.27 Num 16.22
32.28 Jer 34.2, 3
32.29 Jer 21.10; 37.8, 10; 52.13; 19.13
32.30 Jer 2.7; 22.21; 25.7
32.31 2 Kings 23.27; 24.3
32.32 Isa 1.4-6; Dan 9.8
32.33 Jer 2.27; Ezek 8.16; Jer 35.15
32.34 Jer 7.30, 31; Ezek 8.5, 6
32.35 Jer 7.31; 19.5; Lev 18.21; 1 Kings 11.33
32.37 Deut 30.3; Jer 23.3, 6; Zech 14.11

32.16ff Jeremiah went before God in prayer. He had purchased some land; but since he knew the destruction of Jerusalem was at hand, he asked God why he should have bought the land. God responded to Jeremiah's question (vv. 26ff). His people were guilty and judgment would come through the king of Babylon, but God was gracious. He would someday restore his people to the land from which he had dispossessed them and they would once again buy and sell land (vv.

37ff); in this way, Jeremiah's purchase certified God's promise of the restoration.
32.19 God sovereignly orders and works out his purposes and plans. They are wonderful and excellent (Isa 28.29), great and mighty (32.19), unchangeable (Heb 6.16–18), eternally certain (Eph 3.11), and unbreakable or that which cannot be annulled (Isa 14.27). Evildoers neither understand God's plans and purposes nor do they respect or accept them.

to gather them from all the lands to which I drove them in my anger and my wrath and in great indignation; I will bring them back to this place, and I will settle them in safety. 38 They shall be my people, and I will be their God. 39 I will give them one heart and one way, that they may fear me for all time, for their own good and the good of their children after them. 40 I will make an everlasting covenant with them, never to draw back from doing good to them; and I will put the fear of me in their hearts, so that they may not turn from me. 41 I will rejoice in doing good to them, and I will plant them in this land in faithfulness, with all my heart and all my soul.

42 For thus says the LORD: Just as I have brought all this great disaster upon this people, so I will bring upon them all the good fortune that I now promise them. 43 Fields shall be bought in this land of which you are saying, It is a desolation, without human beings or animals; it has been given into the hands of the Chaldeans. 44 Fields shall be bought for money, and deeds shall be signed and sealed and witnessed, in the land of Benjamin, in the places around Jerusalem, and in the cities of Judah, of the hill country, of the Shephelah, and of the Negeb; for I will restore their fortunes, says the LORD.

b. Beyond the exile: restoration of Jerusalem under the righteous Branch

33 The word of the LORD came to Jeremiah a second time, while he was still confined in the court of the guard: 2 Thus says the LORD who made the earth,^{v} the LORD who formed it to establish it — the LORD is his name: 3 Call to me and I will answer you, and will tell you great and hidden things that you have not known. 4 For thus says the LORD, the God of Israel, concerning the houses of this city and the houses of the kings of Judah that were torn down to make a defense against the siege ramps and before the sword:^{w} 5 The Chaldeans are coming in to fight^x and to fill them with the dead bodies of those whom I shall strike down in my anger and my wrath, for I have hidden my face from this city because of all their wickedness. 6 I am going to bring it recovery and healing; I will heal them and reveal to them abundance^w of prosperity and security. 7 I will restore the fortunes of Judah and the fortunes of Israel, and rebuild them as they were at first. 8 I will cleanse them from all the guilt of their sin against me, and I will forgive all the guilt of their sin and rebellion against me. 9 And this city^y shall be to me a name of joy, a praise and a glory before all the nations of the earth who shall hear of all the good that I do for them; they shall fear and tremble because of all the good and all the prosperity I provide for it.

10 Thus says the LORD: In this place of which you say, "It is a waste without human beings or animals," in the towns of Judah and the streets of Jerusalem that are desolate, without inhabitants, human or animal, there shall once more be heard 11 the voice of mirth and the voice of gladness, the voice of the bridegroom and the voice of the bride, the voices of those who sing, as they bring thank offerings to the house of the LORD:

"Give thanks to the LORD of hosts,
　　for the LORD is good,
　　for his steadfast love endures forever!"

For I will restore the fortunes of the land as at first, says the LORD.

Marginal cross-references (left column):

32.38 Jer 30.22; 31.33
32.39 Jer 24.7; Ezek 11.19, 20; 37.25
32.40 Isa 55.3; 31.31, 33; Ezek 39.29
32.41 Deut 30.9; Zeph 3.17; Am 9.15
32.42 Jer 31.28; Zech 8.14, 15; Jer 33.14
32.43 vv. 15, 25
32.44 Jer 17.26; 33.7, 11, 26

33.1 Jer 32.2, 3
33.2 Jer 10.16; 51.19; Ex 15.3
33.3 Ps 50.15; Jer 29.12; 32.17, 27; Isa 48.6
33.4 Jer 32.13, 14, 24
33.5 Isa 8.17; Jer 21.10
33.6 Isa 66.12; Gal 5.22, 23
33.7 Jer 32.44; Am 9.14, 15
33.8 Mic 7.18; Zech 13.1; Heb 9.13, 14
33.9 Isa 62.7; Jer 13.11; Isa 60.5
33.10 Jer 32.43; 26.9; 34.22
33.11 Isa 35.10; 51.3, 11; 1 Chr 16.8, 34; 2 Chr 5.13; Lev 7.12

---

^{v} Gk: Heb *it*　^{w} Meaning of Heb uncertain　^{x} Cn: Heb *They are coming in to fight against the Chaldeans*
^{y} Heb *And it*

33.3 Again and again the Scriptures teach that God is willing and ready to answer those who turn to him in faith. In this instance Jeremiah looked beyond the captivity, foresaw the return to the land, and promised that Jerusalem would come to life again. God's people would once more experience the divine bless- ings of abundance, prosperity, and security. The impossible would become a reality because God is God. **33.11** *as they bring thank offerings.* Jeremiah seems to refer to spiritual sacrifices, not animal offerings, i.e., thanksgivings made with the mouth, or what Hosea calls "the fruit of our lips" (Hos 14.2).

12 Thus says the LORD of hosts: In this place that is waste, without human beings or animals, and in all its towns there shall again be pasture for shepherds resting their flocks. **13** In the towns of the hill country, of the Shephelah, and of the Negeb, in the land of Benjamin, the places around Jerusalem, and in the towns of Judah, flocks shall again pass under the hands of the one who counts them, says the LORD.

14 The days are surely coming, says the LORD, when I will fulfill the promise I made to the house of Israel and the house of Judah. **15** In those days and at that time I will cause a righteous Branch to spring up for David; and he shall execute justice and righteousness in the land. **16** In those days Judah will be saved and Jerusalem will live in safety. And this is the name by which it will be called: "The LORD is our righteousness."

17 For thus says the LORD: David shall never lack a man to sit on the throne of the house of Israel, **18** and the levitical priests shall never lack a man in my presence to offer burnt offerings, to make grain offerings, and to make sacrifices for all time.

19 The word of the LORD came to Jeremiah: **20** Thus says the LORD: If any of you could break my covenant with the day and my covenant with the night, so that day and night would not come at their appointed time, **21** only then could my covenant with my servant David be broken, so that he would not have a son to reign on his throne, and my covenant with my ministers the Levites. **22** Just as the host of heaven cannot be numbered and the sands of the sea cannot be measured, so I will increase the offspring of my servant David, and the Levites who minister to me.

23 The word of the LORD came to Jeremiah: **24** Have you not observed how these people say, "The two families that the LORD chose have been rejected by him," and how they hold my people in such contempt that they no longer regard them as a nation? **25** Thus says the LORD: Only if I had not established my covenant with day and night and the ordinances of heaven and earth, **26** would I reject the offspring of Jacob and of my servant David and not choose any of his descendants as rulers over the offspring of Abraham, Isaac, and Jacob. For I will restore their fortunes, and will have mercy upon them.

C. Encounters between Jeremiah and the kings of Judah

1. Zedekiah condemned for breaking his promise to slaves

34 The word that came to Jeremiah from the LORD, when King Nebuchadrezzar of Babylon and all his army and all the kingdoms of the earth and all the peoples under his dominion were fighting against Jerusalem and all its cities: **2** Thus says the LORD, the God of Israel: Go and speak to King Zedekiah of Judah and say to him: Thus says the LORD: I am going to give this city into the hand of the king of Babylon, and he shall burn it with fire. **3** And you yourself shall not escape from his hand, but shall surely be captured and handed over to him; you shall see the king of Babylon eye to eye and speak with him face to face; and you shall go

---

33.12
Isa 65.10;
Ezek 34.12-14
33.13
Jer 17.26;
Lev 27.32;
Lk 15.4

33.14
Jer 23.5;
Ezek 34.23-25
33.15
Isa 4.2; 11.1;
Zech 3.8;
Ps 72.1-5
33.16
Jer 23.6;
Isa 45.24,
25;
Phil 3.9
33.17
2 Sam 7.16;
1 Kings 2.4;
Lk 1.32, 33
33.18
Deut 18.1;
24.8;
Heb 13.15
33.20
Ps 89.37;
Isa 54.9;
Jer 31.36
33.21
Ps 89.34
33.22
Gen 15.5;
22.17;
Jer 30.19
33.24
Neh 4.2-4;
Ezek 36.2
33.25
Ps 74.16, 17;
Jer 31.35, 36
33.26
Jer 31.37;
Isa 14.1;
Hos 1.7; 2.23

34.1
2 Kings 25.1ff;
Jer 39.1;
1.15;
Dan 2.37, 38
34.2
Jer 22.1, 2;
37.1-4;
Jer 32.29
34.3
Jer 32.4;
2 Kings 25.6,
7;
Jer 39.6, 7

33.15,16 See note on 23.5,6.

33.17 *David shall never lack a man to sit on the throne of the house of Israel.* This refers to what would happen "in those days" (v. 16), i.e., in the Messianic age. God had promised to David an unending royal line (see 2 Sam 7). The line of David continued even after the royal authority was suspended during the exile. Jesus was born of that royal line, fulfilling God's promise to David, for he was ordained by the Father to occupy David's throne (Lk 1.32). Since the eternal Son of God has come, there is no need for other sons of

David to come; the throne God promised is an eternal throne on which the Son of God now sits in the heavenly places.

34.2 God marvelously protected his prophet Jeremiah from harm and danger as he proclaimed God's will. By divine providence, Jeremiah had access to King Zedekiah. One would have supposed that Zedekiah would never have allowed Jeremiah to come into his presence with his message of surrender, especially with the city surrounded by Babylonian troops.

to Babylon. 4 Yet hear the word of the LORD, O King Zedekiah of Judah! Thus says the LORD concerning you: You shall not die by the sword; 5 you shall die in peace. And as spices were burned[z] for your ancestors, the earlier kings who preceded you, so they shall burn spices[a] for you and lament for you, saying, "Alas, lord!" For I have spoken the word, says the LORD.

6   Then the prophet Jeremiah spoke all these words to Zedekiah king of Judah, in Jerusalem, 7 when the army of the king of Babylon was fighting against Jerusalem and against all the cities of Judah that were left, Lachish and Azekah; for these were the only fortified cities of Judah that remained.

8   The word that came to Jeremiah from the LORD, after King Zedekiah had made a covenant with all the people in Jerusalem to make a proclamation of liberty to them — 9 that all should set free their Hebrew slaves, male and female, so that no one should hold another Judean in slavery. 10 And they obeyed, all the officials and all the people who had entered into the covenant that all would set free their slaves, male or female, so that they would not be enslaved again; they obeyed and set them free. 11 But afterward they turned around and took back the male and female slaves they had set free, and brought them again into subjection as slaves. 12 The word of the LORD came to Jeremiah from the LORD: 13 Thus says the LORD, the God of Israel: I myself made a covenant with your ancestors when I brought them out of the land of Egypt, out of the house of slavery, saying, 14 "Every seventh year each of you must set free any Hebrews who have been sold to you and have served you six years; you must set them free from your service." But your ancestors did not listen to me or incline their ears to me. 15 You yourselves recently repented and did what was right in my sight by proclaiming liberty to one another, and you made a covenant before me in the house that is called by my name; 16 but then you turned around and profaned my name when each of you took back your male and female slaves, whom you had set free according to their desire, and you brought them again into subjection to be your slaves. 17 Therefore, thus says the LORD: You have not obeyed me by granting a release to your neighbors and friends; I am going to grant a release to you, says the LORD — a release to the sword, to pestilence, and to famine. I will make you a horror to all the kingdoms of the earth. 18 And those who transgressed my covenant and did not keep the terms of the covenant that they made before me, I will make like[b] the calf when they cut it in two and passed between its parts: 19 the officials of Judah, the officials of Jerusalem, the eunuchs, the priests, and all the people of the land who passed between the parts of the calf 20 shall be handed over to their enemies and to those who seek their lives. Their corpses shall become food for the birds of the air and the wild animals of the earth. 21 And as for King Zedekiah of Judah and his officials, I will hand them over to their enemies and to those who seek their lives, to the army of the king of Babylon, which has withdrawn from you. 22 I am going to command, says the LORD, and will bring them back to this city; and they will fight against it, and take it, and burn it with fire. The towns of Judah I will make a desolation without inhabitant.

z Heb as there was burning   a Heb shall burn   b Cn: Heb lacks like

34.5   so they shall burn spices for you. Jeremiah prophesied that even though Zedekiah would be a captive, he would repent of his sins, die a natural death, and be accorded the type of respect usually shown to Israel's kings, especially to those who had done good. It is better to live and die penitent in a prison than to live and die impenitent in a palace.
34.11   Zedekiah and those who had servants set

them free. But when the siege of Jerusalem was temporarily lifted, they changed their minds and turned back to their sins by bringing the victims back into slavery. These were Hebrew slaves who should have been freed in the seventh year (see Lev 25).
34.17   Because Zedekiah and the slaveholders reversed their stand, God promised to punish them by sword, famine and pestilence.

2. The faithfulness of the Rechabites emphasizes the guilt of Judah

35 The word that came to Jeremiah from the LORD in the days of King Jehoiakim son of Josiah of Judah: 2 Go to the house of the Rechabites, and speak with them, and bring them to the house of the LORD, into one of the chambers; then offer them wine to drink. 3 So I took Jaazaniah son of Jeremiah son of Habazziniah, and his brothers, and all his sons, and the whole house of the Rechabites. 4 I brought them to the house of the LORD into the chamber of the sons of Hanan son of Igdaliah, the man of God, which was near the chamber of the officials, above the chamber of Maaseiah son of Shallum, keeper of the threshold. 5 Then I set before the Rechabites pitchers full of wine, and cups; and I said to them, "Have some wine." 6 But they answered, "We will drink no wine, for our ancestor Jonadab son of Rechab commanded us, 'You shall never drink wine, neither you nor your children; 7 nor shall you ever build a house, or sow seed; nor shall you plant a vineyard, or even own one; but you shall live in tents all your days, that you may live many days in the land where you reside.' 8 We have obeyed the charge of our ancestor Jonadab son of Rechab in all that he commanded us, to drink no wine all our days, ourselves, our wives, our sons, or our daughters, 9 and not to build houses to live in. We have no vineyard or field or seed; 10 but we have lived in tents, and have obeyed and done all that our ancestor Jonadab commanded us. 11 But when King Nebuchadrezzar of Babylon came up against the land, we said, 'Come, and let us go to Jerusalem for fear of the army of the Chaldeans and the army of the Arameans.' That is why we are living in Jerusalem."

12 Then the word of the LORD came to Jeremiah: 13 Thus says the LORD of hosts, the God of Israel: Go and say to the people of Judah and the inhabitants of Jerusalem, Can you not learn a lesson and obey my words? says the LORD. 14 The command has been carried out that Jonadab son of Rechab gave to his descendants to drink no wine; and they drink none to this day, for they have obeyed their ancestor's command. But I myself have spoken to you persistently, and you have not obeyed me. 15 I have sent to you all my servants the prophets, sending them persistently, saying, "Turn now everyone of you from your evil way, and amend your doings, and do not go after other gods to serve them, and then you shall live in the land that I gave to you and your ancestors." But you did not incline your ear or obey me. 16 The descendants of Jonadab son of Rechab have carried out the command that their ancestor gave them, but this people has not obeyed me. 17 Therefore, thus says the LORD, the God of hosts, the God of Israel: I am going to bring on Judah and on all the inhabitants of Jerusalem every disaster that I have pronounced against them; because I have spoken to them and they have not listened, I have called to them and they have not answered.

18 But to the house of the Rechabites Jeremiah said: Thus says the LORD of hosts, the God of Israel: Because you have obeyed the command of your ancestor Jonadab, and kept all his precepts, and done all that he commanded you, 19 therefore thus says the LORD of hosts, the God of Israel: Jonadab son of Rechab shall not lack a descendant to stand before me for all time.

35.1
2 Kings 24.1;
Jer 1.3; 27.20
35.2
2 Kings 10.15;
1 Chr 2.55;
1 Kings 6.5
35.4
Deut 33.1;
1 Kings 12.22;
2 Kings 12.9;
25.18;
1 Chr 9.18,
19
35.5
Am 2.12
35.6
2 Kings 10.15;
1 Chr 2.55;
Lev 10.9;
Lk 1.15
35.7
Gen 25.27;
Heb 11.9;
Ex 20.12;
Eph 6.2, 3
35.8
Prov 1.8, 9;
Eph 6.1;
Col 3.20
35.9
v. 7
35.10
vv. 6, 7
35.11
2 Kings 24.1,
2;
Jer 4.5-7;
8.14
35.13
Isa 28.9-12;
Jer 32.33
35.14
2 Chr 36.15;
Jer 7.13;
25.3;
Isa 30.9;
50.2
35.15
Jer 26.5;
32.33;
Isa 1.16, 17;
Jer 4.1;
18.11; 7.6;
13.10; 22.4;
34.14
35.16
v. 14
35.17
Jer 19.3, 15;
Mic 3.12;
Prov 1.24;
Isa 65.12;
66.4;
Jer 7.13

35.19
Jer 33.17;
15.19

35.2 *Rechabites.* They were a seminomadic people who descended from the Kenites. They refused to drink alcoholic beverages and never were urbanized. **35.5,6** Jeremiah placed wine before the Rechabites, but they refused to drink any of it because their ancestor Jonadab had told them never to do it. Jeremiah was testing them, and they passed the test. God used that illustration to show that he had given his people Israel instructions which they had abandoned. If the

Rechabites were able to keep the pledge of abstinence, Israel could have remained faithful to their covenant with God. Since Israel had not done so, God pronounced judgment on them (vv. 16,17). **35.18** Because of the obedience of the Rechabites to the command of Jonadab, God said they would never lack a descendant to stand before him. If they obeyed Jonadab, how much more would they obey the Lord God.

3. Jehoiakim's arrogance in burning the scroll; the scroll rewritten

36 In the fourth year of King Jehoiakim son of Josiah of Judah, this word came to Jeremiah from the LORD: 2 Take a scroll and write on it all the words that I have spoken to you against Israel and Judah and all the nations, from the day I spoke to you, from the days of Josiah until today. 3 It may be that when the house of Judah hears of all the disasters that I intend to do to them, all of them may turn from their evil ways, so that I may forgive their iniquity and their sin.

4 Then Jeremiah called Baruch son of Neriah, and Baruch wrote on a scroll at Jeremiah's dictation all the words of the LORD that he had spoken to him. 5 And Jeremiah ordered Baruch, saying, "I am prevented from entering the house of the LORD; 6 so you go yourself, and on a fast day in the hearing of the people in the LORD's house you shall read the words of the LORD from the scroll that you have written at my dictation. You shall read them also in the hearing of all the people of Judah who come up from their towns. 7 It may be that their plea will come before the LORD, and that all of them will turn from their evil ways, for great is the anger and wrath that the LORD has pronounced against this people." 8 And Baruch son of Neriah did all that the prophet Jeremiah ordered him about reading from the scroll the words of the LORD in the LORD's house.

9 In the fifth year of King Jehoiakim son of Josiah of Judah, in the ninth month, all the people in Jerusalem and all the people who came from the towns of Judah to Jerusalem proclaimed a fast before the LORD. 10 Then, in the hearing of all the people, Baruch read the words of Jeremiah from the scroll, in the house of the LORD, in the chamber of Gemariah son of Shaphan the secretary, which was in the upper court, at the entry of the New Gate of the LORD's house.

11 When Micaiah son of Gemariah son of Shaphan heard all the words of the LORD from the scroll, 12 he went down to the king's house, into the secretary's chamber; and all the officials were sitting there: Elishama the secretary, Delaiah son of Shemaiah, Elnathan son of Achbor, Gemariah son of Shaphan, Zedekiah son of Hananiah, and all the officials. 13 And Micaiah told them all the words that he had heard, when Baruch read the scroll in the hearing of the people. 14 Then all the officials sent Jehudi son of Nethaniah son of Shelemiah son of Cushi to say to Baruch, "Bring the scroll that you read in the hearing of the people, and come." So Baruch son of Neriah took the scroll in his hand and came to them. 15 And they said to him, "Sit down and read it to us." So Baruch read it to them. 16 When they heard all the words, they turned to one another in alarm, and said to Baruch, "We certainly must report all these words to the king." 17 Then they questioned Baruch, "Tell us now, how did you write all these words? Was it at his dictation?" 18 Baruch answered them, "He dictated all these words to me, and I wrote them with ink on the scroll." 19 Then the officials said to Baruch, "Go and hide, you and Jeremiah, and let no one know where you are."

20 Leaving the scroll in the chamber of Elishama the secretary, they went to the court of the king; and they reported all the words to the king. 21 Then the king sent Jehudi to get the scroll, and he took it from the

36.1
2 Kings 24.1;
Jer 25.1, 3
36.2
vv. 6, 23, 28;
Zech 5.1;
Jer 1.9, 10;
25.9-29; 25.3
36.3
v. 7;
Jer 26.3;
Isa 55.7;
Jer 18.8;
Jon 3.8;
Mk 4.12;
Acts 3.19
36.4
v. 18;
Jer 32.12;
v. 14;
Ezek 2.9
36.5
Jer 32.2; 33.1
36.7
2 Kings 22.13;
Jer 4.4; 21.5
36.8
v. 6
36.9
v. 6;
Esth 4.16;
Jon 3.5
36.10
Jer 26.10
36.11
v. 13
36.12
vv. 20, 25;
Jer 26.22
36.13
2 Kings 22.10;
36.14; v. 21
36.15
v. 21
36.16
v. 24;
Acts 24.25;
Jer 13.18;
Am 7.10, 11
36.18
v. 4
36.19
v. 26;
Jer 26.20-24
36.20
v. 12
36.21
v. 14;
2 Chr 34.18

36.1 *In the fourth year of King Jehoiakim.* Probably in the summer of 605 B.C., shortly after Nebuchadnezzar's victory over the Egyptian army at Carchemish.
36.5 The king had debarred Jeremiah from going to the temple. By doing this he thought he could silence the prophet. But Jeremiah sent Baruch in his stead. He read to the people what God had revealed to Jeremiah.
36.9ff A fast had been proclaimed, presumably a

sign of genuine repentance. Jehoiakim's actions, however, spoke louder than his proclamation of a fast. Baruch, Jeremiah's secretary, used the opportunity to read the words of the prophet Jeremiah to the people. When Jehoiakim heard of this, he summoned Jehudi to read the scroll. When Jehudi read the scroll, the king cut off piece after piece and threw them into the fire until the entire scroll was destroyed. The king and his servants were unafraid; they refused to tear their garments as a sign of repentance (v. 24).

chamber of Elishama the secretary; and Jehudi read it to the king and all the officials who stood beside the king. 22 Now the king was sitting in his winter apartment (it was the ninth month), and there was a fire burning in the brazier before him. 23 As Jehudi read three or four columns, the king^c would cut them off with a penknife and throw them into the fire in the brazier, until the entire scroll was consumed in the fire that was in the brazier. 24 Yet neither the king, nor any of his servants who heard all these words, was alarmed, nor did they tear their garments. 25 Even when Elnathan and Delaiah and Gemariah urged the king not to burn the scroll, he would not listen to them. 26 And the king commanded Jerahmeel the king's son and Seraiah son of Azriel and Shelemiah son of Abdeel to arrest the secretary Baruch and the prophet Jeremiah. But the LORD hid them.

27 Now, after the king had burned the scroll with the words that Baruch wrote at Jeremiah's dictation, the word of the LORD came to Jeremiah: 28 Take another scroll and write on it all the former words that were in the first scroll, which King Jehoiakim of Judah has burned. 29 And concerning King Jehoiakim of Judah you shall say: Thus says the LORD, You have dared to burn this scroll, saying, Why have you written in it that the king of Babylon will certainly come and destroy this land, and will cut off from it human beings and animals? 30 Therefore thus says the LORD concerning King Jehoiakim of Judah: He shall have no one to sit upon the throne of David, and his dead body shall be cast out to the heat by day and the frost by night. 31 And I will punish him and his offspring and his servants for their iniquity; I will bring on them, and on the inhabitants of Jerusalem, and on the people of Judah, all the disasters with which I have threatened them — but they would not listen.

32 Then Jeremiah took another scroll and gave it to the secretary Baruch son of Neriah, who wrote on it at Jeremiah's dictation all the words of the scroll that King Jehoiakim of Judah had burned in the fire; and many similar words were added to them.

4. Jeremiah's arrest and imprisonment

37 Zedekiah son of Josiah, whom King Nebuchadrezzar of Babylon made king in the land of Judah, succeeded Coniah son of Jehoiakim. 2 But neither he nor his servants nor the people of the land listened to the words of the LORD that he spoke through the prophet Jeremiah.

3 King Zedekiah sent Jehucal son of Shelemiah and the priest Zephaniah son of Maaseiah to the prophet Jeremiah saying, "Please pray for us to the LORD our God." 4 Now Jeremiah was still going in and out among the people, for he had not yet been put in prison. 5 Meanwhile, the army of Pharaoh had come out of Egypt; and when the Chaldeans who were besieging Jerusalem heard news of them, they withdrew from Jerusalem.

6 Then the word of the LORD came to the prophet Jeremiah: 7 Thus

c Heb *he*

Cross references:

36.22 Am 3.15
36.23 v. 29
36.24 2 Kings 19.1, 2; 22.11; Isa 36.22; 37.1
36.25 Acts 5.34-39
36.26 1 Kings 19.1ff; Jer 15.20, 21
36.27 vv. 23, 4, 18
36.28 Jer 28.13, 14
36.29 Job 15.24, 25; Isa 45.9; 30.10; Jer 26.9; 32.3; 25.9-11
36.30 2 Kings 24.12-15; Jer 22.30; 22.19
36.31 Jer 23.34; Deut 28.15; Jer 19.15
36.32 vv. 28, 4, 23
37.1 2 Kings 24.17; 2 Chr 36.10; Jer 22.24; Ezek 17.12-21
37.2 2 Chr 36.12, 14
37.3 Jer 21.1, 2; 29.25; 52.24; 1 Kings 13.6; Acts 8.24
37.4 v. 15
37.5 2 Kings 24.7; Ezek 17.15; Jer 34.21
37.7 Jer 21.2; Isa 30.1-3; 31.1-3; Ezek 17.17

36.26 Where and how God hid Jeremiah and Baruch we are not told. God's providence working on behalf of his servants was greater and more effective than the orders and enmity of the king.
36.28 The word of the Lord cannot be destroyed. When Jehoiakim burned that word, Jeremiah, at the command of God, had another scroll prepared. And God added words to those that had been burned by Jehoiakim.
36.30 *He shall have no one to sit upon the throne.* A three-month reign by Jehoiakim's son Jehoiachin (also called Coniah and Jeconiah) evidently did not qualify as "sitting upon the throne," for the Hebrew expression used here implies permanence.
37.1 *Coniah* was the son of Jehoiakim. His name as king was Jehoiachin. He reigned for less than four

months. How Jehoiakim died is not stated. Jehoiachin was taken to Babylon, where he lived for at least thirty-seven years. Nebuchadnezzar appointed Zedekiah as king in Judah after Jehoiachin was taken to Babylon. Zedekiah was his uncle, the brother of Jehoiakim and a son of Josiah. Zedekiah eventually revolted against Nebuchadnezzar, was defeated, and, after his eyes were put out, was sent to Babylon as a prisoner (for this data, see 2 Kings 24–25; 2 Chr 36).
37.2 Even though most of God's people did not hearken unto the words of the Lord, this does not mean that there were no true followers of God left in the land. There always has been a remnant of true believers left among an apostate people so that the gospel is not eliminated and the fire is not quenched.

says the LORD, God of Israel: This is what the two of you shall say to the king of Judah, who sent you to me to inquire of me: Pharaoh's army, which set out to help you, is going to return to its own land, to Egypt. [8] And the Chaldeans shall return and fight against this city; they shall take it and burn it with fire. [9] Thus says the LORD: Do not deceive yourselves, saying, "The Chaldeans will surely go away from us," for they will not go away. [10] Even if you defeated the whole army of Chaldeans who are fighting against you, and there remained of them only wounded men in their tents, they would rise up and burn this city with fire.

[11] Now when the Chaldean army had withdrawn from Jerusalem at the approach of Pharaoh's army, [12] Jeremiah set out from Jerusalem to go to the land of Benjamin to receive his share of property[d] among the people there. [13] When he reached the Benjamin Gate, a sentinel there named Irijah son of Shelemiah son of Hananiah arrested the prophet Jeremiah saying, "You are deserting to the Chaldeans." [14] And Jeremiah said, "That is a lie; I am not deserting to the Chaldeans." But Irijah would not listen to him, and arrested Jeremiah and brought him to the officials. [15] The officials were enraged at Jeremiah, and they beat him and imprisoned him in the house of the secretary Jonathan, for it had been made a prison. [16] Thus Jeremiah was put in the cistern house, in the cells, and remained there many days.

[17] Then King Zedekiah sent for him, and received him. The king questioned him secretly in his house, and said, "Is there any word from the LORD?" Jeremiah said, "There is!" Then he said, "You shall be handed over to the king of Babylon." [18] Jeremiah also said to King Zedekiah, "What wrong have I done to you or your servants or this people, that you have put me in prison? [19] Where are your prophets who prophesied to you, saying, 'The king of Babylon will not come against you and against this land'? [20] Now please hear me, my lord king: be good enough to listen to my plea, and do not send me back to the house of the secretary Jonathan to die there." [21] So King Zedekiah gave orders, and they committed Jeremiah to the court of the guard; and a loaf of bread was given him daily from the bakers' street, until all the bread of the city was gone. So Jeremiah remained in the court of the guard.

5. Jeremiah cast into the muddy cistern; rescued by Ebed-melech

38 Now Shephatiah son of Mattan, Gedaliah son of Pashhur, Jucal son of Shelemiah, and Pashhur son of Malchiah heard the words that Jeremiah was saying to all the people, [2] Thus says the LORD, Those who stay in this city shall die by the sword, by famine, and by pestilence; but those who go out to the Chaldeans shall live; they shall have their lives as a prize of war, and live. [3] Thus says the LORD, This city shall surely be handed over to the army of the king of Babylon and be taken. [4] Then the officials said to the king, "This man ought to be put to death, because

d Meaning of Heb uncertain

Cross references (margin)

37.8
Jer 34.22
37.9
Jer 29.8
37.10
Jer 21.4, 5;
Joel 2.11
37.11
v. 5
37.13
Jer 38.7;
Zech 14.10;
Jer 18.18;
20.10;
Lk 23.2;
Acts 24.5-9,
13
37.14
Jer 40.4-6;
Mt 5.11, 12
37.15
Jer 18.23;
2 Chr 16.10;
18.26
37.16
Jer 38.6
37.17
Jer 38.5;
14-16, 24-27
37.18
Dan 6.22;
Jn 10.32;
Acts 25.8, 11,
25
37.19
Jer 2.28;
6.14; 29.31
37.20
Jer 36.7;
38.26; 18.23
37.21
Jer 32.3;
38.13, 28;
Isa 33.16;
Jer 38.9;
52.6; 39.14,
15
38.1
Jer 37.3;
21.1, 8
38.2
Jer 21.9;
42.17; 45.5
38.3
Jer 21.10;
32.3
38.4
Jer 18.23;
26.11;
1 Kings 18.17;
18; 21.20;
Am 7.10;
Acts 16.20;
Jer 29.7

Study notes

37.8–10 God had ordained that Jerusalem would be set on fire by the Babylonians. So certain was this that even if Judah defeated the Babylonians and only injured enemy soldiers were left, the wounded still would rise up to destroy Jerusalem and burn it.

37.15 God nowhere declares that his prophets will always be protected against the onslaughts of those who spurn his word. Jeremiah was seized by the apostates and imprisoned after he had been beaten. His life was preserved, but his body suffered greatly. But it is better to suffer at the hands of sinners while engaged in the work of God than to suffer at the hands of God for refusing to do his work.

37.20 Jeremiah implored the king not to send him back to the house of Jonathan lest he die there. When

speaking as a mouthpiece for God, Jeremiah was bold. When asking something for himself, he was modest, humble, and uncomplaining. He did not claim that his role as God's messenger entitled him to special treatment.

38.4 The Judeans thought Jeremiah was guilty of betrayal and treason when he advocated surrender to Nebuchadnezzar. His enemies wanted to kill him, but God saved him. Yet he was thrown into an empty cistern with a muddy bottom, into which he sank (vv. 6,11–13). God promises believers grace and strength to put up with whatever occurs so that they can triumph in the midst of adversity (2 Cor 1.3–7; 9.8; Eph 3.20; Phil 4.6,7,19).

he is discouraging the soldiers who are left in this city, and all the people, by speaking such words to them." [5] King Zedekiah said, "Here he is; he is in your hands; for the king is powerless against you." [6] So they took Jeremiah and threw him into the cistern of Malchiah, the king's son, which was in the court of the guard, letting Jeremiah down by ropes. Now there was no water in the cistern, but only mud, and Jeremiah sank in the mud.

[7] Ebed-melech the Ethiopian,[e] a eunuch in the king's house, heard that they had put Jeremiah into the cistern. The king happened to be sitting at the Benjamin Gate, [8] So Ebed-melech left the king's house and spoke to the king, [9] "My lord king, these men have acted wickedly in all they did to the prophet Jeremiah by throwing him into the cistern to die there of hunger, for there is no bread left in the city." [10] Then the king commanded Ebed-melech the Ethiopian,[e] "Take three men with you from here, and pull the prophet Jeremiah up from the cistern before he dies." [11] So Ebed-melech took the men with him and went to the house of the king, to a wardrobe of[f] the storehouse, and took from there old rags and worn-out clothes, which he let down to Jeremiah in the cistern by ropes. [12] Then Ebed-melech the Ethiopian[e] said to Jeremiah, "Just put the rags and clothes between your armpits and the ropes." Jeremiah did so. [13] Then they drew Jeremiah up by the ropes and pulled him out of the cistern. And Jeremiah remained in the court of the guard.

[14] King Zedekiah sent for the prophet Jeremiah and received him at the third entrance of the temple of the LORD. The king said to Jeremiah, "I have something to ask you; do not hide anything from me." [15] Jeremiah said to Zedekiah, "If I tell you, you will put me to death, will you not? And if I give you advice, you will not listen to me." [16] So King Zedekiah swore an oath in secret to Jeremiah, "As the LORD lives, who gave us our lives, I will not put you to death or hand you over to these men who seek your life."

[17] Then Jeremiah said to Zedekiah, "Thus says the LORD, the God of hosts, the God of Israel, If you will only surrender to the officials of the king of Babylon, then your life shall be spared, and this city shall not be burned with fire, and you and your house shall live. [18] But if you do not surrender to the officials of the king of Babylon, then this city shall be handed over to the Chaldeans, and they shall burn it with fire, and you yourself shall not escape from their hand." [19] King Zedekiah said to Jeremiah, "I am afraid of the Judeans who have deserted to the Chaldeans, for I might be handed over to them and they would abuse me." [20] Jeremiah said, "That will not happen. Just obey the voice of the LORD in what I say to you, and it shall go well with you, and your life shall be spared. [21] But if you are determined not to surrender, this is what the LORD has shown me — [22] a vision of all the women remaining in the house of the king of Judah being led out to the officials of the king of Babylon and saying,

38.5	2 Sam 3.39
38.6	Jer 37.21; Acts 16.24; Zech 9.11
38.7	Jer 39.16; 37.13; Am 5.10
38.9	Jer 37.21; 52.6
38.11	v. 6
38.13	Jer 37.21; 39.14, 15
38.14	Jer 21.1, 2; 37.17; 15.11; 42.2-5, 20
38.15	Lk 22.67, 68
38.16	Jer 37.17; Isa 57.16; Zech 12.1; vv. 4-6
38.17	Ps 80.7, 14; 1 Chr 17.24; Ezek 8.4; 2 Kings 24.12; 26.27-30
38.18	Jer 27.8; 32.4; 34.3
38.19	Isa 51.12, 13; Jn 12.42; 19.12, 13; Jer 39.9; 2 Chr 30.10; Neh 4.1
38.20	Jer 11.4, 8; 7.23; Isa 55.3
38.22	Jer 6.12; 8.10; 43.6

[e] Or *Nubian*; Heb *Cushite*   [f] Cn: Heb *to under*

38.6 Jeremiah sank into the mire at the bottom of the cistern. Humanly speaking, he had no bread and no hope for deliverance. He was left to perish. God intervened in the person of Ebed-melech, an Ethiopian, who petitioned the king for his release. The king, either out of compassion or fear that Jeremiah might die, ordered Jeremiah to be lifted from the cistern and placed in the court of the guard (v. 13). **38.14ff** Zedekiah must have had some respect for Jeremiah, for he could not resist sending for him, presumably hoping that this time the prophet would bring him a good word. If there ever was a temptation for a prophet to dilute his message, this would be the

time. Instead, Jeremiah assured the king that Nebuchadnezzar would burn the city unless Zedekiah surrendered. Zedekiah refused to heed Jeremiah's counsel. Nebuchadnezzar besieged the city and took it. He then put out Zedekiah's eyes and shipped him off to Babylon.

38.20–23 God had shown Jeremiah what the alternatives were for the king. If he chose to obey God, he was told what the consequences would be. And if he disobeyed, he knew what God said would happen. God makes the alternatives plain to us by revealing them in the word of God.

'Your trusted friends have seduced you
    and have overcome you;
Now that your feet are stuck in the mud,
    they desert you.'

38.23
Jer 39.6;
41.10

23All your wives and your children shall be led out to the Chaldeans, and you yourself shall not escape from their hand, but shall be seized by the king of Babylon; and this city shall be burned with fire."

24 Then Zedekiah said to Jeremiah, "Do not let anyone else know of this conversation, or you will die. 25If the officials should hear that I have spoken with you, and they should come and say to you, 'Just tell us what you said to the king; do not conceal it from us, or we will put you to death. What did the king say to you?' 26then you shall say to them, 'I was presenting my plea to the king not to send me back to the house of Jonathan to die there.'" 27All the officials did come to Jeremiah and questioned him; and he answered them in the very words the king had commanded. So they stopped questioning him, for the conversation had not been overheard. 28And Jeremiah remained in the court of the guard until the day that Jerusalem was taken.

38.25
vv. 4-6, 27

38.26
Jer 37.15, 20

38.27
1 Sam 10.15,
16; 16.2-5

38.28
Jer 37.21;
39.14

6. The fall of Jerusalem and the capture of Zedekiah; special blessing for Ebed-melech

39.1
2 Kings 25.1-4;
Jer 52.4-7;
Ezek 24.1, 2

39 In the ninth year of King Zedekiah of Judah, in the tenth month, King Nebuchadrezzar of Babylon and all his army came against Jerusalem and besieged it; 2in the eleventh year of Zedekiah, in the fourth month, on the ninth day of the month, a breach was made in the city. 3When Jerusalem was taken,g all the officials of the king of Babylon came and sat in the middle gate: Nergal-sharezer, Samgar-nebo, Sarsechim the Rabsaris, Nergal-sharezer the Rabmag, with all the rest of the officials of the king of Babylon. 4When King Zedekiah of Judah and all the soldiers saw them, they fled, going out of the city at night by way of the king's garden through the gate between the two walls; and they went toward the Arabah. 5But the army of the Chaldeans pursued them, and overtook Zedekiah in the plains of Jericho; and when they had taken him, they brought him up to King Nebuchadrezzar of Babylon, at Riblah, in the land of Hamath; and he passed sentence on him. 6The king of Babylon slaughtered the sons of Zedekiah at Riblah before his eyes; also the king of Babylon slaughtered all the nobles of Judah. 7He put out the eyes of Zedekiah, and bound him in fetters to take him to Babylon. 8The Chaldeans burned the king's house and the houses of the people, and broke down the walls of Jerusalem. 9Then Nebuzaradan the captain of the guard exiled to Babylon the rest of the people who were left in the city, those who had deserted to him, and the people who remained. 10Nebuzaradan the captain of the guard left in the land of Judah some of the poor people who owned nothing, and gave them vineyards and fields at the same time.

11 King Nebuchadrezzar of Babylon gave command concerning Jeremiah through Nebuzaradan, the captain of the guard, saying, 12"Take him, look after him well and do him no harm, but deal with him as he may ask you." 13So Nebuzaradan the captain of the guard, Nebushazban the Rabsaris, Nergal-sharezer the Rabmag, and all the chief officers of the king of Babylon sent 14and took Jeremiah from the court of the guard.

39.2
2 Kings 25.4;
Jer 52.7

39.3
Jer 38.17

39.4
2 Kings 25.4;
Jer 52.7;
Am 2.14;
2 Chr 32.5

39.5
Jer 32.4;
38.18, 23;
Josh 4.13;
2 Kings 23.33

39.6
2 Kings 25.7;
Jer 34.19-21

39.7
2 Kings 25.7;
Jer 52.11;
Ezek 12.13;
Jer 32.5

39.8
2 Kings 25.9,
10;
Jer 38.18;
52.13

39.9
2 Kings 25.11,
20;
Jer 52.12-16;
24.8; 38.19

39.10
2 Kings 25.12;
Jer 52.16

39.11
Jer 1.8;
15.20, 21;
Acts 24.23

39.14
Jer 38.28;
40.1-6;
2 Kings 22.12,
14;
2 Chr 34.20

g This clause has been transposed from 38.28

39.1,2 The siege of Jerusalem began in the ninth year and the tenth month of Zedekiah. During the siege no one could enter or leave the city. Famine began as supplies ran low. The walls were breached by the enemy in the eleventh year of Zedekiah, in the fourth month. Thus the siege was long and exhausting.

39.11,12 Apparently, Nebuchadnezzar was acquainted with the role and activities of Jeremiah. He must have known that the prophet told Judah to submit to the Babylonians. This would have won him the king's favor, though that was not why Jeremiah prophesied in that manner. He had spoken the word of the Lord, and God protected his faithful servant.

They entrusted him to Gedaliah son of Ahikam son of Shaphan to be brought home. So he stayed with his own people.

15 The word of the LORD came to Jeremiah while he was confined in the court of the guard: 16 Go and say to Ebed-melech the Ethiopian: [h] Thus says the LORD of hosts, the God of Israel: I am going to fulfill my words against this city for evil and not for good, and they shall be accomplished in your presence on that day. 17 But I will save you on that day, says the LORD, and you shall not be handed over to those whom you dread. 18 For I will surely save you, and you shall not fall by the sword; but you shall have your life as a prize of war, because you have trusted in me, says the LORD.

III. Prophecies after the fall of Jerusalem (40.1–45.5)

A. Jeremiah's ministry among the remnant in Judah

1. Released by Nebuzaradan, Jeremiah lives in Mizpah with Governor Gedaliah

40 The word that came to Jeremiah from the LORD after Nebuzaradan the captain of the guard had let him go from Ramah, when he took him bound in fetters along with all the captives of Jerusalem and Judah who were being exiled to Babylon. 2 The captain of the guard took Jeremiah and said to him, "The LORD your God threatened this place with this disaster; 3 and now the LORD has brought it about, and has done as he said, because all of you sinned against the LORD and did not obey his voice. Therefore this thing has come upon you. 4 Now look, I have just released you today from the fetters on your hands. If you wish to come with me to Babylon, come, and I will take good care of you; but if you do not wish to come with me to Babylon, you need not come. See, the whole land is before you; go wherever you think it good and right to go. 5 If you remain,[i] then return to Gedaliah son of Ahikam son of Shaphan, whom the king of Babylon appointed governor of the towns of Judah, and stay with him among the people; or go wherever you think it right to go." So the captain of the guard gave him an allowance of food and a present, and let him go. 6 Then Jeremiah went to Gedaliah son of Ahikam at Mizpah, and stayed with him among the people who were left in the land.

7 When all the leaders of the forces in the open country and their troops heard that the king of Babylon had appointed Gedaliah son of Ahikam governor in the land, and had committed to him men, women, and children, those of the poorest of the land who had not been taken into exile to Babylon, 8 they went to Gedaliah at Mizpah—Ishmael son of Nethaniah, Johanan son of Kareah, Seraiah son of Tanhumeth, the sons of Ephai the Netophathite, Jezaniah son of the Maacathite, they and their troops. 9 Gedaliah son of Ahikam son of Shaphan swore to them and their troops, saying, "Do not be afraid to serve the Chaldeans. Stay in the land and serve the king of Babylon, and it shall go well with you. 10 As for me,

h Or Nubian; Heb Cushite   i Syr: Meaning of Heb uncertain

39.16 Jer 38.7, 12; 21.10; Dan 9.12; Zech 1.6
39.17 Ps 41.1, 2; 50.15
39.18 Jer 21.9; 45.5; Ps 34.22; Jer 17.7, 8
40.1 Jer 39.9, 11, 14; 31.15; Eph 6.20
40.2 Jer 22.8, 9; 50.7
40.3 Deut 29.24, 25; Dan 9.11
40.4 Jer 39.11, 12; Gen 20.15
40.5 Jer 39.14; 2 Kings 25.23; v. 4; Jer 52.34
40.6 Jer 39.14; Judg 20.1
40.7 2 Kings 25.23, 24; Jer 39.10; 52.16
40.8 Jer 41.1
40.9 2 Kings 25.24; Jer 27.11; 38.17-20
40.10 v. 6; Jer 35.19; 39.10; v. 12; Jer 48.32

39.16 *Ebed-melech the Ethiopian* had been responsible for delivering Jeremiah from incarceration in the cistern (38.7ff). God did not forget the work of Ebedmelech. Jeremiah was commanded by God to tell him that he would be saved from the sword because "you have trusted in me" (v. 18). Ebed-melech was an alien to God's covenant made with Israel, for he was not a Jew. But he was no alien to the covenant of grace, based on his personal faith in God. This covenant is available to Jew and Gentile alike (cf. Eph 2.8–22). **40.1** Jerusalem had been overthrown. Many of the people had been taken to Babylon, where they would remain for seventy years, until the time of the prophetic word was fulfilled. But some of God's people were left behind in the land. Chs. 40–44 depict the history of these people, their calamities, and their continuing blindness to the commands of God. **40.4** Nebuzaradan suggested that Jeremiah go to Babylon, where he would be well taken care of for the rest of his life. Jeremiah, who was free to make his own choice, elected to remain with those left in the promised land. He stayed with Gedaliah, who was now the governor of Judah, and lived at Mizpah.

I am staying at Mizpah to represent you before the Chaldeans who come to us; but as for you, gather wine and summer fruits and oil, and store them in your vessels, and live in the towns that you have taken over." [11] Likewise, when all the Judeans who were in Moab and among the Ammonites and in Edom and in other lands heard that the king of Babylon had left a remnant in Judah and had appointed Gedaliah son of Ahikam son of Shaphan as governor over them, [12] then all the Judeans returned from all the places to which they had been scattered and came to the land of Judah, to Gedaliah at Mizpah; and they gathered wine and summer fruits in great abundance.

[13] Now Johanan son of Kareah and all the leaders of the forces in the open country came to Gedaliah at Mizpah [14] and said to him, "Are you at all aware that Baalis king of the Ammonites has sent Ishmael son of Nethaniah to take your life?" But Gedaliah son of Ahikam would not believe them. [15] Then Johanan son of Kareah spoke secretly to Gedaliah at Mizpah, "Please let me go and kill Ishmael son of Nethaniah, and no one else will know. Why should he take your life, so that all the Judeans who are gathered around you would be scattered, and the remnant of Judah would perish?" [16] But Gedaliah son of Ahikam said to Johanan of Kareah, "Do not do such a thing, for you are telling a lie about Ishmael."

2. After murdering Gedaliah, Ishmael is routed by Johanan

41 In the seventh month, Ishmael son of Nethaniah son of Elishama, of the royal family, one of the chief officers of the king, came with ten men to Gedaliah son of Ahikam, at Mizpah. As they ate bread together there at Mizpah, [2] Ishmael son of Nethaniah and the ten men with him got up and struck down Gedaliah son of Ahikam son of Shaphan with the sword and killed him, because the king of Babylon had appointed him governor in the land. [3] Ishmael also killed all the Judeans who were with Gedaliah at Mizpah, and the Chaldean soldiers who happened to be there.

[4] On the day after the murder of Gedaliah, before anyone knew of it, [5] eighty men arrived from Shechem and Shiloh and Samaria, with their beards shaved and their clothes torn, and their bodies gashed, bringing grain offerings and incense to present at the temple of the LORD. [6] And Ishmael son of Nethaniah came out from Mizpah to meet them, weeping as he came. As he met them, he said to them, "Come to Gedaliah son of Ahikam." [7] When they reached the middle of the city, Ishmael son of Nethaniah and the men with him slaughtered them, and threw them[j] into a cistern. [8] But there were ten men among them who said to Ishmael, "Do not kill us, for we have stores of wheat, barley, oil, and honey hidden in the fields." So he refrained, and did not kill them along with their companions.

[9] Now the cistern into which Ishmael had thrown all the bodies of the

j Syr: Heb lacks *and threw them*; compare verse 9

Cross references (margin):

40.11 Isa 16.4; 1 Sam 11.1; 12.12; Isa 11.14
40.12 Jer 43.5; v. 10
40.13 v. 8
40.14 Jer 41.10
40.15 1 Sam 26.8; 2 Sam 21.17; Jer 42.2
40.16 Mt 10.16
41.1 2 Kings 25.25; Jer 40.6, 8, 14
41.2 2 Kings 25.25; Jer 40.5
41.5 Gen 33.18; Josh 18.1; 1 Kings 16.24, 29; Jer 16.6; 2 Kings 25.9
41.6 Jer 50.4
41.7 Isa 59.7; Ezek 22.27
41.9 1 Kings 15.22; 2 Chr 16.6

40.11,12 There was rest in Judah under Gedaliah, who was capable and prudent. Jews who had been dispersed all over Palestine returned to Judah and came under the care and control of Gedaliah. Some degree of prosperity came, inasmuch as they gathered a goodly supply of wine and summer fruits.
40.14 A dark cloud hung over the infant state under Gedaliah. Baalis king of the Ammonites wanted to destroy Gedaliah. He employed Ishmael, a Jew of royal stock, to settle in Gedaliah's territory in order to slay the governor. Johanan, a friend of Gedaliah, tried to warn him about the plot, offering to kill Ishmael. But Gedaliah, a peaceful and honorable man, refused the offer and maintained his friend was speaking lies about Ishmael. Johanan's warning, how-

ever, eventually proved to be well-founded.
41.1ff Ishmael and ten of his henchmen visited Gedaliah, ate his bread, and then assassinated him without warning. They did not stop there. They also slew all of the Jews and Chaldeans who were with Gedaliah at the time. For two days the crime went unnoticed by the people, for it was carried out carefully and was artfully concealed.
41.5ff Eighty Jews from various places came to Jerusalem with grain offerings and incense for presentation at the temple. They devoutly had shaven themselves, torn their clothes, and brought offerings. Ishmael and his small band slew them and cast their bodies into a cistern. Then they took some prisoners from among the people and went to the Ammonites.

men whom he had struck down was the large cistern*k* that King Asa had made for defense against King Baasha of Israel; Ishmael son of Nethaniah filled that cistern with those whom he had killed. 10 Then Ishmael took captive all the rest of the people who were in Mizpah, the king's daughters and all the people who were left at Mizpah, whom Nebuzaradan, the captain of the guard, had committed to Gedaliah son of Ahikam. Ishmael son of Nethaniah took them captive and set out to cross over to the Ammonites.

11 But when Johanan son of Kareah and all the leaders of the forces with him heard of all the crimes that Ishmael son of Nethaniah had done, 12 they took all their men and went to fight against Ishmael son of Nethaniah. They came upon him at the great pool that is in Gibeon. 13 And when all the people who were with Ishmael saw Johanan son of Kareah and all the leaders of the forces with him, they were glad. 14 So all the people whom Ishmael had carried away captive from Mizpah turned around and came back, and went to Johanan son of Kareah. 15 But Ishmael son of Nethaniah escaped from Johanan with eight men, and went to the Ammonites. 16 Then Johanan son of Kareah and all the leaders of the forces with him took all the rest of the people whom Ishmael son of Nethaniah had carried away captive*l* from Mizpah after he had slain Gedaliah son of Ahikam — soldiers, women, children, and eunuchs, whom Johanan brought back from Gibeon.*m* 17 And they set out, and stopped at Geruth Chimham near Bethlehem, intending to go to Egypt 18 because of the Chaldeans; for they were afraid of them, because Ishmael son of Nethaniah had killed Gedaliah son of Ahikam, whom the king of Babylon had made governor over the land.

3. Jeremiah warns the remnant not to flee to Egypt

42 Then all the commanders of the forces, and Johanan son of Kareah and Azariah*n* son of Hoshaiah, and all the people from the least to the greatest, approached 2 the prophet Jeremiah and said, "Be good enough to listen to our plea, and pray to the Lord your God for us — for all this remnant. For there are only a few of us left out of many, as your eyes can see. 3 Let the Lord your God show us where we should go and what we should do." 4 The prophet Jeremiah said to them, "Very well: I am going to pray to the Lord your God as you request, and whatever the Lord answers you I will tell you; I will keep nothing back from you." 5 They in their turn said to Jeremiah, "May the Lord be a true and faithful witness against us if we do not act according to everything that the Lord your God sends us through you. 6 Whether it is good or bad, we will obey the voice of the Lord our God to whom we are sending you, in order that it may go well with us when we obey the voice of the Lord our God."

7 At the end of ten days the word of the Lord came to Jeremiah. 8 Then he summoned Johanan son of Kareah and all the commanders of the forces who were with him, and all the people from the least to the

41.10
Jer 40.11, 12;
43.6; 40.7,
14

41.11
Jer 40.7, 8,
13-16
41.12
2 Sam 2.13
41.13
vv. 10, 14

41.15
v. 2

41.16
Jer 42.8;
43.4-7

41.17
2 Sam 19.37,
38;
Jer 42.14
41.18
Jer 42.11, 16;
Lk 12.4, 5;
Jer 40.5

42.1
Jer 40.8, 13;
41.11
42.2
Jer 36.7;
37.20; 19.20;
1 Kings 13.6;
Acts 8.24;
Deut 28.62;
Lam 1.1
42.3
Ps 86.11;
Mic 4.2
42.4
1 Sam 12.23;
1 Kings 22.14;
Jer 23.28;
1 Sam 3.17,
18;
Ps 40.10
42.5
Gen 31.50;
Mic 1.2
42.6
Deut 6.3;
Jer 7.23
42.8
v. 1

---

k Gk: Heb *whom he had killed by the hand of Gedaliah* *l* Cn: Heb *whom he recovered from Ishmael son of Nethaniah* *m* Meaning of Heb uncertain *n* Gk: Heb *Jezaniah*

41.11ff When Johanan learned what had happened, he and his followers pursued Ishmael. Before Ishmael rejoined the Ammonites, a battle broke out and the prisoners taken by Ishmael were released. Ishmael and eight of his followers escaped and went back to the Ammonites.

41.16ff Johanan and his company of people planned to go to Egypt. From the human perspective, this was a reasonable objective. Since Ishmael had slain some Chaldeans, Babylon would not tolerate a captive people slaying their comrades. Vengeance would soon come.

42.1ff Johanan and the people begged Jeremiah to

intervene with God on their behalf. They wanted divine approval of what they had already decided to do. They trusted that God would reveal his will for them through Jeremiah.

42.7 God did not hurry to respond to the request made by Jeremiah. Ten days went by before the prophet received a word from God. The remnant was told to stay in the land, trust God, and not be afraid of Nebuchadnezzar. The rebelliousness of these people manifested itself once again. They had solemnly sworn to obey the voice of God. But when he made his will known, they did the exact opposite and had to suffer the consequences.

42.9 2 Kings 19.4, 6, 20; 22.15	greatest, 9 and said to them, "Thus says the LORD, the God of Israel, to whom you sent me to present your plea before him: 10 If you will only
42.10 Jer 24.6; 31.28; Ezek 36.36; Jon 3.10; 4.2	remain in this land, then I will build you up and not pull you down; I will plant you, and not pluck you up; for I am sorry for the disaster that I have brought upon you. 11 Do not be afraid of the king of Babylon, as you have
42.11 Jer 41.18; Isa 43.5; Rom 8.31	been; do not be afraid of him, says the LORD, for I am with you, to save you and to rescue you from his hand. 12 I will grant you mercy, and he will have mercy on you and restore you to your native soil. 13 But if you
42.12 Ps 106.45, 46	continue to say, 'We will not stay in this land,' thus disobeying the voice of the LORD your God 14 and saying, 'No, we will go to the land of Egypt,
42.13 Jer 44.16	where we shall not see war, or hear the sound of the trumpet, or be hungry
42.14 Jer 41.17; 4.19, 21	for bread, and there we will stay,' 15 then hear the word of the LORD, O remnant of Judah. Thus says the LORD of hosts, the God of Israel: If
42.15 Jer 44.12-14	you are determined to enter Egypt and go to settle there, 16 then the sword
42.16 Jer 44.13, 27; Ezek 11.8	that you fear shall overtake you there, in the land of Egypt; and the famine that you dread shall follow close after you into Egypt; and there you shall
42.17 Jer 44.13, 14, 28	die. 17 All the people who have determined to go to Egypt to settle there shall die by the sword, by famine, and by pestilence; they shall have no remnant or survivor from the disaster that I am bringing upon them.
42.18 Jer 7.20; 33.5; Isa 65.15; Jer 29.18; 22.10, 27	18 "For thus says the LORD of hosts, the God of Israel: Just as my anger and my wrath were poured out on the inhabitants of Jerusalem, so my wrath will be poured out on you when you go to Egypt. You shall become an object of execration and horror, of cursing and ridicule. You
42.19 Deut 17.16; Isa 30.1-7; Neh 9.26, 29, 30	shall see this place no more. 19 The LORD has said to you, O remnant of Judah, Do not go to Egypt. Be well aware that I have warned you today 20 that you have made a fatal mistake. For you yourselves sent me to the
42.20 v. 2	LORD your God, saying, 'Pray for us to the LORD our God, and whatever the LORD our God says, tell us and we will do it.' 21 So I have told you
42.21 Jer 43.1; Ezek 2.7; Jer 43.4	today, but you have not obeyed the voice of the LORD your God in anything that he sent me to tell you. 22 Be well aware, then, that you shall
42.22 Jer 43.11; Hos 9.6	die by the sword, by famine, and by pestilence in the place where you desire to go and settle."

B. Jeremiah's ministry among the refugees in Egypt

1. God's warning rejected, the Jews migrate to Tahpanhes

43.1 Jer 26.8; 51.63; 42.10-18	43 When Jeremiah finished speaking to all the people all these words of the LORD their God, with which the LORD their God had sent him to them, 2 Azariah son of Hoshaiah and Johanan son of Kareah and
43.2 Jer 42.1; 2 Chr 36.13; Jer 42.5	all the other insolent men said to Jeremiah, "You are telling a lie. The LORD our God did not send you to say, 'Do not go to Egypt to settle there';
43.3 Jer 38.4	3 but Baruch son of Neriah is inciting you against us, to hand us over to the Chaldeans, in order that they may kill us or take us into exile in

42.10ff Jeremiah laid before Johanan and his followers what the alternatives were. The little word *if* appears twice (vv. 10,13). He told them what would happen if they stayed in the land and what would take place if they decided to go to Egypt. But he made it plain that it was God's will for them to remain in the land. But since the people had earlier determined to go to Egypt, what God said made no difference to them. It is an insult to God to ask for his will, when a decision has already been made before his answer comes. Whoever prays with a closed mind might just as well not pray. **42.20–22** Jeremiah reminded Johanan and the others that they had sworn to do whatever Jeremiah declared to be the will of God. They refused to do so when they heard what they did not like. So Jeremiah prophesied that they would die in Egypt by the sword, by pestilence, and by famine. One would

suppose that the gravity of the consequences would have occasioned a change of mind. But it was not so. They went and were punished, just as Jeremiah prophesied. **43.2** Jeremiah was accused of being a liar. Since his other prophecies about Jerusalem had been fulfilled in a literal way, it is hard to understand the depravity of these people in discounting Jeremiah's prophecy. They thought Jeremiah was part of a plot to have them killed by the Babylonians or sent down to Babylon as prisoners of war. They refused to believe that if they went to Egypt, they would suffer the fate they thought would happen if they stayed in Judea. But it did in fact occur. The Babylonians invaded Egypt and defeated the Egyptians. Human wisdom is not better than the wisdom of God. His ways are not our ways, and his thoughts are higher than our thoughts. His way is always best.

Babylon." 4 So Johanan son of Kareah and all the commanders of the forces and all the people did not obey the voice of the LORD, to stay in the land of Judah. 5 But Johanan son of Kareah and all the commanders of the forces took all the remnant of Judah who had returned to settle in the land of Judah from all the nations to which they had been driven — 6 the men, the women, the children, the princesses, and everyone whom Nebuzaradan the captain of the guard had left with Gedaliah son of Ahikam son of Shaphan; also the prophet Jeremiah and Baruch son of Neriah. 7 And they came into the land of Egypt, for they did not obey the voice of the LORD. And they arrived at Tahpanhes.

2. Prophecy of the invasion of Egypt by Chaldea

8 Then the word of the LORD came to Jeremiah in Tahpanhes: 9 Take some large stones in your hands, and bury them in the clay pavement[o] that is at the entrance to Pharaoh's palace in Tahpanhes. Let the Judeans see you do it, 10 and say to them, Thus says the LORD of hosts, the God of Israel: I am going to send and take my servant King Nebuchadrezzar of Babylon, and he[p] will set his throne above these stones that I have buried, and he will spread his royal canopy over them. 11 He shall come and ravage the land of Egypt, giving

> those who are destined for pestilence, to pestilence,
> and those who are destined for captivity, to captivity,
> and those who are destined for the sword, to the sword.

12 He[q] shall kindle a fire in the temples of the gods of Egypt; and he shall burn them and carry them away captive; and he shall pick clean the land of Egypt, as a shepherd picks his cloak clean of vermin; and he shall depart from there safely. 13 He shall break the obelisks of Heliopolis, which is in the land of Egypt; and the temples of the gods of Egypt he shall burn with fire.

3. The refugees to perish in Egypt

44 The word that came to Jeremiah for all the Judeans living in the land of Egypt, at Migdol, at Tahpanhes, at Memphis, and in the land of Pathros, 2 Thus says the LORD of hosts, the God of Israel: You yourselves have seen all the disaster that I have brought on Jerusalem and on all the towns of Judah. Look at them; today they are a desolation, without an inhabitant in them, 3 because of the wickedness that they committed, provoking me to anger, in that they went to make offerings and serve other gods that they had not known, neither they, nor you, nor your ancestors. 4 Yet I persistently sent to you all my servants the prophets, saying, "I beg you not to do this abominable thing that I hate!" 5 But they did not listen or incline their ear, to turn from their wickedness and make no offerings to other gods. 6 So my wrath and my anger were poured out and kindled in the towns of Judah and in the streets of Jerusalem; and they became a waste and a desolation, as they still are today. 7 And now thus says the LORD God of hosts, the God of Israel: Why are you doing such great harm to yourselves, to cut off man and woman, child and infant, from the midst of Judah, leaving yourselves without a remnant? 8 Why do you provoke me to anger with the works of your hands, making offerings to other gods in the land of Egypt where you have come to settle?

o Meaning of Heb uncertain p Gk Syr: Heb I q Gk Syr Vg: Heb I

43.4 Jer 42.5, 6, 10-12
43.5 Jer 40.11, 12
43.6 Jer 41.10; 39.10; 40.7
43.7 Jer 44.1
43.8 Jer 2.16; 44.1; 46.14
43.10 Jer 25.9, 11; 27.5, 6; 31.20
43.11 Isa 19.1-25; Jer 44.13; 46.13; Ezek 29.19, 20; Jer 15.2
43.12 Isa 19.1; Jer 46.25; Ezek 30.13
44.1 Jer 46.14; 43.7; Isa 19.13
44.2 Jer 9.11; 34.22; Mic 3.12
44.3 Ezek 8.17, 18; Dan 9.5; Isa 3.8; Jer 19.4; Deut 13.6; 32.17
44.4 2 Chr 36.15; Jer 7.25; 25.4; 26.5; Ezek 8.10
44.5 Jer 11.8, 10; 13.10
44.6 Jer 42.18
44.7 Jer 26.19; Ezek 33.11; Jer 9.21; 51.22
44.8 2 Kings 17.15-17; Jer 25.6, 7; 42.18

43.10 Those who fled from Judah to Egypt thought they would escape from Nebuchadnezzar. Jeremiah now prophesied that Nebuchadnezzar would attack Egypt and destroy it. The Jews would find that they had not escaped from him. God providentially used one bad nation to defeat another one. Nebuchadnezzar would burn the houses of the gods of Egypt and carry many people into captivity.

44.1ff This passage contains no ifs spoken by God. He did not lay before the refugees in Egypt a choice between two opposing possibilities. This is a picture of unrelieved judgment spoken to people whose ancestors disobeyed God and who themselves refused to repent and reform.

Will you be cut off and become an object of cursing and ridicule among all the nations of the earth? 9 Have you forgotten the crimes of your ancestors, of the kings of Judah, of their[r] wives, your own crimes and those of your wives, which they committed in the land of Judah and in the streets of Jerusalem? 10 They have shown no contrition or fear to this day, nor have they walked in my law and my statutes that I set before you and before your ancestors.

11 Therefore thus says the LORD of hosts, the God of Israel: I am determined to bring disaster on you, to bring all Judah to an end. 12 I will take the remnant of Judah who are determined to come to the land of Egypt to settle, and they shall perish, everyone; in the land of Egypt they shall fall; by the sword and by famine they shall perish; from the least to the greatest, they shall die by the sword and by famine; and they shall become an object of execration and horror, of cursing and ridicule. 13 I will punish those who live in the land of Egypt, as I have punished Jerusalem, with the sword, with famine, and with pestilence, 14 so that none of the remnant of Judah who have come to settle in the land of Egypt shall escape or survive or return to the land of Judah. Although they long to go back to live there, they shall not go back, except some fugitives.

15 Then all the men who were aware that their wives had been making offerings to other gods, and all the women who stood by, a great assembly, all the people who lived in Pathros in the land of Egypt, answered Jeremiah: 16 "As for the word that you have spoken to us in the name of the LORD, we are not going to listen to you. 17 Instead, we will do everything that we have vowed, make offerings to the queen of heaven and pour out libations to her, just as we and our ancestors, our kings and our officials, used to do in the towns of Judah and in the streets of Jerusalem. We used to have plenty of food, and prospered, and saw no misfortune. 18 But from the time we stopped making offerings to the queen of heaven and pouring out libations to her, we have lacked everything and have perished by the sword and by famine." 19 And the women said,[s] "Indeed we will go on making offerings to the queen of heaven and pouring out libations to her; do you think that we made cakes for her, marked with her image, and poured out libations to her without our husbands' being involved?"

20 Then Jeremiah said to all the people, men and women, all the people who were giving him this answer: 21 "As for the offerings that you made in the towns of Judah and in the streets of Jerusalem, you and your ancestors, your kings and your officials, and the people of the land, did not the LORD remember them? Did it not come into his mind? 22 The LORD could no longer bear the sight of your evil doings, the abominations that you committed; therefore your land became a desolation and a waste and a curse, without inhabitant, as it is to this day. 23 It is because you burned offerings, and because you sinned against the LORD and did not obey the voice of the LORD or walk in his law and in his statutes and in his decrees, that this disaster has befallen you, as is still evident today."

24 Jeremiah said to all the people and all the women, "Hear the word of the LORD, all you Judeans who are in the land of Egypt, 25 Thus says the LORD of hosts, the God of Israel: You and your wives have accomplished in deeds what you declared in words, saying, 'We are determined to perform the vows that we have made, to make offerings to the queen of heaven and to pour out libations to her.' By all means, keep your vows and make your libations! 26 Therefore hear the word of the LORD, all you

Cross references (left margin)

44.9 Jer 7.9, 10, 17, 18
44.10 Jer 6.15; 8.12; 26.4; 32.23
44.11 Lev 26.17; Jer 21.10; Am 9.4
44.12 Jer 42.15-18, 22
44.13 Jer 11.22; 21.9; 24.10; 42.17, 22
44.14 Jer 22.26, 27; Isa 4.2; 10.20; v. 28; Rom 9.27
44.15 Jer 5.1-5
44.16 Jer 8.6, 12; 13.10
44.17 2 Kings 17.16; Jer 7.18; Hos 2.5-9; Phil 3.19
44.18 Jer 40.12
44.19 Jer 7.18; Num 30.6, 7
44.21 Ezek 8.10, 11; 16.24; Isa 64.9; Jer 14.10; Hos 7.2
44.22 Isa 7.13; Jer 4.4; 21.12; 25.11, 18; 38
44.23 Jer 40.3; vv. 10, 2; Dan 9.11, 12
44.24 Jer 42.15; v. 15; Jer 43.7
44.25 Mt 14.9; Acts 23.12
44.26 Gen 22.16; Am 6.8; Heb 6.13, 18; Ezek 20.39; Jer 5.2

---

r Heb his   s Compare Syr: Heb lacks *And the women said*

44.17 *queen of heaven.* See note on 7.18.
44.18 The Jews maintained that when they had offered incense to other gods and had poured out libations to the queen of heaven, all went well. When they ceased to do these things, circumstances worked against them. Somehow they refused to realize that it was the doing of these things which first occasioned the invasion of Judah by Nebuchadnezzar. Wicked people will always find excuses to evade guilt and justify illicit actions.

Judeans who live in the land of Egypt: Lo, I swear by my great name, says the LORD, that my name shall no longer be pronounced on the lips of any of the people of Judah in all the land of Egypt, saying, 'As the Lord GOD lives.' 27 I am going to watch over them for harm and not for good; all the people of Judah who are in the land of Egypt shall perish by the sword and by famine, until not one is left. 28 And those who escape the sword shall return from the land of Egypt to the land of Judah, few in number; and all the remnant of Judah, who have come to the land of Egypt to settle, shall know whose words will stand, mine or theirs! 29 This shall be the sign to you, says the LORD, that I am going to punish you in this place, in order that you may know that my words against you will surely be carried out: 30 Thus says the LORD, I am going to give Pharaoh Hophra, king of Egypt, into the hands of his enemies, those who seek his life, just as I gave King Zedekiah of Judah into the hand of King Nebuchadrezzar of Babylon, his enemy who sought his life."

C. Encouragement to Baruch, Jeremiah's secretary

45 The word that the prophet Jeremiah spoke to Baruch son of Neriah, when he wrote these words in a scroll at the dictation of Jeremiah, in the fourth year of King Jehoiakim son of Josiah of Judah: 2 Thus says the LORD, the God of Israel, to you, O Baruch: 3 You said, "Woe is me! The LORD has added sorrow to my pain; I am weary with my groaning, and I find no rest." 4 Thus you shall say to him, "Thus says the LORD: I am going to break down what I have built, and pluck up what I have planted — that is, the whole land. 5 And you, do you seek great things for yourself? Do not seek them; for I am going to bring disaster upon all flesh, says the LORD; but I will give you your life as a prize of war in every place to which you may go."

IV. Prophecies against heathen nations (46.1–51.64)

A. Prophecies against Egypt

1. Nebuchadnezzar will crush Neco at Carchemish

46 The word of the LORD that came to the prophet Jeremiah concerning the nations. 2 Concerning Egypt, about the army of Pharaoh Neco, king of Egypt, which was by the river Euphrates at Carchemish and which King Nebuchadrezzar of Babylon defeated in the fourth year of King Jehoiakim son of Josiah of Judah:

3   Prepare buckler and shield,
      and advance for battle!
4   Harness the horses;
      mount the steeds!
    Take your stations with your helmets,
      whet your lances,
      put on your coats of mail!

Side references:
44.27 Jer 1.10; 31.28; Ezek 7.6
44.28 Isa 27.13; vv. 17, 25, 26
44.29 Isa 7.11, 14; 8.18; Prov 19.21; Isa 40.8
44.30 Jer 46.25, 26; Ezek 29.3; 2 Kings 25.4-7; Jer 39.5
45.1 Jer 36.1, 4, 18, 32
45.3 Ps 6.6; 2 Cor 4.1, 16
45.4 Isa 5.5; Jer 11.17; 18.7-10
45.5 1 Kings 3.9, 11; Mt 6.25, 32, 33; Rom 12.16; Jer 25.31; 21.9; 38.2; 39.18
46.1 Jer 25.15-38
46.2 2 Kings 23.29; 2 Chr 35.20; Jer 45.1
46.3 Jer 51.11, 12; Nah 2.1; 3.14
46.4 Ezek 21.9-11; Jer 51.3

44.30 *Pharaoh Hophra.* Hophra, or Apries, ruled Egypt from 588 to 568 B.C. *into the hands of his enemies.* Pharaoh Hophra was killed by Amasis, one of his generals who had revolted and who was then crowned in his place.
45.1 This message, in point of time, follows ch. 36.
45.2ff Faithful Baruch, Jeremiah's secretary, was distressed and discontented, and spoke unadvisedly. God told him to forget seeking great things for himself, for he was bringing evil on all flesh. But in his sovereign mercy, God would give Baruch his life as a "prize of war."

46.1 Beginning with this verse, Jeremiah prophesies a series of judgments against nations other than Judah. This section ends with 51.58.
46.2 *Carchemish* was located on the Euphrates River, sixty miles northeast of Aleppo. The city guarded the main ford over this river and thus was an important military site. Under the kingship of Pharaoh Neco II, Egypt captured the city and harassed the Babylonians. Nebuchadnezzar and his army fell on the city in May or June of 605 B.C., defeating Neco II, whose armies fled to Hamath.

46.5 Isa 42.17; Ezek 39.18; Jer 6.25; 49.29

5 Why do I see them terrified?
They have fallen back;
their warriors are beaten down,
and have fled in haste.
They do not look back—
terror is all around!

says the LORD.

46.6 Isa 30.16; Dan 11.19

6 The swift cannot flee away,
nor can the warrior escape;
in the north by the river Euphrates
they have stumbled and fallen.

46.7 Jer 47.2

7 Who is this, rising like the Nile,
like rivers whose waters surge?

46.8 Isa 37.24; 10.13

8 Egypt rises like the Nile,
like rivers whose waters surge.
It said, Let me rise, let me cover the earth,
let me destroy cities and their inhabitants.

46.9 Jer 47.3; Nah 2.4; 3.9; Isa 66.19

9 Advance, O horses,
and dash madly, O chariots!
Let the warriors go forth:
Ethiopia[t] and Put who carry the shield,
the Ludim, who draw[u] the bow.

46.10 Isa 13.6; Joel 1.15; 2.1; Jer 50.15, 28; Isa 34.6; Zeph 1.7

10 That day is the day of the Lord GOD of hosts,
a day of retribution,
to gain vindication from his foes.
The sword shall devour and be sated,
and drink its fill of their blood.
For the Lord GOD of hosts holds a sacrifice
in the land of the north by the river Euphrates.

46.11 Jer 8.22; 51.8; Isa 47.1; Jer 31.4, 21; 30.13; Ezek 30.21

11 Go up to Gilead, and take balm,
O virgin daughter Egypt!
In vain you have used many medicines;
there is no healing for you.

46.12 Jer 2.36; Nah 3.8-10; Jer 14.2

12 The nations have heard of your shame,
and the earth is full of your cry;
for warrior has stumbled against warrior;
both have fallen together.

2. *Nebuchadnezzar will ravage Memphis and Thebes*

46.13 Isa 19.1; Jer 43.10, 11

13 The word that the LORD spoke to the prophet Jeremiah about the coming of King Nebuchadrezzar of Babylon to attack the land of Egypt:

46.14 Jer 44.1; 43.8; Nah 2.13

14 Declare in Egypt, and proclaim in Migdol;
proclaim in Memphis and Tahpanhes;
Say, "Take your stations and be ready,
for the sword shall devour those around you."
15 Why has Apis fled?[v]
Why did your bull not stand?
—because the LORD thrust him down.

46.16 Lev 26.36, 37; Jer 51.9; 50.16

16 Your multitude stumbled[w] and fell,
and one said to another,[x]
"Come, let us go back to our own people
and to the land of our birth,

[t] Or *Nubia*; Heb *Cush* [u] Cn: Heb *who grasp, who draw* [v] Gk: Heb *Why was it swept away*
[w] Gk: Meaning of Heb uncertain [x] Gk: Heb *and fell one to another and they said*

46.6 The race is not always to the swift nor the battle to the strong (Eccl 9.11). According to the word of God, the swift among the Egyptians would not be able to flee and the mighty warriors would not be able to triumph. God would be the decisive factor in determining the victory.

	because of the destroying sword."	
17	Give Pharaoh, king of Egypt, the name	**46.17** Isa 19.11-16
	"Braggart who missed his chance."	
18	As I live, says the King,	**46.18** Jer 48.15; Ps 89.12; 1 Kings 18.42
	whose name is the LORD of hosts,	
	one is coming	
	like Tabor among the mountains,	
	and like Carmel by the sea.	
19	Pack your bags for exile,	**46.19** Jer 48.18; Isa 20.4; v. 4; Ezek 30.13
	sheltered daughter Egypt!	
	For Memphis shall become a waste,	
	a ruin, without inhabitant.	
20	A beautiful heifer is Egypt—	**46.20** Jer 50.11; v. 24
	a gadfly from the north lights upon her.	
21	Even her mercenaries in her midst	**46.21** v. 5; Ps 37.13; Jer 50.27
	are like fatted calves;	
	they too have turned and fled together,	
	they did not stand;	
	for the day of their calamity has come upon them,	
	the time of their punishment.	
22	She makes a sound like a snake gliding away;	**46.22** Isa 29.4
	for her enemies march in force,	
	and come against her with axes,	
	like those who fell trees.	
23	They shall cut down her forest,	**46.23** Isa 10.34; Jer 21.14; Judg 6.5; Joel 2.25
	says the LORD,	
	though it is impenetrable,	
	because they are more numerous	
	than locusts;	
	they are without number.	
24	Daughter Egypt shall be put to shame;	**46.24** v. 19; Jer 1.15
	she shall be handed over to a people from the north.	

25 The LORD of hosts, the God of Israel, said: See, I am bringing punishment upon Amon of Thebes, and Pharaoh, and Egypt and her gods and her kings, upon Pharaoh and those who trust in him. 26 I will hand them over to those who seek their life, to King Nebuchadrezzar of Babylon and his officers. Afterward Egypt shall be inhabited as in the days of old, says the LORD.

46.25
Jer 43.12;
Ezek 30.14-16;
Jer 44.30;
46.26
Jer 44.30;
Ezek 32.11;
29.11-14

3. Israel will be restored, and the enemy powers will be destroyed

46.27
Isa 41.13;
43.5;
Jer 30.10, 11;
23.3, 4, 6;
50.19
46.28
Isa 8.9, 10;
Jer 1.19;
4.27;
Am 9.8, 9;
Jer 10.24;
30.11

27	But as for you, have no fear, my servant Jacob,
	and do not be dismayed, O Israel;
	for I am going to save you from far away,
	and your offspring from the land of their captivity.
	Jacob shall return and have quiet and ease,
	and no one shall make him afraid.
28	As for you, have no fear, my servant Jacob,

46.20 Egypt is compared to a calf or fair heifer not yet accustomed to the yoke. This may refer to Apis, the bull or calf that the Egyptians worshiped (cf. v. 15).
46.27 Most of the prophecies of Jeremiah were filled with woe for Israel, the object of God's wrath because of its transgressions. Here Jeremiah spoke the hopeful word that God would someday restore Israel after an end had been made to the nations who had plundered them. Israel would not be exterminated, only punished in a just measure; they could look for the day of restoration.

says the LORD,
for I am with you.
I will make an end of all the nations
among which I have banished you,
but I will not make an end of you!
I will chastise you in just measure,
and I will by no means leave you unpunished.

B. *Prophecy against Philistia*

47 The word of the LORD that came to the prophet Jeremiah concerning the Philistines, before Pharaoh attacked Gaza:
2 Thus says the LORD:
See, waters are rising out of the north
and shall become an overflowing torrent;
they shall overflow the land and all that fills it,
the city and those who live in it.
People shall cry out,
and all the inhabitants of the land shall wail.
3 At the noise of the stamping of the hoofs of his stallions,
at the clatter of his chariots, at the rumbling of their wheels,
parents do not turn back for children,
so feeble are their hands,
4 because of the day that is coming
to destroy all the Philistines,
to cut off from Tyre and Sidon
every helper that remains.
For the LORD is destroying the Philistines,
the remnant of the coastland of Caphtor.
5 Baldness has come upon Gaza,
Ashkelon is silenced.
O remnant of their power!*y*
How long will you gash yourselves?
6 Ah, sword of the LORD!
How long until you are quiet?
Put yourself into your scabbard,
rest and be still!
7 How can it*z* be quiet,
when the LORD has given it an order?
Against Ashkelon and against the seashore —
there he has appointed it.

C. *Prophecy against Moab*

48 Concerning Moab.

Thus says the LORD of hosts, the God of Israel:
Alas for Nebo, it is laid waste!
Kiriathaim is put to shame, it is taken;
the fortress is put to shame and broken down;
2 the renown of Moab is no more.

47.1
Jer 25.17, 20;
Am 1.6;
Zeph 2.4
47.2
Isa 14.31;
Jer 46.20, 24;
Isa 8.7;
15.2-5;
Jer 46.12

47.3
Jer 8.16;
Nah 3.2

47.4
Isa 14.31;
23.5, 6, 11;
Joel 3.4;
Zech 9.2-4;
Gen 10.14

47.5
Mic 1.16;
Jer 25.20;
16.6; 41.5

47.6
Jer 12.12;
4.21

47.7
Ezek 14.17;
Mic 6.9

48.1
Isa 15.2;
vv. 22, 23;
Num 32.37

48.2
Isa 16.14;
15.4;
Jer 49.3

y Gk: Heb *their valley*   *z* Gk Vg: Heb *you*

47.1 *before Pharaoh attacked Gaza.* In 609 B.C., the year King Josiah died.
47.4 *Caphtor,* the island of Crete.
47.6,7 Jeremiah longed for peace. He asked when the withdrawn sword would be replaced in its scabbard. The desolations of war were such that peace looked more and more desirable. However, Jeremiah affirmed that war involved the "sword of the LORD." With it he punished enemies and pleaded the cause of his own people.
48.2 See note on Ezek 25.9 for information on the Moabites.

In Heshbon they planned evil against her:
　"Come, let us cut her off from being a nation!"
You also, O Madmen, shall be brought to silence;[a]
　the sword shall pursue you.

3　Hark! a cry from Horonaim,
　　"Desolation and great destruction!"
4　"Moab is destroyed!"
　　her little ones cry out.
5　For at the ascent of Luhith
　　they go[b] up weeping bitterly;
for at the descent of Horonaim
　　they have heard the distressing cry of anguish.
6　Flee! Save yourselves!
　　Be like a wild ass[c] in the desert!

7　Surely, because you trusted in your strongholds[d] and your
　　　treasures,
　　you also shall be taken;
Chemosh shall go out into exile,
　　with his priests and his attendants.
8　The destroyer shall come upon every town,
　　and no town shall escape;
the valley shall perish,
　　and the plain shall be destroyed,
　　as the LORD has spoken.

9　Set aside salt for Moab,
　　for she will surely fall;
her towns shall become a desolation,
　　with no inhabitant in them.

10　Accursed is the one who is slack in doing the work of the
LORD; and accursed is the one who keeps back the sword from bloodshed.

11　Moab has been at ease from his youth,
　　settled like wine[e] on its dregs;
he has not been emptied from vessel to vessel,
　　nor has he gone into exile;
therefore his flavor has remained
　　and his aroma is unspoiled.

12　Therefore, the time is surely coming, says the LORD, when I shall
send to him decanters to decant him, and empty his vessels, and break
his[f] jars in pieces. 13 Then Moab shall be ashamed of Chemosh, as the
house of Israel was ashamed of Bethel, their confidence.

14　How can you say, "We are heroes
　　and mighty warriors"?
15　The destroyer of Moab and his towns has come up,

	48.3 Isa 15.5; vv. 5, 34
	48.5 Isa 15.5
	48.6 Jer 51.6; 17.6
	48.7 Jer 9.23; Num 21.29; 1 Kings 11.33; Jer 49.3
	48.8 Jer 6.26
	48.9 Isa 16.2; Jer 44.22
	48.10 Jer 11.3; 1 Sam 15.3, 9; 1 Kings 20.42; Jer 47.6, 7
	48.11 Jer 22.21; Zech 1.15; Zeph 1.12; Nah 2.2
	48.13 Isa 45.16; v. 39; Hos 10.6; 1 Kings 12.29
	48.14 Isa 10.13-16
	48.15 Jer 50.27; 46.18

---

a The place-name *Madmen* sounds like the Hebrew verb *to be silent*　*b* Cn: Heb *he goes*　*c* Gk Aquila:
Heb *like Aroer*　*d* Gk: Heb *works*　*e* Heb lacks *like wine*　*f* Gk Aquila: Heb *their*

48.5 This is similar to the lament in Isa 15.5.
48.7–11 *Chemosh* was the god of Moab. Here, as
well as in v. 11, the reasons for the demise of Moab
are adduced: (1) they trusted in their wealth and

strength; and (2) they did not reform themselves in
their days of prosperity and peace, for they *settled like
wine on its dregs*, i.e., they were corrupt and had been
sensual and secure in their depravity.

and the choicest of his young men have gone down to
        slaughter,
    says the King, whose name is the LORD of hosts.

48.16
Isa 13.22

16 The calamity of Moab is near at hand
        and his doom approaches swiftly.

48.17
Jer 9.17-20;
Isa 14.5

17 Mourn over him, all you his neighbors,
        and all who know his name;
    say, "How the mighty scepter is broken,
        the glorious staff!"

48.18
Isa 47.1;
Jer 46.19;
v. 8

18 Come down from glory,
        and sit on the parched ground,
        enthroned daughter Dibon!
    For the destroyer of Moab has come up against you;
        he has destroyed your strongholds.

48.19
Deut 2.36;
1 Sam 4.13,
16

19 Stand by the road and watch,
        you inhabitant of Aroer!
    Ask the man fleeing and the woman escaping;
        say, "What has happened?"

48.20
Isa 16.7;
Num 21.13

20 Moab is put to shame, for it is broken down;
        wail and cry!
    Tell it by the Arnon,
        that Moab is laid waste.

48.21
vv. 8, 34;
Josh 13.18
48.24
Am 2.2
48.25
Ps 75.10;
Ezek 30.21
48.26
Jer 25.15, 27
48.27
Zeph 2.8;
Jer 2.26;
18.16

21 Judgment has come upon the tableland, upon Holon, and Jahzah,
and Mephaath, 22 and Dibon, and Nebo, and Beth-diblathaim, 23 and
Kiriathaim, and Beth-gamul, and Beth-meon, 24 and Kerioth, and Bozrah, and all the towns of the land of Moab, far and near. 25 The horn of
Moab is cut off, and his arm is broken, says the LORD.

26 Make him drunk, because he magnified himself against the LORD;
let Moab wallow in his vomit; he too shall become a laughingstock.
27 Israel was a laughingstock for you, though he was not caught among
thieves; but whenever you spoke of him you shook your head!

48.28
Jer 49.16;
Ps 55.6, 7;
Song 2.14

28 Leave the towns, and live on the rock,
        O inhabitants of Moab!
    Be like the dove that nests
        on the sides of the mouth of a gorge.

48.29
Isa 16.6;
Zeph 2.8;
Ps 138.6

29 We have heard of the pride of Moab —
        he is very proud —
    of his loftiness, his pride, and his arrogance,
        and the haughtiness of his heart.

48.30
Isa 37.28;
16.6

30 I myself know his insolence, says the LORD;
        his boasts are false,
        his deeds are false.

48.31
Isa 15.5;
16.7, 11

31 Therefore I wail for Moab;
        I cry out for all Moab;
        for the people of Kir-heres I mourn.

48.32
Isa 16.8, 9;
Num 21.32

32 More than for Jazer I weep for you,
        O vine of Sibmah!
    Your branches crossed over the sea,
        reached as far as Jazer;g
    upon your summer fruits and your vintage
        the destroyer has fallen.

g Two Mss and Isa 16.8: MT the sea of Jazer

48.18 Dibon was the place where the Moabite Stone
was discovered. The site is some thirteen miles east
of the Dead Sea. The Moablite Stone records events of
2 Kings 3 (see note on 2 Kings 3.4-5).

33 Gladness and joy have been taken away
　　from the fruitful land of Moab;
　I have stopped the wine from the wine presses;
　　no one treads them with shouts of joy;
　　the shouting is not the shout of joy.

34　Heshbon and Elealeh cry out;[h] as far as Jahaz they utter their voice, from Zoar to Horonaim and Eglath-shelishiyah. For even the waters of Nimrim have become desolate. 35 And I will bring to an end in Moab, says the LORD, those who offer sacrifice at a high place and make offerings to their gods. 36 Therefore my heart moans for Moab like a flute, and my heart moans like a flute for the people of Kir-heres; for the riches they gained have perished.
37　For every head is shaved and every beard cut off; on all the hands there are gashes, and on the loins sackcloth. 38 On all the housetops of Moab and in the squares there is nothing but lamentation; for I have broken Moab like a vessel that no one wants, says the LORD. 39 How it is broken! How they wail! How Moab has turned his back in shame! So Moab has become a derision and a horror to all his neighbors.

40　For thus says the LORD:
　Look, he shall swoop down like an eagle,
　　and spread his wings against Moab;
41　the towns[i] shall be taken
　　and the strongholds seized.
　The hearts of the warriors of Moab, on that day,
　　shall be like the heart of a woman in labor.
42　Moab shall be destroyed as a people,
　　because he magnified himself against the LORD.
43　Terror, pit, and trap
　　are before you, O inhabitants of Moab!
　　　　　　　　　　　　　says the LORD.
44　Everyone who flees from the terror
　　shall fall into the pit,
　and everyone who climbs out of the pit
　　shall be caught in the trap.
　For I will bring these things[j] upon Moab
　　in the year of their punishment,
　　　　　　　　　　　　　says the LORD.

45　In the shadow of Heshbon
　　fugitives stop exhausted;
　for a fire has gone out from Heshbon,
　　a flame from the house of Sihon;
　it has destroyed the forehead of Moab,
　　the scalp of the people of tumult.[k]
46　Woe to you, O Moab!
　　The people of Chemosh have perished,
　for your sons have been taken captive,
　　and your daughters into captivity.
47　Yet I will restore the fortunes of Moab
　　in the latter days, says the LORD.
　Thus far is the judgment on Moab.

---

h Cn: Heb *From the cry of Heshbon to Elealeh*　*i* Or *Kerioth*　*j* Gk Syr: Heb *bring upon it*　*k* Or *of Shaon*

48.35 If God judged Israel for the worship of idols or false gods, how could he overlook the same idolatry on the part of the heathen Moabites?
48.42 *Moab shall be destroyed.* There may well have been some among the Moabites who believed in the God of Israel (cf. v. 47) and thus were spared destruction, for the fortunes of Moab would be restored in the latter days. This could not happen if all of the Moabites were slain.

48.33
Isa 16.10;
Joel 1.12;
Isa 5.10;
Hag 2.16

48.34
Isa 15.4-6

48.35
Isa 15.2;
16.12;
Jer 7.9; 11.13

48.36
Isa 16.11;
15.7

48.37
Isa 15.2, 3;
Jer 47.5
48.38
Jer 22.28;
25.34
48.39
Ezek 26.16

48.40
Jer 49.22;
Dan 7.4;
Hos 8.1;
Isa 8.8
48.41
Isa 21.3;
Jer 30.6;
49.22, 24;
Mic 4.9

48.42
v. 2;
Ps 83.4;
v. 26;
Isa 37.23
48.43
Isa 24.17,
18;
Lam 3.47
48.44
1 Kings 19.17;
Jer 11.23;
46.21

48.45
v. 2;
Num 21.21,
26, 28, 29;
24.17

48.46
Num 21.29;
v. 7

48.47
Jer 49.6, 39

D. *Prophecies against Ammon, Edom, Damascus, Kedar, and Elam*

1. *The Ammonites to go into captivity*

49 Concerning the Ammonites.

Thus says the LORD:

> Has Israel no sons?
>> Has he no heir?
> Why then has Milcom dispossessed Gad,
>> and his people settled in its towns?

2 Therefore, the time is surely coming,
>> says the LORD,
> when I will sound the battle alarm
>> against Rabbah of the Ammonites;
> it shall become a desolate mound,
>> and its villages shall be burned with fire;
> then Israel shall dispossess those who dispossessed him,
>> says the LORD.

3 Wail, O Heshbon, for Ai is laid waste!
>> Cry out, O daughters[l] of Rabbah!
> Put on sackcloth,
>> lament, and slash yourselves with whips![m]
> For Milcom shall go into exile,
>> with his priests and his attendants.

4 Why do you boast in your strength?
>> Your strength is ebbing,
> O faithless daughter.
> You trusted in your treasures, saying,
>> "Who will attack me?"

5 I am going to bring terror upon you,
>> says the Lord GOD of hosts,
> from all your neighbors,
> and you will be scattered, each headlong,
>> with no one to gather the fugitives.

6 But afterward I will restore the fortunes of the Ammonites, says the LORD.

2. *Edom to be devastated and dispossessed*

7 Concerning Edom.

Thus says the LORD of hosts:

> Is there no longer wisdom in Teman?
>> Has counsel perished from the prudent?
>> Has their wisdom vanished?
8 Flee, turn back, get down low,
>> inhabitants of Dedan!
> For I will bring the calamity of Esau upon him,
>> the time when I punish him.
9 If grape-gatherers came to you,
>> would they not leave gleanings?
> If thieves came by night,

l Or *villages*   *m* Cn: Meaning of Heb uncertain

49.1 See note on Ezek 25.2 for information on the Ammonites.
49.6 As in the case of Moab (48.47), the destruction of the Ammonites was not their final obliteration. God promised to restore their fortunes at a later time.

49.7 See note on Gen 36.9 for information on the Edomites.
49.8 *Dedan* was in northern Arabia and was a flourishing caravan city at the time of Jeremiah and Ezekiel.

Cross references (left margin):
49.1 Ezek 21.28; 25.2; Am 1.13; Zeph 2.8, 9
49.2 Jer 4.19; Ezek 21.20; Isa 14.2
49.3 Jer 48.2; Josh 7.2-5; 8.1-29; Isa 32.11; Jer 4.8; 48.7
49.4 Jer 9.23; 31.22; Ps 62.10; Ezek 28.4, 5
49.5 Jer 48.43, 44; 16.16; 46.5; Lam 4.15
49.6 v. 39; Jer 48.47
49.7 Isa 34.5, 6; Ezek 25.12; Am 1.11, 12; Jer 8.9; v. 20
49.8 v. 30; Jer 25.23; 46.21
49.9 Ob 5

even they would pillage only what they wanted.

10 But as for me, I have stripped Esau bare,
    I have uncovered his hiding places,
    and he is not able to conceal himself.
His offspring are destroyed, his kinsfolk
    and his neighbors; and he is no more.
11 Leave your orphans, I will keep them alive;
    and let your widows trust in me.

12 For thus says the LORD: If those who do not deserve to drink the cup still have to drink it, shall you be the one to go unpunished? You shall not go unpunished; you must drink it. 13 For by myself I have sworn, says the LORD, that Bozrah shall become an object of horror and ridicule, a waste, and an object of cursing; and all her towns shall be perpetual wastes.

14 I have heard tidings from the LORD,
    and a messenger has been sent among the nations:
"Gather yourselves together and come against her,
    and rise up for battle!"
15 For I will make you least among the nations,
    despised by humankind.
16 The terror you inspire
    and the pride of your heart have deceived you,
you who live in the clefts of the rock,[n]
    who hold the height of the hill.
Although you make your nest as high as the eagle's,
    from there I will bring you down,
                  says the LORD.

17 Edom shall become an object of horror; everyone who passes by it will be horrified and will hiss because of all its disasters. 18 As when Sodom and Gomorrah and their neighbors were overthrown, says the LORD, no one shall live there, nor shall anyone settle in it. 19 Like a lion coming up from the thickets of the Jordan against a perennial pasture, I will suddenly chase Edom[o] away from it; and I will appoint over it whomever I choose.[p] For who is like me? Who can summon me? Who is the shepherd who can stand before me? 20 Therefore hear the plan that the LORD has made against Edom and the purposes that he has formed against the inhabitants of Teman: Surely the little ones of the flock shall be dragged away; surely their fold shall be appalled at their fate. 21 At the sound of their fall the earth shall tremble; the sound of their cry shall be heard at the Red Sea.[q] 22 Look, he shall mount up and swoop down like an eagle, and spread his wings against Bozrah, and the heart of the warriors of Edom in that day shall be like the heart of a woman in labor.

3. Damascus to be destroyed

23 Concerning Damascus.

Hamath and Arpad are confounded,
    for they have heard bad news;
they melt in fear, they are troubled like the sea[r]
    that cannot be quiet.
24 Damascus has become feeble, she turned to flee,

n Or of Sela   o Heb him   p Or and I will single out the choicest of his rams: Meaning of Heb uncertain
q Or Sea of Reeds   r Cn: Heb there is trouble in the sea

49.10 Jer 13.26; Mal 1.3; Isa 17.14
49.11 Ps 68.5
49.12 Jer 25.28, 29; 1 Pet 4.17
49.13 1 Kings; Isa 34.6; 34.9-15
49.14 Ob 1-4; Isa 18.2; 30.4; Jer 50.14
49.16 Isa 25.5; 14.13-15; Am 9.2
49.17 Jer 50.13; 1 Kings 9.8; Jer 51.37
49.18 Gen 19.25; Deut 29.23; Am 4.11
49.19 Jer 50.44; 12.5; Isa 46.9
49.20 Jer 50.45; Mal 1.3, 4
49.21 Jer 50.46; Ezek 26.15, 18
49.22 Jer 4.13; 48.40, 41
49.23 2 Chr 16.2; Jer 39.5; Isa 10.9; 57.20
49.24 v. 22; Jer 6.24; 30.6; 48.41

49.13 *by myself I have sworn.* The decree had gone forth from the lips of God, who had sworn by his own name to do this. There is no one else to whom God could take an oath because no one is higher than he. *Bozrah,* a sheep herding center in Edom.

49.23 *Damascus* was the capital city of Aram (Syria). *Hamath* was a city on the Orontes River, more than a hundred miles from Damascus. *Arpad* was some twenty miles northwest of Aleppo.

and panic seized her;
anguish and sorrows have taken hold of her,
    as of a woman in labor.

25 How the famous city is forsaken,[s]
    the joyful town![t]

26 Therefore her young men shall fall in her squares,
    and all her soldiers shall be destroyed in that day,
                                        says the LORD of hosts.

27 And I will kindle a fire at the wall of Damascus,
    and it shall devour the strongholds of Ben-hadad.

4. Kedar and Hazor to be ravaged by Nebuchadrezzar

28 Concerning Kedar and the kingdoms of Hazor that King Nebuchadrezzar of Babylon defeated.

Thus says the LORD:
Rise up, advance against Kedar!
Destroy the people of the east!

29 Take their tents and their flocks,
    their curtains and all their goods;
carry off their camels for yourselves,
    and a cry shall go up: "Terror is all around!"

30 Flee, wander far away, hide in deep places,
    O inhabitants of Hazor!
                                        says the LORD.

For King Nebuchadrezzar of Babylon
    has made a plan against you
    and formed a purpose against you.

31 Rise up, advance against a nation at ease,
    that lives secure,
                                        says the LORD,
    that has no gates or bars,
        that lives alone.

32 Their camels shall become booty,
    their herds of cattle a spoil.
I will scatter to every wind
    those who have shaven temples,
and I will bring calamity
    against them from every side,
                                        says the LORD.

33 Hazor shall become a lair of jackals,
    an everlasting waste;
no one shall live there,
    nor shall anyone settle in it.

5. The Elamites to be dispersed and their rulers slain; a remnant to return

34 The word of the LORD that came to the prophet Jeremiah concerning Elam, at the beginning of the reign of King Zedekiah of Judah.

[s] Vg: Heb *is not forsaken*   [t] Syr Vg Tg: Heb *the town of my joy*

49.28ff *Kedar*, an Arab tribe which came from the stock of Ishmael and lived in the desert east of Palestine. *Hazor*, not the Hazor mentioned in Joshua and Judges (a great city north of the Sea of Galilee), but rather a group of Arab tribes, located east of Palestine in the Arabian Desert, about which little is known.

49.34ff The kingdom of Elam, located in the region that is now the province of Khuzistan in Iran, derived from Elam son of Shem. The Elamites were among the people sent by the Assyrians to settle in Samaria after the demise of the northern kingdom; they participated in the attack on Jerusalem and were among

---

Cross-references (left margin):

49.25
Jer 33.9;
51.41
49.26
Jer 50.30;
51.4;
Am 4.10
49.27
Jer 43.12;
Am 1.3-5;
1 Kings 15.18-20

49.28
Isa 21.16,
17;
Jer 2.10;
Ezek 27.21;
Isa 11.14

49.29
Jer 6.25;
20.3, 10;
46.5

49.30
Jer 25.9

49.31
Isa 47.8;
Ezek 38.11;
Deut 33.28

49.32
Ezek 12.14,
15;
Jer 9.26;
25.23

49.33
Jer 10.22;
Zeph 2.9,
13-15

49.34
Ezek 32.24;
2 Kings 24.17,
18;
Jer 28.1

35 Thus says the LORD of hosts: I am going to break the bow of Elam, the mainstay of their might; 36 and I will bring upon Elam the four winds from the four quarters of heaven; and I will scatter them to all these winds, and there shall be no nation to which the exiles from Elam shall not come. 37 I will terrify Elam before their enemies, and before those who seek their life; I will bring disaster upon them, my fierce anger, says the LORD. I will send the sword after them, until I have consumed them; 38 and I will set my throne in Elam, and destroy their king and officials, says the LORD.

39 But in the latter days I will restore the fortunes of Elam, says the LORD.

E. Prophecies against Babylon

1. Babylon to become an uninhabited waste; the Jews to return home

50 The word that the LORD spoke concerning Babylon, concerning the land of the Chaldeans, by the prophet Jeremiah:

2 Declare among the nations and proclaim,
   set up a banner and proclaim,
   do not conceal it, say:
Babylon is taken,
   Bel is put to shame,
   Merodach is dismayed.
Her images are put to shame,
   her idols are dismayed.

3 For out of the north a nation has come up against her; it shall make her land a desolation, and no one shall live in it; both human beings and animals shall flee away.

4 In those days and in that time, says the LORD, the people of Israel shall come, they and the people of Judah together; they shall come weeping as they seek the LORD their God. 5 They shall ask the way to Zion, with faces turned toward it, and they shall come and join*u* themselves to the LORD by an everlasting covenant that will never be forgotten.

6 My people have been lost sheep; their shepherds have led them astray, turning them away on the mountains; from mountain to hill they have gone, they have forgotten their fold. 7 All who found them have devoured them, and their enemies have said, "We are not guilty, because they have sinned against the LORD, the true pasture, the LORD, the hope of their ancestors."

8 Flee from Babylon, and go out of the land of the Chaldeans, and be like male goats leading the flock. 9 For I am going to stir up and bring against Babylon a company of great nations from the land of the north; and they shall array themselves against her; from there she shall be taken. Their arrows are like the arrows of a skilled warrior who does not return

u Gk: Heb *toward it. Come! They shall join*

49.35
Isa 22.6;
Jer 51.56
49.36
Rev 7.1;
Ezek 5.10;
Am 9.9
49.37
Jer 8.9;
17.18; 6.19;
30.24; 9.16

49.39
Jer 48.47

50.1
Isa 13.1;
Rev 14.8
50.2
Jer 51.27, 31;
Isa 46.1;
Jer 51.44, 47

50.3
Jer 51.48;
9.10;
Zeph 1.3

50.4
Hos 1.11;
Ezra 3.12,
13;
Jer 31.9;
Zech 12.10;
Hos 3.5

50.6
Isa 53.6;
Ezek 34.15,
16;
Jer 23.11-14;
2.20; 3.6, 23;
33.12
50.7
Jer 40.2, 3;
31.23; 14.8;
17.13
50.8
Jer 51.6, 45;
Rev 18.4
50.9
Jer 51.1, 2

---

those who attacked Babylon under Cyrus. God's judgment against the Elamites was not a final judgment, for they were to be restored. Several Elamites were among those who were present at Pentecost when the Holy Spirit was poured out and multitudes were converted.
50.3 See note on Isa 13.20 for information about the demise of Babylon.
50.4 This prophetic word concerns the final regathering of Israel, a promise not yet fulfilled in history.

First the people of Israel must turn to God. Then they will be returned to their land from all parts of the globe. Paul discusses this in Rom 9–11. Christians are not in agreement on how the present state of Israel relates to a prophecy of this nature.
50.9 Jeremiah kept the destruction of Babylon until the last, for it was the last one to experience the wrath of God. Isaiah had foretold its destruction by Cyrus in graphic terms (Isa 45–47).

| | empty-handed. 10Chaldea shall be plundered; all who plunder her shall be sated, says the LORD. |

50.10
Jer 51.24, 35;
Rev 17.16

11   Though you rejoice, though you exult,
        O plunderers of my heritage,
     though you frisk about like a heifer on the grass,
        and neigh like stallions,

50.11
Jer 12.14;
46.20

12   your mother shall be utterly shamed,
        and she who bore you shall be disgraced.
     Lo, she shall be the last of the nations,
        a wilderness, dry land, and a desert.

50.12
Jer 22.6;
51.43

13   Because of the wrath of the LORD she shall not be inhabited,
        but shall be an utter desolation;
     everyone who passes by Babylon shall be appalled
        and hiss because of all her wounds.

50.13
Jer 25.12;
49.17

14   Take up your positions around Babylon,
        all you that bend the bow;
     shoot at her, spare no arrows,
        for she has sinned against the LORD.

50.14
Jer 49.35;
Hab 2.8, 17

15   Raise a shout against her from all sides,
        "She has surrendered;
     her bulwarks have fallen,
        her walls are thrown down."
     For this is the vengeance of the LORD:
        take vengeance on her,
        do to her as she has done.

50.15
Jer 51.14;
1 Chr 29.24;
Ezek 17.18;
Jer 51.44, 58;
46.10

16   Cut off from Babylon the sower,
        and the wielder of the sickle in time of harvest;
     because of the destroying sword
     all of them shall return to their own people,
        and all of them shall flee to their own land.

50.16
Joel 1.11;
Jer 51.9

17   Israel is a hunted sheep driven away by lions. First the king of Assyria devoured it, and now at the end King Nebuchadrezzar of Babylon has gnawed its bones. 18Therefore, thus says the LORD of hosts, the God of Israel: I am going to punish the king of Babylon and his land, as I punished the king of Assyria. 19I will restore Israel to its pasture, and it shall feed on Carmel and in Bashan, and on the hills of Ephraim and in Gilead its hunger shall be satisfied. 20In those days and at that time, says the LORD, the iniquity of Israel shall be sought, and there shall be none; and the sins of Judah, and none shall be found; for I will pardon the remnant that I have spared.

50.17
Jer 2.15;
2 Kings 17.6;
24.10, 14
50.18
Isa 10.12;
Ezek 31.3,
11, 12
50.19
Jer 31.10;
33.12; 31.5
50.20
Jer 31.34;
Mic 7.19;
Isa 1.9;
Jer 33.8

21   Go up to the land of Merathaim;v
        go up against her,
     and attack the inhabitants of Pekodw
        and utterly destroy the last of them,x

                                        says the LORD;
        do all that I have commanded you.

50.21
Ezek 23.23;
Isa 10.6;
44.28; 48.14;
Jer 34.22

22   The noise of battle is in the land,
        and great destruction!

50.22
Jer 51.54-56

23   How the hammer of the whole earth
        is cut down and broken!

50.23
Isa 14.6;
Jer 51.20-24

v Or of Double Rebellion   w Or of Punishment   x Tg: Heb destroy after them

50.20 God promises a day when his people, Israel, would live in perfect harmony with him. Their iniquity would be forgiven and no longer remembered against them. This same truth lies at the heart of the N.T., for justification includes the canceling of our debt of sin and its being cast behind the back of God, to be remembered no more.

How Babylon has become
    a horror among the nations!

24 You set a snare for yourself and you were caught, O Babylon,
    but you did not know it;
  you were discovered and seized,
    because you challenged the Lord.

25 The Lord has opened his armory,
    and brought out the weapons of his wrath,
  for the Lord God of hosts has a task to do
    in the land of the Chaldeans.

26 Come against her from every quarter;
    open her granaries;
  pile her up like heaps of grain, and destroy her utterly;
    let nothing be left of her.

27 Kill all her bulls,
    let them go down to the slaughter.
  Alas for them, their day has come,
    the time of their punishment!

28 Listen! Fugitives and refugees from the land of Babylon are coming to declare in Zion the vengeance of the Lord our God, vengeance for his temple.

29 Summon archers against Babylon, all who bend the bow. Encamp all around her; let no one escape. Repay her according to her deeds; just as she has done, do to her—for she has arrogantly defied the Lord, the Holy One of Israel. 30 Therefore her young men shall fall in her squares, and all her soldiers shall be destroyed on that day, says the Lord.

31 I am against you, O arrogant one,
    says the Lord God of hosts;
  for your day has come,
    the time when I will punish you.

32 The arrogant one shall stumble and fall,
    with no one to raise him up,
  and I will kindle a fire in his cities,
    and it will devour everything around him.

33 Thus says the Lord of hosts: The people of Israel are oppressed, and so too are the people of Judah; all their captors have held them fast and refuse to let them go. 34 Their Redeemer is strong; the Lord of hosts is his name. He will surely plead their cause, that he may give rest to the earth, but unrest to the inhabitants of Babylon.

35 A sword against the Chaldeans, says the Lord,
    and against the inhabitants of Babylon,
    and against her officials and her sages!

36 A sword against the diviners,
    so that they may become fools!
  A sword against her warriors,
    so that they may be destroyed!

37 A sword against her[y] horses and against her[y] chariots,
    and against all the foreign troops in her midst,
    so that they may become women!

y Cn: Heb his

50.24 Jer 48.43, 44; 51.8, 31, 39, 57; Dan 5.30, 31

50.25 Isa 13.5; Jer 51.12, 25, 55

50.26 v. 41; Isa 14.23

50.27 Isa 34.7; Ezek 7.7; Jer 48.44

50.28 Isa 48.20; Jer 51.6; 51.10, 11

50.29 Jer 51.56; Rev 18.6; Isa 47.10

50.30 Isa 13.17, 18; Jer 49.26; 51.56, 57

50.31 Jer 21.13; Nah 2.13

50.32 Isa 10.12-15; Jer 21.14; 49.27

50.33 Isa 14.17; 58.6

50.34 Isa 43.14; Jer 15.21; 31.11; 32.18; 51.19, 36; Isa 14.3-7

50.35 Dan 5.1, 2, 7, 8, 30

50.36 Isa 44.25; Jer 49.22

50.37 Jer 51.21, 22; 25.30; Ezek 30.5; Jer 51.30; Nah 3.13

50.25 When the God of hosts has a task to perform, he does not lack instruments to execute his will— whether other people, other nations, or just himself.

In the case of Babylon, God used Cyrus as his servant. God said, "He shall carry out all my purpose" (Isa 44.28).

A sword against all her treasures,
    that they may be plundered!
38 A drought[z] against her waters,
    that they may be dried up!
For it is a land of images,
    and they go mad over idols.

39 Therefore wild animals shall live with hyenas in Babylon,[a] and ostriches shall inhabit her; she shall never again be peopled, or inhabited for all generations. 40 As when God overthrew Sodom and Gomorrah and their neighbors, says the LORD, so no one shall live there, nor shall anyone settle in her.

41 Look, a people is coming from the north;
    a mighty nation and many kings
are stirring from the farthest parts of the earth.
42 They wield bow and spear,
    they are cruel and have no mercy.
The sound of them is like the roaring sea;
    they ride upon horses,
set in array as a warrior for battle,
    against you, O daughter Babylon!

43 The king of Babylon heard news of them,
    and his hands fell helpless;
anguish seized him,
    pain like that of a woman in labor.

44 Like a lion coming up from the thickets of the Jordan against a perennial pasture, I will suddenly chase them away from her; and I will appoint over her whomever I choose.[b] For who is like me? Who can summon me? Who is the shepherd who can stand before me? 45 Therefore hear the plan that the LORD has made against Babylon, and the purposes that he has formed against the land of the Chaldeans: Surely the little ones of the flock shall be dragged away; surely their[c] fold shall be appalled at their fate. 46 At the sound of the capture of Babylon the earth shall tremble, and her cry shall be heard among the nations.

2. Babylon to be destroyed by the Medes

51 Thus says the LORD:
I am going to stir up a destructive wind[d]
    against Babylon
    and against the inhabitants of Leb-qamai;[e]
2 and I will send winnowers to Babylon,
    and they shall winnow her.
They shall empty her land
    when they come against her from every side
    on the day of trouble.
3 Let not the archer bend his bow,
    and let him not array himself in his coat of mail.
Do not spare her young men;
    utterly destroy her entire army.

Cross references (left margin):

50.38 Jer 51.32, 36, 42, 47, 52
50.39 Isa 13.21, 22; Jer 51.37; Isa 13.20
50.40 Gen 19.25; Jer 49.18; Lk 17.28-30
50.41 cf. v. 3; Jer 6.22; Rev 17.16
50.42 Jer 6.23; Isa 13.18; 5.30
50.43 Jer 51.31; 49.24
50.44 Jer 49.19-21; Isa 46.9; Job 41.10; Jer 49.19
50.45 Isa 14.24; Jer 51.11; 49.20
50.46 Rev 18.9; Ezek 27.28
51.1 Jer 4.11; Hos 13.15
51.2 Isa 41.16; Jer 15.7; Mt 3.12
51.3 Jer 50.14; 46.4; 50.21

---

z Another reading is *A sword* a Heb lacks *in Babylon* b Or *and I will single out the choicest of her rams*: Meaning of Heb uncertain c Syr Gk Tg Compare 49.20: Heb lacks *their* d Or *stir up the spirit of a destroyer* e *Leb-qamai* is a cryptogram for *Kasdim*, Chaldea

---

50.39 God ordained that Babylon would never rise again. The site is currently being excavated and the glories of that ancient city are coming to light by the archaeologists' spades. But there is no evidence that it ever rose from its destroyed state, and presumably never will. God's judgment is irreversible.

4 They shall fall down slain in the land of the Chaldeans,
    and wounded in her streets.
5 Israel and Judah have not been forsaken
    by their God, the LORD of hosts,
though their land is full of guilt
    before the Holy One of Israel.

6 Flee from the midst of Babylon,
    save your lives, each of you!
Do not perish because of her guilt,
    for this is the time of the LORD's vengeance;
    he is repaying her what is due.
7 Babylon was a golden cup in the LORD's hand,
    making all the earth drunken;
the nations drank of her wine,
    and so the nations went mad.
8 Suddenly Babylon has fallen and is shattered;
    wail for her!
Bring balm for her wound;
    perhaps she may be healed.
9 We tried to heal Babylon,
    but she could not be healed.
Forsake her, and let each of us go
    to our own country;
for her judgment has reached up to heaven
    and has been lifted up even to the skies.
10 The LORD has brought forth our vindication;
    come, let us declare in Zion
    the work of the LORD our God.

11 Sharpen the arrows!
    Fill the quivers!
The LORD has stirred up the spirit of the kings of the Medes, because his
purpose concerning Babylon is to destroy it, for that is the vengeance of
the LORD, vengeance for his temple.
12 Raise a standard against the walls of Babylon;
    make the watch strong;
post sentinels;
    prepare the ambushes;
for the LORD has both planned and done
    what he spoke concerning the inhabitants of Babylon.
13 You who live by mighty waters,
    rich in treasures,
your end has come,
    the thread of your life is cut.
14 The LORD of hosts has sworn by himself:
Surely I will fill you with troops like a swarm of locusts,
    and they shall raise a shout of victory over you.

15 It is he who made the earth by his power,
    who established the world by his wisdom,
and by his understanding stretched out the heavens.
16 When he utters his voice there is a tumult of waters in the
    heavens,
    and he makes the mist rise from the ends of the earth.

51.4
Jer 49.26;
50.30, 37
51.5
Isa 54.7, 8;
Jer 33.24-26

51.6
Jer 50.8;
Rev 18.4;
Num 16.26;
Jer 50.15;
25.14
51.7
Rev 17.4;
Jer 25.15;
Rev 14.8;
18.3;
Jer 25.16
51.8
Isa 21.9;
Rev 14.8;
18.2;
Jer 48.20;
Rev 18.9, 11,
19
51.9
Isa 13.14;
Jer 50.16;
Rev 18.5

51.10
Ps 37.6;
Mic 7.9;
Isa 40.2;
Jer 50.28

51.11
Jer 46.4;
Joel 3.9, 10;
Jer 50.3, 9,
28

51.12
Isa 13.2;
Jer 50.2

51.13
Rev 17.1, 15

51.14
Jer 49.13;
Am 6.8;
Nah 3.15;
Jer 50.15
51.15ff
Gen 1.1, 6;
Jer 10.12-16;
Acts 14.15;
Rom 1.20;
Job 9.8;
Ps 104.2;
Isa 40.22
51.16
Ps 18.13;
Jer 10.13;
Ps 135.7

51.11 Whether the Medes knew it or not, it was God who "stirred up the spirit of the kings of the Medes" to destroy Babylon. Humans may do what they want, but ultimately God is in control of their decisions. **51.15–18** These verses are identical with Jer 10.12–16.

He makes lightnings for the rain,
> and he brings out the wind from his storehouses.

51.17
Jer 10.14;
50.2;
Hab 2.18, 19

17 Everyone is stupid and without knowledge;
> goldsmiths are all put to shame by their idols;
> for their images are false,
> and there is no breath in them.

51.18
Jer 10.15

18 They are worthless, a work of delusion;
> at the time of their punishment they shall perish.

51.19
Jer 10.16;
50.34

19 Not like these is the LORD,*f* the portion of Jacob,
> for he is the one who formed all things,
> and Israel is the tribe of his inheritance;
> the LORD of hosts is his name.

51.20
Isa 10.5, 15;
Jer 50.23;
Isa 41.15,
16;
Mic 4.12, 13

20 You are my war club, my weapon of battle:
> with you I smash nations;
>   with you I destroy kingdoms;

51.22
2 Chr 36.17

21 with you I smash the horse and its rider;
> with you I smash the chariot and the charioteer;

22 with you I smash man and woman;
> with you I smash the old man and the boy;
> with you I smash the young man and the girl;

51.23
v. 57

23 with you I smash shepherds and their flocks;
> with you I smash farmers and their teams;
> with you I smash governors and deputies.

51.24
Jer 50.10, 15,
29

24 I will repay Babylon and all the inhabitants of Chaldea before your very eyes for all the wrong that they have done in Zion, says the LORD.

51.25
Jer 50.31;
Zech 4.7;
Rev 8.8

25 I am against you, O destroying mountain,

>   says the LORD,
> that destroys the whole earth;
> I will stretch out my hand against you,
> and roll you down from the crags,
> and make you a burned-out mountain.

51.26
v. 29;
Jer 50.13

26 No stone shall be taken from you for a corner
> and no stone for a foundation,
> but you shall be a perpetual waste,
> says the LORD.

51.27
Isa 13.2;
Jer 50.2;
25.14; 50.41,
42

27 Raise a standard in the land,
> blow the trumpet among the nations;
> prepare the nations for war against her,
> summon against her the kingdoms,
>   Ararat, Minni, and Ashkenaz;
> appoint a marshal against her,
> bring up horses like bristling locusts.

51.28
v. 11
51.29
Jer 8.16;
10.10; 50.46;
Am 8.8;
Isa 13.19,
20; 47.11
51.30
Ps 76.5;
Jer 50.36, 37;
Isa 13.7, 8;
Lam 2.9;
Am 1.5;
Nah 3.13

28 Prepare the nations for war against her,
> the kings of the Medes, with their governors and deputies,
> and every land under their dominion.

29 The land trembles and writhes,
> for the LORD's purposes against Babylon stand,
> to make the land of Babylon a desolation,
> without inhabitant.

30 The warriors of Babylon have given up fighting,

f Heb lacks *the* LORD

51.20 *You,* i.e., Cyrus, who was used of God to conquer Babylon (see Isa 44.28; 45.1).
51.27 *Ararat, Minni, and Ashkenaz.* Ararat is lo-

cated in modern Armenia, Minni southwest of Lake Van, and Ashkenaz south of Lake Urmiah.

they remain in their strongholds;
their strength has failed,
  they have become women;
her buildings are set on fire,
  her bars are broken.

31 One runner runs to meet another,
      and one messenger to meet another,
    to tell the king of Babylon
      that his city is taken from end to end:

32 the fords have been seized,
      the marshes have been burned with fire,
      and the soldiers are in panic.

33 For thus says the LORD of hosts, the God of Israel:
    Daughter Babylon is like a threshing floor
      at the time when it is trodden;
    yet a little while
      and the time of her harvest will come.

34 "King Nebuchadrezzar of Babylon has devoured me,
      he has crushed me;
    he has made me an empty vessel,
      he has swallowed me like a monster;
    he has filled his belly with my delicacies,
      he has spewed me out.

35 May my torn flesh be avenged on Babylon,"
      the inhabitants of Zion shall say.
    "May my blood be avenged on the inhabitants of Chaldea,"
    Jerusalem shall say.

36 Therefore thus says the LORD:
    I am going to defend your cause
      and take vengeance for you.
    I will dry up her sea
      and make her fountain dry;

37 and Babylon shall become a heap of ruins,
      a den of jackals,
    an object of horror and of hissing,
      without inhabitant.

38 Like lions they shall roar together;
      they shall growl like lions' whelps.

39 When they are inflamed, I will set out their drink
      and make them drunk, until they become merry
    and then sleep a perpetual sleep
      and never wake, says the LORD.

40 I will bring them down like lambs to the slaughter,
      like rams and goats.

41 How Sheshach^g is taken,
      the pride of the whole earth seized!
    How Babylon has become
      an object of horror among the nations!

42 The sea has risen over Babylon;
      she has been covered by its tumultuous waves.

43 Her cities have become an object of horror,
      a land of drought and a desert,
    a land in which no one lives,
      and through which no mortal passes.

51.31
2 Chr 30.6;
2 Sam 18.19-31;
Jer 50.24

51.32
Jer 50.37, 38

51.33
Isa 21.10;
41.15;
Hab 3.12;
Isa 17.5-7;
Hos 6.11;
Joel 3.13

51.34
Jer 50.17;
Isa 24.1-3;
Am 8.4

51.35
Ps 137.8;
v. 24

51.36
Ps 140.12;
Jer 50.34;
Rom 12.19;
Jer 50.38

51.37
Isa 13.22;
Jer 50.39;
Rev 18.2
Jer 49.33;
50.13

51.39
Jer 25.27

51.40
Jer 50.27

51.41
Jer 25.26;
Isa 13.19;
Jer 49.25

51.42
Isa 8.7, 8;
Dan 9.26

51.43
Jer 50.12;
Isa 13.20

---

g *Sheshach* is a cryptogram for *Babel*, Babylon

51.44
Isa 46.1;
Jer 50.2;
vv. 34, 58

44 I will punish Bel in Babylon,
    and make him disgorge what he has swallowed.
The nations shall no longer stream to him;
    the wall of Babylon has fallen.

51.45
v. 6;
Jer 50.8;
Rev 18.4;
Acts 2.40
51.46
Jer 46.27, 28;
2 Kings 19.7;
Isa 13.3-5;
19.2

45 Come out of her, my people!
    Save your lives, each of you,
    from the fierce anger of the LORD!
46 Do not be fainthearted or fearful
    at the rumors heard in the land —
one year one rumor comes,
    the next year another,
rumors of violence in the land
    and of ruler against ruler.

51.47
Isa 46.1, 2;
v. 52;
Jer 50.2;
50.12, 35-37

47 Assuredly, the days are coming
    when I will punish the images of Babylon;
her whole land shall be put to shame,
    and all her slain shall fall in her midst.

51.48
Isa 44.23;
49.13;
Rev 12.12;
18.20; vv. 11,
27

48 Then the heavens and the earth,
    and all that is in them,
shall shout for joy over Babylon;
    for the destroyers shall come against them out of the north,
                          says the LORD.

51.49
Jer 50.29

49 Babylon must fall for the slain of Israel,
    as the slain of all the earth have fallen because of Babylon.

51.50
v. 45;
Ps 137.6

50 You survivors of the sword,
    go, do not linger!
Remember the LORD in a distant land,
    and let Jerusalem come into your mind:

51.51
Ps 79.4

51 We are put to shame, for we have heard insults;
    dishonor has covered our face,
for aliens have come
    into the holy places of the LORD's house.

51.52
v. 47;
Jer 50.38

52 Therefore the time is surely coming, says the LORD,
    when I will punish her idols,
and through all her land
    the wounded shall groan.

51.53
Isa 14.12,
13;
Jer 49.16;
Isa 13.3

53 Though Babylon should mount up to heaven,
    and though she should fortify her strong height,
from me destroyers would come upon her,
    says the LORD.

51.54
Jer 50.46

54 Listen! — a cry from Babylon!
    A great crashing from the land of the Chaldeans!

51.55
v. 42

55 For the LORD is laying Babylon waste,
    and stilling her loud clamor.
Their waves roar like mighty waters,
    the sound of their clamor resounds;

51.56
v. 48;
Hab 2.8;
Ps 94.1, 2;
vv. 6, 24

56 for a destroyer has come against her,
    against Babylon;
her warriors are taken,

51.51 *for aliens have come into the holy places of the LORD's house.* The Jews never allowed Gentiles to come into the sanctuary of God. There was a court of the Gentiles beyond which none of them could go. Even Jews who had not gone through the rites of cleansing could not enter the holy places. To do so was punishable by death. It was appalling to think that non-Jews from Babylon had destroyed the holy places of God.

their bows are broken;
for the LORD is a God of recompense,
    he will repay in full.
57 I will make her officials and her sages drunk,
    also her governors, her deputies, and her warriors;
they shall sleep a perpetual sleep and never wake,
    says the King, whose name is the LORD of hosts.

51.57
v. 39;
Ps 76.5, 6;
Jer 46.18;
48.15

58 Thus says the LORD of hosts:
The broad wall of Babylon
    shall be leveled to the ground,
and her high gates
    shall be burned with fire.
The peoples exhaust themselves for nothing,
    and the nations weary themselves only for fire. *h*

51.58
v. 44;
Jer 50.15;
Hab 2.13;
v. 64

59 The word that the prophet Jeremiah commanded Seraiah son of Neriah son of Mahseiah, when he went with King Zedekiah of Judah to Babylon, in the fourth year of his reign. Seraiah was the quartermaster. 60 Jeremiah wrote in a *i* scroll all the disasters that would come on Babylon, all these words that are written concerning Babylon. 61 And Jeremiah said to Seraiah: "When you come to Babylon, see that you read all these words, 62 and say, 'O LORD, you yourself threatened to destroy this place so that neither human beings nor animals shall live in it, and it shall be desolate forever.' 63 When you finish reading this scroll, tie a stone to it, and throw it into the middle of the Euphrates, 64 and say, 'Thus shall Babylon sink, to rise no more, because of the disasters that I am bringing on her.' " *j*
Thus far are the words of Jeremiah.

51.59
Jer 32.12;
28.1
51.60
Jer 30.2, 3;
36.2, 4, 32
51.62
Jer 25.12;
50.3, 39;
v. 43;
Ezek 35.9
51.63
Rev 18.21
51.64
Nah 1.8, 9;
v. 58

V. Historical appendix (52.1–34)

A. Zedekiah's reign

52 Zedekiah was twenty-one years old when he began to reign; he reigned eleven years in Jerusalem. His mother's name was Hamutal daughter of Jeremiah of Libnah. 2 He did what was evil in the sight of the LORD, just as Jehoiakim had done. 3 Indeed, Jerusalem and Judah so angered the LORD that he expelled them from his presence.

52.1
2 Kings 24.18;
2 Chr 36.11-13
52.2
Jer 36.30, 31
52.3
Isa 3.1, 4, 5;
2 Chr 36.13

B. Siege and fall of Jerusalem

Zedekiah rebelled against the king of Babylon. 4 And in the ninth year of his reign, in the tenth month, on the tenth day of the month, King Nebuchadrezzar of Babylon came with all his army against Jerusalem, and they laid siege to it; they built siegeworks against it all around. 5 So the city was besieged until the eleventh year of King Zedekiah. 6 On the ninth day of the fourth month the famine became so severe in the city that there was no food for the people of the land. 7 Then a breach was made in the city wall; *k* and all the soldiers fled and went out from the city by night by the way of the gate between the two walls, by the king's garden, though the Chaldeans were all around the city. They went in the direction of the

52.4
2 Kings 25.1-7;
Jer 39.1;
Ezek 24.1, 2;
Jer 32.24
52.6
Jer 38.9
52.7
Jer 39.2;
39.4-7

h Gk Syr Compare Hab 2.13: Heb *and the nations for fire, and they are weary*   *i* Or *one*   *j* Gk: Heb *on her. And they shall weary themselves*   *k* Heb lacks *wall*

51.60 Apparently Jeremiah himself wrote the prophecy concerning Babylon on a scroll. He told Seraiah to read the word of prophecy, presumably in a public manner, and then to throw the scroll into the Euphrates River, where it would sink — thus signifying the destruction of Babylon.

52.1 Ch. 52 is much the same as 2 Kings 24.18 — 25.30. It is an appendix showing how the prophetic word through Jeremiah was fulfilled. It constitutes a sort of preface to the Lamentations which follow, and it serves as a key to that work.

Arabah. ⁸But the army of the Chaldeans pursued the king, and overtook Zedekiah in the plains of Jericho; and all his army was scattered, deserting him. ⁹Then they captured the king, and brought him up to the king of Babylon at Riblah in the land of Hamath, and he passed sentence on him. ¹⁰The king of Babylon killed the sons of Zedekiah before his eyes, and also killed all the officers of Judah at Riblah. ¹¹He put out the eyes of Zedekiah, and bound him in fetters, and the king of Babylon took him to Babylon, and put him in prison until the day of his death.

12   In the fifth month, on the tenth day of the month — which was the nineteenth year of King Nebuchadrezzar, king of Babylon — Nebuzaradan the captain of the bodyguard who served the king of Babylon, entered Jerusalem. ¹³He burned the house of the LORD, the king's house, and all the houses of Jerusalem; every great house he burned down. ¹⁴All the army of the Chaldeans, who were with the captain of the guard, broke down all the walls around Jerusalem. ¹⁵Nebuzaradan the captain of the guard carried into exile some of the poorest of the people and the rest of the people who were left in the city and the deserters who had defected to the king of Babylon, together with the rest of the artisans. ¹⁶But Nebuzaradan the captain of the guard left some of the poorest people of the land to be vinedressers and tillers of the soil.

17   The pillars of bronze that were in the house of the LORD, and the stands and the bronze sea that were in the house of the LORD, the Chaldeans broke in pieces, and carried all the bronze to Babylon. ¹⁸They took away the pots, the shovels, the snuffers, the basins, the ladles, and all the vessels of bronze used in the temple service. ¹⁹The captain of the guard took away the small bowls also, the firepans, the basins, the pots, the lampstands, the ladles, and the bowls for libation, both those of gold and those of silver. ²⁰As for the two pillars, the one sea, the twelve bronze bulls that were under the sea, and the stands,ˡ which King Solomon had made for the house of the LORD, the bronze of all these vessels was beyond weighing. ²¹As for the pillars, the height of the one pillar was eighteen cubits, its circumference was twelve cubits; it was hollow and its thickness was four fingers. ²²Upon it was a capital of bronze; the height of the capital was five cubits; latticework and pomegranates, all of bronze, encircled the top of the capital. And the second pillar had the same, with pomegranates. ²³There were ninety-six pomegranates on the sides; all the pomegranates encircling the latticework numbered one hundred.

24   The captain of the guard took the chief priest Seraiah, the second priest Zephaniah, and the three guardians of the threshold; ²⁵and from the city he took an officer who had been in command of the soldiers, and seven men of the king's council who were found in the city; the secretary of the commander of the army who mustered the people of the land; and sixty men of the people of the land who were found inside the city. ²⁶Then Nebuzaradan the captain of the guard took them, and brought them to the king of Babylon at Riblah. ²⁷And the king of Babylon struck them down, and put them to death at Riblah in the land of Hamath. So Judah went into exile out of its land.

C. *The deportations*

28   This is the number of the people whom Nebuchadrezzar took into exile: in the seventh year, three thousand twenty-three Judeans; ²⁹in the eighteenth year of Nebuchadrezzar he took into exile from Jerusalem eight hundred thirty-two persons; ³⁰in the twenty-third year of Nebuchadrez-

ˡ Cn: Heb *that were under the stands*

52.13   Before Nebuchadnezzar and his soldiers destroyed Jerusalem and burned the temple, the glory of God had departed from that sacred house. So far as we know, the ark of the covenant was destroyed when the temple was burned.
52.30   If 4,600 is the sum total of the people carried off to Babylon, then the devastation wrought by God's judgment against Judah was extensive. The

zar, Nebuzaradan the captain of the guard took into exile of the Judeans seven hundred forty-five persons; all the persons were four thousand six hundred.

D. *The honor accorded Jehoiachin*

31 In the thirty-seventh year of the exile of King Jehoiachin of Judah, in the twelfth month, on the twenty-fifth day of the month, King Evil-merodach of Babylon, in the year he began to reign, showed favor to King Jehoiachin of Judah and brought him out of prison; 32 he spoke kindly to him, and gave him a seat above the seats of the other kings who were with him in Babylon. 33 So Jehoiachin put aside his prison clothes, and every day of his life he dined regularly at the king's table. 34 For his allowance, a regular daily allowance was given him by the king of Babylon, as long as he lived, up to the day of his death.

52.31
2 Kings 25.27-30;
Gen 40.13

52.33
Gen 41.14,
42;
2 Sam 9.13;
1 Kings 2.7
52.34
2 Sam 9.10

number of God's people had been sharply reduced, but they grew in numbers in Babylon, for the Lord God made them fruitful. The more they were persecuted or oppressed, the more they seemed to grow. And even today, the survival of the Jewish people can be attributed to God's grace.
52.31 *Evil-merodach* was the son and successor of Nebuchadnezzar as king of the Neo-Babylonian Empire (c. 562–560 B.C.). He released Jehoiachin from prison and supplied him with food. Documents found in the ruins of Babylon confirm this. Evil-merodach was assassinated by his brother-in-law, Nerglissar, who ascended to the throne in his place.

INTRODUCTION TO

LAMENTATIONS

Authorship, Date, and Background: The book of Lamentations, until recently, was attributed to Jeremiah the weeping prophet (see introduction to Jeremiah). Various dates and unknown authors have been assigned to the book by those who do not think Jeremiah wrote it. However, the book itself makes clear that the author was an eyewitness who experienced what he was describing. Jeremiah was surely the best qualified to fit the circumstances and to account for the contents of the poems. He was known to have composed laments (2 Chr 35.25). He had been predicting the captivity and the destruction of Jerusalem for forty years before it happened. Beholding the destroyed city, en route to Egypt, his soul must have been moved with anguish over what had happened and the memory remained with him as he wrote the poems between 586 B.C. and 538 B.C.

The book of Lamentations was one of five books included in the Megilloth (see introduction to Esther). Lamentations was read publicly on the ninth of Ab at an annual religious festival. All chapters except ch. 3 have twenty-two verses; ch. 3 has sixty-six. Part of the book follows an alphabetic acrostic. For example, in chs. 1 and 2 each verse starts with a letter of the Hebrew alphabet in order; ch. 5 does not use the acrostic form.

Characteristics and Content: Jeremiah, in writing this book, speaks of Jerusalem's former glories and present desolation. The contrast is marked. He acknowledges the righteousness of God in judgment even as the divine wrath was poured out in vengeance for sin. He accepts suffering with the knowledge that God, who is the author of good and allows evil, responds to the contrite heart. Suffering, however, has its origin in human transgressions and has for its ultimate purpose bringing the people of God to repentance. Jeremiah's description of the siege of Jerusalem is filled with pathos as he portrays the effect on the lives of the inhabitants. Using words like "we," "our," and "us" in the closing chapter, Jeremiah makes confession for the sins of God's people as he beseeches God to restore them to their inheritance.

Outline:

I. Jerusalem desolate and forsaken (1.1–22)

II. God's judgment explained; repentance urged (2.1–22)

III. The prophet's lament and hope (3.1–66)

IV. The condition of Zion, past and present, contrasted (4.1–22)

V. The prayer for mercy amid affliction (5.1–22)

LAMENTATIONS

I. *Jerusalem desolate and forsaken (1.1–22)*

A. *Description of her desolation*

1 How lonely sits the city
　　that once was full of people!
How like a widow she has become,
　　she that was great among the nations!
She that was a princess among the provinces
　　has become a vassal.

2 She weeps bitterly in the night,
　　with tears on her cheeks;
among all her lovers
　　she has no one to comfort her;
all her friends have dealt treacherously with her,
　　they have become her enemies.

3 Judah has gone into exile with suffering
　　and hard servitude;
she lives now among the nations,
　　and finds no resting place;
her pursuers have all overtaken her
　　in the midst of her distress.

4 The roads to Zion mourn,
　　for no one comes to the festivals;
all her gates are desolate,
　　her priests groan;
her young girls grieve,[a]
　　and her lot is bitter.

5 Her foes have become the masters,
　　her enemies prosper,
because the LORD has made her suffer
　　for the multitude of her transgressions;
her children have gone away,
　　captives before the foe.

6 From daughter Zion has departed

a Meaning of Heb uncertain

1.1 Isa 3.26; 54.4; Ezra 4.20; Jer 40.9
1.2 Ps 6.6; Jer 2.25; 4.30
1.3 Jer 13.19; Deut 28.64, 65; 2 Kings 25.4, 5
1.4 Jer 9.11; 10.22; Joel 1.8-13
1.5 Deut 28.43, 44; Jer 30.14, 15; 39.9; 52.28
1.6 Jer 13.18; 2 Kings 25.4, 5

1.1 The northern kingdom of Israel had long since been destroyed. The southern kingdom of Judah was being ruled by the descendants of the house of David. But Judah was following the same path that her northern counterpart had followed, one that had led to divine judgment. Judah and Jerusalem were faced with a similar judgment. The hour for reprieve had passed and destruction and captivity would soon come upon an apostate people.
1.2 *Among all her lovers* refers to Egypt and Israel's other former allies.
1.3 Israel was God's chosen people, separated from the heathen in order not to be defiled. Now Israel sat among those who were aliens to God, with no rest of mind and being ordered about by tyrants.
1.4 No longer were the roads to Jerusalem lined with crowds coming to worship God or celebrate festivals. The priests, who had lost their jobs, sighed, longing for the good old days.

all her majesty.
Her princes have become like stags
    that find no pasture;
they fled without strength
    before the pursuer.

1.7
Ps 42.4;
Isa 5.1-4;
Jer 37.7;
Lam 4.17;
Jer 48.27

7 Jerusalem remembers,
    in the days of her affliction and wandering,
all the precious things
    that were hers in days of old.
When her people fell into the hand of the foe,
    and there was no one to help her,
the foe looked on mocking
    over her downfall.

1.8
1 Kings 8.46;
vv. 5, 20, 17;
Jer 13.22, 26;
vv. 4, 11, 21,
22

8 Jerusalem sinned grievously,
    so she has become a mockery;
all who honored her despise her,
    for they have seen her nakedness;
she herself groans,
    and turns her face away.

1.9
Ezek 24.13;
Deut 32.29;
Isa 47.7;
Jer 13.17, 18;
16.7

9 Her uncleanness was in her skirts;
    she took no thought of her future;
her downfall was appalling,
    with none to comfort her.
"O Lord, look at my affliction,
    for the enemy has triumphed!"

1.10
Isa 64.10,
11;
Jer 51.51;
Deut 23.3

10 Enemies have stretched out their hands
    over all her precious things;
she has even seen the nations
    invade her sanctuary,
those whom you forbade
    to enter your congregation.

1.11
Jer 38.9;
52.6;
1 Sam 30.12

11 All her people groan
    as they search for bread;
they trade their treasures for food
    to revive their strength.
Look, O Lord, and see
    how worthless I have become.

B. Acknowledgment of her sin

1.12
Jer 18.16;
48.27; v. 18;
Jer 30.23, 24;
4.8

12 Is it nothing to you,[b] all you who pass by?
    Look and see
if there is any sorrow like my sorrow,
    which was brought upon me,
which the Lord inflicted
    on the day of his fierce anger.

1.13
Job 30.30;
Hab 3.16;
Job 19.6;
Jer 44.6

13 From on high he sent fire;

[b] Meaning of Heb uncertain

1.8 *have seen her nakedness.* Sin leaves the sinner without adequate covering.
1.9 Jerusalem had been doomed; her fall was terrible to behold. To whom could she turn for help? Jeremiah pleaded with God to look on Jerusalem's affliction, and he expected that he would help her.
1.12 Jerusalem now saw that her plight was not brought about by accident but by design. Great as her sorrow was, the source of that sorrow was God, whose wrath had been poured out on the beloved city.

it went deep into my bones;
  he spread a net for my feet;
    he turned me back;
he has left me stunned,
    faint all day long.

14 My transgressions were bound[c] into a yoke;
    by his hand they were fastened together;
they weigh on my neck,
    sapping my strength;
the Lord handed me over
    to those whom I cannot withstand.

1.14
Deut 28.48;
Isa 47.6;
Jer 28.13, 14;
32.3, 5;
Ezek 25.4, 7

15 The Lord has rejected
    all my warriors in the midst of me;
he proclaimed a time against me
    to crush my young men;
the Lord has trodden as in a wine press
    the virgin daughter Judah.

1.15
Isa 41.2;
Jer 13.24;
18.21;
Isa 28.18;
Mic 7.10;
Rev 14.19

16 For these things I weep;
    my eyes flow with tears;
for a comforter is far from me,
    one to revive my courage;
my children are desolate,
    for the enemy has prevailed.

1.16
Jer 13.17;
14.17;
Lam 2.18;
vv. 2, 9

17 Zion stretches out her hands,
    but there is no one to comfort her;
the Lord has commanded against Jacob
    that his neighbors should become his foes;
Jerusalem has become
    a filthy thing among them.

1.17
Jer 4.31;
2 Kings 24.2-4;
v. 8

18 The Lord is in the right,
    for I have rebelled against his word;
but hear, all you peoples,
    and behold my suffering;
my young women and young men
    have gone into captivity.

1.18
Jer 12.1;
1 Sam 12.14;
v. 12;
Deut 28.32,
41

19 I called to my lovers
    but they deceived me;
my priests and elders
    perished in the city
while seeking food
    to revive their strength.

1.19
Jer 30.14;
14.15;
Lam 2.20

20 See, O Lord, how distressed I am;
    my stomach churns,
    my heart is wrung within me,

1.20
Isa 16.11;
Jer 4.19;
Lam 2.11;
Deut 32.29;
Ezek 7.15

c Meaning of Heb uncertain

1.14 Jerusalem's sins had placed her under a yoke, not for service but for penance, due to her many transgressions. The yoke of Jerusalem's transgressions was a heavy one. For believers, the yoke of Christ is easy and the burden light (Mat. 11.28–30). **1.17** *Zion stretches out her hands.* Zion was throwing up her arms in distress and despair. God had with-drawn from her, so she had no comforter. Her former friends had failed her. **1.19** Jerusalem had called to her lovers, Assyria and Egypt, but they deceived her and turned their eyes from her in the hour of adversity. Priests and elders, who should have been leading the people, died of hunger and served no one.

because I have been very rebellious.
In the street the sword bereaves;
    in the house it is like death.

1.21
Lam 2.15;
Isa 14.5, 6;
Jer 30.16

21 They heard how I was groaning,
    with no one to comfort me.
All my enemies heard of my trouble;
    they are glad that you have done it.
Bring on the day you have announced,
    and let them be as I am.

1.22
Neh 4.4, 5;
Ps 137.7, 8

22 Let all their evil doing come before you;
        and deal with them
    as you have dealt with me
        because of all my transgressions;
    for my groans are many
        and my heart is faint.

II. God's judgment explained; repentance urged (2.1–22)

A. The judgment of the LORD

2.1
Lam 3.43,
44;
Ezek 28.14-16;
Isa 64.11;
Ps 99.5;
132.7

2 How the Lord in his anger
    has humiliated[d] daughter Zion!
He has thrown down from heaven to earth
    the splendor of Israel;
he has not remembered his footstool
    in the day of his anger.

2.2
Ps 21.9;
Lam 3.43;
Mic 5.11, 14;
Isa 25.12;
Ps 89.39

2 The Lord has destroyed without mercy
    all the dwellings of Jacob;
in his wrath he has broken down
    the strongholds of daughter Judah;
he has brought down to the ground in dishonor
    the kingdom and its rulers.

2.3
Ps 75.5, 10;
74.11;
Jer 21.4, 5;
21.14

3 He has cut down in fierce anger
    all the might of Israel;
he has withdrawn his right hand from them
    in the face of the enemy;
he has burned like a flaming fire in Jacob,
    consuming all around.

2.4
Lam 3.12,
13;
Ezek 24.25;
Isa 42.25;
Jer 7.20

4 He has bent his bow like an enemy,
    with his right hand set like a foe;
he has killed all in whom we took pride
    in the tent of daughter Zion;
he has poured out his fury like fire.

2.5
Jer 30.14;
6.26; 9.17-20

5 The Lord has become like an enemy;

d Meaning of Heb uncertain

1.22 This is a prayer of imprecation which declares that God would do to the enemies of Jerusalem what he had done to Jerusalem itself. Our prayers must agree with God's word. When God has pronounced judgment against the nations for their failure to repent and glorify him, we may pray that God's pro- nouncement may be brought to pass.
2.5 *The Lord has become like an enemy.* The God who had been their best friend had become their enemy. His love was no longer present among them and his power to overcome their foes was no longer available. Whoever chooses to live without God must suffer the

he has destroyed Israel.
He has destroyed all its palaces,
    laid in ruins its strongholds,
and multiplied in daughter Judah
    mourning and lamentation.

6 He has broken down his booth like a garden,
    he has destroyed his tabernacle;
  the LORD has abolished in Zion
    festival and sabbath,
  and in his fierce indignation has spurned
    king and priest.

2.6
Jer 7.14;
52.13;
Lam 1.4;
Zeph 3.18;
Lam 4.16,
20; 5.12

7 The Lord has scorned his altar,
    disowned his sanctuary;
  he has delivered into the hand of the enemy
    the walls of her palaces;
  a clamor was raised in the house of the LORD
    as on a day of festival.

2.7
Isa 64.11;
Ezek 7.20-22;
Jer 33.4, 5;
Ps 74.4

8 The LORD determined to lay in ruins
    the wall of daughter Zion;
  he stretched the line;
    he did not withhold his hand from destroying;
  he caused rampart and wall to lament;
    they languish together.

2.8
Jer 5.10;
2 Kings 21.13;
Isa 34.11;
3.26;
Jer 14.2

9 Her gates have sunk into the ground;
    he has ruined and broken her bars;
  her king and princes are among the nations;
    guidance is no more,
  and her prophets obtain
    no vision from the LORD.

2.9
Neh 1.3;
Jer 51.30;
Deut 28.36;
2 Kings 24.15;
2 Chr 15.3;
Jer 14.14;
23.16;
Ezek 7.26

10 The elders of daughter Zion
    sit on the ground in silence;
  they have thrown dust on their heads
    and put on sackcloth;
  the young girls of Jerusalem
    have bowed their heads to the ground.

2.10
Job 2.13;
Isa 3.26;
Am 8.3;
Job 2.12;
Ezek 27.30,
31;
Isa 15.3;
Lam 1.4

11 My eyes are spent with weeping;
    my stomach churns;
  my bile is poured out on the ground
    because of the destruction of my people,
  because infants and babes faint
    in the streets of the city.

2.11
Ps 6.7;
Lam 3.48;
1.20;
Job 16.13;
Ps 22.14;
Lam 4.4

12 They cry to their mothers,
    "Where is bread and wine?"
  as they faint like the wounded
    in the streets of the city,
  as their life is poured out
    on their mothers' bosom.

2.12
Jer 5.17;
Lam 4.4;
Job 30.16

---

consequences of that decision.
2.9 God had always used prophets to whom were
given visions or dreams. Now his people would have
no more prophets and no more visions, for they had
persecuted the prophets he had sent and despised the
visions he had given them.

13 What can I say for you, to what compare you,
        O daughter Jerusalem?
    To what can I liken you, that I may comfort you,
        O virgin daughter Zion?
    For vast as the sea is your ruin;
        who can heal you?

B. *The false prophets of Zion*

14 Your prophets have seen for you
        false and deceptive visions;
    they have not exposed your iniquity
        to restore your fortunes,
    but have seen oracles for you
        that are false and misleading.

15 All who pass along the way
        clap their hands at you;
    they hiss and wag their heads
        at daughter Jerusalem;
    "Is this the city that was called
        the perfection of beauty,
        the joy of all the earth?"

16 All your enemies
        open their mouths against you;
    they hiss, they gnash their teeth,
        they cry: "We have devoured her!
    Ah, this is the day we longed for;
        at last we have seen it!"

17 The LORD has done what he purposed,
        he has carried out his threat;
    as he ordained long ago,
        he has demolished without pity;
    he has made the enemy rejoice over you,
        and exalted the might of your foes.

18 Cry aloud[e] to the Lord!
        O wall of daughter Zion!
    Let tears stream down like a torrent
        day and night!
    Give yourself no rest,
        your eyes no respite!

19 Arise, cry out in the night,
        at the beginning of the watches!
    Pour out your heart like water
        before the presence of the Lord!
    Lift your hands to him
        for the lives of your children,

[e] Cn: Heb *Their heart cried*

2.14 There will always be true and false prophets, and we must learn to distinguish between them (cf. 1 Jn 4.1–6). False prophets tell people what they want to hear, not what they need to hear. They promise good things and easy times, appealing to those whose deeds are evil and who seek to justify themselves. Because they claim to speak in the name of God, they are more welcome with their sweet words than true prophets with their stern and unyielding denouncements of sin.
2.15 Jerusalem was now laid waste and depopulated.

who faint for hunger
    at the head of every street.

20   Look, O Lord, and consider!
    To whom have you done this?
Should women eat their offspring,
    the children they have borne?
Should priest and prophet be killed
    in the sanctuary of the Lord?

2.20
Jer 19.9;
14.15;
Lam 4.13, 16

21   The young and the old are lying
    on the ground in the streets;
my young women and my young men
    have fallen by the sword;
in the day of your anger you have killed them,
    slaughtering without mercy.

2.21
2 Chr 36.17;
Jer 6.11;
Ps 78.62, 63;
Jer 13.14;
Zech 11.6

22   You invited my enemies from all around
    as if for a day of festival;
and on the day of the anger of the Lord
    no one escaped or survived;
those whom I bore and reared
    my enemy has destroyed.

2.22
Ps 31.13;
Jer 6.25;
Hos 9.12, 13

III. *The prophet's lament and hope (3.1–66)*

A. *Lament over Zion's tragic condition*

3   I am one who has seen affliction
    under the rod of God's *f* wrath;
2   he has driven and brought me
    into darkness without any light;
3   against me alone he turns his hand,
    again and again, all day long.

3.1
Job 19.21;
Jer 15.17, 18
3.2
Isa 59.9;
Jer 4.23
3.3
Isa 5.25

4   He has made my flesh and my skin waste away,
    and broken my bones;
5   he has besieged and enveloped me
    with bitterness and tribulation;
6   he has made me sit in darkness
    like the dead of long ago.

3.4
Job 16.8;
Ps 51.8;
Isa 38.13;
Jer 50.17
3.5
Job 19.8;
Jer 23.15
3.6
Ps 88.5, 6

7   He has walled me about so that I cannot escape;
    he has put heavy chains on me;
8   though I call and cry for help,
    he shuts out my prayer;
9   he has blocked my ways with hewn stones,
    he has made my paths crooked.

3.7
Job 3.23;
Jer 40.4
3.8
Job 30.20;
Ps 22.2
3.9
Hos 2.6;
Isa 63.17

10   He is a bear lying in wait for me,
    a lion in hiding;
11   he led me off my way and tore me to pieces;
    he has made me desolate;

3.10
Job 10.16;
Isa 38.13
3.11
Hos 6.1

f Heb *his*

3.2 The word *he* is used many times in vv. 2–16. He, i.e., God, had brought great evils upon Jerusalem. The divine patience had been exhausted, and when that happened, divine judgment fell. It took visible form in the ways described in these verses.

3.9 *he has blocked my ways with hewn stones,* i.e., "he has built a wall that I cannot go through or circle around or climb over." Whatever way Jerusalem sought to go, she was frustrated.

3.12
Ps 7.12, 13;
Job 7.20

12 he bent his bow and set me
as a mark for his arrow.

3.13
Job 6.4

13 He shot into my vitals
the arrows of his quiver;

3.14
Jer 20.7;
Job 30.9

14 I have become the laughingstock of all my people,
the object of their taunt-songs all day long.

3.15
Jer 9.15

15 He has filled me with bitterness,
he has sated me with wormwood.

3.16
Prov 20.17;
Jer 6.26

16 He has made my teeth grind on gravel,
and made me cower in ashes;

3.17
Jer 12.12

17 my soul is bereft of peace;
I have forgotten what happiness is;

3.18
Ps 31.22

18 so I say, "Gone is my glory,
and all that I had hoped for from the Lord."

3.19
Jer 9.15

19 The thought of my affliction and my homelessness
is wormwood and gall!

3.20
Ps 42.5, 6, 11

20 My soul continually thinks of it
and is bowed down within me.

B. *The mercies of God recalled and trust expressed*

3.21
Ps 130.7

21 But this I call to mind,
and therefore I have hope:

3.22
Mal 3.6

22 The steadfast love of the Lord never ceases,*g*
his mercies never come to an end;

3.23
Zeph 3.5

23 they are new every morning;
great is your faithfulness.

3.24
Ps 16.5;
33.18

24 "The Lord is my portion," says my soul,
"therefore I will hope in him."

3.25
Isa 25.9;
30.18; 26.9

25 The Lord is good to those who wait for him,
to the soul that seeks him.

3.26
Ps 37.7; 40.1;
Isa 30.15

26 It is good that one should wait quietly
for the salvation of the Lord.

3.27
Ps 94.12

27 It is good for one to bear
the yoke in youth,

3.28
Jer 15.17

28 to sit alone in silence
when the Lord has imposed it,

3.29
Job 16.15;
Jer 31.17

29 to put one's mouth to the dust
(there may yet be hope),

3.30
Isa 50.6;
Mt 5.39

30 to give one's cheek to the smiter,
and be filled with insults.

3.31
Ps 94.14

31 For the Lord will not
reject forever.

g Syr Tg: Heb *Lord, we are not cut off*

3.16 God had mingled gravel with bread and the teeth of the eater were broken. What was eaten was neither pleasant nor nourishing. Some interpret the phrase "made me cower in ashes" to mean "he has fed me with ashes" (cf. Ps 102.9).
3.18 Jeremiah pictured Jerusalem as saying that God had ceased to be available, and he offered no encouragement to her to come to him. However, no matter how backslidden a people are, God is still the only one who never fails to help those in trouble when they call on him.
3.22,23 Here was a word of hope. Some had been

afflicted by the rod of God's wrath, but because of the Lord's mercies, were not consumed. Therefore they should turn quickly to the God of grace in the hope that restoration would take place. Significantly, in the middle of this most woeful book is a marvellous testimony to God's abiding faithfulness.
3.31,32 Those who are penitent must also be patient until God's deliverance comes. While they wait, they must ever say that God is gracious and merciful. This knowledge produces hope and leads to genuine repentance.

32   Although he causes grief, he will have compassion
      according to the abundance of his steadfast love;
33   for he does not willingly afflict
      or grieve anyone.

34   When all the prisoners of the land
      are crushed under foot,
35   when human rights are perverted
      in the presence of the Most High,
36   when one's case is subverted
      — does the Lord not see it?

37   Who can command and have it done,
      if the Lord has not ordained it?
38   Is it not from the mouth of the Most High
      that good and bad come?
39   Why should any who draw breath complain
      about the punishment of their sins?

C. Israel exhorted to turn to God

40   Let us test and examine our ways,
      and return to the LORD.
41   Let us lift up our hearts as well as our hands
      to God in heaven.
42   We have transgressed and rebelled,
      and you have not forgiven.

43   You have wrapped yourself with anger and pursued us,
      killing without pity;
44   you have wrapped yourself with a cloud
      so that no prayer can pass through.
45   You have made us filth and rubbish
      among the peoples.

46   All our enemies
      have opened their mouths against us;
47   panic and pitfall have come upon us,
      devastation and destruction.
48   My eyes flow with rivers of tears
      because of the destruction of my people.

49   My eyes will flow without ceasing,
      without respite,
50   until the LORD from heaven
      looks down and sees.
51   My eyes cause me grief
      at the fate of all the young women in my city.

3.32 Ps 78.38; Hos 11.8
3.33 Ezek 33.11; Heb 12.10
3.35 Ps 140.12
3.36 Hab 1.13
3.37 Ps 33.9
3.38 Job 2.10; Isa 45.7; Jer 32.42
3.39 Mic 7.9; Heb 12.5, 6
3.40 Ps 119.59; 2 Cor 13.5
3.41 Ps 25.1; 28.2
3.42 Dan 9.5; Jer 5.7, 9
3.43 Lam 2.21; Ps 83.15
3.44 Ps 97.2; v. 8
3.45 1 Cor 4.13
3.46 Lam 2.16
3.47 Isa 24.17; Jer 48.43; Isa 51.19
3.48 Lam 1.16; 2.11, 18
3.49 Ps 77.2
3.50 Isa 63.15

3.37,38 The Babylonians said they would destroy Jerusalem and it came to pass. However, it did not happen because Nebuchadnezzar and his leaders said it, but because God commanded it and commissioned the Chaldeans to do it.
3.38 This verse does not imply that God is the author of sin. It refers to evils such as sickness, punishments for sins, and the like. In this sense, both good and bad are appointed by God. We are to be reconciled to any bad things that come upon us, not because we have sinned, but because God wishes to purify us. And if we suffer because of our transgressions, we must accept the reproof meekly, look to God in repen-

tance, and wait for the hand of God to lift the burden and give us peace of heart.
3.39 Sinful people must not quarrel with God, for his ways are pure, just, holy, and according to truth.
3.42ff Why does bondage continue after the offenders have repented of their sins? Sins are forgiven as soon as sinners have repented and turned from their wicked ways. But the temporal consequences may continue long after a pardon has been granted. In the case of Judah, the seventy years' captivity would not be reduced even one day, in spite of the people's repentance.

3.52
Ps 35.7

52 Those who were my enemies without cause
    have hunted me like a bird;

3.53
Jer 37.16

53 they flung me alive into a pit
    and hurled stones on me;

3.54
Ps 69.2;
Isa 38.10

54 water closed over my head;
    I said, "I am lost."

D. The cry for vengeance against Israel's enemies

3.55
Jon 2.2

55 I called on your name, O LORD,
    from the depths of the pit;

3.56
Ps 116.1, 2

56 you heard my plea, "Do not close your ear
    to my cry for help, but give me relief!"

3.57
Ps 145.18;
Isa 41.10, 14

57 You came near when I called on you;
    you said, "Do not fear!"

3.58
Jer 51.36;
Ps 71.23

58 You have taken up my cause, O Lord,
    you have redeemed my life.

3.59
Jer 18.19, 20;
Ps 35.23

59 You have seen the wrong done to me, O LORD;
    judge my cause.

3.60
Jer 11.19, 20;
18.18

60 You have seen all their malice,
    all their plots against me.

3.61
Lam 5.1

61 You have heard their taunts, O LORD,
    all their plots against me.

3.62
Ezek 36.3

62 The whispers and murmurs of my assailants
    are against me all day long.

3.63
Ps 139.2

63 Whether they sit or rise — see,
    I am the object of their taunt-songs.

3.64
Ps 28.4

64 Pay them back for their deeds, O LORD,
    according to the work of their hands!

3.65
Isa 6.10

65 Give them anguish of heart;
    your curse be on them!

3.66
Ps 8.3

66 Pursue them in anger and destroy them
    from under the LORD's heavens.

IV. The condition of Zion, past and present, contrasted (4.1–22)

A. The effects of the siege

4.1
Ezek 7.19-22;
Jer 52.13, 14

4 How the gold has grown dim,
    how the pure gold is changed!
The sacred stones lie scattered
    at the head of every street.

4.2
Isa 51.18;
30.14;
Jer 19.11

2 The precious children of Zion,
    worth their weight in fine gold —
how they are reckoned as earthen pots,
    the work of a potter's hands!

4.3
Isa 34.13;
49.15;
Job 39.14, 16

3 Even the jackals offer the breast
    and nurse their young,

3.55–57 No matter how deep the pit into which we have fallen, God will hear us if we call upon him. God is good, who quiets the fears of the anxious heart that seeks him in truth.

4.1 The precious stones of the temple were regarded

as holy to the Lord. Now those stones lay scattered, mingled among the common stones. And the smoke of the fire when the temple burned marred the gold of the edifice.

but my people has become cruel,
    like the ostriches in the wilderness.

4   The tongue of the infant sticks
    to the roof of its mouth for thirst;
  the children beg for food,
    but no one gives them anything.

5   Those who feasted on delicacies
    perish in the streets;
  those who were brought up in purple
    cling to ash heaps.

6   For the chastisement[h] of my people has been greater
    than the punishment[i] of Sodom,
  which was overthrown in a moment,
    though no hand was laid on it.[j]

7   Her princes were purer than snow,
    whiter than milk;
  their bodies were more ruddy than coral,
    their hair[j] like sapphire.[k]

8   Now their visage is blacker than soot;
    they are not recognized in the streets.
  Their skin has shriveled on their bones;
    it has become as dry as wood.

9   Happier were those pierced by the sword
    than those pierced by hunger,
  whose life drains away, deprived
    of the produce of the field.

10   The hands of compassionate women
    have boiled their own children;
  they became their food
    in the destruction of my people.

11   The LORD gave full vent to his wrath;
    he poured out his hot anger,
  and kindled a fire in Zion
    that consumed its foundations.

12   The kings of the earth did not believe,
    nor did any of the inhabitants of the world,
  that foe or enemy could enter
    the gates of Jerusalem.

B. *The uselessness of the false prophets*

13   It was for the sins of her prophets

---

h Or *iniquity*   *i* Or *sin*   *j* Meaning of Heb uncertain   *k* Or *lapis lazuli*

4.4
Jer 14.3;
Lam 2.12

4.5
Jer 6.2;
Am 6.3-7;
Ps 113.7

4.6
Ezek 16.48;
Gen 19.23;
Jer 20.16

4.7
Ps 51.7

4.8
Job 30.30;
Lam 5.10;
Ps 102.5

4.9
Jer 15.2;
Ezek 24.23

4.10
Lam 2.20;
2 Kings 6.29;
Deut 28.57

4.11
Jer 7.20;
v. 22;
Deut 32.22;
Jer 21.14

4.12
1 Kings 9.8,
9;
Jer 21.13

4.13
Jer 5.31;
6.13;
Ezek 22.26;
Mic 3.11, 12;
Mt 23.31

4.11,12 The destruction of Jerusalem had been a complete destruction. This event was a surprise to the kings of the earth, for it seemed impossible that this strong and well-fortified city would ever be destroyed. The kings of the nations knew too that Jerusalem was under the protection of the great King who resided in that holy city. They knew that Sennacherib had tried to seize it and had failed dismally when the God of Israel delivered the city from his hands. They could only conclude that the success of Nebuchadnezzar in taking the city had come about because God had given up Jerusalem and commissioned Nebuchadnezzar to seize it.

4.13 It was surprising that the very people who should have guaranteed Jerusalem's survival were the cause of its destruction. The prophets and the priests

and the iniquities of her priests,
who shed the blood of the righteous
in the midst of her.

4.14
Isa 56.10;
59.9, 10;
Jer 19.4; 2.34

14 Blindly they wandered through the streets,
    so defiled with blood
that no one was able
    to touch their garments.

4.15
Lev 13.45;
Jer 49.5

15 "Away! Unclean!" people shouted at them;
    "Away! Away! Do not touch!"
So they became fugitives and wanderers;
    it was said among the nations,
    "They shall stay here no longer."

4.16
Lam 5.12

16 The Lord himself has scattered them,
    he will regard them no more;
no honor was shown to the priests,
    no favor to the elders.

C. *The absence of external help*

4.17
2 Kings 24.7;
Isa 20.5;
Jer 37.7;
Ezek 29.16

17 Our eyes failed, ever watching
    vainly for help;
we were watching eagerly
    for a nation that could not save.

4.18
2 Kings 25.4;
Ezek 7.2, 3;
Am 8.2

18 They dogged our steps
    so that we could not walk in our streets;
our end drew near; our days were numbered;
    for our end had come.

4.19
Deut 28.49;
Jer 4.13;
Hab 1.8

19 Our pursuers were swifter
    than the eagles in the heavens;
they chased us on the mountains,
    they lay in wait for us in the wilderness.

4.20
2 Sam 1.14;
19.21;
Ezek 12.13;
19.4, 8

20 The Lord's anointed, the breath of our life,
    was taken in their pits —
the one of whom we said, "Under his shadow
    we shall live among the nations."

D. *Closing refrain*

4.21
Isa 34.7;
Am 1.11, 12;
Ob 1, 16

21 Rejoice and be glad, O daughter Edom,
    you that live in the land of Uz;
but to you also the cup shall pass;
    you shall become drunk and strip yourself bare.

4.22
Isa 40.2;
Mal 1.3, 4

22 The punishment of your iniquity, O daughter Zion, is
        accomplished,
    he will keep you in exile no longer;
but your iniquity, O daughter Edom, he will punish,
    he will uncover your sins.

---

were among the chief offenders by their sins and iniquities. But the people did not object. They loved "to have it so" (Jer 5.31). Nothing can work greater harm for a church today than for its leaders to sin against God.
4.17 *a nation.* This probably refers to Egypt.

4.21 *O daughter Edom.* The Edomites had always been enemies of Israel. They had sided with Babylon in the months before the fall and destruction of Jerusalem. Edom rejoiced in Jerusalem's fall, but she would be punished by God in the days to come (cf. Ezek 25.12–14; Ob 11–14).

V. *The prayer for mercy amid affliction (5.1–22)*

A. *Acknowledgment of their sin and evil condition*

5 Remember, O Lord, what has befallen us;
    look, and see our disgrace!   5.1 Ps 89.50; 44.13-16

2 Our inheritance has been turned over to strangers,
    our homes to aliens.   5.2 Ps 79.1; Zeph 1.13

3 We have become orphans, fatherless;
    our mothers are like widows.   5.3 Jer 15.8; 18.21

4 We must pay for the water we drink;
    the wood we get must be bought.   5.4 Isa 3.1

5 With a yoke*l* on our necks we are hard driven;
    we are weary, we are given no rest.   5.5 Jer 28.14; Neh 9.36, 37

6 We have made a pact with*m* Egypt and Assyria,
    to get enough bread.   5.6 Jer 2.36; Hos 5.13; 7.11; 9.3

7 Our ancestors sinned; they are no more,
    and we bear their iniquities.   5.7 Jer 14.20; 16.12

8 Slaves rule over us;
    there is no one to deliver us from their hand.   5.8 Neh 5.15; Zech 11.6

9 We get our bread at the peril of our lives,
    because of the sword in the wilderness.   5.9

10 Our skin is black as an oven
    from the scorching heat of famine.   5.10 Lam 4.8

11 Women are raped in Zion,
    virgins in the towns of Judah.   5.11 Isa 13.16; Zech 14.2

12 Princes are hung up by their hands;
    no respect is shown to the elders.   5.12 Lam 4.16

13 Young men are compelled to grind,
    and boys stagger under loads of wood.   5.13 Jer 7.18

14 The old men have left the city gate,
    the young men their music.   5.14 Lam 4.8; Jer 7.34

15 The joy of our hearts has ceased;
    our dancing has been turned to mourning.   5.15 Jer 25.10

16 The crown has fallen from our head;
    woe to us, for we have sinned!   5.16 Ps 89.39; Isa 3.9-11

17 Because of this our hearts are sick,
    because of these things our eyes have grown dim: 5.17 Isa 1.5; Ps 6.7

18 because of Mount Zion, which lies desolate;
    jackals prowl over it.   5.18 Ps 74.2, 3; Neh 4.3

B. *Their prayer for mercy*

19 But you, O Lord, reign forever;
    your throne endures to all generations.   5.19 Ps 9.7; 102.12, 25-27; 45.6

20 Why have you forgotten us completely?
    Why have you forsaken us these many days?   5.20 Ps 13.1

21 Restore us to yourself, O Lord, that we may be restored;
    renew our days as of old —   5.21 Jer 31.18

22 unless you have utterly rejected us,
    and are angry with us beyond measure.   5.22 Jer 7.29; Isa 64.9

l Symmachus: Heb lacks *With a yoke*   *m* Heb *have given the hand to*

5.1ff Jeremiah pictures the calamitous condition of God's people in their captivity. They had lost their homes and were orphans. They suffered the yoke of the oppressor, while slaves ruled over them. They had lost all hope.

5.12 Important officials of Israel had suffered shameful deaths. Perhaps their bodies were hung up after death to public view, for people to revile.

5.19ff Bad as the situation was in Judah, there remained a believing remnant, however small, who were calling on God to remember mercy and to deliver his people from their distress. They addressed God in his sovereign majesty and acknowledged that he reigns eternally. They pleaded for restoration as they recalled better days.

INTRODUCTION TO

EZEKIEL

Authorship, Date, and Background: The author of this book is Ezekiel, whose name means "God strengthens." Buzi, of the priestly family of Zadok, was his father. Ezekiel was born ca. 621 B.C. He was raised in Jerusalem and became a prophet and priest of God during the most difficult period of Judah's history. Judah had been under the yoke of Assyria following the fall of the northern kingdom (Samaria) in 722 B.C. Babylon was to crush Assyria more than a hundred years later. In 605 B.C., after Nebuchadnezzar had defeated the Egyptians and Assyrians at Carchemish, the first deportation of Jews from Judea took place and Daniel was numbered among the victims. A second deportation followed in 597 B.C. and Ezekiel was among those sent to Babylon.

Ezekiel lived in Babylon beside the Chebar river, was married, and had his own home. God called him to his ministry when he had been in Babylon for about five years. He exercised the office of prophet for nearly two decades. His wife died the day the siege of Jerusalem began and he was instructed by God neither to mourn nor weep. Ezekiel's statements about Jerusalem at a time when he was in Babylon have occasioned modern critics to question whether he wrote the book. Evangelicals have always accepted the book as genuine and have found adequate archaeological evidence to support their viewpoint.

Characteristics and Content: The burden of Ezekiel is one of divine judgment on Judah for its sins. In the early part of the prophecy, God commissioned him to be a sentinel on the wall, warning sinners to flee from God's wrath. In various ways he repeatedly warned of the coming destruction of Jerusalem, which was guilty of harlotry, of listening to false prophets, and of failing to put its trust in God.

In the severest terms Ezekiel also pronounced the judgment of God against the surrounding heathen nations. Ammon, Moab, and Philistia received the divine sentence. Tyre was given special attention and its end is described in detail. Egypt's treachery and pride were described, and Ezekiel prophesied that God would use Babylon and its king, Nebuchadnezzar, to destroy her.

In the latter part of his prophecy, Ezekiel foresaw the ultimate restoration of Israel, which he illustrated in his vision of the valley of dry bones. He foretold a time when Israel would turn again to God in repentance and faith, the glory of God would return to a rebuilt temple, the priesthood would be restored, and the Levitical sacrifices would be reinstituted. He provided detailed information about the dimensions and auxiliary buildings and rooms of the new temple. In other words, a ray of hope shines through at the end.

Outline:

I. The divine judgment on Judah and Jerusalem (1.1—24.27)

II. The prophecies against the surrounding nations (25.1—32.32)

III. Israel restored (33.1—39.29)

IV. Israel in the land in the coming age (40.1—48.35)

EZEKIEL

I. *The divine judgment on Judah and Jerusalem (1.1–24.27)*

A. *Introduction*

1. *Superscription*

1 In the thirtieth year, in the fourth month, on the fifth day of the month, as I was among the exiles by the river Chebar, the heavens were opened, and I saw visions of God. 2 On the fifth day of the month (it was the fifth year of the exile of King Jehoiachin), 3 the word of the LORD came to the priest Ezekiel son of Buzi, in the land of the Chaldeans by the river Chebar; and the hand of the LORD was on him there.

2. *The vision of the four living creatures and the four wheels*

4 As I looked, a stormy wind came out of the north: a great cloud with brightness around it and fire flashing forth continually, and in the middle of the fire, something like gleaming amber. 5 In the middle of it was something like four living creatures. This was their appearance: they were of human form. 6 Each had four faces, and each of them had four wings. 7 Their legs were straight, and the soles of their feet were like the sole of a calf's foot; and they sparkled like burnished bronze. 8 Under their wings on their four sides they had human hands. And the four had their faces and their wings thus: 9 their wings touched one another; each of them moved straight ahead, without turning as they moved. 10 As for the appearance of their faces: the four had the face of a human being, the face of a lion on the right side, the face of an ox on the left side, and the face of an eagle; 11 such were their faces. Their wings were spread out above; each creature had two wings, each of which touched the wing of another, while two covered their bodies. 12 Each moved straight ahead; wherever the spirit would go, they went, without turning as they went. 13 In the middle of*a* the living creatures there was something that looked like burning coals of fire, like torches moving to and fro among the living creatures; the fire was bright, and lightning issued from the fire. 14 The living creatures darted to and fro, like a flash of lightning.

15 As I looked at the living creatures, I saw a wheel on the earth beside the living creatures, one for each of the four of them.*b* 16 As for the appearance of the wheels and their construction: their appearance was like the gleaming of beryl; and the four had the same form, their construction being something like a wheel within a wheel. 17 When they moved, they moved in any of the four directions without veering as they moved. 18 Their rims were tall and awesome, for the rims of all four were full of eyes all around. 19 When the living creatures moved, the wheels moved beside them; and when the living creatures rose from the earth, the wheels

---

1.1	Ezek 3.15, 23; Mt 3.16; Acts 7.56
1.2	2 Kings 24.12
1.3	1 Kings 18.46; 2 Kings 3.15
1.4	Isa 21.1
1.5	Rev 4.6; Ezek 10.8, 14
1.6	vv. 10, 23
1.7	Rev 1.15; 2.18
1.8	Ezek 10.8, 21
1.9	vv. 17, 12
1.10	Rev 4.7; Ezek 10.14
1.11	Ezek 10.16, 19; Isa 6.2
1.12	vv. 9, 20
1.13	Ps 104.4; Rev 4.5
1.14	Mt 24.27
1.15	vv. 19-21
1.16	Ezek 10.9-11; Dan 10.6
1.17	v. 12
1.18	Ezek 10.12; Rev 4.6, 8
1.19	Ezek 10.16, 17, 19

---

a Gk OL: Heb *And the appearance of*   *b* Heb *of their faces*

1.1 *the thirtieth year.* Most likely this refers to Ezekiel's age, when at thirty years old he was able to enter upon the full duties of the priesthood (Num 4.2).

1.10 The creatures were four-sided, in that each had four faces made up of a human being, a lion, an ox, and an eagle.

rose. 20 Wherever the spirit would go, they went, and the wheels rose along with them; for the spirit of the living creatures was in the wheels. 21 When they moved, the others moved; when they stopped, the others stopped; and when they rose from the earth, the wheels rose along with them; for the spirit of the living creatures was in the wheels.

22 Over the heads of the living creatures there was something like a dome, shining like crystal,*c* spread out above their heads. 23 Under the dome their wings were stretched out straight, one toward another; and each of the creatures had two wings covering its body. 24 When they moved, I heard the sound of their wings like the sound of mighty waters, like the thunder of the Almighty,*d* a sound of tumult like the sound of an army; when they stopped, they let down their wings. 25 And there came a voice from above the dome over their heads; when they stopped, they let down their wings.

26 And above the dome over their heads there was something like a throne, in appearance like sapphire;*e* and seated above the likeness of a throne was something that seemed like a human form. 27 Upward from what appeared like the loins I saw something like gleaming amber, something that looked like fire enclosed all around; and downward from what looked like the loins I saw something that looked like fire, and there was a splendor all around. 28 Like the bow in a cloud on a rainy day, such was the appearance of the splendor all around. This was the appearance of the likeness of the glory of the LORD.

When I saw it, I fell on my face, and I heard the voice of someone speaking.

3. The commissions of Ezekiel

a. To go to the house of Israel

2 He said to me: O mortal,*f* stand up on your feet, and I will speak with you. 2 And when he spoke to me, a spirit entered into me and set me on my feet; and I heard him speaking to me. 3 He said to me, Mortal, I am sending you to the people of Israel, to a nation*g* of rebels who have rebelled against me; they and their ancestors have transgressed against me to this very day. 4 The descendants are impudent and stubborn. I am sending you to them, and you shall say to them, "Thus says the Lord GOD." 5 Whether they hear or refuse to hear (for they are a rebellious house), they shall know that there has been a prophet among them. 6 And you, O mortal, do not be afraid of them, and do not be afraid of their words, though briers and thorns surround you and you live among scorpions; do not be afraid of their words, and do not be dismayed at their looks, for they are a rebellious house. 7 You shall speak my words to them, whether they hear or refuse to hear; for they are a rebellious house.

c Gk: Heb like the awesome crystal   *d* Traditional rendering of Heb *Shaddai*   *e* Or *lapis lazuli*   *f* Or *son of man*; Heb *ben adam* (and so throughout the book when Ezekiel is addressed)   *g* Syr: Heb to nations

---

1.28 *the likeness of the glory of the LORD.* God is spirit without human form. Here the glory is spoken of as a likeness. When Ezekiel saw it, he fell on his face, awed by the majesty of God.

2.1 *son of man* (NRSV footnote). The phrase stresses Ezekiel's humanity. Despite the many celestial visions Ezekiel had, he was nothing more than a human being. Later this same term came to be applied in a messianic sense to the one who would establish God's rule over all the earth and usher in God's messianic age (e.g., Dan 7.9–13). This messianic usage does not appear in Ezekiel.

2.2 *a spirit entered into me.* The third person of the Trinity appeared. He would appear again and again in Ezekiel, far more than in any other O.T. book. The Spirit came upon Ezekiel, picked him up, and set him

on his feet after he had fallen to the ground.

2.3,4 God's people are called rebellious, impudent, and stubborn. Judah and Jerusalem still stood, though some of the people (including Ezekiel) had already been taken captive to Babylon (cf. 1.1). Just as Jeremiah was doing in the land of Judah, so Ezekiel would forecast the capture and destruction of Jerusalem by Nebuchadnezzar.

2.6,7 God warned Ezekiel that he would face hardships as a prophet. He had to preach whether the people heeded his message or refused to listen and chose to continue in their sins. God had allowed Judah hundreds of years and sent scores of prophets to warn them. God always exercises divine patience in spite of repeated evidences of apostasy.

b. *To eat the scroll*

8 But you, mortal, hear what I say to you; do not be rebellious like that rebellious house; open your mouth and eat what I give you. 9 I looked, and a hand was stretched out to me, and a written scroll was in it. 10 He spread it before me; it had writing on the front and on the back, and written on it were words of lamentation and mourning and woe.

3 He said to me, O mortal, eat what is offered to you; eat this scroll, and go, speak to the house of Israel. 2 So I opened my mouth, and he gave me the scroll to eat. 3 He said to me, Mortal, eat this scroll that I give you and fill your stomach with it. Then I ate it; and in my mouth it was as sweet as honey.

c. *To speak God's message to Israel*

4 He said to me: Mortal, go to the house of Israel and speak my very words to them. 5 For you are not sent to a people of obscure speech and difficult language, but to the house of Israel— 6 not to many peoples of obscure speech and difficult language, whose words you cannot understand. Surely, if I sent you to them, they would listen to you. 7 But the house of Israel will not listen to you, for they are not willing to listen to me; because all the house of Israel have a hard forehead and a stubborn heart. 8 See, I have made your face hard against their faces, and your forehead hard against their foreheads. 9 Like the hardest stone, harder than flint, I have made your forehead; do not fear them or be dismayed at their looks, for they are a rebellious house. 10 He said to me: Mortal, all my words that I shall speak to you receive in your heart and hear with your ears; 11 then go to the exiles, to your people, and speak to them. Say to them, "Thus says the Lord GOD"; whether they hear or refuse to hear.

d. *The visit to Babylon*

12 Then the spirit lifted me up, and as the glory of the LORD rose[h] from its place, I heard behind me the sound of loud rumbling; 13 it was the sound of the wings of the living creatures brushing against one another, and the sound of the wheels beside them, that sounded like a loud rumbling. 14 The spirit lifted me up and bore me away; I went in bitterness in the heat of my spirit, the hand of the LORD being strong upon me. 15 I came to the exiles at Tel-abib, who lived by the river Chebar.[i] And I sat there among them, stunned, for seven days.

e. *The message of the sentinel given*

16 At the end of seven days, the word of the LORD came to me: 17 Mortal, I have made you a sentinel for the house of Israel; whenever you hear a word from my mouth, you shall give them warning from me.

h Cn: Heb and blessed be the glory of the LORD   i Two Mss Syr: Heb Chebar, and to where they lived. Another reading is Chebar, and I sat where they sat

2.8	Isa 50.5; Rev 10.9
2.9	Ezek 8.3; 3.1
2.10	Rev 8.13
3.1	Ezek 2.8, 9
3.3	Rev 10.9, 10; Jer 15.16; Ps 19.10; 119.103
3.4	v. 11
3.5	Jon 1.2; Isa 28.11; 33.19
3.6	Mt 11.21, 23; Acts 13.46-48
3.7	Jn 15.20; Ezek 2.4
3.8	Jer 1.18; 15.20
3.9	Isa 50.7; Mic 3.8; Ezek 2.6
3.10	vv. 1-3
3.11	Ezek 2.5, 7
3.12	Ezek 8.3; Acts 8.39; 2.2
3.13	Ezek 1.24; 10.5, 16, 17
3.14	Jer 6.11; Ezek 1.3; 8.1
3.15	Ezek 1.1; Job 2.13
3.16ff	
3.17	Ezek 33.7-9; Isa 52.8; 56.10; Jer 6.17

2.8 God first opened Ezekiel's eyes and ears. Now he told him to open his mouth and receive the exact word he wanted spoken to his people.

3.1ff Ezekiel was not to speak until he had received the revelation of God. Despite its harshness, the word in his mouth was as sweet as honey.

3.4 Ezekiel was sent to the house of Israel to speak only what God had given him.

3.7 To be forewarned is to be forearmed. God told Ezekiel that his message would not be listened to, not because it was being spoken by Ezekiel but because the people did not want to hear God.

3.12 In 2.2 the Spirit set Ezekiel on his feet. Here the Spirit lifted him up and bore him away (v. 14). In v. 24 the Spirit entered into him. The work of the Spirit in Ezekiel's life is mentioned more times than in any other account in the O.T.

3.14 Ezekiel assumed his role as spokesman for the Lord with a heavy heart, embittered by the knowledge that he would not succeed among these reprobate people.

3.15 The Spirit of God carried him to Babylon where he waited among the captives for God to tell him what to say. He had a twofold message for them when he spoke. The captives would be in Babylon a long time, and they would be joined by many others when Judah and Jerusalem were taken and the city destroyed.

3.16ff God called Ezekiel as a sentinel to sound the alarm whenever danger arose. If he failed to do so, his people would be destroyed and he would be responsible. If, however, the people refused to heed his warnings, he could not be held responsible so long as he did his job. God has given us a similar reponsibility, to warn sinners to flee from the wrath to come.

¹⁸ If I say to the wicked, "You shall surely die," and you give them no warning, or speak to warn the wicked from their wicked way, in order to save their life, those wicked persons shall die for their iniquity; but their blood I will require at your hand. ¹⁹ But if you warn the wicked, and they do not turn from their wickedness, or from their wicked way, they shall die for their iniquity; but you will have saved your life. ²⁰ Again, if the righteous turn from their righteousness and commit iniquity, and I lay a stumbling block before them, they shall die; because you have not warned them, they shall die for their sin, and their righteous deeds that they have done shall not be remembered; but their blood I will require at your hand. ²¹ If, however, you warn the righteous not to sin, and they do not sin, they shall surely live, because they took warning; and you will have saved your life.

f. The commission to confinement

²² Then the hand of the Lord was upon me there; and he said to me, Rise up, go out into the valley, and there I will speak with you. ²³ So I rose up and went out into the valley; and the glory of the Lord stood there, like the glory that I had seen by the river Chebar; and I fell on my face. ²⁴ The spirit entered into me, and set me on my feet; and he spoke with me and said to me: Go, shut yourself inside your house. ²⁵ As for you, mortal, cords shall be placed on you, and you shall be bound with them, so that you cannot go out among the people; ²⁶ and I will make your tongue cling to the roof of your mouth, so that you shall be speechless and unable to reprove them; for they are a rebellious house. ²⁷ But when I speak with you, I will open your mouth, and you shall say to them, "Thus says the Lord God"; let those who will hear, hear; and let those who refuse to hear, refuse; for they are a rebellious house.

B. The coming destruction of Jerusalem

1. The symbol of the siege

And you, O mortal, take a brick and set it before you. On it portray a city, Jerusalem; ² and put siegeworks against it, and build a siege wall against it, and cast up a ramp against it; set camps also against it, and plant battering rams against it all around. ³ Then take an iron plate and place it as an iron wall between you and the city; set your face toward it, and let it be in a state of siege, and press the siege against it. This is a sign for the house of Israel.

2. The symbol of the punishment

⁴ Then lie on your left side, and place the punishment of the house of Israel upon it; you shall bear their punishment for the number of the days that you lie there. ⁵ For I assign to you a number of days, three hundred ninety days, equal to the number of the years of their punishment; and so you shall bear the punishment of the house of Israel. ⁶ When you have completed these, you shall lie down a second time, but on your right side, and bear the punishment of the house of Judah; forty days I assign you, one day for each year. ⁷ You shall set your face toward the siege of Jerusalem, and with your arm bared you shall prophesy against it. ⁸ See,

---

3.23ff Ezekiel saw the glory of God, and the Spirit entered him, set him on his feet, and told him what to do. He was then overtaken by a kind of paralysis in which he lay dumb and bound, incapable of fulfilling the prophetic office until God opened his mouth and filled it with his words.
4.1 *a brick*, i.e., a clay tablet, like those used by the Babylonians for writing. God told Ezekiel to draw a map of Jerusalem on it, along with information about the coming siege against the city.

4.5 *three hundred and ninety days.* Some ancient versions, such as the Septuagint (Greek translation of the O.T.), read, "190 days." If this figure is correct, it would cover the period from 721 B.C. (when Samaria was destroyed) to 536 B.C. If the 390 figure is correct, then the period covers the time from the first apostasy under Jeroboam to the destruction of Jerusalem. Either option is a possibility.

I am putting cords on you so that you cannot turn from one side to the other until you have completed the days of your siege.

3. The symbol of the consequences of the siege

9 And you, take wheat and barley, beans and lentils, millet and spelt; put them into one vessel, and make bread for yourself. During the number of days that you lie on your side, three hundred ninety days, you shall eat it. 10 The food that you eat shall be twenty shekels a day by weight; at fixed times you shall eat it. 11 And you shall drink water by measure, one-sixth of a hin; at fixed times you shall drink. 12 You shall eat it as a barley-cake, baking it in their sight on human dung. 13 The LORD said, "Thus shall the people of Israel eat their bread, unclean, among the nations to which I will drive them." 14 Then I said, "Ah Lord GOD! I have never defiled myself; from my youth up until now I have never eaten what died of itself or was torn by animals, nor has carrion flesh come into my mouth." 15 Then he said to me, "See, I will let you have cow's dung instead of human dung, on which you may prepare your bread."

16 Then he said to me, Mortal, I am going to break the staff of bread in Jerusalem; they shall eat bread by weight and with fearfulness; and they shall drink water by measure and in dismay. 17 Lacking bread and water, they will look at one another in dismay, and waste away under their punishment.

4. The symbol of Jerusalem's fate

a. What will happen to the people

5 And you, O mortal, take a sharp sword; use it as a barber's razor and run it over your head and your beard; then take balances for weighing, and divide the hair. 2 One third of the hair you shall burn in the fire inside the city, when the days of the siege are completed; one third you shall take and strike with the sword all around the city;[j] and one third you shall scatter to the wind, and I will unsheathe the sword after them. 3 Then you shall take from these a small number, and bind them in the skirts of your robe. 4 From these, again, you shall take some, throw them into the fire and burn them up; from there a fire will come out against all the house of Israel.

b. Jerusalem's fate the result of idolatry

5 Thus says the Lord GOD: This is Jerusalem; I have set her in the center of the nations, with countries all around her. 6 But she has rebelled against my ordinances and my statutes, becoming more wicked than the nations and the countries all around her, rejecting my ordinances and not following my statutes. 7 Therefore thus says the Lord GOD: Because you are more turbulent than the nations that are all around you, and have not followed my statutes or kept my ordinances, but have acted according to the ordinances of the nations that are all around you; 8 therefore thus says the Lord GOD: I, I myself, am coming against you; I will execute judgments among you in the sight of the nations. 9 And because of all your

---

4.9
v. 5
4.10
v. 16
4.12
Isa 36.12
4.13
Hos 9.3
4.14
Ezek 9.8;
Acts 10.14;
Ex 22.31;
Lev 17.15;
Deut 14.3;
Isa 65.4
4.16
Lev 26.26;
Isa 3.1;
Ezek 5.16;
14.13; vv. 10,
11;
Ezek 12.19
4.17
Lev 26.39;
Ezek 24.23
5.1
Lev 21.5;
Isa 7.20;
Ezek 44.20
5.2
v. 12;
Ezek 4.2-8;
Lev 26.33
5.3
Jer 39.10
5.4
Jer 41.1, 2;
44.14
5.5
Ezek 4.1;
Lam 1.1
5.6
Ezek 16.47,
48, 51;
Jer 11.10;
Zech 7.11
5.7
2 Chr 33.9;
Ezek 16.47
5.8
Ezek 15.7
5.9
Dan 9.12;
Mt 24.21

---

j Heb it

4.8 *I am putting cords on you*, i.e., God bound Ezekiel in order to carry out the symbol that Jerusalem would be bound by the siege before it capitulated. **4.9ff** Ezekiel was to eat only enough to remain alive, signifying that famine would overtake Jerusalem during the siege. To cook food with human dung was nauseous, so God let him change it to animal dung. *carrion flesh*. The famine would bring the Jews to a place where they would eat anything, even forbidden food, to stay alive (see Lev 11 for the dietary laws referred to here).

5.1ff Ezekiel divided the hair from his head and beard into three parts to prophesy the complete destruction of Jerusalem. It symbolized that one-third of the Jews in Jerusalem would perish by fire, famine, and pestilence, one-third would be slain in the warfare, and one-third would be scattered far and wide. **5.6** Although the nation as a whole had broken God's statutes, this did not mean that all of the people had done so. There was a remnant of faithful people who kept the law of God and loved God with their whole hearts.

abominations, I will do to you what I have never yet done, and the like of which I will never do again. ¹⁰Surely, parents shall eat their children in your midst, and children shall eat their parents; I will execute judgments on you, and any of you who survive I will scatter to every wind. ¹¹Therefore, as I live, says the Lord GOD, surely, because you have defiled my sanctuary with all your detestable things and with all your abominations — therefore I will cut you down;ᵏ my eye will not spare, and I will have no pity. ¹²One third of you shall die of pestilence or be consumed by famine among you; one third shall fall by the sword around you; and one third I will scatter to every wind and will unsheathe the sword after them.

13 My anger shall spend itself, and I will vent my fury on them and satisfy myself; and they shall know that I, the LORD, have spoken in my jealousy, when I spend my fury on them. ¹⁴Moreover I will make you a desolation and an object of mocking among the nations around you, in the sight of all that pass by. ¹⁵You shall beˡ a mockery and a taunt, a warning and a horror, to the nations around you, when I execute judgments on you in anger and fury, and with furious punishments — I, the LORD, have spoken — ¹⁶when I loose against youᵐ my deadly arrows of famine, arrows for destruction, which I will let loose to destroy you, and when I bring more and more famine upon you, and break your staff of bread. ¹⁷I will send famine and wild animals against you, and they will rob you of your children; pestilence and bloodshed shall pass through you; and I will bring the sword upon you. I, the LORD, have spoken.

C. The oracle of the mountains

1. The high places to be destroyed

6 The word of the LORD came to me: ²O mortal, set your face toward the mountains of Israel, and prophesy against them, ³and say, You mountains of Israel, hear the word of the Lord GOD! Thus says the Lord GOD to the mountains and the hills, to the ravines and the valleys: I, I myself will bring a sword upon you, and I will destroy your high places. ⁴Your altars shall become desolate, and your incense stands shall be broken; and I will throw down your slain in front of your idols. ⁵I will lay the corpses of the people of Israel in front of their idols; and I will scatter your bones around your altars. ⁶Wherever you live, your towns shall be waste and your high places ruined, so that your altars will be waste and ruined,ⁿ your idols broken and destroyed, your incense stands cut down, and your works wiped out. ⁷The slain shall fall in your midst; then you shall know that I am the LORD.

2. A remnant to be preserved

8 But I will spare some. Some of you shall escape the sword among the nations and be scattered through the countries. ⁹Those of you who escape shall remember me among the nations where they are carried captive, how I was crushed by their wanton heart that turned away from

5.10
Lev 26.29;
Ezek 12.14;
Zech 2.6

5.11
2 Chr 36.14;
Ezek 7.4, 9;
8.18

5.12
Jer 43.10, 11;
Ezek 12.14

5.13
Lam 4.11;
Ezek 21.17;
36.6

5.14
Lev 26.31,
32;
Neh 2.17

5.15
Deut 28.37;
1 Kings 9.7;
Jer 24.9;
Ezek 25.17

5.16
Deut 32.23,
24;
Ezek 4.16

5.17
Ezek 14.21;
28.23

6.2
Ezek 36.1

6.3
Ezek 36.4, 6

6.4
Lev 26.30

6.5
Jer 8.1, 2

6.6
Lev 26.31;
Zech 13.2

6.7
Ezek 11.10,
12

6.8
Jer 44.28;
Ezek 5.2, 12;
12.16; 14.22

6.9
Jer 51.50;
Ps 78.40;
Isa 7.13;
Ezek 43.24;
20.7, 24;
20.43

ᵏ Another reading is *I will withdraw*   ˡ Gk Syr Vg Tg: Heb *It shall be*   ᵐ Heb *them*   ⁿ Syr Vg Tg: Heb *and be made guilty*

5.10 Jeremiah lamented that mothers ate their own children during the famine caused by the siege of Jerusalem (see Jer 19.9; Lam 4.10). Josephus also affirmed this in his history of the Jews.
5.13 *jealousy.* The Hebrew word used here is translated in the O.T. as "zeal" and "jealousy." Jealousy usually has a negative meaning. But jealousy in God is not the same as jealousy in humans, for God's jealousy has to do with his expectation of exclusive devotion. God will not allow himself to be supplanted

by any other gods, nor will he permit any substitutes in place of himself.
5.17 What happened to Jerusalem, although accomplished by a heathen nation and people, was done by God himself. God can and does accomplish his aims directly or indirectly through nature, nations, angels, or circumstances.
6.8 In the midst of a judgment unto death, God said that he would spare some.

me, and their wanton eyes that turned after their idols. Then they will be loathsome in their own sight for the evils that they have committed, for all their abominations. 10 And they shall know that I am the LORD; I did not threaten in vain to bring this disaster upon them.

3. Israel to know the LORD by his judgments

11 Thus says the Lord GOD: Clap your hands and stamp your foot, and say, Alas for all the vile abominations of the house of Israel! For they shall fall by the sword, by famine, and by pestilence. 12 Those far off shall die of pestilence; those nearby shall fall by the sword; and any who are left and are spared shall die of famine. Thus I will spend my fury upon them. 13 And you shall know that I am the LORD, when their slain lie among their idols around their altars, on every high hill, on all the mountain tops, under every green tree, and under every leafy oak, wherever they offered pleasing odor to all their idols. 14 I will stretch out my hand against them, and make the land desolate and waste, throughout all their settlements, from the wilderness to Riblah.º Then they shall know that I am the LORD.

D. *The oracle of the coming end*

1. *The disaster in the land*

7 The word of the LORD came to me: 2 You, O mortal, thus says the Lord GOD to the land of Israel:
An end! The end has come
    upon the four corners of the land.
3 Now the end is upon you,
    I will let loose my anger upon you;
    I will judge you according to your ways,
    I will punish you for all your abominations.
4 My eye will not spare you, I will have no pity.
    I will punish you for your ways,
    while your abominations are among you.
Then you shall know that I am the LORD.
5 Thus says the Lord GOD:
Disaster after disaster! See, it comes.
6   An end has come, the end has come.
It has awakened against you; see, it comes!
7 Your doomᵖ has come to you,
    O inhabitant of the land.
The time has come, the day is near —
    of tumult, not of reveling on the mountains.
8 Soon now I will pour out my wrath upon you;
    I will spend my anger against you.
I will judge you according to your ways,
    and punish you for all your abominations.
9 My eye will not spare; I will have no pity.
    I will punish you according to your ways,
    while your abominations are among you.
Then you shall know that it is I the LORD who strike.
10 See, the day! See, it comes!
    Your doomᵖ has gone out.

º Another reading is *Diblah*   ᵖ Meaning of Heb uncertain

Cross references (right margin):

6.10 v. 7

6.11 Ezek 21.14; 25.6; 5.12; 7.15
6.12 Dan 9.7; Ezek 5.13
6.13 v. 7; Jer 2.20; Hos 4.13; Isa 57.5
6.14 Isa 5.25; Ezek 14.13; Num 33.46

7.2 Am 8.2; Ezek 11.13; Rev 7.1; 20.8
7.3 vv. 8, 9, 27
7.4 Ezek 5.11; 8.18; 11.21; 6.7
7.5 2 Kings 21.12, 13
7.6 vv. 2, 10
7.7 v. 12; Isa 22.5
7.8 Ezek 20.8, 21; 6.12; v. 3
7.10 v. 7; Isa 10.5

6.11 Ezekiel was commanded to demonstrate his sense of horror and grief by clapping his hands and stamping his feet. Thus the people of God would know how certain would be the evil consequences of their transgressions. When they saw the things Ezek-iel was prophesying come to pass, they would know that God is the Lord.
7.1ff Ezekiel informed the Jews about the final ruin of Jerusalem and the absolute destruction of the land.

11   The rod has blossomed, pride has budded.
     Violence has grown into a rod of wickedness.
   None of them shall remain,
       not their abundance, not their wealth;
       no pre-eminence among them. q

12   The time has come, the day draws near;
       let not the buyer rejoice, nor the seller mourn,
       for wrath is upon all their multitude.
13For the sellers shall not return to what has been sold as long as they
remain alive. For the vision concerns all their multitude; it shall not be
revoked. Because of their iniquity, they cannot maintain their lives. q

2. The desolation of the inhabitants within and without

14   They have blown the horn and made everything ready;
       but no one goes to battle,
       for my wrath is upon all their multitude.

15   The sword is outside, pestilence and famine are inside;
       those in the field die by the sword;
       those in the city—famine and pestilence devour them.

16   If any survivors escape,
       they shall be found on the mountains
       like doves of the valleys,
     all of them moaning over their iniquity.

17   All hands shall grow feeble,
       all knees turn to water.

18   They shall put on sackcloth,
       horror shall cover them.
     Shame shall be on all faces,
       baldness on all their heads.

19   They shall fling their silver into the streets,
       their gold shall be treated as unclean.
     Their silver and gold cannot save them on the day of the wrath of the
LORD. They shall not satisfy their hunger or fill their stomachs with it.
For it was the stumbling block of their iniquity. 20 From their r beautiful
ornament, in which they took pride, they made their abominable images,
their detestable things; therefore I will make of it an unclean thing to
them.

21   I will hand it over to strangers as booty,
       to the wicked of the earth as plunder;
       they shall profane it.

22   I will avert my face from them,
       so that they may profane my treasured s place;
     the violent shall enter it,
       they shall profane it.

23   Make a chain! q
     For the land is full of bloody crimes;
       the city is full of violence.

3. The profaning of the holy places

24   I will bring the worst of the nations
       to take possession of their houses.
     I will put an end to the arrogance of the strong,

q Meaning of Heb uncertain   r Syr Symmachus: Heb its   s Or secret

---

7.11
Jer 6.7; 16.5,
6;
Ezek 24.16,
22

7.12
vv. 5-7, 10;
1 Cor 7.30;
v. 14

7.14
Jer 4.5; v. 12

7.15
Deut 32.25;
Ezek 5.12

7.16
Ezek 6.8;
14.22;
Isa 38.14;
59.11

7.17
Isa 13.7;
Ezek 21.7;
Heb 12.12

7.18
Isa 15.2, 3;
Am 8.10;
Ezek 27.31

7.19
Isa 30.22;
Prov 11.4;
Zeph 1.18;
Ezek 13.5;
14.3, 4

7.20
Jer 7.30

7.21
Ps 74.2-8

7.22
Ezek 39.23,
24

7.23
2 Kings 21.16;
Ezek 9.9;
8.17

7.24
Ezek 21.31;
33.28; 24.21

7.11ff   The Jews could not say that it was not their
fault or that what was happening was an accident.
Their sins had brought this judgment upon them, and
no one else was to blame.
7.15   God declared that his judgment on these sinners would be universal; no one would escape or be
safe anywhere. Whoever was marked for death would
not escape. No one would wail for those who died,
and resistance would do no good.

and their holy places shall be profaned.

25 When anguish comes, they will seek peace,
        but there shall be none.
26 Disaster comes upon disaster,
        rumor follows rumor;
    they shall keep seeking a vision from the prophet;
        instruction shall perish from the priest,
        and counsel from the elders.
27 The king shall mourn,
        the prince shall be wrapped in despair,
        and the hands of the people of the land shall tremble.
    According to their way I will deal with them;
        according to their own judgments I will judge them.
And they shall know that I am the LORD.

E. The vision of abominations in Jerusalem

1. Idolatry in the temple

a. The background of the vision

8 In the sixth year, in the sixth month, on the fifth day of the month, as I sat in my house, with the elders of Judah sitting before me, the hand of the Lord GOD fell upon me there. 2 I looked, and there was a figure that looked like a human being;ᵗ below what appeared to be its loins it was fire, and above the loins it was like the appearance of brightness, like gleaming amber. 3 It stretched out the form of a hand, and took me by a lock of my head; and the spirit lifted me up between earth and heaven, and brought me in visions of God to Jerusalem, to the entrance of the gateway of the inner court that faces north, to the seat of the image of jealousy, which provokes to jealousy. 4 And the glory of the God of Israel was there, like the vision that I had seen in the valley.

b. The image of jealousy

5 Then Godᵘ said to me, "O mortal, lift up your eyes now in the direction of the north." So I lifted up my eyes toward the north, and there, north of the altar gate, in the entrance, was this image of jealousy. 6 He said to me, "Mortal, do you see what they are doing, the great abominations that the house of Israel are committing here, to drive me far from my sanctuary? Yet you will see still greater abominations."

c. The worship of idols and pictures

7 And he brought me to the entrance of the court; I looked, and there was a hole in the wall. 8 Then he said to me, "Mortal, dig through the wall"; and when I dug through the wall, there was an entrance. 9 He said to me, "Go in, and see the vile abominations that they are committing here." 10 So I went in and looked; there, portrayed on the wall all around, were all kinds of creeping things, and loathsome animals, and all the idols of the house of Israel. 11 Before them stood seventy of the elders of the house of Israel, with Jaazaniah son of Shaphan standing among them.

ᵗ Gk: Heb like fire   ᵘ Heb he

Cross-references (right margin):

7.25 Ezek 13.10, 16
7.26 Deut 32.23; Jer 4.20; Ezek 21.7; Ps 74.9; Ezek 20.1, 3
7.27 Ps 35.26; Ezek 26.16; vv. 3, 4, 8; Ezek 18.20
8.1 Ezek 14.1; 20.1; 33.31; 1.3; 3.22
8.2 Ezek 1.4, 27
8.3 Dan 5.5; Ezek 3.12, 14; 11.1; Jer 32.34; Ezek 5.11
8.4 Ezek 1.28
8.5 Zech 5.5; v. 3
8.6 vv. 9, 17; Ezek 5.11 7.22, 24; vv. 11, 14, 16
8.10 Ex 20.4; Ezek 14.3
8.11 Jer 19.1; Num 16.17, 35; Ezek 16.18; 23.41

7.25 *they will seek peace.* When the judgment of God fell, the sinful people would finally seek peace with God so that their lives might be saved. But to no avail. A time comes when the patience of God is exhausted and the door of grace is closed. It is presumptuous for people to assume that they may continue in their evil ways and that God will always answer. Once the divine ear chooses not to hear, there can be no reversal of judgment.
8.1 *The sixth year* was the sixth year of Jehoiachin's

captivity in Babylon (see 1 Kings 24.8–12; 25.27–29).
8.2ff God appeared to Ezekiel in the form of a human, surrounded at the waist by fire. Then the Spirit miraculously took him to Jerusalem and to the temple, where he had a message to bring. *The image of jealousy* was probably an image of a grove or of Baal set up in the house of God. A God who is jealous of his divine prerogatives could not let such apostasy pass unnoticed.

Each had his censer in his hand, and the fragrant cloud of incense was ascending. 12 Then he said to me, "Mortal, have you seen what the elders of the house of Israel are doing in the dark, each in his room of images? For they say, 'The LORD does not see us, the LORD has forsaken the land.' " 13 He said also to me, "You will see still greater abominations that they are committing."

d. The worship of Tammuz

14 Then he brought me to the entrance of the north gate of the house of the LORD; women were sitting there weeping for Tammuz. 15 Then he said to me, "Have you seen this, O mortal? You will see still greater abominations than these."

e. The worship of the sun

16 And he brought me into the inner court of the house of the LORD; there, at the entrance of the temple of the LORD, between the porch and the altar, were about twenty-five men, with their backs to the temple of the LORD, and their faces toward the east, prostrating themselves to the sun toward the east. 17 Then he said to me, "Have you seen this, O mortal? Is it not bad enough that the house of Judah commits the abominations done here? Must they fill the land with violence, and provoke my anger still further? See, they are putting the branch to their nose! 18 Therefore I will act in wrath; my eye will not spare, nor will I have pity; and though they cry in my hearing with a loud voice, I will not listen to them."

2. The slaughter of the idolaters

9 Then he cried in my hearing with a loud voice, saying, "Draw near, you executioners of the city, each with his destroying weapon in his hand." 2 And six men came from the direction of the upper gate, which faces north, each with his weapon for slaughter in his hand; among them was a man clothed in linen, with a writing case at his side. They went in and stood beside the bronze altar.

3 Now the glory of the God of Israel had gone up from the cherub on which it rested to the threshold of the house. The LORD called to the man clothed in linen, who had the writing case at his side; 4 and said to him, "Go through the city, through Jerusalem, and put a mark on the foreheads of those who sigh and groan over all the abominations that are committed in it." 5 To the others he said in my hearing, "Pass through the city after him, and kill; your eye shall not spare, and you shall show no pity. 6 Cut down old men, young men and young women, little children and women, but touch no one who has the mark. And begin at my sanctuary." So they began with the elders who were in front of the house. 7 Then he said to them, "Defile the house, and fill the courts with the slain. Go!" So they

Cross references (left margin):

8.12 Ezek 9.9
8.13 Ezek 9.3
8.14 Ezek 44.4; 46.9
8.16 Ezek 11.1; Jer 2.27; Deut 4.19; Job 31.26; Jer 44.17
8.17 Ezek 9.9; Mic 2.2; Jer 7.18, 19; Ezek 16.26
8.18 Ezek 5.13; 7.4; 9.5, 10; Isa 1.15; Jer 11.11; Mic 3.4; Zech 7.13
9.2 Ezek 10.2; Rev 15.6
9.3 Ezek 8.4; 10.4, 18; 11.22, 23
9.4 Ex 12.7; 1 Pet 4.17; Rev 7.3; 9.4; Ps 119.53, 136; Jer 13.17
9.5 Ezek 5.11; 7.4, 9
9.6 2 Chr 36.17; Rev 9.4; Jer 25.29; Am 3.2; Ezek 8.11, 12, 16
9.7 2 Chr 36.17; Ezek 7.20-22; 6.4

8.12 These evildoers were performing their idolatrous exercise in darkness. They supposed that: (1) because they did it secretly God would not know about it — thus they denied the omniscience of God; and (2) either God could not deliver them or would not do so — thus they had to look to some other god for help. They failed to realize that if God had forsaken them, it was because of their own transgressions, not because God lacked either the power or the desire to save them.

8.14 *Tammuz* was a Babylonian vegetation and fertility god who went to the underworld during the dry season when vegetation withered and streams dried up. Public mourning took place then because, according to Mesopotamian myths, he had been killed and fertility had vanished with him. Jewish women were participating in this idolatrous worship, so strong was

the hold that idolatry had on the people in the holy city.

8.16–18 The priests who had been entrusted to offer true sacrifices to God were themselves practicing abominable wickedness in God's very house. They had sunk so low that they worshiped the sun and had turned their backs toward the temple of the Lord. The jealousy of God to preserve his divine integrity could not allow this wickedness to go unpunished, and the Lord would no longer listen to their prayers.

9.3 *to the threshold of the house* i.e., above the entrance of the temple. For comments on the glory of God, see note on 10.18.

9.4–6 *Those who sigh and groan* were the remnant who disapproved of Jerusalem's idolatry. God had them marked for safety. As God's agent of death proceeded, only they were to be spared.

went out and killed in the city. 8 While they were killing, and I was left alone, I fell prostrate on my face and cried out, "Ah Lord God! will you destroy all who remain of Israel as you pour out your wrath upon Jerusalem?" 9 He said to me, "The guilt of the house of Israel and Judah is exceedingly great; the land is full of bloodshed and the city full of perversity; for they say, 'The Lord has forsaken the land, and the Lord does not see.' 10 As for me, my eye will not spare, nor will I have pity, but I will bring down their deeds upon their heads."

11   Then the man clothed in linen, with the writing case at his side, brought back word, saying, "I have done as you commanded me."

3. *The departure of the Lord from the temple*

10 Then I looked, and above the dome that was over the heads of the cherubim there appeared above them something like a sapphire,^{v} in form resembling a throne. 2 He said to the man clothed in linen, "Go within the wheelwork underneath the cherubim; fill your hands with burning coals from among the cherubim, and scatter them over the city." He went in as I looked on. 3 Now the cherubim were standing on the south side of the house when the man went in; and a cloud filled the inner court. 4 Then the glory of the Lord rose up from the cherub to the threshold of the house; the house was filled with the cloud, and the court was full of the brightness of the glory of the Lord. 5 The sound of the wings of the cherubim was heard as far as the outer court, like the voice of God Almighty^w when he speaks.

6   When he commanded the man clothed in linen, "Take fire from within the wheelwork, from among the cherubim," he went in and stood beside a wheel. 7 And a cherub stretched out his hand from among the cherubim to the fire that was among the cherubim, took some of it and put it into the hands of the man clothed in linen, who took it and went out. 8 The cherubim appeared to have the form of a human hand under their wings.

9   I looked, and there were four wheels beside the cherubim, one beside each cherub; and the appearance of the wheels was like gleaming beryl. 10 And as for their appearance, the four looked alike, something like a wheel within a wheel. 11 When they moved, they moved in any of the four directions without veering as they moved; but in whatever direction the front wheel faced, the others followed without veering as they moved. 12 Their entire body, their rims, their spokes, their wings, and the wheels —the wheels of the four of them—were full of eyes all around. 13 As for the wheels, they were called in my hearing "the wheelwork." 14 Each one had four faces: the first face was that of the cherub, the second face was that of a human being, the third that of a lion, and the fourth that of an eagle.

15   The cherubim rose up. These were the living creatures that I saw by the river Chebar. 16 When the cherubim moved, the wheels moved beside them; and when the cherubim lifted up their wings to rise up from the earth, the wheels at their side did not veer. 17 When they stopped, the

v Or *lapis lazuli*   *w* Traditional rendering of Heb *El Shaddai*

Cross-references (right column):

9.8
1 Chr 21.16;
Josh 7.6;
Ezek 11.13

9.9
Ezek 7.23;
22.29; 8.12

9.10
Isa 65.6;
Ezek 8.18;
7.4; 11.21

10.1
Ezek 1.22,
26;
Rev 4.2
10.2
Ezek 9.2, 3;
v. 13;
Isa 6.6;
Rev 8.5
10.3
Ezek 8.3, 16
10.4
Ezek 1.28;
9.3;
Ex 40.34, 35;
1 Kings 8.10,
11
10.5
Ezek 1.24
10.6
v. 2
10.7
Ezek 1.13

10.8
Ezek 1.8

10.9
Ezek 1.15, 16

10.11
Ezek 1.17;
v. 22
10.12
Rev 4.6, 8;
Ezek 1.18
10.13
v. 2
10.14
Ezek 1.6, 10;
Rev 4.7

10.15
Ezek 1.3, 5
10.16
Ezek 1.19

10.17
Ezek 1.12,
20, 21

10.1 Cherubim in the Scriptures are described as winged creatures of great beauty and power in the service of God. God placed the cherubim on the east side of Eden to keep Adam from eating of the tree of life and living forever (Gen 3.24). In the tabernacle, two cherubim were on either end of the lid or mercy seat of the ark of the covenant. They touched each other with the tips of their wings and bowed before the presence of God (Ex 25.18–21). Figures of cherubim were embroidered on the curtain that separated the most holy place from the holy place (Ex 26.31). John refers to the cherubim as living creatures, four in number, who stand around and in the midst of the throne of God (Rev 4.6,7). The reference to the cherub in 28.14 is understood by many to speak of Satan, whose fall may have been described in Isa 14.12–14.
10.17 The wheels and the cherubim were so interrelated that neither exists apart from the other.

others stopped, and when they rose up, the others rose up with them; for the spirit of the living creatures was in them.

18 Then the glory of the LORD went out from the threshold of the house and stopped above the cherubim. 19 The cherubim lifted up their wings and rose up from the earth in my sight as they went out with the wheels beside them. They stopped at the entrance of the east gate of the house of the LORD; and the glory of the God of Israel was above them.

20 These were the living creatures that I saw underneath the God of Israel by the river Chebar; and I knew that they were cherubim. 21 Each had four faces, each four wings, and underneath their wings something like human hands. 22 As for what their faces were like, they were the same faces whose appearance I had seen by the river Chebar. Each one moved straight ahead.

4. *The ungodly rulers of the nation to be punished*

11 The spirit lifted me up and brought me to the east gate of the house of the LORD, which faces east. There, at the entrance of the gateway, were twenty-five men; among them I saw Jaazaniah son of Azzur, and Pelatiah son of Benaiah, officials of the people. 2 He said to me, "Mortal, these are the men who devise iniquity and who give wicked counsel in this city; 3 they say, 'The time is not near to build houses; this city is the pot, and we are the meat.' 4 Therefore prophesy against them; prophesy, O mortal."

5 Then the spirit of the LORD fell upon me, and he said to me, "Say, Thus says the LORD: This is what you think, O house of Israel; I know the things that come into your mind. 6 You have killed many in this city, and have filled its streets with the slain. 7 Therefore thus says the Lord GOD: The slain whom you have placed within it are the meat, and this city is the pot; but you shall be taken out of it. 8 You have feared the sword; and I will bring the sword upon you, says the Lord GOD. 9 I will take you out of it and give you over to the hands of foreigners, and execute judgments upon you. 10 You shall fall by the sword; I will judge you at the border of Israel. And you shall know that I am the LORD. 11 This city shall not be your pot, and you shall not be the meat inside it; I will judge you at the border of Israel. 12 Then you shall know that I am the LORD, whose statutes you have not followed, and whose ordinances you have not kept, but you have acted according to the ordinances of the nations that are around you."

13 Now, while I was prophesying, Pelatiah son of Benaiah died. Then I fell down on my face, cried with a loud voice, and said, "Ah Lord GOD! will you make a full end of the remnant of Israel?"

14 Then the word of the LORD came to me: 15 Mortal, your kinsfolk, your own kin, your fellow exiles,ˣ the whole house of Israel, all of them, are those of whom the inhabitants of Jerusalem have said, "They have gone far from the LORD; to us this land is given for a possession." 16 Therefore say: Thus says the Lord GOD: Though I removed them far

ˣ Gk Syr: Heb *people of your kindred*

Cross-references (margin)

10.18
v. 4
10.19
11.1, 22

10.20
v. 15;
Ezek 1.22;
1.1
10.21
Ezek 1.6, 8
10.22
Ezek 1.10, 12

11.1
Ezek 3.12,
14; 8.3;
10.19; 8.16
11.2
Isa 30.1;
Mic 2.1
11.3
Ezek 12.22,
27; 2 Pet 3.4;
Jer 1.13;
Ezek 24.3, 6
11.4
Ezek 3.4, 17
11.5
Ezek 2.2;
3.24;
Jer 11.20;
Ezek 38.10
11.6
Ezek 7.23;
22.3, 4
11.7
Ezek 24.3, 6,
10, 11;
Mic 3.3; v. 9
11.9
Ps 106.41;
Ezek 5.8
11.10
2 Kings 25.19-
21;
Jer 52.10;
2 Kings
14.25;
Ezek 6.7
11.11
v. 3
11.12
v. 10;
Ezek 18.8, 9;
8.10, 14, 16
11.13
v. 1;
Ezek 9.8
11.15
Ezek 33.24
11.16
Isa 8.14

Footnotes

10.18 The glory of God had filled the tabernacle (Ex 40.34–38) and the Solomonic temple at its dedication (1 Chr 7.1–3). Now Ezekiel saw God's glory departing from the temple. It hovered over the city and stopped for a time on the Mount of Olives (11.23). God was leaving his people, and once his glory had left, the city was defenseless against its enemies. The glory of God apparently never again returned to the temple, for when the destroyed temple was rebuilt (cf. Ezra 3–6), we do not read of the glory of God filling it, nor is there any reference to the glory of God in the temple in N.T. times. Note, however, 43.1–4, where Ezekiel saw a vision of the final temple being

filled with the glory of God (see note on 43.2).
11.1 Again the Spirit placed Ezekiel in a place where he could see the evils for himself. The leaders of Jerusalem felt safe in the midst of their transgressions and thought only of material things — such as building more houses.
11.5 *Thus says the LORD.* The Spirit of God fell upon Ezekiel and told him what to speak. The Holy Spirit is the divine author of the Scriptures and it is he who spoke through the O.T. prophets (2 Pet 1.20,21). The Trinity is deeply involved in all aspects of the work of God. Thus, whatever the Father says, or Jesus Christ says, or the Holy Spirit says, God says.

away among the nations, and though I scattered them among the countries, yet I have been a sanctuary to them for a little while[y] in the countries where they have gone. 17 Therefore say: Thus says the Lord GOD: I will gather you from the peoples, and assemble you out of the countries where you have been scattered, and I will give you the land of Israel. 18 When they come there, they will remove from it all its detestable things and all its abominations. 19 I will give them one[z] heart, and put a new spirit within them; I will remove the heart of stone from their flesh and give them a heart of flesh, 20 so that they may follow my statutes and keep my ordinances and obey them. Then they shall be my people, and I will be their God. 21 But as for those whose heart goes after their detestable things and their abominations,[a] I will bring their deeds upon their own heads, says the Lord GOD.

5. The glory of the LORD departs from Jerusalem

22 Then the cherubim lifted up their wings, with the wheels beside them; and the glory of the God of Israel was above them. 23 And the glory of the LORD ascended from the middle of the city, and stopped on the mountain east of the city. 24 The spirit lifted me up and brought me in a vision by the spirit of God into Chaldea, to the exiles. Then the vision that I had seen left me. 25 And I told the exiles all the things that the LORD had shown me.

F. The reasons for the fall of Jerusalem

1. Unbelief of the people

a. The sign of the exile's baggage

12 The word of the LORD came to me: 2 Mortal, you are living in the midst of a rebellious house, who have eyes to see but do not see, who have ears to hear but do not hear; 3 for they are a rebellious house. Therefore, mortal, prepare for yourself an exile's baggage, and go into exile by day in their sight; you shall go like an exile from your place to another place in their sight. Perhaps they will understand, though they are a rebellious house. 4 You shall bring out your baggage by day in their sight, as baggage for exile; and you shall go out yourself at evening in their sight, as those do who go into exile. 5 Dig through the wall in their sight, and carry the baggage through it. 6 In their sight you shall lift the baggage on your shoulder, and carry it out in the dark; you shall cover your face, so that you may not see the land; for I have made you a sign for the house of Israel.

7 I did just as I was commanded. I brought out my baggage by day, as baggage for exile, and in the evening I dug through the wall with my

11.17	Jer 24.5; Ezek 28.25; 34.13
11.18	Ezek 37.23; 5.11
11.19	Jer 32.39; Ezek 36.26, 27; 18.31; Zech 7.12; 2 Cor 3.3; Ps 105.45; Ezek 14.11
11.21	Ezek 9.10
11.22	Ezek 1.19; 10.19
11.23	Ezek 8.4; 9.3; Zech 14.4
11.24	Ezek 8.3; 1.1, 3
11.25	Ezek 2.7
12.2	Ezek 2.6-8; Jer 5.21; Mt 13.13, 14
12.3	Jer 26.3; 36.3, 7; 2 Tim 2.25
12.4	Jer 39.4; v. 12
12.6	vv. 12, 13; Isa 8.18; Ezek 4.3; 24.24
12.7	Ezek 24.18; vv. 3-6

---

y Or to some extent z Another reading is a new a Cn: Heb And to the heart of their detestable things and their abominations their heart goes

---

11.18 The captivity, occasioned primarily by Israel's idolatry, cured them of this particular sin. Graven images, the worship of sun and moon, and other flagrant idolatries ceased to exist when Israel returned to the promised land. Jesus never accused the scribes, Pharisees, and Sadducees of worshiping idols, although their many other sins brought about the destruction of Jerusalem and the temple in A.D. 70.
11.24,25 Ezekiel, by the Spirit, was back in Chaldea with the exiles there. *the vision . . . left me,* i.e., it mounted upwards and disappeared from my sight (see

note on Ps 89.19 for information regarding visions). Ezekiel then told the exiles everything he had seen.
12.3 God told Ezekiel to carry his worldly possessions on his shoulders and start a journey. He obeyed, even though he would not learn the full intent of God's purpose until the next morning. He was ready to do anything in order to improve the spiritual state of God's people. God's servants must be willing and ready to perform difficult and inconvenient tasks so that if even one person is converted, the effort is worthwhile.

own hands; I brought it out in the dark, carrying it on my shoulder in their sight.

8 In the morning the word of the LORD came to me: 9 Mortal, has not the house of Israel, the rebellious house, said to you, "What are you doing?" 10 Say to them, "Thus says the Lord GOD: This oracle concerns the prince in Jerusalem and all the house of Israel in it." 11 Say, "I am a sign for you: as I have done, so shall it be done to them; they shall go into exile, into captivity." 12 And the prince who is among them shall lift his baggage on his shoulder in the dark, and shall go out; he[b] shall dig through the wall and carry it through; he shall cover his face, so that he may not see the land with his eyes. 13 I will spread my net over him, and he shall be caught in my snare; and I will bring him to Babylon, the land of the Chaldeans, yet he shall not see it; and he shall die there. 14 I will scatter to every wind all who are around him, his helpers and all his troops; and I will unsheathe the sword behind them. 15 And they shall know that I am the LORD, when I disperse them among the nations and scatter them through the countries. 16 But I will let a few of them escape from the sword, from famine and pestilence, so that they may tell of all their abominations among the nations where they go; then they shall know that I am the LORD.

b. The sign of eating and drinking with quaking

17 The word of the LORD came to me: 18 Mortal, eat your bread with quaking, and drink your water with trembling and with fearfulness; 19 and say to the people of the land, Thus says the Lord GOD concerning the inhabitants of Jerusalem in the land of Israel: They shall eat their bread with fearfulness, and drink their water in dismay, because their land shall be stripped of all it contains, on account of the violence of all those who live in it. 20 The inhabited cities shall be laid waste, and the land shall become a desolation; and you shall know that I am the LORD.

c. The word of the LORD to the house of Israel

21 The word of the LORD came to me: 22 Mortal, what is this proverb of yours about the land of Israel, which says, "The days are prolonged, and every vision comes to nothing"? 23 Tell them therefore, "Thus says the Lord GOD: I will put an end to this proverb, and they shall use it no more as a proverb in Israel." But say to them, The days are near, and the fulfillment of every vision. 24 For there shall no longer be any false vision or flattering divination within the house of Israel. 25 But I the LORD will speak the word that I speak, and it will be fulfilled. It will no longer be delayed; but in your days, O rebellious house, I will speak the word and fulfill it, says the Lord GOD.

26 The word of the LORD came to me: 27 Mortal, the house of Israel is saying, "The vision that he sees is for many years ahead; he prophesies for distant times." 28 Therefore say to them, Thus says the Lord GOD: None of my words will be delayed any longer, but the word that I speak will be fulfilled, says the Lord GOD.

b Gk Syr: Heb they

Cross references (left margin):
12.9 Ezek 2.5; 17.12; 24.19
12.10 Mal 1.1
12.11 v. 6; 2 Kings 25.4-7
12.12 Jer 39.4
12.13 Isa 24.17, 18; Hos 7.12; Jer 52.11; Ezek 17.16
12.14 2 Kings 25.4, 5; Ezek 5.2, 12
12.15 Ezek 6.7, 14
12.16 Ezek 6.8-10; 14.22; Jer 22.8, 9
12.18 Ezek 4.16
12.19 Ezek 4.16; 23.33; Zech 7.14
12.20 Ezek 5.14; 36.3
12.22 Ezek 16.44; 11.3; v. 27; Am 6.3; 2 Pet 3.4
12.23 Joel 2.1; Zeph 1.14
12.24 Ezek 13.23; Zech 13.2-4
12.25 v. 28; Isa 55.11; Dan 9.12; Hab 1.5; v. 2
12.27 v. 22; Dan 10.14; 2 Pet 3.4
12.28 v. 25; Mt 24.48-50

12.10–16 *the prince in Jerusalem,* i.e., King Zedekiah, who would be captured and sent to Babylon. At that time, some of God's people would be cut off. Others would be scattered, that they might bear witness in their captivity to their sins and find restoration after seventy years when they repented. God was not finished with Israel, for they were still the custodians of his revealed word, and from them the Messiah was to come in the fullness of time.
12.22–28 The prophecies Ezekiel gave about the coming destruction had been confirmed by his visions and illustrated by signs. But nothing had happened, and the people assumed that nothing would happen, or that if it did, it would be so far in the future that they did not need to concern themselves about it. They had also concluded that they could no longer trust the true prophets. Now God told them that what had been prophesied so far in advance would indeed come to pass, and that it would be in their days.

2. Heeding false prophets and prophetesses

a. The prophecy against the false prophets

13 The word of the LORD came to me: 2 Mortal, prophesy against the prophets of Israel who are prophesying; say to those who prophesy out of their own imagination: "Hear the word of the LORD!" 3 Thus says the Lord GOD, Alas for the senseless prophets who follow their own spirit, and have seen nothing! 4 Your prophets have been like jackals among ruins, O Israel. 5 You have not gone up into the breaches, or repaired a wall for the house of Israel, so that it might stand in battle on the day of the LORD. 6 They have envisioned falsehood and lying divination; they say, "Says the LORD," when the LORD has not sent them, and yet they wait for the fulfillment of their word! 7 Have you not seen a false vision or uttered a lying divination, when you have said, "Says the LORD," even though I did not speak?

8 Therefore thus says the Lord GOD: Because you have uttered falsehood and envisioned lies, I am against you, says the Lord GOD. 9 My hand will be against the prophets who see false visions and utter lying divinations; they shall not be in the council of my people, nor be enrolled in the register of the house of Israel, nor shall they enter the land of Israel; and you shall know that I am the Lord GOD. 10 Because, in truth, because they have misled my people, saying, "Peace," when there is no peace; and because, when the people build a wall, these prophets*c* smear whitewash on it. 11 Say to those who smear whitewash on it that it shall fall. There will be a deluge of rain,*d* great hailstones will fall, and a stormy wind will break out. 12 When the wall falls, will it not be said to you, "Where is the whitewash you smeared on it?" 13 Therefore thus says the Lord GOD: In my wrath I will make a stormy wind break out, and in my anger there shall be a deluge of rain, and hailstones in wrath to destroy it. 14 I will break down the wall that you have smeared with whitewash, and bring it to the ground, so that its foundation will be laid bare; when it falls, you shall perish within it; and you shall know that I am the LORD. 15 Thus I will spend my wrath upon the wall, and upon those who have smeared it with whitewash; and I will say to you, The wall is no more, nor those who smeared it — 16 the prophets of Israel who prophesied concerning Jerusalem and saw visions of peace for it, when there was no peace, says the Lord GOD.

b. The prophecy against the false prophetesses

17 As for you, mortal, set your face against the daughters of your people, who prophesy out of their own imagination; prophesy against them 18 and say, Thus says the Lord GOD: Woe to the women who sew bands on all wrists, and make veils for the heads of persons of every height, in the hunt for human lives! Will you hunt down lives among my people, and maintain your own lives? 19 You have profaned me among my people for handfuls of barley and for pieces of bread, putting to death

c Heb *they*   d Heb *rain and you*

13.2
Jer 37.19;
v. 17;
Jer 14.14;
23.16, 26;
Am 7.16
13.3
Lam 2.14;
Jer 23.28-32
13.5
Ps 106.23,
30;
Ezek 22.30;
Isa 58.12;
Ezek 7.19
13.6
v. 22;
Ezek 22.28;
Jer 28.15
13.7
Ezek 22.28
13.8
Ezek 21.29;
5.8
13.9
Ezra 2.59,
62;
Neh 7.5;
Ps 69.28;
Ezek 11.10,
12
13.10
Jer 50.6;
8.11; v. 16;
Ezek 22.28
13.11
Ezek 38.22
13.13
v. 11;
Isa 30.30;
Rev 11.19;
16.21
13.14
Mic 1.6; v. 9;
Ezek 14.8
13.16
Ezek 6.14;
Isa 57.21
13.17
Ezek 20.46;
21.2; v. 2
13.18
Ezek 22.25;
2 Pet 2.14
13.19
Ezek 20.39;
Prov 28.21;
Mic 3.5;
Jer 23.14, 17

13.1ff Ezekiel sharply condemned the false prophets, not because he was envious of them or threatened by them, but because they were challenging God and hurting the people. False prophets did not arise in Israel until after the people had rejected and abused the true prophets. Similarly in the days of the Messiah, false messiahs did not arise until after the true Messiah had been rejected. Whenever true preachers of the word of God are rejected, then people become prey to false prophets who speak smooth words and offer easy solutions to sin.
13.3 False prophets, in spite of their claim to come from God, were shown to be pretenders when their prophecies fell to the ground.
13.9,10 God's hand was against the false prophets who preached only peace, telling the people what they wanted to hear, not what God wished to hear. He would seize them and bring them before his bar of divine justice.
13.17 *prophesy out of their own imagination.* The prophetesses were condemned not because they were women or because women should not prophesy; rather, they were judged because they had spoken what they had dreamed up in their own minds. God can speak and has spoken through prophetesses, but never through counterfeits.

persons who should not die and keeping alive persons who should not live, by your lies to my people, who listen to lies.

20 Therefore thus says the Lord GOD: I am against your bands with which you hunt lives;*e* I will tear them from your arms, and let the lives go free, the lives that you hunt down like birds. 21 I will tear off your veils, and save my people from your hands; they shall no longer be prey in your hands; and you shall know that I am the LORD. 22 Because you have disheartened the righteous falsely, although I have not disheartened them, and you have encouraged the wicked not to turn from their wicked way and save their lives; 23 therefore you shall no longer see false visions or practice divination; I will save my people from your hand. Then you will know that I am the LORD.

3. *The idolatry of the elders*

a. *Hypocrisy rebuked*

14 Certain elders of Israel came to me and sat down before me. 2 And the word of the LORD came to me: 3 Mortal, these men have taken their idols into their hearts, and placed their iniquity as a stumbling block before them; shall I let myself be consulted by them? 4 Therefore speak to them, and say to them, Thus says the Lord GOD: Any of those of the house of Israel who take their idols into their hearts and place their iniquity as a stumbling block before them, and yet come to the prophet — I the LORD will answer those who come with the multitude of their idols, 5 in order that I may take hold of the hearts of the house of Israel, all of whom are estranged from me through their idols.

b. *Repentance urged*

6 Therefore say to the house of Israel, Thus says the Lord GOD: Repent and turn away from your idols; and turn away your faces from all your abominations. 7 For any of those of the house of Israel, or of the aliens who reside in Israel, who separate themselves from me, taking their idols into their hearts and placing their iniquity as a stumbling block before them, and yet come to a prophet to inquire of me by him, I the LORD will answer them myself. 8 I will set my face against them; I will make them a sign and a byword and cut them off from the midst of my people; and you shall know that I am the LORD.

9 If a prophet is deceived and speaks a word, I, the LORD, have deceived that prophet, and I will stretch out my hand against him, and will destroy him from the midst of my people Israel. 10 And they shall bear their punishment — the punishment of the inquirer and the punishment of the prophet shall be the same — 11 so that the house of Israel may no longer go astray from me, nor defile themselves any more with all their transgressions. Then they shall be my people, and I will be their God, says the Lord GOD.

c. *The presence of some righteous cannot effect the deliverance of the wicked*

12 The word of the LORD came to me: 13 Mortal, when a land sins against me by acting faithlessly, and I stretch out my hand against it, and break its staff of bread and send famine upon it, and cut off from it human

e Gk Syr: Heb *lives for birds*

14.1ff Some of the spiritual leaders among the exiles inquired of Ezekiel concerning Jerusalem. God knew that in their private lives they worshiped idols and thus were hypocrites. He would answer them according to their sinfulness and give them no hope.
14.6ff God kept urging his people to repent, but he

intended to rid himself of counterfeit prophets and counterfeit saints as a warning to the faithful to keep his ways and walk in his paths. God wanted them to be his people so he might be their God (v. 11).
14.14 The apostasy of Ezekiel's day was so acute that God said even the prayers of Israel's greatest and

---

Marginal references:

13.20 v. 17
13.21 Ps 124.7; v. 9
13.22 Am 5.12; Jer 23.14; Ezek 33.14-16
13.23 v. 6; Ezek 12.24; Mic 3.6; v. 9; Ezek 14.8

14.1 Ezek 8.1; 20.1; 33.31
14.3 Ezek 20.16; 7.19; Jer 11.11; Ezek 20.3, 31
14.4 v. 7
14.5 Isa 1.4; Jer 2.11; Zech 11.8

14.6 Isa 2.20; 30.22; Ezek 18.30; 8.6
14.7 Ex 12.48; 20.10; v. 4
14.8 Jer 44.11; Ezek 15.7; Isa 65.15; Ezek 5.15; 6.7
14.9 1 Kings 22.23; Job 12.16; Jer 4.10; 2 Thess 2.11; Jer 14.15
14.11 Ezek 44.10, 15; 11.20; 37.27

14.13 Ezek 15.8; 6.14; 5.16; vv. 17, 19, 21

beings and animals, 14 even if Noah, Daniel,*f* and Job, these three, were in it, they would save only their own lives by their righteousness, says the Lord God. 15 If I send wild animals through the land to ravage it, so that it is made desolate, and no one may pass through because of the animals; 16 even if these three men were in it, as I live, says the Lord God, they would save neither sons nor daughters; they alone would be saved, but the land would be desolate. 17 Or if I bring a sword upon that land and say, "Let a sword pass through the land," and I cut off human beings and animals from it; 18 though these three men were in it, as I live, says the Lord God, they would save neither sons nor daughters, but they alone would be saved. 19 Or if I send a pestilence into that land, and pour out my wrath upon it with blood, to cut off humans and animals from it; 20 even if Noah, Daniel,*g* and Job were in it, as I live, says the Lord God, they would save neither son nor daughter; they would save only their own lives by their righteousness.

21   For thus says the Lord God: How much more when I send upon Jerusalem my four deadly acts of judgment, sword, famine, wild animals, and pestilence, to cut off humans and animals from it! 22 Yet, survivors shall be left in it, sons and daughters who will be brought out; they will come out to you. When you see their ways and their deeds, you will be consoled for the evil that I have brought upon Jerusalem, for all that I have brought upon it. 23 They shall console you, when you see their ways and their deeds; and you shall know that it was not without cause that I did all that I have done in it, says the Lord God.

G. *The punishment both certain and necessary*

1. *The example of the vine*

15   The word of the Lord came to me:
2   O mortal, how does the wood of the vine surpass all
        other wood —
   the vine branch that is among the trees of the forest?
3   Is wood taken from it to make anything?
        Does one take a peg from it on which to hang any object?
4   It is put in the fire for fuel;
        when the fire has consumed both ends of it
        and the middle of it is charred,
        is it useful for anything?
5   When it was whole it was used for nothing;
        how much less — when the fire has consumed it,
        and it is charred —
        can it ever be used for anything!

6   Therefore thus says the Lord God: Like the wood of the vine among the trees of the forest, which I have given to the fire for fuel, so I will give up the inhabitants of Jerusalem; 7 I will set my face against them; although they escape from the fire, the fire shall still consume them; and you shall know that I am the Lord, when I set my face against them. 8 And I will make the land desolate, because they have acted faithlessly, says the Lord God.

f Or, as otherwise read, *Danel*   *g* Or, as otherwise read, *Danel*

Cross references:
14.14: Jer 15.1-7; Gen 6.8; Dan 1.6; Job 1.1, 5; vv. 16, 18, 20
14.15: Ezek 5.17
14.16: vv. 14, 18, 20; Ezek 18.20
14.17: Ezek 5.12; 21.3, 4; 25.13; Zeph 1.3
14.18: v. 14
14.19: v. 21; Ezek 38.22; 7.8
14.20: v. 14
14.21: Ezek 5.17; Jer 15.2, 3; Rev 6.8
14.22: Ezek 12.16; 7.16; 20.43; 16.54
14.23: Jer 22.8, 9
15.2: Isa 5.1-7; Jer 2.21; Hos 10.1
15.4: v. 6; Ezek 19.14; Jn 15.6
15.6: v. 2; Ezek 17.3-10
15.7: Lev 17.10; Ezek 14.8; Isa 24.18; Ezek 6.7; 7.4; 14.8
15.8: Ezek 14.13

most holy saints — Noah, Daniel, and Job — could not prevail. The best that their godly intercessions could do would be to save only the intercessors themselves. **14.22,23** Jerusalem was marked for ruin, yet in its midst were a few who remained faithful to God. Thus God preserved some who were examples of divine grace. They would go into captivity but their children would be preserved to return to the land at a later date. **15.1ff** No one uses the wood of the grapevine to make furniture. When its usefulness is over, it is fit only for burning. God had given the useless sinners of Jerusalem to the fire for burning. They were good for nothing else.

2. The example of the unfaithful wife

a. The foundling child, Israel

16 The word of the Lord came to me: 2 Mortal, make known to Jerusalem her abominations, 3 and say, Thus says the Lord God to Jerusalem: Your origin and your birth were in the land of the Canaanites; your father was an Amorite, and your mother a Hittite. 4 As for your birth, on the day you were born your navel cord was not cut, nor were you washed with water to cleanse you, nor rubbed with salt, nor wrapped in cloths. 5 No eye pitied you, to do any of these things for you out of compassion for you; but you were thrown out in the open field, for you were abhorred on the day you were born.

6 I passed by you, and saw you flailing about in your blood. As you lay in your blood, I said to you, "Live! 7 and grow up[h] like a plant of the field." You grew up and became tall and arrived at full womanhood;[i] your breasts were formed, and your hair had grown; yet you were naked and bare.

b. Its rescue by God

8 I passed by you again and looked on you; you were at the age for love. I spread the edge of my cloak over you, and covered your nakedness: I pledged myself to you and entered into a covenant with you, says the Lord God, and you became mine. 9 Then I bathed you with water and washed off the blood from you, and anointed you with oil. 10 I clothed you with embroidered cloth and with sandals of fine leather; I bound you in fine linen and covered you with rich fabric.[j] 11 I adorned you with ornaments: I put bracelets on your arms, a chain on your neck, 12 a ring on your nose, earrings in your ears, and a beautiful crown upon your head. 13 You were adorned with gold and silver, while your clothing was of fine linen, rich fabric,[j] and embroidered cloth. You had choice flour and honey and oil for food. You grew exceedingly beautiful, fit to be a queen. 14 Your fame spread among the nations on account of your beauty, for it was perfect because of my splendor that I had bestowed on you, says the Lord God.

c. The whoredom of the rescued foundling

15 But you trusted in your beauty, and played the whore because of your fame, and lavished your whorings on any passer-by.[k] 16 You took some of your garments, and made for yourself colorful shrines, and on them played the whore; nothing like this has ever been or ever shall be.[j] 17 You also took your beautiful jewels of my gold and my silver that I had given you, and made for yourself male images, and with them played the whore; 18 and you took your embroidered garments to cover them, and set my oil and my incense before them. 19 Also my bread that I gave you—I fed you with choice flour and oil and honey—you set it before them as a pleasing odor; and so it was, says the Lord God. 20 You took your sons and your daughters, whom you had borne to me, and these you sacrificed to them to be devoured. As if your whorings were not enough! 21 You slaughtered my children and delivered them up as an offering to them. 22 And in all your abominations and your whorings you did not remember the days of your youth, when you were naked and bare, flailing about in your blood.

h Gk Syr: Heb *Live! I made you a myriad*   *i* Cn: Heb *ornament of ornaments*   *j* Meaning of Heb uncertain   *k* Heb adds *let it be his*

16.1ff In this chapter, Ezekiel shows forth the sins of God's people in detail, using specific illustrations. **16.15** Ezekiel used the illustration of marriage to picture his covenant relationship with Israel. Beautiful Israel had become his bride, but the bride had proved herself to be unfaithful and broke the marriage covenant by committing adultery with the gods of neighboring nations. She had joined them in their pagan worship and took over their pagan lifestyles.

16.2
Ezek 20.4;
22.2; 8.9-17
16.3
Ezek 21.30;
v. 45
16.4
Hos 2.3

16.5
Deut 32.10

16.6
v. 22;
Ex 19.4
16.7
Ex 1.7; v. 22

16.8
Ruth 3.9;
Gen 22.16-18;
Ex 24.7, 8;
19.5;
Jer 2.2
16.10
v. 13

16.11
Ezek 23.40;
Gen 24.22,
47;
Prov 1.9
16.13
Deut 32.13,
14;
1 Sam 10.1
16.14
Ps 50.2;
Lam 2.15

16.15
Isa 57.8;
Jer 2.20;
Ezek 23.3, 8,
11, 12
16.16
v. 10;
Ezek 6.3, 6;
Hos 2.8
16.17
Ezek 7.20
16.18
v. 10
Hos 2.8
16.19
Hos 2.8
16.20
2 Kings 16.3;
Isa 57.5
16.21
2 Kings 17.17;
Jer 19.5
16.22
Hos 11.1;
vv. 4-6

23 After all your wickedness (woe, woe to you! says the Lord GOD),
24 you built yourself a platform and made yourself a lofty place in every
square; 25 at the head of every street you built your lofty place and
prostituted your beauty, offering yourself to every passer-by, and multiplying your whoring. 26 You played the whore with the Egyptians, your
lustful neighbors, multiplying your whoring, to provoke me to anger.
27 Therefore I stretched out my hand against you, reduced your rations,
and gave you up to the will of your enemies, the daughters of the Philistines, who were ashamed of your lewd behavior. 28 You played the whore
with the Assyrians, because you were insatiable; you played the whore
with them, and still you were not satisfied. 29 You multiplied your whoring with Chaldea, the land of merchants; and even with this you were not
satisfied.

30 How sick is your heart, says the Lord GOD, that you did all these
things, the deeds of a brazen whore; 31 building your platform at the head
of every street, and making your lofty place in every square! Yet you were
not like a whore, because you scorned payment. 32 Adulterous wife, who
receives strangers instead of her husband! 33 Gifts are given to all whores;
but you gave your gifts to all your lovers, bribing them to come to you
from all around for your whorings. 34 So you were different from other
women in your whorings: no one solicited you to play the whore; and you
gave payment, while no payment was given to you; you were different.

d. The promised punishment for whoredom

35 Therefore, O whore, hear the word of the LORD: 36 Thus says the
Lord GOD, Because your lust was poured out and your nakedness uncovered in your whoring with your lovers, and because of all your abominable
idols, and because of the blood of your children that you gave to them,
37 therefore, I will gather all your lovers, with whom you took pleasure,
all those you loved and all those you hated; I will gather them against you
from all around, and will uncover your nakedness to them, so that they
may see all your nakedness. 38 I will judge you as women who commit
adultery and shed blood are judged, and bring blood upon you in wrath
and jealousy. 39 I will deliver you into their hands, and they shall throw
down your platform and break down your lofty places; they shall strip you
of your clothes and take your beautiful objects and leave you naked and
bare. 40 They shall bring up a mob against you, and they shall stone you
and cut you to pieces with their swords. 41 They shall burn your houses
and execute judgments on you in the sight of many women; I will stop
you from playing the whore, and you shall also make no more payments.
42 So I will satisfy my fury on you, and my jealousy shall turn away from
you; I will be calm, and will be angry no longer. 43 Because you have not
remembered the days of your youth, but have enraged me with all these
things; therefore, I have returned your deeds upon your head, says the
Lord GOD.

e. The sin worse than that of Sodom and Samaria

Have you not committed lewdness beyond all your abominations?
44 See, everyone who uses proverbs will use this proverb about you, "Like
mother, like daughter." 45 You are the daughter of your mother, who
loathed her husband and her children; and you are the sister of your
sisters, who loathed their husbands and their children. Your mother was

16.24
Isa 57.5, 7;
Jer 2.20; 3.2
16.25
Prov 9.14;
v. 15
16.26
Ezek 8.17;
20.7, 8;
23.19-21
16.27
Ezek 14.13;
20.33, 34;
2 Chr 28.18,
19
16.28
2 Kings 16.7,
10;
2 Chr 28.23
16.29
Ezek 23.14-17
16.30
Jer 3.3
16.31
v. 24;
Isa 52.3
16.33
Isa 30.6;
Hos 8.9, 10

16.36
v. 15;
Ezek 23.10,
18, 29;
Jer 19.5

16.37
Jer 13.22, 26;
Hos 2.10;
Nah 3.5;
Isa 47.3
16.38
Lev 20.10;
Ezek 23.45;
Jer 18.21
16.39
Ezek 21.31;
vv. 24, 31;
Ezek 23.26
16.40
Ezek 23.46,
47;
Jn 8.5, 7
16.41
Deut 13.16;
2 Kings 25.9;
Jer 52.13;
Ezek 23.10,
27
16.42
Ezek 5.13;
Isa 54.9, 10;
Ezek 39.29
16.43
Ps 78.42;
v. 22;
Ezek 6.9;
11.21; 22.31
16.44
Ezek 12.22,
23

16.31 God charged his people with a greater sin than
that of a whore, who expects to be paid for her service.
Israel had engaged in prostitution (see previous note),
but actually paid her customers. No one solicited
God's people to engage in whoredom (v. 34). They
had instead solicited other gods and paid them for
their services. How low Israel had sunk from her
former holy state, when she was the virgin bride of a

covenant-keeping God!
16.35ff God accused Jerusalem of two violations of
his law. She was guilty of idolatry (breaking the first
two commandments of the ten), and of breaking the
first two commandments of the second table by the
murder of her own innocent infants. Because of these
transgressions (which meant they had repudiated the
lawgiver), judgment would fall (v. 43).

a Hittite and your father an Amorite. 46 Your elder sister is Samaria, who lived with her daughters to the north of you; and your younger sister, who lived to the south of you, is Sodom with her daughters. 47 You not only followed their ways, and acted according to their abominations; within a very little time you were more corrupt than they in all your ways. 48 As I live, says the Lord GOD, your sister Sodom and her daughters have not done as you and your daughters have done. 49 This was the guilt of your sister Sodom: she and her daughters had pride, excess of food, and prosperous ease, but did not aid the poor and needy. 50 They were haughty, and did abominable things before me; therefore I removed them when I saw it. 51 Samaria has not committed half your sins; you have committed more abominations than they, and have made your sisters appear righteous by all the abominations that you have committed. 52 Bear your disgrace, you also, for you have brought about for your sisters a more favorable judgment; because of your sins in which you acted more abominably than they, they are more in the right than you. So be ashamed, you also, and bear your disgrace, for you have made your sisters appear righteous.

f. The promise of restoration

53 I will restore their fortunes, the fortunes of Sodom and her daughters and the fortunes of Samaria and her daughters, and I will restore your own fortunes along with theirs, 54 in order that you may bear your disgrace and be ashamed of all that you have done, becoming a consolation to them. 55 As for your sisters, Sodom and her daughters shall return to their former state, Samaria and her daughters shall return to their former state, and you and your daughters shall return to your former state. 56 Was not your sister Sodom a byword in your mouth in the day of your pride, 57 before your wickedness was uncovered? Now you are a mockery to the daughters of Aram[l] and all her neighbors, and to the daughters of the Philistines, those all around who despise you. 58 You must bear the penalty of your lewdness and your abominations, says the LORD.

59 Yes, thus says the Lord GOD: I will deal with you as you have done, you who have despised the oath, breaking the covenant; 60 yet I will remember my covenant with you in the days of your youth, and I will establish with you an everlasting covenant. 61 Then you will remember your ways, and be ashamed when I[m] take your sisters, both your elder and your younger, and give them to you as daughters, but not on account of my[n] covenant with you. 62 I will establish my covenant with you, and you shall know that I am the LORD, 63 in order that you may remember and be confounded, and never open your mouth again because of your shame, when I forgive you all that you have done, says the Lord GOD.

3. The two eagles and the cedar

a. The allegory presented

17 The word of the LORD came to me: 2 O mortal, propound a riddle, and speak an allegory to the house of Israel. 3 Say: Thus says the Lord GOD:

[l] Another reading is *Edom*   [m] Syr: Heb *you*   [n] Heb lacks *my*

16.59,60 Israel's apostasy was so great that his judgment had to be executed. But God would never forget his covenant with his people. Grace, mercy, and love would prevail, for God planned a future restoration for Israel. Someday the nation would be regathered to its ancestral land.
16.62 God promised to reestablish his covenant with his people (cf. v. 60). He would bring glory to himself by being faithful to his covenant promises. Note that the phrase, "You shall know that I am the

LORD,," which elsewhere designated God as the requiter of Israel's sins, is here spoken in mercy, for they would be redeemed. God makes himself known as God both in judgment and in redemption.
17.2ff This chapter uses a parable to tell the story of Zedekiah, who had been set up as king over what was left of Judah after Nebuchadnezzar had destroyed the city and burned the temple. Zedekiah plotted with the Egyptians against Nebuchadnezzar, a treacherous violation of his oath of allegiance that he had

A great eagle, with great wings and long pinions,
　　rich in plumage of many colors,
　　came to the Lebanon.
　　He took the top of the cedar,
4　　broke off its topmost shoot;
　　he carried it to a land of trade,
　　set it in a city of merchants.
5　Then he took a seed from the land,
　　placed it in fertile soil;
　a plant[o] by abundant waters,
　　he set it like a willow twig.
6　It sprouted and became a vine
　　spreading out, but low;
　its branches turned toward him,
　　its roots remained where it stood.
　So it became a vine;
　　it brought forth branches,
　　put forth foliage.

b. The allegory interpreted

7　There was another great eagle,
　　with great wings and much plumage.
　And see! This vine stretched out
　　its roots toward him;
　it shot out its branches toward him,
　　so that he might water it.
　From the bed where it was planted
8　　it was transplanted
　to good soil by abundant waters,
　　so that it might produce branches
　　and bear fruit
　　and become a noble vine.
9Say: Thus says the Lord GOD:
　　Will it prosper?
　Will he not pull up its roots,
　　cause its fruit to rot[o] and wither,
　　its fresh sprouting leaves to fade?
　No strong arm or mighty army will be needed
　　to pull it from its roots.
10　When it is transplanted, will it thrive?
　　When the east wind strikes it,
　　will it not utterly wither,
　　wither on the bed where it grew?
11　　Then the word of the LORD came to me: 12 Say now to the rebellious house: Do you not know what these things mean? Tell them: The king of Babylon came to Jerusalem, took its king and its officials, and brought them back with him to Babylon. 13 He took one of the royal

[o] Meaning of Heb uncertain

17.5
Deut 8.7-9;
Isa 44.4

17.6
v. 14

17.7
v. 15

17.8
v. 5

17.9
vv. 10, 15-21

17.10
v. 15;
Ezek 19.14;
Hos 13.15

17.12
Ezek 2.5;
12.9; v. 3;
2 Kings 24.11-16

17.13
2 Kings 24.15-17;
2 Chr 36.13

sworn in the name of Yahweh. Nebuchadnezzar caught up with Zedekiah, slew his sons before his eyes, blinded him, and brought him to Babylon in chains.
17.3 Riddles and parables can be effective tools in proclaiming God's truth because they drive home the word of God in a manner designed to interest the listeners and compel their attention. Ezekiel told the illustration of the two eagles and the cedar and then gave the interpretation so no one could misunderstand what God had in mind.
17.4 Nebuchadnezzar had come to Judah, captured

Jehoiachin (who was eighteen years old and had reigned for three months), and took him and some of the princes to Babylon. This act is represented by the first eagle who cropped the top, tender branch from the cedar tree and carried it to a land of trade.
17.7 The second eagle, which had great wings and many feathers, is Egypt, with whom Zedekiah contracted an alliance in defiance of his agreement with Nebuchadnezzar, expecting to escape from his grip. God said he would pay the price of his perfidy, be blinded, and be brought to Babylon in chains.

offspring and made a covenant with him, putting him under oath (he had taken away the chief men of the land), 14 so that the kingdom might be humble and not lift itself up, and that by keeping his covenant it might stand. 15 But he rebelled against him by sending ambassadors to Egypt, in order that they might give him horses and a large army. Will he succeed? Can one escape who does such things? Can he break the covenant and yet escape? 16 As I live, says the Lord God, surely in the place where the king resides who made him king, whose oath he despised, and whose covenant with him he broke — in Babylon he shall die. 17 Pharaoh with his mighty army and great company will not help him in war, when ramps are cast up and siege walls built to cut off many lives. 18 Because he despised the oath and broke the covenant, because he gave his hand and yet did all these things, he shall not escape. 19 Therefore thus says the Lord God: As I live, I will surely return upon his head my oath that he despised, and my covenant that he broke. 20 I will spread my net over him, and he shall be caught in my snare; I will bring him to Babylon and enter into judgment with him there for the treason he has committed against me. 21 All the pick*p* of his troops shall fall by the sword, and the survivors shall be scattered to every wind; and you shall know that I, the Lord, have spoken.

c. *The goodly cedar a representation of Messiah*

22   Thus says the Lord God:
    I myself will take a sprig
      from the lofty top of a cedar;
    I will set it out.
    I will break off a tender one
      from the topmost of its young twigs;
    I myself will plant it
      on a high and lofty mountain.
23 On the mountain height of Israel
      I will plant it,
    in order that it may produce boughs and bear fruit,
      and become a noble cedar.
    Under it every kind of bird will live;
      in the shade of its branches will nest
      winged creatures of every kind.
24 All the trees of the field shall know
      that I am the Lord.
    I bring low the high tree,
      I make high the low tree;
    I dry up the green tree
      and make the dry tree flourish.
    I the Lord have spoken;
      I will accomplish it.

H. *The justice of a righteous God*

1. *The person who sins shall die*

18 The word of the Lord came to me: 2 What do you mean by repeating this proverb concerning the land of Israel, "The parents

p Another reading is *fugitives*

Cross references (left margin)

17.14
v. 6;
Ezek 29.14
17.15
2 Kings 24.20;
2 Chr 36.13

17.16
vv. 13, 18, 19;
Jer 52.11;
Ezek 12.13
17.17
Jer 37.7;
Ezek 29.6, 7; 4.2
17.18
Lam 5.6
17.19
Ezek 16.59
17.20
Ezek 12.13;
32.3; 20.36
17.21
2 Kings 25.5, 11;
Ezek 12.14;
6.7, 10

17.22
Isa 11.1;
Jer 23.5;
Zech 3.8;
Ezek 36.36;
20.40

17.23
Isa 2.2, 3;
Ezek 20.40;
Hos 14.5-7;
Mt 13.31, 32

17.24
Ps 96.12;
Ezek 21.26;
19.12; 22.14;
24.14

18.2
Jer 31.29;
Lam 5.7

17.22ff With no descendants of David on the throne, what would happen to the covenant God had made with David, that there should always be a king on the throne? Ezekiel utters a prophecy here about the Messiah King, Jesus Christ, who would come as a root from a dry ground to sit on the throne of his father David in order to establish it forever

(vv. 22–24).
18.2ff *The parents have eaten sour grapes, and the children's teeth are set on edge.* This proverb suggests that to punish children for their parents' sins is as absurd as saying that children should have their teeth set on edge for the grapes their parents had eaten. God answers that accusation by making it plain that each

have eaten sour grapes, and the children's teeth are set on edge"? ³As I live, says the Lord GOD, this proverb shall no more be used by you in Israel. ⁴Know that all lives are mine; the life of the parent as well as the life of the child is mine: it is only the person who sins that shall die.

2. The righteous man shall live

5   If a man is righteous and does what is lawful and right — ⁶if he does not eat upon the mountains or lift up his eyes to the idols of the house of Israel, does not defile his neighbor's wife or approach a woman during her menstrual period, ⁷does not oppress anyone, but restores to the debtor his pledge, commits no robbery, gives his bread to the hungry and covers the naked with a garment, ⁸does not take advance or accrued interest, withholds his hand from iniquity, executes true justice between contending parties, ⁹follows my statutes, and is careful to observe my ordinances, acting faithfully — such a one is righteous; he shall surely live, says the Lord GOD.

3. The wicked son of a righteous man shall die

10   If he has a son who is violent, a shedder of blood, ¹¹who does any of these things (though his father*q* does none of them), who eats upon the mountains, defiles his neighbor's wife, ¹²oppresses the poor and needy, commits robbery, does not restore the pledge, lifts up his eyes to the idols, commits abomination, ¹³takes advance or accrued interest; shall he then live? He shall not. He has done all these abominable things; he shall surely die; his blood shall be upon himself.

4. The righteous son of a wicked man shall live

14   But if this man has a son who sees all the sins that his father has done, considers, and does not do likewise, ¹⁵who does not eat upon the mountains or lift up his eyes to the idols of the house of Israel, does not defile his neighbor's wife, ¹⁶does not wrong anyone, exacts no pledge, commits no robbery, but gives his bread to the hungry and covers the naked with a garment, ¹⁷withholds his hand from iniquity,*r* takes no advance or accrued interest, observes my ordinances, and follows my statutes; he shall not die for his father's iniquity; he shall surely live. ¹⁸As for his father, because he practiced extortion, robbed his brother, and did what is not good among his people, he dies for his iniquity.

19   Yet you say, "Why should not the son suffer for the iniquity of the father?" When the son has done what is lawful and right, and has been careful to observe all my statutes, he shall surely live. ²⁰The person who sins shall die. A child shall not suffer for the iniquity of a parent, nor a parent suffer for the iniquity of a child; the righteousness of the righteous shall be his own, and the wickedness of the wicked shall be his own.

5. The wicked who repent shall live

21   But if the wicked turn away from all their sins that they have committed and keep all my statutes and do what is lawful and right, they

q Heb he   *r* Gk: Heb *the poor*

Cross references
18.3
vv. 11, 20, 30
18.4
Isa 42.5;
v. 20;
Rom 6.23

18.6
Ezek 22.9;
vv. 12, 15;
Lev 18.19;
20.18;
Ezek 22.10
18.7
Ex 22.21;
Lev 19.15;
Deut 24.12,
13;
Lev 19.13
18.8
Ex 22.25;
Lev 25.36,
37;
Deut 23.19;
1.16;
Zech 8.16
18.9
Ezek 20.11;
Am 5.4
18.10
Ex 21.12;
Num 35.31
18.11
vv. 6, 15
18.12
Am 4.1;
Isa 59.6, 7;
Ezek 8.6, 17
18.13
vv. 8, 17;
Ezek 33.4, 5
18.14
Prov 23.24
18.15
vv. 6, 11, 12
18.16
Ps 41.1
18.17
vv. 8, 9, 13,
19, 20
18.18
vv. 10-13;
Ezek 3.18
18.19
Ex 20.5;
Deut 5.9;
2 Kings 23.26
18.20
Deut 24.16;
Isa 3.10, 11;
Rom 2.9
18.21
Ezek 33.12,
19; 3.21

---

one will be accountable for his or her own sins. The soul, be it the parent's or the child's, belongs to God and the soul that sins will die.
18.5 God promises that whoever is righteous will live, for the way the person lives indicates his or her destiny. Those who are saved obey God's laws and show by that action that they are indeed God's people.
18.14 Ezekiel continues his explanation of God's dealing with his people with two illustrations. A wicked son of a pious father will die for his iniquity;

his father's faith cannot save him. So also, a wicked man's righteous son will not die for his father's transgressions; he will be saved because he has followed the Lord, even though his father has not done so.
18.21 Some people who live wicked lives turn from their wicked ways shortly before death and find forgiveness. Their sins will be remembered against them no more. God's grace can take effect the hour before death, even though the sinner may enter into life emptyhanded.

shall surely live; they shall not die. 22 None of the transgressions that they have committed shall be remembered against them; for the righteousness that they have done they shall live. 23 Have I any pleasure in the death of the wicked, says the Lord GOD, and not rather that they should turn from their ways and live? 24 But when the righteous turn away from their righteousness and commit iniquity and do the same abominable things that the wicked do, shall they live? None of the righteous deeds that they have done shall be remembered; for the treachery of which they are guilty and the sin they have committed, they shall die.

6. The way of the LORD is just

25 Yet you say, "The way of the Lord is unfair." Hear now, O house of Israel: Is my way unfair? Is it not your ways that are unfair? 26 When the righteous turn away from their righteousness and commit iniquity, they shall die for it; for the iniquity that they have committed they shall die. 27 Again, when the wicked turn away from the wickedness they have committed and do what is lawful and right, they shall save their life. 28 Because they considered and turned away from all the transgressions that they had committed, they shall surely live; they shall not die. 29 Yet the house of Israel says, "The way of the Lord is unfair." O house of Israel, are my ways unfair? Is it not your ways that are unfair?

7. The command to repent

30 Therefore I will judge you, O house of Israel, all of you according to your ways, says the Lord GOD. Repent and turn from all your transgressions; otherwise iniquity will be your ruin. s 31 Cast away from you all the transgressions that you have committed against me, and get yourselves a new heart and a new spirit! Why will you die, O house of Israel? 32 For I have no pleasure in the death of anyone, says the Lord GOD. Turn, then, and live.

I. Lamentation over the princes of Israel

1. The case of Jehoahaz

19 As for you, raise up a lamentation for the princes of Israel, 2 and say:

What a lioness was your mother
    among lions!
She lay down among young lions,
    rearing her cubs.

3 She raised up one of her cubs,
    he became a young lion,
and he learned to catch prey;
    he devoured humans.

4 The nations sounded an alarm against him;
    he was caught in their pit;

s *Or so that they shall not be a stumbling block of iniquity to you*

18.25 Sinful people often charge God with being unjust. The Scriptures do teach that God's ways are not our ways, but it also says that whatever God does is right (Rom 9.20–24). At the last judgment, every mouth will be stopped and every tongue will have to confess that God's ways are righteous and just and in accordance with truth (Rev 19.2).

18.30ff God urges all sinners to repent for four reasons: (1) repentance is the only way to escape eternal separation from God; (2) whoever will not repent will surely perish; (3) God does not delight in the death of the wicked; (4) those who repent will live forever.

19.1 In picturesque language, Ezekiel tells about Jehoahaz (vv. 1–4), Jehoiachin (vv. 5–9), and Zedekiah (vv. 10–14), three of the last four kings of Judah before the coming of the Messiah, who was to occupy the throne of his father David forever. The fourth king was Jehoiakim, who was king between the time of Jehoahaz and Jehoiachin. We don't know why he was omitted here.

19.2–4 Jehoahaz reigned for three months, then was deposed by the Egyptian Pharaoh and taken to Egypt where he died.

and they brought him with hooks
    to the land of Egypt.

2. The case of Jehoiachin

5 When she saw that she was thwarted,
    that her hope was lost,
  she took another of her cubs
    and made him a young lion.

    19.5
    2 Kings 23.34

6 He prowled among the lions;
    he became a young lion,
  and he learned to catch prey;
    he devoured people.

    19.6
    2 Kings 24.9;
    v. 3

7 And he ravaged their strongholds,ᵗ
    and laid waste their towns;
  the land was appalled, and all in it,
    at the sound of his roaring.

    19.7
    Ezek 12.19;
    30.12

8 The nations set upon him
    from the provinces all around;
  they spread their net over him;
    he was caught in their pit.

    19.8
    2 Kings 24.2;
    v. 4

9 With hooks they put him in a cage,
    and brought him to the king of Babylon;
  they brought him into custody,
    so that his voice should be heard no more
    on the mountains of Israel.

    19.9
    2 Chr 36.6;
    Jer 22.18;
    Ezek 6.2

3. The case of Zedekiah

10 Your mother was like a vine in a vineyardᵘ
    transplanted by the water,
  fruitful and full of branches
    from abundant water.

    19.10
    Ps 80.8-11

11 Its strongest stem became
    a ruler's scepter;ᵛ
  it towered aloft
    among the thick boughs;
  it stood out in its height
    with its mass of branches.

    19.11
    Ezek 31.3;
    Dan 4.11

12 But it was plucked up in fury,
    cast down to the ground;
  the east wind dried it up;
    its fruit was stripped off,
  its strong stem was withered;
    the fire consumed it.

    19.12
    Jer 31.28;
    Ezek 28.17;
    17.10;
    Hos 13.15

13 Now it is transplanted into the wilderness,
    into a dry and thirsty land.

    19.13
    Hos 2.3

14 And fire has gone out from its stem,
    has consumed its branches and fruit,
  so that there remains in it no strong stem,
    no scepter for ruling.

    19.14
    Ezek 15.4;
    Lam 4.20

ᵗ Heb *his widows*   ᵘ Cn: Heb *in your blood*   ᵛ Heb *Its strongest stems became rulers' scepters*

19.5–9 Jehoiachin (also called Jeconiah) reigned three months, after which he was taken to Babylon, where he lived at least thirty-seven years.
19.10–14 Zedekiah reigned eleven years. He was enthroned by Nebuchadnezzar and made a covenant with him, which he broke. Nebuchadnezzar took him prisoner, blinded him, and carried him in chains to

Babylon, where he died in prison.
19.14 *fire has gone out from its stem.* Jerusalem was burned with fire, and Zedekiah, by rebelling against Nebuchadnezzar, was the occasion for this destruction. In other words, the fire that consumed Jerusalem was set by Zedekiah, who was a rod of Judah's branch.

This is a lamentation, and it is used as a lamentation.

J. *The abominations of Israel*

1. *Ezekiel commanded to answer the elders*

20 In the seventh year, in the fifth month, on the tenth day of the month, certain elders of Israel came to consult the Lord, and sat down before me. 2 And the word of the Lord came to me: 3 Mortal, speak to the elders of Israel, and say to them: Thus says the Lord God: Why are you coming? To consult me? As I live, says the Lord God, I will not be consulted by you. 4 Will you judge them, mortal, will you judge them? Then let them know the abominations of their ancestors, 5 and say to them: Thus says the Lord God: On the day when I chose Israel, I swore to the offspring of the house of Jacob — making myself known to them in the land of Egypt — I swore to them, saying, I am the Lord your God. 6 On that day I swore to them that I would bring them out of the land of Egypt into a land that I had searched out for them, a land flowing with milk and honey, the most glorious of all lands. 7 And I said to them, Cast away the detestable things your eyes feast on, every one of you, and do not defile yourselves with the idols of Egypt; I am the Lord your God. 8 But they rebelled against me and would not listen to me; not one of them cast away the detestable things their eyes feasted on, nor did they forsake the idols of Egypt.

2. *Israel's rebellion and idolatry*

Then I thought I would pour out my wrath upon them and spend my anger against them in the midst of the land of Egypt. 9 But I acted for the sake of my name, that it should not be profaned in the sight of the nations among whom they lived, in whose sight I made myself known to them in bringing them out of the land of Egypt. 10 So I led them out of the land of Egypt and brought them into the wilderness. 11 I gave them my statutes and showed them my ordinances, by whose observance everyone shall live. 12 Moreover I gave them my sabbaths, as a sign between me and them so, that they might know that I the Lord sanctify them. 13 But the house of Israel rebelled against me in the wilderness; they did not observe my statutes but rejected my ordinances, by whose observance everyone shall live; and my sabbaths they greatly profaned.

Then I thought I would pour out my wrath upon them in the wilderness, to make an end of them. 14 But I acted for the sake of my name, so that it should not be profaned in the sight of the nations, in whose sight I had brought them out. 15 Moreover I swore to them in the wilderness that I would not bring them into the land that I had given them, a land flowing with milk and honey, the most glorious of all lands, 16 because they rejected my ordinances and did not observe my statutes, and profaned my sabbaths; for their heart went after their idols. 17 Nevertheless my eye spared them, and I did not destroy them or make an end of them in the wilderness.

20.1ff Some of the elders of Judah came to discuss matters with Ezekiel. God graciously spoke to them through Ezekiel, stating his case against them by showing how graciously he had treated them and how they and their fathers had dealt treacherously with him. Yet God would still have mercy and would cause a remnant to repent. At that time he would return them to the land from which they were to be dispossessed. *in the seventh year,* i.e., six years after King Jeconiah was captured.

20.5ff God's charges against Israel covered three pe-

riods of their history. (1) While in Egypt, they had turned from him (vv. 5–9); therefore, God was tempted to leave them in Egypt, but in his grace delivered them anyway. (2) They sinned against God in the wilderness; therefore, he refused to let them enter Canaan for forty years (vv. 10–26). (3) They continued their sinful ways after God brought them into Canaan and gave them every material blessing (vv. 27–32); therefore, God would no longer hear them when they called on him.

18 I said to their children in the wilderness, Do not follow the statutes of your parents, nor observe their ordinances, nor defile yourselves with their idols. 19 I the LORD am your God; follow my statutes, and be careful to observe my ordinances, 20 and hallow my sabbaths that they may be a sign between me and you, so that you may know that I the LORD am your God. 21 But the children rebelled against me; they did not follow my statutes, and were not careful to observe my ordinances, by whose observance everyone shall live; they profaned my sabbaths.

Then I thought I would pour out my wrath upon them and spend my anger against them in the wilderness. 22 But I withheld my hand, and acted for the sake of my name, so that it should not be profaned in the sight of the nations, in whose sight I had brought them out. 23 Moreover I swore to them in the wilderness that I would scatter them among the nations and disperse them through the countries, 24 because they had not executed my ordinances, but had rejected my statutes and profaned my sabbaths, and their eyes were set on their ancestors' idols. 25 Moreover I gave them statutes that were not good and ordinances by which they could not live. 26 I defiled them through their very gifts, in their offering up all their firstborn, in order that I might horrify them, so that they might know that I am the LORD.

27 Therefore, mortal, speak to the house of Israel and say to them, Thus says the Lord GOD: In this again your ancestors blasphemed me, by dealing treacherously with me. 28 For when I had brought them into the land that I swore to give them, then wherever they saw any high hill or any leafy tree, there they offered their sacrifices and presented the provocation of their offering; there they sent up their pleasing odors, and there they poured out their drink offerings. 29 (I said to them, What is the high place to which you go? So it is called Bamah*w* to this day.) 30 Therefore say to the house of Israel, Thus says the Lord GOD: Will you defile yourselves after the manner of your ancestors and go astray after their detestable things? 31 When you offer your gifts and make your children pass through the fire, you defile yourselves with all your idols to this day. And shall I be consulted by you, O house of Israel? As I live, says the Lord GOD, I will not be consulted by you.

3. *God to purge Israel*

32 What is in your mind shall never happen — the thought, "Let us be like the nations, like the tribes of the countries, and worship wood and stone."

33 As I live, says the Lord GOD, surely with a mighty hand and an outstretched arm, and with wrath poured out, I will be king over you. 34 I will bring you out from the peoples and gather you out of the countries where you are scattered, with a mighty hand and an outstretched arm, and with wrath poured out; 35 and I will bring you into the wilderness of the peoples, and there I will enter into judgment with you face to face. 36 As I entered into judgment with your ancestors in the wilderness of the land of Egypt, so I will enter into judgment with you, says the Lord GOD. 37 I will make you pass under the staff, and will bring you within the bond of the covenant. 38 I will purge out the rebels among you, and those who transgress against me; I will bring them out of the land where they reside

w That is *High Place*

20.18	Deut 4.3-6; Zech 1.4; v. 7
20.19	Ex 6.7; 20.2; Deut 5.32
20.20	v. 12
20.21	Num 25.1; vv. 8, 13, 16
20.22	v. 17; Ps 78.38; vv. 9, 14
20.23	Lev 26.33; Deut 28.64; Ps 106.27; Jer 15.4
20.24	vv. 13, 16; Ezek 6.9
20.25	Ps 81.12; Rom 1.24; 2 Thess 2.11
20.26	v. 30; 2 Kings 17.17; 2 Chr 28.3; Ezek 16.20, 21; 6.7
20.27	Ezek 2.7; Rom 2.24; Ezek 18.24; 39.23, 26
20.28	Isa 57.5-7; Ezek 6.13; 16.19
20.30	v. 43; Jer 7.26; 16.12
20.31	Ps 106.37-39; Jer 7.31; Ezek 16.20
20.32	Ezek 11.5; 16.16; Jer 2.25; 44.17
20.33	Jer 21.5
20.34	Jer 42.18; 44.6; Lam 2.4
20.35	Ezek 17.20
20.36	vv. 13, 21; 1 Cor 10.5-10; Deut 32.10
20.37	Lam 17.32; Jer 33.13; Ezek 16.60
20.38	Ezek 34.17; Am 9.9, 10; Jer 44.14; Ezek 6.7

20.18 Children must not imitate bad parents. Among the duties of children to parents are the following: (1) receiving instruction from parents (Prov 1.7–9); (2) honoring parents (Ex 20.12; Heb 12.9); (3) obeying parents (Prov 6.20; Eph 6.1); (4) providing for aged parents (1 Tim 5.4).
20.33ff God spoke of his coming judgment on his

people. He would separate himself from them and later regather them.
20.35 *the wilderness of the peoples,* i.e., the desert judgment hall (the Syro-Arabian deserts), peopled by nomadic tribes. The Israelites returning from Babylon would cross this desert.

as aliens, but they shall not enter the land of Israel. Then you shall know that I am the LORD.

39 As for you, O house of Israel, thus says the Lord GOD: Go serve your idols, everyone of you now and hereafter, if you will not listen to me; but my holy name you shall no more profane with your gifts and your idols.

4. God to show mercy on the obedient

40 For on my holy mountain, the mountain height of Israel, says the Lord GOD, there all the house of Israel, all of them, shall serve me in the land; there I will accept them, and there I will require your contributions and the choicest of your gifts, with all your sacred things. 41 As a pleasing odor I will accept you, when I bring you out from the peoples, and gather you out of the countries where you have been scattered; and I will manifest my holiness among you in the sight of the nations. 42 You shall know that I am the LORD, when I bring you into the land of Israel, the country that I swore to give to your ancestors. 43 There you shall remember your ways and all the deeds by which you have polluted yourselves; and you shall loathe yourselves for all the evils that you have committed. 44 And you shall know that I am the LORD, when I deal with you for my name's sake, not according to your evil ways, or corrupt deeds, O house of Israel, says the Lord GOD.

5. The prophecy against the south

45ˣ The word of the LORD came to me: 46 Mortal, set your face toward the south, preach against the south, and prophesy against the forest land in the Negeb; 47 say to the forest of the Negeb, Hear the word of the LORD: Thus says the Lord GOD, I will kindle a fire in you, and it shall devour every green tree in you and every dry tree; the blazing flame shall not be quenched, and all faces from south to north shall be scorched by it. 48 All

flesh shall see that I the LORD have kindled it; it shall not be quenched. 49 Then I said, "Ah Lord GOD! they are saying of me, 'Is he not a maker of allegories?'"

K. The prophecies of the sharpened sword

1. The sword drawn from the sheath

21 ʸ The word of the LORD came to me: 2 Mortal, set your face toward Jerusalem and preach against the sanctuaries; prophesy against the land of Israel 3 and say to the land of Israel, Thus says the LORD: I am coming against you, and will draw my sword out of its sheath, and will cut off from you both righteous and wicked. 4 Because I will cut off from you both righteous and wicked, therefore my sword shall go out of its sheath against all flesh from south to north; 5 and all flesh shall know that I the LORD have drawn my sword out of its sheath; it shall not be sheathed again. 6 Moan therefore, mortal; moan with breaking heart and bitter grief before their eyes. 7 And when they say to you, "Why do you moan?" you shall say, "Because of the news that has come. Every heart will melt and all hands will be feeble, every spirit will faint and all knees will turn to water. See, it comes and it will be fulfilled," says the Lord GOD.

ˣ Ch 21.1 in Heb   ʸ Ch 21.6 in Heb

20.45ff God now directed his attention specifically to Judah and Jerusalem ("the south"), pronouncing judgment against them. Fire would come upon them and not be quenched.
20.49 *Is he not a maker of allegories?* This charge was meant to ridicule Ezekiel's preaching as too obscure. Those who do not like to hear God's word will always

find something about it to criticize, so that they feel justified in not paying attention.
21.1ff God continued his prediction of the coming disaster on Jerusalem. He told Ezekiel to announce the judgment with moans and a broken heart. The sword of judgment was about to be unsheathed, and nothing could stop this from being done.

2. The sword sharpened

8 And the word of the LORD came to me: 9 Mortal, prophesy and say: Thus says the Lord; Say:

A sword, a sword is sharpened,
  it is also polished;
10 it is sharpened for slaughter,
  honed to flash like lightning!
How can we make merry?
  You have despised the rod,
  and all discipline. z
11 The sword a is given to be polished,
  to be grasped in the hand;
it is sharpened, the sword is polished,
  to be placed in the slayer's hand.
12 Cry and wail, O mortal,
  for it is against my people;
it is against all Israel's princes;
  they are thrown to the sword,
  together with my people.
Ah! Strike the thigh!
13For consider: What! If you despise the rod, will it not happen?z says the Lord GOD.
14 And you, mortal, prophesy;
  strike hand to hand.
Let the sword fall twice, thrice,
  it is a sword for killing.
A sword for great slaughter —
  it surrounds them;
15 therefore hearts melt
  and many stumble.
At all their gates I have set
  the point z of the sword.
Ah! It is made for flashing,
  it is polished b for slaughter.
16 Attack to the right!
  Engage to the left!
  —wherever your edge is directed.
17 I too will strike hand to hand,
  I will satisfy my fury;
  I the LORD have spoken.

3. The sword wielded by Babylon

18 The word of the LORD came to me: 19 Mortal, mark out two roads for the sword of the king of Babylon to come; both of them shall issue from the same land. And make a signpost, make it for a fork in the road leading to a city; 20 mark out the road for the sword to come to Rabbah of the Ammonites or to Judah and to c Jerusalem the fortified. 21 For the king of Babylon stands at the parting of the way, at the fork in the two roads,

z Meaning of Heb uncertain   a Heb It   b Tg: Heb wrapped up   c Gk Syr: Heb Judah in

21.9 Deut 32.41
21.10 Isa 34.5, 6; v. 15
21.11 vv. 15, 19
21.12 Jer 31.19
21.14 Num 24.10; Ezek 6.11; Lev 26.21, 24; Ezek 30.24
21.15 vv. 7, 10
21.17 v. 14; Ezek 22.13; 5.13
21.19 Ezek 4.1-3; v. 15
21.20 Jer 49.2; Ezek 25.5; Am 1.14
21.21 Num 23.23; Prov 16.33; Judg 17.5

21.8ff Jerusalem had despised the rod God used to discipline his people. Now the sword would slaughter them. God would strike his hands and satisfy his anger.
21.9–11 A sword is sharpened and would cut, wound, or kill. It was a sharp and victorious sword against which no one could stand. If it had temporarily rusted in its scabbard, it was now polished and gleaming, flashing like lightning in the sunshine.
21.18ff Babylon would be the agent God used to accomplish Jerusalem's ruin. Kings would be removed from their throne (v. 26); no kings would rule until the coming of the Lord's Messiah, when God would give his Son dominion.
21.21 he inspects the liver. Inspecting the livers of sacrifices was a common form of divination by which ancients thought they could obtain information from the gods. Nebuchadnezzar used this method to get direction about besieging Jerusalem and about marching against Rabbah.

to use divination; he shakes the arrows, he consults the teraphim,[d] he inspects the liver. 22 Into his right hand comes the lot for Jerusalem, to set battering rams, to call out for slaughter, for raising the battle cry, to set battering rams against the gates, to cast up ramps, to build siege towers. 23 But to them it will seem like a false divination; they have sworn solemn oaths; but he brings their guilt to remembrance, bringing about their capture.

24   Therefore thus says the Lord GOD: Because you have brought your guilt to remembrance, in that your transgressions are uncovered, so that in all your deeds your sins appear — because you have come to remembrance, you shall be taken in hand.[e]

4. *The punishment of the prince of Israel*

25   As for you, vile, wicked prince of Israel,
          you whose day has come,
          the time of final punishment,
26   thus says the Lord GOD:
      Remove the turban, take off the crown;
          things shall not remain as they are.
      Exalt that which is low,
          abase that which is high.
27   A ruin, a ruin, a ruin —
          I will make it!
          (Such has never occurred.)
      Until he comes whose right it is;
          to him I will give it.

5. *The sentence against the Ammonites*

28   As for you, mortal, prophesy, and say, Thus says the Lord GOD concerning the Ammonites, and concerning their reproach; say:
      A sword, a sword! Drawn for slaughter,
          polished to consume,[f] to flash like lightning.
29   Offering false visions for you,
          divining lies for you,
      they place you over the necks
          of the vile, wicked ones —
      those whose day has come,
          the time of final punishment.
30   Return it to its sheath!
      In the place where you were created,
          in the land of your origin,
          I will judge you.
31   I will pour out my indignation upon you,
          with the fire of my wrath
      I will blow upon you.
      I will deliver you into brutish hands,
          those skillful to destroy.
32   You shall be fuel for the fire,
          your blood shall enter the earth;
      you shall be remembered no more,
          for I the LORD have spoken.

21.22
Jer 51.14;
Ezek 4.2

21.23
Ezek 17.13,
15, 16, 18;
29.16

21.25
Ezek 7.2, 3,
7; 35.5

21.26
Jer 13.18;
Ezek 16.12;
17.24;
Lk 1.52

21.27
Hag 2.21, 22;
Ps 2.6;
Jer 23.5, 6;
Ezek 34.24;
37.24

21.28
Jer 49.1;
Ezek 25.2, 3;
Zeph 2.8;
Isa 31.8;
Jer 12.12

21.29
Ezek 13.6-9;
22.28; v. 25;
Ezek 35.5

21.30
Jer 47.6, 7;
Ezek 16.3

21.31
Ezek 7.8;
14.19; 22.20,
21;
Jer 6.22, 23;
51.20, 21

21.32
Mal 4.1;
Ezek 25.10

---

d Or the household gods   e Or be taken captive   f Cn: Heb to contain

21.28ff   After God finished the overthrow of Jerusalem, Babylon would destroy the Ammonites, who had delighted in the afflictions that had come to the covenant people of God (see also note on 25.2).

L. *The sins of Jerusalem*

1. *The indictment*

22 The word of the LORD came to me: ²You, mortal, will you judge, will you judge the bloody city? Then declare to it all its abominable deeds. ³You shall say, Thus says the Lord GOD: A city! Shedding blood within itself; its time has come; making its idols, defiling itself. ⁴You have become guilty by the blood that you have shed, and defiled by the idols that you have made; you have brought your day near, the appointed time of your years has come. Therefore I have made you a disgrace before the nations, and a mockery to all the countries. ⁵Those who are near and those who are far from you will mock you, you infamous one, full of tumult.

6 The princes of Israel in you, everyone according to his power, have been bent on shedding blood. ⁷Father and mother are treated with contempt in you; the alien residing within you suffers extortion; the orphan and the widow are wronged in you. ⁸You have despised my holy things, and profaned my sabbaths. ⁹In you are those who slander to shed blood, those in you who eat upon the mountains, who commit lewdness in your midst. ¹⁰In you they uncover their fathers' nakedness; in you they violate women in their menstrual periods. ¹¹One commits abomination with his neighbor's wife; another lewdly defiles his daughter-in-law; another in you defiles his sister, his father's daughter. ¹²In you, they take bribes to shed blood; you take both advance interest and accrued interest, and make gain of your neighbors by extortion; and you have forgotten me, says the Lord GOD.

13 See, I strike my hands together at the dishonest gain you have made, and at the blood that has been shed within you. ¹⁴Can your courage endure, or can your hands remain strong in the days when I shall deal with you? I the LORD have spoken, and I will do it. ¹⁵I will scatter you among the nations and disperse you through the countries, and I will purge your filthiness out of you. ¹⁶And I*g* shall be profaned through you in the sight of the nations; and you shall know that I am the LORD.

2. *The promise of God's wrath*

17 The word of the LORD came to me: ¹⁸Mortal, the house of Israel has become dross to me; all of them, silver,*h* bronze, tin, iron, and lead. In the smelter they have become dross. ¹⁹Therefore thus says the Lord GOD: Because you have all become dross, I will gather you into the midst of Jerusalem. ²⁰As one gathers silver, bronze, iron, lead, and tin into a smelter, to blow the fire upon them in order to melt them; so I will gather you in my anger and in my wrath, and I will put you in and melt you. ²¹I will gather you and blow upon you with the fire of my wrath, and you shall be melted within it. ²²As silver is melted in a smelter, so you shall be melted in it; and you shall know that I the LORD have poured out my wrath upon you.

3. *The indictment extended to all classes*

23 The word of the LORD came to me: ²⁴Mortal, say to it: You are a land that is not cleansed, not rained upon in the day of indignation. ²⁵Its princes*i* within it are like a roaring lion tearing the prey; they have

g Gk Syr Vg: Heb *you*   *h* Transposed from the end of the verse; compare verse 20   *i* Gk: Heb *indignation.* 25A conspiracy of its prophets

22.1ff Ezekiel enumerates Jerusalem's sins explicitly. God had no choice now but to judge them by scattering them among the nations. Their filthiness had to be removed from them; at last they would know that God is the Lord. The Jews did not realize how patient and loving their God had been.

22.23ff All classes of people in Jerusalem had turned away from God and were guilty: princes, prophets, priests, and citizens. God sought to find someone who would intercede for Jerusalem, but there was no one who would speak a good word for Jerusalem or offer a prayer for its deliverance.

22.2
Ezek 20.4;
24.6-9;
Nah 3.1;
Ezek 16.2;
20.4
22.3
vv. 6, 27;
Ezek 23.37,
45
22.4
2 Kings 21.16;
Ezek 24.7, 8;
21.25; 5.14,
15; 16.57
22.5
Isa 22.5
22.6
Isa 1.23
22.7
Deut 27.16;
Ex 22.21, 22
22.8
v. 26;
Lev 19.30;
Ezek 23.38,
39
22.9
Ezek 18.6,
11, 15
22.10
Lev 18.8, 19;
Ezek 18.6
22.11
Ezek 18.11;
Lev 18.15;
18.9
22.12
Mic 7.2, 3;
Lev 25.36;
19.13;
Jer 3.21
22.13
Ezek 21.17;
Isa 33.15;
v. 3
22.14
Ezek 21.7;
24.14
22.15
Deut 4.27;
Zech 4.17;
Ezek 23.27
22.18
Isa 1.22;
Jer 6.28
22.20
v. 21;
Mal 3.2
22.22
Ezek 21.7;
20.8, 33

22.24
Ezek 24.13;
v. 31
22.25
Hos 6.9;
Ps 10.9;
Jer 15.8

devoured human lives; they have taken treasure and precious things; they have made many widows within it. 26 Its priests have done violence to my teaching and have profaned my holy things; they have made no distinction between the holy and the common, neither have they taught the difference between the unclean and the clean, and they have disregarded my sabbaths, so that I am profaned among them. 27 Its officials within it are like wolves tearing the prey, shedding blood, destroying lives to get dishonest gain. 28 Its prophets have smeared whitewash on their behalf, seeing false visions and divining lies for them, saying, "Thus says the Lord GOD," when the LORD has not spoken. 29 The people of the land have practiced extortion and committed robbery; they have oppressed the poor and needy, and have extorted from the alien without redress. 30 And I sought for anyone among them who would repair the wall and stand in the breach before me on behalf of the land, so that I would not destroy it; but I found no one. 31 Therefore I have poured out my indignation upon them; I have consumed them with the fire of my wrath; I have returned their conduct upon their heads, says the Lord GOD.

M. *The whoredom of Oholah (Samaria) and Oholibah (Jerusalem)*

1. *Introduction*

23 The word of the LORD came to me: 2 Mortal, there were two women, the daughters of one mother; 3 they played the whore in Egypt; they played the whore in their youth; their breasts were caressed there, and their virgin bosoms were fondled. 4 Oholah was the name of the elder and Oholibah the name of her sister. They became mine, and they bore sons and daughters. As for their names, Oholah is Samaria, and Oholibah is Jerusalem.

2. *The sin of Oholah*

5 Oholah played the whore while she was mine; she lusted after her lovers the Assyrians, warriors[j] 6 clothed in blue, governors and commanders, all of them handsome young men, mounted horsemen. 7 She bestowed her favors upon them, the choicest men of Assyria all of them; and she defiled herself with all the idols of everyone for whom she lusted. 8 She did not give up her whorings that she had practiced since Egypt; for in her youth men had lain with her and fondled her virgin bosom and poured out their lust upon her. 9 Therefore I delivered her into the hands of her lovers, into the hands of the Assyrians, for whom she lusted. 10 These uncovered her nakedness; they seized her sons and her daughters; and they killed her with the sword. Judgment was executed upon her, and she became a byword among women.

3. *The sin of Oholibah*

11 Her sister Oholibah saw this, yet she was more corrupt than she in her lusting and in her whorings, which were worse than those of her sister. 12 She lusted after the Assyrians, governors and commanders, warriors[j] clothed in full armor, mounted horsemen, all of them handsome young men. 13 And I saw that she was defiled; they both took the same way. 14 But she carried her whorings further; she saw male figures carved on the wall, images of the Chaldeans portrayed in vermilion, 15 with belts

j Meaning of Heb uncertain

23.5ff The sin of *Oholah* (Samaria or Israel) was her entangling alliances and conformity to the religion and lifestyle, first of Assyria (2 Kings 15.19–29) and then of Egypt (2 Kings 17.3–6).

23.11ff *Oholibah* (or the southern kingdom, Judah) also made alliances with Assyria (Isa 7.1–25), Babylon (2 Kings 24.1), and Egypt (Isa 30–31).

L. The sins of Jerusalem

1. The indictment

22 The word of the Lord came to me: 2 You, mortal, will you judge, will you judge the bloody city? Then declare to it all its abominable deeds. 3 You shall say, Thus says the Lord God: A city! Shedding blood within itself; its time has come; making its idols, defiling itself. 4 You have become guilty by the blood that you have shed, and defiled by the idols that you have made; you have brought your day near, the appointed time of your years has come. Therefore I have made you a disgrace before the nations, and a mockery to all the countries. 5 Those who are near and those who are far from you will mock you, you infamous one, full of tumult.

6 The princes of Israel in you, everyone according to his power, have been bent on shedding blood. 7 Father and mother are treated with contempt in you; the alien residing within you suffers extortion; the orphan and the widow are wronged in you. 8 You have despised my holy things, and profaned my sabbaths. 9 In you are those who slander to shed blood, those in you who eat upon the mountains, who commit lewdness in your midst. 10 In you they uncover their fathers' nakedness; in you they violate women in their menstrual periods. 11 One commits abomination with his neighbor's wife; another lewdly defiles his daughter-in-law; another in you defiles his sister, his father's daughter. 12 In you, they take bribes to shed blood; you take both advance interest and accrued interest, and make gain of your neighbors by extortion; and you have forgotten me, says the Lord God.

13 See, I strike my hands together at the dishonest gain you have made, and at the blood that has been shed within you. 14 Can your courage endure, or can your hands remain strong in the days when I shall deal with you? I the Lord have spoken, and I will do it. 15 I will scatter you among the nations and disperse you through the countries, and I will purge your filthiness out of you. 16 And I*g* shall be profaned through you in the sight of the nations; and you shall know that I am the Lord.

2. The promise of God's wrath

17 The word of the Lord came to me: 18 Mortal, the house of Israel has become dross to me; all of them, silver,*h* bronze, tin, iron, and lead. In the smelter they have become dross. 19 Therefore thus says the Lord God: Because you have all become dross, I will gather you into the midst of Jerusalem. 20 As one gathers silver, bronze, iron, lead, and tin into a smelter, to blow the fire upon them in order to melt them; so I will gather you in my anger and in my wrath, and I will put you in and melt you. 21 I will gather you and blow upon you with the fire of my wrath, and you shall be melted within it. 22 As silver is melted in a smelter, so you shall be melted in it; and you shall know that I the Lord have poured out my wrath upon you.

3. The indictment extended to all classes

23 The word of the Lord came to me: 24 Mortal, say to it: You are a land that is not cleansed, not rained upon in the day of indignation. 25 Its princes*i* within it are like a roaring lion tearing the prey; they have

22.2
Ezek 20.4;
24.6-9;
Nah 3.1;
Ezek 16.2;
20.4
22.3
vv. 6, 27;
Ezek 23.37,
45
22.4
2 Kings 21.16;
Ezek 24.7, 8;
21.25; 5.14,
15; 16.57
22.5
Isa 22.5
22.6
Isa 1.23
22.7
Deut 27.16;
Ex 22.21, 22
22.8
v. 26;
Lev 19.30;
Ezek 23.38,
39
22.9
Ezek 18.6,
11, 15
22.10
Lev 18.8, 19;
Ezek 18.6
22.11
Ezek 18.11;
Lev 18.15;
18.9
22.12
Mic 7.2, 3;
Lev 25.36;
19.13;
Jer 3.21
22.13
Ezek 21.17;
Isa 33.15;
v. 3
22.14
Ezek 21.7;
24.14
22.15
Deut 4.27;
Zech 4.17;
Ezek 23.27
22.18
Isa 1.22;
Jer 6.28
22.20
v. 21;
Mal 3.2
22.22
Ezek 21.7;
20.8, 33

22.24
Ezek 24.13;
v. 31
22.25
Hos 6.9;
Ps 10.9;
Jer 15.8

g Gk Syr Vg: Heb *you*   *h* Transposed from the end of the verse; compare verse 20   *i* Gk: Heb *indignation.* 25A conspiracy of its prophets

22.1ff Ezekiel enumerates Jerusalem's sins explicitly. God had no choice now but to judge them by scattering them among the nations. Their filthiness had to be removed from them; at last they would know that God is the Lord. The Jews did not realize how patient and loving their God had been.

22.23ff All classes of people in Jerusalem had turned away from God and were guilty: princes, prophets, priests, and citizens. God sought to find someone who would intercede for Jerusalem, but there was no one who would speak a good word for Jerusalem or offer a prayer for its deliverance.

devoured human lives; they have taken treasure and precious things; they have made many widows within it. 26 Its priests have done violence to my teaching and have profaned my holy things; they have made no distinction between the holy and the common, neither have they taught the difference between the unclean and the clean, and they have disregarded my sabbaths, so that I am profaned among them. 27 Its officials within it are like wolves tearing the prey, shedding blood, destroying lives to get dishonest gain. 28 Its prophets have smeared whitewash on their behalf, seeing false visions and divining lies for them, saying, "Thus says the Lord God," when the Lord has not spoken. 29 The people of the land have practiced extortion and committed robbery; they have oppressed the poor and needy, and have extorted from the alien without redress. 30 And I sought for anyone among them who would repair the wall and stand in the breach before me on behalf of the land, so that I would not destroy it; but I found no one. 31 Therefore I have poured out my indignation upon them; I have consumed them with the fire of my wrath; I have returned their conduct upon their heads, says the Lord God.

M. *The whoredom of Oholah (Samaria) and Oholibah (Jerusalem)*

1. *Introduction*

23 The word of the Lord came to me: 2 Mortal, there were two women, the daughters of one mother; 3 they played the whore in Egypt; they played the whore in their youth; their breasts were caressed there, and their virgin bosoms were fondled. 4 Oholah was the name of the elder and Oholibah the name of her sister. They became mine, and they bore sons and daughters. As for their names, Oholah is Samaria, and Oholibah is Jerusalem.

2. *The sin of Oholah*

5 Oholah played the whore while she was mine; she lusted after her lovers the Assyrians, warriorsʲ 6 clothed in blue, governors and commanders, all of them handsome young men, mounted horsemen. 7 She bestowed her favors upon them, the choicest men of Assyria all of them; and she defiled herself with all the idols of everyone for whom she lusted. 8 She did not give up her whorings that she had practiced since Egypt; for in her youth men had lain with her and fondled her virgin bosom and poured out their lust upon her. 9 Therefore I delivered her into the hands of her lovers, into the hands of the Assyrians, for whom she lusted. 10 These uncovered her nakedness; they seized her sons and her daughters; and they killed her with the sword. Judgment was executed upon her, and she became a byword among women.

3. *The sin of Oholibah*

11 Her sister Oholibah saw this, yet she was more corrupt than she in her lusting and in her whorings, which were worse than those of her sister. 12 She lusted after the Assyrians, governors and commanders, warriorsʲ clothed in full armor, mounted horsemen, all of them handsome young men. 13 And I saw that she was defiled; they both took the same way. 14 But she carried her whorings further; she saw male figures carved on the wall, images of the Chaldeans portrayed in vermilion, 15 with belts

j Meaning of Heb uncertain

23.5ff The sin of *Oholah* (Samaria or Israel) was her entangling alliances and conformity to the religion and lifestyle, first of Assyria (2 Kings 15.19–29) and then of Egypt (2 Kings 17.3–6).

23.11ff *Oholibah* (or the southern kingdom, Judah) also made alliances with Assyria (Isa 7.1–25), Babylon (2 Kings 24.1), and Egypt (Isa 30–31).

around their waists, with flowing turbans on their heads, all of them looking like officers — a picture of Babylonians whose native land was Chaldea. 16 When she saw them she lusted after them, and sent messengers to them in Chaldea. 17 And the Babylonians came to her into the bed of love, and they defiled her with their lust; and after she defiled herself with them, she turned from them in disgust. 18 When she carried on her whorings so openly and flaunted her nakedness, I turned in disgust from her, as I had turned from her sister. 19 Yet she increased her whorings, remembering the days of her youth, when she played the whore in the land of Egypt 20 and lusted after her paramours there, whose members were like those of donkeys, and whose emission was like that of stallions. 21 Thus you longed for the lewdness of your youth, when the Egyptiansᵏ fondled your bosom and caressedˡ your young breasts.

4. The punishment of Oholibah

22 Therefore, O Oholibah, thus says the Lord GOD: I will rouse against you your lovers from whom you turned in disgust, and I will bring them against you from every side: 23 the Babylonians and all the Chaldeans, Pekod and Shoa and Koa, and all the Assyrians with them, handsome young men, governors and commanders all of them, officers and warriors,ᵐ all of them riding on horses. 24 They shall come against you from the northⁿ with chariots and wagons and a host of peoples; they shall set themselves against you on every side with buckler, shield, and helmet, and I will commit the judgment to them, and they shall judge you according to their ordinances. 25 I will direct my indignation against you, in order that they may deal with you in fury. They shall cut off your nose and your ears, and your survivors shall fall by the sword. They shall seize your sons and your daughters, and your survivors shall be devoured by fire. 26 They shall also strip you of your clothes and take away your fine jewels. 27 So I will put an end to your lewdness and your whoring brought from the land of Egypt; you shall not long for them, or remember Egypt any more. 28 For thus says the Lord GOD: I will deliver you into the hands of those whom you hate, into the hands of those from whom you turned in disgust; 29 and they shall deal with you in hatred, and take away all the fruit of your labor, and leave you naked and bare, and the nakedness of your whorings shall be exposed. Your lewdness and your whorings 30 have brought this upon you, because you played the whore with the nations, and polluted yourself with their idols. 31 You have gone the way of your sister; therefore I will give her cup into your hand. 32 Thus says the Lord GOD:

You shall drink your sister's cup,
     deep and wide;
you shall be scorned and derided,
     it holds so much.

33 You shall be filled with drunkenness and sorrow.
A cup of horror and desolation
     is the cup of your sister Samaria;
34 you shall drink it and drain it out,
     and gnaw its sherds,
     and tear out your breasts;

for I have spoken, says the Lord GOD. 35 Therefore thus says the Lord

ᵏ Two Mss: MT *from Egypt*   ˡ Cn: Heb *for the sake of*   ᵐ Compare verses 6 and 12: Heb *officers and called ones*   ⁿ Gk: Meaning of Heb uncertain

Cross references

23.16
v. 20
23.17
vv. 28, 30
23.18
v. 10;
Jer 6.8
23.19
vv. 14, 3
23.20
Ezek 16.26
23.21
v. 3

23.22
v. 28;
Ezek 16.37
23.23
Ezek 21.19;
2 Kings 24.2;
Jer 50.21;
vv. 6, 12
23.24
Ezek 21.15,
19;
Jer 47.3;
Ezek 16.40;
Jer 39.5, 6
23.25
Ezek 8.17,
18;
Zeph 1.18;
v. 47;
Ezek 20.47,
48; 22.20, 21
23.26
Ezek 16.39
23.27
Ezek 16.41;
22.15; vv. 3,
19
23.28
Ezek 16.37
23.29
v. 26;
Ezek 16.39
23.30
vv. 7, 17;
Jer 2.18-20;
Ezek 6.9
23.32
Isa 51.17;
Jer 25.15;
Ezek 22.4, 5

23.33
Jer 25.15, 16,
27;
Ezek 4.16
23.34
Ps 75.8;
Isa 51.17
23.35
Jer 3.21;
Hos 8.14;
1 Kings 14.9;
Neh 9.26

23.22ff After depicting the rottenness of Judah and Jerusalem, God described the indignities which that kingdom would experience at the hands of a nation she had made her lover — Babylon. She had cast God behind her back (v. 35); therefore, God would judge her for her transgressions.

23.32 *You shall drink your sister's cup.* Judah had walked in the same steps as Samaria, committing equally heinous sins. Thus she could expect the same fate as Samaria.

GOD: Because you have forgotten me and cast me behind your back, therefore bear the consequences of your lewdness and whorings.

5. *The judgment of the LORD on Oholah and Oholibah*

23.36
Ezek 20.4;
22.2;
Isa 58.1
23.37
vv. 3, 45;
Ezek 16.20,
21, 36, 45
23.38
Ezek 5.11;
7.20; 22.8
23.39
2 Kings 21.4

23.40
Isa 57.9;
2Ki 9.30;
Jer 4.30;
Ezek 16.13-16
23.41
Esth 1.6;
Am 6.4;
Prov 7.17;
Hos 2.8
23.42
Ezek 16.49;
Jer 51.7;
Ezek 16.11,
12
23.45
Ezek 16.38;
Hos 6.5;
Lev 20.10
23.46
v. 24;
Ezek 16.40;
Jer 15.4;
24.9; 29.18
23.47
Ezek 16.40;
2 Chr 36.17,
19;
Ezek 24.21;
Jer 39.8
23.48
v. 27;
Ezek 22.15;
2 Pet 2.6
23.49
v. 35;
Ezek 6.7;
20.38, 42, 44
24.1
Ezek 1.2;
8.1; 20.1;
26.1
24.2
Isa 8.1;
2 Kings 25.1;
Jer 39.1; 52.4
24.3
Ezek 17.2;
Jer 1.13;
Ezek 11.3
24.4
Ezek 22.19-22;
Mic 3.2, 3
24.5
v. 10

36   The LORD said to me: Mortal, will you judge Oholah and Oholibah? Then declare to them their abominable deeds. 37 For they have committed adultery, and blood is on their hands; with their idols they have committed adultery; and they have even offered up to them for food the children whom they had borne to me. 38 Moreover this they have done to me: they have defiled my sanctuary on the same day and profaned my sabbaths. 39 For when they had slaughtered their children for their idols, on the same day they came into my sanctuary to profane it. This is what they did in my house.

40   They even sent for men to come from far away, to whom a messenger was sent, and they came. For them you bathed yourself, painted your eyes, and decked yourself with ornaments; 41 you sat on a stately couch, with a table spread before it on which you had placed my incense and my oil. 42 The sound of a raucous multitude was around her, with many of the rabble brought in drunken from the wilderness; and they put bracelets on the arms*o* of the women, and beautiful crowns upon their heads. 43 Then I said, Ah, she is worn out with adulteries, but they carry on their sexual acts with her. 44 For they have gone in to her, as one goes in to a whore. Thus they went in to Oholah and to Oholibah, wanton women. 45 But righteous judges shall declare them guilty of adultery and of bloodshed; because they are adulteresses and blood is on their hands.

46   For thus says the Lord GOD: Bring up an assembly against them, and make them an object of terror and of plunder. 47 The assembly shall stone them and with their swords they shall cut them down; they shall kill their sons and their daughters, and burn up their houses. 48 Thus will I put an end to lewdness in the land, so that all women may take warning and not commit lewdness as you have done. 49 They shall repay you for your lewdness, and you shall bear the penalty for your sinful idolatry; and you shall know that I am the Lord GOD.

N. *The allegory of the boiling pot*

24   In the ninth year, in the tenth month, on the tenth day of the month, the word of the LORD came to me: 2 Mortal, write down the name of this day, this very day. The king of Babylon has laid siege to Jerusalem this very day. 3 And utter an allegory to the rebellious house and say to them, Thus says the Lord GOD:

Set on the pot, set it on,
    pour in water also;
4   put in it the pieces,
    all the good pieces, the thigh and the shoulder;
    fill it with choice bones.
5   Take the choicest one of the flock,
    pile the logs*p* under it;
    boil its pieces,*q*
    seethe*r* also its bones in it.

o Heb *hands*   *p* Compare verse 10: Heb *the bones*   *q* Two Mss: Heb *its boilings*   *r* Cn: Heb *its bones seethe*

23.36ff   God spoke about Oholah and Oholibah as one nation, although the northern kingdom had gone into captivity long before this. The remnant left in Samaria gradually drifted toward Judah, so that the two sisters had, in effect, become one nation. Therefore, this judgment of the Lord included not only Judah and Jerusalem but also the remnant of Samaria living in Judah.

24.1   This word from God to Ezekiel took place on the same day that Nebuchadnezzar's siege of Jerusalem began.

24.3   The flesh in the pot was a sign of the miseries Jerusalem was to justly suffer for her transgressions.

6 Therefore thus says the Lord GOD:
   Woe to the bloody city,
      the pot whose rust is in it,
      whose rust has not gone out of it!
   Empty it piece by piece,
      making no choice at all. *s*

7 For the blood she shed is inside it;
      she placed it on a bare rock;
   she did not pour it out on the ground,
      to cover it with earth.

8 To rouse my wrath, to take vengeance,
   I have placed the blood she shed
      on a bare rock,
   so that it may not be covered.

9 Therefore thus says the Lord GOD:
   Woe to the bloody city!
      I will even make the pile great.

10 Heap up the logs, kindle the fire;
      boil the meat well, mix in the spices,
      let the bones be burned.

11 Stand it empty upon the coals,
      so that it may become hot, its copper glow,
      its filth melt in it, its rust be consumed.

12 In vain I have wearied myself; *t*
      its thick rust does not depart.
   To the fire with its rust! *u*

13 Yet, when I cleansed you in your filthy lewdness,
      you did not become clean from your filth;
   you shall not again be cleansed
      until I have satisfied my fury upon you.

14 I the LORD have spoken; the time is coming, I will act. I will not refrain,
I will not spare, I will not relent. According to your ways and your doings
I will judge you, says the Lord GOD.

O. The death of Ezekiel's wife

15 The word of the LORD came to me: 16 Mortal, with one blow I am
about to take away from you the delight of your eyes; yet you shall not
mourn or weep, nor shall your tears run down. 17 Sigh, but not aloud;
make no mourning for the dead. Bind on your turban, and put your
sandals on your feet; do not cover your upper lip or eat the bread of
mourners. *v* 18 So I spoke to the people in the morning, and at evening
my wife died. And on the next morning I did as I was commanded.

19 Then the people said to me, "Will you not tell us what these things
mean for us, that you are acting this way?" 20 Then I said to them: The
word of the LORD came to me: 21 Say to the house of Israel, Thus says
the Lord GOD: I will profane my sanctuary, the pride of your power, the
delight of your eyes, and your heart's desire; and your sons and your
daughters whom you left behind shall fall by the sword. 22 And you shall

24.6
v. 9;
Ezek 22.3;
Mic 7.2;
Joel 3.3;
Nah 3.10

24.7
Ezek 23.37,
45;
Lev 17.13;
Deut 12.16

24.8
Mt 7.2

24.9
v. 6;
Nah 3.1;
Hab 2.12

24.10
v. 5

24.11
Ezek 21.10;
22.15

24.13
Jer 6.28-30;
Ezek 22.24;
5.13; 8.18;
16.42

24.14
1 Sam 15.29;
Isa 55.11;
Ezek 9.10;
18.30; 36.19

24.16
Job 23.2;
Jer 16.5;
22.10; 13.17
24.17
Jer 16.5-7;
2 Sam 15.30;
Mic 3.7

24.19
Ezek 12.9;
37.18
24.21
Jer 7.14;
Ps 27.4;
Jer 6.11;
Ezek 23.47
24.22
Jer 16.6, 7;
v. 17

s Heb *piece, no lot has fallen on it*   *t* Cn: Meaning of Heb uncertain   *u* Meaning of Heb uncertain
v Vg Tg: Heb *of men*

24.6 *Empty it piece by piece.* All the meat in the pot
would be taken out and eaten. There is therefore no
need to cast lots to decide which pieces would be
brought out first.
24.14 The ruin of Jerusalem did not indicate that
every last soul in that city was under the judgment of
God, for some remained faithful to God. Yet when
catastrophe does take place, the innocent often suffer
along with the guilty. They do, however, remain safe

in God's hand (cf. Jn 10.28,29).
24.16 Prophets, like other people, were entitled to
marry. God took Ezekiel's wife from him by death
and ordered him not to show his sorrow. This would
be most unusual, for Ezekiel's wife was "the delight"
of his eyes. This event would finally get the people's
attention (v. 19ff). It symbolized for Jerusalem that
God was going to take from the residents of that city
all that was dearest to them.

do as I have done; you shall not cover your upper lip or eat the bread of mourners.ʷ 23 Your turbans shall be on your heads and your sandals on your feet; you shall not mourn or weep, but you shall pine away in your iniquities and groan to one another. 24 Thus Ezekiel shall be a sign to you; you shall do just as he has done. When this comes, then you shall know that I am the Lord GOD.

25 And you, mortal, on the day when I take from them their stronghold, their joy and glory, the delight of their eyes and their heart's affection, and alsoˣ their sons and their daughters, 26 on that day, one who has escaped will come to you to report to you the news. 27 On that day your mouth shall be opened to the one who has escaped, and you shall speak and no longer be silent. So you shall be a sign to them; and they shall know that I am the LORD.

II. *The prophecies against the surrounding nations* (25.1–32.32)

A. *Ammon*

25 The word of the LORD came to me: 2 Mortal, set your face toward the Ammonites and prophesy against them. 3 Say to the Ammonites, Hear the word of the Lord GOD: Thus says the Lord GOD, Because you said, "Aha!" over my sanctuary when it was profaned, and over the land of Israel when it was made desolate, and over the house of Judah when it went into exile; 4 therefore I am handing you over to the people of the east for a possession. They shall set their encampments among you and pitch their tents in your midst; they shall eat your fruit, and they shall drink your milk. 5 I will make Rabbah a pasture for camels and Ammon a fold for flocks. Then you shall know that I am the LORD. 6 For thus says the Lord GOD: Because you have clapped your hands and stamped your feet and rejoiced with all the malice within you against the land of Israel, 7 therefore I have stretched out my hand against you, and will hand you over as plunder to the nations. I will cut you off from the peoples and will make you perish out of the countries; I will destroy you. Then you shall know that I am the LORD.

B. *Moab*

8 Thus says the Lord GOD: Because Moabʸ said, The house of Judah is like all the other nations, 9 therefore I will lay open the flank of Moab from the townsᶻ on its frontier, the glory of the country, Beth-jeshimoth, Baal-meon, and Kiriathaim. 10 I will give it along with Ammon to the people of the east as a possession. Thus Ammon shall be remembered no more among the nations, 11 and I will execute judgments upon Moab. Then they shall know that I am the LORD.

C. *Edom*

12 Thus says the Lord GOD: Because Edom acted revengefully against the house of Judah and has grievously offended in taking vengeance upon

ʷ Vg Tg: Heb *of men*   ˣ Heb lacks *and also*   ʸ Gk Old Latin: Heb *Moab and Seir*   ᶻ Heb *towns from its towns*

24.23
Job 27.15;
Ps 78.64;
Ezek 33.10
24.24
Ezek 4.3;
12.6, 11;
Jer 17.15;
Ezek 6.7;
25.5
24.25
Jer 11.22
24.26
Ezek 33.21f
24.27
Ezek 3.26,
27; 33.22;
v. 24

25.2
Jer 27.3;
Ezek 21.28;
Am 1.13;
Zeph 2.8, 9
25.3
Prov 17.5;
Ezek 26.2
25.4
Ezek 21.31

25.5
Ezek 21.20;
Isa 17.2;
Zeph 2.14
25.6
Job 27.23;
Lam 2.15;
Zeph 2.8, 10
25.7
Ezek 26.5;
Am 1.14, 15;
Ezek 6.14

25.8
Isa chs. 15,
16;
Jer 48.1;
Am 2.1;
Ezek 35.2, 5
25.9
Num 33.49;
32.3, 38;
32.37
25.10
v. 4;
Ezek 21.32
25.11
Ezek 5.15;
11.9
25.12
Lam 4.21,
22;
Ezek 35.2;
Am 1.11;
Ob 10-16

25.1 Before Ezekiel recorded the fall of Jerusalem and God's promises of restoration, he uttered a series of prophetic oracles against the nations that surrounded the promised land.
25.2 *The Ammonites* were the descendants of Ben-ammi, son of Lot's younger daughter who instigated incest with her father. They became deadly enemies of the true people of God (see Gen 19.33–38).

25.9 *Moab*. The Moabites descended from Lot's elder daughter, who (by incest) gave birth to Moab by her father. The Moabites and the Ammonites were forbidden to enter the congregation of Israel until the tenth generation (see Gen 19.33–38; Deut 23.3).
25.12 *Edom*. See note on Gen 36.9 for information regarding the Edomites.

them, 13 therefore thus says the Lord GOD, I will stretch out my hand against Edom, and cut off from it humans and animals, and I will make it desolate; from Teman even to Dedan they shall fall by the sword. 14 I will lay my vengeance upon Edom by the hand of my people Israel; and they shall act in Edom according to my anger and according to my wrath; and they shall know my vengeance, says the Lord GOD.

D. *Philistia*

15 Thus says the Lord GOD: Because with unending hostilities the Philistines acted in vengeance, and with malice of heart took revenge in destruction; 16 therefore thus says the Lord GOD, I will stretch out my hand against the Philistines, cut off the Cherethites, and destroy the rest of the seacoast. 17 I will execute great vengeance on them with wrathful punishments. Then they shall know that I am the LORD, when I lay my vengeance on them.

E. *Tyre*

1. *Prediction of its doom*

26 In the eleventh year, on the first day of the month, the word of the LORD came to me: 2 Mortal, because Tyre said concerning Jerusalem,

"Aha, broken is the gateway of the peoples;
  it has swung open to me;
I shall be replenished,
  now that it is wasted,"

3 therefore, thus says the Lord GOD:
See, I am against you, O Tyre!
  I will hurl many nations against you,
  as the sea hurls its waves.
4 They shall destroy the walls of Tyre
  and break down its towers.
I will scrape its soil from it
  and make it a bare rock.
5 It shall become, in the midst of the sea,
  a place for spreading nets.
I have spoken, says the Lord GOD.
  It shall become plunder for the nations,
6 and its daughter-towns in the country
  shall be killed by the sword.
Then they shall know that I am the LORD.

2. *Nebuchadnezzar the agent of destruction*

7 For thus says the Lord GOD: I will bring against Tyre from the north King Nebuchadrezzar of Babylon, king of kings, together with horses, chariots, cavalry, and a great and powerful army. 8 Your daughter-towns in the country he shall put to the sword.
He shall set up a siege wall against you,
  cast up a ramp against you,
  and raise a roof of shields against you.

25.13
Am 1.12;
Jer 25.23
25.14
Isa 11.14;
Jer 49.2

25.15
Jer 25.20;
Isa 14.29-31;
Joel 3.4;
2 Chr 28.18
25.16
Zeph 2.4, 5;
1 Sam 30.14;
Jer 47.1-7
25.17
Ezek 5.15;
Ps 9.16

26.2
Isa ch. 23;
Jer 25.22;
Ezek 25.3;
36.2

26.3
Mic 4.11;
Isa 5.30;
Jer 50.42

26.4
Am 1.10

26.5
Ezek 27.32;
29.19

26.6
Ezek 25.5

26.7
Jer 27.3-6;
Ezra 7.12;
Dan 2.37;
Ezek 23.24
26.8
v. 6;
Ezek 21.22;
Jer 6.6; 32.24

25.15 The Philistines descended from Mizraim and were constant opponents of God's people. They worshiped Dagon and other gods. In the Maccabean age they were finally exterminated, according to the prophetic word.
26.2 Isaiah had predicted the fall of Tyre long be-

fore Ezekiel's time (see Isa 23). Nebuchadnezzar was God's instrument to bring about Tyre's downfall, a city built on an island that lay a half mile offshore (see note on 28.2). Nebuchadnezzar besieged mainland Tyre for thirteen years before it capitulated.

26.9
Ezek 21.22

9 He shall direct the shock of his battering rams against
        your walls
    and break down your towers with his axes.

26.10
Jer 4.13;
39.3;
Ezek 27.28

10 His horses shall be so many
        that their dust shall cover you.
    At the noise of cavalry, wheels, and chariots
        your very walls shall shake,
    when he enters your gates
        like those entering a breached city.

26.11
Hab 1.8;
Isa 26.5;
Jer 43.13

11 With the hoofs of his horses
        he shall trample all your streets.
    He shall put your people to the sword,
        and your strong pillars shall fall to the ground.

26.12
v. 5

12 They will plunder your riches
        and loot your merchandise;
    they shall break down your walls
        and destroy your fine houses.
    Your stones and timber and soil
        they shall cast into the water.

26.13
Isa 14.11;
25.10;
Isa 23.16;
Rev 18.22
26.14
vv. 4, 5;
Mal 1.4;
Isa 14.27

13 I will silence the music of your songs;
        the sound of your lyres shall be heard no more.
14 I will make you a bare rock;
        you shall be a place for spreading nets.
    You shall never again be rebuilt,
        for I the LORD have spoken,
        says the Lord GOD.

3. *Lamentation of the princes of the sea*

26.15
v. 18;
Ezek 31.16
26.16
Ezek 27.35;
Jon 3.6;
Job 2.13

15 Thus says the Lord GOD to Tyre: Shall not the coastlands shake
at the sound of your fall, when the wounded groan, when slaughter goes
on within you? 16 Then all the princes of the sea shall step down from their
thrones; they shall remove their robes and strip off their embroidered
garments. They shall clothe themselves with trembling, and shall sit on
the ground; they shall tremble every moment, and be appalled at you.
17 And they shall raise a lamentation over you, and say to you:

26.17
Ezek 27.32;
Rev 18.9;
Isa 23.4;
Ezek 28.2

    How you have vanished[a] from the seas,
        O city renowned,
    once mighty on the sea,
        you and your inhabitants,[b]
    who imposed your[c] terror
        on all the mainland![d]

26.18
v. 15

18 Now the coastlands tremble
        on the day of your fall;
    the coastlands by the sea
        are dismayed at your passing.

4. *Tyre to go down to the Pit*

26.20
Ezek 32.18,
24;
Am 9.2;
Jer 33.9

19 For thus says the Lord GOD: When I make you a city laid waste,
like cities that are not inhabited, when I bring up the deep over you, and
the great waters cover you, 20 then I will thrust you down with those who

a Gk OL Aquila: Heb *have vanished, O inhabited one,*   b Heb *it and its inhabitants*   c Heb *their*
d Cn: Heb *its inhabitants*

26.14 *I will make you a bare rock.* Certain aspects of
vv. 12,14 exceed the actual damage done to Tyre by
Nebuchadnezzar; they foreshadow what happened to
the island settlement through Alexander the Great in
332 B.C.. Unable to take the island by ships, he built
a stone causeway from the mainland to the island.

From that day on its glory was gone and the prophetic
word of God was fulfilled (vv. 4,5,15,21; 27.36;
28.2–9).
26.20 *The land of the living* is an expression for
heaven, where people see the goodness of God and
enjoy eternal happiness. Tyre was not to be numbered

descend into the Pit, to the people of long ago, and I will make you live in the world below, among primeval ruins, with those who go down to the Pit, so that you will not be inhabited or have a place*e* in the land of the living. 21 I will bring you to a dreadful end, and you shall be no more; though sought for, you will never be found again, says the Lord GOD.

26.21
Ezek 27.36;
28.19; v. 14

5. The lamentation over Tyre

a. The beauty and wealth of Tyre

27 The word of the LORD came to me: 2 Now you, mortal, raise a lamentation over Tyre, 3 and say to Tyre, which sits at the entrance to the sea, merchant of the peoples on many coastlands, Thus says the Lord GOD:

O Tyre, you have said,
"I am perfect in beauty."

27.2
Ezek 28.12
27.3
Ezek 28.2;
v. 33;
Ezek 28.12

4 Your borders are in the heart of the seas;
    your builders made perfect your beauty.

27.4
vv. 25-27

5 They made all your planks
    of fir trees from Senir;
they took a cedar from Lebanon
    to make a mast for you.

27.5
Deut 3.9

6 From oaks of Bashan
    they made your oars;
they made your deck of pines*f*
    from the coasts of Cyprus,
    inlaid with ivory.

27.6
Zech 11.2;
Isa 2.13;
Jer 2.10

7 Of fine embroidered linen from Egypt
    was your sail,
    serving as your ensign;
blue and purple from the coasts of Elishah
    was your awning.

8 The inhabitants of Sidon and Arvad
    were your rowers;
skilled men of Zemer*g* were within you,
    they were your pilots.

27.8
1 Kings 9.27

9 The elders of Gebal and its artisans were within you,
    caulking your seams;
all the ships of the sea with their mariners were within you,
    to barter for your wares.

27.9
1 Kings 5.18;
v. 27

b. The armies of Tyre

10 Paras*h* and Lud and Put
    were in your army,
    your mighty warriors;
they hung shield and helmet in you;
    they gave you splendor.

27.10
Ezek 30.5;
38.5; v. 11

11 Men of Arvad and Helech*i*
    were on your walls all around;
    men of Gamad were at your towers.
They hung their quivers all around your walls;
    they made perfect your beauty.

27.11
vv. 3, 8, 10

c. The commerce of Tyre

12 Tarshish did business with you out of the abundance of your great

27.12
2 Chr 20.36;
Isa 23.6, 10;
vv. 18, 33

e Gk: Heb *I will give beauty* *f* Or *boxwood* *g* Cn Compare Gen 10.18: Heb *your skilled men, O Tyre*
h Or *Persia* *i* Or *and your army*

among those in the land of the living.
27.2 God ordered Ezekiel to *raise a lamentation over Tyre* at a time when it was highly prosperous and there

was no reason to suppose it would decay and disappear as a significant city of commerce. Pride and a sense of security against all enemies caused its ruin.

wealth; silver, iron, tin, and lead they exchanged for your wares. 13 Javan, Tubal, and Meshech traded with you; they exchanged human beings and vessels of bronze for your merchandise. 14 Beth-togarmah exchanged for your wares horses, war horses, and mules. 15 The Rhodians[j] traded with you; many coastlands were your own special markets; they brought you in payment ivory tusks and ebony. 16 Edom[k] did business with you because of your abundant goods; they exchanged for your wares turquoise, purple, embroidered work, fine linen, coral, and rubies. 17 Judah and the land of Israel traded with you; they exchanged for your merchandise wheat from Minnith, millet,[l] honey, oil, and balm. 18 Damascus traded with you for your abundant goods—because of your great wealth of every kind—wine of Helbon, and white wool. 19 Vedan and Javan from Uzal[l] entered into trade for your wares; wrought iron, cassia, and sweet cane were bartered for your merchandise. 20 Dedan traded with you in saddlecloths for riding. 21 Arabia and all the princes of Kedar were your favored dealers in lambs, rams, and goats; in these they did business with you. 22 The merchants of Sheba and Raamah traded with you; they exchanged for your wares the best of all kinds of spices, and all precious stones, and gold. 23 Haran, Canneh, Eden, the merchants of Sheba, Asshur, and Chilmad traded with you. 24 These traded with you in choice garments, in clothes of blue and embroidered work, and in carpets of colored material, bound with cords and made secure; in these they traded with you.[m] 25 The ships of Tarshish traveled for you in your trade.

d. The ruin of Tyre

So you were filled and heavily laden
   in the heart of the seas.
26 Your rowers have brought you
   into the high seas.
The east wind has wrecked you
   in the heart of the seas.
27 Your riches, your wares, your merchandise,
   your mariners and your pilots,
your caulkers, your dealers in merchandise,
   and all your warriors within you,
with all the company
   that is with you,
sink into the heart of the seas
   on the day of your ruin.
28 At the sound of the cry of your pilots
   the countryside shakes,
29 and down from their ships
   come all that handle the oar.
The mariners and all the pilots of the sea
   stand on the shore
30 and wail aloud over you,
   and cry bitterly.
They throw dust on their heads
   and wallow in ashes;
31 they make themselves bald for you,
   and put on sackcloth,
and they weep over you in bitterness of soul,
   with bitter mourning.

Cross-references (left margin):

27.13 Gen 10.2; Isa 66.19; Ezek 38.2; Joel 3.3; Rev 18.13
27.14 Gen 10.3; Ezek 38.6
27.15 Gen 10.7; Rev 18.12
27.16 Ezek 28.13; 16.13, 18
27.17 Judg 11.33; Jer 8.22
27.18 Jer 49.23; Ezek 47.16-18; vv. 12, 33
27.20 v. 15
27.21 Jer 25.24; 49.28; Isa 60.7
27.22 Gen 10.7; 1 Kings 10.1, 2; Isa 60.6
27.23 Gen 11.31; 2 Kings 19.12; Am 1.5
27.25 Isa 2.16; 23.14; v. 4
27.26 Ezek 26.19; Ps 48.7; vv. 4, 25, 27
27.27 Prov 11.4; Rev 18.9-19
27.28 Ezek 26.15
27.29 Rev 18.17-19
27.30 Job 2.12; Rev 18.19; Esth 4.1, 3; Jer 6.26
27.31 Jer 16.6; Ezek 29.18; Isa 22.12; 16.9

---

j Gk: Heb *The Dedanites*   *k* Another reading is *Aram*   *l* Meaning of Heb uncertain   *m* Cn: Heb *in your market*

27.13,14 *Javan, Tubal, and Meshech* ... *Beth-togarmah.* These are regions of Asia Minor, now in Turkey.

27.26 Tyre is pictured here as overtaken by an east wind, a reference to Nebuchadnezzar (see notes on 26.2,14).

32 In their wailing they raise a lamentation for you,
        and lament over you:
    "Who was ever destroyed[n] like Tyre
        in the midst of the sea?

27.32
v. 2;
Ezek 26.17;
Rev 18.18

33 When your wares came from the seas,
        you satisfied many peoples;
    with your abundant wealth and merchandise
        you enriched the kings of the earth.

27.33
Rev 18.19

34 Now you are wrecked by the seas,
        in the depths of the waters;
    your merchandise and all your crew
        have sunk with you.

27.34
vv. 26, 27;
Ezek 26.19;
Zech 9.3, 4

35 All the inhabitants of the coastlands
        are appalled at you;
    and their kings are horribly afraid,
        their faces are convulsed.

27.35
Ezek 26.15,
16; 32.10

36 The merchants among the peoples hiss at you;
        you have come to a dreadful end
        and shall be no more forever."

27.36
Jer 18.16;
Zeph 2.15;
Ezek 26.21;
Ps 37.10, 36

F. Prophecies against Tyre and Sidon

1. The pride of Tyre the reason for its ruin

28 The word of the LORD came to me: 2 Mortal, say to the prince of
    Tyre, Thus says the Lord GOD:
Because your heart is proud
    and you have said, "I am a god;
I sit in the seat of the gods,
    in the heart of the seas,"
yet you are but a mortal, and no god,
    though you compare your mind
    with the mind of a god.

28.2
Ezek 27.25-27;
Isa 31.3; v. 6

3   You are indeed wiser than Daniel;[o]
        no secret is hidden from you;

28.3
Dan 1.20

4   by your wisdom and your understanding
        you have amassed wealth for yourself,
    and have gathered gold and silver
        into your treasuries.

28.4
Ezek 27.33

5   By your great wisdom in trade
        you have increased your wealth,
    and your heart has become proud in your wealth.

28.5
Ps 62.10;
Zech 9.3;
Hos 13.6

6   Therefore thus says the Lord GOD:
Because you compare your mind
    with the mind of a god,

28.6
v. 2

7   therefore, I will bring strangers against you,
        the most terrible of the nations;
    they shall draw their swords against the beauty of your wisdom
        and defile your splendor.

28.7
Ezek 26.7;
30.11; 31.12;
32.12; v. 17

8   They shall thrust you down to the Pit,
        and you shall die a violent death
        in the heart of the seas.

28.8
Ezek 32.30;
27.26, 27, 34

9   Will you still say, "I am a god,"
        in the presence of those who kill you,
        though you are but a mortal, and no god,

28.9
v. 2

---

[n] Tg Vg: Heb like silence   [o] Or, as otherwise read, Danel

28.2 *in the heart of the seas.* Tyre was an island fortress just a half mile off the Phoenician coast. It was so strongly fortified that for thirteen years it was able to withstand the siege by Nebuchadnezzar. It was almost impregnable.

in the hands of those who wound you?

28.10
Ezek 31.18;
32.19, 21,
25, 27

10 You shall die the death of the uncircumcised
by the hand of foreigners;
for I have spoken, says the Lord GOD.

2. *The lamentation over Tyre*

28.12
Ezek 27.2;
v. 3;
Ezek 27.3

11 Moreover the word of the LORD came to me: 12 Mortal, raise a lamentation over the king of Tyre, and say to him, Thus says the Lord GOD:

You were the signet of perfection, *p*
full of wisdom and perfect in beauty.

28.13
Ezek 31.8, 9;
36.35

13 You were in Eden, the garden of God;
every precious stone was your covering,
carnelian, chrysolite, and moonstone,
beryl, onyx, and jasper,
sapphire, *q* turquoise, and emerald;
and worked in gold were your settings
and your engravings. *p*
On the day that you were created
they were prepared.

28.14
Ex 25.20;
v. 16;
Ezek 20.40;
Rev 18.16
28.15
Ezek 27.3, 4;
Isa 14.12;
vv. 17, 18

14 With an anointed cherub as guardian I placed you; *p*
you were on the holy mountain of God;
you walked among the stones of fire.

15 You were blameless in your ways
from the day that you were created,
until iniquity was found in you.

28.16
Ezek 27.12ff;
8.17;
Gen 3.24;
v. 14

16 In the abundance of your trade
you were filled with violence, and you sinned;
so I cast you as a profane thing from the mountain of God,
and the guardian cherub drove you out
from among the stones of fire.

28.17
vv. 2, 5;
Ezek 31.10;
27.3, 4;
26.16

17 Your heart was proud because of your beauty;
you corrupted your wisdom for the sake of your splendor.
I cast you to the ground;
I exposed you before kings,
to feast their eyes on you.

28.18
v. 16;
Am 1.9, 10;
Mal 4.3

18 By the multitude of your iniquities,
in the unrighteousness of your trade,
you profaned your sanctuaries.
So I brought out fire from within you;

p Meaning of Heb uncertain   *q* Or *lapis lazuli*

28.12 *raise a lamentation over the king of Tyre*. In this passage (vv. 11–19) some descriptive phrases apply to a human king of Tyre, and some seem to apply to Satan. Therefore great care must be taken to apply these verses with discernment. Some words that can only apply to Satan are: "full of wisdom and perfect in beauty" (v. 12); the "anointed cherub" (v. 14); blameless in all he did from the day he was created by God until iniquity was found in him (v. 15). His heart was filled with pride because of his beauty (v. 17). The Scriptures give Satan many different names, such as (1) "Day Star, son of Dawn" (Isa 14.12); (2) "father of lies" (Jn 8.44); (3) "the ruler of the power of the air" (Eph 2.2); (4) "the god of this world" (2 Cor 4.4; cf. Jn 14.30); (5) the "adversary" (1 Pet 5.8); (6) "the dragon, that ancient serpent, who is the Devil and Satan" (Rev 20.2). His origin is not clear, but light is provided in Isa 14.12–15, Ezek 28.12–19, and Lk 10.18. Satan is: (1) evil (1 Jn 3.8), (2) deceptive and cunning (2 Cor 11.3, 13–15; Rev 12.9), and

(3) the great enemy who rules this world and has many helpers (Lk 8.30; 11.15; Eph 6.12). But Christ has already defeated Satan in principle (Jn 12.31). He will be cast into the lake of fire at the end of time (Rev 20.10). He works to: (1) tempt and seduce the people of God (2 Cor 2.11; 1 Thess 3.5); (2) blind people's eyes to the truth of God (2 Cor 4.3,4); (3) destroy the word of God (Mk 4.15); (4) take up residence in human hearts (Jn 13.27); (5) accuse believers before God (Rev 12.10); and (6) stop God's servants from doing God's will (1 Thess 2.18; 1 Pet 5.8). Believers are told to: (1) resist the devil (Jas 4.7); (2) stay awake and pray (Mt 26.41); and (3) use the shield of faith to stop his flaming arrows (Eph 6.16).
28.14 The cherub here appears to refer to Satan who is to be judged (vv. 16–19) and then cast into the lake of fire (Rev 20.10). The king of Tyre thought of himself as a guardian angel for his people, but if so, he was a fallen angel and ultimately the destroyer of his people.

it consumed you,
and I turned you to ashes on the earth
in the sight of all who saw you.
19 All who know you among the peoples
are appalled at you;
you have come to a dreadful end
and shall be no more forever.

3. Sidon to perish by pestilence and the sword

20 The word of the LORD came to me: 21 Mortal, set your face toward
Sidon, and prophesy against it, 22 and say, Thus says the Lord GOD:
I am against you, O Sidon,
and I will gain glory in your midst.
They shall know that I am the LORD
when I execute judgments in it,
and manifest my holiness in it;
23 for I will send pestilence into it,
and bloodshed into its streets;
and the dead shall fall in its midst,
by the sword that is against it on every side.
And they shall know that I am the LORD.

4. The recovery of the house of Israel

24 The house of Israel shall no longer find a pricking brier or a
piercing thorn among all their neighbors who have treated them with
contempt. And they shall know that I am the Lord GOD.
25 Thus says the Lord GOD: When I gather the house of Israel from
the peoples among whom they are scattered, and manifest my holiness in
them in the sight of the nations, then they shall settle on their own soil
that I gave to my servant Jacob. 26 They shall live in safety in it, and shall
build houses and plant vineyards. They shall live in safety, when I execute
judgments upon all their neighbors who have treated them with contempt.
And they shall know that I am the LORD their God.

G. The prophecies against Egypt

1. The word against Pharaoh

a. Pharaoh's sin of pride

29 In the tenth year, in the tenth month, on the twelfth day of the
month, the word of the LORD came to me: 2 Mortal, set your face
against Pharaoh king of Egypt, and prophesy against him and against all
Egypt; 3 speak, and say, Thus says the Lord GOD:
I am against you,
Pharaoh king of Egypt,
the great dragon sprawling
in the midst of its channels,
saying, "My Nile is my own;
I made it for myself."
4 I will put hooks in your jaws,

28.19	Ezek 26.21; 27.36; Jer 51.64
28.21	Ezek 6.2; 25.2; Isa 23.4, 12; Ezek 32.30
28.22	Ezek 26.3; 39.13; Ps 9.16; v. 26; Ezek 38.16
28.23	Ezek 38.22; Jer 51.52; vv. 24, 26
28.24	Num 33.55; Josh 23.13; Isa 55.13; Ezek 25.6; 36.5
28.25	Isa 11.12; Jer 32.37; Ezek 20.41; Jer 23.8; 27.11; Ezek 37.25
28.26	Jer 23.6; Isa 65.21; Am 9.13, 14
29.2	Ezek 28.21; Jer 44.30; Isa 19.1; Jer 25.19; 46.2, 25
29.3	Jer 44.30; Ezek 28.22; Isa 27.1; 51.9; Ezek 32.2
29.4	2 Kings 19.28; Isa 37.29; Ezek 38.4

28.24ff Again and again God has promised to regather and restore his people Israel. The ultimate fulfillment of this promise will take place at the end of the age. Premillennialists hold that this will be especially true in the millennium, after the return of Christ.
29.2 Egypt and Israel were interlocked in their history in many ways. Abraham had gone to Egypt in a time of famine. Joseph, taken there as a slave, became

a premier in Egypt, and brought his family there. God delivered his people from their bondage in Egypt (Ex 1–14). Later Israel made alliances with Egypt against common enemies. Jesus was taken to Egypt, and out of Egypt God called his Son (Mt 2.15; cf. Hos 11.1). At the end of the age Israel will be a third partner with Egypt and Assyria, and God will say, "Blessed be Egypt my people" (Isa 19.25).

and make the fish of your channels stick to your scales.
I will draw you up from your channels,
   with all the fish of your channels
   sticking to your scales.

29.5
Ezek 32.4-6;
Jer 7.33;
34.20;
Ezek 39.4

5 I will fling you into the wilderness,
   you and all the fish of your channels;
you shall fall in the open field,
   and not be gathered and buried.
To the animals of the earth and to the birds of the air
   I have given you as food.

b. Egypt's judgment

29.6
Isa 36.6

6 Then all the inhabitants of Egypt shall know
   that I am the LORD
because you*r* were a staff of reed
   to the house of Israel;

29.7
Jer 37.5-11;
Ezek 17.17

7 when they grasped you with the hand, you broke,
   and tore all their shoulders;
and when they leaned on you, you broke,
   and made all their legs unsteady.*s*

29.8
Ezek 14.17;
32.11-13
29.9
vv. 10-12, 6,
3

8 Therefore, thus says the Lord GOD: I will bring a sword upon you, and will cut off from you human being and animal; 9 and the land of Egypt shall be a desolation and a waste. Then they shall know that I am the LORD.

c. The desolation and restoration of Egypt

29.10
Ezek 30.12, 6

Because you*t* said, "The Nile is mine, and I made it," 10 therefore, I am against you, and against your channels, and I will make the land of Egypt an utter waste and desolation, from Migdol to Syene, as far as the border of Ethiopia.*u* 11 No human foot shall pass through it, and no animal foot shall pass through it; it shall be uninhabited forty years. 12 I will make the land of Egypt a desolation among desolated countries; and her cities shall be a desolation forty years among cities that are laid waste. I will scatter the Egyptians among the nations, and disperse them among the countries.

29.11
Jer 43.11, 12;
Ezek 32.13
29.12
Ezek 30.7, 26

29.13
Isa 19.22,
23;
Jer 46.26
29.14
Ezek 30.14;
17.6, 14
29.15
v. 14;
Zech 10.11
29.16
Isa 30.2, 3;
36.4, 6;
Jer 14.10;
Hos 8.13;
vv. 6, 9, 21

13 Further, thus says the Lord GOD: At the end of forty years I will gather the Egyptians from the peoples among whom they were scattered; 14 and I will restore the fortunes of Egypt, and bring them back to the land of Pathros, the land of their origin; and there they shall be a lowly kingdom. 15 It shall be the most lowly of the kingdoms, and never again exalt itself above the nations; and I will make them so small that they will never again rule over the nations. 16 The Egyptians*v* shall never again be the reliance of the house of Israel; they will recall their iniquity, when they turned to them for aid. Then they shall know that I am the Lord GOD.

2. Nebuchadnezzar to receive Egypt as his wages

29.18
Jer 27.6;
Ezek 26.7, 8;
27.31

17 In the twenty-seventh year, in the first month, on the first day of the month, the word of the LORD came to me: 18 Mortal, King Nebuchadrezzar of Babylon made his army labor hard against Tyre; every head was made bald and every shoulder was rubbed bare; yet neither he nor his army got anything from Tyre to pay for the labor that he had expended against it. 19 Therefore thus says the Lord GOD: I will give the land of

29.19
Ezek 30.10;
Jer 43.10-13;
Ezek 30.4

r Gk Syr Vg: Heb *they*   *s* Syr: Heb *stand*   *t* Gk Syr Vg: Heb *he*   *u* Or *Nubia*; Heb *Cush*   *v* Heb *It*

29.9 This prophetic promise of the overthrow of Egypt was fulfilled when Nebuchadnezzar invaded that nation in 572 and 568 B.C. Following the conquest of Egypt by the Persian ruler Cambyses (ca.

524 B.C.), Egypt has for the most part been under the control of foreign powers.
29.17 *the twenty-seventh year* i.e., the twenty-seventh year of Jehoiachin's captivity.

Egypt to King Nebuchadrezzar of Babylon; and he shall carry off its wealth and despoil it and plunder it; and it shall be the wages for his army. 20 I have given him the land of Egypt as his payment for which he labored, because they worked for me, says the Lord GOD.

21   On that day I will cause a horn to sprout up for the house of Israel, and I will open your lips among them. Then they shall know that I am the LORD.

3. The nearness of Egypt's doom

a. The LORD's vengeance on Egypt

30 The word of the LORD came to me: 2 Mortal, prophesy, and say, Thus says the Lord GOD:

Wail, "Alas for the day!"
3   For a day is near,
      the day of the LORD is near;
   it will be a day of clouds,
      a time of doom[w] for the nations.
4   A sword shall come upon Egypt,
      and anguish shall be in Ethiopia,[x]
   when the slain fall in Egypt,
      and its wealth is carried away,
      and its foundations are torn down.
5 Ethiopia,[x] and Put, and Lud, and all Arabia, and Libya,[y] and the people of the allied land[z] shall fall with them by the sword.

b. The fall of Egypt's supporters

6   Thus says the LORD:
   Those who support Egypt shall fall,
      and its proud might shall come down;
   from Migdol to Syene
      they shall fall within it by the sword,
   says the Lord GOD.
7   They shall be desolated among other desolated countries,
      and their cities shall lie among cities laid waste.
8   Then they shall know that I am the LORD,
      when I have set fire to Egypt,
      and all who help it are broken.
9   On that day, messengers shall go out from me in ships to terrify the unsuspecting Ethiopians;[a] and anguish shall come upon them on the day of Egypt's doom;[b] for it is coming!

c. The coming of Nebuchadnezzar

10   Thus says the Lord GOD:
   I will put an end to the hordes of Egypt,
      by the hand of King Nebuchadnezzar of Babylon.
11   He and his people with him, the most terrible of the nations,
      shall be brought in to destroy the land;
   and they shall draw their swords against Egypt,
      and fill the land with the slain.
12   I will dry up the channels,
      and will sell the land into the hand of evildoers;
   I will bring desolation upon the land and everything in it
      by the hand of foreigners;

29.20
Isa 45.1-3;
Jer 25.9
29.21
Ps 132.17;
Ezek 24.27;
33.22;
Lk 21.15;
Ezek 6.7; v. 6

30.2
Isa 13.6;
Ezek 21.12;
Joel 1.5, 11, 13
30.3
Ezek 7.7, 12;
Joel 2.1;
Ob 15;
Zeph 1.7;
v. 18
30.4
vv. 11, 5, 9;
Ezek 29.19

30.5
Jer 25.20, 24

30.6
Isa 20.3-6;
Ezek 29.10

30.7
Ezek 29.12
30.8
Ezek 29.6;
9.16; vv. 14, 16, 5, 6
30.9
Isa 18.1, 2;
Ezek 38.11;
32.9, 10

30.10
Ezek 29.19

30.11
Ezek 28.7;
v. 4

30.12
Isa 19.5, 6;
Ezek 29.3, 9

---

w Heb lacks of doom   x Or Nubia; Heb Cush   y Compare Gk Syr Vg: Heb Cub   z Meaning of Heb uncertain   a Or Nubians; Heb Cush   b Heb the day of Egypt

---

30.3   the day of the LORD is near, i.e., the day of God's judgment against Egypt, not the end of the age.

30.5   The neighbors of Egypt, here specified, would also suffer from the invasion of Nebuchadnezzar.

I the LORD have spoken.

d. *The vengeance of the LORD on Egypt*

30.13
Isa 19.1;
Zech 13.2;
v. 16;
Zech 10.11;
Isa 19.16

13 Thus says the Lord GOD:
I will destroy the idols
    and put an end to the images in Memphis;
there shall no longer be a prince in the land of Egypt;
    so I will put fear in the land of Egypt.

30.14
Ezek 29.14;
Ps 78.12, 43;
vv. 15, 16

14 I will make Pathros a desolation,
    and will set fire to Zoan,
    and will execute acts of judgment on Thebes.

30.15
Jer 46.25;
v. 16

15 I will pour my wrath upon Pelusium,
    the stronghold of Egypt,
    and cut off the hordes of Thebes.

30.16
vv. 8, 13-15

16 I will set fire to Egypt;
    Pelusium shall be in great agony;
Thebes shall be breached,
    and Memphis face adversaries by day.

17 The young men of On and of Pi-beseth shall fall by the sword;
    and the cities themselves[c] shall go into captivity.

30.18
Jer 43.8-13;
Ezek 34.27;
v. 3

18 At Tehaphnehes the day shall be dark,
    when I break there the dominion of Egypt,
    and its proud might shall come to an end;
the city[d] shall be covered by a cloud,
    and its daughter-towns shall go into captivity.

30.19
vv. 14, 25, 26

19 Thus I will execute acts of judgment on Egypt.
    Then they shall know that I am the LORD.

e. *The arms of Pharaoh to be broken*

30.21
Ps 10.15;
Jer 46.11

20 In the eleventh year, in the first month, on the seventh day of the month, the word of the LORD came to me: 21 Mortal, I have broken the arm of Pharaoh king of Egypt; it has not been bound up for healing or wrapped with a bandage, so that it may become strong to wield the sword.

30.22
Ezek 29.3;
Ps 37.17
30.23
Ezek 29.12;
v. 26
30.24
vv. 10, 25;
Zech 10.12;
Zeph 2.12;
Ezek 26.15;
21.14, 25
30.25
vv. 24, 22,
11;
Isa 5.25
30.26
Ezek 29.12

22 Therefore thus says the Lord GOD: I am against Pharaoh king of Egypt, and will break his arms, both the strong arm and the one that was broken; and I will make the sword fall from his hand. 23 I will scatter the Egyptians among the nations, and disperse them throughout the lands. 24 I will strengthen the arms of the king of Babylon, and put my sword in his hand; but I will break the arms of Pharaoh, and he will groan before him with the groans of one mortally wounded. 25 I will strengthen the arms of the king of Babylon, but the arms of Pharaoh shall fall. And they shall know that I am the LORD, when I put my sword into the hand of the king of Babylon. He shall stretch it out against the land of Egypt, 26 and I will scatter the Egyptians among the nations and disperse them throughout the countries. Then they shall know that I am the LORD.

4. *The allegory of the great cedar*

a. *Egypt likened to a great cedar*

31.2
Ezek 29.19;
30.10; v. 18

31 In the eleventh year, in the third month, on the first day of the month, the word of the LORD came to me: 2 Mortal, say to Pharaoh king of Egypt and to his hordes:

[c] Heb *and they*   [d] Heb *she*

30.13–19 Ezekiel elaborated on the defeat of Egypt by mentioning the names of major cities and strongholds taken by the Babylonians.
30.20 This took place three months before the fall of Jerusalem.
30.21 A few months before Jerusalem was taken,

Nebuchadnezzar took time off to defeat the Egyptian force that sought to relieve the besieged Jerusalem, thus breaking the arm of Pharaoh.
31.1 This prophecy was spoken a month before Jerusalem fell.

Whom are you like in your greatness?
3   Consider Assyria, a cedar of Lebanon,
     with fair branches and forest shade,
        and of great height,
        its top among the clouds.*e*

4   The waters nourished it,
        the deep made it grow tall,
     making its rivers flow*f*
        around the place it was planted,
     sending forth its streams
        to all the trees of the field.

5   So it towered high
        above all the trees of the field;
     its boughs grew large
        and its branches long,
        from abundant water in its shoots.

6   All the birds of the air
        made their nests in its boughs;
     under its branches all the animals of the field
        gave birth to their young;
     and in its shade
        all great nations lived.

7   It was beautiful in its greatness,
        in the length of its branches;
     for its roots went down
        to abundant water.

8   The cedars in the garden of God could not rival it,
        nor the fir trees equal its boughs;
     the plane trees were as nothing
        compared with its branches;
     no tree in the garden of God
        was like it in beauty.

9   I made it beautiful
        with its mass of branches,
     the envy of all the trees of Eden
        that were in the garden of God.

b. The fall of the cedar into the Pit

10   Therefore thus says the Lord GOD: Because it*g* towered high and
set its top among the clouds,*e* and its heart was proud of its height, 11 I
gave it into the hand of the prince of the nations; he has dealt with it as
its wickedness deserves. I have cast it out. 12 Foreigners from the most
terrible of the nations have cut it down and left it. On the mountains and
in all the valleys its branches have fallen, and its boughs lie broken in all
the watercourses of the land; and all the peoples of the earth went away
from its shade and left it.

13   On its fallen trunk settle
        all the birds of the air,
     and among its boughs lodge
        all the wild animals.

14 All this is in order that no trees by the waters may grow to lofty height
or set their tops among the clouds,*e* and that no trees that drink water
may reach up to them in height.

e Gk: Heb *thick boughs*   *f* Gk: Heb *rivers going*   *g* Syr Vg: Heb *you*

Cross references (right column):

31.3
Nah 3.1ff;
Ezek 17.23;
vv. 5, 10

31.4
Ezek 17.5, 8;
Rev 17.1, 15

31.5
Ps 37.35;
Ezek 17.5

31.6
Ezek 17.23;
Dan 4.12;
Mt 13.32;
Mk 4.32;
Lk 13.19

31.7
vv. 2, 9

31.8
Gen 2.8;
13.10;
Ezek 28.13;
vv. 16, 18

31.9
Ezek 16.14

31.10
Isa 14.13,
14;
Ezek 28.17;
Dan 5.20
31.11
Ezek 30.10,
11;
Nah 3.18
31.12
Ezek 28.7;
Hab 1.6;
Ezek 32.5;
35.8;
Nah 3.17, 18
31.13
Isa 18.6;
Ezek 32.4
31.14
vv. 16, 17;
Ps 63.9;
v. 18;
Ezek 32.24

31.3   Assyria is likened to a great cedar in Lebanon.
This probably refers to the Assyrian empire under
Sennacherib that was unrivaled in its day in extent,
wealth, and power. By implication, Egypt is likened
to Assyria.

31.10ff   Egypt would also be like Assyria in its fall.
So great would be the fall of Egypt that the nations
would quake at the sounds (v. 16). Egypt would go
down to Sheol, to the nether parts of the earth.

For all of them are handed over to death,
    to the world below;
along with all mortals,
    with those who go down to the Pit.

31.15
Ezek 32.7;
Nah 2.10

15 Thus says the Lord GOD: On the day it went down to Sheol I closed the deep over it and covered it; I restrained its rivers, and its mighty waters were checked. I clothed Lebanon in gloom for it, and all the trees of the field fainted because of it. 16 I made the nations quake at the sound of its fall, when I cast it down to Sheol with those who go down to the Pit; and all the trees of Eden, the choice and best of Lebanon, all that were well watered, were consoled in the world below. 17 They also went down to Sheol with it, to those killed by the sword, along with its allies,h those who lived in its shade among the nations.

31.16
Ezek 26.15;
Isa 14.15;
Ezek 32.18;
Isa 14.8;
Ezek 32.31
31.17
Ps 9.17;
Ezek 32.18-20
31.18
Ezek 32.19;
vv. 8, 9, 14;
Ezek 28.10;
32.19, 21

18 Which among the trees of Eden was like you in glory and in greatness? Now you shall be brought down with the trees of Eden to the world below; you shall lie among the uncircumcised, with those who are killed by the sword. This is Pharaoh and all his horde, says the Lord GOD.

5. The lamentation over Pharaoh

a. The evils that shall befall him

32 In the twelfth year, in the twelfth month, on the first day of the month, the word of the LORD came to me: 2 Mortal, raise a lamentation over Pharaoh king of Egypt, and say to him:
    You consider yourself a lion among the nations,
        but you are like a dragon in the seas;
    you thrash about in your streams,
        trouble the water with your feet,
        and foul youri streams.

32.2
Ezek 27.2;
19.3, 6;
38.13; 34.18

3 Thus says the Lord GOD:
    In an assembly of many peoples
        I will throw my net over you;
        and Ij will haul you up in my dragnet.

32.3
Ezek 12.13;
17.20;
Hos 7.12

4 I will throw you on the ground,
        on the open field I will fling you,
    and will cause all the birds of the air to settle on you,
        and I will let the wild animals of the whole earth gorge
            themselves with you.

32.4
Ezek 29.5;
31.13;
Isa 18.6

5 I will strew your flesh on the mountains,
        and fill the valleys with your carcass.k

32.5
Ezek 35.8

6 I will drench the land with your flowing blood
        up to the mountains,
        and the watercourses will be filled with you.

32.6
Ezek 35.6;
Rev 14.20

7 When I blot you out, I will cover the heavens,
        and make their stars dark;
    I will cover the sun with a cloud,
        and the moon shall not give its light.

32.7
Prov 13.9;
Isa 34.4;
13.10;
Joel 2.31;
3.15;
Am 8.9;
Mt 24.29;
Rev 6.12, 13

8 All the shining lights of the heavens
        I will darken above you,

---

h Heb *its arms*   i Heb *their*   j Gk Vg: Heb *they*   k Symmachus Syr Vg: Heb *your height*

31.16,17 Other nations who rejoiced at the fall of Egypt would themselves go the same route at a later date.
32.2 God ordered Ezekiel to begin a lamentation over Egypt. God does not delight in the death of the wicked.
32.3 *I will throw my net over you.* A sovereign God, no matter how big and how strong a nation is, has a net big enough to cover it and strong enough to keep

it enclosed. In this instance the net was the Chaldeans.
32.7,8 This probably alludes to the darkness that came upon Egypt in the contest between Moses and Pharaoh (Ex 10.21–29). The remembrance of this past event might bring some sense to Egypt in the present difficulty and cause her to repent, lest a similar judgment fall again.

and put darkness on your land,

says the Lord GOD.

b. The dispersal of the peoples

9 I will trouble the hearts of many peoples,
     as I carry you captive[l] among the nations,
       into countries you have not known.
10 I will make many peoples appalled at you;
     their kings shall shudder because of you.
When I brandish my sword before them,
     they shall tremble every moment
for their lives, each one of them,
     on the day of your downfall.
11 For thus says the Lord GOD:
The sword of the king of Babylon shall come against you.
12 I will cause your hordes to fall
     by the swords of mighty ones,
     all of them most terrible among the nations.
They shall bring to ruin the pride of Egypt,
     and all its hordes shall perish.
13 I will destroy all its livestock
     from beside abundant waters;
and no human foot shall trouble them any more,
     nor shall the hoofs of cattle trouble them.
14 Then I will make their waters clear,
     and cause their streams to run like oil, says the Lord GOD.
15 When I make the land of Egypt desolate
     and when the land is stripped of all that fills it,
when I strike down all who live in it,
     then they shall know that I am the LORD.
16 This is a lamentation; it shall be chanted.
     The women of the nations shall chant it.
Over Egypt and all its hordes they shall chant it,
     says the Lord GOD.

6. The lamentation over Egypt: the nations Egypt will join in the Pit

17 In the twelfth year, in the first month,[m] on the fifteenth day of the month, the word of the LORD came to me:
18 Mortal, wail over the hordes of Egypt,
     and send them down,
with Egypt[n] and the daughters of majestic nations,
     to the world below,
     with those who go down to the Pit.
19 "Whom do you surpass in beauty?
     Go down! Be laid to rest with the uncircumcised!"
20 They shall fall among those who are killed by the sword. Egypt[o] has been handed over to the sword; carry away both it and its hordes. 21 The mighty chiefs shall speak of them, with their helpers, out of the midst of

---

l Gk: Heb bring your destruction   m Gk: Heb lacks in the first month   n Heb it   o Heb It

---

32.9 The judgment on Egypt would cause surrounding nations to tremble. Aware of their own sins, they knew they were equally worthy of similar punishment at the hands of God.
32.15 When God stripped Egypt bare, it would demonstrate that it was *the* LORD who caused this. Unfortunately nations who refuse to acknowledge God must learn the lesson the hard way and when it is too late.

32.18 Egypt would go down to the pit, joining other nations who would welcome her with pomp and ceremony. "Sheol beneath is stirred up to meet you when you come" (Isa 14.9). Among those mentioned as having come there before Egypt are Assyria, Elam, Meshech, Tubal, Edom, and Sidon (vv. 22–30).

32.9
Ezek 28.19;
Rev 18.10-15;
Ex 15.14-16

32.10
Ezek 27.35;
26.16;
Jer 46.10

32.11
Jer 46.26;
Ezek 30.4

32.12
Ezek 28.7;
31.12; 30.18

32.13
Ezek 29.8, 11

32.15
Ezek 29.12,
19, 20;
Ps 9.16;
Ezek 6.7

32.16
2 Sam 1.17;
2 Chr 35.25;
Ezek 26.17

32.18
vv. 2, 16;
Mic 1.8;
Ezek 26.20;
31.14; v. 24

32.19
Ezek 31.2,
18; 28.10;
vv. 21, 24, 29

32.21
Isa 1.31;
14.9, 10;
vv. 27, 31, 32

Sheol: "They have come down, they lie still, the uncircumcised, killed by the sword."

32.22
Ezek 31.3, 16
32.23
Isa 14.15;
vv. 24-27, 32

22 Assyria is there, and all its company, their graves all around it, all of them killed, fallen by the sword. 23 Their graves are set in the uttermost parts of the Pit. Its company is all around its grave, all of them killed, fallen by the sword, who spread terror in the land of the living.

32.24
Jer 49.34-39;
Ps 27.13;
Isa 38.11;
Jer 11.19;
vv. 25, 30
32.25
Ps 139.8;
vv. 19, 23, 24

24 Elam is there, and all its hordes around its grave; all of them killed, fallen by the sword, who went down uncircumcised into the world below, who spread terror in the land of the living. They bear their shame with those who go down to the Pit. 25 They have made Elam[p] a bed among the slain with all its hordes, their graves all around it, all of them uncircumcised, killed by the sword; for terror of them was spread in the land of the living, and they bear their shame with those who go down to the Pit; they are placed among the slain.

32.26
Gen 10.2;
Ezek 27.13;
38.2; vv. 19,
32
32.27
Isa 14.18,
19, 21, 23

26 Meshech and Tubal are there, and all their multitude, their graves all around them, all of them uncircumcised, killed by the sword; for they spread terror in the land of the living. 27 And they do not lie with the fallen warriors of long ago[q] who went down to Sheol with their weapons of war, whose swords were laid under their heads, and whose shields[r] are upon their bones; for the terror of the warriors was in the land of the living.

32.28
v. 19

28 So you shall be broken and lie among the uncircumcised, with those who are killed by the sword.

32.29
Isa 34.5-15;
Jer 49.7-22;
Ezek 25.13

29 Edom is there, its kings and all its princes, who for all their might are laid with those who are killed by the sword; they lie with the uncircumcised, with those who go down to the Pit.

32.30
Ezek 38.6,
15; 39.2;
28.21

30 The princes of the north are there, all of them, and all the Sidonians, who have gone down in shame with the slain, for all the terror that they caused by their might; they lie uncircumcised with those who are killed by the sword, and bear their shame with those who go down to the Pit.

32.31
vv. 18, 21;
Ezek 31.16
32.32
vv. 19-24

31 When Pharaoh sees them, he will be consoled for all his hordes—Pharaoh and all his army, killed by the sword, says the Lord GOD. 32 For he[s] spread terror in the land of the living; therefore he shall be laid to rest among the uncircumcised, with those who are slain by the sword—Pharaoh and all his multitude, says the Lord GOD.

III. *Israel restored (33.1–39.29)*

A. *The prophet sentinel*

1. *Ezekiel as Israel's sentinel*

33.2
Ezek 3.11;
Jer 12.12;
Zech 13.7;
2 Sam 18.24,
25;
2 Kings 9.17
33.3
Hos 8.1;
Joel 2.1
33.4
Jer 6.17;
Zech 1.4;
Ezek 18.13;
Acts 18.6
33.5
Heb 11.7
33.6
Isa 56.10,
11; v. 8;
Ezek 3.18, 20
33.7
Ezek 3.17-21;
Jer 26.2;
Acts 5.20

33 The word of the LORD came to me: 2 O Mortal, speak to your people and say to them, If I bring the sword upon a land, and the people of the land take one of their number as their sentinel; 3 and if the sentinel sees the sword coming upon the land and blows the trumpet and warns the people; 4 then if any who hear the sound of the trumpet do not take warning, and the sword comes and takes them away, their blood shall be upon their own heads. 5 They heard the sound of the trumpet and did not take warning; their blood shall be upon themselves. But if they had taken warning, they would have saved their lives. 6 But if the sentinel sees the sword coming and does not blow the trumpet, so that the people are not warned, and the sword comes and takes any of them, they are taken away in their iniquity, but their blood I will require at the sentinel's hand.

7 So you, mortal, I have made a sentinel for the house of Israel;

p Heb *it*   *q* Gk Old Latin: Heb *of the uncircumcised*   *r* Cn: Heb *iniquities*   *s* Cn: Heb *I*

33.7 God set Ezekiel as a sentinel to warn the city of its impending destruction if the people refused to repent (cf. 3.17). When sentinels have given warning, they have discharged their trust. They have not only

whenever you hear a word from my mouth, you shall give them warning from me. [8] If I say to the wicked, "O wicked ones, you shall surely die," and you do not speak to warn the wicked to turn from their ways, the wicked shall die in their iniquity, but their blood I will require at your hand. [9] But if you warn the wicked to turn from their ways, and they do not turn from their ways, the wicked shall die in their iniquity, but you will have saved your life.

2. The sentinel's message of righteousness

10 Now you, mortal, say to the house of Israel, Thus you have said: "Our transgressions and our sins weigh upon us, and we waste away because of them; how then can we live?" [11] Say to them, As I live, says the Lord GOD, I have no pleasure in the death of the wicked, but that the wicked turn from their ways and live; turn back, turn back from your evil ways; for why will you die, O house of Israel? [12] And you, mortal, say to your people, The righteousness of the righteous shall not save them when they transgress; and as for the wickedness of the wicked, it shall not make them stumble when they turn from their wickedness; and the righteous shall not be able to live by their righteousness[t] when they sin. [13] Though I say to the righteous that they shall surely live, yet if they trust in their righteousness and commit iniquity, none of their righteous deeds shall be remembered; but in the iniquity that they have committed they shall die. [14] Again, though I say to the wicked, "You shall surely die," yet if they turn from their sin and do what is lawful and right— [15] if the wicked restore the pledge, give back what they have taken by robbery, and walk in the statutes of life, committing no iniquity — they shall surely live, they shall not die. [16] None of the sins that they have committed shall be remembered against them; they have done what is lawful and right, they shall surely live.

17 Yet your people say, "The way of the Lord is not just," when it is their own way that is not just. [18] When the righteous turn from their righteousness, and commit iniquity, they shall die for it.[u] [19] And when the wicked turn from their wickedness, and do what is lawful and right, they shall live by it.[u] [20] Yet you say, "The way of the Lord is not just." O house of Israel, I will judge all of you according to your ways!

3. The tidings of Jerusalem's fall

21 In the twelfth year of our exile, in the tenth month, on the fifth day of the month, someone who had escaped from Jerusalem came to me and said, "The city has fallen." [22] Now the hand of the LORD had been upon me the evening before the fugitive came; but he had opened my mouth by the time the fugitive came to me in the morning; so my mouth was opened, and I was no longer unable to speak.

4. The desolation to come upon the remnant

23 The word of the LORD came to me: [24] Mortal, the inhabitants of these waste places in the land of Israel keep saying, "Abraham was only

Cross references (right margin):
33.8 vv. 14, 6
33.9 Acts 13.40, 41, 46; Ezek 3.19, 21
33.10 Ezek 18.2; 24.23; 37.11
33.11 2 Sam 14.14; Ezek 18.23, 32; 2 Pet 3.9; Ezek 18.30, 31
33.12 Ezek 3.20; 2 Chr 7.14
33.13 Ezek 3.20; 18.24; 2 Pet 2.20, 21
33.14 Ezek 3.18, 19; 18.27
33.15 Lev 6.2, 4, 5; Num 5.6, 7; Lk 19.8; Ezek 20.11
33.16 Ezek 18.22
33.17 Ezek 18.25, 29; v. 20
33.18 Ezek 18.26
33.19 vv. 12, 14
33.20 Ezek 18.25; v. 17
33.21 Ezek 1.2; 24.26; 2 Kings 25.4
33.22 Ezek 1.3; 24.27; Lk 1.64
33.24 Ezek 36.4; Isa 51.2; Acts 7.5

---

t Heb by it   u Heb them

---

delivered their own souls, but also earned their wages. But if they fail to warn the wicked to flee from their wicked ways, their own souls are required of them. Ministers of the gospel should see themselves as sentinels, whose calling is to warn sinners to flee to Christ for salvation and everlasting life.
33.17 The ways of God are just, while the ways of sinners are not. In the end, all who dispute with God will discover that he is right and they are wrong.

33.21 Beginning here, Ezekiel turns from a message of disaster and judgment to a word of promise for Israel in the distant future. God opened the prophet's sealed mouth so that he could speak publicly again.
33.23ff The Jews who remained in the land after the destruction of Jerusalem claimed that if a single individual, Abraham, was given the whole land, they had a right to it. Ezekiel responded by saying that the right to the land depended on obedience, and then he listed their sins (33.25,26).

one man, yet he got possession of the land; but we are many; the land is surely given us to possess." 25 Therefore say to them, Thus says the Lord GOD: You eat flesh with the blood, and lift up your eyes to your idols, and shed blood; shall you then possess the land? 26 You depend on your swords, you commit abominations, and each of you defiles his neighbor's wife; shall you then possess the land? 27 Say this to them, Thus says the Lord GOD: As I live, surely those who are in the waste places shall fall by the sword; and those who are in the open field I will give to the wild animals to be devoured; and those who are in strongholds and in caves shall die by pestilence. 28 I will make the land a desolation and a waste, and its proud might shall come to an end; and the mountains of Israel shall be so desolate that no one will pass through. 29 Then they shall know that I am the LORD, when I have made the land a desolation and a waste because of all their abominations that they have committed.

5. *The people will hear but not heed Ezekiel*

30 As for you, mortal, your people who talk together about you by the walls, and at the doors of the houses, say to one another, each to a neighbor, "Come and hear what the word is that comes from the LORD." 31 They come to you as people come, and they sit before you as my people, and they hear your words, but they will not obey them. For flattery is on their lips, but their heart is set on their gain. 32 To them you are like a singer of love songs,*v* one who has a beautiful voice and plays well on an instrument; they hear what you say, but they will not do it. 33 When this comes — and come it will! — then they shall know that a prophet has been among them.

B. *The prophecy concerning the shepherds of Israel*

1. *Indictment of the shepherds who failed to care for their sheep*

34 The word of the LORD came to me: 2 Mortal, prophesy against the shepherds of Israel: prophesy, and say to them — to the shepherds: Thus says the Lord GOD: Ah, you shepherds of Israel who have been feeding yourselves! Should not shepherds feed the sheep? 3 You eat the fat, you clothe yourselves with the wool, you slaughter the fatlings; but you do not feed the sheep. 4 You have not strengthened the weak, you have not healed the sick, you have not bound up the injured, you have not brought back the strayed, you have not sought the lost, but with force and harshness you have ruled them. 5 So they were scattered, because there was no shepherd; and scattered, they became food for all the wild animals. 6 My sheep were scattered, they wandered over all the mountains and on every high hill; my sheep were scattered over all the face of the earth, with no one to search or seek for them.

7 Therefore, you shepherds, hear the word of the LORD: 8 As I live, says the Lord GOD, because my sheep have become a prey, and my sheep have become food for all the wild animals, since there was no shepherd; and because my shepherds have not searched for my sheep, but the shepherds have fed themselves, and have not fed my sheep; 9 therefore, you shepherds, hear the word of the LORD: 10 Thus says the Lord GOD, I am against the shepherds; and I will demand my sheep at their hand,

v Cn: Heb like a love song

Cross references (left margin):
33.25 Deut 12.16; Ezek 20.24; 22.6, 9
33.26 Ezek 18.6; 22.11
33.27 Ezek 39.4; 1 Sam 13.6; Isa 2.19
33.28 Jer 44.2, 6, 22; Ezek 7.24; 36.34, 35
33.29 Ezek 23.33, 35
33.30 vv. 2, 17; Isa 29.13; 58.2
33.31 Ezek 14.1; 20.1; 8.1; Ps 78.36, 37; Isa 29.13; Mt 13.22
33.33 1 Sam 3.20; Ezek 2.5
34.2 Jer 10.21; vv. 8-10, 14, 15; Jn 10.11; 21.15-17
34.3 Isa 56.11; Zech 11.16; Ezek 22.25, 27
34.4 Zech 11.16; Mt 9.36; Lk 15.4; 1 Pet 5.3
34.5 Jer 10.21; 50.6, 7; Jer 23.2; Mt 9.36
34.8 Acts 20.29; vv. 5, 6, 2
34.10 Ezek 3.18; Heb 13.17; vv. 2, 8

33.30ff The people put on a good show of outward religion and pretended to listen to the prophet, but inwardly they sat at his feet only for entertainment. They heard what he said, but they refused to heed him.
34.2 This prophecy against the shepherds of Israel brought indictment against the princes and magis- trates, and the priests and Levites. They had not fed the sheep, i.e., the people under their charge. Their primary interest was to improve their own condition, not that of the sheep. They were willing to shear the sheep, not to feed them. They left the sheep exposed to the wintry blasts.

and put a stop to their feeding the sheep; no longer shall the shepherds feed themselves. I will rescue my sheep from their mouths, so that they may not be food for them.

2. The Lord the shepherd of the sheep

11   For thus says the Lord God: I myself will search for my sheep, and will seek them out. 12 As shepherds seek out their flocks when they are among their scattered sheep, so I will seek out my sheep. I will rescue them from all the places to which they have been scattered on a day of clouds and thick darkness. 13 I will bring them out from the peoples and gather them from the countries, and will bring them into their own land; and I will feed them on the mountains of Israel, by the watercourses, and in all the inhabited parts of the land. 14 I will feed them with good pasture, and the mountain heights of Israel shall be their pasture; there they shall lie down in good grazing land, and they shall feed on rich pasture on the mountains of Israel. 15 I myself will be the shepherd of my sheep, and I will make them lie down, says the Lord God. 16 I will seek the lost, and I will bring back the strayed, and I will bind up the injured, and I will strengthen the weak, but the fat and the strong I will destroy. I will feed them with justice.

3. The Lord's judgment between sheep and sheep

17   As for you, my flock, thus says the Lord God: I shall judge between sheep and sheep, between rams and goats: 18 Is it not enough for you to feed on the good pasture, but you must tread down with your feet the rest of your pasture? When you drink of clear water, must you foul the rest with your feet? 19 And must my sheep eat what you have trodden with your feet, and drink what you have fouled with your feet?

20   Therefore, thus says the Lord God to them: I myself will judge between the fat sheep and the lean sheep. 21 Because you pushed with flank and shoulder, and butted at all the weak animals with your horns until you scattered them far and wide, 22 I will save my flock, and they shall no longer be ravaged; and I will judge between sheep and sheep.

4. The Messiah as the new shepherd

23   I will set up over them one shepherd, my servant David, and he shall feed them: he shall feed them and be their shepherd. 24 And I, the Lord, will be their God, and my servant David shall be prince among them; I, the Lord, have spoken.

5. The Lord's covenant of peace

25   I will make with them a covenant of peace and banish wild animals from the land, so that they may live in the wild and sleep in the woods securely. 26 I will make them and the region around my hill a blessing; and I will send down the showers in their season; they shall be showers of blessing. 27 The trees of the field shall yield their fruit, and the earth shall yield its increase. They shall be secure on their soil; and they shall know that I am the Lord, when I break the bars of their yoke, and save

---

34.11 The Lord is the chief shepherd, with a concern for and an interest in his sheep. They would be scattered far and wide, but he would search for them, find them, restore them to their land, and sustain them by providing for them. This verse has both an immediate and a long-range fulfillment. The remnant of the Jews would return to Palestine, and at the end of the age there will be the full and final fulfillment of the divine promise, marked by the second advent of Jesus Christ as the glorious victor over sin and death.

34.23 *one shepherd.* This is a specific prophecy about Jesus the Messiah, the son of David. Here he is specifically called *my servant David.* David had died long before this prophetic word was spoken, but it refers to the Davidic covenant, in which God promised that one of David's descendants would always sit on the throne of David. In his sermon in Acts 2, Peter made it clear that Jesus now sits on the throne of his father David and that he will come at last to rule and reign over the whole earth.

34.11
Ezek 11.17;
20.41
34.12
Jn 10.16;
Ezek 30.3;
Joel 2.2
34.13
Isa 65.9, 10;
Jer 23.3;
Ezek 37.22;
Isa 30.25
34.14
Ps 23.1, 2;
Ezek 20.40;
28.25, 26
34.16
Mt 18.11;
Lk 5.32;
Isa 49.26

34.17
Ezek 20.37,
38;
Zech 10.3;
Mt 25.32, 33
34.18
2 Sam 7.19

34.20
v. 17
34.21
Deut 33.17;
Dan 8.4
34.22
vv. 5, 8, 10,
17

34.23
Isa 40.11;
Jer 23.4, 5;
30.9;
Hos 3.5
34.24
Ezek 36.28;
37.27; 37.24,
25;
Hos 3.5
34.25
Isa 11.6-9;
Hos 2.18;
Jer 23.6
34.26
Isa 56.7;
Zech 8.13
34.27
Ps 85.12;
Isa 4.2;
Jer 2.20

them from the hands of those who enslaved them. 28 They shall no more be plunder for the nations, nor shall the animals of the land devour them; they shall live in safety, and no one shall make them afraid. 29 I will provide for them a splendid vegetation so that they shall no more be consumed with hunger in the land, and no longer suffer the insults of the nations. 30 They shall know that I, the LORD their God, am with them, and that they, the house of Israel, are my people, says the Lord GOD. 31 You are my sheep, the sheep of my pasture[w] and I am your God, says the Lord GOD.

C. The prophecy against Mount Seir

35 The word of the LORD came to me: 2 Mortal, set your face against Mount Seir, and prophesy against it, 3 and say to it, Thus says the Lord GOD:

I am against you, Mount Seir;
I stretch out my hand against you
to make you a desolation and a waste.

4 I lay your towns in ruins;
you shall become a desolation,
and you shall know that I am the LORD.

5 Because you cherished an ancient enmity, and gave over the people of Israel to the power of the sword at the time of their calamity, at the time of their final punishment; 6 therefore, as I live, says the Lord GOD, I will prepare you for blood, and blood shall pursue you; since you did not hate bloodshed, bloodshed shall pursue you. 7 I will make Mount Seir a waste and a desolation; and I will cut off from it all who come and go. 8 I will fill its mountains with the slain; on your hills and in your valleys and in all your watercourses those killed with the sword shall fall. 9 I will make you a perpetual desolation, and your cities shall never be inhabited. Then you shall know that I am the LORD.

10 Because you said, "These two nations and these two countries shall be mine, and we will take possession of them,"—although the LORD was there— 11 therefore, as I live, says the Lord GOD, I will deal with you according to the anger and envy that you showed because of your hatred against them; and I will make myself known among you,[x] when I judge you. 12 You shall know that I, the LORD, have heard all the abusive speech that you uttered against the mountains of Israel, saying, "They are laid desolate, they are given us to devour." 13 And you magnified yourselves against me with your mouth, and multiplied your words against me; I heard it. 14 Thus says the Lord GOD: As the whole earth rejoices, I will make you desolate. 15 As you rejoiced over the inheritance of the house of Israel, because it was desolate, so I will deal with you; you shall be desolate, Mount Seir, and all Edom, all of it. Then they shall know that I am the LORD.

D. The restoration of Israel

1. Judgment on Israel's oppressors

36 And you, mortal, prophesy to the mountains of Israel, and say: O mountains of Israel, hear the word of the LORD. 2 Thus says the

Margin cross-references:

34.28 Jer 30.10
34.29 Isa 60.21; Ezek 36.29, 3, 6
34.30 Ezek 36.28; 37.27
34.31 Ps 100.3; Jn 10.11

35.2 Jer 49.7, 8
35.3 Ezek 21.3; Jer 6.12; 15.6; Ezek 25.13; v. 7
35.4 v. 9; Mal 1.3, 4
35.5 Ezek 25.12; Ob 10; Ezek 7.2; 21.25, 29
35.6 Ezek 16.38; 32.6
35.7 Ezek 25.13; 29.11
35.8 Isa 34.5, 6; Ezek 31.12; 32.4, 5
35.9 Jer 49.13; Ezek 6.7; 36.11
35.10 Ezek 36.2, 5; Ps 48.1, 3; Ezek 48.35
35.11 Am 1.11; Mt 7.2; Ps 9.16
35.13 Ezek 36.3; Jer 7.11; 29.23
35.14 Isa 49.13; Jer 51.48
35.15 Jer 50.11; Ob 4, 21; Ezek 6.7

36.1 Ezek 6.2, 3
36.2 Ezek 25.3; Hab 3.19; Ezek 35.10

[w] Gk OL: Heb *pasture, you are people*   [x] Gk: Heb *them*

35.2 *Seir,* i.e., Edom (see note on Gen 36.9).
35.15 The major sin of Edom was its rejoicing over the desolation of Israel. This insulted God, who continued to love Israel and to remember his covenant with that nation. Therefore Edom would be destroyed and other nations would rejoice over its destruction, as Edom did over Israel's.

36.1ff Canaan, Israel's land, had been emptied of its people and was now occupied by enemies of Israel. God proclaimed that he would judge those who had taken over his land and would later return its mountains, hills, watercourses, and valleys to those in whom he delighted.

Lord God: Because the enemy said of you, "Aha!" and, "The ancient heights have become our possession," 3 therefore prophesy, and say: Thus says the Lord God: Because they made you desolate indeed, and crushed you from all sides, so that you became the possession of the rest of the nations, and you became an object of gossip and slander among the people; 4 therefore, O mountains of Israel, hear the word of the Lord God: Thus says the Lord God to the mountains and the hills, the watercourses and the valleys, the desolate wastes and the deserted towns, which have become a source of plunder and an object of derision to the rest of the nations all around; 5 therefore thus says the Lord God: I am speaking in my hot jealousy against the rest of the nations, and against all Edom, who, with wholehearted joy and utter contempt, took my land as their possession, because of its pasture, to plunder it. 6 Therefore prophesy concerning the land of Israel, and say to the mountains and hills, to the watercourses and valleys, Thus says the Lord God: I am speaking in my jealous wrath, because you have suffered the insults of the nations; 7 therefore thus says the Lord God: I swear that the nations that are all around you shall themselves suffer insults.

2. Israel to be returned

8 But you, O mountains of Israel, shall shoot out your branches, and yield your fruit to my people Israel; for they shall soon come home. 9 See now, I am for you; I will turn to you, and you shall be tilled and sown; 10 and I will multiply your population, the whole house of Israel, all of it; the towns shall be inhabited and the waste places rebuilt; 11 and I will multiply human beings and animals upon you. They shall increase and be fruitful; and I will cause you to be inhabited as in your former times, and will do more good to you than ever before. Then you shall know that I am the Lord. 12 I will lead people upon you — my people Israel — and they shall possess you, and you shall be their inheritance. No longer shall you bereave them of children.

13 Thus says the Lord God: Because they say to you, "You devour people, and you bereave your nation of children," 14 therefore you shall no longer devour people and no longer bereave your nation of children, says the Lord God; 15 and no longer will I let you hear the insults of the nations, no longer shall you bear the disgrace of the peoples; and no longer shall you cause your nation to stumble, says the Lord God.

3. Israel's punishment due to idolatry

16 The word of the Lord came to me: 17 Mortal, when the house of Israel lived on their own soil, they defiled it with their ways and their deeds; their conduct in my sight was like the uncleanness of a woman in her menstrual period. 18 So I poured out my wrath upon them for the blood that they had shed upon the land, and for the idols with which they had defiled it. 19 I scattered them among the nations, and they were dispersed through the countries; in accordance with their conduct and their deeds I judged them. 20 But when they came to the nations, wherever they came, they profaned my holy name, in that it was said of them, "These are the people of the Lord, and yet they had to go out of his land." 21 But I had concern for my holy name, which the house of Israel had profaned among the nations to which they came.

36.3
Jer 2.15;
51.34; 18.16;
Ezek 35.13

36.4
Ezek 6.3;
34.28;
Ps 79.4;
Jer 48.27

36.5
Ezek 38.19;
25.12-14;
35.10, 12;
Jer 50.11;
Mic 7.8
36.6
Ps 123.3, 4;
Ezek 34.29
36.7
Ezek 20.6,
15, 23;
Jer 25.9, 15,
29

36.8
v. 4;
Isa 27.6;
Ezek 17.23
36.10
Isa 27.6;
Ezek 37.21,
22; v. 33
36.11
Jer 30.18;
Ezek 16.55;
35.9

36.13
Num 13.32

36.15
Ezek 34.29;
22.4;
Jer 13.16;
18.15

36.17
Lev 18.25,
27, 28;
Jer 2.7
36.18
Ezek 22.20;
16.36, 38;
23.37
36.19
Am 9.9;
Ezek 39.24;
Rom 2.6
36.20
Isa 52.5;
Rom 2.24;
Jer 33.24
36.21
Ps 74.18;
Isa 48.9;
Ezek 20.44

36.16ff The downfall of Israel enabled the pagan nations to scorn Israel and its God. They taunted them by saying that their God could hardly be worthy of devotion, for he had been unable to keep them from these disasters. God made it clear, however, that it was his concern for his holy name that made him destroy Israel (v. 21). And that same concern would cause him to bring his people back (vv. 22–25).

4. The Lord himself to regather Israel

22 Therefore say to the house of Israel, Thus says the Lord God: It is not for your sake, O house of Israel, that I am about to act, but for the sake of my holy name, which you have profaned among the nations to which you came. 23 I will sanctify my great name, which has been profaned among the nations, and which you have profaned among them; and the nations shall know that I am the Lord, says the Lord God, when through you I display my holiness before their eyes. 24 I will take you from the nations, and gather you from all the countries, and bring you into your own land. 25 I will sprinkle clean water upon you, and you shall be clean from all your uncleannesses, and from all your idols I will cleanse you. 26 A new heart I will give you, and a new spirit I will put within you; and I will remove from your body the heart of stone and give you a heart of flesh. 27 I will put my spirit within you, and make you follow my statutes and be careful to observe my ordinances. 28 Then you shall live in the land that I gave to your ancestors; and you shall be my people, and I will be your God. 29 I will save you from all your uncleannesses, and I will summon the grain and make it abundant and lay no famine upon you. 30 I will make the fruit of the tree and the produce of the field abundant, so that you may never again suffer the disgrace of famine among the nations. 31 Then you shall remember your evil ways, and your dealings that were not good; and you shall loathe yourselves for your iniquities and your abominable deeds. 32 It is not for your sake that I will act, says the Lord God; let that be known to you. Be ashamed and dismayed for your ways, O house of Israel.

5. The cities to be inhabited; the waste places rebuilt

33 Thus says the Lord God: On the day that I cleanse you from all your iniquities, I will cause the towns to be inhabited, and the waste places shall be rebuilt. 34 The land that was desolate shall be tilled, instead of being the desolation that it was in the sight of all who passed by. 35 And they will say, "This land that was desolate has become like the garden of Eden; and the waste and desolate and ruined towns are now inhabited and fortified." 36 Then the nations that are left all around you shall know that I, the Lord, have rebuilt the ruined places, and replanted that which was desolate; I, the Lord, have spoken, and I will do it.

6. The people to increase in number

37 Thus says the Lord God: I will also let the house of Israel ask me to do this for them: to increase their population like a flock. 38 Like the flock for sacrifices,^y like the flock at Jerusalem during her appointed festivals, so shall the ruined towns be filled with flocks of people. Then they shall know that I am the Lord.

E. The vision of the dry bones in the valley: Israel to be regathered

37 The hand of the Lord came upon me, and he brought me out by the spirit of the Lord and set me down in the middle of a valley; it was full of bones. 2 He led me all around them; there were very many

^y Heb *flock of holy things*

Cross references (left margin):

36.22
Ps 106.8

36.23
Ezek 20.41;
Ps 126.2;
Ezek 28.25;
39.27
36.24
Ezek 34.13;
37.21
36.25
Isa 52.15;
Heb 10.22;
Zech 13.1
36.26
Ps 51.10;
Ezek 11.19
36.27
Ezek 11.19;
37.14
36.28
Jer 30.22;
Ezek 11.20;
37.27
36.29
Zech 13.1
36.30
Ezek 34.27,
29;
Hos 2.21-23
36.31
Ezek 16.61-63;
20.43; 6.9
36.32
Ezek 20.44;
v. 22

36.33
v. 25;
Zech 8.7, 8;
Isa 58.12;
v. 10
36.34
v. 9
36.35
Isa 51.3;
Ezek 31.9;
Joel 2.3
36.36
Ezek 39.27,
28; 22.14;
37.14

36.38
1 Kings 8.63;
vv. 33-35;
Zech 11.17

37.1
Ezek 1.3;
8.3; 11.24;
Lk 4.1;
Acts 8.39
37.2
v. 11

36.25,26 God promised to cleanse his people from the pollution of sin and to deliver them from the guilt, penalty, and power of sin. He would replace their hearts of stone with new hearts, enabling them to see and think correctly. It would be a soft and tender heart, brought about by his renewing grace. They would then walk according to God's will and commandments, for they would have the Spirit of God in his fullness. By his sanctifying power (v. 27), they would be empowered to live holy lives.

37.1ff What a desolate scene! A valley filled with skeletons of people slain in battle and left for birds to eat the flesh. This is a vision of how Israel would look after God's judgment had taken place.

lying in the valley, and they were very dry. 3 He said to me, "Mortal, can these bones live?" I answered, "O Lord GOD, you know." 4 Then he said to me, "Prophesy to these bones, and say to them: O dry bones, hear the word of the LORD. 5 Thus says the Lord GOD to these bones: I will cause breath[z] to enter you, and you shall live. 6 I will lay sinews on you, and will cause flesh to come upon you, and cover you with skin, and put breath[z] in you, and you shall live; and you shall know that I am the LORD."

7   So I prophesied as I had been commanded; and as I prophesied, suddenly there was a noise, a rattling, and the bones came together, bone to its bone. 8 I looked, and there were sinews on them, and flesh had come upon them, and skin had covered them; but there was no breath in them. 9 Then he said to me, "Prophesy to the breath, prophesy, mortal, and say to the breath:[a] Thus says the Lord GOD: Come from the four winds, O breath,[a] and breathe upon these slain, that they may live." 10 I prophesied as he commanded me, and the breath came into them, and they lived, and stood on their feet, a vast multitude.

11   Then he said to me, "Mortal, these bones are the whole house of Israel. They say, 'Our bones are dried up, and our hope is lost; we are cut off completely.' 12 Therefore prophesy, and say to them, Thus says the Lord GOD: I am going to open your graves, and bring you up from your graves, O my people; and I will bring you back to the land of Israel. 13 And you shall know that I am the LORD, when I open your graves, and bring you up from your graves, O my people. 14 I will put my spirit within you, and you shall live, and I will place you on your own soil; then you shall know that I, the LORD, have spoken and will act, says the LORD."

F. *The union of the two sticks (Israel and Judah)*

15   The word of the LORD came to me: 16 Mortal, take a stick and write on it, "For Judah, and the Israelites associated with it"; then take another stick and write on it, "For Joseph (the stick of Ephraim) and all the house of Israel associated with it"; 17 and join them together into one stick, so that they may become one in your hand. 18 And when your people say to you, "Will you not show us what you mean by these?" 19 say to them, Thus says the Lord GOD: I am about to take the stick of Joseph (which is in the hand of Ephraim) and the tribes of Israel associated with it; and I will put the stick of Judah upon it,[b] and make them one stick, in order that they may be one in my hand. 20 When the sticks on which you write are in your hand before their eyes, 21 then say to them, Thus says the Lord GOD: I will take the people of Israel from the nations among which they have gone, and will gather them from every quarter, and bring them to their own land. 22 I will make them one nation in the land, on the mountains of Israel; and one king shall be king over them all. Never again shall they be two nations, and never again shall they be divided into two kingdoms. 23 They shall never again defile themselves with their idols and their detestable things, or with any of their transgressions. I will save them from all the apostasies into which they have fallen,[c] and will cleanse them. Then they shall be my people, and I will be their God.

24   My servant David shall be king over them; and they shall all have

37.3	Isa 26.19; Deut 32.39; 1 Sam 2.6
37.4	vv. 9, 12; Isa 42.18; Ezek 36.1
37.5	Ps 104.29, 30; vv. 9, 10
37.6	vv. 8-10; Ezek 6.7; 35.12; Joel 2.27; 3.17
37.7	Jer 13.5-7; Ezek 38.19
37.9	Ps 104.30; v. 5; Hos 13.14
37.10	vv. 5, 6; Rev 11.11
37.11	Ezek 36.10; 39.25; Ps 141.7; Isa 49.14
37.12	Isa 26.19; Hos 13.14; v. 25; Ezek 36.24; Am 9.14, 15
37.13	Ezek 6.7; vv. 6, 12
37.14	Ezek 36.27; 39.29; 36.36
37.16	Num 17.2; 2 Chr 11.11-17; 15.9
37.17	vv. 22-24
37.18	Ezek 12.9; 24.19
37.19	Zech 10.6; vv. 16, 17
37.21	Ezek 36.24; 39.27
37.22	Isa 11.13; Jer 3.18; Hos 1.11; Ezek 34.23
37.23	Ezek 11.18; 43.7; 36.25; 36.28
37.24	Jer 30.9; Isa 40.11; Hos 3.5; Ezek 36.27

---

[z] Or *spirit*   [a] Or *wind* or *spirit*   [b] Heb *I will put them upon it*   [c] Another reading is *from all the settlements in which they have sinned*

37.11   The dry bones represented dead Israel. Ezekiel prophesied that God would restore Israel, i.e., bring back life to the dry bones (vv. 11–14). Some see this as fulfilled in Israel's return to the promised land after the captivity; others look on this as a prophecy that will yet be fulfilled.
37.15ff   The Davidic kingdom was divided into two kingdoms after the death of Solomon. That division

has never been overcome; no reunion took place (though see note on 23.36ff). Here God promised that the northern and the southern kingdoms would someday be rejoined in peace, harmony, and goodwill. The two would become one nation before God, undefiled and full of the knowledge of God.
37.24ff   Some think the promises made here to Israel are to be fulfilled in the church, which they believe

37.25
Ezek 28.25;
36.28;
Zech 6.12
37.26
Isa 55.3;
Ezek 36.10;
20.40; 43.7
37.27
Lev 26.11;
Jn 1.14
37.28
Ezek 36.23;
20.12

one shepherd. They shall follow my ordinances and be careful to observe my statutes. 25 They shall live in the land that I gave to my servant Jacob, in which your ancestors lived; they and their children and their children's children shall live there forever; and my servant David shall be their prince forever. 26 I will make a covenant of peace with them; it shall be an everlasting covenant with them; and I will bless[d] them and multiply them, and will set my sanctuary among them forevermore. 27 My dwelling place shall be with them; and I will be their God, and they shall be my people. 28 Then the nations shall know that I the LORD sanctify Israel, when my sanctuary is among them forevermore.

G. The prophecy of Gog and Magog

1. The hordes of Gog to be assembled

38.2
Ezek 39.1;
Rev 20.8
38.3
Ezek 39.1
38.4
2 Kings 19.28;
Ezek 39.2
38.5
Ezek 27.10;
30.4, 5
38.6
Gen 10.2;
Ezek 27.14
38.7
Jer 46.3;
51.12
38.8
Isa 24.22;
Ezek 36.24
38.9
Isa 28.2;
Joel 2.2

38 The word of the LORD came to me: 2 Mortal, set your face toward Gog, of the land of Magog, the chief prince of Meshech and Tubal. Prophesy against him 3 and say: Thus says the Lord GOD: I am against you, O Gog, chief prince of Meshech and Tubal; 4 I will turn you around and put hooks into your jaws, and I will lead you out with all your army, horses and horsemen, all of them clothed in full armor, a great company, all of them with shield and buckler, wielding swords. 5 Persia, Ethiopia,[e] and Put are with them, all of them with buckler and helmet; 6 Gomer and all its troops; Beth-togarmah from the remotest parts of the north with all its troops — many peoples are with you.

7 Be ready and keep ready, you and all the companies that are assembled around you, and hold yourselves in reserve for them. 8 After many days you shall be mustered; in the latter years you shall go against a land restored from war, a land where people were gathered from many nations on the mountains of Israel, which had long lain waste; its people were brought out from the nations and now are living in safety, all of them. 9 You shall advance, coming on like a storm; you shall be like a cloud covering the land, you and all your troops, and many peoples with you.

2. The evil scheme of Gog

38.10
Mic 2.1
38.11
Zech 2.4;
Jer 49.31;
v. 8
38.12
Isa 10.6;
Ezek 29.19;
v. 8
38.13
Ezek 27.22;
27.15;
Nah 2.11-13

10 Thus says the Lord GOD: On that day thoughts will come into your mind, and you will devise an evil scheme. 11 You will say, "I will go up against the land of unwalled villages; I will fall upon the quiet people who live in safety, all of them living without walls, and having no bars or gates"; 12 to seize spoil and carry off plunder; to assail the waste places that are now inhabited, and the people who were gathered from the nations, who are acquiring cattle and goods, who live at the center[f] of the earth. 13 Sheba and Dedan and the merchants of Tarshish and all its

[d] Tg: Heb *give*   [e] Or *Nubia*; Heb *Cush*   [f] Heb *navel*

---

to be the new Israel. Others hold that there must be a literal fulfillment of this prophecy, that Israel and the church are two separate entities with different destinies. Still others think that while Jews and Gentiles comprise the one body (the church), yet Israel will literally be regathered, Christ will rule over them, and the temple will be rebuilt. Much depends on one's view of the millennium (see the note on Rev 20.2 for information on the various millennial views; see also the note on 43.19).
38.2 Chapters 38 and 39 picture, at the end of the age, an attack on Israel by a collusion of wicked powers. They will be defeated by God and Israel will be delivered. Magog is headed up by Gog. That nation, along with Meshech and Tubal, are descendants of the sons of Japheth (Gen 10.2). They have been identified with the Russians, Scythians, Goths, and Cre-

tans, but such identifications are not certain. Gog and Magog are also mentioned in Rev 20.8 as leaders in the final rebellion against God. The size and fearsomeness of the battle can be seen from the statistics connected with it. The weapons of war left after the battle will provide fuel for seven years, and it will take seven months to finish burying the dead. Some premillennialists think there are two battles described here — one at the end of the tribulation and the other at the end of the millennium. Amillennialists take this battle as a symbol of the ongoing struggle of Satan against God's people, the church, a battle that Christ will ultimately win.
38.5,6 Other nations involved in this titanic struggle are allied with those mentioned in v. 2 — possibly people from Iran, Ethiopia, Turkey, and the Ukraine.
38.13 *Sheba and Dedan* are Arab peoples.

young warriors[g] will say to you, "Have you come to seize spoil? Have you assembled your horde to carry off plunder, to carry away silver and gold, to take away cattle and goods, to seize a great amount of booty?"

3. Gog descends on Israel

14 Therefore, mortal, prophesy, and say to Gog: Thus says the Lord GOD: On that day when my people Israel are living securely, you will rouse yourself[h] 15 and come from your place out of the remotest parts of the north, you and many peoples with you, all of them riding on horses, a great horde, a mighty army; 16 you will come up against my people Israel, like a cloud covering the earth. In the latter days I will bring you against my land, so that the nations may know me, when through you, O Gog, I display my holiness before their eyes.

4. The defeat of Gog

17 Thus says the Lord GOD: Are you he of whom I spoke in former days by my servants the prophets of Israel, who in those days prophesied for years that I would bring you against them? 18 On that day, when Gog comes against the land of Israel, says the Lord GOD, my wrath shall be aroused. 19 For in my jealousy and in my blazing wrath I declare: On that day there shall be a great shaking in the land of Israel; 20 the fish of the sea, and the birds of the air, and the animals of the field, and all creeping things that creep on the ground, and all human beings that are on the face of the earth, shall quake at my presence, and the mountains shall be thrown down, and the cliffs shall fall, and every wall shall tumble to the ground. 21 I will summon the sword against Gog[i] in[j] all my mountains, says the Lord GOD; the swords of all will be against their comrades. 22 With pestilence and bloodshed I will enter into judgment with him; and I will pour down torrential rains and hailstones, fire and sulfur, upon him and his troops and the many peoples that are with him. 23 So I will display my greatness and my holiness and make myself known in the eyes of many nations. Then they shall know that I am the LORD.

5. The slaughtered hordes of Gog to be buried

39 And you, mortal, prophesy against Gog, and say: Thus says the Lord GOD: I am against you, O Gog, chief prince of Meshech and Tubal! 2 I will turn you around and drive you forward, and bring you up from the remotest parts of the north, and lead you against the mountains of Israel. 3 I will strike your bow from your left hand, and will make your arrows drop out of your right hand. 4 You shall fall upon the mountains of Israel, you and all your troops and the peoples that are with you; I will give you to birds of prey of every kind and to the wild animals to be devoured. 5 You shall fall in the open field; for I have spoken, says the Lord GOD. 6 I will send fire on Magog and on those who live securely in the coastlands; and they shall know that I am the LORD.

7 My holy name I will make known among my people Israel; and I will not let my holy name be profaned any more; and the nations shall know that I am the LORD, the Holy One in Israel. 8 It has come! It has happened, says the Lord GOD. This is the day of which I have spoken.

g Heb young lions   h Gk: Heb will you not know?   i Heb him   j Heb to or for

38.14
Jer 23.6;
Zech 2.5, 8
38.15
v. 6;
Ezek 39.2
38.16
Ezek 36.23;
39.21

38.17
Isa 34.1-6

38.18
v. 2;
Ps 18.8, 15
38.19
Ezek 36.5, 6;
Nah 1.2;
Hag 2.6, 7;
Rev 16.18
38.20
Jer 4.24;
Hos 4.3;
Nah 1.5, 6;
Zech 14.4
38.21
Ezek 14.17;
Judg 7.22;
1 Sam 14.20;
2 Chr 20.23
38.22
Isa 66.16;
Jer 25.31;
Rev 16.21;
Ps 11.6
38.23
Ezek 36.23;
Ps 9.16;
Ezek 37.28
39.1
Ezek 38.2-4
39.2
Ezek 38.15
39.3
Ezek 30.21-24;
Hos 1.5
39.4
Ezek 38.21;
33.37
39.6
Ezek 38.22;
Am 1.4;
Ps 72.10;
Jer 25.22
39.7
Ezek 36.20-22;
v. 25;
Ezek 20.39;
38.16;
Isa 60.9, 14
39.8
Ezek 38.17

38.14 *when my people Israel are living securely.* God will return Israel to the land, and their safety will come from him as their protector, who is a wall of fire around them.
38.17ff In this final battle God will personally engage the enemy and defeat Gog and his allies. By this he will show his omnipotence and his holiness. The heathen will learn from this that God is God.

39.1ff God reiterates the certainty of the complete destruction of Gog and his partners in crime. He illustrates the vastness of the destruction of the enemy in three ways: (1) their armaments will be used for fuel for seven years; (2) it will take seven months to bury all of the dead; (3) the fowls of the air will feast on the flesh of the unburied dead.

9   Then those who live in the towns of Israel will go out and make fires of the weapons and burn them — bucklers and shields, bows and arrows, handpikes and spears — and they will make fires of them for seven years. 10 They will not need to take wood out of the field or cut down any trees in the forests, for they will make their fires of the weapons; they will despoil those who despoiled them, and plunder those who plundered them, says the Lord GOD.

11   On that day I will give to Gog a place for burial in Israel, the Valley of the Travelers*k* east of the sea; it shall block the path of the travelers, for there Gog and all his horde will be buried; it shall be called the Valley of Hamon-gog.*l* 12 Seven months the house of Israel shall spend burying them, in order to cleanse the land. 13 All the people of the land shall bury them; and it will bring them honor on the day that I show my glory, says the Lord GOD. 14 They will set apart men to pass through the land regularly and bury any invaders*m* who remain on the face of the land, so as to cleanse it; for seven months they shall make their search. 15 As the searchers*m* pass through the land, anyone who sees a human bone shall set up a sign by it, until the buriers have buried it in the Valley of Hamon-gog.*l* 16 (A city Hamonah*n* is there also.) Thus they shall cleanse the land.

6. The sacrificial feast of the LORD

17   As for you, mortal, thus says the Lord GOD: Speak to the birds of every kind and to all the wild animals: Assemble and come, gather from all around to the sacrificial feast that I am preparing for you, a great sacrificial feast on the mountains of Israel, and you shall eat flesh and drink blood. 18 You shall eat the flesh of the mighty, and drink the blood of the princes of the earth — of rams, of lambs, and of goats, of bulls, all of them fatlings of Bashan. 19 You shall eat fat until you are filled, and drink blood until you are drunk, at the sacrificial feast that I am preparing for you. 20 And you shall be filled at my table with horses and charioteers,*o* with warriors and all kinds of soldiers, says the Lord GOD.

21   I will display my glory among the nations; and all the nations shall see my judgment that I have executed, and my hand that I have laid on them. 22 The house of Israel shall know that I am the LORD their God, from that day forward. 23 And the nations shall know that the house of Israel went into captivity for their iniquity, because they dealt treacherously with me. So I hid my face from them and gave them into the hand of their adversaries, and they all fell by the sword. 24 I dealt with them according to their uncleanness and their transgressions, and hid my face from them.

7. The regathering of God's people: Israel shall know the LORD

25   Therefore thus says the Lord GOD: Now I will restore the fortunes of Jacob, and have mercy on the whole house of Israel; and I will be jealous for my holy name. 26 They shall forget*p* their shame, and all the treachery they have practiced against me, when they live securely in their land with no one to make them afraid, 27 when I have brought them back from the peoples and gathered them from their enemies' lands, and through them

k Or of the Abarim   *l* That is, the Horde of Gog   *m* Heb travelers   *n* That is The Horde   *o* Heb chariots
p Another reading is They shall bear

39.21ff The wicked nations will see the glory of God manifested and know that what happened to Israel was the doing of God, as recompense for their transgressions. Israel will also learn the hard lesson that the one who has done all this is the Lord their God.

39.25 Behind the sin, the shame, and the judgments of God, one can discern the merciful face of a tender and loving father whose intention toward Israel is to restore their fortunes. God will wipe out the memory of their sins, and they will fear no more.

have displayed my holiness in the sight of many nations. 28 Then they shall know that I am the Lord their God because I sent them into exile among the nations; and then gathered them into their own land. I will leave none of them behind; 29 and I will never again hide my face from them, when I pour out my spirit upon the house of Israel, says the Lord God.

IV. *Israel in the land in the coming age (40.1–48.35)*

A. *The new temple arrangements*

1. *Introduction*

40 In the twenty-fifth year of our exile, at the beginning of the year, on the tenth day of the month, in the fourteenth year after the city was struck down, on that very day, the hand of the Lord was upon me, and he brought me there. 2 He brought me, in visions of God, to the land of Israel, and set me down upon a very high mountain, on which was a structure like a city to the south. 3 When he brought me there, a man was there, whose appearance shone like bronze, with a linen cord and a measuring reed in his hand; and he was standing in the gateway. 4 The man said to me, "Mortal, look closely and listen attentively, and set your mind upon all that I shall show you, for you were brought here in order that I might show it to you; declare all that you see to the house of Israel."

2. *The east gate of the outer court*

5 Now there was a wall all around the outside of the temple area. The length of the measuring reed in the man's hand was six long cubits, each being a cubit and a handbreadth in length; so he measured the thickness of the wall, one reed; and the height, one reed. 6 Then he went into the gateway facing east, going up its steps, and measured the threshold of the gate, one reed deep.*q* There were 7 recesses, and each recess was one reed wide and one reed deep; and the space between the recesses, five cubits; and the threshold of the gate by the vestibule of the gate at the inner end was one reed deep. 8 Then he measured the inner vestibule of the gateway, one cubit. 9 Then he measured the vestibule of the gateway, eight cubits; and its pilasters, two cubits; and the vestibule of the gate was at the inner end. 10 There were three recesses on either side of the east gate; the three were of the same size; and the pilasters on either side were of the same size. 11 Then he measured the width of the opening of the gateway, ten cubits; and the width of the gateway, thirteen cubits. 12 There was a barrier before the recesses, one cubit on either side; and the recesses were six cubits on either side. 13 Then he measured the gate from the back*r* of the one recess to the back*r* of the other, a width of twenty-five cubits, from wall to wall.*s* 14 He measured*t* also the vestibule, twenty cubits;

q Heb deep, and one threshold, one reed deep   r Gk: Heb roof   s Heb opening facing opening   t Heb made

Cross references (right margin):

39.28 Ezek 34.30; v. 22

39.29 Isa 32.15; Ezek 36.27; 37.14; Joel 2.28; Acts 2.17

40.1 Ezek 33.21; 1.2, 3

40.2 Ezek 8.3; Dan 7.1, 7; Ezek 17.23; Rev 21.10

40.3 Ezek 1.7; Dan 10.6; Ezek 47.3; Rev 11.1; 21.15

40.4 Ezek 44.5; 43.10; Jer 26.2; Acts 20.27

40.5 Ezek 42.20; v. 3

40.6 vv. 20, 26

40.7 vv. 10-16, 21, 29, 33, 36

40.10 v. 7

40.14 vv. 9, 16; 1 Chr 28.6; Isa 62.9; Ezek 42.1

39.29 The indwelling of the Holy Spirit guarantees the presence and the blessing of God. The Spirit of God had departed from Israel, but God promises here that his Spirit will be poured out on the revived house of Israel in the latter days, when Israel turns to God in repentance and in faith looks to Jesus, the true Messiah, for salvation (see the note on Eph 1.13, on the sealing of the Holy Spirit). Again, Christians do not agree on whether this refers to literal Israel or the new Israel of God (the church).

40.1 The remainder of Ezekiel's prophecy was given to him in visions by God, who brought him to the land of Israel for this purpose. Detailed instructions are given for rebuilding the temple and for its services. Israel and God will be in full fellowship with

each other, and Israel's national life will be reconstructed without interruption or discord (see note on 43.19).

40.3 *a man was there.* This was not an angel but Christ himself via Ezekiel's vision. His bronze appearance denotes brightness and strength. In Rev 1.15 Jesus is pictured as having feet of bronze.

40.5 A wall separates the temple from the world and is under divine protection. Christians have bodies that are temples of the Holy Spirit, and as such must be separated from the world and protected by God.

40.6ff Ezekiel describes the large gateway on the east. There were three side rooms serving as guardrooms to control the use of the passageway.

and the gate next to the pilaster on every side of the court.ᵘ 15 From the front of the gate at the entrance to the end of the inner vestibule of the gate was fifty cubits. 16 The recesses and their pilasters had windows, with shuttersᵘ on the inside of the gateway all around; and the vestibules also had windows on the inside all around; and on the pilasters were palm trees.

3. *The thirty chambers about the court*

17 Then he brought me into the outer court; there were chambers there, and a pavement, all around the court; thirty chambers fronted on the pavement. 18 The pavement ran along the side of the gates, corresponding to the length of the gates; this was the lower pavement. 19 Then he measured the distance from the inner front ofᵛ the lower gate to the outer front of the inner court, one hundred cubits.ʷ

4. *The north gate of the outer court*

20 Then he measured the gate of the outer court that faced north—its depth and width. 21 Its recesses, three on either side, and its pilasters and its vestibule were of the same size as those of the first gate; its depth was fifty cubits, and its width twenty-five cubits. 22 Its windows, its vestibule, and its palm trees were of the same size as those of the gate that faced toward the east. Seven steps led up to it; and its vestibule was on the inside.ˣ 23 Opposite the gate on the north, as on the east, was a gate to the inner court; he measured from gate to gate, one hundred cubits.

5. *The south gate of the outer court*

24 Then he led me toward the south, and there was a gate on the south; and he measured its pilasters and its vestibule; they had the same dimensions as the others. 25 There were windows all around in it and in its vestibule, like the windows of the others; its depth was fifty cubits, and its width twenty-five cubits. 26 There were seven steps leading up to it; its vestibule was on the inside.ˣ It had palm trees on its pilasters, one on either side. 27 There was a gate on the south of the inner court; and he measured from gate to gate toward the south, one hundred cubits.

6. *The gates of the inner court*

28 Then he brought me to the inner court by the south gate, and he measured the south gate; it was of the same dimensions as the others. 29 Its recesses, its pilasters, and its vestibule were of the same size as the others; and there were windows all around in it and in its vestibule; its depth was fifty cubits, and its width twenty-five cubits. 30 There were vestibules all around, twenty-five cubits deep and five cubits wide. 31 Its vestibule faced the outer court, and palm trees were on its pilasters, and its stairway had eight steps.

32 Then he brought me to the inner court on the east side, and he measured the gate; it was of the same size as the others. 33 Its recesses, its pilasters, and its vestibule were of the same dimensions as the others; and there were windows all around in it and in its vestibule; its depth was fifty cubits, and its width twenty-five cubits. 34 Its vestibule faced the

40.16
1 Kings 6.4;
vv. 21, 22,
26, 31, 34,
37

40.17
Rev 11.2;
1 Chr 9.26;
2 Chr 31.11;
Ezek 41.6;
45.5
40.19
vv. 23, 27

40.20
v. 6
40.21
vv. 7, 16, 30,
15, 13
40.22
vv. 16, 6, 26,
31, 34, 37,
49
40.23
vv. 19, 27

40.24
v. 21
40.25
vv. 16, 22,
21, 33
40.26
vv. 6, 22, 16

40.27
vv. 23, 32, 19

40.28
vv. 32, 35
40.29
vv. 7, 10, 21,
16, 22, 25

40.30
vv. 16, 21, 25
40.31
vv. 16, 22,
26, 34, 37

40.32
vv. 28-31, 35
40.33
vv. 29, 16, 21

40.34
vv. 16, 22, 37

ᵘ Meaning of Heb uncertain   ᵛ Compare Gk: Heb *from before*   ʷ Heb adds *the east and the north*
ˣ Gk: Heb *before them*

40.20ff Ezekiel describes the gates on the north and the south, much the same as the east gate. It is significant that there is no gate facing the west. Josephus claims that the second temple had no west gate, although 1 Chr 9.24 and 26.8 speak about gates facing west in Solomon's temple. Since the sun rises in the east and sets in the west, this may explain the absence

of a west gate—for the sun will never set on this temple or that kingdom.
40.28 Inside the three outer gates on the east, north, and south, lay the inner court. Inside the inner court were three more gates that led to the temple. A wall surrounded the temple area, and the three inner gates made entrance into the temple area possible.

outer court, and it had palm trees on its pilasters, on either side; and its stairway had eight steps.

35 Then he brought me to the north gate, and he measured it; it had the same dimensions as the others. 36 Its recesses, its pilasters, and its vestibule were of the same size as the others;[y] and it had windows all around. Its depth was fifty cubits, and its width twenty-five cubits. 37 Its vestibule[z] faced the outer court, and it had palm trees on its pilasters, on either side; and its stairway had eight steps.

7. The tables of sacrifice

38 There was a chamber with its door in the vestibule of the gate,[a] where the burnt offering was to be washed. 39 And in the vestibule of the gate were two tables on either side, on which the burnt offering and the sin offering and the guilt offering were to be slaughtered. 40 On the outside of the vestibule[b] at the entrance of the north gate were two tables; and on the other side of the vestibule of the gate were two tables. 41 Four tables were on the inside, and four tables on the outside of the side of the gate, eight tables, on which the sacrifices were to be slaughtered. 42 There were also four tables of hewn stone for the burnt offering, a cubit and a half long, and one cubit and a half wide, and one cubit high, on which the instruments were to be laid with which the burnt offerings and the sacrifices were slaughtered. 43 There were pegs, one handbreadth long, fastened all around the inside. And on the tables the flesh of the offering was to be laid.

8. The chambers for the priests

44 On the outside of the inner gateway there were chambers for the singers in the inner court, one[c] at the side of the north gate facing south, the other at the side of the east gate facing north. 45 He said to me, "This chamber that faces south is for the priests who have charge of the temple, 46 and the chamber that faces north is for the priests who have charge of the altar; these are the descendants of Zadok, who alone among the descendants of Levi may come near to the LORD to minister to him." 47 He measured the court, one hundred cubits deep, and one hundred cubits wide, a square; and the altar was in front of the temple.

9. The vestibule of the temple

48 Then he brought me to the vestibule of the temple and measured the pilasters of the vestibule, five cubits on either side; and the width of the gate was fourteen cubits; and the sidewalls of the gate were three cubits[d] on either side. 49 The depth of the vestibule was twenty cubits, and the width twelve[e] cubits; ten steps led up[f] to it; and there were pillars beside the pilasters on either side.

B. The new temple

1. The nave and the holy place

41 Then he brought me to the nave, and measured the pilasters; on each side six cubits was the width of the pilasters.[g] 2 The width

40.35 Ezek 44.4; 47.2
40.36 vv. 7, 29, 16, 21
40.37 vv. 16, 35
40.38 Ezek 41.10; 42.13;
2 Chr 4.6
40.39 Lev 4.2, 3; 5.6; 6.6; 7.1
40.41 vv. 39, 40
40.42 v. 39; Ex 20.25
40.44 vv. 23, 27, 17, 38; 1 Chr 6.31; 25.1-7
40.45 vv. 17, 38; Lev 8.35; 1 Chr 9.23; 2 Chr 13.11
40.46 vv. 17, 38; Num 18.5; Ezek 44.15; 43.19;
1 Kings 2.35
40.47 vv. 19, 23, 27
40.49 1 Kings 6.3; 2 Kings 7.21; Jer 52.17-23; Rev 3.12
41.1 Ezek 40.2, 3, 17; vv. 21, 23; Ezek 40.9
41.2 1 Kings 6.2, 17; 2 Chr 3.3

---

y One Ms: Compare verses 29 and 33: MT lacks *were of the same size as the others*   z Gk Vg Compare verses 26, 31, 34: Heb *pilasters*   a Cn: Heb *at the pilasters of the gates*   b Cn: Heb *to him who goes up*   c Heb lacks *one*   d Gk: Heb *and the width of the gate was three cubits*   e Gk: Heb *eleven*   f Gk: Heb *and by steps that went up*   g Compare Gk: Heb *tent*

40.44 On the north and south sides of the temple walls, toward the west, were the priests' chambers. The chamber facing south housed the priests who had charge of the temple, and the one facing north housed the priests who had charge of the altar (thus sacrifices took place on the north side).

41.1 The description of the new temple is different from Solomon's temple. There is no reason to suppose that it should be identical with the first temple, for architecture changes from age to age. Some of the

of the entrance was ten cubits; and the sidewalls of the entrance were five cubits on either side. He measured the length of the nave, forty cubits, and its width, twenty cubits. 3 Then he went into the inner room and measured the pilasters of the entrance, two cubits; and the width of the entrance, six cubits; and the sidewalls[h] of the entrance, seven cubits. 4 He measured the depth of the room, twenty cubits, and its width, twenty cubits, beyond the nave. And he said to me, This is the most holy place.

2. *The side chambers*

5 Then he measured the wall of the temple, six cubits thick; and the width of the side chambers, four cubits, all around the temple. 6 The side chambers were in three stories, one over another, thirty in each story. There were offsets[i] all around the wall of the temple to serve as supports for the side chambers, so that they should not be supported by the wall of the temple. 7 The passageway[j] of the side chambers widened from story to story; for the structure was supplied with a stairway all around the temple. For this reason the structure became wider from story to story. One ascended from the bottom story to the uppermost story by way of the middle one. 8 I saw also that the temple had a raised platform all around; the foundations of the side chambers measured a full reed of six long cubits. 9 The thickness of the outer wall of the side chambers was five cubits; and the free space between the side chambers of the temple 10 and the chambers of the court was a width of twenty cubits all around the temple on every side. 11 The side chambers opened onto the area left free, one door toward the north, and another door toward the south; and the width of the part that was left free was five cubits all around.

3. *The building facing the temple on the west*

12 The building that was facing the temple yard on the west side was seventy cubits wide; and the wall of the building was five cubits thick all around, and its depth ninety cubits.

4. *The measurements of the temple and the yard*

13 Then he measured the temple, one hundred cubits deep; and the yard and the building with its walls, one hundred cubits deep; 14 also the width of the east front of the temple and the yard, one hundred cubits.

15 Then he measured the depth of the building facing the yard at the west, together with its galleries[k] on either side, one hundred cubits.

5. *The interior decorations*

The nave of the temple and the inner room and the outer[l] vestibule 16 were paneled,[m] and, all around, all three had windows with recessed[n] frames. Facing the threshold the temple was paneled with wood all around, from the floor up to the windows (now the windows were covered), 17 to the space above the door, even to the inner room, and on the outside. And on all the walls all around in the inner room and the nave there was a pattern.[o] 18 It was formed of cherubim and palm trees, a palm tree between cherub and cherub. Each cherub had two faces: 19 a human face turned toward the palm tree on the one side, and the face of a young lion turned toward the palm tree on the other side. They were carved on

41.3 Ezek 40.16; v. 1 **41.4** 1 Kings 6.20; 2 Chr 3.8
41.5 vv. 6-11 **41.6** 1 Kings 6.5, 6
41.7 1 Kings 6.8
41.8 Ezek 40.5
41.9 v. 11 **41.10** Ezek 40.17
41.11 v. 9
41.12 vv. 13-15; Ezek 42.1
41.13 Ezek 40.47; vv. 13-15 **41.14** Ezek 40.47 **41.15** Ezek 42.1, 10, 13; 40.6; v. 25
41.16 vv. 25, 26; Ezek 40.16; v. 15; Ezek 42.3; 1 Kings 6.15
41.18 1 Kings 6.29; 7.36; Ezek 40.16; 2 Chr 3.5 **41.19** Ezek 1.10; 10.14

h Gk: Heb *width* *i* Gk Compare 1 Kings 6.6: Heb *they entered* *j* Cn: Heb *it was surrounded* *k* Cn: Meaning of Heb uncertain *l* Gk: Heb *of the court* *m* Gk: Heb *the thresholds* *n* Cn Compare Gk 1 Kings 6.4: Meaning of Heb uncertain *o* Heb *measures*

details are difficult for us to understand, and their meaning is variously understood. Nowhere in the account does the vision reveal the time frame when this prophetic word concerning the temple will be fulfilled.

the whole temple all around; 20 from the floor to the area above the door, cherubim and palm trees were carved on the wall. *p*

21 The doorposts of the nave were square. In front of the holy place was something resembling 22 an altar of wood, three cubits high, two cubits long, and two cubits wide; *q* its corners, its base, *r* and its walls were of wood. He said to me, "This is the table that stands before the LORD." 23 The nave and the holy place had each a double door. 24 The doors had two leaves apiece, two swinging leaves for each door. 25 On the doors of the nave were carved cherubim and palm trees, such as were carved on the walls; and there was a canopy of wood in front of the vestibule outside. 26 And there were recessed windows and palm trees on either side, on the sidewalls of the vestibule. *s*

C. *The priests' chambers: north and south*

42 Then he led me out into the outer court, toward the north, and he brought me to the chambers that were opposite the temple yard and opposite the building on the north. 2 The length of the building that was on the north side *t* was *u* one hundred cubits, and the width fifty cubits. 3 Across the twenty cubits that belonged to the inner court, and facing the pavement that belonged to the outer court, the chambers rose *v* gallery *w* by gallery *w* in three stories. 4 In front of the chambers was a passage on the inner side, ten cubits wide and one hundred cubits deep, *x* and its *y* entrances were on the north. 5 Now the upper chambers were narrower, for the galleries *w* took more away from them than from the lower and middle chambers in the building. 6 For they were in three stories, and they had no pillars like the pillars of the outer *z* court; for this reason the upper chambers were set back from the ground more than the lower and the middle ones. 7 There was a wall outside parallel to the chambers, toward the outer court, opposite the chambers, fifty cubits long. 8 For the chambers on the outer court were fifty cubits long, while those opposite the temple were one hundred cubits long. 9 At the foot of these chambers ran a passage that one entered from the east in order to enter them from the outer court. 10 The width of the passage *a* was fixed by the wall of the court.

On the south *b* also, opposite the vacant area and opposite the building, there were chambers 11 with a passage in front of them; they were similar to the chambers on the north, of the same length and width, with the same exits *c* and arrangements and doors. 12 So the entrances of the chambers to the south were entered through the entrance at the head of the corresponding passage, from the east, along the matching wall. *w*

13 Then he said to me, "The north chambers and the south chambers opposite the vacant area are the holy chambers, where the priests who approach the LORD shall eat the most holy offerings; there they shall deposit the most holy offerings—the grain offering, the sin offering, and the guilt offering—for the place is holy. 14 When the priests enter the holy place, they shall not go out of it into the outer court without laying there the vestments in which they minister, for these are holy; they shall put on other garments before they go near to the area open to the people."

41.20 v. 18
41.21 v. 1; 1 Kings 6.33; Ezek 40.9, 14, 16
41.22 Ex 30.1; Rev 8.3; Ezek 44.16; Mal 1.7, 12; Ex 30.8
41.23 1 Kings 6.31-35; vv. 1, 4
41.25 v. 16
41.26 v. 16; Ezek 40.9, 16, 48
42.1 Ezek 40.17, 28; 41.1, 12; vv. 10, 13
42.2 Ezek 41.13
42.3 Ezek 41.10, 16
42.4 Ezek 46.19
42.5 v. 3
42.6 Ezek 41.6
42.7 vv. 10, 12
42.8 Ezek 41.13, 14
42.9 Ezek 44.5; 46.19
42.10 vv. 7, 1, 13; Ezek 40.17
42.11 v. 4
42.13 Lev 7.6; 10.13, 14, 17; Lev 6.25, 29; Num 18.9, 10
42.14 Ezek 44.19; Ex 29.4-9; Zech 3.4, 5

p Cn Compare verse 25: Heb *and the wall*   *q* Gk: Heb lacks *two cubits wide*   *r* Gk: Heb *length*   *s* Cn: Heb *vestibule. And the side chambers of the temple and the canopies*   *t* Gk: Heb *door*   *u* Gk: Heb *before the length*   *v* Heb lacks *the chambers rose*   *w* Meaning of Heb uncertain   *x* Gk Syr: Heb *a way of one cubit*   *y* Heb *their*   *z* Gk: Heb lacks *outer*   *a* Heb lacks *of the passage*   *b* Gk: Heb *east*   *c* Heb *and all their exits*

42.1ff To the north of the temple in the inner court are two blocks of buildings, three stories high. One block is twice the length of the other. They are for the storing of priestly garments and for the priests on duty.

D. *The measurements of the temple area*

15 When he had finished measuring the interior of the temple area, he led me out by the gate that faces east, and measured the temple area all around. 16 He measured the east side with the measuring reed, five hundred cubits by the measuring reed. 17 Then he turned and measured[d] the north side, five hundred cubits by the measuring reed. 18 Then he turned and measured[d] the south side, five hundred cubits by the measuring reed. 19 Then he turned to the west side and measured, five hundred cubits by the measuring reed. 20 He measured it on the four sides. It had a wall around it, five hundred cubits long and five hundred cubits wide, to make a separation between the holy and the common.

E. *The return of the LORD to the temple*

1. *His glory enters the temple*

43 Then he brought me to the gate, the gate facing east. 2 And there, the glory of the God of Israel was coming from the east; the sound was like the sound of mighty waters; and the earth shone with his glory. 3 The[e] vision I saw was like the vision that I had seen when he came to destroy the city, and[f] like the vision that I had seen by the river Chebar; and I fell upon my face. 4 As the glory of the LORD entered the temple by the gate facing east, 5 the spirit lifted me up, and brought me into the inner court; and the glory of the LORD filled the temple.

2. *The message of the LORD*

6 While the man was standing beside me, I heard someone speaking to me out of the temple. 7 He said to me: Mortal, this is the place of my throne and the place for the soles of my feet, where I will reside among the people of Israel forever. The house of Israel shall no more defile my holy name, neither they nor their kings, by their whoring, and by the corpses of their kings at their death.[g] 8 When they placed their threshold by my threshold and their doorposts beside my doorposts, with only a wall between me and them, they were defiling my holy name by their abominations that they committed; therefore I have consumed them in my anger. 9 Now let them put away their idolatry and the corpses of their kings far from me, and I will reside among them forever.

10 As for you, mortal, describe the temple to the house of Israel, and let them measure the pattern; and let them be ashamed of their iniquities. 11 When they are ashamed of all that they have done, make known to them the plan of the temple, its arrangement, its exits and its entrances, and its whole form — all its ordinances and its entire plan and all its laws; and write it down in their sight, so that they may observe and follow the entire plan and all its ordinances. 12 This is the law of the temple: the whole territory on the top of the mountain all around shall be most holy. This is the law of the temple.

3. *The measurements of the altar of burnt offering*

13 These are the dimensions of the altar by cubits (the cubit being one cubit and a handbreadth): its base shall be one cubit high,[h] and one cubit wide, with a rim of one span around its edge. This shall be the height of the altar: 14 From the base on the ground to the lower ledge, two cubits,

42.15
Ezek 40.6;
43.1
42.16
Ezek 40.3

42.20
Ezek 40.5;
Zech 2.5;
Ezek 45.2

43.1
Ezek 10.19;
44.1; 46.1
43.2
Ezek 11.23;
1.24;
Rev 1.15;
18.1;
Ezek 10.4
43.3
Ezek 1.4, 28;
Jer 1.10;
Ezek 1.3;
3.23
43.4
Ezek 10.19;
44.2
43.5
Ezek 3.14;
8.3;
1 Kings 8.10,
11;
Ezek 44.4
43.6
Ezek 1.26;
40.3
43.7
Ps 47.8;
Ezek 1.26;
37.26, 28;
Jer 16.18;
Ezek 6.5, 13
43.8
Ezek 8.3;
23.39; 44.7
43.9
Ezek 18.30,
31
43.10
Ezek 40.4;
v. 11
43.11
Ezek 44.5;
12.3; 11.20;
36.27
43.12
Ezek 40.2

43.13
Ezek 40.5;
41.8

43.14
vv. 17, 20;
Ezek 45.19

---

d Gk: Heb *measuring reed all around. He measured*   *e* Gk: Heb *Like the vision*   *f* Syr: Heb *and the visions*
g Or *on their high places*   *h* Gk: Heb lacks *high*

43.2 The glory of God had departed from the temple (9.3) and from Jerusalem, leaving Judah at the mercy of its enemies. Here the glory returns from the east — the direction to which it went when God's presence left Jerusalem. This return prophesied by Ezekiel refers to God's plan to someday reside among his people once again.

with a width of one cubit; and from the smaller ledge to the larger ledge, four cubits, with a width of one cubit; 15 and the altar hearth, four cubits; and from the altar hearth projecting upward, four horns. 16 The altar hearth shall be square, twelve cubits long by twelve wide. 17 The ledge also shall be square, fourteen cubits long by fourteen wide, with a rim around it half a cubit wide, and its surrounding base, one cubit. Its steps shall face east.

4. Instructions for purifying the altar

18 Then he said to me: Mortal, thus says the Lord GOD: These are the ordinances for the altar: On the day when it is erected for offering burnt offerings upon it and for dashing blood against it, 19 you shall give to the levitical priests of the family of Zadok, who draw near to me to minister to me, says the Lord GOD, a bull for a sin offering. 20 And you shall take some of its blood, and put it on the four horns of the altar, and on the four corners of the ledge, and upon the rim all around; thus you shall purify it and make atonement for it. 21 You shall also take the bull of the sin offering, and it shall be burnt in the appointed place belonging to the temple, outside the sacred area.

22 On the second day you shall offer a male goat without blemish for a sin offering; and the altar shall be purified, as it was purified with the bull. 23 When you have finished purifying it, you shall offer a bull without blemish and a ram from the flock without blemish. 24 You shall present them before the LORD, and the priests shall throw salt on them and offer them up as a burnt offering to the LORD. 25 For seven days you shall provide daily a goat for a sin offering; also a bull and a ram from the flock, without blemish, shall be provided. 26 Seven days shall they make atonement for the altar and cleanse it, and so consecrate it. 27 When these days are over, then from the eighth day onward the priests shall offer upon the altar your burnt offerings and your offerings of well-being; and I will accept you, says the Lord GOD.

F. The rules of the temple

1. The east gate and the prince

44 Then he brought me back to the outer gate of the sanctuary, which faces east; and it was shut. 2 The LORD said to me: This gate shall remain shut; it shall not be opened, and no one shall enter by it; for the LORD, the God of Israel, has entered by it; therefore it shall remain shut. 3 Only the prince, because he is a prince, may sit in it to eat food before the LORD; he shall enter by way of the vestibule of the gate, and shall go out by the same way.

2. The exclusion of the uncircumcised

4 Then he brought me by way of the north gate to the front of the

43.15 Ex 27.2; Lev 9.9; 1 Kings 1.50
43.16 Ex 27.1
43.17 Ex 20.26; Ezek 40.6
43.18 Ezek 2.1; Ex 40.29; Lev 1.5
43.19 1 Kings 2.35; Ezek 44.15; Num 16.5, 40; v. 23; Ezek 45.18, 19
43.21 Ex 29.14; Heb 13.11
43.22 vv. 25, 20, 26
43.23 Ex 29.1
43.24 Lev 2.13; Mk 9.49, 50; Col 4.6
43.25 Ex 29.35, 36; Lev 8.33
43.27 Lev 9.1; 3.1; 17.5; Ezek 20.40
44.1 Ezek 42.14; 43.1
44.2 Ezek 43.4
44.3 Ezek 37.25; Gen 31.54; 1 Cor 10.18; Ezek 46.2, 8
44.4 Ezek 40.20, 40; 3.23; 43.5; 1.28; Rev 15.8

43.19 Chapters 40–48 of Ezekiel are filled with difficulties for interpreters. The prophecies appear to speak of the kingdom age, for nothing remotely resembling these prophecies has as yet appeared. Premillennialists take these prophecies literally; amillennialists, who think there will be no thousand-year kingdom age, do not look for any literal fulfillment of these prophecies, assuming that the church is the new Israel. Perplexing indeed is the question of whether there will be a literal restoration of animal sacrifices, which were done away with by Christ's atoning work at Calvary. Some think these offerings will serve as a memorial, corresponding to the Lord's supper of this present age. Others consider these prophecies as describing in O.T. terms the principle that Christ's

blood will avail wholly during the kingdom age. **44.1–3** The east gate is shut once the Lord has entered it and his glory has rested on the temple and the holy place. A prince is referred to (v. 3), but is not identified. In 45.22 the prince makes a sacrifice for himself and for the people, but in 46.16 he is said to have sons. Therefore it cannot be Jesus Christ. Some think this is the high priest of God or the second in command after the high priest. Either way, he is God's representative. **44.4ff** In earlier times the Jews had profaned the temple by allowing admittance to it by some who were uncircumcised either in heart or in flesh or both. Here the uncircumcised in heart and flesh are forbidden to enter the sanctuary. This would not exclude non-temple; and I looked, and lo! the glory of the LORD filled the temple of the LORD; and I fell upon my face. 5 The LORD said to me: Mortal, mark well, look closely, and listen attentively to all that I shall tell you concerning all the ordinances of the temple of the LORD and all its laws; and mark well those who may be admitted to[i] the temple and all those who are to be excluded from the sanctuary. 6 Say to the rebellious house,[j] to the house of Israel, Thus says the Lord GOD: O house of Israel, let there be an end to all your abominations 7 in admitting foreigners, uncircumcised in heart and flesh, to be in my sanctuary, profaning my temple when you offer to me my food, the fat and the blood. You[k] have broken my covenant with all your abominations. 8 And you have not kept charge of my sacred offerings; but you have appointed foreigners[l] to act for you in keeping my charge in my sanctuary.

3. The exclusion of the idolatrous Levites

9 Thus says the Lord GOD: No foreigner, uncircumcised in heart and flesh, of all the foreigners who are among the people of Israel, shall enter my sanctuary. 10 But the Levites who went far from me, going astray from me after their idols when Israel went astray, shall bear their punishment. 11 They shall be ministers in my sanctuary, having oversight at the gates of the temple, and serving in the temple; they shall slaughter the burnt offering and the sacrifice for the people, and they shall attend on them and serve them. 12 Because they ministered to them before their idols and made the house of Israel stumble into iniquity, therefore I have sworn concerning them, says the Lord GOD, that they shall bear their punishment. 13 They shall not come near to me, to serve me as priest, nor come near any of my sacred offerings, the things that are most sacred; but they shall bear their shame, and the consequences of the abominations that they have committed. 14 Yet I will appoint them to keep charge of the temple, to do all its chores, all that is to be done in it.

4. The service of the levitical descendants of Zadok

15 But the levitical priests, the descendants of Zadok, who kept the charge of my sanctuary when the people of Israel went astray from me, shall come near to me to minister to me; and they shall attend me to offer me the fat and the blood, says the Lord GOD. 16 It is they who shall enter my sanctuary, it is they who shall approach my table, to minister to me, and they shall keep my charge. 17 When they enter the gates of the inner court, they shall wear linen vestments; they shall have nothing of wool on them, while they minister at the gates of the inner court, and within. 18 They shall have linen turbans on their heads, and linen undergarments on their loins; they shall not bind themselves with anything that causes sweat. 19 When they go out into the outer court to the people, they shall remove the vestments in which they have been ministering, and lay them in the holy chambers; and they shall put on other garments, so that they may not communicate holiness to the people with their vestments. 20 They shall not shave their heads or let their locks grow long; they shall only trim the hair of their heads. 21 No priest shall drink wine when he enters the inner court. 22 They shall not marry a widow, or a divorced woman, but

44.5
Ezek 40.4;
43.10, 11

44.6
Ezek 2.5;
3.9; 45.9;
1 Pet 4.3
44.7
Ex 12.43-49;
Lev 26.41;
Deut 10.16;
Jer 4.4; 9.26;
Lev 22.25;
Gen 17.14
44.8
Num 18.7

44.9
v. 7;
Zech 14.21
44.10
2 Kings 23.8,
9;
Ezek 22.26;
Num 18.23
44.11
1 Chr 26.1;
2 Chr 29.34;
Num 16.9
44.12
2 Kings 16.10-16;
Ezek 14.3, 4;
Ps 106.26
44.13
Num 18.3;
2 Kings 23.9;
Ezek 32.30;
39.26
44.14
Num 18.4;
v. 11

44.15
Ezek 40.46;
48.11;
Deut 10.8
44.16
Ezek 41.22;
Mal 1.7, 12
44.17
Ex 28.39, 40,
43; 39.27, 28
44.18
Ex 28.40, 42;
Isa 3.20
44.19
Ezek 42.14;
46.20
44.20
Lev 21.5;
Num 6.5
44.21
Lev 10.9
44.22
Lev 21.7, 13,
14

[i] Cn: Heb *the entrance of* [j] Gk: Heb lacks *house* [k] Gk Syr Vg: Heb *They* [l] Heb lacks *foreigners*

Jews, only those who had not submitted to the laws of the sanctuary. Priests who had defiled God's sanctuary are here demoted to the more ordinary work of Levites, who are not of the priestly order.
44.15 *Zadok*, the son of Ahitub, began the new legitimate priestly line after the line of Eli had been extinguished. His name appears for the first time in 2 Sam 8.17. He descended from Aaron, Eleazar, and Phinehas. The Scriptures do not tell us where his

father or some of his ancestors served as priests. Zadok himself served under David, first as a military leader (1 Chr 12.26-28) and then as priest; he crowned Solomon king.
44.20ff The priests were subject to certain regulations regarding their persons and their marital status. The use of wine before entering the inner court was also forbidden.

only a virgin of the stock of the house of Israel, or a widow who is the widow of a priest. 23 They shall teach my people the difference between the holy and the common, and show them how to distinguish between the unclean and the clean. 24 In a controversy they shall act as judges, and they shall decide it according to my judgments. They shall keep my laws and my statutes regarding all my appointed festivals, and they shall keep my sabbaths holy. 25 They shall not defile themselves by going near to a dead person; for father or mother, however, and for son or daughter, and for brother or unmarried sister they may defile themselves. 26 After he has become clean, they shall count seven days for him. 27 On the day that he goes into the holy place, into the inner court, to minister in the holy place, he shall offer his sin offering, says the Lord GOD.

28   This shall be their inheritance: I am their inheritance; and you shall give them no holding in Israel; I am their holding. 29 They shall eat the grain offering, the sin offering, and the guilt offering; and every devoted thing in Israel shall be theirs. 30 The first of all the first fruits of all kinds, and every offering of all kinds from all your offerings, shall belong to the priests; you shall also give to the priests the first of your dough, in order that a blessing may rest on your house. 31 The priests shall not eat of anything, whether bird or animal, that died of itself or was torn by animals.

G. The land for priests and prince

45   When you allot the land as an inheritance, you shall set aside for the LORD a portion of the land as a holy district, twenty-five thousand cubits long and twenty[m] thousand cubits wide; it shall be holy throughout its entire extent. 2 Of this, a square plot of five hundred by five hundred cubits shall be for the sanctuary, with fifty cubits for an open space around it. 3 In the holy district you shall measure off a section twenty-five thousand cubits long and ten thousand wide, in which shall be the sanctuary, the most holy place. 4 It shall be a holy portion of the land; it shall be for the priests, who minister in the sanctuary and approach the LORD to minister to him; and it shall be both a place for their houses and a holy place for the sanctuary. 5 Another section, twenty-five-thousand cubits long and ten thousand cubits wide, shall be for the Levites who minister at the temple, as their holding for cities to live in.[n]

6   Alongside the portion set apart as the holy district you shall assign as a holding for the city an area five thousand cubits wide, and twenty-five thousand cubits long; it shall belong to the whole house of Israel.

7   And to the prince shall belong the land on both sides of the holy district and the holding of the city, alongside the holy district and the holding of the city, on the west and on the east, corresponding in length to one of the tribal portions, and extending from the western to the eastern boundary 8 of the land. It is to be his property in Israel. And my princes shall no longer oppress my people; but they shall let the house of Israel have the land according to their tribes.

9   Thus says the Lord GOD: Enough, O princes of Israel! Put away

---

m Gk: Heb *ten*   *n* Gk: Heb *as their holding, twenty chambers*

44.23
Lev 10.10;
Mal 2.7
44.24
Deut 17.8, 9;
Ezek 20.12,
20
44.25
Lev 21.1-3
44.26
Num 19.13-19

44.28
Num 18.20;
Deut 10.9;
Josh 13.14,
33
44.29
Num 18.9,
14;
Lev 27.21, 28
44.30
Ex 29.19;
Num 3.13;
15.20;
Neh 10.37;
Mal 3.10
44.31
Ex 22.31;
Lev 22.8
45.1
Ezek 47.21,
22; 48.8
45.2
Ezek 42.20
45.3
Ezek 48.10
45.4
v. 1;
Ezek 48.10,
11
45.5
Ezek 48.13

45.6
Ezek 48.15

45.7
Ezek 46.16-18;
48.21

45.8
Isa 11.3-5;
Jer 23.5;
Ezek 22.27;
46.18;
Josh 11.23
45.9
Ezek 44.6;
Jer 6.7; 22.3;
Neh 5.1-5

44.28 The priests who serve at the altar must obtain their living from the altar, having no other job or source of income except what they get from their priestly service. They do not need farm lands, nor should they be entangled with the affairs of this life.
45.1ff The temple is to be protected by being located within a larger land area measuring some eight square miles. Evidently housing for the priests was related to this provision. The portion for the prince was approximately eight more miles outside the sacred area.
45.9ff Religious and civil authorities must be concerned with fair and just dealings between people. Weights and measures may not be tampered with, in order that people not be cheated. These regulations presuppose the fact that perfection will not yet have come and that sin would still be possible. In a perfected society no laws are needed to prevent wrongdoing.

violence and oppression, and do what is just and right. Cease your evictions of my people, says the Lord God.

H. *Additional instructions*

1. *Honest balances*

10 You shall have honest balances, an honest ephah, and an honest bath.*o* 11 The ephah and the bath shall be of the same measure, the bath containing one-tenth of a homer, and the ephah one-tenth of a homer; the homer shall be the standard measure. 12 The shekel shall be twenty gerahs. Twenty shekels, twenty-five shekels, and fifteen shekels shall make a mina for you.

2. *The grain offerings*

13 This is the offering that you shall make: one-sixth of an ephah from each homer of wheat, and one-sixth of an ephah from each homer of barley, 14 and as the fixed portion of oil,*p* one-tenth of a bath from each cor (the cor,*q* like the homer, contains ten baths); 15 and one sheep from every flock of two hundred, from the pastures of Israel. This is the offering for grain offerings, burnt offerings, and offerings of well-being, to make atonement for them, says the Lord God. 16 All the people of the land shall join with the prince in Israel in making this offering. 17 But this shall be the obligation of the prince regarding the burnt offerings, grain offerings, and drink offerings, at the festivals, the new moons, and the sabbaths, all the appointed festivals of the house of Israel: he shall provide the sin offerings, grain offerings, the burnt offerings, and the offerings of well-being, to make atonement for the house of Israel.

3. *The offerings at sacred seasons*

18 Thus says the Lord God: In the first month, on the first day of the month, you shall take a young bull without blemish, and purify the sanctuary. 19 The priest shall take some of the blood of the sin offering and put it on the doorposts of the temple, the four corners of the ledge of the altar, and the posts of the gate of the inner court. 20 You shall do the same on the seventh day of the month for anyone who has sinned through error or ignorance; so you shall make atonement for the temple.

21 In the first month, on the fourteenth day of the month, you shall celebrate the festival of the passover, and for seven days unleavened bread shall be eaten. 22 On that day the prince shall provide for himself and all the people of the land a young bull for a sin offering. 23 And during the seven days of the festival he shall provide as a burnt offering to the Lord seven young bulls and seven rams without blemish, on each of the seven days; and a male goat daily for a sin offering. 24 He shall provide as a grain offering an ephah for each bull, an ephah for each ram, and a hin of oil to each ephah. 25 In the seventh month, on the fifteenth day of the month and for the seven days of the festival, he shall make the same provision for sin offerings, burnt offerings, and grain offerings, and for the oil.

4. *The new moon and sabbath offerings of the prince*

46 Thus says the Lord God: The gate of the inner court that faces east shall remain closed on the six working days; but on the

---

o A Heb measure of volume *p* Cn: Heb *oil, the bath the oil* *q* Vg: Heb *homer*

45.18 *In the first month, on the first day of the month.* At the beginning of each new year, they must offer a sacrifice for the cleansing of the sanctuary. The Jews date the new year from around the middle of March. **45.25** This event is the festival of tabernacles.

46.1ff Ezekiel here speaks about public worship services on the sabbath, the new moon, and the daily offerings. If this time frame refers to the millennium subsequent to the second advent of Christ, the effects of sin will still be evident, for the Jews are here forbid-

45.10
Lev 19.35,
36;
Prov 11.1
45.11
Isa 5.10
45.12
Ex 30.13;
Lev 27.25;
Num 3.47

45.15
v. 17;
Lev 1.4; 6.30

45.17
Ezek 46.4-12;
1 Kings 8.64;
2 Chr 31.3;
Lev 23.1-44;
Ezek 43.27

45.18
Ezek 46.1, 3,
6;
Lev 16.16
45.19
Ezek 43.20
45.20
Lev 4.27;
16.20; vv. 15,
18

45.21
Ex 12.18;
Lev 23.5, 6;
Num 9.2, 3;
28.16, 17
45.22
Lev 4.14
45.23
Lev 23.8;
Num 28.16-25;
Job 42.8

45.25
Lev 23.34;
Num 29.12;
Deut 16.13

46.1
Ezek 45.17-19

sabbath day it shall be opened and on the day of the new moon it shall
be opened. 2 The prince shall enter by the vestibule of the gate from
outside, and shall take his stand by the post of the gate. The priests shall
offer his burnt offering and his offerings of well-being, and he shall bow
down at the threshold of the gate. Then he shall go out, but the gate shall
not be closed until evening. 3 The people of the land shall bow down at
the entrance of that gate before the LORD on the sabbaths and on the new
moons. 4 The burnt offering that the prince offers to the LORD on the
sabbath day shall be six lambs without blemish and a ram without blemish; 5 and the grain offering with the ram shall be an ephah, and the grain
offering with the lambs shall be as much as he wishes to give, together
with a hin of oil to each ephah. 6 On the day of the new moon he shall
offer a young bull without blemish, and six lambs and a ram, which shall
be without blemish; 7 as a grain offering he shall provide an ephah with
the bull and an ephah with the ram, and with the lambs as much as he
wishes, together with a hin of oil to each ephah. 8 When the prince enters,
he shall come in by the vestibule of the gate, and he shall go out by the
same way.

5. *Entering and leaving the temple*

9 When the people of the land come before the LORD at the appointed
festivals, whoever enters by the north gate to worship shall go out by the
south gate; and whoever enters by the south gate shall go out by the north
gate: they shall not return by way of the gate by which they entered, but
shall go out straight ahead. 10 When they come in, the prince shall come
in with them; and when they go out, he shall go out.

6. *Rules for sacrifice*

11 At the festivals and the appointed seasons the grain offering with
a young bull shall be an ephah, and with a ram an ephah, and with the
lambs as much as one wishes to give, together with a hin of oil to an ephah.
12 When the prince provides a freewill offering, either a burnt offering or
offerings of well-being as a freewill offering to the LORD, the gate facing
east shall be opened for him; and he shall offer his burnt offering or his
offerings of well-being as he does on the sabbath day. Then he shall go
out, and after he has gone out the gate shall be closed.
13 He shall provide a lamb, a yearling, without blemish, for a burnt
offering to the LORD daily; morning by morning he shall provide it. 14 And
he shall provide a grain offering with it morning by morning regularly,
one-sixth of an ephah, and one-third of a hin of oil to moisten the choice
flour, as a grain offering to the LORD; this is the ordinance for all time.
15 Thus the lamb and the grain offering and the oil shall be provided,
morning by morning, as a regular burnt offering.

7. *The prince and the laws of inheritance*

16 Thus says the Lord GOD: If the prince makes a gift to any of his
sons out of his inheritance,[r] it shall belong to his sons, it is their holding
by inheritance. 17 But if he makes a gift out of his inheritance to one of
his servants, it shall be his to the year of liberty; then it shall revert to the
prince; only his sons may keep a gift from his inheritance. 18 The prince
shall not take any of the inheritance of the people, thrusting them out of

46.2 v. 8; Ezek 44.3; 45.9; v. 12
46.3 Lk 1.10; v. 1
46.4 Ezek 45.17
46.5 Ezek 45.24; vv. 7, 11
46.6 v. 1
46.7 v. 5
46.8 Ezek 44.3; v. 2
46.9 Ex 23.14-17; Deut 16.16
46.11 Ezek 45.17; vv. 5, 7
46.12 2 Chr 29.31; Ezek 44.3; v. 2; Ezek 45.17
46.13 Ex 29.38; Num 28.3; Isa 50.4
46.14 Num 28.5
46.15 Ex 29.42; Num 28.6
46.16 2 Chr 21.3
46.17 Lev 27.10
46.18 Ezek 45.8; Mic 2.1, 2; Ezek 34.3-6, 21

[r] Gk: Heb *it is his inheritance*

den to bring blemished animals for sacrifice. However, such sacrifices would be memorial in nature rather than actually atoning, for the work of Christ is a finished work and needs no repeating. If these things occur before the second advent, these sacrifices are seen to symbolize the dedication of the Christian's life to God (see Rom 12.1,2). We will have to wait patiently for the time when the meaning of Ezekiel's prophecies is made plain to us.

46.17 *The year of liberty* refers to the year of jubilee (see Lev 25.13–15).

their holding; he shall give his sons their inheritance out of his own holding, so that none of my people shall be dispossessed of their holding.

8. The kitchens for the temple

19 Then he brought me through the entrance, which was at the side of the gate, to the north row of the holy chambers for the priests; and there I saw a place at the extreme western end of them. 20 He said to me, "This is the place where the priests shall boil the guilt offering and the sin offering, and where they shall bake the grain offering, in order not to bring them out into the outer court and so communicate holiness to the people."

21 Then he brought me out to the outer court, and led me past the four corners of the court; and in each corner of the court there was a court — 22 in the four corners of the court were small*s* courts, forty cubits long and thirty wide; the four were of the same size. 23 On the inside, around each of the four courts*t* was a row of masonry, with hearths made at the bottom of the rows all around. 24 Then he said to me, "These are the kitchens where those who serve at the temple shall boil the sacrifices of the people."

I. The river flowing from the temple

47 Then he brought me back to the entrance of the temple; there, water was flowing from below the threshold of the temple toward the east (for the temple faced east); and the water was flowing down from below the south end of the threshold of the temple, south of the altar. 2 Then he brought me out by way of the north gate, and led me around on the outside to the outer gate that faces toward the east;*u* and the water was coming out on the south side.

3 Going on eastward with a cord in his hand, the man measured one thousand cubits, and then led me through the water; and it was ankle-deep. 4 Again he measured one thousand, and led me through the water; and it was knee-deep. Again he measured one thousand, and led me through the water; and it was up to the waist. 5 Again he measured one thousand, and it was a river that I could not cross, for the water had risen; it was deep enough to swim in, a river that could not be crossed. 6 He said to me, "Mortal, have you seen this?"

Then he led me back along the bank of the river. 7 As I came back, I saw on the bank of the river a great many trees on the one side and on the other. 8 He said to me, "This water flows toward the eastern region and goes down into the Arabah; and when it enters the sea, the sea of stagnant waters, the water will become fresh. 9 Wherever the river goes,*v* every living creature that swarms will live, and there will be very many fish, once these waters reach there. It will become fresh; and everything will live where the river goes. 10 People will stand fishing beside the sea*w* from En-gedi to En-eglaim; it will be a place for the spreading of nets; its fish will be of a great many kinds, like the fish of the Great Sea. 11 But its swamps and marshes will not become fresh; they are to be left for salt. 12 On the banks, on both sides of the river, there will grow all kinds of

Cross references (margin)

46.19
Ezek 42.9, 13

46.20
2 Chr 35.13;
Lev 2.4, 5, 7;
Ezek 44.19

46.24
Ezek 44.11;
v. 20

47.1
Jer 2.13;
Joel 3.18;
Zech 13.1;
14.8;
Rev 22.1
47.2
Ezek 44.1, 2, 4

47.3
Ezek 40.3
47.5
Isa 11.9;
Hab 2.14
47.6
Ezek 2.1;
8.6; 40.4;
44.5
47.7
v. 12;
Rev 22.2
47.8
Deut 3.17;
Isa 35.6, 7;
Josh 3.16
47.9
Jn 4.14;
7.37, 38;
Rev 21.7
47.10
Gen 14.7;
2 Chr 20.2;
Ezek 26.5,
14;
Num 34.6;
Josh 23.4;
Ezek 48.28
47.12
v. 7;
Job 8.16;
Ps 1.3;
Jer 17.8;
Rev 22.2

s Gk Syr Vg: Meaning of Heb uncertain   *t* Heb *the four of them*   *u* Meaning of Heb uncertain   *v* Gk Syr Vg Tg: Heb *the two rivers go*   *w* Heb *it*

46.19ff This is the first mention of the buildings in which the flesh of the offerings is to be boiled. The flesh is holy and is to be eaten by the priests. None is to be taken from there into the outer court.

47.1ff Ezekiel sees a river flowing eastward and having its source from the temple. It becomes a deep river with banks lined with trees, and it sweetens the Dead Sea so that marine life will live in its waters. Some think this vision has a mystical and spiritual meaning and is not to be taken literally. Others understand a

future literal fulfillment. Curiously, this river corresponds to the heavenly one described in Rev 22.1,2 ("the river of the water of life, bright as crystal, flowing from the throne of God and of the Lamb"). Note too Jesus' statement, "Out of the believer's heart shall flow rivers of living water" (Jn 7.38). In all of these instances, the language describes the blessings of God which refresh the souls of believers and provide what they need to become all that they should be.

trees for food. Their leaves will not wither nor their fruit fail, but they will bear fresh fruit every month, because the water for them flows from the sanctuary. Their fruit will be for food, and their leaves for healing."

J. *The boundaries of the land*

13 Thus says the Lord GOD: These are the boundaries by which you shall divide the land for inheritance among the twelve tribes of Israel. Joseph shall have two portions. 14 You shall divide it equally; I swore to give it to your ancestors, and this land shall fall to you as your inheritance.

15 This shall be the boundary of the land: On the north side, from the Great Sea by way of Hethlon to Lebo-hamath, and on to Zedad,ˣ 16 Berothah, Sibraim (which lies between the border of Damascus and the border of Hamath), as far as Hazer-hatticon, which is on the border of Hauran. 17 So the boundary shall run from the sea to Hazar-enon, which is north of the border of Damascus, with the border of Hamath to the north.ʸ This shall be the north side.

18 On the east side, between Hauran and Damascus; along the Jordan between Gilead and the land of Israel; to the eastern sea and as far as Tamar.ᶻ This shall be the east side.

19 On the south side, it shall run from Tamar as far as the waters of Meribath-kadesh, from there along the Wadi of Egyptᵃ to the Great Sea. This shall be the south side.

20 On the west side, the Great Sea shall be the boundary to a point opposite Lebo-hamath. This shall be the west side.

21 So you shall divide this land among you according to the tribes of Israel. 22 You shall allot it as an inheritance for yourselves and for the aliens who reside among you and have begotten children among you. They shall be to you as citizens of Israel; with you they shall be allotted an inheritance among the tribes of Israel. 23 In whatever tribe aliens reside, there you shall assign them their inheritance, says the Lord GOD.

K. *The division of the land*

1. *The land allotted to the north*

48 These are the names of the tribes: Beginning at the northern border, on the Hethlon road,ᵇ from Lebo-hamath, as far as Hazar-enon (which is on the border of Damascus, with Hamath to the north), andᶜ extending from the east side to the west,ᵈ Dan, one portion. 2 Adjoining the territory of Dan, from the east side to the west, Asher, one portion. 3 Adjoining the territory of Asher, from the east side to the west, Naphtali, one portion. 4 Adjoining the territory of Naphtali, from the east side to the west, Manasseh, one portion. 5 Adjoining the territory of Manasseh, from the east side to the west, Ephraim, one portion. 6 Adjoining the territory of Ephraim, from the east side to the west, Reuben, one portion. 7 Adjoining the territory of Reuben, from the east side to the west, Judah, one portion.

2. *The allotment for the priests and Levites*

8 Adjoining the territory of Judah, from the east side to the west, shall

x Gk: Heb *Lebo-zedad,* 16Hamath   y Meaning of Heb uncertain   z Compare Syr: Heb *you shall measure* a Heb lacks *of Egypt*   b Compare 47:15: Heb *by the side of the way*   c Cn: Heb *and they shall be his* d Gk Compare verses 2-8: Heb *the east side the west*

47.13ff The land of Canaan is here guaranteed to the covenant people of God, and its boundaries are set. It shall be divided among the tribes of Israel, and provision is made for aliens who will share their land. At the very least, this typifies the heavenly Canaan, the better country (see Heb 11.16). In this Canaan all distinctions are broken down, for in the body of Christ there is neither Jew nor Gentile.
48.1ff The land north of the temple will be allotted to the seven tribes of Dan, Asher, Naphtali, Manasseh, Ephraim, Reuben, and Judah.
48.8ff See 45.1–8, which also describes the area of

47.13
Num 34.2-12;
Gen 48.5;
1 Chr 5.1;
Ezek 48.4
47.14
Gen 12.7;
Deut 1.8;
Ezek 20.5, 6
47.15
Num 34.8;
Ezek 48.1
47.16
vv. 17, 20;
Ezek 48.1;
v. 18
47.17
Num 34.9;
Ezek 48.1;
v. 16
47.18
v. 16;
Jer 50.19;
Gen 13.10, 11
47.19
Ezek 48.28;
Deut 32.51;
Isa 27.12
47.20
Num 34.6;
vv. 10, 15;
Ezek 48.1;
Am 6.14
47.22
Num 26.55, 56;
Isa 56.6, 7;
Rom 10.12;
Eph 2.12-14;
3.6;
Col 3.11

48.1
Ezek 47.15-17, 20;
Josh 19.40-48
48.2
Josh 19.24-31
48.3
Josh 19.32-39
48.4
Josh 13.29-31;
17.1-11
48.5
Josh 16.5-9;
17.8-10,
14-18
48.6
Josh 13.15-21
48.7
Josh 15.1-63
48.8
Ezek 45.1-6

be the portion that you shall set apart, twenty-five thousand cubits in width, and in length equal to one of the tribal portions, from the east side to the west, with the sanctuary in the middle of it. 9 The portion that you shall set apart for the LORD shall be twenty-five thousand cubits in length, and twenty*e* thousand in width. 10 These shall be the allotments of the holy portion: the priests shall have an allotment measuring twenty-five thousand cubits on the northern side, ten thousand cubits in width on the western side, ten thousand in width on the eastern side, and twenty-five thousand in length on the southern side, with the sanctuary of the LORD in the middle of it. 11 This shall be for the consecrated priests, the descendants*f* of Zadok, who kept my charge, who did not go astray when the people of Israel went astray, as the Levites did. 12 It shall belong to them as a special portion from the holy portion of the land, a most holy place, adjoining the territory of the Levites. 13 Alongside the territory of the priests, the Levites shall have an allotment twenty-five thousand cubits in length and ten thousand in width. The whole length shall be twenty-five thousand cubits and the width twenty*g* thousand. 14 They shall not sell or exchange any of it; they shall not transfer this choice portion of the land, for it is holy to the LORD.

3. The allotment for the city

15 The remainder, five thousand cubits in width and twenty-five thousand in length, shall be for ordinary use for the city, for dwellings and for open country. In the middle of it shall be the city; 16 and these shall be its dimensions: the north side four thousand five hundred cubits, the south side four thousand five hundred, the east side four thousand five hundred, and the west side four thousand five hundred. 17 The city shall have open land: on the north two hundred fifty cubits, on the south two hundred fifty, on the east two hundred fifty, on the west two hundred fifty. 18 The remainder of the length alongside the holy portion shall be ten thousand cubits to the east, and ten thousand to the west, and it shall be alongside the holy portion. Its produce shall be food for the workers of the city. 19 The workers of the city, from all the tribes of Israel, shall cultivate it. 20 The whole portion that you shall set apart shall be twenty-five thousand cubits square, that is, the holy portion together with the property of the city.

4. The allotment for the prince

21 What remains on both sides of the holy portion and of the property of the city shall belong to the prince. Extending from the twenty-five thousand cubits of the holy portion to the east border, and westward from the twenty-five thousand cubits to the west border, parallel to the tribal portions, it shall belong to the prince. The holy portion with the sanctuary of the temple in the middle of it, 22 and the property of the Levites and of the city, shall be in the middle of that which belongs to the prince. The portion of the prince shall lie between the territory of Judah and the territory of Benjamin.

5. The land allotted to the south

23 As for the rest of the tribes: from the east side to the west, Benjamin, one portion. 24 Adjoining the territory of Benjamin, from the east side to the west, Simeon, one portion. 25 Adjoining the territory of Sim-

e Compare 45.1: Heb *ten*   *f* One Ms Gk: Heb *of the descendants*   *g* Gk: Heb *ten*

Canaan devoted to sacred activities. Included are the sanctuary, the portion for the priests and the Levites, the city, and the area assigned to the prince. **48.23ff** The land south of the sacred area will be given to the five tribes of Benjamin, Simeon, Issachar, Zebulun, and Gad. The arrangement differs from that described in Josh 13–17.

eon, from the east side to the west, Issachar, one portion. 26 Adjoining the territory of Issachar, from the east side to the west, Zebulun, one portion. 27 Adjoining the territory of Zebulun, from the east side to the west, Gad, one portion. 28 And adjoining the territory of Gad to the south, the boundary shall run from Tamar to the waters of Meribath-kadesh, from there along the Wadi of Egypt[h] to the Great Sea. 29 This is the land that you shall allot as an inheritance among the tribes of Israel, and these are their portions, says the Lord God.

6. The city named "The Lord is There"

30 These shall be the exits of the city: On the north side, which is to be four thousand five hundred cubits by measure, 31 three gates, the gate of Reuben, the gate of Judah, and the gate of Levi, the gates of the city being named after the tribes of Israel. 32 On the east side, which is to be four thousand five hundred cubits, three gates, the gate of Joseph, the gate of Benjamin, and the gate of Dan. 33 On the south side, which is to be four thousand five hundred cubits by measure, three gates, the gate of Simeon, the gate of Issachar, and the gate of Zebulun. 34 On the west side, which is to be four thousand five hundred cubits, three gates,[i] the gate of Gad, the gate of Asher, and the gate of Naphtali. 35 The circumference of the city shall be eighteen thousand cubits. And the name of the city from that time on shall be, The Lord is There.

h Heb lacks of Egypt   i One Ms Gk Syr: MT their gates three

48.26 Josh 19.10-16
48.27 Josh 13.24-28
48.28 Ezek 47.19, 20
48.29 Ezek 47.13-20
48.30 vv. 31-34
48.31 Rev 21.12, 13
48.35 Jer 23.6; 33.16; 3.17; Joel 3.21; Zech 2.10; Rev 21.3; 22.3

48.35 *The Lord is There*, literally, "Yahweh-Shammah." Where God is, nothing else is needed; where God is, all we need is there too. Here God promises his people that he will dwell among them on earth. This is but a token of the still greater promise that, in eternity, all the people of God shall dwell in the New Jerusalem. However dimly we perceive what is revealed here, and however defective may be our interpretations, the reality as described in Heb 12.22 remains: "But you have come to Mount Zion and to the city of the living God, the heavenly Jerusalem, and to innumerable angels in festal gathering." This is the believer's hope and expectation.

INTRODUCTION TO

DANIEL

Authorship, Date, and Background: Daniel was born to a Judean noble family shortly before Josiah's reformation in 621 B.C. His name means "God is my judge." He was among the first group of Jewish captives taken to Babylon by Nebuchadnezzar in 605 B.C. He lived and ministered in Babylon for a period of approximately sixty years under the kingships of Nebuchadnezzar, Belshazzar, Darius the Mede, and Cyrus. The book was written in Babylon and contains a large segment in the Aramaic language.

For a variety of reasons, liberal scholars beginning with Porphyry (ca. A.D. 260) think that the book was written in 165 B.C., i.e., that the prophetic portions, for the most part, were inscribed after, rather than before, the events took place; thus the author most certainly could not have been Daniel. Both Jewish and evangelical Christian scholars, however, regard Daniel as the author, although he may have been aided by a scribe; the date of the composition was set in the sixth century B.C. Recent evidences, particularly the Dead Sea Scrolls, reinforce the view of Jewish tradition and the early church about Daniel's authorship and the sixth century B.C. composition date.

Daniel wrote to convince his fellow captives that their stay in Babylon was in accord with the plan of God and that it was possible to have a living faith in God despite the captivity. He demonstrated the superiority of Israel's God over the idols of Babylon and assured the Jews that Babylon, the agent of God's judgment, would itself disappear.

Characteristics and Content: Daniel was given a view of history which began with the Jews in captivity and stretched from there to the end of the age. His apocalyptic vision, which had its origin in Nebuchadnezzar's dream, forecasted the rise and fall of four world-empires, along with the rise and permanence of God's eternal and universal kingdom. God's direct intervention in the affairs of people and nations may be seen in the miraculous deliverance of Daniel's three colleagues who were thrown into a furnace of blazing fire when they refused to worship the golden image set up by the king; later Daniel himself was miraculously delivered after being cast into the lions' den.

In the second half of the book, Daniel wrote about the vision of four beasts—a lion, a bear, a leopard, and a fourth one with ten horns. Additional details were given in the vision of the ram and the goat, along with the prophetic interpretation. Then followed a vision of the seventy weeks and the end times. No one can develop a prophetic scheme without reference to the seminal work of Daniel. This book and the Revelation of John in the N.T. have much in common.

Outline:

  I. Daniel and his friends (1.1—6.28)

  II. The final dream and visions (7.1—12.13)

DANIEL

I. Daniel and his friends (1.1–6.28)

A. The training and testing of the remnant

1. The hostages captured

1 In the third year of the reign of King Jehoiakim of Judah, King Nebuchadnezzar of Babylon came to Jerusalem and besieged it. ² The Lord let King Jehoiakim of Judah fall into his power, as well as some of the vessels of the house of God. These he brought to the land of Shinar,*a* and placed the vessels in the treasury of his gods.

2. Daniel and his three friends chosen as students

3 Then the king commanded his palace master Ashpenaz to bring some of the Israelites of the royal family and of the nobility, ⁴ young men without physical defect and handsome, versed in every branch of wisdom, endowed with knowledge and insight, and competent to serve in the king's palace; they were to be taught the literature and language of the Chaldeans. ⁵ The king assigned them a daily portion of the royal rations of food and wine. They were to be educated for three years, so that at the end of that time they could be stationed in the king's court. ⁶ Among them were Daniel, Hananiah, Mishael, and Azariah, from the tribe of Judah. ⁷ The palace master gave them other names: Daniel he called Belteshazzar, Hananiah he called Shadrach, Mishael he called Meshach, and Azariah he called Abednego.

3. The trial of their faith

8 But Daniel resolved that he would not defile himself with the royal rations of food and wine; so he asked the palace master to allow him not to defile himself. ⁹ Now God allowed Daniel to receive favor and compassion from the palace master. ¹⁰ The palace master said to Daniel, "I am

a Gk Theodotion: Heb adds *to the house of his own gods*

1.1
2 Kings 24.1;
2 Chr 36.6
1.2
Jer 27.19, 20;
Isa 11.11;
Zech 5.11

1.3
2 Kings 20.17,
18;
Isa 39.7
1.4
2 Sam 14.25;
Dan 2.4
1.5ff
vv. 8, 18;
1 Kings 10.8;
v. 19
1.6
Ezek 14.14,
20; 28.3
1.7
Dan 4.8;
5.12; 2.49;
3.12

1.8
Deut 32.38;
Ezek 4.13;
Hos 9.3
1.9
Job 5.15, 16;
Ps 106.46;
Prov 16.7
1.10
v. 7

1.1,2 Because of Judah's idolatry, God ordained Babylon to defeat Judah and take it captive. God preserved his people in Babylon and showed them the evils of idolatry. Thus they were prepared to return to Judea, as the people through whom the Messiah would come.
1.3 *The palace master* was the one in charge of the palace slaves.
1.4 *The language of the Chaldeans* was Aramaic; part of Daniel is written in Aramaic (see note on 2.4). The Hebrew lads received instruction in such subjects as history, astronomy, and mathematics. Magic and alchemy were also among the courses of study.
1.5–7 Nebuchadnezzar attempted to make Babylonians—loyal to him and to his court—out of the young Jewish captives. He did this by adopting a threefold plan: (1) new Babylonian names were given them to identify them with Babylon; (2) they were enrolled in a three-year program of indigenization; and (3) they were given the finest Babylonian food.

Daniel complied with the program except where it conflicted with the law of God. God blessed his faithfulness and caused him to prosper in this alien environment.
1.6,7 The four Hebrew young men all had "jah" or "el" in their original names. Both of these were names for the Lord God. Their names were changed when they got to Babylon, and their Babylonian names seem to have had some connections to deities worshiped by these pagans. However, the meaning of their new names is uncertain and there are differences of opinion as to which deities were represented.
1.8 Though the Babylonians had changed Daniel's name, they could not change his nature. He was a Jew and would be so all the days of his life. It would have been an offense for him to eat meat that was not kosher, although that would not apply to wine. Later (in 10.2) we are told that Daniel refused to eat any flesh or drink any wine for a particular time, implying that he was used to eating flesh and drinking wine.

afraid of my lord the king; he has appointed your food and your drink. If he should see you in poorer condition than the other young men of your own age, you would endanger my head with the king." ¹¹ Then Daniel asked the guard whom the palace master had appointed over Daniel, Hananiah, Mishael, and Azariah: ¹² "Please test your servants for ten days. Let us be given vegetables to eat and water to drink. ¹³ You can then compare our appearance with the appearance of the young men who eat the royal rations, and deal with your servants according to what you observe." ¹⁴ So he agreed to this proposal and tested them for ten days. ¹⁵ At the end of ten days it was observed that they appeared better and fatter than all the young men who had been eating the royal rations. ¹⁶ So the guard continued to withdraw their royal rations and the wine they were to drink, and gave them vegetables. ¹⁷ To these four young men God gave knowledge and skill in every aspect of literature and wisdom; Daniel also had insight into all visions and dreams.

4. The reward of their faith

18 At the end of the time that the king had set for them to be brought in, the palace master brought them into the presence of Nebuchadnezzar, ¹⁹ and the king spoke with them. And among them all, no one was found to compare with Daniel, Hananiah, Mishael, and Azariah; therefore they were stationed in the king's court. ²⁰ In every matter of wisdom and understanding concerning which the king inquired of them, he found them ten times better than all the magicians and enchanters in his whole kingdom. ²¹ And Daniel continued there until the first year of King Cyrus.

B. Nebuchadnezzar's dream of the statue and the stone

1. Nebuchadnezzar's forgotten dream

2 In the second year of Nebuchadnezzar's reign, Nebuchadnezzar dreamed such dreams that his spirit was troubled and his sleep left him. ² So the king commanded that the magicians, the enchanters, the sorcerers, and the Chaldeans be summoned to tell the king his dreams. When they came in and stood before the king, ³ he said to them, "I have had such a dream that my spirit is troubled by the desire to understand it." ⁴ The Chaldeans said to the king (in Aramaic),ᵇ "O king, live forever! Tell your servants the dream, and we will reveal the interpretation." ⁵ The king answered the Chaldeans, "This is a public decree: if you do not tell me both the dream and its interpretation, you shall be torn from limb to limb, and your houses shall be laid in ruins. ⁶ But if you do tell me the dream and its interpretation, you shall receive from me gifts and rewards

ᵇ The text from this point to the end of chapter 7 is in Aramaic

---

Cross references (left margin):

1.12 — v. 16
1.15 — Ex 23.25; Prov 10.22
1.16 — v. 12
1.17 — 1 Kings 3.12; Jas 1.5, 17; Dan 2.19; 7.1; 8.1
1.18 — vv. 5, 3, 7
1.19 — Gen 41.46; 1 Kings 10.8; Jer 15.1
1.20 — Dan 2.27, 28, 46, 48; 2.2
1.21 — Dan 6.28; 10.1
2.1 — Gen 41.8; Dan 4.5; Esth 6.1; Dan 6.18
2.2 — Gen 41.8; Ex 7.11; vv. 10, 27; Dan 5.7
2.3 — Gen 40.8; 41.15; Dan 4.5
2.4 — Isa 36.11; 1 Kings 1.31; Dan 3.9; 5.10; 6.6, 21
2.5 — Ezra 6.11; v. 12; Dan 3.29
2.6 — Dan 5.7, 16, 29

1.17 In their academic pursuits God gave these Jewish young men knowledge and skill. They were, of course, diligent in their studies and intent on learning, yet God gave them an unusual capacity that enabled them to surpass others in the classroom. The source of their intellectual gifts was the Father of lights, who gives people the minds to grasp and employ difficult subjects (cf. Jas 1.5,17).

1.20 The Hebrew young men were ten times better than the others in their classes. This was obvious when they were questioned by the king.

1.21 Rulers came and went, but Daniel lived on and served until he was well into his eighties. Despite many testings and conspiracies against him, God delivered him from them all. We are not told anything about his death.

2.1 Unknown to Nebuchadnezzar his dreams came from God. They troubled him so much that he could

not sleep. But he was even more perplexed by the fact that he could not recall what the dreams were, so he resorted to diviners and soothsayers to discover the truth about his dreams.

2.2 *Chaldeans.* This word may be used for the Neo-Babylonians, who established an empire in Mesopotamia under Nabopolassar, or for wise men (astrologers), who were noted for their astral studies.

2.4 The book of Daniel was written in Hebrew and Aramaic. The Aramaic section begins with this verse and continues through 7.28.

2.6 Nebuchadnezzar promised his wise men that if they told him the content of his dreams and the interpretation, he would reward them beyond their wildest imagination. With this promise, they would do all they could to satisfy the king. If they could not do so, it would not be for lack of desire, but of power.

and great honor. Therefore tell me the dream and its interpretation."
7 They answered a second time, "Let the king first tell his servants the dream, then we can give its interpretation." 8 The king answered, "I know with certainty that you are trying to gain time, because you see I have firmly decreed: 9 if you do not tell me the dream, there is but one verdict for you. You have agreed to speak lying and misleading words to me until things take a turn. Therefore, tell me the dream, and I shall know that you can give me its interpretation." 10 The Chaldeans answered the king, "There is no one on earth who can reveal what the king demands! In fact no king, however great and powerful, has ever asked such a thing of any magician or enchanter or Chaldean. 11 The thing that the king is asking is too difficult, and no one can reveal it to the king except the gods, whose dwelling is not with mortals."

2. Daniel interpreting Nebuchadnezzar's dream

a. His request for God to reveal the dream

12 Because of this the king flew into a violent rage and commanded that all the wise men of Babylon be destroyed. 13 The decree was issued, and the wise men were about to be executed; and they looked for Daniel and his companions, to execute them. 14 Then Daniel responded with prudence and discretion to Arioch, the king's chief executioner, who had gone out to execute the wise men of Babylon; 15 he asked Arioch, the royal official, "Why is the decree of the king so urgent?" Arioch then explained the matter to Daniel. 16 So Daniel went in and requested that the king give him time and he would tell the king the interpretation.

17 Then Daniel went to his home and informed his companions, Hananiah, Mishael, and Azariah, 18 and told them to seek mercy from the God of heaven concerning this mystery, so that Daniel and his companions with the rest of the wise men of Babylon might not perish. 19 Then the mystery was revealed to Daniel in a vision of the night, and Daniel blessed the God of heaven.

b. His hymn of thanksgiving

20 Daniel said:
"Blessed be the name of God from age to age,
    for wisdom and power are his.
21 He changes times and seasons,
    deposes kings and sets up kings;
he gives wisdom to the wise
    and knowledge to those who have understanding.
22 He reveals deep and hidden things;
    he knows what is in the darkness,
    and light dwells with him.
23 To you, O God of my ancestors,
    I give thanks and praise,
for you have given me wisdom and power,
    and have now revealed to me what we asked of you,
    for you have revealed to us what the king ordered."

2.7	v. 4
2.9	Esth 4.11; Isa 41.23
2.10	v. 27
2.11	Dan 5.11; Isa 57.15
2.12	v. 5
2.13	Dan 1.19, 20
2.14	v. 24; Jer 52.12, 14
2.15	Dan 3.22; vv. 1-12
2.16	Dan 1.19
2.18	Isa 37.4; Jer 33.3; Dan 9.9
2.19	vv. 22, 27-29; Num 12.6; Job 33.15, 16
2.20	Ps 113.2; Jer 32.19; vv. 21-23
2.21	Esth 1.13; Dan 7.25; Job 12.18; Ps 75.6, 7; Jas 1.5
2.22	Job 12.22; Ps 25.14; 139.11, 12; Isa 45.7; Jer 23.24;
2.23	Dan 5.11, 14; Jas 1.17 Gen 31.42; v. 21; Dan 1.17; vv. 18, 29, 30

2.10   The Chaldeans told the king that no one could recreate forgotten dreams; it was unfair to demand this of them. Nebuchadnezzar furiously ordered all the magicians of Babylon to be executed without exception, including the four Hebrew servants, although they had had no part in the proceedings.
2.16   When Daniel came into the presence of the king, he made no pretense that he had the answer to the king's dream. He only asked for time to get the answer. Joined by his friends, he asked for a word

from God. The "mystery was revealed to Daniel in a vision of the night" (v. 19). For this, he gave all the glory to God.
2.20ff   This prayer is a model of what thanksgiving is. Daniel praised God, who has wisdom and power, sets up and deposes kings, changes times and seasons according to the divine will. This God of his ancestors —and his God—had given him wisdom, power, and knowledge; for this he expressed his thanks.

c. *Before the king, Daniel glorifies God*

2.24
vv. 12-14

24 Therefore Daniel went to Arioch, whom the king had appointed to destroy the wise men of Babylon, and said to him, "Do not destroy the wise men of Babylon; bring me in before the king, and I will give the king the interpretation."

2.25
Gen 41.14;
Dan 1.6;
5.13; 6.13
2.26
Dan 1.7;
vv. 3-7
2.27
vv. 2, 10
2.28
Gen 40.8;
41.16; 49.1;
Isa 2.2;
Mic 4.1;
Dan 4.5
2.29
vv. 22, 28
2.30
Gen 41.16;
Isa 45.3;
Ps 139.2

25 Then Arioch quickly brought Daniel before the king and said to him: "I have found among the exiles from Judah a man who can tell the king the interpretation." 26 The king said to Daniel, whose name was Belteshazzar, "Are you able to tell me the dream that I have seen and its interpretation?" 27 Daniel answered the king, "No wise men, enchanters, magicians, or diviners can show to the king the mystery that the king is asking, 28 but there is a God in heaven who reveals mysteries, and he has disclosed to King Nebuchadnezzar what will happen at the end of days. Your dream and the visions of your head as you lay in bed were these: 29 To you, O king, as you lay in bed, came thoughts of what would be hereafter, and the revealer of mysteries disclosed to you what is to be. 30 But as for me, this mystery has not been revealed to me because of any wisdom that I have more than any other living being, but in order that the interpretation may be known to the king and that you may understand the thoughts of your mind.

d. *Nebuchadnezzar's dream unfolded*

2.31
Dan 7.7;
Hab 1.7
2.32
vv. 38, 39
2.33
vv. 40-43
2.34
Dan 8.25;
Zech 4.6;
Isa 2.9;
60.12
2.35
Ps 1.4;
Hos 13.3;
Ps 37.10, 36;
Isa 2.2, 3
2.36
v. 24

31 "You were looking, O king, and lo! there was a great statue. This statue was huge, its brilliance extraordinary; it was standing before you, and its appearance was frightening. 32 The head of that statue was of fine gold, its chest and arms of silver, its middle and thighs of bronze, 33 its legs of iron, its feet partly of iron and partly of clay. 34 As you looked on, a stone was cut out, not by human hands, and it struck the statue on its feet of iron and clay and broke them in pieces. 35 Then the iron, the clay, the bronze, the silver, and the gold, were all broken in pieces and became like the chaff of the summer threshing floors; and the wind carried them away, so that not a trace of them could be found. But the stone that struck the statue became a great mountain and filled the whole earth.

e. *The four earthly kingdoms and God's eternal kingdom*

2.37
Isa 47.5;
Jer 27.6, 7;
Ezek 26.7;
Ezra 1.2;
Ps 62.11
2.38
Jer 27.6;
Dan 4.21, 22;
v. 32
2.39
v. 32

36 "This was the dream; now we will tell the king its interpretation. 37 You, O king, the king of kings — to whom the God of heaven has given the kingdom, the power, the might, and the glory, 38 into whose hand he has given human beings, wherever they live, the wild animals of the field, and the birds of the air, and whom he has established as ruler over them all — you are the head of gold. 39 After you shall arise another kingdom inferior to yours, and yet a third kingdom of bronze, which shall rule over

---

2.24 Daniel followed protocol and went to Arioch to ask for an audience with the king, to whom he would reveal not only his dream but also the interpretation.
2.28 Daniel dared to tell the king the truth. No magician could discover what the king's dream was, nor could Daniel himself; he owed it all to the God in heaven who reveals secrets. In saying this he cut across all the idols of Nebuchadnezzar's kingdom and proclaimed the superiority of the God of Abraham. He was careful to say that his God was doing this to show the king what would take place in advance of the happenings.
2.31ff Nebuchadnezzar was satisfied with Daniel's record of the dream, for he proceeded without interruption to tell the king he would give him the meaning of the dream which, after all, is more important than the dream itself.
2.36ff In Nebuchadnezzar's dream the four metals stood for four great empires: (1) Nebuchadnezzar's Babylonian Empire (vv. 37,38); (2) the Medo-Persian

Empire, represented by the silver chest and arms (vv. 32,39), whose first great ruler was Cyrus; (3) the Grecian Empire under Alexander the Great and his successors (v. 39); and (4) the Roman Empire, which was the greatest of them all (v. 40). The Roman Empire was sectioned into the Eastern and Western Empires (the two legs). Then ten toes are mentioned; about this there are differences of opinion. Some think it refers to the restoration of the Roman Empire at the close of this age in a confederacy of ten nations, represented by the ten toes. The confederacy will be led by the beast or world conqueror. According to this view, the Rock (Christ) will conquer this confederacy (v. 35) and establish his millennial kingdom. Others hold that the Rock struck its blow by the death and resurrection of Christ, whose kingdom is now filling the whole earth. Christ's kingdom certainly is here now in a spiritual form as he reigns from heaven in the hearts of his people. The final consummation awaits Christ's second advent.

the whole earth. [40] And there shall be a fourth kingdom, strong as iron; just as iron crushes and smashes everything,[c] it shall crush and shatter all these. [41] As you saw the feet and toes partly of potter's clay and partly of iron, it shall be a divided kingdom; but some of the strength of iron shall be in it, as you saw the iron mixed with the clay. [42] As the toes of the feet were part iron and part clay, so the kingdom shall be partly strong and partly brittle. [43] As you saw the iron mixed with clay, so will they mix with one another in marriage,[d] but they will not hold together, just as iron does not mix with clay. [44] And in the days of those kings the God of heaven will set up a kingdom that shall never be destroyed, nor shall this kingdom be left to another people. It shall crush all these kingdoms and bring them to an end, and it shall stand forever; [45] just as you saw that a stone was cut from the mountain not by hands, and that it crushed the iron, the bronze, the clay, the silver, and the gold. The great God has informed the king what shall be hereafter. The dream is certain, and its interpretation trustworthy."

3. Nebuchadnezzar glorifies God and promotes Daniel

46   Then King Nebuchadnezzar fell on his face, worshiped Daniel, and commanded that a grain offering and incense be offered to him. [47] The king said to Daniel, "Truly, your God is God of gods and Lord of kings and a revealer of mysteries, for you have been able to reveal this mystery!" [48] Then the king promoted Daniel, gave him many great gifts, and made him ruler over the whole province of Babylon and chief prefect over all the wise men of Babylon. [49] Daniel made a request of the king, and he appointed Shadrach, Meshach, and Abednego over the affairs of the province of Babylon. But Daniel remained at the king's court.

C. The golden image and the fiery furnace

1. The abomination: the compulsory state religion

3   King Nebuchadnezzar made a golden statue whose height was sixty cubits and whose width was six cubits; he set it up on the plain of Dura in the province of Babylon. [2] Then King Nebuchadnezzar sent for the satraps, the prefects, and the governors, the counselors, the treasurers, the justices, the magistrates, and all the officials of the provinces, to assemble and come to the dedication of the statue that King Nebuchadnezzar had set up. [3] So the satraps, the prefects, and the governors, the counselors, the treasurers, the justices, the magistrates, and all the officials of the provinces, assembled for the dedication of the statue that King Nebuchadnezzar had set up. When they were standing before the statue that Nebuchadnezzar had set up, [4] the herald proclaimed aloud, "You are commanded, O peoples, nations, and languages, [5] that when you hear the sound of the horn, pipe, lyre, trigon, harp, drum, and entire musical ensemble, you are to fall down and worship the golden statue that King Nebuchadnezzar has set up. [6] Whoever does not fall down and worship

c Gk Theodotion Syr Vg: Aram adds *and like iron that crushes*   d Aram *by human seed*

2.40	Dan 7.7, 23
2.41	v. 33
2.44	Ps 2.9; Isa 60.12; 1 Cor 15.24
2.45	Isa 28.16; v. 35; Dan 8.25; v. 29; Mal 1.11; Gen 41.28, 32
2.46	Dan 8.17; Acts 10.25; 14.13; 28.6; Rev 19.10
2.47	Dan 11.36; vv. 22, 28
2.48	v. 6; Dan 4.9; 5.11
2.49	Dan 3.12; Esth 2.19, 21; Dan 3.2
3.1	Isa 46.6; Hab 2.19; v. 30; Dan 2.48
3.2	vv. 3, 27
3.4	Isa 40.9; 58.1; Rev 18.2; Dan 4.1; 6.25
3.5	vv. 7, 10, 15
3.6	vv. 11, 15, 21; Jer 29.22; Rev 14.11

2.46 Nebuchadnezzar was so impressed by what Daniel told him that he bowed before him in an act of worship. He commanded that grain offerings and incense be offered to him. He recognized that what happened was unique and supernatural and thus worthy of adulation. He confessed that Daniel's God is the God of gods and the Lord of kings because he had revealed these mysteries. There is a difference, however, between confessing that God is God and coming to him in faith for salvation. Nebuchadnezzar had "head" knowledge but not saving faith.
2.48,49 Daniel now rose to the heights to become one of the chief rulers of the kingdom under the king

himself. He secured the advancement of his three friends to high positions, for they could help him and he could trust them.
3.1,2 Nebuchadnezzar had learned nothing from his earlier dream and his acknowledgement that Daniel's God was the God of gods. He now erected an image, perhaps of himself, to be worshiped. It was covered with gold and stood around ninety feet high. Idolaters are always seeking new gods to be worshiped. The leaders of the nation gathered for the dedication of the image and the worship of it.
3.6 There was no religious freedom either for natives or foreigners. All were required to bow down

3.7
vv. 4, 5

shall immediately be thrown into a furnace of blazing fire." 7 Therefore, as soon as all the peoples heard the sound of the horn, pipe, lyre, trigon, harp, drum, and entire musical ensemble, all the peoples, nations, and languages fell down and worshiped the golden statue that King Nebuchadnezzar had set up.

2. The accusation and trial of Shadrach, Meshach, and Abednego

3.8
Dan 4.7; 6.12
3.9
Dan 2.4; 5.10
3.10
vv. 4-6;
Dan 6.2;
vv. 5, 7, 15
3.12
Dan 2.49;
1.7; 6.13

8 Accordingly, at this time certain Chaldeans came forward and denounced the Jews. 9 They said to King Nebuchadnezzar, "O king, live forever! 10 You, O king, have made a decree, that everyone who hears the sound of the horn, pipe, lyre, trigon, harp, drum, and entire musical ensemble, shall fall down and worship the golden statue, 11 and whoever does not fall down and worship shall be thrown into a furnace of blazing fire. 12 There are certain Jews whom you have appointed over the affairs of the province of Babylon: Shadrach, Meshach, and Abednego. These pay no heed to you, O king. They do not serve your gods and they do not worship the golden statue that you have set up."

3.13
Dan 2.12;
v. 19
3.14
Isa 46.1;
Jer 50.2; v. 1
3.15
vv. 5, 6;
Ex 5.2;
Isa 36.18-20;
Dan 2.47

13 Then Nebuchadnezzar in furious rage commanded that Shadrach, Meshach, and Abednego be brought in; so they brought those men before the king. 14 Nebuchadnezzar said to them, "Is it true, O Shadrach, Meshach, and Abednego, that you do not serve my gods and you do not worship the golden statue that I have set up? 15 Now if you are ready when you hear the sound of the horn, pipe, lyre, trigon, harp, drum, and entire musical ensemble to fall down and worship the statue that I have made, well and good.*e* But if you do not worship, you shall immediately be thrown into a furnace of blazing fire, and who is the god that will deliver you out of my hands?"

3.16
v. 12
3.17
Ps 27.1, 2;
Isa 26.3, 4;
Jer 15.20, 21
3.18
v. 28

16 Shadrach, Meshach, and Abednego answered the king, "O Nebuchadnezzar, we have no need to present a defense to you in this matter. 17 If our God whom we serve is able to deliver us from the furnace of blazing fire and out of your hand, O king, let him deliver us.*f* 18 But if not, be it known to you, O king, that we will not serve your gods and we will not worship the golden statue that you have set up."

3. The sentence and its execution

3.19
v. 13;
Dan 5.6;
v. 12
3.20
vv. 23-25
3.21
v. 27

19 Then Nebuchadnezzar was so filled with rage against Shadrach, Meshach, and Abednego that his face was distorted. He ordered the furnace heated up seven times more than was customary, 20 and ordered some of the strongest guards in his army to bind Shadrach, Meshach, and Abednego and to throw them into the furnace of blazing fire. 21 So the men were bound, still wearing their tunics,*g* their trousers,*g* their hats, and their other garments, and they were thrown into the furnace of blazing fire. 22 Because the king's command was urgent and the furnace was so

3.22
Ex 12.33;
Dan 2.15

e Aram lacks well and good   f Or If our God whom we serve is able to deliver us, he will deliver us from the furnace of blazing fire and out of your hand, O king.   g Meaning of Aram word uncertain

---

and worship before the golden image; anyone who refused to do so for any reason whatever would be "thrown into a furnace of blazing fire." Under such threats it would take someone of strong conviction to refrain from engaging in idolatrous worship. Those who already worshiped idols had no problem in worshiping another statue. But for the Hebrews, who had always been forbidden to bow before any idol and commanded to worship God alone, it was different. Daniel's three friends were willing to risk death in order to serve the Lord.
3.13 Nebuchadnezzar got angry easily. When he learned that the three Jews did not bow when the

music was played, he was enraged and had them brought before him. He was willing to give them a last chance: bow down and be free; refuse to bow and be consumed in the blazing furnace. He asked them what god would be able to deliver them from such an ordeal.
3.17 Daniel's friends stood for God. They affirmed that God was able to deliver them, and they believed that he would do so. Strongly defying the king, they said that even if God did not choose to deliver them, they would rather die than obey the king. They preferred to risk death rather than to sin.

overheated, the raging flames killed the men who lifted Shadrach, Meshach, and Abednego. 23 But the three men, Shadrach, Meshach, and Abednego, fell down, bound, into the furnace of blazing fire.

3.23
v. 21

4. The miraculous deliverance and the fourth man

24   Then King Nebuchadnezzar was astonished and rose up quickly. He said to his counselors, "Was it not three men that we threw bound into the fire?" They answered the king, "True, O king." 25 He replied, "But I see four men unbound, walking in the middle of the fire, and they are not hurt; and the fourth has the appearance of a god."h 26 Nebuchadnezzar then approached the door of the furnace of blazing fire and said, "Shadrach, Meshach, and Abednego, servants of the Most High God, come out! Come here!" So Shadrach, Meshach, and Abednego came out from the fire. 27 And the satraps, the prefects, the governors, and the king's counselors gathered together and saw that the fire had not had any power over the bodies of those men; the hair of their heads was not singed, their tunicsi were not harmed, and not even the smell of fire came from them. 28 Nebuchadnezzar said, "Blessed be the God of Shadrach, Meshach, and Abednego, who has sent his angel and delivered his servants who trusted in him. They disobeyed the king's command and yielded up their bodies rather than serve and worship any god except their own God. 29 Therefore I make a decree: Any people, nation, or language that utters blasphemy against the God of Shadrach, Meshach, and Abednego shall be torn limb from limb, and their houses laid in ruins; for there is no other god who is able to deliver in this way." 30 Then the king promoted Shadrach, Meshach, and Abednego in the province of Babylon.

3.25
Isa 43.2;
v. 28
3.26
v. 17;
Dan 4.2

3.27
v. 2;
Isa 43.2;
Heb 11.34;
v. 21

3.28
vv. 15, 25;
Acts 5.19;
12.7;
Ps 34.7, 8;
Jer 17.7;
v. 18
3.29
Dan 6.26;
v. 12;
Dan 2.5;
2.47; 6.27
3.30
Dan 2.49

D. Nebuchadnezzar's insanity

1. The frightening dream that could not be interpreted

4 j King Nebuchadnezzar to all peoples, nations, and languages that live throughout the earth: May you have abundant prosperity! 2 The signs and wonders that the Most High God has worked for me I am pleased to recount.

3   How great are his signs,
        how mighty his wonders!
His kingdom is an everlasting kingdom,
        and his sovereignty is from generation to generation.

4 k I, Nebuchadnezzar, was living at ease in my home and prospering in my palace. 5 I saw a dream that frightened me; my fantasies in bed and the visions of my head terrified me. 6 So I made a decree that all the wise men of Babylon should be brought before me, in order that they might tell me the interpretation of the dream. 7 Then the magicians, the enchanters, the Chaldeans, and the diviners came in, and I told them the dream, but they could not tell me its interpretation. 8 At last Daniel came in before

4.1
Dan 6.25
4.2
Dan 3.26

4.3
Dan 6.27;
v. 34;
Dan 2.44;
6.26
4.4
Isa 47.7, 8
4.5
Dan 2.28, 29;
2.1
4.6
Dan 2.2
4.7
Dan 2.2
4.8
Dan 1.7;
2.26;
Dan 5.11, 14

h Aram a son of the gods   i Meaning of Aram word uncertain   j Ch 3.31 in Aram   k Ch 4.1 in Aram

---

3.25 A fourth person appeared in the blazing furnace with Shadrach, Meshach, and Abednego. Nebuchadnezzar said, "The fourth has the appearance of a god." Presumably this was a theophany, an appearance of Jesus Christ in the O.T. Spiritually, we learn that when in difficulty, God's people have the help of Jesus, who has promised to go with us and help us (Heb 2.18). Christ's great promise is that he will never forsake his own (Mt 28.20; Heb 13.5).
3.28 Only a miracle could have kept these faithful Jews from death in the furnace. Nebuchadnezzar seems to have recognized that it was an angel sent by God who performed the miracle. He knew that what had happened was a supernatural event.

3.29 Nebuchadnezzar turned from one extreme to another. Now he ordered death for anyone who spoke against the command of the Hebrews.
4.1 This chapter records a formal statement of the king, a public paper that formed part of the nation's archives.
4.4 Nebuchadnezzar died when he was around forty-five years of age. The madness that came upon him occurred about nine years before his death. Seven of those years were spent in an animal-like state of mind.
4.8 Nebuchadnezzar undoubtedly remembered what Daniel had done for him when he had interpreted his first dream. This time, however, Nebu-

me—he who was named Belteshazzar after the name of my god, and who is endowed with a spirit of the holy gods[l]—and I told him the dream: 9 "O Belteshazzar, chief of the magicians, I know that you are endowed with a spirit of the holy gods[l] and that no mystery is too difficult for you. Hear[m] the dream that I saw; tell me its interpretation.

10[n] Upon my bed this is what I saw;
    there was a tree at the center of the earth,
    and its height was great.

11 The tree grew great and strong,
    its top reached to heaven,
    and it was visible to the ends of the whole earth.

12 Its foliage was beautiful,
    its fruit abundant,
    and it provided food for all.
    The animals of the field found shade under it,
    the birds of the air nested in its branches,
    and from it all living beings were fed.

13 "I continued looking, in the visions of my head as I lay in bed, and there was a holy watcher, coming down from heaven. 14 He cried aloud and said:

'Cut down the tree and chop off its branches,
    strip off its foliage and scatter its fruit.
Let the animals flee from beneath it
    and the birds from its branches.

15 But leave its stump and roots in the ground,
    with a band of iron and bronze,
    in the tender grass of the field.
Let him be bathed with the dew of heaven,
    and let his lot be with the animals of the field
    in the grass of the earth.

16 Let his mind be changed from that of a human,
    and let the mind of an animal be given to him.
    And let seven times pass over him.

17 The sentence is rendered by decree of the watchers,
    the decision is given by order of the holy ones,
    in order that all who live may know
    that the Most High is sovereign over the kingdom of mortals;
he gives it to whom he will
    and sets over it the lowliest of human beings.'

18 "This is the dream that I, King Nebuchadnezzar, saw. Now you, Belteshazzar, declare the interpretation, since all the wise men of my kingdom are unable to tell me the interpretation. You are able, however, for you are endowed with a spirit of the holy gods."[l]

2. Daniel's interpretation and warning

19 Then Daniel, who was called Belteshazzar, was severely distressed for a while. His thoughts terrified him. The king said, "Belteshazzar, do not let the dream or the interpretation terrify you." Belteshazzar answered, "My lord, may the dream be for those who hate you, and its

---

[l] Or a holy, divine spirit   [m] Theodotion: Aram The visions of   [n] Theodotion Syr Compare Gk: Aram adds The visions of my head

---

Cross references (margin)

4.9 Dan 2.48; 5.11; 2.47; 2.4, 5

4.10 vv. 5, 20; Ezek 31.3-6

4.11 vv. 20, 22

4.12 Ezek 31.6, 7; Lam 4.20; Mt 13.32; Lk 13.19

4.13 Dan 7.1; vv. 17, 23; Dan 8.13; Zech 14.5

4.14 Ezek 31.10-14; Mt 3.10; Ezek 31.12, 13

4.15 Job 14.7-9; v. 32

4.16 Dan 7.25; 11.13; 12.7

4.17 Ps 9.16; vv. 2, 25; Dan 5.18, 19; Dan 11.21

4.18 Gen 41.8, 15; Dan 5.8, 15; vv. 7-9

4.19 Dan 7.15, 28; 2 Sam 18.32; Jer 29.7

---

chadnezzar remembered very clearly the contents of his dream, and wanted to know its meaning. So he needed Daniel again.
4.9 *you are endowed with a spirit of the holy gods.* Nebuchadnezzar was a polytheist, thus he could recognize the gods working through Daniel.
4.19 Daniel was distressed and terrified. He knew

the meaning of the dream without having to spend time in prayer, for God had already revealed it to him. He did not want to tell the king the truth, for the punishment God was bringing to Nebuchadnezzar was terrifying even to Daniel. Moreover, he felt a sense of compassion and concern for a king he had served for years.

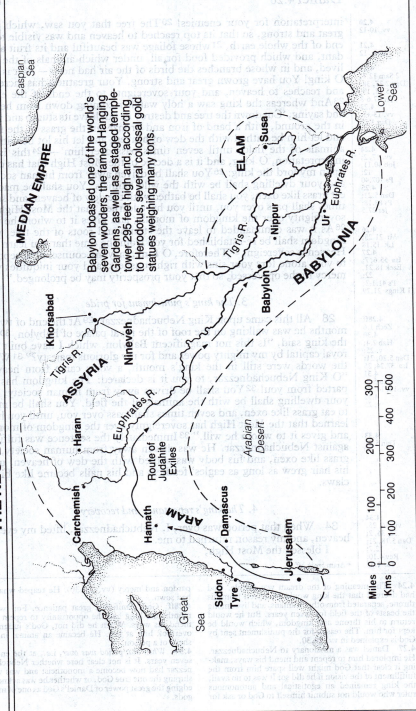

THE NEO-BABYLONIAN EMPIRE 626-539 B.C.

Babylon boasted one of the world's seven wonders, the famed Hanging Gardens, as well as a staged temple-tower 295 feet high and, according to Herodotus, several colossal gold statues weighing many tons.

©1989 The Zondervan Corporation.

4.20
vv. 10-12
4.21
see v. 12
4.22
2 Sam 12.7;
Dan 2.37, 38;
5.18, 19;
Jer 27.6-8
4.23
vv. 13-17;
Dan 5.21

4.24
vv. 17, 2;
Job 40.11,
12;
Ps 107.40
4.25
Dan 5.21;
Ps 83.18;
Jer 27.5

4.26
Mt 21.25;
Lk 15.18
4.27
Isa 55.6, 7;
Ezek 18.21,
22;
Ps 41.1-3;
1 Kings 21.29

4.28ff
Zech 1.6
4.30
Hab 2.4;
v. 25;
Dan 5.20, 21;
Isa 37.24, 25
4.31
Dan 5.5;
vv. 13, 14, 23
4.32
v. 25

4.33
Dan 5.21

4.34
vv. 16, 25,
32, 36, 2;
Dan 5.18, 21;
12.7;
Rev 4.10;
Lk 1.33

interpretation for your enemies! 20 The tree that you saw, which grew great and strong, so that its top reached to heaven and was visible to the end of the whole earth, 21 whose foliage was beautiful and its fruit abundant, and which provided food for all, under which animals of the field lived, and in whose branches the birds of the air had nests — 22 it is you, O king! You have grown great and strong. Your greatness has increased and reaches to heaven, and your sovereignty to the ends of the earth. 23 And whereas the king saw a holy watcher coming down from heaven and saying, 'Cut down the tree and destroy it, but leave its stump and roots in the ground, with a band of iron and bronze, in the grass of the field; and let him be bathed with the dew of heaven, and let his lot be with the animals of the field, until seven times pass over him' — 24 this is the interpretation, O king, and it is a decree of the Most High that has come upon my lord the king: 25 You shall be driven away from human society, and your dwelling shall be with the wild animals. You shall be made to eat grass like oxen, you shall be bathed with the dew of heaven, and seven times shall pass over you, until you have learned that the Most High has sovereignty over the kingdom of mortals, and gives it to whom he will. 26 As it was commanded to leave the stump and roots of the tree, your kingdom shall be re-established for you from the time that you learn that Heaven is sovereign. 27 Therefore, O king, may my counsel be acceptable to you: atone for*o* your sins with righteousness, and your iniquities with mercy to the oppressed, so that your prosperity may be prolonged."

3. The king's punishment for pride

28 All this came upon King Nebuchadnezzar. 29 At the end of twelve months he was walking on the roof of the royal palace of Babylon, 30 and the king said, "Is this not magnificent Babylon, which I have built as a royal capital by my mighty power and for my glorious majesty?" 31 While the words were still in the king's mouth, a voice came from heaven: "O King Nebuchadnezzar, to you it is declared: The kingdom has departed from you! 32 You shall be driven away from human society, and your dwelling shall be with the animals of the field. You shall be made to eat grass like oxen, and seven times shall pass over you, until you have learned that the Most High has sovereignty over the kingdom of mortals and gives it to whom he will." 33 Immediately the sentence was fulfilled against Nebuchadnezzar. He was driven away from human society, ate grass like oxen, and his body was bathed with the dew of heaven, until his hair grew as long as eagles' feathers and his nails became like birds' claws.

4. The king's repentance and recovery

34 When that period was over, I, Nebuchadnezzar, lifted my eyes to heaven, and my reason returned to me.
I blessed the Most High,

o Aram *break off*

4.24 The meaning of the dream was simple. God had decreed that the king would be driven from his throne, separated from other humans, and live among the beasts of the field for seven years. But he would return to his throne and kingdom, which would be kept for him. The reason for the punishment sent by God is explained in vv. 29,30.
4.27 Daniel was a missionary to Nebuchadnezzar. He implored him to repent and mend his ways, making it clear that God might well spare him from the fulfillment of the vision if he did so. It was to no avail; the king remained an egotistical and autonomous ruler who would not submit himself to God or ask for

pardon and mercy (vv. 28–30). He reaped what he had sown.
4.28ff God manifested great patience. For twelve months the king had the opportunity to repent and mend his ways. When he did not, God's judgment overtook him at last. He became an animal in the shape of a person.
4.34 *When that period was over,* i.e., at the end of seven years. It is not clear here whether Nebuchadnezzar had now become a monotheist and was worshiping the one true God, or whether he was acknowledging the great power of Daniel's God as one of many gods.

and praised and honored the one who lives forever.
For his sovereignty is an everlasting sovereignty,
    and his kingdom endures from generation to generation.
35 All the inhabitants of the earth are accounted as nothing,
    and he does what he wills with the host of heaven
    and the inhabitants of the earth.
There is no one who can stay his hand
    or say to him, "What are you doing?"
36 At that time my reason returned to me; and my majesty and splendor
were restored to me for the glory of my kingdom. My counselors and my
lords sought me out, I was re-established over my kingdom, and still more
greatness was added to me. 37 Now I, Nebuchadnezzar, praise and extol
and honor the King of heaven,
    for all his works are truth,
    and his ways are justice;
    and he is able to bring low
        those who walk in pride.

E. Belshazzar's festival and punishment for defying God

1. The profaning of the temple vessels

5 King Belshazzar made a great festival for a thousand of his lords, and
  he was drinking wine in the presence of the thousand.
2 Under the influence of the wine, Belshazzar commanded that they
bring in the vessels of gold and silver that his father Nebuchadnezzar had
taken out of the temple in Jerusalem, so that the king and his lords, his
wives, and his concubines might drink from them. 3 So they brought in
the vessels of gold and silver ᵖ that had been taken out of the temple, the
house of God in Jerusalem, and the king and his lords, his wives, and his
concubines drank from them. 4 They drank the wine and praised the gods
of gold and silver, bronze, iron, wood, and stone.

2. The handwriting on the wall

5 Immediately the fingers of a human hand appeared and began writing on the plaster of the wall of the royal palace, next to the lampstand.
The king was watching the hand as it wrote. 6 Then the king's face turned
pale, and his thoughts terrified him. His limbs gave way, and his knees
knocked together. 7 The king cried aloud to bring in the enchanters, the
Chaldeans, and the diviners; and the king said to the wise men of Babylon,
"Whoever can read this writing and tell me its interpretation shall be
clothed in purple, have a chain of gold around his neck, and rank third
in the kingdom." 8 Then all the king's wise men came in, but they could
not read the writing or tell the king the interpretation. 9 Then King
Belshazzar became greatly terrified and his face turned pale, and his lords
were perplexed.

3. The queen mother turns Belshazzar to Daniel

10 The queen, when she heard the discussion of the king and his

p Theodotion Vg: Aram lacks and silver

4.35 Isa 40.15, 17; Ps 135.6; Isa 43.13; 45.9; Rom 9.20
4.36 vv. 34, 30; Dan 2.31; v. 26
4.37 Ps 33.4, 5; Ex 18.11; Dan 5.20
5.1 Esth 1.3
5.2 Dan 1.2; Jer 52.19; v.23
5.4 v. 23; Rev 9.20
5.5 Dan 4.31; v. 24
5.6 Dan 4.5, 19; Nah 2.10; Ezek 7.17; 21.7
5.7 Isa 47.13; Dan 2.6; Ezek 16.11; Dan 6.2, 3
5.8 Dan 2.10, 27; 4.7
5.9 Isa 21.2-4; Jer 6.24; v. 6
5.10 Dan 2.4; 3.9

5.1 *Belshazzar.* The historicity of Belshazzar has been questioned by some critics. However, recent discoveries prove he was a real person; he was the Chaldean ruler who was reigning when Darius the Mede captured Babylon. Belshazzar's father, Nabonidus, made him coregent and commander of the army whenever he was absent on military ventures. When Daniel interpreted the writing on the wall, Belshazzar made him the third ruler in the king-

dom, i.e., after his father and himself, but before the crown prince, his own son. (v. 29)
5.10 *The queen,* i.e., probably the widow of Nebuchadnezzar. The queen learned of Belshazzar's predicament about the handwriting on the wall. She commended Daniel to him, expressed her judgment of his religious faith, and told him how Nebuchadnezzar had been helped by him in interpreting dreams as one "endowed with a spirit of the holy gods." He

lords, came into the banqueting hall. The queen said, "O king, live forever! Do not let your thoughts terrify you or your face grow pale. 11 There is a man in your kingdom who is endowed with a spirit of the holy gods.*q* In the days of your father he was found to have enlightenment, understanding, and wisdom like the wisdom of the gods. Your father, King Nebuchadnezzar, made him chief of the magicians, enchanters, Chaldeans, and diviners,*r* 12 because an excellent spirit, knowledge, and understanding to interpret dreams, explain riddles, and solve problems were found in this Daniel, whom the king named Belteshazzar. Now let Daniel be called, and he will give the interpretation."

13 Then Daniel was brought in before the king. The king said to Daniel, "So you are Daniel, one of the exiles of Judah, whom my father the king brought from Judah? 14 I have heard of you that a spirit of the gods*s* is in you, and that enlightenment, understanding, and excellent wisdom are found in you. 15 Now the wise men, the enchanters, have been brought in before me to read this writing and tell me its interpretation, but they were not able to give the interpretation of the matter. 16 But I have heard that you can give interpretations and solve problems. Now if you are able to read the writing and tell me its interpretation, you shall be clothed in purple, have a chain of gold around your neck, and rank third in the kingdom."

4. *Daniel announces God's judgment*

17 Then Daniel answered in the presence of the king, "Let your gifts be for yourself, or give your rewards to someone else! Nevertheless I will read the writing to the king and let him know the interpretation. 18 O king, the Most High God gave your father Nebuchadnezzar kingship, greatness, glory, and majesty. 19 And because of the greatness that he gave him, all peoples, nations, and languages trembled and feared before him. He killed those he wanted to kill, kept alive those he wanted to keep alive, honored those he wanted to honor, and degraded those he wanted to degrade. 20 But when his heart was lifted up and his spirit was hardened so that he acted proudly, he was deposed from his kingly throne, and his glory was stripped from him. 21 He was driven from human society, and his mind was made like that of an animal. His dwelling was with the wild asses, he was fed grass like oxen, and his body was bathed with the dew of heaven, until he learned that the Most High God has sovereignty over the kingdom of mortals, and sets over it whomever he will. 22 And you, Belshazzar his son, have not humbled your heart, even though you knew all this! 23 You have exalted yourself against the Lord of heaven! The vessels of his temple have been brought in before you, and you and your lords, your wives and your concubines have been drinking wine from them. You have praised the gods of silver and gold, of bronze, iron, wood, and stone, which do not see or hear or know; but the God in whose power is your very breath, and to whom belong all your ways, you have not honored.

24 "So from his presence the hand was sent and this writing was inscribed. 25 And this is the writing that was inscribed: MENE, MENE, TEKEL, and PARSIN. 26 This is the interpretation of the matter: MENE, God has numbered the days of*t* your kingdom and brought it to an end;

---

q Or *a holy, divine spirit*   *r* Aram adds *the king your father*   *s* Or *a divine spirit*   *t* Aram lacks *the days of*

---

called for Daniel to come at once.
5.11 *Your father, King Nebuchadnezzar.* The Aramaic word for "father" can also mean "predecessor" or even "ancestor" (in this instance, fifth removed, for Nabonidus, not Nebuchadnezzar, was Belshazzar's father). But Nebuchadnezzar might have been Belshazzar's grandfather on his mother's side.

5.17–23 Daniel wanted no rewards for interpreting Belshazzar's sign. He did speak very specifically about the king's sins. First he recounted the sins of Nebuchadnezzar and assigned the same sins to his successor: "You have exalted yourself against the Lord of heaven!" (v. 23).

27 TEKEL, you have been weighed on the scales and found wanting;
28 PERES,[u] your kingdom is divided and given to the Medes and Persians."

5. Daniel rewarded and Belshazzar killed

29 Then Belshazzar gave the command, and Daniel was clothed in purple, a chain of gold was put around his neck, and a proclamation was made concerning him that he should rank third in the kingdom.

30 That very night Belshazzar, the Chaldean king, was killed. 31[v] And Darius the Mede received the kingdom, being about sixty-two years old.

F. Daniel preserved in the lions' den

1. The conspiracy against Daniel

6 It pleased Darius to set over the kingdom one hundred twenty satraps, stationed throughout the whole kingdom, 2 and over them three presidents, including Daniel; to these the satraps gave account, so that the king might suffer no loss. 3 Soon Daniel distinguished himself above all the other presidents and satraps because an excellent spirit was in him, and the king planned to appoint him over the whole kingdom. 4 So the presidents and the satraps tried to find grounds for complaint against Daniel in connection with the kingdom. But they could find no grounds for complaint or any corruption, because he was faithful, and no negligence or corruption could be found in him. 5 The men said, "We shall not find any ground for complaint against this Daniel unless we find it in connection with the law of his God."

6 So the presidents and satraps conspired and came to the king and said to him, "O King Darius, live forever! 7 All the presidents of the kingdom, the prefects and the satraps, the counselors and the governors are agreed that the king should establish an ordinance and enforce an interdict, that whoever prays to anyone, divine or human, for thirty days, except to you, O king, shall be thrown into a den of lions. 8 Now, O king, establish the interdict and sign the document, so that it cannot be changed, according to the law of the Medes and the Persians, which cannot be revoked." 9 Therefore King Darius signed the document and interdict.

[u] The singular of *Parsin* [v] Ch 6.1 in Aram

Cross references (margin):

5.27 Job 31.6; Ps 62.9
5.29 vv. 7, 16
5.30
5.31 Dan 6.1; 9.1
6.1 Esth 1.1; Dan 5.31
6.2 Dan 2.48, 49; Ezra 4.22
6.3 Dan 1.20; 5.12, 14; Esth 10.3
6.4 Gen 43.18; v.22
6.6 v. 21; Neh 2.3; Dan 2.4
6.7 Dan 3.2, 27; Ps 59.3; Dan 3.6; v. 16
6.8 vv. 12, 15; Esth 1.19; 8.8
6.9 Ps 118.9; 146.3

5.28 God had chosen to give Belshazzar's kingdom to the Medes and the Persians. The judgment was certain and its fulfillment imminent—it took place that night.
5.30 Xenophon and Herodotus, ancient Greek historians, wrote about the fall of Babylon. The Euphrates River ran through the center of the city. The Medo-Persian armies strategically diverted the river from its normal channel. Then, while the Babylonians, assuming they were safe, were engaged in carousing and revelry, two Babylonian deserters directed the conquering hosts into the city via the dry bed of the river. The defenders were helpless, and that very night Belshazzar was slain as the invaders overran the city.
5.31 *Darius the Mede.* Darius was made "king" or governor over Chaldea after the defeat of Belshazzar by Cyrus the Great. Darius the Mede must not be confused with Darius the Persian mentioned in Ezra, Haggai, and Zechariah, nor with the one mentioned in Neh 12.22. It seems quite likely that Darius was also known under the name of Gubaru.
6.1 Daniel had the unique capacity of commending himself to kings, a gift that came from God, who used him to accomplish his purposes. He served pagan monarchs with fidelity but without compromising his own faith. He followed the footsteps of Joseph, who faithfully served the Pharaoh. In a complex world today most believers are called upon to labor amid secular and ungodly people who do not know the Lord. This is permissible, as long as they do not compromise their convictions. Darius knew that Daniel would protect the king's interests and serve him well. He became the number one man in the kingdom after the monarch himself. But this gave rise to envy and hatred on the part of those who did not share Daniel's faith in God.
6.9 Some have said that no king would dare do what is reported in vv. 7–9. Thus they consider this story to be legendary. But this is not so. The new Persian rulers of Babylon wanted to consolidate their reign by allowing for no gods other than their own. The unity of the empire would be advanced by getting rid of all the local or regional deities. Worldly wisdom could justify such action on purely political grounds.

2. Daniel detected, tried, and sentenced

6.10
1 Kings 8.48,
49;
Ps 95.6;
55.17;
1 Thess 5.17,
18
6.11
v.6
6.12
Dan 3.8;
Acts 16.19-21

6.13
Dan 1.6;
5.13;
Esth 3.8;
Dan 3.12;
Acts 5.29
6.14
Mk 6.26
6.15
Esth 8.8; v.8

6.16
Jer 38.5;
vv. 7, 20;
Ps 37.39, 40
6.17
Lam 3.55;
Mt 27.66
6.18
2 Sam 12.16,
17;
Esth 6.1;
Dan 2.1

6.20
vv. 26, 27;
Jer 32.17;
Dan 3.17
6.21
Dan 2.4; v. 6
6.22
Acts 12.11;
2 Tim 4.17;
Heb 11.33;
1 Sam 24.10
6.23
vv. 14, 18;
Dan 3.25, 27;
Isa 26.3;
Heb 11.33
6.24
2 Kings 14.6;
Ps 54.5;
Isa 38.13

10 Although Daniel knew that the document had been signed, he continued to go to his house, which had windows in its upper room open toward Jerusalem, and to get down on his knees three times a day to pray to his God and praise him, just as he had done previously. 11 The conspirators came and found Daniel praying and seeking mercy before his God. 12 Then they approached the king and said concerning the interdict, "O king! Did you not sign an interdict, that anyone who prays to anyone, divine or human, within thirty days except to you, O king, shall be thrown into a den of lions?" The king answered, "The thing stands fast, according to the law of the Medes and Persians, which cannot be revoked." 13 Then they responded to the king, "Daniel, one of the exiles from Judah, pays no attention to you, O king, or to the interdict you have signed, but he is saying his prayers three times a day."

14 When the king heard the charge, he was very much distressed. He was determined to save Daniel, and until the sun went down he made every effort to rescue him. 15 Then the conspirators came to the king and said to him, "Know, O king, that it is a law of the Medes and Persians that no interdict or ordinance that the king establishes can be changed."

16 Then the king gave the command, and Daniel was brought and thrown into the den of lions. The king said to Daniel, "May your God, whom you faithfully serve, deliver you!" 17 A stone was brought and laid on the mouth of the den, and the king sealed it with his own signet and with the signet of his lords, so that nothing might be changed concerning Daniel. 18 Then the king went to his palace and spent the night fasting; no food was brought to him, and sleep fled from him.

3. Daniel delivered and his foes punished

19 Then, at break of day, the king got up and hurried to the den of lions. 20 When he came near the den where Daniel was, he cried out anxiously to Daniel, "O Daniel, servant of the living God, has your God whom you faithfully serve been able to deliver you from the lions?" 21 Daniel then said to the king, "O king, live forever! 22 My God sent his angel and shut the lions' mouths so that they would not hurt me, because I was found blameless before him; and also before you, O king, I have done no wrong." 23 Then the king was exceedingly glad and commanded that Daniel be taken up out of the den. So Daniel was taken up out of the den, and no kind of harm was found on him, because he had trusted in his God. 24 The king gave a command, and those who had accused Daniel were brought and thrown into the den of lions—they, their children, and their wives. Before they reached the bottom of the den the lions overpowered them and broke all their bones in pieces.

6.10 The decree of Darius ran counter to the law of God. The age-old question arose: "Shall I obey God or Caesar, when Caesar's law contradicts the law of God?" Some might have wrestled with this question a long time. But Daniel was an old and seasoned believer. He needed no second thoughts; he simply continued his daily devotions in the sight of all, even three times a day. Undoubtedly those who plotted against him did so with the knowledge that Daniel would act exactly the way he did. They knew him and understood the depth of his reverence for God and his obedience to the law of God.
6.14 Darius knew he had been taken in by the plotters, but there was nothing he could do, for his word was pledged and had to be carried out.

6.16 Daniel was cast into the lions' den when he was an old man (probably over eighty). He remained faithful to God (cf. v. 20) and refused to compromise his conscience for material gain throughout his years.
6.20 After a sleepless night of fasting, Darius hastened to the lions' den to see what had happened during the night. He asked the question, "Has your God . . . been able to deliver you?" For Daniel that was no problem. He believed that his God could deliver him. Whether God chose to deliver him or let him die depended on God's will, not on his divine ability. Believers who are in the will of God can know for certain that whatever God does for them will work for good (cf. Rom 8.28).

4. *Darius acknowledges Daniel's God*

25 Then King Darius wrote to all peoples and nations of every language throughout the whole world: "May you have abundant prosperity! 26 I make a decree, that in all my royal dominion people should tremble and fear before the God of Daniel:

For he is the living God,
    enduring forever.
His kingdom shall never be destroyed,
    and his dominion has no end.
27 He delivers and rescues,
    he works signs and wonders in heaven and on earth;
for he has saved Daniel
    from the power of the lions."
28 So this Daniel prospered during the reign of Darius and the reign of Cyrus the Persian.

II. The final dream and visions (7.1–12.13)

A. The vision of the four beasts

1. *The four beasts of Babylon, Persia, Greece, and Rome*

7 In the first year of King Belshazzar of Babylon, Daniel had a dream and visions of his head as he lay in bed. Then he wrote down the dream: [w] 2 I, [x] Daniel, saw in my vision by night the four winds of heaven stirring up the great sea, 3 and four great beasts came up out of the sea, different from one another. 4 The first was like a lion and had eagles' wings. Then, as I watched, its wings were plucked off, and it was lifted up from the ground and made to stand on two feet like a human being; and a human mind was given to it. 5 Another beast appeared, a second one, that looked like a bear. It was raised up on one side, had three tusks [y] in its mouth among its teeth and was told, "Arise, devour many bodies!" 6 After this, as I watched, another appeared, like a leopard. The beast had four wings of a bird on its back and four heads; and dominion was given to it. 7 After this I saw in the visions by night a fourth beast, terrifying and dreadful and exceedingly strong. It had great iron teeth and was devouring, breaking in pieces, and stamping what was left with its feet. It was different from all the beasts that preceded it, and it had ten horns. 8 I was considering the horns, when another horn appeared, a little one, coming up among them; to make room for it, three of the earlier horns were plucked up by the roots. There were eyes like human eyes in this horn, and a mouth speaking arrogantly.

2. *The everlasting kingdom of the Ancient One*

9 As I watched,
    thrones were set in place,

w Q Ms Theodotion: MT adds *the beginning of the words; he said*   *x* Theodotion: Aram *Daniel answered and said, I*   *y* Or *ribs*

Cross references (right margin):
6.25 Ezra 1.1, 2; Esth 3.12; 8.9; Dan 4.1; 1 Pet 1.2
6.26 Dan 3.29; Ps 99.1; Dan 4.34; Ps 93.1, 2; Dan 4.3; 7.14, 27
6.27 v. 22; Dan 4.3
6.28 Ezra 1.1, 2; Dan 1.21; 10.1
7.1 Dan 5.1, 22, 30; 1.17; vv. 7, 13, 15; Jer 36.4, 32
7.3 v. 17; Rev 13.1
7.4 Jer 48.40; Ezek 17.3; Hab 1.8
7.5 Dan 2.39
7.6 v. 12
7.7 Rev 12.3; 13.1; 17.3
7.8 vv. 20, 21; Rev 9.7; vv. 11, 25
7.9 Mk 9.3; Rev 1.14; Ezek 1.13, 26; 10.2, 6

7.1 Daniel speaks now of a dream or vision he had received during the reign of Belshazzar. Chronologically this chapter fits between chs. 4 and 5.
7.4 *like a lion and had eagles' wings*. Archaeologists have found winged lions among the ruins of Nimrud and Babylon. Here they symbolize the Babylonian empire.
7.5 *Another beast*. The total vision comprised four animals: a winged lion, a bear, a leopard, and a fourth animal too dreadful to be described. These animals have been thought to represent Babylon, Media, Persia, and Greece, or possibly Babylon, Medo-Persia,

Greece, and Rome.
7.8 *another horn appeared, a little one*. Horns symbolize power; here they mean kings. Some interpret the fourth kingdom to be Greece and identify the little horn as Antiochus Epiphanes, the Seleucid ruler who tried to halt Jewish worship. Others identify the fourth kingdom as Rome and think the little horn refers to a future antichrist.
7.9–14 *an Ancient One* i.e., Jesus Christ, who sits on the throne of an eternal kingdom. Before him all nations bow. The vision is general, however, not specific. No details can be extracted from it.

and an Ancient One*z* took his throne,
his clothing was white as snow,
and the hair of his head like pure wool;
his throne was fiery flames,
and its wheels were burning fire.
10 A stream of fire issued
and flowed out from his presence.
A thousand thousands served him,
and ten thousand times ten thousand stood attending him.
The court sat in judgment,
and the books were opened.

11 I watched then because of the noise of the arrogant words that the horn was speaking. And as I watched, the beast was put to death, and its body destroyed and given over to be burned with fire. 12 As for the rest of the beasts, their dominion was taken away, but their lives were prolonged for a season and a time. 13 As I watched in the night visions,

I saw one like a human being*a*
coming with the clouds of heaven.
And he came to the Ancient One*b*
and was presented before him.
14 To him was given dominion
and glory and kingship,
that all peoples, nations, and languages
should serve him.
His dominion is an everlasting dominion
that shall not pass away,
and his kingship is one
that shall never be destroyed.

3. The dream explained

15 As for me, Daniel, my spirit was troubled within me,*c* and the visions of my head terrified me. 16 I approached one of the attendants to ask him the truth concerning all this. So he said that he would disclose to me the interpretation of the matter: 17 "As for these four great beasts, four kings shall arise out of the earth. 18 But the holy ones of the Most High shall receive the kingdom and possess the kingdom forever — forever and ever."

19 Then I desired to know the truth concerning the fourth beast, which was different from all the rest, exceedingly terrifying, with its teeth of iron and claws of bronze, and which devoured and broke in pieces, and stamped what was left with its feet; 20 and concerning the ten horns that were on its head, and concerning the other horn, which came up and to make room for which three of them fell out — the horn that had eyes and a mouth that spoke arrogantly, and that seemed greater than the others. 21 As I looked, this horn made war with the holy ones and was prevailing over them, 22 until the Ancient One*b* came; then judgment was given for the holy ones of the Most High, and the time arrived when the holy ones gained possession of the kingdom.

23 This is what he said: "As for the fourth beast,
there shall be a fourth kingdom on earth
that shall be different from all the other kingdoms;

---

z Aram *an Ancient of Days*   *a* Aram *one like a son of man*   *b* Aram *the Ancient of Days*   *c* Aram *troubled in its sheath*

7.13 *one like a human being.* Daniel here prophesies the coming of the Lord Jesus at the end of the age. Traditionally, this phrase is translated "son of man" (cf. footnote NRSV), a title later applied to the Messiah throughout the N.T. Christ's second coming is prophesied repeatedly in the O.T. Christ himself spoke of his second advent (Mt 25.31; Jn 14.3), as did the apostles (Acts 2.30, 1 Tim 6.14) and the angels who spoke God's message to the disciples at the time of the ascension (Acts 1.10,11).

Cross references (left margin):

7.10
Ps 50.3; 97.3;
Isa 30.33;
Rev 5.11;
20.12

7.11
vv. 7, 8;
Rev 19.20
7.12
vv. 3-6

7.13
Ezek 1.26;
Mt 24.30;
26.64;
Mk 13.26;
Lk 21.27;
Rev 1.7, 13

7.14
Ps 2.6-8;
1 Cor 15.27;
Eph 1.22;
Phil 2.9-11;
Ps 72.11;
102.22;
Dan 2.44;
Mic 4.7;
Heb 12.28

7.15
vv. 1, 28
7.16
Rev 5.5;
7.13, 14;
Dan 8.16, 17
7.17
v. 3
7.18
Isa 60.12-14;
Rev 2.26;
20.4
7.19
vv. 7, 8

7.21
Rev 13.7
7.22
vv. 9, 13;
1 Cor 6.2, 3;
v. 18
7.23
vv. 7, 19

it shall devour the whole earth,
    and trample it down, and break it to pieces.

24 As for the ten horns,
    out of this kingdom ten kings shall arise,
        and another shall arise after them.
    This one shall be different from the former ones,
        and shall put down three kings.

25 He shall speak words against the Most High,
    shall wear out the holy ones of the Most High,
    and shall attempt to change the sacred seasons and the law;
    and they shall be given into his power
        for a time, two times,*d* and half a time.

26 Then the court shall sit in judgment,
    and his dominion shall be taken away,
        to be consumed and totally destroyed.

27 The kingship and dominion
    and the greatness of the kingdoms under the whole heaven
        shall be given to the people of the holy ones of the
            Most High;
    their kingdom shall be an everlasting kingdom,
        and all dominions shall serve and obey them.”

28 Here the account ends. As for me, Daniel, my thoughts greatly terrified me, and my face turned pale; but I kept the matter in my mind.

B. *The vision of the ram and the male goat*

1. *The ram of Medo-Persia and the male goat of Greece*

8 In the third year of the reign of King Belshazzar a vision appeared to me, Daniel, after the one that had appeared to me at first. ²In the vision I was looking and saw myself in Susa the capital, in the province of Elam,*e* and I was by the river Ulai.*f* ³I looked up and saw a ram standing beside the river.*g* It had two horns. Both horns were long, but one was longer than the other, and the longer one came up second. ⁴I saw the ram charging westward and northward and southward. All beasts were powerless to withstand it, and no one could rescue from its power; it did as it pleased and became strong.

5 As I was watching, a male goat appeared from the west, coming across the face of the whole earth without touching the ground. The goat had a horn*h* between its eyes. ⁶It came toward the ram with the two horns that I had seen standing beside the river,*g* and it ran at it with savage force. ⁷I saw it approaching the ram. It was enraged against it and struck the ram, breaking its two horns. The ram did not have power to withstand it; it threw the ram down to the ground and trampled upon it, and there was no one who could rescue the ram from its power. ⁸Then the male goat

d Aram *a time, times*   *e* Gk Theodotion: MT Q Ms repeat *in the vision I was looking*   *f* Or *the Ulai Gate*
g Or *gate*   *h* Theodotion: Gk *one horn;* Heb *a horn of vision*

Cross references

7.24
vv. 7, 8;
Rev 17.12

7.25
Isa 37.23;
Dan 8.24, 25;
Rev 13.5;
17.6; 18.24;
Dan 2.21;
12.7;
Rev 12.14

7.26
vv. 10, 22

7.27
vv. 14, 18,
22;
Lk 1.33;
Jn 12.34;
Rev 11.15;
Ps 2.6-12;
Isa 60.12

7.28
v. 15;
Dan 8.27;
Lk 2.19

8.1
Dan 7.1, 15,
28
8.2
Dan 7.2, 15;
Esth 1.2;
Ezek 32.24;
v. 16
8.3
Dan 10.5;
v. 20
8.4
v. 7
8.5
v. 21
8.6
v. 3
8.7
Dan 11.11;
7.7
8.8
2 Chr 26.16;
Dan 5.20;
v. 22;
Dan 7.2;
Rev 7.1

7.24–27 The visions of the *ten horns* parallels the ten toes (2.41,42; see note on 2.36ff). The world ruler of the end of this age will suffer final defeat by Christ (v. 27). The little horn of this verse, which defeats three of the ten kings, should not be confused with the "little horn" of 8.9, which is to emerge from the third kingdom (the Greek empire, established by Alexander the Great). The horn mentioned here will emerge from the fourth kingdom. *another shall arise,* i.e., "another king shall arise." This probably refers to the future antichrist of 2 Thess 2.3,4.
7.28 Daniel kept in mind all that God had revealed to him. He kept the vision in his heart, not to keep it *from* us but to keep it *for* us and to write it down in Scripture. However much the vision may puzzle

us, we can be assured that God is working out his own plan in history.
8.1 Chronologically this chapter precedes ch. 5, for the vision came in the last year of Belshazzar's reign. The vision of ch. 7 came while he was asleep; this one came when he was awake.
8.3 *two horns.* These represent Media and Persia (cf. v. 20).
8.5 *a male goat,* i.e., Greece (cf. v. 21). *a horn between its eyes,* i.e., Alexander the Great.
8.8 *There came up four prominent horns.* The four principal successors of Alexander the Great were Ptolemy I of Egypt, Seleucus of Babylonia, Antigonus of Aram and Asia Minor, and Antipater of Macedonia and Greece.

grew exceedingly great; but at the height of its power, the great horn was broken, and in its place there came up four prominent horns toward the four winds of heaven.

2. The little horn

9 Out of one of them came another[i] horn, a little one, which grew exceedingly great toward the south, toward the east, and toward the beautiful land. 10 It grew as high as the host of heaven. It threw down to the earth some of the host and some of the stars, and trampled on them. 11 Even against the prince of the host it acted arrogantly; it took the regular burnt offering away from him and overthrew the place of his sanctuary. 12 Because of wickedness, the host was given over to it together with the regular burnt offering;[j] it cast truth to the ground, and kept prospering in what it did. 13 Then I heard a holy one speaking, and another holy one said to the one that spoke, "For how long is this vision concerning the regular burnt offering, the transgression that makes desolate, and the giving over of the sanctuary and host to be trampled?"[j] 14 And he answered him,[k] "For two thousand three hundred evenings and mornings; then the sanctuary shall be restored to its rightful state."

3. Gabriel's explanation of the vision

15 When I, Daniel, had seen the vision, I tried to understand it. Then someone appeared standing before me, having the appearance of a man, 16 and I heard a human voice by the Ulai, calling, "Gabriel, help this man understand the vision." 17 So he came near where I stood; and when he came, I became frightened and fell prostrate. But he said to me, "Understand, O mortal,[l] that the vision is for the time of the end."

18 As he was speaking to me, I fell into a trance, face to the ground; then he touched me and set me on my feet. 19 He said, "Listen, and I will tell you what will take place later in the period of wrath; for it refers to the appointed time of the end. 20 As for the ram that you saw with the two horns, these are the kings of Media and Persia. 21 The male goat[m] is the king of Greece, and the great horn between its eyes is the first king. 22 As for the horn that was broken, in place of which four others arose, four kingdoms shall arise from his[n] nation, but not with his power.

23 At the end of their rule,
   when the transgressions have reached their full measure,
   a king of bold countenance shall arise,
      skilled in intrigue.
24 He shall grow strong in power,[o]
      shall cause fearful destruction,
      and shall succeed in what he does.
   He shall destroy the powerful
      and the people of the holy ones.
25 By his cunning

8.9
v. 23;
Dan 11.16,
41
8.10
Rev 12.4
8.11
Dan 11.36,
37;
Josh 5.14;
Dan 11.31;
12.11;
Ezek 46.13,
14
8.13
Dan 4.13, 23;
12.6, 8;
Rev 11.2

8.15
v. 1;
Dan 7.13
8.16
Dan 9.21;
Lk 1.19, 26
8.17
Ezek 1.28;
Rev 1.17
8.18
Dan 10.9, 16,
18;
Ezek 2.2
8.19
Hab 2.3
8.21
v. 5;
Dan 10.20
8.22
v. 8

8.24
Dan 11.36

8.25
Dan 11.21;
v. 11;
Dan 2.34, 45

i Cn Compare 7.8: Heb one   j Meaning of Heb uncertain   k Gk Theodotion Syr Vg: Heb me   l Heb son of man   m Or shaggy male goat   n Gk Theodotion Vg: Heb the   o Theodotion and one Gk Ms: Heb repeats (from 8.22) but not with his power

8.9ff Daniel returns to the ram and he-goat visions (referring to the second and third of the four great kingdoms). In ch. 2, they were the silver and bronze kingdoms; in 7.5,6 they were the bear and leopard kingdoms. The two kingdoms are Medo-Persia and Greece. The little horn, growing slowly at first, is probably Antiochus IV Epiphanes (175–164 B.C.) who, in 168 B.C., profaned the temple and tried to crush the Jewish religion altogether. It also represents the last world dictator (the beast of the Revelation) who is yet to come. *the beautiful land*, i.e., the land of Israel. Israel was attacked by Antiochus Epiphanes, while a later fulfillment of this prophecy is also indicated (see vv. 17,19,23).
8.14 *two thousand three hundred evenings and mornings*, i.e., 1,150 days.
8.23 The literal description here is of one who possesses great shrewdness and intelligence — one who understands riddles and is skilled in intrigues. This probably refers both to Antiochus Epiphanes and to a further fulfillment by the antichrist at the end of human history.

he shall make deceit prosper under his hand,
  and in his own mind he shall be great.
Without warning he shall destroy many
  and shall even rise up against the Prince of princes.
But he shall be broken, and not by human hands.
26The vision of the evenings and the mornings that has been told is true. As for you, seal up the vision, for it refers to many days from now."

27 So I, Daniel, was overcome and lay sick for some days; then I arose and went about the king's business. But I was dismayed by the vision and did not understand it.

C. *The vision of the seventy weeks*

1. *Daniel's promise-claiming prayer*

9 In the first year of Darius son of Ahasuerus, by birth a Mede, who became king over the realm of the Chaldeans — 2 in the first year of his reign, I, Daniel, perceived in the books the number of years that, according to the word of the LORD to the prophet Jeremiah, must be fulfilled for the devastation of Jerusalem, namely, seventy years.

3 Then I turned to the Lord God, to seek an answer by prayer and supplication with fasting and sackcloth and ashes. 4 I prayed to the LORD my God and made confession, saying,

"Ah, Lord, great and awesome God, keeping covenant and steadfast love with those who love you and keep your commandments, 5 we have sinned and done wrong, acted wickedly and rebelled, turning aside from your commandments and ordinances. 6 We have not listened to your servants the prophets, who spoke in your name to our kings, our princes, and our ancestors, and to all the people of the land.

7 "Righteousness is on your side, O Lord, but open shame, as at this day, falls on us, the people of Judah, the inhabitants of Jerusalem, and all Israel, those who are near and those who are far away, in all the lands to which you have driven them, because of the treachery that they have committed against you. 8 Open shame, O LORD, falls on us, our kings, our officials, and our ancestors, because we have sinned against you. 9 To the Lord our God belong mercy and forgiveness, for we have rebelled against him, 10 and have not obeyed the voice of the LORD our God by following his laws, which he set before us by his servants the prophets.

11 "All Israel has transgressed your law and turned aside, refusing to obey your voice. So the curse and the oath written in the law of Moses, the servant of God, have been poured out upon us, because we have sinned against you. 12 He has confirmed his words, which he spoke against us and against our rulers, by bringing upon us a calamity so great that what has been done against Jerusalem has never before been done under the whole heaven. 13 Just as it is written in the law of Moses, all this calamity has come upon us. We did not entreat the favor of the LORD our God, turning from our iniquities and reflecting on his*p* fidelity. 14 So the LORD kept watch over this calamity until he brought it upon us. Indeed, the LORD our God is right in all that he has done; for we have disobeyed his voice.

15 "And now, O Lord our God, who brought your people out of the

p Heb *your*

Cross references

8.26 Dan 10.1; 12.4, 9; 10.14
8.27 Dan 7.28; Hab 3.16
9.1 Dan 5.31; 11.1
9.2 2 Chr 36.21; Jer 29.10; Zech 7.5
9.3 Neh 1.4; Jer 29.12; Jas 4.8
9.4 Deut 7.21; Neh 9.32; Deut 7.9
9.5 Ps 106.6; Lam 1.18, 20; v. 11
9.6 2 Chr 36.15, 16; v. 8
9.7 Jer 23.6; 33.16; Am 9.9
9.8 vv. 6, 5
9.9 Neh 9.17; Ps 130.4
9.10 2 Kings 17.13-15; 18.12
9.11 Isa 1.4-6; Jer 8.5, 10; Deut 27.15
9.12 Isa 44.26; Zech 1.6; Ezek 5.9
9.13 Isa 9.13; Jer 2.30
9.14 Jer 31.28; 44.27; vv. 7, 10
9.15 Ex 6.1, 6; Jer 32.21; Neh 9.10; Jer 32.20

9.2 Daniel obviously had access to the prophecy of Jeremiah and understood its content. Jer 29.10 had expressly foretold the seventy years of captivity, during which time the holy city of Jerusalem would lie desolate. This time was now nearing its end.
9.3 Fearing that the sins of the people might cause God to defer deliverance, Daniel earnestly pleaded with him to end the captivity.
9.9 Two conditions exist that make possible the for-

giveness of sins by God. (1) God's own mercy permits it. Although God is holy and righteous, he is also merciful; his chosen method of atoning for sin vindicated his righteous character and at the same time provided a way of forgiveness for the sinner. (2) The sacrifice of Jesus is the basis for forgiveness (cf. Eph 1.7), for "without the shedding of blood there is no forgiveness of sins" (Heb 9.22).

9.16
1 Sam 12.7;
Ps 31.1;
Zech 8.3

land of Egypt with a mighty hand and made your name renowned even to this day — we have sinned, we have done wickedly. 16 O Lord, in view of all your righteous acts, let your anger and wrath, we pray, turn away from your city Jerusalem, your holy mountain; because of our sins and the iniquities of our ancestors, Jerusalem and your people have become a disgrace among all our neighbors. 17 Now therefore, O our God, listen to the prayer of your servant and to his supplication, and for your own sake, Lord, q let your face shine upon your desolated sanctuary. 18 Incline your ear, O my God, and hear. Open your eyes and look at our desolation and the city that bears your name. We do not present our supplication before you on the ground of our righteousness, but on the ground of your great mercies. 19 O Lord, hear; O Lord, forgive; O Lord, listen and act and do not delay! For your own sake, O my God, because your city and your people bear your name!"

9.17
Num 6.25;
Lam 5.18
9.18
Isa 37.17;
Jer 25.29;
36.7

9.19
Ps 44.23;
74.10, 11

2. Gabriel's appearance and the interpretation

9.20
v. 3;
Isa 58.9; 6.5
9.21
Dan 8.16;
Isa 6.2;
Dan 8.18;
10.10, 16, 18
9.23
Dan 10.12;
Lk 1.28;
Mt 24.15
9.24
Isa 55.10;
Rom 5.10;
Acts 3.14
9.25
Ezra 4.24;
Neh 2.1-8;
3.1;
Jn 1.41;
4.25;
Isa 9.6
9.26
Isa 53.8;
Mk 12.7;
Lk 19.43,
44;
Nah 1.8

20 While I was speaking, and was praying and confessing my sin and the sin of my people Israel, and presenting my supplication before the Lord my God on behalf of the holy mountain of my God — 21 while I was speaking in prayer, the man Gabriel, whom I had seen before in a vision, came to me in swift flight at the time of the evening sacrifice. 22 He came r and said to me, "Daniel, I have now come out to give you wisdom and understanding. 23 At the beginning of your supplications a word went out, and I have come to declare it, for you are greatly beloved. So consider the word and understand the vision:

24 "Seventy weeks are decreed for your people and your holy city: to finish the transgression, to put an end to sin, and to atone for iniquity, to bring in everlasting righteousness, to seal both vision and prophet, and to anoint a most holy place. s 25 Know therefore and understand: from the time that the word went out to restore and rebuild Jerusalem until the time of an anointed prince, there shall be seven weeks; and for sixty-two weeks it shall be built again with streets and moat, but in a troubled time. 26 After

q Theodotion Vg Compare Syr: Heb for the Lord's sake   r Gk Syr: Heb He made to understand
s Or thing or one

9.21 the man Gabriel, i.e., the angel Gabriel who appeared in human form.
9.24 The prophecy of the seventy weeks has been variously interpreted. One conclusion seems self-evident. Each week must be a period of seven years, for a total of 490 years. Daniel divides this period into three parts: the first has seven weeks or forty-nine years, the second has sixty-two weeks or 434 years, and the third has one week or seven years. Some hold that the entire seventy weeks are to follow one upon another without interruption. This interpretation, however, encounters the difficulty that according to the Hebrew text of v. 24, only sixty-nine weeks are to elapse, after which time (cf. v. 26) the anointed one is to be cut off. Others hold that sixty-nine weeks only were fulfilled by the time the anointed one was cut off at Calvary, and that the last week belongs to the period of the great tribulation. Some of the early church fathers held this view. Some of those who hold to the latter view interpret the N.T. church age as an unrevealed mystery during O.T. times, constituting a "parenthesis" until the beginning of the seventieth week. Others who hold this view of the deferment of the seventieth week, however, acknowledge that the N.T. church was quite frequently alluded to in the O.T. The terminus a quo for the commencement of these sixty-nine weeks of years (570 years) is stated to be "from the time that the word [i.e., decree] went out to restore and rebuild Jerusalem" (v. 25). This may refer to a divine decree or to one of three historical edicts: (1) the decree of King Cyrus in 538 B.C. (Ezra 1.1–4); (2) the order of Artaxerxes to Ezra in 457 B.C. (which apparently involved authority to erect the walls of Jerusalem, cf. Ezra 7.6,7; 9.9); (3) the order to Nehemiah in 445 B.C. to carry through the rebuilding of the walls (which Ezra had not been able to accomplish). Of these options, (1) must be ruled out as ending nowhere near to the time of Christ's ministry; (3) comes out too late, unless lunar years are used for the computation. Only (2) comes out right according to regular solar years, for it results in A.D. 27 as the commencement of Christ's ministry. Ezra and Nehemiah render an account of the rebuilding of Jerusalem in forty-nine years and troublous times. Then followed the sixty-two weeks (i.e., years), after which Messiah was cut off for sin. One's view of the remaining week is colored by one's whole scheme of prophetic interpretation. Finally, some hold that all the numbers are used symbolically, as in 12.11,12, and that the passage covers the entire period from Daniel to the final end of history.
9.25 seven weeks; and for sixty-two weeks. This totals 483 years, instead of the 490 years mentioned in v. 24, leaving seven years unaccounted for at the time of Messiah's death. For their future fulfillment, see v. 27 and the book of Revelation. Or possibly the destruction of Jerusalem in A.D. 70 by Titus and the subsequent slaughter of one million Jews during the following three and a half years constitute at least a partial fulfillment of this prophecy.

the sixty-two weeks, an anointed one shall be cut off and shall have nothing, and the troops of the prince who is to come shall destroy the city and the sanctuary. Its*f* end shall come with a flood, and to the end there shall be war. Desolations are decreed. 27 He shall make a strong covenant with many for one week, and for half of the week he shall make sacrifice and offering cease; and in their place*u* shall be an abomination that desolates, until the decreed end is poured out upon the desolator.”

D. The vision of the last days

1. Daniel's vision of an angel

10 In the third year of King Cyrus of Persia a word was revealed to Daniel, who was named Belteshazzar. The word was true, and it concerned a great conflict. He understood the word, having received understanding in the vision.

2 At that time I, Daniel, had been mourning for three weeks. 3 I had eaten no rich food, no meat or wine had entered my mouth, and I had not anointed myself at all, for the full three weeks. 4 On the twenty-fourth day of the first month, as I was standing on the bank of the great river (that is, the Tigris), 5 I looked up and saw a man clothed in linen, with a belt of gold from Uphaz around his waist. 6 His body was like beryl, his face like lightning, his eyes like flaming torches, his arms and legs like the gleam of burnished bronze, and the sound of his words like the roar of a multitude. 7 I, Daniel, alone saw the vision; the people who were with me did not see the vision, though a great trembling fell upon them, and they fled and hid themselves. 8 So I was left alone to see this great vision. My strength left me, and my complexion grew deathly pale, and I retained no strength. 9 Then I heard the sound of his words; and when I heard the sound of his words, I fell into a trance, face to the ground.

10.2
Ezra 9.4, 5;
Neh 1.4
10.4
Dan 8.2;
Gen 2.14
10.5
Dan 12.6, 7;
Rev 1.13;
Jer 10.9
10.6
Mt 17.2;
Rev 1.16, 14;
1.15; 2.18
10.7
2 Kings 6.17;
Acts 9.7;
Ezek 12.18
10.8
Gen 32.24;
Dan 7.28;
8.27
10.9
Dan 8.18

2. Daniel strengthened, encouraged, and promised further revelations

10 But then a hand touched me and roused me to my hands and knees. 11 He said to me, “Daniel, greatly beloved, pay attention to the words that I am going to speak to you. Stand on your feet, for I have now been sent to you.” So while he was speaking this word to me, I stood up trembling. 12 He said to me, “Do not fear, Daniel, for from the first day that you set your mind to gain understanding and to humble yourself before your God, your words have been heard, and I have come because of your words. 13 But the prince of the kingdom of Persia opposed me twenty-one days.

10.10
Jer 1.9;
Dan 9.21;
Rev 1.17
10.11
Dan 9.23
10.12
Rev 1.17;
Dan 9.3,
20-23
10.13
vv. 20, 21;
Dan 12.1;
Jude 9;
Rev 12.7

t Or *His*   *u* Cn: Meaning of Heb uncertain

9.27 What is described as the “abomination that desolates” or its equivalent appears in 9.27; 11.31; 12.11; Mt 24.15; Mk 13.14. It has three different fulfillments. The first occurred under Antiochus Epiphanes in 168 B.C. when the temple was desecrated, the services suspended, a statute of Zeus set up, and the most holy place profaned. A pig was also offered as a sacrifice. The second fulfillment occurred in A.D. 70 under Titus and Vespasian when Roman legions sacked the city, burned the temple, and defiled the sanctuary. The third fulfillment is yet future; it may come during the time of the great tribulation. This verse is regarded by some as a rather comprehensive description of the N.T. antichrist. *he shall make sacrifice and offering cease.* Antiochus Epiphanes, the conquerer, did precisely this. Moreover, in A.D. 70 the temple was itself destroyed and all sacrifices have ended.

10.1 Daniel attested to the truth of the vision he had. It came during the reign of Cyrus, for whom he worked and with whom he was well acquainted.

10.3 In their youth Daniel and his friends ate vegetables and drank only water. Here we note that Daniel's lifestyle had changed, for he had been eating meat and drinking wine.

10.7 The companions of Daniel did not see the vision. Yet something caused them to quake with fear and fly from the scene.

10.11 *I have now been sent to you.* Angels are God's messengers who go where they are sent and speak what they have been told to say. They are utterly faithful, so what the receiver of the message hears can be regarded as trustworthy.

10.13 *the prince of the kingdom of Persia.* The princes in this chapter refer to guardian angels. Nations were thought to have a guardian angel watching over them. Israel regarded *Michael* as its guardian angel.

10.14
Dan 2.28;
8.26;
Hab 2.3
So Michael, one of the chief princes, came to help me, and I left him there with the prince of the kingdom of Persia,^{v} ^{14} and have come to help you understand what is to happen to your people at the end of days. For there is a further vision for those days."

10.15
Ezek 24.27;
Lk 1.20
10.16
Dan 8.15;
v. 10;
Jer 1.9; v. 8
10.17
Isa 6.1-5;
v. 8
15 While he was speaking these words to me, I turned my face toward the ground and was speechless. ^{16} Then one in human form touched my lips, and I opened my mouth to speak, and said to the one who stood before me, "My lord, because of the vision such pains have come upon me that I retain no strength. ^{17} How can my lord's servant talk with my lord? For I am shaking,^{w} no strength remains in me, and no breath is left in me."

10.18
v. 16;
Isa 35.3, 4
10.19
vv. 11, 12;
Judg 6.23
10.20
v. 13;
Dan 8.21;
11.2
10.21
Dan 11.2;
v. 13
11.1ff
Dan 9.1; 5.31
18 Again one in human form touched me and strengthened me. ^{19} He said, "Do not fear, greatly beloved, you are safe. Be strong and courageous!" When he spoke to me, I was strengthened and said, "Let my lord speak, for you have strengthened me." ^{20} Then he said, "Do you know why I have come to you? Now I must return to fight against the prince of Persia, and when I am through with him, the prince of Greece will come. ^{21} But I am to tell you what is inscribed in the book of truth. There is no one with me who contends against these princes except Michael, your

11 prince. ^{1} As for me, in the first year of Darius the Mede, I stood up to support and strengthen him.

3. The interpretation of Daniel's vision

a. From the Persian Empire to the death of Alexander

11.2
Dan 8.26;
8.21
2 "Now I will announce the truth to you. Three more kings shall arise in Persia. The fourth shall be far richer than all of them, and when he has become strong through his riches, he shall stir up all against the kingdom of Greece. ^{3} Then a warrior king shall arise, who shall rule with great dominion and take action as he pleases. ^{4} And while still rising in power, his kingdom shall be broken and divided toward the four winds of heaven, but not to his posterity, nor according to the dominion with which he ruled; for his kingdom shall be uprooted and go to others besides these.

11.3
Dan 8.4, 5,
21
11.4
Dan 8.8, 22;
Ezek 37.9;
Zech 2.6;
Rev 7.1

b. Wars between the Ptolemaic and Seleucid Empires

11.5
vv. 9, 11, 14,
25, 40
5 "Then the king of the south shall grow strong, but one of his officers shall grow stronger than he and shall rule a realm greater than his own

v Gk Theodotion: Heb *I was left there with the kings of Persia* w Gk: Heb *from now*

10.20,21 The angel who came to Daniel had been detained by a superior, evil angel. After coming to Daniel, he returned to fight against the prince of Persia. But he needed help, which was given to him by Michael, who is more powerful than he.

11.1ff This chapter points forward to specific rulers of the Near East during the last few centuries before Christ. The following outline will help one to understand the historical fulfillment of this prophecy: (1) the four kings of v. 2 (although this cannot be stated dogmatically) were the Persian rulers Cyrus, Cambyses, Darius Hystaspes, and Xerxes (Ahasuerus) who attempted the conquest of Greece in 480 B.C.; (2) the mighty king of v. 4 was Alexander the Great who conquered the Persian Empire, ca. 330 B.C.; (3) the division of his kingdom after his death into four parts included Greece, the Asiatic Near East, Egypt, and Asia Minor; (4) the king of the south in v. 5 was Ptolemy I of Egypt (323–285 B.C.) and "one of his princes," his son Ptolemy II (who reigned during the development of the Septuagint and who added various islands and seaport cities to the Egyptian realm); (5) in v. 6 the daughter of Ptolemy II (Berenice) was married to Antiochus II of the Asiatic or Syrian empire; but she and her husband were both murdered by his divorced wife; (6) Bere-

nice's brother, Ptolemy III, avenged her death by invading and pillaging the whole realm of Syria (vv. 7–9); (7) the two sons of v. 10 were Seleucus III and Antiochus III (grandson of Antiochus II), who vigorously pushed down to the borders of Egypt; (8) Ptolemy IV enjoyed a temporary success over Antiochus III at the Battle of Raphia (217 B.C.) and recaptured Palestine from him (vv. 11,12); (9) fifteen years later Antiochus III launched a new and successful counterattack and annexed Palestine ("the beautiful land") to the Seleucid Empire (vv. 13–16); (10) Cleopatra (v. 17) was given in marriage to Ptolemy V by her father Antiochus III; (11) in vv. 18,19 Antiochus invaded Asia Minor and Greece but was defeated by the Romans at Magnesia in 190 B.C.; (13) in vv. 36–45 the primary reference is Antiochus Epiphanes; but many features of this prediction were not fulfilled in his career and can only find fulfilment in the antichrist at the end time.

11.2 *the fourth.* Perhaps this refers to Xerxes (486–465 B.C.), who launched an all-out effort against Greece.

11.3 *a warrior king.* This doubtless was Alexander the Great.

11.5 *the king of the south*, i.e., Ptolemy II.

realm. 6 After some years they shall make an alliance, and the daughter of the king of the south shall come to the king of the north to ratify the agreement. But she shall not retain her power, and his offspring shall not endure. She shall be given up, she and her attendants and her child and the one who supported her.

"In those times 7 a branch from her roots shall rise up in his place. He shall come against the army and enter the fortress of the king of the north, and he shall take action against them and prevail. 8 Even their gods, with their idols and with their precious vessels of silver and gold, he shall carry off to Egypt as spoils of war. For some years he shall refrain from attacking the king of the north; 9 then the latter shall invade the realm of the king of the south, but will return to his own land.

10   "His sons shall wage war and assemble a multitude of great forces, which shall advance like a flood and pass through, and again shall carry the war as far as his fortress. 11 Moved with rage, the king of the south shall go out and do battle against the king of the north, who shall muster a great multitude, which shall, however, be defeated by his enemy. 12 When the multitude has been carried off, his heart shall be exalted, and he shall overthrow tens of thousands, but he shall not prevail. 13 For the king of the north shall again raise a multitude, larger than the former, and after some years^x he shall advance with a great army and abundant supplies.

14   "In those times many shall rise against the king of the south. The lawless among your own people shall lift themselves up in order to fulfill the vision, but they shall fail. 15 Then the king of the north shall come and throw up siegeworks, and take a well-fortified city. And the forces of the south shall not stand, not even his picked troops, for there shall be no strength to resist. 16 But he who comes against him shall take the actions he pleases, and no one shall withstand him. He shall take a position in the beautiful land, and all of it shall be in his power. 17 He shall set his mind to come with the strength of his whole kingdom, and he shall bring terms of peace^y and perform them. In order to destroy the kingdom,^z he shall give him a woman in marriage; but it shall not succeed or be to his advantage. 18 Afterward he shall turn to the coastlands, and shall capture many. But a commander shall put an end to his insolence; indeed,^a he shall turn his insolence back upon him. 19 Then he shall turn back toward the fortresses of his own land, but he shall stumble and fall, and shall not be found.

c. Antiochus Epiphanes's persecution of the Jews

20   "Then shall arise in his place one who shall send an official for the glory of the kingdom; but within a few days he shall be broken, though not in anger or in battle. 21 In his place shall arise a contemptible person

x Heb and at the end of the times years   y Gk: Heb kingdom, and upright ones with him   z Heb it
a Meaning of Heb uncertain

11.6 vv. 13, 15, 40
11.7 vv. 19, 38, 39
11.8 Isa 37.19; 46.1, 2; Jer 43.12, 13
11.10 Isa 8.8; Jer 46.7, 8; Dan 9.26; v. 7
11.11 v. 5; Dan 8.7; vv. 13, 10
11.13 Dan 4.16; 12.7
11.15 Jer 6.6; Ezek 4.2; 17.17
11.16 Dan 8.4, 7; vv. 3, 36; Josh 1.5; vv. 41, 45
11.17 2 Kings 12.17; Ezek 4.3, 7
11.18 Isa 66.19; Jer 31.10; Hos 12.14
11.19 Ps 27.2; Job 20.8; Ezek 26.21
11.20 Isa 60.17
11.21 vv. 24, 32, 34

11.6 the daughter of the king. In 252 B.C. Ptolemy II of Egypt gave his daughter Berenice in marriage to Antiochus II of Aram to conclude a treaty of peace between their two lands. The king of the north is the king of Aram. These prophecies seem to have been fulfilled many years later in the Seleucid wars between Egypt and Aram. **11.7** a branch from her roots, i.e., her brother. Berenice, murdered in Antioch by Antiochus II's former wife Laodice, was the sister of Ptolemy III, who now ascended the Egyptian throne and declared war against the Seleucids to avenge his sister's murder. **11.13** the king of the north, i.e., the Aramean king. Possibly Antiochus III the Great, who was later defeated by the Romans at Magnesia. **11.15** take a well-fortified city. Antiochus defeated Ptolemy's army at Panion (198 B.C.). Following this victory, Seleucid control of Palestine was complete. **11.17** give him a woman in marriage. Antiochus' daughter, Cleopatra, was married off to the Egyptian king. Antiochus wanted to control Egypt but failed to accomplish this aim. **11.18** a commander. Probably the Roman consul Scipio, who defeated Antiochus at Magnesia near Smyrna in 190 B.C. **11.20** in his place. Seleucus IV, successor to Antiochus III, sent Heliodorus to rob and desecrate the temple in Jerusalem. **11.21** In his place shall arise a contemptible person. This may refer to Antiochus IV Epiphanes who, when his brother Seleucus was assassinated, ingratiated himself with the Romans and took over.

on whom royal majesty had not been conferred; he shall come in without warning and obtain the kingdom through intrigue. 22 Armies shall be utterly swept away and broken before him, and the prince of the covenant as well. 23 And after an alliance is made with him, he shall act deceitfully and become strong with a small party. 24 Without warning he shall come into the richest parts[b] of the province and do what none of his predecessors had ever done, lavishing plunder, spoil, and wealth on them. He shall devise plans against strongholds, but only for a time. 25 He shall stir up his power and determination against the king of the south with a great army, and the king of the south shall wage war with a much greater and stronger army. But he shall not succeed, for plots shall be devised against him 26 by those who eat of the royal rations. They shall break him, his army shall be swept away, and many shall fall slain. 27 The two kings, their minds bent on evil, shall sit at one table and exchange lies. But it shall not succeed, for there remains an end at the time appointed. 28 He shall return to his land with great wealth, but his heart shall be set against the holy covenant. He shall work his will, and return to his own land.

29 "At the time appointed he shall return and come into the south, but this time it shall not be as it was before. 30 For ships of Kittim shall come against him, and he shall lose heart and withdraw. He shall be enraged and take action against the holy covenant. He shall turn back and pay heed to those who forsake the holy covenant. 31 Forces sent by him shall occupy and profane the temple and fortress. They shall abolish the regular burnt offering and set up the abomination that makes desolate. 32 He shall seduce with intrigue those who violate the covenant; but the people who are loyal to their God shall stand firm and take action. 33 The wise among the people shall give understanding to many; for some days, however, they shall fall by sword and flame, and suffer captivity and plunder. 34 When they fall victim, they shall receive a little help, and many shall join them insincerely. 35 Some of the wise shall fall, so that they may be refined, purified, and cleansed,[c] until the time of the end, for there is still an interval until the time appointed.

36 "The king shall act as he pleases. He shall exalt himself and consider himself greater than any god, and shall speak horrendous things against the God of gods. He shall prosper until the period of wrath is completed, for what is determined shall be done. 37 He shall pay no respect to the gods of his ancestors, or to the one beloved by women; he shall pay no respect to any other god, for he shall consider himself greater than all. 38 He shall honor the god of fortresses instead of these; a god whom his ancestors did not know he shall honor with gold and silver, with precious stones and costly gifts. 39 He shall deal with the strongest fortresses by the help of a foreign god. Those who acknowledge him he shall make more wealthy, and shall appoint them as rulers over many, and shall distribute the land for a price.

d. The similar event at the time of the end

40 "At the time of the end the king of the south shall attack him. But

b Or among the richest men   c Heb made them white

11.22 *the prince of the covenant*, i.e., "a leader of the priests." Probably Jason, treacherously removed by the Hellenist Menelaus.
11.27 *The two kings.* This probably refers to Antiochus IV and Ptolemy IV.
11.30 *ships of Kittim*, i.e., ships from Cyprus or Roman warships.
11.31 *profane the temple*, by offering pigs on the altar. This event was fulfilled in 168–167 B.C. The *abomination that makes desolate* refers to the placing of a statue of Zeus inside the temple.
11.32 *He shall seduce with intrigue.* Menelaus, the

high priest, conspired with Antiochus against the Jews, who were loyal to God's laws. *But the people who are loyal to their God* perhaps refers to the valiant Maccabees and their sympathizers. However, a further fulfillment may lie in the future.
11.37 *to the one beloved by women*, probably Tammuz-Adonis, whose worship was popular among women (cf. Ezek 8.14).
11.40 *At the time of the end.* The prophecy takes a turn here. Antiochus IV fades from view and the antichrist of the last days becomes the center of attention from this point on.

the king of the north shall rush upon him like a whirlwind, with chariots and horsemen, and with many ships. He shall advance against countries and pass through like a flood. 41 He shall come into the beautiful land, and tens of thousands shall fall victim, but Edom and Moab and the main part of the Ammonites shall escape from his power. 42 He shall stretch out his hand against the countries, and the land of Egypt shall not escape. 43 He shall become ruler of the treasures of gold and of silver, and all the riches of Egypt; and the Libyans and the Ethiopians*d* shall follow in his train. 44 But reports from the east and the north shall alarm him, and he shall go out with great fury to bring ruin and complete destruction to many. 45 He shall pitch his palatial tents between the sea and the beautiful holy mountain. Yet he shall come to his end, with no one to help him.

e. The end of the tribulation and the resurrection of the dead

12 "At that time Michael, the great prince, the protector of your people, shall arise. There shall be a time of anguish, such as has never occurred since nations first came into existence. But at that time your people shall be delivered, everyone who is found written in the book. 2 Many of those who sleep in the dust of the earth*e* shall awake, some to everlasting life, and some to shame and everlasting contempt. 3 Those who are wise shall shine like the brightness of the sky,*f* and those who lead many to righteousness, like the stars forever and ever. 4 But you, Daniel, keep the words secret and the book sealed until the time of the end. Many shall be running back and forth, and evil*g* shall increase."

f. The sealing of the prophecy until the time of the end

5 Then I, Daniel, looked, and two others appeared, one standing on this bank of the stream and one on the other. 6 One of them said to the man clothed in linen, who was upstream, "How long shall it be until the end of these wonders?" 7 The man clothed in linen, who was upstream, raised his right hand and his left hand toward heaven. And I heard him swear by the one who lives forever that it would be for a time, two times, and half a time,*h* and that when the shattering of the power of the holy people comes to an end, all these things would be accomplished. 8 I heard but could not understand; so I said, "My lord, what shall be the outcome of these things?" 9 He said, "Go your way, Daniel, for the words are to remain secret and sealed until the time of the end. 10 Many shall be purified, cleansed, and refined, but the wicked shall continue to act wickedly. None of the wicked shall understand, but those who are wise shall understand. 11 From the time that the regular burnt offering is taken away and the abomination that desolates is set up, there shall be one thousand two hundred ninety days. 12 Happy are those who persevere and attain the thousand three hundred thirty-five days. 13 But you, go your way,*i* and rest; you shall rise for your reward at the end of the days."

d Or *Nubians*; Heb *Cushites*   *e* Or *the land of dust*   *f* Or *dome*   *g* Cn Compare Gk: Heb *knowledge*
h Heb *a time, times, and a half*   *i* Gk Theodotion: Heb adds *to the end*

11.41
Jer 48.47;
49.6

11.43
2 Chr 12.3;
Ezek 30.4, 5;
Nah 3.9

11.45
vv. 16, 41;
Isa 65.25;
66.20;
Dan 9.16, 20

12.1
Dan 10.13,
21; 9.12;
Mt 24.21;
Rev 16.18;
v. 4
12.2
Isa 26.19;
Mt 25.46;
Jn 5.28;
Acts 24.15
12.3
Mt 13.43;
Dan 11.33
12.4
Rev 22.10;
Dan 11.33

12.5
Dan 10.4ff

12.7
Rev 10.5, 6;
Dan 4.34;
7.25;
Rev 12.14;
Lk 21.24;
Rev 10.7
12.8
v. 6
12.9
vv. 13, 4
12.10
Dan 11.35;
Isa 32.6, 7
12.11f
Dan 8.11-14;
9.27; 11.31;
Mt 24.15
12.12
Isa 30.18;
Rev 11.2;
12.6; 13.5
12.13
vv. 9, 4;
Rev 14.13

12.1 God had commissioned Michael to help his people, and they would need his help. He supplied it to those whose names are "written in the book," i.e., the book of life in which the redeemed are listed by name.

12.3 Whoever leads people to Christ will share in the glory of those they have helped to heaven. Only God can save, but the people who lead them to Christ

will have a rich reward. They shall be burning and shining lights, and the memory of their service to God will never be eclipsed.

12.7 *a time, two times, and a half a time*, i.e., three and a half years.

12.11 *one thousand two hundred ninety days*. Three and a half years (v. 7) and thirty extra days.

INTRODUCTION TO
HOSEA

Authorship, Date, and Background: This book is the first of the twelve minor prophets. The author, Hosea (whose name means "salvation"), was the son of Beeri. He lived during the eighth century B.C.; his ministry can be dated from 753 B.C. to around 723 B.C. He was a prophet in the northern kingdom during the reign of Jeroboam and overlapped with Isaiah, Micah, and Amos. It was a time of great prosperity and gross religious apostasy. The northern kingdom had been delivered from its vassalage to Syria, which had declined under Ben-hadad III. Its territory had been expanded to include Damascus, and control of the caravan trade routes brought about the rise of a successful mercantile class. This widened the gap between the rich and the poor even as the mercantile class could now afford the luxuries previously known only by the nobility.

Prosperity brought with it spiritual decline. The Canaanite religion of Baal worship had penetrated Israelite life. It was the most degenerate of all the cults of the area. Baal and his female consort Asherah were fertility deities often worshiped in the form of bulls and cows. Jeroboam I had set up two golden calves, one at Bethel and one at Dan, for the people of the northern kingdom to worship. Drunkenness, prostitution, and violence attended their cultic practices, which were all contrary to the covenant they had with God. God called Hosea to his ministry during the closing days of the northern kingdom before the Assyrian invasion of 722 B.C.

Characteristics and Content: Hosea married a woman of whoredom who proved unfaithful even after her marriage to the prophet. God used this to demonstrate the relation of Israel to himself. He was the faithful husband; Israel was the faithless and adulterous wife. Even as Hosea tenderly dealt with his faithless wife and recovered her from her life of sin, so a loving and tender God was calling Israel to repent of her adultery and return to her God. Hosea's three children were named Jezreel (as a sign of God's punishment of King Jehu's dynasty for their murders), Lo-ruhamah (meaning "no more mercy" to be extended to the northern kingdom), and Lo-ammi (meaning "not mine" or that God has rejected the apostate kingdom of Israel).

All of the tragic consequences experienced by Hosea in his marital disasters were used as signs of Israel's whoredom and departure from the covenant promises made with God years before. He pronounced divine judgment in the name of God, assuring Israel that it would experience captivity and its cities would be destroyed. Its wealth would be taken from the people and their prayers would not be heard. Hosea, however, looked far beyond Israel's present apostasy as he forecasted the time when Israel, because of God's continuing love and faithfulness, would repent and be restored.

Outline:

I. Hosea's marital experiences and their fruits (1.1—3.5)

II. Israel's unfaithfulness to the God of covenant love (4.1—13.16)

III. Forgiveness and blessing in response to repentance (14.1–9)

HOSEA

I. Hosea's marital experiences and their fruits (1.1–3.5)

A. Superscription

1 The word of the LORD that came to Hosea son of Beeri, in the days of Kings Uzziah, Jotham, Ahaz, and Hezekiah of Judah, and in the days of King Jeroboam son of Joash of Israel.

B. Hosea's marriage to Gomer

2 When the LORD first spoke through Hosea, the LORD said to Hosea, "Go, take for yourself a wife of whoredom and have children of whoredom, for the land commits great whoredom by forsaking the LORD." 3 So he went and took Gomer daughter of Diblaim, and she conceived and bore him a son.

4 And the LORD said to him, "Name him Jezreel;[a] for in a little while I will punish the house of Jehu for the blood of Jezreel, and I will put an end to the kingdom of the house of Israel. 5 On that day I will break the bow of Israel in the valley of Jezreel."

6 She conceived again and bore a daughter. Then the LORD said to him, "Name her Lo-ruhamah,[b] for I will no longer have pity on the house of Israel or forgive them. 7 But I will have pity on the house of Judah, and I will save them by the LORD their God; I will not save them by bow, or by sword, or by war, or by horses, or by horsemen."

8 When she had weaned Lo-ruhamah, she conceived and bore a son. 9 Then the LORD said, "Name him Lo-ammi,[c] for you are not my people and I am not your God."[d]

C. The prophecy of restoration

10[e] Yet the number of the people of Israel shall be like the sand of the sea, which can be neither measured nor numbered; and in the place where it was said to them, "You are not my people," it shall be said to them, "Children of the living God." 11 The people of Judah and the people of

---

a That is *God sows*   *b* That is *Not pitied*   *c* That is *Not my people*   *d* Heb *I am not yours*   *e* Ch 2.1 in Heb

---

1.1
Rom 9.25;
2 Kings 5.1-7;
2 Chr 27.1-9;
2 Kings 16.1-20;
2 Chr 28.1-27;
2 Kings 18.1-20;
2 Chr 29.1-32;
2 Kings 13.13;
14.23-29
1.2
Hos 3.1;
Jer 3.1, 12,
14;
Hos 2.5; 3.5
1.4
2 Kings 10.1-14;
15.10
1.5
2 Kings 15.29
1.6
vv. 3, 9;
Hos 2.4
1.7
Isa 30.18;
Jer 25.5, 6;
Zech 9.9, 10
1.9
v. 6
1.10
Gen 32.12;
Jer 33.22;
Rom 9.25-27;
v. 9;
Isa 63.16;
64.8
1.11
Isa 11.12;
Jer 23.5, 6;
Ezek 37.21-24;
Hos 3.5

1.1 Hosea is the first of the twelve minor prophets. The books of the twelve have sometimes been considered to be one book. These prophets are called "minor" because the amount of material contained in each is considerably less than that of the major prophets such as Isaiah, Jeremiah, and Ezekiel. The first nine prophesied before the captivity; the last three wrote after the captivity was over. Jeremiah and Ezekiel repeat some of the material contained in Hosea. It was *the word of the LORD that came to Hosea* that he wrote in the book.
1.2 *a wife of whoredom.* Hosea's marriage to a prostitute served as the background for his message. Just as Gomer was unfaithful to Hosea, so Israel was unfaithful to God.
1.4 *punish . . . for the blood of Jezreel.* Jehu had been party to the deaths of Joram of Israel, Ahaziah of Judah, and Jezebel wife of king Ahab, under orders

from God to execute the family of Ahab (see 1 Kings 21.21; 2 Kings 9.1 – 10.17). But he had exceeded his orders by murdering all the worshipers of Baal (2 Kings 11.18–31). God, in turn, would now punish the house of Jehu.
1.5 *break the bow of Israel in the valley of Jezreel,* a prediction of the Assyrian conquest of Israel twenty-five years later.
1.7 *I will have pity on the house of Judah.* Shortly after defeating Israel, the Assyrian emperor Sennacherib invaded Judah and besieged Jerusalem. He was driven off by the special intervention of God's angel (Isa 36–37).
1.10 Even as Hosea prophesied judgment against Israel, so he also looked to that future day when that nation would be restored to a position of blessing and honor. The new name, "Children of the living God," indicates that this indeed would come to pass.

Israel shall be gathered together, and they shall appoint for themselves one head; and they shall take possession of[f] the land, for great shall be the day of Jezreel.

D. Gomer a symbol of Israel

1. Her adultery

2 [g] Say to your brother,[h] Ammi,[i] and to your sister,[j] Ruhamah.[k]
 2 Plead with your mother, plead —
  for she is not my wife,
   and I am not her husband —
 that she put away her whoring from her face,
  and her adultery from between her breasts,
 3 or I will strip her naked
  and expose her as in the day she was born,
 and make her like a wilderness,
  and turn her into a parched land,
   and kill her with thirst.
 4 Upon her children also I will have no pity,
  because they are children of whoredom.
 5 For their mother has played the whore;
  she who conceived them has acted shamefully.
 For she said, "I will go after my lovers;
  they give me my bread and my water,
   my wool and my flax, my oil and my drink."

2. Gomer's judgment

 6 Therefore I will hedge up her[l] way with thorns;
  and I will build a wall against her,
   so that she cannot find her paths.
 7 She shall pursue her lovers,
  but not overtake them;
 and she shall seek them,
  but shall not find them.
 Then she shall say, "I will go
  and return to my first husband,
   for it was better with me then than now."
 8 She did not know
  that it was I who gave her
 the grain, the wine, and the oil,
  and who lavished upon her silver
   and gold that they used for Baal.
 9 Therefore I will take back
  my grain in its time,
   and my wine in its season;
 and I will take away my wool and my flax,
  which were to cover her nakedness.
 10 Now I will uncover her shame
  in the sight of her lovers,
   and no one shall rescue her out of my hand.

Cross-references (left margin):
- 2.1 v. 23
- 2.2 v. 5; Hos 4.5; Isa 50.1; Hos 1.2
- 2.3 Ezek 16.7, 22, 39; Isa 32.13, 14; Am 8.11
- 2.4 Jer 13.14; Ezek 8.18
- 2.5 Isa 1.21; Jer 3.1, 2, 6; 44.17, 18
- 2.6 Job 3.23; 19.8; Hos 9.6; 10.8
- 2.7 Jer 2.2; 3.1; Ezek 16.8; Hos 13.6
- 2.8 Isa 1.3; Ezek 16.19; Hos 8.4
- 2.9 Hos 8.7; 9.2
- 2.10 Ezek 16.37

---

[f] Heb *rise up from* [g] Ch 2.3 in Heb [h] Gk: Heb *brothers* [i] That is *My people* [j] Gk Vg: Heb *sisters*
[k] That is *Pitied* [l] Gk Syr: Heb *your*

1.11 God promised that Judah and Israel would be brought together again. It was fulfilled in part in Jesus' day when people from Galilee (a part of the territory that formerly belonged to the northern kingdom) along with people from Judea came to know Christ and embraced the gospel. Eleven of the twelve disciples were Galileans. The application of this prophecy to Israel and the Jews today is an issue of debate among Christians.
2.3 God threatened to take away the prosperity of Israel and abandon them to ruin because of their sins (2.3,4,6,7,9–13).

11 I will put an end to all her mirth,
    her festivals, her new moons, her sabbaths,
    and all her appointed festivals.
12 I will lay waste her vines and her fig trees,
    of which she said,
"These are my pay,
    which my lovers have given me."
I will make them a forest,
    and the wild animals shall devour them.
13 I will punish her for the festival days of the Baals,
    when she offered incense to them
and decked herself with her ring and jewelry,
    and went after her lovers,
    and forgot me, says the LORD.

3. *Her restoration promised*

14 Therefore, I will now allure her,
    and bring her into the wilderness,
    and speak tenderly to her.
15 From there I will give her her vineyards,
    and make the Valley of Achor a door of hope.
There she shall respond as in the days of her youth,
    as at the time when she came out of the land of Egypt.
16 On that day, says the LORD, you will call me, "My husband," and no longer will you call me, "My Baal."*m* 17 For I will remove the names of the Baals from her mouth, and they shall be mentioned by name no more. 18 I will make for you*n* a covenant on that day with the wild animals, the birds of the air, and the creeping things of the ground; and I will abolish*o* the bow, the sword, and war from the land; and I will make you lie down in safety. 19 And I will take you for my wife forever; I will take you for my wife in righteousness and in justice, in steadfast love, and in mercy. 20 I will take you for my wife in faithfulness; and you shall know the LORD.
21   On that day I will answer, says the LORD,
    I will answer the heavens
    and they shall answer the earth;
22   and the earth shall answer the grain, the wine, and the oil,
    and they shall answer Jezreel;*p*
23   and I will sow him*q* for myself in the land.
And I will have pity on Lo-ruhamah,*r*
    and I will say to Lo-ammi,*s* "You are my people";
    and he shall say, "You are my God."

4. *Her restoration accomplished*

3 The LORD said to me again, "Go, love a woman who has a lover and is an adulteress, just as the LORD loves the people of Israel, though they turn to other gods and love raisin cakes." 2 So I bought her for fifteen shekels of silver and a homer of barley and a measure of wine.*t* 3 And I

m That is, *"My master"*   *n* Heb *them*   *o* Heb *break*   *p* That is *God sows*   *q* Cn: Heb *her*   *r* That is *Not pitied*   *s* That is *Not my people*   *t* Gk: Heb a *homer of barley and a lethech of barley*

2.11
Jer 7.34;
16.9;
Am 8.10;
Isa 1.13, 14
2.12
v. 5;
Isa 5.5;
Hos 13.8

2.13
Ezek 16.12,
17;
Hos 4.6;
8.14; 13.6

2.14
Ezek 20.33-38

2.15
Ezek 28.25,
26;
Josh 7.26;
Jer 2.2;
Ex 15.1, 2;
Hos 11.1
2.17
Ex 23.13;
Josh 23.7;
Ps 16.4;
Zech 13.2;
v. 13
2.18
Job 5.23;
Isa 11.6-9;
Ps 46.9;
Ezek 34.25
2.19
Isa 62.4, 5;
Jer 3.14;
Isa 1.27
2.20
Hos 6.6; 13.4
2.21
Isa 55.10;
Zech 8.12
2.22
Jer 31.12;
Joel 2.19
2.23
Jer 31.27;
Hos 1.6; 1.9,
10;
Zech 13.9;
Rom 9.25, 26

3.1
Hos 1.2;
2 Sam 6.19;
1 Chr 16.3
3.2
Ruth 4.10

2.14 *I will now allure her.* God still loved faithless Israel. He would take his people away from Canaan and the worship of Baal to the wilderness, where he would speak tenderly to them.
2.18–20 God promised to renew his covenant with them, a covenant they had broken by their infidelity.
3.2 *So I bought her.* The prophet Hosea courted his adulterous wife, seeking reconciliation and beseech-

ing her to leave her wickedness and return to him. This symbolized God's pursuit of Israel, who had engaged in whoredom with pagan gods. In a further spiritual sense, we have all been separated from God and are adulterers and adulteresses, but we have been bought back by God. Hosea paid fifteen shekels of silver, plus barley and wine, for his wife's redemption. God paid for our return to him by the blood of Jesus shed on Calvary.

said to her, "You must remain as mine for many days; you shall not play the whore, you shall not have intercourse with a man, nor I with you." ⁴For the Israelites shall remain many days without king or prince, without sacrifice or pillar, without ephod or teraphim. ⁵Afterward the Israelites shall return and seek the Lᴏʀᴅ their God, and David their king; they shall come in awe to the Lᴏʀᴅ and to his goodness in the latter days.

II. Israel's unfaithfulness to the God of covenant love (4.1–13.16)

A. Israel's adultery

4 Hear the word of the Lᴏʀᴅ, O people of Israel;
  for the Lᴏʀᴅ has an indictment against the inhabitants
    of the land.
There is no faithfulness or loyalty,
  and no knowledge of God in the land.
2 Swearing, lying, and murder,
  and stealing and adultery break out;
    bloodshed follows bloodshed.
3 Therefore the land mourns,
  and all who live in it languish;
together with the wild animals
  and the birds of the air,
    even the fish of the sea are perishing.

4 Yet let no one contend,
  and let none accuse,
    for with you is my contention, O priest.ᵘ
5 You shall stumble by day;
  the prophet also shall stumble with you by night,
    and I will destroy your mother.
6 My people are destroyed for lack of knowledge;
  because you have rejected knowledge,
    I reject you from being a priest to me.
And since you have forgotten the law of your God,
  I also will forget your children.

7 The more they increased,
  the more they sinned against me;
    they changedᵛ their glory into shame.
8 They feed on the sin of my people;
  they are greedy for their iniquity.
9 And it shall be like people, like priest;
  I will punish them for their ways,
    and repay them for their deeds.
10 They shall eat, but not be satisfied;
  they shall play the whore, but not multiply;
because they have forsaken the Lᴏʀᴅ
  to devote themselves to ¹¹whoredom.

Wine and new wine
  take away the understanding.
12 My people consult a piece of wood,

ᵘ Cn: Meaning of Heb uncertain   ᵛ Ancient Heb tradition: MT *I will change*

3.4
Hos 13.10,
11; 2.11;
Ex 28.6;
Judg 17.5;
Zech 10.2
3.5
Jer 50.4, 5;
Ezek 34.23,
24;
Jer 31.9;
Mic 4.1

4.1
Hos 5.1;
12.2;
Mic 6.2;
Isa 59.4;
Jer 7.28;
Hos 6.6; 5.4
4.2
Hos 10.4;
7.3; 6.9; 7.1,
4; 6.8
4.3
Jer 4.28;
Zeph 1.3;
Jer 4.25

4.4
Ezek 3.26;
Deut 17.12
4.5
Hos 5.5;
Ezek 14.3, 7;
Hos 2.2, 5
4.6
v. 1;
Mal 2.7, 8;
Hos 2.13;
8.1, 12

4.7
Hos 10.1;
13.6;
Hab 2.16;
Mal 2.9
4.8
Hos 10.13;
Isa 56.11
4.9
Isa 24.2;
Jer 5.31;
Hos 9.9
4.10
Lev 26.26;
Mic 6.14;
Hos 7.14;
9.17
4.11
Hos 5.4;
Isa 28.7
4.12
Jer 2.27;
Hab 2.19;
Hos 5.4; 9.1

4.8 The priests were greedy for gain derived from their office, and their hearts were not in their duties. Moreover, they encouraged the people in their sins and participated with them.
4.12 *consult a piece of wood.* The Israelites sought guidance from false gods by taking over the arts of

and their divining rod gives them oracles.
For a spirit of whoredom has led them astray,
   and they have played the whore, forsaking their God.

13 They sacrifice on the tops of the mountains,
   and make offerings upon the hills,
under oak, poplar, and terebinth,
   because their shade is good.

Therefore your daughters play the whore,
   and your daughters-in-law commit adultery.

14 I will not punish your daughters when they play the whore,
   nor your daughters-in-law when they commit adultery;
for the men themselves go aside with whores,
   and sacrifice with temple prostitutes;
thus a people without understanding comes to ruin.

15 Though you play the whore, O Israel,
   do not let Judah become guilty.
Do not enter into Gilgal,
   or go up to Beth-aven,
   and do not swear, "As the Lord lives."

16 Like a stubborn heifer,
   Israel is stubborn;
can the Lord now feed them
   like a lamb in a broad pasture?

17 Ephraim is joined to idols—
   let him alone.
18 When their drinking is ended, they indulge in sexual orgies;
   they love lewdness more than their glory.[w]
19 A wind has wrapped them[x] in its wings,
   and they shall be ashamed because of their altars.[y]

B. God's severity toward Israel

5 Hear this, O priests!
   Give heed, O house of Israel!
Listen, O house of the king!
   For the judgment pertains to you;
for you have been a snare at Mizpah,
   and a net spread upon Tabor,
2 and a pit dug deep in Shittim;[z]
   but I will punish all of them.

3 I know Ephraim,
   and Israel is not hidden from me;
for now, O Ephraim, you have played the whore;
   Israel is defiled.
4 Their deeds do not permit them

Cross-references (right margin):

4.13 Jer 3.6; Ezek 6.13; Hos 2.13; 11.2; Am 7.17; Rom 1.28

4.14 v. 18; Deut 23.17; vv. 6, 11

4.15 Am 4.4; 1 Kings 12.28, 29

4.16 Ps 78.8; Isa 5.17; 7.25

4.17 Ps 81.12; v. 4

4.18 vv. 14, 7

4.19 Hos 12.1; 13.15; Isa 1.29

5.1 Hos 4.1; 6.9

5.3 Am 3.2; Hos 6.10

5.4 Hos 4.11, 12

---

w Cn Compare Gk: Meaning of Heb uncertain   x Heb *her*   y Gk Syr: Heb *sacrifices*   z Cn: Meaning of Heb uncertain

---

sorcerers whose predictions were based on how their staffs landed on the ground.
4.17 *Ephraim is joined to idols*, i.e., "is in love with them and has an addiction for them." The nation was beyond repentance, and God had decided to leave them alone.
4.19 *A wind has wrapped them.* A whirlwind would sweep them away. The Assyrian invasion came about twenty years later and the nation of Ephraim com-

pletely disappeared.
5.1 Priests and other classes of society were called to answer the charges against them. This is repeated in different form in v. 8.
5.3,4 The charge was that of spiritual prostitution. They had turned from God, were confirmed in their ways, and delighted in what they were doing. They had broken their marriage vows, i.e., their covenant with God.

to return to their God.
For the spirit of whoredom is within them,
and they do not know the LORD.

5.5
Hos 7.10;
4.5;
Ezek 23.31-35

5 Israel's pride testifies against him;
Ephraim[a] stumbles in his guilt;
Judah also stumbles with them.

5.6
Mic 6.6, 7;
Isa 1.15;
Ezek 8.6

6 With their flocks and herds they shall go
to seek the LORD,
but they will not find him;
he has withdrawn from them.

5.7
Isa 48.8;
Hos 6.7; 2.4,
11, 12

7 They have dealt faithlessly with the LORD;
for they have borne illegitimate children.
Now the new moon shall devour them along with their fields.

5.8
Hos 9.9;
10.9;
Isa 10.29;
30;
Hos 4.15

8 Blow the horn in Gibeah,
the trumpet in Ramah.
Sound the alarm at Beth-aven;
look behind you, Benjamin!

5.9
Isa 37.3;
46.10;
Zech 1.6

9 Ephraim shall become a desolation
in the day of punishment;
among the tribes of Israel
I declare what is sure.

5.10
Deut 19.14;
Ezek 7.8;
Ps 93.3, 4

10 The princes of Judah have become
like those who remove the landmark;
on them I will pour out
my wrath like water.

5.11
Hos 9.16

11 Ephraim is oppressed, crushed in judgment,
because he was determined to go after vanity.[b]

5.12
Ps 39.11;
Prov 12.4

12 Therefore I am like maggots to Ephraim,
and like rottenness to the house of Judah.

5.13
Jer 30.12;
Hos 7.11;
8.9; 10.6;
14.3

13 When Ephraim saw his sickness,
and Judah his wound,
then Ephraim went to Assyria,
and sent to the great king.[c]
But he is not able to cure you
or heal your wound.

5.14
Hos 13.7, 8;
Ps 50.22;
Mic 5.8

14 For I will be like a lion to Ephraim,
and like a young lion to the house of Judah.
I myself will tear and go away;
I will carry off, and no one shall rescue.

5.15
Isa 64.7-9;
Jer 2.27;
Hos 3.5

15 I will return again to my place
until they acknowledge their guilt and seek my face.
In their distress they will beg my favor:

C. Repentance and restoration

6.1
Jer 50.4, 5;
Hos 5.14;
14.4;
Isa 30.26
6.2
Ps 30.5

6 "Come, let us return to the LORD;
for it is he who has torn, and he will heal us;
he has struck down, and he will bind us up.

2 After two days he will revive us;

---

[a] Heb Israel and Ephraim   [b] Gk: Meaning of Heb uncertain   [c] Cn: Heb to a king who will contend

---

5.5 Judah was like Ephraim in her sins. The ten tribes would be carried captive to Assyria and lose their identity, whereas Judah would fall but would rise again after punishment.
5.10 *like those who remove the landmark,* i.e., they were like thieves who changed boundary markers to gain additional land.

5.13 Both kingdoms, when God contended with them, sought relief by making heathen alliances. But this would bring disappointment because only God could heal their sicknesses.
6.1 This plea to turn to the Lord came either from the lips of Hosea or from the people who saw the need to seek help from God for their sins.

on the third day he will raise us up,
   that we may live before him.

3 Let us know, let us press on to know the LORD;
     his appearing is as sure as the dawn;
  he will come to us like the showers,
     like the spring rains that water the earth."

D. Israel's unfaithfulness restated

4 What shall I do with you, O Ephraim?
     What shall I do with you, O Judah?
  Your love is like a morning cloud,
     like the dew that goes away early.

5 Therefore I have hewn them by the prophets,
     I have killed them by the words of my mouth,
  and my^d judgment goes forth as the light.

6 For I desire steadfast love and not sacrifice,
     the knowledge of God rather than burnt offerings.

7 But at^e Adam they transgressed the covenant;
     there they dealt faithlessly with me.

8 Gilead is a city of evildoers,
     tracked with blood.

9 As robbers lie in wait^f for someone,
     so the priests are banded together;^{g}
  they murder on the road to Shechem,
     they commit a monstrous crime.

10 In the house of Israel I have seen a horrible thing;
     Ephraim's whoredom is there, Israel is defiled.

11 For you also, O Judah, a harvest is appointed.

When I would restore the fortunes of my people,

7 ^{1}when I would heal Israel,
    the corruption of Ephraim is revealed,
    and the wicked deeds of Samaria;
  for they deal falsely,
    the thief breaks in,
  and the bandits raid outside.

2 But they do not consider
    that I remember all their wickedness.
  Now their deeds surround them,
    they are before my face.

3 By their wickedness they make the king glad,
    and the officials by their treachery.

4 They are all adulterers;
    they are like a heated oven,
  whose baker does not need to stir the fire,
    from the kneading of the dough until it is leavened.

5 On the day of our king the officials
    became sick with the heat of wine;

6.3
Isa 2.3;
Mic 4.2;
Ps 19.6;
Mic 5.2;
Joel 2.23

6.4
Hos 7.1;
11.8; 13.3

6.5
Jer 1.10, 18;
Heb 4.12;
v. 3

6.6
Mt 9.13;
Ps 50.8, 9;
Hos 2.20

6.7
Hos 8.1; 5.7

6.8
Hos 4.2

6.9
Hos 7.1;
Jer 7.9, 10;
Ezek 22.9;
23.27

6.10
Jer 5.30, 31;
Hos 5.3

6.11
Joel 3.13;
Zeph 2.7

7.1
v. 13;
Hos 6.4;
11.8; 4.2; 6.9

7.2
Hos 8.13;
9.9;
Am 8.7;
Jer 2.19;
Hos 4.9

7.3
v. 5;
Mic 7.3;
Hos 4.2;
11.12;
Rom 1.32

7.4
Jer 9.2; 23.10

7.5
Isa 28.1, 7, 8

---

d Gk Syr: Heb *your*   *e* Cn: Heb *like*   *f* Cn: Meaning of Heb uncertain   *g* Syr: Heb *are a company*

6.4–7 Both Ephraim and Judah had wobbled in their ways and been faithless to their covenant with God. They were like knotty timber which needed to be hewn into proper shape to become useful.
6.7 *like Adam* (NRSV footnote). Even as Adam had broken his covenant with God and died, so had Ephraim violated the conditions of its agreement with God. Therefore they would lose the benefits that ac-

crue to those who keep the covenant.
7.1ff God was eager to heal Ephraim's cancer, which appeared to be fatal, but Ephraim refused to seek his aid. The officials were liars (v. 3) and adulterers (v. 4), drunkenness was epidemic, and their unclean hearts were like heated ovens with a burning desire to sin (vv. 5–7).

he stretched out his hand with mockers.

6 For they are kindled[h] like an oven, their heart burns
    within them;
  all night their anger smolders;
    in the morning it blazes like a flaming fire.

7.7
Ps 21.9;
v. 16;
Isa 64.7

7 All of them are hot as an oven,
    and they devour their rulers.
  All their kings have fallen;
    none of them calls upon me.

7.8
Ps 106.35;
v. 11;
Hos 5.13
7.9
Isa 1.7;
Hos 4.6

8 Ephraim mixes himself with the peoples;
    Ephraim is a cake not turned.
9 Foreigners devour his strength,
    but he does not know it;
  gray hairs are sprinkled upon him,
    but he does not know it.

7.10
Hos 5.5;
vv. 7, 14;
Hos 5.4

10 Israel's pride testifies against[i] him;
     yet they do not return to the LORD their God,
     or seek him, for all this.

7.11
Hos 11.11;
4.6, 11, 14;
v. 16;
Hos 5.13;
8.9; 12.1
7.12
Ezek 12.13

11 Ephraim has become like a dove,
     silly and without sense;
   they call upon Egypt, they go to Assyria.
12 As they go, I will cast my net over them;
     I will bring them down like birds of the air;
   I will discipline them according to the report made to their
     assembly.[j]

7.13
Hos 9.12, 17;
Jer 14.10;
Ezek 34.6;
v. 1;
Mt 23.37

13 Woe to them, for they have strayed from me!
     Destruction to them, for they have rebelled against me!
   I would redeem them,
     but they speak lies against me.

7.14
Jer 3.10;
Am 2.8;
Mic 2.11;
Hos 13.16

14 They do not cry to me from the heart,
     but they wail upon their beds;
   they gash themselves for grain and wine;
     they rebel against me.

7.15
Hos 11.13;
Nah 1.9
7.16
Ps 78.57;
v. 7;
Ezek 23.32

15 It was I who trained and strengthened their arms,
     yet they plot evil against me.
16 They turn to that which does not profit;[k]
     they have become like a defective bow;
   their officials shall fall by the sword
     because of the rage of their tongue.
   So much for their babbling in the land of Egypt.

E. The fruit of Israel's sin

1. God's sentence upon them

8.1
Hos 5.8;
Hab 1.8;
Hos 6.7; 4.6

8 Set the trumpet to your lips!
   One like a vulture[j] is over the house of the LORD,

h Gk Syr: Heb *brought near*   i Or *humbles*   j Meaning of Heb uncertain   k Cn: Meaning of Heb
uncertain

7.7 *they devour their rulers*, i.e., they kill their own kings. This happened to Zechariah, Shallum, and Pekahiah.
7.8 *Ephraim mixes himself with the peoples*. The Israelites associated with and adopted heathen peoples and customs. *a cake not turned*, i.e., like a pancake that is burned on one side and uncooked on the other and is therefore altogether worthless.

7.11 *they call upon Egypt, they go to Assyria*. The royal court of Israel was torn between supporters of a pro-Egyptian alliance and those of a pro-Assyrian alliance. Hosea viewed this as evidence of Israel's failure to trust God.
8.1ff Hosea sets forth the particular sins of Israel in vv. 1,3,12,14: breaking of the covenant, breaking the commandments of God, despising the writings, and

because they have broken my covenant,
    and transgressed my law.
2 Israel cries to me,
    "My God, we — Israel — know you!"
3 Israel has spurned the good;
    the enemy shall pursue him.

4 They made kings, but not through me;
    they set up princes, but without my knowledge.
With their silver and gold they made idols
    for their own destruction.
5 Your calf is rejected, O Samaria.
    My anger burns against them.
How long will they be incapable of innocence?
6   For it is from Israel,
an artisan made it;
    it is not God.
The calf of Samaria
    shall be broken to pieces.*l*

7 For they sow the wind,
    and they shall reap the whirlwind.
The standing grain has no heads,
    it shall yield no meal;
if it were to yield,
    foreigners would devour it.
8 Israel is swallowed up;
    now they are among the nations
    as a useless vessel.
9 For they have gone up to Assyria,
    a wild ass wandering alone;
    Ephraim has bargained for lovers.
10 Though they bargain with the nations,
    I will now gather them up.
They shall soon writhe
    under the burden of kings and princes.

11 When Ephraim multiplied altars to expiate sin,
    they became to him altars for sinning.
12 Though I write for him the multitude of my instructions,
    they are regarded as a strange thing.
13 Though they offer choice sacrifices,*m*
    though they eat flesh,
    the LORD does not accept them.
Now he will remember their iniquity,
    and punish their sins;
    they shall return to Egypt.
14 Israel has forgotten his Maker,
    and built palaces;
and Judah has multiplied fortified cities;
    but I will send a fire upon his cities,
    and it shall devour his strongholds.

8.2
Hos 7.14

8.4
Hos 13.10, 11; 2.8

8.5
v. 6;
Hos 10.5;
13.2;
Jer 13.27
8.6
Hos 13.2

8.7
Hos 10.12, 13;
Isa 66.15;
Nah 1.3

8.8
Jer 51.34;
Hos 13.15

8.9
Hos 7.11;
Jer 2.24;
Ezek 16.3

8.10
Ezek 16.37;
22.40;
Jer 42.2

8.11
Hos 10.1;
12.11
8.12
v. 1;
Hos 4.6
8.13
Jer 7.21;
Hos 7.2;
1 Cor 4.5;
Hos 4.9; 9.7;
9.3, 6

8.14
Hos 2.13;
13.6;
Jer 17.27

---

l Or *shall go up in flames*   *m* Cn: Meaning of Heb uncertain

---

forgetting their God.
8.7ff As a consequence of their sins they would reap the whirlwind, i.e., their foreign alliances would fail to help them (vv. 6,8,10), their sacrifices would do them no good (v. 13), and their cities (which were their home bases) would be laid in ashes (v. 14).

2. *Israel's riches to be taken away*

9.1 Isa 22.12, 13; Hos 10.5; 4.12; Jer 44.17

9 Do not rejoice, O Israel!
Do not exult[n] as other nations do;
for you have played the whore, departing from your God.
You have loved a prostitute's pay
on all threshing floors.

9.2 Hos 2.9

2 Threshing floor and wine vat shall not feed them,
and the new wine shall fail them.

9.3 Jer 2.7; Hos 8.13; Ezek 4.13; Hos 7.11

3 They shall not remain in the land of the LORD;
but Ephraim shall return to Egypt,
and in Assyria they shall eat unclean food.

9.4 Jer 6.20; Hos 5.6; 8.13; Hag 2.14

4 They shall not pour drink offerings of wine to the LORD,
and their sacrifices shall not please him.
Such sacrifices shall be like mourners' bread;
all who eat of it shall be defiled;
for their bread shall be for their hunger only;
it shall not come to the house of the LORD.

9.5 Isa 10.3; Jer 5.31; Joel 1.13
9.6 v. 3; Jer 2.16; Ezek 30.13, 16; Isa 5.6; Hos 10.8

5 What will you do on the day of appointed festival,
and on the day of the festival of the LORD?
6 For even if they escape destruction,
Egypt shall gather them,
Memphis shall bury them.
Nettles shall possess their precious things of silver;[o]
thorns shall be in their tents.

9.7 Jer 10.15; Mic 7.4; Isa 34.8; Jer 16.18; Ezek 14.9, 10
9.8 Hos 5.1
9.9 Isa 31.6; Judg 19.12; Hos 5.8; 10.9; 7.2; 8.13

7 The days of punishment have come,
the days of recompense have come;
Israel cries,[p]
"The prophet is a fool,
the man of the spirit is mad!"
Because of your great iniquity,
your hostility is great.
8 The prophet is a sentinel for my God over Ephraim,
yet a fowler's snare is on all his ways,
and hostility in the house of his God.
9 They have deeply corrupted themselves
as in the days of Gibeah;
he will remember their iniquity,
he will punish their sins.

3. *Israel's population to decline*

9.10 Mic 7.1; Jer 24.2; Num 25.3; Hos 4.14; Jer 11.13

10 Like grapes in the wilderness,

[n] Gk: Heb *To exultation* [o] Meaning of Heb uncertain [p] Cn Compare Gk: Heb *shall know*

9.1ff Israel had no reason to rejoice, for her sins had found her out. Her land would not produce enough food, nor would God's people continue living there. They would be taken from the land and live in Assyria, where their kosher laws would be defunct and they would eat unclean food. They would lack the proper sacrifices and have no altar, and there would be no priests to officiate.
9.6 *Memphis shall bury them.* They would flee for refuge to Egypt, but that would turn out to be a place of death. They expected to find life by their flight from God, only to discover they had inherited death instead.
9.7–9 The day of God's judgment was at hand and would not be delayed. They would learn that their false prophets had been fools and that the word of the true prophets had come to pass. Israel had followed in the steps of their fathers, committing the same kinds of sins.
9.9 *in the days of Gibeah.* See Judg 19.14ff.
9.10 *they came to Baal-peor*, i.e., they forsook the true God and consecrated themselves to Baal-peor, who was the god of Peor (a city of Moab where fertility rites and the worship of Baal abounded). The Moabites invited the Israelites to their temple, though Baal-worship had started among the Israelites long before this (see Num 23; Judg 2.11–13).

I found Israel.
Like the first fruit on the fig tree,
  in its first season,
  I saw your ancestors.
But they came to Baal-peor,
  and consecrated themselves to a thing of shame,
  and became detestable like the thing they loved.

11 Ephraim's glory shall fly away like a bird —
  no birth, no pregnancy, no conception!
12 Even if they bring up children,
  I will bereave them until no one is left.
Woe to them indeed
  when I depart from them!
13 Once I saw Ephraim as a young palm planted in a lovely
    meadow,*q*
  but now Ephraim must lead out his children for slaughter.
14 Give them, O LORD —
  what will you give?
Give them a miscarrying womb
  and dry breasts.

15 Every evil of theirs began at Gilgal;
  there I came to hate them.
Because of the wickedness of their deeds
  I will drive them out of my house.
I will love them no more;
  all their officials are rebels.

16 Ephraim is stricken,
  their root is dried up,
  they shall bear no fruit.
Even though they give birth,
  I will kill the cherished offspring of their womb.
17 Because they have not listened to him,
  my God will reject them;
  they shall become wanderers among the nations.

4. Israel's idols to be destroyed

10 Israel is a luxuriant vine
  that yields its fruit.
The more his fruit increased
  the more altars he built;
as his country improved,
  he improved his pillars.
2 Their heart is false;
  now they must bear their guilt.
The LORD *r* will break down their altars,
  and destroy their pillars.

3 For now they will say:
  "We have no king,

q Meaning of Heb uncertain *r* Heb *he*

Cross references (right margin):

9.11 Hos 4.7; 10.5; v. 14
9.12 v. 16; Hos 7.13
9.13 Ezek 27.3, 4
9.14 v. 11; Lk 23.29
9.15 Hos 4.9; 7.2; 12.2; Isa 1.23
9.16 Hos 5.11; 8.7; v. 12
9.17 Hos 4.10; Deut 28.65
10.1 Ezek 15.1-5; Hos 8.11; 3.4
10.2 1 Kings 18.21; Mt 6.24; Hos 13.16; v. 8
10.3 Ps 12.4

9.13,14 Mothers would cry in anguish for their children. They would nurse them only to have the cruel enemy put them to the sword. Then they would say that the womb that bore no fruit was better than the one that did.
9.15 *Gilgal,* the town where Baal-worship flourished (4.15; 12.11) and where the monarchy was instituted (1 Sam 11.15).
10.1,2 The more they experienced God's loving care, the more prodigal they became in making and serving idols. God would now destroy their idols.

for we do not fear the LORD,
and a king—what could he do for us?"

4 They utter mere words;
with empty oaths they make covenants;
so litigation springs up like poisonous weeds
in the furrows of the field.

5 The inhabitants of Samaria tremble
for the calf[s] of Beth-aven.
Its people shall mourn for it,
and its idolatrous priests shall wail[t] over it,
over its glory that has departed from it.

6 The thing itself shall be carried to Assyria
as tribute to the great king.[u]
Ephraim shall be put to shame,
and Israel shall be ashamed of his idol.[v]

7 Samaria's king shall perish
like a chip on the face of the waters.

8 The high places of Aven, the sin of Israel,
shall be destroyed.
Thorn and thistle shall grow up
on their altars.
They shall say to the mountains, Cover us,
and to the hills, Fall on us.

5. Israel's fortresses to be destroyed

9 Since the days of Gibeah you have sinned, O Israel;
there they have continued.
Shall not war overtake them in Gibeah?

10 I will come[w] against the wayward people to punish them;
and nations shall be gathered against them
when they are punished[x] for their double iniquity.

11 Ephraim was a trained heifer
that loved to thresh,
and I spared her fair neck;
but I will make Ephraim break the ground;
Judah must plow;
Jacob must harrow for himself.

12 Sow for yourselves righteousness;
reap steadfast love;
break up your fallow ground;
for it is time to seek the LORD,
that he may come and rain righteousness upon you.

13 You have plowed wickedness,
you have reaped injustice,
you have eaten the fruit of lies.
Because you have trusted in your power
and in the multitude of your warriors,

14 therefore the tumult of war shall rise against your people,

Cross references (left margin):

10.4 Ezek 17.13-19; Hos 4.2; Deut 31.16, 17

10.5 Hos 8.5, 6; 9.11

10.6 Hos 11.5; 5.13; 4.7; Isa 30.3; Jer 7.24

10.7 Hos 13.11

10.8 v. 5; 1 Kings 12.30; v. 2; Hos 9.6; Lk 23.30; Rev 6.16

10.9 Hos 5.8; 9.9

10.10 Ezek 5.13; Hos 4.9

10.11 Jer 50.11; Hos 4.16; Jer 28.14; Ps 66.12

10.12 Prov 11.18; Jer 4.3; Hos 12.6; 6.3; Isa 44.3; 45.8

10.13 Job 4.8; Gal 6.7, 8; Hos 4.2; 7.3

10.14 Isa 17.3; Hos 13.16

---

[s] Gk Syr: Heb *calves*   [t] Cn: Heb *exult*   [u] Cn: Heb *to a king who will contend*   [v] Cn: Heb *counsel*
[w] Cn Compare Gk: Heb *In my desire*   [x] Gk: Heb *bound*

10.5 These idolaters would tremble and fear, for God would destroy them. In that hour of judgment they would ask the mountains to cover them and the hills to fall on them (v. 8), but it would do no good.
10.9 *the days of Gibeah.* See Judg 19—20.

10.12 Hosea now issued an impassioned plea for God's people to change their ways to a life of righteous living and to seek the Lord. The Lord promised them endless blessings if they did so.
10.14 *Shalman.* Probably Salaman, king of Moab,

and all your fortresses shall be destroyed,
   as Shalman destroyed Beth-arbel on the day of battle
     when mothers were dashed in pieces with their children.

15 Thus it shall be done to you, O Bethel,
   because of your great wickedness.
  At dawn the king of Israel
   shall be utterly cut off.

10.15
v. 7

6. *Israel to be a captive of Assyria*

11 When Israel was a child, I loved him,
    and out of Egypt I called my son.
2 The more I^y called them,
   the more they went from me;^{z}
  they kept sacrificing to the Baals,
   and offering incense to idols.

11.1
Hos 2.15;
12.9, 13;
13.4;
Mt 2.15
11.2
2 Kings 17.13-15;
Hos 2.13;
Isa 65.7;
Jer 18.15

3 Yet it was I who taught Ephraim to walk,
   I took them up in my^a arms;
   but they did not know that I healed them.
4 I led them with cords of human kindness,
   with bands of love.
  I was to them like those
   who lift infants to their cheeks.^{b}
  I bent down to them and fed them.

11.3
Hos 7.15;
Deut 1.31;
Jer 30.17
11.4
Jer 31.2, 3;
Lev 26.13;
Ex 16.32;
Ps 78.25

5 They shall return to the land of Egypt,
   and Assyria shall be their king,
   because they have refused to return to me.
6 The sword rages in their cities,
   it consumes their oracle-priests,
   and devours because of their schemes.
7 My people are bent on turning away from me.
   To the Most High they call,
   but he does not raise them up at all.^{c}

11.5
Hos 10.6;
7.16
11.6
Hos 13.16;
4.16, 17
11.7
Jer 8.5; v. 2

F. *God's tenderness toward Israel*

8 How can I give you up, Ephraim?
   How can I hand you over, O Israel?
  How can I make you like Admah?
   How can I treat you like Zeboiim?
  My heart recoils within me;
   my compassion grows warm and tender.

11.8
Hos 6.4;
Gen 14.8;
Isa 63.15

9 I will not execute my fierce anger;
   I will not again destroy Ephraim;
  for I am God and no mortal,

11.9
Deut 13.17;
Jer 26.3;
Isa 41.14,
16; 55.8, 9;
Mal 3.6

y Gk: Heb *they*   *z* Gk: Heb *them*   *a* Gk Syr Vg: Heb *his*   *b* Or *who ease the yoke on their jaws*
c Meaning of Heb uncertain

---

who invaded Gilead around 740 B.C.

11.1 This verse has a double meaning. God called his son, Jacob (or the people of Israel), out of Egypt in the exodus. Jesus the Messiah was also called out of Egypt — the second fulfillment of this prophetic word (see Mt 2.15).

11.4 *cords of human kindness.* God had brought his people into his service by mild and gentle methods.

11.5 The northern kingdom of Israel lasted for two centuries after the division of the united kingdom following Solomon's death. Hosea prophesied its

downfall. This took place in 722 B.C. when Shalmaneser V and Sargon of Assyria invaded Israel. Israel never recovered from the expulsion of its people as Judah did after her Babylonian captivity. The Scriptures do promise the regathering of all of Israel into a single realm in the last days (14.4–8; Isa 11.13). Some hold that the prophecy of the restoration of the northern kingdom has been fulfilled, at least in part, with Gentile believers becoming God's people, members of the church, God's new Israel.

11.8 *Admah . . . Zeboiim,* cities of the plain that perished with Sodom and Gomorrah (Deut 29.23).

the Holy One in your midst,
and I will not come in wrath.[d]

G. *Israel to be restored*

10 They shall go after the LORD,
who roars like a lion;
when he roars,
his children shall come trembling from the west.

11 They shall come trembling like birds from Egypt,
and like doves from the land of Assyria;
and I will return them to their homes, says the LORD.

H. *Ephraim's unfaithfulness restated; her doom predicted*

1. *The sin of Ephraim*

12[e] Ephraim has surrounded me with lies,
and the house of Israel with deceit;
but Judah still walks[f] with God,
and is faithful to the Holy One.

12 Ephraim herds the wind,
and pursues the east wind all day long;
they multiply falsehood and violence;
they make a treaty with Assyria,
and oil is carried to Egypt.

2. *The judgment on Jacob*

2 The LORD has an indictment against Judah,
and will punish Jacob according to his ways,
and repay him according to his deeds.

3 In the womb he tried to supplant his brother,
and in his manhood he strove with God.

4 He strove with the angel and prevailed,
he wept and sought his favor;
he met him at Bethel,
and there he spoke with him.[g]

5 The LORD the God of hosts,
the LORD is his name!

6 But as for you, return to your God,
hold fast to love and justice,
and wait continually for your God.

3. *Ephraim's sins enlarged on*

7 A trader, in whose hands are false balances,
he loves to oppress.

8 Ephraim has said, "Ah, I am rich,
I have gained wealth for myself;

Cross-references (left margin):

11.10
Hos 6.1-3;
Joel 3.16;
Isa 66.2, 5

11.11
Isa 11.11;
60.8;
Ezek 28.25,
26

11.12
Hos 4.2; 7.3

12.1
2 Kings 17.4;
Isa 30.6

12.2
Mic 6.2;
Hos 4.9

12.3
Gen 25.26;
32.24, 28

12.4
Gen 32.26;
28.12-15

12.5
Ex 3.15

12.6
Mic 6.8;
Hos 6.6;
Mic 7.7

12.7
Am 8.5;
Mic 6.11

12.8
Hos 13.6;
Rev 3.17;
Hos 4.8; 14.1

---

[d] Meaning of Heb uncertain   [e] Ch 12.1 in Heb   [f] Heb *roams* or *rules*   [g] Gk Syr: Heb *us*

12.1 *Ephraim heeds the wind, and pursues the east wind.* The nation of Israel placed vain hopes on human assistance; this was like following the east wind (a destroying wind, good for neither humans nor animals).

12.2ff Hosea referred to Jacob, from whom the Israelites had descended. He recalled three great experiences of Jacob. (1) He caught the heel of his brother in the womb and demonstrated conquering strength. (2) He wrestled with the angel and secured the blessing. (3) He encountered God at Bethel, where the covenant made with Abraham was repeated and renewed. Jacob's God should have been Ephraim's God. Hosea exhorted them to return to that God.

12.7 Ephraim not only farmed the land, but she also was a successful merchant. Yet she used fraud and force to accomplish her ends. She had false weights and balances, took pride in oppression, and loved to engage in it. She thought that what success she had gained came from her own efforts, leaving God out of the picture.

in all of my gain
   no offense has been found in me
   that would be sin."[h]
9 I am the LORD your God
   from the land of Egypt;
   I will make you live in tents again,
   as in the days of the appointed festival.

10 I spoke to the prophets;
   it was I who multiplied visions,
   and through the prophets I will bring destruction.
11 In Gilead[i] there is iniquity,
   they shall surely come to nothing.
   In Gilgal they sacrifice bulls,
   so their altars shall be like stone heaps
   on the furrows of the field.
12 Jacob fled to the land of Aram,
   there Israel served for a wife,
   and for a wife he guarded sheep.[j]
13 By a prophet the LORD brought Israel up from Egypt,
   and by a prophet he was guarded.
14 Ephraim has given bitter offense,
   so his Lord will bring his crimes down on him
   and pay him back for his insults.

4. Ephraim's doom predicted

13 When Ephraim spoke, there was trembling;
   he was exalted in Israel;
   but he incurred guilt through Baal and died.
2 And now they keep on sinning
   and make a cast image for themselves,
   idols of silver made according to their understanding,
   all of them the work of artisans.
   "Sacrifice to these," they say.[k]
   People are kissing calves!
3 Therefore they shall be like the morning mist
   or like the dew that goes away early,
   like chaff that swirls from the threshing floor
   or like smoke from a window.

4 Yet I have been the LORD your God
   ever since the land of Egypt;
   you know no God but me,
   and besides me there is no savior.
5 It was I who fed[l] you in the wilderness,
   in the land of drought.
6 When I fed[m] them, they were satisfied;
   they were satisfied, and their heart was proud;
   therefore they forgot me.
7 So I will become like a lion to them,

12.9
Hos 11.1;
13.4;
Lev 23.42;
Neh 8.17

12.10
2 Kings 17.13;
Jer 7.25;
Ezek 17.2;
20.49

12.11
Hos 6.8;
4.15; 9.15;
10.1, 2

12.12
Gen 28.5;
29.20

12.13
Ex 13.3

12.14
Ezek 18.10-13;
Dan 11.18;
Mic 6.16

13.1
Judg 8.1;
12.1;
Hos 2.8-17

13.2
Isa 46.6;
Hos 8.6

13.3
Hos 6.4;
Dan 2.35;
Ps 68.2

13.4
Hos 12.9;
Isa 43.11

13.5
Deut 2.7;
8.15; 32.10
13.6
Deut 8.12,
14; 32.15;
Hos 2.13;
4.6; 8.14
13.7
Lam 3.10;
Jer 5.6

h Meaning of Heb uncertain   i Compare Syr: Heb *Gilead*   j Heb lacks *sheep*   k Cn Compare Gk: Heb
To these they say sacrifices of people   l Gk Syr: Heb *knew*   m Cn: Heb *according to their pasture*

12.9 God became angry with Ephraim because of his sins. He would pay for them dearly by living again in tents when his cities were destroyed.
12.12 *Israel served for a wife.* Jacob served Laban in order to secure Rachel as his wife. He was deceived and married Leah and then served another seven years in order to marry Rachel too (see Gen 29).

13.1ff Hosea reproved Ephraim for idolatry, a sin forbidden by the second commandment: "You shall not make for yourself an idol . . ." (Ex 20.4). They did not believe that there was no savior but God.
13.5ff Hosea accused Israel of pride, luxury, and lack of discipline. Prosperity was the root of these sins.

like a leopard I will lurk beside the way.

13.8
2 Sam 17.8;
Ps 50.22
8 I will fall upon them like a bear robbed of her cubs,
   and will tear open the covering of their heart;
there I will devour them like a lion,
   as a wild animal would mangle them.

9 I will destroy you, O Israel;
   who can help you?[n]

13.10
2 Kings 17.4;
Hos 8.4
10 Where now is[o] your king, that he may save you?
    Where in all your cities are your rulers,
of whom you said,
    "Give me a king and rulers"?

13.11
1 Sam 8.7;
1 Kings 14.7-10
11 I gave you a king in my anger,
    and I took him away in my wrath.

13.12
Deut 32.34;
Rom 2.5
13.13
Mic 4.9, 10;
Isa 37.3;
66.9
12 Ephraim's iniquity is bound up;
    his sin is kept in store.
13 The pangs of childbirth come for him,
    but he is an unwise son;
for at the proper time he does not present himself
    at the mouth of the womb.

13.14
Ezek 37.12,
13;
1 Cor 15.54,
55;
Rom 11.29
14 Shall I ransom them from the power of Sheol?
    Shall I redeem them from Death?
O Death, where are[p] your plagues?
    O Sheol, where is[p] your destruction?
    Compassion is hidden from my eyes.

13.15
Hos 10.1;
Ezek 17.10;
19.12;
Jer 51.36;
20.5
15 Although he may flourish among rushes,[q]
    the east wind shall come, a blast from the LORD,
    rising from the wilderness;
and his fountain shall dry up,
    his spring shall be parched.
It shall strip his treasury
    of every precious thing.

13.16
Hos 10.2;
7.14;
Isa 13.16;
Hos 10.14;
2 Kings 15.16
16[r] Samaria shall bear her guilt,
    because she has rebelled against her God;
they shall fall by the sword,
    their little ones shall be dashed in pieces,
    and their pregnant women ripped open.

III. Forgiveness and blessing in response to repentance (14.1–9)

A. The call to repent

14.1
Hos 10.12;
14.6;
Joel 2.13
14 Return, O Israel, to the LORD your God,
    for you have stumbled because of your iniquity.

[n] Gk Syr: Heb *for in me is your help* [o] Gk Syr Vg: Heb *I will be* [p] Gk Syr: Heb *I will be* [q] Or *among brothers* [r] Ch 14.1 in Heb

13.9ff God would destroy Ephraim and the blame rested on their own heads. They were guilty, and God now had no compassion on them (v. 14). The east wind, which is a destroying wind, would come. Ephraim would be parched and dried up, her people would fall by the sword, her pregnant women would be ripped open, and her babies dashed to pieces. The wrath of God toward sinners would be terrible to behold, but the righteous did not need to fear, for as a remnant they would be saved by a God of love. **13.11** *I gave you a king . . . and I took him away.* This is probably an allusion to the kings of Israel who were assassinated during the last tempestuous years— Zechariah, Shallum, and Pekahiah. **14.1ff** This chapter is entirely different from the rest of this book. All that precedes it contains rebukes for sins and threats of the outpouring of the wrath of God. Now God exhorted his people to repent, promis-

2 Take words with you
      and return to the LORD;
   say to him,
      "Take away all guilt;
   accept that which is good,
      and we will offer
      the fruit[s] of our lips.

14.2
Mic 7.18, 19;
Heb 13.15

3 Assyria shall not save us;
      we will not ride upon horses;
   we will say no more, 'Our God,'
      to the work of our hands.
   In you the orphan finds mercy."

14.3
Hos 5.13;
Isa 31.1;
Hos 8.6;
13.2;
Ps 10.14

B. The promise of blessing

4 I will heal their disloyalty;
      I will love them freely,
      for my anger has turned from them.

14.4
Zeph 3.17;
Isa 12.1

5 I will be like the dew to Israel;
      he shall blossom like the lily,
      he shall strike root like the forests of Lebanon.[t]

14.5
Job 29.19;
Mt 6.28;
Isa 35.2

6 His shoots shall spread out;
      his beauty shall be like the olive tree,
      and his fragrance like that of Lebanon.

14.6
Ps 52.8;
Song 4.11

7 They shall again live beneath my[u] shadow,
      they shall flourish as a garden;[v]
   they shall blossom like the vine,
      their fragrance shall be like the wine of Lebanon.

14.7
Ps 91.4;
Ezek 17.23;
Hos 2.21, 22

8 O Ephraim, what have I[w] to do with idols?
      It is I who answer and look after you.[x]
   I am like an evergreen cypress;
      your faithfulness[y] comes from me.

14.8
v. 3;
Isa 41.19;
Ezek 17.23

C. The postscript

9 Those who are wise understand these things;
      those who are discerning know them.
   For the ways of the LORD are right,
      and the upright walk in them,
      but transgressors stumble in them.

14.9
Ps 107.43;
Acts 13.10;
Isa 26.7;
1.28

[s] Gk Syr: Heb *bulls*   [t] Cn: Heb *like Lebanon*   [u] Heb *his*   [v] Cn: Heb *they shall grow grain*   [w] Or *What more has Ephraim*   [x] Heb *him*   [y] Heb *your fruit*

ing them mercy if they would do so. In judgment he would wound them so that when they repented he would be able to heal them. It contains a refrain found everywhere in the writings of the prophets: "For the ways of the LORD are right, and the upright walk in them, but transgressors stumble in them" (v. 9). In the end there are only two ways one can walk. One

road leads to life eternal; the other leads to everlasting death.
14.3   Hosea called on Israel to acknowledge that she could not be saved by depending on or associating with such nations as Assyria or Egypt. If there was to be deliverance, it had to come from God, for Israel was a helpless orphan.

INTRODUCTION TO
JOEL

Authorship, Date, and Background: Joel, whose name means "Yahweh is God," was the son of Pethuel and wrote the book which goes by his name. Nothing is known about him or his father. He was from Jerusalem and was well acquainted with the city and the land of Judah. The book cannot be dated either from internal or external evidences and scholars have varied in their suggestions from a pre-exilic date earlier than 800 B.C. to a post-exilic date as late as 350 B.C. The fact that Joel mentioned Edom, Egypt, Philistia, and Phoenicia as contemporary nations at the time of the writing has occasioned conservative scholars to prefer the early date for the composition of the book. Note also similarities with the prophecies of Amos, whose work has been dated in the eighth century B.C.

The background against which the book was written was a locust invasion which devastated the land, leaving behind hunger and destitution for both humans and animals. Such invasions were not uncommon, although they usually did not come from the north. Joel used the invasion to call God's people to repentance and prayer for divine forgiveness. He looked upon the invasion as a divine judgment against the nation.

Characteristics and Content: Joel writes beautifully and descriptively of an actual locust invasion and likens it to the invasion of an army from the north. He called the locusts a vast army and went on to describe the starving priests, the bare fields, the stricken farmers, and the weeping vinedressers. He called for the priests to dress in sackcloth and recommended a fast and the assembling of themselves at the temple to plead with God for help.

From there Joel addressed himself to the future, including a prophecy about the outpouring of God's Spirit on all flesh; this passage was picked up by Peter in his discourse at Pentecost (Acts 2). Many commentators think that part of Joel's prohecy awaits fulfillment at the end of the present age or in what Joel calls "the day of the LORD." At that time, there will be "portents in the heavens and on the earth, blood and fire and columns of smoke. The sun shall be turned to darkness, and the moon to blood, before the great and terrible day of the LORD comes" (2.30,31). In ch. 3, like so many of the other prophets, Joel foresaw future prosperity for Judah and Jerusalem. The people would be delivered by the power of God following severe judgments, at which time God by his power would insure that "Judah shall be inhabited forever, and Jerusalem to all generations" (3.20).

Outline:

I. The plague of locusts (1.1—2.27)

II. The judgment of God and his blessing in the last days (2.28—3.21)

JOEL

I. *The plague of locusts (1.1–2.27)*

A. *Superscription*

1 The word of the LORD that came to Joel son of Pethuel:

2 Hear this, O elders,
   give ear, all inhabitants of the land!
Has such a thing happened in your days,
   or in the days of your ancestors?
3 Tell your children of it,
   and let your children tell their children,
   and their children another generation.

B. *The plague and drought described*

4 What the cutting locust left,
   the swarming locust has eaten.
What the swarming locust left,
   the hopping locust has eaten,
and what the hopping locust left,
   the destroying locust has eaten.

5 Wake up, you drunkards, and weep;
   and wail, all you wine-drinkers,
over the sweet wine,
   for it is cut off from your mouth.
6 For a nation has invaded my land,
   powerful and innumerable;
its teeth are lions' teeth,
   and it has the fangs of a lioness.
7 It has laid waste my vines,
   and splintered my fig trees;
it has stripped off their bark and thrown it down;
   their branches have turned white.

8 Lament like a virgin dressed in sackcloth
   for the husband of her youth.
9 The grain offering and the drink offering are cut off
   from the house of the LORD.

The priests mourn,
   the ministers of the LORD.

1.1
Jer 1.2;
Ezek 1.3;
Hos 1.1;
Acts 2.16
1.2
Hos 4.1; 5.1;
v. 14;
Joel 2.2
1.3
Ps 78.4

1.4
Deut 28.38;
Joel 2.25;
Nah 3.15, 16;
Isa 33.4

1.5
Joel 3.3;
Isa 32.10

1.6
Joel 2.2, 11;
Rev 9.8

1.7
Isa 5.6;
Am 4.9

1.8
v. 13;
Am 8.10
1.9
Joel 2.14, 17

1.2 Joel was about to record something not known in previous experience or recorded in books of history. The elders of the nation were challenged to declare whether they had ever experienced or known of any devastation like that which was about to take place.
1.3 What was going to take place would be so unusual and breathtaking that all generations to come would stand astonished.
1.4 There are many varieties of locusts, four of

which are mentioned here. Their swarms could reach millions if not billions.
1.6 *a nation*, not a nation of human beings, but an unimaginable army of locusts who constituted a nation. They were numberless and had teeth like lions to destroy.
1.7 The locusts ate everything that was edible, including the bark from the trees, which now stood in whiteness against the clear sky.

1.10
Isa 24.4, 7;
Hos 9.2

10 The fields are devastated,
    the ground mourns;
for the grain is destroyed,
    the wine dries up,
    the oil fails.

1.11
Jer 14.3, 4;
Isa 17.11;
Jer 9.12

11 Be dismayed, you farmers,
    wail, you vinedressers,
over the wheat and the barley;
    for the crops of the field are ruined.

1.12
Hab 3.17, 18;
Isa 16.10;
24.11;
Jer 48.33

12 The vine withers,
    the fig tree droops.
Pomegranate, palm, and apple—
    all the trees of the field are dried up;
surely, joy withers away
    among the people.

1.13
v. 8;
Jer 4.8; v. 9;
Joel 2.17;
1 Kings 21.27

13 Put on sackcloth and lament, you priests;
    wail, you ministers of the altar.
Come, pass the night in sackcloth,
    you ministers of my God!
Grain offering and drink offering
    are withheld from the house of your God.

1.14
2 Chr 20.3, 4;
Joel 2.15, 16;
v. 2;
Jon 3.8

14 Sanctify a fast,
    call a solemn assembly.
Gather the elders
    and all the inhabitants of the land
to the house of the Lord your God,
    and cry out to the Lord.

1.15
Jer 30.7;
Isa 13.6, 9;
Joel 2.1, 11,
31
1.16
Isa 3.7;
Deut 12.6, 7;
Ps 43.4

15 Alas for the day!
For the day of the Lord is near,
    and as destruction from the Almighty[a] it comes.
16 Is not the food cut off
    before our eyes,
joy and gladness
    from the house of our God?

1.17
Isa 17.10, 11

17 The seed shrivels under the clods,[b]
    the storehouses are desolate;
the granaries are ruined
    because the grain has failed.

1.18
1 Kings 18.5;
Jer 14.5, 6;
Hos 4.3

18 How the animals groan!
    The herds of cattle wander about
because there is no pasture for them;

a Traditional rendering of Heb Shaddai   b Meaning of Heb uncertain

---

1.12 *The vine withers.* The workers labored, but the fields brought forth no fruit. This was only one of the signs of a future disaster. Joel called for the priests to prepare their hearts in private for their public duty of seeking God's help.
1.13 In good times the people had brought their offerings to the priests from the produce taken from the fields. Now there was nothing for them to eat. The earth was barren and the crops, if any, scanty.
1.14 Joel made it clear that the only hope for the people was to turn to God for help. They had to fast, meet in solemn assembly, and, of course, be ready to admit that what had happened came as a result of their

transgressions.

1.15 *the day of the Lord is near.* This means either the present judgment against Judah and Jerusalem, or that and another judgment at the end of the age. *Alas for the day,* for terrible destruction would come from the hand of God himself.

1.17 The caterpillars had destroyed the corn, the garners were empty, and the seed they planted did not produce its fruit.

1.18 The cattle perished for lack of grass; their groans should touch the hearts of the people on whom this judgment had fallen.

even the flocks of sheep are dazed. [c]

19 To you, O Lord, I cry.
For fire has devoured
the pastures of the wilderness,
and flames have burned
all the trees of the field.
20 Even the wild animals cry to you
because the watercourses are dried up,
and fire has devoured
the pastures of the wilderness.

C. The coming day of the Lord

2 Blow the trumpet in Zion;
sound the alarm on my holy mountain!
Let all the inhabitants of the land tremble,
for the day of the Lord is coming, it is near —
2 a day of darkness and gloom,
a day of clouds and thick darkness!
Like blackness spread upon the mountains
a great and powerful army comes;
their like has never been from of old,
nor will be again after them
in ages to come.

3 Fire devours in front of them,
and behind them a flame burns.
Before them the land is like the garden of Eden,
but after them a desolate wilderness,
and nothing escapes them.

4 They have the appearance of horses,
and like war-horses they charge.
5 As with the rumbling of chariots,
they leap on the tops of the mountains,
like the crackling of a flame of fire
devouring the stubble,
like a powerful army
drawn up for battle.

6 Before them peoples are in anguish,
all faces grow pale. [d]
7 Like warriors they charge,
like soldiers they scale the wall.
Each keeps to its own course,
they do not swerve from [e] their paths.
8 They do not jostle one another,
each keeps to its own track;
they burst through the weapons
and are not halted.
9 They leap upon the city,
they run upon the walls;

1.19
Ps 50.15;
Jer 9.10;
Joel 2.3

1.20
Job 38.41;
Ps 104.21;
1 Kings 17.7;
18.5

2.1
Jer 4.5;
Num 10.9;
Zeph 1.14-16;
vv. 11, 31;
Joel 1.15
2.2
Am 5.18;
Joel 1.6;
Lam 1.12;
Joel 1.2

2.3
Joel 1.19, 20;
Gen 2.8;
Isa 51.3;
Ps 105.34, 35

2.4
Rev 9.7

2.5
Rev 9.9;
Isa 5.24;
30.30

2.6
Isa 13.8;
Nah 2.10;
Jer 30.6
2.7
Isa 5.26, 27;
v. 9

2.9
v. 7;
Jer 9.21;
Jn 10.1

[c] Compare Gk Syr Vg: Meaning of Heb uncertain   [d] Meaning of Heb uncertain   [e] Gk Syr Vg: Heb
they do not take a pledge along

2.1 *The day of the Lord* is yet future, coming at the
end of the age. The prophets saw the ranges of mountains in the distance, but they could not see the valleys
in between. Therefore, they had no way of knowing

how soon the Lord's final judgment would fall.
2.4,5 The locusts appeared like war horses, rumbling chariots, and brands of burning fire that destroyed without leaving anything behind.

they climb up into the houses,
they enter through the windows like a thief.

2.10
Ps 18.7;
Isa 13.10;
Joel 3.15;
Mt 24.29

10 The earth quakes before them,
  the heavens tremble.
The sun and the moon are darkened,
  and the stars withdraw their shining.

2.11
Joel 3.16;
Am 1.2;
vv. 2, 25;
Jer 50.34;
Rev 18.8;
Joel 3.14;
Ezek 22.14

11 The Lord utters his voice
  at the head of his army;
how vast is his host!
  Numberless are those who obey his command.
Truly the day of the Lord is great;
  terrible indeed — who can endure it?

D. *The call to repentance*

2.12
Jer 4.1;
Hos 12.6

12 Yet even now, says the Lord,
  return to me with all your heart,
with fasting, with weeping, and with mourning;

2.13
Ps 34.18;
Isa 57.15;
2 Sam 1.11;
Jon 4.2;
Jer 18.8;
42.10

13   rend your hearts and not your clothing.
Return to the Lord, your God,
  for he is gracious and merciful,
slow to anger, and abounding in steadfast love,
  and relents from punishing.

2.14
Jer 26.3;
Hag 2.19;
Joel 1.9, 13

14 Who knows whether he will not turn and relent,
  and leave a blessing behind him,
a grain offering and a drink offering
  for the Lord, your God?

2.15
Num 10.3;
v. 1;
Jer 36.9;
Joel 1.14

15 Blow the trumpet in Zion;
  sanctify a fast;
call a solemn assembly;

2.16
Ex 19.10, 22;
Ps 19.5

16   gather the people.
Sanctify the congregation;
  assemble the aged;
gather the children,
  even infants at the breast.
Let the bridegroom leave his room,
  and the bride her canopy.

2.17
Ezek 8.16;
Mt 23.35;
Joel 1.9;
Deut 9.26-29;
Isa 37.20;
Ps 44.13;
42.10

17 Between the vestibule and the altar
  let the priests, the ministers of the Lord, weep.
Let them say, "Spare your people, O Lord,
  and do not make your heritage a mockery,
  a byword among the nations.
Why should it be said among the peoples,
  'Where is their God?' "

E. *The promised deliverance following repentance*

2.18
Zech 1.14;
Isa 60.10

18 Then the Lord became jealous for his land,
  and had pity on his people.

2.10 *The sun and the moon are darkened.* Multitudes of locusts clouded sun and moon. And in the last days before the second advent of Christ, a similar or worse situation will prevail.

2.14 Joel saw the judgment coming, but urged the people to repent and turn to God in the hope that he might turn the curse and disaster into blessing. Undoubtedly, had the people heeded Joel's advice, the judgment would have been at least delayed. The same might be said for any nation today that will turn to God.

2.15 *Blow the trumpet in Zion* was the prophet's clear call to humiliation, fasting, prayer, and a complete turning to God for mercy. This was not uncommon; for an example of the effects of this course of action, see 2 Chr 20.

19 In response to his people the LORD said:
      I am sending you
          grain, wine, and oil,
          and you will be satisfied;
      and I will no more make you
          a mockery among the nations.

20 I will remove the northern army far from you,
          and drive it into a parched and desolate land,
      its front into the eastern sea,
          and its rear into the western sea;
      its stench and foul smell will rise up.
          Surely he has done great things!

21 Do not fear, O soil;
          be glad and rejoice,
      for the LORD has done great things!

22 Do not fear, you animals of the field,
          for the pastures of the wilderness are green;
      the tree bears its fruit,
          the fig tree and vine give their full yield.

23 O children of Zion, be glad
          and rejoice in the LORD your God;
      for he has given the early rain*f* for your vindication,
          he has poured down for you abundant rain,
      the early and the later rain, as before.

24 The threshing floors shall be full of grain,
          the vats shall overflow with wine and oil.

25 I will repay you for the years
          that the swarming locust has eaten,
      the hopper, the destroyer, and the cutter,
          my great army, which I sent against you.

26 You shall eat in plenty and be satisfied,
          and praise the name of the LORD your God,
      who has dealt wondrously with you.
          And my people shall never again be put to shame.

27 You shall know that I am in the midst of Israel,
          and that I, the LORD, am your God and there is no other.
      And my people shall never again be put to shame.

II. *The judgment of God and his blessing in the last days* (2.28–3.21)

A. *The promised outpouring of the Spirit*

28*g* Then afterward
          I will pour out my spirit on all flesh;

f Meaning of Heb uncertain   *g* Ch 3.1 in Heb

2.19	Hos 2.21, 22; Ezek 34.29; 36.15
2.20	Jer 1.14, 15; Zech 14.8; Deut 11.24; Isa 34.3; Am 4.10
2.21	Jer 30.10; v. 26
2.22	Ps 65.12, 13
2.23	Ps 149.2; Isa 41.16; Deut 11.14; Jer 5.24; Hos 6.3
2.24	Am 9.13; Mal 3.10
2.25	Joel 1.4
2.26	Isa 62.9; Ps 67.5-7; Isa 25.1; 45.17
2.27	Joel 3.17, 21; Isa 45.1, 21; 49.23
2.28	Acts 2.17-21; Ezek 39.29; Isa 40.5

2.25 Through Joel God promised restoration following repentance. There was yet a period of time to come when blessing and abundance would reign.
2.28 *I will pour out my Spirit upon all flesh.* God had poured out his Spirit upon many people in the O.T. era. A future fulfillment took place at Pentecost.

Peter stated that the outpouring of the Holy Spirit then fulfilled Joel's prophecy (Acts 2.17–21). Some also believe there will be yet another fulfillment of this prophecy, i.e., "in those days" (v. 29), when there will be miraculous signs and frightening physical and meteoric phenomena.

your sons and your daughters shall prophesy,
    your old men shall dream dreams,
    and your young men shall see visions.
29 Even on the male and female slaves,
    in those days, I will pour out my spirit.

30 I will show portents in the heavens and on the earth, blood and fire and columns of smoke. 31 The sun shall be turned to darkness, and the moon to blood, before the great and terrible day of the LORD comes. 32 Then everyone who calls on the name of the LORD shall be saved; for in Mount Zion and in Jerusalem there shall be those who escape, as the LORD has said, and among the survivors shall be those whom the LORD calls.

B. *The restoration of Judah and the judgment of her enemies*

3[h] For then, in those days and at that time, when I restore the fortunes of Judah and Jerusalem, 2 I will gather all the nations and bring them down to the valley of Jehoshaphat, and I will enter into judgment with them there, on account of my people and my heritage Israel, because they have scattered them among the nations. They have divided my land, 3 and cast lots for my people, and traded boys for prostitutes, and sold girls for wine, and drunk it down.

4 What are you to me, O Tyre and Sidon, and all the regions of Philistia? Are you paying me back for something? If you are paying me back, I will turn your deeds back upon your own heads swiftly and speedily. 5 For you have taken my silver and my gold, and have carried my rich treasures into your temples.[i] 6 You have sold the people of Judah and Jerusalem to the Greeks, removing them far from their own border. 7 But now I will rouse them to leave the places to which you have sold them, and I will turn your deeds back upon your own heads. 8 I will sell your sons and your daughters into the hand of the people of Judah, and they will sell them to the Sabeans, to a nation far away; for the LORD has spoken.

9 Proclaim this among the nations:
Prepare war,[j]
    stir up the warriors.
Let all the soldiers draw near,
    let them come up.
10 Beat your plowshares into swords,
    and your pruning hooks into spears;
    let the weakling say, "I am a warrior."

11 Come quickly,[k]
    all you nations all around,
    gather yourselves there.
Bring down your warriors, O LORD.

Cross references (left margin):

2.29 1 Cor 12.13; Gal 3.28

2.30 Mt 24.29; Lk 21.11, 25; Acts 2.19

2.31 Isa 13.9, 10; Mt 24.29; Mal 4.1, 5; Rev 6.12

2.32 Isa 46.13; Mic 4.7; Rom 9.27

3.1 Jer 30.3; Ezek 38.14

3.2 Isa 66.16; Ezek 34.6; 35.10; 36.1-5

3.3 Ob 11; Nah 3.10

3.4 Am 1.9, 10; Ezek 25.12, 17

3.5 2 Kings 12.18; 2 Chr 21.16, 17

3.7 Isa 43.5, 6; Jer 23.8

3.8 Isa 14.2; 60.14; Ezek 23.42; Jer 6.20

3.9 Isa 8.9, 10; Jer 51.27, 28; 6.4; 46.3, 4; Zech 14.2, 3

3.10 Isa 2.4; Mic 4.3; Zech 12.8

3.11 Ezek 38.15, 16; Isa 13.3

---

[h] Ch 4.1 in Heb   [i] Or *palaces*   [j] Heb *sanctify war*   [k] Meaning of Heb uncertain

---

3.1 Though the present circumstances appeared horrendous and unending, they would not be everlasting. God would restore Judah and Jerusalem according to his covenant promise, though no one could date the time with precision.

3.2 *the valley of Jehoshaphat*, or, "the valley where Yahweh judges." The name "Jehoshaphat" means "Yahweh has judged." Joel prophesied that the coming judgment was a reality and would be measured out

to the godless people in that very valley.

3.4ff The nations had wasted the people of God, stolen God's gold and silver, and sold his people into slavery. He would not stand for this forever. These nations would be destroyed and their children delivered over to Judah.

3.9ff God warned the nations to prepare for war against him. He would follow through on this challenge, and they would see who came out victorious.

12 Let the nations rouse themselves,
    and come up to the valley of Jehoshaphat;
for there I will sit to judge
    all the neighboring nations.

13 Put in the sickle,
    for the harvest is ripe.
Go in, tread,
    for the wine press is full.
The vats overflow,
    for their wickedness is great.

14 Multitudes, multitudes,
    in the valley of decision!
For the day of the LORD is near
    in the valley of decision.

15 The sun and the moon are darkened,
    and the stars withdraw their shining.

16 The LORD roars from Zion,
    and utters his voice from Jerusalem,
    and the heavens and the earth shake.
But the LORD is a refuge for his people,
    a stronghold for the people of Israel.

C. Everlasting blessing for God's people

17 So you shall know that I, the LORD your God,
    dwell in Zion, my holy mountain.
And Jerusalem shall be holy,
    and strangers shall never again pass through it.

18 In that day
the mountains shall drip sweet wine,
    the hills shall flow with milk,
and all the stream beds of Judah
    shall flow with water;
a fountain shall come forth from the house of the LORD
    and water the Wadi Shittim.

19 Egypt shall become a desolation
    and Edom a desolate wilderness,
because of the violence done to the people of Judah,
    in whose land they have shed innocent blood.
20 But Judah shall be inhabited forever,
    and Jerusalem to all generations.
21 I will avenge their blood, and I will not clear the guilty,[l]
    for the LORD dwells in Zion.

3.12 Isa 2.4; 3.13
3.13 Mt 13.39; Rev 14.15; Isa 63.3; Rev 14.19
3.14 Isa 34.2-8; Joel 1.15; 2.1
3.15 Joel 2.10, 31
3.16 Am 1.2; Joel 2.11; Hag 2.6; Jer 17.17
3.17 v. 21; Ezek 20.40; Ob 17; Isa 52.1; Nah 1.15
3.18 Am 9.13; Isa 30.25; 35.6; Ezek 47.1-12; Rev 22.1
3.19 Ob 10
3.20 Ezek 37.25; Am 9.15
3.21 Ezek 36.25; v. 17

l Gk Syr: Heb I will hold innocent their blood that I have not held innocent

3.14 The judgment day is coming. It will be a day of decision. Multitudes will be there to hear God pronounce his sentence on them and seal their doom.
3.15 Before the end of time the kingdom of nature will be shaken and changed. The light from sun, moon, and stars will be withdrawn, while the earth and the sky will shake (see also Rev 8.12).
3.17 The time is coming when all people and nations will know that God is Lord, that Zion is his holy mountain, and that Jerusalem is the city of our God. Only the righteous shall pass through that city.
3.18 In that day yet to come the waters will enrich the parched earth, the mountains will yield wine, the hills will flow with milk, and the comforts all people yearn for will be theirs. The paradise lost by Adam will be restored by Jesus Christ.
3.19 Edom and Egypt will be made a desolation. Israel, spiritually revived and right with God, will be favored and blessed with perpetuity.

INTRODUCTION TO

AMOS

Authorship, Date, and Background: Amos gives no identification as to his parentage. His name means "burden" or "burden-bearer." He was from Tekoa, which was approximately five miles south of Bethlehem. Amos was a herdsman and a dresser of sycamore trees (7.14). He prophesied around the middle of the eighth century B.C. and was a contemporary of Isaiah, Micah, and Hosea. Although he came from the southern kingdom of Judah, God called him from his pastoral duties to speak to the northern kingdom of Samaria. At that time, during the reign of Jeroboam II, a large and financially successful mercantile class had come into being in Samaria. They were prosperous but corrupt. The rich got richer and the poor became poorer by the rich oppressing the poor, seizing their lands (it was God's intention that the people of Israel should remain small independent landowners), making serfs of these people, and selling them into slavery.

At the same time, the Canaanite religion had overtaken the northern kingdom, with all of its wicked features such as ritual prostitution, orgies, its fertility cult, and four annual festivals accompanied by drunkenness, idolatry, and violence. Two years before the earthquake, about which we know little, God called Amos to be his prophet, in spite of his having no priestly background and not being a learned scholar. God's ways are not our ways.

Characteristics and Content: Amos came to Samaria first with a message of divine judgment against the surrounding nations. This delighted the people of Samaria, who remembered their suffering under Damascus, the Philistines, Tyre, Moab, Ammon, and Edom. He pronounced God's judgment on his own nation of Judah for their disobedience and their rejection of the law of God. Samaria was also pleased with this message, since they traditionally resented their southern relatives. Then Amos directed the word of judgment against Samaria. He said they had sinned, and God was about to judge them by sending divine retribution upon them. He outlined their sins of sumptuous living, bribery, neglect of the poor, drunkenness, and even their ritual sacrifices which had no internal significance since their hearts were far removed from God. He announced the divine judgment that would follow their impenitence, a judgment fulfilled in 722 B.C., not too many years after Amos completed his short ministry. His visions of a vast swarm of locusts, a great fire, a plumbline, a basket full of ripe fruit, and the smitten temple and slain people were used to dramatize the coming destruction. Yet, like so many of the other prophets, Amos painted a brighter and more hopeful picture toward the end of his diatribe (see 9.11–15).

Outline:

AMOS

I. The prediction of judgment on the surrounding nations (1.1–2.16)

A. Superscription and theme

1 The words of Amos, who was among the shepherds of Tekoa, which he saw concerning Israel in the days of King Uzziah of Judah and in the days of King Jeroboam son of Joash of Israel, two years[a] before the earthquake. 2And he said:

The LORD roars from Zion,
  and utters his voice from Jerusalem;
the pastures of the shepherds wither,
  and the top of Carmel dries up.

1.1
2 Sam 14.2;
2 Kings 14.23-29;
Zech 14.5

1.2
Jer 25.30;
Joel 3.16;
1.18, 19;
Am 9.3

B. Prophecy against Damascus

3 Thus says the LORD:
  For three transgressions of Damascus,
    and for four, I will not revoke the punishment;[b]
  because they have threshed Gilead
    with threshing sledges of iron.
4 So I will send a fire on the house of Hazael,
    and it shall devour the strongholds of Ben-hadad.
5 I will break the gate bars of Damascus,
    and cut off the inhabitants from the Valley of Aven,
  and the one who holds the scepter from Beth-eden;
    and the people of Aram shall go into exile to Kir,
                                             says the LORD.

1.3
Isa 7.8; 8.4;
v. 13

1.4
Jer 49.27;
1 Kings 20.1;
2 Kings 6.24
1.5
Jer 51.30;
2 Kings 16.9;
Am 9.7

C. Prophecy against Gaza (Philistia)

6 Thus says the LORD:
  For three transgressions of Gaza,
    and for four, I will not revoke the punishment;[b]
  because they carried into exile entire communities,

1.6
1 Sam 6.17;
Jer 47.1, 5;
v. 9;
Ob 11

---

a Or *during two years*   *b* Heb *cause it to return*

1.1 Some think that Amos was a cattle-dealer; others that he was a poor shepherd who watched over flocks of his own (see 7.14). He was also a dresser of sycamore trees, which was a poor employment. Why God chose Amos to be his prophet we do not know. Humanly speaking, he would appear to be a very ordinary person. But God who calls also endows, and to whatever occupation God calls anyone. Amos was called to exercise his prophetic office in the northern kingdom. Coming from Tekoa, he was a native of Judah. The earthquake mentioned here is spoken of in Zech 14.5.
1.3 *For three transgressions . . . and for four.* Damascus was guilty of many transgressions. Three and four add up to seven, the perfect number, suggesting that

this nation had filled up the measure of iniquities and was thus ripe for ruin. Amos used the same "three . . . and for four" for the iniquities of the other nations who were facing the judgment of God.
1.5 *the people of Aram shall go . . . to Kir.* Kir was the district to which the captives of Damascus went (2 Kings 16.9) after the victory of Pul, the king of Assyria. Decreeing that the Arameans would go back to Kir as slaves was like saying to the Israelites that they had to go back to Egypt as slaves, for the Arameans had made their exodus from Kir and now were free (9.7).
1.6,7 Gaza was a commercial city, where slaves were bought and sold. There many Israelites were sold into slavery to Edom, their ancient enemy.

to hand them over to Edom.

1.7
Jer 47.1; v. 6
7 So I will send a fire on the wall of Gaza,
 fire that shall devour its strongholds.

1.8
Zeph 2.4;
Zech 9.6;
Ps 81.14;
Ezek 25.16
8 I will cut off the inhabitants from Ashdod,
 and the one who holds the scepter from Ashkelon;
I will turn my hand against Ekron,
 and the remnant of the Philistines shall perish,

        says the Lord GOD.

D. *Prophecy against Tyre (Phoenicia)*

1.9
Isa 23.1-18;
Ezek 26.2-4;
1 Kings 5.1;
9.11-14
9 Thus says the LORD:
For three transgressions of Tyre,
 and for four, I will not revoke the punishment;*c*
because they delivered entire communities over to Edom,
 and did not remember the covenant of kinship.

1.10
Zech 9.4
10 So I will send a fire on the wall of Tyre,
 fire that shall devour its strongholds.

E. *Prophecy against Edom*

1.11
Isa 34.5, 6;
63.1-6;
Jer 49.7-22;
Ob 10-12;
Isa 57.16;
Mic 7.18
11 Thus says the LORD:
For three transgressions of Edom,
 and for four, I will not revoke the punishment;*c*
because he pursued his brother with the sword
 and cast off all pity;
he maintained his anger perpetually,*d*
 and kept his wrath*e* forever.

1.12
Jer 49.7, 20;
Ob 9, 10
12 So I will send a fire on Teman,
 and it shall devour the strongholds of Bozrah.

F. *Prophecy against Ammon*

1.13
Jer 49.1-6;
Ezek 25.2-7;
2 Kings 15.16
13 Thus says the LORD:
For three transgressions of the Ammonites,
 and for four, I will not revoke the punishment;*c*
because they have ripped open pregnant women in Gilead
 in order to enlarge their territory.

1.14
Jer 49.2;
Am 2.2;
Ezek 21.22;
Isa 29.6;
30.30
14 So I will kindle a fire against the wall of Rabbah,
 fire that shall devour its strongholds,
with shouting on the day of battle,
 with a storm on the day of the whirlwind;

1.15
Jer 49.3
15 then their king shall go into exile,
 he and his officials together,

        says the LORD.

G. *Prophecy against Moab*

2.1
Isa chs, 15,
16;
Jer 48;
Zeph 2.8, 9
2 Thus says the LORD:
For three transgressions of Moab,
 and for four, I will not revoke the punishment;*c*
because he burned to lime
 the bones of the king of Edom.

2.2
Jer 48.41, 45
2 So I will send a fire on Moab,

c Heb *cause it to return* *d* Syr Vg: Heb *and his anger tore perpetually* *e* Gk Syr Vg: Heb *and his wrath kept*

1.12 *Teman . . . Bozrah.* Teman was in the north of Edom and Bozrah in the south. The entire country would be devastated.
1.14 *Rabbah*, literally, "the great city," was the capital of the Ammonite nation. Its modern name is Am-

man, the capital city of Jordan.
2.1 God's moral law pertains to all nations, not to Israel alone. Here the Gentile nation Moab committed atrocity against another Gentile nation Edom.

and it shall devour the strongholds of Kerioth,
and Moab shall die amid uproar,
amid shouting and the sound of the trumpet;

3 I will cut off the ruler from its midst,
and will kill all its officials with him,

says the LORD.

2.3
Am 5.7, 12;
6.12;
Ps 2.10;
Isa 40.23;
Jer 48.7

H. *Prophecies against the chosen people*

1. *Judah*

4 Thus says the LORD:
For three transgressions of Judah,
and for four, I will not revoke the punishment;*f*
because they have rejected the law of the LORD,
and have not kept his statutes,
but they have been led astray by the same lies
after which their ancestors walked.

5 So I will send a fire on Judah,
and it shall devour the strongholds of Jerusalem.

2.4
2 Kings 17.19;
Joel 3.2;
Jer 6.19; 8.9;
Dan 9.11;
Isa 28.15;
Jer 16.19;
Ezek 20.13,
16, 18

2.5
Jer 17.27;
Hos 8.14

2. *Israel*

6 Thus says the LORD:
For three transgressions of Israel,
and for four, I will not revoke the punishment;*f*
because they sell the righteous for silver,
and the needy for a pair of sandals —

7 they who trample the head of the poor into the dust of
the earth,
and push the afflicted out of the way;
father and son go in to the same girl,
so that my holy name is profaned;

8 they lay themselves down beside every altar
on garments taken in pledge;
and in the house of their God they drink
wine bought with fines they imposed.

9 Yet I destroyed the Amorite before them,
whose height was like the height of cedars,
and who was as strong as oaks;
I destroyed his fruit above,
and his roots beneath.

10 Also I brought you up out of the land of Egypt,
and led you forty years in the wilderness,
to possess the land of the Amorite.

11 And I raised up some of your children to be prophets
and some of your youths to be nazirites.*g*

2.6
2 Kings 18.12;
Joel 3.3;
Am 5.11, 12;
8.6

2.7
Am 8.4;
5.12;
Lev 20.3;
Hos 4.14

2.8
1 Cor 8.10;
Ex 22.26;
Am 4.1; 6.6

2.9
Deut 2.31;
Num 13.33;
Isa 5.24;
Mal 4.1

2.10
Ex 12.51;
Deut 2.7;
Ex 3.8

2.11
Jer 7.25;
Num 6.2, 3

f Heb *cause it to return*   *g* That is, *those separated* or *those consecrated*

2.4 The nations Amos had condemned thus far had sinned against other peoples. In accusing Judah of sinfulness, he charged this nation with contempt of God's laws — despising them as well as flaunting their disobedience against them. Any rejection of God's law is a rejection of the lawgiver.
2.6 There were few, if any, of the sins of the pagan nations that Israel itself did not commit. The sacred had been so overtaken by the secular that the true faith was virtually abandoned by all except a small minority.

2.8 *lay themselves down ... on garments taken in pledge,* i.e., clothing taken from one's debtors as a guarantee that they would pay back the money loaned. Under Mosaic law, it was illegal to keep pledged clothing of debtors overnight (see Ex 22.26).
2.9 *Amorite.* God dispossessed the Amorites from their land because of their sins and gave it to Israel. Amos said that Israel was now guilty of the same sins that the Amorites had committed.
2.11 *youths to be nazirites.* See note on Judg 13.5.

Is it not indeed so, O people of Israel?

says the LORD.

2.12
Isa 30.10;
Jer 11.21;
Am 7.12, 13;
Mic 2.6

12 But you made the nazirites[h] drink wine,
  and commanded the prophets,
  saying, "You shall not prophesy."

2.13
Joel 3.13

13 So, I will press you down in your place,
  just as a cart presses down
  when it is full of sheaves.[i]

2.14
Isa 30.16,
17;
Jer 9.23;
Ps 33.16
2.15
Jer 51.56;
Ezek 39.3;
Isa 31.3

14 Flight shall perish from the swift,
  and the strong shall not retain their strength,
  nor shall the mighty save their lives;
15 those who handle the bow shall not stand,
  and those who are swift of foot shall not save themselves,
  nor shall those who ride horses save their lives;

2.16
Jer 48.41

16 and those who are stout of heart among the mighty
  shall flee away naked in that day,

says the LORD.

II. *The judgment against Israel (3.1–6.14)*

A. *The relation of Israel to God*

3.1
Jer 8.3;
13.11;
Am 2.10; 9.7

3 Hear this word that the LORD has spoken against you, O people of Israel, against the whole family that I brought up out of the land of Egypt:

3.2
Deut 7.6;
Jer 14.20;
Ezek 20.36;
Lk 12.47;
Rom 2.9

2 You only have I known
  of all the families of the earth;
  therefore I will punish you
  for all your iniquities.

3.3
Lev 26.23, 24

3 Do two walk together
  unless they have made an appointment?

3.4
Hos 11.10

4 Does a lion roar in the forest,
  when it has no prey?
  Does a young lion cry out from its den,
  if it has caught nothing?
5 Does a bird fall into a snare on the earth,
  when there is no trap for it?
  Does a snare spring up from the ground,
  when it has taken nothing?

3.6
Jer 6.1;
Hos 5.8;
Isa 14.24-27;
45.7
3.7
Gen 18.17;
Jn 15.15;
Rev 10.7
3.8
Am 1.2;
Jon 1.1; 3.1;
Jer 20.9;
Acts 4.20

6 Is a trumpet blown in a city,
  and the people are not afraid?
  Does disaster befall a city,
  unless the LORD has done it?
7 Surely the Lord GOD does nothing,
  without revealing his secret
  to his servants the prophets.
8 The lion has roared;

---

[h] That is, *those separated* or *those consecrated*   [i] Meaning of Heb uncertain

---

2.12 Israel seduced nazirites to break their vow not to drink wine. Satan and his cohorts sought to corrupt young minds that were set on mirth, pleasure, and drunkenness. They also threatened the prophets and ordered them not to prophesy. They hated the prophets' messages and did what they could to suppress those who had this gift.
3.1 God now addressed the whole family of Israel, not just the northern tribes.
3.2 *You only have I known.* God bypassed all the

other nations of the earth and chose Israel alone to be his people. This choice obligated the chosen nation to serve faithfully the one who chose them. Every privilege carries with it a corresponding responsibility.
3.3 If two people are at variance, harmony cannot prevail. Where there is no friendship there can be no fellowship. God and his people must first be friends, but sin makes this impossible.
3.4–6 God does not threaten people in order to frighten them, but to bring sinners to their senses.

who will not fear?
The Lord GOD has spoken;
who can but prophesy?

B. The sins of Samaria

9 Proclaim to the strongholds in Ashdod,
and to the strongholds in the land of Egypt,
and say, "Assemble yourselves on Mount Samaria,
and see what great tumults are within it,
and what oppressions are in its midst."

10 They do not know how to do right, says the LORD,
those who store up violence and robbery in their strongholds.

11 Therefore thus says the Lord GOD:
An adversary shall surround the land,
and strip you of your defense;
and your strongholds shall be plundered.

12 Thus says the LORD: As the shepherd rescues from the mouth of
the lion two legs, or a piece of an ear, so shall the people of Israel who
live in Samaria be rescued, with the corner of a couch and part[k] of a bed.

13 Hear, and testify against the house of Jacob,
says the Lord GOD, the God of hosts:

14 On the day I punish Israel for its transgressions,
I will punish the altars of Bethel,
and the horns of the altar shall be cut off
and fall to the ground.

15 I will tear down the winter house as well as the summer house;
and the houses of ivory shall perish,
and the great houses[l] shall come to an end,

says the LORD.

4 Hear this word, you cows of Bashan
who are on Mount Samaria,
who oppress the poor, who crush the needy,
who say to their husbands, "Bring something to drink!"

2 The Lord GOD has sworn by his holiness:
The time is surely coming upon you,
when they shall take you away with hooks,
even the last of you with fishhooks.

3 Through breaches in the wall you shall leave,
each one straight ahead;
and you shall be flung out into Harmon,[k]

says the LORD.

C. Israel's failure to return to God

4 Come to Bethel—and transgress;

j Gk Syr: Heb the mountains of   k Meaning of Heb uncertain   l Or many houses

3.9	Am 1.8; 4.1; 6.1; 8.6
3.10	Jer 4.22; Am 5.7; 6.12; Hab 2.8-11; Zeph 1.9; Zech 5.3, 4
3.11	Am 6.14; 2.14; 2.5
3.12	1 Sam 17.34-37; Am 6.4; Ps 132.3
3.13	Ezek 2.7
3.14	v.2; Am 4.4; 5.5, 6
3.15	Jer 36.22; Judg 3.20; 1 Kings 22.39
4.1	Ps 22.12; Ezek 39.18; Am 3.9; 6.1; 5.11; 8.6; 2.8; 6.6
4.2	Ps 89.25; Am 6.8; 8.7; Isa 37.29; Ezek 38.4; 29.4
4.3	Jer 52.7; Ezek 12.5
4.4	Am 3.14; 5.5; Hos 4.15; Num 28.3, 4; Deut 14.28

3.8 Once God has spoken to a prophet, the prophet can only prophesy. The prophetic impulse is like a fire in the bones.
3.9–15 These verses were directed specifically to Samaria (the northern kingdom). Amos listed their sins: riots in the streets, prisons filled with innocent people, the courts of justice ruled by injustice, and the treasuries replenished by violence and robbery.
3.11 Samaria would be invaded and destroyed and its citizens taken captive by the hands of the enemy. God the Lord had spoken, the God of Israel; he has

the right to pass judgment and the power to execute it.
4.1 *cows of Bashan.* Amos derided the women of Israel, likening them to fat cows. Bashan was a fruitful, grain-producing region.
4.2 *hooks.* Assyrian reliefs portray prisoners who have hooks in their lips.
4.4,5 In effect God said, "Go ahead and multiply your transgressions by multiplying your sacrifices. It will do you no good, for I regard them as an abomination inasmuch as your hearts are not right with me.

to Gilgal — and multiply transgression;
  bring your sacrifices every morning,
    your tithes every three days;

4.5
Lev 7.13;
22.18, 21;
Hos 9.1, 10

5 bring a thank offering of leavened bread,
     and proclaim freewill offerings, publish them;
   for so you love to do, O people of Israel!

says the Lord GOD.

4.6
Isa 3.1;
Jer 14.18;
5.3;
Hag 2.17

6 I gave you cleanness of teeth in all your cities,
     and lack of bread in all your places,
   yet you did not return to me,

says the LORD.

4.7
Deut 11.17;
2 Chr 7.13;
Ex 9.4, 26;
10.22, 23

7 And I also withheld the rain from you
     when there were still three months to the harvest;
   I would send rain on one city,
     and send no rain on another city;
   one field would be rained upon,
     and the field on which it did not rain withered;

4.8
Jer 14.4;
Ezek 4.16;
Jer 3.7

8 so two or three towns wandered to one town
     to drink water, and were not satisfied;
   yet you did not return to me,

says the LORD.

4.9
Deut 28.22;
Hag 2.17;
Joel 1.4;
2.25;
Jer 3.10

9 I struck you with blight and mildew;
     I laid waste[m] your gardens and your vineyards;
       the locust devoured your fig trees and your olive trees;
   yet you did not return to me,

says the LORD.

4.10
Ex 9.3, 6;
Deut 28.27,
60;
Jer 11.22;
18.21; 48.15;
Joel 2.20;
Isa 9.13

10 I sent among you a pestilence after the manner of Egypt;
      I killed your young men with the sword;
    I carried away your horses;[n]
      and I made the stench of your camp go up into your nostrils;
    yet you did not return to me,

says the LORD.

4.11
Isa 13.19;
Zech 3.2;
Jer 23.14

11 I overthrew some of you,
      as when God overthrew Sodom and Gomorrah,
        and you were like a brand snatched from the fire;
    yet you did not return to me,

says the LORD.

4.12
v. 2;
Ezek 13.5
4.13
Jer 10.13;
Ps 139.2;
Dan 2.28;
Jer 13.16;
Mic 1.3;
Am 5.8, 27;
9.6

12 Therefore thus I will do to you, O Israel;
      because I will do this to you,
        prepare to meet your God, O Israel!

13 For lo, the one who forms the mountains, creates the wind,

m Cn: Heb *the multitude of*   *n* Heb *with the captivity of your horses*

What you do will only fill up the measure of your iniquity; then will judgment be executed." Israel had all the right rituals, but there was no heart in them; they were hypocrites.
4.6 Over and over again God had sent Samaria famine, blight, and pestilence, in order to warn them to repent and turn from their wicked ways. Samaria paid no attention to God's warnings, however. In ch. 4 God's words "you did not return to me" appear five times. The arraignment is concluded by the statement that since Israel refused to repent, the nation now had

to prepare to meet God, who would judge them by sending the Assyrian invaders to destroy them.
4.7ff God had tried everything to get the attention of Samaria so that they would repent, but nothing had worked. He sent famine (v. 6), drought (v. 7), blight and mildew (v. 9), and pestilence (v. 10). He overthrew some and spared others (v. 11). Nothing had moved them, so the last word from God was this: "Prepare to meet your God, O Israel!" This is the God of anger, judgment, and unyielding retribution.

reveals his thoughts to mortals,
makes the morning darkness,
and treads on the heights of the earth —
the LORD, the God of hosts, is his name!

D. *The LORD's lamentation over Israel*

5 Hear this word that I take up over you in lamentation, O house of Israel:

2 Fallen, no more to rise,
is maiden Israel;
forsaken on her land,
with no one to raise her up.

3 For thus says the Lord GOD:
The city that marched out a thousand
shall have a hundred left,
and that which marched out a hundred
shall have ten left. *o*

E. *The call to repentance*

4 For thus says the LORD to the house of Israel:
Seek me and live;
5 but do not seek Bethel,
and do not enter into Gilgal
or cross over to Beer-sheba;
for Gilgal shall surely go into exile,
and Bethel shall come to nothing.

6 Seek the LORD and live,
or he will break out against the house of Joseph like fire,
and it will devour Bethel, with no one to quench it.

7 Ah, you that turn justice to wormwood,
and bring righteousness to the ground!

8 The one who made the Pleiades and Orion,
and turns deep darkness into the morning,
and darkens the day into night,
who calls for the waters of the sea,
and pours them out on the surface of the earth,
the LORD is his name,

9 who makes destruction flash out against the strong,
so that destruction comes upon the fortress.

10 They hate the one who reproves in the gate,
and they abhor the one who speaks the truth.

11 Therefore because you trample on the poor
and take from them levies of grain,
you have built houses of hewn stone,
but you shall not live in them;
you have planted pleasant vineyards,
but you shall not drink their wine.

o Heb adds *to the house of Israel*

5.1 Ezek 19.1
5.2 Jer 14.17; Am 8.14; Isa 51.18; Jer 50.32
5.3 Isa 6.13; Am 6.9
5.4 Jer 29.3; Isa 55.3
5.5 Am 4.4; 1 Sam 7.16; 11.14; Am 8.14
5.6 Isa 55.3, 6, 7; v. 14; Deut 4.24; Am 3.14
5.7 Am 6.12
5.8 Job 9.9; 12.22; Isa 42.16; Am 8.9; Ps 104.6-9; Am 9.6; 4.13
5.9 Isa 29.5; Mic 5.11
5.10 Isa 29.21; 1 Kings 22.8; Isa 59.15
5.11 Am 3.9; 8.6; 3.15; 6.11; Mic 6.15

5.1 This chapter begins with the phrase, "Hear this word." God was serious and demanded that the Israelites attend to his word.
5.4 There was still time. Despite their great evils God was waiting for them to seek his face in repen-

tance, so that they might live.
5.5ff The sins of Samaria were many. They had turned to idols (v. 5), executed injustice (v. 7), persecuted God's faithful priests and people (v. 10), and trampled on the poor (v. 11).

5.12
Am 2.6, 7;
Isa 29.21
	12 For I know how many are your transgressions,
	    and how great are your sins —
	you who afflict the righteous, who take a bribe,
	    and push aside the needy in the gate.

5.13 Eccl 3.7	13 Therefore the prudent will keep silent in such a time; for it is an evil time.

5.14
v. 6;
Mic 3.11
	14 Seek good and not evil,
	    that you may live;
	and so the LORD, the God of hosts, will be with you,
	    just as you have said.

5.15
Ps 97.10;
Rom 12.9;
Joel 2.14;
Mic 5.3, 7, 8
	15 Hate evil and love good,
	    and establish justice in the gate;
	it may be that the LORD, the God of hosts,
	    will be gracious to the remnant of Joseph.

5.16
Jer 9.17;
Joel 1.11;
2 Chr 35.25
	16 Therefore thus says the LORD, the God of hosts, the Lord:
	In all the squares there shall be wailing;
	    and in all the streets they shall say, "Alas! alas!"
	They shall call the farmers to mourning,
	    and those skilled in lamentation, to wailing;

5.17
Isa 16.10;
Jer 48.33;
Nah 1.2
	17 in all the vineyards there shall be wailing,
	    for I will pass through the midst of you,
	
	                             says the LORD.

F. The double woe for Israel

1. Exile beyond Damascus

5.18
Isa 5.19;
Joel 1.15;
2.1, 11, 31;
2 Pet 3.4;
Jer 30.7
5.19
Jer 48.44
	18 Alas for you who desire the day of the LORD!
	    Why do you want the day of the LORD?
	It is darkness, not light;
	19 as if someone fled from a lion,
	    and was met by a bear;
	or went into the house and rested a hand against the wall,
	    and was bitten by a snake.

5.20 Isa 13.10; Zeph 1.15	20 Is not the day of the LORD darkness, not light, and gloom with no brightness in it?

5.21
Isa 1.11-16;
Lev 26.31
5.22
Isa 66.3;
Mic 6.6, 7;
Am 4.5
	21 I hate, I despise your festivals,
	    and I take no delight in your solemn assemblies.
	22 Even though you offer me your burnt offerings and grain
	        offerings,
	    I will not accept them;
	and the offerings of well-being of your fatted animals
	    I will not look upon.

5.23
Am 6.4, 5;
8.10
5.24
Jer 22.3;
Ezek 45.9;
Mic 6.8
	23 Take away from me the noise of your songs;
	    I will not listen to the melody of your harps.
	24 But let justice roll down like waters,
	    and righteousness like an ever-flowing stream.

5.14 Judgment was about to fall on Israel, yet God continued to hold forth the olive branch of peace. He implored his people to "hate evil and love good" (v. 15). Although the hour was late, God was still ready to reverse the forces of judgment and bring peace and safety to his people. Sad to say, they spurned these last-minute appeals and were destroyed. Today God speaks the same word of hope to all sinners, assuring them that before the clock strikes twelve he will save them if they repent.
5.18 *Alas for you who desire the day of the LORD!*

Israel regarded this "day" as a time when their enemies would be overcome and they would be vindicated before the world as God's elect people. Amos' bad news was that God's elect people themselves would face judgment.
5.21ff God hated Samaria's festivals, solemn assemblies, offerings, and songs. God had told them that "to obey is better than to sacrifice, and to heed than the fat of rams" (1 Sam 15.22). But they had refused to do this, so he would not listen to them. God desired justice and righteousness.

25 Did you bring to me sacrifices and offerings the forty years in the
wilderness, O house of Israel? 26 You shall take up Sakkuth your king,
and Kaiwan your star-god, your images,[p] which you made for yourselves;
27 therefore I will take you into exile beyond Damascus, says the LORD,
whose name is the God of hosts.

2. *Oppression, desolation, and want predicted*

6 Alas for those who are at ease in Zion,
and for those who feel secure on Mount Samaria,
the notables of the first of the nations,
to whom the house of Israel resorts!
2 Cross over to Calneh, and see;
from there go to Hamath the great;
then go down to Gath of the Philistines.
Are you better[q] than these kingdoms?
Or is your[r] territory greater than their[s] territory,
3 O you that put far away the evil day,
and bring near a reign of violence?

4 Alas for those who lie on beds of ivory,
and lounge on their couches,
and eat lambs from the flock,
and calves from the stall;
5 who sing idle songs to the sound of the harp,
and like David improvise on instruments of music;
6 who drink wine from bowls,
and anoint themselves with the finest oils,
but are not grieved over the ruin of Joseph!
7 Therefore they shall now be the first to go into exile,
and the revelry of the loungers shall pass away.

8 The Lord GOD has sworn by himself
(says the LORD, the God of hosts):
I abhor the pride of Jacob
and hate his strongholds;
and I will deliver up the city and all that is in it.

9 If ten people remain in one house, they shall die. 10 And if a relative,
one who burns the dead,[t] shall take up the body to bring it out of the
house, and shall say to someone in the innermost parts of the house, "Is
anyone else with you?" the answer will come, "No." Then the relative[u]
shall say, "Hush! We must not mention the name of the LORD."

11 See, the LORD commands,
and the great house shall be shattered to bits,
and the little house to pieces.
12 Do horses run on rocks?
Does one plow the sea with oxen?[v]
But you have turned justice into poison
and the fruit of righteousness into wormwood—

5.25 Deut 32.17; Ezek 20.8, 16, 24; Acts 7.42
5.27 2 Kings 17.6; Am 4.13
6.1 Isa 32.9-11; Lk 6.24; Ex 19.5; Am 3.2
6.2 Jer 2.10; Isa 10.9; 2 Kings 18.34; 2 Chr 26.6; Nah 3.8
6.3 Isa 56.12; Am 9.10
6.4 Am 3.15; 3.12; Ezek 34.2, 3
6.5 Isa 5.12; Am 5.23; 1 Chr 23.5
6.6 Am 2.8; 4.1; Gen 37.25; Ezek 9.4
6.7 Am 7.11, 17; Dan 5.4-6, 30; v. 4
6.8 Jer 51.14; Heb 6.13; Deut 32.19; Ps 106.40; Am 3.10, 11; Hos 11.6
6.9 Am 5.3
6.10 Am 5.13; 8.3
6.11 Isa 55.11; Am 3.15
6.12 Isa 59.13, 14; Hos 10.4; Am 5.7

p Heb *your images, your star-god* q Or *Are they better* r Heb *their* s Heb *your* t Or *who makes a burning for him* u Heb *he* v Or *Does one plow them with oxen*

6.1 *at ease*, i.e., full of pride, self-satisfied, and secure. Many of the people supposed they were safe and that God would preserve them as he had often done before. They thought no judgment would or could overtake the elect nation.

6.8 *I abhor the pride of Jacob.* God gave to his people everything the human heart could desire. They were called the chief of the nations; they had the temple, the altar, and the priesthood. But they followed only the forms of worship. They were hypocrites, who did not practice what was preached to them by God. Therefore God loathed, hated, and despised them. His judgment against their wickedness had to follow.

6.13
Ps 75.4, 5

13 you who rejoice in Lo-debar,[w]
  who say, "Have we not by our own strength
    taken Karnaim[x] for ourselves?"

6.14
Jer 5.15;
Am 3.11;
Num 34.8;
1 Kings 8.65

14 Indeed, I am raising up against you a nation,
    O house of Israel, says the Lord, the God of hosts,
  and they shall oppress you from Lebo-hamath
    to the Wadi Arabah.

III. *The five visions of the coming judgment and blessings to follow (7.1–9.15)*

A. *The plague of locusts*

7.1
vv. 4, 7;
Am 8.1;
Joel 1.4;
Am 4.9;
Nah 3.15
7.2
Ex 10.14, 15;
Ezek 9.8;
11.13;
Isa 37.4;
Jer 42.2
7.3
Deut 32.36;
Jer 26.19;
Jon 3.10

7 This is what the Lord God showed me: he was forming locusts at the time the latter growth began to sprout (it was the latter growth after the king's mowings). 2 When they had finished eating the grass of the land, I said,
  "O Lord God, forgive, I beg you!
    How can Jacob stand?
    He is so small!"
3 The Lord relented concerning this;
  "It shall not be," said the Lord.

B. *The fire devouring the deep*

7.4
Isa 66.15,
16;
Am 2.5
7.5
v. 2
7.6
v. 3

4 This is what the Lord God showed me: the Lord God was calling for a shower of fire,[y] and it devoured the great deep and was eating up the land. 5 Then I said,
  "O Lord God, cease, I beg you!
    How can Jacob stand?
    He is so small!"
6 The Lord relented concerning this;
  "This also shall not be," said the Lord God.

C. *The vision of the plumb line: Amos told to leave the land*

7.8
Am 8.2;
Isa 28.17;
34.11;
Lam 2.8;
Mic 7.18
7.9
Hos 10.8;
Mic 1.5;
Isa 63.18;
2 Kings 15.10

7 This is what he showed me: the Lord was standing beside a wall built with a plumb line, with a plumb line in his hand. 8 And the Lord said to me, "Amos, what do you see?" And I said, "A plumb line." Then the Lord said,
  "See, I am setting a plumb line
    in the midst of my people Israel;
    I will never again pass them by;
9 the high places of Isaac shall be made desolate,
    and the sanctuaries of Israel shall be laid waste,
    and I will rise against the house of Jeroboam with the
      sword."

7.10
1 Kings 12.32;
2 Kings 14.23;
Jer 26.8-11

10 Then Amaziah, the priest of Bethel, sent to King Jeroboam of

---

w Or in a thing of nothingness   x Or horns   y Or for a judgment by fire

---

6.14 God can easily bring to pass whatever he needs to do to discipline, chastise, or even destroy a nation. He would now raise up Assyria to do what he wanted done to Israel, and no one could stop him.
7.1 God showed Amos his intention to send locusts over Israel. The prophet prayed for God not to do this, and God agreed not to send them, saying, "It shall not be."

7.4 God showed Amos a judgment by fire. Again he pleaded with God, and God agreed not to do so.
7.7–9 God then gave Amos a vision of a plumb line, an instrument used by surveyors and bricklayers. God would stand on the walls of Israel and cause them to be crushed and ruined. Multitudes would die and the royal house would be destroyed.
7.10 *Amos has conspired*, i.e., "Amos is a traitor."

Israel, saying, "Amos has conspired against you in the very center of the house of Israel; the land is not able to bear all his words. 11 For thus Amos has said,

'Jeroboam shall die by the sword,
    and Israel must go into exile
        away from his land.' "

12And Amaziah said to Amos, "O seer, go, flee away to the land of Judah, earn your bread there, and prophesy there; 13but never again prophesy at Bethel, for it is the king's sanctuary, and it is a temple of the kingdom."

14   Then Amos answered Amaziah, "I am^z no prophet, nor a prophet's son; but I am^z a herdsman, and a dresser of sycamore trees, 15and the LORD took me from following the flock, and the LORD said to me, 'Go, prophesy to my people Israel.'

16   "Now therefore hear the word of the LORD.
    You say, 'Do not prophesy against Israel,
        and do not preach against the house of Isaac.'

17   Therefore thus says the LORD:
    'Your wife shall become a prostitute in the city,
        and your sons and your daughters shall fall by the sword,
    and your land shall be parceled out by line;
you yourself shall die in an unclean land,
    and Israel shall surely go into exile away from its land.' "

D. The basket of summer fruit

1. The vision of Israel's ruin

8 This is what the Lord GOD showed me—a basket of summer fruit.^a 2He said, "Amos, what do you see?" And I said, "A basket of summer fruit."^a Then the LORD said to me,

"The end^b has come upon my people Israel;
    I will never again pass them by.

3   The songs of the temple^c shall become wailings in that day,"
                                            says the Lord GOD;
"the dead bodies shall be many,
    cast out in every place. Be silent!"

2. The lust for money

4   Hear this, you that trample on the needy,
    and bring to ruin the poor of the land,

5   saying, "When will the new moon be over
    so that we may sell grain;
and the sabbath,
    so that we may offer wheat for sale?
We will make the ephah small and the shekel great,

---

^z Or was   ^a Heb qayits   ^b Heb qets   ^c Or palace

Marginal references:

7.11 — vv. 9, 17

7.13 — Am 2.12; 1 Kings 12.32; 13.1
7.14 — 1 Kings 20.35; 2 Kings 2.5; 4.38; 2 Chr 19.2; Am 1.1
7.15 — 2 Sam 7.8; Am 3.8; Jer 7.1; Ezek 2.3, 4
7.16 — Am 2.12; Ezek 21.2; Mic 2.6
7.17 — Jer 29.21; Hos 4.13, 14; Jer 14.16; Ezek 4.13; Hos 9.3

8.2 — Am 7.8; Jer 24.3; Ezek 7.2

8.3 — Am 5.23; 6.9, 10

8.4 — Ps 14.4; Am 5.11, 12
8.5 — 2 Kings 4.23; Neh 13.15, 16; Mic 6.10, 11

The prophet came from Tekoa in Judah and was thus considered a foreigner. His message was unwelcome. Amos was accused of being a troublemaker, and Amaziah, the priest at Bethel, informed him that he should leave Bethel.
7.13 *at Bethel*, i.e., in the capital (see note on Gen 28.19).
7.14 Amos added insult to injury by stating that he was only a layman, a herdsman, and a fruit picker. To suppose that such a common person would have a message from God for Israel was thought to be ridiculous.
8.1 God showed Amos a basket of summer fruit, ready to be consumed. It symbolized that Israel was ripe for ruin because they had failed to repent.

8.3 Israel had built temples for their idols. They went to them singing their ribald songs and committing sexual sins, and went from them to cheat the poor, shortchange the buyers of their wares, and commit every conceivable abomination. God would turn their singing into mourning by scattering dead bodies all over the landscape.
8.4–10 God disclosed what the sins of Israel were. They had no reverence for God; they had only the forms of godliness, not the substance; they cheated; they treated the poor barbarously and without mercy. They had to be punished, and God had taken an oath by himself to do so. It would come when they did not expect it and would turn their laughter into mourning.

and practice deceit with false balances,

6 buying the poor for silver
    and the needy for a pair of sandals,
    and selling the sweepings of the wheat."

7 The LORD has sworn by the pride of Jacob:
    Surely I will never forget any of their deeds.
8 Shall not the land tremble on this account,
    and everyone mourn who lives in it,
and all of it rise like the Nile,
    and be tossed about and sink again, like the Nile of Egypt?

9 On that day, says the Lord GOD,
    I will make the sun go down at noon,
    and darken the earth in broad daylight.
10 I will turn your feasts into mourning,
    and all your songs into lamentation;
I will bring sackcloth on all loins,
    and baldness on every head;
I will make it like the mourning for an only son,
    and the end of it like a bitter day.

3. The famine of the word of God

11 The time is surely coming, says the Lord GOD,
    when I will send a famine on the land;
not a famine of bread, or a thirst for water,
    but of hearing the words of the LORD.
12 They shall wander from sea to sea,
    and from north to east;
they shall run to and fro, seeking the word of the LORD,
    but they shall not find it.

13 In that day the beautiful young women and the young men
    shall faint for thirst.
14 Those who swear by Ashimah of Samaria,
    and say, "As your god lives, O Dan,"
and, "As the way of Beer-sheba lives" —
    they shall fall, and never rise again.

E. The destruction of the sanctuary

9 I saw the LORD standing beside[d] the altar, and he said:
    Strike the capitals until the thresholds shake,
    and shatter them on the heads of all the people;[e]
and those who are left I will kill with the sword;
    not one of them shall flee away,
    not one of them shall escape.

2 Though they dig into Sheol,
    from there shall my hand take them;
though they climb up to heaven,

d Or on   e Heb all of them

8.11,12 The worst of all punishments to come upon Israel would be a famine of the word of God, not of bread and water. No prophets would be sent to them and no visions from God given to guide them. They would run everywhere, searching for a word from God, but they would not find any.
9.2 God is omnipresent. Any who seek to flee from

God and escape his judgment, even by seeking refuge in Sheol, cannot hide from his angry hands. Whoever flees to the outermost parts of the heavens will find they are not beyond the reach of God's avenging hand. What he did to Israel in Amos' day he will do to all those who spurn his grace and mock his law.

from there I will bring them down.

3 Though they hide themselves on the top of Carmel,
    from there I will search out and take them;
and though they hide from my sight at the bottom of the sea,
    there I will command the sea-serpent, and it shall bite them.

4 And though they go into captivity in front of their enemies,
    there I will command the sword, and it shall kill them;
and I will fix my eyes on them
    for harm and not for good.

5 The Lord, GOD of hosts,
he who touches the earth and it melts,
    and all who live in it mourn,
and all of it rises like the Nile,
    and sinks again, like the Nile of Egypt;

6 who builds his upper chambers in the heavens,
    and founds his vault upon the earth;
who calls for the waters of the sea,
    and pours them out upon the surface of the earth —
the LORD is his name.

7 Are you not like the Ethiopians[f] to me,
    O people of Israel? says the LORD.
Did I not bring Israel up from the land of Egypt,
    and the Philistines from Caphtor and the Arameans from
        Kir?

8 The eyes of the Lord GOD are upon the sinful kingdom,
    and I will destroy it from the face of the earth
    —except that I will not utterly destroy the house of Jacob,
                      says the LORD.

9 For lo, I will command,
    and shake the house of Israel among all the nations
as one shakes with a sieve,
    but no pebble shall fall to the ground.

10 All the sinners of my people shall die by the sword,
    who say, "Evil shall not overtake or meet us."

F. The promise of Messianic blessing

1. Restoration of the Davidic kingdom

11 On that day I will raise up
    the booth of David that is fallen,
and repair its[g] breaches,
    and raise up its[h] ruins,
    and rebuild it as in the days of old;

12 in order that they may possess the remnant of Edom
    and all the nations who are called by my name,
    says the LORD who does this.

9.3
Am 1.2;
Jer 16.16, 17;
Isa 27.1

9.4
Lev 26.33;
Ezek 5.12;
Jer 44.11

9.5
Mic 1.4;
Am 8.8

9.6
Ps 104.3;
Am 5.8; 4.13

9.7
Isa 43.3;
Am 2.10;
3.1;
Deut 2.23;
Jer 47.4;
Am 1.5

9.8
Jer 44.27;
vv. 4, 10;
Jer 30.11;
Joel 2.32

9.9
Isa 30.28

9.10
Am 8.14; 6.3

9.11
Acts 15.16,
17;
Ps 80.12;
Isa 63.11;
Jer 46.26

9.12
Ob 19;
Isa 11.14;
43.7

f Or *Nubians*; Heb *Cushites*   g Gk: Heb *their*   h Gk: Heb *his*

9.7 The Israelites thought they were especially favored, since God had delivered them from bondage in Egypt. God reminded them that he had also delivered the Philistines from Caphtor and the Arameans from Kir. God is concerned with all nations, not just his chosen Israel.
9.11 *On that day*, or, "at that time." Amos salted his message of impending judgment with a word of hope and comfort for the future. The day would come when God would restore his people to their land. Some interpret Amos' prophecy to refer to the reinstatement of the house of David to a place of power after the second coming of Christ and the establishment of his millennial kingdom (cf. Lk 1.32; Rev 20).

2. *The productivity of the earth*

9.13
Lev 26.5;
Joel 3.18

13 The time is surely coming, says the LORD,
    when the one who plows shall overtake the one who reaps,
    and the treader of grapes the one who sows the seed;
the mountains shall drip sweet wine,
    and all the hills shall flow with it.

3. *Kingdom blessings*

9.14
Isa 60.4;
Jer 30.18;
Isa 61.4;
Ezek 36.35;
28.26
9.15
Jer 24.6;
31.28;
Isa 60.21;
Jer 32.41;
Ezek 34.28

14 I will restore the fortunes of my people Israel,
    and they shall rebuild the ruined cities and inhabit them;
they shall plant vineyards and drink their wine,
    and they shall make gardens and eat their fruit.
15 I will plant them upon their land,
    and they shall never again be plucked up
    out of the land that I have given them,
                  says the LORD your God.

9.15 When the restoration of God's people takes place, paradise will have been regained. God promises that never again will there be any judgment against them. Cities will be rebuilt, the land will flourish and bring forth its fruit, and even the mountains will drip sweet wine. God has sworn and will not change.

INTRODUCTION TO

OBADIAH

Authorship, Date, and Background: Three of the minor prophets addressed themselves to single nations: Obadiah spoke about Edom, Nahum about Assyria, and Habakkuk about Chaldea. Obadiah (which means "servant of Yahweh") provides no information about himself beyond his name. We know nothing of his background, nor is it possible to date the book with precision. Apparently Obadiah had in mind a time when Jerusalem was invaded and Edom did nothing to assist her. Whether this was the destruction of Jerusalem in 586 B.C. or one of the earlier invasions (e.g., the invasion by Shishak in the time of Jeroboam, see 1 Kings 14.25,26; the invasion by the Philistines and Arabians in the days of Jehoram, see 2 Chron 21.16,17; the invasion by Joash of Israel in the days of Amaziah, see 2 Kings 14.13,14; or the first invasion of Jerusalem by Nebuchadnezzar, see 2 Kings 24.1ff), we do not know. Some conservative scholars date the book as early as the ninth century B.C.; others date it after the fall of Jerusalem under Nebuchadnezzar.

The prophecy was spoken against Edom, whose people descended from Esau, Jacob's brother. Enmity existed between their descendants for generations. The Edomites lived in fortified cities that were almost impregnable; Sela (Petra), Teman, and Bozrah were among their strongholds. Sela was located along an important caravan route and was carved out of rock. During the exodus from Egypt the Edomites forbade the Israelites to pass through their land. This and other actions were included in the condemnation heaped upon Edom by Obadiah as a prophet of God.

Characteristics and Content: Obadiah pointed to the treachery and pride of Edom as besetting sins. He made it plain that God would not stand by idly when his chosen people were being destroyed while their brother, Edom, did nothing to help them. Indeed the Edomites were helping the enemies of Israel, and this was an act that a just God would not overlook. So God, through Obadiah, pronounced divine judgment upon this people and foretold the nation's destruction. Edom would drink the cup of the wrath of God.

At the same time, Obadiah contrasted the end of Edom with God's providential care over his people Israel. Mount Zion would be established in the future; they would have their lands restored to them and would have the Lord as their ruler. And in the end Mount Esau (i.e., the Edomites and their power), would be subject to Mount Zion (i.e., the sons and daughters of the brother whom they were mistreating).

Outline:

I. The judgment against Edom (1–14)

II. The day of the LORD (15–21)

OBADIAH

I. *The judgment against Edom (1–14)*

A. *The fall of Edom predicted*

¹ The vision of Obadiah.

Thus says the Lord GOD concerning Edom:
We have heard a report from the LORD,
  and a messenger has been sent among the nations:
"Rise up! Let us rise against it for battle!"
² I will surely make you least among the nations;
  you shall be utterly despised.
³ Your proud heart has deceived you,
  you that live in the clefts of the rock,[a]
  whose dwelling is in the heights.
You say in your heart,
  "Who will bring me down to the ground?"
⁴ Though you soar aloft like the eagle,
  though your nest is set among the stars,
  from there I will bring you down,
                                                    says the LORD.

B. *Edom's destruction to be complete*

⁵ If thieves came to you,
  if plunderers by night
  —how you have been destroyed!—
  would they not steal only what they wanted?
If grape-gatherers came to you,
  would they not leave gleanings?
⁶ How Esau has been pillaged,
  his treasures searched out!
⁷ All your allies have deceived you,
  they have driven you to the border;
your confederates have prevailed against you;
  those who ate[b] your bread have set a trap for you—
  there is no understanding of it.
⁸ On that day, says the LORD,
  I will destroy the wise out of Edom,
  and understanding out of Mount Esau.
⁹ Your warriors shall be shattered, O Teman,
  so that everyone from Mount Esau will be cut off.

a Or *clefts of Sela* *b* Cn: Heb lacks *those who ate*

Cross-references (left margin):
1 Isa 34.5; Ezek 25.12; Joel 3.19; Jer 49.14; Isa 30.4; Jer 6.4, 5
3 Isa 16.6; Jer 49.16; 2 Kings 14.7; Isa 14.13-15; Rev 18.7
4 Job 20.6; Hab 2.9; Isa 14.13-15
5 Jer 49.9; vv. 9, 10; Isa 17.6
6 Jer 49.10
7 Jer 30.14; 38.22; Ps 41.9; Jer 49.7
8 Job 5.12; Isa 29.14
9 Jer 49.22; Am 1.12; Hab 3.3; v. 5

---

1 *Edom* was a nation southeast of Israel, including Sela (cf. 2 Kings 14.7), the city hewn from rocks. Her southern boundary was on the Gulf of Aqaba. See note on Gen 36.9 for information on the Edomites. **3,4** Edom proudly thought itself impregnable; however, God would bring about its destruction and prove Edom to be wrong.

6 *Esau* is another term for Edom. Esau and Jacob (Israel) were brothers. They were rivals (see Gen 25:19–34; 27) and later their descendants became enemies. *searched out*, i.e., pillaged. **8** *destroy the wise*. Edom was noted for those among her who were wise. Eliphaz, the wisest of Job's three friends, was from Teman, five miles east of Sela.

C. Edom's sins laid bare

10 For the slaughter and violence done to your brother Jacob,
   shame shall cover you,
   and you shall be cut off forever.

11 On the day that you stood aside,
   on the day that strangers carried off his wealth,
   and foreigners entered his gates
   and cast lots for Jerusalem,
   you too were like one of them.

12 But you should not have gloated[c] over[d] your brother
   on the day of his misfortune;
   you should not have rejoiced over the people of Judah
   on the day of their ruin;
   you should not have boasted
   on the day of distress.

13 You should not have entered the gate of my people
   on the day of their calamity;
   you should not have joined in the gloating over Judah's[e]
   disaster
   on the day of his calamity;
   you should not have looted his goods
   on the day of his calamity.

14 You should not have stood at the crossings
   to cut off his fugitives;
   you should not have handed over his survivors
   on the day of distress.

II. The day of the LORD (15–21)

A. The judgment of all nations

15 For the day of the LORD is near against all the nations.
   As you have done, it shall be done to you;
   your deeds shall return on your own head.

16 For as you have drunk on my holy mountain,
   all the nations around you shall drink;
   they shall drink and gulp down,[f]
   and shall be as though they had never been.

B. Deliverance in Zion: the kingdom of the LORD

17 But on Mount Zion there shall be those that escape,
   and it shall be holy;
   and the house of Jacob shall take possession of those who
   dispossessed them.

18 The house of Jacob shall be a fire,
   the house of Joseph a flame,
   and the house of Esau stubble;

10 Ps 137.7; Joel 3.19; Am 1.11

11 Ps 137.7; Joel 3.3; Nah 3.10

12 Mic 4.11; Ezek 35.15; 36.5; Ps 31.18

13 Ezek 35.5, 10; 36.2, 3

15 Ezek 30.3; Joel 1.15; Jer 50.29; Hab 2.8; Ezek 35.11

16 Jer 49.12, 13; 25.15, 16

17 Isa 4.2, 3; Am 9.11-15

18 Isa 10.17; Jer 11.23; Am 1.8

---

c Heb *But do not gloat* (and similarly through verse 14)   d Heb *on the day of*   e Heb *his*   f Meaning of Heb uncertain

---

10ff The sins of Edom are laid bare. They committed violence against the Israelites. They failed to help them in the day of calamity; in fact they found pleasure and satisfaction in their kin's calamities. They insulted them, robbed them, and murdered them. They allied themselves with Israel's enemies. They even refused to help the refugees, returning them to the enemy. Thus, they brought about their own destruction, for whoever strikes at God's people strikes at God.

15,16 The day of God's judgment had come for Edom, as it will come for all the nations in the end. Edom, by way of retribution, would experience the same calamities she created. She had to drink the cup of God's wrath.

17 Not all the children of Jacob would be destroyed, for there would be a remnant. Ultimately a regathered, restored, and triumphant Israel would occupy all the possessions promised to them by God in the covenant.

they shall burn them and consume them,
   and there shall be no survivor of the house of Esau;
                              for the LORD has spoken.

19
Am 9.12;
Isa 11.14;
Zeph 2.7;
Jer 31.5;
32.44

19 Those of the Negeb shall possess Mount Esau,
   and those of the Shephelah the land of the Philistines;
they shall possess the land of Ephraim and the land of Samaria,
   and Benjamin shall possess Gilead.

20
1 Kings 17.9;
Jer 32.44;
33.13

20 The exiles of the Israelites who are in Halah[g]
   shall possess[h] Phoenicia as far as Zarephath;
and the exiles of Jerusalem who are in Sepharad
   shall possess the towns of the Negeb.

21
Neh 9.27;
Ps 22.28;
67.4;
Dan 2.44;
Zech 14.9

21 Those who have been saved[i] shall go up to Mount Zion
   to rule Mount Esau;
and the kingdom shall be the LORD's.

g Cn: Heb *in this army*   h Cn: Meaning of Heb uncertain   i Or *Saviors*

19 Obadiah indicated what the realm of Israel would include and what territories held by other nations would be part of its inheritance. The Negeb formerly belonged to Esau.

20 Halah was one of the places where the Israelite prisoners taken by Assyria were brought (see 2 Kings 17.6; 18.11; 1 Chr 5.26). Apparently it was within reach of Nineveh. *Sepharad* was another such place, though we do not know where it was located.

INTRODUCTION TO

JONAH

Authorship, Date, and Background: The authorship of this book is not plainly stated, but there is no good reason to suppose that it was not Jonah. The use of the third person is no problem since the same approach appears in the Pentateuch of Moses as well as in secular literature (such as the writings of Julius Caesar). Jonah (whose name means "dove") was the son of Amittai; according to 2 Kings 14.25 he lived in Gath-hepher, which was near Nazareth, in the eighth century B.C. Hosea and Amos were contemporaries and Jeroboam II was king.

The book is about Nineveh, the capital city of the Assyrian empire which existed for three centuries. It was a militaristic monarchy detested by the surrounding nations and guilty of depraved and brutal conduct. God was to use Nineveh to punish Samaria, but this nation itself was to disappear from the face of the earth at a later time. Nineveh's insolence and pride offended God, who would judge this country if it did not repent. God ordered Jonah to preach the necessity of repentance to Nineveh with the promise of sudden judgment if the nation failed to respond.

Many modern scholars have always denied that Jonah is history; rather, they argue that it is fiction. They do so because they cannot accept the supernatural, not the least of which is the great fish that swallowed Jonah, who spent three days and three nights inside it. Moreover, the plant that grew and protected Jonah from the heat and the worm which destroyed the plant are unacceptable to those who deny the miraculous. For evangelicals, these facts present no problem.

Characteristics and Content: Jonah received his prophetic call from God to minister to the people of Nineveh. He disobeyed by trying to flee from God's presence and taking a sea voyage in the opposite direction from Nineveh. The omnipresence of God was manifested, for Jonah discovered he could not flee from the divine presence. Following the episode of the three days and nights in the fish's belly, Jonah repented, and was restored and recommissioned to take the same message to the same people as God had originally called him to do. He went to Nineveh and a city-wide revival occurred, reaching to the monarch himself. Jonah was unhappy about the success of his crusade and manifested anger with God. God reproved the prophet by making clear that he cares for all people everywhere and that whoever repents of sin will find mercy from him. The repentance of Nineveh led to the survival of Assyria for another century; it suggests the same need among nations today, and God offers the same promise of forgiveness to those who will repent.

Outline:

I. The disobedient and suffering prophet (1.1–17)

II. The repentant and delivered prophet (2.1–10)

III. The reluctantly obedient prophet (3.1–10)

IV. The God of unlimited mercy (4.1–11)

JONAH

I. *The disobedient and suffering prophet (1.1–17)*

1 Now the word of the Lord came to Jonah son of Amittai, saying, 2 "Go at once to Nineveh, that great city, and cry out against it; for their wickedness has come up before me." 3 But Jonah set out to flee to Tarshish from the presence of the Lord. He went down to Joppa and found a ship going to Tarshish; so he paid his fare and went on board, to go with them to Tarshish, away from the presence of the Lord.

4 But the Lord hurled a great wind upon the sea, and such a mighty storm came upon the sea that the ship threatened to break up. 5 Then the mariners were afraid, and each cried to his god. They threw the cargo that was in the ship into the sea, to lighten it for them. Jonah, meanwhile, had gone down into the hold of the ship and had lain down, and was fast asleep. 6 The captain came and said to him, "What are you doing sound asleep? Get up, call on your god! Perhaps the god will spare us a thought so that we do not perish."

7 The sailors*a* said to one another, "Come, let us cast lots, so that we may know on whose account this calamity has come upon us." So they cast lots, and the lot fell on Jonah. 8 Then they said to him, "Tell us why this calamity has come upon us. What is your occupation? Where do you come from? What is your country? And of what people are you?" 9 "I am a Hebrew," he replied. "I worship the Lord, the God of heaven, who made the sea and the dry land." 10 Then the men were even more afraid, and said to him, "What is this that you have done!" For the men knew that he was fleeing from the presence of the Lord, because he had told them so.

11 Then they said to him, "What shall we do to you, that the sea may quiet down for us?" For the sea was growing more and more tempestuous. 12 He said to them, "Pick me up and throw me into the sea; then the sea will quiet down for you; for I know it is because of me that this great storm has come upon you." 13 Nevertheless the men rowed hard to bring the ship back to land, but they could not, for the sea grew more and more stormy against them. 14 Then they cried out to the Lord, "Please, O Lord, we pray, do not let us perish on account of this man's life. Do not make us guilty of innocent blood; for you, O Lord, have done as it pleased you." 15 So they picked Jonah up and threw him into the sea; and the sea ceased from its raging. 16 Then the men feared the Lord even more, and they offered a sacrifice to the Lord and made vows.

a Heb *They*

1.1 *Jonah son of Amittai* was a prophet in Israel during the kingship of Jeroboam II (2 Kings 14.25).
1.2 It was an honor for Jonah to be chosen by God to represent him as a prophet at Nineveh. He dishonored this call by refusing to go.
1.3 *Tarshish*, probably Tartessus, located in southwest Spain (see also note on 1 Kings 10.22).
1.7 Like most people, Jonah refused to admit his guilt until he had no choice, having been detected by the use of the lot.
1.11 The seamen noted that Jonah was a prophet, so

they asked him for a solution to their problem. It was he who suggested that they toss him overboard, though they resisted this proposal until absolutely necessary.
1.14ff Before throwing Jonah overboard, the seamen pleaded for God's mercy that they might be held guiltless. They perceived that what they experienced had come from the hand of God. God did use Jonah for good in this incident, for the seamen acknowledged that Jonah's God was the true God, and they feared him with great fear.

17[b] But the LORD provided a large fish to swallow up Jonah; and Jonah was in the belly of the fish three days and three nights.

1.17
Jon 4.6;
Mt 12.40;
16.4;
Lk 11.30

II. The repentant and delivered prophet (2.1–10)

2 Then Jonah prayed to the LORD his God from the belly of the fish,
2 saying,
"I called to the LORD out of my distress,
     and he answered me;
out of the belly of Sheol I cried,
     and you heard my voice.

2.1
Ps 130.1
2.2
Ps 18.4-6

3 You cast me into the deep,
     into the heart of the seas,
     and the flood surrounded me;
all your waves and your billows
     passed over me.

2.3
Ps 88.6; 42.7

4 Then I said, 'I am driven away
     from your sight;
how[c] shall I look again
     upon your holy temple?'

2.4
Ps 31.22;
1 Kings 8.38

5 The waters closed in over me;
     the deep surrounded me;
weeds were wrapped around my head

2.5
Ps 69.1;
Lam 3.54

6 at the roots of the mountains.
I went down to the land
     whose bars closed upon me forever;
yet you brought up my life from the Pit,
     O LORD my God.

2.6
Ps 16.10

7 As my life was ebbing away,
     I remembered the LORD;
and my prayer came to you,
     into your holy temple.

2.7
Ps 142.3;
77.10, 11;
18.6

8 Those who worship vain idols
     forsake their true loyalty.

2.8
2 Kings 17.15;
Ps 31;6;
Jer 10.8;
16.19

9 But I with the voice of thanksgiving
     will sacrifice to you;
what I have vowed I will pay.
     Deliverance belongs to the LORD!"

2.9
Ps 50.14;
Hos 14.2;
Heb 13.15;
Job 22.27;
Ps 3.8

10 Then the LORD spoke to the fish, and it spewed Jonah out upon the dry land.

2.10
Jon 1.17

---

b Ch 2.1 in Heb   c Theodotion: Heb surely

1.17 Christ compared his own death and entombment to that of Jonah (Mt 12.40). As Jonah was in the belly of the fish three days and three nights, so Jesus would be three days and three nights in the grave. And as Jonah was delivered from his Sheol (2.2), so Jesus would come forth from the grave alive. Some theorize that Jonah actually died in the belly of the fish and was raised from the dead. Whether he did or not is immaterial, for he was as good as dead in the tomb of the fish. Certainly nothing in the narrative gives credence to the idea that Jonah's imprisonment was not historical.
2.1 It took three days and three nights for God to gain Jonah's attention. *Then*, as a result of his affliction, Jonah began to pray.
2.2 No matter how bad we are and how far we have strayed from the Lord, when we turn to God peni-

tently, he will hear our prayers as he did Jonah's.
2.4 Jonah now admitted that he was out of favor with God, and his prayer was one of confession for his delinquency.
2.8 Those who follow the road of disobedience, as Jonah had done by fleeing from the presence of God, *forsake their true loyalty*; i.e., they have turned away from the true God of mercy to idols who cannot help them. Whatever is not of God is idolatry.
2.9 Jonah swore that he would remain faithful to God if he were delivered, and he offered thanksgiving for God's mercies. The great deliverer is God and God alone. He is the author of salvation.
2.10 Imprisoned for his sin, Jonah was now set free because he had repented and God had been gracious. God spoke to the fish and Jonah was *spewed* out of its belly.

III. *The reluctantly obedient prophet (3.1–10)*

3 The word of the Lord came to Jonah a second time, saying, 2 "Get up, go to Nineveh, that great city, and proclaim to it the message that I tell you." 3 So Jonah set out and went to Nineveh, according to the word of the Lord. Now Nineveh was an exceedingly large city, a three days' walk across. 4 Jonah began to go into the city, going a day's walk. And he cried out, "Forty days more, and Nineveh shall be overthrown!" 5 And the people of Nineveh believed God; they proclaimed a fast, and everyone, great and small, put on sackcloth.

6 When the news reached the king of Nineveh, he rose from his throne, removed his robe, covered himself with sackcloth, and sat in ashes. 7 Then he had a proclamation made in Nineveh: "By the decree of the king and his nobles: No human being or animal, no herd or flock, shall taste anything. They shall not feed, nor shall they drink water. 8 Human beings and animals shall be covered with sackcloth, and they shall cry mightily to God. All shall turn from their evil ways and from the violence that is in their hands. 9 Who knows? God may relent and change his mind; he may turn from his fierce anger, so that we do not perish."

10 When God saw what they did, how they turned from their evil ways, God changed his mind about the calamity that he had said he would bring upon them; and he did not do it.

IV. *The God of unlimited mercy (4.1–11)*

4 But this was very displeasing to Jonah, and he became angry. 2 He prayed to the Lord and said, "O Lord! Is not this what I said while I was still in my own country? That is why I fled to Tarshish at the beginning; for I knew that you are a gracious God and merciful, slow to anger, and abounding in steadfast love, and ready to relent from punishing. 3 And now, O Lord, please take my life from me, for it is better for me to die than to live." 4 And the Lord said, "Is it right for you to be angry?" 5 Then Jonah went out of the city and sat down east of the city, and made a booth for himself there. He sat under it in the shade, waiting to see what would become of the city.

6 The Lord God appointed a bush,[d] and made it come up over Jonah, to give shade over his head, to save him from his discomfort; so Jonah was very happy about the bush. 7 But when dawn came up the next day, God appointed a worm that attacked the bush, so that it withered. 8 When the sun rose, God prepared a sultry east wind, and the sun beat

[d] Heb *qiqayon*, possibly *the castor bean plant*

3.1 Jonah was now recommissioned with his original call to go and proclaim God's message to the city of Nineveh. God gave him a second chance.
3.3 *large city, a three days' walk across,* i.e., so large that it would take three days to walk through it. The Hebrew text makes no distinction between the city proper (the walls of Nineveh were only about eight miles in circumference, accommodating a population of about 175,000 persons) and the administrative district of Nineveh, which was thirty to sixty miles across.
3.4 *Forty days more, and Nineveh shall be overthrown!* This word by Jonah had an implied condition: "unless Nineveh repents." Nineveh did repent and was not overthrown, much to Jonah's displeasure, though a hundred years later the nation returned to its sinful ways and was overthrown.
3.5 The people of Nineveh believed God because they believed Jonah's words. Their response indicated their seriousness, for they not only prayed, they also fasted and put on the garments of penitent

sinners.
3.6ff The king of Nineveh endorsed prayer to Jonah's God, insisted on fasting, sackcloth, and ashes, and ordered his people to turn away from their sins and perform works of righteousness. Otherwise Nineveh would perish.
4.1 Jonah was perhaps the only evangelist who was ever angry that his preaching brought his listeners to repentance.
4.2 *you are a gracious God.* As a loyal Israelite, Jonah preferred to have Nineveh destroyed. He tried to run away because he was afraid his message might save the Ninevites and keep God from destroying the kingdom. Jonah did not understand that God's love goes far beyond national distinctions.
4.3 Jonah preferred to die rather than see his promise of judgment fail to be executed.
4.5 Jonah was so angry that he left the city to sulk, while he waited for a destruction that never took place.

down on the head of Jonah so that he was faint and asked that he might die. He said, "It is better for me to die than to live."

9 But God said to Jonah, "Is it right for you to be angry about the bush?" And he said, "Yes, angry enough to die." 10 Then the LORD said, "You are concerned about the bush, for which you did not labor and which you did not grow; it came into being in a night and perished in a night. 11 And should I not be concerned about Nineveh, that great city, in which there are more than a hundred and twenty thousand persons who do not know their right hand from their left, and also many animals?"

4.9
v. 4

4.11
Jon 1.2; 3.2, 3;
Deut 1.39;
Ps 36.6

4.9 *Is it right for you to be angry?* God patiently reasoned with Jonah to correct him and to humble him. His recovery from the fish's belly did not teach him as much as he should have learned, not the least of which is that God's ways are not our ways and his thoughts are not our thoughts (Isa 55.8,9).

4.11 Jonah was (selfishly) more concerned with the plant that died than he was with the death of Nineveh. God's perspective was the exact opposite: his concern for the city was far greater than the concern for a mere plant.

INTRODUCTION TO

MICAH

Authorship, Date, and Background: Micah, the author of this book, came from Moresheth, which was located some twenty-five miles southwest of Jerusalem. His name means "Who is like Yahweh?" Nothing is said about his ancestry. He prophesied during the reigns of Jotham, Ahaz, and Hezekiah (742 to 687 B.C.). His ministry began earlier than 722 B.C. for his prophecy included a statement about the destruction of Samaria. During the reign of Hezekiah his ministry overlapped with that of the prophet Isaiah, who overshadowed him. Micah witnessed the fall of Samaria, but whether he lived to witness his own nation of Judah surrounded by Sennacherib is not known. In 701 B.C., when Jerusalem was threatened, God's people experienced a remarkable deliverance (see 2 Kings 18; 2 Chr 32; Isa 36).

Micah prophesied during turbulent times. Samaria was wealthy and its mercantile class was exploiting the poor and living in luxury themselves. Judah prospered as well, and sin abounded. When Hezekiah ascended to the throne in Judah, a revival took place. The king reversed the policy of appeasing Assyria, and heathen cult worship in the temple under Ahaz was abolished. Heathen altars, idols, and sacred poles were demolished. All of this delayed the judgment of God against Judah as announced by Micah, but it did not cancel it out. The hearts of the people remained corrupt, and genuine repentance and lasting reformation of life did not come.

Characteristics and Content: Micah announced that God was about to reduce Samaria to a heap of ruins for its transgressions and the failure of its people to repent. Its idols and images were to be destroyed by God and the nation sent off into captivity. He also pronounced divine judgment on Jerusalem, displaying his personal grief by removing his robe and walking barefoot.

The sins of Jerusalem were manifold. Widows were evicted from their homes; travelers were robbed. The rights of inheritance were disregarded. False prophets led the people astray, judges accepted bribes, and priests taught for money. At the same time Micah announced a return of a remnant from captivity in Babylon. Zion indeed would someday be restored. Micah foresaw a ruler in the future whose birthplace would be Bethlehem, a prophecy which is quoted in the N.T. and applied to Jesus the Messiah.

Micah lay down the dictum that God required his people "to do justice, and to love kindness, and to walk humbly with your God" (6.8). But this they were not doing and so judgment had to come. He concluded his prophetic message with a gleam of hope: God would someday gather his people together in the land of promise from among all the nations of the world to which they had gone, and he would establish them securely in their own land. In his concluding prayer, Micah proclaimed, "Who is a God like you, pardoning iniquity. . . ? He will again have compassion upon us; he will tread our iniquities under foot. You will cast all our sins into the depths of the sea. You will show faithfulness to Jacob and unswerving loyalty to Abraham, as you have sworn to our ancestors from the days of old" (7.18–20).

Outline:

I. The pronouncement of judgment on Israel and Judah (1.1—2.13)

II. The judgment followed by restoration and the reign of Messiah (3.1—5.15)

III. Divine punishment followed by divine mercy (6.1—7.20)

Hear, you peoples, all of you;
listen, O earth, and all that is in it,
and let the Lord God be a witness against you,
the Lord from his holy temple.
For lo, the Lord is coming out of his place,
and will come down and tread upon the high places of
the earth.
Then the mountains will melt under him
All this is for the transgression of Jacob
and for the sins of the house of Israel.
What is the transgression of Jacob?

MICAH

I. The pronouncement of judgment on Israel and Judah (1.1–2.13)

A. Introductory heading

1.1
Jer 26.18;
2 Kings 15.5,
7, 32-38;
16.1-20;
18.1-21

1 The word of the LORD that came to Micah of Moresheth in the days of Kings Jotham, Ahaz, and Hezekiah of Judah, which he saw concerning Samaria and Jerusalem.

B. God's anger against Samaria and Judah

1.2
Jer 6.19;
22.29;
Ps 50.7; 11.4

2 Hear, you peoples, all of you;
   listen, O earth, and all that is in it;
and let the Lord GOD be a witness against you,
   the Lord from his holy temple.

1.3
Isa 26.21;
Am 4.13

3 For lo, the LORD is coming out of his place,
   and will come down and tread upon the high places of
      the earth.

1.4
Isa 64.1, 2;
Nah 1.5

4 Then the mountains will melt under him
   and the valleys will burst open,
like wax near the fire,
   like waters poured down a steep place.

1.5
Isa 28.1;
Am 8.14;
2 Chr 34.3, 4

5 All this is for the transgression of Jacob
   and for the sins of the house of Israel.
What is the transgression of Jacob?
   Is it not Samaria?
And what is the high place*a* of Judah?
   Is it not Jerusalem?

1.6
Jer 31.5;
Am 5.11;
Ezek 13.14

6 Therefore I will make Samaria a heap in the open country,
   a place for planting vineyards.
I will pour down her stones into the valley,
   and uncover her foundations.

1.7
Deut 9.21;
2 Chr 34.7;
Isa 23.17

7 All her images shall be beaten to pieces,
   all her wages shall be burned with fire,
   and all her idols I will lay waste;
for as the wages of a prostitute she gathered them,
   and as the wages of a prostitute they shall again be used.

a Heb *what are the high places*

1.1 *which he saw.* Again God used visions to acquaint his prophet with the word he wanted expounded. Many times God spoke; other times he used visions and dreams. Micah saw what the future held in store for Samaria and Jerusalem, i.e., the northern and the southern kingdoms of Israel.
1.2 *Hear, you peoples.* God was addressing the multitudes from his holy temple. If God has a mouth that speaks, we should have ears that hear.
1.5 Micah was a prophet who spoke of God's coming judgment upon both Judah and Samaria. But there was one important difference between the judgments that fell on these kingdoms. The kings of Israel had all been bad; the nation was ripe for judgment long before Judah became ready for similar judgment. Thus Israel fell in 722 B.C., while Jerusalem was destroyed in 586 B.C., 135 years later. God is always patient, extending the time limits for repentance. Then the door of hope is shut and the avenging angel of God is sent to execute his wrath.
1.6 See 2 Kings 17.1–18 for the literal fulfillment of the prophecy that the northern kingdom of Israel would be taken into captivity by Assyria.

8 For this I will lament and wail;
     I will go barefoot and naked;
   I will make lamentation like the jackals,
      and mourning like the ostriches.
9 For her wound[b] is incurable.
     It has come to Judah;
   it has reached to the gate of my people,
      to Jerusalem.

10 Tell it not in Gath,
     weep not at all;
   in Beth-leaphrah
      roll yourselves in the dust.
11 Pass on your way,
     inhabitants of Shaphir,
   in nakedness and shame;
   the inhabitants of Zaanan
      do not come forth;
   Beth-ezel is wailing
      and shall remove its support from you.
12 For the inhabitants of Maroth
     wait anxiously for good,
   yet disaster has come down from the Lord
     to the gate of Jerusalem.
13 Harness the steeds to the chariots,
     inhabitants of Lachish;
   it was the beginning of sin
     to daughter Zion,
   for in you were found
      the transgressions of Israel.
14 Therefore you shall give parting gifts
     to Moresheth-gath;
   the houses of Achzib shall be a deception
     to the kings of Israel.
15 I will again bring a conqueror upon you,
     inhabitants of Mareshah;
   the glory of Israel
     shall come to Adullam.
16 Make yourselves bald and cut off your hair
     for your pampered children;
   make yourselves as bald as the eagle,
     for they have gone from you into exile.

C. The cause of God's anger

1. Their sins described

2 Alas for those who devise wickedness
     and evil deeds[c] on their beds!
   When the morning dawns, they perform it,

[b] Gk Syr Vg: Heb *wounds*   [c] Cn: Heb *work evil*

Cross references (right margin):

1.8 Isa 22.4; 32.11; 13.21, 22

1.9 Jer 30.12, 15; 2 Kings 18.13; v. 12

1.10 2 Sam 1.20

1.11 Ezek 23.29

1.12 Isa 59.9-11; Jer 14.19

1.13 2 Kings 14.19; Isa 36.2

1.14 2 Kings 16.8; Josh 15.44; Jer 15.18

1.15 Josh 15.44; Mic 5.2; Josh 12.15; 2 Sam 23.13

1.16 Isa 15.2; 22.12; Lam 4.5; Am 7.11, 17

2.1 Isa 32.7; Nah 1.11; Hos 7.6, 7; Prov 3.27

1.11 Micah plays with words in vv. 10–14. He bitterly declaimed each town, demonstrating their failures by the use of puns. "Shaphir" sounds like the Hebrew word for "beauty," here contrasted with their shame; *Zaanan* sounds like the verb meaning "to go forth," here contrasted with the fear of its inhabitants to venture outside; *Beth-ezel* sounds like a word for "foundation," which had been taken away from them.

2.1 Micah began to characterize the sinful people. They were covetous, spending their time thinking and planning their evil desires. When they should have been sleeping, they were devising iniquity. When morning came, they carried out the plans they had developed. However gross their sins, they practiced them openly. Even as they had devised all manner of evil, so God would now devise punishment for such haughty sinners.

because it is in their power.
2 They covet fields, and seize them;
  houses, and take them away;
they oppress householder and house,
  people and their inheritance.

2. God's intention to punish

3 Therefore thus says the LORD:
Now, I am devising against this family an evil
  from which you cannot remove your necks;
and you shall not walk haughtily,
  for it will be an evil time.
4 On that day they shall take up a taunt song against you,
  and wail with bitter lamentation,
and say, "We are utterly ruined;
  the LORD *d* alters the inheritance of my people;
how he removes it from me!
  Among our captors *e* he parcels out our fields."
5 Therefore you will have no one to cast the line by lot
  in the assembly of the LORD.

6 "Do not preach" — thus they preach —
  "one should not preach of such things;
  disgrace will not overtake us."
7 Should this be said, O house of Jacob?
  Is the LORD's patience exhausted?
  Are these his doings?
Do not my words do good
  to one who walks uprightly?
8 But you rise up against my people *f* as an enemy;
  you strip the robe from the peaceful, *g*
from those who pass by trustingly
  with no thought of war.
9 The women of my people you drive out
  from their pleasant houses;
from their young children you take away
  my glory forever.
10 Arise and go;
  for this is no place to rest,
because of uncleanness that destroys
  with a grievous destruction. *h*
11 If someone were to go about uttering empty falsehoods,
  saying, "I will preach to you of wine and strong drink,"
  such a one would be the preacher for this people!

3. God's promise of future deliverance

12 I will surely gather all of you, O Jacob,
   I will gather the survivors of Israel;

d Heb he   *e* Cn: Heb the rebellious   *f* Cn: Heb But yesterday my people rose   *g* Cn: Heb from before a garment   *h* Meaning of Heb uncertain

2.2
Am 8.4;
Isa 5.8;
1 Kings 21.1-15

2.3
Am 3.1, 2;
Deut 28.48;
Jer 18.11;
Isa 2.11, 12;
Am 5.13

2.4
Hab 2.6;
Mic 1.8;
Isa 24.3;
Jer 4.13;
6.12; 8.10

2.5
Josh 18.4, 10

2.6
Isa 30.10;
Am 2.12;
7.16;
Mic 3.6; 6.16

2.7
Isa 50.2;
59.1;
Jer 15.16;
Ps 15.2;
84.11

2.8
Jer 12.8;
Mic 3.2, 3;
7.2, 3;
Ps 120.6, 7

2.9
Jer 10.20

2.10
Lev 18.25,
28, 29;
Deut 12.9;
Ps 106.38

2.11
Jer 5.13, 31;
Isa 28.7;
30.10, 11

2.12
Mic 4.6, 7;
5.7, 8; 7.18;
Jer 33.22

2.6 Prophets and seers were an annoyance to these sinners. They rebuked those who spoke words they did not wish to hear and admonished them to keep these things to themselves.
2.12 This verse concerning the return of the people of God to their homeland was partially fulfilled after the seventy years of captivity. But there was no return of the ten tribes of the northern kingdom. Moreover, the return of some of the people of Judah from Babylon was reversed in A.D. 70, when the last dispersion occurred. Many Christians believe that a day when all Israel will be regathered is still coming. Most of the prophets who spoke of the judgment of God against his people also included a word of hope for the future prospects of the children of Jacob at the end of the age.

I will set them together
    like sheep in a fold,
like a flock in its pasture;
    it will resound with people.
13 The one who breaks out will go up before them;
    they will break through and pass the gate,
    going out by it.
Their king will pass on before them,
    the LORD at their head.

II. The judgment followed by restoration and the reign of Messiah (3.1–5.15)

A. Sins denounced and the destruction of Jerusalem foretold

3 And I said:
Listen, you heads of Jacob
    and rulers of the house of Israel!
Should you not know justice?—
2   you who hate the good and love the evil,
who tear the skin off my people,[i]
    and the flesh off their bones;
3 who eat the flesh of my people,
    flay their skin off them,
break their bones in pieces,
    and chop them up like meat[j] in a kettle,
    like flesh in a caldron.

4 Then they will cry to the LORD,
    but he will not answer them;
he will hide his face from them at that time,
    because they have acted wickedly.

5 Thus says the LORD concerning the prophets
    who lead my people astray,
who cry "Peace"
    when they have something to eat,
but declare war against those
    who put nothing into their mouths.
6 Therefore it shall be night to you, without vision,
    and darkness to you, without revelation.
The sun shall go down upon the prophets,
    and the day shall be black over them;
7 the seers shall be disgraced,
    and the diviners put to shame;
they shall all cover their lips,
    for there is no answer from God.
8 But as for me, I am filled with power,
    with the spirit of the LORD,

---

i Heb *from them*   *j* Gk: Heb *as*

2.13 Hos 3.5; Isa 52.12

3.1 Jer 5.4, 5

3.2 Mic 2.8; 7.2, 3; Ezek 22.27

3.3 Ps 14.4; Zeph 3.3; Ezek 34.2, 3; 11.3

3.4 Ps 18.41; Prov 1.28; Isa 1.15; Zech 7.13; Isa 59.2; Mic 7.13

3.5 Isa 56.10; Ezek 13.10; Jer 14.14, 15; Mic 2.11; Jer 6.14; Ezek 13.18, 19

3.6 Isa 8.20, 22; Ezek 13.23; Am 8.9

3.7 Zech 13.4; Isa 44.25; Mic 7.16; 1 Sam 28.6; v. 4

3.8 Isa 61.1, 2; 58.1

3.1 Princes, priests, and prophets are servants of God who are called to do his will. God will reprove the greatest of people, even those in highest authority when they disobey his commandments. Micah was a faithful prophet who reproved the rulers of God's people. He was very specific in enumerating exactly what their sins were. Thus they would have no excuse to claim ignorance of what they had done wrong.

3.8 Most of the prophets spoke with the hope that those who listened would repent and seek the face of the Lord. Often that first required conviction of sin. Before the illness can be treated, it must be diagnosed. Micah boldly claimed that it was the Spirit of God who was with him, who spoke through him, and who endued him with power, judgment, and might to tell Jacob (Judah and Jerusalem) and Israel (Samaria) what their sins were.

and with justice and might,
to declare to Jacob his transgression
    and to Israel his sin.

3.9
v. 1;
Isa 1.23

9 Hear this, you rulers of the house of Jacob
    and chiefs of the house of Israel,
who abhor justice
    and pervert all equity,

3.10
Jer 22.13;
Ezek 22.27;
Hab 2.12

10 who build Zion with blood
    and Jerusalem with wrong!

3.11
Isa 1.23;
Hos 4.18;
Jer 6.13;
Isa 48.2;
Jer 7.4

11 Its rulers give judgment for a bribe,
    its priests teach for a price,
    its prophets give oracles for money;
yet they lean upon the LORD and say,
    "Surely the LORD is with us!
    No harm shall come upon us."

3.12
Jer 26.18;
Mic 4.1, 2

12 Therefore because of you
    Zion shall be plowed as a field;
Jerusalem shall become a heap of ruins,
    and the mountain of the house a wooded height.

B. Promise of the coming of God's kingdom

1. Law and peace

4.1
Isa 2.2–4;
Ezek 17.22;
43.12;
Jer 3.17

4 In days to come
    the mountain of the LORD's house
shall be established as the highest of the mountains,
    and shall be raised up above the hills.
Peoples shall stream to it,

4.2
Zech 2.11;
14.16;
Jer 31.6;
Isa 54.13;
42.1–4;
Zech 14.8, 9

2   and many nations shall come and say:
"Come, let us go up to the mountain of the LORD,
    to the house of the God of Jacob;
that he may teach us his ways
    and that we may walk in his paths."
For out of Zion shall go forth instruction,
    and the word of the LORD from Jerusalem.

4.3
Isa 2.4;
Joel 3.10;
Ps 72.7

3 He shall judge between many peoples,
    and shall arbitrate between strong nations far away;
they shall beat their swords into plowshares,
    and their spears into pruning hooks;
nation shall not lift up sword against nation,
    neither shall they learn war any more;

4.4
1 Kings 4.25;
Zech 3.10;
Isa 1.20;
40.5

4 but they shall all sit under their own vines and under their own
            fig trees,
    and no one shall make them afraid;
for the mouth of the LORD of hosts has spoken.

3.11 *No harm shall come upon us.* These sinners thought that God was with them despite their transgressions. Therefore they rested in the false comfort that nothing could touch them, and that the God who had delivered them in the past would keep them from harm now. How wrong they were!
3.12 Instead of safety and comfort, Zion would *be plowed as a field,* i.e., their buildings in the sacred city would be destroyed and the city would lose its identity.
4.1 In the midst of the certainty of doom and disaster, Micah injected a futuristic note of hope. God had not cast off his people forever. While they waited for restoration, salvation would come to the Gentiles. The first three verses of this chapter are virtually identical to Isa 2.2–4; Isaiah and Micah lived at about the same time (cf. Isa 1.1; Mic 1.1).
4.2 *out of Zion shall go forth instruction.* This looked ahead to the day when Zion would be restored and be the means of blessing to all nations and peoples.
4.3 The peace that humans seek and many seek will never come until the end of the age and the victory of the Messiah over Satan. Then peace will come, the armaments of war will be eliminated, and what can be salvaged will be used for peaceful purposes.

5   For all the peoples walk,
        each in the name of its god,
    but we will walk in the name of the LORD our God
        forever and ever.

4.5
2 Kings 17.29;
Isa 26.8, 13;
Zech 10.12

2. *God's victorious reign*

6   In that day, says the LORD,
        I will assemble the lame
    and gather those who have been driven away,
        and those whom I have afflicted.

4.6
Ezek 34.16;
Zeph 3.19;
Ps 147.2;
Ezek 34.13

7   The lame I will make the remnant,
        and those who were cast off, a strong nation;
    and the LORD will reign over them in Mount Zion
        now and forevermore.

4.7
Mic 2.12;
5.7, 8; 7.18;
Isa 9.6;
Dan 7.14;
Lk 1.33;
Rev 11.15

8   And you, O tower of the flock,
        hill of daughter Zion,
    to you it shall come,
        the former dominion shall come,
        the sovereignty of daughter Jerusalem.

4.8
Mic 2.12;
Isa 1.26;
Zech 9.10

9   Now why do you cry aloud?
        Is there no king in you?
    Has your counselor perished,
        that pangs have seized you like a woman in labor?

4.9
Jer 8.19;
Isa 13.8;
Jer 30.6

10 Writhe and groan,[k] O daughter Zion,
        like a woman in labor;
    for now you shall go forth from the city
        and camp in the open country;
        you shall go to Babylon.
    There you shall be rescued,
        there the LORD will redeem you
        from the hands of your enemies.

4.10
Hos 2.14;
Isa 45.13;
Mic 7.8-12;
Isa 48.20;
52.9-12

11 Now many nations
        are assembled against you,
    saying, "Let her be profaned,
        and let our eyes gaze upon Zion."

4.11
Lam 2.16;
Ob 12;
Mic 7.10

12 But they do not know
        the thoughts of the LORD;
    they do not understand his plan,
        that he has gathered them as sheaves to the threshing floor.

4.12
Isa 55.8;
Rom 11.33;
Isa 21.10

13 Arise and thresh,
        O daughter Zion,
    for I will make your horn iron
        and your hoofs bronze;
        you shall beat in pieces many peoples,

4.13
Isa 41.15;
Dan 2.44;
Zech 4.14

---

k Meaning of Heb uncertain

4.5 *For all the peoples walk, each in the name of its god.* All people are religious, and yet they love, worship, and pray to different gods. The true people of God will not only profess faith in God; they will also walk in his ways.
4.6 The people of God were afflicted, scattered, helpless, and lonely. But God would regather them and all would be well.
4.10 Micah envisioned the Babylonian captivity. That captivity (586–537 B.C.) was two centuries away, but Micah and Isaiah predicted the event long

before it happened. Predictive prophecy supports the reliability of the word of God.
4.12 Jerusalem would be destroyed. The destroyers had their own purpose in mind. But they did not know that providence works in such a way that God's purpose might be quite different from theirs. The enemies of Jerusalem would themselves be smitten by God after they had done his will. God can still use the wicked intentions and deeds of people to further his ultimate purposes for the world, with his own glory in view.

and shall[l] devote their gain to the LORD,
their wealth to the Lord of the whole earth.

5 [m] Now you are walled around with a wall;[n]
siege is laid against us;
with a rod they strike the ruler of Israel
upon the cheek.

3. The coming Messiah and his reign

2[o] But you, O Bethlehem of Ephrathah,
who are one of the little clans of Judah,
from you shall come forth for me
one who is to rule in Israel,
whose origin is from of old,
from ancient days.

3 Therefore he shall give them up until the time
when she who is in labor has brought forth;
then the rest of his kindred shall return
to the people of Israel.

4 And he shall stand and feed his flock in the strength of
the LORD,
in the majesty of the name of the LORD his God.
And they shall live secure, for now he shall be great
to the ends of the earth;

5 and he shall be the one of peace.

If the Assyrians come into our land
and tread upon our soil,[p]
we will raise against them seven shepherds
and eight installed as rulers.

6 They shall rule the land of Assyria with the sword,
and the land of Nimrod with the drawn sword;[q]
they[r] shall rescue us from the Assyrians
if they come into our land
or tread within our border.

7 Then the remnant of Jacob,
surrounded by many peoples,
shall be like dew from the LORD,
like showers on the grass,
which do not depend upon people
or wait for any mortal.

8 And among the nations the remnant of Jacob,
surrounded by many peoples,
shall be like a lion among the animals of the forest,
like a young lion among the flocks of sheep,
which, when it goes through, treads down
and tears in pieces, with no one to deliver.

5.2 This verse is not only prophetic, it has important implications in other ways. Micah prophesied that the Messiah would be born in Bethlehem, and that he would come from the Davidic line, a prophecy that the Jews considered genuine (see Mt 2.5). The prophecy also stated that the Messiah's origin was *from ancient days,* a clear testimony to the existence of the Son of God in O.T. times and thus a hint of the Trinity. The purpose of the Messiah's coming would

be to provide eternal redemption (v. 4).
5.5 *Assyrians.* The area of ancient Assyria is now known as Iraq.
5.7 Micah spoke of those few people of Israel who formed a remnant. On them, in the latter days, would the Spirit be poured out and they would be saved (Rom 9.27). They would be a blessing among many peoples and would be as welcome as the dew of the morning.

Left margin cross-references:

5.1
Jer 5.7;
1 Kings 22.24;
Lam 3.30

5.2
Mt 2.6;
1 Sam 17.12;
23.23;
Lk 2.4;
Isa 9.6

5.3
Mic 4.10;
Hos 11.8;
Isa 10.20-22

5.4
Isa 40.11;
Ezek 34.23;
Isa 52.13;
Lk 1.32

5.5
Isa 9.6;
Rev 11.15;
Isa 8.7, 8

5.6
Nah 2.11-13;
Zeph 2.13;
Gen 10.8;
Isa 37.36, 37

5.7
Mic 2.12;
Deut 32.2;
Hos 14.5

5.8
Mic 4.13;
Zech 10.5;
Hos 5.14;
Ps 50.22

9 Your hand shall be lifted up over your adversaries,
      and all your enemies shall be cut off.

10 In that day, says the Lord,
      I will cut off your horses from among you
      and will destroy your chariots;

11 and I will cut off the cities of your land
      and throw down all your strongholds;

12 and I will cut off sorceries from your hand,
      and you shall have no more soothsayers;

13 and I will cut off your images
      and your pillars from among you,
   and you shall bow down no more
      to the work of your hands;

14 and I will uproot your sacred poles^s from among you
      and destroy your towns.

15 And in anger and wrath I will execute vengeance
      on the nations that did not obey.

III. Divine punishment followed by divine mercy (6.1–7.20)

A. God's complaint against a rebellious people

6   Hear what the Lord says:
      Rise, plead your case before the mountains,
      and let the hills hear your voice.

2 Hear, you mountains, the controversy of the Lord,
      and you enduring foundations of the earth;
   for the Lord has a controversy with his people,
      and he will contend with Israel.

3 "O my people, what have I done to you?
      In what have I wearied you? Answer me!

4 For I brought you up from the land of Egypt,
      and redeemed you from the house of slavery;
   and I sent before you Moses,
      Aaron, and Miriam.

5 O my people, remember now what King Balak of Moab
      devised,
      what Balaam son of Beor answered him,
   and what happened from Shittim to Gilgal,
      that you may know the saving acts of the Lord."

6 "With what shall I come before the Lord,
      and bow myself before God on high?
   Shall I come before him with burnt offerings,
      with calves a year old?

7 Will the Lord be pleased with thousands of rams,
      with ten thousands of rivers of oil?
   Shall I give my firstborn for my transgression,

^s Heb *Asherim*

Cross references

5.9 Ps 10.12; 21.8; Isa 26.11

5.10 Isa 2.7; Hos 14.3; Zech 9.10

5.11 Isa 1.7; Hos 10.14; Am 5.9

5.12 Deut 18.10-12; Isa 2.6

5.13 Zech 13.2; Isa 2.8

5.14 Ex 34.13; Isa 17.8; 27.9

5.15 Ps 149.7; Isa 65.12

6.1 Ps 50.1; Ezek 6.2, 3

6.2 Deut 32.1; Hos 12.2; Isa 1.8; Hos 4.1

6.3 Ps 50.7; Jer 2.5; Isa 43.22, 23

6.4 Ex 12.51; Deut 4.20; 7.8; Ps 77.20; Ex 15.20

6.5 Num 22.5, 6; Rev 2.14; Num 25.1; Josh 4.19; 5.9, 10; Judg 5.11; 1 Sam 12.7

6.6 Ps 40.6-8; 51.16, 17

6.7 2 Kings 16.3; 21.6; Jer 7.31

5.12,13 Some of the greatest evils among the Jews sprang from the practice of sorcery and witchcraft. In the coming days of God's judgment, these would no longer exist, and the idols which normally attended these evil practices would disappear.

6.1 Micah had been talking about a glorious future, but he returned to assail the people for what they were doing at that moment. He ordered them to pay close attention. They were a rebellious people who had dishonored God. His mercies had been many and should have caused them to remain faithful, but they had turned away from him.

6.7 The Jews had become so debased they were offering human sacrifices. This was part of Molech worship. Such practices were forbidden by God (see 2 Kings 16.3; 21.2,6; Jer 7.31; 19.4–6).

the fruit of my body for the sin of my soul?"
8 He has told you, O mortal, what is good;
and what does the LORD require of you
but to do justice, and to love kindness,
and to walk humbly with your God?

9 The voice of the LORD cries to the city
(it is sound wisdom to fear your name):
Hear, O tribe and assembly of the city![t]
10 Can I forget[u] the treasures of wickedness in the house of the wicked,
and the scant measure that is accursed?
11 Can I tolerate wicked scales
and a bag of dishonest weights?
12 Your[v] wealthy are full of violence;
your[w] inhabitants speak lies,
with tongues of deceit in their mouths.
13 Therefore I have begun[x] to strike you down,
making you desolate because of your sins.
14 You shall eat, but not be satisfied,
and there shall be a gnawing hunger within you;
you shall put away, but not save,
and what you save, I will hand over to the sword.
15 You shall sow, but not reap;
you shall tread olives, but not anoint yourselves with oil;
you shall tread grapes, but not drink wine.
16 For you have kept the statutes of Omri[y]
and all the works of the house of Ahab,
and you have followed their counsels.
Therefore I will make you a desolation, and your[z] inhabitants
an object of hissing;
so you shall bear the scorn of my people.

B. *The confession of sin and the hope of mercy*

7 Woe is me! For I have become like one who,
after the summer fruit has been gathered,
after the vintage has been gleaned,
finds no cluster to eat;
there is no first-ripe fig for which I hunger.

6.8 Deut 10.12; 1 Sam 15.22; Hos 6.6; 12.6; Isa 56.1; 57.15; 66.2
6.10 Jer 5.26, 27; Am 3.10; 8.5
6.11 Hos 12.7
6.12 Am 6.3, 4; Mic 2.1, 2; Jer 9.3, 5; Hos 7.13; Am 2.4; Isa 3.8
6.13 Mic 1.9; Isa 1.7; 6.11
6.14 Lev 26.26; Isa 9.20; 30.6
6.15 Deut 28.38; Jer 12.13; Am 5.11; Zeph 1.13
6.16 1 Kings 16.25-33; Jer 7.24; 19.8; 29.18; 51.51
7.1 Isa 24.13; 28.4; Hos 9.10

[t] Cn Compare Gk: Heb *tribe, and who has appointed it yet?* [u] Cn: Meaning of Heb uncertain [v] Heb *Whose* [w] Heb *whose* [x] Gk Syr Vg: Heb *have made sick* [y] Gk Syr Vg Tg: Heb *the statutes of Omri are kept* [z] Heb *its*

6.8 Those who have been redeemed must prove their faith by their works. They must: (1) *do justice* (i.e., render to all their due according to their obligations), (2) *love kindness* (i.e., not only perform acts of kindness but delight in mercy and rejoice in every opportunity to do mercy), and (3) *walk humbly* before their God (i.e., fulfill all the duties of both tables of the law by way of justice and mercy). Some have supposed that one can obtain salvation by living the virtuous life. The setting in which this verse appears, however, says the opposite. God is not addressing the heathen but his covenant people. In Micah's day, the problem was that these people had a dead faith which did not lead to living a holy life. Thus he emphasizes the fruits of true faith, a theme almost identical to the book of James.
6.9 God had just commended justice and mercy to his people. Now he began showing how they had done the exact opposite. This was why he had a controversy with his people and why judgment had to be pronounced.
6.16 *statutes of Omri.* These refer to the statutes that required and enforced the worship of Baal (see 1 Kings 16.25–32; 18.19–40, which describe the life of Omri and Elijah's victory over his son Ahab).
7.1ff Religion was at a low ebb in Israel. In such a context, where can the saints find a refuge? How shall they conduct themselves? Here Micah says that believers must: (1) have an eye to God (v. 7); (2) courageously bear up under the insults and insolences of the enemy (vv. 8–10); (3) bow before God, accepting his rebukes for their own sins (v. 9); (4) expect trouble in this life and make the best of it (vv. 11–13); (5) encourage themselves with God's gracious promises (vv. 14,15); (6) foresee the ruin of the enemies who seem to triumph over them at the moment (vv. 16,17); and (7) live triumphantly in the mercy and grace of God, who is faithful to his covenant promises (vv. 18–20).

2 The faithful have disappeared from the land,
    and there is no one left who is upright;
they all lie in wait for blood,
    and they hunt each other with nets.

3 Their hands are skilled to do evil;
    the official and the judge ask for a bribe,
and the powerful dictate what they desire;
    thus they pervert justice. *a*

4 The best of them is like a brier,
    the most upright of them a thorn hedge.
The day of their *b* sentinels, of their *b* punishment, has come;
    now their confusion is at hand.

5 Put no trust in a friend,
    have no confidence in a loved one;
guard the doors of your mouth
    from her who lies in your embrace;

6 for the son treats the father with contempt,
    the daughter rises up against her mother,
the daughter-in-law against her mother-in-law;
    your enemies are members of your own household.

7 But as for me, I will look to the LORD,
    I will wait for the God of my salvation;
    my God will hear me.

8 Do not rejoice over me, O my enemy;
    when I fall, I shall rise;
when I sit in darkness,
    the LORD will be a light to me.

9 I must bear the indignation of the LORD,
    because I have sinned against him,
until he takes my side
    and executes judgment for me.
He will bring me out to the light;
    I shall see his vindication.

10 Then my enemy will see,
    and shame will cover her who said to me,
    "Where is the LORD your God?"
My eyes will see her downfall; *c*
    now she will be trodden down
    like the mire of the streets.

11 A day for the building of your walls!
    In that day the boundary shall be far extended.

12 In that day they will come to you
    from Assyria to *d* Egypt,
and from Egypt to the River,
    from sea to sea and from mountain to mountain.

13 But the earth will be desolate
    because of its inhabitants,
    for the fruit of their doings.

14 Shepherd your people with your staff,
    the flock that belongs to you,

a Cn: Heb *they weave it*   *b* Heb *your*   *c* Heb lacks *downfall*   *d* One Ms: MT *Assyria and cities of*

7.2
Ps 12.1;
Isa 57.1;
59.7;
Jer 5.26;
Hos 5.1
7.3
Prov 4.16,
17;
Am 5.12;
Mic 3.11
7.4
Ezek 2.6;
28.24;
Nah 1.10;
Isa 10.3;
Hos 9.7;
Isa 22.5
7.5
Jer 9.4
7.6
Ezek 22.7;
Mt 10.21,
35.36;
Lk 12.53
7.7
Hab 2.1;
Ps 130.5; 4.3
7.8
Prov 24.17;
Lam 4.21;
Ps 37.24;
Isa 9.2
7.9
Lam 3.29,
40;
Isa 42.7, 16;
56.1
7.10
Ps 35.26;
Isa 51.23;
Zech 10.5
7.11
Isa 54.11;
Zeph 2.2
7.12
Isa 11.16;
19.23-25
7.13
Jer 25.11;
Mic 6.13;
Isa 3.10, 11;
Mic 3.4
7.14
Mic 5.4;
Ps 23.4;
Jer 50.19;
Am 9.11

7.5,6 Things had gotten so bad in Israel that no one could be trusted, including one's loved ones. The family had ceased to be a family. Discontent, friction, hatred, and abuse were the order of the day.

7.7 When conditions are as bad as those just described, what can a child of faith do? Micah's personal response to this question was to look to God, wait for his salvation, and know that God would hear him.

which lives alone in a forest
in the midst of a garden land;
let them feed in Bashan and Gilead
as in the days of old.

7.15 Ex 3.20; 20.34; Ps 78.12
7.16 Job 21.5; Mic 3.7

15 As in the days when you came out of the land of Egypt,
show us[e] marvelous things.
16 The nations shall see and be ashamed
of all their might;
they shall lay their hands on their mouths;
their ears shall be deaf;

7.17 Ps 72.9; Isa 49.23; Deut 32.24; Ps 18.45; Isa 59.19

17 they shall lick dust like a snake,
like the crawling things of the earth;
they shall come trembling out of their fortresses;
they shall turn in dread to the LORD our God,
and they shall stand in fear of you.

7.18 Ex 34.7, 9; Isa 43.25; Jer 32.41

18 Who is a God like you, pardoning iniquity
and passing over the transgression
of the remnant of your[f] possession?
He does not retain his anger forever,
because he delights in showing clemency.

7.19 Jer 50.20; Isa 38.17; 43.25; Jer 31.34

19 He will again have compassion upon us;
he will tread our iniquities under foot.
You will cast all our[g] sins
into the depths of the sea.

7.20 Lk 1.55, 72; Deut 7.8, 12

20 You will show faithfulness to Jacob
and unswerving loyalty to Abraham,
as you have sworn to our ancestors
from the days of old.

[e] Cn: Heb *I will show him* [f] Heb *his* [g] Gk Syr Vg Tg: Heb *their*

7.18ff Micah ends his book on a joyful note. God was ready and able to pardon the sin of his people. Pardon is the foundation on which all other covenant promises rest. God will renew his favors to those who come to him in repentance. He will turn again and have compassion. Our sins will be cast into the deepest part of the deepest sea, to be remembered against us no more. This message applies to every believer who has backslid from a firm commitment to Christ. We must confess our sins, flee from them, and live according to God's commandments; then all will be well.

INTRODUCTION TO

NAHUM

Authorship, Date, and Background: Like Obadiah, Nahum (whose name means "consolation" or "comfort") announced the downfall of a heathen nation—Assyria and its capital Nineveh. The prophet himself came from Elkosh, the site of which is unknown except that it was undoubtedly in Judea. Apart from the book itself, nothing else is known about the prophet.

The book can be dated with reasonable accuracy. From 3.8 it is apparent that Thebes has been sacked (by Ashurbanipal of Assyria, c. 663 B.C.). The sack and end of the Assyrian empire was to take place shortly. Since that event occurred in 612 B.C., when the Medes and Chaldeans destroyed Nineveh, Nahum's ministry can be dated after 663 B.C. and before 612 B.C. In all probability, Nahum's prophecy was written shortly after the sack of Thebes but before Thebes began to rise again in 654 B.C.

Under the preaching of Jonah, the judgment of God against Nineveh had been suspended because of the nation's repentance. Now there was impending judgment unrelieved by any possibility of repentance. The nation was now ripe for ruin by God. The prophecies of Jonah and Nahum, separated by more than a century and a half, illustrate the mercy and the patience of God in dealing with sinful nations, but also that his tolerance is not without limits.

Characteristics and Content: Nahum's prophecy burns with the white heat of anger against a cruel enemy of God's people. This ruthless military power which had conquered and overthrown other nations would now itself be conquered and overthrown. Judah could rejoice that at last the indignation of God had found expression in the disappearance of a nation which had kept it in a state of vassalage for many years. Nahum saw God as the sovereign ruler of the nations whose omnipotence could not be thwarted. God was slow to anger, but he would not keep his anger forever from resulting in judgment.

In this instance the coming judgment of God was to be final, and Judah would never again need to fear this nation. His graphic picture of Nineveh's overthrow included the siege against the city, its conquest, and its utter ruin by the invading hosts. The Ninevites justly deserved this judgment because they were ruthless plunderers and had been commercial exploiters of many peoples. When the end of Nineveh came, no one would offer any laments over its demise. Worst of all, in the light of God's numerous pronouncements of judgment upon his own people, Nahum cited one clear difference between them and the Assyrians: Judah would leave behind a remnant, whereas no remnant would be left after the destruction of Nineveh—it would perish from the earth forever.

Outline:

NAHUM

I. *The psalm of the Lord's majesty (1.1–15)*

1.1
Isa 13.1;
Hab 1.1;
Nah 2.8; 3.7;
Zeph 2.13

1 An oracle concerning Nineveh. The book of the vision of Nahum of Elkosh.

1.2
Ex 20.5;
Deut 4.24;
32.35, 41;
Ps 94.1

2 A jealous and avenging God is the Lord,
  the Lord is avenging and wrathful;
 the Lord takes vengeance on his adversaries
  and rages against his enemies.

1.3
Ex 34.6, 7;
Ps 103.8;
Isa 29.6;
Ps 104.3

3 The Lord is slow to anger but great in power,
  and the Lord will by no means clear the guilty.

His way is in whirlwind and storm,
  and the clouds are the dust of his feet.

1.4
Ps 106.9;
Isa 33.9

4 He rebukes the sea and makes it dry,
  and he dries up all the rivers;
 Bashan and Carmel wither,
  and the bloom of Lebanon fades.

1.5
Ex 19.18;
Mic 1.4;
Isa 24.1, 20

5 The mountains quake before him,
  and the hills melt;
 the earth heaves before him,
  the world and all who live in it.

1.6
Jer 10.10;
Mal 3.2;
Isa 66.15;
1 Kings 19.11

6 Who can stand before his indignation?
  Who can endure the heat of his anger?
 His wrath is poured out like fire,
  and by him the rocks are broken in pieces.

1.7
1 Chr 16.34;
Ps 28.8

7 The Lord is good,
  a stronghold in a day of trouble;
 he protects those who take refuge in him,

1.8
Isa 28.2, 18;
13.9, 10

8   even in a rushing flood.
 He will make a full end of his adversaries,[a]
  and will pursue his enemies into darkness.

1.9
Ps 2.1;
Isa 28.22

9 Why do you plot against the Lord?

---

a Gk: Heb *of her place*

1.1 *Nineveh* was located on the Tigris River. It was the capital of Assyria, a mighty nation that appeared to be indestructible. Yet Nahum predicted its downfall, and his prediction was fulfilled to the last detail. Under the preaching of Jonah (ca. 770 B.C.) Nineveh had repented, and judgment was averted for more than a century. It was not until 612 B.C. that the Chaldeans and Medes laid siege to Nineveh for two years before it yielded. The destruction was so great that when the Greek historian Xenophon passed by the site two centuries later, the local people could not even tell him its name. In 1885 the site was identified and the ruins were uncovered. Archaeologists have confirmed the biblical account of its destruction from their examination of the ruins.
1.2 God is a God whose justice is inflexible. He is a jealous God — jealous for his own honor, for his

land, and for those who worship him.
1.3–5 Though slow to anger, God does get angry, and when he does, his power over his enemies is irresistible. The wind and the storm bear witness to his might. Seas, rivers, and mountains are controlled by him and demonstrate his strength.
1.6 When God manifests his anger in action, he is a consuming fire. Decades before, the Ninevites learned that he was slow to anger and merciful, but now they would find him implacable in his judgment against them.
1.9ff These verses seem to point both to the great Assyrian Sennacherib and his defeat and to another judgment to follow a century later, when Nineveh would be finished off. The army would be consumed (v. 10). Judgment would come upon the king, who would be cut off, his lineage destroyed, and his gods

He will make an end;
   no adversary will rise up twice.
10 Like thorns they are entangled,
   like drunkards they are drunk;
   they are consumed like dry straw.
11 From you one has gone out
   who plots evil against the LORD,
   one who counsels wickedness.

12 Thus says the LORD,
   "Though they are at full strength and many,[b]
   they will be cut off and pass away.
   Though I have afflicted you,
   I will afflict you no more.
13 And now I will break off his yoke from you
   and snap the bonds that bind you."

14 The LORD has commanded concerning you:
   "Your name shall be perpetuated no longer;
   from the house of your gods I will cut off
   the carved image and the cast image.
   I will make your grave, for you are worthless."

15[c] Look! On the mountains the feet of one
   who brings good tidings,
   who proclaims peace!
   Celebrate your festivals, O Judah,
   fulfill your vows,
   for never again shall the wicked invade you;
   they are utterly cut off.

II. *The siege and fall of Nineveh (2.1–13)*

2 A shatterer[d] has come up against you.
   Guard the ramparts;
   watch the road;
  gird your loins;
   collect all your strength.

2 (For the LORD is restoring the majesty of Jacob,
   as well as the majesty of Israel,
   though ravagers have ravaged them
   and ruined their branches.)

3 The shields of his warriors are red;
   his soldiers are clothed in crimson.
   The metal on the chariots flashes
   on the day when he musters them;
   the chargers[e] prance.
4 The chariots race madly through the streets,

Cross-references (right column):

1.10
2 Sam 23.6;
Mal 4.1

1.11
v. 9;
Ezek 11.2

1.12
Isa 10.16-19,
33, 34; 54.7,
8

1.13
Isa 9.4;
Jer 2.20

1.14
Isa 46.1, 2;
Mic 5.13, 14;
Ezek 32.22,
23

1.15
Isa 40.9;
Ps 52.7;
Rom 10.15;
Lev 23.2, 4;
Isa 52.1;
Joel 3.17;
Isa 29.7, 8

2.1
Jer 51.20-23;
Nah 3.12, 14

2.2
Isa 60.15;
Ezek 37.21-23

2.3
Ezek 23.14,
15;
Job 39.23

2.4
Ezek 26.10;
Jer 4.13

b Meaning of Heb uncertain   *c* Ch 2.1 in Heb   *d* Cn: Heb *scatterer*   *e* Cn Compare Gk Syr: Heb *cypresses*

---

defeated (v. 14). The yoke of this kingdom would be lifted and the oppressed people set free (v. 13). The good news of Nineveh's defeat and retreat would be welcomed, and joy inexpressible would abound everywhere (v. 15).
2.1 Regardless of how well Nineveh armed itself, it would do no good, for everything would be dashed to pieces. Nahum here predicts the events of 612 B.C.,

when Nebuchadnezzar, aided by the Medes, sacked Nineveh, which had appeared to be impregnable.
2.3 Beginning here, Nahum describes the awfulness of the coming conquest. The shields of the armies and their uniforms are crimson with blood. Their chariots look like flaming torches as they dash frantically through the streets. The river gates are opened to allow the invaders to penetrate the stronghold.

they rush to and fro through the squares;
their appearance is like torches,
they dart like lightning.

5 He calls his officers;
they stumble as they come forward;
they hasten to the wall,
and the mantelet^f is set up.

6 The river gates are opened,
the palace trembles.

7 It is decreed^f that the city^g be exiled,
its slave women led away,
moaning like doves
and beating their breasts.

8 Nineveh is like a pool
whose waters^h run away.
"Halt! Halt!" —
but no one turns back.

9 "Plunder the silver,
plunder the gold!
There is no end of treasure!
An abundance of every precious thing!"

10 Devastation, desolation, and destruction!
Hearts faint and knees tremble,
all loins quake,
all faces grow pale!

11 What became of the lions' den,
the cave^i of the young lions,
where the lion goes,
and the lion's cubs, with no one to disturb them?

12 The lion has torn enough for his whelps
and strangled prey for his lionesses;
he has filled his caves with prey
and his dens with torn flesh.

13   See, I am against you, says the Lord of hosts, and I will burn
your^j chariots in smoke, and the sword shall devour your young lions;
I will cut off your prey from the earth, and the voice of your messengers
shall be heard no more.

III. *The reasons for Nineveh's destruction (3.1–19)*

A. *The sin of Nineveh*

3 Ah! City of bloodshed,
utterly deceitful, full of booty —
no end to the plunder!

2 The crack of whip and rumble of wheel,

*f Meaning of Heb uncertain   g Heb it   h Cn Compare Gk: Heb a pool, from the days that she has
become, and they   i Cn: Heb pasture   j Heb her*

2.7–9   Many of the civilians in the city, including
women, would be carried away into exile. The Assyrians would be unable to repel the invaders, and the
wealth of the city would be seized and possessed by
the victors.
2.10ff   Nineveh would be completely and utterly ruined. However much like a lion Nineveh had been, a
stronger lion would come and dash to pieces all who
stood in the way.
2.13   *I am against you.* The Ninevites miscalculated

their situation. A powerful nation of warriors, they
supposed that no combination of hostile powers could
overcome them. That had been true, but now God
entered the picture and declared judgment upon
them. With God against it, Nineveh did not have a
chance for survival.
3.1   Nahum suggests the biblical teaching that humans reap what they sow. Cause and effect will prevail so that the timeless principles of justice and equity have their day.

galloping horse and bounding chariot!

3 Horsemen charging,
        flashing sword and glittering spear,
   piles of dead,
        heaps of corpses,
   dead bodies without end—
        they stumble over the bodies!

4 Because of the countless debaucheries of the prostitute,
        gracefully alluring, mistress of sorcery,
   who enslaves[k] nations through her debaucheries,
        and peoples through her sorcery,

5 I am against you,
        says the LORD of hosts,
   and will lift up your skirts over your face;
   and I will let nations look on your nakedness
        and kingdoms on your shame.

6 I will throw filth at you
        and treat you with contempt,
        and make you a spectacle.

7 Then all who see you will shrink from you and say,
   "Nineveh is devastated; who will bemoan her?"
        Where shall I seek comforters for you?

B. The justness of the judgment

8 Are you better than Thebes[l]
        that sat by the Nile,
   with water around her,
        her rampart a sea,
        water her wall?

9 Ethiopia[m] was her strength,
        Egypt too, and that without limit;
   Put and the Libyans were her[n] helpers.

10 Yet she became an exile,
        she went into captivity;
   even her infants were dashed in pieces
        at the head of every street;
   lots were cast for her nobles,
        all her dignitaries were bound in fetters.

11 You also will be drunken,
        you will go into hiding;[o]
   you will seek
        a refuge from the enemy.

12 All your fortresses are like fig trees

Cross references:

3.3 Hab 3.11; Isa 34.3; 66.16; 2 Kings 19.35

3.4 Isa 23.17; Rev 17.1, 2; Isa 47.9; Rev 18.3

3.5 Nah 2.13; Isa 47.2, 3; Jer 13.22; Ezek 16.37

3.6 Job 9.31; Mal 2.9; Isa 14.16; Jer 51.37

3.7 Jer 51.9; Nah 2.8; Zeph 2.13; Isa 51.19; Jer 15.5

3.8 Jer 46.25; Ezek 30.14-16; Isa 19.6-8

3.9 Isa 20.5; Ezek 27.10; 30.5; 38.5; 2 Chr 12.3; 16.8

3.10 Isa 20.4; 13.16; Hos 13.16; Lam 2.19; Joel 3.3; Ob 11

3.11 Jer 25.27; Isa 2.10, 19

3.12 Isa 28.4; Rev 6.13

---

k Heb sells   l Heb No-amon   m Or Nubia; Heb Cush   n Gk: Heb your   o Meaning of Heb uncertain

---

3.4–7 Nineveh had already been accused of being a city of bloodshed, full of lies and guilty of robbery (v. 1). Now Nahum accuses her of being a prostitute, a mistress of witchcrafts. By this Nahum meant that the Ninevites had taught their conquered peoples to worship their gods and to join them in idolatry. Therefore, God was against the city. Her ruin was guaranteed, and no pity would be shown her. She would become a laughingstock to all who passed by. God would make of her a warning to all nations for all time.
3.8 *Are you better than Thebes?* Thebes was a great city located four hundred miles south of Cairo. The prophet probably had in mind the destruction of Thebes by Ashurbanipal (663 B.C.). If Thebes, the

capital of one of Egypt's greatest dynasties, could be destroyed, why not Nineveh?
3.10 Thebes had thought she was impregnable, but she was not. She had been carried away into exile and her children slain. Lots had been cast for the nobles to see which of the conquerors would take them for their slaves. Nineveh's fate would be the same.
3.12–14 Nineveh's walls would be like ripe figs on a fig tree; shake them and they fall. Her troops would be like frail women. Their city gates would be open to the enemy and the gates themselves burned. In spite of all the preparations to survive the siege by Babylon, fire would devour the city and the sword would kill the inhabitants. The situation was hopeless.

with first-ripe figs —
  if shaken they fall
    into the mouth of the eater.

3.13
Jer 50.37;
51.30;
Ps 147.13

13 Look at your troops:
  they are women in your midst.
The gates of your land
  are wide open to your foes;
  fire has devoured the bars of your gates.

3.14
2 Chr 32.3, 4,
11;
Nah 2.1

14 Draw water for the siege,
  strengthen your forts;
trample the clay,
  tread the mortar,
    take hold of the brick mold!

3.15
v. 13;
Joel 1.4

15 There the fire will devour you,
  the sword will cut you off.
    It will devour you like the locust.

Multiply yourselves like the locust,
  multiply like the grasshopper!

3.16
Isa 23.8

16 You increased your merchants
  more than the stars of the heavens.
  The locust sheds its skin and flies away.

3.17
Jer 51.27;
Rev 9.7

17 Your guards are like grasshoppers,
  your scribes like swarms^p of locusts
settling on the fences
  on a cold day —
when the sun rises, they fly away;
  no one knows where they have gone.

3.18
Ps 76.5, 6;
Isa 56.10;
Jer 51.57;
Nah 2.5;
1 Kings 22.17

18 Your shepherds are asleep,
  O king of Assyria;
  your nobles slumber.
Your people are scattered on the mountains
  with no one to gather them.

3.19
Mic 1.9;
Lam 2.15;
Zeph 2.15

19 There is no assuaging your hurt,
  your wound is mortal.
All who hear the news about you
  clap their hands over you.
For who has ever escaped
  your endless cruelty?

^{p} Meaning of Heb uncertain

3.17–19 Guards and scribes were useless to defend Nineveh. Nobles and shepherds were as good as asleep, and the population would be scattered far and wide. The end had come; Nineveh would be no more forever.

INTRODUCTION TO

HABAKKUK

Authorship, Date, and Background: The prophet Habakkuk, whose name is derived from a Hebrew root meaning "to embrace," was the author of this book. Apart from his name and the fact that he was called a prophet, nothing else is known about him. He lived and prophesied during the closing years of the seventh century B.C. and the early years of the sixth century. Evangelical scholars generally date this book to a period between 605 and 589 B.C. Obadiah had pronounced divine judgment on Edom; Nahum had announced the doom of Assyria; Habakkuk was the third prophet whose ministry was limited to God's judgment on a single Gentile nation— Chaldea (Babylon).

Nineveh had been destroyed by Nabopolassar. Nebuchadnezzar his son reigned from 605 B.C. to 562 B.C. At the battle of Carchemish he defeated the Egyptians and established Babylon as the center of world power in that era. He was God's instrument to execute divine judgment on Judah, bringing about the Babylonian captivity of seventy years.

Characteristics and Content: Habakkuk engaged in a conversation with God about the evils of Judah. The people of Judah were guilty of violence and injustice, and refused to obey the demands of God's law. Habakkuk was disturbed about these conditions and wondered how soon it would be before the judgment of God would fall on his people. He learned that God would use the Chaldeans to punish the people of Judah. He announced that the Chaldeans would spread their terror, seize Judah's possessions, take the people captive, and destroy Jerusalem; Judah's evil would not go on forever unpunished.

However, Habakkuk had serious reservations about the justice of using a nation whose sins were greater than those of Judah. He argued that Chaldea was greedy, covetous, cruel, and idolatrous, and asked God how he could use a more sinful nation to punish a less sinful one. God announced that he would punish the Chaldeans after he had used them to punish Judah. Then Habakkuk made known to all people the good news that the just shall live by their faith (2.2–4). This theme is mentioned by Isaiah and is picked up in the N.T. in Romans, Galatians, and Hebrews. The prophet announced his own faith in God even if troubles beset him, the trees gave forth no fruit, and the earth produced no food. He concluded by saying that if all these evils came upon him, "yet I will rejoice in the LORD; I will exult in the God of my salvation. God, the Lord, is my strength; he makes my feet like the feet of a deer, and makes me tread upon the heights" (3.18,19).

Outline:

I. Habakkuk's first question: why does evil go unpunished? (1.1–4)

II. God's first answer: he will use the Chaldeans to punish (1.5–11)

III. Habakkuk's second question: why will God use the more wicked to punish the less wicked? (1.12—2.1)

IV. God's second answer: the Chaldeans will be punished also (2.2–20)

V. The prayer of Habakkuk (3.1–19)

HABAKKUK

I. Habakkuk's first question: why does evil go unpunished? (1.1–4)

1 The oracle that the prophet Habakkuk saw.

2 O LORD, how long shall I cry for help,
   and you will not listen?
Or cry to you "Violence!"
   and you will not save?
3 Why do you make me see wrongdoing
   and look at trouble?
Destruction and violence are before me;
   strife and contention arise.
4 So the law becomes slack
   and justice never prevails.
The wicked surround the righteous—
   therefore judgment comes forth perverted.

II. God's first answer: he will use the Chaldeans to punish (1.5–11)

5 Look at the nations, and see!
   Be astonished! Be astounded!
For a work is being done in your days
   that you would not believe if you were told.
6 For I am rousing the Chaldeans,
   that fierce and impetuous nation,
who march through the breadth of the earth
   to seize dwellings not their own.
7 Dread and fearsome are they;
   their justice and dignity proceed from themselves.
8 Their horses are swifter than leopards,
   more menacing than wolves at dusk;
   their horses charge.
Their horsemen come from far away;
   they fly like an eagle swift to devour.
9 They all come for violence,
   with faces pressing*a* forward;

a Meaning of Heb uncertain

1.1 Isa 13.1; Nah 1.1
1.2 Ps 13.1, 2; 22.1, 2
1.3 v. 13; Jer 20.8
1.4 Ps 119.126; 22.12; Isa 5.20
1.5 Acts 13.41; Isa 29.9, 14
1.6 2 Kings 24.2; Jer 4.11-13; 5.15; 8.10
1.7 Isa 18.2, 7; Jer 39.5-9
1.8 Jer 4.13; 5.6; Ezek 17.3; Hos 8.1
1.9 Hab 2.5

1.1 Sometimes God uses people to do his work without giving us any knowledge of who they are, where they came from, and who their parents were. We know virtually nothing about Habakkuk except that he was a prophet of God.

1.2 Habakkuk cried out to the Lord for help but nothing happened. His soul was vexed because he identified with the oppressed who suffered from the iniquity and violence of their oppressors.

1.4 When laws on the statute books are not enforced, it is as though there were no laws. Injustice prevails and justice is perverted. Habakkuk recognized this state of affairs among God's people and denounced it.

1.6 *The Chaldeans* were a tribe of people in southern Babylon. Under Nabopolassar, they won their independence from Assyria. Later, under Nebuchadnezzar, they took over all of western Asia, including Judah, which fell in 586 B.C. This was God's first response to Habakkuk's complaint.

1.9 *they gather captives like sand*, i.e., "they shall take a vast number of prisoners."

they gather captives like sand.

1.10
2 Chr 36.6,
10;
Isa 10.9;
14.16;
Jer 32.24;
Ezek 26.8
1.11
Jer 4.11, 12;
2.3;
Dan 4.30

10 At kings they scoff,
and of rulers they make sport.
They laugh at every fortress,
and heap up earth to take it.
11 Then they sweep by like the wind;
they transgress and become guilty;
their own might is their god!

III. Habakkuk's second question: why will God use the more wicked to punish the less wicked? (1.12–2.1)

1.12
Deut 33.27;
Ps 90.2;
Isa 10.5-7;
Deut 32.4

12 Are you not from of old,
O Lord my God, my Holy One?
You[b] shall not die.
O Lord, you have marked them for judgment;
and you, O Rock, have established them for punishment.

1.13
Jer 12.1, 2;
Isa 24.16;
Ps 50.21;
56.1, 2

13 Your eyes are too pure to behold evil,
and you cannot look on wrongdoing;
why do you look on the treacherous,
and are silent when the wicked swallow
those more righteous than they?

1.14
Eccl 9.12

14 You have made people like the fish of the sea,
like crawling things that have no ruler.

1.15
Jer 16.16;
Am 4.2;
Ps 10.9

15 The enemy[c] brings all of them up with a hook;
he drags them out with his net,
he gathers them in his seine;
so he rejoices and exults.
16 Therefore he sacrifices to his net
and makes offerings to his seine;
for by them his portion is lavish,
and his food is rich.

1.17
Isa 19.8;
14.5, 6

17 Is he then to keep on emptying his net,
and destroying nations without mercy?

2.1
Isa 21.8, 11;
Ps 5.3; 85.8

2 I will stand at my watchpost,
and station myself on the rampart;
I will keep watch to see what he will say to me,
and what he[d] will answer concerning my complaint.

---

[b] Ancient Heb tradition: MT *We*   [c] Heb *He*   [d] Syr: Heb *I*

1.10 *they scoff . . . laugh at every fortress*, i.e., "every fort will fall before their attack." The conquering armies were laughing at their victims — at the rulers who were weak and helpless against them. Their defenses were such that a little sand thrown against the walls would create a rampart over which the soldiers could enter the city and destroy it.
1.12 The people of Judah indeed had offended their God, but he is the everlasting God, who will keep his people. His covenant promises are sure. Despite chastisement God will always have a people in the world, for the gates of Sheol (Hades, death) can never prevail against his people (cf. Mt 16.18).
1.13 Wickedness may prosper for a season, but a holy God does not approve of sin, no matter who commits it. Note how even at Calvary, when Jesus Christ became sin for us (cf. 2 Cor 5.21), the face of the Father was turned away from his Son, for he cannot look upon sin. In this second complaint, the

prophet Habakkuk wanted to know why a holy God permitted the triumph of an enemy who was more wicked than the people he was about to overcome.
1.14–16 Judah was like the fish of the sea. As fishermen have every advantage over the fish, so the Chaldeans (Babylonians) would have every advantage over Judah and would capture them.
1.17 Habakkuk asked God whether he would let the Chaldeans go ahead with their wicked designs. Would the nations and their wealth be given over to the fish nets of the Chaldeans? Habakkuk left this question in the hands of his God.
2.1 The prophet assumed the stance of a sentinel who waited patiently to see what God would say. He was willing to listen attentively to the divine words and accept the divine verdict. No matter how dark the days, the believer must not waver, give way to doubts, or distrust God.

IV. *God's second answer: the Chaldeans will be punished also (2.2–20)*

A. *Chaldea is greedy*

2   Then the LORD answered me and said:
Write the vision;
    make it plain on tablets,
    so that a runner may read it.

3   For there is still a vision for the appointed time;
    it speaks of the end, and does not lie.
If it seems to tarry, wait for it;
    it will surely come, it will not delay.

4   Look at the proud!
    Their spirit is not right in them,
    but the righteous live by their faith.*e*

5   Moreover, wealth*f* is treacherous;
    the arrogant do not endure.
They open their throats wide as Sheol;
    like Death they never have enough.
They gather all nations for themselves,
    and collect all peoples as their own.

6   Shall not everyone taunt such people and, with mocking riddles, say
about them,
    "Alas for you who heap up what is not your own!"
How long will you load yourselves with goods taken in
      pledge?

7   Will not your own creditors suddenly rise,
    and those who make you tremble wake up?
Then you will be booty for them.

8   Because you have plundered many nations,
    all that survive of the peoples shall plunder you—
because of human bloodshed, and violence to the earth,
    to cities and all who live in them.

B. *Chaldea is covetous*

9   "Alas for you who get evil gain for your houses,
    setting your nest on high
    to be safe from the reach of harm!"

10   You have devised shame for your house
    by cutting off many peoples;
    you have forfeited your life.

11   The very stones will cry out from the wall,

e Or faithfulness   f Other Heb Mss read wine

Cross references (right margin):

2.2 Deut 27.8; Isa 8.1; Rev 1.19

2.3 Dan 8.17, 19; 10.14; Ezek 12.25; Heb 10.37, 38

2.4 Rom 1.17; Gal 3.11; Heb 10.38, 39

2.5 Prov 20.1; 21.24; 2 Kings 14.10; Jer 25.9

2.6ff Jer 50.13; v. 12; Ezek 18.12; Am 2.8

2.7 Prov 29.1

2.8 Isa 33.1; Zech 2.8; v. 17

2.9 Jer 22.13; Ezek 22.27; Jer 49.16

2.10 2 Kings 9.26; v. 16; Prov 1.18; Jer 26.29

2.11 Josh 24.27; Lk 19.40

2.2 God's message had to be written down to prove that what Habakkuk said would take place and to make God's word easily known to all who could read. The writing had to be legible and the characters large.
2.3 God reminds Habakkuk of the general principle that even though what he has said may not occur as quickly as we might hope, it will take place at the appointed time.
2.4 *the righteous live by their faith.* This is one O.T. instance of the clear biblical teaching that sinners are justified by faith and not by works. This text is quoted in the N.T. (Rom 1.17; Gal 3.11; Heb 10.38,39) as proof that believers are saved by grace through faith alone.
2.5 *Sheol.* See note on Deut 32.22. God charged

Judah's enemy with the desire of the flesh, the desire of the eyes, and pride in riches (see 1 Jn 2.16). That is, they were proud, covetous, and greedy. Such people had enough, but their vain ambitions drove them to further depredations and conquests.
2.8 God assured Habakkuk that the one who had plundered the nations with such violence would also be plundered. Later on, the Medes and Persians would do to Chaldea (Babylon) what no other people had been able to do, and it would be done in a vicious and violent manner.
2.9ff So covetous was Chaldea that it wanted more and more until its kingdom was elevated to the heights of heaven. It would pay any price and commit any deed to accomplish this objective.

and the plaster[g] will respond from the woodwork.

C. *Chaldea is cruel*

2.12
Mic 3.10;
Nah 3.1
12 "Alas for you who build a town by bloodshed,
  and found a city on iniquity!"

2.13
Isa 50.11;
Jer 51.58
13 Is it not from the LORD of hosts
  that peoples labor only to feed the flames,
  and nations weary themselves for nothing?

2.14
Isa 11.9;
Zech 14.8, 9
14 But the earth will be filled
  with the knowledge of the glory of the LORD,
  as the waters cover the sea.

2.15
Isa 28.7, 8;
Hos 7.5
15 "Alas for you who make your neighbors drink,
  pouring out your wrath[h] until they are drunk,
  in order to gaze on their nakedness!"

2.16
v. 10;
Lam 4.21;
Jer 25.15, 27;
Nah 3.6
16 You will be sated with contempt instead of glory.
  Drink, you yourself, and stagger![i]
  The cup in the LORD's right hand
  will come around to you,
  and shame will come upon your glory!

2.17
Zech 11.1;
v. 8;
Jer 51.35
17 For the violence done to Lebanon will overwhelm you;
  the destruction of the animals will terrify you—[j]
  because of human bloodshed and violence to the earth,
  to cities and all who live in them.

D. *Chaldea is idolatrous*

2.18
Isa 42.17;
Jer 2.27, 28;
10.8, 14;
Zech 10.2;
Ps 115.4, 8
18 What use is an idol
  once its maker has shaped it—
  a cast image, a teacher of lies?
  For its maker trusts in what has been made,
  though the product is only an idol that cannot speak!

2.19
Jer 2.27, 28;
1 Kings 18.26-29;
Jer 10.9, 14;
Ps 135.17
19 Alas for you who say to the wood, "Wake up!"
  to silent stone, "Rouse yourself!"
  Can it teach?
  See, it is gold and silver plated,
  and there is no breath in it at all.

2.20
Mic 1.2;
Zeph 1.7;
Zech 2.13
20 But the LORD is in his holy temple;
  let all the earth keep silence before him!

V. *The prayer of Habakkuk (3.1–19)*

A. *"In wrath . . . remember mercy"*

3.2
Job 42.5, 6;
Ps 119.120;
Jer 10.7;
Ps 85.6;
Isa 54.8
3 A prayer of the prophet Habakkuk according to Shigionoth.

2 O LORD, I have heard of your renown,

---

g Or *beam*   *h* Or *poison*   *i* Q Ms Gk: MT *be uncircumcised*   *j* Gk Syr: Meaning of Heb uncertain

---

2.14 God must be honored as the God of equitable justice and invincible power. The defeat of Chaldea by this omnipotent God would manifest the divine glory, and the earth would be filled with the knowledge of it.
2.15,16 Drunkards were indicted—both those who solicited their neighbors to get drunk and those who got drunk themselves. God's punishment for this sin was to make such people drink the cup of God's fury.
2.18ff The Chaldeans were idolatrous. They had many gods whom they beautified, adorned, trusted,

and prayed to; they supposed that their greatness lay in their affection for these idols—even though they could not walk, talk, or breathe. God would strike the idolaters. Thus would all the world stand silent before Israel's God in awe and admiration.
3.1 *Shigionoth.* The meaning of this is obscure; some scholars think it means "mournful dirge." However, the prayer of Habakkuk is one of triumph, and he may have sung it before the Lord.
3.2 God had answered Habakkuk's earlier petition for understanding, and the prophet had heard God's

and I stand in awe, O Lord, of your work.
In our own time revive it;
   in our own time make it known;
   in wrath may you remember mercy.

B. *God dooms the wicked and saves the repentant*

3 God came from Teman,
   the Holy One from Mount Paran.   *Selah*
His glory covered the heavens,
   and the earth was full of his praise.

4 The brightness was like the sun;
   rays came forth from his hand,
   where his power lay hidden.

5 Before him went pestilence,
   and plague followed close behind.

6 He stopped and shook the earth;
   he looked and made the nations tremble.
The eternal mountains were shattered;
   along his ancient pathways
   the everlasting hills sank low.

7 I saw the tents of Cushan under affliction;
   the tent-curtains of the land of Midian trembled.

8 Was your wrath against the rivers,[k] O Lord?
   Or your anger against the rivers,[k]
   or your rage against the sea,[l]
when you drove your horses,
   your chariots to victory?

9 You brandished your naked bow,
   sated[m] were the arrows at your command.[n]   *Selah*
You split the earth with rivers.

10 The mountains saw you, and writhed;
   a torrent of water swept by;
the deep gave forth its voice.
   The sun[o] raised high its hands;

11 the moon[p] stood still in its exalted place,
   at the light of your arrows speeding by,
   at the gleam of your flashing spear.

12 In fury you trod the earth,
   in anger you trampled nations.

13 You came forth to save your people,
   to save your anointed.
You crushed the head of the wicked house,
   laying it bare from foundation to roof.[n]   *Selah*

14 You pierced with their[q] own arrows the head[r] of his warriors,[s]
   who came like a whirlwind to scatter us,[t]

---

k Or against River   *l Or against Sea*   *m Cn: Heb oaths*   *n Meaning of Heb uncertain*   *o Heb It*
p Heb sun, moon   *q Heb his*   *r Or leader*   *s Vg Compare Gk Syr: Meaning of Heb uncertain*   *t Heb me*

3.3
Am 1.12;
Deut 33.2;
Ps 113.4;
48.10

3.4
Ps 18.12;
Job 26.14

3.5
Ex 12.29, 30;
Num 16.46-49

3.6
Ps 35.5;
114.1-6;
Mic 5.2

3.7
Ex 15.14-16;
Judg 7.24, 25

3.8
Ex 7.19, 20;
14.16, 21;
Deut 33.26;
Ps 68.17

3.9
Gen 26.3;
Deut 7.8;
Ps 78.16;
105.41

3.10
Ps 114.1-6;
98.7, 8;
Ex 14.22

3.11
Josh 10.12-14;
Ps 18.9, 11,
14

3.12
Ps 68.7;
Isa 41.15;
Jer 51.33

3.13
Ex 15.2;
Ps 68.19, 20;
110.6;
Ezek 13.14

3.14
Judg 7.22;
Dan 11.40;
Zech 9.14;
Ps 10.8;
64.2-5

---

speech. Fear came over him, as it had Moses, Isaiah, Daniel, and others with similar experiences. He prayed for a revival, a restoration of God himself to sight and sense, and an exhibition of mercy in the midst of wrath. Whenever God's people experience his anger, they must not despair of his mercy, for it is their last and only plea.
3.3 *from Teman . . . from Mount Paran.* Teman was a district of Edom. The language that Habakkuk used to describe the coming of God to deliver his people resembles that used to describe Israel's deliverance from Egypt.
3.3ff Habakkuk drew attention to earlier manifesta-

tions of God's works among his people. He mentioned the glory of God displayed on Mount Sinai, the plagues that Egypt suffered before releasing Israel from its bondage (v. 5), the conquest of Caanan and the expulsion of the heathen (v .6), the dividing of the Red Sea and the Jordan (vv. 8,15), the sun that stood still (v. 11), and the victories of Israel in Caanan over their enemies. The God who performed these deeds does not sleep. Such recollections still serve God's people, for what he has done in ages past, he can do today.
3.7 *Cushan . . . Midian.* These were both Bedouin tribes near Edom.

gloating as if ready to devour the poor who were in hiding.

3.15
Ps 77.19;
Ex 15.8

15 You trampled the sea with your horses,
churning the mighty waters.

3.16
Jer 23.9; 5.15

16 I hear, and I tremble within;
my lips quiver at the sound.
Rottenness enters into my bones,
and my steps tremble*u* beneath me.
I wait quietly for the day of calamity
to come upon the people who attack us.

C. Habakkuk's unwavering faith

3.17ff
Joel 1.18;
Jer 5.17

17 Though the fig tree does not blossom,
and no fruit is on the vines;
though the produce of the olive fails,
and the fields yield no food;
though the flock is cut off from the fold,
and there is no herd in the stalls,

3.18
Isa 61.10;
Ps 46.1-5;
Isa 12.2

18 yet I will rejoice in the LORD;
I will exult in the God of my salvation.

3.19
2 Sam 22.34;
Ps 18.33;
Deut 33.29

19 GOD, the Lord, is my strength;
he makes my feet like the feet of a deer,
and makes me tread upon the heights.*v*

To the leader: with stringed*w* instruments.

u Cn Compare Gk: Meaning of Heb uncertain   *v* Heb *my heights*   *w* Heb *my stringed*

3.16 Habakkuk trembled as he waited for the day of calamity. His body, bones, and lips were affected. His steps tottered and he could hardly walk. But he knew that there was a future triumph ahead. Believers are still certain that a day of triumph is coming, and that when it does, there will be no more trembling, no more punishments, no more dark nights of the soul. It will be an everlasting victory for endless ages.
3.17–19 Habakkuk demonstrated his supreme faith in God by declaring that even if the fruit trees, fig

trees, olive trees, and vines produced no crops, or if the fields yielded no harvest, all animals died, and there were no flocks in the stalls, he would still trust in God. Outward circumstances would never cause him to leave God, his first love. The joy of the Lord is ever the believer's portion, and it is never out of season. Those who trust God will find their strength in him, and he will give speed to their feet and success to their undertakings.

INTRODUCTION TO

ZEPHANIAH

Authorship, Date, and Background: Zephaniah (whose name means "he whom Yahweh has hidden, or protected") was the great-great-grandson of King Hezekiah and thus of royal blood. He was a prince as well as a prophet. He resided in Jerusalem and prophesied during the reign of Josiah (640–609 B.C.). The prophecies of the book were spoken sometime before 621 B.C., since the reform movement of Josiah (621 B.C.) had not yet occurred. Indeed, Zephaniah may have urged reform on King Josiah.

Judah had experienced revival in Hezekiah's day. Yet Isaiah the prophet had revealed that Judah would be taken into captivity in Babylon, a prophecy that Zephaniah must have been familiar with. Manasseh succeeded his father Hezekiah and was responsible for the erection of altars to Baal. He worshiped the hosts of heaven and made sacred poles to Asherah. The people followed him and idolatry existed everywhere. The sins of Judah were as gross as the sins of the inhabitants of Canaan whom God dispossessed of their lands. The Assyrians took evil Manasseh captive to Babylon. He repented and was returned to his kingship, but he was not successful in reversing the evils he had inaugurated. His son Amon followed him and resorted to his father's old ways. He was assassinated when he had been king for less than two years.

Zephaniah's ministry was cast within the context of the evils of his day. God used him to shock the Judeans in their complacency and to point out their sins to them. He warned them of the impending judgment of God as well as the final day of reckoning at the day of the Lord.

Characteristics and Content: Zephaniah opens with the announcement of the final day of judgment. Judah was to be included in this judgment, for she had trusted in her riches and been idolatrous. In the immediate future her houses would be destroyed and her goods taken; therefore Zephaniah urged them to repent. Next Zephaniah spoke of God's impending judgment on the surrounding nations. He would destroy Gaza and the Philistines; Moab and Ammon would experience what happened to Sodom and Gomorrah; Ethiopia and the Assyrians would suffer the wrath of God.

Zephaniah concentrated on the sins of Jerusalem, a city of violence and crime. She would not listen to God's voice; no one could tell her anything; she refused correction; she did not trust in God or seek him. Her leaders, prophets, and judges were guilty before God. But Zephaniah did not stop with the promise of God's vengeance against Judah. He looked beyond that age to a time when God would restore the fortunes of his people. He promised blessings, not only to the remnant from Judah, but also to the whole Israel of the Lord. At that time Jerusalem would be blessed, the Lord would disperse his people's enemies, and the Lord himself, as Israel's king, would live among them. He glowingly ended his prophecy by asserting that God would reverse their captivity: "At that time I will bring you home, at the time when

I gather you; for I will make you renowned and praised among all the peoples of the earth, when I restore your fortunes before your eyes, says the LORD" (3.20).

Outline:

I. The day of the LORD (1.1—2.3)

II. The judgment of the nations (2.4–15)

III. The sin of Jerusalem and the future salvation (3.1–20)

ZEPHANIAH

I. *The day of the Lord (1.1–2.3)*

A. *Introduction*

1 The word of the Lord that came to Zephaniah son of Cushi son of
Gedaliah son of Amariah son of Hezekiah, in the days of King Josiah
son of Amon of Judah.

1.1
2 Kings 22.1-23,
34; 21.18-26

B. *The judgment on Judah*

2 I will utterly sweep away everything
   from the face of the earth, says the Lord.

1.2
Ezek 33.27

3 I will sweep away humans and animals;
   I will sweep away the birds of the air
   and the fish of the sea.
I will make the wicked stumble. *a*
   I will cut off humanity
   from the face of the earth, says the Lord.

1.3
Isa 6.11, 12;
Jer 9.10;
Ezek 7.19

4 I will stretch out my hand against Judah,
   and against all the inhabitants of Jerusalem;
and I will cut off from this place every remnant of Baal
   and the name of the idolatrous priests;*b*

1.4
Ezek 6.14;
Mic 5.13;
Hos 10.5

5 those who bow down on the roofs
   to the host of the heavens;
those who bow down and swear to the Lord,
   but also swear by Milcom;*c*

1.5
Jer 19.13;
5.2, 7; 49.1

6 those who have turned back from following the Lord,
   who have not sought the Lord or inquired of him.

1.6
Isa 1.4;
Jer 2.13;
Isa 9.13;
Hos 7.7

7 Be silent before the Lord God!
   For the day of the Lord is at hand;
the Lord has prepared a sacrifice,
   he has consecrated his guests.

1.7
Hab 2.20;
Zech 2.13;
Isa 13.6;
v. 14;
Isa 34.6;
Jer 46.10

8 And on the day of the Lord's sacrifice
   I will punish the officials and the king's sons
   and all who dress themselves in foreign attire.

1.8
Isa 24.21;
Jer 39.6;
Isa 2.6

a Cn: Heb *sea, and those who cause the wicked to stumble* *b* Compare Gk: Heb *the idolatrous priests with
the priests* *c* Gk Mss Syr Vg: Heb *Malcam* (or, *their king*)

1.1 *Zephaniah* is the last of the minor prophets before the Babylonian captivity and is placed last in
Scripture before the post-exilic prophets. His name
means "The Lord hides," and his great-great-
grandfather was King Hezekiah. Samaria (Israel or
Ephraim) had been destroyed a century earlier. His
ministry revolved around Judah and Jerusalem.
1.2,3 *I will utterly sweep away everything.* Thus begins this prophet, who predicted that Judah and Jerusalem would be destroyed by God. Humans, animals,
birds, and fish would be destroyed in the holocaust.
1.4 The reason for the judgment was idolatry. The
priests themselves were deeply involved in this apostasy.
1.5 *and swear to the Lord, but also swear by Milcom.*

Milcom seems to be identical to the god Baal as the
"king-god" (cf. NRSV footnote). At this point the
Jews professed to love God and also Milcom, swearing
allegiance to the service of both. God would have none
of this (cf. Mt 6.24).
1.7 Zephaniah's prophecy has a double fulfillment.
The first one occurred when Nebuchadnezzar conquered Judah. At the end of the age, the final day of
judgment will come. *the Lord has prepared a sacrifice,*
i.e., the destruction of the people who had rebelled
against him.
1.8 *dress themselves in foreign attire,* i.e., showing
their desire for foreign gods and foreign ways, and
their contempt for the Lord.

9   On that day I will punish
        all who leap over the threshold,
    who fill their master's house
        with violence and fraud.

10 On that day, says the LORD,
        a cry will be heard from the Fish Gate,
    a wail from the Second Quarter,
        a loud crash from the hills.

11 The inhabitants of the Mortar wail,
        for all the traders have perished;
        all who weigh out silver are cut off.

12 At that time I will search Jerusalem with lamps,
        and I will punish the people
    who rest complacently[d] on their dregs,
        those who say in their hearts,
    "The LORD will not do good,
        nor will he do harm."

13 Their wealth shall be plundered,
        and their houses laid waste.
    Though they build houses,
        they shall not inhabit them;
    though they plant vineyards,
        they shall not drink wine from them.

C. *The day of wrath*

14 The great day of the LORD is near,
        near and hastening fast;
    the sound of the day of the LORD is bitter,
        the warrior cries aloud there.

15 That day will be a day of wrath,
        a day of distress and anguish,
    a day of ruin and devastation,
        a day of darkness and gloom,
    a day of clouds and thick darkness,
16   a day of trumpet blast and battle cry
    against the fortified cities
        and against the lofty battlements.

17 I will bring such distress upon people
        that they shall walk like the blind;
        because they have sinned against the LORD,
    their blood shall be poured out like dust,
        and their flesh like dung.

18 Neither their silver nor their gold
        will be able to save them
        on the day of the LORD's wrath;
    in the fire of his passion
        the whole earth shall be consumed;
        for a full, a terrible end

d Heb *who thicken*

Cross references:

1.9 Jer 5.27; Am 3.10

1.10 Am 8.3; 2 Chr 33.14; 34.22; Ezek 6.13

1.11 Jas 5.1; Zeph 2.5; Hos 9.6

1.12 Jer 16.16, 17; Jer 48.11; Am 6.1; Ezek 8.12; 9.9

1.13 Deut 28.30, 39; Am 5.11; Mic 6.15

1.14 Joel 2.1, 11

1.15 Isa 22.5; Jer 30.7; Am 5.18-20

1.16 Jer 4.19; Isa 2.12-15

1.17 Jer 10.18; Isa 59.10; Ps 79.3; Jer 9.22

1.18 Prov 11.4; Zeph 3.8; vv. 2, 3

1.9 *all who leap over the threshold*, i.e., follow a foreign custom associated with idols.
1.11 *Mortar*, a part of Jerusalem where goldsmiths and merchants lived.
1.12 *dregs*, or sediment in wine, here meaning that they were intoxicated with their pleasures — secure, easy, and afraid of nothing.

1.14ff Zephaniah described the evil that was coming on Judah and Jerusalem in the hour of God's wrath against that nation for its sins.
1.18 *Neither their silver nor their gold* would ransom them from the imminent judgment of God. They had hoarded these metals to bail them out in the day of adversity, but it would do them no good.

he will make of all the inhabitants of the earth.

D. *The call to repentance*

2 Gather together, gather,
O shameless nation,
2 before you are driven away
like the drifting chaff,[e]
before there comes upon you
the fierce anger of the LORD,
before there comes upon you
the day of the LORD's wrath.
3 Seek the LORD, all you humble of the land,
who do his commands;
seek righteousness, seek humility;
perhaps you may be hidden
on the day of the LORD's wrath.

II. *The judgment of the nations (2.4–15)*

A. *Gaza and the Philistines*

4 For Gaza shall be deserted,
and Ashkelon shall become a desolation;
Ashdod's people shall be driven out at noon,
and Ekron shall be uprooted.

5 Ah, inhabitants of the seacoast,
you nation of the Cherethites!
The word of the LORD is against you,
O Canaan, land of the Philistines;
and I will destroy you until no inhabitant is left.
6 And you, O seacoast, shall be pastures,
meadows for shepherds
and folds for flocks.
7 The seacoast shall become the possession
of the remnant of the house of Judah,
on which they shall pasture,
and in the houses of Ashkelon
they shall lie down at evening.
For the LORD their God will be mindful of them
and restore their fortunes.

B. *Moab and Ammon*

8 I have heard the taunts of Moab
and the revilings of the Ammonites,
how they have taunted my people
and made boasts against their territory.
9 Therefore, as I live, says the LORD of hosts,
the God of Israel,
Moab shall become like Sodom

e Cn Compare Gk Syr: Heb *before a decree is born; like chaff a day has passed away*

2.1
Joel 1.14;
Jer 3.3; 6.15
2.2
Isa 17.13;
Hos 13.3;
Nah 1.6;
Zeph 1.18

2.3
Am 5.6;
Ps 76.9;
Am 5.14, 15;
Ps 57.1

2.4
Am 1.7, 8;
Zech 9.5-7

2.5
Ezek 25.16;
Am 3.1;
Isa 14.29-31;
Zeph 3.6

2.6
Isa 17.2

2.7
Mic 4.7;
Isa 32.14;
Ps 80.14;
Lk 1.68;
Ps 126.1, 4

2.8
Ezek 25.3, 6, 8;
Jer 49.1

2.9
Isa 15.1-16, 14;
Am 1.13;
Deut 29.23;
Isa 11.14

2.1 *Gather together.* Zephaniah called the shameful nation to a national assembly for the purpose of fasting, praying, and seeking the face of God in repentance in order to avert judgment.
2.4ff Judgment was coming upon the peoples of Gaza, Ashkelon, Ashdod, and Ekron. There was a fifth city of the Philistines known as Gath, but some think this region was under the control of Judah at

this time.
2.5 *Cherethites,* i.e., Cretans.
2.8–11 The Moabites and Ammonites were guilty of the same provocations. They had reviled God's people and rejoiced in their misfortunes. They were worthy of God's judgment, and he would "be terrible against them."

and the Ammonites like Gomorrah,
  a land possessed by nettles and salt pits,
  and a waste forever.
The remnant of my people shall plunder them,
  and the survivors of my nation shall possess them.

2.10
Isa 16.6;
Jer 48.29;
v. 8

10 This shall be their lot in return for their pride,
  because they scoffed and boasted
  against the people of the Lord of hosts.

2.11
Joel 2.11;
Zeph 1.4;
3.9;
Mal 1.11;
Isa 24.15

11 The Lord will be terrible against them;
  he will shrivel all the gods of the earth,
and to him shall bow down,
  each in its place,
  all the coasts and islands of the nations.

C. *Ethiopia and Assyria*

2.12
Isa 18.1

12 You also, O Ethiopians,*f*
  shall be killed by my sword.

2.13
Isa 14.26;
10.12;
Nah 3.7

13 And he will stretch out his hand against the north,
  and destroy Assyria;
and he will make Nineveh a desolation,
  a dry waste like the desert.

2.14
v. 6;
Isa 13.21;
34.11, 14;
Jer 22.14

14 Herds shall lie down in it,
  every wild animal;*g*
the desert owl*h* and the screech owl*h*
  shall lodge on its capitals;
the owl*i* shall hoot at the window,
  the raven*j* croak on the threshold;
for its cedar work will be laid bare.

2.15
Isa 22.2;
47.8; 32.14;
Jer 18.16;
19.8

15 Is this the exultant city
  that lived secure,
that said to itself,
  "I am, and there is no one else"?
What a desolation it has become,
  a lair for wild animals!
Everyone who passes by it
  hisses and shakes the fist.

III. *The sin of Jerusalem and the future salvation (3.1–20)*

A. *The woe on Jerusalem*

3.1
Jer 5.23;
Ezek 23.30;
Jer 6.6

3.2
Jer 22.21;
5.3;
Ps 78.22;
73.28

3 Ah, soiled, defiled,
  oppressing city!
2 It has listened to no voice;
  it has accepted no correction.
It has not trusted in the Lord;
  it has not drawn near to its God.

f Or *Nubians*; Heb *Cushites*   *g* Tg Compare Gk: Heb *nation*   *h* Meaning of Heb uncertain   *i* Cn: Heb *a voice*   *j* Gk Vg: Heb *desolation*

2.12 The Ethiopians had at times been a terror to Israel (see 2 Chr 14.9). Justice would now catch up with them, and the sword of the Lord would slay them.
2.13ff Definitive judgment was also expressed against Nineveh. People would shake their heads in disbelief at the catastrophe.
3.2 Jerusalem was guilty of four sins: (1) God had given his people the law and sent his prophets but

they had not obeyed his voice; (2) God had disciplined them with his word and with a rod but they had refused correction; (3) they had made alliances with other nations and failed to trust the Lord; and (4) God had given them tokens of his presence and established the ordinances by which they could have communion with him, but they had not drawn near to him. Unless and until God's people changed their ways, there was no hope of deliverance; judgment would fall.

3 The officials within it
    are roaring lions;
  its judges are evening wolves
    that leave nothing until the morning.
4 Its prophets are reckless,
    faithless persons;
  its priests have profaned what is sacred,
    they have done violence to the law.
5 The LORD within it is righteous;
    he does no wrong.
  Every morning he renders his judgment,
    each dawn without fail;
  but the unjust knows no shame.

6 I have cut off nations;
    their battlements are in ruins;
  I have laid waste their streets
    so that no one walks in them;
  their cities have been made desolate,
    without people, without inhabitants.
7 I said, "Surely the city[k] will fear me,
    it will accept correction;
  it will not lose sight[l]
    of all that I have brought upon it."
  But they were the more eager
    to make all their deeds corrupt.

B. The deliverance that is to come

1. The call to wait

8 Therefore wait for me, says the LORD,
    for the day when I arise as a witness.
  For my decision is to gather nations,
    to assemble kingdoms,
  to pour out upon them my indignation,
    all the heat of my anger;
  for in the fire of my passion
    all the earth shall be consumed.

9 At that time I will change the speech of the peoples
    to a pure speech,
  that all of them may call on the name of the LORD
    and serve him with one accord.
10 From beyond the rivers of Ethiopia[m]
    my suppliants, my scattered ones,
    shall bring my offering.

11 On that day you shall not be put to shame
    because of all the deeds by which you have rebelled
    against me;
  for then I will remove from your midst

k Heb *it*   *l* Gk Syr: Heb *its dwelling will not be cut off*   *m* Or *Nubia*; Heb *Cush*

3.3
Ezek 22.27;
Hab 1.8

3.4
Hos 9.7;
Ezek 22.26

3.5
vv. 15, 17;
Deut 32.4;
Jer 3.3

3.6
Zeph 1.16;
Isa 6.11;
Zeph 2.5

3.7
v. 2;
Jer 7.7;
Hos 9.9

3.8
Ps 27.14;
Zeph 2.2;
Joel 3.2;
Zeph 1.18

3.9
Isa 19.18;
Ps 22.27;
Zeph 2.11

3.10
Ps 68.31;
Isa 18.1, 7;
60.6, 7

3.11
Isa 45.17;
Joel 2.26, 27;
Isa 2.12;
5.15;
Ezek 20.40

3.8 *Therefore wait for me.* The O.T. prophesied the coming consolation for Israel (cf. Lk 2.25). For hundreds of years faithful Jews waited for the fulfillment of that promise. It came when Jesus was born.
3.9 *a pure speech,* i.e., one which honors the name of God. Purity of worship will replace idolatrous worship, and God will be glorified. This will not take place until after the second advent of Jesus Christ.
3.11ff This description goes far beyond anything known to God's people. According to premillennialists, Zephaniah is describing the millennial age.

your proudly exultant ones,
and you shall no longer be haughty
in my holy mountain.

12 For I will leave in the midst of you
a people humble and lowly.
They shall seek refuge in the name of the LORD —

13 the remnant of Israel;
they shall do no wrong
and utter no lies,
nor shall a deceitful tongue
be found in their mouths.
Then they will pasture and lie down,
and no one shall make them afraid.

2. *The call to rejoice*

14 Sing aloud, O daughter Zion;
shout, O Israel!
Rejoice and exult with all your heart,
O daughter Jerusalem!

15 The LORD has taken away the judgments against you,
he has turned away your enemies.
The king of Israel, the LORD, is in your midst;
you shall fear disaster no more.

16 On that day it shall be said to Jerusalem:
Do not fear, O Zion;
do not let your hands grow weak.

17 The LORD, your God, is in your midst,
a warrior who gives victory;
he will rejoice over you with gladness,
he will renew you[n] in his love;
he will exult over you with loud singing
18 as on a day of festival.[o]
I will remove disaster from you,[p]
so that you will not bear reproach for it.

19 I will deal with all your oppressors
at that time.
And I will save the lame
and gather the outcast,
and I will change their shame into praise
and renown in all the earth.

20 At that time I will bring you home,
at the time when I gather you;
for I will make you renowned and praised
among all the peoples of the earth,
when I restore your fortunes
before your eyes, says the LORD.

[n] Gk Syr: Heb *he will be silent* [o] Gk Syr: Meaning of Heb uncertain [p] Cn: Heb *I will remove from you; they were*

3.17,18 *in his love.* God is love (1 Jn 4.8). The nature of God's love is described in the Scriptures as being sovereign (Deut 7.7; 10.15), everlasting (Jer 31.3), inextinguishable (Rom 8.39), and never-failing (Isa 49.15,16). The full expression of God's love is his sending Jesus Christ, his only Son, to die on Calvary's cross for sinners (Jn 3.16). God's love becomes ours when we are redeemed, for "God's love has been poured into our hearts by the Holy Spirit that has been given to us" (Rom 5.5).

INTRODUCTION TO

HAGGAI

Authorship, Date, and Background: Haggai, the author of this book, was probably born in Babylon during the captivity and returned to Jerusalem with the remnant in 539–538 B.C. The name Haggai is derived from a word meaning "festival," which suggests he may have been born at the time of some Israelite festival. Nothing is known about his family background nor is the name of his father given. He was a contemporary of Zechariah, with whom he shared the common goal to finish the rebuilding of the temple.

The Jewish remnant that returned from Babylon was few in number. Many of those who remained in Babylon had become well-to-do and preferred their present prosperity to an uncertain future in the land their fathers had left in the captivity. Many had likewise become disillusioned with their faith in the God of Abraham. In other words, those who did return to the land were the spiritually acute, religiously motivated to rebuild the temple. They had a hard time at first, due in part to the evil intentions of their hostile neighbors; thus the work was temporarily stopped. When they then began to prosper economically, their interests shifted from spiritual to material things, and for fifteen years they lost interest in working on the temple.

Haggai's prophecies were given in the year 520 B.C. and consisted of four oracles spoken over a period of four months. He addressed them to the forty thousand immigrants who had returned to the land under the edict of King Cyrus of Persia (see Ezra 1). The return was led by Zerubbabel the governor and Joshua the high priest. Following Haggai's prophecies, the work on the temple was resumed in 520 B.C. and its construction was completed in 516 or 515 B.C. (cf. Ezra 5.1,2).

Characteristics and Content: Haggai's first prophecy was directed toward those Jews who were building more elaborate homes while neglecting the temple. He urged them to rebuild the temple and promised the help and blessing of God in material things if they met their spiritual obligations. In the second message Haggai encouraged Zerubbabel and Joshua concerning the presence of the Lord in their midst. He promised them that God would fill his new house with his glory and that its splendor would be greater than that of the first temple. In the next prophecy Haggai said God's people were disobedient and unclean; therefore, God was withholding his blessing from them. If they repented and did what God wanted, he would bless them and the earth would yield a bountiful harvest. Haggai's last oracle was addressed to Zerubbabel, who was like a signet ring upon God's finger. He had been specially chosen by God for his work and God would honor him. This would take place after God had shaken the heavens and the earth and overthrown and destroyed the strength of the kingdoms of the nations (2.22).

Outline:

I. The call to rebuild the temple: the first message (1.1–15)

II. Comfort and hope: the second message (2.1–9)

III. Holiness versus uncleanness and God's blessing: the third message (2.10–19)

IV. Zerubbabel, the servant of the LORD: the fourth message (2.20–23)

HAGGAI

I. *The call to rebuild the temple: the first message (1.1–15)*

A. *Objections and response*

1 In the second year of King Darius, in the sixth month, on the first day of the month, the word of the LORD came by the prophet Haggai to Zerubbabel son of Shealtiel, governor of Judah, and to Joshua son of Jehozadak, the high priest: ² Thus says the LORD of hosts: These people say the time has not yet come to rebuild the LORD's house. ³ Then the word of the LORD came by the prophet Haggai, saying: ⁴ Is it a time for you yourselves to live in your paneled houses, while this house lies in ruins? ⁵ Now therefore thus says the LORD of hosts: Consider how you have fared. ⁶ You have sown much, and harvested little; you eat, but you never have enough; you drink, but you never have your fill; you clothe yourselves, but no one is warm; and you that earn wages earn wages to put them into a bag with holes.

7 Thus says the LORD of hosts: Consider how you have fared. ⁸ Go up to the hills and bring wood and build the house, so that I may take pleasure in it and be honored, says the LORD. ⁹ You have looked for much, and, lo, it came to little; and when you brought it home, I blew it away. Why? says the LORD of hosts. Because my house lies in ruins, while all of you hurry off to your own houses. ¹⁰ Therefore the heavens above you have withheld the dew, and the earth has withheld its produce. ¹¹ And I have called for a drought on the land and the hills, on the grain, the new wine, the oil, on what the soil produces, on human beings and animals, and on all their labors.

B. *The call to rebuild obeyed*

12 Then Zerubbabel son of Shealtiel, and Joshua son of Jehozadak, the high priest, with all the remnant of the people, obeyed the voice of the LORD their God, and the words of the prophet Haggai, as the LORD their God had sent him; and the people feared the LORD. ¹³ Then Haggai, the messenger of the LORD, spoke to the people with the LORD's message, saying, I am with you, says the LORD. ¹⁴ And the LORD stirred up the spirit of Zerubbabel son of Shealtiel, governor of Judah, and the spirit of Joshua son of Jehozadak, the high priest, and the spirit of all the remnant of the people; and they came and worked on the house of the LORD of hosts, their God, ¹⁵ on the twenty-fourth day of the month, in the sixth month.

1.1 Zech 1.1;
1 Chr 3.17;
Ezra 3.2;
Zech 6.11
1.2 v. 15
1.4 2 Sam 7.2;
v. 9
1.5 Lam 3.40
1.6 Deut 28.38;
Mic 6.14;
Zech 8.10
1.7 v. 1
1.8 Ezra 3.7;
Ps 132.13,
14;
Hag 2.7, 9
1.9 v. 6;
Isa 40.7
1.10 Lev 26.19;
Deut 28.23;
1 Kings 8.35
1.11 Mal 3.9-11;
Deut 28.22;
Hag 2.17
1.12 Hag 2.2;
Isa 1.19;
50.10
1.13 Mal 2.7; 3.1;
Mt 28.30;
Rom 8.31
1.14 2 Chr 36.22;
Ezra 1.1; 5.2,
8

1.1 *Haggai* was among the exiles who had returned from Babylon to rebuild the temple in Jerusalem (see Ezra 5.1; 6.14). Haggai directed his message to both the political leader of God's people (Zerubbabel) and the religious leader (Joshua the high priest). Both were held responsible for the failure of the returned remnant to finish building the temple.
1.2 Haggai appeared on the scene some eighteen years after the return of the remnant from Babylon. The rebuilding of the temple had been neglected by the returned exiles. Haggai had a message from God for Zerubbabel and Joshua: begin rebuilding the

house of God.
1.4ff As to whether it was time to rebuild the temple when the people lacked food, God replied that they seemed to have time to build themselves houses and to plant crops. Why didn't they have time to build God's house? God who is over nature had stopped the course of nature as a direct response to their failure to finish the temple.
1.12 Zerubbabel and Joshua got the message, and their response was prompt. Their spirits were stirred up by God, and they began to obey the divine mandate. The people were also inspired to finish the job.

II. *Comfort and hope: the second message (2.1–9)*

2 In the second year of King Darius, ¹in the seventh month, on the twenty-first day of the month, the word of the LORD came by the prophet Haggai, saying: ²Speak now to Zerubbabel son of Shealtiel, governor of Judah, and to Joshua son of Jehozadak, the high priest, and to the remnant of the people, and say, ³Who is left among you that saw this house in its former glory? How does it look to you now? Is it not in your sight as nothing? ⁴Yet now take courage, O Zerubbabel, says the LORD; take courage, O Joshua, son of Jehozadak, the high priest; take courage, all you people of the land, says the LORD; work, for I am with you, says the LORD of hosts, ⁵according to the promise that I made you when you came out of Egypt. My spirit abides among you; do not fear. ⁶For thus says the LORD of hosts: Once again, in a little while, I will shake the heavens and the earth and the sea and the dry land; ⁷and I will shake all the nations, so that the treasure of all nations shall come, and I will fill this house with splendor, says the LORD of hosts. ⁸The silver is mine, and the gold is mine, says the LORD of hosts. ⁹The latter splendor of this house shall be greater than the former, says the LORD of hosts; and in this place I will give prosperity, says the LORD of hosts.

III. *Holiness versus uncleanness and God's blessing: third message (2.10–19)*

10 On the twenty-fourth day of the ninth month, in the second year of Darius, the word of the LORD came by the prophet Haggai, saying: ¹¹Thus says the LORD of hosts: Ask the priests for a ruling: ¹²If one carries consecrated meat in the fold of one's garment, and with the fold touches bread, or stew, or wine, or oil, or any kind of food, does it become holy? The priests answered, "No." ¹³Then Haggai said, "If one who is unclean by contact with a dead body touches any of these, does it become unclean?" The priests answered, "Yes, it becomes unclean." ¹⁴Haggai then said, So is it with this people, and with this nation before me, says the LORD; and so with every work of their hands; and what they offer there is unclean. ¹⁵But now, consider what will come to pass from this day on. Before a stone was placed upon a stone in the LORD's temple, ¹⁶how did you fare?ᵃ When one came to a heap of twenty measures, there were but ten; when one came to the wine vat to draw fifty measures, there were but twenty. ¹⁷I struck you and all the products of your toil with blight and mildew and hail; yet you did not return to me, says the LORD. ¹⁸Consider from this day on, from the twenty-fourth day of the ninth month. Since the day that the foundation of the LORD's temple was laid, consider: ¹⁹Is

ᵃ Gk: Heb *since they were*

Cross references

2.3 — Ezra 3.12; Zech 4.10
2.4 — Zech 8.9; Acts 7.9
2.5 — Ex 29.45, 46; Neh 9.20; Isa 63.11, 14
2.6 — Heb 12.26; Isa 10.25; 29.17; v. 21
2.7 — Dan 2.44; Isa 60.4-9
2.9 — Isa 66.12; Zech 2.5
2.10 — vv. 1, 20
2.11 — Lev 10.10; Deut 33.10; Mal 2.7
2.12 — Ezek 44.19; Mt 23.19
2.13 — Num 19.11, 22
2.14 — Prov 15.8; Isa 1.11-15
2.15 — Hag 1.5; Ezra 3.10; 4.24
2.16 — Hag 1.6, 9; Zech 8.10
2.17 — 1 Kings 8.37; Am 4.9; Isa 9.13
2.18 — Zech 8.9
2.19 — Zech 8.12

2.1ff This chapter contains three sermons by Haggai. (1) The new temple, inferior though it was to Solomon's, would be spiritually greater (vv. 1–9). (2) Because of their response to finish the temple, God would bless them in material things in great measure (vv. 10–19). (3) Haggai assured faithful Zerubbabel that his work would be remembered and appreciated, for he would be numbered among the ancestral line of the Messiah, whose kingdom would have no end (vv. 20–23).
2.4 *I am with you.* God had withheld his blessing from the people while they delayed in finishing the house of God. But now that they obeyed, God was with them to bless them, help them, and reward them for their obedience to his command.
2.5 *My spirit abides among you.* The presence of God's Spirit among them was the surest guarantee

that the work of God would succeed and that the people of God could proceed without fear.
2.6 *I will shake the heavens and the earth.* God would employ physical phenomena and political upheavals to fully execute the divine will. This earthly confusion would be evidence that God was about to act.
2.11 *Ask the priests for a ruling*, i.e., illustrate the answer from the law. If the people did, they would see that sacred things could not communicate holiness to things they touched, and anyone unclean would contaminate whatever he touched.
2.18 *the twenty-fourth day of the ninth month*, i.e., Kislev, equivalent to early December.
2.19 *From this day on I will bless you.* God favors those who obey his law. Those who do God's bidding will never lack God's blessing.

there any seed left in the barn? Do the vine, the fig tree, the pomegranate, and the olive tree still yield nothing? From this day on I will bless you.

IV. Zerubbabel, the servant of the LORD: fourth message (2.20–23)

20 The word of the LORD came a second time to Haggai on the twenty-fourth day of the month: 21 Speak to Zerubbabel, governor of Judah, saying, I am about to shake the heavens and the earth, 22 and to overthrow the throne of kingdoms; I am about to destroy the strength of the kingdoms of the nations, and overthrow the chariots and their riders; and the horses and their riders shall fall, every one by the sword of a comrade. 23 On that day, says the LORD of hosts, I will take you, O Zerubbabel my servant, son of Shealtiel, says the LORD, and make you like a signet ring; for I have chosen you, says the LORD of hosts.

2.20ff
v. 10
2.21
Hag 1.14;
Zech 4.6-10;
Heb 12.26
2.22
Dan 2.44;
Mic 5.10;
Zech 4.6;
2 Chr 20.23
2.23
Song 8.6;
Jer 22.24;
Isa 42.1;
43.10

2.21 *Zerubbabel.* He was heir to the throne of David and thus is listed in the line of David (Mt 1.12; Lk 3.27). He was active in building the new temple, and God promised to give him a house. He was chosen of God and said to be "like a signet ring." (v. 23; a "signet" was a small, official seal). Jeconiah had been as a signet on God's right hand but was removed from that relationship (Jer 22.24); God would now restore the royal line. Jesus Christ is the signet on God's right hand. All power has been given to him (Mt. 28.18).

INTRODUCTION TO

ZECHARIAH

Authorship, Date, and Background: Zechariah (whose name means "God has remembered") was the son of Berechiah and the grandson of Iddo. The latter returned from Babylon with Zerubbabel and Joshua and was in the priestly line. Zechariah may well be the one mentioned in Neh 12.16. He was a contemporary of Haggai and had similar interests in the rebuilding of the temple (see Ezra 5.1,2). His prophetic ministry began in 520 B.C. The historical situation is the same as that described for Haggai. Those who returned to Jerusalem were among the poorer people of the captivity, for the wealthier ones stayed behind. The conditions around Jerusalem and the utter desolation created apathy among the refugees, who became more interested in scratching a living from the unproductive soil than in rebuilding the temple.

Many modern scholars maintain that the second half of this book (chs. 9—14) was written by someone other than Zechariah. Evangelical scholars, on the other hand, have little problem with ascribing the entire book to Zechariah, although it is probable that the latter portion of the book was written much later in his life than the earlier part.

Characteristics and Content: The book of Zechariah is readily divided into two distinct and different segments. The first (chs. 1—8) is historical and dealt with the situation in Jerusalem at the time of its writing. The second half (chs. 9—14) is apocalyptic, having to do with prophecy and the end of the age. Zechariah's first emphasis was on the rebuilding of the temple. With Haggai, he urged the people to complete the unfinished task that had been interrupted. He said God would bless his people if they obeyed him and finished rebuilding. Beginning with 1.7, Zechariah wrote of a series of night visions he received from God. The vision of the red horse showed that God was watching over Judah. The vision of the four animal horns and the four blacksmiths indicated the defeat of Judah's enemies. The measuring line vision revealed what the expanded city of Jerusalem would be like. The dirty-clothed Joshua, reclothed in clean clothes, portrayed the removal of sin and the spiritual reformation of God's people. The gold lampstand whose oil was supplied by two olive trees assured Zerubbabel that God by his Spirit would accomplish his purpose. The scroll flying through the air evidenced God's curse on stealing and lying. The vision of the ephah depicted the removal of sin from Judah to Babylon. The vision of the four chariots referred to God's sovereign control as he patrolled the four corners of the earth.

Zechariah followed up the visions with a section devoted to the consecration of Joshua, who was considered to be a representative of the Messiah (the "Branch"), and another one having to do with fasting as a reminder to the people of the fall of Jerusalem.

Beginning with ch. 9, Zechariah looked to the future. He pronounced God's judgment on the surrounding nations and foresaw the prospects of a triumphant king over Jerusalem. God ultimately would save and protect his own people. Faithless shepherds would be destroyed by judgment. But God would punish his people first for their refusal to accept and follow the true shepherd. Even this abandonment of his people by God was part of the divine plan. Someday Jerusalem would be restored and victorious. Before that happened Jerusalem would be torn apart and many would die, but the coming shepherd would rescue the city and the remnant would acknowledge that the Lord is God. The Mount of Olives would be split and the Lord would become the king of the entire earth. All those who survived would go to Jerusalem to worship the Lord the king, and they would keep the festival of booths. Jerusalem would become the capital city for all the nations of the world.

Outline:

ZECHARIAH

I. *Messages during the building of the temple (1.1–8.23)*

A. *First message: call for national repentance*

1.1
Ezra 4.24;
Hag 1.1;
Neh 12.4, 16
1.3
Isa 31.6;
Mal 3.7;
Jas 4.8
1.4
2 Chr 36.15;
Hos 14.1;
Jer 6.17;
11.7, 8
1.6
Jer 12.16, 17;
Lam 2.17

1 In the eighth month, in the second year of Darius, the word of the LORD came to the prophet Zechariah son of Berechiah son of Iddo, saying: 2 The LORD was very angry with your ancestors. 3 Therefore say to them, Thus says the LORD of hosts: Return to me, says the LORD of hosts, and I will return to you, says the LORD of hosts. 4 Do not be like your ancestors, to whom the former prophets proclaimed, "Thus says the LORD of hosts, Return from your evil ways and from your evil deeds." But they did not hear or heed me, says the LORD. 5 Your ancestors, where are they? And the prophets, do they live forever? 6 But my words and my statutes, which I commanded my servants the prophets, did they not overtake your ancestors? So they repented and said, "The LORD of hosts has dealt with us according to our ways and deeds, just as he planned to do."

B. *Second message: the eight visions of God's care for Israel*

1. *The horsemen among the myrtles*

1.8
Josh 5.13;
Rev 6.4;
Zech 6.2-7
1.9
Zech 2.3; 4.5
1.10
Heb 1.14
1.11
Isa 14.7
1.12
Hab 1.2;
Dan 9.2

7 On the twenty-fourth day of the eleventh month, the month of Shebat, in the second year of Darius, the word of the LORD came to the prophet Zechariah son of Berechiah son of Iddo; and Zechariah*a* said, 8 In the night I saw a man riding on a red horse! He was standing among the myrtle trees in the glen; and behind him were red, sorrel, and white horses. 9 Then I said, "What are these, my lord?" The angel who talked with me said to me, "I will show you what they are." 10 So the man who was standing among the myrtle trees answered, "They are those whom the LORD has sent to patrol the earth." 11 Then they spoke to the angel of the LORD who was standing among the myrtle trees, "We have patrolled the earth, and lo, the whole earth remains at peace." 12 Then the angel of the LORD said, "O LORD of hosts, how long will you withhold mercy from Jerusalem and the cities of Judah, with which you have been angry these

---

a Heb *and he*

1.1 Nine of the minor prophets prophesied before the destruction of Jerusalem. The other three — Haggai, Zechariah and Malachi — prophesied after the captivity ended and appear last in the canon of the O.T. Haggai and Zechariah were contemporaries (see Ezra 5.1; 6.14); both prophesied before Malachi. *the word of the LORD came to the prophet.* Zechariah spoke the word God gave him, not his own words. The Holy Spirit of God was behind it (cf. 2 Pet 1.20,21).
1.2 Before Zechariah talked of mercy, he spoke about repentance. It was law before gospel. God was displeased with the Jews' ancestors and had a complaint against them.
1.3 In the name of God, he urged the returnees to turn to God, so that God could turn to them. He encouraged penitence by calling attention to the misdeeds of their ancestors (v. 4), warning them not to

follow their wicked example.
1.5,6 Prophets and people of the past had died, but the word of God lives forever. What the prophets prophesied and what God threatened came to pass. Since God had done what he threatened, the Jews should pay attention to Zechariah's prophecies directed to them.
1.7 *Shebat.* Equivalent to January — February.
1.9 Some think the rider on the red horse was an O.T. appearance of Christ; he earlier had appeared to Joshua with his sword drawn (Josh 5.13,14).
1.11 The report given to the angel rider on the red horse was that the whole world was at peace and prosperous. However, Jerusalem was surrounded by oppressive enemies and was suffering from internal dissension.

seventy years?" ¹³ Then the LORD replied with gracious and comforting words to the angel who talked with me. ¹⁴ So the angel who talked with me said to me, Proclaim this message: Thus says the LORD of hosts; I am very jealous for Jerusalem and for Zion. ¹⁵ And I am extremely angry with the nations that are at ease; for while I was only a little angry, they made the disaster worse. ¹⁶ Therefore, thus says the LORD, I have returned to Jerusalem with compassion; my house shall be built in it, says the LORD of hosts, and the measuring line shall be stretched out over Jerusalem. ¹⁷ Proclaim further: Thus says the LORD of hosts: My cities shall again overflow with prosperity; the LORD will again comfort Zion and again choose Jerusalem.

2. The four horns and the four smiths

18ᵇ And I looked up and saw four horns. ¹⁹ I asked the angel who talked with me, "What are these?" And he answered me, "These are the horns that have scattered Judah, Israel, and Jerusalem." ²⁰ Then the LORD showed me four blacksmiths. ²¹ And I asked, "What are they coming to do?" He answered, "These are the horns that scattered Judah, so that no head could be raised; but these have come to terrify them, to strike down the horns of the nations that lifted up their horns against the land of Judah to scatter its people."ᶜ

3. The measuring line of Jerusalem

2ᵈ I looked up and saw a man with a measuring line in his hand. ² Then I asked, "Where are you going?" He answered me, "To measure Jerusalem, to see what is its width and what is its length." ³ Then the angel who talked with me came forward, and another angel came forward to meet him, ⁴ and said to him, "Run, say to that young man: Jerusalem shall be inhabited like villages without walls, because of the multitude of people and animals in it. ⁵ For I will be a wall of fire all around it, says the LORD, and I will be the glory within it."

6 Up, up! Flee from the land of the north, says the LORD; for I have spread you abroad like the four winds of heaven, says the LORD. ⁷ Up! Escape to Zion, you that live with daughter Babylon. ⁸ For thus said the LORD of hosts (after his gloryᵉ sent me) regarding the nations that plundered you: Truly, one who touches you touches the apple of my eye.ᶠ ⁹ See now, I am going to raiseᵍ my hand against them, and they shall become plunder for their own slaves. Then you will know that the LORD of hosts has sent me. ¹⁰ Sing and rejoice, O daughter Zion! For lo, I will come and dwell in your midst, says the LORD. ¹¹ Many nations shall join themselves to the LORD on that day, and shall be my people; and I will dwell in your midst. And you shall know that the LORD of hosts has sent me to you. ¹² The LORD will inherit Judah as his portion in the holy land, and will again choose Jerusalem.

13 Be silent, all people, before the LORD; for he has roused himself from his holy dwelling.

ᵇ Ch 2.1 in Heb   ᶜ Heb it   ᵈ Ch 2.5 in Heb   ᵉ Cn: Heb after glory he   ᶠ Heb his eye   ᵍ Or wave

Cross references (margin)

1.13
Zech 4.1;
Isa 40.1, 2
1.14
Zech 8.2
1.15
Ps 123.4;
Am 1.11
1.16
Isa 54.8;
Zech 2.1, 2, 10
1.17
Isa 44.26;
51.3;
Zech 2.12;
3.2

1.20
Isa 44.12;
54.16
1.21
Ps 75.10

2.1
Zech 1.18;
Ezek 40.3
2.2
Ezek 40.3;
Rev 21.15-17
2.4
Ezek 38.11;
Jer 30.19
2.5
Isa 26.1;
Zech 9.8;
Rev 21.23
2.6
Isa 48.20;
Jer 1.14;
Ezek 17.21
2.8
Isa 60.7-9;
Deut 32.10
2.9
Isa 11.15;
Zech 4.9
2.10
Isa 12.6;
Zeph 3.14;
Lev 26.12;
Ezek 37.27
2.12
Deut 32.9;
Zech 1.17
2.13
Hab 2.20;
Ps 78.65;
Isa 51.9

1.14ff God was jealous for Jerusalem and Zion. He was angry with the nations who had plotted evil (1.14,15), and he had come back to Jerusalem with compassion, determined that the temple, the city, and his people would prosper.
1.18ff The four horns were enemy nations. They were overcome by God sending blacksmiths to cut off the horns that were pointed at Judah. This would nullify their power.
2.4 Some consider that this prophecy about a Jerusalem too large to be contained within its walls and to be indwelt by God's glory is yet future. Many Gentiles

are to come to the knowledge of God (v. 11; see Rom 11.13–25).
2.5 a wall of fire. Jerusalem would be safe. As a consuming fire, God would surround the city with his fire and protect it against any and all enemies.
2.6,7 Cyrus' decree, allowing the Jews to return to Palestine, brought back a remnant; however, many chose to remain in the land of their captivity. Zechariah urged them to return to Jerusalem, where the temple was being rebuilt. God would regather the dispersed people and comfort them in the land from which their ancestors had been removed as captives.

4. Joshua as the symbol of the priestly nation

3 Then he showed me the high priest Joshua standing before the angel of the Lord, and Satan[h] standing at his right hand to accuse him. 2 And the Lord said to Satan,[h] "The Lord rebuke you, O Satan![h] The Lord who has chosen Jerusalem rebuke you! Is not this man a brand plucked from the fire?" 3 Now Joshua was dressed with filthy clothes as he stood before the angel. 4 The angel said to those who were standing before him, "Take off his filthy clothes." And to him he said, "See, I have taken your guilt away from you, and I will clothe you with festal apparel." 5 And I said, "Let them put a clean turban on his head." So they put a clean turban on his head and clothed him with the apparel; and the angel of the Lord was standing by.

6 Then the angel of the Lord assured Joshua, saying 7 "Thus says the Lord of hosts: If you will walk in my ways and keep my requirements, then you shall rule my house and have charge of my courts, and I will give you the right of access among those who are standing here. 8 Now listen, Joshua, high priest, you and your colleagues who sit before you! For they are an omen of things to come: I am going to bring my servant the Branch. 9 For on the stone that I have set before Joshua, on a single stone with seven facets, I will engrave its inscription, says the Lord of hosts, and I will remove the guilt of this land in a single day. 10 On that day, says the Lord of hosts, you shall invite each other to come under your vine and fig tree."

5. The lampstand and the two olive trees

4 The angel who talked with me came again, and wakened me, as one is wakened from sleep. 2 He said to me, "What do you see?" And I said, "I see a lampstand all of gold, with a bowl on the top of it; there are seven lamps on it, with seven lips on each of the lamps that are on the top of it. 3 And by it there are two olive trees, one on the right of the bowl and the other on its left." 4 I said to the angel who talked with me, "What are these, my lord?" 5 Then the angel who talked with me answered me, "Do you not know what these are?" I said, "No, my lord." 6 He said to me, "This is the word of the Lord to Zerubbabel: Not by might, nor by power, but by my spirit, says the Lord of hosts. 7 What are you, O great mountain? Before Zerubbabel you shall become a plain; and he shall bring out the top stone amid shouts of 'Grace, grace to it!'"

8 Moreover the word of the Lord came to me, saying, 9 "The hands

h Or *the Accuser;* Heb *the Adversary*

Cross references (left margin):

3.1 Hag 1.1; Ps 109.6
3.2 Jude 9, 23; Am 4.11
3.4 Isa 43.25; Rev 19.8
3.5 Ex 29.6
3.7 1 Kings 3.14; Ezek 44.16; Deut 17.9; Zech 4.14
3.8 Isa 20.3; Ezek 12.11; Isa 4.2; 53.2; Jer 33.15
3.9 Isa 28.16; Zech 4.10; Jer 31.34; Mic 7.18
3.10 1 Kings 4.25; Isa 36.16
4.1 Zech 1.9; 2.3; Dan 8.18
4.2 Ex 25.31; Rev 1.12; Ex 25.37; Rev 4.5
4.3 Rev 11.4
4.5 Zech 1.9
4.6 Hag 2.4, 5; Hos 1.7; Eph 6.17
4.7 Jer 51.25; Ps 118.22; Ezra 3.10, 11

2.13 *Be silent . . . before the* Lord. When standing before the Lord, we must listen, for he is our God and Savior. We must not tell him what he should do or quarrel with him about what he has done.

3.1 *Joshua the high priest* was the son of Jehozadak (see 1 Chr 6.14). Like the Joshua who succeeded Moses in the leadership of Israel, he represents Christ.

3.4 *filthy clothes.* These reflect the sins of the people. Like Christ, Joshua has taken these sins upon himself, although it is only the sacrifice of Christ on Calvary that has atoned for them. Believers today have been given new clothing, the garments of Christ's righteousness (cf. Rom 13.14; Eph 4.24), to replace their own filthy rags.

3.8 *the Branch,* i.e., the Christ. At Christ's first coming the Jews were blinded and could not see him as the Messiah. At the end of the age Israel will receive him by faith and will submit to his rulership (see Rom 11.13–25).

3.9 *the stone.* Christ is not only the Branch; he is also the stone—one which the builders rejected but has now become the cornerstone (see Mt 21.42; 1 Pet 2.7). Having won the victory by his atoning death at

Calvary, he will purge his people from all their transgressions.

4.2 In the vision of the lampstand and the two olive trees, Christ is represented by the lampstand. He, not Jerusalem or any other place, is the center of our unity. Zechariah calls the angel, "my lord" (v. 4), a reference to the deity of Jesus Christ.

4.6 *Zerubbabel* was the governor of Judah, who was given the responsibility for rebuilding the temple (see Hag 1.1; 2.23). *Not by might, nor by power, but by my spirit.* Human might or power is different from the might and power of the Holy Spirit. The former is external and visible, the latter is invisible and apparent only to the eyes of faith. The Spirit of God, for example, had influenced Cyrus to release the captives, and God had worked secretly in the hearts of the captives to accept that decree and return to the land. God's way and will are often carried on successfully when they are working silently, operating without external human force.

4.7 *he shall bring out the top stone,* i.e., "he will finish building this temple."

of Zerubbabel have laid the foundation of this house; his hands shall also complete it. Then you will know that the LORD of hosts has sent me to you. 10 For whoever has despised the day of small things shall rejoice, and shall see the plummet in the hand of Zerubbabel.

"These seven are the eyes of the LORD, which range through the whole earth." 11 Then I said to him, "What are these two olive trees on the right and the left of the lampstand?" 12 And a second time I said to him, "What are these two branches of the olive trees, which pour out the oil*i* through the two golden pipes?" 13 He said to me, "Do you not know what these are?" I said, "No, my lord." 14 Then he said, "These are the two anointed ones who stand by the Lord of the whole earth."

6. *The flying scroll*

5 Again I looked up and saw a flying scroll. 2 And he said to me, "What do you see?" I answered, "I see a flying scroll; its length is twenty cubits, and its width ten cubits." 3 Then he said to me, "This is the curse that goes out over the face of the whole land; for everyone who steals shall be cut off according to the writing on one side, and everyone who swears falsely*j* shall be cut off according to the writing on the other side. 4 I have sent it out, says the LORD of hosts, and it shall enter the house of the thief, and the house of anyone who swears falsely by my name; and it shall abide in that house and consume it, both timber and stones."

7. *The basket of iniquity carried back to Babylon*

5 Then the angel who talked with me came forward and said to me, "Look up and see what this is that is coming out." 6 I said, "What is it?" He said, "This is a basket*k* coming out." And he said, "This is their iniquity*l* in all the land." 7 Then a leaden cover was lifted, and there was a woman sitting in the basket! 8 And he said, "This is Wickedness." So he thrust her back into the basket,*k* and pressed the leaden weight down on its mouth. 9 Then I looked up and saw two women coming forward. The wind was in their wings; they had wings like the wings of a stork, and they lifted up the basket*k* between earth and sky. 10 Then I said to the angel who talked with me, "Where are they taking the basket?"*k* 11 He said to me, "To the land of Shinar, to build a house for it; and when this is prepared, they will set the basket*k* down there on its base."

8. *The four chariots of divine judgment*

6 And again I looked up and saw four chariots coming out from between two mountains—mountains of bronze. 2 The first chariot had red horses, the second chariot black horses, 3 the third chariot white horses, and the fourth chariot dappled gray*m* horses. 4 Then I said to the angel who talked with me, "What are these, my lord?" 5 The angel an-

i Cn: Heb *gold*   *j* The word *falsely* added from verse 4   *k* Heb *ephah*   *l* Gk Compare Syr: Heb *their eye*
m Compare Gk: Meaning of Heb uncertain

4.9
Ezra 3.10;
6.15;
Zech 2.9, 11;
6.15;
Isa 48.16;
Zech 2.8
4.10
Hag 2.3;
Zech 3.9;
Rev 8.2;
Zech 1.10
4.11
v. 3
4.14
Rev 11.4;
Zech 3.1-7;
Mic 4.13

5.1
Ezek 2.9
5.3
Jer 26.6;
Ex 20.15;
Mal 3.8, 9;
v. 4
5.4
Mal 3.5;
Hos 4.2, 3;
Lev 14.45;
Hab 2.9-11

5.5
Zech 1.9, 18
5.6
Lev 19.36;
Am 8.5

5.8
Hos 12.7;
Am 8.5;
Mic 6.11
5.9
v. 5;
Jer 8.7
5.11
Jer 29.5, 28;
Gen 10.10

6.1
Zech 1.18;
5.9; v. 5
6.2
Rev 6.4, 5
6.3
Rev 6.2
6.4
Zech 5.10
6.5
Jer 49.36;
Ezek 37.9;
Mt 24.31;
Rev 7.1

4.14 *the two anointed ones* are Joshua and Zerubbabel—the first having charge of the spiritual affairs of Jerusalem and the other the political affairs of the restored nation. State and church leaders are God's anointed, doing his work for his glory and for the good of the people.
5.1ff A flying scroll, thirty by fifteen feet, was unrolled. It symbolized the terrible judgment of God against sinners. It covered the earth and was directed against those who stole and who swore rashly and profanely.
5.6 *Basket* (ephah–NRSV footnote). In this basket sat a woman, and along with her a leaden weight. She was pressed by the leaden weight and the basket was carried away to some far country. Some think this

refers to the final dispersion of the Jews following the destruction of Jerusalem in A.D. 70 by Titus and Vespasian.
5.11 *the land of Shinar*, i.e., Babylon, which had, by the time of Zechariah, become a symbol for world idolatry and wickedness. Iniquity was symbolically taken from Judah to Babylon.
6.1ff The four chariots of divine judgment were sent abroad to execute God's vengeance. *The north country* (v. 6) seems to picture God's judgment against Babylon, overthrown by the Persians. It may also allude to the end of Babylon in the N.T. (see Rev 11.15; 18.21). *My spirit at rest* (v. 8) means that the judgment of God had been executed and his anger assuaged.

swered me, "These are the four winds[n] of heaven going out, after presenting themselves before the Lord of all the earth. 6 The chariot with the black horses goes toward the north country, the white ones go toward the west country,[o] and the dappled ones go toward the south country." 7 When the steeds came out, they were impatient to get off and patrol the earth. And he said, "Go, patrol the earth." So they patrolled the earth. 8 Then he cried out to me, "Lo, those who go toward the north country have set my spirit at rest in the north country."

9. Sequel: Joshua crowned as a type of the Branch

9 The word of the Lord came to me: 10 Collect silver and gold[p] from the exiles — from Heldai, Tobijah, and Jedaiah — who have arrived from Babylon; and go the same day to the house of Josiah son of Zephaniah. 11 Take the silver and gold and make a crown,[q] and set it on the head of the high priest Joshua son of Jehozadak; 12 say to him: Thus says the Lord of hosts: Here is a man whose name is Branch: for he shall branch out in his place, and he shall build the temple of the Lord. 13 It is he that shall build the temple of the Lord; he shall bear royal honor, and shall sit upon his throne and rule. There shall be a priest by his throne, with peaceful understanding between the two of them. 14 And the crown[r] shall be in the care of Heldai,[s] Tobijah, Jedaiah, and Josiah[t] son of Zephaniah, as a memorial in the temple of the Lord.

15 Those who are far off shall come and help to build the temple of the Lord; and you shall know that the Lord of hosts has sent me to you. This will happen if you diligently obey the voice of the Lord your God.

C. *Third message: the meaning of true piety*

1. *The hypocrisy of extra fasts*

7 In the fourth year of King Darius, the word of the Lord came to Zechariah on the fourth day of the ninth month, which is Chislev. 2 Now the people of Bethel had sent Sharezer and Regem-melech and their men, to entreat the favor of the Lord, 3 and to ask the priests of the house of the Lord of hosts and the prophets, "Should I mourn and practice abstinence in the fifth month, as I have done for so many years?" 4 Then the word of the Lord of hosts came to me: 5 Say to all the people of the land and the priests: When you fasted and lamented in the fifth month and in the seventh, for these seventy years, was it for me that you fasted? 6 And when you eat and when you drink, do you not eat and drink only for yourselves? 7 Were not these the words that the Lord proclaimed by the former prophets, when Jerusalem was inhabited and in prosperity, along with the towns around it, and when the Negeb and the Shephelah were inhabited?

2. *The exile a result of their oppressions*

8 The word of the Lord came to Zechariah, saying: 9 Thus says the

Cross references (left margin)

6.6 Jer 1.14; Ezek 1.4; Dan 11.5
6.7 Zech 1.10
6.8 Ezek 5.13
6.9 Zech 1.1; 7.1; 8.1
6.10 Jer 28.6
6.11 Ezra 3.2; Hag 1.1
6.12 Isa 11.1; Zech 3.8; Isa 53.2
6.13 Isa 9.6; 22.24; 9.7; Ps 110.1, 4
6.14 v. 11
6.15 Isa 57.19; 60.10; Zech 4.9; 3.7
7.1 Zech 1.1, 7; Neh 1.1
7.2 Jer 26.19; Zech 8.21
7.3 Jer 52.12; Zech 8.19; 12.12-14
7.5 Isa 58.5; Zech 8.19; Jer 41.1; Rom 14.6
7.7 Zech 1.4; Jer 22.21; 17.26
7.9 Ezek 18.8; Zech 8.16; Mic 6.8

---

[n] Or *spirits*   [o] Cn: Heb *go after them*   [p] Cn Compare verse 11: Heb lacks *silver and gold*   [q] Gk Mss Syr Tg: Heb *crowns*   [r] Gk Syr: Heb *crowns*   [s] Syr Compare verse 10: Heb *Helem*   [t] Syr Compare verse 10: Heb *Hen*

6.10 Some Jews who remained in Babylon had come with offerings of gold and silver. They were met, not by a priest, but by God's prophet.

6.11 A crown was placed on Joshua's head, the Jews' spiritual leader. Zerubbabel, the political leader, was not crowned.

6.12 The crowning of Joshua represents the crowning of the Branch, i.e., the Messiah, who is priest and king.

6.13 Even as the high priest Joshua rebuilt the tem-

ple in Jerusalem, so shall the Branch, Jesus Christ, build the spiritual temple — the church (see 1 Cor 3.16,17; 2 Cor. 6.16; Eph 2.21,22).

7.1 *Chislev* in this instance is equivalent to late November. *fourth year,* 518 B.C.

7.3 *Should I mourn and practice abstinence?,* i.e., "Should I follow the custom of fasting and mourning during the month of August each year, as I have been doing so long?" This annual event commemorated the destruction of Jerusalem in 587 B.C.

LORD of hosts: Render true judgments, show kindness and mercy to one another; 10 do not oppress the widow, the orphan, the alien, or the poor; and do not devise evil in your hearts against one another. 11 But they refused to listen, and turned a stubborn shoulder, and stopped their ears in order not to hear. 12 They made their hearts adamant in order not to hear the law and the words that the LORD of hosts had sent by his spirit through the former prophets. Therefore great wrath came from the LORD of hosts. 13 Just as, when I u called, they would not hear, so, when they called, I would not hear, says the LORD of hosts, 14 and I scattered them with a whirlwind among all the nations that they had not known. Thus the land they left was desolate, so that no one went to and fro, and a pleasant land was made desolate.

3. God's intention to restore Jerusalem

8 The word of the LORD of hosts came to me, saying: 2 Thus says the LORD of hosts: I am jealous for Zion with great jealousy, and I am jealous for her with great wrath. 3 Thus says the LORD: I will return to Zion, and will dwell in the midst of Jerusalem; Jerusalem shall be called the faithful city, and the mountain of the LORD of hosts shall be called the holy mountain. 4 Thus says the LORD of hosts: Old men and old women shall again sit in the streets of Jerusalem, each with staff in hand because of their great age. 5 And the streets of the city shall be full of boys and girls playing in its streets. 6 Thus says the LORD of hosts: Even though it seems impossible to the remnant of this people in these days, should it also seem impossible to me, says the LORD of hosts? 7 Thus says the LORD of hosts: I will save my people from the east country and from the west country; 8 and I will bring them to live in Jerusalem. They shall be my people and I will be their God, in faithfulness and in righteousness.

9 Thus says the LORD of hosts: Let your hands be strong—you that have recently been hearing these words from the mouths of the prophets who were present when the foundation was laid for the rebuilding of the temple, the house of the LORD of hosts. 10 For before those days there were no wages for people or for animals, nor was there any safety from the foe for those who went out or came in, and I set them all against one another. 11 But now I will not deal with the remnant of this people as in the former days, says the LORD of hosts. 12 For there shall be a sowing of peace; the vine shall yield its fruit, the ground shall give its produce, and the skies shall give their dew; and I will cause the remnant of this people to possess all these things. 13 Just as you have been a cursing among the nations, O house of Judah and house of Israel, so I will save you and you shall be a blessing. Do not be afraid, but let your hands be strong.

14 For thus says the LORD of hosts: Just as I purposed to bring disaster upon you, when your ancestors provoked me to wrath, and I did not relent, says the LORD of hosts, 15 so again I have purposed in these days to do good to Jerusalem and to the house of Judah; do not be afraid.

u Heb he

7.10 Deut 24.17; Jer 7.6; Mic 2.1
7.11 Jer 11.10; 17.23; 5.21; Acts 7.57
7.12 Ezek 11.19; 36.26; Neh 9.29, 30; Dan 9.11
7.13 Prov 1.24; Isa 1.15; Mic 3.4
7.14 Deut 4.27; Jer 23.19; 44.6; Isa 60.15
8.2 Zech 1.14
8.3 Zech 1.16; 2.10, 11; Jer 31.23
8.4 Isa 65.20
8.5 Jer 30.19, 20
8.6 Ps 118.23; Jer 32.17, 27
8.7 Isa 11.11; 43.5, 6; Am 9.14
8.8 Zech 10.10; Ezek 37.25; Zech 2.11
8.9 Hag 2.4; Ezra 5.1
8.10 Hag 1.6
8.11 Ps 103.9; Isa 12.1
8.12 Joel 2.22; Hag 1.10; Isa 61.7
8.13 Jer 42.18; Gen 12.2; Ruth 4.11
8.14 Jer 31.28; Ezek 24.14
8.15 Jer 29.11; v. 13

7.12 The words sent by God through the prophets were not the words of the prophets; they were the words of God, revealed to them by his Spirit. When the people of Israel despised the word of the prophets, they were offending God the sender and resisting the Holy Spirit.
7.13 When the people turn a deaf ear to the words of God, God in turn refuses to listen to their prayers. Why should God answer the prayers of those who profess to own his name but ignore and despise his word?
8.1ff God intended to restore Jerusalem to its former glory. This was accomplished in part in the Maccabean period, many years before the birth of Christ.

According to the premillennial viewpoint, the full glory of which this prophecy speaks awaits the return of Christ and the establishment of his millennial kingdom. Amillennialists see the church of Jesus Christ, i.e., the new Jerusalem of God (cf. Gal 4.26), as the place where God's glory dwells and the place where Jews and Gentiles have become one.
8.11ff Despite economic distress, the danger of traveling away from home, and the hatred of their enemies, God would restore his people and bless them. Judah would, in turn, be a blessing to all nations (v. 13). Therefore they need not fear; they could act confidently and with strength.

16 These are the things that you shall do: Speak the truth to one another, render in your gates judgments that are true and make for peace, 17 do not devise evil in your hearts against one another, and love no false oath; for all these are things that I hate, says the Lord.

4. The nations to seek the Lord in Jerusalem

18 The word of the Lord of hosts came to me, saying: 19 Thus says the Lord of hosts: The fast of the fourth month, and the fast of the fifth, and the fast of the seventh, and the fast of the tenth, shall be seasons of joy and gladness, and cheerful festivals for the house of Judah: therefore love truth and peace.

20 Thus says the Lord of hosts: Peoples shall yet come, the inhabitants of many cities; 21 the inhabitants of one city shall go to another, saying, "Come, let us go to entreat the favor of the Lord, and to seek the Lord of hosts; I myself am going." 22 Many peoples and strong nations shall come to seek the Lord of hosts in Jerusalem, and to entreat the favor of the Lord. 23 Thus says the Lord of hosts: In those days ten men from nations of every language shall take hold of a Jew, grasping his garment and saying, "Let us go with you, for we have heard that God is with you."

II. Messages after the building of the temple (9.1–14.21)

A. Messiah king rejected, triumphant

1. The coming of the king announced

9 An Oracle.

The word of the Lord is against the land of Hadrach
and will rest upon Damascus.
For to the Lord belongs the capital^v of Aram,^w
as do all the tribes of Israel;
2 Hamath also, which borders on it,
Tyre and Sidon, though they are very wise.
3 Tyre has built itself a rampart,
and heaped up silver like dust,
and gold like the dirt of the streets.
4 But now, the Lord will strip it of its possessions
and hurl its wealth into the sea,
and it shall be devoured by fire.

5 Ashkelon shall see it and be afraid;
Gaza too, and shall writhe in anguish;
Ekron also, because its hopes are withered.
The king shall perish from Gaza;
Ashkelon shall be uninhabited;
6 a mongrel people shall settle in Ashdod,
and I will make an end of the pride of Philistia.
7 I will take away its blood from its mouth,

^v Heb eye ^w Cn: Heb of Adam (or of humankind)

Cross-references (margin)

8.16 Zech 7.9; Eph 4.25
8.17 Prov 3.29; Zech 7.10; 5.4; Hab 1.13
8.19 Zech 7.3, 5; Jer 39.2; 52.4; Isa 12.1; v. 16
8.21 Mic 4.1, 2
8.22 Isa 60.3; 66.23; v. 21
8.23 Isa 45.14, 24; 60.14; 1 Cor 14.25; 2 Chr 15.5; Isa 19.2
9.2 Jer 49.23; Ezek 28.3-5, 12, 21
9.3 2 Sam 24.7; Ezek 27.33; 1 Kings 10.21, 27
9.4 Isa 23.1; Ezek 28.18
9.5 Am 1.6-8
9.6 Am 1.6-8
9.7 Ezek 25.15-17

8.16,17 God commanded his people to be truthful, to act justly, to maintain clean hearts, and to keep from making false oaths.
8.20ff Zechariah prophesied a time when inhabitants from many different nations would head for Jerusalem to seek the favor of God. This would transpire, not by human inventions and desires, but by the operation of divine truth and grace through the power of the Spirit. Thus the Jews would be a blessing to all nations, for they would have seen and heard that God was with them. For the two main interpretations of this passage, see note on 8.1ff.
9.1ff Zechariah pronounced God's judgment on Syria, Hamath, Tyre, Sidon, and the Philistines. God used Alexander the Great to fulfill some of these prophecies. While Alexander was destroying surrounding nations and peoples, God moved him to protect the Jews and treat them with favor (v. 8).

and its abominations from between its teeth;
it too shall be a remnant for our God;
it shall be like a clan in Judah,
and Ekron shall be like the Jebusites.

8 Then I will encamp at my house as a guard,
so that no one shall march to and fro;
no oppressor shall again overrun them,
for now I have seen with my own eyes.

9.8
Zech 2.5;
Isa 52.1;
54.14; 60.18

9 Rejoice greatly, O daughter Zion!
Shout aloud, O daughter Jerusalem!
Lo, your king comes to you;
triumphant and victorious is he,
humble and riding on a donkey,
on a colt, the foal of a donkey.

9.9
Zeph 3.14,
15;
Isa 9.6, 7;
Mt 21.5;
Jn 12.15;
Isa 43.3, 11;
57.15

10 He x will cut off the chariot from Ephraim
and the war-horse from Jerusalem;
and the battle bow shall be cut off,
and he shall command peace to the nations;
his dominion shall be from sea to sea,
and from the River to the ends of the earth.

9.10
Hos 1.7;
2.18;
Hag 2.22;
Isa 57.19;
Ps 72.8;
Isa 60.12

2. The program of the king

a. Israel delivered from captivity

11 As for you also, because of the blood of my covenant with you,
I will set your prisoners free from the waterless pit.
12 Return to your stronghold, O prisoners of hope;
today I declare that I will restore to you double.

9.11
Ex 24.8;
Heb 10.29;
Isa 51.14
9.12
Jer 16.19;
17.13;
Isa 61.7

b. Triumph over the Greek oppressor

13 For I have bent Judah as my bow;
I have made Ephraim its arrow.
I will arouse your sons, O Zion,
against your sons, O Greece,
and wield you like a warrior's sword.

9.13
Jer 51.20;
Joel 3.6;
Ps 45.3;
Isa 49.2

14 Then the LORD will appear over them,
and his arrow go forth like lightning;
the Lord GOD will sound the trumpet
and march forth in the whirlwinds of the south.

9.14
Isa 31.5;
Ps 18.14;
Isa 27.13;
21.1; 66.15

15 The LORD of hosts will protect them,
and they shall devour and tread down the slingers; y
they shall drink their blood z like wine,
and be full like a bowl,
drenched like the corners of the altar.

9.15
Isa 37.35;
Zech 12.6;
Job 41.28;
Ps 78.65;
Ex 27.2

16 On that day the LORD their God will save them

9.16
Jer 31.10, 11;
Isa 62.3

x Gk: Heb I   y Cn: Heb the slingstones   z Gk: Heb shall drink

---

9.9 This predicts Christ's triumphal entry into Jerusalem on Palm Sunday (see Mt 21.5; Jn 12.15). As king, he was to be acclaimed by the people who shouted, "Hosanna to the Son of David" (Mt 21.9).
9.10 *from the River to the ends of the earth,* or, to the ends of the land of Palestine. Either interpretation is possible from the Hebrew text, but many other passages indicate Christ's universal rule.
9.11 The covenant of God with Abraham was sealed by the blood of circumcision. The Mosaic covenant of

law was sealed by the blood of animal sacrifices. The new covenant was sealed by the blood of Jesus Christ at Calvary. Without the shedding of blood there is no remission of sin (Heb 9.22), no setting us free from the prison of sin.
9.13 The mention of Greece as a future world power has caused some to suppose that chs. 9–14 were not written by Zechariah. Once predictive prophecy is accepted, however, this poses no problem. Greece was defeated by the Jews during the Maccabean period (2nd century B.C.).

for they are the flock of his people;
for like the jewels of a crown
   they shall shine on his land.

9.17
Jer 31.12, 14

17 For what goodness and beauty are his!
   Grain shall make the young men flourish,
   and new wine the young women.

c. The complete redemption of God's people

10.1
Jer 14.22;
10.13;
Isa 30.23

10 Ask rain from the LORD
   in the season of the spring rain,
from the LORD who makes the storm clouds,
   who gives showers of rain to you,[a]
   the vegetation in the field to everyone.

10.2
Ezek 21.21;
Hos 3.4;
Jer 27.9;
Job 13.4;
Ezek 34.5

2 For the teraphim[b] utter nonsense,
   and the diviners see lies;
the dreamers tell false dreams,
   and give empty consolation.
Therefore the people wander like sheep;
   they suffer for lack of a shepherd.

10.3
Jer 25.34-36;
Ezek 34.12,
17

3 My anger is hot against the shepherds,
   and I will punish the leaders;[c]
for the LORD of hosts cares for his flock, the house of Judah,
   and will make them like his proud war-horse.

10.4
Zech 9.10

4 Out of them shall come the cornerstone,
   out of them the tent peg,
out of them the battle bow,
   out of them every commander.

10.5
2 Sam 22.43;
Hag 2.22

5 Together they shall be like warriors in battle,
   trampling the foe in the mud of the streets;
they shall fight, for the LORD is with them,
   and they shall put to shame the riders on horses.

10.6
v. 12;
Zech 9.16;
8.8; 1.1, 6;
13.9

6 I will strengthen the house of Judah,
   and I will save the house of Joseph.
I will bring them back because I have compassion on them,
   and they shall be as though I had not rejected them;
for I am the LORD their God and I will answer them.

10.7
Zech 9.13,
15;
Isa 54.13

7 Then the people of Ephraim shall become like warriors,
   and their hearts shall be glad as with wine.
Their children shall see it and rejoice,
   their hearts shall exult in the LORD.

10.8
Isa 5.26;
Jer 33.22;
Ezek 36.11

8 I will signal for them and gather them in,
   for I have redeemed them,
and they shall be as numerous as they were before.

10.9
Ezek 6.9

9 Though I scattered them among the nations,
   yet in far countries they shall remember me,
   and they shall rear their children and return.

10.10
Isa 11.11;
Jer 50.19;
Isa 49.19, 20

10 I will bring them home from the land of Egypt,

a Heb *them* b Or *household gods* c Or *male goats*

10.1 Whenever there was no rain, times were bad for the people. God chose to send the rains with reference to the spiritual state of his people. He called on them to pray for the rain, and to pray to him, not to the sun and the stars, as did the heathen. Implicit in this command is what James affirmed: "You do not have, because you do not ask. You ask and do not receive, because you ask wrongly" (Jas 4.2,3).

10.3 The hand of God was over his people in all things, both good and bad. God's anger was displayed in the Babylonian captivity; now his pleasure would be evident in his decision to bless his people who loved and served him.
10.6,7 God owned his people, the twelve tribes of Israel; he was with them in mercy and would save them.

and gather them from Assyria;
I will bring them to the land of Gilead and to Lebanon,
    until there is no room for them.

11 They[d] shall pass through the sea of distress,
    and the waves of the sea shall be struck down,
    and all the depths of the Nile dried up.
The pride of Assyria shall be laid low,
    and the scepter of Egypt shall depart.

12 I will make them strong in the LORD,
    and they shall walk in his name,
                           says the LORD.

3. The rejection of the king

a. The proud in Israel humbled

11 Open your doors, O Lebanon,
    so that fire may devour your cedars!
2 Wail, O cypress, for the cedar has fallen,
    for the glorious trees are ruined!
Wail, oaks of Bashan,
    for the thick forest has been felled!
3 Listen, the wail of the shepherds,
    for their glory is despoiled!
Listen, the roar of the lions,
    for the thickets of the Jordan are destroyed!

b. The good shepherd rejected by his people

4 Thus said the LORD my God: Be a shepherd of the flock doomed to slaughter. 5 Those who buy them kill them and go unpunished; and those who sell them say, "Blessed be the LORD, for I have become rich"; and their own shepherds have no pity on them. 6 For I will no longer have pity on the inhabitants of the earth, says the LORD. I will cause them, every one, to fall each into the hand of a neighbor, and each into the hand of the king; and they shall devastate the earth, and I will deliver no one from their hand.

7 So, on behalf of the sheep merchants, I became the shepherd of the flock doomed to slaughter. I took two staffs; one I named Favor, the other I named Unity, and I tended the sheep. 8 In one month I disposed of the three shepherds, for I had become impatient with them, and they also detested me. 9 So I said, "I will not be your shepherd. What is to die, let it die; what is to be destroyed, let it be destroyed; and let those that are left devour the flesh of one another!" 10 I took my staff Favor and broke it, annulling the covenant that I had made with all the peoples. 11 So it was annulled on that day, and the sheep merchants, who were watching me, knew that it was the word of the LORD. 12 I then said to them, "If it seems right to you, give me my wages; but if not, keep them." So they weighed out as my wages thirty shekels of silver. 13 Then the LORD said to me, "Throw it into the treasury"[e]—this lordly price at which I was

Right margin cross-references:

10.11
Isa 51.9, 10;
19.5-7;
Zeph 2.13;
Ezek 30.13

10.12
Mic 4.5

11.1
Jer 22.6, 7;
Ezek 31.3
11.2
Isa 32.19

11.3
Jer 25.34-36;
50.44

11.4
v. 7
11.5
Jer 50.7;
Hos 12.8
11.6
Jer 13.14;
Zech 14.13;
Mic 5.8

11.7
Zeph 3.12;
Ezek 37.16;
vv. 10, 14
11.8
Hos 5.7
11.9
Jer 15.2;
43.11
11.10
v. 7;
Jer 14.21
11.11
Zeph 3.12
11.12
1 Kings 5.6;
Gen 37.28;
Ex 21.32;
Mt 26.15;
27.9, 10
11.13
Mt 27.9

---

[d] Gk: Heb *He*   [e] Syr: Heb *it to the potter*

10.12 God would strengthen his people, for he was both their strength and their righteousness. *they shall walk in his name*, i.e., they would bring glory to the name of their God.
11.7ff God promised to send the good shepherd for the sheep (cf. Jn 10); but if the shepherd were rejected, the result would be disastrous for those who did so. The staffs *Favor* and *Unity* represent the covenant which would be broken because of transgressions. It was conditioned by obedience, so that disobedience annulled the covenant.

11.12 *thirty shekels of silver*, the price of a slave (Ex 21.32).
11.13 *to the potter* (NRSV footnote). The thirty pieces of silver were as nothing compared to the worth of the one for whom the money was paid. Therefore Zechariah was told to cast it to the potter to buy some clay with it. This is prophetic of Judas Iscariot, who placed a very low value on the Lord Jesus (see Mt 27.3-9). There are still those who profess Jesus to have little value and live as though he is worth only a few small coins.

valued by them. So I took the thirty shekels of silver and threw them into the treasury[f] in the house of the LORD. 14 Then I broke my second staff Unity, annulling the family ties between Judah and Israel.

c. *The false shepherd described*

11.15
Ezek 34.2-4
11.16
Jer 23.2;
Ezek 34.2-6

15   Then the LORD said to me: Take once more the implements of a worthless shepherd. 16 For I am now raising up in the land a shepherd who does not care for the perishing, or seek the wandering,[g] or heal the maimed, or nourish the healthy,[h] but devours the flesh of the fat ones, tearing off even their hoofs.

11.17
Jer 23.1;
Jn 10.12;
Ezek 30.21,
22;
Mic 3.6, 7

17   Oh, my worthless shepherd,
  who deserts the flock!
May the sword strike his arm
  and his right eye!
Let his arm be completely withered,
  his right eye utterly blinded!

B. *The rejected king enthroned*

1. *Repentant Israel triumphant*

a. *Downfall of heathen attackers of Jerusalem*

12.1
Isa 42.5;
57.16;
Heb 12.9

12

An Oracle.

The word of the LORD concerning Israel: Thus says the LORD, who stretched out the heavens and founded the earth and formed the human spirit within: 2 See, I am about to make Jerusalem a cup of reeling for all the surrounding peoples; it will be against Judah also in the siege against Jerusalem. 3 On that day I will make Jerusalem a heavy stone for all the peoples; all who lift it shall grievously hurt themselves. And all the nations of the earth shall come together against it. 4 On that day, says the LORD, I will strike every horse with panic, and its rider with madness. But on the house of Judah I will keep a watchful eye, when I strike every horse of the peoples with blindness. 5 Then the clans of Judah shall say to themselves, "The inhabitants of Jerusalem have strength through the LORD of hosts, their God."

12.2
Isa 51.22,
23;
Zech 14.14
12.3
Dan 2.34, 35,
44, 45;
Mt 21.44;
Zech 14.2
12.4
Ps 76.6;
Ezek 38.4;
Zech 9.10
12.5
Zech 10.6, 12

b. *Israel's power to vanquish all foes*

12.6
Isa 10.17,
18;
Ob 18;
Zech 2.4;
8.3-5
12.7
Jer 30.18;
Am 9.11
12.8
Zech 9.14,
15;
Mic 7.8;
Ps 8.5; 82.6
12.9
v. 3;
Zech 14.2, 3

6   On that day I will make the clans of Judah like a blazing pot on a pile of wood, like a flaming torch among sheaves; and they shall devour to the right and to the left all the surrounding peoples, while Jerusalem shall again be inhabited in its place, in Jerusalem.

7   And the LORD will give victory to the tents of Judah first, that the glory of the house of David and the glory of the inhabitants of Jerusalem may not be exalted over that of Judah. 8 On that day the LORD will shield the inhabitants of Jerusalem so that the feeblest among them on that day shall be like David, and the house of David shall be like God, like the angel of the LORD, at their head. 9 And on that day I will seek to destroy all the nations that come against Jerusalem.

---

[f] Syr: Heb *it to the potter*   [g] Syr Compare Gk Vg: Heb *the youth*   [h] Meaning of Heb uncertain

---

11.16,17 For their punishment, those who rejected the true shepherd would have a false shepherd, who would do the exact opposite of what the true shepherd would do — he would tear and devour the flock.

12.1 Zechariah emphasized the threefold work of the Creator: the heavens, which he stretched out; the earth, which has strong foundations and will not be moved by people; and the human spirit (*ruach*, meaning "spirit" or "wind," not *nephesh*, meaning "animal soul").

12.2ff On a coming day Jerusalem would be besieged by enemy powers, and God would deliver his people from that assault. The strength of those who defended Jerusalem would come from the God of power, who was omnipotent and who would himself intervene in the person of his Son.

12.9 *I will seek to destroy all the nations*, i.e., they would be baffled, broken, and destroyed. What they sought to do to Jerusalem would be done to them. The word *seek* does not mean that God might lack the

c. Repentance of Israel for piercing their king

10 And I will pour out a spirit of compassion and supplication on the house of David and the inhabitants of Jerusalem, so that, when they look on the one[i] whom they have pierced, they shall mourn for him, as one mourns for an only child, and weep bitterly over him, as one weeps over a firstborn. 11 On that day the mourning in Jerusalem will be as great as the mourning for Hadad-rimmon in the plain of Megiddo. 12 The land shall mourn, each family by itself; the family of the house of David by itself, and their wives by themselves; the family of the house of Nathan by itself, and their wives by themselves; 13 the family of the house of Levi by itself, and their wives by themselves; the family of the Shimeites by itself, and their wives by themselves; 14 and all the families that are left, each by itself, and their wives by themselves.

d. Israel cleansed and evil cut off

13 On that day a fountain shall be opened for the house of David and the inhabitants of Jerusalem, to cleanse them from sin and impurity.

2 On that day, says the LORD of hosts, I will cut off the names of the idols from the land, so that they shall be remembered no more; and also I will remove from the land the prophets and the unclean spirit. 3 And if any prophets appear again, their fathers and mothers who bore them will say to them, "You shall not live, for you speak lies in the name of the LORD"; and their fathers and their mothers who bore them shall pierce them through when they prophesy. 4 On that day the prophets will be ashamed, every one, of their visions when they prophesy; they will not put on a hairy mantle in order to deceive, 5 but each of them will say, "I am no prophet, I am a tiller of the soil; for the land has been my possession[j] since my youth." 6 And if anyone asks them, "What are these wounds on your chest?"[k] the answer will be "The wounds I received in the house of my friends."

2. Israel purged, delivered, and triumphant

a. Israel chastened after rejecting the king

7   "Awake, O sword, against my shepherd,
      against the man who is my associate,"
                                    says the LORD of hosts.
   Strike the shepherd, that the sheep may be scattered;
      I will turn my hand against the little ones.
8   In the whole land, says the LORD,
      two-thirds shall be cut off and perish,
      and one-third shall be left alive.
9   And I will put this third into the fire,
      refine them as one refines silver,
      and test them as gold is tested.

	12.10 Isa 44.3; Ezek 39.29; Joel 2.28; Jn 19.34; Rev 1.7; Jer 6.26; Am 8.10
	12.11 2 Kings 23.29
	12.12 Mt 24.30; Rev 1.7
	13.1 Jer 2.13; Heb 9.14; Ps 51.2, 7; Ezek 36.25
	13.2 Ex 23.13; Hos 2.17; Jer 23.14, 15; Ezek 36.25, 29
	13.3 Jer 23.34; Deut 18.20; 13.6-11
	13.4 Mic 3.6, 7; 2 Kings 1.8; Mt 3.4
	13.5 Am 7.14
	13.6 2 Kings 9.24
	13.7 Jer 47.6; Mic 5.2, 4; Jer 23.5, 6; Isa 53.4, 5, 10; Mt 26.31; Isa 1.25
	13.8 Isa 6.13
	13.9 Isa 48.10; 1 Pet 1.6; Zech 10.6; Jer 30.22; Hos 2.23

---

i Heb on me   j Cn: Heb for humankind has caused me to possess   k Heb wounds between your hands

---

power to do this. Rather, it denotes his earnest intention to do this because he is jealous for Zion.
12.10 At the end of the age the Israelites will turn to the Messiah (Rom 11.26). They will mourn for him and weep bitterly over the one whom their ancestors pierced.
12.11 the mourning for Hadad-rimmon in the plain of Megiddo. The reference to grieving was that for King Josiah (see 2 Chr 35.24,25).
13.1 a fountain shall be opened. That fountain is the Lamb of God who takes away the sin of the world. By faith sinners receive the remission of their sins and the fountain of blood becomes the fountain of life.

13.6 these wounds on your chest, possibly self-inflicted cuts, as practiced by false prophets (see 1 Kings 18.28). The wounds I received in the house of my friends. Some think this is a messianic reference to Jesus Christ; others believe this refers to a false prophet who is lying about the reasons for his scars.
13.8 This may be a prophetic word with a double fulfillment. The first fulfillment came with the destruction of Jerusalem in A.D. 70, when unbelieving Jews were cut off (for true believers had already fled the city). For some interpreters, it also refers to the end of the age, when once again Jerusalem will be surrounded and only the righteous will be delivered.

They will call on my name,
and I will answer them.
I will say, "They are my people";
and they will say, "The LORD is our God."

b. *Jerusalem delivered by the LORD*

14 See, a day is coming for the LORD, when the plunder taken from you will be divided in your midst. 2 For I will gather all the nations against Jerusalem to battle, and the city shall be taken and the houses looted and the women raped; half the city shall go into exile, but the rest of the people shall not be cut off from the city. 3 Then the LORD will go forth and fight against those nations as when he fights on a day of battle. 4 On that day his feet shall stand on the Mount of Olives, which lies before Jerusalem on the east; and the Mount of Olives shall be split in two from east to west by a very wide valley; so that one half of the Mount shall withdraw northward, and the other half southward. 5 And you shall flee by the valley of the LORD's mountain,*l* for the valley between the mountains shall reach to Azal;*m* and you shall flee as you fled from the earthquake in the days of King Uzziah of Judah. Then the LORD my God will come, and all the holy ones with him.

6 On that day there shall not be*n* either cold or frost.*o* 7 And there shall be continuous day (it is known to the LORD), not day and not night, for at evening time there shall be light.

8 On that day living waters shall flow out from Jerusalem, half of them to the eastern sea and half of them to the western sea; it shall continue in summer as in winter.

c. *Judah's king supreme over the earth*

9 And the LORD will become king over all the earth; on that day the LORD will be one and his name one.

10 The whole land shall be turned into a plain from Geba to Rimmon south of Jerusalem. But Jerusalem shall remain aloft on its site from the Gate of Benjamin to the place of the former gate, to the Corner Gate, and from the Tower of Hananel to the king's wine presses. 11 And it shall be inhabited, for never again shall it be doomed to destruction; Jerusalem shall abide in security.

12 This shall be the plague with which the LORD will strike all the peoples that wage war against Jerusalem: their flesh shall rot while they are still on their feet; their eyes shall rot in their sockets, and their tongues shall rot in their mouths. 13 On that day a great panic from the LORD shall fall on them, so that each will seize the hand of a neighbor, and the hand of the one will be raised against the hand of the other; 14 even Judah will fight at Jerusalem. And the wealth of all the surrounding nations shall be collected — gold, silver, and garments in great abundance. 15 And a plague like this plague shall fall on the horses, the mules, the camels, the donkeys, and whatever animals may be in those camps.

d. *The nations subjugated and Israel holy*

16 Then all who survive of the nations that have come against Jerusalem shall go up year after year to worship the King, the LORD of hosts, and to keep the festival of booths.*p* 17 If any of the families of the earth

l Heb *my mountains*   *m* Meaning of Heb uncertain   *n* Cn: Heb *there shall not be light*   *o* Compare Gk Syr Vg Tg: Meaning of Heb uncertain   *p* Or *tabernacles*; Heb *succoth*

14.1
Isa 13.9;
Joel 2.1;
Mal 4.1; v. 14
14.2
Zech 12.2, 3;
Isa 13.6;
Zech 13.8
14.3
Zech 9.14, 15
14.4
Ezek 11.23;
Mic 1.3, 4;
Hab 3.6
14.5
Am 1.1;
Isa 66.15,
16;
Mt 25.31;
Jude 14
14.7
Isa 30.26;
Rev 21.23
14.8
Ezek 47.1;
Joel 3.18;
Rev 22.1
14.9
Rev 11.15;
Isa 45.21-24;
Eph 4.5, 6
14.10
Am 9.11;
Zech 12.6;
Jer 37.13;
38.7; 31.38
14.11
Zech 2.4;
Rev 22.3;
Jer 23.5, 6
14.12
Deut 28.21,
22
14.13
1 Sam 14.15,
20;
Zech 11.6;
Ezek 38.21
14.14
Zech 12.2, 5;
Isa 23.18
14.15
v. 12
14.16
Isa 60.6, 7,
9; 66.23; v. 9
14.17
vv. 9, 16;
Am 4.7

14.3ff The second coming of the Lord Jesus is here predicted; he will save Jerusalem (either the literal Jerusalem or the church) from complete destruction.
14.5 *for the valley between the mountains shall reach to Azal,* apparently a hamlet on the eastern outskirts of Jerusalem.

14.9 This verse guarantees that the petition "Your kingdom come" (Mt 6.10) will be answered. At the end of the age Christ's kingdom will extend from shore to shore and his prayer for the unity of believers will prevail (Jn 17.21).

do not go up to Jerusalem to worship the King, the LORD of hosts, there will be no rain upon them. ¹⁸ And if the family of Egypt do not go up and present themselves, then on them shall*q* come the plague that the LORD inflicts on the nations that do not go up to keep the festival of booths.*r* ¹⁹ Such shall be the punishment of Egypt and the punishment of all the nations that do not go up to keep the festival of booths.*r*

20 On that day there shall be inscribed on the bells of the horses, "Holy to the LORD." And the cooking pots in the house of the LORD shall be as holy as*s* the bowls in front of the altar; ²¹ and every cooking pot in Jerusalem and Judah shall be sacred to the LORD of hosts, so that all who sacrifice may come and use them to boil the flesh of the sacrifice. And there shall no longer be traders*t* in the house of the LORD of hosts on that day.

14.18
v. 12

14.19
v. 12

14.20
Ex 28.36-38;
Zech 9.15
14.21
Neh 8.10;
1 Cor 10.31;
Ezek 44.9;
Zech 9.8

q Gk Syr: Heb *shall not*   *r* Or *tabernacles*; Heb *succoth*   *s* Heb *shall be like*   *t* Or *Canaanites*

14.20 *"Holy to the LORD."* This phrase had been engraved on a golden plate worn by the high priest on his forehead (see Ex 28.36; 39.30). At the end of the age it will be written on horses, furniture, etc., when Christ is triumphant. It will be fully manifested by the saints, who as living temples will be sanctified by the Holy Spirit.

INTRODUCTION TO

MALACHI

Authorship, Date, and Background: Malachi was the last of the O.T. writing prophets. His name means "my messenger," and for this reason some have supposed that the author's true name is unknown. The book itself was written after the time of Haggai and Zechariah, for the rebuilt temple was standing, sacrifices were brought to the altar, and the people were subject to the authority of a Persian governor. Therefore the book can be dated somewhere between 450 and 425 B.C.

The people in the land were discouraged. Times were hard; they were experiencing drought and famine, causing them to wonder whether God cared for them. A spirit of apathy, indifference, and spiritual backsliding existed. They had been in the land for almost a hundred years. The walls of Jerusalem and the temple had been rebuilt, but the wicked seemed to prosper while those who walked penitently and kept God's commandments did not. Moveover, the kingdom they were expecting had not yet come and they wondered whether it ever would. It was against this backdrop that Malachi began his prophetic ministry.

Characteristics and Content: Malachi intensely loved his people. He represented great spiritual dynamism, and his words were backed by the conviction that he spoke with the authority of God. In this book, he employed questions and answers to discuss his themes, appealing to reason and using logic to make his case. Always the justice of God was under discussion.

Malachi arraigned the people for being disloyal to God and not keeping his commandments. He used Edom as an illustration to show that cruelty and unfaithfulness would not go unpunished forever. God's people had not yet learned the lessons taught by the captivity. They were again offering blemished sacrifices at the altar and profaning God's name. Even the priests were unfaithful in discharging the duties of their office.

Malachi became angry because the people had intermarried with women from heathen nations. These wives were introducing idolatry, and divorce was common. Malachi insisted that all sacrifices would avail nothing if the hearts of the offerers were not right with their God. God had become weary with this people and would shortly do something about their adulteries, sorceries, lying, failure to bring tithes, and the injustices they heaped on widows, orphans, and aliens. God had his own book of remembrance in which he included the names of those who walked according to his commandments. Contrary to what the people thought, God knew who feared him. They would be saved in the day of God's wrath when the others were destroyed. That great and terrible day of the Lord was pending. However, this divine judgment would be delayed for a season so that a time of mercy might follow, marked by the coming of the prophet Elijah. This, of course, refers to the coming of the Messiah whose forerunner was Elijah, i.e., John the Baptist (see Mt 11.10,14).

Outline:

MALACHI

I. The sin of Israel (1.1–2.17)

A. God's love for Israel shown by the fall of Edom

1 An oracle. The word of the LORD to Israel by Malachi.[a]

2 I have loved you, says the LORD. But you say, "How have you loved us?" Is not Esau Jacob's brother? says the LORD. Yet I have loved Jacob 3 but I have hated Esau; I have made his hill country a desolation and his heritage a desert for jackals. 4 If Edom says, "We are shattered but we will rebuild the ruins," the LORD of hosts says: They may build, but I will tear down, until they are called the wicked country, the people with whom the LORD is angry forever. 5 Your own eyes shall see this, and you shall say, "Great is the LORD beyond the borders of Israel!"

B. The sins of the priesthood

6 A son honors his father, and servants their master. If then I am a father, where is the honor due me? And if I am a master, where is the respect due me? says the LORD of hosts to you, O priests, who despise my name. You say, "How have we despised your name?" 7 By offering polluted food on my altar. And you say, "How have we polluted it?"[b] By thinking that the LORD's table may be despised. 8 When you offer blind animals in sacrifice, is that not wrong? And when you offer those that are lame or sick, is that not wrong? Try presenting that to your governor; will he be pleased with you or show you favor? says the LORD of hosts. 9 And now implore the favor of God, that he may be gracious to us. The fault is yours. Will he show favor to any of you? says the LORD of hosts. 10 Oh, that someone among you would shut the temple[c] doors, so that you would not kindle fire on my altar in vain! I have no pleasure in you, says the LORD of hosts, and I will not accept an offering from your hands. 11 For from the rising of the sun to its setting my name is great among the nations, and in every place incense is offered to my name, and a pure offering; for my name is great among the nations, says the LORD of hosts. 12 But you profane it when you say that the Lord's table is polluted, and the food for it[d] may be despised. 13 "What a weariness this is," you say, and you sniff at me,[e] says the LORD of hosts. You bring what has been taken by violence or is lame or sick, and this you bring as your offering! Shall I accept that from your hand? says the LORD. 14 Cursed be the cheat who has a male in the flock and vows to give it, and yet sacrifices to the Lord

a Or *by my messenger* *b* Gk: Heb *you* *c* Heb lacks *temple* *d* Compare Syr Tg: Heb *its fruit, its food*
e Another reading is *at it*

1.2 God said he loved Israel. But the people were asking why there were no outward evidences of that love. In reply, God said that he loved Jacob and hated Esau his brother, because Esau had rejected God. Jacob was the one with whom the covenant made with Abraham was continued. The outward sign of God's favor toward Israel was marked by his judgment against Edom (Esau's descendants). God's attitude toward Edom was one of perpetual anger (v. 4).

1.8ff Who would bring blind, lame, or sick sacrifices to offer to a great king, let alone to the Lord? Some Israelites were doing this. Furthermore, the priests were serving only for what they got out of their service. To them their work was drudgery. With all this God was offended. But perhaps we who no longer offer animal sacrifices sin as much by our failure to give ourselves wholly over to Jesus Christ as Lord.

1.1
Nah 1.1;
Hab 1.1
1.2
Isa 41.8, 9;
Jer 31.3;
Rom 9.13
1.3
Jer 49.18;
Ezek 35.3-9

1.5
Ps 35.27;
Job 42.8

1.6
Ex 20.12;
Mal 2.10;
Lk 6.46;
Mal 3.5;
2.1-9
1.7
Lev 21.6, 8;
v. 12
1.8
Lev 22.22
1.9
Am 5.22;
Lev 23.34-44
1.10
Isa 1.13;
Jer 14.10-12;
Hos 5.6
1.11
Isa 45.6;
60.3, 5, 6;
Rev 8.3;
Jer 10.6, 7
1.12
Deut 28.15;
v. 7
1.13
Isa 43.22;
61.8;
Lev 22.20
1.14
Lev 22.18-20;
Zech 14.9;
Zeph 2.11

what is blemished; for I am a great King, says the LORD of hosts, and my name is reverenced among the nations.

C. *The warning to the priesthood*

2 And now, O priests, this command is for you. 2 If you will not listen, if you will not lay it to heart to give glory to my name, says the LORD of hosts, then I will send the curse on you and I will curse your blessings; indeed I have already cursed them,*f* because you do not lay it to heart. 3 I will rebuke your offspring, and spread dung on your faces, the dung of your offerings, and I will put you out of my presence.*g*

4 Know, then, that I have sent this command to you, that my covenant with Levi may hold, says the LORD of hosts. 5 My covenant with him was a covenant of life and well-being, which I gave him; this called for reverence, and he revered me and stood in awe of my name. 6 True instruction was in his mouth, and no wrong was found on his lips. He walked with me in integrity and uprightness, and he turned many from iniquity. 7 For the lips of a priest should guard knowledge, and people should seek instruction from his mouth, for he is the messenger of the LORD of hosts. 8 But you have turned aside from the way; you have caused many to stumble by your instruction; you have corrupted the covenant of Levi, says the LORD of hosts, 9 and so I make you despised and abased before all the people, inasmuch as you have not kept my ways but have shown partiality in your instruction.

10 Have we not all one father? Has not one God created us? Why then are we faithless to one another, profaning the covenant of our ancestors? 11 Judah has been faithless, and abomination has been committed in Israel and in Jerusalem; for Judah has profaned the sanctuary of the LORD, which he loves, and has married the daughter of a foreign god. 12 May the LORD cut off from the tents of Jacob anyone who does this — any to witness*h* or answer, or to bring an offering to the LORD of hosts.

13 And this you do as well: You cover the LORD's altar with tears, with weeping and groaning because he no longer regards the offering or accepts it with favor at your hand. 14 You ask, "Why does he not?" Because the LORD was a witness between you and the wife of your youth, to whom you have been faithless, though she is your companion and your wife by covenant. 15 Did not one God make her?*i* Both flesh and spirit are his.*j* And what does the one God*k* desire? Godly offspring. So look to yourselves, and do not let anyone be faithless to the wife of his youth. 16 For I hate*l* divorce, says the LORD, the God of Israel, and covering one's garment with violence, says the LORD of hosts. So take heed to yourselves and do not be faithless.

17 You have wearied the LORD with your words. Yet you say, "How have we wearied him?" By saying, "All who do evil are good in the sight

f Heb *it*   *g* Cn Compare Gk Syr: Heb *and he shall bear you to it*   *h* Cn Compare Gk: Heb *arouse*
i Or *Has he not made one?*   *j* Cn: Heb *and a remnant of spirit was his*   *k* Heb *he*   *l* Cn: Heb *he hates*

2.1ff The priests were accused of despising God and failing to perform their functions properly. They failed to teach correctly or act in accord with the will of God. They broke the agreement God made with Levi when he was chosen for the sacred office of the priesthood. These priests corrupted that office (v. 8). The externals of religion were practiced, but "heart" religion was defiled, so that the externals were of no value.
2.10ff Corrupt conduct always springs from corrupt principles; marriage is the issue in this passage. Judah was married to a strange god because so many of them had married pagans, who had brought their gods into the home and seduced the nation. Moreover, true marriage is a covenant relationship between three par-

ties, the third party being God. Since marriage is permanent, based on the principle of a husband and wife faithfully living together (Gen 2.24), divorce is something God disapproves of and hates. Divine judgment is rendered against anyone who is unfaithful to a spouse (2.15,16).
2.17 *Where is the God of justice?* The concept of justice here is retributive justice, involving the punishing or rewarding of an individual according to what that person deserves. Whatever God does is just. He rightly condemns those who practice evil and who pronounce that what they do is good. This is exactly what the people were doing, and it was appropriate for God to judge them accordingly.

of the LORD, and he delights in them." Or by asking, "Where is the God of justice?"

II. The judgment for sinners and the blessings for the penitent (3.1—4.6)

A. The sending of the Messiah

3 See, I am sending my messenger to prepare the way before me, and the Lord whom you seek will suddenly come to his temple. The messenger of the covenant in whom you delight—indeed, he is coming, says the LORD of hosts. 2 But who can endure the day of his coming, and who can stand when he appears?

For he is like a refiner's fire and like fullers' soap; 3 he will sit as a refiner and purifier of silver, and he will purify the descendants of Levi and refine them like gold and silver, until they present offerings to the LORD in righteousness. *m* 4 Then the offering of Judah and Jerusalem will be pleasing to the LORD as in the days of old and as in former years.

5 Then I will draw near to you for judgment; I will be swift to bear witness against the sorcerers, against the adulterers, against those who swear falsely, against those who oppress the hired workers in their wages, the widow and the orphan, against those who thrust aside the alien, and do not fear me, says the LORD of hosts.

B. The sins of the people

6 For I the LORD do not change; therefore you, O children of Jacob, have not perished. 7 Ever since the days of your ancestors you have turned aside from my statutes and have not kept them. Return to me, and I will return to you, says the LORD of hosts. But you say, "How shall we return?"

8 Will anyone rob God? Yet you are robbing me! But you say, "How are we robbing you?" In your tithes and offerings! 9 You are cursed with a curse, for you are robbing me—the whole nation of you! 10 Bring the full tithe into the storehouse, so that there may be food in my house, and thus put me to the test, says the LORD of hosts; see if I will not open the windows of heaven for you and pour down for you an overflowing blessing. 11 I will rebuke the locust *n* for you, so that it will not destroy the produce of your soil; and your vine in the field shall not be barren, says the LORD of hosts. 12 Then all nations will count you happy, for you will be a land of delight, says the LORD of hosts.

C. The distinction between the good and the evil

13 You have spoken harsh words against me, says the LORD. Yet you say, "How have we spoken against you?" 14 You have said, "It is vain to

m Or *right offerings to the LORD*   *n* Heb *devourer*

3.1
Mt 11.10;
Mk 1.2;
Lk 1.76;
7.27
3.2
Ezek 22.14;
Zech 13.9;
Mt 3.10-12;
1 Cor 3.13-15
3.3
Isa 1.25;
Zech 13.9
3.4
Mal 1.11
3.5
Deut 18.10;
Ezek 22.9-11;
Zech 5.4;
Lev 19.13

3.6
Num 23.19;
Jas 1.17
3.7
Acts 7.51;
Zech 1.3

3.8
Neh 13.10-12
3.9
Mal 2.2
3.10
Prov 3.9, 10;
Ps 78.23-29;
2 Chr 31.10
3.11
Joel 1.4; 2.25
3.12
Isa 61.9;
62.4

3.13
Mal 2.17
3.14
Ps 73.13;
Jer 2.25;
18.12;
Isa 58.3

3.1 God promised the coming of the Messiah and his forerunner, John the Baptist. The Messiah would be a comfort to the afflicted who trusted in him and a terror to evildoers who would be judged and rewarded properly for their transgressions.
3.6 *have not perished.* God and his promises do not change. Yet the redeemed have no claim on the mercy of God and could also perish as do the wicked if they turn from the Lord. But the God of grace and compassion has redeemed his people and promises to keep them for himself. Through the merits of the Messiah, God can declare righteous those who are worthy of death but who turn to him for help. Salvation is by grace and grace alone.
3.8 Tithing—giving God a tenth of one's income—

was established as part of the Mosaic system and was deeply ingrained in the Hebrew tradition, though it existed long before the time of Moses (e.g., Abraham paid tithes to Melchizedek, Gen 14.20). Malachi insisted that to fail to tithe robs God of what rightfully belongs to him. As a result, the divine blessing was withheld. Tithing is not commanded in the N.T. as a legal requirement, but the Christian under grace can hardly do less than the Jew under law. Tithing is the outward sign of an inward commitment that all one has belongs to God, who is entitled to a return on the divine investment in any individual (see note on 1 Cor 16.2).
3.14 *What do we profit by keeping his command?* The question asked is plain: If we cannot expect to get

serve God. What do we profit by keeping his command or by going about as mourners before the LORD of hosts? 15 Now we count the arrogant happy; evildoers not only prosper, but when they put God to the test they escape."

16 Then those who revered the LORD spoke with one another. The LORD took note and listened, and a book of remembrance was written before him of those who revered the LORD and thought on his name. 17 They shall be mine, says the LORD of hosts, my special possession on the day when I act, and I will spare them as parents spare their children who serve them. 18 Then once more you shall see the difference between the righteous and the wicked, between one who serves God and one who does not serve him.

4 ⁰ See, the day is coming, burning like an oven, when all the arrogant and all evildoers will be stubble; the day that comes shall burn them up, says the LORD of hosts, so that it will leave them neither root nor branch. 2 But for you who revere my name the sun of righteousness shall rise, with healing in its wings. You shall go out leaping like calves from the stall. 3 And you shall tread down the wicked, for they will be ashes under the soles of your feet, on the day when I act, says the LORD of hosts.

D. *Conclusion*

1. *The command to obedience*

4 Remember the teaching of my servant Moses, the statutes and ordinances that I commanded him at Horeb for all Israel.

2. *The coming of Elijah before the day of the LORD*

5 Lo, I will send you the prophet Elijah before the great and terrible day of the LORD comes. 6 He will turn the hearts of parents to their children and the hearts of children to their parents, so that I will not come and strike the land with a curse.ᵖ

ᵒ Ch 4.1-6 are Ch 3.19-24 in Heb   ᵖ Or a ban of utter destruction

Cross references (left margin):

3.15
Mal 4.1;
Jer 7.10

3.16
Ps 34.15;
56.8;
Rev 20.12

3.17
1 Pet 2.9;
Isa 26.20
3.18
Gen 18.25;
Am 5.15

4.1
Joel 2.31;
Ob 18;
Am 2.9

4.2
Mal 3.16;
Lk 1.78;
Eph 5.14
4.3
Mic 7.10;
Zech 10.5

4.4
Ex 20.3

4.5
Mt 11.14;
Mk 9.11;
Lk 1.17

---

anything from serving God, why then serve him? This was to be the attitude of the Sadducees in Jesus' day, who denied the resurrection. If there is no resurrection of the dead, and no heaven or Sheol, why serve God in this life? If obedience to the commandments of God yields nothing by way of commendation or reward, it would seem to be a waste of time. It is true that the Bible teaches that we are not saved by obeying commandments (for obedience is not meritorious); yet obedience that follows justification and regeneration is pleasing in the sight of the one who has redeemed us, and he rewards obedient believers at the judgment (Mt 25.31–46; 1 Cor 3.12–15).
3.18 In this world it can be difficult to distinguish between the saved and the lost, the good and the bad. Appearances are deceptive and evil people sometimes look more like saints than the saints do. At the judgment seat of Christ, however, it will be easy to "see the difference between the righteous and the wicked," for then the saints' characters will be both perfected and perfectly discovered; all will then appear in their true colors, and the inner motivations of the heart will be revealed.
4.1 *the day is coming*, i.e., the great and terrible day

of the Lord when the wicked will be identified and their eternal state determined. It will be a day of wrath for them, for a devouring fire will consume them.
4.2 *the sun of righteousness*. This refers to Jesus, the light of the world, the light of people, the light of glory of God.
4.4 The law of Moses is here identified as being the word of God. Moses was simply the one through whom God brought the law. God requires obedience to all of his commandments, for in the keeping of them there is much gain. Saving faith is never alone; it is always accompanied by good works, which include obedience to the law of God (see Jas 2.14–26).
4.5 *I will send you the prophet Elijah*, i.e., "one like the prophet Elijah" (compare with Mt 17.10–12; Lk 1.17). Malachi predicted that Elijah would come *before the great and terrible day of the LORD*. This prophecy has two fulfillments. The first is connected with the birth of Jesus, whose forerunner, John the Baptist, is said to be the representation of Elijah (see Mt 11.14; Lk 1.17; 9.8,19; Jn 1.21). Elijah, along with Moses, appeared at the transfiguration (see Mt 17.1–5; Mk 9.2–13; Lk 9.28–30). The final coming of Elijah is evidently portrayed in Rev 11.3–6.

FROM MALACHI TO CHRIST

Malachi c. 430 B.C.

THE PERSIAN PERIOD
450-330 B.C.

For about 200 years after Nehemiah's time the Persians controlled Judah, but the Jews were allowed to carry on their religious observances and were not interfered with. During this time Judah was ruled by high priests who were responsible to the Jewish government.

Rule of Alexander the Great

THE HELLENISTIC PERIOD
330-166 B.C.

In 333 B.C. the Persian armies stationed in Macedonia were defeated by Alexander the Great. He was convinced that Greek culture was the one force that could unify the world. Alexander permitted the Jews to observe their laws and even granted them exemption from tribute or tax during their sabbath years. The Greek conquest prepared the way for the translation of the OT into Greek (Septuagint version) c. 250 B.C.

Rule
of the
Ptolemies of
Egypt

410	
400 B.C.	
390	
380	
370	
360	
350	
340	
330	334-323 Alexander the Great conquers the East
320	330-328 Alexander's years of power
310	320 Ptolemy (I) Soter conquers Jerusalem; Seleucid dynasty begins
300	311 Seleucus conquers Babylon; Seleucid dynasty begins
290	
280	
270	
260	
250	
240	
230	226 Antiochus III (the Great) of Syria overpowers Palestine
220	223-187 Antiochus becomes Seleucid ruler of Syria
210	
200	198 Antiochus defeats Egypt and gains control of Palestine
190	

THE HASMONEAN PERIOD 166-63 B.C.

When this historical period began, the Jews were being greatly oppressed. The Ptolemies had been tolerant of the Jews and their religious practices but the Seleucid rulers were determined to force Hellenism on them. Copies of the Scriptures were ordered destroyed and laws were enforced with extreme cruelty. The oppressed Jews revolted, led by Judas the Maccabee.

THE ROMAN PERIOD 63 B.C. . . . .

In the year 63 B.C. Pompey, the Roman general, captured Jerusalem, and the provinces of Palestine became subject to Rome. The local government was entrusted part of the time to princes and the rest of the time to procurators who were appointed by the emperors. Herod the Great was ruler of all Palestine at the time of Christ's birth.

Rule of the Seleucids of Syria	
180	
170	175-164 Antiochus (IV) Epiphanes rules Syria; Judaism is prohibited
160	167 Mattathias and his sons rebel against Antiochus; Maccabean revolt begins
150	166-160 Judas Maccabeus's leadership
140	160-143 Jonathan is high priest
130	142 Tower of Jerusalem cleansed
120	142-134 Simon becomes high priest; establishes Hasmonean dynasty
Hasmonean Dynasty	134-104 John Hyrcanus enlarges the independent Jewish state
110	
100	103 Aristobulus's rule
90	102-76 Alexander Janneus's rule
80	75-67 Rule of Salome Alexandra with Hyrcanus II as high priest
70	
60	66-63 Battle between Aristobulus II and Hyrcanus II
50	63 Pompey invades Palestine; Roman rule begins
40	63-40 Hyrcanus II rules but is subject to Rome
Herod the Great rules as king; subject to Rome	40-37 Parthians conquer Jerusalem
30	37 Jerusalem besieged for six months
20	32 Herod defeated
10	19 Herod's temple begun
	16 Herod visits Agrippa
10	4 Herod dies; Archelaus succeeds
20	
A.D. 30	

THE NEW COVENANT
commonly called

The New Testament

of
OUR LORD AND SAVIOR
JESUS CHRIST

New Revised Standard Version

INTRODUCTION TO
THE GOSPEL ACCORDING TO
MATTHEW

Authorship, Date, and Background: The titles attached to the four Gospels, "According to Matthew," "According to Mark," "According to Luke," and "According to John," were not part of the original Gospels. These titles were added later in accord with the tradition of the church that Matthew, Mark, Luke, and John were the authors of these books. Although Matthew is not named in the first Gospel itself and no claim is made in the text for him as the author, the early church agreed that he was the author. Other explanations in support of unknown or known individuals who might have authored the book do not hold up.

Matthew Levi was a tax collector, called by Jesus to be one of the twelve disciples. Virtually nothing is known about him following the resurrection, neither how he lived, where he witnessed, nor how he died. Obviously he was literate, and he was probably a good businessman whose records would be accurate. His imperishable monument is the Gospel according to Matthew. The Jews disliked tax collectors, who paid the Roman government for the right to collect taxes and then extracted as much as they could from the taxpayers. They were regarded as swindlers. For Jesus to eat dinner with one of them was looked upon with great disapproval by the religious leaders of the Jews.

No precise date can be assigned for the writing of this Gospel, although conservative scholars usually assign it to the period between A.D. 50 and 60. Nor is the place where it was written certain. Many think it was composed at Antioch. It addressed itself to both Jews and Gentiles who had become Christians. The Jewish aspect is quite plain; the fact that in Matthew's account Jesus linked his good news closely with the O.T. distinguishes it from the other Gospels. Matthew and Mark are so similar in the details common to both of them that some scholars think Matthew was indebted to Mark for portions of what he wrote. This supposes that Mark was written before Matthew. If the reverse is true, then Mark owed a great deal to Matthew.

Scholars have also sought to uncover the common sources from which all of the Gospel writers got their information, and have asked why there are four Gospels. It makes little difference to Christians whether Matthew got his information firsthand by his own knowledge, from others, from oral tradition, or from the Holy Spirit directly. The Holy Spirit, in any event, is the true author of all Scripture and if he chose to have four Gospels written for different people but containing some materials which are similar, it must be left at that. While there may have been questions about the authorship, the date, and the sources of the information, there never has been any doubt about Matthew's authenticity and its canonicity (i.e., its being a part of the word of God).

Characteristics and Content: Matthew's Gospel tells the story of the life of Jesus. It was designed for teaching, and treats the entire drama of redemption, going back to the O.T. to demonstrate that Jesus is the promised Messiah and that everything predicted about the Messiah was fulfilled in his life, death, resurrection, and ministry. He traces the lineage of Jesus back to Abraham, with whom God made a covenant. He details Jesus' virgin birth and the divine-human natures of his person. Jesus is the Son of David, the King of the Jews, the promised Messiah. His kingdom is not of this world, but he has a kingdom which has come and which will be fully realized in the future in the new Jerusalem. The phrase "the kingdom of heaven" is important in his teaching.

The Gospel records in detail five of Jesus' most important discourses: the sermon on the mount (chs. 5—7); the commissioning of the twelve to take the gospel abroad (ch. 10); the parables of the kingdom (ch. 13); the teaching about the Christian community, the church (Matthew is the only Gospel in which the Gk. word for church, *ekklēsia*, is used, ch. 18); and the prophecies in the Mount of Olives discourse about the closing days of the age (chs. 24—25). The familiar events in the last week of Jesus' life are emphasized, including the incident in the garden of Gethsemane, the betrayal by Judas, the last supper, the appearances before Caiaphas, the Sanhedrin, and Pontius Pilate, followed by his crucifixion, burial, and resurrection. Matthew concludes his account with the great commission, which constitutes the marching orders to the church for that generation and for all succeeding generations until Jesus comes again. His description about baptism "in the name of the Father and of the Son and of the Holy Spirit" (28.19) is among the clearest statements in Scripture about the doctrine of the Trinity.

Outline:

THE GOSPEL ACCORDING TO

MATTHEW

I. *Genealogy and birth of the Messiah (1.1–2.23)*

A. *The genealogy of Jesus (1.1–17; cf. Luke 3.23–38)*

1 An account of the genealogy*a* of Jesus the Messiah,*b* the son of David, the son of Abraham.

2 Abraham was the father of Isaac, and Isaac the father of Jacob, and Jacob the father of Judah and his brothers, 3 and Judah the father of Perez and Zerah by Tamar, and Perez the father of Hezron, and Hezron the father of Aram, 4 and Aram the father of Aminadab, and Aminadab the father of Nahshon, and Nahshon the father of Salmon, 5 and Salmon the father of Boaz by Rahab, and Boaz the father of Obed by Ruth, and Obed the father of Jesse, 6 and Jesse the father of King David.

And David was the father of Solomon by the wife of Uriah, 7 and Solomon the father of Rehoboam, and Rehoboam the father of Abijah, and Abijah the father of Asaph,*c* 8 and Asaph*c* the father of Jehoshaphat, and Jehoshaphat the father of Joram, and Joram the father of Uzziah, 9 and Uzziah the father of Jotham, and Jotham the father of Ahaz, and Ahaz the father of Hezekiah, 10 and Hezekiah the father of Manasseh, and Manasseh the father of Amos,*d* and Amos*d* the father of Josiah, 11 and Josiah the father of Jechoniah and his brothers, at the time of the deportation to Babylon.

12 And after the deportation to Babylon: Jechoniah was the father of Salathiel, and Salathiel the father of Zerubbabel, 13 and Zerubbabel the father of Abiud, and Abiud the father of Eliakim, and Eliakim the father of Azor, 14 and Azor the father of Zadok, and Zadok the father of Achim, and Achim the father of Eliud, 15 and Eliud the father of Eleazar, and Eleazar the father of Matthan, and Matthan the father of Jacob, 16 and Jacob the father of Joseph the husband of Mary, of whom Jesus was born, who is called the Messiah.*e*

17 So all the generations from Abraham to David are fourteen generations; and from David to the deportation to Babylon, fourteen generations; and from the deportation to Babylon to the Messiah,*e* fourteen generations.

B. *The birth of Jesus (1.18–25; Luke 1.26–35; 2.1–7)*

18 Now the birth of Jesus the Messiah*b* took place in this way. When his mother Mary had been engaged to Joseph, but before they lived

---

a Or *birth* *b* Or *Jesus Christ* *c* Other ancient authorities read *Asa* *d* Other ancient authorities read *Amon* *e* Or *the Christ*

1.1
Ps 132.11;
Isa 11.1;
Lk 1.32;
Jn 7.42;
Acts 2.30;
13.23;
Rom 1.3;
Gen 12.3;
22.18;
Gal 3.16
1.2
Gen 21.2, 3;
25.26; 29.35
1.3
Gen 38.27ff;
Ruth 4.18ff;
1 Chr 2.5, 9ff
1.6
1 Sam 16.1;
17.1;
2 Sam 12.24
1.7
1 Chr 3.10
1.10
2 Kings 20.21;
1 Chr 3.13
1.11
2 Kings 24.14-16;
Jer 27.20;
39.9;
Dan 1.2
1.12
1 Chr 3.17,
19
1.16
Lk 1.27

1.17
vv. 11, 12

1.5 The line from which Jesus came was not totally Jewish, for there were female Gentiles who married into that line. *Tamar* (v. 3) was apparently a Canaanite. *Ruth*, the wife of Boaz and the great-grandmother of King David (v. 5), was a Moabite. Most commentators think *Rahab* was the Gentile harlot of Josh 2.1 (see Heb 11.31). Bathsheba is not mentioned by name; she is called *the wife of Uriah* (v. 6), who was a Hittite. These women in the lineage of the Redeemer express the truth that Jesus is the cosmic Christ, the one for all seasons.

1.16 Two genealogies of Jesus appear in the Gospels, one in Matthew and one in Luke. The differences can be explained by the fact that Matthew records the genealogy of Joseph as the legal, not the natural, father of Jesus. Luke traces the genealogy of Jesus through Mary, his mother, which accounts for an almost completely different set of ancestors from Heli to David (Lk 3.23–31). It is assumed that Heli was Joseph's father-in-law. Mary's name is not mentioned before Heli's because Jews did not trace genealogy through a female.

1.19
Deut 24.1

1.21
Lk 2.21;
2.11;
Jn 1.29;
Acts 4.12;
13.3, 38
1.23
Isa 7.14

1.25
Ex 13.2;
Lk 2.21

together, she was found to be with child from the Holy Spirit. 19 Her husband Joseph, being a righteous man and unwilling to expose her to public disgrace, planned to dismiss her quietly. 20 But just when he had resolved to do this, an angel of the Lord appeared to him in a dream and said, "Joseph, son of David, do not be afraid to take Mary as your wife, for the child conceived in her is from the Holy Spirit. 21 She will bear a son, and you are to name him Jesus, for he will save his people from their sins." 22 All this took place to fulfill what had been spoken by the Lord through the prophet:

23   "Look, the virgin shall conceive and bear a son,
    and they shall name him Emmanuel,"

which means, "God is with us." 24 When Joseph awoke from sleep, he did as the angel of the Lord commanded him; he took her as his wife, 25 but had no marital relations with her until she had borne a son;f and he named him Jesus.

C. The visit of the wise men (2.1–12)

2.1
Lk 2.4-7; 1.5
2.2
Jer 23.5;
Zech 9.9;
Mk 15.2;
Jn 1.49

2.5
Jn 7.42

2.6
Mic 5.2;
Jn 21.16

2 In the time of King Herod, after Jesus was born in Bethlehem of Judea, wise meng from the East came to Jerusalem, 2 asking, "Where is the child who has been born king of the Jews? For we observed his star at its rising,h and have come to pay him homage." 3 When King Herod heard this, he was frightened, and all Jerusalem with him; 4 and calling together all the chief priests and scribes of the people, he inquired of them where the Messiahi was to be born. 5 They told him, "In Bethlehem of Judea; for so it has been written by the prophet:

6 'And you, Bethlehem, in the land of Judah,
    are by no means least among the rulers of Judah;
  for from you shall come a ruler
    who is to shepherdj my people Israel.' "

7 Then Herod secretly called for the wise meng and learned from them the exact time when the star had appeared. 8 Then he sent them to

---

f Other ancient authorities read *her firstborn son*   g Or *astrologers*; Gk *magi*   h Or *in the East*   i Or *the Christ*   j Or *rule*

1.19 *her husband*, i.e., her fiancé. *a righteous man*, i.e., a man of stern principle. A Jewish betrothal could be broken only by a divorce; an engaged girl who was pregnant by some other male was stoned to death as an adulteress. Joseph was about to put Mary away quietly, in order to avoid public scandal.

1.20 *when he had resolved to do this.* In his perplexity Joseph did not wish to make a hasty decision. It is better to consider a matter beforehand than to have to repent later. He did not yet know the true facts in the case; the thought of putting Mary away (v. 19) does indicate he believed her to be guilty of adultery. He must have suffered, thinking his beloved had broken faith with him. When God's angel revealed the true situation to him and told him what to do, he was prompt in his obedience and took Mary to wife. Jesus became known as "the carpenter's son" (13.55), rather than the son of a prostitute (though cf. Jn 8.48).

1.21 *Jesus* is the Greek equivalent of the Hebrew name *Jehoshua*, meaning "*Yahweh is salvation.*" The Son of God, born of Mary, is the Lord (Yahweh) God, the Savior.

1.23 The birth of Jesus was a literal fulfillment of Isa 7.14. The Greek word for *virgin* (i.e., *parthenos*), is found in the standard ancient Greek translation of Isaiah. Jesus was unique in that he had no human father. He was conceived in the womb of Mary, who had never had sexual relations with a man, by the supernatural work of the Holy Spirit (cf. Lk 1.35). Through that means he was born the sin-less God-man.

2.1 *King Herod* was the son of Antipater, who wormed his way into the confidence of Julius Caesar. The Romans made him procurator of Judea in 47 B.C. and elevated him to the kingship in 37 B.C., when the last reigning descendant of the Maccabean dynasty, Antigonus, was executed. Herod craftily managed to stay in power despite the changing government of Rome. He was so evil that Augustus said of him, "I would rather be Herod's dog than his son." Herod improved the temple in Jerusalem and was still king when Jesus was born in 5 or 4 B.C. Herod died shortly after the murder of the innocent infants of Bethlehem. *wise men from the East.* The Greek word for this is *magoi*, adopted from an old Persian word *magav.* These men constituted a priestly class that originated in Media. Doubtlessly coming from Persia or Media, these visitors were astrologers, expert in dreams, omens, and prophesying. Having heard about the promise of Messiah in Judea and having seen the new and brilliant star, they were guided by it to the birthplace of Jesus. Their worship prefigured the later submission of many Gentiles to Christ.

2.3 Herod had good reason to be alarmed about the rumor of the birth of Messiah. He and all the Jews supposed that Messiah would come to be king. This would mean the end of his own reign, and he had no intention whatever of permitting anyone to usurp his kingdom.

2.5 *the prophet*, see Mic 5.2.

Bethlehem, saying, "Go and search diligently for the child; and when you have found him, bring me word so that I may also go and pay him homage." 9 When they had heard the king, they set out; and there, ahead of them, went the star that they had seen at its rising,*k* until it stopped over the place where the child was. 10 When they saw that the star had stopped,*l* they were overwhelmed with joy. 11 On entering the house, they saw the child with Mary his mother; and they knelt down and paid him homage. Then, opening their treasure chests, they offered him gifts of gold, frankincense, and myrrh. 12 And having been warned in a dream not to return to Herod, they left for their own country by another road.

2.11
Mt 1.18;
12.46;
Ps 72.10;
Isa 60.2
2.12
Mt 2.22;
Acts 10.22;
Heb 11.7

D. *The flight into Egypt (2.13–18)*

13 Now after they had left, an angel of the Lord appeared to Joseph in a dream and said, "Get up, take the child and his mother, and flee to Egypt, and remain there until I tell you; for Herod is about to search for the child, to destroy him." 14 Then Joseph*m* got up, took the child and his mother by night, and went to Egypt, 15 and remained there until the death of Herod. This was to fulfill what had been spoken by the Lord through the prophet, "Out of Egypt I have called my son."

2.13
v. 19
2.14
Hos 11.1;
Ex 4.22

16 When Herod saw that he had been tricked by the wise men,*n* he was infuriated, and he sent and killed all the children in and around Bethlehem who were two years old or under, according to the time that he had learned from the wise men.*n* 17 Then was fulfilled what had been spoken through the prophet Jeremiah:

18 "A voice was heard in Ramah,
    wailing and loud lamentation,
Rachel weeping for her children;
    she refused to be consoled, because they are no more."

2.18
Jer 31.15

E. *From Egypt to Nazareth (2.19–23; cf. Mark 1.9; Luke 1.26)*

19 When Herod died, an angel of the Lord suddenly appeared in a dream to Joseph in Egypt and said, 20 "Get up, take the child and his mother, and go to the land of Israel, for those who were seeking the child's life are dead." 21 Then Joseph*m* got up, took the child and his mother, and went to the land of Israel. 22 But when he heard that Archelaus was

2.19
Mt 1.20;
v. 13
2.22
v. 12;
Mt 3.13;
Lk 2.39

k Or *in the East* *l* Gk *saw the star* *m* Gk *he* *n* Or *astrologers;* Gk *magi*

2.11 The wise men saw Jesus sometime after his birth, for the family was now in a *house.* King Herod ordered all male infants two years of age and under to be slaughtered (v. 16), for he wished to be assured that among them the infant Jesus was slain. Presumably the astrologers gave Herod the information that led to this slaughter (see note on v. 16).
2.14 *by night,* i.e., that very night. No legions of angels were sent to protect the infant Jesus; Joseph and Mary fled to Egypt.
2.15 Just as Isa 7.14 had a double fulfillment (see note on Isa 7.14), so also does Hos 11.1, quoted here. God had called Israel out of Egypt in the exodus. In referring to that event, Hosea spoke of Israel as God's son. Matthew now picks up this prophecy and assigns it to Jesus, so that the return of Jesus' parents from Egypt with Jesus constitutes a second fulfillment. The N.T. cites a number of events in the earthly career of Jesus as fulfillments of O.T. prophecies. Among them are the following: (1) he would spend part of his childhood in Egypt (Hos 11.1; Mt 2.15); (2) he would suffer and make atonement for sins (Isa 53.4–6; 2 Cor 5.21; 1 Pet 2.24,25); (3) he would ride into Jerusalem on the back of a donkey (Zech 9.9; Mt 21.2,4,5); (4) he would be offered a pain-killer in his

agony on the cross (Ps 69.21; Mt 27.34); (5) he would suffer no broken bones, contrary to the usual procedure connected with crucifixion (Ex 12.46; Ps 34.20; Jn 19.33,36); (6) soldiers would gamble over his garment (Ps 22.18; Mt 27.35); (7) he would utter certain words in his dying agony (Ps 22.1; Mk 15.34); (8) he would rise again from the dead (Ps 16.9,10; Acts 2.25–31).
2.16 Apparently the wise men told Herod the date they had first seen Christ's natal star. This pinpointed the birthdate of the Messiah and gave Herod some idea of the age of the infant. Herod slaughtered all the children two years old and under to be sure he killed the Messiah. It does not mean that Jesus was two years old at this time, only that Herod knew the child could not be more than two.
2.22 *Archelaus* was the son and heir of Herod the Great. The emperor Augustus made him ethnarch (not king) of Samaria, Judea, and Idumea. He was the worst of Herod's sons. The people suffered under him for nine years before he was banished to Vienna by Augustus. After his deportation, Judea was ruled by Roman procurators (such as Pontius Pilate) until A.D. 41.

2.23
Lk 1.26;
Isa 11.1;
Mk 1.24

ruling over Judea in place of his father Herod, he was afraid to go there. And after being warned in a dream, he went away to the district of Galilee. 23 There he made his home in a town called Nazareth, so that what had been spoken through the prophets might be fulfilled, "He will be called a Nazorean."

II. John the Baptist; baptism and temptation of Christ (3.1–4.11)

A. The ministry of John the Baptist
(3.1–12; Mark 1.1–8; Luke 3.2–17; John 1.6–8,19–28)

3.2
Dan 2.44;
Mt 4.7; 10.7
3.3
Isa 40.3;
Mk 1.3;
Lk 3.4;
Jn 1.23;
Lk 1.76
3.4
2 Kings 1.8;
Zech 13.4;
Lev 11.22
3.6
Acts 19.4, 18
3.7
Mt 12.34;
23.33;
Rom 5.9;
1 Thess 1.10
3.8
Acts 26.20
3.9
Jn 8.33, 39;
Acts 13.26;
Rom 4.1, 11,
16
3.10
Mt 7.19
3.11
Acts 1.5;
11.16; 19.4;
Isa 4.4;
Acts 2.3, 4
3.12
Mal 3.3;
Mt 13.30
3.13
Jn 1.31-34

3 In those days John the Baptist appeared in the wilderness of Judea, proclaiming, 2 "Repent, for the kingdom of heaven has come near."o 3 This is the one of whom the prophet Isaiah spoke when he said,
"The voice of one crying out in the wilderness:
  'Prepare the way of the Lord,
    make his paths straight.' "

4 Now John wore clothing of camel's hair with a leather belt around his waist, and his food was locusts and wild honey. 5 Then the people of Jerusalem and all Judea were going out to him, and all the region along the Jordan, 6 and they were baptized by him in the river Jordan, confessing their sins.

7 But when he saw many Pharisees and Sadducees coming for baptism, he said to them, "You brood of vipers! Who warned you to flee from the wrath to come? 8 Bear fruit worthy of repentance. 9 Do not presume to say to yourselves, 'We have Abraham as our ancestor'; for I tell you, God is able from these stones to raise up children to Abraham. 10 Even now the ax is lying at the root of the trees; every tree therefore that does not bear good fruit is cut down and thrown into the fire.

11 "I baptize you withp water for repentance, but one who is more powerful than I is coming after me; I am not worthy to carry his sandals. He will baptize you withp the Holy Spirit and fire. 12 His winnowing fork is in his hand, and he will clear his threshing floor and will gather his wheat into the granary; but the chaff he will burn with unquenchable fire."

B. The baptism of Jesus (3.13–17; Mark 1.9–11; Luke 3.21,22)

13 Then Jesus came from Galilee to John at the Jordan, to be baptized

o Or is at hand   p Or in

3.7 The *Sadducees* were one of the leading Jewish sects of Jesus' day. Their name is thought to be derived from Zadok, a high priest during David's reign. They came mostly from the priestly nobility, whereas the *Pharisees* came from all classes of people. The Sadducees and the Pharisees disliked each other and disagreed in theological matters. The Sadducees objected strenuously to the oral law that the Pharisees accepted and practiced (it was known as "the tradition of the elders"). They accepted the written law of Moses alone. In their theology they were known for what they rejected, such as the bodily resurrection of the dead, future punishments and rewards on the day of judgment, the reality of angels and spirits, and overruling divine providence as against unconditional free will. Though less numerous than the Pharisees, they were equally opposed to Jesus. Jesus refuted the Sadducees on several occasions, although not as often as he denounced the Pharisees (16.1–4,6–12; 22.23–33). The Pharisees were the most influential sect of the day. They believed in rigid separation from anything non-Jewish. Their theology included (1) the

most careful keeping of the law; (2) a belief in the immortality of the soul, the resurrection of the body, and retribution in the afterlife; (3) a belief in the reality of angels and spirits; (4) a belief that God would deliver Israel and restore her earlier glory; and (5) a belief in the doctrine of providence along with free will. Overriding all of this was their belief that Jews earned merit from God by keeping all the major and minor points of the law. They hated Jesus because he did what they rejected (e.g., 9.3,11,14; Lk 5.21). Jesus said they were legalists and condemned their hypocrisy with vigor (e.g., 6.2,5,16; 12.34; 23.33; Mk 7.6).
3.11 *He will baptize you with the Holy Spirit and fire.* This prophetic word was literally fulfilled at Pentecost, when the Holy Spirit filled all of the believers present and tongues as of fire rested on them (Acts 2.1–4). This event marked the beginning of the church. It also conveyed a divine enduement on the early disciples, by which their ministries became a significant force in the spreading of the gospel.

by him. 14 John would have prevented him, saying, "I need to be baptized by you, and do you come to me?" 15 But Jesus answered him, "Let it be so now; for it is proper for us in this way to fulfill all righteousness." Then he consented. 16 And when Jesus had been baptized, just as he came up from the water, suddenly the heavens were opened to him and he saw the Spirit of God descending like a dove and alighting on him. 17 And a voice from heaven said, "This is my Son, the Beloved,q with whom I am well pleased."

3.16
Isa 11.2;
42.1;
Jn 1.32
3.17
Ps 2.7;
Mt 12.18;
17.5;
Mk 9.7;
Lk 9.35

C. The temptation in the wilderness
(4.1–11; Mark 1.12,13; Luke 4.1–13)

4 Then Jesus was led up by the Spirit into the wilderness to be tempted by the devil. 2 He fasted forty days and forty nights, and afterwards he was famished. 3 The tempter came and said to him, "If you are the Son of God, command these stones to become loaves of bread." 4 But he answered, "It is written,

'One does not live by bread alone,
   but by every word that comes from the mouth of God.' "

5 Then the devil took him to the holy city and placed him on the pinnacle of the temple, 6 saying to him, "If you are the Son of God, throw yourself down; for it is written,

'He will command his angels concerning you,'
   and 'On their hands they will bear you up,
so that you will not dash your foot against a stone.' "

7 Jesus said to him, "Again it is written, 'Do not put the Lord your God to the test.' "

8 Again, the devil took him to a very high mountain and showed him all the kingdoms of the world and their splendor; 9 and he said to him, "All these I will give you, if you will fall down and worship me." 10 Jesus said to him, "Away with you, Satan! for it is written,

'Worship the Lord your God,
   and serve only him.' "

11 Then the devil left him, and suddenly angels came and waited on him.

4.2
Ex 34.28;
1 Kings 19.8
4.3
1 Thess 3.5
4.4
Deut 8.3

4.5
Neh 11.1;
Dan 9.24;
Mt 27.53;
Rev 21.10
4.6
Ps 91.11, 12

4.7
Deut 6.16

4.10
1 Chr 21.1;
Deut 6.13

4.11
Mt 26.53;
Lk 22.43;
Heb 1.14

III. Public ministry in Galilee (4.12–18.35)

A. The beginning of Jesus' Galilean ministry
(4.12–17; Mark 1.14,15; Luke 4.14,15; John 4.43–45)

12 Now when Jesusr heard that John had been arrested, he withdrew to Galilee. 13 He left Nazareth and made his home in Capernaum by the sea, in the territory of Zebulun and Naphtali, 14 so that what had been spoken through the prophet Isaiah might be fulfilled:
15 "Land of Zebulun, land of Naphtali,
   on the road by the sea, across the Jordan, Galilee of the
      Gentiles—
16 the people who sat in darkness

4.15
Isa 9.1, 2

4.16
Isa 42.7;
Lk 2.32

q Or my beloved Son   r Gk he

3.15 *fulfill all righteousness*, i.e., although he did not need baptism (for he was without sin), Jesus insisted on being baptized, for this act was by God's divine appointment.
3.16 See note on Lk 3.22 for Jesus' baptism.
4.1 The temptation represents a fight to the death between Jesus and Satan, between the offspring of the woman and the offspring of the serpent (cf. Gen 3.15). Jesus was tempted, his heel bruised; the serpent was repulsed, his head broken.
4.3 Satan hoped to have Jesus despair of his Fa-

ther's goodness, to presume upon his Father's power, and to deny his Father's honor by giving it to Satan. It is the same battle Christians wage today—against the desire of the flesh, the desire of the eyes, and the pride of riches (see 1 Jn 2.16).
4.12,13 From this point on, Capernaum was Jesus' home in Galilee. It was the hometown of Simon and Andrew (Mk 1.29), located at the north end of the Sea of Galilee. The international highway ran through Capernaum; hence, the tax collector's office was located there (9.9; Mk 2.13,14).

have seen a great light,
    and for those who sat in the region and shadow of death
    light has dawned."

Mt 3.2; 10.7 **4.17** [17] From that time Jesus began to proclaim, "Repent, for the kingdom of heaven has come near."[s]

B. The call of James and John
(4.18–25; cf. Mark 1.16–20; Luke 5.1–11)

4.18
Jn 1.35-42

18 As he walked by the Sea of Galilee, he saw two brothers, Simon, who is called Peter, and Andrew his brother, casting a net into the sea — for they were fishermen. [19] And he said to them, "Follow me, and

4.20
Mt 10.28;
Lk 18.28

I will make you fish for people." [20] Immediately they left their nets and followed him. [21] As he went from there, he saw two other brothers, James son of Zebedee and his brother John, in the boat with their father Zebedee, mending their nets, and he called them. [22] Immediately they left the boat and their father, and followed him.

4.23
Mk 1.39;
Lk 4.15, 44;
Mt 9.35;
13.54;
Mk 1.21;
1.34

23 Jesus[t] went throughout Galilee, teaching in their synagogues and proclaiming the good news[u] of the kingdom and curing every disease and every sickness among the people. [24] So his fame spread throughout all Syria, and they brought to him all the sick, those who were afflicted with

4.24
Lk 2.2;
Mt 8.16, 28,
33;
Mk 1.32;
Lk 8.36;
Mt 17.15;
8.6; 9.2, 6

various diseases and pains, demoniacs, epileptics, and paralytics, and he cured them. [25] And great crowds followed him from Galilee, the Decapolis, Jerusalem, Judea, and from beyond the Jordan.

4.25
Mk 3.7, 8;
Lk 6.17

C. The Sermon on the Mount (5.1–7.29; Luke 6.20–49)

1. The Beatitudes (5.1–12; Luke 6.20–23)

5.1
Mk 3.13;
Jn 6.3

5 When Jesus[v] saw the crowds, he went up the mountain; and after he sat down, his disciples came to him. [2] Then he began to speak, and taught them, saying:

5.3
Mk 10.14;
Lk 22.29

3 "Blessed are the poor in spirit, for theirs is the kingdom of heaven.

5.4

4 "Blessed are those who mourn, for they will be comforted.

5.5
Isa 61.2, 3

5 "Blessed are the meek, for they will inherit the earth.

5.6
Isa 55.1, 2

6 "Blessed are those who hunger and thirst for righteousness, for they will be filled.

5.8
Heb 12.14;
1 Jn 3.2

7 "Blessed are the merciful, for they will receive mercy.

8 "Blessed are the pure in heart, for they will see God.

5.9
Rom 8.14

9 "Blessed are the peacemakers, for they will be called children of God.

5.10
1 Pet 3.14
5.11
1 Pet 4.14

10 "Blessed are those who are persecuted for righteousness' sake, for theirs is the kingdom of heaven.

11 "Blessed are you when people revile you and persecute you and

5.12
Acts 7.52;
1 Thess 2.15;
Jas 5.10

utter all kinds of evil against you falsely[w] on my account. [12] Rejoice and

[s] Or is at hand   [t] Gk He   [u] Gk gospel   [v] Gk he   [w] Other ancient authorities lack falsely

---

4.17 The phrase *the kingdom of heaven* is synonymous with the phrase used in Mark and Luke, "the kingdom of God." "Heaven" here is a respectful equivalent to the name of God, which Jews were careful not to employ (Matthew wrote with Jewish readers in mind). Mark and Luke's use of "kingdom of God" was more familiar to a Gentile audience.
4.24 Demon possession is a definite phenomenon. Mk 1.32 and Lk 6.17,18 distinguish between it and bodily ailments. Jesus addressed demons who inhabited people and ordered them to leave (8.32; 17.18; Mk 1.25,34; 9.25). In Lk 8.32 the demons left the possessed and entered a herd of swine. In Mt 8.31 and Mk 9.26 the demons are identified as separate from

the persons they have possessed. Demons are part of the spiritual hierarchy of evil led by Satan.
5.1,2 Many suppose that Jesus delivered the Sermon on the Mount (chapters 5–7) at one time and in one place. Others believe that these three chapters are the creation of Matthew, who collected teachings of Jesus given at different times and under differing circumstances. There is no reason to suppose, however, that Jesus did not repeat many segments of his teaching on a number of occasions, just as ministers preach the same sermon in different places. There is nothing in the text to indicate that this set of sayings was not given at one time.

be glad, for your reward is great in heaven, for in the same way they persecuted the prophets who were before you.

2. What the believer is like (5.13–16)

13 "You are the salt of the earth; but if salt has lost its taste, how can its saltiness be restored? It is no longer good for anything, but is thrown out and trampled under foot.

14 "You are the light of the world. A city built on a hill cannot be hid. 15 No one after lighting a lamp puts it under the bushel basket, but on the lampstand, and it gives light to all in the house. 16 In the same way, let your light shine before others, so that they may see your good works and give glory to your Father in heaven.

3. The righteousness required (5.17–20)

17 "Do not think that I have come to abolish the law or the prophets; I have come not to abolish but to fulfill. 18 For truly I tell you, until heaven and earth pass away, not one letter,ˣ not one stroke of a letter, will pass from the law until all is accomplished. 19 Therefore, whoever breaksʸ one of the least of these commandments, and teaches others to do the same, will be called least in the kingdom of heaven; but whoever does them and teaches them will be called great in the kingdom of heaven. 20 For I tell you, unless your righteousness exceeds that of the scribes and Pharisees, you will never enter the kingdom of heaven.

4. The sixth commandment (5.21–26)

21 "You have heard that it was said to those of ancient times, 'You shall not murder'; and 'whoever murders shall be liable to judgment.' 22 But I say to you that if you are angry with a brother or sister,ᶻ you will be liable to judgment; and if you insultᵃ a brother or sister,ᵇ you will be liable to the council; and if you say, 'You fool,' you will be liable to the hellᶜ of fire. 23 So when you are offering your gift at the altar, if you remember that your brother or sisterᵈ has something against you, 24 leave your gift there before the altar and go; first be reconciled to your brother or sister,ᵈ and then come and offer your gift. 25 Come to terms quickly with your accuser while you are on the way to courtᵉ with him, or your accuser may hand you over to the judge, and the judge to the guard, and you will be thrown into prison. 26 Truly I tell you, you will never get out until you have paid the last penny.

x Gk *one iota* y Or *annuls* z Gk *a brother*; other ancient authorities add *without cause* a Gk *say Raca to* (an obscure term of abuse) b Gk *a brother* c Gk *Gehenna* d Gk *your brother* e Gk lacks *to court*

5.13
Mk 9.50;
Lk 14.34, 35
5.14
Phil 2.15
5.15
Mk 4.21;
Lk 8.16
5.16
1 Pet 2.12

5.17
Rom 3.31;
Gal 3.24
5.18
Lk 16.17
5.19
Jas 2.10

5.21f
Ex 20.13;
Deut 5.17
5.22
1 Jn 3.15;
Jas 2.20

5.23
Mt 8.4;
23.19

5.25
Prov 25.8;
Lk 12.57-59

5.13,14 A handful of salt goes a long way. Christians are as salt, powerfully seasoning with the gospel the places where they live. Christ is the light of the world (Jn 8.12), and his people are the light of the earth. In darkness even the light of a single match can make a great difference. Believers are a light by what they say and how they live.

5.17 The human Jesus was subject to the law of God. He met the demands of the ceremonial law: his circumcision, his presentation in the temple (Lk 2.21ff), and his baptism by John (3.15). In all things Jesus obeyed the law of his Father (Jn 8.46; 1 Pet 2.21–23). But he never put himself into bondage to the legalism that the Pharisees had created by the extravagant interpretations of the law. He also declared himself to be "lord of the sabbath" (12.8). Christ's people are no longer required to keep the ceremonial law, which has been made obsolete by the cross (see Eph 2.15; Col 2.14). Christians, however,

have never been excused from keeping the moral law of God, the ten commandments. They obey them, not in order to merit salvation, but as an indication that their lives have been transformed by the grace of God.
5.21,22 Christ never abrogated the law of murder. He did teach that the believer's righteousness should exceed that of the scribes and Pharisees. They taught that you could hate your enemy in your heart, for there was no sin until you killed that one physically. But Christ said that "heart murder" precedes the actual act. Heart murderers are already guilty before God, even if the fear of retribution restrains them from committing the overt act. Evil in the heart is the root of all outward acts of sin; God condemns both the attitude and the action. *without cause.* This phrase has been relegated to a footnote in the NRSV. However it appears in some ancient Greek N.T. manuscripts. Anger for a right cause is not forbidden in Scripture. God himself is said to be capable of anger.

5. The seventh commandment
(5.27–32; cf. 19.9; Mark 10.11; Luke 16.18)

5.27
Ex 20.14;
Deut 5.18
5.28
Job 31.1;
Prov 6.25
5.29
Mt 18.9;
Mk 9.43-47

27 "You have heard that it was said, 'You shall not commit adultery.' 28 But I say to you that everyone who looks at a woman with lust has already committed adultery with her in his heart. 29 If your right eye causes you to sin, tear it out and throw it away; it is better for you to lose one of your members than for your whole body to be thrown into hell.ᶠ 30 And if your right hand causes you to sin, cut it off and throw it away; it is better for you to lose one of your members than for your whole body to go into hell.ᶠ

5.31
Deut 24.1-4;
Mk 10.11;
12;
Lk 16.18

31 "It was also said, 'Whoever divorces his wife, let him give her a certificate of divorce.' 32 But I say to you that anyone who divorces his wife, except on the ground of unchastity, causes her to commit adultery; and whoever marries a divorced woman commits adultery.

6. The law of oaths (5.33–37)

5.33
Lev 19.12;
Num 30.2;
Deut 23.21;
Mt 23.16
5.34
Jas 5.12;
Isa 66.1

33 "Again, you have heard that it was said to those of ancient times, 'You shall not swear falsely, but carry out the vows you have made to the Lord.' 34 But I say to you, Do not swear at all, either by heaven, for it is the throne of God, 35 or by the earth, for it is his footstool; or by Jerusalem, for it is the city of the great King. 36 And do not swear by your head, for you cannot make one hair white or black. 37 Let your word be 'Yes, Yes' or 'No, No'; anything more than this comes from the evil one.ᵍ

7. The law of retaliation (5.38–42)

5.38
Ex 21.24;
Lev 24.20;
Deut 19.21
5.39
Prov 24.29;
Lk 6.29;
Rom 12.17,
19; 1 Cor 6.7;
1 Pet 3.9
5.42
Deut 15.8;
Lk 6.30

38 "You have heard that it was said, 'An eye for an eye and a tooth for a tooth.' 39 But I say to you, Do not resist an evildoer. But if anyone strikes you on the right cheek, turn the other also; 40 and if anyone wants to sue you and take your coat, give your cloak as well; 41 and if anyone forces you to go one mile, go also the second mile. 42 Give to everyone who begs from you, and do not refuse anyone who wants to borrow from you.

8. The law of love (5.43–48)

5.43
Lev 19.18;
Deut 23.6;
Ps 41.10
5.44
Rom 12.14;
Acts 7.60;
1 Cor 4.12;
1 Pet 2.23
5.45
Job 25.3
5.48
Lev 19.2;
Col 1.28;
Jas 1.4

43 "You have heard that it was said, 'You shall love your neighbor and hate your enemy.' 44 But I say to you, Love your enemies and pray for those who persecute you, 45 so that you may be children of your Father in heaven; for he makes his sun rise on the evil and on the good, and sends rain on the righteous and on the unrighteous. 46 For if you love those who love you, what reward do you have? Do not even the tax collectors do the same? 47 And if you greet only your brothers and sisters,ʰ what more are you doing than others? Do not even the Gentiles do the same? 48 Be perfect, therefore, as your heavenly Father is perfect.

ᶠ Gk Gehenna   ᵍ Or evil   ʰ Gk your brothers

5.27,28 Jesus defines "heart adultery" and physical adultery. To him, adultery is committed when a man looks on a woman with the intent to commit adultery. The Jews of Jesus' day said only the overt act was adultery; a heart filled with adulterous thoughts was still innocent. Jesus' explanation did not change the law of God. He only stated what lay at the heart of the moral law and condemned those whose interpretation opened the door to heart adultery.
5.29,30 Jesus was not telling us to pluck out our eyes or cut off our hands. His main point is that sin is so dangerous that it is preferable to lose the eye and the hand that offend than to give way to sin and perish eternally in it.
5.31 See notes on Deut 24.1 and Mk 10.5ff on divorce.

5.38 This was the law of retaliation, which an injured person might insist on. The principle is that the retaliation should equal the crime. This rule had been instituted by God to prevent people from exacting a greater punishment than was warranted by the injury done. Jesus instructed his followers to go one step further—to love the evildoer and wish him good.
5.44 Jesus corrected the misapprehension the Jews had about the law of love. He made it clear that love exists for enemies as well as friends, for foreigners as well as fellow Jews. Later Paul reiterated the command to love one's enemies, pointing out how Jesus died for us when we were his enemies (Rom 5.8–10).
5.48 The word *perfect* (*teleios*) comes from *telos*, which means "end," "goal," or, "limit." Usually, it signifies "attaining to the end—complete maturity."

D. *The Sermon on the Mount continued: religious observances (6.1–34)*

1. *Giving of alms (6.1–4)*

6 "Beware of practicing your piety before others in order to be seen by them; for then you have no reward from your Father in heaven. 2 "So whenever you give alms, do not sound a trumpet before you, as the hypocrites do in the synagogues and in the streets, so that they may be praised by others. Truly I tell you, they have received their reward. 3 But when you give alms, do not let your left hand know what your right hand is doing, 4 so that your alms may be done in secret; and your Father who sees in secret will reward you.[i]

2. *Praying (6.5–15; cf. Luke 11.1–4)*

5 "And whenever you pray, do not be like the hypocrites; for they love to stand and pray in the synagogues and at the street corners, so that they may be seen by others. Truly I tell you, they have received their reward. 6 But whenever you pray, go into your room and shut the door and pray to your Father who is in secret; and your Father who sees in secret will reward you.[i] 7 "When you are praying, do not heap up empty phrases as the Gentiles do; for they think that they will be heard because of their many words. 8 Do not be like them, for your Father knows what you need before you ask him. 9 "Pray then in this way:

Our Father in heaven,
   hallowed be your name.
10   Your kingdom come.
   Your will be done,
     on earth as it is in heaven.
11   Give us this day our daily bread.[j]
12   And forgive us our debts,
     as we also have forgiven our debtors.
13   And do not bring us to the time of trial,[k]
     but rescue us from the evil one.[l]

14 For if you forgive others their trespasses, your heavenly Father will also forgive you; 15 but if you do not forgive others, neither will your Father forgive your trespasses.

3. *Fasting (6.16–18)*

16 "And whenever you fast, do not look dismal, like the hypocrites, for they disfigure their faces so as to show others that they are fasting.

i Other ancient authorities add openly j Or our bread for tomorrow k Or us into temptation l Or from evil. Other ancient authorities add, in some form, For the kingdom and the power and the glory are yours forever. Amen.

Cross references:
6.1 Mt 23.5
6.2 Rom 12.8
6.4 Col 3.23, 24
6.5 Mk 11.25; Lk 18.10-14
6.6 2 Kings 4.33
6.7 Eccl 5.2; 1 Kings 18.26, 29
6.10 Mt 26.39, 42
6.11 Prov 30.8
6.12 Mt 18.21
6.13 Jn 17.15; 2 Thess 3.3; Jas 1.13
6.14 Mk 11.25, 26; Eph 4.32; Col 3.13
6.15 Mt 18.35
6.16 Isa 58.5

Here, however, the comparison is made between God and his children; hence, the meaning must be expanded to include more than "maturity." This perfection must be a God-like quality of love and kindness even for those who do not deserve it, a quality that is possible for us to attain. This sort of perfectness is not equivalent to absolute sinlessness; rather, it concerns one's intention or attitude to do right. Believers can enjoy the grace from God to maintain an attitude of kindly benevolence and sincere desire for the well-being of others. **6.1** Jesus discusses the three great Christian duties: almsgiving, prayer, and fasting (vv. 1–18). Prayer has to do with our souls, fasting with our bodies, and almsgiving with our possessions. We must perform these duties from the inward person, seeking the approval of God and not the applause of others. **6.9ff** The Lord's Prayer is the model prayer. It begins as all prayer should, with adoration of God Almighty and his interests. It is followed by petitions for our daily needs and requests for the forgiveness of sins. **6.12** Some have seen a legalistic strain in the phrase *forgive us our debts, as we also have forgiven our debtors.* But forgiveness of our sins is never granted by God on the basis of any merit on our part, not even that of forgiving others. Rather, our refusal to forgive others is itself a sin; when we do not forgive others, we demonstrate that we have not repented of our own sin and hence cannot expect forgiveness.

Truly I tell you, they have received their reward. 17 But when you fast, put oil on your head and wash your face, 18 so that your fasting may be seen not by others but by your Father who is in secret; and your Father who sees in secret will reward you.[m]

4. The Christian and the world (6.19–34)

a. True riches (6.19–21)

19 "Do not store up for yourselves treasures on earth, where moth and rust[n] consume and where thieves break in and steal; 20 but store up for yourselves treasures in heaven, where neither moth nor rust[n] consumes and where thieves do not break in and steal. 21 For where your treasure is, there your heart will be also.

b. Light or darkness (6.22,23)

22 "The eye is the lamp of the body. So, if your eye is healthy, your whole body will be full of light; 23 but if your eye is unhealthy, your whole body will be full of darkness. If then the light in you is darkness, how great is the darkness!

c. God or wealth (6.24)

24 "No one can serve two masters; for a slave will either hate the one and love the other, or be devoted to the one and despise the other. You cannot serve God and wealth.[o]

d. Trust or anxiety (6.25–34; cf. Luke 12.22–31)

25 "Therefore I tell you, do not worry about your life, what you will eat or what you will drink,[p] or about your body, what you will wear. Is not life more than food, and the body more than clothing? 26 Look at the birds of the air; they neither sow nor reap nor gather into barns, and yet your heavenly Father feeds them. Are you not of more value than they? 27 And can any of you by worrying add a single hour to your span of life?[q] 28 And why do you worry about clothing? Consider the lilies of the field, how they grow; they neither toil nor spin, 29 yet I tell you, even Solomon in all his glory was not clothed like one of these. 30 But if God so clothes the grass of the field, which is alive today and tomorrow is thrown into the oven, will he not much more clothe you — you of little faith? 31 Therefore do not worry, saying, 'What will we eat?' or 'What will we drink?' or 'What will we wear?' 32 For it is the Gentiles who strive for all these things; and indeed your heavenly Father knows that you need all these things. 33 But strive first for the kingdom of God[r] and his[s] righteousness, and all these things will be given to you as well.

34 "So do not worry about tomorrow, for tomorrow will bring worries of its own. Today's trouble is enough for today.

E. Sermon on the Mount concluded (7.1–29)

1. Judging others (7.1–6; Luke 6.37–42)

7 "Do not judge, so that you may not be judged. 2 For with the judgment you make you will be judged, and the measure you give will be

m Other ancient authorities add *openly*   *n* Gk *eating*   *o* Gk *mammon*   *p* Other ancient authorities lack *or what you will drink*   *q* Or *add one cubit to your height*   *r* Other ancient authorities lack *of God*   *s* Or *its*

6.18
vv. 4, 6

6.19
Prov 23.4;
1 Tim 6.17
Heb 13.5;
Jas 5.1
6.20
Lk 12.33,
34; 18.22;
1 Tim 6.19;
1 Pet 1.4
6.22
Mt 20.15;
Mk 7.22;
Lk 11.34-36

6.24
Lk 16.13

6.25
Ps 55.22;
Phil 4.6;
1 Pet 5.7
6.26
Job 38.41;
Ps 147.9;
Lk 12.24
6.27
Ps 39.5
6.29
1 Kings 10.4-7
6.30
Mt 8.26;
14.31; 16.8

6.32
v. 8

6.33
Mt 19.28;
Mk 10.29,
30;
Lk 18.29, 30

7.1
Mk 4.24;
Rom 2.1;
14.10;
1 Cor 4.3

6.24 *wealth.* In itself, being wealthy is neither bad nor good; how we use our wealth is what makes the difference. Under the Lordship of Christ, wealth is good; not under his Lordship, it becomes an impediment to the Christian life.
6.25 *do not worry.* Anxiety is one of the worst sins a Christian experiences (see note on Ps 37.5).
7.1 The command against judging does not mean

we should never judge. It does mean that we should (1) first judge ourselves (vv. 3–5); (2) never judge rashly; (3) never make our decisions binding on all (Rom 14.1–7); (4) never infer the worst regarding another person's actions (as we are apt to do); (5) never judge a person on the basis of a single act; (6) never judge the hearts of others, for only God knows the heart (1 Cor 4.3–5).

the measure you get. 3 Why do you see the speck in your neighbor's^t eye, but do not notice the log in your own eye? 4 Or how can you say to your neighbor,^u 'Let me take the speck out of your eye,' while the log is in your own eye? 5 You hypocrite, first take the log out of your own eye, and then you will see clearly to take the speck out of your neighbor's^t eye.

6 "Do not give what is holy to dogs; and do not throw your pearls before swine, or they will trample them under foot and turn and maul you.

2. Prayer and the Golden Rule (7.7–12; cf. Luke 11.9–13)

7 "Ask, and it will be given you; search, and you will find; knock, and the door will be opened for you. 8 For everyone who asks receives, and everyone who searches finds, and for everyone who knocks, the door will be opened. 9 Is there anyone among you who, if your child asks for bread, will give a stone? 10 Or if the child asks for a fish, will give a snake? 11 If you then, who are evil, know how to give good gifts to your children, how much more will your Father in heaven give good things to those who ask him!

12 "In everything do to others as you would have them do to you; for this is the law and the prophets.

3. The narrow and the wide gates (7.13,14)

13 "Enter through the narrow gate; for the gate is wide and the road is easy^v that leads to destruction, and there are many who take it. 14 For the gate is narrow and the road is hard that leads to life, and there are few who find it.

4. The test of false prophets (7.15–20)

15 "Beware of false prophets, who come to you in sheep's clothing but inwardly are ravenous wolves. 16 You will know them by their fruits. Are grapes gathered from thorns, or figs from thistles? 17 In the same way, every good tree bears good fruit, but the bad tree bears bad fruit. 18 A good tree cannot bear bad fruit, nor can a bad tree bear good fruit. 19 Every tree that does not bear good fruit is cut down and thrown into the fire. 20 Thus you will know them by their fruits.

5. Profession versus possession (7.21–29)

21 "Not everyone who says to me, 'Lord, Lord,' will enter the kingdom of heaven, but only the one who does the will of my Father in heaven. 22 On that day many will say to me, 'Lord, Lord, did we not prophesy

t Gk brother's   u Gk brother   v Other ancient authorities read for the road is wide and easy

Marginal cross-references

7.6 Prov 9.7, 8; Acts 13.45

7.7 Mk 11.24; Jn 15.7; 16.23, 24; Jas 4.3; 1 Jn 3.22; 5.14, 15

7.8 Jer 29.12, 13

7.12 Lk 6.31; Rom 13.8-10; Gal 5.14

7.13 Lk 13.24

7.15 Jer 23.16; Mt 24.11, 24; Mk 13.22; 2 Pet 2.1; 1 Jn 4.1; Rev 16.13; 19.20; 20.10; Acts 20.29

7.16 Mt 12.33; Mk 3.10; Jas 3.12

7.19 Mt 3.10; Lk 3.9; Jn 15.2, 6

7.21 Hos 8.2 Mt 25.11, 12; Acts 19.13; Rom 2.13; Jas 1.22

7.22 Mt 25.12; Lk 13.25-27

Footnotes

7.7 God speaks to believers through the written word; believers speak to God through prayer. Effective prayer must follow the laws or principles that undergird it: (1) a right relationship to God through Jesus Christ — God promises to answer the prayers of believers; he does not promise to answer the prayers of unbelievers, although he may do so by common grace; (2) a genuine desire to secure from God the petitions addressed to him (1 Sam 1.10,11; 2 Kings 19.14–19; Lk 11.5–10); (3) a confidence in God that leads to asking in simple trust (vv. 7–11; Jas 4.2); (4) a faith that believes that God is able and willing to answer (Mk 11.24; Heb 11:1; 1 Jn 5.14,15); and (5) the confident acceptance of the answer before it has come (Mk 11.24).

7.12 do to others what you would have them do to you. This is the Golden Rule by which we ought to live. There is a four-way test by which we can decide what we should do and how we should think. We must ask: (1) Is it the truth? (2) Is it fair to all concerned?

(3) Will it build good will? (4) Will it be beneficial to all concerned? this is the law and the prophets, i.e., this is the teaching of the law of Moses in a nutshell.

7.15 Scripture abounds with warnings against false prophets (e.g., 24.24; Mk 13.5–7,21,22; Lk 17.23; 21.8; 2 Pet 2.1). They are called treacherous, covetous, crafty, drunken, immoral, and profane. These liars who pretend to be what they are not should be shunned. Their counsel must not be followed.

7.21 The title Lord (kyrios in Greek) is applied to Jesus Christ nearly seven hundred times in the N.T. The earliest Christian confession is that Jesus is both Christ (Messiah) and Lord (e.g., Mt 16.16; Act 2.36; 17.2,3; Rom 10.9; Phil 2.11). As Jesus, he is the Savior; as Christ, he is the anointed one of God; as Lord, he is the master of our lives. Kyrios was used as the equivalent of Yahweh in the ancient Greek translation of the O.T., and this use is continued in the N.T. Thus, Jesus Christ is identified with Yahweh.

in your name, and cast out demons in your name, and do many deeds of power in your name?' 23 Then I will declare to them, 'I never knew you; go away from me, you evildoers.'

24 "Everyone then who hears these words of mine and acts on them will be like a wise man who built his house on rock. 25 The rain fell, the floods came, and the winds blew and beat on that house, but it did not fall, because it had been founded on rock. 26 And everyone who hears these words of mine and does not act on them will be like a foolish man who built his house on sand. 27 The rain fell, and the floods came, and the winds blew and beat against that house, and it fell—and great was its fall!"

28 Now when Jesus had finished saying these things, the crowds were astounded at his teaching, 29 for he taught them as one having authority, and not as their scribes.

F. *Miracles of Jesus (1) (8.1–17)*

1. *The leper cleansed (8.1–4; Mark 1.40–45; Luke 5.12–16)*

8 When Jesus*w* had come down from the mountain, great crowds followed him; 2 and there was a leper*x* who came to him and knelt before him, saying, "Lord, if you choose, you can make me clean." 3 He stretched out his hand and touched him, saying, "I do choose. Be made clean!" Immediately his leprosy*x* was cleansed. 4 Then Jesus said to him, "See that you say nothing to anyone; but go, show yourself to the priest, and offer the gift that Moses commanded, as a testimony to them."

2. *The centurion's servant healed (8.5–13; Luke 7.1–10)*

5 When he entered Capernaum, a centurion came to him, appealing to him 6 and saying, "Lord, my servant is lying at home paralyzed, in terrible distress." 7 And he said to him, "I will come and cure him." 8 The centurion answered, "Lord, I am not worthy to have you come under my roof; but only speak the word, and my servant will be healed. 9 For I also am a man under authority, with soldiers under me; and I say to one, 'Go,' and he goes, and to another, 'Come,' and he comes, and to my slave, 'Do this,' and the slave does it." 10 When Jesus heard him, he was amazed and said to those who followed him, "Truly I tell you, in no one*y* in Israel have I found such faith. 11 I tell you, many will come from east and west and will eat with Abraham and Isaac and Jacob in the kingdom of heaven, 12 while the heirs of the kingdom will be thrown into the outer darkness, where there will be weeping and gnashing of teeth." 13 And to the centurion Jesus said, "Go; let it be done for you according to your faith." And the servant was healed in that hour.

3. *Peter's mother-in-law healed (8.14–17; Mark 1.29–34; Luke 4.28–41)*

14 When Jesus entered Peter's house, he saw his mother-in-law lying in bed with a fever; 15 he touched her hand, and the fever left her, and she got up and began to serve him. 16 That evening they brought to him many who were possessed with demons; and he cast out the spirits with a word, and cured all who were sick. 17 This was to fulfill what had been

---

7.23
Ps 6.8;
Mt 25.12;
Lk 13.25, 27
7.24
Lk 6.47-49;
Jas 1.22-25

7.28
Mt 11.1;
13.53; 19.1;
26.1; 13.54;
Mk 1.22;
6.2;
Lk 4.32;
Jn 7.46

8.2
Mt 9.18;
15.25; 18.26;
20.20;
Jn 9.38
8.4
Lev 14.3, 4,
10;
Mk 3.12;
5.43; 7.36;
8.30; 9.9

8.8
Ps 107.20

8.11
Isa 49.12;
59.19;
Mal 1.11;
Lk 13.29;
Acts 10.45
8.12
Mt 13.42,
50; 22.13;
25.30;
Lk 13.28

8.14
1 Cor 9.5

8.17
Isa 53.4

---

w Gk *he*   *x* The terms *leper* and *leprosy* can refer to several diseases   *y* Other ancient authorities read *Truly I tell you, not even*

8.1ff Matthew presents Christ as Savior (1.21); his credentials are his miracles, which testify to his person and his office. The scope of his miracles shows the magnitude as well as the breadth of his power. He is the master over disease (vv. 1–17; 9.27–34), the master over nature (8.26,27); the master over death (Jn 11.13,43,44; see also Mt 9.18,23–25; Lk 7.12–15);

and the master over devils or demons (Mk 5.12,13; see also Mt 8.28–32; 9.32,33; 15.22–28; 17.14–18; Mk 1.23–27).
8.5ff The centurion was a Gentile, yet he had faith in Christ. Note Jesus' final word: "Go; let it be done for you according to your faith" (v. 13). The servant was healed immediately.

spoken through the prophet Isaiah, "He took our infirmities and bore our diseases."

G. Impulsive and reluctant followers (8.18–22; Luke 9.57–62)

18 Now when Jesus saw great crowds around him, he gave orders to go over to the other side. 19 A scribe then approached and said, "Teacher, I will follow you wherever you go." 20 And Jesus said to him, "Foxes have holes, and birds of the air have nests; but the Son of Man has nowhere to lay his head." 21 Another of his disciples said to him, "Lord, first let me go and bury my father." 22 But Jesus said to him, "Follow me, and let the dead bury their own dead."

H. Miracles of Jesus (2) (8.23–9.8)

1. The storm stilled (8.23–27; Mark 4.36–41; Luke 8.22–25)

23 And when he got into the boat, his disciples followed him. 24 A windstorm arose on the sea, so great that the boat was being swamped by the waves; but he was asleep. 25 And they went and woke him up, saying, "Lord, save us! We are perishing!" 26 And he said to them, "Why are you afraid, you of little faith?" Then he got up and rebuked the winds and the sea; and there was a dead calm. 27 They were amazed, saying, "What sort of man is this, that even the winds and the sea obey him?"

2. Demons cast out (8.28–9.1; Mark 5.1–20; Luke 8.26–39)

28 When he came to the other side, to the country of the Gadarenes,ᶻ two demoniacs coming out of the tombs met him. They were so fierce that no one could pass that way. 29 Suddenly they shouted, "What have you to do with us, Son of God? Have you come here to torment us before the time?" 30 Now a large herd of swine was feeding at some distance from them. 31 The demons begged him, "If you cast us out, send us into the herd of swine." 32 And he said to them, "Go!" So they came out and entered the swine; and suddenly, the whole herd rushed down the steep bank into the sea and perished in the water. 33 The swineherds ran off, and on going into the town, they told the whole story about what had happened to the demoniacs. 34 Then the whole town came out to meet Jesus; and when they saw him, they begged him to leave their neighborhood. 9 1 And after getting into a boat he crossed the sea and came to his own town.

3. A paralytic healed and forgiven (9.2–8; Mark 2.1–12; Luke 5.17–26)

2 And just then some people were carrying a paralyzed man lying on a bed. When Jesus saw their faith, he said to the paralytic, "Take heart,

ᶻ Other ancient authorities read *Gergesenes*; others, *Gerasenes*

Cross-references (right margin):

8.18 Mk 4.35; Lk 8.22

8.22 Mt 9.9; Jn 1.43; 21.19

8.26 Mt 6.30; 14.31; 16.8; Ps 65.7; 89.9; 107.29

8.29 Judg 11.12; 2 Sam 16.10; Mk 1.24; Jn 2.4

8.34 see 1 Kings 17.18; Lk 5.8; Acts 16.39

9.1 Mt 4.13

9.2 Mt 9.22; Mk 6.50; 10.49; Acts 23.11

8.17 Healing is included in the work of Jesus Christ as redeemer. The Bible does not indicate that we become sick because we sin, nor does God intend to heal every sick person and remove every malady. God continues to be involved in healing today. All Christians agree that prayer is effective; not all Christians agree, however, if the gift of miraculous healing is still present.
8.20 *Son of Man.* Jesus referred to himself as the Son of Man more than eighty times in the Gospels. This term describes his office as the Messiah. Jesus avoided describing himself as "Messiah" because the people of his day attached improper connotations to it; they thought of the Messiah as an irresistible military conqueror who would smite Rome and restore the political empire of King David. As a messianic term, "Son of Man" was first used in Dan 7.13, where

it was applied to a heavenly figure who received everlasting rulership over all from the Ancient One. Jesus gave this title its full messianic and redemptive significance.
8.22 The command *follow me* takes precedence over all else in our lives.
8.29 Even demons knew that Jesus was the Christ, yet they hated him. Those who called Jesus the *Son of God* defiantly said they wanted nothing to do with the Savior. They also expressed fear that Christ would torment them *before the time.* They knew what many unbelievers do not know, that there is a time when the wicked will be tormented.
9.2 *your sins are forgiven.* Jesus had the power to forgive sins, not just to declare that they had been forgiven. Since God alone can forgive sins, Jesus was declaring here that he was God.

son; your sins are forgiven." 3 Then some of the scribes said to themselves, "This man is blaspheming." 4 But Jesus, perceiving their thoughts, said, "Why do you think evil in your hearts? 5 For which is easier, to say, 'Your sins are forgiven,' or to say, 'Stand up and walk'? 6 But so that you may know that the Son of Man has authority on earth to forgive sins" — he then said to the paralytic — "Stand up, take your bed and go to your home." 7 And he stood up and went to his home. 8 When the crowds saw it, they were filled with awe, and they glorified God, who had given such authority to human beings.

I. Matthew called (9.9–13; Mark 2.13–17; Luke 5.27–32)

9   As Jesus was walking along, he saw a man called Matthew sitting at the tax booth; and he said to him, "Follow me." And he got up and followed him.

10   And as he sat at dinner[a] in the house, many tax collectors and sinners came and were sitting[b] with him and his disciples. 11 When the Pharisees saw this, they said to his disciples, "Why does your teacher eat with tax collectors and sinners?" 12 But when he heard this, he said, "Those who are well have no need of a physician, but those who are sick. 13 Go and learn what this means, 'I desire mercy, not sacrifice.' For I have come to call not the righteous but sinners."

J. The question about fasting (9.14–17; Mark 2.18–22; Luke 5.33–39)

14   Then the disciples of John came to him, saying, "Why do we and the Pharisees fast often,[c] but your disciples do not fast?" 15 And Jesus said to them, "The wedding guests cannot mourn as long as the bridegroom is with them, can they? The days will come when the bridegroom is taken away from them, and then they will fast. 16 No one sews a piece of unshrunk cloth on an old cloak, for the patch pulls away from the cloak, and a worse tear is made. 17 Neither is new wine put into old wineskins; otherwise, the skins burst, and the wine is spilled, and the skins are destroyed; but new wine is put into fresh wineskins, and so both are preserved."

K. Miracles of Jesus (3) (9.18–34)

1. The hemorrhages stopped and the dead raised (9.18–26; Mark 5.21–43; Luke 8.40–56)

18   While he was saying these things to them, suddenly a leader of the synagogue[d] came in and knelt before him, saying, "My daughter has just died; but come and lay your hand on her, and she will live." 19 And Jesus got up and followed him, with his disciples. 20 Then suddenly a woman who had been suffering from hemorrhages for twelve years came up behind him and touched the fringe of his cloak, 21 for she said to herself, "If I only touch his cloak, I will be made well." 22 Jesus turned, and seeing her he said, "Take heart, daughter; your faith has made you well." And

9.4
Mt 12.25;
Lk 6.8; 9.47;
11.17

9.8
Mt 5.16;
15.31;
Lk 7.16;
13.13; 17.15;
23.47;
Jn 15.8;
Acts 4.21;
11.18; 21.20

9.11
Mt 11.19;
Gal 2.15

9.13
Hos 6.6;
Mic 6.6-8;
Mt 12.7;
1 Tim 1.15

9.14
Lk 18.12
9.15
Jn 3.29;
Acts 13.2, 3;
14.23
9.16
Lk 5.36

9.18
Mt 8.2;
Jn 9.38
9.20
Mt 14.36;
Mk 3.10
9.21
see Lk 6.19
9.22
Mk 10.52;
Lk 7.50;
17.19; 18.42;
Mt 9.9;
15.28

---

a Gk reclined   b Gk were reclining   c Other ancient authorities lack often   d Gk lacks of the synagogue

---

9.10   tax collectors and sinners. The sinners were ordinary Jews who did not keep all the minute prescriptions of the ceremonial laws — especially those dealing with food and social customs — that the Pharisees prized so highly. The Pharisees criticized Jesus for eating and drinking with both kinds of people and for befriending them. It was against this self-righteousness that Jesus told the story about the Pharisee and the tax collector who went to the temple to

pray (Lk 18.9–14).
9.18ff   The raising of the dead occurs rarely in the Bible. Of the various miracles performed by Jesus, he did this only a few times. There have been no empirically verified evidences for this sort of miracle in our generation. This does not rule out the possibility of that type of miracle, however; it only means some kinds of miracles are more common than others.

instantly the woman was made well. 23 When Jesus came to the leader's house, and saw the flute players and the crowd making a commotion, 24 he said, "Go away; for the girl is not dead but sleeping." And they laughed at him. 25 But when the crowd had been put outside, he went in and took her by the hand, and the girl got up. 26 And the report of this spread throughout that district.

2. Sight to the blind and speech to the mute (9.27–34)

27 As Jesus went on from there, two blind men followed him, crying loudly, "Have mercy on us, Son of David!" 28 When he entered the house, the blind men came to him; and Jesus said to them, "Do you believe that I am able to do this?" They said to him, "Yes, Lord." 29 Then he touched their eyes and said, "According to your faith let it be done to you." 30 And their eyes were opened. Then Jesus sternly ordered them, "See that no one knows of this." 31 But they went away and spread the news about him throughout that district.

32 After they had gone away, a demoniac who was mute was brought to him. 33 And when the demon had been cast out, the one who had been mute spoke; and the crowds were amazed and said, "Never has anything like this been seen in Israel." 34 But the Pharisees said, "By the ruler of the demons he casts out the demons."*e*

L. The need for workers (9.35–38)

35 Then Jesus went about all the cities and villages, teaching in their synagogues, and proclaiming the good news of the kingdom, and curing every disease and every sickness. 36 When he saw the crowds, he had compassion for them, because they were harassed and helpless, like sheep without a shepherd. 37 Then he said to his disciples, "The harvest is plentiful, but the laborers are few; 38 therefore ask the Lord of the harvest to send out laborers into his harvest."

M. The names and mission of the Twelve (10.1–15; Mark 6.7–13; Luke 9.1–16)

10 Then Jesus*f* summoned his twelve disciples and gave them authority over unclean spirits, to cast them out, and to cure every disease and every sickness. 2 These are the names of the twelve apostles: first, Simon, also known as Peter, and his brother Andrew; James son of Zebedee, and his brother John; 3 Philip and Bartholomew; Thomas and Matthew the tax collector; James son of Alphaeus, and Thaddaeus;*g* 4 Simon the Cananaean, and Judas Iscariot, the one who betrayed him.

5 These twelve Jesus sent out with the following instructions: "Go nowhere among the Gentiles, and enter no town of the Samaritans, 6 but go rather to the lost sheep of the house of Israel. 7 As you go, proclaim the good news, 'The kingdom of heaven has come near.'*h* 8 Cure the sick, raise the dead, cleanse the lepers,*i* cast out demons. You received without payment; give without payment. 9 Take no gold, or silver, or copper in your belts, 10 no bag for your journey, or two tunics, or sandals, or a staff; for laborers deserve their food. 11 Whatever town or village you enter, find

e Other ancient authorities lack this verse   *f* Gk *he*   *g* Other ancient authorities read *Lebbaeus*, or *Lebbaeus called Thaddaeus*   *h* Or *is at hand*   *i* The terms *leper* and *leprosy* can refer to several diseases

9.23
see
2 Chr 35.25;
Jer 9.17;
16.6;
Ezek 24.17
9.24
see Jn 11.13;
Acts 20.10

9.27
Mt 15.22;
Mk 10.47,
48;
Lk 18.38, 39
9.29
see v. 22;
Mt 8.13
9.30
Mt 8.4; 17.9
9.31
Mk 7.36
9.32
Mt 12.22-24;
Lk 11.14

9.34
Mt 12.24;
Mk 3.22;
Lk 11.15

9.35
Mk 6.6;
Lk 13.22
9.36
Mk 6.34;
Ezek 34.5;
Zech 10.2
9.37
Lk 10.2;
Jn 4.35

10.1
Mk 3.13-15;
Lk 6.14-16;
Acts 1.13

10.4
Lk 6.15;
Acts 1.13;
Jn 13.26
10.5
Lk 9.52;
Acts 8.5, 25
10.6
Mt 15.24;
Ezek 34.5
10.7
Mt 3.2;
Lk 10.9
10.10
1 Cor 9.7;
1 Tim 5.18

9.38 Jesus urged his followers to pray that God would send forth laborers into the harvest fields. By this he suggests that there are some things that do not happen because believers have not prayed. Moreover, if we do pray, we can be sure that God will affirmatively answer this prayer. Through this prayer we become able to fulfill the Great Commission (Mt 28.19).

10.7,8 *is at hand* (footnote NRSV). Jesus sent forth the twelve to preach the gospel and gave them power to raise the dead, cast out demons, etc. These signs of the kingdom were meant to show the multitudes that the message of the disciples was from God and should be believed.

out who in it is worthy, and stay there until you leave. 12 As you enter the house, greet it. 13 If the house is worthy, let your peace come upon it; but if it is not worthy, let your peace return to you. 14 If anyone will not welcome you or listen to your words, shake off the dust from your feet as you leave that house or town. 15 Truly I tell you, it will be more tolerable for the land of Sodom and Gomorrah on the day of judgment than for that town.

10.14
Lk 10.10,
11;
Acts 13.51;
18.6
10.15
Mt 11.22

N. *The servant and suffering*
(10.16–23; cf. Mark 13.9–13; Luke 21.12–19)

10.16
Lk 10.3;
Rom 16.19
10.18
Acts 25.24-26

16 "See, I am sending you out like sheep into the midst of wolves; so be wise as serpents and innocent as doves. 17 Beware of them, for they will hand you over to councils and flog you in their synagogues; 18 and you will be dragged before governors and kings because of me, as a testimony to them and the Gentiles. 19 When they hand you over, do not worry about how you are to speak or what you are to say; for what you are to say will be given to you at that time; 20 for it is not you who speak, but the Spirit of your Father speaking through you. 21 Brother will betray brother to death, and a father his child, and children will rise against parents and have them put to death; 22 and you will be hated by all because of my name. But the one who endures to the end will be saved. 23 When they persecute you in one town, flee to the next; for truly I tell you, you will not have gone through all the towns of Israel before the Son of Man comes.

10.20
2 Sam 23.2;
Jn 16.7-11;
Acts 4.8
10.22
Lk 21.17;
Dan 12.12;
Mt 24.13;
Mk 13.13

O. *The servant's encouragement (10.24–33; cf. Luke 12.2–9)*

10.24
Lk 6.40;
Jn 13.16;
15.20
10.25
Mt 12.24;
Mk 3.22;
Lk 11.15
10.26
Mk 4.22;
Lk 8.17;
12.2, 3
10.28
Isa 8.12, 13;
Heb 10.31
10.30
Lk 21.18;
Acts 27.34

24 "A disciple is not above the teacher, nor a slave above the master; 25 it is enough for the disciple to be like the teacher, and the slave like the master. If they have called the master of the house Beelzebul, how much more will they malign those of his household!

26 "So have no fear of them; for nothing is covered up that will not be uncovered, and nothing secret that will not become known. 27 What I say to you in the dark, tell in the light; and what you hear whispered, proclaim from the housetops. 28 Do not fear those who kill the body but cannot kill the soul; rather fear him who can destroy both soul and body in hell.*j* 29 Are not two sparrows sold for a penny? Yet not one of them will fall to the ground apart from your Father. 30 And even the hairs of your head are all counted. 31 So do not be afraid; you are of more value than many sparrows.

10.32
Rom 10.9;
2 Tim 2.12;
Rev 3.5

32 "Everyone therefore who acknowledges me before others, I also will acknowledge before my Father in heaven; 33 but whoever denies me before others, I also will deny before my Father in heaven.

P. *The servant and the cross (10.34–39)*

10.34
Lk 12.51-53;
Mk 13.12

34 "Do not think that I have come to bring peace to the earth; I have not come to bring peace, but a sword.

j Gk Gehenna

10.20 Jesus promised that when his followers were brought before magistrates and kings, the Spirit of their Father would be with them. The Spirit would give them the proper words to say, guaranteeing that they would say the right thing at the right time. Such testimony would be effective.

10.25 *Beelzebul*, a Greek word derived from the Philistine deity *Be-el-zebul* ("lord of the flies"; see note on 2 Kings 1.2). In Aramaic this word means "lord of the high house" or "lord of the temple." In Jesus' day the people believed Beelzebul to be the leader of the demons; i.e., it was simply another name for Satan. Jesus was accused by the Pharisees of being

a co-worker with Beelzebul in casting out demons from people (12.24,27; Mk 3.22; Lk 11.15,18,19). **10.28** The Scriptures teach four things about *hell*, or *Gehenna* (NRSV footnote): (1) it is a prepared place (25.41); (2) it is a place which endures forever (25.46; Isa 33.14; Rev 20.10); (3) it is a place of suffering (Mk 9.47–49); (4) it is a place of fire and sulphur (Rev 14.10; 20.15).

10.34,35 Jesus and his gospel are great dividers. Families are torn apart when some believe and others do not. Whoever puts even a loved one before the Son of God is not worthy of the Savior. We can expect the sword, which is always the symbol of division, disaf-

35 For I have come to set a man against his father,
   and a daughter against her mother,
   and a daughter-in-law against her mother-in-law;
36 and one's foes will be members of one's own household.
37 Whoever loves father or mother more than me is not worthy of me; and
whoever loves son or daughter more than me is not worthy of me; 38 and
whoever does not take up the cross and follow me is not worthy of me.
39 Those who find their life will lose it, and those who lose their life for
my sake will find it.

Q. The servant and the reward (10.40–11.1)

40 "Whoever welcomes you welcomes me, and whoever welcomes me
welcomes the one who sent me. 41 Whoever welcomes a prophet in the
name of a prophet will receive a prophet's reward; and whoever welcomes
a righteous person in the name of a righteous person will receive the
reward of the righteous; 42 and whoever gives even a cup of cold water to
one of these little ones in the name of a disciple—truly I tell you, none
of these will lose their reward."

11 Now when Jesus had finished instructing his twelve disciples, he
went on from there to teach and proclaim his message in their
cities.

R. John the Baptist's last message (11.2–19; Luke 7.18–35)

2 When John heard in prison what the Messiah[k] was doing, he sent
word by his[l] disciples 3 and said to him, "Are you the one who is to come,
or are we to wait for another?" 4 Jesus answered them, "Go and tell John
what you hear and see: 5 the blind receive their sight, the lame walk, the
lepers[m] are cleansed, the deaf hear, the dead are raised, and the poor have
good news brought to them. 6 And blessed is anyone who takes no offense
at me."
7 As they went away, Jesus began to speak to the crowds about John:
"What did you go out into the wilderness to look at? A reed shaken by
the wind? 8 What then did you go out to see? Someone[n] dressed in soft
robes? Look, those who wear soft robes are in royal palaces. 9 What then
did you go out to see? A prophet?[o] Yes, I tell you, and more than a
prophet. 10 This is the one about whom it is written,
   'See, I am sending my messenger ahead of you,
      who will prepare your way before you.'
11 Truly I tell you, among those born of women no one has arisen greater

k Or *the Christ* *l* Other ancient authorities read *two of his* *m* The terms *leper* and *leprosy* can refer to
several diseases *n* Or *Why then did you go out? To see someone* *o* Other ancient authorities read *Why
then did you go out? To see a prophet?*

Cross references:
10.35 Mic 7.6
10.36 Mic 7.6
10.37 Lk 14.26
10.38 Mt 16.24
10.39 Mt 16.25; Lk 17.33; Jn 12.25
10.40 Lk 9.48; Jn 12.44; Gal 4.14
10.42 Mt 25.40; Heb 6.10
11.2 Mt 14.3; Mk 6.17; Lk 9.7ff
11.3 Jn 11.27
11.5 Isa 35.4-6; 61.1; Lk 4.18, 19
11.6 Isa 8.14, 15; Rom 9.32; 1 Pet 2.8
11.7 Mt 3.1
11.9 Lk 1.76
11.10 Mal 3.1; Mk 1.2

---

fection, and even judgment.
10.40,41 Jesus assures us that some who hear us will
reject our message, but others will receive it. Whoever welcomes Christ's ambassadors welcomes him,
and whoever rejects his ambassadors rejects him.
There is a suitable reward awaiting those who serve
Christ faithfully.
11.3 *Are you the one who is to come, or are we to wait
for another?* John had baptized Jesus and had witnessed the endorsement of Jesus as Messiah by the
Father and the Holy Spirit. Now he was in jail, despondent and without the help of the Messiah whom
he had announced to all people. Doubtless he expected the Messiah to deliver him. Thus he sent his
disciples with the question addressed to Jesus, so that
he might be reassured that indeed he was the Messiah.
Jesus performed miracles before those disciples and
sent them back to tell John that his credentials

showed he was the Messiah (probably thinking of Isa
61.1–3). Shortly thereafter John was killed, and Jesus
was moving steadily toward Jerusalem, toward Calvary.
11.11 Jesus said that the least in the kingdom of
heaven are greater than John the Baptist. While this
statement is enigmatic, what he meant was probably
this: as great and good as John was, he was still in the
flesh, full of infirmity and imperfections, whereas the
lowest saint in the kingdom of heaven was already
glorified and "greater than" any saint still on earth.
Dispensationalists think this refers to the position of
John the Baptist under the old dispensation, which
has been superseded since the crucifixion and resurrection of Jesus and the outpouring of the Holy
Spirit. The saints in the new dispensation occupy
a higher position than that of John under the old
one.

than John the Baptist; yet the least in the kingdom of heaven is greater
than he. 12 From the days of John the Baptist until now the kingdom of
heaven has suffered violence,[p] and the violent take it by force. 13 For all
the prophets and the law prophesied until John came; 14 and if you are
willing to accept it, he is Elijah who is to come. 15 Let anyone with ears[q]
listen!

16 "But to what will I compare this generation? It is like children
sitting in the marketplaces and calling to one another,

17 'We played the flute for you, and you did not dance;
we wailed, and you did not mourn.'

18 For John came neither eating nor drinking, and they say, 'He has a
demon'; 19 the Son of Man came eating and drinking, and they say, 'Look,
a glutton and a drunkard, a friend of tax collectors and sinners!' Yet
wisdom is vindicated by her deeds."[r]

S. *The judgment of the unrepentant (11.20–24; cf. Luke 10.12–15)*

20 Then he began to reproach the cities in which most of his deeds
of power had been done, because they did not repent. 21 "Woe to you,
Chorazin! Woe to you, Bethsaida! For if the deeds of power done in you
had been done in Tyre and Sidon, they would have repented long ago in
sackcloth and ashes. 22 But I tell you, on the day of judgment it will be
more tolerable for Tyre and Sidon than for you. 23 And you, Capernaum,
will you be exalted to heaven?
No, you will be brought down to Hades.
For if the deeds of power done in you had been done in Sodom, it would
have remained until this day. 24 But I tell you that on the day of judgment
it will be more tolerable for the land of Sodom than for you."

T. *Jesus who reveals the Father (11.25–30; cf. Luke 10.21,22)*

25 At that time Jesus said, "I thank[s] you, Father, Lord of heaven
and earth, because you have hidden these things from the wise and the
intelligent and have revealed them to infants; 26 yes, Father, for such was
your gracious will.[t] 27 All things have been handed over to me by my
Father; and no one knows the Son except the Father, and no one knows
the Father except the Son and anyone to whom the Son chooses to reveal
him.

28 "Come to me, all you that are weary and are carrying heavy burdens, and I will give you rest. 29 Take my yoke upon you, and learn from
me; for I am gentle and humble in heart, and you will find rest for your
souls. 30 For my yoke is easy, and my burden is light."

U. *Jesus the Lord of the sabbath (12.1–8; Mark 2.23–28; Luke 6.1–5)*

12 At that time Jesus went through the grainfields on the sabbath;
his disciples were hungry, and they began to pluck heads of grain
and to eat. 2 When the Pharisees saw it, they said to him, "Look, your
disciples are doing what is not lawful to do on the sabbath." 3 He said to

11.14 Mal 4.5; Mt 17.12; Lk 1.17
11.15 Mt 13.9, 43; Mk 4.23; Rev 13.9
11.19 Mt 9.11; Lk 15.2
11.21 Jon 3.7, 8
11.22 v. 24; Mt 10.15
11.23 Isa 14.13; Lam 2.1
11.24 Mt 10.15
11.25 1 Cor 1.26-29
11.27 Mt 28.18; Jn 3.35; 13.3; 17.2
11.28 see Jer 31.25; Jn 7.37
11.29 Jn 13.15; Phil 2.5; 1 Pet 2.21; 1 Jn 2.6; Jer 6.16
12.1 Deut 23.25
12.2 v. 10; Lk 13.14; 14.3; Jn 5.10; 7.23; 9.16
12.3 1 Sam 21.6

[p] Or *has been coming violently* [q] Other ancient authorities add *to hear* [r] Other ancient authorities read *children* [s] Or *praise* [t] Or *for so it was well-pleasing in your sight*

11.18 *He has a demon.* Those who reject the gospel will use every excuse possible to justify their unbelief. John came as a mourner who neither ate nor drank, and he was rejected. Jesus came eating and drinking, and he was rejected.
11.21 *Tyre and Sidon* were cities destroyed by God for their wickedness. *Sidon* is called "Sodom" in v. 23.
11.29 Believers have a yoke for their necks and a crown for their heads. The former signifies identification with Christ in his death and the accompanying sufferings; the latter signifies participation in Christ's glory, when believers shall wear crowns on their heads and enjoy everlasting blessedness (1 Cor 9.25; 2 Tim 4.8). Becoming a Christian does not deliver anyone from suffering, but such is a momentary affliction when compared to the glory that shall be revealed (2 Cor 4.17).

them, "Have you not read what David did when he and his companions were hungry? 4 He entered the house of God and ate the bread of the Presence, which it was not lawful for him or his companions to eat, but only for the priests. 5 Or have you not read in the law that on the sabbath the priests in the temple break the sabbath and yet are guiltless? 6 I tell you, something greater than the temple is here. 7 But if you had known what this means, 'I desire mercy and not sacrifice,' you would not have condemned the guiltless. 8 For the Son of Man is lord of the sabbath."

12.4
Ex 25.30;
Lev 24.5, 9
12.5
Num 28.9, 10
12.6
vv. 41, 42
12.7
Hos 6.6;
Mt 9.13

V. The healing of the withered hand on the sabbath
(12.9–14; Mark 3.1–6; Luke 6.6–11)

9 He left that place and entered their synagogue; 10 a man was there with a withered hand, and they asked him, "Is it lawful to cure on the sabbath?" so that they might accuse him. 11 He said to them, "Suppose one of you has only one sheep and it falls into a pit on the sabbath; will you not lay hold of it and lift it out? 12 How much more valuable is a human being than a sheep! So it is lawful to do good on the sabbath." 13 Then he said to the man, "Stretch out your hand." He stretched it out, and it was restored, as sound as the other. 14 But the Pharisees went out and conspired against him, how to destroy him.

12.10
Lk 13.14;
14.3;
Jn 9.16
12.11
Lk 14.5
12.12
Mt 10.31

12.14
Mt 27.1;
Mk 3.6;
Lk 6.11;
Jn 5.18;
11.53

W. Jesus heals many (12.15–21; Mark 3.7–12; cf. Luke 6.17–19)

15 When Jesus became aware of this, he departed. Many crowds[u] followed him, and he cured all of them, 16 and he ordered them not to make him known. 17 This was to fulfill what had been spoken through the prophet Isaiah:

18 "Here is my servant, whom I have chosen,
　　my beloved, with whom my soul is well pleased.
I will put my Spirit upon him,
　　and he will proclaim justice to the Gentiles.
19 He will not wrangle or cry aloud,
　　nor will anyone hear his voice in the streets.
20 He will not break a bruised reed
　　or quench a smoldering wick
until he brings justice to victory.
21 　And in his name the Gentiles will hope."

12.15
Mt 10.23;
19.2
12.16
Mt 9.30

12.18
Isa 42.1-4

u Other ancient authorities lack *crowds*

12.3–5 In response to his critics, Jesus often referred to the O.T. Scriptures to explain and justify his conduct. Here he referred to two incidents. (1) David and his followers ate the bread which was reserved for the priests (1 Sam 21.1–6), indicating that human need comes before ceremonial regulations. (2) The priests worked on the sabbath by offering sacrifices, proving that if they could break one law to keep another, so Jesus could breach the sabbath law in the larger interests of the kingdom of God.
12.4 See note on Mk 2.25ff regarding *the bread of the Presence.*
12.6 *something greater than the temple is here.* The glory of God had rested on the tabernacle and on the Solomonic temple; in Jesus dwelt the whole fullness of deity bodily (Jn 1.14; Col 2.9). Since Jesus as God was present among them, the temple took on new significance. Without that presence it was a barren and useless heap of stones.
12.11 This verse asks a rhetorical question. To the

Pharisees, the implied answer would be, "Of course we would."
12.12 The Jews performed works of necessity and mercy on the sabbath. They watered and fed their animals and rescued those that fell into pits. They thought more of their property than they did of suffering humanity. Jewish respect for the law had turned into legalism. There are still people today who are more concerned about do's and don'ts than about the spirit of God's law.
12.18–21 *I will put my Spirit upon him.* Christ had the Spirit without measure (Jn 3.34), was filled with the Spirit (Lk 4.1), and he offered himself on Calvary by the eternal Spirit (Heb 9.14). *in his name the Gentiles will hope.* Just as in the O.T. Israel was called to hope in God (e.g., Ps 42.5,11; 131.3), so the nations are now called to hope in God's servant Jesus. In other words, Christ is God, equal in power and glory with the Father (Jn 17.5,24; Phil 2.6).

X. *Jesus answers the Pharisees' slander*
(12.22–37; Mark 3.20–30; Luke 11.14–23)

22 Then they brought to him a demoniac who was blind and mute; and he cured him, so that the one who had been mute could speak and see. 23 All the crowds were amazed and said, "Can this be the Son of David?" 24 But when the Pharisees heard it, they said, "It is only by Beelzebul, the ruler of the demons, that this fellow casts out the demons." 25 He knew what they were thinking and said to them, "Every kingdom divided against itself is laid waste, and no city or house divided against itself will stand. 26 If Satan casts out Satan, he is divided against himself; how then will his kingdom stand? 27 If I cast out demons by Beelzebul, by whom do your own exorcists*v* cast them out? Therefore they will be your judges. 28 But if it is by the Spirit of God that I cast out demons, then the kingdom of God has come to you. 29 Or how can one enter a strong man's house and plunder his property, without first tying up the strong man? Then indeed the house can be plundered. 30 Whoever is not with me is against me, and whoever does not gather with me scatters. 31 Therefore I tell you, people will be forgiven for every sin and blasphemy, but blasphemy against the Spirit will not be forgiven. 32 Whoever speaks a word against the Son of Man will be forgiven, but whoever speaks against the Holy Spirit will not be forgiven, either in this age or in the age to come.

33 "Either make the tree good, and its fruit good; or make the tree bad, and its fruit bad; for the tree is known by its fruit. 34 You brood of vipers! How can you speak good things, when you are evil? For out of the abundance of the heart the mouth speaks. 35 The good person brings good things out of a good treasure, and the evil person brings evil things out of an evil treasure. 36 I tell you, on the day of judgment you will have to give an account for every careless word you utter; 37 for by your words you will be justified, and by your words you will be condemned."

Y. *Warning against seeking signs (12.38–45; Luke 11.29–32)*

38 Then some of the scribes and Pharisees said to him, "Teacher, we wish to see a sign from you." 39 But he answered them, "An evil and adulterous generation asks for a sign, but no sign will be given to it except the sign of the prophet Jonah. 40 For just as Jonah was three days and three nights in the belly of the sea monster, so for three days and three nights the Son of Man will be in the heart of the earth. 41 The people of Nineveh will rise up at the judgment with this generation and condemn it, because they repented at the proclamation of Jonah, and see, something greater than Jonah is here! 42 The queen of the South will rise up at the judgment with this generation and condemn it, because she came from the ends of the earth to listen to the wisdom of Solomon, and see, something greater than Solomon is here!

43 "When the unclean spirit has gone out of a person, it wanders through waterless regions looking for a resting place, but it finds none. 44 Then it says, 'I will return to my house from which I came.' When it

v Gk *sons*

12.24 The Pharisees believed in miracles and regarded what Jesus did as miraculous. But they attributed the miracle to Beelzebul, i.e., Satan (see note on 10.25). By this accusation they were blaspheming, because they attributed to Satan what was the true work of God. They posited that Jesus was in league with Satan himself and had derived his power from him.
12.31,32 See note on Mk 3.29 regarding the sin against the Holy Spirit.
12.36 What we say tells others what we really think.

Whether words are good or bad depend upon our intended meaning. Idle or careless words will be judged (see note on 2 Cor 5.10 for a look at Christ's judgment).
12.40 Jonah is an O.T. representation of Christ, though with a difference: Jonah was imprisoned in the fish for his own sins; Christ was imprisoned in hell for our sins. Jesus' words here can be used to support the historicity of Jonah's imprisonment, for Jesus refers to Jonah in connection with the queen of Sheba, a historical figure.

comes, it finds it empty, swept, and put in order. 45 Then it goes and brings along seven other spirits more evil than itself, and they enter and live there; and the last state of that person is worse than the first. So will it be also with this evil generation."

Z. Christ's true kindred (12.46–50; Mark 3.31–35; Luke 8.19–21)

46 While he was still speaking to the crowds, his mother and his brothers were standing outside, wanting to speak to him. 47 Someone told him, "Look, your mother and your brothers are standing outside, wanting to speak to you."*w* 48 But to the one who had told him this, Jesus*x* replied, "Who is my mother, and who are my brothers?" 49 And pointing to his disciples, he said, "Here are my mother and my brothers! 50 For whoever does the will of my Father in heaven is my brother and sister and mother."

AA. Jesus teaches in parables (13.1–52)

1. The sower (13.1–23)

a. The story of the sower (13.1–9; Mark 4.1–9; Luke 8.4–8)

13 That same day Jesus went out of the house and sat beside the sea. 2 Such great crowds gathered around him that he got into a boat and sat there, while the whole crowd stood on the beach. 3 And he told them many things in parables, saying: "Listen! A sower went out to sow. 4 And as he sowed, some seeds fell on the path, and the birds came and ate them up. 5 Other seeds fell on rocky ground, where they did not have much soil, and they sprang up quickly, since they had no depth of soil. 6 But when the sun rose, they were scorched; and since they had no root, they withered away. 7 Other seeds fell among thorns, and the thorns grew up and choked them. 8 Other seeds fell on good soil and brought forth grain, some a hundredfold, some sixty, some thirty. 9 Let anyone with ears*y* listen!"

b. The reason for parables (13.10–17; Mark 4.10–12; Luke 8.9–10)

10 Then the disciples came and asked him, "Why do you speak to them in parables?" 11 He answered, "To you it has been given to know the secrets*z* of the kingdom of heaven, but to them it has not been given. 12 For to those who have, more will be given, and they will have an abundance; but from those who have nothing, even what they have will be taken away. 13 The reason I speak to them in parables is that 'seeing they do not perceive, and hearing they do not listen, nor do they understand.' 14 With them indeed is fulfilled the prophecy of Isaiah that says:
'You will indeed listen, but never understand,
    and you will indeed look, but never perceive.
15 For this people's heart has grown dull,
        and their ears are hard of hearing,
            and they have shut their eyes;
    so that they might not look with their eyes,
        and listen with their ears,

w Other ancient authorities lack verse 47   x Gk he   y Other ancient authorities add to hear
z Or mysteries

12.45	2 Pet 2.20
12.46	Mt 13.55; Mk 6.3; Jn 2.12; 7.3, 5; Acts 1.4; 1 Cor 9.5; Gal 1.9
12.50	Jn 15.14
13.2	Lk 5.3
13.8	Gen 26.12
13.9	Mt 11.15
13.11	Mt 11.25; 19.11; Jn 6.65; 1 Cor 2.10; 1 Jn 2.27
13.12	Mt 25.29; Lk 19.26
13.13	Jer 5.21; Ezek 12.2
13.14	Isa 6.9, 10; Ezek 12.2; Jn 12.40; Acts 28.26, 27; Rom 11.8
13.15	Heb 5.11

13.3 A parable is an earthly story with a heavenly meaning. The story uses the language and figures of that day. No parable should be pressed beyond its central meaning, which is usually easy to discern; the details may not be separated from that central thought. Thus, for example, in the parable of the mustard seed (vv. 31,32) the main point relates to the growth of the kingdom. The details about the seed, the tree, and the birds are incidental.

13.10ff *Why do you speak to them in parables?* Jesus responded to this question by saying that his disciples could find the explanation of parables simply by asking him. But to those who rejected him, the spiritual meaning of the parables would be unclear. Such people might find parables interesting fables, but they would have no other meaning for them.

and understand with their heart and turn—
and I would heal them.'
16But blessed are your eyes, for they see, and your ears, for they hear.
17Truly I tell you, many prophets and righteous people longed to see what
you see, but did not see it, and to hear what you hear, but did not hear
it.

c. The parable of the sower explained
(13.18–23; Mark 4.13–20; Luke 8.11–15)

18 "Hear then the parable of the sower. 19When anyone hears the
word of the kingdom and does not understand it, the evil one comes and
snatches away what is sown in the heart; this is what was sown on the path.
20As for what was sown on rocky ground, this is the one who hears the
word and immediately receives it with joy; 21yet such a person has no root,
but endures only for a while, and when trouble or persecution arises on
account of the word, that person immediately falls away.*a* 22As for what
was sown among thorns, this is the one who hears the word, but the cares
of the world and the lure of wealth choke the word, and it yields nothing.
23But as for what was sown on good soil, this is the one who hears the
word and understands it, who indeed bears fruit and yields, in one case
a hundredfold, in another sixty, and in another thirty."

2. The wheat and the weeds (13.24–30; cf. Mark 4.26–29)

24 He put before them another parable: "The kingdom of heaven may
be compared to someone who sowed good seed in his field; 25but while
everybody was asleep, an enemy came and sowed weeds among the wheat,
and then went away. 26So when the plants came up and bore grain, then
the weeds appeared as well. 27And the slaves of the householder came and
said to him, 'Master, did you not sow good seed in your field? Where,
then, did these weeds come from?' 28He answered, 'An enemy has done
this.' The slaves said to him, 'Then do you want us to go and gather them?'
29But he replied, 'No; for in gathering the weeds you would uproot the
wheat along with them. 30Let both of them grow together until the
harvest; and at harvest time I will tell the reapers, Collect the weeds first
and bind them in bundles to be burned, but gather the wheat into my
barn.'"

3. The mustard seed
(13.31,32; Mark 4.30–32; Luke 13.18,19)

31 He put before them another parable: "The kingdom of heaven is
like a mustard seed that someone took and sowed in his field; 32it is the
smallest of all the seeds, but when it has grown it is the greatest of shrubs
and becomes a tree, so that the birds of the air come and make nests in
its branches."

4. The yeast (13.33–35; Luke 13.20,21)

33 He told them another parable: "The kingdom of heaven is like

a Gk *stumbles*

13.16
Mt 16.17;
Lk 10.23,
24;
Jn 20.29
13.17
Heb 11.13;
1 Pet 1.10, 11

13.19
Mt 4.23

13.21
Mt 11.6
13.22
Rom 12.2;
1 Cor 1.20;
2 Cor 4.4;
Gal 1.4;
Eph 2.2;
Mt 19.23;
1 Tim 6.9,
10, 17
13.23
v. 8

13.24
Lk 13.18, 20

13.30
Mt 3.12

13.31
see Isa 2.2,
3;
Mic 4.1
13.32
Ps 104.12;
Ezek 17.23;
31.6;
Dan 4.12

13.33
Gen 18.6;
Gal 5.9

13.19 *the evil one,* i.e., Satan.
13.30 The parable of the weeds among the wheat
teaches that there are always true and false believers
in the church, and we cannot always distinguish between them. The presence of false believers does
harm Christ's body, but harm may also come from
human efforts to remove them, especially if mistakes
are made and the true are excluded. Unbelievers, of
course, should be excluded if they can be positively
identified. But the final separation will be made by

the judge of all, the Lord Jesus, who makes no mistakes.
13.31,32 This parable's central teaching is the
growth and spread of the gospel throughout the
world. Just as the tiny mustard seed becomes a giant
tree (see note on 17.20), so the gospel, which begins
slowly, will flourish in the end. The existence of the
Christian church all around the globe represents a
partial fulfillment of this prophetic word.
13.33 Yeast is generally used in the Bible in an evil

yeast that a woman took and mixed in with[b] three measures of flour until all of it was leavened."

34 Jesus told the crowds all these things in parables; without a parable he told them nothing. 35 This was to fulfill what had been spoken through the prophet:[c]

"I will open my mouth to speak in parables;
     I will proclaim what has been hidden from the foundation of
          the world."[d]

5. The wheat and the weeds explained (13.36–43)

36 Then he left the crowds and went into the house. And his disciples approached him, saying, "Explain to us the parable of the weeds of the field." 37 He answered, "The one who sows the good seed is the Son of Man; 38 the field is the world, and the good seed are the children of the kingdom; the weeds are the children of the evil one, 39 and the enemy who sowed them is the devil; the harvest is the end of the age, and the reapers are angels. 40 Just as the weeds are collected and burned up with fire, so will it be at the end of the age. 41 The Son of Man will send his angels, and they will collect out of his kingdom all causes of sin and all evildoers, 42 and they will throw them into the furnace of fire, where there will be weeping and gnashing of teeth. 43 Then the righteous will shine like the sun in the kingdom of their Father. Let anyone with ears[e] listen!

6. The hidden treasure (13.44)

44 "The kingdom of heaven is like treasure hidden in a field, which someone found and hid; then in his joy he goes and sells all that he has and buys that field.

7. The pearl (13.45)

45 "Again, the kingdom of heaven is like a merchant in search of fine pearls; 46 on finding one pearl of great value, he went and sold all that he had and bought it.

8. The dragnet (13.47–53)

47 "Again, the kingdom of heaven is like a net that was thrown into the sea and caught fish of every kind; 48 when it was full, they drew it ashore, sat down, and put the good into baskets but threw out the bad. 49 So it will be at the end of the age. The angels will come out and separate the evil from the righteous 50 and throw them into the furnace of fire, where there will be weeping and gnashing of teeth. 51 "Have you understood all this?" They answered, "Yes." 52 And he said to them, "Therefore every scribe who has been trained for the king-

---

13.34
Mk 4.33, 34
13.35
Ps 78.2;
Rom 16.25,
26; 1 Cor 2.7;
Eph 3.9;
Col 1.26

13.38
Mt 24.14;
28.19;
Lk 24.47;
Jn 8.44; 1 Jn
3.10
13.39
Joel 3.13;
Mt 24.3;
28.20;
Rev 14.15
13.40
1 Cor 10.11;
Heb 9.26
13.41
Mt 24.31
13.42
Mt 8.12;
v. 50;
Mt 24.51;
25.30;
Lk 13.28
13.43
Dan 12.3;
Mt 11.15
13.44
see Phil 3.7,
8;
Isa 55.1

13.47
Mt 22.10

13.49
Mt 25.32
13.50
v. 42

---

b Gk hid in   c Other ancient authorities read the prophet Isaiah   d Other ancient authorities lack of the world   e Other ancient authorities add to hear

---

sense. It refers to (1) the doctrines of the Pharisees and Sadducees (16.6,12); (2) ungodly people who claim to be true followers (1 Cor 5.6,7); (3) false teachers (Gal 5.8,9); and (4) malice and evil (1 Cor 5.8). Only in this parable does yeast have a positive connotation, symbolizing the silent permeating power of the kingdom that requires only a small amount in the dough to be effective.
13.34,35 The meaning of Jesus' stories was apparently unclear both to the multitudes and to his own disciples. Note Mark's comment: Jesus "explained everything in private to his disciples" (Mk 4.34).
13.44 The central teaching of this illustration is that the gospel has such value that a person should give up everything to possess that which is the greatest of all things (16.26). Some hold, however, that the discov-

erer of the treasure is Christ himself, who gave his all to purchase the church.
13.45,46 The story of the pearl is similar to that of the hidden treasure. When a pearl merchant finds a pearl of real value, he will sell all he has and buy that one pearl. Salvation is the pearl of great price, though it costs us nothing! Jesus paid it all. Another interpretation is that Jesus is referring to himself as the purchaser; he paid all he had in order to buy the church for himself.
13.47ff The net represents the kingdom of heaven. Just as a net cast into the sea catches a mixed company of fishes, so in the kingdom of heaven are a mixed company of people. At the end of the age, the good will be separated out. This story makes it clear that not all people will be saved.

13.53
Mt 7.28;
11.1; 19.1;
26.1
dom of heaven is like the master of a household who brings out of his treasure what is new and what is old." 53 When Jesus had finished these parables, he left that place.

BB. *Second rejection of Jesus at Nazareth (13.54–58; Mark 6.1–6; Luke 4.16–30)*

13.54
Mt 4.23;
7.28
13.55
Lk 3.23;
Jn 6.42

13.57
Jn 4.44
54 He came to his hometown and began to teach the people*f* in their synagogue, so that they were astounded and said, "Where did this man get this wisdom and these deeds of power? 55 Is not this the carpenter's son? Is not his mother called Mary? And are not his brothers James and Joseph and Simon and Judas? 56 And are not all his sisters with us? Where then did this man get all this?" 57 And they took offense at him. But Jesus said to them, "Prophets are not without honor except in their own country and in their own house." 58 And he did not do many deeds of power there, because of their unbelief.

CC. *Death of John the Baptist (14.1–12; Mark 6.14–29; Luke 9.7–9)*

14.1
Mk 8.15;
Lk 3.1, 19;
8.3; 13.31;
23.7, 8;
Acts 4.27;
12.1
14.3
Lk 3.19, 20
14.4
Lev 18.16;
20.21
14.5
Mt 21.26;
Lk 20.6
14 At that time Herod the ruler*g* heard reports about Jesus; 2 and he said to his servants, "This is John the Baptist; he has been raised from the dead, and for this reason these powers are at work in him." 3 For Herod had arrested John, bound him, and put him in prison on account of Herodias, his brother Philip's wife,*h* 4 because John had been telling him, "It is not lawful for you to have her." 5 Though Herod*i* wanted to put him to death, he feared the crowd, because they regarded him as a prophet. 6 But when Herod's birthday came, the daughter of Herodias danced before the company, and she pleased Herod 7 so that he promised on oath to grant her whatever she might ask. 8 Prompted by her mother, she said, "Give me the head of John the Baptist here on a platter." 9 The king was grieved, yet out of regard for his oaths and for the guests, he commanded it to be given; 10 he sent and had John beheaded in the prison. 11 The head was brought on a platter and given to the girl, who brought it to her mother. 12 His disciples came and took the body and buried it; then they went and told Jesus.

DD. *The five thousand fed (14.13–21; Mark 6.30–44; Luke 9.10–17; John 6.1–13; cf. Matt. 15.32–38)*

14.14
Mt 9.36
13 Now when Jesus heard this, he withdrew from there in a boat to a deserted place by himself. But when the crowds heard it, they followed him on foot from the towns. 14 When he went ashore, he saw a great crowd; and he had compassion for them and cured their sick. 15 When it

f Gk *them*   *g* Gk *tetrarch*   *h* Other ancient authorities read *his brother's wife*   *i* Gk *he*

13.54 *He came to his hometown.* Everyone knew that Jesus performed mighty deeds and spoke words of wisdom. Since he did not have the benefit of advanced education, they wondered how he was able to think and speak as he did and where he got the power to perform miracles. They were puzzled especially because Jesus came from a common family. Joseph was a humble carpenter; his mother was a simple village girl. The obvious explanation is that Jesus was of divine origin; he was the Son of God. Already at twelve years old his knowledge of the Scriptures startled the learned teachers in the temple (Lk 2.41–52).
13.55 See note on Mk 6.3 regarding the family of Jesus.
14.1 This Herod was Herod Antipas, the son of Herod the Great by Malthace, a Samaritan woman.

Born ca. 20 B.C., he now ruled over Galilee and Perea. Apparently he believed in the resurrection of the dead, a doctrine affirmed by the Pharisees and denied by the Sadducees, for he thought Jesus was a resurrected John performing greater miracles than ever before and bringing him more trouble. He was reproached by his own guilty conscience for having killed John (vv. 3–12). Jesus faced a problem: he knew that Herod would do to him what he had done to John. Thus he went away until the time appointed by his Father. Sometimes God's servants should flee rather than remain and be martyred.
14.3 See note on Lk 1.57 regarding John the Baptist and his life. See also note on Mk 6.17 about Philip, the brother of Herod Antipas.

was evening, the disciples came to him and said, "This is a deserted place, and the hour is now late; send the crowds away so that they may go into the villages and buy food for themselves." 16 Jesus said to them, "They need not go away; you give them something to eat." 17 They replied, "We have nothing here but five loaves and two fish." 18 And he said, "Bring them here to me." 19 Then he ordered the crowds to sit down on the grass. Taking the five loaves and the two fish, he looked up to heaven, and blessed and broke the loaves, and gave them to the disciples, and the disciples gave them to the crowds. 20 And all ate and were filled; and they took up what was left over of the broken pieces, twelve baskets full. 21 And those who ate were about five thousand men, besides women and children.

14.17
Mt 16.9
14.19
1 Sam 9.13;
Mt 15.36;
Mk 14.22;
Lk 24.30

EE. *Jesus walks on the sea (14.22–36; Mark 6.45–52; John 6.15–21)*

22 Immediately he made the disciples get into the boat and go on ahead to the other side, while he dismissed the crowds. 23 And after he had dismissed the crowds, he went up the mountain by himself to pray. When evening came, he was there alone, 24 but by this time the boat, battered by the waves, was far from the land,*j* for the wind was against them. 25 And early in the morning he came walking toward them on the sea. 26 But when the disciples saw him walking on the sea, they were terrified, saying, "It is a ghost!" And they cried out in fear. 27 But immediately Jesus spoke to them and said, "Take heart, it is I; do not be afraid."

28 Peter answered him, "Lord, if it is you, command me to come to you on the water." 29 He said, "Come." So Peter got out of the boat, started walking on the water, and came toward Jesus. 30 But when he noticed the strong wind,*k* he became frightened, and beginning to sink, he cried out, "Lord, save me!" 31 Jesus immediately reached out his hand and caught him, saying to him, "You of little faith, why did you doubt?" 32 When they got into the boat, the wind ceased. 33 And those in the boat worshiped him, saying, "Truly you are the Son of God."

34 When they had crossed over, they came to land at Gennesaret. 35 After the people of that place recognized him, they sent word throughout the region and brought all who were sick to him, 36 and begged him that they might touch even the fringe of his cloak; and all who touched it were healed.

14.23
Lk 6.12;
9.28

14.26
see Lk 24.37
14.27
Mt 9.2; 17.7;
28.10;
Rev 1.17

14.31
Mt 6.30;
8.26; 16.8
14.33
Ps 2.7;
Mt 16.16;
26.63;
Lk 4.41;
Jn 11.27;
Acts 8.37;
Rom 1.4
14.36
Mt 9.20;
Mk 3.10

FF. *Ceremonial and real defilement (15.1–20; Mark 7.1–23)*

15 Then Pharisees and scribes came to Jesus from Jerusalem and said, 2 "Why do your disciples break the tradition of the elders? For they do not wash their hands before they eat." 3 He answered them, "And why do you break the commandment of God for the sake of your

15.2
Lk 11.38

j Other ancient authorities read *was out on the sea*   *k* Other ancient authorities read *the wind*

14.16 *you give them something to eat.* Earlier Jesus had given his disciples power to cast out demons, raise the dead, and heal the sick. Now he instructed them to feed the hungry, but they stood about puzzled and hesitant. They represent believers who have the power of the Holy Spirit available to them but who do not take advantage of that power for the glory of God and the progress of the gospel.

14.22 Jesus sent his disciples ahead of him by ship, where a storm overtook them. Earlier, in another storm, they had trusted Jesus who was with them, asleep in the back of the boat (7.23–27; Mk 4.35–41). The master was training them to walk by faith, not by sight.

14.28ff Peter wanted to be with Jesus, so he asked permission to walk on the water. But when he began to look at the waves, he forgot to keep looking at Jesus

and began to sink as terror overtook him. He turned to the right source for help, appealing to Jesus to save him. Jesus did so, but rebuked him for his lack of faith. Peter represents those believers who start their pilgrim journey filled with joy and hope, but are then caught up in a terrifying situation from which there appears to be no deliverance. Then faith is tested in the fire and proved to be true or false.

15.2 God commanded only the priests to wash before eating (Lev 22.1–16). The teachers of the law broadened this command to all Jews. This is legalism at work. Jesus censured them by taking a different law, the one about honoring parents, and showed how their expansion of it made it different from the intention of the lawgiver. This can happen today when believers make traditions not found in Scripture normative for all.

15.4
Ex 20.12;
Deut 5.16;
Eph 6.2
15.5
Ex 21.17;
Lev 20.9;
Deut 27.16

15.9
Col 2.18-22

15.11
Acts 10.14,
15; 1 Tim 4.3

15.13
Isa 60.21;
Jn 15.2;
1 Cor 3.9ff
15.14
Mt 23.16;
Lk 6.39;
Rom 2.19
15.15
Mt 13.36
15.16
Mt 16.9
15.18
Mt 12.34;
Jas 3.6
15.19
Gal 5.19-21;
1 Cor 6.9, 10;
Rom 14.14

15.22
Mt 9.27;
4.24

15.24
Mt 10.6, 23
15.25
Mt 8.2;
18.26; 20.20;
Jn 9.38
15.28
Mt 9.22, 28;
Mk 10.52;
Lk 7.50;
17.19

15.30
Lk 7.22

tradition? 4 For God said,[l] 'Honor your father and your mother,' and, 'Whoever speaks evil of father or mother must surely die.' 5 But you say that whoever tells father or mother, 'Whatever support you might have had from me is given to God,'[m] then that person need not honor the father.[n] 6 So, for the sake of your tradition, you make void the word[o] of God. 7 You hypocrites! Isaiah prophesied rightly about you when he said:

8   'This people honors me with their lips,
         but their hearts are far from me;
9   in vain do they worship me,
         teaching human precepts as doctrines.' "

10   Then he called the crowd to him and said to them, "Listen and understand: 11 it is not what goes into the mouth that defiles a person, but it is what comes out of the mouth that defiles." 12 Then the disciples approached and said to him, "Do you know that the Pharisees took offense when they heard what you said?" 13 He answered, "Every plant that my heavenly Father has not planted will be uprooted. 14 Let them alone; they are blind guides of the blind.[p] And if one blind person guides another, both will fall into a pit." 15 But Peter said to him, "Explain this parable to us." 16 Then he said, "Are you also still without understanding? 17 Do you not see that whatever goes into the mouth enters the stomach, and goes out into the sewer? 18 But what comes out of the mouth proceeds from the heart, and this is what defiles. 19 For out of the heart come evil intentions, murder, adultery, fornication, theft, false witness, slander. 20 These are what defile a person, but to eat with unwashed hands does not defile."

GG. *Journey toward Tyre and Sidon (15.21–28; Mark 7.24–30)*

21   Jesus left that place and went away to the district of Tyre and Sidon. 22 Just then a Canaanite woman from that region came out and started shouting, "Have mercy on me, Lord, Son of David; my daughter is tormented by a demon." 23 But he did not answer her at all. And his disciples came and urged him, saying, "Send her away, for she keeps shouting after us." 24 He answered, "I was sent only to the lost sheep of the house of Israel." 25 But she came and knelt before him, saying, "Lord, help me." 26 He answered, "It is not fair to take the children's food and throw it to the dogs." 27 She said, "Yes, Lord, yet even the dogs eat the crumbs that fall from their masters' table." 28 Then Jesus answered her, "Woman, great is your faith! Let it be done for you as you wish." And her daughter was healed instantly.

HH. *Many people healed (15.29–31; Mark 7.31–37)*

29   After Jesus had left that place, he passed along the Sea of Galilee, and he went up the mountain, where he sat down. 30 Great crowds came

l Other ancient authorities read *commanded, saying*   *m* Or *is an offering*   *n* Other ancient authorities add *or the mother*   *o* Other ancient authorities read *law* ; others, *commandment*   *p* Other ancient authorities lack *of the blind*

15.7,8 Jesus describes here the sin of hypocrisy, that of speaking pious words with our lips but not really believing them in our hearts. The Pharisees were guilty of this sin.
15.11 *it is what comes out of the mouth that defiles.* What indicates the pollution of sin in our lives is not eating food with unwashed hands, but speaking ungodly words from unsanctified hearts.
15.27 *even the dogs eat the crumbs that fall from their masters' table.* Jesus' statement to the Canaanite woman that he should not take children's food and throw it to the dogs could have produced silence and discouragement (v. 26). Yet she persevered, insisting

that even dogs could eat the crumbs that fell from the children's plates to the ground. Jesus commended the mother's faith and healed her daughter. God is the God of the whole earth, for Jews and Gentiles alike can claim him and his promises.
15.30,31 This account of Christ's wholesale healing demonstrates his goodness. He invited all to come to him, rich and poor, young and old. He never complained of crowds nor looked with contempt upon those who were needy. He healed all sorts of sicknesses. Nothing baffled him and no disease went untreated. Likewise, no soul seeking salvation will be rejected.

to him, bringing with them the lame, the maimed, the blind, the mute, and many others. They put them at his feet, and he cured them, 31 so that the crowd was amazed when they saw the mute speaking, the maimed whole, the lame walking, and the blind seeing. And they praised the God of Israel.

II. The four thousand fed (15.32–39; Mark 8.1–9)

32   Then Jesus called his disciples to him and said, "I have compassion for the crowd, because they have been with me now for three days and have nothing to eat; and I do not want to send them away hungry, for they might faint on the way." 33 The disciples said to him, "Where are we to get enough bread in the desert to feed so great a crowd?" 34 Jesus asked them, "How many loaves have you?" They said, "Seven, and a few small fish." 35 Then ordering the crowd to sit down on the ground, 36 he took the seven loaves and the fish; and after giving thanks he broke them and gave them to the disciples, and the disciples gave them to the crowds. 37 And all of them ate and were filled; and they took up the broken pieces left over, seven baskets full. 38 Those who had eaten were four thousand men, besides women and children. 39 After sending away the crowds, he got into the boat and went to the region of Magadan.*q*

JJ. The Pharisees and Sadducees demand a sign from heaven (16.1–12; Mark 8.11–21)

16   The Pharisees and Sadducees came, and to test Jesus*r* they asked him to show them a sign from heaven. 2 He answered them, "When it is evening, you say, 'It will be fair weather, for the sky is red.' 3 And in the morning, 'It will be stormy today, for the sky is red and threatening.' You know how to interpret the appearance of the sky, but you cannot interpret the signs of the times.*s* 4 An evil and adulterous generation asks for a sign, but no sign will be given to it except the sign of Jonah." Then he left them and went away.

5   When the disciples reached the other side, they had forgotten to bring any bread. 6 Jesus said to them, "Watch out, and beware of the yeast of the Pharisees and Sadducees." 7 They said to one another, "It is because we have brought no bread." 8 And becoming aware of it, Jesus said, "You of little faith, why are you talking about having no bread? 9 Do you still not perceive? Do you not remember the five loaves for the five thousand, and how many baskets you gathered? 10 Or the seven loaves for the four thousand, and how many baskets you gathered? 11 How could you fail to perceive that I was not speaking about bread? Beware of the yeast of the Pharisees and Sadducees!" 12 Then they understood that he had not told them to beware of the yeast of bread, but of the teaching of the Pharisees and Sadducees.

KK. Peter's confession (16.13–20; Mark 8.27–30; Luke 9.18–21)

13   Now when Jesus came into the district of Caesarea Philippi, he asked his disciples, "Who do people say that the Son of Man is?" 14 And they said, "Some say John the Baptist, but others Elijah, and still others

Cross references
15.31 Mt 9.8
15.32 Mt 9.36
15.36 Mt 14.19; 1 Sam 9.13
16.1 Mt 12.38; Lk 11.16, 29; 12.54-56
16.4 Jon 3.4, 5; Mt 12.39
16.6 Lk 12.1
16.8 Mt 6.30; 8.26; 14.31
16.9 Mt 14.17-21
16.10 Mt 15.34-38
16.14 Mt 14.2; Jn 1.21

---

q Other ancient authorities read *Magdala* or *Magdalan*   *r* Gk *him*   *s* Other ancient authorities lack *2When it is . . . of the times*

16.1   In this instance, the Pharisees and Sadducees were companions in their opposition to Jesus Christ, though on most issues they disagreed with each other. The only thing that held them together was a common enemy.
16.4   The Pharisees and Sadducees were persistent in asking for a supernatural sign from heaven to confirm Jesus' claim to be the Messiah. They had already dismissed his miracles. Jesus gave them no sign except the sign of Jonah, a reference to his own death and resurrection as the greatest sign of his Lordship (cf. Phil 2.6–11).

Jeremiah or one of the prophets." 15 He said to them, "But who do you say that I am?" 16 Simon Peter answered, "You are the Messiah,[t] the Son of the living God." 17 And Jesus answered him, "Blessed are you, Simon son of Jonah! For flesh and blood has not revealed this to you, but my Father in heaven. 18 And I tell you, you are Peter,[u] and on this rock[v] I will build my church, and the gates of Hades will not prevail against it. 19 I will give you the keys of the kingdom of heaven, and whatever you bind on earth will be bound in heaven, and whatever you loose on earth will be loosed in heaven." 20 Then he sternly ordered the disciples not to tell anyone that he was[w] the Messiah.[t]

16.16
Mt 14.33;
Jn 6.69;
11.27
16.17
1 Cor 15.50;
Gal 1.6;
Eph 6.12
16.18
Jn 1.42
16.19
Mt 18.18;
Jn 20.23
16.20
Mk 3.12;
5.43; 7.36;
9.9

LL. Christ foretells his death, resurrection, and second coming
(16.21–28; Mark 8.31–9.1; Luke 9.22–27)

16.21
Mt 17.22,
23; 20.17-19;
Lk 17.25

21   From that time on, Jesus began to show his disciples that he must go to Jerusalem and undergo great suffering at the hands of the elders and chief priests and scribes, and be killed, and on the third day be raised. 22 And Peter took him aside and began to rebuke him, saying, "God forbid it, Lord! This must never happen to you." 23 But he turned and said to Peter, "Get behind me, Satan! You are a stumbling block to me; for you are setting your mind not on divine things but on human things."

16.24
Mt 10.38,
39;
Lk 14.27;
17.33;
Jn 12.25
16.27
Mt 10.33;
Lk 12.9;
1 Jn 2.18;
Rom 2.6;
Rev 22.12
16.28
Mt 10.23;
1 Cor 16.22;
1 Thess
4.15-18;
Rev 1.7;
Jas 5.7

24   Then Jesus told his disciples, "If any want to become my followers, let them deny themselves and take up their cross and follow me. 25 For those who want to save their life will lose it, and those who lose their life for my sake will find it. 26 For what will it profit them if they gain the whole world but forfeit their life? Or what will they give in return for their life?

27   "For the Son of Man is to come with his angels in the glory of his Father, and then he will repay everyone for what has been done. 28 Truly I tell you, there are some standing here who will not taste death before they see the Son of Man coming in his kingdom."

[t] Or the Christ   [u] Gk Petros   [v] Gk petra   [w] Other ancient authorities add Jesus

---

16.18 This verse has been used to support the notion that the church is founded on Peter. Such a view overlooks the play on words in the Greek text that Christ made. He first said, "You are Peter" (Greek, petros, which means rock or "rock-man"), and then he said, "on this rock" (Greek, petra, which also means rock but is morphologically feminine). Two views of Christ's play on words have been advanced. One is that when he said, "on this rock I will build my church," he pointed to himself as being that rock, on which he would build the church. In the other view, the rock was Peter's confession that Jesus was the Christ, the Son of the living God; on that confession Christ would build his church. In either case the church is built on Christ (1 Cor 3.11). Paul says that the church is "built upon the foundation of the apostles and prophets, with Christ Jesus himself as the cornerstone" (Eph 2.20). Whatever may have been the role of the apostles and prophets, Jesus, the chief cornerstone, is the one on whom the church is founded. Because Christ is the all-powerful one, *the gates of Hades will not prevail against* the church. All authority belongs to the ascended Christ, who reigns in glory over the church.

16.19 *The keys of the kingdom*, here given to Peter as a representative of the disciples, were later given to all the apostles and to the church for all ages (cf. 18.18; Jn 20.23). The power of the keys does not allow one to forgive sins by one's own self. The phrase *will be bound . . . will be loosed* is actually "will have been bound . . . will have been loosed." That is, God in heaven does the binding and the loosing. Apostles and ministers of the gospel can announce the binding and loosing but not initiate them. Peter used this power in Acts 2 when he proclaimed the good news and assured the hearers that their sins would be forgiven if they repented. But he did not say nor could he say, "I forgive your sins." Only God can do that.

16.23 In v. 17 Jesus said to Peter, "Blessed are you." Now he rebuked him pointedly. Jesus had informed his disciples about his coming death. Peter, perhaps innocently, attempted to deter Jesus from fulfilling his unique mission. Jesus regarded any interference with the will of his Father as satanic in origin.

16.24 Self-denial means the radical giving up of self to Christ. It means being crucified with Christ, i.e., having the old selfish ego (Gal 2.20) put to death. The believer is dead to the world, dead to the old life, dead to self, and alive to God (cf. Rom 6.6–13; Col 3.1–4). Taking up one's cross similarly means putting one's old self and all that it means to death.

16.26 This verse should be understood two ways. (1) Its meaning in terms of this present world: However much of this world's goods a person gains, it is of no advantage to that person at death. We come into this world with nothing and we leave with nothing (cf. 1 Tim 6.7,8). (2) Its meaning in terms of the world to come: The loss of the immortal soul cannot be regained after death by having owned much wealth in the whole world. How many riches a person has makes no difference with God on the judgment day; no one can purchase salvation.

MM. *The transfiguration (17.1–13; Mark 9.2–13; Luke 9.28–36)*

17 Six days later, Jesus took with him Peter and James and his brother John and led them up a high mountain, by themselves. 2 And he was transfigured before them, and his face shone like the sun, and his clothes became dazzling white. 3 Suddenly there appeared to them Moses and Elijah, talking with him. 4 Then Peter said to Jesus, "Lord, it is good for us to be here; if you wish, I* will make three dwellings*y* here, one for you, one for Moses, and one for Elijah." 5 While he was still speaking, suddenly a bright cloud overshadowed them, and from the cloud a voice said, "This is my Son, the Beloved;*z* with him I am well pleased; listen to him!" 6 When the disciples heard this, they fell to the ground and were overcome by fear. 7 But Jesus came and touched them, saying, "Get up and do not be afraid." 8 And when they looked up, they saw no one except Jesus himself alone.

9 As they were coming down the mountain, Jesus ordered them, "Tell no one about the vision until after the Son of Man has been raised from the dead." 10 And the disciples asked him, "Why, then, do the scribes say that Elijah must come first?" 11 He replied, "Elijah is indeed coming and will restore all things; 12 but I tell you that Elijah has already come, and they did not recognize him, but they did to him whatever they pleased. So also the Son of Man is about to suffer at their hands." 13 Then the disciples understood that he was speaking to them about John the Baptist.

NN. *The epileptic boy cured (17.14–21; Mark 9.14–29; Luke 9.37–43)*

14 When they came to the crowd, a man came to him, knelt before him, 15 and said, "Lord, have mercy on my son, for he is an epileptic and he suffers terribly; he often falls into the fire and often into the water. 16 And I brought him to your disciples, but they could not cure him." 17 Jesus answered, "You faithless and perverse generation, how much longer must I be with you? How much longer must I put up with you? Bring him here to me." 18 And Jesus rebuked the demon,*a* and it*b* came out of him, and the boy was cured instantly. 19 Then the disciples came to Jesus privately and said, "Why could we not cast it out?" 20 He said to them, "Because of your little faith. For truly I tell you, if you have faith the size of a*c* mustard seed, you will say to this mountain, 'Move from here to there,' and it will move; and nothing will be impossible for you."*d*

OO. *Jesus again foretells his death and resurrection (17.22,23; Mark 9.30–32; Luke 9.43–45)*

22 As they were gathering*e* in Galilee, Jesus said to them, "The Son of Man is going to be betrayed into human hands, 23 and they will kill him, and on the third day he will be raised." And they were greatly distressed.

PP. *The coin in the fish's mouth (17.24–27)*

24 When they reached Capernaum, the collectors of the temple tax*f*

17.1
Mt 26.37;
Mk 5.37;
13.2

17.5
2 Pet 1.17;
Mt 3.17;
Isa 42.1;
Acts 3.22, 23

17.7
Mt 14.27

17.9
Mt 8.4;
16.20;
Mk 3.12;
5.43; 7.36
17.10
Mal 4.5;
Mt 11.14
17.11
Mal 4.6;
Lk 1.16, 17
17.12
Mt 11.14;
14.3, 10;
16.21

17.15
Mt 4.24

17.20
Mt 21.21;
Mk 11.23;
Lk 17.6;
1 Cor 12.9

17.22
Mt 16.21;
20.17;
Lk 18.31;
24.6, 7

17.24
Ex 30.13;
38.26

x Other ancient authorities read *we*   y Or *tents*   z Or *my beloved Son*   a Gk it or *him*   b Gk *the demon*
c Gk *faith as a grain of*   d Other ancient authorities add verse 21, *But this kind does not come out except
by prayer and fasting*   e Other ancient authorities read *living*   f Gk *didrachma*

17.2 See note on Mk 9.2.
17.9 Had Jesus' three disciples disclosed what had happened at the transfiguration, Jesus' death on the cross would have appeared wholly out of accord with the vision. But after his resurrection they were free to tell of it; Christ's resurrection and subsequent glory would be the positive proof needed to explain what happened on the mount of transfiguration.
17.11 See note on Mal 4.5 regarding Elijah.

17.20 *faith the size of a mustard seed.* This seed was the smallest planted by the Jews of Jesus' day, yet the bush grew to be eight to twelve feet high and birds made their nests in its branches. Surely the smallest amount of faith will be richly rewarded, for even small faith is real faith.
17.24ff *Does your teacher not pay the temple tax?* Every free Jewish male over twenty years of age was required to pay the yearly half-shekel temple tax (cf.

came to Peter and said, "Does your teacher not pay the temple tax?"ᵍ
25 He said, "Yes, he does." And when he came home, Jesus spoke of it first, asking, "What do you think, Simon? From whom do kings of the earth take toll or tribute? From their children or from others?" 26 When Peterʰ said, "From others," Jesus said to him, "Then the children are free. 27 However, so that we do not give offense to them, go to the sea and cast a hook; take the first fish that comes up; and when you open its mouth, you will find a coin;ⁱ take that and give it to them for you and me."

17.25
Rom 13.7;
Mt 22.17, 19

17.27
Mt 5.29, 30;
18.6, 8;
Lk 17.2;
Jn 6.61;
1 Cor 8.13

QQ. Discourse on humility (18.1–9; Mark 9.33–37; Luke 9.46–48)

18 At that time the disciples came to Jesus and asked, "Who is the greatest in the kingdom of heaven?" 2 He called a child, whom he put among them, 3 and said, "Truly I tell you, unless you change and become like children, you will never enter the kingdom of heaven. 4 Whoever becomes humble like this child is the greatest in the kingdom of heaven. 5 Whoever welcomes one such child in my name welcomes me.

6 "If any of you put a stumbling block before one of these little ones who believe in me, it would be better for you if a great millstone were fastened around your neck and you were drowned in the depth of the sea. 7 Woe to the world because of stumbling blocks! Occasions for stumbling are bound to come, but woe to the one by whom the stumbling block comes!

8 "If your hand or your foot causes you to stumble, cut it off and throw it away; it is better for you to enter life maimed or lame than to have two hands or two feet and to be thrown into the eternal fire. 9 And if your eye causes you to stumble, tear it out and throw it away; it is better for you to enter life with one eye than to have two eyes and to be thrown into the hellʲ of fire.

18.3
Mt 19.14;
Mk 10.15;
Lk 18.17;
1 Pet 2.2
18.4
Mt 20.27;
23.11
18.5
Mt 10.40;
Lk 18.17
18.6
Lk 17.1, 2
18.7
Lk 17.1;
1 Cor 11.19
18.8
Mt 5.29, 30;
Mk 9.43, 45
18.9
Mt 5.29;
Mk 9.47;
Mt 17.27

RR. The lost sheep (18.10–14; Luke 15.4–7)

10 "Take care that you do not despise one of these little ones; for, I tell you, in heaven their angels continually see the face of my Father in heaven.ᵏ 12 What do you think? If a shepherd has a hundred sheep, and one of them has gone astray, does he not leave the ninety-nine on the mountains and go in search of the one that went astray? 13 And if he finds it, truly I tell you, he rejoices over it more than over the ninety-nine that never went astray. 14 So it is not the will of yourˡ Father in heaven that one of these little ones should be lost.

18.10
Ps 34.7;
Acts 12.11;
Heb 1.14

SS. The treatment of offenders (18.15–35)

1. Church discipline (18.15–20)

15 "If another member of the churchᵐ sins against you,ⁿ go and

18.15
Lev 19.17;
Lk 17.3;
Gal 6.1;
Jas 5.19, 20

ᵍ Gk didrachma ʰ Gk he ⁱ Gk stater; the stater was worth two didrachmas ʲ Gk Gehenna ᵏ Other ancient authorities add verse 11, For the Son of Man came to save the lost ˡ Other ancient authorities read my ᵐ Gk If your brother ⁿ Other ancient authorities lack against you

---

Ex 30.11–16). The Greek coin equivalent to the Hebrew half-shekel was the double drachma (didrachma); the "coin" referred to in v. 27 was a stater, worth two didrachmas (see NRSV footnote).

18.3 become like children, who are harmless, inoffensive, and trusting. Christ's disciples are to imitate the virtues of a child, shunning the vices of adults whose values mark them off as lacking moral excellence.

18.9 The word translated hell here is Gehenna, the Aramaic form of the Hebrew Gehinnom, meaning "the valley of Hinnom." In the O.T. the valley of Hinnom

was the place where infants were sacrificed and where the repulsive idol of Molech was worshiped. These perversions occurred during the reigns of Ahaz and Manasseh. King Josiah converted that area into a city dump where fire smoldered continually. Thus it became a fitting symbol for hell. The N.T. used the word Gehenna to describe the place to which unrepentant sinners go. Its fire is unquenchable and the torment unending. Bible readers may be confused when translators use the English word hell for both Hades and Gehenna. The NRSV, when using the word hell, indicates in footnotes when it is Gehenna.

point out the fault when the two of you are alone. If the member listens
to you, you have regained that one.[o] 16 But if you are not listened to, take
one or two others along with you, so that every word may be confirmed
by the evidence of two or three witnesses. 17 If the member refuses to listen
to them, tell it to the church; and if the offender refuses to listen even to
the church, let such a one be to you as a Gentile and a tax collector.
18 Truly I tell you, whatever you bind on earth will be bound in heaven,
and whatever you loose on earth will be loosed in heaven. 19 Again, truly
I tell you, if two of you agree on earth about anything you ask, it will be
done for you by my Father in heaven. 20 For where two or three are
gathered in my name, I am there among them."

18.16 Deut 19.15; Jn 8.17; 2 Cor 13.1; Heb 10.28
18.17 1 Cor 6.1-6; 2 Thess 3.6, 14
18.18 Mt 16.19; Jn 20.23
18.19 Mt 5.24; 1 Jn 5.14

2. *The law of forgiveness* (18.21–35)

21 Then Peter came and said to him, "Lord, if another member of the
church[p] sins against me, how often should I forgive? As many as seven
times?" 22 Jesus said to him, "Not seven times, but, I tell you, seventy-
seven[q] times.
23 "For this reason the kingdom of heaven may be compared to a king
who wished to settle accounts with his slaves. 24 When he began the
reckoning, one who owed him ten thousand talents[r] was brought to him;
25 and, as he could not pay, his lord ordered him to be sold, together with
his wife and children and all his possessions, and payment to be made.
26 So the slave fell on his knees before him, saying, 'Have patience with
me, and I will pay you everything.' 27 And out of pity for him, the lord
of that slave released him and forgave him the debt. 28 But that same slave,
as he went out, came upon one of his fellow slaves who owed him a
hundred denarii;[s] and seizing him by the throat, he said, 'Pay what you
owe.' 29 Then his fellow slave fell down and pleaded with him, 'Have
patience with me, and I will pay you.' 30 But he refused; then he went and
threw him into prison until he would pay the debt. 31 When his fellow
slaves saw what had happened, they were greatly distressed, and they went
and reported to their lord all that had taken place. 32 Then his lord
summoned him and said to him, 'You wicked slave! I forgave you all that
debt because you pleaded with me. 33 Should you not have had mercy on

18.21 Gen 4.24; Lk 17.4
18.22 Mt 6.14; Mk 11.25; Col 3.13
18.23 Mt 25.19
18.25 Lk 7.42; 2 Kings 4.1; Neh 5.5, 8
18.26 Mt 8.2

[o] Gk *the brother* [p] Gk *if my brother* [q] Or *seventy times seven* [r] A talent was worth more than fifteen years' wages of a laborer [s] The denarius was the usual day's wage for a laborer

18.17 *let such a one be to you as a Gentile and a tax collector.* i.e., "let that person be excommunicated." In addition to establishing the church (16.18), God also ordained its government and order. Church discipline is s gift from God and excommunication is one means whereby discipline is to be enforced. The rules are simple enough: (1) a Christian who has something against anyone should first confront that person privately; (2) if this does not effect a positive result, the offended party is to go to the offender accompanied by two or three witnesses; (3) if the first two steps do not work, the offended person is to take the matter to the church. If the guilty person will not repent and refuses to accept discipline, then he or she is to be excommunicated. This action cuts the guilty off from the fellowship or communion of the church (hence our word, "ex-communicate") and from the ordinances or sacraments. God wants churches to (1) maintain sound doctrine; (2) maintain order (1 Cor 11.34; Titus 1.5); and (3) rebuke and deal with offenders (1 Tim 5.20; 2 Tim 4.2). Believers should accept the church's correction and submit to its discipline (2 Cor 10.8; 13.10; Heb 13.17). The purpose of excommunication is to bring the guilty to repentance (cf. 1 Cor 5.5). That penalty is often the very means by which repentance takes place.

18.22 *seventy times seven* (footnote NRSV). On what basis does Jesus say we should forgive anyone this many times? God has forgiven us and will forgive us an unlimited number of times. We are commanded to forgive those who have sinned against us just as many times as God has forgiven us.

18.23ff The basic teaching of this parable is the absolute necessity of an attitude of forgiveness. The unmerciful debtor owed the king a great sum of money, and his debt was freely forgiven him. Then this person refused to forgive a fellow servant's debt, one which was insignificant when compared to the debt the king had forgiven him. He wickedly pressed for payment and jailed the one who owed him that small sum. The lesson is plain: we have been forgiven our sins, which is the heaviest of all debts; therefore, we should forgive others, whose debts are small by comparison.

18.24ff *ten thousand talents.* This is hyperbole for effect. The sum of money involved was unimaginable; it could never be repaid (note NRSV footnote). So is the debt of sinners to God, yet God willingly forgives any who come to him. We should in turn have mercy on anyone who owes us a token debt, especially when balanced against our own incalculable one.

18.28 *a hundred denarii,* approximately $1,500-$2,500 (note NRSV footnote).

your fellow slave, as I had mercy on you?' 34 And in anger his lord handed him over to be tortured until he would pay his entire debt. 35 So my heavenly Father will also do to every one of you, if you do not forgive your brother or sister[t] from your heart."

18.35
Mt 6.14;
Mk 11.26;
Jas 2.13

IV. *From Galilee to Jerusalem (19.1–20.34)*

A. *Jesus goes to Judea (19.1,2)*

19.1
Mk 10.1;
Jn 10.40
19.2
Mt 4.23

19 When Jesus had finished saying these things, he left Galilee and went to the region of Judea beyond the Jordan. 2 Large crowds followed him, and he cured them there.

B. *Jesus' teaching on marriage (19.3–12; Mark 10.2–12)*

19.3
Mt 5.31
19.4
Gen 1.27; 5.2
19.5
Gen 2.24;
1 Cor 6.16;
Eph 5.31
19.7
Deut 24.1-4;
Mt 5.31
19.9
Mk 5.32;
Lk 16.18;
1 Cor 7.10-13

3 Some Pharisees came to him, and to test him they asked, "Is it lawful for a man to divorce his wife for any cause?" 4 He answered, "Have you not read that the one who made them at the beginning 'made them male and female,' 5 and said, 'For this reason a man shall leave his father and mother and be joined to his wife, and the two shall become one flesh'? 6 So they are no longer two, but one flesh. Therefore what God has joined together, let no one separate." 7 They said to him, "Why then did Moses command us to give a certificate of dismissal and to divorce her?" 8 He said to them, "It was because you were so hard-hearted that Moses allowed you to divorce your wives, but from the beginning it was not so. 9 And I say to you, whoever divorces his wife, except for unchastity, and marries another commits adultery."[u]

19.11
1 Cor 7.7-9

10 His disciples said to him, "If such is the case of a man with his wife, it is better not to marry." 11 But he said to them, "Not everyone can accept this teaching, but only those to whom it is given. 12 For there are eunuchs who have been so from birth, and there are eunuchs who have been made eunuchs by others, and there are eunuchs who have made themselves eunuchs for the sake of the kingdom of heaven. Let anyone accept this who can."

C. *Jesus blesses little children* *(19.13–15; Mark 10.13–16; Luke 18.15–17)*

19.14
Mt 18.3;
1 Cor 14.20;
1 Pet 2.2

13 Then little children were being brought to him in order that he might lay his hands on them and pray; the disciples spoke sternly to those who brought them; 14 but Jesus said, "Let the little children come to me, and do not stop them; for it is to such as these that the kingdom of heaven belongs." 15 And he laid his hands on them and went on his way.

D. *The rich young ruler* *(19.16–30; Mark 10.17–31; Luke 18.18–30)*

19.16
Lev 18.5;
Lk 10.25

16 Then someone came to him and said, "Teacher, what good deed

---

[t] Gk *brother* [u] Other ancient authorities read *except on the ground of unchastity, causes her to commit adultery*; others add at the end of the verse *and he who marries a divorced woman commits adultery*

19.3 See note on Mk 10.5ff regarding divorce.
19.10 The disciples of Jesus introduced the notion that it might be better for no one to marry. Jesus said that it is only good for some not to marry. Everyone must decide individually whether he or she has that gift (cf. 1 Cor 7.7). Whoever does not have the gift of continence should not hesitate to get married, rather than be aflame with passion (1 Cor 7.9).
19.16ff This young man was concerned about his spiritual condition, believed in eternal life, knew his life lacked meaning, and sought to know what to do

in order to secure eternal life. When Jesus told him to keep the commandments, he proudly asserted that he had done so from his youth. He was mistaken, but Jesus took him at his word and continued the discussion in order to uncover his basic problem. When he told him to sell his worldly possessions, give the money to the poor, and follow him, the rich young ruler left sorrowfully, for he valued his worldly possessions more than he valued Jesus. Whatever comes between us and Jesus will keep us from eternal life.

must I do to have eternal life?" 17 And he said to him, "Why do you ask me about what is good? There is only one who is good. If you wish to enter into life, keep the commandments." 18 He said to him, "Which ones?" And Jesus said, "You shall not murder; You shall not commit adultery; You shall not steal; You shall not bear false witness; 19 Honor your father and mother; also, You shall love your neighbor as yourself." 20 The young man said to him, "I have kept all these;*v* what do I still lack?" 21 Jesus said to him, "If you wish to be perfect, go, sell your possessions, and give the money*w* to the poor, and you will have treasure in heaven; then come, follow me." 22 When the young man heard this word, he went away grieving, for he had many possessions.

23 Then Jesus said to his disciples, "Truly I tell you, it will be hard for a rich person to enter the kingdom of heaven. 24 Again I tell you, it is easier for a camel to go through the eye of a needle than for someone who is rich to enter the kingdom of God." 25 When the disciples heard this, they were greatly astounded and said, "Then who can be saved?" 26 But Jesus looked at them and said, "For mortals it is impossible, but for God all things are possible."

27 Then Peter said in reply, "Look, we have left everything and followed you. What then will we have?" 28 Jesus said to them, "Truly I tell you, at the renewal of all things, when the Son of Man is seated on the throne of his glory, you who have followed me will also sit on twelve thrones, judging the twelve tribes of Israel. 29 And everyone who has left houses or brothers or sisters or father or mother or children or fields, for my name's sake, will receive a hundredfold,*x* and will inherit eternal life. 30 But many who are first will be last, and the last will be first.

E. *Parable of the landowner (20.1–16)*

20 "For the kingdom of heaven is like a landowner who went out early in the morning to hire laborers for his vineyard. 2 After agreeing with the laborers for the usual daily wage,*y* he sent them into his vineyard. 3 When he went out about nine o'clock, he saw others standing idle in the marketplace; 4 and he said to them, 'You also go into the vineyard, and I will pay you whatever is right.' So they went. 5 When he went out again about noon and about three o'clock, he did the same. 6 And about five o'clock he went out and found others standing around; and he said to them, 'Why are you standing here idle all day?' 7 They said to him, 'Because no one has hired us.' He said to them, 'You also go into the vineyard.' 8 When evening came, the owner of the vineyard said to his manager, 'Call the laborers and give them their pay, beginning with the last and then going to the first.' 9 When those hired about five o'clock came, each of them received the usual daily wage.*y* 10 Now when the first came, they thought they would receive more; but each of them also

---

19.18
Ex 20.13;
Deut 5.17;
Rom 13.9;
Jas 2.11
19.19
Lev 19.18;
Mt 22.39;
Rom 13.9;
Gal 5.14
19.21
Mt 6.20;
Lk 12.33;
16.9;
Acts 2.45;
4.34, 35
19.23
Mt 13.22;
1 Cor 1.26;
1 Tim 6.9, 10

19.26
Gen 18.14;
Job 42.2;
Jer 32.17;
Zech 8.6
19.27
Mt 4.20;
Lk 5.11
19.28
Mt 20.21;
Lk 22.28-30;
Rev 3.21

19.30
Mt 20.16;
Lk 13.30

20.1
Mt 13.24;
21.28, 33

20.8
Lev 19.3;
Deut 24.15

---

v Other ancient authorities add *from my youth*　*w* Gk lacks *the money*　*x* Other ancient authorities read *manifold*　*y* Gk *a denarius*

19.17 See note on Mk 10.18.
19.24 *for a camel to go through the eye of a needle.* This figure of speech (hyperbole) indicates how difficult it is for the rich who pride themselves on their material possessions to repent and accept Christ as their Savior (see also Mk 10.25 and Lk 18.25).
19.27 *we have left everything and followed you. What then will we have?* The disciples indeed had left everything to follow Jesus, but it was not really very much. Peter seems to imply that leaving all put Christ in debt to them. He wanted to know what they would get for doing so. He failed to realize that Jesus himself had forsaken all in order to redeem him. We do not forsake all *in order to* get a reward, even though leaving everything to follow Jesus will result in a reward. God

rewards those who serve him without thought of a reward.
19.28 *at the renewal of all things,* i.e., at the second advent of Jesus Christ, when the heavens and the earth will be regenerated (cf. Rom 8.18–21; Eph 1.10).
20.1ff In this illustration, each laborer, no matter how long he worked, received the same pay. God's saving grace has nothing to do with our years of service to him or the work of our hands. The dying thief was just as well off as a person who has been a believer for many years. The sinner who comes to God at the eleventh hour is just as blessed as the one who came at daybreak (see also note on Deut 15.3).

received the usual daily wage.[z] 11 And when they received it, they grumbled against the landowner, 12 saying, 'These last worked only one hour, and you have made them equal to us who have borne the burden of the day and the scorching heat.' 13 But he replied to one of them, 'Friend, I am doing you no wrong; did you not agree with me for the usual daily wage?[z] 14 Take what belongs to you and go; I choose to give to this last the same as I give to you. 15 Am I not allowed to do what I choose with what belongs to me? Or are you envious because I am generous?'[a] 16 So the last will be first, and the first will be last."[b]

F. Christ foretells his crucifixion and resurrection
(20.17–19; Mark 10.32–34; Luke 18.31–34)

17 While Jesus was going up to Jerusalem, he took the twelve disciples aside by themselves, and said to them on the way, 18 "See, we are going up to Jerusalem, and the Son of Man will be handed over to the chief priests and scribes, and they will condemn him to death; 19 then they will hand him over to the Gentiles to be mocked and flogged and crucified; and on the third day he will be raised."

G. Ambition of James and John (20.20–28; Mark 10.35–45)

20 Then the mother of the sons of Zebedee came to him with her sons, and kneeling before him, she asked a favor of him. 21 And he said to her, "What do you want?" She said to him, "Declare that these two sons of mine will sit, one at your right hand and one at your left, in your kingdom." 22 But Jesus answered, "You do not know what you are asking. Are you able to drink the cup that I am about to drink?"[c] They said to him, "We are able." 23 He said to them, "You will indeed drink my cup, but to sit at my right hand and at my left, this is not mine to grant, but it is for those for whom it has been prepared by my Father."

24 When the ten heard it, they were angry with the two brothers. 25 But Jesus called them to him and said, "You know that the rulers of the Gentiles lord it over them, and their great ones are tyrants over them. 26 It will not be so among you; but whoever wishes to be great among you must be your servant, 27 and whoever wishes to be first among you must be your slave; 28 just as the Son of Man came not to be served but to serve, and to give his life a ransom for many."

H. Healing two blind men near Jericho
(20.29–34; Mark 10.46–52; Luke 18.35–43)

29 As they were leaving Jericho, a large crowd followed him. 30 There were two blind men sitting by the roadside. When they heard that Jesus was passing by, they shouted, "Lord,[d] have mercy on us, Son of David!" 31 The crowd sternly ordered them to be quiet; but they shouted even more loudly, "Have mercy on us, Lord, Son of David!" 32 Jesus stood still and called them, saying, "What do you want me to do for you?" 33 They said to him, "Lord, let our eyes be opened." 34 Moved with compassion, Jesus touched their eyes. Immediately they regained their sight and followed him.

Cross references (left margin):

20.12 Jon 4.8; Lk 12.55; Jas 1.11
20.13 Mt 22.12; 26.50
20.15 Deut 15.9; Mt 6.23; Mk 7.22
20.16 Mt 19.30
20.18 Mt 16.21
20.19 Mt 16.21; 27.2; Acts 2.23; 3.13
20.20 Mt 4.21; 8.2; 9.18; Jn 9.38
20.21 Mt 19.28
20.22 Mt 26.39, 42; Lk 22.42; Jn 18.11
20.23 Acts 12.2; Rev 1.9; Mt 25.34
20.24 Lk 22.24, 25
20.25 Lk 22.25-27
20.26 Mt 23.11; Mk 9.35; Lk 9.48
20.28 Jn 13.4; Phil 2.7; Jn 13.14; Isa 53.10; 1 Tim 2.6; Titus 2.14; 1 Pet 1.19; Mt 26.28; Heb 9.28
20.30 Mt 9.27

---

[z] Gk a *denarius* [a] Gk *is your eye evil because I am good?* [b] Other ancient authorities add *for many are called but few are chosen* [c] Other ancient authorities add *or to be baptized with the baptism that I am baptized with?* [d] Other ancient authorities lack *Lord*

20.20 See the note on Mk 10.35ff regarding the petition of James, John, and their mother for status and power in Jesus' coming kingdom.
20.25ff Christ contrasts the ambition of the unregenerate who covet power, glory, and self-aggrandizement with that of converted people who do not live for self, but for God. The saved seek to glorify God and are characterized by self-sacrificing love. Jesus himself did not come to be served but to serve; we should do the same by seeking to serve God and others.

V. The last week in Jerusalem (21.1–28.15)

A. The triumphal entry
(21.1–11; Mark 11.1–11; Luke 19.29–44; John 12.12–19)

21 When they had come near Jerusalem and had reached Bethphage, at the Mount of Olives, Jesus sent two disciples, 2 saying to them, "Go into the village ahead of you, and immediately you will find a donkey tied, and a colt with her; untie them and bring them to me. 3 If anyone says anything to you, just say this, 'The Lord needs them.' And he will send them immediately.*" 4 This took place to fulfill what had been spoken through the prophet, saying,

5   "Tell the daughter of Zion,
     Look, your king is coming to you,
       humble, and mounted on a donkey,
         and on a colt, the foal of a donkey."

6 The disciples went and did as Jesus had directed them; 7 they brought the donkey and the colt, and put their cloaks on them, and he sat on them. 8 A very large crowd*f* spread their cloaks on the road, and others cut branches from the trees and spread them on the road. 9 The crowds that went ahead of him and that followed were shouting,

   "Hosanna to the Son of David!
   Blessed is the one who comes in the name of the Lord!
   Hosanna in the highest heaven!"

10 When he entered Jerusalem, the whole city was in turmoil, asking, "Who is this?" 11 The crowds were saying, "This is the prophet Jesus from Nazareth in Galilee."

B. Second cleansing of the temple
(21.12–17; Mark 11.15–19; Luke 19.45–48; cf. John 2.13–22)

12   Then Jesus entered the temple*g* and drove out all who were selling and buying in the temple, and he overturned the tables of the money changers and the seats of those who sold doves. 13 He said to them, "It is written,

   'My house shall be called a house of prayer';
   but you are making it a den of robbers."

14   The blind and the lame came to him in the temple, and he cured them. 15 But when the chief priests and the scribes saw the amazing things that he did, and heard*h* the children crying out in the temple, "Hosanna to the Son of David," they became angry 16 and said to him, "Do you hear what these are saying?" Jesus said to them, "Yes; have you never read,

   'Out of the mouths of infants and nursing babies
     you have prepared praise for yourself'?"

17 He left them, went out of the city to Bethany, and spent the night there.

C. The barren fig tree (21.18–22; Mark 11.12–14,20–25)

18   In the morning, when he returned to the city, he was hungry. 19 And seeing a fig tree by the side of the road, he went to it and found

---

e Or *'The Lord needs them and will send them back immediately.'*   *f* Or *Most of the crowd*   *g* Other ancient authorities add *of God*   *h* Gk lacks *heard*

21.1ff See note on Lk 19.28ff regarding the triumphal entry into Jerusalem.
21.2 Jesus instructed two unnamed disciples to find and bring him two animals, a donkey and her colt. The prophetic word would not have been fulfilled if they had brought only one donkey (see Zech 9.9). Exact fulfillments such as these confirm for us that God will fulfill all prophecies, especially those that concern the last days.
21.9 The word *Hosanna*, meaning "Save, we beseech you," is used six times in the Gospels.
21.12 According to Jn 2, Jesus used a whip to drive out the money changers, though no mention of that is made here.
21.19 *seeing a fig tree.* This type of fig tree produced fruit before or at the same time the leaves came out.

21.5
Isa 62.11;
Zech 9.9

21.8
2 Kings 9.13
21.9
Ps 118.26;
v. 15;
Mt 23.39

21.11
Jn 6.14;
7.40;
Acts 3.22;
Mk 6.15;
Lk 13.33

21.12
Ex 30.13;
Deut 14.25
21.13
Isa 56.7;
Jer 7.11

21.15
v. 9;
Lk 19.39
21.16
Ps 8.2

nothing at all on it but leaves. Then he said to it, "May no fruit ever come from you again!" And the fig tree withered at once. 20 When the disciples saw it, they were amazed, saying, "How did the fig tree wither at once?" 21 Jesus answered them, "Truly I tell you, if you have faith and do not doubt, not only will you do what has been done to the fig tree, but even if you say to this mountain, 'Be lifted up and thrown into the sea,' it will be done. 22 Whatever you ask for in prayer with faith, you will receive."

D. *Christ's authority challenged*
(21.23–27; Mark 11.27–33; Luke 20.1–8)

23 When he entered the temple, the chief priests and the elders of the people came to him as he was teaching, and said, "By what authority are you doing these things, and who gave you this authority?" 24 Jesus said to them, "I will also ask you one question; if you tell me the answer, then I will also tell you by what authority I do these things. 25 Did the baptism of John come from heaven, or was it of human origin?" And they argued with one another, "If we say, 'From heaven,' he will say to us, 'Why then did you not believe him?' 26 But if we say, 'Of human origin,' we are afraid of the crowd; for all regard John as a prophet." 27 So they answered Jesus, "We do not know." And he said to them, "Neither will I tell you by what authority I am doing these things.

E. *Parable of the two sons (21.28–32)*

28 "What do you think? A man had two sons; he went to the first and said, 'Son, go and work in the vineyard today.' 29 He answered, 'I will not'; but later he changed his mind and went. 30 The father[i] went to the second and said the same; and he answered, 'I go, sir'; but he did not go. 31 Which of the two did the will of his father?" They said, "The first." Jesus said to them, "Truly I tell you, the tax collectors and the prostitutes are going into the kingdom of God ahead of you. 32 For John came to you in the way of righteousness and you did not believe him, but the tax collectors and the prostitutes believed him; and even after you saw it, you did not change your minds and believe him.

F. *Parable of the wicked tenants*
(21.33–46; Mark 12.1–12; Luke 20.9–19)

33 "Listen to another parable. There was a landowner who planted a vineyard, put a fence around it, dug a wine press in it, and built a watchtower. Then he leased it to tenants and went to another country. 34 When the harvest time had come, he sent his slaves to the tenants to collect his produce. 35 But the tenants seized his slaves and beat one, killed another, and stoned another. 36 Again he sent other slaves, more than the

i Gk *He*

Cross references (left margin)

21.21 Mt 17.20; Lk 17.6; Jas 1.6
21.22 Mt 7.7; Jn 14.13, 14; 16.23; Jas 5.16
21.23 Acts 4.7; 7.27
21.26 Mt 14.5; Mk 6.20
21.28 v. 33; Mt 20.21
21.31 Lk 7.29, 50
21.32 Mt 3.1ff; Lk 7.29, 30; 3.12, 13
21.33 Ps 80.8; Isa 5.1-7; Mt 25.14, 15
21.34 Mt 22.3
21.35 2 Chr 24.21; Mt 23.34, 37; Heb 11.36, 37

Thus, if a tree were good, there should be fruit with the leaves. The fuller meaning of Jesus' statement is an attack on the Jews, who had nothing but leaves, no fruit. Since the fig tree symbolized Israel (Hos 9.10; Joel 1.7), this curse pronounced judgment upon Israel.

21.21 After cursing the fig tree, Jesus informed his disciples that if they had faith and did not doubt, greater things than the cursing of this tree could be done by them through prayer. Doubt is the enemy of faith; James said that those whose faith wavers will not receive anything from the Lord (Jas 1.6,7).

21.22 See note on Mt 7.7 on the principles of prayer and faith.

21.25 Jesus trapped his enemies in a dilemma. His question about the baptism of John implied that John's authority was divine, just as his was. If his enemies denied John's authority they would risk offending the people who believed John had divine authority. And if they affirmed his authority, then they should regard Jesus as having divine authority because John declared that Jesus did come from God and had authority (Jn 4.31,32).

21.28ff Matthew alone records this parable, in the context of the questioning of Jesus' authority by the chief priests and elders. Jesus spoke the story of the two sons in the vineyard to show the spiritual ineptness of the Jewish leaders who refused to say that John's baptism was of God; even the lowly publicans and the harlots knew the story and accepted it as true.

21.33 See note on Lk 20.9ff on the wicked tenants.

first; and they treated them in the same way. 37 Finally he sent his son to them, saying, 'They will respect my son.' 38 But when the tenants saw the son, they said to themselves, 'This is the heir; come, let us kill him and get his inheritance.' 39 So they seized him, threw him out of the vineyard, and killed him. 40 Now when the owner of the vineyard comes, what will he do to those tenants?" 41 They said to him, "He will put those wretches to a miserable death, and lease the vineyard to other tenants who will give him the produce at the harvest time."

42   Jesus said to them, "Have you never read in the scriptures:

'The stone that the builders rejected
    has become the cornerstone;*j*
this was the Lord's doing,
    and it is amazing in our eyes'?

43 Therefore I tell you, the kingdom of God will be taken away from you and given to a people that produces the fruits of the kingdom.*k* 44 The one who falls on this stone will be broken to pieces; and it will crush anyone on whom it falls."*l*

45   When the chief priests and the Pharisees heard his parables, they realized that he was speaking about them. 46 They wanted to arrest him, but they feared the crowds, because they regarded him as a prophet.

G. *Parable of the wedding banquet (22.1–14; Luke 14.15–24)*

22 Once more Jesus spoke to them in parables, saying: 2 "The kingdom of heaven may be compared to a king who gave a wedding banquet for his son. 3 He sent his slaves to call those who had been invited to the wedding banquet, but they would not come. 4 Again he sent other slaves, saying, 'Tell those who have been invited: Look, I have prepared my dinner, my oxen and my fat calves have been slaughtered, and everything is ready; come to the wedding banquet.' 5 But they made light of it and went away, one to his farm, another to his business, 6 while the rest seized his slaves, mistreated them, and killed them. 7 The king was enraged. He sent his troops, destroyed those murderers, and burned their city. 8 Then he said to his slaves, 'The wedding is ready, but those invited were not worthy. 9 Go therefore into the main streets, and invite everyone you find to the wedding banquet.' 10 Those slaves went out into the streets and gathered all whom they found, both good and bad; so the wedding hall was filled with guests.

11   "But when the king came in to see the guests, he noticed a man there who was not wearing a wedding robe, 12 and he said to him, 'Friend, how did you get in here without a wedding robe?' And he was speechless. 13 Then the king said to the attendants, 'Bind him hand and foot, and throw him into the outer darkness, where there will be weeping and gnashing of teeth.' 14 For many are called, but few are chosen."

H. *Three questions by the Jewish rulers (22.15–40)*

1. *Taxes to the emperor (22.15–22; Mark 12.13–17; Luke 20.19–26)*

15   Then the Pharisees went and plotted to entrap him in what he said. 16 So they sent their disciples to him, along with the Herodians, saying,

j Or keystone   *k Gk the fruits of it*   *l Other ancient authorities lack verse 44*

Cross-references (right margin):

21.38 Ps 2.8; Heb 1.2; Mt 26.3; 27.1

21.41 Mt 8.11; Acts 13.46; 18.6; 28.28

21.42 Ps 118.22, 23; Acts 4.11; 1 Pet 2.7

21.43 Mt 8.12

21.46 vv. 26, 11

22.2 Mt 13.24

22.3 Mt 21.34

22.4 Mt 21.36

22.7 Lk 19.27

22.8 Mt 10.11, 13

22.10 Mt 13.47

22.11 2 Cor 5.3; Eph 4.24; Col 3.10, 12; Rev 3.4; 16.15; 19.8

22.12 Mt 20.13; 26.50

22.13 Mt 8.12; Lk 13.28

22.16 Mk 3.6; 8.15

21.42 This verse, taken from Ps 118.22, apparently hints at a Jewish story that a stone carved out for the temple was discarded when no place could be found for it. Then it was discovered that it was the chief cornerstone of the building. The rejection of this key stone by the builders exemplifies the type of abuse Jesus received from the Jews.
22.2 See note on Lk 14.16ff about the parable of the wedding banquet.

22.16 The Herodians (mentioned also in Mk 3.6; 12.13) were a political party that attached itself to Herod's dynasty. Archelaus, Herod's son, became the ethnarch of Judea but was deposed (ca. A.D. 7) and replaced by Roman governors. The Herodians wanted the return of the Herodian dynasty to Judea. The Herodians and the Pharisees joined forces against Jesus, whom they considered their greatest enemy. Their alliance was one of convenience, its sole pur-

"Teacher, we know that you are sincere, and teach the way of God in accordance with truth, and show deference to no one; for you do not regard people with partiality. 17 Tell us, then, what you think. Is it lawful to pay taxes to the emperor, or not?" 18 But Jesus, aware of their malice, said, "Why are you putting me to the test, you hypocrites? 19 Show me the coin used for the tax." And they brought him a denarius. 20 Then he said to them, "Whose head is this, and whose title?" 21 They answered, "The emperor's." Then he said to them, "Give therefore to the emperor the things that are the emperor's, and to God the things that are God's." 22 When they heard this, they were amazed; and they left him and went away.

2. The Sadducees and the resurrection
(22.23–33; Mark 12.18–27; Luke 20.27–38)

23 The same day some Sadducees came to him, saying there is no resurrection;*m* and they asked him a question, saying, 24 "Teacher, Moses said, 'If a man dies childless, his brother shall marry the widow, and raise up children for his brother.' 25 Now there were seven brothers among us; the first married, and died childless, leaving the widow to his brother. 26 The second did the same, so also the third, down to the seventh. 27 Last of all, the woman herself died. 28 In the resurrection, then, whose wife of the seven will she be? For all of them had married her."

29 Jesus answered them, "You are wrong, because you know neither the scriptures nor the power of God. 30 For in the resurrection they neither marry nor are given in marriage, but are like angels*n* in heaven. 31 And as for the resurrection of the dead, have you not read what was said to you by God, 32 'I am the God of Abraham, the God of Isaac, and the God of Jacob'? He is God not of the dead, but of the living." 33 And when the crowd heard it, they were astounded at his teaching.

3. The great commandment
(22.34–40; Mark 12.28–34)

34 When the Pharisees heard that he had silenced the Sadducees, they gathered together, 35 and one of them, a lawyer, asked him a question to test him. 36 "Teacher, which commandment in the law is the greatest?" 37 He said to him, " 'You shall love the Lord your God with all your heart, and with all your soul, and with all your mind.' 38 This is the greatest and first commandment. 39 And a second is like it: 'You shall love your neighbor as yourself.' 40 On these two commandments hang all the law and the prophets."

I. Christ's unanswerable question
(22.41–46; Mark 12.35–37; Luke 20.41–44)

41 Now while the Pharisees were gathered together, Jesus asked them this question: 42 "What do you think of the Messiah?*o* Whose son is he?" They said to him, "The son of David." 43 He said to them, "How is it then that David by the Spirit*p* calls him Lord, saying,

m Other ancient authorities read *who say that there is no resurrection*   *n* Other ancient authorities add *of God*   *o* Or *Christ*   *p* Gk *in spirit*

Margin references:
22.17 Mt 17.25
22.21 Rom 13.7
22.23 Acts 23.8
22.24 Deut 25.5
22.29 Jn 20.9
22.32 Ex 3.6, 16; Acts 7.32; Heb 11.16
22.33 Mt 7.28
22.35 Lk 7.30; 10.25; 11.45; 14.3
22.37 Deut 6.5
22.39 Lev 19.18; Mt 19.19; Rom 13.9; Gal 5.14; Jas 2.8
22.40 Mt 7.12
22.42 Mt 9.27

pose being the disposal of Jesus.
22.21 See note on Mk 12.17.
22.23 See note on Lk 20.27ff for information about the Sadducees and the resurrection.
22.25 See note on Deut 25.5–10 for comments on levirate marriage.
22.32 When God spoke to Moses he said, "I *am* the God of Abraham . . . Isaac, and . . . Jacob." He did

not say, "I *was*." Therefore, Jesus insisted, Abraham, Isaac, and Jacob were alive when God said this, even though they had died and their bodies were buried years earlier. To Jesus, the Sadducees were denying what the Bible clearly taught, that the soul of a believer is immortal and will be raised to life at some later date.
22.43 See notes on Mk 12.35,36.

JEWISH SECTS

PHARISEES

Their roots can be traced to the second century B.C. — to the Hasidim.
1. Along with the Torah, they accepted as equally inspired and authoritative, all material contained within the oral tradition.
2. On free will and determination, they held to a mediating view that made it impossible for either free will or the sovereignty of God to cancel out the other.
3. They accepted a rather developed hierarchy of angels and demons.
4. They taught that there was a future for the dead.
5. They believed in the immortality of the soul and in reward and retribution after death.
6. They were champions of human equality.
7. The emphasis of their teaching was ethical rather than theological.

SADDUCEES

They probably had their beginning during the Hasmonean period (166-63 B.C.). Their demise occurred c. A.D. 70 with the fall of Jerusalem.
1. They denied that the oral law was authoritative and binding.
2. They interpreted Mosaic law more literally than did the Pharisees.
3. They were very exacting in Levitical purity.
4. They attributed all to free will.
5. They argued there is neither resurrection of the dead nor a future life.
6. They rejected a belief in angels and demons.
7. They rejected the idea of a spiritual world.
8. Only the books of Moses were canonical Scripture.

ESSENES

They probably originated among the Hasidim, along with the Pharisees, from whom they later separated (I Maccabees 2:42; 7:13). They were a group of very strict and zealous Jews who took part with the Maccabeans in a revolt against the Syrians, c. 165-155 B.C.
1. They followed a strict observance of the purity laws of the Torah.
2. They were notable for their communal ownership of property.
3. They had a strong sense of mutual responsibility.
4. Daily worship was an important feature along with a daily study of their sacred scriptures.
5. Solemn oaths of piety and obedience had to be taken.
6. Sacrifices were offered on holy days and during sacred seasons.
7. Marriage was not condemned in principle but was avoided.
8. They attributed all that happened to fate.

ZEALOTS

They originated during the reign of Herod the Great c. 6 B.C. and ceased to exist in A.D. 73 at Masada.
1. They opposed payment of tribute for taxes to a pagan emperor, saying that allegiance was due only to God.
2. They held a fierce loyalty to the Jewish traditions.
3. They were opposed to the use of the Greek language in Palestine.
4. They prophesied the coming of the time of salvation.

22.44
Ps 110.1;
Acts 2.34;
Heb 1.13;
10.13
22.46
Mk 12.34;
Lk 20.40

44 'The Lord said to my Lord,
   "Sit at my right hand,
      until I put your enemies under your feet" '?
45 If David thus calls him Lord, how can he be his son?" 46 No one was able to give him an answer, nor from that day did anyone dare to ask him any more questions.

J. The warning against Pharisaism
(23.1–12; Mark 12.38–40; Luke 20.45–47)

23.2
Ezra 7.6, 25;
Neh 8.4

23.4
Lk 11.46;
Acts 15.10;
Gal 6.13
23.5
Mt 6.1, 2, 5,
16;
Deut 6.8
23.6
Lk 11.43;
14.7; 20.46
23.8
Jas 3.1
23.9
Mal 1.6
23.11
Mt 20.26
23.12
Lk 14.11;
18.14;
Jas 4.6;
1 Pet 5.5

23 Then Jesus said to the crowds and to his disciples, 2 "The scribes and the Pharisees sit on Moses' seat; 3 therefore, do whatever they teach you and follow it; but do not do as they do, for they do not practice what they teach. 4 They tie up heavy burdens, hard to bear,*q* and lay them on the shoulders of others; but they themselves are unwilling to lift a finger to move them. 5 They do all their deeds to be seen by others; for they make their phylacteries broad and their fringes long. 6 They love to have the place of honor at banquets and the best seats in the synagogues, 7 and to be greeted with respect in the marketplaces, and to have people call them rabbi. 8 But you are not to be called rabbi, for you have one teacher, and you are all students.*r* 9 And call no one your father on earth, for you have one Father — the one in heaven. 10 Nor are you to be called instructors, for you have one instructor, the Messiah.*s* 11 The greatest among you will be your servant. 12 All who exalt themselves will be humbled, and all who humble themselves will be exalted.

K. The woes upon the Pharisees (23.13–36)

23.13
Lk 11.52

13 "But woe to you, scribes and Pharisees, hypocrites! For you lock people out of the kingdom of heaven. For you do not go in yourselves, and when others are going in, you stop them.*t* 15 Woe to you, scribes and Pharisees, hypocrites! For you cross sea and land to make a single convert, and you make the new convert twice as much a child of hell*u* as yourselves.

23.16
v. 24;
Mt 15.14;
5.33-35
23.17
Ex 30.29

23.19
Ex 29.37

16 "Woe to you, blind guides, who say, 'Whoever swears by the sanctuary is bound by nothing, but whoever swears by the gold of the sanctuary is bound by the oath.' 17 You blind fools! For which is greater, the gold or the sanctuary that has made the gold sacred? 18 And you say, 'Whoever swears by the altar is bound by nothing, but whoever swears by the gift that is on the altar is bound by the oath.' 19 How blind you are! For which is greater, the gift or the altar that makes the gift sacred? 20 So whoever swears by the altar, swears by it and by everything on it; 21 and

q Other ancient authorities lack *hard to bear*   *r* Gk *brothers*   *s* Or *the Christ*   *t* Other authorities add here (or after verse 12) verse 14, *Woe to you, scribes and Pharisees, hypocrites! For you devour widows' houses and for the sake of appearance you make long prayers; therefore you will receive the greater condemnation*   *u* Gk *Gehenna*

23.2ff Nowhere else in the Gospels does Jesus speak so scorchingly about other people. He recognized the legitimacy of the office of the scribes and Pharisees, but made it clear that bad people can occupy good offices. Although the Pharisees boasted of their orthodoxy and their good deeds, what they said and how they acted did not agree. Jesus therefore called them "hypocrites" (i.e., stage-players in religion), and their practices should not be followed.
23.5 *phylacteries*, or "prayer boxes," were small leather cases containing strips of vellum on which were written the words from Ex 13.1–16; Deut 6.4–9; 11.13–21. Two such cases (called *tephillim*, "prayers") were carried, one on the forehead and the other on the arm, in literal compliance with Ex 13.16; Deut 6.8; 11.18. *Fringes* were the four tassels, one at

each corner of the cloak, that symbolized religious devotion (Num 15.38–41). Jesus said the Pharisees did this in order to parade their piety before other people, and he condemned the practice.
23.16 One item that Jesus condemned in the scribes and Pharisees was their permitting people to violate their vows by following certain procedures. Taking an oath by the temple allowed for exemptions; but if it was taken by the gold of the temple, it was binding. To Jesus, the gold was sanctified by the temple, not the temple by the gold. Thus taking an oath by the temple was binding because the oath was taken before the one who lives in it (God). Moreover, no one may break one of God's commandments on the ground that to keep it would violate an oath.

whoever swears by the sanctuary, swears by it and by the one who dwells in it; 22 and whoever swears by heaven, swears by the throne of God and by the one who is seated upon it.

23 "Woe to you, scribes and Pharisees, hypocrites! For you tithe mint, dill, and cummin, and have neglected the weightier matters of the law: justice and mercy and faith. It is these you ought to have practiced without neglecting the others. 24 You blind guides! You strain out a gnat but swallow a camel!

25 "Woe to you, scribes and Pharisees, hypocrites! For you clean the outside of the cup and of the plate, but inside they are full of greed and self-indulgence. 26 You blind Pharisee! First clean the inside of the cup,[v] so that the outside also may become clean.

27 "Woe to you, scribes and Pharisees, hypocrites! For you are like whitewashed tombs, which on the outside look beautiful, but inside they are full of the bones of the dead and of all kinds of filth. 28 So you also on the outside look righteous to others, but inside you are full of hypocrisy and lawlessness.

29 "Woe to you, scribes and Pharisees, hypocrites! For you build the tombs of the prophets and decorate the graves of the righteous, 30 and you say, 'If we had lived in the days of our ancestors, we would not have taken part with them in shedding the blood of the prophets.' 31 Thus you testify against yourselves that you are descendants of those who murdered the prophets. 32 Fill up, then, the measure of your ancestors. 33 You snakes, you brood of vipers! How can you escape being sentenced to hell?[w] 34 Therefore I send you prophets, sages, and scribes, some of whom you will kill and crucify, and some you will flog in your synagogues and pursue from town to town, 35 so that upon you may come all the righteous blood shed on earth, from the blood of righteous Abel to the blood of Zechariah son of Barachiah, whom you murdered between the sanctuary and the altar. 36 Truly I tell you, all this will come upon this generation.

L. The lament over Jerusalem (23.37–39; Luke 13.34–35)

37 "Jerusalem, Jerusalem, the city that kills the prophets and stones those who are sent to it! How often have I desired to gather your children together as a hen gathers her brood under her wings, and you were not willing! 38 See, your house is left to you, desolate.[x] 39 For I tell you, you will not see me again until you say, 'Blessed is the one who comes in the name of the Lord.' "

M. The Olivet discourse (24.1–25.46; Mark 13; Luke 21)

1. The course of this age (24.1–14; Mark 13.3–13; Luke 21.5–19)

24 As Jesus came out of the temple and was going away, his disciples came to point out to him the buildings of the temple. 2 Then he asked them, "You see all these, do you not? Truly I tell you, not one stone will be left here upon another; all will be thrown down."

3 When he was sitting on the Mount of Olives, the disciples came to him privately, saying, "Tell us, when will this be, and what will be the

Cross-references (right margin):
23.22 Ps 11.4; Mt 5.34
23.23 Mt 11.42; Lev 27.30; Mic 6.8
23.24 v. 16
23.25 Mk 7.4; Lk 11.39
23.27 Lk 11.44; Acts 23.3
23.29 Lk 11.47, 48
23.31 Acts 7.51, 52
23.32 1 Thess 2.16
23.33 Mt 3.7; 5.22
23.34 Lk 11.49; 2 Chr 36.15, 16
23.35 Gen 4.8; Heb 11.4; Zech 1.1; 2 Chr 24.21
23.36 Mt 10.23; 24.34
23.37 2 Chr 24.21
23.39 Ps 118.26; Mt 21.9
24.1 Mk 13.1
24.2 Mt 26.61; 27.39, 40; Lk 19.44; Jn 2.19

---

v Other ancient authorities add *and of the plate*　w Gk *Gehenna*　x Other ancient authorities lack *desolate*

23.35 *Zechariah,* the author of the O.T. book of Zechariah (cf. Zech 1.1). Some have argued that the Zechariah here is the one murdered in 2 Chr 24.20–22. Since the book of 2 Chronicles appears last in the Hebrew Bible, the phrase *from the blood of righteous Abel to the blood of Zechariah* means essentially "from the first to the last murder in the O.T." **24.2ff** Though some N.T. prophecies (such as the destruction of Jerusalem) have already taken place,

others await fulfillment. The Olivet discourse of Jesus (chs. 23–25) and the book of Revelation contain much prophecy which yet remains to be fulfilled. **24.3** Jesus' disciples asked him two separate questions: (1) *when will this be?,* i.e., the destruction of the temple buildings; (2) *what will be the sign of your coming and of the end of the age?* Presumably Matthew did not record everything that Jesus said on these two questions.

sign of your coming and of the end of the age?" 4 Jesus answered them, "Beware that no one leads you astray. 5 For many will come in my name, saying, 'I am the Messiah!'*y* and they will lead many astray. 6 And you will hear of wars and rumors of wars; see that you are not alarmed; for this must take place, but the end is not yet. 7 For nation will rise against nation, and kingdom against kingdom, and there will be famines*z* and earthquakes in various places: 8 all this is but the beginning of the birth pangs.

9 "Then they will hand you over to be tortured and will put you to death, and you will be hated by all nations because of my name. 10 Then many will fall away,*a* and they will betray one another and hate one another. 11 And many false prophets will arise and lead many astray. 12 And because of the increase of lawlessness, the love of many will grow cold. 13 But the one who endures to the end will be saved. 14 And this good news*b* of the kingdom will be proclaimed throughout the world, as a testimony to all the nations; and then the end will come.

2. The great tribulation (24.15–28; Mark 13.14–23; Luke 21.20–24)

15 "So when you see the desolating sacrilege standing in the holy place, as was spoken of by the prophet Daniel (let the reader understand), 16 then those in Judea must flee to the mountains; 17 the one on the housetop must not go down to take what is in the house; 18 the one in the field must not turn back to get a coat. 19 Woe to those who are pregnant and to those who are nursing infants in those days! 20 Pray that your flight may not be in winter or on a sabbath. 21 For at that time there will be great suffering, such as has not been from the beginning of the world until now, no, and never will be. 22 And if those days had not been cut short, no one would be saved; but for the sake of the elect those days will be cut short. 23 Then if anyone says to you, 'Look! Here is the Messiah!'*y* or 'There he is!' — do not believe it. 24 For false messiahs*c* and false prophets will appear and produce great signs and omens, to lead astray, if possible, even the elect. 25 Take note, I have told you beforehand. 26 So, if they say to you, 'Look! He is in the wilderness,' do not go out. If they say, 'Look! He is in the inner rooms,' do not believe it. 27 For as the lightning comes from the east and flashes as far as the west, so will be the coming of the Son of Man. 28 Wherever the corpse is, there the vultures will gather.

3. The coming of the Son of Man
(24.29–31; Mark 13.24–27; Luke 21.25–28)

29 "Immediately after the suffering of those days
the sun will be darkened,
    and the moon will not give its light;
the stars will fall from heaven,
    and the powers of heaven will be shaken.

y Or *the Christ*   *z* Other ancient authorities add *and pestilences*   *a* Or *stumble*   *b* Or *gospel*   *c* Or *christs*

24.12 *the love of many will grow cold.* This implies, of course, that at one time the love of many for the Lord was hot. During the tribulation, many will lose their initial affection for God (cf. Rev 2:1–7). This is a serious warning to all as the end of the age approaches.

24.14 The coming of the Lord is here related to the preaching of the gospel to all the world. So long as Jesus tarries, the great commission must continue to be carried out.

24.15 *the desolating sacrilege.* The Greek phrase used here is nearly an exact rendering of Dan 9.27 in the Septuagint (the Greek version of the O.T.). The first fulfillment of this prophecy occurred in 165 B.C.,

when Antiochus IV (Epiphanes) sacrificed a pig on the altar before the temple of Jerusalem. Here Jesus spoke of a future event. Some think this was fulfilled in A.D. 70, when the temple and the holy city were destroyed by the Romans. Others believe this prophecy remains to be fulfilled at the end of the age. Those who hold the latter view usually tie the words of Daniel and Jesus to those of Paul in 2 Thess 2.8–12, where he wrote about the lawless one, a person whom Paul definitely related to the second coming of Jesus (see note on Dan 9.27).

24.17 *housetop,* i.e., "rooftop." Rooftops, being flat, were used as porches at that time (see Acts 10.9).

Cross-references (left margin)

24.4 Jer 29.8; 2 Thess 2.3
24.5 vv. 11, 23, 24; 1 Jn 2.18
24.7 Isa 19.2; Hag 2.22; Zech 14.13
24.9 Mt 10.17, 22; Jn 15.18; 16.2
24.10 Mt 11.6
24.11 Mt 7.15; Acts 20.29; 1 Tim 4.1
24.13 Mt 10.22; Rev 2.7
24.14 Rom 10.18; Col 1.6, 23
24.15 Dan 9.27; 11.31; 12.11; Acts 21.28; 1 Cor 15.52; 1 Thess 4.16
24.21 Dan 12.1; Joel 2.2
24.22 Isa 65.8, 9
24.23 Lk 17.23; 21.8
24.24 2 Thess 2.9–11; Rev 13.13
24.27 Lk 17.24
24.29 Isa 13.10; Ezek 32.7; Joel 2.10; Rev 8.12

30 Then the sign of the Son of Man will appear in heaven, and then all the tribes of the earth will mourn, and they will see 'the Son of Man coming on the clouds of heaven' with power and great glory. 31 And he will send out his angels with a loud trumpet call, and they will gather his elect from the four winds, from one end of heaven to the other.

24.30
Dan 7.13;
Mt 16.27;
Rev 1.7
24.31
Isa 27.13;
Zech 9.14

4. The parable of the fig tree
(24.32–35; Mark 13.28–31; Luke 21.29–33)

32 "From the fig tree learn its lesson: as soon as its branch becomes tender and puts forth its leaves, you know that summer is near. 33 So also, when you see all these things, you know that he*d* is near, at the very gates. 34 Truly I tell you, this generation will not pass away until all these things have taken place. 35 Heaven and earth will pass away, but my words will not pass away.

24.33
Jas 5.9
24.34
Mt 16.28;
23.36
24.35
Mt 5.18

5. Watchfulness (24.36–44; Mark 13.32–37; Luke 21.34–36)

36 "But about that day and hour no one knows, neither the angels of heaven, nor the Son,*e* but only the Father. 37 For as the days of Noah were, so will be the coming of the Son of Man. 38 For as in those days before the flood they were eating and drinking, marrying and giving in marriage, until the day Noah entered the ark, 39 and they knew nothing until the flood came and swept them all away, so too will be the coming of the Son of Man. 40 Then two will be in the field; one will be taken and one will be left. 41 Two women will be grinding meal together; one will be taken and one will be left. 42 Keep awake therefore, for you do not know on what day*f* your Lord is coming. 43 But understand this: if the owner of the house had known in what part of the night the thief was coming, he would have stayed awake and would not have let his house be broken into. 44 Therefore you also must be ready, for the Son of Man is coming at an unexpected hour.

24.37
Gen 6.5;
7.6-23;
Lk 17.26, 27
24.40
Lk 17.34, 35
24.42
Mt 25.13;
Lk 12.40
24.43
1 Thess 5.2;
2 Pet 3.10;
Rev 3.3;
16.15
24.44
1 Thess 5.6

6. Faithful and unfaithful slaves (24.45–51; Luke 12.42–46)

45 "Who then is the faithful and wise slave, whom his master has put in charge of his household, to give the other slaves*g* their allowance of food at the proper time? 46 Blessed is that slave whom his master will find at work when he arrives. 47 Truly I tell you, he will put that one in charge of all his possessions. 48 But if that wicked slave says to himself, 'My master is delayed,' 49 and he begins to beat his fellow slaves, and eats and drinks with drunkards, 50 the master of that slave will come on a day when he does not expect him and at an hour that he does not know. 51 He will cut him in pieces*h* and put him with the hypocrites, where there will be weeping and gnashing of teeth.

24.45
Mt 25.21, 23
24.46
Rev 16.15
24.49
Lk 21.34
24.51
Mt 8.12;
13.42, 50;
25.30

d Or it   *e* Other ancient authorities lack nor the Son   *f* Other ancient authorities read at what hour
g Gk to give them   *h* Or cut him off

24.31 with a loud trumpet call. The sound of the trumpet is connected with many events in the history of Israel: the giving of the law (Ex 19.13,16); the calling of assemblies (Num 10.2); the praise of God (Ps 81.3); offering sacrifices (Num 10.10); proclaiming the year of jubilee (Lev 25.9). According to the N.T., when the last trumpet sounds, sinners will experience the just judgment of God and the saints will enter their eternal jubilee (1 Cor 15.52; 1 Thess 4.16).
24.34 A generation in the O.T. was measured as forty years. There is a question about whether Jesus

was talking about the generation of people who were alive at his time, or the generation of people who would be living at the time of the second advent. If the former is correct, then Jesus was saying that these things would happen not more than forty years after his death and resurrection. Seeing that Jerusalem was destroyed in A.D. 70, Christ's contemporaries did live to the fulfillment of these things. In the latter case, however, Jesus meant that the generation of those living at the time of the beginning of the signs characterizing the end times would live to see the fulfillment of them all.

7. The parable of the ten bridesmaids (25.1–13)

25 "Then the kingdom of heaven will be like this. Ten bridesmaids[i] took their lamps and went to meet the bridegroom.[j] 2 Five of them were foolish, and five were wise. 3 When the foolish took their lamps, they took no oil with them; 4 but the wise took flasks of oil with their lamps. 5 As the bridegroom was delayed, all of them became drowsy and slept. 6 But at midnight there was a shout, 'Look! Here is the bridegroom! Come out to meet him.' 7 Then all those bridesmaids[i] got up and trimmed their lamps. 8 The foolish said to the wise, 'Give us some of your oil, for our lamps are going out.' 9 But the wise replied, 'No! there will not be enough for you and for us; you had better go to the dealers and buy some for yourselves.' 10 And while they went to buy it, the bridegroom came, and those who were ready went with him into the wedding banquet; and the door was shut. 11 Later the other bridesmaids[i] came also, saying, 'Lord, lord, open to us.' 12 But he replied, 'Truly I tell you, I do not know you.' 13 Keep awake therefore, for you know neither the day nor the hour.[k]

8. The parable of the talents (25.14–30)

14 "For it is as if a man, going on a journey, summoned his slaves and entrusted his property to them; 15 to one he gave five talents,[l] to another two, to another one, to each according to his ability. Then he went away. 16 The one who had received the five talents went off at once and traded with them, and made five more talents. 17 In the same way, the one who had the two talents made two more talents. 18 But the one who had received the one talent went off and dug a hole in the ground and hid his master's money. 19 After a long time the master of those slaves came and settled accounts with them. 20 Then the one who had received the five talents came forward, bringing five more talents, saying, 'Master, you handed over to me five talents; see, I have made five more talents.' 21 His master said to him, 'Well done, good and trustworthy slave; you have been trustworthy in a few things, I will put you in charge of many things; enter into the joy of your master.' 22 And the one with the two talents also came forward, saying, 'Master, you handed over to me two talents; see, I have made two more talents.' 23 His master said to him, 'Well done, good and trustworthy slave; you have been trustworthy in a few things, I will put you in charge of many things; enter into the joy of your master.' 24 Then the one who had received the one talent also came forward, saying, 'Master, I knew that you were a harsh man, reaping where you did not sow, and gathering where you did not scatter seed; 25 so I was afraid, and I went and hid your talent in the ground. Here you have what is yours.' 26 But his master replied, 'You wicked and lazy slave! You knew, did you, that I reap where I did not sow, and gather where I did not scatter? 27 Then you ought to have invested my money with the bankers, and on my return I would have received what was my own with interest. 28 So take the talent from him, and give it to the one with the ten talents. 29 For to all those who have, more will be given, and they will have an abundance; but from those who have nothing, even what they have will be taken away. 30 As

i Gk virgins   j Other ancient authorities add and the bride   k Other ancient authorities add in which the Son of Man is coming   l A talent was worth more than fifteen years' wages of a laborer

---

25.1ff This parable teaches Christians that they must be watchful and ready for the coming of the Lord. The five foolish bridesmaids were careless, assuming they had plenty of time to get ready for that event.
25.14ff This parable teaches that God has given talents or abilities to people according to his good plea-

sure. Whether many or few, they must use them properly with care and zeal. The servant with one talent failed to do so, then charged his master with greediness and cruelty. Christ's response to that senseless charge was that if the servant knew the master was so rapacious, the least he could have done was put out the money at interest.

for this worthless slave, throw him into the outer darkness, where there will be weeping and gnashing of teeth.'

9. The judgment (25.31–46)

31 "When the Son of Man comes in his glory, and all the angels with him, then he will sit on the throne of his glory. 32 All the nations will be gathered before him, and he will separate people one from another as a shepherd separates the sheep from the goats, 33 and he will put the sheep at his right hand and the goats at the left. 34 Then the king will say to those at his right hand, 'Come, you that are blessed by my Father, inherit the kingdom prepared for you from the foundation of the world; 35 for I was hungry and you gave me food, I was thirsty and you gave me something to drink, I was a stranger and you welcomed me, 36 I was naked and you gave me clothing, I was sick and you took care of me, I was in prison and you visited me.' 37 Then the righteous will answer him, 'Lord, when was it that we saw you hungry and gave you food, or thirsty and gave you something to drink? 38 And when was it that we saw you a stranger and welcomed you, or naked and gave you clothing? 39 And when was it that we saw you sick or in prison and visited you?' 40 And the king will answer them, 'Truly I tell you, just as you did it to one of the least of these who are members of my family,^{m} you did it to me.' 41 Then he will say to those at his left hand, 'You that are accursed, depart from me into the eternal fire prepared for the devil and his angels; 42 for I was hungry and you gave me no food, I was thirsty and you gave me nothing to drink, 43 I was a stranger and you did not welcome me, naked and you did not give me clothing, sick and in prison and you did not visit me.' 44 Then they also will answer, 'Lord, when was it that we saw you hungry or thirsty or a stranger or naked or sick or in prison, and did not take care of you?' 45 Then he will answer them, 'Truly I tell you, just as you did not do it to one of the least of these, you did not do it to me.' 46 And these will go away into eternal punishment, but the righteous into eternal life."

N. The trial and condemnation of Jesus (26.1–27.26)

1. The plot to kill Jesus
(26.1–5,14–16; Mark 14.1–2,10–11; Luke 22.1–6)

26 When Jesus had finished saying all these things, he said to his disciples, 2 "You know that after two days the Passover is coming, and the Son of Man will be handed over to be crucified."

3 Then the chief priests and the elders of the people gathered in the palace of the high priest, who was called Caiaphas, 4 and they conspired to arrest Jesus by stealth and kill him. 5 But they said, "Not during the festival, or there may be a riot among the people."

2. Anointing of Jesus by Mary of Bethany
(26.6–13; Mark 14.3–9; John 12.1–8)

6 Now while Jesus was at Bethany in the house of Simon the leper,^{n} 7 a woman came to him with an alabaster jar of very costly ointment, and she poured it on his head as he sat at the table. 8 But when the disciples

^{m} Gk these my brothers ^{n} The terms leper and leprosy can refer to several diseases

25.31
Mt 16.27;
19.28
25.32
Ezek 34.17,
20
25.34
Lk 12.32;
1 Cor 6.9;
15.50;
Gal 5.21;
Rev 13.8;
17.8
25.35
Isa 58.7;
Ezek 18.7;
Jas 1.27;
Heb 13.2
25.36
Jas 2.15, 16;
2 Tim 1.16
25.40
Prov 14.31;
19.17;
Mt 10.42;
Heb 6.10
25.41
Mt 7.23;
Mk 9.48;
Lk 16.24;
Jude 7;
2 Pet 2.4

25.45
Prov 14.31;
17.5
25.46
Dan 12.2;
Jn 5.29;
Rom 2.7;
Gal 6.8

26.1
Mt 7.28;
11.1; 13.53;
19.1
26.2
Jn 13.1
26.3
Ps 2.2;
Jn 11.47-53
26.4
Mt 12.14
26.5
Mt 27.24

26.6
Mt 21.17

25.46 *Eternal punishment* or eternal death results from the failure to seek the face of God and to embrace Jesus Christ as Savior (Rom 6.16,21; 8.13). It differs from physical death, which saved and unsaved alike experience, and comes in its final form at the last judgment (see note on Rev 20.11,12). It is variously designated in Scripture as (1) "shame and everlasting contempt" (Dan 12.2); (2) "destruction" (Rom 9.22); (3) God's "wrath that is coming" (1 Thess 1.10); (4) "the second death" (Rev 2.11); and (5) the place "where their worm never dies, and the fire is never quenched" (Mk 9.48). Christ alone is the one through whom sinners may escape this awful end (Jn 3.16; 8.51; Acts 4.12).

saw it, they were angry and said, "Why this waste? 9 For this ointment could have been sold for a large sum, and the money given to the poor." 10 But Jesus, aware of this, said to them, "Why do you trouble the woman? She has performed a good service for me. 11 For you always have the poor with you, but you will not always have me. 12 By pouring this ointment on my body she has prepared me for burial. 13 Truly I tell you, wherever this good news*o* is proclaimed in the whole world, what she has done will be told in remembrance of her."

<small>26.11
Deut 15.11
26.12
Jn 19.40</small>

3. The bargain of Judas Iscariot (26.14–16, vv. 1–5)

14 Then one of the twelve, who was called Judas Iscariot, went to the chief priests 15 and said, "What will you give me if I betray him to you?" They paid him thirty pieces of silver. 16 And from that moment he began to look for an opportunity to betray him.

<small>26.15
Ex 21.32
Zech 11.12</small>

4. The Last Supper (26.17–35)

a. The passover prepared (26.17–19; Mark 14.12–16; Luke 22.7–13)

17 On the first day of Unleavened Bread the disciples came to Jesus, saying, "Where do you want us to make the preparations for you to eat the Passover?" 18 He said, "Go into the city to a certain man, and say to him, 'The Teacher says, My time is near; I will keep the Passover at your house with my disciples.' " 19 So the disciples did as Jesus had directed them, and they prepared the Passover meal.

<small>26.18
Jn 7.6, 8;
12.23; 13.1;
17.1
26.19
Deut 16.5-8</small>

b. The passover eaten
(26.20–25; Mark 14.17–21; Luke 22.14–18; see John 13.1–30)

20 When it was evening, he took his place with the twelve;*p* 21 and while they were eating, he said, "Truly I tell you, one of you will betray me." 22 And they became greatly distressed and began to say to him one after another, "Surely not I, Lord?" 23 He answered, "The one who has dipped his hand into the bowl with me will betray me. 24 The Son of Man goes as it is written of him, but woe to that one by whom the Son of Man is betrayed! It would have been better for that one not to have been born." 25 Judas, who betrayed him, said, "Surely not I, Rabbi?" He replied, "You have said so."

<small>26.23
Ps 41.9;
Lk 22.21;
Jn 13.18;
Isa 53;
Dan 9.26;
Lk 24.25;
Acts 17.2, 3;
1 Cor 15.3</small>

c. The Lord's Supper instituted
(26.26–29; Mark 14.22–25; Luke 22.19–24)

26 While they were eating, Jesus took a loaf of bread, and after blessing it he broke it, gave it to the disciples, and said, "Take, eat; this is my body." 27 Then he took a cup, and after giving thanks he gave it to them, saying, "Drink from it, all of you; 28 for this is my blood of the*q*

<small>26.26
1 Cor 10.16;
11.23-25
26.28
Ex 24.6-8;
Mt 20.28;
Mk 1.4;
Heb 9.20</small>

o Or *gospel*   *p* Other ancient authorities add *disciples*   *q* Other ancient authorities add *new*

26.14 *Judas Iscariot.* The name *Judas* is the Greek form of Judah; *Iscariot* may have been the Hellenized form for the town of Kerioth. He was the only disciple from Judea; all the others were from Galilee. In the lists of the disciples, his name always appears last. He was covetous and dishonest, willing to sell Jesus to his enemies for a few pieces of silver. Jesus knew Judas would betray him even before he chose him as a disciple, and said that "it would have been better for that one not to have been born" (v. 24). The Bible gives two accounts of his death (Mt 27.3-10; Acts 1.16-20). The apparent discrepancy in these two accounts can be reconciled by the fact that Matthew's statement means no more than that he went away in despair and suffocated, while Luke adds that he fell on his face and burst open, spilling out his bowels. Judas' life warns any who would betray Christ (e.g.,

see Heb 6.6).
26.26 See note on Mk 14.22ff regarding the Eucharist or Lord's supper.
26.28 At the heart of the gospel is *the forgiveness of sins.* The apostles, standing before the hostile high priest, said God exalted Jesus so that the people of Israel could have their sins forgiven (Acts 5.31); in Antioch of Pisidia Paul said, "through this man forgiveness of sins is proclaimed" (Acts 13.38). Forgiveness of sins is a divine, not a human, prerogative: "If we confess our sins, he who is faithful and just will forgive us our sins" (1 Jn 1.9). When God forgives sins they are forgotten, cast behind his back forever (Isa 38.17). He forgives *all* our sins save one—blaspheming the Holy Spirit (12.31; Mk 3.29; 1 Jn 5.16), the only one who can bring about repentance and faith.

covenant, which is poured out for many for the forgiveness of sins. 29 I tell you, I will never again drink of this fruit of the vine until that day when I drink it new with you in my Father's kingdom."

d. Peter's denial foretold
(26.30–35; Mark 14.27–31; Luke 22.31–34; see John 14–17)

30 When they had sung the hymn, they went out to the Mount of Olives.

31 Then Jesus said to them, "You will all become deserters because of me this night; for it is written,

'I will strike the shepherd,
    and the sheep of the flock will be scattered.'

32 But after I am raised up, I will go ahead of you to Galilee." 33 Peter said to him, "Though all become deserters because of you, I will never desert you." 34 Jesus said to him, "Truly I tell you, this very night, before the cock crows, you will deny me three times." 35 Peter said to him, "Even though I must die with you, I will not deny you." And so said all the disciples.

5. Jesus in Gethsemane (26.36–56)

a. Jesus' agony
(26.36–46; Mark 14.32–42; Luke 22.39–46; cf. John 18.1)

36 Then Jesus went with them to a place called Gethsemane; and he said to his disciples, "Sit here while I go over there and pray." 37 He took with him Peter and the two sons of Zebedee, and began to be grieved and agitated. 38 Then he said to them, "I am deeply grieved, even to death; remain here, and stay awake with me." 39 And going a little farther, he threw himself on the ground and prayed, "My Father, if it is possible, let this cup pass from me; yet not what I want but what you want." 40 Then he came to the disciples and found them sleeping; and he said to Peter, "So, could you not stay awake with me one hour? 41 Stay awake and pray that you may not come into the time of trial;r the spirit indeed is willing, but the flesh is weak." 42 Again he went away for the second time and prayed, "My Father, if this cannot pass unless I drink it, your will be done." 43 Again he came and found them sleeping, for their eyes were heavy. 44 So leaving them again, he went away and prayed for the third time, saying the same words. 45 Then he came to the disciples and said to them, "Are you still sleeping and taking your rest? See, the hour is at hand, and the Son of Man is betrayed into the hands of sinners. 46 Get up, let us be going. See, my betrayer is at hand."

b. Jesus' betrayal and arrest
(26.47–56; Mark 14.43–50; Luke 22.47–53; John 18.1–11)

47 While he was still speaking, Judas, one of the twelve, arrived; with him was a large crowd with swords and clubs, from the chief priests and the elders of the people. 48 Now the betrayer had given them a sign, saying, "The one I will kiss is the man; arrest him." 49 At once he came

26.30
Mk 14.26

26.31
Jn 16.32;
Mt 11.6;
Zech 13.7

26.32
Mt 28.7, 10, 16
26.34
Jn 13.38
26.35
Jn 13.37

26.37
Mt 4.21

26.38
Jn 12.27
26.39
Jn 12.27;
Mt 20.22;
Jn 6.38;
Phil 2.8
26.40
v. 38
26.41
Mt 6.13;
Lk 11.4
26.42
Jn 4.34;
5.30; 6.38

26.45
v. 18;
Jn 12.23, 27;
13.1; 17.1

26.49
v. 25

r Or into temptation

26.39 The cup of which Jesus spoke has been the subject of much discussion. One school of thought says that Jesus prayed for some other way to save sinners than for him to die. But Calvary was God's only way, and Jesus accepted it without hesitation or qualification (cf. "not what I want but what you want"). Others hold that Jesus always prayed according to the will of the Father. In his humanity he feared that Satan might kill him in the Garden of Gethsemane before he made atonement on the cross. Thus, he

was prepared to die in the garden, if the Father so willed. His prayer was answered; he was able to go to Calvary. The most likely view is that Jesus, knowing what suffering eternal death for sin meant, shrank from the imminent experience of bearing the sins of the world, because the Father would turn his face from him when he became sin for us (cf. 2 Cor 5.21). In this view, the cup meant separation from the Father (cf. 27.46, "My God, my God, why have you forsaken me?"). He left the garden victoriously.

26.50
Mt 20.13;
22.12

26.52
Gen 9.6;
Rev 13.10
26.53
2 Kings 6.17;
Dan 7.10
26.54
v. 24;
Lk 24.25,
44, 46
26.56
v. 54

up to Jesus and said, "Greetings, Rabbi!" and kissed him. 50 Jesus said to him, "Friend, do what you are here to do." Then they came and laid hands on Jesus and arrested him. 51 Suddenly, one of those with Jesus put his hand on his sword, drew it, and struck the slave of the high priest, cutting off his ear. 52 Then Jesus said to him, "Put your sword back into its place; for all who take the sword will perish by the sword. 53 Do you think that I cannot appeal to my Father, and he will at once send me more than twelve legions of angels? 54 But how then would the scriptures be fulfilled, which say it must happen in this way?" 55 At that hour Jesus said to the crowds, "Have you come out with swords and clubs to arrest me as though I were a bandit? Day after day I sat in the temple teaching, and you did not arrest me. 56 But all this has taken place, so that the scriptures of the prophets may be fulfilled." Then all the disciples deserted him and fled.

6. Jesus before Caiaphas
(26.57–68; Mark 14.53–65; cf. Luke 22.54; John 18.12–14,19–25)

26.58
Jn 18.15

26.60
Ps 27.12;
35.11;
Acts 6.13;
Deut 19.15
26.61
Mt 27.40
26.63
Isa 53.7;
Mt 27.12,
14;
Lev 5.1;
Jn 18.33
26.64
Ps 110.1;
Dan 7.13;
Mt 16.27, 28
26.65
Num 14.6;
Acts 14.14;
Lev 24.16
26.66
Jn 19.7
26.67
Isa 53.3;
Mt 27.30;
Jn 19.3

57 Those who had arrested Jesus took him to Caiaphas the high priest, in whose house the scribes and the elders had gathered. 58 But Peter was following him at a distance, as far as the courtyard of the high priest; and going inside, he sat with the guards in order to see how this would end. 59 Now the chief priests and the whole council were looking for false testimony against Jesus so that they might put him to death, 60 but they found none, though many false witnesses came forward. At last two came forward 61 and said, "This fellow said, 'I am able to destroy the temple of God and to build it in three days.' " 62 The high priest stood up and said, "Have you no answer? What is it that they testify against you?" 63 But Jesus was silent. Then the high priest said to him, "I put you under oath before the living God, tell us if you are the Messiah,^{s} the Son of God." 64 Jesus said to him, "You have said so. But I tell you,

From now on you will see the Son of Man
    seated at the right hand of Power
    and coming on the clouds of heaven."

65 Then the high priest tore his clothes and said, "He has blasphemed! Why do we still need witnesses? You have now heard his blasphemy. 66 What is your verdict?" They answered, "He deserves death." 67 Then they spat in his face and struck him; and some slapped him, 68 saying, "Prophesy to us, you Messiah!^{s} Who is it that struck you?"

^{s} Or Christ

26.49 *kissed*, i.e., embraced and kissed, the greeting still used among people in Eastern countries (see note on Mk 14.45 for information about Judas' betrayal of Jesus).

26.57 *Caiaphas the high priest* was son-in-law of Annas, who had previously served as high priest. Valerius Gratus, the predecessor of Pontius Pilate, had appointed him to the office, where he stayed until his removal by Vitellius in A.D. 37. Caiaphas hated Christ and recommended the action that led to Calvary (Jn 11.49–53). Jesus stood silent before him until he demanded in the name of God to know whether Jesus was the Christ (v. 63). Jesus said that he was (v. 64). Unable to convict Jesus by the testimony of perjurers, Caiaphas then accused Jesus of blasphemy and condemned him to be crucified.

26.59 *The . . . council*, i.e., the Sanhedrin or the Jewish Supreme Court, was the highest ecclesiastical and political body among the Jews. The origin of this body is obscure. Jewish tradition speaks of two Sanhedrins. (1) The Little Sanhedrin had twenty-three members and judged cases other than those reserved for the highest body. If the lower courts could not arrive at a decision, the case was referred to the other Sanhedrin. (2) The Sanhedrin in Jerusalem was generally referred to as the Great Sanhedrin. It had seventy-one members, called "elders," who usually were chosen from among the chief priests and the scribes. Exactly how they were chosen is unknown. Tradition has it that prospective candidates had to be learned, humble, and popular with the people. The Sanhedrin was led by a president. The high priest, Caiaphas, seems to have been the presiding officer during the trial of Jesus, but this does not mean that the high priest was generally the president. Any decisions it made were binding. This court met in the chambers of the Hall of Hewn Stone in Jerusalem. They sat in a semicircle so that all could see each other. In cases involving life or death, the younger members voted first so they could not be influenced by their elders. No fewer than twenty-three members had to be present when such a case arose. If a verdict was reached by a majority of one, the number of court members had to be increased. Only when the full court was in session could a person be declared guilty by a majority of one.

7. Peter's denial of Jesus
(26.69–75; Mark 14.66–72; Luke 22.55–63; John 18.15–18,25–27)

69 Now Peter was sitting outside in the courtyard. A servant-girl came to him and said, "You also were with Jesus the Galilean." 70 But he denied it before all of them, saying, "I do not know what you are talking about." 71 When he went out to the porch, another servant-girl saw him, and she said to the bystanders, "This man was with Jesus of Nazareth."*t* 72 Again he denied it with an oath, "I do not know the man." 73 After a little while the bystanders came up and said to Peter, "Certainly you are also one of them, for your accent betrays you." 74 Then he began to curse, and he swore an oath, "I do not know the man!" At that moment the cock crowed. 75 Then Peter remembered what Jesus had said: "Before the cock crows, you will deny me three times." And he went out and wept bitterly.

26.75
v. 34;
Jn 13.38

8. Jesus delivered to Pilate by the council
(27.1–2; Mark 15.1; Luke 23.1; John 18.28)

27 When morning came, all the chief priests and the elders of the people conferred together against Jesus in order to bring about his death. 2 They bound him, led him away, and handed him over to Pilate the governor.

27.2
Mt 20.19;
Acts 3.13

9. The death of Judas Iscariot (27.3–10; cf. Acts 1.16–20)

3 When Judas, his betrayer, saw that Jesus*u* was condemned, he repented and brought back the thirty pieces of silver to the chief priests and the elders. 4 He said, "I have sinned by betraying innocent*v* blood." But they said, "What is that to us? See to it yourself." 5 Throwing down the pieces of silver in the temple, he departed; and he went and hanged himself. 6 But the chief priests, taking the pieces of silver, said, "It is not lawful to put them into the treasury, since they are blood money." 7 After conferring together, they used them to buy the potter's field as a place to bury foreigners. 8 For this reason that field has been called the Field of Blood to this day. 9 Then was fulfilled what had been spoken through the prophet Jeremiah,*w* "And they took*x* the thirty pieces of silver, the price of the one on whom a price had been set,*y* on whom some of the people of Israel had set a price, 10 and they gave*z* them for the potter's field, as the Lord commanded me."

27.3
Mt 26.14, 15
27.4
v. 24
27.5
Acts 1.18

27.8
Acts 1.19
27.9f
Zech 11.12,
13

10. Jesus before Pontius Pilate
(27.11–26; Mark 15.2–15; Luke 23.3–25; John 18.29–40)

a. Jesus questioned (27.11–14)

11 Now Jesus stood before the governor; and the governor asked him, "Are you the King of the Jews?" Jesus said, "You say so." 12 But when he was accused by the chief priests and elders, he did not answer. 13 Then Pilate said to him, "Do you not hear how many accusations they make

27.12
Mt 26.63;
Jn 19.9
27.13
Mt 26.62;
Jn 19.10

t Gk the Nazorean   *u* Gk he   *v* Other ancient authorities read *righteous*   *w* Other ancient authorities read *Zechariah* or *Isaiah*   *x* Or *I took*   *y* Or *the price of the precious One*   *z* Other ancient authorities read *I gave*

26.69ff See note on Mk 14.71 regarding Peter's denial of Christ.

27.1 *conferred together against Jesus in order to bring about his death.* They did not have the authority themselves to execute Jesus, so they sought to induce the Roman government to sentence him to death.

27.9,10 Much of this quotation comes from Zech 11.12,13, but Matthew attributes it to Jeremiah. Is this an error? In comparing these passages it can be seen that Zechariah contains no reference to "the pot-

ter's field"; the whole point of the quotation, however, has to do with the field purchased with Judas' money. Jer 32.6–9 does refer to a field Jeremiah purchased, and Jer 19.1–13 gives an account about a potter's vessel and the field of Topeth, which became a place of burial. Matthew combines sources in this quotation and assigns it to Jeremiah since he was the better known prophet and because "the potter's field" is the main point of his prophecy.

against you?" 14 But he gave him no answer, not even to a single charge, so that the governor was greatly amazed.

15 Now at the festival the governor was accustomed to release a prisoner for the crowd, anyone whom they wanted. 16 At that time they had a notorious prisoner, called Jesus*a* Barabbas. 17 So after they had gathered, Pilate said to them, "Whom do you want me to release for you, Jesus*a* Barabbas or Jesus who is called the Messiah?"*b* 18 For he realized that it was out of jealousy that they had handed him over. 19 While he was sitting on the judgment seat, his wife sent word to him, "Have nothing to do with that innocent man, for today I have suffered a great deal because of a dream about him." 20 Now the chief priests and the elders persuaded the crowds to ask for Barabbas and to have Jesus killed. 21 The governor again said to them, "Which of the two do you want me to release for you?" And they said, "Barabbas." 22 Pilate said to them, "Then what should I do with Jesus who is called the Messiah?"*b* All of them said, "Let him be crucified!" 23 Then he asked, "Why, what evil has he done?" But they shouted all the more, "Let him be crucified!"

b. Barabbas released and Jesus delivered (27.24–26)

24 So when Pilate saw that he could do nothing, but rather that a riot was beginning, he took some water and washed his hands before the crowd, saying, "I am innocent of this man's blood;*c* see to it yourselves." 25 Then the people as a whole answered, "His blood be on us and on our children!" 26 So he released Barabbas for them; and after flogging Jesus, he handed him over to be crucified.

O. The crucifixion and burial of Jesus (27.27–66)

1. Jesus crowned with thorns (27.27–31; Mark 15.16–20; cf. John 19.2,3)

27 Then the soldiers of the governor took Jesus into the governor's headquarters,*d* and they gathered the whole cohort around him. 28 They stripped him and put a scarlet robe on him, 29 and after twisting some thorns into a crown, they put it on his head. They put a reed in his right hand and knelt before him and mocked him, saying, "Hail, King of the Jews!" 30 They spat on him, and took the reed and struck him on the head. 31 After mocking him, they stripped him of the robe and put his own clothes on him. Then they led him away to crucify him.

2. Jesus crucified (27.32–44; Mark 15.21–32; Luke 23.32–43; John 19.17–24)

32 As they went out, they came upon a man from Cyrene named Simon; they compelled this man to carry his cross. 33 And when they came to a place called Golgotha (which means Place of a Skull), 34 they offered him wine to drink, mixed with gall; but when he tasted it, he would not drink it. 35 And when they had crucified him, they divided his clothes among themselves by casting lots;*e* 36 then they sat down there and kept

a Other ancient authorities lack *Jesus*   *b* Or *the Christ*   *c* Other ancient authorities read *this righteous blood*, or *this righteous man's blood*   *d* Gk *the praetorium*   *e* Other ancient authorities add *in order that what had been spoken through the prophet might be fulfilled, "They divided my clothes among themselves, and for my clothing they cast lots."*

27.14
1 Tim 6.13

27.19
Acts 12.21;
v. 24

27.20
Acts 3.14

27.24
Mt 26.5;
Deut 21.6-8;
Ps 26.6; v. 19
27.25
Josh 2.19;
Acts 5.28
27.26
Isa 53.5

27.27
Jn 18.28, 33;
Acts 10.1
27.29
Ps 69.19;
Isa 53.3

27.30
Mt 26.67;
Mk 10.34;
14.65
27.31
Isa 53.7

27.32
Heb 13.12

27.34
Ps 69.21
27.35
Ps 22.18
27.36
v. 54

27.16   See note on Mk 15.7 about Barabbas.
27.33   See note on Jn 19.17 regarding Calvary (Golgotha).
27.37   Each Gospel records something about the sign that hung over the cross of Jesus. A convicted criminal usually carried a sign on the way to be exe-

cuted, inscribed with the crime. When the execution took place, the sign was hung around the neck of the victim or nailed to the cross. Jesus' official crime was insubordination to Rome. The full inscription (for no Gospel writer gives the charge in its entirety) seems to have been: "This is Jesus of Nazareth, the King of

watch over him. 37 Over his head they put the charge against him, which read, "This is Jesus, the King of the Jews."

38   Then two bandits were crucified with him, one on his right and one on his left. 39 Those who passed by derided[f] him, shaking their heads 40 and saying, "You who would destroy the temple and build it in three days, save yourself! If you are the Son of God, come down from the cross." 41 In the same way the chief priests also, along with the scribes and elders, were mocking him, saying, 42 "He saved others; he cannot save himself.[g] He is the King of Israel; let him come down from the cross now, and we will believe in him. 43 He trusts in God; let God deliver him now, if he wants to; for he said, 'I am God's Son.' " 44 The bandits who were crucified with him also taunted him in the same way.

3. The death of Christ
(27.45–56; Mark 15.33–41; Luke 23.41–49; John 19.28–37)

45   From noon on, darkness came over the whole land[h] until three in the afternoon. 46 And about three o'clock Jesus cried with a loud voice, "Eli, Eli, lema sabachthani?" that is, "My God, my God, why have you forsaken me?" 47 When some of the bystanders heard it, they said, "This man is calling for Elijah." 48 At once one of them ran and got a sponge, filled it with sour wine, put it on a stick, and gave it to him to drink. 49 But the others said, "Wait, let us see whether Elijah will come to save him."[i] 50 Then Jesus cried again with a loud voice and breathed his last.[j] 51 At that moment the curtain of the temple was torn in two, from top to bottom. The earth shook, and the rocks were split. 52 The tombs also were opened, and many bodies of the saints who had fallen asleep were raised. 53 After his resurrection they came out of the tombs and entered the holy city and appeared to many. 54 Now when the centurion and those with him, who were keeping watch over Jesus, saw the earthquake and what took place, they were terrified and said, "Truly this man was God's Son!"[k]

55   Many women were also there, looking on from a distance; they had followed Jesus from Galilee and had provided for him. 56 Among them were Mary Magdalene, and Mary the mother of James and Joseph, and the mother of the sons of Zebedee.

27.38 Isa 53.12
27.39 Ps 22.7; 109.25
27.40 Mt 26.61; Acts 6.14; Jn 2.19
27.42 Jn 1.49; 12.13
27.43 Ps 22.8

27.45 Am 8.9
27.46 Ps 22.1

27.48 Ps 69.21

27.51 Ex 26.31; Heb 9.3; v. 54

27.54 Mt 3.17; 17.5

27.55 Lk 8.2, 3
27.56 Mk 15.40, 47; Lk 24.10

---

f Or blasphemed   g Or is he unable to save himself?   h Or earth   i Other ancient authorities add And another took a spear and pierced his side, and out came water and blood   j Or gave up his spirit   k Or a son of God

---

the Jews." According to Jn 19.20, it was written in Hebrew (or Aramaic, the local Jewish language), Greek (the universal language of the day), and Latin (the legal language of the ruling nation, Rome). Differences in the Gospel accounts may be explained by the following facts: Matthew recorded the inscription from Aramaic ("This is Jesus, the King of the Jews"), Mark and Luke from Latin ("The King of the Jews" in Mark 15.26; "This is the King of the Jews" in Lk 23.38), and John from Greek ("Jesus of Nazareth, the King of the Jews" in Jn 19.19). While the accounts are not identical, they faithfully represent the differences of the versions which were tacked on the cross. **27.38** See note on Lk 23.33 on the different accounts of the two bandits. **27.50** Christ was not killed by Satan or the Roman soldiers. He had earlier affirmed that no one could take his life, for he had the power to lay it down and to take it up again (see Jn 10.14–18). His atoning death was a voluntary sacrifice, freely done in obedience to the will of the Father. **27.51** The tearing of the curtain that sealed off the

Holy of Holies in the temple meant several things: (1) full atonement had been made, so that an earthly sanctuary for sacrifice and atonement was no longer necessary (Heb 10.19,20); (2) Christ offered his blood on the mercy seat of the Holy of Holies, going through the torn curtain, and later in the heavenly sanctuary after the resurrection, where he is now seated at the right hand of the Father (Heb 9.12,24); (3) the high priestly ministry of Jesus made a human priesthood forever unnecessary between people and God (Heb 7.23–28); (4) all Christians have immediate access to God the Father, without any intermediaries needed except Christ himself (Rom 5.2; Eph 2.18; 3.21). **27.52,53** Matthew alone records this miracle of the resurrection of some dead believers during Christ's passion and resurrection. We do not know how many were raised, nor do we know whether they died later and were reburied or whether they ascended into heaven in their bodies with Jesus in his ascension. According to the NRSV, these dead came out of their graves *after* the Lord's resurrection, then went into Jerusalem and appeared to many people.

4. Jesus laid in the tomb
(27.57–61; Mark 15.42–47; Luke 23.50–56; John 19.38–42)

27.57
Acts 13.29

57 When it was evening, there came a rich man from Arimathea, named Joseph, who was also a disciple of Jesus. 58 He went to Pilate and asked for the body of Jesus; then Pilate ordered it to be given to him. 59 So Joseph took the body and wrapped it in a clean linen cloth 60 and laid it in his own new tomb, which he had hewn in the rock. He then rolled a great stone to the door of the tomb and went away. 61 Mary Magdalene and the other Mary were there, sitting opposite the tomb.

27.60
Mt 28.2;
Mk 16.4

5. The tomb sealed and guarded (27.62–66)

27.63
Mt 16.21;
17.23; 20.19;
Mk 8.31;
10.34;
Lk 9.22;
18.33; 24.6,
7;
Jn 2.19
27.66
v. 60;
Mt 28.11-15

62 The next day, that is, after the day of Preparation, the chief priests and the Pharisees gathered before Pilate 63 and said, "Sir, we remember what that impostor said while he was still alive, 'After three days I will rise again.' 64 Therefore command the tomb to be made secure until the third day; otherwise his disciples may go and steal him away, and tell the people, 'He has been raised from the dead,' and the last deception would be worse than the first." 65 Pilate said to them, "You have a guard[l] of soldiers; go, make it as secure as you can."[m] 66 So they went with the guard and made the tomb secure by sealing the stone.

P. The resurrection of Jesus Christ
(28.1–10; Mark 16.1–8; Luke 24.1–11; John 20.1–18)

28.1
Lk 8.2;
Mt 27.56
28.2
Mt 27.51, 60
28.3
Dan 7.9;
10.6;
Mk 9.3;
Jn 20.12;
Acts 1.10
28.5
v. 10;
Mt 14.27
28.6
Mt 12.40;
16.21; 17.23;
20.19
28.7
Mt 26.32;
v. 16
28.9
Jn 20.14-18
28.10
Rom 8.29;
Heb 2.11

28 After the sabbath, as the first day of the week was dawning, Mary Magdalene and the other Mary went to see the tomb. 2 And suddenly there was a great earthquake; for an angel of the Lord, descending from heaven, came and rolled back the stone and sat on it. 3 His appearance was like lightning, and his clothing white as snow. 4 For fear of him the guards shook and became like dead men. 5 But the angel said to the women, "Do not be afraid; I know that you are looking for Jesus who was crucified. 6 He is not here; for he has been raised, as he said. Come, see the place where he[n] lay. 7 Then go quickly and tell his disciples, 'He has been raised from the dead,'[o] and indeed he is going ahead of you to Galilee; there you will see him.' This is my message for you." 8 So they left the tomb quickly with fear and great joy, and ran to tell his disciples. 9 Suddenly Jesus met them and said, "Greetings!" And they came to him, took hold of his feet, and worshiped him. 10 Then Jesus said to them, "Do not be afraid; go and tell my brothers to go to Galilee; there they will see me."

Q. The bribing of the soldiers (28.11–15)

28.11
Mt 27.65, 66

11 While they were going, some of the guard went into the city and told the chief priests everything that had happened. 12 After the priests[p] had assembled with the elders, they devised a plan to give a large sum of money to the soldiers, 13 telling them, "You must say, 'His disciples came

---

l Or *Take a guard*   *m* Gk *you know how*   *n* Other ancient authorities read *the Lord*   *o* Other ancient authorities lack *from the dead*   *p* Gk *they*

27.66 *sealing the stone.* This was done by stringing a cord across the rock, then sealing the cord at each end with clay.
28.6 Christ's resurrection fulfilled O.T. prophecy (Ps 16.10) and Jesus' own statements (20.19; Jn 10.18). While there is no record of unbelievers seeing him, various believers attest to its factuality: (1) the eleven apostles, to whom "he presented himself alive . . . by many convincing proofs" (Acts 1.3); (2) the apostle Paul (Acts 9.3–8; 1 Cor 15.8; Gal 1.12); (3) five hundred Christian believers (1 Cor 15.6); and

(4) Thomas the doubter, who had to see for himself (Jn 20.24–29). According to Paul in 1 Cor 15, the Christian faith stands or falls on the bodily resurrection of Jesus, for it guarantees that (1) Jesus was truly the Son of God (Rom 1.4); (2) God the Father accepted what Jesus did at Calvary on the basis of the resurrection (Rom 4.25); (3) the risen Christ pleads for his people before the Father (Rom 8.34); (4) believers have the hope of eternal life (1 Pet 1.3–5); and (5) believers will also rise and have resurrected bodies like that of Jesus (1 Cor 15.49; Phil 3.21; 1 Jn 3.2).

by night and stole him away while we were asleep.' [14] If this comes to the governor's ears, we will satisfy him and keep you out of trouble." [15] So they took the money and did as they were directed. And this story is still told among the Jews to this day.

VI. The appearance in Galilee; the great commission (28.16–20; Mark 16.15–18)

16   Now the eleven disciples went to Galilee, to the mountain to which Jesus had directed them. [17] When they saw him, they worshiped him; but some doubted. [18] And Jesus came and said to them, "All authority in heaven and on earth has been given to me. [19] Go therefore and make disciples of all nations, baptizing them in the name of the Father and of the Son and of the Holy Spirit, [20] and teaching them to obey everything that I have commanded you. And remember, I am with you always, to the end of the age." [q]

[q] Other ancient authorities add *Amen*

28.14
Mt 27.2
28.16
v. 7;
Mt 26.32
28.18
Dan 7.13, 14;
Lk 10.22;
Phil 2.9, 10;
1 Pet 3.22
28.19
Lk 24.47;
Acts 1.8
28.20
Acts 2.42;
Mt 18.20;
Acts 18.10

28.19 Jesus' command here is the basis for water baptism, which has been accepted and practiced by the church through the ages. While virtually all Christians agree on the need for water baptism, they differ widely on all other aspects of it. Some believe that immersion constitutes the only mode of baptism; others hold to pouring or sprinkling. Some baptize infants on the grounds that it replaces the rite of circumcision. Others refuse to baptize until the individual is old enough to make a credible personal profession of faith. Some call baptism a sacrament, which conveys grace; others call it a symbol. According to Jesus, baptism is to be administered "in the name of the Father and of the Son and of the Holy Spirit." Modern critics claim this formula is falsely ascribed to Jesus and that it represents later church tradition, for nowhere in the book of Acts is baptism performed with the name of the Trinity. Evangelicals accept this verse as Jesus' words and agree that the Trinitarian formula was spoken by the Son of God himself (see note on Acts 2.38).

INTRODUCTION TO
THE GOSPEL ACCORDING TO
MARK

Authorship, Date, and Background: Tradition has identified John Mark as the author of the second Gospel. The text itself does not mention him by name. Mark came from a well-to-do family. His mother, Mary, was a friend of the apostles. Some think Mary's home was the site of the Last Supper and the home in which the disciples gathered to wait for Pentecost. It was definitely the place in which the Christians gathered to pray for the release of Peter from prison and where he came when he was set free (Acts 12.12ff). Barnabas was Mark's cousin and a fellow missionary.

Acts 12.25 states that Paul and Barnabas ministered in Antioch, and when they left that city they were accompanied by Mark as their assistant. Acts 13.1–5 details how Paul and Barnabas were called by the Holy Spirit and sent by the church on their first missionary journey. When Paul and Barnabas landed at Perga, Mark deserted them and returned to Jerusalem (Acts 13.13). Whatever the reason for the desertion, Paul was disillusioned with Mark. Later, when Barnabas and Paul were at Antioch following the Jerusalem conference, they agreed to go on a preaching mission to Asia Minor. Barnabas wanted to take Mark with them, but Paul dissented. This broke up the team. Barnabas took Mark and went to Cyprus; Paul took Silas and went to Syria and Cilicia (Acts 15.34–41). Some time afterwards, Paul and Mark were reconciled. Paul paid tribute to him and described him as his traveling companion (Col 4.10; Philem 24; 2 Tim 4.11).

The apostle Peter spoke of Mark as his son in 1 Pet 5.13. This is important because the names of Mark and Peter have been connected together with the Gospel of Mark. Mark had not been a follower or companion of Jesus; he was probably too young at the time. But he was closely associated with Peter, and his Gospel is thought to be a written account of what Peter preached, penned either before or after Peter's death. Many scholars think that the Gospel was composed in Rome before the fall of Jerusalem in A.D. 70 (perhaps as early as A.D. 50), and that it was intended for non-Jewish believers. Many scholars think it was the first Gospel to be written, and that Matthew and Luke both used Mark as one of their chief sources for their own writings. Probably all of them had access to the oral traditions which included much of the same material. Since some scholars still regard Matthew's Gospel as the earliest, Mark may have been indebted to him or both of them to others. The date is not so important. What is important is that all of the Gospels were produced under the aegis of the Holy Spirit.

Characteristics and Content: Mark's Gospel is not a biography. Nothing is said about the birth, genealogy, or early life of Jesus; rather, Mark concentrates on his public ministry. He does this in narrative style, paying attention to details in an action-packed, vivid, and colorful account of Jesus' last years. He does not concentrate so much on what Jesus said as on what he did, especially his miracles. He pictures Jesus as the Son of God and the mighty overcomer of disease, demons, and death. The Greek word translated "immediately," "at once," and "soon" is used more than forty times.

Mark explains Jewish customs—this indicates that the Gospel was intended for a non-Jewish audience. Mark starts by declaring, "The beginning of the good news of Jesus Christ, the Son of God" (1.1). The effect of his writing is sharpened and reinforced by the use of active rather than passive verbs. Much of what he says sounds as though it could have been taken from Peter's preaching, the substance of which he tries to preserve for the reader. At the same time, Mark's Gospel is full of basic doctrine. Almost from the beginning he makes it clear that Jesus is pressing toward his goal—the cross of Calvary and the salvation of sinners through faith in him.

The ending of Mark's Gospel (16.9–20) is not found in the two oldest Greek manuscripts. It is included in later manuscripts, and in other early manuscripts it appears with variations and partial omissions. These endings vary in style from the rest of the Gospel. Yet without the ending, the Gospel seems to conclude very abruptly. This is the only major textual problem for the book.

Outline:

I. The beginning of the good news (1.1–13)

II. Public ministry in Galilee (1.14—9.50)

III. From Galilee to Jerusalem (10.1–52)

IV. The last week in Jerusalem (11.1—16.8)

V. Appearances of the risen Christ (16.9–20)

THE GOSPEL ACCORDING TO

MARK

I. *The beginning of the good news (1.1–13)*

A. *The ministry of John the Baptist*
(1.1–8; Matt. 3.1–12; Luke 3.2–17; John 1.6–8,19–28)

1.1
Mt 4.3
1.2
Mal 3.1;
Mt 11.10;
Lk 7.27
1.3
Isa 40.3

1 The beginning of the good news*a* of Jesus Christ, the Son of God.*b*
2 As it is written in the prophet Isaiah,*c*
"See, I am sending my messenger ahead of you,*d*
　　who will prepare your way;
3 the voice of one crying out in the wilderness:
　　'Prepare the way of the Lord,
　　make his paths straight,' "

1.4
Acts 13.24;
Lk 1.77

4John the baptizer appeared*e* in the wilderness, proclaiming a baptism of repentance for the forgiveness of sins. 5And people from the whole Judean countryside and all the people of Jerusalem were going out to him,

1.6
Lev 11.22

and were baptized by him in the river Jordan, confessing their sins. 6Now John was clothed with camel's hair, with a leather belt around his waist,

1.7
Acts 13.25

and he ate locusts and wild honey. 7He proclaimed, "The one who is more powerful than I is coming after me; I am not worthy to stoop down and

1.8
Acts 1.5;
Isa 44.3;
Joel 2.28

untie the thong of his sandals. 8I have baptized you with*f* water; but he will baptize you with*f* the Holy Spirit."

B. *The baptism of Jesus (1.9–11; Matt. 3.13–17; Luke 3.21,22)*

1.9
Mt 2.23
1.10
Jn 1.32
1.11
Ps 2.7;
Isa 42.1

9 In those days Jesus came from Nazareth of Galilee and was baptized by John in the Jordan. 10And just as he was coming up out of the water, he saw the heavens torn apart and the Spirit descending like a dove on him. 11And a voice came from heaven, "You are my Son, the Beloved;*g* with you I am well pleased."

C. *The temptation of Jesus (1.12,13; Matt. 4.1–11; Luke 4.1–13)*

12 And the Spirit immediately drove him out into the wilderness.

a Or *gospel*　*b* Other ancient authorities lack *the Son of God*　*c* Other ancient authorities read *in the prophets*　*d* Gk *before your face*　*e* Other ancient authorities read *John was baptizing*　*f* Or *in*　*g* Or *my beloved Son*

1.1 Mark begins with the gospel of Jesus Christ, who had John the Baptist as his forerunner and herald. Mark said nothing about Jesus' ancestry or about his birth. Nor did he do what John did—give us information about the pre-incarnate Christ, the Logos (or Word). Mark was not an apostle, and most of what he wrote appears in Matthew or in Luke. His testimony gives added witness to the truth of the O.T. and N.T. Whether his Gospel preceded or followed Matthew's is of no great significance.
1.2 *my messenger*, i.e., John the Baptist. See note on Lk 1.57 for information about the life of John.
1.4 *for the forgiveness of sins*. The baptism of John, which certainly included the need for repentance along with the promise of the forgiveness of sins, was not full Christian baptism. The Christian church did not yet exist; John did not baptize in the name of the Trinity; he never baptized with the Holy Spirit, who

had not yet been given (see Jn 7.39). In Acts 18.25 we read that Apollos knew only the baptism of John, and in 19.1–7 Paul came across several disciples of John who had been baptized before Jesus' death. Paul rebaptized them in the name of Jesus and laid hands on them to receive the gift of the Holy Spirit.
1.8 *with water*, or, "in water" (NRSV footnote); *with the Holy Spirit*, or, "in the Holy Spirit" (NRSV footnote). The correct translation of the Greek word (which is the same in both instances) has been a matter of controversy among Christians.
1.10 See note on Lk 3.22 on the baptism of Jesus by John.
1.12,13 See notes on Lk 4.1,2 on the temptation of Jesus. *Angels* are sent to do God's will or to communicate it to people. The Hebrew (*mal'akh*) and Greek (*angellos*) both mean "messenger." Angels constitute a high order of beings who stand in the presence of

13 He was in the wilderness forty days, tempted by Satan; and he was with the wild beasts; and the angels waited on him.

II. *Public ministry in Galilee (1.14–9.50)*

A. *The beginning of Jesus' Galilean ministry*
(1.14,15; Matt. 4.12–17; Luke 4.14,15; John 4.43–45)

14   Now after John was arrested, Jesus came to Galilee, proclaiming the good news[h] of God,[i] 15 and saying, "The time is fulfilled, and the kingdom of God has come near;[j] repent, and believe in the good news."[h]

B. *The call of the first four disciples*
(1.16–20; Matt. 4.18–22; Luke 5.1–11; cf. John 1.40–42)

16   As Jesus passed along the Sea of Galilee, he saw Simon and his brother Andrew casting a net into the sea—for they were fishermen. 17 And Jesus said to them, "Follow me and I will make you fish for people." 18 And immediately they left their nets and followed him. 19 As he went a little farther, he saw James son of Zebedee and his brother John, who were in their boat mending the nets. 20 Immediately he called them; and they left their father Zebedee in the boat with the hired men, and followed him.

C. *The unclean spirit cast out (1.21–28; Luke 4.31–37)*

21   They went to Capernaum; and when the sabbath came, he entered the synagogue and taught. 22 They were astounded at his teaching, for he taught them as one having authority, and not as the scribes. 23 Just then there was in their synagogue a man with an unclean spirit, 24 and he cried out, "What have you to do with us, Jesus of Nazareth? Have you come to destroy us? I know who you are, the Holy One of God." 25 But Jesus rebuked him, saying, "Be silent, and come out of him!" 26 And the unclean spirit, convulsing him and crying with a loud voice, came out of him. 27 They were all amazed, and they kept on asking one another, "What is this? A new teaching—with authority! He[k] commands even the unclean spirits, and they obey him." 28 At once his fame began to spread throughout the surrounding region of Galilee.

D. *Peter's mother-in-law healed*
(1.29–31; Matt. 8.14–17; Luke 4.38–41)

29   As soon as they[l] left the synagogue, they entered the house of Simon and Andrew, with James and John. 30 Now Simon's mother-in-law was in bed with a fever, and they told him about her at once. 31 He came

---

1.14 Mt 4.23
1.15 Gal 4.4; Eph 1.10; Acts 20.21

1.18 Mt 19.27

1.21 Mt 4.23
1.22 Mt 7.28
1.24 Mt 8.29; Mk 10.47; 14.67; Jn 6.69; Acts 3.14
1.25 v. 34
1.27 Mk 10.24, 32

1.29 vv. 21, 23

---

h Or *gospel*   i Other ancient authorities read *of the kingdom*   j Or *is at hand*   k Or *A new teaching! With authority he*   l Other ancient authorities read *he*

God. The term "angel" includes evil ones who, along with Satan, fell from glory. In Rev 1–3 the term seems to apply to pastors—God's messengers to the seven churches in Asia. Occasionally in the O.T., God himself appears in angelic form (Gen 16.7–14; 22.11–19; Ex 3.2–4; Judg 2.1; 6.1–14; 13.3; see Ex 24.10 for note on "theophany"). According to the Bible, angels (1) are created beings (Neh 9.6; Col 1.16); (2) are innumerable (Heb 12.22; Rev 5.11); (3) are above the laws of matter, i.e., can pass through closed doors and iron gates (Acts 12.7); (4) are spirits of divine service (Heb 1.14); (5) differ in rank and power (they are divided into such classes as angels, archangels, principalities, and powers; see Dan 10.12–21; Col 1.16); (6) are more intelligent than

humans (2 Sam 14.20); and (7) excel in power (2 Sam 24.16; 2 Kings 19.35; Ps 103.20; Mt 28.2,4; 2 Pet 2.11; Rev 20.1–3).
1.23 This was Jesus' first contact with a demon-possessed person. No appeal was made to him to do anything, either by the one who was possessed or by those attending the synagogue. The demon himself challenged Jesus, who promptly exorcised him by saying, "Be silent, and come out of him!" (v. 25). The demon obeyed immediately. The bystanders got the message: even demons obey the Son of God.
1.30,31 Jesus was Peter's guest. When he found Peter's mother-in-law sick of a fever, he healed her. Wherever Christ comes, he comes to do good.

and took her by the hand and lifted her up. Then the fever left her, and she began to serve them.

E. *The sick healed; demons cast out*
(1.32–34; Matt. 8.16–17; Luke 4.40–41)

32 That evening, at sunset, they brought to him all who were sick or possessed with demons. 33 And the whole city was gathered around the door. 34 And he cured many who were sick with various diseases, and cast out many demons; and he would not permit the demons to speak, because they knew him.

F. *First preaching tour in Galilee*
(1.35–39; cf. Luke 4.42–44)

35 In the morning, while it was still very dark, he got up and went out to a deserted place, and there he prayed. 36 And Simon and his companions hunted for him. 37 When they found him, they said to him, "Everyone is searching for you." 38 He answered, "Let us go on to the neighboring towns, so that I may proclaim the message there also; for that is what I came out to do." 39 And he went throughout Galilee, proclaiming the message in their synagogues and casting out demons.

G. *The leper cleansed (1.40–45; Matt. 8.1–4; Luke 5.12–16)*

40 A leper[m] came to him begging him, and kneeling[n] he said to him, "If you choose, you can make me clean." 41 Moved with pity,[o] Jesus[p] stretched out his hand and touched him, and said to him, "I do choose. Be made clean!" 42 Immediately the leprosy[m] left him, and he was made clean. 43 After sternly warning him he sent him away at once, 44 saying to him, "See that you say nothing to anyone; but go, show yourself to the priest, and offer for your cleansing what Moses commanded, as a testimony to them." 45 But he went out and began to proclaim it freely, and to spread the word, so that Jesus[p] could no longer go into a town openly, but stayed out in the country; and people came to him from every quarter.

H. *A paralytic healed and forgiven*
(2.1–12; Matt. 9.1–8; Luke 5.17–26)

2 When he returned to Capernaum after some days, it was reported that he was at home. 2 So many gathered around that there was no longer room for them, not even in front of the door; and he was speaking the word to them. 3 Then some people[q] came, bringing to him a paralyzed man, carried by four of them. 4 And when they could not bring him to Jesus because of the crowd, they removed the roof above him; and after having dug through it, they let down the mat on which the paralytic lay. 5 When Jesus saw their faith, he said to the paralytic, "Son, your sins are forgiven." 6 Now some of the scribes were sitting there, questioning in their hearts, 7 "Why does this fellow speak in this way? It is blasphemy! Who can forgive sins but God alone?" 8 At once Jesus perceived in his spirit that they were discussing these questions among themselves; and he said to

Marginal references

1.32 Mk 4.24
1.34 Mt 4.23; Mk 3.12; Acts 16.17, 18
1.35 Mt 14.23; Lk 5.16
1.38 Isa 61.1
1.39 Mt 4.23-25
1.40 Mk 10.17
1.44 Lev 13.49; 14.2-32
1.45 Lk 5.15; Mt 28.15; Mk 2.13; Lk 5.17; Jn 6.2
2.2 v. 13
2.3 Mt 4.24
2.7 Isa 43.25

---

m The terms *leper* and *leprosy* can refer to several diseases   *n* Other ancient authorities lack *kneeling*   *o* Other ancient authorities read *anger*   *p* Gk *he*   *q* Gk *they*

1.35 As a human being, Jesus prayed to his Father in heaven. If he needed to pray, so do we. He prayed long before daybreak, choosing a solitary place where no one could observe him and where there would be no distraction. And when he finished praying, he went back to his work. Prayer never excuses us from our ordinary duties; rather, it should help us meet those obligations.

1.40 See note on Mt 8.1.
2.1ff See note on Lk 5.17.
2.7 The scribes asked the right question about Jesus and the forgiveness of sins. If God alone can do this, Jesus either was God or was guilty of blasphemy. They concluded wrongly, however, that Jesus was not God.

them, "Why do you raise such questions in your hearts? 9 Which is easier, to say to the paralytic, 'Your sins are forgiven,' or to say, 'Stand up and take your mat and walk'? 10 But so that you may know that the Son of Man has authority on earth to forgive sins" — he said to the paralytic — 11 "I say to you, stand up, take your mat and go to your home." 12 And he stood up, and immediately took the mat and went out before all of them; so that they were all amazed and glorified God, saying, "We have never seen anything like this!"

2.12
Mt 9.33

I. *Matthew called (2.13–17; Matt. 9.9–13; Luke 5.27–32)*

13 Jesus*r* went out again beside the sea; the whole crowd gathered around him, and he taught them. 14 As he was walking along, he saw Levi son of Alphaeus sitting at the tax booth, and he said to him, "Follow me." And he got up and followed him.

2.13
Mk 1.45
2.14
Mt 8.22

15 And as he sat at dinner*s* in Levi's*t* house, many tax collectors and sinners were also sitting*u* with Jesus and his disciples — for there were many who followed him. 16 When the scribes of*v* the Pharisees saw that he was eating with sinners and tax collectors, they said to his disciples, "Why does he eat*w* with tax collectors and sinners?" 17 When Jesus heard this, he said to them, "Those who are well have no need of a physician, but those who are sick; I have come to call not the righteous but sinners."

2.16
Acts 23.9
2.17
Lk 19.10;
1 Tim 1.15

J. *The question about fasting (2.18–22; Matt. 9.14–17; Luke 5.33–39)*

18 Now John's disciples and the Pharisees were fasting; and people*x* came and said to him, "Why do John's disciples and the disciples of the Pharisees fast, but your disciples do not fast?" 19 Jesus said to them, "The wedding guests cannot fast while the bridegroom is with them, can they? As long as they have the bridegroom with them, they cannot fast. 20 The days will come when the bridegroom is taken away from them, and then they will fast on that day.

2.20
Lk 17.22

21 "No one sews a piece of unshrunk cloth on an old cloak; otherwise, the patch pulls away from it, the new from the old, and a worse tear is made. 22 And no one puts new wine into old wineskins; otherwise, the wine will burst the skins, and the wine is lost, and so are the skins; but one puts new wine into fresh wineskins."*y*

K. *Jesus the Lord of the sabbath (2.23–28; Matt. 12.1–8; Luke 6.1–5)*

23 One sabbath he was going through the grainfields; and as they made their way his disciples began to pluck heads of grain. 24 The Pharisees said to him, "Look, why are they doing what is not lawful on the sabbath?" 25 And he said to them, "Have you never read what David did when he and his companions were hungry and in need of food? 26 He

2.23
Deut 23.25

2.26
1 Sam 21.1-6;
2 Sam 8.17;
Ex 29.32, 33;
Lev 24.9

r Gk *He*　*s* Gk *reclined*　*t* Gk *his*　*u* Gk *reclining*　*v* Other ancient authorities read *and*　*w* Other ancient authorities add *and drink*　*x* Gk *they*　*y* Other ancient authorities lack *but one puts new wine into fresh wineskins*

2.18 People, including the apostles (Acts 13.1-3), fasted in Jesus' day. The early Christians, however, did not fast regularly as a Christian duty. When asked by his disciples why he did not fast, Jesus said that fasting was an expression of sorrow and was not in keeping with the intense joy his disciples shared with him. In Mt 6.16–18 Jesus was critical of a fasting that was only for show and that looked for the approval of people. He endorsed secret fasting only, in which one seeks to glorify God. Present-day Christians might well engage in fasting from time to time.

2.21,22 See note on Lk 5.36ff.
2.25ff In obedience to Lev 24.5–9 the priests prepared twelve loaves of bread every week, laying them before the Lord on the table every sabbath (cf. Ex 25.30; 35.13; 39.36). When they did this, the priests could then eat the old loaves if they wished. But no one else was allowed to eat the sacred bread.
2.26 Some critics have said Jesus was mistaken here when he referred to Abiathar, for 1 Sam 21.1–6 states that Ahimelech, the father of Abiathar, gave the sacred bread to David. But according to Mark, the only

entered the house of God, when Abiathar was high priest, and ate the bread of the Presence, which it is not lawful for any but the priests to eat, and he gave some to his companions." 27 Then he said to them, "The sabbath was made for humankind, and not humankind for the sabbath; 28 so the Son of Man is lord even of the sabbath."

2.27
Ex 23.12;
Deut 5.14

L. Jesus heals on the sabbath (3.1–6; Matt. 12.9–14; Luke 6.6–11)

3.1
Mk 1.21, 39
3.2
Lk 14.1;
20.20;
Mt 12.10

3 Again he entered the synagogue, and a man was there who had a withered hand. 2 They watched him to see whether he would cure him on the sabbath, so that they might accuse him. 3 And he said to the man who had the withered hand, "Come forward." 4 Then he said to them, "Is it lawful to do good or to do harm on the sabbath, to save life or to kill?" But they were silent. 5 He looked around at them with anger; he was grieved at their hardness of heart and said to the man, "Stretch out your hand." He stretched it out, and his hand was restored. 6 The Pharisees went out and immediately conspired with the Herodians against him, how to destroy him.

3.6
Mt 12.14;
22.16;
Mk 12.13

M. Jesus heals many (3.7–12; Matt. 12.15–21; cf. Luke 6.17–19)

3.7
Mt 4.25
3.8
Mt 11.21

7 Jesus departed with his disciples to the sea, and a great multitude from Galilee followed him; 8 hearing all that he was doing, they came to him in great numbers from Judea, Jerusalem, Idumea, beyond the Jordan, and the region around Tyre and Sidon. 9 He told his disciples to have a boat ready for him because of the crowd, so that they would not crush him; 10 for he had cured many, so that all who had diseases pressed upon him to touch him. 11 Whenever the unclean spirits saw him, they fell down before him and shouted, "You are the Son of God!" 12 But he sternly ordered them not to make him known.

3.10
Mt 4.23;
Mk 5.29, 34;
6.56; 8.22
3.11
Mk 1.23, 24;
Lk 4.41;
Mt 14.33
3.12
Mk 1.25, 34

N. The appointing of the Twelve (3.13–19; Matt. 10.1–4; Luke 6.12–16)

3.13
Mt 5.1;
Lk 9.1

13 He went up the mountain and called to him those whom he wanted, and they came to him. 14 And he appointed twelve, whom he also named apostles,z to be with him, and to be sent out to proclaim the message, 15 and to have authority to cast out demons. 16 So he appointed the twelve:a Simon (to whom he gave the name Peter); 17 James son of Zebedee and John the brother of James (to whom he gave the name Boanerges, that is, Sons of Thunder); 18 and Andrew, and Philip, and

3.16
Jn 1.42

z Other ancient authorities lack *whom he also named apostles*   a Other ancient authorities lack *So he appointed the twelve*

---

thing Jesus said was that the incident took place "when Abiathar was high priest," who served jointly with his father before his father died.
2.27 God rested on the seventh day (Gen 2.2). This is the first mention of the sabbath in Scripture. In Israel the seventh day (Saturday) was the sabbath and as such was incorporated into the Mosaic law (Ex 20.9–11). The Jews became litigious about the sabbath, adding all sorts of restrictions and regulations that made matters cumbersome. They even figured exactly how far one could travel on the sabbath before it became work and a violation of the law (note the phrase "a sabbath day's journey" in Acts 1.12). Jesus has provided us with two principles relative to work on the sabbath: (1) *The sabbath was made for humankind, and not humankind for the sabbath*; and (2) works of mercy and of necessity are permissible on the sabbath. For example, to pluck grain for food was a necessity; to save the life of an animal from a pit was a work of mercy, as was the healing of a sick person

(Mt 12.1–8; Lk 6.1–5; 13.10–17).
3.1ff The only question here was whether it was right or wrong to heal on the sabbath day. Such an "act of mercy" was not forbidden, but those who hated Jesus wished to use this healing against him by calling it an "act of work" on the sabbath day.
3.11 *unclean spirits*, i.e., demons. These demons knew about Jesus Christ and were fully aware of his divine sonship; nevertheless, they were not and could not be saved. Similarly, people may profess faith in all the doctrines of the Christian faith without being regenerated (cf. Jas 2.19).
3.14 Though Jesus had many followers, the special group whom he chose were to become the apostles in the church after Pentecost. From the beginning he knew that Judas Iscariot would betray him, and he was chosen in accord with the plan of God from whom nothing is hidden. Judas was later replaced by Matthias (Acts 1.26). Paul was also called by God to be an apostle (Rom 1.1).

Bartholomew, and Matthew, and Thomas, and James son of Alphaeus, and Thaddaeus, and Simon the Cananaean, 19and Judas Iscariot, who betrayed him.

O. *Jesus answers the slander of the Pharisees*
(3.20–27; Matt. 12.22–45; Luke 11.14–23)

Then he went home; 20and the crowd came together again, so that they could not even eat. 21When his family heard it, they went out to restrain him, for people were saying, "He has gone out of his mind." 22And the scribes who came down from Jerusalem said, "He has Beelzebul, and by the ruler of the demons he casts out demons." 23And he called them to him, and spoke to them in parables, "How can Satan cast out Satan? 24If a kingdom is divided against itself, that kingdom cannot stand. 25And if a house is divided against itself, that house will not be able to stand. 26And if Satan has risen up against himself and is divided, he cannot stand, but his end has come. 27But no one can enter a strong man's house and plunder his property without first tying up the strong man; then indeed the house can be plundered.

3.20
Mk 6.31
3.21
Jn 10.20;
Acts 26.24
3.22
Mt 9.34;
10.25;
Jn 7.20;
8.48, 52
3.23
Mk 4.2ff
3.27
Isa 49.24, 25

P. *The unforgivable sin (3.28–30)*

28 "Truly I tell you, people will be forgiven for their sins and whatever blasphemies they utter; 29but whoever blasphemes against the Holy Spirit can never have forgiveness, but is guilty of an eternal sin" — 30for they had said, "He has an unclean spirit."

3.28
Lk 12.10

Q. *Christ's true kindred (3.31–35; Matt. 12.46–50; Luke 8.19–21)*

31 Then his mother and his brothers came; and standing outside, they sent to him and called him. 32A crowd was sitting around him; and they said to him, "Your mother and your brothers and sisters[b] are outside, asking for you." 33And he replied, "Who are my mother and my brothers?" 34And looking at those who sat around him, he said, "Here are my mother and my brothers! 35Whoever does the will of God is my brother and sister and mother."

3.31
Mt 12.46;
Lk 8.19

R. *Jesus teaches in parables (4.1–34)*

1. *Parable of the sower (4.1–9; Matt. 13.1–9; Luke 8.4–8)*

4 Again he began to teach beside the sea. Such a very large crowd gathered around him that he got into a boat on the sea and sat there, while the whole crowd was beside the sea on the land. 2He began to teach them many things in parables, and in his teaching he said to them: 3"Listen! A sower went out to sow. 4And as he sowed, some seed fell on the path, and the birds came and ate it up. 5Other seed fell on rocky ground, where it did not have much soil, and it sprang up quickly, since it had no depth of soil. 6And when the sun rose, it was scorched; and since it had no root, it withered away. 7Other seed fell among thorns, and the thorns grew up and choked it, and it yielded no grain. 8Other seed fell

4.1
Mk 2.13; 3.7
4.2
Mk 3.23

4.8
Jn 15.5;
Col 1.6

---

b Other ancient authorities lack *and sisters*

3.22 *Beelzebul.* See note on Mt 10.25.
3.29 Blaspheming *against the Holy Spirit* is the unpardonable sin. It consists in the constant, conscious, and deliberate rejection of the Spirit's witness to Christ's deity and his power to save. Inasmuch as only the Holy Spirit can convince and convert sinners (Jn 16.7–11), any final rejection of his witness and wooing makes it impossible for such a person to be saved.
3.35 We may claim as our brothers and sisters those

who are related to us by the blood of Christ, through which we all are adopted into the family of God. Such people are closer to us than relatives and earthly family members who do not know the Savior.
4.3ff The elements in each part of the parable are the same — the seed, the sower, and the soil. It is always the same seed and the same sower; only the soil is different. That is, four kinds of people hear the good news, but only one of the four responds in such a way as to produce acceptable fruit.

into good soil and brought forth grain, growing up and increasing and yielding thirty and sixty and a hundredfold." 9 And he said, "Let anyone with ears to hear listen!"

4.9
Mt 11.15

2. The reason for parables (4.10–12; Matt. 13.10–17; Luke 8.9–10)

10 When he was alone, those who were around him along with the twelve asked him about the parables. 11 And he said to them, "To you has been given the secret[c] of the kingdom of God, but for those outside, everything comes in parables; 12 in order that

'they may indeed look, but not perceive,
    and may indeed listen, but not understand;
so that they may not turn again and be forgiven.'"

4.11
1 Cor 5.12;
Col 4.5;
1 Thess 4.12;
1 Tim 3.7
4.12
Isa 6.9;
Jn 12.40;
Acts 28.26;
Rom 11.8

3. The parable of the sower explained (4.13–20; Matt. 13.18–23; Luke 8.11–15)

13 And he said to them, "Do you not understand this parable? Then how will you understand all the parables? 14 The sower sows the word. 15 These are the ones on the path where the word is sown: when they hear, Satan immediately comes and takes away the word that is sown in them. 16 And these are the ones sown on rocky ground: when they hear the word, they immediately receive it with joy. 17 But they have no root, and endure only for a while; then, when trouble or persecution arises on account of the word, immediately they fall away.[d] 18 And others are those sown among the thorns: these are the ones who hear the word, 19 but the cares of the world, and the lure of wealth, and the desire for other things come in and choke the word, and it yields nothing. 20 And these are the ones sown on the good soil: they hear the word and accept it and bear fruit, thirty and sixty and a hundredfold."

4.15
Mk 2.23, 26

4. The parable of the lamp (4.21–25; cf. Matt. 5.15; Luke 8.16; 11.33)

21 He said to them, "Is a lamp brought in to be put under the bushel basket, or under the bed, and not on the lampstand? 22 For there is nothing hidden, except to be disclosed; nor is anything secret, except to come to light. 23 Let anyone with ears to hear listen!" 24 And he said to them, "Pay attention to what you hear; the measure you give will be the measure you get, and still more will be given you. 25 For to those who have, more will be given; and from those who have nothing, even what they have will be taken away."

4.22
Mt 10.26;
Lk 8.17;
12.2
4.23
Mt 11.15
4.24
Mt 7.2;
Lk 6.38
4.25
Mt 13.12;
25.29;
Lk 8.18;
19.26

5. The parable of growing seed (4.26–29)

26 He also said, "The kingdom of God is as if someone would scatter seed on the ground, 27 and would sleep and rise night and day, and the seed would sprout and grow, he does not know how. 28 The earth produces of itself, first the stalk, then the head, then the full grain in the head.

4.26
Mt 13.24

c Or mystery   d Or stumble

4.11,12 Clearly Jesus used illustrations or parables in order to hide the truth, not to reveal it. The words of Jesus summarize what God said to Isaiah regarding Israel's rejection of Isaiah's message (Isa 6.9,10). At that time, Israel's unwillingness to repent and accept God's forgiveness was the result of its rejection of the word of God mediated through Isaiah. This pattern was being duplicated in Christ's ministry when the Jews rejected his teaching (cf. Mt 13.13–15).
4.15 Among the works of Satan are the following: (1) he seeks to destroy the preached word of God; (2) he blinds people's eyes to the truth of the gospel (2 Cor 4.3,4); (3) he tempts the people of God (1 Cor

7.5; 2 Cor 2.11; 1 Thess 3.5); (4) he molests and harasses God's servants in countless ways (1 Thess 2.18; 1 Pet 5.8); (5) he enters into people and uses them as his tools (Mt 12.27,28,43–45; Jn 13.27); and (6) he accuses people before God (Job 1.8–11; Zech 3.1; Rev 12.10).
4.26ff The central teaching of this illustration is the law of growth. After planting, the seed may not sprout for some time. The kingdom of God is like that. Though its beginning was small in Jerusalem, it now extends around the whole earth. God alone knows how to bring forth an abundant harvest from the gospel seed.

29 But when the grain is ripe, at once he goes in with his sickle, because the harvest has come."

4.29
Rev 14.15

6. The parable of the mustard seed
(4.30–34; Matt. 13.31,32; Luke 13.18,19)

30 He also said, "With what can we compare the kingdom of God, or what parable will we use for it? 31 It is like a mustard seed, which, when sown upon the ground, is the smallest of all the seeds on earth; 32 yet when it is sown it grows up and becomes the greatest of all shrubs, and puts forth large branches, so that the birds of the air can make nests in its shade."

33 With many such parables he spoke the word to them, as they were able to hear it; 34 he did not speak to them except in parables, but he explained everything in private to his disciples.

4.30
Mt 13.24

4.33
Jn 16.12
4.34
Mt 13.34;
Jn 16.25

S. The storm stilled (4.35–41; Matt. 8.23–27; Luke 8.22–25)

35 On that day, when evening had come, he said to them, "Let us go across to the other side." 36 And leaving the crowd behind, they took him with them in the boat, just as he was. Other boats were with him. 37 A great windstorm arose, and the waves beat into the boat, so that the boat was already being swamped. 38 But he was in the stern, asleep on the cushion; and they woke him up and said to him, "Teacher, do you not care that we are perishing?" 39 He woke up and rebuked the wind, and said to the sea, "Peace! Be still!" Then the wind ceased, and there was a dead calm. 40 He said to them, "Why are you afraid? Have you still no faith?" 41 And they were filled with great awe and said to one another, "Who then is this, that even the wind and the sea obey him?"

4.36
Mk 5.2, 21

4.40
Mt 14.31,
32;
Mk 16.14

T. Demons cast out (5.1–20; Matt. 8.28–34; Luke 8.26–39)

5 They came to the other side of the sea, to the country of the Gerasenes.ᵉ 2 And when he had stepped out of the boat, immediately a man of the tombs with an unclean spirit met him. 3 He lived among the tombs; and no one could restrain him any more, even with a chain; 4 for he had often been restrained with shackles and chains, but the chains he wrenched apart, and the shackles he broke in pieces; and no one had the strength to subdue him. 5 Night and day among the tombs and on the mountains he was always howling and bruising himself with stones. 6 When he saw Jesus from a distance, he ran and bowed down before him; 7 and he shouted at the top of his voice, "What have you to do with me, Jesus, Son of the Most High God? I adjure you by God, do not torment me." 8 For he had said to him, "Come out of the man, you unclean spirit!" 9 Then Jesusᶠ asked him, "What is your name?" He replied, "My name is Legion; for we are many." 10 He begged him earnestly not to send them out of the country. 11 Now there on the hillside a great herd of swine was feeding; 12 and the unclean spiritsᵍ begged him, "Send us into the swine;

5.2
Mt 4.1; 1.23

5.6
Mt 4.9;
18.26
5.7
Mt 8.29; 4.3;
Lk 8.28;
Acts 16.17;
Heb 7.1

ᵉ Other ancient authorities read Gergesenes; others, Gadarenes   ᶠ Gk he   ᵍ Gk they

4.30ff See note on Mt 13.31,32.

4.38 do you not care that we are perishing? However much we may sympathize with the fear and distress of the disciples, it remains clear that they did not yet understand the true nature of Jesus and his unfailing concern for them. Their question expressed doubt about Jesus' care for their welfare. We should never question for a single moment the solicitude of Jesus for us or doubt his power to help us in times of difficulty.

4.39 Be still! i.e., "be muzzled," as one would muzzle a dog to keep it from barking and biting.

5.1ff See note on Lk 8.29ff.

5.9 Legion, i.e., the largest military unit of the Roman army, numbering from three to six thousand men. Its use here simply means that a whole group of demons inhabited this man.

5.11 If those who owned the swine were Jews, they were in violation of the Mosaic law, though they may have been Gentiles. When Jesus commanded the demons to enter the swine, it was appropriate for evil spirits to occupy unclean rather than clean animals. Some criticize Jesus here, maintaining that he had no right to let the demons enter the swine and rush to their death. Since he was creator of all things, however, he owned them and could dispose of them according to his will.

let us enter them." 13 So he gave them permission. And the unclean spirits came out and entered the swine; and the herd, numbering about two thousand, rushed down the steep bank into the sea, and were drowned in the sea.

14 The swineherds ran off and told it in the city and in the country. Then people came to see what it was that had happened. 15 They came to Jesus and saw the demoniac sitting there, clothed and in his right mind, the very man who had had the legion; and they were afraid. 16 Those who had seen what had happened to the demoniac and to the swine reported it. 17 Then they began to beg Jesus[h] to leave their neighborhood. 18 As he was getting into the boat, the man who had been possessed by demons begged him that he might be with him. 19 But Jesus[i] refused, and said to him, "Go home to your friends, and tell them how much the Lord has done for you, and what mercy he has shown you." 20 And he went away and began to proclaim in the Decapolis how much Jesus had done for him; and everyone was amazed.

U. The woman with hemorrhages healed and Jairus's daughter raised (5.21–43; Matt. 9.18–26; Luke 8.40–56)

21 When Jesus had crossed again in the boat[j] to the other side, a great crowd gathered around him; and he was by the sea. 22 Then one of the leaders of the synagogue named Jairus came and, when he saw him, fell at his feet 23 and begged him repeatedly, "My little daughter is at the point of death. Come and lay your hands on her, so that she may be made well, and live." 24 So he went with him.

And a large crowd followed him and pressed in on him. 25 Now there was a woman who had been suffering from hemorrhages for twelve years. 26 She had endured much under many physicians, and had spent all that she had; and she was no better, but rather grew worse. 27 She had heard about Jesus, and came up behind him in the crowd and touched his cloak, 28 for she said, "If I but touch his clothes, I will be made well." 29 Immediately her hemorrhage stopped; and she felt in her body that she was healed of her disease. 30 Immediately aware that power had gone forth from him, Jesus turned about in the crowd and said, "Who touched my clothes?" 31 And his disciples said to him, "You see the crowd pressing in on you; how can you say, 'Who touched me?'" 32 He looked all around to see who had done it. 33 But the woman, knowing what had happened to her, came in fear and trembling, fell down before him, and told him the whole truth. 34 He said to her, "Daughter, your faith has made you well; go in peace, and be healed of your disease."

35 While he was still speaking, some people came from the leader's house to say, "Your daughter is dead. Why trouble the teacher any further?" 36 But overhearing[k] what they said, Jesus said to the leader of the synagogue, "Do not fear, only believe." 37 He allowed no one to follow him except Peter, James, and John, the brother of James. 38 When they came to the house of the leader of the synagogue, he saw a commotion, people weeping and wailing loudly. 39 When he had entered, he said to them, "Why do you make a commotion and weep? The child is not dead

Cross references (left margin)
5.15 vv. 16, 18; Mt 4.24; v. 9
5.18 Acts 16.39
5.20 Mk 7.31; Mt 4.25
5.21 Mt 9.1
5.22 Lk 8.49; 13.14; Acts 13.15; 18.8, 17
5.23 Mk 6.5; 7.32; 8.23; Acts 9.17; 28.8
5.25 Lev 15.25
5.29 v. 34
5.30 Lk 5.17
5.34 Lk 7.50; 8.48; Acts 16.36; Jas 2.16
5.35 v. 22
5.36 Lk 8.50
5.37 Mt 17.1; 26.37
5.38 v. 22
5.39 Jn 11.11

---

h Gk him   i Gk he   j Other ancient authorities lack *in the boat*   k Or *ignoring*; other ancient authorities read *hearing*

5.22   See note on Lk 8.41ff.
5.25ff   This woman was an outcast because of her hemorrhages. She could not come into the temple, participate in any religious ceremonies, or touch other persons without making them ceremonially unclean; she could not even live with her husband. But she was healed when she touched the fringe of Jesus' clothes. He required her to come forward and affirmed that she was healed because of her faith, manifested in

touching his garment. Moreover, he wanted the crowd to know that she was no longer an outcast, for her ceremonial defilement had been removed. So we who are unclean by our sins are made whole in Jesus Christ and our defilement disappears.
5.38   *weeping and wailing loudly.* These were professional mourners who were paid for their services by the family.

but sleeping." 40 And they laughed at him. Then he put them all outside, and took the child's father and mother and those who were with him, and went in where the child was. 41 He took her by the hand and said to her, "Talitha cum," which means, "Little girl, get up!" 42 And immediately the girl got up and began to walk about (she was twelve years of age). At this they were overcome with amazement. 43 He strictly ordered them that no one should know this, and told them to give her something to eat.

5.41
Lk 7.14;
Acts 9.40

5.43
Mt 8.4

V. Second rejection of Jesus at Nazareth
(6.1–6; Matt. 13.53–58; Luke 4.16–30)

6 He left that place and came to his hometown, and his disciples followed him. 2 On the sabbath he began to teach in the synagogue, and many who heard him were astounded. They said, "Where did this man get all this? What is this wisdom that has been given to him? What deeds of power are being done by his hands! 3 Is not this the carpenter, the son of Mary*l* and brother of James and Joses and Judas and Simon, and are not his sisters here with us?" And they took offense*m* at him. 4 Then Jesus said to them, "Prophets are not without honor, except in their hometown, and among their own kin, and in their own house." 5 And he could do no deed of power there, except that he laid his hands on a few sick people and cured them. 6 And he was amazed at their unbelief.

6.2
Mt 4.23;
7.28;
Mk 1.21

6.3
Mt 12.46;
11.6

6.4
Jn 4.44
6.5
Mt 5.23;
7.32; 8.23
6.6
Mt 9.35;
Lk 13.22

W. The mission of the Twelve (6.7–13; Matt. 10.1–15; Luke 9.1–6)

Then he went about among the villages teaching. 7 He called the twelve and began to send them out two by two, and gave them authority over the unclean spirits. 8 He ordered them to take nothing for their journey except a staff; no bread, no bag, no money in their belts; 9 but to wear sandals and not to put on two tunics. 10 He said to them, "Wherever you enter a house, stay there until you leave the place. 11 If any place will not welcome you and they refuse to hear you, as you leave, shake off the dust that is on your feet as a testimony against them." 12 So they went out and proclaimed that all should repent. 13 They cast out many demons, and anointed with oil many who were sick and cured them.

6.7
Mk 3.13;
Lk 10.1

6.12
Mt 11.1;
Lk 9.6
6.13
Jas 5.14

X. John the Baptist beheaded (6.14–29; Matt. 14.1–12;
Luke 9.7–9)

14 King Herod heard of it, for Jesus'*n* name had become known. Some were*o* saying, "John the baptizer has been raised from the dead; and for this reason these powers are at work in him." 15 But others said, "It is Elijah." And others said, "It is a prophet, like one of the prophets

6.15
Mt 16.14;
Mk 8.28;
Mt 21.11

l Other ancient authorities read *son of the carpenter and of Mary*　*m* Or *stumbled*　*n* Gk *his*　*o* Other ancient authorities read *He was*

6.1 *his hometown*, i.e., Nazareth.
6.3 Jesus was called a *carpenter*, a "carpenter's son" (Mt 13.55), and "Joseph's son" (Lk 4.22). Calling him *the son of Mary* was probably intended as a slur, since men were commonly called the sons of their fathers, not their mothers. In this verse Jesus' sisters are mentioned, but their names are not given. The names of Jesus' brothers are stated: *James and Joses and Judas and Simon* (see Jn 7.3–10; Acts 1.14). In Gal 1.19, Paul mentions "James the Lord's brother," and in Gal 2.9 he is called one of the "pillars" of the church (the same James of Acts 12.17; 15.13–21; 1 Cor 15.7). It seems apparent that Jesus' brothers did not believe in him until after his resurrection (cf. Jn 7.5). Most Protestants believe that the sisters and brothers of Jesus referred to here were the children of Joseph and Mary. Later theories that these were chil-

dren of Joseph by an earlier marriage or that they were cousins of Jesus have no Biblical basis.
6.7 By sending forth the twelve two by two, Jesus was increasing his own ministry sixfold. If every dedicated Christian were to win one other person to Christ in a year, it would not be long before the church would form the largest group of people on the earth.
6.11 *shake off the dust*, i.e., break off any relationship and refuse to accept responsibility for whatever happens after that.
6.12 Repentance is emphasized as essential throughout the N.T. The four Gospels constantly reiterate this theme, as do Acts (Acts 2.38; 17.30; 20.21) and the epistles (Rom 2.4; 2 Cor 7.9,10; 2 Pet 3.9).
6.14 See note on Lk 1.57.

6.16
Lk 3.19

of old." 16 But when Herod heard of it, he said, "John, whom I beheaded, has been raised."

17 For Herod himself had sent men who arrested John, bound him, and put him in prison on account of Herodias, his brother Philip's wife, because Herod*p* had married her. 18 For John had been telling Herod, "It is not lawful for you to have your brother's wife." 19 And Herodias had a grudge against him, and wanted to kill him. But she could not, 20 for Herod feared John, knowing that he was a righteous and holy man, and he protected him. When he heard him, he was greatly perplexed;*q* and yet he liked to listen to him. 21 But an opportunity came when Herod on his birthday gave a banquet for his courtiers and officers and for the leaders of Galilee. 22 When his daughter Herodias*r* came in and danced, she pleased Herod and his guests; and the king said to the girl, "Ask me for whatever you wish, and I will give it." 23 And he solemnly swore to her, "Whatever you ask me, I will give you, even half of my kingdom." 24 She went out and said to her mother, "What should I ask for?" She replied, "The head of John the baptizer." 25 Immediately she rushed back to the king and requested, "I want you to give me at once the head of John the Baptist on a platter." 26 The king was deeply grieved; yet out of regard for his oaths and for the guests, he did not want to refuse her. 27 Immediately the king sent a soldier of the guard with orders to bring John's*s* head. He went and beheaded him in the prison, 28 brought his head on a platter, and gave it to the girl. Then the girl gave it to her mother. 29 When his disciples heard about it, they came and took his body, and laid it in a tomb.

6.18
Lev 18.16;
20.21
6.20
Mt 21.26

6.21
Esth 1.3;
2.18

6.23
Esth 5.3, 6;
7.2

Y. *The five thousand fed (6.30–44; Matt. 14.13–21; Luke 9.10–17; John 6.1–13; cf. Matt. 15.32–39)*

30 The apostles gathered around Jesus, and told him all that they had done and taught. 31 He said to them, "Come away to a deserted place all by yourselves and rest a while." For many were coming and going, and they had no leisure even to eat. 32 And they went away in the boat to a deserted place by themselves. 33 Now many saw them going and recognized them, and they hurried there on foot from all the towns and arrived ahead of them. 34 As he went ashore, he saw a great crowd; and he had compassion for them, because they were like sheep without a shepherd; and he began to teach them many things. 35 When it grew late, his disciples came to him and said, "This is a deserted place, and the hour is now very late; 36 send them away so that they may go into the surrounding country and villages and buy something for themselves to eat." 37 But he answered them, "You give them something to eat." They said to him, "Are we to go and buy two hundred denarii*t* worth of bread, and give it to them to eat?" 38 And he said to them, "How many loaves have you? Go and see." When they had found out, they said, "Five, and two fish." 39 Then he ordered them to get all the people to sit down in groups on the green grass. 40 So they sat down in groups of hundreds and of fifties. 41 Taking the five loaves and the two fish, he looked up to heaven, and blessed and broke the loaves, and gave them to his disciples to set before the people; and he divided the two fish among them all. 42 And all ate and were filled; 43 and they took up twelve baskets full of broken pieces and

6.31
Mk 3.20

6.32
v. 45

6.34
Mt 9.36

6.37
2 Kings 4.42-44

6.38
Mt 15.34;
Mk 8.5

6.41
Mt 26.26;
Mk 14.22;
Lk 24.30, 31

p Gk he   *q* Other ancient authorities read *he did many things*   *r* Other ancient authorities read *the daughter of Herodias herself*   *s* Gk his   *t* The denarius was the usual day's wage for a laborer

6.17 The Philip mentioned here was the brother of Herod Antipas, the tetrarch of Galilee and son of Herod the Great and Mariamne (the daughter of Simon the high priest). He should not be confused with the Philip who was the ruler of Ituraea (Lk 3.1).
6.26 *regard for his oaths.* One who took an oath did

that which was considered irreversible. This was true in pagan nations as well as among the Jews.
6.37 *two hundred denarii,* i.e., more than half a year's wages (cf. NRSV footnote). See the note on Mt 14.16 for the explanation of the phrase, *You give them something to eat.*

of the fish. 44 Those who had eaten the loaves numbered five thousand men.

Z. Jesus walks on the sea
(6.45–52; Matt. 14.22–32; John 6.15–21)

45 Immediately he made his disciples get into the boat and go on ahead to the other side, to Bethsaida, while he dismissed the crowd. 46 After saying farewell to them, he went up on the mountain to pray. 47 When evening came, the boat was out on the sea, and he was alone on the land. 48 When he saw that they were straining at the oars against an adverse wind, he came towards them early in the morning, walking on the sea. He intended to pass them by. 49 But when they saw him walking on the sea, they thought it was a ghost and cried out; 50 for they all saw him and were terrified. But immediately he spoke to them and said, "Take heart, it is I; do not be afraid." 51 Then he got into the boat with them and the wind ceased. And they were utterly astounded, 52 for they did not understand about the loaves, but their hearts were hardened.

AA. Jesus' ministry at Gennesaret (6.53–56; Matt. 14.34–36)

53 When they had crossed over, they came to land at Gennesaret and moored the boat. 54 When they got out of the boat, people at once recognized him, 55 and rushed about that whole region and began to bring the sick on mats to wherever they heard he was. 56 And wherever he went, into villages or cities or farms, they laid the sick in the marketplaces, and begged him that they might touch even the fringe of his cloak; and all who touched it were healed.

BB. Ceremonial and real defilement: the Pharisees rebuked
(7.1–23; Matt. 15.1–20)

7 Now when the Pharisees and some of the scribes who had come from Jerusalem gathered around him, 2 they noticed that some of his disciples were eating with defiled hands, that is, without washing them. 3 (For the Pharisees, and all the Jews, do not eat unless they thoroughly wash their hands,ᵘ thus observing the tradition of the elders; 4 and they do not eat anything from the market unless they wash it;ᵛ and there are also many other traditions that they observe, the washing of cups, pots, and bronze kettles.ʷ) 5 So the Pharisees and the scribes asked him, "Why do your disciples not liveˣ according to the tradition of the elders, but eat with defiled hands?" 6 He said to them, "Isaiah prophesied rightly about you hypocrites, as it is written,

'This people honors me with their lips,
    but their hearts are far from me;
7 in vain do they worship me,
    teaching human precepts as doctrines.'

8 You abandon the commandment of God and hold to human tradition."

9 Then he said to them, "You have a fine way of rejecting the commandment of God in order to keep your tradition! 10 For Moses said,

---

Cross references (right margin):

6.45 v. 32; Mt 11.21; Mk 8.22
6.48 Mt 13.35; 24.43
6.50 Mt 9.2
6.51 v. 32
6.52 Mk 8.17, 18; 3.5
6.53 Jn 6.24, 25
6.56 Mk 3.10; Mt 9.20
7.3 v. 5; Acts 10.14, 28; 11.8
7.4 Mt 23.25; Lk 11.39
7.5 vv. 3, 8, 9, 13; Gal 1.14
7.6 Isa 29.13
7.8 vv. 5, 9, 13
7.9 vv. 5, 8, 13
7.10 Ex 20.12; Deut 5.6; Ex 21.17; Lev 20.9

ᵘ Meaning of Gk uncertain   ᵛ Other ancient authorities read and when they come from the marketplace, they do not eat unless they purify themselves   ʷ Other ancient authorities add and beds   ˣ Gk walk

---

6.44 *five thousand men.* This does not mean the crowd was only male. Women and children were not counted here, so that many more than five thousand must have been fed (cf. Mt 14.21; 15:38).
6.48 In the Greco-Roman system of calculation, the night watch was divided into four segments of three hours each (from six o'clock in the evening to six o'clock in the morning). Jesus appeared here *early in*

the morning, i.e., in the last watch, between three and six in the morning.
7.1 See note on Mt 3.7.
7.5 *defiled hands.* This does not necessarily mean their hands were dirty, only that they had not been washed in accordance with the religious rituals and therefore were ceremonially unclean.
7.6ff See note on Mt 15.7,8.

'Honor your father and your mother'; and, 'Whoever speaks evil of father
or mother must surely die.' [11] But you say that if anyone tells father or
mother, 'Whatever support you might have had from me is Corban' (that
is, an offering to God[y])— [12] then you no longer permit doing anything
for a father or mother, [13] thus making void the word of God through your
tradition that you have handed on. And you do many things like this."

14 Then he called the crowd again and said to them, "Listen to me,
all of you, and understand: [15] there is nothing outside a person that by
going in can defile, but the things that come out are what defile."[z]

17 When he had left the crowd and entered the house, his disciples
asked him about the parable. [18] He said to them, "Then do you also fail
to understand? Do you not see that whatever goes into a person from
outside cannot defile, [19] since it enters, not the heart but the stomach, and
goes out into the sewer?" (Thus he declared all foods clean.) [20] And he
said, "It is what comes out of a person that defiles. [21] For it is from within,
from the human heart, that evil intentions come: fornication, theft, murder, [22] adultery, avarice, wickedness, deceit, licentiousness, envy, slander, pride, folly. [23] All these evil things come from within, and they defile
a person."

CC. Journey toward Tyre and Sidon: the Syrophoenician woman's daughter healed (7.24–30; Matt. 15.21–28)

24 From there he set out and went away to the region of Tyre.[a] He
entered a house and did not want anyone to know he was there. Yet he
could not escape notice, [25] but a woman whose little daughter had an
unclean spirit immediately heard about him, and she came and bowed
down at his feet. [26] Now the woman was a Gentile, of Syrophoenician
origin. She begged him to cast the demon out of her daughter. [27] He said
to her, "Let the children be fed first, for it is not fair to take the children's
food and throw it to the dogs." [28] But she answered him, "Sir,[b] even the
dogs under the table eat the children's crumbs." [29] Then he said to her,
"For saying that, you may go—the demon has left your daughter." [30] So
she went home, found the child lying on the bed, and the demon gone.

DD. A deaf mute healed (7.31–37; Matt. 15.29–31)

31 Then he returned from the region of Tyre, and went by way of
Sidon towards the Sea of Galilee, in the region of the Decapolis. [32] They
brought to him a deaf man who had an impediment in his speech; and they
begged him to lay his hand on him. [33] He took him aside in private, away
from the crowd, and put his fingers into his ears, and he spat and touched
his tongue. [34] Then looking up to heaven, he sighed and said to him,
"Ephphatha," that is, "Be opened." [35] And immediately his ears were
opened, his tongue was released, and he spoke plainly. [36] Then Jesus[c]
ordered them to tell no one; but the more he ordered them, the more
zealously they proclaimed it. [37] They were astounded beyond measure,

Marginal references:
7.11 Mt 23.18
7.13 vv. 5, 8, 9
7.17 Mk 9.28
7.19 Rom 14.1-12; Col 2.16; Lk 11.41; Acts 10.15; 11.9
7.22 Mt 6.23; 20.15
7.24 Mt 11.21
7.32 Mk 5.23; Mt 9.32; Lk 11.14
7.33 Mk 8.23
7.34 Mk 6.41; 8.12
7.35 Isa 35.5, 6
7.36 Mk 1.44; 5.43

---

y Gk lacks *to God*   z Other ancient authorities add verse 16, *"Let anyone with ears to hear listen"*
a Other ancient authorities add *and Sidon*   b Or *Lord*; other ancient authorities prefix *Yes*   c Gk *he*

7.11 *Corban.* Some Jews vowed money to God and
were declared to be free from using any of it for the
support of their needy, aging parents. It was probably
an excuse to violate the commandment to honor father and mother.
7.20 Sin is centered in the human heart, not the
stomach. What people eat does not make them sinners, but what comes out from within them (i.e., from
their hearts) is what defiles them. The sins Jesus
refers to are internal, springing from the heart: murder, theft, fornication, adultery, pride, etc.

7.30 This demon was cast out by Jesus from a distance. He never saw the girl nor did he touch her. His
divine power over demons was effective whether the
victims were near him or far away. His word was
sufficient.
7.33ff Sometimes Jesus healed in strange and unusual ways. Here, he poked his finger in the ears of
a deaf man with a speech impediment, then spat on
his finger and touched his tongue. The man was instantly and perfectly healed, to the amazement of the
crowd.

saying, "He has done everything well; he even makes the deaf to hear and the mute to speak."

EE. The four thousand fed (8.1–10; Matt. 15.32–39)

8 In those days when there was again a great crowd without anything to eat, he called his disciples and said to them, 2 "I have compassion for the crowd, because they have been with me now for three days and have nothing to eat. 3 If I send them away hungry to their homes, they will faint on the way—and some of them have come from a great distance." 4 His disciples replied, "How can one feed these people with bread here in the desert?" 5 He asked them, "How many loaves do you have?" They said, "Seven." 6 Then he ordered the crowd to sit down on the ground; and he took the seven loaves, and after giving thanks he broke them and gave them to his disciples to distribute; and they distributed them to the crowd. 7 They had also a few small fish; and after blessing them, he ordered that these too should be distributed. 8 They ate and were filled; and they took up the broken pieces left over, seven baskets full. 9 Now there were about four thousand people. And he sent them away. 10 And immediately he got into the boat with his disciples and went to the district of Dalmanutha.*d*

8.2
Mt 9.36

8.5
Mk 6.38

8.7
Mt 14.19;
Mk 6.41

FF. The Pharisees seek a sign from heaven (8.11–21; Matt. 16.1–10)

11 The Pharisees came and began to argue with him, asking him for a sign from heaven, to test him. 12 And he sighed deeply in his spirit and said, "Why does this generation ask for a sign? Truly I tell you, no sign will be given to this generation." 13 And he left them, and getting into the boat again, he went across to the other side.

14 Now the disciples*e* had forgotten to bring any bread; and they had only one loaf with them in the boat. 15 And he cautioned them, saying, "Watch out—beware of the yeast of the Pharisees and the yeast of Herod."*f* 16 They said to one another, "It is because we have no bread." 17 And becoming aware of it, Jesus said to them, "Why are you talking about having no bread? Do you still not perceive or understand? Are your hearts hardened? 18 Do you have eyes, and fail to see? Do you have ears, and fail to hear? And do you not remember? 19 When I broke the five loaves for the five thousand, how many baskets full of broken pieces did you collect?" They said to him, "Twelve." 20 "And the seven for the four thousand, how many baskets full of broken pieces did you collect?" And they said to him, "Seven." 21 Then he said to them, "Do you not yet understand?"

8.11
Mt 12.38,
39;
Lk 11.29;
Jn 6.30
8.12
Mk 7.34

8.15
Lk 12.1;
Mk 16.4;
12.13

8.17
Mk 6.52;
Isa 6.9, 10

8.19
Mt 14.20;
Mk 6.43;
Lk 9.17;
Jn 6.13
8.20
vv. 6-9;
Mt 15.37
8.21
Mk 6.52

GG. The blind man healed near Bethsaida (8.22–26)

22 They came to Bethsaida. Some people*g* brought a blind man to him and begged him to touch him. 23 He took the blind man by the hand and led him out of the village; and when he had put saliva on his eyes and

8.22
Mt 11.21;
Mk 6.45;
Lk 9.10
8.23
Mk 7.33;
5.23

d Other ancient authorities read Mageda or Magdala   e Gk they   f Other ancient authorities read the Herodians   g Gk They

---

8.2 A great crowd had gathered to listen to Jesus and remained with him for three days without food. Note the incredible zeal of those who are moved by the word of God and would rather do without food than miss what Jesus was saying. Unlike the religious leaders, the common people appreciated Jesus and listened to him, and he fed them out of compassion and concern.
8.8 *seven baskets.* In the feeding of the five thousand the baskets were much smaller than those mentioned

here. These were large, like the one used to let Paul down the wall in his escape from Damascus (Acts 9.25).
8.10 *Dalmanutha* seems to have been a town on the western shore of the Sea of Galilee. Its precise location is unknown.
8.11 *to test him.* The Pharisees were saying in effect, "If we see the sign, then we will believe in you" (see also note on Mt 16.4).

laid his hands on him, he asked him, "Can you see anything?" 24 And the man[h] looked up and said, "I can see people, but they look like trees, walking." 25 Then Jesus[h] laid his hands on his eyes again; and he looked intently and his sight was restored, and he saw everything clearly. 26 Then he sent him away to his home, saying, "Do not even go into the village."[i]

HH. Peter's confession (8.27–30; Matt. 16.13–20; Luke 9.18–21)

27 Jesus went on with his disciples to the villages of Caesarea Philippi; and on the way he asked his disciples, "Who do people say that I am?" 28 And they answered him, "John the Baptist; and others, Elijah; and still others, one of the prophets." 29 He asked them, "But who do you say that I am?" Peter answered him, "You are the Messiah."[j] 30 And he sternly ordered them not to tell anyone about him.

II. Jesus foretells his death, resurrection, and second coming (8.31–9.1; Matt. 16.21–28; Luke 9.22–27)

31 Then he began to teach them that the Son of Man must undergo great suffering, and be rejected by the elders, the chief priests, and the scribes, and be killed, and after three days rise again. 32 He said all this quite openly. And Peter took him aside and began to rebuke him. 33 But turning and looking at his disciples, he rebuked Peter and said, "Get behind me, Satan! For you are setting your mind not on divine things but on human things."

34 He called the crowd with his disciples, and said to them, "If any want to become my followers, let them deny themselves and take up their cross and follow me. 35 For those who want to save their life will lose it, and those who lose their life for my sake, and for the sake of the gospel,[k] will save it. 36 For what will it profit them to gain the whole world and forfeit their life? 37 Indeed, what can they give in return for their life? 38 Those who are ashamed of me and of my words[l] in this adulterous and sinful generation, of them the Son of Man will also be ashamed when he comes in the glory of his Father with the holy angels." 9 1 And he said to them, "Truly I tell you, there are some standing here who will not taste death until they see that the kingdom of God has come with[m] power."

JJ. The transfiguration (9.2–13; Matt. 17.1–8; Luke 9.28–36)

2 Six days later, Jesus took with him Peter and James and John, and led them up a high mountain apart, by themselves. And he was transfigured before them, 3 and his clothes became dazzling white, such as no one[n] on earth could bleach them. 4 And there appeared to them Elijah with Moses, who were talking with Jesus. 5 Then Peter said to Jesus, "Rabbi, it is good for us to be here; let us make three dwellings,[o] one for you, one for Moses, and one for Elijah." 6 He did not know what to say, for they were terrified. 7 Then a cloud overshadowed them, and from

Marginal cross-references (left column):
8.26 Mt 8.4
8.27 Jn 6.66-69
8.28 Mk 6.14
8.29 Jn 6.69; 11.27
8.30 Mk 9.9
8.32 Jn 18.20
8.33 Mt 4.10
8.34 Mt 10.38; Lk 14.27
8.35 Mt 10.39; Lk 17.33; Jn 12.25
8.38 Mt 10.33; Lk 12.9; Mt 8.20; Mk 13.26
9.1 Mt 24.30; 25.31; Mk 13.30; Lk 22.18
9.2 Mk 5.37; 13.3
9.3 Mt 28.3
9.5 Mt 23.7
9.7 2 Pet 1.17, 18; Mk 1.11

h Gk he i Other ancient authorities add or tell anyone in the village j Or the Christ k Other ancient authorities read lose their life for the sake of the gospel l Other ancient authorities read and of mine m Or in n Gk no fuller o Or tents

8.29 See note on Mt 16.18.
8.32 *He said all this quite openly.* In this case, Jesus did not speak obliquely, in parables, or indirectly. However prejudiced the disciples might have been, they could not have misunderstood what he was saying to them. Peter, out of a misplaced love, wanted to shield the Savior from this horrible fate (v. 31). Jesus rebuked him strongly and emphatically.
9.2 The first three Gospels have an account of Christ's transfigured glory, each one containing unique details. The event probably occurred on

Mount Hermon. Moses and Elijah appeared in person and three of Jesus' disciples witnessed their presence (Lk 9.32). Christ's radiance was only a foretaste of his glory, but the event strengthened the disciples. They heard the voice of God from the cloud (v. 7). The sudden disappearance of Moses and Elijah, leaving only Jesus, meant that in him O.T. law and prophets were fulfilled. Peter never forgot that moment, for years later he drew attention to his being an eyewitness of Christ's splendor and glory (2 Pet 1.16–18).

the cloud there came a voice, "This is my Son, the Beloved;*p* listen to him!" 8 Suddenly when they looked around, they saw no one with them any more, but only Jesus.

9   As they were coming down the mountain, he ordered them to tell no one about what they had seen, until after the Son of Man had risen from the dead. 10 So they kept the matter to themselves, questioning what this rising from the dead could mean. 11 Then they asked him, "Why do the scribes say that Elijah must come first?" 12 He said to them, "Elijah is indeed coming first to restore all things. How then is it written about the Son of Man, that he is to go through many sufferings and be treated with contempt? 13 But I tell you that Elijah has come, and they did to him whatever they pleased, as it is written about him."

KK. *The demoniac boy cured (9.14–29; Matt. 17.14–21; Luke 9.37–43)*

14   When they came to the disciples, they saw a great crowd around them, and some scribes arguing with them. 15 When the whole crowd saw him, they were immediately overcome with awe, and they ran forward to greet him. 16 He asked them, "What are you arguing about with them?" 17 Someone from the crowd answered him, "Teacher, I brought you my son; he has a spirit that makes him unable to speak; 18 and whenever it seizes him, it dashes him down; and he foams and grinds his teeth and becomes rigid; and I asked your disciples to cast it out, but they could not do so." 19 He answered them, "You faithless generation, how much longer must I be among you? How much longer must I put up with you? Bring him to me." 20 And they brought the boy*q* to him. When the spirit saw him, immediately it convulsed the boy,*q* and he fell on the ground and rolled about, foaming at the mouth. 21 Jesus*r* asked the father, "How long has this been happening to him?" And he said, "From childhood. 22 It has often cast him into the fire and into the water, to destroy him; but if you are able to do anything, have pity on us and help us." 23 Jesus said to him, "If you are able! — All things can be done for the one who believes." 24 Immediately the father of the child cried out,*s* "I believe; help my unbelief!" 25 When Jesus saw that a crowd came running together, he rebuked the unclean spirit, saying to it, "You spirit that keeps this boy from speaking and hearing, I command you, come out of him, and never enter him again!" 26 After crying out and convulsing him terribly, it came out, and the boy was like a corpse, so that most of them said, "He is dead." 27 But Jesus took him by the hand and lifted him up, and he was able to stand. 28 When he had entered the house, his disciples asked him privately, "Why could we not cast it out?" 29 He said to them, "This kind can come out only through prayer."*t*

LL. *Jesus again foretells his death and resurrection (9.30–32; Matt. 17.22–23; Luke 9.43–45)*

30   They went on from there and passed through Galilee. He did not want anyone to know it; 31 for he was teaching his disciples, saying to them, "The Son of Man is to be betrayed into human hands, and they will kill him, and three days after being killed, he will rise again." 32 But they did not understand what he was saying and were afraid to ask him.

p Or *my beloved Son*   *q* Gk *him*   *r* Gk *He*   *s* Other ancient authorities add *with tears*   *t* Other ancient authorities add *and fasting*

9.9
Mk 5.43;
7.36; 8.30
9.11
Mt 11.14
9.12
Ps 22.6;
Lk 23.11;
Phil 2.7
9.13
Mt 11.14;
Lk 1.17

9.15
Mk 14.33;
16.5, 6

9.20
Mk 1.26

9.23
Mk 11.23;
Lk 17.6;
Jn 11.40
9.25
v. 15

9.28
Mk 7.17

9.31
Mt 16.21;
Mk 8.31
9.32
Jn 12.16

9.11 *Elijah must come first.* See note on Mal 4.5.
9.23 *All things can be done for the one who believes.* This statement may not be extended beyond its immediate frame of reference. For example, all humans must die (Rom 6:23), and this passage may not be understood to mean that if we truly believe, we will be able to escape death. The key point in Jesus' statement is "the one who believes." Effective faith always rests on the will of God. To claim "by faith" that which is not the will of God as revealed in Scripture is wrong.

MM. Discourse on humility (9.33–50; Matt. 18.1–5; Luke 9.46–48)

33 Then they came to Capernaum; and when he was in the house he asked them, "What were you arguing about on the way?" 34 But they were silent, for on the way they had argued with one another who was the greatest. 35 He sat down, called the twelve, and said to them, "Whoever wants to be first must be last of all and servant of all." 36 Then he took a little child and put it among them; and taking it in his arms, he said to them, 37 "Whoever welcomes one such child in my name welcomes me, and whoever welcomes me welcomes not me but the one who sent me."

38 John said to him, "Teacher, we saw someone[u] casting out demons in your name, and we tried to stop him, because he was not following us." 39 But Jesus said, "Do not stop him; for no one who does a deed of power in my name will be able soon afterward to speak evil of me. 40 Whoever is not against us is for us. 41 For truly I tell you, whoever gives you a cup of water to drink because you bear the name of Christ will by no means lose the reward.

42 "If any of you put a stumbling block before one of these little ones who believe in me,[v] it would be better for you if a great millstone were hung around your neck and you were thrown into the sea. 43 If your hand causes you to stumble, cut it off; it is better for you to enter life maimed than to have two hands and to go to hell,[w] to the unquenchable fire.[x] 45 And if your foot causes you to stumble, cut it off; it is better for you to enter life lame than to have two feet and to be thrown into hell.[w,x] 47 And if your eye causes you to stumble, tear it out; it is better for you to enter the kingdom of God with one eye than to have two eyes and to be thrown into hell,[w] 48 where their worm never dies, and the fire is never quenched.

49 "For everyone will be salted with fire.[y] 50 Salt is good; but if salt has lost its saltiness, how can you season it?[z] Have salt in yourselves, and be at peace with one another."

III. From Galilee to Jerusalem (10.1–52)

A. Jesus goes to Judea (10.1)

10 He left that place and went to the region of Judea and[a] beyond the Jordan. And crowds again gathered around him; and, as was his custom, he again taught them.

B. Jesus teaches about marriage (10.2–12; Matt. 19.3–12)

2 Some Pharisees came, and to test him they asked, "Is it lawful for a man to divorce his wife?" 3 He answered them, "What did Moses

[u] Other ancient authorities add *who does not follow us* [v] Other ancient authorities lack *in me*
[w] Gk *Gehenna* [x] Verses 44 and 46 (which are identical with verse 48) are lacking in the best ancient authorities [y] Other ancient authorities either add or substitute *and every sacrifice will be salted with salt* [z] Or *how can you restore its saltiness?* [a] Other ancient authorities lack *and*

9.38ff Jesus rebuked sectarianism here. The fact that someone is not a member of a specific denomination does not mean that one cannot love Christ, honor him, and do his work.
9.43ff See note on Mt 5.29,30.
9.47 Jesus here contrasts the kingdom of God with *hell* (or *Gehenna* , see NRSV footnote; see also note on Mt 18.9). Scripture teaches that the inhabitants of this place include (1) the devil, the beast, and the false prophet (Rev 19.20; 20.10); (2) the fallen angels (2 Pet 2.4); (3) the wicked (Ps 9.17); (4) anyone whose name is not written in the Lamb's book of life (Rev 20.15); and (5) those who refuse to do the will of God (Mt 7.21). To deny the existence of hell repudiates the teaching of Scripture, including that of

the Lord Jesus, and undermines the reality of heaven, hell's opposite. Scripture clearly teaches that people will go to the lake of fire unless they accept Jesus Christ as their Savior.
9.49 *For everyone will be salted with fire.* Numerous explanations have been given for this phrase. Many commentators perceive this as an allusion to Lev 2.13, which states that cereal offerings were to be offered with "the salt of the covenant." Note too that salt is a preservative and fire is often used as a purifier.
10.1 *left that place,* i.e., Capernaum. Mentioned here so quietly, this was his final farewell to Galilee. He never returned until after his death and resurrection (cf. 16.7).

command you?" 4 They said, "Moses allowed a man to write a certificate of dismissal and to divorce her." 5 But Jesus said to them, "Because of your hardness of heart he wrote this commandment for you. 6 But from the beginning of creation, 'God made them male and female.' 7 'For this reason a man shall leave his father and mother and be joined to his wife,[b] 8 and the two shall become one flesh.' So they are no longer two, but one flesh. 9 Therefore what God has joined together, let no one separate."

10   Then in the house the disciples asked him again about this matter. 11 He said to them, "Whoever divorces his wife and marries another commits adultery against her; 12 and if she divorces her husband and marries another, she commits adultery."

C. Jesus blesses little children
(10.13–16; Matt. 19.13–15; Luke 18.15–17)

13   People were bringing little children to him in order that he might touch them; and the disciples spoke sternly to them. 14 But when Jesus saw this, he was indignant and said to them, "Let the little children come to me; do not stop them; for it is to such as these that the kingdom of God belongs. 15 Truly I tell you, whoever does not receive the kingdom of God as a little child will never enter it." 16 And he took them up in his arms, laid his hands on them, and blessed them.

D. The rich young ruler: the peril of riches
(10.17–31; Matt. 19.16–30; Luke 18.18–30)

17   As he was setting out on a journey, a man ran up and knelt before him, and asked him, "Good Teacher, what must I do to inherit eternal life?" 18 Jesus said to him, "Why do you call me good? No one is good but God alone. 19 You know the commandments: 'You shall not murder; You shall not commit adultery; You shall not steal; You shall not bear false witness; You shall not defraud; Honor your father and mother.'" 20 He said to him, "Teacher, I have kept all these since my youth." 21 Jesus, looking at him, loved him and said, "You lack one thing; go, sell what you own, and give the money[c] to the poor, and you will have treasure in heaven; then come, follow me." 22 When he heard this, he was shocked and went away grieving, for he had many possessions.

23   Then Jesus looked around and said to his disciples, "How hard it will be for those who have wealth to enter the kingdom of God!" 24 And the disciples were perplexed at these words. But Jesus said to them again, "Children, how hard it is[d] to enter the kingdom of God! 25 It is easier for a camel to go through the eye of a needle than for someone who is rich to enter the kingdom of God." 26 They were greatly astounded and said to one another,[e] "Then who can be saved?" 27 Jesus looked at them and said, "For mortals it is impossible, but not for God; for God all things are possible."

28   Peter began to say to him, "Look, we have left everything and followed you." 29 Jesus said, "Truly I tell you, there is no one who has left house or brothers or sisters or mother or father or children or fields, for my sake and for the sake of the good news,[f] 30 who will not receive

Side references:

10.4 Deut 24.1-4; Mt 5.31; 19.7
10.6 Gen 1.27; 5.2
10.7 Gen 2.24; 1 Cor 6.16

10.11 Mt 5.32; Lk 16.18; Rom 7.3; 1 Cor 7.10, 11

10.15 Mt 18.3; 1 Cor 14.20; 1 Pet 2.2
10.16 Mk 9.36

10.17 Mk 1.40; Lk 10.25; Eph 1.18
10.19 Ex 20.12-16; Deut 5.16-20
10.21 Mt 6.20; Lk 12.33; Acts 2.35; 4.34, 35

10.23 Mt 19.23; Lk 18.24
10.24 Ps 52.7; 62.10; 1 Tim 6.17

10.27 Jer 32.17

10.28 Mt 4.20-22
10.29 Mt 6.33

---

b Other ancient authorities lack *and be joined to his wife*   c Gk lacks *the money*   d Other ancient authorities add *for those who trust in riches*   e Other ancient authorities read *to him*   f Or *gospel*

10.5ff The teachings of Jesus on divorce are found here and in Mt 5.27–32; 19.3–9; Lk 16.18. Paul stated that his teaching on divorce came directly from Jesus (1 Cor 7.10,11). Divorce is everywhere forbidden, except when adultery is involved (see notes on Gen 2.24; Deut 24.1).
10.17 See note on Mt 19.16ff.

10.18 The rich young man called Jesus *good*, while Jesus said only God can be called good. The implication is plain: "If you call me good, call me God, for that is who I am."
10.25 *eye of a needle* probably refers to a Jerusalem gate that was so narrow it was difficult for a loaded camel to pass through.

a hundredfold now in this age — houses, brothers and sisters, mothers and children, and fields, with persecutions — and in the age to come eternal life. 31 But many who are first will be last, and the last will be first."

10.31
Mt 20.16;
Lk 13.30

E. *Christ foretells his crucifixion and resurrection (10.32–34; Matt. 20.17–19; Luke 18.31–34)*

10.32
Mk 8.31;
9.31;
Lk 9.22

32 They were on the road, going up to Jerusalem, and Jesus was walking ahead of them; they were amazed, and those who followed were afraid. He took the twelve aside again and began to tell them what was to happen to him, 33 saying, "See, we are going up to Jerusalem, and the Son of Man will be handed over to the chief priests and the scribes, and they will condemn him to death; then they will hand him over to the Gentiles; 34 they will mock him, and spit upon him, and flog him, and kill him; and after three days he will rise again."

10.34
Mt 26.67;
27.30;
Mk 14.65

F. *Ambition of James and John (10.35–45; Matt. 20.20–28)*

35 James and John, the sons of Zebedee, came forward to him and said to him, "Teacher, we want you to do for us whatever we ask of you." 36 And he said to them, "What is it you want me to do for you?" 37 And they said to him, "Grant us to sit, one at your right hand and one at your left, in your glory." 38 But Jesus said to them, "You do not know what you are asking. Are you able to drink the cup that I drink, or be baptized with the baptism that I am baptized with?" 39 They replied, "We are able." Then Jesus said to them, "The cup that I drink you will drink; and with the baptism with which I am baptized, you will be baptized; 40 but to sit at my right hand or at my left is not mine to grant, but it is for those for whom it has been prepared."

10.37
Mt 19.28;
Lk 22.30
10.38
Lk 12.50;
Jn 18.11
10.39
Acts 12.2;
Rev 1.9;
10.41;
Lk 22.25-27

41 When the ten heard this, they began to be angry with James and John. 42 So Jesus called them and said to them, "You know that among the Gentiles those whom they recognize as their rulers lord it over them, and their great ones are tyrants over them. 43 But it is not so among you; but whoever wishes to become great among you must be your servant, 44 and whoever wishes to be first among you must be slave of all. 45 For the Son of Man came not to be served but to serve, and to give his life a ransom for many."

10.43
Mt 9.35

10.45
Jn 13.14;
1 Tim 2.5, 6

G. *Bartimaeus receives his sight (10.46–52; Matt. 20.29–34; Luke 18.35–43)*

46 They came to Jericho. As he and his disciples and a large crowd were leaving Jericho, Bartimaeus son of Timaeus, a blind beggar, was sitting by the roadside. 47 When he heard that it was Jesus of Nazareth, he began to shout out and say, "Jesus, Son of David, have mercy on me!" 48 Many sternly ordered him to be quiet, but he cried out even more loudly, "Son of David, have mercy on me!" 49 Jesus stood still and said, "Call him here." And they called the blind man, saying to him, "Take heart; get up, he is calling you." 50 So throwing off his cloak, he sprang up and came to Jesus. 51 Then Jesus said to him, "What do you want me to do for you?" The blind man said to him, "My teacher,^{g} let me see

10.47
Mt 9.27

10.51
Jn 20.16;
Mt 23.7

g Aramaic *Rabbouni*

10.35ff In Mt 20.21 the mother of James and John asked for her sons to be seated on the left and the right hands of Jesus in his kingdom. Here James and John made the request themselves. We can assume that both the mother and the sons asked the same petition of Jesus and received the same sort of reply. Note how prayer can be used and abused. Jesus bypassed the

petition by saying it is not part of his role to make that decision. It belonged to his Father, to whom he was obedient and from whom he would not take what was not his to do. James and John's request was based on a serious sinful inclination — the desire for power and status. Such desires display a spirit of worldliness. **10.42** See note on Mt 20.25ff.

again." 52 Jesus said to him, "Go; your faith has made you well." Immediately he regained his sight and followed him on the way.

10.52
Mt 9.22;
Mk 5.34;
Lk 7.50;
8.48; 17.19

IV. The last week in Jerusalem (11.1–16.8)

A. The triumphal entry
(11.1–11; Matt. 21.1–11; Luke 19.29–44; John 12.12–19)

11 When they were approaching Jerusalem, at Bethphage and Bethany, near the Mount of Olives, he sent two of his disciples 2 and said to them, "Go into the village ahead of you, and immediately as you enter it, you will find tied there a colt that has never been ridden; untie it and bring it. 3 If anyone says to you, 'Why are you doing this?' just say this, 'The Lord needs it and will send it back here immediately.' " 4 They went away and found a colt tied near a door, outside in the street. As they were untying it, 5 some of the bystanders said to them, "What are you doing, untying the colt?" 6 They told them what Jesus had said; and they allowed them to take it. 7 Then they brought the colt to Jesus and threw their cloaks on it; and he sat on it. 8 Many people spread their cloaks on the road, and others spread leafy branches that they had cut in the fields. 9 Then those who went ahead and those who followed were shouting,

"Hosanna!
Blessed is the one who comes in the name of the Lord!
10   Blessed is the coming kingdom of our ancestor David!
Hosanna in the highest heaven!"

11   Then he entered Jerusalem and went into the temple; and when he had looked around at everything, as it was already late, he went out to Bethany with the twelve.

11.1
Mt 21.17

11.4
Mk 14.16

11.9
Ps 118.26;
Mt 23.39

11.11
Mt 21.10,
11, 17

B. The barren fig tree
(11.12–14,20–25; Matt. 21.18–22)

12   On the following day, when they came from Bethany, he was hungry. 13 Seeing in the distance a fig tree in leaf, he went to see whether perhaps he would find anything on it. When he came to it, he found nothing but leaves, for it was not the season for figs. 14 He said to it, "May no one ever eat fruit from you again." And his disciples heard it.

11.12
Lk 13.6-9

C. Second cleansing of the temple
(11.15–19; Matt. 21.12–17; Luke 19.45–48; cf. John 2.13–22)

15   Then they came to Jerusalem. And he entered the temple and began to drive out those who were selling and those who were buying in the temple, and he overturned the tables of the money changers and the seats of those who sold doves; 16 and he would not allow anyone to carry anything through the temple. 17 He was teaching and saying, "Is it not written,

'My house shall be called a house of prayer for all the nations'?

11.17
Isa 56.7;
Jer 7.11

11.1 *Bethphage* (meaning "place of unripe figs") was a village on the Mount of Olives near or on the road from Jericho to Jerusalem. It was probably less than a mile from Jerusalem and might, therefore, be considered a suburb. *Bethany* (probably meaning "house of dates or figs") was about two miles southeast of Jerusalem (Jn 11.18). Lazarus and his sisters, Martha and Mary, lived there (Jn 11.1). See note on Lk 19.28ff for additional information on the triumphal entry of Jesus into Jerusalem.
11.12–14 In Matthew's account we are told that the fig tree withered at once and would never again bear fruit (Mt 21.18). Christ has power over all of nature,

including the trees of the field.
11.15ff Multitudes gathered at Jerusalem each year to offer animal sacrifices at the special Jewish festivals. Coming from afar, they had to buy the animals at the temple. Animal vendors offered ritually clean animals for a good price. Money merchants exchanged currencies so that these Jews could pay the annual half-shekel poll tax. Such transactions were taking place in the court of the Gentiles where non-Jews were allowed to worship. This bazaar-like business atmosphere made worship virtually impossible and ignored God's word that his house was to be "a house of prayer for all nations" (Isa 56.7).

But you have made it a den of robbers."

11.18
Mt 21.46;
7.28;
Mk 1.22;
Lk 4.32

18 And when the chief priests and the scribes heard it, they kept looking for a way to kill him; for they were afraid of him, because the whole crowd was spellbound by his teaching. 19 And when evening came, Jesus and his disciples^h went out of the city.

D. *The power of faith (11.20–25)*

11.20
Mt 21.19
11.21
Mt 23.7
11.22
Mt 17.20
11.23
Mt 21.21;
Lk 17.6
11.24
Mt 7.7;
Jn 14.13, 14;
15.7; 16.23,
24;
Jas 1.5, 6
11.25
Mt 6.14, 15;
Col 3.13

20 In the morning as they passed by, they saw the fig tree withered away to its roots. 21 Then Peter remembered and said to him, "Rabbi, look! The fig tree that you cursed has withered." 22 Jesus answered them, "Have^i faith in God. 23 Truly I tell you, if you say to this mountain, 'Be taken up and thrown into the sea,' and if you do not doubt in your heart, but believe that what you say will come to pass, it will be done for you. 24 So I tell you, whatever you ask for in prayer, believe that you have received^j it, and it will be yours.

25 "Whenever you stand praying, forgive, if you have anything against anyone; so that your Father in heaven may also forgive you your trespasses."^k

E. *Christ's authority challenged*
(11.27–33; Matt. 21.23–27; Luke 20.1–8)

27 Again they came to Jerusalem. As he was walking in the temple, the chief priests, the scribes, and the elders came to him 28 and said, "By what authority are you doing these things? Who gave you this authority to do them?" 29 Jesus said to them, "I will ask you one question; answer me, and I will tell you by what authority I do these things. 30 Did the baptism of John come from heaven, or was it of human origin? Answer me." 31 They argued with one another, "If we say, 'From heaven,' he will say, 'Why then did you not believe him?' 32 But shall we say, 'Of human origin'?"—they were afraid of the crowd, for all regarded John as truly a prophet. 33 So they answered Jesus, "We do not know." And Jesus said to them, "Neither will I tell you by what authority I am doing these things."

11.32
Mt 14.5

F. *Parable of the wicked tenants*
(12.1–12; Matt. 21.33–46; Luke 20.9–19)

12.1
Isa 5.1-7

12 Then he began to speak to them in parables. "A man planted a vineyard, put a fence around it, dug a pit for the wine press, and built a watchtower; then he leased it to tenants and went to another country. 2 When the season came, he sent a slave to the tenants to collect from them his share of the produce of the vineyard. 3 But they seized him, and beat him, and sent him away empty-handed. 4 And again he sent another slave to them; this one they beat over the head and insulted. 5 Then he sent another, and that one they killed. And so it was with many others; some they beat, and others they killed. 6 He had still one other, a beloved son. Finally he sent him to them, saying, 'They will respect my son.' 7 But those tenants said to one another, 'This is the heir; come, let us kill him, and the inheritance will be ours.' 8 So they seized him, killed him, and threw him out of the vineyard. 9 What then will the owner of

12.6
cf. Heb 1.1-3

---

h Gk *they*: other ancient authorities read *he*   *i* Other ancient authorities read *"If you have*   *j* Other ancient authorities read *are receiving*   *k* Other ancient authorities add verse 26, *"But if you do not forgive, neither will your Father in heaven forgive your trespasses."*

11.24ff   See notes on Mt 7.7 for the principles which govern prayer.
11.27   Christ often taught as he walked, following the custom of the Greek schools of philosophy. The

Jewish leaders questioned his authority (see note on Mt 21.25).
12.1ff   See note on Lk 20.9ff.

the vineyard do? He will come and destroy the tenants and give the vineyard to others. 10 Have you not read this scripture:

'The stone that the builders rejected
    has become the cornerstone;[l]
11 this was the Lord's doing,
    and it is amazing in our eyes'?"

12 When they realized that he had told this parable against them, they wanted to arrest him, but they feared the crowd. So they left him and went away.

G. Three questions by the Jewish rulers (12.13–34)

1. Paying taxes to the emperor
(12.13–17; Matt. 22.15–22; Luke 20.20–26)

13 Then they sent to him some Pharisees and some Herodians to trap him in what he said. 14 And they came and said to him, "Teacher, we know that you are sincere, and show deference to no one; for you do not regard people with partiality, but teach the way of God in accordance with truth. Is it lawful to pay taxes to the emperor, or not? 15 Should we pay them, or should we not?" But knowing their hypocrisy, he said to them, "Why are you putting me to the test? Bring me a denarius and let me see it." 16 And they brought one. Then he said to them, "Whose head is this, and whose title?" They answered, "The emperor's." 17 Jesus said to them, "Give to the emperor the things that are the emperor's, and to God the things that are God's." And they were utterly amazed at him.

2. The Sadducees and the resurrection
(12.18–27; Matt. 22.23–33; Luke 20.27–38)

18 Some Sadducees, who say there is no resurrection, came to him and asked him a question, saying, 19 "Teacher, Moses wrote for us that if a man's brother dies, leaving a wife but no child, the man[m] shall marry the widow and raise up children for his brother. 20 There were seven brothers; the first married and, when he died, left no children; 21 and the second married the widow[n] and died, leaving no children; and the third likewise; 22 none of the seven left children. Last of all the woman herself died. 23 In the resurrection[o] whose wife will she be? For the seven had married her."

24 Jesus said to them, "Is not this the reason you are wrong, that you know neither the scriptures nor the power of God? 25 For when they rise from the dead, they neither marry nor are given in marriage, but are like angels in heaven. 26 And as for the dead being raised, have you not read in the book of Moses, in the story about the bush, how God said to him, 'I am the God of Abraham, the God of Isaac, and the God of Jacob'? 27 He is God not of the dead, but of the living; you are quite wrong."

3. The great commandment (12.28–34; Matt. 22.34–40)

28 One of the scribes came near and heard them disputing with one

12.10
Ps 118.22, 23;
Acts 4.11;
1 Pet 2.7

12.12
Mt 21.45, 46;
Mk 11.18;
Mt 22.22

12.13
Mk 3.6;
Lk 11.54

12.17
Rom 13.7

12.19
Deut 25.5

12.25
1 Cor 15.42, 49, 52
12.26
Ex 3.6

12.28
Lk 10.25-28;
20.39

---

l Or *keystone*   *m* Gk *his brother*   *n* Gk *her*   *o* Other ancient authorities add *when they rise*

12.10 *The stone that the builders rejected.* See note on Mt 21.42.
12.13 *Herodians.* See note on Mt 22.16.
12.14 See note on Lk 20.20.
12.17 God's due takes precedence over the emperor's due when one is forced to choose between them.
12.18 See note on Lk 20.27ff.
12.24 *you know neither the scriptures.* Jesus maintained that the O.T. taught about the resurrection and that those who read the Scriptures should have

known it. We are responsible for all that the Bible contains, whether we know all of it or not.
12.26 Jesus provided a unique interpretation of the O.T. here. Had God said to Moses in Ex 3.6, "I *was* the God of Abraham," that would have meant that Abraham and the other ancestors had ceased to exist; "I am" meant they are alive and God was still their God.
12.28 *scribes.* See note on 2 Sam 8.17 regarding scribes in the O.T. In the N.T., the scribes were often Pharisees (Acts 23.9); were the teachers of the O.T. law (Mt 22.35); were O.T. experts (v. 35; Mt 2.4;

another, and seeing that he answered them well, he asked him, "Which commandment is the first of all?" 29 Jesus answered, "The first is, 'Hear, O Israel: the Lord our God, the Lord is one; 30 you shall love the Lord your God with all your heart, and with all your soul, and with all your mind, and with all your strength.' 31 The second is this, 'You shall love your neighbor as yourself.' There is no other commandment greater than these." 32 Then the scribe said to him, "You are right, Teacher; you have truly said that 'he is one, and besides him there is no other'; 33 and 'to love him with all the heart, and with all the understanding, and with all the strength,' and 'to love one's neighbor as oneself,'—this is much more important than all whole burnt offerings and sacrifices." 34 When Jesus saw that he answered wisely, he said to him, "You are not far from the kingdom of God." After that no one dared to ask him any question.

12.29
Deut 6.4

12.31
Lev 19.18;
Rom 13.9;
Gal 5.14;
Jas 2.8

12.32
Deut 4.39;
Isa 45.6, 14;
46.9

12.33
1 Sam 15.22;
Hos 6.6;
Mic 6.6-8

12.34
Mt 22.46

H. Christ's unanswerable question
(12.35–37; Matt. 22.41–46; Luke 20.41–44)

12.35
Mt 26.55;
9.27

12.36
Ps 110.1;
Acts 2.34, 35;
Heb 1.13

12.37
Jn 12.9

35 While Jesus was teaching in the temple, he said, "How can the scribes say that the Messiah⁰⁰ is the son of David? 36 David himself, by the Holy Spirit, declared,

'The Lord said to my Lord,

"Sit at my right hand,

until I put your enemies under your feet." '

37 David himself calls him Lord; so how can he be his son?" And the large crowd was listening to him with delight.

I. Jesus' warning against the scribes
(12.38–40; Matt. 23.1–12; Luke 20.45–47)

12.38
Lk 11.43

38 As he taught, he said, "Beware of the scribes, who like to walk around in long robes, and to be greeted with respect in the marketplaces, 39 and to have the best seats in the synagogues and places of honor at banquets! 40 They devour widows' houses and for the sake of appearance say long prayers. They will receive the greater condemnation."

J. The widow's penny (12.41–44)

12.41
Jn 8.20;
2 Kings 12.9

12.43
2 Cor 8.12

41 He sat down opposite the treasury, and watched the crowd putting money into the treasury. Many rich people put in large sums. 42 A poor widow came and put in two small copper coins, which are worth a penny. 43 Then he called his disciples and said to them, "Truly I tell you, this poor widow has put in more than all those who are contributing to the treasury. 44 For all of them have contributed out of their abundance; but she out of her poverty has put in everything she had, all she had to live on."

⁰⁰ Or the Christ

17.10); were filled with pride (v. 38); sat on Moses' seat (Mt 23.2); were condemned by Jesus (Mt 23.15); helped to secure Christ's condemnation (Lk 23.10); and persecuted the N.T. saints (Acts 4.5,18,21; 6.12).

12.29ff The twofold law of love (love toward God, and love toward all people including enemies) governs all Christian conduct. But even love must work in concert with the principles of righteousness, holiness, and justice. A loving person, for example, will never do something expressly forbidden in God's law (i.e., it is never loving to commit adultery or tell a lie, however compelling the circumstances might appear

to be). Love must be concerned with both the physical and spiritual well-being of other people.

12.35 According to Jesus, the scribes were defective in their teaching. They did teach that the Messiah was to be the Son of David, but they did not explain how and why David called that Son "Lord." Obviously, by calling him Lord, David knew that his coming Son was the Son of God and as such was worthy of being his Lord. The Messiah is God, a truth not taught by the scribes.

12.36 *The Lord said to my Lord.* The first use of "Lord" means "God"; the second "Lord" means "Messiah."

K. *The Olivet discourse (13.1–37; Matt. 24; Luke 21)*

1. *Course of the present age (13.1–13; Matt. 24.1–14; Luke 21.5–19)*

13 As he came out of the temple, one of his disciples said to him,
"Look, Teacher, what large stones and what large buildings!"
2 Then Jesus asked him, "Do you see these great buildings? Not one stone
will be left here upon another; all will be thrown down."
3 When he was sitting on the Mount of Olives opposite the temple,
Peter, James, John, and Andrew asked him privately, 4 "Tell us, when
will this be, and what will be the sign that all these things are about to
be accomplished?" 5 Then Jesus began to say to them, "Beware that no
one leads you astray. 6 Many will come in my name and say, 'I am he!'[p]
and they will lead many astray. 7 When you hear of wars and rumors of
wars, do not be alarmed; this must take place, but the end is still to come.
8 For nation will rise against nation, and kingdom against kingdom; there
will be earthquakes in various places; there will be famines. This is but
the beginning of the birth pangs.
9 "As for yourselves, beware; for they will hand you over to councils;
and you will be beaten in synagogues; and you will stand before governors
and kings because of me, as a testimony to them. 10 And the good news[q]
must first be proclaimed to all nations. 11 When they bring you to trial and
hand you over, do not worry beforehand about what you are to say; but
say whatever is given you at that time, for it is not you who speak, but
the Holy Spirit. 12 Brother will betray brother to death, and a father his
child, and children will rise against parents and have them put to death;
13 and you will be hated by all because of my name. But the one who
endures to the end will be saved.

13.2 Lk 19.44; Mk 14.58; 15.29; Acts 6.14
13.3 Mk 5.37; 9.2
13.5 Eph 5.6; 1 Thess 2.3
13.6 Jn 8.24
13.9 Mt 10.17
13.11 Mt 10.19; Lk 12.11
13.12 Mic 7.6; Mt 10.21
13.13 Jn 15.21; Mt 10.22; Rev 2.10

2. *The great tribulation (13.14–23; Matt. 24.15–28; Luke 21.20–24)*

14 "But when you see the desolating sacrilege set up where it ought
not to be (let the reader understand), then those in Judea must flee to the
mountains; 15 the one on the housetop must not go down or enter the
house to take anything away; 16 the one in the field must not turn back
to get a coat. 17 Woe to those who are pregnant and to those who are
nursing infants in those days! 18 Pray that it may not be in winter. 19 For
in those days there will be suffering, such as has not been from the
beginning of the creation that God created until now, no, and never will
be. 20 And if the Lord had not cut short those days, no one would be saved;
but for the sake of the elect, whom he chose, he has cut short those days.
21 And if anyone says to you at that time, 'Look! Here is the Messiah!'[r]
or 'Look! There he is!'—do not believe it. 22 False messiahs[s] and
false prophets will appear and produce signs and omens, to lead
astray, if possible, the elect. 23 But be alert; I have already told you everything.

13.14 Dan 9.27; 11.31; 12.11
13.17 Lk 23.29
13.19 Dan 9.26; 12.1; Joel 2.2
13.21 Lk 17.23; 21.8
13.22 Mt 7.15; Jn 4.48
13.23 2 Pet 3.17

[p] Gk *I am* [q] Gk *gospel* [r] Or *the Christ* [s] Or *christs*

13.1ff See note on Mt 24.2ff regarding the Olivet discourse.
13.7 *but the end is still to come.* Jesus nowhere taught that his second advent would be shortly after his ascension. The time lag is indeterminate (cf. vv. 32–33). Believers should therefore live as though he were coming today; at the same time, they should make proper preparations for their earthly life as though he were not coming for a long time.
13.11 Christ prophesied that his followers would suffer persecution and be called upon to speak to their own defense. The Holy Spirit would supply them with words in the hour of their need. We are not capable in ourselves of doing and saying the right things under such circumstances.
13.20 *for the sake of the elect.* God has his elect, for he knows who are his own, and he will preserve them despite the seductive approaches of their enemy. Yet Jesus warned that even the elect should take heed and be careful, for dangers lie before them and they would be exposed to the wiles of the devil.

3. The second coming of Christ
(13.24–27; Matt. 24.29–31; Luke 21.25–28)

13.24
Zeph 1.15

24 "But in those days, after that suffering,
    the sun will be darkened,
    and the moon will not give its light,
25 and the stars will be falling from heaven,
    and the powers in the heavens will be shaken.

13.26
Dan 7.13;
Mt 16.27;
Mk 14.62;
1 Thess 4.16;
2 Thess 1.7,
10

26 Then they will see 'the Son of Man coming in clouds' with great power and glory. 27 Then he will send out the angels, and gather his elect from the four winds, from the ends of the earth to the ends of heaven.

4. The parable of the fig tree
(13.28–31; Matt. 24.32–35; Luke 21.29–33)

28 "From the fig tree learn its lesson: as soon as its branch becomes tender and puts forth its leaves, you know that summer is near. 29 So also, when you see these things taking place, you know that he[t] is near, at the very gates.

13.30
Mk 9.1
13.31
Mt 5.18;
Lk 16.17

30 Truly I tell you, this generation will not pass away until all these things have taken place. 31 Heaven and earth will pass away, but my words will not pass away.

5. Watchfulness (13.32–37; Matt. 24.32–35; Luke 21.29–33)

13.32
Acts 1.7
13.33
Eph 6.18;
Col 4.2;
1 Thess 5.6
13.34
Mt 25.14
13.35
Lk 12.35-40

32 "But about that day or hour no one knows, neither the angels in heaven, nor the Son, but only the Father. 33 Beware, keep alert;[u] for you do not know when the time will come. 34 It is like a man going on a journey, when he leaves home and puts his slaves in charge, each with his work, and commands the doorkeeper to be on the watch. 35 Therefore, keep awake—for you do not know when the master of the house will come, in the evening, or at midnight, or at cockcrow, or at dawn, 36 or else he may find you asleep when he comes suddenly. 37 And what I say to you I say to all: Keep awake."

L. The plot to kill Jesus
(14.1,2,10,11; Matt. 26.1–5,14–16; Luke 22.1–6)

14.1
Jn 11.55;
13.1;
Mt 12.14

14 It was two days before the Passover and the festival of Unleavened Bread. The chief priests and the scribes were looking for a way to arrest Jesus[v] by stealth and kill him; 2 for they said, "Not during the festival, or there may be a riot among the people."

M. Jesus anointed by Mary of Bethany
(14.3–9; Matt. 26.6–13; John 12.1–8)

14.3
Lk 7.37-39;
Mt 21.17

3 While he was at Bethany in the house of Simon the leper,[w] as he

---

[t] Or it   [u] Other ancient authorities add *and pray*   [v] Gk *him*   [w] The terms *leper* and *leprosy* can refer to several diseases

---

13.24,25 The disruption of sun, moon, and stars will take place before the second coming of Jesus. This should assure all believers who remain alive until Christ's coming that Christ has not come and will not come until these disturbances of nature occur first.
13.35–37 Jesus enjoins his people to be watchful. The Greek word *grēgoreō* means to "be awake," "keep awake," "be alert and on guard," or "watch out." We must be courageous (1 Cor 16.13), prayerful (Lk 21.36; Eph 6.18), and thankful (Col 4.2) as we watch. Blessings await those who stay awake (Rev 16.15). We must expect the coming of the Lord at any time, since we know not the day nor the hour (Mt 24.42; 25.13).

14.1 *The Passover* was celebrated on the fourteenth day of Nisan (March-April). All males over age twelve were to go to Jerusalem for this observance. The Passover was a single day commemorating Israel's deliverance from Egypt on the night that the angel of death slew the firstborn of every household except those whose doors had been sprinkled with blood. It looked forward to Calvary and the shed blood of Christ. The Passover was followed by the seven-day festival of unleavened bread, when no yeast was used. This festival commemorated Israel's flight from Egypt. The Passover and the festival of unleavened bread were generally celebrated as one festival (see also note on Ex 12.11–13).
14.3 See note on Lk 7.36ff.

sat at the table, a woman came with an alabaster jar of very costly ointment of nard, and she broke open the jar and poured the ointment on his head. 4 But some were there who said to one another in anger, "Why was the ointment wasted in this way? 5 For this ointment could have been sold for more than three hundred denarii,ˣ and the money given to the poor." And they scolded her. 6 But Jesus said, "Let her alone; why do you trouble her? She has performed a good service for me. 7 For you always have the poor with you, and you can show kindness to them whenever you wish; but you will not always have me. 8 She has done what she could; she has anointed my body beforehand for its burial. 9 Truly I tell you, wherever the good newsʸ is proclaimed in the whole world, what she has done will be told in remembrance of her."

N. The bargain of Judas Iscariot (14.10,11)

10 Then Judas Iscariot, who was one of the twelve, went to the chief priests in order to betray him to them. 11 When they heard it, they were greatly pleased, and promised to give him money. So he began to look for an opportunity to betray him.

O. The Last Supper (14.12–25)

1. The passover prepared (14.12–16; Matt. 26.17–19; Luke 22.7–13)

12 On the first day of Unleavened Bread, when the Passover lamb is sacrificed, his disciples said to him, "Where do you want us to go and make the preparations for you to eat the Passover?" 13 So he sent two of his disciples, saying to them, "Go into the city, and a man carrying a jar of water will meet you; follow him, 14 and wherever he enters, say to the owner of the house, 'The Teacher asks, Where is my guest room where I may eat the Passover with my disciples?' 15 He will show you a large room upstairs, furnished and ready. Make preparations for us there." 16 So the disciples set out and went to the city, and found everything as he had told them; and they prepared the Passover meal.

2. The passover eaten (14.17–21; Matt. 26.20–25; Luke 22.14–18; see John 13.1–30)

17 When it was evening, he came with the twelve. 18 And when they had taken their places and were eating, Jesus said, "Truly I tell you, one of you will betray me, one who is eating with me." 19 They began to be distressed and to say to him one after another, "Surely, not I?" 20 He said to them, "It is one of the twelve, one who is dipping breadᶻ into the bowlᵃ with me. 21 For the Son of Man goes as it is written of him, but woe to that one by whom the Son of Man is betrayed! It would have been better for that one not to have been born."

3. The Lord's Supper instituted (14.22–25; Matt. 26.26–29; Luke 22.19–24)

22 While they were eating, he took a loaf of bread, and after blessing

14.7 Deut 15.11

14.8 Jn 19.20

14.10 Lk 22.3, 4; Jn 6.71

14.12 Ex 12.11

14.18 vv. 44, 45

14.22 Mk 6.41; 8.6; Lk 24.30; 1 Cor 11.23-25

ˣ The denarius was the usual day's wage for a laborer   ʸ Or *gospel*   ᶻ Gk lacks *bread*   ᵃ Other ancient authorities read *same bowl*

14.5 The cost of the ointment would have equaled the yearly pay of a lower-class worker. Matthew says that "his disciples were indignant" (26.8). That is, Judas Iscariot was not alone in his objections to the use of the expensive aromatic ointment. Jesus endorsed Mary's act. All believers, under the Holy Spirit, are responsible for what they do with what God has given.

14.10 See note on Mt 26.14.
14.13 See note on Lk 22.10.
14.22ff The Lord's Supper, or Eucharist, was instituted by Christ and is recorded in the three synoptic Gospels. Paul states specifically that the Supper was instituted by Christ (1 Cor 11.23ff). It brought to fulfillment the meaning of the Passover meal celebrated according to Ex 12.21-28 (cf. 1 Cor 5.7,8). It

it he broke it, gave it to them, and said, "Take; this is my body." 23 Then he took a cup, and after giving thanks he gave it to them, and all of them drank from it. 24 He said to them, "This is my blood of the[b] covenant, which is poured out for many. 25 Truly I tell you, I will never again drink of the fruit of the vine until that day when I drink it new in the kingdom of God."

14.23
1 Cor 10.16

14.24
Ex 24.8;
Heb 9.20

P. Peter's denial foretold
(14.26–31; Matt. 26.30–35; Luke 22.31–34; see John 14–17)

26 When they had sung the hymn, they went out to the Mount of Olives. 27 And Jesus said to them, "You will all become deserters; for it is written,

'I will strike the shepherd,
and the sheep will be scattered.'

28 But after I am raised up, I will go before you to Galilee." 29 Peter said to him, "Even though all become deserters, I will not." 30 Jesus said to him, "Truly I tell you, this day, this very night, before the cock crows twice, you will deny me three times." 31 But he said vehemently, "Even though I must die with you, I will not deny you." And all of them said the same.

14.26
Mt 21.1
14.27
Zech 13.7

14.28
Mk 16.7
14.29
Jn 13.37, 38
14.30
vv. 66-72;
Jn 13.38

Q. Jesus in Gethsemane (14.32–52)

1. His agony (14.32–42; Matt. 26.36–46; Luke 22.39–46; cf. John 18.1)

32 They went to a place called Gethsemane; and he said to his disciples, "Sit here while I pray." 33 He took with him Peter and James and John, and began to be distressed and agitated. 34 And he said to them, "I am deeply grieved, even to death; remain here, and keep awake." 35 And going a little farther, he threw himself on the ground and prayed that, if it were possible, the hour might pass from him. 36 He said, "Abba,[c] Father, for you all things are possible; remove this cup from me; yet, not what I want, but what you want." 37 He came and found them sleeping; and he said to Peter, "Simon, are you asleep? Could you not keep awake one hour? 38 Keep awake and pray that you may not come into the time of trial;[d] the spirit indeed is willing, but the flesh is weak." 39 And again he went away and prayed, saying the same words. 40 And once more he came and found them sleeping, for their eyes were very heavy; and they did not know what to say to him. 41 He came a third time and said to them, "Are you still sleeping and taking your rest? Enough! The hour has come; the Son of Man is betrayed into the hands of sinners. 42 Get up, let us be going. See, my betrayer is at hand."

14.34
Jn 12.27
14.35
v. 41
14.36
Rom 8.15;
Gal 4.6;
Jn 5.30; 6.38

14.38
Mt 6.13;
Lk 11.4;
Rom 7.23;
Gal 5.17
14.41
v. 35;
Jn 13.1

2. Jesus' betrayal and arrest
(14.43–52; Matt. 26.47–56; Luke 22.47–53; John 18.1–11)

43 Immediately, while he was still speaking, Judas, one of the twelve,

---

b Other ancient authorities add *new*   c Aramaic for *Father*   d Or *into temptation*

---

is to be celebrated by the church until the return of the Lord. Paul urges self-examination on the part of every communicant in the meal. Only professing Christians who are making a sincere effort to live a life dedicated to God should sit at the table of the Lord; those who do not discern the Lord's body bring judgment against themselves (1 Cor 11.27–30). Some churches believe in the actual presence of Christ in the elements; some believe in his spiritual presence; others hold that Christ is present only symbolically. One's view is determined by how these words are interpreted: "This is my body" and "This is my blood." Some celebrate the Lord's Supper daily, some weekly, some monthly, and some quarterly.
14.26 Jesus and his disciples sang, probably using psalms of rejoicing and praise. Though surrounded by their enemies, they were not afraid to fulfill the duty of singing psalms (cf. Acts 16.25).
14.36 *this cup.* See note on Mt 26.39.
14.37 Jesus did not ask his closest friends to watch with him all night—only for a single hour. And they failed him miserably in this momentous hour.

arrived; and with him there was a crowd with swords and clubs, from the chief priests, the scribes, and the elders. 44 Now the betrayer had given them a sign, saying, "The one I will kiss is the man; arrest him and lead him away under guard." 45 So when he came, he went up to him at once and said, "Rabbi!" and kissed him. 46 Then they laid hands on him and arrested him. 47 But one of those who stood near drew his sword and struck the slave of the high priest, cutting off his ear. 48 Then Jesus said to them, "Have you come out with swords and clubs to arrest me as though I were a bandit? 49 Day after day I was with you in the temple teaching, and you did not arrest me. But let the scriptures be fulfilled." 50 All of them deserted him and fled.

51   A certain young man was following him, wearing nothing but a linen cloth. They caught hold of him, 52 but he left the linen cloth and ran off naked.

R. Jesus before Caiaphas
(14.53–65; Matt. 26.57–68; cf. Luke 22.54; John 18.12–14, 19–25)

53   They took Jesus to the high priest; and all the chief priests, the elders, and the scribes were assembled. 54 Peter had followed him at a distance, right into the courtyard of the high priest; and he was sitting with the guards, warming himself at the fire. 55 Now the chief priests and the whole council were looking for testimony against Jesus to put him to death; but they found none. 56 For many gave false testimony against him, and their testimony did not agree. 57 Some stood up and gave false testimony against him, saying, 58 "We heard him say, 'I will destroy this temple that is made with hands, and in three days I will build another, not made with hands.' " 59 But even on this point their testimony did not agree. 60 Then the high priest stood up before them and asked Jesus, "Have you no answer? What is it that they testify against you?" 61 But he was silent and did not answer. Again the high priest asked him, "Are you the Messiah,[e] the Son of the Blessed One?" 62 Jesus said, "I am; and

'you will see the Son of Man
    seated at the right hand of the Power,'
and 'coming with the clouds of heaven.' "

63 Then the high priest tore his clothes and said, "Why do we still need witnesses? 64 You have heard his blasphemy! What is your decision?" All of them condemned him as deserving death. 65 Some began to spit on him, to blindfold him, and to strike him, saying to him, "Prophesy!" The guards also took him over and beat him.

S. Peter's denial of Jesus
(14.66–72; Matt. 26.69–75; Luke 22.55–62; John 18.15–18, 25–27)

66   While Peter was below in the courtyard, one of the servant-girls of the high priest came by. 67 When she saw Peter warming himself, she stared at him and said, "You also were with Jesus, the man from Nazareth." 68 But he denied it, saying, "I do not know or understand what you

[e] Or the Christ

Cross references (right margin):

14.45 Mt 23.7

14.49 Mk 12.35; Isa 53.7ff; Lk 19.47; Jn 18.19-21
14.50 Ps 88.8; v. 7

14.54 v. 68; Mt 26.3; Jn 18.18

14.58 Mk 15.29; Jn 2.19; Acts 6.14

14.61 Isa 53.7

14.62 Dan 7.13; Mt 24.30; Mk 13.26

14.63 Num 14.6; Acts 14.14
14.64 Lev 24.16
14.65 Mk 10.34; Esth 7.8; Lk 22.64

14.66 vv. 30, 54
14.67 v. 54; Mk 1.24
14.68 v. 54

14.44 *kiss*, the usual oriental greeting even to this day.
14.45 Judas Iscariot had been with Jesus for two and a half years. He had watched him and was aware of his sinless life. He had heard the Savior's words of grace. He had seen him perform matchless miracles beyond anything ever known to us. He had eaten with him, prayed with him, and heard him tell of his coming death and resurrection. None of this affected him sufficiently to keep him from selling the Son of God for thirty pieces of silver. He served as the treasurer

of the disciples and was a thief (Jn 12.4–7). He knew all about hell, yet never turned from his sins to receive the gift of life.
14.47 *one of those*, i.e., Peter (see Jn 18.10).
14.49 *let the scriptures be fulfilled.* Jesus was fully aware that every prophetic word of the O.T. had to be fulfilled. He left nothing undone in his life to keep any Scripture from being fulfilled.
14.61 *did not answer.* This fulfilled Isa 53.7: "He did not open his mouth."

are talking about." And he went out into the forecourt.*f* Then the cock crowed.*g* 69 And the servant-girl, on seeing him, began again to say to the bystanders, "This man is one of them." 70 But again he denied it. Then after a little while the bystanders again said to Peter, "Certainly you are one of them; for you are a Galilean." 71 But he began to curse, and he swore an oath, "I do not know this man you are talking about." 72 At that moment the cock crowed for the second time. Then Peter remembered that Jesus had said to him, "Before the cock crows twice, you will deny me three times." And he broke down and wept.

14.70
v. 68;
Acts 2.7

14.72
v. 30

T. *Jesus before Pontius Pilate*
(15.1–15; Matt. 27.11–26; Luke 23.3–25; John 18.29–40)

1. *Pilate questions Jesus (15.1–5)*

15.1
Mt 5.22;
Lk 22.66;
23.1;
Jn 18.28

15 As soon as it was morning, the chief priests held a consultation with the elders and scribes and the whole council. They bound Jesus, led him away, and handed him over to Pilate. 2 Pilate asked him, "Are you the King of the Jews?" He answered him, "You say so." 3 Then the chief priests accused him of many things. 4 Pilate asked him again, "Have you no answer? See how many charges they bring against you." 5 But Jesus made no further reply, so that Pilate was amazed.

15.5
Isa 53.7

2. *Pilate releases Barabbas and delivers Jesus (15.6–15)*

15.6
Mt 27.15;
Lk 23.17;
Jn 18.39

6 Now at the festival he used to release a prisoner for them, anyone for whom they asked. 7 Now a man called Barabbas was in prison with the rebels who had committed murder during the insurrection. 8 So the crowd came and began to ask Pilate to do for them according to his custom. 9 Then he answered them, "Do you want me to release for you the King of the Jews?" 10 For he realized that it was out of jealousy that the chief priests had handed him over. 11 But the chief priests stirred up the crowd to have him release Barabbas for them instead. 12 Pilate spoke to them again, "Then what do you wish me to do*h* with the man you call*i* the King of the Jews?" 13 They shouted back, "Crucify him!" 14 Pilate asked them, "Why, what evil has he done?" But they shouted all the more, "Crucify him!" 15 So Pilate, wishing to satisfy the crowd, released Barabbas for them; and after flogging Jesus, he handed him over to be crucified.

15.11
Acts 3.14

15.15
Jn 19.1, 16

f Or *gateway*   *g* Other ancient authorities lack *Then the cock crowed*   *h* Other ancient authorities read *what should I do*   *i* Other ancient authorities lack *the man you call*

14.71 It was bad enough that Peter denied his Lord. It was still worse that he did so by taking an oath in the name of God. He perjured himself when he testified to that which he knew was untrue. It was a sad spectacle, but it had one positive aspect — the glory of God's grace was made greater by the fact that Peter was restored (Jn 21.15–17) and became an ardent witness to Jesus after Pentecost. This fact opens the door of hope to all sinners, no matter what they have done or how bad they are.

15.1 *Pilate* was the Roman procurator (governor) over the territory formerly ruled by Herod's son, Archelaus. Judea, Idumea, and Samaria were part of that territory. Nothing is known of Pontius Pilate's origins, although procurators usually came from the Roman equestrian class. Pilate's rule began about the time John the Baptist started preaching. He was responsible for the financial administration of the territory and for the collection of taxes. The Jewish Sanhe-

drin exercised great power, except that it did not have the right to impose a death sentence without an appeal to the procurator, who then carried out executions. Pilate and the Jews were often at odds with each other. In the case of Jesus, Pilate wanted to release him, but he finally capitulated to their demands that Jesus be crucified, putting aside any sense of justice and moral rectitude for personal and political reasons. After ten years' service he was removed from the procuratorship.

15.7 *Barabbas* was a well-known revolutionary who probably led the revolt mentioned in Lk 23.18,19,25. In Jn 18.40 he is called a "bandit" (Gk. *lēstēs*), a word used by Josephus to describe rebels against Roman authority. The same word is used to describe the two thieves crucified on either side of Jesus. We know nothing more about Barabbas than is found in Scripture. Some manuscripts call him "Jesus Barabbas."

U. *The crucifixion and burial of Jesus (15.16–47)*

1. *Jesus crowned with thorns*
(15.16–20; Matt. 27.27–31; cf. John 19.2,3)

16   Then the soldiers led him into the courtyard of the palace (that is, the governor's headquarters[j]); and they called together the whole cohort. 17 And they clothed him in a purple cloak; and after twisting some thorns into a crown, they put it on him. 18 And they began saluting him, "Hail, King of the Jews!" 19 They struck his head with a reed, spat upon him, and knelt down in homage to him. 20 After mocking him, they stripped him of the purple cloak and put his own clothes on him. Then they led him out to crucify him.

2. *Jesus crucified*
(15.21–32; Matt. 27.32–44; Luke 23.32–43; John 19.17–24)

21   They compelled a passer-by, who was coming in from the country, to carry his cross; it was Simon of Cyrene, the father of Alexander and Rufus. 22 Then they brought Jesus[k] to the place called Golgotha (which means the place of a skull). 23 And they offered him wine mixed with myrrh; but he did not take it. 24 And they crucified him, and divided his clothes among them, casting lots to decide what each should take.

25   It was nine o'clock in the morning when they crucified him. 26 The inscription of the charge against him read, "The King of the Jews." 27 And with him they crucified two bandits, one on his right and one on his left.[l] 29 Those who passed by derided[m] him, shaking their heads and saying, "Aha! You who would destroy the temple and build it in three days, 30 save yourself, and come down from the cross!" 31 In the same way the chief priests, along with the scribes, were also mocking him among themselves and saying, "He saved others; he cannot save himself. 32 Let the Messiah,[n] the King of Israel, come down from the cross now, so that we may see and believe." Those who were crucified with him also taunted him.

3. *The death of Jesus*
(15.33–41; Matt. 27.45–50; Luke 23.44–49; John 19.28–37)

33   When it was noon, darkness came over the whole land[o] until three in the afternoon. 34 At three o'clock Jesus cried out with a loud voice, "Eloi, Eloi, lema sabachthani?" which means, "My God, my God, why have you forsaken me?"[p] 35 When some of the bystanders heard it, they said, "Listen, he is calling for Elijah." 36 And someone ran, filled a sponge with sour wine, put it on a stick, and gave it to him to drink, saying, "Wait, let us see whether Elijah will come to take him down." 37 Then Jesus gave a loud cry and breathed his last. 38 And the curtain of the

15.16 Acts 10.1
15.21 Lk 23.26; Rom 16.13
15.24 Ps 22.18
15.29 Ps 22.7; Mk 13.2; 14.58; Jn 2.19
15.31 Ps 22.8
15.32 vv. 26, 27
15.34 Ps 22.1
15.36 Ps 69.21
15.38 Heb 10.19, 20

j Gk the praetorium   k Gk him   l Other ancient authorities add verse 28, And the scripture was fulfilled that says, "And he was counted among the lawless."   m Or blasphemed   n Or the Christ   o Or earth p Other ancient authorities read made me a reproach

15.21 *Simon of Cyrene* was probably a Jew from North Africa, who had business dealings in Jerusalem at this time. He is said to be the father of Alexander and Rufus, men known to the readers of Mark's Gospel.
15.22 *Golgotha.* See note on Jn 19.17.
15.23 This concoction may have been offered to dull the pain, but Jesus refused this escape from his sufferings.
15.26 *inscription.* See note on Mt 27.37.
15.27 See note on Lk 23.33.
15.34 *Eloi, Eloi, lema sabachthani.* Jesus spoke in

Aramaic. The onlookers misunderstood his first two words and thought he was calling for the prophet Elijah. Jesus died in the darkness, for the light of God's face was withdrawn from his Son and from the earth. Jesus was made sin for us (2 Cor 5.21); he endured the wrath of God and the absence of the Father for the first and last time. That is why he cried out in his suffering and distress, "My God, my God, why have you forsaken me?"
15.38 *curtain.* A heavy curtain hung in front of the most Holy Place, a place in the temple reserved by God for himself; the curtain separated him from sin-

15.39
Mk 1.11; 9.7

temple was torn in two, from top to bottom. 39 Now when the centurion, who stood facing him, saw that in this way he[q] breathed his last, he said, "Truly this man was God's Son!"[r]

15.40
Ps 38.11;
Jn 19.25;
Mk 16.1
15.41
Lk 8.1-3

40   There were also women looking on from a distance; among them were Mary Magdalene, and Mary the mother of James the younger and of Joses, and Salome. 41 These used to follow him and provided for him when he was in Galilee; and there were many other women who had come up with him to Jerusalem.

4. Jesus laid in the tomb
(15.42–47; Matt. 27.57–61; Luke 23.50–56; John 19.38–42)

15.42
Deut 21.22,
23;
Mt 27.62
15.43
Acts 13.50;
17.12;
Lk 2.25, 38

42   When evening had come, and since it was the day of Preparation, that is, the day before the sabbath, 43 Joseph of Arimathea, a respected member of the council, who was also himself waiting expectantly for the kingdom of God, went boldly to Pilate and asked for the body of Jesus. 44 Then Pilate wondered if he were already dead; and summoning the centurion, he asked him whether he had been dead for some time.

15.45
v. 39

45 When he learned from the centurion that he was dead, he granted the body to Joseph. 46 Then Joseph[s] bought a linen cloth, and taking down the body,[t] wrapped it in the linen cloth, and laid it in a tomb that had been hewn out of the rock. He then rolled a stone against the door of the tomb. 47 Mary Magdalene and Mary the mother of Joses saw where the body[t] was laid.

V. The resurrection of Jesus Christ
(16.1–8; Matt. 28.1–10; Luke 24.1–11; John 20.1–18)

16.1
Lk 23.56;
Jn 19.39

16 When the sabbath was over, Mary Magdalene, and Mary the mother of James, and Salome bought spices, so that they might go and anoint him. 2 And very early on the first day of the week, when the sun had risen, they went to the tomb. 3 They had been saying to one another, "Who will roll away the stone for us from the entrance to the tomb?" 4 When they looked up, they saw that the stone, which was very large, had already been rolled back. 5 As they entered the tomb, they saw a young man, dressed in a white robe, sitting on the right side; and they were alarmed. 6 But he said to them, "Do not be alarmed; you are looking for Jesus of Nazareth, who was crucified. He has been raised; he is not here. Look, there is the place they laid him. 7 But go, tell his disciples and Peter that he is going ahead of you to Galilee; there you will see him, just as he told you." 8 So they went out and fled from the tomb, for terror and amazement had seized them; and they said nothing to anyone, for they were afraid.[u]

16.3
Mk 15.46

16.5
Mk 9.15

16.6
v. 5;
Mk 1.24
16.7
Mk 14.28;
Jn 21.1-23

THE SHORTER ENDING OF MARK

[[And all that had been commanded them they told briefly to those

---

[q] Other ancient authorities add *cried out and*   [r] Or *a son of God*   [s] Gk *he*   [t] Gk *it*   [u] Some of the most ancient authorities bring the book to a close at the end of verse 8. One authority concludes the book with the shorter ending; others include the shorter ending and then continue with verses 9-20. In most authorities verses 9-20 follow immediately after verse 8, though in some of these authorities the passage is marked as being doubtful.

---

ful humankind. Now it was split from above, showing that Christ's death for sin had opened up access to the holy God (cf. Rom 5.1,2).
15.43 *Joseph of Arimathaea* was a member of the Sanhedrin. He placed the body of Jesus in his own unused tomb. As one of those who was looking for the kingdom of God, he may indeed have been a believer in Jesus Christ. His conduct set him apart from most of the scribes, Pharisees, and Sadducees.

16.1ff   The three women who came to anoint the body of Jesus with spices spoke about the problem of moving the large, heavy stone that closed over Jesus' tomb. The empty tomb came as a surprise to them. Like the disciples, they did not understand Jesus' predictions that he would rise from the dead on the third day (8.31; 9.31; 10.34).
16.6   See note on Mt 28.6.

around Peter. And afterward Jesus himself sent out through them, from east to west, the sacred and imperishable proclamation of eternal salvation.*v*⟧

THE LONGER ENDING OF MARK

V. *Appearances of the risen Christ (16.9–20)*

9 ⟦Now after he rose early on the first day of the week, he appeared first to Mary Magdalene, from whom he had cast out seven demons. 10 She went out and told those who had been with him, while they were mourning and weeping. 11 But when they heard that he was alive and had been seen by her, they would not believe it.

16.9
Jn 20.11-18

12 After this he appeared in another form to two of them, as they were walking into the country. 13 And they went back and told the rest, but they did not believe them.

16.12
Lk 24.13-35

14 Later he appeared to the eleven themselves as they were sitting at the table; and he upbraided them for their lack of faith and stubbornness, because they had not believed those who saw him after he had risen.*w* 15 And he said to them, "Go into all the world and proclaim the good news*x* to the whole creation. 16 The one who believes and is baptized will be saved; but the one who does not believe will be condemned. 17 And these signs will accompany those who believe: by using my name they will cast out demons; they will speak in new tongues; 18 they will pick up snakes in their hands,*y* and if they drink any deadly thing, it will not hurt them; they will lay their hands on the sick, and they will recover."

16.14
Lk 24.36-38;
Jn 20.26

16.15
Mt 28.18-20;
Lk 24.47, 48

19 So then the Lord Jesus, after he had spoken to them, was taken up into heaven and sat down at the right hand of God. 20 And they went out and proclaimed the good news everywhere, while the Lord worked with them and confirmed the message by the signs that accompanied it.*v*⟧

16.19
Lk 24.50,
51;
Acts 1.9-11

v Other ancient authorities add *Amen*   *w* Other ancient authorities add, in whole or in part, *And they excused themselves, saying, "This age of lawlessness and unbelief is under Satan, who does not allow the truth and power of God to prevail over the unclean things of the spirits. Therefore reveal your righteousness now"—thus they spoke to Christ. And Christ replied to them, "The term of years of Satan's power has been fulfilled, but other terrible things draw near. And for those who have sinned I was handed over to death, that they may return to the truth and sin no more, that they may inherit the spiritual and imperishable glory of righteousness that is in heaven."*   *x* Or *gospel*   *y* Other ancient authorities lack *in their hands*

16.9ff Many scholars think vv. 9–20 do not belong to the original text of Mark because it is absent in the two of the oldest manuscripts. Some evangelicals, however, do accept this passage as authentic.
16.15 Christ delivers the Great Commission four other times in the N.T. (Mt 28.18–20; Lk 24.44–49; Jn 20.21; and Acts 1.8). The evangelization of the entire world is the church's primary mission. Before

Christ returns to earth the good news will have been preached to all the world, though the Bible makes it plain that not all people will believe.
16.17 *new tongues.* Some ancient manuscripts omit "new." Jesus specifically enjoins his followers to cast out demons in his name. The book of Acts has several references to this occurring in the early church (e.g., Acts 5.16; 16.16–18; 19.11–17).

INTRODUCTION TO

THE GOSPEL ACCORDING TO

LUKE

Authorship, Date, and Background: The Gospel according to Luke and The Acts of the Apostles were obviously written by the same person (compare the first few verses of both works). The unvarying tradition of the early church assigned the authorship to Luke, called "the beloved physician" by Paul (Col 4.14). Luke was not an apostle nor did he personally witness most of the events he wrote about. At the time he wrote there were already in existence many garbled accounts of the life of Jesus, both oral and perhaps written. Luke intended to write about Jesus only after having carefully checked the sources to make sure of their accuracy (1.1–4). He was a companion of Paul and had the benefit not only of the witness of other apostles who were with Jesus from the beginning, but of Paul, who had received his knowledge of the gospel by special revelation from God (Gal 1.11,12).

Luke was a Gentile Christian converted in Antioch less than fifteen years after Pentecost. The "we" of Acts 16.10 indicates that Luke joined Paul at Troas. He may have been a leader of the church at Philippi, rejoining Paul when he returned to that city on his third missionary journey (Acts 20.6, another "we" section). Luke was well-educated, wrote flawless Greek, and was well versed in the culture of the Roman world. He was with Paul when the latter wrote 2 Timothy, for he wrote, "Only Luke is with me" (2 Tim 4.11). In other words, Luke was no armchair historian, but a full-fledged missionary.

The place where this Gospel was composed is unknown, although it was somewhere in the Hellenistic world outside Palestine. The date is also uncertain. Some scholars think it was written before the fall of Jerusalem in A.D. 70, and others during the period from A.D. 80 to 90. Probably A.D. 60 is the best approximate date for its composition. It was addressed to Theophilus, a wealthy citizen of Antioch who likely held a government position. He may or may not have been a Christian at this point, for the Gospel seems directed to convince him of the truth of Jesus as God's Son and the Savior of the world. Apparently Luke expected Theophilus to distribute this writing widely. In any event, it was intended for all people everywhere, even though specifically directed to Theophilus.

Characteristics and Content: Luke's Gospel has been called "the most beautiful book ever written." In its pages Luke traces the ancestry of Jesus back to Adam, son of God (3.23–38). He has all humanity in view and makes clear God's interest in all people everywhere. He writes in an orderly and precise fashion, but behind the human author lies the Holy Spirit who inspired Luke to put on paper what God wanted written. Thus, while Luke uses some material similar to that found in Mark and Matthew, he has a different purpose in mind. Non-Jews in particular find Luke's Gospel best suited to their needs.

Luke contains material not found in any other Gospel. The parables of the rich man and Lazarus, the good Samaritan, the rich man who gloated over his wealth, the sharp accountant who looked after himself, the self-righteous Pharisee and the tax collector, and the lost son are told with great skill. The names of Zechariah, Elizabeth, Simeon, Anna, Zacchaeus, and Cleopas do not appear anywhere else. The account of Jesus' post-resurrection appearance at Emmaus is a powerful story. The birth of Christ is enriched by hymns which are well known in the church: the *Magnificat* of Mary (1.46–55), the *Benedictus* of John's father Zechariah (1.67–79), the *Gloria in Excelsis* chanted by the angels (2.14), and the *Nunc Dimittis* spoken by Simeon when he cradled Jesus in his arms (2.25–32).

Luke writes doctrinally to show that Jesus is God incarnate, who came to seek and to save the lost. More references to the person and work of the Holy Spirit appear in Luke than in the first two Gospels together. He supplies more information about faithful women believers than any other Gospel writer and praises them. Luke identifies himself with the lower classes, even though he himself was of upper class origin. He says a great deal about poverty and wealth and pictures Jesus as a champion of the poor and distressed.

Outline:

   I. Introduction (1.1–4)

  II. Birth and childhood of John the Baptist and of Jesus (1.5—2.52)

 III. The ministry of John the Baptist (3.1–20)

 IV. The baptism and temptation of Jesus (3.21—4.13)

  V. Public ministry in Galilee (4.14—9.50)

 VI. The journey to Jerusalem (9.51—19.27)

 VII. The last week in Jerusalem (19.28—24.53)

THE GOSPEL ACCORDING TO

LUKE

I. *Introduction (1.1–4)*

1 Since many have been undertaken to set down an orderly account of the events that have been fulfilled among us, 2 just as they were handed on to us by those who from the beginning were eyewitnesses and servants of the word, 3 I too decided, after investigating everything carefully from the very first,[a] to write an orderly account for you, most excellent Theophilus, 4 so that you may know the truth concerning the things about which you have been instructed.

1.2
Heb 2.3;
1 Pet 5.1;
2 Pet 1.16;
1 Jn 1.1;
Mk 1.1;
Jn 15.27
1.3
Acts 11.4;
18.23; 1.1
1.4
Jn 20.31

II. *Birth and childhood of John the Baptist and of Jesus (1.5–2.52)*

A. *Birth of John the Baptist foretold (1.5–25)*

1.5
Mt 2.1;
1 Chr 24.10
1.6
Gen 7.1;
1 Kings 9.4;
2 Kings 20.3

5 In the days of King Herod of Judea, there was a priest named Zechariah, who belonged to the priestly order of Abijah. His wife was a descendant of Aaron, and her name was Elizabeth. 6 Both of them were righteous before God, living blamelessly according to all the commandments and regulations of the Lord. 7 But they had no children, because Elizabeth was barren, and both were getting on in years.

1.8
1 Chr 24.19;
2 Chr 8.14
1.9
Ex 30.7, 8;
1 Chr 23.13;
2 Chr 29.11
1.10
Lev 16.17
1.13
vv. 30, 60, 63
1.14
v. 58
1.15
Num 6.3;
Judg 13.4;
Lk 7.33;
Jer 1.5;
Gal 1.15
1.16
Mal 4.5, 6
1.17
Mt 11.14;
17.13
1.18
Gen 17.17;
v. 34

8 Once when he was serving as priest before God and his section on duty, 9 he was chosen by lot, according to the custom of the priesthood, to enter the sanctuary of the Lord and offer incense. 10 Now at the time of the incense offering, the whole assembly of the people was praying outside. 11 Then there appeared to him an angel of the Lord, standing at the right side of the altar of incense. 12 When Zechariah saw him, he was terrified; and fear overwhelmed him. 13 But the angel said to him, "Do not be afraid, Zechariah, for your prayer has been heard. Your wife Elizabeth will bear you a son, and you will name him John. 14 You will have joy and gladness, and many will rejoice at his birth, 15 for he will be great in the sight of the Lord. He must never drink wine or strong drink; even before his birth he will be filled with the Holy Spirit. 16 He will turn many of the people of Israel to the Lord their God. 17 With the spirit and power of Elijah he will go before him, to turn the hearts of parents to their children, and the disobedient to the wisdom of the righteous, to make ready a people prepared for the Lord." 18 Zechariah said to the angel, "How will I know that this is so? For I am an old man, and my wife is

a Or *for a long time*

1.3 *most excellent Theophilus.* The name means "one who loves God."
1.5 Both Zechariah and Elizabeth were members of the tribe of Levi and came from the line of Aaron. Many descendants of Levi were not eligible for the priesthood; according to Mosaic law only the "sons of Aaron" could be priests (Ex 28.1; Lev 21.1; Num 3.10). *Herod.* See note on Mt 2.1 on Herod the Great.
1.6 *Both of them were righteous before God.* Like Abraham their ancestor, they had been justified by their faith and were regenerated. They also lived righteous lives in accordance with the law of God. Also

like Abraham and Sarah, they had no children.
1.10 *incense offering.* See note on Ex 30.1.
1.11 *an angel.* This was Gabriel (v. 19).
1.13 *your prayer has been heard.* No doubt he and Elizabeth had prayed for children for a long time. Their prayers were heard, even though the answer was delayed in accordance with the plan of God.
1.17 *Elijah.* See note on Mal 4.5. *to turn the hearts of parents to their children, and the disobedient to the wisdom of the righteous.* John would soften adult hearts to become like little children's and change disobedient minds to the wisdom of faith.

getting on in years." ¹⁹ The angel replied, "I am Gabriel. I stand in the presence of God, and I have been sent to speak to you and to bring you this good news. ²⁰ But now, because you did not believe my words, which will be fulfilled in their time, you will become mute, unable to speak, until the day these things occur."

21   Meanwhile the people were waiting for Zechariah, and wondered at his delay in the sanctuary. ²² When he did come out, he could not speak to them, and they realized that he had seen a vision in the sanctuary. He kept motioning to them and remained unable to speak. ²³ When his time of service was ended, he went to his home.

24   After those days his wife Elizabeth conceived, and for five months she remained in seclusion. She said, ²⁵ "This is what the Lord has done for me when he looked favorably on me and took away the disgrace I have endured among my people."

B. *The birth of Jesus foretold: the annunciation*
(1.26–38; Matt. 1.18–25)

26   In the sixth month the angel Gabriel was sent by God to a town in Galilee called Nazareth, ²⁷ to a virgin engaged to a man whose name was Joseph, of the house of David. The virgin's name was Mary. ²⁸ And he came to her and said, "Greetings, favored one! The Lord is with you."ᵇ ²⁹ But she was much perplexed by his words and pondered what sort of greeting this might be. ³⁰ The angel said to her, "Do not be afraid, Mary, for you have found favor with God. ³¹ And now, you will conceive in your womb and bear a son, and you will name him Jesus. ³² He will be great, and will be called the Son of the Most High, and the Lord God will give to him the throne of his ancestor David. ³³ He will reign over the house of Jacob forever, and of his kingdom there will be no end." ³⁴ Mary said to the angel, "How can this be, since I am a virgin?"ᶜ ³⁵ The angel said to her, "The Holy Spirit will come upon you, and the power of the Most High will overshadow you; therefore the child to be bornᵈ will be holy; he will be called Son of God. ³⁶ And now, your relative Elizabeth in her old age has also conceived a son; and this is the sixth month for her who was said to be barren. ³⁷ For nothing will be impossible with God." ³⁸ Then Mary said, "Here am I, the servant of the Lord; let it be with me according to your word." Then the angel departed from her.

C. *Mary visits Elizabeth*
(1.39–45)

39   In those days Mary set out and went with haste to a Judean town in the hill country, ⁴⁰ where she entered the house of Zechariah and greeted Elizabeth. ⁴¹ When Elizabeth heard Mary's greeting, the child leaped in her womb. And Elizabeth was filled with the Holy Spirit ⁴² and exclaimed with a loud cry, "Blessed are you among women, and blessed is the fruit of your womb. ⁴³ And why has this happened to me, that the

---

1.19 Dan 8.16; 9.21-23; Mt 18.10
1.20 Ezek 3.26; 24.27
1.22 v. 62
1.25 Gen 30.23; Isa 4.1
1.26 Mt 2.23
1.27 Mt 1.16; v. 19
1.28 Dan 9.23; 10.19
1.31 Isa 7.14; Lk 2.21
1.32 Mk 5.7; Isa 9.6, 7; Jer 23.5; Rev 3.7
1.33 Dan 2.44; 7.14, 27; Mt 28.18; Heb 1.8
1.35 v. 32; Mk 1.24; Mt 4.3
1.37 Gen 18.14; Jer 32.17; Mt 19.26; Mk 10.27; Lk 18.27; Rom 4.21
1.39 v. 65
1.41 v. 67
1.42 Judg 5.24; Lk 11.27, 28
1.43 Lk 2.11

ᵇ Other ancient authorities add *Blessed are you among women*   ᶜ Gk *I do not know a man*   ᵈ Other ancient authorities add *of you*

1.19 Gabriel, Michael, and Satan are the only angels named in the Bible. Satan, of course, is a fallen angel; the other two, archangels of God.
1.27 *a virgin engaged to . . . Joseph.* See note on 2.5.
1.35 To believe the doctrine of the virgin birth of Jesus is important for three reasons: (1) the word of God clearly asserts it; (2) it undergirds the supernatural and miraculous; and (3) any denial of it destroys the whole fabric of the Christian faith by weakening the reality of the incarnation (God manifest in the flesh).

1.38 God does not violate the integrity of the human person. The Holy Spirit would not have come upon Mary without her consent. Here Mary responded positively to the message of the angel Gabriel and was willing to be *the servant of the Lord.*
1.41 Elizabeth was filled with the Holy Spirit, as were Mary (cf. v. 35), Zechariah (v. 67), and John the Baptist (while he was still in his mother's womb, v. 15). This foreshadowed the day when all believers would be filled with the Holy Spirit (Acts 2:1–4).

mother of my Lord comes to me? 44 For as soon as I heard the sound of your greeting, the child in my womb leaped for joy. 45 And blessed is she who believed that there would be*e* a fulfillment of what was spoken to her by the Lord."

D. *The song of Mary (1.46–56)*

46   And Mary*f* said,
"My soul magnifies the Lord,
47   and my spirit rejoices in God my Savior,
48   for he has looked with favor on the lowliness of his servant.
         Surely, from now on all generations will call me blessed;
49   for the Mighty One has done great things for me,
         and holy is his name.
50   His mercy is for those who fear him
         from generation to generation.
51   He has shown strength with his arm;
         he has scattered the proud in the thoughts of their hearts.
52   He has brought down the powerful from their thrones,
         and lifted up the lowly;
53   he has filled the hungry with good things,
         and sent the rich away empty.
54   He has helped his servant Israel,
         in remembrance of his mercy,
55   according to the promise he made to our ancestors,
         to Abraham and to his descendants forever."

56   And Mary remained with her about three months and then returned to her home.

E. *Birth of John the Baptist (1.57–66)*

57   Now the time came for Elizabeth to give birth, and she bore a son. 58 Her neighbors and relatives heard that the Lord had shown his great mercy to her, and they rejoiced with her.

59   On the eighth day they came to circumcise the child, and they were going to name him Zechariah after his father. 60 But his mother said, "No; he is to be called John." 61 They said to her, "None of your relatives has this name." 62 Then they began motioning to his father to find out what name he wanted to give him. 63 He asked for a writing tablet and wrote, "His name is John." And all of them were amazed. 64 Immediately his mouth was opened and his tongue freed, and he began to speak, praising God. 65 Fear came over all their neighbors, and all these things were talked about throughout the entire hill country of Judea. 66 All who heard them pondered them and said, "What then will this child become?" For, indeed, the hand of the Lord was with him.

e Or believed, for there will be   f Other ancient authorities read Elizabeth

Marginal references

1.46 — 1 Sam 2.1-10; Ps 34.2, 3
1.47 — Ps 35.9; 1 Tim 1.1; 2.3; Titus 2.10; Jude 25
1.48 — Ps 138.6; Lk 11.27
1.49 — Ps 71.19; 111.9
1.50 — Ps 103.17
1.51 — Ps 98.1; Isa 40.10; Ps 33.10; 1 Pet 5.5
1.52 — Job 5.11
1.53 — Ps 34.10
1.54 — Ps 98.3
1.55 — Gen 17.19; Ps 132.11; Gal 3.16
1.58 — Gen 19.19
1.59 — Gen 17.12; Lev 12.3
1.62 — v. 22
1.63 — v. 13
1.64 — v. 20
1.66 — Lk 2.19, 51; Gen 39.2; Acts 11.21

Study notes

1.47 *rejoices in God my Savior.* This profession by Mary makes it plain that Mary was not born without original sin, for she expresses the need for a divine Savior. How a sinful woman could bear a sinless son is part of the miracle of the incarnation.
1.57 Jesus said, "No one has arisen greater than John the Baptist" (Mt 11.11), yet little is known about his life. Aside from the Bible, only Josephus, the Jewish historian, says anything about him. Scripture tells us he was the son of Elizabeth and Zechariah. He was six months older than Jesus, born in an unnamed town in the hill country of Judea (v. 39). He was the forerunner who announced the coming of the Messiah, and his ministry was prophetic. He preached about the coming kingdom, stressing repentance and confession of sin. He baptized Jesus. Herod imprisoned him (ca. A.D. 28) because he preached against Herod's marriage to his brother Philip's wife, Herodias. Herodias and her daughter Salome forced Herod to behead John (Mk 6.14ff).
1.59,60 Circumcision, a sign of the old covenant, was performed on the eighth day after the birth of male babies, at which time they were named. This boy was named John, which means "God is gracious."
1.62 *motioning to his father.* Zechariah was apparently both deaf and speechless, for he had not heard what his wife had said.

F. The song of Zechariah (1.67–80)

67 Then his father Zechariah was filled with the Holy Spirit and spoke this prophecy:
68 "Blessed be the Lord God of Israel,
　for he has looked favorably on his people and redeemed them.
69 He has raised up a mighty savior[g] for us
　in the house of his servant David,
70 as he spoke through the mouth of his holy prophets from of old,
71 that we would be saved from our enemies and from the hand of all who hate us.
72 Thus he has shown the mercy promised to our ancestors,
　and has remembered his holy covenant,
73 the oath that he swore to our ancestor Abraham,
　to grant us 74 that we, being rescued from the hands of our enemies,
　might serve him without fear, 75 in holiness and righteousness before him all our days.
76 And you, child, will be called the prophet of the Most High;
　for you will go before the Lord to prepare his ways,
77 to give knowledge of salvation to his people
　by the forgiveness of their sins.
78 By the tender mercy of our God,
　the dawn from on high will break upon[h] us,
79 to give light to those who sit in darkness and in the shadow of death,
　to guide our feet into the way of peace."
80 The child grew and became strong in spirit, and he was in the wilderness until the day he appeared publicly to Israel.

G. The birth of Jesus the Christ (2.1–7; Matt. 1.18–25)

2 In those days a decree went out from Emperor Augustus that all the world should be registered. 2 This was the first registration and was taken while Quirinius was governor of Syria. 3 All went to their own towns to be registered. 4 Joseph also went from the town of Nazareth in Galilee to Judea, to the city of David called Bethlehem, because he was descended from the house and family of David. 5 He went to be registered with Mary, to whom he was engaged and who was expecting a child. 6 While they were there, the time came for her to deliver her child. 7 And she gave birth to her firstborn son and wrapped him in bands of cloth, and laid him in a manger, because there was no place for them in the inn.

g Gk a horn of salvation　h Other ancient authorities read has broken upon

---

Cross-references (margin):

1.67 v. 41; Joel 2.28
1.68 Ps 72.18; 111.9; Lk 7.16
1.69 Ps 18.2; 89.17; 132.17; Ezek 29.21
1.70 Jer 23.5; Dan 9.24; Acts 3.21; Rom 1.2; Mic 7.20; Ps 105.8, 9; 106.45; Ezek 16.60
1.74 Rom 6.18; Heb 9.14
1.75 Eph 4.24; Titus 2.12
1.76 Mal 3.1; 4.5; Mt 11.9, 10
1.77 Mk 1.4
1.79 Mt 9.2; Mk 4.16; Acts 26.18
1.80 Lk 2.40, 52
2.1 Lk 3.1
2.4 Lk 1.27

1.67 Zechariah was filled with the Holy Spirit. See note on v. 41.

1.73 the oath. When God swore to Abraham that he would keep the divine covenant, he swore by himself, since there was no one greater by whom God could swear (see note on Heb 6.17).

2.1ff Luke was an able historian who grounds his historical account of Jesus in world history. Though the accuracy of Quirinius as governor of Syria has been widely questioned by critics of the Bible, there is no good reason to maintain that Luke was erroneous.

2.5 to whom he was engaged. Mary and Joseph were engaged but not yet married. That period of engagement was not the same as engagement in modern America, for it was a legal arrangement that could only be broken by divorce. Mary's pregnancy would have been construed as adultery and she could have been stoned to death. God protected her in her innocence and used Joseph as her shield against any charge of misconduct (see note on Mt 1.19).

2.6 the time came for her to deliver her child. Jesus, the Prince of Peace, was born in the fullness of time (cf. Gal 4.4). It came during a time of universal peace and when the whole world was united under the Greek language. At that time, Judah was under Roman control, so that the sceptre had departed from Israel (cf. Gen 49.10).

2.7 bands of cloth, i.e., clean cloths wrapped around the newborn child according to the custom of that day. A manger was a feeding trough for animals. If Jesus was born in a cave (as some suppose), it was probably cut out of a rock wall.

H. *The angels and the shepherds (2.8–20)*

8 In that region there were shepherds living in the fields, keeping watch over their flock by night. **9** Then an angel of the Lord stood before them, and the glory of the Lord shone around them, and they were terrified. **10** But the angel said to them, "Do not be afraid; for see — I am bringing you good news of great joy for all the people: **11** to you is born this day in the city of David a Savior, who is the Messiah,[i] the Lord. **12** This will be a sign for you: you will find a child wrapped in bands of cloth and lying in a manger." **13** And suddenly there was with the angel a multitude of the heavenly host,[j] praising God and saying,

14   "Glory to God in the highest heaven,
        and on earth peace among those whom he favors!"[k]

15 When the angels had left them and gone into heaven, the shepherds said to one another, "Let us go now to Bethlehem and see this thing that has taken place, which the Lord has made known to us." **16** So they went with haste and found Mary and Joseph, and the child lying in the manger. **17** When they saw this, they made known what had been told them about this child; **18** and all who heard it were amazed at what the shepherds told them. **19** But Mary treasured all these words and pondered them in her heart. **20** The shepherds returned, glorifying and praising God for all they had heard and seen, as it had been told them.

I. *The circumcision (2.21)*

21 After eight days had passed, it was time to circumcise the child; and he was called Jesus, the name given by the angel before he was conceived in the womb.

J. *The presentation in the temple (2.22–28)*

22 When the time came for their purification according to the law of Moses, they brought him up to Jerusalem to present him to the Lord **23** (as it is written in the law of the Lord, "Every firstborn male shall be designated as holy to the Lord"), **24** and they offered a sacrifice according to what is stated in the law of the Lord, "a pair of turtledoves or two young pigeons."

25 Now there was a man in Jerusalem whose name was Simeon;[l] this man was righteous and devout, looking forward to the consolation of Israel, and the Holy Spirit rested on him. **26** It had been revealed to him by the Holy Spirit that he would not see death before he had seen the Lord's Messiah.[m] **27** Guided by the Spirit, Simeon[n] came into the temple; and when the parents brought in the child Jesus, to do for him what was customary under the law, **28** Simeon[o] took him in his arms and praised God, saying,

---

2.9 Lk 1.11; Acts 5.19
2.10 Mt 14.27
2.11 Jn 4.42; Mt 1.16; 16.16; Lk 1.43; Acts 2.36
2.12 1 Sam 2.34; 2 Kings 19.29; Isa 7.14
2.13 Dan 7.10; Rev 5.11
2.14 Isa 57.19; Lk 1.79; Rom 5.1; Eph 1.9; Phil 2.13
2.19 v. 51
2.20 Mt 9.8
2.21 Lk 1.59; 1.31
2.22 Lev 12.2-6
2.23 Ex 13.2, 12; Num 3.13
2.25 v. 38; Lk 23.51
2.26 Ps 89.48; Heb 11.5
2.27 v. 22

---

[i] Or *the Christ*   [j] Gk *army*   [k] Other ancient authorities read *peace, goodwill among people*   [l] Gk *Symeon*
[m] Or *the Lord's Christ*   [n] Gk *In the Spirit, he*   [o] Gk *he*

2.10 *all the people.* Even though Scripture clearly teaches that not all people will be saved, all must be reached with the good news. Thus the gospel is universal. Various passages of the Bible imply the importance of missionary outreach to all people: (1) the universal message at the birth of Jesus (cf. vv. 29–32); (2) the missionary thrust of the Lord's prayer ("your will be done, on earth as it is in heaven," Mt 6.10); (3) the great commission of our Lord (Mt 28.18–20; Mk 16.15; Lk 24.45–49; Jn 20.21; Acts 1:8); and (4) the first apostolic sermon ("for you . . . and . . . everyone whom the Lord our God calls to him," Acts 2.39).
2.14,15 The angels chanted their hallelujah song of praise. God received the honor and people gained the joy of the Savior's birth. The shepherds went immedi-

ately to Bethlehem. They went in faith, for they did not say, "Let us go and see *if*," but "Let us go and see *this thing*." After doing so, they spread the good news abroad for all to hear.
2.21 Through this rite of circumcision, Jesus identified himself with God's covenant people. He did not need circumcision (i.e., the cutting away of human flesh), because although he was made after the likeness of sinful flesh, he himself was without sin.
2.25 *Simeon* is nowhere else mentioned in the Bible. He was righteous and devout, waiting with expectancy for the coming of the Messiah. Best of all, he was taught, led, and filled by the Holy Spirit. *the consolation of Israel*, i.e., the Messiah, who would bring God's people comfort.

K. The song of Simeon (2.29–35)

29 "Master, now you are dismissing your servant[p] in peace,
        according to your word;
30 for my eyes have seen your salvation,
31   which you have prepared in the presence of all peoples,
32 a light for revelation to the Gentiles
        and for glory to your people Israel."

33 And the child's father and mother were amazed at what was being
said about him. 34 Then Simeon[q] blessed them and said to his mother
Mary, "This child is destined for the falling and the rising of many in
Israel, and to be a sign that will be opposed 35 so that the inner thoughts
of many will be revealed—and a sword will pierce your own soul too."

L. The adoration of Anna (2.36–40)

36 There was also a prophet, Anna[r] the daughter of Phanuel, of the
tribe of Asher. She was of a great age, having lived with her husband seven
years after her marriage, 37 then as a widow to the age of eighty-four. She
never left the temple but worshiped there with fasting and prayer night
and day. 38 At that moment she came, and began to praise God and to
speak about the child[s] to all who were looking for the redemption of
Jerusalem.
39 When they had finished everything required by the law of the
Lord, they returned to Galilee, to their own town of Nazareth. 40 The
child grew and became strong, filled with wisdom; and the favor of God
was upon him.

M. The boy Jesus in the temple (2.41–52)

41 Now every year his parents went to Jerusalem for the festival of
the Passover. 42 And when he was twelve years old, they went up as usual
for the festival. 43 When the festival was ended and they started to return,
the boy Jesus stayed behind in Jerusalem, but his parents did not know
it. 44 Assuming that he was in the group of travelers, they went a day's
journey. Then they started to look for him among their relatives and
friends. 45 When they did not find him, they returned to Jerusalem to
search for him. 46 After three days they found him in the temple, sitting
among the teachers, listening to them and asking them questions. 47 And
all who heard him were amazed at his understanding and his answers.
48 When his parents[t] saw him they were astonished; and his mother said
to him, "Child, why have you treated us like this? Look, your father and
I have been searching for you in great anxiety." 49 He said to them, "Why
were you searching for me? Did you not know that I must be in my
Father's house?"[u] 50 But they did not understand what he said to them.
51 Then he went down with them and came to Nazareth, and was obedient
to them. His mother treasured all these things in her heart.

[p] Gk slave   [q] Gk Symeon   [r] Gk Hanna   [s] Gk him   [t] Gk they   [u] Or be about my Father's interests?

2.29 v. 26
2.30 Isa 52.10; Lk 3.6
2.32 Isa 42.6; 49.6; Acts 13.47; 26.23
2.34 Mt 21.44; 1 Cor 1.23, 24; 2 Cor 2.16; 1 Pet 2.7, 8
2.36 Acts 21.9; Josh 19.24; 1 Tim 5.9
2.37 Acts 13.3; 1 Tim 5.5
2.38 v. 25; Lk 24.21
2.39 v. 51
2.40 v. 52; Lk 1.80
2.41 Ex 23.15; Deut 16.1-6
2.47 Mt 7.28; Mk 1.22; Lk 4.22, 32; Jn 7.15, 46
2.48 Mk 3.31-35
2.49 Jn 2.16
2.50 Mk 9.32; Lk 9.45
2.51 vv. 19, 39

2.34,35 Simeon spoke a prophetic word to Mary
about her son. He was *destined for the falling and the
rising of many in Israel.* Jesus would be a suffering
servant, and a sword would pass through Mary's own
soul too. This prophetic word was fulfilled when she
saw him dying on the cross.
2.36 *Anna* was a prophet whose work was like that
of the male prophets. She belonged to the tribe of
Asher, one of the ten tribes dispersed in the Assyrian
captivity. While the tribe never returned officially to
Palestine, her family had come back and had remembered their genealogy. She probably was more than
one hundred years old when Joseph and Mary
brought Jesus to the temple. Anna was a devout and

saintly woman who joined in praise to God for Jesus,
whom she looked upon as the Messiah.
2.41ff Luke records the only incident of Jesus between his birth and the beginning of his public ministry at age thirty. He sat in the temple among the
teachers of the law, who were amazed at his understanding and questions.
2.49ff *Did you not know. . . .?* Even at this tender age
Jesus had an inner awareness about himself, his relationship with God, and his role as Savior of the world.
What he said made an indelible impression on the
mind and heart of Mary, for she "treasured all these
things in her heart."

2.52
v. 40;
1 Sam 2.26
52 And Jesus increased in wisdom and in years,^{v} and in divine and human favor.

III. *The ministry of John the Baptist*
(3.1–20; Matt. 3.1–12; Mark 1.1–8; John 1.6–8, 19–28)

3.1
Mt 27.2;
14.1
3 In the fifteenth year of the reign of Emperor Tiberius, when Pontius Pilate was governor of Judea, and Herod was ruler^w of Galilee, and his brother Philip ruler^w of the region of Ituraea and Trachonitis, and Lysanias ruler^w of Abilene, 2 during the high priesthood of Annas and Caiaphas, the word of God came to John son of Zechariah in the wilderness. 3 He went into all the region around the Jordan, proclaiming a baptism of repentance for the forgiveness of sins, 4 as it is written in the book of the words of the prophet Isaiah,

3.2
Jn 11.49;
18.13;
Acts 4.6;
Mt 26.3
3.4
Isa 40.3-5

"The voice of one crying out in the wilderness:
'Prepare the way of the Lord,
make his paths straight.
5 Every valley shall be filled,
and every mountain and hill shall be made low,
and the crooked shall be made straight,
and the rough ways made smooth;
6 and all flesh shall see the salvation of God.' "

3.6
Ps 98.2;
Isa 52.10;
Lk 2.30
3.7
Mt 12.34;
23.33
3.8
Jn 8.33, 39
3.9
Mt 7.19;
Heb 6.7, 8

7 John said to the crowds that came out to be baptized by him, "You brood of vipers! Who warned you to flee from the wrath to come? 8 Bear fruits worthy of repentance. Do not begin to say to yourselves, 'We have Abraham as our ancestor'; for I tell you, God is able from these stones to raise up children to Abraham. 9 Even now the ax is lying at the root of the trees; every tree therefore that does not bear good fruit is cut down and thrown into the fire."

3.10
Acts 2.37
3.11
Jas 2.15, 16
3.12
Lk 7.29
3.13
Lk 19.8
3.14
Ex 23.1;
Lev 19.11

10 And the crowds asked him, "What then should we do?" 11 In reply he said to them, "Whoever has two coats must share with anyone who has none; and whoever has food must do likewise." 12 Even tax collectors came to be baptized, and they asked him, "Teacher, what should we do?" 13 He said to them, "Collect no more than the amount prescribed for you." 14 Soldiers also asked him, "And we, what should we do?" He said to them, "Do not extort money from anyone by threats or false accusation, and be satisfied with your wages."

3.15
Acts 13.25

3.16
Acts 1.5;
11.16; 19.4
3.17
Isa 30.24;
Mic 4.12;
Mt 13.30

15 As the people were filled with expectation, and all were questioning in their hearts concerning John, whether he might be the Messiah,^{x} 16 John answered all of them by saying, "I baptize you with water; but one who is more powerful than I is coming; I am not worthy to untie the thong of his sandals. He will baptize you with^y the Holy Spirit and fire. 17 His winnowing fork is in his hand, to clear his threshing floor and to gather the wheat into his granary; but the chaff he will burn with unquenchable fire."

---

v Or *in stature*   *w* Gk *tetrarch*   *x* Or *the Christ*   *y* Or *in*

2.52 In his humanity, Jesus developed in human wisdom, human stature, and human associations.
3.1 *Tiberius*, the adopted son of the emperor Augustus, reigned from A.D. 14–37. *Pilate*. See note on Mk 15.1.
3.2 *the word of God came to John*. The word of God had come to the prophets of old. It now came to John, though we are not told how. Whether he got it through his father, from an angel, in a dream, by a vision, or through a voice from heaven, we do not know. When God's word came, John began to preach it in the power of the Holy Spirit.
3.3 *proclaiming a baptism of repentance for the forgiveness of sins*. John assured the listeners that their sins

would be pardoned and their lives changed if they repented. If they refused to repent, however, they would face "the wrath to come" (v. 7).
3.4 *The voice of one crying out in the wilderness.* John fulfilled Isa 40.3, for through him the proud were humbled, the humble enriched, sinners converted, difficulties removed, and all flesh could see the salvation of the Lord.
3.16 *I am not worthy to untie the thong of his sandals,* i.e., "I am not worthy of being his slave." *He will baptize.* John said he baptized with water but Jesus would baptize with the Holy Spirit and fire. This prophecy was fulfilled at Pentecost when the Holy Spirit came upon the followers of Jesus (see Acts 2).

18 So, with many other exhortations, he proclaimed the good news to the people. 19 But Herod the ruler,[z] who had been rebuked by him because of Herodias, his brother's wife, and because of all the evil things that Herod had done, 20 added to them all by shutting up John in prison.

3.19
Mt 14.3, 4;
Mk 6.17, 18

IV. The baptism and temptation of Jesus (3.21–4.13)

A. The baptism of Jesus (3.21,22; Matt. 3.13–17; Mark 1.9–11)

21 Now when all the people were baptized, and when Jesus also had been baptized and was praying, the heaven was opened, 22 and the Holy Spirit descended upon him in bodily form like a dove. And a voice came from heaven, "You are my Son, the Beloved;[a] with you I am well pleased."[b]

3.21
Lk 5.16;
6.12; 9.18,
28; 11.1
3.22
Ps 2.7;
Isa 42.1;
Lk 9.35;
Acts 10.38;
2 Pet 1.17

B. The genealogy of Jesus (3.23–38; cf. Matt. 1.1–17)

23 Jesus was about thirty years old when he began his work. He was the son (as was thought) of Joseph son of Heli, 24 son of Matthat, son of Levi, son of Melchi, son of Jannai, son of Joseph, 25 son of Mattathias, son of Amos, son of Nahum, son of Esli, son of Naggai, 26 son of Maath, son of Mattathias, son of Semein, son of Josech, son of Joda, 27 son of Joanan, son of Rhesa, son of Zerubbabel, son of Shealtiel,[c] son of Neri, 28 son of Melchi, son of Addi, son of Cosam, son of Elmadam, son of Er, 29 son of Joshua, son of Eliezer, son of Jorim, son of Matthat, son of Levi, 30 son of Simeon, son of Judah, son of Joseph, son of Jonam, son of Eliakim, 31 son of Melea, son of Menna, son of Mattatha, son of Nathan, son of David, 32 son of Jesse, son of Obed, son of Boaz, son of Sala,[d] son of Nahshon, 33 son of Amminadab, son of Admin, son of Arni,[e] son of Hezron, son of Perez, son of Judah, 34 son of Jacob, son of Isaac, son of Abraham, son of Terah, son of Nahor, 35 son of Serug, son of Reu, son of Peleg, son of Eber, son of Shelah, 36 son of Cainan, son of Arphaxad, son of Shem, son of Noah, son of Lamech, 37 son of Methuselah, son of Enoch, son of Jared, son of Mahalaleel, son of Cainan, 38 son of Enos, son of Seth, son of Adam, son of God.

3.23
Mt 4.17;
Acts 1.1;
Jn 8.57;
Lk 1.27

3.27
Mt 1.12

3.31
2 Sam 5.14;
1 Chr 3.5
3.32
Ruth 4.18ff;
1 Chr 2.10ff
3.34
Gen 11.24, 26
3.36
Gen 11.12;
5.6ff
3.38
Gen 5.1, 2

C. The wilderness temptation of Jesus (4.1–13; Matt. 4.1–11; Mark 1.12,13)

4 Jesus, full of the Holy Spirit, returned from the Jordan and was led by the Spirit in the wilderness, 2 where for forty days he was tempted by the devil. He ate nothing at all during those days, and when they were over, he was famished. 3 The devil said to him, "If you are the Son of God,

4.1
v. 14;
Lk 2.27
4.2
Ex 34.28;
1 Kings 19.8

z Gk tetrarch a Or my beloved Son b Other ancient authorities read You are my Son, today I have begotten you c Gk Salathiel d Other ancient authorities read Salmon e Other ancient authorities read Amminadab, son of Aram; others vary widely

---

3.20 Luke mentions the imprisonment of John before he mentions the baptism of Jesus by John. He does this to finish the historical data about John, although his imprisonment occurred one year after the baptism of Jesus.
3.22 In the baptism of Jesus we note the obvious presence of the Trinity. The Father spoke, acknowledging Jesus as his Son. The Holy Spirit descended upon Jesus in the form of a dove. This event marked the beginning of the public ministry of Jesus.
3.23–38 Luke traces Jesus' genealogy through Mary, whereas Matthew traced it through Joseph, his legal father. In accordance with Jewish legal custom, Luke calls Joseph the son of Heli (i.e., he was the husband of Heli's daughter). Luke carefully notes that Jesus was not really Joseph's physical son. For

Luke to trace Mary's genealogy is appropriate, for he shows a consistent interest in the women who followed Jesus. Matthew traces the genealogy of Jesus to Abraham, while Luke takes it all the way back to Adam.
4.1 was led by the Spirit. Not only Jesus but all those who believe in him can experience being led by the Spirit (Rom 8.9–16). When we are so led, we can be confident that we are safe in the will of God and that we will be sustained and helped by his divine power.
4.2 Though Jesus was tempted by the devil (Mt 4.1; Mk 1.12,13), he never sinned (2 Cor 5.21; Heb 4.15; 1 Jn 3.5). In his humanity he could have sinned but did not. In his deity, however, it was impossible for him to sin.

4.4
Deut 8.3
command this stone to become a loaf of bread." 4 Jesus answered him, "It is written, 'One does not live by bread alone.' "

5 Then the devil^f led him up and showed him in an instant all the kingdoms of the world. 6 And the devil^f said to him, "To you I will give their glory and all this authority; for it has been given over to me, and I give it to anyone I please. 7 If you, then, will worship me, it will all be yours." 8 Jesus answered him, "It is written,

4.6
Jn 12.31;
14.30; 1 Jn
5.19
4.8
Deut 6.13

'Worship the Lord your God,
and serve only him.' "

9 Then the devil^f took him to Jerusalem, and placed him on the pinnacle of the temple, saying to him, "If you are the Son of God, throw yourself down from here, 10 for it is written,

4.10
Ps 91.11, 12

'He will command his angels concerning you,
to protect you,'

11 and

'On their hands they will bear you up,
so that you will not dash your foot against a stone.' "

4.12
Deut 6.16
4.13
Jn 14.30;
Heb 4.15

12 Jesus answered him, "It is said, 'Do not put the Lord your God to the test.' " 13 When the devil had finished every test, he departed from him until an opportune time.

V. Public ministry in Galilee (4.14–9.50)

A. Jesus returns to Galilee
(4.14,15; Matt. 4.12–17; Mark 1.14,15; John 4.43–45)

4.14
Mt 9.26
4.15
Mt 9.35;
11.1

14 Then Jesus, filled with the power of the Spirit, returned to Galilee, and a report about him spread through all the surrounding country. 15 He began to teach in their synagogues and was praised by everyone.

B. Jesus' first rejection at Nazareth (4.16–30)

4.16
Mt 13.54;
Mk 6.1;
Acts 13.14-16

16 When he came to Nazareth, where he had been brought up, he went to the synagogue on the sabbath day, as was his custom. He stood up to read, 17 and the scroll of the prophet Isaiah was given to him. He unrolled the scroll and found the place where it was written:

4.18
Isa 61.1, 2;
Mt 12.18

18 "The Spirit of the Lord is upon me,
because he has anointed me
to bring good news to the poor.
He has sent me to proclaim release to the captives
and recovery of sight to the blind,
to let the oppressed go free,

4.19
Lev 25.10
4.20
v. 17
4.22
Ps 45.2;
Mt 13;54,
55;
Mk 6.2, 3;
Jn 6.42; 7.15

19 to proclaim the year of the Lord's favor."

20 And he rolled up the scroll, gave it back to the attendant, and sat down. The eyes of all in the synagogue were fixed on him. 21 Then he began to say to them, "Today this scripture has been fulfilled in your hearing." 22 All spoke well of him and were amazed at the gracious words that came

^f Gk he

4.4ff In this threefold temptation certain truths are evident: (1) Jesus would make no compact with the devil; (2) he would perform no miracles until he began preaching, for miracles ratified what he taught; (3) he would work no miracles for himself because he came to suffer, not to please himself; (4) he gladly delayed the proof of his being the Son of God until the proper time; (5) he would not act independently from his Father.
4.13 Christ emerged the victor here. The devil left to work out other plans to entrap and defeat Jesus, having failed to induce him to sin.
4.14ff Jesus, filled with the power of the Spirit, now

began his public ministry, teaching the people and healing them of their diseases.
4.19 *to proclaim the year of the Lord's favor,* i.e., "to give blessings to all who come to him." This phrase implied his own incarnation and atoning death on the cross. When Jesus closed the scroll of Isaiah, he stopped before adding "and the day of vengeance of our God" (Isa 61.2). Christ was proclaiming salvation here, though he knew that at his second advent God's wrath awaited all who refused to believe in him (cf. Mt 13.40–42,49,50; 25.1–46).
4.22 *Is not this Joseph's son?* The listeners heard things they never heard before. They found it diffi-

from his mouth. They said, "Is not this Joseph's son?" 23 He said to them, "Doubtless you will quote to me this proverb, 'Doctor, cure yourself!' And you will say, 'Do here also in your hometown the things that we have heard you did at Capernaum.' " 24 And he said, "Truly I tell you, no prophet is accepted in the prophet's hometown. 25 But the truth is, there were many widows in Israel in the time of Elijah, when the heaven was shut up three years and six months, and there was a severe famine over all the land; 26 yet Elijah was sent to none of them except to a widow at Zarephath in Sidon. 27 There were also many lepers[g] in Israel in the time of the prophet Elisha, and none of them was cleansed except Naaman the Syrian." 28 When they heard this, all in the synagogue were filled with rage. 29 They got up, drove him out of the town, and led him to the brow of the hill on which their town was built, so that they might hurl him off the cliff. 30 But he passed through the midst of them and went on his way.

C. Jesus performing miracles at Capernaum (4.31–44)

1. The casting out of the unclean spirit (4.31–37; Mark 1.21–28)

31 He went down to Capernaum, a city in Galilee, and was teaching them on the sabbath. 32 They were astounded at his teaching, because he spoke with authority. 33 In the synagogue there was a man who had the spirit of an unclean demon, and he cried out with a loud voice, 34 "Let us alone! What have you to do with us, Jesus of Nazareth? Have you come to destroy us? I know who you are, the Holy One of God." 35 But Jesus rebuked him, saying, "Be silent, and come out of him!" When the demon had thrown him down before them, he came out of him without having done him any harm. 36 They were all amazed and kept saying to one another, "What kind of utterance is this? For with authority and power he commands the unclean spirits, and out they come!" 37 And a report about him began to reach every place in the region.

2. Peter's mother-in-law healed (4.38,39; Matt. 8.14–17; Mark 1.29–34)

38 After leaving the synagogue he entered Simon's house. Now Simon's mother-in-law was suffering from a high fever, and they asked him about her. 39 Then he stood over her and rebuked the fever, and it left her. Immediately she got up and began to serve them.

3. Healing the sick; casting out demons (4.40–44; Matt. 8.16–17; Mark 1.32–34)

40 As the sun was setting, all those who had any who were sick with various kinds of diseases brought them to him; and he laid his hands on each of them and cured them. 41 Demons also came out of many, shouting, "You are the Son of God!" But he rebuked them and would not allow them to speak, because they knew that he was the Messiah.[h]

42 At daybreak he departed and went into a deserted place. And the crowds were looking for him; and when they reached him, they wanted

g The terms *leper* and *leprosy* can refer to several diseases   h Or *the Christ*

4.23
Mk 1.21ff;
2.1ff; v. 16
4.24
Mt 13.57;
Mk 6.4;
Jn 4.44
4.25
1 Kings 17.1,
8-16; 18.1;
Jas 5.17, 18
4.27
2 Kings 5.1-14
4.29
Num 15.35;
Acts 7.58;
Heb 13.12
4.30
Jn 8.49;
10.39

4.31
Mt 4.13
4.32
Mt 7.28;
Mk 11.18;
Jn 7.46
4.34
v. 41;
Ps 16.10;
Dan 9.24
4.35
vv. 39, 41;
Mt 8.26;
Mk 4.39;
Lk 8.24
4.36
v. 32
4.37
v. 14

4.39
vv. 35, 41

4.40
Mk 5.23;
Mt 4.23
4.41
Mt 4.3; 8.4

4.42
Mk 1.35-38

---

cult to believe that a son of Joseph could say these things. God, through Joseph, had covered Mary's virgin birth with dignity and kept her from scandal, public disgrace, and humiliation.
4.28–30 From the beginning we hear how "he came to what was his own, and his own people did not accept him" (Jn 1.11). The Jews could not stand hearing that God was interested in the Gentiles and would save some of them. Jesus escaped from their wrath because his hour had not yet come.

4.32 *he spoke with authority.* The word "authority" (Gk. *exousia*) indicates that Jesus exercised the authority of absolute truth, for he was God. The Jewish scribes and rabbis appealed only to the traditions of their human ancestors. But Jesus' authority came from God and his words were final. From them there was no appeal.
4.36 Christ cast out devils, who knew full well that he was God, with authority and power. He muzzled them and delivered the victims unhurt (cf. v. 41).

to prevent him from leaving them. 43 But he said to them, "I must proclaim the good news of the kingdom of God to the other cities also; for I was sent for this purpose." 44 So he continued proclaiming the message in the synagogues of Judea. *i*

4.44
Mt 4.18-22;
Mk 1.16-20;
Jn 1.40-42

D. The call of the first disciples
(5.1–11; Matt. 4.18–22; Mark 1.16–20)

5 Once while Jesus*j* was standing beside the lake of Gennesaret, and the crowd was pressing in on him to hear the word of God, 2 he saw two boats there at the shore of the lake; the fishermen had gone out of them and were washing their nets. 3 He got into one of the boats, the one belonging to Simon, and asked him to put out a little way from the shore. Then he sat down and taught the crowds from the boat. 4 When he had finished speaking, he said to Simon, "Put out into the deep water and let down your nets for a catch." 5 Simon answered, "Master, we have worked all night long but have caught nothing. Yet if you say so, I will let down the nets." 6 When they had done this, they caught so many fish that their nets were beginning to break. 7 So they signaled their partners in the other boat to come and help them. And they came and filled both boats, so that they began to sink. 8 But when Simon Peter saw it, he fell down at Jesus' knees, saying, "Go away from me, Lord, for I am a sinful man!" 9 For he and all who were with him were amazed at the catch of fish that they had taken; 10 and so also were James and John, sons of Zebedee, who were partners with Simon. Then Jesus said to Simon, "Do not be afraid; from now on you will be catching people." 11 When they had brought their boats to shore, they left everything and followed him.

5.3
Mt 13.1, 2;
Mk 4.1
5.4
Jn 21.6
5.5
Lk 8.24, 45;
9.33, 49;
17.13

5.10
Mt 14.27
5.11
v. 28;
Mt 19.29

E. The leper cleansed (5.12–16; Matt. 8.1–4; Mark 1.40–45)

12 Once, when he was in one of the cities, there was a man covered with leprosy. *k* When he saw Jesus, he bowed with his face to the ground and begged him, "Lord, if you choose, you can make me clean." 13 Then Jesus*j* stretched out his hand, touched him, and said, "I do choose. Be made clean." Immediately the leprosy*k* left him. 14 And he ordered him to tell no one. "Go," he said, "and show yourself to the priest and, as Moses commanded, make an offering for your cleansing, for a testimony to them." 15 But now more than ever the word about Jesus*l* spread abroad; many crowds would gather to hear him and to be cured of their diseases. 16 But he would withdraw to deserted places and pray.

5.12
Lk 17.11-19

5.15
Mt 9.26;
Lk 4.14, 37
5.16
Mt 14.23;
Mk 6.46;
Lk 3.21;
6.12; 9.18,
28; 11.1

F. A paralytic healed and forgiven
(5.17–26; Matt. 9.1–8; Mark 2.1–12)

17 One day, while he was teaching, Pharisees and teachers of the law

5.17
Mt 15.1;
Mk 5.30;
Lk 6.19

i Other ancient authorities read *Galilee* *j* Gk *he* *k* The terms *leper* and *leprosy* can refer to several diseases *l* Gk *him*

5.1 *Gennesaret,* i.e., the Sea of Galilee.
5.11 *they left everything.* Christ called Peter, James, and John. So powerful and effective was that call that they surrendered everything to the Lordship of Jesus, not knowing where it would lead them or what they might be called upon to do or to suffer.
5.12 Leprosy was a common disease among the Jews. It was transmissible and incurable at that time. Lepers were cut off from their people, could not occupy the office of the priesthood, and were obliged to shout out that they were unclean (Lev 13.45). The priests acted as the physicians to diagnose the disease and to watch it carefully. Leprosy from the biblical perspective is representative of sin, which cuts people off from God until cleansed. Jesus is the only cure for the leprosy of sin.
5.14 Jesus honored the Jewish law by commanding the healed leper to show himself to the priest and get clearance, since he was no longer leprous. That such a person could be made instantaneously whole was nothing short of a miracle. The priest, upon seeing this, should have known that Jesus was no mere human being.
5.17 *Pharisees and teachers of the law,* i.e., Jews in positions of authority who heard of Jesus' fame and came to investigate.

were sitting near by (they had come from every village of Galilee and Judea and from Jerusalem); and the power of the Lord was with him to heal.*m* 18 Just then some men came, carrying a paralyzed man on a bed. They were trying to bring him in and lay him before Jesus;*n* 19 but finding no way to bring him in because of the crowd, they went up on the roof and let him down with his bed through the tiles into the middle of the crowd*o* in front of Jesus. 20 When he saw their faith, he said, "Friend,*p* your sins are forgiven you." 21 Then the scribes and the Pharisees began to question, "Who is this who is speaking blasphemies? Who can forgive sins but God alone?" 22 When Jesus perceived their questionings, he answered them, "Why do you raise such questions in your hearts? 23 Which is easier, to say, 'Your sins are forgiven you,' or to say, 'Stand up and walk'? 24 But so that you may know that the Son of Man has authority on earth to forgive sins" — he said to the one who was paralyzed — "I say to you, stand up and take your bed and go to your home." 25 Immediately he stood up before them, took what he had been lying on, and went to his home, glorifying God. 26 Amazement seized all of them, and they glorified God and were filled with awe, saying, "We have seen strange things today."

G. The call of Levi (Matthew)
(5.27–32; Matt. 9.9–13; Mark 2.13–17)

27   After this he went out and saw a tax collector named Levi, sitting at the tax booth; and he said to him, "Follow me." 28 And he got up, left everything, and followed him.

29   Then Levi gave a great banquet for him in his house; and there was a large crowd of tax collectors and others sitting at the table*q* with them. 30 The Pharisees and their scribes were complaining to his disciples, saying, "Why do you eat and drink with tax collectors and sinners?" 31 Jesus answered, "Those who are well have no need of a physician, but those who are sick; 32 I have come to call not the righteous but sinners to repentance."

H. The question about fasting
(5.33–39; Matt. 9.14–17; Mark 2.18–22)

33   Then they said to him, "John's disciples, like the disciples of the Pharisees, frequently fast and pray, but your disciples eat and drink." 34 Jesus said to them, "You cannot make wedding guests fast while the bridegroom is with them, can you? 35 The days will come when the bridegroom will be taken away from them, and then they will fast in those days." 36 He also told them a parable: "No one tears a piece from a new garment and sews it on an old garment; otherwise the new will be torn, and the piece from the new will not match the old. 37 And no one puts new wine into old wineskins; otherwise the new wine will burst the skins and will be spilled, and the skins will be destroyed. 38 But new wine must

---

m Other ancient authorities read *was present to heal them*   *n* Gk *him*   *o* Gk *into the midst*   *p* Gk *Man*   *q* Gk *reclining*

Cross-references:

5.19 Mt 24.17
5.20 Lk 7.48, 49
5.21 Isa 43.25
5.26 Lk 7.16
5.28 v. 11
5.29 Lk 15.1
5.30 Acts 23.9
5.32 1 Tim 1.15
5.33 Lk 7.18; Jn 3.25, 26
5.35 Lk 9.22; 17.22

5.21 *Who can forgive sins, but God alone?* Jesus had the power on earth to forgive sins and his healings were proof of that power. The Jewish leaders asked the right question here. If God alone can forgive sins and Jesus did this, then he must be God.

5.27 *Levi*, i.e., Matthew, a tax collector who became one of Jesus' disciples (cf. Mt 10.3). Tax collectors were looked upon as extortioners by the Jews, and they hated them (3.13; 18.11; 19.8). Some became quite wealthy (19.2). Jesus was criticized for associating with them (Mt 9.11; 11.19). Some of them responded to the preaching of John the Baptist and were baptized (3.12; 7.29; Mt 21.32). Some of them heard Jesus and became believers (15.1; Mt 21.31; Mk 2.15).

5.35 *will be taken away from them.* This oblique expression refers to the death of Jesus Christ.

5.36ff The parables of the new garment and the new wine in old wineskins teach the same lesson. The kingdom of God cannot be mixed with the old legalistic Jewish system. The truth of this was demonstrated after Pentecost when the church and synagogue finally had to be separated, for the Jewish community continued to trust in works of merit while the church preached the message of grace.

be put into fresh wineskins. ³⁹ And no one after drinking old wine desires new wine, but says, 'The old is good.' "^r

I. Jesus the Lord of the sabbath
(6.1–5; Matt. 12.1–8; Mark 2.23–28)

6 One sabbath^s while Jesus^t was going through the grainfields, his disciples plucked some heads of grain, rubbed them in their hands, and ate them. ² But some of the Pharisees said, "Why are you doing what is not lawful^u on the sabbath?" ³ Jesus answered, "Have you not read what David did when he and his companions were hungry? ⁴ He entered the house of God and took and ate the bread of the Presence, which it is not lawful for any but the priests to eat, and gave some to his companions?" ⁵ Then he said to them, "The Son of Man is lord of the sabbath."

J. Jesus heals on the sabbath
(6.6–11; Matt. 12.9–14; Mark 3.1–6)

6 On another sabbath he entered the synagogue and taught, and there was a man there whose right hand was withered. ⁷ The scribes and the Pharisees watched him to see whether he would cure on the sabbath, so that they might find an accusation against him. ⁸ Even though he knew what they were thinking, he said to the man who had the withered hand, "Come and stand here." He got up and stood there. ⁹ Then Jesus said to them, "I ask you, is it lawful to do good or to do harm on the sabbath, to save life or to destroy it?" ¹⁰ After looking around at all of them, he said to him, "Stretch out your hand." He did so, and his hand was restored. ¹¹ But they were filled with fury and discussed with one another what they might do to Jesus.

K. The choosing of the Twelve
(6.12–16; Matt. 10.1–4; Mark 3.13–19)

12 Now during those days he went out to the mountain to pray; and he spent the night in prayer to God. ¹³ And when day came, he called his disciples and chose twelve of them, whom he also named apostles: ¹⁴ Simon, whom he named Peter, and his brother Andrew, and James, and John, and Philip, and Bartholomew, ¹⁵ and Matthew, and Thomas, and James son of Alphaeus, and Simon, who was called the Zealot, ¹⁶ and Judas son of James, and Judas Iscariot, who became a traitor.

L. Sermon on the Mount: Beatitudes and other teachings
(6.17–26; cf. Matt. 5–7)

17 He came down with them and stood on a level place, with a great

---

^r Other ancient authorities read *better*; others lack verse 39 ^s Other ancient authorities read *On the second first sabbath* ^t Gk *he* ^u Other ancient authorities add *to do*

6.1 *sabbath.* See note on Mk 2.27.
6.3 See note on Mt 12.3–5.
6.12 Jesus spent time alone with his Father in prayer before he chose his disciples. Believers too should make their decisions after prayer.
6.13 *apostles,* literally, "ones sent forth." Apostles are ambassadors serving the one who sent them. There seem to be two distinct uses of this word in the New Testament. One is a more general use, designating certain individuals sent out as missionaries, such as Barnabas, James, Andronicus, and Junia (Acts 14.14; Rom 16.7; 1 Cor 15.7; Gal 1.19). The other refers to the office of apostle (cf. 1 Cor 12.28; Eph 4.11), an office that no longer continues, for one of the

qualifications was that they must have seen the risen Lord Jesus face to face (24.48; Acts 1.8,22; 1 Cor 9.1). Apostles had to be called or appointed by the Holy Spirit himself, for no mere person could endow anyone with this authority. The apostles performed miracles and signs that testified to their authenticity (2 Cor 12.11,12).
6.17ff Up to this point Jesus preached mainly in the synagogues. Now he went out in the open. Multitudes came to hear him and all who needed healing were healed. This stands in marked contrast with those today who claim the gift of healing; only a few here and there are healed. Furthermore, healers today must seek the power of God, whereas Jesus had this power in himself.

crowd of his disciples and a great multitude of people from all Judea, Jerusalem, and the coast of Tyre and Sidon. 18They had come to hear him and to be healed of their diseases; and those who were troubled with unclean spirits were cured. 19And all in the crowd were trying to touch him, for power came out from him and healed all of them.

20   Then he looked up at his disciples and said:
"Blessed are you who are poor,
      for yours is the kingdom of God.
21 "Blessed are you who are hungry now,
      for you will be filled.
"Blessed are you who weep now,
      for you will laugh.
22 "Blessed are you when people hate you, and when they exclude you, revile you, and defame you*v* on account of the Son of Man. 23Rejoice in that day and leap for joy, for surely your reward is great in heaven; for that is what their ancestors did to the prophets.
24 "But woe to you who are rich,
      for you have received your consolation.
25 "Woe to you who are full now,
      for you will be hungry.
"Woe to you who are laughing now,
      for you will mourn and weep.
26 "Woe to you when all speak well of you, for that is what their ancestors did to the false prophets.

M. *The law of love (6.27–36; Matt. 5.43–48)*

27   "But I say to you that listen, Love your enemies, do good to those who hate you, 28bless those who curse you, pray for those who abuse you. 29If anyone strikes you on the cheek, offer the other also; and from anyone who takes away your coat do not withhold even your shirt. 30Give to everyone who begs from you; and if anyone takes away your goods, do not ask for them again. 31Do to others as you would have them do to you.

32   "If you love those who love you, what credit is that to you? For even sinners love those who love them. 33If you do good to those who do good to you, what credit is that to you? For even sinners do the same. 34If you lend to those from whom you hope to receive, what credit is that to you? Even sinners lend to sinners, to receive as much again. 35But love your enemies, do good, and lend, expecting nothing in return.*w* Your reward will be great, and you will be children of the Most High; for he is kind to the ungrateful and the wicked. 36Be merciful, just as your Father is merciful.

N. *Judging others (6.37–45; Matt. 7.1–5)*

37   "Do not judge, and you will not be judged; do not condemn, and you will not be condemned. Forgive, and you will be forgiven; 38give, and it will be given to you. A good measure, pressed down, shaken together, running over, will be put into your lap; for the measure you give will be the measure you get back."

v Gk *cast out your name as evil*   *w* Other ancient authorities read *despairing of no one*

6.19	Mt 9.21; 14.36; Mk 3.10; Lk 5.17
6.21	Isa 61.3
6.22	1 Pet 4.14; Jn 9.22; 16.2
6.23	Acts 5.41; Col 1.24; Mal 4.2; Acts 7.51
6.24	Jas 5.1; Lk 16.25
6.25	Isa 65.13; Prov 14.13
6.26	Jn 15.19
6.27	v. 35; Rom 12.20
6.28	Lk 23.34; Acts 7.60
6.30	Deut 15.7, 8, 10; Prov 21.26
6.31	Mt 7.12
6.35	vv. 27, 30
6.37	Rom 2.1
6.38	Mk 4.24; Jas 2.13

6.20ff This section is an abbreviated version of Mt 5–7. Probably both accounts were summaries of Jesus' sermon on the mount. The longer Matthean account can be read in a few minutes, even though Jesus undoubtedly spoke far longer. Together, the Gospels give us just a small portion of everything Jesus said and did in the nearly three years of his public ministry (cf. Jn 21.25).
6.24 *woe to you who are rich,* not because they were rich but because they trusted in their riches instead

of trusting in God.
6.27ff Jesus expanded on the law of love as taught in the O.T. Some of his ideas on the subject were considered unorthodox. Paul enlarged on this theme in 1 Cor 13.
6.37 *Forgive, and you will be forgiven,* The failure to forgive others is a sin itself, and until others are forgiven, we will not be forgiven (see also note on Mt 6.12).

6.39
Mt 15.4
6.40
Mt 10.24;
Jn 13.16;
15.20

6.43
Mt 7.16, 18,
20
6.44
Mt 12.33
6.45
Mt 12.34,
35;
Mk 7.20

6.46
Mt 7.21
6.47
Jas 1.22-25

7.1
Mt 7.28

7.9
v. 50

7.11
1 Kings 17.17-24;
2 Kings 4.32-37;
Mk 5.21-24,
35-43;
Jn 11.1-44

39 He also told them a parable: "Can a blind person guide a blind person? Will not both fall into a pit? 40 A disciple is not above the teacher, but everyone who is fully qualified will be like the teacher. 41 Why do you see the speck in your neighbor's[x] eye, but do not notice the log in your own eye? 42 Or how can you say to your neighbor,[y] 'Friend,[y] let me take out the speck in your eye,' when you yourself do not see the log in your own eye? You hypocrite, first take the log out of your own eye, and then you will see clearly to take the speck out of your neighbor's[x] eye.

43 "No good tree bears bad fruit, nor again does a bad tree bear good fruit; 44 for each tree is known by its own fruit. Figs are not gathered from thorns, nor are grapes picked from a bramble bush. 45 The good person out of the good treasure of the heart produces good, and the evil person out of evil treasure produces evil; for it is out of the abundance of the heart that the mouth speaks.

O. The parable of the two houses (6.46–49; Matt. 7.24–27)

46 "Why do you call me 'Lord, Lord,' and do not do what I tell you? 47 I will show you what someone is like who comes to me, hears my words, and acts on them. 48 That one is like a man building a house, who dug deeply and laid the foundation on rock; when a flood arose, the river burst against that house but could not shake it, because it had been well built.[z] 49 But the one who hears and does not act is like a man who built a house on the ground without a foundation. When the river burst against it, immediately it fell, and great was the ruin of that house."

P. The centurion's servant healed (7.1–10; Matt. 8.5–13)

7 After Jesus[a] had finished all his sayings in the hearing of the people, he entered Capernaum. 2 A centurion there had a slave whom he valued highly, and who was ill and close to death. 3 When he heard about Jesus, he sent some Jewish elders to him, asking him to come and heal his slave. 4 When they came to Jesus, they appealed to him earnestly, saying, "He is worthy of having you do this for him, 5 for he loves our people, and it is he who built our synagogue for us." 6 And Jesus went with them, but when he was not far from the house, the centurion sent friends to say to him, "Lord, do not trouble yourself, for I am not worthy to have you come under my roof; 7 therefore I did not presume to come to you. But only speak the word, and let my servant be healed. 8 For I also am a man set under authority, with soldiers under me; and I say to one, 'Go,' and he goes, and to another, 'Come,' and he comes, and to my slave, 'Do this,' and the slave does it." 9 When Jesus heard this he was amazed at him, and turning to the crowd that followed him, he said, "I tell you, not even in Israel have I found such faith." 10 When those who had been sent returned to the house, they found the slave in good health.

Q. The raising of the widow's son (7.11–17)

11 Soon afterwards[b] he went to a town called Nain, and his disciples and a large crowd went with him. 12 As he approached the gate of the

[x] Gk brother's   [y] Gk brother   [z] Other ancient authorities read founded upon the rock   [a] Gk he   [b] Other ancient authorities read Next day

6.41 We who want to pick out the speck of dust in another's eye may have a two-by-four in our own. Before we reform others we must first reform ourselves.
6.47,48 Jesus distinguishes between a true and false profession of faith. The rock, or good foundation, symbolizes those who come to Jesus Christ for salvation (cf. 1 Cor 3.11; 1 Pet 2.7,8). Those who build on sand have no foundation, even if works of righteousness abound.

7.2 centurion, a noncommissioned Roman army officer.
7.9 A sharp contrast is drawn between the Gentile centurion who believed in Jesus and the Jews who exhibited unbelief.
7.11ff Many incidents, including the raising of the widow's son, appear only in the Gospel of Luke. Others are the story of Lazarus and the rich man, the parables of the lost sheep, the lost coin, and the lost son, and the story of the good Samaritan.

town, a man who had died was being carried out. He was his mother's only son, and she was a widow; and with her was a large crowd from the town. ¹³When the Lord saw her, he had compassion for her and said to her, "Do not weep." ¹⁴Then he came forward and touched the bier, and the bearers stood still. And he said, "Young man, I say to you, rise!" ¹⁵The dead man sat up and began to speak, and Jesusᶜ gave him to his mother. ¹⁶Fear seized all of them; and they glorified God, saying, "A great prophet has risen among us!" and "God has looked favorably on his people!" ¹⁷This word about him spread throughout Judea and all the surrounding country.

R. John the Baptist's last message (7.18–35; Matt. 11.2–19)

18   The disciples of John reported all these things to him. So John summoned two of his disciples ¹⁹and sent them to the Lord to ask, "Are you the one who is to come, or are we to wait for another?" ²⁰When the men had come to him, they said, "John the Baptist has sent us to you to ask, 'Are you the one who is to come, or are we to wait for another?'" ²¹Jesusᵈ had just then cured many people of diseases, plagues, and evil spirits, and had given sight to many who were blind. ²²And he answered them, "Go and tell John what you have seen and heard: the blind receive their sight, the lame walk, the lepersᵉ are cleansed, the deaf hear, the dead are raised, the poor have good news brought to them. ²³And blessed is anyone who takes no offense at me."

24   When John's messengers had gone, Jesusᶜ began to speak to the crowds about John:ᶠ "What did you go out into the wilderness to look at? A reed shaken by the wind? ²⁵What then did you go out to see? Someoneᵍ dressed in soft robes? Look, those who put on fine clothing and live in luxury are in royal palaces. ²⁶What then did you go out to see? A prophet? Yes, I tell you, and more than a prophet. ²⁷This is the one about whom it is written,

'See, I am sending my messenger ahead of you,
   who will prepare your way before you.'

²⁸I tell you, among those born of women no one is greater than John; yet the least in the kingdom of God is greater than he." ²⁹(And all the people who heard this, including the tax collectors, acknowledged the justice of God,ʰ because they had been baptized with John's baptism. ³⁰But by refusing to be baptized by him, the Pharisees and the lawyers rejected God's purpose for themselves.)

31   "To what then will I compare the people of this generation, and what are they like? ³²They are like children sitting in the marketplace and calling to one another,

'We played the flute for you, and you did not dance;
   we wailed, and you did not weep.'

³³For John the Baptist has come eating no bread and drinking no wine, and you say, 'He has a demon'; ³⁴the Son of Man has come eating and drinking, and you say, 'Look, a glutton and a drunkard, a friend of tax

---

ᶜ Gk he   ᵈ Gk He   ᵉ The terms leper and leprosy can refer to several diseases   ᶠ Gk him   ᵍ Or Why then did you go out? To see someone   ʰ Or praised God

---

7.13
v. 19;
Lk 10.1;
11.1, 39;
12.42; 13.15;
17.5, 6; 18.6;
19.8; 22.61;
24.34
7.14
Lk 8.54;
Jn 11.43;
Acts 9.40
7.16
Lk 1.65;
Jn 6.14;
Lk 1.68

7.21
Mt 4.23;
Mk 3.10
7.22
Isa 29.18,
19; 35.5, 6;
Lk 4.18

7.27
Mal 3.1;
Mk 1.2

7.29
Mt 21.32;
Lk 3.12
7.30
Mt 22.35;
Acts 20.27

7.33
Lk 1.15
7.34
Lk 5.29;
15.1, 2

7.20 John the Baptist was in jail and depressed, perhaps wondering why Jesus, his cousin and his Lord, had not come to help him. He sought for reassurance that the one he had baptized was indeed the Messiah. In response, Jesus performed many mighty miracles and indicated that these should give John rest of spirit and mind.
7.23 Jesus warned John the Baptist not to reject or condemn him because of a wrong idea of what the divine Messiah was supposed to do. Jesus did the right things the right way at the right time.

7.31ff Jesus likened the Pharisees and teachers of the law to two groups of children. One group played a wedding song and expected the second group to dance to their tune. The second group played a funeral dirge, and the first group would not weep with them. The Pharisees rejected John the Baptist because he was an ascetic. They then rejected Jesus because he acted the opposite way. No matter which way God offered them eternal life, they turned it down.

collectors and sinners!' 35 Nevertheless, wisdom is vindicated by all her children.''

S. *Jesus anointed: the sinful woman forgiven (7.36–50)*

7.36ff
Mt 26.6-13;
Mk 14.3-9;
Jn 12.1-8

36   One of the Pharisees asked Jesus[i] to eat with him, and he went into the Pharisee's house and took his place at the table. 37 And a woman in the city, who was a sinner, having learned that he was eating in the Pharisee's house, brought an alabaster jar of ointment. 38 She stood behind him at his feet, weeping, and began to bathe his feet with her tears and to dry them with her hair. Then she continued kissing his feet and anointing them with the ointment.

7.39
v. 16;
Lk 24.19;
Jn 6.14

39 Now when the Pharisee who had invited him saw it, he said to himself, "If this man were a prophet, he would have known who and what kind of woman this is who is touching him — that she is a sinner."

7.41
Mt 18.28

40 Jesus spoke up and said to him, "Simon, I have something to say to you." "Teacher," he replied, "speak." 41 "A certain creditor had two debtors; one owed five hundred denarii,[j] and the other fifty. 42 When they could not pay, he canceled the debts for both of them. Now which of them will love him more?" 43 Simon answered, "I suppose the one for whom he canceled the greater debt." And Jesus[k] said to him, "You have judged rightly."

7.44
Gen 18.4;
19.2; 43.24;
Judg 19.21;
1 Tim 5.10

44 Then turning toward the woman, he said to Simon, "Do you see this woman? I entered your house; you gave me no water for my feet, but she has bathed my feet with her tears and dried them with her hair.

7.46
Ps 23.5

45 You gave me no kiss, but from the time I came in she has not stopped kissing my feet. 46 You did not anoint my head with oil, but she has anointed my feet with ointment. 47 Therefore, I tell you, her sins, which were many, have been forgiven; hence she has shown great love. But the one to whom little is forgiven, loves little."

7.48
Mt 9.2;
Mk 2.5;
Lk 5.20
7.50
Mt 9.22;
Mk 5.34;
Lk 8.48

48 Then he said to her, "Your sins are forgiven." 49 But those who were at the table with him began to say among themselves, "Who is this who even forgives sins?" 50 And he said to the woman, "Your faith has saved you; go in peace."

T. *Christ's companions on his second preaching tour (8.1–3)*

8.1
Mt 4.23

8.2
Mt 27.55, 56

8   Soon afterwards he went on through cities and villages, proclaiming and bringing the good news of the kingdom of God. The twelve were with him, 2 as well as some women who had been cured of evil spirits and infirmities: Mary, called Magdalene, from whom seven demons had gone out, 3 and Joanna, the wife of Herod's steward Chuza, and Susanna, and many others, who provided for them[l] out of their resources.

U. *Parable of the sower (8.4–8; Matt. 13.1–8; Mark 4.1–9)*

4   When a great crowd gathered and people from town after town came to him, he said in a parable: 5 "A sower went out to sow his seed; and as he sowed, some fell on the path and was trampled on, and the birds of the air ate it up. 6 Some fell on the rock; and as it grew up, it withered

---

i Gk *him*   j The denarius was the usual day's wage for a laborer   k Gk *he*   l Other ancient authorities read *him*

7.36ff   This incident must not be confused with a similar one that occurred in Bethany of Judea during the closing week of Jesus' life and ministry (Mk 14.3-9; Jn 12.1-8), for this one occurred during Jesus' Galilean ministry. The sinful woman is unnamed, whereas in Bethany the woman was Mary, the sister of Martha and Lazarus. In this incident the host is Simon the Pharisee; in Bethany it was Simon the leper. Jesus' concluding statements in each incident are quite different. No evidence exists for supposing that this sinful woman was Mary Magdalene (cf. note on 8.2).

7.41ff   The point of this parable is that the more we have been forgiven, the more gratitude we should express to the Lord. Jesus knew that this woman had been saved by faith and was expressing her changed life in outward fashion. Her works showed the reality of her saving faith.

8.2   *Magdalene* means "of the town of Magdala." This town was a fishing village on the west bank of the Sea of Galilee. Jesus delivered Mary from demon possession. Nowhere in Scripture does it say or suggest that she was guilty of immorality or prostitution.

8.5   See note on Mk 4.3ff.

for lack of moisture. 7 Some fell among thorns, and the thorns grew with it and choked it. 8 Some fell into good soil, and when it grew, it produced a hundredfold." As he said this, he called out, "Let anyone with ears to hear listen!"

V. *The reason for parables (8.9,10; Matt. 13.1–17; Mark 4.10–12)*

9   Then his disciples asked him what this parable meant. 10 He said, "To you it has been given to know the secrets*m* of the kingdom of God; but to others I speak*n* in parables, so that

    'looking they may not perceive,
      and listening they may not understand.'

W. *The parable of the sower explained (8.11–18; Matt. 13.18–23; Mark 4.13–20)*

11   "Now the parable is this: The seed is the word of God. 12 The ones on the path are those who have heard; then the devil comes and takes away the word from their hearts, so that they may not believe and be saved. 13 The ones on the rock are those who, when they hear the word, receive it with joy. But these have no root; they believe only for a while and in a time of testing fall away. 14 As for what fell among the thorns, these are the ones who hear; but as they go on their way, they are choked by the cares and riches and pleasures of life, and their fruit does not mature. 15 But as for that in the good soil, these are the ones who, when they hear the word, hold it fast in an honest and good heart, and bear fruit with patient endurance.

16   "No one after lighting a lamp hides it under a jar, or puts it under a bed, but puts it on a lampstand, so that those who enter may see the light. 17 For nothing is hidden that will not be disclosed, nor is anything secret that will not become known and come to light. 18 Then pay attention to how you listen; for to those who have, more will be given; and from those who do not have, even what they seem to have will be taken away."

X. *Christ's true kindred (8.19–21; Matt. 12.46–50; Mark 3.31–35)*

19   Then his mother and his brothers came to him, but they could not reach him because of the crowd. 20 And he was told, "Your mother and your brothers are standing outside, wanting to see you." 21 But he said to them, "My mother and my brothers are those who hear the word of God and do it."

Y. *The storm stilled (8.22–25; Matt. 8.23–27; Mark 4.36–41)*

22   One day he got into a boat with his disciples, and he said to them, "Let us go across to the other side of the lake." So they put out, 23 and while they were sailing he fell asleep. A windstorm swept down on the lake, and the boat was filling with water, and they were in danger. 24 They went to him and woke him up, shouting, "Master, Master, we are perishing!" And he woke up and rebuked the wind and the raging waves; they ceased, and there was a calm. 25 He said to them, "Where is your faith?"

m Or *mysteries*   *n* Gk lacks *I speak*

8.16   These words, spoken to the disciples, constitute advice to those who preach the gospel. Whoever has the gift to do so must minister the gospel. They are like lighted candles, giving light to those in darkness.
8.19   Jesus had brothers and sisters. James and Judas (Jude), both writers of N.T. books, were his brothers, as were Joseph and Simon (Mt 13.55,56). Jesus was the eldest child and had a large responsibility in the well-being of his mother, brothers, and

sisters before he began his public ministry.
8.21   Faithful hearers of the word of God always become faithful doers of the work of God.
8.24   In this incident Jesus demonstrated his power over nature. The disciples, though accustomed to storms, were frightened by the fierceness of this one. Fears can be silenced by calling on the Lord Jesus. When they did this, Jesus commanded the waves to be still, and a great calm came over the waters.

8.8
Mt 11.15

8.10
Isa 6.9, 10;
Jer 5.21;
Ezek 12.2

8.11
1 Thess 2.13;
1 Pet 1.23

8.16
Mt 5.15;
Mk 4.21;
Lk 11.33
8.17
Mt 10.26;
Mk 4.22;
Lk 12.2
8.18
Mt 13.12;
25.29;
Lk 19.26

8.21
Lk 11.28;
Jn 15.14

8.22
Mk 6.47-52;
Jn 6.16-21

8.24
Lk 5.5; 4.39

They were afraid and amazed, and said to one another, "Who then is this, that he commands even the winds and the water, and they obey him?"

Z. Demons cast out (8.26–39; Matt. 8.28–34; Mark 5.1–20)

26 Then they arrived at the country of the Gerasenes,^{o} which is opposite Galilee. 27 As he stepped out on land, a man of the city who had demons met him. For a long time he had worn^p no clothes, and he did not live in a house but in the tombs. 28 When he saw Jesus, he fell down before him and shouted at the top of his voice, "What have you to do with me, Jesus, Son of the Most High God? I beg you, do not torment me"— 29 for Jesus^q had commanded the unclean spirit to come out of the man. (For many times it had seized him; he was kept under guard and bound with chains and shackles, but he would break the bonds and be driven by the demon into the wilds.) 30 Jesus then asked him, "What is your name?" He said, "Legion"; for many demons had entered him. 31 They begged him not to order them to go back into the abyss.

32 Now there on the hillside a large herd of swine was feeding; and the demons^r begged Jesus^s to let them enter these. So he gave them permission. 33 Then the demons came out of the man and entered the swine, and the herd rushed down the steep bank into the lake and was drowned.

34 When the swineherds saw what had happened, they ran off and told it in the city and in the country. 35 Then people came out to see what had happened, and when they came to Jesus, they found the man from whom the demons had gone sitting at the feet of Jesus, clothed and in his right mind. And they were afraid. 36 Those who had seen it told them how the one who had been possessed by demons had been healed. 37 Then all the people of the surrounding country of the Gerasenes^o asked Jesus^s to leave them; for they were seized with great fear. So he got into the boat and returned. 38 The man from whom the demons had gone begged that he might be with him; but Jesus^q sent him away, saying, 39 "Return to your home, and declare how much God has done for you." So he went away, proclaiming throughout the city how much Jesus had done for him.

AA. The woman with hemorrhages healed and Jairus's daughter raised
(8.40–56; Matt. 9.18–26; Mark 5.21–43)

40 Now when Jesus returned, the crowd welcomed him, for they were all waiting for him. 41 Just then there came a man named Jairus, a leader of the synagogue. He fell at Jesus' feet and begged him to come to his house, 42 for he had an only daughter, about twelve years old, who was dying.

As he went, the crowds pressed in on him. 43 Now there was a woman who had been suffering from hemorrhages for twelve years; and though she had spent all she had on physicians,^{t} no one could cure her. 44 She came up behind him and touched the fringe of his clothes, and immedi-

---

Marginal references:
- 8.28 / Mk 1.24
- 8.31 / Rom 10.7; Rev 20.1, 3
- 8.33 / vv. 22, 23
- 8.35 / Lk 10.39
- 8.36 / Mt 4.24
- 8.37 / Acts 16.39

---

^{o} Other ancient authorities read *Gadarenes*; others, *Gergesenes* ^{p} Other ancient authorities read *a man of the city who had had demons for a long time met him. He wore* ^{q} Gk *he* ^{r} Gk *they* ^{s} Gk *him* ^{t} Other ancient authorities lack *and though she had spent all she had on physicians*

8.29ff Unclean spirits had great power over the bodies of those they inhabited. These spirits in this story were so strong that they broke the chains and fetters with which the demon-possessed man was bound. When he was delivered and in his right mind, multitudes came to see him. Instead of sensing the greatness of Jesus and opening their hearts to him, they were afraid (v. 37) and urged him to leave as quickly as possible.

8.41ff Jairus was a ruler of the synagogue. He knew

about Jesus and his healings, but he did not ask him to speak a healing word at a distance. He wanted Jesus to come to his home and cure his dying daughter. The report that the girl was dead made the case seem hopeless. But Jesus told him to have faith, a faith that should be bold and daring. The healing of the woman with the issue of blood for twelve years undoubtedly encouraged Jairus. When Jesus spoke a word to Jairus' daughter, her spirit returned to her body.

ately her hemorrhage stopped. 45 Then Jesus asked, "Who touched me?" When all denied it, Peter[u] said, "Master, the crowds surround you and press in on you." 46 But Jesus said, "Someone touched me; for I noticed that power had gone out from me." 47 When the woman saw that she could not remain hidden, she came trembling; and falling down before him, she declared in the presence of all the people why she had touched him, and how she had been immediately healed. 48 He said to her, "Daughter, your faith has made you well; go in peace."

49   While he was still speaking, someone came from the leader's house to say, "Your daughter is dead; do not trouble the teacher any longer." 50 When Jesus heard this, he replied, "Do not fear. Only believe, and she will be saved." 51 When he came to the house, he did not allow anyone to enter with him, except Peter, John, and James, and the child's father and mother. 52 They were all weeping and wailing for her; but he said, "Do not weep; for she is not dead but sleeping." 53 And they laughed at him, knowing that she was dead. 54 But he took her by the hand and called out, "Child, get up!" 55 Her spirit returned, and she got up at once. Then he directed them to give her something to eat. 56 Her parents were astounded; but he ordered them to tell no one what had happened.

BB. *The mission of the Twelve (9.1–6; Matt. 10.1–15; Mark 6.7–13)*

9 Then Jesus[v] called the twelve together and gave them power and authority over all demons and to cure diseases, 2 and he sent them out to proclaim the kingdom of God and to heal. 3 He said to them, "Take nothing for your journey, no staff, nor bag, nor bread, nor money — not even an extra tunic. 4 Whatever house you enter, stay there, and leave from there. 5 Wherever they do not welcome you, as you are leaving that town shake the dust off your feet as a testimony against them." 6 They departed and went through the villages, bringing the good news and curing diseases everywhere.

CC. *Death of John the Baptist (9.7–9; Matt. 14.1–12; Mark 6.14–39)*

7   Now Herod the ruler[w] heard about all that had taken place, and he was perplexed, because it was said by some that John had been raised from the dead, 8 by some that Elijah had appeared, and by others that one of the ancient prophets had arisen. 9 Herod said, "John I beheaded; but who is this about whom I hear such things?" And he tried to see him.

DD. *The five thousand fed (9.10–17; Matt. 14.13–21; Mark 6.30–44; John 6.1–13; cf. Matt. 15.32–38)*

10   On their return the apostles told Jesus[x] all they had done. He took them with him and withdrew privately to a city called Bethsaida. 11 When the crowds found out about it, they followed him; and he welcomed them, and spoke to them about the kingdom of God, and healed those who needed to be cured.

12   The day was drawing to a close, and the twelve came to him and said, "Send the crowd away, so that they may go into the surrounding

Cross-references column:
8.45 Lk 5.5
8.46 Lk 5.17; 6.19
8.48 Lk 7.50; 17.19; 18.42
8.49 v. 41
8.52 Lk 23.27; Jn 11.11, 13
8.54 Lk 7.14; Jn 11.43
8.56 Mt 8.4; Mk 3.12; 7.36; Lk 9.21
9.1 Mk 3.13, 14
9.2 Lk 10.1, 9
9.3 Lk 10.4; 22.35
9.5 Acts 13.51
9.7 v. 19
9.8 Mt 16.14
9.9 Lk 23.8
9.10 v. 17

---

[u] Other ancient authorities add *and those who were with him*   [v] Gk *he*   [w] Gk *tetrarch*   [x] Gk *him*

9.1 Jesus sent his disciples forth and gave them power to preach, heal, and cast out devils. They were to go as they were, without a change of clothing or a second pair of shoes. Nor were they to take money or food; rather they had to trust God to care for them. In this manner they would learn that God takes care of his ambassadors and supplies their needs.

9.10ff The four Gospels all report the feeding of the five thousand. Mark writes that the grass was green, suggesting that the feeding took place shortly before the Passover (March-April). Jesus blessed the food before distributing it. No food was wasted, for whatever was left over was gathered and kept.

villages and countryside, to lodge and get provisions; for we are here in a deserted place." ¹³But he said to them, "You give them something to eat." They said, "We have no more than five loaves and two fish — unless we are to go and buy food for all these people." ¹⁴For there were about five thousand men. And he said to his disciples, "Make them sit down in groups of about fifty each." ¹⁵They did so and made them all sit down. ¹⁶And taking the five loaves and the two fish, he looked up to heaven, and blessed and broke them, and gave them to the disciples to set before the crowd. ¹⁷And all ate and were filled. What was left over was gathered up, twelve baskets of broken pieces.

EE. Peter's confession and Christ's death and resurrection foretold (9.18–27; Matt. 16.13–28; Mark 8.27–9.1)

18 Once when Jesusʸ was praying alone, with only the disciples near him, he asked them, "Who do the crowds say that I am?" ¹⁹They answered, "John the Baptist; but others, Elijah; and still others, that one of the ancient prophets has arisen." ²⁰He said to them, "But who do you say that I am?" Peter answered, "The Messiahᶻ of God."

21 He sternly ordered and commanded them not to tell anyone, ²²saying, "The Son of Man must undergo great suffering, and be rejected by the elders, chief priests, and scribes, and be killed, and on the third day be raised."

23 Then he said to them all, "If any want to become my followers, let them deny themselves and take up their cross daily and follow me. ²⁴For those who want to save their life will lose it, and those who lose their life for my sake will save it. ²⁵What does it profit them if they gain the whole world, but lose or forfeit themselves? ²⁶Those who are ashamed of me and of my words, of them the Son of Man will be ashamed when he comes in his glory and the glory of the Father and of the holy angels. ²⁷But truly I tell you, there are some standing here who will not taste death before they see the kingdom of God."

FF. The transfiguration (9.28–36; Matt. 17.1–8; Mark 9.2–13)

28 Now about eight days after these sayings Jesusʸ took with him Peter and John and James, and went up on the mountain to pray. ²⁹And while he was praying, the appearance of his face changed, and his clothes became dazzling white. ³⁰Suddenly they saw two men, Moses and Elijah, talking to him. ³¹They appeared in glory and were speaking of his departure, which he was about to accomplish at Jerusalem. ³²Now Peter and his companions were weighed down with sleep; but since they had stayed awake,ᵃ they saw his glory and the two men who stood with him. ³³Just as they were leaving him, Peter said to Jesus, "Master, it is good for us to be here; let us make three dwellings,ᵇ one for you, one for Moses, and

ʸ Gk he   ᶻ Or The Christ   ᵃ Or but when they were fully awake   ᵇ Or tents

---

9.13 *You give them something to eat.* Earlier Jesus had sent his disciples to preach and heal and had given them authority and power (v. 1). Now he tells them to exercise this power to feed the hungry multitudes. The disciples had the power, but were either unaware of it or did not have the faith to meet the challenge. Likewise since Pentecost, the Holy Spirit has empowered believers; few, however, make full use the power available to them.
9.18ff When Jesus was alone with his disciples and praying, he asked them who the crowds said he was. They responded with a number of suggestions: Elijah, John the Baptist, and others. When he asked them who *they* thought he was, Peter declared Jesus to be "the Messiah of God." This opened the door for

Jesus to tell them what it meant to be the Christ. He then foretold his rejection, death, and resurrection, though they failed to understand the full implications of this prediction.
9.20 See note on Mt 16.19 regarding Peter, the church, and the keys to the kingdom.
9.23ff Jesus now informed his disciples that they were not to prevent his suffering but rather to prepare for their own. He wanted them to give wholehearted allegiance to him; their souls were at stake. Matthew and Mark speak about losing one's soul, whereas Luke speaks of a person losing oneself, for the soul is the self. The whole world is not worth the price of the soul.
9.28ff See note on Mk 9.2.

one for Elijah"—not knowing what he said. [34] While he was saying this, a cloud came and overshadowed them; and they were terrified as they entered the cloud. [35] Then from the cloud came a voice that said, "This is my Son, my Chosen;[c] listen to him!" [36] When the voice had spoken, Jesus was found alone. And they kept silent and in those days told no one any of the things they had seen.

9.35
2 Pet 1.17,
18;
Mt 3.17
9.36
Mt 17.9

GG. *The unclean spirit cast out of the boy* (9.37–42; Matt. 17.14–21; Mark 9.14–29)

37 On the next day, when they had come down from the mountain, a great crowd met him. [38] Just then a man from the crowd shouted, "Teacher, I beg you to look at my son; he is my only child. [39] Suddenly a spirit seizes him, and all at once he[d] shrieks. It convulses him until he foams at the mouth; it mauls him and will scarcely leave him. [40] I begged your disciples to cast it out, but they could not." [41] Jesus answered, "You faithless and perverse generation, how much longer must I be with you and bear with you? Bring your son here." [42] While he was coming, the demon dashed him to the ground in convulsions. But Jesus rebuked the unclean spirit, healed the boy, and gave him back to his father. [43] And all were astounded at the greatness of God.

9.43
2 Pet 1.16

HH. *Jesus again foretells His death and resurrection* (9.43–45; Matt. 17.22–23; Mark 9.30–32)

While everyone was amazed at all that he was doing, he said to his disciples, [44] "Let these words sink into your ears: The Son of Man is going to be betrayed into human hands." [45] But they did not understand this saying; its meaning was concealed from them, so that they could not perceive it. And they were afraid to ask him about this saying.

9.44
v. 22
9.45
Lk 2.50;
18.34

II. *Discourse on humility* (9.46–50; Matt. 18.1–5; Mark 9.33–37)

46 An argument arose among them as to which one of them was the greatest. [47] But Jesus, aware of their inner thoughts, took a little child and put it by his side, [48] and said to them, "Whoever welcomes this child in my name welcomes me, and whoever welcomes me welcomes the one who sent me; for the least among all of you is the greatest."

49 John answered, "Master, we saw someone casting out demons in your name, and we tried to stop him, because he does not follow with us." [50] But Jesus said to him, "Do not stop him; for whoever is not against you is for you."

9.48
Mt 10.40;
Jn 12.44;
13.20;
Mt 23.11, 12
9.49
Mk 9.38
9.50
Mt 12.30

---

c *Other ancient authorities read* my Beloved   d *Or* it

9.37ff An unnamed person's only son was torn, bruised, and possessed of an evil spirit. Jesus' disciples had been unable to help this one, for they apparently lacked the necessary faith, though not the power (cf. vv. 1–6). The man then appealed to the Master. So Jesus healed the lad in a manner that left everyone astounded.
9.45 *they could not perceive it.* Perhaps their inability to see and understand was because they were expecting a messianic kingdom under Jesus in which they would be sitting in seats of authority and lording it over others. Indeed they began to argue about which of them would be greatest in that kingdom. Like them, we all too often lack understanding and wonder whether what God is doing is the right thing.
9.46 So sharp was the argument among the disciples that nothing would satisfy any of them short of being

greatest in Christ's kingdom. Thus, Jesus had to teach them the lesson of humility.
9.47 *aware of their inner thoughts.* Jesus knew then, and knows now, the thoughts and intentions of every heart. We should be careful about our thought lives, lest we fall into the same trap as the disciples.
9.50 *whoever is not against you is for you.* Lk 11.23 seems to say the exact opposite: "Whoever is not with me is against me." Both statements are true when the context is understood. Here Jesus refers to those who are for him but who are not openly associated with the twelve disciples. They are not opponents of Jesus but friends who believe in him and seek to serve him. In 11.23 Jesus refers to those who are not his followers in any true sense, and thus are against him. There can be no neutrality about our relationship to Jesus. Either we are for him or against him.

VI. The journey to Jerusalem (9.51–19.27)

A. Samaritan opposition (9.51–55)

9.51
Lk 13.22;
17.11; 18.31;
19.11, 28
9.52
Mt 10.5;
Jn 4.4
9.54
Mk 3.17;
1 Kings 1.10,
12

51 When the days drew near for him to be taken up, he set his face to go to Jerusalem. 52 And he sent messengers ahead of him. On their way they entered a village of the Samaritans to make ready for him; 53 but they did not receive him, because his face was set toward Jerusalem. 54 When his disciples James and John saw it, they said, "Lord, do you want us to command fire to come down from heaven and consume them?"ᵉ 55 But he turned and rebuked them. 56 Thenᶠ they went on to another village.

B. Impulsive and reluctant followers (9.57–62; Matt. 8.18–22)

9.59
Mt 8.21, 22

57 As they were going along the road, someone said to him, "I will follow you wherever you go." 58 And Jesus said to him, "Foxes have holes, and birds of the air have nests; but the Son of Man has nowhere to lay his head." 59 To another he said, "Follow me." But he said, "Lord, first let me go and bury my father." 60 But Jesusᵍ said to him, "Let the dead bury their own dead; but as for you, go and proclaim the kingdom of God." 61 Another said, "I will follow you, Lord; but let me first say farewell to those at my home." 62 Jesus said to him, "No one who puts a hand to the plow and looks back is fit for the kingdom of God."

C. The mission of the seventy (10.1–24)

10.1
Mt 10.1;
Mk 6.7;
Lk 9.1, 2,
51, 52
10.2
Mt 9.37, 38;
Jn 4.35
10.3
Mt 10.16
10.4
Mt 10.9, 10;
Mk 6.8;
Lk 9.3
10.5
Mk 10.12
10.7
Mt 10.10;
1 Cor 9.14;
1 Tim 5.18
10.9
Mt 3.2; 10.7
10.11
Mt 10.14;
Mk 6.11;
Lk 9.5
10.12
Mt 10.15;
11.24
10.13
Mt 11.21;
Lk 6.24-26
10.15
Mt 11.23

10 After this the Lord appointed seventyʰ others and sent them on ahead of him in pairs to every town and place where he himself intended to go. 2 He said to them, "The harvest is plentiful, but the laborers are few; therefore ask the Lord of the harvest to send out laborers into his harvest. 3 Go on your way. See, I am sending you out like lambs into the midst of wolves. 4 Carry no purse, no bag, no sandals; and greet no one on the road. 5 Whatever house you enter, first say, 'Peace to this house!' 6 And if anyone is there who shares in peace, your peace will rest on that person; but if not, it will return to you. 7 Remain in the same house, eating and drinking whatever they provide, for the laborer deserves to be paid. Do not move about from house to house. 8 Whenever you enter a town and its people welcome you, eat what is set before you; 9 cure the sick who are there, and say to them, 'The kingdom of God has come near to you.'ⁱ 10 But whenever you enter a town and they do not welcome you, go out into its streets and say, 11 'Even the dust of your town that clings to our feet, we wipe off in protest against you. Yet know this: the kingdom of God has come near.'ʲ 12 I tell you, on that day it will be more tolerable for Sodom than for that town.

13 "Woe to you, Chorazin! Woe to you, Bethsaida! For if the deeds of power done in you had been done in Tyre and Sidon, they would have repented long ago, sitting in sackcloth and ashes. 14 But at the judgment it will be more tolerable for Tyre and Sidon than for you. 15 And you, Capernaum,

ᵉ Other ancient authorities add *as Elijah did* ᶠ Other ancient authorities read *rebuked them, and said, "You do not know what spirit you are of,* ⁵⁶*for the Son of Man has not come to destroy the lives of human beings but to save them." Then* ᵍ Gk *he* ʰ Other ancient authorities read *seventy-two* ⁱ Or *is at hand for you* ʲ Or *is at hand*

10.1 The sending of the seventy indicates the growing numbers of those who followed Jesus. Luke alone records this incident.
10.12 *on that day*, i.e., the day of judgment. Other Scripture passages indicate there will be two judgments. One is the believers' judgment; the other is the judgment of the great white throne (Rev 20.11ff). The latter is the one referred to here, for it is the final judgment, symbolized by the fire that destroyed Sodom.

10.13,14 Christ pronounced doom on Chorazin, Bethsaida, and Capernaum — cities where much of his evangelizing work had been done. They enjoyed greater privileges than did Tyre and Sidon, yet only a few in these cities repented. Their punishment would be greater than that pronounced upon Tyre and Sidon, who did not have the opportunity to hear Christ.

will you be exalted to heaven?

No, you will be brought down to Hades.

16 "Whoever listens to you listens to me, and whoever rejects you rejects me, and whoever rejects me rejects the one who sent me."

17 The seventy*k* returned with joy, saying, "Lord, in your name even the demons submit to us!" 18 He said to them, "I watched Satan fall from heaven like a flash of lightning. 19 See, I have given you authority to tread on snakes and scorpions, and over all the power of the enemy; and nothing will hurt you. 20 Nevertheless, do not rejoice at this, that the spirits submit to you, but rejoice that your names are written in heaven."

21 At that same hour Jesus*l* rejoiced in the Holy Spirit*m* and said, "I thank*n* you, Father, Lord of heaven and earth, because you have hidden these things from the wise and the intelligent and have revealed them to infants; yes, Father, for such was your gracious will.*o* 22 All things have been handed over to me by my Father; and no one knows who the Son is except the Father, or who the Father is except the Son and anyone to whom the Son chooses to reveal him."

23 Then turning to the disciples, Jesus*l* said to them privately, "Blessed are the eyes that see what you see! 24 For I tell you that many prophets and kings desired to see what you see, but did not see it, and to hear what you hear, but did not hear it."

D. *The good Samaritan (10.25–37)*

25 Just then a lawyer stood up to test Jesus.*p* "Teacher," he said, "what must I do to inherit eternal life?" 26 He said to him, "What is written in the law? What do you read there?" 27 He answered, "You shall love the Lord your God with all your heart, and with all your soul, and with all your strength, and with all your mind; and your neighbor as yourself." 28 And he said to him, "You have given the right answer; do this, and you will live."

29 But wanting to justify himself, he asked Jesus, "And who is my neighbor?" 30 Jesus replied, "A man was going down from Jerusalem to Jericho, and fell into the hands of robbers, who stripped him, beat him, and went away, leaving him half dead. 31 Now by chance a priest was going down that road; and when he saw him, he passed by on the other side. 32 So likewise a Levite, when he came to the place and saw him, passed by on the other side. 33 But a Samaritan while traveling came near him; and when he saw him, he was moved with pity. 34 He went to him and bandaged his wounds, having poured oil and wine on them. Then he put him on his own animal, brought him to an inn, and took care of him.

	10.16 Mt 10.40; Mk 9.37; Lk 9.48; Jn 13.20
	10.17 v. 1
	10.18 Jn 12.31; Rev 9.1; 12.8, 9
	10.19 Acts 28.5
	10.20 Ex 32.32; Ps 69.28; Dan 12.1; Phil 4.3; Heb 12.23; Rev 13.8; 21.27
	10.21 Mt 11.25; 1 Cor 1.26-29
	10.22 Mt 28.18; Jn 3.35; 17.2
	10.23 Mt 13.16
	10.24 1 Pet 1.10
	10.25 Mt 19.16; Mk 10.17; Lk 18.18
	10.27 Deut 6.5; Lev 19.18; Rom 13.9; Gal 5.14; Jas 2.8
	10.28 Lev 18.5; Mt 19.17
	10.29 Lk 16.15
	10.33 Lk 9.52; Jn 4.9

---

k Other ancient authorities read *seventy-two*   *l* Gk *he*   *m* Other authorities read *in the spirit*   *n* Or *praise*
o Or *for so it was well-pleasing in your sight*   *p* Gk *him*

10.15 *Hades* (Gk. *hadēs* or *haidēs*) means "not to be seen" and is the N.T. equivalent for the O.T. *sheol. Sheol* was the general abode of the dead, both good and bad. As used in the N.T., *Hades* may mean an actual place (e.g., 16.23) or the state of death itself (e.g., Acts 2.27–31). The idea of hell as the everlasting abode of the wicked dead is expressed by "the lake of fire" (Rev 20.15) or by "Gehenna" (see note on Mt 18.9).

10.17ff The seventy returned, declaring that their ministry was successful to the extent that even demons were subjected to them. Jesus agreed with their words and stated that he saw Satan fall as lightning from heaven (cf. also Jn 12.31). He repeated and enlarged their commission, for they would now have power to tread on serpents and scorpions and not be hurt. Nevertheless, having their names written down in heaven is better than having power over demons.

10.30ff Only Luke records the story of the good Samaritan, which must be understood within the context in which Jesus told it. When an expert in Moses' law asked Jesus what he needed to do to inherit eternal life, Jesus gave him the summary of the law: love God with your whole heart and love your neighbor as yourself. The Jews of Jesus' day considered only their fellow Jews to be their neighbors. When the legal expert asked Jesus to tell him who his neighbor was, Jesus used the illustration of the good Samaritan, not only answering the question who was a neighbor (i.e., anyone nearby), but also giving instructions on how to act neighborly. When pressed by Jesus, the Jew had to admit that the Samaritan loved his neighbor while the Jews did not. Note, however, that Jesus did not say that the Samaritan was saved by his good works.

35 The next day he took out two denarii,*q* gave them to the innkeeper, and said, 'Take care of him; and when I come back, I will repay you whatever more you spend.' 36 Which of these three, do you think, was a neighbor to the man who fell into the hands of the robbers?" 37 He said, "The one who showed him mercy." Jesus said to him, "Go and do likewise."

E. *Jesus visits Mary and Martha (10.38–42)*

10.38
Jn 11.1;
12.2, 3
10.39
Lk 8.35;
Acts 22.3

10.42
Ps 27.4

38 Now as they went on their way, he entered a certain village, where a woman named Martha welcomed him into her home. 39 She had a sister named Mary, who sat at the Lord's feet and listened to what he was saying. 40 But Martha was distracted by her many tasks; so she came to him and asked, "Lord, do you not care that my sister has left me to do all the work by myself? Tell her then to help me." 41 But the Lord answered her, "Martha, Martha, you are worried and distracted by many things; 42 there is need of only one thing.*r* Mary has chosen the better part, which will not be taken away from her."

F. *Jesus' discourse on prayer (11.1–13; cf. Matt. 6.5–15)*

11.1
Mk 1.35;
Lk 3.21

11 1 He was praying in a certain place, and after he had finished, one of his disciples said to him, "Lord, teach us to pray, as John taught his disciples." 2 He said to them, "When you pray, say:

Father,*s* hallowed be your name.
Your kingdom come.*t*

11.4
Mt 18.35;
Mk 11.25

3   Give us each day our daily bread.*u*
4   And forgive us our sins,
        for we ourselves forgive everyone indebted to us.
     And do not bring us to the time of trial."*v*

5 And he said to them, "Suppose one of you has a friend, and you go to him at midnight and say to him, 'Friend, lend me three loaves of bread; 6 for a friend of mine has arrived, and I have nothing to set before him.' 7 And he answers from within, 'Do not bother me; the door has already been locked, and my children are with me in bed; I cannot get up and give you anything.' 8 I tell you, even though he will not get up and give him anything because he is his friend, at least because of his persistence he will get up and give him whatever he needs.

11.8
Lk 18.1-6

9 "So I say to you, Ask, and it will be given you; search, and you will find; knock, and the door will be opened for you. 10 For everyone who asks receives, and everyone who searches finds, and for everyone who knocks, the door will be opened. 11 Is there anyone among you who, if your child asks for*w* a fish, will give a snake instead of a fish? 12 Or if the child asks for an egg, will give a scorpion? 13 If you then, who are evil, know how to give good gifts to your children, how much more will the heavenly Father give the Holy Spirit*x* to those who ask him!"

11.9
Mt 7.7-11;
18.19; 21.22;
Mk 11.24;
Jas 1.5-8;
1 Jn 5.14, 15

q The denarius was the usual day's wage for a laborer   *r* Other ancient authorities read *few things are necessary, or only one*   *s* Other ancient authorities read *Our Father in heaven*   *t* A few ancient authorities read *Your Holy Spirit come upon us and cleanse us.* Other ancient authorities add *Your will be done, on earth as in heaven*   *u* Or *our bread for tomorrow*   *v* Or *us into temptation.* Other ancient authorities add *but rescue us from the evil one* (or *from evil*)   *w* Other ancient authorities add *bread, will give a stone; or if your child asks for*   *x* Other ancient authorities read *the Father give the Holy Spirit from heaven*

10.40 In this story about Mary and Martha, Jesus insisted that a right balance must be maintained between the life of active service and that of quiet meditation and communion with the Lord. Serving Jesus a meal was not as important as sitting at his feet and learning what he had to teach.
11.1 *to pray.* See note on Mt 7.7.

11.8 Here and in 18.1–6 Jesus encourages persistence in prayer. We are never to let God go until the answers have come.
11.12 *will give a scorpion?* This is a hypothetical question, the answer to which is self-evident. No parent would give a child a scorpion instead of bread.

G. Jesus answers the slander of the Pharisees
(11.14–28; Matt. 12.22–45; Mark 3.20–30)

14 Now he was casting out a demon that was mute; when the demon had gone out, the one who had been mute spoke, and the crowds were amazed. 15 But some of them said, "He casts out demons by Beelzebul, the ruler of the demons." 16 Others, to test him, kept demanding from him a sign from heaven. 17 But he knew what they were thinking and said to them, "Every kingdom divided against itself becomes a desert, and house falls on house. 18 If Satan also is divided against himself, how will his kingdom stand? —for you say that I cast out the demons by Beelzebul. 19 Now if I cast out the demons by Beelzebul, by whom do your exorcists*y* cast them out? Therefore they will be your judges. 20 But if it is by the finger of God that I cast out the demons, then the kingdom of God has come to you. 21 When a strong man, fully armed, guards his castle, his property is safe. 22 But when one stronger than he attacks him and overpowers him, he takes away his armor in which he trusted and divides his plunder. 23 Whoever is not with me is against me, and whoever does not gather with me scatters.

24 "When the unclean spirit has gone out of a person, it wanders through waterless regions looking for a resting place, but not finding any, it says, 'I will return to my house from which I came.' 25 When it comes, it finds it swept and put in order. 26 Then it goes and brings seven other spirits more evil than itself, and they enter and live there; and the last state of that person is worse than the first."

27 While he was saying this, a woman in the crowd raised her voice and said to him, "Blessed is the womb that bore you and the breasts that nursed you!" 28 But he said, "Blessed rather are those who hear the word of God and obey it!"

H. Warning against seeking signs
(11.29–32; Matt. 12.38–42)

29 When the crowds were increasing, he began to say, "This generation is an evil generation; it asks for a sign, but no sign will be given to it except the sign of Jonah. 30 For just as Jonah became a sign to the people of Nineveh, so the Son of Man will be to this generation. 31 The queen of the South will rise at the judgment with the people of this generation and condemn them, because she came from the ends of the earth to listen to the wisdom of Solomon, and see, something greater than Solomon is here! 32 The people of Nineveh will rise up at the judgment with this generation and condemn it, because they repented at the proclamation of Jonah, and see, something greater than Jonah is here!

I. The parable of the lighted lamp (11.33–36)

33 "No one after lighting a lamp puts it in a cellar,*z* but on the lampstand so that those who enter may see the light. 34 Your eye is the lamp of your body. If your eye is healthy, your whole body is full of light;

11.14	Mt 9.32-34
11.16	Mt 16.1; Mk 8.11
11.17	Jn 2.25
11.20	Ex 8.19
11.23	Lk 9.50
11.26	Heb 10.26; 2 Pet 2.20
11.27	Lk 23.29
11.28	Lk 8.21; Jn 15.14
11.29	Mt 16.4; Mk 8.12; v. 16
11.31	1 Kings 10.1; 2 Chr 9.1
11.32	Jon 3.5
11.33	Mt 5.15; Mk 4.21; Lk 8.16
11.34	Mt 6.22, 23

y Gk sons *z* Other ancient authorities add or under the bushel basket

---

11.15 *Beelzebul,* i.e., Satan (see note on Mt 10.25).
11.16 *a sign from heaven,* i.e., something spectacular to prove that he was the Messiah.
11.21,22 *When a strong man, fully armed, guards his castle.* This refers to Satan, who thinks all is well because of his armor. But that which Satan trusts in will be taken from him by One stronger than he.
11.29 See note on Mt 12.40.
11.31 *queen of the South,* i.e., the queen of Sheba.
11.32 *something greater than Jonah is here!* Nineveh repented at the preaching of Jonah. Now Christ, who

is greater, has come; but the Jewish nation to whom he preached would not learn from Nineveh. They refused to repent.
11.34 *Your eye is the lamp of your body.* When the eye is sound and the light is shining, we can see where we are and know how to walk and do our work. When the eye is blinded, the whole body is wrapped in darkness. Applied spiritually, although Christ, the light of the world, keeps shining, the wrong inner nature of sinners keeps them from seeing that light.

but if it is not healthy, your body is full of darkness. 35 Therefore consider whether the light in you is not darkness. 36 If then your whole body is full of light, with no part of it in darkness, it will be as full of light as when a lamp gives you light with its rays."

J. Pharisaism exposed and denounced (11.37–54)

11.37
Lk 7.36;
14.1
11.38
Mk 7.3, 4
11.39
Mt 23.25, 26
11.41
Lk 12.33;
Mk 7.19;
Titus 1.15
11.42
Mt 23.23;
Lk 18.12
11.43
Mt 23.6, 7;
Mk 12.38,
39;
Lk 20.46
11.44
Mt 23.27
11.46
Mt 23.4
11.47
Mt 23.29-32;
Acts 7.51-53

11.49
Mt 23.34-36;
1 Cor 1.24;
Col 2.3

11.51
Gen 4.8;
2 Chr 24.20,
21
11.52
Mt 23.13

11.54
Mk 12.13

37 While he was speaking, a Pharisee invited him to dine with him; so he went in and took his place at the table. 38 The Pharisee was amazed to see that he did not first wash before dinner. 39 Then the Lord said to him, "Now you Pharisees clean the outside of the cup and of the dish, but inside you are full of greed and wickedness. 40 You fools! Did not the one who made the outside make the inside also? 41 So give for alms those things that are within; and see, everything will be clean for you.

42 "But woe to you Pharisees! For you tithe mint and rue and herbs of all kinds, and neglect justice and the love of God; it is these you ought to have practiced, without neglecting the others. 43 Woe to you Pharisees! For you love to have the seat of honor in the synagogues and to be greeted with respect in the marketplaces. 44 Woe to you! For you are like unmarked graves, and people walk over them without realizing it."

45 One of the lawyers answered him, "Teacher, when you say these things, you insult us too." 46 And he said, "Woe also to you lawyers! For you load people with burdens hard to bear, and you yourselves do not lift a finger to ease them. 47 Woe to you! For you build the tombs of the prophets whom your ancestors killed. 48 So you are witnesses and approve of the deeds of your ancestors; for they killed them, and you build their tombs. 49 Therefore also the Wisdom of God said, 'I will send them prophets and apostles, some of whom they will kill and persecute,' 50 so that this generation may be charged with the blood of all the prophets shed since the foundation of the world, 51 from the blood of Abel to the blood of Zechariah, who perished between the altar and the sanctuary. Yes, I tell you, it will be charged against this generation. 52 Woe to you lawyers! For you have taken away the key of knowledge; you did not enter yourselves, and you hindered those who were entering."

53 When he went outside, the scribes and the Pharisees began to be very hostile toward him and to cross-examine him about many things, 54 lying in wait for him, to catch him in something he might say.

K. Warning against the yeast of the Pharisees (12.1–12)

12.1
Mt 16.6;
Mk 8.15;
Mt 16.12
12.2
Mt 10.26,
27;
Mk 4.22;
Lk 8.17;
Eph 5.13
12.4
Mt 10.28-33;
Jn 15.14, 15
12.5
Heb 10.31

12 Meanwhile, when the crowd gathered by the thousands, so that they trampled on one another, he began to speak first to his disciples, "Beware of the yeast of the Pharisees, that is, their hypocrisy. 2 Nothing is covered up that will not be uncovered, and nothing secret that will not become known. 3 Therefore whatever you have said in the dark will be heard in the light, and what you have whispered behind closed doors will be proclaimed from the housetops.

4 "I tell you, my friends, do not fear those who kill the body, and after that can do nothing more. 5 But I will warn you whom to fear: fear him who, after he has killed, has authority*a* to cast into hell.*b* Yes, I tell you,

a Or power   *b* Gk Gehenna

11.51 See note on Mt 23.35.
12.1 In warning against the hypocrisy of the Pharisees, Jesus wanted his disciples to know he was opposed to the same sin among his followers. Good people must be warned against this sin and remember that someday everything they do will be revealed.
12.5 Hell (Gk. gehenna, see note on Mt 18.9). Those who do not believe in the reality of hell usually entertain one of three views: (1) annihilationism — God is too loving to permit sinners to suffer forever; therefore he annihilates their souls at some point after physical death; (2) restorationism — God cannot condemn sinners to eternal punishment forever, so he ultimately restores them to fellowship with himself in heaven, no matter how long it takes; (3) presentism — sinners experience their heaven or hell here on earth during this life, with rewards or retribution meted out in the here and now. The Bible, however, teaches the reality of the eternal gehenna, symbolized by the lake of fire (Rev 19.20; 20.14,15).

fear him! 6 Are not five sparrows sold for two pennies? Yet not one of them is forgotten in God's sight. 7 But even the hairs of your head are all counted. Do not be afraid; you are of more value than many sparrows.

8 "And I tell you, everyone who acknowledges me before others, the Son of Man also will acknowledge before the angels of God; 9 but whoever denies me before others will be denied before the angels of God. 10 And everyone who speaks a word against the Son of Man will be forgiven; but whoever blasphemes against the Holy Spirit will not be forgiven. 11 When they bring you before the synagogues, the rulers, and the authorities, do not worry about how[c] you are to defend yourselves or what you are to say; 12 for the Holy Spirit will teach you at that very hour what you ought to say."

L. Parable of the rich fool: covetousness (12.13–21)

13 Someone in the crowd said to him, "Teacher, tell my brother to divide the family inheritance with me." 14 But he said to him, "Friend, who set me to be a judge or arbitrator over you?" 15 And he said to them, "Take care! Be on your guard against all kinds of greed; for one's life does not consist in the abundance of possessions." 16 Then he told them a parable: "The land of a rich man produced abundantly. 17 And he thought to himself, 'What should I do, for I have no place to store my crops?' 18 Then he said, 'I will do this: I will pull down my barns and build larger ones, and there I will store all my grain and my goods. 19 And I will say to my soul, Soul, you have ample goods laid up for many years; relax, eat, drink, be merry.' 20 But God said to him, 'You fool! This very night your life is being demanded of you. And the things you have prepared, whose will they be?' 21 So it is with those who store up treasures for themselves but are not rich toward God."

M. Trust or anxiety (12.22–34; cf. Matt. 6.25–34)

22 He said to his disciples, "Therefore I tell you, do not worry about your life, what you will eat, or about your body, what you will wear. 23 For life is more than food, and the body more than clothing. 24 Consider the ravens: they neither sow nor reap, they have neither storehouse nor barn, and yet God feeds them. Of how much more value are you than the birds! 25 And can any of you by worrying add a single hour to your span of life?[d] 26 If then you are not able to do so small a thing as that, why do you worry about the rest? 27 Consider the lilies, how they grow: they neither toil nor spin;[e] yet I tell you, even Solomon in all his glory was not clothed like one of these. 28 But if God so clothes the grass of the field, which is alive today and tomorrow is thrown into the oven, how much more will he clothe you—you of little faith! 29 And do not keep striving for what you are to eat and what you are to drink, and do not keep worrying. 30 For it is the nations of the world that strive after all these things, and your Father knows that you need them. 31 Instead, strive for his[f] kingdom, and these things will be given to you as well.

32 "Do not be afraid, little flock, for it is your Father's good pleasure

12.7 Mt 12.12; Lk 21.18; Acts 27.34
12.8 Mk 8.38; 2 Tim 2.12; 1 Jn 2.23
12.10 Mt 12.31, 32; Mk 3.28, 29
12.11 Mt 10.19; Mk 13.11; Lk 21.14
12.14 Mic 6.8; Rom 2.1, 3
12.19 Eccl 11.9; Jas 5.5
12.20 Jer 17.11; Job 27.8; Ps 39.6
12.21 v. 33
12.24 Job 38.41
12.25 Ps 39.5
12.27 1 Kings 10.4-7
12.30 Mt 6.8
12.32 Jn 21.15-17

c Other ancient authorities add or what d Or add a cubit to your stature e Other ancient authorities read Consider the lilies; they neither spin nor weave f Other ancient authorities read God's

12.16ff Worldliness concerns itself with this life and its material aspects. Christ warned against an attitude of covetousness. Scripture does not teach that wealth per se is evil, but when wealth becomes an end in itself it is a snare and a sin. Wealthy believers must take special precautions, for material possessions constitute a powerful source of temptation (see Mt 6.20, 32–34; 19.16–24; 1 Tim 6.6–10, 17–19).
12.22 Jesus had far more disciples than the twelve who comprised the inner circle. Here he spoke to a larger gathering of disciples about the problem of anxiety—a sign of a lack of faith.
12.23 God has already done for believers the greater thing by giving them eternal life. He can also do the lesser; he will provide food and drink for his people so that they need not be anxious about the things of this life.
12.28 grass . . . is thrown into the oven. Since wood was scarce, the Jews often used dry grass in their ovens.

12.33
Mt 19.21;
Mk 6.20
12.34
Mt 6.21

to give you the kingdom. 33 Sell your possessions, and give alms. Make purses for yourselves that do not wear out, an unfailing treasure in heaven, where no thief comes near and no moth destroys. 34 For where your treasure is, there your heart will be also.

N. Exhortation to vigilance (12.35–40)

12.35
Mt 25.1-13;
Mk 13.33-37;
Eph 6.14
12.37
Mt 24.42,
46;
Lk 17.8;
Jn 13.4

35 "Be dressed for action and have your lamps lit; 36 be like those who are waiting for their master to return from the wedding banquet, so that they may open the door for him as soon as he comes and knocks. 37 Blessed are those slaves whom the master finds alert when he comes; truly I tell you, he will fasten his belt and have them sit down to eat, and he will come and serve them. 38 If he comes during the middle of the night, or near dawn, and finds them so, blessed are those slaves.

12.39
Mt 24.43;
1 Thess 5.2;
2 Pet 3.10;
Rev 3.3;
16.15
12.40
Mt 24.44;
Mk 13.33;
Lk 21.36

39 "But know this: if the owner of the house had known at what hour the thief was coming, he^g would not have let his house be broken into. 40 You also must be ready, for the Son of Man is coming at an unexpected hour."

O. Faithful and unfaithful servants (12.41–48; Matt. 24.45–51)

12.42
Lk 7.13

41 Peter said, "Lord, are you telling this parable for us or for everyone?" 42 And the Lord said, "Who then is the faithful and prudent manager whom his master will put in charge of his slaves, to give them their allowance of food at the proper time? 43 Blessed is that slave whom his master will find at work when he arrives. 44 Truly I tell you, he will put that one in charge of all his possessions. 45 But if that slave says to himself, 'My master is delayed in coming,' and if he begins to beat the other slaves, men and women, and to eat and drink and get drunk, 46 the master of that slave will come on a day when he does not expect him and at an hour that he does not know, and will cut him in pieces,^{h} and put him with the unfaithful. 47 That slave who knew what his master wanted, but did not prepare himself or do what was wanted, will receive a severe beating.

12.47
Num 15.30;
Deut 25.2
12.48
Lev 5.17

48 But the one who did not know and did what deserved a beating will receive a light beating. From everyone to whom much has been given, much will be required; and from the one to whom much has been entrusted, even more will be demanded.

P. Christ the great divider (12.49–59)

12.50
Mk 10.38;
Jn 12.27
12.51
Mt 10.34-36;
v. 49
12.53
Mic 7.6;
Mt 10.21

49 "I came to bring fire to the earth, and how I wish it were already kindled! 50 I have a baptism with which to be baptized, and what stress I am under until it is completed! 51 Do you think that I have come to bring peace to the earth? No, I tell you, but rather division! 52 From now on five in one household will be divided, three against two and two against three; 53 they will be divided:

father against son
  and son against father,
    mother against daughter
      and daughter against mother,
        mother-in-law against her daughter-in-law
          and daughter-in-law against mother-in-law."

12.54
Mt 16.2

54 He also said to the crowds, "When you see a cloud rising in the

---

^{g} Other ancient authorities add *would have watched and* ^{h} Or *cut him off*

12.33 *give alms.* The verb tense used here means to give again and again, every time God brings us into touch with someone in need.
12.42ff This parable stresses the necessity for faithfully discharging one's obligations as a servant of the Lord. Jesus warned that the delay in the return of the master would be no excuse for slothfulness or taking

one's ease. When the master returned, he would reward faithfulness and fittingly punish a lack of it.
12.53 Jesus affirmed that the effect of gospel preaching would be divisive, even reaching into private families. Unbelievers in the family would become angry with, persecute, and condemn relatives who followed Jesus.

west, you immediately say, 'It is going to rain'; and so it happens. 55 And
when you see the south wind blowing, you say, 'There will be scorching
heat'; and it happens. 56 You hypocrites! You know how to interpret the
appearance of earth and sky, but why do you not know how to interpret
the present time?

57 "And why do you not judge for yourselves what is right? 58 Thus,
when you go with your accuser before a magistrate, on the way make an
effort to settle the case,[i] or you may be dragged before the judge, and
the judge hand you over to the officer, and the officer throw you in prison.
59 I tell you, you will never get out until you have paid the very last
penny."

Q. Jesus' call to repentance (13.1–9)

13 At that very time there were some present who told him about the
Galileans whose blood Pilate had mingled with their sacrifices.
2 He asked them, "Do you think that because these Galileans suffered in
this way they were worse sinners than all other Galileans? 3 No, I tell you;
but unless you repent, you will all perish as they did. 4 Or those eighteen
who were killed when the tower of Siloam fell on them — do you think that
they were worse offenders than all the others living in Jerusalem? 5 No,
I tell you; but unless you repent, you will all perish just as they did."

6 Then he told this parable: "A man had a fig tree planted in his
vineyard; and he came looking for fruit on it and found none. 7 So he said
to the gardener, 'See here! For three years I have come looking for fruit
on this fig tree, and still I find none. Cut it down! Why should it be
wasting the soil?' 8 He replied, 'Sir, let it alone for one more year, until
I dig around it and put manure on it. 9 If it bears fruit next year, well and
good; but if not, you can cut it down.'"

R. A woman healed on the sabbath (13.10–17)

10 Now he was teaching in one of the synagogues on the sabbath.
11 And just then there appeared a woman with a spirit that had crippled
her for eighteen years. She was bent over and was quite unable to stand
up straight. 12 When Jesus saw her, he called her over and said, "Woman,
you are set free from your ailment." 13 When he laid his hands on her,
immediately she stood up straight and began praising God. 14 But the
leader of the synagogue, indignant because Jesus had cured on the sabbath, kept saying to the crowd, "There are six days on which work ought
to be done; come on those days and be cured, and not on the sabbath day."
15 But the Lord answered him and said, "You hypocrites! Does not each
of you on the sabbath untie his ox or his donkey from the manger, and
lead it away to give it water? 16 And ought not this woman, a daughter of
Abraham whom Satan bound for eighteen long years, be set free from this
bondage on the sabbath day?" 17 When he said this, all his opponents were
put to shame; and the entire crowd was rejoicing at all the wonderful
things that he was doing.

i Gk settle with him

Marginal references

12.55 Mt 20.12
12.56 Mt 16.3
12.58 Mt 5.25, 26
12.59 Mk 12.42

13.1 Mt 27.2
13.2 Jn 9.2, 3
13.4 Lk 11.4
13.6 Mt 21.19
13.7 Mt 3.10; 7.19; Lk 3.9

13.11 v. 16
13.13 Mk 5.23
13.14 Ex 20.9; Lk 6.7; 14.3
13.15 Lk 7.13; 14.5
13.16 Lk 19.9

13.1 *Galileans whose blood Pilate had mingled with
their sacrifices.* This is the only information we have
about this event. Apparently Pilate's soldiers murdered some Jews in the act of offering sacrifices and
mixed their blood with that of their offerings. Perhaps
Pilate feared an insurrection by these Jews.
13.6ff The parable of the barren fig tree refers primarily to the nation of Israel (see Hos 9.10; Joel 1.7).
For many centuries God looked for Israel to bear
fruits worthy of repentance (cf. 3.8), but nothing had
happened. Now Israel was rejecting God's Son. Their
long-suffering God would grant more time for Israel
to repent and turn to him at last. But if they persisted
in their refusal to turn to God, they would be cut off.
13.11 This woman, with an infirmity for eighteen
years, did not ask Jesus for anything. Instead he saw
her, felt compassion for her in her plight, and cured
her immediately. In his anger at Jesus, the ruler of the
synagogue forgot that works of mercy and necessity
are permissible on the sabbath. The entire crowd had
greater spiritual insight than he did, for they praised
and glorified God for what Jesus had done.

S. *Parable of the mustard seed (13.18,19; Matt. 13.31,32; Mark 4.30–32)*

18 He said therefore, "What is the kingdom of God like? And to what should I compare it? 19 It is like a mustard seed that someone took and sowed in the garden; it grew and became a tree, and the birds of the air made nests in its branches."

T. *Parable of the yeast (13.20,21; Matt. 13.31,32)*

20 And again he said, "To what should I compare the kingdom of God? 21 It is like yeast that a woman took and mixed in with[j] three measures of flour until all of it was leavened."

U. *The narrow door (13.22–30)*

22 Jesus[k] went through one town and village after another, teaching as he made his way to Jerusalem. 23 Someone asked him, "Lord, will only a few be saved?" He said to them, 24 "Strive to enter through the narrow door; for many, I tell you, will try to enter and will not be able. 25 When once the owner of the house has got up and shut the door, and you begin to stand outside and to knock at the door, saying, 'Lord, open to us,' then in reply he will say to you, 'I do not know where you come from.' 26 Then you will begin to say, 'We ate and drank with you, and you taught in our streets.' 27 But he will say, 'I do not know where you come from; go away from me, all you evildoers!' 28 There will be weeping and gnashing of teeth when you see Abraham and Isaac and Jacob and all the prophets in the kingdom of God, and you yourselves thrown out. 29 Then people will come from east and west, from north and south, and will eat in the kingdom of God. 30 Indeed, some are last who will be first, and some are first who will be last."

V. *Jesus sends a message to Herod and weeps over Jerusalem (13.31–35)*

31 At that very hour some Pharisees came and said to him, "Get away from here, for Herod wants to kill you." 32 He said to them, "Go and tell that fox for me,[l] 'Listen, I am casting out demons and performing cures today and tomorrow, and on the third day I finish my work. 33 Yet today, tomorrow, and the next day I must be on my way, because it is impossible for a prophet to be killed outside of Jerusalem.' 34 Jerusalem, Jerusalem, the city that kills the prophets and stones those who are sent to it! How often have I desired to gather your children together as a hen gathers her brood under her wings, and you were not willing! 35 See, your house is left to you. And I tell you, you will not see me until the time comes when[m] you say, 'Blessed is the one who comes in the name of the Lord.' "

W. *Jesus heals on the sabbath (14.1–6)*

14 On one occasion when Jesus[n] was going to the house of a leader of the Pharisees to eat a meal on the sabbath, they were watching him closely. 2 Just then, in front of him, there was a man who had dropsy. 3 And Jesus asked the lawyers and Pharisees, "Is it lawful to cure people

13.22 Lk 9.51
13.24 Mt 7.13
13.25 Mt 25.10-12; 7.23
13.27 Mt 7.23; 25.41
13.28 Mt 8.11, 12
13.30 Mt 19.30; Mk 10.31
13.32 Heb 2.10; 7.28
13.34 Mt 23.37-39; Lk 19.41
13.35 Ps 118.26; Mt 21.9; Lk 19.38
14.1 Mk 3.2
14.3 Mt 12.10; Mk 3.4; Lk 6.9

[j] Gk *hid in* [k] Gk *He* [l] Gk lacks *for me* [m] Other ancient authorities lack *the time comes when* [n] Gk *he*

13.19 See note on Mt 13.31,32.
13.20,21 See note on Mt 13.33.
13.22ff Salvation is through a narrow door, i.e., through Jesus Christ alone, who is the door (Jn 10.7). There is no other way to eternal life (Jn 14.6). All other doors lead to darkness and everlasting separation from the true God.
13.32 *tell that fox.* Christ was not terrified by the thought that Herod sought his life. By calling him a fox, Jesus spoke plainly that Herod was a man of insignificance and cunning.
14.1 *the sabbath.* See note on Mk 2.27.
14.3 Jesus confounded his critics by asking whether it was lawful to heal on the sabbath. They could not

younger of them said to his father, 'Father, give me the share of the property that will belong to me.' So he divided his property between them. 13 A few days later the younger son gathered all he had and traveled to a distant country, and there he squandered his property in dissolute living. 14 When he had spent everything, a severe famine took place throughout that country, and he began to be in need. 15 So he went and hired himself out to one of the citizens of that country, who sent him to his fields to feed the pigs. 16 He would gladly have filled himself with*u* the pods that the pigs were eating; and no one gave him anything. 17 But when he came to himself he said, 'How many of my father's hired hands have bread enough and to spare, but here I am dying of hunger! 18 I will get up and go to my father, and I will say to him, "Father, I have sinned against heaven and before you; 19 I am no longer worthy to be called your son; treat me like one of your hired hands."' 20 So he set off and went to his father. But while he was still far off, his father saw him and was filled with compassion; he ran and put his arms around him and kissed him. 21 Then the son said to him, 'Father, I have sinned against heaven and before you; I am no longer worthy to be called your son.'*v* 22 But the father said to his slaves, 'Quickly, bring out a robe — the best one — and put it on him; put a ring on his finger and sandals on his feet. 23 And get the fatted calf and kill it, and let us eat and celebrate; 24 for this son of mine was dead and is alive again; he was lost and is found!' And they began to celebrate.

25 "Now his elder son was in the field; and when he came and approached the house, he heard music and dancing. 26 He called one of the slaves and asked what was going on. 27 He replied, 'Your brother has come, and your father has killed the fatted calf, because he has got him back safe and sound.' 28 Then he became angry and refused to go in. His father came out and began to plead with him. 29 But he answered his father, 'Listen! For all these years I have been working like a slave for you, and I have never disobeyed your command; yet you have never given me even a young goat so that I might celebrate with my friends. 30 But when this son of yours came back, who has devoured your property with prostitutes, you killed the fatted calf for him!' 31 Then the father*w* said to him, 'Son, you are always with me, and all that is mine is yours. 32 But we had to celebrate and rejoice, because this brother of yours was dead and has come to life; he was lost and has been found.' "

BB. *Parable of the dishonest manager (16.1–13)*

16 Then Jesus*w* said to the disciples, "There was a rich man who had a manager, and charges were brought to him that this man was squandering his property. 2 So he summoned him and said to him, 'What is this that I hear about you? Give me an accounting of your management, because you cannot be my manager any longer.' 3 Then the manager said to himself, 'What will I do, now that my master is taking the position away from me? I am not strong enough to dig, and I am ashamed to beg. 4 I have decided what to do so that, when I am dismissed as manager, people may welcome me into their homes.' 5 So, summoning his master's debtors one by one, he asked the first, 'How much do you owe my master?' 6 He

u Other ancient authorities read *filled his stomach with*   *v* Other ancient authorities add *Treat me like one of your hired servants*   *w* Gk *he*

15.20
Gen 45.14;
46.29;
Acts 20.37
15.21
Ps 51.4
15.22
Zech 3.4;
Gen 41.42

15.24
v. 32;
1 Tim 5.6;
Eph 2.1; 5.14

15.30
v. 12

15.32
v. 24

16.1
Lk 15.13

and the lost coin become a lost son; the shepherd and the woman become the father. The prodigal son who left his father's house to live in sin repented and returned to be received with joy by his father. The reaction of the elder brother was like that of the Pharisees and scribes (cf. vv. 1,2).
15.20 What stands out in this parable is the incredible mercy shown by the loving father when his son returned.

15.32 The conversion of a single soul is the raising of that soul from the dead. It pleases God and should please the whole family of God.
16.1ff This parable was told in the presence of the Pharisees (cf. v. 14). The point is plain: if unsaved people spend all their time looking to their material interests and promoting their own welfare, believers should use their energies and talents to advance their spiritual interests — the only ones of lasting value.

answered, 'A hundred jugs of olive oil.' He said to him, 'Take your bill, sit down quickly, and make it fifty.' 7 Then he asked another, 'And how much do you owe?' He replied, 'A hundred containers of wheat.' He said to him, 'Take your bill and make it eighty.' 8 And his master commended the dishonest manager because he had acted shrewdly; for the children of this age are more shrewd in dealing with their own generation than are the children of light. 9 And I tell you, make friends for yourselves by means of dishonest wealth *x* so that when it is gone, they may welcome you into the eternal homes. *y*

10 "Whoever is faithful in a very little is faithful also in much; and whoever is dishonest in a very little is dishonest also in much. 11 If then you have not been faithful with the dishonest wealth, *x* who will entrust to you the true riches? 12 And if you have not been faithful with what belongs to another, who will give you what is your own? 13 No slave can serve two masters; for a slave will either hate the one and love the other, or be devoted to the one and despise the other. You cannot serve God and wealth." *x*

CC. *Jesus answers the Pharisees (16.14–18)*

14 The Pharisees, who were lovers of money, heard all this, and they ridiculed him. 15 So he said to them, "You are those who justify yourselves in the sight of others; but God knows your hearts; for what is prized by human beings is an abomination in the sight of God.

16 "The law and the prophets were in effect until John came; since then the good news of the kingdom of God is proclaimed, and everyone tries to enter it by force. *z* 17 But it is easier for heaven and earth to pass away, than for one stroke of a letter in the law to be dropped.

18 "Anyone who divorces his wife and marries another commits adultery, and whoever marries a woman divorced from her husband commits adultery.

DD. *The rich man and Lazarus (16.19–31)*

19 "There was a rich man who was dressed in purple and fine linen and who feasted sumptuously every day. 20 And at his gate lay a poor man named Lazarus, covered with sores, 21 who longed to satisfy his hunger with what fell from the rich man's table; even the dogs would come and lick his sores. 22 The poor man died and was carried away by the angels to be with Abraham. *a* The rich man also died and was buried. 23 In Hades, where he was being tormented, he looked up and saw Abraham far away with Lazarus by his side. *b* 24 He called out, 'Father Abraham, have mercy on me, and send Lazarus to dip the tip of his finger in water and cool my tongue; for I am in agony in these flames.' 25 But Abraham said, 'Child, remember that during your lifetime you received your good things, and Lazarus in like manner evil things; but now he is comforted here, and you are in agony. 26 Besides all this, between you and us a great chasm has been fixed, so that those who might want to pass from here to you cannot do so, and no one can cross from there to us.' 27 He said, 'Then, father, I beg you to send him to my father's house — 28 for I have five brothers — that he may warn them, so that they will not also come into

16.8
Jn 12.36;
Eph 5.8;
1 Thess 5.5
16.9
Mt 6.19, 24;
19.21;
Lk 11.41;
12.33
16.10
Mt 25.21;
Lk 19.17
16.11
v. 9
16.13
Mt 6.24

16.14
2 Tim 3.2;
Lk 23.35
16.15
Lk 10.29;
1 Sam 16.7;
Prov 21.2;
Acts 1.24
16.16
Mt 11.12,
13; 4.23
16.17
Isa 40.8;
Mt 5.17, 18;
Lk 21.33
16.18
Mt 5.31, 32;
19.19;
Mk 10.11;
1 Cor 7.10,
11

16.20
Acts 3.2

16.22
Jn 13.23
16.23
Mt 11.23
16.24
v. 30;
Mt 25.41
16.25
Lk 6.24

---

x Gk *mammon*   *y* Gk *tents*   *z* Or *everyone is strongly urged to enter it*   *a* Gk *to Abraham's bosom*   *b* Gk *in his bosom*

16.11 The truly rich are those who are rich in faith. The riches of the world are deceitful and uncertain.
16.18 See note on Mk 10.5ff.
16.19ff Some think this is a parable; others believe it is a true story. In either event it teaches two lessons: (1) wealth and one's social status are no guarantee of eternal life; and (2) the Scriptures have supplied sin-

ners with all the information they need to keep them from everlasting destruction.
16.23 *Hades*, i.e., that part of Hades where unbelievers go to await the final judgment. The rich man is conscious; he is already suffering. He receives no second chance, nor can he communicate with the living.

this place of torment.' 29 Abraham replied, 'They have Moses and the prophets; they should listen to them.' 30 He said, 'No, father Abraham; but if someone goes to them from the dead, they will repent.' 31 He said to him, 'If they do not listen to Moses and the prophets, neither will they be convinced even if someone rises from the dead.' "

16.29
Lk 4.17;
Jn 5.45-47;
Acts 15.21
16.30
Lk 3.8; 19.9

EE. *Jesus' teaching on forgiveness and faith (17.1–10)*

17   Jesus*c* said to his disciples, "Occasions for stumbling are bound to come, but woe to anyone by whom they come! 2 It would be better for you if a millstone were hung around your neck and you were thrown into the sea than for you to cause one of these little ones to stumble. 3 Be on your guard! If another disciple*d* sins, you must rebuke the offender, and if there is repentance, you must forgive. 4 And if the same person sins against you seven times a day, and turns back to you seven times and says, 'I repent,' you must forgive."

17.1
Mt 18.6, 7;
Mk 9.42;
1 Cor 11.19
17.2
1 Cor 8.12
17.3
Mt 18.15
17.4
Mt 18.21, 22

5   The apostles said to the Lord, "Increase our faith!" 6 The Lord replied, "If you had faith the size of a*e* mustard seed, you could say to this mulberry tree, 'Be uprooted and planted in the sea,' and it would obey you.

17.5
Mk 6.30
17.6
Mt 17.20;
21.21;
Mk 9.23;
Lk 7.13

7   "Who among you would say to your slave who has just come in from plowing or tending sheep in the field, 'Come here at once and take your place at the table'? 8 Would you not rather say to him, 'Prepare supper for me, put on your apron and serve me while I eat and drink; later you may eat and drink'? 9 Do you thank the slave for doing what was commanded? 10 So you also, when you have done all that you were ordered to do, say, 'We are worthless slaves; we have done only what we ought to have done!' "

17.8
Lk 12.37

FF. *The healing of the ten lepers (17.11–19)*

11   On the way to Jerusalem Jesus*f* was going through the region between Samaria and Galilee. 12 As he entered a village, ten lepers*g* approached him. Keeping their distance, 13 they called out, saying, "Jesus, Master, have mercy on us!" 14 When he saw them, he said to them, "Go and show yourselves to the priests." And as they went, they were made clean. 15 Then one of them, when he saw that he was healed, turned back, praising God with a loud voice. 16 He prostrated himself at Jesus'*h* feet and thanked him. And he was a Samaritan. 17 Then Jesus asked, "Were not ten made clean? But the other nine, where are they? 18 Was none of them found to return and give praise to God except this foreigner?" 19 Then he said to him, "Get up and go on your way; your faith has made you well."

17.11
Lk 9.51, 52;
Jn 4.3, 4
17.12
Lev 13.46
17.14
Lev 13.2;
14.2;
Mt 8.4
17.15
Mt 9.8
17.16
Mt 10.5

17.19
Mt 9.22;
Mk 5.34;
Lk 7.50;
8.48; 18.42

GG. *The coming of the kingdom (17.20,21)*

20   Once Jesus*f* was asked by the Pharisees when the kingdom of God was coming, and he answered, "The kingdom of God is not coming with things that can be observed; 21 nor will they say, 'Look, here it is!' or 'There it is!' For, in fact, the kingdom of God is among*i* you."

17.20
Lk 19.11;
Acts 1.6
17.21
v. 23

c Gk *He* *d* Gk *your brother* *e* Gk *faith as a grain of* *f* Gk *he* *g* The terms *leper* and *leprosy* can refer to several diseases *h* Gk *his* *i* Or *within*

17.3   To forgive those who offend us is one of our greatest reponsibilities; vengeance is wrong. We must be willing to forgive freely, even seven times a day — which suggests an indefinite number.
17.7   Those who serve Christ must be humble slaves who admit they do not merit any favor with God. Those who do all they are commanded are not worthy of special notice, for they have done no more than they ought to have done.
17.12   The Jews supposed that leprosy was inflicted

on people as a punishment for a particular sin. The ten lepers asked Jesus for mercy without mentioning their leprosy. Jesus did not tell them they were healed. Rather, he said for them to show themselves to the priests, who would look to see whether they were unclean. While en route to see the priests, their leprosy vanished. Only one, a Samaritan, returned to give thanks and praise God.
17.21   *among you.* This means there is an already existing spiritual reality in the hearts of humans.

HH. *Christ's second coming (17.22–37)*

22 Then he said to the disciples, "The days are coming when you will long to see one of the days of the Son of Man, and you will not see it. 23 They will say to you, 'Look there!' or 'Look here!' Do not go, do not set off in pursuit. 24 For as the lightning flashes and lights up the sky from one side to the other, so will the Son of Man be in his day.*j* 25 But first he must endure much suffering and be rejected by this generation. 26 Just as it was in the days of Noah, so too it will be in the days of the Son of Man. 27 They were eating and drinking, and marrying and being given in marriage, until the day Noah entered the ark, and the flood came and destroyed all of them. 28 Likewise, just as it was in the days of Lot: they were eating and drinking, buying and selling, planting and building, 29 but on the day that Lot left Sodom, it rained fire and sulfur from heaven and destroyed all of them 30 — it will be like that on the day that the Son of Man is revealed. 31 On that day, anyone on the housetop who has belongings in the house must not come down to take them away; and likewise anyone in the field must not turn back. 32 Remember Lot's wife. 33 Those who try to make their life secure will lose it, but those who lose their life will keep it. 34 I tell you, on that night there will be two in one bed; one will be taken and the other left. 35 There will be two women grinding meal together; one will be taken and the other left."*k* 37 Then they asked him, "Where, Lord?" He said to them, "Where the corpse is, there the vultures will gather."

II. *Parable of the widow and the judge (18.1–8)*

18 Then Jesus*l* told them a parable about their need to pray always and not to lose heart. 2 He said, "In a certain city there was a judge who neither feared God nor had respect for people. 3 In that city there was a widow who kept coming to him and saying, 'Grant me justice against my opponent.' 4 For a while he refused; but later he said to himself, 'Though I have no fear of God and no respect for anyone, 5 yet because this widow keeps bothering me, I will grant her justice, so that she may not wear me out by continually coming.' "*m* 6 And the Lord said, "Listen to what the unjust judge says. 7 And will not God grant justice to his chosen ones who cry to him day and night? Will he delay long in helping them? 8 I tell you, he will quickly grant justice to them. And yet, when the Son of Man comes, will he find faith on earth?"

JJ. *Parable of the Pharisee and the tax collector (18.9–14)*

9 He also told this parable to some who trusted in themselves that they were righteous and regarded others with contempt: 10 "Two men went up to the temple to pray, one a Pharisee and the other a tax collector. 11 The Pharisee, standing by himself, was praying thus, 'God, I thank you that

---

j Other ancient authorities lack *in his day* *k* Other ancient authorities add verse 36, "Two will be in the field; one will be taken and the other left." *l* Gk *he* *m* Or *so that she may not finally come and slap me in the face*

Those who have Jesus as king of their lives show it in their daily actions. In its outward form, the kingdom of God will come with the second advent of Jesus. **17.26,27** Until the time of Jesus' coming many people will be fully absorbed in worldly activities and concern for the material aspects of life. They will take no precautions for the return of the Son of God and will not be prepared for it. Therefore the judgment will overtake them suddenly and unexpectedly, and they will have no opportunity to find deliverance. **18.1ff** The faithful people of God should persist in

prayer when they do not receive an immediate answer. **18.9ff** *be merciful to me.* This parable shows the difference between the self-righteous Pharisee who boasted of his good works and the cheating tax collector who knew he was wicked and who sought the mercy of God without any works of righteousness. **18.12** *I fast twice a week.* The law of Moses required fasting one day in the year in connection with the day of atonement (see Lev 16.29ff; cf. Acts 27.9). The

I am not like other people: thieves, rogues, adulterers, or even like this tax collector. 12 I fast twice a week; I give a tenth of all my income.' 13 But the tax collector, standing far off, would not even look up to heaven, but was beating his breast and saying, 'God, be merciful to me, a sinner!' 14 I tell you, this man went down to his home justified rather than the other; for all who exalt themselves will be humbled, but all who humble themselves will be exalted."

KK. *Jesus and the little children*
(18.15–17; Matt. 19.13–15; Mark 10.13–16)

15 People were bringing even infants to him that he might touch them; and when the disciples saw it, they sternly ordered them not to do it. 16 But Jesus called for them and said, "Let the little children come to me, and do not stop them; for it is to such as these that the kingdom of God belongs. 17 Truly I tell you, whoever does not receive the kingdom of God as a little child will never enter it."

LL. *The rich young ruler*
(18.18–30; Matt. 19.16–30; Mark 10.17–31)

18 A certain ruler asked him, "Good Teacher, what must I do to inherit eternal life?" 19 Jesus said to him, "Why do you call me good? No one is good but God alone. 20 You know the commandments: 'You shall not commit adultery; You shall not murder; You shall not steal; You shall not bear false witness; Honor your father and mother.' " 21 He replied, "I have kept all these since my youth." 22 When Jesus heard this, he said to him, "There is still one thing lacking. Sell all that you own and distribute the money[n] to the poor, and you will have treasure in heaven; then come, follow me." 23 But when he heard this, he became sad; for he was very rich. 24 Jesus looked at him and said, "How hard it is for those who have wealth to enter the kingdom of God! 25 Indeed, it is easier for a camel to go through the eye of a needle than for someone who is rich to enter the kingdom of God."

26 Those who heard it said, "Then who can be saved?" 27 He replied, "What is impossible for mortals is possible for God."

28 Then Peter said, "Look, we have left our homes and followed you." 29 And he said to them, "Truly I tell you, there is no one who has left house or wife or brothers or parents or children, for the sake of the kingdom of God, 30 who will not get back very much more in this age, and in the age to come eternal life."

MM. *Christ foretells his crucifixion and resurrection*
(18.31–34; Matt. 20.17–19; Mark 10.32–34)

31 Then he took the twelve aside and said to them, "See, we are going up to Jerusalem, and everything that is written about the Son of Man by the prophets will be accomplished. 32 For he will be handed over to the Gentiles; and he will be mocked and insulted and spat upon. 33 After they have flogged him, they will kill him, and on the third day he will rise again." 34 But they understood nothing about all these things; in fact, what he said was hidden from them, and they did not grasp what was said.

---

n Gk lacks *the money*

18.12	Mt 9.14; Lk 11.42
18.13	Lk 23.48
18.14	Mt 23.12; Lk 14.11; 1 Pet 5.6
18.17	Mt 18.3
18.18	Lk 10.25
18.20	Ex 20.12-16; Deut 5.16-20; Rom 13.9
18.22	Lk 12.33; Mt 19.21
18.24	Prov 11.28
18.27	Gen 18.14; Job 42.2; Jer 32.17; Lk 1.37
18.28	Lk 5.11
18.30	Mt 12.32
18.31	Lk 9.51; Ps 22
18.32	Mt 16.21; 27.2; Lk 23.1
18.34	Mk 9.32; Lk 9.45

Pharisee here fasted two days a week; not even oral tradition required that. He was proud of the fact that he exceeded the requirements of the law. The Pharisees and the disciples of John the Baptist often fasted

(5.33; Matt 9.14; Mk 2.18; see note on Mk 2.18 on fasting).
18.18ff See note on Mt 19.16ff.
18.19 See note on Mk 10.18.

NN. *Healing the blind man near Jericho*
(18.35–43; Matt. 20.29–34; Mark 10.46–52)

35 As he approached Jericho, a blind man was sitting by the roadside begging. 36 When he heard a crowd going by, he asked what was happening. 37 They told him, "Jesus of Nazareth*o* is passing by." 38 Then he shouted, "Jesus, Son of David, have mercy on me!" 39 Those who were in front sternly ordered him to be quiet; but he shouted even more loudly, "Son of David, have mercy on me!" 40 Jesus stood still and ordered the man to be brought to him; and when he came near, he asked him, 41 "What do you want me to do for you?" He said, "Lord, let me see again." 42 Jesus said to him, "Receive your sight; your faith has saved you." 43 Immediately he regained his sight and followed him, glorifying God; and all the people, when they saw it, praised God.

OO. *The conversion of Zaccheus (19.1–10)*

19 He entered Jericho and was passing through it. 2 A man was there named Zacchaeus; he was a chief tax collector and was rich. 3 He was trying to see who Jesus was, but on account of the crowd he could not, because he was short in stature. 4 So he ran ahead and climbed a sycamore tree to see him, because he was going to pass that way. 5 When Jesus came to the place, he looked up and said to him, "Zacchaeus, hurry and come down; for I must stay at your house today." 6 So he hurried down and was happy to welcome him. 7 All who saw it began to grumble and said, "He has gone to be the guest of one who is a sinner." 8 Zacchaeus stood there and said to the Lord, "Look, half of my possessions, Lord, I will give to the poor; and if I have defrauded anyone of anything, I will pay back four times as much." 9 Then Jesus said to him, "Today salvation has come to this house, because he too is a son of Abraham. 10 For the Son of Man came to seek out and to save the lost."

PP. *The parable of the pounds (19.11–27)*

11 As they were listening to this, he went on to tell a parable, because he was near Jerusalem, and because they supposed that the kingdom of God was to appear immediately. 12 So he said, "A nobleman went to a distant country to get royal power for himself and then return. 13 He summoned ten of his slaves, and gave them ten pounds,*p* and said to them, 'Do business with these until I come back.' 14 But the citizens of his country hated him and sent a delegation after him, saying, 'We do not want this man to rule over us.' 15 When he returned, having received royal power, he ordered these slaves, to whom he had given the money, to be summoned so that he might find out what they had gained by trading. 16 The first came forward and said, 'Lord, your pound has made ten more pounds.' 17 He said to him, 'Well done, good slave! Because you have been trustworthy in a very small thing, take charge of ten cities.' 18 Then the second came, saying, 'Lord, your pound has made five pounds.' 19 He said

Marginal references (left column):
18.38
Mt 9.27
18.39
v. 38

18.42
Mt 9.22;
Mk 5.34;
Lk 17.19
18.43
Mt 9.8;
Lk 13.17

19.1
Lk 18.35

19.4
1 Kings 10.27;
1 Chr 27.28;
Isa 9.10

19.7
Mt 9.11;
Lk 5.30
19.8
Lk 7.13;
3.14;
Ex 22.1;
Lev 6.5;
Num 5.7;
2 Sam 12.6
19.9
Lk 3.8;
13.16;
Rom 4.16;
Gal 3.7
19.10
Mt 18.11
19.11
Acts 1.6
19.12
Mt 25.14-30;
Mk 13.34

19.17
Lk 16.10

o Gk *the Nazorean*   *p* The mina, rendered here by *pound*, was about three months' wages for a laborer

---

18.35 *Jericho.* There were two Jerichos: one was the site of a Canaanite city (cf. Josh 2); the new Jericho had been a recently built Herodian city.
19.1 Only Luke tells the story about Zacchaeus, a Jewish tax collector who had others working under him. He was rich, which probably means that he extorted money from the taxpayers. Nonetheless, he was determined to see Jesus. Without Zacchaeus saying a word to Jesus, Jesus told him that he would stay at his house. For a Jew to enter the house of a tax collector was unheard of, and the Jews were angry with Jesus. Yet salvation came to this despised person, for Jesus came to save the lost.

19.11ff This story, in which Jesus pictured himself as the nobleman who went away and left all to his slaves, has the same messages as the parable of the talents in Mt 25.14ff. (1) Diligence receives its rich reward; laziness is punished. In God's kingdom, a fatal destiny awaits those who are not truly the Lord's slaves and who refuse to let him reign over them. (2) The kingdom of God will not appear immediately, for the king went into a far country to get royal power for himself. That is, Christ must first go to heaven and sit at the right hand of the Father; at the end of the age he will return.

to him, 'And you, rule over five cities.' 20 Then the other came, saying, 'Lord, here is your pound. I wrapped it up in a piece of cloth, 21 for I was afraid of you, because you are a harsh man; you take what you did not deposit, and reap what you did not sow.' 22 He said to him, 'I will judge you by your own words, you wicked slave! You knew, did you, that I was a harsh man, taking what I did not deposit and reaping what I did not sow? 23 Why then did you not put my money into the bank? Then when I returned, I could have collected it with interest.' 24 He said to the bystanders, 'Take the pound from him and give it to the one who has ten pounds.' 25 (And they said to him, 'Lord, he has ten pounds!') 26 'I tell you, to all those who have, more will be given; but from those who have nothing, even what they have will be taken away. 27 But as for these enemies of mine who did not want me to be king over them — bring them here and slaughter them in my presence.' "

VII. The last week in Jerusalem (19.28–24.53)

A. The triumphal entry
(19.28–40; Matt. 21.1–11; Mark 11.1–11; John 12.12–19)

28 After he had said this, he went on ahead, going up to Jerusalem. 29 When he had come near Bethphage and Bethany, at the place called the Mount of Olives, he sent two of the disciples, 30 saying, "Go into the village ahead of you, and as you enter it you will find tied there a colt that has never been ridden. Untie it and bring it here. 31 If anyone asks you, 'Why are you untying it?' just say this, 'The Lord needs it.' " 32 So those who were sent departed and found it as he had told them. 33 As they were untying the colt, its owners asked them, "Why are you untying the colt?" 34 They said, "The Lord needs it." 35 Then they brought it to Jesus; and after throwing their cloaks on the colt, they set Jesus on it. 36 As he rode along, people kept spreading their cloaks on the road. 37 As he was now approaching the path down from the Mount of Olives, the whole multitude of the disciples began to praise God joyfully with a loud voice for all the deeds of power that they had seen, 38 saying,

"Blessed is the king
   who comes in the name of the Lord!
   Peace in heaven,
      and glory in the highest heaven!"

39 Some of the Pharisees in the crowd said to him, "Teacher, order your disciples to stop." 40 He answered, "I tell you, if these were silent, the stones would shout out."

B. Jesus weeps over Jerusalem (19.41–44)

41 As he came near and saw the city, he wept over it, 42 saying, "If you, even you, had only recognized on this day the things that make for peace! But now they are hidden from your eyes. 43 Indeed, the days will come upon you, when your enemies will set up ramparts around you and surround you, and hem you in on every side. 44 They will crush you to the ground, you and your children within you, and they will not leave

against him.

19.28ff Jesus' triumphal entry into Jerusalem is recorded in all four Gospels, an event which fulfilled the prophecy of Zech 9.9. It took place on the first day of the week of Christ's passion, when he was to be rejected and crucified. He came into Jerusalem as king and conqueror; this was a preview of his second advent, when he will come in power and great glory. This was the last opportunity for the Jews to face up to his royal claims and make their decision for or

19.41 Luke alone records the fact that Jesus' entry into Jerusalem was interrupted briefly as he stopped to weep over the city and bemoan the fact that the Jews would not surrender to his claims. His tears were a sign of Jerusalem's appointed doom that occurred in A.D. 70 as a direct consequence of the Jewish rejection of the Messiah.

19.21 Mt 25.24 | 19.22 2 Sam 1.16; Job 15.6; Mt 25.26 | 19.26 Mt 13.12; Lk 8.18 | 19.28 Mk 10.32; Mt 21.17; Lk 21.37 | 19.32 Lk 22.13 | 19.36 2 Kings 9.13 | 19.38 Ps 118.26; Lk 13.35; 2.14 | 19.39 Mt 21.15, 16 | 19.40 Hab 2.11 | 19.41 Lk 13.34, 35 | 19.43 Isa 29.3; Jer 6.6; Ezek 4.2; Lk 21.20 | 19.44 Mt 24.2; Mk 13.2; Lk 21.6; 1 Pet 2.12

within you one stone upon another; because you did not recognize the time of your visitation from God."*q*

C. *Second cleansing of the temple*
(19.45–48; Matt. 21.12–17; Mark 11.15–19; cf. John 2.13–22)

19.46
Isa 56.7

45 Then he entered the temple and began to drive out those who were selling things there; 46 and he said, "It is written,

'My house shall be a house of prayer';

but you have made it a den of robbers."

19.47
Mt 26.55;
Mk 11.18;
Jn 7.19

47 Every day he was teaching in the temple. The chief priests, the scribes, and the leaders of the people kept looking for a way to kill him; 48 but they did not find anything they could do, for all the people were spellbound by what they heard.

D. *Christ's authority challenged*
(20.1–8; Matt. 21.23–27; Mark 11.27–33)

20.1
Mt 26.55;
Lk 8.1
20.2
Jn 2.18;
Acts 4.7; 7.27

20 One day, as he was teaching the people in the temple and telling the good news, the chief priests and the scribes came with the elders 2 and said to him, "Tell us, by what authority are you doing these things? Who is it who gave you this authority?" 3 He answered them, "I will also ask you a question, and you tell me: 4 Did the baptism of John come from heaven, or was it of human origin?" 5 They discussed it with one another, saying, "If we say, 'From heaven,' he will say, 'Why did you

20.6
Mt 14.5;
Lk 7.29

not believe him?' 6 But if we say, 'Of human origin,' all the people will stone us; for they are convinced that John was a prophet." 7 So they answered that they did not know where it came from. 8 Then Jesus said to them, "Neither will I tell you by what authority I am doing these things."

E. *Parable of the wicked tenants*
(20.9–18; Matt. 21.33–46; Mark 12.1–12)

20.9
Isa 5.1-7;
Mt 25.14

9 He began to tell the people this parable: "A man planted a vineyard, and leased it to tenants, and went to another country for a long time. 10 When the season came, he sent a slave to the tenants in order that they might give him his share of the produce of the vineyard; but the tenants beat him and sent him away empty-handed. 11 Next he sent another slave; that one also they beat and insulted and sent away empty-handed. 12 And he sent still a third; this one also they wounded and threw out. 13 Then the owner of the vineyard said, 'What shall I do? I will send my beloved son; perhaps they will respect him.' 14 But when the tenants saw him, they discussed it among themselves and said, 'This is the heir; let us kill him so that the inheritance may be ours.' 15 So they threw him out of the vineyard and killed him. What then will the owner of the vineyard do to

20.16
Lk 19.27;
Rom 3.4, 6,
31
20.17
Ps 118.22,
23; 1 Pet 2.6

them? 16 He will come and destroy those tenants and give the vineyard to others." When they heard this, they said, "Heaven forbid!" 17 But he looked at them and said, "What then does this text mean:

'The stone that the builders rejected

q Gk lacks *from God*

19.45 Jesus loved the purity of the temple more than its wealth and for the second time, he cleansed it (see Jn 2.13–22). This house of prayer was being profaned by those who bought and sold there (see note on Mk 11.15ff).
20.2 It is not unusual for people to question what is obvious. Christ's miracles showed by what authority he did his works. The Jews knew his authority was divine and not human. Thus when Jesus asked them

about John and his authority, they were stumped. By questioning Jesus' authority the chief priests, scribes, and elders lost their own authority.
20.9ff This parable of the wicked tenants symbolized the Jewish nation and its rejection of God's Messiah. Jesus warned of the dire consequences of this decision — not only would they be cast out, but their inheritance would be given over to Gentiles, who would be offered the kingdom.

has become the cornerstone'?"[r]
18 Everyone who falls on that stone will be broken to pieces; and it will crush anyone on whom it falls." 19 When the scribes and chief priests realized that he had told this parable against them, they wanted to lay hands on him at that very hour, but they feared the people.

20.18
Isa 8.14, 15
20.19
Lk 19.47

F. Paying taxes to the emperor
(20.19–26; Matt. 22.15–22; Mark 12.13–17)

20 So they watched him and sent spies who pretended to be honest, in order to trap him by what he said, so as to hand him over to the jurisdiction and authority of the governor. 21 So they asked him, "Teacher, we know that you are right in what you say and teach, and you show deference to no one, but teach the way of God in accordance with truth. 22 Is it lawful for us to pay taxes to the emperor, or not?" 23 But he perceived their craftiness and said to them, 24 "Show me a denarius. Whose head and whose title does it bear?" They said, "The emperor's." 25 He said to them, "Then give to the emperor the things that are the emperor's, and to God the things that are God's." 26 And they were not able in the presence of the people to trap him by what he said; and being amazed by his answer, they became silent.

20.21
Jn 3.2

20.25
Rom 13.7;
Lk 23.2

G. The Sadducees and the resurrection
(20.27–40; Matt. 22.23–33; Mark 12.18–27)

27 Some Sadducees, those who say there is no resurrection, came to him 28 and asked him a question, "Teacher, Moses wrote for us that if a man's brother dies, leaving a wife but no children, the man[s] shall marry the widow and raise up children for his brother. 29 Now there were seven brothers; the first married, and died childless; 30 then the second 31 and the third married her, and so in the same way all seven died childless. 32 Finally the woman also died. 33 In the resurrection, therefore, whose wife will the woman be? For the seven had married her."

34 Jesus said to them, "Those who belong to this age marry and are given in marriage; 35 but those who are considered worthy of a place in that age and in the resurrection from the dead neither marry nor are given in marriage. 36 Indeed they cannot die anymore, because they are like angels and are children of God, being children of the resurrection. 37 And the fact that the dead are raised Moses himself showed, in the story about the bush, where he speaks of the Lord as the God of Abraham, the God of Isaac, and the God of Jacob. 38 Now he is God not of the dead, but of the living; for to him all of them are alive." 39 Then some of the scribes answered, "Teacher, you have spoken well." 40 For they no longer dared to ask him another question.

20.27
Acts 23.6, 8
20.28
Deut 25.5

20.36
Rom 8.16,
17; 1 Jn 3.1,
2
20.37
Ex 3.6
20.38
Rom 6.10, 11
20.40
Mt 22.46;
Mk 12.34

[r] Or keystone   [s] Gk his brother

20.20 Jesus' enemies wanted to deliver him over to the power and authority of the Roman government, for only the governor could condemn him to death. They needed some legitimate claim against him, so they asked whether it was lawful for the free-born sons of Abraham to pay tribute to the emperor. If Jesus said it was wrong, they could deliver him to the Roman government for treason. If he said it was right, the Jews would be angry, for they thought the Messiah should free them from Rome's yoke. The questioners admitted that the coin they gave Jesus had the emperor's image on it. Since they had no problem using the emperor's money as an instrument of commerce, Jesus replied, they ought to pay tribute to the one who gave them this convenience. But the Jews were not to be bound by the claims of the emperor's religion, for only God has the authority to say, "Give me your heart."

20.27ff Some Sadducees. The Sadducees usually stood in opposition to the Pharisees, but when it came to Jesus they were in league with each other to rid themselves of him. The Sadducees did not believe in the resurrection of the dead, yet they asked Jesus a question about that issue in order to entrap him. They supposed that Jesus could not answer their question and that this would further their cause against the doctrine of the bodily resurrection. But as usual the Son of God used Scripture to support his answer and left them confounded.

H. *Christ's unanswerable question*
(20.41–44; Matt. 22.41–46; Mark 12.35–37)

41   Then he said to them, "How can they say that the Messiah[t] is David's son? 42 For David himself says in the book of Psalms,

'The Lord said to my Lord,
  "Sit at my right hand,
43   until I make your enemies your footstool." '

44 David thus calls him Lord; so how can he be his son?"

I. *Warning against the scribes*
(20.45–47; Matt. 23.1–12; Mark 12.38–40)

45   In the hearing of all the people he said to the[u] disciples, 46 "Beware of the scribes, who like to walk around in long robes, and love to be greeted with respect in the marketplaces, and to have the best seats in the synagogues and places of honor at banquets. 47 They devour widows' houses and for the sake of appearance say long prayers. They will receive the greater condemnation."

J. *The widow's offering (21.1–4)*

21 He looked up and saw rich people putting their gifts into the treasury; 2 he also saw a poor widow put in two small copper coins. 3 He said, "Truly I tell you, this poor widow has put in more than all of them; 4 for all of them have contributed out of their abundance, but she out of her poverty has put in all she had to live on."

K. *The Olivet discourse (21.5–38; Matt. 24; Mark 13)*

1. *The course of this age (21.5–19; Matt. 24.1–14; Mark 13.3–13)*

5   When some were speaking about the temple, how it was adorned with beautiful stones and gifts dedicated to God, he said, 6 "As for these things that you see, the days will come when not one stone will be left upon another; all will be thrown down."

7   They asked him, "Teacher, when will this be, and what will be the sign that this is about to take place?" 8 And he said, "Beware that you are not led astray; for many will come in my name and say, 'I am he!'[v] and, 'The time is near!'[w] Do not go after them.

9   "When you hear of wars and insurrections, do not be terrified; for these things must take place first, but the end will not follow immediately." 10 Then he said to them, "Nation will rise against nation, and kingdom against kingdom; 11 there will be great earthquakes, and in various places famines and plagues; and there will be dreadful portents and great signs from heaven.

12   "But before all this occurs, they will arrest you and persecute you; they will hand you over to synagogues and prisons, and you will be brought before kings and governors because of my name. 13 This will give you an opportunity to testify. 14 So make up your minds not to prepare your defense in advance; 15 for I will give you words[x] and a wisdom that

Side references (left margin):

20.42
Ps 110.1;
Acts 2.34

20.46
Lk 11.43

21.1
Mk 12.41-44
21.2
Mk 12.42

21.5
Mk 13.1
21.6
Lk 19.44

21.8
Mk 13.21;
Lk 17.23

21.10
2 Chr 15.6;
Isa 19.2

21.12
Jn 16.2

21.13
Phil 1.12
21.14
Lk 12.11, 12
21.15
Lk 12.12

---

t Or *the Christ*   *u* Other ancient authorities read *his*   *v* Gk *I am*   *w* Or *at hand*   *x* Gk *a mouth*

20.42ff   *The Lord said to my Lord.* The first use of Lord in Ps 110.1 means "God"; the second one means "Messiah" (who would be the Son of David). Jesus' question was this: If David calls his son Lord, how then can he be his son? The answer is: (1) Christ as God was David's Lord; (2) Christ as man was David's son (see note on Mk 12.35).
20.46   Jesus accused the scribes of being proud, hypocritical, covetous, and oppressive; they used religion

as a cloak for crime. Their pretended piety constituted a double iniquity, for which they had to pay.
21.7   See note on Mt 24.3.
21.15   The disciples of Jesus, then and now, need not be afraid about what to say when they stand before Jewish or pagan authorities. Christ through the Spirit will tell them what to say and their testimony will not be overthrown or disproved. They may not be acquitted because their persecutors, filled with hatred, will

none of your opponents will be able to withstand or contradict. 16 You will be betrayed even by parents and brothers, by relatives and friends; and they will put some of you to death. 17 You will be hated by all because of my name. 18 But not a hair of your head will perish. 19 By your endurance you will gain your souls.

2. The destruction of Jerusalem
(21.20–24; Matt. 24.15–28; Mark 13.14–23)

20 "When you see Jerusalem surrounded by armies, then know that its desolation has come near.ʸ 21 Then those in Judea must flee to the mountains, and those inside the city must leave it, and those out in the country must not enter it; 22 for these are days of vengeance, as a fulfillment of all that is written. 23 Woe to those who are pregnant and to those who are nursing infants in those days! For there will be great distress on the earth and wrath against this people; 24 they will fall by the edge of the sword and be taken away as captives among all nations; and Jerusalem will be trampled on by the Gentiles, until the times of the Gentiles are fulfilled.

3. The second coming of Christ
(21.25–28; Matt. 24.29–31; Mark 13.24–27)

25 "There will be signs in the sun, the moon, and the stars, and on the earth distress among nations confused by the roaring of the sea and the waves. 26 People will faint from fear and foreboding of what is coming upon the world, for the powers of the heavens will be shaken. 27 Then they will see 'the Son of Man coming in a cloud' with power and great glory. 28 Now when these things begin to take place, stand up and raise your heads, because your redemption is drawing near."

4. The parable of the fig tree
(21.29–33; Matt. 24.32–35; Mark 13.28–31)

29 Then he told them a parable: "Look at the fig tree and all the trees; 30 as soon as they sprout leaves you can see for yourselves and know that summer is already near. 31 So also, when you see these things taking place, you know that the kingdom of God is near. 32 Truly I tell you, this generation will not pass away until all things have taken place. 33 Heaven and earth will pass away, but my words will not pass away.

5. Watchfulness (21.34–38; Matt. 24.36–51; Mark 13.32–37)

34 "Be on guard so that your hearts are not weighed down with dissipation and drunkenness and the worries of this life, and that day does not catch you unexpectedly, 35 like a trap. For it will come upon all who live on the face of the whole earth. 36 Be alert at all times, praying that you may have the strength to escape all these things that will take place, and to stand before the Son of Man."

37 Every day he was teaching in the temple, and at night he would go out and spend the night on the Mount of Olives, as it was called. 38 And all the people would get up early in the morning to listen to him in the temple.

y Or is at hand

21.16
Lk 12.52, 53

21.17
Mt 10.22
21.18
Mt 10.30;
Lk 12.7
21.19
Rev 2.7

21.20
Lk 19.43
21.21
Lk 17.31

21.22
Isa 63.4;
Dan 9.24-27;
Zech 11.1

21.24
Isa 63.18;
Dan 8.13;
9.27; 12.7;
Rom 11.25;
Rev 11.2

21.25
2 Pet 3.10, 12

21.27
Rev 1.7;
14.14
21.28
Lk 18.7

21.31
Mt 3.2

21.33
Lk 16.17

21.34
Mk 4.19;
Lk 12.45;
1 Thess 5.6, 7
21.36
Lk 18.1

21.37
Lk 19.47;
Mk 11.19

condemn them even if they can prove nothing against them. Some will be imprisoned, beaten, or put to death.
21.20–24 Jesus' prophecy about Jerusalem's destruction was literally fulfilled in A.D. 70 when Titus and the Roman legions captured it. Josephus, the Jewish historian, describes the taking of the city in some detail in his *Wars of the Jews*, Books V and VI. After A.D. 70, Jerusalem was trampled on by the Gentiles (v. 24). Some think the recent return of the Jews to Israel and their control of Jerusalem marks the end of "the times of the Gentiles" and the fulfillment of this prophetic word.

L. The plot to kill Jesus
(22.1–6; Matt. 26.1–5,14–16; Mark 14.1–2,10–11)

22.1
Jn 11.47-53
22.2
Mt 12.14

22 Now the festival of Unleavened Bread, which is called the Passover, was near. 2 The chief priests and the scribes were looking for a way to put Jesus[z] to death, for they were afraid of the people.

22.3
Jn 13.2

3 Then Satan entered into Judas called Iscariot, who was one of the twelve; 4 he went away and conferred with the chief priests and officers of the temple police about how he might betray him to them. 5 They were

22.5
Zech 11.12

greatly pleased and agreed to give him money. 6 So he consented and began to look for an opportunity to betray him to them when no crowd was present.

M. The Last Supper (22.7–30)

1. The passover prepared (22.7–13; Matt. 26.17–19; Mark 14.12–16)

22.7
Ex 12.18-20;
Deut 16.5-8
22.8
Lk 19.29;
Acts 3.1

7 Then came the day of Unleavened Bread, on which the Passover lamb had to be sacrificed. 8 So Jesus[a] sent Peter and John, saying, "Go and prepare the Passover meal for us that we may eat it." 9 They asked him, "Where do you want us to make preparations for it?" 10 "Listen," he said to them, "when you have entered the city, a man carrying a jar of water will meet you; follow him into the house he enters 11 and say to the owner of the house, 'The teacher asks you, "Where is the guest room, where I may eat the Passover with my disciples?"' 12 He will show you a large room upstairs, already furnished. Make preparations for us there." 13 So they went and found everything as he had told them; and they prepared the Passover meal.

2. The passover eaten and the Lord's Supper instituted
(22.14–30; Matt. 26.20–29; Mark 14.17–25; see John 13.1–30)

14 When the hour came, he took his place at the table, and the apostles with him. 15 He said to them, "I have eagerly desired to eat this

22.16
Lk 14.15;
Rev 19.9

Passover with you before I suffer; 16 for I tell you, I will not eat it[b] until it is fulfilled in the kingdom of God." 17 Then he took a cup, and after giving thanks he said, "Take this and divide it among yourselves; 18 for I tell you that from now on I will not drink of the fruit of the vine until the kingdom of God comes." 19 Then he took a loaf of bread, and when he had given thanks, he broke it and gave it to them, saying, "This is my body, which is given for you. Do this in remembrance of me." 20 And he did the same with the cup after supper, saying, "This cup that is poured

22.21
Mt 26.21-24;
Mk 14.18-21;
Jn 13.21-30
22.22
Acts 2.23;
4.28
22.24
Mk 9.34;
Lk 9.46
22.25
Mt 20.25-28;
Mk 10.42-45
22.26
Lk 9.48;
1 Pet 5.5
22.27
Lk 12.37

out for you is the new covenant in my blood.[c] 21 But see, the one who betrays me is with me, and his hand is on the table. 22 For the Son of Man is going as it has been determined, but woe to that one by whom he is betrayed!" 23 Then they began to ask one another which one of them it could be who would do this.

24 A dispute also arose among them as to which one of them was to be regarded as the greatest. 25 But he said to them, "The kings of the Gentiles lord it over them; and those in authority over them are called benefactors. 26 But not so with you; rather the greatest among you must become like the youngest, and the leader like one who serves. 27 For who

---

z Gk him   a Gk he   b Other ancient authorities read *never eat it again*   c Other ancient authorities lack, in whole or in part, verses 19b-20 (*which is given . . . in my blood*)

22.2 The chief priests and scribes feared the people who saw in Jesus what they missed in their own religious leaders.
22.3 See note on Mt 26.14.
22.10 Women carried pitchers on their heads; men carried water skins. Here a man carried a pitcher; he

was thus easily identifiable by Jesus' disciples. This was either a prearranged signal or an evidence of Jesus' miraculous knowledge.
22.15 See notes on Ex 12.11–13 and Mk 14.1.
22.17 See note on Mk 14.22ff for varying views about the Eucharist (the Lord's Supper).

is greater, the one who is at the table or the one who serves? Is it not the one at the table? But I am among you as one who serves.

28 "You are those who have stood by me in my trials; 29and I confer on you, just as my Father has conferred on me, a kingdom, 30so that you may eat and drink at my table in my kingdom, and you will sit on thrones judging the twelve tribes of Israel.

N. Peter's denial foretold
(22.31–38; Matt. 26.30–35; Mark 14.27–31; see John 14–17)

31 "Simon, Simon, listen! Satan has demanded*d* to sift all of you like wheat, 32but I have prayed for you that your own faith may not fail; and you, when once you have turned back, strengthen your brothers." 33And he said to him, "Lord, I am ready to go with you to prison and to death!" 34Jesus*e* said, "I tell you, Peter, the cock will not crow this day, until you have denied three times that you know me."

35 He said to them, "When I sent you out without a purse, bag, or sandals, did you lack anything?" They said, "No, not a thing." 36He said to them, "But now, the one who has a purse must take it, and likewise a bag. And the one who has no sword must sell his cloak and buy one. 37For I tell you, this scripture must be fulfilled in me, 'And he was counted among the lawless'; and indeed what is written about me is being fulfilled." 38They said, "Lord, look, here are two swords." He replied, "It is enough."

O. Jesus in Gethsemane (22.39–53)

1. His agony (22.39–46; Matt. 26.36–46; Mark 14.32–43; cf. John 18.1)

39 He came out and went, as was his custom, to the Mount of Olives; and the disciples followed him. 40When he reached the place, he said to them, "Pray that you may not come into the time of trial."*f* 41Then he withdrew from them about a stone's throw, knelt down, and prayed, 42"Father, if you are willing, remove this cup from me; yet, not my will but yours be done." [[43Then an angel from heaven appeared to him and gave him strength. 44In his anguish he prayed more earnestly, and his sweat became like great drops of blood falling down on the ground.]]*g* 45When he got up from prayer, he came to the disciples and found them sleeping because of grief, 46and he said to them, "Why are you sleeping? Get up and pray that you may not come into the time of trial."*f*

2. Jesus' betrayal and arrest
(22.47–53; Matt. 26.47–56; Mark 14.43–50; John 18.1–11)

47 While he was still speaking, suddenly a crowd came, and the one called Judas, one of the twelve, was leading them. He approached Jesus to kiss him; 48but Jesus said to him, "Judas, is it with a kiss that you are betraying the Son of Man?" 49When those who were around him saw what was coming, they asked, "Lord, should we strike with the sword?" 50Then one of them struck the slave of the high priest and cut off his right ear. 51But Jesus said, "No more of this!" And he touched his ear and

---

d Or *has obtained permission*   *e* Gk *He*   *f* Or *into temptation*   *g* Other ancient authorities lack verses 43 and 44

22.32 Intercessory prayer consists of asking God's help on behalf of other people. In the Bible we are commanded to intercede for others, including kings and those in authority (1 Tim 2.1,2); pray for ministers of the gospel (2 Cor 1.11; Phil 1.19); pray for those who persecute us (Mt 5.44); and pray for friends (Job 42.8).
22.42 *this cup.* See note on Mt 26.39.
22.47 *He approached Jesus to kiss him.* This is still the traditional greeting among men in eastern lands (see the note on Mk 14.45 on the betrayal of Jesus).

22.28
Heb 2.18;
4.15
22.29
Lk 12.32;
2 Tim 2.12
22.30
Lk 14.15;
Rev 19.9;
Mt 19.28;
Rev 3.21

22.31
Job 1.6-12;
Am 9.9
22.32
Jn 17.9, 15;
21.15-17

22.35
Mt 10.9;
Lk 9.3; 10.4

22.37
Isa 53.12;
Mk 15.28

22.39
Lk 21.37
22.40
Mt 6.13

22.42
Mk 10.38;
Jn 5.30;
18.11

22.46
v. 40

22.49
v. 38

22.52
vv. 4, 37
22.53
Jn 12.27

healed him. 52 Then Jesus said to the chief priests, the officers of the temple police, and the elders who had come for him, "Have you come out with swords and clubs as if I were a bandit? 53 When I was with you day after day in the temple, you did not lay hands on me. But this is your hour, and the power of darkness!"

P. Peter's denial of Jesus
(22.54–71; Matt. 26.69–75; Mark 14.66–72; John 18.15–18,25–27)

22.54
Mt 26.58;
Mk 14.54

54   Then they seized him and led him away, bringing him into the high priest's house. But Peter was following at a distance. 55 When they had kindled a fire in the middle of the courtyard and sat down together, Peter sat among them. 56 Then a servant-girl, seeing him in the firelight, stared at him and said, "This man also was with him." 57 But he denied it, saying, "Woman, I do not know him." 58 A little later someone else, on seeing him, said, "You also are one of them." But Peter said, "Man, I am not!" 59 Then about an hour later still another kept insisting, "Surely this man also was with him; for he is a Galilean." 60 But Peter said, "Man, I do not know what you are talking about!" At that moment, while he was still

22.61
v. 34

speaking, the cock crowed. 61 The Lord turned and looked at Peter. Then Peter remembered the word of the Lord, how he had said to him, "Before the cock crows today, you will deny me three times." 62 And he went out and wept bitterly.

22.63
Mt 26.67,
68;
Mk 14.65;
Jn 18.22, 23
22.66
Mt 27.1;
Mk 15.1
22.67
Mt 26.63-66;
Mk 14.61-63;
Jn 18.19-21
22.70
Mt 27.11;
Lk 23.3

63   Now the men who were holding Jesus began to mock him and beat him; 64 they also blindfolded him and kept asking him, "Prophesy! Who is it that struck you?" 65 They kept heaping many other insults on him.

66   When day came, the assembly of the elders of the people, both chief priests and scribes, gathered together, and they brought him to their council. 67 They said, "If you are the Messiah,*h* tell us." He replied, "If I tell you, you will not believe; 68 and if I question you, you will not answer. 69 But from now on the Son of Man will be seated at the right hand of the power of God." 70 All of them asked, "Are you, then, the Son of God?" He said to them, "You say that I am." 71 Then they said, "What further testimony do we need? We have heard it ourselves from his own lips!"

Q. Jesus before Pontius Pilate
(23.1–25; Matt. 27.11–26; Mark 15.2–15; John 18.29–40)

1. Pilate questions Jesus (23.1–5)

23.1
Mt 27.2;
Mk 15.1;
Jn 18.28
23.2
Lk 20.22;
Jn 19.12
23.3
Lk 22.70;
1 Tim 6.13
23.4
1 Pet 2.22

23   Then the assembly rose as a body and brought Jesus*i* before Pilate. 2 They began to accuse him, saying, "We found this man perverting our nation, forbidding us to pay taxes to the emperor, and saying that he himself is the Messiah, a king."*j* 3 Then Pilate asked him, "Are you the king of the Jews?" He answered, "You say so." 4 Then Pilate said to the chief priests and the crowds, "I find no basis for an accusation against this man." 5 But they were insistent and said, "He stirs up the people by teaching throughout all Judea, from Galilee where he began even to this place."

h Or the Christ   *i* Gk him   *j* Or is an anointed king

22.61 *The Lord turned and looked at Peter.* By this look Jesus indicated several things. (1) It reproved Peter for having denied his Lord. (2) It manifested compassion, for Jesus knew how weak Peter was. (3) It perhaps conveyed to Peter a hint of grace, which later enabled him to repent and be restored.
22.62 *wept bitterly.* Weeping may occur because one

is caught or because one is genuinely sorry for doing wrong. The latter was the case here, for Peter's weeping was followed by repentance and restoration.
23.3 *You say so.* This is an enigmatic statement. It may mean, "Can you prove it?" Or, "Have you any evidence?" Or, "It is as you say. I am, but over Israel and not as a rival to Rome."

2. Pilate sends Jesus to Herod (23.6–12)

6 When Pilate heard this, he asked whether the man was a Galilean. 7 And when he learned that he was under Herod's jurisdiction, he sent him off to Herod, who was himself in Jerusalem at that time. 8 When Herod saw Jesus, he was very glad, for he had been wanting to see him for a long time, because he had heard about him and was hoping to see him perform some sign. 9 He questioned him at some length, but Jesus[k] gave him no answer. 10 The chief priests and the scribes stood by, vehemently accusing him. 11 Even Herod with his soldiers treated him with contempt and mocked him; then he put an elegant robe on him, and sent him back to Pilate. 12 That same day Herod and Pilate became friends with each other; before this they had been enemies.

23.7
Lk 3.1
23.8
Lk 9.9;
Mt 14.1;
Mk 6.14

23.11
Mk 15.17-19;
Jn 19.2, 3
23.12
Acts 4.27

3. Pilate wants to free Jesus (23.13–17)

13 Pilate then called together the chief priests, the leaders, and the people, 14 and said to them, "You brought me this man as one who was perverting the people; and here I have examined him in your presence and have not found this man guilty of any of your charges against him. 15 Neither has Herod, for he sent him back to us. Indeed, he has done nothing to deserve death. 16 I will therefore have him flogged and release him."[l]

23.14
vv. 2, 4

23.16
Mt 27.26;
Mk 15.15;
Jn 19.1

4. Pilate releases Barabbas and delivers Jesus (23.18–25)

18 Then they all shouted out together, "Away with this fellow! Release Barabbas for us!" 19 (This was a man who had been put in prison for an insurrection that had taken place in the city, and for murder.) 20 Pilate, wanting to release Jesus, addressed them again; 21 but they kept shouting, "Crucify, crucify him!" 22 A third time he said to them, "Why, what evil has he done? I have found in him no ground for the sentence of death; I will therefore have him flogged and then release him." 23 But they kept urgently demanding with loud shouts that he should be crucified; and their voices prevailed. 24 So Pilate gave his verdict that their demand should be granted. 25 He released the man they asked for, the one who had been put in prison for insurrection and murder, and he handed Jesus over as they wished.

23.18
Mt 27.20-23;
Mk 15.11-14;
Jn 18.38-40;
19.14, 15;
Acts 3.13, 14
23.22
v. 16

R. The crucifixion and burial of Jesus (23.26–56)

1. Jesus on the way to Calvary (23.26–31; see Matt. 27.32; Mark 15.21)

26 As they led him away, they seized a man, Simon of Cyrene, who was coming from the country, and they laid the cross on him, and made him carry it behind Jesus. 27 A great number of the people followed him, and among them were women who were beating their breasts and wailing for him. 28 But Jesus turned to them and said, "Daughters of Jerusalem, do not weep for me, but weep for yourselves and for your children. 29 For the days are surely coming when they will say, 'Blessed are the barren, and the wombs that never bore, and the breasts that never nursed.' 30 Then they will begin to say to the mountains, 'Fall on us'; and to the hills, 'Cover us.' 31 For if they do this when the wood is green, what will happen when it is dry?"

23.26
Jn 19.17
23.27
Lk 8.52
23.28
Lk 19.41-44;
21.23, 24
23.30
Isa 2.19;
Hos 10.8;
Rev 6.16
23.31
Ezek 20.47

k Gk *he* *l* Here, or after verse 19, other ancient authorities add verse 17, *Now he was obliged to release someone for them at the festival*

23.16 If Jesus was innocent of the charges, Pilate's offer to chastise him before releasing him was motivated by political equivocation and personal enhancement of his career. **23.18** See note on Mk 15.7. **23.26** See note on Mk 15.21.

2. Jesus crucified
(23.32–38; Matt. 27.32–44; Mark 15.21–32; John 19.17–24)

23.32
Isa 53.12

32 Two others also, who were criminals, were led away to be put to death with him. 33 When they came to the place that is called The Skull, they crucified Jesus[m] there with the criminals, one on his right and one on his left. ⟦34 Then Jesus said, "Father, forgive them; for they do not know what they are doing."⟧[n] And they cast lots to divide his clothing. 35 And the people stood by, watching; but the leaders scoffed at him, saying, "He saved others; let him save himself if he is the Messiah[o] of God, his chosen one!" 36 The soldiers also mocked him, coming up and offering him sour wine, 37 and saying, "If you are the King of the Jews, save yourself!" 38 There was also an inscription over him,[p] "This is the King of the Jews."

23.34
Ps 22.18;
Acts 7.60
23.35
Ps 22.17
23.36
Ps 69.21;
Mt 27.48

3. The penitent criminal (23.39–43)

23.39
vv. 35, 37

39 One of the criminals who were hanged there kept deriding[q] him and saying, "Are you not the Messiah?[o] Save yourself and us!" 40 But the other rebuked him, saying, "Do you not fear God, since you are under the same sentence of condemnation? 41 And we indeed have been condemned justly, for we are getting what we deserve for our deeds, but this man has done nothing wrong." 42 Then he said, "Jesus, remember me when you come into[r] your kingdom." 43 He replied, "Truly I tell you, today you will be with me in Paradise."

23.41
vv. 4, 14, 22
23.43
2 Cor 12.3, 4;
Rev 2.7

4. The death of Jesus
(23.44–49; Matt. 27.45–50; Mark 15.33–41; John 19.28–37)

23.45
Ex 26.31-35;
Heb 9.8;
10.19
23.46
Ps 31.5;
1 Pet 2.23
23.47
Mt 27.54
23.49
Ps 38.11;
Lk 8.2

44 It was now about noon, and darkness came over the whole land[s] until three in the afternoon, 45 while the sun's light failed;[t] and the curtain of the temple was torn in two. 46 Then Jesus, crying with a loud voice, said, "Father, into your hands I commend my spirit." Having said this, he breathed his last. 47 When the centurion saw what had taken place, he praised God and said, "Certainly this man was innocent."[u] 48 And when all the crowds who had gathered there for this spectacle saw what had taken place, they returned home, beating their breasts. 49 But all his acquaintances, including the women who had followed him from Galilee, stood at a distance, watching these things.

5. Jesus laid in the tomb
(23.50–56; Matt. 27.57–61; Mark 15.42–47; John 19.38–42)

50 Now there was a good and righteous man named Joseph, who,

m Gk *him* n Other ancient authorities lack the sentence *Then Jesus . . . what they are doing* o *Or the Christ* p Other ancient authorities add *written in Greek and Latin and Hebrew* (that is, *Aramaic*) q *Or blaspheming* r Other ancient authorities read *in* s *Or earth* t *Or the sun was eclipsed*. Other ancient authorities read *the sun was darkened* u *Or righteous*

23.33 Jesus died between two bandits. Both of these were sinners, but they died different deaths. One bandit died *in* his sin, while the other died *to* sin, having been forgiven by Christ. Jesus himself had committed no sin, but the sin of the world was laid on him. Thus he died *for* sin (see note on Jn 19.17).
23.34ff The order in which Christ spoke his seven last sayings on the cross is as follows: (1) the word of forgiveness: "Father, forgive them; for they do not know what they are doing"; (2) the word of salvation: "Truly I tell you, today you will be with me in Paradise" (v. 43); (3) the word of affection: "Woman, here is your son. . . . Here is your mother" (Jn 19.26,27);

(4) the word of despair: "My God, my God, why have you forsaken me?" (Mt 27.46; Mk 15.34); (5) the word of physical torment: "I am thirsty" (Jn 19.28); (6) the word of triumph: "It is finished" (Jn 19.30); and (7) the word of committal: "Father, into your hands I commend my spirit" (v. 46).
23.43 *Paradise.* This word is actually a Persian loan word and appears only two other times in the N.T. (2 Cor 12.4; Rev 2.7). Originally it meant an enclosed park or a pleasure ground. In the Septuagint it was used as a term for the garden of Eden, and in the intertestamental times it meant a superterrestrial place of happiness. As used here, it can mean "heaven" or "the presence of God."

though a member of the council, 51 had not agreed to their plan and action. He came from the Jewish town of Arimathea, and he was waiting expectantly for the kingdom of God. 52 This man went to Pilate and asked for the body of Jesus. 53 Then he took it down, wrapped it in a linen cloth, and laid it in a rock-hewn tomb where no one had ever been laid. 54 It was the day of Preparation, and the sabbath was beginning. v 55 The women who had come with him from Galilee followed, and they saw the tomb and how his body was laid. 56 Then they returned, and prepared spices and ointments.

On the sabbath they rested according to the commandment.

S. The resurrection of Jesus Christ
(24.1–11; Matt. 28.1–10; Mark 16.1–8; John 20.1–18)

24 But on the first day of the week, at early dawn, they came to the tomb, taking the spices that they had prepared. 2 They found the stone rolled away from the tomb, 3 but when they went in, they did not find the body. w 4 While they were perplexed about this, suddenly two men in dazzling clothes stood beside them. 5 The women x were terrified and bowed their faces to the ground, but the men y said to them, "Why do you look for the living among the dead? He is not here, but has risen. z 6 Remember how he told you, while he was still in Galilee, 7 that the Son of Man must be handed over to sinners, and be crucified, and on the third day rise again." 8 Then they remembered his words, 9 and returning from the tomb, they told all this to the eleven and to all the rest. 10 Now it was Mary Magdalene, Joanna, Mary the mother of James, and the other women with them who told this to the apostles. 11 But these words seemed to them an idle tale, and they did not believe them. 12 But Peter got up and ran to the tomb; stooping and looking in, he saw the linen cloths by themselves; then he went home, amazed at what had happened. a

T. The walk to Emmaus (24.13–35)

13 Now on that same day two of them were going to a village called Emmaus, about seven miles b from Jerusalem, 14 and talking with each other about all these things that had happened. 15 While they were talking and discussing, Jesus himself came near and went with them, 16 but their eyes were kept from recognizing him. 17 And he said to them, "What are you discussing with each other while you walk along?" They stood still, looking sad. c 18 Then one of them, whose name was Cleopas, answered him, "Are you the only stranger in Jerusalem who does not know the things that have taken place there in these days?" 19 He asked them, "What things?" They replied, "The things about Jesus of Nazareth, d who was a prophet mighty in deed and word before God and all the people, 20 and how our chief priests and leaders handed him over to be condemned to death and crucified him. 21 But we had hoped that he was the one to redeem Israel. e Yes, and besides all this, it is now the third day since these things took place. 22 Moreover, some women of our group astounded us. They were at the tomb early this morning, 23 and when they did not

Cross-references (right margin):
23.51 Lk 2.25
23.54 Mt 27.62
23.55 v. 49
23.56 Mk 16.1; Ex 12.16; 20.10
24.1 Lk 23.56
24.4 Acts 1.10; 12.7
24.6 Mt 17.22, 23; Mk 9.30, 31; Lk 9.22
24.8 Jn 2.22
24.9 v. 46
24.10 Lk 8.1-3
24.11 v. 35
24.15 v. 36
24.16 Jn 21.4
24.18 Jn 19.25
24.19 Mt 21.11; Lk 7.16; 13.33; Acts 3.22
24.20 Lk 23.13
24.21 Lk 1.68
24.22 vv. 9, 10

v Gk was dawning   w Other ancient authorities add of the Lord Jesus   x Gk They   y Gk but they
z Other ancient authorities lack He is not here, but has risen   a Other ancient authorities lack verse 12
b Gk sixty stadia; other ancient authorities read a hundred sixty stadia   c Other ancient authorities read
walk along, looking sad?"   d Other ancient authorities read Jesus the Nazorean   e Or to set Israel free

23.54 the day of Preparation, i.e., Friday (cf. Mk 15.42; Jn 19.31,42). All necessary preparations had to be made in advance of the sabbath, which began at sundown and which permitted no work. The burial of Jesus, therefore, had to be carried out before sundown on Friday. **24.1ff** See note on Mt 28.6.

24.4 two men. Some have supposed a discrepancy here, for Matthew and Mark mention only one angel (Mt 28.5; Mk 16.5), while John does not report any angel. But the problem is readily resolved: Matthew and Mark did not say there was only one angel. Luke simply gives us more complete information.

RESURRECTION APPEARANCES

Event	Date	Matthew	Mark	Luke	John	Acts	I Corinthians
At the empty tomb outside Jerusalem	Early Sunday morning	28:1-10	16:1-8	24:1-12	20:1-9		
To Mary Magdalene at the tomb	Early Sunday morning		16:9-11		20:11-18		
To two travelers on the road to Emmaus	Sunday at midday		16:12-13	24:13-32			
To Peter in Jerusalem	During the day on Sunday			24:34			15:5
To the ten disciples in the upper room	Sunday evening			24:36-43	20:19-25		
To the eleven disciples in the upper room	One week later		16:14		20:26-31		15:5
To seven disciples fishing on the Sea of Galilee	One day at daybreak				21:1-23		
To the eleven disciples on the mountain in Galilee	Some time later	28:16-20	16:15-18				
To more than 500	Some time later						15:6
To James	Some time later						15:7
At the Ascension on the Mt. of Olives	Forty days after the resurrection			24:44-51		1:3-8	

© 1989 The Zondervan Corporation.

find his body there, they came back and told us that they had indeed seen
a vision of angels who said that he was alive. 24 Some of those who were
with us went to the tomb and found it just as the women had said; but
they did not see him." 25 Then he said to them, "Oh, how foolish you are,
and how slow of heart to believe all that the prophets have declared! 26 Was
it not necessary that the Messiah*f* should suffer these things and then
enter into his glory?" 27 Then beginning with Moses and all the prophets,
he interpreted to them the things about himself in all the scriptures.

28   As they came near the village to which they were going, he walked
ahead as if he were going on. 29 But they urged him strongly, saying, "Stay
with us, because it is almost evening and the day is now nearly over." So
he went in to stay with them. 30 When he was at the table with them, he
took bread, blessed and broke it, and gave it to them. 31 Then their eyes
were opened, and they recognized him; and he vanished from their sight.
32 They said to each other, "Were not our hearts burning within us*g* while
he was talking to us on the road, while he was opening the scriptures to
us?" 33 That same hour they got up and returned to Jerusalem; and they
found the eleven and their companions gathered together. 34 They were
saying, "The Lord has risen indeed, and he has appeared to Simon!"
35 Then they told what had happened on the road, and how he had been
made known to them in the breaking of the bread.

U. Christ appears to the ten in Jerusalem
(24.36–43; John 20.19–25)

36   While they were talking about this, Jesus himself stood among
them and said to them, "Peace be with you."*h* 37 They were startled and
terrified, and thought that they were seeing a ghost. 38 He said to them,
"Why are you frightened, and why do doubts arise in your hearts? 39 Look
at my hands and my feet; see that it is I myself. Touch me and see; for
a ghost does not have flesh and bones as you see that I have." 40 And when
he had said this, he showed them his hands and his feet.*i* 41 While in their
joy they were disbelieving and still wondering, he said to them, "Have you
anything here to eat?" 42 They gave him a piece of broiled fish, 43 and he
took it and ate in their presence.

V. The great commission
(24.44–49; cf. Matt. 28.18–20; John 20.21; Acts 1.8)

44   Then he said to them, "These are my words that I spoke to you
while I was still with you—that everything written about me in the law
of Moses, the prophets, and the psalms must be fulfilled." 45 Then he
opened their minds to understand the scriptures, 46 and he said to them,

f Or *the Christ*   *g* Other ancient authorities lack *within us*   *h* Other ancient authorities lack *and said to
them, "Peace be with you."*   *i* Other ancient authorities lack verse 40

24.24 v. 12
24.26 Heb 2.10; 1 Pet 1.11
24.27 Gen 3.15; Num 21.9; Deut 18.15; Isa 7.14; 9.6; 40.10, 11; ch. 53; Ezek 34.23; Dan 9.24; Mic 7.20; Mal 3.1
24.28 Mk 6.48
24.30 Mt 14.19
24.33 Acts 1.14
24.34 1 Cor 15.5
24.37 Mk 6.49
24.39 Jn 20.27
24.41 Jn 21.5
24.43 Acts 10.41
24.44 Mt 16.21; Mk 8.31; Lk 9.22; 18.31
24.46 Isa 50.6; Hos 6.2; 1 Cor 15.3, 4

24.31 *he vanished from their sight.* Jesus, in his resurrected body, was able to disappear at will. He could
pass through doors (Jn 20.26) and come and go as he
pleased. On the other hand, Jesus performed the normal bodily act of eating food (vv. 42,43). Jesus' resurrection body had different properties, and so will ours
(cf. Phil 3.20,21).
24.39 Jesus told his disciples that he was not a spirit.
He had hands and feet and invited them to feel him.
He also took a piece of broiled fish and ate it (vv.
42,43). Whoever denies the bodily resurrection of
Jesus does so against the expressed affirmation of it
in Scripture.
24.45ff Everywhere in the Bible the resurrection of
Christ is treated as a bodily resurrection. Many have
denied this teaching, offering such explanations as:
(1) the "swoon theory," which claims Jesus died later

— he did not really die on the cross; (2) the "fraud
theory" — that the disciples stole his body and lied
about the resurrection; (3) the "hallucination theory"
— that the excited disciples saw visions but not the
real Jesus; and (4) the "wrong-tomb theory" — that
the disciples went to the wrong tomb. Jesus' empty
tomb nullifies all of these notions, for the *belief* in
Christ's resurrection arose out of the *fact* of his resurrection. Moreover, the bodily resurrection of Christ
was necessary in order to (1) make the forgiveness of
sins possible (1 Cor 15.17); (2) fulfill the biblical
prophecies of the resurrection (vv. 45,46); (3) make
justification of sinners possible (Rom 4.25; 8.34); and
(4) lay a solid foundation for the Christian's hope
(1 Cor 15.19). Christ's resurrection was accomplished
by the power of God (Acts 2.24; Rom 8.11; Eph
1.19,20) and by Christ himself (Jn 2.19; 10.18).

24.47
Acts 5.31;
13.38;
Mt 28.19
24.48
Acts 1.8
24.49
Jn 14.16;
Acts 1.4

"Thus it is written, that the Messiah[j] is to suffer and to rise from the dead on the third day, 47 and that repentance and forgiveness of sins is to be proclaimed in his name to all nations, beginning from Jerusalem. 48 You are witnesses[k] of these things. 49 And see, I am sending upon you what my Father promised; so stay here in the city until you have been clothed with power from on high."

W. Christ's ascension
(24.50–53; Mark 16.19–20; cf. Acts 1.9–11)

24.50
Acts 1.12
24.51
2 Kings 2.11

24.53
Acts 2.46

50   Then he led them out as far as Bethany, and, lifting up his hands, he blessed them. 51 While he was blessing them, he withdrew from them and was carried up into heaven.[l] 52 And they worshiped him, and[m] returned to Jerusalem with great joy; 53 and they were continually in the temple blessing God.[n]

---

j Or the Christ   *k* Or nations. Beginning from Jerusalem 48you are witnesses   *l* Other ancient authorities lack *and was carried up into heaven*   *m* Other ancient authorities lack *worshiped him, and*   *n* Other ancient authorities add *Amen*

24.47   The great commission presented here has three parts: (1) the good news the disciples were to preach (the death and resurrection of Jesus and the promise of the forgiveness of sins upon repentance); (2) the people they were to reach (all nations, beginning from Jerusalem); and (3) the power they would

have to make their work effective (the Holy Spirit, see next note).
24.49   *what my Father promised.* According to Acts 1.4,5 the promise was the baptism of the Holy Spirit.
24.50   *as far as Bethany.* Bethany was approximately a mile away, across the valley on the Mount of Olives.

INTRODUCTION TO
THE GOSPEL ACCORDING TO
JOHN

Authorship, Date, and Background: The authorship of the fourth Gospel cannot be determined from the material in the book itself, for no author is named directly. But there are enough hints to draw the conclusion that John, the son of Zebedee and Salome (who was probably the sister of Mary, the mother of Jesus), was the author. The writer was a Palestinian Jew and an eyewitness who was familiar with Jewish customs and traditions. The early church regarded John as the author and contrary claims have scant evidence to displace this view. His name never appears in the Gospel, though on several occasion one of Jesus' closest disciples (undoubtedly John) is called "the disciple whom Jesus loved" (13.23; 19.26; 20.2; 21.7,20,24).

John was with Jesus on numerous occasions. The Lord called him and his brother the "Sons of Thunder" (Mk 3.17), for they were prejudiced, brash, and belligerent. They were ready to reprimand a man who was casting out demons successfully, simply because he was not one of them. Jesus forbade them (9.49,50). Moreover, they asked Jesus one time when they were in a Samaritan village: "Lord, do you want us to command fire to come down from heaven and consume them?" (Lk 9.52–55). Jesus rebuked them. They had their mother ask Jesus that her sons might sit on two thrones next to his throne in his kingdom (Mt 20.20ff). Jesus refused this request. It was John who sat so close to Jesus at the last supper. And it was he who was to become known later as the apostle of love. He also authored 1, 2, and 3 John and Revelation, the last book of Scripture.

In all probability the book was written in Ephesus (Asia Minor) and can be dated in the last decade of the first century (A.D. 90–95). The date is important because this Gospel is quite different from Matthew, Mark, and Luke. These have been called the "synoptic Gospels" (meaning having the same or common views); John's work does not fit this pattern. The simplest explanation is that he was familiar with the other Gospels, and the Holy Spirit wanted him to fill in some of the gaps and to stress more specifically what the other Gospels hinted at but did not say explicitly. It was unnecessary for him to repeat what was already known and widely read. Moreover, some time had passed since the writing of the other Gospels, and the theology of the church was developing. John had something to contribute to this development.

Characteristics and Content: John presents Jesus as true God and a true human being. At least five times he repeats his witness and that of others, together with the teaching of Jesus himself, about the deity of Jesus: (1) He "was God" (1.1,2); (2) "before Abraham was, I am" (8.58); (3) "The Father and I are one" (10.30); (4) "Whoever has seen me has seen the Father" (14.9); (5) Thomas said, "My Lord and my God!" (20.28). He also emphasizes the humanity of Jesus when he speaks of him as tired, hungry, troubled, loyal to his friends, loving, and brave. John shows that Jesus, as the God-man, was functionally subordinate to his Father, who sent him into this world. He was obedient to the Father and he always did his Father's will, even unto death on the cross. Moreover, he accomplished the Father's work, which was to bring life to sinful people (10.10).

John states his purpose for writing the book explicitly: "Now Jesus did many other signs in the presence of his disciples, which are not written in this book. But these are written so that you may come to believe that Jesus is the Messiah, the Son of God, and that through believing you may have life in his name" (20.30,31). In these verses John uses three of the words which constitute the dominant motif of the work: (1) miracles or signs; (2) faith or believing on Jesus; (3) life, which is the result of faith in him. John thus declares that sinners need not believe without evidence. He presents seven miracles or signs as evidence and expects that as a result of them, sinners ought to have faith in Jesus. These seven signs are: (1) changing water into wine (2.1–11); (2) healing the government official's son (4.46–54); (3) healing the paralyzed man (5.1–9); (4) feeding the five thousand (6.1–14); (5) walking on the water (6.16–21); (6) healing the man born blind (9.1–12); (7) raising Lazarus from the dead (11.1–46). Five of these seven miracles do not appear in the other Gospels. All seven were performed publicly to help people or were for the benefit of other people.

John also records the seven "I ams" of Jesus (in addition to "I am" standing by itself, 8.58): (1) "I am the bread of life" (6.35); (2) "I am the light of the world" (8.12); (3) "I am the gate for the sheep" (10.7); (4) "I am the good shepherd" (10.11,14); (5) "I am the resurrection and the life" (11.25); (6) "I am the way, and the truth, and the life" (14.6); (7) "I am the true vine" (15.1).

Outline:

I. Prologue (1.1–18)

II. Revelation to old Israel: the public ministry (1.19—12.50)

III. Revelation to new Israel: disclosures to the disciples (13.1—20.29)

IV. Conclusion (20.30,31)

V. Epilogue (21.1–25)

THE GOSPEL ACCORDING TO

JOHN

I. Prologue (1.1–18)

A. The eternal Word (1.1–5)

1 In the beginning was the Word, and the Word was with God, and the Word was God. ² He was in the beginning with God. ³ All things came into being through him, and without him not one thing came into being. What has come into being ⁴ in him was life,ᵃ and the life was the light of all people. ⁵ The light shines in the darkness, and the darkness did not overcome it.

B. The ministry of John the Baptist
(1.6–8; see vv. 19–28; Matt. 3.1–12; Mark 1.1–8; Luke 3.2–17)

6 There was a man sent from God, whose name was John. ⁷ He came as a witness to testify to the light, so that all might believe through him. ⁸ He himself was not the light, but he came to testify to the light. ⁹ The true light, which enlightens everyone, was coming into the world.ᵇ

C. The first coming of Jesus Christ and his rejection (1.9–13)

10 He was in the world, and the world came into being through him; yet the world did not know him. ¹¹ He came to what was his own,ᶜ and his own people did not accept him. ¹² But to all who received him, who believed in his name, he gave power to become children of God, ¹³ who were born, not of blood or of the will of the flesh or of the will of man, but of God.

D. The witness of John the Baptist to the incarnate Word
(1.14–18)

14 And the Word became flesh and lived among us, and we have seen

---

a Or ³through him. And without him not one thing came into being that has come into being. ⁴In him was life
b Or He was the true light that enlightens everyone coming into the world *c* Or to his own home

---

1.1
Col 1.17;
1 Jn 1.1;
Phil 2.6
1.3
Col 1.16;
Heb 1.2
1.4
Jn 5.26;
11.25; 14.6
1.5
Jn 3.19; 9.5;
12.46

1.7
Acts 19.4

1.8
v. 20
1.9
Isa 49.6;
1 Jn 2.8

1.10
Col 1.16;
Heb 1.2
1.12
Gal 3.26;
Jn 3.18; 1 Jn
5.13
1.13
Jn 3.5, 6;
Jas 1.18;
1 Pet 1.23

1.14
Rom 1.3;
Gal 4.4;
1 Tim 3.16;
Heb 2.14

1.1 *In the beginning,* i.e., before anything else existed. *the Word,* i.e., Christ, the wisdom and power of God, God's personal expression of himself to humankind. Christ was the incarnate Word, in contrast to the written Word, the Bible. The incarnate Word is eternal and is both with God, yet distinct from God. The Word is identical in essence to God the Father and to God the Holy Spirit. The Word had a role in creation (Col 1.16; Heb 1.2; 11.3). The Word became flesh (i.e., God became human); Jesus is thus the God-man. "For in him the whole fullness of deity dwells bodily" (Col 2.9). The incarnate Word is made known to people through the written Word.
1.12 *who believed in his name,* i.e., who trusted in him to save them. At least four benefits come to those who are regenerated: (1) they become children of God (see also Rom 9.26); (2) they become "a new creation" (2 Cor 5.17; Gal 6.15); (3) they are given God's own character, i.e., they "become participants of the

divine nature" (2 Pet 1.4); and (4) they share Christ's triumph and power over sin and the world (1 Jn 3.9; 5.4,18).
1.14 *the Word became flesh,* i.e., God's Son became human (cf. Gal 4.4,5; Phil 2.6,7). This is called the *incarnation,* a word that derives from the Latin and means "in the flesh." The incarnation is the act whereby the second person of the Trinity, the Son of God, took on real human flesh. He was one person with two natures — a perfectly divine nature and a perfectly human (albeit sinless) nature. Not only did he have all the attributes of deity (see note on v. 1), but as human he had all the attributes of the first Adam, or humanity. His two natures are separate and distinct, yet without fusion or mixture (cf. Acts 3.22; Gal 4.4; 1 Tim 2.5; Heb 2.14,17,18; 4.15). The resurrected and ascended Lord Jesus will forever be the God-man in a body (cf. Acts 1.11). His second advent will also be in bodily form.

his glory, the glory as of a father's only son,*d* full of grace and truth.

1.15
v. 30
15 (John testified to him and cried out, "This was he of whom I said, 'He who comes after me ranks ahead of me because he was before me.' ")

1.16
Eph 1.23;
Col 1.19
1.17
Rom 3.24
1.18
Ex 33.20;
Jn 6.46; 1 Jn
4.9
16 From his fullness we have all received, grace upon grace. 17 The law indeed was given through Moses; grace and truth came through Jesus Christ. 18 No one has ever seen God. It is God the only Son,*e* who is close to the Father's heart,*f* who has made him known.

II. Revelation to old Israel: the public ministry (1.19–12.50)

A. John's witness to himself (1.19–28)

1.20
Jn 3.28;
Lk 3.15, 16
1.21
Mt 11.14;
16.14;
Deut 18.15
1.23
Mt 3.1;
Mk 1.3;
Lk 3.4;
Isa 40.3
19 This is the testimony given by John when the Jews sent priests and Levites from Jerusalem to ask him, "Who are you?" 20 He confessed and did not deny it, but confessed, "I am not the Messiah."*g* 21 And they asked him, "What then? Are you Elijah?" He said, "I am not." "Are you the prophet?" He answered, "No." 22 Then they said to him, "Who are you? Let us have an answer for those who sent us. What do you say about yourself?" 23 He said,

"I am the voice of one crying out in the wilderness,
'Make straight the way of the Lord,'"

as the prophet Isaiah said.

1.26
Acts 1.5
1.27
vv. 15, 30
1.28
Jn 3.26;
10.40
24 Now they had been sent from the Pharisees. 25 They asked him, "Why then are you baptizing if you are neither the Messiah,*g* nor Elijah, nor the prophet?" 26 John answered them, "I baptize with water. Among you stands one whom you do not know, 27 the one who is coming after me; I am not worthy to untie the thong of his sandal." 28 This took place in Bethany across the Jordan where John was baptizing.

B. John's witness to Jesus (1.29–34)

1.29
Isa 53.7;
1 Pet 1.19
1.30
vv. 15, 27
1.32
Mt 3.16;
Mk 1.10;
Lk 3.22
1.33
Mt 3.11;
Acts 1.5
29 The next day he saw Jesus coming toward him and declared, "Here is the Lamb of God who takes away the sin of the world! 30 This is he of whom I said, 'After me comes a man who ranks ahead of me because he was before me.' 31 I myself did not know him; but I came baptizing with water for this reason, that he might be revealed to Israel." 32 And John testified, "I saw the Spirit descending from heaven like a dove, and it remained on him. 33 I myself did not know him, but the one who sent me

d Or *the Father's only Son*   *e* Other ancient authorities read *It is an only Son, God*, or *It is the only Son*   *f* Gk *bosom*   *g* Or *the Christ*

1.17 *Grace* (Gk. *charis*, also meaning "favor") is the unearned favor of God, given freely to those who deserve the exact opposite. Grace is an attribute of God (Ex 22.27; 33.19; Neh 9.17; 1 Pet 5.10). We are justified by grace (Rom 3.24; Titus 3.7); saved by grace (Eph 1.7,8); elected by grace (Rom 11.5,6); given faith by grace (Acts 18.27; Eph 2.8,9); given spiritual gifts by grace (Rom 12.6); and provided with strength, comfort, and hope through grace (2 Cor 12.9; 2 Thess 2.16).

1.18 God is spirit (cf. 4.24). As such, he is invisible and nonmaterial. Yet Scripture says that humans have beheld God or his presence (e.g., Gen 32.30; Ex 24.9, 10; Judg 13.22; Isa 6.1; Dan 7.9). How do we explain this? (1) Sometimes God momentarily assumed human form in order to communicate with people; these appearances are called "theophanies." (2) On other occasions God sent angels or the "angel of the Lord" to act for him. (3) A third alternative is that the language of some appearances seems symbolic, as when Isaiah evidently saw a vision (Isa 6.1). Since the advent of Jesus, all who have seen him have seen the

Father (14.9). With the Scriptures and with Christ, believers today need no other supernatural manifestations of God.

1.21 *Are you the prophet?* This prophet (see also v. 25; 6.14; 7.40; Acts 3.22,23; 7.37) is the one spoken about by Moses in Deut 18.15,18. It does not refer to John the Baptist, but to Jesus Christ.

1.30 *because he was before me.* Since John the Baptist was six months older than Jesus, this statement refers to Christ's preincarnate existence as the eternal God. This may have been revealed to John directly by the Spirit or else by the Spirit's teaching through the O.T.

1.32 *John testified*, i.e., bore witness. John did not bear witness to Jesus of himself, for he was sent by God. Somehow God had told John that the one on whom he saw the Holy Spirit coming and remaining was the Son of God. Thus John was prevented from making any mistake. John baptized Jesus with water but affirmed that Jesus would baptize with the Holy Spirit.

to baptize with water said to me, 'He on whom you see the Spirit descend and remain is the one who baptizes with the Holy Spirit.' 34 And I myself have seen and have testified that this is the Son of God."[h]

1.34
v. 49

C. Andrew and Peter follow Jesus (1.35–42)

35 The next day John again was standing with two of his disciples, 36 and as he watched Jesus walk by, he exclaimed, "Look, here is the Lamb of God!" 37 The two disciples heard him say this, and they followed Jesus. 38 When Jesus turned and saw them following, he said to them, "What are you looking for?" They said to him, "Rabbi" (which translated means Teacher), "where are you staying?" 39 He said to them, "Come and see." They came and saw where he was staying, and they remained with him that day. It was about four o'clock in the afternoon. 40 One of the two who heard John speak and followed him was Andrew, Simon Peter's brother. 41 He first found his brother Simon and said to him, "We have found the Messiah" (which is translated Anointed[i]). 42 He brought Simon[j] to Jesus, who looked at him and said, "You are Simon son of John. You are to be called Cephas" (which is translated Peter[k]).

1.35
v. 29
1.36
v. 29
1.38
v. 49

1.40
Mt 4.18-22;
Mk 1.16-20;
Lk 5.2-11
1.41
Dan 9.25;
Jn 4.25
1.42
Jn 21.15-17;
1 Cor 15.5;
Mt 16.18

D. Philip and Nathanael follow Jesus (1.43–51)

43 The next day Jesus decided to go to Galilee. He found Philip and said to him, "Follow me." 44 Now Philip was from Bethsaida, the city of Andrew and Peter. 45 Philip found Nathanael and said to him, "We have found him about whom Moses in the law and also the prophets wrote, Jesus son of Joseph from Nazareth." 46 Nathanael said to him, "Can anything good come out of Nazareth?" Philip said to him, "Come and see." 47 When Jesus saw Nathanael coming toward him, he said of him, "Here is truly an Israelite in whom there is no deceit!" 48 Nathanael asked him, "Where did you get to know me?" Jesus answered, "I saw you under the fig tree before Philip called you." 49 Nathanael replied, "Rabbi, you are the Son of God! You are the King of Israel!" 50 Jesus answered, "Do you believe because I told you that I saw you under the fig tree? You will see greater things than these." 51 And he said to him, "Very truly, I tell you,[l] you will see heaven opened and the angels of God ascending and descending upon the Son of Man."

1.43
Mt 10.3;
Jn 6.5, 7;
12.21, 22;
14.8, 9
1.44
Jn 12.21
1.45
Jn 21.2;
Lk 24.27;
Mt 2.23;
Lk 2.4
1.46
Jn 7.41, 42
1.47
Ps 32.2; 73.1;
Rom 9.4, 6
1.49
vv. 38, 34;
Mt 2.2;
Mk 15.32;
Jn 12.13
1.51
Gen 28.12;
Mt 3.16;
Lk 3.21;
Mt 8.20

E. The first miracle: water made into wine (2.1–12)

2 On the third day there was a wedding in Cana of Galilee, and the mother of Jesus was there. 2 Jesus and his disciples had also been invited to the wedding. 3 When the wine gave out, the mother of Jesus said to him, "They have no wine." 4 And Jesus said to her, "Woman, what concern is that to you and to me? My hour has not yet come." 5 His mother said to the servants, "Do whatever he tells you." 6 Now standing there were six stone water jars for the Jewish rites of purification, each holding

2.1
Jn 4.46; 21.2

2.4
Jn 19.26;
7.6, 30; 8.20
2.6
Mk 7.3, 4;
Jn 3.25

[h] Other ancient authorities read is God's chosen one   [i] Or Christ   [j] Gk him   [k] From the word for rock in Aramaic (kepha) and Greek (petra), respectively   [l] Both instances of the Greek word for you in this verse are plural

1.40,41 He first found his own brother Simon. Andrew was the first disciple of Jesus. And he was the first missionary, for he brought Simon to Jesus. Nothing is more beautiful than to bring our own families to Jesus Christ for salvation.
1.45 Philip, like Andrew, also came to Christ, and he did the same thing Andrew did—he shared his faith with someone else and brought him to Jesus. He told Nathanael, We have found him. The "we" is significant, for Philip came from the same town as Andrew and Peter. Already the nucleus for the twelve people Jesus would bring into the closest communion

with himself was forming. Nathanael's realization of Jesus' omnipresence brought him to faith in the Savior (vv. 48,49).
2.4 Woman. As human, Jesus was close to Mary his mother; as God, he was distant from her. He was both her son and her Savior. She had to learn from the beginning of his public ministry that her son had begun his task as Messiah. Yet Jesus never forgot his mother, as the tender scene at Calvary indicates. He gave her over to his disciple to care for her after his departure from this world (see 19.26).

twenty or thirty gallons. 7 Jesus said to them, "Fill the jars with water." And they filled them up to the brim. 8 He said to them, "Now draw some out, and take it to the chief steward." So they took it. 9 When the steward tasted the water that had become wine, and did not know where it came from (though the servants who had drawn the water knew), the steward called the bridegroom 10 and said to him, "Everyone serves the good wine first, and then the inferior wine after the guests have become drunk. But you have kept the good wine until now." 11 Jesus did this, the first of his signs, in Cana of Galilee, and revealed his glory; and his disciples believed in him.

12   After this he went down to Capernaum with his mother, his brothers, and his disciples; and they remained there a few days.

F. Cleansing of the temple
(2.13–25; cf. Matt. 21.12–17; Mark 11.15–19; Luke 19.45–48)

13   The Passover of the Jews was near, and Jesus went up to Jerusalem. 14 In the temple he found people selling cattle, sheep, and doves, and the money changers seated at their tables. 15 Making a whip of cords, he drove all of them out of the temple, both the sheep and the cattle. He also poured out the coins of the money changers and overturned their tables. 16 He told those who were selling the doves, "Take these things out of here! Stop making my Father's house a marketplace!" 17 His disciples remembered that it was written, "Zeal for your house will consume me." 18 The Jews then said to him, "What sign can you show us for doing this?" 19 Jesus answered them, "Destroy this temple, and in three days I will raise it up." 20 The Jews then said, "This temple has been under construction for forty-six years, and will you raise it up in three days?" 21 But he was speaking of the temple of his body. 22 After he was raised from the dead, his disciples remembered that he had said this; and they believed the scripture and the word that Jesus had spoken.

23   When he was in Jerusalem during the Passover festival, many believed in his name because they saw the signs that he was doing. 24 But Jesus on his part would not entrust himself to them, because he knew all people 25 and needed no one to testify about anyone; for he himself knew what was in everyone.

G. Jesus' discourse with Nicodemus: the new birth (3.1–21)

3 Now there was a Pharisee named Nicodemus, a leader of the Jews. 2 He came to Jesus*m* by night and said to him, "Rabbi, we know that you are a teacher who has come from God; for no one can do these signs that you do apart from the presence of God." 3 Jesus answered him, "Very

m Gk *him*

Cross-references (margin):

2.9 — Jn 4.46
2.11 — Jn 1.14
2.12 — Mt 4.13; 12.46
2.13 — Jn 6.4; 11.55; Deut 16.1-6; Lk 2.41
2.16 — Lk 2.49
2.17 — Ps 69.9
2.18 — Mt 12.38
2.19 — Mt 26.61; 27.40; Mk 14.58
2.21 — 1 Cor 6.19
2.22 — Lk 24.8; Jn 12.16; 14.26
2.23 — v. 13
2.25 — Jn 6.61, 64; 13.11
3.1 — Jn 7.50; 19.39; Lk 23.13; Jn 7.26
3.2 — Jn 9.16, 33; Acts 2.22; 10.38
3.3 — Titus 3.5; Jas 1.18; 1 Pet 1.23; 1 Jn 3.9

2.11 *Signs* (Gk. *semeion*) is used in the Gospel of John to describe Christ's miracles—2.23; 3.2; 4.54; 6.2,14; 7.31; 9.16; 11.47; 12.18). These signs had the specific purpose of bringing people to salvation in Jesus as God's Son (see 20.30,31). Christ's miracles were unique in that he performed them through the power inherent within him.

2.14ff Every year thousands of dispersed Jews came to Jerusalem for the Passover. They could not bring along animals for sacrifice, but they brought different kinds of currency, which they could exchange for local money and use to purchase animals. Thus the temple site itself was filled with money changers and animal dealers, a situation that infuriated Jesus. Some scholars say this cleansing of the temple is the same as that recorded in the Synoptic Gospels. However, the first three Gospels speak of the cleansing of the temple as having occurred shortly before Christ's cru-

cifixion. If John's account is the same, he was incorrect in assigning it to the beginning of Jesus' ministry rather than to the end of it. The best solution is to see two temple cleansings; John alone records the first one.

2.23 *Passover.* See notes on Ex 12.11-13 and Mk 14.1.

3.3 *born anew* (NRSV footnote). Once-born persons die twice—they die in the flesh and they die in the spirit. Twice-born persons die once—they die in the flesh but their souls live on forever. That is, regeneration or the "new birth" is the impartation of divine life into the believers' souls. All Christians must be twice-born: the first time from a mother's womb, then again by the Spirit of God to new life. The new birth comes through the redemption of Jesus Christ, whose blood was shed for this purpose (1 Pet 1.17–23).

truly, I tell you, no one can see the kingdom of God without being born from above."ⁿ 4 Nicodemus said to him, "How can anyone be born after having grown old? Can one enter a second time into the mother's womb and be born?" 5 Jesus answered, "Very truly, I tell you, no one can enter the kingdom of God without being born of water and Spirit. 6 What is born of the flesh is flesh, and what is born of the Spirit is spirit.ᵒ 7 Do not be astonished that I said to you, 'Youᵖ must be born from above.'ᑫ 8 The windᵒ blows where it chooses, and you hear the sound of it, but you do not know where it comes from or where it goes. So it is with everyone who is born of the Spirit." 9 Nicodemus said to him, "How can these things be?" 10 Jesus answered him, "Are you a teacher of Israel, and yet you do not understand these things?

11 "Very truly, I tell you, we speak of what we know and testify to what we have seen; yet youʳ do not receive our testimony. 12 If I have told you about earthly things and you do not believe, how can you believe if I tell you about heavenly things? 13 No one has ascended into heaven except the one who descended from heaven, the Son of Man.ˢ 14 And just as Moses lifted up the serpent in the wilderness, so must the Son of Man be lifted up, 15 that whoever believes in him may have eternal life.ᵗ

16 "For God so loved the world that he gave his only Son, so that everyone who believes in him may not perish but may have eternal life. 17 "Indeed, God did not send the Son into the world to condemn the world, but in order that the world might be saved through him. 18 Those who believe in him are not condemned; but those who do not believe are condemned already, because they have not believed in the name of the only Son of God. 19 And this is the judgment, that the light has come into the world, and people loved darkness rather than light because their deeds were evil. 20 For all who do evil hate the light and do not come to the light, so that their deeds may not be exposed. 21 But those who do what is true come to the light, so that it may be clearly seen that their deeds have been done in God."ᵗ

H. *Jesus baptizes in Judea (3.22–24)*

22 After this Jesus and his disciples went into the Judean countryside, and he spent some time there with them and baptized. 23 John also was baptizing at Aenon near Salim because water was abundant there; and people kept coming and were being baptized 24 — John, of course, had not yet been thrown into prison.

I. *John's testimony to Jesus (3.25–36)*

25 Now a discussion about purification arose between John's disciples and a Jew.ᵘ 26 They came to John and said to him, "Rabbi, the one who was with you across the Jordan, to whom you testified, here he is baptizing, and all are going to him." 27 John answered, "No one can receive

ⁿ Or *born anew*　ᵒ The same Greek word means both *wind* and *spirit*　ᵖ The Greek word for *you* here is plural　ᑫ Or *anew*　ʳ The Greek word for *you* here and in verse 12 is plural　ˢ Other ancient authorities add *who is in heaven*　ᵗ Some interpreters hold that the quotation concludes with verse 15　ᵘ Other ancient authorities read *the Jews*

3.5　Eph 5.26; Titus 3.5
3.6　Jn 1.13; 1 Cor 15.50
3.8　1 Cor 2.11
3.9　Jn 6.52, 60
3.10　Lk 2.46
3.11　Jn 7.16, 17
3.13　Prov 30.4; Acts 2.34; Rom 10.6; Eph 4.9
3.14　Num 21.9; Jn 8.28; 12.34
3.15　v. 36; Jn 20.21; 1 Jn 5.11-13
3.16　Rom 5.8; 1 Jn 4.9
3.17　Jn 5.36, 38; 8.15; 12.47; 1 Jn 4.14
3.18　Jn 5.24; 1 Jn 4.9
3.19　Jn 1.4; 8.12
3.20　Eph 5.11, 13
3.21　1 Jn 1.6
3.22　Jn 4.2
3.24　Mt 4.12; 14.3
3.25　Jn 2.6
3.26　Jn 1.7, 28
3.27　1 Cor 4.7; Heb 5.4

3.5 *without being born of water and Spirit*, i.e., without being born physically and spiritually. "Born of water" means the normal process observed during every human birth, although many believe this phrase refers to water baptism. Regarding water baptism, some Christians teach that new life is imparted by baptism (the doctrine of "baptismal regeneration"). Others hold to "believer's baptism," by which baptism is performed as a symbol that the recipient already has saving faith and is born again. Still others hold that while baptism, particularly infant baptism, does not save the recipient, it is a means of grace and

constitutes a sacrament of God's covenant with his people. Regarding "born of . . . Spirit," the Holy Spirit through the word of God convicts, converts, and regenerates the sinner (see 16.8–11; Rom 8.9–11,14–16).
3.14 See note on Num 21.9. The brass serpent was representative of Christ. Like the serpent, he was to be lifted up in death. The serpent was effective only when those who had been bitten lifted their eyes to look at it, though it was God who saved, not the serpent itself. Whoever looks to Jesus will be saved and live forever.

anything except what has been given from heaven. 28 You yourselves are my witnesses that I said, 'I am not the Messiah,[v] but I have been sent ahead of him.' 29 He who has the bride is the bridegroom. The friend of the bridegroom, who stands and hears him, rejoices greatly at the bridegroom's voice. For this reason my joy has been fulfilled. 30 He must increase, but I must decrease."[w]

31 The one who comes from above is above all; the one who is of the earth belongs to the earth and speaks about earthly things. The one who comes from heaven is above all. 32 He testifies to what he has seen and heard, yet no one accepts his testimony. 33 Whoever has accepted his testimony has certified[x] this, that God is true. 34 He whom God has sent speaks the words of God, for he gives the Spirit without measure. 35 The Father loves the Son and has placed all things in his hands. 36 Whoever believes in the Son has eternal life; whoever disobeys the Son will not see life, but must endure God's wrath.

J. Jesus in Samaria (4.1–6)

4 Now when Jesus[y] learned that the Pharisees had heard, "Jesus is making and baptizing more disciples than John" 2 — although it was not Jesus himself but his disciples who baptized — 3 he left Judea and started back to Galilee. 4 But he had to go through Samaria. 5 So he came to a Samaritan city called Sychar, near the plot of ground that Jacob had given to his son Joseph. 6 Jacob's well was there, and Jesus, tired out by his journey, was sitting by the well. It was about noon.

K. Jesus' discourse with the woman of Samaria (4.7–38)

7 A Samaritan woman came to draw water, and Jesus said to her, "Give me a drink." 8 (His disciples had gone to the city to buy food.) 9 The Samaritan woman said to him, "How is it that you, a Jew, ask a drink of me, a woman of Samaria?" (Jews do not share things in common with Samaritans.)[z] 10 Jesus answered her, "If you knew the gift of God, and who it is that is saying to you, 'Give me a drink,' you would have asked him, and he would have given you living water." 11 The woman said to him, "Sir, you have no bucket, and the well is deep. Where do you get that living water? 12 Are you greater than our ancestor Jacob, who gave us the well, and with his sons and his flocks drank from it?" 13 Jesus said to her, "Everyone who drinks of this water will be thirsty again, 14 but those who drink of the water that I will give them will never be thirsty. The water that I will give will become in them a spring of water gushing up to eternal life." 15 The woman said to him, "Sir, give me this water, so that I may never be thirsty or have to keep coming here to draw water."

16 Jesus said to her, "Go, call your husband, and come back." 17 The woman answered him, "I have no husband." Jesus said to her, "You are right in saying, 'I have no husband'; 18 for you have had five husbands,

[v] Or the Christ   [w] Some interpreters hold that the quotation continues through verse 36   [x] Gk set a seal   to   [y] Other ancient authorities read the Lord   [z] Other ancient authorities lack this sentence

---

4.5,6 The Samaritan village of *Sychar* (now Askar) was on the east slope of Mount Ebal, not far from Mount Gerazim, where the Samaritans had built a temple. This temple had been torn down by John Hyrcanus in 128 B.C. The Samaritan Passover was held on Mount Gerazim each year near the ruins of the temple. But the Samaritans probably worshiped regularly at the foot of Gerazim, near Shechem. The Samaritans were a numerous people in Jesus' day. They were a mixed breed of the union of Jews with Assyrians. After the fall of Samaria in 722 B.C., the land of the northern kingdom was repopulated by Gentiles from the Assyrian Empire, who intermarried with Jews and formed the Samaritans. Because they repre-

sented the mixture of pagans and Jews, the Jews had no intercourse with them and hated them. The scribes and Pharisees suspected Jesus of treason because he ministered to Samaritans.

4.18ff The Samaritan woman at the well was sinful. She knew about the Messiah and believed he would come. Jesus did not hesitate to identify himself as the one she was looking for (v. 26). Like Andrew and Philip (1.40–46), she received Christ and went back to the village to tell its residents about Jesus, not just that they would rejoice with her, but that they would come to know Christ. The upshot of the incident was that "many Samaritans from that city believed in him because of the woman's testimony" (v. 39).

and the one you have now is not your husband. What you have said is true!" 19 The woman said to him, "Sir, I see that you are a prophet. 20 Our ancestors worshiped on this mountain, but you*a* say that the place where people must worship is in Jerusalem." 21 Jesus said to her, "Woman, believe me, the hour is coming when you will worship the Father neither on this mountain nor in Jerusalem. 22 You worship what you do not know; we worship what we know, for salvation is from the Jews. 23 But the hour is coming, and is now here, when the true worshipers will worship the Father in spirit and truth, for the Father seeks such as these to worship him. 24 God is spirit, and those who worship him must worship in spirit and truth." 25 The woman said to him, "I know that Messiah is coming" (who is called Christ). "When he comes, he will proclaim all things to us." 26 Jesus said to her, "I am he,*b* the one who is speaking to you."

27 Just then his disciples came. They were astonished that he was speaking with a woman, but no one said, "What do you want?" or, "Why are you speaking with her?" 28 Then the woman left her water jar and went back to the city. She said to the people, 29 "Come and see a man who told me everything I have ever done! He cannot be the Messiah,*c* can he?" 30 They left the city and were on their way to him.

31 Meanwhile the disciples were urging him, "Rabbi, eat something." 32 But he said to them, "I have food to eat that you do not know about." 33 So the disciples said to one another, "Surely no one has brought him something to eat?" 34 Jesus said to them, "My food is to do the will of him who sent me and to complete his work. 35 Do you not say, 'Four months more, then comes the harvest'? But I tell you, look around you, and see how the fields are ripe for harvesting. 36 The reaper is already receiving*d* wages and is gathering fruit for eternal life, so that sower and reaper may rejoice together. 37 For here the saying holds true, 'One sows and another reaps.' 38 I sent you to reap that for which you did not labor. Others have labored, and you have entered into their labor."

L. *The conversion of Samaritans (4.39–42)*

39 Many Samaritans from that city believed in him because of the woman's testimony, "He told me everything I have ever done." 40 So when the Samaritans came to him, they asked him to stay with them; and he stayed there two days. 41 And many more believed because of his word. 42 They said to the woman, "It is no longer because of what you said that we believe, for we have heard for ourselves, and we know that this is truly the Savior of the world."

M. *Jesus returns to Galilee*
(4.43–45; Matt. 4.12–17; Mark 1.14,15; Luke 4.14,15)

43 When the two days were over, he went from that place to Galilee 44 (for Jesus himself had testified that a prophet has no honor in the prophet's own country). 45 When he came to Galilee, the Galileans welcomed him, since they had seen all that he had done in Jerusalem at the festival; for they too had gone to the festival.

a The Greek word for *you* here and in verses 21 and 22 is plural   *b* Gk *I am*   *c* Or *the Christ*
d Or *35. . . the fields are already ripe for harvesting.* 36The reaper is receiving

---

4.21–23 Jesus sets out here one of the basic responses required of all believers — to worship God in spirit and in truth (see also Mt 4.10).
4.24 *God is spirit*, for he is an infinite and eternal mind, an intelligent being, incorporeal, immaterial, invisible, and incorruptible.
4.35 Jesus wanted his disciples to know that they could not just sit around and wait for "the right time" to begin God's harvest. The right time to begin was

now, for the fields were already ripe unto harvest. Jesus' disciples had not sown the seed; all they needed to do was harvest the crop.
4.39 From the seemingly insignificant incident of an immoral woman's testimony, Jesus spent two days in Samaria and multitudes were converted. They acknowledged that the woman's testimony inspired them to believe; faith came when they met and talked with the Savior himself (v. 42).

Cross-reference column:

4.19 Lk 7.39
4.20 Deut 11.29; Josh 8.33; Lk 9.53
4.21 Mal 1.11; 1 Tim 2.8
4.22 2 Kings 17.28-41; Isa 2.3; Rom 3.1, 2; 9.4, 5
4.23 Jn 5.25; Phil 3.3
4.24 Phil 3.3
4.25 Jn 1.41; Mt 1.16
4.26 Mt 26.63, 64; Mk 14.61, 62; Jn 8.24
4.27 v. 8
4.29 vv. 17, 18; Jn 7.26, 31
4.32 Mt 4.4
4.34 Jn 5.30; 6.38; 17.4; 19.30
4.35 Mt 9.37; Lk 10.2
4.36 Rom 1.13; v. 14
4.37 Job 31.8; Mic 6.15
4.39 v. 29
4.42 1 Jn 4.14; 1 Tim 4.10; 2 Tim 1.10
4.43 v. 40
4.44 Mt 13.57; Mk 1.65; Lk 4.24
4.45 Jn 2.23

N. *The healing of the official's son (4.46–54)*

4.46
Jn 2.1-11

46 Then he came again to Cana in Galilee where he had changed the water into wine. Now there was a royal official whose son lay ill in Capernaum. 47 When he heard that Jesus had come from Judea to Galilee,

4.47
vv. 3, 54

he went and begged him to come down and heal his son, for he was at the point of death. 48 Then Jesus said to him, "Unless you*e* see signs and

4.48
Dan 4.2;
Mk 13.22;
Acts 2.19, 22,
43; 4.30;
Rom 15.19;
Heb 2.4

wonders you will not believe." 49 The official said to him, "Sir, come down before my little boy dies." 50 Jesus said to him, "Go; your son will live." The man believed the word that Jesus spoke to him and started on his way. 51 As he was going down, his slaves met him and told him that his child was alive. 52 So he asked them the hour when he began to recover, and they said to him, "Yesterday at one in the afternoon the fever left him."

4.53
Acts 11.14

53 The father realized that this was the hour when Jesus had said to him, "Your son will live." So he himself believed, along with his whole household.

4.54
Jn 2.11

54 Now this was the second sign that Jesus did after coming from Judea to Galilee.

O. *Jesus heals at Bethesda on the sabbath (5.1–9a)*

5 After this there was a festival of the Jews, and Jesus went up to Jerusalem.

5.2
Neh 3.1;
12.39

2 Now in Jerusalem by the Sheep Gate there is a pool, called in Hebrew*f* Beth-zatha,*g* which has five porticoes. 3 In these lay many invalids — blind, lame, and paralyzed.*h* 5 One man was there who had been ill for thirty-eight years. 6 When Jesus saw him lying there and knew that he had been there a long time, he said to him, "Do you want to be made well?" 7 The sick man answered him, "Sir, I have no one to put me into the pool when the water is stirred up; and while I am making my way,

5.8
Mt 9.6;
Mk 2.11;
Lk 5.24
5.9
Jn 9.14

someone else steps down ahead of me." 8 Jesus said to him, "Stand up, take your mat and walk." 9 At once the man was made well, and he took up his mat and began to walk.

P. *Jesus' relationship to his Father (5.9b–24)*

5.10
vv. 15, 16;
Neh 13.19;
Jer 17.21;
Mt 12.2;
Mk 2.24;
Jn 7.23; 9.16

Now that day was a sabbath. 10 So the Jews said to the man who had been cured, "It is the sabbath; it is not lawful for you to carry your mat." 11 But he answered them, "The man who made me well said to me, 'Take up your mat and walk.'" 12 They asked him, "Who is the man who said to you, 'Take it up and walk'?" 13 Now the man who had been healed did not know who it was, for Jesus had disappeared in*i* the crowd that was

5.14
Mk 2.5;
Jn 8.11

there. 14 Later Jesus found him in the temple and said to him, "See, you have been made well! Do not sin any more, so that nothing worse happens to you." 15 The man went away and told the Jews that it was Jesus who had made him well. 16 Therefore the Jews started persecuting Jesus,

5.17
Jn 9.4; 14.10
5.18
Jn 7.1, 19;
10.30, 33

because he was doing such things on the sabbath. 17 But Jesus answered them, "My Father is still working, and I also am working." 18 For this

e Both instances of the Greek word for *you* in this verse are plural   *f* That is, *Aramaic*   *g* Other ancient authorities read *Bethesda*, others *Bethsaida*   *h* Other ancient authorities add, wholly or in part, *waiting for the stirring of the water;* 4*for an angel of the Lord went down at certain seasons into the pool, and stirred up the water; whoever stepped in first after the stirring of the water was made well from whatever disease that person had.*   *i* Or *had left because of*

4.46ff John alone reports the healing of the royal official's son, the second miracle Jesus performed. The official said, "Come"; our Lord said, "Go." That was all that was needed; our Lord could heal from a distance without even laying on hands.
5.3 In many places where the Savior went he healed all who were ailing. Here we see *many invalids — blind, lame, and paralyzed.* John records the healing of only one of them, though Jesus may have healed more. Or perhaps the others had no faith in Jesus' power to heal.

5.16 Almost from the beginning of Jesus' ministry, he encountered legalistic Jews who criticized Jesus for healing on the sabbath day. When this person who had been ill for thirty-eight years was healed, one would suppose the Jews would have praised God for the healing. Instead they began immediately to persecute the one who had performed the miracle.
5.18 *equal to God.* Jesus claimed a number of times to be God. In this incident the Jews understood what

reason the Jews were seeking all the more to kill him, because he was not only breaking the sabbath, but was also calling God his own Father, thereby making himself equal to God.

19 Jesus said to them, "Very truly, I tell you, the Son can do nothing on his own, but only what he sees the Father doing; for whatever the Father*j* does, the Son does likewise. 20 The Father loves the Son and shows him all that he himself is doing; and he will show him greater works than these, so that you will be astonished. 21 Indeed, just as the Father raises the dead and gives them life, so also the Son gives life to whomever he wishes. 22 The Father judges no one but has given all judgment to the Son, 23 so that all may honor the Son just as they honor the Father. Anyone who does not honor the Son does not honor the Father who sent him. 24 Very truly, I tell you, anyone who hears my word and believes him who sent me has eternal life, and does not come under judgment, but has passed from death to life.

Q. The two resurrections (5.25–29)

25 "Very truly, I tell you, the hour is coming, and is now here, when the dead will hear the voice of the Son of God, and those who hear will live. 26 For just as the Father has life in himself, so he has granted the Son also to have life in himself; 27 and he has given him authority to execute judgment, because he is the Son of Man. 28 Do not be astonished at this; for the hour is coming when all who are in their graves will hear his voice 29 and will come out — those who have done good, to the resurrection of life, and those who have done evil, to the resurrection of condemnation.

R. The Father's witness to the Son (5.30–47)

30 "I can do nothing on my own. As I hear, I judge; and my judgment is just, because I seek to do not my own will but the will of him who sent me. 31 "If I testify about myself, my testimony is not true. 32 There is another who testifies on my behalf, and I know that his testimony to me is true. 33 You sent messengers to John, and he testified to the truth. 34 Not that I accept such human testimony, but I say these things so that you may be saved. 35 He was a burning and shining lamp, and you were willing to rejoice for a while in his light. 36 But I have a testimony greater than John's. The works that the Father has given me to complete, the very works that I am doing, testify on my behalf that the Father has sent me. 37 And the Father who sent me has himself testified on my behalf. You have never heard his voice or seen his form, 38 and you do not have his word abiding in you, because you do not believe him whom he has sent. 39 "You search the scriptures because you think that in them you have eternal life; and it is they that testify on my behalf. 40 Yet you refuse to

j Gk that one

5.19	Jn 8.28; 12.49; 14.10
5.20	Jn 3.35; 14.12
5.21	Rom 4.17; 8.11; Jn 11.25
5.22	Jn 9.39; Acts 17.31
5.23	Lk 10.16; 1 Jn 2.23
5.24	Jn 3.18; 12.44; 20.31; 1 Jn 5.13; 3.14
5.25	Jn 4.21; 6.60; 8.43, 47
5.26	Jn 6.57
5.27	Acts 10.42; 17.31
5.29	Dan 12.2; Acts 24.15; Mt 25.46
5.30	Jn 8.16; 4.34; 6.38
5.31	Jn 8.14
5.32	Jn 8.18
5.33	Jn 1.7, 15, 19, 27, 32
5.34	1 Jn 5.9
5.35	2 Pet 1.19; Mt 21.26
5.36	1 Jn 5.9; Jn 10.25; 14.11; 15.24
5.37	Jn 8.18; Deut 4.12; 1 Tim 1.17
5.38	Jn 3.17
5.39	Lk 24.25, 27; Acts 13.27

Jesus was saying: he made himself equal to God. Either he was guilty of blasphemy and he deserved to die, or his claim was true and they should worship him. Jesus' deity is always the dividing line between those who believe in him and those who disbelieve. **5.24** *does not come under judgment.* Scripture speaks of three major judgments of God: (1) the judgment of the sins of those who accept Christ as Savior — a judgment that took place once for all by the death of Jesus on the cross (Rom 8.1); (2) the judgment of believers at the judgment seat of Christ — when rewards will be handed out after we have given an accounting for our lives (Rom 14.10; 2 Cor 5.10); and (3) the judgment of unbelievers (the great white throne judgment of

Rev 20.11) — the books will be opened and all impenitent sinners will be thrown into the lake of fire. **5.31** Jesus elsewhere stated that his own witness or testimony to himself *was* sufficient (8.14). But here he acceded to the demands of the rabbis for some verification of his claims. The verse may well be phrased: "If I bear witness to myself without other witnesses, it does not measure up to the legal requirement." Then Christ offered other witnesses to himself: (1) God his Father (vv. 36,37); (2) John the Baptist (v. 33); (3) his miraculous works (v. 36); (4) the word of God (v. 39); (5) the prophecy of Moses (v. 46; cf. Deut 18.19). In other words, the unbelief of the Jews was not caused by a lack of witnesses.

come to me to have life. 41 I do not accept glory from human beings. 42 But I know that you do not have the love of God in[k] you. 43 I have come in my Father's name, and you do not accept me; if another comes in his own name, you will accept him. 44 How can you believe when you accept glory from one another and do not seek the glory that comes from the one who alone is God? 45 Do not think that I will accuse you before the Father; your accuser is Moses, on whom you have set your hope. 46 If you believed Moses, you would believe me, for he wrote about me. 47 But if you do not believe what he wrote, how will you believe what I say?"

S. *The five thousand fed (6.1–14; Matt. 14.13–21; Mark 6.30–44; Luke 9.10–17; cf. Matt. 15.32–38)*

6 After this Jesus went to the other side of the Sea of Galilee, also called the Sea of Tiberias.[l] 2 A large crowd kept following him, because they saw the signs that he was doing for the sick. 3 Jesus went up the mountain and sat down there with his disciples. 4 Now the Passover, the festival of the Jews, was near. 5 When he looked up and saw a large crowd coming toward him, Jesus said to Philip, "Where are we to buy bread for these people to eat?" 6 He said this to test him, for he himself knew what he was going to do. 7 Philip answered him, "Six months' wages[m] would not buy enough bread for each of them to get a little." 8 One of his disciples, Andrew, Simon Peter's brother, said to him, 9 "There is a boy here who has five barley loaves and two fish. But what are they among so many people?" 10 Jesus said, "Make the people sit down." Now there was a great deal of grass in the place; so they[n] sat down, about five thousand in all. 11 Then Jesus took the loaves, and when he had given thanks, he distributed them to those who were seated; so also the fish, as much as they wanted. 12 When they were satisfied, he told his disciples, "Gather up the fragments left over, so that nothing may be lost." 13 So they gathered them up, and from the fragments of the five barley loaves, left by those who had eaten, they filled twelve baskets. 14 When the people saw the sign that he had done, they began to say, "This is indeed the prophet who is to come into the world."

T. *Jesus walks on the sea (6.15–21; Matt. 14.22–32; Mark 6.45–52)*

15 When Jesus realized that they were about to come and take him by force to make him king, he withdrew again to the mountain by himself.

16 When evening came, his disciples went down to the sea, 17 got into a boat, and started across the sea to Capernaum. It was now dark, and Jesus had not yet come to them. 18 The sea became rough because a strong wind was blowing. 19 When they had rowed about three or four miles,[o] they saw Jesus walking on the sea and coming near the boat, and they were terrified. 20 But he said to them, "It is I;[p] do not be afraid." 21 Then they wanted to take him into the boat, and immediately the boat reached the land toward which they were going.

---

k Or among   l Gk of Galilee of Tiberias   m Gk Two hundred denarii; the denarius was the usual day's wage for a laborer   n Gk the men   o Gk about twenty-five or thirty stadia   p Gk I am

---

6.1 John carefully refrained from simply repeating what the other three Gospel writers wrote. The feeding of the five thousand is the only miracle recorded in all four Gospels. He probably included this one because it provided a necessary backdrop for the conversation that follows.
6.12 *Gather up the fragments left over.* If Jesus, who supplied this large amount of food, was concerned that what was left be gathered up and used for human

consumption, how much more should Christians be careful not to be wasteful.
6.15 These well-fed people now wanted to forcibly make Jesus king. Then they would not have to work any more to get food, and Jesus could possibly deliver them from the yoke of the Romans. In his humility and self-denial, Jesus squelched their designs by withdrawing to the mountains.

U. Jesus' discourse on the bread of life (6.22–40)

22 The next day the crowd that had stayed on the other side of the sea saw that there had been only one boat there. They also saw that Jesus had not got into the boat with his disciples, but that his disciples had gone away alone. 23 Then some boats from Tiberias came near the place where they had eaten the bread after the Lord had given thanks.*q* 24 So when the crowd saw that neither Jesus nor his disciples were there, they themselves got into the boats and went to Capernaum looking for Jesus.

25 When they found him on the other side of the sea, they said to him, "Rabbi, when did you come here?" 26 Jesus answered them, "Very truly, I tell you, you are looking for me, not because you saw signs, but because you ate your fill of the loaves. 27 Do not work for the food that perishes, but for the food that endures for eternal life, which the Son of Man will give you. For it is on him that God the Father has set his seal." 28 Then they said to him, "What must we do to perform the works of God?" 29 Jesus answered them, "This is the work of God, that you believe in him whom he has sent." 30 So they said to him, "What sign are you going to give us then, so that we may see it and believe you? What work are you performing? 31 Our ancestors ate the manna in the wilderness; as it is written, 'He gave them bread from heaven to eat.' " 32 Then Jesus said to them, "Very truly, I tell you, it was not Moses who gave you the bread from heaven, but it is my Father who gives you the true bread from heaven. 33 For the bread of God is that which*r* comes down from heaven and gives life to the world." 34 They said to him, "Sir, give us this bread always."

35 Jesus said to them, "I am the bread of life. Whoever comes to me will never be hungry, and whoever believes in me will never be thirsty. 36 But I said to you that you have seen me and yet do not believe. 37 Everything that the Father gives me will come to me, and anyone who comes to me I will never drive away; 38 for I have come down from heaven, not to do my own will, but the will of him who sent me. 39 And this is the will of him who sent me, that I should lose nothing of all that he has given me, but raise it up on the last day. 40 This is indeed the will of my Father, that all who see the Son and believe in him may have eternal life; and I will raise them up on the last day."

V. The Jews dispute Jesus' claim (6.41–59)

41 Then the Jews began to complain about him because he said, "I am the bread that came down from heaven." 42 They were saying, "Is not this Jesus, the son of Joseph, whose father and mother we know? How can he now say, 'I have come down from heaven'?" 43 Jesus answered them, "Do not complain among yourselves. 44 No one can come to me unless drawn by the Father who sent me; and I will raise that person up on the last day. 45 It is written in the prophets, 'And they shall all be taught by God.' Everyone who has heard and learned from the Father comes to

Cross references:
6.22 vv. 2, 16ff
6.23 vv. 1, 11
6.24 Mt 14.34; Mk 6.53
6.26 vv. 24, 30
6.27 Isa 55.2; v. 54; Jn 4.14; 3.35
6.29 1 Jn 3.23; Jn 3.17
6.30 Mt 12.38; Mk 8.11
6.31 Ex 16.15; Num 11.8; Neh 9.15; Ps 78.24
6.33 v. 50
6.34 Jn 4.15
6.35 vv. 48, 51; Jn 4.14
6.36 v. 26
6.37 v. 39; Jn 17.2
6.38 Jn 4.34; 5.30
6.39 Jn 10.28; 17.12; 18.9
6.40 vv. 27, 47, 54; Jn 3.15, 16
6.42 Lk 4.22; Jn 7.27, 28; vv. 38, 62
6.44 Jer 31.3; Hos 11.4; Jn 12.32
6.45 Isa 54.13; Jer 31.34; Heb 8.10; 10.16

q Other ancient authorities lack after the Lord had given thanks   *r Or* he who

---

6.27 *Do not work for the food that perishes,* i.e., "do not make the concerns of this present life your chief care and pursuit." Jesus took the concern his followers had for the bodily aspect of life and turned their attention to the spiritual side of life, i.e., to the necessity of caring for the soul, that part of us that never perishes.
6.30 Following Jesus' feeding of the five thousand, he spoke to the people about the food that endures to eternal life. They asked him for a sign that they might see and believe. They did not realize that we see *after* we believe, not before. The people had reversed the divine order.

6.35 *I am the bread of life.* Bread is used figuratively to illustrate that just as bread sustains physical life, Jesus sustains the spiritual life of the believer. Those who come in faith to Jesus as the bread of life will find their spiritual hunger satisfied.
6.42 It is easy to understand why the Jews were puzzled over the words of Jesus concerning his descent from heaven, for they knew him as the son of Mary and Joseph. They had heard of angels coming down from heaven but never of a person doing so. Since they refused to accept the proofs Jesus gave them of his messiahship (see note on 5.31), they were left in the dark.

6.46
Jn 1.18;
5.37; 7.29;
8.19
6.47
Jn 3.16, 18,
36; 5.24;
11.26
6.48
vv. 35, 51
6.49
v. 31
6.50
v. 33
6.51
Heb 10.10
6.52
Jn 9.16;
10.19
6.53
Mt 26.26, 28
6.54
Jn 4.14
6.56
Jn 15.4; 1 Jn
3.24; 4.15,
16
6.57
Jn 3.17
6.58
vv. 49-51

me. 46 Not that anyone has seen the Father except the one who is from God; he has seen the Father. 47 Very truly, I tell you, whoever believes has eternal life. 48 I am the bread of life. 49 Your ancestors ate the manna in the wilderness, and they died. 50 This is the bread that comes down from heaven, so that one may eat of it and not die. 51 I am the living bread that came down from heaven. Whoever eats of this bread will live forever; and the bread that I will give for the life of the world is my flesh."

52 The Jews then disputed among themselves, saying, "How can this man give us his flesh to eat?" 53 So Jesus said to them, "Very truly, I tell you, unless you eat the flesh of the Son of Man and drink his blood, you have no life in you. 54 Those who eat my flesh and drink my blood have eternal life, and I will raise them up on the last day; 55 for my flesh is true food and my blood is true drink. 56 Those who eat my flesh and drink my blood abide in me, and I in them. 57 Just as the living Father sent me, and I live because of the Father, so whoever eats me will live because of me. 58 This is the bread that came down from heaven, not like that which your ancestors ate, and they died. But the one who eats this bread will live forever." 59 He said these things while he was teaching in the synagogue at Capernaum.

W. The questioning disciples (6.60–65)

6.60
v. 66
6.61
Mt 11.6
6.62
Jn 3.13; 17.5
6.63
2 Cor 3.6
6.64
Jn 2.25
6.65
vv. 37, 44;
Jn 3.27

60 When many of his disciples heard it, they said, "This teaching is difficult; who can accept it?" 61 But Jesus, being aware that his disciples were complaining about it, said to them, "Does this offend you? 62 Then what if you were to see the Son of Man ascending to where he was before? 63 It is the spirit that gives life; the flesh is useless. The words that I have spoken to you are spirit and life. 64 But among you there are some who do not believe." For Jesus knew from the first who were the ones that did not believe, and who was the one that would betray him. 65 And he said, "For this reason I have told you that no one can come to me unless it is granted by the Father."

X. Peter's great affirmation (6.66–71)

6.66
v. 60
6.67
Mt 10.2
6.68
Mt 16.16;
Acts 5.20
6.69
Mk 8.29;
Lk 9.20
6.70
Jn 15.16, 19;
13.27
6.71
Jn 13.26;
Mk 14.10

66 Because of this many of his disciples turned back and no longer went about with him. 67 So Jesus asked the twelve, "Do you also wish to go away?" 68 Simon Peter answered him, "Lord, to whom can we go? You have the words of eternal life. 69 We have come to believe and know that you are the Holy One of God." s 70 Jesus answered them, "Did I not choose you, the twelve? Yet one of you is a devil." 71 He was speaking of Judas son of Simon Iscariot, t for he, though one of the twelve, was going to betray him.

s Other ancient authorities read *the Christ, the Son of the living God*   t Other ancient authorities read *Judas Iscariot son of Simon;* others, *Judas son of Simon from Karyot* (Kerioth)

6.53 Jesus used a physical figure of speech in order to teach a great spiritual truth: people should believe on him as the bread of life (see note on v. 35). Since the Lord's Supper was not yet instituted, this must refer to a spiritual eating and drinking, not a sacramental one.

6.59 Jesus did not proclaim his doctrine to a closed gathering of people. He taught openly in the synagogue, where the religious leaders had every opportunity to hear him and to gauge the truth of what he said.

6.60 Many of Jesus' disciples (i.e., followers other than the small group of his twelve disciples) were offended by what Jesus said about eating his flesh.

Because they thought in terms of cannibalism, it was a hard saying for them to accept. But they failed to admit that they did not understand, nor did they ask Jesus to explain what he meant and to open their eyes to his truth.

6.64 Jesus knew from the beginning everyone who would believe on him and everyone who would not. He could infallibly distinguish between those whose love was real and those whose love was counterfeit.

6.68 *to whom can we go?* Peter, acting as spokesman for the twelve, made it clear that if Jesus was not their choice, they had no other alternative. If Jesus could not save them, then no one else could. Jesus is the way, the truth, and the life (14.6).

Y. Jesus and the festival of Booths (7.1–13)

7 After this Jesus went about in Galilee. He did not wish[u] to go about in Judea because the Jews were looking for an opportunity to kill him. 2 Now the Jewish festival of Booths[v] was near. 3 So his brothers said to him, "Leave here and go to Judea so that your disciples also may see the works you are doing; 4 for no one who wants[w] to be widely known acts in secret. If you do these things, show yourself to the world." 5 (For not even his brothers believed in him.) 6 Jesus said to them, "My time has not yet come, but your time is always here. 7 The world cannot hate you, but it hates me because I testify against it that its works are evil. 8 Go to the festival yourselves. I am not[x] going to this festival, for my time has not yet fully come." 9 After saying this, he remained in Galilee.

10 But after his brothers had gone to the festival, then he also went, not publicly but as it were[y] in secret. 11 The Jews were looking for him at the festival and saying, "Where is he?" 12 And there was considerable complaining about him among the crowds. While some were saying, "He is a good man," others were saying, "No, he is deceiving the crowd." 13 Yet no one would speak openly about him for fear of the Jews.

Z. Jesus teaches in the temple (7.14–36)

14 About the middle of the festival Jesus went up into the temple and began to teach. 15 The Jews were astonished at it, saying, "How does this man have such learning,[z] when he has never been taught?" 16 Then Jesus answered them, "My teaching is not mine but his who sent me. 17 Anyone who resolves to do the will of God will know whether the teaching is from God or whether I am speaking on my own. 18 Those who speak on their own seek their own glory; but the one who seeks the glory of him who sent him is true, and there is nothing false in him.

19 "Did not Moses give you the law? Yet none of you keeps the law. Why are you looking for an opportunity to kill me?" 20 The crowd answered, "You have a demon! Who is trying to kill you?" 21 Jesus answered them, "I performed one work, and all of you are astonished. 22 Moses gave you circumcision (it is, of course, not from Moses, but from the patriarchs), and you circumcise a man on the sabbath. 23 If a man receives circumcision on the sabbath in order that the law of Moses may not be broken, are you angry with me because I healed a man's whole body on the sabbath? 24 Do not judge by appearances, but judge with right judgment."

25 Now some of the people of Jerusalem were saying, "Is not this the man whom they are trying to kill? 26 And here he is, speaking openly, but they say nothing to him! Can it be that the authorities really know that this is the Messiah?[a] 27 Yet we know where this man is from; but when the Messiah[a] comes, no one will know where he is from." 28 Then Jesus

7.1	Jn 5.18
7.2	Lev 23.34; Deut 16.16
7.3	Mt 12.46; Mk 3.31
7.5	Mk 3.21
7.6	Mt 26.18; vv. 8, 30
7.7	Jn 15.18, 19; 3.19, 20
7.8	v. 6
7.11	Jn 11.56
7.12	vv. 40-43
7.13	Jn 9.22; 12.42; 19.38
7.14	v. 28
7.15	Mt 13.54; Mk 6.2; Lk 4.22
7.16	Jn 3.11; 8.28; 12.49
7.17	Jn 8.43
7.18	Jn 5.41; 8.50
7.19	Ex 24.3; Jn 1.17; 11.53
7.20	Jn 8.48; 10.20
7.22	Lev 12.3; Gen 17.10
7.23	Mk 3.5
7.24	Lev 19.15; Jn 8.15
7.26	v. 48
7.27	Mt 13.55; Mk 6.3; Lk 4.22
7.28	Jn 8.14; 8.26; 1.18

u Other ancient authorities read *was not at liberty*   v Or *Tabernacles*   w Other ancient authorities read *wants it*   x Other ancient authorities add *yet*   y Other ancient authorities lack *as it were*   z Or *this man know his letters*   a Or *the Christ*

7.2 *festival of Booths.* This was the O.T. festival that began on the fifteenth day of the seventh month (September-October) and lasted eight days. It commemorated the wilderness life of the Hebrews when they left Egypt. At this festival, priests drew water from the pool of Siloam and poured it out upon the altar of the temple (see 7.37–39; see note on Ex 23.16).

7.5 At this stage, Jesus' brothers did not believe in him. Grace does not run automatically in the family line. Being born in a Christian family is a good thing, but it is no guarantee of salvation. Each of us has to make an individual decision.

7.14,15 Jesus was an enigma to those who listened to him at the temple. The people knew he had not been a student in the schools of the prophets, nor had he received the education of the rabbis. But he had received the Spirit without measure (3.34), so that he did not need to receive knowledge from humans.

7.21–23 All male infants were circumcised on the eighth day after birth. If the baby was born on the sabbath, circumcision was performed the following sabbath despite the prohibition against work on that day. Jesus argued that if the Jews could violate the sabbath law in order to keep the law of circumcision, it was far more reasonable to allow for healing on the sabbath.

cried out as he was teaching in the temple, "You know me, and you know where I am from. I have not come on my own. But the one who sent me is true, and you do not know him. 29 I know him, because I am from him, and he sent me." 30 Then they tried to arrest him, but no one laid hands on him, because his hour had not yet come. 31 Yet many in the crowd believed in him and were saying, "When the Messiah[b] comes, will he do more signs than this man has done?"[c]

32 The Pharisees heard the crowd muttering such things about him, and the chief priests and Pharisees sent temple police to arrest him. 33 Jesus then said, "I will be with you a little while longer, and then I am going to him who sent me. 34 You will search for me, but you will not find me; and where I am, you cannot come." 35 The Jews said to one another, "Where does this man intend to go that we will not find him? Does he intend to go to the Dispersion among the Greeks and teach the Greeks? 36 What does he mean by saying, 'You will search for me and you will not find me' and 'Where I am, you cannot come'?"

AA. The last day of the festival (7.37–52)

37 On the last day of the festival, the great day, while Jesus was standing there, he cried out, "Let anyone who is thirsty come to me, 38 and let the one who believes in me drink. As[d] the scripture has said, 'Out of the believer's heart[e] shall flow rivers of living water.'" 39 Now he said this about the Spirit, which believers in him were to receive; for as yet there was no Spirit,[f] because Jesus was not yet glorified.

40 When they heard these words, some in the crowd said, "This is really the prophet." 41 Others said, "This is the Messiah."[b] But some asked, "Surely the Messiah[b] does not come from Galilee, does he? 42 Has not the scripture said that the Messiah[b] is descended from David and comes from Bethlehem, the village where David lived?" 43 So there was a division in the crowd because of him. 44 Some of them wanted to arrest him, but no one laid hands on him.

45 Then the temple police went back to the chief priests and Pharisees, who asked them, "Why did you not arrest him?" 46 The police answered, "Never has anyone spoken like this!" 47 Then the Pharisees replied, "Surely you have not been deceived too, have you? 48 Has any one of the authorities or of the Pharisees believed in him? 49 But this crowd, which does not know the law—they are accursed." 50 Nicodemus, who had gone to Jesus[g] before, and who was one of them, asked, 51 "Our law does not judge people without first giving them a hearing to find out what they are doing, does it?" 52 They replied, "Surely you are not also from Galilee, are you? Search and you will see that no prophet is to arise from Galilee."

BB. The woman caught in adultery (7.53—8.11)

8 ⟦53 Then each of them went home, 1 while Jesus went to the Mount of Olives. 2 Early in the morning he came again to the temple.

---

b Or the Christ   c Other ancient authorities read is doing   d Or come to me and drink. 38 The one who believes in me, as   e Gk out of his belly   f Other ancient authorities read for as yet the Spirit (others, Holy Spirit) had not been given   g Gk him

---

Cross-references (left margin):

7.29 Mt 11.27; Jn 10.15
7.30 Mt 21.46; Jn 8.20
7.31 Jn 8.30; Mt 12.23
7.33 Jn 13.33; 16.16-19
7.34 Jn 8.21; 13.33
7.35 Jas 1.1; 1 Pet 1.1
7.37 Lev 23.36; Isa 55.1; Rev 22.17
7.38 Isa 12.3; Jn 4.10, 14
7.39 Joel 2.28; Acts 2.17, 33; Jn 20.22; 12.23
7.40 Mt 21.11; Jn 1.21
7.41 Jn 1.46
7.42 Jer 23.5; Mic 5.2; Mt 2.5; Lk 2.4
7.43 Jn 9.16; 10.19
7.44 v. 30
7.46 Mt 7.28, 29
7.47 v. 12
7.48 Jn 12.42
7.51 Deut 17.6; 19.15

7.30 *his hour had not yet come.* "His hour" occurs frequently in John's Gospel. The reason the multitude could not lay hands on Jesus was not that they lacked the desire to do so, or that they talked without intending to act. Rather, God hindered them from doing what they wanted because he had a timetable for his Son, and nothing could interfere with the divine plan.
7.38 There is no direct quotation to be found in Scripture for the phrase *out of his belly shall flow rivers of living water* (NRSV footnote). The Scripture that

the Lord referred to was not a specific O.T. text, but the general message of such passages as Isa 12.3; 44.3; 58.11; Ezek 47.1–12; Joel 3.18.
7.53—8.11 In this story, the scribes and Pharisees were guilty of misapplying God's law. They brought only the woman, not the accomplice in her crime, while the law demanded that both parties be stoned, if guilty. When Jesus called for witnesses to cast the first stone, the Pharisees and the woman's other accusers disappeared. They knew their case was illegal. When the woman was set free, Jesus told her to go and

All the people came to him and he sat down and began to teach them. 3 The scribes and the Pharisees brought a woman who had been caught in adultery; and making her stand before all of them, 4 they said to him, "Teacher, this woman was caught in the very act of committing adultery. 5 Now in the law Moses commanded us to stone such women. Now what do you say?" 6 They said this to test him, so that they might have some charge to bring against him. Jesus bent down and wrote with his finger on the ground. 7 When they kept on questioning him, he straightened up and said to them, "Let anyone among you who is without sin be the first to throw a stone at her." 8 And once again he bent down and wrote on the ground. *h* 9 When they heard it, they went away, one by one, beginning with the elders; and Jesus was left alone with the woman standing before him. 10 Jesus straightened up and said to her, "Woman, where are they? Has no one condemned you?" 11 She said, "No one, sir." *i* And Jesus said, "Neither do I condemn you. Go your way, and from now on do not sin again." *j*

8.5
Lev 20.10;
Deut 22.22

8.7
Deut 17.7;
Rom 2.1

8.9
Rom 2.22

8.11
Jn 3.18; 5.14

CC. *Jesus the light of the world: the claim and the testimony (8.12–20)*

12 Again Jesus spoke to them, saying, "I am the light of the world. Whoever follows me will never walk in darkness but will have the light of life." 13 Then the Pharisees said to him, "You are testifying on your own behalf; your testimony is not valid." 14 Jesus answered, "Even if I testify on my own behalf, my testimony is valid because I know where I have come from and where I am going, but you do not know where I come from or where I am going. 15 You judge by human standards; *k* I judge no one. 16 Yet even if I do judge, my judgment is valid; for it is not I alone who judge, but I and the Father *l* who sent me. 17 In your law it is written that the testimony of two witnesses is valid. 18 I testify on my own behalf, and the Father who sent me testifies on my behalf." 19 Then they said to him, "Where is your Father?" Jesus answered, "You know neither me nor my Father. If you knew me, you would know my Father also." 20 He spoke these words while he was teaching in the treasury of the temple, but no one arrested him, because his hour had not yet come.

8.12
Jn 1.4; 9.5;
12.35
8.13
Jn 5.31
8.14
Jn 18.37;
13.3; 16.28;
7.28; 9.29
8.15
Jn 7.24; 3.17
8.16
Jn 5.30
8.17
Deut 17.6;
Mt 18.16
8.18
Jn 5.37
8.19
Jn 14.7; 16.3
8.20
Mk 12.41;
Jn 7.30

DD. *Jesus warns against unbelief (8.21–30)*

21 Again he said to them, "I am going away, and you will search for me, but you will die in your sin. Where I am going, you cannot come." 22 Then the Jews said, "Is he going to kill himself? Is that what he means by saying, 'Where I am going, you cannot come'?" 23 He said to them, "You are from below, I am from above; you are of this world, I am not of this world. 24 I told you that you would die in your sins, for you will die in your sins unless you believe that I am he." *m* 25 They said to him, "Who are you?" Jesus said to them, "Why do I speak to you at all? *n* 26 I have much to say about you and much to condemn; but the one who sent me is true, and I declare to the world what I have heard from him." 27 They did not understand that he was speaking to them about the

8.21
Jn 7.34

8.23
Jn 3.31;
17.14
8.24
Mk 13.6;
Jn 4.26;
13.19
8.26
Jn 7.28;
3.32; 15.15

h Other ancient authorities add the sins of each of them   i Or Lord   j The most ancient authorities lack 7.53—8.11; other authorities add the passage here or after 7.36 or after 21.25 or after Luke 21.38, with variations of text; some mark the passage as doubtful.   k Gk according to the flesh   l Other ancient authorities read he   m Gk I am   n Or What I have told you from the beginning

to sin no more.
8.12 A worthy Christian walk is characterized by certain inward and outward qualities. Some of the inward qualities are purity, or walking as children of the light (Eph 5.8,8; 1 Jn 1.6,7; 2.11); sincerity or integrity (2 Cor 4.2); obedience to God (2 Jn 6); faith, not sight (2 Cor 5.7); and living in the truth (3 Jn 3,4). The outward characteristics are outward honesty

(Rom 13.12,13; 1 Thess 4.11,12); acting carefully (Eph 5.15,16); walking wisely (Col 4.5,6); and manifesting love (Eph 5.2).
8.24 Jesus declared himself to be God and asserted that salvation depended on believing in him. Those who do not believe in him will die in their sins and thus lose all hope of eternal life.

8.28
Jn 3.14;
12.32; 5.19;
3.11
8.29
Jn 4.34;
5.30; 6.38
8.30
Jn 7.31;
10.42; 11.45

Father. 28 So Jesus said, "When you have lifted up the Son of Man, then you will realize that I am he,[o] and that I do nothing on my own, but I speak these things as the Father instructed me. 29 And the one who sent me is with me; he has not left me alone, for I always do what is pleasing to him." 30 As he was saying these things, many believed in him.

EE. The true descendants of Abraham (8.31–59)

8.31
Jn 15.7; 2 Jn
9
8.32
Rom 8.2;
Jas 2.12
8.33
Mt 3.9
8.34
Rom 6.16;
2 Pet 2.19
8.35
Gal 4.30
8.37
vv. 39, 40
8.38
Jn 5.19, 30;
14.10, 24

31 Then Jesus said to the Jews who had believed in him, "If you continue in my word, you are truly my disciples; 32 and you will know the truth, and the truth will make you free." 33 They answered him, "We are descendants of Abraham and have never been slaves to anyone. What do you mean by saying, 'You will be made free'?"

34 Jesus answered them, "Very truly, I tell you, everyone who commits sin is a slave to sin. 35 The slave does not have a permanent place in the household; the son has a place there forever. 36 So if the Son makes you free, you will be free indeed. 37 I know that you are descendants of Abraham; yet you look for an opportunity to kill me, because there is no place in you for my word. 38 I declare what I have seen in the Father's presence; as for you, you should do what you have heard from the Father."[p]

8.39
Rom 9.7;
Gal 3.7
8.40
v. 26
8.41
Isa 63.16;
64.8
8.42
1 Jn 5.1;
Jn 16.27, 28;
17.8; 7.28
8.44
1 Jn 3.8;
vv. 38, 41;
1 Jn 2.4;
Mt 12.34

39 They answered him, "Abraham is our father." Jesus said to them, "If you were Abraham's children, you would be doing[q] what Abraham did, 40 but now you are trying to kill me, a man who has told you the truth that I heard from God. This is not what Abraham did. 41 You are indeed doing what your father does." They said to him, "We are not illegitimate children; we have one father, God himself." 42 Jesus said to them, "If God were your Father, you would love me, for I came from God and now I am here. I did not come on my own, but he sent me. 43 Why do you not understand what I say? It is because you cannot accept my word. 44 You are from your father the devil, and you choose to do your father's desires. He was a murderer from the beginning and does not stand in the truth, because there is no truth in him. When he lies, he speaks according to his own nature, for he is a liar and the father of lies. 45 But because I tell the truth, you do not believe me. 46 Which of you convicts me of sin? If I tell the truth, why do you not believe me? 47 Whoever is from God hears the words of God. The reason you do not hear them is that you are not from God."

8.47
1 Jn 4.6
8.48
v. 52;
Jn 7.20;
10.20
8.50
Jn 5.41
8.51
Jn 14.23;
15.20; 17.6;
Mt 16.28;
Heb 11.5
8.52
Jn 7.20;
14.23; 15.20;
17.6

48 The Jews answered him, "Are we not right in saying that you are a Samaritan and have a demon?" 49 Jesus answered, "I do not have a demon; but I honor my Father, and you dishonor me. 50 Yet I do not seek my own glory; there is one who seeks it and he is the judge. 51 Very truly, I tell you, whoever keeps my word will never see death." 52 The Jews said

o Gk I am   p Other ancient authorities read you do what you have heard from your father   q Other ancient authorities read If you are Abraham's children, then do

---

8.28 lifted up, i.e., lifted up on the cross. Jesus was fully aware that the cross would be the eventual means of his death (cf. Mk 8.31; 9:31; 10:33; Jn 3.14,15).
8.31ff All the Jews were children of Abraham after the flesh but not all were children of Abraham according to faith (cf. Rom 9.6–9). Jesus promised that faith in him would set them free from slavery. Some Jews took exception to these words (v. 33), for they thought they were free by virtue of their being children of Abraham. He informed them that, as sinners, they were slaves to sin, and that he had the power to set them free from that bondage. Moreover, Jesus agreed that they were descendants of Abraham (v. 37), but it would avail them nothing, for they did not have Abraham's faith.
8.39 you would be doing what Abraham did, i.e., the

Jews would show an interest in the covenant God made with Abraham and his offspring. Since Jesus was the one who fulfilled this covenant (cf. Gal 3.15, 16), this would entail faith in him as Savior and obedience to him as Lord, neither of which the Jews had at this moment.
8.42 Jesus made the astounding claim that the Jews did not have God as their Father for two reasons: (1) They did not love Jesus himself; whoever does not love Jesus is accursed (1 Cor 16.22). (2) They did not understand Jesus' speech, which was divine and intelligible to those who were familiar with the voice of God in the O.T. In plainest words, they did not speak the language of the family of God.
8.44 the devil. See note on Ezek 28.12. Everyone is either a child of God or a child of the devil (see 1 Jn 3.10).

to him, "Now we know that you have a demon. Abraham died, and so did the prophets; yet you say, 'Whoever keeps my word will never taste death.' 53 Are you greater than our father Abraham, who died? The prophets also died. Who do you claim to be?" 54 Jesus answered, "If I glorify myself, my glory is nothing. It is my Father who glorifies me, he of whom you say, 'He is our God,' 55 though you do not know him. But I know him; if I would say that I do not know him, I would be a liar like you. But I do know him and I keep his word. 56 Your ancestor Abraham rejoiced that he would see my day; he saw it and was glad." 57 Then the Jews said to him, "You are not yet fifty years old, and have you seen Abraham?"r 58 Jesus said to them, "Very truly, I tell you, before Abraham was, I am." 59 So they picked up stones to throw at him, but Jesus hid himself and went out of the temple.

FF. *Jesus heals the man born blind (9.1–12)*

9 As he walked along, he saw a man blind from birth. 2 His disciples asked him, "Rabbi, who sinned, this man or his parents, that he was born blind?" 3 Jesus answered, "Neither this man nor his parents sinned; he was born blind so that God's works might be revealed in him. 4 Wes must work the works of him who sent met while it is day; night is coming when no one can work. 5 As long as I am in the world, I am the light of the world." 6 When he had said this, he spat on the ground and made mud with the saliva and spread the mud on the man's eyes, 7 saying to him, "Go, wash in the pool of Siloam" (which means Sent). Then he went and washed and came back able to see. 8 The neighbors and those who had seen him before as a beggar began to ask, "Is this not the man who used to sit and beg?" 9 Some were saying, "It is he." Others were saying, "No, but it is someone like him." He kept saying, "I am the man." 10 But they kept asking him, "Then how were your eyes opened?" 11 He answered, "The man called Jesus made mud, spread it on my eyes, and said to me, 'Go to Siloam and wash.' Then I went and washed and received my sight." 12 They said to him, "Where is he?" He said, "I do not know."

GG. *The Pharisees question the healed man (9.13–23)*

13 They brought to the Pharisees the man who had formerly been blind. 14 Now it was a sabbath day when Jesus made the mud and opened his eyes. 15 Then the Pharisees also began to ask him how he had received his sight. He said to them, "He put mud on my eyes. Then I washed, and now I see." 16 Some of the Pharisees said, "This man is not from God, for he does not observe the sabbath." But others said, "How can a man who

8.53
Jn 4.12
8.54
v. 50;
Jn 16.14
8.55
Jn 7.28, 29;
15.10
8.56
Mt 13.17;
Heb 11.13
8.58
Jn 1.1; 17.5,
24;
Rev 1.8
8.59
Jn 10.31;
11.8; 12.36

9.2
v. 34;
Lk 13.2;
Ex 20.5;
Ezek 18.20
9.3
Jn 11.4
9.4
Jn 11.9;
12.35
9.5
Jn 1.4; 8.12;
12.46
9.6
Mk 7.33;
8.23
9.7
v. 11;
Lk 13.4;
Jn 11.37
9.11
v. 7

9.14
Jn 5.9
9.15
v. 10
9.16
Mt 12.2;
Jn 7.43;
10.19

---

r Other ancient authorities read *has Abraham seen you?*   s Other ancient authorities read *I*   t Other ancient authorities read *us*

8.58 *before Abraham was, I am.* This is one of Jesus' clearest statements about his eternal existence (see also Isa 9.6; Jn 1.1,2). He attributed to himself the name of Yahweh as revealed to Moses in Ex 3.14, and (judging from their reaction) that is how his hearers understood these words. They were not ready to accept what he said, for to do so meant they would have to worship him.
9.1ff A common opinion, apparently shared by Jesus' disciples, was that sickness came as a result of sin. Since this man was blind from birth, obviously his own sin had not been the cause of the "punishment." So the question was whether his blindness was

a punishment for his parents' sins. Jesus replied that sickness is not always the result of sin. This man was born blind so that God's work might be demonstrated through healing him.
9.16 *How can a man who is a sinner perform such signs?* This excellent question produced a division among the Jewish leaders. Miracles did not move those who were steeped in their unbelief. The blind man's eyes were opened by Jesus, but their blind hearts remained darkened; and they refused the remedy by which they too could see spiritually (cf. vv. 40,41).

9.17
v. 15;
Mt 21.11

9.18
v. 22

9.22
Jn 7.13;
12.42; v. 34;
Lk 6.22

9.23
v. 21

is a sinner perform such signs?" And they were divided. 17 So they said again to the blind man, "What do you say about him? It was your eyes he opened." He said, "He is a prophet."

18   The Jews did not believe that he had been blind and had received his sight until they called the parents of the man who had received his sight 19 and asked them, "Is this your son, who you say was born blind? How then does he now see?" 20 His parents answered, "We know that this is our son, and that he was born blind; 21 but we do not know how it is that now he sees, nor do we know who opened his eyes. Ask him; he is of age. He will speak for himself." 22 His parents said this because they were afraid of the Jews; for the Jews had already agreed that anyone who confessed Jesus^u to be the Messiah^v would be put out of the synagogue. 23 Therefore his parents said, "He is of age; ask him."

HH. *The Pharisees question the healed man a second time (9.24–34)*

9.24
Josh 7.19;
1 Sam 6.5;
v. 16

9.27
v. 15;
Jn 5.25
9.28
Jn 5.45
9.29
Jn 8.14

9.31
Job 27.8, 9;
Ps 34.15;
66.18;
Prov 15.29;
28.9;
Isa 1.15;
Jer 11.11;
Zech 7.13
9.33
v. 16
9.34
v. 2

24   So for the second time they called the man who had been blind, and they said to him, "Give glory to God! We know that this man is a sinner." 25 He answered, "I do not know whether he is a sinner. One thing I do know, that though I was blind, now I see." 26 They said to him, "What did he do to you? How did he open your eyes?" 27 He answered them, "I have told you already, and you would not listen. Why do you want to hear it again? Do you also want to become his disciples?" 28 Then they reviled him, saying, "You are his disciple, but we are disciples of Moses. 29 We know that God has spoken to Moses, but as for this man, we do not know where he comes from." 30 The man answered, "Here is an astonishing thing! You do not know where he comes from, and yet he opened my eyes. 31 We know that God does not listen to sinners, but he does listen to one who worships him and obeys his will. 32 Never since the world began has it been heard that anyone opened the eyes of a person born blind. 33 If this man were not from God, he could do nothing." 34 They answered him, "You were born entirely in sins, and are you trying to teach us?" And they drove him out.

II. *Jesus seeks the outcast (9.35–41)*

9.35
Mt 14.33;
16.16;
Mk 1.1;
Jn 10.36
9.36
Rom 10.14
9.37
Jn 4.26
9.38
Mt 28.9
9.39
Jn 5.22, 27;
3.19;
Mt 13.13;
15.14
9.40
Rom 2.19
9.41
Jn 15.22, 24

35   Jesus heard that they had driven him out, and when he found him, he said, "Do you believe in the Son of Man?"^w 36 He answered, "And who is he, sir?^x Tell me, so that I may believe in him." 37 Jesus said to him, "You have seen him, and the one speaking with you is he." 38 He said, "Lord,^x I believe." And he worshiped him. 39 Jesus said, "I came into this world for judgment so that those who do not see may see, and those who do see may become blind." 40 Some of the Pharisees near him heard this and said to him, "Surely we are not blind, are we?" 41 Jesus said to them, "If you were blind, you would not have sin. But now that you say, 'We see,' your sin remains.

u Gk *him*   v Or *the Christ*   w Other ancient authorities read *the Son of God*   x *Sir* and *Lord* translate the same Greek word

9.22 The Pharisees did not think Jesus to be the Messiah for two reasons: (1) his teachings were contrary to their traditions; (2) they expected the Messiah to come in pomp and splendor, but Jesus came in lowliness and humility. Understandably, therefore, they agreed to disfellowship anyone who professed faith in Jesus as the Messiah, for such persons were considered apostates. To Jesus, however, his miraculous deeds should have convinced them that he was the Messiah (cf. 20.30,31).

9.34 *And they drove him out.* The man healed of his blindness was cast out of the synagogue. Good people may well be denied the comfort of the church, but it is better to be cast out of the fellowship than to remain and surrender true convictions. This man's sufferings were similar to those of the apostles in Acts.
9.38 *he worshiped him.* It would have been blasphemous for Jesus to accept this worship, which belongs only to God, if he were not God.

JJ. *Jesus' discourse on the good shepherd* (10.1–18)

10 "Very truly, I tell you, anyone who does not enter the sheepfold by the gate but climbs in by another way is a thief and a bandit. 2 The one who enters by the gate is the shepherd of the sheep. 3 The gatekeeper opens the gate for him, and the sheep hear his voice. He calls his own sheep by name and leads them out. 4 When he has brought out all his own, he goes ahead of them, and the sheep follow him because they know his voice. 5 They will not follow a stranger, but they will run from him because they do not know the voice of strangers." 6 Jesus used this figure of speech with them, but they did not understand what he was saying to them.

7 So again Jesus said to them, "Very truly, I tell you, I am the gate for the sheep. 8 All who came before me are thieves and bandits; but the sheep did not listen to them. 9 I am the gate. Whoever enters by me will be saved, and will come in and go out and find pasture. 10 The thief comes only to steal and kill and destroy. I came that they may have life, and have it abundantly.

11 "I am the good shepherd. The good shepherd lays down his life for the sheep. 12 The hired hand, who is not the shepherd and does not own the sheep, sees the wolf coming and leaves the sheep and runs away—and the wolf snatches them and scatters them. 13 The hired hand runs away because a hired hand does not care for the sheep. 14 I am the good shepherd. I know my own and my own know me, 15 just as the Father knows me and I know the Father. And I lay down my life for the sheep. 16 I have other sheep that do not belong to this fold. I must bring them also, and they will listen to my voice. So there will be one flock, one shepherd. 17 For this reason the Father loves me, because I lay down my life in order to take it up again. 18 No one takes[y] it from me, but I lay it down of my own accord. I have power to lay it down, and I have power to take it up again. I have received this command from my Father."

KK. *The Jews divided (10.19–21)*

19 Again the Jews were divided because of these words. 20 Many of them were saying, "He has a demon and is out of his mind. Why listen to him?" 21 Others were saying, "These are not the words of one who has a demon. Can a demon open the eyes of the blind?"

10.2 Mk 6.34; vv. 11, 12
10.3 vv. 16, 27, 9
10.4 v. 3
10.6 Jn 16.25
10.7 Jer 23.1, 2; Ezek 34.2
10.10 Jn 5.40
10.11 Isa 40.11; Ezek 34.11-16, 23; Heb 13.20; 1 Pet 5.4; Rev 7.17; 1 Jn 3.16; Jn 15.13
10.12 Zech 11.16, 17
10.14 vv. 11, 27
10.15 Mt 11.27
10.16 Isa 56.8; Jn 11.52; Eph 2.14; 1 Pet 2.25
10.17 Isa 53.7, 8, 12
10.18 Jn 2.19; 15.10; Heb 5.8
10.19 Jn 7.43; 9.16
10.20 Jn 7.20; 8.48; Mk 3.21
10.21 Jn 9.32, 33; Ex 4.11

---

y Other ancient authorities read *has taken*

10.1ff Jesus' story of the good shepherd is an allegory, not a parable (see note on Mt 13.3 regarding the definition of a parable). An allegory differs from a parable in one important way: *all* the details of an allegory are significant. In the allegory of the good shepherd all of the details are important: Jesus is the shepherd of the sheep. He is the door. The sheep enter the kingdom through the door. Jesus, the shepherd, died for his sheep. And whoever is not a true sheep cannot enter the door.
10.11 Christ is called *the good shepherd* here, "the great shepherd" in Heb 13.20, and "the chief shepherd" in 1 Pet 5.4. The good shepherd died for his sheep, the great shepherd enables the sheep to do God's will, and the chief shepherd is coming again with his reward for the sheep. That is, as the good shepherd Christ's work is finished, as the great shepherd his work is present, and as the chief shepherd his work is future.
10.16 *there will be one flock, one shepherd.* Jesus

promised that Jews and Gentiles would be incorporated into the one church of which he was the shepherd. That is, the one church has one head, Christ (cf. Eph 1.22; Col 1.18); it is guided and led by the one Spirit (Eph 4.3,4); and it is commanded to have love for all members of the flock (1 Jn 3.11–24).
10.20 *He has a demon and is out of his mind.* John did not report as many of the healings as the other Gospel writers did. For example, he did not record any of the miracles in which Jesus cast out demons. But he did record several of the times when Jesus was accused of having a demon and being insane, of imagining things (7.20), and of speaking wildly (8.48–52).
10.22 *The festival of the Dedication* started after 168 B.C. The temple had been violated by Antiochus Epiphanes, who offered a pig on the altar (cf. Dan 11.31). When Judas Maccabeus recaptured the city, he had the temple cleansed of its idolatry. This festival commemorated the rededication of the temple.

LL. *Jesus the Christ, the Son of God (10.22–42)*

22 At that time the festival of the Dedication took place in Jerusalem. It was winter, 23 and Jesus was walking in the temple, in the portico of Solomon. 24 So the Jews gathered around him and said to him, "How long will you keep us in suspense? If you are the Messiah,*z* tell us plainly." 25 Jesus answered, "I have told you, and you do not believe. The works that I do in my Father's name testify to me; 26 but you do not believe, because you do not belong to my sheep. 27 My sheep hear my voice. I know them, and they follow me. 28 I give them eternal life, and they will never perish. No one will snatch them out of my hand. 29 What my Father has given me is greater than all else, and no one can snatch it out of the Father's hand.*a* 30 The Father and I are one."

31 The Jews took up stones again to stone him. 32 Jesus replied, "I have shown you many good works from the Father. For which of these are you going to stone me?" 33 The Jews answered, "It is not for a good work that we are going to stone you, but for blasphemy, because you, though only a human being, are making yourself God." 34 Jesus answered, "Is it not written in your law,*b* 'I said, you are gods'? 35 If those to whom the word of God came were called 'gods'—and the scripture cannot be annulled— 36 can you say that the one whom the Father has sanctified and sent into the world is blaspheming because I said, 'I am God's Son'? 37 If I am not doing the works of my Father, then do not believe me. 38 But if I do them, even though you do not believe me, believe the works, so that you may know and understand*c* that the Father is in me and I am in the Father." 39 Then they tried to arrest him again, but he escaped from their hands.

40 He went away again across the Jordan to the place where John had been baptizing earlier, and he remained there. 41 Many came to him, and they were saying, "John performed no sign, but everything that John said about this man was true." 42 And many believed in him there.

Cross references (margin):
- 10.23 Acts 3.11; 5.12
- 10.25 Jn 5.36
- 10.26 Jn 8.47
- 10.27 vv. 4, 14
- 10.28 Jn 17.2, 3; 1 Jn 2.25; Jn 6.37, 39
- 10.29 Jn 14.28; 17.2, 6ff
- 10.30 Jn 17.21ff
- 10.31 Jn 8.59
- 10.33 Jn 5.18
- 10.34 Ps 82.6
- 10.36 Jn 6.69; 3.17; Jn 5.17, 18
- 10.37 Jn 15.24
- 10.38 Jn 14.10, 11; 17.21
- 10.39 Jn 7.30; 8.59
- 10.40 Jn 1.28
- 10.41 Jn 2.11; 3.30
- 10.42 Jn 7.31; 11.45

z Or *the Christ*　*a* Other ancient authorities read *My Father who has given them to me is greater than all, and no one can snatch them out of the Father's hand*　*b* Other ancient authorities read *in the law*　*c* Other ancient authorities lack *and understand*; others read *and believe*

According to the apocryphal books of the Maccabees, the festival lasted eight days in the winter month of Chislev (December); today it is called Hanukkah. **10.28** *Eternal life* is promised to all who receive Christ as Savior (1.12). Believers may know of a certainty that they have eternal life (1 Jn 5.13), and are assured they will never perish. They are "protected by the power of God through faith for a salvation . . ." (1 Pet 1.5). **10.30** One of the crucial teachings of the Bible is that Jesus is God (see note on 8.58). Here he declared he was one with the Father. In Jn 14.9 he said, "Whoever has seen me has seen the Father." In Mt 11.27 he said, "No one knows the Son except the Father, and no one knows the Father except the Son and anyone to whom the Son chooses to reveal him." When the high priest asked, "Are you the Messiah, the Son of the Blessed One?" Jesus responded, "I am; and 'you will see the Son of Man seated at the right hand of the Power,' and 'coming with the clouds of heaven' " (Mk 14.61,62). The high priest declared this to be blasphemy, for Jesus claimed to be God (Mk 14.64). If Jesus is not God, he was a notorious liar, the worst enemy of the human soul. **10.35** *word of God.* The sixty-six books that make up the Bible are called the canon ("canon" means

"rod" or "rule"); these books constitute the authoritative books of God's revelation. The canon of the O.T. was well known in Jesus' day and consisted of the thirty-nine books we have in our Bibles. Jesus placed his stamp of approval on the O.T. Scriptures, called them the word of God, and said that they *cannot be annulled.* He even asserted that the smallest particle of the word cannot be destroyed without the heavens and the earth first being destroyed (Mt 5.17,18). Jesus, in other words, witnessed to a trustworthy Bible. His Lordship requires that Christians believe what Jesus taught. The books now in the N.T. began as separate books sent to and used by various churches in the Greco-Roman world. Copies were made and circulated widely. The Gospels were written to tell new believers about Jesus the Messiah and to prepare them for baptism and Christian service. Gradually the twenty-seven books which presently comprise the N.T. were accepted and acknowledged to be God's word. Lists of these canonical letters and Gospels were drawn up, possibly as a safeguard against spurious apocryphal "Gospels" and so-called "apostolic letters" produced by Gnostics and other heretics. The authority of a few of the N.T. books was questioned at first, but gradually all that are in our present canon were accepted as normative.

MM. The raising of Lazarus (11.1–57)

1. Jesus hears of Lazarus' death (11.1–6)

11 Now a certain man was ill, Lazarus of Bethany, the village of Mary and her sister Martha. 2 Mary was the one who anointed the Lord with perfume and wiped his feet with her hair; her brother Lazarus was ill. 3 So the sisters sent a message to Jesus,d "Lord, he whom you love is ill." 4 But when Jesus heard it, he said, "This illness does not lead to death; rather it is for God's glory, so that the Son of God may be glorified through it." 5 Accordingly, though Jesus loved Martha and her sister and Lazarus, 6 after having heard that Lazaruse was ill, he stayed two days longer in the place where he was.

2. Jesus goes to Lazarus' home (11.7–16)

7 Then after this he said to the disciples, "Let us go to Judea again." 8 The disciples said to him, "Rabbi, the Jews were just now trying to stone you, and are you going there again?" 9 Jesus answered, "Are there not twelve hours of daylight? Those who walk during the day do not stumble, because they see the light of this world. 10 But those who walk at night stumble, because the light is not in them." 11 After saying this, he told them, "Our friend Lazarus has fallen asleep, but I am going there to awaken him." 12 The disciples said to him, "Lord, if he has fallen asleep, he will be all right." 13 Jesus, however, had been speaking about his death, but they thought that he was referring merely to sleep. 14 Then Jesus told them plainly, "Lazarus is dead. 15 For your sake I am glad I was not there, so that you may believe. But let us go to him." 16 Thomas, who was called the Twin,f said to his fellow disciples, "Let us also go, that we may die with him."

3. Jesus talks with Martha: "the resurrection and the life" (11.17–27)

17 When Jesus arrived, he found that Lazaruse had already been in the tomb four days. 18 Now Bethany was near Jerusalem, some two milesg away, 19 and many of the Jews had come to Martha and Mary to console them about their brother. 20 When Martha heard that Jesus was coming, she went and met him, while Mary stayed at home. 21 Martha said to Jesus, "Lord, if you had been here, my brother would not have died. 22 But even now I know that God will give you whatever you ask of him." 23 Jesus said to her, "Your brother will rise again." 24 Martha said to him, "I know that he will rise again in the resurrection on the last day." 25 Jesus said to her, "I am the resurrection and the life.h Those who believe in me, even though they die, will live, 26 and everyone who lives and believes

11.1	Mk 11.1; Lk 10.38
11.2	Mk 14.3; Lk 7.38; Jn 12.3
11.3	Lk 7.13
11.4	v. 40; Jn 9.3
11.7	Jn 10.40
11.8	Jn 10.31
11.9	Lk 13.33; Jn 9.4; 12.35
11.11	v. 3; Mt 27.52; Mk 5.39; Acts 7.60
11.13	Mt 9.24; Lk 8.52
11.16	Mt 10.3; Jn 20.24-28
11.17	v. 39
11.18	v. 1
11.19	Job 2.11
11.21	vv. 2, 32
11.22	Jn 9.31
11.24	Dan 12.2; Jn 5.28, 29; Acts 24.15
11.25	Jn 1.4; 5.26; 14.6; 3.36
11.26	Jn 6.47; 8.51

d Gk him   e Gk he   f Gk Didymus   g Gk fifteen stadia   h Other ancient authorities lack and the life

11.3 Mary and Martha sent for Jesus when their brother Lazarus was dying. Their relationship to Jesus was more than that of friends. They believed on him, knew that he performed miracles, and confidently sought his help in the hour of trial. Trials make sickness and death come to all people, including Christians. But we have God for our helper, as Mary and Martha had Jesus, the God-man, for their helper.

11.11 has fallen asleep. The disciples misunderstood Jesus, believing that Lazarus was ill and restless, but finally fallen asleep, and was recovering. But Jesus corrected their misunderstanding: "Lazarus is dead" (11.14). Jesus can raise the dead just as easily as he can heal the sick. Life and death are under the control of the Son of God.

11.17 had already been in the tomb four days. By this time the body was in a state of decay, so that no one could question whether Lazarus was really dead. Jesus knew very well what he was doing and why he delayed coming until his friend was dead. He also intended to use the occasion to instruct Martha, not only about the resurrection of the dead, but, more importantly, that he himself was and is the resurrection and the life.

11.24 Martha, like many Jews, professed to believe in the resurrection of the dead. Jesus gently took her from that conviction to the necessity of believing in him. He pressed her to tell him whether she believed him to be the Christ, the Son of God. Martha's response in the affirmative is a confession that all believers must make.

11.27
Mt 16.16;
Jn 6.14

in me will never die. Do you believe this?" 27 She said to him, "Yes, Lord, I believe that you are the Messiah,[i] the Son of God, the one coming into the world."

4. *Jesus talks with Mary (11.28–37)*

11.28
Mt 26.18;
Lk 22.11
11.30
v. 20
11.31
v. 19
11.32
v. 21
11.33
v. 38;
Jn 12.27;
13.21
11.35
Lk 19.41
11.37
Jn 9.6, 7

28 When she had said this, she went back and called her sister Mary, and told her privately, "The Teacher is here and is calling for you." 29 And when she heard it, she got up quickly and went to him. 30 Now Jesus had not yet come to the village, but was still at the place where Martha had met him. 31 The Jews who were with her in the house, consoling her, saw Mary get up quickly and go out. They followed her because they thought that she was going to the tomb to weep there. 32 When Mary came where Jesus was and saw him, she knelt at his feet and said to him, "Lord, if you had been here, my brother would not have died." 33 When Jesus saw her weeping, and the Jews who came with her also weeping, he was greatly disturbed in spirit and deeply moved. 34 He said, "Where have you laid him?" They said to him, "Lord, come and see." 35 Jesus began to weep. 36 So the Jews said, "See how he loved him!" 37 But some of them said, "Could not he who opened the eyes of the blind man have kept this man from dying?"

5. *Jesus raises Lazarus from the dead (11.38–44)*

11.38
v. 33;
Mt 27.60;
Mk 15.46;
Lk 24.2;
Jn 20.1
11.39
v. 17
11.40
vv. 4, 23
11.41
Jn 17.1;
Mt 11.25
11.42
Jn 12.30;
3.17
11.44
Jn 19.40;
20.7

38 Then Jesus, again greatly disturbed, came to the tomb. It was a cave, and a stone was lying against it. 39 Jesus said, "Take away the stone." Martha, the sister of the dead man, said to him, "Lord, already there is a stench because he has been dead four days." 40 Jesus said to her, "Did I not tell you that if you believed, you would see the glory of God?" 41 So they took away the stone. And Jesus looked upward and said, "Father, I thank you for having heard me. 42 I knew that you always hear me, but I have said this for the sake of the crowd standing here, so that they may believe that you sent me." 43 When he had said this, he cried with a loud voice, "Lazarus, come out!" 44 The dead man came out, his hands and feet bound with strips of cloth, and his face wrapped in a cloth. Jesus said to them, "Unbind him, and let him go."

6. *The Pharisees plot to kill Jesus (11.45–57)*

11.45
v. 19;
Jn 2.23
11.47
v. 57;
Mt 26.3

45 Many of the Jews therefore, who had come with Mary and had seen what Jesus did, believed in him. 46 But some of them went to the Pharisees and told them what he had done. 47 So the chief priests and the Pharisees called a meeting of the council, and said, "What are we to do? This man is performing many signs. 48 If we let him go on like this, everyone will believe in him, and the Romans will come and destroy both our holy place[j] and our nation." 49 But one of them, Caiaphas, who was high priest that year, said to them, "You know nothing at all! 50 You do not understand that it is better for you to have one man die for the people than to have the whole nation destroyed." 51 He did not say this on his own, but being high priest that year he prophesied that Jesus was about to die for the nation, 52 and not for the nation only, but to gather into one the

11.49
Mt 26.3;
Jn 18.13, 14
11.50
Jn 18.14

11.52
Isa 49.6;
Jn 10.16

i Or *the Christ j* Or *our temple*; Greek *our place*

11.35 Scripture never says Jesus laughed, although we can imagine that he had a robust sense of humor and that he undoubtedly expressed his pleasure with laughter. But here the Bible records his grief over Lazarus' death (see also Lk 19.41).
11.41,42 Jesus' prayer teaches us to call God our Father when we pray, to praise him when we come with our requests, and to rest in the certainty that God hears and answers prayer. The Father always an-

swered Jesus' requests.
11.45ff Many Jews believed as a result of the raising of Lazarus, while others were irritated, unsettled, and hostile. Some of these went to the Pharisees, who they knew felt the same, and told them about the latest exploits of Jesus. A special council meeting was called, which had for its one purpose the destruction of Jesus and his ministry.

dispersed children of God. 53 So from that day on they planned to put him to death.

54 Jesus therefore no longer walked about openly among the Jews, but went from there to a town called Ephraim in the region near the wilderness; and he remained there with the disciples.

55 Now the Passover of the Jews was near, and many went up from the country to Jerusalem before the Passover to purify themselves. 56 They were looking for Jesus and were asking one another as they stood in the temple, "What do you think? Surely he will not come to the festival, will he?" 57 Now the chief priests and the Pharisees had given orders that anyone who knew where Jesus^k was should let them know, so that they might arrest him.

NN. *Jesus anointed by Mary of Bethany*
(12.1–11; Matt. 26.6–13; Mark 14.3–9)

12 Six days before the Passover Jesus came to Bethany, the home of Lazarus, whom he had raised from the dead. 2 There they gave a dinner for him. Martha served, and Lazarus was one of those at the table with him. 3 Mary took a pound of costly perfume made of pure nard, anointed Jesus' feet, and wiped them^l with her hair. The house was filled with the fragrance of the perfume. 4 But Judas Iscariot, one of his disciples (the one who was about to betray him), said, 5 "Why was this perfume not sold for three hundred denarii^m and the money given to the poor?" 6 (He said this not because he cared about the poor, but because he was a thief; he kept the common purse and used to steal what was put into it.) 7 Jesus said, "Leave her alone. She bought it^n so that she might keep it for the day of my burial. 8 You always have the poor with you, but you do not always have me."

9 When the great crowd of the Jews learned that he was there, they came not only because of Jesus but also to see Lazarus, whom he had raised from the dead. 10 So the chief priests planned to put Lazarus to death as well, 11 since it was on account of him that many of the Jews were deserting and were believing in Jesus.

OO. *The triumphal entry*
(12.12–19; Matt. 21.1–11; Mark 11.1–11; Luke 19.29–44)

12 The next day the great crowd that had come to the festival heard that Jesus was coming to Jerusalem. 13 So they took branches of palm trees and went out to meet him, shouting,

"Hosanna!

Blessed is the one who comes in the name of the Lord—
    the King of Israel!"

14 Jesus found a young donkey and sat on it; as it is written:

15 "Do not be afraid, daughter of Zion.
    Look, your king is coming,
        sitting on a donkey's colt!"

---

k Gk *he*   l Gk *his feet*   m Three hundred denarii would be nearly a year's wages for a laborer
n Gk lacks *She bought it*

11.53
Mt 26.4
11.54
Jn 7.1;
2 Chr 13.19
11.55
Mt 26.1, 2;
Mk 14.1;
Lk 22.1;
Jn 12.1;
Num 9.10;
2 Chr 30.17, 18
11.56
Jn 7.11

12.1
Lk 7.37-39;
Jn 11.55
12.2
Lk 10.38
12.3
Jn 11.2;
Mk 14.3
12.4
Jn 6.71
12.6
Jn 13.29;
Lk 8.3
12.7
Jn 19.40

12.8
Mt 26.11;
Mk 14.7
12.9
Mk 12.37;
Mt 11.43, 44

12.11
v. 18;
Jn 11.45

12.13
Ps 118.25, 26;
Jn 1.49

12.15
Zech 9.9

11.54 Jesus withdrew from walking openly and working miracles among the Jews, not because he was afraid or had lost his courage, but as a mark of his displeasure against Jerusalem for its rejection of him. Furthermore, his removal would make the cruelty of his enemies even more inexcusable, for they could no longer blame him for making public appearances and performing miracles that upset them. He would not reenter Jerusalem until the hour came for him to be lifted up from the earth.

12.2ff At the feast that Mary, Martha, and Lazarus of Bethany made for Jesus, Mary anointed Jesus' feet with a costly ointment. The criticism of Judas Iscariot that the money so spent would have been better used to feed the poor (v. 5) was hypocritical, for he was a thief who stole from the money bag entrusted to him. Within a short time Judas would sell his own soul to Satan (13.2,27; Lk 22.3) and his master to Jewish enemies for a few pieces of silver.
12.12ff See note on Lk 19.28ff.

16His disciples did not understand these things at first; but when Jesus was glorified, then they remembered that these things had been written of him and had been done to him. 17 So the crowd that had been with him when he called Lazarus out of the tomb and raised him from the dead continued to testify.*o* 18 It was also because they heard that he had performed this sign that the crowd went to meet him. 19 The Pharisees then said to one another, "You see, you can do nothing. Look, the world has gone after him!"

PP. *Christ sought by the Gentiles: his last public discourse (12.20–36)*

20 Now among those who went up to worship at the festival were some Greeks. 21 They came to Philip, who was from Bethsaida in Galilee, and said to him, "Sir, we wish to see Jesus." 22 Philip went and told Andrew; then Andrew and Philip went and told Jesus. 23 Jesus answered them, "The hour has come for the Son of Man to be glorified. 24 Very truly, I tell you, unless a grain of wheat falls into the earth and dies, it remains just a single grain; but if it dies, it bears much fruit. 25 Those who love their life lose it, and those who hate their life in this world will keep it for eternal life. 26 Whoever serves me must follow me, and where I am, there will my servant be also. Whoever serves me, the Father will honor.

27 "Now my soul is troubled. And what should I say — 'Father, save me from this hour'? No, it is for this reason that I have come to this hour. 28 Father, glorify your name." Then a voice came from heaven, "I have glorified it, and I will glorify it again." 29 The crowd standing there heard it and said that it was thunder. Others said, "An angel has spoken to him." 30 Jesus answered, "This voice has come for your sake, not for mine. 31 Now is the judgment of this world; now the ruler of this world will be driven out. 32 And I, when I am lifted up from the earth, will draw all people*p* to myself." 33 He said this to indicate the kind of death he was to die. 34 The crowd answered him, "We have heard from the law that the Messiah*q* remains forever. How can you say that the Son of Man must be lifted up? Who is this Son of Man?" 35 Jesus said to them, "The light is with you for a little longer. Walk while you have the light, so that the darkness may not overtake you. If you walk in the darkness, you do not know where you are going. 36 While you have the light, believe in the light, so that you may become children of light."

QQ. *The cause of unbelief (12.37–43)*

After Jesus had said this, he departed and hid from them. 37 Although he had performed so many signs in their presence, they did not believe in him. 38 This was to fulfill the word spoken by the prophet Isaiah:

o Other ancient authorities read *with him began to testify that he had called. . .from the dead*   *p* Other ancient authorities read *all things*   *q* Or *the Christ*

12.16 Jesus' disciples (including John) did not understand the meaning and significance of the triumphal entry of Jesus into the holy city. Despite their having been with the teacher for more than two years, they still had much to learn. Later the Holy Spirit recalled to their memory some of these things, which then became clear to them.

12.24 Some Greeks (probably Gentile proselytes) warmly attended Jesus in what was his last public preaching. To them he spoke of his approaching death and burial by the figure of a grain of wheat, which must first die and then produce new life. So he, the Savior of the world, must die and be buried, and from that death would come forth a bountiful harvest

of life for those who put their trust in him.

12.31 *the ruler of this world,* i.e., Satan. Jesus never denied that Satan had power over the present ungodly world (cf. 14.30; 16.11; Mt 4.8–10; Lk 4.5–8). Here, however, Jesus made the stupendous claim that he would soon be victorious over the devil and terminate his power on earth. This was accomplished by his death and resurrection, which resulted in freeing sinners from Satan's grip (v. 32).

12.32 *from the earth,* i.e., on the cross.

12.38 *to whom has the arm of the Lord been revealed?* i.e., "Who will accept God's mighty miracles as proof?" The question is from Isa 53.1.

"Lord, who has believed our message,
 and to whom has the arm of the Lord been revealed?"
39 And so they could not believe, because Isaiah also said,
40 "He has blinded their eyes
  and hardened their heart,
 so that they might not look with their eyes,
  and understand with their heart and turn —
  and I would heal them."
41 Isaiah said this because[r] he saw his glory and spoke about him. 42 Nevertheless many, even of the authorities, believed in him. But because of the Pharisees they did not confess it, for fear that they would be put out of the synagogue; 43 for they loved human glory more than the glory that comes from God.

RR. A summary of Jesus' claims (12.44–50)

44 Then Jesus cried aloud: "Whoever believes in me believes not in me but in him who sent me. 45 And whoever sees me sees him who sent me. 46 I have come as light into the world, so that everyone who believes in me should not remain in the darkness. 47 I do not judge anyone who hears my words and does not keep them, for I came not to judge the world, but to save the world. 48 The one who rejects me and does not receive my word has a judge; on the last day the word that I have spoken will serve as judge, 49 for I have not spoken on my own, but the Father who sent me has himself given me a commandment about what to say and what to speak. 50 And I know that his commandment is eternal life. What I speak, therefore, I speak just as the Father has told me."

III. Revelation to new Israel: disclosures to the disciples (13.1–20.29)

A. Washing the disciples' feet (13.1–20)

13 Now before the festival of the Passover, Jesus knew that his hour had come to depart from this world and go to the Father. Having loved his own who were in the world, he loved them to the end. 2 The devil had already put it into the heart of Judas son of Simon Iscariot to betray him. And during supper 3 Jesus, knowing that the Father had given all things into his hands, and that he had come from God and was going to God, 4 got up from the table,[s] took off his outer robe, and tied a towel around himself. 5 Then he poured water into a basin and began to wash the disciples' feet and to wipe them with the towel that was tied around him. 6 He came to Simon Peter, who said to him, "Lord, are you going to wash my feet?" 7 Jesus answered, "You do not know now what I am doing, but later you will understand." 8 Peter said to him, "You will never wash my feet." Jesus answered, "Unless I wash you, you have no share with me." 9 Simon Peter said to him, "Lord, not my feet only but also my

r Other ancient witnesses read *when* s Gk *from supper*

Cross references (marginal column):

12.40 Isa 6.9, 10; Mt 13.14
12.41 Isa 6.1
12.42 Jn 7.48, 13; 9.22
12.43 Jn 5.44
12.44 Mt 10.40; Jn 5.24
12.45 Jn 14.9
12.46 Jn 1.4; 3.19; 8.12; 9.5
12.47 Jn 3.17
12.48 Lk 10.16; Mt 10.15
12.49 Jn 14.31
12.50 Jn 8.28
13.1 Jn 11.55; 12.23; 16.28
13.2 Jn 6.70, 71; Mk 14.10
13.3 Mt 28.18; Heb 2.8; Jn 8.42; 16.28
13.4 Lk 22.27
13.5 Lk 7.44
13.8 Jn 3.5; 9.7

12.40 *He*, i.e., God. The Greek here is a paraphrase of Isa 6.10.
12.42 Apparently some of the chief authorities believed Jesus to be the Messiah, but were afraid to say so publicly. The Pharisees had controlling power and would have put them out of the synagogue (cf. 9.22). To such people, the applause of the Jews was more important than the approval of God. Going along with the crowd is both an ancient and a modern practice.
12.50 This verse is a fitting summary of the ministry of Jesus. He delivered the message given him by the Father and kept back nothing that was profitable for people to hear. He set us an example of supreme obedience to the Father.
13.2 Judas opened his heart so that the prince of demons possessed him — body, soul, and spirit (see note on 12.2ff).
13.5 Jesus washed the disciples' feet to show his disciples that he loved them, to demonstrate the emptying of himself, to teach them about spiritual washing (which is more important than physical washing), and to provide the disciples with his example of humility and service.

hands and my head!" 10 Jesus said to him, "One who has bathed does not need to wash, except for the feet,ᵗ but is entirely clean. And youᵘ are clean, though not all of you." 11 For he knew who was to betray him; for this reason he said, "Not all of you are clean."

12 After he had washed their feet, had put on his robe, and had returned to the table, he said to them, "Do you know what I have done to you? 13 You call me Teacher and Lord—and you are right, for that is what I am. 14 So if I, your Lord and Teacher, have washed your feet, you also ought to wash one another's feet. 15 For I have set you an example, that you also should do as I have done to you. 16 Very truly, I tell you, servantsᵛ are not greater than their master, nor are messengers greater than the one who sent them. 17 If you know these things, you are blessed if you do them. 18 I am not speaking of all of you; I know whom I have chosen. But it is to fulfill the scripture, 'The one who ate my breadʷ has lifted his heel against me.' 19 I tell you this now, before it occurs, so that when it does occur, you may believe that I am he.ˣ 20 Very truly, I tell you, whoever receives one whom I send receives me; and whoever receives me receives him who sent me."

B. Jesus dismisses Judas Iscariot, his betrayer (13.21–30; Matt. 26.21–25; Mark 14.18–21; Luke 22.21–23)

21 After saying this Jesus was troubled in spirit, and declared, "Very truly, I tell you, one of you will betray me." 22 The disciples looked at one another, uncertain of whom he was speaking. 23 One of his disciples—the one whom Jesus loved—was reclining next to him; 24 Simon Peter therefore motioned to him to ask Jesus of whom he was speaking. 25 So while reclining next to Jesus, he asked him, "Lord, who is it?" 26 Jesus answered, "It is the one to whom I give this piece of bread when I have dipped it in the dish."ʸ So when he had dipped the piece of bread, he gave it to Judas son of Simon Iscariot.ᶻ 27 After he received the piece of bread,ᵃ Satan entered into him. Jesus said to him, "Do quickly what you are going to do." 28 Now no one at the table knew why he said this to him. 29 Some thought that, because Judas had the common purse, Jesus was telling him, "Buy what we need for the festival"; or, that he should give something to the poor. 30 So, after receiving the piece of bread, he immediately went out. And it was night.

C. Jesus announces his departure (13.31–35)

31 When he had gone out, Jesus said, "Now the Son of Man has been glorified, and God has been glorified in him. 32 If God has been glorified in him,ᵇ God will also glorify him in himself and will glorify him at once. 33 Little children, I am with you only a little longer. You will look for me; and as I said to the Jews so now I say to you, 'Where I am going, you cannot come.' 34 I give you a new commandment, that you love one another. Just as I have loved you, you also should love one another. 35 By this everyone will know that you are my disciples, if you have love for one another."

ᵗ Other ancient authorities lack *except for the feet*   ᵘ The Greek word for *you* here is plural   ᵛ Gk *slaves*   ʷ Other ancient authorities read *ate bread with me*   ˣ Gk *I am*   ʸ Gk *dipped it*   ᶻ Other ancient authorities read *Judas Iscariot son of Simon*; others, *Judas son of Simon from Karyot* (Kerioth)   ᵃ Gk *After the piece of bread*   ᵇ Other ancient authorities lack *If God has been glorified in him*

13.14 Some Christians take this command of Jesus literally and practice foot washing in the church. Others hold that it is figurative for an attitude of service and humility among believers.
13.23 *One of his disciples—the one whom Jesus loved.* Most commentators believe this disciple to be John, the writer of this book. *was reclining next to him.* The

custom of the period was to recline around a table, leaning on the left elbow.
13.27 Satan as one of God's creatures can be in only one place at a time. But he has a horde of fallen angels who assist him and do his bidding. In the case of Judas Iscariot, Scripture says that Satan himself entered into his heart and took possession of him.

D. *Peter's denial foretold (13.36–38)*

36 Simon Peter said to him, "Lord, where are you going?" Jesus answered, "Where I am going, you cannot follow me now; but you will follow afterward." **37** Peter said to him, "Lord, why can I not follow you now? I will lay down my life for you." **38** Jesus answered, "Will you lay down your life for me? Very truly, I tell you, before the cock crows, you will have denied me three times.

E. *Christ comforts his disciples (14.1–31)*

1. *The way, and the truth, and the life (14.1–14)*

14 "Do not let your hearts be troubled. Believe[c] in God, believe also in me. **2** In my Father's house there are many dwelling places. If it were not so, would I have told you that I go to prepare a place for you?[d] **3** And if I go and prepare a place for you, I will come again and will take you to myself, so that where I am, there you may be also. **4** And you know the way to the place where I am going."[e] **5** Thomas said to him, "Lord, we do not know where you are going. How can we know the way?" **6** Jesus said to him, "I am the way, and the truth, and the life. No one comes to the Father except through me. **7** If you know me, you will know[f] my Father also. From now on you do know him and have seen him."

8 Philip said to him, "Lord, show us the Father, and we will be satisfied." **9** Jesus said to him, "Have I been with you all this time, Philip, and you still do not know me? Whoever has seen me has seen the Father. How can you say, 'Show us the Father'? **10** Do you not believe that I am in the Father and the Father is in me? The words that I say to you I do not speak on my own; but the Father who dwells in me does his works. **11** Believe me that I am in the Father and the Father is in me; but if you do not, then believe me because of the works themselves. **12** Very truly, I tell you, the one who believes in me will also do the works that I do and, in fact, will do greater works than these, because I am going to the Father. **13** I will do whatever you ask in my name, so that the Father may be glorified in the Son. **14** If in my name you ask me[g] for anything, I will do it.

2. *The promise of the Holy Spirit (14.15–24)*

15 "If you love me, you will keep[h] my commandments. **16** And I will

13.36	Jn 21.18; 2 Pet 1.14
13.37	Mt 26.33-35; Mk 14.29-31; Lk 22.33, 34
13.38	Jn 18.27
14.1	Jn 16.23, 24
14.2	Jn 13.33
14.3	Jn 12.26
14.5	Jn 11.16
14.6	Jn 10.9; 8.32; 1.4; 11.25
14.7	Jn 8.19
14.9	Jn 12.45
14.10	Jn 10.38; 5.19; 12.49
14.11	Jn 5.36; 10.38
14.12	Mt 21.21; Lk 10.17
14.13	Jn 15.7, 16; 16.23; Jas 1.5
14.15	Jn 15.10; 1 Jn 5.3
14.16	Jn 15.26; 16.7; 1 Jn 2.1

---

c Or You believe d Or If it were not so, I would have told you; for I go to prepare a place for you e Other ancient authorities read Where I am going you know, and the way you know f Other ancient authorities read If you had known me, you would have known g Other ancient authorities lack me h Other ancient authorities read me, keep

---

13.37 We can give Peter the benefit of the doubt that his intention to lay down his life for Jesus was genuine. He correctly believed that it would be better to die with Jesus than to live without him. In carrying out this intention he failed miserably; yet would we have done any better?

14.6 Jesus affirmed, "I am the way to God; I am the truth about God; I am the life of God." Those who want to know God must come to him through Jesus Christ, and through him alone. All other ways are dead-end streets that lead no place except to darkness and everlasting night.

14.11 *I am in the Father and the Father is in me.* Whoever knows Jesus as the Christ, the Son of God, knows God the Father as well. Jesus gives two reasons for this: (1) he said so and we must believe what he said; (2) his works corroborate his words and we must believe him for his works' sake.

14.12 *greater works than these.* Subsequent history confirms this saying of Jesus. For example, Jesus had healed people with the hem of his garment, while

Peter did with his shadow (Acts 5.15) and Paul by handkerchiefs that had touched him (Acts 19.12). Christ performed miracles for two or three years in one country, but his followers have done miracles in his name for many ages throughout the world.

14.13 Great is the power of prayer; nowhere is this truth spoken more broadly and in such an all-encompassing way. We must pray if we need help. We must ask in Jesus' name, for it has great power. He promises that we will receive what we ask for. And the goal of all this is the glory of God the Father in and through his Son, Jesus Christ.

14.15,16 In Jn 14–16 five passages are written about the Holy Spirit; in four of them he is called *Advocate* (Gk. *parakletos*). The verb *parakaleo*, from which the noun is formed, means "to encourage," "to exhort," or "to comfort." Thus *parakletos* refers to someone who takes our part or intercedes on our behalf to help us. The Holy Spirit came from the Father (15.26) at the request of the Son (14.16) and in Jesus' name (14.26). But Jesus also said he would ask the Father, and he will give you another Advocate,[i] to be with you forever. [17] This is the Spirit of truth, whom the world cannot receive, because it neither sees him nor knows him. You know him, because he abides with you, and he will be in[j] you.

[18] "I will not leave you orphaned; I am coming to you. [19] In a little while the world will no longer see me, but you will see me; because I live, you also will live. [20] On that day you will know that I am in my Father, and you in me, and I in you. [21] They who have my commandments and keep them are those who love me; and those who love me will be loved by my Father, and I will love them and reveal myself to them." [22] Judas (not Iscariot) said to him, "Lord, how is it that you will reveal yourself to us, and not to the world?" [23] Jesus answered him, "Those who love me will keep my word, and my Father will love them, and we will come to them and make our home with them. [24] Whoever does not love me does not keep my words; and the word that you hear is not mine, but is from the Father who sent me.

3. The promise of peace (14.25–31)

[25] "I have said these things to you while I am still with you. [26] But the Advocate,[i] the Holy Spirit, whom the Father will send in my name, will teach you everything, and remind you of all that I have said to you. [27] Peace I leave with you; my peace I give to you. I do not give to you as the world gives. Do not let your hearts be troubled, and do not let them be afraid. [28] You heard me say to you, 'I am going away, and I am coming to you.' If you loved me, you would rejoice that I am going to the Father, because the Father is greater than I. [29] And now I have told you this before it occurs, so that when it does occur, you may believe. [30] I will no longer talk much with you, for the ruler of this world is coming. He has no power over me; [31] but I do as the Father has commanded me, so that the world may know that I love the Father. Rise, let us be on our way.

F. Christit the true vine (15.1–17)

15 "I am the true vine, and my Father is the vinegrower. [2] He removes every branch in me that bears no fruit. Every branch that bears fruit he prunes[k] to make it bear more fruit. [3] You have already been cleansed[k] by the word that I have spoken to you. [4] Abide in me as I abide in you. Just as the branch cannot bear fruit by itself unless it abides in the vine, neither can you unless you abide in me. [5] I am the vine, you are the branches. Those who abide in me and I in them bear much fruit, because apart from me you can do nothing. [6] Whoever does not abide in me is thrown away like a branch and withers; such branches are gathered,

14.17
Jn 16.13;
1 Jn 4.6;
1 Cor 2.14
14.18
vv. 3, 28
14.19
Jn 7.33;
16.16; 6.57
14.20
Jn 10.38
14.21
1 Jn 2.5; 5.3
14.22
Acts 1.13;
10.14, 41
14.23
1 Jn 2.24;
Rev 3.20
14.24
Jn 7.16;
8.28; 12.49

14.26
Jn 15.26;
16.7, 13;
1 Jn 2.20, 27
14.27
Jn 16.33;
Phil 4.7;
Col 3.15
14.28
vv. 3, 18;
Jn 5.18;
10.29, 30;
Phil 2.6
14.29
Jn 13.19
14.30
Jn 12.31
14.31
Jn 10.18;
12.49; 18.1

15.1
Isa 5.1-7;
Ezek 19.10
15.3
Jn 13.10;
17.17;
Eph 5.26
15.4
1 Jn 2.6
15.5
v. 16
15.6
v. 2

---

[i] Or *Helper* [j] Or *among* [k] The same Greek root refers to pruning and cleansing

---

send the Advocate (15.26). From these passages the church has concluded that the Spirit came from the Father and the Son. For the work of the Holy Spirit, see note on 16.14.

14.16–18 *another Advocate.* Jesus promised to pray to the Father for the coming of the Holy Spirit after he left this earth. He is the Spirit of truth, who will abide with us and in us forever. The coming of the Holy Spirit is tantamount to the coming of Jesus to our hearts, for the Spirit mediates to us the presence of Jesus. That is, experientially speaking, to have the Spirit is to have Christ (cf. Rom 8.9–11).

14.26 The *Advocate* or helper will teach us all things and will bring back to our memories spiritual things we have forgotten.

14.27 *my peace I give to you.* When Christ was about to leave the world, he made (as it were) his will. His soul he commended to his Father (Lk 23.46); his mother he left to the care of John (19.26,27); but what should he leave to his disciples? He left them in possession of his peace, so that they need not be afraid.

15.2 Just as fruit trees are expected to produce fruit, so regenerated Christians are expected to bear fruit in their lives. Fruitlessness is abnormal, so that branches that bear no fruit are lopped off. And those branches that bear fruit are pruned so that they may bear more fruit. But, as Jesus indicates, bearing fruit is not an end in itself. The goal of the Christian life is abiding in loving fellowship with God.

thrown into the fire, and burned. 7 If you abide in me, and my words abide in you, ask for whatever you wish, and it will be done for you. 8 My Father is glorified by this, that you bear much fruit and become*l* my disciples. 9 As the Father has loved me, so I have loved you; abide in my love. 10 If you keep my commandments, you will abide in my love, just as I have kept my Father's commandments and abide in his love. 11 I have said these things to you so that my joy may be in you, and that your joy may be complete.

12 "This is my commandment, that you love one another as I have loved you. 13 No one has greater love than this, to lay down one's life for one's friends. 14 You are my friends if you do what I command you. 15 I do not call you servants*m* any longer, because the servant*n* does not know what the master is doing; but I have called you friends, because I have made known to you everything that I have heard from my Father. 16 You did not choose me but I chose you. And I appointed you to go and bear fruit, fruit that will last, so that the Father will give you whatever you ask him in my name. 17 I am giving you these commands so that you may love one another.

G. *The hatred of the world (15.18–16.4)*

18 "If the world hates you, be aware that it hated me before it hated you. 19 If you belonged to the world,*o* the world would love you as its own. Because you do not belong to the world, but I have chosen you out of the world—therefore the world hates you. 20 Remember the word that I said to you, 'Servants*p* are not greater than their master.' If they persecuted me, they will persecute you; if they kept my word, they will keep yours also. 21 But they will do all these things to you on account of my name, because they do not know him who sent me. 22 If I had not come and spoken to them, they would not have sin; but now they have no excuse for their sin. 23 Whoever hates me hates my Father also. 24 If I had not done among them the works that no one else did, they would not have sin. But now they have seen and hated both me and my Father. 25 It was to fulfill the word that is written in their law, 'They hated me without a cause.'

26 "When the Advocate*q* comes, whom I will send to you from the Father, the Spirit of truth who comes from the Father, he will testify on my behalf. 27 You also are to testify because you have been with me from the beginning.

16 "I have said these things to you to keep you from stumbling. 2 They will put you out of the synagogues. Indeed, an hour is coming when those who kill you will think that by doing so they are offering worship to God. 3 And they will do this because they have not known the Father or me. 4 But I have said these things to you so that when their hour comes you may remember that I told you about them.

l Or *be*   *m* Gk *slaves*   *n* Gk *slave*   *o* Gk *were of the world*   *p* Gk *Slaves*   *q* Or *Helper*

15.7
Jn 14.13;
16.23
15.8
Mt 5.16;
Jn 8.31
15.10
Jn 14.15, 23
15.11
Jn 17.13
15.12
Jn 13.34
15.13
Rom 5.7, 8;
Jn 10.11
15.14
Mt 12.50
15.15
Jn 8.26
15.16
Jn 6.70;
14.13
15.18
1 Jn 3.13
15.19
Jn 17.14
15.20
Mt 10.24;
Lk 6.40;
Jn 13.16
15.21
Mt 12.24;
Lk 6.40;
Jn 13.16
15.22
Jn 9.41;
Rom 1.20
15.23
1 Jn 2.23
15.24
Jn 5.36
15.25
Ps 35.19;
69.4
15.26
Jn 14.16, 17,
26; 1 Jn 2.1
15.27
Lk 24.48;
Acts 2.32;
3.15; 5.32;
10.39; 13.31;
1 Jn 4.14
16.1
Jn 15.18-27;
Mt 11.6
16.2
Jn 9.22;
Acts 26.9, 10;
Isa 66.5;
Rev 6.9
16.3
Jn 15.21;
17.25; 1 Jn
3.1
16.4
Jn 13.19;
15.27

15.9ff *As the Father has loved me, so I have loved you.* Jesus refers to four love relationships here: (1) the Father loves the Son; (2) Jesus uses the Father's love for himself as the pattern of Jesus' love for his disciples, the demonstration of which is found in his death for his friends (v. 13); (3) the disciples are to love him and to abide in his love (v. 10); and (4) the disciples are to love one another (v. 17). Elsewhere Scripture declares that Jesus loves the church, his body (Eph 5.25), and that nothing can separate us from his love (Rom 8.35).
15.18ff There are two kinds of people: the children of God and the children of the world (see note on 8.44). The children of the world hate the children of God, because the latter are not of the world but belong to Jesus Christ, whom the world hates. This hatred stems from ignorance, for the children of the world do not know God, the one who sent Jesus.
15.24 The greatest sin of the children of the world is that they see Christ and his mighty works, but deny him and hate him. At the same time, they hate the Father who sent him, in spite of all the evidence around them that testifies to his existence—such as the beauty of nature, the providence of God, and the appearance of his Son Jesus Christ. Therefore, those who hate God and Jesus Christ are without excuse (cf. Rom 1.18-23).

H. The departure of Jesus and the coming of the Holy Spirit (16.5–11)

"I did not say these things to you from the beginning, because I was with you. 5 But now I am going to him who sent me; yet none of you asks me, 'Where are you going?' 6 But because I have said these things to you, sorrow has filled your hearts. 7 Nevertheless I tell you the truth: it is to your advantage that I go away, for if I do not go away, the Advocate[r] will not come to you; but if I go, I will send him to you. 8 And when he comes, he will prove the world wrong about[s] sin and righteousness and judgment: 9 about sin, because they do not believe in me; 10 about righteousness, because I am going to the Father and you will see me no longer; 11 about judgment, because the ruler of this world has been condemned.

I. The illuminating power of the Holy Spirit (16.12–15)

12 "I still have many things to say to you, but you cannot bear them now. 13 When the Spirit of truth comes, he will guide you into all the truth; for he will not speak on his own, but will speak whatever he hears, and he will declare to you the things that are to come. 14 He will glorify me, because he will take what is mine and declare it to you. 15 All that the Father has is mine. For this reason I said that he will take what is mine and declare it to you.

J. Jesus' farewell to his disciples (16.16–33)

16 "A little while, and you will no longer see me, and again a little while, and you will see me." 17 Then some of his disciples said to one another, "What does he mean by saying to us, 'A little while, and you will no longer see me, and again a little while, and you will see me'; and 'Because I am going to the Father'?" 18 They said, "What does he mean by this 'a little while'? We do not know what he is talking about." 19 Jesus knew that they wanted to ask him, so he said to them, "Are you discussing among yourselves what I meant when I said, 'A little while, and you will no longer see me, and again a little while, and you will see me'? 20 Very truly, I tell you, you will weep and mourn, but the world will rejoice; you will have pain, but your pain will turn into joy. 21 When a woman is in labor, she has pain, because her hour has come. But when her child is

[r] Or Helper [s] Or convict the world of

Marginal references:

16.5 Jn 7.33; 13.36; 14.5
16.7 Jn 7.39; 14.16, 26; 15.26
16.9 Jn 15.22
16.10 Acts 3.14; 7.52; 17.31; 1 Pet 3.18
16.11 Jn 12.31
16.12 Mk 4.33
16.13 Jn 14.17, 26
16.14 Jn 7.39
16.15 Jn 17.10
16.16 Jn 7.33; 14.18-24; 13.3
16.17 vv. 16, 5
16.19 Mk 9.32
16.20 Lk 23.27; Jn 20.20
16.21 1 Thess 5.3

16.7 *it is to your advantage that I go away.* This refers to Jesus' ascension, which was necessary in order for him (1) to make possible the coming of the Holy Spirit; (2) to fulfill his own prophetic word (14.28; 16.5; 20.17); (3) to make possible the further work of Jesus — preparing a place for his people and interceding for them (14.2,3; Heb 7.25; 9.24); and (4) to enter the Holy Place in heaven with his blood in order to secure eternal redemption (Heb 9.11,12). The Holy Spirit could not come until the work of Jesus on earth was completed. That is, only after Christ had satisfied the demands of divine justice by dying, rising again, ascending into heaven, and sitting at the right hand of the Father, could the age of the Holy Spirit on earth commence.

16.8 *he will prove the world wrong about sin and righteousness and judgment.* "Sin" here consists in the refusal to accept Christ and his message. "Righteousness" indicates that Christ's death was not a defeat but a victory, for the Father vindicated his Son's mission and accepted what he had done as the basis on which to forgive sin and impute righteousness to believers. "Judgment" indicates that the life, death, and resurrection of Jesus Christ constitute the basis on which God condemned the ruler of this world's darkness.

16.12,13 The revelation of God is progressive. Christ revealed to his disciples many things not revealed in the O.T. But he left untold some things that were to be revealed by the Holy Spirit after his ascension. By promising the Holy Spirit to guide his disciples "into all the truth" (v. 13), Jesus was pre-authenticating the N.T. God's revelation was complete when the apostles died and the canon of Scripture was closed.

16.14 The Holy Spirit has a distinct ministry. Among the works he performs are the following: (1) he glorifies Christ; (2) he speaks as directed by Jesus (vv. 13–15) and bears witness to him (15.26); (3) he convicts people of sin (v. 8); (4) he regenerates sinners (3.15); (5) he indwells the hearts of all believers (14.16,17) and produces his fruit in their lives (1 Cor 3.16; Gal 5.22,23); (6) he seals and marks believers (Eph 1.13; see note on Eph 4.30); (7) he leads and guides believers (Acts 8.29; 13.2,4); (8) he prompts believers to worship and pray (Jn 4.24; Eph 6.18; Jude 20); (9) he empowers believers for testimony (Acts 1.8); (10) he teaches believers (14.26; 16.13) and enables them to understand the Scriptures (1 Cor 2.12); and (11) he gives life to believers' dead bodies in the resurrection (Rom 8.11).

born, she no longer remembers the anguish because of the joy of having brought a human being into the world. 22 So you have pain now; but I will see you again, and your hearts will rejoice, and no one will take your joy from you. 23 On that day you will ask nothing of me.*t* Very truly, I tell you, if you ask anything of the Father in my name, he will give it to you.*u* 24 Until now you have not asked for anything in my name. Ask and you will receive, so that your joy may be complete.

25 "I have said these things to you in figures of speech. The hour is coming when I will no longer speak to you in figures, but will tell you plainly of the Father. 26 On that day you will ask in my name. I do not say to you that I will ask the Father on your behalf; 27 for the Father himself loves you, because you have loved me and have believed that I came from God.*v* 28 I came from the Father and have come into the world; again, I am leaving the world and am going to the Father."

29 His disciples said, "Yes, now you are speaking plainly, not in any figure of speech! 30 Now we know that you know all things, and do not need to have anyone question you; by this we believe that you came from God." 31 Jesus answered them, "Do you now believe? 32 The hour is coming, indeed it has come, when you will be scattered, each one to his home, and you will leave me alone. Yet I am not alone because the Father is with me. 33 I have said this to you, so that in me you may have peace. In the world you face persecution. But take courage; I have conquered the world!"

K. Christ's intercessory prayer (17.1–26)

1. The prayer to be glorified (17.1–5)

17 After Jesus had spoken these words, he looked up to heaven and said, "Father, the hour has come; glorify your Son so that the Son may glorify you, 2 since you have given him authority over all people,*w* to give eternal life to all whom you have given him. 3 And this is eternal life, that they may know you, the only true God, and Jesus Christ whom you have sent. 4 I glorified you on earth by finishing the work that you gave me to do. 5 So now, Father, glorify me in your own presence with the glory that I had in your presence before the world existed.

2. The prayer for the disciples (17.6–19)

6 "I have made your name known to those whom you gave me from the world. They were yours, and you gave them to me, and they have kept your word. 7 Now they know that everything you have given me is from you; 8 for the words that you gave to me I have given to them, and they have received them and know in truth that I came from you; and they have believed that you sent me. 9 I am asking on their behalf; I am not asking on behalf of the world, but on behalf of those whom you gave me, because they are yours. 10 All mine are yours, and yours are mine; and I have been glorified in them. 11 And now I am no longer in the world, but they are

16.22	vv. 6, 16
16.23	Mt 7.7; Jn 14.13; 15.16
16.24	Jn 15.11
16.25	Jn 10.6; Mt 13.34
16.27	Jn 14.21, 23
16.28	Jn 13.3
16.29	v. 25
16.30	Jn 8.42
16.32	Mt 26.31; Mk 14.27
16.33	Jn 14.27; Col 1.20; Rom 8.37; Rev 3.21
17.1	Jn 12.23; 13.32
17.2	Dan 7.14; Heb 2.8; Jn 6.37
17.3	Jn 5.44; 3.34; 6.29, 57
17.4	Jn 13.31; 4.34; 14.31
17.5	Jn 1.1; Phil 2.6
17.6	Jn 6.37, 39
17.8	Jn 8.28; 16.27
17.9	Lk 22.32; Jn 14.16
17.10	Jn 16.15
17.11	Jn 13.1; 7.33; Rev 19.12; Jn 10.30

t Or will ask me no question   *u Other ancient authorities read Father, he will give it to you in my name*   *v Other ancient authorities read the Father*   *w Gk flesh*

16.33 Jesus promised that his followers would suffer persecution. Why God permits suffering and allows tribulation is a deep mystery. For the believer three kinds of afflictions need to be defined: (1) some trials happen to us simply because we are human—such as sickness, bereavement, death, etc.; (2) some trials come from Satan by God's permission (Job 1; 2; Lk 13.11–16); (3) some trials are sent by God to purify his people (Mal 3.2,3; Jn 15.2) and to conform them to the image of Jesus his Son (Rom 8.28,29). It is not always clear to us from which source a problem may have come.

17.1 Addressing his prayer to their common Father, Jesus begins a family prayer, for his disciples were part of his family. Just as dying Jacob prayed for the twelve patriarchs (Gen 49) and Moses for the twelve tribes (Deut 33), so Jesus prays for the twelve apostles. This prayer, made by our high priest, was a preface to his redeeming death and is illustrative of his present intercession in heaven (cf. Rom 8.34; Heb 7.25; 9.24).

in the world, and I am coming to you. Holy Father, protect them in your name that you have given me, so that they may be one, as we are one. 12 While I was with them, I protected them in your name that^x you have given me. I guarded them, and not one of them was lost except the one destined to be lost,^{y} so that the scripture might be fulfilled. 13 But now I am coming to you, and I speak these things in the world so that they may have my joy made complete in themselves.^{z} 14 I have given them your word, and the world has hated them because they do not belong to the world, just as I do not belong to the world. 15 I am not asking you to take them out of the world, but I ask you to protect them from the evil one.^{a} 16 They do not belong to the world, just as I do not belong to the world. 17 Sanctify them in the truth; your word is truth. 18 As you have sent me into the world, so I have sent them into the world. 19 And for their sakes I sanctify myself, so that they also may be sanctified in truth.

3. The prayer for the church (17.20–26)

20 "I ask not only on behalf of these, but also on behalf of those who will believe in me through their word, 21 that they may all be one. As you, Father, are in me and I am in you, may they also be in us,^{b} so that the world may believe that you have sent me. 22 The glory that you have given me I have given them, so that they may be one, as we are one, 23 I in them and you in me, that they may become completely one, so that the world may know that you have sent me and have loved them even as you have loved me. 24 Father, I desire that those also, whom you have given me, may be with me where I am, to see my glory, which you have given me because you loved me before the foundation of the world.

25 "Righteous Father, the world does not know you, but I know you; and these know that you have sent me. 26 I made your name known to them, and I will make it known, so that the love with which you have loved me may be in them, and I in them."

L. Jesus' betrayal and arrest
(18.1–11; Matt. 26.47–56; Mark 14.43–50; Luke 22.27–53)

18 After Jesus had spoken these words, he went out with his disciples across the Kidron valley to a place where there was a garden, which he and his disciples entered. 2 Now Judas, who betrayed him, also

Cross references (left margin):

17.12 Heb 2.13; Jn 6.39; 18.9; 6.70
17.14 Jn 15.19; 8.23
17.15 Mt 6.13
17.16 v. 14
17.17 Jn 15.3
17.18 Jn 20.21
17.19 Jn 15.13
17.21 Jn 10.38
17.22 Jn 14.20
17.24 Jn 12.26; Mt 25.34; v. 5
17.25 Jn 15.21; 16.3; 7.29; Jn 16.27
17.26 v. 6; Jn 15.9
18.1 2 Sam 15.23
18.2 Lk 21.37; 22.39

---

^{x} Other ancient authorities read *protected in your name those whom* ^{y} Gk *except the son of destruction* ^{z} Or *among themselves* ^{a} Or *from evil* ^{b} Other ancient authorities read *be one in us*

17.14 Christians are not *of* the world, though Christ clearly stated they were to be *in* the world (vv. 15,18). Christians are the salt of the earth and the light of the world (Mt 5.13–16). While in the world believers must have victory *over* the world (see 1 Jn 2.15) and must not be conformed *to* the world (Rom 12.2).

17.17 *Sanctify them.* Sanctification is the work of the Holy Spirit in the lives of believers. The use of the written Word of God is essential to sanctification. So are the means of grace such as prayer, worship, the use of the ordinances or sacraments, and the communion of the saints. God uses chastisement to improve the character of the saints (Heb 12.10). Equally important is the will, whereby believers separate themselves from unrighteousness (2 Cor 6.17).

17.21 The communion of the saints lies at the heart of Christ's prayer in this chapter. The people of God are to be united with each other in life and experience because they are united with him. The communion of the saints suggests (1) the fellowship we have with God through Jesus Christ by the Spirit (1 Jn 1.3); (2) the fellowship by promise with the saints already

in glory with whom we are also united (Heb 12.22–24); and (3) the fellowship with all other believers who are still on earth (Gal 2.9,10; 1 Jn 1.7). The unity believers enjoy as members of the mystical body of Christ must find expression in concrete forms in the churches on earth. Saints should pray for one another (2 Cor 1.11; Eph 6.18); exhort one another (Col 3.16; Heb 10.25); and comfort and edify one another (1 Thess 4.18; 5.11). The outward expression of inner unity is shown when the saints gather for the public worship of God, celebrate the Eucharist, and practice baptism.

17.23 *I in them, and you in me, that they may become completely one.* This is a threefold truth: (1) believers have union with Christ; (2) believers have union with God through Jesus Christ; (3) believers have union with each other as a result of their union in God and in Christ.

18.1 Christ was about to fulfill the third responsibility of a priest. Priests were to teach, to pray, and to offer sacrifices. Christ had finished both his teaching and his praying ministries. Now he would become an offering for sin.

knew the place, because Jesus often met there with his disciples. ³ So Judas brought a detachment of soldiers together with police from the chief priests and the Pharisees, and they came there with lanterns and torches and weapons. ⁴ Then Jesus, knowing all that was to happen to him, came forward and asked them, "Whom are you looking for?" ⁵ They answered, "Jesus of Nazareth."ᶜ Jesus replied, "I am he."ᵈ Judas, who betrayed him, was standing with them. ⁶ When Jesusᵉ said to them, "I am he,"ᵈ they stepped back and fell to the ground. ⁷ Again he asked them, "Whom are you looking for?" And they said, "Jesus of Nazareth."ᶜ ⁸ Jesus answered, "I told you that I am he.ᵈ So if you are looking for me, let these men go." ⁹ This was to fulfill the word that he had spoken, "I did not lose a single one of those whom you gave me." ¹⁰ Then Simon Peter, who had a sword, drew it, struck the high priest's slave, and cut off his right ear. The slave's name was Malchus. ¹¹ Jesus said to Peter, "Put your sword back into its sheath. Am I not to drink the cup that the Father has given me?"

18.3
Acts 1.16

18.4
Jn 6.64;
13.1, 11; v. 7

18.7
v. 4

18.9
Jn 17.12

18.11
Mt 20.22

M. Jesus before the Jewish authorities
(18.12–14; see vv. 19–24)

12   So the soldiers, their officer, and the Jewish police arrested Jesus and bound him. ¹³ First they took him to Annas, who was the father-in-law of Caiaphas, the high priest that year. ¹⁴ Caiaphas was the one who had advised the Jews that it was better to have one person die for the people.

18.13
Mt 26.57;
Mk 14.53;
Lk 22.54
18.14
Jn 11.49-51

N. Peter's denial of Jesus (18.15–18; vv. 25–27; Matt. 26.69–75;
Mark 14.66–72; Luke 22.55–62)

15   Simon Peter and another disciple followed Jesus. Since that disciple was known to the high priest, he went with Jesus into the courtyard of the high priest, ¹⁶ but Peter was standing outside at the gate. So the other disciple, who was known to the high priest, went out, spoke to the woman who guarded the gate, and brought Peter in. ¹⁷ The woman said to Peter, "You are not also one of this man's disciples, are you?" He said, "I am not." ¹⁸ Now the slaves and the police had made a charcoal fire because it was cold, and they were standing around it and warming themselves. Peter also was standing with them and warming himself.

18.15
Mt 26.58;
Mk 14.54;
Lk 22.54

18.17
v. 25

18.18
Mk 14.54,
67;
Jn 21.9

O. Jesus before the Jewish authorities
(18.19–27; see vv. 12–14)

19   Then the high priest questioned Jesus about his disciples and about his teaching. ²⁰ Jesus answered, "I have spoken openly to the world; I have always taught in synagogues and in the temple, where all the Jews come together. I have said nothing in secret. ²¹ Why do you ask me? Ask those who heard what I said to them; they know what I said." ²² When he had said this, one of the police standing nearby struck Jesus on the face, saying, "Is that how you answer the high priest?" ²³ Jesus answered, "If I have spoken wrongly, testify to the wrong. But if I have spoken rightly,

18.19
Mt 26.59-68;
Mk 14.55-65;
Lk 22.63-71
18.20
Mt 26.55;
Jn 7.26
18.22
v. 3;
Jn 19.3
18.23
Mt 5.39;
Acts 23.2-5

ᶜ Gk the Nazorean   ᵈ Gk I am   ᵉ Gk he

18.6   *they stepped back and fell to the ground.* Jesus could have struck these men dead, or summoned the angels of heaven to rescue him (Mt 26.52,53), or even have had the ground swallow them up as it did Korah (Num 16.31ff). By only striking them to the ground, he possibly intended them to see their need for repentance and to give them time to repent. In any case,

Jesus' action here demonstrated that no one could take his life from him; he would lay it down of himself voluntarily (Jn 10.17,18).
18.10   Only John records it was Peter who did this (cf. Mt 26.51; Mk 14.47; Lk 22.45,50).
18.15ff   See note on Mk 14.71.

18.24
v. 13

18.25
v. 18

18.26
v. 10

18.27
Jn 13.38 why do you strike me?" 24 Then Annas sent him bound to Caiaphas the high priest.

25 Now Simon Peter was standing and warming himself. They asked him, "You are not also one of his disciples, are you?" He denied it and said, "I am not." 26 One of the slaves of the high priest, a relative of the man whose ear Peter had cut off, asked, "Did I not see you in the garden with him?" 27 Again Peter denied it, and at that moment the cock crowed.

P. Jesus before Pontius Pilate
(18.28–19.16; Matt. 27.11–16; Mark 15.2–15; Luke 23.3–25)

1. Pilate demands the indictment (18.28–32)

18.28
Mt 27.1, 2;
Mk 15.1;
Lk 23.1;
Jn 11.55;
Acts 11.3 28 Then they took Jesus from Caiaphas to Pilate's headquarters.ᶠ It was early in the morning. They themselves did not enter the headquarters,ᶠ so as to avoid ritual defilement and to be able to eat the Passover. 29 So Pilate went out to them and said, "What accusation do you bring against this man?" 30 They answered, "If this man were not a criminal, we would not have handed him over to you." 31 Pilate said to them, "Take him yourselves and judge him according to your law." The Jews replied, "We are not permitted to put anyone to death." 32 (This was to fulfill what Jesus had said when he indicated the kind of death he was to die.)

18.32
Mt 20.19;
Jn 12.32, 33

2. Pilate's first questioning of Jesus (18.33–38)

18.33
vv. 28, 29;
Jn 19.9;
Lk 23.3 33 Then Pilate entered the headquartersᶠ again, summoned Jesus, and asked him, "Are you the King of the Jews?" 34 Jesus answered, "Do you ask this on your own, or did others tell you about me?" 35 Pilate replied, "I am not a Jew, am I? Your own nation and the chief priests have handed you over to me. What have you done?" 36 Jesus answered, "My kingdom is not from this world. If my kingdom were from this world, my followers would be fighting to keep me from being handed over to the Jews. But as it is, my kingdom is not from here." 37 Pilate asked him, "So you are a king?" Jesus answered, "You say that I am a king. For this I was born, and for this I came into the world, to testify to the truth. Everyone who belongs to the truth listens to my voice." 38 Pilate asked him, "What is truth?"

18.36
Mt 26.53;
Lk 17.21;
Jn 6.15

18.37
Jn 8.47; 1 Jn
3.19; 4.6

18.38
Jn 19.4, 6

3. The people demand Barabbas (18.39–40)

After he had said this, he went out to the Jews again and told them, "I find no case against him. 39 But you have a custom that I release someone for you at the Passover. Do you want me to release for you the King of the Jews?" 40 They shouted in reply, "Not this man, but Barabbas!" Now Barabbas was a bandit.

18.39
Mt 27.15-18,
20-23;
Mk 15.6-15;
Lk 23.18-25
18.40
Acts 3.14

ᶠ Gk the praetorium

18.24 *Caiaphas.* See note on Mt 26.57.
18.28 *to avoid ritual defilement.* By Jewish law, entering the house of a Gentile was a serious offense.
18.32 *he indicated the kind of death he was to die,* i.e., this fulfilled Jesus' prediction concerning crucifixion as the method of his execution (see 3.14; 8.28; 12.32,34; Mt 20.19). Normal Jewish execution was by stoning (cf. 8.5; Acts 7.58,59).
18.36 *My kingdom.* Christ is king, though his kingdom is not of this world system. His is a spiritual and eternal kingdom. A kingship implies three things: (1) the king must be sovereign; (2) he must have a people to rule over; and (3) he must have a territory

under his control. Spiritually, Christ has all of these now. He is seated at the right hand of the Father on his throne (Acts 2.34; Heb 1.3; Rev 3.21), he has a people in the church who are his subjects, and the Father has given him authority. He came to wrest the kingdoms of this world of darkness from their rulers and to present them to the Father at the end of time. He fights against Satan, ruler of this present world (12.31). His second coming will mark his visible glory and irresistible power as the King of kings and Lord of the whole universe (Phil 2.10,11; Rev 19.16).
18.40 *Barabbas.* See note on Mk 15.7.

4. *Pilate scourges Jesus and questions him again (19.1–12)*

19 Then Pilate took Jesus and had him flogged. ²And the soldiers wove a crown of thorns and put it on his head, and they dressed him in a purple robe. ³They kept coming up to him, saying, "Hail, King of the Jews!" and striking him on the face. ⁴Pilate went out again and said to them, "Look, I am bringing him out to you to let you know that I find no case against him." ⁵So Jesus came out, wearing the crown of thorns and the purple robe. Pilate said to them, "Here is the man!" ⁶When the chief priests and the police saw him, they shouted, "Crucify! Crucify him!" Pilate said to them, "Take him yourselves and crucify him; I find no case against him." ⁷The Jews answered him, "We have a law, and according to that law he ought to die because he has claimed to be the Son of God."

8 Now when Pilate heard this, he was more afraid than ever. ⁹He entered his headquarters*ᵍ* again and asked Jesus, "Where are you from?" But Jesus gave him no answer. ¹⁰Pilate therefore said to him, "Do you refuse to speak to me? Do you not know that I have power to release you, and power to crucify you?" ¹¹Jesus answered him, "You would have no power over me unless it had been given you from above; therefore the one who handed me over to you is guilty of a greater sin." ¹²From then on Pilate tried to release him, but the Jews cried out, "If you release this man, you are no friend of the emperor. Everyone who claims to be a king sets himself against the emperor."

5. *Pilate delivers Jesus (19.13–16)*

13 When Pilate heard these words, he brought Jesus outside and sat*ʰ* on the judge's bench at a place called The Stone Pavement, or in Hebrew*ⁱ* Gabbatha. ¹⁴Now it was the day of Preparation for the Passover; and it was about noon. He said to the Jews, "Here is your King!" ¹⁵They cried out, "Away with him! Away with him! Crucify him!" Pilate asked them, "Shall I crucify your King?" The chief priests answered, "We have no king but the emperor." ¹⁶Then he handed him over to them to be crucified.

Q. *The crucifixion and burial of Jesus (19.17–42)*

1. *Jesus crucified*
(19.17–27; Matt. 27.32–44; Mark 15.21–32; Luke 23.32–43)

So they took Jesus; ¹⁷and carrying the cross by himself, he went out to what is called The Place of the Skull, which in Hebrew*ⁱ* is called

19.1 Mt 27.26
19.2 Mt 27.27-30; Mk 15.16-19
19.3 Jn 18.22
19.4 v. 6; Jn 18.38
19.5 v. 2
19.6 Acts 3.13
19.7 Lev 24.16; Mt 26.63-66; Jn 5.18; 10.33
19.9 Isa 53.7; Mt 27.12, 14
19.11 Rom 13.11; Jn 18.28ff
19.12 Lk 23.2
19.13 Mt 27.19
19.14 Mt 27.62; Mk 15.25; vv. 19, 21
19.16 Mt 27.26; Mk 15.15; Lk 23.25
19.17 Lk 23.26

ᵍ Gk the praetorium   ʰ Or seated him   ⁱ That is, Aramaic

19.1 *had him flogged.* Flogging was a dreadful punishment. The Romans normally used a weapon weighted by pieces of bone and metal. Some victims even died during flogging. Jesus was flogged, then forced to carry his cross, and at last fastened to the cross to die. His suffering for us is beyond human imagination.
19.10 Pilate was disturbed that Jesus refused to answer his question. It appeared as an affront to him who had great power and was accustomed to having people answer him quickly. Perhaps he was thinking that since he knew Jesus was innocent and wished to set him free (Lk 23.20), Jesus ought to speak in his own defense and thus help Pilate acquit him. But Jesus would not and could not do this, for he had come to die. Boastfully and arrogantly Pilate asked Jesus a question: "Do you not know that I have power to release you, and power to crucify you?" In reply, Jesus indicated that no one has authority or power except it be given by God. Every ruler is under a

higher power and rules only by divine consent (Rom 13.1–5).
19.11 *the one.* Some think Jesus meant Caiaphas the high priest, under whose direction the Jews handed Jesus over to Pilate. If so, Caiaphas gave the orders for Jesus' arrest and condemnation. Others think Jesus meant Judas Iscariot, who betrayed (handed over) Jesus to the Jews.
19.17 *The Place of the Skull, which in Hebrew is called Golgotha.* The location of Golgotha, or Calvary, cannot be known with certainty. Two locations are possible. The traditional site is now within the old city of Jerusalem where the Church of the Holy Sepulchre now stands. Those who favor this site claim it lay outside the city walls when Christ was crucified. The other location is known as Gordon's Calvary. The site was suggested by Otto Thenius in 1842 and declared in 1885 by General Charles Gordon to be the site of the crucifixion.

Golgotha. [18] There they crucified him, and with him two others, one on either side, with Jesus between them. [19] Pilate also had an inscription written and put on the cross. It read, "Jesus of Nazareth,[j] the King of the Jews." [20] Many of the Jews read this inscription, because the place where Jesus was crucified was near the city; and it was written in Hebrew,[k] in Latin, and in Greek. [21] Then the chief priests of the Jews said to Pilate, "Do not write, 'The King of the Jews,' but, 'This man said, I am King of the Jews.' " [22] Pilate answered, "What I have written I have written." [23] When the soldiers had crucified Jesus, they took his clothes and divided them into four parts, one for each soldier. They also took his tunic; now the tunic was seamless, woven in one piece from the top. [24] So they said to one another, "Let us not tear it, but cast lots for it to see who will get it." This was to fulfill what the scripture says,

> "They divided my clothes among themselves,
>   and for my clothing they cast lots."

[25] And that is what the soldiers did.

Meanwhile, standing near the cross of Jesus were his mother, and his mother's sister, Mary the wife of Clopas, and Mary Magdalene. [26] When Jesus saw his mother and the disciple whom he loved standing beside her, he said to his mother, "Woman, here is your son." [27] Then he said to the disciple, "Here is your mother." And from that hour the disciple took her into his own home.

2. The death of Jesus
(19.28–37; Matt. 27.45–50; Mark 15.33–41; Luke 23.44–49)

[28] After this, when Jesus knew that all was now finished, he said (in order to fulfill the scripture), "I am thirsty." [29] A jar full of sour wine was standing there. So they put a sponge full of the wine on a branch of hyssop and held it to his mouth. [30] When Jesus had received the wine, he said, "It is finished." Then he bowed his head and gave up his spirit.

[31] Since it was the day of Preparation, the Jews did not want the bodies left on the cross during the sabbath, especially because that sabbath was a day of great solemnity. So they asked Pilate to have the legs of the crucified men broken and the bodies removed. [32] Then the soldiers came and broke the legs of the first and of the other who had been crucified with him. [33] But when they came to Jesus and saw that he was already dead, they did not break his legs. [34] Instead, one of the soldiers pierced his side with a spear, and at once blood and water came out. [35] (He who saw this has testified so that you also may believe. His testimony is true, and he knows[l] that he tells the truth.) [36] These things occurred so that the scripture might be fulfilled, "None of his bones shall be broken." [37] And again another passage of scripture says, "They will look on the one whom they have pierced."

Margin references:
19.21 — v. 14
19.24 — Ex 28.32; Ps 22.18
19.25 — Mt 27.55, 56; Mk 15.40, 41; Lk 23.49; 24.18; Jn 20.1, 18
19.26 — Jn 13.23; 20.2; 21.20; 2.4
19.28 — Jn 13.1; 17.4; Ps 69.21
19.30 — Jn 17.4
19.31 — Deut 21.23; Ex 12.16
19.32 — v. 18
19.34 — 1 Jn 5.6, 8
19.35 — Jn 15.27; 21.24
19.36 — Ex 12.46; Num 9.12; Ps 34.20
19.37 — Zech 12.10

j Gk the Nazorean   *k* That is, Aramaic   *l* Or there is one who knows

---

19.18 See note on Lk 23.33.
19.25 Four faithful women stood beside the cross of Jesus: (1) Mary, Jesus' mother, whose presence the other Gospel writers fail to mention; (2) Mary's sister, probably named Salome (Mk 15.40), the wife of Zebedee and mother of John and James (Mt 27.56); (3) Mary, Cleopas' wife, the mother of James the younger and Joses (Mt 27.56; Mk 15.40); and (4) Mary Magdalene (Mt 27.56; Mk 15.40).
19.26 Despite his intense suffering Jesus did not forget his human mother. He made provision for her after his death by turning her over to John (a nephew of hers), who was to be like a son to her. When God removes one of our supports he often raises up another to take its place. John accepted this responsibil-

ity and Mary was assured of help all the days of her life.
19.28ff See note on Lk 23.34ff for the seven sayings of Christ on the cross.
19.30 *It is finished.* The work given to Jesus by the Father was now completed. Nothing more needed to be added to it and nothing could be taken away from it. *he bowed his head and gave up his spirit.* Those who died by crucifixion normally raised their heads at the end to gasp for breath and then dropped them when they died. Jesus bowed his head before he died as a sign of his submission to the Father's will, and to show he gave his life by his own volition and not because he was powerless.

3. Jesus laid in the tomb
(19.38–42; Matt. 27.57–61; Mark 15.42–47; Luke 23.50–56)

38 After these things, Joseph of Arimathea, who was a disciple of Jesus, though a secret one because of his fear of the Jews, asked Pilate to let him take away the body of Jesus. Pilate gave him permission; so he came and removed his body. 39 Nicodemus, who had at first come to Jesus by night, also came, bringing a mixture of myrrh and aloes, weighing about a hundred pounds. 40 They took the body of Jesus and wrapped it with the spices in linen cloths, according to the burial custom of the Jews. 41 Now there was a garden in the place where he was crucified, and in the garden there was a new tomb in which no one had ever been laid. 42 And so, because it was the Jewish day of Preparation, and the tomb was nearby, they laid Jesus there.

19.39
Jn 3.1; 7.50
19.40
Jn 11.44;
Mt 26.12;
Jn 20.5, 7;
Lk 24.12
19.42
vv. 14, 31,
20, 41

R. The resurrection of Jesus Christ
(20.1–10; Matt. 28.1–10; Mark 16.1–8; Luke 24.1–11)

20 Early on the first day of the week, while it was still dark, Mary Magdalene came to the tomb and saw that the stone had been removed from the tomb. 2 So she ran and went to Simon Peter and the other disciple, the one whom Jesus loved, and said to them, "They have taken the Lord out of the tomb, and we do not know where they have laid him." 3 Then Peter and the other disciple set out and went toward the tomb. 4 The two were running together, but the other disciple outran Peter and reached the tomb first. 5 He bent down to look in and saw the linen wrappings lying there, but he did not go in. 6 Then Simon Peter came, following him, and went into the tomb. He saw the linen wrappings lying there, 7 and the cloth that had been on Jesus' head, not lying with the linen wrappings but rolled up in a place by itself. 8 Then the other disciple, who reached the tomb first, also went in, and he saw and believed; 9 for as yet they did not understand the scripture, that he must rise from the dead. 10 Then the disciples returned to their homes.

20.1
Mt 27.60, 66
20.2
Jn 13.23;
19.26; 21.7,
20, 24
20.3
Lk 24.12
20.5
Jn 19.40
20.8
v. 4
20.9
Mt 22.29;
Lk 24.26, 46

S. Jesus appears to Mary Magdalene (20.11–18)

11 But Mary stood weeping outside the tomb. As she wept, she bent over to look[m] into the tomb; 12 and she saw two angels in white, sitting where the body of Jesus had been lying, one at the head and the other at the feet. 13 They said to her, "Woman, why are you weeping?" She said to them, "They have taken away my Lord, and I do not know where they have laid him." 14 When she had said this, she turned around and saw Jesus standing there, but she did not know that it was Jesus. 15 Jesus said to her, "Woman, why are you weeping? Whom are you looking for?"

20.11
Mk 16.5;
v. 5
20.12
Mt 28.2, 3;
Mk 16.5;
Lk 24.4
20.13
v. 2
20.14
Mt 28.9;
Jn 21.4
20.15
v. 13

m Gk lacks to look

20.1 *the first day of the week,* i.e., early Sunday morning. See note on Mt 28.6.
20.2 *the other disciple, the one whom Jesus loved,* i.e., John (see note on 13.23).
20.6,7 The presence of linen wrappings lying there and the head cloth rolled up in a place by itself seem to indicate that Jesus miraculously came through the grave clothes when he rose from the dead.
20.8 *and believed.* John, the author of this Gospel, believed that Jesus had risen from the dead and was alive forevermore.
20.9 *for as yet they did not understand the scripture.* The O.T. spoke of the resurrection of the Messiah (Ps 16.10). Jesus himself told his disciples he would rise from the dead (Lk 18.33). Despite this, the disciples did not understand these predictions. After the resurrection Jesus opened their minds that they might un-

derstand the O.T., and he revealed to them all the Scriptures that spoke concerning him (Lk 24.44,45).
20.11ff The chronology of Christ's resurrection appearances seems to be as follows: (1) to Mary Magdalene and the other women (Mt 28.9; Mk 16.9,10; Jn 20.11–18); (2) to the disciples on the road to Emmaus (Mk 16.12; Lk 24.13–15); (3) to Peter (Lk 24.34; 1 Cor 15.5); (4) to the ten disciples in the upper room (Jn 20.19); (5) to the eleven in the upper room with Thomas present (Mk 16.14; Lk 24.36; Jn 20.26); (6) to the disciples at the Sea of Tiberias (Jn 21.1–24); (7) to the eleven on a mountain in Galilee (Mt 28.16–20); (8) to five hundred of the brethren (1 Cor 15.6); (9) to James (1 Cor 15.7); (10) to all of the apostles (1 Cor 15.7); (11) to those present when he ascended into heaven (Mk 16.19; Lk 24.50,51; Acts 1.3–12).

Supposing him to be the gardener, she said to him, "Sir, if you have carried him away, tell me where you have laid him, and I will take him away." 16 Jesus said to her, "Mary!" She turned and said to him in Hebrew,[n] "Rabbouni!" (which means Teacher). 17 Jesus said to her, "Do not hold on to me, because I have not yet ascended to the Father. But go to my brothers and say to them, 'I am ascending to my Father and your Father, to my God and your God.'" 18 Mary Magdalene went and announced to the disciples, "I have seen the Lord"; and she told them that he had said these things to her.

20.17
Mt 28.10;
v. 27;
Jn 7.33

20.18
Lk 24.10, 13

T. Jesus appears to the ten in Jerusalem (20.19–25; Luke 24.36–43)

19 When it was evening on that day, the first day of the week, and the doors of the house where the disciples had met were locked for fear of the Jews, Jesus came and stood among them and said, "Peace be with you." 20 After he said this, he showed them his hands and his side. Then the disciples rejoiced when they saw the Lord. 21 Jesus said to them again, "Peace be with you. As the Father has sent me, so I send you." 22 When he had said this, he breathed on them and said to them, "Receive the Holy Spirit. 23 If you forgive the sins of any, they are forgiven them; if you retain the sins of any, they are retained." 24 But Thomas (who was called the Twin[o]), one of the twelve, was not with them when Jesus came. 25 So the other disciples told him, "We have seen the Lord." But he said to them, "Unless I see the mark of the nails in his hands, and put my finger in the mark of the nails and my hand in his side, I will not believe."

20.19
Lk 24.36-39;
vv. 21, 26

20.20
Lk 24.39,
40;
Jn 16.20, 22

20.21
Mt 28.19;
Jn 17.18, 19

20.23
Mt 16.19;
18.18

20.24
Jn 11.16

20.25
v. 20

U. Jesus appears to Thomas and the ten (20.26–29)

26 A week later his disciples were again in the house, and Thomas was with them. Although the doors were shut, Jesus came and stood among them and said, "Peace be with you." 27 Then he said to Thomas, "Put your finger here and see my hands. Reach out your hand and put it in my side. Do not doubt but believe." 28 Thomas answered him, "My Lord and my God!" 29 Jesus said to him, "Have you believed because you have seen me? Blessed are those who have not seen and yet have come to believe."

20.26
v. 21

20.27
v. 25;
Lk 24.40

20.29
1 Pet 1.8

IV. Conclusion (20.30,31)

30 Now Jesus did many other signs in the presence of his disciples, which are not written in this book. 31 But these are written so that you may come to believe[p] that Jesus is the Messiah,[q] the Son of God, and that through believing you may have life in his name.

20.30
Jn 21.25
20.31
Jn 19.35;
3.15

[n] That is, *Aramaic*   [o] Gk *Didymus*   [p] Other ancient authorities read *may continue to believe*   [q] Or the *Christ*

20.17 *Do not hold on to me,* i.e., "do not detain me; go tell the others what you have seen." The nature of the risen Christ was different from his nature before his resurrection. Later, however, Jesus invited his disciples to touch and handle him (v.27; cf. Lk 24.39, 40).

20.22 *Receive the Holy Spirit.* The relationship between this verse and the Pentecost event (Acts 1–2) is unclear. Some see this verse as the moment in which the disciples were regenerated. Others think it means the disciples were sealed and indwelt by the Spirit here and were filled later. Still others consider this to be a prophecy of Pentecost (cf. Acts 1.4,5).

20.28 *my God.* A watershed question in Christian doctrine is: Is Jesus God? Scripture states definitively that Jesus Christ is God manifest in the flesh. He is eternally preexistent (1.1,2; Isa 9.6; Heb 13.8; Rev 22.13), the only Son of God (10.30; 14.9; Mt 11.27; Mk 14.61,62). The N.T. clearly refers to him as God (Titus 2.13; 1 Jn 5.20). The following attributes of deity are assigned to him: (1) holiness (8.46; 2 Cor 5.21; Heb 7.26); (2) omnipresence (Mt 18.20; 28.20); (3) omnipotence (Mt 28.18; Heb 1.3; Rev 1.8); (4) immutability (Heb 1.11,12; 13.8); (5) divine creative activity (1.3; 1 Cor 8.6; Col 1.16,17; Heb 1.10); (6) his right to be worshiped (Mt 2.11; 14.33; 28.9; Phil 2.10; Heb 1.6); (7) his right and power to forgive sins (1.29; Mk 2.5–10; Lk 24.47; Acts 10.43; 1 Jn 1.7). Denial of Christ's deity destroys the basic structure of the Christian faith.

V. Epilogue: (21.1–25)

A. Jesus appears to the disciples at the Sea of Tiberias (21.1–14)

21 After these things Jesus showed himself again to the disciples by the Sea of Tiberias; and he showed himself in this way. ²Gathered there together were Simon Peter, Thomas called the Twin,ʳ Nathanael of Cana in Galilee, the sons of Zebedee, and two others of his disciples. ³Simon Peter said to them, "I am going fishing." They said to him, "We will go with you." They went out and got into the boat, but that night they caught nothing.

4 Just after daybreak, Jesus stood on the beach; but the disciples did not know that it was Jesus. ⁵Jesus said to them, "Children, you have no fish, have you?" They answered him, "No." ⁶He said to them, "Cast the net to the right side of the boat, and you will find some." So they cast it, and now they were not able to haul it in because there were so many fish. ⁷That disciple whom Jesus loved said to Peter, "It is the Lord!" When Simon Peter heard that it was the Lord, he put on some clothes, for he was naked, and jumped into the sea. ⁸But the other disciples came in the boat, dragging the net full of fish, for they were not far from the land, only about a hundred yardsˢ off.

9 When they had gone ashore, they saw a charcoal fire there, with fish on it, and bread. ¹⁰Jesus said to them, "Bring some of the fish that you have just caught." ¹¹So Simon Peter went aboard and hauled the net ashore, full of large fish, a hundred fifty-three of them; and though there were so many, the net was not torn. ¹²Jesus said to them, "Come and have breakfast." Now none of the disciples dared to ask him, "Who are you?" because they knew it was the Lord. ¹³Jesus came and took the bread and gave it to them, and did the same with the fish. ¹⁴This was now the third time that Jesus appeared to the disciples after he was raised from the dead.

B. Jesus questions Peter (21.15–23)

15 When they had finished breakfast, Jesus said to Simon Peter, "Simon son of John, do you love me more than these?" He said to him, "Yes, Lord; you know that I love you." Jesus said to him, "Feed my lambs." ¹⁶A second time he said to him, "Simon son of John, do you love me?" He said to him, "Yes, Lord; you know that I love you." Jesus said to him, "Tend my sheep." ¹⁷He said to him the third time, "Simon son of John, do you love me?" Peter felt hurt because he said to him the third time, "Do you love me?" And he said to him, "Lord, you know every-

ʳ Gk Didymus   ˢ Gk two hundred cubits

Cross-references (right margin):
21.1 Jn 20.19, 26; 6.1
21.2 Jn 11.16; 1.45;
21.3 Mt 4.21; Mk 1.19; Lk 5.10
21.3 Lk 5.5
21.4 Jn 20.14
21.5 Lk 24.41
21.6 Lk 5.4, 6, 7
21.7 Jn 13.23; 20.2; v. 20
21.9 vv. 10, 13
21.13 v. 9
21.14 Jn 20.19, 26
21.15 Jn 13.37; Mt 26.33; Mk 14.29
21.16 Mt 2.6; Acts 20.28; 1 Pet 5.2; Rev 7.17
21.17 Jn 16.30; v. 16

21.1 *Sea of Tiberias*, also known as Lake Gennesaret, the Sea of Galilee, and the Lake of Tiberias.
21.2 *the sons of Zebedee*, i.e., James and John.
21.3 *I am going fishing.* After the resurrection, the disciples were at a loss what to do. Jesus had not yet given them instructions to wait in Jerusalem for the outpouring of the Holy Spirit. Consequently, these men, who had been busy with Jesus for almost three years, decided to return to what had been their trade before they became disciples.
21.6 This incident repeated what the disciples had experienced before. According to Luke, Peter, James, and John had fished all night and caught nothing. Jesus told them to cast in their nets and they reaped a large harvest of fish. Then they became followers of Jesus (Lk 5.1–8). Now at the end of Jesus' time on earth the same thing happened. The disciples were fishing and again they caught nothing. Jesus appeared and told them to cast in their nets, and when they did they caught many fish. Peter, remembering the first occasion, sensed immediately that it

was the Lord. By this incident Jesus probably implied that the time for them to catch people had come (Lk 5.10).
21.7 *That disciple whom Jesus loved*, i.e., John (see note on 13.23).
21.15–17 *do you love me more than these?* There is an ambiguity as to what this question means. Some think it means: "Do you love me more than you love these other disciples?" Others: "Do you love me more than these other disciples love me?" And still others: "Do you love me more than your boats, nets, and fish?" Two different Greek words are used for *love* in this section. The first two times Jesus used the word *agapaō*, meaning high, devoted love. When Peter refused to use that word in his answer, Jesus turns to the word he did use, *phileō*, a lower form of love having to do with the love of friendship. Peter accepted this word and maintained that he loved Jesus this way. Peter was humbler now than earlier in his life and was making no claim to superior love.

thing; you know that I love you." Jesus said to him, "Feed my sheep. [18] Very truly, I tell you, when you were younger, you used to fasten your own belt and to go wherever you wished. But when you grow old, you will stretch out your hands, and someone else will fasten a belt around you and take you where you do not wish to go." [19] (He said this to indicate the kind of death by which he would glorify God.) After this he said to him, "Follow me."

[20] Peter turned and saw the disciple whom Jesus loved following them; he was the one who had reclined next to Jesus at the supper and had said, "Lord, who is it that is going to betray you?" [21] When Peter saw him, he said to Jesus, "Lord, what about him?" [22] Jesus said to him, "If it is my will that he remain until I come, what is that to you? Follow me!" [23] So the rumor spread in the community[t] that this disciple would not die. Yet Jesus did not say to him that he would not die, but, "If it is my will that he remain until I come, what is that to you?"[u]

C. The authentication of the author (21.24,25)

[24] This is the disciple who is testifying to these things and has written them, and we know that his testimony is true. [25] But there are also many other things that Jesus did; if every one of them were written down, I suppose that the world itself could not contain the books that would be written.

---

[t] Gk *among the brothers*   [u] Other ancient authorities lack *what is that to you*

21.19
2 Pet 1.14

21.20
v. 7;
Jn 13.25

21.22
Mt 16.27,
28; 25.31;
1 Cor 4.5;
11.26;
Rev 2.25;
3.11; 22.7,
20
21.23
Acts 1.15

21.24
Jn 15.27;
19.35
21.25
Jn 20.30

21.21 Curious Peter, having been told what would happen to him later in life, became very curious about John and asked Jesus about him. Jesus told him, in effect, "It is none of your business. All you need to do is follow me." When believers follow Jesus, they will be kept busy enough. Those who want to know the will of God for everybody else are distracted from the will of God for themselves, for God does not tell us what his will is for others.
21.25 Even though everything Jesus said and did could fill more books that we could ever read, God has made known to us all we need to know about Jesus — enough to accept him as our Savior and Lord.

INTRODUCTION TO

THE

ACTS

OF THE APOSTLES

Authorship, Date, and Background: The Acts of the Apostles and Luke's Gospel were written by the same person (see introduction to Luke). Luke has been identified with both books from the earliest days, and while neither book has any author's identification in the text, there is no reason for supposing the books were written by anyone else. The date for the book lies somewhere between A.D. 64 and 72. Tradition has it that Luke died shortly after Paul was executed and therefore Acts ends with Paul's imprisonment in Rome. The two years spent there gave Luke sufficient time to do his research work in tracing down what happened as the gospel was preached throughout the Roman empire. There is good reason to believe that the good news was preached in North Africa and in the regions to the east of Palestine and perhaps as far as India and maybe even China. Luke did not write about that aspect of the gospel's progress. He confined his attention to Palestine, Asia Minor (now Turkey), Macedonia, Greece, and Rome.

In so short a book as The Acts of the Apostles it would be impossible to do more than give the briefest account of all that transpired following the ascension of Jesus Christ and the beginning of the church at Pentecost. So Luke limited his account largely to the ministries of Peter and Paul. For this reason, some say the title could well be The Acts of Peter and Paul. Others have suggested it should be titled The Acts of the Holy Spirit, and still others The Acts of the Church. When all is taken into account, however, The Acts of the Apostles appears to be the appropriate title.

In these discussions it should be remembered that the ultimate author of all Scripture is the Holy Spirit, who selected and used the writers to accomplish the divine purpose (see 2 Tim 3.16; 2 Pet 1.20,21). In doing this, while we have not been told everything that happened, we can know that what we are told is trustworthy and dependable theologically and factually. Moreover, in Luke's case he certainly knew by personal experience some of what he wrote about. He no doubt gathered information from such people as Silas, Titus, Timothy, Apollos, John Mark, and Barnabas. The Holy Spirit aided him in the choice and selection of his material and kept him from saying what is not true.

Characteristics and Content: Luke provides the link which connects the four Gospels with all of the other apostolic writings found in the N.T. This book is really the bridge, the absence of which would leave us immeasurably poorer and in the dark about the earliest days of the church. Luke commences with the ascension, recording another statement of Jesus' command to take the good news to the ends of the earth (1.8). Then comes Pentecost, the birthday of the church. On that occasion the disciples of Jesus received the power the Master had promised and were enabled to go forth preaching the word and performing miracles to attest to the truth of what they proclaimed.

The sermons Luke records are strikingly similar in content. Again and again the core of the messages claims that Jesus Christ fulfilled the Scriptures by dying for people's sins and rising again, and that he is now exalted in heaven at the throne of his Father. This Jesus, they claim, is the Lord and Christ (the Messiah), who is for Jew and Gentile alike. They urge people everywhere to repent, accept Christ by faith, be baptized, receive the gift of the Holy Spirit, and enjoy God's promise to participate in the new age that began at Pentecost and that would reach its consummation with the return of Jesus in righteousness to judge the world. The resurrection of Jesus lies at the heart of the apostolic good news.

Luke also emphasizes the person and work of the Holy Spirit—the one who brings conviction of sin, righteousness, and judgment (cf. Jn 16.8). He sends forth workers into the harvest field (see Acts 13) and directs the missionary enterprise (cf. 16.6). Sin is judged immediately in the early church to show that no one can play fast and loose with God and with truth (cf. the Ananias and Sapphira episode in ch. 5). Peter spoke of their sin as one in which they were lying to the Holy Spirit (5.3). Luke records how believers are filled with the Holy Spirit and this makes all the difference in their lives and ministry.

This book comes to a conclusion at a time when the Roman empire had been evangelized, churches established, elders and deacons selected, and the basic order of the church set up.

Outline:

I. Jerusalem (1.1—8.3)

II. Judea, Samaria, and on to Antioch of Syria (8.4—12.25)

III. Throughout the Roman empire with Paul (13.1—28.31)

THE
ACTS
OF THE APOSTLES

I. Jerusalem (1.1–8.3)

A. Introduction

1. Preface

1 In the first book, Theophilus, I wrote about all that Jesus did and taught from the beginning ²until the day when he was taken up to heaven, after giving instructions through the Holy Spirit to the apostles whom he had chosen. ³After his suffering he presented himself alive to them by many convincing proofs, appearing to them during forty days and speaking about the kingdom of God. ⁴While staying*a* with them, he ordered them not to leave Jerusalem, but to wait there for the promise of the Father. "This," he said, "is what you have heard from me; ⁵for John baptized with water, but you will be baptized with*b* the Holy Spirit not many days from now."

2. The ascension

6 So when they had come together, they asked him, "Lord, is this the time when you will restore the kingdom to Israel?" ⁷He replied, "It is not for you to know the times or periods that the Father has set by his own authority. ⁸But you will receive power when the Holy Spirit has come upon you; and you will be my witnesses in Jerusalem, in all Judea and Samaria, and to the ends of the earth." ⁹When he had said this, as they were watching, he was lifted up, and a cloud took him out of their sight. ¹⁰While he was going and they were gazing up toward heaven, suddenly two men in white robes stood by them. ¹¹They said, "Men of Galilee, why do you stand looking up toward heaven? This Jesus, who has been taken up from you into heaven, will come in the same way as you saw him go into heaven."

a Or *eating*   *b* Or *by*

1.1
Lk 1.1-4
1.2
Mt 28.19
1.3
Mt 28.17;
Lk 24.34,
36;
1 Cor 15.5-7
1.4
Lk 24.49;
Jn 14.16
1.5
Acts 11.16

1.6
Mt 24.3
1.7
Mt 24.36;
Mk 13.32
1.8
Acts 2.1-4;
Lk 24.48;
Jn 15.27
1.9
Lk 24.51;
v. 2
1.10
Lk 24.4;
Jn 20.12
1.11
Mt 24.30;
Mk 13.26;
Jn 14.3

1.1 *In the first book*, i.e., the Gospel of Luke (see note on Lk 1.3).

1.3 Christ remained on earth for forty days following his resurrection. He wanted (1) to verify his resurrection by many appearances, in order to silence those who would deny the miracle; (2) to instruct his disciples in the great truths of Scripture concerning his life and ministry and so prevent false teachers from making inroads among the apostles; and (3) to pave the way for the Holy Spirit's work of instruction and confirmation (Jn 14.26).

1.6 *is this the time when you will restore the kingdom to Israel?* That is, "Will you now make the nation of the Jews what it used to be under the kingly reigns of David and Solomon?"

1.8 This is the fifth statement of the great commission (see notes on Mk 16.15; Lk 24.47). The mission

of the church is to preach the good news to every creature. When this is completed, Jesus Christ will return again in power and great glory.

1.9 The ascension occurred at the Mount of Olives near Bethany (Lk 24.50) in the presence of the eleven apostles and two white-robed men (either angels or perhaps Moses and Elijah, who were with Jesus in his transfiguration, Lk 9.30). The two men assured the apostles that Jesus would return the same way as they had just seen him go into heaven. That is, Christ's return will be personal and visible. He will come "with his mighty angels in flaming fire " (2 Thess 1.7,8); "with all his saints" (1 Thess 3.13); "like a thief in the night" (1 Thess 5.2; 2 Pet 3.10; Rev 16.15); "in his glory" (Mt 25.31); "with a cry of command . . . and with the sound of God's trumpet" (1 Thess 4.16); and "suddenly" (Mk 13.36).

B. *The origin of the church*

1. *The disciples in prayer*

12   Then they returned to Jerusalem from the mount called Olivet, which is near Jerusalem, a sabbath day's journey away. ¹³When they had entered the city, they went to the room upstairs where they were staying, Peter, and John, and James, and Andrew, Philip and Thomas, Bartholomew and Matthew, James son of*c* James. ¹⁴All these were constantly devoting themselves to prayer, together with certain women, including Mary the mother of Jesus, as well as his brothers.

2. *The replacement of Judas Iscariot*

15   In those days Peter stood up among the believers*d* (together with the crowd numbered about one hundred twenty persons) and said, ¹⁶"Friends,*e* the scripture had to be fulfilled, which the Holy Spirit through David foretold concerning Judas, who became a guide for those who arrested Jesus— ¹⁷for he was numbered among us and was allotted his share in this ministry." ¹⁸(Now this man acquired a field with the reward of his wickedness; and falling headlong,*f* he burst open in the middle and all his bowels gushed out. ¹⁹This became known to all the residents of Jerusalem, so that the field was called in their language Hakeldama, that is, Field of Blood.) ²⁰"For it is written in the book of Psalms,

'Let his homestead become desolate,
   and let there be no one to live in it';

and

'Let another take his position of overseer.'

²¹So one of the men who have accompanied us during all the time that the Lord Jesus went in and out among us, ²²beginning from the baptism of John until the day when he was taken up from us—one of these must become a witness with us to his resurrection." ²³So they proposed two, Joseph called Barsabbas, who was also known as Justus, and Matthias. ²⁴Then they prayed and said, "Lord, you know everyone's heart. Show us which one of these two you have chosen ²⁵to take the place*g* in this ministry and apostleship from which Judas turned aside to go to his own place." ²⁶And they cast lots for them, and the lot fell on Matthias; and he was added to the eleven apostles.

C. *The outpouring of the Holy Spirit*

1. *The gift of the Spirit*

2   When the day of Pentecost had come, they were all together in one place. ²And suddenly from heaven there came a sound like the rush of a violent wind, and it filled the entire house where they were sitting.

c Or *the brother of*   *d* Gk *brothers*   *e* Gk *Men, brothers*   *f* Or *swelling up*   *g* Other ancient authorities read *the share*

Marginal references:

1.13
Acts 9.37, 39;
20.8;
Mt 10.2-4;
Mk 3.16-19;
Lk 6.14-16
1.14
Acts 2.1, 46;
Lk 23.49,
55;
Mt 12.46

1.15
Jn 21.23;
Acts 6.3; 9.30
1.16
Jn 13.18
1.17
Jn 6.70, 71;
v. 25;
Acts 20.24;
21.19
1.18
Mt 27.3-10;
26.14, 15
1.20
Ps 69.25;
109.8

1.21
Lk 24.3
1.22
Mk 1.1; v. 8;
Acts 2.32

1.24
1 Sam 16.7;
Jer 17.10;
Acts 15.8;
Rom 8.27
1.26
Lev 16.8

2.1
Lev 23.15;
Deut 16.9;
Acts 1.14
2.2
Acts 4.31

1.15 Peter, in company with the one hundred and twenty, addressed the issue of Judas Iscariot, now dead. His death left only eleven of the twelve apostles. But why choose anyone to fill Judas' place? Because they knew the Scripture (Ps 109.8) and fulfilled it.
1.26 *Matthias* was chosen by lot to replace Judas Iscariot as an apostle. The main function of the office of apostle was to witness to Jesus' resurrection. Throughout Acts Christ's resurrection is emphasized (2.32; 3.15; 4.2,10,33; 5.30–32; 10.29–41; 13.30, 31). The apostles preached that God had exalted the resurrected Christ and enthroned him as Savior and Lord. Christ's ascension and appointment to the seat at the right hand of the Father demonstrates the Father's acceptance of the saving work of Christ.
2.1 *Pentecost* (Gk. *pentekostē*), meaning "fiftieth day," was celebrated on the seventh day of Sivan (May-June), fifty days after the Passover. It was one of the three festivals at which all males were supposed to congregate. Pentecost was also known as the festival of weeks, the day of the first fruits, and the festival of harvest (see note on Lev 23.15,16). The day of Pentecost marks the beginning of the Christian church. Pentecost was a miraculous event that came

3 Divided tongues, as of fire, appeared among them, and a tongue rested on each of them. 4 All of them were filled with the Holy Spirit and began to speak in other languages, as the Spirit gave them ability.

5 Now there were devout Jews from every nation under heaven living in Jerusalem. 6 And at this sound the crowd gathered and was bewildered, because each one heard them speaking in the native language of each. 7 Amazed and astonished, they asked, "Are not all these who are speaking Galileans? 8 And how is it that we hear, each of us, in our own native language? 9 Parthians, Medes, Elamites, and residents of Mesopotamia, Judea and Cappadocia, Pontus and Asia, 10 Phrygia and Pamphylia, Egypt and the parts of Libya belonging to Cyrene, and visitors from Rome, both Jews and proselytes, 11 Cretans and Arabs — in our own languages we hear them speaking about God's deeds of power." 12 All were amazed and perplexed, saying to one another, "What does this mean?" 13 But others sneered and said, "They are filled with new wine."

2. Peter's Pentecostal sermon

14 But Peter, standing with the eleven, raised his voice and addressed them, "Men of Judea and all who live in Jerusalem, let this be known to you, and listen to what I say. 15 Indeed, these are not drunk, as you suppose, for it is only nine o'clock in the morning. 16 No, this is what was spoken through the prophet Joel:

17 'In the last days it will be, God declares,
   that I will pour out my Spirit upon all flesh,
      and your sons and your daughters shall prophesy,
   and your young men shall see visions,
      and your old men shall dream dreams.
18 Even upon my slaves, both men and women,
   in those days I will pour out my Spirit;
      and they shall prophesy.
19 And I will show portents in the heaven above
   and signs on the earth below,
      blood, and fire, and smoky mist.
20 The sun shall be turned to darkness
   and the moon to blood,
      before the coming of the Lord's great and glorious day.
21 Then everyone who calls on the name of the Lord shall
      be saved.'

22 "You that are Israelites,[h] listen to what I have to say: Jesus of Nazareth,[i] a man attested to you by God with deeds of power, wonders, and signs that God did through him among you, as you yourselves know — 23 this man, handed over to you according to the definite plan and foreknowledge of God, you crucified and killed by the hands of those outside the law. 24 But God raised him up, having freed him from death,[j] because

---

h Gk Men, Israelites   i Gk the Nazorean   j Gk the pains of death

2.4
Acts 4.8, 31;
9.17; 13.9,
52;
1 Cor 12.10,
11; 14.21
2.5
Acts 8.2
2.7
v. 12;
Acts 1.11
2.9
1 Pet 1.1;
Acts 6.9;
16.6;
Rom 16.5;
1 Cor 16.19;
2 Cor 1.8
2.12
v. 7
2.13
1 Cor 14.23

2.15
1 Thess 5.7

2.17
Joel 2.28-32;
Zech 12.10;
Jn 7.38;
Acts 10.45;
21.9

2.18
Acts 21.4, 9,
10

2.20
Mt 24.29;
Mk 13.24;
Lk 21.25
2.21
Rom 10.13
2.22
Jn 3.2;
Acts 10.38;
Jn 4.48
2.23
Mt 26.24;
Lk 22.22;
Acts 3.18;
4.28; 3.13
2.24
Acts 3.15;
Rom 4.24;
2 Cor 4.14;
Eph 1.20;
Col 2.12;
Heb 13.20;
1 Pet 1.21

---

suddenly, accompanied by several signs: (1) the wind, filling the place and revealing the presence of the Holy Spirit; (2) the tongues, signifying the preaching of the good news to all nations; and (3) the fire, symbolizing the power and zeal given to those who obeyed Christ in taking the gospel to the ends of the earth.
2.4 *other languages,* i.e., languages given to them by the Holy Spirit which they did not know themselves.
2.8 Some think the miracle at Pentecost was a miracle of hearing, i.e., that the disciples spoke just one language and that the people gathered were given the gift of understanding the disciples' language. It seems clear from the text, however, that it was a miracle of speaking, that the disciples were given the gift of speaking in the languages of the other peoples present.
2.17 *The last days* began with the first advent of Jesus Christ and will end with his second coming. How long this period will last is nowhere stated in Scripture.
2.23 Scripture teaches various aspects of Christ's work on Calvary: (1) its necessity for our redemption (17.3; Lk 24.46); (2) its ordination by God (2.23); (3) its voluntary action by Jesus himself (Mt 26.53; Jn 10.17,18); and (4) its acceptability to the Father as a true and saving sacrifice (Eph 5.2; 1 Thess 5.10).

COUNTRIES OF PEOPLE MENTIONED AT PENTECOST

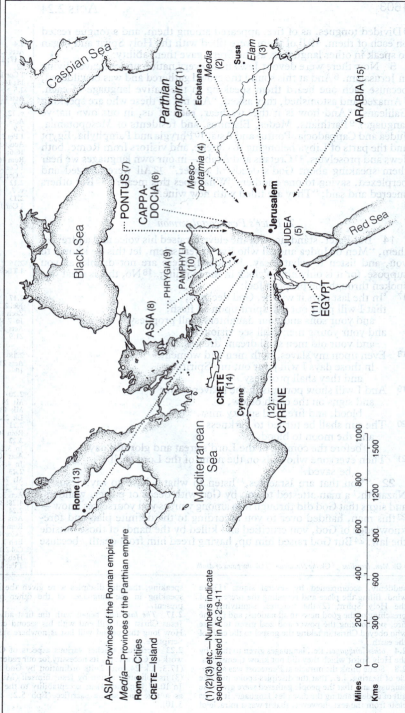

Caspian Sea

Parthian empire

Ecbatana •
Media (2)

Susa
Elam (3)

ARABIA (15)

PONTUS (7)

CAPPA-
DOCIA (6)

Black Sea

Meso-
potamia (4)

• Jerusalem

JUDEA (5)

Red Sea

PHRYGIA (9)

PAMPHYLIA (10)

ASIA (8)

EGYPT (11)

Mediterranean Sea

CRETE (14)

Cyrene

CYRENE (12)

Rome (13)

Miles 0   200   400   600   800   1000
Kms   0   300   600   900   1200 1500

ASIA—Provinces of the Roman empire
Media—Provinces of the Parthian empire
Rome—Cities
CRETE—Island

(1) (2) (3) etc.—Numbers indicate
sequence listed in Ac 2:9-11

it was impossible for him to be held in its power. 25 For David says
concerning him,

'I saw the Lord always before me,
　　for he is at my right hand so that I will not be shaken;
26　therefore my heart was glad, and my tongue rejoiced;
　　moreover my flesh will live in hope.
27　For you will not abandon my soul to Hades,
　　or let your Holy One experience corruption.
28　You have made known to me the ways of life;
　　you will make me full of gladness with your presence.'

29　"Fellow Israelites,[k] I may say to you confidently of our ancestor
David that he both died and was buried, and his tomb is with us to this
day. 30 Since he was a prophet, he knew that God had sworn with an oath
to him that he would put one of his descendants on his throne. 31 Foreseeing this, David[l] spoke of the resurrection of the Messiah,[m] saying,

'He was not abandoned to Hades,
　　nor did his flesh experience corruption.'

32 This Jesus God raised up, and of that all of us are witnesses. 33 Being
therefore exalted at[n] the right hand of God, and having received from the
Father the promise of the Holy Spirit, he has poured out this that you both
see and hear. 34 For David did not ascend into the heavens, but he himself
says,

'The Lord said to my Lord,
　　"Sit at my right hand,
35　　until I make your enemies your footstool."'

36 Therefore let the entire house of Israel know with certainty that God
has made him both Lord and Messiah,[o] this Jesus whom you crucified."

3. The first ingathering of souls

37　Now when they heard this, they were cut to the heart and said to
Peter and to the other apostles, "Brothers,[k] what should we do?" 38 Peter
said to them, "Repent, and be baptized every one of you in the name of
Jesus Christ so that your sins may be forgiven; and you will receive the
gift of the Holy Spirit. 39 For the promise is for you, for your children,
and for all who are far away, everyone whom the Lord our God calls to
him." 40 And he testified with many other arguments and exhorted them,
saying, "Save yourselves from this corrupt generation." 41 So those who
welcomed his message were baptized, and that day about three thousand
persons were added. 42 They devoted themselves to the apostles' teaching
and fellowship, to the breaking of bread and the prayers.

4. The fellowship of believers

43　Awe came upon everyone, because many wonders and signs were

k Gk Men, brothers　l Gk he　m Or the Christ　n Or by　o Or Christ

2.25 Ps 16.8-11
2.27 Mt 11.23; Acts 13.35
2.29 Acts 7.8, 9; 13.36; 1 Kings 2.10; Neh 3.16
2.30 2 Sam 7.12, 13; Ps 132.11; Rom 1.3
2.31 Ps 16.10
2.32 v. 24; Acts 1.8
2.33 Acts 5.31; 1.4; Jn 7.39; 14.26; 15.26; Acts 10.45
2.34 Ps 110.1; Mt 22.44
2.37 Lk 3.10; Acts 9.6; 16.30
2.38 Lk 24.47; Acts 3.19; 5.31; 8.12, 16; 22.16
2.39 Isa 57.19; Joel 2.32; Acts 10.45; Eph 2.13
2.43 Acts 5.12

2.34 David died and was buried; he did not ascend
into heaven to sit at the right hand of God, for his
body still lay in the grave. Thus the words quoted
from David (Ps 110.1) were not spoken about himself, but applied to God's Son, Jesus Christ. He is now
exalted *by* God *to* God's right hand as the supreme
ruler over the entire cosmos. This exaltation of Jesus
formed an integral part of the apostolic message — and
of the gospel message today.
2.38 Water baptism upon profession of faith is commanded here. It normally precedes admission to the
fellowship of the church and is required by most
denominations (see note on Mt 28.19). We must not
confuse it with the baptism of the Spirit, which the
church experienced here on Pentecost.
2.41 The "greater works" of the disciples, prophe-

sied and promised by Jesus Christ in Jn 14.12, began
to be fulfilled. Peter, empowered by the Spirit, saw
three thousand people respond to the gospel invitation. This was far more than the total number of
people who had remained faithful to Christ up to this
point (1.15).
2.42 *the breaking of bread,* i.e., the Eucharist or the
Lord's Supper, one of the two ordinances or sacraments of most churches.
2.43 *many wonders and signs.* The power of the Holy
Spirit worked effectively, so that the hearers had corroborating evidence to support the spoken word of
the disciples. These miracles functioned in the same
way as the miracles of Jesus had done (cf. Jn
20.30–31).

2.44
Acts 4.32, 34

2.46
Acts 5.42;
20.7;
1 Cor 10.16
2.47
Acts 4.33;
Rom 14.18;
Acts 5.14;
11.24

being done by the apostles. 44 All who believed were together and had all things in common; 45 they would sell their possessions and goods and distribute the proceeds*p* to all, as any had need. 46 Day by day, as they spent much time together in the temple, they broke bread at home*q* and ate their food with glad and generous*r* hearts, 47 praising God and having the goodwill of all the people. And day by day the Lord added to their number those who were being saved.

D. *The church at work in Jerusalem*

1. *Peter's second sermon: healing of the lame man*

3.1
Acts 2.46;
Ps 55.17
3.2
Acts 14.8;
Lk 16.20;
v. 10
3.4
Acts 10.4
3.6
Acts 4.10

3 One day Peter and John were going up to the temple at the hour of prayer, at three o'clock in the afternoon. 2 And a man lame from birth was being carried in. People would lay him daily at the gate of the temple called the Beautiful Gate so that he could ask for alms from those entering the temple. 3 When he saw Peter and John about to go into the temple, he asked them for alms. 4 Peter looked intently at him, as did John, and said, "Look at us." 5 And he fixed his attention on them, expecting to receive something from them. 6 But Peter said, "I have no silver or gold, but what I have I give you; in the name of Jesus Christ of Nazareth,*s* stand up and walk." 7 And he took him by the right hand and raised him up; and immediately his feet and ankles were made strong. 8 Jumping up, he stood and began to walk, and he entered the temple with them, walking and leaping and praising God. 9 All the people saw him walking and praising God, 10 and they recognized him as the one who used to sit and ask for alms at the Beautiful Gate of the temple; and they were filled with wonder and amazement at what had happened to him.

3.9
Acts 4.16, 21
3.10
Jn 9.8

3.11
Lk 22.8;
Jn 10.23;
Acts 5.12

11   While he clung to Peter and John, all the people ran together to them in the portico called Solomon's Portico, utterly astonished. 12 When Peter saw it, he addressed the people, "You Israelites,*t* why do you wonder at this, or why do you stare at us, as though by our own power or piety we had made him walk? 13 The God of Abraham, the God of Isaac, and the God of Jacob, the God of our ancestors has glorified his servant*u* Jesus, whom you handed over and rejected in the presence of Pilate, though he had decided to release him. 14 But you rejected the Holy and Righteous One and asked to have a murderer given to you, 15 and you killed the Author of life, whom God raised from the dead. To this we are witnesses. 16 And by faith in his name, his name itself has made this man strong, whom you see and know; and the faith that is through Jesus*v* has given him this perfect health in the presence of all of you.

3.13
Isa 52.13;
Acts 5.30;
Mt 27.2;
Acts 2.23;
Lk 23.4
3.14
Mk 1.24;
Acts 4.27;
7.52;
Mk 15.11;
Lk 23.18-25
3.15
Acts 5.31;
2.24, 32

p Gk *them*   *q* Or *from house to house*   *r* Or *sincere*   *s* Gk *the Nazorean*   *t* Gk *Men, Israelites*   *u* Or *child*
v Gk *him*

2.47 The body of Christ comprises those who have been regenerated and baptized, i.e., those who have made a credible profession of faith. Not all who profess Christ have truly been regenerated, and some who are not church members may indeed be born again. God knows the hearts of all people. The word for "church" (Gk. *ecclēsia*) is used in the N.T. to refer both to local congregations and to the church universal (e.g., 1 Cor 1.2; 2 Cor 1.1; Gal 1.2; Eph 1.22). Dispensationalists distinguish between Israel and the church; they use Eph 3.5, where it says that the church which had its beginnings at Pentecost was a mystery hidden from the ages and only then made known to people. On the other hand, Acts 7.38 mentions Israel as the *ecclēsia* in the wilderness, and many view the church as the new Israel of God (cf. Gal 6.16). In any event, the Calvary event is something to which the people of Israel looked forward to and to which the church since Pentecost looks back. The

saints of both the O.T. and the N.T. have been redeemed only by Christ's sacrifice.
3.6 Peter and John had no alms to give the cripple. But they had something else far more valuable to give—power in the name of Jesus, by which they healed the man for Christ's glory.
3.14,15 Peter forthrightly charged the Jews of Jerusalem with handing Jesus over to the Romans for execution. They could not escape their responsibility nor shrug off their guilt. This does not mean, however, that we may hold the Jews of our day responsible for what their ancestors did. The Bible gives no basis for anti-Semitism, for it breaches the second table of the law, which requires that we love our neighbors (including our enemies) as ourselves. All of us are at fault for the death of Jesus, since he was nailed to the cross for our sins and for the sins of the whole world (1 Jn 2.2).

17 "And now, friends,[w] I know that you acted in ignorance, as did also your rulers. 18 In this way God fulfilled what he had foretold through all the prophets, that his Messiah[x] would suffer. 19 Repent therefore, and turn to God so that your sins may be wiped out, 20 so that times of refreshing may come from the presence of the Lord, and that he may send the Messiah[y] appointed for you, that is, Jesus, 21 who must remain in heaven until the time of universal restoration that God announced long ago through his holy prophets. 22 Moses said, 'The Lord your God will raise up for you from your own people[w] a prophet like me. You must listen to whatever he tells you. 23 And it will be that everyone who does not listen to that prophet will be utterly rooted out of the people.' 24 And all the prophets, as many as have spoken, from Samuel and those after him, also predicted these days. 25 You are the descendants of the prophets and of the covenant that God gave to your ancestors, saying to Abraham, 'And in your descendants all the families of the earth shall be blessed.' 26 When God raised up his servant,[z] he sent him first to you, to bless you by turning each of you from your wicked ways."

2. The beginning of opposition

a. Peter and John arrested

4 While Peter and John[a] were speaking to the people, the priests, the captain of the temple, and the Sadducees came to them, 2 much annoyed because they were teaching the people and proclaiming that in Jesus there is the resurrection of the dead. 3 So they arrested them and put them in custody until the next day, for it was already evening. 4 But many of those who heard the word believed; and they numbered about five thousand.

b. Peter's defense before the council

5 The next day their rulers, elders, and scribes assembled in Jerusalem, 6 with Annas the high priest, Caiaphas, John,[b] and Alexander, and all who were of the high-priestly family. 7 When they had made the prisoners[c] stand in their midst, they inquired, "By what power or by what name did you do this?" 8 Then Peter, filled with the Holy Spirit, said to them, "Rulers of the people and elders, 9 if we are questioned today because of a good deed done to someone who was sick and are asked how this man has been healed, 10 let it be known to all of you, and to all the people of Israel, that this man is standing before you in good health by the name of Jesus Christ of Nazareth,[d] whom you crucified, whom God raised from the dead. 11 This Jesus[e] is

'the stone that was rejected by you, the builders;
    it has become the cornerstone.'[f]

12 There is salvation in no one else, for there is no other name under heaven given among mortals by which we must be saved."

c. Peter and John set free

13 Now when they saw the boldness of Peter and John and realized

3.17 Lk 23.34; Acts 13.27
3.18 Acts 2.23; Lk 24.27; Acts 17.3; 26.23
3.21 Acts 1.11; Mt 17.11; Lk 1.70
3.22 Deut 18.15; Acts 7.37
3.23 Deut 18.19
3.25 Acts 2.39; Rom 9.4, 8; Gen 12.3; 28.14
3.26 Acts 13.46; 2.24; v. 22
4.1 Lk 22.4; Mt 3.7; Acts 6.12
4.2 Acts 17.18; 23.8
4.3 Acts 5.18
4.4 Acts 2.41
4.5 Lk 23.13
4.6 Lk 3.2; Mt 26.3
4.8 Acts 13.9; Lk 23.13; v. 5
4.10 Acts 3.6; 2.24
4.11 Ps 118.22; Isa 28.16; Mt 21.42
4.12 Mt 1.21; Acts 10.43; 1 Tim 2.5, 6
4.13 v. 31; Mt 11.25; 1 Cor 1.27

w Gk brothers   x Or his Christ   y Or the Christ   z Or child   a Gk While they   b Other ancient authorities read Jonathan   c Gk them   d Gk the Nazorean   e Gk This   f Or keystone

3.17ff Peter gave his listeners and their leaders the benefit of the doubt — they may have crucified Jesus in ignorance. He hastened to inform them that a free pardon could be theirs; they must repent of their sins and believe on the very Messiah they executed.
3.19 Repentance followed by conversion results in pardon and forgiveness of sins (Isa 55.7) and the gift of the Holy Spirit (2.38).
4.1 The Sadducees. See note on Mt 3.7.
4.8 filled. The Greek word used here is in the aorist passive tense, suggesting that Peter was given imme-

diate inspiration by the Holy Spirit for this occasion, as a fulfillment of the promise of Jesus in Mt 10.19,20 (see also note on 6.5). We need not fear about what to say when we are forced to appear before kings and rulers. The same Holy Spirit will help us and give us the right words.
4.13 uneducated and ordinary men. To the members of the Sanhedrin, these Galileans were nonprofessional teachers and therefore to be scorned. Since they had no special training, their persuasive eloquence was most astonishing but fully in accord

that they were uneducated and ordinary men, they were amazed and recognized them as companions of Jesus. 14 When they saw the man who had been cured standing beside them, they had nothing to say in opposition. 15 So they ordered them to leave the council while they discussed the matter with one another. 16 They said, "What will we do with them? For it is obvious to all who live in Jerusalem that a notable sign has been done through them; we cannot deny it. 17 But to keep it from spreading further among the people, let us warn them to speak no more to anyone in this name." 18 So they called them and ordered them not to speak or teach at all in the name of Jesus. 19 But Peter and John answered them, "Whether it is right in God's sight to listen to you rather than to God, you must judge; 20 for we cannot keep from speaking about what we have seen and heard." 21 After threatening them again, they let them go, finding no way to punish them because of the people, for all of them praised God for what had happened. 22 For the man on whom this sign of healing had been performed was more than forty years old.

d. The report to the church

23 After they were released, they went to their friends[g] and reported what the chief priests and the elders had said to them. 24 When they heard it, they raised their voices together to God and said, "Sovereign Lord, who made the heaven and the earth, the sea, and everything in them, 25 it is you who said by the Holy Spirit through our ancestor David, your servant:[h]

'Why did the Gentiles rage,
    and the peoples imagine vain things?
26 The kings of the earth took their stand,
    and the rulers have gathered together
    against the Lord and against his Messiah.'[i]

27 For in this city, in fact, both Herod and Pontius Pilate, with the Gentiles and the peoples of Israel, gathered together against your holy servant[h] Jesus, whom you anointed, 28 to do whatever your hand and your plan had predestined to take place. 29 And now, Lord, look at their threats, and grant to your servants[j] to speak your word with all boldness, 30 while you stretch out your hand to heal, and signs and wonders are performed through the name of your holy servant[h] Jesus." 31 When they had prayed, the place in which they were gathered together was shaken; and they were all filled with the Holy Spirit and spoke the word of God with boldness.

32 Now the whole group of those who believed were of one heart and soul, and no one claimed private ownership of any possessions, but everything they owned was held in common. 33 With great power the apostles gave their testimony to the resurrection of the Lord Jesus, and great grace was upon them all. 34 There was not a needy person among them, for as many as owned lands or houses sold them and brought the proceeds of what was sold. 35 They laid it at the apostles' feet, and it was distributed

4.15
Mt 5.22
4.16
Jn 11.47;
Acts 3.7-10

4.18
Acts 5.40
4.19
Acts 5.28, 29
4.20
Acts 1.8; 2.32

4.24
2 Kings 19.15

4.25
Ps 2.1;
Acts 1.16

4.26
Heb 1.9
4.27
v. 30;
Lk 4.18;
Jn 10.36;
Mt 14.1;
Lk 23.12
4.28
Acts 2.23
4.29
vv. 13, 31;
Acts 9.27;
13.46; 28.31
4.30
Acts 2.43;
5.12; 3.6, 16;
v. 27
4.31
Acts 2.2, 4;
v. 29
4.32
Acts 5.12;
2.44
4.33
Acts 1.8; 1.22
4.34
Acts 2.45
4.35
v. 37;
Acts 5.2;
2.45; 6.1

g Gk their own   h Or child   i Or his Christ   j Gk slaves

with the teaching office of the Holy Spirit and the promise of Christ (Lk 12.11,12).
4.19,20 Peter and John were denied freedom to proclaim Christ publicly. Being men of principle, they refused to obey the ban and insisted they would do what God commanded and what was right, regardless of the consequences.
4.31 *shaken . . . filled with the Holy Spirit.* Once again, the apostles received a fresh infilling of the Spirit of God, enabling them to discharge their obligations to God by speaking his word with boldness. This infilling was unrelated to their being sealed and indwelt by the Spirit; this had already occurred and was not repeatable.
4.32 *no one claimed private ownership of any posses-*

sions. This passage does not support the notion that community of property was required in the early church. In every case the act of selling property and of giving the proceeds for the work of the church was voluntary. No coercion was applied. Peter clearly said that Ananias' property belonged to him, and once he sold it he was free to do as he pleased with the money (5.4). When money was given, it was used only to help those in need, not shared among all the saints. The donations were simply expressions of Christian love and concern. Any group of Christians has the right to engage in communal living, but they have no right to force anyone else to follow their pattern, nor do they have a biblical right to seize property by law or by force.

to each as any had need. 36 There was a Levite, a native of Cyprus, Joseph, to whom the apostles gave the name Barnabas (which means "son of encouragement"). 37 He sold a field that belonged to him, then brought the money, and laid it at the apostles' feet.

3. Discipline in the church

a. Ananias

5 But a man named Ananias, with the consent of his wife Sapphira, sold a piece of property; 2 with his wife's knowledge, he kept back some of the proceeds, and brought only a part and laid it at the apostles' feet. 3 "Ananias," Peter asked, "why has Satan filled your heart to lie to the Holy Spirit and to keep back part of the proceeds of the land? 4 While it remained unsold, did it not remain your own? And after it was sold, were not the proceeds at your disposal? How is it that you have contrived this deed in your heart? You did not lie to us[k] but to God!" 5 Now when Ananias heard these words, he fell down and died. And great fear seized all who heard of it. 6 The young men came and wrapped up his body,[l] then carried him out and buried him.

b. Sapphira

7 After an interval of about three hours his wife came in, not knowing what had happened. 8 Peter said to her, "Tell me whether you and your husband sold the land for such and such a price." And she said, "Yes, that was the price." 9 Then Peter said to her, "How is it that you have agreed together to put the Spirit of the Lord to the test? Look, the feet of those who have buried your husband are at the door, and they will carry you out." 10 Immediately she fell down at his feet and died. When the young men came in they found her dead, so they carried her out and buried her beside her husband. 11 And great fear seized the whole church and all who heard of these things.

4. The first persecution

a. Converts multiplied

12 Now many signs and wonders were done among the people through the apostles. And they were all together in Solomon's Portico. 13 None of the rest dared to join them, but the people held them in high esteem. 14 Yet more than ever believers were added to the Lord, great numbers of both men and women, 15 so that they even carried out the sick into the streets, and laid them on cots and mats, in order that Peter's shadow might fall on some of them as he came by. 16 A great number of people would also gather from the towns around Jerusalem, bringing the sick and those tormented by unclean spirits, and they were all cured.

b. The apostles imprisoned

17 Then the high priest took action; he and all who were with him

---

4.37
v. 35;
Acts 5.2

5.2
Acts 4.37

5.3
Deut 23.21;
Lk 22.3;
Jn 13.2, 7;
v. 9

5.5
vv. 10, 11

5.6
Jn 19.40

5.8
v. 2

5.9
v. 3

5.10
v. 5

5.11
v. 5;
Acts 19.17

5.12
Acts 2.43;
3.11; 4.32

5.13
Acts 2.47;
4.21

5.14
Acts 2.47;
11.24

5.15
Mt 9.21;
14.36;
Acts 19.12 2

5.17
Acts 15.5; 4.1

---

[k] Gk *to men*   [l] Meaning of Gk uncertain

5.3,4 When Ananias lied to the apostles, he actually lied to the Holy Spirit, an act that Peter declared was lying to God. The Holy Spirit is the third person of the Trinity. As God, he has all the attributes of deity; he is united with the Father and the Son and is equal to them. The Holy Spirit is eternal (Heb 9.14), omniscient (1 Cor 2.10), omnipresent (Ps 139.7–13), and omnipotent (Lk 1.35; Rom 15.19). He authored Scripture (2 Pet 1.20,21), had a part in creation (Gen 1.2), and participates in the redemption of sinners (Rom 8.9–11).
5.5 Judgment begins with the household of God (1 Pet 4.17). Here that judgment was executed when

Ananias *fell down and died.*
5.9 *you have agreed together to put the Spirit of the Lord to the test.* In effect Peter was asking Sapphira: "Did you think you could get away with this sin so that even the Holy Spirit would be unable to detect you? By your actions you have challenged the Holy Spirit."
5.16 *they were all cured.* Christ had given his apostles the power through the Holy Spirit to cure people. Though healings undoubtedly occur today, what distinguished the work of the apostles was that *all* were cured. This does not happen today; in fact very few are healed.

5.18
Acts 4.3
5.19
Acts 12.7;
16.26
5.20
Jn 6.63, 68
5.21
Acts 4.5, 6;
vv. 27, 34, 41

5.24
Acts 4.1

5.26
Acts 4.21

5.28
Acts 4.18;
2.33, 36;
3.15; 7.52;
Mt 23.35;
27.25
5.29
Acts 4.19
5.30
Acts 3.13, 15;
22.14; 10.39;
13.29;
Gal 3.13;
1 Pet 2.24
5.31
Acts 2.33;
Heb 2.10;
Acts 3.15
5.32
Lk 24.48;
Jn 15.26;
Rom 8.16
5.33
Acts 2.37;
7.54

5.38
Mt 15.13

5.39
Acts 7.51;
9.5; 11.17

(that is, the sect of the Sadducees), being filled with jealousy, 18 arrested the apostles and put them in the public prison. 19 But during the night an angel of the Lord opened the prison doors, brought them out, and said, 20 "Go, stand in the temple and tell the people the whole message about this life." 21 When they heard this, they entered the temple at daybreak and went on with their teaching.

When the high priest and those with him arrived, they called together the council and the whole body of the elders of Israel, and sent to the prison to have them brought. 22 But when the temple police went there, they did not find them in the prison; so they returned and reported, 23 "We found the prison securely locked and the guards standing at the doors, but when we opened them, we found no one inside." 24 Now when the captain of the temple and the chief priests heard these words, they were perplexed about them, wondering what might be going on. 25 Then someone arrived and announced, "Look, the men whom you put in prison are standing in the temple and teaching the people!" 26 Then the captain went with the temple police and brought them, but without violence, for they were afraid of being stoned by the people.

27 When they had brought them, they had them stand before the council. The high priest questioned them, 28 saying, "We gave you strict orders not to teach in this name,*m* yet here you have filled Jerusalem with your teaching and you are determined to bring this man's blood on us." 29 But Peter and the apostles answered, "We must obey God rather than any human authority.*n* 30 The God of our ancestors raised up Jesus, whom you had killed by hanging him on a tree. 31 God exalted him at his right hand as Leader and Savior that he might give repentance to Israel and forgiveness of sins. 32 And we are witnesses to these things, and so is the Holy Spirit whom God has given to those who obey him."

c. The counsel of Gamaliel

33 When they heard this, they were enraged and wanted to kill them. 34 But a Pharisee in the council named Gamaliel, a teacher of the law, respected by all the people, stood up and ordered the men to be put outside for a short time. 35 Then he said to them, "Fellow Israelites,*o* consider carefully what you propose to do to these men. 36 For some time ago Theudas rose up, claiming to be somebody, and a number of men, about four hundred, joined him; but he was killed, and all who followed him were dispersed and disappeared. 37 After him Judas the Galilean rose up at the time of the census and got people to follow him; he also perished, and all who followed him were scattered. 38 So in the present case, I tell you, keep away from these men and let them alone; because if this plan or this undertaking is of human origin, it will fail; 39 but if it is of God, you will not be able to overthrow them—in that case you may even be found fighting against God!"

---

m Other ancient authorities read *Did we not give you strict orders not to teach in this name?*   *n* Gk than men   *o* Gk Men, Israelites

---

5.19 God intervened here by sending his angel to open the prison doors and free the imprisoned followers of Jesus. This was not an act performed by a secret supporter of the apostles among the temple police, as some maintain.
5.32 The disciples testified that their sole source of power was the Spirit of God, who was working in them to accomplish the divine purpose. This same power is available to believers today.
5.34 *Gamaliel* was a well-known teacher under whom Saul of Tarsus studied (22.3). He was a rabbi who belonged to the liberal group of Jewish teachers who followed the interpretations of Hillel (a deeply respected rabbi who died shortly before the time of Jesus).

5.36 *Theudas* had led a revolt against the Roman authorities. Apparently, no other extant material refers to this man, although Josephus, the Jewish historian, *does* speak of a revolt led by a man named Theudas in A.D. 44. Since the name was common, it may well be that two revolutionary leaders had the same name.
5.37 *Judas the Galilean* is mentioned by Josephus as a bandit in the days of King Herod. He had led a revolt against the census being carried out by Quirinius in A.D. 6, though some question whether the Judas of this verse is the same person. Judas was defeated, but his movement—the Zealots—pressed on. This revolutionary party was dedicated to overthrowing Roman power by force of arms.

They were convinced by him, ⁴⁰and when they had called in the apostles, they had them flogged. Then they ordered them not to speak in the name of Jesus, and let them go. ⁴¹As they left the council, they rejoiced that they were considered worthy to suffer dishonor for the sake of the name. ⁴²And every day in the temple and at home*p* they did not cease to teach and proclaim Jesus as the Messiah. *q*

5. The first deacons

6 Now during those days, when the disciples were increasing in number, the Hellenists complained against the Hebrews because their widows were being neglected in the daily distribution of food. ²And the twelve called together the whole community of the disciples and said, "It is not right that we should neglect the word of God in order to wait on tables.*r* ³Therefore, friends,*s* select from among yourselves seven men of good standing, full of the Spirit and of wisdom, whom we may appoint to this task, ⁴while we, for our part, will devote ourselves to prayer and to serving the word." ⁵What they said pleased the whole community, and they chose Stephen, a man full of faith and the Holy Spirit, together with Philip, Prochorus, Nicanor, Timon, Parmenas, and Nicolaus, a proselyte of Antioch. ⁶They had these men stand before the apostles, who prayed and laid their hands on them.

7 The word of God continued to spread; the number of the disciples increased greatly in Jerusalem, and a great many of the priests became obedient to the faith.

6. The first martyrdom

a. The arrest of Stephen

8 Stephen, full of grace and power, did great wonders and signs among the people. ⁹Then some of those who belonged to the synagogue of the Freedmen (as it was called), Cyrenians, Alexandrians, and others of those from Cilicia and Asia, stood up and argued with Stephen. ¹⁰But they could not withstand the wisdom and the Spirit*t* with which he spoke. ¹¹Then they secretly instigated some men to say, "We have heard him speak blasphemous words against Moses and God." ¹²They stirred up the people as well as the elders and the scribes; then they suddenly confronted him, seized him, and brought him before the council. ¹³They set up false witnesses who said, "This man never stops saying things against this holy place and the law; ¹⁴for we have heard him say that this Jesus of Nazareth*u* will destroy this place and will change the customs

p Or from house to house   q Or the Christ   r Or keep accounts   s Gk brothers   t Or spirit   u Gk the Nazorean

---

5.40
Mt 10.17;
Mk 13.9
5.41
1 Pet 4.13,
16;
Jn 15.21
5.42
Acts 2.46;
8.35; 11.20;
17.18;
Gal 1.16

6.1
Acts 2.41, 47;
9.29; 11.20;
4.35

6.3
Jn 21.23;
Acts 1.15

6.5
Acts 11.19,
24; 8.5, 26;
21.8
6.6
Acts 1.24;
8.17; 9.17;
13.3;
1 Tim 4.14;
5.22;
2 Tim 1.6
6.7
Acts 12.24;
19.20;
Acts 13.8;
14.22;
Gal 1.23;
6.10

6.10
Lk 21.15;
Acts 5.39
6.11
Mt 26.59, 60

6.13
Acts 7.58;
21.28
6.14
Mt 26.61;
15.1; 21.21;
26.3; 28.17

5.42 Publicly and privately the apostles taught and preached despite the ban placed on those activities by the Jewish religious leaders. They obeyed God rather than these human leaders.
6.1 The *Hellenists* and the *Hebrews* may be distinguished as follows: the former were Jews who spoke Greek and followed some of the Greek customs; the latter were conservative Jews who spoke Hebrew (or Aramaic), refused to keep Greek customs, and were probably natives of Jerusalem. A certain tension between these diverse groups in the early church is not surprising.
6.3 The deacons to be selected had to meet three qualifications: (1) be men of good standing; (2) have the gift of wisdom; and, most important, (3) be full of the Holy Spirit. It seems apparent that not all of the believers in that day were full of the Spirit. If they had been, there would have been no need to specify this

as a qualification. Since all believers have been sealed and indwelt by the Spirit (Rom 8.9–11; Eph 1.14), it follows that the filling of the Spirit was something additional. Frequently this infilling takes place in the lives of believers subsequent to their conversion, when certain conditions have been met.
6.5 *full . . . of the Holy Spirit.* This phrase, indicating the abiding infilling of the Spirit in Stephen, has different connotations than the "filling of the Holy Spirit" (see note on 4.8). *Nicolaus*, one of the first seven deacons, was a Gentile who had become a Jewish proselyte at Antioch and had now become a Christian.

6.8 *full of grace and power*, i.e., Stephen had a strong faith, reinforced by the powerful presence of the Holy Spirit in his heart and life.

6.9 *synagogue.* See note on 13.5.

that Moses handed on to us." [15] And all who sat in the council looked intently at him, and they saw that his face was like the face of an angel.

b. The defense of Stephen

7.2
Acts 22.1;
Ps 29.3;
Gen 11.31;
15.7

7.3
Gen 12.1
7.4
Gen 12.5
7.5
Gen 12.7;
17.8; 26.3

7.6
Gen 15.13,
14;
Ex 12.40
7.7
Ex 3.12
7.8
Gen 17.9-11;
21.2-4;
25.26;
29.31ff

7.9
Gen 37.4, 11,
28; 39.2, 21,
23
7.10
Gen 41.37;
42.6
7.11
Gen 41.54
7.12
Gen 42.1, 2
7.13
Gen 45.1-4
7.14
Gen 45.9, 10;
46.26, 27;
Deut 10.22
7.15
Gen 46.5;
49.33;
Ex 1.6
7.16
Gen 23.16;
33.19;
Josh 24.32
7.17
Ex 1.7-9;
Ps 105.24, 25
7.19
Ex 1.10, 11,
15-22

7.22
1 Kings 4.30;
Isa 19.11

7 Then the high priest asked him, "Are these things so?" [2] And Stephen replied:

"Brothers[v] and fathers, listen to me. The God of glory appeared to our ancestor Abraham when he was in Mesopotamia, before he lived in Haran, [3] and said to him, 'Leave your country and your relatives and go to the land that I will show you.' [4] Then he left the country of the Chaldeans and settled in Haran. After his father died, God had him move from there to this country in which you are now living. [5] He did not give him any of it as a heritage, not even a foot's length, but promised to give it to him as his possession and to his descendants after him, even though he had no child. [6] And God spoke in these terms, that his descendants would be resident aliens in a country belonging to others, who would enslave them and mistreat them during four hundred years. [7] 'But I will judge the nation that they serve,' said God, 'and after that they shall come out and worship me in this place.' [8] Then he gave him the covenant of circumcision. And so Abraham[w] became the father of Isaac and circumcised him on the eighth day; and Isaac became the father of Jacob, and Jacob of the twelve patriarchs.

[9] "The patriarchs, jealous of Joseph, sold him into Egypt; but God was with him, [10] and rescued him from all his afflictions, and enabled him to win favor and to show wisdom when he stood before Pharaoh, king of Egypt, who appointed him ruler over Egypt and over all his household. [11] Now there came a famine throughout Egypt and Canaan, and great suffering, and our ancestors could find no food. [12] But when Jacob heard that there was grain in Egypt, he sent our ancestors there on their first visit. [13] On the second visit Joseph made himself known to his brothers, and Joseph's family became known to Pharaoh. [14] Then Joseph sent and invited his father Jacob and all his relatives to come to him, seventy-five in all; [15] so Jacob went down to Egypt. He himself died there as well as our ancestors, [16] and their bodies[x] were brought back to Shechem and laid in the tomb that Abraham had bought for a sum of silver from the sons of Hamor in Shechem.

[17] "But as the time drew near for the fulfillment of the promise that God had made to Abraham, our people in Egypt increased and multiplied [18] until another king who had not known Joseph ruled over Egypt. [19] He dealt craftily with our race and forced our ancestors to abandon their infants so that they would die. [20] At this time Moses was born, and he was beautiful before God. For three months he was brought up in his father's house; [21] and when he was abandoned, Pharaoh's daughter adopted him and brought him up as her own son. [22] So Moses was instructed in all the wisdom of the Egyptians and was powerful in his words and deeds.

---

v Gk Men, brothers   w Gk he   x Gk they

7.2ff Stephen's detailed defense of himself is broken off rather abruptly at v. 50. Evidently his enemies would not listen to him any further. Justice presupposes that the defendant has a right to state his case fully and fairly. In his discourse Stephen quoted from the Septuagint rather than from the Hebrew text of Scripture, just as we quote from English translations rather than from the Hebrew and the Greek originals. **7.6** *four hundred years.* Ex 12.40 says four hundred thirty years. "Four hundred" may be a round number here. Rabbinical tradition reckoned 400 years from Isaac's birth to the Exodus. Paul's 430-year figure (Gal 3.17) spans the divine promise from Abraham to the Exodus. Depending on the starting point, either figure is correct.

7.16 Some have supposed that Stephen made a mistake here. In the O.T. we read that Abraham purchased a field from Ephron the Hittite; it included what was called the cave of Machpelah, where he buried Sarah and where he, Isaac, and Jacob were also buried (Gen 23.17ff; 50.13). It was Jacob who made a land purchase from the children of Hamor, Shechem's father (Gen 33.19). At least two explanations have been offered. Some claim that the field Jacob purchased was the same field Abraham had bought, but that the land had changed hands at least once before Jacob repurchased it. Others simply claim that Stephen is compressing the history of the O.T. in order to get quickly to his main point, expressed in vv. 48–53.

23 "When he was forty years old, it came into his heart to visit his relatives, the Israelites.*y* 24 When he saw one of them being wronged, he defended the oppressed man and avenged him by striking down the Egyptian. 25 He supposed that his kinsfolk would understand that God through him was rescuing them, but they did not understand. 26 The next day he came to some of them as they were quarreling and tried to reconcile them, saying, 'Men, you are brothers; why do you wrong each other?' 27 But the man who was wronging his neighbor pushed Moses*z* aside, saying, 'Who made you a ruler and a judge over us? 28 Do you want to kill me as you killed the Egyptian yesterday?' 29 When he heard this, Moses fled and became a resident alien in the land of Midian. There he became the father of two sons.

30 "Now when forty years had passed, an angel appeared to him in the wilderness of Mount Sinai, in the flame of a burning bush. 31 When Moses saw it, he was amazed at the sight; and as he approached to look, there came the voice of the Lord: 32 'I am the God of your ancestors, the God of Abraham, Isaac, and Jacob.' Moses began to tremble and did not dare to look. 33 Then the Lord said to him, 'Take off the sandals from your feet, for the place where you are standing is holy ground. 34 I have surely seen the mistreatment of my people who are in Egypt and have heard their groaning, and I have come down to rescue them. Come now, I will send you to Egypt.'

35 "It was this Moses whom they rejected when they said, 'Who made you a ruler and a judge?' and whom God now sent as both ruler and liberator through the angel who appeared to him in the bush. 36 He led them out, having performed wonders and signs in Egypt, at the Red Sea, and in the wilderness for forty years. 37 This is the Moses who said to the Israelites, 'God will raise up a prophet for you from your own people*a* as he raised me up.' 38 He is the one who was in the congregation in the wilderness with the angel who spoke to him at Mount Sinai, and with our ancestors; and he received living oracles to give to us. 39 Our ancestors were unwilling to obey him; instead, they pushed him aside, and in their hearts they turned back to Egypt, 40 saying to Aaron, 'Make gods for us who will lead the way for us; as for this Moses who led us out from the land of Egypt, we do not know what has happened to him.' 41 At that time they made a calf, offered a sacrifice to the idol, and reveled in the works of their hands. 42 But God turned away from them and handed them over to worship the host of heaven, as it is written in the book of the prophets:

'Did you offer to me slain victims and sacrifices
    forty years in the wilderness, O house of Israel?
43 No; you took along the tent of Moloch,

y Gk *his brothers, the sons of Israel*   *z* Gk *him*   *a* Gk *your brothers*

7.23	Ex 2.11, 12
7.30	Ex 3.1, 2
7.32	Ex 3.6
7.33	Ex 3.5; Josh 5.15
7.34	Ex 3.7
7.35	Ex 14.19
7.36	Ex 12.41; 14.21
7.37	Deut 18.15, 18; Acts 3.22
7.38	Ex 19.17; Isa 63.9; Rom 3.2; Heb 5.12; 1 Pet 4.11
7.40	Ex 32.1, 23
7.41	Ex 32.4, 6; Ps 106.19
7.42	Ezek 20.25, 39; Am 5.25, 26

7.25 *they did not understand.* Stephen had been accused of blaspheming Moses (6.13,14). He in turn asked his listeners to look at what their ancestors had done to Moses, whom they did not understand when he tried to deliver them from their enemies. He warned them to take heed not to reject the one whom God had sent to deliver them from a worse Egypt. If they rejected Stephen's word from God, they would suffer a worse punishment than did their ancestors who died in the wilderness and did not enter the promised land.
7.30ff Rather than blaspheming Moses, Stephen favored him and quoted him with approbation. God had called Moses and sent him to deliver Israel from Egypt. Israel refused to obey Moses and went so far as to make a golden calf. Stephen argued that the Jews' treatment of himself was similar to the treatment accorded Moses by their ancestors, and thus they were guilty of the same kind of sin.
7.37 *as he raised me up,* i.e., "much like me." Jesus

occupied the offices of prophet, priest, and king. Here he is the prophet promised by Moses in Deut 18.15. As prophet, Jesus came to declare God's will, reveal God's person, and point people to God the Father by indicating that all have sinned and need a Savior. As priest (Heb 8.1), Jesus filled the office both of the one who offered the sacrifice and the one who was the sacrifice (the Lamb of God); he entered the Most Holy Place as a priest and sprinkled the blood (his own) on the mercy seat of God. As king, he inherited the throne of his father David. He who was rejected by the Jews and given a crown of thorns, a reed, and a cross, was raised from the dead and is now "exalted at the right hand of God" (2.33). From there he will someday come to judge the living and the dead as King of kings and Lord of lords (Rev 19.16), "and he will reign forever and ever" (Rev 11.15).
7.43 *Moloch* and *Rephan.* In Hebrew their names are *Sakkuth* and *Kaiwan* (Am 5.26), the former a Canaanite deity, the latter believed to be one of the

and the star of your god Rephan,
the images that you made to worship;
so I will remove you beyond Babylon.'

7.44
Ex 25.9, 40

44 "Our ancestors had the tent of testimony in the wilderness, as God[b] directed when he spoke to Moses, ordering him to make it according to the pattern he had seen. 45 Our ancestors in turn brought it in with Joshua when they dispossessed the nations that God drove out before our ancestors. And it was there until the time of David, 46 who found favor with God and asked that he might find a dwelling place for the house of Jacob.[c] 47 But it was Solomon who built a house for him. 48 Yet the Most High does not dwell in houses made with human hands;[d] as the prophet says,

7.45
Josh 3.14-17;
Ps 44.2
7.46
2 Sam 7.8-16;
Ps 132.1-5
7.48
1 Kings 8.27;
2 Chr 2.6

49 'Heaven is my throne,
and the earth is my footstool.
What kind of house will you build for me, says the Lord,
or what is the place of my rest?
50 Did not my hand make all these things?'

7.49
Isa 66.1, 2;
Mt 5.34, 35

51 "You stiff-necked people, uncircumcised in heart and ears, you are forever opposing the Holy Spirit, just as your ancestors used to do. 52 Which of the prophets did your ancestors not persecute? They killed those who foretold the coming of the Righteous One, and now you have become his betrayers and murderers. 53 You are the ones that received the law as ordained by angels, and yet you have not kept it."

7.51
Lev 26.41;
Jer 6.10; 9.26
7.52
2 Chr 36.16;
Mt 23.31,
37;
Acts 3.14
7.53
Ex 20.1;
Heb 2.2

c. The stoning of Stephen

54 When they heard these things, they became enraged and ground their teeth at Stephen.[e] 55 But filled with the Holy Spirit, he gazed into heaven and saw the glory of God and Jesus standing at the right hand of God. 56 "Look," he said, "I see the heavens opened and the Son of Man standing at the right hand of God!" 57 But they covered their ears, and with a loud shout all rushed together against him. 58 Then they dragged him out of the city and began to stone him; and the witnesses laid their coats at the feet of a young man named Saul. 59 While they were stoning Stephen, he prayed, "Lord Jesus, receive my spirit." 60 Then he knelt down and cried out in a loud voice, "Lord, do not hold this sin against them." When he had said this, he died.[f] 8 And Saul approved of their killing him.

7.55
Acts 6.5
7.56
Mt 3.16;
Dan 7.13
7.58
Lk 4.29;
Lev 24.16;
Deut 13.9, 10
7.59
Acts 9.14
7.60
Acts 9.40
8.1
Acts 7.58;
11.19

d. The scattering of the church

That day a severe persecution began against the church in Jerusalem, and all except the apostles were scattered throughout the countryside of Judea and Samaria. 2 Devout men buried Stephen and made loud lamenta-

8.2
Gen 23.2;
50.10;
2 Sam 3.31

b Gk he   c Other ancient authorities read for the God of Jacob   d Gk with hands   e Gk him   f Gk fell asleep

gods of ancient Egypt.
7.51 Stephen accused his listeners of resisting the Holy Spirit as their ancestors had done. That is, when the Jews in the O.T. resisted the prophets, they were resisting the Holy Spirit, who guided the prophets (cf. 2 Pet 1.20,21). Whoever persecutes or tries to silence those who speak under the influence of the Holy Spirit is guilty of the same sin.
7.52 Nothing Stephen said could have angered his listeners more than his accusation that they were betrayers and murderers of Jesus the Messiah. We must never forget, however, that Jews and Gentiles are equally responsible for the death of Jesus (see note on 3.14,15).
7.58 began to stone him. The Mishnah (a Jewish writing of the second century) relates that after a person

was convicted and sentenced to die by stoning, he would be taken to the stoning place outside the court. Before the actual execution the victim was called upon to make a confession. As he got close to the stoning place, his garments were removed. Then one of the witnesses would push the accused into a twelve-foot-deep pit. If this did not kill the victim, a second witness would drop a large stone on him. If he still lived, he would then be stoned by all the members of the congregation of Israel. Saul (Paul) was present at Stephen's death and approved the stoning.
8.1 See note on 13.9.
8.2 Devout men. It is not clear whether these were Christians who braved the persecution or whether they were godly and sympathetic Jews.

tion over him. ³But Saul was ravaging the church by entering house after house; dragging off both men and women, he committed them to prison.

8.3
Acts 7.58;
22.4; 25.10,
11;
1 Cor 15.9;
Gal 1.13;
Phil 3.6;
1 Tim 1.13

II. *Judea, Samaria, and on to Antioch of Syria (8.4–12.25)*

A. *The ministry of Philip*

1. *Philip at Samaria*

4 Now those who were scattered went from place to place, proclaiming the word. ⁵Philip went down to the city*g* of Samaria and proclaimed the Messiah*h* to them. ⁶The crowds with one accord listened eagerly to what was said by Philip, hearing and seeing the signs that he did, ⁷for unclean spirits, crying with loud shrieks, came out of many who were possessed; and many others who were paralyzed or lame were cured. ⁸So there was great joy in that city.

8.4
v. 1;
Acts 15.35
8.5
Acts 6.5
8.7
Mt 4.24

2. *Conversion of Simon the sorcerer*

9 Now a certain man named Simon had previously practiced magic in the city and amazed the people of Samaria, saying that he was someone great. ¹⁰All of them, from the least to the greatest, listened to him eagerly, saying, "This man is the power of God that is called Great." ¹¹And they listened eagerly to him because for a long time he had amazed them with his magic. ¹²But when they believed Philip, who was proclaiming the good news about the kingdom of God and the name of Jesus Christ, they were baptized, both men and women. ¹³Even Simon himself believed. After being baptized, he stayed constantly with Philip and was amazed when he saw the signs and great miracles that took place.

8.9
Acts 13.6;
5.36
8.10
Acts 14.11;
28.6
8.12
Acts 1.3; 2.38
8.13
v. 6;
Acts 19.11

14 Now when the apostles at Jerusalem heard that Samaria had accepted the word of God, they sent Peter and John to them. ¹⁵The two went down and prayed for them that they might receive the Holy Spirit ¹⁶(for as yet the Spirit had not come*i* upon any of them; they had only been baptized in the name of the Lord Jesus). ¹⁷Then Peter and John*j* laid their hands on them, and they received the Holy Spirit. ¹⁸Now when Simon saw that the Spirit was given through the laying on of the apostles' hands, he offered them money, ¹⁹saying, "Give me also this power so that anyone on whom I lay my hands may receive the Holy Spirit." ²⁰But Peter said to him, "May your silver perish with you, because you thought you could obtain God's gift with money! ²¹You have no part or share in this,

8.14
v. 1
8.15
Acts 2.38
8.16
Acts 19.2;
Mt 28.19;
Acts 10.48;
19.5
8.17
Acts 6.6; 2.4
8.20
Acts 2.38;
Mt 10.8;
2 Kings 5.16
8.21
Ps 78.37

g Other ancient authorities read *a city*   *h* Or *the Christ*   *i* Gk *fallen*   *j* Gk *they*

8.4 *those who were scattered,* i.e., the believers. The primary mission of the church is to proclaim the good news of salvation in Jesus. This mission can be accomplished by (1) evangelism through direct oral presentation or mass communication media; (2) medical missions, by which the healing of people's bodies opens the door to bringing healing to their souls through gospel witnessing; (3) education, by which people interested in improving themselves can be reached by the gospel; and (4) literary work (the translation of the Bible or parts of it, or the writing of books, articles, and tracts and their dissemination), by which people can come to know Christ.

8.9ff *Simon,* a magician, was thought to manifest the power of God. Following his dubious conversion he tried to buy the power of the Holy Spirit from the apostles so that he could convey it to others by laying on his hands (v. 19). No doubt he wanted this power to increase his authority and enlarge his prestige among the people. He was severely rebuked by Peter, who urged him to repent of his sin (v. 22). The word "simony" (buying or selling important church positions) is derived from this incident.

8.10 *This man is the power of God that is called Great.* The Samaritans attributed to Simon the great power of God, when actually his power came from Satan. In other words, devils may be mistaken for deities. This sort of thing will occur especially at the end of the age (Rev 13.2–5).

8.13 Miracles are effects in nature that cannot be attributed to any recognized operation of nature and are thus indicative of a superhuman power; they stand in contrast to God's providence (see note on Prov 16.33). Miracles are much rarer than God's providences, for God does not do supernaturally what can be done naturally. For example, a person generally recovers from sickness by providence, not by miracle. At times, however, God may choose to use a miracle in the healing of an individual, as a sign of his great power.

8.17ff *they received the Holy Spirit.* The receiving of the Holy Spirit must have been accompanied by some sign or signs that impressed Simon the sorcerer. Whatever it was, he wanted it and offered money if the apostles would give him that power.

for your heart is not right before God. 22 Repent therefore of this wickedness of yours, and pray to the Lord that, if possible, the intent of your heart may be forgiven you. 23 For I see that you are in the gall of bitterness and the chains of wickedness." 24 Simon answered, "Pray for me to the Lord, that nothing of what you *k* have said may happen to me."

25 Now after Peter and John *l* had testified and spoken the word of the Lord, they returned to Jerusalem, proclaiming the good news to many villages of the Samaritans.

3. Conversion of the Ethiopian eunuch

26 Then an angel of the Lord said to Philip, "Get up and go toward the south *m* to the road that goes down from Jerusalem to Gaza." (This is a wilderness road.) 27 So he got up and went. Now there was an Ethiopian eunuch, a court official of the Candace, queen of the Ethiopians, in charge of her entire treasury. He had come to Jerusalem to worship 28 and was returning home; seated in his chariot, he was reading the prophet Isaiah. 29 Then the Spirit said to Philip, "Go over to this chariot and join it." 30 So Philip ran up to it and heard him reading the prophet Isaiah. He asked, "Do you understand what you are reading?" 31 He replied, "How can I, unless someone guides me?" And he invited Philip to get in and sit beside him. 32 Now the passage of the scripture that he was reading was this:

"Like a sheep he was led to the slaughter,
    and like a lamb silent before its shearer,
        so he does not open his mouth.
33 In his humiliation justice was denied him.
    Who can describe his generation?
        For his life is taken away from the earth."

34 The eunuch asked Philip, "About whom, may I ask you, does the prophet say this, about himself or about someone else?" 35 Then Philip began to speak, and starting with this scripture, he proclaimed to him the good news about Jesus. 36 As they were going along the road, they came to some water; and the eunuch said, "Look, here is water! What is to prevent me from being baptized?" *n* 38 He commanded the chariot to stop, and both of them, Philip and the eunuch, went down into the water, and Philip *o* baptized him. 39 When they came up out of the water, the Spirit of the Lord snatched Philip away; the eunuch saw him no more, and went on his way rejoicing. 40 But Philip found himself at Azotus, and as he was

Margin references:

8.23 Isa 58.6; Heb 12.15
8.25 Lk 16.28; v. 40
8.26 Acts 5.19; v. 5
8.27 Ps 68.31; Zeph 3.10; Jn 12.20
8.29 Acts 10.19; 11.12; 13.2; 20.23; 21.11
8.32 Isa 53.7, 8
8.35 Mt 5.2; Lk 24.27; Acts 17.2; 18.28; 5.42
8.36 Acts 10.47
8.39 1 Kings 18.12; 2 Kings 2.16; Ezek 3.12, 14

k The Greek word for *you* and the verb *pray* are plural   *l* Gk *after they*   *m* Or *go at noon*   *n* Other ancient authorities add all or most of verse 37, *And Philip said, "If you believe with all your heart, you may." And he replied, "I believe that Jesus Christ is the Son of God."*   *o* Gk *he*

8.23 *you are in the gall of bitterness.* Simon was odious and abominable to God, and his end would be as bitter as gall.
8.26ff Philip was directed first by an angel to start his journey toward the south. Then the Holy Spirit commanded him to join himself to the chariot of the Ethiopian eunuch (v. 29). Neither the Spirit nor the angel explained the Scripture to the eunuch; this duty was reserved for the church, i.e., the human followers of Jesus. Wherever and whenever anyone sincerely wants to know God, God will in one way or another make himself known. Philip's witness was marked by humility, obedience, enthusiasm, boldness, guidance by the Spirit, and knowledge of the word of God. He preached Jesus, pressed for a decision, and followed the eunuch's commitment by water baptism. This passage illustrates what personal witnessing is all about. Christ has commanded the church to be a witnessing body. All witnessing must be done through the instrumentality and power of the Holy Spirit. Every believer is called to be a witness; who-

ever fails this call can become spiritually stagnant.
8.27 The Ethiopian eunuch had gone to Jerusalem to worship in the temple as a proselyte. He became a Christian under the witness of Philip and was the second Gentile convert mentioned in Acts (cf. note on 6.5).
8.29 The Holy Spirit spearheads the Christian mission: (1) he directs God's servants where, when, and what they are to do or preach (8.29; 10.19,20; 16.6,7; 1 Cor 2.13); (2) he chooses and commissions workers for service (13.2; 20.28); (3) he communicates God's truth to people (1.16; 1 Pet 1.11,12; 2 Pet 1.21); (4) he teaches the church the truth about Jesus (Jn 14.26; 1 Cor 12.3); (5) he testifies to the Son and magnifies him (Jn 15.26; 16.14); and (6) he reproves sinners and convicts them of their guilt (Jn 16.8).
8.39 Philip was miraculously transported by the Spirit of God from his place beside the eunuch to another destination. This would have provided the eunuch convincing proof that what had happened indeed proceeded from a miracle-working God.

passing through the region, he proclaimed the good news to all the towns until he came to Caesarea.

B. The conversion of Saul (Paul)

1. His call on the Damascus road

9 Meanwhile Saul, still breathing threats and murder against the disciples of the Lord, went to the high priest 2 and asked him for letters to the synagogues at Damascus, so that if he found any who belonged to the Way, men or women, he might bring them bound to Jerusalem. 3 Now as he was going along and approaching Damascus, suddenly a light from heaven flashed around him. 4 He fell to the ground and heard a voice saying to him, "Saul, Saul, why do you persecute me?" 5 He asked, "Who are you, Lord?" The reply came, "I am Jesus, whom you are persecuting. 6 But get up and enter the city, and you will be told what you are to do." 7 The men who were traveling with him stood speechless because they heard the voice but saw no one. 8 Saul got up from the ground, and though his eyes were open, he could see nothing; so they led him by the hand and brought him into Damascus. 9 For three days he was without sight, and neither ate nor drank.

2. His baptism by Ananias

10 Now there was a disciple in Damascus named Ananias. The Lord said to him in a vision, "Ananias." He answered, "Here I am, Lord." 11 The Lord said to him, "Get up and go to the street called Straight, and at the house of Judas look for a man of Tarsus named Saul. At this moment he is praying, 12 and he has seen in a vision*p* a man named Ananias come in and lay his hands on him so that he might regain his sight." 13 But Ananias answered, "Lord, I have heard from many about this man, how much evil he has done to your saints in Jerusalem; 14 and here he has authority from the chief priests to bind all who invoke your name." 15 But the Lord said to him, "Go, for he is an instrument whom I have chosen to bring my name before Gentiles and kings and before the people of Israel; 16 I myself will show him how much he must suffer for the sake of my name." 17 So Ananias went and entered the house. He laid his hands on Saul*q* and said, "Brother Saul, the Lord Jesus, who appeared to you on your way here, has sent me so that you may regain your sight and be filled with the Holy Spirit." 18 And immediately something like scales fell from his eyes, and his sight was restored. Then he got up and was baptized, 19 and after taking some food, he regained his strength.

3. His preaching at Damascus

For several days he was with the disciples in Damascus, 20 and immediately he began to proclaim Jesus in the synagogues, saying, "He is the Son of God." 21 All who heard him were amazed and said, "Is not this the man who made havoc in Jerusalem among those who invoked this name? And has he not come here for the purpose of bringing them bound before the

9.1 Acts 8.3; 22.4-16; 26.9-18
9.3 Acts 22.6; 26.12; 1 Cor 15.8
9.4 Acts 22.7; 26.14
9.7 Acts 22.9; 26.13, 14
9.8 Acts 22.11; Gal 1.17
9.10 Acts 22.12
9.11 Acts 21.39; 22.3
9.14 v. 21; Acts 7.59; 1 Cor 1.2; 2 Tim 2.22
9.15 Acts 13.2; Eph 3.7, 8; Gal 2.7, 8; Acts 25.22, 23; 26.1
9.16 Acts 20.23; 21.11; 2 Cor 11.23
9.17 Acts 22.12, 13; 8.17; 2.4; 4.31
9.19 Acts 26.20
9.21 Acts 8.3; Gal 1.13, 23

p Other ancient authorities lack in a vision   q Gk him

9.2 *the Way.* In Acts Christians were called the people of "the Way" (see also 19.9,23; 24.14,22). In 18.26 it is called "the Way of God," and in 16.17 "a way of salvation." Jesus said, "I am the way" (Jn 14.6); by faith in him people become followers of that way.
9.16 This prophetic word was fulfilled in the life and ministry of Paul. A partial description of Paul's sufferings is recorded in 2 Cor 11.23ff. Salvation does not guarantee exemption from suffering. As believ-

ers, we have only the certainty of grace to bear whatever God allows.
9.17 It is here, subsequent to his conversion, that Paul was filled with the Holy Spirit. His entire life from that moment forward indicates that, unlike persons such as Samson, he never lost the fullness of the Spirit. Though Paul did speak in tongues (1 Cor. 14.18), nothing is said whether he spoke in tongues at this time.

9.22
Acts 18.28

9.23
Acts 23.12;
25.3
9.24
2 Cor 11.32,
33

9.26
Acts 22.17;
Gal 1.17, 18
9.27
Acts 4.36;
vv. 20, 22

9.29
Acts 6.1;
11.20;
2 Cor 11.26
9.31
Acts 8.1

9.32
v. 13

9.34
Acts 3.6, 16;
4.10
9.35
1 Chr 5.16;
Acts 11.21

9.36
Jn 1.3;
1 Tim 2.10;
Titus 3.8
9.37
Acts 1.13
9.38
Acts 11.26
9.39
Acts 6.1

chief priests?" 22 Saul became increasingly more powerful and confounded the Jews who lived in Damascus by proving that Jesus*r* was the Messiah.*s*

4. His escape from the Jews

23 After some time had passed, the Jews plotted to kill him, 24 but their plot became known to Saul. They were watching the gates day and night so that they might kill him; 25 but his disciples took him by night and let him down through an opening in the wall,*t* lowering him in a basket.

5. His reception in Jerusalem

26 When he had come to Jerusalem, he attempted to join the disciples; and they were all afraid of him, for they did not believe that he was a disciple. 27 But Barnabas took him, brought him to the apostles, and described for them how on the road he had seen the Lord, who had spoken to him, and how in Damascus he had spoken boldly in the name of Jesus. 28 So he went in and out among them in Jerusalem, speaking boldly in the name of the Lord. 29 He spoke and argued with the Hellenists; but they were attempting to kill him. 30 When the believers*u* learned of it, they brought him down to Caesarea and sent him off to Tarsus.

31 Meanwhile the church throughout Judea, Galilee, and Samaria had peace and was built up. Living in the fear of the Lord and in the comfort of the Holy Spirit, it increased in numbers.

C. The ministry of Peter

1. Aeneas healed

32 Now as Peter went here and there among all the believers,*v* he came down also to the saints living in Lydda. 33 There he found a man named Aeneas, who had been bedridden for eight years, for he was paralyzed. 34 Peter said to him, "Aeneas, Jesus Christ heals you; get up and make your bed!" And immediately he got up. 35 And all the residents of Lydda and Sharon saw him and turned to the Lord.

2. Tabitha raised from the dead

36 Now in Joppa there was a disciple whose name was Tabitha, which in Greek is Dorcas.*w* She was devoted to good works and acts of charity. 37 At that time she became ill and died. When they had washed her, they laid her in a room upstairs. 38 Since Lydda was near Joppa, the disciples, who heard that Peter was there, sent two men to him with the request, "Please come to us without delay." 39 So Peter got up and went with them; and when he arrived, they took him to the room upstairs. All the widows stood beside him, weeping and showing tunics and other clothing that

r Gk that this *s* Or the Christ *t* Gk through the wall *u* Gk brothers *v* Gk all of them *w* The name Tabitha in Aramaic and the name Dorcas in Greek mean a gazelle

9.23ff Apparently the Jews of Damascus and the local government were annoyed with Paul and with his persistent preaching of Jesus. These enemies sought to kill him, but Paul escaped (cf. 2 Cor. 11.32,33). The city gates were guarded, so he could not pass through them. But he was in a house built on the city wall; this facilitated his escape. The disciples placed him in a large basket, tied a rope to its handle, then lowered Paul to the ground outside the wall.
9.26 *They were all afraid of him* because they feared that he might be putting on an act that was insincere, and then would entrap them and bring them to their

death. Such fears of one who have been such a notorious persecutor of the church were understandable. **9.34** In this miracle Peter called on the power of Jesus Christ and said, *Jesus Christ heals you.* During the time of Jesus and the early apostles miracles were abundant, just as they were in the critical times of Moses in Egypt and of Elijah and Elisha. At the end of the age, miracles both by Satan and believers may increase dramatically in number.
9.38ff The raising of Tabitha (Dorcas) created quite a stir, so that *many believed in the Lord.* No one could deny that the power of God was at work—the God who alone could bring the dead back to life.

Dorcas had made while she was with them. 40 Peter put all of them outside, and then he knelt down and prayed. He turned to the body and said, "Tabitha, get up." Then she opened her eyes, and seeing Peter, she sat up. 41 He gave her his hand and helped her up. Then calling the saints and widows, he showed her to be alive. 42 This became known throughout Joppa, and many believed in the Lord. 43 Meanwhile he stayed in Joppa for some time with a certain Simon, a tanner.

9.40
Mt 9.25;
Acts 7.60;
Mk 5.41, 42
9.41
v. 13
9.43
Acts 10.6

3. The conversion of Cornelius

a. Cornelius' vision

10 In Caesarea there was a man named Cornelius, a centurion of the Italian Cohort, as it was called. 2 He was a devout man who feared God with all his household; he gave alms generously to the people and prayed constantly to God. 3 One afternoon at about three o'clock he had a vision in which he clearly saw an angel of God coming in and saying to him, "Cornelius." 4 He stared at him in terror and said, "What is it, Lord?" He answered, "Your prayers and your alms have ascended as a memorial before God. 5 Now send men to Joppa for a certain Simon who is called Peter; 6 he is lodging with Simon, a tanner, whose house is by the seaside." 7 When the angel who spoke to him had left, he called two of his slaves and a devout soldier from the ranks of those who served him, 8 and after telling them everything, he sent them to Joppa.

10.2
vv. 22, 35
10.3
Acts 9.10;
3.1; 5.19
10.4
Acts 3.4;
Rev 8.4;
Mt 26.13
10.6
Acts 9.43

b. Peter's vision

9 About noon the next day, as they were on their journey and approaching the city, Peter went up on the roof to pray. 10 He became hungry and wanted something to eat; and while it was being prepared, he fell into a trance. 11 He saw the heaven opened and something like a large sheet coming down, being lowered to the ground by its four corners. 12 In it were all kinds of four-footed creatures and reptiles and birds of the air. 13 Then he heard a voice saying, "Get up, Peter; kill and eat." 14 But Peter said, "By no means, Lord; for I have never eaten anything that is profane or unclean." 15 The voice said to him again, a second time, "What God has made clean, you must not call profane." 16 This happened three times, and the thing was suddenly taken up to heaven.

10.9
Acts 11.5-14;
Mt 24.17
10.10
Acts 22.17
10.11
Acts 7.56;
Rev 19.11
10.14
Acts 9.5;
Lev 11.4;
20.25;
Deut 14.3, 7;
Ezek 4.14
10.15
v. 28;
Mt 15.11;
Rom 14.14,
17, 20;
1 Cor 10.25;
1 Tim 4.4;
Titus 1.15

c. The sending for Peter

17 Now while Peter was greatly puzzled about what to make of the vision that he had seen, suddenly the men sent by Cornelius appeared. They were asking for Simon's house and were standing by the gate. 18 They called out to ask whether Simon, who was called Peter, was staying there. 19 While Peter was still thinking about the vision, the Spirit

10.17
v. 3
10.19
Acts 11.12

10.1ff The conversion of the Roman centurion Cornelius, his household, and his friends, began a new phase in the spread of the good news (cf. Peter's comments in 15.7–9). But it would not have happened without a specific vision from God that caused Peter to preach to a Gentile.

10.2,3 *devout man who feared God.* Cornelius devotedly followed the Jewish way of life, except for circumcision. God sent an angel so that this Gentile could know the Messiah. The angel appeared in a vision that disturbed him but supplied him with the information he needed in order to hear the gospel and so obtain eternal life.

10.10ff For Peter to go to the home of Cornelius, some sort of earthshaking revelation from God was required. Jews did not enter Gentile homes even if the people in the house were God-fearing, and they certainly did not eat together, for Jewish orthodoxy dictated that Jews could not eat nonkosher food. Only by a special vision from Jesus himself was Peter con-

vinced to visit Cornelius (see note on v. 14).

10.12 We do not know whether the animals, reptiles, and birds were all unclean or whether there was a mixture of both clean and unclean creatures, though the latter is more likely. God intended to show that his grace was sufficient for both Jew and Gentile. What he declares to be clean, we may not call unclean.

10.14 *By no means, Lord.* This suggests that Jesus personally appeared to Peter and that Peter recognized his voice.

10.16 *This happened three times.* Either the vision came three times to assure Peter that God was certainly behind it, or possibly Peter said no to God twice and only after the third appearance of the vision was he willing to accept its message. God often has respect for our weakness; therefore, when we doubt the first call of God, he will give a second witness to assure us that it is from him.

10.19 *While Peter was still thinking.* An adequate understanding of the O.T. would have convinced Pe-

10.20
Acts 15.7

10.22
v. 2;
Acts 11.14

10.23
v. 45;
Acts 11.12

10.26
Acts 24.14,
15;
Rev 19.10
10.28
Jn 4.9;
18.28;
Acts 11.3;
15.8, 9

10.30
Acts 1.10;
Mt 28.3;
Mk 16.5;
Lk 24.4
10.34
Deut 10.17;
Rom 2.11;
Eph 6.9;
Col 3.25;
1 Pet 1.17
10.35
Acts 15.9
10.36
Isa 57.19;
Mt 28.18;
Rom 10.12;
Eph 1.20, 22
10.38
Acts 2.22;
Jn 3.2
10.39
Lk 24.48;
Acts 5.30
10.40
Acts 2.24
10.41
Jn 14.17, 22;
21.13
10.42
Mt 28.19,
20;
Rom 14.9;
2 Cor 5.10;
1 Pet 4.5
10.43
Isa 53.11;
Acts 26.22;
15.9;
Rom 10.11;
Gal 3.22
10.44
Acts 4.31;
8.15, 16;
11.15; 15.8

said to him, "Look, three[x] men are searching for you. [20] Now get up, go down, and go with them without hesitation; for I have sent them." [21] So Peter went down to the men and said, "I am the one you are looking for; what is the reason for your coming?" [22] They answered, "Cornelius, a centurion, an upright and God-fearing man, who is well spoken of by the whole Jewish nation, was directed by a holy angel to send for you to come to his house and to hear what you have to say." [23] So Peter[y] invited them in and gave them lodging.

d. *Peter's visit to Cornelius*

The next day he got up and went with them, and some of the believers[z] from Joppa accompanied him. [24] The following day they came to Caesarea. Cornelius was expecting them and had called together his relatives and close friends. [25] On Peter's arrival Cornelius met him, and falling at his feet, worshiped him. [26] But Peter made him get up, saying, "Stand up; I am only a mortal." [27] And as he talked with him, he went in and found that many had assembled; [28] and he said to them, "You yourselves know that it is unlawful for a Jew to associate with or to visit a Gentile; but God has shown me that I should not call anyone profane or unclean. [29] So when I was sent for, I came without objection. Now may I ask why you sent for me?"

[30] Cornelius replied, "Four days ago at this very hour, at three o'clock, I was praying in my house when suddenly a man in dazzling clothes stood before me. [31] He said, 'Cornelius, your prayer has been heard and your alms have been remembered before God. [32] Send therefore to Joppa and ask for Simon, who is called Peter; he is staying in the home of Simon, a tanner, by the sea.' [33] Therefore I sent for you immediately, and you have been kind enough to come. So now all of us are here in the presence of God to listen to all that the Lord has commanded you to say."

e. *Peter's sermon to Cornelius*

[34] Then Peter began to speak to them: "I truly understand that God shows no partiality, [35] but in every nation anyone who fears him and does what is right is acceptable to him. [36] You know the message he sent to the people of Israel, preaching peace by Jesus Christ—he is Lord of all. [37] That message spread throughout Judea, beginning in Galilee after the baptism that John announced: [38] how God anointed Jesus of Nazareth with the Holy Spirit and with power; how he went about doing good and healing all who were oppressed by the devil, for God was with him. [39] We are witnesses to all that he did both in Judea and in Jerusalem. They put him to death by hanging him on a tree; [40] but God raised him on the third day and allowed him to appear, [41] not to all the people but to us who were chosen by God as witnesses, and who ate and drank with him after he rose from the dead. [42] He commanded us to preach to the people and to testify that he is the one ordained by God as judge of the living and the dead. [43] All the prophets testify about him that everyone who believes in him receives forgiveness of sins through his name."

f. *The baptism of Cornelius*

[44] While Peter was still speaking, the Holy Spirit fell upon all who

[x] One ancient authority reads *two*; others lack the word   [y] Gk *he*   [z] Gk *brothers*

---

ter that God is the God of the Gentiles too (see Isa 42.6,7). *the Spirit said to him.* We do not know whether this was an audible voice or an inward persuasion of the Spirit. In any event, Peter obeyed the command to visit Cornelius.
10.33   *all of us are here . . . to listen.* Cornelius and his relatives and close friends were gathered together, prepared to listen to the word of God—an attentive audience indeed. This field was truly ripe to harvest

and only needed Peter to explain the way of salvation.
10.38   *God anointed Jesus of Nazareth with the Holy Spirit.* This was the fulfillment of Isa 61.1ff (cf. Lk 4.16–21). In his humanity Jesus was anointed by the Spirit and filled with the Spirit. So believers today can have the Spirit's anointing (see 1 Jn 2.27 and 2 Cor 1.21,22).
10.44-46   *the Holy Spirit fell upon all.* This has rightly been called the Gentile Pentecost. The Gen-

heard the word. 45 The circumcised believers who had come with Peter were astounded that the gift of the Holy Spirit had been poured out even on the Gentiles, 46 for they heard them speaking in tongues and extolling God. Then Peter said, 47 "Can anyone withhold the water for baptizing these people who have received the Holy Spirit just as we have?" 48 So he ordered them to be baptized in the name of Jesus Christ. Then they invited him to stay for several days.

g. Peter's defense of Gentile evangelization

11 Now the apostles and the believers[a] who were in Judea heard that the Gentiles had also accepted the word of God. 2 So when Peter went up to Jerusalem, the circumcised believers[b] criticized him, 3 saying, "Why did you go to uncircumcised men and eat with them?" 4 Then Peter began to explain it to them, step by step, saying, 5 "I was in the city of Joppa praying, and in a trance I saw a vision. There was something like a large sheet coming down from heaven, being lowered by its four corners; and it came close to me. 6 As I looked at it closely I saw four-footed animals, beasts of prey, reptiles, and birds of the air. 7 I also heard a voice saying to me, 'Get up, Peter; kill and eat.' 8 But I replied, 'By no means, Lord; for nothing profane or unclean has ever entered my mouth.' 9 But a second time the voice answered from heaven, 'What God has made clean, you must not call profane.' 10 This happened three times; then everything was pulled up again to heaven. 11 At that very moment three men, sent to me from Caesarea, arrived at the house where we were. 12 The Spirit told me to go with them and not to make a distinction between them and us.[c] These six brothers also accompanied me, and we entered the man's house. 13 He told us how he had seen the angel standing in his house and saying, 'Send to Joppa and bring Simon, who is called Peter; 14 he will give you a message by which you and your entire household will be saved.' 15 And as I began to speak, the Holy Spirit fell upon them just as it had upon us at the beginning. 16 And I remembered the word of the Lord, how he had said, 'John baptized with water, but you will be baptized with the Holy Spirit.' 17 If then God gave them the same gift that he gave us when we believed in the Lord Jesus Christ, who was I that I could hinder God?" 18 When they heard this, they were silenced. And they praised God, saying, "Then God has given even to the Gentiles the repentance that leads to life."

D. Barnabas at Antioch

19 Now those who were scattered because of the persecution that took place over Stephen traveled as far as Phoenicia, Cyprus, and Antioch, and they spoke the word to no one except Jews. 20 But among them were some men of Cyprus and Cyrene who, on coming to Antioch, spoke to the Hellenists[d] also, proclaiming the Lord Jesus. 21 The hand of the Lord was with them, and a great number became believers and turned to the Lord.

a Gk brothers　b Gk lacks believers　c Or not to hesitate　d Other ancient authorities read Greeks

Cross references

10.45 v. 23; Acts 11.18
10.47 Acts 8.36; 11.17
10.48 1 Cor 1.17; Acts 2.38; 8.16; 19.5
11.2 Acts 10.45
11.3 Acts 10.28; Gal 2.12
11.4 Lk 1.3
11.5 Acts 10.9-32
11.9 Acts 10.15
11.12 Acts 8.29; 15.9; 10.23
11.13 Acts 10.30
11.15 Acts 10.44; 2.4
11.16 Mt 3.11; Jn 1.26, 33; Acts 1.5; Joel 2.28; 3.18
11.17 Acts 10.45, 47
11.18 Rom 10.12, 13; 2 Cor 7.10
11.19 Acts 8.1, 4
11.20 Acts 4.36; 6.5; 13.1; 5.42
11.21 Lk 1.66; Acts 2.47; 9.35

Commentary

tiles spoke with tongues and extolled God, convincing Peter that this was from God and that the Gentiles, like believing Jews, were heirs of the kingdom. Such an outpouring of the Spirit on Gentiles amazed Peter and his companions.

10.47,48 The converts were born again, sealed, and indwelt by the Spirit before they were baptized with water. Those who reject the notion of baptismal regeneration point to this text, while the proponents of that doctrine use Jn 3.5 to support their view.

11.1–3 The Gentiles received the Word of God, believed on Jesus, and were baptized. But they were not circumcised. The first ecumenical council had not yet taken place (Acts 15), so the circumcision ques-

tion was open for debate. The early church was plagued by legalism, particularly as it related to circumcision (see Paul's letter to the Galatians).

11.4ff Peter defended his evangelizing the Gentiles without circumcising them by recounting what had happened to him in the conversion of Cornelius. The fact that the Holy Spirit had come upon those Gentiles validated his ministry and confirmed the fact that the gospel was for uncircumcised Gentiles as well as for circumcised Jews.

11.21 *The hand of the Lord was with them.* Those who preached were ordinary believers, not apostles or ordained ministers. Yet God worked in them and through them, and many believed. Lay witnesses to

11.23
Acts 13.43;
14.22
11.24
Acts 6.5;
v. 21;
Acts 5.14
11.25
Acts 9.11, 30
11.26
Acts 26.28

22 News of this came to the ears of the church in Jerusalem, and they sent Barnabas to Antioch. 23 When he came and saw the grace of God, he rejoiced, and he exhorted them all to remain faithful to the Lord with steadfast devotion; 24 for he was a good man, full of the Holy Spirit and of faith. And a great many people were brought to the Lord. 25 Then Barnabas went to Tarsus to look for Saul, 26 and when he had found him, he brought him to Antioch. So it was that for an entire year they met with *e* the church and taught a great many people, and it was in Antioch that the disciples were first called "Christians."

11.27
Acts 18.22;
1 Cor 12.28
11.28
Acts 21.10
11.29
Rom 15.26;
1 Cor 16.1;
2 Cor 9.1
11.30
Acts 12.25;
14.23

27 At that time prophets came down from Jerusalem to Antioch. 28 One of them named Agabus stood up and predicted by the Spirit that there would be a severe famine over all the world; and this took place during the reign of Claudius. 29 The disciples determined that according to their ability, each would send relief to the believers *f* living in Judea; 30 this they did, sending it to the elders by Barnabas and Saul.

E. Herod's persecution

1. Martyrdom of James; imprisonment of Peter

12.2
Mt 4.21;
20.23
12.3
Acts 24.27;
Ex 12.15;
23.15
12.5
Eph 6.18;
1 Thess 5.17

12 About that time King Herod laid violent hands upon some who belonged to the church. 2 He had James, the brother of John, killed with the sword. 3 After he saw that it pleased the Jews, he proceeded to arrest Peter also. (This was during the festival of Unleavened Bread.) 4 When he had seized him, he put him in prison and handed him over to four squads of soldiers to guard him, intending to bring him out to the people after the Passover. 5 While Peter was kept in prison, the church prayed fervently to God for him.

2. Deliverance of Peter

12.6
Acts 21.33
12.7
Acts 5.19;
16.26

6 The very night before Herod was going to bring him out, Peter, bound with two chains, was sleeping between two soldiers, while guards in front of the door were keeping watch over the prison. 7 Suddenly an

e Or were guests of   f Gk brothers

Jesus Christ have led many to know Christ. God accomplishes what he wants however he is pleased to do so.

11.22 Barnabas was officially delegated by the church to investigate the situation at Antioch. Ministers and evangelists do have a responsibility to a larger body of believers, to which they give an accounting and under whose direction they serve (cf. 13.1–4).
11.26 *Christians.* This is the first instance in which believers are called Christians, a word that appears only two other times in the N.T. (26.28; 1 Pet 4.16). In Antioch the word may have been used as a slur.
11.27 This is the first mention of Christian prophets in the N.T. John the Baptist and Jesus were called prophets (cf. Lk 1.76; 13.33). Besides Agabus (see next note), Luke refers to prophets in the church at Antioch (13.1); Judas and Silas are called prophets (15.32), and the four unmarried daughters of Philip prophesied (21.9). Prophets are mentioned in 1 Cor 11.4,5; 12.28; 14.29–32,37; Eph 4.11; we do not know whether the prophets referred to in Eph 2.20 and 3.5 are O.T. or N.T. prophets.
11.28 *Agabus,* who came from Jerusalem, prophesied the coming famine; later he predicted that Paul would be shackled and bound over to the Gentiles (21.10,11). The gift of prophecy was not limited to the apostles. Tradition says that Agabus was one of the seventy (Lk 10.1–20) and that he was later martyred. *Claudius* was the Roman emperor in A.D. 41–54. He was a nephew of the emperor Tiberius

and a grandson of Livia, the wife of Augustus. Agrippina, his last wife, was his niece. He adopted her son Nero, who succeeded him as emperor.
11.30 The relief for the hungry in Judea was limited to the Christian community. Obviously the small group of Christians could not send enough money to feed all those suffering in the famine. Christian mercy begins with helping those who belong to Jesus; after that, we must help those who are outside the kingdom (cf. Gal 6.10). *elders.* This is the first mention of elders in the N.T. church. Other references to elders in the Jerusalem church include 15.2,4,6,22,23; 16.4; 21.18. References to elders elsewhere include 14.23; 20.17. Outside of the Acts they are mentioned in 1 Tim 4.14; 5.17–19; Titus 1.5; Jas 5.14; 1 Pet 5.1,5; 2 Jn 1; 3 Jn 1. Of their origin, nothing is said. Probably the office was taken from the Jewish pattern of elders in the synagogue (see note on Titus 1.5ff).
12.1 *Herod* Agrippa I was a grandson of Herod the Great. Born in 11 B.C., he was educated in Rome and made tetrarch of Iturea, Trachonitis, and Gaulinitis in A.D. 37 by Emperor Gaius. Gaius also gave him the title of king. Then he was made ruler over Galilee and Perea; later Emperor Claudius extended his kingdom to include Judea and Samaria.
12.2 *He had James . . . killed with the sword.* James was the first of the apostles to suffer martyrdom. God did not reveal why he permitted James to die and Peter to live. James' brother John outlived all of the apostles.

angel of the Lord appeared and a light shone in the cell. He tapped Peter on the side and woke him, saying, "Get up quickly." And the chains fell off his wrists. 8 The angel said to him, "Fasten your belt and put on your sandals." He did so. Then he said to him, "Wrap your cloak around you and follow me." 9 Peter[g] went out and followed him; he did not realize that what was happening with the angel's help was real; he thought he was seeing a vision. 10 After they had passed the first and the second guard, they came before the iron gate leading into the city. It opened for them of its own accord, and they went outside and walked along a lane, when suddenly the angel left him. 11 Then Peter came to himself and said, "Now I am sure that the Lord has sent his angel and rescued me from the hands of Herod and from all that the Jewish people were expecting."

3. The testimony of Peter

12 As soon as he realized this, he went to the house of Mary, the mother of John whose other name was Mark, where many had gathered and were praying. 13 When he knocked at the outer gate, a maid named Rhoda came to answer. 14 On recognizing Peter's voice, she was so overjoyed that, instead of opening the gate, she ran in and announced that Peter was standing at the gate. 15 They said to her, "You are out of your mind!" But she insisted that it was so. They said, "It is his angel." 16 Meanwhile Peter continued knocking; and when they opened the gate, they saw him and were amazed. 17 He motioned to them with his hand to be silent, and described for them how the Lord had brought him out of the prison. And he added, "Tell this to James and to the believers."[h] Then he left and went to another place.

4. Herod's punishment of the guards

18 When morning came, there was no small commotion among the soldiers over what had become of Peter. 19 When Herod had searched for him and could not find him, he examined the guards and ordered them to be put to death. Then he went down from Judea to Caesarea and stayed there.

5. Herod's death

20 Now Herod[i] was angry with the people of Tyre and Sidon. So they came to him in a body; and after winning over Blastus, the king's chamberlain, they asked for a reconciliation, because their country depended on the king's country for food. 21 On an appointed day Herod put on his royal robes, took his seat on the platform, and delivered a public address to them. 22 The people kept shouting, "The voice of a god, and not of a mortal!" 23 And immediately, because he had not given the glory to God, an angel of the Lord struck him down, and he was eaten by worms and died.

24 But the word of God continued to advance and gain adherents. 25 Then after completing their mission Barnabas and Saul returned to[j] Jerusalem and brought with them John, whose other name was Mark.

g Gk He   h Gk brothers   i Gk he   j Other ancient authorities read from

---

12.9
Acts 9.10

12.10
Acts 16.26

12.11
Lk 15.17;
Dan 3.28;
6.22;
2 Cor 1.10;
2 Pet 2.9

12.12
Acts 15.37;
v. 5

12.13
Jn 18.16, 17

12.14
Lk 24.41

12.15
Gen 48.16;
Mt 18.10

12.17
Acts 13.16;
19.33; 21.40

12.19
Acts 16.27;
27.42

12.20
Mt 11.21;
1 Kings 5.9,
11;
Ezek 27.17

12.23
1 Sam 25.38;
2 Sam 24.17

12.24
Acts 6.7;
19.20

12.25
Acts 13.5; 13;
15.37

12.10 Skeptics suppose that Peter was secretly delivered by human hand. Scripture, however, makes it plain that the iron gate leading to the city opened of itself; it was a miraculous act.
12.13ff A strange scene indeed! Rhoda responded to Peter's knocking at the gate; she recognized the apostle's voice but refused to open the gate. She ran to tell the others who were praying for Peter. They refused to believe that their prayers had been answered, in-

sisted that Rhoda was out of her mind, and preferred to believe that Peter was dead and that an angel was making use of his name. But God had indeed performed the unexpected!
12.24 The more the church was persecuted, the more it grew by God's grace, just as Israel in Egypt grew greatly. Here the death of James multiplied the number of believers.

III. *Throughout the Roman empire with Paul (13.1–28.31)*

A. First missionary journey

1. *The call of Paul and Barnabas*

13.1
Acts 11.22-26

13 Now in the church at Antioch there were prophets and teachers: Barnabas, Simeon who was called Niger, Lucius of Cyrene, Manaen a member of the court of Herod the ruler,[k] and Saul. 2 While they were worshiping the Lord and fasting, the Holy Spirit said, "Set apart for me Barnabas and Saul for the work to which I have called them." 3 Then after fasting and praying they laid their hands on them and sent them off.

13.2
Acts 9.15;
22.21; 14.26
13.3
Acts 6.65;
14.26

2. *Their ministry on Cyprus*

13.4
vv. 2, 3;
Acts 4.36
13.5
Acts 9.20
13.6
Acts 8.9
13.7
vv. 8, 12
13.8
Acts 8.9;
vv. 7, 12;
Acts 6.7
13.9
Acts 4.8
13.10
Mt 13.38;
Jn 8.44;
Hos 14.9
13.11
Ex 9.3
13.12
vv. 7, 8;
Acts 8.25

4 So, being sent out by the Holy Spirit, they went down to Seleucia; and from there they sailed to Cyprus. 5 When they arrived at Salamis, they proclaimed the word of God in the synagogues of the Jews. And they had John also to assist them. 6 When they had gone through the whole island as far as Paphos, they met a certain magician, a Jewish false prophet, named Bar-Jesus. 7 He was with the proconsul, Sergius Paulus, an intelligent man, who summoned Barnabas and Saul and wanted to hear the word of God. 8 But the magician Elymas (for that is the translation of his name) opposed them and tried to turn the proconsul away from the faith. 9 But Saul, also known as Paul, filled with the Holy Spirit, looked intently at him 10 and said, "You son of the devil, you enemy of all righteousness, full of all deceit and villainy, will you not stop making crooked the straight paths of the Lord? 11 And now listen — the hand of the Lord is against you, and you will be blind for a while, unable to see the sun." Immediately mist and darkness came over him, and he went about groping for someone to lead him by the hand. 12 When the proconsul saw what had happened, he believed, for he was astonished at the teaching about the Lord.

3. *Their ministry to Perga and Antioch*

13.13
Acts 15.38

13 Then Paul and his companions set sail from Paphos and came to Perga in Pamphylia. John, however, left them and returned to Jerusalem; 14 but they went on from Perga and came to Antioch in Pisidia. And on the sabbath day they went into the synagogue and sat down. 15 After the reading of the law and the prophets, the officials of the synagogue sent them a message, saying, "Brothers, if you have any word of exhortation

13.14
Acts 14.19,
21; 16.13

[k] Gk *tetrarch*

13.1 *Teachers* as a distinct group are referred to here and in 1 Cor 12.28,29; Eph 4.11; Heb 5.12; Jas 3.1. Paul called himself a teacher in 1 Tim 2.7 and 2 Tim 1.11, and his teaching ministry is mentioned in 11.26; 15.35; 18.11; 20.20; 28.31.
13.2ff The missionary call for Paul and Barnabas came when the gathered people of God were worshiping and fasting; there the Holy Spirit made his will known. The church laid hands on them and sent them away. Missionaries should be certain that the Spirit of God has called them and then look to the church to ratify the call and send them forth. This does not negate, however, the responsibility that all of us have been given to witness to those around us.
13.5 A *synagogue* (Gk. *synagōgē*) means literally "a place where people gather together." The origin of the Jewish synagogue is hazy, but it can probably be traced to the fact that the dispersion of the Jews left them without a temple. Synagogues were established in order to worship God. The services included the

reading and exposition of the O.T., prayer, praise, and thanksgiving (see 13.15; 15.21; Mt 6.5; Lk 4.16–21). Paul usually began his preaching in the synagogues of the cities he visited, telling worshipers about Jesus the Messiah.
13.6 The *Bar-Jesus* of this verse is called Elymas in v. 8. This man saw the gospel as a threat, for he had power with Sergius Paulus the proconsul and thought that if the latter became a Christian, he would lose his influence. Paul, filled with the Spirit, rebuked him and said he would be blinded. This happened immediately, and what Elymas feared took place: Sergius Paulus became a Christian.
13.9 Saul was the apostle's Hebrew name, possibly named after the most famous Benjaminite, King Saul (cf. Phil 3.5); Paul was his Greek name.
13.13 John Mark appears to have left Paul and Barnabas without giving them a reason or seeking their consent. This was to have repercussions later on in the relationship between Barnabas and Paul (15.36–40).

for the people, give it." 16 So Paul stood up and with a gesture began to speak:

"You Israelites,*l* and others who fear God, listen. 17 The God of this people Israel chose our ancestors and made the people great during their stay in the land of Egypt, and with uplifted arm he led them out of it. 18 For about forty years he put up with*m* them in the wilderness. 19 After he had destroyed seven nations in the land of Canaan, he gave them their land as an inheritance 20 for about four hundred fifty years. After that he gave them judges until the time of the prophet Samuel. 21 Then they asked for a king; and God gave them Saul son of Kish, a man of the tribe of Benjamin, who reigned for forty years. 22 When he had removed him, he made David their king. In his testimony about him he said, 'I have found David, son of Jesse, to be a man after my heart, who will carry out all my wishes.' 23 Of this man's posterity God has brought to Israel a Savior, Jesus, as he promised; 24 before his coming John had already proclaimed a baptism of repentance to all the people of Israel. 25 And as John was finishing his work, he said, 'What do you suppose that I am? I am not he. No, but one is coming after me; I am not worthy to untie the thong of the sandals*n* on his feet.'

26 "My brothers, you descendants of Abraham's family, and others who fear God, to us*o* the message of this salvation has been sent. 27 Because the residents of Jerusalem and their leaders did not recognize him or understand the words of the prophets that are read every sabbath, they fulfilled those words by condemning him. 28 Even though they found no cause for a sentence of death, they asked Pilate to have him killed. 29 When they had carried out everything that was written about him, they took him down from the tree and laid him in a tomb. 30 But God raised him from the dead; 31 and for many days he appeared to those who came up with him from Galilee to Jerusalem, and they are now his witnesses to the people. 32 And we bring you the good news that what God promised to our ancestors 33 he has fulfilled for us, their children, by raising Jesus; as also it is written in the second psalm,

'You are my Son;
　today I have begotten you.'

34 As to his raising him from the dead, no more to return to corruption, he has spoken in this way,

'I will give you the holy promises made to David.'

35 Therefore he has also said in another psalm,

'You will not let your Holy One experience corruption.'

36 For David, after he had served the purpose of God in his own generation, died,*p* was laid beside his ancestors, and experienced corruption; 37 but he whom God raised up experienced no corruption. 38 Let it be known to you therefore, my brothers, that through this man forgiveness of sins is proclaimed to you; 39 by this Jesus*q* everyone who believes is set free from all those sins*r* from which you could not be freed by the

13.17
Deut 7.6-8

13.18
Ex 16.35;
Deut 1.31
13.19
Deut 7.1;
Josh 19.51
13.20
Judg 2.16;
1 Sam 3.20
13.21
1 Sam 8.5;
10.1
13.22
1 Sam 13.14;
15.23, 26
13.23
Isa 11.1;
Mt 1.21;
Rom 11.26
13.24
Mt 3.1;
Lk 3.3
13.25
Mt 3.11;
Lk 3.16
13.27
Lk 23.13;
Acts 3.17;
Lk 24.27
13.28
Mt 27.22
13.29
Lk 18.31;
Mt 27.59
13.30
Mt 28.6
13.31
Mt 28.16;
Lk 24.48
13.32
Gen 3.15;
Rom 4.13
13.33
Ps 2.7
13.34
Isa 55.3

13.35
Ps 16.10;
Acts 2.27
13.36
Acts 2.29;
1 Kings 2.10
13.38
Lk 24.47

13.39
Rom 3.28;
Acts 10.43

---

l Gk Men, Israelites　*m* Other ancient authorities read cared for　*n* Gk untie the sandals　*o* Other ancient authorities read you　*p* Gk fell asleep　*q* Gk this　*r* Gk all

---

13.23–25 Jesus was one of David's posterity and the Savior according to divine promise. Since many of the Jews believed that John the Baptist was a prophet, Paul injected him into the picture and spoke of his preaching of the need for repentance. Nonetheless, John refused to dignify himself as that prophet who should come; rather, he pointed to the true prophet, Jesus Christ.
13.27 The Jews condemned Jesus because they did not recognize him as the Savior. They knew and read the words of the prophets, but their hearts were so darkened that they could not understand the word of God. No one can make sense out of the Scriptures

without the help of the Holy Spirit.
13.30,31 *God raised him from the dead.* David was dead and his body still lay in his tomb. But Jesus is alive, for God raised him back to life. Many saw him in his resurrection and witnessed to that truth. To the apostle, the resurrection fulfilled the O.T. promise of God (vv. 34,35; see Ps 16.10; Isa 55.3). The resurrection is the main pillar by which the whole fabric of the gospel is maintained.
13.38–41 Paul closed his message by imploring his listeners to receive the forgiveness of their sins in and through Jesus Christ and by warning them against the sin of unbelief.

law of Moses. 40 Beware, therefore, that what the prophets said does not happen to you:

41 'Look, you scoffers!

Be amazed and perish,
  for in your days I am doing a work,
    a work that you will never believe, even if someone
      tells you.' "

42 As Paul and Barnabas[s] were going out, the people urged them to speak about these things again the next sabbath. 43 When the meeting of the synagogue broke up, many Jews and devout converts to Judaism followed Paul and Barnabas, who spoke to them and urged them to continue in the grace of God.

44 The next sabbath almost the whole city gathered to hear the word of the Lord.[t] 45 But when the Jews saw the crowds, they were filled with jealousy; and blaspheming, they contradicted what was spoken by Paul. 46 Then both Paul and Barnabas spoke out boldly, saying, "It was necessary that the word of God should be spoken first to you. Since you reject it and judge yourselves to be unworthy of eternal life, we are now turning to the Gentiles. 47 For so the Lord has commanded us, saying,

'I have set you to be a light for the Gentiles,
  so that you may bring salvation to the ends of the earth.' "

48 When the Gentiles heard this, they were glad and praised the word of the Lord; and as many as had been destined for eternal life became believers. 49 Thus the word of the Lord spread throughout the region. 50 But the Jews incited the devout women of high standing and the leading men of the city, and stirred up persecution against Paul and Barnabas, and drove them out of their region. 51 So they shook the dust off their feet in protest against them, and went to Iconium. 52 And the disciples were filled with joy and with the Holy Spirit.

4. Their ministry at Iconium

14 The same thing occurred in Iconium, where Paul and Barnabas[s] went into the Jewish synagogue and spoke in such a way that a great number of both Jews and Greeks became believers. 2 But the unbelieving Jews stirred up the Gentiles and poisoned their minds against the brothers. 3 So they remained for a long time, speaking boldly for the Lord, who testified to the word of his grace by granting signs and wonders to be done through them. 4 But the residents of the city were divided; some sided with the Jews, and some with the apostles. 5 And when an attempt was made by both Gentiles and Jews, with their rulers, to mistreat them and to stone them, 6 the apostles[s] learned of it and fled to Lystra and Derbe, cities of Lycaonia, and to the surrounding country; 7 and there they continued proclaiming the good news.

5. Their ministry at Lystra

8 In Lystra there was a man sitting who could not use his feet and had

[s] Gk they   [t] Other ancient authorities read God

13.45,46 The success of Paul's preaching aroused the envy and hatred of some Jews, who contradicted all he said and went so far as to blaspheme the name Paul preached. This rejection by the Jews led Paul and Barnabas to turn with the same gospel to the Gentiles.
14.6 When Paul and Barnabas learned that the enemies of the gospel intended to do them bodily harm, they fled from Iconium to Lystra and Derbe. Instead of seeking martyrdom by remaining in Iconium, they prudently left the city. God did not intend for his people to seek martyrdom, though they were to wel-

come it and submit to it when there was nothing they could do about it. In the will of God we are to preserve our lives as long as we can.
14.8,9 Both Peter (3.1–8) and Paul healed a man crippled from birth. The two incidents differed in that this one had faith, whereas the first one expected from Peter nothing but alms, yet God graciously healed him. Paul had the spiritual gift of discernment (1 Cor 12.10) and sensed the faith of that man. He commanded him to do what he had never done before: stand up on his feet and walk.

Cross references (left margin):
13.40 Jn 6.45
13.41 Hab 1.5
13.42 v. 14
13.43 Acts 11.23; 14.22
13.45 Acts 18.6; 1 Pet 4.4; Jude 10
13.46 v. 26; Acts 3.26; 18.6; 28.28
13.47 Isa 49.6; Lk 2.32
13.48 Acts 2.47; Rom 3.28ff
13.51 Mt 10.14; Mk 6.11; Lk 9.5; Acts 18.6
13.52 Acts 2.4
14.1 Acts 13.51; 13.5; 2.47; 18.4
14.3 Heb 2.4; Jn 4.48
14.4 Acts 17.4, 5; v. 14
14.5 2 Tim 3.11
14.6 Mt 10.23
14.8 Acts 3.2

never walked, for he had been crippled from birth. 9 He listened to Paul as he was speaking. And Paul, looking at him intently and seeing that he had faith to be healed, 10 said in a loud voice, "Stand upright on your feet." And the man^u sprang up and began to walk. 11 When the crowds saw what Paul had done, they shouted in the Lycaonian language, "The gods have come down to us in human form!" 12 Barnabas they called Zeus, and Paul they called Hermes, because he was the chief speaker. 13 The priest of Zeus, whose temple was just outside the city,^v brought oxen and garlands to the gates; he and the crowds wanted to offer sacrifice. 14 When the apostles Barnabas and Paul heard of it, they tore their clothes and rushed out into the crowd, shouting, 15 "Friends,^w why are you doing this? We are mortals just like you, and we bring you good news, that you should turn from these worthless things to the living God, who made the heaven and the earth and the sea and all that is in them. 16 In past generations he allowed all the nations to follow their own ways; 17 yet he has not left himself without a witness in doing good—giving you rains from heaven and fruitful seasons, and filling you with food and your hearts with joy." 18 Even with these words, they scarcely restrained the crowds from offering sacrifice to them.

19   But Jews came there from Antioch and Iconium and won over the crowds. Then they stoned Paul and dragged him out of the city, supposing that he was dead. 20 But when the disciples surrounded him, he got up and went into the city. The next day he went on with Barnabas to Derbe.

6. Their return to Antioch

21   After they had proclaimed the good news to that city and had made many disciples, they returned to Lystra, then on to Iconium and Antioch. 22 There they strengthened the souls of the disciples and encouraged them to continue in the faith, saying, "It is through many persecutions that we must enter the kingdom of God." 23 And after they had appointed elders for them in each church, with prayer and fasting they entrusted them to the Lord in whom they had come to believe.

24   Then they passed through Pisidia and came to Pamphylia. 25 When they had spoken the word in Perga, they went down to Attalia. 26 From there they sailed back to Antioch, where they had been commended to the grace of God for the work^x that they had completed. 27 When they arrived, they called the church together and related all that God had done with them, and how he had opened a door of faith for the Gentiles. 28 And they stayed there with the disciples for some time.

B. The Jerusalem conference

1. The problem stated

15   Then certain individuals came down from Judea and were teaching the brothers, "Unless you are circumcised according to the

---

^u Gk he   ^v Or The priest of Zeus-Outside-the-City   ^w Gk Men   ^x Or committed in the grace of God to the work

---

14.9
Acts 3.4;
10.4;
Mt 9.28, 29
14.11
Acts 8.10;
28.6

14.15
Acts 10.26;
Jas 5.17;
1 Sam 12.21;
Jer 14.22;
1 Cor 8.4;
Gen 1.1;
Ps 146.6;
Rev 14.7
14.16
Ps 81.12;
Acts 17.30;
1 Pet 4.3
14.17
Acts 17.27;
Rom 1.20;
Deut 11.14;
Job 5.10;
Ps 65.10
14.19
Acts 13.45;
2 Cor 11.25;
2 Tim 3.11
14.20
vv. 22, 28

14.22
Acts 11.23;
13.43;
Jn 16.33;
1 Thess 3.3;
2 Tim 3.12
14.23
Titus 1.5;
Acts 11.30;
13.3; 20.32
14.26
Acts 11.19;
13.1, 3;
15.40
14.27
Acts 15.4, 12;
21.19;
1 Cor 16.9;
2 Cor 2.12;
Col 4.3

15.1
v. 24;
Gal 2.12;
v. 5;
Gal 5.2;
Acts 6.14

14.12 The residents of Lystra looked on Barnabas and Paul as gods, and planned to offer sacrifices to them. The apostles tore their clothes, repulsed by the insult this was to their God in heaven, and stated plainly that they were just like other mortals (14.15). The main difference between them and these pagans lay in the fact that Barnabas and Paul were regenerated believers.
14.19 Here at Lystra Paul experienced stoning, the only time he was stoned (see 2 Cor 11.25; vv.23–33 gives a long list of Paul's sufferings). The ones who stoned him dragged him out of the city and left him for dead. It is not impossible that Paul really was dead

and that God revived him to continue his ministry. He was given grace to bear what God called him to endure. He stands as a model for those who must suffer in the will of God, knowing that God loves them and will deliver them through death, if not before.
14.27,28 Paul and his small band returned to Antioch of Syria, from where they had been sent on their missionary tour, and reported what had happened and how God had opened the door of faith for the Gentiles. When God opens a door, no one can shut it. They spent some time in Antioch with their friends in the church.
15.1 The enemies of the gospel caught up with Paul

15.2
v. 7;
Gal 2.2;
Acts 11.30

custom of Moses, you cannot be saved." 2 And after Paul and Barnabas had no small dissension and debate with them, Paul and Barnabas and some of the others were appointed to go up to Jerusalem to discuss this question with the apostles and the elders. 3 So they were sent on their way by the church, and as they passed through both Phoenicia and Samaria, they reported the conversion of the Gentiles, and brought great joy to all the believers.*y* 4 When they came to Jerusalem, they were welcomed by the church and the apostles and the elders, and they reported all that God had done with them. 5 But some believers who belonged to the sect of the Pharisees stood up and said, "It is necessary for them to be circumcised and ordered to keep the law of Moses."

15.3
Acts 20.38;
Rom 15.24;
1 Cor 16.6,
11;
Acts 14.27

15.4
v. 12;
Acts 14.27

2. The council deciding

6 The apostles and the elders met together to consider this matter. 7 After there had been much debate, Peter stood up and said to them, "My brothers,*z* you know that in the early days God made a choice among you, that I should be the one through whom the Gentiles would hear the message of the good news and become believers. 8 And God, who knows the human heart, testified to them by giving them the Holy Spirit, just as he did to us; 9 and in cleansing their hearts by faith he has made no distinction between them and us. 10 Now therefore why are you putting God to the test by placing on the neck of the disciples a yoke that neither our ancestors nor we have been able to bear? 11 On the contrary, we believe that we will be saved through the grace of the Lord Jesus, just as they will."

15.7
Acts 10.19,
20; 20.24

15.8
Acts 1.24;
10.44, 47

15.9
Acts 10.28,
34, 43; 11.12

15.10
Mt 23.4;
Gal 5.1

15.11
Rom 3.24;
Eph 2.5-8;
Titus 2.11;
3.4, 5

12 The whole assembly kept silence, and listened to Barnabas and Paul as they told of all the signs and wonders that God had done through them among the Gentiles. 13 After they finished speaking, James replied, "My brothers,*z* listen to me. 14 Simeon has related how God first looked favorably on the Gentiles, to take from among them a people for his name. 15 This agrees with the words of the prophets, as it is written,

15.12
Jn 4.48;
Acts 14.27

15.13
Acts 12.17

15.15
Acts 13.40

15.16
Am 9.11, 12;
Jer 12.15

16   'After this I will return,
          and I will rebuild the dwelling of David, which has fallen;
          from its ruins I will rebuild it,
          and I will set it up,
17   so that all other peoples may seek the Lord —

y Gk *brothers*   *z* Gk *Men, brothers*

---

and Barnabas at Antioch. Coming from Jerusalem they insisted that Gentiles had to be circumcised and keep the law of Moses in order to be saved. This created no small dissension among the believers and for Paul and Barnabas.

15.2 Paul and Barnabas were appointed to go to Jerusalem to settle the question of circumcision and keeping the law in a conference with the apostles and elders of the church there. The case for the gospel would be strengthened if the apostles and elders in Jerusalem confirmed what Paul and Barnabas taught. It was generally agreed that the apostles and elders in Jerusalem were the ones who could best decide the issue.

15.4,5 Paul and Barnabas received a royal welcome in Jerusalem and gave a full report of what God had done on their missionary journey. They were embraced as believers and were shown love and friendship. Some Pharisees who had become Christians immediately challenged Paul by insisting upon the necessity to circumcise all who believed on Jesus. Thus the debate began.

15.6ff After much debate, Peter stood up to address the assembly. Again he testified how the Holy Spirit had come on Gentile believers who had not been cir-

cumcised (cf. 10.44–48). If by giving the Holy Spirit God showed he was satisfied with believers who were not circumcised, why should the church not accept this? Refusing to do so would be an offense to God and to Gentile believers. Christ came to proclaim liberty to the captives, not bondage to the law.

15.13ff Up to this point Paul, Barnabas, and Peter had their say, agreeing with each other that circumcision is not necessary for salvation. Now James, the leader of the church in Jerusalem, entered the fray and spoke on behalf of these brothers, supporting their view ("Simeon" in v. 14 means Peter). After giving Scripture (Am 9.11,12) to support his view, James rendered a definitive judgment that God did not insist on circumcision as essential to salvation. But James went on to suggest that Gentiles stay away from things polluted by idols, from fornication, from things strangled, and from blood. Thus James made some allowance for sensitivities of the Pharisees until they had matured in the faith. Abstaining from fornication is clearly mentioned elsewhere in the N.T. (e.g., 1 Cor 6.18; 1 Thes 4.3); the concern over Jewish food laws and eating meat sacrificed to idols remained an issue of debate (see 1 Cor 8–10; Rom 14:1 – 15.6).

even all the Gentiles over whom my name has been called.
Thus says the Lord, who has been making these things
18 known from long ago.'*a*
19 Therefore I have reached the decision that we should not trouble those
Gentiles who are turning to God, 20 but we should write to them to abstain
only from things polluted by idols and from fornication and from whatever
has been strangled*b* and from blood. 21 For in every city, for generations
past, Moses has had those who proclaim him, for he has been read aloud
every sabbath in the synagogues."

3. The decision communicated

22   Then the apostles and the elders, with the consent of the whole
church, decided to choose men from among their members*c* and to send
them to Antioch with Paul and Barnabas. They sent Judas called Barsabbas, and Silas, leaders among the brothers, 23 with the following letter:
"The brothers, both the apostles and the elders, to the believers*d* of
Gentile origin in Antioch and Syria and Cilicia, greetings. 24 Since we have
heard that certain persons who have gone out from us, though with no
instructions from us, have said things to disturb you and have unsettled
your minds,*e* 25 we have decided unanimously to choose representatives*f*
and send them to you, along with our beloved Barnabas and Paul, 26 who
have risked their lives for the sake of our Lord Jesus Christ. 27 We have
therefore sent Judas and Silas, who themselves will tell you the same
things by word of mouth. 28 For it has seemed good to the Holy Spirit and
to us to impose on you no further burden than these essentials: 29 that you
abstain from what has been sacrificed to idols and from blood and from
what is strangled*g* and from fornication. If you keep yourselves from
these, you will do well. Farewell."

30   So they were sent off and went down to Antioch. When they
gathered the congregation together, they delivered the letter. 31 When its
members*h* read it, they rejoiced at the exhortation. 32 Judas and Silas,
who were themselves prophets, said much to encourage and strengthen
the believers.*d* 33 After they had been there for some time, they were sent
off in peace by the believers*d* to those who had sent them.*i* 35 But Paul
and Barnabas remained in Antioch, and there, with many others, they
taught and proclaimed the word of the Lord.

C. Second missionary journey

1. Asia Minor

a. Separation of Paul and Barnabas

36   After some days Paul said to Barnabas, "Come, let us return and
visit the believers*d* in every city where we proclaimed the word of the

---

a Other ancient authorities read *things.* 18*Known to God from of old are all his works.'* *b* Other ancient
authorities lack *and from whatever has been strangled* *c* Gk *from among them* *d* Gk *brothers* *e* Other
ancient authorities add *saying, 'You must be circumcised and keep the law,'* *f* Gk *men* *g* Other ancient
authorities lack *and from what is strangled* *h* Gk *When they* *i* Other ancient authorities add verse 34,
But it seemed good to Silas to remain there

Cross-references (right margin):

15.20
v. 29;
1 Cor 8.7-13;
10.7, 8,
14-28;
Rev 2.14, 20;
Gen 9.4;
Lev 3.17;
Deut 12.16,
23
15.21
Acts 13.15;
2 Cor 3.14,
15
15.22
Acts 11.20;
vv. 27, 32, 40
15.23
vv. 1, 41;
Acts 23.26;
Jas 1.1
15.24
v. 1;
Gal 1.7; 5.10
15.26
Acts 14.19;
1 Cor 15.30
15.29
v. 20;
Acts 21.25;
Lev 17.14
15.33
Acts 16.36;
1 Cor 16.11;
Heb 11.31
15.36ff
Acts 13.4, 13,
14, 51; 14.1,
6, 24, 25

15.22 The conference in Jerusalem did not end until
James had unanimous agreement of the apostles, elders, and the whole church for the verdict he rendered. The Jerusalem leaders sent a delegation back
to the Gentile believers in Antioch with a letter. Judas
and Silas, leading men from Jerusalem, brought the
letter that supported the views of Paul and Barnabas.
15.29 With the sending of this letter, the first
ecumenical church council ever held came to its conclusion. The Holy Spirit conveyed his will through
the apostles and elders, who felt assured that he had
spoken to them (see especially v. 28). Decisions made

apart from such a conviction are often wrong. Believers cannot go it alone, however sensible and prudent
they think their conclusions to be. The Holy Spirit is
both teacher and leader.
15.36ff Paul and Barnabas had a difference of opinion over John Mark. When they could not agree, they
separated, Paul taking Silas with him and Barnabas
taking Mark. Paul and Barnabas transcended their
difficulties without resorting to hostility. This solution establishes a pattern for us in facing conflicts with
others. Later, Paul and John Mark worked together
again (Philem 24; 2 Tim 4.11).

15.37
Acts 12.12
15.38
Acts 13.13

15.41
Acts 16.5

16.1
Acts 14.6;
19.22;
Rom 16.21;
1 Cor 4.17;
2 Tim 1.2;
1.5
16.3
Gal 2.3
16.4
Acts 15.28,
29; 15.2;
11.30
16.5
Acts 15.41

16.6
Acts 18.23;
2.9
16.7
v. 8;
Lk 24.49;
Rom 8.9;
Gal 4.6
16.8
v. 11;
2 Cor 2.12;
2 Tim 4.13
16.9
Acts 9.10;
18.5; 20.1, 3;
27.2
16.10
2 Cor 2.13

16.11
v. 8;
2 Tim 4.13
16.12
Phil 1.1;
Acts 18.5;
19.21, 22,
29; 20.1, 3;
27.2
16.13
Acts 13.14
16.14
Lk 24.45
16.15
Acts 11.14;
Lk 24.29

Lord and see how they are doing." 37 Barnabas wanted to take with them John called Mark. 38 But Paul decided not to take with them one who had deserted them in Pamphylia and had not accompanied them in the work. 39 The disagreement became so sharp that they parted company; Barnabas took Mark with him and sailed away to Cyprus. 40 But Paul chose Silas and set out, the believers[j] commending him to the grace of the Lord. 41 He went through Syria and Cilicia, strengthening the churches.

b. Selection of Timothy

16 Paul[k] went on also to Derbe and to Lystra, where there was a disciple named Timothy, the son of a Jewish woman who was a believer; but his father was a Greek. 2 He was well spoken of by the believers[j] in Lystra and Iconium. 3 Paul wanted Timothy to accompany him; and he took him and had him circumcised because of the Jews who were in those places, for they all knew that his father was a Greek. 4 As they went from town to town, they delivered to them for observance the decisions that had been reached by the apostles and elders who were in Jerusalem. 5 So the churches were strengthened in the faith and increased in numbers daily.

c. The Macedonian call

6 They went through the region of Phrygia and Galatia, having been forbidden by the Holy Spirit to speak the word in Asia. 7 When they had come opposite Mysia, they attempted to go into Bithynia, but the Spirit of Jesus did not allow them; 8 so, passing by Mysia, they went down to Troas. 9 During the night Paul had a vision: there stood a man of Macedonia pleading with him and saying, "Come over to Macedonia and help us." 10 When he had seen the vision, we immediately tried to cross over to Macedonia, being convinced that God had called us to proclaim the good news to them.

2. The Macedonian ministry

a. At Philippi

11 We set sail from Troas and took a straight course to Samothrace, the following day to Neapolis, 12 and from there to Philippi, which is a leading city of the district[l] of Macedonia and a Roman colony. We remained in this city for some days. 13 On the sabbath day we went outside the gate by the river, where we supposed there was a place of prayer; and we sat down and spoke to the women who had gathered there. 14 A certain woman named Lydia, a worshiper of God, was listening to us; she was from the city of Thyatira and a dealer in purple cloth. The Lord opened her heart to listen eagerly to what was said by Paul. 15 When she and her household were baptized, she urged us, saying, "If you have judged me to be faithful to the Lord, come and stay at my home." And she prevailed upon us.

---

j Gk brothers   k Gk He   l Other authorities read a city of the first district

---

16.3 Paul had argued strongly that circumcision was no longer required (Gal 2.3–5); yet here he had Timothy circumcised. Principle did not require it to be done, but expediency made it appropriate. Had he not done so, the progress of the gospel would have been set back and evangelization made more difficult. Scripture does lay down the maxim that what is wrong in principle should never be done, however expedient it may appear to be. But many acts are not wrong in principle and may be done or not done, depending on the circumstances (cf. 1 Cor 9 and notes).
16.6 The apostolic band was forbidden by the Holy

Spirit to preach the word in Asia. We do not know whether this was by way of inward persuasion of the Spirit or caused by external circumstances. Either way, they knew they were being led by the Spirit. **16.10** Here, for the first time, the word "we" becomes part of the narrative voice in Acts. This means that Luke, the author of the book, had joined himself to Paul in his ministry. He went with Paul from Troas to Philippi, but he left the party when they left Philippi (v. 40). The other "we" section of Acts begins in Philippi several years later (20.5) and continues through much of the remainder of the book.

16 One day, as we were going to the place of prayer, we met a slave-girl who had a spirit of divination and brought her owners a great deal of money by fortune-telling. 17 While she followed Paul and us, she would cry out, "These men are slaves of the Most High God, who proclaim to you[m] a way of salvation." 18 She kept doing this for many days. But Paul, very much annoyed, turned and said to the spirit, "I order you in the name of Jesus Christ to come out of her." And it came out that very hour.

19 But when her owners saw that their hope of making money was gone, they seized Paul and Silas and dragged them into the marketplace before the authorities. 20 When they had brought them before the magistrates, they said, "These men are disturbing our city; they are Jews 21 and are advocating customs that are not lawful for us as Romans to adopt or observe." 22 The crowd joined in attacking them, and the magistrates had them stripped of their clothing and ordered them to be beaten with rods. 23 After they had given them a severe flogging, they threw them into prison and ordered the jailer to keep them securely. 24 Following these instructions, he put them in the innermost cell and fastened their feet in the stocks.

25 About midnight Paul and Silas were praying and singing hymns to God, and the prisoners were listening to them. 26 Suddenly there was an earthquake, so violent that the foundations of the prison were shaken; and immediately all the doors were opened and everyone's chains were unfastened. 27 When the jailer woke up and saw the prison doors wide open, he drew his sword and was about to kill himself, since he supposed that the prisoners had escaped. 28 But Paul shouted in a loud voice, "Do not harm yourself, for we are all here." 29 The jailer[n] called for lights, and rushing in, he fell down trembling before Paul and Silas. 30 Then he brought them outside and said, "Sirs, what must I do to be saved?" 31 They answered, "Believe on the Lord Jesus, and you will be saved, you and your household." 32 They spoke the word of the Lord[o] to him and to all who were in his house. 33 At the same hour of the night he took them and washed their wounds; then he and his entire family were baptized without delay. 34 He brought them up into the house and set food before them; and he and his entire household rejoiced that he had become a believer in God.

35 When morning came, the magistrates sent the police, saying, "Let those men go." 36 And the jailer reported the message to Paul, saying, "The magistrates sent word to let you go; therefore come out now and go in peace." 37 But Paul replied, "They have beaten us in public, uncondemned, men who are Roman citizens, and have thrown us into prison; and now are they going to discharge us in secret? Certainly not! Let them come and take us out themselves." 38 The police reported these words to the magistrates, and they were afraid when they heard that they were Roman citizens; 39 so they came and apologized to them. And they took them out and asked them to leave the city. 40 After leaving the prison they went to Lydia's home; and when they had seen and encouraged the brothers and sisters[p] there, they departed.

16.16 Deut 18.11; 1 Sam 28.3, 7
16.17 Mk 5.7
16.19 Acts 19.25, 26; 15.40; 17.6, 7; Jas 2.6
16.20 Acts 17.6
16.22 2 Cor 11.23, 25; 1 Thess 2.2
16.23 vv. 27, 36
16.24 Jer 20.2, 3
16.25 Eph 5.19
16.26 Acts 4.31; 5.19; 12.7, 10
16.27 Acts 12.19
16.30 Acts 2.37; 9.6; 22.10
16.31 Jn 3.16, 36; 6.47; 1 Jn 5.10
16.33 v. 25
16.34 Acts 11.14
16.36 vv. 23, 27
16.37 Acts 22.25-27
16.38 Acts 22.29
16.39 Mt 8.34
16.40 v. 14

---

m Other ancient authorities read *to us*   n Gk *He*   o Other ancient authorities read *word of God*
p Gk *brothers*

16.18 Paul successfully exorcised the demon who had inhabited the slave girl, performing this action in the name of the Lord Jesus Christ. Though the concept of demons entering an individual can be abused, many cases of demon possession and exorcism are genuine. **16.26** Paul and Silas, jailed in Philippi, were beaten and their feet put in stocks. Yet they prayed and sang praises to God. The earthquake that occasioned their release has been questioned, but it was clearly a natural event that was occasioned by God's supernatural intervention and accomplished his purpose to free his servants. **16.37** Paul did not hesitate to claim his rights as a Roman citizen and to demand the protection of the law. Christians should not refuse to use their rights to protect their own persons.

b. *At Thessalonica*

17 After Paul and Silas*q* had passed through Amphipolis and Apollonia, they came to Thessalonica, where there was a synagogue of the Jews. 2 And Paul went in, as was his custom, and on three sabbath days argued with them from the scriptures, 3 explaining and proving that it was necessary for the Messiah*r* to suffer and to rise from the dead, and saying, "This is the Messiah,*r* Jesus whom I am proclaiming to you." 4 Some of them were persuaded and joined Paul and Silas, as did a great many of the devout Greeks and not a few of the leading women. 5 But the Jews became jealous, and with the help of some ruffians in the marketplaces they formed a mob and set the city in an uproar. While they were searching for Paul and Silas to bring them out to the assembly, they attacked Jason's house. 6 When they could not find them, they dragged Jason and some believers*s* before the city authorities,*t* shouting, "These people who have been turning the world upside down have come here also, 7 and Jason has entertained them as guests. They are all acting contrary to the decrees of the emperor, saying that there is another king named Jesus." 8 The people and the city officials were disturbed when they heard this, 9 and after they had taken bail from Jason and the others, they let them go.

c. *At Beroea*

10 That very night the believers*s* sent Paul and Silas off to Beroea; and when they arrived, they went to the Jewish synagogue. 11 These Jews were more receptive than those in Thessalonica, for they welcomed the message very eagerly and examined the scriptures every day to see whether these things were so. 12 Many of them therefore believed, including not a few Greek women and men of high standing. 13 But when the Jews of Thessalonica learned that the word of God had been proclaimed by Paul in Beroea as well, they came there too, to stir up and incite the crowds. 14 Then the believers*s* immediately sent Paul away to the coast, but Silas and Timothy remained behind. 15 Those who conducted Paul brought him as far as Athens; and after receiving instructions to have Silas and Timothy join him as soon as possible, they left him.

3. The ministry in Greece

a. *At Athens*

16 While Paul was waiting for them in Athens, he was deeply distressed to see that the city was full of idols. 17 So he argued in the synagogue with the Jews and the devout persons, and also in the marketplace*u* every day with those who happened to be there. 18 Also some

q Gk *they*   *r* Or *the Christ*   *s* Gk *brothers*   *t* Gk *politarchs*   *u* Or *civic center*; Gk *agora*

Cross-references (left margin):

17.1 Acts 27.2; 1 Thess 1.1; 2 Thess 1.1
17.2 Acts 9.20; 13.14; 16.13; 19.8
17.3 Lk 24.26, 46; Acts 18.28; Gal 3.1
17.4 Acts 15.22, 27, 32, 40
17.5 v. 13; Rom 16.21
17.6 Acts 16.19, 20
17.7 Lk 23.2; Jn 19.12
17.9 v. 5
17.10 v. 14; Acts 20.4; v. 2
17.11 Isa 34.16; Lk 16.29; Jn 5.39
17.14 vv. 6, 10; Acts 16.1
17.15 Acts 15.3; vv. 16, 21, 22; Acts 18.5
17.16 2 Pet 2.8
17.18 1 Cor 4.10; Acts 4.2

17.2 Following his usual custom Paul went to the synagogue and preached the gospel for three weeks to the Jews, emphasizing the death and resurrection of Jesus as the promised Messiah. Paul also must have preached to Gentile idolaters, for he later wrote that they turned from idols to God (1 Thess 1.9).

17.5ff Paul and Silas encountered severe persecution in Thessalonica. The unbelieving Jews used people of the basest sort to attack Christianity. They persecuted Paul's followers who, they claimed, were public enemies that presented a danger to the state. Upset, the rulers of the city responded with appropriate measures. Thereupon Paul and Silas practiced what Jesus taught (Mt 10.14) by fleeing from Thessalonica and going to Beroea. There they were well received, and many Jews and Gentiles believed.

17.13 The wicked Jewish opponents of Paul in Thessalonica learned what was happening in Beroea. They sent an embassy there to put out the light of the gospel and to warn the Jews there that Paul was a deceiver. The tense situation was relieved when Paul's friends took him to Athens. Silas and Timothy were to join him in Athens. Timothy went to Thessalonica in order to bring back word to Paul about the progress of the faith there.

17.18 *Epicureans* followed the teaching of Epicurus (born 342 B.C.), a resident of Athens in the later years of his life. He taught that pleasure was the supreme good in life and that people should pursue it unabashedly. The *Stoics*, followers of Zeno (ca. 278 B.C.) charged that this teaching led to sloth and sensuality; they stressed indifference to pain or pleasure as well as the need for the courage never to submit or yield. Paul's message cut across the teachings of both groups and appeared to them to be novel.

Epicurean and Stoic philosophers debated with him. Some said, "What does this babbler want to say?" Others said, "He seems to be a proclaimer of foreign divinities." (This was because he was telling the good news about Jesus and the resurrection.) 19 So they took him and brought him to the Areopagus and asked him, "May we know what this new teaching is that you are presenting? 20 It sounds rather strange to us, so we would like to know what it means." 21 Now all the Athenians and the foreigners living there would spend their time in nothing but telling or hearing something new.

22   Then Paul stood in front of the Areopagus and said, "Athenians, I see how extremely religious you are in every way. 23 For as I went through the city and looked carefully at the objects of your worship, I found among them an altar with the inscription, 'To an unknown god.' What therefore you worship as unknown, this I proclaim to you. 24 The God who made the world and everything in it, he who is Lord of heaven and earth, does not live in shrines made by human hands, 25 nor is he served by human hands, as though he needed anything, since he himself gives to all mortals life and breath and all things. 26 From one ancestor[v] he made all nations to inhabit the whole earth, and he allotted the times of their existence and the boundaries of the places where they would live, 27 so that they would search for God[w] and perhaps grope for him and find him—though indeed he is not far from each one of us. 28 For 'In him we live and move and have our being'; as even some of your own poets have said,

'For we too are his offspring.'

29 Since we are God's offspring, we ought not to think that the deity is like gold, or silver, or stone, an image formed by the art and imagination of mortals. 30 While God has overlooked the times of human ignorance, now he commands all people everywhere to repent, 31 because he has fixed a day on which he will have the world judged in righteousness by a man whom he has appointed, and of this he has given assurance to all by raising him from the dead."

32   When they heard of the resurrection of the dead, some scoffed; but others said, "We will hear you again about this." 33 At that point Paul left them. 34 But some of them joined him and became believers, including Dionysius the Areopagite and a woman named Damaris, and others with them.

b. At Corinth

18 After this Paul[x] left Athens and went to Corinth. 2 There he found a Jew named Aquila, a native of Pontus, who had recently come

v Gk *From one*; other ancient authorities read *From one blood*   w Other ancient authorities read *the Lord*
x Gk *he*

17.19
Acts 23.19;
v. 22

17.24
Isa 42.5;
Acts 14.15;
Mt 11.25;
Acts 7.48
17.25
Ps 50.10-12;
Isa 42.5;
57.16;
Zech 12.1
17.26
Mal 2.10;
Deut 32.8
17.27
Rom 1.20;
Acts 14.17
17.28
Col 1.17;
Heb 1.3;
Epimenides;
Aratus,
haenomena, 5
17.29
Isa 40.18ff
17.30
v. 23;
Acts 14.16;
Rom 3.25;
Lk 24.47;
Titus 2.11,
12; 1 Pet 1.14
17.31
Mt 10.15;
Acts 10.42;
Lk 22.22;
Acts 22.4
17.34
vv. 19, 22

18.1
Acts 17.15;
1 Cor 1.2
18.2
Rom 16.3;
1 Cor 16.19;
2 Tim 4.19;
Acts 11.28

17.26   The entire human race has descended from Adam and Eve, our first parents. Since this is so, racism is in itself sinful. God makes no distinction based on the color of a person's skin; neither should the Christian.
17.30   Repentance is essential to salvation. But repentance in and of itself does not save. It merely brings the sinner to a place where God's forgiving grace meets him. True repentance comprises five parts: (1) a change of mind (Mt 21.28,29); (2) genuine heart sorrow for sin (Lk 18.9–14); (3) confession of sin (Lk 15.18; 18.13); (4) forsaking one's sins (Prov 28.13; Isa 55.7; Jn 8.11); and (5) turning to God as Savior and Lord (1 Thess 1.9).
18.1ff   Paul came to Corinth after a rather bad experience in Athens. Corinth was to be a better mission

field, for many there came to know Christ. Corinth was a very wicked city; in fact, "to corinthianize" was a phrase used to denote how evil a city or people could become. Corinth was the least likely city to experience a spiritual awakening. But that made no difference to God, for his word can break down the hardest heart. As in many other cities, the Jews in Corinth turned against Paul, so he turned from them to the Gentiles and reaped a bountiful harvest. He met up with Aquila and Priscilla, who joined with him in preaching the good news. This Jewish Christian couple had left Rome because Emperor Claudius banished all Jews from Rome. At this period in the history of the church, Gentiles did not distinguish between Jews and Christians, for Christianity appeared to them as a Jewish sect.

from Italy with his wife Priscilla, because Claudius had ordered all Jews to leave Rome. Paul[y] went to see them, 3 and, because he was of the same trade, he stayed with them, and they worked together — by trade they were tentmakers. 4 Every sabbath he would argue in the synagogue and would try to convince Jews and Greeks.

5 When Silas and Timothy arrived from Macedonia, Paul was occupied with proclaiming the word,[z] testifying to the Jews that the Messiah[a] was Jesus. 6 When they opposed and reviled him, in protest he shook the dust from his clothes[b] and said to them, "Your blood be on your own heads! I am innocent. From now on I will go to the Gentiles." 7 Then he left the synagogue[c] and went to the house of a man named Titius[d] Justus, a worshiper of God; his house was next door to the synagogue. 8 Crispus, the official of the synagogue, became a believer in the Lord, together with all his household; and many of the Corinthians who heard Paul became believers and were baptized. 9 One night the Lord said to Paul in a vision, "Do not be afraid, but speak and do not be silent; 10 for I am with you, and no one will lay a hand on you to harm you, for there are many in this city who are my people." 11 He stayed there a year and six months, teaching the word of God among them.

12 But when Gallio was proconsul of Achaia, the Jews made a united attack on Paul and brought him before the tribunal. 13 They said, "This man is persuading people to worship God in ways that are contrary to the law." 14 Just as Paul was about to speak, Gallio said to the Jews, "If it were a matter of crime or serious villainy, I would be justified in accepting the complaint of you Jews; 15 but since it is a matter of questions about words and names and your own law, see to it yourselves; I do not wish to be a judge of these matters." 16 And he dismissed them from the tribunal. 17 Then all of them[e] seized Sosthenes, the official of the synagogue, and beat him in front of the tribunal. But Gallio paid no attention to any of these things.

c. The return to Antioch

18 After staying there for a considerable time, Paul said farewell to the believers[f] and sailed for Syria, accompanied by Priscilla and Aquila. At Cenchreae he had his hair cut, for he was under a vow. 19 When they reached Ephesus, he left them there, but first he himself went into the synagogue and had a discussion with the Jews. 20 When they asked him to stay longer, he declined; 21 but on taking leave of them, he said, "I[g] will return to you, if God wills." Then he set sail from Ephesus.

---

y Gk *He*   z Gk *with the word*   a Or *the Christ*   b Gk *reviled him, he shook out his clothes*   c Gk *left there*
d Other ancient authorities read *Titus*   e Other ancient authorities read *all the Greeks*   f Gk *brothers*
g Other ancient authorities read *I must at all costs keep the approaching festival in Jerusalem, but I*

18.3 The highly educated Paul had been apprenticed as a leatherworker (here called a *tentmaker*), enabling him to support himself. Many rabbis did not think it proper to receive payment for their teaching, so they practiced a trade in addition to their teaching of the law. Rabbi Gamaliel III insisted that the study of the Torah should always be combined with some secular occupation.
18.7 When he left the Jews and the synagogue, Paul went to the house of Gentile believer Titius Justus, who lived next door to the synagogue. Then Crispus, the ruler of the synagogue, was converted and many in Corinth heard the word of God, believed on Jesus Christ, and were baptized.
18.9–11 The Lord visited Paul in a vision, telling him that he had many people in Corinth. Their names were written in the book of life even before they knew

it. God promised Paul much fruit, so he stayed in Corinth for a year and a half, preaching and teaching the word of God.
18.12 *Achaia* was a Roman province, of which Corinth was the capital. Gallio was its proconsul (v. 14), appointed to that position by Emperor Claudius in July, A.D. 51. Gallio was the brother of the famous philosopher Seneca.
18.19 *Ephesus.* Paul stopped at Ephesus for the first time at the end of his second missionary journey. He preached the good news for a short while and went on to Antioch in Syria, his home base. The Holy Spirit had previously forbade him to preach in the Roman province of Asia, of which Ephesus was the capital. On his third missionary journey Paul returned to Ephesus, where he spent nearly three years (19.1,8–10; 20.1).

D. Third missionary journey

1. At Galatia and Phrygia

22 When he had landed at Caesarea, he went up to Jerusalem[h] and greeted the church, and then went down to Antioch. 23 After spending some time there he departed and went from place to place through the region of Galatia[i] and Phrygia, strengthening all the disciples.

18.22
Acts 11.19
18.23
Acts 16.6;
14.22; 15.32, 41

2. At Ephesus

a. The preaching of Apollos

24 Now there came to Ephesus a Jew named Apollos, a native of Alexandria. He was an eloquent man, well-versed in the scriptures. 25 He had been instructed in the Way of the Lord; and he spoke with burning enthusiasm and taught accurately the things concerning Jesus, though he knew only the baptism of John. 26 He began to speak boldly in the synagogue; but when Priscilla and Aquila heard him, they took him aside and explained the Way of God to him more accurately. 27 And when he wished to cross over to Achaia, the believers[j] encouraged him and wrote to the disciples to welcome him. On his arrival he greatly helped those who through grace had become believers, 28 for he powerfully refuted the Jews in public, showing by the scriptures that the Messiah[k] is Jesus.

18.24
Acts 19.1;
1 Cor 1.12;
3.5, 6; 4.6;
Titus 3.13
18.25
Rom 12.11;
Acts 19.3
18.27
vv. 12, 18
18.28
Acts 9.22;
17.3; v. 5

b. Paul's and John's disciples

19 While Apollos was in Corinth, Paul passed through the interior regions and came to Ephesus, where he found some disciples. 2 He said to them, "Did you receive the Holy Spirit when you became believers?" They replied, "No, we have not even heard that there is a Holy Spirit." 3 Then he said, "Into what then were you baptized?" They answered, "Into John's baptism." 4 Paul said, "John baptized with the baptism of repentance, telling the people to believe in the one who was to come after him, that is, in Jesus." 5 On hearing this, they were baptized in the name of the Lord Jesus. 6 When Paul had laid his hands on them, the Holy Spirit came upon them, and they spoke in tongues and prophesied — 7 altogether there were about twelve of them.

19.1
1 Cor 1.12;
3.5, 6;
Acts 18.1,
19-24
19.3
Acts 18.25
19.4
Mt 3.11;
Acts 13.24,
25
19.6
Acts 6.6;
8.17; 2.4;
10.46

c. Paul in the synagogue and the hall of Tyrannus

8 He entered the synagogue and for three months spoke out boldly, and argued persuasively about the kingdom of God. 9 When some stubbornly refused to believe and spoke evil of the Way before the congregation, he left them, taking the disciples with him, and argued daily in the lecture hall of Tyrannus.[l] 10 This continued for two years, so that all the residents of Asia, both Jews and Greeks, heard the word of the Lord.

19.8
Acts 17.2;
18.4; 1.3;
28.23
19.9
Acts 14.4;
2 Tim 1.15;
Acts 9.2;
v. 30
19.10
Acts 20.31;
vv. 22, 26,
27;
Acts 13.12

h Gk went up   i Gk the Galatian region   j Gk brothers   k Or the Christ   l Other ancient authorities read of a certain Tyrannus, from eleven o'clock in the morning to four in the afternoon

18.24ff Apollos was a scholarly and eloquent preacher, who knew the O.T. Scriptures well. He may have been a disciple of John the Baptist. He believed Jesus was the Messiah and zealously shared this knowledge with others. But he was not fully informed concerning the Christian faith and knew little or nothing about the Holy Spirit. After receiving instruction from Aquila and Priscilla, Apollos went to Corinth to minister there (cf. 1 Cor 3.5,6).
19.1 Paul, now on his third and last missionary journey, came to Ephesus. In this city was a temple to Artemis (see note on v. 24ff). From Ephesus the gospel spread out to the surrounding region, including the seven churches of Revelation (see Rev 1.11; 2; 3).

19.2 when you became believers. Paul found twelve disciples in Ephesus and asked them whether they have received the Holy Spirit. Even though they indicated they had never heard of the Holy Spirit, Paul regarded them as true believers. After telling them about Jesus and the Spirit, Paul baptized them in the name of Jesus and they received the gift of tongues and prophecy.
19.9 The hall of Tyrannus was probably a lecture hall or building for hire. Paul used this room regularly for a period of two years, where he was able to preach and speak without interference. He enjoyed a wide hearing in what was apparently a well situated and spacious accommodation.

d. Miracles by Paul

11 God did extraordinary miracles through Paul, 12 so that when the handkerchiefs or aprons that had touched his skin were brought to the sick, their diseases left them, and the evil spirits came out of them. 13 Then some itinerant Jewish exorcists tried to use the name of the Lord Jesus over those who had evil spirits, saying, "I adjure you by the Jesus whom Paul proclaims." 14 Seven sons of a Jewish high priest named Sceva were doing this. 15 But the evil spirit said to them in reply, "Jesus I know, and Paul I know; but who are you?" 16 Then the man with the evil spirit leaped on them, mastered them all, and so overpowered them that they fled out

of the house naked and wounded. 17 When this became known to all residents of Ephesus, both Jews and Greeks, everyone was awestruck; and the name of the Lord Jesus was praised. 18 Also many of those who became believers confessed and disclosed their practices. 19 A number of those who practiced magic collected their books and burned them publicly; when the value of these books[m] was calculated, it was found to come to

fifty thousand silver coins. 20 So the word of the Lord grew mightily and prevailed.

e. Paul's future plans

21 Now after these things had been accomplished, Paul resolved in the Spirit to go through Macedonia and Achaia, and then to go on to Jerusalem. He said, "After I have gone there, I must also see Rome." 22 So he sent two of his helpers, Timothy and Erastus, to Macedonia, while he himself stayed for some time longer in Asia.

f. Demetrius and the riot at Ephesus

23 About that time no little disturbance broke out concerning the Way. 24 A man named Demetrius, a silversmith who made silver shrines of Artemis, brought no little business to the artisans. 25 These he gathered together, with the workers of the same trade, and said, "Men, you know that we get our wealth from this business. 26 You also see and hear that

not only in Ephesus but in almost the whole of Asia this Paul has persuaded and drawn away a considerable number of people by saying that gods made with hands are not gods. 27 And there is danger not only that this trade of ours may come into disrepute but also that the temple of the great goddess Artemis will be scorned, and she will be deprived of her

majesty that brought all Asia and the world to worship her."

28 When they heard this, they were enraged and shouted, "Great is Artemis of the Ephesians!" 29 The city was filled with the confusion; and people[n] rushed together to the theater, dragging with them Gaius and Aristarchus, Macedonians who were Paul's travel companions. 30 Paul

[m] Gk them   [n] Gk they

19.12 The *handkerchiefs or aprons* were sweat rags that Paul tied around his head and waist while working at his trade. Healings and exorcisms resulted from placing them on the afflicted; they remind us of Jesus' miracle of a woman who touched the fringe of his cloak (Mk 5.25–34).

19.14ff *Sceva*, described as a high priest, could not have functioned in this capacity in Asia Minor. He may have exercised that office in Jerusalem, or he may have been a member of a high-priestly family or the head of one of the twenty-four courses of priests. His sons tried to exorcise demons by using the name of Jesus. Apparently they worked together, but since they did not have the authority of either Jesus or Paul, they failed miserably. As a result of their failure the true faith advanced, the church was revived, and believers who still practiced the occult gave up their magic books and burned them publicly. Truth pre-

vailed over error.

19.24ff *Artemis* was an Ephesian goddess. She was a fertility goddess whose statue was supposed to have dropped down out of heaven. Her temple at Ephesus was one of the seven wonders of the ancient world. *Demetrius, a silversmith,* owed his living to the manufacture of idols of Artemis. As a result of Paul's preaching, Demetrius' business and that of other silversmiths was severely affected. Consequently he gathered a mob and started a riot, claiming that Paul had been persuading people not to worship the goddess and was thus degrading her and her temple.

19.30ff Paul wanted to enter the theater and speak to the crowd assembled there, but his friends, both Christian and non-Christian, would not let him do this, fearing that the angry mob would tear him to bits. The Jews joined the unbelieving Gentiles and appointed Alexander to speak against Paul. When the

wished to go into the crowd, but the disciples would not let him; 31 even
some officials of the province of Asia,[o] who were friendly to him, sent
him a message urging him not to venture into the theater. 32 Meanwhile,
some were shouting one thing, some another; for the assembly was in
confusion, and most of them did not know why they had come together.
33 Some of the crowd gave instructions to Alexander, whom the Jews had
pushed forward. And Alexander motioned for silence and tried to make
a defense before the people. 34 But when they recognized that he was a
Jew, for about two hours all of them shouted in unison, "Great is Artemis
of the Ephesians!" 35 But when the town clerk had quieted the crowd, he
said, "Citizens of Ephesus, who is there that does not know that the city
of the Ephesians is the temple keeper of the great Artemis and of the statue
that fell from heaven?[p] 36 Since these things cannot be denied, you ought
to be quiet and do nothing rash. 37 You have brought these men here who
are neither temple robbers nor blasphemers of our[q] goddess. 38 If therefore Demetrius and the artisans with him have a complaint against anyone,
the courts are open, and there are proconsuls; let them bring charges there
against one another. 39 If there is anything further[r] you want to know,
it must be settled in the regular assembly. 40 For we are in danger of being
charged with rioting today, since there is no cause that we can give to
justify this commotion." 41 When he had said this, he dismissed the
assembly.

3. *Paul's last visit to Macedonia and Achaia*

20 After the uproar had ceased, Paul sent for the disciples; and after
encouraging them and saying farewell, he left for Macedonia.
2 When he had gone through those regions and had given the believers[s]
much encouragement, he came to Greece, 3 where he stayed for three
months. He was about to set sail for Syria when a plot was made against
him by the Jews, and so he decided to return through Macedonia. 4 He
was accompanied by Sopater son of Pyrrhus from Beroea, by Aristarchus
and Secundus from Thessalonica, by Gaius from Derbe, and by Timothy,
as well as by Tychicus and Trophimus from Asia. 5 They went ahead and
were waiting for us in Troas; 6 but we sailed from Philippi after the days
of Unleavened Bread, and in five days we joined them in Troas, where
we stayed for seven days.

4. *Troas and Miletus*

7 On the first day of the week, when we met to break bread, Paul was
holding a discussion with them; since he intended to leave the next day,
he continued speaking until midnight. 8 There were many lamps in the
room upstairs where we were meeting. 9 A young man named Eutychus,

19.32 Acts 21.34
19.33 1 Tim 1.20; 2 Tim 4.14; Acts 12.17
19.35 Acts 18.19
19.37 Rom 2.22
19.38 Acts 13.7
20.1 Acts 11.26; 1 Cor 16.5; 1 Tim 1.3
20.3 v. 19; Acts 23.12; 25.3; 2 Cor 11.26
20.4 Acts 19.29; 27.2; 16.1; Eph 6.21; Col 4.7; 2 Tim 4.12; Titus 3.12; Acts 21.29; 2 Tim 4.20
20.6 Acts 16.8; 2 Cor 2.12; 2 Tim 4.13
20.7 1 Cor 16.2; Rev 1.10
20.8 Acts 1.13

[o] Gk *some of the Asiarchs* [p] Meaning of Gk uncertain [q] Other ancient authorities read *your* [r] Other ancient authorities read *about other matters* [s] Gk *given them*

Ephesians noted that he was a Jew, they would not hear him, for they knew that both Jews and Christians were against their idol worship.
19.35 The town clerk brought order out of chaos. He warned the crowd that their riotous conduct was illegal. He dismissed them and the riot ended. Paul's personal ministry in Ephesus also ended at this point. At some point during his stay in Ephesus, he almost lost his life (2 Cor 1.8–11).
20.1–3 Paul left Ephesus, having spent more time there than in any other place where he had ministered. He did not leave Ephesus because he was frightened, but for two reasons: (1) he was convinced it was God's will; (2) he was taking a collection for Jerusalem and wanted to bring the money there (cf. Rom 15.25–31; 2 Cor 8; 9). Paul probably wrote his first letter to the Corinthians before leaving Ephesus; his description of fighting with beasts at Ephesus (1 Cor 15.32) may be an account of the riot involving the silversmiths and the goddess Artemis. From Ephesus he went to Macedonia to visit the churches at Philippi and Thessalonica, and there he wrote 2 Corinthians. Then he spent three months in Corinth (Greece), from where he wrote Romans.
20.7ff Paul went to Troas, where Luke rejoined him (the "we" section begins again). It took five days to get to Troas by sea, and he remained in Troas for seven days. While there he preached an all-night long sermon. A man named Eutychus, sitting in a window, fell asleep and dropped to his death. The incident interrupted Paul's discourse, but the undaunted apostle embraced the dead body and raised it back to life by the power of God.

20.10
1 Kings 17.21;
Mt 9.23, 24

who was sitting in the window, began to sink off into a deep sleep while Paul talked still longer. Overcome by sleep, he fell to the ground three floors below and was picked up dead. 10 But Paul went down, and bending over him took him in his arms, and said, "Do not be alarmed, for his life is in him." 11 Then Paul went upstairs, and after he had broken bread and eaten, he continued to converse with them until dawn; then he left. 12 Meanwhile they had taken the boy away alive and were not a little comforted.

13 We went ahead to the ship and set sail for Assos, intending to take Paul on board there; for he had made this arrangement, intending to go by land himself. 14 When he met us in Assos, we took him on board and went to Mitylene. 15 We sailed from there, and on the following day we arrived opposite Chios. The next day we touched at Samos, and ᶠ the day after that we came to Miletus. 16 For Paul had decided to sail past Ephesus, so that he might not have to spend time in Asia; he was eager to be in Jerusalem, if possible, on the day of Pentecost.

20.15
v. 17;
2 Tim 4.20
20.16
Acts 18.19;
21.4, 12;
19.21; 2.1;
1 Cor 16.8

5. Paul's defense before the Ephesian elders

17 From Miletus he sent a message to Ephesus, asking the elders of the church to meet him. 18 When they came to him, he said to them:

"You yourselves know how I lived among you the entire time from the first day that I set foot in Asia, 19 serving the Lord with all humility and with tears, enduring the trials that came to me through the plots of the Jews. 20 I did not shrink from doing anything helpful, proclaiming the message to you and teaching you publicly and from house to house, 21 as I testified to both Jews and Greeks about repentance toward God and faith toward our Lord Jesus. 22 And now, as a captive to the Spirit,ᵘ I am on my way to Jerusalem, not knowing what will happen to me there, 23 except that the Holy Spirit testifies to me in every city that imprisonment and persecutions are waiting for me. 24 But I do not count my life of any value to myself, if only I may finish my course and the ministry that I received from the Lord Jesus, to testify to the good news of God's grace.

25 "And now I know that none of you, among whom I have gone about proclaiming the kingdom, will ever see my face again. 26 Therefore I declare to you this day that I am not responsible for the blood of any of you, 27 for I did not shrink from declaring to you the whole purpose of God. 28 Keep watch over yourselves and over all the flock, of which the Holy Spirit has made you overseers, to shepherd the church of Godᵛ that he obtained with the blood of his own Son. ʷ 29 I know that after I have gone, savage wolves will come in among you, not sparing the flock. 30 Some even from your own group will come distorting the truth in order to entice the disciples to follow them. 31 Therefore be alert, remembering that for three years I did not cease night or day to warn everyone with

20.17
Acts 11.30
20.18
Acts 18.19;
19.1, 10
20.20
v. 27
20.21
Acts 18.5;
2.38; 24.24;
26.18
20.22
v. 16
20.23
Acts 21.4, 11
20.24
Acts 21.13;
2 Cor 4.16;
Acts 1.17;
2 Cor 4.1;
Gal 1.1;
Titus 1.3
20.25
v. 38
20.26
Acts 18.6;
2 Cor 7.2
20.27
v. 20;
Acts 13.36
20.28
1 Tim 4.16;
1 Pet 5.2;
1 Cor 12.28;
1 Pet 1.19;
20.29;
Mt 7.15
20.31
Acts 19.10

ᶠ Other ancient authorities add *after remaining at Trogyllium*   ᵘ Or *And now, bound in the spirit*   ᵛ Other ancient authorities read *of the Lord*   ʷ Or *with his own blood*; Gk *with the blood of his Own*

20.16 Since Paul was anxious to celebrate Pentecost in Jerusalem, he decided to bypass Ephesus on his journey back to the holy city. The ship stopped at Miletus and Paul sent a note to the Ephesian elders to visit with him at Miletus. The elders and their families came to Miletus to see him off to Jerusalem.

20.18 Paul spoke to his dear friends from Ephesus and reminded them of his style of ministry. He knew that suffering awaited him in the days ahead, but he was under the compulsion of the Holy Spirit to continue his journey. In spite of the dangers that lay ahead, he courageously determined to continue, without concern for his life. He was convinced that he would never see these friends again.

20.24 At Iconium Paul had fled for his life. Here he stated that he did not count his life of any value to himself. Self-preservation was not important to Paul; doing the will of God was. He was under the control of the Spirit, and although he knew what this would mean in the future, he was perfectly willing to suffer death for the cause of Christ with the assurance that, if that happened, it would be God's will.

20.28 *the flock . . . the church.* The church is given several names in the N.T., each one descriptive of its function, position, and relation to Christ: his body (Eph 1.22,23; Col 1.24); the flock of God (1 Pet 5.2); God's field, God's building (1 Cor 3.9); God's temple (1 Cor. 3.16; 2 Cor 6.16); and the bride at the marriage supper of the Lamb (Rev 21.9).

tears. ³²And now I commend you to God and to the message of his grace, a message that is able to build you up and to give you the inheritance among all who are sanctified. ³³I coveted no one's silver or gold or clothing. ³⁴You know for yourselves that I worked with my own hands to support myself and my companions. ³⁵In all this I have given you an example that by such work we must support the weak, remembering the words of the Lord Jesus, for he himself said, 'It is more blessed to give than to receive.'"

36 When he had finished speaking, he knelt down with them all and prayed. ³⁷There was much weeping among them all; they embraced Paul and kissed him, ³⁸grieving especially because of what he had said, that they would not see him again. Then they brought him to the ship.

6. Paul travels to Caesarea

21 When we had parted from them and set sail, we came by a straight course to Cos, and the next day to Rhodes, and from there to Patara.ˣ ²When we found a ship bound for Phoenicia, we went on board and set sail. ³We came in sight of Cyprus; and leaving it on our left, we sailed to Syria and landed at Tyre, because the ship was to unload its cargo there. ⁴We looked up the disciples and stayed there for seven days. Through the Spirit they told Paul not to go on to Jerusalem. ⁵When our days there were ended, we left and proceeded on our journey; and all of them, with wives and children, escorted us outside the city. There we knelt down on the beach and prayed ⁶and said farewell to one another. Then we went on board the ship, and they returned home.

7 When we had finishedʸ the voyage from Tyre, we arrived at Ptolemais; and we greeted the believersᶻ and stayed with them for one day. ⁸The next day we left and came to Caesarea; and we went into the house of Philip the evangelist, one of the seven, and stayed with him. ⁹He had four unmarried daughtersᵃ who had the gift of prophecy. ¹⁰While we were staying there for several days, a prophet named Agabus came down from Judea. ¹¹He came to us and took Paul's belt, bound his own feet and hands with it, and said, "Thus says the Holy Spirit, 'This is the way the Jews in Jerusalem will bind the man who owns this belt and will hand him over to the Gentiles.'" ¹²When we heard this, we and the people there urged him not to go up to Jerusalem. ¹³Then Paul answered, "What are you doing, weeping and breaking my heart? For I am ready not only to be bound but even to die in Jerusalem for the name of the Lord Jesus." ¹⁴Since he would not be persuaded, we remained silent except to say, "The Lord's will be done."

15 After these days we got ready and started to go up to Jerusalem. ¹⁶Some of the disciples from Caesarea also came along and brought us to

---

x Other ancient authorities add *and Myra*   y Or *continued*   z Gk *brothers*   a Gk *four daughters, virgins,*

Cross references (right margin):

20.32 Acts 14.23; 9.31; 26.18; Eph 1.18; Col 1.12; 3.24; 1 Pet 1.4
20.33 1 Cor 9.12; 2 Cor 7.2; 11.9; 12.17
20.34 Acts 18.3
20.35 Rom 15.1
20.36 Acts 9.40; 21.5
20.37 Gen 45.14
20.38 v. 25; Acts 15.3
21.2 Acts 11.19
21.4 v. 11; Acts 20.23
21.5 Acts 20.36
21.7 Acts 12.20; 1.15
21.8 Eph 4.11; 2 Tim 4.5; Acts 6.5; 8.26, 40
21.9 Acts 2.17; Lk 2.36
21.10 Acts 11.28
21.11 v. 33; Acts 20.23
21.13 Acts 20.24
21.14 Mt 26.42; Lk 22.42
21.16 vv. 3, 4

20.33 Without boasting, Paul commended himself as an example of indifference to the world. He never sought worldly wealth, he worked for a living while he preached, and by his work he earned enough to support others as well as himself. His apt conclusion was summarized in a quotation from Jesus (recorded only here): "It is more blessed to give than to receive." He had given much and received little, and he was happy to do so.

20.36ff Paul and his friends wept together, prayed together, embraced each other, and kissed each other. They brought him to the ship on which he would sail eastward to accomplish his mission in Jerusalem and experience whatever was to befall him.

21.8 *Philip.* Philip had been one of those chosen to be a deacon (6.5), but he also was an evangelist. After Stephen's death Philip had great success preaching in Samaria. He was responsible for the conversion of the

Ethiopian eunuch (8.26ff; see note on 8.27). When Paul stayed at his home, he had settled in Caesarea. He had four daughters who prophesied, i.e., they were female preachers.

21.12 Paul's companions and the saints at Caesarea, having heard the prophecy of Agabus, tried to keep Paul from going to Jerusalem. Paul, however, was fixed in his determination to go and refused to be dissuaded by his friends. The advice and counsel of friends should never stop believers from proceeding along the course laid out by the Holy Spirit.

21.16 *Mnason* was a friend of Paul mentioned only in this verse. He was a Cypriot, was probably Jewish, and as an early disciple was probably converted at Pentecost or shortly thereafter. His fidelity to the faith was exemplary and his hospitality in taking Paul and others into his home outstanding.

the house of Mnason of Cyprus, an early disciple, with whom we were to stay.

E. Paul a prisoner in Jerusalem, Caesarea, and Rome

1. Paul in Jerusalem

17 When we arrived in Jerusalem, the brothers welcomed us warmly. 18 The next day Paul went with us to visit James; and all the elders were present. 19 After greeting them, he related one by one the things that God had done among the Gentiles through his ministry. 20 When they heard it, they praised God. Then they said to him, "You see, brother, how many thousands of believers there are among the Jews, and they are all zealous for the law. 21 They have been told about you that you teach all the Jews living among the Gentiles to forsake Moses, and that you tell them not to circumcise their children or observe the customs. 22 What then is to be done? They will certainly hear that you have come. 23 So do what we tell you. We have four men who are under a vow. 24 Join these men, go through the rite of purification with them, and pay for the shaving of their heads. Thus all will know that there is nothing in what they have been told about you, but that you yourself observe and guard the law. 25 But as for the Gentiles who have become believers, we have sent a letter with our judgment that they should abstain from what has been sacrificed to idols and from blood and from what is strangled [b] and from fornication." 26 Then Paul took the men, and the next day, having purified himself, he entered the temple with them, making public the completion of the days of purification when the sacrifice would be made for each of them.

2. Paul's imprisonment

a. His arrest

27 When the seven days were almost completed, the Jews from Asia, who had seen him in the temple, stirred up the whole crowd. They seized him, 28 shouting, "Fellow Israelites, help! This is the man who is teaching everyone everywhere against our people, our law, and this place; more than that, he has actually brought Greeks into the temple and has defiled this holy place." 29 For they had previously seen Trophimus the Ephesian with him in the city, and they supposed that Paul had brought him into the temple. 30 Then all the city was aroused, and the people rushed together. They seized Paul and dragged him out of the temple, and immediately the doors were shut. 31 While they were trying to kill him, word came to the tribune of the cohort that all Jerusalem was in an uproar. 32 Immediately he took soldiers and centurions and ran down to them. When they saw the tribune and the soldiers, they stopped beating Paul. 33 Then the tribune came, arrested him, and ordered him to be bound with two chains; he inquired who he was and what he had done. 34 Some in the crowd shouted one thing, some another; and as he could not learn the facts because of the uproar, he ordered him to be brought into the barracks.

[b] Other ancient authorities lack *and from what is strangled*

21.20ff James and others played a mediating role in the ongoing controversy about Paul. A number of Jewish believers still functioned under the law and remained unhappy with Paul who, they thought, opposed the circumcision of their children and taught that the customs they accepted should be abrogated. So James and the others asked Paul to show his allegiance to Moses and the law by going to the temple and showing himself publicly with four others who were ending their nazirite vows. Paul agreed to do this.
21.23 See note on Num 6.1,2.

21.27ff Trophimus, a Gentile Christian (v. 29), had accompanied Paul to Jerusalem. As a Gentile he could enter the court of the Gentiles, but he could not go beyond the barrier separating it from the inner court of the temple. The penalty for doing so was death. Signs were posted in Greek and Latin to warn Gentiles to stay out. It was falsely reported that Paul had taken a Gentile into the inner court where the sacrifices were offered. The people were aroused and this occasioned the closing of the temple gates. The presence of a Gentile would mean that the temple had been defiled.

Margin cross-references:

21.17 Acts 15.4
21.18 Acts 12.17; 15.13
21.19 Acts 14.27; 1.17; 20.24
21.20 Acts 22.3; Rom 10.2; Gal 1.14
21.21 v. 28; 1 Cor 7.18, 19
21.23 Acts 18.18
21.24 v. 26; Acts 24.18
21.25 Acts 15.20, 29
21.26 Num 6.13; Acts 24.18

21.27 Acts 24.18; 26.21
21.28 Acts 24.5, 6

21.29 Acts 20.4; 18.19
21.30 Acts 26.21; 16.19

21.32 Acts 23.27

21.33 Acts 20.23; v. 11
21.34 Acts 19.32; v. 37

35 When Paul^c came to the steps, the violence of the mob was so great that he had to be carried by the soldiers. 36 The crowd that followed kept shouting, "Away with him!"

b. His defense

37 Just as Paul was about to be brought into the barracks, he said to the tribune, "May I say something to you?" The tribune^d replied, "Do you know Greek? 38 Then you are not the Egyptian who recently stirred up a revolt and led the four thousand assassins out into the wilderness?" 39 Paul replied, "I am a Jew, from Tarsus in Cilicia, a citizen of an important city; I beg you, let me speak to the people." 40 When he had given him permission, Paul stood on the steps and motioned to the people for silence; and when there was a great hush, he addressed them in the Hebrew^e language, saying:

22 "Brothers and fathers, listen to the defense that I now make before you."

2 When they heard him addressing them in Hebrew,^e they became even more quiet. Then he said:

3 "I am a Jew, born in Tarsus in Cilicia, but brought up in this city at the feet of Gamaliel, educated strictly according to our ancestral law, being zealous for God, just as all of you are today. 4 I persecuted this Way up to the point of death by binding both men and women and putting them in prison, 5 as the high priest and the whole council of elders can testify about me. From them I also received letters to the brothers in Damascus, and I went there in order to bind those who were there and to bring them back to Jerusalem for punishment.

6 "While I was on my way and approaching Damascus, about noon a great light from heaven suddenly shone about me. 7 I fell to the ground and heard a voice saying to me, 'Saul, Saul, why are you persecuting me?' 8 I answered, 'Who are you, Lord?' Then he said to me, 'I am Jesus of Nazareth^f whom you are persecuting.' 9 Now those who were with me saw the light but did not hear the voice of the one who was speaking to me. 10 I asked, 'What am I to do, Lord?' The Lord said to me, 'Get up and go to Damascus; there you will be told everything that has been assigned to you to do.' 11 Since I could not see because of the brightness of that light, those who were with me took my hand and led me to Damascus.

12 "A certain Ananias, who was a devout man according to the law and well spoken of by all the Jews living there, 13 came to me; and standing beside me, he said, 'Brother Saul, regain your sight!' In that very hour I regained my sight and saw him. 14 Then he said, 'The God of our ancestors has chosen you to know his will, to see the Righteous One and to hear his own voice; 15 for you will be his witness to all the world of what you have seen and heard. 16 And now why do you delay? Get up, be baptized, and have your sins washed away, calling on his name.'

17 "After I had returned to Jerusalem and while I was praying in the temple, I fell into a trance 18 and saw Jesus^g saying to me, 'Hurry and get out of Jerusalem quickly, because they will not accept your testimony about me.' 19 And I said, 'Lord, they themselves know that in every synagogue I imprisoned and beat those who believed in you. 20 And while

c Gk he   d Gk He   e That is, Aramaic   f Gk the Nazorean   g Gk him

21.36	Lk 23.18; Jn 19.15; Acts 22.22
21.37	v. 34
21.38	Acts 5.36; Mt 24.26
21.39	Acts 9.11; 22.3
21.40	Acts 12.17; 22.2; 26.14
22.1	Acts 7.2
22.2	Acts 21.40
22.3	Acts 21.39; 20.4; Lk 10.39; Acts 26.5; 21.20
22.4	Acts 8.3; 26.9-11; Phil 3.6; 1 Tim 1.13
22.5	Lk 22.66; Acts 4.5; 9.2; 26.10, 12
22.6	Acts 9.3; 26.12, 13
22.9	Acts 9.7; 26.13
22.10	Acts 16.30
22.11	Acts 9.8
22.12	Acts 9.17; 10.22
22.14	Acts 3.13; 5.30; 9.15; 26.16; 1 Cor 9.1; 15.8; Acts 7.52
22.15	Acts 23.11; 26.16
22.16	Acts 2.38; Heb 10.22; Acts 9.14; Rom 10.13
22.17	Acts 9.26; 10.10
22.19	v. 4; Acts 8.3; 26.11; Mt 10.17
22.20	Lk 11.48; Acts 8.1; Rom 1.32

21.38 Josephus, the Jewish historian, refers to this *Egyptian*, whose followers congregated on the Mount of Olives in A.D. 54 to watch the walls of Jerusalem fall. Felix routed the revolters, although the Egyptian himself escaped.
22.3 *Gamaliel*. See note on 5.34.
22.8 Paul had not seen Jesus during his earthly ministry, but, as he testified here, he did see the resur-

rected Jesus (cf. also 1 Cor 15.8). This was essential for one who held the office of an apostle (1 Cor 9.1).
22.12 *Ananias* was a believer whom God chose to minister to Paul during his three days of blindness. Despite his fears (see 9.13,14) Ananias obeyed God's orders. Tradition has it that he was bishop of Damascus and one of the seventy (Lk 12.1ff) and he died a martyr.

the blood of your witness Stephen was shed, I myself was standing by, approving and keeping the coats of those who killed him.' 21 Then he said to me, 'Go, for I will send you far away to the Gentiles.' "

22 Up to this point they listened to him, but then they shouted, "Away with such a fellow from the earth! For he should not be allowed to live." 23 And while they were shouting, throwing off their cloaks, and tossing dust into the air, 24 the tribune directed that he was to be brought into the barracks, and ordered him to be examined by flogging, to find out the reason for this outcry against him. 25 But when they had tied him up with thongs,*h* Paul said to the centurion who was standing by, "Is it legal for you to flog a Roman citizen who is uncondemned?" 26 When the centurion heard that, he went to the tribune and said to him, "What are you about to do? This man is a Roman citizen." 27 The tribune came and asked Paul,*i* "Tell me, are you a Roman citizen?" And he said, "Yes." 28 The tribune answered, "It cost me a large sum of money to get my citizenship." Paul said, "But I was born a citizen." 29 Immediately those who were about to examine him drew back from him; and the tribune also was afraid, for he realized that Paul was a Roman citizen and that he had bound him.

c. *His trial before the council*

30 Since he wanted to find out what Paul*j* was being accused of by the Jews, the next day he released him and ordered the chief priests and the entire council to meet. He brought Paul down and had him stand before them.

23 While Paul was looking intently at the council he said, "Brothers,*k* up to this day I have lived my life with a clear conscience before God." 2 Then the high priest Ananias ordered those standing near him to strike him on the mouth. 3 At this Paul said to him, "God will strike you, you whitewashed wall! Are you sitting there to judge me according to the law, and yet in violation of the law you order me to be struck?" 4 Those standing nearby said, "Do you dare to insult God's high priest?" 5 And Paul said, "I did not realize, brothers, that he was high priest; for it is written, 'You shall not speak evil of a leader of your people.' "

6 When Paul noticed that some were Sadducees and others were Pharisees, he called out in the council, "Brothers, I am a Pharisee, a son of Pharisees. I am on trial concerning the hope of the resurrection*l* of the dead." 7 When he said this, a dissension began between the Pharisees and the Sadducees, and the assembly was divided. 8 (The Sadducees say that there is no resurrection, or angel, or spirit; but the Pharisees acknowledge all three.) 9 Then a great clamor arose, and certain scribes of the Pharisees' group stood up and contended, "We find nothing wrong with this man. What if a spirit or an angel has spoken to him?" 10 When the dissension became violent, the tribune, fearing that they would tear Paul to pieces,

22.21
Acts 9.15

22.22
Acts 21.36;
25.24
22.23
Acts 7.58;
2 Sam 16.13
22.24
Acts 21.34
22.25
Acts 16.37

22.29
vv. 24, 25

22.30
Acts 23.28;
21.33

23.1
Acts 22.30;
24.16;
2 Cor 1.12;
2 Tim 1.3
23.2
Jn 18.22
23.3
Mt 23.27;
Lev 19.35;
Deut 25.1, 2;
Jn 7.51
23.5
Ex 22.28
23.6
Acts 26.5;
Phil 3.5;
Acts 24.15,
16; 26.8
23.8
Mt 22.23;
Mk 12.18;
Lk 20.27
23.9
Acts 25.25;
26.31; 22.7,
17, 18
23.10
Acts 21.34

---

h Or *up for the lashes*   *i* Gk *him*   *j* Gk *he*   *k* Gk *Men, brothers*   *l* Gk *concerning hope and resurrection*

22.21ff By referring to the Gentiles and claiming that God had directly commissioned him to preach to them, Paul inflamed the mob more than ever.
22.24 The *tribune* ordered flogging for Paul, a dreadful and often fatal punishment given to criminals. He did not yet know that Paul was a Roman citizen.
22.25 Paul held Roman citizenship. If both parents were Roman citizens, the children were automatically Roman citizens. If the woman in a marriage was not a Roman citizen, the offspring were not. People could also become Roman citizens by purchasing it or by receiving it as a grant for services rendered. Roman citizens could not be flogged or put to death without the right of appeal to the emperor. Once an appeal was

granted, no further steps could be taken until the emperor had acted (cf. 25.11,12), although not all appeals to the emperor were granted. While waiting for his trial, the accused could be housed with a friend who vouched for his appearance, kept in a common jail, placed in the custody of a soldier to whom he was chained, or permitted to live in his own lodgings.
23.1ff Paul now stood before the Sanhedrin (see note on Mt 26.59). He was unafraid to stand before this august body and give a fair account of his conduct. When Paul maintained his innocence, the high priest Ananias ordered him to be struck, presumably because he thought Paul was lying.
23.6 See note on Mt 3.7.

ordered the soldiers to go down, take him by force, and bring him into the barracks. 11 That night the Lord stood near him and said, "Keep up your courage! For just as you have testified for me in Jerusalem, so you must bear witness also in Rome."

d. His removal to Caesarea

12 In the morning the Jews joined in a conspiracy and bound themselves by an oath neither to eat nor drink until they had killed Paul. 13 There were more than forty who joined in this conspiracy. 14 They went to the chief priests and elders and said, "We have strictly bound ourselves by an oath to taste no food until we have killed Paul. 15 Now then, you and the council must notify the tribune to bring him down to you, on the pretext that you want to make a more thorough examination of his case. And we are ready to do away with him before he arrives."

16 Now the son of Paul's sister heard about the ambush; so he went and gained entrance to the barracks and told Paul. 17 Paul called one of the centurions and said, "Take this young man to the tribune, for he has something to report to him." 18 So he took him, brought him to the tribune, and said, "The prisoner Paul called me and asked me to bring this young man to you; he has something to tell you." 19 The tribune took him by the hand, drew him aside privately, and asked, "What is it that you have to report to me?" 20 He answered, "The Jews have agreed to ask you to bring Paul down to the council tomorrow, as though they were going to inquire more thoroughly into his case. 21 But do not be persuaded by them, for more than forty of their men are lying in ambush for him. They have bound themselves by an oath neither to eat nor drink until they kill him. They are ready now and are waiting for your consent." 22 So the tribune dismissed the young man, ordering him, "Tell no one that you have informed me of this."

23 Then he summoned two of the centurions and said, "Get ready to leave by nine o'clock tonight for Caesarea with two hundred soldiers, seventy horsemen, and two hundred spearmen. 24 Also provide mounts for Paul to ride, and take him safely to Felix the governor." 25 He wrote a letter to this effect:

26 "Claudius Lysias to his Excellency the governor Felix, greetings. 27 This man was seized by the Jews and was about to be killed by them, but when I had learned that he was a Roman citizen, I came with the guard and rescued him. 28 Since I wanted to know the charge for which they accused him, I had him brought to their council. 29 I found that he was accused concerning questions of their law, but was charged with nothing deserving death or imprisonment. 30 When I was informed that there would be a plot against the man, I sent him to you at once, ordering his accusers also to state before you what they have against him. *m*"

31 So the soldiers, according to their instructions, took Paul and brought him during the night to Antipatris. 32 The next day they let the

m Other ancient authorities add *Farewell*

23.11	Acts 18.9; 19.21; 28.23
23.12	vv. 21, 30; Acts 25.3
23.14	v. 21
23.15	Acts 22.30
23.16	Acts 21.34; v. 10
23.18	Eph 3.1
23.20	vv. 14, 15
23.21	vv.12, 14
23.23	v. 33
23.24	Acts 24.1, 3, 10; 25.14
23.26	Acts 24.3; 15.23
23.27	Acts 21.32, 33; 22.25-29
23.28	Acts 22.30
23.29	Acts 18.15; 25.19; 26.31
23.30	vv. 20, 21; Acts 24.19; 25.16
23.32	v. 23

23.11 The risen Lord supernaturally visited his servant Paul, fulfilling Mt 28.20, "I am with you always." Jesus encouraged Paul, "Keep up your courage!" Those who trust the Savior have nothing to fear, not even death itself. Scripture speaks of five instances when the Lord appeared to Paul: on the Damascus road (9.5; 22.8; 26.15); on his first visit to Jerusalem (22.17,18); in Corinth (18.9,10); when Paul was struggling with his thorn in the flesh (2 Cor 12.7-9); and on his last visit to Jerusalem (23.11).
23.16 Nowhere else in the Scriptures is any reference made to Paul's relatives. When his nephew

learned of his uncle's predicament, he informed Paul, who in turn sent him to the tribune with the information.
23.24 *Felix* had been appointed governor of Judea by Claudius Caesar and exercised military and civil authority over that region. His wife Drusilla (24.24) was Jewish, the youngest daughter of Herod Agrippa I; she had left her husband Azizus, king of Emesa, for Felix. They lived in Caesarea. Felix was hated by the Jews, so by leaving Paul in jail (24.27), he was trying to win Jewish favor. Rioting by the Jews and charges of mismanagement leveled against him eventually resulted in his being recalled to Rome.

23.33
vv. 23, 24, 26

23.34
Acts 21.39

23.35
Acts 24.19;
25.16; 24.27

24.1
Acts 23.2, 30,
35

24.3
Acts 23.26;
26.25

24.5
Acts 16.20;
17.6; 21.28
24.6
Acts 21.28

24.9
1 Thess 2.16
24.10
Acts 23.24

24.11
Acts 21.26
24.12
Acts 25.8;
28.17
24.13
Acts 25.7
24.14
Acts 9.2;
v. 5;
Acts 3.13;
26.22; 28.23
24.15
Acts 23.6;
28.20;
Dan 12.2;
Jn 5.28, 29
24.16
Acts 23.1
24.17
Acts 11.29,
30;
Rom 15.25-28;
2 Cor 8.1-4;
Gal 2.10
24.18
Acts 21.26,
27
24.19
Acts 23.30
24.21
Acts 23.6
24.23
Acts 23.35;
28.16; 23.16;
27.3

horsemen go on with him, while they returned to the barracks. 33 When they came to Caesarea and delivered the letter to the governor, they presented Paul also before him. 34 On reading the letter, he asked what province he belonged to, and when he learned that he was from Cilicia, 35 he said, "I will give you a hearing when your accusers arrive." Then he ordered that he be kept under guard in Herod's headquarters. [n]

e. *Paul's defense at Caesarea*

(1) PAUL BEFORE FELIX

24 Five days later the high priest Ananias came down with some elders and an attorney, a certain Tertullus, and they reported their case against Paul to the governor. 2 When Paul [o] had been summoned, Tertullus began to accuse him, saying:

"Your Excellency, [p] because of you we have long enjoyed peace, and reforms have been made for this people because of your foresight. 3 We welcome this in every way and everywhere with utmost gratitude. 4 But, to detain you no further, I beg you to hear us briefly with your customary graciousness. 5 We have, in fact, found this man a pestilent fellow, an agitator among all the Jews throughout the world, and a ringleader of the sect of the Nazarenes. [q] 6 He even tried to profane the temple, and so we seized him. [r] 8 By examining him yourself you will be able to learn from him concerning everything of which we accuse him."

9 The Jews also joined in the charge by asserting that all this was true.

10 When the governor motioned to him to speak, Paul replied:

"I cheerfully make my defense, knowing that for many years you have been a judge over this nation. 11 As you can find out, it is not more than twelve days since I went up to worship in Jerusalem. 12 They did not find me disputing with anyone in the temple or stirring up a crowd either in the synagogues or throughout the city. 13 Neither can they prove to you the charge that they now bring against me. 14 But this I admit to you, that according to the Way, which they call a sect, I worship the God of our ancestors, believing everything laid down according to the law or written in the prophets. 15 I have a hope in God — a hope that they themselves also accept — that there will be a resurrection of both [s] the righteous and the unrighteous. 16 Therefore I do my best always to have a clear conscience toward God and all people. 17 Now after some years I came to bring alms to my nation and to offer sacrifices. 18 While I was doing this, they found me in the temple, completing the rite of purification, without any crowd or disturbance. 19 But there were some Jews from Asia — they ought to be here before you to make an accusation, if they have anything against me. 20 Or let these men here tell what crime they had found when I stood before the council, 21 unless it was this one sentence that I called out while standing before them, 'It is about the resurrection of the dead that I am on trial before you today.'"

22 But Felix, who was rather well informed about the Way, adjourned the hearing with the comment, "When Lysias the tribune comes down, I will decide your case." 23 Then he ordered the centurion to keep him

---

[n] Gk *praetorium* [o] Gk *he* [p] Gk lacks *Your Excellency* [q] Gk *Nazoreans* [r] Other ancient authorities add *and we would have judged him according to our law.* 7 But the chief captain Lysias came and with great violence took him out of our hands, 8 commanding his accusers to come before you. [s] Other ancient authorities read *of the dead, both of*

24.1ff *Tertullus* was an attorney hired by the Jews to state their case against Paul. He was probably a Hellenistic Jew with a common Roman name. He tried to flatter Felix and then sought to show that Paul was an enemy of two elements Felix was assigned to protect — the public peace and the Jewish religion. He charged that Paul was guilty of sedition (i.e., he was like those Jews throughout the empire who wanted to overthrow Roman control of Jerusalem).

24.22 Felix justly deferred action on Paul's case because the Roman tribune Lysias was not present to testify. This was important because Tertullus had implied Lysias was guilty of misconduct. Felix also was familiar with the Way, and this may have had something to do with the deferment.

24.23 Felix made sure that Paul would not run away, but he left him enough freedom so that his friends had access to him. In other words, Felix did

in custody, but to let him have some liberty and not to prevent any of his friends from taking care of his needs.

24 Some days later when Felix came with his wife Drusilla, who was Jewish, he sent for Paul and heard him speak concerning faith in Christ Jesus. 25 And as he discussed justice, self-control, and the coming judgment, Felix became frightened and said, "Go away for the present; when I have an opportunity, I will send for you." 26 At the same time he hoped that money would be given him by Paul, and for that reason he used to send for him very often and converse with him.

27 After two years had passed, Felix was succeeded by Porcius Festus; and since he wanted to grant the Jews a favor, Felix left Paul in prison.

(2) PAUL BEFORE FESTUS

25 Three days after Festus had arrived in the province, he went up from Caesarea to Jerusalem 2 where the chief priests and the leaders of the Jews gave him a report against Paul. They appealed to him 3 and requested, as a favor to them against Paul,ᵗ to have him transferred to Jerusalem. They were, in fact, planning an ambush to kill him along the way. 4 Festus replied that Paul was being kept at Caesarea, and that he himself intended to go there shortly. 5 "So," he said, "let those of you who have the authority come down with me, and if there is anything wrong about the man, let them accuse him."

6 After he had stayed among them not more than eight or ten days, he went down to Caesarea; the next day he took his seat on the tribunal and ordered Paul to be brought. 7 When he arrived, the Jews who had gone down from Jerusalem surrounded him, bringing many serious charges against him, which they could not prove. 8 Paul said in his defense, "I have in no way committed an offense against the law of the Jews, or against the temple, or against the emperor." 9 But Festus, wishing to do the Jews a favor, asked Paul, "Do you wish to go up to Jerusalem and be tried there before me on these charges?" 10 Paul said, "I am appealing to the emperor's tribunal; this is where I should be tried. I have done no wrong to the Jews, as you very well know. 11 Now if I am in the wrong and have committed something for which I deserve to die, I am not trying to escape death; but if there is nothing to their charges against me, no one can turn me over to them. I appeal to the emperor." 12 Then Festus, after he had conferred with his council, replied, "You have appealed to the emperor; to the emperor you will go."

(3) FESTUS AND AGRIPPA

13 After several days had passed, King Agrippa and Bernice arrived at Caesarea to welcome Festus. 14 Since they were staying there several days, Festus laid Paul's case before the king, saying, "There is a man here who was left in prison by Felix. 15 When I was in Jerusalem, the chief priests and the elders of the Jews informed me about him and asked for a sentence against him. 16 I told them that it was not the custom of the

ᵗ Gk him

24.25
Gal 5.23;
Acts 10.42

24.27
Acts 25.1, 4,
9, 14; 12.3;
23.35

25.2
Acts 24.1;
v. 15
25.3
Acts 23.12,
15
25.4
Acts 24.23

25.7
Mk 15.3;
Lk 23.2, 10;
Acts 24.5, 13
25.8
Acts 6.13;
24.12; 28.17
25.9
Acts 24.27;
v. 20

25.11
v. 25;
Acts 26.32;
28.19

25.14
Acts 24.27
25.15
Acts 24.1;
v. 2
25.16
vv. 4, 5

not regard the charges against Paul so grievous, for if he had been an insurrectionist he would have kept him under tight guard.
24.27 Justice was not speedy, for Paul waited for two years in prison without a trial. Meanwhile, Felix was replaced by Porcius Festus (ca. A.D. 57–60).
25.1ff We know little about *Festus* except that he inherited a bad situation and tried to keep the Jews within bounds. Festus suggested that Paul stand trial before his own people, whereupon Paul appealed to the emperor for trial (see note on 22.25). This came as a welcome relief to Festus, who gladly allowed him his request.
25.2,3 God's law forbade lying. This did not, how-

ever, deter the chief priests and leaders of the Jews from asking Festus to remit Paul to Jerusalem for trial, when they really intended to have him killed en route. For them, the end would justify the means.
25.11 Paul did not object to capital punishment, for he readily agreed that if he was guilty of the charges he was willing to be executed.
25.13 This *Agrippa* was Herod Agrippa II. He was seventeen when his father, Herod Agrippa I, died (see ch. 12). He sought, though without success, to build up the kingdom and to reconcile Judaism and Hellenism. The apostle Paul appeared before him and his sister Bernice, of whom history has little good to say.

Romans to hand over anyone before the accused had met the accusers face to face and had been given an opportunity to make a defense against the charge. 17 So when they met here, I lost no time, but on the next day took my seat on the tribunal and ordered the man to be brought. 18 When the accusers stood up, they did not charge him with any of the crimes[u] that I was expecting. 19 Instead they had certain points of disagreement with him about their own religion and about a certain Jesus, who had died, but whom Paul asserted to be alive. 20 Since I was at a loss how to investigate these questions, I asked whether he wished to go to Jerusalem and be tried there on these charges.[v] 21 But when Paul had appealed to be kept in custody for the decision of his Imperial Majesty, I ordered him to be held until I could send him to the emperor." 22 Agrippa said to Festus, "I would like to hear the man myself." "Tomorrow," he said, "you will hear him."

23 So on the next day Agrippa and Bernice came with great pomp, and they entered the audience hall with the military tribunes and the prominent men of the city. Then Festus gave the order and Paul was brought in. 24 And Festus said, "King Agrippa and all here present with us, you see this man about whom the whole Jewish community petitioned me, both in Jerusalem and here, shouting that he ought not to live any longer. 25 But I found that he had done nothing deserving death; and when he appealed to his Imperial Majesty, I decided to send him. 26 But I have nothing definite to write to our sovereign about him. Therefore I have brought him before all of you, and especially before you, King Agrippa, so that, after we have examined him, I may have something to write — 27 for it seems to me unreasonable to send a prisoner without indicating the charges against him."

(4) PAUL BEFORE AGRIPPA

26 Agrippa said to Paul, "You have permission to speak for yourself." Then Paul stretched out his hand and began to defend himself:

2 "I consider myself fortunate that it is before you, King Agrippa, I am to make my defense today against all the accusations of the Jews, 3 because you are especially familiar with all the customs and controversies of the Jews; therefore I beg of you to listen to me patiently.

4 "All the Jews know my way of life from my youth, a life spent from the beginning among my own people and in Jerusalem. 5 They have known for a long time, if they are willing to testify, that I have belonged to the strictest sect of our religion and lived as a Pharisee. 6 And now I stand here on trial on account of my hope in the promise made by God to our ancestors, 7 a promise that our twelve tribes hope to attain, as they earnestly worship day and night. It is for this hope, your Excellency,[w] that I am accused by Jews! 8 Why is it thought incredible by any of you that God raises the dead?

9 "Indeed, I myself was convinced that I ought to do many things against the name of Jesus of Nazareth.[x] 10 And that is what I did in Jerusalem; with authority received from the chief priests, I not only locked up many of the saints in prison, but I also cast my vote against them when they were being condemned to death. 11 By punishing them often in all the synagogues I tried to force them to blaspheme; and since I was so furiously enraged at them, I pursued them even to foreign cities.

12 "With this in mind, I was traveling to Damascus with the authority

---

u Other ancient authorities read *with anything*   v Gk *on them*   w Gk *O king*   x Gk *the Nazorean*

26.8 Paul's argument turned on the fact that, as a Pharisee, he believed in the resurrection of the dead (cf. 23.6–9). From the viewpoint of the Pharisees, it is obvious that while they believed in a doctrine of the resurrection, there was one resurrection they did not believe in — that of Jesus Christ. They refused to be-

lieve he was the Messiah.

26.11 *force them to blaspheme*, i.e., to say that Jesus was a deceiver and that they would now renounce their faith in him as Lord. The Jews would not have thought this to be blasphemous, but Christians would.

and commission of the chief priests, [13] when at midday along the road, your Excellency,[y] I saw a light from heaven, brighter than the sun, shining around me and my companions. [14] When we had all fallen to the ground, I heard a voice saying to me in the Hebrew[z] language, 'Saul, Saul, why are you persecuting me? It hurts you to kick against the goads.' [15] I asked, 'Who are you, Lord?' The Lord answered, 'I am Jesus whom you are persecuting. [16] But get up and stand on your feet; for I have appeared to you for this purpose, to appoint you to serve and testify to the things in which you have seen me[a] and to those in which I will appear to you. [17] I will rescue you from your people and from the Gentiles — to whom I am sending you [18] to open their eyes so that they may turn from darkness to light and from the power of Satan to God, so that they may receive forgiveness of sins and a place among those who are sanctified by faith in me.'

19   "After that, King Agrippa, I was not disobedient to the heavenly vision, [20] but declared first to those in Damascus, then in Jerusalem and throughout the countryside of Judea, and also to the Gentiles, that they should repent and turn to God and do deeds consistent with repentance. [21] For this reason the Jews seized me in the temple and tried to kill me. [22] To this day I have had help from God, and so I stand here, testifying to both small and great, saying nothing but what the prophets and Moses said would take place: [23] that the Messiah[b] must suffer, and that, by being the first to rise from the dead, he would proclaim light both to our people and to the Gentiles."

24   While he was making this defense, Festus exclaimed, "You are out of your mind, Paul! Too much learning is driving you insane!" [25] But Paul said, "I am not out of my mind, most excellent Festus, but I am speaking the sober truth. [26] Indeed the king knows about these things, and to him I speak freely; for I am certain that none of these things has escaped his notice, for this was not done in a corner. [27] King Agrippa, do you believe the prophets? I know that you believe." [28] Agrippa said to Paul, "Are you so quickly persuading me to become a Christian?"[c] [29] Paul replied, "Whether quickly or not, I pray to God that not only you but also all who are listening to me today might become such as I am — except for these chains."

30   Then the king got up, and with him the governor and Bernice and those who had been seated with them; [31] and as they were leaving, they said to one another, "This man is doing nothing to deserve death or imprisonment." [32] Agrippa said to Festus, "This man could have been set free if he had not appealed to the emperor."

3. Paul sent to Rome

a. The embarkation and voyage

27   When it was decided that we were to sail for Italy, they transferred Paul and some other prisoners to a centurion of the Augustan

---

y Gk O king   z That is, Aramaic   a Other ancient authorities read *the things that you have seen*   b Or the Christ   c Or *Quickly you will persuade me to play the Christian*

26.24 Festus exclaimed that Paul had cracked his brain by too much studying, for he was talking like an insane person. He simply did not understand what Paul was trying to say. Paul was certain, however, that Agrippa, who was familiar with the Jewish customs and doctrine, did comprehend his position.
26.28 *Are you so quickly persuading me to become a Christian?* Some read Agrippa's statement as ironical, "Do you really think that in such a short time you could convince me to become a Christian?" Others think he was almost ready to believe that Jesus Christ was the Messiah, but stopped short of salvation by

refusing to take Jesus Christ into his heart.
26.32 Perhaps Paul had made a mistake in appealing to the emperor. Yet since King Agrippa knew Paul was not guilty of any crime punishable under Roman law, he should have set him free by asking him to reverse his appeal to the emperor. Politically, however, this would have again created problems with the Jews.
27.1 A centurion commanded a hundred soldiers. This large number of soldiers was assigned to assure that Paul and the other prisoners on board the ship got to Rome safely for trial.

26.14
Acts 9.7;
21.40

26.16
Ezek 2.1;
Dan 10.11;
Acts 22.14,
15
26.17
Jer 1.8, 19;
Acts 22.21
26.18
Isa 35.5;
42.7;
Eph 5.8;
Col 1.13;
1 Pet 2.9;
Lk 24.47;
Acts 2.38;
20.32
26.20
Acts 9.19-29;
22.17-20;
13.46; 9.15;
3.19;
Mt 3.8;
Lk 3.8
26.21
Acts 21.30,
31
26.22
Lk 24.27,
44;
Acts 24.14
26.23
Mt 26.24;
1 Cor 15.20;
Col 1.18;
Rev 1.5;
Lk 2.32
26.24
2 Kings 9.11;
Jn 10.20;
1Cor 1.23
26.25
Acts 23.26;
24.3
26.30
Acts 25.33
26.31
Acts 23.29
26.32
Acts 28.18;
25.11

27.1
Acts 25.12,
25; 10.1

Cohort, named Julius. 2 Embarking on a ship of Adramyttium that was about to set sail to the ports along the coast of Asia, we put to sea, accompanied by Aristarchus, a Macedonian from Thessalonica. 3 The next day we put in at Sidon; and Julius treated Paul kindly, and allowed him to go to his friends to be cared for. 4 Putting out to sea from there, we sailed under the lee of Cyprus, because the winds were against us. 5 After we had sailed across the sea that is off Cilicia and Pamphylia, we came to Myra in Lycia. 6 There the centurion found an Alexandrian ship bound for Italy and put us on board. 7 We sailed slowly for a number of days and arrived with difficulty off Cnidus, and as the wind was against us, we sailed under the lee of Crete off Salmone. 8 Sailing past it with difficulty, we came to a place called Fair Havens, near the city of Lasea.

9 Since much time had been lost and sailing was now dangerous, because even the Fast had already gone by, Paul advised them, 10 saying, "Sirs, I can see that the voyage will be with danger and much heavy loss, not only of the cargo and the ship, but also of our lives." 11 But the centurion paid more attention to the pilot and to the owner of the ship than to what Paul said. 12 Since the harbor was not suitable for spending the winter, the majority was in favor of putting to sea from there, on the chance that somehow they could reach Phoenix, where they could spend the winter. It was a harbor of Crete, facing southwest and northwest.

13 When a moderate south wind began to blow, they thought they could achieve their purpose; so they weighed anchor and began to sail past Crete, close to the shore. 14 But soon a violent wind, called the northeaster, rushed down from Crete.*d* 15 Since the ship was caught and could not be turned head-on into the wind, we gave way to it and were driven. 16 By running under the lee of a small island called Cauda*e* we were scarcely able to get the ship's boat under control. 17 After hoisting it up they took measures*f* to undergird the ship; then, fearing that they would run on the Syrtis, they lowered the sea anchor and so were driven. 18 We were being pounded by the storm so violently that on the next day they began to throw the cargo overboard, 19 and on the third day with their own hands they threw the ship's tackle overboard. 20 When neither sun nor stars appeared for many days, and no small tempest raged, all hope of our being saved was at last abandoned.

21 Since they had been without food for a long time, Paul then stood up among them and said, "Men, you should have listened to me and not have set sail from Crete and thereby avoided this damage and loss. 22 I urge you now to keep up your courage, for there will be no loss of life among you, but only of the ship. 23 For last night there stood by me an angel of the God to whom I belong and whom I worship, 24 and he said, 'Do not be afraid, Paul; you must stand before the emperor; and indeed, God has granted safety to all those who are sailing with you.' 25 So keep up your courage, men, for I have faith in God that it will be exactly as I have been told. 26 But we will have to run aground on some island."

b. The shipwreck

27 When the fourteenth night had come, as we were drifting across the sea of Adria, about midnight the sailors suspected that they were nearing land. 28 So they took soundings and found twenty fathoms; a little farther on they took soundings again and found fifteen fathoms. 29 Fearing that we might run on the rocks, they let down four anchors from the stern

d Gk it   *e* Other ancient authorities read *Clauda*   *f* Gk helps

27.9   *The Fast* referred to here is the only one prescribed by the Mosaic law and occurred on the Day of Atonement (the tenth day of Tishri, i.e., September/October). If this incident took place in A.D. 59, the Day of Atonement was on or near October 5.
27.23   God used angels on many occasions to bring

messages to his servants. The angel here assured Paul that the passengers on board the ship would all be saved if they followed his advice. God's angels still stand ready to do his bidding among his people (cf. Heb 1.14).
27.28   *twenty fathoms.* A fathom is six feet.

and prayed for day to come. 30 But when the sailors tried to escape from the ship and had lowered the boat into the sea, on the pretext of putting out anchors from the bow, 31 Paul said to the centurion and the soldiers, "Unless these men stay in the ship, you cannot be saved." 32 Then the soldiers cut away the ropes of the boat and set it adrift.

33 Just before daybreak, Paul urged all of them to take some food, saying, "Today is the fourteenth day that you have been in suspense and remaining without food, having eaten nothing. 34 Therefore I urge you to take some food, for it will help you survive; for none of you will lose a hair from your heads." 35 After he had said this, he took bread; and giving thanks to God in the presence of all, he broke it and began to eat. 36 Then all of them were encouraged and took food for themselves. 37 (We were in all two hundred seventy-six*g* persons in the ship.) 38 After they had satisfied their hunger, they lightened the ship by throwing the wheat into the sea.

39 In the morning they did not recognize the land, but they noticed a bay with a beach, on which they planned to run the ship ashore, if they could. 40 So they cast off the anchors and left them in the sea. At the same time they loosened the ropes that tied the steering-oars; then hoisting the foresail to the wind, they made for the beach. 41 But striking a reef,*h* they ran the ship aground; the bow stuck and remained immovable, but the stern was being broken up by the force of the waves. 42 The soldiers' plan was to kill the prisoners, so that none might swim away and escape; 43 but the centurion, wishing to save Paul, kept them from carrying out their plan. He ordered those who could swim to jump overboard first and make for the land, 44 and the rest to follow, some on planks and others on pieces of the ship. And so it was that all were brought safely to land.

c. The stopover at Malta

28 After we had reached safety, we then learned that the island was called Malta. 2 The natives showed us unusual kindness. Since it had begun to rain and was cold, they kindled a fire and welcomed all of us around it. 3 Paul had gathered a bundle of brushwood and was putting it on the fire, when a viper, driven out by the heat, fastened itself on his hand. 4 When the natives saw the creature hanging from his hand, they said to one another, "This man must be a murderer; though he has escaped from the sea, justice has not allowed him to live." 5 He, however, shook off the creature into the fire and suffered no harm. 6 They were expecting him to swell up or drop dead, but after they had waited a long time and saw that nothing unusual had happened to him, they changed their minds and began to say that he was a god.

7 Now in the neighborhood of that place were lands belonging to the leading man of the island, named Publius, who received us and entertained us hospitably for three days. 8 It so happened that the father of Publius lay sick in bed with fever and dysentery. Paul visited him and cured him by praying and putting his hands on him. 9 After this happened, the rest of the people on the island who had diseases also came and were

27.30	v. 16
27.34	1 Kings 1.52; Mt 10.30; Lk 12.7; 21.18
27.35	1 Sam 9.13; Mt 15.36; Mk 8.6; Jn 6.11; 1 Tim 4.3, 4
27.36	vv. 22, 25
27.38	v. 18
27.39	Acts 28.1
27.40	v. 29
27.41	2 Cor 11.25
27.42	Acts 12.19
27.43	v. 3
27.44	vv. 22, 31
28.1	Acts 27.26, 39
28.2	Rom 1.14; 1 Cor 14.11; Col 3.11
28.4	Lk 13.2, 4
28.5	Lk 10.19
28.6	Acts 14.11
28.8	Jas 5.14, 15; Mk 5.23

---

g Other ancient authorities read *seventy-six*; others, *about seventy-six*   *h* Gk *place of two seas*

27.30 The sailors were thinking only of themselves, in spite of the fact that the rule of sea has always been that sailors must look first to the passengers, even if they drown as a consequence. Paul intervened and the soldiers cut the rope of the small boat they had lowered for themselves.

27.38ff Hoping possibly to beach the ship as soon as it was light, the mariners dropped overboard everything they could to lighten the ship so that it could be steered as close to the shore as possible. But the ship struck a reef, became stuck, and was wrecked. The passengers and crew had to make their way to shore

as best they could. All escaped, as Paul said they would.

28.3ff The incident of the viper falls in line with Mk 16.18. Paul was doing the will of God and was under divine protection. The bystanders were understandably impressed, although Paul then had to remind them that he was no god. Paul's healing of the father of Publius added to the excitement. No doubt Paul used the occasion to proclaim the gospel, for wherever Paul was he told people about Jesus (cf. Phil 1.12–14).

cured. ¹⁰They bestowed many honors on us, and when we were about to sail, they put on board all the provisions we needed.

28.11
Acts 27.6

11 Three months later we set sail on a ship that had wintered at the island, an Alexandrian ship with the Twin Brothers as its figurehead. ¹²We put in at Syracuse and stayed there for three days; ¹³then we weighed anchor and came to Rhegium. After one day there a south wind sprang up, and on the second day we came to Puteoli. ¹⁴There we found believersⁱ and were invited to stay with them for seven days. And so we came to Rome. ¹⁵The believersⁱ from there, when they heard of us, came as far as the Forum of Appius and Three Taverns to meet us. On seeing them, Paul thanked God and took courage.

28.14
Acts 1.15

16 When we came into Rome, Paul was allowed to live by himself, with the soldier who was guarding him.

28.16
Acts 24.23;
27.3

d. The arrival at Rome

17 Three days later he called together the local leaders of the Jews. When they had assembled, he said to them, "Brothers, though I had done nothing against our people or the customs of our ancestors, yet I was arrested in Jerusalem and handed over to the Romans. ¹⁸When they had examined me, the Romansʲ wanted to release me, because there was no reason for the death penalty in my case. ¹⁹But when the Jews objected, I was compelled to appeal to the emperor—even though I had no charge to bring against my nation. ²⁰For this reason therefore I have asked to see you and speak with you,ᵏ since it is for the sake of the hope of Israel that I am bound with this chain." ²¹They replied, "We have received no letters from Judea about you, and none of the brothers coming here has reported or spoken anything evil about you. ²²But we would like to hear from you what you think, for with regard to this sect we know that everywhere it is spoken against."

28.17
Acts 13.50;
25.8; 6.14
28.18
Acts 22.24;
26.31, 32;
23.29
28.19
Acts 25.11
28.20
Acts 26.6, 7,
29;
Eph 3.1; 4.1;
6.20;
2 Tim 1.16
28.21
Acts 22.5
28.22
Acts 24.14;
1 Pet 2.12;
4.14

23 After they had set a day to meet with him, they came to him at his lodgings in great numbers. From morning until evening he explained the matter to them, testifying to the kingdom of God and trying to convince them about Jesus both from the law of Moses and from the prophets. ²⁴Some were convinced by what he had said, while others refused to believe. ²⁵So they disagreed with each other; and as they were leaving, Paul made one further statement: "The Holy Spirit was right in saying to your ancestors through the prophet Isaiah,

28.23
Acts 17.3;
19.8

28.24
Acts 14.4

26 'Go to this people and say,
   You will indeed listen, but never understand,
      and you will indeed look, but never perceive.
27 For this people's heart has grown dull,
      and their ears are hard of hearing,
         and they have shut their eyes;
   so that they might not look with their eyes,
      and listen with their ears,
         and understand with their heart and turn—

28.26
Isa 6.9, 10;
Mt 13.14,
15;
Rom 11.8

ⁱ Gk brothers   ʲ Gk they   ᵏ Or I have asked you to see me and speak with me

28.13,14 The ship now disembarked the passengers and the prisoners at Puteoli, where they stayed for seven days. Believers in Christ greeted them, but we do not know how they had heard the good news or when they had become Christians. From there they had to make their journey to Rome on foot.

28.17 Paul was now in Rome, where there was a Jewish community. Earlier Claudius Caesar had driven all Jews from Rome (18.2), but after his death a number of them returned to Rome. Paul called the Jewish leaders together to explain his case before them. Some had heard about Paul and Christianity, but no one from Jerusalem had yet come to press charges against him.

28.23,24 Paul the prisoner was still Paul the missionary—still keeping the faith and finishing his course (cf. 2 Tim 4.7). The results were the same as usual: some believed and some did not. He worked from morning to evening, eagerly seeking to persuade them to accept Jesus as the Messiah spoken of in their own Scriptures.

28.26ff Paul affirmed that Isaiah's words were from the Holy Spirit, for the prophet had been under the control of the Spirit and received his message from the Spirit (see Isa 6.9,10; 61.1-3). Paul went on to state that since the Jews had rejected the message of the gospel, God had turned to the Gentiles, who were willing to listen and to embrace the Lord Jesus.

and I would heal them.'

28Let it be known to you then that this salvation of God has been sent to the Gentiles; they will listen."[l]

30 He lived there two whole years at his own expense[m] and welcomed all who came to him, 31proclaiming the kingdom of God and teaching about the Lord Jesus Christ with all boldness and without hindrance.

[l] Other ancient authorities add verse 29, *And when he had said these words, the Jews departed, arguing vigorously among themselves*   [m] Or *in his own hired dwelling*

28.28
Mt 21.41,
43;
Acts 13.46,
47;
Rom 11.11
28.31
v. 23;
Eph 6.19;
2 Tim 2.9

28.30 How Paul supported himself we are not told. Whether it was from gifts he was given or work that he performed is not known. In our last view of him in Acts, Paul was still witnessing and speaking forth the word of truth. The book ends without telling us what happened to him, though tradition has it that Paul was released from prison after appearing before the emperor (cf. 2 Tim 4.16,17).

INTRODUCTION TO
THE LETTER OF PAUL TO THE
ROMANS

Authorship, Date, and Background: Romans was written by Paul about A.D. 56–57. He had completed his third missionary tour and was in Corinth where he composed the letter carried to Rome by Phoebe (16.1), a deacon of the church of Cenchreae. The letter was addressed to friends, not to a church at Rome. Indeed, how the church at Rome got started is not known, although at Pentecost there were visitors in Jerusalem from that city who probably returned to Rome to proclaim the good news and to spread the faith. At the time of writing, there were more Gentile believers in Rome than Jewish converts. Paul was on his way to Jerusalem with funds for the saints, but he expected to visit Rome in the days ahead, something he had longed to do earlier but had been prevented from doing. He hoped to use Rome as the base of operations for a trip to Spain.

In his letter to the Romans, Paul sets forth the Christian faith in a systematic fashion; thus it is comparable to Galatians in that both are theological and didactic. Romans is notably lacking in data having to do with the end of the age (eschatology); rather, it consists of an exposition of foundational truths essential to a full-orbed gospel. This letter, by way of an introduction, was written in order to open the door for Paul's future visit which, unknown to him, would come two years later in chains and not in freedom. At this point, he yearned to visit his friends there, instruct them in the holy faith, and go from Rome to Spain for evangelistic outreach with their help and prayers.

Characteristics and Content: Paul presents, in orderly fashion, the essential elements of the gospel, having for its central motif the concept of salvation (justification) by faith alone without good works. The gospel is "the power of God for salvation to everyone who has faith" (1.16). All need this good news, for Jews and non-Jews are guilty before God. Jesus Christ is the sinner's only hope; by his death and resurrection and through faith in him, heaven's doors are opened for the redeemed to enter in. The grace (i.e., the favor) of God is freely offered. How it is obtained, what it involves, and what the consequences are, are spelled out by Paul. Paul contrasts law and grace in a powerful manner. He discusses the person and the work of the Holy Spirit: believers are indwelt by the Spirit; the Spirit raised Jesus from the dead; believers are led by the Spirit, are aided by the Spirit in prayer, are the first-fruits of the Spirit, and call God "Father" by the Spirit's witness. To believers is given the assurance that "all things work together for good" (8.28). Our salvation is certain, for the Scriptures tell us that nothing can separate us from the love of God through Christ Jesus our Lord.

Chs. 9—11 constitute a parenthesis (an interruption of the line of thought) in which Paul deals with Israel and God's purpose for his people, a purpose which is certain to be executed because God is sovereign.

In ch. 12 Paul speaks about the Christian in a holistic manner, insisting that the true Christian life consists in the body being given to God as a living sacrifice and the mind being renewed or transformed to reflect the mind of Christ. He orders

Christians to be subject to governing authorities (ch. 13), along with additional ethical teachings summed up in the second table of the law ("Love your neighbor as yourself"). Paul shares his future plans with his readers and closes the letter with commendations and a doxology. There has been some question about whether ch. 16 belongs to the letter, since one ancient manuscript has the benediction of 16.25–27 at the end of ch. 15. There is, however, no good reason for supposing it was not part of the original letter.

Outline:

THE LETTER OF PAUL TO THE
ROMANS

I. Introduction (1.1–17)

A. Greeting

1 Paul, a servant^a of Jesus Christ, called to be an apostle, set apart for the gospel of God, 2which he promised beforehand through his prophets in the holy scriptures, 3the gospel concerning his Son, who was descended from David according to the flesh 4and was declared to be Son of God with power according to the spirit^b of holiness by resurrection from the dead, Jesus Christ our Lord, 5through whom we have received grace and apostleship to bring about the obedience of faith among all the Gentiles for the sake of his name, 6including yourselves who are called to belong to Jesus Christ,

7 To all God's beloved in Rome, who are called to be saints:
Grace to you and peace from God our Father and the Lord Jesus Christ.

B. Prayer of thanksgiving

8 First, I thank my God through Jesus Christ for all of you, because your faith is proclaimed throughout the world. 9For God, whom I serve with my spirit by announcing the gospel^c of his Son, is my witness that without ceasing I remember you always in my prayers, 10asking that by God's will I may somehow at last succeed in coming to you. 11For I am longing to see you so that I may share with you some spiritual gift to strengthen you — 12or rather so that we may be mutually encouraged by each other's faith, both yours and mine. 13I want you to know, brothers and sisters,^d that I have often intended to come to you (but thus far have been prevented), in order that I may reap some harvest among you as I have among the rest of the Gentiles. 14I am a debtor both to Greeks and to barbarians, both to the wise and to the foolish 15 — hence my eagerness to proclaim the gospel to you also who are in Rome.

C. Theme

16 For I am not ashamed of the gospel; it is the power of God for salvation to everyone who has faith, to the Jew first and also to the Greek.

a Gk *slave*   *b* Or *Spirit*   *c* Gk *my spirit in the gospel*   *d* Gk *brothers*

1.1
1 Cor 1.1;
Acts 9.15;
2 Cor 11.7
1.2
Acts 26.6;
Gal 3.8
1.3
Jn 1.14
1.4
Acts 13.33;
Heb 9.14
1.5
Gal 1.16;
Acts 6.7; 9.15
1.7
1 Cor 1.2, 3;
Gal 1.3;
Eph 1.2

1.8
Phil 1.3;
Acts 16.19
1.9
Phil 1.8;
Acts 24.14;
Eph 1.16
1.10
Rom 15.32
1.11
Rom 15.23
1.13
Rom 15.22

1.14
1 Cor 9.16;
Acts 28.2
1.15
Rom 12.18;
15.20

1.16
2 Tim 1.8;
1 Cor 1.18;
Acts 3.26;
Rom 2.9

1.1 *a servant of Jesus Christ.* Paul considers himself as Christ's slave (*doulos*). He does not use the word for hired servant (*misthios* or *diakonos*), who had certain rights; such servants were paid for their labor and were free to leave their employment. Slaves were not free nor did they have any privileges. Paul considers all Christians as Christ's slaves (6.18,19) and as slaves to one another (2 Cor 4.5).
1.3,4 Romans was written to explain the gospel, at the center of which is Christ. Paul witnesses to the divine and human natures of the Lord Jesus Christ. He was born in the line of David according to the flesh (i.e., his humanity). At the same time he was God's Son, proved by his resurrection (i.e., his deity).
1.7 *saints* (Gk. *hagioi*, from *hagios*, meaning "set apart," "separated to God," "holy"). This designates those who have been regenerated and are set apart and

indwelt by the Holy Spirit to live a holy life. All believers are saints and should strive to become more and more like Jesus, even though perfection cannot be attained until after death. *God our Father.* God is the Creator of all persons, but he is not the Father of all. He is the Father only of those who believe. Nor are all people the children of God; only those who have been regenerated are God's children. All people are divided into two classes — those who are in the family of God and those who are not (see note on Jn 8.44). When unbelievers are born again, they are adopted as members of God's family.
1.11ff Paul wants to visit the Roman church as the apostle to the Gentiles (cf. 15.15–24), to edify them and receive encouragement for his own faith. *barbarians*, i.e., those who did not speak the same language as the Romans.

17 For in it the righteousness of God is revealed through faith for faith; as it is written, "The one who is righteous will live by faith."[e]

II. The world's need of God (1.18–3.20)

A. The Gentiles: guilty before God

18 For the wrath of God is revealed from heaven against all ungodliness and wickedness of those who by their wickedness suppress the truth. 19 For what can be known about God is plain to them, because God has shown it to them. 20 Ever since the creation of the world his eternal power and divine nature, invisible though they are, have been understood and seen through the things he has made. So they are without excuse; 21 for though they knew God, they did not honor him as God or give thanks to him, but they became futile in their thinking, and their senseless minds were darkened. 22 Claiming to be wise, they became fools; 23 and they exchanged the glory of the immortal God for images resembling a mortal human being or birds or four-footed animals or reptiles.

24 Therefore God gave them up in the lusts of their hearts to impurity, to the degrading of their bodies among themselves, 25 because they exchanged the truth about God for a lie and worshiped and served the creature rather than the Creator, who is blessed forever! Amen.

26 For this reason God gave them up to degrading passions. Their women exchanged natural intercourse for unnatural, 27 and in the same way also the men, giving up natural intercourse with women, were consumed with passion for one another. Men committed shameless acts with men and received in their own persons the due penalty for their error.

28 And since they did not see fit to acknowledge God, God gave them up to a debased mind and to things that should not be done. 29 They were filled with every kind of wickedness, evil, covetousness, malice. Full of envy, murder, strife, deceit, craftiness, they are gossips, 30 slanderers, God-haters,[f] insolent, haughty, boastful, inventors of evil, rebellious toward parents, 31 foolish, faithless, heartless, ruthless. 32 They know God's decree, that those who practice such things deserve to die — yet they not only do them but even applaud others who practice them.

B. God's principles of judgment

2 Therefore you have no excuse, whoever you are, when you judge others; for in passing judgment on another you condemn yourself,

e Or The one who is righteous through faith will live f Or God-hated

1.17
Rom 3.21;
Gal 3.11;
Heb 10.38

1.18ff
Eph 5.6;
Col 3.6
1.19
Acts 14.17
1.20
Ps 19.1-6

1.21
Jer 2.5;
Eph 4.17, 18

1.22
Jer 10.14
1.23
Ps 106.20;
Jer 2.11;
Acts 17.29
1.24
Eph 4.18, 19;
1 Pet 4.3
1.25
Isa 44.20;
Jer 10.14;
Rom 9.5
1.26
Lev 18.22;
Eph 4.19;
1 Thess 4.5
1.27
Lev 18.22;
20.13
1.28
Eph 4.19

1.30
Ps 5.5;
2 Tim 3.2
1.31
2 Tim 3.3
1.32
Rom 6.21;
Acts 8.1;
22.20

2.1
Rom 1.20;
2 Sam 12.5-7;
Mt 7.1, 2

1.16 In the term *salvation*, (Gk. *sōtēria*, meaning "safety" or "soundness") are included other doctrinal components such as justification, regeneration, sanctification, glorification, redemption, grace, and forgiveness. Salvation is (1) of the Lord (Ps 37.39); (2) by and through the saving work of Jesus Christ (Acts 4.12; Gal 1.4; Heb 2.10; 5.9); and (3) not of works by sinners, lest they should boast (11.6; Eph 2.9; 2 Tim 1.9; Titus 3.5). Salvation is past, present, and future. Believers have been delivered from their guilt and the penalty of sin (Eph 2.8); they are now being delivered from the power of sin (1 Cor 15.2); they will at last be delivered from God's wrath and conformed to the glorious image of God's sinless Son (5.10,11; 8.29). **1.18ff** The human race retrogressed after the fall. People turned from serving one God to serving idols and from purity to adultery, fornication, and perverse sins against nature itself. At last "God gave them up . . . to things that should not be done" (v. 28). Bodies and minds that once were holy have become depraved with no hope of improvement apart from regeneration

and sanctification. **1.24** *God gave them up.* Paul uses this phrase three times (vv. 24,26,28): (1) he gave them up to using sexual relations in a wrong fashion, i.e., fornication and adultery; (2) he gave them up to using sexual relations in a perverse way, i.e., homosexual conduct; and (3) he gave them up to a debased mind, so that they called evil good and defended those who did the things described in vv. 24–32. **1.28ff** The consequences of sin are (1) degradation, for sinners' natures are corrupted, their desires polluted, their spiritual sights blinded, and their wills set in opposition to God's will; (2) condemnation as the inevitable consequences (3.19); and (3) separation from God, which is death (5.21; 6.23; cf. Ezek 18.4; Eph 2.1). **2.1** In ch. 1 Paul has shown that the Gentiles are under sin and condemnation. Now he shows that the Jews are also in the same predicament, even though they exhibit self-conceit by supposing that the Gentiles are guilty and they are not.

because you, the judge, are doing the very same things. 2 You say,^{g} "We know that God's judgment on those who do such things is in accordance with truth." 3 Do you imagine, whoever you are, that when you judge those who do such things and yet do them yourself, you will escape the judgment of God? 4 Or do you despise the riches of his kindness and forbearance and patience? Do you not realize that God's kindness is meant to lead you to repentance? 5 But by your hard and impenitent heart you are storing up wrath for yourself on the day of wrath, when God's righteous judgment will be revealed. 6 For he will repay according to each one's deeds: 7 to those who by patiently doing good seek for glory and honor and immortality, he will give eternal life; 8 while for those who are self-seeking and who obey not the truth but wickedness, there will be wrath and fury. 9 There will be anguish and distress for everyone who does evil, the Jew first and also the Greek, 10 but glory and honor and peace for everyone who does good, the Jew first and also the Greek. 11 For God shows no partiality.

12 All who have sinned apart from the law will also perish apart from the law, and all who have sinned under the law will be judged by the law. 13 For it is not the hearers of the law who are righteous in God's sight, but the doers of the law who will be justified. 14 When Gentiles, who do not possess the law, do instinctively what the law requires, these, though not having the law, are a law to themselves. 15 They show that what the law requires is written on their hearts, to which their own conscience also bears witness; and their conflicting thoughts will accuse or perhaps excuse them 16 on the day when, according to my gospel, God, through Jesus Christ, will judge the secret thoughts of all.

C. The Jews: guilty before God

17 But if you call yourself a Jew and rely on the law and boast of your relation to God 18 and know his will and determine what is best because you are instructed in the law, 19 and if you are sure that you are a guide to the blind, a light to those who are in darkness, 20 a corrector of the foolish, a teacher of children, having in the law the embodiment of knowledge and truth, 21 you, then, that teach others, will you not teach yourself? While you preach against stealing, do you steal? 22 You that forbid adultery, do you commit adultery? You that abhor idols, do you rob temples? 23 You that boast in the law, do you dishonor God by

Cross references (left margin):

2.4 Eph 1.7; 2.7; Rom 11.22; 3.25; Ex 34.6; 2 Pet 3.9
2.5 Deut 32.34; Jude 6
2.6 Mt 16.27; 1 Cor 3.8; 2 Cor 5.10
2.8 Gal 5.20; 2 Thess 2.12
2.9 1 Pet 4.17
2.10 1 Pet 1.7; v. 9
2.11 Deut 10.17; Gal 2.6; Eph 6.9
2.12 Rom 3.19; 1 Cor 9.21
2.13 Jas 1.22, 23, 25
2.14ff v. 15
2.15 vv. 14, 27
2.16 Eccl 12.14; 1 Cor 4.5; Acts 10.42; 1 Tim 1.11
2.17 v. 23; Mic 3.11; Rom 9.4
2.18 Phil 1.10
2.20 Rom 6.17; 2 Tim 1.13
2.21 Mt 23.3, 4
2.22 Acts 19.37
2.23 v. 17

^{g} Gk lacks *You say*

2.4ff The Jews are guilty of having slighted God's goodness and have provoked God's wrath against them. Since God will judge people by their works and the Jews do not obey the truth, God will bring ruin to Jewish sinners as well as to Gentile sinners. God does not show partiality; he does not judge sinning Gentiles and excuse sinning Jews (v. 11).
2.12–15 *the law.* The law of God is the revealed expression of the will of God. That will is imperfectly manifested in conscience (see next note) but perfectly in the word of God, the Scriptures. The judicial and ceremonial laws of the O.T. were given to a specific people, the Jews, and for a specific period in their history. The ten commandments constitute the moral law (Ex 20.2–17; Deut 5.6–21), and it is timeless, for it concerns itself with the permanent relations of people with respect to marriage, sex, property, filial obedience, etc. Faith in Christ does not release anyone from the demands of God's moral law. *will ever perish.* The condition of those who die without ever having heard of Christ is a serious theological problem. Scripture seems to assign them to everlasting punishment on the basis of the light they have, however limited. Thus one who knows neither Christ nor the

moral law still has the light of conscience. There is no biblical warrant for the belief that there is a second chance for those who have never heard the word of God.
2.15 *conscience.* God gave Adam a conscience that was uncorrupted before he sinned. After his sin it was depraved and corrupted, but not totally erased. Conscience serves as a witness to truth (Prov 20.27), but moral choice tells whether it has been obeyed (Josh 24.15). People's own consciences accuse them of sin (Gen 42.21; 2 Sam 24.10; Mt 27.3) and will condemn them when the books are opened. Every mouth will be silenced and God's judgments will be seen to be true and just (Rev 20.12–15). Believers who are walking in the Spirit repent of and confess any known sin. In this way it is possible to have a blameless conscience (9.1; 14.22; Acts 24.16).
2.17ff The Jews had more knowledge or light than the Gentiles since they had the revealed word of God, but they sinned against their knowledge and their profession. They preached better in the pulpit than they lived outside of it. Their sins occasioned unbelievers to blaspheme the name of God (v. 24).

breaking the law? 24 For, as it is written, "The name of God is blasphemed among the Gentiles because of you."

25 Circumcision indeed is of value if you obey the law; but if you break the law, your circumcision has become uncircumcision. 26 So, if those who are uncircumcised keep the requirements of the law, will not their uncircumcision be regarded as circumcision? 27 Then those who are physically uncircumcised but keep the law will condemn you that have the written code and circumcision but break the law. 28 For a person is not a Jew who is one outwardly, nor is true circumcision something external and physical. 29 Rather, a person is a Jew who is one inwardly, and real circumcision is a matter of the heart — it is spiritual and not literal. Such a person receives praise not from others but from God.

3 Then what advantage has the Jew? Or what is the value of circumcision? 2 Much, in every way. For in the first place the Jews[h] were entrusted with the oracles of God. 3 What if some were unfaithful? Will their faithlessness nullify the faithfulness of God? 4 By no means! Although everyone is a liar, let God be proved true, as it is written,

"So that you may be justified in your words,
    and prevail in your judging."[i]

5 But if our injustice serves to confirm the justice of God, what should we say? That God is unjust to inflict wrath on us? (I speak in a human way.) 6 By no means! For then how could God judge the world? 7 But if through my falsehood God's truthfulness abounds to his glory, why am I still being condemned as a sinner? 8 And why not say (as some people slander us by saying that we say), "Let us do evil so that good may come"? Their condemnation is deserved!

D. The world: guilty before God

9 What then? Are we any better off?[j] No, not at all; for we have already charged that all, both Jews and Greeks, are under the power of sin, 10 as it is written:

"There is no one who is righteous, not even one;
11   there is no one who has understanding,
        there is no one who seeks God.
12 All have turned aside, together they have become worthless;
        there is no one who shows kindness,
            there is not even one."
13 "Their throats are opened graves;
        they use their tongues to deceive."
    "The venom of vipers is under their lips."
14 "Their mouths are full of cursing and bitterness."
15 "Their feet are swift to shed blood;
16   ruin and misery are in their paths,
17   and the way of peace they have not known."
18 "There is no fear of God before their eyes."
19 Now we know that whatever the law says, it speaks to those who

h Gk they   i Gk when you are being judged   j Or at any disadvantage?

Cross-references (right margin):

2.24 — Isa 52.5
2.25 — Gal 5.3
2.26 — 1 Cor 7.19; Eph 2.11; Rom 8.4
2.27 — Mt 12.41
2.28 — Mt 3.9; Jn 8.39; Rom 9.6; Gal 6.15
2.29 — Col 2.11; 1 Pet 3.4
3.2 — Deut 4.8; Ps 147.19
3.3 — Heb 4.2; 2 Tim 2.13
3.4 — Jn 3.33; Ps 116.11; 51.4
3.5 — Rom 6.19; Gal 3.15
3.6 — Gen 18.25
3.7 — v. 4
3.8 — Rom 6.1
3.9 — Gal 3.22
3.10 — Ps 14.1-3
3.13 — Ps 5.9
3.14 — Ps 10.7; 140.3
3.15 — Isa 59.7, 8
3.18 — Ps 36.1
3.19 — Jn 10.34; Rom 2.12

Study notes (bottom):

2.25ff Paul agrees that circumcision has value if Jews keep the law. But if they are circumcised and still break the law, their circumcision has no value and they are no better off than the uncircumcised Gentiles. True circumcision is of the heart, not the flesh; it is spiritual, not literal.
3.1,2 The Jews do have some advantages over the Gentiles. To them God gave the O.T., *the oracles of God,* in their own language. They had the true means of salvation but not a monopoly on it, for God's good news was meant for the Gentiles too.
3.3 Although many Jews were unfaithful, this could neither annul what God said nor lead God to be un-

faithful to himself or to his promises.
3.5,6 This question was being asked: if our sins actually serve to demonstrate God's justice, why should he punish sin? Paul responds by saying that if God were not to inflict punishment, then God could not judge anyone. But God has revealed that he will indeed judge everyone for their sins.
3.9ff Paul concludes this section of Romans by drawing together a number of O.T. texts to point out that all people are guilty and corrupt — Jew and Gentile alike. The whole world is guilty before God; there is no hope for anyone were it not for the good news Paul will soon announce.

are under the law, so that every mouth may be silenced, and the whole world may be held accountable to God. 20 For "no human being will be justified in his sight" by deeds prescribed by the law, for through the law comes the knowledge of sin.

III. Justification by faith alone (3.21–8.39)

A. The means of salvation: faith

21 But now, apart from law, the righteousness of God has been disclosed, and is attested by the law and the prophets, 22 the righteousness of God through faith in Jesus Christ[k] for all who believe. For there is no distinction, 23 since all have sinned and fall short of the glory of God; 24 they are now justified by his grace as a gift, through the redemption that is in Christ Jesus, 25 whom God put forward as a sacrifice of atonement[l] by his blood, effective through faith. He did this to show his righteousness, because in his divine forbearance he had passed over the sins previously committed; 26 it was to prove at the present time that he himself is righteous and that he justifies the one who has faith in Jesus.[m]

27 Then what becomes of boasting? It is excluded. By what law? By that of works? No, but by the law of faith. 28 For we hold that a person is justified by faith apart from works prescribed by the law. 29 Or is God the God of Jews only? Is he not the God of Gentiles also? Yes, of Gentiles also, 30 since God is one; and he will justify the circumcised on the ground of faith and the uncircumcised through that same faith. 31 Do we then overthrow the law by this faith? By no means! On the contrary, we uphold the law.

B. The Old Testament proof: Abraham saved by faith

4 What then are we to say was gained by[n] Abraham, our ancestor according to the flesh? 2 For if Abraham was justified by works, he has something to boast about, but not before God. 3 For what does the

k Or through the faith of Jesus Christ l Or a place of atonement m Or who has the faith of Jesus n Other ancient authorities read say about

Marginal references

3.20 Ps 143.2; Acts 13.39; Gal 2.16; Rom 7.7

3.21 Rom 1.17; 9.30; 1.2; Acts 10.43
3.22 Rom 10.12; Gal 3.28; Col 3.11
3.23 Gal 3.22
3.24 Rom 4.16; Eph 1.7; 2.8; Col 1.14; Heb 9.12, 15
3.25 1 Jn 2.2; Heb 9.14, 28; 1 Pet 1.19
3.27 Rom 2.17, 23; 4.2;
1 Cor 1.29-31; Eph 2.9
3.28 Acts 13.39; Eph 2.9
3.29 Rom 9.24; Acts 10.34, 35
3.30 Gal 3.8
4.2 1 Cor 1.31
4.3 Gen 15.6; Gal 3.6; Jas 2.23

3.20 God has several purposes to his moral law: to demonstrate his own moral perfection, to show sinners their guilt and take away their excuses, to provide a standard for the governing of human society, and to provide a guide for believers as to how their conduct will please and glorify God.

3.22 Righteousness, as it pertains to people, refers to keeping God's will, law, and moral standards perfectly. This no one has ever done except Christ; therefore, no one else has ever been truly righteous (vv. 10,23). God, however, imputes perfect righteousness to all those who believe in his Son; this act is called "justification." The means whereby we are justified is faith in Jesus Christ. The Holy Spirit empowers justified believers so that they can live righteously, in accord with the will of God; this is called "sanctification." Righteousness as it pertains to God stresses his attribute of perfection and carries with it the assurance that he will do what he has promised. God's righteousness also expresses itself in his wrath or holy displeasure against all iniquity or unrighteousness.

3.23 All humans, irrespective of race, color, or creed, are sinners. No one can escape sin's guilt; Jews and Gentiles alike are guilty (cf. 1.18). Sin is the lack of conformity to the will of God, a violation of the moral law as written in the hearts of all creatures and revealed in the word of God. The Hebrew term for sin means "to deviate from the way"; the Greek term indicates "a missing of the mark" or "a going aside from." Sin could not exist unless there were a norm

or standard against which the acts of people could be measured or judged. Sin exists both in overt acts and in the attitude of the heart. Guilt normally supposes the intention is present to do evil. Though people are unable to read the intentions of each other's hearts, God knows the hearts of all people infallibly (1 Chr 28.9; Heb 4.13).

3.25 sacrifice of atonement (Gk. hilastērion, also appearing in Heb 9.5 as "mercy seat"). God was rightfully angry with sinners (1.18ff); the sacrifice of Christ on the cross satisfied his demands that sin be paid for. Thus the sinner is reconciled to God by Christ's atoning death.

3.27ff boasting. No human being has any reason to boast before God. The fact that God saves us by his grace excludes that possibility. Furthermore, the principle of salvation by faith alone also precludes boasting, for God justifies Jew and Gentile alike only through the act of faith, not because of any works they have done.

4.1ff The Jews regarded Abraham as their father, and rightly so. But Paul shows them that Abraham was justified neither by circumcision nor by works. "Abraham believed God, and it was reckoned to him as righteousness" (v. 3, quoting Gen 15.6), and this took place before he was circumcised (v. 10). Thus circumcision followed his justification as a sign. Moreover faith of necessity excludes works, for if salvation is by works, then faith is not necessary.

scripture say? "Abraham believed God, and it was reckoned to him as righteousness." [4] Now to one who works, wages are not reckoned as a gift but as something due. [5] But to one who without works trusts him who justifies the ungodly, such faith is reckoned as righteousness. [6] So also David speaks of the blessedness of those to whom God reckons righteousness apart from works:

7 "Blessed are those whose iniquities are forgiven,
 and whose sins are covered;
8 blessed is the one against whom the Lord will not reckon sin."

9 Is this blessedness, then, pronounced only on the circumcised, or also on the uncircumcised? We say, "Faith was reckoned to Abraham as righteousness." [10] How then was it reckoned to him? Was it before or after he had been circumcised? It was not after, but before he was circumcised. [11] He received the sign of circumcision as a seal of the righteousness that he had by faith while he was still uncircumcised. The purpose was to make him the ancestor of all who believe without being circumcised and who thus have righteousness reckoned to them, [12] and likewise the ancestor of the circumcised who are not only circumcised but who also follow the example of the faith that our ancestor Abraham had before he was circumcised.

13 For the promise that he would inherit the world did not come to Abraham or to his descendants through the law but through the righteousness of faith. [14] If it is the adherents of the law who are to be the heirs, faith is null and the promise is void. [15] For the law brings wrath; but where there is no law, neither is there violation.

16 For this reason it depends on faith, in order that the promise may rest on grace and be guaranteed to all his descendants, not only to the adherents of the law but also to those who share the faith of Abraham (for he is the father of all of us, [17] as it is written, "I have made you the father of many nations") — in the presence of the God in whom he believed, who gives life to the dead and calls into existence the things that do not exist. [18] Hoping against hope, he believed that he would become "the father of many nations," according to what was said, "So numerous shall your descendants be." [19] He did not weaken in faith when he considered his own body, which was already*o* as good as dead (for he was about a hundred years old), or when he considered the barrenness of Sarah's womb. [20] No distrust made him waver concerning the promise of God, but he grew strong in his faith as he gave glory to God, [21] being fully convinced that God was able to do what he had promised. [22] Therefore his faith*p* "was reckoned to him as righteousness." [23] Now the words, "it was reckoned to him," were written not for his sake alone, [24] but for ours also. It will be reckoned to us who believe in him who raised Jesus our Lord from

4.4	Rom 11.6
4.7	Ps 32.1, 2
4.8	2 Cor 5.19
4.9	Rom 3.30; v. 3
4.11	Gen 17.10; Lk 19.9
4.13	Gen 17.4-6; Gal 3.29
4.14	Gal 3.18
4.15	Rom 3.20; 7.8, 10, 11; Gal 3.10
4.16	Rom 3.24; 9.8; 15.8
4.17	Gen 17.5; 1 Cor 1.28
4.18	Gen 15.5
4.19	Gen 17.17; Heb 11.11
4.21	Gen 18.14; Heb 11.19
4.23	Rom 15.4; 1 Cor 9.10; 10.11
4.24	Rom 10.9; Acts 2.24

o Other ancient authorities lack *already* *p* Gk *Therefore it*

4.6 *blessedness.* When we trust Christ for salvation God reckons us to be righteous, not because we have any inherent righteousness, but because the righteousness of Christ is imputed to us. Christ bore the sinner's guilt and punishment (Isa 53.5,11; 2 Cor 5.21; Gal 3.13) and Christ's righteousness is placed on our account (1 Cor 1.30; 2 Cor 5.21; Phil 3.9). In sum, Christ has taken our guilt and given us his righteousness.
4.11 *Circumcision* was the seal of the Abrahamic covenant. Yet circumcision did not save. The Jews of Paul's day had all been circumcised, but that did not mean that they were saved. Abraham himself was saved before he was circumcised (see note on v. 1ff). In the N.T., water baptism is the seal of the new covenant. But not all baptized people are saved, just as not all circumcised people were saved in Paul's time. Moreover, uncircumcised and unbaptized peo-

ple can and do get to heaven. For example, the dying thief was not baptized, yet he was with Jesus in paradise (Lk 23.43). Water baptism is important, but ultimately faith alone determines the destiny of all.
4.13ff Abraham was justified four hundred years before the law was given, and his justification did not come through the law but through faith. What was true for Abraham was true for his descendants, and it remains true for all people today.
4.18 Abraham believed God in hope and even when all hope seemed futile. Reason and experience told him that the promise of a son by Sarah at ninety years old could not happen, but in spite of this he believed. His hope sprang from his belief in God's all-sufficiency and that he would and could do what he had promised. This pattern of faith and hope in God applies today as well.

the dead, 25 who was handed over to death for our trespasses and was raised for our justification.

C. The results of justification by faith

5 Therefore, since we are justified by faith, we*q* have peace with God through our Lord Jesus Christ, 2 through whom we have obtained access*r* to this grace in which we stand; and we*s* boast in our hope of sharing the glory of God. 3 And not only that, but we*s* also boast in our sufferings, knowing that suffering produces endurance, 4 and endurance produces character, and character produces hope, 5 and hope does not disappoint us, because God's love has been poured into our hearts through the Holy Spirit that has been given to us.

6 For while we were still weak, at the right time Christ died for the ungodly. 7 Indeed, rarely will anyone die for a righteous person — though perhaps for a good person someone might actually dare to die. 8 But God proves his love for us in that while we still were sinners Christ died for us. 9 Much more surely then, now that we have been justified by his blood, will we be saved through him from the wrath of God.*t* 10 For if while we were enemies, we were reconciled to God through the death of his Son, much more surely, having been reconciled, will we be saved by his life. 11 But more than that, we even boast in God through our Lord Jesus Christ, through whom we have now received reconciliation.

D. Christ the ground of our salvation

12 Therefore, just as sin came into the world through one man, and death came through sin, and so death spread to all because all have sinned — 13 sin was indeed in the world before the law, but sin is not reckoned when there is no law. 14 Yet death exercised dominion from Adam to Moses, even over those whose sins were not like the transgression of Adam, who is a type of the one who is to come.

15 But the free gift is not like the trespass. For if the many died through the one man's trespass, much more surely have the grace of God and the free gift in the grace of the one man, Jesus Christ, abounded for

q Other ancient authorities read *let us*   *r* Other ancient authorities add *by faith*   *s* Or *let us*   *t* Gk *the wrath*

4.25 *our justification* (Gk. *dikaiōsis*). This word appears only twice in the N.T., while the verb *dikaioō* ("to justify") appears almost forty times. Justification is by grace and excludes works of all kinds (11.6; Gal 2.16,21; 3.10,21; 5.3,4; Eph 2.8,9; Phil 3.9). It has to do with the believer's relationship to God through the imputation of the righteousness of Jesus Christ. It is more than a pardon, for a pardon does not extinguish guilt. By the blood of Christ the demands of God's law have been fully met and satisfied so that the believers' situation is just as though they had never sinned. In other words, through justification the slate of God's claim against us as a result of our sin is wiped clean. This is in contrast to regeneration, through which a change takes place within the human heart. Both justification and regeneration must take place for salvation to be genuine.
5.1 *peace.* Sin is the obstacle that causes war between people and God. When sin is taken care of by faith in Christ and justification, the cause of the war is removed, enmity ceases, and peace begins. All believers have made their peace with God through the blood of the cross.
5.3 *suffering produces endurance.* Endurance results from testing, from being tried and not being found wanting. Without suffering there is little possibility that the believer can attain endurance. And without endurance, the Christian character God wants for us

is not developed.
5.9,10 *justified by his blood.* Without the shedding of blood there is no forgiveness of sin (Heb 9.22); the blood makes atonement for the soul (Lev 17.11). Thus the shed blood of Christ justifies the believer. *reconciled.* In addition to justification, we are reconciled to God by Christ's death and saved by his life. Christ's death removes God's anger against us for our sin and restores our relationship with him.
5.12ff In this passage Paul outlines two opposite states of existence: life versus death. In Adam there is sin, condemnation, and death; in Christ there is righteousness, justification, and eternal life. In Christ, Adam's situation, which we have inherited, is reversed. The comparison is not precise, however, because grace far exceeds anyone's sin and condemnation.
5.14 Adam was our common father, the representative of all of us. What he did may be said to have been done by us in him. By this one man sin entered the human race. Christ is the second Adam and the representative of all the elect. What he did may be said to have been done by us in him. In this way Adam functions as a type of Jesus Christ.
5.15 If guilt and wrath can be communicated, so can grace and love. If there is power and efficacy in the sin of people, there is greater power and efficacy in the righteousness and grace of Jesus Christ.

the many. 16 And the free gift is not like the effect of the one man's sin. For the judgment following one trespass brought condemnation, but the free gift following many trespasses brings justification. 17 If, because of the one man's trespass, death exercised dominion through that one, much more surely will those who receive the abundance of grace and the free gift of righteousness exercise dominion in life through the one man, Jesus Christ.

18 Therefore just as one man's trespass led to condemnation for all, so one man's act of righteousness leads to justification and life for all. 19 For just as by the one man's disobedience the many were made sinners, so by the one man's obedience the many will be made righteous. 20 But law came in, with the result that the trespass multiplied; but where sin increased, grace abounded all the more, 21 so that, just as sin exercised dominion in death, so grace might also exercise dominion through justification u leading to eternal life through Jesus Christ our Lord.

E. *The believer's life in Christ*

1. *United in his death*

6 What then are we to say? Should we continue in sin in order that grace may abound? 2 By no means! How can we who died to sin go on living in it? 3 Do you not know that all of us who have been baptized into Christ Jesus were baptized into his death? 4 Therefore we have been buried with him by baptism into death, so that, just as Christ was raised from the dead by the glory of the Father, so we too might walk in newness of life.

5 For if we have been united with him in a death like his, we will certainly be united with him in a resurrection like his. 6 We know that our old self was crucified with him so that the body of sin might be destroyed, and we might no longer be enslaved to sin. 7 For whoever has died is freed from sin. 8 But if we have died with Christ, we believe that we will also live with him. 9 We know that Christ, being raised from the dead, will never die again; death no longer has dominion over him. 10 The death he died, he died to sin, once for all; but the life he lives, he lives to God. 11 So you also must consider yourselves dead to sin and alive to God in Christ Jesus.

12 Therefore, do not let sin exercise dominion in your mortal bodies, to make you obey their passions. 13 No longer present your members to sin as instruments v of wickedness, but present yourselves to God as those who have been brought from death to life, and present your members to God as instruments v of righteousness. 14 For sin will have no dominion over you, since you are not under law but under grace.

u Or *righteousness*   v Or *weapons*

5.17
2 Tim 2.12;
Rev 22.5

5.18
v. 12;
Rom 4.25
5.19
v. 12;
Rom 11.32;
Phil 2.8
5.20
Rom 7.7, 8;
Gal 3.19;
1 Tim 1.14
5.21
vv. 12, 14;
Jn 1.17;
Rom 6.23

6.1
Rom 3.5, 8;
v. 15
6.2
Rom 7.4, 6;
Gal 2.19;
Col 3.3;
1 Pet 2.24
6.3
Acts 2.38;
8.16; 19.5
6.4
Col 2.12;
Gal 6.15;
Eph 4.22-24;
Col 3.10
6.6
Eph 4.22;
Col 3.9;
Gal 2.20;
Rom 7.24
6.9
Rev 1.18
6.10
Heb 7.27
6.11
v. 2;
Gal 2.19
6.12
v. 14
6.13
Rom 7.5;
Col 3.5;
Rom 12.1
6.14
Rom 8.2;
Gal 5.18

5.18,19 Adam's sin was disobedience. What he did was evil because it was forbidden by God. By God's judicial act we are made sinners along with Adam, for we are his posterity. In a similar pattern, through the obedience and the righteousness of Jesus Christ many are made righteous. The free gift is offered to all, though it is received only by those who believe. Some have interpreted v. 18 as teaching universalism, the doctrine that all humans will be saved through Christ just as all are lost in Adam. But this interpretation presses the analogy beyond what Paul meant. Nowhere do the Scriptures say that eventually everyone will obtain eternal life.

5.21 By God's grace through Jesus Christ our Lord, righteousness is applied to all who believe in order to justify them, and it is implanted within their hearts in order to sanctify them.

6.1ff Some people suppose that the doctrine of grace releases them from the obligation to keep the law of

God. This error is known as "antinomianism" (meaning "against the moral law") and leads to the conclusion that the more one sins, the more God's grace abounds. Paul refutes that view in this chapter (see also 3.8) by showing that salvation includes deliverance from the power of sin and death, not continued bondage to it.

6.2 *died to sin.* Death to sin should result in holiness of life. In this chapter Paul exhorts all believers to live a new life of holiness in Jesus Christ.

6.11ff *alive to God in Christ Jesus.* Through dying with Jesus Christ and rising again with him, we have a new life in God and a new delight in him for whom we live, yielding to him our eyes, ears, tongues, hands, etc.

6.14 *sin will have no dominion over you.* The glorious freedom we have in Christ means Christians can live victoriously. They can obey God from the heart, experience complete dedication, and enjoy God's grace,

2. Slaves to righteousness

15 What then? Should we sin because we are not under law but under grace? By no means! 16 Do you not know that if you present yourselves to anyone as obedient slaves, you are slaves of the one whom you obey, either of sin, which leads to death, or of obedience, which leads to righteousness? 17 But thanks be to God that you, having once been slaves of sin, have become obedient from the heart to the form of teaching to which you were entrusted, 18 and that you, having been set free from sin, have become slaves of righteousness. 19 I am speaking in human terms because of your natural limitations. *w* For just as you once presented your members as slaves to impurity and to greater and greater iniquity, so now present your members as slaves to righteousness for sanctification.

20 When you were slaves of sin, you were free in regard to righteousness. 21 So what advantage did you then get from the things of which you now are ashamed? The end of those things is death. 22 But now that you have been freed from sin and enslaved to God, the advantage you get is sanctification. The end is eternal life. 23 For the wages of sin is death, but the free gift of God is eternal life in Christ Jesus our Lord.

3. Married to Christ

7 Do you not know, brothers and sisters*x* — for I am speaking to those who know the law — that the law is binding on a person only during that person's lifetime? 2 Thus a married woman is bound by the law to her husband as long as he lives; but if her husband dies, she is discharged from the law concerning the husband. 3 Accordingly, she will be called an adulteress if she lives with another man while her husband is alive. But if her husband dies, she is free from that law, and if she marries another man, she is not an adulteress.

4 In the same way, my friends,*x* you have died to the law through the body of Christ, so that you may belong to another, to him who has been raised from the dead in order that we may bear fruit for God. 5 While we were living in the flesh, our sinful passions, aroused by the law, were at work in our members to bear fruit for death. 6 But now we are discharged from the law, dead to that which held us captive, so that we are slaves not under the old written code but in the new life of the Spirit.

4. The Christian struggle

7 What then should we say? That the law is sin? By no means! Yet, if it had not been for the law, I would not have known sin. I would not have known what it is to covet if the law had not said, "You shall not covet." 8 But sin, seizing an opportunity in the commandment, produced in me all kinds of covetousness. Apart from the law sin lies dead. 9 I was

w Gk the weakness of your flesh   *x* Gk brothers

6.16
Rom 11.2;
Mt 6.24;
Jn 8.34;
2 Pet 2.19
6.17
Rom 1.8;
2 Tim 1.13
6.18
Jn 8.32;
Rom 8.2
6.19
Rom 3.5;
6.13; 12.1

6.20
Mt 6.24;
Jn 8.34
6.21
Rom 7.5; 8.6,
13, 21
6.22
Jn 8.32;
1 Cor 7.22;
1 Pet 2.16
6.23
Rom 5.12;
5.21;
Gal 6.7, 8

7.2
1 Cor 7.39

7.3
Mt 5.32

7.4
Rom 6.2, 11;
Gal 2.19;
Col 1.22
7.5
Rom 6.13,
21;
Gal 5.19;
Jas 1.15
7.6
Rom 2.29;
2 Cor 3.6

7.7
Ex 20.17;
Deut 5.21;
Rom 3.20;
5.20
7.8
v. 11;
1 Cor 15.56

which alone makes such a life possible. Indeed, if there is no evidence of this new life in one who professes to be a Christian, the question may be rightly asked whether such a person has really been regenerated.
6.16 We are slaves to the master we obey. There are only two choices: God or Satan. Once Christians have been so gloriously delivered from obedience and slavery to Satan, they would be fools to return to that manner of life.
6.23 Sinners merit *death* as their wages. But saints do not merit eternal life. It is a *free gift* through Jesus Christ.
7.4 *you may belong to another.* We were married to the law by our transgressions. But in salvation we have died to the law and been released from our bondage to Satan. Now we are married to Jesus Christ. As

members of this new order, we must demonstrate to the world what the new life in Christ is all about.
7.7ff The whole import of the following verses depends on whether Paul is speaking of life before or after conversion. Scholars have argued strenuously for both interpretations (see note on 7.14ff). The war Paul refers to in his own life leads some to believe he was emphasizing the acute sense of one's own sin and the impotence, humanly speaking, to gain victory over it. Whatever the problem and however deep the sense of despair (cf. v. 24), Paul makes a sharp turnabout in ch. 8, which is the key to the life of victory. Paul, who cannot gain victory in the flesh, knows that victory is in Christ through the power of the Holy Spirit. Therefore, holiness is not only a possibility and a duty; it is our hope and it can be attained.

once alive apart from the law, but when the commandment came, sin revived 10 and I died, and the very commandment that promised life proved to be death to me. 11 For sin, seizing an opportunity in the commandment, deceived me and through it killed me. 12 So the law is holy, and the commandment is holy and just and good.

13 Did what is good, then, bring death to me? By no means! It was sin, working death in me through what is good, in order that sin might be shown to be sin, and through the commandment might become sinful beyond measure.

14 For we know that the law is spiritual; but I am of the flesh, sold into slavery under sin.y 15 I do not understand my own actions. For I do not do what I want, but I do the very thing I hate. 16 Now if I do what I do not want, I agree that the law is good. 17 But in fact it is no longer I that do it, but sin that dwells within me. 18 For I know that nothing good dwells within me, that is, in my flesh. I can will what is right, but I cannot do it. 19 For I do not do the good I want, but the evil I do not want is what I do. 20 Now if I do what I do not want, it is no longer I that do it, but sin that dwells within me.

21 So I find it to be a law that when I want to do what is good, evil lies close at hand. 22 For I delight in the law of God in my inmost self, 23 but I see in my members another law at war with the law of my mind, making me captive to the law of sin that dwells in my members. 24 Wretched man that I am! Who will rescue me from this body of death? 25 Thanks be to God through Jesus Christ our Lord!

So then, with my mind I am a slave to the law of God, but with my flesh I am a slave to the law of sin.

5. Life in the Spirit

a. Holiness a possibility

8 There is therefore now no condemnation for those who are in Christ Jesus. 2 For the law of the Spiritz of life in Christ Jesus has set youa free from the law of sin and of death. 3 For God has done what the law, weakened by the flesh, could not do: by sending his own Son in the likeness of sinful flesh, and to deal with sin,b he condemned sin in the flesh, 4 so that the just requirement of the law might be fulfilled in us, who walk not according to the flesh but according to the Spirit.z 5 For those who live according to the flesh set their minds on the things of the flesh, but those who live according to the Spiritz set their minds on the things of the Spirit.z 6 To set the mind on the flesh is death, but to set the mind

---

Cross references (right margin):

7.10 Lev 18.5; Rom 10.5; Gal 3.12
7.12 1 Tim 1.8
7.15 Gal 5.17
7.16 v. 12
7.17 v. 20
7.18 v. 25
7.19 v. 15
7.20 v. 17
7.21 vv. 23, 25
7.22 Ps 1.2; 2 Cor 4.16; Eph 3.16
7.23 Gal 5.17
7.24 Rom 6.6; 8.2
7.25 1 Cor 15.57
8.1 Rom 5.16
8.2 1 Cor 15.45; Rom 6.14, 18;
8.3 Jn 8.32, 36
8.3 Acts 13.39; Heb 7.18; Phil 2.7; Heb 2.14
8.4 Gal 5.16, 25
8.5 Gal 5.19-25
8.6 Rom 6.21; Gal 6.8

---

y Gk sold under sin   z Or spirit   a Here the Greek word you is singular number; other ancient authorities read me or us   b Or and as a sin offering

---

7.12 the law is holy . . . just and good. The law is God's will, and it is consonant with the rules of justice. It has for its grand design reaching people and aiding them to come to God and receive eternal life.
7.13 Sin perverts the law. The commandments (illustrated by the commandment not to covet), which were ordained to life and happiness, pointed out our sin and certified our death. The same sun that softens wax, hardens clay.
7.14ff This passage points out the difficulty interpreters face, for there are two things that seem paradoxical. On the one hand, Paul seems to be speaking about a convicted soul that is still unregenerate, for his reference to someone "sold into slavery under sin" (v. 14) can hardly mean a regenerate believer. On the other hand, he seems to be talking about a renewed, sanctified soul still in a state of imperfection, for his reference to those who delight in the law of God and serve the law of God (vv. 22,25) can hardly mean those who are dead in trespasses and sin.

7.15 For believers to say they have no sin is a lie (see 1 Jn 1.8). All believers do struggle in their hearts against the remainders of indwelling corruption. Truly regenerate persons groan under these struggles, mourn over them, and hate sin in any form. But in the end believers cannot fail, for ch. 8 refers to the possibility of a victorious life.
7.22 Regenerate people have new minds, which *delight in the law of God*. They consent to it and struggle to obey it.
7.25 In our ongoing struggle against sin, Paul reassures us that Christ is all-sufficient. In the midst of his complaint Paul begins to praise the one through whom God has spared us and pardoned us.
8.1 All people deserve condemnation (cf. 3.23; 6.23), but we as believers will not experience it. We have the unspeakable privilege of being among those to whom God speaks the words of this verse. Christ is our advocate, who removes our condemnation so that God is pleased with us.

on the Spirit*c* is life and peace. 7 For this reason the mind that is set on the flesh is hostile to God; it does not submit to God's law — indeed it cannot, 8 and those who are in the flesh cannot please God.

9 But you are not in the flesh; you are in the Spirit,*c* since the Spirit of God dwells in you. Anyone who does not have the Spirit of Christ does not belong to him. 10 But if Christ is in you, though the body is dead because of sin, the Spirit*c* is life because of righteousness. 11 If the Spirit of him who raised Jesus from the dead dwells in you, he who raised Christ*d* from the dead will give life to your mortal bodies also through*e* his Spirit that dwells in you.

b. Holiness a duty

12 So then, brothers and sisters,*f* we are debtors, not to the flesh, to live according to the flesh — 13 for if you live according to the flesh, you will die; but if by the Spirit you put to death the deeds of the body, you will live. 14 For all who are led by the Spirit of God are children of God. 15 For you did not receive a spirit of slavery to fall back into fear, but you have received a spirit of adoption. When we cry, "Abba!*g* Father!" 16 it is that very Spirit bearing witness*h* with our spirit that we are children of God, 17 and if children, then heirs, heirs of God and joint heirs with Christ — if, in fact, we suffer with him so that we may also be glorified with him.

6. The future glory

a. A sure hope

18 I consider that the sufferings of this present time are not worth comparing with the glory about to be revealed to us. 19 For the creation waits with eager longing for the revealing of the children of God; 20 for the creation was subjected to futility, not of its own will but by the will of the one who subjected it, in hope 21 that the creation itself will be set free from its bondage to decay and will obtain the freedom of the glory of the children of God. 22 We know that the whole creation has been groaning in labor pains until now; 23 and not only the creation, but we ourselves, who have the first fruits of the Spirit, groan inwardly while we

c Or *spirit*   *d* Other ancient authorities read *the Christ* or *Christ Jesus* or *Jesus Christ*   *e* Other ancient authorities read *on account of*   *f* Gk *brothers*   *g* Aramaic for *Father*   *h* Or 15 a spirit of adoption, by which we cry, "Abba! Father!" 16 The Spirit itself bears witness

---

8.6 *set the mind . . . set the mind.* There are two kinds of mind — the spiritual mind and the fleshly mind. Each leads to a different end; the mind of the Spirit leads to life and peace, the mind of the flesh to death. Those who have a spiritual mind do not walk after the flesh. Anyone who professes Christ and then walks after the flesh must ask two questions: (1) Am I truly regenerated? (2) If I am regenerated, how can I be sanctified so that my life corresponds to my claim to be a Christian?
8.9 Whoever is regenerated is sealed by the Holy Spirit (cf. Eph 1.13) and indwelt by the same Spirit. Whoever does not have the Spirit does not have Christ and lives in a state of darkness and separation from God.
8.10 One of the benefits of regeneration is spiritual life, but the body remains under the sentence of death. Believers will die in the flesh but not in the spirit. There is a future bodily resurrection in which the body will be reunited by the Spirit with the soul (v. 11), be clothed in glory (Phil 3.21), and become immortal (1 Cor 15.42–49).
8.11 It was the Holy Spirit who raised Christ from the dead. The same Spirit is the agent who gives life to sinners dead in their trespasses.
8.13 Paul and James were in full agreement that the

regenerated children of God must live differently. Faith without works is a dead faith (Jas 2.14ff), and those who have true faith manifest that change by the way they think and live.
8.16 *it is that very Spirit bearing witness with our spirit.* The world of the unregenerate cannot understand what is taught here, because they do not know the Spirit of God. The great certainty of our salvation comes from the witness of the Holy Spirit with our spirits. *Children of God* are those who have received Christ as Savior and Lord and have been regenerated, for "to all who received him . . . he gave power to become children of God" (Jn 1.12). Only Christ by nature is a child of God, but sinners can be adopted into the family of God via the new birth.
8.17 Believers are joint heirs with Jesus Christ, who is their older brother. All that belongs to him belongs also to those who are his brothers and sisters through redemption (cf. 1 Cor 3.21–23).
8.22 By his transgression Adam not only condemned his descendants to sin and death, but his act also brought the bondage of decay to all nonhuman life and to nature itself. Fortunately, redemption is cosmic; all things will be reconstituted (cf. 2 Pet 3.10–13) and no longer subject to futility and decay.

wait for adoption, the redemption of our bodies. ²⁴For in[i] hope we were saved. Now hope that is seen is not hope. For who hopes[j] for what is seen? ²⁵But if we hope for what we do not see, we wait for it with patience.

b. *A sure help*

26   Likewise the Spirit helps us in our weakness; for we do not know how to pray as we ought, but that very Spirit intercedes[k] with sighs too deep for words. ²⁷And God,[l] who searches the heart, knows what is the mind of the Spirit, because the Spirit[m] intercedes for the saints according to the will of God.[n]

28   We know that all things work together for good[o] for those who love God, who are called according to his purpose. ²⁹For those whom he foreknew he also predestined to be conformed to the image of his Son, in order that he might be the firstborn within a large family.[p] ³⁰And those whom he predestined he also called; and those whom he called he also justified; and those whom he justified he also glorified.

c. *A certain salvation*

31   What then are we to say about these things? If God is for us, who is against us? ³²He who did not withhold his own Son, but gave him up for all of us, will he not with him also give us everything else? ³³Who will bring any charge against God's elect? It is God who justifies. ³⁴Who is to condemn? It is Christ Jesus, who died, yes, who was raised, who is at the right hand of God, who indeed intercedes for us.[q] ³⁵Who will separate us from the love of Christ? Will hardship, or distress, or persecution, or famine, or nakedness, or peril, or sword? ³⁶As it is written,

"For your sake we are being killed all day long;
   we are accounted as sheep to be slaughtered."

³⁷No, in all these things we are more than conquerors through him who loved us. ³⁸For I am convinced that neither death, nor life, nor angels, nor rulers, nor things present, nor things to come, nor powers, ³⁹nor height, nor depth, nor anything else in all creation, will be able to separate us from the love of God in Christ Jesus our Lord.

IV. *Jew and Gentile in the plan of God (9.1–11.36)*

A. *Paul's sorrow for Israel*

9   I am speaking the truth in Christ—I am not lying; my conscience confirms it by the Holy Spirit—²I have great sorrow and unceasing

i Or *by*   *j* Other ancient authorities read *awaits*   *k* Other ancient authorities add *for us*   *l* Gk *the one*
m Gk *he* or *it*   *n* Gk *according to God*   *o* Other ancient authorities read *God makes all things work together*
for good, or *in all things God works for good*   *p* Gk *among many brothers*   *q* Or *Is it Christ Jesus . . . for us?*

8.26
Mt 20.22;
Eph 6.18
8.27
Ps 139.1, 2;
Lk 16.15;
Rev 2.23
8.28
v. 32
8.29
Rom 11.2;
1 Pet 1.2, 20;
Eph 1.5, 11;
Phil 3.21;
Heb 1.6
8.30
Eph 1.5, 11;
Rom 9.24;
1 Cor 6.11
8.31
Rom 4.1;
Ps 118.6
8.32
Jn 3.16;
Rom 5.8;
4.25
8.33
Lk 18.7;
Isa 50.8, 9
8.34
Col 3.1;
Heb 1.3;
7.25; 9.24;
1 Jn 2.1
8.36
Ps 44.22;
2 Cor 4.11
8.37
1 Cor 15.57;
Rev 1.5
8.38
Eph 1.21;
1 Pet 3.22

9.1
2 Cor 1.23;
11.10;
1 Tim 2.7

8.24   Christian *hope,* based on the reliable promises of God, constitutes confidence that the day will arrive when what we hope for comes to pass. The lack of hope is sin, for it denies what God and Scripture affirm. Hope is reinforced by reading the Word of God, by prayer, and by the infilling of the Holy Spirit.
8.26   Believers are imperfect in their prayer lives, for often we do not know what to ask for nor how to pray. The Spirit in the word of God and in the believers' hearts helps. He teaches us how to pray, what to pray for, and even takes over for us with sighs too deep for words. When the Spirit's strength is added to our weakness, we are unconquerable.
8.28   The phrase *we know* is the basis of the believer's certainty. There are no ifs, ands, or buts about that certainty.
8.29   *he also predestined.* Predestination with respect to salvation is an act of God done in accordance with his will. The attempt to undercut predestination by

saying that it is based on foreknowledge (i.e., that God foresees what people will do and then ordains that they do it) is inconsistent, for predestination then loses all credible meaning. We must admit we are faced with a mystery here, in which God works out his sovereign will while at the same time preserving human free choice. Thus people may act freely to accept or reject Jesus Christ; yet only the Holy Spirit can move them to accept him, and their response to God's grace is foreknown and foreordained in the mind and will of God.
8.38,39   Paul is fully and strongly convinced that nothing living or dead, animate or inanimate, can breach the believer's defense and separate him from the God to whom he is attached by faith through Jesus Christ. This is God's solemn promise, and his word cannot be broken by anyone or anything.
9.1ff   Paul interrupts his argument to speak in chs. 9—11 about Israel and its future. Beginning with

9.3
Ex 32.32

9.4
Acts 3.25;
Ps 147.19;
Heb 9.1
9.5
Col 1.16-19;
Jn 1.1;
Rom 1.25

9.6
Num 23.19;
Rom 2.28,
29;
Gal 6.16
9.7
Gal 4.23;
Heb 11.18
9.8
Rom 8.14;
Gal 3.29;
4.28
9.9
Gen 18.10
9.10
Gen 25.21
9.11
Rom 4.17;
8.28
9.12
Gen 25.23
9.13
Mal 1.2, 3
9.14
2 Chr 19.7
9.15
Ex 33.19
9.16
Eph 2.8
9.17
Ex 9.16

9.19
2 Chr 20.6;
Job 23.13;
Dan 4.35
9.20
Isa 29.16;
64.8
9.21
2 Tim 2.20

anguish in my heart. 3 For I could wish that I myself were accursed and cut off from Christ for the sake of my own people,[r] my kindred according to the flesh. 4 They are Israelites, and to them belong the adoption, the glory, the covenants, the giving of the law, the worship, and the promises; 5 to them belong the patriarchs, and from them, according to the flesh, comes the Messiah,[s] who is over all, God blessed forever.[t] Amen.

B. The unbelief of the Jew not God's fault

6 It is not as though the word of God had failed. For not all Israelites truly belong to Israel, 7 and not all of Abraham's children are his true descendants; but "It is through Isaac that descendants shall be named for you." 8 This means that it is not the children of the flesh who are the children of God, but the children of the promise are counted as descendants. 9 For this is what the promise said, "About this time I will return and Sarah shall have a son." 10 Nor is that all; something similar happened to Rebecca when she had conceived children by one husband, our ancestor Isaac. 11 Even before they had been born or had done anything good or bad (so that God's purpose of election might continue, 12 not by works but by his call) she was told, "The elder shall serve the younger." 13 As it is written,

"I have loved Jacob,
    but I have hated Esau."

14 What then are we to say? Is there injustice on God's part? By no means! 15 For he says to Moses,

"I will have mercy on whom I have mercy,
    and I will have compassion on whom I have compassion."

16 So it depends not on human will or exertion, but on God who shows mercy. 17 For the scripture says to Pharaoh, "I have raised you up for this very purpose of showing my power in you, so that my name may be proclaimed in all the earth." 18 So then he has mercy on whomever he chooses, and he hardens the heart of whomever he chooses.

19 You will say to me then, "Why then does he still find fault? For who can resist his will?" 20 But who indeed are you, a human being, to argue with God? Will what is molded say to the one who molds it, "Why have you made me like this?" 21 Has the potter no right over the clay, to make out of the same lump one object for special use and another for

[r] Gk my brothers   [s] Or the Christ   [t] Or Messiah, who is God over all, blessed forever; or Messiah. May he who is God over all be blessed forever

"therefore" in ch. 12 Paul picks up where he left off at the end of ch. 8. One might do well to temporarily skip the reading of chs. 9 — 11, go to ch. 12, and later return to these chapters.
9.3 *I could wish*, i.e., he would if he could, but he knows that he cannot be accursed for the sake of Israel his people. So intense is his affection for the children of Abraham that he would willingly lose his own eternal life if they could gain salvation by his losing it.
9.4 It is ironical that the Israelites, in spite of having received from God everything anyone could want, rejected the one who gave them so much.
9.5 *Messiah . . . God blessed forever.* According to the construction in the Greek, this is one of the clearest verses in the Bible that confirms the deity of Jesus Christ. He is God Almighty, the second person of the holy Trinity.
9.6ff Paul notes the difference between those who belong to Israel by physical birth and those who are part of spiritual Israel. Not all who were born into Jewish families belonged to spiritual Israel. But all who share Abraham's faith in God, whether Jew or Gentile, are the real spiritual descendants of Abraham. Thus Gentile Christians are true children of Abraham.

9.13 *I have loved Jacob, but I have hated Esau.* Jacob had been chosen by God to be Abraham's promised heir through whom the Messiah should come. This was done while Esau and Jacob were in their mother's womb and before either had done good or evil. Everything was done "so that God's purpose of election might continue" (v. 11). For example, God called Mary to be the mother of the historical Jesus, and John the Baptist to be Christ's forerunner, and Jeremiah to be his prophet before any of them were conceived. The reference here to loving Jacob and hating Esau (quoted from Mal 1.2,3) does not refer to them as individuals but to the Israelites (the descendants of Jacob) and the Edomites (the descendants of Esau). The Edomites were hated by God for their sins against him.
9.21 This verse must be understood within the larger context of all the teachings of Scripture about human capability and responsibility. People are not merely impotent organisms, automatons void of responsibility either for their actions or for their ultimate destiny. The merciful God has freely opened the gate of life to all who respond to the gospel invitation (cf. v. 16). He has extended mercy to all; humans, of their own volition, may take it or leave it.

ordinary use? 22 What if God, desiring to show his wrath and to make known his power, has endured with much patience the objects of wrath that are made for destruction; 23 and what if he has done so in order to make known the riches of his glory for the objects of mercy, which he has prepared beforehand for glory — 24 including us whom he has called, not from the Jews only but also from the Gentiles? 25 As indeed he says in Hosea,

> "Those who were not my people I will call 'my people,'
> and her who was not beloved I will call 'beloved.' "

26 "And in the very place where it was said to them, 'You are not
> my people,'
> there they shall be called children of the living God."

27 And Isaiah cries out concerning Israel, "Though the number of the children of Israel were like the sand of the sea, only a remnant of them will be saved; 28 for the Lord will execute his sentence on the earth quickly and decisively."[u] 29 And as Isaiah predicted,

> "If the Lord of hosts had not left survivors[v] to us,
> we would have fared like Sodom
> and been made like Gomorrah."

30 What then are we to say? Gentiles, who did not strive for righteousness, have attained it, that is, righteousness through faith; 31 but Israel, who did strive for the righteousness that is based on the law, did not succeed in fulfilling that law. 32 Why not? Because they did not strive for it on the basis of faith, but as if it were based on works. They have stumbled over the stumbling stone, 33 as it is written,

> "See, I am laying in Zion a stone that will make people
> stumble, a rock that will make them fall,
> and whoever believes in him[w] will not be put to shame."

C. God's rejection the fault of the Jews

10 Brothers and sisters,[x] my heart's desire and prayer to God for them is that they may be saved. 2 I can testify that they have a zeal for God, but it is not enlightened. 3 For, being ignorant of the righteousness that comes from God, and seeking to establish their own, they have not submitted to God's righteousness. 4 For Christ is the end of the law so that there may be righteousness for everyone who believes.

5 Moses writes concerning the righteousness that comes from the law, that "the person who does these things will live by them." 6 But the righteousness that comes from faith says, "Do not say in your heart, 'Who will ascend into heaven?' " (that is, to bring Christ down) 7 "or 'Who will descend into the abyss?' " (that is, to bring Christ up from the dead). 8 But what does it say?

> "The word is near you,
> on your lips and in your heart"

u Other authorities read *for he will finish his work and cut it short in righteousness, because the Lord will make the sentence shortened on the earth*   *v* Or *descendants*; Gk *seed*   *w* Or *trusts in it*
x Gk *Brothers*

Cross references (right margin):

9.22 Rom 2.4
9.23 Eph 3.16; Rom 8.29, 30
9.24 Rom 3.29
9.25 Hos 2.23; 1 Pet 2.10
9.26 Hos 1.10
9.27 Isa 10.22, 23; Gen 22.17; Hos 1.10
9.29 Isa 1.4; 13.19; Jer 50.40
9.30 Rom 10.6; Gal 2.16; Heb 11.7
9.31 Rom 10.2, 3; Gal 5.4
9.32 1 Pet 2.6, 8
9.33 Isa 28.16; Mt 21.42; Rom 10.11
10.2 Acts 21.20
10.3 Rom 1.17; Phil 3.9
10.4 Gal 3.24; Rom 7.1-4
10.5 Neh 9.29; Ezek 20.11, 13, 21; Rom 7.10
10.7 Heb 13.20
10.8 Deut 30.14

9.23 Nothing required God to make salvation available to sinners. He owed them nothing; sinners owed him everything and they could not pay. By his free grace he offers life both to the Jew and to the Gentile, for both are under condemnation (cf. 3.23).
9.30ff The Gentiles did not follow after righteousness nor did they seek a remedy for their desperate condition. But God extended gospel benefits to them through faith, and many responded and were made righteous. On the other hand, the Jews followed after the law of righteousness and talked much about justification and holiness, but they did not attain them, for they sought it by their own works. They rejected Christ, who was sent to remedy their condition. He became a stumbling block to them, a rock over which they tripped and fell. But to them God also extended the good news in the person of Jesus; they must turn to him if they wish to attain righteousness.
10.3 Self-righteousness undercuts God's own righteousness by inserting a spurious substitute in its place, a human righteousness that gives them no standing in the sight of God (Isa 64.6; Mk 10.18). It comes from the false view that humans in themselves can be righteous with God or can make themselves righteous by their own efforts.

10.9 Mt 10.32; Lk 12.8; Acts 16.31	(that is, the word of faith that we proclaim); 9 because[y] if you confess with your lips that Jesus is Lord and believe in your heart that God raised him from the dead, you will be saved. 10 For one believes with the heart and so is justified, and one confesses with the mouth and so is saved. 11 The scripture says, "No one who believes in him will be put to shame." 12 For there is no distinction between Jew and Greek; the same Lord is Lord of all and is generous to all who call on him. 13 For, "Everyone who calls on the name of the Lord shall be saved."

10.11
Isa 28.16;
Rom 9.33
10.12
Rom 3.22,
29;
Gal 3.28;
Acts 10.36
10.13
Joel 2.32;
Acts 2.21
10.15
Isa 52.7

14 But how are they to call on one in whom they have not believed? And how are they to believe in one of whom they have never heard? And how are they to hear without someone to proclaim him? 15 And how are they to proclaim him unless they are sent? As it is written, "How beautiful are the feet of those who bring good news!" 16 But not all have obeyed the good news;[z] for Isaiah says, "Lord, who has believed our message?" 17 So faith comes from what is heard, and what is heard comes through the word of Christ.[a]

10.16
Heb 4.2;
Isa 53.1;
Jn 12.38
10.17
Gal 3.2, 5;
Col 3.16
10.18
Ps 19.4;
Col 1.6, 23;
1 Thess 1.8

18 But I ask, have they not heard? Indeed they have; for

"Their voice has gone out to all the earth,
    and their words to the ends of the world."

10.19
Deut 32.21;
Rom 11.11

19 Again I ask, did Israel not understand? First Moses says,

"I will make you jealous of those who are not a nation;
    with a foolish nation I will make you angry."

10.20
Isa 65.1;
Rom 9.30

20 Then Isaiah is so bold as to say,

"I have been found by those who did not seek me;
    I have shown myself to those who did not ask for me."

10.21
Isa 65.2

21 But of Israel he says, "All day long I have held out my hands to a disobedient and contrary people."

D. Israel's rejection not final

1. The remnant

11.1
1 Sam 12.22;
Jer 31.37;
2 Cor 11.22;
Phil 3.5
11.2
Ps 94.19;
1 Kings 19.10;
Rom 8.29
11.4
1 Kings 19.18
11.5
2 Kings 19.4;
Rom 9.27

11 I ask, then, has God rejected his people? By no means! I myself am an Israelite, a descendant of Abraham, a member of the tribe of Benjamin. 2 God has not rejected his people whom he foreknew. Do you not know what the scripture says of Elijah, how he pleads with God against Israel? 3 "Lord, they have killed your prophets, they have demolished your altars; I alone am left, and they are seeking my life." 4 But what is the divine reply to him? "I have kept for myself seven thousand who have not bowed the knee to Baal." 5 So too at the present time there is a

y Or namely, that   z Or gospel   a Or about Christ; other ancient authorities read of God

---

10.9,10 These two verses contain that which is basic and essential to salvation from sin. Those who hear that Jesus is Lord, believe that in their hearts, and confess him with their lips can be sure that they have eternal life. Such people are saved.
10.13 Regardless of what position we may have on human free choice, this verse (quoting Joel 2.32) says clearly that whoever calls on the name of the Lord shall be saved. Evangelism and missionary outreach have one main task: to exhort whoever hears to come to salvation in Christ. Why some respond to the invitation and others do not is not the business of the evangelist or the missionary. That belongs to the secret counsels of God.
10.15 *unless they are sent.* All believers must pray that the Lord of the harvest will send forth laborers into the harvest fields (Lk 10.2). And all believers should say in their hearts, "Here am I; send me!" (cf. Isa 6.8), and then do as the Spirit leads.
11.1ff *has God rejected his people?* i.e., "Has God totally and finally rejected Israel?" or, "Are all the

Israelites abandoned to God's wrath and eternal ruin?" Indeed many of them have been cast off, but not all. There is a remnant according to grace who will be saved (v. 5), though their salvation will be by grace apart from works (v. 6). Both Jews and Gentiles come to God the same way: by faith alone. Many evangelical Christians hold that the church is the new Israel; they do not distinguish Israel as uniquely different from the church, for to them, the saved of all ages are members of the church, the body of Christ. Dispensationalists, on the other hand, hold to seven dispensations or covenants. In their thinking there are two separate and distinct peoples of God: Israel and the church. They are premillennial and generally believe in the secret, pretribulational rapture of the church. World evangelization will be completed by the Jews subsequent to the rapture of the church. They maintain that while all Scripture is written to us, not all Scripture is for us in this age. For example, the sermon on the mount applies to Israel, not the church, and thus many do not pray the Lord's Prayer.

remnant, chosen by grace. [6] But if it is by grace, it is no longer on the basis of works, otherwise grace would no longer be grace. [b]

7　What then? Israel failed to obtain what it was seeking. The elect obtained it, but the rest were hardened, [8] as it is written,

"God gave them a sluggish spirit,
　　eyes that would not see
　　and ears that would not hear,
down to this very day."

[9] And David says,

"Let their table become a snare and a trap,
　　a stumbling block and a retribution for them;
[10]　let their eyes be darkened so that they cannot see,
　　and keep their backs forever bent."

2. Israel's future salvation

11　So I ask, have they stumbled so as to fall? By no means! But through their stumbling [c] salvation has come to the Gentiles, so as to make Israel [d] jealous. [12] Now if their stumbling [c] means riches for the world, and if their defeat means riches for Gentiles, how much more will their full inclusion mean!

13　Now I am speaking to you Gentiles. Inasmuch then as I am an apostle to the Gentiles, I glorify my ministry [14] in order to make my own people [e] jealous, and thus save some of them. [15] For if their rejection is the reconciliation of the world, what will their acceptance be but life from the dead! [16] If the part of the dough offered as first fruits is holy, then the whole batch is holy; and if the root is holy, then the branches also are holy.

17　But if some of the branches were broken off, and you, a wild olive shoot, were grafted in their place to share the rich root [f] of the olive tree, [18] do not boast over the branches. If you do boast, remember that it is not you that support the root, but the root that supports you. [19] You will say, "Branches were broken off so that I might be grafted in." [20] That is true. They were broken off because of their unbelief, but you stand only through faith. So do not become proud, but stand in awe. [21] For if God did not spare the natural branches, perhaps he will not spare you. [g] [22] Note then the kindness and the severity of God: severity toward those who have fallen, but God's kindness toward you, provided you continue in his kindness; otherwise you also will be cut off. [23] And even those of Israel, [h] if they do not persist in unbelief, will be grafted in, for God has the power to graft them in again. [24] For if you have been cut from what is by nature a wild olive tree and grafted, contrary to nature, into a cultivated olive tree, how much more will these natural branches be grafted back into their own olive tree.

25　So that you may not claim to be wiser than you are, brothers and

	11.6 Rom 4.4
	11.7 Rom 9.18, 31
	11.8 Isa 29.10; Deut 29.4; Mt 13.13, 14
	11.9 Ps 69.22, 23
	11.11 Acts 13.46; Rom 10.19 **11.12** v. 25
	11.13 Acts 9.15; Rom 15.16 **11.14** Rom 10.19; 1 Cor 7.16; 9.22 **11.15** Lk 15.24, 32 **11.16** Lev 23.10; Num 15.18 **11.17** Jer 11.17; Acts 2.39; Eph 2.11, 12 **11.20** Rom 12.16; 2 Cor 1.24
	11.22 1 Cor 15.2; Heb 3.6; Jn 15.2 **11.23** 2 Cor 3.16
	11.25 1 Cor 2.7-10; Eph 3.3-5, 9; Rom 9.18

b Other ancient authorities add *But if it is by works, it is no longer on the basis of grace, otherwise work would no longer be work*　c Gk *transgression*　d Gk *them*　e Gk *my flesh*　f Other ancient authorities read *the richness*　g Other ancient authorities read *neither will he spare you*　h Gk lacks *of Israel*

11.11 Paul preached to the Jews first (cf. the book of Acts). When they rejected the gospel, he turned to the Gentiles (e.g., Acts 13.44–48). Thus Israel is directly responsible for the gospel being preached to the Gentiles. But it does not mean that had Israel accepted the gospel the Gentiles would have been left to themselves. Isaiah had prophesied that the good news was for the Gentiles as well as for the Jews (Isa 49.6; cf. Lk 2.30–32).
11.17 Paul's use of *the olive tree* revolves around faith and unbelief. The Jews who were part of God's olive tree had been removed because of their unbelief; Gentiles who came from wild olive trees were being grafted into the stock of Israel because of their faith. Any Jews who do repent and return to God may be

regrafted into the true tree, and Gentiles can be removed if they abandon their faith. Figures usually break down at some point and are not fully adequate to explain the truths at hand. Thus, this analogy does not fully explain the paradox of human freedom and God's sovereign election.
11.25,26 People are brought to God individually. Nowhere is God said to save nations as such. However, God did choose Israel and used that nation to be a channel for his purposes. But each Israelite was saved or lost depending upon his or her personal response to God's good news of and provision for redemption. God is now bringing in his redeemed from every nation, tribe, people, and language (Rev 7.9). *all Israel will be saved.* This means that substan-

11.26
Isa 59.20, 21

11.27
Isa 27.9

11.28
Deut 7.8;
10.15;
Rom 5.10;
9.5
11.29
Num 23.19
11.30
Eph 2.2
11.32
Rom 3.9;
Gal 3.22, 23

11.33
Eph 3.8;
Ps 92.5
11.34
Isa 40.13,
14;
1 Cor 2.16;
Job 36.22

11.36
1 Cor 8.6;
Heb 2.10;
Rom 16.27;
Heb 13.21

12.1
2 Cor 10.1, 2;
Rom 6.13,
16, 19;
1 Pet 2.5
12.2
1 Pet 1.14;
1 Jn 2.15;
Eph 4.23;
5.10

12.3
Rom 15.15;
2 Cor 10.13;
Eph 4.7
12.4
1 Cor 12.12-14;
Eph 4.4, 16
12.6
1 Cor 7.7;
12.4, 10;
1 Pet 4.10, 11

sisters,[i] I want you to understand this mystery: a hardening has come upon part of Israel, until the full number of the Gentiles has come in. 26 And so all Israel will be saved; as it is written,

"Out of Zion will come the Deliverer;
    he will banish ungodliness from Jacob."
27 "And this is my covenant with them,
    when I take away their sins."

28 As regards the gospel they are enemies of God[j] for your sake; but as regards election they are beloved, for the sake of their ancestors; 29 for the gifts and the calling of God are irrevocable. 30 Just as you were once disobedient to God but have now received mercy because of their disobedience, 31 so they have now been disobedient in order that, by the mercy shown to you, they too may now[k] receive mercy. 32 For God has imprisoned all in disobedience so that he may be merciful to all.

3. Paul's concluding doxology

33 O the depth of the riches and wisdom and knowledge of God! How unsearchable are his judgments and how inscrutable his ways!
34 "For who has known the mind of the Lord?
    Or who has been his counselor?"
35 "Or who has given a gift to him,
    to receive a gift in return?"
36 For from him and through him and to him are all things. To him be the glory forever. Amen.

V. Ethical teaching (12.1–15.13)

A. The call to full surrender

12 I appeal to you therefore, brothers and sisters,[i] by the mercies of God, to present your bodies as a living sacrifice, holy and acceptable to God, which is your spiritual[l] worship. 2 Do not be conformed to this world,[m] but be transformed by the renewing of your minds, so that you may discern what is the will of God — what is good and acceptable and perfect.[n]

B. The use of God's gifts

3 For by the grace given to me I say to everyone among you not to think of yourself more highly than you ought to think, but to think with sober judgment, each according to the measure of faith that God has assigned. 4 For as in one body we have many members, and not all the members have the same function, 5 so we, who are many, are one body in Christ, and individually we are members one of another. 6 We have gifts

i Gk brothers j Gk lacks of God k Other ancient authorities lack now l Or reasonable m Gk age
n Or what is the good and acceptable and perfect will of God

tial numbers of the Jews will turn to God in Christ before the end of the age. They will be saved the same way everyone else is — by faith in Christ.
12.1,2 In ch. 1 Paul spoke holistically about people, stating that people commit all kinds of sexual and other sins because their minds have been corrupted. Thus he unified mind and body, for the body merely expresses what is in the mind. Now in ch. 12 Paul ties mind and body together in the new relationship in Jesus Christ. We must lay our bodies on the altar of sacrifice to God just as Abraham tied his son Isaac to the altar. At the same time, our minds must be renewed and transformed.
12.3 think of yourself. All believers should have a good self-image based on the fact that they are a new

creation in Christ Jesus. Unfortunately, some believers wrongly think of themselves as worthless. On the other hand, others fall into the sin of thinking more highly of themselves than they ought. We should have a sober, realistic view of ourselves, a view that neither downgrades nor exalts ourselves beyond the truth.
12.6 God by his Spirit gives believers different gifts. All of us must use these gifts, some directly in matters related to the church, others in callings such as medicine, law, business, etc. Whoever is given the gift of making money has received that gift from the Spirit and should use that means to glorify God. Men and women who work in factories are likewise gifted by the Spirit and should work as unto God. God's gifts are not to be abused, misused, or unused.

that differ according to the grace given to us: prophecy, in proportion to faith; 7 ministry, in ministering; the teacher, in teaching; 8 the exhorter, in exhortation; the giver, in generosity; the leader, in diligence; the compassionate, in cheerfulness.

C. Christian conduct in personal relationships

9 Let love be genuine; hate what is evil, hold fast to what is good; 10 love one another with mutual affection; outdo one another in showing honor. 11 Do not lag in zeal, be ardent in spirit, serve the Lord.*o* 12 Rejoice in hope, be patient in suffering, persevere in prayer. 13 Contribute to the needs of the saints; extend hospitality to strangers.

14 Bless those who persecute you; bless and do not curse them. 15 Rejoice with those who rejoice, weep with those who weep. 16 Live in harmony with one another; do not be haughty, but associate with the lowly;*p* do not claim to be wiser than you are. 17 Do not repay anyone evil for evil, but take thought for what is noble in the sight of all. 18 If it is possible, so far as it depends on you, live peaceably with all. 19 Beloved, never avenge yourselves, but leave room for the wrath of God;*q* for it is written, "Vengeance is mine, I will repay, says the Lord." 20 No, "if your enemies are hungry, feed them; if they are thirsty, give them something to drink; for by doing this you will heap burning coals on their heads." 21 Do not be overcome by evil, but overcome evil with good.

D. Christian conduct in relation to the state

13 Let every person be subject to the governing authorities; for there is no authority except from God, and those authorities that exist have been instituted by God. 2 Therefore whoever resists authority resists what God has appointed, and those who resist will incur judgment. 3 For rulers are not a terror to good conduct, but to bad. Do you wish to have no fear of the authority? Then do what is good, and you will receive its approval; 4 for it is God's servant for your good. But if you do what is wrong, you should be afraid, for the authority*r* does not bear the sword in vain! It is the servant of God to execute wrath on the wrongdoer. 5 Therefore one must be subject, not only because of wrath but also because of conscience. 6 For the same reason you also pay taxes, for the authorities are God's servants, busy with this very thing. 7 Pay to all what is due them—taxes to whom taxes are due, revenue to whom revenue is due, respect to whom respect is due, honor to whom honor is due.

E. The call to love

8 Owe no one anything, except to love one another; for the one who loves another has fulfilled the law. 9 The commandments, "You shall not commit adultery; You shall not murder; You shall not steal; You shall not

o Other ancient authorities read *serve the opportune time*   *p* Or *give yourselves to humble tasks*   *q* Gk *the wrath*   *r* Gk *it*

12.7 1 Cor 12.28; 14.26
12.8 Acts 15.32; Mt 6.1-3; 1 Tim 5.17; 2 Cor 9.7

12.12 Heb 10.32, 36; Acts 1.14
12.13 Rom 15.25; Heb 13.2
12.14 Mt 5.44; Lk 6.28
12.16 Rom 15.5; 11.25
12.17 Prov 20.22; 2 Cor 8.21
12.18 Mk 9.50; Rom 14.19
12.19 Lev 19.18; Heb 10.30
12.20 Prov 25.21, 22; Mt 5.44; Lk 6.27
13.1 Titus 3.1; 1 Pet 2.13; Jn 19.11; Dan 2.21
13.2 Titus 3.1
13.3 1 Pet 2.14
13.4 1 Thess 4.6
13.5 Eccl 8.2; 1 Pet 2.19
13.7 Mt 22.21; Mk 12.17; Lk 20.25

13.8 Gal 5.14; Col 3.14; Jas 2.8
13.9 Ex 20.13, 14; Mt 19.19

12.11 *be ardent in spirit.* Spirit-filled believers will be aglow with the Spirit. Their lives will conform to the will of God, and they will bring forth the fruit of the Spirit (cf. Gal 5.22,23).
12.18 Christians must endeavor to live peaceably with everyone, believers and unbelievers alike. But we must not promote peace at any price, especially if doing so requires that we go against our consciences as shaped by God's word.
13.1ff Governments are ordained of God, receive their authority from God, and must be obeyed. They bear the sword and must execute vengeance on wrongdoers, and they are entitled to gather taxes from the citizenry (cf. 1 Pet 2.13–17). Citizens should nei-

ther cringe before government nor be slaves to it. As patriots they should love their country. Only as long as their God-given rights of religious and political liberty exist are they compelled to obey the government. When, however, the emperor's laws require Christians to break God's laws, they must resist the emperor and obey God.
13.9,10 Scripture lays down three specific principles regarding the law of love: (1) "Love your neighbor as yourself"; (2) "Love does no wrong to a neighbor"; (3) "do to others as you would have them do to you" (Mt 7.12). All this is based on the commandment to love God first.

covet"; and any other commandment, are summed up in this word, "Love your neighbor as yourself." 10 Love does no wrong to a neighbor; therefore, love is the fulfilling of the law.

F. *Hope, the Christian motivation*

11 Besides this, you know what time it is, how it is now the moment for you to wake from sleep. For salvation is nearer to us now than when we became believers; 12 the night is far gone, the day is near. Let us then lay aside the works of darkness and put on the armor of light; 13 let us live honorably as in the day, not in reveling and drunkenness, not in debauchery and licentiousness, not in quarreling and jealousy. 14 Instead, put on the Lord Jesus Christ, and make no provision for the flesh, to gratify its desires.

G. *The Christian and matters of conscience*

1. *Not to judge*

14 Welcome those who are weak in faith,ˢ but not for the purpose of quarreling over opinions. 2 Some believe in eating anything, while the weak eat only vegetables. 3 Those who eat must not despise those who abstain, and those who abstain must not pass judgment on those who eat; for God has welcomed them. 4 Who are you to pass judgment on servants of another? It is before their own lord that they stand or fall. And they will be upheld, for the Lordᵗ is able to make them stand.

5 Some judge one day to be better than another, while others judge all days to be alike. Let all be fully convinced in their own minds. 6 Those who observe the day, observe it in honor of the Lord. Also those who eat, eat in honor of the Lord, since they give thanks to God; while those who abstain, abstain in honor of the Lord and give thanks to God.

7 We do not live to ourselves, and we do not die to ourselves. 8 If we live, we live to the Lord, and if we die, we die to the Lord; so then, whether we live or whether we die, we are the Lord's. 9 For to this end Christ died and lived again, so that he might be Lord of both the dead and the living.

10 Why do you pass judgment on your brother or sister?ᵘ Or you, why do you despise your brother or sister?ᵘ For we will all stand before the judgment seat of God. ᵛ 11 For it is written,

"As I live, says the Lord, every knee shall bow to me,
and every tongue shall give praise toʷ God."

12 So then, each of us will be accountable to God. ˣ

13.11ff
1 Cor 7.29,
30; 15.34;
Eph 5.14;
1 Thess 5.5,
6
13.12
1 Jn 2.8;
Eph 5.11;
1 Thess 5.8
13.13
1 Thess 4.12;
Gal 5.21;
Eph 5.18
13.14
Gal 3.27;
Eph 4.24;
Gal 5.16
14.1
1 Cor 8.9;
9.22
14.2
1 Tim 4.4;
Titus 1.15
14.3
Col 2.16
14.4
Jas 4.12
14.5
Gal 4.10
14.6
1 Cor 10.31;
1 Tim 4.3
14.7
2 Cor 5.15;
Gal 2.20;
Phil 1.20, 21
14.8
Phil 1.20
14.9
2 Cor 5.15;
Acts 10.36
14.10
2 Cor 5.10
14.11
Isa 45.23;
Phil 2.10, 11
14.12
Mt 12.36;
1 Pet 4.5

ˢ Or *conviction*   ᵗ Other ancient authorities read *for God*   ᵘ Gk *brother*   ᵛ Other ancient authorities read *of Christ*   ʷ Or *confess*   ˣ Other ancient authorities lack *to God*

13.11ff Believers should be motivated by their expectation of the return of the Lord. This does not mean that Paul expected the imminent coming of Christ, for, as ch. 11 shows, he expected a long interval between the first and the second coming. In another sense, the Lord comes to each person through physical death. Since death may occur at any time — and surely not more than a few decades ahead in Paul's own life — we should be hard at work, for when it does come, we will work no more.

14.2 Apparently the Romans were divided over the question of eating meats and vegetables or eating only vegetables. This was a problem unique to that time. But there will always be differences of opinion about secondary matters for which the Bible gives no explicit instructions. We must bear with one another and not make our own opinions a matter of absolute

principle. Live and let live is a good injunction about such matters (see next note).

14.8 Biblical rules governing Christian conduct turn on two foci: general principles and specific commands. Among the general principles are the following: (1) we must respect others (1 Thess 4.11,12); (2) we must be fully pleasing to God (Col 1.10); (3) we must walk in the Spirit (Gal 5.25); (4) we must walk in newness of life (6.4); and (5) we must walk worthy of our calling (Eph 4.1). God's specific commands include (1) controlling the body (1 Cor 9.27); (2) forgiving those who wrong us (12.17–20); (3) subduing anger (4.26; Jas 1.19); (4) having no fellowship with sinners (Ps 1.1; 2 Thess 3.6); and (5) living peaceably with all people (12.18; Heb 12.14).

2. Not to be a stumbling block

13 Let us therefore no longer pass judgment on one another, but resolve instead never to put a stumbling block or hindrance in the way of another.*y* 14 I know and am persuaded in the Lord Jesus that nothing is unclean in itself; but it is unclean for anyone who thinks it unclean. 15 If your brother or sister*z* is being injured by what you eat, you are no longer walking in love. Do not let what you eat cause the ruin of one for whom Christ died. 16 So do not let your good be spoken of as evil. 17 For the kingdom of God is not food and drink but righteousness and peace and joy in the Holy Spirit. 18 The one who thus serves Christ is acceptable to God and has human approval. 19 Let us then pursue what makes for peace and for mutual upbuilding. 20 Do not, for the sake of food, destroy the work of God. Everything is indeed clean, but it is wrong for you to make others fall by what you eat; 21 it is good not to eat meat or drink wine or do anything that makes your brother or sister*z* stumble.*a* 22 The faith that you have, have as your own conviction before God. Blessed are those who have no reason to condemn themselves because of what they approve. 23 But those who have doubts are condemned if they eat, because they do not act from faith;*b* for whatever does not proceed from faith*b* is sin.*c*

3. To follow Christ's example

15 We who are strong ought to put up with the failings of the weak, and not to please ourselves. 2 Each of us must please our neighbor for the good purpose of building up the neighbor. 3 For Christ did not please himself; but, as it is written, "The insults of those who insult you have fallen on me." 4 For whatever was written in former days was written for our instruction, so that by steadfastness and by the encouragement of the scriptures we might have hope. 5 May the God of steadfastness and encouragement grant you to live in harmony with one another, in accordance with Christ Jesus, 6 so that together you may with one voice glorify the God and Father of our Lord Jesus Christ.

7 Welcome one another, therefore, just as Christ has welcomed you, for the glory of God. 8 For I tell you that Christ has become a servant of the circumcised on behalf of the truth of God in order that he might confirm the promises given to the patriarchs, 9 and in order that the Gentiles might glorify God for his mercy. As it is written,

"Therefore I will confess*d* you among the Gentiles,
    and sing praises to your name";

10 and again he says,

"Rejoice, O Gentiles, with his people";

11 and again,

"Praise the Lord, all you Gentiles,
    and let all the peoples praise him";

y Gk *of a brother* *z* Gk *brother* *a* Other ancient authorities add *or be upset or be weakened*
b Or *conviction* *c* Other authorities, some ancient, add here 16.25-27 *d* Or *thank*

14.13
Mt 7.1;
1 Cor 8.13
14.14
Acts 10.15;
1 Cor 8.7
14.15
Eph 5.2;
1 Cor 8.11
14.16
1 Cor 10.30
14.17
1 Cor 8.8;
Rom 15.13
14.18
2 Cor 8.21
14.19
Ps 34.14;
Heb 12.14;
Rom 15.2
14.20
v. 15;
1 Cor 8.9-12
14.21
1 Cor 8.13
14.22
1 Jn 3.21

15.1
Rom 14.1;
Gal 6.1, 2
15.2
1 Cor 10.33;
Rom 14.19
15.3
Ps 69.9;
2 Cor 8.9
15.4
Rom 4.23,
24;
2 Tim 3.16,
17
15.5
Rom 12.16;
1 Cor 1.10
15.6
Rev 1.6
15.7
Rom 14.1
15.8
Mt 15.24;
Acts 3.25, 26;
Rom 3.3;
2 Cor 1.20
15.9
Ps 18.49;
2 Sam 22.50
15.10
Deut 32.43
15.11
Ps 117.1

14.14 To Paul, no food is unclean in itself. Some Roman believers felt differently and were abstaining from certain kinds of food, especially meat (v. 2). Paul calls them weak or immature Christians and warns them not to pass judgment on those who have not followed their example (vv. 3,4,10), since the latter had eaten with thanksgiving to God. Paul commends those believers who did not feel bound by such scruples, but he warns them not to despise weaker believers. They should not injure the weak by their example, for weak saints who considered something as impure would be injured in their consciences and thus sin against God if they ate of it.
14.21 When it comes to decisions about personal conduct, three general rules will help us make proper

choices: (1) zeal in doing those things about which all agree; (2) liberty in making choices in matters of indifference; and (3) deference toward those who are weak, tender, and easily influenced.
14.23 Whenever you have doubt about an activity, do not do it. This is a good principle to follow when we are uncertain as to whether we should or should not do something. Always give God the benefit of the doubt.
15.1,2 Christian living includes putting up with the faults, failures, and bad habits of other Christians who may be ill-taught or stubbornly opinionated. Mature believers should meekly and pleasingly put up with their neighbors, so long as this does not involve them personally in sin.

12and again Isaiah says,
"The root of Jesse shall come,
     the one who rises to rule the Gentiles;
in him the Gentiles shall hope."
13May the God of hope fill you with all joy and peace in believing, so that
you may abound in hope by the power of the Holy Spirit.

VI. Conclusion and postscript (15.14–16.27)

A. Paul's reasons for writing

14 I myself feel confident about you, my brothers and sisters,[e] that
you yourselves are full of goodness, filled with all knowledge, and able to
instruct one another. 15Nevertheless on some points I have written to you
rather boldly by way of reminder, because of the grace given me by God
16to be a minister of Christ Jesus to the Gentiles in the priestly service
of the gospel of God, so that the offering of the Gentiles may be acceptable,
sanctified by the Holy Spirit. 17In Christ Jesus, then, I have reason to
boast of my work for God. 18For I will not venture to speak of anything
except what Christ has accomplished[f] through me to win obedience from
the Gentiles, by word and deed, 19by the power of signs and wonders,
by the power of the Spirit of God,[g] so that from Jerusalem and as far
around as Illyricum I have fully proclaimed the good news[h] of Christ.
20Thus I make it my ambition to proclaim the good news,[h] not where
Christ has already been named, so that I do not build on someone else's
foundation, 21but as it is written,
"Those who have never been told of him shall see,
     and those who have never heard of him shall understand."

B. Paul's future plans

22 This is the reason that I have so often been hindered from coming
to you. 23But now, with no further place for me in these regions, I desire,
as I have for many years, to come to you 24when I go to Spain. For I do
hope to see you on my journey and to be sent on by you, once I have
enjoyed your company for a little while. 25At present, however, I am
going to Jerusalem in a ministry to the saints; 26for Macedonia and Achaia
have been pleased to share their resources with the poor among the saints
at Jerusalem. 27They were pleased to do this, and indeed they owe it to
them; for if the Gentiles have come to share in their spiritual blessings,
they ought also to be of service to them in material things. 28So, when
I have completed this, and have delivered to them what has been collected,[i] I will set out by way of you to Spain; 29and I know that when
I come to you, I will come in the fullness of the blessing[j] of Christ.

30 I appeal to you, brothers and sisters,[e] by our Lord Jesus Christ
and by the love of the Spirit, to join me in earnest prayer to God on my

e Gk brothers   f Gk speak of those things that Christ has not accomplished   g Other ancient authorities read
of the Spirit or of the Holy Spirit   h Or gospel   i Gk have sealed to them this fruit   j Other ancient
authorities add of the gospel

15.13 Paul entreats God, the author of all hope, to
fill the Romans with faith, joy, and peace, and he calls
upon the Holy Spirit to enable his readers not simply
to have hope but to abound in it.
15.19 Paul does not hesitate to declare that he had
performed signs and wonders through the power
of the Holy Spirit, which had convinced skeptics
and helped to bring them to Christ (cf. Acts
19.11ff).
15.23ff Paul is planning to visit Spain to preach the
good news, and he expects to stop in Rome to encourage the saints there. We have no record that he ever

fulfilled this desire, though he did come to Rome
under different circumstances (see Acts 28). Right
now he has an important task to perform — to go to
Jerusalem with the offering taken by believers for the
aid of the poor saints in that territory.
15.30 Those who do not pray for themselves and for
others should not expect others to pray for them. Paul
entreats the Romans to pray for him, i.e., to join him
in his own prayers for himself, and particularly that
he might come to them in Rome. Paul in turn has
already prayed to God with thankgiving for the Roman saints (1.8,9).

behalf, 31 that I may be rescued from the unbelievers in Judea, and that my ministry*k* to Jerusalem may be acceptable to the saints, 32 so that by God's will I may come to you with joy and be refreshed in your company. 33 The God of peace be with all of you. *l* Amen.

C. Commendations and greetings

16 I commend to you our sister Phoebe, a deacon*m* of the church at Cenchreae, 2 so that you may welcome her in the Lord as is fitting for the saints, and help her in whatever she may require from you, for she has been a benefactor of many and of myself as well.

3 Greet Prisca and Aquila, who work with me in Christ Jesus, 4 and who risked their necks for my life, to whom not only I give thanks, but also all the churches of the Gentiles. 5 Greet also the church in their house. Greet my beloved Epaenetus, who was the first convert*n* in Asia for Christ. 6 Greet Mary, who has worked very hard among you. 7 Greet Andronicus and Junia,*o* my relatives*p* who were in prison with me; they are prominent among the apostles, and they were in Christ before I was. 8 Greet Ampliatus, my beloved in the Lord. 9 Greet Urbanus, our co-worker in Christ, and my beloved Stachys. 10 Greet Apelles, who is approved in Christ. Greet those who belong to the family of Aristobulus. 11 Greet my relative*q* Herodion. Greet those in the Lord who belong to the family of Narcissus. 12 Greet those workers in the Lord, Tryphaena and Tryphosa. Greet the beloved Persis, who has worked hard in the Lord. 13 Greet Rufus, chosen in the Lord; and greet his mother — a mother to me also. 14 Greet Asyncritus, Phlegon, Hermes, Patrobas, Hermas, and the brothers and sisters*r* who are with them. 15 Greet Philologus, Julia, Nereus and his sister, and Olympas, and all the saints who are with them. 16 Greet one another with a holy kiss. All the churches of Christ greet you.

17 I urge you, brothers and sisters,*r* to keep an eye on those who cause dissensions and offenses, in opposition to the teaching that you have learned; avoid them. 18 For such people do not serve our Lord Christ, but their own appetites,*s* and by smooth talk and flattery they deceive the hearts of the simple-minded. 19 For while your obedience is known to all, so that I rejoice over you, I want you to be wise in what is good and guileless in what is evil. 20 The God of peace will shortly crush Satan under your feet. The grace of our Lord Jesus Christ be with you.*t*

21 Timothy, my co-worker, greets you; so do Lucius and Jason and Sosipater, my relatives.*p*

22 I Tertius, the writer of this letter, greet you in the Lord.*u*

23 Gaius, who is host to me and to the whole church, greets you. Erastus, the city treasurer, and our brother Quartus, greet you.*v*

Cross-references

15.32 Rom 1.10; Acts 18.21; 1 Cor 16.18
15.33 Rom 16.20; 2 Cor 13.11; Phil 4.9; Heb 13.20
16.1 Acts 18.18
16.2 Phil 2.29; Rom 15.15, 31
16.3 Acts 18.2; 2 Tim 4.19
16.5 1 Cor 16.15, 19; Col 4.15
16.9 2 Cor 5.17
16.10 2 Cor 5.17
16.11 vv. 7, 21; 1 Cor 1.11
16.15 vv. 2, 14
16.16 1 Cor 16.20; 2 Cor 13.12; 1 Thess 5.26
16.17 1 Tim 1.3; 6.3; Gal 1.8, 9; 2 Thess 3.6, 14; 2 Jn 10
16.18 Phil 3.19; Col 2.4
16.19 Rom 1.8; Mt 10.16; 1 Cor 14.20
16.20 Rom 15.33; Gen 3.15; 1 Cor 16.23; 1 Thess 5.28
16.21 Acts 16.1; 13.1; 17.5; 20.4; vv. 7, 11

Textual notes

k Other ancient authorities read *my bringing of a gift* *l* One ancient authority adds 16.25-27 here *m* Or *minister* *n* Gk *first fruits* *o* Or *Junias*; other ancient authorities read *Julia* *p* Or *compatriots* *q* Or *compatriot* *r* Gk *brothers* *s* Gk *their own belly* *t* Other ancient authorities lack this sentence *u* Or *I Tertius, writing this letter in the Lord, greet you* *v* Other ancient authorities add verse 24, The grace of our Lord Jesus Christ be with all of you. Amen.

Study notes

16.1 This is the Bible's only mention of *Phoebe, a deacon.* We may assume from this the right and privilege for churches to have women deacons, although we have no way of knowing whether Phoebe filled a definite office or was simply serving the Christian community. Nowhere does Scripture set up the specific office of woman deacon, but by inference this verse surely allows for such an office.
16.3 See note on 2 Tim 4.19.
16.7 Andronicus and Junia were Paul's cousins. They had come to Christ before him. Some think they were husband and wife; others think they were both males. Since Paul mentions being in prision a number of times (2 Cor 11.23), it appears that these two were fellow-prisoners in one of those imprisonments.
16.8ff Paul had many good friends and close acquaintances, in Rome and elsewhere. Their names dot the Scriptures even though we know little about many of them. Christians friends are our brothers and sisters in Christ.
16.22 *Tertius* was either a secretary who wrote as Paul dictated or a scribe who copied from what may have been Paul's otherwise illegible handwriting.

D. *Doxology*

25 Now to God[w] who is able to strengthen you according to my gospel and the proclamation of Jesus Christ, according to the revelation of the mystery that was kept secret for long ages 26 but is now disclosed, and through the prophetic writings is made known to all the Gentiles, according to the command of the eternal God, to bring about the obedience of faith — 27 to the only wise God, through Jesus Christ, to whom[x] be the glory forever! Amen.[y]

[w] Gk *the one*   [x] Other ancient authorities lack *to whom*. The verse then reads, *to the only wise God be the glory through Jesus Christ forever. Amen.*   [y] Other ancient authorities lack 16.25-27 or include it after 14.23 or 15.33; others put verse 24 after verse 27

16.25,26 Throughout the era of the O.T., God did not plainly reveal that in Christ he would someday have the good news preached to Gentiles. But that time had now come, and God revealed that mystery to Paul (see also Eph 3.3–6). Paul also suggests that the Holy Spirit is making this mystery known through new *prophetic writings*, including Paul's own writings as part of the revealed word of God.

CORINTHIANS

Authorship, Date, and Background: The Corinthian church was founded by Paul on his second missionary circuit (Acts 18.1ff). He was assisted in this task by Aquila and Priscilla, and later by Silas and Timothy. Paul went to Corinth from Athens (where his ministry had not resulted in the founding of a church). His disappointment at Athens was softened by what happened at Corinth, where a strong and very gifted church came into being. It was largely a Gentile church, although Paul began his ministry in the synagogue and some Jews were converted. That synagogue ministry was brought to a halt when some Jews appealed to Gallio the proconsul (governor) for help in stopping the apostle, who was persuading "people to worship God in ways that are contrary to the law" (Acts 18.13). Gallio ruled in favor of Paul, and he continued his evangelism in the home of Titius Justus (often thought to be the Gaius of 1.14; cf. Rom. 16.23), whose house was next door to the synagogue and to which he had gone before the trial. He spent the better part of two years in the city. Paul went from Corinth to Jerusalem via Ephesus and returned there after ministering in other parts of Asia Minor. He was in Ephesus when he wrote his first letter to the church at Corinth (5.9,10). That letter has been lost, although some scholars believe that portions of it may be included in both 1 and 2 Corinthians. Either through a personal visit or by a letter, Paul learned from those of the household of Chloe of some difficulties in the Corinthian church. Later Stephanas, Fortunatus, and Achaicus (16.17) brought a letter to the apostle from the church, in which they requested a response to certain specific questions. It was this combination of incidents which led to the writing of 1 Corinthians. It was probably written in the winter of A.D. 55 at the height of his Ephesian ministry.

Characteristics and Content: Corinth was a bustling metropolis, an important commercial and maritime city. It had a vile reputation for licentiousness and immorality of all sorts. The Greek verb "corinthianize" means "to behave as they do in Corinth." Since most of the converts coming from this environment were unfamiliar with the O.T. lifestyle, they needed instruction and help as they moved from the ethical standards of paganism to those of the Christian life. Numerous problems beset these young believers. Thus Paul's letter addresses itself to specific difficulties in the church. The church was divided into warring factions. A case of flagrant immorality had arisen. Christians were suing each other. Marriage and divorce problems troubled the church. Paul's authority was being questioned. Questions about food offered to idols as well as the role of women, the Lord's supper, and spiritual gifts continually plagued the congregation. Above all, the bodily resurrection of Jesus from the dead was under assault. Paul addresses himself to these issues and in so doing lays down guidelines which have remained for the instruction of the church of Jesus Christ through the ages.

This letter is marked by three outstanding segments, the absence of any one of which would leave us markedly poorer. The first has to do with the Lord's supper (11.17ff); here we find the earliest account of its celebration and Paul's instruction concerning it; the second is the great hymn of love in which Paul states that all of the gifts of the Corinthian church shrink into insignificance if love is missing (ch. 13); the third is the magnificent defense for the bodily resurrection of Jesus Christ, the truth or falsity of which establishes or undercuts the foundation of the Christian faith (ch. 15).

Outline:

THE FIRST LETTER OF PAUL TO THE
CORINTHIANS

I. Introduction (1.1–9)

A. Greeting

1 Paul, called to be an apostle of Christ Jesus by the will of God, and our brother Sosthenes,

2 To the church of God that is in Corinth, to those who are sanctified in Christ Jesus, called to be saints, together with all those who in every place call on the name of our Lord Jesus Christ, both their Lord[a] and ours:

3 Grace to you and peace from God our Father and the Lord Jesus Christ.

B. Thanksgiving

4 I give thanks to my[b] God always for you because of the grace of God that has been given you in Christ Jesus, 5 for in every way you have been enriched in him, in speech and knowledge of every kind — 6 just as the testimony of[c] Christ has been strengthened among you — 7 so that you are not lacking in any spiritual gift as you wait for the revealing of our Lord Jesus Christ. 8 He will also strengthen you to the end, so that you may be blameless on the day of our Lord Jesus Christ. 9 God is faithful; by him you were called into the fellowship of his Son, Jesus Christ our Lord.

II. Divisions (1.10–4.21)

A. Exhortation to unity

10 Now I appeal to you, brothers and sisters,[d] by the name of our Lord Jesus Christ, that all of you be in agreement and that there be no divisions among you, but that you be united in the same mind and the same purpose. 11 For it has been reported to me by Chloe's people that there are quarrels among you, my brothers and sisters.[e] 12 What I mean is that each of you says, "I belong to Paul," or "I belong to Apollos," or "I belong to Cephas," or "I belong to Christ." 13 Has Christ been divided? Was Paul crucified for you? Or were you baptized in the name of Paul? 14 I thank God[f] that I baptized none of you except Crispus and Gaius,

---

a Gk *theirs* *b* Other ancient authorities lack *my* *c* Or *to* *d* Gk *brothers* *e* Gk *my brothers* *f* Other ancient authorities read *I am thankful*

1.1 *Sosthenes.* The Sosthenes of Acts 18.17 was the successor to Crispus as ruler of the synagogue in Corinth. He was beaten by the mob before the tribunal subsequent to the dismissal of charges against Paul by Gallio. That Sosthenes may be the one spoken of here, in which case he had become a Christian.
1.5 The Corinthian church was especially gifted by the Holy Spirit with speech and knowledge. Some have the ability to speak but have nothing to say. Others have something to say but do not know how to speak. In Corinth the people had something to say and they had the gift of speech so that they could say it well.
1.10 Schism in the church generally has to do with

marginal matters, not those which are foundational to the Christian faith. Schism breaks the unity of the body and is condemned as contrary to his will (v. 13; 12.13; Jn 17.21–23). It usually exposes the carnality of believers (3.1–3). God commands believers to avoid fellowship with those who create dissension in the body (Rom 16.17). But when apostasy is involved, the situation is quite different, for apostates must be excommunicated from the fellowship.
1.14 The Corinthians took great pride in who performed the rite of water baptism for them. They bragged that it was worth more if an apostle did it than if it were done by a person of lesser stature. Paul speaks against this attitude.

1.1
Rom 1.1;
2 Cor 1.1;
Eph 1.1;
Col 1.1;
Acts 18.17
1.2
Acts 18.1;
Rom 1.7;
Acts 7.59
1.3
Rom 1.7

1.4
Rom 1.8
1.5
2 Cor 9.11;
8.7
1.6
2 Tim 1.8;
Rev 1.2
1.7
Phil 3.20;
Titus 2.13;
2 Pet 3.12
1.9
Isa 49.7;
1 Jn 1.3

1.10
2 Cor 13.11;
Rom 12.16

1.13
2 Cor 11.4;
Mt 28.19;
Acts 2.38
1.14
Acts 18.8;
Rom 16.23

¹⁵so that no one can say that you were baptized in my name. ¹⁶(I did baptize also the household of Stephanas; beyond that, I do not know whether I baptized anyone else.) ¹⁷For Christ did not send me to baptize but to proclaim the gospel, and not with eloquent wisdom, so that the cross of Christ might not be emptied of its power.

B. The wisdom of the world and the foolishness of God

18 For the message about the cross is foolishness to those who are perishing, but to us who are being saved it is the power of God. ¹⁹For it is written,

"I will destroy the wisdom of the wise,
    and the discernment of the discerning I will thwart."

²⁰Where is the one who is wise? Where is the scribe? Where is the debater of this age? Has not God made foolish the wisdom of the world? ²¹For since, in the wisdom of God, the world did not know God through wisdom, God decided, through the foolishness of our proclamation, to save those who believe. ²²For Jews demand signs and Greeks desire wisdom, ²³but we proclaim Christ crucified, a stumbling block to Jews and foolishness to Gentiles, ²⁴but to those who are the called, both Jews and Greeks, Christ the power of God and the wisdom of God. ²⁵For God's foolishness is wiser than human wisdom, and God's weakness is stronger than human strength.

26 Consider your own call, brothers and sisters:ᵍ not many of you were wise by human standards,ʰ not many were powerful, not many were of noble birth. ²⁷But God chose what is foolish in the world to shame the wise; God chose what is weak in the world to shame the strong; ²⁸God chose what is low and despised in the world, things that are not, to reduce to nothing things that are, ²⁹so that no oneⁱ might boast in the presence of God. ³⁰He is the source of your life in Christ Jesus, who became for us wisdom from God, and righteousness and sanctification and redemption, ³¹in order that, as it is written, "Let the one who boasts, boast inʲ the Lord."

2 When I came to you, brothers and sisters,ᵍ I did not come proclaiming the mysteryᵏ of God to you in lofty words or wisdom. ²For I decided to know nothing among you except Jesus Christ, and him crucified. ³And I came to you in weakness and in fear and in much trembling. ⁴My speech and my proclamation were not with plausible words of wisdom,ˡ but with a demonstration of the Spirit and of power, ⁵so that your faith might rest not on human wisdom but on the power of God.

C. True wisdom the gift of God

6 Yet among the mature we do speak wisdom, though it is not a wisdom of this age or of the rulers of this age, who are doomed to perish. ⁷But we speak God's wisdom, secret and hidden, which God decreed before the ages for our glory. ⁸None of the rulers of this age understood

---

g Gk brothers   *h* Gk according to the flesh   *i* Gk no flesh   *j* Or of   *k* Other ancient authorities read testimony   *l* Other ancient authorities read the persuasiveness of wisdom

---

1.22,23 Jews and Greeks both rejected Jesus but for different reasons. The Jews required a sign, for they thought the Messiah would be a great prince who worked political wonders. Because Jesus did not fulfill their expectations, they rejected, despised, and hated him. The Greeks looked at Christ from the perspective of the wisdom of the world. They laughed at the idea of a crucified Savior and mocked unlearned and uneducated disciples who proclaimed Jesus as Redeemer, so they rejected Jesus too. Thus Paul preached a Jesus who was a stumbling block to the Jews and foolishness to the Gentiles.

1.30 Christ alone is our righteousness (see notes on Rom 3.21—4.25). Those who wish to boast of salvation should boast only of the righteousness they have in Christ.

2.1ff Paul affirms that he did not come to preach in wisdom or in eloquent speech. He wanted to preach nothing among them except the simple message of Jesus Christ and him crucified. Our faith should be founded on the power of God, not on human wisdom.

2.7 *God's wisdom, secret and hidden.* Paul is not opposed to wisdom as such, but only a human wisdom that rejects divine wisdom.

this; for if they had, they would not have crucified the Lord of glory. 9 But, as it is written,

"What no eye has seen, nor ear heard,
    nor the human heart conceived,
what God has prepared for those who love him" —

10 these things God has revealed to us through the Spirit; for the Spirit searches everything, even the depths of God. 11 For what human being knows what is truly human except the human spirit that is within? So also no one comprehends what is truly God's except the Spirit of God. 12 Now we have received not the spirit of the world, but the Spirit that is from God, so that we may understand the gifts bestowed on us by God. 13 And we speak of these things in words not taught by human wisdom but taught by the Spirit, interpreting spiritual things to those who are spiritual.[m]

14 Those who are unspiritual[n] do not receive the gifts of God's Spirit, for they are foolishness to them, and they are unable to understand them because they are spiritually discerned. 15 Those who are spiritual discern all things, and they are themselves subject to no one else's scrutiny. 16 "For who has known the mind of the Lord
    so as to instruct him?"
But we have the mind of Christ.

3 And so, brothers and sisters,[o] I could not speak to you as spiritual people, but rather as people of the flesh, as infants in Christ. 2 I fed you with milk, not solid food, for you were not ready for solid food. Even now you are still not ready, 3 for you are still of the flesh. For as long as there is jealousy and quarreling among you, are you not of the flesh, and behaving according to human inclinations? 4 For when one says, "I belong to Paul," and another, "I belong to Apollos," are you not merely human?

D. The apostles: co-workers together

5 What then is Apollos? What is Paul? Servants through whom you came to believe, as the Lord assigned to each. 6 I planted, Apollos watered, but God gave the growth. 7 So neither the one who plants nor the one who waters is anything, but only God who gives the growth. 8 The one who plants and the one who waters have a common purpose, and each will receive wages according to the labor of each. 9 For we are God's servants, working together; you are God's field, God's building.

10 According to the grace of God given to me, like a skilled master builder I laid a foundation, and someone else is building on it. Each builder must choose with care how to build on it. 11 For no one can lay any foundation other than the one that has been laid; that foundation is

m Or interpreting spiritual things in spiritual language, or comparing spiritual things with spiritual
n Or natural   o Gk brothers

2.9
Isa 64.4;
65.17

2.10
Mt 16.17;
Eph 3.3, 5;
Jn 14.26
2.11
Prov 20.27;
Jer 17.9
2.12
Rom 8.15;
1 Cor 1.27
2.13
1 Cor 1.17
2.14
1 Cor 1.18;
Jas 3.15

2.16
Isa 40.13;
Jn 15.15

3.1
1 Cor 2.15;
Rom 7.14;
1 Cor 2.14;
Heb 5.13
3.2
Heb 5.12, 13;
1 Pet 2.2
3.3
1 Cor 1.11;
Gal 5.20;
Jas 3.16
3.4
1 Cor 1.12

3.8
Ps 62.12;
Gal 6.4, 5
3.9
2 Cor 6.1;
Isa 61.3;
Eph 2.20-22;
1 Pet 2.5
3.10
Rom 12.3;
15.20;
1 Cor 15.10
3.11
Isa 28.6;
Eph 2.20

2.10ff Human beings cannot understand the true meaning of the Bible by themselves. The Holy Spirit must illumine their minds so they can understand God's salvation; he goes on to illumine the minds of believers so they can grasp the deeper truths of God's Word.

2.14 *those who are unspiritual* (Gk. *psychikos*). This word refers to natural, fallen people who are dead in trespasses and sins (Eph 2.1,12). They must be distinguished from people of the flesh (Gk. *sarkinos*; see next note).

3.1 Christians fall into one of two classes: they are either fleshly or spiritual, i.e., they are either babies or mature. Baby Christians live as people of the flesh (Gk. *sarkinos*), desiring to please themselves. They are not fully yielded to Christ as Lord and do not walk in full fellowship with God. They are not filled with the Spirit as they should be (Eph 5.18), nor do their lives

reflect the fruit of the Spirit (Gal 5.22,23).

3.5-9 Ministers, i.e., preachers of the good news, are servants of God, not masters of people. They are only agents of God, not objects of faith in whom people should trust. Different ministers have different tasks: Paul planted and Apollos watered, but it was God who gave the increase. All the glory belongs to God and none to humans. God's servants are not in competition with each other; rather they should be united in aim and purpose.

3.10 *a skilled master builder*, i.e., a chief worker, not the designer, who is God. As God's worker Paul lays a foundation, and the only foundation for the Christian church is the unique faith in Jesus Christ. The foundation is not a system of doctrinal truths (as important as that is) but a person. The goal of all doctrine is to bring us to faith in the person of Jesus Christ.

3.13
1 Cor 4.5;
2 Thess
1.7-10
3.14
1 Cor 4.5;
9.17
3.15
Job 23.10;
Jude 23
3.16
1 Cor 6.19;
2 Cor 6.16

3.18
Isa 5.21;
1 Cor 8.2
3.19
Job 5.13;
1 Cor 1.20
3.20
Ps 94.11

3.21
1 Cor 4.6;
Rom 8.32
3.23
1 Cor 15.23;
2 Cor 10.7;
Gal 3.29

4.1
2 Cor 6.4;
1 Cor 9.17;
Rom 11.25;
16.25
4.4
2 Cor 1.12;
Rom 2.13
4.5
Rom 2.1;
2 Cor 10.18;
Rom 2.29

4.6
1 Cor 1.19,
31; 3.19, 20;
1.12; 3.4
4.7
Rom 12.3, 6

Jesus Christ. 12 Now if anyone builds on the foundation with gold, silver, precious stones, wood, hay, straw— 13 the work of each builder will become visible, for the Day will disclose it, because it will be revealed with fire, and the fire will test what sort of work each has done. 14 If what has been built on the foundation survives, the builder will receive a reward. 15 If the work is burned up, the builder will suffer loss; the builder will be saved, but only as through fire.

16 Do you not know that you are God's temple and that God's Spirit dwells in you?_p_ 17 If anyone destroys God's temple, God will destroy that person. For God's temple is holy, and you are that temple.

18 Do not deceive yourselves. If you think that you are wise in this age, you should become fools so that you may become wise. 19 For the wisdom of this world is foolishness with God. For it is written,

"He catches the wise in their craftiness,"

20 and again,

"The Lord knows the thoughts of the wise,
　　that they are futile."

21 So let no one boast about human leaders. For all things are yours, 22 whether Paul or Apollos or Cephas or the world or life or death or the present or the future— all belong to you, 23 and you belong to Christ, and Christ belongs to God.

E. *The ministry judged by God*

4 Think of us in this way, as servants of Christ and stewards of God's mysteries. 2 Moreover, it is required of stewards that they be found trustworthy. 3 But with me it is a very small thing that I should be judged by you or by any human court. I do not even judge myself. 4 I am not aware of anything against myself, but I am not thereby acquitted. It is the Lord who judges me. 5 Therefore do not pronounce judgment before the time, before the Lord comes, who will bring to light the things now hidden in darkness and will disclose the purposes of the heart. Then each one will receive commendation from God.

F. *The humility of the apostles*

6 I have applied all this to Apollos and myself for your benefit, brothers and sisters,_q_ so that you may learn through us the meaning of the saying, "Nothing beyond what is written," so that none of you will be puffed up in favor of one against another. 7 For who sees anything

p In verses 16 and 17 the Greek word for you is plural q Gk brothers

---

3.14 Compare this with the note on 2 Cor 5.10 on the judgment seat of Christ. The doctrine of rewards has nothing whatever to do with salvation, for this is attained by faith alone and springs from God's grace. God determines rewards according to the works of believers, performed from the moment of their regeneration. Some Christians will enter heaven with the smell of smoke on their garments because all of their works will be tested and burned up. Any reward we receive springs from God's grace, for no works are perfect and all are lacking at some point. God mercifully accepts the intentions of the heart. We must not despise the reward (see Heb 11.26), but the motivation for the reward should be the desire to glorify God.

3.16 Our bodies are temples of the Holy Spirit. Just as God's Shekinah glory came into the Holy Place of the tabernacle in the wilderness and in the temple (Ex 40.34; 2 Chr 7.1), so the Spirit indwells believers. Since our bodies now form the Spirit's temple, we must not defile them in any way. This serves as a great

incentive for living a life of holiness.

3.21 *let no one boast about human leaders.* The ministry is a wonderful calling, and faithful ministers are a blessing to church and people. However, whoever honors human beings with praise that belongs to God is in error, and whoever receives such praise takes away from God the glory that belongs only to him.

4.1,2 Paul is God's steward, as are all ministers of the gospel. Their main responsibility is to be trustworthy. They must not lay down requirements for the laity that do not have God's approval, and they must faithfully feed them with the wholesome food of true doctrine.

4.4 Even though Paul may think himself to be without fault, that does not make it so and acquit him of any wrongdoing. God sees the heart, and the inner thoughts and motivations that may be unknown to us are known to him. The day will come when all hidden things will be brought to light and the purposes of our hearts disclosed. Then every person will receive God's verdict of either commendation or disapproval.

different in you?*r* What do you have that you did not receive? And if you received it, why do you boast as if it were not a gift?

8 Already you have all you want! Already you have become rich! Quite apart from us you have become kings! Indeed, I wish that you had become kings, so that we might be kings with you! 9 For I think that God has exhibited us apostles as last of all, as though sentenced to death, because we have become a spectacle to the world, to angels and to mortals. 10 We are fools for the sake of Christ, but you are wise in Christ. We are weak, but you are strong. You are held in honor, but we in disrepute. 11 To the present hour we are hungry and thirsty, we are poorly clothed and beaten and homeless, 12 and we grow weary from the work of our own hands. When reviled, we bless; when persecuted, we endure; 13 when slandered, we speak kindly. We have become like the rubbish of the world, the dregs of all things, to this very day.

G. The appeal of Paul

14 I am not writing this to make you ashamed, but to admonish you as my beloved children. 15 For though you might have ten thousand guardians in Christ, you do not have many fathers. Indeed, in Christ Jesus I became your father through the gospel. 16 I appeal to you, then, be imitators of me. 17 For this reason I sent*s* you Timothy, who is my beloved and faithful child in the Lord, to remind you of my ways in Christ Jesus, as I teach them everywhere in every church. 18 But some of you, thinking that I am not coming to you, have become arrogant. 19 But I will come to you soon, if the Lord wills, and I will find out not the talk of these arrogant people but their power. 20 For the kingdom of God depends not on talk but on power. 21 What would you prefer? Am I to come to you with a stick, or with love in a spirit of gentleness?

III. Sexual morality (5.1–7.40)

A. Incest at Corinth

5 It is actually reported that there is sexual immorality among you, and of a kind that is not found even among pagans; for a man is living with his father's wife. 2 And you are arrogant! Should you not rather have mourned, so that he who has done this would have been removed from among you?

3 For though absent in body, I am present in spirit; and as if present I have already pronounced judgment 4 in the name of the Lord Jesus on the man who has done such a thing.*t* When you are assembled, and my spirit is present with the power of our Lord Jesus, 5 you are to hand this

r Or *Who makes you different from another?* *s* Or *am sending* *t* Or *on the man who has done such a thing in the name of the Lord Jesus*

4.8
Rev 3.17, 18
4.9
1 Cor 15.31;
2 Cor 11.23;
Rom 8.36;
Heb 10.33
4.10
1 Cor 1.18;
Acts 17.18;
1 Cor 3.18
4.11
Rom 8.35;
2 Cor 11.23-27
4.12
Acts 18.3;
1 Pet 3.9;
Jn 15.20;
Rom 8.35
4.14
1 Thess 2.11
4.15
1 Cor 1.30;
Philem 10
4.16
Phil 3.17;
1 Thess 1.6;
2 Thess 3.9
4.19
Acts 19.21;
2 Cor 1.15;
Rom 15.32
4.20
1 Thess 1.5
4.21
2 Cor 1.23;
13.10
5.1
Lev 18.8;
Deut 22.30;
2 Cor 7.12
5.2
1 Cor 4.18;
2 Cor 7.7
5.3
Col 2.5
5.4
2 Thess 3.6;
2 Cor 2.10
5.5
1 Tim 1.20

4.9 *as though sentenced to death.* In this figure of speech Paul is comparing himself to the gladiatorial contests in Roman amphitheatres. Humans were forced to fight with wild animals or to cut each other down. Victors were not freed but kept to fight another day, so the day came for almost every victor to suffer defeat. In like figure, Paul and others like him are made a spectacle to the world. They suffer by being weak, despised, hungry, thirsty, poorly clothed, beaten, homeless, reviled, persecuted, and slandered, like the rubbish of the world.
4.17 No matter how committed believers are, they must constantly be reminded of things they are apt to forget. Paul is therefore sending Timothy to the Corinthians to remind them of the teachings and life principles Paul taught them.
4.21 Paul gives the Corinthians a choice: either they

must make things right so that he can come in a spirit of gentleness, or he will come with a heavy hand to censure sinners, chastise them, and use his apostolic authority in a way he preferred not to do.
5.1 The Corinthian church was uniquely gifted by God, but it also had hangovers from earlier days when they were living the immoral Corinthian life. Though the believers in this church are justified, they are not yet sufficiently sanctified. One of the church members is living with his step-mother, i.e., he has either married her or he is living with her as his concubine. Paul says that even the heathen object to such a lifestyle and urges the church to practice discipline in this case.
5.5 *hand this man over to Satan.* Since this is an extreme case, it requires extreme measures. Paul wants this guilty party, by an act of extraordinary

man over to Satan for the destruction of the flesh, so that his spirit may
be saved in the day of the Lord.[u]

B. *The duty to perform*

6 Your boasting is not a good thing. Do you not know that a little yeast
leavens the whole batch of dough? 7 Clean out the old yeast so that you
may be a new batch, as you really are unleavened. For our paschal lamb,
Christ, has been sacrificed. 8 Therefore, let us celebrate the festival, not
with the old yeast, the yeast of malice and evil, but with the unleavened
bread of sincerity and truth.

C. *The command to follow*

9 I wrote to you in my letter not to associate with sexually immoral
persons— 10 not at all meaning the immoral of this world, or the greedy
and robbers, or idolaters, since you would then need to go out of the
world. 11 But now I am writing to you not to associate with anyone who
bears the name of brother or sister[v] who is sexually immoral or greedy,
or is an idolater, reviler, drunkard, or robber. Do not even eat with such
a one. 12 For what have I to do with judging those outside? Is it not those
who are inside that you are to judge? 13 God will judge those outside.
"Drive out the wicked person from among you."

D. *Lawsuits and the Christian*

6 When any of you has a grievance against another, do you dare to take
it to court before the unrighteous, instead of taking it before the
saints? 2 Do you not know that the saints will judge the world? And if the
world is to be judged by you, are you incompetent to try trivial cases? 3 Do
you not know that we are to judge angels—to say nothing of ordinary
matters? 4 If you have ordinary cases, then, do you appoint as judges those
who have no standing in the church? 5 I say this to your shame. Can it be
that there is no one among you wise enough to decide between one
believer[v] and another, 6 but a believer[v] goes to court against a believer[v]
—and before unbelievers at that?
7 In fact, to have lawsuits at all with one another is already a defeat
for you. Why not rather be wronged? Why not rather be defrauded? 8 But
you yourselves wrong and defraud—and believers[w] at that.

E. *Kingdom standards*

9 Do you not know that wrongdoers will not inherit the kingdom of
God? Do not be deceived! Fornicators, idolaters, adulterers, male prostitutes, sodomites, 10 thieves, the greedy, drunkards, revilers, robbers—
none of these will inherit the kingdom of God. 11 And this is what some

5.6 Jas 4.16; Gal 5.9
5.7 1 Pet 1.19
5.8 Deut 16.3; Mk 8.15
5.9 2 Cor 6.14; Eph 5.11; 2 Thess 3.14
5.10 1 Cor 10.27
5.11 2 Thess 3.6; 1 Cor 10.7, 14, 20, 21
5.12 Mk 4.11; 1 Cor 6.1-4
5.13 Deut 13.5; 21.21
6.1 Mt 18.17
6.2 Dan 7.22; Mt 19.28; Lk 22.30
6.4 1 Cor 5.12
6.5 1 Cor 15.34; Acts 1.15
6.6 2 Cor 6.14, 15
6.7 Mt 5.39, 40; Rom 12.17
6.8 1 Thess 4.6
6.9 Gal 5.21; 1 Tim 1.10; Rev 22.15
6.11 Eph 2.2; Col 3.7; Titus 3.3

[u] Other ancient authorities add *Jesus* [v] Gk *brother* [w] Gk *brothers*

power, given over to Satan—not to destroy him, but to deliver him from his sin, even if it means the destruction of his body. He wants to be sure that his spirit is saved.

5.7 *our paschal lamb, Christ.* Christ fulfilled the O.T. type of the sacrificial lamb offered as an atoning sacrifice (see note on Ex 12.11–13).

5.11 Paul lays down the dictum that believers should break fellowship with those who are guilty of sexual sins, greed, worship of idols, drunkenness, and theft. He categorically states they must be put out of the church. Evidently he regards these sins as contagious and wishes to keep the saints from being infected.

6.2ff *Do you not know. . . ?* Paul uses the phrase six times. The Corinthians feel that they are so smart and so wise that Paul (ironically) wants to know why, if they are so wise, they do not know the things he is telling them. His teaching is plain: Christians must not go to secular or civil courts to settle disputes among themselves. The church should act as mediator and the parties involved should accept its verdict. He hammers home the truth that recourse to law courts by Christians against one another is a sure sign of defeat in their Christian life and walk (v. 7). It is better to suffer wrong or injury and leave the situation in the hands of God.

6.11 In justification God does something *for* sinners. This has to do with their legal standing with him; they become righteous by the imputation of Christ's righteousness. In sanctification God does something *in* believers; it has to do with character and conduct. Sanctification is the work of the triune God —Father, Son, and Holy Spirit (Rom 15.16; 1 Thess

of you used to be. But you were washed, you were sanctified, you were justified in the name of the Lord Jesus Christ and in the Spirit of our God.

F. *Chastity*

12 "All things are lawful for me," but not all things are beneficial. "All things are lawful for me," but I will not be dominated by anything. 13 "Food is meant for the stomach and the stomach for food,"ˣ and God will destroy both one and the other. The body is meant not for fornication but for the Lord, and the Lord for the body. 14 And God raised the Lord and will also raise us by his power. 15 Do you not know that your bodies are members of Christ? Should I therefore take the members of Christ and make them members of a prostitute? Never! 16 Do you not know that whoever is united to a prostitute becomes one body with her? For it is said, "The two shall be one flesh." 17 But anyone united to the Lord becomes one spirit with him. 18 Shun fornication! Every sin that a person commits is outside the body; but the fornicator sins against the body itself. 19 Or do you not know that your body is a templeʸ of the Holy Spirit within you, which you have from God, and that you are not your own? 20 For you were bought with a price; therefore glorify God in your body.

G. *Marriage and celibacy*

1. *Principles of marriage*

7 Now concerning the matters about which you wrote: "It is well for a man not to touch a woman." 2 But because of cases of sexual immorality, each man should have his own wife and each woman her own husband. 3 The husband should give to his wife her conjugal rights, and likewise the wife to her husband. 4 For the wife does not have authority over her own body, but the husband does; likewise the husband does not have authority over his own body, but the wife does. 5 Do not deprive one another except perhaps by agreement for a set time, to devote yourselves to prayer, and then come together again, so that Satan may not tempt you because of your lack of self-control. 6 This I say by way of concession, not of command. 7 I wish that all were as I myself am. But each has a particular gift from God, one having one kind and another a different kind.

8 To the unmarried and the widows I say that it is well for them to remain unmarried as I am. 9 But if they are not practicing self-control, they should marry. For it is better to marry than to be aflame with passion.

x The quotation may extend to the word *other*   y Or *sanctuary*

Margin references:

6.12 1 Cor 10.23
6.13 Mt 15.17; Eph 5.23
6.14 Rom 6.5, 8; 8.11;
2 Cor 4.14; Eph 1.19
6.15 Rom 12.5; 1 Cor 12.27
6.16 Gen 2.4; Mt 19.5; Eph 5.31
6.17 Jn 17.21-23; Gal 2.20
6.18 Rom 6.12; Heb 13.4; 1 Thess 4.4
6.19 Jn 2.21; Rom 14.7, 8
6.20 1 Cor 7.23; 1 Pet 1.18, 19; Rev 5.9
7.1 vv. 8, 26
7.3 1 Pet 3.7
7.5 Ex 19.15; 1 Sam 21.4, 5; 1 Thess 3.5
7.6 2 Cor 8.8
7.7 v. 8; 1 Cor 9.5; 12.11; Mt 19.12
7.8 vv. 1, 26
7.9 1 Tim 5.14

5.23; Heb 2.11). In sanctification believers put off the old self, put on the new, and are conformed to the image of Jesus Christ (Rom 6.11,12; 8.28,29; Col 3.3–14; 1 Thess 4.3).

6.12–20 Apparently the Corinthians agreed that adultery was wrong, but not fornication. As the appetite that demands food finds satisfaction by eating, so they may have thought that the sexual appetite of the unmarried can be satisfied by fornication. They may have misconstrued Paul's teaching about freedom or liberty to include the appropriateness of fornication. Paul corrects their error, showing that the sex act joins two bodies into a single relationship. To fornicate is immoral; it is a sin against the Holy Spirit, who dwells in the Christian's body. God must be glorified in all believers' bodies, and fornication does not do this.

7.2 God intended marriage to be a union of one man and one woman for life; polygamy was not his intention (Gen 2.24; Mk 10.6–8). As Christ is the head of the body, so the husband is the head of the wife (Eph 5.23). Husbands must support, protect, and care for

their wives. They are to love them (Eph 5.25), be thoughtful of their needs (1 Pet 3.7), be faithful to them (Mal 2.14), and stay married (no divorce except for unchastity, Mt 19.3–9).

7.5 Many a marriage has ended by the failure of one partner to provide sexual satisfaction to the other. It is legitimate for a married couple to interrupt this aspect of the marital bond for a season if there is agreement by both parties. But Paul advises them to come together again lest Satan tempt one or both of the spouses to seek sexual satisfaction outside the marriage. Adultery for any reason is never condoned in Scripture.

7.7 The continuation of life requires marriage and propagation. Since most people do not have the gift of continence, they should marry and have offspring. But God gives some of his people (such as Paul himself) the gift of continence. For them the single state is in accord with the will of God. Paul wishes all of God's children had his gift, but acknowledges that for those who do not have this gift, it is better to marry than to be aflame with passion (v. 9).

2. The Christian and divorce

7.10
Mal 2.14;
Mt 5.32;
19.3-9;
Mk 10.11;
Lk 16.18
7.12
v. 6;
2 Cor 11.17

7.14
Mal 2.15

7.15
Rom 14.19;
1 Cor 14.33
7.16
1 Pet 3.1

10 To the married I give this command — not I but the Lord — that the wife should not separate from her husband [11] (but if she does separate, let her remain unmarried or else be reconciled to her husband), and that the husband should not divorce his wife.

12 To the rest I say — I and not the Lord — that if any believer[z] has a wife who is an unbeliever, and she consents to live with him, he should not divorce her. [13] And if any woman has a husband who is an unbeliever, and he consents to live with her, she should not divorce him. [14] For the unbelieving husband is made holy through his wife, and the unbelieving wife is made holy through her husband. Otherwise, your children would be unclean, but as it is, they are holy. [15] But if the unbelieving partner separates, let it be so; in such a case the brother or sister is not bound. It is to peace that God has called you.[a] [16] Wife, for all you know, you might save your husband. Husband, for all you know, you might save your wife.

3. The status quo

7.17
Rom 12.3;
1 Cor 4.17;
14.33;
2 Cor 8.18;
11.28
7.18
Acts 15.1, 2
7.19
Gal 5.6; 6.15;
Rom 2.25
7.20
v. 24

7.22
Jn 8.32, 36;
Philem 16;
Eph 6.6
7.23
1 Cor 6.20

17 However that may be, let each of you lead the life that the Lord has assigned, to which God called you. This is my rule in all the churches. [18] Was anyone at the time of his call already circumcised? Let him not seek to remove the marks of circumcision. Was anyone at the time of his call uncircumcised? Let him not seek circumcision. [19] Circumcision is nothing, and uncircumcision is nothing; but obeying the commandments of God is everything. [20] Let each of you remain in the condition in which you were called.

21 Were you a slave when called? Do not be concerned about it. Even if you can gain your freedom, make use of your present condition now more than ever.[b] [22] For whoever was called in the Lord as a slave is a freed person belonging to the Lord, just as whoever was free when called is a slave of Christ. [23] You were bought with a price; do not become slaves of human masters. [24] In whatever condition you were called, brothers and sisters,[c] there remain with God.

4. Counsel to the unmarried

7.25
2 Cor 8.8, 10;
1 Tim 1.13,
16
7.26
vv. 1, 8

7.29
Rom 13.11,
12; v. 31

25 Now concerning virgins, I have no command of the Lord, but I give my opinion as one who by the Lord's mercy is trustworthy. [26] I think that, in view of the impending[d] crisis, it is well for you to remain as you are. [27] Are you bound to a wife? Do not seek to be free. Are you free from a wife? Do not seek a wife. [28] But if you marry, you do not sin, and if a virgin marries, she does not sin. Yet those who marry will experience distress in this life,[e] and I would spare you that. [29] I mean, brothers and sisters,[c] the appointed time has grown short; from now on, let even those who have wives be as though they had none, [30] and those who mourn as though they were not mourning, and those who rejoice as though they were not rejoicing, and those who buy as though they had no possessions,

---

z Gk brother a Other ancient authorities read us b Or avail yourself of the opportunity c Gk brothers
d Or present e Gk in the flesh

7.15 See note on Deut 24.1.
7.21 Freedom is better than slavery. Therefore, slaves would do well to obtain their freedom if they can. Yet Paul does not condemn slavery per se, nor does he say it is wrong for a Christian of his day to have slaves. Christians have therefore been divided on the issue of slavery, but Scripture implicitly indicates that slavery is not something to be endorsed by believers.
7.26 Paul is not a woman-hater, nor does he belittle marriage. Rather, he elevates it to the highest possible

position. Paul does not say here that being single is best for all humans in all times. By way of advice, because God has not given a specific command, he thinks it wise for those who have the gift of continence to remain single so as to devote themselves wholly to the service of God. The *impending crisis* may cause some to deny Christ in order to save their wives and children from torture and death. Or his advice may be based on the possibility of the imminent coming of the Lord. But he does not intend to bind all Christians of all ages by this statement.

31 and those who deal with the world as though they had no dealings with it. For the present form of this world is passing away.

32 I want you to be free from anxieties. The unmarried man is anxious about the affairs of the Lord, how to please the Lord; 33 but the married man is anxious about the affairs of the world, how to please his wife, 34 and his interests are divided. And the unmarried woman and the virgin are anxious about the affairs of the Lord, so that they may be holy in body and spirit; but the married woman is anxious about the affairs of the world, how to please her husband. 35 I say this for your own benefit, not to put any restraint upon you, but to promote good order and unhindered devotion to the Lord.

5. Asceticism and marriage

36 If anyone thinks that he is not behaving properly toward his fiancée,ᶠ if his passions are strong, and so it has to be, let him marry as he wishes; it is no sin. Let them marry. 37 But if someone stands firm in his resolve, being under no necessity but having his own desire under control, and has determined in his own mind to keep her as his fiancée,ᶠ he will do well. 38 So then, he who marries his fiancéeᶠ does well; and he who refrains from marriage will do better.

6. Counsel to widows

39 A wife is bound as long as her husband lives. But if the husband dies,ᵍ she is free to marry anyone she wishes, only in the Lord. 40 But in my judgment she is more blessed if she remains as she is. And I think that I too have the Spirit of God.

IV. Christian liberty (8.1–11.1)

A. Food sacrificed to idols

8 Now concerning food sacrificed to idols: we know that "all of us possess knowledge." Knowledge puffs up, but love builds up. 2 Anyone who claims to know something does not yet have the necessary knowledge; 3 but anyone who loves God is known by him.

4 Hence, as to the eating of food offered to idols, we know that "no idol in the world really exists," and that "there is no God but one." 5 Indeed, even though there may be so-called gods in heaven or on earth — as in fact there are many gods and many lords — 6 yet for us there is one God, the Father, from whom are all things and for whom we exist, and one Lord, Jesus Christ, through whom are all things and through whom we exist.

7 It is not everyone, however, who has this knowledge. Since some have become so accustomed to idols until now, they still think of the food they eat as food offered to an idol; and their conscience, being weak, is defiled. 8 "Food will not bring us close to God."ʰ We are no worse off if we do not eat, and no better off if we do. 9 But take care that this liberty of yours does not somehow become a stumbling block to the weak. 10 For if others see you, who possess knowledge, eating in the temple of an idol, might they not, since their conscience is weak, be encouraged to the point of eating food sacrificed to idols? 11 So by your knowledge those weak

---

ᶠ Gk virgin   ᵍ Gk falls asleep   ʰ The quotation may extend to the end of the verse

---

8.1ff In ancient Corinth parts of the animals sacrificed to idols found their way into the meat markets for sale to the public (see 10.25). Some believers there felt that eating meat of this kind was idolatrous, since the animal had been dedicated to an idol. Paul says that idols are nothing; thus, eating meat offered to

them is wrong in itself. But since weaker consciences are offended by this act of eating, believers should abstain from food offered to idols for the sake of the weaker person's conscience.
8.9 See notes on 10.23; Acts 16.3; Rom 14.
8.11ff Paul so values the soul of a brother or sister

7.31
1 Cor 9.18;
1 Jn 2.17
7.32
1 Tim 5.5
7.34
Lk 10.40

7.38
Heb 13.4

7.39
Rom 7.2;
2 Cor 6.14
7.40
v. 25

8.1
Acts 15.20;
Rom 15.14;
14.3, 10
8.2
1 Cor 3.18;
13.8, 9, 12;
1 Tim 6.4
8.3
Gal 4.9;
Rom 8.29
8.5
1 Cor 10.19;
Deut 6.4;
Eph 4.6
8.6
Mal 2.10;
Rom 11.36;
Phil 2.11
8.7
1 Cor 10.28;
Rom 14.14
8.8
Rom 14.17
8.9
Gal 5.13;
Rom 14.1,
13, 20
8.10
1 Cor 10.28,
32
8.11
Rom 14.15,
20

believers for whom Christ died are destroyed.*i* 12 But when you thus sin against members of your family,*j* and wound their conscience when it is weak, you sin against Christ. 13 Therefore, if food is a cause of their falling,*k* I will never eat meat, so that I may not cause one of them*l* to fall.

B. *The law of expediency*

1. *Christian rights acknowledged*

9 Am I not free? Am I not an apostle? Have I not seen Jesus our Lord? Are you not my work in the Lord? 2 If I am not an apostle to others, at least I am to you; for you are the seal of my apostleship in the Lord.

3 This is my defense to those who would examine me. 4 Do we not have the right to our food and drink? 5 Do we not have the right to be accompanied by a believing wife,*m* as do the other apostles and the brothers of the Lord and Cephas? 6 Or is it only Barnabas and I who have no right to refrain from working for a living? 7 Who at any time pays the expenses for doing military service? Who plants a vineyard and does not eat any of its fruit? Or who tends a flock and does not get any of its milk?

8 Do I say this on human authority? Does not the law also say the same? 9 For it is written in the law of Moses, "You shall not muzzle an ox while it is treading out the grain." Is it for oxen that God is concerned? 10 Or does he not speak entirely for our sake? It was indeed written for our sake, for whoever plows should plow in hope and whoever threshes should thresh in hope of a share in the crop. 11 If we have sown spiritual good among you, is it too much if we reap your material benefits? 12 If others share this rightful claim on you, do not we still more?

Nevertheless, we have not made use of this right, but we endure anything rather than put an obstacle in the way of the gospel of Christ. 13 Do you not know that those who are employed in the temple service get their food from the temple, and those who serve at the altar share in what is sacrificed on the altar? 14 In the same way, the Lord commanded that those who proclaim the gospel should get their living by the gospel.

2. *Christian rights surrendered*

15 But I have made no use of any of these rights, nor am I writing this so that they may be applied in my case. Indeed, I would rather die than that — no one will deprive me of my ground for boasting! 16 If I proclaim the gospel, this gives me no ground for boasting, for an obligation is laid on me, and woe to me if I do not proclaim the gospel! 17 For if I do this of my own will, I have a reward; but if not of my own will, I am entrusted with a commission. 18 What then is my reward? Just this: that in my proclamation I may make the gospel free of charge, so as not to make full use of my rights in the gospel.

i Gk *the weak brother . . . is destroyed*   *j* Gk *against the brothers*   *k* Gk *my brother's falling*   *l* Gk *cause my brother*   *m* Gk *a sister as wife*

that he will gladly deny himself something he considers legitimate, if it means someone else's conscience is not troubled and that no one stumbles in his or her faith.

9.1 Paul has served the Corinthians well and they owe their salvation to his faithful preaching. He is therefore deeply agitated when some questioned whether he was really an apostle. He insists that those who have come to Christ through his preaching are a seal of his apostleship; to question him on this is most ungrateful.

9.3ff Paul defends the right of ministers to receive wages for their services (see also Gal 6.6). Soldiers of war cannot be expected to support themselves when they serve in the army; those who receive benefit from their services must support them. A shepherd has a right to the milk of the flock, and whoever tends a vineyard has a right to eat of its fruit. Paul supports his position by words from Moses: "You shall not muzzle an ox while it is treading out the grain" (Deut 25.4). If God cares enough for animals to let them feed from what they are working on, does he not also care for preachers, intending that their listeners should support them?

9.14 Though Paul insists on his right to a salary (see previous note), he consistently refused to accept one. He supported himself by tent-making, so that no one could accuse him of ministering to make money.

19 For though I am free with respect to all, I have made myself a slave to all, so that I might win more of them. **20** To the Jews I became as a Jew, in order to win Jews. To those under the law I became as one under the law (though I myself am not under the law) so that I might win those under the law. **21** To those outside the law I became as one outside the law (though I am not free from God's law but am under Christ's law) so that I might win those outside the law. **22** To the weak I became weak, so that I might win the weak. I have become all things to all people, that I might by all means save some. **23** I do it all for the sake of the gospel, so that I may share in its blessings.

3. The true race

24 Do you not know that in a race the runners all compete, but only one receives the prize? Run in such a way that you may win it. **25** Athletes exercise self-control in all things; they do it to receive a perishable wreath, but we an imperishable one. **26** So I do not run aimlessly, nor do I box as though beating the air; **27** but I punish my body and enslave it, so that after proclaiming to others I myself should not be disqualified.

C. The evil of self-indulgence illustrated

10 I do not want you to be unaware, brothers and sisters,[n] that our ancestors were all under the cloud, and all passed through the sea, **2** and all were baptized into Moses in the cloud and in the sea, **3** and all ate the same spiritual food, **4** and all drank the same spiritual drink. For they drank from the spiritual rock that followed them, and the rock was Christ. **5** Nevertheless, God was not pleased with most of them, and they were struck down in the wilderness.

6 Now these things occurred as examples for us, so that we might not desire evil as they did. **7** Do not become idolaters as some of them did; as it is written, "The people sat down to eat and drink, and they rose up to play." **8** We must not indulge in sexual immorality as some of them did, and twenty-three thousand fell in a single day. **9** We must not put Christ[o] to the test, as some of them did, and were destroyed by serpents. **10** And do not complain as some of them did, and were destroyed by the destroyer. **11** These things happened to them to serve as an example, and they were written down to instruct us, on whom the ends of the ages have come. **12** So if you think you are standing, watch out that you do not fall. **13** No testing has overtaken you that is not common to everyone. God is

n Gk brothers   o Other ancient authorities read the Lord

9.19
Gal 5.13;
Mt 18.15;
1 Pet 3.1
9.20
Acts 16.3;
21.23;
Rom 11.14;
Gal 2.19
9.21
Rom 2.12,
14;
Gal 3.2;
1 Cor 7.22

9.24
2 Tim 4.7;
Heb 12.1
9.25
Eph 6.12;
1 Tim 6.12
9.27
Rom 8.13;
Col 3.5;
Rom 6.18
10.1
Ex 13.21;
14.22, 29;
Rom 1.13
10.3
Ex 16.4, 35
10.4
Ex 17.6;
Num 20.11
10.5
Num 14.29,
30;
Heb 3.17
10.6
Num 11.4,
34;
Ps 106.14
10.7
Ex 32.4, 6
10.8
Num 25.1ff
10.9
Num 21.5, 6
10.10
Num 16.41,
49;
Ex 12.23
10.11
Rom 13.11;
Phil 4.5
10.12
Rom 11.20
10.13
2 Pet 2.9

9.19ff Paul is free in Christ, that is, he is in bondage to no one. Yet he surrenders his freedom in many instances so that he may win unbelievers to Christ. It is biblically permissible and methodologically sound to identify with people where they are and in what they do, so long as the Christian conscience is not defiled.

9.24 It was true that in the Isthmian games only the winner received the garland. But this is not so for Christians. We are encouraged to run, and all those who do will receive a winner's crown (cf. 2 Tim 4.7, 8). We cannot fail as long as we keep on running.

10.1–4 Using Israel as an illustration, Paul warns the Corinthians that God's covenant of grace, freely offered to all, does not mean that all will inherit the covenant promises. He argues that all God's benefits bestowed on Israel came from Christ whether they were aware of it or not. These benefits were granted to everyone, good and bad alike. All experienced safety from the pillar of cloud and all were delivered from Egypt. The same principles that applied to the Israelites apply to the new covenant and thus to the Corinthians (see next note).

10.5 Although all of these Israelites experienced the outward, material blessing of God, God was not pleased with all of them. Most of them did not share in the spiritual blessings of God. Virtually all of the adults who left Egypt died in the desert, never entering the promised land. Paul uses this illustration to warn the Corinthians that those who sin freely against God will not inherit eternal life, even though they might identify themselves as Christians.

10.8 This incident is often confused with the account in Num 25.9 of the death of 24,000 at Shittim. It really refers to the golden calf plague of Ex 32 (cf. v. 7, quoting Ex 32.6). Though the Exodus account gives no number of people who died after the apostasy of the golden calf, by the inspiration of the Spirit Paul does give the number.

10.10 Grumbling and complaining are sins against God. They arise from a bitter dislike of adverse circumstances, either resulting from sin or sent by God to purify and test us. We must not complain, for God is provoked when we do.

10.13 No believer who falls into sin may ever say, "I couldn't help it; it wasn't my fault." God assures

faithful, and he will not let you be tested beyond your strength, but with the testing he will also provide the way out so that you may be able to endure it.

D. *Participation in idol festivals prohibited*

14 Therefore, my dear friends,*p* flee from the worship of idols. 15 I speak as to sensible people; judge for yourselves what I say. 16 The cup of blessing that we bless, is it not a sharing in the blood of Christ? The bread that we break, is it not a sharing in the body of Christ? 17 Because there is one bread, we who are many are one body, for we all partake of the one bread. 18 Consider the people of Israel;*q* are not those who eat the sacrifices partners in the altar? 19 What do I imply then? That food sacrificed to idols is anything, or that an idol is anything? 20 No, I imply that what pagans sacrifice, they sacrifice to demons and not to God. I do not want you to be partners with demons. 21 You cannot drink the cup of the Lord and the cup of demons. You cannot partake of the table of the Lord and the table of demons. 22 Or are we provoking the Lord to jealousy? Are we stronger than he?

E. *The basic principles summed up*

23 "All things are lawful," but not all things are beneficial. "All things are lawful," but not all things build up. 24 Do not seek your own advantage, but that of the other. 25 Eat whatever is sold in the meat market without raising any question on the ground of conscience, 26 for "the earth and its fullness are the Lord's." 27 If an unbeliever invites you to a meal and you are disposed to go, eat whatever is set before you without raising any question on the ground of conscience. 28 But if someone says to you, "This has been offered in sacrifice," then do not eat it, out of consideration for the one who informed you, and for the sake of conscience — 29 I mean the other's conscience, not your own. For why should my liberty be subject to the judgment of someone else's conscience? 30 If I partake with thankfulness, why should I be denounced because of that for which I give thanks?

31 So, whether you eat or drink, or whatever you do, do everything for the glory of God. 32 Give no offense to Jews or to Greeks or to the church of God, 33 just as I try to please everyone in everything I do, not seeking my own advantage, but that of many, so that they may be saved.

11 1 Be imitators of me, as I am of Christ.

V. *Public worship (11.2–14.40)*

A. *The veiling of women*

2 I commend you because you remember me in everything and main-

p Gk *my beloved*　*q* Gk *Israel according to the flesh*

us that we will never be tempted in ways and manners not common to other humans, nor will we ever be tempted in a way that cannot be resisted or overcome. Therefore, believers who sin are always at fault and have no one to blame except themselves.
10.23 The law of love is basic to all human relationships — love for God and love for others. In the Christian's relationships to others, two principles govern conduct: (1) whatever is stated as wrong in principle, i.e., whatever is explicitly forbidden, must be shunned; (2) the principle of expediency governs all other decisions in relation to others. Anything that is questionable or has the appearance of evil or that may cause a weaker believer to take offense or stumble must be avoided. In matters of expediency believ-

ers forego that which they do not think to be wrong in principle but which they give up out of love for God and their fellow believers.
10.31–33 Paul lays down two principles by which we are to govern our choices: (1) we must do that which is for the glory of God; and (2) we must be concerned about the well-being of others. Note how Paul refers to glorifying God in the ordinary things of life. If we make a habit of doing this, we will also glorify him in the spiritual and the extraordinary affairs of life.
11.2 *maintain the traditions just as I handed them on to you.* Before the N.T. was written, traditions about Jesus were passed around by word of mouth. 1 Corinthians was written perhaps ten years earlier than any

tain the traditions just as I handed them on to you. 3But I want you to understand that Christ is the head of every man, and the husband*r* is the head of his wife,*s* and God is the head of Christ. 4Any man who prays or prophesies with something on his head disgraces his head, 5but any woman who prays or prophesies with her head unveiled disgraces her head—it is one and the same thing as having her head shaved. 6For if a woman will not veil herself, then she should cut off her hair; but if it is disgraceful for a woman to have her hair cut off or to be shaved, she should wear a veil. 7For a man ought not to have his head veiled, since he is the image and reflection*t* of God; but woman is the reflection*t* of man. 8Indeed, man was not made from woman, but woman from man. 9Neither was man created for the sake of woman, but woman for the sake of man. 10For this reason a woman ought to have a symbol of*u* authority on her head,*v* because of the angels. 11Nevertheless, in the Lord woman is not independent of man or man independent of woman. 12For just as woman came from man, so man comes through woman; but all things come from God. 13Judge for yourselves: is it proper for a woman to pray to God with her head unveiled? 14Does not nature itself teach you that if a man wears long hair, it is degrading to him, 15but if a woman has long hair, it is her glory? For her hair is given to her for a covering. 16But if anyone is disposed to be contentious—we have no such custom, nor do the churches of God.

B. *The Lord's Supper*

17 Now in the following instructions I do not commend you, because when you come together it is not for the better but for the worse. 18For, to begin with, when you come together as a church, I hear that there are divisions among you; and to some extent I believe it. 19Indeed, there have to be factions among you, for only so will it become clear who among you are genuine. 20When you come together, it is not really to eat the Lord's supper. 21For when the time comes to eat, each of you goes ahead with your own supper, and one goes hungry and another becomes drunk. 22What! Do you not have homes to eat and drink in? Or do you show contempt for the church of God and humiliate those who have nothing? What should I say to you? Should I commend you? In this matter I do not commend you!

23 For I received from the Lord what I also handed on to you, that the Lord Jesus on the night when he was betrayed took a loaf of bread, 24and when he had given thanks, he broke it and said, "This is my body

11.3
Eph 1.22;
4.15; 5.23;
1 Cor 3.23
11.4
Acts 13.1;
1 Thess 5.20
11.5
Acts 21.9;
Deut 21.12

11.7
Gen 1.26

11.8
Gen 2.21-23
11.9
Gen 2.18
11.10
Gen 24.65
11.12
2 Cor 5.18;
Rom 11.36
11.13
Lk 12.57

11.16
1 Cor 7.17

11.17
vv. 2, 22
11.18
1 Cor 1.10-12
11.19
Mt 18.7;
Lk 17.1;
1 Tim 4.1;
Deut 13.3;
1 Jn 2.19
11.21
2 Pet 2.13;
Jude 12
11.22
1 Cor 10.32;
Jas 2.6

11.23
1 Cor 15.3;
Mt 26.26-28;
Mk 14.22-24;
Lk 22.17-20

r The same Greek word means *man* or *husband*   *s* Or *head of the woman*   *t* Or *glory*   *u* Gk lacks *a symbol of*   *v* Or *have freedom of choice regarding her head*

of the Gospels and twenty years after Christ's ascension. Meanwhile, oral transmission of what Christ did and said was common. Elsewhere Paul declares that whatever traditions he passed on were true (2 Thess 2.15–3.6). Inspiration of the Bible by the Holy Spirit means that among all the traditions known in the early church, only those that were accurate and historical became part of the written word of God, so that any tradition not found in Scripture is not necessarily binding on the Christian conscience.
11.5 Evidently Paul is saying that it is permissible for women to pray or to prophesy publicly; his only restriction is that they must have their heads covered. Should this custom continue today or was it simply a cultural pattern which no longer should be practiced? Some churches have generally insisted that women wear hats; others have not. It seems apparent that women may do either. Liberty at this point is important since at best it is a secondary matter.
11.16 The apostle concludes that since the wearing of a head covering for women was the common cus-

tom of the churches, women should follow that custom. His focus is not on whether this or other customs may be changed or how to make such changes.
11.17–22 The Lord's Supper in the early church was accompanied by a love feast, a fellowshp meal to set a context of Christian love. In the church at Corinth the love feast degenerated into schism and disorder. Some of those who attended got drunk, while others despised their poorer brothers and sisters by refusing to share what they brought with them. Paul accuses them of treating the celebration of the Supper contemptuously by their scandalous conduct at the love feast. He disapproves of this and judges them strongly.
11.23 The Lord's Supper was instituted without Paul's being there. How then can he instruct the church about its observance? He carefully points out that his knowledge about the celebration was given to him by divine revelation from Jesus Christ.
11.24 *Do this . . . in remembrance of me.* The Supper is a memorial remembrance of Christ's redeeming

that is for[w] you. Do this in remembrance of me." 25 In the same way he took the cup also, after supper, saying, "This cup is the new covenant in my blood. Do this, as often as you drink it, in remembrance of me." 26 For as often as you eat this bread and drink the cup, you proclaim the Lord's death until he comes.

27 Whoever, therefore, eats the bread or drinks the cup of the Lord in an unworthy manner will be answerable for the body and blood of the Lord. 28 Examine yourselves, and only then eat of the bread and drink of the cup. 29 For all who eat and drink[x] without discerning the body,[y] eat and drink judgment against themselves. 30 For this reason many of you are weak and ill, and some have died.[z] 31 But if we judged ourselves, we would not be judged. 32 But when we are judged by the Lord, we are disciplined[a] so that we may not be condemned along with the world.

33 So then, my brothers and sisters,[b] when you come together to eat, wait for one another. 34 If you are hungry, eat at home, so that when you come together, it will not be for your condemnation. About the other things I will give instructions when I come.

C. The use of spiritual gifts

1. The gifts of the Spirit

a. The source of spiritual gifts

12 Now concerning spiritual gifts,[c] brothers and sisters,[b] I do not want you to be uninformed. 2 You know that when you were pagans, you were enticed and led astray to idols that could not speak. 3 Therefore I want you to understand that no one speaking by the Spirit of God ever says "Let Jesus be cursed!" and no one can say "Jesus is Lord" except by the Holy Spirit.

b. Varieties of gifts

4 Now there are varieties of gifts, but the same Spirit; 5 and there are varieties of services, but the same Lord; 6 and there are varieties of activities, but it is the same God who activates all of them in everyone. 7 To each is given the manifestation of the Spirit for the common good. 8 To one is given through the Spirit the utterance of wisdom, and to another the utterance of knowledge according to the same Spirit, 9 to another faith by the same Spirit, to another gifts of healing by the one Spirit, 10 to another the working of miracles, to another prophecy, to another the discernment of spirits, to another various kinds of tongues, to another the interpreta-

---

w Other ancient authorities read *is broken for* *x* Other ancient authorities add *in an unworthy manner,* *y* Other ancient authorities read *the Lord's body* *z* Gk *fallen asleep* *a* Or *When we are judged, we are being disciplined by the Lord* *b* Gk *brothers* *c* Or *spiritual persons*

---

work on Calvary. The participants must eat the bread and drink the cup, and do so in a worthy manner. Churches interpret the meaning of the bread and cup in different ways (see note on Mk 14.22ff).

11.28ff Some Corinthians were celebrating the Eucharist (the Lord's Supper) in an unworthy manner. God sent judgment on them and many became ill because of their abuse of the Supper (v. 30). Paul enjoins them (and us) to examine themselves *before* celebrating the Supper.

12.1 Many times the Scriptures speak to issues after a problem has developed. The Corinthian church abounded in spiritual gifts, but abuses arose among those who were not yet mature in the faith and who had not advanced greatly in their sanctification. Paul had to instruct them about spiritual gifts and their proper use.

12.3 *no one speaking by the Spirit of God ever says "Let*

Jesus be cursed!" Jews and Gentiles blasphemed Jesus as an imposter and angrily denounced him. Paul insists that those who blaspheme or disown the Son of God cannot do this if they are controlled by the Spirit. No one who blasphemes Christ has the Spirit, and such a blasphemer is thus under the sentence of death by God unless and until such people receive Christ and are given the gift of the Spirit.

12.8 Some say that the sign gifts (healing, tongues, miracles, etc.) ceased at the end of the apostolic age. Nowhere does Scripture affirm this notion. However, others give the impression that these gifts abound. This too is incorrect. In the O.T. and N.T. healings were infrequent and occurred in only a few special instances (e.g., through Moses, Elijah and Elisha, Jesus, and the apostles). We must not exaggerate their occurrence.

tion of tongues. **11** All these are activated by one and the same Spirit, who allots to each one individually just as the Spirit chooses.

c. Unity in diversity

12 For just as the body is one and has many members, and all the members of the body, though many, are one body, so it is with Christ. **13** For in the one Spirit we were all baptized into one body — Jews or Greeks, slaves or free — and we were all made to drink of one Spirit.

14 Indeed, the body does not consist of one member but of many. **15** If the foot would say, "Because I am not a hand, I do not belong to the body," that would not make it any less a part of the body. **16** And if the ear would say, "Because I am not an eye, I do not belong to the body," that would not make it any less a part of the body. **17** If the whole body were an eye, where would the hearing be? If the whole body were hearing, where would the sense of smell be? **18** But as it is, God arranged the members in the body, each one of them, as he chose. **19** If all were a single member, where would the body be? **20** As it is, there are many members, yet one body. **21** The eye cannot say to the hand, "I have no need of you," nor again the head to the feet, "I have no need of you." **22** On the contrary, the members of the body that seem to be weaker are indispensable, **23** and those members of the body that we think less honorable we clothe with greater honor, and our less respectable members are treated with greater respect; **24** whereas our more respectable members do not need this. But God has so arranged the body, giving the greater honor to the inferior member, **25** that there may be no dissension within the body, but the members may have the same care for one another. **26** If one member suffers, all suffer together with it; if one member is honored, all rejoice together with it.

d. Specific gifts

27 Now you are the body of Christ and individually members of it. **28** And God has appointed in the church first apostles, second prophets, third teachers; then deeds of power, then gifts of healing, forms of assistance, forms of leadership, various kinds of tongues. **29** Are all apostles? Are all prophets? Are all teachers? Do all work miracles? **30** Do all possess gifts of healing? Do all speak in tongues? Do all interpret? **31** But strive for the greater gifts. And I will show you a still more excellent way.

2. The way of love

a. Love superior

13 If I speak in the tongues of mortals and of angels, but do not have love, I am a noisy gong or a clanging cymbal. **2** And if I have

12.11
2 Cor 10.13;
Heb 2.4

12.12
Rom 12.4;
Gal 3.16
12.13
Eph 2.18;
Gal 3.28;
Col 3.11;
Jn 7.37-39

12.18
vv. 28, 11

12.20
v. 14

12.27
Eph 1.23;
4.12;
Col 1.18, 24;
Eph 5.30;
Rom 12.5
12.28
Eph 4.11;
2.30; 3.5;
Rom 12.6, 8;
vv. 9, 10
12.30
v. 10
12.31
1 Cor 14.1,
39
13.2
Acts 13.1;
1 Cor 14.1;
Mt 7.22;
1 Cor 12.9;
Mt 17.20;
21.21

12.11 The Holy Spirit gives different gifts to different people. None of the gifts described in the preceding verses is given to all believers. The Corinthian church was specially enthralled with the gift of tongues. Paul carefully places that gift in the lowest order of enumeration. When he says the Corinthians must "strive for the greater gifts" (v. 31), he means that there are more important gifts than speaking in tongues. All believers who want to receive gifts must remember that they are given according to God's will.
12.28 Regarding the gifts God has given believers, the functions vary but together they enable the church to operate effectively. Note how all three persons of the Trinity are involved in giving these gifts. In Eph 4.11 Paul refers to these as gifts of *Christ* (apostles, prophets, evangelists, pastors and teachers). Here are the gifts of *God*. In vv. 8ff they are gifts given by the *Spirit*. Every genuine call to an office carries with it the divine ability to discharge the duties of that office.

12.30 *Do all speak in tongues?* The N.T. refers to the gift of tongues several times. At Pentecost one of the miracles that attested to the advent of the Spirit was the gift of tongues, where the languages spoken were known languages of the various peoples who had come from afar to Jerusalem (Acts 2.1–11). Here the gift of tongues (expanded on in ch. 14) appears to be ecstatic utterances rather than known languages. Such tongues-speaking benefits primarily the person who has the gift. Paul states that the use of tongues in the church must conform to certain requirements: (1) not more than two or three shall speak (14.27); (2) they must speak in order, one at a time (14.27); (3) there must be an interpreter (14.27,28); (4) women should be silent (14.34). Some do not believe that speaking in tongues belongs to this present age. It cannot, however, be ruled out as a matter of principle, though Paul classifies it as a lesser gift (14.5). Speaking in tongues is not needed as a sign of regeneration or of sanctification.

13.3
Mt 6.2

prophetic powers, and understand all mysteries and all knowledge, and if I have all faith, so as to remove mountains, but do not have love, I am nothing. 3 If I give away all my possessions, and if I hand over my body so that I may boast,*d* but do not have love, I gain nothing.

b. *Love defined*

13.4
Prov 10.12;
1 Pet 4.8
13.5
1 Cor 10.24;
2 Cor 5.19
13.6
2 Jn 4
13.7
Rom 15.1;
1 Cor 9.12
13.8
vv. 1, 2
13.9
1 Cor 8.2

4 Love is patient; love is kind; love is not envious or boastful or arrogant 5 or rude. It does not insist on its own way; it is not irritable or resentful; 6 it does not rejoice in wrongdoing, but rejoices in the truth. 7 It bears all things, believes all things, hopes all things, endures all things.

c. *Love imperishable*

8 Love never ends. But as for prophecies, they will come to an end; as for tongues, they will cease; as for knowledge, it will come to an end. 9 For we know only in part, and we prophesy only in part; 10 but when the complete comes, the partial will come to an end. 11 When I was a child, I spoke like a child, I thought like a child, I reasoned like a child; when I became an adult, I put an end to childish ways. 12 For now we see in a mirror, dimly,*e* but then we will see face to face. Now I know only in part; then I will know fully, even as I have been fully known. 13 And now faith, hope, and love abide, these three; and the greatest of these is love.

13.12
2 Cor 5.7;
Phil 3.12;
1 Jn 3.2;
1 Cor 8.3
13.13
1 Cor 16.14

3. *The worth and use of spiritual gifts*

a. *Prophecy versus tongues*

14.1
1 Cor 16.14;
12.31; 12.1;
13.2
14.2
Acts 10.46;
1 Cor 12.10,
28, 30; 13.1
14.3
vv. 5, 12, 17,
26;
Acts 4.36
14.5
Num 11.29

14 Pursue love and strive for the spiritual gifts, and especially that you may prophesy. 2 For those who speak in a tongue do not speak to other people but to God; for nobody understands them, since they are speaking mysteries in the Spirit. 3 On the other hand, those who prophesy speak to other people for their upbuilding and encouragement and consolation. 4 Those who speak in a tongue build up themselves, but those who prophesy build up the church. 5 Now I would like all of you to speak in tongues, but even more to prophesy. One who prophesies is greater than one who speaks in tongues, unless someone interprets, so that the church may be built up.

14.6
v. 26;
1 Cor 12.8;
Rom 6.17

6 Now, brothers and sisters,*f* if I come to you speaking in tongues, how will I benefit you unless I speak to you in some revelation or knowledge or prophecy or teaching? 7 It is the same way with lifeless instruments that produce sound, such as the flute or the harp. If they do not give distinct notes, how will anyone know what is being played? 8 And if the bugle gives an indistinct sound, who will get ready for battle? 9 So with yourselves; if in a tongue you utter speech that is not intelligible, how will anyone know what is being said? For you will be speaking into the air.

14.8
Num 10.9
14.9
1 Cor 9.26

d Other ancient authorities read *body to be burned*   *e* Gk *in a riddle*   *f* Gk *brothers*

13.1 *love*, (Gk. *agapē*). Beginning with this verse Paul compares love with such gifts as tongues, prophetic powers, understanding mysteries, knowledge, faith, and giving goods to feed the poor. His final conclusion is that where love is lacking, none of these gifts will benefit the one doing these things.

13.8 This verse cannot be used to support the notion that prophecy and tongues passed away at the end of the apostolic age and therefore no longer exist. The time when these things cease will be the time of Christ's return in glory and power.

13.13 *Faith, hope, and love* are the three most important graces. But two of the three are temporal and are needed only in this present life. Faith and hope will disappear when we get to heaven (cf. Rom 8.24, 25; 2 Cor 5.6–8). But love will remain forever.

14.1 Love is an aspect of the fruit of the Spirit (Gal 5.22,23), available to all Christians. Paul elevates it above the spiritual gifts, though he does not rule out or underestimate these gifts. In ch. 14 he teaches which gifts we should prefer and by what rules we should make comparisons. Those who rule out some of the spiritual gifts and retain others do the church an injustice. At the same time, some gifts are more useful and valuable than others and we need to follow Paul's order of importance when we seek for gifts from the Spirit.

14.4 Speaking in tongues is rewarding and helpful to the one who has this gift. But those who have the gift of prophecy can do more than those who use tongues, for they will edify the church, whereas tongues-speakers edify only themselves. Whatever usefulness tongues may have for the people who speak them, they sound like gibberish to others, for they hear only sounds without sense.

10 There are doubtless many different kinds of sounds in the world, and nothing is without sound. 11 If then I do not know the meaning of a sound, I will be a foreigner to the speaker and the speaker a foreigner to me. 12 So with yourselves; since you are eager for spiritual gifts, strive to excel in them for building up the church.

13 Therefore, one who speaks in a tongue should pray for the power to interpret. 14 For if I pray in a tongue, my spirit prays but my mind is unproductive. 15 What should I do then? I will pray with the spirit, but I will pray with the mind also; I will sing praise with the spirit, but I will sing praise with the mind also. 16 Otherwise, if you say a blessing with the spirit, how can anyone in the position of an outsider say the "Amen" to your thanksgiving, since the outsider does not know what you are saying? 17 For you may give thanks well enough, but the other person is not built up. 18 I thank God that I speak in tongues more than all of you; 19 nevertheless, in church I would rather speak five words with my mind, in order to instruct others also, than ten thousand words in a tongue.

20 Brothers and sisters,g do not be children in your thinking; rather, be infants in evil, but in thinking be adults. 21 In the law it is written,

"By people of strange tongues
    and by the lips of foreigners
I will speak to this people;
    yet even then they will not listen to me,"

says the Lord. 22 Tongues, then, are a sign not for believers but for unbelievers, while prophecy is not for unbelievers but for believers. 23 If, therefore, the whole church comes together and all speak in tongues, and outsiders or unbelievers enter, will they not say that you are out of your mind? 24 But if all prophesy, an unbeliever or outsider who enters is reproved by all and called to account by all. 25 After the secrets of the unbeliever's heart are disclosed, that person will bow down before God and worship him, declaring, "God is really among you."

b. Rules regarding the use of spiritual gifts

26 What should be done then, my friends?g When you come together, each one has a hymn, a lesson, a revelation, a tongue, or an interpretation. Let all things be done for building up. 27 If anyone speaks in a tongue, let there be only two or at most three, and each in turn; and let one interpret. 28 But if there is no one to interpret, let them be silent in church and speak to themselves and to God. 29 Let two or three prophets speak, and let the others weigh what is said. 30 If a revelation is made to someone else sitting nearby, let the first person be silent. 31 For you can all prophesy one by one, so that all may learn and all be encouraged. 32 And the spirits of prophets are subject to the prophets, 33 for God is a God of disorder but of peace.

(As in all the churches of the saints, 34 women should be silent in the churches. For they are not permitted to speak, but should be subordinate, as the law also says. 35 If there is anything they desire to know, let them ask their husbands at home. For it is shameful for a woman to speak in

g Gk brothers

14.11
Acts 28.2
14.12
vv. 4, 5, 17, 26

14.15
Eph 5.19;
Col 3.16
14.16
1 Chr 16.36;
Ps 106.48;
Mt 15.36;
1 Cor 11.24
14.17
Rom 14.19

14.20
Eph 4.14;
Heb 5.12, 13;
Ps 131.2;
Rom 16.19;
1 Pet 2.2
14.21
Jn 10.34;
Isa 28.11, 12
14.22
v. 1
14.23
Acts 2.13

14.25
Jn 4.19;
Lk 17.16;
Isa 45.14;
Zech 8.23

14.26
1 Cor 12.7-10;
2 Cor 12.19;
Eph 4.12

14.29
1 Cor 12.10

14.32
1 Jn 4.1
14.33
v. 40;
1 Cor 4.17;
11.16
14.34
1 Tim 2.11,
12; 1 Pet 3.1;
Gen 3.16

14.15 Those who pray in public should pray intelligibly, not in a language the people do not understand, i.e., a language foreign to those who listen.
14.26 The Spirit may give believers a hymn, a lesson, a revelation, a tongue, or an interpretation. These are not given for show but for edification. The main principle is that all things must be done for building up the church, requiring (among other things) a sense of proper order (v. 40).
14.34,35 Paul here appears to prohibit women from speaking in church services, although earlier he recognized that women may have the gift of prophecy (11.5). The vexing question remains whether this prohibition is binding at all times and in all places. Churches vary widely on this subject. Some ordain women to the gospel ministry; others do not ordain women but permit them to speak in the worship services; others prohibit them from participating in any official capacity in a worship setting. The Scriptures do not speak explicitly enough to settle the issue for the satisfaction of all.

church.*h* 36 Or did the word of God originate with you? Or are you the only ones it has reached?)

37 Anyone who claims to be a prophet, or to have spiritual powers, must acknowledge that what I am writing to you is a command of the Lord. 38 Anyone who does not recognize this is not to be recognized. 39 So, my friends,*i* be eager to prophesy, and do not forbid speaking in tongues; 40 but all things should be done decently and in order.

VI. *The resurrection (15.1–58)*

A. *The fact of the resurrection*

15 Now I would remind you, brothers and sisters,*j* of the good news*k* that I proclaimed to you, which you in turn received, in which also you stand, 2 through which also you are being saved, if you hold firmly to the message that I proclaimed to you — unless you have come to believe in vain.

3 For I handed on to you as of first importance what I in turn had received: that Christ died for our sins in accordance with the scriptures, 4 and that he was buried, and that he was raised on the third day in accordance with the scriptures, 5 and that he appeared to Cephas, then to the twelve. 6 Then he appeared to more than five hundred brothers and sisters*j* at one time, most of whom are still alive, though some have died.*l* 7 Then he appeared to James, then to all the apostles. 8 Last of all, as to one untimely born, he appeared also to me. 9 For I am the least of the apostles, unfit to be called an apostle, because I persecuted the church of God. 10 But by the grace of God I am what I am, and his grace toward me has not been in vain. On the contrary, I worked harder than any of them — though it was not I, but the grace of God that is with me. 11 Whether then it was I or they, so we proclaim and so you have come to believe.

B. *The necessity of the resurrection*

12 Now if Christ is proclaimed as raised from the dead, how can some of you say there is no resurrection of the dead? 13 If there is no resurrection of the dead, then Christ has not been raised; 14 and if Christ has not been raised, then our proclamation has been in vain and your faith has been in vain. 15 We are even found to be misrepresenting God, because we testified of God that he raised Christ — whom he did not raise if it is true that the dead are not raised. 16 For if the dead are not raised, then Christ has not been raised. 17 If Christ has not been raised, your faith is futile and you are still in your sins. 18 Then those also who have died*l* in Christ have

h Other ancient authorities put verses 34-35 after verse 40   *i* Gk *my brothers*   *j* Gk *brothers*   *k* Or *gospel*   *l* Gk *fallen asleep*

14.37ff The Spirit does not contradict himself by saying one thing to one person and something different to another. If anyone thinks the Spirit has said something different from what the Spirit has told Paul, Paul says that that other person must not be recognized.

15.1ff Paul reiterates the fundamental truths of the Christian faith: Christ died, was buried, and rose again the third day. The theological meaning of this statement is expanded elsewhere in the Pauline writings.

15.4 The resurrection of Jesus from the dead distinguishes the Christian faith from all other religions and cults, for none of them claims that their founder died and rose again in the same body. Buddha, Mohammed, Zoroaster, Confucius, Lao-Tze and the others are dead and gone; only Jesus is said to be alive

forevermore. So crucial is this teaching that Paul argues that if Christ did not rise from the dead, the Christian faith has no foundation on which to rest (vv. 12–19).

15.9 Humility causes Paul to affirm that he is the least of the apostles, certainly the last to be chosen. And he does not feel worthy, for he at one time severely persecuted the church. But in spiritual gifts, service to Christ, and sufferings for the faith, Paul is in no sense inferior to any of the other apostles.

15.12ff Paul's argument for the necessity of believing the bodily resurrection of Jesus Christ is unassailable. If Christ arose, the Christian faith is real; if he didn't, the faith means nothing. A dead Christ results in a dead and useless faith. If the Christian hope does not avail beyond the grave, we have nothing to look forward to, including our salvation.

perished. 19 If for this life only we have hoped in Christ, we are of all people most to be pitied.

C. The assurance of the resurrection

20 But in fact Christ has been raised from the dead, the first fruits of those who have died. *m* 21 For since death came through a human being, the resurrection of the dead has also come through a human being; 22 for as all die in Adam, so all will be made alive in Christ. 23 But each in his own order: Christ the first fruits, then at his coming those who belong to Christ. 24 Then comes the end, *n* when he hands over the kingdom to God the Father, after he has destroyed every ruler and every authority and power. 25 For he must reign until he has put all his enemies under his feet. 26 The last enemy to be destroyed is death. 27 For "God *o* has put all things in subjection under his feet." But when it says, "All things are put in subjection," it is plain that this does not include the one who put all things in subjection under him. 28 When all things are subjected to him, then the Son himself will also be subjected to the one who put all things in subjection under him, so that God may be all in all.

D. The logic of the resurrection

29 Otherwise, what will those people do who receive baptism on behalf of the dead? If the dead are not raised at all, why are people baptized on their behalf?

30 And why are we putting ourselves in danger every hour? 31 I die every day! That is as certain, brothers and sisters, *p* as my boasting of you—a boast that I make in Christ Jesus our Lord. 32 If with merely human hopes I fought with wild animals at Ephesus, what would I have gained by it? If the dead are not raised,

"Let us eat and drink,
    for tomorrow we die."

33 Do not be deceived:

"Bad company ruins good morals."

34 Come to a sober and right mind, and sin no more; for some people have no knowledge of God. I say this to your shame.

E. The nature of the resurrection body

35 But someone will ask, "How are the dead raised? With what kind of body do they come?" 36 Fool! What you sow does not come to life unless it dies. 37 And as for what you sow, you do not sow the body that is to be, but a bare seed, perhaps of wheat or of some other grain. 38 But God gives it a body as he has chosen, and to each kind of seed its own body. 39 Not all flesh is alike, but there is one flesh for human beings, another for animals, another for birds, and another for fish. 40 There are both heavenly bodies and earthly bodies, but the glory of the heavenly is one thing, and that of the earthly is another. 41 There is one glory of the sun,

---

m Gk *fallen asleep*   *n* Or *Then come the rest*   *o* Gk *he*   *p* Gk *brothers*

15.19
2 Tim 3.12

15.20
1 Pet 1.3;
v. 23;
Acts 26.23;
Rev 1.5
15.21
Rom 5.12
15.24
Dan 7.14, 27
15.25
Ps 110.1
15.26
2 Tim 1.10;
Rev 20.14
15.27
Ps 8.6;
Mt 28.18;
Heb 2.8
15.28
Phil 3.21;
1 Cor 3.23

15.30
2 Cor 11.26
15.31
Rom 8.36;
2 Cor 4.10;
11.23
15.32
2 Cor 1.8;
Lk 12.19

15.34
1 Thess 4.5;
1 Cor 6.5

15.35
Rom 9.19;
Ezek 37.3
15.36
Jn 12.24
15.38
Gen 1.11

15.18 *have fallen asleep in Christ* (NRSV footnote). This refers to the physical body, which sleeps in the grave. But the spirits of the saints go to be with the Lord. They exist in a state of bliss (Lk 16.19ff), having joyful fellowship with Christ as they await their resurrection bodies (1 Thess 4.13ff; Rev 20.4–6).

15.22 Because of his sin the first Adam brought death to his descendants. The second man, the last Adam, brings life and immortality by his death for sin and his resurrection to everlasting life. Jesus Christ brought death to death. Because he who did this lives,

we also shall live forever.

15.29 While the meaning of this verse is unclear to us, it must have been quite clear to the Corinthians. Some have used it to support the view that we can undergo water baptism for relatives long since dead and that by vicarious baptism they will obtain the forgiveness of sins and inherit eternal life. This notion supposes that those who are saved in this manner do not exercise personal faith; this contradicts every Scripture that speaks of faith alone as the only way to be justified by God.

and another glory of the moon, and another glory of the stars; indeed, star differs from star in glory.

42 So it is with the resurrection of the dead. What is sown is perishable, what is raised is imperishable. 43 It is sown in dishonor, it is raised in glory. It is sown in weakness, it is raised in power. 44 It is sown a physical body, it is raised a spiritual body. If there is a physical body, there is also a spiritual body. 45 Thus it is written, "The first man, Adam, became a living being"; the last Adam became a life-giving spirit. 46 But it is not the spiritual that is first, but the physical, and then the spiritual. 47 The first man was from the earth, a man of dust; the second man is*q* from heaven. 48 As was the man of dust, so are those who are of the dust; and as is the man of heaven, so are those who are of heaven. 49 Just as we have borne the image of the man of dust, we will*r* also bear the image of the man of heaven.

F. The Christian's confidence

50 What I am saying, brothers and sisters,*s* is this: flesh and blood cannot inherit the kingdom of God, nor does the perishable inherit the imperishable. 51 Listen, I will tell you a mystery! We will not all die,*t* but we will all be changed, 52 in a moment, in the twinkling of an eye, at the last trumpet. For the trumpet will sound, and the dead will be raised imperishable, and we will be changed. 53 For this perishable body must put on imperishability, and this mortal body must put on immortality. 54 When this perishable body puts on imperishability, and this mortal body puts on immortality, then the saying that is written will be fulfilled:
"Death has been swallowed up in victory."
55 "Where, O death, is your victory?
    Where, O death, is your sting?"
56 The sting of death is sin, and the power of sin is the law. 57 But thanks be to God, who gives us the victory through our Lord Jesus Christ.
58 Therefore, my beloved,*u* be steadfast, immovable, always excelling in the work of the Lord, because you know that in the Lord your labor is not in vain.

VII. Personal matters (16.1–24)

A. The contribution for the poor

16 Now concerning the collection for the saints: you should follow the directions I gave to the churches of Galatia. 2 On the first day

q Other ancient authorities add *the Lord*   *r* Other ancient authorities read *let us*   *s* Gk *brothers*   *t* Gk *fall asleep*   *u* Gk *beloved brothers*

15.42 The bodies of all people are mortal. Christ's resurrected body was the same body that lay in the grave, with this exception—it became immortal. Mortality was the consequence of the fall of Adam (cf. Gen 2.16,17; 3.19). Immortality is the gift of God through the death and resurrection of Christ. The new or changed body will be perfect and incorruptible.

15.47 *The first man . . . the second man.* God's covenant between himself and the first Adam was conditioned on Adam's perfect obedience; this was thus a covenant of works (Gen 2.16,17). When Adam sinned he broke the covenant and, as representative and progenitor of the whole human race, plunged the world into sin (Rom 5.12–19). Christ, the last Adam (v. 45), kept God's law perfectly, thus fulfilling the terms of the covenant. By his death he paid the penalty of death for sin and set sinners free from the law of sin and of death (Rom 8.1,2). Even as guilt was imputed to the entire human race by Adam's sin, so

righteousness is imputed to those who believe in Jesus.

15.51ff This passage unfolds a mystery: not all believers will die in the flesh, for some will remain alive until the coming of the Lord Jesus Christ. Christ will catch them up into the clouds, and they will be miraculously changed in their physical being "in the twinkling of an eye" (see 1 Thess 4.13–18).

15.58 Because Jesus arose from the dead, believers must be *steadfast, immovable, always excelling in the work of the Lord.* Because he lives, believers also live — in time and in eternity.

16.2 The principles for giving money to the Lord include (1) giving regularly — *on the first day of every week* (the Lord's Day); (2) participation by all believers — *each of you*; (3) giving proportionately — depending on *whatever extra you earn*; (4) preventive — *so that collections need not be taken when I come* (see also note on Mal 3.8).

of every week, each of you is to put aside and save whatever extra you earn, so that collections need not be taken when I come. 3 And when I arrive, I will send any whom you approve with letters to take your gift to Jerusalem. 4 If it seems advisable that I should go also, they will accompany me.

B. Paul's itinerary

5   I will visit you after passing through Macedonia — for I intend to pass through Macedonia — 6 and perhaps I will stay with you or even spend the winter, so that you may send me on my way, wherever I go. 7 I do not want to see you now just in passing, for I hope to spend some time with you, if the Lord permits. 8 But I will stay in Ephesus until Pentecost, 9 for a wide door for effective work has opened to me, and there are many adversaries.

10   If Timothy comes, see that he has nothing to fear among you, for he is doing the work of the Lord just as I am; 11 therefore let no one despise him. Send him on his way in peace, so that he may come to me; for I am expecting him with the brothers.

12   Now concerning our brother Apollos, I strongly urged him to visit you with the other brothers, but he was not at all willing *v* to come now. He will come when he has the opportunity.

C. Concluding exhortations, greetings, and benediction

13   Keep alert, stand firm in your faith, be courageous, be strong. 14 Let all that you do be done in love.

15   Now, brothers and sisters, *w* you know that members of the household of Stephanas were the first converts in Achaia, and they have devoted themselves to the service of the saints; 16 I urge you to put yourselves at the service of such people, and of everyone who works and toils with them. 17 I rejoice at the coming of Stephanas and Fortunatus and Achaicus, because they have made up for your absence; 18 for they refreshed my spirit as well as yours. So give recognition to such persons.

19   The churches of Asia send greetings. Aquila and Prisca, together with the church in their house, greet you warmly in the Lord. 20 All the brothers and sisters *w* send greetings. Greet one another with a holy kiss.

21   I, Paul, write this greeting with my own hand. 22 Let anyone be accursed who has no love for the Lord. Our Lord, come! *x* 23 The grace of the Lord Jesus be with you. 24 My love be with all of you in Christ Jesus. *y*

v Or it was not at all God's will for him   w Gk brothers   x Gk Marana tha. These Aramaic words can also be read Maran atha, meaning Our Lord has come   y Other ancient authorities add Amen

16.3
2 Cor 8.18, 19

16.5
Acts 19.21
16.6
Acts 15.3
16.7
Acts 18.21

16.10
Acts 16.1; 19.22;
1 Cor 15.58
16.11
1 Tim 4.12;
Acts 15.33
16.12
Acts 18.24;
1 Cor 1.12; 3.5, 6

16.13
Phil 1.27;
2 Thess 2.15;
Eph 6.10
16.14
1 Cor 14.1
16.15
Rom 16.5;
2 Cor 8.4;
Heb 6.10
16.16
Heb 13.1
16.17
2 Cor 7.6, 7;
11.9
16.18
2 Cor 7.13;
Phil 2.29
16.19
Acts 16.6;
Rom 16.5
16.22
Eph 6.24;
Rom 9.3
16.23
Rom 16.20

16.5   Paul expects to leave Asia soon and come to Corinth, where he plans to spend some time. He hopes they will assist him in expediting his future plans by way of encouragement and provision.
16.10   Timothy will come to Corinth before Paul does. He wants the church to receive Timothy well, not despise him, and cooperate with him as he corrects the difficulties in the Corinthian church. He pleads with them to speed Timothy on his way to rejoin the apostle. He especially hopes Timothy will come in peace, i.e., bring the good news that all is well in the church.

16.17   Stephanas and Fortunatus and Achaicus were the three members of a delegation that brought a letter from the Corinthian church (see 7.1) to Paul, who was then in Ephesus. Stephanas had been baptized by Paul; he and his family were the first converts of Achaia (v. 15; 1.16). The family was active in the ministry.
16.22   Let anyone be accursed who has no love for the Lord. Those who do not love the Lord Jesus are doomed; they are under a most weighty and awful curse (Gk. anathema).

INTRODUCTION TO
THE SECOND LETTER OF PAUL TO THE
CORINTHIANS

Authorship, Date, and Background: The letter known to us as 2 Corinthians was written by Paul in A.D. 56. It was probably composed in Macedonia and sent to Corinth. Paul had hoped 1 Corinthians (his second letter to them, see introduction to 1 Corinthians) would correct the problems of the young church. Instead, the situation deteriorated and the apostle was severely alienated from these believers. The pressures were both internal and external. Internally, someone in the congregation led a revolt against the apostle, a revolt which included other church members. Externally, a group of Jewish Christians came from Jerusalem claiming to represent the other apostles. They purported to bring with them information which undercut both the apostolic commission and the authority of Paul with the congregation (11.4,5,12,13,20–23). All of this, plus the fact that 1 Corinthians had not solved the problems, caused Paul to make a hasty journey to Corinth; he was rebuffed and humiliated (2.1; cf. 12.14; 13.1), and the situation worsened. Upon his return he wrote another letter (his third) to Corinth (2.3,4,9; 7.8,12). It was a stern communication delivered by Titus (7.6–8), who was instructed to return with a response as soon as possible. First Paul waited for Titus at Troas. Then he moved on to Macedonia where Titus arrived to tell him that the crisis was over; the Corinthian church had been reconciled to Paul.

Paul now wrote his fourth letter to the Corinthian church, a letter we now call 2 Corinthians. Some scholars have claimed that chs. 10—13 are part of the third or stern letter which was incorporated into the fourth letter. But the manuscript evidence does not warrant this conclusion. In all probability the third letter is no longer in existence.

Characteristics and Content: 2 Corinthians is not a theological treatise *per se*, nor does it have the systematic and ordered appearance characteristic of 1 Corinthians. In this letter, the apostle runs the gamut of human emotions: despair, joy, ecstatic elation, sarcasm, and even angry threats. One sees in it deep currents of a pastor's sense of rejection by his beloved children whom he has brought to Christ, followed by a sense of relief and joy when the crisis is over and the dissidents have been reconciled to him. Even though the letter is after the fact, Paul makes a passionate and detailed response to the attacks leveled against his apostolic commission and authority. Later in the letter, he defends his authority in relation to his person.

Speaking biographically, Paul recounts his own background and with deep emotion rightfully boasts of his sufferings for the sake of Jesus. He glories in the sober reality that he supports himself and does not look to his churches for financial help. He rebukes the false teachers sharply who attacked his personhood and discloses that God, who has given him an exalted state and ministry, has also given him a thorn in the flesh to keep him humble. Why did God allow all of these dreadful circumstances to cloud the life of this servant? In 12.9, Paul answers that God did this in order to make him depend on his grace. Furthermore, in Romans (the next letter Paul wrote), he testifies for the comfort of believers in all ages who are called upon to suffer: "No, in all these things we are more than conquerers through him who loved us" (Rom 8.37).

Outline:

THE SECOND LETTER OF PAUL TO THE

CORINTHIANS

I. Introduction (1.1–11)

A. Greeting

1.1
Col 1.1;
1 Tim 1.1;
1 Cor 1.1

1 Paul, an apostle of Christ Jesus by the will of God, and Timothy our brother,

To the church of God that is in Corinth, including all the saints throughout Achaia:

1.2
Rom 1.7;
1 Cor 1.3;
Gal 1.3

2 Grace to you and peace from God our Father and the Lord Jesus Christ.

B. Thanksgiving

1.3
Eph 1.3;
1 Pet 1.3;
Rom 15.5
1.4
2 Cor 7.6, 7, 13
1.5
2 Cor 4.10;
Col 1.24
1.6
2 Cor 4.15
1.7
Rom 8.17;
2 Tim 2.12
1.8
Acts 19.23;
1 Cor 15.32
1.9
Jer 17.5, 7
1.10
2 Pet 2.9
1.11
Rom 15.30;
Phil 1.19;
2 Cor 4.15

3 Blessed be the God and Father of our Lord Jesus Christ, the Father of mercies and the God of all consolation, 4 who consoles us in all our affliction, so that we may be able to console those who are in any affliction with the consolation with which we ourselves are consoled by God. 5 For just as the sufferings of Christ are abundant for us, so also our consolation is abundant through Christ. 6 If we are being afflicted, it is for your consolation and salvation; if we are being consoled, it is for your consolation, which you experience when you patiently endure the same sufferings that we are also suffering. 7 Our hope for you is unshaken; for we know that as you share in our sufferings, so also you share in our consolation.

8 We do not want you to be unaware, brothers and sisters,*a* of the affliction we experienced in Asia; for we were so utterly, unbearably crushed that we despaired of life itself. 9 Indeed, we felt that we had received the sentence of death so that we would rely not on ourselves but on God who raises the dead. 10 He who rescued us from so deadly a peril will continue to rescue us; on him we have set our hope that he will rescue us again, 11 as you also join in helping us by your prayers, so that many will give thanks on our*b* behalf for the blessing granted us through the prayers of many.

II. The defense of the ministry (1.12–7.16)

A. Paul's change of plans

1.12
2 Cor 2.17;
1 Cor 2.4, 13

12 Indeed, this is our boast, the testimony of our conscience: we have

---

a Gk brothers   *b* Other ancient authorities read *your*

1.2 *the Lord Jesus Christ.* Jesus means "Savior"; Christ means "the anointed one"; Lord means "master." For the believer Jesus is Savior and Lord. Lordship means that Jesus Christ has the undivided possession and control of the Christian who comes under that Lordship. One can be regenerated or born again without being under the Lordship of Christ. Jesus is Lord theologically, but he is not Lord in the Christian's experience until, by an act of will, the believer chooses to come under Christ's Lordship.
1.3 *the Father of our Lord Jesus Christ.* God is the Father of Jesus Christ in his divine nature from all eternity. He is the Father of the human Jesus through the womb of the virgin Mary, who was supernaturally

impregnated by the Holy Spirit (Mt 1.20; Lk 1.30–35).
1.11 Paul thanks the Corinthians for the help they have given him through their prayers. Other believers will also give thanks to God for the effectiveness of the Corinthian prayers. Paul assuredly believes that God answers the petitions of his people.
1.12 This marks the beginning of Paul's defense of himself and of his actions for which he had been maligned by some. The criticisms against the apostle were: (1) he cared little for the church because he did not keep his promises about visiting that church; (2) he was no speaker, no leader, just a person of insignificant appearance who lacked spirituality;

behaved in the world with frankness[c] and godly sincerity, not by earthly wisdom but by the grace of God—and all the more toward you. 13 For we write you nothing other than what you can read and also understand; I hope you will understand until the end— 14 as you have already understood us in part—that on the day of the Lord Jesus we are your boast even as you are our boast.

15 Since I was sure of this, I wanted to come to you first, so that you might have a double favor;[d] 16 I wanted to visit you on my way to Macedonia, and to come back to you from Macedonia and have you send me on to Judea. 17 Was I vacillating when I wanted to do this? Do I make my plans according to ordinary human standards,[e] ready to say "Yes, yes" and "No, no" at the same time? 18 As surely as God is faithful, our word to you has not been "Yes and No." 19 For the Son of God, Jesus Christ, whom we proclaimed among you, Silvanus and Timothy and I, was not "Yes and No"; but in him it is always "Yes." 20 For in him every one of God's promises is a "Yes." For this reason it is through him that we say the "Amen," to the glory of God. 21 But it is God who establishes us with you in Christ and has anointed us, 22 by putting his seal on us and giving us his Spirit in our hearts as a first installment.

B. The reason for the change of plans

23 But I call on God as witness against me: it was to spare you that I did not come again to Corinth. 24 I do not mean to imply that we lord it over your faith; rather, we are workers with you for your joy, because you stand firm in the faith. 2 ¹ So I made up my mind not to make you another painful visit. 2 For if I cause you pain, who is there to make me glad but the one whom I have pained? 3 And I wrote as I did, so that when I came, I might not suffer pain from those who should have made me rejoice; for I am confident about all of you, that my joy would be the joy of all of you. 4 For I wrote you out of much distress and anguish of heart and with many tears, not to cause you pain, but to let you know the abundant love that I have for you.

C. Forgiveness of the penitent offender

5 But if anyone has caused pain, he has caused it not to me, but to some extent—not to exaggerate it—to all of you. 6 This punishment by the majority is enough for such a person; 7 so now instead you should forgive and console him, so that he may not be overwhelmed by excessive sorrow. 8 So I urge you to reaffirm your love for him. 9 I wrote for this reason: to test you and to know whether you are obedient in everything.

c Other ancient authorities read holiness   d Other ancient authorities read pleasure   e Gk according to the flesh

1.14
1 Cor 1.8
1.15
1 Cor 4.19;
Rom 1.11;
15.29
1.16
1 Cor 16.5-7
1.17
2 Cor 10.2, 3
1.18
1 Cor 1.9;
2 Cor 2.17
1.19
Mt 16.16;
1 Thess 1.1;
Heb 13.8
1.20
Rom 15.8, 9;
1 Cor 14.16
1.21
1 Cor 1.8;
1 Jn 2.20, 27
1.22
Eph 1.13
1.23
Gal 1.20;
1 Cor 4.21;
2 Cor 2.3
1.24
1 Pet 5.3;
Rom 11.20;
1 Cor 15.1
2.1
2 Cor 1.23
2.2
2 Cor 7.8
2.3
2 Cor 12.21;
7.16; 8.22
2.4
2 Cor 7.8, 9,
12
2.5
1 Cor 5.1, 2
2.6
1 Cor 5.4, 5
2.7
Gal 6.1;
Eph 4.32
2.9
Phil 2.22;
2 Cor 7.15;
10.6

---

(3) he had a way of insinuating himself into favor with people and was deceitful; (4) he obtained money in underhanded ways because he accepted no monetary support.
1.22 Paul mentions two important truths about the work of the Holy Spirit. He seals every believer, i.e., all believers bear the mark of God upon themselves; he indwells believers so that they have the Spirit in their hearts as a first installment of God's blessings, a pledge that more is to come.
1.23 Paul explains why he did not come to Corinth as he had earlier promised. Thus he answers one of the objections against him (see note on v. 12): he wanted to spare them, for the time was not ripe for his visit.
2.4 Paul affirms his sorrow, joy, sympathy, anguish, and love for the people of the Corinthian church. This answers the charge that he did not care

for the Corinthians (see note on 1.12).
2.5–11 Paul proposes certain principles about dealing with those who need to be disciplined. (1) No church should fail to discipline offending members. (2) Discipline is not a decision to be made by one person but by the whole church. (3) The purpose of discipline is not penal but the restoration of the offender. (4) A repentant brother or sister should in turn be forgiven and treated with affection. (5) Severity and lack of sympathy may drive a sinner to desperation and place that one under the power of Satan.
2.6 Paul is possibly referring here to the incestuous person who had been excommunicated for sin (see 1 Cor 5). The punishment was effective, for the offender had repented. Paul orders the church to restore this person, reverse the excommunication, and forgive the offender. They must renew and confirm their love for him.

10 Anyone whom you forgive, I also forgive. What I have forgiven, if I have forgiven anything, has been for your sake in the presence of Christ. 11 And we do this so that we may not be outwitted by Satan; for we are not ignorant of his designs.

D. Paul's vindication of his ministry

1. A triumphant ministry

12 When I came to Troas to proclaim the good news of Christ, a door was opened for me in the Lord; 13 but my mind could not rest because I did not find my brother Titus there. So I said farewell to them and went on to Macedonia.

14 But thanks be to God, who in Christ always leads us in triumphal procession, and through us spreads in every place the fragrance that comes from knowing him. 15 For we are the aroma of Christ to God among those who are being saved and among those who are perishing; 16 to the one a fragrance from death to death, to the other a fragrance from life to life. Who is sufficient for these things? 17 For we are not peddlers of God's word like so many;*f* but in Christ we speak as persons of sincerity, as persons sent from God and standing in his presence.

2. A commended ministry

3 Are we beginning to commend ourselves again? Surely we do not need, as some do, letters of recommendation to you or from you, do we? 2 You yourselves are our letter, written on our*g* hearts, to be known and read by all; 3 and you show that you are a letter of Christ, prepared by us, written not with ink but with the Spirit of the living God, not on tablets of stone but on tablets of human hearts.

3. A ministry of glory

4 Such is the confidence that we have through Christ toward God. 5 Not that we are competent of ourselves to claim anything as coming from us; our competence is from God, 6 who has made us competent to be ministers of a new covenant, not of letter but of spirit; for the letter kills, but the Spirit gives life.

7 Now if the ministry of death, chiseled in letters on stone tablets,*h* came in glory so that the people of Israel could not gaze at Moses' face because of the glory of his face, a glory now set aside, 8 how much more will the ministry of the Spirit come in glory? 9 For if there was glory in the ministry of condemnation, much more does the ministry of justification abound in glory! 10 Indeed, what once had glory has lost its glory

f Other ancient authorities read *like the others*   *g* Other ancient authorities read *your*   *h* Gk *on stones*

Cross references (left margin):

2.11 — Mt 4.10; Lk 22.31; 2 Cor 4.4; 1 Pet 5.8

2.12 — Acts 16.8; 1 Cor 16.9
2.13 — 2 Cor 7.5, 6; Mk 6.46; Rom 15.26
2.14 — Rom 6.17; Eph 5.2; Phil 4.18; 1 Cor 12.8
2.15 — Eph 5.2; Phil 4.18; 2 Cor 4.3
2.16 — Jn 9.39; 1 Pet 2.7
2.17 — 2 Cor 4.2; 1.12; 12.19
3.1 — 2 Cor 5.12; 12.11; Acts 18.27
3.2 — 1 Cor 9.2
3.3 — Jer 31.33; Ezek 11.19

3.4 — Eph 3.12
3.5 — 2 Cor 2.16; 1 Cor 15.10
3.6 — Heb 8.6, 8; Gal 3.10; Jn 6.63
3.7 — Ex 34.29-35
3.9 — v. 7; Rom 1.17; 3.21

2.12 Starting with this verse Paul engages in a systematic defense of his ministry. He answers the various charges leveled against him by those who were suspicious (see note on 1.12). It does happen that even the best of God's servants are misunderstood and libeled and their motives impugned. God delivers them in the midst of such experiences, though not from them. Paul's prayers provided him with the power to be an overcomer in the midst of trials.
2.14 God always causes us to triumph in Christ. On the surface this may not always appear to be true, espcially when saints are persecuted, imprisoned, and even murdered. But when such people willingly and persistently endure these things, they show their victory in Christ.
3.1,2 *You yourselves are our letter.* Some Jews who opposed Paul had apparently come with letters from Jerusalem recommending themselves to the Corinthians. Paul apologizes for seeming to recommend himself, especially since the Corinthians themselves are his own best letters written on his heart.
3.6 Paul contrasts the old and the new covenants. Important to the new covenant is the Holy Spirit's coming in mighty power. Thus the ministry of people through the preaching of the gospel is accompanied by the ministry of the Spirit who produces spiritual and eternal life as the fruit of preaching.
3.7,8 Moses' face shone with the brightness of the glory of God when he came off the mountain. Yet this was related to law. Now that the Spirit has come, the message of the gospel has a greater and eternally enduring brightness and glory that outshines anything Moses ever experienced.

because of the greater glory; 11for if what was set aside came through glory, much more has the permanent come in glory!

12 Since, then, we have such a hope, we act with great boldness, 13not like Moses, who put a veil over his face to keep the people of Israel from gazing at the end of the glory thatⁱ was being set aside. 14But their minds were hardened. Indeed, to this very day, when they hear the reading of the old covenant, that same veil is still there, since only in Christ is it set aside. 15Indeed, to this very day whenever Moses is read, a veil lies over their minds; 16but when one turns to the Lord, the veil is removed. 17Now the Lord is the Spirit, and where the Spirit of the Lord is, there is freedom. 18And all of us, with unveiled faces, seeing the glory of the Lord as though reflected in a mirror, are being transformed into the same image from one degree of glory to another; for this comes from the Lord, the Spirit.

4. An honest ministry

4 Therefore, since it is by God's mercy that we are engaged in this ministry, we do not lose heart. 2We have renounced the shameful things that one hides; we refuse to practice cunning or to falsify God's word; but by the open statement of the truth we commend ourselves to the conscience of everyone in the sight of God. 3And even if our gospel is veiled, it is veiled to those who are perishing. 4In their case the god of this world has blinded the minds of the unbelievers, to keep them from seeing the light of the gospel of the glory of Christ, who is the image of God. 5For we do not proclaim ourselves; we proclaim Jesus Christ as Lord and ourselves as your slaves for Jesus' sake. 6For it is the God who said, "Let light shine out of darkness," who has shone in our hearts to give the light of the knowledge of the glory of God in the face of Jesus Christ.

5. A tried ministry

7 But we have this treasure in clay jars, so that it may be made clear that this extraordinary power belongs to God and does not come from us. 8We are afflicted in every way, but not crushed; perplexed, but not driven to despair; 9persecuted, but not forsaken; struck down, but not destroyed; 10always carrying in the body the death of Jesus, so that the life of Jesus may also be made visible in our bodies. 11For while we live, we are always being given up to death for Jesus' sake, so that the life of Jesus may be made visible in our mortal flesh. 12So death is at work in us, but life in you.

13 But just as we have the same spirit of faith that is in accordance with scripture — "I believed, and so I spoke" — we also believe, and so we speak, 14because we know that the one who raised the Lord Jesus will raise us also with Jesus, and will bring us with you into his presence.

ⁱ Gk of what

3.12
2 Cor 7.4;
Eph 6.19
3.13
v. 7;
Ex 34.33
3.14
Rom 11.7;
Acts 13.15;
v. 6
3.16
Rom 11.23
3.17
1 Cor 15.45;
Isa 61.1, 2;
Jn 8.32
3.18
1 Cor 13.12;
2 Cor 4.4, 6;
Rom 8.29

4.1
2 Cor 3.6;
1 Cor 7.25
4.2
2 Cor 2.17
4.3
2 Cor 2.12;
3.14;
1 Cor 1.18
4.4
Jn 12.31;
Col 1.15;
Jn 1.18
4.5
1 Cor 1.13,
23; 9.19
4.6
Gen 1.3;
2 Pet 1.19

4.7
2 Cor 5.1;
1 Cor 2.5
4.8
2 Cor 7.5;
6.12
4.9
Jn 15.20;
Heb 13.5;
Ps 37.24
4.10
Gal 6.17;
Rom 8.17
4.11
Rom 8.36
4.12
2 Cor 13.9
4.13
Ps 116.10
4.14
1 Thess 4.14

3.16,17 A veil covered Moses' face and continues to cover the words of Moses, i.e., O.T. law; but it is removed in Jesus Christ. Having Christ produces liberty; bondage to the law and the absolute necessity of obedience to it are gone. The believer enters into a glorious freedom.
4.2 Ministers of the gospel are all too often criticized as crafty adulterers of the word of God. Paul defends himself and his colleagues by asserting that they performed God's work by good means suitable to a good end. The use of bad means for good ends is everywhere forbidden in the Scriptures.
4.6 Wherever God and his word are not, there is darkness. But God is overcoming the darkness in the souls of people by bringing them the light of the knowledge of the glory of God in the face of Jesus Christ. Thus

the church is to take Jesus, the light of the world, to the ends of the earth that sinners may not sit in darkness forever.
4.7 Ministers are weak, but their God is strong. The divine strength is demonstrated more through human weakness, so that the weaker the human vessel the stronger the power of God appears (cf. 12.7–10).
4.10 Paul's sufferings constituted a continual process of death. They were gradually killing him and one day would kill him. He had the consolation and joy of knowing that he was sharing an experience with Jesus Christ, who had been subjected to a gradual dying until at last he went to the cross of Calvary.
4.13 His faith kept Paul from fainting. He quotes David (Ps 116.10), from whose words he gained strength and whose example he wished to imitate.

15 Yes, everything is for your sake, so that grace, as it extends to more and more people, may increase thanksgiving, to the glory of God.
16 So we do not lose heart. Even though our outer nature is wasting away, our inner nature is being renewed day by day. 17 For this slight momentary affliction is preparing us for an eternal weight of glory beyond all measure, 18 because we look not at what can be seen but at what cannot be seen; for what can be seen is temporary, but what cannot be seen is eternal.

6. *A courageous ministry*

5 For we know that if the earthly tent we live in is destroyed, we have a building from God, a house not made with hands, eternal in the heavens. 2 For in this tent we groan, longing to be clothed with our heavenly dwelling— 3 if indeed, when we have taken it off[j] we will not be found naked. 4 For while we are still in this tent, we groan under our burden, because we wish not to be unclothed but to be further clothed, so that what is mortal may be swallowed up by life. 5 He who has prepared us for this very thing is God, who has given us the Spirit as a guarantee.
6 So we are always confident; even though we know that while we are at home in the body we are away from the Lord— 7 for we walk by faith, not by sight. 8 Yes, we do have confidence, and we would rather be away from the body and at home with the Lord. 9 So whether we are at home or away, we make it our aim to please him. 10 For all of us must appear before the judgment seat of Christ, so that each may receive recompense for what has been done in the body, whether good or evil.

7. *A dedicated and reconciling ministry*

11 Therefore, knowing the fear of the Lord, we try to persuade others; but we ourselves are well known to God, and I hope that we are also well known to your consciences. 12 We are not commending ourselves to you again, but giving you an opportunity to boast about us, so that you may be able to answer those who boast in outward appearance and not in the heart. 13 For if we are beside ourselves, it is for God; if we are in our right mind, it is for you. 14 For the love of Christ urges us on, because we are convinced that one has died for all; therefore all have died. 15 And

j Other ancient authorities read put it on

Cross references

4.16
Rom 7.22;
Col 3.10
4.17
Rom 8.18;
1 Pet 1.6
4.18
Rom 8.24;
Heb 11.1

5.1
2 Pet 1.13, 14
5.2
Rom 8.23;
v. 4
5.4
1 Cor 15.53,
54
5.5
Rom 8.23;
2 Cor 1.22
5.6
Heb 11.13,
14
5.7
1 Cor 13.12
5.8
Phil 1.23
5.10
Rom 14.10;
Eph 6.8

5.11
Heb 10.31;
Jude 23;
2 Cor 4.2
5.12
2 Cor 3.1;
1.14
5.13
2 Cor 11.1,
16, 17
5.14
Acts 18.5;
Rom 5.15;
Gal 2.20
5.15
Rom 14.7-9

4.17,18 Faith looks at life from the long view, not the short one of the present situation. Since afflictions are temporary and limited, wise Christians look at things unseen, which are eternal. They know that what lies before them is infinitely greater than anything they dreamed of. In light of this, whatever they suffer here and now means nothing.
5.1ff Paul refers to the body as a tent. At death the spirit is separated from this tent and awaits a heavenly body prepared by God for all of his people. Paul is anxious to inherit that new body so as to escape the bodiless state when he dies, confident of the Christian hope that mortality will eventually be swallowed up and endless life in the new body come.
5.7 *for we walk by faith.* Faith is for this world, sight for the world to come. It is our Christian duty to walk by faith until we come to live by sight in eternity. The walk by faith provides confidence for every day (v. 8).
5.10 *the judgment seat of Christ.* Many Christians distinguish this judgment of Christ from the great white throne judgment (Rev 20.11ff). To them, the former is a judgment before which all believers stand and at which their works will be judged, while the latter is a judgment at which only unbelievers will

appear before being consigned forever to the lake of fire. The believer's judgment occurs at the coming of the Lord (see also 1 Cor 4.5; 2 Tim 4.8; Rev 22.12). At this time (1) all believers must appear before the judgment seat (v. 10; Rom 14.10); (2) all will give account of themselves (Rom 14.12); (3) the good deeds and the bad ones will be reviewed (v. 10); (4) rewards will be determined according to our deeds (Rev 22.12); (5) some will receive no reward but will be saved "only as through fire" (1 Cor 3.12–15).
5.11 The apostle continues his defense against evil attacks. Some thought he was not what he claimed to be (see note on 1.12). Here he says that his basis for ministry is the terror of facing God in the judgment. God knows what lies inside him and he does not fear standing before God. He hopes that what God knows about him the Corinthians will also know to be true of him.
5.14 *the love of Christ urges us on.* Paul is not saying that it is *his* love toward Christ that directs him, although that is quite true; rather, it is Christ's love toward him and his fellow-workers. This love, which motivated Christ to die on the cross, is the love that motivates them to preach the good news and causes them to endure all things.

he died for all, so that those who live might live no longer for themselves, but for him who died and was raised for them.

16 From now on, therefore, we regard no one from a human point of view;[k] even though we once knew Christ from a human point of view,[k] we know him no longer in that way. 17 So if anyone is in Christ, there is a new creation: everything old has passed away; see, everything has become new! 18 All this is from God, who reconciled us to himself through Christ, and has given us the ministry of reconciliation; 19 that is, in Christ God was reconciling the world to himself,[l] not counting their trespasses against them, and entrusting the message of reconciliation to us. 20 So we are ambassadors for Christ, since God is making his appeal through us; we entreat you on behalf of Christ, be reconciled to God. 21 For our sake he made him to be sin who knew no sin, so that in him we might become the righteousness of God.

6 As we work together with him,[m] we urge you also not to accept the grace of God in vain. 2 For he says,
"At an acceptable time I have listened to you,
and on a day of salvation I have helped you."
See, now is the acceptable time; see, now is the day of salvation! 3 We are putting no obstacle in anyone's way, so that no fault may be found with our ministry, 4 but as servants of God we have commended ourselves in every way: through great endurance, in afflictions, hardships, calamities, 5 beatings, imprisonments, riots, labors, sleepless nights, hunger; 6 by purity, knowledge, patience, kindness, holiness of spirit, genuine love, 7 truthful speech, and the power of God; with the weapons of righteousness for the right hand and for the left; 8 in honor and dishonor, in ill repute and good repute. We are treated as impostors, and yet are true; 9 as unknown, and yet are well known; as dying, and see—we are alive; as punished, and yet not killed; 10 as sorrowful, yet always rejoicing; as poor, yet making many rich; as having nothing, and yet possessing everything.

8. An exhorting ministry

a. A call for sympathy

11 We have spoken frankly to you Corinthians; our heart is wide open to you. 12 There is no restriction in our affections, but only in yours. 13 In return—I speak as to children—open wide your hearts also.

b. A command to separation

14 Do not be mismatched with unbelievers. For what partnership is there between righteousness and lawlessness? Or what fellowship is there between light and darkness? 15 What agreement does Christ have with

k Gk according to the flesh   l Or God was in Christ reconciling the world to himself   m Gk As we work together

5.16
2 Cor 11.18;
Phil 3.4;
Jn 8.15
5.17
Rom 16.7;
Gal 5.6;
Rev 21.4, 5
5.18
Col 1.20;
Rom 5.10
5.20
2 Cor 3.6;
Eph 6.20;
2 Cor 6.1
5.21
1 Pet 2.22;
1 Jn 3.5;
Gal 3.13
6.1
1 Cor 3.9;
2 Cor 5.20;
Heb 12.15
6.2
Isa 49.8
6.3
Rom 14.13;
1 Cor 9.12;
10.32

6.5
2 Cor 11.23

6.7
2 Cor 4.2;
10.4;
Eph 6.11, 13
6.9
Rom 8.36;
2 Cor 1.8-10;
4.10, 11
6.10
Rom 8.32;
1 Cor 3.21

6.11
Ezek 33.22;
2 Cor 7.3;
Isa 60.5
6.13
1 Cor 4.14

6.14
Deut 7.2, 3;
1 Cor 5.9, 10;
Eph 5.7, 11;
1 Jn 1.6

5.17 For believers, the *new creation* means they have become "brand new persons" in Jesus Christ by regeneration or the new birth (Eph 2.10); for the universe, the *new creation* means a new heaven and a new earth (Isa 65.17; Rom 8.20,21; 2 Pet 3.13).
5.18 *reconciled us to himself.* Reconciliation occurred through the death of God's Son (Rom 5.10; Col 1.22), i.e., through his blood on the cross (Col 1.20; Eph 2.16). Paul uses reconciliation and justification as synonymous (see also Rom 5). Reconciliation is the work of God, not humans; we secure it by faith, which grants us peace with God and immediate access to him (Eph 2.16–18).
6.1,2 God initiates grace and works to make grace effective. Paul and all Christian workers cooperate with God by proclaiming what he has done and by entreating sinners not to accept God's grace in vain.

Isaiah (Isa 49.8, quoted here) had said that in due time God would hear the cry of those who called on him for help and would deliver them. That time has now come in the gospel age through the ministry of Paul and other evangelists.

6.7 "Weapons of righteousness" consist of an offensive weapon, the sword (carried in the right hand), and a defensive weapon, a shield (carried in the left hand); see Eph 6.11,13–17.

6.8 *as imposters,* i.e., some had said that Paul and his company were imposters. In vv. 9,10 Paul cites his experiences and characteristics and those of his associates in order to refute this charge.

6.11ff Paul has been candid and open with the Corinthians, expressing deep affection for them. He begs them to love him in return (cf. 7.2).

Beliar? Or what does a believer share with an unbeliever? 16 What agreement has the temple of God with idols? For we[n] are the temple of the living God; as God said,
"I will live in them and walk among them,
    and I will be their God,
    and they shall be my people.

17 Therefore come out from them,
    and be separate from them, says the Lord,
and touch nothing unclean;
    then I will welcome you,

18 and I will be your father,
    and you shall be my sons and daughters,
    says the Lord Almighty."

7 Since we have these promises, beloved, let us cleanse ourselves from every defilement of body and of spirit, making holiness perfect in the fear of God.

c. A plea for fellowship

2 Make room in your hearts[o] for us; we have wronged no one, we have corrupted no one, we have taken advantage of no one. 3 I do not say this to condemn you, for I said before that you are in our hearts, to die together and to live together. 4 I often boast about you; I have great pride in you; I am filled with consolation; I am overjoyed in all our affliction.

d. The joy of good news

5 For even when we came into Macedonia, our bodies had no rest, but we were afflicted in every way — disputes without and fears within. 6 But God, who consoles the downcast, consoled us by the arrival of Titus, 7 and not only by his coming, but also by the consolation with which he was consoled about you, as he told us of your longing, your mourning, your zeal for me, so that I rejoiced still more. 8 For even if I made you sorry with my letter, I do not regret it (though I did regret it, for I see that I grieved you with that letter, though only briefly). 9 Now I rejoice, not because you were grieved, but because your grief led to repentance; for you felt a godly grief, so that you were not harmed in any way by us. 10 For

godly grief produces a repentance that leads to salvation and brings no regret, but worldly grief produces death. 11 For see what earnestness this

godly grief has produced in you, what eagerness to clear yourselves, what indignation, what alarm, what longing, what zeal, what punishment! At every point you have proved yourselves guiltless in the matter. 12 So

although I wrote to you, it was not on account of the one who did the wrong, nor on account of the one who was wronged, but in order that your

---

[n] Other ancient authorities read you [o] Gk lacks in your hearts

---

6.17 God commands his people to be separated from unbelievers and from the world. Like Christ, we are in the world but not of the world (cf. Jn 17.11–16). Christians must shun any compromising relationships with nonbelievers. We are not to marry unbelievers, nor choose them for intimate companions, nor have cordial fellowship with them. But separation is not only *from* something; believers must be separated *to* God. They must hold fast to what is good and flee from what is evil (cf. Rom 12.9).
7.1 This verse is the proper ending for 6.14–18. In the light of the promises stated, believers need to be cleansed from their sins by sorrow, confession, and restitution. They must make holiness the one great desire of their hearts and press on toward the goal of being like Jesus Christ.
7.2ff Paul stresses his confidence in the Corinthians, that they will continue to accept him as their

leader and not follow the imposters who have been undermining his position.
7.8 Paul refers to a stern letter he had written to the church at Corinth (see also v. 12). Many believe that this letter has been lost, though some hold that chs. 10–13 constitute this letter. In any case, Paul did not hesitate to take corrective action on behalf of the church whenever it was necessary.
7.12ff The earlier letter of Paul was written with the good intention of helping the church, even though he may have appeared to be severe. His concern went far beyond the guilty believer to the church itself. The church must not allow the crime to go unnoticed or the scandal unheeded. Any church that refuses to exercise discipline by reproof and admonition will itself suffer serious loss, and its spiritual state will worsen.

zeal for us might be made known to you before God. 13 In this we find comfort.

In addition to our own consolation, we rejoiced still more at the joy of Titus, because his mind has been set at rest by all of you. 14 For if I have been somewhat boastful about you to him, I was not disgraced; but just as everything we said to you was true, so our boasting to Titus has proved true as well. 15 And his heart goes out all the more to you, as he remembers the obedience of all of you, and how you welcomed him with fear and trembling. 16 I rejoice, because I have complete confidence in you.

III. The collection for the saints (8.1–9.15)

A. The Macedonian example

8 We want you to know, brothers and sisters,p about the grace of God that has been granted to the churches of Macedonia; 2 for during a severe ordeal of affliction, their abundant joy and their extreme poverty have overflowed in a wealth of generosity on their part. 3 For, as I can testify, they voluntarily gave according to their means, and even beyond their means, 4 begging us earnestly for the privilegeq of sharing in this ministry to the saints — 5 and this, not merely as we expected; they gave themselves first to the Lord, and, by the will of God, to us, 6 so that we might urge Titus that, as he had already made a beginning, so he should also complete this generous undertakingr among you. 7 Now as you excel in everything — in faith, in speech, in knowledge, in utmost eagerness, and in our love for yous — so we want you to excel also in this generous undertaking.r

B. The example of Jesus

8 I do not say this as a command, but I am testing the genuineness of your love against the earnestness of others. 9 For you know the generous actt of our Lord Jesus Christ, that though he was rich, yet for your sakes he became poor, so that by his poverty you might become rich. 10 And in this matter I am giving my advice: it is appropriate for you who began last year not only to do something but even to desire to do something — 11 now finish doing it, so that your eagerness may be matched by completing it according to your means. 12 For if the eagerness is there, the gift is acceptable according to what one has — not according to what one does not have. 13 I do not mean that there should be relief for others and pressure on you, but it is a question of a fair balance between 14 your present abundance and their need, so that their abundance may be for your need, in order that there may be a fair balance. 15 As it is written,

"The one who had much did not have too much,
    and the one who had little did not have too little."

p Gk brothers   q Gk grace   r Gk this grace   s Other ancient authorities read your love for us   t Gk the grace

7.13	v. 6; 1 Cor 16.18
7.14	vv. 4, 6
7.15	2 Cor 2.9; Phil 2.12
7.16	2 Thess 3.4
8.1	Acts 16.9
8.2	2 Cor 9.11
8.3	1 Cor 16.2
8.4	Acts 24.17; Rom 15.25, 26, 31; 2 Cor 9.1
8.6	v. 17; 2 Cor 12.18; vv. 16, 23, 10
8.7	2 Cor 9.8; 1 Cor 1.5; 12.13
8.8	1 Cor 7.6
8.9	2 Cor 13.14; Phil 2.6, 7
8.10	1 Cor 7.25; 2 Cor 9.2; 1 Cor 16.2, 3
8.11	2 Cor 9.2
8.12	Mk 12.43, 44; Lk 21.3
8.14	2 Cor 9.12
8.15	Ex 16.18

8.1 This section of Paul's letter (8.1 — 9.15) refers to the generous Macedonian offering taken for the relief of Christians in Jerusalem, which Paul used to motivate the Christians in Corinth to give liberally. Salvation should touch both our pocketbooks and our souls. Paul's care in the way the money was to be carried indicates his fiscal integrity. The gift itself was designed to express the unity of the faith between Jews and Gentiles (Rom 15.25–27).
8.5 they gave themselves first to the Lord. Believers ought to give themselves wholeheartedly to the Lord, though not all do so. Such giving includes all we have, for God to use as he chooses. But in doing so, we only give back to God what belongs to him in the first

place.
8.9 In urging the Corinthians to help the poor saints, Paul uses Christ as an illustration. Jesus became poor in two ways. First, he gave up his glory with the Father in heaven to become a human being. Second, he was literally poor in the things of this world. He was born into a poor family, lived a poor life, died in poverty, and was buried in a borrowed grave. Yet all this demeaning of himself has worked to our advantage, for through his poverty we have acquired great riches — both the riches of a new relationship to God and the riches of heaven as joint heirs with Jesus Christ (Rom 8.15–17).

C. *The coming of Titus and the messengers*

16 But thanks be to God who put in the heart of Titus the same eagerness for you that I myself have. [17] For he not only accepted our appeal, but since he is more eager than ever, he is going to you of his own accord. [18] With him we are sending the brother who is famous among all the churches for his proclaiming the good news;[u] [19] and not only that, but he has also been appointed by the churches to travel with us while we are administering this generous undertaking[v] for the glory of the Lord himself[w] and to show our goodwill. [20] We intend that no one should blame us about this generous gift that we are administering, [21] for we intend to do what is right not only in the Lord's sight but also in the sight of others. [22] And with them we are sending our brother whom we have often tested and found eager in many matters, but who is now more eager than ever because of his great confidence in you. [23] As for Titus, he is my partner and co-worker in your service; as for our brothers, they are messengers[x] of the churches, the glory of Christ. [24] Therefore openly before the churches, show them the proof of your love and of our reason for boasting about you.

D. *Appeal to their generosity*

9 Now it is not necessary for me to write you about the ministry to the saints, [2] for I know your eagerness, which is the subject of my boasting about you to the people of Macedonia, saying that Achaia has been ready since last year; and your zeal has stirred up most of them. [3] But I am sending the brothers in order that our boasting about you may not prove to have been empty in this case, so that you may be ready, as I said you would be; [4] otherwise, if some Macedonians come with me and find that you are not ready, we would be humiliated — to say nothing of you — in this undertaking.[y] [5] So I thought it necessary to urge the brothers to go on ahead to you, and arrange in advance for this bountiful gift that you have promised, so that it may be ready as a voluntary gift and not as an extortion.

E. *God's reward of the liberal giver*

6 The point is this: the one who sows sparingly will also reap sparingly, and the one who sows bountifully will also reap bountifully. [7] Each of you must give as you have made up your mind, not reluctantly or under compulsion, for God loves a cheerful giver. [8] And God is able to provide you with every blessing in abundance, so that by always having enough

u Or *the gospel*   *v* Gk *this grace*   *w* Other ancient authorities lack *himself*   *x* Gk *apostles*   *y* Other ancient authorities add *of boasting*

Cross-references (margin)

8.17
v. 6
8.18
2 Cor 12.18
8.19
1 Cor 16.3, 4;
vv. 4, 6, 11
8.21
Rom 12.17;
14.18
8.23
Phil 2.25
8.24
2 Cor 7.14;
9.2
9.1
2 Cor 8.4
9.2
2 Cor 7.4;
Rom 15.26;
Acts 18.12;
2 Cor 8.10
9.3
1 Cor 16.2
9.4
Rom 15.26
9.5
Gen 33.11;
1 Sam 25.27;
Phil 4.17;
2 Cor 12.17,
18
9.6
Gal 6.7, 9
9.7
Deut 15.7,
10;
Ex 25.2;
Rom 12.8;
2 Cor 8.12
9.8
Eph 3.20;
Phil 4.19

8.18 Who the brother referred to here is, we do not know, although some have suggested it was Luke. Apparently this individual was well known and a splendid evangelist. The rolls of heaven are filled with unnamed warriors of the cross whose names have been lost but who are known of God.

8.23 Paul began his letter by identifying Timothy with himself. Now he makes reference to faithful Titus, who is leading a party to accept the Corinthian offering for the poor saints in Jerusalem. Paul deliberately chooses Titus and others (probably Luke and Apollos) because they have an unblemished reputation. No one can thereby accuse him of personal interest or the desire for personal gain in this effort. He wants to avoid all appearance of evil because of certain charges levelled against him (see note on 1.12).

9.1ff Paul tells the Corinthians that he has boasted of their liberal giving to others. He urges them to justify his confidence in them so that he and his co-workers will not be humiliated by any failure on the part of the Corinthians to match the expectation created by his words.

9.5ff Sometimes the Spirit gives individuals and churches the special gift of giving (cf. Rom 12.8). These principles of giving are outlined here: (1) giving should be bountiful; (2) giving should be deliberate, i.e., by thought and design; (3) giving should be done cheerfully, not under compulsion.

9.6 The more seed farmers plant in their fields, the more crops they will reap at harvest time. Paul applies this obvious principle to the spiritual realm of giving; giving should be liberal. God promises that those who share liberally of their means will also reap a generous harvest in the divine kingdom when the accounts are balanced and the rewards are handed out.

of everything, you may share abundantly in every good work. ⁹As it is written,

"He scatters abroad, he gives to the poor;
    his righteousness*z* endures forever."

¹⁰He who supplies seed to the sower and bread for food will supply and multiply your seed for sowing and increase the harvest of your righteousness.*z* ¹¹You will be enriched in every way for your great generosity, which will produce thanksgiving to God through us; ¹²for the rendering of this ministry not only supplies the needs of the saints but also overflows with many thanksgivings to God. ¹³Through the testing of this ministry you glorify God by your obedience to the confession of the gospel of Christ and by the generosity of your sharing with them and with all others, ¹⁴while they long for you and pray for you because of the surpassing grace of God that he has given you. ¹⁵Thanks be to God for his indescribable gift!

IV. *Paul's personal defense and appeal (10.1–13.10)*

A. *Paul replies to the charge of weakness and cowardice*

10 I myself, Paul, appeal to you by the meekness and gentleness of Christ—I who am humble when face to face with you, but bold toward you when I am away!— ²I ask that when I am present I need not show boldness by daring to oppose those who think we are acting according to human standards.*a* ³Indeed, we live as human beings,*b* but we do not wage war according to human standards;*a* ⁴for the weapons of our warfare are not merely human,*c* but they have divine power to destroy strongholds. We destroy arguments ⁵and every proud obstacle raised up against the knowledge of God, and we take every thought captive to obey Christ. ⁶We are ready to punish every disobedience when your obedience is complete.

7 Look at what is before your eyes. If you are confident that you belong to Christ, remind yourself of this, that just as you belong to Christ, so also do we. ⁸Now, even if I boast a little too much of our authority, which the Lord gave for building you up and not for tearing you down, I will not be ashamed of it. ⁹I do not want to seem as though I am trying to frighten you with my letters. ¹⁰For they say, "His letters are weighty and strong, but his bodily presence is weak, and his speech contemptible." ¹¹Let such people understand that what we say by letter when absent, we will also do when present.

B. *Paul stays within the limits of God's appointments*

12 We do not dare to classify or compare ourselves with some of those who commend themselves. But when they measure themselves by one

9.9
Ps 112.9

9.10
Isa 55.10;
Hos 10.12
9.11
1 Cor 1.5, 11
9.12
2 Cor 8.14
9.13
2 Cor 8.4;
Rom 15.31;
Mt 9.8;
2 Cor 2.12
9.15
2 Cor 2.14;
Rom 5.15, 16

10.1
Gal 5.2;
Rom 12.1
10.2
1 Cor 4.21;
2 Cor 13.2,
10
10.3
v. 2
10.4
1 Tim 1.18;
2 Tim 2.3;
Acts 7.22;
1 Cor 2.5;
Jer 1.10
10.5
1 Cor 1.19;
Isa 2.11, 12;
2 Cor 9.13
10.6
2 Cor 2.9
10.7
Jn 7.24;
1 Cor 1.12;
14.37
10.8
2 Cor 7.4;
13.10
10.10
1 Cor 2.3;
Gal 4.13, 14;
1 Cor 1.17

10.12
2 Cor 3.1;
5.12

---

z Or *benevolence*   *a* Gk *according to the flesh*   *b* Gk *in the flesh*   *c* Gk *fleshly*

9.10 God graciously gives us so much; therefore, we can give to others. Givers are never losers, for God promises to enrich them in everything.
9.15 *his indescribable gift.* Some interpreters understand this as the gift of grace given to the Corinthians, making them able and willing to help the poor saints. A better understanding is to see this as a reference to Jesus Christ as God's gift, a gift so great that it defies anyone's ability to express it with words.
10.1,2 Previously Paul used "we" in this letter. Now he turns to the more personal word "I." He is speaking for himself about some of the personal problems he has had with the Corinthians. Because he wishes to avoid severity, he asks them not to give him any occasion that will require it.
10.4 The doctrines of the gospel and the discipline

of the church are the weapons of our warfare. Because they come from God, outward force must never be used. Believers can depend on the power of truth, the humility of wisdom, and the persuasive power of the Holy Spirit to do the work.
10.7ff Paul now reasons with the Corinthians against those who have despised him, maligned him, and judged him. He begs them not to judge the gift by the package in which it is wrapped. Some people may be learned who have not learned Christ and may appear virtuous when they have no virtue in their hearts. Paul resumes using "we," including his co-workers with him. Paul's opponents should remember that he and his workers are equally ministers of Christ, just as they claim to be.

10.13
v. 15
10.14
2 Cor 2.12
10.15
Rom 15.20;
2 Thess 1.3
10.17
Jer 9.24;
1 Cor 1.31
10.18
Rom 2.29;
1 Cor 4.5
11.1
vv. 16, 17,
21;
2 Cor 5.13
11.2
Hos 2.19;
Eph 5.26, 27;
2 Cor 4.14
11.3
Gen 3.4;
Jn 8.44
11.4
1 Cor 3.11;
Rom 8.15;
Gal 1.6-8
11.5
2 Cor 12.11;
Gal 2.6
11.6
1 Cor 1.17;
Eph 3.4;
2 Cor 4.2
11.7
2 Cor 12.13;
1 Cor 9.18
11.8
Phil 4.15, 18
11.9
2 Cor 12.13,
14
11.10
Rom 9.1;
1 Cor 9.15;
Acts 18.12
11.11
2 Cor 12.15
11.12
1 Cor 9.12
11.13
Gal 1.7;
2 Pet 2.1;
Phil 3.2
11.15
Phil 3.19

another, and compare themselves with one another, they do not show good sense. 13 We, however, will not boast beyond limits, but will keep within the field that God has assigned to us, to reach out even as far as you. 14 For we were not overstepping our limits when we reached you; we were the first to come all the way to you with the good news*d* of Christ. 15 We do not boast beyond limits, that is, in the labors of others; but our hope is that, as your faith increases, our sphere of action among you may be greatly enlarged, 16 so that we may proclaim the good news*d* in lands beyond you, without boasting of work already done in someone else's sphere of action. 17 "Let the one who boasts, boast in the Lord." 18 For it is not those who commend themselves that are approved, but those whom the Lord commends.

C. Paul's fear of false teachers

11 I wish you would bear with me in a little foolishness. Do bear with me! 2 I feel a divine jealousy for you, for I promised you in marriage to one husband, to present you as a chaste virgin to Christ. 3 But I am afraid that as the serpent deceived Eve by its cunning, your thoughts will be led astray from a sincere and pure*e* devotion to Christ. 4 For if someone comes and proclaims another Jesus than the one we proclaimed, or if you receive a different spirit from the one you received, or a different gospel from the one you accepted, you submit to it readily enough. 5 I think that I am not in the least inferior to these super-apostles. 6 I may be untrained in speech, but not in knowledge; certainly in every way and in all things we have made this evident to you.

D. Paul's self-support

7 Did I commit a sin by humbling myself so that you might be exalted, because I proclaimed God's good news*f* to you free of charge? 8 I robbed other churches by accepting support from them in order to serve you. 9 And when I was with you and was in need, I did not burden anyone, for my needs were supplied by the friends*g* who came from Macedonia. So I refrained and will continue to refrain from burdening you in any way. 10 As the truth of Christ is in me, this boast of mine will not be silenced in the regions of Achaia. 11 And why? Because I do not love you? God knows I do!

12 And what I do I will also continue to do, in order to deny an opportunity to those who want an opportunity to be recognized as our equals in what they boast about. 13 For such boasters are false apostles, deceitful workers, disguising themselves as apostles of Christ. 14 And no wonder! Even Satan disguises himself as an angel of light. 15 So it is not

---

d Or *the gospel*   *e* Other ancient authorities lack *and pure*   *f* Gk *the gospel of God*   *g* Gk *brothers*

10.17,18 Quoting from Jer 9.24, Paul instructs ministers to be careful to give God all the glory for their work and success, for in and of themselves they are nothing. Those who commend themselves are not thereby commended; the only commendation that counts is what comes from God.

11.1ff Paul now becomes bold in his statements because he fears that the loyalty of his beloved Corinthians may be corrupted. He is jealous for their sake and does not want them to be wooed away, like Eve, from their devotion to Christ and become unfaithful or adulterous. He apologizes for the forceful language he is about to use, but feels forced to do so by his opponents. His jealousy is a godly jealousy.

11.7 The Corinthians could never say Paul preached to them for the money they gave him. He was self-supporting, and any funds from others were supplied "by the friends who came from Macedonia." Though

a Christian worker deserves to be paid (cf. 1 Cor 9.4–12; 1 Tim 5.17,18), Paul himself never asked the Corinthians for money to support him.

11.12 Paul gives the real reason why he refused financial help from the Corinthians: those who opposed him wanted money; indeed, they demanded it. He says, in effect, "Let them do as I do—preach for nothing." His enemies, who were claiming equality with him, could not match him in this.

11.13 The N.T. age saw counterfeit apostles who gave the impression of being true servants of Jesus Christ. They were as industrious and generous in promoting error as the apostles were in preaching truth. They sought as much to undermine the faith as true believers sought to establish it. What was true then is equally true today and will always be until the end of the age (cf. Mk 13.5,6,21–23).

strange if his ministers also disguise themselves as ministers of righteousness. Their end will match their deeds.

E. Paul's rightful boasting

1. The necessity for it

16 I repeat, let no one think that I am a fool; but if you do, then accept me as a fool, so that I too may boast a little. 17 What I am saying in regard to this boastful confidence, I am saying not with the Lord's authority, but as a fool; 18 since many boast according to human standards,*h* I will also boast. 19 For you gladly put up with fools, being wise yourselves! 20 For you put up with it when someone makes slaves of you, or preys upon you, or takes advantage of you, or puts on airs, or gives you a slap in the face. 21 To my shame, I must say, we were too weak for that!

2. The grounds for it

But whatever anyone dares to boast of — I am speaking as a fool — I also dare to boast of that. 22 Are they Hebrews? So am I. Are they Israelites? So am I. Are they descendants of Abraham? So am I. 23 Are they ministers of Christ? I am talking like a madman — I am a better one: with far greater labors, far more imprisonments, with countless floggings, and often near death. 24 Five times I have received from the Jews the forty lashes minus one. 25 Three times I was beaten with rods. Once I received a stoning. Three times I was shipwrecked; for a night and a day I was adrift at sea; 26 on frequent journeys, in danger from rivers, danger from bandits, danger from my own people, danger from Gentiles, danger in the city, danger in the wilderness, danger at sea, danger from false brothers and sisters;*i* 27 in toil and hardship, through many a sleepless night, hungry and thirsty, often without food, cold and naked. 28 And, besides other things, I am under daily pressure because of my anxiety for all the churches. 29 Who is weak, and I am not weak? Who is made to stumble, and I am not indignant?

30 If I must boast, I will boast of the things that show my weakness. 31 The God and Father of the Lord Jesus (blessed be he forever!) knows that I do not lie. 32 In Damascus, the governor*j* under King Aretas guarded the city of Damascus in order to*k* seize me, 33 but I was let down in a basket through a window in the wall,*l* and escaped from his hands.

12 It is necessary to boast; nothing is to be gained by it, but I will go on to visions and revelations of the Lord. 2 I know a person in Christ who fourteen years ago was caught up to the third heaven — whether in the body or out of the body I do not know; God knows. 3 And

---

h Gk according to the flesh   *i* Gk brothers   *j* Gk ethnarch   *k* Other ancient authorities read and wanted to
l Gk through the wall

11.16
v. 1
11.17
1 Cor 7.6, 12, 25;
Acts 9.24, 25
11.18
Phil 3.3, 4

11.21
2 Cor 10.10;
Phil 3.4

11.22
Acts 6.1;
Phil 3.5;
Rom 9.4
11.23
1 Cor 15.10;
Acts 16.23;
2 Cor 6.5
11.24
Deut 25.3
11.25
Acts 16.22;
14.19
11.26
Acts 9.23;
14.5; 21.31;
Gal 2.4
11.27
1 Thess 2.9;
1 Cor 4.11;
2 Cor 6.5
11.29
1 Cor 9.22
11.30
1 Cor 2.3
11.31
Gal 1.20;
Rom 9.5
11.32
Acts 9.24, 25
12.1
Co 11.30;
v. 7;
Gal 1.12; 2.2
12.2
Rom 16.7;
Eph 4.10;
2 Cor 11.11

11.16ff Paul will soon boast about what he has suffered for the sake of Christ. He carefully notes that the Lord Jesus did not directly reveal to him that he should do this, so he hopes they will not regard this as folly. The circumstances of his case make this step necessary. Paul's list of suffering makes his case of being under the Lordship of Christ airtight. No one can accuse anyone who has suffered this much of being in the ministry for money, since there are much easier ways of making money. Only dedication to the living God can explain why Paul lived and suffered as he did.
11.24 Paul was whipped five times by the Jews. Deut 25.1–3 limited the beating to forty lashes by the whip. Lest a mistake be made, the Jews stopped at thirty-nine, so as not to break the law. Offenders were stripped of their clothes and bound to two pillars by their outstretched hands. The minister of the syna-

gogue used a triple-thonged lash, and Scripture was read as the beating was given.
11.31 So deeply moved is Paul that he calls upon God as his witness to what he has just said. That is, Paul is taking an oath before the omniscient God that everything he says is the truth.
12.2 *Heaven,* used more than 275 times in the N.T., has a variety of references. It denotes God's dwelling place (1 Kings 8.30; Mt 6.9), God's throne (Isa 66.1; also Acts 7.49), and God's creation (Rev 10.6). As the Mediator, Christ entered into heaven (Acts 3.21,22; Heb 6.19,20; 9.11, 24). All the holy angels are in heaven (Mt 18.10; 24.36), and all of the wicked are forever excluded from heaven (Gal 5.21; Rev 22.15). Believers must lay up treasure in heaven (Mt 6.20; Lk 12.33), and heaven holds the priceless gift of eternal life which the saints will inherit in the resurrection (1 Pet 1.4).

12.4
Lk 23.43

12.6
2 Cor 10.8;
11.16

12.8
Mt 26.44
12.9
Phil 4.13;
2 Cor 11.30;
1 Pet 4.14
12.10
Rom 5.3;
2 Cor 6.4;
2 Thess 1.4

12.11
2 Cor 11.1, 5
12.12
Rom 15.18,
19
12.13
1 Cor 9.12,
18;
2 Cor 11.7
12.14
2 Cor 13.1;
1 Cor 10.24,
33; 4.14, 15;
Prov 19.14
12.15
Phil 2.17;
1 Thess 2.8
12.18
2 Cor 8.6, 16,
18

12.19
Rom 9.1;
2 Cor 10.8
12.20
2 Cor 2.1-4;
1 Cor 1.11;
3.3

I know that such a person—whether in the body or out of the body I do not know; God knows— 4was caught up into Paradise and heard things that are not to be told, that no mortal is permitted to repeat. 5On behalf of such a one I will boast, but on my own behalf I will not boast, except of my weaknesses. 6But if I wish to boast, I will not be a fool, for I will be speaking the truth. But I refrain from it, so that no one may think better of me than what is seen in me or heard from me, 7even considering the exceptional character of the revelations. Therefore, to keep*m* me from being too elated, a thorn was given me in the flesh, a messenger of Satan to torment me, to keep me from being too elated.*n* 8Three times I appealed to the Lord about this, that it would leave me, 9but he said to me, "My grace is sufficient for you, for power*o* is made perfect in weakness." So, I will boast all the more gladly of my weaknesses, so that the power of Christ may dwell in me. 10Therefore I am content with weaknesses, insults, hardships, persecutions, and calamities for the sake of Christ; for whenever I am weak, then I am strong.

F. The marks of a true apostle

11 I have been a fool! You forced me to it. Indeed you should have been the ones commending me, for I am not at all inferior to these super-apostles, even though I am nothing. 12The signs of a true apostle were performed among you with utmost patience, signs and wonders and mighty works. 13How have you been worse off than the other churches, except that I myself did not burden you? Forgive me this wrong!

14 Here I am, ready to come to you this third time. And I will not be a burden, because I do not want what is yours but you; for children ought not to lay up for their parents, but parents for their children. 15I will most gladly spend and be spent for you. If I love you more, am I to be loved less? 16Let it be assumed that I did not burden you. Nevertheless (you say) since I was crafty, I took you in by deceit. 17Did I take advantage of you through any of those whom I sent to you? 18I urged Titus to go, and sent the brother with him. Titus did not take advantage of you, did he? Did we not conduct ourselves with the same spirit? Did we not take the same steps?

G. The appeal for repentance

19 Have you been thinking all along that we have been defending ourselves before you? We are speaking in Christ before God. Everything we do, beloved, is for the sake of building you up. 20For I fear that when I come, I may find you not as I wish, and that you may find me not as you wish; I fear that there may perhaps be quarreling, jealousy, anger,

---

m Other ancient authorities read *To keep*   *n* Other ancient authorities lack *to keep me from being too elated*   *o* Other ancient authorities read *my power*

12.7 Paul does not say specifically what his thorn in the flesh was. It was a messenger from Satan, which means that God permitted Satan to do this even as he permitted Job to suffer under Satan. Even though the thorn was not removed, Satan was defeated, because it enabled Paul to experience the surpassing grace and power of God, thereby bringing glory to God.
12.8 *Three times I appealed to the Lord.* This may simply mean *often.* God answered Paul's prayer by saying no. But God stood by Paul and gave him his grace, enabling him to bear the infirmity in a manner by which God was glorified. Even though God does not take away from us some of the physical burdens he has sent, we like Paul can glory in our infirmities, knowing that God produces strength out of our weaknesses.
12.12 *signs and wonders and mighty works.* God gave the apostles outward, confirming indicators to show

they were what they said they were and to keep their listeners from claiming that they could not tell whether the apostles were speaking the truth. These miraculous signs were sufficient and beyond question, so that those who refused to acknowledge Jesus would have no excuse in the day of judgment.
12.15 The love of Paul for the Corinthians did not abate, but increased more and more. He was willing to continue serving them and teaching them, even if the more he loved them, the less they returned love to him.
12.20 Paul warns the Corinthians of his fears that the sinners among them will not repent and thus the problems will persist. In that event he will come to reprove and rebuke them, and they will discover that he is a far more severe man than they ever realized (cf. 13.10).

selfishness, slander, gossip, conceit, and disorder. [21] I fear that when I come again, my God may humble me before you, and that I may have to mourn over many who previously sinned and have not repented of the impurity, sexual immorality, and licentiousness that they have practiced.

13 This is the third time I am coming to you. "Any charge must be sustained by the evidence of two or three witnesses." [2] I warned those who sinned previously and all the others, and I warn them now while absent, as I did when present on my second visit, that if I come again, I will not be lenient — [3] since you desire proof that Christ is speaking in me. He is not weak in dealing with you, but is powerful in you. [4] For he was crucified in weakness, but lives by the power of God. For we are weak in him,[p] but in dealing with you we will live with him by the power of God.

5 Examine yourselves to see whether you are living in the faith. Test yourselves. Do you not realize that Jesus Christ is in you? — unless, indeed, you fail to meet the test! [6] I hope you will find out that we have not failed. [7] But we pray to God that you may not do anything wrong — not that we may appear to have met the test, but that you may do what is right, though we may seem to have failed. [8] For we cannot do anything against the truth, but only for the truth. [9] For we rejoice when we are weak and you are strong. This is what we pray for, that you may become perfect. [10] So I write these things while I am away from you, so that when I come, I may not have to be severe in using the authority that the Lord has given me for building up and not for tearing down.

V. Conclusion (13.11–14)

A. Exhortations and greetings

11 Finally, brothers and sisters,[q] farewell.[r] Put things in order, listen to my appeal,[s] agree with one another, live in peace; and the God of love and peace will be with you. [12] Greet one another with a holy kiss. All the saints greet you.

B. Benediction

13 The grace of the Lord Jesus Christ, the love of God, and the communion of[t] the Holy Spirit be with all of you.

p Other ancient authorities read with him   q Gk brothers   r Or rejoice   s Or encourage one another   t Or and the sharing in

13.2ff *I will not be lenient.* The apostle means business and speaks forthrightly. If he comes and finds things out of order, he will spare no one and they will know that Christ is speaking in him. Jesus was crucified in weakness, and Paul preaches in weakness, but both the Son of God and the apostle have the power of God working in and through them.
13.5 *Examine yourselves.* This exhortation is important, for there are people who make false professions of faith in Christ either deliberately or unwittingly. Paul wants all of us to examine ourselves to be certain that we are not reprobates, but are firmly grounded on the true rock, Jesus Christ.
13.11 When the people of God love each other truly, live in peace, have one mind, and endure their sufferings gracefully, they can be sure that the God of love and peace will be present among them.
13.13 Paul concludes this epistle with his apostolic benediction based on the Trinity; he pronounces upon them the grace of Christ, the love of the Father,

and the communion of the Holy Spirit. The word "Trinity" does not appear in Scripture. However, Christianity has always been trinitarian. This doctrine asserts that God is one in essence, subsisting in three persons, the Father, the Son, and the Holy Spirit, from all eternity. All three persons of the Trinity share the same divine attributes. Each has a unique task to perform: God the Father sent Jesus the Son; God the Son died on Calvary's cross; the Father and the Son sent God the Holy Spirit, who seals and indwells every believer. Salvation too is the work of the Trinity (see 2 Thess 2.13,14; Titus 3.4–6). Numerous other passages of the Bible refer to all three persons in the same breath. At the baptism of Jesus, for example, the Holy Spirit appeared as a dove and the Father's voice was heard (Mt 3.16,17). In Mt 28.19 God commands believers to be baptized into the name of the Father and of the Son and of the Holy Spirit. See also Rom 8.9; 1 Cor 12.3–6; Eph 4.4–6; 1 Pet 1.2; Jude 20,21; Rev 1.4,5.

12.21
2 Cor 2.1, 4;
13.2;
Gal 5.19

13.1
2 Cor 12.14;
Deut 19.15;
Mt 18.16

13.3
Mt 10.20;
1 Cor 5.4;
2 Cor 9.8;
10.4
13.4
Phil 2.7, 8;
1 Pet 3.18;
Rom 6.4, 8;
v. 9
13.5
Jn 6.6;
1 Cor 11.28;
9.27

13.9
2 Cor 11.30;
12.10
13.10
2 Cor 2.3;
Titus 1.13;
2 Cor 10.8

13.11
Rom 15.33;
Eph 6.23

13.12b
Phil 4.22

INTRODUCTION TO
THE LETTER OF PAUL TO THE
GALATIANS

Authorship, Date, and Background: The conversion of Paul on the road to Damascus occurred around A.D. 32; the letter he wrote to the Galatians was composed after he had been in the ministry fifteen or more years. He was known as the apostle to the Gentiles, i.e., to the non-Jews. One of the great questions of that day had to do with the relationship of new converts to Judaism. Though the O.T. clearly taught that salvation is by faith alone, Judaism insisted on the necessity of circumcision and the keeping of the law as part of the process of salvation. Some Jewish Christians and non-Jews who had been circumcised and who adhered to the law followed this Jewish line of thinking, insisting that faith alone is insufficient for salvation. Known as the Judaizers, they followed Paul wherever he evangelized, teaching that converts must keep the law and be circumcised. This was true in the region of Galatia where Paul's ministry had been quite successful. Paul had to answer this challenge to salvation by faith alone. Any concession at this point would destroy the entire faith.

The dating of Galatians depends in large measure on the question of the destination of the letter—whether it was addressed to the Christians of South Galatia or North Galatia. Paul visited South Galatia on his first missionary expedition, and since some feel the letter to the Galatians does not mention the first missionary council at Jerusalem, they suppose it was composed around A.D. 49 and sent to South Galatia. This would make it the earliest of Paul's writings. Others, however, date the letter A.D. 55–56, since Acts 16.6 and 18.23 specifically mention visits to Galatia by Paul on his second and third journeys, which occurred after the Jerusalem conference (Acts 15). Whether the letter was written in A.D. 49 or A.D. 55–56 is not of great importance, for the Pauline authorship is not in question and the contents of the letter have universal and enduring value. In any event, both Galatians and Romans constitute the most systematic theological presentation of the gospel with all of its implications. They are the most highly didactic (teaching) books in the N.T., and all of the other letters in the N.T. must be understood in the light of these.

Characteristics and Content: Galatians has been called the *Magna Charta* of Christian freedom. For the apostle Paul the issue at stake is the most important one relating to his preaching of the gospel: "Is a sinner saved by faith alone or by a combination of faith plus works?" Stated another way, it involves a choice between faith or works, between grace or law. The Judaizers were saying that new believers should be circumcised and observe Jewish laws and customs. Paul rightly sees that the principle involved is of such magnitude that to compromise the issue will result in the loss of the true gospel and bring believers into a slavery from which the same gospel is supposed to free them. He claims in Galatians that the gospel he knows has not come from human beings, but from God by way of direct revelation. In a forceful manner and without apology, Paul asserts that sinners are justified by faith rather than by the works of the law. Anyone who mixes in works as a basis for salvation is preaching another gospel, and Paul places a solemn curse on anyone who does this.

He goes on to summarize the gospel he preaches. Later Paul will reaffirm and expand the central truths of Galatians in his letter to the Romans.

What Paul does not say is of equal importance, for some maintain that the apostles James and Paul are in sharp disagreement. It is true that for Paul, sinners are saved by faith alone, but saving faith is *always* accompanied by good works; in other words, the saved person produces the fruits of righteousness which are displayed in a transformed and holy life.

Outline:

I. Introduction (1.1–10)

II. Paul's apostolic authority (1.11–2.21)

III. Paul's doctrine of justification (3.1–4.31)

IV. The effect of Christian freedom (5.1–6.10)

V. Conclusion (6.11–18)

THE LETTER OF PAUL TO THE
GALATIANS

I. *Introduction (1.1–10)*

A. *Greeting*

Paul an apostle — sent neither by human commission nor from human authorities, but through Jesus Christ and God the Father, who raised him from the dead — 2 and all the members of God's family*a* who are with me,

To the churches of Galatia:

3 Grace to you and peace from God our Father and the Lord Jesus Christ, 4 who gave himself for our sins to set us free from the present evil age, according to the will of our God and Father, 5 to whom be the glory forever and ever. Amen.

B. *The occasion of the letter*

6 I am astonished that you are so quickly deserting the one who called you in the grace of Christ and are turning to a different gospel — 7 not that there is another gospel, but there are some who are confusing you and want to pervert the gospel of Christ. 8 But even if we or an angel*b* from heaven should proclaim to you a gospel contrary to what we proclaimed to you, let that one be accursed! 9 As we have said before, so now I repeat, if anyone proclaims to you a gospel contrary to what you received, let that one be accursed!

10 Am I now seeking human approval, or God's approval? Or am I trying to please people? If I were still pleasing people, I would not be a servant*c* of Christ.

II. *Paul's apostolic authority (1.11–2.21)*

A. *Of divine origin*

11 For I want you to know, brothers and sisters,*d* that the gospel that was proclaimed by me is not of human origin; 12 for I did not receive it

1.1
2 Cor 1.1;
vv. 11, 12;
Acts 9.6; 2.24
1.2
Phil 4.21;
1 Cor 16.1
1.3
Rom 1.7
1.4
Rom 4.25;
Gal 2.20;
2 Cor 4.4
1.5
Rom 16.27
1.6
Gal 5.8;
2 Cor 11.4
1.7
Acts 15.24;
Gal 5.10
1.8
2 Cor 11.4,
14;
Rom 9.3
1.9
Rom 16.17
1.10
1 Thess 2.4
1.11
1 Cor 15.1
1.12
vv. 1, 16;
Eph 3.3

a Gk *all the brothers*   *b* Or *a messenger*   *c* Gk *slave*   *d* Gk *brothers*

1.1ff The three essential themes of this letter are included in the opening greeting: (1) Paul's apostolic authority; (2) the doctrine of justification by faith alone; and (3) the life believers should live, i.e., their sanctification.
1.4 Jesus died on the cross to redeem us. Three principles underlie his death: (1) the principle of "covering," by which the believer's sins are covered over by Christ's blood so that they are no longer seen by God (Rom 4.7); (2) the principle of reconciliation through a sacrifice of atonement, i.e., through the payment of the penalty for sin by Jesus Christ, divine justice has been vindicated and the sinner brought back into fellowship with God (Eph 2.16; Col 1.20); (3) the principle of substitution, by which Jesus Christ died the death believers should have died, i.e., he died in their place (2 Cor 5.21; 1 Pet 2.24).
1.6 Paul writes as one deeply moved by the possibility that his beloved Galatians have defected from grace. He pronounces a curse (see next note) on anyone who preaches a different message from his, especially on those who argue in favor of circumcision as necessary for salvation. To him, grace and works cannot be mixed as part of the process of salvation.
1.8 *let that one be accursed.* The Greek word used here is *anathema*; it refers to an "object devoted to destruction" and is also used in Acts 23.12–14; Rom 9.3; 1 Cor 12.3; 16.22. Traditionally, an anathema is a pronouncement against an individual by an ecclesiastical body, accompanied by excommunication.
1.12 The disciples who associated with Jesus on earth could say they had received their knowledge of the good news by direct revelation, for it came from the Lord Jesus himself. Paul did not personally know the human Jesus. Normally he would have received his knowledge of the good news through other human beings, but Paul affirms that he obtained it, not from other humans, but directly from Jesus Christ through

from a human source, nor was I taught it, but I received it through a revelation of Jesus Christ. 13 You have heard, no doubt, of my earlier life in Judaism. I was violently persecuting the church of God and was trying to destroy it. 14 I advanced in Judaism beyond many among my people of the same age, for I was far more zealous for the traditions of my ancestors. 15 But when God, who had set me apart before I was born and called me through his grace, was pleased 16 to reveal his Son to me,*e* so that I might proclaim him among the Gentiles, I did not confer with any human being, 17 nor did I go up to Jerusalem to those who were already apostles before me, but I went away at once into Arabia, and afterwards I returned to Damascus.

B. Independent of the apostles

18 Then after three years I did go up to Jerusalem to visit Cephas and stayed with him fifteen days; 19 but I did not see any other apostle except James the Lord's brother. 20 In what I am writing to you, before God, I do not lie! 21 Then I went into the regions of Syria and Cilicia, 22 and I was still unknown by sight to the churches of Judea that are in Christ; 23 they only heard it said, "The one who formerly was persecuting us is now proclaiming the faith he once tried to destroy." 24 And they glorified God because of me.

C. Accepted by the church

2 Then after fourteen years I went up again to Jerusalem with Barnabas, taking Titus along with me. 2 I went up in response to a revelation. Then I laid before them (though only in a private meeting with the acknowledged leaders) the gospel that I proclaim among the Gentiles, in order to make sure that I was not running, or had not run, in vain. 3 But even Titus, who was with me, was not compelled to be circumcised, though he was a Greek. 4 But because of false believers*f* secretly brought in, who slipped in to spy on the freedom we have in Christ Jesus, so that they might enslave us — 5 we did not submit to them even for a moment, so that the truth of the gospel might always remain with you. 6 And from those who were supposed to be acknowledged leaders (what they actually were makes no difference to me; God shows no partiality) — those leaders contributed nothing to me. 7 On the contrary, when they saw that I had been entrusted with the gospel for the uncircumcised, just as Peter had been entrusted with the gospel for the circumcised 8 (for he who worked through Peter making him an apostle to the circumcised also worked through me in sending me to the Gentiles), 9 and when James and Cephas and John, who were acknowledged pillars, recognized the grace that had been given to me, they gave to Barnabas and me the right hand of fellowship, agreeing that we should go to the Gentiles and they to the circumcised. 10 They asked only one thing, that we remember the poor, which was actually what I was*g* eager to do.

D. Demonstrated in conflict with Peter

11 But when Cephas came to Antioch, I opposed him to his face,

e Gk in me   f Gk false brothers   g Or had been

1.13
Acts 8.3; 9.21
1.14
Acts 22.3;
Col 2.8
1.15
Isa 49.1, 5;
Jer 1.5;
Acts 9.15;
Rom 1.1
1.16
Acts 9.20;
Eph 6.12

1.18
Acts 9.22, 23, 26, 27
1.19
Mt 13.55
1.21
Acts 9.30
1.22
1 Thess 2.14;
Rom 16.7

2.1
Acts 15.2
2.2
Acts 15.12;
Gal 1.6;
Phil 2.16
2.3
2 Cor 2.13;
Acts 16.3;
1 Cor 9.21
2.4
Acts 15.1;
2 Cor 11.26
2.5
v. 14;
Col 1.5
2.6
Gal 6.3;
Rom 2.11;
2 Cor 12.11
2.7
1 Thess 2.4;
Acts 13.46
2.9
Rom 12.3;
Gal 1.16

2.10
Acts 11.29, 30; 24.17

2.11
Acts 11.10

---

special revelation. He was taught by the risen Lord who appeared to him and was called by him to be an apostle.
1.15,16 In the sovereignty of God, Paul was set apart by God for salvation and service before he was born. He was called by grace, which brought about his conversion; at that same time Christ was revealed *in* him (footnote NRSV), not simply *to* him.
1.18 *Cephas,* Peter's name in Aramaic. Both Peter

and Cephas mean "rock" (cf. Mt 16.18).
2.3 Paul wanted to make it clear that keeping the ceremonial law contributed nothing to salvation. Consequently he refused to have Titus, a non-Jew who worked together with him, circumcised.
2.7–9 Peter and Paul preached essentially the same gospel; Paul was called to preach to the Gentiles; Peter to the Jews.
2.11 Peter was not rebuked by Paul because of

2.12
Acts 11.2, 3
2.13
v. 1
2.14
vv. 5, 9, 11

2.15
Phil 3.4, 5;
Mt 9.11
2.16
Acts 13.39;
Rom 1.17;
3.20
2.17
v. 15;
Gal 3.21

2.19
Rom 8.2;
6.14;
2 Cor 5.15;
1 Thess 5.10
2.20
1 Pet 4.2;
Eph 5.2;
Titus 2.14
2.21
Gal 3.21

3.1
Gal 1.2; 5.7;
1 Cor 1.23
3.2
Acts 2.38;
Rom 10.16,
17
3.3
Gal 4.9;
Heb 7.16
3.4
1 Cor 15.2
3.5
Phil 1.19;
1 Cor 12.10;
Rom 10.17
3.6
Gen 15.6;
Rom 4.3;
Jas 2.23
3.7
v. 9
3.8
Gen 12.3;
Acts 3.25
3.9
Rom 4.16;
v. 7

because he stood self-condemned; [12] for until certain people came from James, he used to eat with the Gentiles. But after they came, he drew back and kept himself separate for fear of the circumcision faction. [13] And the other Jews joined him in this hypocrisy, so that even Barnabas was led astray by their hypocrisy. [14] But when I saw that they were not acting consistently with the truth of the gospel, I said to Cephas before them all, "If you, though a Jew, live like a Gentile and not like a Jew, how can you compel the Gentiles to live like Jews?"[h]

15 We ourselves are Jews by birth and not Gentile sinners; [16] yet we know that a person is justified[i] not by the works of the law but through faith in Jesus Christ.[j] And we have come to believe in Christ Jesus, so that we might be justified by faith in Christ,[k] and not by doing the works of the law, because no one will be justified by the works of the law. [17] But if, in our effort to be justified in Christ, we ourselves have been found to be sinners, is Christ then a servant of sin? Certainly not! [18] But if I build up again the very things that I once tore down, then I demonstrate that I am a transgressor. [19] For through the law I died to the law, so that I might live to God. I have been crucified with Christ; [20] and it is no longer I who live, but it is Christ who lives in me. And the life I now live in the flesh I live by faith in the Son of God,[l] who loved me and gave himself for me. [21] I do not nullify the grace of God; for if justification[m] comes through the law, then Christ died for nothing.

III. *Paul's doctrine of justification (3.1–4.31)*

A. The Galatians deceived

3 You foolish Galatians! Who has bewitched you? It was before your eyes that Jesus Christ was publicly exhibited as crucified! [2] The only thing I want to learn from you is this: Did you receive the Spirit by doing the works of the law or by believing what you heard? [3] Are you so foolish? Having started with the Spirit, are you now ending with the flesh? [4] Did you experience so much for nothing? — if it really was for nothing. [5] Well then, does God[n] supply you with the Spirit and work miracles among you by your doing the works of the law, or by your believing what you heard?

B. The witness of Abraham

6 Just as Abraham "believed God, and it was reckoned to him as righteousness," [7] so, you see, those who believe are the descendants of Abraham. [8] And the scripture, foreseeing that God would justify the Gentiles by faith, declared the gospel beforehand to Abraham, saying, "All the Gentiles shall be blessed in you." [9] For this reason, those who believe are blessed with Abraham who believed.

h Some interpreters hold that the quotation extends into the following paragraph   i Or reckoned as righteous; and so elsewhere   j Or the faith of Jesus Christ   k Or the faith of Christ   l Or by the faith of the Son of God   m Or righteousness   n Gk he

---

heresy but because of hypocrisy (v. 13). Peter failed to practice what he himself believed in principle. While Peter never taught that anyone could be saved by circumcision (see v. 14), he was refusing to fellowship with uncircumcised Gentiles because of pressure put on him by circumcised Hebrew Christians. He probably did not wish to offend prospective Jewish converts. To Paul this surrendered the basic principle that salvation is purely of grace without obedience to the ritual law of Moses. It is true that we must be concerned for weaker people's consciences, but when this leads to a betrayal of the good news it is wrong.
2.16 From beginning to end the believer's life depends on faith. The entire Scripture testifies to this truth: the believer lives by faith (v. 20), is kept by

faith and stands firm through it (1 Pet 1.5), resists the devil and overcomes him by faith (Eph 6.12; 1 Pet 5.8,9), and walks by faith (2 Cor 5.7).
2.19,20 Paul here employs several amazing paradoxes concerning his relationship to Jesus Christ. He is crucified, yet he lives. He is dead to the world and to the law, yet he is alive to God and Jesus Christ. He lives and yet not he.
3.1–5 Paul preached the cross of Christ to the Galatians. When they received Christ, they were given the Spirit by faith, not by the works of the law. Paul warns them not to go back to the principle of law as that in which they place their confidence.
3.6 For God's covenant with Abraham, see note on Gen 12.2.

C. Faith without works

10 For all who rely on the works of the law are under a curse; for it is written, "Cursed is everyone who does not observe and obey all the things written in the book of the law." 11 Now it is evident that no one is justified before God by the law; for "The one who is righteous will live by faith."o 12 But the law does not rest on faith; on the contrary, "Whoever does the works of the lawp will live by them." 13 Christ redeemed us from the curse of the law by becoming a curse for us — for it is written, "Cursed is everyone who hangs on a tree" — 14 in order that in Christ Jesus the blessing of Abraham might come to the Gentiles, so that we might receive the promise of the Spirit through faith.

D. The Abrahamic covenant

15 Brothers and sisters,q I give an example from daily life: once a person's willr has been ratified, no one adds to it or annuls it. 16 Now the promises were made to Abraham and to his offspring;s it does not say, "And to offsprings,"t as of many; but it says, "And to your offspring,"s that is, to one person, who is Christ. 17 My point is this: the law, which came four hundred thirty years later, does not annul a covenant previously ratified by God, so as to nullify the promise. 18 For if the inheritance comes from the law, it no longer comes from the promise; but God granted it to Abraham through the promise.

E. The function of the law

19 Why then the law? It was added because of transgressions, until the offsprings would come to whom the promise had been made; and it was ordained through angels by a mediator. 20 Now a mediator involves more than one party; but God is one. 21 Is the law then opposed to the promises of God? Certainly not! For if a law had been given that could make alive, then righteousness would indeed come through the law. 22 But the scripture has imprisoned all things under the power of sin, so that what was promised through faith in Jesus Christu might be given to those who believe.

F. The superiority of faith over law

23 Now before faith came, we were imprisoned and guarded under the law until faith would be revealed. 24 Therefore the law was our disciplinarian until Christ came, so that we might be justified by faith. 25 But now that faith has come, we are no longer subject to a disciplinarian, 26 for in Christ Jesus you are all children of God through faith. 27 As many of you as were baptized into Christ have clothed yourselves with Christ. 28 There

o Or The one who is righteous through faith will live   p Gk does them   q Gk Brothers   r Or covenant (as in verse 17)   s Gk seed   t Gk seeds   u Or through the faith of Jesus Christ

3.10
Deut 27.26
3.11
Gal 2.16;
Hab 2.4;
Heb 10.38
3.12
Lev 18.5;
Rom 10.5
3.13
Gal 4.5;
Acts 5.30;
Deut 21.23
3.14
Rom 4.9;
Joel 2.28;
Acts 2.33
3.15
Heb 9.17
3.16
Gen 12.3;
13.15;
Acts 3.25
3.17
Ex 12.40;
Rom 4.13
3.18
Rom 4.14;
8.17
3.19
Acts 7.53;
Deut 5.5
3.20
Heb 8.6;
9.15; 12.24
3.21
Gal 2.17, 21
3.22
Rom 3.9-19;
11.32
3.23
Rom 11.32
3.24
Rom 10.4;
1 Cor 4.15;
Gal 2.16
3.26
Jn 1.12;
Rom 8.14
3.27
Rom 6.3;
13.14
3.28
Col 3.11;
Jn 10.16;
Eph 2.14, 15

3.10 All people fall under the curse and condemnation of God who has given us the law, for no one has ever been able to keep the whole law of God. In fact, the breaking of a single commandment makes people guilty of having broken the whole law of God. Sinners could be saved if they kept the whole law of God. But since everyone sins and falls short of God's glory (Rom 3.23), another way had to be found for humans to be saved. That way was Christ, who became a curse for us by dying the accursed death of the cross; by faith in him believers are redeemed from the curse of the law.
3.11 See note on Hab 2.4 for salvation by faith alone.
3.24 God's law is good but it cannot save. It is designed to show us our deficiencies, but it cannot deliver us from them. It enlightens us but does not empower us. It reveals what we ought to be like and tells what we ought to do, but it cannot make us what we should be or give us strength to do what we know we should. The law, in other words, points out our need for Jesus Christ as the way of salvation God has provided.
3.28 no longer Jew or Greek . . . no longer male and female. All who believe are baptized into Christ; in him there are no distinctions. Jews and Gentiles can come to him with no distinction. So can male and female. So can black and white. So can slave and master. Salvation does not eliminate these earthly distinctions, but it stresses unity among humans in Christ rather than diversity. In heaven racial distinctions, national barriers, sexual discrimination, and all other biases will cease.

is no longer Jew or Greek, there is no longer slave or free, there is no longer male and female; for all of you are one in Christ Jesus. 29 And if you belong to Christ, then you are Abraham's offspring, *v* heirs according to the promise.

4 My point is this: heirs, as long as they are minors, are no better than slaves, though they are the owners of all the property; 2 but they remain under guardians and trustees until the date set by the father. 3 So with us; while we were minors, we were enslaved to the elemental spirits *w* of the world. 4 But when the fullness of time had come, God sent his Son, born of a woman, born under the law, 5 in order to redeem those who were under the law, so that we might receive adoption as children. 6 And because you are children, God has sent the Spirit of his Son into our *x* hearts, crying, "Abba! *y* Father!" 7 So you are no longer a slave but a child, and if a child then also an heir, through God. *z*

G. Appeal against a return to slavery

8 Formerly, when you did not know God, you were enslaved to beings that by nature are not gods. 9 Now, however, that you have come to know God, or rather to be known by God, how can you turn back again to the weak and beggarly elemental spirits? *a* How can you want to be enslaved to them again? 10 You are observing special days, and months, and seasons, and years. 11 I am afraid that my work for you may have been wasted.

12 Friends, *b* I beg you, become as I am, for I also have become as you are. You have done me no wrong. 13 You know that it was because of a physical infirmity that I first announced the gospel to you; 14 though my condition put you to the test, you did not scorn or despise me, but welcomed me as an angel of God, as Christ Jesus. 15 What has become of the goodwill you felt? For I testify that, had it been possible, you would have torn out your eyes and given them to me. 16 Have I now become your enemy by telling you the truth? 17 They make much of you, but for no good purpose; they want to exclude you, so that you may make much of them. 18 It is good to be made much of for a good purpose at all times, and not only when I am present with you. 19 My little children, for whom I am again in the pain of childbirth until Christ is formed in you, 20 I wish I were present with you now and could change my tone, for I am perplexed about you.

21 Tell me, you who desire to be subject to the law, will you not listen

---

v Gk *seed*   *w* Or *the rudiments*   *x* Other ancient authorities read *your*   *y* Aramaic for *Father*   *z* Other ancient authorities read *an heir of God through Christ*   *a* Or *beggarly rudiments*   *b* Gk *Brothers*

Cross references (left margin):

3.29
1 Cor 3.23;
Gal 4.28

4.3
Col 2.8, 20;
Heb 5.12
4.4
Eph 1.10;
Mt 5.17
4.5
Eph 1.7;
Jn 1.12;
Eph 1.5
4.6
Rom 5.5;
8.15

4.8
Eph 2.12;
1 Thess 4.5;
Rom 1.25;
1 Cor 12.2
4.9
1 Cor 8.3;
Col 2.20
4.10
Rom 14.5
4.11
1 Thess 3.5
4.12
Gal 6.18
4.13
1 Cor 2.3
4.14
Mt 10.40;
Lk 10.16
4.16
Am 5.10

4.18
vv. 13, 14
4.19
1 Jn 2.1;
1 Cor 4.15;
Eph 4.13

4.21
Lk 16.29

4.1 Paul now uses the illustration of a child under age to signify the O.T. dispensation. It was an age of darkness and bondage when compared to the liberty and light under the gospel. In the fullness of time God put an end to the era of the law and brought in the gospel; i.e., the old covenant gave way to the new covenant in Jesus Christ. He came to redeem those who were under the law, which could not save.

4.5 *adoption* (Gk. *huiothesia*) is a N.T. word used only by Paul. Through a new birth (i.e., regeneration) believers are adopted into the family of God and become his sons and daughters. Adoption has privileges and responsibilities, for God has ordained that believers should become like his Son (Rom 8.29). Adopted children (1) are objects of the Father's love (Jn 17.23); (2) bear God's image (Rom 8.29; 2 Pet 1.4); (3) are indwelt by God's Spirit (v. 6); (4) have his name (1 Jn 3.1); (5) are disciplined and trained by the Father (Heb 12.5–11); and (6) are God's heirs who share his treasures (Rom 8.17; 1 Pet 1.4). God's sons and daughters are responsible to do the Father's will, embrace the Father's teaching, and witness to the

Father's love.

4.13 Nobody knows what Paul's bodily ailment was (mentioned only here and in 2 Cor 12.7–10). We may suppose that it was chronic, painful, and repulsive to others as well as humiliating and debilitating to the apostle himself. Malaria, epilepsy, migraine, and ophthalmia have all been suggested.

4.17ff Paul here warns against the false teachers, the Judaizers, who want to bring the Galatians under the law from which they have been delivered. The Judaizers are more interested in themselves than in the Galatians, though they pretend to be interested in order to seduce them. So great is his concern for the Galatians that he says he experiences the pain of childbirth for them. They are his little children, and he continues to mother them until Christ is fully formed in them.

4.21ff Paul illustrates the difference between those who trust Christ and those who trust the law by the allegory (v. 24) of Isaac and Ishmael. Ishmael, the son of a slave, represents Sinai and the law, which leads to bondage and death. But Isaac was the son of promto the law? 22 For it is written that Abraham had two sons, one by a slave woman and the other by a free woman. 23 One, the child of the slave, was born according to the flesh; the other, the child of the free woman, was born through the promise. 24 Now this is an allegory: these women are two covenants. One woman, in fact, is Hagar, from Mount Sinai, bearing children for slavery. 25 Now Hagar is Mount Sinai in Arabia*c* and corresponds to the present Jerusalem, for she is in slavery with her children. 26 But the other woman corresponds to the Jerusalem above; she is free, and she is our mother. 27 For it is written,

"Rejoice, you childless one, you who bear no children,
    burst into song and shout, you who endure no birth pangs;
for the children of the desolate woman are more numerous
    than the children of the one who is married."

28 Now you,*d* my friends,*e* are children of the promise, like Isaac. 29 But just as at that time the child who was born according to the flesh persecuted the child who was born according to the Spirit, so it is now also. 30 But what does the scripture say? "Drive out the slave and her child; for the child of the slave will not share the inheritance with the child of the free woman." 31 So then, friends,*e* we are children, not of the slave but of the free woman. 1 For freedom Christ has set us free. Stand firm, therefore, and do not submit again to a yoke of slavery.

IV. *The effect of Christian liberty (5.1–6.10)*

A. *Liberty threatened by legalism*

2 Listen! I, Paul, am telling you that if you let yourselves be circumcised, Christ will be of no benefit to you. 3 Once again I testify to every man who lets himself be circumcised that he is obliged to obey the entire law. 4 You who want to be justified by the law have cut yourselves off from Christ; you have fallen away from grace. 5 For through the Spirit, by faith, we eagerly wait for the hope of righteousness. 6 For in Christ Jesus neither circumcision nor uncircumcision counts for anything; the only thing that counts is faith working*f* through love.

7 You were running well; who prevented you from obeying the truth? 8 Such persuasion does not come from the one who calls you. 9 A little yeast leavens the whole batch of dough. 10 I am confident about you in the Lord that you will not think otherwise. But whoever it is that is confusing you will pay the penalty. 11 But my friends,*e* why am I still being persecuted if I am still preaching circumcision? In that case the offense of the cross has been removed. 12 I wish those who unsettle you would castrate themselves!

c Other ancient authorities read *For Sinai is a mountain in Arabia*   *d* Other ancient authorities read *we*
e Gk *brothers*   *f* Or *made effective*

Side refs: 4.22 Gen 16.15; 21.2, 9; 4.23 Rom 9.7; Gen 18.10; Heb 11.11; 4.24 Deut 33.2; 4.26 Isa 2.2; Heb 12.22; Rev 3.12; 4.27 Isa 54.1; 4.28 Acts 3.25; Rom 9.8; 4.29 Gen 21.9; 4.30 Gen 21.10-12; 5.1 Jn 8.32; Acts 15.10; 5.2 Acts 15.1; 5.3 Gal 3.10; 5.4 Heb 12.15; 2 Pet 3.17; 5.5 Rom 8.23, 24; 2 Tim 4.8; 5.6 1 Cor 7.19; Jas 2.18; 5.7 1 Cor 9.24; Gal 3.1; 5.8 Gal 1.6; 5.9 1 Cor 5.6; 5.10 2 Cor 2.3; Gal 1.7; 5.11 Gal 4.29; 6.12; 1 Cor 1.23

ise; he represents Jerusalem, which is free and has life. Christ is the true heir of the covenant made by God with Abraham and his offspring, and so are all those who belong to him. The son of the slave will not inherit what belongs to the son of the promise.
5.1 *Christ has set us free.* Christians obtain liberty through Jesus' work (4.3–5; Col 1.13). True liberty consists in freedom from the law (Rom 7.6; 8.2), from the curse of the law (3.13), from the fear of death (Heb 2.15), from sin (Rom 6.7,18), and from the O.T. ceremonial laws (4.3; Col 2.20). But liberty must not become license; we must not be antinomians (see note on Rom 6.1ff). Liberty brings believers by voluntary choice into total submission to Jesus Christ and his will for us. The grand paradox of Scripture is that those who are slaves of Jesus Christ (see notes on Rom 1.1; 6.16) have the greatest freedom.

5.2 The Judaizers said that one must be circumcised and keep the law in order to be saved. To Paul, those who do this forfeit all rights in Jesus Christ. Christ will not benefit them, for ultimately they are relying on themselves rather than on the Lord.
5.5 *the hope of righteousness.* The hope of righteousness is the happiness we know we will receive in the world to come. But this must be qualified by two facts. (1) This hope is ours by faith, not by the works of the law. (2) This belongs to us through the Spirit, who is the author of salvation, our teacher, and the source of our hope.
5.6 If we are in Christ by faith, neither circumcision nor uncircumcision has any value. In other words, circumcision is a matter of indifference. In Christ the law no longer exercises dominion over us.

B. *Freedom defined*

5.13
1 Cor 8.9;
1 Pet 2.16;
1 Cor 9.19
5.14
Lev 19.18;
Mt 7.12;
22.39;
Rom 13.8

13　For you were called to freedom, brothers and sisters;*g* only do not use your freedom as an opportunity for self-indulgence,*h* but through love become slaves to one another. 14 For the whole law is summed up in a single commandment, "You shall love your neighbor as yourself." 15 If, however, you bite and devour one another, take care that you are not consumed by one another.

C. *Liberty in practice*

5.16
Rom 8.4;
vv. 24, 25;
Eph 2.3
5.17
Rom 7.15-23
5.18
Rom 6.14
5.19
Eph 5.3;
Col 3.5
5.21
1 Cor 6.9

16　Live by the Spirit, I say, and do not gratify the desires of the flesh. 17 For what the flesh desires is opposed to the Spirit, and what the Spirit desires is opposed to the flesh; for these are opposed to each other, to prevent you from doing what you want. 18 But if you are led by the Spirit, you are not subject to the law. 19 Now the works of the flesh are obvious: fornication, impurity, licentiousness, 20 idolatry, sorcery, enmities, strife, jealousy, anger, quarrels, dissensions, factions, 21 envy,*i* drunkenness, carousing, and things like these. I am warning you, as I warned you before: those who do such things will not inherit the kingdom of God.

5.22
Eph 5.9;
Col 3.12-15;
1 Cor 13.7
5.24
Rom 6.6
5.25
Rom 8.4
5.26
Phil 2.3

22　By contrast, the fruit of the Spirit is love, joy, peace, patience, kindness, generosity, faithfulness, 23 gentleness, and self-control. There is no law against such things. 24 And those who belong to Christ Jesus have crucified the flesh with its passions and desires. 25 If we live by the Spirit, let us also be guided by the Spirit. 26 Let us not become conceited, competing against one another, envying one another.

D. *Exhortations and warnings*

6.2
Rom 15.1;
Jas 2.8
6.3
Rom 12.3;
1 Cor 8.2;
2 Cor 3.5
6.4
1 Cor 11.28;
Phil 1.26
6.6
1 Cor 9.11
6.7
1 Cor 6.9;
Job 13.9
6.8
Hos 8.7;
Jas 3.18
6.9
1 Cor 15.58;
Heb 3.6;
Rev 2.10
6.10
Jn 9.4;
Titus 3.8;
Eph 2.19

6　My friends,*j* if anyone is detected in a transgression, you who have received the Spirit should restore such a one in a spirit of gentleness. Take care that you yourselves are not tempted. 2 Bear one another's burdens, and in this way you will fulfill*k* the law of Christ. 3 For if those who are nothing think they are something, they deceive themselves. 4 All must test their own work; then that work, rather than their neighbor's work, will become a cause for pride. 5 For all must carry their own loads.

6　Those who are taught the word must share in all good things with their teacher.

7　Do not be deceived; God is not mocked, for you reap whatever you sow. 8 If you sow to your own flesh, you will reap corruption from the flesh; but if you sow to the Spirit, you will reap eternal life from the Spirit. 9 So let us not grow weary in doing what is right, for we will reap at harvest time, if we do not give up. 10 So then, whenever we have an opportunity,

g Gk *brothers*　*h* Gk *the flesh*　*i* Other ancient authorities add *murder*　*j* Gk *Brothers*　*k* Other ancient authorities read *in this way fulfill*

5.13,14 Believers are called to freedom, but we must not make this an occasion to serve the passions of our human nature. That is, we are freed from the curse of the law but not from the moral law of God. God's will for how we relate to other people is summarized in Lev 19.18: we must love our neighbors as we love ourselves.

5.22ff The true evidence of a holy or sanctified life becomes evident when the fruit of the Spirit is manifested in the believer's life.

5.25 If Christians claim to have received the Spirit of Christ, the only way the world can tell this is by their living a Spirit-filled life. This is the inheritance and the privilege of all who have accepted Jesus as Savior and Lord (cf. Acts 2.38).

6.1 *restore such a one.* It is the responsibility of Spirit-filled Christians to restore those who have gone astray. What an erring brother or sister must do to be

brought back into fellowship with God is confess the sin (1 Jn 1.9); apply the blood of Jesus for cleansing (1 Jn 1.7); and, in some cases, make repayment or restitution (Lk 19.8,9).

6.2 The law of Christ is the law of love. We fulfill this law when we bear one another's burdens, which means to comfort, counsel, and assist other believers as our circumstances allow. We must exercise a spirit of forgiveness and sympathy.

6.6 Paul expects believers to take good care of their ministers in the material things of life (cf. 1 Cor 9.4–14;; 1 Tim 5.17,18).

6.7ff There is a law of retribution written large in the universe, and no one can escape it: we shall reap as we have sown. For those who have done well, there will be a reward; for those who have done evil, punishment.

let us work for the good of all, and especially for those of the family of faith.

V. Conclusion (6.11–18)

A. Liberty and the cross

11 See what large letters I make when I am writing in my own hand! 12 It is those who want to make a good showing in the flesh that try to compel you to be circumcised — only that they may not be persecuted for the cross of Christ. 13 Even the circumcised do not themselves obey the law, but they want you to be circumcised so that they may boast about your flesh. 14 May I never boast of anything except the cross of our Lord Jesus Christ, by which[l] the world has been crucified to me, and I to the world. 15 For[m] neither circumcision nor uncircumcision is anything; but a new creation is everything! 16 As for those who will follow this rule — peace be upon them, and mercy, and upon the Israel of God.

B. The cost of liberty

17 From now on, let no one make trouble for me; for I carry the marks of Jesus branded on my body.

C. The benediction

18 May the grace of our Lord Jesus Christ be with your spirit, brothers and sisters.[n] Amen.

l Or through whom   m Other ancient authorities add in Christ Jesus   n Gk brothers

6.12
Mt 23.27, 28;
Acts 15.1;
Gal 5.11
6.13
Rom 2.25;
Phil 3.3
6.14
Gal 2.20;
Rom 6.2, 6
6.15
2 Cor 5.17

6.17
2 Cor 1.5

6.14 The Judaizers gloried in the law and circumcision. Paul gloried in the cross of Christ, and in nothing else. The cross was the basis of his hope and the sole content of his preaching (cf. 1 Cor 2.2).
6.15 True religion and salvation do not consist in circumcision or uncircumcision. Paul knows that people are neither helped nor hurt by circumcision (unless they make it necessary to salvation). The only thing that counts is being a new creation through faith in Christ (cf. 2 Cor 5.17), whereby we are justified before God.

INTRODUCTION TO
THE LETTER OF PAUL TO THE
EPHESIANS

Authorship, Date, and Background: Ephesians is one of the four "prison epistles" (also Colossians, Philippians, and Philemon). Since Paul was in prison a number of times, the question arises which of the many imprisonments was the locale from which these letters were sent to their destinations. Despite the difference of opinion, Rome is the most likely city, and the date of writing is A.D. 60–61.

Modern liberal scholars almost without exception think Paul did not write Ephesians. Evangelicals have generally thought he did. The case for non-Pauline authorship is tenuous, and the weight of evidence falls in favor of Pauline authorship. The most important fact is that the letter itself claims to be Pauline, for the salutation begins: "Paul, an apostle" (1.1). Thus, to say Paul did not write the letter is to disregard what the Bible itself says. To suppose that someone else would claim to be Paul, however high the motive, given the fact that God is the author of Scripture, is not credible. Any who maintain that what the Bible says is true must conclude that Paul indeed was the author of the letter.

Some of the ancient manuscripts leave out the phrase "in Ephesus"; this raises the question to whom the letter was addressed. A number of evangelical scholars say it was an "encyclical letter," by which is meant a letter probably intended for a number of churches in Asia, Ephesus included. Tychicus was Paul's messenger who brought the letter from Rome to Asia (6.21). Aristarchus, Epaphras, Luke, Demas, and Mark, were with Paul at the time of writing (cf. Col 4.7ff). The letter represents Paul's maturest thinking about the church. It also overlaps at points with Colossians, written during the same period.

Characteristics and Content: Ephesians comes at a point in time when many new churches have come into being. Paul, no doubt, has given great thought to the nature of the church, and under the guidance of the Holy Spirit he writes something unique. In this letter he talks about the church as a universal phenomenon, whereas in his other letters the word "church" refers to a local congregation. Ephesians presents an overview of God's plan of the ages. Paul speaks about the purpose of God from before the beginning of the world, and the certainty that the divine intention will be realized through Jesus Christ via the apostles and prophets.

Paul calls the church "his body,"i.e., the body of Christ (1.23). He also proclaims that it is the bride or wife of Christ (5.22ff) and the dwelling place (temple) of the Holy Spirit (2.19–22). Christ is the head over the church and all believers, Jew and Gentile alike, are members of the body. This church includes believers of all ages, even those yet to come into it. Believers hear the good news that there is something beyond this earthly sphere—the "heavenly places" (1.3; 2.6; 3.10). This view of the church finds its fullest disclosure in Ephesians.

Ephesians also treats the work of the Holy Spirit in the lives of believers. In it we learn that believers are "marked with the seal of the promised Holy Spirit." (1.13); that Jew and Gentile have access to God the Father through the Holy Spirit (2.18); that the revelation of God's mystery of the ages has come to apostles and prophets by the Holy Spirit (3.5); that Paul prays that God may "grant that you may be strengthened in your inner being with power through his Spirit" (3.16); that we are to be careful not to "grieve the Holy Spirit of God" by the way we live (4.30); that we ought to, and therefore can, "be filled with the Spirit" (5.18); and that we should pray "in the Spirit at all times in every prayer and supplication" (6.18)

In Ephesians, believers are marked off as members of the new humanity, a world-wide family of redeemed sons and daughters who have peace with God and should be at peace with each other, rejoicing in and making use of the unfathomable riches we have in Jesus Christ.

Outline:

   I. Greeting (1.1,2)

  II. Doctrinal affirmations (1.3—3.21)

 III. Practical exhortations (4.1—6.20)

 IV. Conclusion (6.21—24)

THE LETTER OF PAUL TO THE
EPHESIANS

I. Greeting (1.1,2)

1.1 2 Cor 1.1; 1 Cor 1.1; Phil 1.1; Col 1.1, 2 **1.2** Rom 1.7	**1** Paul, an apostle of Christ Jesus by the will of God, To the saints who are in Ephesus and are faithful*a* in Christ Jesus: 2 Grace to you and peace from God our Father and the Lord Jesus Christ.

II. Doctrinal affirmations (1.3–3.21)

A. The origin of the church

1.3 2 Cor 1.3; Eph 2.6; 3.10; 6.12 **1.4** Eph 5.27; Col 1.22; Eph 4.2, 15, 16 **1.5** Rom 8.29f **1.7** Col 1.14 **1.9** Rom 16.25 **1.10** Gal 4.4; Col 1.16, 20 **1.11** Eph 3.11; Rom 9.11; Heb 6.17 **1.12** vv. 6, 14 **1.13** Col 1.5; Eph 4.30 **1.14** 2 Cor 1.22; Acts 20.32	3 Blessed be the God and Father of our Lord Jesus Christ, who has blessed us in Christ with every spiritual blessing in the heavenly places, 4 just as he chose us in Christ*b* before the foundation of the world to be holy and blameless before him in love. 5 He destined us for adoption as his children through Jesus Christ, according to the good pleasure of his will, 6 to the praise of his glorious grace that he freely bestowed on us in the Beloved. 7 In him we have redemption through his blood, the forgiveness of our trespasses, according to the riches of his grace 8 that he lavished on us. With all wisdom and insight 9 he has made known to us the mystery of his will, according to his good pleasure that he set forth in Christ, 10 as a plan for the fullness of time, to gather up all things in him, things in heaven and things on earth. 11 In Christ we have also obtained an inheritance,*c* having been destined according to the purpose of him who accomplishes all things according to his counsel and will, 12 so that we, who were the first to set our hope on Christ, might live for the praise of his glory. 13 In him you also, when you had heard the word of truth, the gospel of your salvation, and had believed in him, were marked with the seal of the promised Holy Spirit; 14 this*d* is the pledge of our inheritance toward redemption as God's own people, to the praise of his glory.

a Other ancient authorities lack *in Ephesus*, reading *saints who are also faithful* *b* Gk *in him* *c* Or *been made a heritage* *d* Other ancient authorities read *who*

1.3 *in the heavenly places* (or "the heavenlies," from the Greek *hoi epouranioi*; see 1.20; 2.6; 3.10; 6.12). This is the spiritual realm where Christ now reigns, his sacrifice having been accepted by the Father, where believers enjoy every spiritual blessing, and where Christians wage their warfare against the forces of Satan (6.12).
1.4 *he chose us.* The Scriptural doctrine of election is the outworking of God's power to effect what he chooses. Election is always according to God's sovereign purpose (v. 11; Rom 9.10–13). We are elected or chosen (1) to be adopted as sons and daughters of God (v. 5); (2) to obtain eternal glory (Rom 8.21); (3) to do good works (2.10); and (4) to become like Jesus (Rom 8.29). The relationship of election to salvation has been debated among Christians. Some maintain that the number of the elect is limited and that all of the elect come to know Jesus as Savior. Others say that if only those who are elected are saved, then Christ's redemption was limited. Still others reply that the call to salvation is universal and that the divine intention is to save all; therefore, election po-

tentially involves everyone, even when all do not accept Christ. Many teach that God's election is based on his foreknowledge (Rom 8.29), in the sense that God foresees who will believe in Jesus and chooses them on that basis. Regardless of one's view, Scripture is clear on two basic principles: (1) humans are free moral agents; (2) God sovereignly works out all things according to his own good pleasure.
1.7 Redemption includes the forgiveness of sins (cf. Col 1.14); justification or right standing with God (Rom 3.24); adoption into the family of God (Gal 4.4,5); and purification (Titus 2.14).
1.13 *the seal.* Whoever receives Jesus Christ as Savior is sealed by the Holy Spirit of God as a pledge or guarantee that we are his and that we will someday secure the full possession of that salvation (see also 2 Cor 1.22). Christ was the first one on whom "God the Father has set his seal" (Jn 6.27), done at his baptism when the Spirit rested on him. In addition to being sealed, believers are indwelt by the Spirit (1 Cor 3.16) and should be filled with the Spirit (5.18).

B. *Prayer for the Ephesians*

15 I have heard of your faith in the Lord Jesus and your love*e* toward all the saints, and for this reason 16 I do not cease to give thanks for you as I remember you in my prayers. 17 I pray that the God of our Lord Jesus Christ, the Father of glory, may give you a spirit of wisdom and revelation as you come to know him, 18 so that, with the eyes of your heart enlightened, you may know what is the hope to which he has called you, what are the riches of his glorious inheritance among the saints, 19 and what is the immeasurable greatness of his power for us who believe, according to the working of his great power. 20 God*f* put this power to work in Christ when he raised him from the dead and seated him at his right hand in the heavenly places, 21 far above all rule and authority and power and dominion, and above every name that is named, not only in this age but also in the age to come. 22 And he has put all things under his feet and has made him the head over all things for the church, 23 which is his body, the fullness of him who fills all in all.

C. *The building of the church*

2 You were dead through the trespasses and sins 2 in which you once lived, following the course of this world, following the ruler of the power of the air, the spirit that is now at work among those who are disobedient. 3 All of us once lived among them in the passions of our flesh, following the desires of flesh and senses, and we were by nature children of wrath, like everyone else. 4 But God, who is rich in mercy, out of the great love with which he loved us 5 even when we were dead through our trespasses, made us alive together with Christ*g* — by grace you have been saved — 6 and raised us up with him and seated us with him in the heavenly places in Christ Jesus, 7 so that in the ages to come he might show the immeasurable riches of his grace in kindness toward us in Christ Jesus. 8 For by grace you have been saved through faith, and this is not your own doing; it is the gift of God — 9 not the result of works, so that no one may boast. 10 For we are what he has made us, created in Christ Jesus for good works, which God prepared beforehand to be our way of life.

11 So then, remember that at one time you Gentiles by birth,*h* called "the uncircumcision" by those who are called "the circumcision" — a physical circumcision made in the flesh by human hands — 12 remember

e Other ancient authorities lack *and your love*   *f* Gk *He*   *g* Other ancient authorities read *in Christ*   *h* Gk *in the flesh*

1.15 Col 1.4; Eph 3.18
1.16 Rom 1.8, 9; Col 1.3, 9
1.17 Jn 20.17; Col 1.9
1.18 Acts 26.18; Eph 4.4
1.19 Col 1.29; Eph 6.10
1.20 Acts 2.24; Heb 1.3
1.21 Phil 2.9, 10
1.22 Mt 28.18; Eph 4.15; 5.23
1.23 Rom 12.5; Col 2.17
2.1 v. 5; Jn 5.24
2.2 Eph 6.12; 5.6
2.3 Gal 5.16, 17; Rom 2.14; 5.10
2.4 Rom 10.12
2.5 vv. 1, 8
2.6 Eph 1.20
2.7 Titus 3.4
2.8 Gal 2.16; v. 5
2.9 Rom 3.20, 28; 2 Tim 1.9
2.10 Eph 4.24; Titus 2.14
2.11 Rom 2.28; Col 2.11
2.12 1 Thess 4.5; Gal 4.8

1.22,23 *the church, which is his body.* The church universal includes all believers of all ages, from the beginning of time until the consummation of the age. It is the body of Christ, known only to God and yet is manifested in visible forms. The Scriptures uphold the unity of the church (Jn 17.11), but this is a spiritual unity, independent of all ecclesiastical organizations. Today there are many churches, including Roman Catholic, Eastern Orthodox, Lutheran, Anglican, Methodist, Presbyterian, Reformed, Baptist, etc. There is little likelihood that all of the churches that call themselves Christian will ever become one undivided church, although some insist that the visible churches should become one visibly as well as spiritually. Unity must always be based on the truth of God (4.4,14–16). (1) Christ's church was purchased with his blood (Acts 20.28); (2) all believers are baptized into the body (1 Cor 12.13); (3) it is a spiritual organism with many members (1 Cor 12.12); and (4) all members of the body are subject to Christ (5.24).

2.6 Paul says that believers sit with Christ in the heavenly realms right now, already sharing in his royal status and his sovereign power. Their life is hidden with Christ in God (Col 3.3), and their true citizenship is in heaven (Phil 3.20). They work to advance his kingdom on earth by their worship, prayers, witness, and missionary outreach.

2.8 *this is not your own doing.* Salvation is secured by faith alone; this excludes any and all human works of righteousness. True saving faith always has in it three elements, each of which is necessary: (1) knowledge, for no one is saved without knowing something (Rom 10.17); (2) mental consent to the knowledge, i.e., one is convinced in his or her mind that the good news is true; and (3) laying hold of Christ by a personal act of the will — i.e., receiving Jesus Christ as one's Savior (Jn 1.12). Moreover, true faith is never alone; it is always accompanied by good works, done as the fruit of faith. The absence of good works subsequent to salvation leaves open the question whether one has truly been regenerated.

2.12 *having no hope and without God.* To be without Christ is to be without God, and to be without God means having no ultimate hope in life. In other words, it is impossible to get to heaven through any other religion or by any other road. Christianity is the only true faith, and without it people are lost.

that you were at that time without Christ, being aliens from the commonwealth of Israel, and strangers to the covenants of promise, having no hope and without God in the world. 13 But now in Christ Jesus you who once were far off have been brought near by the blood of Christ. 14 For he is our peace; in his flesh he has made both groups into one and has broken down the dividing wall, that is, the hostility between us. 15 He has abolished the law with its commandments and ordinances, that he might create in himself one new humanity in place of the two, thus making peace, 16 and might reconcile both groups to God in one body[i] through the cross, thus putting to death that hostility through it.[j] 17 So he came and proclaimed peace to you who were far off and peace to those who were near; 18 for through him both of us have access in one Spirit to the Father. 19 So then you are no longer strangers and aliens, but you are citizens with the saints and also members of the household of God, 20 built upon the foundation of the apostles and prophets, with Christ Jesus himself as the cornerstone.[k] 21 In him the whole structure is joined together and grows into a holy temple in the Lord; 22 in whom you also are built together spiritually[l] into a dwelling place for God.

D. *The function of the church*

3 This is the reason that I Paul am a prisoner for[m] Christ Jesus for the sake of you Gentiles — 2 for surely you have already heard of the commission of God's grace that was given me for you, 3 and how the mystery was made known to me by revelation, as I wrote above in a few words, 4 a reading of which will enable you to perceive my understanding of the mystery of Christ. 5 In former generations this mystery[n] was not made known to humankind, as it has now been revealed to his holy apostles and prophets by the Spirit: 6 that is, the Gentiles have become fellow heirs, members of the same body, and sharers in the promise in Christ Jesus through the gospel.

7 Of this gospel I have become a servant according to the gift of God's grace that was given me by the working of his power. 8 Although I am the very least of all the saints, this grace was given to me to bring to the Gentiles the news of the boundless riches of Christ, 9 and to make everyone see[o] what is the plan of the mystery hidden for ages in[p] God who created all things; 10 so that through the church the wisdom of God in its rich variety might now be made known to the rulers and authorities in the heavenly places. 11 This was in accordance with the eternal purpose that he has carried out in Christ Jesus our Lord, 12 in whom we have access to God in boldness and confidence through faith in him.[q] 13 I pray therefore that you[r] may not lose heart over my sufferings for you; they are your glory.

14 For this reason I bow my knees before the Father,[s] 15 from whom every family[t] in heaven and on earth takes its name. 16 I pray that,

---

i Or reconcile both of us in one body for God   j Or in him, or in himself   k Or keystone   l Gk in the Spirit   m Or of   n Gk it   o Other ancient authorities read to bring to light   p Or by   q Or the faith of him   r Or I   s Other ancient authorities add of our Lord Jesus Christ   t Gk fatherhood

---

2.18 Through Jesus Christ, i.e., in his name and by virtue of his atoning sacrifice, all believers have access to the holy presence of Almighty God. They draw near to him by the Spirit.
3.1 *I Paul am a prisoner for Christ Jesus.* When he wrote this letter, Paul was in prison for having preached Christ. But he is a prisoner in another sense: as Christ's servant, he has come under the total control of Christ. He is a prisoner *of* Christ (cf. NRSV footnote).
3.5 *this mystery . . . revealed.* Jews and Gentiles are one body in Christ and are thus fellow-heirs in the kingdom. In the O.T. God had hinted that this was

his plan (e.g., Gen 12.2,3), but only now is this mystery fully revealed. Revelation is progressive, and some things hidden in former ages have now been made clear.
3.8 Paul magnifies his office as an apostle privileged to preach the gospel, and at the same time he humbly speaks of himself as the very least of all the saints (see also 1 Tim 1.12–17).
3.12 Through Christ, justified and righteous sinners can come to God by faith, without fear. God will not reject those who come, but will receive them, hear them, and help them (see note on 2.18).

according to the riches of his glory, he may grant that you may be strengthened in your inner being with power through his Spirit, 17 and that Christ may dwell in your hearts through faith, as you are being rooted and grounded in love. 18 I pray that you may have the power to comprehend, with all the saints, what is the breadth and length and height and depth, 19 and to know the love of Christ that surpasses knowledge, so that you may be filled with all the fullness of God.

20   Now to him who by the power at work within us is able to accomplish abundantly far more than all we can ask or imagine, 21 to him be glory in the church and in Christ Jesus to all generations, forever and ever. Amen.

III. Practical exhortations (4.1–6.20)

A. The unity of the church

4 I therefore, the prisoner in the Lord, beg you to lead a life worthy of the calling to which you have been called, 2 with all humility and gentleness, with patience, bearing with one another in love, 3 making every effort to maintain the unity of the Spirit in the bond of peace. 4 There is one body and one Spirit, just as you were called to the one hope of your calling, 5 one Lord, one faith, one baptism, 6 one God and Father of all, who is above all and through all and in all.

7   But each of us was given grace according to the measure of Christ's gift. 8 Therefore it is said,
   "When he ascended on high he made captivity itself a captive;
   he gave gifts to his people."
9 (When it says, "He ascended," what does it mean but that he had also descended ᵘ into the lower parts of the earth? 10 He who descended is the same one who ascended far above all the heavens, so that he might fill all things.) 11 The gifts he gave were that some would be apostles, some prophets, some evangelists, some pastors and teachers, 12 to equip the saints for the work of ministry, for building up the body of Christ, 13 until all of us come to the unity of the faith and of the knowledge of the Son of God, to maturity, to the measure of the full stature of Christ. 14 We must no longer be children, tossed to and fro and blown about by every wind of doctrine, by people's trickery, by their craftiness in deceitful scheming. 15 But speaking the truth in love, we must grow up in every way into him who is the head, into Christ, 16 from whom the whole body, joined and knit together by every ligament with which it is equipped, as each part is working properly, promotes the body's growth in building itself up in love.

B. The moral standards of the church

17   Now this I affirm and insist on in the Lord: you must no longer live as the Gentiles live, in the futility of their minds. 18 They are darkened

ᵘ Other ancient authorities add *first*

3.17
Jn 14.23;
Col 1.23
3.18
Eph 1.18;
Job 11.8, 9
3.19
Col 2.10;
Eph 1.23
3.20
Rom 16.25
3.21
Rom 11.36

4.1
Eph 3.1;
Col 1.10
4.2
Col 3.12;
Eph 1.4
4.3
Col 3.14
4.4
1 Cor 12.12;
Eph 2.16;
1.18
4.6
Rom 11.36
4.7
Rom 12.3
4.8
Ps 68.18;
Judg 5.12;
Col 2.15
4.9
Jn 3.13
4.11
1 Cor 12.28
4.12
2 Cor 13.9;
Eph 1.23;
1 Cor 12.27
4.13
Col 2.2;
1 Cor 14.20;
Col 1.28
4.14
1 Cor 14.20;
Jas 1.6;
Eph 6.11
4.15
2 Cor 4.2;
Eph 1.22;
Col 1.18
4.17
Col 3.7;
1 Pet 4.3;
Rom 1.21
4.18
Eph 2.1, 12;
2 Cor 3.14

3.20   God *is able* to accomplish abundantly far more than all we can ask or imagine. He is also *willing* to do this. The God many Christians worship is too small. We need to understand that he is greater than we can possibly imagine.
4.3,4   Believers constitute one body, and we must be eager to keep the unity of that body. Unity, however, can exist in the midst of diversity (see note on 1.22,23).
4.11,12   The visible church must have organization and leadership. Christ through the Holy Spirit provides the church with leaders: apostles, prophets, evangelists, pastors, and teachers. Their basic task is

to equip the saints to build up Christ's body, i.e., to encourage believers, strengthen them, and show them how to be conformed to the image of Christ.
4.14   Paul here emphasizes the importance of correct doctrine. Every Christian should know the great doctrines of the faith, for peace without agreement in the essential truths of Scripture will destroy the foundations of the faith, and believers who are doctrinally ignorant become a ripe target for false teachers. But doctrine is not sufficient, for doctrine without love is mere formalism. Right doctrine and love should go hand in hand.

in their understanding, alienated from the life of God because of their ignorance and hardness of heart. 19 They have lost all sensitivity and have abandoned themselves to licentiousness, greedy to practice every kind of impurity. 20 That is not the way you learned Christ! 21 For surely you have heard about him and were taught in him, as truth is in Jesus. 22 You were taught to put away your former way of life, your old self, corrupt and deluded by its lusts, 23 and to be renewed in the spirit of your minds, 24 and to clothe yourselves with the new self, created according to the likeness of God in true righteousness and holiness.

25　So then, putting away falsehood, let all of us speak the truth to our neighbors, for we are members of one another. 26 Be angry but do not sin; do not let the sun go down on your anger, 27 and do not make room for the devil. 28 Thieves must give up stealing; rather let them labor and work honestly with their own hands, so as to have something to share with the needy. 29 Let no evil talk come out of your mouths, but only what is useful for building up,*v* as there is need, so that your words may give grace to those who hear. 30 And do not grieve the Holy Spirit of God, with which you were marked with a seal for the day of redemption. 31 Put away from you all bitterness and wrath and anger and wrangling and slander, together with all malice, 32 and be kind to one another, tenderhearted, forgiving one another, as God in Christ has forgiven you.*w* 1 Therefore be imitators of God, as beloved children, 2 and live in love, as Christ loved us*x* and gave himself up for us, a fragrant offering and sacrifice to God.

3　But fornication and impurity of any kind, or greed, must not even be mentioned among you, as is proper among saints. 4 Entirely out of place is obscene, silly, and vulgar talk; but instead, let there be thanksgiving. 5 Be sure of this, that no fornicator or impure person, or one who is greedy (that is, an idolater), has any inheritance in the kingdom of Christ and of God.

6　Let no one deceive you with empty words, for because of these things the wrath of God comes on those who are disobedient. 7 Therefore do not be associated with them. 8 For once you were darkness, but now in the Lord you are light. Live as children of light — 9 for the fruit of the light is found in all that is good and right and true. 10 Try to find out what is pleasing to the Lord. 11 Take no part in the unfruitful works of darkness, but instead expose them. 12 For it is shameful even to mention what such people do secretly; 13 but everything exposed by the light becomes visible, 14 for everything that becomes visible is light. Therefore it says,

"Sleeper, awake!
　Rise from the dead,
　　and Christ will shine on you."

15　Be careful then how you live, not as unwise people but as wise, 16 making the most of the time, because the days are evil. 17 So do not be foolish, but understand what the will of the Lord is. 18 Do not get drunk

v Other ancient authorities read building up faith　w Other ancient authorities read us　x Other ancient authorities read you

---

4.25ff Beginning in v. 17, Paul defines in clear terms what right conduct is. In these verses he bans lying, anger, stealing, and corrupt use of the tongue. These must have been some of the common sins of the Ephesians.

4.30 *do not grieve the Holy Spirit of God.* The Spirit of God is grieved when we sin against God's law. Fellowship between Christ and us is thus interrupted, and we lose the Spirit's power and fullness. Elsewhere the Scriptures speak of quenching the Spirit (see note on 1 Thess 5.19), insulting the Spirit (Heb 10.29), and opposing the Spirit (Acts 7.51).

5.3ff Living in love (v. 2) means shunning fornication, impurity, greed, obscenity, vulgar talk, and the like. The Ephesian Christians must not associate with such people (v. 7). Paul goes on to indicate his delight that although these new believers were once living in darkness, they now have experienced the light of the gospel and are living as children of light (vv. 8,9).

5.18 Every believer is sealed with the Holy Spirit when born again (see note on 1.13). But not all believers are spiritual Christians; some are mere infants in Christ, living a life in the flesh (1 Cor 3.1–3). Thus Paul instructs believers to be filled with the Holy Spirit, establishing Christian maturity or the Spirit-filled life as the objective for every believer. This can be attained by (1) confessing all known sins (2 Cor 7.1; 1 Jn 1.7–9); (2) giving oneself over to God in

with wine, for that is debauchery; but be filled with the Spirit, 19 as you sing psalms and hymns and spiritual songs among yourselves, singing and making melody to the Lord in your hearts, 20 giving thanks to God the Father at all times and for everything in the name of our Lord Jesus Christ.

C. The Christian household

21 Be subject to one another out of reverence for Christ.

22 Wives, be subject to your husbands as you are to the Lord. 23 For the husband is the head of the wife just as Christ is the head of the church, the body of which he is the Savior. 24 Just as the church is subject to Christ, so also wives ought to be, in everything, to their husbands.

25 Husbands, love your wives, just as Christ loved the church and gave himself up for her, 26 in order to make her holy by cleansing her with the washing of water by the word, 27 so as to present the church to himself in splendor, without a spot or wrinkle or anything of the kind — yes, so that she may be holy and without blemish. 28 In the same way, husbands should love their wives as they do their own bodies. He who loves his wife loves himself. 29 For no one ever hates his own body, but he nourishes and tenderly cares for it, just as Christ does for the church, 30 because we are members of his body. y 31 "For this reason a man will leave his father and mother and be joined to his wife, and the two will become one flesh." 32 This is a great mystery, and I am applying it to Christ and the church. 33 Each of you, however, should love his wife as himself, and a wife should respect her husband.

6 Children, obey your parents in the Lord, z for this is right. 2 "Honor your father and mother" — this is the first commandment with a promise: 3 "so that it may be well with you and you may live long on the earth."

4 And, fathers, do not provoke your children to anger, but bring them up in the discipline and instruction of the Lord.

5 Slaves, obey your earthly masters with fear and trembling, in single-ness of heart, as you obey Christ; 6 not only while being watched, and in order to please them, but as slaves of Christ, doing the will of God from the heart. 7 Render service with enthusiasm, as to the Lord and not to men and women, 8 knowing that whatever good we do, we will receive the same again from the Lord, whether we are slaves or free.

9 And, masters, do the same to them. Stop threatening them, for you know that both of you have the same Master in heaven, and with him there is no partiality.

D. The church's warfare

10 Finally, be strong in the Lord and in the strength of his power.

y Other ancient authorities add of his flesh and of his bones z Other ancient authorities lack in the Lord

5.18
Prov 20.1;
Lk 1.15
5.19
Col 3.16;
Acts 16.25
5.20
Ps 34.1;
Heb 13.15

5.22
Gen 3.16;
Eph 6.5
5.23
1 Cor 11.3;
Col 1.18;
Eph 1.23
5.24
Col 3.18
5.25
Col 3.19
5.26
Titus 3.5
5.27
Col 1.22;
Eph 1.4
5.28
v. 25
5.30
1 Cor 6.15;
Eph 1.23
5.31
Gen 2.24;
Mt 19.5;
1 Cor 6.16
5.32
Col 3.19;
1 Pet 3.6
6.1
Col 3.20
6.2
Deut 5.16
6.4
Col 3.21;
Gen 18.19
6.5
Col 3.22;
1 Tim 6.1;
Phil 2.12;
1 Chr 29.17
6.7
Col 3.23
6.9
Lev 25.43;
Jn 13.13;
Col 3.25

6.10
1 Cor 16.13;
Eph 1.19

total sacrifice (Rom 6.13; 12.1); (3) asking God to fill one's heart and believing he will fill those who confess their sins and surrender their lives to him (Rom 4.20–22); (4) embracing the promise that the Holy Spirit has filled them; and (5) going out to live as those who have been filled with the Holy Spirit.

5.22 See note on Titus 2.4.

5.23ff This passage sets forth most clearly the teach-ing that the church is the bride of Christ. The idea of God being married to his people is implicit in Isaiah (see Isa 54.5,6) and in Hosea, who denounced the spiritual adultery of Israel. Jesus used the analogy of the bridegroom in his teachings (Mt 9.15; 25.1–13; Lk 5.34,35). In Revelation, John likened the new Jerusalem to a bride adorned for her husband.

6.1 Citing the O.T. law, Paul commands children to

obey their parents. But when the orders of parents conflict with the laws of God, even children are not required to obey. Obedience is "in the Lord." If a parent orders a child to steal, lie, or cheat, this is contrary to the express will of God and should not be complied with (see also note on Ezek 20.18).

6.5ff Christian slaves have two masters: one is their earthly master and the other their heavenly master, Jesus Christ. They must therefore serve their earthly master as though they are serving Christ, in singleness of heart, doing the will of God. Beginning at v. 9 Paul admonishes Christian masters to treat their slaves ac-cording to the rules of God, for both slaves and mas-ters belong to the same master, who shows no partial-ity in favor of or against either of them.

6.10ff God's children are soldiers; Jesus is the com-

6.11
1 Cor 16.21
6.12
1 Cor 9.25;
Rom 8.38

6.13
2 Cor 10.4;
Eph 5.16
6.14
Isa 11.5;
59.17
6.15
Isa 52.7
6.16
1 Jn 5.4
6.17
Isa 59.17;
Heb 4.12
6.18
Lk 18.1;
Mt 26.41;
Phil 1.4
6.19
Acts 4.29;
2 Cor 3.12
6.20
2 Cor 5.20;
Phil 1.20

6.21
Acts 20.4

6.23
1 Pet 5.14;
Gal 5.6

¹¹ Put on the whole armor of God, so that you may be able to stand against the wiles of the devil. ¹² For our*a* struggle is not against enemies of blood and flesh, but against the rulers, against the authorities, against the cosmic powers of this present darkness, against the spiritual forces of evil in the heavenly places. ¹³ Therefore take up the whole armor of God, so that you may be able to withstand on that evil day, and having done everything, to stand firm. ¹⁴ Stand therefore, and fasten the belt of truth around your waist, and put on the breastplate of righteousness. ¹⁵ As shoes for your feet put on whatever will make you ready to proclaim the gospel of peace. ¹⁶ With all of these,*b* take the shield of faith, with which you will be able to quench all the flaming arrows of the evil one. ¹⁷ Take the helmet of salvation, and the sword of the Spirit, which is the word of God.

18   Pray in the Spirit at all times in every prayer and supplication. To that end keep alert and always persevere in supplication for all the saints. ¹⁹ Pray also for me, so that when I speak, a message may be given to me to make known with boldness the mystery of the gospel,*c* ²⁰ for which I am an ambassador in chains. Pray that I may declare it boldly, as I must speak.

IV. Conclusion (6.21–24)

21   So that you also may know how I am and what I am doing, Tychicus will tell you everything. He is a dear brother and a faithful minister in the Lord. ²² I am sending him to you for this very purpose, to let you know how we are, and to encourage your hearts.

23   Peace be to the whole community,*d* and love with faith, from God the Father and the Lord Jesus Christ. ²⁴ Grace be with all who have an undying love for our Lord Jesus Christ.*e*

a Other ancient authorities read *your*   *b* Or *In all circumstances*   *c* Other ancient authorities lack *of the gospel*   *d* Gk *to the brothers*   *e* Other ancient authorities add *Amen*

---

manding officer; the cross is the banner; Satan is the great adversary. Here God indicates how the soldiers of the cross must be armored and how they are to fight. God has provided spiritual armor to protect Christians and has placed in their hands a sword, the word of God, with which to conquer and overcome evil.
6.11 *the devil.* See note on Ezek 28.12.
6.18 God gives various instructions on prayer in the Bible. Among them are: (1) pray to God the Father (Heb 11.6); (2) pray in the name of Jesus (see Jn 14.6); (3) pray in the Spirit (v. 18); (4) pray according to the will of God (1 Jn 5.14,15); (5) pray in faith (3:20; Jas 1.6); (6) pray earnestly (Lk 6.12); and (7) pray without display or hypocrisy (Mt 6.5). Elements in prayer include: adoration of God; thanksgiving to God; confession of one's sin; petition (praying for one's own needs); intercession (praying for the needs of others).
6.19 *Pray also for me.* Paul does not ask the Ephesians to pray for his physical deliverance from prison. Rather, he asks for boldness so that he may proclaim the good news which has been entrusted to him. Implicit in this request is the principle that believers should share their faith whatever their temporal situation is.
6.21 Tychicus, described by Paul as a "beloved brother, a faithful minister, and a fellow servant in the Lord" (Col 4.7), was a good friend and able helper of Paul. When Paul was imprisoned, it was Tychicus who delivered letters to the Ephesians and the Colossians. He encouraged these Christian believers and informed them concerning the welfare of the apostle (cf. Col 4.8). Later Paul sent Tychicus to Ephesus to minister there when Paul was in jail in Rome (2 Tim 4.12).

INTRODUCTION TO

THE LETTER OF PAUL TO THE

PHILIPPIANS

Authorship, Date, and Background: It has been universally recognized that Paul wrote this letter to the Christians in Philippi, and there are no good reasons to question it. It is a "prison letter" (see introduction to Ephesians). This letter was composed around A.D. 60-61, possibly from Rome. Other cities (e.g., Ephesus and Caesarea) have also been suggested; if either of these is correct, the date of writing would be earlier.

A special relationship developed between Paul and the Philippian church. He came to Philippi on his second missionary journey, believing that God had specifically called him and his co-workers to preach in Macedonia. Paul had a vision involving "a man of Macedonia pleading with him and saying, 'Come over to Macedonia and help us.' " Paul took this vision to mean "that God had called us to proclaim the good news to them" (Acts 16.9,10). Thus Paul began his missionary work in Europe. Many were converted and churches were founded in Europe as a result of his prompt response to that vision. Philippi had few Jewish residents, not enough to form a synagogue. Thus the church became a Gentile church, which had for its early members Lydia, the Roman jailer, and probably the demon-possessed slave girl whose deliverance brought about the beatings of Paul and Silas (Acts 16.11ff). Clement, Euodia, and Syntyche (4.2,3) were won to Christ either at this time or later. When Paul departed from Philippi, Luke remained there to carry on the ministry (see Acts 16.11–40).

Paul had close ties with this church. He visited Philippi at the end of his third missionary tour, prior to spending the winter at Corinth (Acts 20.1-3; 2 Cor 11.9). With the coming of spring he returned to Philippi where he spent the passover season among these beloved friends (Acts 20.3,6). This letter of Philippians is one of the most personal ones that he wrote.

Characteristics and Content: Paul writes a letter to his beloved friends at Philippi who have assisted him materially in the spread of the gospel by their gifts for his work. "I rejoice in the Lord greatly that now at last you have revived your concern for me" (4.10). Paul well knows that those who have helped him will be properly rewarded as though they themselves had preached the good news to the people he has reached.

Several key words occur throughout this short letter. One is "the gospel," which he refers to nine times: the Philippians have helped him in the spread of the gospel (1.5), his imprisonment furthers the gospel (1.12), the brethren are more bold to speak the word of God (1.14), the Philippians strive "for the faith of the gospel" (1.27), and he appreciates the women who labored with him in the gospel (4.3). A second key idea of this letter has to do with joy and rejoicing. Paul prays for them with joy (1.4); he will continue to live for their joy (1.25); he urges them to unity, to be of the same mind, to fulfill his joy (2.2); and he tells them, "Rejoice in the Lord, always; again I will say, Rejoice" (4.4; cf. 3.1).

Paul speaks about advancing the faith in the midst of suffering, even as he faces death. He exhorts us to live a holy life, holds forth Jesus as our example, and defines the believers' Christian duties. Along with exhortations, he mentions he will send Timothy and Epaphroditus to them. The latter has been sick unto death, but God has preserved him. He closes with the admonition that they always be full of joy (4.4), thanks them for their gift, and assures them that God will give them peace (4.7), power (4.13), and provision (4.19).

Outline:

I. Introduction (1.1–11)

II. Paul's personal circumstances (1.12–30)

III. The Christian life (2.1–18)

IV. The coming of Timothy and Epaphroditus (2.19–30)

V. Exhortation and doctrine (3.1–4.9)

VI. Acknowledgement of the Philippian gift (4.10–20)

VII. Conclusion (4.21–23)

THE LETTER OF PAUL TO THE

PHILIPPIANS

I. Introduction (1.1–11)

A. Greeting

1 Paul and Timothy, servants*a* of Christ Jesus,
To all the saints in Christ Jesus who are in Philippi, with the bishops*b* and deacons:*c*

2 Grace to you and peace from God our Father and the Lord Jesus Christ.

B. Thanksgiving and prayer

3 I thank my God every time I remember you, 4 constantly praying with joy in every one of my prayers for all of you, 5 because of your sharing in the gospel from the first day until now. 6 I am confident of this, that the one who began a good work among you will bring it to completion by the day of Jesus Christ. 7 It is right for me to think this way about all of you, because you hold me in your heart,*d* for all of you share in God's grace*e* with me, both in my imprisonment and in the defense and confirmation of the gospel. 8 For God is my witness, how I long for all of you with the compassion of Christ Jesus. 9 And this is my prayer, that your love may overflow more and more with knowledge and full insight 10 to help you to determine what is best, so that in the day of Christ you may be pure and blameless, 11 having produced the harvest of righteousness that comes through Jesus Christ for the glory and praise of God.

II. Paul's personal circumstances (1.12–30)

12 I want you to know, beloved,*f* that what has happened to me has actually helped to spread the gospel, 13 so that it has become known throughout the whole imperial guard*g* and to everyone else that my imprisonment is for Christ; 14 and most of the brothers and sisters,*f* having been made confident in the Lord by my imprisonment, dare to speak the word*h* with greater boldness and without fear.

15 Some proclaim Christ from envy and rivalry, but others from goodwill. 16 These proclaim Christ out of love, knowing that I have been put here for the defense of the gospel; 17 the others proclaim Christ out of selfish ambition, not sincerely but intending to increase my suffering

a Gk *slaves*   *b* Or *overseers*   *c* Or *overseers and helpers*   *d* Or *because I hold you in my heart*   *e* Gk *in grace*
f Gk *brothers*   *g* Gk *whole praetorium*   *h* Other ancient authorities read *word of God*

1.1
2 Cor 1.1;
Acts 16.1;
1 Cor 1.2
1.2
1 Pet 1.2

1.3
1 Cor 1.4
1.4
Rom 1.9
1.5
Acts 2.42;
16.17
1.6
v. 10
1.7
2 Pet 1.13;
2 Cor 7.3;
vv. 13, 14, 17
1.8
Rom 1.9;
Gal 1.20
1.9
1 Thess 3.12;
Col 1.9

1.13
Phil 4.22

1.14
v. 7

1.15
Phil 2.3
1.16
1 Cor 9.17;
v. 12
1.17
Phil 2.3

1.1 *bishops and deacons.* See notes on 1 Tim 3.8; Titus 1.5ff.
1.6 The *good work* referred to here begins with regeneration and springs from the grace of God who gives life in Jesus Christ to those who are dead in trespasses and sins (Eph 2.1). God, who begins this good work, will not rest until the work is completed *by the day of Jesus Christ,* i.e., at his second advent.
1.12 Some might suppose that when a servant of God is laid up for any reason, this hinders God's work, but Paul here affirms that even his apparent defeats and disasters actually furthered the work of God.

1.13 *The imperial guard* was a select group of soldiers organized first by Augustus in 2 B.C. Numbering nine or ten thousand men, they were attached to the emperor's palace and to the palaces of provincial governors and procurators.
1.15ff Paul suffered from false friends as well as open enemies. They considered him a rival, were envious of his apostleship and success, and hoped to add affliction to what he was already suffering. But his mind and heart were at ease for one reason: at least they were preaching Christ, and in this he rejoiced. Let God judge the motivation that directed their actions.

in my imprisonment. 18 What does it matter? Just this, that Christ is proclaimed in every way, whether out of false motives or true; and in that I rejoice.

Yes, and I will continue to rejoice, 19 for I know that through your prayers and the help of the Spirit of Jesus Christ this will turn out for my deliverance. 20 It is my eager expectation and hope that I will not be put to shame in any way, but that by my speaking with all boldness, Christ will be exalted now as always in my body, whether by life or by death. 21 For to me, living is Christ and dying is gain. 22 If I am to live in the flesh, that means fruitful labor for me; and I do not know which I prefer. 23 I am hard pressed between the two: my desire is to depart and be with Christ, for that is far better; 24 but to remain in the flesh is more necessary for you. 25 Since I am convinced of this, I know that I will remain and continue with all of you for your progress and joy in faith, 26 so that I may share abundantly in your boasting in Christ Jesus when I come to you again.

27 Only, live your life in a manner worthy of the gospel of Christ, so that, whether I come and see you or am absent and hear about you, I will know that you are standing firm in one spirit, striving side by side with one mind for the faith of the gospel, 28 and are in no way intimidated by your opponents. For them this is evidence of their destruction, but of your salvation. And this is God's doing. 29 For he has graciously granted you the privilege not only of believing in Christ, but of suffering for him as well — 30 since you are having the same struggle that you saw I had and now hear that I still have.

III. The Christian life (2.1–18)

A. Christ our example

2 If then there is any encouragement in Christ, any consolation from love, any sharing in the Spirit, any compassion and sympathy, 2 make my joy complete: be of the same mind, having the same love, being in full accord and of one mind. 3 Do nothing from selfish ambition or conceit, but in humility regard others as better than yourselves. 4 Let each of you look not to your own interests, but to the interests of others. 5 Let the same mind be in you that was[i] in Christ Jesus,

6 who, though he was in the form of God,
    did not regard equality with God
    as something to be exploited,
7 but emptied himself,
    taking the form of a slave,
    being born in human likeness.
And being found in human form,
8 he humbled himself
    and became obedient to the point of death —
    even death on a cross.

9 Therefore God also highly exalted him

[i] Or that you have

Cross references (margin)

1.19 2 Cor 1.11
1.20 Rom 8.19; 5.5; Eph 6.19
1.23 2 Cor 5.8; 2 Tim 4.6
1.26 2 Cor 1.14; 5.12
1.28 2 Thess 1.5; Rom 8.17
1.29 Mt 5.12; Acts 14.22
1.30 1 Thess 2.2; Col 2.1; Acts 16.19
2.1 2 Cor 13.14; Col 3.12
2.2 Jn 3.29; Rom 12.16; 1 Pet 3.8
2.3 Gal 5.26; Rom 12.10; 1 Pet 5.5
2.4 Rom 15.1, 2
2.5 Mt 11.29; 1 Pet 2.21
2.6 Jn 1.1; 2 Cor 4.4; Jn 5.18
2.7 Jn 1.14; Gal 4.4; Heb 2.17
2.8 Mt 26.39; Jn 10.18; Heb 5.8
2.9 Acts 2.33; Heb 2.9; Eph 1.20, 21

1.20 Believers must affirm, as Paul did here, that our sole objective in life is to glorify Christ, even if this must be done by death. While we should never seek martyrdom, we should have a spirit of willingness to endure it, if it is the will of God.

2.7 *emptied himself.* This is the doctrine of *kenosis* (literally, "emptying"), a theological term applied to the incarnation of Christ. Taking the form of a slave, our Lord divested himself of some aspects pertaining to his divine state and assumed such human limitations as being hungry and thirsty and requiring sleep. It was a self-assumed limitation consistent with being a true human. Thus Jesus was the God-man — having in one person a truly human nature and a truly divine nature. We will never fully understand this great mystery, but it is one that pervades the Scriptures (cf. Mt 27.46; Mk 13.32; Lk 2.40–52; Jn 17.4; 2 Cor 8.9; Heb 4.15; 5.7,8).

and gave him the name
 that is above every name,
10 so that at the name of Jesus
  every knee should bend,
  in heaven and on earth and under the earth,
11 and every tongue should confess
  that Jesus Christ is Lord,
  to the glory of God the Father.

2.10
Mt 28.18;
Rom 14.11

2.11
Jn 13.13;
Acts 2.36

B. Duties of Christians

12 Therefore, my beloved, just as you have always obeyed me, not only in my presence, but much more now in my absence, work out your own salvation with fear and trembling; 13 for it is God who is at work in you, enabling you both to will and to work for his good pleasure.

14 Do all things without murmuring and arguing, 15 so that you may be blameless and innocent, children of God without blemish in the midst of a crooked and perverse generation, in which you shine like stars in the world. 16 It is by your holding fast to the word of life that I can boast on the day of Christ that I did not run in vain or labor in vain. 17 But even if I am being poured out as a libation over the sacrifice and the offering of your faith, I am glad and rejoice with all of you — 18 and in the same way you also must be glad and rejoice with me.

2.12f
Phil 1.5;
Eph 6.5
2.13
2 Cor 3.5
2.14
1 Cor 10.10;
Rom 14.1
2.15
Mt 5.45;
Eph 5.1; 5.8
2.16
2 Cor 1.14;
1 Thess 2.19
2.17
2 Tim 4.6;
Rom 15.16;
Col 1.24

IV. *The coming of Timothy and Epaphroditus (2.19–30)*

19 I hope in the Lord Jesus to send Timothy to you soon, so that I may be cheered by news of you. 20 I have no one like him who will be genuinely concerned for your welfare. 21 All of them are seeking their own interests, not those of Jesus Christ. 22 But Timothy's[j] worth you know, how like a son with a father he has served with me in the work of the gospel. 23 I hope therefore to send him as soon as I see how things go with me; 24 and I trust in the Lord that I will also come soon.

25 Still, I think it necessary to send to you Epaphroditus — my brother and co-worker and fellow soldier, your messenger[k] and minister to my need; 26 for he has been longing for[l] all of you, and has been distressed because you heard that he was ill. 27 He was indeed so ill that he nearly died. But God had mercy on him, and not only on him but on me also, so that I would not have one sorrow after another. 28 I am the more eager to send him, therefore, in order that you may rejoice at seeing him again, and that I may be less anxious. 29 Welcome him then in the Lord with all joy, and honor such people, 30 because he came close to death for the work of Christ,[m] risking his life to make up for those services that you could not give me.

2.19
Rom 16.21
2.20
1 Cor 16.10
2.21
1 Cor 10.24;
13.5
2.22
1 Cor 4.17;
1 Tim 1.2
2.24
Phil 1.25
2.25
Phil 4.18;
Philem 2
2.26
Phil 1.8

2.29
1 Cor 16.18;
1 Tim 5.17
2.30
1 Cor 16.17

j Gk *his*   *k* Gk *apostle*   *l* Other ancient authorities read *longing to see*   *m* Other ancient authorities read *of the Lord*

2.12,13 Paul speaks in one breath both of the sovereignty of God and of the free agency of believers. We are responsible for living the Christian life, yet it is really God who is working in us. How these two apparently contradictory ideas can both be true is impossible for us to understand, though it is expressed repeatedly in the Scriptures.
2.14 The Christian's testimony is enhanced by an equable temper and proper behavior. Paul specifies two things here: we should cheerfully do the will of God, not grumbling against it; and we should not engage in useless disputes with fellow believers and so destroy our harmony and unity.

2.19–24 Paul planned to send Timothy to them to find out how they were faring. He praised his assistant by saying that he had been tried and proven to be a worthy servant of the Lord. Timothy cared for the Philippians more than he cared for himself.
2.25ff *Epaphroditus* was a highly respected member of the Philippian church. He had brought an offering to Paul from the church and was commissioned to stay with the apostle to help him. He became ill, probably from overextending himself to fulfill his ministry. Following a slow recovery, he was sent by Paul back to Philippi, being commended as a brother, co-worker, and fellow soldier.

V. *Exhortation and doctrine (3.1–4.9)*

A. *The example of Paul*

3 Finally, my brothers and sisters,[n] rejoice[o] in the Lord.

To write the same things to you is not troublesome to me, and for you it is a safeguard. 2 Beware of the dogs, beware of the evil workers, beware of those who mutilate the flesh![p] 3 For it is we who are the circumcision, who worship in the Spirit of God[q] and boast in Christ Jesus and have no confidence in the flesh — 4 even though I, too, have reason for confidence in the flesh.

If anyone else has reason to be confident in the flesh, I have more: 5 circumcised on the eighth day, a member of the people of Israel, of the tribe of Benjamin, a Hebrew born of Hebrews; as to the law, a Pharisee; 6 as to zeal, a persecutor of the church; as to righteousness under the law, blameless.

7 Yet whatever gains I had, these I have come to regard as loss because of Christ. 8 More than that, I regard everything as loss because of the surpassing value of knowing Christ Jesus my Lord. For his sake I have suffered the loss of all things, and I regard them as rubbish, in order that I may gain Christ 9 and be found in him, not having a righteousness of my own that comes from the law, but one that comes through faith in Christ,[r] the righteousness from God based on faith. 10 I want to know Christ[s] and the power of his resurrection and the sharing of his sufferings by becoming like him in his death, 11 if somehow I may attain the resurrection from the dead.

12 Not that I have already obtained this or have already reached the goal;[t] but I press on to make it my own, because Christ Jesus has made me his own. 13 Beloved,[u] I do not consider that I have made it my own;[v] but this one thing I do: forgetting what lies behind and straining forward to what lies ahead, 14 I press on toward the goal for the prize of the heavenly[w] call of God in Christ Jesus. 15 Let those of us then who are mature be of the same mind; and if you think differently about anything, this too God will reveal to you. 16 Only let us hold fast to what we have attained.

B. *Warning against antinomianism*

17 Brothers and sisters,[u] join in imitating me, and observe those who live according to the example you have in us. 18 For many live as enemies of the cross of Christ; I have often told you of them, and now I tell you even with tears. 19 Their end is destruction; their god is the belly; and their glory is in their shame; their minds are set on earthly things. 20 But our citizenship[x] is in heaven, and it is from there that we are expecting a

---

n Gk *my brothers*   o Or *farewell*   p Gk *the mutilation*   q Other ancient authorities read *worship God in spirit*   r Or *through the faith of Christ*   s Gk *him*   t Or *have already been made perfect*   u Gk *Brothers*   v Other ancient authorities read *my own yet*   w Gk *upward*   x Or *commonwealth*

3.1 *rejoice in the Lord.* Paul encourages the Philippians to be happy and content with what they have in the Lord Jesus and in his grace. The more we rejoice in Jesus, the more we will desire to serve him and the less likely will be the chance of falling away from him.
3.3 True circumcision is not of the flesh but of the spirit (cf. Rom 2.25–29). True Christians worship in the Spirit, rejoice in Jesus Christ, and do not place confidence for salvation in their obedience to God's law.
3.7 Paul grew up a high-class Jew steeped in Judaism. At one time he had placed his confidence for salvation in being a circumcised Hebrew, a member of the tribe of Benjamin, a Pharisee who kept the law

blamelessly, and a persecutor of Christians. All these things he now considered worthless and useless when compared with what he had in Jesus Christ. Believers should say the same thing; whatever fame, fortune, attainments, and place in the community we have are nothing when compared to our standing in Jesus Christ.
3.20 *citizenship* (Gk. *politeuma*). The Christian has two citizenships: one on earth and the other in heaven. The citizenship of this world, where Satan rules, is transitory; heavenly citizenship, under the rule of God, is eternal. We wait for the coming of the Lord's kingdom on earth and the triumph of the crucified one over the principalities and powers.

3.1
Phil 4.4

3.2
Gal 5.15;
2 Cor 11.13
3.3
Rom 2.28,
29;
Gal 6.14, 15
3.5
Rom 11.1;
2 Cor 11.22
3.6
Acts 22.3;
Rom 10.5;
Lk 1.6
3.7
Mt 13.44;
Lk 14.33
3.8
Eph 4.13;
2 Pet 1.3
3.9
Rom 10.5;
9.30
3.10
Rom 6.3-5;
8.17
3.11
Acts 26.7
3.12
1 Tim 6.12;
1 Cor 13.10;
Acts 9.5, 6
3.13
Lk 9.62;
1 Cor 9.24
3.14
Heb 6.1;
2 Tim 1.9
3.15
1 Cor 2.6;
Gal 5.10
3.16
Rom 12.16;
Gal 6.16
3.17
1 Cor 4.16;
1 Pet 5.3
3.18
Acts 20.31;
Gal 6.14
3.19
2 Cor 11.15;
Rom 16.18;
6.21; 8.5, 6
3.20
Eph 2.19;
Col 3.1;
1 Cor 1.7

Savior, the Lord Jesus Christ. 21 He will transform the body of our humiliation[y] that it may be conformed to the body of his glory,[z] by the power that also enables him to make all things subject to himself. 4 1 Therefore, my brothers and sisters,[a] whom I love and long for, my joy and crown, stand firm in the Lord in this way, my beloved.

C. Exhortation concluded

2 I urge Euodia and I urge Syntyche to be of the same mind in the Lord. 3 Yes, and I ask you also, my loyal companion,[b] help these women, for they have struggled beside me in the work of the gospel, together with Clement and the rest of my co-workers, whose names are in the book of life. 4 Rejoice[c] in the Lord always; again I will say, Rejoice.[c] 5 Let your gentleness be known to everyone. The Lord is near. 6 Do not worry about anything, but in everything by prayer and supplication with thanksgiving let your requests be made known to God. 7 And the peace of God, which surpasses all understanding, will guard your hearts and your minds in Christ Jesus.

8 Finally, beloved,[d] whatever is true, whatever is honorable, whatever is just, whatever is pure, whatever is pleasing, whatever is commendable, if there is any excellence and if there is anything worthy of praise, think about[e] these things. 9 Keep on doing the things that you have learned and received and heard and seen in me, and the God of peace will be with you.

VI. Acknowledgment of the Philippian gift (4.10–20)

10 I rejoice[f] in the Lord greatly that now at last you have revived your concern for me; indeed, you were concerned for me, but had no opportunity to show it.[g] 11 Not that I am referring to being in need; for I have learned to be content with whatever I have. 12 I know what it is to have little, and I know what it is to have plenty. In any and all circumstances I have learned the secret of being well-fed and of going hungry, of having plenty and of being in need. 13 I can do all things through him who strengthens me. 14 In any case, it was kind of you to share my distress. 15 You Philippians indeed know that in the early days of the gospel, when I left Macedonia, no church shared with me in the matter of giving and receiving, except you alone. 16 For even when I was in Thessalonica, you sent me help for my needs more than once. 17 Not that I seek the gift, but I seek the profit that accumulates to your account. 18 I have been paid in full and have more than enough; I am fully satisfied, now that I have received from Epaphroditus the gifts you sent, a fragrant offering, a sacrifice acceptable and pleasing to God. 19 And my God will fully satisfy

y Or our humble bodies   z Or his glorious body   a Gk my brothers   b Or loyal Syzygus   c Or Farewell
d Gk brothers   e Gk take account of   f Gk I rejoiced   g Gk lacks to show it

3.21 1 Cor 15.43; Col 3.4; Eph 1.19
4.1 Phil 1.8; 1 Cor 16.13; Phil 1.27
4.2 Phil 2.2
4.3 Rom 16.3; Lk 10.20; Rev 3.5
4.4 Rom 12.12; Phil 3.1
4.5 Heb 10.37; Jas 5.8, 9
4.6 Mt 6.25; Eph 6.18
4.7 Jn 14.27; Col 3.15; 1 Pet 1.5
4.8 1 Pet 2.12; 1 Thess 5.22
4.9 Phil 3.17; Rom 15.33
4.11 1 Tim 6.6
4.12 1 Cor 4.11; 2 Cor 11.9
4.13 Jn 15.5; 2 Cor 12.9
4.14 Phil 1.7
4.15 2 Cor 11.8, 9
4.16 Acts 17.1; 1 Thess 2.9
4.17 Titus 3.14
4.18 Phil 2.25; 2 Cor 2.14
4.19 Ps 23.1; 2 Cor 9.8; Eph 1.7

4.2 Euodia and Syntyche, two female believers, were influential in the church at Philippi, where women were prominent (see Acts 16.12–15). But they had had a serious disagreement with each other, though we are not told of the cause of their estrangement. Paul wanted to bring them together again. Anything that separates us from our fellow believers should be dealt with as quickly as possible (cf. Mt 5.23–25).
4.3 Clement is singled out here from among the rest of Paul's co-workers. Presumably Paul hoped that he would be the one to help Euodia and Syntyche reconcile their differences. Paul held all three in respect as those whose names were included in the book of life.

4.6 Prayerlessness brings nothing but worry and insecurity, whereas prayer with thanksgiving brings a peace that passes all human understanding. This peace is independent of all outward circumstances, springing from the love of God for his people, for they know that he will answer their prayers according to his will and for their good (cf. Rom 8.28).
4.13 Paul speaks of three great promises of God in this chapter: the *peace* of God, which surpasses all understanding (v. 7), the *power* of God, by which we can do whatever God wants us to do (v. 13), and the *provision* of God, which satisfies every need of ours (v. 19).

4.20
Gal 1.4;
Rom 11.36

every need of yours according to his riches in glory in Christ Jesus. 20 To our God and Father be glory forever and ever. Amen.

VII. *Conclusion (4.21–23)*

21   Greet every saint in Christ Jesus. The friends[h] who are with me greet you. 22 All the saints greet you, especially those of the emperor's household.

23   The grace of the Lord Jesus Christ be with your spirit.[i]

[h] Gk brothers   [i] Other ancient authorities add *Amen*

4.22   *those of the emperor's household*, i.e., the Christian converts who belonged to the emperor's court. There were believers in the emperor's family, and these saints in high places were willing to join with

Paul in sending greetings to their fellow Christians in Philippi. All barriers made by humans are broken down in the light of our salvation in Christ.

INTRODUCTION TO

THE LETTER OF PAUL TO THE

COLOSSIANS

Authorship, Date, and Background: Colossians is another of Paul's "prison letters" (see introduction to Ephesians). This one was undoubtedly written from the same place that Ephesians was—likely Rome. The date for its composition is A.D. 60–61. Similarities between Colossians and Ephesians have occasioned some to suppose that Colossians was written by someone other than Paul. However, such similarities should be expected when the two letters were sent to two different churches in different localities at about the same time.

The town of Colossae was located in Asia Minor (Turkey) in the Lycus Valley, not far from Laodicea and Hierapolis. It had been a thriving commercial city, but declined as Hierapolis and Laodicea grew in importance. It was noted for its glossy black wool taken from sheep which grazed in the surrounding hills. Paul had never visited Colossae, although the church there was founded during the time of his Ephesian ministry. Since Epaphras was a native of this city, it was probably he who preached there and started the church (see Acts 19.10; Col 4.12). Philemon and his slave Onesimus came from that city, and Paul told Philemon to have a room ready for him when he visited Colossae as he hoped to do (Philem 22). He also sent Philemon greetings from Epaphras, whom he identified as his fellow prisoner (Philem 23).

The Colossian church had been deeply infiltrated by teachings foreign to the Christian faith. Some Christians there were syncretists, adding to Christianity elements from non-Christian sources such as Gnosticism, paganism, and Judaic speculative philosophy. Some worshiped angelic powers, some said asceticism was essential to salvation, and still others had an inordinate liking for knowledge and wisdom of a secret sort. As a result, the person and work of Jesus Christ were downgraded. These wrong customs in the church occasioned the writing of this letter by Paul, in which he set forth clearly and passionately the correct view of Jesus Christ and his preeminence.

Characteristics and Content: Paul's hymn or prayer of praise to Jesus Christ stands out in the Colossian letter (1.15–20). Whether Paul writes this himself, gets it from an earlier Christian liturgy, or receives it directly from the Holy Spirit makes no difference. It clearly assigns to Jesus Christ expressions which belong to deity alone—i.e., to God. Paul's superb and dazzling statement sums up his teaching about Jesus, when he says, "For in him the whole fulness of deity dwells bodily" (2.9). This is the Jesus he describes in ch. 1 as bearing "the image of the invisible God," as the one through whom all things were created, as the one who by his power holds everything together, as the head of the body, the church, so "that he might come to have first place in everything" (1.15–20).

Paul goes on to destroy the idea of a syncretistic faith by showing that Jesus and Jesus alone is all the believer needs; nothing can or should be added to what he has done and what he commands. He warns the Colossians against the errors which have crept into their midst and sweeps away the legalism to which they have become attached. Paul urges them to stop doing things which hinder them and to put on those things which mark them as true believers in Christ. He carefully delineates what the relationships should be between husbands and wives, parents and children, and masters and slaves. The letter closes with exhortations, a commendation both of Tychicus and Onesimus, and greetings from Luke and Demas. He asks that they pass his letter on to the church at Laodicea; this suggests that group faced similar problems. He also speaks of a letter he has written to Laodicea; this is no longer extant, though some think it may be Ephesians.

Outline:

THE LETTER OF PAUL TO THE

COLOSSIANS

I. Introduction (1.1–14)

A. Greeting

1 Paul, an apostle of Christ Jesus by the will of God, and Timothy our brother,

2 To the saints and faithful brothers and sisters*a* in Christ in Colossae:

Grace to you and peace from God our Father.

B. Thanksgiving

3 In our prayers for you we always thank God, the Father of our Lord Jesus Christ, 4 for we have heard of your faith in Christ Jesus and of the love that you have for all the saints, 5 because of the hope laid up for you in heaven. You have heard of this hope before in the word of the truth, the gospel 6 that has come to you. Just as it is bearing fruit and growing in the whole world, so it has been bearing fruit among yourselves from the day you heard it and truly comprehended the grace of God. 7 This you learned from Epaphras, our beloved fellow servant.*b* He is a faithful minister of Christ on your*c* behalf, 8 and he has made known to us your love in the Spirit.

C. Apostolic prayer

9 For this reason, since the day we heard it, we have not ceased praying for you and asking that you may be filled with the knowledge of God's*d* will in all spiritual wisdom and understanding, 10 so that you may lead lives worthy of the Lord, fully pleasing to him, as you bear fruit in every good work and as you grow in the knowledge of God. 11 May you be made strong with all the strength that comes from his glorious power, and may you be prepared to endure everything with patience, while joyfully 12 giving thanks to the Father, who has enabled*e* you*f* to share in the inheritance of the saints in the light. 13 He has rescued us from the power of darkness and transferred us into the kingdom of his beloved Son, 14 in whom we have redemption, the forgiveness of sins.*g*

1.1
Eph 1.1

1.2
Rom 1.7

1.3
Eph 1.16
1.4
Eph 1.15;
Gal 5.6
1.5
1 Thess 5.8;
1 Pet 1.4
1.6
Mt 24.14;
Jn 15.16
1.7
Philem 23;
Col 4.7
1.8
Rom 15.30

1.9
Eph 1.15-17;
Rom 12.2
1.10
Eph 4.1;
1 Thess 4.1;
Rom 1.13
1.11
Eph 3.16;
4.2;
Acts 5.41
1.12
Eph 5.20;
1.11
1.13
Eph 6.12;
2 Pet 1.11

a Gk *brothers* *b* Gk *slave* *c* Other ancient authorities read *our* *d* Gk *his* *e* Other ancient authorities read *called* *f* Other ancient authorities read *us* *g* Other ancient authorities add *through his blood*

1.1 In Philippians Paul called himself a servant (slave) of Jesus Christ. Here he calls himself an apostle. He had a divine call to that high office and he enjoyed three outward evidences as seals of the apostleship: (1) he had seen the risen Christ (1 Cor 9.1,2); (2) he was an inspired witness to the resurrection of Jesus Christ (Gal 1.1–9); and (3) he had the gift of performing miracles (2 Cor 12.12).
1.3–5 Paul begins with a prayer of thanksgiving for the three major graces manifested in the lives of the Colossians: (1) faith in Christ; (2) love of the Christian community; (3) the hope laid up for them in heaven.
1.7 *Epaphras* (mentioned also in 4.12; Philem 23) is

called a *beloved fellow servant*, i.e., a faithful fellow-slave of Jesus, one who may have founded the church at Colossae. He suffered with Paul during part of his first Roman imprisonment and may have been imprisoned with him as an accomplice in the case.
1.9,10 Paul prays for knowledge, which has as its goal leading a life worthy of the Lord. Knowing and doing go hand in hand; right actions always come from right thinking.
1.13 The picture used to explain the relationship between Christ and his people is that of king and kingdom. The believer has been delivered from the power of darkness and been transferred to the kingdom of God's dear Son.

II. Christian doctrine (1.15–3.4)

A. The person and work of Christ

15 He is the image of the invisible God, the firstborn of all creation; 16 for in*h* him all things in heaven and on earth were created, things visible and invisible, whether thrones or dominions or rulers or powers — all things have been created through him and for him. 17 He himself is before all things, and in*h* him all things hold together. 18 He is the head of the body, the church; he is the beginning, the firstborn from the dead, so that he might come to have first place in everything. 19 For in him all the fullness of God was pleased to dwell, 20 and through him God was pleased to reconcile to himself all things, whether on earth or in heaven, by making peace through the blood of his cross.

21 And you who were once estranged and hostile in mind, doing evil deeds, 22 he has now reconciled*i* in his fleshly body*j* through death, so as to present you holy and blameless and irreproachable before him — 23 provided that you continue securely established and steadfast in the faith, without shifting from the hope promised by the gospel that you heard, which has been proclaimed to every creature under heaven. I, Paul, became a servant of this gospel.

B. The ministry of Paul

24 I am now rejoicing in my sufferings for your sake, and in my flesh I am completing what is lacking in Christ's afflictions for the sake of his body, that is, the church. 25 I became its servant according to God's commission that was given to me for you, to make the word of God fully known, 26 the mystery that has been hidden throughout the ages and generations but has now been revealed to his saints. 27 To them God chose to make known how great among the Gentiles are the riches of the glory of this mystery, which is Christ in you, the hope of glory. 28 It is he whom we proclaim, warning everyone and teaching everyone in all wisdom, so that we may present everyone mature in Christ. 29 For this I toil and struggle with all the energy that he powerfully inspires within me.

C. Paul's concern for them

2 For I want you to know how much I am struggling for you, and for those in Laodicea, and for all who have not seen me face to face. 2 I want their hearts to be encouraged and united in love, so that they may have all the riches of assured understanding and have the knowledge of God's mystery, that is, Christ himself,*k* 3 in whom are hidden all the treasures of wisdom and knowledge. 4 I am saying this so that no one may deceive you with plausible arguments. 5 For though I am absent in body, yet I am with you in spirit, and I rejoice to see your morale and the firmness of your faith in Christ.

6 As you therefore have received Christ Jesus the Lord, continue to live your lives*l* in him, 7 rooted and built up in him and established in the faith, just as you were taught, abounding in thanksgiving.

h Or by   *i* Other ancient authorities read *you have now been reconciled*   *j* Gk *in the body of his flesh*
k Other ancient authorities read *of the mystery of God, both of the Father and of Christ*   *l* Gk *to walk*

1.15ff Christ was involved in the creation of all things in heaven and on earth, as was God the Father (Gen 1.1) and God the Holy Spirit (Job 33.4).
1.22 God commands us to a life of holiness and gives us grace to make it possible. Some hold that it is possible for us to reach a state of sinless perfection; others hold that sinless perfection is not attainable in this life, but it does come, at death, through glorification. Between these two is the view that admits we can

sin, but that we can also fight against and overcome sin.
1.26,27 Christ comes to live in our hearts when we are regenerated (cf. Eph 3.17). This union with Christ includes two things: (1) we become members of his body and partakers of the divine nature as we feed on him (Jn 6.56) and as his Word abides in us (Jn 15.7); and (2) we grow in grace and fruitfulness as we abide in him (Jn 15.5ff).

D. The sufficiency of Christ

8 See to it that no one takes you captive through philosophy and empty deceit, according to human tradition, according to the elemental spirits of the universe,[m] and not according to Christ. 9 For in him the whole fullness of deity dwells bodily, 10 and you have come to fullness in him, who is the head of every ruler and authority. 11 In him also you were circumcised with a spiritual circumcision,[n] by putting off the body of the flesh in the circumcision of Christ; 12 when you were buried with him in baptism, you were also raised with him through faith in the power of God, who raised him from the dead. 13 And when you were dead in trespasses and the uncircumcision of your flesh, God[o] made you[p] alive together with him, when he forgave us all our trespasses, 14 erasing the record that stood against us with its legal demands. He set this aside, nailing it to the cross. 15 He disarmed[q] the rulers and authorities and made a public example of them, triumphing over them in it.

E. Asceticism and ritual condemned

16 Therefore do not let anyone condemn you in matters of food and drink or of observing festivals, new moons, or sabbaths. 17 These are only a shadow of what is to come, but the substance belongs to Christ. 18 Do not let anyone disqualify you, insisting on self-abasement and worship of angels, dwelling[r] on visions,[s] puffed up without cause by a human way of thinking,[t] 19 and not holding fast to the head, from whom the whole body, nourished and held together by its ligaments and sinews, grows with a growth that is from God.

20 If with Christ you died to the elemental spirits of the universe,[m] why do you live as if you still belonged to the world? Why do you submit to regulations, 21 "Do not handle, Do not taste, Do not touch"? 22 All these regulations refer to things that perish with use; they are simply human commands and teachings. 23 These have indeed an appearance of wisdom in promoting self-imposed piety, humility, and severe treatment of the body, but they are of no value in checking self-indulgence.[u]

F. The true center of the Christian life

3 So if you have been raised with Christ, seek the things that are above, where Christ is, seated at the right hand of God. 2 Set your minds on things that are above, not on things that are on earth, 3 for you have died, and your life is hidden with Christ in God. 4 When Christ who is your[v] life is revealed, then you also will be revealed with him in glory.

2.8
1 Cor 8.9;
1 Tim 6.20;
Gal 4.3
2.9
Jn 1.14;
Col 1.19
2.10
Eph 1.21, 22
2.11f
Rom 2.29;
Phil 3.3;
Rom 6.6;
Gal 5.24
2.12
Rom 6.4, 5;
Acts 2.24
2.13
Eph 2.1
2.14
Eph 2.15
2.15
Gen 3.15;
Isa 53.12;
Eph 6.12
2.16
Rom 14.3;
14.17; 14.5;
Gal 4.10, 11
2.17
Heb 8.5
2.18
Phil 3.14;
v. 23
2.19
Eph 1.22;
4.16
2.20
Rom 6.3, 5;
Gal 4.3, 9
2.22
1 Cor 6.13;
Isa 29.13;
Titus 1.14
2.23
Rom 13.14;
1 Tim 4.8

3.1
Ps 110.1;
Rom 8.34
3.2
Phil 3.19, 20
3.3
Rom 6.2;
2 Cor 5.14
3.4
1 Jn 3.2;
Jn 14.6

m Or the rudiments of the world n Gk a circumcision made without hands o Gk he p Other ancient authorities read made us; others, made q Or divested himself of r Other ancient authorities read not dwelling s Meaning of Gk uncertain t Gk by the mind of his flesh u Or are of no value, serving only to indulge the flesh v Other authorities read our

2.11,12 These verses are used by those who practice infant baptism, to establish the teaching that baptism has replaced circumcision as the sign of God's covenant with us. They argue that since infants were circumcised in the O.T., so also should infants now be baptized in water. Those who disagree with infant baptism maintain that the connection made here between circumcision and baptism is merely spiritual and has nothing to say about who should be baptized. **2.20** This passage and the book of Hebrews make plain that the ceremonial law with its prohibition against handling, tasting, and touching (especially unclean things) has forever been abolished (see also

Acts 10; 15). Under the new covenant, the laws for blood sacrifices and dietary matters need not be followed any longer, for Jesus has set us free. **3.1** *if you have been raised with Christ.* The gospel message preached by the apostles stressed the resurrection of Christ as the climax of God's redemptive work. In their preaching, they continually emphasized the fact that Christ had been raised from the dead (e.g., Acts 2.24–32; 3.14; 4.10; 10.40,41; 13.30, 31; 17.31). **3.3,4** Christ is the believer's entire life, and he lives in every believer (cf. Gal 2.20). All will someday appear with him in glory.

III. The Christian life (3.5–4.6)

A. The transformed walk

5 Put to death, therefore, whatever in you is earthly: fornication, impurity, passion, evil desire, and greed (which is idolatry). 6 On account of these the wrath of God is coming on those who are disobedient. w 7 These are the ways you also once followed, when you were living that life. x 8 But now you must get rid of all such things — anger, wrath, malice, slander, and abusive y language from your mouth. 9 Do not lie to one another, seeing that you have stripped off the old self with its practices 10 and have clothed yourselves with the new self, which is being renewed in knowledge according to the image of its creator. 11 In that renewal z there is no longer Greek and Jew, circumcised and uncircumcised, barbarian, Scythian, slave and free; but Christ is all and in all!

12 As God's chosen ones, holy and beloved, clothe yourselves with compassion, kindness, humility, meekness, and patience. 13 Bear with one another and, if anyone has a complaint against another, forgive each other; just as the Lord a has forgiven you, so you also must forgive. 14 Above all, clothe yourselves with love, which binds everything together in perfect harmony. 15 And let the peace of Christ rule in your hearts, to which indeed you were called in the one body. And be thankful. 16 Let the word of Christ b dwell in you richly; teach and admonish one another in all wisdom; and with gratitude in your hearts sing psalms, hymns, and spiritual songs to God. c 17 And whatever you do, in word or deed, do everything in the name of the Lord Jesus, giving thanks to God the Father through him.

B. The Christian family

18 Wives, be subject to your husbands, as is fitting in the Lord. 19 Husbands, love your wives and never treat them harshly.

20 Children, obey your parents in everything, for this is your acceptable duty in the Lord. 21 Fathers, do not provoke your children, or they may lose heart. 22 Slaves, obey your earthly masters d in everything, not only while being watched and in order to please them, but wholeheartedly, fearing the Lord. d 23 Whatever your task, put yourselves into it, as done for the Lord and not for your masters, e 24 since you know that from the Lord you will receive the inheritance as your reward; you serve f the Lord Christ. 25 For the wrongdoer will be paid back for whatever wrong has been done, and there is no partiality. 4 1 Masters, treat your slaves justly and fairly, for you know that you also have a Master in heaven.

Cross-references (left margin)

3.5 Rom 6.13; Eph 5.3, 5
3.6 Rom 1.18; Eph 5.6
3.7 Eph 2.2
3.8 Eph 4.22, 29
3.9 Eph 4.25; 4.22
3.10 Rom 12.2; Eph 4.23; 2.10
3.11 Gal 3.28; Eph 1.23
3.12 Gal 5.22, 23; Phil 2.3; 2 Cor 6.6
3.13 Eph 4.2, 32
3.14 Eph 4.3
3.15 Phil 4.7; 1 Cor 7.15; Eph 4.4
3.16 Eph 5.19
3.17 1 Cor 10.31; Eph 5.20
3.18 Eph 5.22–6.9
3.19 Eph 5.25
3.20 Eph 6.1
3.21 Eph 6.4
3.22 Eph 6.5, 6; Philem 16
3.24 Eph 6.8; 1 Cor 7.22
3.25 Eph 6.8, 9; Acts 10.34
4.1 Lev 25.43, 53; Eph 6.9

w Other ancient authorities lack on those who are disobedient (Gk the children of disobedience)   x Or living among such people   y Or filthy   z Gk its creator, 11 where   a Other ancient authorities read just as Christ   b Other ancient authorities read of God, or of the Lord   c Other ancient authorities read to the Lord   d In Greek the same word is used for master and Lord   e Gk not for men   f Or you are slaves of, or be slaves of

3.5ff The holy life expected of the Christian involves putting off certain sinful activities (vv. 5–9) and putting on other actions (vv. 12–17). The picture used is that of putting off an old dirty garment and putting on a new clean one. Only when the sins of the flesh have been put to death can a Christlike life come alive. This is what sanctification is all about.

3.18ff Beginning here Paul repeats in abbreviated form what he wrote to the church at Ephesus about husbands and wives, children and parents, and slaves and masters (Eph 5.22 — 6.9).

3.18,19 Wives must be subject to the authority of their husbands. In other words, authority is essential to social and domestic order. Yet it is not unlimited, for a wife is not required to submit to anything that violates her conscience or requires any action contrary to the will of God. A wife is protected by the command to husbands that they love their wives. Love makes tyranny, unkindness, selfishness, and cruelty in the marriage relationship impossible. A wife has a right to support, sympathy, and protection.

3.22 The Scriptures lay down three broad principles governing the relationships between masters and servants (slaves) (or employers and employees): (1) servants must obey their masters and serve them well (cf. Eph 6.5–7; 1 Pet 2.18–20); (2) masters must treat their servants in a proper manner (Eph 6.9); and (3) masters and servants alike are servants of God.

C. Prayer

2 Devote yourselves to prayer, keeping alert in it with thanksgiving.
3 At the same time pray for us as well that God will open to us a door for
the word, that we may declare the mystery of Christ, for which I am in
prison, 4 so that I may reveal it clearly, as I should.

D. Conduct

5 Conduct yourselves wisely toward outsiders, making the most of the
time.ᵍ 6 Let your speech always be gracious, seasoned with salt, so that
you may know how you ought to answer everyone.

IV. Conclusion (4.7–18)

A. Regarding Tychicus and Onesimus

7 Tychicus will tell you all the news about me; he is a beloved brother,
a faithful minister, and a fellow servantʰ in the Lord. 8 I have sent him
to you for this very purpose, so that you may know how we areⁱ and that
he may encourage your hearts; 9 he is coming with Onesimus, the faithful
and beloved brother, who is one of you. They will tell you about everything here.

B. Greetings from friends and final instructions

10 Aristarchus my fellow prisoner greets you, as does Mark the cousin
of Barnabas, concerning whom you have received instructions—if he
comes to you, welcome him. 11 And Jesus who is called Justus greets you.
These are the only ones of the circumcision among my co-workers for the
kingdom of God, and they have been a comfort to me. 12 Epaphras, who
is one of you, a servantʰ of Christ Jesus, greets you. He is always wrestling
in his prayers on your behalf, so that you may stand mature and fully
assured in everything that God wills. 13 For I testify for him that he has
worked hard for you and for those in Laodicea and in Hierapolis. 14 Luke,
the beloved physician, and Demas greet you. 15 Give my greetings to the
brothers and sistersʲ in Laodicea, and to Nympha and the church in her
house. 16 And when this letter has been read among you, have it read also
in the church of the Laodiceans; and see that you read also the letter from
Laodicea. 17 And say to Archippus, "See that you complete the task that
you have received in the Lord."

18 I, Paul, write this greeting with my own hand. Remember my
chains. Grace be with you.ᵏ

ᵍ Or *opportunity*   ʰ Gk *slave*   ⁱ Other authorities read *that I may know how you are*   ʲ Gk *brothers*
ᵏ Other ancient authorities add *Amen*

4.2 If v. 2 is to be connected with what precedes it
about masters and servants, masters are to pray with
their servants daily and to continue in prayer, implying concern for the soul as well as the body.
4.7 *Tychicus.* See note on Eph 6.21.
4.10 *Aristarchus.* See note on Philem 24.

4.12 *Epaphras.* See note on 1.7.
4.17 *Archippus* (also mentioned in Philem 2) was
entrusted with some form of ministry, and Paul encourages him to fulfill that ministry. He may have
been a son of Philemon.

4.2
Rom 12.12;
Eph 6.18;
Phil 2.7
4.3
Eph 6.19;
1 Cor 16.9;
Eph 6.20

4.5
Eph 5.15, 16
4.6
Eph 4.29;
Mk 9.50;
1 Pet 3.15

4.7
Eph 6.21, 22

4.9
Philem 10

4.10
Acts 19.29;
15.37; 4.36
4.11
Acts 11.2;
Rom 16.3
4.12
Col 1.7;
Rom 15.30;
Phil 3.15
4.13
Col 2.1
4.14
2 Tim 4.10,
11;
Philem 24
4.15
Rom 16.5
4.17
Philem 2;
2 Tim 4.5

4.18
1 Cor 16.21;
Heb 13.3;
13.25

INTRODUCTION TO
THE FIRST LETTER OF PAUL TO THE
THESSALONIANS

Authorship, Date, and Background: On his second missionary tour, Paul visited Thessalonica around A.D. 49. He had walked from the city of Philippi to Thessalonica along the Egnatian highway. He and his colleagues spent three sabbaths in the synagogue at Thessalonica preaching the gospel. Apparently they then spent several months more in the city and established a church. Thessalonica, a free city, had been founded by Cassander. He named it for his wife, the half-sister of Alexander the Great. It was a flourishing seaport and a successful commercial center. In this pagan city, some Jews and a number of Gentiles came to faith in Jesus Christ. The Jews who did not respond to the gospel persecuted Paul, forcing him to flee the city (Acts 17.5ff). He went to Beroea, where the Jews willingly inquired into the truth of Paul's message.

When the reports of Paul's success elsewhere became known in Thessalonica, the unbelieving Jews came to Beroea to foment a riot. Paul left there and eventually arrived in Athens. Silas and Timothy remained in Beroea to help the infant church. From Athens, Paul went to Corinth where he was to plant another church. While in Corinth, Timothy brought a report of certain happenings in the church at Thessalonica, a church about which the apostle was deeply concerned. He had planned to revisit the church (cf. 2.17,18).

1 and 2 Thessalonians were written ca. A.D. 50–51, within a short time of each other; Corinth was the city in which they were composed. These two letters comprise the earliest epistles of Paul found in the N.T. Some think Galatians may have been written earlier, but this seems unlikely. The Thessalonian church was in turmoil because of divisions between Jewish converts who were steeped in the Jewish way of life and the Gentile believers who had come out of paganism and were quite casual about sexual and other matters. It is possible that Paul may have received a letter from the Thessalonian church, and that his own letters to them were a response.

Characteristics and Content: Paul writes to the Thessalonians to assure them of his love and to praise them for their steadfastness in standing up to the persecution which had come their way from the unbelieving Jews. He also wishes to correct certain errors which have crept into the infant church and to strengthen the believers for the future conflicts he knows they will experience. Since his own personhood has been attacked, he defends himself against the charges by affirming that his motivation was good and his conduct appropriate. He speaks about the great fundamentals of the Christian faith, one of which is holy living. He wants the Thessalonians to separate themselves from the flagrant immorality that surrounds them. The church members are also upset over the fate of Christians who have departed this life prior to the coming of the Lord; Paul assures them that the dead in Christ will be raised to everlasting life at the coming of the Lord Jesus. He insists that the true church will be caught up in the air to be with Jesus, though he does not say whether this will happen before the great tribulation, in the middle of it, or after the church has gone through it (see note on 4.15).

Paul instructs believers to be busy about the ordinary tasks of life, since their expectation of the immediate return of Christ had caused some to grow careless about daily duties. He urges them to honor the elders who labor among them (5.12), and cautions believers not to quench the Spirit or to despise those who prophesy (5.19,20).

Outline:

I. Personal matters (1.1—3.13)

II. Exhortation and instruction (4.1—5.28)

THE FIRST LETTER OF PAUL TO THE

THESSALONIANS

I. *Personal matters (1.1–3.13)*

A. *Greeting*

1.1
2 Thess 1.1;
2 Cor 1.19;
Acts 16.1;
17.1;
Rom 1.7

1 Paul, Silvanus, and Timothy,
To the church of the Thessalonians in God the Father and the Lord Jesus Christ:
Grace to you and peace.

B. *Thanksgiving for them*

1.2
2 Thess 1.3;
Rom 1.8, 9
1.3
2 Thess 1.11;
1.3
1.5
2 Thess 2.14;
Col 2.2;
2 Thess 3.7
1.6
1 Cor 4.16;
11.1;
Acts 17.5-10;
13.52
1.8
Rom 10.18;
1.8; 2 Thess
1.4
1.9
1 Cor 12.2;
Gal 4.8
1.10
2 Pet 3.12;
Acts 2.24;
Rom 5.9

2 We always give thanks to God for all of you and mention you in our prayers, constantly 3 remembering before our God and Father your work of faith and labor of love and steadfastness of hope in our Lord Jesus Christ. 4 For we know, brothers and sisters *a* beloved by God, that he has chosen you, 5 because our message of the gospel came to you not in word only, but also in power and in the Holy Spirit and with full conviction; just as you know what kind of persons we proved to be among you for your sake. 6 And you became imitators of us and of the Lord, for in spite of persecution you received the word with joy inspired by the Holy Spirit, 7 so that you became an example to all the believers in Macedonia and in Achaia. 8 For the word of the Lord has sounded forth from you not only in Macedonia and Achaia, but in every place your faith in God has become known, so that we have no need to speak about it. 9 For the people of those regions *b* report about us what kind of welcome we had among you, and how you turned to God from idols, to serve a living and true God, 10 and to wait for his Son from heaven, whom he raised from the dead — Jesus, who rescues us from the wrath that is coming.

C. *Paul's work among them*

2.1
1 Thess 1.5,
9
2.2
Acts 16.22;
1 Thess 1.5;
Phil 1.30
2.3
2 Cor 7.2
2.4
2 Cor 2.17;
Gal 2.7; 1.10
2.5
Acts 20.33;
Rom 1.9

2 You yourselves know, brothers and sisters, *a* that our coming to you was not in vain, 2 but though we had already suffered and been shamefully mistreated at Philippi, as you know, we had courage in our God to declare to you the gospel of God in spite of great opposition. 3 For our appeal does not spring from deceit or impure motives or trickery, 4 but just as we have been approved by God to be entrusted with the message of the gospel, even so we speak, not to please mortals, but to please God who tests our hearts. 5 As you know and as God is our witness, we never

a Gk *brothers*   *b* Gk *For they*

1.1 *Silvanus* (see also 2 Thess 1.1; 2 Cor 1.19; 1 Pet 5.12). This is the latinized form of Silas (see Acts 15.22 – 18.5). He was a trusted companion of Paul on his second missionary journey.
1.2,3 Thanksgiving in prayer involves the adoration of God, who is the object of our worship and praise. We must never stop thanking God for his goodness to us. Paul thanks God for the Thessalonians' faith at work, their love put into practice, and their steadfast hope.
1.5ff The gospel in Thessalonica was proclaimed in the power of the Holy Spirit and with much convic-

tion; it was received with joy by the Thessalonians in spite of persecution; it was put into practice in their imitating the apostles and the Lord; it was noticed by their neighbors, for they became an example to believers in Macedonia and Achaia.
2.1ff Paul reminds the readers of his manner of preaching among them. He acted with courage and resolution (v. 2), with great simplicity and godly sincerity (v. 3), without either flattery or greed (v. 5), and without desire for personal praise (v. 6). This is an excellent model for preachers today.

came with words of flattery or with a pretext for greed; 6 nor did we seek praise from mortals, whether from you or from others, 7 though we might have made demands as apostles of Christ. But we were gentle[c] among you, like a nurse tenderly caring for her own children. 8 So deeply do we care for you that we are determined to share with you not only the gospel of God but also our own selves, because you have become very dear to us.

9   You remember our labor and toil, brothers and sisters;[d] we worked night and day, so that we might not burden any of you while we proclaimed to you the gospel of God. 10 You are witnesses, and God also, how pure, upright, and blameless our conduct was toward you believers. 11 As you know, we dealt with each one of you like a father with his children, 12 urging and encouraging you and pleading that you lead a life worthy of God, who calls you into his own kingdom and glory.

D. Paul's reception by them

13   We also constantly give thanks to God for this, that when you received the word of God that you heard from us, you accepted it not as a human word but as what it really is, God's word, which is also at work in you believers. 14 For you, brothers and sisters,[d] became imitators of the churches of God in Christ Jesus that are in Judea, for you suffered the same things from your own compatriots as they did from the Jews, 15 who killed both the Lord Jesus and the prophets,[e] and drove us out; they displease God and oppose everyone 16 by hindering us from speaking to the Gentiles so that they may be saved. Thus they have constantly been filling up the measure of their sins; but God's wrath has overtaken them at last.[f]

E. Timothy's mission among them

17   As for us, brothers and sisters,[d] when, for a short time, we were made orphans by being separated from you—in person, not in heart—we longed with great eagerness to see you face to face. 18 For we wanted to come to you—certainly I, Paul, wanted to again and again—but Satan blocked our way. 19 For what is our hope or joy or crown of boasting before our Lord Jesus at his coming? Is it not you? 20 Yes, you are our glory and joy!

3   Therefore when we could bear it no longer, we decided to be left alone in Athens; 2 and we sent Timothy, our brother and co-worker for God in proclaiming[g] the gospel of Christ, to strengthen and encourage you for the sake of your faith, 3 so that no one would be shaken by these persecutions. Indeed, you yourselves know that this is what we are destined for. 4 In fact, when we were with you, we told you beforehand that we were to suffer persecution; so it turned out, as you know. 5 For this reason, when I could bear it no longer, I sent to find out about your faith; I was afraid that somehow the tempter had tempted you and that our labor had been in vain.

c Other ancient authorities read infants   d Gk brothers   e Other ancient authorities read their own prophets   f Or completely or forever   g Gk lacks proclaiming

Cross references

2.6
2 Cor 4.5;
1 Cor 9.1, 2
2.7
v. 11;
Gal 4.19
2.8
2 Cor 12.15;
1 Jn 3.16
2.9
Acts 20.34;
2 Thess 3.8;
2 Cor 12.13
2.10
1 Thess 1.5.
2 Cor 1.12
2.11
1 Cor 4.14;
v. 7
2.12
Eph 4.1;
1 Pet 5.10
2.13
1 Thess 1.2;
Gal 4.14
2.14
Acts 17.5;
2 Thess 1.4
2.15
Acts 2.23;
7.52
2.16
Acts 9.23;
13.45, 50ff;
Mt 23.32
2.17
1 Cor 5.3;
1 Thess 3.10
2.18
Rom 15.22;
1.13
2.19
2 Cor 1.14;
Phil 4.1;
1 Thess 3.13
2.20
2 Cor 1.14
3.1
v. 5;
Acts 17.15
3.2
2 Cor 1.1;
Col 1.1
3.3
Acts 9.16;
14.22
3.4
Acts 20.24;
1 Thess 2.14
3.5
1 Cor 11.3;
Gal 2.2

2.7ff Paul summarizes his ministry among the Thessalonians: (1) he was like a nurse to children (v. 7); (2) he manifested a deep care for them (v. 8); (3) he took no wages from them (v. 9); and (4) his behavior and that of those who accompanied him was blameless and without offense (v. 10). In other words, Paul correlated his preaching with an exemplary lifestyle.
2.9 See 1 Cor 9.3–18; 2 Cor 11.7 and notes.
2.13 In Paul's mind, the words he preached and wrote are the true words of God (see also 1 Cor 11.23ff; 14.37; 15.1–4; Gal 1.11,12).

2.18 *Satan blocked our way.* Perhaps humans were responsible for Paul's inability to do what he thought was God's will. If so, it still was caused by Satan, for he works through humans to obstruct and defeat the work of God.
3.1 Paul, Silas, and Timothy had to leave Thessalonica because of persecution (Acts 17.1–10). Paul had sent Timothy back to them to find out how they were doing and to strengthen them in the faith. This demonstrated his genuine pastoral concern for the children of God.

F. The good report from them

6 But Timothy has just now come to us from you, and has brought us the good news of your faith and love. He has told us also that you always remember us kindly and long to see us — just as we long to see you. **7** For this reason, brothers and sisters,[h] during all our distress and persecution we have been encouraged about you through your faith. **8** For we now live, if you continue to stand firm in the Lord. **9** How can we thank God enough for you in return for all the joy that we feel before our God because of you? **10** Night and day we pray most earnestly that we may see you face to face and restore whatever is lacking in your faith.

G. Paul's prayer for them

11 Now may our God and Father himself and our Lord Jesus direct our way to you. **12** And may the Lord make you increase and abound in love for one another and for all, just as we abound in love for you. **13** And may he so strengthen your hearts in holiness that you may be blameless before our God and Father at the coming of our Lord Jesus with all his saints.

II. Exhortation and instruction (4.1–5.28)

A. Exhortation to purity

4 Finally, brothers and sisters,[h] we ask and urge you in the Lord Jesus that, as you learned from us how you ought to live and to please God (as, in fact, you are doing), you should do so more and more. **2** For you know what instructions we gave you through the Lord Jesus. **3** For this is the will of God, your sanctification: that you abstain from fornication; **4** that each one of you know how to control your own body[i] in holiness and honor, **5** not with lustful passion, like the Gentiles who do not know God; **6** that no one wrong or exploit a brother or sister[j] in this matter, because the Lord is an avenger in all these things, just as we have already told you beforehand and solemnly warned you. **7** For God did not call us to impurity but in holiness. **8** Therefore whoever rejects this rejects not human authority but God, who also gives his Holy Spirit to you.

B. Exhortation to love and work

9 Now concerning love of the brothers and sisters,[h] you do not need to have anyone write to you, for you yourselves have been taught by God to love one another; **10** and indeed you do love all the brothers and sisters[h] throughout Macedonia. But we urge you, beloved,[h] to do so more and more, **11** to aspire to live quietly, to mind your own affairs, and to work with your hands, as we directed you, **12** so that you may behave properly toward outsiders and be dependent on no one.

C. Comfort about the saved who have died

13 But we do not want you to be uninformed, brothers and sisters,[h]

Cross references (left margin):

3.6 Acts 18.5; 1 Thess 1.3
3.7 2 Cor 1.4
3.8 Phil 4.1
3.9 1 Thess 1.2
3.10 2 Tim 1.3; 2 Cor 13.9
3.11 2 Thess 3.5
3.12 1 Thess 4.1, 10
3.13 1 Cor 1.8; 1 Thess 2.19; 4.17
4.1 Phil 1.27; 1 Thess 2.12; Col 1.10
4.3 1 Cor 6.18; Col 3.5
4.4 1 Cor 7.2; 1 Pet 3.7
4.5 Col 3.5; Eph 4.17; 1 Cor 15.34
4.6 1 Cor 6.8; Heb 13.4
4.7 Lev 11.44; 1 Pet 1.15; 1 Thess 2.3
4.8 Rom 5.5
4.9 Rom 12.10; 1 Thess 5.1
4.10 1 Thess 1.7; 3.12
4.11 Eph 4.28; 2 Thess 3.10-12
4.12 Rom 13.13
4.13 Eph 2.12

---

h Gk *brothers*   *i* Or *how to take a wife for himself*   *j* Gk *brother*

3.6ff To Paul's great satisfaction, Timothy returned to tell him that the Thessalonians were keeping the faith and continuing in their love of the apostle. He assures them that he is praying constantly for them. **3.13** Paul asserts that the Lord will surely come in his glory, and when he does, the saints will come with him. They do not need to fear that day, for through the forgivenss of their sins they are blameless before God and do not need to fear the everlasting punishment reserved for the ungodly.

4.1 As in all his writing, Paul ties faith together with a transformed life by which true disciples of Jesus demonstrate the genuineness of their conversion. **4.3,4** It is God's will for us to be sanctified (see note on 1 Cor 6.11), which means having holiness in the heart and purity in the body. Paul is especially concerned about immorality among the believers, for an immoral life means an absence of holiness in the heart. **4.9** See notes on Rom 13.9,10; 1 Cor 10.23.

about those who have died,*k* so that you may not grieve as others do who have no hope. 14 For since we believe that Jesus died and rose again, even so, through Jesus, God will bring with him those who have died.*k* 15 For this we declare to you by the word of the Lord, that we who are alive, who are left until the coming of the Lord, will by no means precede those who have died.*k* 16 For the Lord himself, with a cry of command, with the archangel's call and with the sound of God's trumpet, will descend from heaven, and the dead in Christ will rise first. 17 Then we who are alive, who are left, will be caught up in the clouds together with them to meet the Lord in the air; and so we will be with the Lord forever. 18 Therefore encourage one another with these words.

D. The sudden coming of the Lord

5 Now concerning the times and the seasons, brothers and sisters,*l* you do not need to have anything written to you. 2 For you yourselves know very well that the day of the Lord will come like a thief in the night. 3 When they say, "There is peace and security," then sudden destruction will come upon them, as labor pains come upon a pregnant woman, and there will be no escape! 4 But you, beloved,*l* are not in darkness, for that day to surprise you like a thief; 5 for you are all children of light and children of the day; we are not of the night or of darkness. 6 So then let us not fall asleep as others do, but let us keep awake and be sober; 7 for those who sleep sleep at night, and those who are drunk get drunk at night. 8 But since we belong to the day, let us be sober, and put on the breastplate of faith and love, and for a helmet the hope of salvation. 9 For God has destined us not for wrath but for obtaining salvation through our Lord Jesus Christ, 10 who died for us, so that whether we are awake or asleep we may live with him. 11 Therefore encourage one another and build up each other, as indeed you are doing.

E. Practical exhortations

12 But we appeal to you, brothers and sisters,*l* to respect those who labor among you, and have charge of you in the Lord and admonish you; 13 esteem them very highly in love because of their work. Be at peace among yourselves. 14 And we urge you, beloved,*l* to admonish the idlers, encourage the fainthearted, help the weak, be patient with all of them. 15 See that none of you repays evil for evil, but always seek to do good to

k Gk fallen asleep   *l* Gk brothers

4.14
1 Cor 15.13, 23
4.15
1 Kings 13.17; 20.35;
1 Cor 15.51, 52
4.16
Mt 24.31;
1 Cor 15.23;
2 Thess 2.1
4.17
1 Cor 15.52;
Acts 1.9;
Rev 11.12;
Jn 12.26

5.1
Acts 1.7;
1 Thess 4.9
5.2
1 Cor 1.8;
2 Pet 3.10
5.3
Hos 13.13
5.4
Acts 26.18;
1 Jn 2.8
5.6
Rom 13.11;
1 Pet 1.13
5.7
Acts 2.15;
2 Pet 2.13
5.8
Eph 6.14, 23, 17
5.9
2 Thess 2.13, 14;
Rom 14.9
5.10
2 Cor 5.15
5.12
1 Tim 5.17;
Heb 13.17
5.14
2 Thess 3.11;
Rom 14.1
5.15
Rom 12.17;
1 Pet 3.9;
Gal 6.10;
2.13, 14;
Rom 14.9

4.13 *about those who have died.* The Scriptures speak about those who die as having fallen asleep in Jesus (see NRSV footnote). Does this teach (as some maintain) "soul-sleep," that the dead in Christ have no conscious life? The primary focus of this phrase refers to the body, which lies in the grave to await the day of resurrection. The spirit at death, while separated from the body, goes to be with Jesus in glory. It is alive and awaits reunion with a resurrected body. **4.15** *until the coming of the Lord.* Paul is speaking about the coming of the Lord (Gk. *parousia*). The *parousia* of Jesus is related to the catching away of living believers and of deceased believers who are raised from their graves—a teaching known as "the rapture" of the church (from Latin *raptus*, meaning "being caught away"). The rapture will be marked by the cry of command or mighty shout from the Lord, the soul-stirring cry of the archangel, and the great trumpet call of God. Premillennialists hold that the rapture sets the stage for Christ's millennial kingdom (see note on Rev 20.2). Within this interpretation, there are three views commonly held about the relation of the rapture to the great tribulation: (1) pretribulation rapturists believe that the church will be

caught away into the air before the great tribulation begins (see Mt 24.15ff; Rev 7.14); (2) midtribulation rapturists believe the church will be exposed to the wrath of wicked people but will be caught away just before the second half of the tribulation when God pours out his wrath on humankind; (3) posttribulation rapturists believe the church will go through the tribulation but will be miraculously preserved by the power of God, just as the children of Israel were preserved from the plagues in Egypt. None of these three views is *explicitly* taught in the Scriptures (see also note on Rev 7.14). **5.1** Paul warns against setting any timetable for the second coming of the Lord, for it will come as unexpectedly as a thief in the night. Since no one knows when his coming will take place, believers must always be ready (vv. 6–8; Mt 24.42; 25.13; Mk 13.33–37; Lk 12.35–38). **5.6ff** What should believers do while they wait for Christ's coming? They must be watchful and sober, must not sleep spiritually or get drunk, must be temperate and moderate, and must be armed with faith, hope, and love. The reason for this is that they are not destined to experience the wrath of God but salvation.

one another and to all. [16]Rejoice always, [17]pray without ceasing, [18]give thanks in all circumstances; for this is the will of God in Christ Jesus for you. [19]Do not quench the Spirit. [20]Do not despise the words of prophets,[m] [21]but test everything; hold fast to what is good; [22]abstain from every form of evil.

F. Conclusion

[23] May the God of peace himself sanctify you entirely; and may your spirit and soul and body be kept sound[n] and blameless at the coming of our Lord Jesus Christ. [24]The one who calls you is faithful, and he will do this.

[25] Beloved,[o] pray for us.

[26] Greet all the brothers and sisters[p] with a holy kiss. [27]I solemnly command you by the Lord that this letter be read to all of them.[q]

[28] The grace of our Lord Jesus Christ be with you.[r]

[m] Gk *despise prophecies*   [n] Or *complete*   [o] Gk *Brothers*   [p] Gk *brothers*   [q] Gk *to all the brothers*   [r] Other ancient authorities add *Amen*

5.19 *Do not quench the Spirit* (see the note on Eph 4.30, where Paul says believers must not grieve the Holy Spirit). Here Paul is saying something quite different. The Holy Spirit has given us gifts (e.g., speaking in tongues, prophecy, healing, etc.). Paul cautions us not to dampen, smother, or quench those gifts. Rather, we must use them in the service of our Lord and for the building up of the church (1 Cor 14.26).

5.23 *spirit and soul and body.* In many passages, the Bible speaks of humans as being composed of body and soul; is Paul suggesting here that we are made up of three parts? No final answer can be given. We do know that the Hebrews looked upon human beings as a single living unit, not as a combination of parts. The O.T. uses words such as *flesh, heart, soul,* and *spirit,* but never discusses formally any relationship between these words; they are often interchangeable. At the same time, it is true that some things that are indefinite in the O.T. are more definite in the N.T. Suffice it to say that the Bible indicates people exist after death, at least for a time, as disembodied persons who are conscious and for whom pain or pleasure are realities (Lk 16.19ff; 2 Cor 5.1–8; Phil 1.23; Rev 7.14–17).

Introduction to 2 Thessalonians

Outline:

I. G

II. Personal matters (1-12)

III. The day of the Lord (2:1-1)

IV. Exhortations (3:1-1

INTRODUCTION TO
THE SECOND LETTER OF PAUL TO THE
THESSALONIANS

Authorship, Date, and Background: See the introduction to 1 Thessalonians. This second letter was written shortly after 1 Thessalonians by Paul at Corinth (A.D. 50–51). Paul had written the first letter to instruct believers about matters having to do with the second coming of the Lord Jesus. Apparently they misunderstood what he had said. His emphasis on the imminence of the Lord's coming resulted in some of them thinking that the day of the Lord had already started. Others thought he was coming so soon that they stopped work and waited idly. They had missed the point that Jesus will come as a thief in the night and at a time when people do not expect him. Thus Paul received disheartening news from Thessalonica about this situation, and he sent out this second letter to straighten them out.

One statement in this letter seems to suggest that the Thessalonians had been led astray by wrong teaching from unauthentic sources. He begs them not to be shaken or alarmed, "either by spirit or by word or by letter, as though from us, to the effect that the day of the Lord is already here" (2.2). The speed with which Paul writes the second letter after having composed the first one indicates his deep concern for the believers, his distaste for false doctrine, and his pastoral heart which demands immediate action.

Characteristics and Content: One of Paul's main emphases in this letter is that the day of the Lord has not yet started and that there are definite signs that will precede the end of this age. It is not clear to us today what some of the signs are, though they must have been clear to the Thessalonians. The first sign is the appearance of "the lawless one," who will cause many others to rebel against God. It will be a period of sudden and rapidly accelerating apostasy from godliness. Second, this person will not appear until the one who is restraining him is removed. Who the restrainer is, Paul does not say. Some have thought this refers to the Holy Spirit, whose presence they think will someday be withdrawn amd cause society to crumble because his restraining power will no longer hold things together. But commentators disagree on this view. Believers had best be tentative in their efforts to identify "the restrainer." Finally, the coming lawless one "opposes and exalts himself above every so-called god or object of worship, so that he takes his seat in the temple of God, declaring himself to be God" (2.4). He "uses all power, signs, lying wonders, and every kind of wicked deception" (2.9,10). Obviously this had not occurred at the time Paul wrote his letter. Nor has it occurred at any time since then. Therefore, until this happens, we can know that any reports of the Lord's return are untrue. Meanwhile we must keep on doing the will of God, yet expect him to come at any time.

Outline:

THE SECOND LETTER OF PAUL TO THE

THESSALONIANS

I. Greeting (1.1,2)

1 Paul, Silvanus, and Timothy,
To the church of the Thessalonians in God our Father and the Lord Jesus Christ:
2 Grace to you and peace from God our[a] Father and the Lord Jesus Christ.

II. Personal matters (1.3–12)

A. Thanksgiving

3 We must always give thanks to God for you, brothers and sisters,[b] as is right, because your faith is growing abundantly, and the love of everyone of you for one another is increasing. 4 Therefore we ourselves boast of you among the churches of God for your steadfastness and faith during all your persecutions and the afflictions that you are enduring.

B. Encouragement to endure

5 This is evidence of the righteous judgment of God, and is intended to make you worthy of the kingdom of God, for which you are also suffering. 6 For it is indeed just of God to repay with affliction those who afflict you, 7 and to give relief to the afflicted as well as to us, when the Lord Jesus is revealed from heaven with his mighty angels 8 in flaming fire, inflicting vengeance on those who do not know God and on those who do not obey the gospel of our Lord Jesus. 9 These will suffer the punishment of eternal destruction, separated from the presence of the Lord and from the glory of his might, 10 when he comes to be glorified by his saints and to be marveled at on that day among all who have believed, because our testimony to you was believed. 11 To this end we always pray for you, asking that our God will make you worthy of his call and will fulfill by his power every good resolve and work of faith, 12 so that the name of our Lord Jesus may be glorified in you, and you in him, according to the grace of our God and the Lord Jesus Christ.

a Other ancient authorities read *the*   *b* Gk *brothers*

1.1
1 Thess 1.1;
2 Cor 1.19;
Acts 16.1
1.2
Rom 1.7;
1 Cor 1.3

1.3
1 Thess 1.2;
3.12
1.4
2 Cor 7.14;
1 Thess 1.3;
2.14

1.5
Phil 1.28;
1 Thess 2.14
1.6
Col 3.25;
Rev 6.10
1.7
1 Thess 4.16;
Jude 14
1.8
Gal 4.8;
Rom 2.8
1.9
Phil 3.19;
2 Pet 3.7;
2 Thess 2.8
1.10
Jn 17.10;
1 Cor 3.13;
1.6
1.11
v. 5; 1 Thess
1.3
1.12
Phil 2.9ff

1.1 See note on 1 Thess 1.1.
1.3,4 In 1 Thess 1.3 Paul gave thanks for the faith, love, and steadfast hope of the Thessalonians. Here he gives thanks for their growth in these graces. Their faith grew exceedingly, and their love to God and the saints increased, and their steadfastness persisted in spite of, or because of, their persecution and tribulations.
1.8 *inflicting vengeance.* God's wrath is consistent with his holiness, righteousness, and justice. When all is said and done, we have no right to question how God upholds his justice (cf. Rom 9.19–29). God's

wrath means the imposition of penal judgment on sinners who have broken his laws; its basis is God's love for his moral universe. Those who trample down the moral law must pay for their wickedness. The wrath of God against the sins of those who believe was satisfied by the death of Christ on Calvary. Sometimes his wrath is poured out on people and nations in time (e.g., the destruction of Nineveh, Jerusalem, Rome). But his wrath may also be delayed until the final days—"the great day of their wrath" (Rev 6.17; 11.18; 19.15).

III. *The day of the Lord (2.1–17)*

A. *Events preceding the day of the Lord*

2 As to the coming of our Lord Jesus Christ and our being gathered together to him, we beg you, brothers and sisters,*c* 2 not to be quickly shaken in mind or alarmed, either by spirit or by word or by letter, as though from us, to the effect that the day of the Lord is already here. 3 Let no one deceive you in any way; for that day will not come unless the rebellion comes first and the lawless one*d* is revealed, the one destined for destruction.*e* 4 He opposes and exalts himself above every so-called god or object of worship, so that he takes his seat in the temple of God, declaring himself to be God. 5 Do you not remember that I told you these things when I was still with you? 6 And you know what is now restraining him, so that he may be revealed when his time comes. 7 For the mystery of lawlessness is already at work, but only until the one who now restrains it is removed. 8 And then the lawless one will be revealed, whom the Lord Jesus*f* will destroy*g* with the breath of his mouth, annihilating him by the manifestation of his coming. 9 The coming of the lawless one is apparent in the working of Satan, who uses all power, signs, lying wonders, 10 and every kind of wicked deception for those who are perishing, because they refused to love the truth and so be saved. 11 For this reason God sends them a powerful delusion, leading them to believe what is false, 12 so that all who have not believed the truth but took pleasure in unrighteousness will be condemned.

B. *Thanksgiving and exhortation*

13 But we must always give thanks to God for you, brothers and sisters*c* beloved by the Lord, because God chose you as the first fruits*h* for salvation through sanctification by the Spirit and through belief in the truth. 14 For this purpose he called you through our proclamation of the good news,*i* so that you may obtain the glory of our Lord Jesus Christ. 15 So then, brothers and sisters,*c* stand firm and hold fast to the traditions that you were taught by us, either by word of mouth or by our letter.

16 Now may our Lord Jesus Christ himself and God our Father, who loved us and through grace gave us eternal comfort and good hope, 17 comfort your hearts and strengthen them in every good work and word.

c Gk *brothers*   *d* Gk *the man of lawlessness*; other ancient authorities read *the man of sin*   *e* Gk *the son of destruction*   *f* Other ancient authorities lack *Jesus*   *g* Other ancient authorities read *consume*   *h* Other ancient authorities read *from the beginning*   *i* Or *through our gospel*

2.1 1 Thess 4.15-17; Mk 13.27
2.2 Eph 5.6; 2 Thess 3.17; 1 Cor 1.8
2.3 Eph 5.6-8; Dan 7.25; 8.25; 11.36; Rev 13.5ff; Jn 17.12
2.4 1 Cor 8.5; Isa 14.13, 14; Ezek 28.2
2.7 Rev 17.5, 7
2.8 Dan 7.10; Rev 19.15
2.9 Mt 24.24; Jn 4.48
2.10 1 Cor 1.18
2.11 Rom 1.28; Mt 24.5; 1 Tim 4.1
2.12 Rom 1.32
2.13 Eph 1.4; 1 Pet 1.2
2.14 1 Pet 5.10
2.15 1 Cor 16.13; 11.2
2.16 1 Thess 3.11; Jn 3.16
2.17 1 Thess 3.2; 2 Thess 3.3

2.3 Before the second coming of Christ certain events must take place: (1) the gospel will be preached to all the world for a witness (Mt 24.14); (2) the great tribulation will occur; and (3) the lawless one will rise for a short period of time. Wickedness will be unrestrained as the power of the Holy Spirit is lifted (v. 7); the human race will experience great misfortune. Other prophetic references to this period include Dan 7.8ff; 9.27; Mt 24.15ff; Rev 13.2–10.
2.7 This verse does not indicate who the restrainer is who holds back lawlessness and the lawless one. Some have suggested it is the Holy Spirit, removed from the world at the end of the age. Others think he remains but lifts his restraining power, at which time the wicked will do what they had wanted to do but had been restrained from doing by the Holy Spirit. In any event the time is coming when restraints against sin and wickedness will be lifted and people will be free to do as they please.
2.9 See note on Ex 8.7.
2.10–12 These verses proclaim both the sins and the ruin of God's enemies. Because they do not love truth, they do not believe it. And because they do not believe truth, they take great pleasure in their unrighteousness. God's grace toward them is withdrawn, and they are given over to Satan to be his deluded assistants.
2.13ff The saints have been chosen or elected by God from before the foundation of the world (cf. Eph 1.4) to be saved. Their call is made effectual by the inward operation of the Holy Spirit in their hearts. Paul now exhorts them to stand fast in the traditions of the apostles in which they were taught. Those oral traditions have now been recorded in the Scriptures as a written record of God's truth. We are bound only by that written word of God.

IV. *Exhortations (3.1–18)*

A. *To pray*

3 Finally, brothers and sisters,[j] pray for us, so that the word of the Lord may spread rapidly and be glorified everywhere, just as it is among you, 2 and that we may be rescued from wicked and evil people; for not all have faith. 3 But the Lord is faithful; he will strengthen you and guard you from the evil one.[k] 4 And we have confidence in the Lord concerning you, that you are doing and will go on doing the things that we command. 5 May the Lord direct your hearts to the love of God and to the steadfastness of Christ.

B. *To work*

6 Now we command you, beloved,[j] in the name of our Lord Jesus Christ, to keep away from believers who are[l] living in idleness and not according to the tradition that they[m] received from us. 7 For you yourselves know how you ought to imitate us; we were not idle when we were with you, 8 and we did not eat anyone's bread without paying for it; but with toil and labor we worked night and day, so that we might not burden any of you. 9 This was not because we do not have that right, but in order to give you an example to imitate. 10 For even when we were with you, we gave you this command: Anyone unwilling to work should not eat. 11 For we hear that some of you are living in idleness, mere busybodies, not doing any work. 12 Now such persons we command and exhort in the Lord Jesus Christ to do their work quietly and to earn their own living. 13 Brothers and sisters,[n] do not be weary in doing what is right.

14 Take note of those who do not obey what we say in this letter; have nothing to do with them, so that they may be ashamed. 15 Do not regard them as enemies, but warn them as believers.[o]

C. *Prayer, greetings, and benediction*

16 Now may the Lord of peace himself give you peace at all times in all ways. The Lord be with all of you.

17 I, Paul, write this greeting with my own hand. This is the mark in every letter of mine; it is the way I write. 18 The grace of our Lord Jesus Christ be with all of you.[p]

---

j Gk *brothers*   k Or *from evil*   l Gk *from every brother who is*   m Other ancient authorities read *you*
n Gk *Brothers*   o Gk *a brother*   p Other ancient authorities add *Amen*

Cross-references:
3.1 1 Thess 4.1; 5.25; 1.8
3.2 Rom 15.31
3.3 1 Cor 1.9; 1 Thess 5.24; 2 Pet 2.9
3.4 2 Cor 2.3; Gal 5.10
3.5 1 Chr 29.18
3.6 1 Cor 5.4, 11; 2 Thess 2.15
3.7 1 Thess 1.6
3.8 1 Thess 2.9; Acts 18.3; Eph 4.28
3.9 1 Cor 9.4ff
3.10 1 Thess 4.11
3.11 1 Tim 5.13
3.12 1 Thess 4.1, 11; Eph 4.28
3.13 Gal 6.9
3.14 Mt 18.17
3.15 Gal 6.1; 1 Thess 5.14
3.16 Rom 15.33; Ruth 2.4
3.17 1 Cor 16.21
3.18 Rom 16.20; 1 Thess 5.28

3.1 Paul asks the Thessalonians to pray for him and his small band. He has always remembered them in his prayers and does not want them to forget him in their prayers. The communion of saints and the unity of the body are kept by praying together and by praying for each other when absent from each other.

3.6 The church must break fellowship with any who walk in a disorderly manner. This includes those who have broken away from the teaching of Paul. He commands the Thessalonians to break fellowship with those who refuse to obey his instructions in this letter (see note on vv. 14,15).

3.10 *Anyone unwilling to work should not eat.* Paul is not talking about people who through no fault of their own — such as unemployment or illness — are unable to work. Rather, he is referring to those who, because they think Christ is about to return, have quit their jobs and become lazy, sponging off the rest of the believers for their daily necessities.

3.14,15 Paul instructs the church as to how believers should respond to disorderly members in their midst. There must first be sufficient evidence of their wrongdoing. Then the disorderly must be admonished in a friendly fashion, with the expectation that they will mend their ways. If any continue in their wrong conduct, the true believers must withdraw from them and no longer keep company with them. They must hate their sins but love the sinners, pray for them, and work toward their recovery and full return as brothers and sisters in Christ.

3.16 *The Lord be with all of you.* Christians can desire nothing better for themselves and their families and friends than to experience the continual gracious presence of the Lord with them.

INTRODUCTION TO

THE FIRST LETTER OF PAUL TO

TIMOTHY

Authorship, Date, and Background: The three letters 1 Timothy, 2 Timothy, and Titus are known as the Pastorals. They were obviously written by the same person and around the same time. From the second century until the nineteenth century it was commonly accepted that the apostle Paul wrote these letters. The dates of their writing must have been before his traditional execution date, in the early A.D. 60s. Beginning in the nineteenth century, critical scholars have attacked the Pauline authorship vigorously and have generally concluded that the letters were written after Paul's death; many have supposed they were written in the second century. Some say a disciple wrote the letters in the name of his teacher and that this involved no deception since this was done occasionally in the secular world. Others think a later admirer of Paul put them in their present form with a view to preserving Pauline traditions and to sustain the impact of Paul's authority by attaching his name to them. Other scholars reject Pauline authorship on the grounds that the letters do not contain some things that Paul would have included if he had written them. They overlook the fact that the Holy Spirit is the divine author of Scripture and that he worked through humans. Moreover, for critics to state what *must* have been included in order for these letters to be considered genuinely Pauline is to place themselves in a position of authority which belongs to the Holy Spirit and not to the critics.

It is quite correct that Acts does not include some of the details of Paul's life and ministry mentioned in the Pastorals. But it seems apparent that Paul suffered two Roman imprisonments. Between the two, he was free to travel so that his mission with Titus to Crete, a winter spent at Nicopolis, and the period when he visited Asia Minor and left Trophimus ill at Miletus occurred subsequent to his release from his first Roman imprisonment referred to in Acts 28. 2 Timothy, however, places him back in Rome as a prisoner awaiting his execution. If these personal details not recorded in Acts were inventions of someone who wrote these letters in Paul's name, it throws open the whole question of biblical authority and truthfulness, calling into doubt the gospel itself. Those who trust the word of God can live comfortably with the claim of these letters that Paul is the author.

Characteristics and Content: Timothy, to whom this letter is addressed, was born in Lystra to a Jewish mother and a Greek father. He had been raised in the Jewish faith and worked together with Paul in his early years. Paul had Timothy circumcised (Acts 16.3), not because circumcision was a necessity but to avoid controversy and in the larger interests of Timothy's ministry. Timothy was immature and timid, not forceful. He suffered from a weak stomach. Paul assigned him to a ministry at Ephesus (1.3). The letter was designed to encourage him and to strengthen him for that ministry, as well as to help the church members understand that he had the apostolic authority of Paul behind him. Paul was probably traveling at the time of the writing and was himself actively engaged in ministry. The church which Timothy pastored was troubled by some who were teaching wrong doctrines and myths (1.3,4).

The burden of the letter is to communicate to Timothy pastoral advice on the operation and conduct of a local congregation. In the course of doing this, Paul speaks about women at worship, the offices of bishop and deacon, the coming apostasy, and Timothy's relationships to widows, elders, backsliders, slaves, and lovers of money. Paul's concluding advice to Timothy is to flee from sin, pursue righteousness, fight the good fight, and keep the commandment of Jesus Christ.

Outline:

   I. Greeting (1.1,2)

  II. Instructions for the church and church officers (1.3—3.16)

 III. Instructions to Timothy (4.1—6.21)

THE FIRST LETTER OF PAUL TO
TIMOTHY

I. Greeting (1.1,2)

1.1
Acts 9.15;
Col 1.27
1.2
Acts 16.1;
2 Tim 1.2

1 Paul, an apostle of Christ Jesus by the command of God our Savior and of Christ Jesus our hope,

2 To Timothy, my loyal child in the faith:

Grace, mercy, and peace from God the Father and Christ Jesus our Lord.

II. *Instructions for the church and church officers (1.3–3.16)*

A. *The problem at Ephesus: unsound doctrine*

1.3
Acts 20.1;
Gal 1.6, 7
1.4
Titus 1.14;
1 Tim 6.4
1.5
2 Tim 2.22
1.6
Titus 1.10
1.7
Jas 3.1;
1 Tim 6.4
1.8
Rom 7.12
1.9
Gal 3.19;
1 Pet 4.18
1.10
2 Tim 4.3;
Titus 1.9
1.11
Gal 2.7

3 I urge you, as I did when I was on my way to Macedonia, to remain in Ephesus so that you may instruct certain people not to teach any different doctrine, 4 and not to occupy themselves with myths and endless genealogies that promote speculations rather than the divine training*a* that is known by faith. 5 But the aim of such instruction is love that comes from a pure heart, a good conscience, and sincere faith. 6 Some people have deviated from these and turned to meaningless talk, 7 desiring to be teachers of the law, without understanding either what they are saying or the things about which they make assertions.

8 Now we know that the law is good, if one uses it legitimately. 9 This means understanding that the law is laid down not for the innocent but for the lawless and disobedient, for the godless and sinful, for the unholy and profane, for those who kill their father or mother, for murderers, 10 fornicators, sodomites, slave traders, liars, perjurers, and whatever else is contrary to the sound teaching 11 that conforms to the glorious gospel of the blessed God, which he entrusted to me.

B. *The testimony of Paul*

1.12
2 Cor 12.9;
Col 1.25
1.13
Acts 8.3
1.14
Rom 5.20;
2 Tim 1.13
1.15
2 Tim 2.11;
Titus 3.8

12 I am grateful to Christ Jesus our Lord, who has strengthened me, because he judged me faithful and appointed me to his service, 13 even though I was formerly a blasphemer, a persecutor, and a man of violence. But I received mercy because I had acted ignorantly in unbelief, 14 and the grace of our Lord overflowed for me with the faith and love that are in Christ Jesus. 15 The saying is sure and worthy of full acceptance, that Christ Jesus came into the world to save sinners — of whom I am the

a Or *plan*

1.1,2 Most of Paul's letters were addressed to churches. Four were sent to individuals: Timothy (two letters), Titus, and Philemon. Titus and Timothy were evangelists (2 Tim 4.5), not apostles. Timothy was Paul's own child in the faith, i.e., he had been converted under the ministry of the apostle (see Acts 16.1–3).
1.4 *Myths* are false teachings (see also 4.7; 2 Tim 4.4; Titus 1.14), some of which are dealt with by Paul in his letters; they are called godless and silly. In this sense myths are still present, e.g., those teachings that say that Jesus is not God, that he did not rise from the dead in his human body, and that his death was not substitutionary. We cannot be sure that *endless*

genealogies are (see also Titus 3.9). Some think they had to do with Gnosticism and the notion that someone lower than God through many creative acts created the world. In any event these notions created controversy and were to be avoided in order to prevent dissension in the church.
1.8 The law may be used rightly or wrongly. The Jews used the law to oppose the gospel of Jesus Christ, setting it up against justification by faith alone.
1.9,10 The law does not exist primarily for the righteous but to point out sin and keep sinners in check. Here Paul lists some notorious breaches of the law, most of which violate parts of the second table of the law — love of one's neighbor.

foremost. 16 But for that very reason I received mercy, so that in me, as the foremost, Jesus Christ might display the utmost patience, making me an example to those who would come to believe in him for eternal life. 17 To the King of the ages, immortal, invisible, the only God, be honor and glory forever and ever.[b] Amen.

C. The exhortation to Timothy

18 I am giving you these instructions, Timothy, my child, in accordance with the prophecies made earlier about you, so that by following them you may fight the good fight, 19 having faith and a good conscience. By rejecting conscience, certain persons have suffered shipwreck in the faith; 20 among them are Hymenaeus and Alexander, whom I have turned over to Satan, so that they may learn not to blaspheme.

D. Public prayer

2 First of all, then, I urge that supplications, prayers, intercessions, and thanksgivings be made for everyone, 2 for kings and all who are in high positions, so that we may lead a quiet and peaceable life in all godliness and dignity. 3 This is right and is acceptable in the sight of God our Savior, 4 who desires everyone to be saved and to come to the knowledge of the truth. 5 For
there is one God;
there is also one mediator between God and humankind,
Christ Jesus, himself human,
6   who gave himself a ransom for all
—this was attested at the right time. 7 For this I was appointed a herald and an apostle (I am telling the truth,[c] I am not lying), a teacher of the Gentiles in faith and truth.

E. The position of women

8 I desire, then, that in every place the men should pray, lifting up holy hands without anger or argument; 9 also that the women should dress themselves modestly and decently in suitable clothing, not with their hair braided, or with gold, pearls, or expensive clothes, 10 but with good works, as is proper for women who profess reverence for God. 11 Let a woman[d] learn in silence with full submission. 12 I permit no woman[d] to teach or to have authority over a man;[e] she is to keep silent. 13 For Adam was formed first, then Eve; 14 and Adam was not deceived, but the woman was deceived and became a transgressor. 15 Yet she will be saved through childbearing, provided they continue in faith and love and holiness, with modesty.

---

b Gk to the ages of the ages   *c* Other ancient authorities add in Christ   *d* Or wife   *e* Or her husband

Cross references

1.16
v. 13;
Eph 2.7
1.17
Col 1.15;
Rom 11.36

1.18
1 Tim 4.14;
2 Tim 2.2, 3
1.19
1 Tim 6.12, 21
1.20
2 Tim 2.17; 4.14

2.2
Ezra 6.10;
Rom 13.1
2.3
Rom 12.2;
1 Tim 4.10
2.4
Jn 3.16;
2 Tim 2.25
2.5
Gal 3.20;
Heb 9.15
2.6
Mk 10.45;
1 Cor 1.6;
Gal 4.4
2.7
Eph 3.7, 8;
Gal 1.16

2.8
Ps 134.2
2.9
1 Pet 3.3

2.11
1 Cor 14.34

2.13
Gen 1.27;
1 Cor 11.8
2.14
Gen 3.6;
2 Cor 11.3
2.15
1 Tim 1.14

1.18 *fight the good fight.* The Christian life is a battle that lasts until death. It is directed against such enemies as Satan (2 Cor 2.11; Eph 6.11,12), the flesh (Rom 7.23; Gal 5.17; 1 Pet 2.11), the world (Jn 16.33; 1 Jn 5.4,5), and death (1 Cor 15.26; Heb 2.14,15). Believers are called upon to be well armed (Eph 6.14–18), watchful (1 Pet 5.8), and always exercising faith (1 Tim 1.18,19). Final victory is ours, and along with it are eternal rewards (Rom 16.20; 2 Tim 4.8; Rev 2.17; 3.5; 21.7).
1.20 *whom I have turned over to Satan,* means that remedial discipline, probably excommunication from the fellowship of the church, had been applied (see 1 Cor 5.5).

2.5 A mediator is one who stands between two opposing parties. Christ is the only mediator who stands between guilty sinners and the righteous God. By his blood he has broken down the wall of hostility between God and sinful people and between Jew and Gentile (Eph 2.14). We have direct and immediate access to God the Father through the mediator (Rom 5.2; Eph 2.18; 3.12). This passage eliminates all angels, saints, priests, or anyone else as mediators.
2.11 *Let a woman learn in silence.* See note on 1 Cor 14.34,35.
2.13 Some scholars disbelieve the historicity of Adam and Eve, but Paul obviously accepts Gen 1—3 as literal and factual, not myth or saga.

F. The office of bishop

3 The saying is sure:*f* whoever aspires to the office of bishop*g* desires a noble task. 2 Now a bishop*h* must be above reproach, married only once,*i* temperate, sensible, respectable, hospitable, an apt teacher, 3 not a drunkard, not violent but gentle, not quarrelsome, and not a lover of money. 4 He must manage his own household well, keeping his children submissive and respectful in every way — 5 for if someone does not know how to manage his own household, how can he take care of God's church? 6 He must not be a recent convert, or he may be puffed up with conceit and fall into the condemnation of the devil. 7 Moreover, he must be well thought of by outsiders, so that he may not fall into disgrace and the snare of the devil.

G. The office of deacon

8 Deacons likewise must be serious, not double-tongued, not indulging in much wine, not greedy for money; 9 they must hold fast to the mystery of the faith with a clear conscience. 10 And let them first be tested; then, if they prove themselves blameless, let them serve as deacons. 11 Women*j* likewise must be serious, not slanderers, but temperate, faithful in all things. 12 Let deacons be married only once,*k* and let them manage their children and their households well; 13 for those who serve well as deacons gain a good standing for themselves and great boldness in the faith that is in Christ Jesus.

14 I hope to come to you soon, but I am writing these instructions to you so that, 15 if I am delayed, you may know how one ought to behave in the household of God, which is the church of the living God, the pillar and bulwark of the truth. 16 Without any doubt, the mystery of our religion is great:

He*l* was revealed in flesh,
vindicated*m* in spirit,*n*
seen by angels,
proclaimed among Gentiles,
believed in throughout the world,
taken up in glory.

III. Instructions to Timothy (4.1–6.21)

A. Of false doctrine

4 Now the Spirit expressly says that in later*o* times some will renounce the faith by paying attention to deceitful spirits and teachings of demons, 2 through the hypocrisy of liars whose consciences are seared

f Some interpreters place these words at the end of the previous paragraph. Other ancient authorities read *The saying is commonly accepted*   *g* Or *overseer*   *h* Or *an overseer*   *i* Gk *the husband of one wife*   *j* Or *Their wives*, or *Women deacons*   *k* Gk *be husbands of one wife*   *l* Gk *Who*; other ancient authorities read *God*; others, *Which*   *m* Or *justified*   *n* Or *by the Spirit*   *o* Or *the last*

3.1ff It is no sin to aspire to attain the office of *bishop* (overseer or elder, see note on Titus 1.5ff), provided that the one who does this realizes it is a task, not simply a position of privilege. Those who seek this office for their own honor or financial gain are guilty of greed.
3.2 *married only once.* Since the priests of the O.T. were permitted to remarry after the death of a wife, there is no reason to suppose that the rule here is not the same. Paul seems to mean that no one should be an elder who has divorced his wife and married another woman, or who has more than one wife, i.e., a polygamist (cf. NRSV footnote, "husband of one wife").
3.8 The N.T. prescribes two offices for the congre-

gation: bishops or elders (see note on v. 1), and *deacons.* The word *deacon* (Gk. *diakonos*) means "one who serves." The diaconate began in order to free the apostles to preach the word and to pray (see Acts 6.1–6). Temporal affairs, such as caring for the poor, were entrusted to the deacons. Deacons, like elders or bishops, were ordained by the laying on of hands.
3.11 From the Greek it is impossible to say whether this verse applies to wives of deacons or to women deacons in the church. Rom 16.1 specifically states that Phoebe was a deacon (see note on that verse). Thus the office is open to women.
3.16 See notes on Jn 1.14 and Phil 2.7.
4.1 *in later times*, presumably the end times preceding the return of Christ.

with a hot iron. 3 They forbid marriage and demand abstinence from foods, which God created to be received with thanksgiving by those who believe and know the truth. 4 For everything created by God is good, and nothing is to be rejected, provided it is received with thanksgiving; 5 for it is sanctified by God's word and by prayer.

4.3
1 Cor 7.28;
Heb 13.4;
Gen 1.29;
Rom 14.6
4.4
Rom 14.14

B. On godly living

6 If you put these instructions before the brothers and sisters,*p* you will be a good servant*q* of Christ Jesus, nourished on the words of the faith and of the sound teaching that you have followed. 7 Have nothing to do with profane myths and old wives' tales. Train yourself in godliness, 8 for, while physical training is of some value, godliness is valuable in every way, holding promise for both the present life and the life to come. 9 The saying is sure and worthy of full acceptance. 10 For to this end we toil and struggle,*r* because we have our hope set on the living God, who is the Savior of all people, especially of those who believe.

4.6
2 Cor 11.23;
1 Tim 1.10;
2 Tim 3.10
4.7
2 Tim 2.16;
Heb 5.14
4.8
1 Tim 6.6;
Ps 37.4;
Rom 8.28
4.10
1 Cor 4.11;
1 Tim 2.4

C. On faithful service

11 These are the things you must insist on and teach. 12 Let no one despise your youth, but set the believers an example in speech and conduct, in love, in faith, in purity. 13 Until I arrive, give attention to the public reading of scripture,*s* to exhorting, to teaching. 14 Do not neglect the gift that is in you, which was given to you through prophecy with the laying on of hands by the council of elders.*t* 15 Put these things into practice, devote yourself to them, so that all may see your progress. 16 Pay close attention to yourself and to your teaching; continue in these things, for in doing this you will save both yourself and your hearers.

4.11
1 Tim 5.7;
6.2
4.12
Titus 2.7;
1 Pet 5.3;
1 Tim 1.14
4.14
2 Tim 1.6;
1 Tim 1.18;
5.22;
Acts 6.6
4.16
Acts 20.28;
Ezek 33.9

D. On pastoral duties

1. Widows

5 Do not speak harshly to an older man,*u* but speak to him as to a father, to younger men as brothers, 2 to older women as mothers, to younger women as sisters — with absolute purity.

3 Honor widows who are really widows. 4 If a widow has children or grandchildren, they should first learn their religious duty to their own family and make some repayment to their parents; for this is pleasing in God's sight. 5 The real widow, left alone, has set her hope on God and continues in supplications and prayers night and day; 6 but the widow*v* who lives for pleasure is dead even while she lives. 7 Give these commands as well, so that they may be above reproach. 8 And whoever does not provide for relatives, and especially for family members, has denied the faith and is worse than an unbeliever.

5.1
Lev 19.32

5.3
vv. 5, 16
5.4
Eph 6.1, 2
5.5
vv. 3, 16;
1 Cor 7.32;
Lk 2.37
5.6
Jas 5.5
5.7
1 Tim 4.11
5.8
Gal 6.10;
Titus 1.16

p Gk *brothers*   *q* Or *deacon*   *r* Other ancient authorities read *suffer reproach*   *s* Gk *to the reading*   *t* Gk *by the presbytery*   *u* Or *an elder, or a presbyter*   *v* Gk *she*

4.3 *They forbid marriage.* By this statement Paul clearly establishes the legitimacy of marriage; since the letter is directed to Timothy, it also means that evangelists, along with prophets and apostles (see 1 Cor 9.5), have the right to marry. Some, however, are given the gift of continence (1 Cor 7.7,25–35); for them the single state is the will of God.
4.14 *Do not neglect the gift that is in you.* Whoever neglects the gifts that God has given will discover that unused gifts wither.
4.16 Those interested in saving souls must first see to it that their own souls are saved and that they are living a God-fearing life. The dangers of an unconverted minister cannot be overemphasized.
5.1 One of the difficult tasks of the ministry is to

rebuke. Paul cautions Timothy about how to do this. Older men (or elders in the church) must be rebuked tenderly. Younger men must be addressed as brothers in Christ, lovingly and tenderly. Older women must be approached as though they were Timothy's mother, and younger women as if they were his own sisters.
5.3ff *Widows* occupied an important place in the early church. They were financially helpless unless their children or grandchildren supported them. Thus the churches made provision for widows, but Paul wanted to be sure only the needy ones who had no other means of support were helped. He gives detailed instructions on this subject (vv. 3–16).

5.10
Acts 16.15;
Heb 13.2;
Lk 7.44;
v. 16

5.13
2 Thess 3.11;
Titus 1.11

5.14
1 Cor 7.9;
Titus 2.5
5.16
vv. 3, 5

9 Let a widow be put on the list if she is not less than sixty years old and has been married only once;[w] 10 she must be well attested for her good works, as one who has brought up children, shown hospitality, washed the saints' feet, helped the afflicted, and devoted herself to doing good in every way. 11 But refuse to put younger widows on the list; for when their sensual desires alienate them from Christ, they want to marry, 12 and so they incur condemnation for having violated their first pledge. 13 Besides that, they learn to be idle, gadding about from house to house; and they are not merely idle, but also gossips and busybodies, saying what they should not say. 14 So I would have younger widows marry, bear children, and manage their households, so as to give the adversary no occasion to revile us. 15 For some have already turned away to follow Satan. 16 If any believing woman[x] has relatives who are really widows, let her assist them; let the church not be burdened, so that it can assist those who are real widows.

2. Elders

5.17
Phil 2.29;
Rom 12.8;
Acts 28.10
5.18
1 Cor 9.9;
Lev 19.13;
Deut 24.14,
15;
Mt 10.10
5.19
Deut 19.15
5.20
Titus 1.13;
Deut 13.11
5.21
1 Tim 6.13;
2 Tim 2.14
5.22
Acts 6.6;
2 Tim 1.6;
Eph 5.11
5.23
1 Tim 3.8

17 Let the elders who rule well be considered worthy of double honor,[y] especially those who labor in preaching and teaching; 18 for the scripture says, "You shall not muzzle an ox while it is treading out the grain," and, "The laborer deserves to be paid." 19 Never accept any accusation against an elder except on the evidence of two or three witnesses. 20 As for those who persist in sin, rebuke them in the presence of all, so that the rest also may stand in fear. 21 In the presence of God and of Christ Jesus and of the elect angels, I warn you to keep these instructions without prejudice, doing nothing on the basis of partiality. 22 Do not ordain[z] anyone hastily, and do not participate in the sins of others; keep yourself pure.

23 No longer drink only water, but take a little wine for the sake of your stomach and your frequent ailments.

24 The sins of some people are conspicuous and precede them to judgment, while the sins of others follow them there. 25 So also good works are conspicuous; and even when they are not, they cannot remain hidden.

3. Slaves

6.1
Titus 2.9;
1 Pet 2.18;
Titus 2.5, 8
6.2
Gal 3.28;
Philem 16;
1 Tim 4.11

6 Let all who are under the yoke of slavery regard their masters as worthy of all honor, so that the name of God and the teaching may not be blasphemed. 2 Those who have believing masters must not be disrespectful to them on the ground that they are members of the church;[a] rather they must serve them all the more, since those who benefit by their service are believers and beloved.[b]

---

w Gk the wife of one husband   x Other ancient authorities read believing man or woman; others, believing man   y Or compensation   z Gk Do not lay hands on   a Gk are brothers   b Or since they are believers and beloved, who devote themselves to good deeds

---

5.17 The duties of elders are twofold: to rule the church well and to preach and teach God's word and doctrine. They must not be lazy but work zealously in this office to which they have been called by the Holy Spirit. Such servants of God are worthy of double honor—public esteem and adequate provision in the material things of life.
5.20 If sins are public and known to people, the rebuke should also be public. Simply censuring a minister may be insufficient for correction. Other steps would be suspension from the ministry, removal from the ministry by deposing a bishop or elder, and finally excommunication from the communion of the church itself.
5.23 Evidently Paul was concerned about Timothy's health. He was not physically strong and appar-ently had stomach problems. Nothing is said here about healing. Many of God's servants have to bear physical infirmities from which they are not delivered in this life. Paul's suggestion that Timothy use a little wine may imply that he was drinking contaminated water.
6.1,2 all who are under the yoke of slavery. Paul is speaking about believers who are slaves (Gk. douloi); they must honor, respect, and obey their masters. If they do not, then the name of the God they profess to worship is defamed. If a Christian slave has a believing master, this does not give the slave the right to be be disrespectful. Paul respected the civil law and the social patterns of his day and did not militate against the law of slavery.

E. *Warning against false teachers*

Teach and urge these duties. 3 Whoever teaches otherwise and does not agree with the sound words of our Lord Jesus Christ and the teaching that is in accordance with godliness, 4 is conceited, understanding nothing, and has a morbid craving for controversy and for disputes about words. From these come envy, dissension, slander, base suspicions, 5 and wrangling among those who are depraved in mind and bereft of the truth, imagining that godliness is a means of gain.*c* 6 Of course, there is great gain in godliness combined with contentment; 7 for we brought nothing into the world, so that*d* we can take nothing out of it; 8 but if we have food and clothing, we will be content with these. 9 But those who want to be rich fall into temptation and are trapped by many senseless and harmful desires that plunge people into ruin and destruction. 10 For the love of money is a root of all kinds of evil, and in their eagerness to be rich some have wandered away from the faith and pierced themselves with many pains.

F. *Exhortation to Timothy*

11 But as for you, man of God, shun all this; pursue righteousness, godliness, faith, love, endurance, gentleness. 12 Fight the good fight of the faith; take hold of the eternal life, to which you were called and for which you made*e* the good confession in the presence of many witnesses. 13 In the presence of God, who gives life to all things, and of Christ Jesus, who in his testimony before Pontius Pilate made the good confession, I charge you 14 to keep the commandment without spot or blame until the manifestation of our Lord Jesus Christ, 15 which he will bring about at the right time—he who is the blessed and only Sovereign, the King of kings and Lord of lords. 16 It is he alone who has immortality and dwells in unapproachable light, whom no one has ever seen or can see; to him be honor and eternal dominion. Amen.

G. *The use of wealth*

17 As for those who in the present age are rich, command them not to be haughty, or to set their hopes on the uncertainty of riches, but rather on God who richly provides us with everything for our enjoyment. 18 They are to do good, to be rich in good works, generous, and ready to share, 19 thus storing up for themselves the treasure of a good foundation for the future, so that they may take hold of the life that really is life.

H. *Final charge and benediction*

20 Timothy, guard what has been entrusted to you. Avoid the profane chatter and contradictions of what is falsely called knowledge; 21 by professing it some have missed the mark as regards the faith.

Grace be with you.*f*

c Other ancient authorities add *Withdraw yourself from such people*   *d* Other ancient authorities read *world—it is certain that*   *e* Gk *confessed*   *f* The Greek word for *you* here is plural; in other ancient authorities it is singular. Other ancient authorities add *Amen*

6.10 In itself money is neither good nor bad. Nor is it wrong for a believer to be wealthy. But many people have even been turned away from God because of their *love of money*, a sin related to greed. It is often the first step toward all kinds of sins. More crimes have been committed for money than for almost any other reason. Pride in riches is forbidden and the wealthy must use their money "to do good" (vv. 17, 18).

6.12 *the good confession in the presence of many witnesses*, i.e., the confession Timothy made in public at the time of his baptism.
6.17 The rich, not the poor, are apt to be haughty. But riches are uncertain, for in the twinkling of an eye God, who provided them in the first place, can remove them. Setting one's hope on God instead of riches assures an individual of the blessing and enjoyment of God.

6.3 2 Tim 1.13; Titus 1.1
6.4 1 Cor 8.2; 2 Tim 2.14
6.5 1 Cor 11.16; Titus 1.11; 2 Pet 2.3
6.6 Phil 4.11; Heb 13.5
6.7 Job 1.21
6.8 Heb 13.5
6.9 1 Tim 3.7; 1.19
6.10 1 Tim 3.3; Jas 5.19
6.12 1 Cor 9.25, 26; 1 Tim 1.18; Heb 13.23
6.13 1 Tim 5.21; Jn 18.37
6.14 Phil 1.6; 2 Thess 2.8
6.15 1 Tim 1.11, 17; Rev 17.14; 19.16
6.16 1 Tim 1.17; Jn 1.18; Eph 3.21
6.17 Lk 12.20, 21; 1 Tim 4.10; Acts 14.17
6.18 1 Tim 5.10; Rom 12.8, 13
6.20 2 Tim 1.14; 2.16

INTRODUCTION TO
THE SECOND LETTER OF PAUL TO
TIMOTHY

Authorship, Date, and Background: See the introduction to 1 Timothy. Paul had now come close to the end of his earthly pilgrimage. He was a prisoner at Rome, writing the last of his letters which we have in the Bible. We do not know whether he ever visited Spain (cf. Rom 15.23,24) between his first and second imprisonments. He did, however, stop at Crete, Corinth, Miletus, and Troas. The order of these stops is unknown. Evidently he was arrested suddenly and unexpectedly, for his travel plans were interrupted. He had left books at Troas, hoping to return for them later, but never did. He may have been arrested by the authorities either at Troas or Nicopolis. The reason for Paul's seizure is not stated. Some have suggested that it was due to the pique of Alexander the coppersmith, whom Paul mentions in 4.14 and who may be the same person talked about in Acts 19.33. It is possible that Alexander and his fellow traders, whose businesses were hurt by the response of the people to the gospel, may have witnessed against Paul to the Roman authorities. Since Paul warns Timothy against Alexander, he must have been operating within the same general area where Timothy was located.

Characteristics and Content: 2 Timothy makes clear how intimate the relationship is between Paul and Timothy, whom he addresses as "my beloved child." Paul speaks about Timothy's background and family, his ordination to the gospel ministry, and his own teaching ministry to this younger colleague. Paul mentions his constant prayers for Timothy and his desire to draw Timothy closer to himself in his imprisonment. Whereas in his first Roman imprisonment he had other colleagues with him (see Col 4.7ff), he now seems isolated and in need of Christian fellowship. He urgently desires to strengthen Timothy for the work he will have to undertake alone, for Paul expects his own immediate death (4.6–8). He wants Timothy to approach his task as a soldier of Jesus Christ who is willing to lay down his life for the Lord and the faith.

Paul envisions difficult days to come (3.1ff). This prophetic statement has been partially fulfilled in some of the dark days in the history of the church, and it will be one of the chief characteristics of the closing days of this age before the coming of the Lord Jesus. The only way by which the spirit of antichrist can be overcome, in that age and in any age, is by the knowledge and use of the holy Scriptures, "that are able to instruct you for salvation through faith in Christ Jesus" (3.15). His final charge to Timothy (4.1–8) is a masterpiece. No one should consider the Christian ministry unless his life and outlook conform to the standard Paul lays down for that office.

Outline:

　I.　Greeting (1.1,2)

　II.　Appeal and exhortation to Timothy (1.3—2.13)

　III.　Sound doctrine, right conduct, and false teaching (2.14—4.8)

　IV.　Conclusion (4.9–22)

THE SECOND LETTER OF PAUL TO

TIMOTHY

I. Greeting (1.1,2)

I. Greeting (1.1,2)

II. Appeal and exhortation to Timothy (1.3—2.13)

III. Sound doctrine, right conduct, and false teaching (2.14—4.8)

IV. Conclusion (4.9—22)

1.1
2 Cor 1.1;
Eph 3.6;
Titus 1.2
1.2
1 Tim 1.2

1 Paul, an apostle of Christ Jesus by the will of God, for the sake of the promise of life that is in Christ Jesus,
2 To Timothy, my beloved child:
Grace, mercy, and peace from God the Father and Christ Jesus our Lord.

II. Appeal and exhortation to Timothy (1.3–2.13)

1.3
Rom 1.8, 9;
1 Thess 1.2,
21;
Acts 20.37
1.4
2 Tim 4.9
1.5
1 Tim 1.5;
Acts 16.1
1.6
1 Tim 4.14
1.7
Rom 8.15;
Jn 14.27
1.8
Rom 1.16;
Eph 3.1;
? Tim 2.3, 9;
4.5
1.9
Heb 3.1;
Rom 16.25
1.10
Eph 1.9;
1 Cor 15.54
1.11
1 Tim 2.7
1.12
Titus 3.8;
1 Tim 6.20
1.13
Titus 1.9;
Rom 2.20;
1 Tim 1.14
1.14
Rom 8.9, 11
1.15
Acts 19.10;
2 Tim 4.10,
11, 16
1.16
2 Tim 4.19

3 I am grateful to God—whom I worship with a clear conscience, as my ancestors did—when I remember you constantly in my prayers night and day. 4 Recalling your tears, I long to see you so that I may be filled with joy. 5 I am reminded of your sincere faith, a faith that lived first in your grandmother Lois and your mother Eunice and now, I am sure, lives in you. 6 For this reason I remind you to rekindle the gift of God that is within you through the laying on of my hands; 7 for God did not give us a spirit of cowardice, but rather a spirit of power and of love and of self-discipline.

8 Do not be ashamed, then, of the testimony about our Lord or of me his prisoner, but join with me in suffering for the gospel, relying on the power of God, 9 who saved us and called us with a holy calling, not according to our works but according to his own purpose and grace. This grace was given to us in Christ Jesus before the ages began, 10 but it has now been revealed through the appearing of our Savior Christ Jesus, who abolished death and brought life and immortality to light through the gospel. 11 For this gospel I was appointed a herald and an apostle and a teacher,*a* 12 and for this reason I suffer as I do. But I am not ashamed, for I know the one in whom I have put my trust, and I am sure that he is able to guard until that day what I have entrusted to him.*b* 13 Hold to the standard of sound teaching that you have heard from me, in the faith and love that are in Christ Jesus. 14 Guard the good treasure entrusted to you, with the help of the Holy Spirit living in us.

15 You are aware that all who are in Asia have turned away from me, including Phygelus and Hermogenes. 16 May the Lord grant mercy to the household of Onesiphorus, because he often refreshed me and was not

a Other ancient authorities add *of the Gentiles* *b* Or *what has been entrusted to me*

1.3 With thanksgiving to God, Paul remembered Timothy in his prayers night and day. Prayer was Paul's constant business, and he never forgot his friends when he prayed.

1.4 *Recalling your tears.* We do not know whether these tears were shed when Timothy and Paul parted for each to perform his ministry, or whether Timothy shed tears while ministering. Godly ministers may have occasion to weep much over the spiritual condition of their parishioners.

1.5 Lois and Eunice, Timothy's grandmother and mother, were godly women who greatly influenced this young man. We know little about them except the role they played in leading Timothy to Christ. One of the frequent ways in which people become believers

is through the influence of godly homes.

1.6 *rekindle the gift of God,* i.e., stir it up like the fire under the embers. Extraordinary gifts were conferred on Timothy when Paul laid his hands on him (cf. 1 Tim 4.14), though the gift did not come from Paul but from God, the author of all gifts.

1.10 The first appearing of Jesus refers to his incarnation; his second appearing (cf. Titus 2.13) refers to his coming again in power and great glory.

1.15 This is the only mention of Phygelus and Hermogenes, two men who deserted Paul. The church has always had those whose professions turned out to be false. Note the contrast of this to Onesiphorus (v. 16), who was a faithful and devout believer.

ashamed of my chain; 17 when he arrived in Rome, he eagerly[c] searched for me and found me 18 — may the Lord grant that he will find mercy from the Lord on that day! And you know very well how much service he rendered in Ephesus.

2 You then, my child, be strong in the grace that is in Christ Jesus; 2 and what you have heard from me through many witnesses entrust to faithful people who will be able to teach others as well. 3 Share in suffering like a good soldier of Christ Jesus. 4 No one serving in the army gets entangled in everyday affairs; the soldier's aim is to please the enlisting officer. 5 And in the case of an athlete, no one is crowned without competing according to the rules. 6 It is the farmer who does the work who ought to have the first share of the crops. 7 Think over what I say, for the Lord will give you understanding in all things.

8 Remember Jesus Christ, raised from the dead, a descendant of David — that is my gospel, 9 for which I suffer hardship, even to the point of being chained like a criminal. But the word of God is not chained. 10 Therefore I endure everything for the sake of the elect, so that they may also obtain the salvation that is in Christ Jesus, with eternal glory. 11 The saying is sure:

If we have died with him, we will also live with him;
12　if we endure, we will also reign with him;
　　if we deny him, he will also deny us;
13　if we are faithless, he remains faithful —
　　for he cannot deny himself.

III. Sound doctrine, right conduct, and false teaching (2.14–4.8)

A. Personal counsel to Timothy

14 Remind them of this, and warn them before God[d] that they are to avoid wrangling over words, which does no good but only ruins those who are listening. 15 Do your best to present yourself to God as one approved by him, a worker who has no need to be ashamed, rightly explaining the word of truth. 16 Avoid profane chatter, for it will lead people into more and more impiety, 17 and their talk will spread like gangrene. Among them are Hymenaeus and Philetus, 18 who have swerved from the truth by claiming that the resurrection has already taken place. They are upsetting the faith of some. 19 But God's firm foundation

c Or *promptly*　d Other ancient authorities read *the Lord*

1.18
2 Thess 1.10;
Heb 6.10

2.1
2 Tim 1.2;
Eph 6.10
2.2
2 Tim 1.13;
1 Tim 6.12;
1.18; 1.12
2.3
1 Tim 1.18
2.4
2 Pet 2.20
2.5
1 Cor 9.25
2.8
Acts 2.24;
Mt 1.1;
Rom 2.16
2.9
Acts 9.16;
Phil 1.7;
Acts 28.31
2.10
Eph 3.13;
2 Cor 1.6
2.12
1 Pet 4.13;
Mt 10.33
2.13
Rom 3.3;
Num 23.19

2.14
1 Tim 5.21;
6.4
2.15
Jas 1.12
2.16
1 Tim 4.7
2.17
1 Tim 1.20
2.18
1 Cor 15.12
2.19
Isa 28.16,
17;
1 Tim 3.15;
Jn 10.14;
1 Cor 1.2

2.12,13 Paul sets up two operating principles characteristic of Jesus. He is faithful both to his promises and to his threatenings. If we prove faithful, he will be faithful to us; if we prove faithless he still remains faithful, but he will institute judgment against us and refuse to affirm us before his Father.
2.15 The quality of the Christian life is related to one's knowledge and use of the word of God. The reasons for studying the word include the following: (1) it is, in part, the source of faith (Rom 10.17); (2) it makes possible a holy life (Ps 119.11); (3) it provides light and guidance (Ps 119.105); (4) the Holy Spirit uses it to bring conviction of sin (Jn 16.8,9) and to accomplish the work of sanctification (Eph 6.17); and (5) it keeps the believer from error and provides a standard by which to measure the opinions of people (3.16,17).
2.18 Scripture indicates there are different kinds of error. Some errors spring from ignorance (Acts 19.1–6). Others come from failure to understand the

word of God correctly (cf. disagreements about baptism, church government, and the like); in many of these issues the Bible is not crystal clear. Here Paul refers to serious error which upsets the faith of some, though Paul does not call it apostasy (cf. Acts 21.21; 2 Thess 2.3,4). As another form of error, apostasy dissolves any relation one might have had with God in Jesus Christ. Normally, it includes a denial of the deity of Christ or of his atoning work on Calvary (Phil 3.18; 2 Pet 2.1; 1 Jn 4.1–3). Peter (2 Pet 2) and Jude both describe apostates. They are to be dealt with forthrightly (3.9; Rom 16.17,18; 2 Jn 10) when their views have been tested by Scripture. The end of the age will be marked by widespread departure from the faith (3.1–3,5).
2.19 *The Lord knows those who are his.* God knows who his people are and owns them so that he will never lose them (cf. Jn 10.28,29). Believers can rest on this promise of God.

stands, bearing this inscription: "The Lord knows those who are his," and, "Let everyone who calls on the name of the Lord turn away from wickedness."

20 In a large house there are utensils not only of gold and silver but also of wood and clay, some for special use, some for ordinary. 21 All who cleanse themselves of the things I have mentioned*e* will become special utensils, dedicated and useful to the owner of the house, ready for every good work. 22 Shun youthful passions and pursue righteousness, faith, love, and peace, along with those who call on the Lord from a pure heart. 23 Have nothing to do with stupid and senseless controversies; you know that they breed quarrels. 24 And the Lord's servant*f* must not be quarrelsome but kindly to everyone, an apt teacher, patient, 25 correcting opponents with gentleness. God may perhaps grant that they will repent and come to know the truth, 26 and that they may escape from the snare of the devil, having been held captive by him to do his will.*g*

B. The coming of apostasy

3 You must understand this, that in the last days distressing times will come. 2 For people will be lovers of themselves, lovers of money, boasters, arrogant, abusive, disobedient to their parents, ungrateful, unholy, 3 inhuman, implacable, slanderers, profligates, brutes, haters of good, 4 treacherous, reckless, swollen with conceit, lovers of pleasure rather than lovers of God, 5 holding to the outward form of godliness but denying its power. Avoid them! 6 For among them are those who make their way into households and captivate silly women, overwhelmed by their sins and swayed by all kinds of desires, 7 who are always being instructed and can never arrive at a knowledge of the truth. 8 As Jannes and Jambres opposed Moses, so these people, of corrupt mind and counterfeit faith, also oppose the truth. 9 But they will not make much progress, because, as in the case of those two men,*h* their folly will become plain to everyone.

C. The defense of the faith

10 Now you have observed my teaching, my conduct, my aim in life, my faith, my patience, my love, my steadfastness, 11 my persecutions, and my suffering the things that happened to me in Antioch, Iconium, and Lystra. What persecutions I endured! Yet the Lord rescued me from all of them. 12 Indeed, all who want to live a godly life in Christ Jesus will be persecuted. 13 But wicked people and impostors will go from bad to worse, deceiving others and being deceived. 14 But as for you, continue in what you have learned and firmly believed, knowing from whom you learned it, 15 and how from childhood you have known the sacred writings that are able to instruct you for salvation through faith in Christ Jesus. 16 All

e Gk *of these things*   *f* Gk *slave*   *g* Or *by him, to do his* (that is, God's) *will*   *h* Gk lacks *two men*

2.22 *Shun youthful passions.* With age, the attraction of youthful lusts will diminish—not necessarily because we have complete victory over them but because they tend to lose their appeal. But the elderly have their own temptations, such as concentration on financial security and personal comfort.
3.1 *in the last days distressing times will come.* Though the church always faces times of distress, a heightening of wickedness will occur in the last days. It should not be cause for undue alarm, for it is a necessary precursor of the return of Jesus.
3.8 According to Jewish tradition, Jannes and Jambres were Egyptian magicians who opposed Moses before Pharaoh (Ex 7.11; 9.11). Their names are found in ancient Jewish writings and in Christian apocryphal works.

3.11,12 Paul does not speak of his sufferings and difficulties to deter believers from serving Christ. Since all believers will be subjected to afflictions, Paul wants to assure us that God will be with us and sustain us. We can therefore take courage and pursue our calling with great determination. Under persecutions true believers grow stronger.
3.16 *inspired by God.* The Bible is "God-breathed" or "God-inspired" (Gk. *theopneustos*). God the Holy Spirit used people to write Scripture (2 Pet 1.20,21). From the earliest days the church has believed and taught that the Bible is free from error as a whole and in its parts. The prophets, the apostles, and Jesus all taught that the Bible is the word of God and can be trusted at all points. It is trustworthy precisely because it was inspired by the Holy Spirit, even as Jesus

scripture is inspired by God and is[i] useful for teaching, for reproof, for correction, and for training in righteousness, [17] so that everyone who belongs to God may be proficient, equipped for every good work.

D. The charge to preach sound doctrine

4 In the presence of God and of Christ Jesus, who is to judge the living and the dead, and in view of his appearing and his kingdom, I solemnly urge you: [2] proclaim the message; be persistent whether the time is favorable or unfavorable; convince, rebuke, and encourage, with the utmost patience in teaching. [3] For the time is coming when people will not put up with sound doctrine, but having itching ears, they will accumulate for themselves teachers to suit their own desires, [4] and will turn away from listening to the truth and wander away to myths. [5] As for you, always be sober, endure suffering, do the work of an evangelist, carry out your ministry fully.

[6] As for me, I am already being poured out as a libation, and the time of my departure has come. [7] I have fought the good fight, I have finished the race, I have kept the faith. [8] From now on there is reserved for me the crown of righteousness, which the Lord, the righteous judge, will give me on that day, and not only to me but also to all who have longed for his appearing.

IV. Conclusion (4.9–22)

[9] Do your best to come to me soon, [10] for Demas, in love with this present world, has deserted me and gone to Thessalonica; Crescens has gone to Galatia,[j] Titus to Dalmatia. [11] Only Luke is with me. Get Mark and bring him with you, for he is useful in my ministry. [12] I have sent Tychicus to Ephesus. [13] When you come, bring the cloak that I left with Carpus at Troas, also the books, and above all the parchments. [14] Alexander the coppersmith did me great harm; the Lord will pay him back for his deeds. [15] You also must beware of him, for he strongly opposed our message.

[16] At my first defense no one came to my support, but all deserted me. May it not be counted against them! [17] But the Lord stood by me and gave me strength, so that through me the message might be fully proclaimed and all the Gentiles might hear it. So I was rescued from the lion's mouth. [18] The Lord will rescue me from every evil attack and save me for his heavenly kingdom. To him be the glory forever and ever. Amen.

[19] Greet Prisca and Aquila, and the household of Onesiphorus.

---

[i] Or *Every scripture inspired by God is also*   [j] Other ancient authorities read *Gaul*

Cross-references (side column)

3.17 1 Tim 6.11; 2 Tim 2.21
4.1 1 Tim 5.21; Acts 10.42
4.2 1 Tim 5.20; Titus 1.13; 1 Tim 4.13
4.3 2 Tim 3.1, 6; 1 Tim 1.10
4.5 Acts 21.8
4.6 Phil 2.17; 1.23
4.7 Phil 3.14; 1 Tim 6.12
4.8 Jas 1.12; 1 Pet 5.4; 2 Tim 1.12
4.10 Col 4.14; 1 Jn 2.15
4.11 2 Tim 1.15; Col 4.14; Acts 12.12
4.14 Acts 19.33; Rom 12.19; Ps 119.98, 99
4.16 Acts 7.60
4.17 Acts 23.11; 2 Pet 2.9
4.18 Ps 121.7; Rom 11.36
4.19 Acts 18.2

Notes

was sinless because he was conceived by the same Spirit. Inspiration is plenary and verbal, i.e., all of the Bible is inspired and inspiration extends to the very words of Scripture. A few think the Bible was dictated; most hold that the writers were free to use their own style and manner, but were superintended by the Spirit, who kept them from error. Both views hold that inerrancy pertains to the original manuscripts (the *autographa*), agreeing that ancient copyists made minor mistakes in transmitting the text. Some believe that inerrancy is limited to matters of faith and practice and does not extend to historical and scientific phenomena as recorded in the Bible. They think such errors in minor matters do not impair the essential message of the Bible, nor do they destroy Christian faith. All too often, however, this view of limited inerrancy had led to unlimited errancy.
4.7 See note on 1 Tim 1.18.
4.8 *longed for his appearing.* The N.T. as a whole stresses the need for eager expectancy of the coming

of the Lord Jesus at the end of history. Believers should show their love for his coming by demonstrating it in their lives (vv. 7,8); look or wait for his coming (1 Cor 1.7; Phil 3.20; 1 Thess 1.10; Titus 2.13); be ready for his coming (Mt 24.44; Lk 12.40); wait patiently for his coming (Jas 5.7,8); and pray for his coming (Rev 22.20).
4.10 *Demas.* How awful that someone should have his name written indelibly into the sacred record as one who so loved this present evil world that he forsook the calling of God.
4.14 *Alexander the coppersmith.* All believers should live in the light of the truth that their works will be judged and that they will be rewarded according to what they have done.
4.19 *Prisca* was the wife of Aquila; both were true followers of Jesus Christ and personal friends of the apostle Paul. They fled from Rome to Corinth when Claudius expelled the Jews in A.D. 52 (Acts 18.2). They ministered in Ephesus (Acts 18.18–26), and

4.20
Acts 19.22
4.21
v. 9
4.22
Gal 6.18;
Philem 25

20 Erastus remained in Corinth; Trophimus I left ill in Miletus. 21 Do your best to come before winter. Eubulus sends greetings to you, as do Pudens and Linus and Claudia and all the brothers and sisters. *k*

22 The Lord be with your spirit. Grace be with you. *l*

k Gk *all the brothers*   *l* The Greek word for *you* here is plural. Other ancient authorities add *Amen*

from there returned to Rome (cf. Rom 16.3,4). As Paul now writes to Timothy, they have returned to Ephesus (cf. 1 Tim 1.3).

4.20 *Erastus* may be the same person as is mentioned in Acts 19.22; the Erastus of Rom 16.23 (the city treasurer) is probably a different individual. For *Trophimus*, see the note on Acts 21.27ff.

Introduction to Titus

Outline:

I. Greeting (1.1-)

II. Church organization (1.5-16)

III. The Christian life (2.1–3.11)

IV. Personal matters and benediction (3.12-15

INTRODUCTION TO
THE LETTER OF PAUL TO
TITUS

Authorship, Date, and Background: See the introduction to 1 Timothy for the question of authorship and date. The letter to Titus was written between 1 and 2 Timothy. Paul, together with Titus, ministered to the people of Crete. When he finished his ministry, he left Titus behind to solidify the work by organizing the churches and correcting errors which abounded among the converts. He intended to send Artemas or Tychicus to Crete. Upon the arrival of one or the other in Crete to replace Titus, Paul wanted Titus then to meet him at Nicopolis, where he expected to spend the winter.

At the time Paul wrote to Titus, the gospel at Crete had not yet produced mature believers. The church was not properly organized and its members lived irregular lives. The older women were gossipy and overindulged in wine; the men were lazy and careless; the young women were not working hard enough and were apt to neglect their families and be flirtatious. The Cretans failed to relate the gospel of grace to an earthly life of good works, something Paul was careful to insist on.

Titus, to whom this letter was addressed, was a longtime companion of Paul. He is named in 2 Corinthians, Galatians, and 2 Timothy, though not in Acts. He was a Gentile who was not circumcised and whom Paul refused to have circumcised since, in this instance, it would have been a concession to the legalism which Paul was fighting (Gal 2.1–3). Titus was an ideal pastor and one to whom Paul could entrust the difficult mission among the Cretans.

Characteristics and Content: Paul calls Titus "my loyal child in the faith we share" (1.4). He says he left him in Crete to strengthen each of its churches and to "appoint elders in every town" (1.5). Paul has great confidence in Titus, for he counsels Titus on how to work out the problems of a difficult pastorate. Titus is more doctrinal than 1 Timothy. Two passages stand out in particular: 2.11–14 and 3.4–7. In them Paul speaks about the deity of Jesus Christ, his atonement as a substitute for us, the universality of salvation for all who receive Christ, salvation by faith without works, the coming of the Holy Spirit, sanctification, and God as a God of love and grace. Especially important is Paul's reference to the return of Jesus to earth from heaven. Paul's emphasis on "sound doctrine" (i.e., being strong in the true faith, 1.9; 2.1) indicates that there was a body of truth generally regarded as foundational to the Christian faith; deviations from that norm must be vigorously opposed. Paul closes with an instruction to Titus to come to Nicopolis to spend the winter with him (3.12).

Outline:

I. Greeting (1.1–4)

II. Church organization (1.5–16)

III. The Christian life (2.1—3.11)

IV. Personal matters and benediction (3.12–15)

THE LETTER OF PAUL TO

TITUS

I. Greeting (1.1–4)

1 Paul, a servant[a] of God and an apostle of Jesus Christ, for the sake of the faith of God's elect and the knowledge of the truth that is in accordance with godliness, 2 in the hope of eternal life that God, who never lies, promised before the ages began — 3 in due time he revealed his word through the proclamation with which I have been entrusted by the command of God our Savior,

4 To Titus, my loyal child in the faith we share:
Grace[b] and peace from God the Father and Christ Jesus our Savior.

II. Church organization (1.5–16)

A. Qualifications for elders

5 I left you behind in Crete for this reason, so that you should put in order what remained to be done, and should appoint elders in every town, as I directed you: 6 someone who is blameless, married only once,[c] whose children are believers, not accused of debauchery and not rebellious. 7 For a bishop,[d] as God's steward, must be blameless; he must not be arrogant or quick-tempered or addicted to wine or violent or greedy for gain; 8 but he must be hospitable, a lover of goodness, prudent, upright, devout, and self-controlled. 9 He must have a firm grasp of the word that is trustworthy in accordance with the teaching, so that he may be able both to preach with sound doctrine and to refute those who contradict it.

B. Exposé of false teachers

10 There are also many rebellious people, idle talkers and deceivers, especially those of the circumcision; 11 they must be silenced, since they are upsetting whole families by teaching for sordid gain what it is not right to teach. 12 It was one of them, their very own prophet, who said, "Cretans are always liars, vicious brutes, lazy gluttons." 13 That testimony is true. For this reason rebuke them sharply, so that they may become sound in the faith, 14 not paying attention to Jewish myths or to commandments of those who reject the truth. 15 To the pure all things are pure, but to the corrupt and unbelieving nothing is pure. Their very minds and consciences are corrupted. 16 They profess to know

---

a Gk *slave*   *b* Other ancient authorities read *Grace, mercy,*   *c* Gk *husband of one wife*   *d* Or *an overseer*

1.1	Rom 1.1; 2 Cor 1.1; 1 Tim 2.4; 6.3
1.2	2 Tim 1.1; Rom 16.25
1.3	2 Tim 1.10; 1 Thess 2.4
1.4	2 Cor 2.13; Eph 1.2; 1 Tim 1.2
1.5	Acts 27.7; 14.23; 11.30
1.6	1 Tim 3.2-4
1.7	1 Cor 4.1; Eph 5.18
1.8	1 Tim 3.2; 2 Tim 3.3
1.9	1 Tim 1.19;
1.10	
1.10	1 Tim 1.6; Acts 11.2
1.11	2 Tim 3.6; 1 Tim 6.5
1.12	Acts 17.28
1.13	2 Cor 13.10; Titus 2.2
1.14	1 Tim 1.4; Isa 29.13
1.15	Lk 11.39, 41; Rom 14.23
1.16	1 Jn 2.4; 2 Tim 3.5, 8

1.2 *in the hope of eternal life.* Christian hope is not wishful thinking, but it is based on the promises of God, who cannot lie. And God's plan to give eternal life was promised *before* the world began.
1.5ff The words "elder" (Gk. *presbuteros*) and "bishop" (Gk. *episkopos,* "overseer") are used interchangeably in the N.T. (cf. vv. 5,7). The plural is normally used; there is no record of a single bishop or elder in any N.T. church, although a single person like Diotrephes did usurp controlling authority over a local church (3 Jn 9). The qualifications for the office are laid down here and in 1 Tim 3.1–7. The call comes from the Holy Spirit but it must be ratified by the church; hands were to be laid on one called to this office (v. 5; Acts 14.23). The Spirit's call also meant the endowment by the Spirit with the gifts necessary to discharge the duties of the office (1 Cor 12.28; Eph 4.11). The functions of the office include (1) rulership (1 Tim 5.17); (2) preaching of the word and keeping the people sound in the faith (v. 9; 1 Tim 5.17); and (3) caring for the flock like a shepherd (Acts 20.28; 1 Pet 5.2).
1.10ff Titus must avoid or reject bad teachers who entertain false notions not in accord with the truth. He is to rebuke them sharply. Paul hopes they will be correctable, become sound in the faith, and no longer give heed to fables and to commandments which have no warrant in the Scriptures (v. 14).

God, but they deny him by their actions. They are detestable, disobedient, unfit for any good work.

III. *The Christian life (2.1–3.11)*

A. *Among Christians*

2 But as for you, teach what is consistent with sound doctrine. 2 Tell the older men to be temperate, serious, prudent, and sound in faith, in love, and in endurance.

3 Likewise, tell the older women to be reverent in behavior, not to be slanderers or slaves to drink; they are to teach what is good, 4 so that they may encourage the young women to love their husbands, to love their children, 5 to be self-controlled, chaste, good managers of the household, kind, being submissive to their husbands, so that the word of God may not be discredited.

6 Likewise, urge the younger men to be self-controlled. 7 Show yourself in all respects a model of good works, and in your teaching show integrity, gravity, 8 and sound speech that cannot be censured; then any opponent will be put to shame, having nothing evil to say of us.

9 Tell slaves to be submissive to their masters and to give satisfaction in every respect; they are not to talk back, 10 not to pilfer, but to show complete and perfect fidelity, so that in everything they may be an ornament to the doctrine of God our Savior.

B. *In the light of the blessed hope*

11 For the grace of God has appeared, bringing salvation to all,*e* 12 training us to renounce impiety and worldly passions, and in the present age to live lives that are self-controlled, upright, and godly, 13 while we wait for the blessed hope and the manifestation of the glory of our great God and Savior,*f* Jesus Christ. 14 He it is who gave himself for us that he might redeem us from all iniquity and purify for himself a people of his own who are zealous for good deeds.

15 Declare these things; exhort and reprove with all authority.*g* Let no one look down on you.

C. *Faith and works*

3 Remind them to be subject to rulers and authorities, to be obedient, to be ready for every good work, 2 to speak evil of no one, to avoid quarreling, to be gentle, and to show every courtesy to everyone. 3 For we ourselves were once foolish, disobedient, led astray, slaves to various passions and pleasures, passing our days in malice and envy, despicable, hating one another. 4 But when the goodness and loving kindness of God our Savior appeared, 5 he saved us, not because of any works of righteousness that we had done, but according to his mercy, through the water*h*

---

e Or *has appeared to all, bringing salvation*   *f* Or *of the great God and our Savior*   *g* Gk *commandment*
h Gk *washing*

2.1ff Paul commands Titus to preach and teach sound doctrine to old men, old women, young women (who will be taught by old ones), and young men. But faith must be accompanied by Christian works. Titus must therefore himself do good works and thus be a model against whom no charges of hypocrisy can be leveled (vv. 7,8).
2.4 Wives have certain obligations to their husbands, such as to love them, to live with them until death parts them (Rom 7.2,3), to be submissive to them (v. 5; Eph 5.22), to respect them (Eph 5.33), and to respond to their sexual needs (1 Cor 7.3–5).
2.13 The coming of our glorious God and Savior is

the church's blessed hope. But that hope includes all of the events connected with the return of the Lord, not just what some call the rapture of the church (see note on 1 Thess 4.15).
3.1 Christians must have respect for government and obey rulers and authorities (see note on Rom 13.1ff). Although in general Christians should not speak evil of anyone, there are times when they must address forthrightly the sins of wicked people.
3.5 *Rebirth and renewal* are inward and spiritual. Although it is expressed outwardly by the sign and seal of water baptism, regeneration as such is the renewing work of the Holy Spirit in the believer.

2.1
Titus 1.9
2.2
Titus 1.13
2.3
1 Tim 3.8
2.5
1 Cor 14.34;
Eph 5.22;
1 Tim 6.1
2.7
1 Tim 4.12
2.8
1 Tim 6.3
2.9
Eph 6.5
2.10
Mt 5.16
2.11
Rom 5.15;
1 Tim 2.4
2.12
Titus 3.3;
2 Tim 3.12
2.13
2 Thess 2.8;
2 Pet 1.1
2.14
1 Tim 2.6;
Heb 9.14;
Ex 19.5;
Eph 2.10
3.1
Rom 13.1;
2 Tim 2.21
3.2
Eph 4.31;
2 Tim 2.24,
25
3.3
1 Cor 6.11;
1 Pet 4.3
3.4
Titus 2.11;
1 Tim 2.3
3.5
Rom 3.20;
Eph 5.26;
Rom 12.2

of rebirth and renewal by the Holy Spirit. 6 This Spirit he poured out on us richly through Jesus Christ our Savior, 7 so that, having been justified by his grace, we might become heirs according to the hope of eternal life. 8 The saying is sure.

I desire that you insist on these things, so that those who have come to believe in God may be careful to devote themselves to good works; these things are excellent and profitable to everyone. 9 But avoid stupid controversies, genealogies, dissensions, and quarrels about the law, for they are unprofitable and worthless. 10 After a first and second admonition, have nothing more to do with anyone who causes divisions, 11 since you know that such a person is perverted and sinful, being self-condemned.

IV. *Personal matters and benediction (3.12–15)*

12 When I send Artemas to you, or Tychicus, do your best to come to me at Nicopolis, for I have decided to spend the winter there. 13 Make every effort to send Zenas the lawyer and Apollos on their way, and see that they lack nothing. 14 And let people learn to devote themselves to good works in order to meet urgent needs, so that they may not be unproductive.

15 All who are with me send greetings to you. Greet those who love us in the faith.

Grace be with all of you. *i*

i Other ancient authorities add *Amen*

3.6
Rom 5.5
3.7
Rom 3.24;
8.17, 24
3.8
1 Tim 1.15;
Titus 2.14
3.9
1 Tim 1.4;
2 Tim 2.14
3.10
Rom 16.17

3.12
Acts 20.4;
2 Tim 4.9, 10
3.13
Acts 18.24
3.14
v. 8

3.15
Col 4.18

3.7 Christians are not only justified; they also have assurance from God concerning the many blessings of justification. Among them are (1) the assurance of salvation itself (Isa 12.2; Jn 3.17; Acts 16.30,31); (2) the certainty of eternal life (1 Jn 5.13); (3) peace with God (Rom 5.1); (4) freedom from condemnation (Rom 8.1,33,34); (5) the guarantee of a glorious resurrection (Phil 3.21); (6) the promise of a kingdom (Heb 12.28); (7) the gift of a crown in heaven (2 Tim 4.7,8); (8) joint-heirship with Jesus (3.7; Rom 8.17); and (9) the assurance of glorification (Rom 8.30).
3.10 Paul tells Titus how to deal with *anyone who causes divisions*. Such people must be admonished at least twice with the hope of bringing them back to the true faith. If and when this does not happen, they must be cast out of the communion, and all believers

should be warned to have nothing to do with them. The Greek word for "division" (*hairesis*) is used in various ways in the N.T. In Acts it simply means a party within a group and is thus neutral (e.g., Acts 15.5; 24.5). In Paul's writing it has a negative connotation, implying schism (e.g., 1 Cor 11.19; Gal 5.20). Peter uses it to denote heretical doctrine (2 Pet 2.1). The early church Fathers thought of it in connection with erroneous doctrine. In popular terminology today the word means doctrinal departure from orthodoxy, such as the denial of Christ's deity, the Trinity, the virgin birth, etc.
3.12ff Paul is sending Artemas or Tychicus to Crete to replace Titus as resident minister. Titus himself is likely an evangelist and not a settled minister, so Paul wants him to rejoin him at Nicopolis to assist him there.

INTRODUCTION TO
THE LETTER OF PAUL TO
PHILEMON

Authorship, Date, and Background: Philemon is the shortest of Paul's letters. It is one of the "prison letters" (see introduction to Ephesians) and was written from Rome during the same period as the other letters (around A.D. 60–61). Slavery had long been a recognized institution, even in Israelite society. Moses had given explicit instructions concerning it, for even slaves had some rights and protection under Jewish law. Nowhere does the N.T. specifically speak against it, though there is general agreement that the principles of the N.T. were responsible for the elimination of slavery. Paul, for example, taught that in Christ there is neither slave nor free (Col 3.11).

The letter addressed to Philemon arose out of a situation in which his slave Onesimus had fled with some of his master's money or property. Apparently he came into contact with Paul, who brought him to salvation through Jesus Christ. What should Onesimus do now that he was a Christian, inasmuch as his master Philemon was a believer? Since salvation includes repentance and restitution, it was apparent that Onesimus could do nothing else than return to his master and resume his role as a slave. Philemon had the right of life and death over Onesimus and could have had him executed for his actions. It was against this background that the apostle Paul wrote not only to Philemon but also to the church which met in his home. This made the letter something more than a personal note to a friend. It brought the church into the picture and with it the moral persuasion of other believers who would watch the decision Philemon was called upon to make.

Characteristics and Content: The letter centers on the motif of forgiveness. Onesimus had committed a crime, probably theft (v. 18). But Paul pleads for compassion for him and even offers to pay back whatever Onesimus has stolen. He notes that the relationship of Onesimus to Philemon has changed from that of a slave to "a beloved brother" (16). Paul himself really wants to retain Onesimus, but sends him back because it is the right thing to do. He asks Philemon to treat Onesimus kindly, confident that he will do so (21). The letter breathes out Paul's unspoken hope that Philemon will set him free. By adding greetings from his other fellow workers, he lets Philemon know that they are also watching to see how he will react to the apostle's appeal.

Outline:

I. Greeting (1–3)

II. Paul's love for Philemon (4–7)

III. Appeal for Onesimus (8–22)

IV. Greetings and benediction (23–25)

THE LETTER OF PAUL TO

PHILEMON

I. Greeting (1–3)

1 Paul, a prisoner of Christ Jesus, and Timothy our brother,[a]
To Philemon our dear friend and co-worker, 2 to Apphia our sister,[b]
to Archippus our fellow soldier, and to the church in your house:
3 Grace to you and peace from God our Father and the Lord Jesus
Christ.

1
Eph 3.1;
2 Cor 1.1;
Phil 2.25
2
Col 4.17;
Phil 2.25;
Rom 16.5

II. Paul's love for Philemon (4–7)

4 When I remember you[c] in my prayers, I always thank my God
5 because I hear of your love for all the saints and your faith toward the
Lord Jesus. 6 I pray that the sharing of your faith may become effective
when you perceive all the good that we[d] may do for Christ. 7 I have indeed
received much joy and encouragement from your love, because the hearts
of the saints have been refreshed through you, my brother.

4
Rom 1.8, 9
5
Eph 1.15;
Col 1.4
7
v. 20;
2 Cor 7.13

III. Appeal for Onesimus (8–22)

8 For this reason, though I am bold enough in Christ to command you
to do your duty, 9 yet I would rather appeal to you on the basis of
love—and I, Paul, do this as an old man, and now also as a prisoner of
Christ Jesus.[e] 10 I am appealing to you for my child, Onesimus, whose
father I have become during my imprisonment. 11 Formerly he was useless
to you, but now he is indeed useful[f] both to you and to me. 12 I am
sending him, that is, my own heart, back to you. 13 I wanted to keep him
with me, so that he might be of service to me in your place during my
imprisonment for the gospel; 14 but I preferred to do nothing without your
consent, in order that your good deed might be voluntary and not something forced. 15 Perhaps this is the reason he was separated from you for
a while, so that you might have him back forever, 16 no longer as a slave
but more than a slave, a beloved brother—especially to me but how much
more to you, both in the flesh and in the Lord.
17 So if you consider me your partner, welcome him as you would

10
Col 4.9;
1 Cor 4.14,
15
13
Phil 1.7
14
1 Pet 5.2;
2 Cor 9.7
16
Mt 23.8;
1 Tim 6.2;
Col 3.22
17
2 Cor 8.23

---

a Gk *the brother* *b* Gk *the sister* *c* From verse 4 through verse 21, *you* is singular *d* Other ancient
authorities read *you* (plural) *e* Or *as an ambassador of Christ Jesus, and now also his prisoner*
f The name Onesimus means *useful* or (compare verse 20) *beneficial*

---

1 *Paul, a prisoner of Christ Jesus.* No one is distinguished simply because he is in jail, as Paul was
when he wrote this letter. But being a prisoner for
the true faith and for preaching the gospel is true
glory.
2 Although this letter is entitled *Philemon*, Paul also
addressed Apphia, Archippus, and the church which
was in Philemon's house. No doubt Paul wanted these
people to know what his request for Onesimus was,
for Philemon would be under added pressure to ac-
cede to Paul's petition.
8 Philemon is so noted for his Christian life and
deeds (vv. 4–7) that Paul is giving his friend another
opportunity to demonstrate the reality of his faith and
life in Christ by freeing Onesimus or at least by receiving him back without reprisal.

9ff Paul could order Philemon to free Onesimus,
but he prefers to plead his case on the basis of love,
not commandment. He pictures himself as an aged
saint in prison whose load has been lightened by
Onesimus' services to him.
12 Paul's appeal for Onesimus arises in part from
the fact that this slave had found Christ under his
ministry. Therefore he has more than an ordinary
interest in his situation.
15 As a runaway slave, Onesimus was worthy of
death. Paul argues that since he has found Christ,
Onesimus is coming back to Philemon not simply as
a slave, but as a beloved brother in Christ. Both of
them are now brothers in Christ. Thus, for Philemon
to treat Onesimus simply as a runaway slave would be
incongruent with his testimony as a Christian.

welcome me. 18 If he has wronged you in any way, or owes you anything, charge that to my account. 19 I, Paul, am writing this with my own hand: I will repay it. I say nothing about your owing me even your own self. 20 Yes, brother, let me have this benefit from you in the Lord! Refresh my heart in Christ. 21 Confident of your obedience, I am writing to you, knowing that you will do even more than I say.

22   One thing more—prepare a guest room for me, for I am hoping through your prayers to be restored to you.

IV. *Greetings and benediction (23–25)*

23   Epaphras, my fellow prisoner in Christ Jesus, sends greetings to you,g 24 and so do Mark, Aristarchus, Demas, and Luke, my fellow workers.
25   The grace of the Lord Jesus Christ be with your spirit. h

g Here *you* is singular   h Other ancient authorities add *Amen*

21
2 Cor 2.3

22
Acts 28.23;
Phil 1.25;
2.24;
2 Cor 1.11

23
Col 1.7
24
Acts 12.12;
Col 4.10
25
2 Tim 4.22

---

23   *Epaphras.* See note on Col 1.7.
24   *Aristarchus,* one of Paul's followers from Thessalonica (Acts 20.4), was imprisoned with the apostle (Col 4.10) and may have been martyred in Rome under Nero. *Demas* later deserted Paul because he loved this present world (see 2 Tim 4.10).

INTRODUCTION TO
THE LETTER TO THE
HEBREWS

Authorship, Date, and Background: We do not know with any certainty who the author of Hebrews was. No name is given, nor does the letter supply details which would enable anyone to make a positive identification. For these reasons, a number of different people have been suggested as the author; for example, Paul, Barnabas, and Apollos. We do know that the letter was not written by Timothy, for the author names him as just having been released from jail. If Paul were the author, he would hardly have spoken of Timothy as "brother" when he usually called him "son." Apparently the author was a Jew, for he was familar with the O.T. (especially the Septuagint translation) and was a man of high literary skills.

The letter came from the second generation era of Christians (see 5.12,13; 10.32). Since persecution was seen as imminent but had not yet come, and since the author wrote as though the temple was still standing, it appears that the letter can probably be dated before the sack of Jerusalem (A.D. 70). That would make it the mid to late 60s.

The book of Hebrews does not state to whom it was written. But a reconstruction of the history of the times leads to the conclusion that the Christian church was moving away from the synagogue, and that questions were being asked about the relation of Christianity to Judaism and about how Jesus Christ fit into the picture of the O.T. sacrificial system. Indeed, there was a need for a book like Hebrews to explain more fully how God's plan moved from the O.T. to the N.T. and how Jesus Christ fulfilled the O.T. prophetic word.

Characteristics and Content: Hebrews centers around the use of the word "better." The Son, Jesus Christ, is better than the angels, whom the Jews greatly respected and feared. He is better than Moses, and his priesthood is better than that of Aaron, the founding father of the priesthood. Jesus is linked to the Melchizedek priesthood, which existed before the Aaronic priesthood, and to the Jewish ancestor Abraham, who paid tithes to Melchizedek. Jesus is the center of the new covenant which is better than the old covenant, for the old one was temporary and the new one is eternal. Nowhere else in the N.T. is the new covenant explained more fully. Christ is the better sacrifice since the blood of bulls and goats could never take away sin forever. These sacrifices had to be repeated again and again, while the sacrifice of Jesus is a once-for-all sacrifice which took away sin permanently and never needs to be repeated. Moreover, the writer shows that faith is the better way. No one can faultlessly keep the whole law of God. All the law can do is condemn people (cf. Galatians). But faith is the excellent way in which God makes it possible for humans to come to him for salvation and eternal life.

The author defines faith succinctly (11.1) and then illustrates it profusely in the lives of the O.T. saints, all of whom were saved by faith and not by works. The roster of believers includes some whose works indeed were suspect but who, in spite of their actions, were saved by their faith. God's deliverance is the end result of faith. The writer closes the letter with admonitions and sounds forth the divine promise of a kingdom which cannot be destroyed (12.28). In the last chapter, he reiterates the eternal nature of Jesus Christ who is the same yesterday, today, and forever (13.8), and concludes with the magnificent benediction in which it is asserted that Christ, the great shepherd of the sheep, has risen from the dead, and the new and everlasting agreement between God and sinners by virtue of Christ's atonement on the cross is available to all who will come.

Typology (the study of how the O.T. points forward to the coming of Jesus Christ) finds a central place in this letter. We find how the O.T. promises are finally and forever fulfilled in the N.T. in the person of Jesus. The author speaks of all three persons of the Trinity, the Father, the Son, and the Holy Spirit, in a way which advances this doctrine noticeably.

Outline:

THE LETTER TO THE
HEBREWS

I. Introduction: Christ — the final revelation of God (1.1–4)

1 Long ago God spoke to our ancestors in many and various ways by the prophets, 2 but in these last days he has spoken to us by a Son,*a* whom he appointed heir of all things, through whom he also created the worlds. 3 He is the reflection of God's glory and the exact imprint of God's very being, and he sustains*b* all things by his powerful word. When he had made purification for sins, he sat down at the right hand of the Majesty on high, 4 having become as much superior to angels as the name he has inherited is more excellent than theirs.

1.2
Gal 4.4;
Heb 2.3;
Ps 2.8;
Jn 1.3;
1 Cor 8.6
1.3
Jn 1.14;
Col 1.17;
Heb 7.27; 8.1
1.4
Eph 1.21;
Phil 2.9, 10

II. Christ — better than the angels (1.5–2.18)

A. Christ the Son of God

5 For to which of the angels did God ever say,
"You are my Son;
   today I have begotten you"?
Or again,
"I will be his Father,
   and he will be my Son"?
6 And again, when he brings the firstborn into the world, he says,
"Let all God's angels worship him."
7 Of the angels he says,
"He makes his angels winds,
   and his servants flames of fire."
8 But of the Son he says,
"Your throne, O God, is*c* forever and ever,
   and the righteous scepter is the scepter of your*d* kingdom.
9 You have loved righteousness and hated wickedness;
   therefore God, your God, has anointed you
   with the oil of gladness beyond your companions."
10 And,
"In the beginning, Lord, you founded the earth,
   and the heavens are the work of your hands;
11 they will perish, but you remain;
   they will all wear out like clothing;
12 like a cloak you will roll them up,
   and like clothing*e* they will be changed.

1.5
Ps 2.7

1.6
Heb 10.5;
Deut 32.43
1.7
Ps 104.4

1.8
Ps 45.6, 7

1.9
Phil 2.9;
Isa 61.1, 3

1.10
Ps 102.25

1.11
Isa 34.4

1.12
Heb 13.8

a Or *the Son*   *b* Or *bears along*   *c* Or *God is your throne*   *d* Other ancient authorities read *his*   *e* Other ancient authorities lack *like clothing*

1.1ff The opening verses of Hebrews contain seven great theological themes: (1) theism — there is a God; (2) revelation — God has revealed himself through the prophets and through his Son; (3) incarnation — God became a human being in Jesus Christ; (4) creation — God created all things through Christ; (5) providence — God sustains all things by his powerful word; (6) redemption — Christ by his mediatorship and atoning death made salvation possible; (7) ascension — the Lord Jesus has ascended into heaven and is seated at the right hand of the Father.
1.3 *sat down.* See note on 10.12.
1.5 Although angels are great in power and position, they are subject to Jesus Christ and worship and glorify the Father, the Son, and the Holy Spirit. No angel has ever been called the Son of God.
1.8,9 Christ holds a sceptre of power and authority in his hand. He is a king, and he rules over a kingdom of people and angels (cf. 1 Pet 3.22).

> But you are the same,
> and your years will never end."

1.13
Ps 110.1;
Heb 10.13

13But to which of the angels has he ever said,
> "Sit at my right hand
> until I make your enemies a footstool for your feet"?

1.14
Ps 103.20;
Heb 5.9

14Are not all angels*f* spirits in the divine service, sent to serve for the sake of those who are to inherit salvation?

B. *Christ the human being*

1. *Warning against rejecting God's revelation*

2.2
Heb 1.1;
Acts 7.53;
Heb 10.28,
35
2.3
Heb 10.29;
1.1;
Lk 1.2
2.4
Jn 4.48;
1 Cor 12.4;
Eph 1.5

2 Therefore we must pay greater attention to what we have heard, so that we do not drift away from it. 2For if the message declared through angels was valid, and every transgression or disobedience received a just penalty, 3how can we escape if we neglect so great a salvation? It was declared at first through the Lord, and it was attested to us by those who heard him, 4while God added his testimony by signs and wonders and various miracles, and by gifts of the Holy Spirit, distributed according to his will.

2. *The kingdom conferred on Christ*

2.5
Heb 6.5
2.6
Ps 8.4-6

5 Now God*g* did not subject the coming world, about which we are speaking, to angels. 6But someone has testified somewhere,
> "What are human beings that you are mindful of them,*h*
> or mortals, that you care for them?*i*
> 7 You have made them for a little while lower*j* than the angels;
> you have crowned them with glory and honor,*k*
> 8 subjecting all things under their feet."

2.8
Mt 28.18;
1 Cor 15.27;
15.25
2.9
Phil 2.7-9;
Acts 2.33;
Jn 3.16; 1 Jn
2.2

Now in subjecting all things to them, God*g* left nothing outside their control. As it is, we do not yet see everything in subjection to them, 9but we do see Jesus, who for a little while was made lower*l* than the angels, now crowned with glory and honor because of the suffering of death, so that by the grace of God*m* he might taste death for everyone.

3. *Christ as truly human*

2.10
Lk 24.46;
Rom 11.36;
Acts 3.15;
5.31;
Lk 13.32
2.11
Heb 10.10;
Acts 17.26;
Jn 20.17
2.12
Ps 22.22
2.13
Isa 8.17, 18;
Jn 10.29

10 It was fitting that God,*g* for whom and through whom all things exist, in bringing many children to glory, should make the pioneer of their salvation perfect through sufferings. 11For the one who sanctifies and those who are sanctified all have one Father.*n* For this reason Jesus*g* is not ashamed to call them brothers and sisters,*o* 12saying,
> "I will proclaim your name to my brothers and sisters,*o*
> in the midst of the congregation I will praise you."
13And again,
> "I will put my trust in him."

f Gk *all of them*   *g* Gk *he*   *h* Gk *What is man that you are mindful of him?*   *i* Gk *or the son of man that you care for him?* In the Hebrew of Psalm 8.4-6 both *man* and *son of man* refer to all humankind   *j* Or *them only a little lower*   *k* Other ancient authorities add *and set them over the works of your hands*   *l* Or *who was made a little lower*   *m* Other ancient authorities read *apart from God*   *n* Gk *are all of one*
o Gk *brothers*

1.14 As to their nature angels are spirits, i.e., they have no bodies. As to their work they are in divine service, i.e., they serve God and do his will, particularly ministering to the people of God as those who will inherit salvation (cf. Ps 91.11).
2.2 *the message declared through angels* refers to the law given to Israel on Mount Sinai. Angels were involved in the giving of the law (see Acts 7.38,53; Gal 3.19; cf. Deut 33.2).
2.3 *so great a salvation.* The gospel reveals our great Savior and shows us how we can be saved from sin and

restored to God's favor and holy living. Those who despise this great salvation are condemned already. The Lord Jesus was the first one to speak the good news plainly and clearly.
2.9 *the suffering of death.* The cross was necessary to accomplish God's plan of redeeming sinners. There was no other way by which they are saved.
2.11 Union with Christ means that we are all his brothers and sisters, and he is not ashamed to call us that.

And again,
"Here am I and the children whom God has given me."

4. Christ as true sacrifice for humankind

14 Since, therefore, the children share flesh and blood, he himself likewise shared the same things, so that through death he might destroy the one who has the power of death, that is, the devil, 15 and free those who all their lives were held in slavery by the fear of death. 16 For it is clear that he did not come to help angels, but the descendants of Abraham. 17 Therefore he had to become like his brothers and sisters*p* in every respect, so that he might be a merciful and faithful high priest in the service of God, to make a sacrifice of atonement for the sins of the people. 18 Because he himself was tested by what he suffered, he is able to help those who are being tested.

III. Christ—better than Moses and Joshua (3.1—4.13)

A. Christ as Lord superior to Moses as servant

3 Therefore, brothers and sisters,*p* holy partners in a heavenly calling, consider that Jesus, the apostle and high priest of our confession, 2 was faithful to the one who appointed him, just as Moses also "was faithful in all*q* God's*r* house." 3 Yet Jesus*s* is worthy of more glory than Moses, just as the builder of a house has more honor than the house itself. 4 (For every house is built by someone, but the builder of all things is God.) 5 Now Moses was faithful in all God's*r* house as a servant, to testify to the things that would be spoken later. 6 Christ, however, was faithful over God's*r* house as a son, and we are his house if we hold firm*t* the confidence and the pride that belong to hope.

B. Christ's rest superior to that of Moses and Joshua

1. Introduction

7 Therefore, as the Holy Spirit says,
"Today, if you hear his voice,
8 do not harden your hearts as in the rebellion,
 as on the day of testing in the wilderness,
9 where your ancestors put me to the test,
 though they had seen my works 10 for forty years.
Therefore I was angry with that generation,
 and I said, 'They always go astray in their hearts,

p Gk brothers   *q* Other ancient authorities lack *all*   *r* Gk his   *s* Gk this one   *t* Other ancient authorities add *to the end*

Cross-references:
2.14 Mt 16.17; Jn 1.14; 1 Cor 15.54-57; 1 Jn 3.8
2.15 Rom 8.15; 2 Tim 1.7
2.17 Phil 2.7; Heb 4.15; 5.1, 2; 1 Jn 2.2; 4.10
2.18 Heb 4.15
3.1 Heb 2.11; Phil 3.14; Rom 15.8; Heb 10.21
3.3 2 Cor 3.7-11
3.4 Eph 2.10; Heb 1.2
3.5 Num 12.7; Ex 14.31; Deut 18.18, 19
3.6 Heb 1.2; 1 Cor 3.16; Rom 5.2; Col 1.23
3.7 Heb 9.8; Ps 95.7
3.9 Acts 7.36

2.14 *he himself likewise shared the same things*, i.e., Jesus Christ, who is God, became human. He did not possess the nature of angels but of humankind. He united his divine nature with human nature in himself.

2.17 *Make a sacrifice of atonement for the sins of the people* is translated elsewhere as "make expiation" or "propitiation" for our sins. It comes from the Greek word *hilaskomai*, which means "to propitiate" or "to make atonement." At Calvary Christ atoned for the sins of humankind. His death accomplished at least three things: (1) our sins were covered (the O.T. word *kaphar* means "to cover over" or "atone for," see Lev 16); (2) we were reconciled, i.e., the broken relationship between us and God was reestablished (cf. 2 Cor 5.18–21); (3) Jesus was our substitute, i.e., he stood in the place of sinners and paid the penalty for our transgressions (cf. Isa 53.4–6). The shedding of blood was basic to the atonement (9.22). The cross is a once-for-all sacrifice that becomes effective when claimed by faith.

3.1,2 *holy partners*, i.e., those holy in principle through the new birth and holy in conduct and life. *consider that Jesus . . . was faithful.* The writer wants the holy partners to think about Jesus, the apostle and high priest of their profession.

3.5,6 No one in the O.T. was considered closer to God than Moses (cf. Ex 33.7–11,18–23), but Hebrews points out he was only a servant in God's house, while Jesus is the Son. The house is the church of God made up of all believers, and Christ is the master of that house as well as its maker.

3.7 What the psalmist said (Ps 95.7), the Holy Spirit said; conversely, what the Holy Spirit said, the psalmist said. Scripture is thus both human and divine, though the ultimate author is the Holy Spirit.

and they have not known my ways.'
11 As in my anger I swore,
'They will not enter my rest.' "

2. The necessity of persevering faith to enter Christ's rest

12 Take care, brothers and sisters,ᵘ that none of you may have an evil, unbelieving heart that turns away from the living God. 13 But exhort one another every day, as long as it is called "today," so that none of you may be hardened by the deceitfulness of sin. 14 For we have become partners of Christ, if only we hold our first confidence firm to the end. 15 As it is said,

"Today, if you hear his voice,
do not harden your hearts as in the rebellion."

16 Now who were they who heard and yet were rebellious? Was it not all those who left Egypt under the leadership of Moses? 17 But with whom was he angry forty years? Was it not those who sinned, whose bodies fell in the wilderness? 18 And to whom did he swear that they would not enter his rest, if not to those who were disobedient? 19 So we see that they were unable to enter because of unbelief.

3. Warning against missing Christ's rest as typified by Canaan rest

4 Therefore, while the promise of entering his rest is still open, let us take care that none of you should seem to have failed to reach it. 2 For indeed the good news came to us just as to them; but the message they heard did not benefit them, because they were not united by faith with those who listened.ᵛ 3 For we who have believed enter that rest, just as Godʷ has said,

"As in my anger I swore,
'They shall not enter my rest,' "

though his works were finished at the foundation of the world. 4 For in one place it speaks about the seventh day as follows, "And God rested on the seventh day from all his works." 5 And again in this place it says, "They shall not enter my rest." 6 Since therefore it remains open for some to enter it, and those who formerly received the good news failed to enter because of disobedience, 7 again he sets a certain day — "today" — saying through David much later, in the words already quoted,

"Today, if you hear his voice,
do not harden your hearts."

8 For if Joshua had given them rest, Godʷ would not speak later about another day. 9 So then, a sabbath rest still remains for the people of God;

ᵘ Gk brothers   ᵛ Other ancient authorities read it did not meet with faith in those who listened   ʷ Gk he

---

3.11
Heb 4.3, 5

3.12
Heb 12.25;
9.14
3.13
Heb 10.24,
25;
Eph 4.22
3.14
v. 6
3.15
v. 7
3.16
Num 14.2
3.17
Num 14.29;
Ps 106.26
3.18
Num 14.23;
Heb 4.6
3.19
Jn 3.36

4.1
Heb 12.15
4.2
1 Thess 2.13

4.3
Ps 95.11;
Heb 3.11

4.4
Gen 2.2;
Ex 20.11
4.5
Ps 95.11;
Heb 3.11
4.6
Heb 3.18, 19
4.7
Ps 95.7, 8;
Heb 3.7, 8

4.8
Josh 22.4;
Heb 1.1

3.12 *Take care.* This warning is spoken in reference to the kind of sin that kept the Israelites from entering the land of Canaan. The Israelites repudiated Moses and were punished for it; how much more will Christians be punished if they spurn Christ who is greater than Moses.
3.17ff *with whom was he angry?* God was angry with the Israelites for sinning against him by their unbelief and idolatry. When divine patience is exhausted, judgment must fall.
4.2 *Good news* (Gk. *euaggelion*) means "good tidings, good message, gospel." In the N.T. the following expressions are representative ways of speaking about this good news: (1) good news of peace (Eph 2.17); (2) the good news about God's mighty kindness and love (Acts 20.24); (3) the good news about the kingdom (Mt 24.14); and (4) the eternal gospel (Rev 14.6). On the basis of different usages, some

have supposed there are different gospels. Such distinctions are unwarranted. In all ages sinners have been saved by the good news of salvation by faith — whether looking forward to Calvary or looking back to it. Abraham was saved by the gospel (Gal 3.8), just as everyone else in the N.T. was. The bottom line of the good news is that the incarnate Son of God died and rose again for our justification.
4.9 *sabbath rest . . . for the people of God.* The first rest in Scripture came on the seventh day of creation, at which time God rested (Gen 2.3). The second rest was the one promised to Israel in Canaan, but they could not enter it because of their unbelief (v. 2; Ps 95.11). The third rest is that of Jesus, when he entered the land of eternal rest after finishing the work of redemption. These rests prefigure the believers' ultimate rest, into which they will someday enter.

10 for those who enter God's rest also cease from their labors as God did from his. 11 Let us therefore make every effort to enter that rest, so that no one may fall through such disobedience as theirs.

12 Indeed, the word of God is living and active, sharper than any two-edged sword, piercing until it divides soul from spirit, joints from marrow; it is able to judge the thoughts and intentions of the heart. 13 And before him no creature is hidden, but all are naked and laid bare to the eyes of the one to whom we must render an account.

IV. Christ—better than the Aaronic priesthood (4.14—7.28)

A. Christ the way of approach to God

14 Since, then, we have a great high priest who has passed through the heavens, Jesus, the Son of God, let us hold fast to our confession. 15 For we do not have a high priest who is unable to sympathize with our weaknesses, but we have one who in every respect has been tested^x as we are, yet without sin. 16 Let us therefore approach the throne of grace with boldness, so that we may receive mercy and find grace to help in time of need.

B. Christ, God's appointed high priest

5 Every high priest chosen from among mortals is put in charge of things pertaining to God on their behalf, to offer gifts and sacrifices for sins. 2 He is able to deal gently with the ignorant and wayward, since he himself is subject to weakness; 3 and because of this he must offer sacrifice for his own sins as well as for those of the people. 4 And one does not presume to take this honor, but takes it only when called by God, just as Aaron was.

5 So also Christ did not glorify himself in becoming a high priest, but was appointed by the one who said to him,

"You are my Son,
　　today I have begotten you";

6 as he says also in another place,

"You are a priest forever,
　　according to the order of Melchizedek."

7 In the days of his flesh, Jesus^y offered up prayers and supplications, with loud cries and tears, to the one who was able to save him from death, and he was heard because of his reverent submission. 8 Although he was a Son, he learned obedience through what he suffered; 9 and having been

x Or tempted　y Gk he

4.10
v. 4
4.11
Heb 3.18
4.12
Jer 23.29;
Eph 6.17;
1 Cor 14.24,
25
4.13
Ps 33.13-15;
Job 26.6

4.14
Heb 3.1;
7.26; 10.23
4.15
Heb 2.18;
2 Cor 5.21;
1 Pet 2.22
4.16
Eph 2.18

5.1
Heb 8.3, 4;
7.27
5.2
Heb 2.18;
Jas 5.19;
Heb 7.28
5.3
Heb 7.27; 9.7
5.4
2 Chr 26.18;
Ex 28.1
5.5
Jn 8.54;
Ps 2.7;
Heb 1.1, 5
5.6
Ps 110.4;
Heb 7.17
5.7
Mt 26.39,
53; 27.46;
Mk 14.36;
15.34
5.8
Heb 3.6;
Phil 2.8
5.9
Heb 2.10

4.10,11 True believers do not rely on their own works of righteousness by trying to keep the law. Believers in Christ and his righteousness enter into the grace of rest here and the glory of rest hereafter. **4.15** Sinlessness exists only when the inward motivations and the outward acts are perfect in the sight of God. Jesus is the only human being who ever lived of whom it can be said that he exhibited a sinless and absolutely holy life. The Scriptures bear witness to this in the following ways: (1) Jesus' own witness (Jn 8.46; see also Jn 8.29; 17.19); (2) the witness of others (Mt 27.4,19; Lk 23.41; Jn 18.38); and (3) the witness of the apostles (v. 15; 7.26; 2 Cor 5.21; 1 Pet 2.21,22; 1 Jn 3.5). **5.1** The high priest was ordained by God to offer sacrifices for himself and for others. He was a sinner whose own transgressions were covered by the blood of bulls and goats first (cf. 7.27; 9.6,7). Then he offered sacrifices for others. He functioned as a medi-

ator between God and sinners. This high priest prefigured Jesus, the divine and sinless high priest whose own blood made atonement for the sins of humankind (9.11-14). **5.4ff** Christ is our high priest, not after the order of Aaron but after the order of Melchizedek, who preceded Aaron (see v. 10; 6.20-7.28). Just as earlier the author stressed the superiority of Christ to Moses (see note on 3.5,6), so now he stresses how, in the manner of his call and in the holiness of his person, Christ far surpasses Aaron, the first high priest of God to offer sacrifices in the tent in the wilderness. **5.8** *he learned obedience through what he suffered.* Even though Christ was God's Son, he had to learn obedience in his humanity. He was tempted in all points as we are, yet he never sinned (4.15) but always did the Father's will. Thus he did what the first Adam did not do. All of this was part of his duty as our mediator.

5.10
vv. 5, 6

made perfect, he became the source of eternal salvation for all who obey him, [10] having been designated by God a high priest according to the order of Melchizedek.

C. Exhortation to lay hold of Christ and his redemption

1. The immature reproved

5.12
Gal 4.3;
Heb 6.1;
Acts 7.38;
1 Cor 3.2
5.13
1 Cor 3.1
5.14
Isa 7.15

[11] About this[z] we have much to say that is hard to explain, since you have become dull in understanding. [12] For though by this time you ought to be teachers, you need someone to teach you again the basic elements of the oracles of God. You need milk, not solid food; [13] for everyone who lives on milk, being still an infant, is unskilled in the word of righteousness. [14] But solid food is for the mature, for those whose faculties have been trained by practice to distinguish good from evil.

2. A warning advanced

6.1
Phil 3.12-14;
Heb 5.12;
9.14
6.2
Acts 19.3, 4;
6.6; 17.31,
32
6.3
Acts 18.21
6.4ff
Heb 10.26,
32;
Eph 2.8;
Gal 3.2, 5
6.5
Heb 2.5
6.6
Heb 10.26-29
6.7
Ps 65.10
6.8
Gen 3.17, 18

6 Therefore let us go on toward perfection,[a] leaving behind the basic teaching about Christ, and not laying again the foundation: repentance from dead works and faith toward God, [2] instruction about baptisms, laying on of hands, resurrection of the dead, and eternal judgment. [3] And we will do[b] this, if God permits. [4] For it is impossible to restore again to repentance those who have once been enlightened, and have tasted the heavenly gift, and have shared in the Holy Spirit, [5] and have tasted the goodness of the word of God and the powers of the age to come, [6] and then have fallen away, since on their own they are crucifying again the Son of God and are holding him up to contempt. [7] Ground that drinks up the rain falling on it repeatedly, and that produces a crop useful to those for whom it is cultivated, receives a blessing from God. [8] But if it produces thorns and thistles, it is worthless and on the verge of being cursed; its end is to be burned over.

3. True believers encouraged

6.10
Mt 10.42;
25.40;
2 Thess 1.6,
7; 1 Thess
1.3;
Rom 15.25
6.11
Heb 3.6, 14;
Col 2.2

[9] Even though we speak in this way, beloved, we are confident of better things in your case, things that belong to salvation. [10] For God is not unjust; he will not overlook your work and the love that you showed for his sake[c] in serving the saints, as you still do. [11] And we want each

---

[z] Or him   [a] Or toward maturity   [b] Other ancient authorities read let us do   [c] Gk for his name

---

5.12 Some believers are babies who need milk (i.e., the simple, plain message of God's truth). Some, such as these Hebrew Christians, need to be taught the basics over and over again, for they so easily forget what they have learned. The author chides them for not becoming mature adults in Christ.

6.1,2 The writer wants babies in Christ to grow up into maturity. To do this they must remember the following six foundational principles: (1) repentance from dead works; (2) faith toward God; (3) the doctrine of baptism, which constitutes the sign and seal of the covenant (see note on Rom 4.11); (4) the laying on of hands in connection with the ordination of ministers; (5) the resurrection of the dead; (6) eternal judgment, which promises life to the righteous and separation from God to the unrighteous.

6.4ff Can a saved person lose his or her salvation? Theologians have differed on this question through the centuries. Historically, the controversy took its most famous shape after the Reformation when Jacob Arminius, a Dutch theologian who opposed the teaching of John Calvin, taught that salvation can be lost;

the Calvinists insisted on the doctrine of God's preservation of all true believers. To Arminians, vv. 4,5 mean the person was truly born again and has lost his salvation. Note this, however; logically v. 4 implies that if salvation were to be lost, it would be impossible for that person to be born again, lose it, and then be born again *again*. This much is clear: whoever openly and consciously rejects Jesus Christ is unregenerate even if he seemed to have been saved earlier. The Arminian would say he had lost his salvation; the Calvinist that he never had it. Either way, the result is identical.

6.11 *the full assurance of hope.* Some have strong hope; others have weak hope. We all need the full assurance of hope and must be careful to promote that hope through the grace of God. Hope is based on faith, and some who had this hope have now inherited what they hoped for (v. 12). We must follow their example. The author goes on to encourage us to lay hold of the hope set before us (v. 18). If we do not, we have no one to blame except ourselves.

one of you to show the same diligence so as to realize the full assurance of hope to the very end, 12 so that you may not become sluggish, but imitators of those who through faith and patience inherit the promises.

4. *God's covenant promise unchanging*

13 When God made a promise to Abraham, because he had no one greater by whom to swear, he swore by himself, 14 saying, "I will surely bless you and multiply you." 15 And thus Abraham,*d* having patiently endured, obtained the promise. 16 Human beings, of course, swear by someone greater than themselves, and an oath given as confirmation puts an end to all dispute. 17 In the same way, when God desired to show even more clearly to the heirs of the promise the unchangeable character of his purpose, he guaranteed it by an oath, 18 so that through two unchangeable things, in which it is impossible that God would prove false, we who have taken refuge might be strongly encouraged to seize the hope set before us. 19 We have this hope, a sure and steadfast anchor of the soul, a hope that enters the inner shrine behind the curtain, 20 where Jesus, a forerunner on our behalf, has entered, having become a high priest forever according to the order of Melchizedek.

D. *Christ's Melchizedek priesthood surpasses the Levitical*

1. *The priority of the Melchizedek priesthood*

7 This "King Melchizedek of Salem, priest of the Most High God, met Abraham as he was returning from defeating the kings and blessed him"; 2 and to him Abraham apportioned "one-tenth of everything." His name, in the first place, means "king of righteousness"; next he is also king of Salem, that is, "king of peace." 3 Without father, without mother, without genealogy, having neither beginning of days nor end of life, but resembling the Son of God, he remains a priest forever.

4 See how great he is! Even*e* Abraham the patriarch gave him a tenth of the spoils. 5 And those descendants of Levi who receive the priestly office have a commandment in the law to collect tithes*f* from the people, that is, from their kindred,*g* though these also are descended from Abraham. 6 But this man, who does not belong to their ancestry, collected tithes*f* from Abraham and blessed him who had received the promises. 7 It is beyond dispute that the inferior is blessed by the superior. 8 In the one case, tithes are received by those who are mortal; in the other, by one of whom it is testified that he lives. 9 One might even say that Levi himself, who receives tithes, paid tithes through Abraham, 10 for he was still in the loins of his ancestor when Melchizedek met him.

---

d Gk *he*   *e* Other ancient authorities lack *Even*   *f* Or *a tenth*   *g* Gk *brothers*

6.17 God, unlike humans, does not change, for he is immutable. From eternity to eternity this is so (Ps 90.1). It is the foundation on which the faith of all believers rests. Whatever God has promised to do, he does. For our own certainty, God reinforces his promises by a divine oath made by himself and to himself. **7.1–3** Melchizedek was a Canaanite king who reigned in Salem and who worshiped the true God (Gen 14.17–24). He was therefore a Gentile in the kingdom of God. He was raised up by God to be a representative of Christ and was honored as such by Abraham. The expression "without father, without mother" (v. 3) means no more than that Melchizedek's parentage has been kept hidden from us so he might typify Christ, who had no human father according to his human nature and no mother according to his divine nature. **7.4** When Abraham paid tithes to Melchizedek, he paid tithes to Jesus Christ who is represented in Melchizedek (see next note). In other words, Jesus is superior to Abraham, the first ancestor of the Jews. **7.9** Abraham paid tithes to Melchizedek, and by implication, Levi was paying these tithes in his grandfather Abraham before his conception. In other words, descendants of Levi (e.g., Aaron, the high priest), who regularly received tithes, themselves paid tithes to Jesus. Thus the author of Hebrews has demonstrated how Jesus is superior to the priesthood of Aaron.

6.12 Heb 10.36

6.13 Gen 22.16, 17; Lk 1.73

6.16 Gal 3.15; Ex 22.11

6.17 Heb 11.9; Ps 110.4

6.18 Titus 1.2; Heb 7.19

6.19 Lev 16.2; Heb 9.7

6.20 Heb 4.14; 5.6

7.1 Gen 14.18-20

7.3 vv. 6, 28

7.4 Gen 14.20

7.5 Num 18.21, 26

7.6 Gen 14.19; Rom 4.13

7.8 Heb 5.6; 6.20

2. The transitory priesthood of Aaron versus the eternal priesthood of Christ

7.11
vv. 18, 19;
Heb 8.7;
10.1; v. 17

11 Now if perfection had been attainable through the levitical priesthood — for the people received the law under this priesthood — what further need would there have been to speak of another priest arising according to the order of Melchizedek, rather than one according to the order of Aaron? 12 For when there is a change in the priesthood, there is

7.13
vv. 14, 11

necessarily a change in the law as well. 13 Now the one of whom these things are spoken belonged to another tribe, from which no one has ever served at the altar. 14 For it is evident that our Lord was descended from Judah, and in connection with that tribe Moses said nothing about priests.

7.14
Isa 11.1;
Mt 1.3;
Lk 3.33;
Rom 1.3;
Rev 5.5
7.16
Heb 9.10, 14
7.17
Ps 110.4;
Heb 5.6;
6.20; v.21

15 It is even more obvious when another priest arises, resembling Melchizedek, 16 one who has become a priest, not through a legal requirement concerning physical descent, but through the power of an indestructible life. 17 For it is attested of him,

"You are a priest forever,
    according to the order of Melchizedek."

7.18
Rom 8.3;
Gal 4.9
7.19
Acts 13.39;
Rom 3.20;
Gal 2.16;
Heb 9.9;
6.18; 8.6;
4.16

18 There is, on the one hand, the abrogation of an earlier commandment because it was weak and ineffectual 19 (for the law made nothing perfect); there is, on the other hand, the introduction of a better hope, through which we approach God.

3. The superior efficacy of Christ's priesthood

7.21
Ps 110.4

20 This was confirmed with an oath; for others who became priests took their office without an oath, 21 but this one became a priest with an oath, because of the one who said to him,

"The Lord has sworn
    and will not change his mind,
'You are a priest forever' " —

7.22
Heb 8.6;
9.15; 12.24
7.24
v. 28
7.25
v. 19;
Rom 8.34;
Heb 9.24
7.26
Heb 4.15; 8.1
7.27
Heb 5.1, 3;
9.12;
Eph 5.2;
Heb 9.14, 28
7.28
Heb 5.2; 1.2;
2.10

22 accordingly Jesus has also become the guarantee of a better covenant.

23 Furthermore, the former priests were many in number, because they were prevented by death from continuing in office; 24 but he holds his priesthood permanently, because he continues forever. 25 Consequently he is able for all time to save[h] those who approach God through him, since he always lives to make intercession for them.

26 For it was fitting that we should have such a high priest, holy, blameless, undefiled, separated from sinners, and exalted above the heavens. 27 Unlike the other[i] high priests, he has no need to offer sacrifices day after day, first for his own sins, and then for those of the people; this he did once for all when he offered himself. 28 For the law appoints as high

---

h Or able to save completely   i Gk lacks other

7.12 *a change in the priesthood . . . a change in the law.* The tribe of the priesthood was changed from Levi to Judah, when Jesus was born as our high priest. Levi and the law went together, while Jesus and the good news go hand in hand. The O.T. priesthood was weak, imperfect, and could not save. Christ's priesthood is perfect, has power, and takes away sin.

7.17 The quotation from Ps 110.4 comes from the lips of David. When he wrote this by the help of the Spirit, he would not have known that the author of Hebrews would appropriate it and claim it to be fulfilled in Jesus Christ, who came from the seed of David but whose priesthood sprang from Melchizedek.

7.21 *The Lord has sworn and will not change his mind.* The God of the covenant does what is permanent and effective, not what is temporary and provisional. The divine purposes will be fulfilled, sinners will be brought into fellowship with God, and their sins will

be forgiven.

7.26 Jesus Christ, as opposed to all the high priests from the tribe of Levi, is precisely the high priest sinners need. The O.T. priests were sinners and they eventually died. Christ, on the other hand, is sinless — he was born without original sin and remained undefiled throughout his life. And he now lives forever, exalted above the heavens, even above the angels, because of his personal holiness and dignity.

7.28 Jesus, the Son, is God and shares divine attributes, such as the following: holiness (v. 26; Jn 8.46; 2 Cor 5.21); eternity (Mic 5.2; Jn 1.1; 8.58; 17.5,24; Col 1.17); omnipotence (1.3; Mt 28.18; Rev 1.8); omniscience (Mt 9.4; Jn 6.64; 16.30; see also Jn 2.24; 18.4; Col 2.3); immutability (1.11,12; 13.8); omnipresence (Mt 28.20; Jn 3.13; see also Mt 18.20; Eph 1.23); creative activity (Jn 1.3; Col 1.16,17; see also 1 Cor 8.6; Heb 1.8,10); power to forgive sins (Mk 2.5,7–10; see also Lk 24.47; Jn 1.29; Acts 10.43; 1 Jn

priests those who are subject to weakness, but the word of the oath, which came later than the law, appoints a Son who has been made perfect forever.

V. Christ — his better covenant (8.1–10.18)

A. The old and the new covenants

1. The new covenant better than the old

8 Now the main point in what we are saying is this: we have such a high priest, one who is seated at the right hand of the throne of the Majesty in the heavens, [2] a minister in the sanctuary and the true tent[j] that the Lord, and not any mortal, has set up. [3] For every high priest is appointed to offer gifts and sacrifices; hence it is necessary for this priest also to have something to offer. [4] Now if he were on earth, he would not be a priest at all, since there are priests who offer gifts according to the law. [5] They offer worship in a sanctuary that is a sketch and shadow of the heavenly one; for Moses, when he was about to erect the tent,[j] was warned, "See that you make everything according to the pattern that was shown you on the mountain." [6] But Jesus[k] has now obtained a more excellent ministry, and to that degree he is the mediator of a better covenant, which has been enacted through better promises. [7] For if that first covenant had been faultless, there would have been no need to look for a second one.

2. The new covenant based on superior promises

[8] God[l] finds fault with them when he says:
"The days are surely coming, says the Lord,
    when I will establish a new covenant with the house of Israel
    and with the house of Judah;
[9] not like the covenant that I made with their ancestors,
    on the day when I took them by the hand to lead them out
        of the land of Egypt;
for they did not continue in my covenant,
    and so I had no concern for them, says the Lord.
[10] This is the covenant that I will make with the house of Israel
    after those days, says the Lord:
I will put my laws in their minds,
    and write them on their hearts,
and I will be their God,
    and they shall be my people.
[11] And they shall not teach one another
    or say to each other, 'Know the Lord,'
for they shall all know me,
    from the least of them to the greatest.
[12] For I will be merciful toward their iniquities,
    and I will remember their sins no more.' "

j Or *tabernacle*   k Gk *he*   l Gk *He*

8.1	Heb 2.17; 1.3
8.2	Heb 9.11, 24
8.3	Heb 5.1; 9.14
8.4	Heb 5.1
8.5	Col 2.17; Heb 9.23; 10.1; Ex 25.40; Heb 11.7; 12.25
8.6	1 Tim 2.5; Heb 7.22
8.7	Heb 7.11, 18
8.8	Jer 31.31-34
8.9	Ex 19.5, 6
8.10	Heb 10:16; 2 Cor 3.3; Zech 8.8
8.11	Isa 54.13; Jn 6.45; 1 Jn 2.27
8.12	Heb 10.17

1.7); the right to be worshiped (Mt 8.2; Phil 2.10). See note on 10.12.
8.1 *one who is seated.* See note on 10.12.
8.8 The *new covenant* is superior to the old one. Under the old covenant believers were given symbols and types. Under the new covenant the historical Jesus, who died and rose again, is the reality to whom the symbols pointed. Sinners put their trust in him as Savior and Lord and receive the Holy Spirit, who takes up his residence in the hearts of the faithful. Israel misused the old covenant by falling into legalism, attempting to save themselves by works. Salva-

tion, then and now, is by faith alone through God's free grace. By the old covenant sins were covered; now sins are removed.
8.10ff This quote from Jer 31 points out the extraordinary provisions of the new covenant. God gave the law *to* the Israelites, but he now puts his laws *in* the minds and *on* the hearts of those who believe in Christ. God has become our God, we are his people, and our sins are remembered against us no more (see note on 10.17).

8.13
2 Cor 5.17
13In speaking of "a new covenant," he has made the first one obsolete. And what is obsolete and growing old will soon disappear.

B. Old and new covenant sacrifices compared

1. The temporary Levitical sacrifices

9.1
Ex 25.8
9.2
Ex 25.8, 9,
23-39
9.3
Ex 26.31-33
9.4
Ex 30.1-5;
25.10ff;
16.32, 33;
Num 17.10
9.5
Ex 25.17ff
9.6
Num 28.3
9.7
Lev 16.11ff;
Ex 30.10;
Heb 5.2, 3
9.8
Heb 10.19,
20;
Jn 14.6
9.9
Heb 11.19;
5.1;
Gal 3.21
9.10
Lev 11.2ff;
Col 2.16;
Heb 7.16
9.11ff
Heb 2.17;
10.1; 8.2
9.12
Heb 7.27;
10.4
9.13
Num 19.9,
17, 18
9.14
1 Jn 1.7;
1 Pet 3.18;
Titus 2.14

9 Now even the first covenant had regulations for worship and an earthly sanctuary. **2**For a tent*m* was constructed, the first one, in which were the lampstand, the table, and the bread of the Presence;*n* this is called the Holy Place. **3**Behind the second curtain was a tent*m* called the Holy of Holies. **4**In it stood the golden altar of incense and the ark of the covenant overlaid on all sides with gold, in which there were a golden urn holding the manna, and Aaron's rod that budded, and the tablets of the covenant; **5**above it were the cherubim of glory overshadowing the mercy seat.*o* Of these things we cannot speak now in detail.

6 Such preparations having been made, the priests go continually into the first tent*m* to carry out their ritual duties; **7**but only the high priest goes into the second, and he but once a year, and not without taking the blood that he offers for himself and for the sins committed unintentionally by the people. **8**By this the Holy Spirit indicates that the way into the sanctuary has not yet been disclosed as long as the first tent*m* is still standing. **9**This is a symbol*p* of the present time, during which gifts and sacrifices are offered that cannot perfect the conscience of the worshiper, **10**but deal only with food and drink and various baptisms, regulations for the body imposed until the time comes to set things right.

2. The eternal heavenly sacrifice of Christ

11 But when Christ came as a high priest of the good things that have come,*q* then through the greater and perfect*r* tent*m* (not made with hands, that is, not of this creation), **12**he entered once for all into the Holy Place, not with the blood of goats and calves, but with his own blood, thus obtaining eternal redemption. **13**For if the blood of goats and bulls, with the sprinkling of the ashes of a heifer, sanctifies those who have been defiled so that their flesh is purified, **14**how much more will the blood of Christ, who through the eternal Spirit*s* offered himself without blemish to God, purify our*t* conscience from dead works to worship the living God!

m Or tabernacle   *n* Gk the presentation of the loaves   *o* Or the place of atonement   *p* Gk parable   *q* Other ancient authorities read good things to come   *r* Gk more perfect   *s* Other ancient authorities read Holy Spirit   *t* Other ancient authorities read your

9.2 *a tent.* See note on Ex 25.9. Since there were no windows in the tent, the *lampstand* provided light. It signified God as Israel's light and pointed ahead to Christ as the light of the world to sinners sitting in darkness. In that light, we eat the bread of life.
9.4 *the golden altar of incense.* According to the O.T., this altar was stationed in front of the curtain. Thus the writer was speaking proleptically here, for he sees it now subsequent to Christ's atoning sacrifice at Calvary (at which time the curtain was rent in two, Mk 15.38); i.e., the altar of incense now stands before the ark since the curtain is gone. Nothing now separates believers from the Holy of Holies to which they, as priests of God, have access in Christ (see note on 10.20). *The ark of the covenant,* overlaid with pure gold, represents Christ's perfect obedience in which he fulfilled all righteousness. The golden pot contained manna, reminding the reader of God's miraculous provision for them. Aaron's rod represents Christ our high priest.
9.5 *The cherubim* represent the angels of God who rejoice in the merits and work of Christ. They chant

his eternal praises and overshadow the mercy seat, which symbolizes Jesus Christ and his righteousness as that which provides a covering for all of our sins.
9.8–10 *The Holy Spirit indicates* that the O.T. institutions (such as the tent and the high priesthood) were external and temporary arrangements, imposed until the coming of Christ. They anticipated their fulfillment in Christ, who exceeds them in every way. In other words, just as Christ is superior to the angels (ch.1), Moses (ch. 3), Abraham and Levi (ch. 7), and the old covenant (ch. 8), so he is superior to all the O.T. religious institutions.
9.11ff Christ is our great *high priest.* The Jewish high priest ministered at the altar, a function he shared with other priests. But he alone entered into the most Holy Place once a year with blood to make atonement for himself and for the sins of the people. Yet he is inferior to Christ, whose priestly work on the cross has earned our eternal salvation once and for all (vv. 25–28). Christ is also our mediator, the one who stands between us and a holy God, and we can approach God boldly only through him.

3. The new covenant fulfilled in Christ's death

a. The covenant validated by the death of the testator

15 For this reason he is the mediator of a new covenant, so that those who are called may receive the promised eternal inheritance, because a death has occurred that redeems them from the transgressions under the first covenant.ᵘ 16 Where a willᵘ is involved, the death of the one who made it must be established. 17 For a willᵘ takes effect only at death, since it is not in force as long as the one who made it is alive. 18 Hence not even the first covenant was inaugurated without blood. 19 For when every commandment had been told to all the people by Moses in accordance with the law, he took the blood of calves and goats,ᵛ with water and scarlet wool and hyssop, and sprinkled both the scroll itself and all the people, 20 saying, "This is the blood of the covenant that God has ordained for you." 21 And in the same way he sprinkled with the blood both the tentʷ and all the vessels used in worship. 22 Indeed, under the law almost everything is purified with blood, and without the shedding of blood there is no forgiveness of sins.

b. Christ the sufficient offering for sin

23 Thus it was necessary for the sketches of the heavenly things to be purified with these rites, but the heavenly things themselves need better sacrifices than these. 24 For Christ did not enter a sanctuary made by human hands, a mere copy of the true one, but he entered into heaven itself, now to appear in the presence of God on our behalf. 25 Nor was it to offer himself again and again, as the high priest enters the Holy Place year after year with blood that is not his own; 26 for then he would have had to suffer again and again since the foundation of the world. But as it is, he has appeared once for all at the end of the age to remove sin by the sacrifice of himself. 27 And just as it is appointed for mortals to die once, and after that the judgment, 28 so Christ, having been offered once to bear the sins of many, will appear a second time, not to deal with sin, but to save those who are eagerly waiting for him.

4. The superiority and finality of the new covenant

a. Christ the once-for-all sacrifice

10 Since the law has only a shadow of the good things to come and not the true form of these realities, itˣ can never, by the same sacrifices that are continually offered year after year, make perfect those who approach. 2 Otherwise, would they not have ceased being offered, since the worshipers, cleansed once for all, would no longer have any consciousness of sin? 3 But in these sacrifices there is a reminder of sin year

9.15
1 Tim 2.5;
Heb 3.1; 7.22

9.17
Gal 3.15
9.18
Ex 24.6
9.19
Ex 24.65ff;
Lev 14.4, 7

9.20
Ex 24.8;
Mt 26.28
9.21
Lev 8.15
9.22
Lev 17.11

9.23
Heb 8.5

9.24
Heb 6.20;
8.2; 7.25;
1 Jn 2.1
9.25
v. 7;
Heb 10.19
9.26
Heb 4.3;
7.27; 1.2

9.27
Gen 3.19;
2 Cor 5.10
9.28
Rom 6.10;
1 Pet 2.24;
Titus 2.13

10.1
Heb 9.9, 11,
23

10.3
Heb 9.7

ᵘ The Greek word used here means both *covenant* and *will*   ᵛ Other ancient authorities lack *and goats*
ʷ Or *tabernacle*   ˣ Other ancient authorities read *they*

9.22 No one can be saved apart from *the shedding of blood*; we have no choice but to accept the way God decided to make salvation possible. Note here how the work of Christ is far superior to the work of the Levitical priesthood. The animals to be slain for the sacrifices could not offer themselves by consent; Christ gave himself voluntarily. The priests offered the blood of animals; Christ offered his own blood. His blood is far superior because the blood of bulls and goats could never bring salvation; only the blood of Christ could do that. In other words, the sins of the O.T. saints were remitted only in that the blood of bulls and goats looked forward to the blood of Christ.
9.28 When Christ comes again many purposes in the plan of God will be brought to conclusion: (1) our salvation will be completed (cf. 1 Pet 1.5); (2) Christ

will reign in heaven and on earth as absolute King of kings (Rev 11.15); (3) he will destroy the power and reign of death (1 Cor 15.25,26); (4) he will be admired and praised by all the saints (2 Thess 1.10); (5) every dark and hidden thing will be revealed (1 Cor 4.5); (6) the final judgment of the living and the dead will take place (Jn 5.22; 2 Tim 4.1; Jude 15; Rev 20.11–13); (7) the dead saints will rise first (1 Thess 4.16); (8) the living saints will be caught up together with the risen dead saints in the clouds (1 Thess 4.17); and (9) the lawless one will be destroyed (2 Thess 2.8).
10.1 *the law has only a shadow.* Law has now been replaced by gospel. In Christ we now have the substance of what was previously only a representaion of the reality.

10.4
Mic 6.6, 7
10.5
Ps 40.6-8;
Heb 1.6;
1 Pet 2.24

10.7
Jer 36.2

10.8
vv. 5, 6;
Mk 12.33
10.9
v. 7
10.10
Jn 17.19;
Heb 7.27;
1 Pet 2.24

10.11
Heb 5.1; v. 4
10.12
Heb 1.3
10.13
Ps 110.1.
Heb 1.13
10.14
v. 1
10.15
Heb 3.7
10.16
Jer 31.33, 34

10.17
Heb 8.12

10.19
Eph 2.18;
Heb 9.8, 12
10.20
Heb 9.8, 3
10.21
Heb 2.17;
1 Tim 3.15

after year. 4 For it is impossible for the blood of bulls and goats to take away sins. 5 Consequently, when Christ[y] came into the world, he said,

"Sacrifices and offerings you have not desired,
 but a body you have prepared for me;
6 in burnt offerings and sin offerings
 you have taken no pleasure.
7 Then I said, 'See, God, I have come to do your will, O God'
 (in the scroll of the book[z] it is written of me)."

8 When he said above, "You have neither desired nor taken pleasure in sacrifices and offerings and burnt offerings and sin offerings" (these are offered according to the law), 9 then he added, "See, I have come to do your will." He abolishes the first in order to establish the second. 10 And it is by God's will[a] that we have been sanctified through the offering of the body of Jesus Christ once for all.

b. The evidence of his finished work

11 And every priest stands day after day at his service, offering again and again the same sacrifices that can never take away sins. 12 But when Christ[b] had offered for all time a single sacrifice for sins, "he sat down at the right hand of God," 13 and since then has been waiting "until his enemies would be made a footstool for his feet." 14 For by a single offering he has perfected for all time those who are sanctified. 15 And the Holy Spirit also testifies to us, for after saying,

16 "This is the covenant that I will make with them
 after those days, says the Lord:
I will put my laws in their hearts,
 and I will write them on their minds,"

17 he also adds,

"I will remember[c] their sins and their lawless deeds no more."

18 Where there is forgiveness of these, there is no longer any offering for sin.

VI. Faith — the better way (10.19–12.29)

A. Exhortation to hold firm

1. Our access to God the ground of our hope

19 Therefore, my friends,[d] since we have confidence to enter the sanctuary by the blood of Jesus, 20 by the new and living way that he opened for us through the curtain (that is, through his flesh), 21 and since

y Gk he   z Meaning of Gk uncertain   a Gk by that will   b Gk this one   c Gk on their minds and I will remember   d Gk Therefore, brothers

10.7–9 Christ came to do the Father's will. He was ready and willing to provide redemption; it was his delight to do this.
10.10 *we have been sanctified* (from Gk. *hagiasmos*, which comes from *hagios*, meaning "holy"). Sanctification is an action of the Holy Spirit whereby he makes believers holy by destroying their sinful nature and implanting Christian graces within them (see Gal 5.16–25). Upon conversion believers are set apart from the world as God's possession, and in principle they are already wholly sanctified in the sight of God. But sanctification also involves a process in which believers die more and more to self and live more and more to God.
10.12 *sat down* (cf. 1.3; 8.1). The tabernacle and the temple had no seats, and the priests had to perform their work standing. This symbolized their work was never finished. Furthermore, the high priest entered the most Holy Place year after year. However, when Christ atoned for our sins, he entered the heavenly

sanctuary with his blood and *sat down* at the right hand of the Father — signifying the Father was satisfied with the work he did and that it was finished once and for all.
10.17 Our sins, when covered by the blood of Christ, are forgiven. They are remembered no more; put away by God (2 Sam 12.13); cast behind God's back (Isa 38.17); blotted out (Isa 43.25); cast into the depths of the sea (Mic 7.19); and removed as far as the east is from the west (Ps 103.12).
10.20 *by the new and living way.* Salvation is made possible only by the offering of the flesh of the Son of God in death. His salvation is (1) the only way of salvation; (2) the new way, for it supersedes the old covenant and the law; and (3) the living way, for were we to come to God by any other way we would die, not live. The flesh of our Savior is represented in the O.T. by the curtain which partitioned off the most Holy Place; through it we as priests can approach God.

we have a great priest over the house of God, 22 let us approach with a true heart in full assurance of faith, with our hearts sprinkled clean from an evil conscience and our bodies washed with pure water. 23 Let us hold fast to the confession of our hope without wavering, for he who has promised is faithful. 24 And let us consider how to provoke one another to love and good deeds, 25 not neglecting to meet together, as is the habit of some, but encouraging one another, and all the more as you see the Day approaching.

2. The judgment for failure to hold firm

26 For if we willfully persist in sin after having received the knowledge of the truth, there no longer remains a sacrifice for sins, 27 but a fearful prospect of judgment, and a fury of fire that will consume the adversaries. 28 Anyone who has violated the law of Moses dies without mercy "on the testimony of two or three witnesses." 29 How much worse punishment do you think will be deserved by those who have spurned the Son of God, profaned the blood of the covenant by which they were sanctified, and outraged the Spirit of grace? 30 For we know the one who said, "Vengeance is mine, I will repay." And again, "The Lord will judge his people." 31 It is a fearful thing to fall into the hands of the living God.

3. Future reward for those who endure

32 But recall those earlier days when, after you had been enlightened, you endured a hard struggle with sufferings, 33 sometimes being publicly exposed to abuse and persecution, and sometimes being partners with those so treated. 34 For you had compassion for those who were in prison, and you cheerfully accepted the plundering of your possessions, knowing that you yourselves possessed something better and more lasting. 35 Do not, therefore, abandon that confidence of yours; it brings a great reward. 36 For you need endurance, so that when you have done the will of God, you may receive what was promised. 37 For yet

"in a very little while,
　the one who is coming will come and will not delay;
38　but my righteous one will live by faith.
　My soul takes no pleasure in anyone who shrinks back."

39 But we are not among those who shrink back and so are lost, but among those who have faith and so are saved.

B. Definition and illustration of faith

1. Faith defined

11 Now faith is the assurance of things hoped for, the conviction of things not seen. 2 Indeed, by faith[e] our ancestors received approval. 3 By faith we understand that the worlds were prepared by the word of God, so that what is seen was made from things that are not visible.[f]

e Gk by this　f Or was not made out of visible things

Cross-references
10.22　Heb 4.16; Eph 3.12; Heb 9.14; Ezek 36.25
10.23　Heb 4.14; 1 Cor 1.9
10.24　Heb 13.1; Titus 3.8
10.25　Acts 2.42; Heb 3.13; Phil 4.5
10.26　Num 15.30; 2 Pet 2.20
10.27　Heb 9.27; Isa 26.11
10.28　Deut 17.2-6; Heb 2.2
10.29　Heb 2.3; 6.6; 13.20; Eph 4.30; Heb 6.4
10.30　Deut 32.35, 36; Rom 12.19
10.32　Heb 6.4; Phil 1.29, 30
10.33　1 Cor 4.9; 1 Thess 2.14
10.34　Heb 9.15
10.35　Heb 2.2
10.36　Lk 21.19; Col 3.24
10.37　Hab 2.3, 4; Lk 18.8
10.38　Rom 1.17; Gal 3.11
10.39　2 Pet 2.20; Acts 16.30
11.1　Rom 8.24; 2 Cor 4.18; 5.7
11.2　vv. 4, 39
11.3　Gen 1.1; Jn 1.3; Heb 6.5

10.25 The church is a community of believers who are commanded to meet together for worship, to celebrate the Lord's Supper, to baptize new believers, and to have fellowship one with another. The word of God is to be preached for the edification of believers and offerings are to be gathered. All Christians should unite with a church and attend its services regularly. 10.26ff The author here gives good reasons why we should avoid apostasy: (1) because apostasy means we willfully persist in sin after we have received the truth and for that there is no more sacrifice; (2) because an awful fate of divine judgment awaits such people; and (3) because the O.T. reminds us how God executed the judgment of death against those who broke the inferior law of Moses.
10.35 The author encourages believers to persevere because of the reward they will someday receive. God will liberally reward all who truly seek to follow him and obey his commandments.
11.1 See note on Eph 2.8 for a definition of faith.

2. Faith of the early patriarchs

4 By faith Abel offered to God a more acceptable[g] sacrifice than Cain's. Through this he received approval as righteous, God himself giving approval to his gifts; he died, but through his faith[h] he still speaks. [5] By faith Enoch was taken so that he did not experience death; and "he was not found, because God had taken him." For it was attested before he was taken away that "he had pleased God." [6] And without faith it is impossible to please God, for whoever would approach him must believe that he exists and that he rewards those who seek him. [7] By faith Noah, warned by God about events as yet unseen, respected the warning and built an ark to save his household; by this he condemned the world and became an heir to the righteousness that is in accordance with faith.

3. The faith of Abraham and his descendants

8 By faith Abraham obeyed when he was called to set out for a place that he was to receive as an inheritance; and he set out, not knowing where he was going. [9] By faith he stayed for a time in the land he had been promised, as in a foreign land, living in tents, as did Isaac and Jacob, who were heirs with him of the same promise. [10] For he looked forward to the city that has foundations, whose architect and builder is God. [11] By faith he received power of procreation, even though he was too old — and Sarah herself was barren — because he considered him faithful who had promised.[i] [12] Therefore from one person, and this one as good as dead, descendants were born, "as many as the stars of heaven and as the innumerable grains of sand by the seashore."

13 All of these died in faith without having received the promises, but from a distance they saw and greeted them. They confessed that they were strangers and foreigners on the earth, [14] for people who speak in this way make it clear that they are seeking a homeland. [15] If they had been thinking of the land that they had left behind, they would have had opportunity to return. [16] But as it is, they desire a better country, that is, a heavenly one. Therefore God is not ashamed to be called their God; indeed, he has prepared a city for them.

17 By faith Abraham, when put to the test, offered up Isaac. He who had received the promises was ready to offer up his only son, [18] of whom he had been told, "It is through Isaac that descendants shall be named for you." [19] He considered the fact that God is able even to raise someone from the dead — and figuratively speaking, he did receive him back. [20] By faith Isaac invoked blessings for the future on Jacob and Esau. [21] By faith Jacob, when dying, blessed each of the sons of Joseph, "bowing in worship over the top of his staff." [22] By faith Joseph, at the end of his life, made mention of the exodus of the Israelites and gave instructions about his burial.[j]

---

g Gk *greater*   h Gk *through it*   i Or *By faith Sarah herself, though barren, received power to conceive, even when she was too old, because she considered him faithful who had promised.*   j Gk *his bones*

Cross-references (margin)

11.4 Gen 4.4, 10; 1 Jn 3.12; Heb 12.24
11.5 Gen 5.21-24
11.6 Heb 7.19
11.7 Gen 6.13-22
11.8 Gen 12.1-4; Acts 7.2-4
11.9 Gen 12.8; 18.1, 9; Heb 6.17
11.10 Heb 12.22; 13.14; Rev 21.2
11.11 Gen 17.19; 18.11-14; 21.2
11.12 Rom 4.19; Gen 22.17; 32.12
11.13 Gen 23.4; Ps 39.12
11.16 Ex 3.6, 15; Phil 3.20; Heb 13.14
11.17 Gen 22.1-10; Jas 2.21
11.18 Gen 21.12; Rom 9.7
11.19 Rom 4.21
11.21 Gen 48.5, 16, 20
11.22 Gen 50.24, 25; Ex 13.19

11.4ff All the saints mentioned in this chapter are examples of people who had faith. They may be divided into two classes: those whose names and exploits are mentioned and those whose names but not their exploits are stated. The account is also interesting because of those whose names are omitted and those who are named. For example, Adam, Elijah, and Elisha are not specifically named. Samson and Jephthah represent some who, humanly speaking, rank below some of the unnamed. Two women are mentioned: Sarah and Rahab.

11.5 See note on Gen 5.24.

11.7 Noah received a divine revelation by God. He was faithful in communicating God's message to those around him, though only his family entered the ark; all other listeners to his preaching were lost (2 Pet 2.5).

11.8 A major component of Abraham's faith consisted in his going out without *knowing where he was going.* He had an implicit trust in God and lived as an alien, keeping his eye on his true home, the heavenly Canaan.

11.19 Abraham was willing to offer Isaac but was kept from doing so by a command from God. He believed that if he did offer his son, God would raise Isaac from the dead. In principle, he did receive Isaac back from death, just as God raised his own Son back to life.

4. The faith of Moses the deliverer

23 By faith Moses was hidden by his parents for three months after his birth, because they saw that the child was beautiful; and they were not afraid of the king's edict. [k] 24 By faith Moses, when he was grown up, refused to be called a son of Pharaoh's daughter, 25 choosing rather to share ill-treatment with the people of God than to enjoy the fleeting pleasures of sin. 26 He considered abuse suffered for the Christ [l] to be greater wealth than the treasures of Egypt, for he was looking ahead to the reward. 27 By faith he left Egypt, unafraid of the king's anger; for he persevered as though [m] he saw him who is invisible. 28 By faith he kept the Passover and the sprinkling of blood, so that the destroyer of the firstborn would not touch the firstborn of Israel. [n]

5. The faith of the Israelites and Rahab

29 By faith the people passed through the Red Sea as if it were dry land, but when the Egyptians attempted to do so they were drowned. 30 By faith the walls of Jericho fell after they had been encircled for seven days. 31 By faith Rahab the prostitute did not perish with those who were disobedient, [o] because she had received the spies in peace.

6. The faith of the judges and prophets

32 And what more should I say? For time would fail me to tell of Gideon, Barak, Samson, Jephthah, of David and Samuel and the prophets — 33 who through faith conquered kingdoms, administered justice, obtained promises, shut the mouths of lions, 34 quenched raging fire, escaped the edge of the sword, won strength out of weakness, became mighty in war, put foreign armies to flight. 35 Women received their dead by resurrection. Others were tortured, refusing to accept release, in order to obtain a better resurrection. 36 Others suffered mocking and flogging, and even chains and imprisonment. 37 They were stoned to death, they were sawn in two, [p] they were killed by the sword; they went about in skins of sheep and goats, destitute, persecuted, tormented — 38 of whom the world was not worthy. They wandered in deserts and mountains, and in caves and holes in the ground.

39 Yet all these, though they were commended for their faith, did not receive what was promised, 40 since God had provided something better so that they would not, apart from us, be made perfect.

C. Faith and the believer

1. Christ our example

12 Therefore, since we are surrounded by so great a cloud of witnesses, let us also lay aside every weight and the sin that clings so closely, [q] and let us run with perseverance the race that is set before us, 2 looking to Jesus the pioneer and perfecter of our faith, who for the sake

k Other ancient authorities add By faith Moses, when he was grown up, killed the Egyptian, because he observed the humiliation of his people (Gk brothers) l Or the Messiah m Or because n Gk would not touch them o Or unbelieving p Other ancient authorities add they were tempted q Other ancient authorities read sin that easily distracts

Cross-references (right margin):

11.23 Ex 2.2; 1.16
11.24 Ex 2.10
11.25 v. 37
11.26 Heb 13.13; 2.2
11.27 Ex 12.50, 51; v. 13
11.28 Ex 12.21
11.29 Ex 14.21-31
11.30 Josh 6.12-21
11.31 Josh 2.9ff; 6.23; Jas 2.25
11.33 2 Sam 7.11; Judg 14.5; 1 Sam 17.34; Dan 6.22
11.34 2 Kings 20.7; Judg 15.8
11.35 1 Kings 17.22; Acts 22.25
11.36 Jer 20.2
11.37 1 Kings 21.13; Acts 7.58; 2 Kings 1.8
11.38 1 Kings 18.4
11.40 Heb 5.9
12.1 1 Cor 9.24; Heb 10.36
12.2 Phil 2.8, 9; Heb 1.3, 13; 1 Pet 3.22

11.27 *as though he saw him who is invisible.* God is spirit and thus has no parts and is not a material being. He is invisible to the physical eye but not to the eye of faith; yet he is no less real because he is invisible. Moses saw God by faith and this enabled him to endure.

11.32–38 The writer now speaks of great deliverances that came to many saints who trusted in God (vv. 32–35a). He then goes on (vv. 35b–38) to speak of others who, for their faith, suffered greatly and

found deliverance in death rather than in life as martyrs for the faith. They were just as much heroes of faith and in the will of God as those who performed great exploits for God.

12.1ff The great *cloud of witnesses* is made up of two parties: those who did great exploits by faith (ch. 11), and Jesus the Redeemer. We must live as they did and run the kind of race they ran, with patience and persistence.

of[r] the joy that was set before him endured the cross, disregarding its shame, and has taken his seat at the right hand of the throne of God.

2. Discipline for spiritual development

3 Consider him who endured such hostility against himself from sinners,[s] so that you may not grow weary or lose heart. 4 In your struggle against sin you have not yet resisted to the point of shedding your blood. 5 And you have forgotten the exhortation that addresses you as children —
"My child, do not regard lightly the discipline of the Lord,
    or lose heart when you are punished by him;
6 for the Lord disciplines those whom he loves,
    and chastises every child whom he accepts."
7 Endure trials for the sake of discipline. God is treating you as children; for what child is there whom a parent does not discipline? 8 If you do not have that discipline in which all children share, then you are illegitimate and not his children. 9 Moreover, we had human parents to discipline us, and we respected them. Should we not be even more willing to be subject to the Father of spirits and live? 10 For they disciplined us for a short time as seemed best to them, but he disciplines us for our good, in order that we may share his holiness. 11 Now, discipline always seems painful rather than pleasant at the time, but later it yields the peaceful fruit of righteousness to those who have been trained by it.

3. Exhortation to endure

12 Therefore lift your drooping hands and strengthen your weak knees, 13 and make straight paths for your feet, so that what is lame may not be put out of joint, but rather be healed.
14 Pursue peace with everyone, and the holiness without which no one will see the Lord. 15 See to it that no one fails to obtain the grace of God; that no root of bitterness springs up and causes trouble, and through it many become defiled. 16 See to it that no one becomes like Esau, an immoral and godless person, who sold his birthright for a single meal. 17 You know that later, when he wanted to inherit the blessing, he was rejected, for he found no chance to repent,[t] even though he sought the blessing[u] with tears.

4. Final warning against apostasy

18 You have not come to something[v] that can be touched, a blazing fire, and darkness, and gloom, and a tempest, 19 and the sound of a trumpet, and a voice whose words made the hearers beg that not another word be spoken to them. 20 (For they could not endure the order that was given, "If even an animal touches the mountain, it shall be stoned to death." 21 Indeed, so terrifying was the sight that Moses said, "I tremble with fear.") 22 But you have come to Mount Zion and to the city of the living God, the heavenly Jerusalem, and to innumerable angels in festal

12.3
Mt 10.24;
Gal 6.9
12.4
Heb 10.32-34;
1 Cor 10.13
12.5
Prov 3.11, 12
12.6
Ps 94.12;
Jas 1.12
12.7
Deut 8.5
12.8
1 Pet 5.9
12.9
Lk 18.2;
Num 16.22;
Isa 38.16
12.10
2 Pet 1.4
12.11
1 Pet 1.6;
Jas 3.17, 18

12.12
Isa 35.3
12.13
Prov 4.26;
Gal 6.1
12.14
Rom 14.19;
6.22;
Mt 5.8
12.15
Gal 5.4;
Deut 29.18;
Heb 3.12
12.16
Gen 25.33
12.17
Gen 27.30-40

12.18
Ex 19.12-22;
Deut 4.11
12.19
Ex 20.19;
Deut 5.5
12.20
Ex 19.12, 13
12.21
Ex 19.16
12.22
Phil 3.20;
Gal 4.26

[r] Or *who instead of*   [s] Other ancient authorities read *such hostility from sinners against themselves*   [t] Or *no chance to change his father's mind*   [u] Gk *it*   [v] Other ancient authorities read *a mountain*

12.4 The Scriptures indicate several ways by which temptation can be overcome: (1) resisting temptation in faith (Eph 6.16; 1 Pet 5.8,9); (2) guarding against temptation (Mt 26.41); (3) employing the resources of prayer (Mt 6.13); (4) not letting Satan use other believers as instruments of evil (Rom 14.13); and (5) helping to restore a fallen believer who repents (see note on Gal 6.1).
12.6ff Coming to Christ is no guarantee that our problems will cease; in fact, they may just be beginning. First, Satan goes after God's people in an effort to undo the work of Christ (cf. Job 1; Lk 22.31,32).

Second, God himself wants us to be perfect as his Son is perfect. To this end he must discipline us (cf. Jn 15.2). Discipline is hard to bear, but afterwards "it yields the peaceful fruit of righteousness" (v. 11).
12.16 See note on Gen 25.25.
12.22 *the city of the living God.* The entire human race forms a worldwide city, but it will someday fade away. When history ends, believers will live in the city of God, the new Jerusalem (see note on Rev 21.2). Life began in the garden of Eden and will end in the city God himself has built.

gathering, 23 and to the assembly[w] of the firstborn who are enrolled in heaven, and to God the judge of all, and to the spirits of the righteous made perfect, 24 and to Jesus, the mediator of a new covenant, and to the sprinkled blood that speaks a better word than the blood of Abel.

25 See that you do not refuse the one who is speaking; for if they did not escape when they refused the one who warned them on earth, how much less will we escape if we reject the one who warns from heaven! 26 At that time his voice shook the earth; but now he has promised, "Yet once more I will shake not only the earth but also the heaven." 27 This phrase, "Yet once more," indicates the removal of what is shaken — that is, created things — so that what cannot be shaken may remain. 28 Therefore, since we are receiving a kingdom that cannot be shaken, let us give thanks, by which we offer to God an acceptable worship with reverence and awe; 29 for indeed our God is a consuming fire.

VII. Conclusion (13.1–25)

A. Exhortations and warnings

1. General Christian obligations

13 Let mutual love continue. 2 Do not neglect to show hospitality to strangers, for by doing that some have entertained angels without knowing it. 3 Remember those who are in prison, as though you were in prison with them; those who are being tortured, as though you yourselves were being tortured.[x] 4 Let marriage be held in honor by all, and let the marriage bed be kept undefiled; for God will judge fornicators and adulterers. 5 Keep your lives free from the love of money, and be content with what you have; for he has said, "I will never leave you or forsake you." 6 So we can say with confidence,

"The Lord is my helper;
I will not be afraid.
What can anyone do to me?"

2. Living an obedient life

7 Remember your leaders, those who spoke the word of God to you; consider the outcome of their way of life, and imitate their faith. 8 Jesus Christ is the same yesterday and today and forever. 9 Do not be carried away by all kinds of strange teachings; for it is well for the heart to be strengthened by grace, not by regulations about food,[y] which have not benefited those who observe them. 10 We have an altar from which those who officiate in the tent[z] have no right to eat. 11 For the bodies of those animals whose blood is brought into the sanctuary by the high priest as a sacrifice for sin are burned outside the camp. 12 Therefore Jesus also suffered outside the city gate in order to sanctify the people by his own blood. 13 Let us then go to him outside the camp and bear the abuse he

w Or angels, and to the festal gathering 23 and assembly   x Gk were in the body   y Gk not by foods
z Or tabernacle

12.23
Lk 10.20;
Phil 3.12
12.24
1 Tim 2.5;
Gen 4.10;
Heb 11.4
12.25
Heb 2.2, 3;
8.5; 11.7
12.26
Ex 19.18;
Hag 2.6
12.27
1 Cor 7.31;
2 Pet 3.10
12.28
Dan 2.44;
Heb 13.15
12.29
Deut 4.24

13.1
Rom 12.10;
1 Thess 4.9;
1 Pet 1.22
13.2
1 Pet 4.9;
Gen 18.3
13.3
Mt 25.36;
Col 4.18
13.4
1 Cor 6.9;
Rev 22.15
13.5
Phil 4.11;
Deut 31.6, 8;
Josh 1.5

13.7
v. 17;
Heb 6.12
13.8
Heb 1.12
13.9
Eph 4.14;
Col 2.7, 16
13.10
1 Cor 9.13;
10.18
13.11
Ex 29.14;
Lev 16.27
13.12
Jn 19.17
13.13
Heb 11.26

12.25ff When God speaks he expects us to listen and to act appropriately. We know that those who did not obey in the old covenant did not escape his anger. Nor shall we escape, if we follow in their footsteps. True believers have received the kingdom of God's grace and glory, which is so firmly founded that it can never be shaken (v. 28).
13.1ff This chapter forms a practical part of Hebrews. If God is our God, how then shall we live? By demonstrating love for brothers and sisters, giving hospitality, exuding sympathy, living purely and chastely, and avoiding immorality and adultery.

13.4 See note on 1 Cor 7.26.
13.5 The reason we can be content with little or nothing in this life is the promise of God, *I will never leave you or forsake you* (see also note on 1 Tim 6.10).
13.7 *your leaders.* These are ministers, God's guides and rulers for the church, those who minister the word of God. We must pray for them, listen to their teaching, and follow it as they faithfully expound it.
13.8 The author ascribes to Jesus Christ two characteristics of God; his eternity and his unchangeableness.

13.14
Phil 3.20;
Heb 10.34;
12.22
13.15
1 Pet 2.5;
Isa 57.9;
Hos 14.2
13.17
Isa 62.6;
Acts 20.28

13.18
1 Thess 5.25;
Acts 24.16
13.19
Philem 22

13.20
Rom 15.33;
Zech 9.11
13.21
1 Pet 5.10;
Phil 2.13

13.23
1 Thess 3.2;
1 Tim 6.12
13.24
v. 7
13.25
Col 4.18;
Titus 3.15

endured. 14 For here we have no lasting city, but we are looking for the city that is to come. 15 Through him, then, let us continually offer a sacrifice of praise to God, that is, the fruit of lips that confess his name. 16 Do not neglect to do good and to share what you have, for such sacrifices are pleasing to God.

17 Obey your leaders and submit to them, for they are keeping watch over your souls and will give an account. Let them do this with joy and not with sighing — for that would be harmful to you.

3. Request for prayer

18 Pray for us; we are sure that we have a clear conscience, desiring to act honorably in all things. 19 I urge you all the more to do this, so that I may be restored to you very soon.

B. Personal references and benedictions

20 Now may the God of peace, who brought back from the dead our Lord Jesus, the great shepherd of the sheep, by the blood of the eternal covenant, 21 make you complete in everything good so that you may do his will, working among us*a* that which is pleasing in his sight, through Jesus Christ, to whom be the glory forever and ever. Amen.

22 I appeal to you, brothers and sisters,*b* bear with my word of exhortation, for I have written to you briefly. 23 I want you to know that our brother Timothy has been set free; and if he comes in time, he will be with me when I see you. 24 Greet all your leaders and all the saints. Those from Italy send you greetings. 25 Grace be with all of you.*c*

a Other ancient authorities read *you*   *b* Gk *brothers*   *c* Other ancient authorities add *Amen*

13.17 Even more specifically than in v. 7, the writer here commands believers to submit to their faithful leaders and to do so joyfully.
13.20,21 In this closing benediction God is called *the God of peace*, Jesus Christ is named *the great shep-*

herd (see note on Jn 10.11) who was brought back from the dead, salvation is said to come through *the blood of the eternal covenant*, and a prayer is offered for the perfection of the saints through the work of Jesus Christ. All glory be to the Savior!

JAMES

Authorship, Date, and Background: The letter of James opens with the statement, "James, a servant of God and of the Lord Jesus Christ" (1.1). This immediately establishes the author as James—the James who is none other than the brother of the Lord Jesus (cf. Mk 6.3; Gal 1.19). Many in the Catholic tradition understand the word *brother* to mean "cousin," though this is unlikely. Others think he was the son of Joseph by a former marriage, in which event he would have been Jesus' stepbrother. Most, however, accept James as the son of Joseph and Mary and thus the half-brother of Jesus. He was converted after the resurrection of the Lord Jesus (cf. 1 Cor 15.7) and was among those who waited for the coming of the Holy Spirit on the day of Pentecost (Acts 1.14). Later he became the leader of the church in Jerusalem (Acts 12.19; 15.13; 21.18; Gal 2.9).

The letter best fits the period between A.D. 45 and 50. The city of Jerusalem had not yet been seized and destroyed. Jews from around the Roman empire returned to Jerusalem for the Jewish festivals, so that addressing the letter "to the twelve tribes in the Dispersion" (1.1) indicates that they had been dispersed before the fall of Jerusalem. In other words, the letter was not directed to Gentile Christians but to Jews who had become Christians, who knew the O.T., and who kept the law. James himself (see Gal 2.12), was well known for his strict adherence to the law. At the time of writing, Jewish Christians did not fully understand their freedom in Christ. Indeed not until the Council at Jerusalem were the question of circumcision as part of the process of salvation for Gentile converts and the requirement to follow all the Jewish customs and ceremonies decided (Acts 15.5). The result was to break the yoke of legalism and to set free both Gentiles and Jews.

James' primary purpose in this letter was to set forth ethical standards of the Christian life. It was, therefore, an intensely practical letter and did not delve too deeply into other aspects of theology.

Characteristics and Content: Many Bible students have supposed that what James said about faith and works differs substantively from what Paul said. It was because of this notion that Martin Luther, who so strongly taught salvation by faith alone without works, could call the letter of James "a strawy epistle." He missed the point that James' letter makes. Basically there is no difference between the teaching of Paul and James (see note on 2.14ff). Both Paul and James believed that saving faith is always accompanied by good works. James' statement in 2.24 that "a person is justified by works and not by faith alone," simply means that the proof of real salvation must be seen in the life of obedience, i.e., of works commanded and ordained of God. James proves this from the O.T. life of Abraham (see note on 2.21). His final conclusion is that while faith without works is dead, it cannot be said that works of any kind are necessary to salvation or that works can save anyone.

The letter of James should be understood within its larger context because the author lays down ethical principles about various aspects of the Christian life, e.g., lawsuits, relations between employers and employees, giving rich people special seats in houses of worship, the use of the tongue, peacemaking, slander, and evil desires. The concluding chapter is rich in its promises about divine help for the sick when they are anointed with oil and prayed over. The prophet Elijah illustrates the power of prayer and challenges Christians of all ages.

Outline:

THE LETTER OF

JAMES

I. Greeting (1.1)

1 James, a servant[a] of God and of the Lord Jesus Christ,
To the twelve tribes in the Dispersion:
Greetings.

1.1
Acts 12.17;
Titus 1.1;
Acts 26.7;
Deut 32.26;
Jn 7.35;
1 Pet 1.1

II. True religion (1.2–27)

A. Evidenced by patience in temptation

2 My brothers and sisters,[b] whenever you face trials of any kind, consider it nothing but joy, 3 because you know that the testing of your faith produces endurance; 4 and let endurance have its full effect, so that you may be mature and complete, lacking in nothing.

5 If any of you is lacking in wisdom, ask God, who gives to all generously and ungrudgingly, and it will be given you. 6 But ask in faith, never doubting, for the one who doubts is like a wave of the sea, driven and tossed by the wind; 7, 8 for the doubter, being double-minded and unstable in every way, must not expect to receive anything from the Lord.

9 Let the believer[c] who is lowly boast in being raised up, 10 and the rich in being brought low, because the rich will disappear like a flower in the field. 11 For the sun rises with its scorching heat and withers the field; its flower falls, and its beauty perishes. It is the same way with the rich; in the midst of a busy life, they will wither away.

12 Blessed is anyone who endures temptation. Such a one has stood the test and will receive the crown of life that the Lord[d] has promised to those who love him. 13 No one, when tempted, should say, "I am being tempted by God"; for God cannot be tempted by evil and he himself tempts no one. 14 But one is tempted by one's own desire, being lured and enticed by it; 15 then, when that desire has conceived, it gives birth to sin, and that sin, when it is fully grown, gives birth to death. 16 Do not be deceived, my beloved.[e]

17 Every generous act of giving, with every perfect gift, is from above, coming down from the Father of lights, with whom there is no variation or shadow due to change.[f] 18 In fulfillment of his own purpose he gave us birth by the word of truth, so that we would become a kind of first fruits of his creatures.

1.2
Mt 5.12;
Heb 10.34;
1 Pet 1.6
1.3
Rom 5.3
1.4
Col 4.12;
1 Thess 5.23
1.5
1 Kings 3.9;
Prov 2.3;
1 Jn 5.14
1.6
Mk 11.24
1.7
Jas 4.8
1.10
1 Cor 7.31;
1 Pet 1.24
1.11
Isa 40.6-8;
Ps 102.4, 11
1.12
Heb 12.5;
Jas 2.5

1.15
Job 15.35;
Ps 7.14;
Rom 6.21, 23
1.16
1 Cor 6.9;
v. 19
1.17
Jn 3.27;
Mal 3.6
1.18
Jn 1.13;
Eph 1.12;
Rev 14.4

---

a Gk slave   b Gk brothers   c Gk brother   d Gk he; other ancient authorities read God   e Gk my beloved brothers   f Other ancient authorities read variation due to a shadow of turning

---

1.1 James was a half brother of Jesus (Gal 1.19), though he never mentions that. But he does call himself a servant (or slave) of the Lord Jesus. He addresses this letter to the Jews of the Dispersion, including both saved and lost Jews.
1.2 See note on Job 1.14.
1.5 Wisdom is the gift of God and we should pray for it. It is available to everyone. As believers we can come as often as we wish and will receive what we ask for. God does not reproach those who ask for wisdom.
1.12 The crown of life is promised to all who love the Lord and persevere in their Christian faith.
1.13ff Being tempted (from Gk. peirazō) has two

meanings in the N.T. (1) In vv. 2,6, it means trials such as all Christians undergo simply because they are alive. God allows trials to mature and perfect us as his people. (2) In v. 13 it means solicitation to evil, something God never does. Thus we can never blame God for our sinful acts, for evil comes from within us (cf. Mk 7.20–23). Satan himself is the great tempter (1 Chr 21.1; Mt 4.1; Jn 13.2), and we must pray to God to deliver us from the power of the evil one (Mt 6.13).
1.17 Rather than being one who tempts us to sin, God is the author and fountain of everything good. As the Father of lights, he is unchangeable.

B. Evidenced by conduct

19 You must understand this, my beloved:*g* let everyone be quick to listen, slow to speak, slow to anger; 20 for your anger does not produce God's righteousness. 21 Therefore rid yourselves of all sordidness and rank growth of wickedness, and welcome with meekness the implanted word that has the power to save your souls.

22 But be doers of the word, and not merely hearers who deceive themselves. 23 For if any are hearers of the word and not doers, they are like those who look at themselves*h* in a mirror; 24 for they look at themselves and, on going away, immediately forget what they were like. 25 But those who look into the perfect law, the law of liberty, and persevere, being not hearers who forget but doers who act—they will be blessed in their doing.

26 If any think they are religious, and do not bridle their tongues but deceive their hearts, their religion is worthless. 27 Religion that is pure and undefiled before God, the Father, is this: to care for orphans and widows in their distress, and to keep oneself unstained by the world.

III. True faith (2.1–3.12)

A. Evidenced by impartiality

2 My brothers and sisters,*i* do you with your acts of favoritism really believe in our glorious Lord Jesus Christ?*j* 2 For if a person with gold rings and in fine clothes comes into your assembly, and if a poor person in dirty clothes also comes in, 3 and if you take notice of the one wearing the fine clothes and say, "Have a seat here, please," while to the one who is poor you say, "Stand there," or, "Sit at my feet,"*k* 4 have you not made distinctions among yourselves, and become judges with evil thoughts? 5 Listen, my beloved brothers and sisters.*l* Has not God chosen the poor in the world to be rich in faith and to be heirs of the kingdom that he has promised to those who love him? 6 But you have dishonored the poor. Is it not the rich who oppress you? Is it not they who drag you into court? 7 Is it not they who blaspheme the excellent name that was invoked over you?

8 You do well if you really fulfill the royal law according to the scripture, "You shall love your neighbor as yourself." 9 But if you show partiality, you commit sin and are convicted by the law as transgressors. 10 For whoever keeps the whole law but fails in one point has become accountable for all of it. 11 For the one who said, "You shall not commit adultery," also said, "You shall not murder." Now if you do not commit adultery but if you murder, you have become a transgressor of the law. 12 So speak and so act as those who are to be judged by the law of liberty. 13 For judgment will be without mercy to anyone who has shown no mercy; mercy triumphs over judgment.

g Gk my beloved brothers   h Gk at the face of his birth   i Gk My brothers   j Or hold the faith of our glorious Lord Jesus Christ without acts of favoritism   k Gk Sit under my footstool   l Gk brothers

1.19ff *be quick to listen.* We must hear the word eagerly and obey it carefully. Truth must be received in the heart and expressed in the life.
1.26,27 James gives three tests of true faith: bridling the tongue, caring for needy people, and keeping oneself unstained by the world.
2.1 All believers are one in Jesus Christ. Distinctions such as male and female, Jew and Gentile, slave and free no longer apply (cf. Gal 3.29; Col 3.11). Christians should never show favoritism based on position, power, race, color, wealth, or popularity.

2.8 Love is called *the royal law*, for it comes from the King of kings. Love of one's neighbor summarizes the second table of the law (the last six of the ten commandments).
2.10 A single sin, however small and insignificant, automatically causes sinners to breach the whole law of God and brings them under God's condemnation and disqualifies us from heaven. The Scriptures do indeed indicate that there are greater and lesser sins, but from God's perspective, any and all sins offend him.

B. *Evidenced by works*

14   What good is it, my brothers and sisters,*m* if you say you have faith but do not have works? Can faith save you? 15 If a brother or sister is naked and lacks daily food, 16 and one of you says to them, "Go in peace; keep warm and eat your fill," and yet you do not supply their bodily needs, what is the good of that? 17 So faith by itself, if it has no works, is dead.

18   But someone will say, "You have faith and I have works." Show me your faith apart from your works, and I by my works will show you my faith. 19 You believe that God is one; you do well. Even the demons believe—and shudder. 20 Do you want to be shown, you senseless person, that faith apart from works is barren? 21 Was not our ancestor Abraham justified by works when he offered his son Isaac on the altar? 22 You see that faith was active along with his works, and faith was brought to completion by the works. 23 Thus the scripture was fulfilled that says, "Abraham believed God, and it was reckoned to him as righteousness," and he was called the friend of God. 24 You see that a person is justified by works and not by faith alone. 25 Likewise, was not Rahab the prostitute also justified by works when she welcomed the messengers and sent them out by another road? 26 For just as the body without the spirit is dead, so faith without works is also dead.

C. *Evidenced by words*

3   Not many of you should become teachers, my brothers and sisters,*m* for you know that we who teach will be judged with greater strictness. 2 For all of us make many mistakes. Anyone who makes no mistakes in speaking is perfect, able to keep the whole body in check with a bridle. 3 If we put bits into the mouths of horses to make them obey us, we guide their whole bodies. 4 Or look at ships: though they are so large that it takes strong winds to drive them, yet they are guided by a very small rudder wherever the will of the pilot directs. 5 So also the tongue is a small member, yet it boasts of great exploits.

How great a forest is set ablaze by a small fire! 6 And the tongue is a fire. The tongue is placed among our members as a world of iniquity; it stains the whole body, sets on fire the cycle of nature,*n* and is itself set on fire by hell.*o* 7 For every species of beast and bird, of reptile and sea creature, can be tamed and has been tamed by the human species, 8 but no one can tame the tongue—a restless evil, full of deadly poison. 9 With it we bless the Lord and Father, and with it we curse those who are made in the likeness of God. 10 From the same mouth come blessing and cursing. My brothers and sisters,*p* this ought not to be so. 11 Does a spring pour forth from the same opening both fresh and brackish water? 12 Can a fig tree, my brothers and sisters,*q* yield olives, or a grapevine figs? No more can salt water yield fresh.

m Gk *brothers*   *n* Or *wheel of birth*   *o* Gk *Gehenna*   *p* Gk *My brothers*   *q* Gk *my brothers*

2.14 Mt 7.26; Jas 1.22ff
2.15 Lk 3.11
2.16 1 Jn 3.17, 18
2.18 Jas 3.13
2.19 Deut 6.4; Mt 8.29; Lk 4.34
2.20 v. 17
2.21 Gen 22.9
2.22 Heb 11.17
2.23 Gen 15.6; Rom 4.3; 2 Chr 20.7; Isa 41.8
2.25 Josh 2.1ff; Heb 11.31
2.26 v. 20
3.1 Mt 23.8; Lk 6.37
3.2 1 Kings 8.46; 1 Pet 3.10; Mt 12.37; Jas 1.26
3.3 Ps 32.9
3.5 Prov 12.18; Ps 12.3
3.6 Prov 16.27; Mt 15.11, 18, 19
3.8 Ps 140.3; Rom 3.13
3.9 Gen 1.26
3.12 Mt 7.16

2.14ff Some maintain that James' and Paul's teachings about faith and works are at variance, but this is not so. James argues that when sinners are saved by faith alone, saving faith is never alone, for it is *always* accompanied by good works which demonstrate that faith. Thus if one's life does not show forth any good works, the question must be asked whether this person has genuine faith. Paul has the same position (e.g., 2 Cor 5.17; see note on Rom 8.13). A regenerated individual becomes a brand new person inside and will act like one, so that a profession of faith cannot be considered valid if the so-called new believer's life remains unchanged.

2.21 Abraham was justified by faith (Gen 15.6) long before he offered Isaac on the altar (Gen 22). This illustrates the principle that works inevitably follow regeneration and conversion as a proof of their validity.

3.7 All the animals, fish, and birds can be tamed but not the tongue, except by the grace and help of the Almighty. The God who prepared a great fish to swallow Jonah and eject him out three days later, closed the mouths of lions before Daniel, and tamed ravens to feed Elijah, can certainly enable us to control our tongues, if we but ask.

3.9 *who are made in the likeness of God.* To use the same tongue that blesses God to curse, slander, and revile people is contradictory, for it is equivalent to blessing and cursing God at the same time. James follows this up with several illustrations from nature.

IV. *True wisdom (3.13–5.18)*

A. *True versus false wisdom*

3.13
Gal 6.4;
Jas 2.18
3.14
Rom 2.8;
v. 16;
1 Tim 2.4;
Jas 5.19
3.15
Jas 1.17;
1 Tim 4.1
3.16
Gal 5.20
3.17
1 Cor 2.6;
Rom 12.9;
1 Pet 1.22
3.18
Prov 11.18;
Isa 32.17
4.1
Titus 3.9;
Rom 7.23

13 Who is wise and understanding among you? Show by your good life that your works are done with gentleness born of wisdom. 14 But if you have bitter envy and selfish ambition in your hearts, do not be boastful and false to the truth. 15 Such wisdom does not come down from above, but is earthly, unspiritual, devilish. 16 For where there is envy and selfish ambition, there will also be disorder and wickedness of every kind. 17 But the wisdom from above is first pure, then peaceable, gentle, willing to yield, full of mercy and good fruits, without a trace of partiality or hypocrisy. 18 And a harvest of righteousness is sown in peace for*r* those who make peace.

B. *Worldly friendship*

4.3
Ps 18.41;
1 Jn 3.22;
5.14
4.4
Jas 1.27;
1 Jn 2.15;
Jn 15.19
4.5
Gen 6.5;
Num 11.29
4.6
Ps 138.6;
Prov 3.34
4.7
1 Pet 5.6-9
4.8
2 Chr 15.2;
Isa 1.16;
Jas 1.8
4.9
Lk 6.25
4.10
Mt 23.12

4 Those conflicts and disputes among you, where do they come from? Do they not come from your cravings that are at war within you? 2 You want something and do not have it; so you commit murder. And you covet*s* something and cannot obtain it; so you engage in disputes and conflicts. You do not have, because you do not ask. 3 You ask and do not receive, because you ask wrongly, in order to spend what you get on your pleasures. 4 Adulterers! Do you not know that friendship with the world is enmity with God? Therefore whoever wishes to be a friend of the world becomes an enemy of God. 5 Or do you suppose that it is for nothing that the scripture says, "God*t* yearns jealously for the spirit that he has made to dwell in us"? 6 But he gives all the more grace; therefore it says,

"God opposes the proud,
    but gives grace to the humble."

7 Submit yourselves therefore to God. Resist the devil, and he will flee from you. 8 Draw near to God, and he will draw near to you. Cleanse your hands, you sinners, and purify your hearts, you double-minded. 9 Lament and mourn and weep. Let your laughter be turned into mourning and your joy into dejection. 10 Humble yourselves before the Lord, and he will exalt you.

C. *Slander*

4.11
1 Pet 2.1

11 Do not speak evil against one another, brothers and sisters.*u* Whoever speaks evil against another or judges another, speaks evil against the law and judges the law; but if you judge the law, you are not a doer of the law but a judge. 12 There is one lawgiver and judge who is able to save and to destroy. So who, then, are you to judge your neighbor?

4.12
Mt 10.28;
Rom 14.4

D. *False confidence*

4.13
Prov 27.1
4.14
Job 7.7;
Ps 102.3
4.15
Acts 18.21

13 Come now, you who say, "Today or tomorrow we will go to such and such a town and spend a year there, doing business and making money." 14 Yet you do not even know what tomorrow will bring. What is your life? For you are a mist that appears for a little while and then vanishes. 15 Instead you ought to say, "If the Lord wishes, we will live and

---

r Or *by*   *s* Or *you murder and you covet*   *t* Gk *He*   *u* Gk *brothers*

3.15ff There are two kinds of wisdom. One comes from above (i.e., from God) and the other from below (i.e., from the devil). Believers can tell what kind of wisdom they have by the type of life they live.
4.2 Many sins have their origin in covetousness (cf. 1 Tim 6.10). For example, Satan coveted the power of the Creator. Virtually all wars begin by one nation's coveting what another nation possesses. Judas Iscar-

iot coveted money (see Jn 12.6). The corruption found among people in public life is frequently caused by the same sin.
4.11 See note on Ex 23.1.
4.15 Believers should make all of their plans provisionally because no one knows what tomorrow will bring. What we plan to do is always contingent on the will of God, which is unknown to us but controls our

do this or that." [16] As it is, you boast in your arrogance; all such boasting is evil. [17] Anyone, then, who knows the right thing to do and fails to do it, commits sin.

E. The end of the oppressor

5 Come now, you rich people, weep and wail for the miseries that are coming to you. [2] Your riches have rotted, and your clothes are moth-eaten. [3] Your gold and silver have rusted, and their rust will be evidence against you, and it will eat your flesh like fire. You have laid up treasure*v* for the last days. [4] Listen! The wages of the laborers who mowed your fields, which you kept back by fraud, cry out, and the cries of the harvesters have reached the ears of the Lord of hosts. [5] You have lived on the earth in luxury and in pleasure; you have fattened your hearts in a day of slaughter. [6] You have condemned and murdered the righteous one, who does not resist you.

F. The patience of the saints

[7] Be patient, therefore, beloved,*w* until the coming of the Lord. The farmer waits for the precious crop from the earth, being patient with it until it receives the early and the late rains. [8] You also must be patient. Strengthen your hearts, for the coming of the Lord is near.*x* [9] Beloved,*y* do not grumble against one another, so that you may not be judged. See, the Judge is standing at the doors! [10] As an example of suffering and patience, beloved,*w* take the prophets who spoke in the name of the Lord. [11] Indeed we call blessed those who showed endurance. You have heard of the endurance of Job, and you have seen the purpose of the Lord, how the Lord is compassionate and merciful.

G. The avoidance of oaths

[12] Above all, my beloved,*w* do not swear, either by heaven or by earth or by any other oath, but let your "Yes" be yes and your "No" be no, so that you may not fall under condemnation.

H. Prayer for the sick and confession of sins

[13] Are any among you suffering? They should pray. Are any cheerful? They should sing songs of praise. [14] Are any among you sick? They should call for the elders of the church and have them pray over them, anointing them with oil in the name of the Lord. [15] The prayer of faith will save the sick, and the Lord will raise them up; and anyone who has committed sins will be forgiven. [16] Therefore confess your sins to one another, and pray for one another, so that you may be healed. The prayer of the righteous is powerful and effective. [17] Elijah was a human being like us, and he

v Or *will eat your flesh, since you have stored up fire*   *w* Gk *brothers*   *x* Or *is at hand*   *y* Gk *Brothers*

4.16
1 Cor 5.6
4.17
Lk 12.47;
Jn 9.41

5.1
Lk 6.24
5.2
5.3
Job 13.28;
Mt 6.20
5.3
vv. 7, 8
5.4
Lev 19.13;
Deut 24.15;
Rom 9.29
5.5
Am 6.1;
Jer 12.3;
25.34

5.7
Deut 11.14;
Jer 5.24
5.8
1 Pet 4.7
5.9
Jas 4.11, 12;
Mt 24.33
5.10
Mt 5.12
5.11
Mt 5.10;
Job 1.21, 22;
42.10;
Num 14.18

5.12
Mt 5.34-37

5.13
v. 10;
Ps 50.15;
Col 3.16
5.14
Mk 6.13
5.16
Mt 3.6;
1 Pet 2.24;
Jn 9.31
5.17
Acts 14.15;
1 Kings 17.1;
Lk 4.25

---

actions.
5.1–6 James is not addressing Christian brothers and sisters here, but unbelieving Jews in the Dispersion (cf. 1.1). He accuses them of covetousness, oppression, sensuality, voluptuousness, and persecution. He warns them that they will face miseries, for their riches will rot, their gold and silver will rust, and they shall be eaten up as by fire. This is what will happen to those who spurn the grace of God.
5.7ff Now addressing believing Jews, James encourages them to be patient and to persevere in the faith, for the Lord is coming and "the Judge is standing at the doors!" They should look to the example of Job, who suffered the loss of children, wealth, and health, but triumphed in the end.
5.14ff *Are any among you sick?* It is indisputable that God can and does heal people miraculously. To some

God gives the gift of a faith that heals, but this is not promised to all. Beyond this, there is the grace of faith, which can always be claimed by the believer. All believers can and should pray for healing, but they should also employ medical means, for these too are gifts of God. And we should include the proviso, "If it be God's will" (cf. 4.15). Paul himself prayed earnestly for healing, but God denied his request for a specific reason (see 2 Cor 12.7–9).
5.16 Confessing sins to one another is a hazardous practice if those to whom we make the confession cannot keep secrets. Great care must be exercised as to when and how we do it. Properly used, the admonition is valuable and has good therapeutic potential.
5.17 James refers to Elijah and his prayers in order to encourage us, for our prayers can have equal power

5.18
1 Kings 18.42, 45

prayed fervently that it might not rain, and for three years and six months it did not rain on the earth. 18 Then he prayed again, and the heaven gave rain and the earth yielded its harvest.

V. Conclusion (5.19,20)

5.19
Mt 18.15
5.20
Rom 11.14;
1 Pet 4.8

19 My brothers and sisters,z if anyone among you wanders from the truth and is brought back by another, 20 you should know that whoever brings back a sinner from wandering will save the sinner'sa soul from death and will cover a multitude of sins.

z Gk My brothers   a Gk his

and bring about good results—for us, for our loved ones, and for our nation. Nothing lies beyond the power of God to change, and prayer is the divinely ordained method to make God's power available to us.

5.19,20 James is not referring to people who have ceased to be believers. Rather he refers to those who have slipped into error in their daily Christian lives. We should be concerned about the spiritual condition of a backslidden brother or sister, and we should engage in restoring such people in a spirit of gentleness (cf. Gal 6.1).

INTRODUCTION TO
THE FIRST LETTER OF
PETER

Authorship, Date, and Background: 1 Peter was written by the apostle Peter. This view has been challenged in the modern era even though it was the view of the church through the ages. Objections to his authorship have been based on linguistic, theological, and historical considerations. However, Peter identified Silvanus as his secretary (5.12), and this could well explain anything giving the appearance of being un-Petrine. Certainly the internal evidences affirm the Petrine authorship of the letter, and his identification of John Mark's presence with him (5.13) also attests to it. The whole letter gives the appearance of an eyewitness to the events described. Thus one can confidently insist that Peter was indeed the author.

At the end of the letter, Peter's greeting from the church in Babylon has been generally understood to refer to Rome. There are evidences which confirm the opinion that Peter was martyred in Rome under Nero around A.D. 65–67. This does not mean that he founded the church at Rome, only that he was there at the end of his life. Thus the letter was written in Rome and sent to "the exiles of the Dispersion in Pontus, Galatia, Cappadocia, Asia, and Bithynia" (1.1). Most of these addressees were Jews in these territories who had been converted to Christ. Other references in the letter suggest that at least a few of them were Gentile converts. Possibly Peter had preached to them at one time in his life. This may be one reason for Paul's not having evangelized in some of these areas (Acts 16.7), since he sought to go where Christ had not been preached (Rom 15.20). Now persecution had come and would grow worse in the years ahead. The situation required some word from the apostle by way of comfort and encouragement. This came in the letter.

Characteristics and Content: The basic theme of 1 Peter is a living hope in the midst of persecution and suffering. More than a dozen times Peter refers to persecution: "In this you rejoice, even if now for a little while you have had to suffer various trials" (1.6); "it is a credit to you if . . . you endure pain while suffering unjustly" (2.19); "even if you do suffer for doing what is right, you are blessed" (3.14); "it is better to suffer for doing good . . . than to suffer for doing evil" (3.17). These all indicate persecution then or in the future, and Peter encourages them to meet it with the knowledge that victory would be theirs at last.

The letter clearly teaches the sovereignty of God both with respect to the choice of Jesus Christ as the slain Lamb from before the foundation of the world (1.20) and these believers as chosen of God (1.2; 2.9). Suffering is part of the believer's identification with Christ and his suffering. This is a privilege and points to future joy and gladness. The repeated mention of Christ's suffering bears all the earmarks of one who was there when it happened. In staccato-like fashion, the apostle uses imperatives to tell believers what they are to do. Nowhere else in the N.T. letters will this be found to the same degree. Thus Peter says: be holy (1.15); conduct yourselves honorably (2.12); accept the authority of every human institution (2.13); honor everyone (2.17); wives, accept the authority of your husbands (3.1); husbands, show consideration for your wives (3.7); have unity of spirit (3.8); be serious and discipline yourselves (4.7); and rejoice (4.13).

Peter's conclusion fits in with his certainty that they will be persecuted. He says believers must be careful to watch out for Satan's attacks and to stand firm when he does attack. They are to trust the Lord and know that other believers around the world are also being persecuted. But after they have suffered they can be absolutely certain that God will give them his eternal glory. He will restore, support, and establish them (5.10). Why then should Christians fear anything or anyone?

Outline:

I. Greeting (1.1,2)

II. The blessings of the redeemed (1.3—2.10)

III. The duties of believers (2.11—4.11)

IV. Constancy in trial (4.12—5.11)

V. Conclusion and benediction (5.12—14)

THE FIRST LETTER OF

PETER

I. Greeting (1.1,2)

1 Peter, an apostle of Jesus Christ,
To the exiles of the Dispersion in Pontus, Galatia, Cappadocia, Asia, and Bithynia, 2 who have been chosen and destined by God the Father and sanctified by the Spirit to be obedient to Jesus Christ and to be sprinkled with his blood:
May grace and peace be yours in abundance.

II. The blessings of the redeemed (1.3–2.10)

A. The risen Christ

3 Blessed be the God and Father of our Lord Jesus Christ! By his great mercy he has given us a new birth into a living hope through the resurrection of Jesus Christ from the dead, 4 and into an inheritance that is imperishable, undefiled, and unfading, kept in heaven for you, 5 who are being protected by the power of God through faith for a salvation ready to be revealed in the last time. 6 In this you rejoice,[a] even if now for a little while you have had to suffer various trials, 7 so that the genuineness of your faith — being more precious than gold that, though perishable, is tested by fire — may be found to result in praise and glory and honor when Jesus Christ is revealed. 8 Although you have not seen[b] him, you love him; and even though you do not see him now, you believe in him and rejoice with an indescribable and glorious joy, 9 for you are receiving the outcome of your faith, the salvation of your souls.

B. The witness of the prophets

10 Concerning this salvation, the prophets who prophesied of the grace that was to be yours made careful search and inquiry, 11 inquiring about the person or time that the Spirit of Christ within them indicated when it testified in advance to the sufferings destined for Christ and the subsequent glory. 12 It was revealed to them that they were serving not themselves but you, in regard to the things that have now been announced to you through those who brought you good news by the Holy Spirit sent from heaven — things into which angels long to look!

C. Exhortation to a holy life

13 Therefore prepare your minds for action;[c] discipline yourselves;

---

a Or Rejoice in this   *b* Other ancient authorities read *known*   *c* Gk *gird up the loins of your mind*

1.1
2 Pet 2.1;
Acts 2.5, 9
1.2
2 Thess 2.13;
Heb 10.22;
2 Pet 1.2

1.3
2 Cor 1.3;
Jas 1.18;
1 Cor 15.20
1.4
Col 3.24
1.5
Jn 10.28
1.6
Rom 5.2;
1 Pet 5.10;
Jas 1.2
1.7
Jas 1.3;
Ps 66.10;
Rom 2.7
1.8
1 Jn 4.20;
Jn 20.29
1.9
Rom 6.22

1.10
Mt 13.17;
26.24
1.11
2 Pet 1.21;
Isa ch. 53
1.12
Dan 9.24;
Eph 3.10

1.13
Eph 6.14;
1 Thess 5.6

1.2 *Chosen and destined* means that God knows everything from eternity. He knew who would be saved before creation began. Foreknowledge must be related to the doctrine of election (see note on Eph 1.4). *to be sprinkled with his blood.* This phrase relates back to the O.T. ritual of sprinkling the blood of a killed animal on the altar, by which the offerer received the benefit of the sacrifice. The sprinkled blood of Christ does four things for us: (1) it justifies us (Rom 5.19); (2) it seals us with God's covenant promise, of which the Lord's Supper is a sign (Lk 22.20); (3) it cleanses us from all sin (1 Jn 1.7); and (4) it enables us to become citizens of the kingdom of heaven (Heb 10.19).
1.12 The effectiveness of the ministries of God's people depends upon the Holy Spirit, sent down from heaven by the Father and the ascended Lord Jesus Christ. The surest guarantee for a spiritually successful Christian life and ministry is unalterably connected with being filled with the Holy Spirit.

set all your hope on the grace that Jesus Christ will bring you when he is revealed. [14] Like obedient children, do not be conformed to the desires that you formerly had in ignorance. [15] Instead, as he who called you is holy, be holy yourselves in all your conduct; [16] for it is written, "You shall be holy, for I am holy."

[17] If you invoke as Father the one who judges all people impartially according to their deeds, live in reverent fear during the time of your exile. [18] You know that you were ransomed from the futile ways inherited from your ancestors, not with perishable things like silver or gold, [19] but with the precious blood of Christ, like that of a lamb without defect or blemish. [20] He was destined before the foundation of the world, but was revealed at the end of the ages for your sake. [21] Through him you have come to trust in God, who raised him from the dead and gave him glory, so that your faith and hope are set on God.

[22] Now that you have purified your souls by your obedience to the truth[d] so that you have genuine mutual love, love one another deeply[e] from the heart.[f] [23] You have been born anew, not of perishable but of imperishable seed, through the living and enduring word of God.[g] [24] For

"All flesh is like grass
  and all its glory like the flower of grass.
The grass withers,
  and the flower falls,
[25] but the word of the Lord endures forever."

That word is the good news that was announced to you.

2 Rid yourselves, therefore, of all malice, and all guile, insincerity, envy, and all slander. [2] Like newborn infants, long for the pure, spiritual milk, so that by it you may grow into salvation — [3] if indeed you have tasted that the Lord is good.

D. Christ our cornerstone

[4] Come to him, a living stone, though rejected by mortals yet chosen and precious in God's sight, and [5] like living stones, let yourselves be built[h] into a spiritual house, to be a holy priesthood, to offer spiritual sacrifices acceptable to God through Jesus Christ. [6] For it stands in scripture:

"See, I am laying in Zion a stone,
  a cornerstone chosen and precious;
  and whoever believes in him[i] will not be put to shame."

[7] To you then who believe, he is precious; but for those who do not believe,

"The stone that the builders rejected
  has become the very head of the corner,"

[8] and

"A stone that makes them stumble,
  and a rock that makes them fall."

They stumble because they disobey the word, as they were destined to do.

---

d Other ancient authorities add *through the Spirit*   *e* Or *constantly*   *f* Other ancient authorities read *a pure heart*   *g* Or *through the word of the living and enduring God*   *h* Or *you yourselves are being built*   *i* Or *it*

1.18 *Ransomed* (GK. *lutroō*) means "to buy back from bondage" or "to redeem." The need for being redeemed springs from our bondage to Satan and to sin (Jn 8.34; Rom 6.17,23). It is God who ransoms us by his grace. God has done this through the meritorious death of Jesus Christ (1 Cor 1.30; Gal 3.13; 4.4,5; Eph 1.7; Titus 2.14). Like salvation, redemption is past, present, and future: we have been redeemed; we are being redeemed; and we will be redeemed. The final redemption occurs when that which we have embraced by faith becomes a historical reality.
1.23 *have been born anew.* See note on Jn 3.3.

2.5 *holy priesthood.* All those who are united to Christ by faith are priests unto God (see also 2.9; Rev 1.6). Under the old covenant, believers required a priest to mediate between them and God at the altar. The high priest was their mediator in the Most Holy Place. Jesus Christ has become our high priest (Heb 4.14; 5.10; 7.27; 9.11); we now may go directly to God through him without any human mediator. This N.T. truth, the priesthood of *all* believers, includes both laity and clergy. The term "priest" is never applied to an apostle or elder in any church except as part of this universal priesthood.

9 But you are a chosen race, a royal priesthood, a holy nation, God's own people,[j] in order that you may proclaim the mighty acts of him who called you out of darkness into his marvelous light.
10 Once you were not a people,
    but now you are God's people;
once you had not received mercy,
    but now you have received mercy.

III. The duties of believers (2.11–4.11)

A. The Christian and unbelievers

11 Beloved, I urge you as aliens and exiles to abstain from the desires of the flesh that wage war against the soul. 12 Conduct yourselves honorably among the Gentiles, so that, though they malign you as evildoers, they may see your honorable deeds and glorify God when he comes to judge.[k]

B. The Christian and the state

13 For the Lord's sake accept the authority of every human institution,[l] whether of the emperor as supreme, 14 or of governors, as sent by him to punish those who do wrong and to praise those who do right. 15 For it is God's will that by doing right you should silence the ignorance of the foolish. 16 As servants[m] of God, live as free people, yet do not use your freedom as a pretext for evil. 17 Honor everyone. Love the family of believers.[n] Fear God. Honor the emperor.

C. Slaves and their masters

18 Slaves, accept the authority of your masters with all deference, not only those who are kind and gentle but also those who are harsh. 19 For it is a credit to you if, being aware of God, you endure pain while suffering unjustly. 20 If you endure when you are beaten for doing wrong, what credit is that? But if you endure when you do right and suffer for it, you have God's approval. 21 For to this you have been called, because Christ also suffered for you, leaving you an example, so that you should follow in his steps.

D. Christ our great example

22 "He committed no sin,
    and no deceit was found in his mouth."
23 When he was abused, he did not return abuse; when he suffered, he did not threaten; but he entrusted himself to the one who judges justly. 24 He

---

2.9
Deut 10.15;
Acts 26.18

2.10
Hos 1.9, 10

2.11
Rom 12.1;
Ps 39.12;
Gal 5.16;
Jas 4.1
2.12
Phil 2.15;
1 Pet 3.16;
Mt 5.16

2.13
Rom 13.1
2.14
Rom 13.4, 3
2.15
1 Pet 3.17;
Titus 2.8
2.16
Gal 5.1;
1 Cor 7.22
2.17
Rom 12.10;
Heb 13.1

2.18
Eph 6.5
2.19
Rom 13.5

2.20
1 Pet 3.17

2.21
Mt 16.24;
Acts 14.22

2.22
Isa 53.9
2.23
Isa 53.7;
Heb 12.3;
Lk 23.46
2.24
Heb 9.28;
Rom 6.2;
Isa 53.5

---

j Gk a people for his possession   k Gk God on the day of visitation   l Or every institution ordained for human beings   m Gk slaves   n Gk Love the brotherhood

---

2.11 *aliens and exiles.* Believers are in the world but are not to be of the world (see note on Jn 17.14). Our real world is heaven, and as aliens we are moving toward our true homes. On the way to glory we must never settle into this world and adopt its values as our own.

2.17 *Love the family of believers.* The Scriptures place some limitations on the notion of brotherhood and sisterhood. Certainly all people are brothers and sisters in the sense that they have descended from Adam and Eve, their common ancestors. Yet the Scriptures speak of a unique family of God brought into being by regeneration and adoption. Believers are therefore related to God and to each other as children and heirs of God. In the biblical sense, only believers are said to be children of God and brothers and sisters of one another.

2.22 *He committed no sin.* If Jesus had sinned, (1) he could not have been the Son of God; (2) he could not have been our sacrifice for sin (since he would have needed a sacrifice for his own sinfulness); (3) there would be no secure foundation on which to rest the Christian faith; (4) he could not have been the prototype of perfect redeemed people.

2.24 *Christ was sacrificed for sin instead of us;* he was our substitute. He actually bore *our* sins in his own body on the tree. Three principles are inherent in God's plan of redemption. (1) Sinners are lost, separated from God because of their sins (Rom 1.18; 3.19; 6.23). (2) The God of grace provided a substitute for sinners in the person of his Son, to be our sin-bearer (Isa 53.6; 2 Cor 5.21). He has bridged the chasm that separated them from a holy God. Since the death of Christ no further sacrifices for sin are

himself bore our sins in his body on the cross,[o] so that, free from sins, we might live for righteousness; by his wounds[p] you have been healed. 25 For you were going astray like sheep, but now you have returned to the shepherd and guardian of your souls.

E. The husband and the wife

3 Wives, in the same way, accept the authority of your husbands, so that, even if some of them do not obey the word, they may be won over without a word by their wives' conduct, 2 when they see the purity and reverence of your lives. 3 Do not adorn yourselves outwardly by braiding your hair, and by wearing gold ornaments or fine clothing; 4 rather, let your adornment be the inner self with the lasting beauty of a gentle and quiet spirit, which is very precious in God's sight. 5 It was in this way long ago that the holy women who hoped in God used to adorn themselves by accepting the authority of their husbands. 6 Thus Sarah obeyed Abraham and called him lord. You have become her daughters as long as you do what is good and never let fears alarm you.

7 Husbands, in the same way, show consideration for your wives in your life together, paying honor to the woman as the weaker sex,[q] since they too are also heirs of the gracious gift of life — so that nothing may hinder your prayers.

F. Christian conduct in review

8 Finally, all of you, have unity of spirit, sympathy, love for one another, a tender heart, and a humble mind. 9 Do not repay evil for evil or abuse for abuse; but, on the contrary, repay with a blessing. It is for this that you were called — that you might inherit a blessing. 10 For

"Those who desire life
    and desire to see good days,
let them keep their tongues from evil
    and their lips from speaking deceit;
11 let them turn away from evil and do good;
    let them seek peace and pursue it.
12 For the eyes of the Lord are on the righteous,
    and his ears are open to their prayer.
But the face of the Lord is against those who do evil."

G. The Christian and persecution

13 Now who will harm you if you are eager to do what is good? 14 But even if you do suffer for doing what is right, you are blessed. Do not fear what they fear,[r] and do not be intimidated, 15 but in your hearts sanctify Christ as Lord. Always be ready to make your defense to anyone who demands from you an accounting for the hope that is in you; 16 yet do it with gentleness and reverence.[s] Keep your conscience clear, so that, when you are maligned, those who abuse you for your good conduct in Christ may be put to shame. 17 For it is better to suffer for doing good, if suffering should be God's will, than to suffer for doing evil. 18 For Christ also suffered[t] for sins once for all, the righteous for the unrighteous, in

o Or carried up our sins in his body to the tree   p Gk bruise   q Gk vessel   r Gk their fear   s Or respect
t Other ancient authorities read died

---

needed. (3) The Father accepted the finished work of the Son, thus securing for those who believe the forgiveness of sins, peace, and fellowship with God (Rom 5.1,6,8,10).
3.3–5 Though the Bible does not prohibit the use of jewelry and other outward adornments, it does establish principles on this issue. True adornment consists in spiritual qualities of a gentle and quiet spirit. Atti-

tude of heart plus outward modesty in dress and adornment go hand in hand.
3.14 *suffer for doing what is right.* Christians are called upon to do right even if that act involves suffering for them. Standing up for what the Bible teaches may easily produce suffering, reproach, and character assassination. What is worse, however, is to do nothing when error abounds and action is called for.

order to bring you[u] to God. He was put to death in the flesh, but made alive in the spirit, 19 in which also he went and made a proclamation to the spirits in prison, 20 who in former times did not obey, when God waited patiently in the days of Noah, during the building of the ark, in which a few, that is, eight persons, were saved through water. 21 And baptism, which this prefigured, now saves you—not as a removal of dirt from the body, but as an appeal to God for[v] a good conscience, through the resurrection of Jesus Christ, 22 who has gone into heaven and is at the right hand of God, with angels, authorities, and powers made subject to him.

3.19 1 Pet 4.6 **3.20** Gen 6.3, 5; Heb 11.7; Gen 8.18 **3.21** Titus 3.5; Heb 9.14; 1 Pet 1.3 **3.22** Rom 8.34, 38

H. Exhortation to duty

4 Since therefore Christ suffered in the flesh,[w] arm yourselves also with the same intention (for whoever has suffered in the flesh has finished with sin), 2 so as to live for the rest of your earthly life[x] no longer by human desires but by the will of God. 3 You have already spent enough time in doing what the Gentiles like to do, living in licentiousness, passions, drunkenness, revels, carousing, and lawless idolatry. 4 They are surprised that you no longer join them in the same excesses of dissipation, and so they blaspheme.[y] 5 But they will have to give an accounting to him who stands ready to judge the living and the dead. 6 For this is the reason the gospel was proclaimed even to the dead, so that, though they had been judged in the flesh as everyone is judged, they might live in the spirit as God does.

7 The end of all things is near;[z] therefore be serious and discipline yourselves for the sake of your prayers. 8 Above all, maintain constant love for one another, for love covers a multitude of sins. 9 Be hospitable to one another without complaining. 10 Like good stewards of the manifold grace of God, serve one another with whatever gift each of you has received. 11 Whoever speaks must do so as one speaking the very words of God; whoever serves must do so with the strength that God supplies, so that God may be glorified in all things through Jesus Christ. To him belong the glory and the power forever and ever. Amen.

4.1 1 Pet 3.18; Gal 5.24 **4.2** Gal 2.20; Rom 6.11 **4.3** Eph 4.17 **4.4** 1 Pet 3.16 **4.5** Acts 10.42; 2 Tim 4.1 **4.6** 1 Pet 3.19 **4.7** Rom 13.11; 1 Pet 1.13 **4.8** Heb 13.1; 1 Cor 13.7 **4.9** Heb 13.2; 2 Cor 9.7 **4.10** Rom 12.6, 7; 1 Cor 4.1 **4.11** Eph 6.10; 5.20; 1 Tim 6.16

IV. Constancy in trial (4.12–5.11)

A. Exhortation to steadfastness

12 Beloved, do not be surprised at the fiery ordeal that is taking place among you to test you, as though something strange were happening to you. 13 But rejoice insofar as you are sharing Christ's sufferings, so that you may also be glad and shout for joy when his glory is revealed. 14 If

4.12 1 Pet 1.6, 7 **4.13** Phil 3.10; Rom 8.17 **4.14** Mt 5.11

[u] Other ancient authorities read us   [v] Or a pledge to God from   [w] Other ancient authorities add for us; others, for you   [x] Gk rest of the time in the flesh   [y] Or they malign you   [z] Or is at hand

3.19 Some have interpreted this verse as meaning that during the time between his crucifixion and resurrection Christ preached to the lost souls in Hades (see note on Lk 10.15) so that they might have a second opportunity to be saved. This view runs contrary to all other Scriptures that explicitly preclude the possibility of a second chance (e.g., Lk 16.25; Heb 9.27). Others think this verse means that Christ was in Noah by the Holy Spirit when Noah preached to those doomed by the flood. Still others translate the phrase "in which" as "by which" and interpret Christ's death and resurrection itself as a proclamation of victory to the forces of evil (symbolized by the flood victims).
4.1–3 Even as Christ died to save us, we must die to sin in our personal lives. Negatively, we must not live in the flesh; positively, we must be conformed to

the revealed will of God (cf. Rom 12.1), so that "licentiousness, passions, drunkenness, revels, carousing, and lawless idolatry" lose their hold on us.
4.4 Wicked friends cannot understand it when their comrades, upon conversion, turn their backs on the old habits of sin. They see the new life in Christ as tedious and boring. Not infrequently they will make fun of their old friends as they seek to turn them back to their old ways.
4.12 We are not told specifically what the fiery ordeal is to which we will be subjected. It is a general statement, and each age must interpret for itself which situations test our faith in God and our human patience, strength, and sincerity. Believers should never be surprised that these ordeals come. The surprise would be if there were none.

you are reviled for the name of Christ, you are blessed, because the spirit of glory,[a] which is the Spirit of God, is resting on you. [b] 15 But let none of you suffer as a murderer, a thief, a criminal, or even as a mischief maker. 16 Yet if any of you suffers as a Christian, do not consider it a disgrace, but glorify God because you bear this name. 17 For the time has come for judgment to begin with the household of God; if it begins with us, what will be the end for those who do not obey the gospel of God? 18 And

> "If it is hard for the righteous to be saved,
>   what will become of the ungodly and the sinners?"

19 Therefore, let those suffering in accordance with God's will entrust themselves to a faithful Creator, while continuing to do good.

B. Exhortation to faithfulness

5 Now as an elder myself and a witness of the sufferings of Christ, as well as one who shares in the glory to be revealed, I exhort the elders among you 2 to tend the flock of God that is in your charge, exercising the oversight,[c] not under compulsion but willingly, as God would have you do it[d] — not for sordid gain but eagerly. 3 Do not lord it over those in your charge, but be examples to the flock. 4 And when the chief shepherd appears, you will win the crown of glory that never fades away. 5 In the same way, you who are younger must accept the authority of the elders.[e] And all of you must clothe yourselves with humility in your dealings with one another, for

> "God opposes the proud,
>   but gives grace to the humble."

6 Humble yourselves therefore under the mighty hand of God, so that he may exalt you in due time. 7 Cast all your anxiety on him, because he cares for you. 8 Discipline yourselves, keep alert.[f] Like a roaring lion your adversary the devil prowls around, looking for someone to devour. 9 Resist him, steadfast in your faith, for you know that your brothers and sisters[g] in all the world are undergoing the same kinds of suffering. 10 And after you have suffered for a little while, the God of all grace, who has called you to his eternal glory in Christ, will himself restore, support, strengthen, and establish you. 11 To him be the power forever and ever. Amen.

V. Conclusion and benediction (5.12–14)

12 Through Silvanus, whom I consider a faithful brother, I have written this short letter to encourage you and to testify that this is the true

4.15 1 Thess 4.11
4.16 Acts 5.41
4.17 Jer 25.29; Mal 3.5
4.18 Prov 11.31; Lk 23.31
4.19 2 Tim 1.12
5.1 Lk 24.48; 1 Pet 1.5, 7; Rev 1.9
5.2 Jn 21.16; 1 Cor 9.17; 1 Tim 3.3, 8; Titus 1.7
5.3 Ezek 34.4; Phil 3.17
5.4 Heb 13.20; 2 Tim 4.8
5.5 Jas 4.6; Isa 57.15
5.6 Jas 4.10
5.7 Ps 37.5; Mt 6.25; Heb 13.5
5.8 Lk 21.34; Job 1.7
5.9 Jas 4.7; Col 2.5; Acts 14.22
5.10 Heb 13.21; 2 Thess 2.17
5.12 2 Cor 1.19; Heb 13.22

---

a Other ancient authorities add *and of power*   b Other ancient authorities add *On their part he is blasphemed, but on your part he is glorified*   c Other ancient authorities lack *exercising the oversight*   d Other ancient authorities lack *as God would have you do it*   e Or *of those who are older*   f Or *be vigilant*   g Gk *your brotherhood*

4.15ff There is a kind of suffering that comes to the saints as a result of their own sins and shortcomings. But God also allows believers to suffer as part of his will for them. They are to be more concerned for their souls than for their bodies. Therefore they must entrust their souls to God and engage in the kind of life that is designed to glorify him.

5.1 See note on Titus 1.5ff.

5.4 See note on Jn 10.11.

5.5,6 *Humility* solves many of life's problems. Pride always affects the believer adversely, for God and pride are at odds and God will put down the proud at his pleasure. God's grace enables a believer to be humble, and those who are humble will sooner or later be exalted.

5.7 Anxiety is a great threat to peace of mind and constancy of Christian conduct (see note on Ps 37.5).

5.8 Peter warns believers that the devil (see note on Ezek 28.12) is always busy seeking to destroy the work of God. Believers must resist Satan by being steadfast in the holy faith (cf. Eph 6.10–20).

5.12 *Silvanus* (see note on 1 Thess 1.1). *the true grace of God.* Peter's main purpose in writing this letter is to assure believers that the doctrine of salvation he taught is the true account of the grace of God. Therefore he earnestly exhorts them to stand fast in this grace.

grace of God. Stand fast in it. [13] Your sister church[h] in Babylon, chosen together with you, sends you greetings; and so does my son Mark. [14] Greet one another with a kiss of love.

Peace to all of you who are in Christ.[i]

[h] Gk *She who is*   [i] Other ancient authorities add *Amen*

5.13
Acts 12.12
5.14
Rom 16.16;
Eph 6.23

THE SECOND LETTER OF

Characteristics and Content: This letter serves to remind believers of the alluring nature of the gospel, castigates the false teachers who bring in destructive heresies, and indicates that heresy is usually accompanied by corrupt and immoral behavior on the part of those who spread it. In ch. 2, a chapter similar to Jude, the author describes the kind of people these heretics are and the sort of lives they live. Believers are warned to be pure and urged to grow in the grace and the knowledge of Jesus Christ. Peter emphasizes the certainty of punishment for unbelief, just as God cast out the wicked angels from his presence and he executed divine judgment upon evil people in Noah's time. Peter also presents Sodom and Gomorrah as example of cities, and Balaam as an example of a man, who suffered for their misdeeds.

INTRODUCTION TO
THE SECOND LETTER OF
PETER

Authorship, Date, and Background: Five books of the N.T. were written specifically to combat the rising tide of heresy. These short writings are 2 Peter, Jude, and 1, 2, and 3 John. All of them were composed after A.D. 60. Wherever truth exists, error always follows. This has been a fact in the history of the Christian church. By A.D. 60, false doctrines had crept into and were being propagated in the church. In the case of 2 Peter, the apostle chose to stress the need for believers to have true knowledge to offset error. He wanted to stimulate strong faith and to encourage believers that the expected coming of the Lord was no fantasy even though that coming was delayed beyond the time they had in mind for it. Churches always need to be reminded of the truths on which their faith rests.

The great problem surrounding 2 Peter has to do with authorship. Many modern scholars refuse to accept the Petrine authorship of the letter. They do so despite the claim of the letter itself that Peter was the author (see 1.1). The author spoke of his imminent death and stated this was shown to him by the Lord Jesus (1.14; cf. Jn 21.18). He claimed to have been with Jesus on the holy mountain during the transfiguration (1.17,18). He had already written one letter to them, i.e., 1 Peter (3.1). He spoke about the apostle Paul as though he were still alive and called him a wise and beloved brother (3.15). To those who accept the word of God at face value, all of this should be sufficient to accept the Petrine authorship of the letter. The opinion that some unknown writer composed the letter between A.D. 100 and 150, long after the death of Peter, would make the letter a forgery. Part of their argument is that both letters are combating a heresy more in keeping with second century history than first, but this is very difficult to substantiate. It is true that there is an overlapping of portions of this letter with that of Jude, which was definitely written after Peter's death. The argument that Peter in his letter was indebted to Jude turns out to be quite the opposite; it was Jude who was indebted to 2 Peter instead. The conclusion is therefore warranted that 2 Peter was written at Rome and composed about A.D. 65-67, just prior to Peter's death.

Characteristics and Content: This letter serves to remind believers of the unchanging nature of the gospel, castigates the false teachers who bring in destructive heresies, and indicates that heresy is usually accompanied by corrupt and immoral behavior on the part of those who spread it. In ch. 2, a chapter similar to Jude, the author describes the kind of people these heretics are and the sort of lives they live. Believers are warned to be pure and urged to grow in the grace and the knowledge of Jesus Christ. Peter emphasizes the certainty of punishment for unbelief, just as God cast out the wicked angels from his presence and he executed divine judgment upon evil people in Noah's time. Peter also presents Sodom and Gomorrah as examples of cities, and Balaam as an example of a man, who suffered for their misdeeds.

In response to those mocking the Christians because the end of the age had not yet come, Peter insists that God's judgment is delayed so that people may repent. But he envisions a day when the earth and the heavens will be burned with fire, at which time the godless will perish (3.7). In the place of the destroyed universe there will emerge "new heavens and a new earth, where righteousness is at home" (3.13). Thus his letter contains both the certain threat of judgment for the wicked and the sure promise of deliverance and happiness for those who believe in Jesus.

Outline:

be envisions ... heavens will be blurred with fire, at which time the guilt ... in the blaze of the destroyed universe there will emerge ... new earth, where righteousness is at home" (3.13). Thus his letter contains both ... hment of judgment for the wicked and the sure promise of deliverance and happiness for those who believe in Jesus.

THE SECOND LETTER OF
PETER

I. Greeting (1.1,2)

1.1
Rom 1.1;
1 Pet 1.1;
Rom 1.12;
3.21-26;
Titus 2.13
1.2
1 Pet 1.2;
vv. 3, 8

1 Simeon*a* Peter, a servant*b* and apostle of Jesus Christ,
To those who have received a faith as precious as ours through the righteousness of our God and Savior Jesus Christ:*c*
2 May grace and peace be yours in abundance in the knowledge of God and of Jesus our Lord.

II. True knowledge (1.3–21)

A. The growth of true knowledge

1.3
1 Pet 1.5;
1 Thess 2.12
1.4
2 Cor 7.1;
Eph 4.24;
1 Jn 3.2;
2 Pet 2.18-20
1.5
2 Pet 3.18;
Col 2.3
1.6
Acts 24.26;
Lk 21.19;
v. 3
1.7
1 Thess 3.12
1.8
Jn 15.2;
Titus 3.14
1.9
1 Jn 2.11;
Eph 5.26;
1 Jn 1.7

3 His divine power has given us everything needed for life and godliness, through the knowledge of him who called us by*d* his own glory and goodness. 4 Thus he has given us, through these things, his precious and very great promises, so that through them you may escape from the corruption that is in the world because of lust, and may become participants of the divine nature. 5 For this very reason, you must make every effort to support your faith with goodness, and goodness with knowledge, 6 and knowledge with self-control, and self-control with endurance, and endurance with godliness, 7 and godliness with mutual*e* affection, and mutual*e* affection with love. 8 For if these things are yours and are increasing among you, they keep you from being ineffective and unfruitful in the knowledge of our Lord Jesus Christ. 9 For anyone who lacks these things is short-sighted and blind, and is forgetful of the cleansing of past sins. 10 Therefore, brothers and sisters,*f* be all the more eager to confirm your call and election, for if you do this, you will never stumble. 11 For in this way, entry into the eternal kingdom of our Lord and Savior Jesus Christ will be richly provided for you.

B. The ground of true knowledge

1.12
1 Jn 2.21
1.13
2 Cor 5.1
1.14
2 Tim 4.6;
Jn 21.18, 19
1.16
1 Tim 1.4;
Mt 17.1;
Mk 9.2

12 Therefore I intend to keep on reminding you of these things, though you know them already and are established in the truth that has come to you. 13 I think it right, as long as I am in this body,*g* to refresh your memory, 14 since I know that my death*h* will come soon, as indeed our Lord Jesus Christ has made clear to me. 15 And I will make every effort so that after my departure you may be able at any time to recall these things.

16 For we did not follow cleverly devised myths when we made

---

a Other ancient authorities read *Simon*   *b* Gk *slave*   *c* Or *of our God and the Savior Jesus Christ*   *d* Other ancient authorities read *through*   *e* Gk *brotherly*   *f* Gk *brothers*   *g* Gk *tent*   *h* Gk *the putting off of my tent*

1.1 In his first epistle Peter uses only the name Peter in the introduction (1 Pet 1.1); here we have *Simon Peter.* Simon was the name given to him at his circumcision; the name Peter was given to him by Christ (Jn 1.42). He probably used "Simon" here to emphasize his Jewishness to his Jewish Christian friends.
1.4 *precious and very great promises.* Scripture contains almost 5,000 different promises made by God for his people. Believers can claim with assurance any and all of the promises of God, for what God promises

he performs or fulfills. He always keeps his word (cf. 2 Cor 1.20). *participants of the divine nature.* Believers are renewed in the spirit of their mind, after the image of God, in knowledge, righteousness, and holiness (see Eph 4.23,24; Col 3.10).
1.12 Ministers are to be good "reminders." They must remind their brothers and sisters what their beliefs are and what duties are expected of them.
1.16 There were many myths and fables abroad in Peter's day. Non-Christian religions were filled with

known to you the power and coming of our Lord Jesus Christ, but we had been eyewitnesses of his majesty. 17 For he received honor and glory from God the Father when that voice was conveyed to him by the Majestic Glory, saying, "This is my Son, my Beloved,*i* with whom I am well pleased." 18 We ourselves heard this voice come from heaven, while we were with him on the holy mountain.

19 So we have the prophetic message more fully confirmed. You will do well to be attentive to this as to a lamp shining in a dark place, until the day dawns and the morning star rises in your hearts. 20 First of all you must understand this, that no prophecy of scripture is a matter of one's own interpretation, 21 because no prophecy ever came by human will, but men and women moved by the Holy Spirit spoke from God.*j*

III. False teachers (2.1–22)

A. The inroads of error

2 But false prophets also arose among the people, just as there will be false teachers among you, who will secretly bring in destructive opinions. They will even deny the Master who bought them—bringing swift destruction on themselves. 2 Even so, many will follow their licentious ways, and because of these teachers*k* the way of truth will be maligned. 3 And in their greed they will exploit you with deceptive words. Their condemnation, pronounced against them long ago, has not been idle, and their destruction is not asleep.

B. Punishment of error

4 For if God did not spare the angels when they sinned, but cast them into hell*l* and committed them to chains*m* of deepest darkness to be kept until the judgment; 5 and if he did not spare the ancient world, even though he saved Noah, a herald of righteousness, with seven others, when he brought a flood on a world of the ungodly; 6 and if by turning the cities of Sodom and Gomorrah to ashes he condemned them to extinction*n* and made them an example of what is coming to the ungodly;*o* 7 and if he rescued Lot, a righteous man greatly distressed by the licentiousness of the lawless 8 (for that righteous man, living among them day after day, was tormented in his righteous soul by their lawless deeds that he saw and heard), 9 then the Lord knows how to rescue the godly from trial, and to keep the unrighteous under punishment until the day of judgment 10 —

i Other ancient authorities read *my beloved Son*   *j* Other ancient authorities read *but moved by the Holy Spirit saints of God spoke*   *k* Gk *because of them*   *l* Gk *Tartaros*   *m* Other ancient authorities read *pits*   *n* Other ancient authorities lack *to extinction*   *o* Other ancient authorities read *an example to those who were to be ungodly*

1.17
Mt 3.17;
Lk 9.35
1.18
Mt 17.6
1.19
1 Pet 1.10,
11;
Ps 119.105;
Rev 22.16
1.20f
Rom 12.6
1.21
2 Tim 3.16;
1 Pet 1.11;
Acts 1.16

2.1
1 Tim 4.1;
Jude 18;
1 Cor 6.20

2.3
1 Tim 6.5;
2 Cor 2.17;
Deut 32.35

2.4
Jude 6;
Jn 8.44;
Rev 20.1, 2
2.5
Gen 7.1;
Heb 11.7;
1 Pet 3.20
2.6
Gen 19.24;
Jude 7;
Num 26.10
2.7
Gen 19.16;
2 Pet 3.17
2.9
1 Cor 10.13;
Jude 6

2.10
2 Pet 3.3;
Jude 8;
Titus 1.7

---

them. Peter insists upon the historicity of the Christian faith and defends it as based upon the experience of himself and James and John, who were with the Lord Jesus Christ at his transfiguration as eyewitnesses of his majesty. They heard God confirm the fact that Jesus was the divine Son to whom they should listen (see note on Mk 9.2).

1.19ff Scripture is authoritative, for it sits in judgment on us, not we on it. It is revelatory, for it tells us what we cannot otherwise know. It is inspired, for the Holy Spirit is the true author of Scripture (see note on 2 Tim 3.16). And it is without error, a doctrine that springs from an authoritative, revelatory, and inspired word of God. Here Peter carefully states that holy men and women of God were used to write the Scriptures. The Holy Spirit moved on them, in them, and through them so that what they delivered was the mind and the will of God. Prophecy did not come from them but from the Holy Spirit, who influ-

enced them to say and write what God wanted said and written. Thus the word of God is trustworthy in all of its parts.

2.1 Peter assures us that false prophets and teachers will arise in the church. They will teach destructive heresies under the cloak of so-called truth. They will deny the Lord who bought them by denying essential truths such as the deity of Jesus Christ. Many will follow them, and the teachers will exploit them for their own ends. But God promises swift destruction on such teachers.

2.4ff If God punished sinning angels, the world in Noah's day, and the people of Sodom and Gomorrah, who then can escape the wrath of God against sin? Peter encourages believers by assuring them that even as God rescued Lot, so he will sustain and rescue faithful believers, who live in the midst of a sinful world.

especially those who indulge their flesh in depraved lust, and who despise authority.

C. Character and conduct of deceivers

2.11
Jude 9
2.12
Jude 10

Bold and willful, they are not afraid to slander the glorious ones,^{p} 11 whereas angels, though greater in might and power, do not bring against them a slanderous judgment from the Lord.^{q} 12 These people, however, are like irrational animals, mere creatures of instinct, born to be caught and killed. They slander what they do not understand, and when those creatures are destroyed,^{r} they also will be destroyed, 13 suffering^s the penalty for doing wrong. They count it a pleasure to revel in the daytime. They are blots and blemishes, reveling in their dissipation^t while they feast with you. 14 They have eyes full of adultery, insatiable for sin. They entice unsteady souls. They have hearts trained in greed. Accursed children! 15 They have left the straight road and have gone astray, following the road of Balaam son of Bosor,^{u} who loved the wages of doing wrong, 16 but was rebuked for his own transgression; a speechless donkey spoke with a human voice and restrained the prophet's madness.

2.13
Rom 13.13;
Jude 12;
1 Cor 11.20,
21
2.14
v. 18;
Jude 11; v. 3;
Eph 2.3
2.15
Num 22.5, 7;
Jude 11
2.16
Num 22.21,
23, 28, 30,
31

D. Evil consequences of their deception

2.17
Jude 12, 13
2.18
Jude 16
2.19f
Jn 8.34;
Rom 6.16
2.20
Mt 12.45;
Lk 11.26;
2 Pet 1.2
2.21
Heb 6.4ff;
2 Pet 3.2;
Jude 3
2.22
Prov 26.11

17 These are waterless springs and mists driven by a storm; for them the deepest darkness has been reserved. 18 For they speak bombastic nonsense, and with licentious desires of the flesh they entice people who have just^v escaped from those who live in error. 19 They promise them freedom, but they themselves are slaves of corruption; for people are slaves to whatever masters them. 20 For if, after they have escaped the defilements of the world through the knowledge of our Lord and Savior Jesus Christ, they are again entangled in them and overpowered, the last state has become worse for them than the first. 21 For it would have been better for them never to have known the way of righteousness than, after knowing it, to turn back from the holy commandment that was passed on to them. 22 It has happened to them according to the true proverb,

"The dog turns back to its own vomit,"

and,

"The sow is washed only to wallow in the mud."

IV. The second coming of Christ (3.1–18)

A. The promise of his coming

3.3
1 Tim 4.1;
Jude 18;
2 Pet 2.10
3.4
Isa 5.9;
Jer 17.15;
Ezek 12.22;
Mt 24.48;
Acts 7.60;
Mt 10.6

3 This is now, beloved, the second letter I am writing to you; in them I am trying to arouse your sincere intention by reminding you 2 that you should remember the words spoken in the past by the holy prophets, and the commandment of the Lord and Savior spoken through your apostles. 3 First of all you must understand this, that in the last days scoffers will come, scoffing and indulging their own lusts 4 and saying,

^{p} Or *angels*; Gk *glories* ^{q} Other ancient authorities read *before the Lord*; others lack the phrase ^{r} Gk *in their destruction* ^{s} Other ancient authorities read *receiving* ^{t} Other ancient authorities read *love-feasts* ^{u} Other ancient authorities read *Beor* ^{v} Other ancient authorities read *actually*

2.15 *The road of Balaam* (cf. Jude 11) is the way of compromise. Balaam used his God-given prophetic gift for personal advancement, because of his greed for money. While professing to serve God, he was advancing his own self-interest. This kind of person will experience divine condemnation (see also notes on Num 22.5,11; Rev 2.14).
3.3 *scoffers*. These are people who live and talk as they please, not as God pleases. They acknowledge no master except themselves. By their scoffing they seek to deliver God's people from what they think are

foolish convictions and a senseless way of life.
3.4 *Where is the promise of his coming?* The longer Jesus delays his return, the more unbelievers raise their voices to disclaim his second coming. Surely, they say, we should see signs of that coming. Since they see none, they assert that he is not coming at all. Peter responds by saying that a thousand years are as a day in the mind of God (v. 8). Why should finite minds think it strange that Jesus has not yet returned? Furthermore, God is exercising patience that those who have not yet come to faith in Jesus will

"Where is the promise of his coming? For ever since our ancestors died,[w] all things continue as they were from the beginning of creation!" 5 They deliberately ignore this fact, that by the word of God heavens existed long ago and an earth was formed out of water and by means of water, 6 through which the world of that time was deluged with water and perished. 7 But by the same word the present heavens and earth have been reserved for fire, being kept until the day of judgment and destruction of the godless.

B. The time and circumstances

8 But do not ignore this one fact, beloved, that with the Lord one day is like a thousand years, and a thousand years are like one day. 9 The Lord is not slow about his promise, as some think of slowness, but is patient with you,[x] not wanting any to perish, but all to come to repentance. 10 But the day of the Lord will come like a thief, and then the heavens will pass away with a loud noise, and the elements will be dissolved with fire, and the earth and everything that is done on it will be disclosed.[y]

11 Since all these things are to be dissolved in this way, what sort of persons ought you to be in leading lives of holiness and godliness, 12 waiting for and hastening[z] the coming of the day of God, because of which the heavens will be set ablaze and dissolved, and the elements will melt with fire? 13 But, in accordance with his promise, we wait for new heavens and a new earth, where righteousness is at home.

C. The concluding exhortation

14 Therefore, beloved, while you are waiting for these things, strive to be found by him at peace, without spot or blemish; 15 and regard the patience of our Lord as salvation. So also our beloved brother Paul wrote to you according to the wisdom given him, 16 speaking of this as he does in all his letters. There are some things in them hard to understand, which the ignorant and unstable twist to their own destruction, as they do the other scriptures. 17 You therefore, beloved, since you are forewarned, beware that you are not carried away with the error of the lawless and lose your own stability. 18 But grow in the grace and knowledge of our Lord and Savior Jesus Christ. To him be the glory both now and to the day of eternity. Amen.[a]

3.5 Gen 1.6, 9; Heb 11.3; Ps 24.2; Col 1.17
3.6 Gen 7.21, 22
3.7 v. 10; 2 Thess 1.7; 1 Cor 3.13
3.8 Ps 90.4
3.9 Heb 10.37; Isa 30.18; 1 Pet 3.20; Rom 2.4
3.10 Mt 24.43; 1 Thess 5.2; Mt 24.35; Rev 21.1
3.12 1 Cor 1.7; Titus 2.13; Ps 50.3; Isa 34.4; v. 10
3.13 Isa 65.17; 66.22; Rev 21.1
3.14 2 Pet 1.10; 1 Cor 15.58; Phil 2.15
3.15 v. 9; 1 Cor 3.10; Eph 3.3
3.16 v. 14; Heb 5.11; 2 Pet 2.14; v. 2
3.17 1 Cor 10.12; 2 Pet 2.18; Rev 2.5

w Gk our fathers fell asleep   x Other ancient authorities read on your account   y Other ancient authorities read will be burned up   z Or earnestly desiring   a Other ancient authorities lack Amen

do so before it is too late (v. 9).
3.5ff Peter refers to the great flood in which the world, except for the family of Noah, perished (Gen 6–8). This happened by the word of God. The same powerful word that created the world can also destroy it. A final day for judging the world is coming. It will result in the purgation of the heavens and the earth, though the time of that coming event is unknown to us.
3.9 The good news for sinful people is that Christ has delayed his coming in order to reach out to sinners that they may repent, be converted, and have their sins blotted out. When he does come, the day of opportunity will be over and the gates of heaven shut.
3.10 The phrase the day of the Lord appears in Acts 2.20 ("the Lord's great and glorious day"); 1 Cor 5.5; 1 Thess 5.2. It refers to Christ's second advent, reiterating what is found in the O.T. prophets (e.g., Joel 2.1; Zeph 1.7). Of this advent three things can be said: (1) Christ's coming is certain, although the

time is known to God alone (Mk 13.32); (2) Christ's coming will be sudden, unexpected, and with no advance warning (1 Thess 5.1–3); (3) Christ's coming will be a day of solemn judgment (Acts 17.31). Peter relates this phrase to the passing away of the heavens and the dissolving of the elements with fire (cf. v. 12).
3.13,14 Peter exhorts the people of God to live lives of purity and godliness while they wait for the Lord's coming. They can wait because they have the promise of new heavens and a new earth where righteousness prevails and sin is banished. This hope is based on the promise of God alone, and he does not lie.
3.15,16 Peter speaks highly of Paul, calling him a beloved brother who had wisdom and whose writings were difficult for Jews to understand because what he said went against the grain of their traditional teachings. Already in Peter's day, unstable and unlearned people were twisting his words to their own destruction.

INTRODUCTION TO

THE FIRST LETTER OF

JOHN

Authorship, Date, and Background: The authorship of 1 John as well as 2 and 3 John has been questioned because none of the letters names the author specifically. Most scholars agree that the same person wrote all three letters, for their form and vocabulary are virtually identical. Tradition has associated John, the son of Zebedee, with them, the same John who wrote the Gospel of John and later Revelation. With this tradition most evangelical scholars have agreed. The date for these three letters has been set around A.D. 90, prior to the persecution by Domitian which resulted in John's banishment from Ephesus to Patmos in A.D. 95, followed by his return to Ephesus around A.D. 97. John died around the turn of the century.

The letters do not tell us much about whom they were written to. Undoubtedly they were originally intended for Ephesus and the surrounding area; later they were sent and read elsewhere whenever Christian communities were threatened by Gnosticism. We do know the purpose of 1 John. Gnosticism (from the Gk. word meaning "knowledge") had come in like a flood and was seriously challenging the Christian faith. Three errors lay at the heart of this heresy. The most important one denied the incarnation (God becoming human in Jesus Christ). Gnosticism could not reconcile Christ's deity with Jesus' humanity. So the real humanity of Jesus was submerged, making him, in effect, a being without a real body. A key Gnostic, Cerinthus, later said Jesus was an ordinary human being on whom the Logos (Word, i.e., the divine nature) came at his baptism and from whom it departed before his death on Calvary. Thus only the human Jesus died on the cross.

The second Gnostic error centered around human dualism. To them, Christians had saved souls in sinful bodies. The soul was so separated from the body that immorality and spiritual accommodation to evil were true only of the body, not of the soul. Thus a Gnostic could sin freely without damaging his soul. The third error claimed that only those who had been initiated into Gnosticism and knew its secrets had the true light. 1 John was written to combat these serious errors threatening the life of the church.

Characteristics and Content: 1 John has no introduction, no named author, no prayer of thanksgiving, and no concluding greeting. Largely because of these omissions the letter has been thought of as an encyclical or circular document intended for wide circulation, perhaps to be read in all of the churches in the region of Ephesus. John writes in a homiletical tone and uses repetition and parallelism for effect. It is quite apparent that he is a leader who has apostolic authority and does not hesitate to use it.

The letter is not organized as tightly as a treatise like Romans, yet three dominant ideas are set forth powerfully and dogmatically. The first is that God is *light* (1.5) in whom there is no darkness. The children of God are to walk in the light. To do less than this is to deny the light. The second idea is that God is *life*; that is, believers have eternal life through Jesus Christ, commencing at conversion and continuing forever. Believers are to live the life of God in Christ by the Holy Spirit who dwells in each believer and teaches each one what is right (2.24–29). Third, God is *love* (4.8). John argues that whoever knows God must love because God is love. Whoever does not love does not have God. All believers must dwell in love. All of these things are true because Jesus came in the flesh. Whoever does not believe what God has said about his Son calls God a liar (5.10,11). The closing admonition is always appropriate: "Little children, keep yourselves from idols" (5.21).

Outline:

I. Introduction (1.1–4)

II. Assurance and walking in the light (1.5—2.29)

III. Assurance and abiding in love (3.1—4.21)

IV. Faith and certainty (5.1–12)

V. Conclusion (5.13–21)

THE FIRST LETTER OF
JOHN

I. Introduction (1.1–4)

1.1
Jn 1.1, 14;
2 Pet 1.16;
Jn 20.27
1.2
Jn 1.1-4;
Rom 16.26;
Jn 21.24
1.3
Acts 4.20;
1 Cor 1.9
1.4
1 Jn 2.1;
Jn 3.29

1 We declare to you what was from the beginning, what we have heard, what we have seen with our eyes, what we have looked at and touched with our hands, concerning the word of life — 2 this life was revealed, and we have seen it and testify to it, and declare to you the eternal life that was with the Father and was revealed to us — 3 we declare to you what we have seen and heard so that you also may have fellowship with us; and truly our fellowship is with the Father and with his Son Jesus Christ. 4 We are writing these things so that our[a] joy may be complete.

II. Assurance and walking in the light (1.5–2.28)

A. The test of righteousness

1.5
1 Jn 3.11
1.6
2 Cor 6.14;
Jn 8.55; 3.21
1.7
Heb 9.14;
1 Pet 1.19;
Rev 1.5
1.8
Job 15.14;
Prov 20.9;
Jas 3.2; 1 Jn
2.4
1.9
Ps 51.2
1.10
1 Jn 5.10;
2.14
2.1
Rom 8.34;
Heb 7.25
2.2
Rom 3.25;
Jn 1.29
2.5
Jn 14.23;
1 Jn 4.12, 13
2.6
Jn 15.4;
1 Pet 2.21

5 This is the message we have heard from him and proclaim to you, that God is light and in him there is no darkness at all. 6 If we say that we have fellowship with him while we are walking in darkness, we lie and do not do what is true; 7 but if we walk in the light as he himself is in the light, we have fellowship with one another, and the blood of Jesus his Son cleanses us from all sin. 8 If we say that we have no sin, we deceive ourselves, and the truth is not in us. 9 If we confess our sins, he who is faithful and just will forgive us our sins and cleanse us from all unrighteousness. 10 If we say that we have not sinned, we make him a liar, and his word is not in us.

2 My little children, I am writing these things to you so that you may not sin. But if anyone does sin, we have an advocate with the Father, Jesus Christ the righteous; 2 and he is the atoning sacrifice for our sins, and not for ours only but also for the sins of the whole world.

3 Now by this we may be sure that we know him, if we obey his commandments. 4 Whoever says, "I have come to know him," but does not obey his commandments, is a liar, and in such a person the truth does not exist; 5 but whoever obeys his word, truly in this person the love of God has reached perfection. By this we may be sure that we are in him: 6 whoever says, "I abide in him," ought to walk just as he walked.

a Other ancient authorities read *your*

1.1 Though Jesus existed from all eternity, he was a real person. He was seen by John and others, who were eye-witnesses to his glory. They touched him and knew that he was real. They heard him with their ears as he spoke the words of life. Everything they said and wrote about him was based on factual data.
1.7ff Christians do sin after they have been converted and thus must be cleansed from their sins day by day. John says this cleansing (1) is accomplished through the blood of Christ (v. 7), (2) requires confession of our sins to God (v. 9), and (3) removes from us every wrong we have done (v. 9).
2.1 *we have an advocate with the Father.* An advocate (Gk. *paraklētos*, literally, "the one called alongside in order to help") is one who pleads on our behalf. Christ is our advocate before the Father with respect to our sins. When we sin, repent, and confess our transgressions, Jesus Christ the righteous pleads his blood for us before the Father. His blood covers all our sins and brings us back into full fellowship with God. The same Greek word is used for the Holy Spirit four times in the Gospel of John, translated there as "Advocate" (Jn 14.16,26; 15.26; 16.7).
2.4 John reiterates the testimony of Paul and James about the proper relationship between faith and works. James said that faith without works is dead (Jas 2.17,20,26). Paul indicates that rewards will be based on our good and bad deeds (2 Cor 5.10). To John, whoever does not keep the commandments of Jesus is a liar and the truth is not in such a person. Thus faith in Christ without good deeds (i.e., keeping the commandments) is not real.

B. The test of love

7 Beloved, I am writing you no new commandment, but an old commandment that you have had from the beginning; the old commandment is the word that you have heard. 8 Yet I am writing you a new commandment that is true in him and in you, because[b] the darkness is passing away and the true light is already shining. 9 Whoever says, "I am in the light," while hating a brother or sister,[c] is still in the darkness. 10 Whoever loves a brother or sister[d] lives in the light, and in such a person[e] there is no cause for stumbling. 11 But whoever hates another believer[f] is in the darkness, walks in the darkness, and does not know the way to go, because the darkness has brought on blindness.

12 I am writing to you, little children,
    because your sins are forgiven on account of his name.
13 I am writing to you, fathers,
    because you know him who is from the beginning.
I am writing to you, young people,
    because you have conquered the evil one.
14 I write to you, children,
    because you know the Father.
I write to you, fathers,
    because you know him who is from the beginning.
I write to you, young people,
    because you are strong
    and the word of God abides in you,
    and you have overcome the evil one.

15 Do not love the world or the things in the world. The love of the Father is not in those who love the world; 16 for all that is in the world — the desire of the flesh, the desire of the eyes, the pride in riches — comes not from the Father but from the world. 17 And the world and its desire[g] are passing away, but those who do the will of God live forever.

C. The test of true belief

18 Children, it is the last hour! As you have heard that antichrist is coming, so now many antichrists have come. From this we know that it is the last hour. 19 They went out from us, but they did not belong to us; for if they had belonged to us, they would have remained with us. But by going out they made it plain that none of them belongs to us. 20 But you have been anointed by the Holy One, and all of you have knowledge.[h] 21 I write to you, not because you do not know the truth, but because you know it, and you know that no lie comes from the truth. 22 Who is the liar but the one who denies that Jesus is the Christ?[i] This is the antichrist, the one who denies the Father and the Son. 23 No one who denies the Son has the Father; everyone who confesses the Son has the Father also. 24 Let what you heard from the beginning abide in you. If what you heard from the beginning abides in you, then you will abide in the Son and in the

Cross references (right margin)

2.7 1 Jn 3.2; 2 Jn 5; 1 Jn 3.11
2.8 Eph 5.8; 1 Thess 5.5; Jn 1.9
2.9 2 Pet 1.9
2.10 1 Jn 3.14; v. 11
2.11 Jn 12.35
2.12 Lk 24.47
2.13 1 Jn 1.1; v. 14
2.14 1 Jn 1.1; Eph 6.10; Jn 5.38
2.15 Rom 12.2; Mt 6.24; Jas 4.4
2.16 Rom 13.14; Prov 27.20; Jas 4.16
2.17 1 Cor 7.31
2.18 1 Pet 4.7; 1 Jn 4.1, 3
2.19 Acts 20.30; Mt 24.24; 1 Cor 11.19
2.20 2 Cor 1.21; Acts 3.14; Jn 14.26
2.21 2 Pet 1.12; 1 Jn 3.19
2.23 Jn 14.7
2.24 2 Jn 6; Jn 14.23

---

b Or that   c Gk hating a brother   d Gk loves a brother   e Or in it   f Gk hates a brother   g Or the desire for it   h Other ancient authorities read you know all things   i Or the Messiah

---

2.9ff One essential aspect of the Spirit's fruit is love (cf. Gal 5.22). Those who hate their brothers and sisters are in darkness, for hatred is disobedience to the great commandment that we should love one another. Those who are loveless show that their profession of faith cannot be genuine. Such people cannot know where they are going, because hatred has blinded them.
2.16 John here defines three great sins of worldliness: the desire of the flesh, the desire of the eyes, the pride in riches. The first has to do with pleasure, by which bodily desires are satisfied; the second has to do with covetousness, which springs from the eye and has to do with the desire for things; the third has to do with worldly ambition, which craves honor and applause.
2.18 The Bible distinguishes the antichrist from many antichrists and from the spirit of the antichrist (4.3). Here John does not have in mind the antichrist, but all those who make common cause with him and whose evil spirit they imitate. Since they deny the basic truths of the gospel they are called antichrists (see also note on 4.3).

Father. 25 And this is what he has promised us,[j] eternal life.

26 I write these things to you concerning those who would deceive you. 27 As for you, the anointing that you received from him abides in you, and so you do not need anyone to teach you. But as his anointing teaches you about all things, and is true and is not a lie, and just as it has taught you, abide in him.[k]

28 And now, little children, abide in him, so that when he is revealed we may have confidence and not be put to shame before him at his coming.

III. Assurance and abiding in love (2.29–4.21)

A. Obedience in action

29 If you know that he is righteous, you may be sure that everyone who does right has been born of him. 1 See what love the Father has given us, that we should be called children of God; and that is what we are. The reason the world does not know us is that it did not know him. 2 Beloved, we are God's children now; what we will be has not yet been revealed. What we do know is this: when he[k] is revealed, we will be like him, for we will see him as he is. 3 And all who have this hope in him purify themselves, just as he is pure.

4 Everyone who commits sin is guilty of lawlessness; sin is lawlessness. 5 You know that he was revealed to take away sins, and in him there is no sin. 6 No one who abides in him sins; no one who sins has either seen him or known him. 7 Little children, let no one deceive you. Everyone who does what is right is righteous, just as he is righteous. 8 Everyone who commits sin is a child of the devil; for the devil has been sinning from the beginning. The Son of God was revealed for this purpose, to destroy the works of the devil. 9 Those who have been born of God do not sin, because God's seed abides in them;[l] they cannot sin, because they have been born of God. 10 The children of God and the children of the devil are revealed in this way: all who do not do what is right are not from God, nor are those who do not love their brothers and sisters.[m]

B. Love in action

11 For this is the message you have heard from the beginning, that we should love one another. 12 We must not be like Cain who was from the evil one and murdered his brother. And why did he murder him? Because his own deeds were evil and his brother's righteous. 13 Do not be astonished, brothers and sisters,[n] that the world hates you. 14 We know that we have passed from death to life because we love one another. Whoever does not love abides in death. 15 All who hate a brother or sister[m]

j Other ancient authorities read *you*   *k* Or *it*   *l* Or *because the children of God abide in him*   *m* Gk *his brother*   *n* Gk *brothers*

2.27 An *anointing* abides in believers and teaches them all things. This anointing is from the Holy Spirit, by whom believers have an inward witness and confirmation of the divine truths they have received. The Spirit is the constant witness to Jesus Christ in the hearts of his people. Since the Spirit is truth (5.6), he can teach them only what is true, including all things necessary to their knowledge of God in Jesus Christ.
3.1 *we should be called children of God.* God the Father has adopted as his children all those, and only those, who have come to Jesus Christ in faith (cf. Jn 1.12). Jesus calls them his brothers and sisters and confers on them the power and dignity of the children of God. Though by nature all people are heirs of sin and guilt and are children of corruption, by grace God is not ashamed to have us call him Father (cf. Mt 6.9).

3.2 *we will be like him,* i.e., like Jesus Christ. Only three people ever lived who had sinless minds: Adam, Eve, and Jesus. The first two lost their sinless state; only Jesus remained without sin, and it is that distinguished him in his humanity from all other people. The day is coming when believers will regain sinless minds.
3.10 Unbelievers are *children of the devil.* Such children neglect true religion and give no place to God. Neither do they have any use for the children of God, despising, hating, and persecuting them.
3.15 John's primary focus here is the relationship of a believer towards a fellow-believer. Any believer who hates another Christian commits "heart-murder," even though he or she does not kill physically. Hatred is inconsistent with a true life in Christ; therefore, such persons do not have eternal life in themselves.

Marginal references:

2.25 Jn 17.3
2.26 2 Jn 7
2.27 Jn 14.26, 17
2.28 1 Jn 3.2, 21; 4.17; Mk 8.38; 1 Thess 2.19
2.29 1 Jn 3.7, 9; 4.7
3.1 Jn 1.12; 16.3
3.2 Rom 8.15; 2 Cor 4.17; Rom 8.29; 2 Pet 1.4; 2 Cor 3.18
3.4 Rom 4.15; 1 Jn 5.17
3.5 Isa 53.5, 6; 2 Cor 5.21
3.7 1 Jn 2.1, 26, 29
3.8 Jn 8.44; 16.11; Heb 2.14
3.9 1 Jn 5.18; 1 Pet 1.23
3.10 1 Jn 2.29
3.11 1 Jn 1.5; Jn 13.34, 35; 2 Jn 5
3.13 Jn 15.18
3.14 Jn 5.24; 1 Jn 2.9, 11
3.15 Mt 5.21, 22; Jn 8.44; Gal 5.20, 21

are murderers, and you know that murderers do not have eternal life abiding in them. 16We know love by this, that he laid down his life for us—and we ought to lay down our lives for one another. 17How does God's love abide in anyone who has the world's goods and sees a brother or sister*o* in need and yet refuses help?

18 Little children, let us love, not in word or speech, but in truth and action. 19And by this we will know that we are from the truth and will reassure our hearts before him 20whenever our hearts condemn us; for God is greater than our hearts, and he knows everything. 21Beloved, if our hearts do not condemn us, we have boldness before God; 22and we receive from him whatever we ask, because we obey his commandments and do what pleases him.

23 And this is his commandment, that we should believe in the name of his Son Jesus Christ and love one another, just as he has commanded us. 24All who obey his commandments abide in him, and he abides in them. And by this we know that he abides in us, by the Spirit that he has given us.

C. Faith in action

4 Beloved, do not believe every spirit, but test the spirits to see whether they are from God; for many false prophets have gone out into the world. 2By this you know the Spirit of God: every spirit that confesses that Jesus Christ has come in the flesh is from God, 3and every spirit that does not confess Jesus*p* is not from God. And this is the spirit of the antichrist, of which you have heard that it is coming; and now it is already in the world. 4Little children, you are from God, and have conquered them; for the one who is in you is greater than the one who is in the world. 5They are from the world; therefore what they say is from the world, and the world listens to them. 6We are from God. Whoever knows God listens to us, and whoever is not from God does not listen to us. From this we know the spirit of truth and the spirit of error.

D. The source of love

7 Beloved, let us love one another, because love is from God; everyone who loves is born of God and knows God. 8Whoever does not love does not know God, for God is love. 9God's love was revealed among us in this way: God sent his only Son into the world so that we might live through him. 10In this is love, not that we loved God but that he loved us and sent his Son to be the atoning sacrifice for our sins. 11Beloved, since God loved us so much, we also ought to love one another. 12No one has ever seen God; if we love one another, God lives in us, and his love is perfected in us.

13 By this we know that we abide in him and he in us, because he has given us of his Spirit. 14And we have seen and do testify that the Father

o Gk brother   *p* Other ancient authorities read *does away with Jesus* (Gk *dissolves Jesus*)

3.16
Jn 3.16;
13.1; 15.13
3.17
Deut 15.7;
1 Jn 4.20
3.18
Rom 12.9;
Jas 1.22
3.19
1 Jn 2.21
3.20
1 Cor 4.4
3.21
1 Jn 5.14
3.22
Mt 7.7;
21.22; 1 Jn
2.3
3.23
1 Jn 2.8
3.24
Rom 8.9;
1 Jn 4.13

4.1
Mt 24.4;
2 Pet 2.1;
1 Jn 2.18
4.2
1 Cor 12.3;
1 Jn 2.23
4.3
2 Jn 7; 1 Jn
2.22; 2 Thess
2.7
4.4
1 Jn 5.4
4.5
Jn 3.31;
15.19
4.6
Jn 8.47;
1 Cor 14.37;
Jn 14.17;
1 Tim 4.1
4.7
1 Jn 3.10, 11
4.8
v. 16
4.9
Jn 3.16; 1 Jn
5.11
4.10
Rom 5.8, 10;
1 Jn 2.2
4.11
Jn 3.16;
15.12
4.12
Jn 1.18;
1 Tim 6.16;
1 Jn 2.5
4.13
1 Jn 3.24

3.18 John, like James, insists on the necessity of good works. Love is simply a matter of lip service but should be seen and known in actions. To speak beautiful words means nothing if they are not accompanied by good works.
3.22 Those who have a good conscience toward God will not desire anything contrary to the honor and glory of God. They will depend on God, who will give them the good things they ask (see Ps 84.11).
4.1 Wherever truth exists, falsehood always appears. Thus we must examine everything that claims to come from the Spirit of God. Since John knows that many false prophets have gone out into the world, he instructs us as to the need for testing whether the spirits are genuinely from God. Our basis of comparison is the Bible; whatever is not in agreement with it must be rejected.
4.3 *antichrist.* (see also 2.18,22). Some of the antichrists at one time belonged to the Christian fellowship. Their error, for which they left the fellowship, was a denial of the reality of the incarnation, which was also a repudiation of the Father. This heresy was a direct result of Gnostic teaching (see Introduction; see note on 2 Jn 7).
4.10 God first loved us when we had no love for him (cf. Rom 5.6–10). He demonstrated his love by the giving of his Son to be the atoning sacrifice for our sins. God is love, and that love is boundless, incomprehensible, mysterious, and unsearchable.

has sent his Son as the Savior of the world. 15 God abides in those who confess that Jesus is the Son of God, and they abide in God. 16 So we have known and believe the love that God has for us.

God is love, and those who abide in love abide in God, and God abides in them. 17 Love has been perfected among us in this: that we may have boldness on the day of judgment, because as he is, so are we in this world. 18 There is no fear in love, but perfect love casts out fear; for fear has to do with punishment, and whoever fears has not reached perfection in love. 19 We love*q* because he first loved us. 20 Those who say, "I love God," and hate their brothers or sisters,*r* are liars; for those who do not love a brother or sister*s* whom they have seen, cannot love God whom they have not seen. 21 The commandment we have from him is this: those who love God must love their brothers and sisters*r* also.

IV. *Faith and certainty (5.1–12)*

A. *Victory through faith*

5 Everyone who believes that Jesus is the Christ*t* has been born of God, and everyone who loves the parent loves the child. 2 By this we know that we love the children of God, when we love God and obey his commandments. 3 For the love of God is this, that we obey his commandments. And his commandments are not burdensome, 4 for whatever is born of God conquers the world. And this is the victory that conquers the world, our faith. 5 Who is it that conquers the world but the one who believes that Jesus is the Son of God?

B. *Faith through the Son*

6 This is the one who came by water and blood, Jesus Christ, not with the water only but with the water and the blood. And the Spirit is the one that testifies, for the Spirit is the truth. 7 There are three that testify:*u* 8 the Spirit and the water and the blood, and these three agree. 9 If we receive human testimony, the testimony of God is greater; for this is the testimony of God that he has testified to his Son. 10 Those who believe in the Son of God have the testimony in their hearts. Those who do not believe in God*v* have made him a liar by not believing in the testimony that God has given concerning his Son. 11 And this is the testimony: God gave us eternal life, and this life is in his Son. 12 Whoever has the Son has life; whoever does not have the Son of God does not have life.

V. *Conclusion (5.13–21)*

13 I write these things to you who believe in the name of the Son of God, so that you may know that you have eternal life.

q Other ancient authorities add *him*; others add *God*   *r* Gk *brothers*   *s* Gk *brother*   *t* Or *the Messiah*   *u* A few ancient authorities read (with variations) 7 *There are three that testify in heaven, the Father, the Word, and the Holy Spirit, and these three are one.* 8 *And there are three that testify on earth:*   *v* Other ancient authorities read *in the Son*

4.18 We must distinguish between "the fear of God" and "being afraid of God." Fear as reverential trust toward the infinite God (a common theme in the O.T.) is appropriate. But we do not need to be afraid of him, for this implies a sense of guilt for sins. Perhaps a better word for fear here is dread; i.e., perfect love casts out dread.
5.4 *conquers the world.* We who are born of God are born *for* God. This makes possible the spiritual and intellectual conquest of the world. Faith is the means by which believers conquer.
5.6 *the Spirit is the one that testifies, for the Spirit is the truth.* God the Holy Spirit witnesses to our hearts that

Jesus is Lord and that the Bible is God's infallible word. Indeed the words of the Scriptures were "not taught by human wisdom but taught by the Spirit" (1 Cor 2.13).
5.13 *that you may know.* Some Christians do not have the assurance of faith and lack confidence in their salvation. John has written his epistle that all may know (i.e., be certain) that they have eternal life. Since God is speaking through John, confidence in his word assures the weakest of hearts and minds that they can know with certainty that they have eternal life.

14 And this is the boldness we have in him, that if we ask anything according to his will, he hears us. ¹⁵And if we know that he hears us in whatever we ask, we know that we have obtained the requests made of him. ¹⁶If you see your brother or sister*w* committing what is not a mortal sin, you will ask, and God*x* will give life to such a one—to those whose sin is not mortal. There is sin that is mortal; I do not say that you should pray about that. ¹⁷All wrongdoing is sin, but there is sin that is not mortal.

18 We know that those who are born of God do not sin, but the one who was born of God protects them, and the evil one does not touch them. ¹⁹We know that we are God's children, and that the whole world lies under the power of the evil one. ²⁰And we know that the Son of God has come and has given us understanding so that we may know him who is true;*y* and we are in him who is true, in his Son Jesus Christ. He is the true God and eternal life.

21 Little children, keep yourselves from idols.*z*

w Gk *your brother*   *x* Gk *he*   *y* Other ancient authorities read *know the true God*   *z* Other ancient authorities add *Amen*

5.14
1 Jn 3.21, 22;
Mt 7.7
5.16
Jas 5.15;
Heb 6.4, 6
5.17
1 Jn 3.4
5.18
1 Jn 3.9;
Jn 14.30
5.19
1 Jn 4.6;
Gal 1.4
5.20
Lk 24.45;
Jn 17.3;
Rev 3.7
5.21
1 Cor 10.14

5.14,15 These verses contain one of the greatest of all promises in the Scriptures. If we make our petitions and intercessions according to the will of God, God hears us. And if God hears us we can be absolutely certain that we will get what we have prayed for. In many cases, we can discern the will of God from Scripture, so that when we pray according to that word we know that our prayers will be answered in the affirmative.

5.18 *those who are born of God do not sin.* This statement, as it stands, seems to contradict 1.8. The clause might better be translated, "no one born of God makes sin a habit of life." Those who deliberately and with malicious forethought sin and keep on sinning have reason to question whether they have really been born of God.

INTRODUCTION TO
THE SECOND LETTER OF
JOHN

Authorship, Date, and Background: 2 and 3 John were both written by "the elder." The question of authorship depends upon identifying who "the elder" was. Clearly, 1, 2, and 3 John were written by the same person (see introduction to 1 John). Some modern scholars do not think it was the apostle John, but as far as the ancient church is concerned, it was John, the son of Zebedee. Evangelical scholars generally agree that the Gospel of John and these three letters were all composed by the apostle. All three letters were undoubtedly written in the city of Ephesus around A.D. 90.

John wrote the letter to "the elect lady," but whether this is the correct translation of the Greek remains an open question. It could be translated "the lady Eclecta," "the elect Cyria," or "the elect lady," depending upon whether the greeting is a proper name. Interpretation takes over at this point, for it is also possible that the term "lady" is a figurative expression applied to a church whose members can easily be called her "children." The problem has not been resolved.

Though the addressee of the letter is an open question, the content is not. John addresses the problem of false teachers in the church and of believers being subverted. John not only warns his readers; he also wants them to be vigilant so they will not be swept away by the error of Gnosticism (see introduction to 1 John).

Characteristics and Content: The church has been plagued by false doctrine throughout the ages. Wrong teachings always dilute the witness of believers, bring ill effects to those who accept them, and result in decay and decline in the Christian's personal life. The person of Jesus Christ is at issue here in 2 John, particularly whether Jesus became a true human being with a body like ours (v. 7). John stresses the true humanity of Christ, making plain that Christianity is based upon propositions which are forever true. Any departure from such central truths of the faith produces shipwreck, and John forbids believers even to invite such heretics into their homes or to encourage them in any way. We can tell who such people are by what they teach and by the type of lives they live; those who do not love are not true believers, however much they profess faith in doctrine.

Outline:

   I. Greeting (1–3)

  II. Counsel and warnings (4–11)

 III. Conclusion (12,13)

THE SECOND LETTER OF
JOHN

I. *Greeting (1–3)*

1 The elder to the elect lady and her children, whom I love in the truth, and not only I but also all who know the truth, **2** because of the truth that abides in us and will be with us forever:

3 Grace, mercy, and peace will be with us from God the Father and from*a* Jesus Christ, the Father's Son, in truth and love.

II. *Counsel and warnings (4–11)*

4 I was overjoyed to find some of your children walking in the truth, just as we have been commanded by the Father. **5** But now, dear lady, I ask you, not as though I were writing you a new commandment, but one we have had from the beginning, let us love one another. **6** And this is love, that we walk according to his commandments; this is the commandment just as you have heard it from the beginning — you must walk in it.

7 Many deceivers have gone out into the world, those who do not confess that Jesus Christ has come in the flesh; any such person is the deceiver and the antichrist! **8** Be on your guard, so that you do not lose what we*b* have worked for, but may receive a full reward. **9** Everyone who does not abide in the teaching of Christ, but goes beyond it, does not have God; whoever abides in the teaching has both the Father and the Son. **10** Do not receive into the house or welcome anyone who comes to you and does not bring this teaching; **11** for to welcome is to participate in the evil deeds of such a person.

III. *Conclusion (12,13)*

12 Although I have much to write to you, I would rather not use paper and ink; instead I hope to come to you and talk with you face to face, so that our joy may be complete.

13 The children of your elect sister send you their greetings.*c*

a Other ancient authorities add *the Lord*   *b* Other ancient authorities read *you*   *c* Other ancient authorities add *Amen*

1
3 Jn 1; 1 Jn 3.18;
Jn 8.32
2
2 Pet 1.12;
1 Jn 1.8
3
1 Tim 1.2
4
3 Jn 3, 4
5
1 Jn 2.7;
3.11
6
1 Jn 2.5;
2.24
7
1 Jn 4.1-3;
2.22
8
Mk 13.9;
1 Cor 3.8;
Heb 10.32
9
1 Jn 2.23
10
Rom 16.17
11
1 Tim 5.22
12
3 Jn 13, 14;
1 Jn 1.4
13
v. 1

1ff *The elect lady* is probably a woman of eminent birth and education (cf. Acts 16.14; 17.4; 1 Cor 1.26). Not all Christians were poor and uneducated. John rejoices in her influence, particularly on her children (v. 4), who have the truth and are walking in it. Thus wherever these children go, they so live that their faith can be seen by all.
5,6 John reiterates the truth that words and actions belong together. Love means walking in the commandments of Jesus. When we obey his commandments we are walking in the faith.
7 An early Gnostic heresy, Docetism, held that Jesus' body was not real flesh and blood; it was a purely spiritual body. John affirms that Jesus came in the flesh and was a real human being composed of flesh and blood (cf. 1 Jn 4.2,3). Whoever affirms this heresy cannot be of God, and whoever is not of God is not a regenerate believer.
10,11 Those who deny the faith are out to destroy the soul. Such people must not be welcomed into the home or the church. Whoever does so becomes a partaker of the wicked one's deeds.
12 Some things are better spoken than written. John is still able to travel, so he hopes to see this sister shortly and speak at length with her.

INTRODUCTION TO
THE THIRD LETTER OF
JOHN

Authorship, Date, and Background: Like 1 and 2 John, tradition has it that 3 John was written by the apostle John (see introduction to 1 John). The opening greeting identifies the author as "the elder," like 2 John (see introduction to 2 John). Assuming Johannine authorship, it was written sometime around A.D. 90. The absence of any reference to the Roman persecutions in any of the three letters by John suggests all were written before emperor Trajan's time and probably before the last years of Domitian, whose reign ended in A.D. 96.

3 John is more administrative than theological. It was addressed to Gaius, a pastor or a leader in the church (possibly the one mentioned in Acts 19.29; 20.4; Rom 16.23; 1 Cor 1.14), though where his church was located is not stated. In those days, traveling prophets, evangelists, and teachers went from church to church. They were taken care of by the churches to which they went and were helped on their way to the next station. It appears that Gaius knew Diotrephes, also mentioned in the letter. Gaius was a beloved and faithful servant of the Lord, whereas Diotrephes refused to help the traveling visitors, withstood the authority of the elder, and used the occasion to speak against him. Moreover, those members of the congregation who wished to help the visiting preachers were put out of the church.

Characteristics and Content: John evidently has authority over several churches and is angry at Diotrephes for his insubordination. He expects to visit the church and put things right. He wants to encourage faithful Gaius and to commend Demetrius whose reputation is excellent and who clings to the truth. Implied in the letter is the Gnostic problem mentioned in 1 John, a heresy agitating the churches and destroying the true gospel. Beloved Gaius must not let the evil influence of Diotrephes influence him. John emphasizes one aspect of the faith which is always pertinent to believers. He says, "Whoever does good is from God; whoever does evil has not seen God" (v. 11).

Outline:

   I. Greeting (1–4)

  II. Encouragement for Gaius (5–8)

 III. Reproof for Diotrephes (9,10)

 IV. Commendation for Demetrius (11,12)

  V. Conclusion (13–15)

THE THIRD LETTER OF
JOHN

I. *Greeting (1–4)*

1 The elder to the beloved Gaius, whom I love in truth.

2 Beloved, I pray that all may go well with you and that you may be in good health, just as it is well with your soul. 3 I was overjoyed when some of the friends[a] arrived and testified to your faithfulness to the truth, namely how you walk in the truth. 4 I have no greater joy than this, to hear that my children are walking in the truth.

1
2 Jn 1
3
2 Jn 4; vv. 5, 10
4
1 Cor 4.15;
Philem 10

II. *Encouragement for Gaius (5–8)*

5 Beloved, you do faithfully whatever you do for the friends,[a] even though they are strangers to you; 6 they have testified to your love before the church. You will do well to send them on in a manner worthy of God; 7 for they began their journey for the sake of Christ,[b] accepting no support from non-believers.[c] 8 Therefore we ought to support such people, so that we may become co-workers with the truth.

5
Rom 12.13;
Heb 13.2
6
Acts 15.3;
Titus 3.13
7
Acts 5.41;
20.33, 35

III. *Reproof for Diotrephes (9,10)*

9 I have written something to the church; but Diotrephes, who likes to put himself first, does not acknowledge our authority. 10 So if I come, I will call attention to what he is doing in spreading false charges against us. And not content with those charges, he refuses to welcome the friends,[a] and even prevents those who want to do so and expels them from the church.

9
2 Jn 9
10
2 Jn 12; v. 5;
Jn 9.34

IV. *Commendation for Demetrius (11,12)*

11 Beloved, do not imitate what is evil but imitate what is good. Whoever does good is from God; whoever does evil has not seen God. 12 Everyone has testified favorably about Demetrius, and so has the truth itself. We also testify for him,[d] and you know that our testimony is true.

11
Ps 37.27;
1 Jn 2.29;
3.6, 9
12
1 Tim 3.7;
Jn 21.24

---

a Gk *brothers*   *b* Gk *for the sake of the name*   *c* Gk *the Gentiles*   *d* Gk lacks *for him*

---

2 John rejoices that Gaius is prospering in spiritual matters and wants him to prosper equally in physical health. Grace and health are two of God's best gifts.
6 Gaius was a man of faith, sincere in his religious convictions, devoted to God, and charitable, who was providing hospitality to traveling evangelists. The brothers and sisters in his church testified to his goodness.
9 Compared to Gaius, Diotrephes was a disaster.

Apparently he was a proud and ambitious minister in the church, who had no use for the apostle's authority and talked against him. He excommunicated people at will, and lacked the graces displayed by Gaius.
12 A third person mentioned by John is Demetrius. All good people held him in esteem. He was a firm believer in whom John has confidence. Therefore he can recommend him highly and claim that his testimony is true and should be trusted.

V. *Conclusion (13–15)*

2 Jn 12
1 Pet 5.14

13 I have much to write to you, but I would rather not write with pen and ink; **14** instead I hope to see you soon, and we will talk together face to face.

15 Peace to you. The friends send you their greetings. Greet the friends there, each by name.

13,14 John stops writing, since he expects to see these people in person soon; he prefers that to pen and ink.

INTRODUCTION TO
THE LETTER OF
JUDE

Introduction to Jude

I. Introduction (1-4)

Authorship, Date, and Background: Jude was the brother of James (v. 1), the leader of the Jerusalem church (see introduction to James). In Mk 6.3 both of them are called the brothers of Jesus. Jude, like James, came to know Jesus the Christ as Savior subsequent to the resurrection, though he was never as important in the early church as James. His letter in its style, vocabulary, and terseness is similar to James' letter. The date of Jude is important because parts of it are similar to 2 Peter (especially vv. 17,18, verbatim quotations from 2 Pet 3.3). Since the letter of Jude was almost certainly written after the destruction of Jerusalem when Peter was already dead, Peter could not have copied from Jude but vice versa (see introduction to 2 Peter). Evangelical scholars have generally accepted Jude as the author.

Nothing in the letter indicates specifically for whom it was intended. It was probably composed outside of Palestine and was intended for the Jews of the Dispersion (i.e., Jews living throughout the Roman empire) who had come to the knowledge of Jesus Christ and were associated with the church. Jude's illustrations from the O.T. involving obscure figures, plus his use of extrabiblical quotations, suggests that his readers were familiar with these literary Jewish sources. The heresy Jude was combating was somehow connected with Gnosticism (see introduction to 1 John), for false teachers were allowing for fleshly indulgence in all kinds of licentious sins on the basis that body and spirit were regarded as separate and unrelated.

Characteristics and Content: Jude articulates the foundational truths of the Christian faith as though they are well established and unchanging. He addresses his readers as "beloved," and has for his purpose the need to urge them to "contend for the faith that was once for all entrusted to the saints" (v. 3). In doing so, he presents them with the consequences that fall on those who depart from the faith. First he speaks about Israel, who had been saved out of Egypt; when they distrusted God he destroyed them (v. 5). He recalls God's awful judgment on the fallen angels who have been chained up in prisons, waiting for the judgment day (v. 6). As if this were not enough, he cites the judgment of God against Sodom and Gomorrah, which were destroyed by fire and thus continue to be a warning to us (v. 7). These are sobering illustrations.

Jude goes on to write about specific individuals who experienced the wrath of God: Cain, Balaam, and Korah (v. 11). He quotes with approval from the noncanonical book of Enoch about the coming of the Lord with his holy ones to render judgment and mete out punishment to the wicked; he also quotes from the *Assumption of Moses* about the dispute between Michael and Satan over the body of Moses. These quotations from extrabiblical sources simply illustrate the point Jude makes; they are not designed to give them canonical status. He warns his readers to be careful and assures them that God "is able to keep you from falling, and to make you stand without blemish in the presence of his glory with rejoicing" (v. 24).

Outline:

I. Introduction (1–4)

II. Character and doom of false teachers (5–16)

III. Admonition to hold the true faith (17–23)

IV. Benediction (24,25)

THE LETTER OF
JUDE

I. Introduction (1–4)

1 Jude,[a] a servant[b] of Jesus Christ and brother of James,
To those who are called, who are beloved[c] in[d] God the Father and kept safe for[d] Jesus Christ:
2 May mercy, peace, and love be yours in abundance.
3 Beloved, while eagerly preparing to write to you about the salvation we share, I find it necessary to write and appeal to you to contend for the faith that was once for all entrusted to the saints. 4 For certain intruders have stolen in among you, people who long ago were designated for this condemnation as ungodly, who pervert the grace of our God into licentiousness and deny our only Master and Lord, Jesus Christ.[e]

II. Character and doom of false teachers (5–16)

5 Now I desire to remind you, though you are fully informed, that the Lord, who once for all saved[f] a people out of the land of Egypt, afterward destroyed those who did not believe. 6 And the angels who did not keep their own position, but left their proper dwelling, he has kept in eternal chains in deepest darkness for the judgment of the great day. 7 Likewise, Sodom and Gomorrah and the surrounding cities, which, in the same manner as they, indulged in sexual immorality and pursued unnatural lust,[g] serve as an example by undergoing a punishment of eternal fire.

8 Yet in the same way these dreamers also defile the flesh, reject authority, and slander the glorious ones.[h] 9 But when the archangel Michael contended with the devil and disputed about the body of Moses, he did not dare to bring a condemnation of slander[i] against him, but said, "The Lord rebuke you!" 10 But these people slander whatever they do not understand, and they are destroyed by those things that, like irrational animals, they know by instinct. 11 Woe to them! For they go the way of Cain, and abandon themselves to Balaam's error for the sake of gain, and perish in Korah's rebellion. 12 These are blemishes[j] on your love-feasts,

a Gk *Judas* b Gk *slave* c Other ancient authorities read *sanctified* d Or *by* e Or *the only Master and our Lord Jesus Christ* f Other ancient authorities read *though you were once for all fully informed, that Jesus* (or *Joshua*) *who saved* g Gk *went after other flesh* h Or *angels*; Gk *glories* i Or *condemnation for blasphemy* j Or *reefs*

1
Acts 1.13;
1 Pet 1.5

2
1 Pet 1.2;
2 Pet 1.2
3
Titus 1.4;
1 Tim 6.12
4
Gal 2.4;
2 Pet 2.1;
Rom 9.22;
2 Pet 2.1

5
Num 14.29;
Ps 106.26
6
Jn 8.44;
2 Pet 2.4;
Rev 20.10
7
2 Pet 2.6;
Gen 19.24
8
2 Pet 2.10
9
Dan 10.13;
Zech 3.2
10
2 Pet 2.12;
Phil 3.19
11
Gen 4.3-8;
1 Jn 3.12;
Num 22.7;
2 Pet 2.15;
Num 16.1-3,
31-35
12
2 Pet 2.13;
1 Cor 11.20ff;
Eph 4.14;
Mt 15.13

---

1 Jude chooses to name himself as the brother of James, who was a half brother of Jesus. Thus Jude was also a half brother of the Lord after the flesh. But he does not press his family claim; instead, he identifies himself as a servant or slave of Jesus Christ — as must all who have been redeemed through the blood of Jesus Christ.
3 Error is dangerous, so those who have the true faith must contend for it earnestly. But defending the truth should always be done in a lawful manner. All too often ungodly people cause divisions and widen breaches merely to advance and promote their own selfish, ambitious, and covetous ends.
6 *angels.* These angels were obviously sinless and unfallen at one time, but they sinned, were expelled from heaven, and were consigned to "eternal chains in deepest darkness" (cf. 2 Pet 2.4) where they await

the last judgment and their final punishment. They will be cast into the lake of fire with their leader, Satan (Mt 25.41; Rev 20.7–15).
9 The dispute over the body of Moses is recounted in the Jewish apocryphal book titled *The Assumption of Moses.* According to some of the early church fathers, Satan tried to claim the body of Moses for two reasons. (1) He, Satan, was the lord of matter; to this the angel replied that God is Lord of all, for he created matter. (2) Moses was a murderer and therefore his body belonged to Satan; to this accusation the angel said, "The Lord rebuke you," and Satan fled (cf. Zech 3.2).
11 *Balaam's error.* See note on 2 Pet 2.15. This differs from the teaching of Balaam (see note on Rev 2.14).

while they feast with you without fear, feeding themselves.[k] They are waterless clouds carried along by the winds; autumn trees without fruit, twice dead, uprooted; 13 wild waves of the sea, casting up the foam of their own shame; wandering stars, for whom the deepest darkness has been reserved forever.

14 It was also about these that Enoch, in the seventh generation from Adam, prophesied, saying, "See, the Lord is coming[l] with ten thousands of his holy ones, 15 to execute judgment on all, and to convict everyone of all the deeds of ungodliness that they have committed in such an ungodly way, and of all the harsh things that ungodly sinners have spoken against him." 16 These are grumblers and malcontents; they indulge their own lusts; they are bombastic in speech, flattering people to their own advantage.

III. Admonition to hold the true faith (17–23)

17 But you, beloved, must remember the predictions of the apostles of our Lord Jesus Christ; 18 for they said to you, "In the last time there will be scoffers, indulging their own ungodly lusts." 19 It is these worldly people, devoid of the Spirit, who are causing divisions. 20 But you, beloved, build yourselves up on your most holy faith; pray in the Holy Spirit; 21 keep yourselves in the love of God; look forward to the mercy of our Lord Jesus Christ that leads to[m] eternal life. 22 And have mercy on some who are wavering; 23 save others by snatching them out of the fire; and have mercy on still others with fear, hating even the tunic defiled by their bodies.[n]

IV. Benediction (24,25)

24 Now to him who is able to keep you from falling, and to make you stand without blemish in the presence of his glory with rejoicing, 25 to the only God our Savior, through Jesus Christ our Lord, be glory, majesty, power, and authority, before all time and now and forever. Amen.

[k] Or *without fear. They are shepherds who care only for themselves* [l] Gk *came* [m] Gk *Christ to* [n] Gk *by the flesh.* The Greek text of verses 22-23 is uncertain at several points

Cross-references (left margin)

13   Isa 57.20; Phil 3.19; 2 Pet 2.17

14   Gen 5.18; Deut 33.2; Dan 7.10

15   2 Pet 2.6ff; 1 Tim 1.9

16   2 Pet 2.18

17   2 Pet 3.2

18   1 Tim 4.1; 2 Pet 2.1

19   1 Cor 2.14, 15; Jas 3.15

20   Col 2.7; Eph 6.18

21   Titus 2.13; 2 Pet 3.12

23   Am 4.11; Zech 3.2-5

24   Rom 16.25; Eph 3.20; Col 1.22

25   1 Tim 1.17; Rom 11.36

---

14 The phrase *the seventh generation from Adam* appears in Enoch 60.8. The noncanonical book of Enoch contains portions that can be dated from the beginning of the Christian era, including the statement quoted here.

20 *pray in the Holy Spirit.* This involves submitting ourselves to the guidance and the teaching of the Holy Spirit. Faith, fervency, and persistence constitute the right spirit for prayer. Whenever we truly pray in the Holy Spirit, great results will come.

24,25 According to this apostolic benediction, God is both willing and able to keep us from falling. And of those given to Jesus by the Father, none shall be lost (Jn 6.39). Our Redeemer promises to present us before the Father as faultless, for he has become sin for us (2 Cor 5.21).

INTRODUCTION TO

THE

REVELATION

TO JOHN

Authorship, Date, and Background: Appropriately placed at the end of the N.T., the book of Revelation closes the canon of Scripture. The closing of the canon means that there is no new revelation given to us by God. The O.T. and N.T. are all there is. The next revelation will be the revealing of the Son of God from heaven when Jesus comes the second time.

Revelation itself claims to have come from God to John. When all of the scholarly claims have been examined, it boils down to the conclusion that John, the son of Zebedee, the brother of James, and the author of the Gospel of John and the three letters of John, wrote the book. He was an apostle, an eyewitness, and an aged saint. The book itself was written during the time of the persecution by Domitian, which places it in the last decade of the first century (ca. A.D. 96).

John had been imprisoned on the island of Patmos. The stated reason for his exile there was his preaching "of the word of God and the testimony of Jesus" (1.9). It must be remembered that he was an eyewitness who had been with Jesus throughout the days of his ministry on this earth. Christianity, once regarded as a cult under the umbrella of Judaism, no longer enjoyed this protection. It was regarded as a new religion, and the stubborn refusal of Christians to bow before the emperor, who set himself up as God, occasioned their persecution. Toleration was no longer possible. The church was placed on the defensive, a situation which was to continue until Constantine's day. Thus it was written at a time when Christians were inclined toward despair because of the persecution. Their despair was offset only by the expectation of being saved by divine intervention on their behalf.

Revelation is the only completely apocalyptic book in the N.T. It discloses things otherwise hidden which could only be made known by revelation from God. Its style of writing is similar to that of Daniel in the O.T. Times of persecution usually produced apocalyptic books—literature with strange dreams and visions of a symbolic nature, with celestial beings and demonic powers fighting against each other, with the assurance of the victory of right over wrong, and with the certainty that the righteous would be delivered and the wicked judged. As an apocalyptic book, it contains much prophecy.

Characteristics and Content: The big question about Revelation is: What does it all mean? The first three chapters are plain enough. They include the prologue, the vision, the portrait, and the messages to the seven churches of Asia. These were actual churches. John evaluates their strengths and weaknesses and warns them that their lampstands may be removed. Beginning with ch. 4, John writes about the seven seals, the seven trumpets, the seven signs, and the seven bowls. These are followed by the coming of Christ the conqueror, the binding of Satan, the millennial reign of the Lord, the last rebellion, the final judgment, and the new heavens and the new earth. The consummation of human history brings with it the total end of evil and the total victory of God and good forever and ever. The real problem has to do with interpretation. What do these things mean? There have been at least four schools of thought.

The *Preterist School* holds that all of Revelation pertains only to the events of that day in symbolic form. Nothing in the book is futuristic; i.e., it has no predictive prophecy. This view commends itself to many modern scholars who do not accept the possibility of predictive prophecy.

The second is the *Idealist School,* which holds that the book simply gives us a picture of the ongoing struggle between good and evil characteristic of all ages. This school does not think the symbols can be attached to any specific historical events. The emphasis is on ethical and spiritual truths, not on historical happenings. By spiritualizing the book, it dehistoricizes it so that there is no climax to history when Jesus comes to sit on a visible throne in all of his glory.

The third school is known as the *Historicist School,* which claims that the book discloses in broad outline form the future course of history from the descent of the Holy Spirit to the second coming of Jesus. Major events in history since the age of the apostles are made known through the symbols in the book. For example, the seven seals are thought to represent the division of the Roman empire and its dissolution; the coming of the locusts is thought to represent the invasions of Europe by the Muslims. The advocates of this view are not agreed about the meaning of each symbol.

The fourth school is the *Futurist School,* which holds generally that the first three chapters of Revelation are historical and the remaining portions of the book, beginning with ch. 4, have to do with the period at the end of the age known as the great tribulation. These events are regarded as literally as possible and are thought to be wholly future.

In addition to these four schools, many Christians combine two of them together. For example, some Bible scholars take a basically futurist view, but also hold that one of John's main goals was to shape the ethical conduct of the Christians to whom he was writing (the idealist view).

Broadly speaking, most Christians today adhere to one of three interpretations of eschatology (the doctrine of what will happen in the end times), each of which is related to the understanding of ch. 20 (see also notes on that chapter). The three views are known as the postmillennial, the amillennial, and the premillennial view.

Postmillennialism teaches that through the efforts of Christians, Satan will be bound during this present age. The church will progress and an earthly millennium (literally, a thousand-year age of righteousness) will be brought into existence, at the end of which Jesus Christ will return. This view presents an optimistic account of the triumph of righteousness quite at variance with the experience of history.

Amillennialism interprets ch. 20 in such a way as to foreclose any possibility of a future millennium of peace and righteousness after the coming of the Lord. To most amillennialists, we are presently in the millennium, for Christ reigns right now at God's right hand and controls the activities of Satan. It may not seem at times that he is in control, but the believer knows that he is. Amillennialists do allow for significant catastrophic events connected with the end of this age (the great tribulation), immediately preceding the coming of Christ. At that time, history as we know it will end, the final judgment will take place, and the eternal age will begin.

The premillennialist believes the course of history moves inevitably toward the climax of the age, the rapture of the church, the great tribulation, and the second coming of Jesus (all of which are described in great detail in this book). The closing days of the age will witness the great tribulation such as the world has never seen. At the end of this period Jesus will come again and establish his thousand-year (millennial) kingdom of righteousness on earth. Satan will be bound during this time but loosed at the end of it to commence the final episode in the history of humanity. Christ will be triumphant; the devil and his hosts, including the unsaved, will be consigned to the lake of fire, while the righteous saints will live and reign with Christ in the city of God, the new Jerusalem, which comes down from God out of heaven.

Outline:

I. Introduction (1.1–20)

II. The messages to the seven churches (2.1—3.22)

III. The things that shall be (4.1—22.5)

IV. Epilogue (22.6–21)

THE
REVELATION
TO JOHN

I. *Introduction (1.1–20)*

A. *The source of the revelation*

1.1
Jn 12.49;
Rev 22.16
1.2
1 Cor 1.6;
Rev 12.17
1.3
Lk 11.28;
Rev 22.10

1 The revelation of Jesus Christ, which God gave him to show his servants*a* what must soon take place; he made*b* it known by sending his angel to his servant*c* John, 2 who testified to the word of God and to the testimony of Jesus Christ, even to all that he saw.

3 Blessed is the one who reads aloud the words of the prophecy, and blessed are those who hear and who keep what is written in it; for the time is near.

B. *The greeting*

1.4
Jn 1.1;
Rev 3.1; 4.5
1.5
Rev 3.14;
Col 1.18;
Ps 89.27;
Rev 17.14;
Jn 13.34;
Heb 9.14
1.6
1 Pet 2.5;
Rev 5.10;
Rom 11.36
1.7
Zech 12.10

4 John to the seven churches that are in Asia:

Grace to you and peace from him who is and who was and who is to come, and from the seven spirits who are before his throne, 5 and from Jesus Christ, the faithful witness, the firstborn of the dead, and the ruler of the kings of the earth.

To him who loves us and freed*d* us from our sins by his blood, 6 and made*b* us to be a kingdom, priests serving*e* his God and Father, to him be glory and dominion forever and ever. Amen.

7   Look! He is coming with the clouds;
　　　every eye will see him,
　　even those who pierced him;
　　　and on his account all the tribes of the earth will wail.
So it is to be. Amen.

1.8
Rev 21.6;
4.8; 16.7

8   "I am the Alpha and the Omega," says the Lord God, who is and who was and who is to come, the Almighty.

C. *The voice and the vision*

1.9
Phil 4.14;
2 Tim 2.12
1.10
Rev 4.1, 2
1.11
vv. 8, 17

9   I, John, your brother who share with you in Jesus the persecution and the kingdom and the patient endurance, was on the island called Patmos because of the word of God and the testimony of Jesus.*f* 10 I was in the spirit*g* on the Lord's day, and I heard behind me a loud voice like a trumpet 11 saying, "Write in a book what you see and send it to the seven

---

a Gk *slaves*　*b* Gk *and he made*　*c* Gk *slave*　*d* Other ancient authorities read *washed*　*e* Gk *priests to*
f Or *testimony to Jesus*　*g* Or *in the Spirit*

1.1 *Revelation* differs from *inspiration* (see note on 2 Tim 3.16). Revelation is the self-disclosure of God and the disclosure to people of that which they could not know by themselves. Some Scriptures (such as this book) were written by people with immediate access to the information; some used written documents or oral tradition as their source of information (see Lk 1.1–4). Irrespective of their source, Bible writers, through the Holy Spirit, chose the right material and gave us a trustworthy Bible.
1.2 John was the recipient of this revelation. He received it from the angel, who was acting under the direction of Jesus Christ, who received it from the Father.

1.4 *who is and who was and who is to come.* The Father here is spoken of in terms of his eternal being (cf. Ex 3.14,15). *The seven spirits* indicates the Holy Spirit in terms of his perfection and completeness, symbolized by the number seven.
1.8 *I am Alpha and Omega,* i.e., "I am the A and the Z." This has to do with God's almighty power, not his eternity of existence. All events from the beginning to the end of history are controlled by him.
1.11 The letters to the seven churches are addressed to literal churches in existence at the time John wrote. They refer to conditions that existed in those and other churches of the age, but also apply to similar conditions in the churches of Jesus Christ in later

churches, to Ephesus, to Smyrna, to Pergamum, to Thyatira, to Sardis, to Philadelphia, and to Laodicea."

12 Then I turned to see whose voice it was that spoke to me, and on turning I saw seven golden lampstands, 13 and in the midst of the lampstands I saw one like the Son of Man, clothed with a long robe and with a golden sash across his chest. 14 His head and his hair were white as white wool, white as snow; his eyes were like a flame of fire, 15 his feet were like burnished bronze, refined as in a furnace, and his voice was like the sound of many waters. 16 In his right hand he held seven stars, and from his mouth came a sharp, two-edged sword, and his face was like the sun shining with full force.

17 When I saw him, I fell at his feet as though dead. But he placed his right hand on me, saying, "Do not be afraid; I am the first and the last, 18 and the living one. I was dead, and see, I am alive forever and ever; and I have the keys of Death and of Hades. 19 Now write what you have seen, what is, and what is to take place after this. 20 As for the mystery of the seven stars that you saw in my right hand, and the seven golden lampstands: the seven stars are the angels of the seven churches, and the seven lampstands are the seven churches.

II. The messages to the seven churches (2.1–3.22)

A. The message to Ephesus

2 "To the angel of the church in Ephesus write: These are the words of him who holds the seven stars in his right hand, who walks among the seven golden lampstands:

2 "I know your works, your toil and your patient endurance. I know that you cannot tolerate evildoers; you have tested those who claim to be apostles but are not, and have found them to be false. 3 I also know that you are enduring patiently and bearing up for the sake of my name, and that you have not grown weary. 4 But I have this against you, that you have abandoned the love you had at first. 5 Remember then from what you have fallen; repent, and do the works you did at first. If not, I will come to you and remove your lampstand from its place, unless you repent. 6 Yet this is to your credit: you hate the works of the Nicolaitans, which I also hate. 7 Let anyone who has an ear listen to what the Spirit is saying to the churches. To everyone who conquers, I will give permission to eat from the tree of life that is in the paradise of God.

B. The message to Smyrna

8 "And to the angel of the church in Smyrna write: These are the words of the first and the last, who was dead and came to life:

9 "I know your affliction and your poverty, even though you are rich. I know the slander on the part of those who say that they are Jews and are not, but are a synagogue of Satan. 10 Do not fear what you are about

1.12 Ex 25.27; Zech 4.2
1.13 Ezek 1.26; Dan 7.13; 10.5
1.14 Dan 7.9; 10.6; Rev 19.12
1.15 Dan 10.6; Ezek 43.2
1.16 Rev 2.1; 3.1; Heb 4.12; Rev 2.12, 16
1.17 Ezek 1.28; Dan 8.18; 10.10; Isa 41.4
1.18 Rom 6.9; Rev 4.9; 20.1
1.20 Zech 4.2

2.1 Rev 1.16; 1.13
2.2 Rev 3.1, 8; 1 Jn 4.1; 2 Cor 11.13
2.3 Jn 15.21
2.4 Mt 24.12
2.5 vv. 16, 22, 2; Rev 1.20
2.6 v. 15
2.7 Mt 11.15; Rev 3.6, 13; 22.2, 14; Gen 2.9
2.8 Rev 1.11, 17, 18
2.9 Rev 1.9; Jas 2.5; Rev 3.9
2.10 Rev 3.10; Dan 1.12

---

ages. Some interpreters think the seven churches represent seven successive epochs of church history from the beginning to the end of the present age of the Holy Spirit. This view has serious defects, particularly since it identifies the Protestant Reformation with the Sardis church, said to be more dead than alive (3.1)! It is true that in the end times, the evils mentioned in these letters will intensify, particularly the lukewarmness, nakedness, and shame of the Laodicean church.
2.1 Ephesus was a strategic center in the Roman world. Paul established a church there (Acts 19). The city was in a state of decline for some centuries. It had once been a seaport, but silt from the river around which the city was built eventually left Ephesus seven

miles inland from the Mediterranean Sea. Its enormous pagan temple was one of the wonders of the world. Today it is a vast archaeological dig, being gradually uncovered to reveal the ancient splendor of a pagan metropolis.
2.6 The Nicolaitans were a heretical group tolerated by the church of Pergamum (v. 15), but rejected by the church at Ephesus. They stressed Christian liberty to such an extent that they allowed for gross immorality and idolatry.
2.8 Smyrna (now called Izmir) is the only one of the seven churches of Asia that is alive and flourishing today. It lies at the head of the gulf into which the Hermus River flows. How the Christian faith came into Smyrna is not known.

2.11
Rev 20.14;
21.8

to suffer. Beware, the devil is about to throw some of you into prison so that you may be tested, and for ten days you will have affliction. Be faithful until death, and I will give you the crown of life. 11 Let anyone who has an ear listen to what the Spirit is saying to the churches. Whoever conquers will not be harmed by the second death.

C. The message to Pergamum

2.12
Rev 1.11, 16
2.13
Rev 14.12;
v. 9
2.14
Num 24.14;
2 Pet 2.15;
Jude 11;
1 Cor 8.9;
10.19, 20;
6.13
2.15
v. 6
2.16
2 Thess 2.8;
Rev 1.16
2.17
Jn 6.49, 50;
Isa 62.2;
Rev 19.12

12 "And to the angel of the church in Pergamum write: These are the words of him who has the sharp two-edged sword:

13 "I know where you are living, where Satan's throne is. Yet you are holding fast to my name, and you did not deny your faith in meʰ even in the days of Antipas my witness, my faithful one, who was killed among you, where Satan lives. 14 But I have a few things against you: you have some there who hold to the teaching of Balaam, who taught Balak to put a stumbling block before the people of Israel, so that they would eat food sacrificed to idols and practice fornication. 15 So you also have some who hold to the teaching of the Nicolaitans. 16 Repent then. If not, I will come to you soon and make war against them with the sword of my mouth. 17 Let anyone who has an ear listen to what the Spirit is saying to the churches. To everyone who conquers I will give some of the hidden manna, and I will give a white stone, and on the white stone is written a new name that no one knows except the one who receives it.

D. The message to Thyatira

2.18
Rev 1.11, 14,
15
2.19
v. 2
2.20
1 Kings 16.31;
21.25;
2 Kings 9.7;
Acts 15.20
2.21
Rom 2.4;
Rev 9.20
2.22
Rev 17.2;
18.9
2.23
Jer 11.20;
Acts 1.24;
Rom 8.27;
Ps 62.12
2.24
Acts 15.28

18 "And to the angel of the church in Thyatira write: These are the words of the Son of God, who has eyes like a flame of fire, and whose feet are like burnished bronze:

19 "I know your works — your love, faith, service, and patient endurance. I know that your last works are greater than the first. 20 But I have this against you: you tolerate that woman Jezebel, who calls herself a prophet and is teaching and beguiling my servantsⁱ to practice fornication and to eat food sacrificed to idols. 21 I gave her time to repent, but she refuses to repent of her fornication. 22 Beware, I am throwing her on a bed, and those who commit adultery with her I am throwing into great distress, unless they repent of her doings; 23 and I will strike her children dead. And all the churches will know that I am the one who searches minds and hearts, and I will give to each of you as your works deserve. 24 But to the rest of you in Thyatira, who do not hold this teaching, who have not learned what some call 'the deep things of Satan,' to you I say, I do not lay on you any other burden; 25 only hold fast to what you have until I

ʰ Or *deny my faith*   ⁱ Gk *slaves*

2.12 *Pergamum* was the capital city of the Roman province of Pergamum in Asia. It was a center for pagan worship. The imperial cult built around the Roman emperor required citizens to burn a pinch of incense at the foot of his statue. The Nicolaitans (v. 15) thought a little compromise would preserve the faith and keep anti-Christian sentiment at a minimum, but to the apostles, no compromise was permissible. They resisted it vigorously.
2.14 *The teaching of Balaam* must be distinguished from the error of Balaam (see note on 2 Pet 2.15). Balaam taught King Balak to entice Israel to worship idols, to marry his unbelieving subjects, and to partake of their ritual prostitution (Num 31.15,16). All too often Christians who have married unbelievers have lost their spirituality and backslidden from the true faith.
2.18 *Thyatira* was founded by Seleucus I, a general

of Alexander, who located the city on a valley road between the Hermus and Caicus rivers, twenty miles southeast of Pergamum. It was a commercial center engaged in vigorous trade. The trade guilds were pagan in orientation and their social events were interlaced with pagan rituals, making it difficult for Christians to stay in business if they refused to participate in the social excesses. The Nicolaitans sought a compromise, but it was rejected by John, who demanded maintaining Christian principles.
2.20 Jezebel's teaching at Thyatira was the same as that of Balaam (v. 14) — to practice immorality and eat food sacrificed to idols. Sins of idolatry and immorality commonly went together in pagan religions. We do not know whether this was a real Jezebel or simply a title applied to a woman whose life resembled that of Jezebel in the O.T. (cf. 1 Kings 16.31; 2 Kings 9.22).

come. ²⁶To everyone who conquers and continues to do my works to the end,

    I will give authority over the nations;
²⁷ to rule^j them with an iron rod,
    as when clay pots are shattered—
²⁸even as I also received authority from my Father. To the one who conquers I will also give the morning star. ²⁹Let anyone who has an ear listen to what the Spirit is saying to the churches.

E. The message to Sardis

3 "And to the angel of the church in Sardis write: These are the words of him who has the seven spirits of God and the seven stars:

"I know your works; you have a name of being alive, but you are dead. ²Wake up, and strengthen what remains and is on the point of death, for I have not found your works perfect in the sight of my God. ³Remember then what you received and heard; obey it, and repent. If you do not wake up, I will come like a thief, and you will not know at what hour I will come to you. ⁴Yet you have still a few persons in Sardis who have not soiled their clothes; they will walk with me, dressed in white, for they are worthy. ⁵If you conquer, you will be clothed like them in white robes, and I will not blot your name out of the book of life; I will confess your name before my Father and before his angels. ⁶Let anyone who has an ear listen to what the Spirit is saying to the churches.

F. The message to Philadelphia

7 "And to the angel of the church in Philadelphia write:
These are the words of the holy one, the true one,
    who has the key of David,
    who opens and no one will shut,
      who shuts and no one opens:
8 "I know your works. Look, I have set before you an open door, which no one is able to shut. I know that you have but little power, and yet you have kept my word and have not denied my name. ⁹I will make those of the synagogue of Satan who say that they are Jews and are not, but are lying—I will make them come and bow down before your feet, and they will learn that I have loved you. ¹⁰Because you have kept my word of patient endurance, I will keep you from the hour of trial that is coming on the whole world to test the inhabitants of the earth. ¹¹I am coming soon; hold fast to what you have, so that no one may seize your crown. ¹²If you conquer, I will make you a pillar in the temple of my God; you will never go out of it. I will write on you the name of my God, and the name of the city of my God, the new Jerusalem that comes down from my God out of heaven, and my own new name. ¹³Let anyone who has an ear listen to what the Spirit is saying to the churches.

j Or to shepherd

2.26
Heb 3.6;
Ps 2.8;
Rev 3.21
2.27
Rev 12.5;
Isa 30.14;
Jer 19.11
2.28
Rev 22.16

3.1
Rev 1.4, 16;
2.2;
1 Tim 5.6

3.3
1 Thess 5.2,
6; 2 Pet 3.10

3.4
Acts 1.15;
Jude 23;
Rev 6.11;
7.9, 13
3.5
Mt 10.32
3.6
Rev 2.7

3.7
Acts 3.14;
1 Jn 5.20;
Isa 22.22

3.8
Acts 14.27;
Rev 2.13
3.9
Rev 2.9;
Isa 49.23;
43.4
3.10
2 Pet 2.9;
Rev 16.14;
6.10; 17.8
3.11
Rev 22.7, 12,
20; 2.25, 10
3.12
Gal 2.9;
Rev 22.4;
21.2
3.13
v. 6

3.1 *Sardis* is associated with the name of Croesus, who brought wealth and prosperity to this ancient capital and royal seat. Rome made it an administrative center for Roman Asia. The worship of Cybele along with the emperor cult was prominent there. *the words of him who has the seven spirits of God.* This refers to Jesus Christ, the one anointed by the Holy Spirit at his baptism; on him the Holy Spirit abides in all his power and perfection (symbolized by the number seven).
3.2ff This church manifested no spiritual fruit: sinners were not being saved, the church members were

not being sanctified, and the needy were being neglected. There were a few, however, who lived a God-fearing life (v. 4).
3.7,8 *Philadelphia*, a significant center of influence, was built on the fault line of a major volcanic area. It has disappeared into history. There was an active synagogue in the city, whose members persecuted those who became Christians; further severe trials could be expected. Note that no word of reproof is spoken to the church of this city. *the key of David.* This key symbolizes Christ's rule and authority, which covers heaven and earth.

G. *The message to Laodicea*

3.14
Isa 65.16
3.15
v. 1
3.17
Hos 12.8;
Zech 11.5;
1 Cor 4.8
3.18
Isa 55.1;
Mt 13.44;
Rev 7.13
3.19
Prov 3.11;
Heb 12.5, 6;
Rev 2.5
3.20
Mt 24.33;
Lk 12.36;
Jn 14.23
3.21
Rev 2.7;
Mt 19.28;
Rev 5.5
3.22
Rev 2.7

14 "And to the angel of the church in Laodicea write: The words of the Amen, the faithful and true witness, the origin[k] of God's creation: 15 "I know your works; you are neither cold nor hot. I wish that you were either cold or hot. 16 So, because you are lukewarm, and neither cold nor hot, I am about to spit you out of my mouth. 17 For you say, 'I am rich, I have prospered, and I need nothing.' You do not realize that you are wretched, pitiable, poor, blind, and naked. 18 Therefore I counsel you to buy from me gold refined by fire so that you may be rich; and white robes to clothe you and to keep the shame of your nakedness from being seen; and salve to anoint your eyes so that you may see. 19 I reprove and discipline those whom I love. Be earnest, therefore, and repent. 20 Listen! I am standing at the door, knocking; if you hear my voice and open the door, I will come in to you and eat with you, and you with me. 21 To the one who conquers I will give a place with me on my throne, just as I myself conquered and sat down with my Father on his throne. 22 Let anyone who has an ear listen to what the Spirit is saying to the churches."

III. *The things that shall be (4.1–22.5)*

A. *The heavenly worship*

4.1
Rev 1.10;
11.12; 1.19
4.2
Rev 1.10;
Isa 6.1;
Ezek 1.26-28;
Dan 7.9
4.4
Rev 11.16;
3.4, 5
4.5
Rev 8.5;
16.18; 1.4;
Zech 4.2
4.6
Rev 15.2;
Ezek 1.5
4.7
Ezek 1.10;
10.14
4.8
Isa 6.2; 3;
Rev 1.8, 4
4.9
Ps 47.8;
Rev 10.6;
15.7
4.10
Rev 5.8, 14;
vv. 2, 9, 4

4 After this I looked, and there in heaven a door stood open! And the first voice, which I had heard speaking to me like a trumpet, said, "Come up here, and I will show you what must take place after this." 2 At once I was in the spirit,[l] and there in heaven stood a throne, with one seated on the throne! 3 And the one seated there looks like jasper and carnelian, and around the throne is a rainbow that looks like an emerald. 4 Around the throne are twenty-four thrones, and seated on the thrones are twenty-four elders, dressed in white robes, with golden crowns on their heads. 5 Coming from the throne are flashes of lightning, and rumblings and peals of thunder, and in front of the throne burn seven flaming torches, which are the seven spirits of God; 6 and in front of the throne there is something like a sea of glass, like crystal.

Around the throne, and on each side of the throne, are four living creatures, full of eyes in front and behind: 7 the first living creature like a lion, the second living creature like an ox, the third living creature with a face like a human face, and the fourth living creature like a flying eagle. 8 And the four living creatures, each of them with six wings, are full of eyes all around and inside. Day and night without ceasing they sing,

"Holy, holy, holy,
    the Lord God the Almighty,
    who was and is and is to come."

9 And whenever the living creatures give glory and honor and thanks to the one who is seated on the throne, who lives forever and ever, 10 the twenty-four elders fall before the one who is seated on the throne and

k Or *beginning*   *l* Or *in the Spirit*

3.14 *Laodicea* became an important military outpost and trading center during the period of the Roman supremacy. Its wealth came from its famous black sheep and a salve used to treat diseases of the eye. John's remedy to the Laodiceans for their spiritual poverty, blindness, and nakedness related directly to their earthly wealth, eye-salve, and clothing industry.
4.1 *Come up here* is understood by some in the dispensational tradition to mean the pretribulation rapture of the church. There are problems with this view, for these words were spoken to John, not the church. The word "church" is not used again until the end of Revelation.

4.2,3 The *one seated on the throne* is God Almighty. The jasper stone may symbolize God's holiness, the carnelian stone his divine wrath, and the rainbow his unfailing mercy.
4.6 *four living creatures.* Commentators differ on the meaning of the four creatures. They seem to be angelic beings, described with animal-like comparisons to denote their strength (a lion), their service (an ox), their intelligence (a human), and their speed (a flying eagle).
4.8 The praises of these creatures start with the holiness of God, go on to stress his omnipotence, and end with his eternity.

worship the one who lives forever and ever; they cast their crowns before the throne, singing,

11   "You are worthy, our Lord and God,
       to receive glory and honor and power,
   for you created all things,
       and by your will they existed and were created."

4.11
Rev 5.12;
Gen 1.1;
Eph 3.9;
Rev 10.6

B. Prelude to the seven seals:
the scroll opened and the Lamb adored

5 Then I saw in the right hand of the one seated on the throne a scroll written on the inside and on the back, sealed*m* with seven seals; 2 and I saw a mighty angel proclaiming with a loud voice, "Who is worthy to open the scroll and break its seals?" 3 And no one in heaven or on earth or under the earth was able to open the scroll or to look into it. 4 And I began to weep bitterly because no one was found worthy to open the scroll or to look into it. 5 Then one of the elders said to me, "Do not weep. See, the Lion of the tribe of Judah, the Root of David, has conquered, so that he can open the scroll and its seven seals."

6 Then I saw between the throne and the four living creatures and among the elders a Lamb standing as if it had been slaughtered, having seven horns and seven eyes, which are the seven spirits of God sent out into all the earth. 7 He went and took the scroll from the right hand of the one who was seated on the throne. 8 When he had taken the scroll, the four living creatures and the twenty-four elders fell before the Lamb, each holding a harp and golden bowls full of incense, which are the prayers of the saints. 9 They sing a new song:
"You are worthy to take the scroll
   and to open its seals,
for you were slaughtered and by your blood you ransomed
      for God
   saints from*n* every tribe and language and people and
      nation;
10 you have made them to be a kingdom and priests serving*o* our
      God,
   and they will reign on earth."

11 Then I looked, and I heard the voice of many angels surrounding the throne and the living creatures and the elders; they numbered myriads of myriads and thousands of thousands, 12 singing with full voice,
"Worthy is the Lamb that was slaughtered
   to receive power and wealth and wisdom and might
   and honor and glory and blessing!"

5.1
vv. 7, 13;
Ezek 2.9, 10;
Isa 29.11;
Dan 12.4
5.2
Rev 10.1

5.5
Gen 49.9;
Heb 7.14;
Isa 11.1, 10;
Rom 15.12;
Rev 22.16
5.6
Rev 4.6;
Isa 53.7;
Rev 13.8;
Zech 3.9;
4.10;
Rev 4.5
5.7
v. 1
5.8
Rev 14.2;
Ps 141.2
5.9
Ps 40.3;
Rev 4.11;
1 Cor 6.20;
Heb 9.12

5.10
Ex 19.6;
Isa 61.6

5.11
Dan 7.10;
Heb 12.22
5.12
Rev 4.11

m Or written on the inside, and sealed on the back   *n Gk ransomed for God from*   *o Gk priests to*

4.11 *You are worthy.* This phrase was traditionally used to salute the emperor in a triumphal procession; *O Lord* was added by Domitian, emperor at this time. Christians, however, owe their allegiance to the Lord God Almighty.
5.1ff The scroll is in the hands of Christ, who has all authority in heaven and on earth (cf. Mt 28.18). He rules throughout history to insure the continuance of the church and the establishment of God's kingdom everywhere. The scroll is written on both sides, with no room for any additions. It contains all the decrees of God and outlines all that will transpire until the end of this present age. John did not know what was written on the scroll, for the testimony was sealed until Jesus Christ began opening its seals.
5.5 This text contains two allusions to O.T. Scriptures prophesying the coming Messiah. One is Gen 49.9,10, which speaks of a lion's whelp and of the

sceptre not departing from Judah until Shiloh comes (cf. footnote NRSV). The other is Isa 11.1: "a shoot shall come out from the stump of Jesse."
5.6 See note on 3.1.
5.8 See note on Ex 30.1.
5.9,10 *They sing a new song.* It is new, for it goes beyond creation to redemption and exalts Jesus Christ, who is worthy because (1) he was slaughtered (i.e., he paid it all for sinners on the cross of Calvary); (2) he has ransomed sinners by his shed blood; (3) he has redeemed people from "every tribe and language and people and nation" (i.e., he is a universal Redeemer); (4) he has made the saved priests and kings unto their God; (5) they shall reign on earth with him.
5.11ff In this song of praise the participants are living creatures, elders, angels, and all creation. They worship God on his throne and the Lamb that was slain; both are God Almighty.

5.13 Phil 2.10; v. 3; 1 Tim 6.16; Rev 1.6; 6.16; 7.10

13 Then I heard every creature in heaven and on earth and under the earth
and in the sea, and all that is in them, singing,
"To the one seated on the throne and to the Lamb
be blessing and honor and glory and might
forever and ever!"

5.14 Rev 19.4; 4.9, 10

14 And the four living creatures said, "Amen!" And the elders fell down
and worshiped.

C. *The vision of the seven seals*

1. *The first seal: the white horse*

6.1 Rev 5.5-7, 1; 14.2; 19.6
6.2 Zech 6.3; Rev 19.11; Zech 6.11; Rev 14.14

6 Then I saw the Lamb open one of the seven seals, and I heard one
of the four living creatures call out, as with a voice of thunder,
"Come!"[p] 2 I looked, and there was a white horse! Its rider had a bow;
a crown was given to him, and he came out conquering and to conquer.

2. *The second seal: the red horse*

6.3 Rev 4.7
6.4 Zech 6.2

3 When he opened the second seal, I heard the second living creature
call out, "Come!"[p] 4 And out came[q] another horse, bright red; its rider
was permitted to take peace from the earth, so that people would slaughter
one another; and he was given a great sword.

3. *The third seal: the black horse*

6.5 Rev 4.7; Zech 6.2
6.6 Rev 4.6, 7; 9.4

5 When he opened the third seal, I heard the third living creature call
out, "Come!"[p] I looked, and there was a black horse! Its rider held a pair
of scales in his hand, 6 and I heard what seemed to be a voice in the midst
of the four living creatures saying, "A quart of wheat for a day's pay,[r]
and three quarts of barley for a day's pay,[r] but do not damage the olive
oil and the wine!"

4. *The fourth seal: the pale green horse*

6.7 Rev 4.7
6.8 Zech 6.3; Hos 13.14; Ezek 5.12

7 When he opened the fourth seal, I heard the voice of the fourth
living creature call out, "Come!"[p] 8 I looked and there was a pale green
horse! Its rider's name was Death, and Hades followed with him; they
were given authority over a fourth of the earth, to kill with sword, famine,
and pestilence, and by the wild animals of the earth.

5. *The fifth seal: the martyrs*

6.9 Rev 14.18; 16.7; 20.4; 1.9; 12.17
6.10 Zech 1.12; Ps 79.5; Rev 3.7; 19.2
6.11 Rev 3.5; 7.9; 14.13; Heb 11.40

9 When he opened the fifth seal, I saw under the altar the souls of
those who had been slaughtered for the word of God and for the testimony
they had given; 10 they cried out with a loud voice, "Sovereign Lord, holy
and true, how long will it be before you judge and avenge our blood on
the inhabitants of the earth?" 11 They were each given a white robe and
told to rest a little longer, until the number would be complete both of
their fellow servants[s] and of their brothers and sisters,[t] who were soon
to be killed as they themselves had been killed.

6. *The sixth seal: signs in the heavens*

6.12 Rev 16.18; Mt 24.29; Joel 2.31; Acts 2.20

12 When he opened the sixth seal, I looked, and there came a great

[p] Or *"Go!"* [q] Or *went* [r] Gk *a denarius* [s] Gk *slaves* [t] Gk *brothers*

6.2 The white horse represents peace, which comes and goes during the course of this present age. The peace disappears when the second horse, the red one, appears, taking peace from the earth (i.e., war follows peace).

6.5 The black horse symbolizes famine, followed by the pale horse, which represents death, for death always follows war (the red horse) and famine.

6.9 The four horses give way to a scene in heaven where the souls of the martyrs who have died for the true faith cry out for vengeance against their murderers.

6.12ff What the details of this passage mean is difficult to determine, though the general theme is clear.

earthquake; the sun became black as sackcloth, the full moon became like blood, 13 and the stars of the sky fell to the earth as the fig tree drops its winter fruit when shaken by a gale. 14 The sky vanished like a scroll rolling itself up, and every mountain and island was removed from its place. 15 Then the kings of the earth and the magnates and the generals and the rich and the powerful, and everyone, slave and free, hid in the caves and among the rocks of the mountains, 16 calling to the mountains and rocks, "Fall on us and hide us from the face of the one seated on the throne and from the wrath of the Lamb; 17 for the great day of their wrath has come, and who is able to stand?"

7. Interlude

a. The sealing of God's servants

7 After this I saw four angels standing at the four corners of the earth, holding back the four winds of the earth so that no wind could blow on earth or sea or against any tree. 2 I saw another angel ascending from the rising of the sun, having the seal of the living God, and he called with a loud voice to the four angels who had been given power to damage earth and sea, 3 saying, "Do not damage the earth or the sea or the trees, until we have marked the servants[u] of our God with a seal on their foreheads."

4 And I heard the number of those who were sealed, one hundred forty-four thousand, sealed out of every tribe of the people of Israel:

5 From the tribe of Judah twelve thousand sealed,
    from the tribe of Reuben twelve thousand,
    from the tribe of Gad twelve thousand,
6 from the tribe of Asher twelve thousand,
    from the tribe of Naphtali twelve thousand,
    from the tribe of Manasseh twelve thousand,
7 from the tribe of Simeon twelve thousand,
    from the tribe of Levi twelve thousand,
    from the tribe of Issachar twelve thousand,
8 from the tribe of Zebulun twelve thousand,
    from the tribe of Joseph twelve thousand,
    from the tribe of Benjamin twelve thousand sealed.

b. The white-robed saints from the great ordeal

9 After this I looked, and there was a great multitude that no one could count, from every nation, from all tribes and peoples and languages, standing before the throne and before the Lamb, robed in white, with palm branches in their hands. 10 They cried out in a loud voice, saying, "Salvation belongs to our God who is seated on the throne, and
    to the Lamb!"
11 And all the angels stood around the throne and around the elders and

u Gk *slaves*

6.13 Rev 8.10; 9.1; Isa 34.4
6.14 Isa 34.4; Jer 3.23; 4.24; Rev 16.10
6.15 Isa 2.10, 19
6.16 Hos 10.8; Lk 23.30; Rev 9.6
6.17 Zeph 1.14; Rev 16.14; Ps 76.7
7.1 Rev 9.4
7.3 Rev 6.6; Ezek 9.4; Rev 22.4
7.4ff Rev 9.16; 14.1
7.9 Rom 11.25; Rev 5.9; 3.5, 18; 4.4; 6.11
7.10 Ps 3.8; Rev 12.10; 19.1; 5.13
7.11 Rev 4.6

The impenitent, i.e., all classes of society, seek to escape their doom but cannot do so. The great day of the wrath of God has come, and they are terrified.
6.16 God and Christ are again linked together in cosmic power, coming in judgment against all classes of people.
7.1ff Six of the seven seals were opened in ch. 6. Before the seventh seal is opened there is an interlude, showing four angels covering the four corners of the earth and holding the four winds. The judgment that is about to fall is universal; no one can escape except the chosen believers who are made secure by God (v. 3). Their sealing comes before the judgment itself and guarantees their preservation when the seventh seal is opened.

7.4–8 *one hundred forty-four thousand* (see also 14.1, 3). The tribe of Dan is replaced by Manasseh, one of Joseph's sons. Ephraim, the brother of Manasseh, is also omitted, though the tribe of Joseph is present. The omission is curious since Ephraim was one of the most significant of the Jewish tribes. The number, 144,000, is probably not an exact number. Some think it represents the complete number of Jews, known to and elected by God, who will come to Christ during the great tribulation.
7.9ff The scene changes from earth to heaven, where God's people are assured that their sacrifices are not in vain. After the tribulation has passed, God will reward his faithful people. All the difficulties and martyrdoms of life are transitory and give way to victory and perfection.

the four living creatures, and they fell on their faces before the throne and worshiped God, 12 singing,

> "Amen! Blessing and glory and wisdom
> and thanksgiving and honor
> and power and might
> be to our God forever and ever! Amen."

13 Then one of the elders addressed me, saying, "Who are these, robed in white, and where have they come from?" 14 I said to him, "Sir, you are the one that knows." Then he said to me, "These are they who have come out of the great ordeal; they have washed their robes and made them white in the blood of the Lamb.

15 For this reason they are before the throne of God,
> and worship him day and night within his temple,
> and the one who is seated on the throne will shelter them.
16 They will hunger no more, and thirst no more;
> the sun will not strike them,
> nor any scorching heat;
17 for the Lamb at the center of the throne will be their shepherd,
> and he will guide them to springs of the water of life,
> and God will wipe away every tear from their eyes."

8. The seventh seal: making ready the seven trumpets

8 When the Lamb opened the seventh seal, there was silence in heaven for about half an hour. 2 And I saw the seven angels who stand before God, and seven trumpets were given to them.

3 Another angel with a golden censer came and stood at the altar; he was given a great quantity of incense to offer with the prayers of all the saints on the golden altar that is before the throne. 4 And the smoke of the incense, with the prayers of the saints, rose before God from the hand of the angel. 5 Then the angel took the censer and filled it with fire from the altar and threw it on the earth; and there were peals of thunder, rumblings, flashes of lightning, and an earthquake.

6 Now the seven angels who had the seven trumpets made ready to blow them.

D. The seven trumpets

1. The first trumpet: hail, fire, and blood

7 The first angel blew his trumpet, and there came hail and fire, mixed with blood, and they were hurled to the earth; and a third of the earth was burned up, and a third of the trees were burned up, and all green grass was burned up.

2. The second trumpet: the sea becomes blood

8 The second angel blew his trumpet, and something like a great

Cross references (left margin):

7.12 Rev 5.12-14
7.13 v. 9
7.14 Mt 24.21; Zech 3.3-5; Heb 9.14; 1 Jn 1.7
7.15 Isa 4.5, 6; Rev 21.3
7.16 Isa 49.10; Ps 121.5, 6; Rev 21.4
7.17 Ps 23.1; Jn 10.11, 14; Isa 25.8
8.1 Rev 6.1
8.2 1 Cor 15.52; 1 Thess 4.16
8.3 Rev 7.2; 5.8; Ex 30.1; Rev 6.9
8.4 Ps 141.2
8.5 Lev 16.12; Rev 4.5; 6.12
8.6 v. 2
8.7 Ezek 38.22; Rev 9.4
8.8 Jer 51.25; Rev 16.3

7.14 *The great ordeal* (often translated "the great tribulation") is that period of time just prior to the return of the Lord Jesus when great trials, afflictions, and even martyrdom will come to believers, either those who belonged to Christ before the tribulation began or those who are converted during the tribulation. Some divide this period into two segments. During the first half, the wrath of the wicked will be poured out on the earth; during the second half, the wrath of God will be poured out. For the three views of the relationship of the rapture of the church to the great tribulation, see note on 1 Thess 4.15.
8.1 The *silence* designates an interruption for a short time before the contents of the seventh seal are revealed. The end will not come until they have been

made known. The seven trumpets and the seven bowls constitute the contents of the seventh seal.
8.3,4 See note on Ex 30.1.
8.6 *The seven trumpets* constitute the divine judgments of Almighty God against sinners in the world before the return of Christ. These occur at the end of the age and are only partial, for only a third of the people of the earth are affected.
8.7ff The first four trumpets concern God's judgment on the natural elements: the earth, the sea, the rivers, and the heavenly bodies.
8.8,9 The events connected with the trumpets' judgments parallel some of God's judgments on the Egyptians just before Israel was delivered from its bondage to Pharaoh. The events connected with the

mountain, burning with fire, was thrown into the sea. 9 A third of the sea became blood, a third of the living creatures in the sea died, and a third of the ships were destroyed.

3. The third trumpet: the falling star

10 The third angel blew his trumpet, and a great star fell from heaven, blazing like a torch, and it fell on a third of the rivers and on the springs of water. 11 The name of the star is Wormwood. A third of the waters became wormwood, and many died from the water, because it was made bitter.

4. The fourth trumpet: the darkening of the sun, moon, and stars

12 The fourth angel blew his trumpet, and a third of the sun was struck, and a third of the moon, and a third of the stars, so that a third of their light was darkened; a third of the day was kept from shining, and likewise the night.

13 Then I looked, and I heard an eagle crying with a loud voice as it flew in midheaven, "Woe, woe, woe to the inhabitants of the earth, at the blasts of the other trumpets that the three angels are about to blow!"

5. The fifth trumpet: the opening of the bottomless pit

9 And the fifth angel blew his trumpet, and I saw a star that had fallen from heaven to earth, and he was given the key to the shaft of the bottomless pit; 2 he opened the shaft of the bottomless pit, and from the shaft rose smoke like the smoke of a great furnace, and the sun and the air were darkened with the smoke from the shaft. 3 Then from the smoke came locusts on the earth, and they were given authority like the authority of scorpions of the earth. 4 They were told not to damage the grass of the earth or any green growth or any tree, but only those people who do not have the seal of God on their foreheads. 5 They were allowed to torture them for five months, but not to kill them, and their torture was like the torture of a scorpion when it stings someone. 6 And in those days people will seek death but will not find it; they will long to die, but death will flee from them.

7 In appearance the locusts were like horses equipped for battle. On their heads were what looked like crowns of gold; their faces were like human faces, 8 their hair like women's hair, and their teeth like lions' teeth; 9 they had scales like iron breastplates, and the noise of their wings was like the noise of many chariots with horses rushing into battle. 10 They have tails like scorpions, with stingers, and in their tails is their power to harm people for five months. 11 They have as king over them the angel of the bottomless pit; his name in Hebrew is Abaddon,v and in Greek he is called Apollyon.w

12 The first woe has passed. There are still two woes to come.

v That is, Destruction   w That is, Destroyer

8.10 Isa 14.12; Rev 9.1; 16.4
8.11 Jer 9.15; 23.15
8.12 Rev 6.12, 13
8.13 Rev 14.6; 19.17; 9.12; 11.14
9.1 Rev 8.10; Lk 8.31; Rev 17.8; 20.1
9.2 Gen 19.28; Ex 19.18; Joel 2.2, 10
9.3 Ex 10.12-15; v. 10
9.4 Rev 6.6; 8.7; 7.2, 3
9.5 vv. 10, 3
9.6 Job 3.21; Jer 8.3; Rev 6.16
9.7 Joel 2.4; Nah 3.17; Dan 7.8
9.8 Joel 1.6
9.9 Joel 2.5
9.10 vv. 5, 19
9.11 Eph 2.2; v. 1
9.12 Rev 8.13

---

second trumpet recall the first plague of God against Egypt when the Nile became blood.
8.10,11 The events connected with the third trumpet are similar to the experience the Israelites had with the bitter waters of Marah (Ex 15.23). But here the sweet waters are made bitter, whereas at Marah the bitter water was made sweet.
8.12,13 The result of the fourth trumpet is like the ninth plague of God on Egypt, when darkness came. It is a partial judgment by way of warning, not a judgment of destruction. Worse judgments (the last three trumpets) are soon to come (v. 13).
9.1 The fifth trumpet resembles what happened in Egypt even more closely than the first four trumpets (see note on 8.8,9). Locusts come on the scene, though this invasion originates in the bottomless pit. They torture but do not kill people.
9.4 The locusts are commanded not to touch those who have the seal of God on their foreheads. Thus the people of God are supernaturally preserved from this plague.

6. The sixth trumpet: the four angels released

13   Then the sixth angel blew his trumpet, and I heard a voice from the four^x horns of the golden altar before God, 14 saying to the sixth angel who had the trumpet, "Release the four angels who are bound at the great river Euphrates." 15 So the four angels were released, who had been held ready for the hour, the day, the month, and the year, to kill a third of humankind. 16 The number of the troops of cavalry was two hundred million; I heard their number. 17 And this was how I saw the horses in my vision: the riders wore breastplates the color of fire and of sapphire^y and of sulfur; the heads of the horses were like lions' heads, and fire and smoke and sulfur came out of their mouths. 18 By these three plagues a third of humankind was killed, by the fire and smoke and sulfur coming out of their mouths. 19 For the power of the horses is in their mouths and in their tails; their tails are like serpents, having heads; and with them they inflict harm.

20   The rest of humankind, who were not killed by these plagues, did not repent of the works of their hands or give up worshiping demons and idols of gold and silver and bronze and stone and wood, which cannot see or hear or walk. 21 And they did not repent of their murders or their sorceries or their fornication or their thefts.

7. The second interlude

a. John eats the scroll

10   And I saw another mighty angel coming down from heaven, wrapped in a cloud, with a rainbow over his head; his face was like the sun, and his legs like pillars of fire. 2 He held a little scroll open in his hand. Setting his right foot on the sea and his left foot on the land, 3 he gave a great shout, like a lion roaring. And when he shouted, the seven thunders sounded. 4 And when the seven thunders had sounded, I was about to write, but I heard a voice from heaven saying, "Seal up what the seven thunders have said, and do not write it down." 5 Then the angel whom I saw standing on the sea and the land
        raised his right hand to heaven
6   and swore by him who lives forever and ever,
who created heaven and what is in it, the earth and what is in it, and the sea and what is in it: "There will be no more delay, 7 but in the days when the seventh angel is to blow his trumpet, the mystery of God will be fulfilled, as he announced to his servants^z the prophets."

8   Then the voice that I had heard from heaven spoke to me again, saying, "Go, take the scroll that is open in the hand of the angel who is standing on the sea and on the land." 9 So I went to the angel and told him to give me the little scroll; and he said to me, "Take it, and eat it; it will be bitter to your stomach, but sweet as honey in your mouth." 10 So

---

x Other ancient authorities lack *four*   y Gk *hyacinth*   z Gk *slaves*

9.13
Ex 30.1-3;
Rev 8.3
9.14
Rev 16.12
9.15
v. 18
9.16
Rev 5.11; 7.4
9.17
v. 18;
Rev 11.5

9.18
vv. 15, 17

9.20
Deut 31.29;
1 Cor 10.20;
Ps 115.4;
135.15;
Dan 5.23
9.21
Rev 2.21;
18.23; 17.2,
5

10.1
Rev 5.2;
Mt 17.2;
Rev 1.16, 15

10.3
Isa 31.4;
Rev 4.5
10.4
Dan 8.26;
12.4, 9;
Rev 22.10
10.5
Ex 6.8;
Dan 12.7
10.6
Rev 4.11;
14.7; 16.17
10.7
Rev 11.15;
Rom 16.25
10.8
v. 4

10.9
Jer 15.16;
Ezek 2.8
10.10
Ezek 3.3

9.13 The sixth trumpet sounds and four destroying angels are released to do the bidding of God. They bring the retributive justice of God and execute divine judgment against unbelievers. The ruin and devastation of the invading troops mark this scene in which a third of humankind are killed and the remainder are warned about their impending judgment. The terrifying account of the angelic judgment does not cause impenitent sinners to change their ways or abandon their ungodly living. They refuse to repent (v. 20,21). Note that what happens comes at a specific hour, day, month, and year (v. 15). God's timetable is at work and nothing can hinder it or stop it from happening.
10.1 Before the seventh seal was broken, there was an interlude (see note on 7.1ff). Now, before the

seventh trumpet sounds, there is another interlude. In it John eats a little open scroll, which tastes sweet in his mouth, but is bitter in his stomach (vv. 9,10). The fact that it must remain sealed (v. 4) seems to indicate that more has been revealed to him than he is permitted to disclose. It is followed by the story of the two witnesses.
10.4 *The seven thunders* are a mystery to us. Since they are sealed, it is useless for us to conjecture what they mean.
10.7 *the mystery of God.* This is something previously concealed from God's people but is now revealed and made plain. It denotes the purpose of God to consummate history, solve the problems of humankind and nations, and bless the world by the fulfillment of God's redemptive purpose.

I took the little scroll from the hand of the angel and ate it; it was sweet as honey in my mouth, but when I had eaten it, my stomach was made bitter.

11 Then they said to me, "You must prophesy again about many peoples and nations and languages and kings."

b. *The two witnesses*

11 Then I was given a measuring rod like a staff, and I was told, "Come and measure the temple of God and the altar and those who worship there, 2 but do not measure the court outside the temple; leave that out, for it is given over to the nations, and they will trample over the holy city for forty-two months. 3 And I will grant my two witnesses authority to prophesy for one thousand two hundred sixty days, wearing sackcloth."

4 These are the two olive trees and the two lampstands that stand before the Lord of the earth. 5 And if anyone wants to harm them, fire pours from their mouth and consumes their foes; anyone who wants to harm them must be killed in this manner. 6 They have authority to shut the sky, so that no rain may fall during the days of their prophesying, and they have authority over the waters to turn them into blood, and to strike the earth with every kind of plague, as often as they desire.

7 When they have finished their testimony, the beast that comes up from the bottomless pit will make war on them and conquer them and kill them, 8 and their dead bodies will lie in the street of the great city that is prophetically[a] called Sodom and Egypt, where also their Lord was crucified. 9 For three and a half days members of the peoples and tribes and languages and nations will gaze at their dead bodies and refuse to let them be placed in a tomb; 10 and the inhabitants of the earth will gloat over them and celebrate and exchange presents, because these two prophets had been a torment to the inhabitants of the earth.

11 But after the three and a half days, the breath[b] of life from God entered them, and they stood on their feet, and those who saw them were terrified. 12 Then they[c] heard a loud voice from heaven saying to them, "Come up here!" And they went up to heaven in a cloud while their enemies watched them. 13 At that moment there was a great earthquake, and a tenth of the city fell; seven thousand people were killed in the earthquake, and the rest were terrified and gave glory to the God of heaven.

14 The second woe has passed. The third woe is coming very soon.

8. *The seventh trumpet: the consummation*

15 Then the seventh angel blew his trumpet, and there were loud voices in heaven, saying,

a Or *allegorically*; Gk *spiritually*   *b* Or *the spirit*   *c* Other ancient authorities read *I*

Cross-references (margin)

10.11
Rev 11.1;
Ezek 37.4, 9

11.1
Ezek 40.3;
Rev 21.15
11.2
Ezek 40.17;
Lk 21.24;
Rev 13.5
11.3
Rev 19.10;
12.6
11.4
Ps 52.8;
Jer 11.16;
Zech 4.3;
Mt 11.14
11.5
2 Kings 1.10;
Jer 5.14;
Num 16.29
11.6
1 Kings 17.1;
Ex 7.17, 19
11.7
Rev 13.1;
9.1, 2;
Dan 7.21
11.8
Rev 14.8;
Isa 1.9;
Heb 13.12
11.10
Rev 3.10;
Esth 9.19, 22

11.11
Ezek 37.5, 9,
10, 14
11.12
Rev 4.1;
2 Kings 2.11;
Acts 1.9
11.13
Rev 6.12;
14.7; 16.11

11.14
Rev 9.12

11.15
Rev 10.7;
16.17; 19.1;
12.10;
Dan 2.44;
7.14, 27

Study notes

11.1ff This chapter informs us that God's people will be empowered for witness and will bear a faithful testimony. Many of them will even seal their testimony with their blood. Though they will not be delivered from such persecution, they will be delivered from the evil one by their martyrdom, resulting in glorious resurrection to endless life.
11.3 The two witnesses, who are to prophesy for 1,260 days or three and a half years, are identified with Elijah and Moses. Elijah kept the rain from falling for this length of time, and Moses called down the plagues on Egypt. These two men are named together in Mal 4.4,5 and appeared at Christ's transfiguration (Mk 9.4). God will sustain them in their work, and if any oppose them, they have power to devour their enemies by a fire that comes out of their mouths. They can keep rain from falling, turn waters into blood, and let plagues loose among the peoples. Their ministry is so terrifying that one wonders how and why anyone would not hear their message, repent, and turn to God for forgiveness.
11.7 When the two witnesses have finished their work, and only then, can they be martyred by the beast that ascends out of the bottomless pit. What will be true for them is true for God's people today. No one can take their lives from them unless and until they have finished the work God has entrusted to them.
11.12 *Come up here!* Those who hold to a midtribulation rapture of the church (see note on 1 Thess 4.15) think that event occurs at this time.
11.15ff While John has much more to say in this

"The kingdom of the world has become the kingdom of
    our Lord
      and of his Messiah,[d]
    and he will reign forever and ever."

16 Then the twenty-four elders who sit on their thrones before God
fell on their faces and worshiped God, 17 singing,

"We give you thanks, Lord God Almighty,
    who are and who were,
    for you have taken your great power
      and begun to reign.

18 The nations raged,
    but your wrath has come,
    and the time for judging the dead,
    for rewarding your servants,[e] the prophets
      and saints and all who fear your name,
      both small and great,
    and for destroying those who destroy the earth."

19 Then God's temple in heaven was opened, and the ark of his
covenant was seen within his temple; and there were flashes of lightning,
rumblings, peals of thunder, an earthquake, and heavy hail.

E. *Several mystic figures*

1. *The woman with child, the dragon, and the male child*

12 A great portent appeared in heaven: a woman clothed with the
sun, with the moon under her feet, and on her head a crown of
twelve stars. 2 She was pregnant and was crying out in birth pangs, in the
agony of giving birth. 3 Then another portent appeared in heaven: a great
red dragon, with seven heads and ten horns, and seven diadems on his
heads. 4 His tail swept down a third of the stars of heaven and threw them
to the earth. Then the dragon stood before the woman who was about to
bear a child, so that he might devour her child as soon as it was born. 5 And
she gave birth to a son, a male child, who is to rule[f] all the nations with
a rod of iron. But her child was snatched away and taken to God and to
his throne; 6 and the woman fled into the wilderness, where she has a place
prepared by God, so that there she can be nourished for one thousand two
hundred sixty days.

2. *The angel Michael*

7 And war broke out in heaven; Michael and his angels fought against
the dragon. The dragon and his angels fought back, 8 but they were

d Gk *Christ*   *e* Gk *slaves*   *f* Or *to shepherd*

11.16
Rev 4.4; 5.8
11.17
Rev 1.8; 19.6

11.18
Ps 2.1;
Dan 7.9, 10;
Rev 10.7;
19.5

11.19
Rev 15.5, 8;
8.5; 16.21

12.2
Isa 66.7;
Gal 4.19
12.3
Rev 13.1;
Dan 7.7;
Rev 19.12
12.4
Rev 8.7, 12;
Dan 8.10
12.5
Ps 2.9;
Rev 2.27;
2 Cor 12.2
12.6
Rev 11.3

12.7
Dan 10.13;
Rev 20.2

---

book, the seventh trumpet marks the climax or final
goal of God's purpose. His kingdom has come on
earth as it is in heaven. What the people of God had
longed and prayed for now comes to pass. When the
seventh seal is opened, there is a period of silence in
heaven; when the seventh trumpet sounds, great
voices from heaven are heard, chanting the praise of
God. All creation is brought back under the rule and
reign of its rightful Lord and King. This reign of God
and of his Christ will be forever and forever.
11.17 *who are and who were.* Those who sing here do
not need to add, "who are to come" (cf. 1.4) for he
has now come and is there. Those who sing here look
upon the start of the universal and eternal reign of the
King.
11.19 The heavenly temple is opened and the ark of
the covenant is now visible because God has finished
his work. This symbolizes that we now have perfect
access to God. We perceive his glory as we never

perceived it before, and we understand the meaning
of grace beyond anything we ever dreamed possible.
12.1 The woman clothed with the sun and with the
moon under her feet represents all God's people. She
is watched carefully by the dragon, i.e., Satan, the
arch-enemy of God and Christ. The male child represents the Lord Jesus Christ, who is to rule over the
cosmos. When the child is caught up to God and his
throne, the woman flees into the wilderness, where
God protects her. God always protects and keeps his
people against the onslaughts of Satan.
12.7ff There is a great war in heaven between Satan
with the fallen angels and Michael with the good
angels. Satan is dethroned; he and his angels are cast
down to earth to persecute the people of God. But
here again he is ineffective because God protects
his people as a whole, even though individual believers can become the victims of Satan's hatred and
power.

defeated, and there was no longer any place for them in heaven. 9 The great dragon was thrown down, that ancient serpent, who is called the Devil and Satan, the deceiver of the whole world — he was thrown down to the earth, and his angels were thrown down with him.

10 Then I heard a loud voice in heaven, proclaiming,

"Now have come the salvation and the power
    and the kingdom of our God
    and the authority of his Messiah,*g*
for the accuser of our comrades*h* has been thrown down,
    who accuses them day and night before our God.

11 But they have conquered him by the blood of the Lamb
    and by the word of their testimony,
for they did not cling to life even in the face of death.

12 Rejoice then, you heavens
    and those who dwell in them!
But woe to the earth and the sea,
    for the devil has come down to you
with great wrath,
    because he knows that his time is short!"

13 So when the dragon saw that he had been thrown down to the earth, he pursued*i* the woman who had given birth to the male child. 14 But the woman was given the two wings of the great eagle, so that she could fly from the serpent into the wilderness, to her place where she is nourished for a time, and times, and half a time. 15 Then from his mouth the serpent poured water like a river after the woman, to sweep her away with the flood. 16 But the earth came to the help of the woman; it opened its mouth and swallowed the river that the dragon had poured from his mouth. 17 Then the dragon was angry with the woman, and went off to make war on the rest of her children, those who keep the commandments of God and hold the testimony of Jesus.

3. The beast from the sea

18 Then the dragon*j* took his stand on the sand of the seashore.

13

1 And I saw a beast rising out of the sea, having ten horns and seven heads; and on its horns were ten diadems, and on its heads were blasphemous names. 2 And the beast that I saw was like a leopard, its feet were like a bear's, and its mouth was like a lion's mouth. And the dragon gave it his power and his throne and great authority. 3 One of its heads seemed to have received a death-blow, but its mortal wound*k* had been healed. In amazement the whole earth followed the beast. 4 They worshiped the dragon, for he had given his authority to the beast, and they worshiped the beast, saying, "Who is like the beast, and who can fight against it?"

5 The beast was given a mouth uttering haughty and blasphemous words, and it was allowed to exercise authority for forty-two months. 6 It

g Gk *Christ*   *h* Gk *brothers*   *i* Or *persecuted*   *j* Gk *Then he*; other ancient authorities read *Then I stood*
k Gk *the plague of its death*

12.9 Gen 3.1, 4; Rev 20.2, 3, 8, 10; Jn 12.31

12.10 Rev 11.15; Job 1.9-11; Zech 3.1

12.11 Rom 16.20; Lk 14.26

12.12 Ps 96.11; Isa 49.13; Rev 18.20; 8.13; 10.6

12.13 vv. 3, 5

12.14 Ex 19.4; Dan 7.25; 12.7

12.15 Isa 59.19

12.17 Gen 3.15; Rev 11.7; 14.12; 1.2, 9

13.1 Dan 7.1-6; Rev 17.3

13.2 Rev 16.10

13.3 Rev 17.8

13.4 Rev 18.18

13.5 Dan 7.8, 11, 25; Rev 11.2

13.6 Rev 12.12

12.9 The precise time when this happened or will happen is not clear. One thing is sure: in the struggle between God and Satan this malign spirit will be defeated because of Christ's victory at Calvary (Jn 12.31) and his resurrection on Easter Sunday.
12.13ff Satan can no longer oppose Jesus Christ, for his power has been diminished. But Satan seeks to persecute the church (represented by the woman), who is given a refuge in the wilderness. The phrase "for a time, and times, and half a time" (v. 14) is a period of three and a half years prior to the time of Jesus' second coming.
13.1 The dragon of ch. 12 and the two beasts of ch.

13 constitute a trinity of evil. Under their awful assaults the saints of God experience persecution probably worse than anything suffered by God's people before. That trinity of evil is offset by the Trinity of God — the Father, the Son, and the Holy Spirit — who are victorious over the trinity of evil.
13.2 The beast from the sea represents the power of paganism, which is worldwide and has extensive control over the nations. This beast has the savageness and agility of a leopard, the overwhelming power of a bear, and the petrifying snarl of a lion. The dragon has given power to this beast so that people worship it. This beast exercises political power over the world.

opened its mouth to utter blasphemies against God, blaspheming his name
and his dwelling, that is, those who dwell in heaven. 7 Also it was allowed
to make war on the saints and to conquer them.[l] It was given authority
over every tribe and people and language and nation, 8 and all the inhabitants of the earth will worship it, everyone whose name has not been
written from the foundation of the world in the book of life of the Lamb
that was slaughtered.[m]

9 Let anyone who has an ear listen:

10 If you are to be taken captive,
       into captivity you go;
   if you kill with the sword,
       with the sword you must be killed.

Here is a call for the endurance and faith of the saints.

4. The beast from the earth

11 Then I saw another beast that rose out of the earth; it had two horns
like a lamb and it spoke like a dragon. 12 It exercises all the authority of
the first beast on its behalf, and it makes the earth and its inhabitants
worship the first beast, whose mortal wound[n] had been healed. 13 It
performs great signs, even making fire come down from heaven to earth
in the sight of all; 14 and by the signs that it is allowed to perform on behalf
of the beast, it deceives the inhabitants of earth, telling them to make an
image for the beast that had been wounded by the sword[o] and yet lived;
15 and it was allowed to give breath[p] to the image of the beast so that the
image of the beast could even speak and cause those who would not
worship the image of the beast to be killed. 16 Also it causes all, both small
and great, both rich and poor, both free and slave, to be marked on the
right hand or the forehead, 17 so that no one can buy or sell who does not
have the mark, that is, the name of the beast or the number of its name.
18 This calls for wisdom: let anyone with understanding calculate the
number of the beast, for it is the number of a person. Its number is six
hundred sixty-six.[q]

5. The Lamb on Mount Zion

14 Then I looked, and there was the Lamb, standing on Mount Zion!
And with him were one hundred forty-four thousand who had his
name and his Father's name written on their foreheads. 2 And I heard a
voice from heaven like the sound of many waters and like the sound of
loud thunder; the voice I heard was like the sound of harpists playing on
their harps; 3 and they sing a new song before the throne and before the
four living creatures and before the elders. No one could learn that song
except the one hundred forty-four thousand who have been redeemed
from the earth. 4 It is these who have not defiled themselves with women,
for they are virgins; these follow the Lamb wherever he goes. They have

13.7
Dan 7.21;
Rev 11.7; 5.9
13.8
Phil 4.3;
Rev 3.5;
17.8; 5.6

13.9
Mk 4.23;
Rev 2.7
13.10
Isa 33.1;
Mt 26.52;
Rev 14.12

13.11
Rev 11.7
13.12
vv. 4, 14;
Rev 14.9, 11;
v. 3
13.13
Mt 24.24;
Rev 16.14;
1 Kings 18.38;
Rev 20.9
13.14
Rev 12.9;
2 Thess 2.9,
10
13.15
Dan 3.5;
Rev 16.2
13.16
Rev 11.18;
19.5, 18;
14.9
13.17
Rev 14.9, 11.
15.2
13.18
Rev 17.9;
15.2; 21.17

14.1
Rev 5.6;
Ps 2.6;
Rev 3.12; 7.3
14.2
Rev 1.15; 5.8

14.3
Rev 5.9; v. 1

14.4
2 Cor 11.2;
Rev 3.4; 5.9;
Jas 1.18

[l] Other ancient authorities lack this sentence   [m] Or written in the book of life of the Lamb that was
slaughtered from the foundation of the world   [n] Gk whose plague of its death   [o] Or that had received the
plague of the sword   [p] Or spirit   [q] Other ancient authorities read six hundred sixteen

13.11 The beast from the earth, with two horns like
a lamb and speech like a dragon, is the false prophet
who encourages humankind to worship the first
beast. He performs what appear to be miraculous acts
and is a religious rather than a civil power. The mark
of his name is 666. He represents the antichrist, a false
Christ who is at enmity with the true Christ while
pretending to be good.
14.1 The number 144,000 is enigmatic (see note on
7.4–8). Commentators differ as to its meaning. Some
think it is a figure of speech denoting the entire

church. Others think they are martyrs who have
sealed their testimony with their blood. The statement that they "have not defiled themselves with
women" is also a matter of uncertain interpretation.
The event seems to be placed in heaven, for the Lamb
is present, as are some of the people of God. Since it
follows hard on the emergence of the two beasts from
the sea and earth, it may well depict the suffering of
a persecuted church whose members have on their
foreheads the mark of God rather than the number
666.

been redeemed from humankind as first fruits for God and the Lamb, 5 and in their mouth no lie was found; they are blameless.

6. Interlude: the angelic messages

6　Then I saw another angel flying in midheaven, with an eternal gospel to proclaim to those who live[r] on the earth — to every nation and tribe and language and people. 7 He said in a loud voice, "Fear God and give him glory, for the hour of his judgment has come; and worship him who made heaven and earth, the sea and the springs of water."

8　Then another angel, a second, followed, saying, "Fallen, fallen is Babylon the great! She has made all nations drink of the wine of the wrath of her fornication."

9　Then another angel, a third, followed them, crying with a loud voice, "Those who worship the beast and its image, and receive a mark on their foreheads or on their hands, 10 they will also drink the wine of God's wrath, poured unmixed into the cup of his anger, and they will be tormented with fire and sulfur in the presence of the holy angels and in the presence of the Lamb. 11 And the smoke of their torment goes up forever and ever. There is no rest day or night for those who worship the beast and its image and for anyone who receives the mark of its name."

12　Here is a call for the endurance of the saints, those who keep the commandments of God and hold fast to the faith of[s] Jesus.

13　And I heard a voice from heaven saying, "Write this: Blessed are the dead who from now on die in the Lord." "Yes," says the Spirit, "they will rest from their labors, for their deeds follow them."

14　Then I looked, and there was a white cloud, and seated on the cloud was one like the Son of Man, with a golden crown on his head, and a sharp sickle in his hand! 15 Another angel came out of the temple, calling with a loud voice to the one who sat on the cloud, "Use your sickle and reap, for the hour to reap has come, because the harvest of the earth is fully ripe." 16 So the one who sat on the cloud swung his sickle over the earth, and the earth was reaped.

17　Then another angel came out of the temple in heaven, and he too had a sharp sickle. 18 Then another angel came out from the altar, the angel who has authority over fire, and he called with a loud voice to him who had the sharp sickle, "Use your sharp sickle and gather the clusters of the vine of the earth, for its grapes are ripe." 19 So the angel swung his sickle over the earth and gathered the vintage of the earth, and he threw it into the great wine press of the wrath of God. 20 And the wine press was

r Gk sit　　s Or to their faith in

14.5
Ps 32.2;
Zeph 3.13;
Eph 5.27

14.6
Rev 8.13;
3.10; 5.9
14.7
Rev 15.4;
11.13; 4.11;
8.10

14.8
Isa 21.9;
Jer 51.8;
Rev 18.2;
17.5; 18.10
14.9
Rev 13.14-16

14.10
Isa 51.17;
Jer 25.15;
Rev 18.6;
20.10; 19.20
14.11
Isa 34.10;
Rev 19.3;
4.8; 13.17

14.12
Rev 13.10;
12.17
14.13
Rev 20.6;
1 Cor 15.18;
1 Thess 4.16

14.14
Dan 7.13;
Rev 1.13; 6.2
14.15
Joel 3.13;
Jer 51.33;
Rev 13.12

14.18
Rev 16.8;
Joel 3.13

14.19
Rev 19.15

14.20
Isa 63.3;
Heb 13.12;
Rev 11.8

14.6ff In the interlude between vv. 1–5 and vv. 14–20 three angels appear, each with a message. The first one, with the everlasting gospel, speaks of God's mercy and justice, announcing that divine judgment is about to fall. The second one (v. 8) looks toward the doom of Babylon (see next note). The third angel speaks of the wrath of God directed against those who worship the beast and have his mark on the forehead or the hand. The saints are called upon to endure; those who persevere unto death are called blessed (see v. 13).
14.8 Babylon (see 16.17–21 and 17.1–8). To identify Babylon here with any known city or nation with certainty is impossible. Widespread disagreement exists about this. Some identify Babylon with Jerusalem. Others think it to be an ecclesiastical system. The Reformers thought it was the Roman papacy. Later expositors thought it to be apostate Christendom at the end of this age. The most favored identification of Babylon is with Rome, the capital city where

the emperor of Rome resided when Revelation was written. In 17.4,5, Babylon the Great is pictured as a woman arrayed in purple and scarlet. Of her it is said, "The woman you saw is the great city that rules over the kings of the earth" (17.18). Revelation describes the final fall of Babylon. In 16.17–21 John sees it about to be destroyed, and in ch. 18 Babylon has fallen. Whatever the final identification of this city, Babylon kills faithful Christians and seduces people under its dominion, sharing its wealth with the merchants of the earth, who in the end suffer with it.
14.14ff This segment is climactic. The church of God is to be delivered and the enemies of God destroyed. The wheat and the tares have grown together; now is the time of harvest and vintage. The avenging angel uses his sickle to cut and gather the vintage to be thrown into the wine press (symbolizing God's wrath). At last, the victory of God over his enemies will be fulfilled.

trodden outside the city, and blood flowed from the wine press, as high as a horse's bridle, for a distance of about two hundred miles.[t]

F. The seven bowls of God's wrath

1. Preliminary vision in heaven

15 Then I saw another portent in heaven, great and amazing: seven angels with seven plagues, which are the last, for with them the wrath of God is ended.

2 And I saw what appeared to be a sea of glass mixed with fire, and those who had conquered the beast and its image and the number of its name, standing beside the sea of glass with harps of God in their hands. 3 And they sing the song of Moses, the servant[u] of God, and the song of the Lamb:

"Great and amazing are your deeds,
Lord God the Almighty!
Just and true are your ways,
King of the nations![v]
4 Lord, who will not fear
and glorify your name?
For you alone are holy.
All nations will come
and worship before you,
for your judgments have been revealed."

5 After this I looked, and the temple of the tent[w] of witness in heaven was opened, 6 and out of the temple came the seven angels with the seven plagues, robed in pure bright linen,[x] with golden sashes across their chests. 7 Then one of the four living creatures gave the seven angels seven golden bowls full of the wrath of God, who lives forever and ever; 8 and the temple was filled with smoke from the glory of God and from his power, and no one could enter the temple until the seven plagues of the seven angels were ended.

16 Then I heard a loud voice from the temple telling the seven angels, "Go and pour out on the earth the seven bowls of the wrath of God."

2. The first bowl: sores on humans

2 So the first angel went and poured his bowl on the earth, and a foul and painful sore came on those who had the mark of the beast and who worshiped its image.

15.1
Rev 12.1, 3;
16.1;
Lev 26.21;
Rev 14.10
15.2
Rev 4.6;
13.14, 15;
5.8
15.3
Deut 32.3, 4;
Ps 111.2;
145.17;
Hos 14.9
15.4
Jer 10.7;
Isa 66.23
15.5
Rev 11.19;
Num 1.50
15.6
Rev 14.15;
v. 1;
Rev 1.13
15.7
Rev 4.6, 9;
10.6
15.8
Ex 40.34;
1 Kings 8.10;
Isa 6.4
16.1
Rev 15.1
16.2
Rev 8.7;
Ex 9.9-11;
Rev 13.15-17

[t] Gk one thousand six hundred stadia   [u] Gk slave   [v] Other ancient authorities read the ages   [w] Or tabernacle   [x] Other ancient authorities read stone

---

15.1 Chs. 15 and 16 constitute a surprise in Revelation. Instead of going on immediately to speak of the victory of the Lamb, John recapitulates and enlarges on what he has already described. The seven bowls of wrath are the elements contained in the seventh seal. Seven angels with seven plagues will come upon unbelievers. They are dispatched by a voice from the temple telling them to go about their work.
15.3 *they sing.* These are the company of the redeemed, standing by the sea of glass with the harps of God in their hands. They sing the song of Moses and of the Lamb. The former refers back to the song sung by Moses and the Israelites after their redemption from Egypt (Ex 15). The song of the Lamb undoubtedly refers to the completed redemption of God's people.

15.5ff The seven angels with the seven plagues emerge from the temple of God in heaven with seven golden bowls full of the wrath of God. *The tent of witness* refers to the law of God housed in the Most Holy Place. When they leave the temple, the smoke from the glory of God and from his power fills the temple so that no one can enter until the work of the seven angels is completed.
16.2ff The first six bowls are poured out in rapid succession. Some hold that the church has been removed and only tribulation saints (i.e., those who have come to salvation after the rapture) and unbelievers are here. Others hold that the church will go through the great tribulation but will be supernaturally preserved from the wrath of God (see note on 1 Thess 4.15).

3. The second bowl: the sea becomes like blood

3 The second angel poured his bowl into the sea, and it became like
the blood of a corpse, and every living thing in the sea died.

4. The third bowl: rivers and springs become blood

4 The third angel poured his bowl into the rivers and the springs of
water, and they became blood. 5 And I heard the angel of the waters say,
  "You are just, O Holy One, who are and were,
      for you have judged these things;
6 because they shed the blood of saints and prophets,
      you have given them blood to drink.
  It is what they deserve!"
7 And I heard the altar respond,
  "Yes, O Lord God, the Almighty,
      your judgments are true and just!"

5. The fourth bowl: fierce heat of the sun

8 The fourth angel poured his bowl on the sun, and it was allowed to
scorch people with fire; 9 they were scorched by the fierce heat, but
they cursed the name of God, who had authority over these plagues, and
they did not repent and give him glory.

6. The fifth bowl: darkness

10 The fifth angel poured his bowl on the throne of the beast, and its
kingdom was plunged into darkness; people gnawed their tongues in
agony, 11 and cursed the God of heaven because of their pains and sores,
and they did not repent of their deeds.

7. The sixth bowl: the foul spirits prepare for Harmagedon

12 The sixth angel poured his bowl on the great river Euphrates, and
its water was dried up in order to prepare the way for the kings from the
east. 13 And I saw three foul spirits like frogs coming from the mouth of
the dragon, from the mouth of the beast, and from the mouth of the false
prophet. 14 These are demonic spirits, performing signs, who go abroad
to the kings of the whole world, to assemble them for battle on the great
day of God the Almighty. 15 ("See, I am coming like a thief! Blessed is
the one who stays awake and is clothed,ʸ not going about naked and
exposed to shame.") 16 And they assembled them at the place that in
Hebrew is called Harmagedon.

8. The seventh bowl: lightning, thunder, and an earthquake

17 The seventh angel poured his bowl into the air, and a loud voice

y Gk and keeps his robes

16.3	Rev 8.8, 9; Ex 17.17-21
16.4	Rev 8.10; Ex 7.17-21
16.5	Rev 15.3; 11.17; 15.4
16.6	Rev 17.6; 18.24; Isa 49.26
16.7	Rev 6.9; 14.18; 15.3; 19.2
16.8	Rev 8.12; 14.18
16.9	Rev 2.21; 11.13
16.10	Rev 13.2; 9.2; 11.10
16.11	vv. 9, 21; Rev 11.13; 2.21
16.12	Rev 9.14; Isa 41.2
16.13	Rev 12.3; 13.1; 19.20
16.14	1 Tim 4.1; Rev 13.13; 3.10; 17.14
16.15	1 Thess 5.2; 2 Cor 5.3
16.16	Rev 19.19; 9.11; 2 Kings 23.29, 30
16.17	Eph 2.2; Rev 11.15; 14.15; 21.6

16.5ff In the narrative of the trumpets (8.6 — 11.15) there are no voices explaining the happenings. Here, when the third bowl is poured out, two voices are heard: one is that of the angel of the waters and the other that of the prophets and martyrs whose intercessions have come to the altar of God (v. 7). Both rejoice in this just judgment and proclaim the righteousness of the Lord God.

16.13ff As with the seals and the trumpets, there is an interruption between the sixth and seventh bowl. It specifies that the nations of the earth are to be gathered together for the last and great battle of the age, the battle of Harmagedon. Then comes the seventh bowl.

16.16 Harmagedon is the place where the last great

battle of the age will be fought between good and evil (see note on 2 Chr 35.22 for location of Harmagedon), and it is also the name of the battle itself. Evil will be defeated and destroyed. God will triumph. Premillennialists believe that this triumph of Christ will bring about his thousand-year reign on earth and the binding of Satan. Amillennialists hold that this battle will be the beginning of the end of history and will be followed immediately by the final judgment and the start of the new age.

16.17ff The seventh bowl is poured into the air. Cosmic judgments follow, in which the great city is split into three parts, islands disappear, hail falls, lightning flashes, and the earth quakes.

16.18
Rev 4.5;
6.12;
Dan 12.1
16.19
Rev 17.18;
14.8; 18.5;
14.10
16.20
Rev 6.14
16.21
Rev 11.19;
Ex 9.23

came out of the temple, from the throne, saying, "It is done!" 18 And there came flashes of lightning, rumblings, peals of thunder, and a violent earthquake, such as had not occurred since people were upon the earth, so violent was that earthquake. 19 The great city was split into three parts, and the cities of the nations fell. God remembered great Babylon and gave her the wine-cup of the fury of his wrath. 20 And every island fled away, and no mountains were to be found; 21 and huge hailstones, each weighing about a hundred pounds,z dropped from heaven on people, until they cursed God for the plague of the hail, so fearful was that plague.

G. The judgment of Babylon

1. The great whore

17.1
Rev 21.9;
16.19; 19.2;
Jer 51.13
17.2
Rev 18.3;
14.8
17.3
Rev 12.3, 6,
14
17.4
Jer 51.7;
Rev 18.16;
18.6
17.5
2 Thess 2.7;
Rev 14.8;
16.19; 18.9
17.6
Rev 18.24;
13.15; 12.11

17 Then one of the seven angels who had the seven bowls came and said to me, "Come, I will show you the judgment of the great whore who is seated on many waters, 2 with whom the kings of the earth have committed fornication, and with the wine of whose fornication the inhabitants of the earth have become drunk." 3 So he carried me away in the spirita into a wilderness, and I saw a woman sitting on a scarlet beast that was full of blasphemous names, and it had seven heads and ten horns. 4 The woman was clothed in purple and scarlet, and adorned with gold and jewels and pearls, holding in her hand a golden cup full of abominations and the impurities of her fornication; 5 and on her forehead was written a name, a mystery: "Babylon the great, mother of whores and of earth's abominations." 6 And I saw that the woman was drunk with the blood of the saints and the blood of the witnesses to Jesus.

2. The mystery of the whore and the beast explained

17.7
vv. 5, 3, 9
17.8
Rev 11.7;
13.10; 3.10;
13.3, 8

When I saw her, I was greatly amazed. 7 But the angel said to me, "Why are you so amazed? I will tell you the mystery of the woman, and of the beast with seven heads and ten horns that carries her. 8 The beast that you saw was, and is not, and is about to ascend from the bottomless pit and go to destruction. And the inhabitants of the earth, whose names have not been written in the book of life from the foundation of the world, will be amazed when they see the beast, because it was and is not and is to come.

17.9
Rev 13.18
17.11
v. 8
17.12
Dan 7.20;
Rev 13.1;
18.10, 17, 19
17.13
v. 17
17.14
Rev 16.14;
1 Tim 6.15;
Rev 19.16;
Mt 22.14

9 "This calls for a mind that has wisdom: the seven heads are seven mountains on which the woman is seated; also, they are seven kings, 10 of whom five have fallen, one is living, and the other has not yet come; and when he comes, he must remain only a little while. 11 As for the beast that was and is not, it is an eighth but it belongs to the seven, and it goes to destruction. 12 And the ten horns that you saw are ten kings who have not yet received a kingdom, but they are to receive authority as kings for one hour, together with the beast. 13 These are united in yielding their power and authority to the beast; 14 they will make war on the Lamb, and the

z Gk weighing about a talent   a Or in the Spirit

16.21 Instead of repenting, wicked people blaspheme the name of God. Great calamities will not bring such people to repentance unless the grace of God works repentance in their hearts. Those who are so hardened that they will not repent will experience utter destruction.

17.1 In chs. 17 and 18 John paints a picture that graphically describes Babylon (the great whore) and the beast. He describes the relationship between these two (see next note) and announces the impending destruction of both. The great whore is Babylon, drunk with the blood of the saints and martyrs. Many think she represents imperial Rome, a city marked by idolatry, cruelty, and godlessness, and a persecutor of the true faith (see also note on Isa 13.20).

17.7ff The great whore and the beast with seven heads and ten horns collaborate to rule the world. Babylon at first appears to control the beast, but then, after having served the purpose of the beast, Babylon is destroyed by it. She is made naked and desolate, and her flesh is eaten and the city burned. The religious system is overthrown by the beast, who may well be the lawless one referred to in 2 Thess 2.3,4. If so, he will destroy all true religion and require all people to worship him.

17.11,12 The number seven represents completeness and ten is the number of the world. It appears that seven here symbolizes the apostate religious hierarchy in league with the political power symbolized by the ten horns.

Lamb will conquer them, for he is Lord of lords and King of kings, and those with him are called and chosen and faithful."

15   And he said to me, "The waters that you saw, where the whore is seated, are peoples and multitudes and nations and languages. ¹⁶ And the ten horns that you saw, they and the beast will hate the whore; they will make her desolate and naked; they will devour her flesh and burn her up with fire. ¹⁷ For God has put it into their hearts to carry out his purpose by agreeing to give their kingdom to the beast, until the words of God will be fulfilled. ¹⁸ The woman you saw is the great city that rules over the kings of the earth."

3. The doom of Babylon announced

18 After this I saw another angel coming down from heaven, having great authority; and the earth was made bright with his splendor. ² He called out with a mighty voice,

"Fallen, fallen is Babylon the great!
    It has become a dwelling place of demons,
a haunt of every foul spirit,
    a haunt of every foul bird,
    a haunt of every foul and hateful beast.ᵇ
3 For all the nations have drunkᶜ
    of the wine of the wrath of her fornication,
    and the kings of the earth have committed fornication with her,
        and the merchants of the earth have grown rich from the
            powerᵈ of her luxury."

4. The call to come out of Babylon

4   Then I heard another voice from heaven saying,
"Come out of her, my people,
    so that you do not take part in her sins,
    and so that you do not share in her plagues;
5 for her sins are heaped high as heaven,
    and God has remembered her iniquities.
6 Render to her as she herself has rendered,
    and repay her double for her deeds;
    mix a double draught for her in the cup she mixed.
7 As she glorified herself and lived luxuriously,
    so give her a like measure of torment and grief.
Since in her heart she says,
    'I rule as a queen;
I am no widow,
    and I will never see grief,'
8 therefore her plagues will come in a single day —
    pestilence and mourning and famine —
and she will be burned with fire;
    for mighty is the Lord God who judges her."

ᵇ Other ancient authorities lack the words *a haunt of every foul beast* and attach the words *and hateful* to the previous line so as to read *a haunt of every foul and hateful bird*   ᶜ Other ancient authorities read *She has made all nations drink*   ᵈ Or *resources*

17.17 God uses wicked people to accomplish his divine plan. He has supreme power and is in full control of this entire situation. All the forces of darkness on earth and hell are subject to him, as he directs events toward the consummation of all things.
18.1ff Babylon is about to fall, and God calls for his people to flee the city (vv. 4–8). Its punishment is certain.
18.2,3 Babylon is guilty of having corrupted the nations. Kings have shared in her wantonness and merchants have grown rich in their trade through her. All will share her doom and be rewarded according to their works.

17.15
Isa 8.7;
Rev 5.9; 13.7
17.16
Rev 18.17,
19;
Ezek 16.37,
39;
Rev 19.18;
8.8
17.17
2 Thess 2.11;
Rev 10.7
17.18
Rev 16.19

18.1
Rev 17.1;
10.1;
Ezek 43.2
18.2
Rev 14.8;
Isa 13.21,
22;
Jer 50.39

18.3
Rev 14.8;
Jer 25.15, 27

18.4
Isa 48.20;
Jer 50.8;
2 Cor 6.17

18.5
Jer 51.9;
Rev 16.19
18.6
Ps 137.8;
Jer 50.15;
Rev 14.10;
16.19
18.7
Ezek 28.2-8;
Isa 47.7, 8;
Zeph 2.15

18.8
Isa 47.9;
Rev 17.16;
Jer 50.34;
Rev 11.17

5. *The lament of the world over Babylon*

18.9
Rev 17.2;
Jer 50.46;
v. 18;
Rev 19.3
18.10
vv. 15, 17,
16, 19

9   And the kings of the earth, who committed fornication and lived in luxury with her, will weep and wail over her when they see the smoke of her burning; [10] they will stand far off, in fear of her torment, and say,

"Alas, alas, the great city,
    Babylon, the mighty city!
For in one hour your judgment has come."

18.11
v. 3;
Ezek 27.27
18.12
Rev 17.4
18.13
Ezek 27.13

11   And the merchants of the earth weep and mourn for her, since no one buys their cargo anymore, [12] cargo of gold, silver, jewels and pearls, fine linen, purple, silk and scarlet, all kinds of scented wood, all articles of ivory, all articles of costly wood, bronze, iron, and marble, [13] cinnamon, spice, incense, myrrh, frankincense, wine, olive oil, choice flour and wheat, cattle and sheep, horses and chariots, slaves—and human lives.[e]

14   "The fruit for which your soul longed
        has gone from you,
    and all your dainties and your splendor
    are lost to you,
        never to be found again!"

18.15
Ezek 27.36,
31
18.16
Rev 17.4

[15] The merchants of these wares, who gained wealth from her, will stand far off, in fear of her torment, weeping and mourning aloud,

16   "Alas, alas, the great city,
        clothed in fine linen,
    in purple and scarlet,
    adorned with gold,
        with jewels, and with pearls!

18.17
Rev 17.16;
Isa 23.14;
Ezek 27.29
18.18
Ezek 27.30;
Rev 13.4
18.19
Josh 7.6;
Job 2.12;
Ezek 27.30

17   For in one hour all this wealth has been laid waste!"

And all shipmasters and seafarers, sailors and all whose trade is on the sea, stood far off [18] and cried out as they saw the smoke of her burning, "What city was like the great city?"

[19] And they threw dust on their heads, as they wept and mourned, crying out,

"Alas, alas, the great city,
    where all who had ships at sea
    grew rich by her wealth!
For in one hour she has been laid waste."

6. *Heaven's rejoicing over Babylon's fall*

18.20
Isa 44.23;
Jer 51.48;
Rev 19.2

20   Rejoice over her, O heaven, you saints and apostles and prophets! For God has given judgment for you against her.

7. *Babylon's doom symbolically portrayed*

18.21
Jer 51.63;
Rev 12.8

21   Then a mighty angel took up a stone like a great millstone and threw it into the sea, saying,
"With such violence Babylon the great city
    will be thrown down,

e Or chariots, and human bodies and souls

18.9,10 The kings of the earth lament the fall of Babylon. Though they position themselves afar off lest they share the same fate, they will not escape, for there is no sign of repentance.
18.11ff The merchants weep and mourn over the judgment against Babylon, not because of its sinfulness but because Babylon was their chief market. In a single hour all is destroyed and they have no market for their goods.
18.17ff A third lamentation is heard from shipmasters whose maritime interests are impaired by the loss of Babylon.

18.20 While the whole world mourns the loss of Babylon, all heaven rejoices that judgment has come at last. We can be sure that a day will come for Babylon, just as it will at the end of the age for all humankind.
18.21-24 A mighty angel takes a huge millstone and drops it into the ocean. Just as that stone sinks to rise no more, so shall this happen to Babylon. All music is stilled, commerce ceases, lights go out, and marriages stop. The only thing left are the bloodstains of the saints and the prophets who have been murdered.

22 and will be found no more;
    and the sound of harpists and minstrels and of flutists and
        trumpeters
        will be heard in you no more;
    and an artisan of any trade
        will be found in you no more;
    and the sound of the millstone
        will be heard in you no more;
23 and the light of a lamp
        will shine in you no more;
    and the voice of bridegroom and bride
        will be heard in you no more;
    for your merchants were the magnates of the earth,
        and all nations were deceived by your sorcery.
24 And in you*f* was found the blood of prophets and of saints,
        and of all who have been slaughtered on earth."

8. *Praise to God for judgment: the marriage supper of the Lamb*

19 After this I heard what seemed to be the loud voice of a great
multitude in heaven, saying,

"Hallelujah!
Salvation and glory and power to our God,
2   for his judgments are true and just;
    he has judged the great whore
        who corrupted the earth with her fornication,
    and he has avenged on her the blood of his servants."*g*
3 Once more they said,

"Hallelujah!
The smoke goes up from her forever and ever."
4 And the twenty-four elders and the four living creatures fell down and
worshiped God who is seated on the throne, saying,

"Amen. Hallelujah!"

5   And from the throne came a voice saying,

"Praise our God,
    all you his servants,*g*
and all who fear him,
    small and great."

6 Then I heard what seemed to be the voice of a great multitude, like the
sound of many waters and like the sound of mighty thunderpeals, crying
out,

"Hallelujah!
For the Lord our God
    the Almighty reigns.
7   Let us rejoice and exult
        and give him the glory,

---

f Gk her   *g* Gk slaves

Cross references (right column):

18.22 Isa 24.8; Ezek 26.13; Jer 25.10

18.23 Jer 25.10; 7.34; 16.9; Isa 23.8; Nah 3.4

18.24 Rev 17.6; Jer 51.49

19.1 Rev 11.15; 4.11; 7.10, 12; 12.10

19.2 Deut 32.43; Rev 6.10

19.3 Isa 34.10; Rev 14.11

19.4 Rev 4.4, 6; 5.14

19.5 Ps 134.1; Rev 11.18; 20.12

19.6 Rev 11.15, 17; 14.2

19.7 Mt 22.2; 25.10; 2 Cor 11.2; Eph 5.32; Rev 21.2, 9

19.1–8 This section contains four "Hallelujahs," a word meaning "Praise the Lord." Up to this point there has been music on earth and in heaven, but now a "Hallelujah Chorus" is sung. In all of the N.T. the word "Hallelujah" never appears until here. The first two "Hallelujahs" celebrate the end of Babylon, for the harlot has been judged forever (vv. 2,3; see notes on v. 4 and v. 6 for the third and fourth "Hallelujahs").

19.2 There are at least three bases on which God renders judgment: (1) he judges according to truth (cf. also 16.7), and there can be no concealment because he is omniscient (Ps 139.1–6); (2) he makes no exceptions and will give each one whatever his or her

deeds deserve (Eccl 12.14; Rom 2.11); (3) he judges the motives as well as the external conduct (Rom 2.16; 1 Cor 4.5).

19.4 The third "Hallelujah" is sung by the twenty-four elders and the four living creatures.

19.6 The fourth "Hallelujah," a grand oratorio in which all the choirs of heaven join, celebrates the marriage supper of the Lamb.

19.7 The marriage supper or the wedding banquet of the Lamb apparently precedes the second coming of Christ, since it is mentioned first. The saints attend the supper, i.e., the saved of all ages, including believers who died before and after Calvary.

19.8
Rev 15.4

19.9
v. 10;
Rev 1.19;
Lk 14.15;
Rev 21.5
19.10
Rev 22.8;
Acts 10.26;
Rev 22.9;
12.17

19.11
Rev 15.5;
6.2; 3.14;
Isa 11.4
19.12
Rev 1.14;
6.2; 2.17
19.13
Isa 63.2, 3;
Jn 1.1
19.14
v. 8
19.15
Isa 11.4;
2 Thess 2.8;
Ps 2.9;
Rev 2.27;
14.19, 20
19.16
Dan 2.47;
Rev 17.14
19.17
Rev 8.13;
Ezek 39.17
19.18
Ezek 39.18-20;
Rev 11.18
19.19
Rev 11.7;
16.14, 16
19.20
Rev 16.13;
13.12ff;
Dan 7.11;
Rev 20.10;
14.10; 21.8
19.21
vv. 11, 19,
15, 17
20.1
Rev 10.1;
1.18; 9.1
20.2
2 Pet 2.4;
Jude 6;
Rev 12.9

for the marriage of the Lamb has come,
  and his bride has made herself ready;
8 to her it has been granted to be clothed
  with fine linen, bright and pure" —
for the fine linen is the righteous deeds of the saints.

9 And the angel said[h] to me, "Write this: Blessed are those who are invited to the marriage supper of the Lamb." And he said to me, "These are true words of God." 10 Then I fell down at his feet to worship him, but he said to me, "You must not do that! I am a fellow servant[i] with you and your comrades[j] who hold the testimony of Jesus.[k] Worship God! For the testimony of Jesus[k] is the spirit of prophecy."

H. The defeat of the beast and the false prophet

11 Then I saw heaven opened, and there was a white horse! Its rider is called Faithful and True, and in righteousness he judges and makes war. 12 His eyes are like a flame of fire, and on his head are many diadems; and he has a name inscribed that no one knows but himself. 13 He is clothed in a robe dipped in[l] blood, and his name is called The Word of God. 14 And the armies of heaven, wearing fine linen, white and pure, were following him on white horses. 15 From his mouth comes a sharp sword with which to strike down the nations, and he will rule[m] them with a rod of iron; he will tread the wine press of the fury of the wrath of God the Almighty. 16 On his robe and on his thigh he has a name inscribed, "King of kings and Lord of lords."

17 Then I saw an angel standing in the sun, and with a loud voice he called to all the birds that fly in midheaven, "Come, gather for the great supper of God, 18 to eat the flesh of kings, the flesh of captains, the flesh of the mighty, the flesh of horses and their riders — flesh of all, both free and slave, both small and great." 19 Then I saw the beast and the kings of the earth with their armies gathered to make war against the rider on the horse and against his army. 20 And the beast was captured, and with it the false prophet who had performed in its presence the signs by which he deceived those who had received the mark of the beast and those who worshiped its image. These two were thrown alive into the lake of fire that burns with sulfur. 21 And the rest were killed by the sword of the rider on the horse, the sword that came from his mouth; and all the birds were gorged with their flesh.

I. The binding of Satan

20 Then I saw an angel coming down from heaven, holding in his hand the key to the bottomless pit and a great chain. 2 He seized

---

h Gk *he said*   *i* Gk *slave*   *j* Gk *brothers*   *k* Or *to Jesus*   *l* Other ancient authorities read *sprinkled with*
m Or *will shepherd*

19.13 The Bible is the word of God written; Jesus is the Word of God incarnate. He comes as the conquering Lord with a sharp sword to take vengeance on the enemies of God. The beast and the false prophet are taken captive and thrown alive into the lake of fire that burns with sulphur (see also 20.2 for the binding of Satan). The people of God of all ages have nothing now to fear. The victory has been won, and God has triumphed over evil forever.
20.2 Generally, Christians have entertained one of three views regarding the millennium (which literally means a period of a thousand years). (1) Postmillennialism looks for a thousand-year period of peace and plenty brought in by the church whereby the preached gospel conquers the world. At the end of the thousand years Christ will return to earth and the new heaven and the new earth will be established and eternity will begin. St. Augustine was a proponent of

postmillennialism and many evangelical scholars a hundred years ago promoted the view. Some Bible believers accept this view today, especially in the light of the decline of optimism about the human race. (2) Amillennialism says there is no literal thousand-year earthly kingdom before or after the coming of the Lord which will mark the beginning of the new heaven and the new earth and eternity. Some amillenarians hold that the thousand years of 20.2 constitute the entire period between the first and the second coming of Christ. In general they do not look for a literal fulfillment of the O.T. prophecies concerning Israel's restoration, the creation of a new temple, and a time of peace and prosperity for the Jews. Rather, the church is the new Israel, and all O.T prophecies point to Christ and the church. (3) Premillennialism looks for the start of the millennium at the second coming of Christ. At the end of that time, Satan (who

the dragon, that ancient serpent, who is the Devil and Satan, and bound him for a thousand years, 3 and threw him into the pit, and locked and sealed it over him, so that he would deceive the nations no more, until the thousand years were ended. After that he must be let out for a little while.

J. The millennial reign of Christ

4 Then I saw thrones, and those seated on them were given authority to judge. I also saw the souls of those who had been beheaded for their testimony to Jesus[n] and for the word of God. They had not worshiped the beast or its image and had not received its mark on their foreheads or their hands. They came to life and reigned with Christ a thousand years. 5 (The rest of the dead did not come to life until the thousand years were ended.) This is the first resurrection. 6 Blessed and holy are those who share in the first resurrection. Over these the second death has no power, but they will be priests of God and of Christ, and they will reign with him a thousand years.

K. The loosing of Satan

7 When the thousand years are ended, Satan will be released from his prison 8 and will come out to deceive the nations at the four corners of the earth, Gog and Magog, in order to gather them for battle; they are as numerous as the sands of the sea. 9 They marched up over the breadth of the earth and surrounded the camp of the saints and the beloved city. And fire came down from heaven[o] and consumed them. 10 And the devil who had deceived them was thrown into the lake of fire and sulfur, where the beast and the false prophet were, and they will be tormented day and night forever and ever.

L. The great white throne judgment

11 Then I saw a great white throne and the one who sat on it; the earth and the heaven fled from his presence, and no place was found for them. 12 And I saw the dead, great and small, standing before the throne, and books were opened. Also another book was opened, the book of life. And the dead were judged according to their works, as recorded in the books. 13 And the sea gave up the dead that were in it, Death and Hades gave up the dead that were in them, and all were judged according to what they had done. 14 Then Death and Hades were thrown into the lake of fire. This

n Or for the testimony of Jesus o Other ancient authorities read from God, out of heaven, or out of heaven from God

20.3 Dan 6.17; Rev 12.9
20.4 Dan 7.9, 22, 27; Rev 6.9; 13.12, 15, 16
20.5 Lk 14.14; Phil 3.11; 1 Thess 4.16
20.6 Rev 14.13; 2.11; 21.8; 1.6
20.7 v. 2
20.8 Ezek 38.2; 39.1; Rev 16.14; Heb 11.12
20.9 Ezek 38.9, 22; 39.6
20.10 vv. 3, 8
20.11f Rev 4.2; 21.1; Dan 2.35; Rev 12.8
20.12 Mt 16.27; Rev 2.3; 22.12
20.13 Rev 6.8; Isa 26.19; Rev 2.23
20.14 1 Cor 15.26; Rev 6.8

has been bound for a thousand years) will be loosed and a great rebellion will be brought into being. Then he will be cast into the lake of fire forever. On the relationship of the tribulation to the establishment of the millennium, see note on 1 Thess 4.15. Differing views of the millennium do not constitute grounds for division among Christians, since all believe in the coming of the Lord and the establishment of his eternal kingdom.
20.5 Some commentators think this *first resurrection* includes only those martyrs mentioned in v. 4. These then participate in Christ's thousand-year reign, after which the general resurrection of the other dead takes place. Premillennialists generally understand that the first resurrection occurs at Christ's second advent and includes *all* the righteous dead, plus those who are alive at his coming, who will then reign with Christ on earth for a thousand years. At the end of this time the second resurrection of the unbelieving dead will occur. Amillennialists generally view the first resur-

rection as the resurrection that believers experience in Christ at the time of conversion (cf. Rom 6.5; Eph 2.4,5). We should recognize that no view is without problems of interpretation.
20.10 After Satan is bound for a thousand years, he is loosed for a time; then, after the battle of Gog and Magog, he is thrown into the lake of fire to suffer forever (for comments on Satan, see note on Ezek 28.12).
20.11,12 According to the premillennial view, the last judgment, that of the *great white throne*, will take place at the end of the thousand years, at which time the wicked dead will be raised and judged. The passage refers to books, one of which is the book of life (cf. 3.5; 13.8). We do not know how many other books there are, though one must contain human works. Those who do not have their names inscribed in the book of life will be cast into the lake of fire; there will be no higher court of appeal.

is the second death, the lake of fire; 15 and anyone whose name was not found written in the book of life was thrown into the lake of fire.

M. The new heaven and the new earth

21 Then I saw a new heaven and a new earth; for the first heaven and the first earth had passed away, and the sea was no more. 2 And I saw the holy city, the new Jerusalem, coming down out of heaven from God, prepared as a bride adorned for her husband. 3 And I heard a loud voice from the throne saying,

"See, the home*p* of God is among mortals.
He will dwell*q* with them;
they will be his peoples,*r*
and God himself will be with them;*s*
4 he will wipe every tear from their eyes.
Death will be no more;
mourning and crying and pain will be no more,
for the first things have passed away."

5 And the one who was seated on the throne said, "See, I am making all things new." Also he said, "Write this, for these words are trustworthy and true." 6 Then he said to me, "It is done! I am the Alpha and the Omega, the beginning and the end. To the thirsty I will give water as a gift from the spring of the water of life. 7 Those who conquer will inherit these things, and I will be their God and they will be my children. 8 But as for the cowardly, the faithless,*t* the polluted, the murderers, the fornicators, the sorcerers, the idolaters, and all liars, their place will be in the lake that burns with fire and sulfur, which is the second death."

N. The new Jerusalem

1. The city

9 Then one of the seven angels who had the seven bowls full of the seven last plagues came and said to me, "Come, I will show you the bride, the wife of the Lamb." 10 And in the spirit*u* he carried me away to a great, high mountain and showed me the holy city Jerusalem coming down out of heaven from God. 11 It has the glory of God and a radiance like a very rare jewel, like jasper, clear as crystal. 12 It has a great, high wall with twelve gates, and at the gates twelve angels, and on the gates are inscribed the names of the twelve tribes of the Israelites; 13 on the east three gates,

p Gk the tabernacle *q* Gk will tabernacle *r* Other ancient authorities read *people*
s Other ancient authorities add *and be their God* *t* Or *the unbelieving* *u* Or *in the Spirit*

21.1
Isa 65.17;
2 Pet 3.13;
Rev 20.11
21.2
Heb 11.10;
12.22;
Rev 3.12
21.3
Ezek 37.27;
2 Cor 6.16;
Rev 7.15

21.4
Rev 7.17;
1 Cor 15.26;
Rev 20.14;
Isa 35.10;
65.19
21.5
Rev 4.9;
20.11;
Isa 43.19;
Rev 19.9
21.6
Rev 16.17;
1.8; 22.13;
Jn 4.10
21.7
Rev 2.7; v. 3
21.8
Heb 12.14;
Rev 22.15;
19.20; 2.11

21.9
Rev 15.1, 6,
7; 20.14ff
21.10
Rev 1.10;
Ezek 40.2;
Rev 17.3
21.11
Rev 15.8;
22.5; 4.6
21.12
Ezek 48.31-34

20.15 Unrepentant sinners will be *thrown into the lake of fire.* Some have challenged whether these souls will consciously experience eternal punishment, either by assuming that all humankind will ultimately be saved or that unrepentant sinners will be annihilated and cease to exist. But the doctrine of eternal, conscious punishment is clearly indicated in the Scriptures by such expressions as (1) eternal fire (Mt 25.41); (2) the fire is never quenched (Mk 9.48); and (3) the lake that burns with fire and sulphur (21.8). Furthermore, the Greek term for the adjective "eternal" is the same, whether it modifies "life" or "death," and the phrase 'forever and ever' (literally, "unto the ages of the ages") is used both for endless life and for endless death (cf. 1.18; 11.15; 14.11; 20.10). If the one is conscious, the other is as well. **21.2** The *holy city, the new Jerusalem,* coming down from God out of heaven, is the final abode of the saints. This eternal habitation becomes theirs after the judgment of the great white throne (20.11ff). This chapter describes its boundaries, structures, and in-

habitants. The description is only symbolic, but the saints can rest assured that the reality defies description and meets the highest expectations of all who inhabit the city. **21.5** *I am making all things new.* The cosmos was stained with the sin of Satan and of Adam. Following the cosmic victory of Jesus Christ in his cross, resurrection, and ascension, all residual elements of the fall will be removed and the universe return to its prefall perfection for all eternity (see Mt 19.28; 2 Pet 3.10–13)). This will occur at the final stage of the second advent, when Satan is finally defeated. **21.6** *I am the Alpha and the Omega, the beginning and the end.* The will and the power of God Almighty created all things seen and unseen. Now the pleasure and the glory of the creator, sustainer, and redeemer are fulfilled. Sinless perfection has come and God is all in all. **21.9** *the bride, the wife of the Lamb,* i.e., the church of God—at last triumphant, perfected, and glorious in holiness.

on the north three gates, on the south three gates, and on the west three gates. 14 And the wall of the city has twelve foundations, and on them are the twelve names of the twelve apostles of the Lamb.

2. Its measurements

15 The angel[v] who talked to me had a measuring rod of gold to measure the city and its gates and walls. 16 The city lies foursquare, its length the same as its width; and he measured the city with his rod, fifteen hundred miles;[w] its length and width and height are equal. 17 He also measured its wall, one hundred forty-four cubits[x] by human measurement, which the angel was using. 18 The wall is built of jasper, while the city is pure gold, clear as glass. 19 The foundations of the wall of the city are adorned with every jewel; the first was jasper, the second sapphire, the third agate, the fourth emerald, 20 the fifth onyx, the sixth carnelian, the seventh chrysolite, the eighth beryl, the ninth topaz, the tenth chrysoprase, the eleventh jacinth, the twelfth amethyst. 21 And the twelve gates are twelve pearls, each of the gates is a single pearl, and the street of the city is pure gold, transparent as glass.

3. Its light

22 I saw no temple in the city, for its temple is the Lord God the Almighty and the Lamb. 23 And the city has no need of sun or moon to shine on it, for the glory of God is its light, and its lamp is the Lamb. 24 The nations will walk by its light, and the kings of the earth will bring their glory into it. 25 Its gates will never be shut by day — and there will be no night there. 26 People will bring into it the glory and the honor of the nations. 27 But nothing unclean will enter it, nor anyone who practices abomination or falsehood, but only those who are written in the Lamb's book of life.

4. Its blessings

22 Then the angel[y] showed me the river of the water of life, bright as crystal, flowing from the throne of God and of the Lamb 2 through the middle of the street of the city. On either side of the river is the tree of life[z] with its twelve kinds of fruit, producing its fruit each month; and the leaves of the tree are for the healing of the nations. 3 Nothing accursed will be found there any more. But the throne of God and of the Lamb will be in it, and his servants[a] will worship him; 4 they will see his face, and his name will be on their foreheads. 5 And there will be no more night; they need no light of lamp or sun, for the Lord God will be their light, and they will reign forever and ever.

IV. Epilogue (22.6–21)

A. Testimony to the truth of the revelation

6 And he said to me, "These words are trustworthy and true, for the Lord, the God of the spirits of the prophets, has sent his angel to show his servants[a] what must soon take place."

v Gk He   w Gk twelve thousand stadia   x That is, almost seventy-five yards   y Gk he   z Or the Lamb.
2 In the middle of the street of the city, and on either side of the river, is the tree of life   a Gk slaves

21.22,23 The new Jerusalem does not need either the sun or the moon to light it, nor is there any temple. God and his Son are the temple and the light of the city. God is light (1 Jn 1.5), and wherever God is, no light is needed.
21.27 The city's residents comprise those whose names are written in the Lamb's book of life, and no others. Those who lived unrepentant lives of wicked-

ness are excluded from the city and are assigned to their final destiny in the lake of fire (see v. 8).
22.2 the tree of life. Adam could have but did not eat of the fruit of the tree of life. When he sinned he no longer had access to the tree of life. Now at the end of the age in the new Jerusalem, the tree of life is there for the people of God, who will eat of its fruit forever and live forever.

Cross-references

21.14
Mt 16.18;
Eph 2.20

21.15
Rev 11.1

21.18
vv. 11, 19, 21;
Rev 4.6
21.19
Isa 54.11, 12; vv. 11, 18;
Rev 4.3
21.20
Rev 4.3
21.21
vv. 15, 25, 18

21.22
Jn 4.21, 23;
Rev 1.8; 5.6
21.23
Isa 24.23;
60.19, 20;
Rev 22.5
21.24
Isa 60.3, 5
21.25
Isa 60.11;
Zech 14.7;
Rev 22.5
21.27
Isa 52.1;
Joel 3.17;
Rev 22.14;
3.5
22.1
Ezek 47.1;
Zech 14.8;
Rev 4.6
22.2
Gen 2.9;
Rev 2.7;
Ezek 47.12
22.3
Zech 14.11;
Rev 7.15
22.4
Mt 5.8;
Rev 14.1
22.5
Rev 21.25, 23;
Dan 7.27

22.6
Rev 1.1;
19.19; 21.5

22.7
Rev 3.11; 1.3

7 "See, I am coming soon! Blessed is the one who keeps the words of the prophecy of this book."

22.8
Rev 1.1;
19.10
22.9
Rev 19.10;
1.1; vv. 10,
18, 19;
Rev 21.2

8 I, John, am the one who heard and saw these things. And when I heard and saw them, I fell down to worship at the feet of the angel who showed them to me; 9 but he said to me, "You must not do that! I am a fellow servant[b] with you and your comrades[c] the prophets, and with those who keep the words of this book. Worship God!"

B. The distinction drawn

22.10
Dan 8.26;
Rev 1.3
22.11
Dan 12.10;
Ezek 3.27

10 And he said to me, "Do not seal up the words of the prophecy of this book, for the time is near. 11 Let the evildoer still do evil, and the filthy still be filthy, and the righteous still do right, and the holy still be holy."

22.12
Isa 40.10;
Jer 17.10;
Rev 2.23
22.13
Rev 1.8, 17;
21.6
22.15
Gal 5.19ff;
Col 3.6;
Phil 3.2

12 "See, I am coming soon; my reward is with me, to repay according to everyone's work. 13 I am the Alpha and the Omega, the first and the last, the beginning and the end."

14 Blessed are those who wash their robes,[d] so that they will have the right to the tree of life and may enter the city by the gates. 15 Outside are the dogs and sorcerers and fornicators and murderers and idolaters, and everyone who loves and practices falsehood.

C. The invitation given

22.16
Rev 1.1; 5.5;
Zech 6.12;
2 Pet 1.19;
Rev 2.28
22.17
Rev 2.7;
21.2;
Isa 55.1;
Rev 21.6
22.18
Deut 4.2;
Prov 30.6;
Rev 15.6;
16.21

16 "It is I, Jesus, who sent my angel to you with this testimony for the churches. I am the root and the descendant of David, the bright morning star."
17   The Spirit and the bride say, "Come."
        And let everyone who hears say, "Come."
        And let everyone who is thirsty come.
        Let anyone who wishes take the water of life as a gift.
18 I warn everyone who hears the words of the prophecy of this book: if anyone adds to them, God will add to that person the plagues described in this book; 19 if anyone takes away from the words of the book of this prophecy, God will take away that person's share in the tree of life and in the holy city, which are described in this book.

22.20

20 The one who testifies to these things says, "Surely I am coming soon."
    Amen. Come, Lord Jesus!

D. The benediction

21 The grace of the Lord Jesus be with all the saints. Amen.[e]

b Gk *slave*   *c* Gk *brothers*   *d* Other ancient authorities read *do his commandments*   *e* Other ancient authorities lack *all*; others lack *the saints*; others lack *Amen*

22.11ff At the end of this age evil will become stronger than ever. Instead of turning to God, evildoers will flee even further from him. There is not one word about universal salvation. But there is always the invitation, even to the worst sinner, to come to Christ before it is too late (v. 17).
22.13 Revelation opens with Jesus portrayed as the Alpha and the Omega (1.8), and it closes with the same refrain. The entire book is about the reigning Christ who waits at the Father's right hand for that moment when he will come the second time in power and great glory.
22.16 The Scriptures assert one final time the deity and humanity of Christ. As God Christ was David's root and as man David's descendant.

22.18 John warns one and all about the dangers that can spring from tampering with the word of God. The specific reference here has to do with the book of Revelation. But by inference we can extend it to the totality of Scripture. For if it is wrong to tamper with Revelation, it is equally wrong to tamper with anything else that is the word of God.
22.20 John expresses his fervent hope that Christ will come shortly as promised. Revelation closes the Bible as Genesis opened it. The garden in which Adam lived and from which he was ejected because of his sin has been replaced by the new Jerusalem, where the inhabitants regain the paradise that Adam lost.

Index to the Annotations

This index provides a listing of all subjects discussed in the commentary notes, together with the Scripture reference and page number of that note.

Concordance to the NRSV

This concordance to the New Revised Standard Version of the Bible began with the one found in the RSV Harper Study Bible. Each verse used in that earlier concordance was examined for changes that scholars made in the NRSV text, and these changes have been incorporated in this concordance.

The RSV Harper Study Bible concordance was the product of extensive research. Incorporated into it were (a) Bible verses relating to approximately three hundred carefully selected doctrinal and practical topics (such as *grace*, *justify*, *redemption*, *faith*, *hope*, *love*, etc.), and (b) the favorite Bible verses and golden texts from several Sunday School curriculum courses. In other words, almost any verse that the average user might want to look up should be found within this concordance.

Note the following features of this concordance:

1. For each verse quoted, an italicized single letter is used to designate the word entry.

2. The texts chosen for each word entry have been placed in Bible book order.

3. Occasionally the verses under a word entry contain different forms of that entry (for example, under the word ABIDE, they contain "abide," "abides," or "abode"); the alternative forms have been placed in parentheses after the key word entry. The context given in each verse will clue the reader which form of the word entry fits the italicized letter.

4. Many Bible names have been placed in a paragraph style, giving the most important references to events in that person's life.

5. Sometimes a verse is taken from a footnote reading rather than the main text of the NRSV. When this is the case, the verse reference has an "n" after it.

A concordance of this type is naturally limited and cannot be expected to meet the needs of every user. Nevertheless, in the extent of coverage, relevance of inclusion, and objectivity of selection, it should prove to be a valuable tool for Bible reading, study, and comprehension.

AARON

Brother of Moses, Ex 4.14; 7.1; commended for his eloquence, Ex 4.14; chosen to assist Moses, Ex 4.16,27-28; co-leader with Moses, Ex 5.1; 8.25; supported Moses' arms, Ex 17.12; set apart as priest, Ex 28; Heb 5.4; made a golden calf, Ex 32; Acts 7.40-41; found fault with Moses, Num 12; his rod budded, Num 17; Heb 9.4; with Moses disobedient at Meribah, Num 20.10-53; died on Mount Hor, Num 20.26-29.

ABANDON (ABANDONED)

Deut	4.31 a merciful God, he will neither *a* you
	29.25 they *a* the covenant of the LORD, the
	32.15 He *a* God who made him, and scoffed
2 Kings	22.17 Because they have *a* me and have made
2 Chr	12. 1 he *a* the law of the LORD, he and all
	13.10 the LORD is our God, and we have not *a*
Ps	37.33 The LORD will not *a* them to their
Isa	54. 7 For a brief moment I *a* you, but with
Jer	22. 9 "Because they *a* the covenant of the
Acts	2.27 you will not *a* my soul to Hades, or let
Rev	2. 4 you, that you have *a* the love you had

ABASE

Job	40.11 look on all who are proud, and *a* them.
Ezek	21.26 that which is low, *a* that which is high.

ABEL

Gen	4. 2 Now *A* was a keeper of sheep, and Cain
	4. 8 Cain said to his brother *A*, "Let us go
	4.25 for me another child instead of *A*,
Mt	23.35 from the blood of righteous *A* to the
Heb	11. 4 By faith *A* offered to God a more
	12.24 a better word than the blood of *A*.

ABHOR

Job	19.19 All my intimate friends *a* me, and those
	30.10 They *a* me, they keep aloof from me;

ABHORRENT

Deut	12.31 every *a* thing that the LORD hates
	17. 1 for that is *a* to the LORD your God.
1 Sam	27.12 "He has made himself utterly *a* to his

ABIATHAR

1 Sam	22.20 Ahitub, *A*, escaped and fled after David.
	23. 6 When *A* . . . fled to David at Keilah, he

ABIDE

1 Sam	30.	7 David said to the priest *A* son of
2 Sam	15.29	So Zadok and *A* carried the ark of God
	20.25	was secretary; Zadok and *A* were priests;
Mk	2.26	when *A* was high priest, and ate the

ABIDE (ABIDES ABODE)

Gen	6.	3 My spirit shall not *a* in mortals forever,
Ps	15.	1 O LORD, who may *a* in your tent? Who
	68.16	at the mount that God desired for his *a*,
	91.	1 who *a* in the shadow of the Almighty,
Prov	3.33	but he blesses the *a* of the righteous.
Hag	2.	5 My spirit *a* among you; do not fear. For
Jn	15.	4 *A* in me, as I *a* in you. Just as the
1 Cor	13.13	So faith, hope, and love *a*, these three;
1 Jn	2.24	*a* in you, then you will *a* in the Son
	3.	6 No one who *a* in him sins; no one who
2 Jn		2 because of the truth that *a* in us and

ABILITY

Ex	31.	3 I have filled him . . . with *a*,
Mt	25.15	another one, to each according to his *a*.

ABIMELECH

Gen	20.	2 King *A* of Gerar sent and took Sarah.

ABISHAI

Sought to kill Saul, 1 Sam 26.5-9; pursued Abner, 2 Sam 2.18,24; desired to kill Shimei, 2 Sam 16.9-11; 19.21; one of David's key warriors, 2 Sam 23.18-19; slew the Edomites, 1 Chr 18.12.

ABLE

Num	13.30	it, for we are well *a* to overcome it."
	14.16	is because the LORD was not *a* to bring
Josh	23.	9 no one has been *a* to withstand you to
1 Sam	6.20	"Who is *a* to stand before the LORD, this
2 Chr	25.	9 "The LORD is *a* to give you much more
Dan	3.17	is *a* to deliver us from the furnace of
	6.20	been *a* to deliver you from the lions?"
Mt	3.	9 God is *a* from these stones to raise up
	9.28	"Do you believe that I am *a* to do this?"
	20.22	Are you *a* to drink the cup that I am
Lk	12.26	you are not *a* to do so small a thing
2 Cor	9.	8 And God is *a* to provide you with every
Eph	3.20	within us is *a* to accomplish abundantly
Heb	2.18	suffered, he is *a* to help those who are

ABNER

Captain of Saul's host, 1 Sam 14.50; made Ish-bosheth king, 2 Sam 2.8-11; fought David's forces, 2 Sam 2.12-32; made a league with David, 2 Sam 3.6-21; slain by Joab, 2 Sam 3.22-30; mourned by David, 2 Sam 3.31-39.

ABOLISH (ABOLISHED)

Hos	2.18	I will *a* the bow, the sword, and war
2 Tim	1.10	Jesus, who *a* death and brought life and

ABOMINABLE

Ps	14.	1 They are corrupt, they do *a* deeds; there

ABOMINATION (ABOMINATIONS)

Lev	18.30	my charge not to commit any of these *a*
Prov	6.16	seven that are an *a* to him: haughty
	11.	1 A false balance is an *a* to the LORD, but
	17.15	are both alike an *a* to the LORD.
	20.23	Differing weights are an *a* to the LORD,
	28.	9 to the law, even one's prayer is an *a*.
Isa	1.13	offerings is futile; incense is an *a* to me.
Ezek	8.	9 "Go in, and see the vile *a* that they are
	11.18	it all its detestable things and all its *a*.
	16.	2 make known to Jerusalem her *a*,
Dan	9.27	in their place shall be an *a* that
	11.31	and set up the *a* that makes desolate.
Mal	2.11	*a* has been committed in Israel and in
Rev	17.	4 a golden cup full of *a* and and the

ABOUND (ABOUNDED ABOUNDS)

Ps	72.	7 may righteousness flourish and peace *a*,
Prov	28.20	The faithful will *a* with blessings, but

Rom	3.	7 God's truthfulness *a* to his glory,
	5.20	where sin increased, grace *a* all the

ABRAHAM

Born, Gen 11.26; married Sarai, Gen 11.29; migrated from Ur to Haran, Gen 11.31; called by God, Gen 12.1-5; Heb 11.8; went to Egypt, Gen 12.10-20; separated from Lot, Gen 13.7-11; rescued Lot, Gen 14.13-16; God's covenant with him, Gen 15.18; 17.1-21; Ishmael is born to him, Gen 16.15-16; entertained angels, Gen 18.1-21; interceded for Sodom, Gen 18.22-33; banished Hagar and Ishmael, Gen 21.9-21; offered up Isaac, Gen 22.1-14; buried Sarah, Gen 23; married Keturah, Gen 25.1; death and burial, Gen 25.8-10.

Gen	17.	5 your name shall be *A*; for I have made
	20.	1 *A* journeyed toward . . . the Negeb
	22.	1 God tested *A*. He said to him, "*A*!" And
Mt	3.	9 'We have *A* as our ancestor'; for I tell
Lk	16.22	carried away by the angels to be with *A*.
Jn	8.58	truly, I tell you, before *A* was, I am."
Heb	11.	8 By faith *A* obeyed when he was called

ABSALOM

Third son of David, 2 Sam 3.3; avenged Tamar and fled, 2 Sam 13.20-39; returned to Jerusalem, 2 Sam 14.23-33; conspired against David, 2 Sam 15.1-12; slain by Joab, 2 Sam 18.9-17; mourned by David, 2 Sam 18.33.

ABSENT

1 Cor	5.	3 though *a* in body, I am present in spirit;
Col	2.	5 though I am *a* in body, yet I am with

ABSTAIN

Acts	15.20	write to them to *a* only from things
1 Thess	5.22	what is good; *a* from every form of evil.

ABUNDANCE

Ps	37.16	one has than the *a* of many wicked.
	105.	40 and gave them food from heaven in *a*.
Mt	12.34	For out of the *a* of the heart the mouth
Mk	12.15	life does not consist in the *a* of
Lk	21.	4 have contributed out of their *a*, but she
2 Cor	9.	8 to provide you with every blessing in *a*,

ABUNDANT (ABUNDANTLY)

Gen	30.30	before I came, and it has increased *a*;
Jn	10.10	that they may have life, and have it *a*.
2 Cor	8.	2 their *a* joy and their extreme poverty

ABUSE

Ex	22.22	You shall not *a* any widow or orphan.

ACCEPT (ACCEPTED)

Gen	4.	7 If you do well, will you not be *a*? But if
Deut	33.11	substance, and *a* the work of his hands;
2 Kings	5.26	Is this a time to *a* money and to *a*
Job	42.	8 I will *a* his prayer not to deal with you
Prov	2.	1 child, if you *a* my words and treasure
Jer	14.12	and grain offering, I do not *a* them;
Ezek	43.27	offerings of well-being; and I will *a* you,
Hos	14.	2 away all guilt; *a* that which is good,
Am	5.22	and grain offerings, I will not *a* them;
Mt	19.12	heaven. Let anyone *a* this who can.
Lk	4.24	no prophet is *a* in the prophet's
Jn	5.43	my Father's name and you do not *a* me;
Acts	22.18	they will not *a* your testimony about
1 Pet	2.13	For the Lord's sake *a* the authority of
	3.	1 *a* the authority of your husbands, so

ACCEPTABLE

Lev	22.20	a blemish, for it will not be *a* for you.
2 Cor	6.	2 "At an *a* time I have listened to you,

ACCESS

Rom	5.	2 through whom we have obtained *a* to
Eph	2.18	him both of us have *a* in one Spirit
	3.12	in whom we have *a* to God in boldness

ACCORD

Zeph	3.	9 of the LORD and serve him with one *a.*
Acts	8.	6 with one *a* listened eagerly to what was

ACCOUNT (ACCOUNTS ACCOUNTING)

Mt	1.	1 An *a* of the genealogy of Jesus the
	12.36	you will have to give an *a* for every
	18.23	who wished to settle *a* with his slaves.
Lk	16.	2 Give me an *a* of your management,
Philem		18 owes you anything, charge that to my *a.*

ACCOUNTABLE

Rom	14.12	So then, each of us will be a to God.

ACCURSED

Isa	65.20	short of a hundred will be considered *a.*
Jer	48.10	*A* is the one who is slack in doing the
Rom	9.	3 For I could wish that I myself were *a*
1 Cor	16.22	Let anyone be *a* who has no love for
Gal	1.	8 to what you received, let that one be *a*!

ACCUSATION (ACCUSATIONS)

Mt	27.13	how many *a* they make against you?"
Lk	23.	4 crowds, "I find no basis for an *a* against
Jn	18.29	them and said, "What *a* do you bring

ACCUSE (ACCUSED)

Jer	2.	9 *a* you, and I *a* your children's children.
Hos	4.	4 Yet let no one contend, let none *a,*
Zech	3.	1 standing at his right hand to *a* him.
Mt	12.10	the sabbath?" so that they might *a* him.
	27.12	when he was *a* by the chief priests and
Mk	15.	3 the chief priests *a* him of many things.
Acts	23.28	charge for which they had *a* him, I had

ACCUSER

Mt	5.25	Come to terms quickly with your *a*
Lk	12.58	when you go with your *a* before the

ACHAIA

Acts	18.12	Gallio was proconsul of *A,* the Jews
	19.21	Spirit to go through Macedonia and *A,*
Rom	15.26	Macedonia and *A* have been pleased to
2 Cor	9.	2 saying that *A* has been ready since last
1 Thess	1.	7 all the believers in Macedonia and in *A.*

ACKNOWLEDGE (ACKNOWLEDGED ACKNOWLEDGES)

Deut	4.35	that you would *a* that the LORD is God;
	4.39	So *a* today and take to heart that the
Job	40.14	Then I will also *a* to you that your own
Ps	32.	5 Then I *a* my sin to you, and I did not
Prov	3.	6 In all your ways *a* him, and he will
Jer	3.13	Only *a* your guilt, that you have
	14.20	We *a* our wickedness, O LORD, the
Dan	11.39	who *a* him he shall make more wealthy,
Hos	5.15	until they *a* their guilt and seek my
Mt	10.32	who *a* me before others, I will also *a*
Lk	12.	8 who *a* me before others, the Son of

ACQUIRED

Ex	15.16	until the people whom you *a* passed by.
Ruth	4.	9 I have *a* from the hand of Naomi all
	4.10	I have *a* Ruth the Moabite . . . to be my
Eccl	1.16	"I have *a* great wisdom, surpassing all

ACQUIT (ACQUITTED)

Deut	5.11	not *a* anyone who misuses his name.
Isa	5.23	who *a* the guilty for a bribe, and deprive
1 Cor	4.	4 against myself, but I am not thereby *a.*

ACQUITTAL

Ps	69.27	guilt; may they have no *a* from you.

ACT (ACTED ACTING ACTS)

Ps	119.126	It is time for the LORD to *a,* for your law
Jer	22.	3 Thus says the LORD: *A* with justice and
Ezek	20.14	But I *a* for the sake of my name, so
Mic	3.	4 time, because they have *a* wickedly.

Lk	6.47	to me, hears my words and *a* on them.
2 Cor	10.	2 to oppose those who think we are *a*
Jas	2.12	so *a* as those who are to be judged by

ACTION (ACTIONS)

1 Sam	2.	3 knowledge, and by him *a* are weighed.
Dan	11.32	their God shall stand firm and take *a.*
1 Jn	3.18	in word or speech, but in truth and *a.*

ACTIVATES

1 Cor	12.	6 is the the same God who *a* all of them

ACTS (n)

Ps	103.	7 to Moses, his *a* to the people of Israel.
Prov	20.11	make themselves known by their *a,*

ADAM

Gen	3.21	God made garments of skins for *A* and
	5.	1 This is a list of the descendants of *A.*
	5.	3 When *A* had lived one hundred thirty
Lk	3.38	Enos, son of Seth, son of *A,* son of God.
Rom	5.14	death exercised dominion from *A* to
1 Cor	15.22	as all die in *A,* so all will be made alive
	15.45	"The first man, *A,* became a living
1 Tim	2.13	For *A* was formed first, then Eve; and *A*

ADD (ADDED ADDS)

Gen	30.24	"May the LORD *a* to me another son!"
Deut	4.	2 You must neither *a* anything to what I
	12.32	I command you; do not *a* to it
Prov	30.	6 Do not *a* to his words, or else he will
Heb	2.	4 God *a* his testimony by signs and
Rev	22.18	this book: if any one *a* to them, God

ADMIRED

Esth	2.15	Now Esther was *a* by all who saw her.

ADMITTED

Deut	23.	1 is cut off shall be *a* to the assembly

ADMONISH

1 Cor	4.14	ashamed, but to *a* you as my beloved
1 Thess	5.14	we urge you, beloved to *a* the idlers,

ADMONITION

Prov	15.31	The ear that heeds wholesome *a* will

ADOPTION

Rom	8.23	groan inwardly while we wait for *a,* the
	8.15	fear, but you have received a spirit of *a.*
	9.	4 Israelites, and to them belong the *a,* the
Gal	4.	5 so that we might receive *a* as children.

ADORNED

Prov	14.18	The simple are *a* with folly, but the
Rev	21.	2 prepared as a bride *a* for her husband.

ADULTERERS

Hos	7.	4 They are all *a*; they are like a heated
Mal	3.	5 against the sorcerers, against the *a,*
Jas	4.	4 *A*! Do you not know that friendship

ADULTERESS

Hos	3.	1 a woman who has a lover and is an *a,*
Rom	7.	3 an *a* if she lives with another man

ADULTERY (ADULTERIES)

Ex	20.14	You shall not commit *a.*
Lev	20.10	If a man commits *a* with a wife of his
Deut	5.18	Neither shall you commit *a.*
Prov	6.32	But he who commits *a* has no sense; he
Jer	3.	8 for all the *a* of that faithless one, Israel,
	5.	7 I fed them to the full, they committed *a*
	13.27	your abominations, your *a* and your
Mt	5.27	it was said, 'You shall not commit *a.*'
	5.28	committed *a* with her in his heart.
	19.	9 and marries another, commits *a.*
Mk	7.21	come fornication, theft, murder, *a,*
	10.11	marries another, commits *a* against her;
Lk	16.18	his wife and marries another commits *a,*

Jn	8.	3 a woman who had been caught in *a*;
2 Pet	2.14	They have eyes full of *a*, insatiable for

ADVANCE (ADVANCED)

Esth	2.	9 and *a* her and her maids to the best
Acts	12.24	But the word of God continued to *a* and

ADVANTAGE

Job	35.	3 If you ask, "What *a* have I? How am I
Eccl	3.19	humans have no *a* over the animals; for
	5.	9 this is an *a* for a land: a king for a
	7.11	an *a* to those who see the sun.
Rom	3.	1 Then what *a* has the Jew? Or what is
1 Cor	10.33	everything I do, not seeking my own *a*,

ADVERSARY (ADVERSARIES)

Ezra	4.	1 When the *a* of Judah and Benjamin
Ps	27.12	Do not give me up to the will of my *a*;
Am	3.	1 An *a* shall surround the land, and strip

ADVERSITY

Ps	10.	6 all generations we shall not meet *a*."
Prov	24.10	If you faint in the day of *a*, your
Isa	48.10	I have tested you in the furnace of *a*.

ADVICE

Num	31.16	These women here, on Balaam's *a*,
1 Kings	12.	8 But he disregarded the *a* that the older
2 Chr	10.	8 he rejected the *a* that the older men
Ps	1.	1 who do not follow the *a* of the wicked,
Prov	8.14	I have good *a* and sound wisdom; I have
	12.	5 just; the *a* of the wicked is treacherous.
	19.20	Listen to *a* and accept instruction, that
Eccl	4.13	foolish king, who will no longer take *a*.
2 Cor	8.10	in this matter I am giving my *a*: it is

ADVOCATE

Jn	14.16	and he will give you another *A*, to be
	15.26	"When the *A* comes, whom I will send
	16.	7 go away, the *A* will not come to you;
1 Jn	2.	1 we have an *a* with the Father, Jesus

AFFLICT (AFFLICTED)

Deut	28.27	Lord will *a* you with the boils of Egypt,
Job	34.28	to him, and he heard the cry of the *a* —
	36.	6 wicked alive, but gives the *a* their right.
Ps	9.12	he does not forget the cry of the *a*.
	34.	2 in the Lord; let the *a* hear and be glad.
	94.	5 people, O Lord, and *a* your heritage.
Isa	53.	7 *a*, yet he did not open his mouth; like a
	58.10	hungry and satisfy the needs of the *a*,
Mic	4.	6 driven away, and those whom I have *a*.
Nah	1.12	I have *a* you, I will *a* you no more.
2 Cor	1.	6 If we are being *a*, it is for your
	4.	8 We are *a* in every way, but not crushed;

AFFLICTION (AFFLICTIONS)

Gen	16.11	for the Lord has given heed to your *a*.
	29.32	the Lord has looked upon my *a*;
	31.42	God saw my *a* and the labor of my
Deut	16.	3 the bread of *a* — because you came out
	28.59	your offspring with severe and lasting *a*
Job	30.16	within me; days of *a* have taken hold
Ps	22.24	For he did not despise or abhor the *a* of
	34.19	Many are the *a* of the righteous; but the
Isa	30.20	bread of adversity and the water of *a*,
Lam	3.	1 I am one who has seen *a* under the rod
2 Cor	1.	4 who consoles us in all our *a*, so that we
	6.	4 way: through great endurance, in *a*,
	7.	4 consolation; I am overjoyed in all our *a*.
Col	1.24	completing what is lacking in Christ's *a*
Rev	2.	9 "I know your *a* and your poverty, even

AFFORD

Lev	27.	8 to what each one making a vow can *a*.

AFRAID

Gen	3.10	I was *a*, because I was naked; and I hid
	32.	7 Then Jacob was greatly *a* and

Gen	43.18	Now the men were *a* because they were
Ex	2.14	Then Moses was *a* and thought, "Surely
	3.	6 his face, for he was *a* to look at God.
	14.13	"Do not be *a*, stand firm, and see the
Num	12.	8 Why then were you not *a* to speak
Deut	13.11	Then all Israel shall hear and be *a*, and
	17.13	All the people shall hear and be *a*, and
1 Sam	18.12	Saul was *a* of David, because the Lord
2 Sam	1.14	"Were you not *a* to lift your hand to
2 Kings	25.24	Do not be *a* because of the Chaldean
1 Chr	13.12	David was *a* of God that day; he said,
2 Chr	20.	3 Jehoshaphat was *a*; he set himself to
Ezra	4.	4 of Judah, and made them *a* to build,
Ps	3.	6 I am not *a* of ten thousands of people
	27.	1 of my life; of whom shall I be *a*?
	56.	3 when I am *a*, I put my trust in you.
	119.120	of you, and I am *a* of your judgments.
Isa	10.24	do not be *a* of the Assyrians when they
	12.	2 salvation; I will trust, and will not be *a*,
	41.10	do not be *a*, for I am your God; I will
Jer	36.24	was *a*, nor did they tear their garments.
Zeph	3.13	down, and no one shall make them *a*.
Zech	8.13	Do not be *a*, but let your hands be
Mt	1.20	do not be *a* to take Mary as your wife,
	10.31	So do not be *a*; you are of more value
	28.	5 angel said to the women, "Do not be *a*;
Mk	6.50	said, "Take heart, it is I; do not be *a*."
	11.18	to kill him; for they were *a* of him,
Lk	19.21	for I was *a* of you, because you are a
Jn	9.22	this because they were *a* of the Jews;
	12.15	"Do not be *a*, daughter of Zion. Look,
	14.27	be troubled, and do not let them be *a*.
	19.	8 when Pilate heard this, he was more *a*
Acts	9.26	disciples; and they were all *a* of him,
	27.24	'Do not be *a*, Paul; you must stand
Heb	11.23	and they were not *a* of the king's edict.

AFFRONT

Prov	17.	9 who forgives an *a* fosters friendship,

AGE (AGES)

Prov	8.23	*A* ago I was set up, at the first, before
Mt	13.40	fire, so it will be at the end of the *a*.

AGED

Job	12.12	Is wisdom with the *a*, and
	15.10	gray-haired and the *a* are on our side,
	29.	8 withdrew, and the *a* rose up and stood;

AGITATED

Mk	14.33	John, and began to be distressed and *a*.

AGONY

Isa	13.	8 Pangs and *a* will seize them; they will

AGREE (AGREED)

Gen	23.16	Abraham *a* with Ephron; and Abraham
Dan	1.14	So he *a* to this proposal and tested
Mt	18.19	if two of you *a* on earth about anything
	20.13	did you not *a* with me for the usual
Mk	14.56	him, and their testimony did not *a*.
Acts	5.	9 you have *a* together to put the Spirit of
Rom	7.16	I do not want, I *a* that the law is good.

AGREEABLE

Lev	10.19	would it have been *a* to the Lord?

AGREEMENT

Isa	28.15	death, and with Sheol we have an *a*;
2 Cor	6.15	What *a* does Christ have with Belial? Or
	6.16	What *a* has the temple of God with

AGRIPPA

Acts	25.13	King *A* and Bernice arrived at Caesarea
	26.	1 *A* said to Paul, "You have permission to
	26.27	King *A*, do you believe the prophets? I

AH

Isa	5.	8 *A*, you who join house to house, who

Isa 5.11 *A*, you who rise early in the morning in

AHAB
1 Kings 16.28 in Samaria; his son *A* succeeded him.
17. 1 Elijah . . . said to *A*, "As the LORD the
18.17 When *A* saw Elijah, *A* said to him, "Is it
21. 2 And *A* said to Naboth, "Give me your
21.29 you seen how *A* has humbled himself
Jer 29.22 make you like Zedekiah and *A*, whom

AI
Gen 12. 8 tent, with Bethel on the west and *A* on
13. 3 at the beginning, between Bethel and *A*,
Josh 7. 2 sent men from Jericho to *A*, which is
8. 1 go up now to *A*. See, I have handed

AID
Ps 22.19 away! O my help, come quickly to my *a*!

AILMENT
Lk 13.12 "Woman, you are set free from your *a*."

AIM
2 Tim 3.10 my teaching, my conduct, my *a* in life,

ALARM (ALARMED)
Num 10. 5 When you blow an *a*, the camps on the
Ps 31.22 I had said in my *a*, "I am driven far
Mk 13. 7 wars and rumors of wars, do not be *a*;

ALERT
Lk 12.37 the master finds *a* when he comes;
21.36 Be *a* at all times, praying that you may
1 Cor 16.13 Keep *a*, stand firm in your faith, be
Col 4. 2 yourselves to prayer, keeping *a* in it

ALEXANDRIA (ALEXANRIAN)
Acts 18.24 a Jew named Apollos, a native of *A*,
27. 6 *A* ship bound for Italy, and put us on
28.11 an *A* ship with the Twin Brothers as its

ALIEN (ALIENS)
Gen 12.10 down to Egypt to reside there as an *a*,
19. 9 " This fellow came here as an *a*, and he
Ex 23. 9 You shall not oppress a resident *a*; you
Lev 19.10 shall leave them for the poor and the *a*:
19.34 You shall love the *a* as yourself, for you
23.22 shall leave them for the poor and the *a*:
24.22 one law for the *a* and for the citizen;
Num 15.16 You and the *a* who resides with you
Deut 24.17 You shall not deprive a resident *a* or an
1 Chr 29.15 we are *a* and transients before you, as
Ps 39.12 I am your passing guest, an *a*, like all
105. 23 Jacob lived as an *a* in the land of Ham.
119. 19 I live as an *a* in the land; do not hide
Isa 1. 7 your very presence *a* devour your land;
Jer 51.51 *a* have come into the holy places of the
Zech 7.10 oppress the widow, the orphan, the *a*,
1 Pet 2.11 Beloved, I urge you as *a* and exiles to

ALIVE
Deut 4. 4 to the LORD your God are all *a* today.
Lk 15.24 son of mine was dead and is *a* again;
Acts 25.19 died, but whom Paul asserted to be *a*.
Rom 6.11 dead to sin and *a* to God in Christ
1 Cor 15.22 Adam, so all will be made *a* in Christ.
Eph 2. 5 made us *a* together with Christ—

ALL
1 Chr 29.14 For *a* things come from you, and of
1 Cor 13. 3 If I give away *a* my possessions, and if I
Heb 7.25 he is able for *a* time to save those

ALLEGORY (ALLEGORIES)
Ezek 17. 2 propound a riddle, and speak an *a* to
20.49 saying of me, 'Is he not a maker of *a*?' "
24. 3 And utter an *a* to the rebellious house
Gal 4.24 this is an *a*; these women are two

ALLIANCE
1 Kings 15.19 "Let there be an *a* between me and you,

ALLIED
Isa 7. 2 that Aram had *a* itself with Ephraim,

ALLOTMENT
Num 18.20 Aaron: You shall have no *a* in their

ALLY
Prov 18.19 An *a* offended is stronger than a city;

ALMIGHTY
Gen 17. 1 "I am God *A*; walk before me, and be
48. 3 "God *A* appeared to me at Luz in the
Isa 13. 6 it will come like destruction from the *A*!
Rev 19. 6 For the Lord our God the *A* reigns.

ALMOND (ALMONDS)
Num 17. 8 produced blossoms, and bore ripe *a*.
Eccl 12. 5 the *a* tree blossoms, the grasshopper
Jer 1.11 And I said, "I see a branch of an *a* tree."

ALMS
Mt 6. 2 So whenever you give *a*, do not sound a
Lk 11.41 give for *a* those things that are within;
Acts 10. 4 your *a* have ascended as a memorial

ALONE
Gen 2.18 not good that the man should be *a*; I
Job 7.19 me for a while, let me *a* till I swallow
Lk 18.19 me good? No one is good but God *a*.
Jn 16.32 will leave me *a*. Yet I am not *a* because
Jas 2.24 is justified by works and not by faith *a*.

ALTAR (ALTARS)
Gen 8.20 Then Noah built an *a* to the LORD, and
12. 7 So he built there an *a* to the LORD, who
13.18 and there he built an *a* to the LORD.
22. 9 Abraham built an *a* there and laid the
26.25 So he built an *a* there, called on the
33.20 There he erected an *a* and called it
35. 1 Make an *a* there to the God who
Ex 17.15 And Moses built an *a* and called it, The
27. 1 You shall make the *a* of acacia wood,
30. 1 make an *a* on which to offer incense;
38. 1 He made the *a* of burnt offering also of
Deut 7. 5 deal with them: break down their *a*,
12. 3 Break down their *a*, smash their pillars,
12.27 and the blood, on the *a* of the LORD
27. 5 you shall build an *a* there to the LORD
Josh 8.30 Joshua built on Mount Ebal an *a* to the
22.11 had built an *a* at the frontier of the
22.23 building an *a* to turn away from
1 Sam 14.35 Saul built an *a* to the LORD; it was the
1 Kings 1.50 and went to grasp the horns of the *a*.
18.30 he repaired the *a* of the LORD that had
2 Kings 16.10 he saw the *a* that was at Damascus.
21. 3 he erected a for Baal, made a sacred
2 Chr 4. 1 He made an *a* of bronze, twenty cubits
Ps 43. 4 Then I will go to the *a* of God, to God
Isa 6. 6 coal that had been taken from the *a*
19.19 an *a* to the LORD in the center of the
Ezek 43.13 are the dimensions of the *a* by cubits
Am 9. 1 I saw the LORD standing beside the *a*,
Mt 5.23 when you are offering your gift at the *a*,
Acts 17.23 an *a* with the inscription, 'To an
Heb 13.10 We have an *a* from which those who

AMALEK (AMALEKITES)
Ex 17.13 And Joshua defeated *A* and his people
Num 24.20 "First among the nations was *A*, but its
1 Sam 15. 2 "I will punish the *A* for what they did in
15.32 "Bring Agag king of the *A* here to me."
1 Chr 4.43 they destroyed the remnant of the *A*

AMAZED (AMAZING)
Isa 29.14 will again do *a* things with this people,
Mt 8.10 When Jesus heard him, he was *a* and

Mt	8.27 they were *a*, saying, "What sort of man
	9.33 mute spoke; and the crowds were *a* and
	22.22 When they heard this, they were *a*; and
Mk	5.20 had done for him; and everyone was *a*
	6. 6 And he was *a* at their unbelief. Then he
	12.17 God's." And they were utterly *a* at him.
	15. 5 no further reply, so that Pilate was *a*.
Lk	2.18 all who heard it were *a* at what the
	7. 9 When Jesus heard this he was *a* at him,
Acts	2.12 All were *a* and perplexed, saying to one
	4.13 they were *a* and they recognized them
	8.13 Philip and was *a* when he saw the signs
Rev	15. 3 "Great and *a* are your deeds, Lord God
	17. 7 angel said to me, "Why are you so *a*?

AMAZEMENT

Gen	43.33 the men looked at one another in *a*.
Mk	5.42 At this they were overcome with *a*.

AMBASSADOR (AMBASSADORS)

Isa	18. 2 sending *a* by the Nile in vessels of
Ezek	17.15 against him by sending *a* to Egypt,
2 Cor	5.20 So we are *a* for Christ, since God is
Eph	6.20 of the gospel, I am an *a* in chains.

AMBUSH

Josh	8. 9 they went to the place of *a*, and lay
2 Chr	20.22 the LORD set an *a* against the

AMEN

Ps	41.13 from everlasting to everlasting. *A* and *A*.
1 Cor	14.16 in the position of an outsider say the "*A*"
Rev	3.14 "The words of the *A*, the faithful and

AMEND

Jer	7. 3 *A* your ways and your doings, and let
	26.13 Now therefore *a* your ways and your

AMMONITES

Gen	19.38 Ben-ammi; he is the ancestor of the *A*
Deut	2.19 you approach the frontier of the *A*,
1 Sam	11.11 and cut down the *A* until the heat of
2 Chr	26. 8 *A* paid tribute to Uzziah, and his fame
Isa	11.14 and Moab, and the *A* shall obey them.

AMOS

Am	1. 1 The words of *A*, who was among the
	7.10 "*A* has conspired against you in the very
	7.14 *A* answered Amaziah, "I am no prophet,
	8. 2 fruit. He said, "*A*, what do you see?"

ANATHOTH

Josh	21.18 *A* with its pasture lands, and Almon
1 Kings	2.26 "Go to *A*, to your estate; for you deserve
Isa	10.30 Listen, O Laishah! Answer her, O *A*!
Jer	1. 1 of the priests who were in *A* in the land
	29.27 have you not rebuked Jeremiah of *A*
	32. 7 "Buy my field that is at *A*, for the right

ANCESTOR (ANCESTORS)

Gen	17. 5 you the *a* of a multitude of nations.
1 Chr	5.25 transgressed against the God of their *a*,
Ps	44. 1 our *a* have told us, what deeds you
Rom	4.11 was to make him the *a* of all who

ANCESTRAL

1 Kings 21. 3 that I should give you my *a* inheritance."

ANDREW

Mt	4.18 Peter, and *A* his brother, casting a net
	10. 2 also known as Peter, and his brother *A*;
Mk	13. 3 James, John and *A* asked him privately,
Jn	1.40 speak and followed him, was *A*, Simon
	6. 8 disciples, *A*, Simon Peter's brother, said
	12.22 and told *A*; then *A* and Philip went
Acts	1.13 Peter, and John, and James, and *A*,

ANGEL

Gen	21.17 the *a* of God called to Hagar from

Gen	24. 7 he will send his *a* before you, and you
Ex	23.20 I am going to send an *a* in front of you,
	33. 2 I will send an *a* before you, and I will
Num	20.16 voice, and sent an *a* and brought us out
1 Sam	29. 9 blameless in my sight as an *a* of God;
2 Sam	14.17 my lord the king is like the *a* of God,
	19.27 my lord the king is like the *a* of God;
1 Kings 13.18 an *a* spoke to me by the word of the
	19. 5 an *a* touched him, and said to him,
Dan	3.28 who has sent his *a* and delivered his
	6.22 sent his *a* and shut the lions' mouths
Hos	12. 4 He strove with the *a* and prevailed, he
Zech	1. 9 a who talked with me said to me, "I will
Lk	1.30 The *a* said to her, "Do not be afraid,
	22.43 an *a* from heaven appeared to him and
Jn	12.29 Others said, "An *a* has spoken to him."
Acts	6.15 that his face was like the face of an *a*.
	7.30 an *a* appeared to him in the wilderness
	10. 3 in which he clearly saw an *a* of God
	23. 8 there is no resurrection, or *a*, or spirit;
	27.23 stood by me an *a* of the God to whom I
2 Cor	11.14 wonder! Satan disguises himself as an *a*
Gal	1. 8 even if we or an *a* from heaven should
Rev	3. 7 to the *a* of the church in Philadelphia
	10. 1 another mighty *a* coming down from
	18.21 a mighty *a* took up a stone like a great
	19.17 I saw an *a* standing in the sun, and
	22.16 "It is I, Jesus, who sent my *a* to you

ANGELS

Gen	19. 1 The two *a* came to Sodom in the
	19.15 the *a* urged Lot, saying, "Get up, take
	28.12 the *a* of God were ascending and
	32. 1 on his way and the *a* of God met him;
Ps	78.25 Mortals ate of the bread of *a*; he sent
	91.11 he will command his *a* concerning you
	103. 20 Bless the LORD, O you his *a*, you
	148. 2 Praise him, all his *a*; praise him, all his
Mt	4. 6 'He will command his *a* concerning
	4.11 suddenly *a* came and waited on him.
	13.39 end of the age, and the reapers are *a*.
	18.10 in heaven their *a* continually see the
	24.31 he will send out his *a* with a loud
Mk	1.13 wild beasts; and the *a* waited on him.
Lk	4.10 will command his *a* concerning you,
	9.26 glory of the Father and of the holy *a*,
	12. 9 others will be denied before the *a*
	15.10 joy in the presence of the *a* of God over
Jn	1.51 opened and the *a* of God ascending
	20.12 the tomb and she saw two *a* in white,
Acts	7.53 law as ordained by *a*, and yet you have
Rom	8.38 death, nor life, nor *a*, nor rulers, nor
1 Cor	4. 9 become a spectacle to the world, to *a*
	6. 3 Do you not know that we are to judge *a*
	11.10 authority on her head, because of the *a*.
	13. 1 in the tongues of mortals and of *a*,
Col	2.18 on self-abasement and worship of *a*,
Heb	2. 7 them for a little while lower than the *a*;
1 Pet	1.12 into which *a* long to look!
2 Pet	2. 4 if God did not spare the *a* when they
Jude	6 the *a* who did not keep their own
Rev	7. 1 I saw four *a* standing at the four corners
	9.14 "Release the four *a* who are bound at

ANGEL OF THE LORD

Gen	16. 7 The *a* found her by a spring of water in
	22.11 the *a* called to him from heaven, and
Ex	3. 2 There the *a* appeared to him in a flame
Num	22.23 The donkey saw the *a* standing in the
	22.31 of Balaam, and he saw the *a* standing
Judg	6.11 *a* came and sat under the oak at
	13. 3 the *a* appeared to the woman and said
2 Kings	1. 3 *a* said to Elijah the Tishbite, "Get
	19.35 That very night the *a* set out and struck
1 Chr	21.16 The *a* was then standing by the
Ps	34. 7 The *a* encamps around those who fear
Isa	37.36 Then the *a* set out and struck down one

Mt	1.20 an *a* appeared to him in a dream,
	28. 2 for an *a*, descending from heaven, came
Lk	1.11 there appeared to him an *a*, standing at
	2. 9 an *a* stood before them, and the glory
Jn	5. 4 for an *a* went down at certain seasons
Acts	5.19 the night an *a* opened the prison doors,
	8.26 an *a* said to Philip, "Get up and go
	12. 7 *a* appeared and a light shone in the

ANGER (ANGERED)

Gen	27.45 until your brother's *a* against you turns
Ex	4.14 Then the *a* of the LORD was kindled
	32.19 dancing, Moses' *a* burned hot, and he
Num	11. 1 the LORD heard it and his *a* was kindled.
	12. 9 the *a* of the LORD was kindled against
	22.22 God's *a* was kindled because he was
	25. 4 in order that the fierce *a* of the LORD
	32.14 the LORD's fierce *a* against Israel!
Judg	8. 3 said this, their *a* against him subsided.
	10. 7 *a* of the LORD was kindled against Israel,
1 Sam	20.30 Then Saul's *a* was kindled against
2 Sam	24. 1 the *a* of the LORD was kindled against
1 Kings	15.30 because of the *a* to which he provoked
1 Chr	13.10 *a* of the LORD was kindled against
Ezra	5.12 because our ancestors had *a* the God
Job	20.23 God will send his fierce *a* into them,
Ps	69.24 and let your burning *a* overtake them.
	78.31 the *a* of God rose against them and he
	103. 8 and gracious, slow to *a* and abounding
	106. 32 They *a* the LORD at the waters of
Prov	14.29 is slow to *a* has great understanding,
	15.18 who are slow to *a* calm contention.
	16.32 One who is slow to *a* is better than the
	19.12 A king's *a* is like the growling of a lion,
	20. 2 dread *a* of a king is like the growling
	21.14 A gift in secret averts *a*; and a
Eccl	7. 9 Do not be quick to *a*, for *a* lodges in
Isa	5.25 the *a* of the LORD was kindled against
	9.21 his *a* has not turned away; and his hand
	10. 5 Ah, Assyria, the rod of my *a* — the club
	42.25 poured upon them the heat of his *a* and
Jer	4. 8 "The fierce *a* of the LORD has not turned
	23.20 *a* of the LORD will not turn back until
Lam	2. 1 How the Lord in his *a* has humiliated
	2.22 and on the day of the *a* of the LORD no
Dan	9.16 let your *a* and wrath, we pray, turn
Hos	8. 5 rejected, O Samaria. My *a* burns against
	11. 9 I will not execute my fierce *a*; I will not
Nah	1. 3 The LORD is slow to *a* but great in
	1. 6 Who can endure the heat of his *a*? His
Mk	3. 5 He looked around at them with *a*, he

ANGRY

Gen	30. 2 Jacob became very *a* with Rachel and
	44.18 do not be *a* with your servant; for you
Lev	10.16 He was *a* with Eleazar and Ithamar,
Deut	1.37 Even with me the LORD was *a* on your
2 Sam	19.42 Why then are you *a* over this matter?
2 Kings	5.11 Naaman became *a* and went away,
2 Chr	16.10 Asa was *a* with the seer, and put him in
	25.15 LORD was *a* with Amaziah and sent him
Ps	4. 4 When you are *a*, do not sin; ponder it
	60. 1 defenses; you have been *a*; now restore
	112. 10 The wicked see it and are *a*; they gnash
Prov	22.14 pit; he with whom the LORD is *a* falls
	25.23 rain, and a backbiting tongue, *a* looks.
Song	1. 6 My mother's sons were *a* with me; they
Jer	3. 5 will he be *a* for ever, will he be
Jon	4. 4 LORD said, "Is it right for you to be *a*?"
Zech	1. 2 LORD was very *a* with your ancestors.
Mt	5.22 if you are *a* with a brother or sister, you
	26. 8 when the disciples saw it, they were *a*
Mk	10.41 began to be *a* with James and John.
Lk	15.28 he became *a* and refused to go in. His
Rom	10.19 with a foolish nation I will make you *a*."
Eph	4.26 Be *a* but do not sin; do not let the sun
Heb	3.10 I was *a* with that generation, and I said,

ANGUISH

Gen	42.21 not listen. That is why this *a* has come
Ps	119.143 Trouble and *a* have come upon me, but
Isa	53.11 his *a* he shall see light; he shall find
Dan	12. 1 There shall be a time of *a*, such as has
Zeph	1.15 a day of wrath, a day of distress and *a*,
Rom	2. 9 There will be *a* and distress for
Lk	22.44 in his *a* he prayed more earnestly, and

ANIMAL (ANIMALS)

Gen	1.25 God made the wild *a* of the earth of
Ex	22.19 "Whoever lies with an *a* shall be put to
Lev	11. 2 all the land *a*, these . . . you may eat.
Deut	7.22 the wild *a* would become too numerous
Job	5.23 field, and the wild *a* shall be at peace
	12. 7 ask the *a*, and they will teach you; the
Ps	49.12 pomp; they are like the *a* that perish.
	104. 20 night, when all the *a* of the forest come
Eccl	3.18 them to show that they are but *a*.
Dan	4.25 your dwelling shall be with the wild *a*.
1 Cor	15.32 hopes I fought with wild *a* at Ephesus?

ANNIHILATE

Deut	20.17 You shall *a* them — the Hittites and the

ANNOUNCED

Gal	4.13 infirmity that I first *a* the gospel to you;

ANNUL (ANNULLED)

Jn	10.35 — and the scripture cannot be *a* —
Gal	3.17 does not *a* a covenant previously

ANOINT (ANOINTED) (v)

Gen	31.13 the God of Bethel, where you *a* a pillar
Ex	28.41 and shall *a* them and ordain them and
	30.26 With it you shall *a* the tent of meeting
	30.30 You shall *a* Aaron and his sons, and
Lev	8.12 oil on Aaron's head, and *a* him, to
Ruth	3. 3 Wash and *a* yourself, and put on your
1 Sam	9.16 you shall *a* him to be ruler over my
	10. 1 "The LORD has *a* you ruler over his
	16. 3 you shall *a* for me the one whom I
	16.12 LORD said, "Rise and *a* him; for this is
1 Kings	1.39 a Solomon. Then they blew the
2 Kings	9. 3 says the LORD: I *a* you king over Israel.'
	11.12 proclaimed him king, and *a* him; they
1 Chr	14. 8 Philistines heard that David had been *a*
	29.22 they *a* him as LORD's prince, and Zadok
Ps	23. 5 you *a* my head with oil, my cup
	45. 7 your God, has *a* you with the oil of
	89.20 servant David; with my holy oil I have *a*
Isa	61. 1 is upon me, because the LORD has *a* me;
Dan	9.24 prophet, and to *a* a most holy place.
Mk	6.13 and *a* with oil many who were sick and
	14. 8 she has *a* my body beforehand for its
	16. 1 spices, so that they might go and *a* him.
Lk	4.18 because he has *a* me to bring good
	7.38 his feet and *a* them with the ointment.
Jn	11. 2 Mary was the one who *a* the Lord with
	12. 3 pure nard, *a* Jesus' feet and wiped them
Acts	4.27 your holy servant Jesus, whom you *a*,
	10.38 how God *a* Jesus of Nazareth with the
2 Cor	1.21 in Christ and has *a* us, by putting his
1 Jn	2.20 But you have been *a* by the Holy One,
Rev	3.18 and salve to *a* your eyes so that you

ANOINTED (ANOINTING) (n and adj)

1 Sam	2.35 go in and out before my *a* one forever.
	16. 6 "Surely the LORD's *a* is now before the
	24.10 against my lord; for he is the LORD's *a*.'
	26. 9 can raise his hand against the LORD's *a*,
	26.16 kept watch over your lord, the LORD's *a*.
2 Sam	1.14 lift your hand to destroy the LORD's *a*?
	22.51 and shows steadfast love to his *a*, to
1 Chr	16.22 "Do not touch my *a* ones; do my
Ps	2. 2 together, against the LORD and his *a*,
	18.50 king, and shows steadfast love to his *a*,
	28. 8 people; he is the saving refuge of his *a*.

Ps	84.	9 O God; look on the face of your *a*.
	105.	15 saying, "Do not touch my *a* ones; do my
	132.	10 not turn away the face of your *a* one.
Isa	45.	1 Thus says the LORD to his *a*, to Cyrus,
Ezek	28.	14 With an *a* cherub as guardian I placed
Dan	9.	25 Jerusalem until the time of an *a* prince,
Hab	3.	13 to save your people, to save your *a*.
Zech	4.	14 the two *a* ones who stand by the Lord
1 Jn	2.	27 the *a* that you received from him abides

ANSWER (n)

Gen	41.	16 I; God will give Pharaoh a favorable *a*."
Job	32.	3 friends because they had found no *a*,
Ps	119.	42 shall have an *a* for those who taunt me,
Prov	15.	1 A soft *a* turns away wrath, but a harsh
	16.	1 the *a* of the tongue is from the LORD.
	18.	13 If one gives *a* before hearing, it is folly
Song	5.	6 him; I called him, but he gave no *a*.
Lk	23.	9 some length, but Jesus gave him no *a*.

ANSWER (ANSWERED ANSWERS)

Gen	35.	3 an altar there to the God who *a* me in
1 Sam	6.	of the LORD, the LORD did not *a* him,
1 Kings	18.24 the god who *a* by fire is indeed God."	
2 Kings	18.36 king's command was, "Do not *a* him."	
Job	9.	14 How then can I *a* him, choosing my
	30.20 I cry to you and you do not *a* me; I	
	31.35 is my signature! let the Almighty *a* me!)	
	33.13 saying 'He will *a* none of my words'?	
	38.	1 the LORD *a* Job out of the whirlwind:
	42.	1 Then Job *a* the LORD; "I know that you
Ps	4.	1 A me when I call, O God of my right!
	20.	1 The LORD *a* you in the day of trouble!
	27.	7 cry aloud, be gracious to me and *a* me!
	81.	7 I *a* you in the secret place of thunder; I
	91.15 When they call to me, I will *a* them; I	
Prov	1.28 they will call upon me, but I will not *a*;	
	26.	4 Do not *a* fools according to their folly,
Isa	30.19 of your cry; when he hears it, he will *a*	
	65.24 Before they call I will *a*, while they are	
Jer	7.13 and when I called you, you did not *a*,	
	33.	3 Call to me and I will *a* you, and will tell
Hos	2.21 I will *a* the heavens and they shall *a* the	
Mic	6.	3 you? In what have I wearied you? *A* me!

ANSWERABLE

1 Cor	11.27 will be *a* for the body and blood	

ANTICHRIST

1 Jn	2.18 As you have heard that *a* is coming, so	
	2.22 This is the *a*, the who denies the Father	
	4.	3 this is the spirit of the *a*, of which you
2 Jn		7 such person is the deceiver and the *a*.

ANTIOCH

Acts	11.19 Phoenicia and Cyprus and *A*, and they	
	11.26 in *A* the disciples were first called	
	13.	1 the church at *A* there were prophets
	13.14 on from Perga and came to *A* of Pisidia.	
	14.19 Jews came there from *A* and Iconium	
	14.26 From there they sailed to *A*, where they	
	15.35 Paul and Barnabas remained in *A*, and	
	18.22 the church, and then went down to *A*.	
Gal	2.11 But when Cephas came to *A*, I opposed	
2 Tim	3.11 the things that happened to me at *A*,	

ANXIETY

Prov	12.25 *A* weighs down the human heart, but a	
2 Cor	11.28 because of my *a* for all the churches.	
1 Pet	5.	7 Cast all your *a* on him, because he

ANXIOUS

1 Cor	7.32 The unmarried man is *a* about the Lord,	

APOLLOS

Acts	18.24 came to Ephesus a Jew named *A*, a	
	19.	1 While *A* was in Corinth, Paul passed
1 Cor	1.12 "I belong to Paul," or "I belong to *A*,"	

1 Cor	3.	4 to Paul," and another, "I belong to *A*,"
	16.12 concerning our brother *A*, I strongly	
Titus	3.13 Zenas the lawyer and *A* on their way,	

APOSTASIES

Jer	2.19 punish you, and your *a* will convict you.	
	14.	7 our *a* indeed are many, and we have

APOSTLE (APOSTLES)

Mk	6.30 The *a* gathered around Jesus, and told	
Lk	9.10 On their return the *a* told Jesus all they	
	22.14 place at the table, and the *a* with him.	
Acts	1.	2 through the Holy Spirit to the *a*
	11.	1 the *a* and the believers who were in
Rom	11.13 then as I am an *a* to the Gentiles,	
1 Cor	1.	1 Paul, called to be an *a* of Christ Jesus
	9.	1 Am I not free? Am I not an *a*? Have I
	12.28 God has appointed in the church first *a*,	
2 Cor	11.	5 in the least inferior to these super-*a*.
Gal	1.	1 Paul an *a*—neither sent by human
Eph		5 now been revealed to his holy *a* and
	4.11 gave were that some should be *a*, some	
1 Tim	1.	1 Paul, an *a* of Christ Jesus by the
2 Tim	1.11 I was appointed a herald and an *a*	
2 Pet	3.	2 Lord and Savior spoken through your *a*.
Jude		17 remember the predictions of the *a* of
Rev	2.	2 who claim to be *a* but are not, and have
	21.14 names of the twelve *a* of the Lamb.	

APOSTLESHIP

Acts	1.25 ministry and *a* from which Judas turned	
Rom	1.	5 whom we have received grace and *a*

APPALLED

Ezra	9.	3 hair from my head and beard, and sat *a*.
Job	17.	8 The upright are *a* at this, and the
Ps	40.15 Let those be *a* because of their shame	

APPEAL (APPEALING)

Mt	26.53 you think that I cannot *a* to my Father,	
Acts	25.11 me over to them. I *a* to the emperor."	
Rom	12.	1 I *a* to you, therefore, brothers and
1 Cor	4.16 I *a* to you, then, be imitators of me.	
2 Cor	5.20 since God making his *a* through us;	
	13.11 Put things in order, listen to my *a*,	
1 Pet	3.21 as an *a* to God for a good conscience,	
2 Cor	10.	1 I myself, Paul, *a* to you by the
Philem		10 I am *a* to you for my child, Onesimus,

APPEAR (APPEARED)

Gen	18.	1 The LORD *a* to Abraham by the oaks of
	26.	2 The LORD *a* to Isaac and said, "Do not
	48.	3 "God Almighty *a* to me at Luz in the
Ex	3.	2 There the angel of the LORD *a* to him in
	16.10 the glory of the LORD *a* in the cloud.	
	23.17 all your males shall *a* before the Lord	
Num	16.19 the glory of the LORD *a* to the whole	
Deut	31.15 the LORD *a* at the tent in a pillar of	
Judg	6.12 angel of the LORD *a* to him and said to	
2 Chr	1.	7 God *a* to Solomon, and said to him,
	7.12 the LORD *a* to Solomon in the night and	
Isa	1.12 When you come to *a* before me, who	
Jer	31.	3 the LORD *a* to him from far away. I have
Mt	24.30 sign of the Son of Man will *a* in heaven,	
Mk	16.9n the week, he *a* first to Mary Magdalene,	
Lk	9.31 They *a* in glory and were speaking of	
	19.11 kingdom of God was to *a* immediately.	
Acts	7.	2 God of glory *a* to our father Abraham
2 Cor	5.10 all of us must *a* before the judgment	
Heb	9.24 itself, now to *a* in the presence of God	
	9.26 he has *a* once for all at the end of the	
	9.28 the sins of many, will *a* a second time,	

APPEARANCE

Mt	23.14n for the sake of *a* you make long prayers;	
Mk	12.40 and for the sake of *a* say long prayers.	

APPEARING

2 Tim 4. 8 also to all who have longed for his *a*.

APPLAUD

Rom 1.32 but even *a* others who practice them.

APPLE (APPLES)

Deut 32.10 him, guarded him as the *a* of his eye.
Ps 17. 8 Guard me as the *a* of the eye; hide me
Prov 7. 2 keep my teachings as the *a* of your eye;
25.11 A word fitly spoken is like *a* of gold in a
Song 2. 3 As an *a* tree among the trees of the
Zech 2. 8 touches you touches the *a* of my eye.

APPLY

Prov 23.12 *A* your mind to instruction and your ear

APPOINT (APPOINTED)

2 Sam 7.10 I will *a* a place for my people Israel and
2 Chr 11.15 and had *a* his own priests for the high
Neh 5.14 I was *a* to be their governor in the land
Job 30.23 death, and to the house *a* for all living.
Ps 7. 6 O my God; you have *a* a judgment.
Jon 4. 6 The Lᴏʀᴅ God *a* a bush, and made it
4. 7 God *a* a worm that attacked the bush,
Mk 3.14 he *a* twelve, whom he also named
Lk 10. 1 this the Lord *a* seventy others and sent
Jn 15.16 I chose you. And I *a* you to go and bear
Acts 3.20 may send the Messiah *a* for you, that is,
2 Tim 1.11 For this gospel I was *a* a herald and an
Heb 1. 2 us by a Son, whom he *a* the heir of all

APPROACH

Jer 30.21 for who would otherwise dare to *a* me?
Ezek 42.13 where the priests who *a* the Lᴏʀᴅ shall
Heb 10.22 let us *a* with a true heart in full

APPROVAL

Rom 13. 3 what is good, and you will receive its *a*;
Heb 11. 2 by faith our ancestors received *a*.

APPROVED (APPROVING)

1 Sam 18. 5 the people, even the servants of Saul, *a*.
Eccl 9. 7 for God has long ago *a* what you do.
Acts 8. 1 Saul *a* of their killing him. That day a
22.20 I myself was standing by, *a* and keeping
2 Tim 2.15 yourself to God as one *a* by him,

AQUILA

Acts 18. 2 There he found a Jew named *A*, a
18.18 Syria, accompanied by Priscilla and *A*.
18.26 when Priscilla and *A* heard him, they
Rom 16. 3 Greet Prisca and *A*, who work with me
1 Cor 16.19 *A* and Prisca, together with the church
2 Tim 4.19 Greet Prisca and *A*, and the household

ARABIA

1 Kings 10.15 and from all the kings of *A* and the
Gal 1.17 but I went away at once into *A*; and
4.25 Hagar is Mount Sinai in *A* and

ARAM (ARAMEANS)

2 Kings 5. 1 of the army of the king of *A*,
6.23 the *A* no longer came raiding into the
Isa 7. 8 the head of *A* is Damascus, and the
Am 9. 7 from Caphtor and the *A* from Kir?

ARARAT

Gen 8. 4 ark came to rest on the mountains of *A*.

ARBITRATE

Mic 4. 3 and shall *a* between strong nations

ARCHANGEL (ARCHANGEL'S)

1 Thess 4.16 with the *a* call, and with the sound of
Jude 9 when the *a* Michael contended with the

ARGUE (ARGUED ARGUES ARGUING)

Isa 3.13 The Lᴏʀᴅ rises to *a* his case; he stands

Job 13. 3 and I desire to *a* my case with God.
40. 2 Anyone who *a* with God must respond."
Prov 25. 9 A your case with your neighbor directly,
Mk 9.33 "What were you *a* about on the way?"
11.31 They *a* with one another, "If we say,
Acts 9.29 He spoke and *a* with the Hellenists; but
17. 2 on three sabbath days *a* with them from
17.17 he *a* in the synagogue with the Jews
18. 4 sabbath he would *a* in the synagogue

ARGUMENT (ARGUMENTS)

2 Cor 10. 4 We destroy *a* and every proud obstacle
Col 2. 4 one may deceive you with plausible *a*.
1 Tim 2. 8 up holy hands without anger or *a*;

ARIMATHEA

Mt 27.57 came a rich man from *A*, named
Jn 19.38 things, Joseph of *A*, who was a disciple

ARISE

Num 10.35 Moses would say, "*A*, O Lᴏʀᴅ, let your
Isa 60. 1 *A*, shine; for your light has come, and

ARK

Gen 6.14 Make yourself an *a* of cypress wood;
8. 4 the *a* came to rest on the mountains of
Ex 25.10 They shall make an *a* of acacia wood;
37. 1 Bezalel made the *a* of acacia wood; it
Num 10.33 with the *a* of the covenant of the Lᴏʀᴅ
Josh 3. 3 "When you see the *a* of the covenant of
6.11 the *a* of the Lᴏʀᴅ went around the city,
Judg 20.27 (for the *a* of the covenant of God was
1 Sam 4. 3 Let us bring the *a* of the covenant of
4.11 The *a* of God was captured; and the two
5. 2 Philistines took the *a* of God and
6.13 they looked up and saw the *a*, they
6.19 when they greeted the *a* of the Lᴏʀᴅ;
14.18 to Ahijah, "Bring the *a* of God here."
2 Sam 6. 2 to bring up from there the *a* of God,
15.24 Levites, carrying the *a* of the covenant
1 Chr 13. 3 let us bring again the *a* of our God to
16. 1 They brought in the *a* of God, and set it
2 Chr 5. 4 came, and the Levites carried the *a*.
Jer 3.16 no more say, "The *a* of the covenant of
Heb 9. 4 of incense and the *a* of the covenant
Rev 11.19 *a* of his covenant was seen within his

ARM (ARMS)

2 Chr 32. 8 With him is an *a* of flesh; but with us is
Job 40. 9 Have you an *a* like God, and can you
Ps 44. 3 nor did their own *a* give them victory;
98. 1 and his holy *a* have gotten him victory.
Isa 40.10 with might, and his *a* rules for him;
Mk 9.36 them; and taking it in his *a*, he said
10.16 he took them up in his *a*, laid his
Jn 12.38 and to whom has the *a* of the Lord

ARMOR

1 Sam 17.38 Saul clothed David with his *a*; he put a
Eph 6.11 Put on the whole *a* of God, so that you

ARMY (ARMIES)

Josh 5.14 as commander of the *a* of the Lᴏʀᴅ I
2 Kings 25. 5 the *a* of the Chaldeans pursued
1 Chr 12.22 there was a great *a*, like an *a* of God.
Ps 27. 3 Though an *a* encamp against me, my
44. 9 us, and have not gone out with our *a*.
Joel 2.25 my great *a*, which I sent against you.

AROMA

2 Cor 2.15 we are the *a* of Christ to God among

AROUSED

Jer 32.31 This city has *a* my anger and wrath,

ARRESTED

Mt 4.12 Jesus heard that John had been *a*,
Mk 1.14 after John was *a*, Jesus came to Galilee,

ARROGANCE
Jas 4.16 you boast in your *a*; all such boasting is

ARROGANT
Ps	36.11 Do not let the foot of the *a* tread on me,
	119.51 The *a* utterly deride me, but I do not
	119.78 Let the *a* be put to shame, because
Prov	16. 5 All those who are *a* are an abomination
Mal	3.15 Now we count the *a* happy; evildoers
1 Cor	4.18 am not coming to you, have become *a*,
	5. 2 And you are *a*! Should you not rather

ARROGANTLY
Dan 8.11 against the prince of the host it acted *a*;

ARROW (ARROWS)
1 Sam	20.20 I will shoot three *a* to the side of it, as
2 Kings	13.17 "The LORD's *a* of victory, the *a* of victory
Job	6. 4 For the *a* of the Almighty are in me; my
Ps	7.13 weapons, making his *a* fiery shafts.
	18.14 he sent out his *a*, and scattered them;
	38. 2 your *a* have sunk into me, and your
	45. 5 Your *a* are sharp in the heart of the
Prov	7.23 the trap until an *a* pierces its entrails.
Isa	5.28 their *a* are sharp, all their bows bent,
Ezek	5.16 deadly *a* of famine, *a* for destruction.

ARTISAN (ARTISANS)
Isa 41. 7 The *a* encourages the goldsmith, and
44.11 and the *a* too are merely human.

ASCEND (ASCENDED ASCENDING)
Judg	13.20 angel of the LORD *a* in the flame of the
Ps	24. 3 Who shall *a* the hill of the LORD? And
	68.18 You *a* the high mount, leading captives
	139. 8 If I *a* to heaven, you are there; if I make
Prov	30. 4 Who has *a* to heaven and come down?
Isa	14.13 "I will *a* to heaven; I will raise my
Jn	3.13 No one has *a* into heaven except the
	6.62 were to see the Son of man *a* to where
	20.17 because I have not yet *a* to the Father.
Rom	10. 6 in your heart, 'Who will *a* into heaven?' "
Eph	4. 9 "He *a*," what does it mean but that he

ASHAMED
Gen	2.25 wife were both naked, and were not *a*.
Ezra	9. 6 "O my God, I am too *a* and embarrassed
Ps	25. 3 be *a* who are wantonly treacherous.
	34. 5 radiant; so your faces shall never be *a*.
Jer	6.15 yet they were not *a*, they did not know
	8.12 they were not at all *a*, they did not
	12.13 shall be *a* of their harvests because of
Mk	8.38 Those who are *a* of me and of my words
Lk	9.26 Those who are *a* of me and of my
Rom	1.16 I am not *a* of the gospel; it is the power
1 Cor	4.14 I am not writing this to make you *a*,
2 Tim	1. 8 Do not be *a*, then, of the testimony
	1.12 But I am not *a*, for I know the one in

ASHER
Gen	30.13 call me happy"; so she named him *A*.
Num	1.13 from *A*, Pagiel son of Ochran;
Deut	33.24 And of *A* he said, Most blessed of sons
Judg	5.17 *A* sat still at the coast of the sea,

ASHES
Gen	18.27 to the Lord, I who am but dust and *a*.
Job	13.12 Your maxims are proverbs of *a*, your
	30.19 and I have become like dust and *a*.

ASIA
Acts	2. 9 Judea and Cappadocia, Pontus and *A*,
	6. 9 those from Cilicia and *A*, stood up and
	16. 6 the Holy Spirit to speak the word in *A*.
	19.10 all the residents of *A*, both Jews and
	19.27 her majesty that brought all *A* and the
Rom	16. 5 was the first convert in *A* for Christ.
1 Cor	16.19 The churches of *A* send greetings.

1 Pet	1. 1 Galatia, Cappadocia, *A*, and Bithynia,
Rev	1. 4 to the seven churches that are in *A*:

ASK (ASKED ASKING)
Ex	11. 2 that every man is to *a* his neighbor
	12.35 They had *a* the Egyptians for jewelry of
1 Sam	1.20 for she said, "I have *a* him of the LORD."
1 Kings	3. 5 God said, "*A* what I should give you."
2 Chr	1. 7 said to him, "*A* what I should give you."
Ps	2. 8 *A* of me, and I will make the nations
	27. 4 One thing I *a* of the LORD, that will I
	106.15 he gave them what they *a*, but sent a
Prov	30. 7 Two things I *a* of you; do not deny
Isa	1.12 who *a* this from your hand? Trample my
	7.11 to Ahaz, saying, *A* a sign of the LORD
	65. 1 be sought out by those who did not *a*,
Jer	50. 5 They shall *a* the way to Zion, with faces
Zech	10. 1 *A* rain from the LORD in the season of
Mt	6. 8 knows what you need before you *a* him.
	7. 7 "*A*, and it will be given you; search, and
	9.38 *a* the Lord of the harvest to send out
	21.22 Whatever you *a* for in prayer with faith,
	27.58 to Pilate and *a* for the body of Jesus;
Mk	6.22 the girl, "*A* me for whatever you wish,
	10.35 you to do for us whatever we *a* of you."
Lk	10. 2 laborers are few; therefore *a* the Lord of
	11. 9 I say to you, *A*, and it will be given you;
	11.13 give the Holy Spirit to those who *a*
	23.52 to Pilate and *a* for the body of Jesus.
Jn	14.13 I will do whatever you *a* in my name, so
	14.16 And I will *a* the Father, and he will give
	15. 7 and my words abide in you, *a* for
	16.24 *A* and you will receive, so that your joy
	17. 9 I am *a* on their behalf; I am not *a* on
	17.15 world, but I *a* that you protect them
	17.20 "I *a* not only on behalf of these, but
Eph	3.20 far more than all that we *a* or
Jas	1. 5 any of you is lacking wisdom, *a* God,
	4. 2 You do not have, because you do not *a*.
1 Jn	3.22 we receive from him whatever we *a*,
	5.14 if we *a* anything according to his will,
	5.16 not a mortal sin, you will *a*, and God

ASLEEP
1 Kings	18.27 or perhaps he is *a* and must be
Mt	8.24 swamped by the waves; but he was *a*.
Mk	4.38 he was in the stern, *a* on the cushion;
	13.36 else he may find you *a* when he comes
Lk	8.23 and while they were sailing he fell *a*. A
Jn	11.11 "Our friend Lazarus has fallen *a*, but I
1 Thess	5. 6 then let us not fall *a* as others do, but

ASSEMBLE (ASSEMBLED)
Gen	49. 2 *A* and hear, O sons of Jacob, listen to
Lev	8. 3 *a* the whole congregation at the
Num	1.18 they *a* the whole congregation together.
1 Kings	8. 1 Solomon *a* the elders of Israel and all
2 Chr	5. 2 Solomon *a* the elders of Israel and all
Neh	9. 1 people of Israel were *a* with fasting and
Isa	45.20 *A* yourselves and come together, draw
Ezek	11.17 and *a* you out of the countries where
	39. 1 to all the wild animals: *A* and come,
1 Cor	5. 4 When you are *a*, and my spirit is

ASSEMBLY
Lev	23.36 it is a solemn *a*; you shall not work at
1 Chr	29.20 David said to the whole *a*, "Bless the
2 Chr	23. 3 the whole *a* made a covenant with the
Ps	7. 7 Let the *a* of the peoples be gathered
	149. 1 song, his praise in the *a* of the faithful.
Joel	2.15 fast; call a solemn *a*; gather the people.
Acts	19.39 it must be settled in the regular *a*.
Heb	12.23 to the *a* of the firstborn who are
Jas	2. 2 and in fine clothes comes into your *a*,

ASSURANCE
Acts 17.31 he has given *a* to all by raising him
Heb 6.11 to realize the full *a* of hope to the very

Heb   11. 1 faith is the *a* of things hoped for, the

ASSYRIA

Gen   2.14 river is Tigris, which flows east of *A*.
2 Kings 15.29 King Tiglath-pileser of *A* came and
       19.20 to me about King Sennacherib of *A*.
Isa   7.18 and for the bee that is in the land of *A*.
Hos   7.11 they call upon Egypt, they go to *A*.
       14. 3 *A* shall not save us; we will not ride

ASTONISHED

2 Chr   7.21 exalted, everyone passing by will be *a*,
Dan   3.24 King Nebuchadnezzar was *a* and rose
Mt   7.28 the crowds were *a* at his teaching.

ASTOUNDED

Lk   4.32 They were *a* at his teaching, because he

ASTRAY

Ps   58. 3 The wicked go *a* from the womb; they
       95.10 "They are a people whose hearts go *a*,
      119. 67 Before I was humbled when I went *a*;
Isa   9.16 those who lead this people led them *a*,
Hos   4.12 a spirit of whoredom has led them *a*,
Mt   24. 5 Messiah,' and they will lead many *a*.
Mk   13. 5 "Beware that no one leads you *a*. Many
Lk   21. 8 "Beware that you are not led *a*; for

ASUNDER

Ps   2. 3 "Let us burst their bonds *a*, and cast

ATHENS (ATHENIANS)

Acts   17.15 conducted Paul brought him as far as *A*;
       17.22 "*A*, I see how extremely religious you
       18. 1 After this Paul left *A* and went to
1 Thess 3. 1 longer, we decided to be left alone in *A*;

ATONE (ATONED)

Prov   16. 6 loyalty and faithfulness iniquity is *a* for,
Dan   9.24 to put an end to sin, and to *a* for

ATONEMENT

Ex   29.36 shall offer a bull as a sin offering for *a*.
       32.30 perhaps I can make *a* for your sin."
Lev   1. 4 shall be acceptable in your behalf as *a*
        8.15 he consecrated it, to make *a* for it.
        9. 7 make *a* for yourself and for the people;
       14.18 priest shall make *a* on his behalf before
       16.34 everlasting statute for you, to make *a*
       17.11 for, as life, it is the blood that makes *a*.
       23.27 of this seventh month is the day of *a*.
Num   16.46 the congregation and make *a* for them.
       31.50 perhaps a for ourselves before the LORD.
2 Chr 29.24 at the altar, to make *a* for all Israel.
Ezek   45.20 so you shall make *a* for the temple.

ATTACK

Isa   7. 1 of Israel went up to *a* Jerusalem,

ATTEND

Jer   9.25 when I will *a* to all those who are

ATTENTION

Acts   18.17 But Gallio paid no *a* to these things.
       27.11 centurion paid more *a* to the pilot and
Heb   2. 1 pay greater *a* to what we have heard,

ATTENTIVE

Neh   1.11 Lord, let your ear be *a* to the prayer of
Prov   4.20 My child, be *a* to my words; incline
        5. 1 My child, be *a* to my wisdom, incline

ATTESTED

Acts   2.22 of Nazareth, a man *a* to you by God
Rom   3.21 been disclosed, and is *a* by the law and
Heb   11. 5 it was *a* before he was taken away that

ATTORNEY

Acts   24. 1 elders and an *a*, a certain Tertullus,

AUTHORITIES

Rom   13. 1 every person be subject to governing *a*;
Titus   3. 1 them to be be subject to rulers and *a*,

AUTHORITY

Isa   9. 6 given to us; *a* rests upon his shoulders;
       22.21 I will commit your *a* to his hand, and
Mt   7.29 taught them as one having *a*, and not
        8. 9 I also am a man under *a*, with soldiers
        9. 6 Son of man has *a* on earth to forgive
       21.23 "By what *a* are you doing these things,
       28.18 "All *a* in heaven and on earth has been
Mk   1.22 he taught them as one having *a*, and
        2.10 Son of Man has *a* on earth to forgive
        3.15 and to have *a* to cast out demons.
       11.28 "By what *a* are you doing these things?
Lk   4. 6 you I will give their glory and all this *a*;
        4.36 with *a* and power he commands the
        5.24 that the Son of Man has *a* on earth
       10.19 I have given you *a* to tread on snakes
       20. 2 by what *a* are you doing these things?
Jn   5.27 has given him *a* to execute judgment,
Acts   9.14 he has *a* from the chief priests to bind
Rom   13. 1 there is no *a* except from God, and
2 Cor 10. 8 if I boast a little too much of our *a*,
Rev   2.26 the end, I will give *a* over the nations,
       12.10 of our God and the *a* of his Messiah,
       13. 2 it his power and his throne and great *a*.

AVARICE

Mk   7.22 adultery, *a*, wickedness, deceit,

AVENGE (AVENGED)

2 Kings 9. 7 that I may *a* on Jezebel the blood
Isa   1.24 my enemies, and *a* myself on my foes!
Joel   3.21 I will *a* their blood, and I will not clear
Rom   12.19 never *a* yourselves, but leave room for
Rev   19. 2 and he has *a* on her the blood of his

AVENGER

Num   35.12 shall be for you a refuge from the *a*,
1 Thess 4. 6 because the Lord is an *a* in all these

AVOID

Prov   4.15 not walk in the way of evildoers. *A* it;
       14.27 so that one may *a* the snares of death.
2 Tim   2.16 *A* such profane chatter, for it will lead
Titus   3. 2 of no one, to *a* quarreling, to be gentle,

AWAKE (AWAKES)

Ps   57. 8 *A*, my soul! *A*, O harp and lyre! I will *a*
       73.20 They are like a dream when one *a*, an
Isa   52. 1 *A*, *a*, put on your strength, O Zion! Put
Mt   24.42 Keep *a* therefore, for you do not know
       25.13 Keep *a* therefore, for you know neither
       26.38 remain here, and stay *a* with me."
       26.42 Stay *a* and pray that you may not come
Mk   14.34 even to death; remain here, and keep *a*."
Rev   16.15 Blessed is the one who stays *a* and is

AWAKEN

Song   8. 4 do not stir up or *a* love until it is ready!
Jn   11.11 asleep, but I am going there to *a* him."

AWARE

1 Pet   2.19 if, being *a* of God, you endure pain

AWE

Ps   33. 8 of the world stand in *a* of him.
      119.161 but my heart stands in *a* of your words.
Mt   9. 8 crowds saw it, they were filled with *a*,

AX (AXES)

2 Kings 6. 5 a log, his *a* head fell into the water;
1 Chr 20. 3 to work with saws and iron picks and *a*.
Ps   74. 5 they hacked the wooden trellis with *a*.
Isa   10.15 Shall the *a* vaunt itself over the one
Mt   3.10 now the *a* is lying at the root of the
Lk   3. 9 Even now the *a* is lying at the root of

AZAZEL

Lev 16. 8 lot for the Lord and the other lot for A.

B

BAAL (BAALS)

Judg 2.13 abandoned the Lord, and worshiped B
6.31 "Will you contend for B? Or will you
10.13 our God and have worshiped the B."
1 Kings 16.31 and went and served B, and worshiped
2 Kings 17.16 all the host of heaven, and served B.
Jer 2. 8 the prophets prophesied by B, and went
Hos 2. 8 her silver and gold that they used for B.

BABEL

Gen 11. 9 Therefore it was called B, because there

BABES (BABIES)

Ps 8. 2 Out of the mouths of b and infants you
Isa 3. 4 princes, and b shall rule over them.
Mt 21.16 of the mouth of infants and nursing b

BABYLON (BABYLONIA)

2 Kings 17.24 king of Assyria brought people from B,
1 Chr 9. 1 Judah was taken into exile in B because
Ezra 1.11 were brought up from B to Jerusalem.
Ps 137. 1 By the rivers of B — there we sat down
Isa 48.20 Go out from B, flee from Chaldea,
Mt 1.11 at the time of the deportation to B.
1 Pet 5.13 Your sister church in B, chosen together
Rev 14. 8 fallen is B the great! She has made all

BACK (BACKS)

Ps 18.40 You have made my enemies turn their b
Isa 38.17 you have cast all my sins behind your b.

BACKSLIDING

Jer 8. 5 away turned away in perpetual b?

BALAAM

Num 22. 5 He sent messengers to B son of Beor at
23. 1 Then B said to Balak, "Build me seven
24. 1 Now B saw that it pleased the Lord to
31. 8 they also slew B the son of Beor with
Mic 6. 5 what B the son of Beor answered him,
2 Pet 2.15 gone astray, following the road of B, son
Rev 2.14 who hold to the teaching of B, who

BALANCE (BALANCES)

Job 6. 2 and all my calamity laid in the b!
Prov 11. 1 A false b is an abomination to the Lord,
Isa 40.12 in scales and the hills in a b?
Ezek 5. 1 and your beard; then take b for
Hos 12. 7 A trader, in whose hands are false b, he

BALDHEAD

2 Kings 2.23 at him, saying, "Go away, b! Go away, b!"

BAND

Jer 9. 2 they are all adulterers, a b of traitors.

BANDIT (BANDITS)

Mk 14.48 clubs to arrest me as though I were a b?
15.27 with him they crucified two b, one of
Jn 18.40 but Barabbas!" Now Barabbas was a b.
2 Cor 11.26 from rivers, danger from b, danger from

BANDS

Lk 2. 7 wrapped him in b of cloth, and laid him

BANISH

Eccl 11.10 B anxiety from your mind, and put away

BANQUET (BANQUETING)

Song 2. 4 He brought me to the b house, and his
Dan 5.10 lords, came into the b hall. The queen
Lk 5.29 Levi gave a great b for him in his house;

BAPTISM (BAPTISMS)

Mt 21.25 Did the b of John come from heaven, or

Mk 10.38 with the b that I am baptized with?"
11.30 Did the b of John come from heaven, or
Lk 3. 3 proclaiming a b of repentance for the
12.50 I have a b with which to be baptized,
20. 4 Did the b of John come from heaven, or
1 Cor 15.29 do who receive b on behalf of the dead?
Eph 4. 5 one Lord, one faith, one b, one God
Col 2.12 when you were buried with him in b,
Heb 6. 2 toward God, with instruction about b,
9.10 only with food and drink and various b,
1 Pet 3.21 b, which then prefigured, now saves

BAPTIZE (BAPTIZED BAPTIZING)

Mt 3. 6 they were b by him in the river Jordan,
3.11 "I b you with water for repentance, but
28.19 b them in the name of the Father
Mk 16.16 The one who believes and is b will be
Lk 3.16 "I b you with water; but one who is
7.29 justice of God, because they had been b
Jn 1.26 John answered them, "I b with water.
3.23 John also was b at Aenon near Salim
4. 1 "Jesus is making and b more disciples
Acts 1. 5 you will be b with the Holy Spirit not
8.12 they were b, both men and women.
8.38 down into the water, and Philip b him.
9.18 restored. Then he got up and was b,
16.15 When she and her household were b,
22.16 Get up and be b, and have your sins
Rom 6. 3 have been b into Christ Jesus were b
1 Cor 1.13 Or were you b in the name of Paul?
1.17 Christ did not send me to b but to
10. 2 all were b into Moses in the cloud and
12.13 Spirit we were all b into one body—
Gal 3.27 b into Christ have clothed yourselves

BAPTIZER

Mk 1. 4 John the b appeared in the wilderness,
6.14 saying, "John the b has been raised

BARABBAS

Mt 27.21 to release for you?" And they said, "B."
Mk 15. 7 a man called B was in prison with the
15.11 to have him release B for them instead.
15.15 satisfy the crowd, released B for them;
Jn 18.40 in reply, "Not this man, but B!" Now B

BAREFOOT

2 Sam 15.30 with his head covered and walking b;
Isa 20. 3 Isaiah has walked naked and b for three

BARNABAS

Benevolent, Acts 4.36-37; introduced Paul to the apostles, Acts 9.26-27; preached at Antioch, Acts 11.22-24; ministered with Paul at Antioch, Acts 11.25-26; took relief offerings to Judea, Acts 11.29-30; accompanied Paul on his first missionary journey, Acts 13.1—14.28; attended the Council of Jerusalem, Acts 15.1-31; separated from Paul, Acts 15.36-41.

BARNS

Prov 3.10 then your b will be filled with plenty,
Mt 6.26 neither sow nor reap nor gather into b,
Lk 12.18 I will pull down my b, and build larger

BARREN

Gen 11.30 Now Sarai was b; she had no child.
29.31 he opened her womb; but Rachel was b.
Judg 13. 2 Manoah; and his wife was b, having
Ps 113. 9 He gives the b woman a home, making
Isa 54. 1 Sing, O b one who did not bear; burst
Lk 1. 7 Elizabeth was b, and both were getting

BARRIERS

Isa 59. 2 your iniquities have been b between you

BARTHOLOMEW

Mt 10. 3 Philip and B; Thomas and Matthew the
Lk 6.14 and John, and Philip, and B, and
Acts 1.13 Philip and Thomas, B and Matthew,

BARUCH

Jer	32.12	I gave the deed of purchase to *B* son of
	36. 4	and *B* wrote on a scroll at Jeremiah's
	36.18	*B* answered them, "He dictated all these
	43. 3	but *B* son of Neraiah is inciting you
	45. 1	the prophet Jeremiah spoke to *B* son of

BASIN

Ex	30.18	You shall make a bronze *b* with a
	38. 8	He made the bronze *b* with its stand of

BASKET (BASKETS)

Ex	2. 3	she got a papyrus *b* for him, and
Jer	24. 1	two *b* of figs placed before the temple
Am	8. 1	God showed me — a *b* of summer fruit.
Mt	13.48	put the good into *b* but threw out the
	14.20	over of the broken pieces, twelve *b* full.
	15.37	the broken pieces left over, seven *b* full.
Mk	8.19	how many *b* full of broken pieces did
Acts	9.25	in the wall, lowering him in a *b*.
2 Cor	11.33	I was let down in a *b* through a window

BATHED (BATHING)

2 Sam	11. 2	that he saw from the roof a woman *b*;
Ezek	16. 9	Then I *b* you with water and washed off

BATHSHEBA

Taken by David, 2 Sam 11.1-5; gave birth to Solomon, 2 Sam 12.24; interceded for Solomon's succession on the throne, 1 Kings 1.15-31; petitioned for Adonijah, 1 Kings 2.12-25.

BATTLE

Num	31. 7	They did *b* against Midian, as the Lord
1 Sam	4.16	"I have just come from the *b*; I fled
1 Kings	8.44	"If you people go out to *b* against their
2 Chr	20.15	for the *b* is not yours but God's.
1 Cor	14. 8	sound, who will get ready for *b*?
Rev	16.14	to assemble them for *b* on the great day

BEAR (BEARS) (n)

1 Sam	17.34	whenever a lion or a *b* came, and took a
2 Kings	2.24	Then two she-*b* came out of the woods
Dan	7. 5	a second one, that looked like a *b*.

BEAR (BEARS BORE) (v)

Gen	4.13	"My punishment is greater than I can *b*!
	43. 9	you, then let me *b* the blame forever.
	44.32	then I shall *b* the blame in the sight of
Ex	28.12	Aaron shall *b* their names before the
	28.30	Aaron shall *b* the judgment of the
Num	18. 1	shall *b* responsibility for the offenses
Esth	8. 6	how can I *b* to see the calamity that is
Ps	55.12	enemies who taunt me — I could *b* that;
	68.19	Blessed be the Lord, who daily *b* us up;
Isa	53.11	and he shall *b* their iniquities.
Jer	44.22	longer *b* the sight of your evil doings,
Gal	6. 2	*B* one another's burdens, and in this
1 Pet	2.24	He himself *b* our sins in his body on

BEAST

Rev	13.11	Then I saw another *b* that rose out of
	17. 8	*b* that you saw was, and is not, and is

BEATINGS

Isa	1. 5	Why do you seek further *b*? Why do you

BEAUTIFUL

Gen	12.11	that you are a woman *b* in appearance;
2 Sam	11. 2	woman bathing; the woman was very *b*.
Esth	2. 7	the girl was fair and *b*, and when her
Ps	48. 2	His holy mountain, *b* in elevation, is
Song	1. 5	I am black and *b*, O daughters of
	6. 4	You are *b* as Tirzah, my love, comely as
Isa	4. 2	day the branch of the Lord shall be *b*
Jer	13.20	flock that was given you, your *b* flock?
Ezek	16.13	You grew exceedingly *b*, fit to be a

BEAUTIFY

Jer	4.30	In vain you *b* yourself. Your lovers

BEAUTY

Ps	27. 4	to behold the *b* of the Lord, and to
	45.11	house, and the king will desire your *b*.
Prov	6.25	Do not desire her *b* in your heart, and
	31.30	Charm is deceitful, and *b* is vain, but a
Ezek	27. 3	Tyre, you have said, "I am perfect in *b*."
	28.17	Your heart was proud because of your *b*;
1 Pet	3. 4	lasting *b* of a gentle and quiet spirit,

BED (BEDS)

Job	7.13	When I say, "My *b* will comfort me, my
Isa	28.20	the *b* is too short to stretch oneself on
Am	6. 4	Alas for those who lie upon *b* of ivory,
Mt	9. 6	"Stand up, take your *b* and go to your
Lk	5.19	him down with his *b* through the tiles

BEE (BEES)

Deut	1.44	out against you and chased you as *b* do.
Judg	14. 8	a swarm of *b* in the body of the lion,
Isa	7.18	for the *b* that is in the land of Assyria.

BEELZEBUL

Mt	12.24	"It is only by *B*, the ruler of demons,
Mk	3.22	"He has *B*, and by the ruler of the

BEER-SHEBA

Gen	21.14	wandered about in the wilderness of *B*.
	21.32	When they had made a covenant at *B*,
	22.19	together to *B*; and Abraham lived at *B*.
	46. 1	and came to *B*, he offered sacrifices to
1 Sam	3.20	all Israel from Dan to *B* knew that
1 Chr	21. 2	number Israel, from *B* to Dan, and bring
Am	5. 5	not enter into Gilgal or cross over to *B*;

BEFITS

Ps	33. 1	O you righteous. Praise *b* the upright.

BEG

Gal	4.12	Friends, I *b* you, become as I am, for I

BEGGAR

Mk	10.46	a blind *b*, was sitting by the roadside.
Jn	9. 8	those who had seen him before as a *b*,

BEGINNING

Gen	1. 1	In the *b* when God created the heavens
Ex	12. 2	shall mark for you the *b* of months;
Ps	111.10	The fear of the Lord is the *b* of wisdom;
Prov	1. 7	The fear of the Lord is the *b* of
	4. 7	The *b* of wisdom is this: Get wisdom,
Mt	24. 8	all this is but the *b* of the birthpangs.
Mk	1. 1	The *b* of the good news of Jesus Christ,
Jn	1. 1	In the *b* was the Word, and the Word

BEGUILING

Rev	2.20	and is teaching and *b* my servants

BEHAVE (BEHAVED BEHAVING)

1 Cor	3. 3	and *b* according to human inclinations?
	7.36	he is not *b* properly toward his fiancee,
2 Cor	1.12	we have *b* in the world with frankness
1 Tim	3.15	ought to *b* in the household of God,

BEHAVIOR

1 Sam	21.13	he changed his *b* before them; he

BEHEADED

Mt	14.10	he sent and had John *b* in the prison.
Mk	6.16	it, he said, "John, whom I *b*, has been

BEHEMOTH

Job	40.15	"Look at *B*, which I made just as I

BEHOLD

Ps	17.15	As for me, I shall *b* your face in
	46. 8	Come, *b* the works of the Lord; see
	97. 6	and all the peoples *b* his glory.

BEINGS

Job	1. 6	One day the heavenly *b* came to present
	38. 7	and all the heavenly *b* shouted for joy?

BELIEVE

Gen	45.26	He was stunned; he could not *b* them.
Ex	4. 5	"so that they may *b* that the LORD, the
2 Chr	20.20	you will be established; *b* his prophets,"
Job	9.16	I do not *b* that he would listen to my
Ps	27.13	I *b* that I shall see the goodness of the
	119. 66	for I *b* in your commandments.
Prov	14.15	The simple *b* everything, but the clever
	26.25	an enemy speaks graciously, do not *b*
Isa	43.10	that you may know and *b* me and
Jer	12. 6	do not *b* them, though they speak
Hab	1. 5	that you would not *b* if you were told.
Mt	9.28	"Do you *b* that I am able to do this?"
	21.25	to us, 'Why then did you not *b* him?'
	27.42	the cross now, and we will *b* in him.
Mk	1.15	near; repent, and *b* in the good news."
	5.36	of the synagogue, "Do not fear, only *b*."
	11.24	ask for in prayer, *b* that you receive it,
	13.21	or 'Look! There he is!' —do not *b* it.
	16.11	had been seen by her, they would not *b*
Lk	1.20	because you did not *b* my words, which
	8.13	no root, they *b* for a while and in a
	8.50	not fear. Only *b*, and she shall be saved."
	20. 5	he will say, 'Why did you not *b* him?'
	22.67	He replied, "If I tell you, you will not *b*;
	24.25	how slow of heart to *b* all that the
Jn	1. 7	light, so that all might *b* through him.
	3.18	who *b* in him are not condemned;
	4.42	we *b*, for we have heard for ourselves,
	5.46	If you believed Moses, you would *b* me,
	6.69	We have come to *b* and know that you
	9.35	he said, "Do you *b* in the Son of man?"
	10.26	but you do not *b*, because you do not
	10.38	though you do not *b* me, *b* the works,
	11.15	glad I was not there, so that you may *b*.
	12.37	in their presence, they did not *b* in him.
	14. 1	be troubled. *B* in God, *b* also in me.
	17.20	on behalf of those who will *b* in me
	19.35	has testified so that you also may *b*.
	20.25	and my hand in his side, I will not *b*."
	20.29	have not seen and yet have come to *b*."
Acts	8.37n	Philip said, "If you *b* with all your heart,
	15.11	we *b* that we will be saved through the
	16.31	"*B* in the Lord Jesus, and you will be
	26.27	King Agrippa, do you *b* the prophets? I
Rom	3.22	faith in Jesus Christ for all who *b*.
	10. 9	and *b* in your heart that God raised him
1 Cor	1.21	our proclamation, to save those who *b*.
Heb	11. 6	approach him must *b* that he exists
1 Jn	5.10	Those who *b* in the Son of God have

BELIEVED (BELIEVES BELIEVING)

Gen	15. 6	And he *b* the LORD; and the LORD
Ex	4.31	The people *b*; and when they heard that
	14.31	*b* in the LORD and in his servant Moses.
Ps	106. 12	Then they *b* his words; they sang his
Isa	53. 1	Who has *b* what we have heard? And to
Mk	9.23	things can be done for the one who *b*."
	16.16n	The one who *b* and is baptized will be
Lk	1.45	blessed is she who *b* that there would
Jn	2.22	they *b* the scripture and the word that
	3.15	up, that whoever *b* in him may have
	4.39	Many Samaritans from that city *b* in
	4.50	The man *b* the word that Jesus spoke to
	4.53	will live." So he himself *b*, along with his
	5.24	anyone who hears my word and *b* him
	7. 5	(For not even his brothers *b* in him.)
	7.31	Yet many in the crowd *b* in him and
	11.45	and had seen what Jesus did, *b* in him.
	20. 8	first, also went in, and he saw and *b*;
Acts	4. 4	many of those who heard the word *b*;
	9.42	throughout Joppa, and many *b* in the
	10.43	everyone who *b* in him receives

Acts	13.12	saw what had happened, he *b*,
	17.12	Many of them therefore *b*, including not
Rom	9.33	whoever *b* in him will not be put to
	10.11	one who *b* in him will be put to shame."
1 Cor	13. 7	It bears all things, *b* all things, hopes
Gal	3. 6	Just as Abraham "*b* God, and it was
Phil	1.29	not only of *b* in Christ, but of suffering
Titus	3. 8	so that those who have *b* in God may
1 Jn	5. 1	who *b* that Jesus is the Christ has been

BELIEVER (BELIEVERS)

Acts	5.14	more than ever *b* were added to the
	9.30	when the *b* learned of it, they brought
	11.21	a great number became *b* and turned to
	11.29	send relief to the *b* living in Judea;
	14. 1	of both Jews and Greeks became *b*.
	15. 3	and brought great joy to all the *b*.
	16. 1	son of a Jewish woman who was a *b*;
	17.34	him and became *b*, including Dionysius
	18. 8	official of the synagogue, became a *b*
1 Cor	6. 6	but a *b* goes to court against a *b*
	8.11	So by your knowledge those weak *b* for
1 Thess	2.13	word, which is also at work in you *b*.
2 Thess	3.15	them as enemies, but warn them as *b*.
1 Jn	2.11	Whoever hates another *b* is in the

BELLY

Gen	3.14	upon your *b* you shall go, and dust shall
Jon	2. 2	me; out of the *b* of Sheol I cried,

BELONG (BELONGED BELONGS)

Ps	82. 8	the earth; for all the nations *b* to you!
Mic	7.14	with your staff, the flock that *b* to you,
Rom	7. 4	you may *b* to another, to him who has
Col	2.20	you live as if you still *b* to the world?

BELOVED

Deut	33.12	The *b* of the LORD rests in safety—the
Neh	13.26	he was *b* by his God, and God made
Ps	127. 2	anxious toil; for he gives sleep to his *b*.
Song	1.14	My *b* is to me a cluster of henna
	2.16	My *b* is mine and I am his; he pastures
	5. 9	What is your *b* more than another's, O
	6. 3	I am my beloved's and my *b* is mine; he
	8. 5	the wilderness, leaning upon her *b*?
Dan	10.11	He said to me, "Daniel, greatly *b*, pay
Mt	3.17	"This is my Son, the *B*, with whom I am
	17. 5	"This is my Son, the *B*; with whom I am
Mk	1.11	"You are my Son, the *B*; with you I am
	9. 7	"This is my Son, the *B*; listen to him."
	12. 6	still one other, a *b* son. Finally he sent
Lk	3.22	"You are my Son, the *B*; with you I am
Rom	9.25	and her who was not *b* I will call '*b*.' "
	11.28	as regards election they are *b*, for the
	16. 8	Greet Ampliatus, my *b* in the Lord.
Eph	1. 6	that he freely bestowed on us in the *B*.
1 Tim	6. 2	by their service are believers and *b*.
2 Pet	1.17	"This is my Son, my *B*, with whom I am
Jude	20	you, *b*, build yourselves up on your

BELTS

Job	12.21	princes, and looses the *b* of the strong.
Isa	11. 5	Righteousness shall be the *b* around his
Mt	3. 4	hair with a leather *b* around his waist,
Mk	6. 8	no bread, no bag, no money in their *b*;
Acts	21.11	us and took Paul's *b*, and bound his

BEND

Phil	2.10	the name of Jesus every knee should *b*,

BENEFICIAL

1 Cor	6.12	lawful for me," but not all things are *b*.
	10.23	are lawful," but not all things are *b*.

BENEFIT (BENEFITS)

Ps	103. 2	my soul, and do not forget all his *b*—
1 Cor	7.35	I say this for your own *b*, not to put any
Gal	5. 2	Christ will be of no *b* to you.

BEN-HADAD I

King of Syria, 1 Kings 15.18; made alliance with Asa, 1 Kings 15.19; ravaged cities in northern Israel, 1 Kings 15.20-21. (See also 2 Chr 16.4.)

BEN-HADAD II

King of Syria, 1 Kings 20.1; besieged Samaria, 1 Kings 20.1; defeated twice by Ahab, 1 Kings 20.2-30; granted conditions of peace, 1 Kings 20.31-34.

BEN-HADAD III

King of Syria, 2 Kings 13.3,24; oppressed cities of Israel, 2 Kings 13.3-13; defeated by Jehoahaz, king of Israel, 2 Kings 13.22-25.

BENJAMIN

Born, Gen 35.16-18; brought to Egypt, Gen 43; accused of theft but interceded for by Judah, Gen 44; blessed by Jacob, Gen 49.27.

Tribe of Benjamin: blessed by Moses, Deut 33.12; allotted its territory, Josh 18.11-28; decimated almost to extinction, Judg 20; rebuilt through new wives and families, Judg 21; Saul, the first king of Israel, and Paul, the apostle, from this tribe, 1 Sam 9.1; Phil 3.5.

BEREAVE (BEREAVED)

Gen	42.36	"I am the one you have b of children:
Jer	15. 7	have b them, I have destroyed my
Hos	9.12	I will b them until no one is left.

BESET

Ps	109. 3	They b me with words of hate, and

BESIDE

Ps	23. 2	pastures; he leads me b still waters;

BESIEGE (BESIEGED)

Deut	20.12	war against you, then you shall b it;
	28.52	It shall b you in all your towns until
2 Chr	6.28	if their enemies b them in any of the
Eccl	9.14	it. A great king came against it and b it,
Isa	1. 8	in a cucumber field, like a b city.
Jer	52. 5	city was b untill the eleventh year of

BEST

Phil	1.10	insight to help you determine what is b,

BESTIR

Ps	35.23	Wake up! B yourself for my defense, for

BESTOWED

Acts	28.10	They b many honors on us, and when
1 Cor	2.12	we may understand the gifts b on us
Eph	1. 6	glorious grace which he freely b on us

BETHANY

Mt	21.17	out of the city to B and lodged there.
	26. 6	while Jesus was at B in the house of
Lk	19.29	come near Bethphage and B, at the
	24.50	led them out as far as B, and lifting up
Jn	11. 1	a certain man was ill, Lazarus of B, the
	12. 1	Jesus came to B, the home of Lazarus,

BETHEL

Gen	12. 8	east of B, and pitched his tent, with B
	28.19	He called that place B; but the name of
	31.13	I am the God of B, where you anointed
Josh	8. 9	ambush, and lay between B and Ai, so
1 Sam	7.16	He went on a circuit year by year to B,
1 Kings	12.29	He set one in B, and the other he put
	13.11	there lived an old prophet in B. One of
Ezra	2.28	Of B and Ai, two hundred twenty-three.
Am	4. 4	Come to B—and transgress; to
	7.10	Then Amaziah, the priest of B, sent to
	7.13	never again prophesy at B, for it is the

BETHLEHEM

Gen	35.19	on the way to Ephrath (that is, B),
Ruth	1.19	until they came to B. When they came

1 Sam	16. 4	the LORD commanded, and came to B.
	17.15	from Saul to his father's sheep at B.
2 Sam	23.16	drew water from the well of B that was
Mic	5. 2	But you, O B of Ephrathah, who are
Mt	2. 1	after Jesus was born in B of Judea, wise
	2. 6	'And you, B, in the land of Judah, are
Lk	2. 4	to the city of David called B, because
Jn	7.42	comes from B, the village where David

BETHSAIDA

Mt	11.21	Woe to you, B! For if the deeds of
Mk	6.45	and go on ahead to the other side, to B,
	8.22	They came to B. Some people brought a
Lk	9.10	withdrew privately to a city called B.

BETRAY (BETRAYED BETRAYING)

Mt	17.22	"The Son of Man is going to be b into
	26.16	to look for an opportunity to b him.
	26.24	that one by whom the Son of man is b!
	26.45	the Son of Man is b into the hands of
	27. 4	"I have sinned in b innocent blood." But
Mk	3.19	and Judas Iscariot, who b him.
	13.12	Brother will b brother to death, and a
	14.11	to look for an opportunity to b him.
	14.18	"Truly I tell you, one of you will b me,
	14.41	the Son of Man is b into the hands of
Lk	21.16	You will be b even by parents and
	22. 4	about how he might b him to them.
Jn	13.11	For he knew who was to b him; for this
	18. 2	Judas, who b him, also knew the place,
1 Cor	11.23	on the night when he was b took a

BETTER

Job	35. 3	How am I b off than if I had sinned?
Eccl	3.12	nothing b for them than to be happy
Phil	2. 3	but in humility regard others b than
Heb	8. 6	he is the mediator of a b covenant,
	9.23	themselves need b sacrifices than these.

BEWARE

Eccl	12.12	Of anything beyond these, my child, b.
Mt	7.15	"B of false prophets, who come to you
	16. 6	out, and b of the yeast of the Pharisees
Mk	8.15	out—b of the yeast of the Pharisees
	12.38	"B of the scribes, who like to walk

BIND (BINDS BOUND)

Gen	44.30	then, as his life is b up in the boy's life,
Job	26. 8	He b up the waters in his thick clouds,
Ps	147. 3	bokenhearted, and b up their wounds.
Prov	6.21	B them upon your heart always; tie
Ezek	34.16	the strayed, and I will b up the injured,
Mt	16.19	whatever you b on earth will be bound
	18.18	whatever you b on earth will be bound
1 Cor	7.27	Are you b to a wife? Do not seek to be

BIRD (BIRDS BIRD'S)

Gen	1.20	let b fly above the earth across the
Deut	22. 6	If you come on a b nest, in any tree or
Ps	11. 1	to me, "Flee like a b to the mountains;
	102. 7	I lie awake; like a lonely b on the
	124. 7	have escaped like a b from the snare
Prov	1.17	the net baited while the b is looking on;
Isa	31. 5	Like b hovering overhead, so the LORD
Jer	12. 9	Are the b of prey all around her? Go,
Am	3. 5	Does a b fall into a snare on the earth,
Mt	8.20	have holes, and b of the air have nests;
	13.32	b of the air come and make nests in its
Mk	4.32	so that the b of the air can make nests
Lk	9.58	and b of the air have nests; but the Son
	13.19	the b of the air made nests in its

BIRTH

Deut	32.18	you forgot the God who gave you b.
Ezek	16. 3	Your origin and your b were in the land
Mt	1.18	Now the b of Jesus the Messiah took

BIRTHRIGHT

Gen	25.31 Jacob said, "First sell me your *b*."
	27.36 He took away my *b*; and look, now he
	43.33 the firstborn according to his *b* and the

BISHOP (BISHOPS)

Phil	1. 1 who are in Philippi, with the *b* and
1 Tim	3. 1 whoever aspires to the office of *b*
Titus	1. 7 a *b*, as God's steward, must be

BIT

2 Kings	19.28 in your nose and my *b* in your mouth,
Isa	37.29 in your nose and my *b* in your mouth;

BITTER

Gen	26.35 they made life *b* for Isaac and Rebekah.
Jer	4.18 This is your doom; how *b* it is! It has
Rev	10. 9 it will be *b* to your stomach, but sweet

BITTERNESS

Num	5.18 shall have the water of *b* that brings the
Job	10. 1 I will speak in the *b* of my soul.
	21.25 Another dies in *b* of soul, never having
Prov	14.10 The heart knows its own *b*, and no

BLACK

Song	1. 5 I am *b* and beautiful, O daughters of

BLAME

Gen	43. 9 you, then let me bear the *b* forever.
	44.32 then I will bear the *b* in the sight of my
2 Cor	8.20 no one should *b* us about this generous

BLAMELESS (BLAMELESSLY)

Gen	6. 9 a righteous man, *b* in his generation;
	17. 1 Almighty; walk before me, and be *b*.
Job	1. 1 That man was *b* and upright, one who
	8.20 God will not reject a *b* person, nor take
	9.20 me; though I am *b*, he would prove
Ps	18.25 loyal; with the *b* you show yourself *b*;
	37.37 Mark the *b*, and behold the upright, for
	119. 1 Happy are those whose way is *b*, who
	119. 80 May my heart be *b* in your statutes, so
Ezek	28.15 You were *b* in your ways from the day
Lk	1. 6 living *b* according to all the
1 Cor	1. 8 that you may be *b* on the day of our
Phil	3. 6 as to righteousness under the law, *b*.

BLASPHEME (BLASPHEMED BLASPHEMES BLASPHEMING)

Lev	24.11 Israelite woman's son *b* the Name in a
Ezek	20.27 In this again your fathers *b* me, by
Mt	9. 3 said to themselves, "This man is *b*."
Mk	3.29 whoever *b* against the Holy Spirit can
Acts	26.11 synagogues I tried to force them to *b*;
Rom	2.24 "The name of God is *b* among the
Rev	13. 6 God, *b* his name and his dwelling,

BLASPHEMER

1 Tim	1.13 though I was formerly a *b*, a persecutor,

BLASPHEMOUS

Acts	6.11 "We have heard him speak *b* words
Rev	13. 1 and on its heads were *b* names.

BLASPHEMY (BLASPHEMIES)

Mt	12.31 every sin and *b*, but *b* against the Spirit
	26.65 witnesses? You have now heard his *b*.
Mk	14.64 have heard his *b*! What is your
Lk	5.21 "Who is this who is speaking *b*? Who
Jn	10.33 we are going to stone you, but for *b*;

BLAZING

Deut	4.11 while the mountain was *b* up to the

BLEMISH

Lev	21.18 no one who has a *b* shall draw near,
Num	19. 2 without defect, in which there is no *b*
	28. 3 two male lambs a year old without *b*,

2 Sam	14.25 of his head there was no *b* in him;

BLESS (BLESSING) (v)

Gen	12. 2 and I will *b* you, and make your name
	22.17 I will indeed *b* you, and I will make you
	27. 4 to eat, so that I may *b* you before I die."
	32.26 I will not let you go, unless you *b* me."
	49.25 by the Almighty who will *b* you with
Num	6.24 The LORD *b* you and keep you;
Deut	7.13 he will love you, *b* you, and multiply
Judg	5. 2 offer themselves willingly— *b* the LORD!
Ruth	2. 4 you." They answered, "The LORD *b* you."
1 Chr	4.10 "Oh that you would *b* me and enlarge
	17.27 please you to *b* the house of your
Neh	9. 5 "Stand up and *b* the LORD your God
Ps	29.11 May the LORD *b* his people with peace!
	34. 1 I will *b* the LORD at all times; his praise
	66. 8 *B* our God, O peoples, let the sound of
	103. 1 *B* the LORD, O my soul; and all that is
Hag	2.19 nothing? From this day on I will *b* you.
Lk	24.53 were continually in the temple *b* God.
Rom	12.14 *B* those who persecute you; *b* and do
1 Cor	4.12 When reviled, we *b*; when persecuted,
Heb	6.14 himself, saying, "I will surely *b* you and

BLESSED (v and adj)

Gen	1.22 And God *b* them, saying, "Be fruitful
	9. 1 God *b* Noah and his sons, and said to
	18.18 nations of the earth shall be *b* in him?
	24. 1 and the LORD had *b* Abraham in all
	24.27 he said, "*B* be the LORD, the God of my
	27.29 and *b* be everyone who blesses you!"
	39. 5 the LORD *b* the Egyptian's house for
	47. 7 before Pharaoh, and Jacob *b* Pharaoh.
Num	22.12 not curse the people, for they are *b*."
	23.20 a command to bless; he has *b*, and I
	24. 9 *B* is everyone who blesses you, and
Deut	33. 1 with Moses the man of God *b* the
Josh	17.14 people, whom all along the LORD *b*?"
Judg	5.24 "Most *b* of women be Jael, the wife of
	13.24 The boy grew, and the LORD *b* him.
Ruth	2.19 *B* be the man who took notice of you."
2 Sam	6.11 the LORD *b* Obed-edom and all his
1 Kings	8.56 "*B* be the LORD, who has given rest to
1 Chr	13.14 *b* the household of Obed-edom and all
	16.36 *B* be the LORD, the God of Isreal, from
2 Chr	20.26 of Beracah, for there they *b* the LORD;
Job	1.21 taken away; *b* be the name of the LORD."
	42.12 LORD *b* the latter days of Job more than
Isa	30.18 God of justice; *b* are all those who wait
	61. 9 they are a people whom the LORD has *b*.
Jer	17. 7 *B* are those who trust in the LORD,
Dan	2.19 night, and Daniel *b* the God of heaven.
Mt	5. 3 "*B* are the poor in spirit, for theirs is
	13.16 *b* are your eyes, for they see, and your
	14.19 and *b* and broke the loaves, and gave
	21. 9 *B* is the one who comes in the name of
	24.46 is that slave whom his master will
	25.34 "Come, you that are *b* of my Father,
Mk	10.16 laid his hands on them, and *b* them.
	11. 9 "Hosanna! *B* is the one who comes in
	14.61 the Messiah, the Son of the *B* One?"
Lk	1.42 "*B* are you among women, and *b* is the
	1.68 "*B* be the Lord God of Israel, for he has
	6.20 "*B* are you who are poor, for yours is
	10.23 "*B* are the eyes that see what you see!
	11.27 "*B* is the womb that bore you and the
	12.38 and finds them so, *b* are those slaves!
	13.35 "*B* is the one who comes in the name
	19.38 "*B* is the King who comes in the name
	24.50 and, lifting up his hands, he *b* them.
Jn	13.17 you are *b* if you do them.
	20.29 *B* are those who have not seen and yet
Acts	20.35 said, 'It is more *b* to give than to
Rom	9. 5 Messiah, who is over all, God *b* forever.
1 Cor	7.40 she is more *b* if she remains as she is.
Gal	3. 8 "All the Gentiles shall be *b* in you."

BLESSING

Eph	1. 3 who has *b* us in Christ with every
Jas	5.11 we call *b* those who showed endurance.
1 Pet	3.14 suffer for doing what is right, you are *b*.
Rev	14.13 "Write this: *B* are the dead who from
	22. 7 *B* is the one who keeps the words of
	22.14 *B* are those who wash their robes, so

BLESSING (BLESSINGS)

Gen	22.18 of the earth gain *b* for themselves,
Lev	25.21 I will order my *b* upon you in the sixth
Deut	11.26 I am setting before you today a *b* and a
	23. 5 God turned the curse into a *b* for you,
	27.12 shall stand on Mount Gerizim for the *b*
	28. 2 all these *b* shall come upon you and
Josh	8.34 all the words of the law, *b* and curses,
Ps	21. 3 For you meet him with rich *b*; you set a
Prov	10.22 The *b* of the LORD makes rich, and he
	11.11 By the *b* of the upright a city is exalted,
Isa	19.24 Assyria, a *b* in the midst of the earth,
	65.16 whoever invokes a *b* in the land shall
Ezek	34.26 their season; they shall be showers of *b*.
	44.30 order that a *b* may rest on your house.
Mal	3.10 pour down for you an overflowing *b*.
Rom	15.29 come in the fullness of the *b* of Christ.
1 Cor	10.16 The cup of *b* which we bless, is it not a
Jas	3.10 the same mouth come *b* and cursing.

BLIND (n and adj)

Deut	28.29 at noon as *b* people grope in darkness,
2 Sam	5. 8 to attack the lame and the *b*, those
Job	29.15 I was eyes to the *b*, and feet to those
Ps	146. 8 LORD opens the eyes of the *b*. The LORD
Isa	29.18 darkness the eyes of the *b* shall see.
	35. 5 Then the eyes of the *b* shall be opened,
	42. 7 the nations, to open the eyes that are *b*,
	42.16 I will lead the *b* by a road they do not
	42.19 Who is *b* but my servant, or deaf like
	43. 8 the people who are *b*, yet have eyes,
	56.10 Israel's sentinels are *b*, they are all
	59.10 We grope like the *b* along a wall,
Mal	1. 8 When you offer *b* animals in sacrifice, is
Mt	9.27 two *b* men followed him, crying loudly,
	11. 5 the *b* receive their sight, the lame walk,
	12.22 brought to him a demoniac who was *b*
	15.14 them alone; they are *b* guides of the *b*.
	15.30 the lame, the maimed, the *b*, the mute,
	20.30 two *b* men sitting by the roadside.
	23.16 "Woe to you, *b* guides, who say,
Mk	8.22 Some people brought a *b* man to him
	10.51 And the *b* man said to him, "My
Lk	4.18 and recovering of sight to the *b*,
	6.39 "Can a *b* person guide a *b* person? Will
	7.21 had given sight to many who were *b*.
	14.13 poor, the crippled, the lame, and the *b*,
	18.35 Jericho, a *b* man was sitting by the
Jn	9. 1 along, he saw a man *b* from birth.
	9.20 this is our son, and that he was born *b*;
	9.25 know, that though I was *b*, now I see."
	9.39 and those who do see may become *b*."
	10.21 Can a demon open the eyes of the *b*?"
Rom	2.19 you are a guide to the *b*, a light to
2 Pet	1. 9 lacks these things is nearsighted and *b*,
Rev	3.17 wretched, pitiable, poor, *b*, and naked.

BLIND (BLINDED BLINDS) (v)

Deut	16.19 for a bribe *b* the eyes of the wise and
1 Sam	12. 3 I taken a bribe to *b* my eyes with it?
2 Cor	4. 4 god of this world has *b* the minds of the

BLINDLY

Lam	4.14 *b* they wandered through the streets, so

BLINDNESS

Gen	19.11 they struck with *b* the men who were at
2 Kings	6.18 said, "Strike this people, please, with *b*."
Zech	12. 4 horse with panic, and its rider with *b*.
1 Jn	2.11 because the darkness has brought on *b*.

BLOOD

Gen	4.10 your brother's *b* is crying out to me
	9. 4 not eat flesh with its life, that is, its *b*.
	9. 6 Whoever sheds the *b* of a human, by a
	42.22 now there comes a reckoning for his *b*."
Ex	7.17 in the Nile, and it shall be turned to *b*.
	24. 8 "See the *b* of the covenant that the
	29.12 shall take some of the *b* of the bull and
Lev	16.14 He shall take some of the *b* of the bull,
	17.11 life, it is the *b* that makes atonement.
Deut	12.16 The *b*, however, you must not eat; you
1 Sam	14.32 and the troops ate them with the *b*.
Ps	105. 29 He turned their waters into *b*, and
Ezek	3.18 but their *b* I will require at your hand.
Mt	23.30 in shedding the *b* of the prophets.'
	23.35 from the *b* of righteous Abel to the *b* of
	26.28 this is my *b* of the covenant, which is
	27.24 saying, "I am innocent of this man's *b*;
Mk	14.24 "This is my *b* of the covenant, which is
Lk	11.51 from the *b* of Abel to the *b* of
	22.20 out for you is the new covenant in my *b*
Jn	6.53 of Man and drink his *b*, you have no life
Acts	1.19 Hakeldama, that is, Field of *B*.)
	18. 6 "Your *b* be upon your heads! I am
Rom	5. 9 we have been justified by his *b*, will we
1 Cor	15.50 flesh and *b* cannot inherit the kingdom
Eph	1. 7 we have redemption through his *b*, the
	2.13 been brought near by the *b* of Christ.
Heb	9. 7 and not without taking the *b* that he
	9.12 but his own *b*, thus obtaining eternal
	10.19 to enter the sanctuary by the *b* of Jesus,
	10.29 profaned the *b* of the covenant by
1 Pet	1.19 with the precious *b* of Christ, like that
1 Jn	1. 7 the *b* of Jesus his Son cleanses us from
	5. 6 only but with the water and the *b*.
Rev	7.14 made them white in the *b* of the Lamb.
	11. 6 over the waters to turn them into *b*,
	12.11 conquered him by the *b* of the Lamb
	19. 2 and he has avenged on her the *b* of his

BLOODSHED

Isa	5. 7 he expected justice, but saw *b*;
Jer	48.10 one who keeps back the sword from *b*.

BLOT (BLOTS BLOTTED)

Ex	32.32 if not, *b* me out of the book that you
Deut	9.14 and *b* out their name from under
	25.19 shall *b* out the remembrance of Amalek
	29.20 LORD will *b* out their names from under
2 Kings	14.27 had not said he would *b* out the name
Ps	51. 1 mercy *b* out my transgressions.
	109. 14 not let the sin of his mother be *b* out.
Isa	6. 7 guilt has departed and your sin is *b* out."
	43.25 I am He who *b* out your transgressions
Jer	18.23 do not *b* out their sin from your sight.

BLOW

Num	10. 5 When you *b* an alarm, the camp on the
Song	4.16 O south wind! *B* upon my garden,

BOAST (BOASTING) (n)

Ps	34. 2 My soul makes its *b* in the LORD; let the
Rom	3.27 Then what becomes of *b*? It is
2 Cor	7.14 true, so our *b* to Titus has proved true
	8.24 of your love and of our reason for *b*
	11.10 this *b* of mine shall not be silenced in

BOAST (BOASTED BOASTS) (v)

Ps	10. 3 the wicked *b* of the desires of their
	38.16 rejoice over me, those who *b* against
	44. 8 In God we have *b* continually, and we
Prov	20.14 says the buyer, then goes away and *b*.
	25.14 rain is one who *b* of a gift never given.
	27. 1 Do not *b* about tomorrow, for you do
Jer	9.24 let those who *b* in this, that they
Rom	2.17 the law and *b* of your relation to God
	2.23 You that *b* in the law, do you dishonor

Rom	5. 2 and we *b* in our hope of sharing the
	5.11 we even *b* in God through our Lord
	11.18 do not *b* over the branches. If you do *b*,
1 Cor	1.31 written, "Let one who *b*, *b* in the Lord."
	3.21 So let no one *b* about human leaders.
2 Cor	7. 4 I often *b* about you; I have great pride
	10.17 "Let the one who *b*, *b* in the Lord." For
	11.21 as a fool— I also dare to *b* of that.
Gal	6.14 I never *b* of anything except the cross
Eph	2. 9 result of works, so that no one may *b*.
Jas	1. 9 Let the believer who is lowly in being

BOAT

Mt	4.22 they left the *b* and their father, and
Mk	3. 9 He told his disciples to have a *b* ready
Lk	8.22 day he got into a *b* with his disciples,
Jn	6.21 and immediately the *b* reached the land

BODILY

| Lk | 3.22 Spirit descended on him in *b* form like |
| Col | 2. 9 the whole fullness of deity dwells *b*, |

BODY (BODIES)

Gen	47.18 of my lord but our *b* and our lands.
1 Sam	31.12 took the *b* of Saul and the *b* of his sons
Isa	37.36 morning dawned, they were all dead *b*.
Mt	10.28 Do not fear those who can kill the *b*
	26.26 and said, "Take, eat; this is my *b*."
	27.58 to Pilate and asked for the *b* of Jesus;
Mk	6.29 about it, they came and took his *b*,
	14.22 to them, and said, "Take; this is my *b*."
	15.43 to Pilate and asked for the *b* of Jesus.
Lk	22.19 saying, "This is my *b*, which is given for
Jn	2.21 he was speaking of the temple of his *b*.
Rom	12. 4 as in one *b* we have many members,
1 Cor	6.13 *b* is meant not for fornication but for
	6.15 that your *b* are members of Christ?
	6.19 your *b* is a temple of the Holy Spirit
	12.12 For just as the *b* is one and has many
	12.24 God has so arranged the *b*, giving the
	12.27 Now you are the *b* of Christ and
	15.35 With what kind of *b* do they come?"
Gal	6.17 the marks of Jesus branded on my *b*.
Eph	1.23 the church, which is his *b*, the fullness
	4. 4 There is one *b* and one Spirit, just as
	4.16 the whole *b*, joined and knit together by
	5.30 because we are members of his *b*.
Phil	3.21 transform the *b* of our humiliation that
Col	1.18 He is the head of the *b*, the church; he
	2.19 head, from whom the whole *b*,
Heb	10. 5 but a *b* you have prepared for me;
Jude	9 disputed about the *b* of Moses, he did
Rev	11. 8 dead *b* will lie in the street of the great

BOG

| Ps | 40. 2 from the desolate pit, out of the miry *b*, |

BOIL (v)

| Deut | 14.21 shall not *b* a kid in its mother's milk. |

BOILS (n)

| Ex | 9. 9 shall cause festering *b* on humans and |
| Deut | 28.27 Lord will afflict you with the *b* of Egypt, |

BOLD

| Prov | 21.29 The wicked put on a *b* face, but the |

BOLDNESS

Acts	4.13 when they saw the *b* of Peter and John
	4.29 servants to speak thy word with all *b*,
	28.31 about the Lord Jesus Christ with all *b*
2 Cor	3.12 have such a hope, we act with great *b*,
Eph	3.12 have access to God in *b* and confidence
Phil	1.14 dare to speak the word with greater *b*
1 Jn	4.17 we may have *b* on the day of judgment,
	5.14 this is the *b* we have in him, that if we

BOND (BONDS)

| Ps | 69.33 does not despise his own that are in *b*. |

| Isa | 58. 6 to loose the *b* of injustice, to undo the |
| Eph | 4. 3 the unity of the Spirit in the *b* of peace. |

BONE (BONES)

Gen	50.25 comes to you, you shall carry up my *b*
Ex	13.19 Moses took with him the *b* of Joseph
Num	9.12 of it until morning, nor break a *b* of it;
Josh	24.32 The *b* of Joseph, which the Israelites
2 Kings	13.21 man touched the *b* of Elisha, he came
1 Chr	11. 1 and said, "See, we are your *b* and flesh.
Ps	22.17 I can count all my *b*. They stare and
	34.20 He keeps all their *b*; not one of them
Jer	8. 1 the *b* of the kings of Judah, the *b* of its
Ezek	37. 7 a rattling, and the *b* came together,
Jn	19.36 fulfilled, "None of his *b* shall be broken."

BOOK (BOOKS)

Ex	24. 7 took the *b* of the covenant, and read it
Num	21.14 is said in the *B* of the Wars of the Lord,
Deut	31.26 "Take this *b* of the law and put it
Josh	1. 8 This *b* of the law shall not depart out of
	8.31 is written in the *b* of the law of Moses,
2 Kings	22. 8 I have found the *b* of the law in the
	23. 2 all the words of the *b* of the covenant
2 Chr	34.16 Shaphan brought the *b* to the king, and
Neh	7. 5 I found the *b* of the genealogy of those
	8. 1 Ezra to bring the *b* of the law of Moses
Job	19.23 down! O that they were inscribed in a *b*!
Ps	139. 16 In your *b* were written, all the days that
Eccl	12.12 Of making many *b* there is no end, and
Isa	30. 8 them on a tablet, inscribe it in a *b*,
	34.16 Seek and read from the *b* of the Lord:
Jer	25.13 everything written in this *b*, which
Dan	7.10 in judgment, and the *b* were opened.
	9. 2 perceived in the *b* the number of years
	10.21 you what is inscribed in the *b* of truth.
	12. 1 everyone who is found written in the *b*.
Mal	3.16 a *b* of remembrance was written before
Jn	20.30 are not written in this *b*. But these
	21.25 itself could not contain the *b* that
Acts	19.19 magic collected their *b* and burned
Phil	4. 3 whose names are in the *b* of life.
2 Tim	4.13 also the *b*, and above all the
Rev	1.11 "Write in a *b* what you see and send it
	3. 5 I will not blot your name out of the *b* of
	13. 8 of the world in the *b* of life of the Lamb
	20.12 Also another *b* was opened, the *b* of
	21.27 who are written in the Lamb's *b* of life.

BOOTH (BOOTHS)

Gen	33.17 a house, and made *b* for his cattle;
Lev	23.34 there shall be the festival of *b* to the
	23.42 You shall live in *b* for seven days; all
Deut	16.13 You shall keep the festival of *b* for
Neh	8.14 Israel should live in *b* during the festival
Am	9.11 I will raise up the *b* of David that has
Jon	4. 5 city, and made a *b* for himself there.
Jn	7. 2 Now the Jewish festival of *B* was near

BOOTY

| Num | 31.32 The *b* remaining from the spoil that the |

BORN

1 Kings	13. 2 'A son shall be *b* to the house of David,
Job	14. 1 "A mortal *b* of woman, few of days, and
	25. 4 How can one *b* of woman be pure?
Eccl	3. 2 time to be *b*, and a time to die, a time
Isa	9. 6 For a child has been *b* for us, a son is
Jer	1. 5 before you were *b* I consecrated you;
Mt	1.16 husband of Mary, of whom Jesus was *b*,
	2. 1 after Jesus was *b* in Bethlehem of
	11.11 among those *b* of women no one has
Lk	1.35 child to be *b* will be holy; he will be
Jn	1.13 of God, who were *b*, not of blood or
	3. 5 God without being *b* from above.
	9.34 "You were *b* entirely in sins, and you
	16.21 her child is *b*, she no longer remembers
1 Pet	1.23 You have been *b* anew, not of

BORROW

1 Jn	3.	9 Those who have been *b* of God do not
	5.18	know that those *b* of God do not sin,

BORROW

2 Kings	4.	3 "Go outside, *b* vessels from all your
Ps	37.21	The wicked *b*, and do not pay back, but
Mt	5.42	do not refuse anyone who wants to *b*

BORROWER

Prov	22.	7 and the *b* is the slave of the lender.
Isa	24.	2 as with the lender, so with the *b*; as

BOSOM

Prov	6.27	Can fire be carried in the *b* without
Isa	40.11	in his arms, and carry them in his *b*,
	66.11	deeply with delight from her glorious *b*.

BOTHER (BOTHERING)

Lk	11.	7 "Do not *b* me; the door has already
	18.	5 because this widow keeps *b* me, I will

BOTTLE

Ps	33.	7 gathered the waters of the sea as in a *b*;
	56.	8 of my tossings; put my tears in your *b*.

BOUGH (BOUGHS)

Gen	49.22	Joseph is a fruitful *b*, a fruitful *b* by a
Ezek	31.12	have fallen, and its *b* lie broken in all

BOUNDARY (BOUNDARIES)

Deut	19.14	not remove your neighbor's *b* marker,
	32.	8 he fixed the *b* of the peoples according

BOUNDLESS

Eph	3.	8 to the Gentiles the news of the *b* riches

BOUNDS

Ps	74.17	You have fixed all the *b* of the earth;

BOUNTY

Ps	65.11	You crown the year with your *b*; your
	116.	12 I return to the LORD for all his *b* to me?

BOW (n)

Gen	9.13	I set my *b* in the cloud, and it shall be
	21.20	and became an expert with the *b*.
Ps	44.	6 For not in my *b* do I trust, nor can my
	46.	9 he breaks the *b*, and shatters the spear;
Hos	1.	5 On that day I will break the *b* of Israel

BOW (BOWED BOWING)

Gen	33.	6 they and their children, and *b* down;
	42.	6 Joseph's brothers came and *b*
	43.28	And they *b* their heads and did
	49.	8 your father's sons shall *b* down before
Ex	23.24	you shall not *b* down to their gods, or
Deut	5.	9 You shall not *b* down to them or
	26.10	and *b* down before the LORD your God.
1 Kings	19.18	all the knees that have not *b* to Baal,
2 Kings	4.37	and fell at his feet, *b* to the ground;
Ps	5.	7 I will *b* down toward your holy temple
	81.	9 you shall not *b* down to a foreign god.
	86.	9 you have made shall come and *b* down
Zeph	1.	5 who *b* down on the roofs to the host of
Jn	19.30	Then he *b* his head and gave up his
Rev	3.	9 and *b* down before your feet, and they

BOWL (BOWLS)

2 Kings	2.20	"Bring me a new *b*, and put salt in it."
Mt	26.23	has dipped his hand in the *b* with me,
Rev	16.	1 earth the seven *b* of the wrath of God."

BOY (BOYS)

Gen	44.34	to my father if the *b* is not with me?
	48.16	bless the *b*; and in them let my name
1 Sam	20.21	Then I will send the *b*, saying, 'Go, find
	17.33	to fight against him; for you are just a *b*
2 Kings	5.14	was restored like the flesh of a young *b*,
2 Chr	34.	3 while he was still a *b*, he began to seek
Prov	22.15	Folly is bound up in the heart of a *b*,

Isa	3.	4 I will make *b* their princes, and babes
Jer	1.	6 know how to speak, for I am only a *b*."
Zech	8.	5 city shall be of *b* and girls playing in its
Jn	6.	9 is a *b* here who has five barley loaves

BRANCH (BRANCHES)

Isa	4.	2 day the *b* of the LORD shall be beautiful
	11.	1 and a *b* shall grow out of his roots.
Jer	23.	5 I will raise up for David a righteous *B*,
	33.15	I will cause a righteous *B* to spring up
Zech	3.	8 I am going to bring my servant the *B*.
Mk	11.	8 and others spread leafy *b* that they had
Jn	12.13	So they took *b* of palm trees and went
	15.	2 He removes every *b* in me that bears no
Rom	11.18	do not boast over the *b*. If you do boast,

BREACH

Ps	106.	23 Moses, his chosen one, stood in the *b*
Ezek	22.30	stand in the *b* before me on behalf of

BREAD

Ex	16.	4 I am going to rain *b* from heaven for
Deut	8.	3 one does not live by *b* alone, but by
1 Sam	21.	6 no *b* there except the *b* of the Presence,
Prov	4.17	For they eat the *b* of wickedness and
	22.	9 are blessed, for they share their *b* with
Eccl	11.	1 Send out your *b* upon the waters, for
Isa	3.	1 all support of *b*, and all support of
Jer	37.21	loaf of *b* was given him daily from the
Ezek	4.17	Lacking *b* and water, they will look at
Mt	4.	3 these stones to become loaves of *b*."
	12.	4 of God and ate the *b* of the Presence,
	15.33	"Where are we to get enough *b* in the
	26.26	Jesus took a loaf of *b*, and after
Mk	8.	4 can one feed these people with *b* here
	14.22	he took a loaf of *b*, and after blessing it
Lk	4.	3 this stone to become a loaf of *b*."
	22.19	he took a loaf of *b*, and when he had
	24.30	he took *b*, blessed and broke it, and
Jn	6.32	not Moses who gave you the *b* from
	6.35	"I am the *b* of life; Whoever comes to
	13.26	the one to whom I give this piece of *b*
	21.13	Jesus came and took the *b* and gave it
Acts	20.	7 of the week, when we met to break *b*,
1 Cor	10.16	The *b* that we break, is it not a sharing
	11.23	when he was betrayed took a loaf of *b*,

BREAK (BREAKING BROKE BROKEN)

Gen	17.14	from his people; he has *b* my covenant."
Num	9.12	of it until morning, nor *b* a bone of it;
Deut	7.	5 *b* down their altars, smash their pillars,
Ezra	9.14	shall we *b* your commandments again
Job	16.12	at ease, and he *b* me in two; he seized
	17.11	My days are past, my plans are *b* off,
Ps	34.20	their bones; not one of them will be *b*.
	102.	23 He has *b* my strength in midcourse; he
	119.126	LORD to act, for your law has been *b*.
Prov	18.14	sickness; a *b* spirit—who can bear?
Jer	19.11	So will I *b* this people and this city, as
	33.20	If any of you could *b* my covenant with
Hos	8.	1 have *b* my covenant, and transgressed
Jn	19.33	already dead, they did not *b* his legs.
Acts	21.13	are you doing, weeping and *b* my heart?
Rom	2.27	code and circumcision but *b* the law.

BREASTPLATE

Isa	59.17	He put on righteousness like a *b*, and a
Eph	6.14	and put on the *b* of righteousness.
1 Thess	5.	8 and put on the *b* of faith and love,

BREASTS

Song	4.	5 Your two *b* are like two fawns, twins of
Isa	32.12	Beat upon your *b* for the present fields,

BREATH

Job	32.	8 the *b* of the Almighty, that makes for
Ps	18.15	rebuke, O LORD, at the blast of the *b* of
	33.	6 and all their host by the *b* of his mouth.

Ps	62. 9 Those of low estate are but a *b*, those
	94.11 thoughts, that they are but an empty *b*.
	144. 4 They are like a *b*; their days are like a
	146. 4 their *b* departs they return to the earth;
Eccl	3.19 They all have the same *b*, and humans
	11. 5 as you do not know how the *b* comes
	12. 7 and the *b* returns to God who gave it.
Isa	11. 4 and with the *b* of his lips he shall kill
	40. 7 fades, when the *b* of the LORD blows
Ezek	37. 5 to these bones: I will cause *b* to enter
	37. 9 "Prophesy to the *b*, prophesy, mortal,
Rev	13.15 to give *b* to the image of the beast

BREATHE (BREATHED BREATHES BREATHING)

Gen	2. 7 *b* into his nostrils the breath of life; and
Ps	27.12 against me, and they are *b* out violence.
	150. 6 Let everything that *b* praise the LORD!
Acts	9. 1 Saul, still *b* threats and murder against

BREEZE

| Gen | 3. 8 the garden at the time of the evening *b*, |

BRIBE (BRIBES)

Ex	23. 8 take no *b*, for a *b* blinds the officials,
Deut	16.19 not accept *b*, for a *b* blinds the eyes
1 Sam	8. 3 gain; they took *b* and perverted justice.
	12. 3 from whose hand have I taken a *b* to
Ps	26.10 and whose right hands are full of *b*.
Prov	15.27 but those who hate *b* will live.
	17. 8 A *b* is like a magic stone in the eyes of
Am	5.12 who take a *b*, and push aside the needy
Mic	3.11 Its rulers give judgment for a *b*, its
	7. 3 the official and the judge ask for a *b*,

BRIBERY

| Job | 15.34 and fire consumes the tents of *b*. |

BRICK (BRICKS)

Gen	11. 3 "Come, let us make *b*, and burn them
Ex	5. 7 longer give the people straw to make *b*,
Isa	9.10 "The *b* have fallen, but we will build
Ezek	4. 1 take a *b* and set it before you. On it

BRIDE

Song	4. 9 sister, my *b*, you have ravished my heart
Isa	61.10 garland, and as a *b* adorns herself with
Jer	2.32 forget her ornaments, or a *b* her attire?
	7.34 mirth and gladness, the voice of the *b*
Rev	21. 2 from God, prepared as a *b* adorned for
	21. 9 I will show you the *b*, the wife of the

BRIDEGROOM

Ex	4.26 "Truly you are a *b* of blood to me!"
Ps	19. 5 which comes out like a *b* from his
Mt	9.15 mourn as long as the *b* is with them,
Mk	2.19 cannot fast while the *b* is with them
Lk	5.34 wedding guests fast while the *b* is with
Jn	3.29 The friend of the *b*, who stands and

BRIDESMAIDS

| Mt | 25. 1 Ten *b* took their lamps and went to |

BRIDLE

Ps	32. 9 temper must be curbed with bit and *b*,
Jas	1.26 are religious, and do not *b* their tongues
	3. 2 keep the whole body in check with a *b*.

BRIGHT (BRIGHTER)

Job	11.17 your life will be *b* than the noonday; its
Acts	26.13 a light from heaven, *b* than the sun,
Rev	22.16 of David, the *b* morning star."

BRING (BRINGING BRINGS BROUGHT)

Gen	28.15 will *b* you back to this land; for I will
	45.19 wives, and *b* your father, and come.
Ex	13.11 "When the LORD has *b* you into the land
Num	24. 8 God *b* him out of Egypt, is like the
	27. 5 Moses *b* their case before the LORD.
Job	33.30 to *b* back their soul from the Pit, so

Ps	64. 9 they will tell what God has *b* about,
Isa	49.22 they shall *b* your sons in their bosom,
	52. 7 announces peace, who *b* good news,
	60. 5 abundance of the sea shall be *b* to you,
	61. 1 he has sent me to *b* good news to the
Jer	21. 1 I will *b* them together into the center of
Am	5.25 Did you *b* to me sacrifices and offerings
Nah	1.15 the feet of one who *b* good tidings,
Mal	3.10 B the full tithe into the storehouse, so
Mt	6.13 And do not *b* us to the time of trial, but
	10.34 the earth; I have not come to *b* peace,
Lk	2.10 —I am *b* you good news of great joy for
	4.18 me to *b* good news to the poor.
Jn	1.42 He *b* Simon to Jesus, who looked at
Jas	5.19 from the truth and is *b* back by another,

BROKENHEARTED

| Ps | 34.18 The LORD is near to the *b*, and saves the |
| Isa | 61. 1 to the oppressed, to bind up the *b*, to |

BRONZE

Gen	4.22 who made all kinds of *b* and iron tools.
Num	21. 9 Moses made a serpent of *b*, and put it
Jer	15.20 you to this people a fortified wall of *b*;
Dan	2.32 of silver, its middle and thighs of *b*,

BROOD

| Mt | 23.37 as a hen gathers her *b* under her wings, |
| Lk | 3. 7 "You *b* of vipers! Who warned you to |

BROOKS

| Jer | 31. 9 I will let them walk by *b* of water, in a |

BROTHER (BROTHERS BROTHER'S)

Gen	4. 8 Cain rose up against his *b* Abel, and
	20.16 I have given your *b* a thousand pieces of
	27.45 until your *b* anger against you turns
	37.11 So his *b* were jealous of him, but his
	37.27 lay our hands on him, for he is our *b*,
	45. 4 "I am your *b*, Joseph, whom you sold
	49. 8 Judah, your *b* shall praise you; your
Num	20.14 "Thus says your *b* Israel: You know all
Deut	25. 5 Her husband's *b* shall go in to her,
Judg	9. 5 house at Ophrah, and killed his *b*
1 Sam	17.22 the ranks, and went and greeted his *b*.
1 Kings	2.15 has turned about and become my *b*,
	13.30 mourned over him, saying, "Alas, my *b*!"
	20.32 he said, "Is he still live? He is my *b*."
1 Chr	5. 2 Judah became prominent among his *b*
Ps	22.22 will tell of your name to my *b* and
Mal	1. 2 you loved us?" Is not Esau Jacob's *b*?
Mt	5.22 if you are angry with a *b* or sister, you
	10.21 B will betray *b* to death, and a father
	12.46 his mother and his *b* were standing
	12.50 the will of my Father in heaven is my *b*,
	13.55 are not his *b* James and Joseph and
	20.24 it, they were angry with the two *b*.
	28.10 go and tell my *b* to go to Galilee; there
Mk	3.35 does the will of God is my *b* and sister
	12.19 widow and raise up children for his *b*.
	13.12 B will betray *b* to death, and a father
Lk	8.20 mother and your *b* are standing outside,
Jn	7. 5 (For not even his *b* believed in him.)
Acts	7.13 Joseph made himself known to his *b*,
	7.26 you are *b*; why do you wrong each
	9.17 hands on Saul and said, "*B* Saul, the
Rom	14.10 Why do you pass judgment on your *b* or
	14.21 that makes your *b* or sister stumble.
1 Cor	5.11 with anyone who bears the name of *b* or
2 Cor	8.18 we are sending the *b* who is famous
Gal	1.19 apostle except James the Lord's *b*.
1 Thess	4. 6 that no one wrong or exploit a *b* or
Philem	16 but more than a slave, a beloved *b*
1 Jn	3.17 sees a *b* or sister in need, yet refuses to
	4.20 "I love God," and hates their *b* or sisters,

BRUISED

| Isa | 42. 3 a *b* reed he will not break, and a dimly |

BUCKET

Isa 40.15 the nations are like a drop from a *b*,

BUILD (BUILDING BUILDS BUILT)

1 Kings	6.	1 he began to *b* the house of the LORD.
1 Chr	17.12	He shall *b* a house for me, and I will
	22.19	Go and *b* the sanctuary of the LORD God
2 Chr	2.	6 who is able to *b* him a house, since
Neh	2.18	to me. Then they said, "Let us start *b*!"
Ps	127.	1 Unless the LORD *b* the house, those who
Prov	9.	1 Wisdom has *b* her house, she has hewn
	14.	1 The wise woman *b* her house, but the
	24.	3 By wisdom a house is *b*, and by
Eccl	2.	4 works; I *b* houses and planted vineyards
Isa	61.	4 They shall *b* up the ancient ruins, they
Jer	29.	5 *B* houses and live in them; plant
Dan	4.30	magnificent Babylon, which I have *b* as
Hab	2.12	for you who *b* a town by bloodshed,
Hag	1.	8 hills and bring wood and *b* the house,
Mal	1.	4 They may *b*, but I will tear down, until
Mt	16.18	on this rock I will *b* my church, and the
Lk	6.48	like a man *b* a house, who dug deeply
	14.30	fellow began to *b*, and was not able
Acts	20.32	a message that is able to *b* you up and
1 Cor	10.23	are lawful," but not all things *b* up.
	14.12	to excel in them for *b* up the church.
	14.26	Let all things be done for *b* up. If
2 Cor	10.	8 which the Lord gave for *b* you up
	12.19	do, beloved, is for the sake of *b* you up.
Eph	2.20	household of God, *b* upon the
1 Thess	5.11	one another and *b* up each other,
Jude	20	beloved, *b* yourselves up on most holy

BUILDERS

Ps	118.	22 The stone that the *b* rejected has
Lk	20.17	stone that the *b* rejected has become

BUILDING (BUILDINGS)

Mk	13.	1 what large stones and what large *b*!"
1 Cor	3.	9 together; you are God's field, God's *b*.

BULWARK (BULWARKS)

Ps	8.	2 you have founded a *b* because of your
Isa	26.	1 city; he sets up victory like walls and *b*.
Jer	50.15	surrendered; her *b* have fallen, her walls

BURDEN (BURDENS) (n)

Num	11.11	that you lay the *b* of all this people on
Ps	38.	4 my head; they weigh like a *b* too heavy
	55.22	Cast your *b* on the LORD, and he will
	66.11	us into the net; you laid *b* on our backs;
Isa	9.	4 the yoke of their *b*, and the bar across
	10.27	On that day his *b* will be removed from
Jer	17.21	that you do not bear a *b* on the sabbath
	23.33	asks you, "What is the *b* of the LORD?
	23.36	the *b* is everyone's own word, and so
Mt	11.30	For my yoke is easy, and my *b* is light."
	20.12	equal to us who have borne the *b* of the
	23.	4 They tie up heavy *b*, hard to bear, and
Lk	11.46	you load people with *b* hard to bear,
Acts	15.28	impose on you no further *b* than these
Gal	6.	2 Bear one another's *b*, and in this way
Rev	2.24	I say, I do not lay upon you any other *b*;

BURDEN (BURDENED BURDENING)

Isa	43.24	But you have *b* me with your sins; you
2 Cor	11.	9 and will continue to refrain from *b* you
	12.13	except that I myself did not *b* you?
2 Thess	3.	8 day, so that we might not *b* any of you.

BURIAL

Mk 14. 8 anointed my body beforehand for its *b*.

BURN (BURNED BURNING)

Josh	11.11	who breathed, and he *b* Hazor with fire.
Ps	38.	7 my loins are filled with *b*, and there is
	39.	3 While I mused, the fire *b*; then I spoke
Jer	20.	9 like a *b* fire shut up in my bones,

Jer	36.25	urged the king not to *b* the scroll, he
	39.	8 Chaldeans *b* the king's house and the
	52.13	He *b* the house of the LORD, the king's
Lam	2.	3 he has *b* like a flaming fire in Jacob,
Mt	13.30	first and bind them in bundles to be *b*,
Lk	24.32	"Were not our hearts *b* within us while
Acts	19.19	their books and *b* them publicly;
1 Cor	3.15	If the work is *b* up, the builder will

BURNT OFFERING (BURNT OFFERINGS)

Gen	8.20	clean bird, and offered *b* on the altar.
	22.	7 are here, but where is the lamb for a *b*?"
Ex	29.18	it is a *b* to the LORD; it is a pleasing
Lev	1.	3 If the offering is a *b* from the herd, you
	1.17	the wood that is on the fire; it is a *b*,
	6.	9 This is the ritual of the *b*. The *b* itself
Judg	13.16	if you want to prepare a *b*, then offer it
1 Sam	7.	9 lamb and offered it as a whole *b*
	13.12	so I forced myself, and offered the *b*."
	15.22	Has the LORD as great delight in *b* and
2 Sam	24.24	I will not offer *b* to the LORD my God
2 Kings	3.27	succeed him, and offered him as a *b*
1 Chr	16.40	to offer *b* to the LORD on the altar of the
	21.26	and presented *b* and offerings of
Ezra	3.	4 and offered the daily *b* by number
Ps	40.	6 ear. *B* and sin offering you have not
	50.	8 you; your *b* are continually before me.
	51.16	if I were to give a *b*, you would not be
Isa	1.11	I have had enough of *b* of rams and the
Jer	7.21	Add your *b* to your sacrifices, and eat
Ezek	46.12	provides a freewill offering, either a *b*
Dan	8.11	it took the regular *b* away from him and
Mic	6.	6 Shall I come before him with *b*, with

BURY (BURIED)

Gen	23.19	Abraham *b* Sarah his wife in the cave of
	35.29	and his sons Esau and Jacob *b* him.
	47.29	truly with me. Do not *b* me in Egypt.
Deut	34.	6 He was *b* in a valley in the land of
Mt	8.21	"Lord, first let me go and *b* my father."
Lk	9.59	"Lord, first let me go and *b* my father."
Rom	6.	4 we have been *b* with him by baptism
1 Cor	15.	4 he was *b*, and that he was raised on the
Col	2.12	when you were *b* with him in baptism,

BUSH

Ex	3.	2 to him in a flame of fire out of a *b*;
Jon	4.	6 God appointed a *b*, and made it come
Lk	20.37	showed, in the story about the *b*,
Acts	7.30	Sinai, in the flame of a burning *b*.

BUSHEL

Mt	5.15	lighting a lamp puts it under a *b* basket,
Mk	4.21	brought in to be put under a *b* basket,

BUSY

1 Kings	20.40	While your servant was *b* here and
Ps	141.	4 to *b* myself with wicked deeds in

BUSYBODIES

2 Thess	3.11	in idleness, mere *b*, not doing any work.
1 Tim	5.13	not merely idle, but also gossips and *b*,

BUY (BOUGHT)

Ex	21.	2 When you *b* a male Hebrew slave, he
2 Sam	24.24	"No, but I will *b* them from you for a
1 Chr	21.24	"No; I will *b* them for the full price. I
Neh	5.	8 have *b* back our Jewish kindred who
Hos	3.	2 I *b* her for fifteen shekels of silver and a
1 Cor	6.20	you were *b* with a price; therefore
	7.23	You were *b* with a price; do not become
2 Pet	2.	1 even deny the Master who *b* them—

BUYER

Deut 28.68 female slaves, but there will be no *b*.

BYWORD

Deut	28.37	and a *b* among all the peoples where
2 Chr	7.20	make it a proverb and a *b* among all

Job	17.	6 "He has made me a *b* of the peoples,
Ps	44.14	have made us a *b* among the nations,

C

CAESAREA

Mt	16.13	came into the district of *C* Philippi,
Mk	8.27	disciples to the villages of *C* Philippi;
Acts	8.40	to all the towns until he came to *C*.
	10.	1 In *C* there was a man named Cornelius,
	11.11	three men, sent to me from *C*, arrived
	18.22	When he had landed at *C*, he went up
	23.33	When they came to *C* and delivered the
	25.	4 replied that Paul was being kept at *C*,

CAIAPHAS

High priest, Mt 26.3, 57; Lk 3.2; Jn 18.13; prophesied that Jesus should die, 11.49-53; 18.14; took part in the trial of Jesus, Mt 26.62-66 (Mk 14.60-64; Jn 18.19-24,28); present at examination of Peter and John, Acts 4.6-21.

CAIN (CAIN'S)

Gen	4.	1 Eve, and she conceived and bore *C*,
	4.	3 *C* brought to the LORD an offering of the
	4.	8 *C* rose up against his brother Abel, and
	4.16	*C* went away from the presence of the
	4.25	instead of Abel, for *C* had killed him."
Heb	11.	4 God a more acceptable sacrifice than *C*.
1 Jn	3.12	not be like *C* who was from the evil one
Jude		11 they go the way of *C*, and abandon

CAKE (CAKES)

Gen	18.	6 of choice flour, knead it, and make *c*."
Hos	7.	8 the peoples; Ephraim is a *c* not turned.

CALAMITY

Job	6.30	my tongue? Cannot my taste discern *c*?
Ps	18.18	They confronted me in the day of my *c*;
Prov	1.26	I also will laugh at your *c*; I will mock
Jer	48.16	The *c* of Moab is near at hand and his
Dan	9.14	So the LORD kept watch over this *c* until
Ob		13 gate of my people on the day of their *c*;

CALEB

Sent with the spies, Num 13.16; exhorted the people, Num 13.30; 14.6-10; was promised entrance into Canaan, Num 14.22-38 (32.10-12; Deut 1.34-36); Num 26.65; received Hebron as an inheritance, Josh 14.6-15; 15.13-19; Judg 1.20.

CALF (CALVES)

Gen	18.	7 herd, and took a *c*, tender and good,
Ex	32.	4 it in a mold, and cast an image of a *c*;
	32.24	it into the fire, and out came this *c*!"
1 Kings	12.28	took counsel, and made two *c* of gold.
Ps	106.	19 They made a *c* at Horeb and worshiped
Hos	13.	2 to these," they say. People are kissing *c*!
Lk	15.23	get the fatted *c* and kill it, and let us
Acts	7.41	they made a *c*, offered a sacrifice to the

CALL (CALLING CALLS)

Job	13.22	Then *c*, and I will answer; or let me
	14.15	You would *c*, and I would answer you;
Ps	50.	4 He *c* to the heavens above and to the
	53.	4 they eat bread, and do not *c* upon God?
	55.16	But I *c* upon God; and the LORD will
	80.18	us life, and we will *c* on your name.
	91.15	When they *c* to me, I will answer them;
	102.	2 answer me speedily in the day when I *c*.
	105.	1 give thanks to the LORD, *c* on his name,
	116.	2 I will *c* on him as long as I live.
	145.	18 the LORD is near to all who *c* on him, to
Prov	8.	1 Does not wisdom *c*, does not
Isa	45.	3 I *c* you by your name, I surname you,
	55.	6 be found, *c* upon him while he is near;
	64.	7 There is no one who *c* upon your name,
	65.24	Before they *c* I will answer, while they

Jer	3.19	I thought you would *c* me, My Father,
	33.	3 *C* to me and I will answer you, and will
Joel	2.15	sanctify a fast; *c* a solemn assembly;
	2.32	who *c* on the name of the LORD
Mk	10.49	to him, "Take heart; get up, he is *c* you."
	15.35	it, they said "Listen, he is *c* for Elijah."
Lk	15.	6 he *c* together his friends and neighbors,
Jn	10.	3 his voice. He *c* his own sheep by name
Acts	2.21	who *c* on the name of the Lord
Rom	10.12	all and is generous to all who *c* on him.
	10.14	how are they to *c* on one in whom they
	11.29	gifts and the *c* of God are irrevocable.
1 Cor	1.26	Consider your own *c*, brothers and
2 Tim	2.22	who *c* upon the Lord from a pure heart.
2 Pet	1.10	eager to confirm your *c* and election,

CALLED

Gen	13.	4 there Abram *c* on the name of the LORD.
	22.14	So Abraham *c* that place "The LORD will
Ex	3.	4 God *c* to him out of the bush, "Moses,
Judg	16.28	Then Samson *c* to the LORD and said,
1 Sam	3.	4 the Lord *c*, "Samuel! Samuel!" and he
Prov	1.24	Because I have *c* and you refused, have
Song	5.	6 him; I *c* him, but he gave no answer.
Isa	41.	9 earth, and *c* from its farthest corners,
	42.	6 the LORD, I have *c* you in righteousness,
	49.	1 The LORD *c* me before I was born, while
Jer	35.17	I have *c* to them and they have not
Mt	2.15	prophet, "Out of Egypt have I *c* my son."
Mk	3.13	the hills, and *c* to him those whom he
	6.	7 He *c* the twelve and began to send
Lk	1.32	and will be *c* the Son of the Most High,
	9.	1 Jesus *c* the twelve together and gave
Acts	11.26	the disciples were first *c* "Christians."
	28.17	he *c* together the local leaders of the
Rom	1.	6 yourselves who are *c* to belong to Jesus
	8.30	whom he predestined he also *c*; and
1 Cor	1.24	to those who are *c*, both Jews and
	7.15	It is to peace that God has *c* you.
Gal	1.	6 quickly deserting the one who *c* you in
	5.13	you were *c* to freedom, brothers and
Heb	5.	4 it only when *c* by God, just as Aaron
	11.	8 faith Abraham obeyed when he was *c*
Jas	2.23	and he was *c* the friend of God.
Jude		1 To those who are *c*, who are beloved in

CALM

Mt	8.26	and the sea; and there was a dead *c*.
Mk	4.39	wind ceased, and there was a dead *c*.
Lk	8.24	waves; they ceased, and there was a *c*.

CAMEL (CAMELS CAMEL'S)

Gen	24.10	the servant took ten of his master's *c*
Mt	3.	4 John wore clothing of *c* hair with a
	19.24	easier for a *c* to go through the eye of a
	23.24	You strain out a gnat but swallow a *c*!
Mk	10.25	It is easier for a *c* to go through the eye
Lk	18.25	easier for a *c* to go through the eye of a

CAMP

Num	2.	2 The Israelites shall *c* each in their
	4.	5 When the *c* is to set out, Aaron and his
	5.	2 put out of the *c* everyone who is

CANA

Jn	2.	1 there was a wedding in *C* in Galilee,
	4.46	he came again to *C* in Galilee where he
	21.	2 the Twin, Nathanael of *C* in Galilee,

CANAAN (CANAANITE)

Gen	9.22	Ham, the father of *C*, saw the
	9.25	"Cursed be *C*; lowest of slaves shall he
	11.31	the Chaldeans to go into the land of *C*;
	12.	5 they set forth to go to the land of *C*.
	42.	5 the famine had reached the land of *C*.
Ex	6.	4 with them, to give them the land of *C*,
Deut	32.49	view the land of *C*, which I am giving to
Ps	106.	38 whom they sacrificed to the idols of *C*;

Mt 15.22 a *C* woman from that region came out

CANCELED

Lk 7.42 they could not pay, he *c* the debts

CAPABLE

Prov 31.10 A *c* wife who can find? She is far more

CAPERNAUM

Mt 4.13 left Nazareth and made his home in *C*
8. 5 When he entered *C*, a centurion came
11.23 and you *C*, will you be exalted to
17.24 When they reaced *C*, the collectors of
Mk 2. 1 When he returned to *C* after some days,
Lk 7. 1 the hearing of the people, he entered *C*.
10.15 you *C*, will you be exalted to heaven?
Jn 4.46 a royal official whose son lay ill in *C*.
6.59 he was teaching in the synagogue at *C*.

CAPTIVE (CAPTIVES)

Gen 14.14 that his nephew had been taken *c*,
Deut 21.11 you see among the *c* a beautiful woman
Ezra 2. 1 province who came from those *c* exiles
Ps 68.18 the high mount, leading *c* in thy train,
Isa 20. 4 of Assyria lead away the Egyptians as *c*
52. 2 from your neck, O *c* daughter Zion!
Jer 13.17 the LORD's flock has been taken *c*.
20. 4 he shall carry them *c* to Babylon, and
Lk 21.24 be taken away as *c* among all nations;
Rom 7.23 making me *c* to the law of sin that
2 Cor 10. 5 and we take every thought *c* to obey
Eph 4. 8 on high he made captivity itself a *c*;
Rev 13.10 If you are to be taken *c*, into captivity

CAPTIVITY

Isa 46. 2 the burden, but themselves go into *c*.
Jer 15. 2 famine, and those destined for *c*, to *c*.
22.22 and your lovers shall go into *c*;
Ezek 39.23 Israel went into *c* for their iniquity,

CAPTORS

Ps 137. 3 our *c* asked us for songs, and our
Isa 14. 2 will take captive those who were their *c*,

CARE (CARED CARES)

Deut 32.10 *c* for him, guarded him as the apple of
Ps 8. 4 of them, mortals that you *c* for them?
142. 4 refuge remains to me; no one *c* for me.
Jer 30.17 an outcast: "It is Zion, no one *c* for her!"
Mk 4.38 do you not *c* that we are perishing?"
4.19 but the *c* of the world, and the lure of
Lk 8.14 they are choked by the *c* and riches and
10.34 him to an inn, and took *c* of him.
1 Cor 3.10 must choose with *c* how to build it.
12.25 but the members may have the same *c*
Heb 2. 6 them, or mortals, that you *c* for them?

CAREFUL

Deut 5.32 You must therefore be *c* to do as the
2 Kings 10.31 Jehu was not *c* to follow the law of the

CARELESS

Prov 14.16 the fool throws off restraint and is *c*.
Mt 12.36 have to give an account for every *c* word

CARMEL

Josh 12.22 one; the king of Jokneam in *C*, one;
1 Sam 15.12 "Saul went to *C*, where he set up a
25. 5 "Go up to *C*, and go to Nabal, and greet
1 Kings 18.19 all Israel assemble for me at Mount *C*,
Song 7. 5 Your head crowns you like *C*, and your
Isa 35. 2 to it, the majesty of *C* and Sharon.

CARPENTER (CARPENTER'S)

Isa 44.13 The *c* stretches a line, marks it out with
Mt 13.55 Is not this the *c* son? Is not his mother
Mk 6. 3 Is not this the *c*, the son of Mary and

CARRY (CARRIED CARRIES CARRYING)

Gen 50.25 comes to you, you shall *c* up my bones
Deut 1.31 your God *c* you, just as one *c* a child,
2 Kings 24.14 He *c* away all Jerusalem, all the
2 Chr 36. 7 Nebuchadnezzar also *c* some of the
Ps 49.17 when they die they will *c* nothing away;
Eccl 5.15 for their toil, which they may *c* away
Isa 46. 4 even when you turn gray I will *c* you.
63. 9 he lifted them up and *c* them all the
Jer 20. 5 and seize them, and *c* them to Babylon,
Mk 15.21 to *c* his cross; it was Simon of Cyrene,
Lk 14.27 Whoever does not *c* the cross and follow
24.51 from them and was *c* up into heaven.
Jn 19.17 *c* the cross by himself, he went out to
Acts 13.29 they had *c* out all that was written
2 Cor 4.10 always *c* in the body the death of Jesus,
Rev 17.17 to *c* out his purpose by agreeing to give

CASE

Num 27. 5 Moses brought their *c* before the LORD.
Job 13.18 I have indeed prepared my *c*; I know
23. 4 I would lay my *c* before him, and fill my
Prov 18.17 one who first states a *c* seems right,
25. 9 Argue your *c* with your neighbor
Isa 41.21 Set forth your *c*, says the LORD; bring
Jn 18.38 and told them, "I find no *c* against him.
19. 4 you know that I find no *c* against him."
19. 6 crucify him; I find no *c* against him."
Acts 25.14 Festus laid Paul's *c* before the king,

CAST (CASTING CASTS)

Gen 21.10 "*C* out this slave woman with her son;
2 Kings 21.14 I will *c* off the remnant of my heritage,
Ps 42. 5 Why are you *c* down, O my soul, and
43. 5 Why are you *c* down, O my soul, and
55.22 *C* your burden on the LORD, and he will
Prov 21.12 wicked; he *c* the wicked down to ruin.
Jer 7.15 I will *c* you out of my sight, just as I *c*
Mk 3.15 and to have authority to *c* out demons.
3.22 and by the ruler of the demons he *c* out
9.28 privately, "Why could we not *c* it out?"
Lk 9.49 we saw a man *c* out demons in your
11.15 "He *c* out demons by Beelzebul, the
Jn 21. 6 "*C* the net to the right side of the boat,

CASTLE

Lk 11.21 a strong man, fully armed, guards his *c*,

CATCH (CATCHES CATCHING CAUGHT)

Jer 5.26 they set a trap; they *c* human beings.
Lk 5.10 from now on you will be *c* people."
1 Cor 3.19 "He *c* the wise in their craftiness,
2 Cor 12. 2 ago was *c* up to the third heaven—
1 Thess 4.17 will be *c* up in the clouds together with

CATTLE

Gen 1.25 God made . . . the *c* of every kind, and
Job 18. 3 Why are we counted as *c*? Why are we

CAUSE

Job 5. 8 seek God, to God I would commit my *c*.
Ps 35. 7 without *c* they hid their net for me;
69. 4 my head those who hate me without *c*;
119.154 Plead my *c* and redeem me; give me life
140. 12 LORD maintains the *c* of the needy, and
Prov 23.11 strong; he will plead their *c* against you.
Isa 51.22 God who pleads the *c* of his people:
Jer 5.28 they do not judge with justice the *c* of
Jn 15.25 their law, 'They hated me without a *c*.'

CAVE (CAVES)

Gen 19.30 Zoar; so he lived in a *c* with his two
23.19 buried Sarah his wife in the *c* of the
25. 9 buried him in the *c* of Machpelah, in
49.29 Bury me with my ancestors—in the *c*
50.13 buried him in the *c* of the field at
1 Sam 13. 6 people hid themselves in *c* and in holes
22. 1 and there escaped to the *c* of Adullam;

1 Kings 18. 4 hundred prophets, hid them fifty to a *c*,
          19. 9 At that place he came to a *c*, and spent
Isa   2.19 Enter the *c* of the rocks and the holes

CEASE (CEASED CEASES CEASING)

1 Sam   7. 8 "Do not *c* to cry out to the LORD our
       12.23 against the LORD by *c* to pray for you;
Ezra   4.23 and by force and power made them *c*.
Job   3.17 There the wicked *c* from troubling, and
Ps   46. 9 He makes wars *c* to the end of the
Prov 22.10 goes out; quarreling and abuse will *c*.
Isa   1.16 *c* to do evil, learn to do good; seek
Lam   3.22 The steadfast love of the LORD never *c*,
Dan   9.27 he shall make sacrifice and offering *c*;
Jon   1.15 the sea; and the sea *c* from its raging.
Mk   6.51 into the boat with them and the wind *c*.
Rev   4. 8 Day and night without *c* they sing,

CEDAR (CEDARS)

Judg 9.15 bramble and devour the *c* of Lebanon.'
Ps   29. 5 voice of the LORD breaks the *c*; the LORD
Song 1.17 the beams of our house are *c*, our
Isa   2.13 against all the *c* of Lebanon, lofty and
       9.10 down, but we will put *c* in their place."
Ezek 31. 3 Consider Assyria, a *c* of Lebanon, with

CELLAR

Lk   11.33 lighting a lamp puts it in a *c*, but on

CENSUS

Num   1. 2 Take a *c* of the whole congregation of
      26. 2 Take a *c* of the whole congregation of
Acts   5.37 rose up at the time of the *c* and got

CENTURION

Mt   8. 5 a *c* came to him, appealing to him and
     27.54 *c* and those with him, who were
Mk   15.39 Now when the *c*, who stood facing him,
Lk   7. 2 A *c* there had a slave whom he valued
     23.47 When the *c* saw what had taken place,

CEPHAS

1 Cor 15. 5 that he appeared to *C*, then to the

CERTIFIED

Jn   3.33 testimony has *c* this, that God is true.

CHAFF

Job 21.18 wind, and like *c* that the storm carries
Ps   1. 4 are not so but are like *c* which the wind
     35. 5 them be like *c* before the wind, with
Isa   17.13 they will flee far away, chased like *c* on
     29. 5 the multitude of tyrants like flying *c*.
     33.11 You conceive *c*, you bring forth stubble;
     41.15 and you shall make the hills like *c*.
Dan   2.35 broken in pieces and became like the *c*
Hos   13. 3 like *c* that swirls from the threshing
Mt   3.12 but the *c* he will burn with . . . fire.
Lk   3.17 but the *c* he will burn with . . . fire.

CHAIN (CHAINS)

Mk   5. 3 restrain him anymore, even with a *c*;
Acts 26.29 become as I am—except for these *c*."
     28.20 of Israel that I am bound with this *c*."
2 Tim 1.16 me and was not ashamed of my *c*;

CHANGE (CHANGED)

Gen 31.41 and you have *c* my wages ten times.
     35. 2 purify yourselves, and *c* your clothes;
Ex   13.17 they may *c* their minds and return to
     32.12 *c* your mind and do not bring disaster
Num 23.19 or a mortal, that he should *c* his mind.
Esth   9. 1 which had been *c* to a day when the
Ps 102. 26 a garment. You *c* them like clothing,
Jer   2.11 Has a nation *c* its gods, even though
    13.23 Can Ethiopians *c* their skin or leopards
    18. 8 turns from its evil, I will *c* my mind
    26.13 the LORD will *c* his mind about the
    26.19 did not the LORD *c* his mind about the

Dan   4.16 his mind be *c* from that of a human,
Hos   4. 7 me; they *c* their glory into shame.
Mal   3. 6 For I the LORD do not *c*; therefore you,
Mt   18. 3 unless you *c* and become like children,
    21.29 not'; but later he *c* his mind and went.
1 Cor 15.51 We will not all die, but we will all be *c*,
Heb   7.21 Lord has sworn and will not *c* his mind,

CHANNELS

Job 28.10 They cut out *c* in the rocks, and their
Ps   18.15 the *c* of the sea were seen, and the

CHARACTER

Rom 5. 4 endurance produces *c*, and *c* produces
Heb   6.17 the unchangeable *c* of his purpose,

CHARGE (CHARGED CHARGES)

Gen 28. 1 Jacob and blessed him, and *c* him,
Deut 3.28 But *c* Joshua, and encourage and
    33. 4 Moses *c* us with the law, as a
1 Kings 2. 1 to die drew near, he *c* Solomon his son,
Neh   5. 7 I brought *c* against the nobles and the
Ezra   1. 2 he has *c* me to build him a house at
Mt   27.37 over his head they put the *c* against
Mk   13.34 he leaves home and puts his slaves in *c*,
Lk   11.50 may be *c* with the blood of all
Acts 25. 7 bringing many serious *c* against him,
    25.18 they did not *c* him with any of the
    25.27 without indicating the *c* against
Rom 3. 9 for we have already *c* that all, both Jews
    8.33 will bring any *c* against God's elect?

CHARIOT (CHARIOTS)

Josh 17.16 who live in the plain have *c* of iron,
2 Kings 2.11 a *c* of fire and horses of fire separated
    6.17 of horses and *c* of fire round all Elisha.
Ps   20. 7 Some take pride in *c*, and some in
Isa   31. 1 who rely on horses, who trust in *c*
Joel   2. 5 As with the rumbling of *c*, they leap on
Nah   2. 4 The *c* race madly through the streets,
Hab   3. 8 you drove your horses, your *c* to victory?
Zech 6. 1 up and saw four *c* came out from

CHARM

Isa   47.11 upon you, which you cannot *c* away;

CHARMER (CHARMERS)

Ps   58. 5 it does not hear the voice of *c* or of the
Eccl 10.11 charmed, there is no advantage in a *c*.

CHASE (CHASED)

Lev   26. 7 You shall give *c* to your enemies, and
Deut 1.44 out against you and *c* you as bees do.
Neh 13.28 the Horonite; I *c* him away from me.

CHASTENING

Isa   26.16 poured out a prayer when your *c* was on

CHASTISE

Ps   39.11 You *c* mortals in punishment for sin,
Jer   30.11 I will *c* you in just measure, and I will
    46.28 I will *c* you in just measure, and I will

CHEAT

Lev   25.17 You shall not *c* one another, but you

CHEDORLAOMER

Gen 14. 1 King Arioch of Ellasar, King *C* of Elam,

CHEEK (CHEEKS)

1 Kings 22.24 up to Micaiah, slapped him on the *c*,
2 Chr 18.23 up to Micaiah, slapped him on the *c*,
Song 1.10 Your *c* are comely with ornaments, your
Isa   50. 6 my *c* to those who pulled out the beard;
Lam   3.30 to give one's *c* to the smiter, and be
Mt   5.39 if anyone strikes you on the right *c*,

CHEER

Job   9.27 my sad countenance and be of good *c*,'

25

CHEERFUL

Prov	15.13 A glad heart makes a *c* countenance,
	17.22 A *c* heart is a good medicine, but a
2 Cor	9. 7 compulsion, for God loves a *c* giver.

CHEERFULNESS

Rom	12. 8 in diligence; the compassionate, in *c*.

CHERISHED

Ps	66.18 If I had *c* iniquity in my heart, the Lord
Ezek	35. 5 Because you *c* an ancient enmity, and

CHERUB (CHERUBIM)

Gen	3.24 of the garden of Eden he placed the *c*,
Ex	25.18 You shall make two of gold; you shall
	26. 1 make them with *c* skillfully worked
2 Sam	22.11 He rode on a *c*, and flew; he was seen
1 Kings	6.23 he made two *c* of olivewood, each ten
Isa	37.16 Israel, who are enthroned above the *c*,
Ezek	9. 3 God of Israel had gone up from the *c*
	10. 3 Now the *c* were standing on the south
	28.14 With an anointed *c* as guardian I placed
Heb	9. 5 above it were the *c* of glory

CHEST

Zech	13. 6 "What are these wounds on your *c*?" the

CHEW (CHEWS)

Lev	11.26 or does not *c* the cud is unclean
Deut	14. 6 and *c* the cud, among the animals, you

CHILD

Ruth	4.16 Naomi took the *c* and laid him in her
1 Kings	3. 7 although I am only a little *c*; I do not
Ps	131. 2 like a weaned *c* with its mother; my
Prov	2. 1 My *c*, if you accept my words and
	10. 1 A wise *c* makes a glad father but a
	23.19 Hear, my *c*, and be wise, and direct
	23.26 My *c*, give me your heart, and let your
	27.11 Be wise, my *c*, and make my heart glad,
	29.15 a mother is disgraced by a neglected *c*.
Isa	9. 6 For a *c* has been born for us, a son is
	11. 6 together, and a little *c* shall lead them.
Ezek	18.20 A *c* shall not suffer for the iniquity of a
Hos	11. 1 Israel was a *c*, I loved him, and out of
Mt	1.18 found to be with *c* from the Holy Spirit.
	2. 8 "Go and search diligently for the *c*; and
	7. 9 who if your *c* asks for bread, will give a
	18. 2 He called a *c*, whom he put among
Mk	9.36 he took a little *c* and put it among
	13.12 brother to death, and a father his *c*,
Lk	1.41 greeting, the *c* leaped in her womb.
	1.66 said, "What then will this *c* become?"
	1.76 you, *c*, will be called the prophet of the
	1.80 the *c* grew and became strong in spirit,
	2.40 the *c* grew and became strong, filled
	2.48 his mother said to him, "*C*, why have
	11.11 if your *c* asks for a fish, will give a
	8.54 by the hand and called out, "*C*, get up!"
	9.47 thoughts, took a little *c* and put it by
1 Cor	13.11 I was a *c*, I spoke like a *c*, I thought
Gal	4. 7 but a *c*, and if a *c* then also an heir,
1 Tim	1. 2 To Timothy, my loyal *c* in the faith:
2 Tim	1. 2 To Timothy, my beloved *c*: Grace,
Heb	12. 5 "My *c*, do not regard lightly the
1 Jn	5. 1 who loves the parent loves the *c*.
Rev	12. 4 that he might devour her *c* as soon as it

CHILDBEARING

1 Tim	2.15 she will be saved through *c*, provided

CHILDHOOD

2 Tim	3.15 how from *c* you have known the sacred

CHILDLESS

Gen	15. 2 what will you give me, for I continue *c*,
Gal	4.27 "Rejoice, you *c* one, you who bear no

CHILDREN (CHILDREN'S)

Gen	18.19 chosen him, that he may charge his *c*
	33. 5 "The *c* whom God has graciously given
Ex	12.26 when your *c* ask you, "What do you
Num	14.18 the iniquity of the parents upon the *c*
Deut	1.39 your *c*, who today do not yet know right
	4.10 on the earth, and may teach their *c* so";
	6. 7 Recite them to your *c* and talk about
	11. 2 Remember today that it was not your *c*
	12.25 go well with you and your *c* after you,
	32.46 give them as a command to your *c*,
1 Kings	9. 6 you or your *c*, and do not keep my
2 Kings	14. 6 nor *c* be put to death for the parents;
2 Chr	6.16 if only your *c* keep to their way, to walk
	25. 4 he did not put their *c* to death,
Job	8. 4 If your *c* sinned against him, he
Ps	89.30 If his *c* forsake my law and do not
	103. 17 fear him, and his righteousness to *c c*,
	128. 3 your *c* will be like olive shoots around
	128. 6 May you see your *c c*! Peace be upon
Prov	4. 1 Listen, *c*, to a father's instruction, and
	13.22 good leave an inheritance to their *c c*,
	13.24 Those who spare the rod hate their *c*,
	17.25 Foolish *c* are a grief to their father and
	19.26 their mother are *c* who cause shame
	20.11 Even *c* make themselves known by their
	22. 6 Train *c* in the right way, and when old,
	29.17 Discipline your *c*, and they will give
	31.28 Her *c* rise up and call her happy; her
Isa	1. 2 I reared *c* and brought them up, but
	8.18 I and the *c* whom the LORD has given
	30. 9 rebellious people, faithless *c*, *c* who will
	49.20 The *c* born in the time of your
	54.13 All your *c* shall be taught by the LORD,
	66. 8 as Zion was in labor she delivered her *c*.
Jer	31.29 grapes, and the *c* teeth are set on edge."
Ezek	5.10 midst, and *c* shall eat their parents;
	18. 2 grapes, and the *c* teeth are set on edge"?
	23.39 they had slaughtered their *c* for their
Hos	1.10 be said to them, "*C* of the living God."
Joel	1. 3 Tell your *c* of it, and let your *c* tell their
Mal	4. 6 will turn the hearts of parents to their *c*
Mt	2.16 and he sent and killed all the *c*
	3. 9 these stones to raise up *c* to Abraham.
	5. 9 for they will be called *c* of God.
	7.11 know how to give good gifts to your *c*,
	17.26 Jesus said to him, "Then the *c* are free.
	19.13 Then little *c* were being brought to him
	19.14 "Let the little *c* come to me, and do not
	21.15 heard the *c* crying out in the temple,
Mk	7.27 said to her, "Let the *c* be fed first, for it
	10.14 "Let the little *c* come to me; do not
Lk	1.17 to turn the hearts of parents to their *c*,
	3. 8 is able from these stones to raise up *c*
	6.35 and you will be *c* of the Most High;
	7.32 like *c* sitting in the marketplace and
	16. 8 the *c* of this age are more shrewd in
	18.16 "Let the little *c* come to me, and do not
Jn	1.12 he gave power to become *c* of God,
	8.39 "If you were Abraham's *c*, you would be
	12.36 so that you may become *c* of light."
	13.33 Little *c*, I am with you only a little
Acts	2.39 promise is for you, for your *c*, and for
Rom	8.14 led by the Spirit of God are *c* of God.
	8.16 we are *c* of God, and if *c*, then heirs,
	9. 8 but the *c* of the promise are counted
1 Cor	7.14 Otherwise, your *c* would be unclean,
	14.20 do not be *c* in your thinking; rather, be
2 Cor	12.14 *c* ought not to lay up for their parents,
Gal	3.26 Jesus you are all *c* of God through faith.
	4.28 my friends, are *c* of promise, like Isaac.
Eph	1. 5 adoption as his *c* through Jesus Christ,
	2. 3 and we were by nature *c* of wrath,
	4.14 We must no longer be *c*, tossed to and
	6. 1 *C*, obey your parents in the Lord, for
Phil	2.15 *c* of God without blemish in the midst

Col	3.20 *C*, obey your parents in everything, for
1 Thess	5. 5 you are all *c* of light and *c* of the day;
1 Pet	1.14 Like obedient *c*, do not be conformed
1 Jn	2.18 *C*, it is the last hour! As you have heard
	3. 1 us, that we should be called *c* of God;
2 Jn	4 some of your *c* walking in the truth,

CHOKE (CHOKED)

Mt	13.22 lure of wealth *c* the word, and it yields
Mk	4. 7 thorns, the thorns grew up and *c* it,
	4.19 other things come in and *c* the word,
Lk	8. 7 and the thorns grew up and *c* it.
	8.14 their way, they are *c* by the cares of

CHOOSE (CHOOSES CHOOSING)

Num	16. 7 man whom the LORD *c* shall be the holy
	17. 5 staff of the man whom I *c* shall sprout;
Deut	12. 5 God will *c* out of all your tribes as his
	14.24 LORD your God will *c* to set his name
	17.15 a king whom the LORD your God will *c*.
	30.19 *C* life so that you and your descendants
Josh	24.15 *c* this day whom you will serve, whether
1 Sam	17. 8 *C* a man for yourselves, and let him
2 Sam	24.12 Three things I offer you; *c* one of them,
1 Chr	21.10 Three things I offer you; *c* one of them,
Ps	16. 4 who *c* another god multiply their
	25.12 will teach them the way they should *c*.
	65. 4 Happy are those whom you *c* and bring
Prov	1.29 and did not *c* the fear of the LORD,
Isa	7.15 how to refuse the evil and *c* the good.
	58. 5 Is such the fast that I *c*, a day to
Zech	1.17 comfort Zion and again *c* Jerusalem.
Mt	20.15 to do what I *c* with what belongs
Mk	1.40 he said to him, "If you *c*, you can make
Jn	15.16 You did not *c* me, but I chose you. And
Acts	15.25 to *c* representatives and send them to
Heb	11.25 daughter, *c* rather to share ill-treatment

CHORAZIN

Mt	11.21 "Woe to you, *C*! Woe to you, Bethsaida!
Lk	10.13 "Woe to you, *C*! Woe to you, Bethsaida!

CHOSE (CHOSEN) (v)

Gen	13.11 So Lot *c* for himself all the plain of the
	18.19 No, for I have *c* him, that he may
Ex	18.25 Moses *c* able men from all Israel and
Num	1.16 were the ones *c* from the congregation,
Deut	4.37 your ancestors, he *c* their descendants
	7. 7 the LORD set his heart on you and *c* you,
	18. 5 LORD your God has *c* Levi out of all your
1 Sam	2.28 I *c* him out of all the tribes of Israel to
	10.24 see the one one whom the LORD has *c*?
1 Kings	3. 8 midst of the people whom you have *c*,
	11.13 the sake of Jerusalem, which I have *c*."
2 Kings	23.27 I will reject this city that I have *c*,
1 Chr	28.10 LORD has *c* you to build a house as the
2 Chr	29.11 for the LORD has *c* you to stand in his
Ps	47. 4 He *c* our heritage for us, the pride of
	78.68 But he *c* the tribe of Judah, Mount
	119. 30 I have *c* the way of faithfulness; I set
	119.173 to help me, for I have *c* your precepts.
Prov	22. 1 A good name is to be *c* rather than
Isa	41. 8 my servant, Jacob, whom I have *c*,
	43.10 my servant whom I have *c*, so that you
	49. 7 the Holy One of Israel, who has *c* you."
	66. 3 These have *c* their own ways, and in
Jer	33.24 "The two families that the LORD *c* have
Hag	2.23 you like a signet ring; for I have *c* you,
Mt	12.18 Here is my servant, whom I have *c*, my
	22.14 For many are called, but few are *c*."
Lk	6.13 and *c* twelve of them, whom he also
	14. 7 how the guests *c* the places of honor,
Jn	13.18 I know whom I have *c*. But it is to
Acts	6. 5 they *c* Stephen, a man full of faith and
	9.15 instrument whom I have *c* to bring my
	22.14 ancestors has *c* you to know his will,
1 Cor	1.27 God *c* what is foolish in the world to

1 Cor	12.18 members in the body, each one as he *c*.
Eph	1. 4 just as he *c* us in Christ before the
1 Thess	1. 4 beloved by God, that he has *c* you,
2 Thess	2.13 God *c* you as the first fruits for
1 Pet	1. 2 who have been *c* and destined by God

CHOSEN (n and adj)

1 Chr	16.13 Israel, children of Jacob, his *c* ones.
Ps	89. 3 "I have made a covenant with my *c* one,
	105. 43 out with joy, his *c* ones with singing.
	106. 23 had not Moses, his *c* one, stood in the
Isa	42. 1 my *c*, in whom my soul delights;
	45. 4 Jacob, and Israel my *c*, I call you
	65. 9 my *c* shall inherit it, and my servants
	65.22 my *c* shall long enjoy the work of their
Lk	9.35 said, "This is my Son, my *C*; listen to
Col	3.12 As God's *c* ones, holy and beloved,
1 Pet	2. 9 you are a *c* race, a royal priesthood, a

CHRISTIAN (CHRISTIANS)

Acts	11.26 that the disciples were first called "*C*.
	26.28 quickly persuading me to become a *C*?"
1 Pet	4.16 Yet if any of you suffers as a *C*, do not

CHURCH (CHURCHES)

Mt	16.18 on this rock I will build my *c*, and the
	18.17 to listen to them, tell it to the *c*;
Acts	9.31 the *c* throughout Judea, Galilee, and
	11.22 News of this came to the ears of the *c*
	12. 1 upon some who belonged to the *c*.
	12. 5 Peter was kept in prison, the *c* prayed
	16. 5 So the *c* were strengthened in the faith
Rom	16. 5 Greet also the *c* in their house.
1 Cor	10.32 to Jews or to Greeks or to the *c* of God,
	12.28 God has appointed in the *c* first
	14. 4 but those who prophesy build up the *c*.
	15. 9 an apostle, because I persecuted the *c*
2 Cor	8. 1 has been granted to the *c* of Macedonia;
Eph	1.22 head over all things for the *c*, which is
	3.21 to him be glory in the *c* and in Christ
	5.24 Just as the *c* is subject to Christ, so
1 Tim	3. 5 how can he take care of God's *c*?
	5.16 let the *c* not be burdened, so that it can
Philem	2 soldier, and to the *c* in your house:
3 Jn	10 to do so and expels them from the *c*.
Rev	1. 4 John to the seven *c* that are in Asia:
	2.23 all the *c* will know that I am the one

CIRCLE

Prov	8.27 there, when he drew a *c* on the face of
Isa	40.22 is he who sits above the *c* of the earth,

CIRCUMCISE (CIRCUMCISED)

Gen	17.10 you: Every male among you shall be *c*.
	34.24 and every male was *c*, all who went out
Deut	10.16 *C*, then, the foreskin of your heart, and
	30. 6 God will *c* your heart and the heart of
Josh	5. 3 made flint knives and *c* the Israelites
Jer	4. 4 *C* yourselves to the LORD, remove the
Jn	7.22 and you *c* a man on the sabbath.
Acts	11. 2 the *c* believers criticized him,
	15. 1 "Unless you are *c* according to the
Gal	2. 3 with me, was not compelled to be *c*,
Col	2.11 were *c* with a spiritual circumcision,

CIRCUMCISION

Ex	4.26 she said, "A bridegroom of blood by *c*."
Rom	2.26 their uncircumcision be regarded as *c*?
	4.11 He received the sign of *c* as a seal of
1 Cor	7.19 *C* is nothing, and uncircumcision is
Gal	5. 6 in Christ Jesus neither *c* nor
Eph	2.11 by those who are called "the *c*"—

CISTERN (CISTERNS)

Prov	5.15 Drink water from your own *c*, flowing
Jer	2.13 water, and dug out *c* for themselves,
	38. 6 and threw him into the *c* of Malchiah,

CITIZENSHIP

Phil	3.20	But our c is in heaven, and it is from

CITY (CITIES)

Num	35.	6 the Levites shall include six c of refuge,
Deut	19.	2 you shall set apart three c in the land
Josh	6.	3 You shall march around the c, all the
	20.	2 'Appoint the c of refuge, of which I
2 Kings	25.	4 a breach was made in the c wall; the
Ps	46.	4 whose streams make glad the c of God,
	48.	1 to be praised in the c of our God.
Prov	11.	10 blessing of the upright a c is exalted,
Eccl	9.	14 a little c with few people in it. A great
Isa	1.	26 shall be called the c of righteousness,
Jer	39.	2 the month, a breach was made in the c.
Lam	1.	1 How lonely sits the c that once was full
Ezek	33.	21 came to me and said, "The c has fallen."
Dan	9.	19 because your c and your people bear
Zech	8.	3 Jerusalem shall be called the faithful c,
Mt	5.	14 world. A c built on a hill cannot be hid.
Mk	1.	33 the whole c was gathered around the
Lk	19.	19 said to him, 'And you, rule over five c.'
Acts	17.	16 to see that the c was full of idols.
Heb	11.	10 he looked forward to the c that has
Rev	3.	12 God, and the name of the c of my God,
	21.	2 the holy c, new Jerusalem, coming
	21.	15 of gold to measure the c and its gates

CLAIMS

1 Cor	14.	37 Anyone who c to be a prophet, or to

CLAN

Num	27.	4 of our father be taken away from his c

CLAY

Job	10.	9 that you have fashioned me like c;
	13.	12 ashes, your defenses are defenses of c.
	33.	6 are; I too was formed from a piece of c.
Isa	29.	16 Shall the potter be regarded as the c?
	45.	9 Does the c say to the one who fashions
	64.	8 we are the c, and you are our potter; we
Jer	18.	6 Just like the c in the potter's hand, so

CLEAN

Gen	7.	2 with you seven pairs of all c animals,
Deut	14.	11 You may eat any c birds.
2 Kings	5.	14 the flesh of a young boy, and he was c.
Job	14.	4 Who can bring a c thing out of an
	15.	14 What are mortals that they can be c? Or
	25.	4 How can one born of woman be c?
	33.	9 You say, "I am c, without transgression;
Ps	24.	4 Those who have c hands and pure
	73.	13 in vain I have kept my heart c and
Prov	20.	9 Who can say, "I have made my heart c;
Isa	1.	16 Wash yourselves; make yourselves c;
Jer	13.	27 long will it be before you are made c?
Mt	8.	2 if you choose, you can make me c."
	23.	25 you c the outside of the cup and of the
Mk	1.	40 "If you choose, you can make me c."
Lk	5.	12 if you choose, you can make me c."
	11.	41 and see, everything will be c for you.
	17.	14 And as they went they were made c
Acts	10.	15 "What God has made c, you must not
	11.	9 'What God has made c, you must not
Rom	14.	20 Everything is indeed c, but it is wrong

CLEANNESS

Ps	18.	20 according to the c of my hands he

CLEANSE (CLEANSED CLEANSES CLEANSING)

Lev	14.	11 The priest who c shall set the person to
Num	8.	6 from among the Israelites and c them.
Deut	32.	43 hate him, and c the land for his people.
2 Chr	29.	16 part of the house of the LORD to c it,
Job	9.	30 with soap and c my hands with lye,
Ps	51.	2 my iniquity, and c me from my sin.
Prov	20.	30 Blows that wound c away evil; beatings
Isa	4.	4 and c the bloodstains of Jerusalem from

Jer	33.	8 I will c them from all the guilt of their
Ezek	22.	24 You are a land that is not c, not rained
	36.	25 from all your idols I will c you. A new
	37.	23 and will c them. Then they shall be my
Dan	11.	35 they may be refined, purified, and c,
Mt	10.	8 the sick, raise the dead, c the lepers,
Lk	4.	27 none of them was c, except Naaman
Jn	15.	3 You have already been c by the word
2 Cor	7.	1 let us c ourselves from every defilement
Eph	5.	26 to make her holy by c her with the
Jas	4.	8 C your hands, you sinners, and purify

CLEAR (CLEARED)

Gen	44.	16 can we speak? How can we c ourselves?
Ps	19.	12 their errors? C me from hidden faults.
	80.	9 You c the ground for it; it took deep
Lk	3.	17 to c his threshing floor, and to gather

CLEFT-FOOTED

Lev	11.	3 and is c and chews the cud —such you

CLING (CLINGS)

Gen	2.	24 his father and mother and c to his wife,
Job	19.	20 My bones c to my skin and flesh, and I
Ps	119.	25 My soul c to the dust; revive me
	119.	31 I c to your decrees, O LORD; let me not
Rev	12.	11 for they did not c to life even in the

CLOAK (CLOAKS)

Ruth	3.	9 spread your c over your servant, for you
1 Sam	24.	4 stealthily cut off a corner of Saul's c.
Ezek	16.	8 and I spread the edge of my c over you,
Mt	5.	40 and take your coat, give your c as well;
	21.	8 A very large crowd spread their c on the
Mk	2.	21 a piece of unshrunk cloth on an old c;
	5.	27 him in the crowd and touched his c.
	6.	56 might touch even the fringe of his c;
	11.	8 Many people spread their c on the road,
Lk	19.	36 kept spreading their c on the road.
2 Tim	4.	13 When you come, bring the c that I left

CLOTH

Isa	64.	6 our righteous deeds are like a filthy c.
Mt	9.	16 a piece of unshrunk c on an old cloak,
Lk	2.	7 son and wrapped him in bands of c,

CLOTHE (CLOTHED CLOTHES)

Gen	3.	21 for the man and his wife, and c them.
2 Chr	28.	15 with the booty they c all that were
Job	29.	14 I put on righteousness, and it c me; my
Ps	30.	11 off my sackcloth and c me with joy,
Isa	22.	21 will c him with your robe and bind your
Zech	3.	5 a clean turban on his head and c him
Mt	6.	30 if God so c the grass of the field, which
	6.	29 all his glory was not c like one of these.
Mk	5.	15 saw the demoniac sitting there, c and in
	15.	17 they c him in a purple cloak; and after
Lk	8.	35 feet of Jesus, c and in his right mind;
	12.	27 all his glory was not c like one of these.
	12.	28 if God so c the grass of the field, which
2 Cor	5.	2 to be c with our heavenly dwelling—
Eph	4.	24 and to c yourselves with a new self,
Col	3.	12 c yourselves with compassion, kindness,
Rev	16.	15 is the one who stays awake and is c,

CLOTHES (CLOTHING)

Deut	8.	4 The c on your back did not wear out
Job	31.	19 I have seen anyone perish for lack of c,
Ps	22.	18 they divide my c among themselves, and
Prov	25.	20 Like a moth in c or a worm in wood,
	27.	26 lambs will provide your c, and the goats
Mt	6.	25 than food, and the body more than c?
	7.	15 prophets, who come to you in sheep's c
	17.	2 sun, and his c became dazzling white.
	27.	35 they divided his c among themselves by
Mk	15.	24 divided his c among them, casting lots
Lk	8.	44 touched the fringe of his c, and
	23.	34 doing. And they cast lots to divide his c.

Jn	19.24 themselves, and for my *c* they cast lots."
Acts	9.39 and other *c* that Dorcas had made
1 Pet	3. 3 by wearing gold ornaments or fine *c*;

CLOUD (CLOUDS)

Gen	9.13 I set my bow in the *c*, and it shall be a
Ex	13.21 a pillar of *c* by day, to lead them along
	40.34 Then the *c* covered the tent of meeting,
Num	9.15 the *c* covered the tabernacle, the tent of
	12. 5 LORD came down in a pillar of *c*, and
Deut	31.15 the pillar of *c* stood at the entrance to
Isa	4. 5 over its places of assembly a *c* by day
Mt	17. 5 suddenly a bright *c* overshadowed them,
Mk	9. 7 Then a *c* overshadowed them, and from
Acts	1. 9 up, and a *c* took him out of their sight.
1 Cor	10. 2 all were baptized into Moses in the *c*

COAL (COALS)

Ps	18. 8 glowing *c* flamed forth from him.
	140. 10 Let burning *c* fall on them! Let them be
Prov	25.22 you will heap *c* of fire on their heads,
Isa	6. 6 seraphs flew to me, holding a live *c* that
Rom	12.20 you will heap burning *c* on their heads."

COAT (COATS)

Mt	5.40 sue you and take your *c*, give your cloak
Lk	3.11 "Whoever has two *c* must share with
	6.29 takes away your *c* do not withhold even
Acts	22.20 and keeping the *c* of those who killed

COAX

Judg	14.15 said to Samson's wife, "*C* your husband
	16. 5 "*C* him, and find out what makes his

COCK

Mt	26.74 the man!" At that moment the *c* crowed.
Mk	14.30 before the *c* crows twice, you will deny
	14.68 into the forecourt. Then the *c* crowed.
Lk	22.34 Peter, the *c* will not crow this day, until
	22.60 he was still speaking, the *c* crowed.
Jn	13.38 before the *c* crows, you will have denied

COIN (COINS)

Mt	17.27 you open its mouth you will find a *c*;
Mk	12.42 came and put in two small copper *c*,
Lk	21. 2 a poor widow put in two small copper *c*.

COLD

Mt	24.12 the love of many will grow *c*.
Rev	3.16 are lukewarm, and neither *c* nor hot,

COLLECT (COLLECTED)

Gen	47.14 Joseph *c* all the money to be found in
Mt	13.41 they will *c* out of his kingdom all

COLLECTION

1 Cor	16. 1 concerning the *c* for the saints: you

COLT

Zech	9. 9 and riding on a donkey, on a *c*, the foal
Mk	11. 2 you will find tied there a *c* that has
Lk	19.30 will find tied there a *c* that has never

COME

Gen	24.31 "*C* in, O blessed of the LORD. Why do
Num	10.29 *c* with us, and we will treat you well;
Ps	66.16 *C* and hear, all you who fear God, and I
	100. 2 *C* into his presence with singing.
Prov	2.19 those who go to her never *c* back, nor
	25. 7 for it is better to be told, "*C* up here,"
Song	7.11 *C*, my beloved, let us go forth into the
Isa	1.18 *C* now, let us argue it out, says the
	2. 3 *C*, let us go up to the mountain of the
	2. 5 of Jacob, *c*, let us walk in the light
	26.20 *C*, my people, enter your chambers, and
	35. 4 recompense. He will *c* and save you."
	55. 1 you that have no money, *c*, buy and eat!
Jer	2.27 their trouble they say, "*C* and save us!"
Hos	6. 1 "*C*, let us return to the LORD; for it is he

Mic	4. 2 "*C*, let us go up to the mountain of the
Mal	3. 1 you seek will suddenly *c* to his temple;
Mt	6.10 Your kingdom *c*, Your will be done, on
	8. 9 to another, '*C*,' and he *c*, and to my
	11. 3 "Are you the one who is to *c*, or are we
	11.28 *C* to me, all you that are weary and are
	24. 5 For many will *c* in my name, saying, 'I
Mk	6.31 "*C* away to a deserted place all by
	13. 6 Many will *c* in my name and say, 'I am
Jn	1.39 He said to them, "*C* and see." They came
	4.29 "*C* and see a man who told me
	7.28 I am from. I have not *c* on my own.
	7.37 "Let anyone who is thirsty *c* to me, and
	11.43 cried with a loud voice, "Lazarus, *c* out!"
Acts	1.11 will *c* in the same way as you saw him
	16. 9 "*C* over to Macedonia and help us."
Rom	15.23 years, to *c* to you when I go to Spain.
1 Cor	16.22 has no love for the Lord. Our Lord, *c*!
2 Tim	4. 9 Do your best to *c* to me soon, for
Heb	12.22 But you have *c* to Mount Zion and to
Rev	18. 4 "*C* out of her, my people, so that you
	22.17 Spirit and the Bride say, "*C*." And let

COMES (CAME COMING)

1 Sam	28.13 a divine being *c* up out of the ground."
2 Sam	19.15 king *c* back to the Jordan; and Judah *c*
Ps	50. 3 God *c*, and does not keep silence,
	96.13 for he is *c*, he is *c* to judge the earth.
	118. 26 Blessed is the one who *c* in the name of
Isa	63. 1 "Who is this that *c* from Edom, from
Dan	6. 6 and satraps conspired and *c* to the king
Mal	4. 1 the day is *c*, burning like an oven, when
	4. 5 the great and terrible day of the LORD *c*.
Mt	21. 9 Blessed is the one who *c* in the name of
	23.39 'Blessed is the one who *c* in the name
	24.42 not know on what day your Lord is *c*.
	25.31 "When the Son of Man *c* in his glory,
	26.64 of Power and *c* on the clouds of heaven."
Mk	3.13 whom he wanted, and they *c* to him.
	8.38 also be ashamed when he *c* in the glory
	10.45 Son of Man *c* not to be served but to
	13.26 they will see the Son of man *c* in clouds
	14.62 and '*c* with the clouds of heaven.' "
Lk	12.40 Son of Man is *c* at an unexpected hour."
	13.35 the one who *c* in the name of the Lord!' "
	21.27 'Son of Man *c* in a cloud' with power
Jn	6.35 "Whoever *c* to me will never be hungry,
	6.37 who *c* to me I will never drive away;
	12.13 Blessed is the one who *c* in the name of
	14.18 not leave you orphaned; I am *c* to you.
1 Cor	11.26 proclaim the Lord's death until he *c*.
2 Cor	13. 1 This is the third time I am *c* to you.
Heb	10.37 the one who is *c* one will come and
Jude	14 "See, the Lord is *c* with ten thousands
Rev	1. 7 Look! he is *c* with the clouds; every eye
	3.11 I am *c* soon; hold fast to what you have,
	22.12 I am *c* soon, my reward is with me, to
	22.20 these things says, "Surely I am *c* soon."

COMELY

Song	6. 4 my love, *c* as Jerusalem, terrible as an

COMFORT (n)

Ps	119. 50 This is my *c* in my distress, that your
2 Cor	7.13 to you before God. In this we find *c*.
2 Thess	2.16 grace gave us eternal *c* and good hope,

COMFORT (COMFORTED COMFORTS)

Gen	24.67 So Isaac was *c* after his mother's death.
	37.35 sought to *c* him; but he refused to be *c*,
Job	2.11 together to go and console and *c* him.
	21.34 will you *c* me with empty nothings?
Ps	23. 4 your rod and your staff—they *c* me.
	77. 2 wearying; my soul refuses to be *c*.
	86.17 you, LORD, have helped me and *c* me.
Isa	12. 1 your anger turned away, and you *c* me.
	40. 1 *C*, O *c* my people, says your God. Speak

Isa	49.13 For the LORD has *c* his people, and will
	51. 3 For the LORD will *c* Zion; he will *c* all
	51.12 I am he who *c* you; why then are you
	52. 9 for the LORD has *c* his people, he has
	61. 2 of our God; to *c* all who mourn;
	66.13 As a mother *c* her child, so I will *c* you;
Lam	1. 2 all her lovers she has no one to *c* her;
Lk	16.25 but now he is *c* here, and you are in

COMFORTERS

Job	16. 2 such things; miserable *c* are you all.
Ps	69.20 was none; and for *c*, but I found none.
Nah	3. 7 her? Where shall I seek *c* for you?

COMING (n)

Mt	24. 3 what will be the sign of your *c* and of
	24.27 so will be the *c* of the Son of Man.
	24.37 so will be the *c* of the Son of Man.
Lk	12.45 'My master is delayed in *c*.' and if he
1 Cor	15.23 fruits, then at his *c* those who belong to
1 Thess	2.19 boasting before our Lord Jesus at his *c*?
	3.13 at the *c* of our Lord Jesus with all his
	4.15 who are alive, who are left until the *c* of
	5.23 and blameless at the *c* of our Lord
2 Thess	2. 1 As to the *c* of our Lord Jesus Christ and
Jas	5. 7 beloved, until the *c* of the Lord.
2 Pet	1.16 to you the power and *c* of our Lord
	3. 4 "Where is the promise of his *c*? For ever
1 Jn	2.28 be put to shame before him at his *c*.

COMMAND (n)

Num	9.18 At the *c* of the LORD the Israelites would
	20.24 you rebelled against my *c* at the waters
	22.18 I could not go beyond the *c* of the LORD
Ps	68.11 The Lord gives the *c*; great is the
Eccl	8. 2 Keep the king's *c* because of your
1 Cor	7.10 To the married I give *c* —not I but the
	14.37 what I am writing to you is a *c* of the

COMMAND (COMMANDED COMMANDS)

Gen	2.16 God *c* the man, "You may freely eat of
	6.22 did this; he did all that God *c* him.
Ex	7. 2 You shall speak all that I *c* you, and
	39.32 just as the LORD had *c* Moses.
Lev	8.36 did all the things that the LORD *c*
Deut	4.13 his covenant, which he *c* you to
	28. 8 LORD will *c* the blessing upon you in
Josh	1. 9 I hereby *c* you: Be strong and
	11.15 As the LORD *c* . . . Moses, so Moses *c*
Ps	33. 9 it came to be; he *c*, and it stood firm.
	148. 5 LORD, for he *c* and they were created.
Jer	1. 7 and you shall speak whatever I *c* you.
	11. 4 to my voice, and do all that I *c* you.
	26. 2 to them all the words that I *c* you;
Mt	4. 6 'He will *c* his angels concerning you,'
	28.20 them to obey everything I have *c* you.
Lk	8.25 this, that he *c* even the winds and the
	9.54 do you want us to *c* fire to come down
Jn	15.14 You are my friends if you do what I *c*
1 Cor	9.14 Lord *c* that those who proclaim the
1 Tim	6.17 age are rich, *c* them not to be haughty,

COMMANDER (COMMANDERS COMMANDER'S)

Gen	21.22 with Phicol the *c* of his army, said to
Deut	20. 9 then the *c* shall take charge of them.
	33.21 for there a *c* allotment was reserved; he
Josh	5.14 as *c* of the army of the LORD have I now

COMMANDMENT (COMMANDMENTS)

Ex	34.28 the words of the covenant, the ten *c*.
Lev	27.34 These are the *c* that the LORD gave to
Deut	4.13 you to observe, that is, the ten *c*.
1 Kings	2. 3 keeping his statutes, his *c*, his
Ezra	9.14 shall we break your *c* again and
Ps	119.151 near, O LORD, and all your *c* are true.
Prov	4. 4 fast to my words; keep my *c*, and live;
	13.13 who respect the *c* will be rewarded.
Eccl	12.13 Fear God, and keep his *c*; for that is the

Mt	19.17 you wish to enter into life, keep the *c*."
Jn	13.34 I give you a new *c*, that you love one
Rom	7.12 law is holy, and the *c* is holy and just
1 Jn	2. 7 no new *c*, but an old *c* that you have
	5. 3 his *c*. And his *c* are not burdensome,
2 Jn	5 though I were writing you a new *c*, but

COMMEND (COMMENDED COMMENDS)

Prov	12. 8 One is *c* for good sense, but a perverse
Eccl	8.15 I *c* enjoyment, for there is nothing
Lk	16. 8 his master *c* the dishonest manager
	23.46 "Father, into your hands I *c* my spirit!"
Acts	20.32 now I *c* you to God and to the message
Rom	16. 1 I *c* to you our sister Phoebe, a deacon
2 Cor	3. 1 Are we beginning to *c* ourselves again?
	10.12 with some of those who *c* themselves.
	10.18 approved, but those whom the Lord *c*.

COMMISSION

1 Cor	9.17 of my own will, I am entrusted with a *c*.
Eph	3. 2 of the *c* of God's grace that was given
Col	1.25 became its servant according to God's *c*

COMMIT (COMMITTED)

Josh	22.31 you have not *c* this treachery against
1 Kings	15. 3 he *c* all the sins that his father did
Neh	2.18 they *c* themselves to the common good.
Job	5. 8 God, and to God I would *c* my cause.
Ps	31. 5 Into your hand I *c* my spirit; you have
	37. 5 C your way to the LORD; trust in him
Prov	16. 3 C your work to the LORD, and your plans
Jer	20.12 them, for to you have I *c* my cause.
Ezek	17.20 for the treason he has *c* against me.
Dan	9. 7 of the treachery that they have *c*

COMMON

Acts	2.44 were together and had all things in *c*;
	4.32 everything they owned was held in *c*.
1 Cor	10.13 overtaken you that is not *c* to everyone.

COMMONWEALTH

Eph	2.12 Christ, being aliens from the *c* of Israel,

COMMUNE

Ps	77. 6 I *c* with my heart in the night; I

COMMUNION

2 Cor	13.13 and the *c* of the Holy Spirit be with all

COMMUNITY

Jn	21.23 rumor spread in the *c* that this disciple

COMPANION (COMPANIONS)

Josh	14. 8 my *c* who went up with me made the
Judg	14.20 Samson's wife was given to his *c*, who
Job	6.15 My *c* are treacherous like a torrent-bed,
Ps	119. 63 I am a *c* of all who fear you, of those
Prov	13.20 wise, but the *c* of fools suffers harm.
	28. 7 but *c* of gluttons shame their parents.
Song	8.13 my *c* are listening for your voice;
Mal	2.14 though she is your *c* and your wife by
Phil	4. 3 Yes, and I ask you, my loyal *c*, help

COMPANY

Ps	50.18 see one, and you keep *c* with adulterers.
	111. 1 in the *c* of the upright, in the
Jer	15.17 I did not sit in the *c* of merrymakers,
1 Cor	15.33 be deceived: "Bad *c* ruins good morals."

COMPARE (COMPARED)

Ps	40. 5 none can *c* with you. Were I to proclaim
	89. 6 who in the skies can be *c* to the LORD?
Isa	46. 5 and *c* me, as though we were alike?
Mt	11.16 to what will I *c* this generation? It is
2 Cor	10.12 We do not dare to classify or *c* ourselves

COMPASSION

Deut	13.17 show you *c*, and in his *c* multiply you,
Judg	21. 6 Israelites had *c* for Benjamin their kin,

Judg	21.15	people had c on Benjamin because the
2 Kings	13.23	gracious to them and had c on them;
2 Chr	30. 9	kindred and your children will find c
	36.15	he had c on his people and on his
Ps	103. 13	As a father has c on his children, so the
	135. 14	his people, and have c on his servants.
Isa	14. 1	the LORD will have c on Jacob and will
	54. 7	you, but with great c I will gather you.
Jer	12.15	them up, I will again have c on them,
Dan	1. 9	allowed Daniel to receive favor and c
Mic	7.19	He will again have c upon us; he will
Zech	12.10	I will pour out a spirit of c and
Mt	9.36	he saw the crowds, he had c for them,
	14.14	and he had c for them and cured their
	15.32	"I have c for the crowd, because they
	20.34	Moved with c, Jesus touched their eyes.
Mk	6.34	he saw a great crowd; and he had c on
	8. 2	"I have c for the crowd, because they
Lk	7.13	he had c for her and said to her, and
	15.20	father saw him and was filled with c;
Heb	10.34	For you had c for those who were in

COMPASSIONATE

Ex	22.27	cries out to me, I will listen, for I am c.
Ps	78.38	he, being c, forgave their iniquity, and
Jas	5.11	Lord, how the Lord is c and merciful.

COMPEL (COMPELLED)

Mt	27.32	they c this man to carry his cross.
Lk	14.23	and lanes, and c the people to come in,
Gal	2. 3	with me, was not c to be circumcised,
	2.14	Jew, how can you c the Gentiles to live

COMPETE

Jer	12. 5	you, how will you c with horses?
1 Cor	9.24	in a race the runners all c, but only one

COMPETENT

2 Cor	3. 5	Not that we are c of ourselves to claim

COMPLAIN (COMPLAINED)

Gen	21.25	Abraham c to Abimelech about a well
Ex	16. 2	the Israelites c against Moses and Aaron
Num	11. 1	people c in the hearing of the LORD
	14. 2	Israelites c against Moses and Aaron;
	14.27	long shall this wicked congregation c
Job	7.11	of my spirit; I will c in the bitterness of
Jn	6.41	the Jews began to c about him because
Acts	6. 1	Hellenists c against the Hebrews
1 Cor	10.10	do not c as some of them did, and were

COMPLAINT

Job	23. 2	"Today also my c is bitter; his hand is
Ps	55.17	and at noon I utter my c and moan, and
	142. 2	I pour out my c before him; I tell my
Dan	6. 4	to find grounds for c against Daniel
Hab	2. 1	what he will answer concerning my c.

COMPLETE (COMPLETED COMPLETING)

Gen	15.16	the iniquity of the Amorites is not yet c."
Jn	5.36	that the Father has given me to c,
Rom	15.28	when I have c this, and have delieveed
2 Cor	8.11	by c it according to your means.
Jas	1. 4	so that you may be mature and c,

COMPLETELY

Jn	17.23	that they may become c one, so that

COMPLETION

Jas	2.22	faith was brought to c by the works,

COMPREHEND

Job	37. 5	he does great things that we cannot c.
Eph	3.18	I pray that you may have power to c,

COMPUTE

Lev	25.50	They shall c with the purchaser the

CONCEAL (CONCEALED CONCEALS)

Job	31.33	if I have c my transgressions as others
Prov	12.23	One who is clever c knowledge, but the
	25. 2	It is the glory of God to c things, but
	28.13	No one who c transgressions will

CONCEIT

Job	37.24	regard any who are wise in their own c."

CONCEITED

1 Tim	6. 4	is c, understanding nothing, and has a

CONCEIVE (CONCEIVED)

Gen	4. 1	his wife Eve, and she c and bore Cain,
Ps	35.20	they c deceitful words against those

CONCERNED

Jon	4.10	LORD said, "You are c about the bush,
Phil	2.20	will be genuinely c for your welfare.

CONCOCT

Prov	16.27	Scoundrels c evil, and their speech is

CONCUBINE (CONCUBINES)

Judg	19. 2	his c became angry with him, and she
2 Sam	16.22	Absalom went in to his father's c in the

CONDEMN (CONDEMNED CONDEMNS)

Job	34.29	When he is quiet, who can c? When he
	40. 8	you c me that you may be justified?
Ps	34.22	those who take refuge in him will be c.
	37.33	or let them be c when they are brought
	94.21	righteous, and c the innocent to death.
	109. 31	to save them from those who would c
Prov	12. 2	LORD, but those who devise evil he c.
Mt	20.18	scribes, and they will c him to death;
Mk	10.33	scribes, and they will c him to death,
Lk	11.32	judgment with this generation and c it;
Jn	3.17	not to c the world, but in order that
	8.10	where are they? Has no one c you?"
Rom	8.34	Who is to c? Is it Christ Jesus, who
Col	2.16	do not let anyone c you in the matters
1 Jn	3.21	if our hearts do not c us, we have

CONDEMNATION

Rom	5.18	as one man's trespass led to c for all,
	8. 1	is now no c for those who are in Christ

CONDITION

1 Cor	7.20	you remain in the c in which you were

CONDUCT

Job	11. 4	you say, "My c is pure, and I am clean
Ps	112. 5	lend, who c their affairs with justice.
Prov	10.23	wise c is a pleasure to a person of
Col	4. 5	C yourselves wisely toward outsiders,
1 Pet	2.12	C yourselves honorably among the
	3.16	those who abuse you for your good c in

CONDUIT

2 Kings	18.17	and stood by the c of the upper pool,
	20.20	how he made the pool and the c and
Isa	36. 2	He stood by the c of the upper pool on

CONFERRED

Mt	27. 1	and elders of the people c together
Lk	22.29	on you just as my Father has c on me,

CONFESS (CONFESSED CONFESSES CONFESSING)

Lev	5. 5	you shall c the sin that you have
	26.40	But if they c their iniquity and the
Num	5. 7	c the sin that has been committed. The
1 Kings	8.33	turn again to you, c your name, pray
Ps	32. 5	"I will c my transgressions to the LORD,"
Prov	28.13	but one who c and forsakes them will
Mt	3. 6	by him in the river Jordan, c their sins.
Mk	1. 5	by him in the river Jordan, c their sins.
Jn	1.20	He c and did not deny it, but c, "I am

Jn	9.22	anyone who *c* Jesus to be the Messiah
Acts	19.18	many of those who became believers *c*
Rom	10. 9	if you *c* with your lips that Jesus is
	10.10	one *c* with the mouth and is so saved.
	15. 9	I will *c* you among the Gentiles,
Phil	2.11	every tongue should *c* that Jesus Christ
Heb	11.13	They *c* that they were strangers and
Jas	5.16	*c* your sins to one another, and pray for
1 Jn	1. 9	we *c* our sins, he who is faithful and
	4.15	abides in those who *c* that Jesus is the
Rev	3. 5	I will *c* your name before my Father and

CONFESSION

Ezra	10. 1	Ezra prayed and made *c*, weeping and
	10.11	Now make *c* to the LORD the God of
Dan	9. 4	made *c*, saying, "Ah, Lord, great and
1 Tim	6.13	made the good *c*, I charge you to keep
Heb	4.14	Son of God, let us hold fast to our *c*.

CONFIDENCE

2 Kings	18.19	of Assyria: On what do you base this *c*
Prov	3.26	the LORD will be your *c* and will keep
	11.13	who is trustworthy in spirit keeps a *c*.
Isa	36. 4	On what do you base this *c* of yours?
Mic	7. 5	in a friend, have no *c* in a loved one;
Phil	3. 4	I, too, have reason for *c* in the flesh,
2 Thess	3. 4	we have *c* in the Lord concerning you,

CONFIDENT

Ps	27. 3	war rise up against me, yet I will be *c*.
2 Cor	5. 6	So we are always *c*; even though we
	10. 7	If you are *c* that you belong to Christ,
Gal	5.10	I am *c* about you in the Lord that you
Phil	1. 6	I am *c* of this, that the one who began
Heb	6. 9	beloved, we are *c* of better things in

CONFIRMS (CONFIRMED)

Ps	119.106	I have sworn an oath and *c* it, to
Isa	44.26	who *c* the word of his servant, and
Mt	18.16	every word may be *c* by the evidence of
Mk	16.20	*n c* the message by the signs that

CONFLICTS

Jas	4. 1	Those *c* and disputes among you, where

CONFORMED

Rom	12. 2	Do not be *c* to this world but be
Phil	3.21	it may be *c* to the body of his glory,
1 Pet	1.14	do not be *c* to the desires that you

CONFRONT

Deut	31.21	this song shall *c* them as a witness,
Ps	17.13	Rise up, O LORD, *c* them, overthrow

CONFUSING

Gal	1. 7	but there are some who are *c* you and

CONFUSION

Ex	23.27	will throw into *c* all the people against
Esth	3.15	but the city of Susa was thrown into *c*.

CONFUTED

Job	32.12	there was in fact no one that *c* Job, no

CONGREGATION

Lev	4.13	If the whole *c* of Israel errs
Num	1. 2	Take a census of the whole *c* of
	35.24	the *c* shall judge between the slayer and
Ps	22.22	and sisters; in the midst of the *c* I will
	26.12	level ground; in the great *c* I will bless
	40.10	and your faithfulness from the great *c*.
	107. 32	Let them extol him in the *c* of the
Acts	7.38	in the *c* in the wilderness with the
Heb	2.12	in the midst of the *c* I will praise

CONQUER (CONQUERED CONQUERING CONQUERS)

Jn	16.33	But take courage; I have *c* the world!"
Heb	11.33	who through faith *c* kingdoms,

1 Jn	4. 4	you are from God, and have *c* them; for
	5. 4	And this is the victory that *c* the world,
Rev	2.17	To everyone who *c* I will give some of
	3. 5	If you *c* you will be clothed like them in
	3.21	one who *c*, I will give a place with me
	5. 5	Judah, the Root of David, has *c*, so that
	6. 2	to him, and he came out *c* and to *c*.
	12.11	have *c* him by the blood of the Lamb
	15. 2	those who had *c* the beast and its
	17.14	the Lamb will *c* them, for he is Lord of
	21. 7	who *c* will inherit these things, and I

CONQUERORS

Rom	8.37	we are more than *c* through him who

CONSCIENCE

Acts	23. 1	I have lived my life with a clear *c* before
	24.16	I do my best always to have a clear *c*
Rom	2.15	to which their own *c* also bears witness;
	9. 1	— I am not lying; my *c* confirms it by
	13. 5	because of wrath but also because of *c*.
1 Cor	8.10	since their *c* is weak, be encouraged to
	10.29	I mean the other's *c*, not your own. For
1 Tim	1.19	good fight, having faith and a good *c*.
2 Tim	1. 3	God — whom I worship with a clear *c*,
Heb	9. 9	cannot perfect the *c* of the worshiper,
1 Pet	3.16	Keep your *c* clear, so that, when you
	3.21	but as an appeal to God for a good *c*,

CONSCIENTIOUS

2 Chr	29.34	— for the Levites were more *c* than the

CONSECRATE (CONSECRATED CONSECRATES CONSECRATING)

Ex	13. 2	"*C* to me all the firstborn; whatever is
	19.10	"Go to the people and *c* them today and
	28.41	ordain them and *c* them, so that they
	29. 1	is what you shall do to them to *c* them,
Lev	8.10	and all that was in it, and *c* them.
	20. 7	*C* yourselves therefore, and be holy; for
	27.14	If a person *c* a house to the LORD, the
Num	8.17	in the land of Egypt I *c* them for myself,
Deut	15.19	herd and flock you shall *c* to the LORD
1 Chr	29. 5	will offer willingly, *c* themselves today
Jer	1. 5	you, and before you were born I *c* you;

CONSECRATION

Num	6. 7	their *c* to God is upon the head.

CONSENT (CONSENTED CONSENTS)

Prov	1.10	child, if sinners entice you, do not *c*.
Lk	22. 6	he *c* and began to look for a way to
Acts	15.22	elders, with the *c* of the whole church,
1 Cor	7.12	and she *c* to live with him, he should

CONSIDER (CONSIDERED CONSIDERS)

Judg	19.30	until this day? *C* it, take counsel, and
Ruth	1. 6	the LORD had *c* his people and given
1 Sam	12.24	for *c* what great things he has done for
Job	1. 8	to Satan, "Have you *c* my servant Job?
	37.14	stop and *c* the wondrous works of God.
Ps	41. 1	Happy are those who *c* the poor;
	90.11	Who *c* the power of your anger? Your
	119. 95	to destroy me, but I *c* your decrees.
Prov	6. 6	you lazybones; *c* its ways, and be wise.
	24.32	Then I saw and *c* it; I looked and
Isa	44.19	No one *c*, nor is there knowledge or
Hag	1. 5	*C* how you have fared. You have sown
	2.15	But now, *c* what will come to pass from
Mt	6.28	*C* the lilies of the field, how they grow;
Lk	12.24	*C* the ravens: they neither sow nor reap,
Acts	20.24	I do not *c* my life of any value to
Rom	6.11	you also must *c* yourselves dead to sin
Heb	3. 1	that Jesus, the apostle and high priest
	10.24	let us *c* how to provoke one another to
	11.11	barren — because he *c* him faithful who
	11.19	He *c* the fact that God is able even to
	12. 3	*C* him who endured such hostility

Jas 1. 2 trials of any kind, *c* it nothing but joy,

CONSIGNED

Isa 38.10 I am *c* to the gates of Sheol for the

CONSISTENT (CONSISTENTLY)

Gal 2.14 they were not acting *c* with the truth
Titus 2. 1 teach what is *c* with sound doctrine.

CONSOLATION (CONSOLATIONS)

Job 15.11 Are the *c* of God too small for you, or
21. 2 to my words, and let this be your *c*.
Jer 16. 7 anyone give them the cup of *c* to drink
Ezek 16.54 you have done, becoming a *c* to them.
Zech 10. 2 tell false dreams, and give empty *c*.
Lk 2.25 looking forward to the *c* of Israel,
2 Cor 1. 3 Father of mercies and God of all *c*,

CONSOLE (CONSOLED)

Ezek 14.22 you will be *c* for the evil that I have
Jn 11.19 to Martha and Mary to *c* them about
2 Cor 7. 6 downcast, *c* us by the arrival of Titus,

CONSPIRACY

2 Sam 15.12 The *c* grew in strength, and the people
Isa 8.12 Do not call *c* all that this people call *c*,
Acts 23.13 more than forty who joined in this *c*.

CONSPIRE (CONSPIRED)

Gen 37.18 came near to them, they *c* to kill him.
1 Kings 16. 9 his his servant Zimri . . . *c* against him.
Ps 2. 1 Why do the nations *c*, and the peoples
Am 7.10 "Amos has *c* against you in the very

CONSTRAINS

Job 32.18 full of words; the spirit within me *c* me.

CONSULT (CONSULTED CONSULTS)

1 Chr 13. 1 David *c* with the commanders of the
Isa 8.19 if the people say to you, "*C* the ghosts
31. 1 to the Holy One of Israel or *c* the LORD!
Ezek 14. 3 them; shall I let myself be *c* by them?
20. 3 Why are you coming? To *c* me? As I
21.21 shakes the arrows, he *c* the teraphim,
Hos 4.12 My people *c* a piece of wood, and their

CONSUME (CONSUMED CONSUMES CONSUMING)

Num 16.21 so that I may *c* them in a moment.
Job 1.16 the sheep and the servants, and *c* them;
20.26 them; what is left in their tent will be *c*.
Ps 59.13 *c* them in wrath, *c* them until they are
90. 7 For we are *c* by your anger; by your
Mt 6.20 where neither moth nor rust *c* and
Heb 12.29 and awe; for indeed our God is a *c* fire.

CONTAIN

1 Kings 8.27 and the highest heaven cannot *c* you,
Jn 21.25 world itself could not *c* the books that

CONTEMPLATE

Isa 52.15 which they had not heard they shall *c*.

CONTEMPT

Gen 16. 4 she looked with *c* on her mistress.
Esth 1.17 to look with *c* upon their husbands,
Job 12. 5 Those at ease have *c* for misfortune, but
Isa 9. 1 he brought into *c* the land of Zebulun
Lk 18. 9 righteous and regarded others with *c*:
1 Cor 11.22 Or do you show *c* for the church of God

CONTEND

Judg 6.31 "Will you *c* for Baal? Or will you defend
Job 10. 2 me; let me know why you *c* against me.
13.19 Who is there that will *c* with me? For
Ps 35. 1 *C*, O LORD, with those who *c* with me;
Isa 49.25 I will *c* with those who *c* with you, and
Hos 4. 4 Yet let no one *c*, and let none accuse,
Jude 3 appeal to you to *c* for the faith that was

CONTENT

Josh 7. 7 Would that we had been *c* to settle
2 Cor 12.10 Therefore I am *c* with weaknesses,
Phil 4.11 need; for I have learned to be *c* with
1 Tim 6. 8 and clothing, we will be *c* with these.

CONTENTIOUS

Prov 21.19 land than with a *c* and fretful wife.
27.15 on a rainy day and a *c* wife are alike;

CONTINUALLY

Ps 34. 1 his praise shall *c* be in my mouth.

CONTINUE (CONTINUED)

Ps 36.10 O *c* your steadfast love to those who
Jer 31. 3 I have *c* my faithfulness to you.
Jn 8.31 "If you *c* in my word, you are truly my
Acts 13.43 them and urged them to *c* in the grace
Rom 6. 1 we *c* in sin that grace may abound?
Phil 1.25 I will remain and *c* with all of you for
2 Tim 3.14 for you, *c* in what you have learned and

CONTRIBUTIONS

2 Chr 31.12 Faithfully brought in the *c*, the tithes

CONTRITE

Ps 51.17 a broken and *c* heart, O God, you will
Isa 66. 2 to the humble and *c* in spirit, who

CONTRITION

Jer 44.10 They have shown no *c* or fear to this

CONTROL (CONTROLLED)

Gen 45. 1 Joseph could no longer *c* himself before
Prov 16.32 one whose temper is *c* than one who
1 Cor 7.37 necessity but having his desire under *c*,
1 Thess 4. 4 you know how to *c* your body in
Heb 2. 8 them, God left nothing outside their *c*.

CONTROVERSY

Mic 6. 2 Hear, you mountains, the *c* of the LORD,

CONVERT (CONVERTS)

Mt 23.15 cross sea and land to make a single *c*,
Rom 16. 5 Epaenetus, who was the first *c* in Asia
1 Cor 16.15 were the first *c* in Achaia, and
1 Tim 3. 6 He must not be a recent *c*, or he may

CONVICT (CONVICTS)

Jer 2.19 you, and your apostasies will *c* you.
Jn 8.46 Which of you *c* me of sin? If I tell the
Jude 15 to *c* everyone of all the deeds of

CONVINCE (CONVINCED)

Acts 18. 4 and would try to *c* Jews and Greeks.
Rom 4.21 fully *c* that God was able to do what he
8.38 I am *c* that neither death, nor life, nor
14. 5 Let all be fully *c* in their own minds.

CONVOCATION

Lev 23. 3 is a sabbath of complete rest, a holy *c*;
Num 28.26 of weeks, you shall have a holy *c*;

COOKED

2 Kings 6.29 we *c* my son and ate him. The next day

COOL

Prov 17.27 who is *c* in spirit has understanding.

COPY

Josh 8.32 wrote on the stones a *c* of the law
Esth 4. 8 Mordecai also gave him a *c* of the

CORBAN

Mk 7.11 might have had from me is *C*' (that is,

CORD (CORDS)

Ps 18. 4 The *c* of death encompassed me, the
129. 4 he has cut the *c* of the wicked.
Eccl 4.12 A threefold *c* is not quickly broken.

Eccl	12.	6 before the silver c is snapped, and the
Hos	11.	4 I led them with c of human kindness,

CORINTH

Acts	18.	1 this Paul left Athens and went to C.
	19.	1 While Apollos was at C, Paul passed
1 Cor	1.	2 church of God that is in C, to those

CORNELIUS

Acts	10.	1 there was a man named C, a centurion
	10.	3 of God coming in and saying to him, "C."
	10.24	C was expecting them and had called
	10.31	'C, your prayer has been heard and

CORNER

Acts	26.26	his notice, for this was not done in a c.
1 Pet	2.	7 has become the very head of the c,"

CORNERSTONE

Eph	2.20	with Christ Jesus himself as the c,
1 Pet	2.	6 Zion a stone, a c chosen and precious;

CORPSE

Mt	24.28	Wherever the c is, there the vultures

CORRECT

Jer	10.24	C me, O Lord, but in just measure; not

CORRECTION

Jer	2.30	down your children; they accepted no c.
	5.	3 them, but they refused to take c.
Zeph	3.	2 to no voice; it has accepted no c.
	3.	7 the city will fear me, it will accept c;

CORRUPT (CORRUPTED)

Gen	6.11	Now the earth was c in God's sight, and
Hos	9.	9 They have deeply c themselves as in the
Mal	2.	8 you have c the covenant of Levi,

CORRUPTION

Dan	6.	4 find no grounds for complaint or any c,
Acts	2.27	or let your Holy One experience c.
	13.35	not let your Holy One experience c.'

CORRUPTLY

Deut	4.16	do not act c by making an idol for

COST

2 Sam	24.24	to the Lord my God that c me nothing."
1 Chr	21.24	offer burnt offerings that c me nothing."
Ezra	6.	4 timber; let the c be paid from the royal
Lk	14.28	not first sit down and estimate the c,

COUNCIL (COUNCILS)

Job	15.	8 Have you listened in the c of God? And
Ps	82.	1 God has taken his place in the divine c;
	89.	7 a God feared in the c of the holy ones,
Jer	23.18	For who has stood in the c of the Lord
Mt	10.17	they will hand you over to c and flog
Lk	23.50	though a member of the c, had not

COUNSEL (COUNSELED COUNSELS)

Ex	18.19	Now listen to me. I will give you c, and
2 Sam	17.	7 time the c which Ahithophel has given
Job	26.	2 you have c one who has no wisdom,
	38.	2 "Who is this that darkens c by words
Ps	2.	2 the rulers take c together, against the
	33.10	brings the c of the nations to nothing;
	33.11	c of the Lord stands forever, the
	73.24	You guide me with your c, and
	106.	13 his works; they did not wait for his c.
Prov	15.22	Without c, plans go wrong, but with
Isa	11.	2 the spirit of c and might, the spirit of
	28.29	Lord of hosts; he is wonderful in c, and
Jer	7.24	evil will they walked in their own c,
	18.18	from the priest, nor c from the wise,
	32.19	of hosts, great in c and mighty in deed;
Dan	4.27	O king, let my c be acceptable to you:
Eph	1.11	all things according to his c and will,

COUNSELOR (COUNSELORS)

2 Chr	22.	3 his mother was his c in doing wickedly.
	25.16	"Have we made you a royal c? Stop!
Ps	119.	24 decrees are my delight, they are my c.
Isa	1.26	at the first, your c as at the beginning.
	3.	3 dignitary, c and the skillful magician
	9.	6 and he is named Wonderful C, Mighty
	40.13	Lord, or as his c has instructed him?
	41.28	among these there is no c who, when I
Mic	4.	9 Has your c perished, that pangs have

COUNT (COUNTED COUNTING)

Gen	15.	5 c the stars, if you are able to c them."
Num	23.10	Who can c the dust of Jacob, or number
2 Sam	24.	1 "Go, c the people of Israel and Judah."
Ps	90.12	So teach us to c our days that we may
	139.	18 I try to c them—they are more than
Mk	15.28	n says, "And he was c among the lawless."
Lk	22.37	'And he was c among the lawless'; and
2 Cor	5.19	world to himself, not c their trespasses

COUNTENANCE

Gen	4.	5 So Cain was very angry, and his c fell.
Job	29.24	light of my c they did not extinguish.
Prov	15.13	A glad heart makes a cheerful c, but by

COUNTRY

Heb	11.16	they desire a better c, that is, a

COURAGE

1 Sam	4.	9 Take c, and be men, O Philistines, in
1 Chr	28.20	"Be strong and of good c, and act. Do
2 Chr	15.	8 he took c, and put away the abominable
Ps	27.14	be strong, and let your heart take c;
	31.24	Be strong, and let your heart take c, all
Ezek	22.14	Can your c endure, or can your hands
Jn	16.33	But take c; I have conquered
Acts	23.11	"Keep up your c! For just as you have
	27.22	I urge you now to keep up your c, for
	27.25	So keep up your c, men, for I have faith
	28.15	them, Paul thanked God and took c.

COURAGEOUS (COURAGEOUSLY)

Josh	1.	6 Be strong and c; for you shall put this
	1.	9 Be strong and c; do not be frightened or
	10.25	be strong and c; for thus the Lord will
2 Sam	10.12	Be strong, and let us be c for the sake
2 Chr	19.11	Deal c, and may the Lord be with the
1 Cor	16.13	stand firm in your faith, be c, be strong.

COURSE

Ps	19.	5 like a strong man runs its c with joy.
Acts	20.24	if only I may finish my c and the

COURT

Ex	27.	9 You shall make the c of the tabernacle.
1 Cor	4.	3 be judged by you or by any human c.
	6.	1 do you dare to take it to c before the

COVENANT

Gen	6.18	I will establish my c with you; and you
	9.	9 I am establishing my c with you and
	17.	2 I will make my c between me and you,
	21.27	Abimelech, and the two men made a c.
	26.28	and us, and let us make a c with you,
	31.44	Come now, let us make a c, you and I;
Ex	2.24	God remembered his c with Abraham,
	6.	4 I also established my c with them, to
	23.32	You shall make no c with them and
	24.	8 "See the blood of the c that the Lord
	25.16	You shall put into the ark the c that I
	34.28	wrote . . . the words of the c, the ten
Lev	26.	9 you; and I will maintain my c with you.
	26.25	you, executing vengeance for the c;
	26.42	I will remember also my c with Isaac,
Num	25.12	say, 'I hereby grant him my c of peace.
Deut	4.31	he will not forget the c with your
	5.	3 our ancestors did the Lord make this c,

Deut	7.	2 Make no c with them and show them
	7.	9 the faithful God who maintains c loyalty
	7.12	God will maintain with you the c loyalty
	17.	2 the LORD your God, and transgress his c
	29.	1 These are the words of the c that the
	29.12	to enter into the c of the LORD your
	29.25	it is because they abandoned the c of
	33.	9 observed your word, and kept your c.
Josh	24.25	So Joshua made a c with the people
Judg	2.	1 I said, 'I will never break my c with
	2.	2 do not make a c with the inhabitants of
1 Sam	18.	3 Jonathan made a c with David, because
	20.	8 brought your servant into a sacred c
2 Sam	3.21	they may make a c with you, and that
	5.	3 David made a c with them at Hebron
	23.	5 he has made with me an everlasting c,
1 Kings	8.23	keeping c and showing steadfast love for
	19.10	Israelites have forsaken your c, thrown
2 Kings	11.	4 He made a c with them and put them
	23.	2 book of the c that had been found in
	23.	3 book. All the people joined in the c.
1 Chr	16.15	Remember his c forever, the word that
2 Chr	6.14	keeping c in steadfast love with your
	15.12	They entered into a c to seek the LORD,
	21.	7 of the c that he had made with David,
	34.31	his place and made a c before the LORD,
Ezra	10.	3 let us make a c with our God to send
Ps	25.10	for those who keep his c and
	25.14	and he makes his c known to them.
	44.17	not forgotten you, or be false to your c.
	50.	5 faithful ones, who made a c with me by
	55.20	on a friend and violated a c with me.
	74.20	Have regard for your c, for the dark
	78.37	toward him; they were not true to his c.
	83.	5 accord; against they they make a c—
	89.	3 "I have made a c with my chosen one,
	103.	18 to those who keep his c and remember
	105.	10 a statute, to Israel as an everlasting c,
	106.	45 their sake he remembered his c, and
	132.	12 If your sons keep my c and my decrees
Prov	2.17	of her youth and forgets her sacred c;
Isa	28.18	your c with death will be annulled,
	42.	6 I have given you as a c to the people, a
	59.21	as for me, this is my c with them, says
	61.	8 I will make an everlasting c with them.
Jer	11.10	the house of Judah have broken the c
	14.21	and do not break your c with us.
	22.	9 "Because they abandoned the c of the
	31.31	when I will make a new c with the
	32.40	I will make an everlasting c with them,
	33.21	then could my c with my servant David
	50.	5 c that will never be forgotten.
Ezek	16.60	yet I will remember my c with you in
	17.14	that by keeping his c it might stand.
	37.26	I will make a c of peace with them; it
Dan	9.27	He shall make a strong c with many for
	11.28	his heart shall be set against the holy c.
Hos	6.	7 But at Adam they transgressed the c;
Mal	2.	4 to you, that my c with Levi may hold,
	2.14	is your companion and your wife by c.
Mt	26.28	this is my blood of the c, which is
Mk	14.24	"This is my blood of the c, which is
Lk	1.72	and has remembered his holy c,
Acts	3.25	of the prophets and of the c
	7.	8 Then he gave him the c of circumcision.
Rom	11.27	"And this is my c with them, when I
1 Cor	11.25	"This cup is the new c in my blood. Do
2 Cor	3.	6 competent to be ministers of a new c,
	3.14	when they hear the reading of the old c,
Gal	3.17	does not annul a c previously ratified by
Heb	7.22	also become the guarantee of a better c.
	8.	8 when I will establish a new c with the
	9.15	reason he is the mediator of a new c,
	10.16	is the c that I will make with them
Rev	11.19	the ark of his c was seen within his

COVENANTS

Hos	10.	4 words; with empty oaths they make c;
Eph	2.12	strangers to the c of promise, having no

COVER (COVERED COVERING COVERS)

Gen	7.20	mountains, c them fifteen cubits deep.
Ex	33.22	I will c you with my hand until I have
Num	9.15	the cloud c the tabernacle, the tent of
	16.42	the cloud had c it, and the glory of the
Ps	5.12	LORD; you c them with favor as a shield.
	91.	4 he will c you with his pinions, and
Prov	10.12	stirs up strife, but love c all offenses.
Isa	6.	2 with two they c their faces, and with
	11.	9 of the LORD as the waters c the sea.
Hos	10.	8 They shall say to the mountains, C us,
Mt	10.26	nothing is c up that will not be
Lk	12.	2 Nothing is c up that will not be
	23.30	'Fall on us'; and to the hills, 'C us.'

COVERING (n)

Ps	18.11	He made darkness his c around him, his
Isa	28.20	on it, and the c too narrow to wrap

COVET (COVETED)

Ex	20.17	You shall not c your neighbor's house;
Deut	5.21	Neither shall you c your neighbor's
Josh	7.21	fifty shekels, then I c them and took
Mic	2.	2 They c fields, and seize them; houses,
Acts	20.33	I c no one's silver or gold or clothing.
Rom	7.	7 the law had not said, "You shall not c."
	13.	9 You shall not steal, You shall not c,"

COVETOUSNESS

Isa	57.17	Because of their wicked c I was angry; I
Rom	1.29	kind of wickedness, evil, c, malice.
	7.	8 produced in me all kinds of c.

CO-WORKERS

Col	4.11	among my c for the kingdom of God,
3 Jn		8 that we may become c with the truth.

CRAFT

Isa	2.16	Tarshish, and against all the beautiful c.

CRAFTINESS

Job	5.13	He takes the wise in their own c; and
1 Cor	3.19	written, "He catches the wise in their c,"
Eph	4.14	by their c in deceitful scheming.

CRAFTY

Job	5.12	He frustrates the devices of the c, so
	15.	5 and you choose the tongue of the c.

CRAVING (CRAVINGS)

Prov	21.25	The c of the lazy person is fatal, for lazy
Jas	4.	1 they come from your c that are at war

CREATE (CREATED CREATES)

Gen	1.	1 when God c the heavens and the earth,
	1.21	God c the great sea monsters and every
	1.27	God c humankind in his own image, in
Deut	32.	6 Is not he your father, who c you, who
Ps	51.10	C in me a clean heart, O God, and put
	104.	30 you send forth your Spirit, they are c;
	148.	5 for he commanded and they were c.
Prov	8.22	The LORD c me at the beginning of his
Isa	4.	5 Then the LORD will c over the whole site
	40.26	your eyes on high and see: who c these?
	41.20	this, the Holy One of Israel has c it.
	42.	5 says God, the LORD, who c the heavens
	43.	7 whom I c for my glory, whom I formed
	45.	7 I form light and c darkness, I make
	45.18	thus says the LORD, who c the heavens
	65.17	For I am about to c new heavens and a
Jer	31.22	For the LORD has c a new thing on the
Am	4.13	c the wind, and reveals his thoughts to
Eph	2.10	us, c in Christ Jesus for good works,
Col	1.16	—all things have been c through him

1 Tim	4.	4 For everything *c* by God is good, and
Rev	4.11	to you *c* all things, and by your will
	10.	6 who *c* heaven and what is in it, the

CREATION

Mk	13.19	not been from the beginning of the *c*
Rom	8.21	the *c* itself will be set free from its
	8.22	the whole *c* has been groaning in labor
2 Cor	5.17	if anyone is in Christ, there is a new *c:*
Gal	6.15	is anything; but a new *c* is everything!
2 Pet	3.	4 as they were from the beginning of *c*!"

CREATOR

Eccl	12.	1 Remember your *C* in the days of your
Isa	40.28	God, *C* of the ends of the earth.
	43.15	Holy One, the *C* of Israel, your King.
Rom	1.25	served the creature rather than the *C,*

CREATURES

Gen	1.20	waters bring forth swarms of living *c,*
Ezek	10.17	for the spirit of the living *c* was in
Rev	4.	6 four living *c,* full of eyes in front and

CREDIT

Deut	24.13	it will be to your *c* before the LORD your

CREDITOR (CREDITORS)

Deut	15.	2 every *c* shall remit the claim that is
Isa	50.	1 Or which of my *c* is it to whom I have
Lk	7.41	"A certain *c* had two debtors; one owed

CREEPING

Gen	1.24	cattle and *c* things and wild animals of

CRETE

Acts	27.12	It was a harbor of *C*, facing southwest
Titus	1.	5 I left you behind in *C* for this reason, so

CRIME (CRIMES)

Gen	50.17	I beg you, forgive the *c* of your brothers
Deut	24.16	only for their own *c* may persons be put
Judg	9.56	God repaid Abimelech for the *c* he
Ezek	7.23	the land is full of bloody *c*; the city is

CRIMINAL

Judg	20.	3 us, how did this *c* act come about?"

CRIMSON

Josh	2.18	tie this *c* cord in the window through

CRINGE (CRINGING)

Ps	18.44	obeyed me; foreigners came *c* to me.
	66.	3 great power, your enemies *c* before you.

CRIPPLED

Acts	14.	8 walked, for he had been *c* from birth.
2 Sam	4.	4 Jonathan had a son who was *c* in his
	9.	3 a son of Jonathan; he is *c* in his feet."

CRISIS

1 Cor	7.26	in view of the impending *c*, it is well for

CROOKED

Prov	2.15	those whose paths are *c*, and who are
Eccl	1.15	What is *c* cannot be made straight, and
	7.13	can make straight what he has made *c*?
Isa	59.	8 Their roads they have made *c*; no one

CROPS

Lk	12.17	I do, for I have no place to store my *c*?'
2 Tim	2.	6 ought to have the first share of the *c*.

CROSS

Mt	10.38	whoever does not take the *c* and follow
	16.24	and take up their *c* and follow me.
	27.32	they compelled this man to carry his *c*.
Mk	8.34	deny themselves and take up their *c*
	15.21	to carry his *c*; it was Simon of Cyrene,
	15.30	yourself, and come down from the *c*!"
Lk	9.23	themselves and take up their *c* daily

Lk	14.27	does not carry the *c* and follow me
	23.26	laid the *c* on him, and made him carry
Jn	19.17	and carrying the *c* by himself, he went
1 Cor	1.17	so that the *c* of Christ be emptied of its
Gal	5.11	the offense of the *c* has been removed.
	6.12	they may not be persecuted for the *c*
	6.14	I never boast of anything except the *c*
Phil	2.	8 the point of death—even death on a *c*.
	3.18	many live as enemies of the *c* of Christ;
Col	2.14	He set this aside, nailing it to the *c*.
Heb	12.	2 endured the *c*, disregarding its shame,
1 Pet	2.24	bore our sins in his body on the *c*,

CROSS-EXAMINE

Lk	11.53	to *c* him about many things, lying in

CROSSING

Josh	3.17	entire nation finished *c* over the Jordan.

CROWD (CROWDS)

Mt	4.25	And great *c* followed him from Galilee,
Mk	8.	2 "I have compassion on the *c*, because
	12.37	The large *c* was listening to him with

CROWN (CROWNED)

2 Chr	23.11	out the king's son, put the *c* on him,
Ps	8.	5 God, and *c* them with glory and honor.
	21.	3 rich blessings; you set a *c* of fine gold
	65.11	You *c* the year with your bounty; your
Prov	4.	9 she will bestow on you a beautiful *c*."
	12.	4 A good wife is the *c* of her husband, but
	16.31	Gray hair is a *c* of glory; it is gained in
Isa	62.	3 You shall be a *c* of beauty in the hand
Lam	5.16	*c* has fallen from our head; woe to us,
Ezek	16.12	ears, and a beautiful *c* upon your head.
Zech	6.11	make a *c*, and set it on the head of the
2 Tim	4.	8 reserved for me the *c* of righteousness,
Rev	3.11	have so that no one may seize your *c*.
	14.14	Son of Man, with a golden *c* on his

CROWS

Mk	14.30	very night, before the cock *c* twice, you

CRUCIBLE

Prov	17.	3 The *c* is for silver, and the furnace is for

CRUCIFY (CRUCIFIED)

Mt	20.19	to be mocked and flogged and *c*;
	23.34	some of whom you will kill and *c*, and
	27.22	All of them said, "Let him be *c*."
	27.35	when they had *c* him, they divided his
	28.	5 you are looking for Jesus who was *c*.
Mk	15.13	They shouted back, "*C* him!"
	15.20	him. Then they led him out to *c* him.
	16.	6 for Jesus of Nazareth, who was *c*.
Lk	23.21	but they kept shouting, "*C*, *c*, him!"
	23.33	The Skull, they *c* Jesus there with the
Jn	19.	6 saw him, they shouted, "*C* him, *c* him!"
	19.10	to release you, and power to *c* you?"
	19.18	There they *c* him, and with him two
Acts	2.23	you *c* and killed by the hands of those
Rom	6.	6 our old self was *c* with him so that the
1 Cor	1.13	been divided? Was Paul *c* for you?
	2.	2 you except Jesus Christ and him *c*.
	2.	8 had, they would not have *c* the Lord
2 Cor	13.	4 For he was *c* in weakness, but lives by
Gal	2.19	I have been *c* with Christ; and it is no
	3.	1 Jesus Christ was publicly exhibited as *c*!
	6.14	by which the world has been *c* to me,
Rev	11.	8 and Egypt, where also their Lord was *c*.

CRUEL (CRUELLY)

Job	30.21	You have turned *c* to me; with the
	39.16	It deals *c* with its young, as if they were
Prov	11.17	but the *c* do themselves harm.

CRUMBS

Mt	15.27	yet even the dogs eat the *c* that fall
Mk	7.28	under the table eat the children's *c*."

CRUSH (CRUSHED)

Job	20.19	they have c and abandoned the poor,
Ps	18.29	By you I can c a troop; and by my God I
Lam	1.15	a time against me to c my young men;
Mk	3. 9	crowd, so that they would not c him;
Lk	20.18	and it will c anyone on whom it falls."
Rom	16.20	The God of peace will shortly c Satan

CRY (CRIED CRYING)

Gen	4.10	Listen, your brother's blood is c out to
	27.34	Esau heard his father's words, he c out
Ex	2. 6	the child. He was c, and she took pity
	22.23	c out to me, I will surely heed their c;
Lev	13.45	upper lip and c out, "Unclean, unclean."
1 Sam	7. 9	Samuel c out to the LORD for Israel, and
	5.11	Samuel was angry; and he c out to the
Job	19. 7	Even when I c out, 'Violence!' I am not
Ps	5. 2	Listen to the sound of my c, my King
	18. 6	to my God I c for help. From his temple
	88. 1	when, at night, I c out in your presence,
	99. 6	his name. They c to the LORD, and he
	102. 1	prayer, O LORD; let my c come to you.
	107.28	they c to the LORD in their trouble,
	119.145	With my whole heart I c; answer me, O
	120. 1	In my distress I c to the LORD, that he
	130. 1	Out of the depths I c to you, O LORD.
Isa	42. 2	He will not c or lift up his voice, or
Jon	1. 2	that great city, and c against it;
Mt	12.19	He will not wrangle or c aloud, nor will

CUNNING

2 Cor	4. 2	we refuse to practice c or to falsify

CUP

Gen	44. 2	Put my c, the silver c, in the top of the
Ps	11. 6	wind shall be the portion of their c.
	16. 5	LORD is my chosen portion and my c;
	23. 5	anoint head with oil; my c overflows.
	75. 8	For in the hand of the LORD there is a c
	116. 13	I will lift up the c of salvation and call
Isa	51.17	the c of his wrath, who have drunk to
Jer	25.28	And if they refuse to accept the c from
Hab	2.16	The c in the LORD's right hand will
Mt	10.42	whoever gives even a c of cold water to
	20.22	Are you able to drink the c that I am
	23.25	you clean the outside of the c and of
	26.27	Then he took a c, and after giving
	26.39	if it is possible, let this c pass from me;
Mk	9.41	whoever gives you a c of water to drink
	10.38	Are you able to drink the c that I drink,
	14.23	Then he took a c, and after giving
	14.36	are possible; remove this c from me;
Lk	11.39	you Pharisees clean the outside of the c
	22.17	he took a c, and after giving thanks he
	22.42	you are willing, remove this c from me;
Jn	18.11	the c that the Father has given me?"
1 Cor	10.16	The c of blessing which we bless, is it
	11.25	"This c is the new covenant in my
Rev	16.19	her the wine-c of the fury of his wrath.

CUPBEARER

Gen	40. 9	So the chief c told his dream to Joseph,

CURDS

Gen	18. 8	he took c and milk and the calf that he
Isa	7.15	He shall eat c and honey by the time he

CURE (CURED CURING)

Mt	4.23	c every disease and every sickness
	8.16	with a word, and c all who were sick.
	10. 8	C the sick, raise the dead, cleanse the
	12.15	followed him, and he c all of them.
	14.14	compassion for them and c their sick,
	17.16	disciples, but they could not c him."
Lk	4.23	to me this proverb, 'Doctor, c yourself!'
	4.40	his hands on each of them and c them.
	7.21	Jesus had just then c many people of
	8. 2	as some women who had been c of evil

CURE

(continued right column)

Lk	13.14	come on those days and be c, and not
	14. 3	"Is it lawful to c people on the sabbath,
Acts	28. 8	him and c him by praying and putting
	28. 9	who had diseases also came and were c.

CURSE (CURSES CURSING CURSINGS) (n)

Deut	11.26	before you today a blessing and a c—
	21.23	anyone hung on a tree is under God's c.
	27.13	shall stand on Mount Ebal for the c:
Josh	8.34	the words of the law, blessings and c,
Prov	3.33	The LORD's c is on the house of the
Jer	25.18	a waste, an object of hissing and a c,
Zech	5. 3	"This is the c that goes out over the
	8.13	you have been a c among the nations,
Mal	2. 2	then I will send the c on you and I will
Rom	3.14	"Their mouths are full of c and
Gal	3.10	on the works of the law are under a c;
Jas	3.10	the same mouth come blessing and c.

CURSE (CURSED CURSES CURSING) (v)

Gen	3.14	c are you among all animals and among
	4.11	you are c from the ground, which has
	12. 3	and the one who c you I will c; and in
	49. 7	C be their anger, for it is fierce, and
Ex	21.17	Whoever c father or mother shall be put
Num	22. 6	Come now, c this people for me, since
	23. 8	How can I c whom God has not c? How
Josh	6.26	"C before the LORD be anyone who tries
1 Sam	14.24	"C be anyone who eats food before it is
2 Sam	16. 5	was Shimei son of Gera; he came out c.
1 Kings	21.13	saying, "Naboth c God and the king."
2 Kings	2.24	and saw them, he c them in the name
Job	1.11	he has, and he will c you to your face."
	2. 9	in your integrity? C God, and die."
	3. 1	his mouth and c the day of his birth.
Ps	109. 17	He loved to c; let curses come on him.
Prov	20.20	If you c father or mother, your lamp will
Eccl	10.20	Do not c the king, even in your thought,
Jer	17. 5	C are those who trust in mere mortals
	20.14	C be the day on which I was born! The
Mk	11.21	"Rabbi, look! The fig tree that you c has
Lk	6.28	bless those who c you, pray for those
1 Cor	12. 3	Spirit of God ever says "Let Jesus be c!"
Gal	3.13	"C is everyone who hangs on a tree"
Rev	16. 9	they c the name of God, who had

CURTAIN (CURTAINS)

Ex	26. 1	make the tabernacle with ten c of fine
Lev	2	into the sanctuary inside the c before
Mt	27.51	the c of the temple was torn in two,
Mk	15.38	the c of the temple was torn in two,
Lk	23.45	failed; and the c of the temple was torn
Heb	9. 3	Behind the second c was a tent called
	10.20	the c (that is, through his flesh),

CUSH

Gen	2.13	that flows around the whole land of C.

CUSTOM (CUSTOMS)

Ezra	7.24	shall not be lawful to impose tribute, c,
Jer	10. 3	For the c of the peoples are false: a tree
Lk	4.16	on the sabbath day, as was his c.

CUT

1 Kings	18.28	aloud, and c themselves with swords
Isa	14.22	will c off from Babylon name and
Dan	9.26	an anointed one shall be c off and shall
Mk	9.43	If your hand causes you to sin, c it off;
Acts	2.37	they heard this, they were c to the heart

CYMBALS (CYMBALS)

Ps	150. 5	Praise him with clanging c; praise him
1 Cor	13. 1	love, I am a noisy gong or a clanging c.

CYPRUS

Acts	4.36	a Levite, a native of C, Joseph, to whom
	11.19	Stephen traveled as far as Phoenicia, C
	13. 4	and from there they sailed to C.

CYRUS

Acts 15.39 Mark with him and sailed away to C.
27. 4 sailed under the lee of C, because the

CYRUS

Ezra 1. 1 In the first year of King C of Persia, in
4. 3 as King C of Persia has commanded
5.13 King C of Babylon, in the first year of
Isa 44.28 who says of C, "He is my shepherd, and
45. 1 says the LORD to his anointed, to C,
Dan 1.21 there until the first year of King C.

D

DAILY

Lk 9.23 and take up their cross d and follow
11. 3 Give us each day our d bread.

DAMASCUS

Gen 14.15 pursued them to Hobah, north of D.
2 Sam 8. 6 put garrisons among the Arameans of D;
Isa 7. 8 For the head of Aram is D, and the
Zech 9. 1 land of Hadrach and will rest upon D.
Acts 9. 2 him for letters to the synagogues at D,
22.10 'Get up and go to D; there you will be
2 Cor 11.32 under King Aretas guarded the city of D
Gal 1.17 Arabia, and afterwards I returned to D.

DAN (Son of Jacob)

Born, Gen 30.6; blessed by Jacob, Gen 49.16-17.
Tribe of Dan: blessed by Moses, Deut 33.22; allotted
territory, Josh 19.40-48; migrated north, Judg 18; became center of idolatry, 1 Kings 12.28-30.

DAN (the city)

Gen 14.14 them, and went in pursuit as far as D.
Judg 18.29 They named the city D, after their
20. 1 came out, from D to Beersheba,
1 Sam 3.20 all Israel from D to Beersheba knew

DANCE (DANCED DANCING)

Ex 32.19 and the d, Moses' anger burned hot,
Judg 21.21 young women of Shiloh come out to d
2 Sam 6.14 David d before the LORD with all his
Ps 30.11 You have turned my mourning into d;
Lam 5.15 our d has been turned to mourning.
Mt 11.17 the flute for you and you did not d;
14. 6 the daughter of Herodias d before the
Mk 6.22 his daughter Herodias came in and d,
Lk 7.32 the flute for you, and you did not d;

DANGER

1 Cor 15.30 we putting ourselves in d every hour?

DANIEL (BELTESHAZZAR)

Trained in the king's palace, Dan 1.1-7; abstained from
the king's food, Dan 1.8-16; interpreted Nebuchadnezzar's dreams, Dan 2; 4; interpreted the handwriting on
the wall, Dan 5.10-29; delivered from the lion's den, Dan
6; visions and dreams, Dan 7 — 8; 10 — 12; prayed for his
people, Dan 9.

DARE

Rom 5. 7 person someone might actually d to die.
1 Cor 6. 1 do you d take it to court before the

DARIUS

Ezra 4. 5 of Persia and until the reign of King D
6. 1 Then King D made a decree, and they
Dan 5.31 D the Mede received the kingdom,
6.28 Daniel prospered during the reign of D
Hag 1. 1 In the second year of King D, in the
Zech 1. 1 eighth month, in the second year of D,

DARK

Job 24.16 In the d they dig through houses; by
Mt 10.27 What I say to you in the d, tell in the
2 Pet 1.19 to this as a lamp shining in a d place,

DARKEN (DARKENED DARKENS)

Job 38. 2 "Who is this that d counsel by words
Eccl 12. 2 the stars are d and the clouds return
Am 8. 9 noon, and d the earth in broad daylight.
Mk 13.24 the sun will be d, and the moon will

DARKEST

Ps 23. 4 though I walk through the d valley,

DARKNESS

Gen 1. 5 light Day, and the d he called Night.
15.12 and terrifying d descended upon him.
Ex 10.21 may be d over the land of Egypt, a d
Job 10.21 return, to the land of gloom and deep d,
24.17 are friends with the terrors of deep d.
Ps 44.19 of jackals, and covered us with deep d.
139. 12 even the d is not dark to you; the night
Isa 8.22 earth, but will see only distress and d,
Jer 13.16 the LORD your God before he brings d,
Joel 2. 2 it is near — a day of d and gloom, a day
Mt 6.23 If then the light in you is d, how great
22.13 throw him into the outer d, where there
25.30 throw him into the outer d, where there
27.45 noon on, d came over the whole land
Mk 15.33 was noon, d came over the whole land
Lk 23.44 noon, and d came over the whole land
1 Pet 2. 9 called you out of d into his marvelous

DAUGHTER (DAUGHTERS)

Gen 20.12 the d of my father but not the d of my
Ruth 1.12 Turn back, my d, go your way, for I am
Esth 2. 7 Mordecai adopted her as his own d.
Ps 144. 12 our d like corner pillars, cut for the
Isa 3.17 with scabs the heads of the d of Zion,
Zech 9. 9 greatly, O d Zion! Shout aloud, O d
Mt 9.18 "My d has just died; but come and lay
21. 5 "Tell the d of Zion, Look, your king is
Mk 5.23 "My little d is at the point of death.
7.29 may go — the demon has left your d."
Lk 8.42 he had an only d, about twelve years
Acts 7.21 abandoned, Pharaoh's d adopted him
Heb 11.24 to be called the son of Pharaoh's d,

DAVID

Anointed by Samuel, 1 Sam 16.1-13; played the harp
for Saul, 1 Sam 16.14-23; killed Goliath, 1 Sam 17; won
Jonathan's friendship, 1 Sam 18.1-4; incurred Saul's jealousy, 1 Sam 18.5-9; married Michal, 1 Sam 18.20-29; fled
from Saul, 1 Sam 19 — 22; fought the Philistines, 1 Sam
23; spared Saul at En-gedi, 1 Sam 24; David and Abigail,
1 Sam 25; spared Saul at Ziph, 1 Sam 26; lived among the
Philistines, 1 Sam 27.1 — 28.2; 29; defeated the Amalekites, 1 Sam 30; made king over Judah, 2 Sam 2.1-7; made
king over Israel, 2 Sam 5.1-16; brought the ark to Jerusalem, 2 Sam 6; God's covenant with David, 2 Sam 7;
extended his kingdom, 2 Sam 8; David and Bath-sheba,
2 Sam 11.1 — 12.25; fled Absalom's revolt, 2 Sam 15 — 16;
returned to Jerusalem, 2 Sam 19; David's song, 2 Sam
22.1 — 23.7; numbered Israel and Judah, 2 Sam 24;
charged Solomon, 1 Kings 2.1-9; died, 1 Kings 2.10-12.
(See also 1 Chr 11 — 29.)

Ps 78.70 He chose his servant D, and took him
Jer 23. 5 when I will raise up for D a righteous
Ezek 34.23 over them one shepherd, my servant D,
Mt 12. 3 Have you not read what D did when he
Mk 2.25 "Have you never read what D did when
Lk 1.32 will give him the throne of his father D,
Acts 2.25 For D says concerning him, 'I saw the
Rom 1. 3 who was descended from D according to
Rev 5. 5 of Judah, the Root of D, has conquered,

DAWN

Ps 119.147 I rise before d and cry for help; I put
Isa 58. 8 light shall break forth like the d, and
Lk 1.78 our God, the d from on high will break

DAWNING

Mt	28. 1 as the first day of the week was *d*, Mary

DAY (DAYS)

Gen	1. 5 God called the light *D*, and the
	2. 3 God blessed the seventh *d* and hallowed
Deut	33.25 and as your *d*, so is your strength.
Josh	10.14 There has been no *d* like it before or
2 Kings	7. 9 This is a *d* of good news; if we are
Job	15.23 They know that a *d* of darkness is ready
Ps	19. 2 *D* to *d* pours forth speech, and night to
	42. 8 By *d* the LORD commands his steadfast
	74.16 Yours is the *d*, yours also the night; you
	90.12 So teach us to count our *d* that we may
	102. 11 My *d* are like an evening shadow; I
	118. 24 This is the *d* that the LORD has made;
	145. 2 Every *d* I will bless you, and praise your
Isa	2.12 LORD of hosts has a *d* against all that is
	11.10 On that *d* the root of Jesse shall stand
	12. 1 You will say in that *d*: "I will give
	13. 6 Wail, for the *d* of the LORD is near; it
	34. 8 the LORD has a *d* of vengeance, a year of
	37. 3 "This *d* is a *d* of distress, of rebuke, and
Jer	46.10 That *d* is the *d* of the Lord GOD of
Ezek	30. 3 a *d* is near, the *d* of the LORD is near;
Joel	1.15 for the *d*! For the *d* of the LORD is near,
	2.11 the *d* of the LORD is great; terrible
Am	5.18 Why do you want the *d* of the LORD? It
Zeph	1.14 great *d* of the LORD is near, near and
Zech	14. 1 a *d* is coming for the LORD, when the
Mal	3. 2 who can endure the *d* of his coming,
	4. 1 the *d* is coming, burning like an oven,
Mk	13.32 "But about that *d* or hour no one
Jn	8.56 rejoiced that he would see my *d*;
Acts	5.42 every *d* in the temple and at home they
Rom	13.13 let us live honorably as in the *d*, not in
1 Cor	15.31 in danger every hour? I die every *d*!
	16. 2 On the first *d* of every week, each of
2 Cor	1.14 on the *d* of the Lord Jesus we are your
	6. 2 you, on a *d* of salvation I have helped
Phil	1. 6 bring it to completion by the *d* of Jesus
1 Thess	5. 2 the *d* of the Lord will come like a thief
Heb	10.25 the more as you see the *D* approaching.
2 Pet	3.10 the *d* of the Lord will come like a thief,

DEACONS

Phil	1. 1 are in Philippi, with the bishops' and *d*:
1 Tim	3. 8 *D* likewise must be serious, not

DEAD

Num	14.29 your *d* bodies shall fall in this very
	16.48 He stood between the *d* and the living;
2 Kings	19.35 dawned, they were all *d* bodies.
Eccl	9. 3 live, and after that they go to the *d*.
Mt	8.22 me, and let the *d* bury their own *d*."
	9.24 away; for the girl is not *d* but sleeping."
	11. 5 the deaf hear, the *d* are raised, and the
	22.32 He is not God of the *d*, but of the
Mk	5.39 weep? The child is not *d* but sleeping."
	15.44 Pilate wondered if he were already *d*;
Lk	8.49 "Your daughter is *d*; do not trouble the
	9.60 "Let the *d* bury their own *d*; but as for
	15.24 son of mine was *d*, and is alive again;
Acts	14.19 out of the city, supposing that he was *d*.
	20. 9 below and was picked up *d*. But Paul
Rom	8.10 though the body is *d* because of sin, the
1 Cor	15.29 who receive baptism on behalf of the *d*?
Eph	2. 1 You were *d* through the trespasses and
Jude	12 autumn trees without fruit, twice *d*,
Rev	3. 1 a name of being alive, but you are *d*.
	14.13 Blessed are the *d* who from now on die
	20.12 I saw the *d*, great and small, standing

DEAF

Lev	19.14 You shall not revile the *d* or put a
Isa	29.18 In that day the *d* shall hear the words
Mk	7.32 They brought to him a *d* man who had

Mk	7.37 makes the *d* hear and the dumb speak."

DEAL (DEALT)

Gen	12.16 for her sake he *d* well with Abram; and
	21. 1 The LORD *d* with Sarah as he had said,
Ps	103. 10 not *d* with us according to our sins,
	147. 20 has not *d* thus with any other nation;

DEAR

Ps	39.11 sin, consuming like a moth what is *d*
	102. 14 For your servants hold its stones *d*, and

DEATH

Num	11.15 going to treat me, put me to *d* at once
	23.10 Let me die the *d* of the upright, and let
Deut	30.15 life and prosperity, *d* and adversity.
2 Sam	15.21 whether for *d* or for life, there also your
	22. 6 me, the snares of *d* confronted me.
Job	38.17 Have the gates of *d* been revealed to
Ps	116. 3 The snares of *d* encompassed me; the
	116. 15 of the LORD is the *d* of his faithful ones.
Prov	14.12 to a person, but its end is the way to *d*.
Jer	21. 8 you the way of life and the way of *d*.
Ezek	18.32 I have no pleasure in the *d* of anyone,
Hos	13.14 from *D*? O *D*, where are your plagues?
Mk	5.23 daughter is at the point of *d*. Come and
	14.55 testimony against Jesus to put him to *d*;
Lk	1.79 sit darkness and in the shadow of *d*,
	9.27 some standing here who will not taste *d*
	22. 2 looking for a way to put Jesus to *d*,
Jn	12.33 to indicate the kind of *d* he was to die.
	21.19 to indicate the kind of *d* by which he
Rom	5.14 *d* excercised dominion from Adam to
	8.13 you put to *d* the deeds of the body,
	8.38 I am sure that neither *d*, nor life, nor
1 Cor	15.54 be fulfilled: "*D* has been swallowed up
	15.55 "Where, O *d*, is your victory? Where, O
2 Cor	2.16 to the one a fragrance from *d* to *d*, to
Col	3. 5 Put to *d*, therefore, whatever in you is
2 Tim	1.10 Christ Jesus, who abolished *d* and
2 Pet	1.14 since I know that my *d* will come soon,
Rev	2.11 will not be harmed by the second *d*.

DEBORAH

Judg	4. 4 *D*, a prophetess, the wife of Lappidoth,
	4.14 *D* said to Barak, "Up! For this is the day
	5. 1 Then *D* and Barak . . . sang on that day,

DEBT (DEBTS)

1 Sam	22. 2 in distress, and everyone who was in *d*,
2 Kings	4. 7 "Go sell the oil and pay your *d*, and you
Neh	10.31 year and the exaction of every *d*.
Mt	18.27 released him and forgave him the *d*.

DEBTORS

Lk	7.41 "A certain creditor had two *d*; one owed
	16. 5 summoning his master's *d* one by one,
Rom	8.12 we are *d*, not to the flesh, to live

DECEIT

Job	15.35 forth evil and their heart prepares *d*."
	27. 4 and my tongue will not utter *d*.
Ps	10. 7 mouths are filled with cursing and *d*
	17. 1 give ear to my prayer from lips free of *d*.
	32. 2 and in whose spirit there is no *d*.
	34.13 evil, and your lips from speaking *d*.
	50.19 rein for evil, and your tongue frames *d*.
Prov	12.20 *D* is in the mind of those who plan evil,
Isa	53. 9 and there was no *d* in his mouth.
Jer	14.14 and the *d* of their own minds.
Am	8. 5 and practice with false balances,
Mk	7.22 wickedness, *d*, licentiousness, envy,
Jn	1.47 truly an Israelite in whom there is no *d*!"
Rom	1.29 Full of envy, murder, strife, *d*, craftiness
2 Cor	12.16 since I was crafty, I took you in by *d*.
1 Thess	2. 3 our appeal does not spring from *d* or

DECEITFUL

Ps	5. 6 the LORD abhors the bloodthirsty and *d*.
	52. 4 love all words that devour, O *d* tongue.
Prov	31.30 Charm is *d*, and beauty is vain, but a
Nah	3. 1 City of bloodshed, utterly *d*, full of
2 Cor	11.13 boasters are false apostles, *d* workers,
Eph	4.14 by their craftiness in *d* scheming.

DECEITFULNESS

Heb	3.13 of you may be hardened by the *d* of sin.

DECEIVE (DECEIVED DECEIVES DECEIVING)

Gen	29.25 for Rachel? Why then have you *d* me?"
Lev	6. 2 trespass against the LORD by a *d*
Josh	9.22 "Why did you *d* us, saying, 'We are very
1 Sam	19.17 "Why have you *d* me like this, and let
1 Kings	13.18 and drink water." But he was *d* him.
2 Kings	18.29 'Do not let Hezekiah *d* you, for he will
Job	12.16 wisdom; the *d* and the deceiver are his.
	13. 9 you *d* him, as one person *d* another?
Prov	26.19 one who *d* his neighbor and says, "I am
Jer	4.10 GOD, how utterly you have *d* this people
	9. 5 They all *d* their neighbors, and no one
	37. 9 Do not *d* yourselves, saying, "The
Lam	1.19 I called to my lovers but they *d* me; my
Jn	7.12 were saying, "No, he is *d* the crowd."
	7.47 "Surely, you have not been *d* too, have
Rom	16.18 by smooth talk and flattery they will *d*
1 Cor	6. 9 Do not be *d*! Fornicators, idolaters,
	15.33 Do not be *d*: "Bad company ruins good
2 Cor	11. 3 afraid that as the serpent *d* Eve by its
Gal	6. 7 Do not be *d*; God is not mocked, for
Eph	5. 6 Let no one *d* you with empty words, for
Col	2. 4 may *d* you with plausible arguments.
2 Thess	2. 3 Let no one *d* you in any way; for that
1 Tim	2.14 Adam was not *d*, but the woman was *d*
Rev	18.23 and all nations were *d* by your sorcery.

DECEIVER (DECEIVERS)

Titus	1.10 rebellious people, idle talkers and *d*,
2 Jn	7 such person is the *d* and the antichrist.
Rev	12. 9 and Satan, the *d* of the whole world

DECENTLY

1 Cor	14.40 but all things should be done *d* and in

DECIDE (DECIDED)

1 Chr	21.12 Now *d* what answer I shall return to the
2 Chr	2. 1 Solomon *d* to build a temple for the
Isa	11. 4 and *d* with equity for the meek of the
1 Cor	2. 2 I *d* to know nothing among you except

DECISION (DECISIONS)

Deut	17. 8 If any judicial *d* is too difficult for you
	17. 9 they shall announce to you the *d* in the
Prov	16.10 Inspired *d* are on the lips of a king; his
Joel	3.14 multitudes, in the valley of *d*! For the
Acts	16. 4 the *d* that had been reached by the

DECLARE (DECLARED)

1 Chr	16.24 *D* his glory among the nations, his
Ps	96. 3 *D* his glory among the nations his
	145. 6 proclaimed, and I will *d* your greatness.
Isa	48. 3 "The former things I *d* long ago, they
	66.19 shall *d* my glory among the nations.
Mt	7.23 Then I will *d* to them, 'I never knew
Jn	16.13 and he will *d* to you the things that are
Rom	1. 4 and was *d* to be Son of God with power

DECREE (DECREED DECREES)

Ezra	6. 8 I make a *d* regarding what you shall do
Job	20.29 God, the heritage *d* for him by God."
Ps	2. 7 I will tell of the *d* of the LORD: He said
	19. 7 the *d* of the LORD are sure, making wise
	78. 5 He established a *d* in Jacob, and
	93. 5 Your *d* are very sure; holiness befits
	99. 7 they kept his *d*, and the statutes that he
Isa	10. 1 Ah, you who make iniquitous *d*, who

Dan	4.24 O king, and it is a *d* of the Most High
	6.26 I make a *d*, that in all my royal
	9.24 "Seventy weeks are *d* for your people
Lk	2. 1 *d* went out from Emperor Augustus that
Acts	17. 7 acting contrary to the *d* of the emperor,
1 Cor	2. 7 hidden, which God *d* before the ages

DEDICATE (DEDICATED)

2 Sam	8.11 these also King David *d* to the LORD,
1 Kings	7.51 the things that David his father had *d*,
	8.63 of Israel *d* the house of the LORD.
1 Chr	26.27 From booty won in battles they *d* gifts
2 Chr	2. 4 my God and *d* it to him for offering

DEDICATION

Num	7.10 presented offerings for the *d* of the altar
Ezra	6.17 They offered at the *d* of this house of
Neh	12.27 at the *d* of the wall of Jerusalem they
Dan	3. 2 and come to the *d* of the statue
Jn	10.22 time the festival of the *D* took place

DEED (DEEDS)

Deut	11. 7 seen every great *d* that the LORD did.
Judg	6.13 where are all his wonderful *d* that our
Job	34.11 according to their *d* he will repay
Ps	150. 2 Praise him for his mighty *d*; praise him
Eccl	12.14 God will bring every *d* into judgment,
Jer	25.14 I will repay them according to their *d*
Lk	23.41 are getting what we deserve for our *d*,
Jn	3.19 than light because their *d* were evil.
Rom	3.20 in his sight" by *d* prescribed by the law,
	8.13 you put to death the *d* of the body
Rev	14.13 their labors, for their *d* follow them."

DEEP

Job	11. 7 "Can you find out the *d* things of God?
Ps	42. 7 *D* calls to *d* at the thunder of your
	92. 5 O LORD! Your thoughts are very *d*!
	104. 6 You cover it with the *d* as a garment;
Prov	8.28 he established the fountains of the *d*,
Dan	2.22 He reveals *d* and hidden things; he
Lk	5. 4 into the *d* water and let down your nets
Rev	2.24 what some call 'the *d* things of Satan,'

DEFEAT

1 Cor	6. 7 at all with one another is already a *d*

DEFECT

Dan	1. 4 young men without physical *d* and

DEFEND

2 Kings	19.34 For I will *d* this city to save it, for my
	20. 6 I will *d* this city for my own sake and
Ps	45. 4 for the cause of truth and to *d* the right;
Prov	31. 9 righteously, *d* the rights of the poor
Isa	37.35 I will *d* this city to save it, for my own
Lk	12.11 worry about how you are to *d* yourselves

DEFENSE

Acts	22. 1 fathers, listen to the *d* that I now make
Phil	1. 7 in the *d* and confirmation of the gospel.

DEFENSELESS

Ps	141. 8 in you I seek refuge; leave me not *d*.

DEFER (DEFERRED)

Lev	19.32 rise before the aged, and to the old;
Prov	13.12 Hope *d* makes the heart sick, but a
Isa	48. 9 For my name's sake I *d* my anger, for

DEFILE (DEFILED DEFILES DEFILING)

Lev	15.31 in their uncleanness by *d* my tabernacle
	18.24 Do not *d* yourselves in any of these
Num	19.13 not purify themselves, *d* the tabernacle
	19.20 they have *d* the sanctuary of the LORD.
	35.34 You shall not *d* the land in which you
Neh	13.29 they have *d* the priesthood, the
Ps	79. 1 they have *d* your holy temple; they have
Jer	2. 7 But when you entered you *d* my land,

Ezek	5.11	you have *d* my sanctuary with all your
	20.31	you *d* yourselves with all your idols to
	23.38	they have *d* my sanctuary on the same
	37.23	They shall never again *d* themselves
	43. 8	they were *d* my holy name by their
Dan	1. 8	not *d* himself with the royal rations of
Hos	5. 3	you have played the whore; Israel is *d*.
Mt	15.18	from the heart, and this is what *d*.
Mk	7.15	*d*, the things that come out are what *d*."
	7.20	is what comes out of a person that *d*.
1 Cor	8. 7	and their conscience, being weak, is *d*.

DEFRAUD (DEFRAUDED)

Lev	6. 2	robbery, or if you have *d* his neighbor,
	19.13	You shall not *d* your neighbor; you shall
Lk	19. 8	if I have *d* anyone of anything I will pay
1 Cor	6. 7	be wronged? Why not rather be *d*?

DEFY

1 Sam	17.10	"Today I *d* the ranks of Israel! Give me

DEGRADING

Rom	1.24	to impurity, to the *d* of their bodies

DELAY

Hab	2. 3	for it; it will surely come, it will not *d*.

DELIGHT (DELIGHTS) (n)

Gen	3. 6	for food, and that it was a *d* to the eyes,
Deut	28.63	as the LORD took *d* in making you
	30. 9	will again take *d* in prospering you,
1 Sam	19. 1	son Jonathan took great *d* in David.
	15.22	"Has the LORD as great *d* in burnt
Job	27.10	Will they take *d* in the Almighty? Will
	34. 9	profits one nothing to take *d* in God.'
Ps	1. 2	but their *d* is in the law of the LORD,
	36. 8	give them drink from the river of your *d*.
	37. 4	Take *d* in the LORD, and he will give you
	51.16	For you have no *d* in sacrifice; if I were
	119. 77	that I may live; for your law is my *d*.
Prov	8.30	I was daily his *d*, rejoicing before him
	11.20	but those of blameless ways are his *d*.
	15. 8	but the prayer of the upright is his *d*.
	16.13	Righteous lips are the *d* of a king, and
Song	2. 3	With great *d* I sat in his shadow, and
Ezek	24.16	take away from you the *d* of your eyes;

DELIGHT (DELIGHTED DELIGHTS) (v)

2 Sam	22.20	he delivered me, because he *d* in me.
1 Kings	10. 9	be the LORD your God, who has *d* in you
Job	22.26	you will *d* yourself in the Almighty,
Ps	5. 4	you are not a God who *d* in wickedness;
	37.23	firm by the LORD, when he *d* in our way;
	40. 8	I *d* to do your will, O my God; your law
	44. 3	of your countenance, for you *d* in them.
	51.19	then you will *d* in right sacrifices, in
	112. 1	who greatly *d* in his commandments.
Prov	1.22	How long will scoffers *d* in their
	3.12	loves, as a father the son in whom he *d*.
Isa	1.11	I do not *d* in the blood of bulls, or of
	55. 2	is good, and *d* yourselves in rich food.
	58. 2	they seek me and *d* to know my ways,
	62. 4	for the LORD in you, and your land
Mic	7.18	because he *d* in showing clemency.
Mal	3. 1	the covenant in whom you *d*—indeed,
Rom	7.22	I *d* in the law of God, in my inmost

DELIVER

Gen	32.11	*D* me, please, from the hand of my
Ex	3. 8	I have come down to *d* them from the
	5.23	done nothing at all to *d* your people."
	25.22	I will *d* to you all my commands for the
Josh	2.13	to them, and *d* our lives from death."
Judg	7. 7	hundred men that lapped I will *d* you,
Ps	3. 7	Rise up, O LORD! *D* me, O my God! For
	6. 4	Turn, O LORD, save my life; *d* me for the
	33.19	to *d* their soul from death, and to keep
	59. 1	*D* me from my enemies, O my God;

Eccl	8. 8	wickedness *d* those who practice it.
Isa	43.13	is no one who can *d* from my hand;
	50. 2	redeem? Or have I no power to *d*?
Jer	1. 8	of them, for I am with you to *d* you,
Dan	3.17	serve is able to *d* us from the furnace
	6.16	God, whom you faithfully serve, *d* you!"

DELIVERS (DELIVERED DELIVERING)

Gen	14.20	Most High, who has *d* your enemies
Ex	18. 9	to Israel, in *d* them from the Egyptians.
Judg	2.18	he *d* them from the hand of their
	6. 9	I *d* you from the hand of the Egyptians,
	7. 2	me, saying, 'My own hand has *d* me.'
2 Sam	19. 9	"The king *d* us from the hands of our
	22.18	He *d* me from my strong enemy, from
	22.20	place; he *d* me, because he delighted
Job	29.12	because I *d* the poor who cried, and the
Ps	18.17	He *d* me from my strong enemy, and
	33.16	a warrior is not *d* by his great strength.
	34. 4	me, and *d* me from all my fears.
	54. 7	For he has *d* me from every trouble,
	106. 10	of the foe, and *d* them from the hand of
	107. 6	and he *d* them from their distress;
	116. 8	For you have *d* my soul from death, my
	138. 7	your hand, and your right hand *d* me.
Prov	11. 4	wrath, but righteousness *d* from death.
	11. 8	The righteous are *d* from trouble, and
Eccl	9.15	man, and he by his wisdom *d* the city.
Dan	12. 1	But at that time your people shall be *d*,
Rom	15.28	*d* to them what has been collected,

DELIVERANCE

Ex	14.13	stand firm, and see the *d* that the LORD
1 Sam	11. 9	time the sun is hot, you shall have *d*.' "
	11.13	today the LORD has brought *d* to Israel."
Ps	3. 8	*D* belongs to the LORD; may your
	9.14	of daughter Zion, rejoice in your *d*.
	22.31	proclaim his *d* to a people yet unborn,
	32. 7	you surround me with glad cries of *d*.
	53. 6	O that *d* for Israel would come from
Isa	46.13	I bring near my *d*, it is not far off, and
	51. 5	I will bring near my *d* swiftly, my
Jon	2. 9	vowed I will pay. *D* belongs to the LORD!"
Phil	1.19	Jesus Christ this will turn out for my *d*.

DELIVERER

Judg	3. 9	LORD raised up a *d* for the Israelites,
2 Sam	22. 2	LORD is my rock, my fortress, and my *d*,
Ps	18. 2	LORD is my rock, my fortress, and my *d*,
	140. 7	O LORD, my LORD, my strong *d*, you have

DELUDED

Isa	44.20	a *d* mind has led him astray, and he

DELUSION

Isa	41.29	No, they are all a *d*; their works are
2 Thess	2.11	reason God sends them a powerful *d*,

DEMANDED

Lk	12.20	very night your life is being *d* of you.
	12.48	been entrusted, even more will be *d*.

DEMON (DEMONS)

Mt	15.22	David, my daughter is tormented by a *d*."
Mk	1.34	various diseases, and cast out many *d*;
	3.22	and by the ruler of the *d* he casts out *d*."
	9.38	someone casting out *d* in your name,
Lk	7.33	no wine, and you say, 'He has a *d*';
	11.14	casting out a *d* that was mute; when
Jn	7.20	crowd answered, "You have a *d*! Who is
1 Cor	10.20	pagans sacrifice, they sacrifice to and
1 Tim	4. 1	to deceitful spirits and teachings of *d*,
Jas	2.19	well. Even the *d* believe—and shudder.
Rev	9.20	or give up worshiping *d* and idols of
	18. 2	It has become a dwelling place of *d*,

DEMONSTRATION

1 Cor	2. 4	but with a *d* of the Spirit and of power,

DEN

Jer	7.11 become a *d* of robbers in your sight?
Mt	21.13 but you are making it a *d* of robbers."

DENARIUS

Mk	12.15 to the test? Bring me a *d*, and let me
Lk	20.24 "Show me a *d*. Whose head and whose

DENOUNCED

Dan	3. 8 came forward and *d* the Jews.

DENY (DENIED DENIES)

Ezra	8.21 that we might *d* ourselves before our
Mt	10.33 others, I also will *d* before my Father
	16.24 let them *d* themselves and take up their
	26.34 cock crows, you will *d* me three times."
	26.70 he *d* it before all of them, saying, "I do
Mk	8.34 let them *d* themselves and take up their
	14.30 crows twice, you will *d* me three times."
	14.68 he *d* it, saying, "I do not know or
Lk	12. 9 whoever *d* me before others will be
	22.34 have *d* three times that you know me."
	22.57 But he *d* it, saying, "Woman, I do not
Jn	18.25 are you?" He *d* it and said, "I am not."
1 Tim	5. 8 has *d* the faith and is worse than an
2 Tim	2.12 with him; if we *d* him, he also will *d*
Titus	1.16 God, but they *d* him by their actions.
2 Pet	2. 1 They will even *d* the Master who bought
1 Jn	2.22 antichrist, the one who *d* the Father
Rev	2.13 my name, and you did not *d* your faith

DEPART (DEPARTED)

Ps	18.21 and have not wickedly *d* from my God.
	34.14 *D* from evil, and do good; seek peace,
Isa	52.11 *D*, *d*, go out from there! Touch no
Mt	25.41 *d* from me into the eternal fire prepared

DEPARTURE

Lk	9.31 in glory and were speaking of his *d*,
2 Pet	1.15 after my *d* you may be able at any time

DEPRAVED

1 Tim	6. 5 among those who are *d* in mind

DEPRIVE

Isa	5.23 and *d* the innocent of their rights!
1 Cor	7. 5 Do not *d* one another except perhaps by
	9.15 —no one will *d* me of my ground for

DEPTHS

Ps	130. 1 Out of the *d* I cry to you, O Lord. Lord,
1 Cor	2.10 searches everything, even the *d* of God.

DERBE

Acts	14. 6 of it and fled to Lystra and *D*, cities
	16. 1 Paul went on also to *D* and to Lystra,
	20. 4 by Gaius of *D*, and by Timothy, as well

DERIDED

Mt	27.39 Those who passed by *d* him, shaking
Mk	15.29 Those who passed by *d* him, shaking

DESCEND (DESCENDED)

Ex	34. 5 The Lord *d* in the cloud and stood with
Lk	3.22 the Holy Spirit *d* upon him in bodily
1 Thess	4.16 will *d* from heaven, and the dead in
Heb	7.14 evident that our Lord was *d* from Judah;

DESCENDANTS

Gen	5. 1 This is a list of the *d* of Adam. When
	10. 1 These are the *d* of Noah's sons, Shem,
Deut	4.40 well-being and that of your *d* after you,
Ps	89. 4 'I will establish your *d* forever, and
Rom	4.18 was said, "So numerous shall your *d* be."
	9. 7 is through Isaac that *d* shall be named
Gal	3. 7 who believe are the *d* of Abraham.

DESERT

Ps	107. 4 Some wandered in *d* wastes, finding no

Isa	21.13 the scrub of the *d* plain you will lodge,
	35. 6 in the wilderness, and streams in the *d*;
	41.19 I will set in the *d* the cyprus, the plane
	42.11 *d* and the towns lift up their voice, the
	51. 3 her *d* like the garden of the Lord; joy

DESERTED (DESERTING)

Mt	14.13 from there in a boat to a *d* place
	26.56 Then all the disciples *d* him and fled.
Mk	6.31 "Come away to a *d* place all by
	14.50 All of them *d* him and fled.
Gal	1. 6 are so quickly *d* the one called you
2 Tim	4.10 has *d* me and gone to Thessalonica;

DESERTERS

Mt	26.31 "You will all become *d* because of me

DESERVE (DESERVED DESERVES DESERVING)

Deut	19. 6 although a death sentence was not *d*,
Mt	10.10 or a staff; for laborers *d* their food.
	26.66 verdict?" They answered, "He *d* death."
Mk	14.64 All of them condemned him as *d* death.
1 Tim	5.18 "The laborer *d* to be paid." Never accept
Rev	16. 6 them blood to drink. It is what they *d*!"

DESIGNATED

Heb	5.10 having been *d* by God a high priest

DESIGNS

2 Cor	2.11 Satan; for we are not ignorant of his *d*.

DESIRE (DESIRES) (n)

Gen	3.16 your *d* shall be for your husband, and
Deut	12. 8 today, all of us according to our own *d*,
1 Sam	9.20 And on whom is all Israel's *d* fixed, if
2 Sam	23. 5 cause to prosper all my help and my *d*?
2 Chr	9.12 granted the queen of Sheba every *d* that
Job	17.11 plans are broken off, the *d* of my heart.
Ps	10.17 Lord, you will hear the *d* of the meek;
	37. 4 and he will give you the *d* of your heart.
	140. 8 Grant not, O Lord, the *d* of the wicked;
	145.16 your hand, satisfying the *d* of every
	145.19 He fulfills the *d* of all who fear him; he
Prov	10.24 the *d* of the righteous will be granted.
	11.23 The *d* of the righteous ends only in
	13.12 sick, but a *d* fulfilled is a tree of life.
	13.19 A *d* realized is sweet to the soul, but to
Eccl	6. 9 sight of eyes than the wandering of *d*;
	12. 5 and *d* fails; because all must go to their
Song	7.10 I am my beloved's, and his *d* is for me.
Isa	26. 8 name and your renown are the soul's *d*.
Rom	10. 1 and sisters, my heart's *d* and prayer
Eph	2. 3 following the *d* of flesh and senses, and
1 Jn	2.16 the *d* of the flesh, the *d* of the eyes, the

DESIRE (DESIRED DESIRES) (v)

Esth	1. 8 of his palace to do as each one *d*.
Job	21.14 'Leave us alone! We do not *d* to know
Ps	19.10 More to be *d* are they than gold, even
	40. 6 Sacrifice and offering you do not *d*; but
	45.11 house, and the king will *d* your beauty.
	51. 6 You *d* truth in the inward being;
	73.25 And there is nothing on earth that I *d*
Prov	6.25 Do not *d* her beauty in your heart, and
	21.10 The souls of the wicked *d* evil; their
Isa	53. 2 in his appearance that we should *d* him.
Lk	10.24 and kings *d* to see what you see!
	22.15 eagerly *d* to eat this passover with you
Gal	4.21 me, you who *d* to be subject to the law,
	5.17 the flesh *d* is opposed to the Spirit,

DESOLATE

Ps	68. 6 God gives the *d* a home to live in; he
Isa	1. 7 aliens devour your land; it is *d*, as
	24. 1 to lay waste the earth and make it *d*,
Mt	23.38 See, your house is left to you, *d*.

DESOLATION

Jer	4.27 The whole land shall be a *d*; yet I will

Lk   21.20 armies, know that its *d* has come near.

DESPERATE

Ps   88.15 youth up. I suffer your terrors; I am *d*.

DESPISE (DESPISED DESPISING)

Gen   25.34 his way. Thus Esau *d* his birthright.
Num   6.16 the LORD; and she *d* him in her heart.
          14.11 How long will this people *d* me? And
          15.31 Because of having *d* the word of the
          16.30 know that these men have *d* the LORD."
2 Kings   17.15 They *d* his statutes, and his covenant
2 Chr   36.16 the messengers of God, *d* his words,
Neh   4. 4 Hear, O our God, for we are *d*; turn
Job   5.17 therefore do not *d* the discipline of the
          19.18 Even young children *d* me; when I rise,
          42. 6 therefore I *d* myself, and repent in dust
Ps   22. 6 not human; scorned by others, and *d*
          106. 24 Then they *d* the pleasant land, having
          119.141 I am small and *d*, yet I do not forget
Prov   1. 7 fools *d* wisdom and instruction.
          3.11 My child, do not *d* the LORD's discipline
          13.13 Those who *d* the word bring destruction
Isa   1. 4 who have *d* the Holy One of Israel, who
          5.24 and have *d* the word of the Holy One
          49. 7 to one deeply *d*, abhorred by the
          52. 5 continually, all day long my name is *d*.
          53. 3 He was *d* and rejected by others; a man
Jer   4.30 you beautify yourself. Your lovers *d* you;
          49.15 among the nations, *d* by humankind.
Am   5.21 I hate, I *d* your festivals, and I take no
Zech   4.10 whoever has *d* the day of small things
Mt   6.24 be devoted to the one and *d* the other.
          18.10 you do not *d* one of these little ones;
Lk   16.13 be devoted to the one and *d* the other.
1 Cor   1.28 God chose what is low and *d* in the
          16.11 let no one *d* him. Send him on his way
Gal   4.14 you did not scorn or *d* me, but
2 Pet   2.10 in depraved lust, and who *d* authority.

DESPOILED

Ps   12. 5 "Because the poor are *d*, because the

DESTINE (DESTINED)

Isa   65.12 I will *d* you to the sword, and all of you
Acts   13.48 many as had been *d* for eternal life
Eph   1. 5 He *d* us for adoption as his children
1 Thess   5. 9 For God has *d* us not for wrath but for
1 Pet   1.20 He was *d* before the foundation of the

DESTITUTE

Ps   102. 17 He will regard the prayer of the *d*, and
Heb   11.37 and goats, *d*, persecuted, tormented—

DESTROY (DESTROYED DESTROYING DESTROYS)

Gen   20. 4 "Lord, will you *d* an innocent people?
Num   33.52 *d* all their figured stones, *d* all their
Deut   7. 2 them, then you must utterly *d* them.
Josh   11.20 that they might be utterly *d*, and might
1 Sam   15. 3 and utterly *d* all that they have;
2 Kings   8.19 LORD would not *d* Judah, for the sake of
Ps   57. 1 take refuge, until the *d* storms pass by.
          101. 8 by morning I will *d* all the wicked
Prov   1.32 and the complacency of fools *d* them;
          14.11 The house of the wicked is *d*, but the
Jer   5.17 they shall *d* with the sword your
Lam   2. 2 The Lord has *d* without mercy all the
Ezek   9. 8 will you *d* all who remain of Israel as
Hos   4. 6 My people are *d* for lack of knowledge;
Mt   26.61 'I am able to *d* the temple of God and
Mk   12. 9 He will come and *d* the tenants, and
          14.58 "We heard him say, 'I will *d* this temple
Lk   12.33 no thief comes near and no moth *d*.
Jn   2.19 "*D* this temple, and in three days I will
1 Cor   3.17 If anyone *d* God's temple, God will *d*
2 Thess   2. 8 whom the Lord Jesus will *d* with the
Heb   2.14 through death he might *d* the one who

2 Pet   2.12 creatures are *d*, they also will be *d*,
Rev   11.18 great, and for *d* those who *d* the earth."

DESTROYERS

Jer   22. 7 I will prepare *d* against you, all with

DESTRUCTION

Prov   16.18 Pride goes before *d*, and a haughty
Isa   28.22 have heard a decree of *d* from the Lord
Lam   2.11 ground because of the *d* of my people,
1 Cor   5. 5 man over to Satan for the *d* of the flesh,

DETERMINE (DETERMINED)

1 Sam   20. 7 angry, then know that evil is *d* by him.
2 Chr   25.16 "I know that God has *d* to destroy you,
Esth   7. 7 saw that the king had *d* to destroy him.
Job   14. 5 Since their days are *d*, and the number
Dan   11.36 completed, for what is *d* shall be done.
Lk   22.22 Son of Man is going as it has been *d*,
Rom   2.18 know his will and *d* what is best
1 Cor   7.37 and has *d* in his own mind to keep her
Phil   1.10 full insight to help you *d* what is best,

DETEST

Num   21. 5 no water, and we *d* this miserable food."

DETESTABLE

Lev   11.10 that are in the waters, they are *d* to you
Ezek   20. 7 Cast away the *d* things your eyes feast
Hos   9.10 and become *d* like the thing they loved.

DEVIL

Mt   4. 1 the wilderness to be tempted by the *d*.
          13.39 enemy who sowed them is the *d*; the
Lk   8.12 the *d* comes and takes away the word
Jn   8.44 You are from your father the *d*, and you
          13. 2 The *d* had already put it into the heart
Eph   4.27 and do not make room for the *d*.
Jas   4. 7 to God. Resist the *d*, and he will flee
1 Pet   5. 8 roaring lion your adversary the *d* prowls
1 Jn   3. 8 *d* has been sinning from the beginning.
          3. 8 purpose, to destroy the works of the *d*.
Rev   2.10 Beware, the *d* is about to throw some of
          12.12 the *d* has come down to you with great
          20.10 the *d* who had deceived them was

DEVIOUS

Jer   17. 9 The heart is *d* above all else; it is

DEVISE

Prov   24. 2 for their minds *d* violence, and their
Ezek   11. 2 these are the men who *d* iniquity and
Mic   2. 1 Alas for those who *d* wickedness and

DEVOTE (DEVOTED)

Lev   27.28 every *d* thing is most holy to the LORD.
Num   18.14 Every *d* thing in Israel shall be yours.
Josh   6.18 to covet and take any of the *d* things
          7. 1 broke faith in regard to the *d* things;
Ezek   44.29 and every *d* thing in Israel shall be
Mic   4.13 and shall *d* their gain to the LORD,
Titus   3. 8 may be careful to *d* themselves to good

DEVOTION

1 Chr   29. 3 because of my *d* to the house of my
Acts   11.23 faithful to the Lord with steadfast *d*;
2 Cor   11. 3 from a sincere and pure *d* to Christ.

DEVOUR (DEVOURED DEVOURING DEVOURS)

2 Sam   2.26 "Is the sword to keep *d* forever? Do you
Prov   21.20 the house of the wise, but the fool *d* it.
Isa   1.20 and rebel, you shall be *d* by the sword;
          9.20 satisfied; they *d* the flesh of their own
Jer   30.16 Therefore all who *d* you shall be *d*, and
Hos   7. 7 are as an oven, and they *d* their rulers.
Mt   23.14n For you *d* widows' houses and for the

DEVOUT

Lk   2.25 Simeon, this man was righteous and *d*,

Acts	2. 5 there were *d* Jews from every nation
	10. 2 He was a *d* man who feared God with
	22.12 certain Ananias, who was a *d* man

DEW

Judg	6.37 if there is *d* on the fleece alone, and it
Ps	133. 3 It is like the *d* of Hermon, which falls
Prov	3.20 open, and the clouds drop down the *d*.
	19.12 but his favor is like *d* on the grass.
Hos	6. 4 cloud, like the *d* that goes away early.
	13. 3 mist or like the *d* that goes away early,
	14. 5 I will be as the *d* to Israel; he shall

DIE (DIES DYING)

Gen	2.17 in the day that you eat of it you shall *d*."
Num	16.29 If these people *d* a natural death, or if a
	26.65 them, "They shall *d* in the wilderness."
Deut	4.22 I am going to *d* in this land without
	32.50 you shall *d* there on the mountain
Judg	16.30 said, "Let me *d* with the Philistines."
Job	3.11 "Why did I not *d* at birth, come forth
	12. 2 the people, and wisdom will *d* with you.
	14.10 But mortals *d*, and are laid low; humans
	21.23 One *d* in full prosperity, being wholly at
Ps	41. 5 wonder in malice when I shall *d*,
	118. 17 I shall not *d*, but I shall live, and
Prov	10.21 feed many, but fools *d* for lack of sense.
	19.16 who are heedless of their ways will *d*.
Eccl	2.16 How can the wise *d* just like fools?
Ezek	33.11 evil ways; why will you *d*, O house of
Mk	14.31 "Even though I must *d* with you, I will
Jn	8.24 for you will *d* in your sins unless you
	11.16 us also go, that we may *d* with him."
	12.24 grain; but if it *d*, it bears much fruit.
	21.23 that this disciple would not *d*.
Rom	6. 9 raised from the dead, will never *d* again;
	14. 8 if we *d*, we *d* to the Lord; so then,
1 Cor	15.31 in danger every hour? I *d* every day!
2 Cor	6. 9 as *d*, and see—we are alive; as
Phil	1.21 to me, living is Christ, and *d* is gain.

DIED

Gen	7.21 all flesh *d* that moved on the earth,
	25. 8 Abraham . . . *d* in a good old age, an old
	35.29 Isaac . . . *d* and was gathered to his
Ex	2.23 After a long time the king of Egypt *d*.
Deut	34. 5 Then Moses . . . *d* there in the land of
Josh	24.29 Joshua son of Nun . . . *d*, being one
1 Sam	31. 6 Saul and his three sons . . . *d* together
2 Sam	18.33 Would that I had *d* instead of you, O
1 Kings	22.37 So the king *d*, and was brought to
2 Kings	4.20 child sat on her lap till noon, and he *d*.
1 Chr	10.13 Saul *d* for his unfaithfulness; he was
Ezek	24.18 the morning, and at evening my wife *d*.
Lk	7.12 a man who had *d* was being carried out.
Acts	7.60 them." When he had said this, he *d*.
Rom	5. 6 the right time Christ *d* for the ungodly.
	6. 2 can we who *d* to sin go on living in it?
	7. 4 you have *d* to the law through the body
	7.10 and I *d*, and the very commandment
1 Cor	8.11 for whom Christ *d* are destroyed.
	11.30 you are weak and ill, and some have *d*.
	15. 3 that Christ *d* for our sins in accordance
	15. 6 are still alive, though some have *d*.
2 Cor	5.14 that one has *d* for all; therefore all have
Gal	2.19 through the law I *d* to the law, so that I
1 Thess	4.13 about those who have *d*, so that you
Rev	16. 3 and every living thing in the sea *d*.

DIFFERENCE

| Ezek | 44.23 people the *d* between the holy and the |

DIFFERENT

| 1 Cor | 4. 7 who sees anything *d* in you? What do |
| Gal | 1. 6 Christ and are turning to a *d* gospel— |

DIG (DIGS DUG)

| Gen | 26.22 moved from there and *d* another well, |

Prov	26.27 Whoever *d* a pit will fall into it, and a
Eccl	10. 8 Whoever *d* a pit will fall into it; and
Mt	25.18 went off and *d* a hole in the ground
Lk	16. 3 I am not strong enough to *d*, and I am

DILIGENT (DILIGENTLY)

Deut	11.22 If you will *d* observe this entire
	28.58 If you do not *d* observe all the words of
Prov	12.24 The hand of the *d* will rule, while the
	13. 4 while the appetite of the *d* is richly
	21. 5 The plans of the *d* lead surely to

DIM

| Ps | 69. 3 is parched. My eyes grow *d* with waiting |

DINE

| Gen | 43.16 ready, for the men are to *d* with me |
| Lk | 11.37 a Pharisee asked him to *d* with him; so |

DINNER

Prov	15.17 Better is a *d* of vegetables where love is
Mt	22. 4 I have prepared my *d*, my oxen and my
Lk	14.12 or *d*, do not invite your friends or your
	14.16 gave a great *d*, and invited many.

DIPPED

| Mt | 26.23 "The one who has *d* his hand into the |
| Jn | 13.26 of bread when I have *d* it in the dish." |

DIRECT (DIRECTED DIRECTS)

1 Sam	7. 3 *D* your heart to the LORD, and serve him
1 Chr	29.18 people, and *d* their hearts toward you.
Ps	119.128 I *d* my steps by all your precepts; I hate
Prov	16. 9 plans the way, but the LORD *d* the steps.
Isa	40.13 Who has *d* the Spirit of the LORD, or as
Mt	28.16 mountain to which Jesus had *d* them.
Acts	10.22 was *d* by a holy angel to send for you to

DIRECTION

| Josh | 9.14 and did not ask *d* from the LORD. |

DISAPPOINTED

| Job | 41. 9 Any hope of capturing it will be *d*; were |

DISASTER

Prov	24.22 for *d* comes from them suddenly, and
Jer	17.18 bring on them the day of *d*; destroy
	44.11 I am determined to bring *d* on you, to
Am	3. 6 Does *d* befall a city, unless the LORD has
Zeph	3.15 in your midst; you shall fear *d* no more.

DISCERN (DISCERNED DISCERNING)

1 Kings	3. 9 able to *d* between good and evil;
Ps	139. 2 I rise up; you *d* my thoughts from far
Rom	12. 2 you may *d* what is the will of God—
1 Cor	1.19 the discernment of the *d* I will thwart."
	2.14 them because they are spiritually *d*.
	11.29 who eat and drink without *d* the body,

DISCERNMENT

| 1 Cor | 1.19 wise, and the *d* of the discerning I will |

DISCHARGED

| Rom | 7. 2 her husband dies she is *d* from the law |
| | 7. 6 But now we are *d* from the law, dead to |

DISCIPLE (DISCIPLES)

Isa	8.16 seal the teaching among my *d*.
Mt	10. 1 Jesus summoned his twelve *d* and gave
	10.24 "A *d* is not above the teacher, nor a
	14.19 *d*, and the *d* gave them to the crowds.
	15. 2 "Why do your *d* break the tradition of
	17.16 I brought him to your *d*, but they could
	21. 1 the Mount of Olives, Jesus sent two *d*,
	28. 7 tell his *d*, 'He has been raised from the
	28.19 Go therefore and make *d* of all nations,
Mk	3. 7 Jesus departed with his *d* to the sea,
	6.45 he made his *d* get into the boat and go
	8. 6 gave them to his *d* to distribute and

Mk	9.31 he was teaching his *d*, saying to them, 10.13 them, and the *d* spoke sternly to them.
Lk	6.40 A *d* is not above the teacher, but 7.18 John summoned two of his *d* and sent 9.16 broke them, and gave them to the *d* to 14.33 cannot become my *d* if you do not give 17. 3 your guard! If another *d* sins, rebuke the 19.29 he sent two of the *d*, saying, "Go into 22.39 of Olives; and the *d* followed him.
Jn	2.11 his glory; and his *d* believed in him. 3.25 arose between John's *d* and a Jew. 6.66 many of his *d* turned back and no 8.31 in my word, you are truly my *d*; 9.28 are his *d*, but we are *d* of Moses. 13.35 that you are my *d*, if you have love for 15. 8 you bear much fruit and become my *d*. 19.26 Jesus saw his mother and the *d* whom 19.38 Joseph of Arimathea, who was a *d* of 20. 2 went to Simon Peter and the other *d*, 20.19 where the *d* had met were locked for 21. 4 the *d* did not know that it was Jesus.
Acts	9.10 was a *d* at Damascus named Ananias.

DISCIPLINARIAN

Gal	3.24 the law was our *d* until Christ came, so 3.25 come, we are no longer subject to a *d*,

DISCIPLINE (n)

Job	5.17 do not despise the *d* of the Almighty.
Ps	50.17 For you hate *d*, and you cast my words
Prov	3.11 do not despise the Lord's *d* or be weary 15.10 There is severe *d* for one who forsakes 23.13 Do not withhold *d* from your children; if
Heb	12. 5 do not regard lightly the *d* of the Lord, 12.11 *d* always seems painful rather than

DISCIPLINE (DISCIPLINED DISCIPLINES)

Deut	4.36 he made you hear his voice to *d* you.
	8. 5 as a parent *d* a child so the Lord your
1 Kings	12.11 My father *d* you with whips, but I will *d*
Ps	6. 1 in your anger, nor *d* me in your wrath. 38. 1 in your anger, nor *d* me in your wrath! 94.10 He who *d* the nations, he teaches 94.12 Happy are those whom you *d*, O Lord,
Prov	19.18 *D* your children while there is hope; do 29.17 *D* your children, and they will give you
Jer	31.18 "You *d* me, and I took the *d*; I was like
Hos	7.12 I will *d* them according to the report
1 Cor	11.32 we are *d* so that we may not be
Heb	12. 9 we had human parents to *d* us, and we
1 Pet	1.13 your minds for action; *d* yourselves;
Rev	3.19 I reprove and *d* those whom I love. Be

DISCLOSED

Mk	4.22 there is nothing hidden, except to be *d*;

DISCORD

Prov	6.19 falsely, and one who sows *d* in a family.

DISCOURAGE

Num	32. 7 Why will you *d* the hearts of the

DISCOVER

Ps	44.21 to a strange god, would not God *d* this?

DISCRETION

1 Chr	22.12 may the Lord grant you *d* and

DISEASE (DISEASED DISEASES)

Ex	15.26 I will not bring upon you any of the *d*
Deut	7.15 all the dread *d* of Egypt that you
1 Kings	15.23 But in his old age he was *d* in his feet.
2 Chr	16.12 yet even in his *d* he did not seek the 21.18 him in his bowels with an incurable *d*.
Ps	106. 15 but sent a wasting *d* among them.
Mt	4.23 curing every *d* and every sickness 8.17 "He took our infirmities and bore our *d*."
Mk	3.10 so that all who had *d* pressed upon him 5.29 her body that she was healed of her *d*.

Lk	6.18 to hear him and to be healed of their *d*;

DISGRACE

Josh	5. 9 rolled away from you the *d* of Egypt."
2 Kings	19. 3 is a day of distress, of rebuke, and of *d*;
Job	10.15 for I am filled with *d* and look upon my
Ps	44.15 All day long my *d* is before me, and
Prov	3.35 will inherit honor, but stubborn fools, *d*.
	18. 3 comes also; and with dishonor comes *d*.
Jer	31.19 because I bore the *d* of my youth."
Ezek	22. 4 I have made you a *d* to the nations,
Mt	1.19 and unwilling to expose her to public *d*,
Lk	1.25 me and took away the *d* I have endured

DISGRACEFUL

Deut	22.21 she committed a *d* act in Israel by
1 Cor	11. 6 if it is *d* for a woman to have her hair

DISGUISE (DISGUISED DISGUISING)

1 Kings	14. 2 said to his wife, "Go, *d* yourself, 20.38 the road, *d* himself with a bandage over
2 Chr	18.29 "I will *d* myself and go into battle, but 35.22 him, but *d* himself in order to fight
2 Cor	11.13 workers, *d* themselves as apostles

DISH

Lk	11.39 the *d*, but inside you are full of greed

DISHONEST

Ex	18.21 God, are trustworthy, and hate *d* gain;
Jer	22.17 eyes and heart are only on your *d* gain,
Ezek	22.13 together at the *d* gain you have made,
Lk	16. 8 master commended the *d* manager 16.11 not been faithful with the *d* wealth,

DISHONOR

Ps	109. 29 May my accusers be clothed with *d*;
Jer	2.25 in our shame, and let our *d* cover us; 14.21 sake; do not *d* your glorious throne;

DISINHERIT

Num	14.12 strike them with pestilence and *d* them,

DISLOYALTY

Hos	14. 4 I will heal their *d*; I will love them

DISMAYED

Job	21. 6 When I think of it I am *d*, and
Dan	8.27 But I was *d* by the vision and did not

DISOBEDIENCE

Rom	5.19 just as by one man's *d* many were made

DISOBEDIENT

Lk	1.17 the *d* to the wisdom of the righteous, to
Acts	26.19 that, King Agrippa, I was not *d* to the
Rom	10.21 long I have held out my hands to a *d*
Eph	2. 2 is now at work among those who are *d*.
Titus	3. 3 For we ourselves were once foolish, *d*,
Heb	3.18 his rest, if not to those who were *d*?

DISOBEY (DISOBEYED)

Deut	17.12 anyone who presumes to *d* the priest
1 Kings	13.21 "Because you have *d* the word of the 13.26 "It is the man of God who *d* the word of
Prov	24.21 the king, and do not *d* either of them;
Lk	15.29 and I never *d* your command; yet you

DISORDER

1 Cor	14.33 God is a God not of *d* but of peace.

DISPLAYED

Ps	77.14 have *d* your might among the peoples.

DISPERSE (DISPERSED)

Isa	11.12 of Israel, and gather the *d* of Judah
Ezek	22.15 and *d* you through the countries, 36.19 and they were *d* through the countries;

DISPERSION

| Jn | 7.35 intend to go to the *D* among the Greeks |
| 1 Pet | 1. 1 To the exiles of the *D* in Pontus, |

DISPLEASE (DISPLEASED DISPLEASING)

Gen	38.10 he did was *d* in the sight of the LORD,
	48.17 hand on the head of Ephraim, it *d* him;
Num	22.34 if it is *d* to you, I will return home."
1 Sam	8. 6 But the thing *d* Samuel when they said,
2 Sam	11.27 things that David had done *d* the LORD.
1 Kings	1. 6 had never at any time *d* him by asking,
1 Chr	21. 7 God was *d* with this thing, and he
Prov	24.18 or else the LORD will see it and be *d*,
Isa	59.15 The LORD saw it, and it *d* him that there
Jon	4. 1 very *d* to Jonah, and he became angry.
1 Thess	2.15 they *d* God and oppose everyone by

DISPLEASURE

| Num | 14.34 forty years, and you shall know my *d*." |

DISPOSSESS (DISPOSSESSED)

| Deut | 9. 1 go in and *d* nations larger and mightier |
| Acts | 7.45 with Joshua when they *d* the nations |

DISPUTE (DISPUTES)

Deut	19.17 then both parties to the *d* shall appear
Eccl	6.10 they are not able to *d* with those who
Lk	22.24 A *d* also arose among them as to which
2 Cor	7. 5 every way —*d* without and fear within.

DISQUALIFY (DISQUALIFIED)

| 1 Cor | 9.27 to others I myself should not be *d*. |
| Col | 2.18 Do not let anyone *d* you, insisting on |

DISREPUTE

| Acts | 19.27 that this trade of ours may come into *d* |
| 1 Cor | 4.10 You are held in honor, but we in *d*. To |

DISSENSION (DISSENSIONS)

Rom	16.17 keep an eye on those who cause *d* and
1 Cor	12.25 there may be no *d* within the body, but
Titus	3. 9 genealogies, *d*, and quarrels

DISSOLVED

| 2 Pet | 3.10 elements will be *d* with fire, and the |
| | 3.11 all these things are to be *d* in this way, |

DISTANCE

| Lk | 22.54 house. But Peter was following at a *d*. |

DISTINCT

| Ex | 33.16 way, we shall be *d*, I and your people, |

DISTINCTION (DISTINCTIONS)

Ex	8.23 I will make a *d* between my people and
	11. 7 know that the LORD makes a *d* between
Lev	11.47 to make a *d* between the unclean and
	20.25 make a *d* between the clean animal and
Ezek	22.26 have made no *d* between the holy and
Acts	15. 9 has made no *d* between them and us.
Rom	3.22 for all who believe. For there is no *d*,
	10.12 there is no *d* between Jew and Greek;
Jas	2. 4 have you not made *d* among yourselves,

DISTINGUISH (DISTINGUISHED)

Lev	10.10 You are to *d* between the holy and the
Song	5.10 and ruddy, *d* among ten thousand.
Ezek	44.23 how to *d* between the unclean and
Dan	6. 3 Daniel *d* himself above all the other
Heb	5.14 trained by practice to *d* good from evil.

DISTRACTED

| Lk | 10.41 Martha, you are worried and *d* by many |

DISTRESS

Deut	4.30 In your *d*, when all these things have
Judg	10.14 them deliver you in the time of your *d*."
1 Sam	22. 2 Everyone who was in *d*, and everyone
2 Sam	16.12 be that the LORD will look upon my *d*,

2 Kings	14.26 LORD saw that the *d* of Israel was very
2 Chr	15. 4 but when in their *d* they turned to the
	28.22 of his *d* he became yet more faithless
	33.12 he was in *d* he entreated the favor
Neh	9. 9 saw the *d* of our ancestors in Egypt and
Ps	4. 1 You gave me room when I was in *d*. Be
	107. 6 and he delivered them from their *d*;
	116. 3 hold on me; I suffered *d* and anguish.
	120. 1 In my *d* I cry to the LORD, that he may
Prov	1.27 when *d* and anguish come upon you.
Isa	8.22 earth, but will see only *d* and darkness.
	26.16 LORD, in *d* they sought you, they poured
	63. 9 he became their savior in all their *d*.
Jer	30. 7 none like it; it is a time of *d* for Jacob;
Jon	2. 2 I called to the LORD out of my *d*, and he
Lk	21.23 For there will be great *d* on the earth
1 Cor	7.28 who marry will experience *d* in this life,
2 Cor	2. 4 I wrote you out of much *d* and anguish
Rev	2.22 I am throwing into great *d*, unless they

DISTRESSED (DISTRESSING)

Gen	21.11 The matter was very *d* to Abraham on
	45. 5 And now do not be *d*, or angry with
1 Sam	1.10 She was deeply *d* and prayed to the
Dan	4.19 was called Beltashazzar, was severely *d*
	6.14 heard the charge, he was very much *d*.
Mt	17.23 will be raised." And they were greatly *d*.
2 Pet	2. 7 Lot, a righteous man greatly *d* by the

DISTRIBUTED

| Josh | 13.32 the inheritances that Moses *d* in the |
| Heb | 2. 4 by gifts of the Holy Spirit, *d* according |

DISTURBED

1 Sam	28.15 said to Saul, "Why have you *d* me by
Jn	11.38 Then Jesus, again greatly *d*, came to the
Acts	17. 8 and the city officials were *d* when they

DIVIDE (DIVIDED DIVIDES DIVIDING)

Ex	14.21 into dry land; and the waters were *d*.
Num	31.27 *D* the booty into two parts, between the
Josh	19.51 of meeting. So they finished *d* the land.
2 Sam	1.23 In life and in death they were not *d*;
1 Kings	3.25 "*D* the living boy in two; then give half
Neh	9.11 you *d* the sea before them, so that they
Isa	53.12 and he shall *d* the spoil with the strong;
Ezek	37.22 and never again shall they be *d* into two
Mt	12.25 every kingdom *d* against itself is laid
Mk	3.24 If a kingdom is *d* against itself, that
	15.24 him, and *d* his clothes among them.
Lk	11.17 every kingdom *d* against itself becomes
	12.13 "Teacher, tell my brother to *d* the
	12.53 one household will be *d*, father against
	22.17 "Take this, and *d* it among yourselves;
Jn	10.19 Again the Jews were *d* because of these
	19.24 "They *d* my clothes among themselves,
1 Cor	1.13 Has Christ been *d*? Was Paul crucified
Heb	4.12 piercing until it *d* soul from spirit,

DIVINATION

Gen	30.27 I have learned by *d* that the LORD has
Num	22. 7 departed with fees for *d* in their hand;
Ezek	12.24 longer be any false vision or flattering *d*
Acts	16.16 slave girl who had a spirit of *d* and

DIVINE

| 2 Pet | 1. 4 become participants of the *d* nature. |

DIVISION (DIVISIONS)

1 Chr	24. 1 The *d* of the sons of Aaron were these.
Lk	12.51 the earth? No, I tell you, but rather *d*;
1 Cor	1.10 and that there be no *d* among you,
	11.18 I hear that there are *d* among you;

DIVORCE (DIVORCES)

Deut	24. 1 he writes her a certificate of *d*, puts it
Jer	3. 8 I had sent her away with a decree of *d*;
Mt	19. 7 whoever *d* his wife, except for

Mk	10.	4 a certificate of dismissal and to *d* her."
1 Cor	7.13	to live with her, she should not *d* him.

DO (DONE)

Gen	2.	3 rested from all the work that he had *d*
2 Chr	29.36	of what God had *d* for the people;
Eccl	9.	7 God has long ago approved what you *d*.
Isa	63.	7 because of all that the LORD has *d* for
Zeph	2.	3 of the land, who *d* his commands;
Mt	7.12	as you would have them *d* to you;
	16.27	will repay everyone for what has been *d*.
Acts	21.19	that God had *d* among the Gentiles

DOCTOR

Lk	4.23	to me this proverb, '*D*, cure yourself!'

DOCTRINE (DOCTRINES)

Mk	7.	7 me, teaching human precepts as *d*.'
Eph	4.14	fro and blown about by every wind of *d*,
1 Tim	1.	3 people not to teach any different *d*,
Titus	1.	9 to preach with sound *d* and to refute
	2.10	may be an ornament to the *d* of God

DOCUMENT

Isa	29.11	for you like the words of a sealed *d*.

DOERS

Rom	2.13	the *d* of the law who will be justified.
Jas	1.22	But be *d* of the word, and not merely

DOG (DOGS)

Judg	7.	5 who lap with their tongues, as a *d* laps,
2 Sam	9.	8 should look upon a dead *d* such as I?"
1 Kings	21.19	Naboth, *d* will also lick up your blood."
2 Kings	8.13	"What is your servant, who is a mere *d*,
Ps	59.	6 evening they come back, howling like *d*
Prov	26.17	who takes a passing *d* by the ears.
Eccl	9.	4 for a living *d* is better than a dead
Isa	56.10	they are all silent *d* that cannot bark;
Mt	7.	6 "Do not give what is holy to *d*; and do
	15.26	children's food and throw it to the *d*."
Mk	7.28	even the *d* under the table eat the
Lk	16.21	the *d* would come and lick his sores.
Phil	3.	2 Beware of the *d*, beware of the evil
2 Pet	2.22	"The *d* turns back to its own vomit,"

DOME

Gen	1.	6 "Let there be a *d* in the midst of the

DOMINATED

1 Cor	6.12	for me," but I will not be *d* by anything.

DOMINION

Ps	22.28	For *d* belongs to the LORD, and he rules
	72.	8 May he have *d* from sea to sea, and
	103.	22 all his works, in all places of his *d*.
Ezek	30.18	dark, when I break there the *d* of Egypt,
Dan	6.26	be destroyed, and his *d* has no end.
Zech	9.10	nations; his *d* shall be from sea to sea,
Rom	5.21	grace also might exercise *d* through
	6.	9 again; death no longer has *d* over him.
	6.12	Do not let sin exercise *d* in your mortal

DONKEY (DONKEY'S)

Num	22.23	The *d* saw the angel of the LORD
	22.28	mouth of the *d*, and it said to Balaam,
Mt	21.	5 humble, and mounted on an *d*, and on
Jn	12.15	your king is coming, sitting on a *d* colt!"
2 Pet	2.16	a speechless *d* spoke with human voice

DOOR (DOORS)

Ps	24.	7 O gates! and be lifted up, O ancient *d*!
Prov	18.16	A gift opens *d*; it gives access to the
Isa	45.	2 I will break in pieces the *d* of bronze
Hos	2.15	make the Valley of Achor a *d* of hope.
Lk	12.	3 have whispered behind closed *d* will be
	13.24	"Strive to enter through the narrow *d*;
	13.25	knock at the *d*, saying, 'Lord, open to
Acts	14.27	opened a *d* of faith for the Gentiles.

1 Cor	16.	9 a wide *d* for effective work has opened
Col	4.	3 God will open to us a *d* for the word,
Rev	3.	8 Look, I have set before you an open *d*,
	3.20	I am standing at the *d*, knocking; if you
	4.	1 and there in heaven a *d* stood open!

DOORKEEPER

Ps	84.10	I would rather be a *d* in the house of

DOORPOSTS

Ex	12.	7 blood and put it on the two *d* and the

DORCAS

Acts	9.36	name was Tabitha, which in Greek is *D*.
	9.39	other clothing that *D* had made while

DOUBLE

Gen	43.15	they took *d* the money with them, as
2 Kings	2.	9 let me inherit a *d* share of your spirit."
Ps	12.	2 with flattering lips and a *d* heart they
Isa	40.	2 from the LORD's hand *d* for all her sins.
Zech	9.12	I declare that I will restore to you *d*.

DOUBT (DOUBTS)

Deut	28.66	Your life shall hang in *d* before you;
Mt	21.21	if you have faith and do not *d*, not only
Mk	11.23	sea and if you do not *d* in your heart,
Jn	20.27	put it in my side. Do not *d* but believe."
Rom	14.23	those who have *d* are condemned if

DOVE (DOVES)

Gen	8.	8 he sent out a *d* from him, to see if the
Ps	55.	6 "O that I had wings like a *d*! I would fly
Song	5.12	His eyes are like *d* beside springs of
Hos	7.11	Ephraim has become like a *d*, silly and
Mt	3.16	the Spirit of God descending like a *d*
Lk	3.22	upon him in bodily form like a *d*,
Jn	1.32	Spirit descending from heaven like a *d*,

DOWNFALL

Prov	29.16	but the righteous will look upon their *d*.
Ezek	32.10	each one of them, on the day of your *d*.

DOWNTRODDEN

Ps	74.21	Do not let the *d* be put to shame; let
	147.	6 The LORD lifts up the *d*, he casts the

DRAGON

Ezek	32.	2 but you are like a *d* in the seas;
Rev	12.	3 a great red *d*, with seven heads and ten

DRAW (DRAWN DREW)

Gen	24.11	time when women go out to *d* water.
	24.19	"I will *d* for your camels also, until they
Ps	18.16	took me; he *d* me out of mighty waters.
	30.	1 you, O LORD, for you have *d* me up,
	69.18	*D* near to me, redeem me, set me free
Song	1.	4 *D* me after you, let us make haste. The
Isa	34.	1 *D* near, O nations, to hear, O peoples,
Acts	7.17	as the time *d* near for the fulfillment of
Jas	4.	8 *D* near to God and he will *d* near to

DRAWERS

Josh	9.21	hewers of wood and *d* of water for all

DREAD

Isa	7.16	before whose two kings you are in *d*
	8.12	and do not fear what it fears or be in *d*.

DREAM (DREAMED DREAMS)

Gen	28.12	he *d* that there was a ladder set up on
	31.24	God came to Laban . . . in a *d* by night,
	37.	5 Joseph had a *d*, and when he told it to
	40.	5 One night they both *d* —the cupbearer
	41.	8 Pharaoh told them his *d*, but there was
	42.	9 Joseph also remembered the *d* that he
Num	12.	6 them in visions; I speak to you in *d*.
Deut	13.	1 or those who divine by *d* appear among
Judg	7.13	"I had a *d*; and in it a cake of barley

DREAMER

1 Kings	3.	5 the Lord appeared to Solomon in a *d*
Eccl	5.	7 With many *d* come vanities and a
Isa	29.	8 a hungry person *d* of eating and wakes
Jer	23.28	Let the prophet who has a *d* tell the *d*,
Dan	2.	1 Nebuchadnezzar *d* such *d* that his spirit
Joel	2.28	your old men shall *d d*, and your young
Mt	1.20	of the Lord appeared to him in a *d*
	27.19	a great deal because of a *d* about him."
Acts	2.17	see visions, and your old men shall *d d*.

DREAMER

Gen	37.19	said to one another, "Here comes this *d*.

DRENCH

Ezek	32.	6 I will *d* the land with your flowing

DRINK (n)

Ps	36.	8 and you give them *d* from the river of
Prov	31.	6 Give strong *d* to one who is perishing,
Lk	1.15	He must never drink wine or strong *d*,
Jn	4.	7 and Jesus said to her, "Give me a *d*."
Titus	2.	3 not to be slanderers or slaves to *d*;

DRINK (DRANK DRINKING)

Gen	19.32	Come, let us make our father *d* wine,
	24.14	say, '*D*, and I will water your camels'
Lev	10.	8 D no wine nor strong drink, neither you
2 Sam	23.15	that someone would give me water to *d*
Ps	60.	3 given us wine to *d* that made us reel.
	110.	7 He will *d* from the stream by the path;
Prov	5.15	*D* water from your own cistern, flowing
	25.21	if they are thirsty, give them water to *d*;
Song	5.	1 Eat, friends, *d*, and be drunk with love.
Jer	25.17	nations to whom the Lord sent me *d* it:
	35.	6 But they answered, "We will *d* no wine,
Hab	2.15	for you who make your neighbors *d*,
Mt	11.18	John came neither eating nor *d*, and
	24.38	before the flood they were eating and *d*,
	27.34	they offered him wine to *d*, mixed with
Mk	14.23	it to them, and all of them *d* from it.
Lk	7.33	*d* no wine; and you say, 'He has a
	12.29	eat and what you are to *d*, and do not
Jn	4.14	those who *d* of the water that I will give
1 Cor	10.	4 they *d* from the spiritual rock that
	10.31	So, whether you eat or *d*, or whatever
	11.26	this bread and the cup, you proclaim
	12.13	we were all made to *d* of one Spirit.
1 Tim	5.23	No longer *d* only water, but take a little

DRIVE (DRIVES DRIVING DROVE)

Gen	31.18	and he *d* away all his livestock, all the
Ex	14.21	the Lord *d* the sea back by a strong
Judg	1.27	Manasseh did not *d* out the inhabitants
2 Kings	9.20	son of Nimshi; for he *d* like a maniac."
Ps	35.	5 with the angel of the Lord *d* them on.
	44.	2 with your own hand *d* out the nations,
Isa	59.19	stream that the wind of the Lord *d* on.
Mt	21.12	and *d* out all who were selling and
Jn	9.34	trying to teach us?" And they *d* him out.

DROSS

Ps	119.119	the wicked of the earth you count as *d*;
Prov	25.	4 Take away the *d* from the silver, and
Isa	1.22	Your silver has become *d*, your wine is
	1.25	I will smelt away your *d* as with lye and

DROUGHT

Hag	1.11	I have called for a *d* on the land and

DROWNED

Mt	18.	6 your neck and you were *d* in the depth
Mk	5.13	into the sea, and were *d* in the sea.
Lk	8.33	the steep bank into the lake and was *d*.

DRUNK

Gen	9.21	wine and became *d*, and he lay
2 Sam	11.13	in his presence and he made him *d*;
Isa	29.	9 Be *d*, but not with wine; stagger, but
	51.17	wrath, who have *d* to the dregs the bowl

Acts	2.15	Indeed, these men are not *d*, as you

DRUNKARD (DRUNKARDS)

Ps	69.12	gate, and the *d* make songs about me.
Isa	19.14	Egypt stagger in all its doings as a *d*
	28.	1 the proud garland of the *d* of Ephraim,
Mt	11.19	a glutton and a *d*, a friend of tax
	24.49	slaves, and eats and drinks with *d*,
Lk	7.34	'Look, a glutton and a *d*, a friend of tax
1 Cor	5.11	or is an idolater, reviler, *d*, or robber.

DRUNKENNESS

Eccl	10.17	time— for strength, and not for *d*!
Ezek	23.33	You shall be filled with *d* and sorrow. A

DRY (DRIED DRYING)

Gen	8.13	saw that the face of the ground was *d*.
Josh	2.10	heard how the Lord *d* up the water of
	3.17	the priests . . . stood on *d* ground in the
Isa	44.27	deep, "Be *d*— I will *d* up your rivers";
Joel	1.12	the trees of the field are *d* up;

DUE

Rom	4.	4 reckoned as a gift but as something *d*.

DULL

Acts	28.27	For this people's heart has grown *d*,
Heb	5.11	you have become *d* in understanding.

DUST

Gen	2.	7 Lord God formed man from the *d* of the
	3.14	and *d* you shall eat all the days of your
	3.19	you are *d*, and to *d* you shall return."
	13.16	your offspring like the *d* of the earth;
	18.27	to the Lord, I who am but *d* and ashes.
Job	34.15	together, and all mortals return to *d*.
	38.38	when the *d* runs into a mass and the
Ps	90.	3 You turn us back to *d*, and say, "Turn
	103.	14 made; he remembers that we are *d*.
	104.	29 breath, they die and return to their *d*.
Eccl	3.20	all are from the *d*, and all turn to *d*
	12.	7 the *d* returns to the earth as it was, and
Mt	10.14	shake off the *d* from your feet as you
Lk	10.11	*d* of your town that clings to our feet,

DUTY

Deut	25.	5 performing the *d* of a husband's brother
1 Tim	5.	4 first learn their religious *d* to their own

DWELL (DWELLS)

Ex	29.45	I will *d* among the Israelites, and I will
1 Kings	6.13	I will *d* among the children of Israel,
	8.27	will God indeed *d* on the earth? Even
Ps	23.	6 I shall *d* in the house of the Lord my
Isa	33.	5 The Lord is exalted, he *d* on high; he
Jn	14.10	own; but the Father who *d* in me does
Rom	7.17	I that do it, but sin that *d* within me.
1 Cor	3.16	temple and that God's Spirit *d* in you?
Eph	3.17	Christ may *d* in your hearts through
Jas	4.	5 for the spirit that he has made to *d*
Rev	21.	3 He will *d* with them as their God; they

DWELLING (DWELLINGS)

Job	23.	3 him, that I might come even to his *d*!
Ps	43.	3 me to your holy hill and to your *d*!
	78.60	He abandoned his *d* at Shiloh, the tent
Isa	11.10	of him, and his *d* shall be glorious.
Mt	17.	4 I will make three *d* here, one for you,
Mk	9.	5 let us make three *d*, one for you, one
Lk	9.33	let us make three *d*, one for you, one
Acts	28.30	n his own hired *d* and welcome all who

DWELLING PLACE

Deut	33.27	n The eternal God is a *d*, he shatters
Ps	84.	1 How lovely is your *d*, O Lord of hosts!
	90.	1 Lord, you have been our *d* in all
	132.	5 for the Lord, a *d* for the Mighty One
	132.	7 "Let us go to his *d*; let us worship at his
Ezek	37.27	My *d* shall be with them; and I will be

DWINDLED

| Isa | 24. 6 inhabitants of the earth *d*, and few |

E

EAGER (EAGERNESS)

Rom	1.15 —hence my *e* to proclaim the gospel to
1 Cor	14.39 friends, be *e* to prophesy, and do not
2 Cor	8.16 heart of Titus the same *e* for you that I

EAGLE (EAGLES)

Lev	11.13 they are an abomination: the *e*, the
Job	39.27 it at your command that the *e* mounts
Prov	30.19 I do not understand: the way of an *e* in
Isa	40.31 they shall mount up with wings like *e*,
Ezek	10.14 of a lion, and the fourth that of an *e*.
	17. 2 A great *e*, with great wings and long

EAR (EARS)

Ex	21. 6 his master shall pierce his *e* with an
Job	42. 5 heard of you by the hearing of the *e*,
Ps	34.15 and his *e* are open to their cry.
	40. 6 but you have given me an open *e*.
	94. 9 who planted the *e*, does he not hear?
	135. 17 they have *e*, but they do not hear, and
Prov	2. 2 making your *e* attentive to wisdom and
Jer	5.21 not see, who have *e*, but do not hear.
Ezek	12. 2 who have *e* to hear but do not hear;
Mt	13. 9 Let anyone with *e*, listen!"
	26.51 of the high priest, cutting off his *e*.
Mk	4. 9 said, Let anyone with *e* to hear listen!
	4.23 Let anyone with *e* to hear listen!"
	14.47 of the high priest, cutting off his *e*.
Lk	14.35 away. Let anyone with *e* to hear listen!
	22.50 of the high priest and cut off his right *e*.
Jn	18.10 priest's slave, and cut off his right *e*.
1 Cor	2. 9 "What no eye has seen, nor *e* heard, nor
	12.16 And if the *e* would say, "Because I am
Rev	2.29 Let anyone who had an *e* listen to what

EARN

| 1 Cor | 16. 2 aside and save whatever extra you *e*, |

EARTH

Gen	1. 1 God created the heavens and the *e*,
	1.10 God called the dry land *E*, and the
Josh	3.11 Lord of all the *e* is going to pass before
Job	26. 7 the void, and hangs the *e* upon nothing.
Ps	24. 1 The *e* is the Lord's and all that is in it,
	33. 5 the *e* is full of the steadfast love of the
	65. 9 You visit the *e* and water it, you greatly
Isa	6. 3 of hosts; the whole *e* is full of his glory."
Jer	4.27 Because of this the *e* shall mourn, and
Ezek	34.27 fruit, and the *e* shall yield its increase.
Hab	2.20 holy temple; let all the *e* keep silence
	3.12 In fury you trod the *e*, in anger you
Zeph	3. 8 my passion all the *e* shall be consumed.
Mt	27.51 The *e* shook, and the rocks were split.
Mk	4.28 The *e* produces of itself, first the stalk,
1 Cor	10.26 for "the *e* and its fullness are the
	15.47 first man was from the *e*, a man of dust;
2 Pet	3.13 wait for a new heavens and a new *e*,
Rev	6. 4 was permitted to take peace from the *e*,

EARTHLY

| 2 Cor | 1.12 not by *e* wisdom but by the grace of |
| | 5. 1 if the *e* tent we live in is destroyed, we |

EARTHQUAKE (EARTHQUAKES)

1 Kings	19.11 after the wind an *e*, but the Lord was
Isa	29. 6 with thunder and *e* and great noise,
Am	1. 1 Joash of Israel, two years before the *e*.
Mt	28. 2 suddenly there was a great *e*; for an
Mk	13. 8 there will be *e* in various places; there
Lk	21.11 there will be great *e*, and in various
Acts	16.26 there was an *e*, so violent that the
Rev	16.18 of thunder, and a violent *e*, such as

EASE

Job	3.26 I am not at *e*, nor am I quiet; I have no
Ps	73.12 are the wicked; always at *e*, they
Am	6. 1 Alas for those who are at *e* in Zion, and

EAST

Mt	2. 1 wise men from the *E* came to
	8.11 many will come from *e* and west and
Lk	13.29 people will come from *e* and west,

EASY (EASIER)

Mt	7.13 the road is *e* that leads to destruction,
	9. 5 which is *e*, to say, 'Your sins are
	11.30 For my yoke is *e*, and my burden is

EAT (ATE EATEN EATING)

Gen	2.17 tree of knowledge . . . you shall not *e*,
	43.32 the Egyptians could not *e* with the
Ex	12.15 days you shall *e* unleavened bread,
	32. 6 the people sat down to *e* and drink, and
Lev	7.26 You must not *e* any blood whatever,
	19.26 You shall not *e* anything with its blood
Deut	12. 7 you shall *e* in the presence of the Lord
1 Sam	9.24 guests." So Saul *a* with Samuel that day.
	14.32 and the troops *a* them with the blood.
Ps	14. 4 all the evildoers who *e* up my people as
Prov	23. 1 you sit down to *e* with a ruler, observe
Isa	1.19 you shall *e* the good of the land;
	22.13 wine. "Let us *e* and drink, for tomorrow
Jer	15.16 Your words were found, and I *a* them,
Ezek	2. 8 open your mouth and *e* what I give you.
	3. 1 *e* this scroll, and go, speak to the house
Dan	4.33 from human society, *a* grass like oxen,
Mt	9.11 "Why does your teacher *e* with tax
	15.38 Those who had *e* were four thousand
	24.38 before the flood they were *e* and
	26.26 and said, "Take, *e*; this is my body."
Mk	14.14 guest room where I may *e* the Passover
Lk	5.30 "Why do you *e* and drink with tax
	12.19 many years; relax, *e*, drink, be merry.'
	17.27 They were *e* and drinking, and marrying
	24.43 and he took it and *a* in their presence.
Jn	4.31 were urging him, "Rabbi, *e* something."
Acts	10.13 voice saying, "Get up, Peter; kill and *e*."
	11. 7 to me, 'Get up, Peter; kill and *e*.'
Rom	14. 3 Those who *e* must not despise those
1 Cor	10.27 whatever is set before you without
	10.31 So, whether you *e* or drink, or whatever
	15.32 "Let us *e* and drink, for tomorrow we
2 Thess	3.10 anyone unwilling to work should not *e*.
Rev	3.20 I will come in to you and *e* with you,

EBENEZER

| 1 Sam | 7.12 and named it *E*; for he said, "Thus far |

EDEN

Gen	2. 8 God planted a garden in *E*, in the east;
Isa	51. 3 and will make her wilderness like *E*,
Ezek	28.13 You were in *E*, the garden of God; every
Joel	2. 3 them the land is like the garden of *E*,

EDOM (EDOMITES)

Gen	25.30 famished!" (Therefore he was called *E*.)
	36. 9 descendants of Esau, ancestor of the *E*,
Num	20.21 *E* refused to give Israel passage through
2 Sam	8.14 He put garrisons in *E*; throughout all *E*
Ps	108. 9 is my washbasin; on *E* I hurl my shoe;
Isa	63. 1 "Who is this that comes from *E*, from
Am	9.12 that they may possess the remnant of *E*

EGYPT

Gen	12.10 Abram went down to *E* to reside there
	37.28 of silver. And they took Joseph to *E*.
	41.33 wise, and set him over the land of *E*.
	45.13 father how greatly I am honored in *E*,
Ex	7. 4 I will lay my hand upon *E* and bring my
	13.14 of hand the Lord brought us out of *E*,
1 Kings	3. 1 alliance with Pharaoh king of *E*;

Hos	11. 1 him, and out of *E* I called my son.
Mt	2.13 and flee to *E*, and remain there until I
	2.15 "Out of *E* have I called my son."
Heb	11.26 greater wealth than the treasures of *E*,

ELDER (ELDERS)

Gen	25.23 the other, the *e* shall serve the younger."
Lev	4.15 The *e* of the congregation shall lay their
Num	11.16 "Gather for me seventy of the *e* of
Ruth	4. 2 Boaz took ten men of the *e* of the city,
Prov	31.23 city gates, taking his seat among the *e*
Mt	16.21 great suffering at the hands of the *e*
Lk	7. 3 sent some Jewish *e* to him, asking him
Acts	20.17 asking the *e* of the church to meet him.
Rom	9.12 was told, "The *e* will serve the younger."
1 Tim	4.14 laying on of hands by the council of *e*.
	5.17 Let the *e* who rule well be considered
Titus	1. 5 and should appoint *e* in every town, as I
Jas	5.14 sick? They should call for the *e* of the
1 Pet	5. 1 I exhort the *e* among you to tend the
2 Jn	1 The *e* to the elect lady and her
3 Jn	1 The *e* to the beloved Garius, whom I
Rev	4. 4 on the thrones were twenty-four *e*,
	19. 4 the twenty-four *e* and the four living

ELECT

Mt	24.22 for the sake of the *e* those days will be
	24.31 they will gather his *e* from the four
Mk	13.20 but for the sake of the *e*, whom he
	13.27 gather his *e* from the four winds, from
Rom	8.33 will bring any charge against God's *e*?
	11. 7 The *e* obtained it, but the rest were
2 Tim	2.10 endure everything for the sake of the *e*,

ELECTION

Rom	9.11 that God's purpose of *e* might continue,
	11.28 as regards *e* they are beloved, for the
2 Pet	1.10 more eager to confirm your call and *e*,

ELEMENTS

2 Pet	3.10 the *e* will be dissolved with fire, and the
	3.12 dissolved, and the *e* will melt with fire!

ELEVEN

Mk	16.14 Later he appeared to the *e* themselves
Lk	24.33 found the *e* and their companions

ELI

1 Sam	1. 3 where two sons of *E* . . . were priests of
	1. 9 Now *E* the priest was sitting on the seat
	1.25 bull, and they brought the child to *E*.
	2.11 LORD, in the presence of the priest *E*.
	3. 1 was ministering to the LORD under *E*.
	4.11 and the two sons of *E* . . . died.
	4.15 *E* was ninety-eight years old and his

ELIJAH

Predicted the drought, 1 Kings 17.1; fed by ravens, 1 Kings 17.2-7; fed by the widow of Zarephath, 1 Ki 17.8-16; revived the son of the widow, 1 Kings 17.17-24; met Ahab, 1 Kings 18.1-19; triumphed over the prophets of Baal, 1 Kings 18.20-40; prayed for rain, 1 Kings 18.41-46; fled to Mount Horeb, 1 Kings 19.1-8; heard the still small voice, 1 Kings 19.9-18; chose Elisha, 1 Kings 19.19-21; reproved Ahab, 1 Kings 21.17-29; called fire from heaven, 2 Kings 1.3-16; taken up into heaven, 2 Kings 2.1-11.

Mal	4. 5 I will send you the prophet *E* before the
Mt	11.14 to accept it, he is *E* who is to come.
	17. 3 appeared to them Moses and *E*, talking
Mk	9.13 I tell you that *E* has come, and they did
	15.35 it, they said, "Listen, he is calling for *E*."
Lk	1.17 With the spirit and power of *E* he will
	9.54n heaven and consume them as *E* did?"
Jn	1.21 "What then? Are you *E*?" He said, "I am
Jas	5.17 *E* was a human being like us, and he

ELISHA

Called, 1 Kings 19.19-21; succeeded Elijah, 2 Kings 2.1-15; purified the water, 2 Kings 2.19-22; cursed the children, 2 Kings 2.23-25; prophesied victory over the Moabites, 2 Kings 3; increased the widow's oil, 2 Kings 4.1-7; restored the life of the Shunammite's son, 2 Kings 4.8-37; purified the pot of stew, 2 Kings 4.38-41; fed a multitude, 2 Kings 4.42-44; healed Naaman's leprosy, 2 Kings 5; caused Syrians' blindness, 2 Kings 6.8-23; promised food in time of famine, 2 Kings 6.24—7.2; prophesied Hazael's cruelty, 2 Kings 8.7-15; anointed Jehu, 2 Kings 9.1-10; prophesied victory over Syria, 2 Kings 13.14-19; death and burial, 2 Kings 13.20; bones of Elisha, 2 Kings 13.21.

ELIZABETH

Lk	1. 5 of Aaron, and her name was *E*.
	1.13 your wife *E* will bear you a son, and you
	1.40 the house of Zechariah and greeted *E*.

ELOQUENT

Ex	4.10 O my Lord, I have never been *e*, neither
1 Cor	1.17 the gospel, and not with *e* wisdom,

EMBLEMS

Ps	74. 7 holy place; they set up their *e* there.

EMBRACED

Gen	48.10 him; and he kissed them and *e* them.
Song	2. 6 my head, and that his right hand *e* me!

EMMANUEL (see IMMANUEL)

EMMAUS

Lk	24.13 of them were going to a village called *E*,

EMPEROR (EMPEROR'S)

Mt	22.21 "Give therefore to the *e* the things that
Jn	19.12 to be a king sets himself against the *e*."
Acts	25.10 "I am appealing to the *e* tribunal; this is
Phil	4.22 you especially those of the *e* household.

EMPTY

Job	35.13 God does not hear an *e* cry, nor does
Mt	6. 7 do not heap up *e* phrases as the

ENABLE

Eccl	6. 2 yet God does not *e* them to enjoy these

ENCAMP (ENCAMPS)

Job	19.12 against me, and *e* round about my tent.
Ps	27. 3 Though an army *e* against me, my heart
	34. 7 The angel of the LORD *e* around those
Isa	29. 3 like David I will *e* against you; I will

ENCOMPASSES

Jer	31.22 thing on the earth: a woman *e* a man.

ENCOURAGE (ENCOURAGED)

Deut	1.38 *e* him, for he is the one who will secure
	3.28 charge Joshua, and *e* and strengthen
2 Chr	32. 8 were by the words of King Hezekiah
Job	16. 5 I could *e* you with my mouth, and the
Ezek	13.22 you have *e* the wicked not to turn from
Eph	6.22 know how we are, and to *e* your hearts.
Col	2. 2 I want their hearts to be *e* and united
1 Thess	4.18 *e* one another with these words.
Titus	2. 4 *e* the young women to love their

ENCOURAGEMENT

Acts	4.36 Barnabas (which means "son of *e*").
Phil	2. 1 If then there is any *e* in Christ, any

END (ENDS) (n)

Gen	6.13 determined to make an *e* of all flesh,
Ps	2. 8 and the *e* of the earth your possession.
	19. 4 and their words to the *e* of the world.
	39. 4 "LORD, let me know my *e*, and what is
	90. 9 our years come to an *e* like a sigh.
Eccl	4. 8 yet there is no *e* to all their toil, and
	12.13 The *e* of the matter; all has been heard.
Lam	4.18 our *e* drew near; our days were

Ezek	7. 2 An *e*! The *e* has come upon the four
Dan	11.45 shall come to his *e*, with no one to help
Am	8. 2 The *e* has come upon my people Israel;
Mt	24. 3 of your coming and of the *e* of the age?"
	24.14 the nations; and then the *e* will come.
	28.20 am with you always, to the *e* of the age."
Jn	13. 1 in the world, he loved them to the *e*.
Acts	1. 8 and Samaria, and to the *e* of the earth."
Rom	10. 4 For Christ is the *e* of the law so that
1 Cor	13. 8 as for knowledge, it will come to an *e*.
Heb	6.16 as confirmation puts an *e* to all dispute.
1 Pet	4. 7 The *e* of all things is near; therefore be
	4.17 what will be the *e* for those who do not

END (ENDS) (v)

Mt	26.58 guards in order to see how this would *e*.
1 Cor	13. 8 Love never *e*; But as for prophesies,
Heb	1.12 the same, and your years will never *e*."

ENDURANCE

Lk	21.19 By your *e* you will gain your souls.
Rom	5. 4 produces *e*, and *e* produces character,
2 Cor	6. 4 every way: through great *e*, in
Heb	10.36 For you need *e*, so that when you have
Jas	1. 3 the testing of your faith produces *e*.
2 Pet	1. 6 and self-control with *e*, and *e* with
Rev	14.12 Here is a call for the *e* of the saints,

ENDURE (ENDURED ENDURES)

Job	8.15 if one lays hold of it, it will not *e*.
Ps	72.17 May his name *e* forever, his fame
	100. 5 his steadfast love *e* forever, and his
	102. 26 They will perish, but you *e*; they will all
	111. 3 work, and his righteousness *e* forever.
	118. 2 Israel say, "His steadfast love *e* forever."
	136. 2 of gods, for his steadfast love *e* forever.
Ezek	22.14 Can your courage *e*, or can your hands
Nah	1. 6 Who can *e* the heat of his anger? His
Mal	3. 2 who can *e* the day of his coming, and
Mt	10.22 But the one who *e* to the end will be
	24.13 But the one who *e* to the end will be
Mk	4.17 have no root and *e* only for a while;
	13.13 the one who *e* to the end will be saved.
Jn	6.27 for the food that *e* for eternal life,
1 Cor	13. 7 all things, hopes all things, *e* all things.
	10.13 way out so that you may be able to *e* it.
2 Tim	2.12 if we *e*, we will also reign with him; if
Heb	12. 2 *e* the cross, disregarding its shame, and
Jas	1.12 Blessed is anyone who *e* temptation.
1 Pet	2.20 If you *e* when you are beaten for doing

ENEMY (ENEMIES)

Lev	26.32 devastate the land, so that your *e* who
Deut	28.25 cause you to be defeated before your *e*;
Judg	5.31 "So perish all your *e*, O Lord! But may
1 Kings	21.20 to Elijah, "Have you found me, O my *e*?"
Esth	9.22 the Jews gained relief from their *e*,
Job	13.24 hide your face, and count me as your *e*?
Ps	72. 9 before him, and his *e* will lick the dust.
	92. 9 your *e*, O Lord, for your *e* shall perish;
Prov	16. 7 he causes even their *e* to be at peace
	24.17 Do not rejoice when your *e* fall, and do
	25.21 If your *e* are hungry, give them bread to
Mt	5.43 love your neighbor and hate your *e*.'
	22.44 until I put your *e* under your feet' "?
Lk	6.27 Love your *e*, do good to those who hate
Rom	12.20 "if your *e* are hungry, feed them; if they
1 Cor	15.26 The last *e* to be destroyed is death. For
Gal	4.16 become your *e* by telling you the truth?
Phil	3.18 many live as *e* of the cross; I have often

ENGAGE (ENGAGED)

Ex	22.16 a man seduces a virgin who is not *e*
Deut	2. 5 not to *e* in battle with them, for I will
	20. 7 Has anyone become *e* to a woman but
Mt	1.18 Mary had been *e* to Joseph, but before
Lk	1.27 to a virgin *e* to a man whose name was
	2. 5 registered with Mary, to whom he was *e*

ENGRAVE

Ex	28.11 you shall *e* the two stones with the
Zech	3. 9 seven facets, I will *e* its inscription,

ENJOY

Isa	65.22 and my chosen shall long *e* the work of
Heb	11.25 of God than to *e* the fleeting pleasures

ENJOYMENT

Eccl	2.24 to eat and drink and find *e* in their toil.
	5.18 fitting is to eat and drink and find *e* in

ENLARGE (ENLARGED)

Ps	119. 32 for you *e* my understanding.
Isa	54. 2 *E* the sight of your tent, and let the
2 Cor	10.15 of action among you may be greatly *e*,

ENLIGHTENED

Rom	10. 2 they have a zeal for God, but it is not *e*.
Heb	10.32 after you had been *e*, you endured a

ENLIGHTENING

Ps	19. 8 of the Lord is clear, *e* the eyes;

ENOCH

Gen	4.18 To *E* was born Irad; and Irad was the
	5.18 years he became the father of *E*.
	5.22 *E* walked with God after the birth of
	5.24 *E* walked with God; then he was no
Lk	3.37 of Methuselah, son of *E*, son of Jared,
Heb	11. 5 By faith *E* was taken so that he did not
Jude	14 It was also about these that *E*, in the

ENRAGED

Isa	8.21 when they are hungry, they will be *e*
	34. 2 Lord is *e* against all the nations, and

ENRICH (ENRICHED)

1 Sam	17.25 the king will greatly *e* the man who kills
1 Cor	1. 5 in every way you have been *e* in him, in
2 Cor	9.11 You will be *e* in every way for your great

ENROLLED

Num	1.19 So he *e* them in the wilderness of Sinai.
	2.33 the Levites were not *e* among the other
Heb	12.23 of the firstborn who are *e* in heaven,

ENSIGNS

Num	2. 2 under *e* by their ancestral houses; they

ENSLAVED

Rom	6. 6 and we might no longer be *e* to sin.
Gal	4. 3 while we were minors, we were *e* to the

ENTANGLED

2 Sam	22. 6 the cords of Sheol *e* me; the snares of
Ps	18. 5 the cords of Sheol *e* me; the snares of

ENTER (ENTERED)

Gen	7.13 day Noah with his sons . . . *e* the ark,
Ex	40.35 Moses was not able to *e* the tent of
Num	20.24 For he shall not *e* the land that I have
Deut	29.12 to *e* into the covenant of the Lord your
Ps	95.11 anger I swore, "They shall not *e* my rest."
	100. 4 *E* his gates with thanksgiving, and his
Isa	26.20 Come, my people, *e* your chambers, and
Mt	5.20 you will never *e* the kingdom of
	7.13 "*E* through the narrow gate; for the gate
	7.21 to me, 'Lord, Lord,' will *e* the kingdom
	19.24 hard for a rich person to *e* the kingdom
Mk	3.27 no one can *e* a strong man's house and
	10.23 who have wealth to *e* the kingdom
Lk	11.52 you did not *e* yourselves, and you
Jn	3. 5 no one can *e* the kingdom of God

ENTHRONED

Ps	9. 7 But the Lord sits *e* forever, he has
	80. 1 You who are *e* upon the cherubim,
	123. 1 eyes, O you who are *e* in the heavens!

ENTICE (ENTICED)

1 Kings	22.20 Lord said, 'Who will e Ahab, so that he
2 Chr	18.21 Lord said, "You are to e him, and you
Job	31. 9 "If my heart has been e by a woman,
Prov	1.10 child, if sinners e you, do not consent.
	16.29 The violent e their neighbors, and lead
Jer	20. 7 O Lord, you have e me, and I was e;

ENTREAT (ENTREATED)

Judg	13. 8 Manoah e the Lord, and said, "O Lord, I
Zech	7. 2 to e the favor of the Lord, and to ask
2 Cor	5.20 we e you on behalf of Christ, be

ENTREATY

2 Chr	33.19 His prayer, and how God received his e,
Ezra	8.23 God for this, and he listened to our e.

ENTRUST (ENTRUSTED ENTRUSTING)

Num	12. 7 Moses; he is e with all my house.
Lk	16.11 who will e to you the true riches?
Jn	2.24 his part would not e himself to them,
Rom	3. 2 place the Jews were e with the oracles
1 Cor	9.17 my own will, I am e with a commission.
2 Cor	5.19 and e to us the message of
1 Tim	6.20 Timothy, guard what has been e to you.
2 Tim	1.12 to guard until that day what I e to him.
	2. 2 many witnesses e to faithful people
1 Pet	4.19 will e themselves to a faithful Creator,

ENVIOUS

Ps	37. 1 do not be e of wrongdoers, for they will
	73. 3 For I was e of the arrogant; I saw the
1 Cor	13. 4 love is kind; love is not e or boastful or

ENVOY (ENVOYS)

2 Chr	32.31 the e of the officials of Babylon,
Prov	13.17 brings trouble, but a faithful e, healing.
Isa	33. 7 the streets; the e of peace weep bitterly.

ENVY (ENVIED)

Gen	26.14 so that the Philistines e him.
	30. 1 bore Jacob no children, she e her sister;
Prov	3.31 Do not e the violent and do not choose
	23.17 Do not let your heart e sinners, but
	24. 1 Do not e the wicked, nor desire to be

EPHESUS

Acts	18.19 When they reached E, he left them
	19. 1 to E, where he found some disciples.
	20.16 For Paul had decided to sail past E, so
1 Cor	15.32 hopes I fought with wild animals at E,
1 Tim	1. 3 remain in E so that you may instruct
Rev	2. 1 "To the angel of the church in E write:

EPHRAIM (EPHRAIMITES)

Gen	41.52 The second he named E, "For God has
	48. 1 him his two sons, Manasseh and E.
Num	7.48 son of Ammihud, the leader of the E:
Judg	1.29 E did not drive out the Canaanites who
Ps	78.67 he did not choose the tribe of E;
Hos	4.17 E is joined to idols— let him alone.
	7. 8 E mixes himself with the peoples; E is
	11. 8 How can I give you up, E? How can I

EPILEPTIC (EPILEPTICS)

Mt	4.24 demoniacs, e, and paralytics, and he
	17.15 have mercy on my son, for he is an e

EQUAL

Jn	5.18 thereby making himself e with God.

EQUITY

Ps	98. 9 righteousness, and the peoples with e.
	99. 4 lover of justice, you have established e;

ERECT (ERECTED)

Gen	33.20 There he e an altar and called it
Lev	26. 1 idols and e no carved images or pillars,

ERR

Prov	14.22 Do they not e that plan evil? Those who

ERROR (ERRORS)

Lev	5.18 atonement on your behalf for the e that
Num	15.25 sin offering before the Lord, that the
Job	19. 4 I have erred, my e remains with me.
Ps	19.12 But who can detect their e? Clear me
Eccl	10. 5 sun, as great an e as if it proceeded
Rom	1.27 own persons the due penalty for their e.

ESAU

Born, Gen 25.24-26; sold his birthright, Gen 25.29-34; married Hittite women, Gen 26.34; lost Isaac's blessing, Gen 27.30-40; hated Jacob, Gen 27.41; married Mahalath, Gen 28.9; reconciled with Jacob, Gen 33.1-15.

ESCAPE (ESCAPED ESCAPES)

1 Sam	22.20 named Abiathar, e and fled after David.
Esth	4.13 palace you will e any more than all the
Ps	124. 7 We have e like a bird from the snare of
Eccl	7.26 one who pleases God e her, but the
Jer	44.14 to settle in the land of Egypt shall e
Ezek	24.26 on that day, one who has e will come to
	33.21 someone who has e from Jerusalem
Ob	17 be those that e, and it shall be holy;
1 Thess	5. 3 woman, and there will be no e!
Heb	2. 3 how can we e if we neglect so great a
2 Pet	2.20 they have e the defilements of the world

ESTABLISH (ESTABLISHED ESTABLISHES)

Gen	17. 7 I will e my covenant between me and
	17.21 my covenant I will e with Isaac, whom
Deut	28. 9 Lord will e you as his holy people, as he
	29.13 that he may e you today as his people,
	32. 6 created you, who made you and e you?
2 Sam	5.12 perceived that the Lord had e him king
	7.12 your body, and I will e his kingdom.
1 Kings	2.12 David, and his kingdom was firmly e.
	9. 5 I will e your royal throne over Israel
1 Chr	17.14 and his throne shall be e forever.
Ps	8. 3 the moon and the stars that you have e;
	74.16 night; you e the luminaries and the sun.
	99. 4 King, lover of justice, you have equity;
Prov	3.19 by understanding he e the heavens;
Isa	2. 2 Lord's house shall be e as the highest
	9. 7 his kingdom. He will e and uphold it
	16. 5 throne shall be e in steadfast love in
Jer	10.12 power, who e the world by his wisdom,
	51.15 power, who e the world by his wisdom,
2 Cor	1.21 it is God who e us with you in Christ
1 Pet	5.10 restore, support, strengthen, and e you.

ESTATE

Prov	20.21 An e quickly acquired in the beginning

ESTEEM

1 Thess	5.13 e them very highly in love because of

ESTHER

Esth	2. 7 is E, his cousin, for she had neither
	9.32 The command of Queen E fixed these

ETERNAL

Mt	18. 8 feet and to be thrown into the e fire.
	19.16 good deed must I do to have e life?"
	19.29 a hundredfold, and will inherit e life.
	25.41 depart from me into the e fire prepared
Mk	3.29 have forgiveness, but is guilty of an e sin"
	10.17 what must I do to inherit e life?"
Lk	10.25 said, "what must I do to inherit e life?"
	16. 9 may welcome you into the e homes.
Jn	3.16 him may not perish but may have e life.
	12.25 life in this world will keep it for e life.
	12.50 I know that his commandment is e life.
	17. 2 people, to give e life to all whom you
Acts	13.46 to be unworthy of e life, we are now
	13.48 as had been destined for e life became

Rom 2. 7 and immortality, he will give *e* life;
5.21 justification leading to *e* life through
2 Cor 4.18 but what cannot be seen is *e*.
Titus 1. 2 in hope of *e* life that God, who never
1 Jn 2.25 this is what he has promised us, *e* life.
5.13 that you may know that you have *e* life.
5.20 Christ. He is the true God and *e* life.

ETERNITY
Isa 57.15 the high and lofty one who inhabits *e*,

ETHIOPIA (ETHIOPIAN)
Ps 68.31 Egypt; let *E* hasten to stretch out its
Isa 43. 3 *E* and Seba in exchange for you.
Acts 8.27 an *E* eunuch, a court official of the

EUNUCH (EUNUCHS)
Mt 19.12 *e* who have made themselves *e* for the
Acts 8.27 an Ethiopian *e*, a court official of the

EUPHRATES
Gen 2.14 of Assyria. And the fourth river is the *E*.
15.18 the river of Egypt to . . . the river *E*,
Josh 1. 4 the river *E*, all the land of the Hittites,
24. 2 lived beyond the *E* and served other
Jer 13. 4 go now to the *E*, and hide it there in a
Rev 16.12 poured his bowl on the great river *E*,

EVANGELIST (EVANGELISTS)
Acts 21. 8 we went into the house of Philip the *e*,
Eph 4.11 some prophets, some *e*, some pastors
2 Tim 4. 5 do the work of an *e*, carry out your

EVE
Gen 3.20 The man named his wife *E*, because she
4. 1 Now the man knew his wife *E*, and she
2 Cor 11. 3 afraid that as the serpent deceived *E*
1 Tim 2.13 For Adam was formed first, then *E*; and

EVENING
Mt 8.16 That *e* they brought to him many who
Mk 1.32 That *e*, at sundown, they brought to
14.17 When it was *e*, he came with the

EVERLASTING
Gen 9.16 remember the *e* covenant between God
17. 7 for an *e* covenant, to be God to you and
21.33 on the name of the LORD, the *E* God.
Ps 139. 24 way in me, and lead me in the way *e*.
145. 13 Your kingdom is an *e* kingdom, and
Isa 9. 6 Mighty God, *E* Father, Prince
26. 4 for in the LORD GOD you have an *e* rock.
60.19 LORD will be your *e* light, and your God
Ezek 16.60 I will establish with you an *e* covenant.
Dan 12. 2 of the earth shall awake, some to life,
Hab 1.12 Are you not from of *e*, O LORD my God,

EVIL
Deut 13. 5 you shall purge the *e* from your midst.
Judg 4. 1 Israelites again did what was *e* in the
10. 6 Israelites again did what was *e* in the
1 Sam 20. 7 that *e* has been determined by him.
1 Kings 11. 6 Solomon did what was *e* in the sight of
16.25 Omri did what was *e* in the sight of the
2 Chr 33. 6 He did much *e* in the sight of the LORD,
33. 9 that they did more *e* than the nations
Neh 9.28 had rest, they again did *e* before you,
Ps 7.14 See how they conceive *e*, and are
28. 4 and according to the *e* of their deeds;
35. 4 confounded who devise *e* against me.
91.10 no *e* shall befall you, no scourge come
140. 11 in the land; let *e* speedily hunt down
Prov 6.18 plans, feet that hurry to run to *e*,
Eccl 8.11 the human heart is fully set to do *e*.
Isa 5.20 Ah, you who call *e* good and good *e*,
Jer 9. 3 for they proceed from *e* to *e*, and they
16.10 pronounced all this great *e* against us?
Ezek 33.11 turn back, turn back from your *e* ways;
Dan 12. 4 back and forth, and *e* shall increase."

Nah 1.11 gone out who plots *e* against the LORD,
Mt 7.11 If you then, who are *e*, know how to
12.45 brings along seven other spirits more *e*
13.49 and separate the *e* from the righteous
15.19 out of the heart come *e* intentions,
27.23 he asked, "Why, what *e* has he done?"
Mk 15.14 asked them, "Why, what *e* has he done?"
Lk 11.13 who are *e*, know how to give good gifts
11.26 seven other spirits more *e* than itself,
Jn 7. 7 I testify against it that its works are *e*.
17.15 ask you to protect them from the *e* one.
Acts 23. 5 'You shall not speak *e* of a leader of
Rom 2. 9 and distress for everyone who does *e*,
3. 8 "Let us do *e* so that good may come?"
7.19 but the *e* I do not want is what I do.
1 Cor 5. 8 the old yeast, the yeast of malice and *e*,
Eph 4.29 Let no *e* talk come out of your mouths,
1 Thess 5.15 See that none of you repays *e* for *e*, but
1 Tim 6.10 of money is the root of all kinds of *e*,
Titus 3. 2 every good work, to speak *e* of no one,
1 Jn 2.13 because you have conquered the *e* one.

EVILDOER (EVILDOERS)
Prov 4.14 and do not walk in the way of *e*.
Mt 7.23 knew you; go away from me, you *e*.'
Lk 13.27 come from; go away from me, all you *e*!'
Rev 22.11 Let the *e* still do evil, and the filthy still

EXALT (EXALTED EXALTING EXALTS)
Ex 9.17 You are still *e* yourself against my
Josh 3. 7 "This day I will begin to *e* you in the
4.14 On that day the LORD *e* Joshua in the
1 Kings 1. 5 Now Adonijah son of Haggith *e* himself,
1 Chr 29.25 The LORD highly *e* Solomon in the sight
Job 36.22 See, God is *e* in his power; who is a
Ps 18.46 rock, and *e* be the God of my salvation,
35.26 let those who *e* themselves against me
46.10 among the nations, I am *e* in the earth."
57. 5 Be *e*, O God, above the heavens. Let
108. 5 Be *e*, O God, above the heavens, and let
138. 2 for you have *e* your name and your word
148. 13 for his name alone is *e*; his glory is
Prov 4. 8 Prize her highly, and she will *e* you; she
14.34 Righteousness *e* a nation, but sin is a
Isa 2.11 humbled; and the LORD alone will be *e*
Ezek 21.26 *E* that which is low, abase that which is
Lk 14.11 all who *e* themselves will be humbled,
Acts 5.31 God *e* him at his right hand as Leader
Phil 1.20 Christ will be *e* now as always in my
2. 9 Therefore God also highly *e* him and

EXAMINE (EXAMINED EXAMINES)
Ezra 10.16 month they sat down to *e* the matter.
Prov 5.21 of the LORD, and he *e* all their paths.
Lam 3.40 Let us test and *e* our ways, and return
Lk 23.14 I have *e* him in your presence and have
Acts 12.19 find him, he *e* the guards and ordered
17.11 eagerly and *e* the scriptures every day
22.24 and ordered him to be *e* by flogging,
1 Cor 9. 3 is my defense to those who would *e* me.
11.28 *E* yourselves, and then only eat of the
2 Cor 13. 5 *E* yourselves to see whether you are

EXAMPLE (EXAMPLES)
Jn 13.15 I have set you an *e*, that you also
1 Cor 10. 6 these things occurred as *e* for us, so
10.11 happened to them to serve as an *e*,
1 Thess 1. 7 so that you became an *e* to all the
2 Thess 3. 9 but in order to give you an *e* to imitate.
1 Tim 1.16 the utmost patience, making me an *e* to
4.12 but set the believers an *e* in speech and
1 Pet 2.21 also suffered for you, leaving you an *e*,
5. 3 in your charge, but be *e* to the flock.

EXCEEDS
Mt 5.20 unless your righteousness *e* that of the

EXCELLENCY

Acts	26. 7	for this hope, your *E*, that I am accused

EXCELLENT

Isa	28.29	wonderful in counsel, and *e* in wisdom.
Dan	5.12	an *e* spirit, knowledge, and
1 Cor	12.31	And I will show you a still more *e* way.
Jas	2. 7	they who blaspheme that *e* name that

EXCHANGED

Ps	106. 20	They *e* the glory of God for the image of
Rom	1.26	Their women *e* natural intercourse for

EXCUSE (EXCUSES)

Lk	14.18	they all alike began to make *e*. The first
Jn	15.22	but now they have no *e* for their sin.
Rom	1.20	they are without *e*; for though they

EXECUTE

Isa	66.16	by fire will the LORD *e* judgment, and by
Mic	5.15	wrath I will *e* vengeance on the nations

EXHORTATION

Acts	15.31	members read it, they rejoiced at the *e*.
Rom	12. 8	the exhorter, in *e*; the giver, in
Heb	13.22	bear with my word of *e*, for I have

EXILE (EXILED)

2 Kings	17.23	Israel was *e* from their own land to
Isa	5.13	my people go into *e* without knowledge;
Jer	40. 1	Judah who were being *e* to Babylon.
	52.30	of the guard took into *e* of the Judeans
Ezek	12. 4	their sight, as those who do go into *e*.

EXPECTATION

Prov	11.23	in good; the *e* of the wicked in wrath.
Lk	3.15	people were filled with *e*, and all were

EXPECTED (EXPECTING)

Isa	5. 7	he *e* justice, but saw bloodshed;
Phil	3.20	it is from there that we are *e* a Savior,

EXPERIENCE

Gal	3. 4	Did you *e* so much for nothing? — if it

EXPIATION

2 Sam	21. 3	How shall I make *e*, that you may bless

EXPLAIN (EXPLAINED)

Gen	41.24	there was no one who could *e* it to me."
Mk	4.34	he *e* everything in private to his
Acts	18.26	him aside and *e* the way of God to him
	28.23	to evening he *e* the matter to them,

EXPOSE (EXPOSED)

Jn	3.20	light, so that their deeds may not be *e*.
Eph	5.11	works of darkness, but instead *e* them.

EXPOUND

Deut	1. 5	Moses undertook to *e* this law as

EXTEND (EXTENDS)

Isa	11.11	the Lord will *e* his hand yet a second
2 Cor	4.15	so that grace, as it *e* to more and more

EXTERNAL

Rom	2.28	nor is true circumcision something *e* or

EXTOL

Ps	99. 5	*E* the LORD our God; worship at his
Song	1. 4	we will *e* your love more than wine;

EXULT

Ps	94. 3	wicked, how long shall the wicked *e*?
Jer	11.15	flesh avert your doom? Can you then *e*?
Zeph	3.14	Rejoice and *e* with all your heart, O
Zech	10. 7	rejoice, their hearts shall *e* in the LORD.

EXULTANT

Ps	68. 4	name is the LORD — be *e* before him.

EYE

Ex	21.24	*e* for *e*, tooth for tooth, hand for hand,
Lev	24.20	*e* for *e*, tooth for tooth; the injury
Deut	19.21	life for life, *e* for *e*, tooth for tooth,
Job	42. 5	of the ear, but now my *e* sees you;
Ps	32. 8	I will counsel you with my *e* upon you.
	33.18	the *e* of the LORD is on those who fear
Isa	64. 4	no *e* has seen any God besides you,
Mt	5.29	If your right *e* causes you to sin, tear it
	5.38	it was said, 'An *e* for an *e* and a tooth
	6.22	if your *e* is healthy, your whole body
	7. 3	you see the speck in your neighbor's *e*,
	18. 9	if your *e* causes you to stumble, tear it
Mk	9.47	if your *e* causes you to stumble, tear it
Lk	11.34	Your *e* is the lamp of your body. If your
1 Cor	2. 9	"What no *e* has seen, nor ear heard, nor

EYES

Num	10.31	and you will serve as *e* for us.
Deut	11.12	The *e* of the LORD your God are always
	29. 4	understand, or *e* to see, or ears to hear.
Judg	17. 6	did what was right in their own *e*.
	21.25	did what was right in their own *e*.
1 Kings	1.20	the *e* of all Israel are on you to tell
	8.29	that your *e* may be open night and day
2 Kings	6.17	he may see." So the LORD opened the *e*
2 Chr	6.20	May your *e* may be open day and night
	16. 9	the *e* of the LORD range throughout the
	20.12	know what to do, but our *e* are on you."
Job	28.10	in the rocks, their *e* see every precious
	32. 1	because he was righteous in his own *e*.
Ps	6. 7	My *e* waste away because of grief; they
	11. 4	His *e* behold, his gaze examines
	115. 5	but do not speak; *e*, but do not see.
	119. 18	Open my *e*, so that I may behold
	119.136	My *e* shed streams of tears because
	121. 1	I lift up my *e* to the hills — from where
	123. 1	To you I lift up my *e*, O you who are
	135. 16	speak; they have *e*, but they do not see;
	139. 16	Your *e* beheld my unformed substance.
	145. 15	The *e* of all look to you, and you give
Prov	4.25	Let your *e* look directly forward, and
	15. 3	The *e* of the LORD are in every place,
	22.12	The *e* of the LORD keep watch over
	30.12	are those who are pure in their own *e*
Isa	6.10	and shut their *e*, so that they may not
	29.10	he has closed your *e*, you prophets, and
	32. 3	Then the *e* of those who have sight will
	33.17	Your *e* will see the king in his beauty;
	37.17	and hear; open your *e*, O LORD, and see;
	49.18	Lift up your *e* all around and see; they
Jer	5.21	people, who have *e*, but do not see,
	9. 1	of water, and my *e* a fountain of tears,
	24. 6	I will set my *e* upon them for good, and
Am	9. 8	*e* of the Lord GOD are upon the sinful
Hab	1.13	Your *e* are too pure to behold evil, and
Lk	10.23	are the *e* that see what you see!
	24.31	their *e* were opened, and they
Rom	11. 8	*e* that would not see and ears that
2 Cor	10. 7	Look at what is before your *e*. If you are
Gal	4.15	have torn out your *e* and given them
Heb	4.13	laid bare to the *e* of the one to whom
1 Pet	3.12	the *e* of the Lord are on the righteous,
Rev	3.18	and salve to anoint your *e* so that you

EYEWITNESSES

Lk	1. 2	who from the beginning were *e* and
2 Pet	1.16	but we had been *e* of his majesty.

EZEKIEL

Called, Ezek 2—3. Visions: cherubim, Ezek 1; 10; abominations in Jerusalem, Ezek 8—9; valley of dry bones, Ezek 37; the temple, Ezek 40.1—47.12; division of land, 47.13—48.35. Prophecies: against Israel, Ezek 4—7; 11—12; 14—24; 33; against false prophets, Ezek 13; 34; against other nations, Ezek 25—32; 35; 38—39; of restoration, Ezek 11.14-20; 34; 36; 39.23-29.

EZRA

Ezra	7. 6 *E* went up from Babylonia. He was a
	7.10 For *E* had set his heart to study the law
	10. 1 While *E* prayed and made confession,
Neh	8. 1 They told *E* the scribe to bring the book

F

FACE (FACES)

Ex	33.11 the Lord used to speak to Moses *f* to *f*,
	33.23 my back; but my *f* shall not be seen."
	34.29 the skin of his *f* shone because he has
Num	6.25 the Lord make his *f* to shine upon you,
Deut	5. 4 Lord spoke with you *f* to *f* at the
	34.10 like Moses, whom the Lord knew *f* to *f*.
2 Kings	14. 8 "Come, let us look one another in the *f*."
Ezra	9.15 though no one can *f* you because of
Ps	4. 6 Let the light of your *f* shine on us,
	24. 6 who seek the *f* of the God of Jacob.
	27. 8 Your *f*, Lord, do I seek. Do not hide
	31.16 Let your *f* shine on your servant; save
	34.16 The *f* of the Lord is against evildoers, to
	67. 1 us and make his *f* to shine upon us,
	119.135 Make your *f* shine upon your servant,
Song	2.14 let me see your *f*, let me hear your
Mt	6.16 hypocrites, for they disfigure their *f* so
2 Cor	3. 7 Israel could not gaze at Moses' *f*

FACTIONS

1 Cor	11.19 there have to be *f* among you, so it will

FAIL (FAILED)

Josh	23.14 not one thing has *f* of all the good
1 Sam	17.32 "Let no one's heart *f* because of him;
1 Kings	2. 4 not *f* you a successor on the throne
Job	19.14 and my close friends have *f* me;

FAINT

Song	5. 8 beloved, tell him this: I am *f* with love.
Isa	7. 4 and do not let your heart be *f* because
	40.29 He gives power to the *f*, and strengthens
	42. He will not *f* or be crushed until he has
Lam	1.13 me back; he has left me stunned, *f*
Mt	15.32 hungry, for they might *f* on the way.
Mk	8. 3 to their homes, they will *f* on the way;

FAIR (FAIREST)

Prov	1. 9 for they are a *f* garland for your head,
Song	1. 8 If you do not know, O *f* among women,

FAITH

Deut	32.51 because both of you broke *f* with me
Josh	7. 1 Israelites broke *f* in regard to the
Ps	78.22 Israel, because they had no *f* in God,
Isa	7. 9 If you do not stand firm in *f*, you shall
Hab	2. 4 them, but the righteous live by their *f*.
Mt	8.10 in no one in Israel have I found such *f*.
	8.13 it be done for you according to your *f*."
	8.26 "Why are you afraid, you of little *f*?"
	15.28 "Woman, great is your *f*! Let it be done
	17.20 said to them, "Because of your little *f*.
	21.21 if you have *f* and do not doubt, not only
Mk	2. 5 when Jesus saw their *f*, he said to the
	4.40 are you afraid? Have you still no *f*?"
	5.34 "Daughter, your *f* has made you well; go
	11.22 Jesus answered them, "Have *f* in God.
Lk	5.20 When he saw their *f* he said, "Friend,
	7. 9 not even in Israel have I found such *f*."
	8.48 "Daughter, your *f* has made you well; go
	12.28 will he clothe you—you of little *f*?
	17. 5 said to the Lord, "Increase our *f*!"
	17.19 on your way; your *f* has made you well."
	18. 8 of Man comes, will he find *f* on earth?"
	18.42 your sight; your *f* has saved you."
	22.32 prayed for you that your own *f* may not
Acts	14. 9 and seeing that he had *f* to be healed,
	14.27 had opened a door of *f* for the Gentiles.
	20.21 God and *f* toward our Lord Jesus.

Acts	26.18 those who are sanctified by *f* in me.'
	27.25 for I have *f* in God that it will be
Rom	1. 8 because your *f* is proclaimed throughout
	1.16 God for salvation to everyone who has *f*
	3.31 Do we then overthrow the law by this *f*?
	4.16 For this reason it depends on *f*, in order
	4.19 He did not weaken in *f* when he
	5. 1 since we are justified by *f*, we have
	12. 3 according to the measure of *f* that God
	14. 1 Welcome those who are weak in *f*, but
	14.23 whatever does not proceed from *f* is sin.
1 Cor	12. 9 to another *f* by the same Spirit, to
2 Cor	4.13 we have the same spirit of *f* that is in
Gal	1.23 the *f* he once tried to destroy."
	2.16 that we may be justified by *f* in Christ,
	5. 6 the only thing that counts is *f* working
	6.10 especially for those of the family of *f*.
Eph	1.15 I have heard of your *f* in the Lord Jesus
	2. 8 by grace you have been saved through *f*,
	6.16 take the shield of *f*, with which you will
Col	1. 4 we have heard of your *f* in Christ Jesus
1 Thess	1. 3 your work of *f* and labor of love and
	3. 7 encouraged about you through your *f*.
1 Tim	3.13 themselves and great boldness in the *f*
	5. 8 has denied the *f* and is worse than an
	6.12 Fight the good fight of the *f*; take hold
2 Tim	1. 5 I am reminded of your sincere *f*, a *f* that
Philem	6 sharing of your *f* may become effective
Heb	4. 2 not united in *f* with those who listened.
	10.38 but my righteous one will live by *f*.
	11. 1 Now *f* is the assurance of things hoped
	11.33 who through *f* conquered kingdoms,
	13. 7 of their way of life, and imitate their *f*.
Jas	2.18 and I by my works will show you my *f*.
	2.22 You see that *f* was active along with his
1 Pet	1. 7 the genuineness of your *f*— being more
Jude	3 you to contend for the *f* that was once
Rev	14.12 of God and hold fast to the *f* of Jesus.

FAITHFUL

1 Sam	2.35 I will raise up for myself a *f* priest, who
	22.14 among your servants is so *f* as David?
2 Chr	31.20 he did what was good and right and *f*
Neh	7. 2 —for he was a *f* man and feared God
	9. 8 you found his heart *f* before you, and
Ps	4. 3 the Lord has set apart the *f* for himself;
	16.10 up to Sheol, or let the *f* one see the Pit.
	30. 4 O you his *f* ones, and give thanks to his
	31.23 The Lord preserves the *f*, but
	32. 6 let all who are *f* offer prayer to you;
	37.28 justice; he will not forsake his *f* ones.
	50. 5 "Gather to me my *f* ones, who made a
	78. 8 steadfast, whose spirit was not *f* to God.
	79. 2 the flesh of your *f* to the wild animals
	101. 6 I will look with favor on the *f* in the
	116. 15 of the Lord is the death of his *f* ones.
Prov	2. 8 and preserving the way of his *f* ones.
Isa	1.21 How the *f* city has become a whore! She
	25. 1 things, plans formed of old, *f* and sure.
Dan	6. 4 he was *f*, and no negligence or
Hos	11.12 Judah still walks with God, and is *f* to
Mt	24.45 "Who then is the *f* and wise slave,
Lk	12.42 is the *f* and prudent manager whom his
	16.10 whoever is *f* in a very little is *f* also in
Acts	11.23 them all to remain *f* to the Lord
1 Cor	1. 9 God is *f*; by him you were called into
	10.13 God is *f*, and he will not let you be
Col	1. 7 He is a *f* minister of Christ on your
1 Thess	5.24 The one who calls you is *f*, and he will
2 Thess	3. 3 But the Lord is *f*; he will strengthen you
2 Tim	2. 2 entrust to *f* people who will be able to
Heb	11.11 barren— because he considered him *f*
Rev	2.10 Be *f* until death, and I will give you the
	19.11 horse! Its rider is called *F* and True,

FAITHFULNESS

Ps	36. 5 to the heavens, your *f* to the clouds.

Ps	40.10	I have spoken of your *f* and your
	57.10	heavens; your *f* extends to the clouds.
	85.11	*F* will spring up from the ground, and
	88.11	in the grave, or your *f* in Abaddon?
	89. 2	forever; your *f* is as firm as the heavens.
	89.33	my steadfast love, or be false to my *f*.
	92. 2	in the morning, and your *f* by night,
	117. 2	us, and the *f* of the LORD endures
	119. 90	Your *f* endures to all generations; you
	119.138	decrees in righteousnsss and in all *f*.
	143. 1	give ear to my supplications in your *f*;
Jer	31. 3	therefore I have continued my *f* to you.
Lam	3.23	are new every morning; great is your *f*.
Hos	4. 1	There is no *f* or loyalty, and no

FAITHLESS (FAITHLESSLY)

Ezek	15. 8	desolate, because they have acted *f*,
Prov	13.15	favor, but the way of the *f* is their ruin.
Jer	3. 6	seen what she did, that *f* one, Israel,
Mt	17.17	"You *f* and perverse generation, how
Lk	9.41	"You *f* and perverse generation, how
Rev	21. 8	as for the cowardly, the *f*, the polluted,

FAITHLESSNESS

Ezra	9. 2	in this *f* the officials and leaders have
Rom	3. 3	Will their *f* nullify the faithfulness of

FALL (FALLEN FELL)

Num	14. 5	Moses and Aaron *f* on their faces before
	16. 4	When Moses heard it, he *f* on his face.
	16.22	They *f* on their faces, and said, "O God,
	16.45	in a moment." And they *f* on their faces.
1 Sam	3.19	let none of his words *f* to the ground.
	25.23	*f* before David on her face, bowing to
2 Sam	1.25	How the mighty have *f* in the midst of
Ps	37.24	we stumble, we shall not *f* headlong,
	53. 3	They have all *f* away, they are all alike
	106. 26	would make them *f* in the wilderness,
	141. 10	Let the wicked *f* into their own nets,
Prov	24.17	Do not rejoice when your enemies *f*,
Isa	14.12	How you are *f* from heaven, O Day Star,
	21. 9	"*F*, *f* is Babylon; and all the images of
Jer	51. 8	Suddenly Babylon has *f* and is
Hos	10. 8	Cover us, and to the hills, *F* on us.
Mic	7. 8	when I *f*, I shall rise; when I sit in
Mt	24.10	Then many will *f* away, and they will
Mk	4.17	of the word, immediately they *f* away.
Rom	11.11	So I ask, have they stumbled so as to *f*?
Gal	5. 4	from Christ; you have *f* away from grace.
Heb	4.11	one may *f* through such disobedience
	6. 6	the age to come, and then have *f* away,
1 Pet	2. 8	stumble, and a rock that makes them *f*."
Rev	1.17	saw him, I *f* at his feet as though dead.
	14. 8	"*F*, *f* is Babylon the great! She has made

FALLING (n)

Lk	2.34	this child is set for the *f* and the rising
1 Cor	8.13	if food is a cause of their *f*, I will never

FALSE (FALSELY)

Gen	21.23	swear . . . that you will not deal *f* with
Deut	32. 5	his degenerate children have dealt *f*
2 Chr	26.16	he was *f* to the LORD his God, and
Job	31.28	judges, for I should have been *f* to God
Ps	119. 29	Put *f* ways far from me; and graciously
	119.104	therefore I hate every *f* way.
Prov	6.19	lying witness who testifies *f*, and one
Jer	51.17	for their images are *f*; and there is no
Hos	10. 2	Their heart is *f*; now they must bear
Mt	7.15	"Beware of *f* prophets, who come to you
	24.24	For *f* messiahs and *f* prophets will
Phil	1.18	way, whether out of *f* motives or true;
2 Thess	2.11	leading them to believe what is *f*,

FALSEHOOD

Job	21.34	is nothing left of your answers but *f*."
Ps	62. 4	They take pleasure in *f*; they bless with
	119.163	I hate and abhor *f*, but I love your law.

Prov	30. 8	Remove far from me *f* and lying; give
Isa	5.18	who drag iniquity along with cords of *f*,
Ezek	13. 6	They have envisioned *f* and lying
Eph	4.25	putting away *f*, let all of us speak the

FALSIFY

2 Cor	4. 2	to practice cunning or to *f* God's word;

FAME

Mk	1.28	At once his *f* began to spread

FAMILY (FAMILIES)

Gen	12. 3	in you all the *f* of the earth shall be
Job	19.13	"He has put my *f* far from me, and my
	22. 6	pledges from your *f* for no reason,
Ps	107. 41	distress, and makes their *f* like flocks.
Jer	31. 1	I will be the God of all the *f* of Israel,
Am	3. 2	have I known of all the *f* of the earth;
Mt	25.40	of these who are members of my *f*, you
Gal	6.10	all, especially for those of the *f* of faith.

FAMINE

Gen	12.10	there was a *f* in the land. So Abram
	41.30	them there will arise seven years of *f*,
	47.20	fields, because *f* was severe upon them;
Ruth	1. 1	judges ruled there was a *f* in the land,
2 Sam	21. 1	a *f* in the days of David for three years,
1 Kings	18. 2	to Ahab. The *f* was severe in Samaria
2 Kings	6.25	continued, *f* in Samaria became so great
	25. 3	the *f* became so severe in the city that
1 Chr	21.12	either three years of *f*; or three months
Job	5.20	In *f* he will redeem you from death, and
Ps	105. 16	When he summoned *f* against the land,
Jer	14.15	"Sword and *f* shall not come on this
	24.10	I will send sword, *f*, and pestilence
Lam	5.10	as an oven from the scorching heat of *f*.
Am	8.11	not a *f* of bread, or a thirst for water,
Acts	11.28	would be a severe *f* over all the world;

FAR

Lk	15.20	while he was still *f* off, his father saw

FAST (FASTING) (n)

2 Chr	20. 3	proclaimed a *f* throughout all Judah.
Ezra	8.21	I proclaimed a *f* there, at the river
Neh	9. 1	people of Israel were assembled with *f*
Esth	4. 3	mourning among the Jews, with *f* and
	4.16	hold a *f* on my behalf, and neither eat
Ps	109. 24	My knees are weak through *f*; my body
Joel	2.12	return to me with all your heart, with *f*,
Jon	3. 5	believed God; they proclaimed a *f*,
Zech	8.19	The *f* of the fourth month, and the *f* of
Mt	17.21	n not come out except by prayer and *f*."
Mk	9.29	n can come out only through prayer and *f*."

FAST (FASTED FASTING) (v)

1 Sam	7. 6	They *f* that day, and said, "We have
Neh	1. 4	for days, *f* and praying before the God
Isa	58. 3	"Why do we *f*, but you do not see? Why
Zech	7. 5	seventy years, was it for me that you *f*?
Mt	4. 2	He *f* forty days and forty nights, and
	6.16	so as to show others that they are *f*.
	9.14	*f* often, but your disciples do not *f*?"
Mk	2.18	Pharisees *f*, but your disciples do not *f*?"
Lk	5.33	frequently *f* and pray, but your disciples

FATAL

Jer	17.16	service, nor have I desired the *f* day.

FATE

Eccl	3.19	the *f* of humans and the *f* of animals is
	9. 2	since the same *f* comes to all, to the

FATHER (FATHERS FATHER'S)

Gen	2.24	Therefore a man leaves his *f* and his
	5. 3	Adam . . . became the *f* of a son in his
	50. 5	let me go up, so that I may bury my *f*;
Deut	32. 6	Is not he your *f*, who created you, who
1 Sam	2.25	would not listen to the voice of their *f*;

1 Sam	22.	3 "Pray let my *f* and my mother come to
2 Sam	7.14	I will be his *f*, and he shall be a son to
1 Kings	1.	6 His *f* had never at any time displeased
1 Chr	17.13	I will be a *f* to him, and he shall be a
Job	29.16	I was a *f* to the needy, and I
	38.28	"Has the rain a *f*, or who has begotten
Ps	27.10	If my *f* and my mother forsake me, the
	68.	5 *F* of the orphans and protector of
	103.	13 As a *f* has compassion for his children,
Prov	1.	8 Hear, my child, your *f* instruction, and
	10.	1 A wise child makes a glad *f*, but a
	23.22	Listen to your *f* who begot you, and do
	28.24	Anyone who robs *f* or mother and says,
Isa	64.	8 Yet, O LORD, you are our *F*; we are the
Mal	2.10	Have we not all one *f*? Has not one God
Mt	5.45	that you may be children of your *F* in
	5.48	therefore, as your heavenly *F* is perfect.
	6.	9 in this way: Our *F* in heaven, hallowed
	7.21	only the one who does the will of my *F*
	10.32	I also will acknowledge before my *F* in
	10.37	Whoever loves *f* or mother more than
	19.	5 a man shall leave his *f* and mother and
	23.	9 call no man your *f* on earth, for you
Mk	7.11	you say that if anyone tells *f* or mother,
	10.	7 leave his *f* and mother and be joined
Lk	2.49	know that I must be in my *F* house?"
	9.59	"Lord, first let me go and bury my *f*."
	11.13	heavenly *F* give the Holy Spirit to those
	12.53	will be divided, *f* against son and son
	14.26	to me and does not hate *f* and mother,
Jn	12.49	but the *F* who sent me has himself
1 Cor	4.15	I became your *f* through the gospel.
2 Cor	6.18	I will be your *f*, and you will be my sons
Eph	6.	4 *F*, do not provoke your children to
Col	3.21	*F*, do not provoke your children, or they
Heb	7.	3 Without *f*, without mother, without
Jas	1.17	coming down from the *F* of lights, with
1 Jn	2.13	I am writing to you, *f*, because you

FAULT

1 Sam	29.	3 to me I have found no *f* in him to this
Rom	9.19	"Why then does he still find *f*? For who
2 Cor	6.	3 so that no *f* may be found with our
Heb	8.	8 God finds *f* with them when he says:

FAVOR

Gen	6.	8 But Noah found *f* in the sight of the
	18.	3 if I find *f* with you, do not pass by your
	32.	5 in order that I may find *f* in your sight.' "
	33.	8 answered, "To find *f* with my lord."
Ex	3.21	I will bring this people into such *f* with
	11.	3 The LORD gave the people *f* in the sight
	12.36	The LORD had given the people *f* in the
	33.12	and you have also found *f* in my sight.'
Lev	26.	9 I will look with *f* upon you and make
Num	11.15	if I have found *f* in your sight—and do
Judg	6.17	If now I have found *f* with you, then
Ruth	2.10	"Why have I found *f* in your sight, that
2 Sam	14.22	knows that I have found *f* in your sight,
	15.25	If I find *f* in the eyes of the LORD, he
Ezra	9.	8 for a brief moment *f* has been shown by
Esth	5.	8 If I have won the king's *f*, and if it
Job	20.10	children will seek the *f* of the poor,
Ps	84.11	sun and shield; he bestows *f* and honor.
	90.17	Let the *f* of the Lord our God be upon
	115.	12 the people of Tyre will seek your *f* with
Prov	3.	4 So you will find *f* and good repute in
	3.34	scornful, but to the humble he shows *f*.
	11.27	Whoever diligently seeks good seeks *f*,
	16.15	his *f* is like the clouds that bring the
	18.22	good thing, and obtains *f* from the LORD.
Eccl	10.12	words spoken by the wise bring them *f*,
Isa	60.10	you down, but in my *f* I have had mercy
Jer	16.13	day and night, for I will show you no *f*.
Lk	1.30	Mary, for you have found *f* with God.
	2.40	and the *f* of God was upon him.
	2.52	in years, and in divine and human *f*.

Acts	7.46	David, who found *f* with God and asked
	24.27	to grant the Jews a *f*, Felix left Paul in
2 Cor	1.15	first, so that you might have a double *f*;

FAVORABLE

1 Kings	22.	8 he never prophesies anything *f* about
	22.13	with one accord are *f* to the king;
Ps	85.	1 LORD, you were *f* to your land; you

FAVORED

Lk	1.28	"Greetings, *f* one! The Lord is with you."

FEAR (FEARS) (n)

Ex	14.10	In great *f* the Israelites cried out to the
Deut	2.25	to put the dread and *f* of you upon the
2 Chr	20.29	The *f* of God came on all the kingdoms
	26.	5 who instructed him in the *f* of God;
Esth	8.17	because the *f* of the Jews had fallen
Job	28.28	the *f* of the Lord, that is wisdom;
Ps	2.11	Serve the LORD with *f*, with trembling
	19.	9 the *f* of the LORD is pure, enduring
	36.	1 there is no *f* of God before their eyes.
Prov	1.	7 The *f* of the LORD is the beginning of
	9.10	The *f* of the LORD is the beginning of
	14.27	The *f* of the LORD is a fountain of life,
	19.23	The *f* of the LORD is life indeed; filled
	29.25	The *f* of others lays a snare, but one
Isa	8.13	let him be your *f*, and let him be your
Mt	14.26	"It is a ghost!" And they cried out for *f*.
Jn	20.19	had met were locked for *f* of the Jews,
Rom	3.18	"There is no *f* of God before their eyes."
	13.	3 you wish to have no *f* of the authority?
1 Cor	2.	3 and in *f* and in much trembling.
2 Cor	5.11	knowing the *f* of the Lord, we try to
	7.	5 way—disputes without and *f* within.
	7.15	welcomed him with *f* and trembling.
1 Jn	4.18	There is no *f* in love, but perfect love

FEAR (FEARED FEARS) (v)

Gen	42.18	"Do this and you will live, for I *f* God:
Ex	1.17	because the midwives *f* God, he gave
	9.20	of Pharaoh who *f* the word of the LORD
	18.21	among all the people, men who *f* God,
Num	14.	9 and the LORD is with us; do not *f* them.
Deut	1.21	promised you; do not *f* or be dismayed."
	5.29	to *f* me and to keep all my
	6.	2 may *f* the LORD your God all the days of
	31.	8 or forsake you. Do not *f* or be dismayed."
Josh	8.	1 the LORD said to Joshua, "Do not *f* or be
1 Sam	15.24	because I *f* the people and obeyed their
2 Chr	20.15	says the LORD to you: 'Do not *f* or be
Ps	25.14	of the LORD is for those who *f* him,
	46.	2 we will not *f*, though the earth
	102.	15 The nations will *f* the name of the LORD,
	111.	5 He provides food for those who *f* him;
	119.	38 your promise, which is for those who *f*
Prov	3.	7 own eyes; *f* the LORD, and turn away
	24.21	My child, *f* the LORD and the king, and
	31.30	but a woman who *f* the LORD is to be
Eccl	5.	7 and a multitude of words; but *f* God.
	8.12	it will be well with those who *f* God,
	12.13	*F* God, and keep his commandments;
Isa	41.10	do not *f*, for I am with you, do not be
	50.10	Who among you *f* the LORD and obeys
Jer	5.24	say in their hearts, "Let us *f* the LORD
	33.	9 they shall *f* and tremble because of all
	46.27	have no *f*, my servant Jacob, and do not
Dan	6.26	tremble and *f* before the God of Daniel:
Mt	14.	5 he *f* the crowd, because they regarded
Mk	6.20	Herod *f* John, knowing he was a
Lk	1.50	His mercy is for those who *f* him from
	12.	5 I will warn you whom to *f*: *f* him who,
Acts	10.	2 He was a devout man who *f* God with
Rev	15.	4 Lord, who will not *f* and glorify your

FEAST (FEASTED FEASTING FEASTS)

Esth	9.17	they rested and made that a day of *f*
Ps	36.	8 They *f* on the abundance of your house,

Ps	63.	5 My soul is satisfied with a rich f, and
Isa	25.	6 for all peoples a f of rich food, a f of
Lam	4.	5 Those who f on delicacies perish in the
Am	8.10	I will turn your f into mourning, and all

FEEBLE

Neh	4.	2 "What are these f Jews doing? Will they
Isa	13.	7 Therefore all hands will be f, and every

FEED (FED)

Ex	16.32	may see the food with which I f you
Deut	8.16	and f you in the wilderness with manna
1 Kings	17.	9 commanded a widow there to f you."
Prov	10.21	The lips of the righteous f many, but
Isa	40.11	He will f his flock like a shepherd; he
	58.14	I will f you with the heritage of your
	61.	5 Strangers shall stand and f your flocks,
Jer	50.19	and it shall f on Camel and in Bashan,
Ezek	34.	2 Should not shepherds f the sheep? You
Hos	13.	5 I who f you in the wilderness, in the
Mic	5.	4 he shall stand and f his flock in the
Mk	8.	4 "How can one f these people with bread
Jn	21.17	you." Jesus said to him, "F my sheep.

FELLOW

Gen	19.	9 "This f came here as an alien, and he
Ex	2.13	"Why do you strike your f Hebrew?"
Acts	22.22	then they shouted, "Away with such a f
Eph	3.	6 the Gentiles are f heirs, members of the
Phil	2.25	co-worker and f soldier, your messenger

FELLOWSHIP

Acts	2.42	the apostles' teaching and f, to the
1 Cor	1.	9 by him you were called into the f of his
Gal	2.	9 to Barnabas and me the right hand of f,
1 Jn	1.	3 that you also may have f with us; and

FESTIVAL (FESTIVALS)

Ex	23.14	in a year you shall hold a f for me.
Lev	23.	2 These are the appointed f of the LORD
	23.41	You shall keep it as a f to the LORD
Num	29.39	offer to the LORD at your appointed f,
1 Kings	8.65	Solomon held the f at that time, and all
Dan	5.	1 King Belshazzar made a great f for a
Mt	26.	5 "Not during the f, or there may be a riot
	27.15	Now at the f the governor was
Mk	15.	6 Now at the f he used to release a
Lk	2.41	to Jerusalem for the f of the Passover.
	22.	1 the f of Unleavened Bread which is

FEVER

Mk	1.30	mother-in-law was in bed with a f,
Lk	4.38	was suffering from a high f,
Jn	4.52	at one in the afternoon the f left him."
Acts	28.	8 father of Publius lay sick in bed with f

FEW

Eccl	5.	2 earth; therefore let your words be f.
Mt	7.14	leads to life, and there are f who find it.
Lk	13.23	him, "Lord, will only a f be saved?"

FIELD

Isa	5.	8 who add f to f, until there is room for
Jer	32.	7 "Buy my f that is at Anathoth, for the
Mt	13.44	of heaven is like treasure hidden in a f,
Acts	1.19	the f was called in their language
1 Cor	3.	9 you are God's f, God's building.

FIERCE

Song	8.	6 strong as death, passion f as the grave.

FIG TREE (FIG TREES)

Song	2.13	The f puts forth its figs, and the vines
Isa	34.	4 on a vine, or fruit withering on a f.
Joel	1.	7 waste my vines, and splintered my f;
Hab	3.17	Though the f does not blossom, and no
Mic	4.	4 their own vines and under their own f,
Mt	21.19	you again!" And the f withered at once.
Mk	11.13	Seeing in the distance a f in leaf, he

Mk	13.28	"From the f learn its lesson: as soon as
Lk	13.	6 A man had a f planted in his vineyard;
	21.29	"Look at the f and all the trees; as soon
Jn	1.48	"I saw you under the f before Philip
Jas	3.12	Can a f, my brothers and sister, yield

FIGHT (FIGHTING)

Ex	14.14	The LORD will f for you, and you have
Deut	1.30	God . . . is the one who will f for you,
	20.	4 God who goes before you, to f for you
2 Chr	11.	4 LORD: You shall not go up or f against
Isa	31.	4 the LORD of hosts will come down to f
	58.	4 Look, you fast only to quarrel and to f
Jer	1.19	They will f against you; but they shall
	21.	5 I myself will f against you with
Zech	14.14	other; even Judah will f at Jerusalem.
Jn	18.36	my followers would be f, to keep me
Acts	5.39	you may even be found f against God!"
1 Tim	1.19	following them, you may f the good f.
	6.12	F the good f of the faith; take hold of

FIGS

Jer	8.13	grapes on the vine, nor f on the fig tree;
	24.	1 The LORD showed me two baskets of f

FILL (FILLED)

Gen	1.22	multiply and f the waters in the seas,
	1.28	multiply, and f the earth and subdue it;
Ex	40.35	the glory of the LORD f the tabernacle.
Num	14.21	all the earth shall be f with the glory of
Deut	14.29	in your towns, may come and eat their f
1 Kings	8.11	for the glory of the LORD f the house of
2 Kings	24.	4 he f Jerusalem with innocent blood, and
2 Chr	5.14	glory of the LORD f the house of God.
Prov	7.18	Come, let us take our f of love until
Isa	27.	6 shoots, and f the whole world with fruit.
Ezek	43.	5 and the glory of the LORD f the temple.
	44.	4 lo! the glory of the LORD f the temple
Hab	2.14	the earth will be f with the knowledge
Lk	1.53	he has f the hungry with good things,
	3.	5 Every valley shall be f, and every
Jn	2.	7 said to them, "F the jars with water."
	6.26	because you ate your f of the loaves.
Acts	2.	4 All of them were f with the Holy Spirit
	5.28	you have f Jerusalem with your teaching
Eph	5.18	is debauchery; but be f with the Spirit,

FINAL

Ezek	21.25	come, the time of your f punishment,

FIND (FINDS FOUND)

Num	32.23	and be sure your sin will f you out.
Deut	4.29	you will f him if you search after him
	32.10n	He f him in a desert land, in a howling
1 Sam	25.28	evil shall not be f in you so long as you
2 Chr	34.15	Shaphan, "I have f the book of the law
Neh	8.14	they f it written in the law, which the
Job	23.	3 Oh, that I knew where I might f him,
	33.24	down into the Pit; I have f a ransom;
Prov	8.35	For whoever f me f life and obtains
	18.22	He who f a wife f a good thing, and
Song	3.	4 when I f him whom my soul loves.
Jer	15.16	Your words were f, and I ate them, and
	29.14	I will let you f me, says the LORD, and I
Lk	15.	9 Rejoice with me, for I have f the coin
	15.24	and is alive again; he was lost, and is f.
Jn	1.41	said to him, "We have f the Messiah"
	1.45	"We have f him about whom Moses in
	9.35	had driven him out, and when he f him,
Rev	20.15	not f written in the book of life was

FINE

Ex	2.	2 that he was a f child, she hid him three

FINGER (FINGERS)

Ex	8.19	said to Pharaoh, "This is the f of God!"
	31.18	of stone, written with the f of God.
Deut	9.10	stone tablets written with the f of God;

Ps	8.	3 at your heavens, the work of your *f*,
Dan	5.	5 the *f* of a human hand appeared and
Mt	23.	4 are unwilling to lift a *f* to move them.
Lk	11.20	if it is by the *f* of God that I cast out
	11.46	do not lift one *f* to ease them.

FINISH (FINISHED FINISHING)

Gen	2.	1 Thus the heavens and the earth were *f*,
1 Kings	6.14	So Solomon built the house, and *f* it.
1 Chr	28.20	the service of the house of the LORD is *f*.
Ezra	6.15	and this house was *f* on the third day of
Neh	6.15	So the wall was *f* on the twenty-fifth
Dan	9.24	to *f* the transgression, to put an end to
Lk	13.32	and on the third day I *f* my work.
Jn	17.	4 on earth by *f* the work that you gave
	19.30	he said, "It is *f*." Then he bowed his
Acts	20.24	if only I may *f* my course and the
2 Tim	4.	7 good fight, I have *f* the race, I have kept
1 Pet	4.	1 has suffered in the flesh has *f* with sin),

FIRE

Gen	19.24	and Gomorrah sulfur and *f* from the
Lev	9.24	*F* came out from the LORD and
	10.	1 they offered unholy *f* before the LORD,
Deut	4.12	the LORD spoke to you out of the *f*.
	4.24	the LORD your God is a devouring *f*, a
	5.	4 to face at the mountain, out of the *f*.
Josh	8.19	took it, and at once set the city on *f*.
Judg	1.	8 put it to the sword and set the city on *f*.
1 Kings	18.38	Then the *f* of the LORD fell and
	19.12	a *f*, but the LORD was not in the *f*;
2 Kings	2.11	a chariot of *f* and horses of *f* separated
2 Chr	7.	1 Solomon had ended his prayer, *f* came
Ps	66.12	we went through *f* and through water;
	83.14	As *f* consumes the forest, as the flame
Prov	26.20	For lack of wood the *f* goes out, and
Isa	43.	2 when you walk through *f* you shall not
	66.24	not die, their *f* shall not be quenched,
Jer	20.	9 like a burning *f* shut up in my bones;
	23.29	Is not my word like *f*, says the LORD,
	36.23	the entire scroll was consumed in the *f*
Lam	1.13	"From on high he sent *f*; it went deep
Dan	3.25	walking in the middle of the *f*,
Mt	3.10	fruit is cut down and thrown into the *f*.
	3.11	baptize you with the Holy Spirit and *f*.
	25.41	depart from me into the eternal *f*
Lk	3.16	baptize you with the Holy Spirit and *f*.
	9.54	do you want us to command *f* to come
	12.49	"I came to bring *f* to the earth, and how
Jn	21.	9 ashore, they saw a charcoal *f* there,
Acts	28.	5 shook off the creature into the *f* and
1 Cor	3.13	be revealed with *f*, and the *f* will test
	3.15	will be saved, but only as through *f*.
2 Thess	1.	8 with his mighty angels in flaming *f*,
Heb	12.29	for indeed our God is a consuming *f*.
Jas	3.	6 And the tongue is a *f*. The tongue is
Jude		7 undergoing a punishment of eternal *f*.
		23 others by snatching them out of the *f*;
Rev	21.	8 will be in the lake that burns with *f*

FIRMAMENT

Ps	19.	1 God; and the *f* proclaims his handiwork.

FIRST

Isa	41.	4 I, the LORD, am *f*, and will be with the
Mt	6.33	strive *f* for the kingdom of God and his
	19.30	many who are *f* will be last, and the last
Mk	9.35	"Whoever wants to be *f* must be last of
Lk	9.59	"Lord, *f* let me go and bury my father."
Rom	16.	5 who was the *f* convert in Asia
1 Cor	15.47	The *f* man was from the earth, a man of
	16.15	were the *f* converts in Achaia,
2 Cor	8.	5 they gave themselves *f* to the Lord and,
3 Jn		9 Diotrephes, who likes to put himself *f*,
Rev	1.17	not be afraid; I am the *f* and the last,
	20.	5 were ended.) This is the *f* resurrection.

FIRST FRUITS

Ex	34.26	For if your ground you shall bring to
Lev	2.14	a grain offering of *f* to the LORD, you
	23.10	shall bring the sheaf of the *f* of your
Num	28.26	On the day of the *f*, when you offer a
Prov	3.	9 and with the *f* of all your produce.
Rom	11.16	dough offered as *f* is holy, then the
1 Cor	15.20	the dead, the *f* of those who have died.
2 Thess	3.13	God chose you as the *f* for salvation
Jas	1.18	we would become a kind of *f* of his

FIRSTBORN

Ex	11.	5 Every *f* in the land of Egypt shall die,
Num	3.45	the Levites as substitutes for all the *f*
	8.17	For all the *f* among the Israelites are
Ps	78.51	He struck all the *f* in Egypt, the first
	89.27	I will make him the *f*, the highest of the
Col	1.15	the invisible God, the *f* of all creation;

FIRSTLING

Lev	27.26	A *f* of animals . . . which as a *f* belongs

FISH

Gen	1.26	let them have dominion over the *f* of
Ex	7.21	the *f* in the river died. The river stank
Isa	19.	8 Those who *f* will mourn; all who cast
Jon	1.17	provided a large *f* to swallow up Jonah;
	2.10	spoke to the *f*, and it spewed Jonah out
Mt	7.10	Or if the child asks for a *f*, will give a
	14.17	nothing here but five loaves and two *f*."
	15.34	They said, "Seven, and a few small *f*."
	17.27	take the first *f* that comes up; and when
Mk	1.17	me, and I will make you *f* for people."
	6.38	found out, they said, "Five, and two *f*."
	8.	7 They had also a few small *f*; and after
Lk	11.11	if your child asks for a *f*, will give a
Jn	6.	9 who has five barley loaves and two *f*.
	21.	6 haul it in because there were so many *f*.

FISHERMEN

Jer	16.16	I am now sending for many *f*, says the
Mk	1.16	a net in the sea — for they were *f*.

FIVE

Mt	16.	9 you not remember the *f* loaves for the *f*
Mk	6.38	found out, they said, "*F*, and two fish."
	6.44	loaves were numbered *f* thousand men.
Lk	9.13	"We have no more than *f* loaves and two
Jn	4.18	for you have had *f* husbands, and the

FIXED

Lk	4.20	of all in the synagogue were *f* on him.
Acts	17.31	because he has *f* a day on which he will

FLAME

Isa	10.17	become a fire, and his Holy One a *f*;
	43.	2 and the *f* shall not consume you.

FLASHES

Song	8.	6 as the grave. Its *f* are *f* of fire, a raging
Rev	4.	5 from the throne are *f* of lightning,

FLATTER (FLATTERING FLATTERS)

Job	32.22	For I do not know how to *f*— or my
Ps	12.	2 other; with *f* lips and a double heart
	36.	2 For they *f* themselves in their own eyes
Prov	26.28	its victims, and a *f* mouth works ruin.
	28.23	favor than one who *f* with the tongue.
	29.	5 Whoever *f* a neighbor is spreading a net

FLAVOR

Job	6.	6 is there any *f* in the juice of mallows?

FLEE (FLED)

Ex	2.15	But Moses *f* from Pharaoh. He settled
Deut	19.	5 the killer may *f* to one of these cities
1 Kings	2.29	"Joab has *f* to the tent of the LORD and
Ps	11.	1 how can you say to me, "*F* like a bird to
	143.	9 my enemies; I have *f* to you for refuge.

Prov	28.	1 The wicked *f* when no one pursues, but
Jer	6.	1 *F* for safety, O children of Benjamin,
Jon	1.	3 Jonah set out to *f* to Tarshish from the
Zech	14.	5 you shall *f* as you *f* from the earthquake
Mt	2.13	child and his mother, and *f* to Egypt,
	10.23	you in one town, *f* to the next;
Lk	3.	7 Who warned you to *f* from the wrath
	21.21	those in Judea must *f* to the mountains,
1 Cor	10.14	dear friends, *f* from the worship of idols.

FLEECE

Judg	6.37	I am going to lay a *f* of wool on the

FLEET

1 Kings	9.26	Solomon built a *f* of ships at
	10.11	Moreover, the *f* of Hiram, which carried

FLEETING

Ps	39.	4 my days; let me know how *f* my life is.
Heb	11.25	God than to enjoy the *f* pleasures of sin.

FLESH

1 Chr	11.	1 and said, "See, we are your bone and *f.*
2 Chr	32.	8 With him is an arm of *f*; but with us is
Job	19.26	destroyed, then in my *f* I shall see God,
Ps	145.	21 and all *f* will bless his holy name
Mt	26.41	indeed is willing, but the *f* is weak."
Mk	14.38	indeed is willing, but the *f* is weak."
Lk	3.	6 and all *f* shall see the salvation of God.' "
Jn	1.14	the Word became *f* and lived among us,
	6.51	give for the life of the world is my *f.*
	6.63	the spirit that gives life; the *f* is useless.
Rom	7.14	but I am of the *f*, sold into slavery
	7.18	good dwells within me, that is, in my *f.*
	8.	3 his own Son in the likeness of sinful *f*,
	8.	6 To set the mind on the *f* is death, but
	8.	9 But you are not in the *f*, you are in the
	9.	5 according to the *f*, comes the Messiah,
1 Cor	3.	1 but rather as people of the *f*, as infants
	5.	5 to Satan for the destruction of the *f*,
	15.39	Not all *f* is alike, but there is one *f* for
	15.50	*f* and blood cannot inherit the kingdom
2 Cor	12.	7 a thorn was given me in the *f*, a
Gal	5.17	the *f* desires is opposed to the Spirit,
Phil	3.	4 too, have reason for confidence in the *f.*

FLESHPOTS

Ex	16.	3 when we sat by the *f* and ate our fill of

FLOAT (FLOATED)

Gen	7.18	and the ark *f* on the face of the waters.
2 Kings	6.	6 threw it in there, and made the iron *f.*

FLOCK

Gen	30.41	the stronger of the *f* were breeding,
Ps	68.10	your *f* found a dwelling in it; in your
	77.20	You lead your people like a *f* by the
	79.13	Then we your people, the *f* of your
Isa	40.11	He will feed his *f* like a shepherd; he
Ezek	36.38	Like the *f* for sacrifices, like the *f* at
Lk	12.32	"Do not be afraid, little *f*, for it is the
1 Pet	5.	2 among you to tend to the *f* of God

FLOGGED (FLOGGING)

Mt	20.19	to be mocked and *f* and crucified,
	27.26	and after *f* Jesus, he handed him over
Lk	18.33	After they have *f* him, they will kill him,
	23.16	therefore have him *f* and release him."
Jn	19.	1 Then Pilate took Jesus and had him *f*
Acts	22.24	ordered him to be examined by *f*, to

FLOOD (FLOODS)

Gen	6.17	I am going to bring a *f* of waters on the
	9.11	never again shall there be a *f* to destroy
Ps	6.	6 every night I *f* my bed with my tears.
	29.10	The LORD sits enthroned over the *f*; the
Mt	7.27	The rain fell, and the *f* came, and the
Lk	17.27	ark, and the *f* came and destroyed all

FLOWING

Rev	22.	1 as crystal, *f* from the throne of God

FLOWER (FLOWERS)

Job	14.	2 comes up like a *f* and withers, flees like
Song	2.12	The *f* appear on the earth, the time of
Isa	40.	7 The grass withers, the *f* fades, when the

FLY (FLIES)

Ex	8.21	I will send swarms of *f* on you, your
Eccl	10.	1 Dead *f* make the perfumer's ointment
Isa	7.18	that day the LORD will whistle for the *f*

FOES

2 Sam	24.13	will you flee three months before your *f*
Ps	3.	1 O LORD, how many are my *f*! Many are
	108.	13 it is he who will tread down our *f.*
Mt	10.36	and one's *f* will be members of one's

FOLD

Jer	50.	6 have gone, they have forgotten their *f.*
Jn	10.16	sheep, that do not belong to this *f.*

FOLLOW

Lev	20.23	You shall not *f* the practices of the
	26.	3 If you *f* my statutes and keep my
Deut	5.33	You must *f* exactly the path that the
	13.	4 your God you shall *f*, him alone you
1 Sam	8.	3 his sons did not *f* in his ways, but
1 Kings	18.21	If the LORD is God, *f* him; but if Baal,
2 Kings	10.31	Jehu was not careful to *f* the law of the
Ps	38.20	my adversaries because I *f* after good.
Eccl	11.	9 *F* the inclination of your heart and the
Ezek	11.20	they may *f* my statutes and keep my
	20.19	your God; *f* my statutes, and be careful
	37.24	They shall *f* my ordinances and be
Mt	4.19	*f* me, and I will make you fish for
	8.19	"Teacher, I will *f* you wherever you go."
	8.22	"*F* me, and let the dead bury their own
	9.	9 tax booth; and he said to him, "*F* me."
Mk	2.14	tax booth; and he said to him, "*F* me."
	5.37	allowed no one to *f* him except Peter,
	15.41	These used to *f* him and provided for
Lk	5.27	tax booth; and he said to him, "*F* me."
	9.23	and take up their cross daily and *f*
	9.49	him, because he does not *f* with us."
	9.57	to him, "I will *f* you wherever you go."
	18.22	treasure in heaven; then come, *f* me."
Jn	1.43	He found Philip and said to him, "*F* me."
	10.	4 the sheep *f* him, because they know his
	10.27	my voice. I know them, and they *f* me.
	12.26	Whoever serves me, must *f* me, and
	13.37	"Lord, why can I not *f* you now? I will
	21.19	God.) After this he said to him, "*F* me."
Rom	4.12	who also *f* the example of the faith that

FOLLOWED (FOLLOWING)

Num	32.12	for they have unreservedly *f* the LORD.'
Josh	14.	8 yet I wholeheartedly *f* the LORD my God.
2 Kings	17.15	they *f* the nations that were around
Jer	9.14	but have stubbornly *f* their own hearts
Ezek	11.12	whose statutes you have not *f*, and
Mic	6.16	of Ahab, and you have *f* their counsels.
Mt	26.58	Peter was *f* him at a distance, as far as
Mk	1.18	they left their nets and *f* him.
	10.28	we have left everything and *f* you."
	14.54	Peter had *f* him at a distance, right into
Lk	18.28	we have left our homes and *f* you."
	22.54	house. But Peter was *f* at a distance.
Jn	1.40	John speak, and *f* him was Andrew,
	18.15	Peter and another disciple *f* Jesus.

FOLLOWERS

Mt	16.24	"If any want to become my *f*, let them
Mk	8.34	"If any want to become my *f*, let them

FOLLY (FOLLIES)

1 Sam	25.25	Nabal is his name, and *f* is with him;

Ps	73.	7 fatness; their hearts overflow with *f*.
Prov	24.	9 The devising of *f* is sin, and the scoffer
	26.11	his vomit is a fool who reverts to his *f*.

FOOD (FOODS)

Gen	1.29	in its fruit; you shall have them for *f*.
	3.	6 woman saw that the tree was good for *f*,
Num	21.	5 no *f* and no water, and we detest this
Lam	4.	4 children beg for *f*, but no one gives
Mt	15.26	It is not fair to take the children's *f* and
Mk	7.27	not fair to take the children's *f* and
Lk	12.23	For life is more than *f*, and the body
Jn	4.32	"I have *f* to eat that you do not know
1 Cor	6.13	"*F* is meant for the stomach and the
	9.	4 not have the right to our *f* and drink?
1 Tim	4.	3 marriage and demand abstinence from *f*,
	6.	8 have *f* and clothing, we will be content

FOOL (FOOLS)

1 Sam	26.21	I have been a *f*, and have made a great
2 Sam	3.33	saying, "Should Abner die as a *f* dies?
Job	5.	2 Surely vexation kills the *f*, and jealousy
Ps	14.	1 *F* say in their hearts, "There is no God."
	49.10	*f* and dolt perish together and leave
	53.	1 *F* say in their hearts, "There is no God."
Prov	10.	8 but a babbling *f* will come to ruin.
	13.16	intelligently, but the *f* displays folly.
	14.	7 Leave the presence of a *f*, for there you
	14.	9 *F* mock at the guilt offering, but the
	16.22	has it, but folly is the punishment of
	17.12	of its cubs than to confront a *f* in folly.
	24.	7 Wisdom is too high for *f*; in the gate
	26.	1 in harvest, so honor is not fitting for a *f*.
	26.	5 Answer *f* according to their folly, or they
Eccl	2.15	happens to the *f* will happen to me
	4.	5 *F* fold their hands, and consume their
	7.17	not be too wicked, and do not be a *f*;
Isa	35.	8 no traveler, not even *f*, shall go astray.
Mt	5.22	if you say, 'You *f*!' you will be liable to
Lk	11.40	You *f*! Did not the one who made the
	12.20	'you *f*! This very night your life is being
Rom	1.22	Claiming to be wise, they became *f*, and
1 Cor	4.10	We are *f* for the sake of Christ, but you

FOOLISH

Isa	44.25	the wise, and makes their knowledge *f*;
Jer	4.22	"For my people are *f*, they do not know
Mt	7.26	will be like a *f* man who built his house
Lk	24.25	"Oh, how *f* you are, and how slow of

FOOLISHNESS

1 Cor	1.21	through the *f* of our proclamation,
	2.14	of God's Spirit, for they are *f* to them,

FOOT (FEET)

Ps	2.12	with trembling kiss his *f*, or he will be
	8.	6 you have put all things under their *f*,
	119.	59 of your ways, turn my *f* to your decrees;
	119.105	Your word is a lamp to my *f* and a light
	121.	3 He will not let your *f* be moved, he who
Song	7.	1 How graceful are your *f* in sandals, O
Nah	1.15	mountains the *f* of one who brings good
Mt	22.44	until I put your enemies under your *f*" '?
	28.	9 him, took hold of his *f*, and worshiped
Mk	9.45	if your *f* causes you to stumble, cut it
	12.36	until I put your enemies under your *f*." '
Lk	7.38	to bathe his *f* with her tears and to dry
	10.39	Mary, who sat at the Lord's *f* and
	24.39	Look at my hands and my *f*; see that it
Jn	12.	3 anointed Jesus' *f* and wiped them with
	13.	5 began to wash the disciples' *f* and to
Rom	3.15	Their *f* are swift to shed blood, ruin and
1 Cor	12.15	If the *f* would say, "Because I am not a
	15.25	he has put all his enemies under his *f*.

FOOT-RUNNERS

Jer	12.	5 If you have raced *f* and they have

FOOTSTOOL

Ps	110.	1 hand until I make your enemies your *f*."
Isa	66.	1 is my throne and the earth is my *f*;
Lk	20.43	hand, until I make your enemies a *f*." '
Acts	2.35	hand, until I make your enemies your *f*." '
Heb	10.13	"until his enemies would be made a *f*

FORBEARANCE

Rom	3.25	in his divine *f* he passed over the sins

FORBID (FORBIDDEN)

1 Cor	14.39	and do not *f* speaking in tongues;
Acts	16.	6 been *f* by the Holy Spirit to speak the

FORCE (FORCED FORCES)

Deut	33.27	the ancient gods, shatters the *f* of old;
1 Sam	13.12	so I *f* myself, and offered the burnt
Prov	12.24	while the lazy will be put to *f* labor.
Mt	11.12	violence, and the violent take it by *f*.
Jn	6.15	and take him by *f* to make him king,
2 Cor	12.11	I have been a fool! You *f* me to it.

FOREHEAD (FOREHEADS)

Ezek	3.	7 have a hard *f* and a stubborn heart.
	9.	4 and put a mark on the *f* of the those
Rev	13.16	to be marked on the right hand or the *f*,

FOREIGN

Ezra	10.11	have trespassed and married *f* women,
Ps	137.	4 we sing the LORD's song in a *f* land?

FOREIGNER (FOREIGNERS)

Deut	23.20	On loans to a *f* you may charge interest,
1 Kings	8.41	"Likewise when a *f*, who is not of your
Ezek	44.	7 to all your abominations in admitting *f*,
Lk	17.18	and give praise to God except this *f*?"
1 Cor	14.11	of a sound, I will be a *f* to the speaker

FOREKNEW

Rom	8.29	those whom he *f* he also predestined to
	11.	2 has not rejected his people whom he *f*.

FOREKNOWLEDGE

Acts	2.23	definite plan and *f* of God, you crucified

FORFEIT (FORFEITED)

Deut	22.	9 the whole yield will have to be *f*, both
Mk	8.36	to gain the whole world and *f* their life?

FORGET (FORGETS FORGETTING FORGOT FORGOTTEN)

Gen	40.23	did not remember Joseph, but *f* him.
Deut	4.31	he will not *f* the covenant with your
	6.12	take care that you do not *f* the LORD,
	8.11	Take care that you do not *f* the LORD, by
Judg	3.	7 *f* the LORD their God, and worshiping
1 Sam	12.	9 they *f* the LORD their God; and he sold
Ps	10.11	They think in their heart, "God has *f*, he
	42.	9 to God, my rock, "Why have you *f* me?
	44.24	Why do you *f* our affliction and
	44.17	come upon us, yet we have not *f* you
	45.10	*f* your people and your father's house,
	74.19	animals; do not *f* the life of your poor
	77.	9 Has God *f* to be gracious? Has he in
	103.	2 my soul, and do not *f* all his benefits—
	106.13	But they soon *f* his works; they did not
	119.	16 in your statutes; I will not *f* your word.
	137.	5 If I *f* you, O Jerusalem, let my right
Prov	2.17	of her youth and *f* her sacred covenant;
	3.	1 My child, do not *f* my teaching, but let
	31.	7 let them drink and *f* their poverty, and
Isa	17.10	you have *f* the God of your salvation,
	44.21	my servant; O Israel, you will not be *f*
	49.14	has forsaken me, my Lord has *f* me."
	51.13	You have *f* the LORD, your Maker, who
	65.11	the LORD, who *f* my holy mountain,
Jer	2.32	Yet my people have *f* me, days without
	13.25	because you have *f* me and trusted
	18.15	But my people have *f* me, they burn

Jer	23.27	plan to make my people *f* my name
	30.14	All your lovers have *f* you; they care
	50. 6	they have gone, they have *f* their fold.
Lam	5.20	Why have you *f* us completely? Why
Hos	4. 6	you have *f* the law of your God, I also
Mk	8.14	the disciples had *f* to bring bread; and
Lk	12. 6	Yet not one of them is *f* in God's sight.
Phil	3.13	I do; *f* what lies behind and straining

FORGIVE

Gen	50.17	I beg you, *f* the crime of your brothers
Ex	32.32	if you will only *f* their sin —but if not,
Num	14.19	*F* the iniquity of this people according
	14.20	said, "I do *f*, just as you have asked;
	30. 8	bound herself; and the LORD will *f* her.
Josh	24.19	God; he will not *f* your transgressions
1 Sam	25.28	Please *f* the trespass of your servant; for
1 Kings	8.30	heaven your dwelling place; heed and *f*.
	8.39	*f*, and act, and render to all whose
2 Chr	6.21	heaven your dwelling place; hear and *f*.
	7.14	and will *f* their sin and heal their land.
Ps	25.18	and my trouble, and *f* all my sins.
	79. 9	deliver us, and *f* our sins, for your
	85. 2	You *f* the iniquity of your people; you
Isa	2. 9	is brought low--do not *f* them!
Jer	31.34	for I will *f* their iniquity, and remember
	33. 8	I will *f* all the guilt of their sin and
	36. 3	so that I may *f* their iniquity and their
Mt	6.12	And *f* us our debts, as we also have
	6.15	not *f* others, neither will your Father *f*
	18.35	one of you, if you do not *f* your brother
Mk	2. 7	Who can *f* sins but God alone?"
	11.25	Whenever you stand praying, *f*, if you
Lk	6.37	condemned. *F*, and you will be forgiven;
	11. 4	And *f* us our sins, for we ourselves *f*
	17. 3	and if there is repentance you must *f*.
	23.34	Jesus said, "Father, *f* them; for they do
Jn	20.23	If you *f* the sins of any, they are
2 Cor	2. 7	instead you should *f* and console him,
1 Jn	1. 9	and just will *f* us our sins and cleanse

FORGIVES (FORGAVE FORGIVEN FORGIVING)

Ex	34. 7	*f* iniquity and transgression and sin, yet
Lev	4.20	for them, and they shall be *f*.
	19.22	the sin he committed shall be *f* him.
Num	14.18	love, *f* iniquity and transgression,
	15.25	of the Israelites, and they shall be *f*;
Ps	32. 1	are those whose transgression is *f*,
	78.38	being compassionate, *f* their iniquity,
	99. 8	you were a *f* God to them, but an
	103. 3	who *f* all your iniquity, who heals all
Prov	17. 9	One who *f* an affront fosters friendship,
Isa	33.24	the people who live there will be *f* their
Lam	3.42	and rebelled, and you have not *f*.
Mt	9. 2	"Take heart, son; your sins are *f*."
	12.31	will be *f* for every sin and blasphemy,
	18.27	slave released him and *f* him the debt.
	18.32	You wicked slave! I *f* you all that debt
Mk	2. 5	to the paralytic, "Son, your sins are *f*."
	3.28	people will be *f* for their sins and
Lk	5.20	he said, "Friend, your sins are *f* you."
	12.10	a word against the Son of Man will be *f*;
Acts	2.38	Jesus Christ so that your sins may be *f*;
	8.22	the intent of your heart may be *f*
Rom	4. 7	are those whose iniquities are *f*,
Eph	4.32	one another, as God in Christ has *f* you.
Col	2.13	when he *f* us all our trespasses, erasing
1 Jn	2.12	your sins are *f* on account of his name.

FORGIVENESS

Ps	130. 4	But there is *f* with you, so that you may
Dan	9. 9	the Lord our God belong mercy and *f*,
Acts	10.43	everyone who believes in him receives *f*
	13.38	that through this man *f* of sins is
	26.18	so that they may receive *f* of sins and a
Col	1.14	we have redemption, the *f* of sins.
Heb	9.22	the shedding of blood there is no *f*

FORK

Jer	15. 7	winnowed them with a winnowing *f*
Lk	3.17	winnowing *f* is in his hand, to clear his

FORM (FORMED FORMS)

Gen	2. 7	God *f* man from the dust of the ground,
	2.19	God *f* every animal of the field and
Job	33. 6	are; I too was *f* from a piece of clay.
Isa	43. 1	you, O Jacob, he who *f* you, O Israel:
	44. 2	who made you, who *f* you in the womb
Jer	1. 5	"Before I *f* you in the womb I knew you,
Am	4.13	lo, the one who *f* the mountains,
Gal	4.19	of childbirth until Christ be *f* in you,
Acts	14.11	gods have come down to us in human *f*!"
1 Cor	7.31	the present *f* of this world is passing
Phil	2. 6	though he was in the *f* of God, did not
2 Tim	3. 5	holding to the outward *f* of godliness

FORMER

Isa	41.22	Tell us the *f* things, what they are, so
	48. 3	The *f* things I declared long ago, they

FORNICATION

Acts	15.20	to abstain only from . . . *f* and from

FORNICATORS

1 Cor	6. 9	Do not be deceived! *F*, idolaters,

FORSAKE (FORSAKEN FORSAKING)

Deut	31. 8	with you; he will not fail you or *f* you.
Josh	1. 5	be with you; I will not fail you or *f* you.
1 Sam	8. 8	*f* me and serving other gods, so also
1 Kings	9. 9	'Because they have *f* the LORD their
	11.33	because he has *f* me, worshiped Astarte
	18.18	because you have *f* the commandments
1 Chr	28. 9	but if you *f* him, he will abandon you
2 Chr	7.19	if you turn aside and *f* my statutes and
Ps	9.10	O LORD, have not *f* those who seek you.
	22. 1	My God, my God, why have you *f* me?
	27. 9	Do not cast me off, do not *f* me, O God
	37.25	yet I have not seen the righteous *f* or
	37.28	justice; he will not *f* his faithful ones.
	71.11	and seize that person whom God has *f*,
	94.14	For the LORD will not *f* his people; he
	119. 8	your statutes; do not utterly *f* me.
Prov	3. 3	not let loyalty and faithfulness *f* you;
	6.20	and do not *f* your mother's teaching.
Isa	1. 4	deal corruptly, who have *f* the LORD,
	1.28	who *f* the LORD shall be consumed.
	2. 6	you have *f* the ways of your people, O
	55. 7	let the wicked *f* their way, and the
Jer	1.16	them, for all their wickedness in *f* me;
	2.17	brought this upon yourself by *f* the LORD
	5.19	you have *f* me and served foreign gods
	16.11	It is because your ancestors have *f* me,
Ezek	8.12	not see us, the LORD has *f* the land."
Am	5. 2	maiden Israel; *f* on her land, with no
Mt	27.46	"My God, my God, why have you *f* me?"
Mk	15.34	"My God, my God, why have you *f* me?"
2 Cor	4. 9	persecuted, but not *f*; struck down, but

FORTRESS

Ps	31. 2	of refuge for me, a strong *f* to save me.
	31. 3	You are indeed my rock and my *f*; for
	59. 9	watch for you; for you, O God, are my *f*.
	144. 2	my rock and my *f*, my stronghold and
Prov	10.15	The wealth of the rich is their *f*; the
Dan	11.38	strongest *f* by the help of a foreign god.

FORTUNES

Deut	30. 3	God will restore your *f* and have
Job	42.10	LORD restored the *f* of Job, when he had
Ps	14. 7	When the LORD restores the *f* of his
	53. 6	When God restores the *f* of his people,
	85. 1	your land; you restored the *f* of Jacob.
	126. 1	When the LORD restored the *f* of Zion,
Jer	31.23	and in its towns when I restore their *f*:
	33. 7	I will restore the *f* of Judah and the *f* of

Am	9.14	I will restore the *f* of my people Israel,
Zeph	2. 7	be mindful of them and restore their *f*.
	3.20	when I restore your *f* before your eyes,

FORTY

Gen	7. 4	rain upon the earth *f* days and *f* nights;
Ex	24.18	on the mountain *f* days and *f* nights.
Num	14.33	shepherds in the wilderness for *f* years,
Deut	2. 7	These *f* years the LORD your God has
	9.11	At the end of *f* days and *f* nights the
	25. 3	*F* lashes may be given but not more; if
	29. 5	I have led you *f* years in the wilderness.

FOUNDATION (FOUNDATIONS)

Ezra	3. 6	But the *f* of the temple of the LORD was
	3.11	because the *f* of the house of the LORD
Job	38. 4	were you when I laid the *f* of the earth?
Ps	11. 3	If the *f* are destroyed, what can the
	18. 7	the earth reeled and rocked; the *f* also
	102. 25	Long ago you laid the *f* of the earth,
Isa	24.18	opened, and the *f* of the earth tremble.
	28.16	See, I am laying in Zion a *f* stone, a
	40.21	not understood from the *f* of the earth?
	54.11	antimony, and lay your *f* with sapphires.
Hag	2.18	the day that the *f* of the LORD's temple
Mt	13.35	been hidden from the *f* of the world."
Rom	15.20	that I do not build on someone else's *f*,
1 Cor	3.11	no one can lay any *f* other than the one
2 Tim	2.19	But God's firm *f* stands, bearing this

FOUNDED

Ps	24. 2	he has *f* it upon the seas, and
Prov	3.19	The LORD by wisdom *f* the earth; by

FOUNTAIN (FOUNTAINS)

Gen	7.11	all the *f* of the great deep burst forth,
Ps	36. 9	with you is the *f* of life; in your light we
Prov	14.27	The fear of the LORD is a *f* of life, so
	16.22	Wisdom is a *f* of life to one who has it,
	18. 4	waters; the *f* of wisdom is a gushing
	25.26	Like a muddied spring or a polluted *f*
Eccl	12. 6	pitcher is broken at the *f*, and the
Song	4.12	my bride, a garden locked, a *f* sealed.
Jer	2.13	they have forsaken me, the *f* of living
	9. 1	of water, and my eyes a *f* of tears,
	17.13	forsaken the LORD, the *f* of living water, the LORD.
Joel	3.18	a *f* shall come forth from the house of
Zech	13. 1	that day a *f* shall be opened for the

FOX (FOXES)

Judg	15. 4	and caught three hundred *f*, and took
Neh	4. 3	*f* going up on it would break
Song	2.15	Catch us the *f*, the little *f*, that spoil the
Mt	8.20	"*F* have holes, and birds of the air have
Lk	9.58	"*F* have holes, and birds of the air have
	13.32	"Go and tell that *f* for me, 'Listen, I am

FRAGRANCE

Song	7.13	The mandrakes give forth *f*, and over
2 Cor	2.14	the *f* that comes from knowing him.

FRANKINCENSE

Isa	60. 6	They shall bring gold and *f*, and shall
Mt	2.11	they offered him gifts of gold, *f*, and

FREE (FREED)

Gen	44.10	my slave, but the rest of you shall go *f*.
Ex	21. 5	children; I will not go out a *f* person,"
Num	32.22	and be *f* of obligation to the LORD and
Deut	15.13	a male slave out from you a *f* person
Ps	146. 7	The LORD sets the prisoners *f*; the LORD
Ezek	13.20	and let the lives go *f*, the lives that you
Lk	1.64	his tongue *f*, and he began to speak,
Jn	8.32	the truth and the truth will make you *f*.'
	8.36	So if the Son makes you *f*, you will be *f*
Acts	13.39	you could not be *f* by the law of Moses.
Rom	5.15	But the *f* gift is not like the trespass.
	6. 7	For whoever has died is *f* from sin. But

Rom	6.18	you, having been set *f* from sin, have
1 Cor	7.39	the husband dies, she is *f* to marry
	9. 1	Am I not *f*? Am I not an apostle? Have I
2 Cor	11. 7	God's good news to you *f* of charge?
Gal	1. 4	our sins to set us *f* from the present evil
	3.28	or Greek, there is no longer slave or *f*,
Heb	2.15	*f* those who all their lives were held in
Rev	1. 5	us and *f* us from our sins by his blood,

FREEDOM

Rom	8.21	and will obtain the *f* of glory of the
1 Cor	7.21	Even if you can gain your *f*, make use
2 Cor	3.17	the Spirit of the Lord is, there is *f*.
Gal	2. 4	in to spy on the *f* we have in Christ
	5. 1	For *f* Christ has set us free. Stand firm,
	5.13	you were called to *f*, brothers and
1 Pet	2.16	yet do not use your *f* as pretext for evil.
2 Pet	2.19	They promise them *f*, but they

FREELY

Gen	2.16	"You may *f* eat of every tree of the
Prov	11.24	Some give *f*, yet grow all the richer;

FREEWILL OFFERING (FREEWILL OFFERINGS)

Lev	7.16	or a *f*, it shall be eaten on the day that
Deut	16.10	contributing a *f* in proportion to the
Ezra	1. 4	animals, besides *f* for the house of God
	2.68	of families made *f* for the house of God,

FRIEND (FRIENDS)

Ex	33.11	face to face, as one speaks to a *f*.
Judg	5.31	may your *f* be like the sun as it rises in
2 Chr	20. 7	to the descendants of your *f* Abraham?
Job	6.14	"Those who withhold kindness from a *f*
	6.27	the orphan, and bargain over your *f*.
	16.20	My *f* scorn me; my eye pours out tears
	19.14	relatives and my close *f* have failed me;
	42.10	of Job when he had prayed for his *f*;
Ps	35.14	my bosom, as though I grieved for my *f*
	41. 9	Even my bosom *f* in whom I trusted,
	55.13	my equal, my companion, my familiar *f*.
	88.18	have caused *f* and neighbor to shun me;
Prov	16.28	strife, and a whisperer separates close *f*.
	17.17	A *f* loves at all times, and kinsfolk are
	18.24	Some *f* play at friendship but a true *f*
	19. 4	Wealth brings many *f*, but the poor are
	19. 6	generous, and everyone is a *f* to a giver
	22.24	Make no *f* with those given to anger,
	27. 6	Well meant are the wounds a *f* inflicts,
Jer	3. 4	"My father, you are the *f* of my
Mic	7. 5	Put no trust in a *f*, have no confidence
Mt	11.19	a *f* of tax collectors and sinners!'
	20.13	'*F*, I am doing you no wrong; did you
	26.50	to him, "*F*, do what you are here to do."
Mk	5.19	"Go home to your *f*, and tell them how
Lk	7.34	and a drunkard, a *f* of tax collectors and
	11. 5	'*F*, lend me three loaves of bread; for a
	12. 4	my *f*, do not fear those who kill the
	14.10	say to you, '*F*, move up higher'; then
	16. 9	make *f* by means of dishonest wealth so
Jn	11.11	"Our *f* Lazarus has fallen asleep, but I
	15.13	this, to lay down one's life for one's *f*.
	19.12	this man, you are no *f* of the emperor,
2 Cor	11. 9	needs were supplied by the *f* who came
Jas	2.23	and he was called the *f* of God.

FRIENDSHIP

Job	29. 4	when the *f* of God was upon my tent;
Ps	25.14	The *f* of the LORD is for those who fear
Jas	4. 4	know that *f* with the world is enmity

FRIGHTENED

Dan	4. 5	I saw a dream that *f* me. My fantasies
Mt	2. 3	When king Herod heard this, he was *f*,
Lk	24.38	"Why are you *f*, and why do doubts arise

FRINGE

Mt	9.20	him and touched the *f* of his cloak,

Mt	14.	36 might touch even the *f* of his cloak;

FROGS

Ex	8.	2 I will plague your whole country with *f*.
Ps	105.	30 Their land swarmed with *f*, even in the

FRUIT (FRUITS)

Num	13.	26 and showed them the *f* of the land.
Deut	30.	9 in the *f* of your body, in the *f* of your
Ps	1.	3 water, which yield their *f* in its season,
Prov	1.	31 they shall eat the *f* of their way
	8.	19 My *f* is better than gold, even fine gold,
	11.	30 The *f* of the righteous is a tree of life,
Song	4.	13 of pomegranates with all choicest *f*,
Jer	21.	14 you according to the *f* of your doings,
Mic	6.	7 the *f* of my body for the sin of my soul?"
Hab	3.	17 not blossom, and no *f* is on the vines;
Mt	7.	16 You will know them by their *f*. Are
	21.	43 that produces the *f* of the kingdom."
Mk	4.	20 hear the word and accept it and bear *f*,
	11.	14 "May no one ever eat *f* from you again."
Lk	1.	42 and blessed is the *f* of your womb!
	3.	9 not bear good *f* is cut down and thrown
	6.	43 "No good tree bears bad *f*, nor again
	8.	15 and bear *f* with patient endurance.
Jn	12.	24 grain; but if it dies, it bears much *f*.
	15.	5 abide in me and I in them bear much *f*,
Gal	5.	22 the *f* of the Spirit is love, joy, peace,
Col	1.	10 as you bear *f* in every good work and as
Heb	12.	11 it yields the peaceful *f* of righteousness
Rev	18.	14 *f* for which your soul longed has gone
	22.	2 twelve kinds of *f*, producing its *f* each

FRUSTRATE (FRUSTRATES)

Ezra	4.	5 they bribed officials to *f* their plan
Job	5.	12 He *f* the devices of the crafty, so that

FUGITIVE

Gen	4.	12 you will be a *f* and a wanderer on the

FULFILL (FULFILLED FULFILLING FULFILLS)

Gen	26.	3 I will *f* the oath that I swore to your
Deut	9.	5 to *f* the promise which the LORD made
1 Kings	2.	27 thus *f* the word of the LORD that he had
2 Chr	6.	10 the LORD has *f* his promise that he
	36.	21 to *f* the word of the LORD by the mouth
Ps	20.	5 May the LORD *f* all your petitions.
	138.	8 The LORD will *f* his purpose for me; your
	145.	19 He *f* the desire of all who fear him; he
Jer	28.	6 may the LORD *f* the words that you have
	33.	14 I will *f* the promise I made to the house
Mt	3.	15 for us in this way to *f* all righteousness."
	5.	17 I have come not to abolish but to *f*.
	8.	17 *f* what had been spoken through the
	21.	4 took place to *f* what had been spoken
	26.	56 scriptures of the prophets might be *f*."
Mk	1.	15 "The time is *f*, and the kingdom of God
	14.	49 arrest me. But let the scriptures be *f*."
	15.	28n the scripture was *f* that says, "And he
Lk	1.	1 the events that have been *f* among us,
	4.	21 "Today this scripture has been *f* in your
	22.	16 I will not eat it until it is *f* in the
	24.	44 the prophets, and the psalms must be *f*."
Jn	3.	29 For this reason my joy has been *f*.
	17.	12 be lost, so that the scripture might be *f*.
	19.	24 get it. This was to *f* what the scripture
Rom	9.	31 the law, did not succeed in *f* that law.
	13.	8 who loves one another has *f* the law.

FULL

Isa	6.	3 hosts; the whole earth is *f* of his glory."
Rom	11.	25 until the *f* number of the Gentiles
Jas	1.	4 let endurance have its *f* effect, so that

FULLY

Lk	6.	40 everyone who is *f* qualified will be like

FULLERS'

Mal	3.	2 he is like refiner's fire and like *f* soap;

FULLNESS

Jn	1.	16 From his *f* have we all received, grace
Rom	15.	29 you, I will come in the *f* of the blessing
Gal	4.	4 But when the *f* of time had come, God
Eph	3.	19 you may be filled with all the *f* of God.
Col	2.	9 in him the whole *f* of deity dwells
	2.	10 you have come to *f* in him, who is the

FURNACE

Ps	12.	6 that are pure, silver refined in a *f*
	21.	9 You will make them like a fiery *f* when
Prov	27.	21 is for silver, and the *f* is for gold,
Isa	31.	9 is in Zion, and whose *f* is in Jerusalem.
	48.	10 I have tested you in the *f* of adversity.
Dan	3.	19 He ordered the *f* heated up seven times
Mt	13.	42 they will throw them into the *f* of fire,

FURY

Isa	42.	13 a soldier, like a warrior he stirs up his *f*;
Ezek	21.	17 strike hand to hand, I will satisfy my *f*;
Lk	6.	11 they were filled with *f* and discussed

FUTILE

Isa	1.	13 courts no more; bringing offerings is *f*;
Rom	1.	21 they became *f* in their thinking, and
1 Cor	15.	17 your faith is *f* and you are still in your

FUTILITY

Rom	8.	20 creation was subjected to *f*, not of its
Eph	4.	17 Gentiles live, in the *f* of their minds.

G

GABRIEL

Dan	8.	16 "G, help this man understand the
	9.	21 in prayer, the man *G*, whom I had seen
Lk	1.	19 "I am *G*. I stand in the presence of God,
	1.	26 In the sixth month the angel *G* was

GAD

Gen	30.	11 "Good fortune!" so she named him *G*.
	46.	16 The children of *G*: Ziphion, Haggi,
Deut	33.	20 he said: Blessed be the enlargement of *G*!

GADITES

Num	32.	33 Moses gave to them—to the *G* and to

GAIN (GAINED GAINING)

Ps	119.	36 my heart to your decrees, and not to *g*.
Prov	1.	3 for *g* instruction in wise dealing,
	9.	9 righteous and they will *g* in learning.
Eccl	1.	3 What do people *g* from all the toil at
	2.	11 was nothing to be *g* under the sun.
	5.	16 go and what *g* do they have for toiling
Mic	4.	13 devote their *g* to the LORD, their wealth
Hab	2.	9 Alas for you who get evil *g* for your
Mt	16.	26 it profit them if they *g* the whole world
Lk	9.	25 them if they *g* the whole world, but lose
	19.	15 find out what that had *g* by trading.
2 Cor	12.	1 to boast; nothing is to be *g* by it, but I
Phil	1.	21 to me, living is Christ and dying is *g*.
	3.	8 as rubbish, in order that I may *g* Christ

GALATIA

Acts	16.	6 through the region of Phrygia and *G*,
	18.	23 through the region of *G* and Phrygia,
1 Cor	16.	1 directions I gave to the churches of *G*.
Gal	1.	2 To the churches of *G*: Grace to you and
1 Pet	1.	1 exiles of the Dispersion in Pontus, *G*,

GALILEAN

Mt	26.	69 said, "You also were with Jesus the *G*."
Mk	14.	70 you are one of them; for you are a *G*."
Lk	23.	6 he asked whether the man was a *G*.

GALILEE

Josh	20. 7	they set apart Kedesh in *G* in the hill
Isa	9. 1	the land beyond the Jordan, *G* of the
Mt	2.22	he went away to the district of *G*.
	4.12	has been arrested, he withdrew to *G*.
	4.15	across the Jordan, *G* of the Gentiles—
Mk	3. 7	a great multitude from *G* followed him;
	16. 7	he is going ahead of you to *G*; there you
Lk	2. 4	went up from the town of Nazareth in *G*
Jn	2. 1	there was a wedding in Cana in *G*, and
	4. 3	he left Judea and started back to *G*.
	7.52	you not also from *G*, are you? Search
Acts	1.11	"Men of *G*, why do you stand looking

GALLIO

Acts	18.12	But when *G* was proconsul of Achaia,
	18.17	But *G* paid no attention to any of these

GALLOWS

Esth	5.14	"Let a *g* fifty cubits high be made, and

GAMALIEL

Acts	5.34	Pharisee in the council named *G*, a
	22. 3	brought up in this city at the feet of *G*,

GAME

Gen	27. 3	go out to the field, and hunt *g* for me.

GAP

Neh	6. 1	the wall and there was no *g* left in it

GARDEN

Gen	2. 8	God planted a *g* in Eden, in the east;
	13.10	everywhere like the *g* of the LORD,
Song	4.12	A *g* locked is my sister, my bride, a *g*
Isa	1.30	leaf withers, and like a *g* without water.
Ezek	28.13	You were in Eden, the *g* of God; every
	31. 8	The cedars in the *g* of God could not
	36.35	desolate has become like the *g* of Eden;
Joel	2. 3	them the land is like the *g* of Eden,
Jn	19.41	where he was crucified, and in the *g*

GARDENER

Jn	20.15	Supposing him to be the *g*, she said to

GARLAND

Isa	28. 1	the proud *g* of the drunkards of
	28. 5	the LORD of hosts will be a *g* of glory,

GARLIC

Num	11. 5	the leeks, the onions, and the *g*;

GARMENT (GARMENTS)

Gen	3.21	God made *g* of skins for the man and
	39.13	saw that he had left his *g* in her hand,
Deut	22. 5	nor shall a man put on a woman's *g*;
Job	13.28	rotten thing, like a *g* that is moth-eaten.
Prov	20.16	Take the *g* of the one who has given
Eccl	9. 8	Let your *g* be always white; do not let
Song	5. 3	I had put off my *g*, how could I put it
Lk	5.36	"No one tears a piece from a new *g* and

GATE (GATES)

Neh	2.13	down and its *g* that had been destroyed
Job	38.17	Have the *g* of death been revealed to
Ps	24. 7	Lift up your heads, O *g*! and be lifted
	122. 2	standing within your *g*, O Jerusalem.
Isa	26. 2	Open the *g*, so that the righteous nation
Mk	13.29	you know that he is near, at the very *g*.
Jn	10. 7	I tell you, I am the *g* for the sheep.
	10. 9	I am the *g*; whoever enters by me will
Heb	13.12	Jesus also suffered outside the city *g* in

GATEWAY

Gen	19. 1	Lot was sitting in the *g* of Sodom.

GATHER (GATHERED GATHERING GATHERS)

Gen	1. 9	"Let the waters . . . be *g* together into
	41.35	Let them *g* all the food of these good

Ex	16.16	"*G* as much of it as each of you needs,
Num	15.32	found a man *g* sticks on the sabbath
Deut	30. 4	there the LORD your God will *g* you,
Ps	106. 47	God, and *g* us from among the nations,
	107. 3	and *g* in from the lands, from the east
Prov	10. 5	A child who *g* in summer is prudent,
Eccl	2. 8	I also *g* for myself silver and gold and
Isa	49. 5	him, and that Israel might be *g* to him,
	56. 8	who *g* the outcasts of Israel, I will
Jer	4. 5	and say, "*G* together, and let us go
	9.22	the reaper, and no one shall *g* them."
	23. 3	I myself will *g* the remnant of my flock
	29.14	*g* you from all the nations and all the
	31.10	who scattered Israel will *g* him, and will
	32.37	I am going to *g* them from all the lands
Ezek	22.19	dross, I will *g* you into the midst of
Joel	3.11	nations all around, *g* yourselves there.
Mic	7. 1	who, after the summer fruit has been *g*,
Zeph	3.19	I will save the lame and *g* the outcast,
Mt	12.30	whoever does not *g* with me scatters.
	18.20	two or three are *g* in my name, I am
Mk	13.27	and *g* his elect from the four winds,
Lk	11.23	whoever does not *g* with me scatters.
	13.34	I have *g* your children together as a hen
Jn	6.12	"*G* up the fragments left over, so that
	11.52	to *g* into one the dispersed children of
Eph	1.10	of time, to *g* up all things in him,

GAZA

Gen	10.19	extended from Sidon . . . as far as *G*,
Judg	1.18	Judah took *G* with its territory,
	16. 1	Samson went to *G*, where he saw a
Zech	9. 5	shall see it and be afraid; *G* too,
Acts	8.26	that goes down from Jerusalem to *G*."

GENEALOGY (GENEALOGIES)

Mt	1. 1	An account of the *g* of Jesus the
1 Tim	1. 4	with myths and endless *g* that promote
Heb	7. 3	father, without mother, without *g*,

GENERATION (GENERATIONS)

Gen	2. 4	are the *g* of the heavens and the earth
Ps	100. 5	forever, and his faithfulness to all *g*.
Eccl	1. 4	A *g* goes, and a *g* comes, but the earth
Mt	12.39	evil and adulterous *g* asks for a sign,
Mk	8.38	words in this adulterous and sinful *g*,

GENEROUS (GENEROUSLY)

Ps	112. 5	It is well with those who deal *g* and
Acts	2.46	ate their food with glad and *g* hearts,
2 Cor	8. 9	For you know the *g* act of our Lord
1 Tim	6.18	good, to be rich in good works, *g*, and

GENTILE (GENTILES)

Mt	10. 5	"Go nowhere among the *G*, and enter
Mk	7.26	the woman was a *G*, of Syrophoenician
Acts	4.25	'Why did the *G* rage, and the peoples
	11.18	even to the *G* the repentance that leads
Gal	3. 8	that God would justify the *G* by faith,

GENTLE

Mt	11.29	I am *g* and humble in heart, and you
1 Thess	2. 7	we were *g* among you, like a nurse
Titus	3. 2	avoid quarrelling, to be *g*, and to show
1 Pet	3. 4	lasting beauty of a *g* and quiet spirit,

GENTLENESS

1 Cor	4.21	a stick, or with love in a spirit of *g*?
2 Cor	10. 1	you by the meekness and *g* of Christ—
Gal	6. 1	restore such a one in a spirit of *g*.
Eph	4. 2	called, with all humility and *g*, with

GENUINENESS

1 Pet	1. 7	so that the *g* of your faith, —being more

GET (GETTING GOT)

Lk	15.27	he has *g* him back safe and sound.'
	18.30	who will not *g* back very much more in
	23.41	we are *g* what we deserve for our deeds,

GETHSEMANE

Mt	26.36 went with them to a place called *G*;
Mk	14.32 They went a place which was called *G*;

GHOST

Mt	14.26 they were terrified, saying, "It is a *g*!"
Mk	6.49 on the sea, they thought it was a *g*,
Lk	24.37 and thought that they were seeing a *g*.

GIBEAH

Judg	19.12 of Israel; but we will continue on to *G*."
1 Sam	10.26 Saul also went to his home at *G*, and
	14.16 Saul's lookouts in *G* of Benjamin were
Isa	10.29 Ramah trembles, *G* of Saul has fled.

GIDEON

Judg	6.11 as his son *G* was beating out wheat in
	7. 1 (that is, *G*) and all the troops that were
	7.19 *G* and the hundred who were with him
	8. 4 Then *G* came to the Jordan and crossed
	8.23 *G* said to them, "I will not rule over
	8.32 *G* the son of Joash died at a good old
Heb	11.32 time would fail me to tell of *G*, Barak,

GIFT (GIFTS)

Gen	33.11 Please accept my *g* that I brought you,
Num	8.19 I have given the Levites as a *g* to Aaron
1 Sam	2.20 by this woman for the *g* that she made
Ps	45.12 of Tyre will seek your favor with *g*,
	68.18 receiving *g* among the people, even
	68.29 at Jerusalem kings bear *g* to you.
	72.10 the kings of Sheba and Seba bring *g*.
Prov	18.16 A *g* opens doors; it gives access to the
	21.14 A *g* in secret averts anger; and a
Eccl	3.13 God's *g* that all should eat and drink
Isa	1.23 Everyone loves a bribe and runs after *g*.
Mt	7.11 If you . . . know how to give good *g* to
Lk	11.13 who are evil, know how to give good *g*
	21. 1 people putting their *g* into the treasury;
Acts	2.38 you will receive the *g* of the Holy Spirit.
	8.20 you could obtain *g* of God with money!
	11.17 then God gave them the same *g* that he
Rom	4. 4 wages are not reckoned as a *g* but as
	6.23 but the free *g* of God is eternal life in
	12. 6 We have *g* that differ according to the
1 Cor	7. each has a particular *g* from God, one
	12. 4 there are varieties of *g*, but the same
	14. 1 love and strive for the spiritual *g*,
	16. 3 with letters to take your *g* to Jerusalem.
2 Cor	9.15 be to God for his indescribable *g*!
Eph	3. 7 according to the *g* of God's grace
	4. 7 according to the measure of Christ's *g*.
Phil	4.17 Not that I seek the *g*; but I seek the
1 Tim	4.14 Do not neglect the *g* that is in you,
Heb	2. 4 and by *g* of the Holy Spirit, distributed
1 Pet	4.10 serve one another with whatever *g* each

GILEAD

Gen	31.21 his face toward the hill country of *G*.
Deut	3.15 To Machir I gave *G*.
	34. 1 him the whole land: *G* as far as Dan,
Josh	12. 2 of the Ammonites, that is, half of *G*,
Ps	60. 7 *G* is mine, and Manasseh is mine;
Jer	8.22 Is there no balm in *G*? Is there no

GILGAL

Josh	4.19 they camped in *G* on the east border of
	10. 9 having marched up all night from *G*.
1 Sam	7.16 on a circuit year by year to Bethel, *G*,
	13. 4 were called out to join Saul at *G*.
Am	4. 4 to *G*—and multiply transgression;

GIRD (GIRDED)

Ex	29. 5 and *g* him with the decorated band of
2 Sam	22.40 For you *g* me with strength for the
Ps	45. 3 *G* your sword on your thigh, O mighty

GIRL (GIRLS GIRL'S)

Judg	19. 4 the *g* father, made him stay, and he
2 Kings	5. 2 had taken a young *g* captive from the
Ps	68.25 between them *g* playing tambourines:
Prov	30.19 seas, and the way of a man with a *g*.
Zech	8. 5 city shall be of boys and *g* playing in its
Mt	9.24 away; for the *g* is not dead but sleeping."

GIVE

Gen	13.15 all the land that you see I will *g* to you
Ex	22.29 firstborn of your sons you shall *g* to me.
	30.15 *g* more, and the poor shall not *g* less,
Deut	1.35 the good land which I swore to *g* to
	6.10 to Jacob, to *g* you—a land with fine,
	28.65 Lord will *g* you a trembling heart,
Judg	8. 5 "Please *g* some loaves of bread to my
1 Sam	28.19 the Lord will *g* Israel along with you
2 Kings	12.11 They would *g* the money that was
Ps	16.10 you do not *g* me up to Sheol, or let
	105. 11 "To you I will *g* the land of Canaan as
	119. 34 *G* me understanding, that I may keep
Prov	21.26 covet, but the righteous *g* and do not
	23.26 My child, *g* me your heart, and let your
Hos	11. 8 How can I *g* you up, Ephraim? How can
Mt	6.11 *G* us this day our daily bread.
	14.16 go away; you *g* them something to eat."
	16.19 I *g* you the keys of the kingdom of
	22.21 "*G* therefore to the emperor the things
Mk	6.37 them, "You *g* them something to eat."
	12.17 them, "*G* to the emperor the things that
Lk	6.38 *g*, and it will be given to you. A good
	14.33 my disciple if you do not *g* up all of
	20.25 "Then *g* to the emperor the things that
Jn	4. 7 and Jesus said to her, "*G* me a drink."
	6.34 said to him, "Sir, *g* us this bread always."
	10.28 I *g* them eternal life, and they will never
	14.16 he will *g* you another Advocate, to be
Acts	20.35 said, 'It is more blessed to *g* than to
Rom	8.32 will he not with him also *g* us
1 Cor	7. 3 husband should *g* to his wife her
Eph	1.17 of glory, may *g* you a spirit of wisdom

GIVES (GAVE GIVEN GIVING)

Num	21.34 of him, for I have *g* him into your hand,
Deut	2.33 our God *g* him over to us; and we
2 Chr	13.16 and God *g* them into their hands.
Judg	16.23 "Our god has *g* Samson our enemy into
Job	1.21 the Lord *g*, and the Lord has taken
	35.10 is God my Maker, who *g* strength
Ps	37.21 the righteous are generous and keep *g*;
	68.11 The Lord *g* the command; great is the
	136. 25 who *g* food to all flesh, for his steadfast
Prov	2. 6 For the Lord *g* wisdom; from his mouth
	12.26 The righteous *g* good advice to friends,
	28.27 Whoever *g* to the poor lack nothing, but
Eccl	2.26 the one who pleases him God *g* wisdom
	12. 7 and the breath returns to God who *g* it.
Mt	13.12 For to those who have, more will be *g*,
	15. 5 might have had from me is *g* to God,'
Mk	4.25 For those who have, more will be *g*; and
Lk	8.18 to those who have, more will be *g*; and
	12.48 whom much has been *g*, much will be
Jn	5.22 one but has *g* all judgment to the Son,
2 Cor	9. 9 "He scatters abroad, he *g* to the poor;
Gal	1. 4 Christ, who *g* himself for our sins to set
	2.20 who loved me and *g* himself for me.
Phil	4.15 shared with me in the matter of *g*
1 Jn	3.24 in us, by the Spirit that he has *g* us.

GLAD

Ps	9. 2 I will be *g* and exult in you; I will sing
	40.16 may all who seek you rejoice and be *g*
	46. 4 a river whose streams make *g* the city of
	105. 38 Egypt was *g* when they departed, for
	122. 1 I was *g* when they said to me, "Let us
Prov	15.13 A *g* heart makes a cheerful
Isa	25. 9 let us be *g* and rejoice in his salvation.

GLADNESS

Isa 65.18 But be g and rejoice forever in what I
Phi1 2.17 of your faith, I am g and rejoice with all

GLADNESS

Esth 9.19 of Adar as a day of g and feasting,
Ps 4. 7 You have put more g in my heart more
 100. 2 Worship the LORD with g; come into his
Isa 16.10 Joy and g are taken away from the
 61. 3 ashes, the oil of g instead of mourning,
Jer 7.34 to an end the sound of mirth and g,

GLORIFY (GLORIFIED)

Ezra 7.27 of the king to g the house of the LORD
Ps 50.15 I will deliver you, and you shall g me."
Isa 44.23 redeemed Jacob, and will be g in Israel.
 49. 3 my servant, Israel, in whom I will be g."
 55. 5 the Holy One of Israel, for he has g you.
 60. 7 my altar, and I will g my glorious house.
Lk 5.26 they g God and were filled with awe,
 7.16 they g God, saying, "A great prophet has
Jn 7.39 no Spirit, because Jesus was not yet g.
 12.28 Father, g your name." Then a voice came
 13.31 said, "Now the Son of Man has been g
 14.13 so that the Father may be g in the Son.
 15. 8 Father is g by this, that you bear much
 17. 1 the hour has come; g your Son so that
Rom 11.13 apostle to the Gentiles. I g my ministry
1 Cor 6.20 a price; therefore g God in your body.
Rev 15. 4 who will not fear and g your name?

GLORIOUS (GLORIOUSLY)

Ps 87. 3 G things are spoken of you, O city of
Isa 12. 5 praises to the LORD, for he has done g;

GLORY

Ex 16. 7 you shall see the g of the LORD, because
 24.16 The g of the LORD settled on Mount
 40.34 the g of the LORD filled the tabernacle,
Num 14.21 shall be filled with the g of the LORD
 16.19 the g of the LORD appeared to the whole
Deut 5.24 God has shown us his g and greatness,
Josh 7.19 give g to the LORD God of Israel and
1 Sam 4.21 "The g has departed from Israel,"
 15.29 the G of Israel will not recant or change
1 Kings 8.11 for the g of the LORD filled the house of
1 Chr 16.24 Declare his g among the nations, his
 29.11 are the greatness, the power, the g,
2 Chr 5.14 for the g of the LORD filled the house of
Ps 8. 1 You have set your g above the heavens.
 19. 1 heavens are telling the g of God; and
 21. 5 His g is great through your help;
 29. 1 beings, ascribe to the LORD g and
 97. 6 and all the peoples behold his g.
 106. 47 to your holy name and g in your praise.
 115. 1 but to your name give g, for the sake of
Isa 24.15 Therefore in the east give g to the LORD;
 35. 2 The g of Lebanon shall be given to it,
 35. 2 They shall see the g of the LORD, the
 40. 5 the g of the LORD shall be revealed,
 42. 8 my I give to no other, nor my praise
Jer 33. 9 a g before all the nations of the earth
Ezek 1.28 of the likeness of the g of the LORD.
 3.12 me up, and as the g of the LORD rose
 3.23 and the g of the LORD stood there, like
 9. 3 the g of the God of Israel had gone up
 10.18 the g of the LORD went out from the
 28.22 O Sidon, and I will gain in your midst
 39.21 I will display my g among the nations;
 43. 2 And there, the g of the God of Israel
Dan 7.14 was given dominion and g and kingship,
Hab 2.14 the knowledge of the g of the LORD,
Mt 24.30 of heaven' with power and great g.
Lk 2.14 "G to God in the highest heaven , and
Jn 5.41 I do accept g from human beings.
 7.18 speak on their own seek their own g;
 8.50 Yet I do not seek my own g; there is
 11. 4 lead to death; rather it is for God's g,

Jn 12.43 for they loved human g more than the g
 17. 5 with the g that I had in your presence
 17.24 to see my g which you have given me
Rom 1.23 exchanged the g of the immortal God
 3.23 sinned and fall short of the g of God;
 8.18 not worth comparing with the g about
 11.36 things. To him be the g forever. Amen.
1 Cor 15.43 It is sown in dishonor, it is raised in g.
2 Cor 3.11 more has the permanent come in g.
Phil 3.21 may be conformed to the body of his g,
Col 1.27 which is Christ in you, the hope of g.
2 Thess 1. 9 of the Lord and from the g of his might,
 2.14 that you may obtain the g of our Lord
2 Pet 1. 3 of him who called by his own g
Rev 7.12 "Amen! Blessing and g and wisdom and
 14. 7 "Fear God and give him g, for the hour

GNASH (GNASHED GNASHING)

Job 16. 9 and hated me; he has g his teeth at me;
Ps 35.16 and more, g at me with their teeth.
Lam 2.16 they hiss, they g their teeth, they cry:
Mt 24.51 there will be weeping and g of teeth.

GNAT (GNATS)

Ex 8.16 become g throughout the whole land
Mt 23.24 guides, You strain out a g but swallow

GO (GOING)

Gen 7. 1 "G into the ark, you and all your
 24.58 "Will you g with this man?" She said, "I
Ex 5. 1 'Let my people g, so that they may
 9.13 'Let my people g, so that they may
Num 14. 4 choose a captain, and g back to Egypt."
2 Kings 5.10 "G, wash in the Jordan seven times, and
Ps 143. 8 Teach me the way I should g, for to you
Eccl 5.15 they shall g again, naked as they came,
Isa 2. 3 "Come, let us g up to the mountain of
 6. 9 "G, and say to this people: 'Keep
 48.20 G out from Babylon, flee from Chaldea,
Jer 42. 3 show us where we should g and what
Hos 11.10 They shall g after the LORD, who roars
Am 7.15 LORD said to me, 'G, prophesy to my
Mic 4. 2 "Come, let us g up to the mountain of
Mal 3.14 or by g about as mourners before the
Mt 6. 6 whenever you pray, g into your room
 28. 7 Then g quickly and tell his disciples,
 28.19 G therefore and make disciples of all
Mk 5.19 "G home to your friends, and tell them
 16. 7 But g, tell his disciples and Peter that
 16.15n "G into all the world and proclaim the
Lk 9.60 as for you, g and proclaim the kingdom
Jn 6.68 "Lord, to whom can we g? You have the

GOADS

Eccl 12.11 sayings of the wise are like g, and like
Acts 26.14 me? It hurts you to kick against the g.'

GOAL

Phil 3.12 this or have already reached the g;

GOAT-DEMONS

Lev 17. 7 no longer offer their sacrifices for g,
2 Chr 11.15 for the high places, and for the g,
Isa 34.14 with hyenas, g shall call to each other;

GOD

Gen 1. 1 when G created the heavens and
 3. 5 and you will be like G, knowing good
 8. 1 G remembered Noah and all the wild
 50.25 "When G comes to you, you shall carry
Ex 2.24 G heard their groaning, and G
 13.17 G did not lead them by way of the land
Josh 10.42 the LORD G of Israel fought for Israel.
2 Sam 7.23 on earth whose G went to redeem it as
1 Kings 8.28 O LORD my G, heeding the cry and the
 11.23 G raised up another adversary against
2 Chr 36.15 The LORD, the G of their ancestors, sent
 36.16 they kept mocking the messengers of G,

Ps	8.	5 have made them a little lower than *G*,
	22.	1 *G*, my *G*, why have you forsaken me?
Isa	12.	2 the LORD *G* is my strength and my
	26.	4 LORD *G* you have an everlasting rock.
	40.	1 O comfort my people, says your *G*.
Dan	3.	25 the fourth has the appearance of a *g*."
Hag	1.	14 the house of the LORD of hosts, their *G*,
Mal	3.	8 Will anyone rob *G*? Yet you are robbing
Mk	15.	34 "My *G*, my *G*, why have you forsaken
Jn	20.	28 answered him. "My Lord and my *G*!"
Acts	2.	32 This Jesus *G* raised up, and of that all
	28.	6 minds and began to say that he was a *g*.
1 Cor	14.	33 for *G* is not a *G* of disorder but of
2 Cor	4.	4 case the *g* of this world has blinded
Eph	2.	4 But *G*, who is rich in mercy, out of the
	2.	8 your own doing; it is the gift of *G*—
	4.	24 created according to the likeness of *G*
	5.	1 be imitators of *G*, as beloved children,
Titus	2.	11 the grace of *G* has appeared, bringing
	2.	13 the glory of our great *G* and Savior
Rev	21.	22 its temple is the Lord *G* the Almighty
	22.	1 as crystal, flowing from the throne of *G*

GODLESS

Job	8.	13 forget God; hope of the *g* shall perish.
	13.	16 that the *g* shall not come before him.
	20.	5 the joy of the *g* is but for a moment?
	27.	8 For what is the hope of the *g* when God
	36.	13 "The *g* in heart cherish anger; they do
Prov	11.	9 the *g* would destroy their neighbors,
Isa	9.	17 for everyone was *g* and an evildoer, and
	10.	6 Against a *g* nation I send him, and
	33.	14 are afraid; trembling has seized the *g*:

GODLINESS

1 Tim	6.	3 teaching that is in accordance with *g*,
	6.	5 imagining that *g* is a means of gain.
2 Tim	3.	5 holding the outward form of *g* but
2 Pet	1.	7 *g* with mutual affection, and mutual

GODLY

Ps	12.	1 there is no longer anyone who is *g*; the
	52.	1 one, of mischief done against the *g*?
2 Tim	3.	12 all who want to live a *g* life in Christ

GODS

Gen	31.	19 Rachel stole her father's household *g*.
	31.	30 father's house, why did you steal my *g*?"
	31.	34 Rachel had taken the household *g* and
1 Kings	20.	23 "Their *g* are *g* of the hills, and so they
Ps	82.	6 "You are *g*, children of the Most High,
Isa	37.	19 have hurled their *g* into the fire; though
Jer	5.	19 served foreign *g* in your land, so you
	16.	20 Can mortals make for themselves *g*?
Dan	4.	8 is endowed with a spirit of the holy *g*—
Acts	7.	40 saying to Aaron, "Make *g* for us who
1 Cor	8.	5 though there may be so-called *g* in

GOLD

Gen	2.	11 whole land of Havilah, where there is *g*;
Num	31.	52 all the *g* of the offering that they
Job	22.	25 if the Almighty is your *g* and your
	31.	24 "If I have made *g* my trust, or called
Ps	19.	10 More to be desired are they than *g*,
Prov	8.	10 and knowledge rather than choice *g*;
	25.	11 spoken is like apples of *g* in a setting of
Isa	60.	6 They shall bring *g* and frankincense,
Lam	4.	1 How the *g* has grown dim, how the pure
Dan	2.	32 head of that statue was of fine *g*, its
Acts	3.	6 "I have no silver and *g*, but what I have
Rev	21.	18 while the city is pure *g*, clear as glass.

GOLGOTHA

Mt	27.	33 they came to a place called *G* (which
Mk	15.	22 brought Jesus to the place called *G*
Jn	19.	17 the Skull, which in Hebrew is called *G*.

GOLIATH

1 Sam	17.	4 of the Philistines, a champion named *G*,
	17.	23 the Philistine of Gath, *G* by name, came
	21.	9 "The sword of *G* the Philistine, whom

GOMORRAH

Gen	13.	10 before the LORD had destroyed . . . *G*.
	14.	10 as kings of Sodom and *G* fled, some fell
	19.	24 the LORD rained on . . . *G* sulfur and fire
Deut	29.	23 like the destruction of Sodom and *G*,
Isa	1.	9 been like Sodom, and become like *G*.
Mt	10.	15 of Sodom and *G* than for that town.
Jude		6 Likewise, Sodom and *G* and the

GOOD

Gen	1.	4 God saw that the light was *g*; and God
	1.	31 he had made, and indeed, it was very *g*.
Deut	1.	23 The plan seemed *g* to me, and I
1 Chr	19.	13 may the LORD do what seems *g* to him."
Ps	14.	3 perverse; there is no one that does *g*,
	16.	2 my Lord; I have no *g* apart from you."
	25.	8 *G* and upright is the LORD; therefore he
	37.	27 Depart from evil, and do *g*; so you shall
	92.	1 It is *g* to give thanks to the LORD, to
133.		1 *g* and pleasant it is when kindred live
Prov	31.	12 She does him *g*, and not harm, all the
Eccl	7.	1 *g* name is better than precious
Isa	5.	20 you who call evil *g* and *g* evil, who put
	48.	17 God, who teaches you for your own *g*,
Hos	14.	2 accept that which is *g*, and we will offer
Am	5.	15 Hate evil, and love *g*, and establish
Mic	3.	2 you who hate the *g* and love the evil,
Mt	13.	8 Other seeds fell on *g* soil and brought
	13.	48 put the *g* into baskets but threw out the
	25.	21 "Well done, *g* and trustworthy slave; you
Mk	4.	8 Other seed fell into *g* soil and brought
	10.	18 call me *g*? No one is but God alone.
Lk	6.	9 is it lawful to do *g* or to do harm on the
	8.	8 Some fell into *g* soil, and when it grew,
	9.	33 "Master, it is *g* for us to be here; let us
Jn	1.	46 "Can anything *g* come out of Nazareth?"
Rom	3.	8 "Let us do evil so that *g* may come?"
	7.	18 I know that nothing *g* dwells within me,
	8.	28 all things work together for *g* for those
	14.	16 do not let your *g* be spoken of as evil.
	16.	19 I want you to be wise in what is *g* and
1 Pet	2.	3 you have tasted that the Lord is *g*.

GOOD NEWS

Mt	26.	13 wherever this *g* is proclaimed in the
Mk	1.	1 The beginning of the *g* of Jesus Christ,
	1.	14 into Galilee, proclaiming the *g* of God,
	13.	10 the *g* must first be preached to all
Acts	14.	7 there they continued proclaiming the *g*.
	20.	24 Jesus, to testify to the *g* of God's grace.
1 Cor	15.	1 of the *g* that I proclaimed to you, which
2 Cor	10.	14 all the way to you with the *g* of Christ.

GOODNESS

Ps	23.	6 Surely *g* and mercy shall follow me all
	31.	19 O how abundant is your *g*, that you
Zech	9.	17 what *g* and beauty are his! Grain shall
2 Pet	1.	5 support your faith with *g*, and *g* with

GOSPEL

Mt	24.	14n this *g* of the kingdom will be
	26.	13n wherever this *g* is proclaimed in the
Mk	1.	1n The beginning of the *g* of Jesus Christ,
	1.	14n into Galilee, proclaiming the *g* of God,
	13.	10n the *g* must first be preached to all
	14.	9n wherever the *g* is proclaimed in the
	16.	15n world and proclaim the *g* to the whole
Rom	1.	1 an apostle, set apart for the *g* of God,
	1.	16 I am not ashamed of the *g*; it is the
	2.	16 day when, according to my *g*, God,
	16.	25 to strengthen you according to my *g*
2 Cor	9.	13 to the confession of the *g* of Christ

Gal	1.	6 and are turning to a different *g*—
	1.11	the *g* that was proclaimed by me is not
	2.	7 with the *g* for the uncircumcised,
Eph	1.13	word of truth, the *g* of your salvation,
	6.15	you ready to proclaim the *g* of peace;
Phil	1.27	your life in a manner worthy of the *g*
Col	1.23	from the hope promised by the *g*
1 Thess	1.	5 of the *g* came to you not in word only,
1 Tim	1.11	teaching that conforms to the glorious *g*
2 Tim	1.	8 but join with me in suffering for the *g*,
1 Pet	4.	6 *g* was proclaimed even to the dead, so
Rev	14.	6 angel . . . with an eternal *g* to proclaim

GOSSIP (GOSSIPS)

Prov	11.13	A *g* goes about telling secrets, but on
	20.19	A *g* reveals secrets; therefore do not
Rom	1.29	strife, deceit, craftiness, they are *g*,
1 Tim	5.13	they are not merely idle, but also *g* and

GOVERNOR (GOVERNORS)

Gen	42.	6 Joseph was *g* over the land; it was he
Neh	5.14	I was appointed to be their *g* in the
Jer	40.	7 Gedaliah son of Ahikam *g* in the
Mal	1.	8 wrong? Try presenting that to your *g*;
Mk	13.	9 you will stand before *g* and kings

GRACE

Ps	45.	2 of men; *g* is poured upon your lips;
Jer	31.	2 found *g* in the wilderness; when Israel
Zech	4.	7 top stone amid shouts of '*G*, *g* to it!' "
Jn	1.14	a father's only son, full of *g* and truth.
Acts	4.33	Jesus, and great *g* was upon them all.
	13.43	urged them to continue in the *g* of God.
	14.	3 testified to the word of his *g*, by
	14.26	commended to the *g* of God for the
	15.40	commending him to the *g* of the Lord.
Rom	1.	5 through whom we have received *g* and
	3.24	they are now justified by his *g* as a gift,
	4.16	in order that the promise may rest on *g*
	5.	2 access to this *g* in which we stand,
	5.15	much more surely have the *g* of God
	5.20	but where sin increased, *g* abounded all
	6.	1 we continue in sin in order that *g*
	15.15	because of the *g* given me by God
1 Cor	3.10	According to the *g* of God given to me,
	15.10	by the *g* of God I am what I am, and
2 Cor	4.15	so that *g*, as it extends to more and
	12.	9 "My *g* is sufficient for you, for power is
	13.13	The *g* of the Lord Jesus Christ, the love
Gal	1.	6 the one who called you in the *g*
	5.	4 Christ; you have fallen away from *g*.
Eph	1.	7 according to the riches of his *g*
	2.	7 show the immeasurable riches of his *g*
2 Thess	2.16	and through *g* gave us eternal comfort
1 Tim	1.14	the *g* of our Lord overflowed for me
Titus	2.11	For the *g* of God has appeared, bringing
	3.	7 so that, having been justified by his *g*,
Heb	4.16	approach the throne of *g* with boldness,
	13.	9 for the heart to be strengthened by *g*,
Jas	4.	6 But he gives all the more *g*; therefore it
1 Pet	4.10	Like good stewards of the manifold *g* of
	5.	5 the proud, but gives *g* to the humble."
	5.10	God of all *g*, who has called you to his
2 Pet	3.18	grow in the *g* and knowledge of our
Jude		4 who pervert the *g* of our God into

GRACEFUL

Song	7.	1 How *g* are your feet in sandals, O

GRACIOUS

Num	6.25	face shine upon you, and be *g* to you;
2 Kings	13.23	the Lord was *g* to them and had
Ps	67.	1 May God be *g* to us and bless us, and
	103.	8 The Lord is merciful and *g*, slow to
	145.	8 The Lord is *g* and merciful, slow to
	147.	1 praises to our God; for he is *g*, and a
Prov	22.11	love a pure heart and are *g* in speech
Isa	33.	2 O Lord, be *g* to us; we wait for you. Be

Joel	2.13	your God, for he is *g* and merciful,
Lk	4.22	were amazed at the *g* words that came
Col	4.	6 Let your speech always be *g*, seasoned

GRAIN

Prov	14.	4 Where there are no oxen, there is no *g*;
Mk	4.28	the head, then the full *g* in the head.
Lk	6.	1 his disciples plucked some heads of *g*,
Acts	7.12	Jacob heard that there was *g* in Egypt,
1 Cor	15.37	perhaps of wheat or of some other *g*.

GRAIN OFFERING

Lev	2.	1 When anyone brings a *g* to the Lord,
	6.14	This is the ritual of the *g*: The sons of

GRAINFIELDS

Mt	12.	1 Jesus through the *g* on the sabbath; his

GRANT (GRANTED)

1 Sam	1.17	God of Israel *g* your petition you have
2 Chr	9.12	Solomon *g* to the queen of Sheba every
Prov	10.24	but the desire of the righteous will be *g*.
Acts	27.24	God has *g* safety to all those who are

GRAPES

Num	13.23	a branch with a single cluster of *g*,
Isa	5.	2 he expected it to yield *g*, but it yielded
Jer	31.29	say: "The parents have eaten sour *g*,
Ezek	18.	2 parents have eaten sour *g*, and the
Hos	9.10	Like *g* in the wilderness, I found Israel.
Am	9.13	reaps, and the treader of *g* the one who

GRASS

Ps	37.	2 they will soon fade like the *g*, and
	103.	15 As for mortals, their days are like *g*;
Isa	5.24	as dry *g* sinks down in the flame, so
	40.	6 All people are *g*, and their constancy is
Dan	4.33	from human society, ate *g* like oxen,
Lk	12.28	if God so clothes the *g* of the field,
1 Pet	1.24	"All flesh is like *g* and all its glory like
Rev	8.	7 up, and all green *g* was burnt up.

GRASSHOPPERS

Num	13.33	to ourselves we seemed like *g*, and so
Isa	40.22	the earth, and its inhabitants are like *g*;
Nah	3.17	Your guards are like *g*, your scribes like

GRAVE (GRAVES)

Ps	49.14	straight to the *g* they descend, and their
Ezek	32.23	Its company is all around its *g*, all of
	37.12	your *g*, and bring you up from your *g*,
Lk	11.44	you are like unmarked *g*, and people
Jn	5.28	all who are in their *g* will hear his voice

GREAT (GREATER GREATEST)

2 Sam	5.10	David became *g* and *g*, for the Lord, the
	7.22	you are *g*, O Lord God; for there is no
1 Chr	11.	9 David became *g* and *g*, for the Lord of
	17.19	you have done all these *g* deeds,
Job	37.23	find him; he is *g* in power and justice,
Ps	40.16	say continually, "*G* is the Lord!"
	70.	4 your salvation say evermore, "God is *g*!"
Eccl	2.	9 So I became *g* and surpassed all who
Jer	45.	5 you, do you seek *g* things for yourself?
Joel	2.21	rejoice, for the Lord has done *g* things!
Mal	1.	5 this, and you shall say, "*G* is the Lord
Mt	5.19	them will be called *g* in the kingdom
	12.	6 something *g* than the temple is here.
	12.42	see, something *g* than Solomon is here.
	15.28	"Woman, *g* is your faith! Let it be done
	18.	1 asked, "Who is the *g* in the kingdom
Mk	9.34	argued with one another who was the *g*.
Lk	1.15	he will be *g* in the sight of the Lord. He
	22.24	of them was to be regarded as the *g*.
1 Cor	13.13	these three; and the *g* of these is love.
Rev	2.19	that your last works are *g* than the first.
	18.16	"Alas, alas, the *g* city, clothed in fine

GREATNESS

Deut	3.24	only begun to show your servant your *g*
Ps	145.	3 to be praised; his *g* is unsearchable.
	150.	2 him according to his surpassing *g*!
Ezek	31.	2 hordes: Whom are you like in your *g*?
	38.23	I will display my *g* and my holiness and

GREECE

Dan	8.21	The male goat is the king of *G*, and the
	11.	2 stir up all against the kingdom of *G*.
Zech	9.13	sons, O Zion, against your sons, O *G*,
Acts	20.	2 he came to *G*, where he stayed for three

GREED

Lk	12.15	Be on your guard against all kinds of *g*;
1 Thess	2.	5 words of flattery or with a pretext for *g*;
2 Pet	2.	3 in their *g* they will exploit you with
	2.14	souls. They have hearts trained in *g*.

GREEDY

1 Sam	2.29	"Why then look with *g* eye at my
Prov	1.19	is the end of all who are *g* for gain;
Jer	6.13	of them, everyone is *g* for unjust gain;
	8.10	greatest everyone is *g* for unjust gain;
1 Cor	5.11	or sister who is sexually immoral or *g*,
	6.10	thieves, the *g*, drunkards, revilers,
Eph	5.	5 one who is *g* (that is, an idolater), has

GREEK (GREEKS)

Jn	12.20	to worship at the festival were some *G*.
Acts	14.	1 of both Jews and *G* became believers.
	16.	1 was a believer; but his father was a *G*.
	19.10	of Asia, both Jews and *G* heard the
	20.21	as I testified to both Jews and to *G*
Rom	1.14	I am a debtor both to *G* and to
1 Cor	1.22	demand signs and *G* desire wisdom,

GREET (GREETED GREETING)

1 Sam	6.19	when they *g* the ark of the LORD; and he
Mt	23.	7 to be *g* with respect in the
Mk	12.38	and to be *g* with respect in the
Lk	1.29	pondered what sort of *g* this might be.
	1.41	When Elizabeth heard Mary's *g*,
	11.43	be *g* with respect in the marketplaces.
Rom	16.16	*G* one another with a holy kiss. All the
1 Cor	16.21	I, Paul, write this *g* with my own hand.
Heb	11.13	from a distance they saw and *g* them.

GRIEF

Prov	14.13	the heart is sad, and the end of joy is *g*.
	17.25	Foolish children are a *g* to their father
2 Cor	7.10	godly *g* produces a repentance that

GRIEVE (GRIEVED GRIEVING)

Gen	6.	6 on the earth, and it *g* him to his heart.
1 Sam	16.	1 "How long will you *g* over Saul? I have
Ps	78.40	the wilderness and *g* him in the desert!
Isa	63.10	But they rebelled and *g* his holy spirit!
Am	6.	6 but are not *g* over the ruin of Joseph!
Mt	14.	9 The king was *g*; yet out of regard for his
Mk	3.	5 he was *g* at their hardness of heart and
	10.22	went away *g*; for he had many
	14.34	"I am deeply *g*, even to death; remain
Eph	4.30	do not *g* the Holy Spirit of God, with
1 Thess	4.13	so that you may not *g* as others do who

GROAN (GROANING GROANS)

Ps	79.11	the *g* of the prisoners come before you;
Prov	29.	2 but when the wicked rule, the people *g*.
Ezek	30.24	of Pharaoh, and he will *g* before him
Joel	1.18	How the animals *g*! The herds of cattle
Acts	7.34	are in Egypt and have heard their *g*,

GROPE

Job	5.14	and *g* at noonday as in the night.
	12.25	They *g* in the dark without light; he
Isa	59.10	We *g* like the blind along a wall,

GROUND

Judg	16.21	shackles; and he *g* at the mill in prison.
Lk	23.22	in him no *g* for the sentence of death;
Acts	7.54	enraged and *g* their teeth at Stephen.

GROUPS

Mk	6.39	all the people to sit down in *g* on the

GROW (GREW)

1 Sam	2.21	the boy Samuel *g* up in the presence of
	3.19	As Samuel *g* up, the LORD was with him
Isa	9.	7 His authority shall *g* continually, and
	53.	2 he *g* up before him like a young plant,
Lk	1.80	The child *g* and became strong in spirit,
	2.40	The child *g* and became strong, filled
Acts	19.20	So the word of the Lord *g* mightily and

GRUMBLED

Deut	1.27	you *g* in your tents and said, "It is
Ps	106.	25 They *g* in their tents, and did not obey

GUARANTEE

2 Cor	5.	5 God, who has given us the Spirit as a *g*.

GUARD (GUARDS)

1 Sam	2.	9 He will *g* the feet of his faithful ones,
Neh	4.	9 to our God, and set a *g* as a protection
Job	7.12	the Dragon, that you set a *g* over me?
Ps	91.11	his angels concerning you to *g* you
	97.10	he *g* the lives of his faithful; he rescues
	140.	4 *G* me, O LORD, from the hands of the
	141.	3 Set a *g* over my mouth, O LORD; keep
Prov	2.11	over you; and understanding will *g* you.
	4.	6 keep you; love her, and she will *g* you.
	13.	3 Those who *g* their mouths preserve their
Eccl	5.	1 *G* your steps when you go to the house
Mt	5.25	to the judge, and the judge to the *g*,
Phil	4.	7 will *g* your hearts and your minds in
1 Tim	6.20	*g* what has been entrusted to you.

GUARDIAN (GUARDIANS)

Gal	4.	2 they remain under *g* and trustees until
1 Cor	4.15	might have ten thousand *g* in Christ,
1 Pet	2.25	to the shepherd and *g* of your souls.

GUEST (GUESTS)

Ps	39.12	For I am your passing *g*, an alien, like
Zeph	1.	7 a sacrifice, he has consecrated his *g*.
Mt	22.10	bad; so wedding hall was filled with *g*.
Lk	22.11	"Where is the *g* room, where I may eat

GUIDANCE

Job	37.12	They turn round and round by his *g*, to
Prov	11.14	Where there is no *g*, a nation falls, but
	24.	6 for by wise *g* you can wage your war,

GUIDE (GUIDED GUIDES)

Deut	32.12	the LORD alone *g* him; no foreign god
Ps	31.	3 for your name's sake lead me and *g*
	48.14	and ever. He will be our *g* forever.
	67.	4 people with equity and *g* the nations
	73.24	You *g* me with your counsel, and
	78.52	sheep, and *g* them in the wilderness
Isa	42.16	they have not known I will *g* them.
	58.11	The LORD will *g* you continually, and
Mt	15.14	if one blind person *g* another, both will
Lk	6.39	"Can a blind person *g* a blind person?
Jn	16.13	truth comes he will *g* you into all truth;
Acts	1.16	Judas, who became a *g* for those who
Rom	2.19	are sure that you are a *g* to the blind,
Gal	5.25	the Spirit, let us also be *g* by the Spirit.

GUILE

Prov	26.26	though hatred is covered with *g*, the

GUILT

Lev	4.22	"When a ruler sins, . . . and incurs *g*,
1 Chr	21.	3 this? Why should he bring *g* on Israel?"
Ps	25.11	O LORD, pardon my *g*, for it is great.

Ezek	16.49 This was the *g* of your sister Sodom:
Hos	13. 1 in Israel; but he incurred *g* through Baal
Zech	3. 9 I will remove the *g* of this land in a

GUILT OFFERING
Lev	7. 1 This is the ritual of the *g*. It is most

GUILTLESS
2 Sam	3.28 kingdom are forever *g* before the LORD
2 Cor	7.11 point you have proved yourselves *g* in

GUILTY
Lev	5. 4 know it , you shall in any of these be *g*.
Ps	68.21 of those who walk in their *g* ways.
Isa	5.23 who acquit the *g* for a bribe, and
	50. 9 who helps me; who will declare me *g*?
Jer	3 All who ate of it were held *g*; disaster
	12. 1 Why does the way of the *g* prosper?
Ezek	22. 4 have become *g* by the blood that you
Hos	4.15 O Israel, do not let Judah become *g*.
Lk	23.14 have not found this man *g* of any of

H

HABAKKUK
Hab	1. 1 The oracle that the prophet *H* saw. O
	3. 1 A prayer of the prophet *H* according to

HADES
Mt	16.18 and the gates of *H* will not prevail
Lk	16.23 In *H*, where he was being tormented, he
Acts	2.27 For you will not abandon my soul to *H*,
Rev	6. 8 was Death, and *H* followed with him;
	20.14 Death and *H* were thrown into the lake

HAGAR
Gen	16. 1 Egyptian slave-girl whose name was *H*,
	16.15 *H* bore Abram a son; and Abram named
	21. 9 Sarah saw the son of *H* the Egyptian,
	21.14 and a skin of water, and gave it to *H*,
Gal	4.24 is *H*, from Mount Sinai, bearing

HAGGAI
Ezra	5. 1 Now the prophets, *H* and Zechariah son
	6.14 the prophesying of the prophet *H*
Hag	1. 1 came by the prophet *H* to Zerubbabel
	2. 1 of the LORD came by the prophet *H*,

HAIL (HAILSTONES)
Ex	9.18 I will cause the heaviest *h* to fall that
Josh	10.11 more who died because of the *h* than

HAIR (HAIRS)
Ps	40.12 they are more than the *h* of my head,
Prov	23. 7 like a *h* in the throat, so are they. "Eat
Isa	3.24 and instead of well-set *h*, baldness:
Mt	10.30 even the *h* of your head are all counted.
Lk	7.38 her tears and to dry them with her *h*.
	12. 7 even the *h* of your head are all counted.
1 Cor	11.15 if a woman has long *h*, it is her glory?

HALLOW (HALLOWED)
Gen	2. 3 God blessed the seventh day and *h* it,
Ezek	20.20 and *h* my sabbaths that they may be a
Mt	6. 9 Our Father in heaven, *h* be your name.
Lk	11. 2 "Father, *h* be your name. Your kingdom

HAMATH
Isa	36.19 Where are the gods of *H* and Arpad?
Am	6. 2 and see; from there go to *H* the great;

HAMMER
Judg	4.21 and took a *h* in her hand, and went
1 Kings	6. 7 so that neither *h* nor axe nor any tool
Jer	23.29 like fire, says the LORD, and like a *h*
	50.23 the *h* of the whole earth is cut down

HAND (n)
Gen	9. 2 the sea; into your *h* they are delivered.
	48.17 saw that his father laid his right *h* on

Ex	3.19 you go unless compelled by a mighty *h*.
	4. 2 "What is that in your *h*?" He said, "A
	15.12 You stretched out your right *h*, the
	17.11 whenever he lowered his *h*, Amalek
Lev	4.24 lay his *h* upon the head of of the goat;
Num	21.34 of him, for I have given him into your *h*,
Deut	2.15 the LORD's own *h* was against them, to
	4.34 by war, by a mighty *h* and an
	5.15 from there with a mighty *h* and an
	26. 8 brought us out of Egypt with a mighty *h*
1 Sam	5. 6 The *h* of the LORD was heavy on the
	12.15 then the *h* of the LORD will be against
	18.17 "I will not raise a *h* against him; let the
	23.16 there he strengthened his *h* through the
2 Sam	3.18 Israel from the *h* of the Philistines
	24.14 let us fall into the *h* of the LORD, for his
1 Chr	4.10 and that your *h* might be with me, and
Ezra	7.28 I took courage, for the *h* of the LORD my
Job	8.20 person, nor take the *h* of evildoers.
	12. 9 does not know that the *h* of the LORD
	19.21 for the *h* of God has touched me!
	40.14 your own right *h* can give you victory.
Ps	31.15 My times are in your *h*; deliver me from
	32. 4 day and night your *h* was heavy on me;
	74.11 why do you keep your *h* in your bosom?
	104. 28 when you open your *h*, they are filled
	106. 10 them from the *h* of the enemy.
	118. 16 right *h* of the LORD is exalted; the right
Eccl	9. 1 their deeds are in the *h* of God; whether
	9.10 Whatever your *h* finds to do, do with
Isa	5.25 away, and his *h* is stretched out still.
	8.11 to me while his *h* was strong upon me,
	9.12 turned away; his *h* is stretched out still.
	9.17 turned away; his *h* is stretched out still.
	14.27 His *h* is stretched out, and who will
	40.12 the waters in the hollow of his *h*
	59. 1 See, the LORD's *h* is not too short to
Ezek	3.14 my spirit, the *h* of the LORD was being
	3.22 *h* of the LORD was upon me there; and
	13. 9 My *h* will be against the prophets who
	20.33 a mighty *h* and an outstretched arm,
	25.16 stretch out my *h* against the Philistines,
	33.22 *h* of the LORD had been upon me the
	37. 1 The *h* of the LORD came upon me, and
Dan	5. 5 fingers of a human *h* appeared and
Mt	3.12 His winnowing fork is in his *h*, and he
	5.30 if your right *h* causes you to sin, cut if
	6. 3 left *h* know what your right *h* is doing,
	18. 8 "If your *h* or your foot causes you to
Mk	3. 5 said to the man, "Stretch out your *h*." He
	9.43 If your *h* causes you to stumble, cut it
Lk	6. 6 man there whose right *h* was withered.
	6.10 He did so, and the *h* was restored.
Jn	20.25 of the nails and my *h* in his side, I will
Acts	11.21 The *h* of the Lord was with them, and a
	13.11 the *h* of the Lord is against you, and
1 Cor	5. 5 you are to *h* this man over to Satan for
2 Thess	3.17 Paul, write this greeting with my own *h*.

HANDS (n)
Num	27.23 he laid his *h* on him and commissioned
Job	10. 8 Your *h* fashioned and made me; and
	34.19 poor, for they are all the work of his *h*?
Ps	24. 4 who have clean *h* and pure hearts, who
	115. 7 They have *h*, but do not feel; feet, but
Prov	31.20 and reaches out her *h* to the needy.
Jer	32.28 this city into the *h* of the Chaldeans
Mt	15.20 to eat with unwashed *h* does not defile."
Mk	7. 2 his disciples were eating with defiled *h*,
Lk	15.19 son; treat me like one of your hired *h*."
	24.39 Look at my *h* and my feet; see that it is
Jn	13. 9 feet only but also my *h* and my head!"
	20.20 he showed them his *h* and his side.
	20.25 I see the mark of the nails in his *h*,
Rom	10.21 I have held out my *h* to a disobedient
2 Cor	5. 1 a house not made with *h*, eternal in the
1 Jn	1. 1 have looked at and touched with our *h*,

HANDED

Deut	3. 2 for I have *h* him over to you, along with
Mt	11.27 "All things have been *h* over to me by
	20.18 the Son of Man will be *h* over to the
	26. 2 of Man will be *h* over to be crucified.
	27. 2 led him away, and *h* him over to Pilate
Mk	15. 1 led him away and *h* him over to Pilate.
Lk	18.32 he will be *h* over to the Gentiles; and

HANDSOME

Ps	45. 2 You are the most *h* of men; grace is

HANG (HANGED HANGING HANGS HUNG)

Deut	21.23 for anyone *h* on a tree is under God's
2 Sam	17.23 set his house in order, and *h* himself;
	18.10 told Joab, "I saw Absalom *h* in an oak."
Esth	6. 4 to the king about having Mordecai *h*
	7. 9 And the king said, "*H* him on that."
Job	26. 7 the void, and *h* the earth upon nothing.
Ps	137. 2 On the willows there we *h* up our harps.
Mt	27. 5 departed; and he went and *h* himself.
Acts	10.39 put him to death by *h* him on a tree;

HANNAH

1 Sam	1. 2 two wives; the name of the one was *H*,
	1.13 *H* was praying silently; only her lips
	2. 1 *H* prayed and said, "My heart exults in
	2.21 the LORD took note of *H*; she conceived

HAPPY

Deut	24. 5 at home one year, to be *h* with the wife
	33.29 *H* are you, O Israel! Who is like you, a
1 Kings	10. 8 *H* are your wives! *H* are these your
2 Chr	9. 7 *H* are your people! *H* are these your
Job	5.17 "How *h* is the one whom God reproves;
Ps	1. 1 *H* are those who do not follow the
	32. 1 *H* are those whose transgression is
	34. 8 is good; *h* are those who take refuge
	41. 1 *H* are those who consider the poor; the
	127. 5 *H* is the man who has his quiver full of
	144. 15 *H* are the people whose God is the
	146. 5 *H* are those whose help is the God of
Prov	3.13 *H* are those who find wisdom, and
	8.32 to me: *h* are those who keep my ways.
	28.14 *H* is the one who is never without fear,
	31.28 Her children rise up and call her *h*; her
Mal	3.15 we count the arrogant *h*; evildoers not

HARD (HARDER)

Jer	32.17 arm! Nothing is too *h* for you.
Mt	7.14 road is *h* that leads to life, and there
1 Cor	15.10 I worked *h* than any of them—
2 Pet	3.16 some things in them *h* to understand,

HARDEN (HARDENED HARDENS)

Ex	4.21 but I will *h* his heart, so that he will
	7. 3 I will *h* Pharaoh's heart, and I will
	8.32 But Pharaoh *h* his heart this time also,
Deut	2.30 LORD your God had *h* his spirit and
Josh	11.20 it was the LORD's doing to *h* their hearts
1 Sam	6. 6 Why should you *h* your hearts as the
Ps	95. 8 Do not *h* your hearts, as at Meribah, as
Isa	63.17 stray from your ways and *h* our heart,
Dan	5.20 spirit was *h* so that he acted proudly, he
Mk	6.52 the loaves, but their hearts were *h*.
Jn	12.40 has blinded their eyes and *h* their heart,
Rom	9.18 and he *h* the heart of whomever he
	11. 7 elect obtained it, but the rest were *h*,
2 Cor	3.14 But their minds were *h*. Indeed, to this
Heb	3. 8 do not *h* your hearts as in the rebellion,

HARDENING

Rom	11.25 a *h* has come upon part of Israel, until

HARD-HEARTED

Deut	15. 7 do not be *h* or tight-fisted toward your
Mt	19. 8 because you were so *h* that Moses

HARDNESS

Mk	3. 5 he was grieved at their *h* of heart and
	10. 5 "Because of your *h* of heart he wrote
Eph	4.18 of their ignorance and *h* of heart.

HARDSHIP

Rom	8.35 Will *h*, or distress, or persecution, or

HARM

Gen	44.29 one also from me, and *h* comes to him,
Jer	25. 6 of your hands. Then I will do you no *h*."
	39.12 look after him well and do him no *h*,
Lk	6. 9 to do good or to do *h* on the sabbath,
Acts	16.28 "Do not *h* yourself, for we are all here."

HARMAGEDON

Rev	16.16 at the place that in Hebrew is called *H*.

HARMONY

Rom	15. 5 grant you to live in *h* with one another,
Col	3.14 binds everything together in perfect *h*.

HARP (HARPS)

Ps	108. 2 Awake, O *h* and lyre! I will awake the
	137. 2 On the willows there we hung up our *h*.
1 Cor	14. 7 notes, such as the flute or the *h*.
Rev	5. 8 each holding a *h* and golden bowls full
	14. 2 the sound of harpists playing on their *h*,

HARSH (HARSHLY)

Ruth	1.21 when the LORD dealt *h* with me and the
Mt	25.24 I knew that you were a *h* man, reaping

HARVEST (HARVESTS)

Gen	8.22 as the earth endures, seedtime and *h*,
Lev	23.10 and you reap its *h*, you shall bring the
Prov	25.13 snow in the time of *h* are faithful
Isa	9. 3 rejoice before you as with joy at the *h*,
	16. 9 for the shout over your fruit *h* and your
Jer	5.17 They shall eat up your *h* and your food;
	8.20 "The *h* is past, the summer is ended,
	12.13 They shall be ashamed of their *h*
Joel	3.13 Put in the sickle, for the *h* is ripe. Go
Mt	9.37 "The *h* is plentiful, but the laborers are
	13.30 both of them grow together until the *h*;
Mk	4.29 the sickle, because the *h* has come."
Lk	10. 2 of the *h* to send out laborers into his *h*.
Jn	4.35 'Four months more, then comes the *h*'?
Rom	1.13 that I may reap some *h* among you
2 Cor	9.10 increase the *h* of your righteousness.
Phil	1.11 having produced the *h* of righteousness
Rev	14.15 because the *h* of the earth is fully ripe."

HASTE

Ps	38.22 Make *h* to help me, O Lord, my
	70. 1 deliver me. O LORD, make *h* to help me!
Lk	2.16 went with *h*, and found Mary and

HATE (HATED HATES)

Gen	27.41 Now Esau *h* Jacob because of the
Ps	26. 5 I *h* the company of evildoers, and will
	68. 1 let those who *h* him flee before
	69. 4 are those who *h* me without cause;
	101. 3 I *h* the work of those who fall away; it
	106. 41 so that those who *h* them ruled them.
	119.113 I *h* the doubled-minded, but I love your
Prov	6.16 six things that the LORD *h*, seven that
	19. 7 If the poor are *h* even by their kin, how
Eccl	2.18 I *h* all my toil in which I had toiled
Jer	44. 4 to do this abominable thing that I *h*!"
Am	5.15 *H* evil and love good, and establish
Mal	1. 3 I have loved Jacob but have *h* Esau; I
Mt	10.22 you will be *h* by all because of my
	24. 9 you will be *h* by all nations because of
Mk	13.13 you will be *h* by all because of my
Lk	6.22 "Blessed are you when people *h* you,
	14.26 comes to me and does not *h* father and
	21.17 You will be *h* by all because of my

Jn	15.18 "If the world *h* you, be aware that it *h*
	15.25 their law, 'They *h* me without a cause.'
	17.14 and the world has *h* them because they
Rom	7.15 what I want, but I do the very thing I *h*.
	9.13 "I have loved Jacob, but I have *h* Esau."
	12. 9 *h* what is evil, hold fast to what is good;
Eph	5.29 no one ever *h* his own body, but he
Heb	1. 9 loved righteousness and *h* wickedness;
1 Jn	4.20 say, "I love God," and *h* their brothers or

HATRED

Num	35.20 if someone pushes another from *h*, or
Ps	25.19 foes, and with what violent *h* they hate
Prov	8.13 fear of the Lord is *h* of evil. Pride and

HAUGHTY

Prov	6.17 *h* eyes, a lying tongue, and hands that
Isa	3.16 Because the daughters of Zion are *h*
	5.15 low, and the eyes of the *h* are humbled.
Jer	13.15 Hear and give ear; do not be *h*, for the
Rom	12.16 do not be *h*, but associate with the

HAWK

Lev	11.16 the sea gull, the *h* of any kind;
Job	39.26 "Is it by your wisdom that the *h* soars,

HEAD

Gen	28.11 of the place, he put it under his *h*
1 Sam	17.51 killed him; then he cut off his *h* with it.
2 Kings	4.19 He complained to his father, "Oh, my *h*,
Song	7. 5 Your *h* crowns you like Carmel, and
Mt	14. 8 "Give me the *h* of John the Baptist here
Mk	6.28 brought his *h* on a platter, and gave it
Jn	13. 9 feet only but also my hands and my *h*!"
1 Cor	11. 3 Christ is the *h* of every man, and the
Eph	1.22 and has made him the *h* over all things
	5.23 the husband is the *h* of the wife just as
Col	1.18 He is the *h* of the body, the church; he

HEAL (HEALED HEALS)

Gen	20.17 prayed to God; and God *h* Abimelech,
Ex	15.26 Egyptians; for I am the Lord who *h* you."
Num	12.13 cried to the Lord, "O God, please *h* her."
Deut	32.39 I kill and I make alive; I wound and I *h*;
2 Chr	7.14 will forgive their sin and *h* their land.
Ps	30. 2 to you for help, and you have *h* me.
	41. 4 me; *h* me, for I have sinned against you."
	103. 3 your iniquity, who *h* all your diseases,
	107. 20 he sent out his word and *h* them, and
	147. 3 He *h* the brokenhearted, and binds up
Isa	30.26 and *h* the wounds inflicted by his blow.
	53. 5 us whole, and by his bruises we are *h*.
	57.19 near, says the Lord; and I will *h* them.
Jer	3.22 children, I will *h* your faithlessness.
	17.14 *H* me, O Lord, and I shall be *h*; save
	30.17 health to you, and your wounds I will *h*,
	33. 6 I will *h* them and reveal to them
	51. 9 We tried to *h* Babylon, but she could
Hos	5.13 is not able to cure you or *h* your wound.
	7. 1 when I would *h* Israel, the corruption of
	11. 3 but they did not know that I *h* them.
	14. 4 I will *h* their disloyalty; I will love them
Mt	13.15 heart and turn — and I would *h* them.'
Mk	6.56 cloak; and all who touched it were *h*.
Lk	6.18 hear him and to be *h* of their diseases;
	8.47 and how she had been immediately *h*;
	9. 2 proclaim the kingdom of God and to *h*.
	22.51 this!" And he touched his ear and *h* him.
Jn	4.47 him to come down and *h* his son,
	5.13 man who had been *h* did not know who
Acts	14. 9 and seeing that he had faith to be *h*,
1 Pet	2.24 by his wounds you have been *h*.

HEALING

Prov	3. 8 It will be *h* for your flesh and a
	29. 1 will suddenly be broken beyond *h*.
Jer	8.15 find no good, for a time of *h*, but found
	14.19 us down so that there is no *h* for us?

Jer	46.11 many medicines; there is no *h* for you.
Ezek	47.12 will be for food, and their leaves for *h*."
Mal	4. 2 shall rise, with *h* in its wings.
1 Cor	12. 9 to another gifts of *h* by the one Spirit,
	12.28 then deeds of power, then gifts of *h*,
Rev	22. 2 of the trees are for the *h* of the nations.

HEALTH (HEALTHY)

Ps	38. 3 is no *h* in my bones because of my sin.
Prov	16.24 to the soul and *h* to the body.
Jer	30.17 For I will restore *h* to you, and your
Lk	11.34 when your eye is *h*, your whole body is
Acts	3.16 Jesus has given him this perfect *h* in
3 Jn	2 well with you and that you may be in *h*,

HEAP

Josh	3.13 cut off; they shall stand in a single *h*."
Job	27.16 Though they *h* up silver like dust, and
Ps	39. 6 they *h* up, and do not know who
Prov	25.22 you will *h* coals of fire on their heads,
Jer	9.11 I will make Jerusalem a *h* of ruins, a

HEAR (HEARD HEARS)

Gen	21.17 God *h* the voice of the boy; and the
Ex	2.24 God *h* their groaning, and God
Deut	4.10 I will let them *h* my words, so that they
	5. 1 *H*, O Israel, the statutes and ordinances
	6. 4 *H*, O Israel: The Lord is our God, the
	31.12 that they may *h* and learn to fear the
2 Sam	5.24 When you *h* the sound of marching in
	22. 7 From his temple he *h* my voice, and my
1 Kings	8.39 then *h* in heaven your dwelling place,
2 Kings	19.16 Incline your ear, O Lord, and *h*; open
2 Chr	6.27 may you *h* in heaven, forgive the sin of
	7.12 "I have *h* your prayer, and have chosen
	33.13 received his entreaty, and *h* his plea,
Neh	8. 9 people wept when they *h* the words of
Job	42. 4 '*H*, and I will speak; I will question
Ps	6. 9 The Lord has *h* my supplication; the
	34.17 the righteous cry for help, the Lord *h*,
	49. 1 *H* this, all peoples; give ear, all
Prov	1. 8 *H*, my child, your father's instruction,
Isa	1. 2 *H*, O heavens, and listen, O earth; for
	33.13 *H*, you who are far away, what I have
	40.28 Have you not known? Have you not *h*?
	64. 4 From ages past no one has *h*, no ear
	66. 8 Who has *h* of such a thing? Who has
Jer	18. 2 and there I will let you *h* my words."
	31.18 I *h* Ephraim pleading: "You disciplined
Ezek	3.27 Let those who will *h*, *h*; and let those
	12. 2 see, who have ears to *h*, but do not *h*;
	33.31 and they *h* your words, but they will not
Mic	1. 2 *H*, you peoples, all of you; listen, O
Mt	11. 4 "Go and tell John what you *h* and see:
Mk	4.24 to them, "Pay attention to what you *h*;
Lk	6.18 They had come to *h* him and to be
	7.22 tell John what you have seen and *h*:
Jn	5.24 anyone who *h* my word and believes
	10. 3 the sheep *h* his voice. He calls his own
	12.47 I do not judge anyone who *h* my words
Acts	4.20 about what we have seen and *h*."
	10.44 the Holy Spirit fell on all who *h*
	19.10 of Asia, both Jews and Greeks, *h* the
Rom	10.14 And how are they to *h* without someone
	15.21 and those who have never *h* of him
1 Jn	1. 1 what we have *h*, what we have seen
Rev	1. 3 blessed are those who *h* and who keep

HEARING (n)

Gen	23.10 Abraham in the *h* of the Hittites,
Neh	13. 1 the book of Moses in the *h* of the
1 Cor	12.17 were an eye, where would the *h* be?

HEART

Gen	8.21 the inclination of the human *h* is evil
Ex	28.30 judgment . . . on his *h* before the Lord
	35. 5 let whoever is of a generous *h* bring the
Deut	6. 5 love the Lord your God with all your *h*,

Deut	7. 7	people that the LORD set his *h* on you
	10.12	serve the LORD your God with all your *h*
	10.15	yet the LORD set his *h* in love on your
	17.17	for himself, or else his *h* will turn away;
	28.65	LORD will give you a trembling *h*, failing
	30. 6	God will circumcise your *h* and the *h*
	30.14	mouth and in your *h* for you to observe.
1 Sam	7. 3	Direct your *h* to the LORD, and serve
	10. 9	God gave him another *h*; and all these
	13.14	has sought out a man after his own *h*;
	16. 7	but the LORD looks on the *h*."
	25.37	his *h* died within him; he became like a
2 Sam	17.10	whose *h* is like the *h* of a lion, will
	24.10	David was stricken to the *h* because he
1 Kings	3. 6	in uprightness of *h* toward you; and you
	8.48	if they repent with all their *h* and soul
	11. 9	with Solomon, because his *h* had turned
	15.14	the *h* of Asa was true to the LORD all his
2 Kings	14.10	your *h* has lifted you up. Be content
	22.19	because your *h* was penitent and you
	23.25	turned to the LORD with all his *h*, with
1 Chr	28. 9	him with single mind and willing *h*;
	29.17	I know, my God, that you search the *h*,
2 Chr	16. 9	to strengthen those whose *h* is true
	17. 6	His *h* was courageous in the ways of the
	25.19	your *h* has lifted you up in boastfulness.
	32.25	his *h* was proud. Therefore wrath came
Ezra	6.22	turned the *h* of the king of Assyria to
	7.10	Ezra had set his *h* to study the law of
Neh	2. 2	sick? This can only be sadness of the *h*."
	2.12	had put into my *h* to do for Jerusalem.
Job	11.13	"If you direct your *h* rightly, you will
	23.16	God has made my *h* faint; the Almighty
	31. 9	"If my *h* has been enticed by a woman,
	36.13	"The godless in *h* cherish anger; they do
Ps	19. 8	of the LORD are right, rejoicing the *h*;
	44.21	this? For he knows the secrets of the *h*.
	45. 1	My *h* overflows with a goodly theme; I
	51.10	Create in me a clean *h*, O God, and put
	55.21	than butter, but with a *h* set on war;
	57. 7	My *h* is steadfast, O God, my *h* is
	69.20	Insults have broken my *h*, so that I am
	77. 6	I commune with my *h* in the night; I
	78.18	They tested God in their *h* by
	101. 2	I will walk with integrity of *h* within my
	102. 4	My *h* is stricken and withered like grass;
	104.15	wine to gladden the human *h*, oil to
	108. 1	My *h* is steadfast, O God, my *h* is
	109.22	needy, and my *h* is pierced within me.
	119.11	I treasure your word in my *h*, so that I
	143. 4	within me; my *h* within me is appalled.
Prov	2.10	wisdom will come into your *h*, and
	3. 3	write them on the tablet of your *h*.
	4.23	Keep your *h* with all vigilance, for from
	6.18	a *h* that devises wicked plans, feet that
	18.12	Before destruction one's *h* is haughty,
	20. 9	Who can say, I have made my *h* clean; I
	21. 1	king's *h* is a stream of water in the
	23.26	My child, give me your *h*, and let your
	26.23	vessel are smooth lips with an evil *h*.
	27.19	face, so one human *h* reflects another.
Eccl	5. 2	nor let your *h* be quick to utter a word
	10. 2	The *h* of the wise inclines to the right,
Song	8. 6	Set me as a seal upon your *h*, as a seal
Isa	1. 5	head is sick, and the whole *h* faint.
	38. 3	you in faithfulness with a whole *h*,
	42.25	burned him, but he did not take it to *h*.
	63.17	stray from your ways and harden our *h*,
Jer	3.10	did not return to me with her whole *h*,
	3.15	give you shepherds after my own *h*, who
	4.14	Jerusalem, wash your *h* clean of
	4.19	My *h* is beating wildly; I cannot keep
	17. 9	The *h* is devious above all else; it is
	32.39	I will give them one *h* and one way,
Ezek	11.19	I will give them one *h*, and put a new
	16.30	How sick is your *h*, says the Lord GOD,
	28. 2	Because your *h* is proud and you have

Ezek	33.31	lips, but their *h* is set on their gain.
	36.26	remove from your body the *h* of stone
	44. 7	uncircumcised in *h* and flesh,
Dan	5.22	his son, have not humbled your *h*,
Hos	10. 2	Their *h* is false; now they must bear
Joel	2.12	return to me with all your *h*, with
Am	2.16	who are stout of *h* among the mighty
Mt	5. 8	"Blessed are the pure in *h*, for they will
	5.28	committed adultery with her in his *h*.
	6.21	treasure is, there your *h* will be also.
	9. 2	"Take *h*, son; your sins are forgiven."
	13.15	this people's *h* has grown dull, and their
	14.27	said, "Take *h*, it is I; do not be afraid."
	15.19	out of the *h* come evil intentions,
Mk	6.50	said, "Take *h*, it is I; do not be afraid."
	7.21	it is . . . from the human *h*, that evil
	10. 5	"Because of your hardness of *h* he wrote
	12.30	love the Lord your God with all your *h*,
Lk	2.19	words and pondered them in her *h*.
	2.51	treasured all these things in her *h*.
	6.45	out of the good treasure of the *h*
Jn	1.18	only Son, who is close to the Father's *h*,
	7.38	"Out of the believer's *h* shall flow rivers
Acts	1.24	"Lord, you know everyone's *h*. Show us
	2.26	therefore my *h* was glad, and my tongue
	4.32	who believed were of one *h* and soul,
	7.23	came into his *h* to visit his relatives, the
	7.51	people, uncircumcised in *h* and ears,
	8.21	this, for your *h* is not right before God.
	13.22	son of Jesse, to be a man after my *h*,
	15. 8	God who knows the human *h* testified
	16.14	Lord opened her *h* to listen eagerly to
	21.13	you doing, weeping and breaking my *h*?
	28.27	For this people's *h* has grown dull, and
Rom	8.27	God, who searches the *h*, knows what is
	9. 2	sorrow and unceasing anguish in my *h*.
	10. 9	believe in your *h* that God raised him
1 Cor	2. 9	ear heard, nor the human *h* conceived,
2 Cor	4. 1	in this ministry, we do not lose *h*.
	6.11	to you Corinthians; our *h* is wide open
	7.15	his *h* goes out all the more to you, as
1 Tim	1. 5	is love that comes from a pure *h*,
Heb	4.12	the thoughts and intentions of the *h*.
1 Pet	1.22	love one another deeply from the *h*.

HEARTS

Ex	25. 2	from all those whose *h* prompt them to
Josh	5. 1	they had crossed over, their *h* melted,
	24.23	you, and incline your *h* to the LORD,
2 Sam	15. 6	so Absalom stole the *h* of the people of
1 Kings	18.37	and that you have turned their *h* back."
Ps	14. 1	Fools say in their *h*, "There is no God."
	24. 4	who have clean hands and pure *h*,
	53. 1	Fools say in their *h*, there is no God."
	95. 8	Do not harden your *h*, as at Meribah, as
	112. 8	Their *h* are steady, they will not be
Isa	29.13	their lips, while their *h* are far from me,
	51. 7	who have kept my teaching in your *h*;
Jer	17. 5	whose *h* turn away from the LORD.
	31.33	them and I will write it on their *h*;
Zech	7.12	They made their *h* adamant in order not
Mal	4. 6	He will turn the *h* of parents to
Mt	15. 8	their lips, but their *h* are far from me;
Mk	2. 8	do you raise such question in your *h*?
	6.52	the loaves, but their *h* were hardened.
	7. 6	their lips, but their *h* are far from me;
	8.17	or understand? Are your *h* hardened?
Lk	1.17	turn the *h* of parents to their children,
	24.32	"Were not our *h* burning within us while
Jn	12.40	blinded their eyes and hardened their *h*,
	14. 1	"Do not let your *h* be troubled. Believe
	14.27	Do not let your *h* be troubled, and do
Rom	2.15	the law requires is written on their *h*,
2 Thess	3. 5	May the Lord direct your *h* to the love
Heb	3. 8	do not harden your *h* as in the
	3.10	'They always go astray in their *h*, and
	4. 7	hear his voice, do not harden your *h*."

Heb	8.10 their minds, and write them on their *h*,
1 Jn	3.20 whenever our *h* condemn us; for God is
Rev	2.23 am the one who searches minds and *h*,

HEAVEN (HEAVENS)

Ex	16. 4 I am going to rain bread from *h* for you;
	20.22 yourselves that I spoke with you from *h*.
Deut	30.12 It is not in *h*, that you should say, "Who
1 Kings	8.27 Even *h* and the highest *h* cannot
2 Chr	6.18 and the highest *h* cannot contain you,
Ps	19. 1 The *h* are telling the glory of God; and
	103. 11 as the *h* are high above the earth, so
	119. 89 forever; your word is firmly fixed in *h*.
	139. 8 I ascend to *h*, you are there; if I make
Isa	14.12 How you are fallen from *h*, O Day Star,
	24. 4 and withers; the *h* languish together
	66. 1 *H* is my throne and the earth is my
Hag	1.10 *h* above you have withheld the dew, and
Mt	5.18 until *h* and earth pass away, not one
	6. 9 "Pray then in this way: Our father in *h*,
Mk	1.10 he saw the *h* torn apart and the Spirit
	13.31 *H* and earth will pass away, but my
	16.19n Jesus . . . was taken up into *h* and sat
Lk	21.26 for the powers of the *h* will be shaken.
	21.33 *H* and earth will pass away, but my
Acts	9. 3 suddenly a light from *h* flashed
1 Cor	15.49 also bear the image of the man of *h*.
2 Cor	12. 2 ago was caught up to the third *h*—
1 Pet	3.22 Christ, who has gone into *h* and is at
2 Pet	3. 5 by the word of God *h* existed long ago
	3.13 we wait for new *h* and a new earth,
Rev	4. 1 and there in *h* a door stood open!
	19. 1 voice of a great multitude in *h*, saying,
	21. 1 I saw a new *h* and a new earth; for the

HEAVENLY

Jn	3.12 you believe if I tell you about *h* things?
2 Cor	5. 2 to be clothed with our *h* dwelling—
Eph	1. 3 every spiritual blessing in the *h* places,

HEAVY

1 Kings	14. 6 For I am charged with *h* tidings for you.
Ps	32. 4 day and night your hand was *h* on me;
Eccl	6. 1 the sun, and it lies *h* upon humankind:
Mt	11.28 are weary and are carrying *h* burdens,

HEBRON

Gen	13.18 by the oaks of Mamre, which are at *H*;
Judg	1.10 against the Canaanites who lived in *H*
2 Sam	2.11 that David was king in *H* over the house

HEED (HEEDED)

Ex	5. 2 Who is the LORD, that I should *h* him
Deut	4.30 return to the LORD your God and *h* him.
	7.12 If you *h* these ordinances, by diligently
	13. 8 you must not yield to or *h* any such
Judg	6.10 But you have not given *h* to my voice."
1 Sam	12.15 if you will not *h* the voice of the LORD,
2 Chr	11. 4 they *h* the word of the LORD and turned
Ps	31. 7 you have taken *h* of my adversities;
Prov	1.23 Give *h* to my reproof; I will pour out my
Eccl	9.17 words of the wise are more to be *h*
Jer	8. 6 I have given *h* and listened, but they do
	11. 3 Cursed be anyone who does not *h* the
	26. 5 to *h* the words of my servants the

HEEL

Gen	3.15 your head, and you will strike his *h*."
	25.26 out, with his hand gripping Esau's *h*;
Ps	41. 9 my bread, has lifted the *h* against me.

HEIFER

Gen	15. 9 "Bring me a *h* three years old, a female
Num	19. 2 to bring you a red *h* without defect, in
Judg	14.18 "If you had not plowed with my *h*, you

HEIGHT

Rom	8.39 nor *h*, nor depth, nor anything else in

HEIR (HEIRS)

Gen	15. 3 and so a slave . . . is to be my *h*."
Jer	49. 1 Has Israel no sons? Has he no *h*? Why
Mt	21.38 'This is the *h*; come, let us kill him and
Mk	12. 7 'This is the *h*; come, let us kill him, and
Lk	20.14 'This is the *h*; let us kill him so that
Rom	8.17 if children, then *h*, *h* of God and joint *h*
Gal	4. 1 *h*, as long as they are minors, are no
Eph	3. 6 the Gentiles have become fellow *h*,
Heb	11. 7 world and became an *h* to righteousness

HELL

Mt	5.22 fool!' you will be liable to the *h* of fire.
	5.29 your whole body to be thrown into *h*.
	18. 9 eyes and to be thrown into the *h* of fire.
Lk	12. 5 has killed, has authority to cast into *h*.

HELLENISTS

Acts	6. 1 *H* complained against the Hebrews
	9.29 spoke and argued with the *H*; but they

HELMET

Isa	59.17 and a *h* of salvation on his head;
Eph	6.17 Take the *h* of salvation, and the sword
1 Thess	5. 8 love, and for a *h* the hope of salvation.

HELP (n)

2 Sam	22.36 salvation, and your *h* made me great.
Ps	18.35 supported me; your *h* made me great.
	42. 5 God; for I shall again praise him, my *h*
	42.11 God; for I shall again praise him, my *h*
	70. 5 You are my *h* and my deliverer; O LORD,
	121. 2 My *h* comes from the LORD, who made
Isa	30. 7 Egypt's *h* is worthless and empty,
Acts	26.22 To this day I have had *h* from God, and
Phil	4.16 I was in in Thessalonica, you sent me *h*

HELP (HELPED HELPS) (v)

Ex	2.19 "An Egyptian *h* us against the
Deut	28.31 your enemies, without anyone to *h* you.
2 Kings	14.26 bond or free, and no one to *h* Israel.
2 Chr	14.11 *H* us, O LORD our God, for we rely on
	26. 7 God *h* him against the Philistines,
Ps	106. 4 people; *h* me when you deliver them;
	107. 12 labor; they fell down, with none to *h*.
	109. 26 *H* me, O LORD my God! Save me
Isa	49. 8 you, on a day of salvation I have *h* you;
	50. 7 The Lord GOD *h* me; therefore I have
Hos	13. 9 destroy you, O Israel; who can *h* you?
Mt	15.25 knelt before him, saying, "Lord, *h* me."

HELPER

Gen	2.18 I will make him a *h* as his partner."
Ps	10.14 and you have been the *h* of the orphan.
	30.10 be gracious to me! O LORD, be my *h*!"
Heb	13. 6 "The Lord is my *h*, I will not be afraid.

HELPLESS

Jer	6.24 our hands fall *h*; anguish has taken hold

HEM

Ps	139. 5 You *h* me in, behind and before, and lay

HEMORRHAGES

Mk	5.25 been suffering from *h* for twelve years,
Lk	8.43 been suffering from *h* for twelve years;

HERALD

2 Chr	36.22 Persia so that he sent a *h* throughout
Ezra	1. 1 Persia so that he sent a *h* throughout
1 Tim	2. 7 right time. For this I was appointed a *h*

HERE

Isa	40. 9 to the cities of Judah, "*H* is your God!"

HERITAGE

1 Kings	8.53 to be your *h*, just as you promised
Job	31. 2 and my *h* from the Almighty on high?
Ps	2. 8 I will make the nations your *h*, and the

Ps	16.	6 in pleasant places; I have a goodly *h*.
	33.12	people whom he has chosen as his *h*.
	94.14	his people; he will not abandon his *h*;
Jer	12.	7 my house, I have abandoned my *h*;
	17.	4 By your own act you shall lose the *h*
	50.11	though you exult, O plunderers of my *h*,

HERMON

Deut	3.	8 Jordan, from Wadi Arnon to Mount *H*
	4.48	as far as Mount Sirion (that is, H),
Josh	11.17	the valley of Lebanon below Mount *H*.
	12.	1 from the Wadi Arnon to Mount *H*, with
Ps	89.12	them; Tabor and *H* joyously praise
	133.	3 It is like the dew of *H*, which falls on
Song	4.	8 Amana, from the peak of Senir and *H*,

HEROD

Mt	2.	1 In the time of King *H*, after Jesus was
	2.13	for *H* is about to search for the child, to
	2.16	When *H* saw that he had been tricked
	2.19	When *H* died, an angel of the Lord
	14.	1 At that time *H* the ruler heard reports
Mk	6.14	King *H* heard of it, for Jesus' name had
	8.15	of the Pharisees and the yeast of *H*."
Lk	3.	1 and *H* was ruler of Galilee, and his
	13.31	away from here, for *H* wants to kill you."
	23.	7 he sent him off to *H*, who was himself
Acts	4.27	in this city, both *H* and Pontius Pilate,
	12.	1 King *H* laid violent hands upon some
	12.20	Now *H* was angry with the people of
	12.21	day *H* put on his royal robes, took his

HEZEKIAH

2 Kings	16.20	city of David; his son *H* succeeded him.
	19.14	*H* received the letter from the hand of
	20.	1 In those days *H* became sick and was at
2 Chr	30.	1 *H* sent word to all Israel and Judah,
	30.18	But *H* had prayed for them, saying,
	32.30	*H* closed the upper outlet of the waters
Isa	39.	1 envoys with letters and a present to *H*,

HIDE (HID HIDDEN HIDES HIDING)

Gen	3.	8 the man and his wife *h* themselves from
	18.17	"Shall I *h* from Abraham what I am
Ex	2.	2 a fine baby, she *h* him three months.
	2.12	he killed the Egyptian and *h* him in the
	3.	6 Moses *h* his face, for he was afraid to
Josh	2.	4 woman took the two men and *h* them.
1 Sam	3.17	Do not *h* it from me. May God do so to
	10.22	"See, he has *h* himself among the
2 Chr	22.11	—*h* him from Athaliah, so that she did
Ps	10.	1 do you *h* yourself in times of trouble?
	13.	1 forever? How long will you *h* your face
	17.	8 eye; *h* me in the shadow of your wings,
	19.12	their error? Clear me from *h* faults.
	27.	5 he will *h* me in his shelter in the day of
	27.	9 Do not *h* your face from me. Do not
	30.	7 you *h* your face; I was dismayed.
	40.10	I have not *h* your saving help within my
	55.	1 do not *h* yourself from my supplication.
	89.46	O Lord? Will you *h* yourself forever?
	104.	29 When you *h* your face, they are
	119.114	You are my *h* place and my shield; I
Prov	27.	5 Better is open rebuke than *h* love.
Isa	1.15	your hands, I will *h* my eyes from you;
	2.10	*h* in the dust from the terror of the
	32.	2 will be like a *h* place from the wind,
	40.27	"My way is *h* from the Lord, and my
	45.15	you are a God who *h* himself, O God of
	49.	2 in the shadow of his hand he *h* me;
	64.	5 because you *h* yourself we transgressed.
	65.16	former troubles are forgotten and are *h*
Jer	13.	5 So I went, and *h* it by the Euphrates, as
	36.26	prophet Jeremiah. But the Lord *h* them.
Ezek	39.29	I will never again *h* my face from them,
Am	9.	3 they *h* themselves on the top of Carmel,
Mt	5.14	A city built on a hill cannot be *h*.

Mt	25.18	the ground and *h* his master's money.
Mk	4.22	For there is nothing *h*, except to be
Lk	8.17	nothing is *h* that will not be disclosed,
	10.21	have *h* these things from the wise and
Heb	4.13	before him no creature is *h*, but all are

HIGH (HIGHER)

Ezra	9.	6 our iniquities have risen *h* than our
Eccl	10.	6 folly is set in many *h* places, and the
Ezek	17.24	low the *h* tree, I make *h* the low tree;

HIGH PRIEST

Mk	2.26	when Abiathar was *h*, and ate the bread
	14.53	They took Jesus to the *h*; and all the
Jn	18.19	the *h* questioned Jesus about his
Acts	5.17	Then the *h* took action; he and all who
	23.	4 "Do you dare to insult God's *h*?" And
Heb	2.17	be a merciful and faithful *h* in the
	3.	1 Jesus, the apostle and *h* of our
	4.14	have a great *h* who has passed through
	5.	5 did not glorify himself in becoming a *h*,

HIGHWAY (HIGHWAYS)

Ps	84.	5 you, in whose heart are the *h* to Zion.
Isa	11.16	so there shall be a *h* from Assyria for
	19.23	there will be a *h* from Egypt to Assyria,
	35.	8 A *h* shall be there, and it shall be called
	49.11	a road, and my *h* shall be raised up.

HILL (HILLS)

Deut	2.	3 skirting this *h* country long enough.
1 Kings	20.23	"Their gods are gods of the *h*, and so
Ps	24.	3 Who shall ascend the *h* of the Lord?

HINDER

1 Sam	14.	6 nothing can *h* the Lord from saving by

HIP

Gen	32.25	him on the *h* socket; and Jacob's *h*

HIRAM

2 Sam	5.11	King *H* of Tyre sent messengers to
1 Kings	5.	1 Now *H* king of Tyre sent his servants to
	7.13	King Solomon invited and received *H*
	7.40	*H* also made the pots, the shovels, and
	9.12	when *H* came from Tyre to see the
1 Chr	14.	1 King *H* of Tyre sent messengers to

HIRED

Deut	23.	4 because they *h* against you Balaam son
2 Chr	24.12	they *h* masons and carpenters to restore
Lk	15.19	son; treat me like one of your *h* hands."

HITTITE (HITTITES)

Gen	15.20	the *H*, the Perizzites, the Rephaim,
	23.10	Ephron the *H* answered Abraham in the
Ex	3.	8 country of the Canaanites, the *H*, the
	23.23	brings you to the Amorites, the *H*, the
Deut	7.	1 away many nations before you—the *H*,
1 Kings	9.20	who were left of the Amorites, the *H*,
2 Kings	7.	6 has hired against us the kings of the *H*
Ezra	9.	1 from the Canaanites, the *H*, the

HOLD (HELD HOLDING)

Gen	17.	8 the land of Canaan, for a perpetual *h*;
	48.	4 offspring after you for a perpetual *h*.'
Deut	30.20	God, obeying him, and *h* fast to him;
Josh	22.	5 to *h* fast to him, and to serve him with
	23.	8 but *h* fast to the Lord your God, as you
Job	27.	6 I *h* fast my righteousness, and will not
Ps	119.101	I *h* back my feet from every evil way, in
Isa	65.	2 I *h* out my hands all day long to a
Jer	26.	2 I command you; do not *h* back a word.
Ezek	44.28	give them no *h* in Israel; I am their *h*.
Jn	20.17	"Do not *h* on to me, because I have not
Rom	3.28	we *h* that a person is justified by faith
	12.	9 hate what is evil, *h* fast to what is good;

HOLE (HOLES)

Ezek	8.	7 I looked, and there was a *h* in the wall.
Hag	1.	6 wages to put them into a bag with *h*.

HOLINESS

Ex	15.11	Who is like you, majestic in *h*, awesome
Ps	93.	5 very sure; *h* befits your house, O Lord,
Ezek	20.41	I will manifest my *h* among you in the
	36.23	you I display my *h* before their eyes.
	38.16	through you, O Gog, I display my *h*
Lk	1.75	serve him without fear, in *h* and
2 Cor	7.	1 making *h* perfect in the fear of God.
Eph	4.24	of God in true righteousness and *h*.
1 Thess	4.	7 did not call us to impurity but in *h*.
Heb	12.14	and the *h* without which no one will

HOLLOW

Isa	40.12	the waters in the *h* of his hand

HOLY

Ex	3.	5 on which you are standing is *h* ground."
	19.	6 me a priestly kingdom and a *h* nation.
	26.33	for you the *h* place from the most *h*.
	28.36	engraving of a signet, "*H* to the Lord."
	39.30	engraving of a signet, "*H* to the Lord."
Lev	10.	3 who are near me I will show myself *h*,
	10.10	distinguish between the *h* and the
	11.44	therefore, and be *h*, for I am *h*.
	19.	2 You shall be *h*, for I the Lord your God
	20.26	You shall be *h* to me; for I the Lord am
	21.	6 They shall be *h* to their God, and not
	22.	2 that they may not profane my *h* name;
Num	4.20	not go in to look on the *h* things even
	6.	5 they shall be *h*; they shall let the locks
	16.	3 All the congregation are *h*, everyone of
Deut	5.12	Observe the sabbath day and keep it *h*,
	7.	6 For you are a people *h* to the Lord your
	14.	2 For you are a people *h* to the Lord your
	23.14	your camp must be *h*, so that he may
1 Sam	2.	2 "There is no *H* One like the Lord, no
Ezra	8.28	"You are *h* to the Lord, and the vessels
Neh	13.22	the gates, to keep the sabbath day *h*.
Job	5.	1 To which of the *h* ones will you turn?
Ps	16.	3 As for the *h* ones in the land, they are
	22.	3 Yet you are *h*, enthroned on the praises
	30.	4 ones, and give thanks to his *h* name.
	34.	9 O fear the Lord, you his *h* ones, for
	48.	1 in the city of our God. His *h* mountain,
	96.	9 Worship the Lord in *h* splendor; tremble
	99.	3 your great and awesome name. *H* is he!
	134.	2 Lift up your hands to the *h* place, and
Isa	5.16	God shows himself *h* by righteousness.
	6.	3 "*H*, *h*, *h* is the Lord of hosts; the earth
	8.13	of hosts, him you shall regard as *h*;
	35.	8 there, and it shall be called the *H* Way;
	62.	9 gather it shall drink it in my *h* courts.
	62.12	They shall be called, "The *H* People,
Jer	2.	3 Israel was *h* to the Lord, the first fruits
	17.22	but keep the sabbath day *h*, as I
	51.51	aliens have come into the *h* places of
Ezek	42.20	between the *h* and the common.
Dan	7.18	the *h* ones of the Most High shall
	7.27	given to the people of the *h* ones of the
	8.13	Then I heard a *h* one speaking, and
	8.24	powerful and the people of the *h* ones.
	12.	7 the shattering of the power of the *h*
Zech	14.	5 will come, and all the *h* ones with him.
Mt	7.	6 "Do not give what is *h* to dogs; and do
	24.15	sacrilege standing in the *h* place,
Mk	6.20	that he was a righteous and *h* man,
Lk	2.23	first born male shall be designated as *h*
Acts	7.33	the place where you are standing is *h*
Rom	7.12	So the law is *h*, and the commandment
	12.	1 bodies as a living sacrifice, *h* and
1 Cor	7.14	the unbelieving husband is made *h*
	7.34	so that they may be *h* in body and in
Eph	1.	4 of the world to be *h* and blameless

Eph	5.26	in order to make her *h*, by cleansing her
	5.27	that she may be *h* and without blemish.
Heb	7.26	such a high priest, *h*, blameless,
1 Pet	1.15	called you is *h*, be *h* yourselves in all
Jude	14	coming with ten thousand of his *h* ones,
Rev	3.	7 These are the words of the *h* one, the
	4.	8 "*H*, *h*, *h*, is the Lord God the Almighty,
	21.	2 I saw the *h* city, the new Jerusalem,

HOLY ONE

Prov	9.10	and knowledge of the *H* is insight.
Isa	41.14	Lord; your Redeemer is the *H* of Israel.
	43.14	Lord, your Redeemer, the *H* of Israel:
Hab	1.12	not from of old, O Lord my God, my *H*?
Jn	6.69	and know that you are the *H* of God."
Acts	13.35	not let your *H* experience corruption.'

HOLY SPIRIT

Ps	51.11	and do not take your *h* from me.
Mt	1.18	was found to be with child from the *H*.
Mk	1.	8 but he will baptize you with the *H*."
Eph	1.13	with the seal of the promised *H*,
2 Pet	1.21	men and women moved by the *H* spoke

HOME

Ps	68.	6 God gives the desolate a *h* to live in; he
Mk	5.19	"Go *h* to your friends, and tell them
	8.26	he sent him away to his *h*, saying, "Do
Lk	8.39	"Return to your *h*, and declare how
Jn	14.23	to them and make our *h* with them.
	19.27	hour the disciple took her to his own *h*.
1 Cor	11.34	If you are hungry, eat at *h*, so that when
	14.35	know, let them ask their husbands at *h*.
2 Cor	5.	6 while we are at *h* in the body we are
Rev	21.	3 "See, the *h* of God is among mortals.

HOMELAND

Heb	11.14	make it clear that they are seeking a *h*.

HOMETOWN

Mk	6.	1 He left that place and came to his *h*,

HONEST

Lev	19.36	You shall have *h* balances, *h* weights, an
Deut	25.15	You shall have only a full and *h* weight;
Prov	16.11	*H* balances and scales are the Lord's;
Ezek	45.10	You shall have *h* balances, an *h* ephah,
Lk	8.15	hold it fast in an *h* and good heart

HONESTY

Gen	30.33	So my *h* will answer for me later, when

HONEY

Ex	3.	8 land, a land flowing with milk and *h*,
	16.31	taste of it was like wafers made with *h*.
Deut	32.13	he nursed him with *h* from the crags,
1 Sam	14.29	because I tasted a little of this *h*.
Ps	19.10	sweeter also than *h*, and drippings of
	81.16	wheat and with *h* from the rock I would
	119.103	your words to my taste, sweeter than *h*
Prov	24.13	My child, eat *h*, for it is good, and the
Song	4.11	*h* and milk are under your tongue;
Isa	7.15	He shall eat curds and *h* by the time he
Ezek	3.	3 and in my mouth it was as sweet as *h*.
Rev	10.10	sweet as *h* in my mouth, but when I

HONOR (n)

Num	22.17	I will surely do you great *h*, and
2 Sam	6.22	spoken, by them I shall be held in *h*."
2 Chr	1.11	not asked for possessions, wealth, *h*,
Esth	6.	3 "What *h* or distinction has been
Ps	96.	6 *H* and majesty are before him; strength
	104.	1 are very great. You are clothed with *h*
Prov	15.33	in wisdom, and humility goes before *h*.
	29.23	one who is lowly in spirit will obtain *h*.
Dan	2.	6 from me gifts and rewards and great *h*.
Mt	13.57	"Prophets are not without *h* except in
Mk	6.	4 "Prophets are not without *h*, except in
Lk	14.	7 how the guests chose the places of *h*,

Rom	2. 7 doing good seek for glory and *h* and
	12.10 outdo one another in showing *h*.
	13. 7 respect is due, *h* to whom *h* is due.
1 Cor	4.10 You are held in *h*, but we in disrepute.
2 Cor	6. 8 in *h* and dishonor, in ill repute and
1 Tim	6.16 see; to him be *h* and eternal dominion.

HONOR (HONORED HONORS) (v)

Gen	34.19 he was the most *h* of all his family.
Ex	20.12 *H* your father and your mother, so that
Deut	5.16 *H* your father and your mother, as the
1 Sam	2.30 those who *h* me I will *h*, and those who
	15.30 "I have sinned; yet *h* me now before the
1 Chr	4. 9 Jabez was *h* more than his brothers;
Ps	50.23 thanksgiving as their sacrifice *h* me;
Prov	3. 9 *H* the LORD with your substance and
Isa	29.13 and *h* me with their lips, while their
	43.23 offerings, or *h* me with your sacrifices.
	58.13 if you *h* it, not going your own ways,
Jer	30.19 I will make them *h*, and they shall not
Dan	11.38 He shall *h* the god of fortresses instead
Mal	1. 6 A son *h* his father, and servants their
Mt	15. 4 God said, '*H* your father and your
	15. 8 'This people *h* me with their lips, but
	19.19 *H* your father and mother; also, You
Mk	7.10 said, "*H* your father and your mother';
Lk	14.10 will be *h* in the presence of all who sit
Jn	5.23 all may *h* the Son, just as they *h* the
	8.49 I *h* my father, and you dishonor me.
Eph	6. 2 is right. "*H* your father and mother"—
Phil	2.29 Lord with all joy, and *h* such people,
1 Tim	5. 3 *H* widows who are really widows. If a

HONORABLE

Phil	4. 8 is true, whatever is *h*, whatever is just,

HOPE (n)

Ezra	10. 2 but even now there is *h* for Israel in
Job	5.16 So the poor have *h*, and injustice shuts
	13.15 See, he will kill me; I have no *h*; but I
	14.19 the earth; you destroy the *h* of mortals.
	17.15 where then is my *h*? Who will see my *h*?
	19.10 gone, he has uprooted my *h* like a tree.
	27. 8 what is the *h* of the godless when God
Ps	65. 5 you are the *h* of all the ends of the
	78. 7 so that they should set their *h* in God,
	146. 5 God of Jacob, whose *h* is in the LORD
Prov	10.28 The *h* of the righteous ends in gladness,
	13.12 *H* deferred makes the heart sick, but a
	19.18 your children while there is *h*;
	29.20 There is more *h* for a fool than for
Isa	20. 5 because of Ethiopia their *h* and Egypt
Jer	14.22 We set our *h* on you, for it is you who
	31.17 There is *h* for your future, says the
Ezek	37.11 bones are dried up, and our *h* is lost;
Hos	2.15 make the Valley of Achor a door of *h*.
Acts	28.20 since it is for the sake of the *h* of Israel
Rom	4.18 Hoping against *h*, he believed that he
	12.12 Rejoice in *h*, be patient in suffering,
1 Cor	15.19 for in this life only we have *h* in Christ,
Eph	1.12 who were the first to set our *h* on Christ
	1.18 is the *h* to which he has called you,
Col	1. 5 of the *h* laid up for you in heaven.
	1.23 from the *h* promised by the gospel
	1.27 which is Christ in you, the *h* of glory.
1 Thess	1. 3 love and steadfastness of *h* in our Lord
	2.19 what is our *h* or joy or crown of
Titus	2.13 godly, while we wait for the blessed *h*,
Heb	6.18 encouraged to seize the *h* set before us.
	10.23 us hold fast the confession of our *h*
1 Pet	1. 3 has given us a new birth into a living *h*
1 Jn	3. 3 who have this *h* in him purify

HOPE (HOPED HOPES) (v)

Ps	33.18 him, on those who *h* in his steadfast
	33.22 LORD, be upon us even as we *h* in you.
	42. 5 within me? *H* in God; for I shall again

Ps	43. 5 *H* in God; for I shall again praise him,
	56. 6 steps. As they have *h* to have my life,
	71.14 But I will *h* continually, and will praise
	119. 74 rejoice, because I have *h* in your word.
	119.166 I *h* for your salvation, O LORD, and I
Lam	3.18 and all that I had *h* for from the LORD."
Mt	12.21 And in his name will the Gentiles *h*."
Lk	6.34 to those from whom you *h* to receive,
	24.21 we had *h* that he was the one to
Rom	8.24 is not hope. For who *h* for what is seen?
	15.12 Gentiles; in him the Gentiles shall *h*."
1 Cor	15.19 for in this life only we have *h* in Christ,

HORN (HORNS)

1 Kings	1.50 up and went to grasp the *h* of the altar.
	2.28 the LORD and grasped the *h* of the altar.
Jer	48.25 The *h* of Moab is cut off, and his arm is
Ezek	29.21 I will cause a *h* to sprout up for the
Dan	3. 5 when you hear the sound of the *h*, pipe,
	7. 7 that preceded it, and it had ten *h*.
	8. 3 two *h*. Both *h* were long, but one was
Zech	1.18 I looked up and saw four *h*. I asked the
Rev	17.12 the ten *h* that you saw are ten kings

HORSE (HORSES)

Deut	17.16 he must not acquire many *h* for himself,
Josh	11. 6 you shall hamstring their *h*, and burn
1 Kings	10.28 Solomon's import of *h* was from Egypt
2 Chr	1.16 Solomon's *h* were imported from Egypt
	9.25 Solomon had four thousand stalls for *h*
Job	39.18 aloft, it laughs at the *h* and its rider.
Ps	32. 9 Do not be like a *h* or a mule, without
	33.17 The war *h* is a vain hope for victory,
Prov	21.31 *h* is made ready for the day of battle,
	26. 3 A whip for the *h*, a bridle for the
Am	6.12 Do *h* run on rocks? Does one plow the
Zech	1. 8 the night I saw a man riding on a red *h*!
	6. 2 The first chariot had red *h*, the second
Jas	3. 3 put bits into the mouths of *h* to make

HOSANNAH

Mt	21.15 "*H* to the Son of David!" they became
Mk	11. 9 shouting, "*H*! Blessed is the one who

HOSEA

Hos	1. 1 word of the LORD that came to *H* son of
Rom	9.25 As indeed he says in *H*, "Those who

HOSPITABLE

1 Tim	3. 2 temperate, sensible, respectable, *h*, an
Titus	1. 8 he must be *h*, a lover of goodness,
1 Pet	4. 9 Be *h* to one another without

HOSPITALITY

Rom	12.13 of the saints; extend *h* to strangers.

HOSTILE

Rom	8. 7 that is set on the flesh is *h* to God;
Col	1.21 were once estranged and *h* in mind,

HOSTILITY

Deut	15. 9 view your needy neighbor with *h* and

HOSTS

2 Sam	7.26 'The LORD is God over Israel'; and
Ps	24.10 is this King of glory? The LORD of *h*,
Isa	1. 9 If the LORD of *h* had not left us a few

HOUR

Mt	20.12 'These last worked only one *h*, and you
	25.13 for you know neither the day nor the *h*.
Mk	13.32 about that day or *h* no one knows,
	14.35 possible, the *h* might pass from him.
	14.41 The *h* has come; the Son of man is
Lk	22.53 But this is your *h*, and the power of
Jn	4.21 me, the *h* is coming when you will
	7.30 him, because his *h* had not yet come.
	12.23 "The *h* has come for the Son of Man to
	12.27 I say— 'Father, save me from this *h*'?

Jn	16.32 The *h* is coming, indeed it has come,

HOUSE (HOUSES)

Lev	27.14 If a person consecrates a *h* to the LORD,
Deut	8.12 eaten your fill and built fine *h* and live
2 Sam	7.11 to you that the LORD will make you a *h*.
2 Kings	25. 9 burned the *h* of the LORD, the king's *h*,
1 Chr	17. 5 I have not lived in a *h* since the day I
	17.10 to you that the LORD will build you a *h*.
	22. 5 and the *h* that is to be built for the
	28. 2 planned to build a *h* of rest for the ark
2 Chr	5.14 for the glory of the LORD filled the *h* of
	22.12 hidden in the *h* of God, while Athaliah
	24. 4 Joash decided to restore the *h* of
	29.18 "We have cleansed all the *h* of the LORD,
Ezra	3.11 the foundation of the *h* of the LORD
	6.15 this *h* was finished on the third day of
Neh	13.11 said, "Why is the *h* of God forsaken?"
Job	8.14 is gossamer, a spider's *h* their trust.
Ps	42. 4 led them in procession to the *h* of God,
	52. 8 like a green olive tree in the *h* of God.
	69. 9 zeal for your *h* that has consumed me;
	84.10 be a doorkeeper in the *h* of my God
	92.13 They are planted in the *h* of the LORD,
	122. 1 to me, "Let us go to the *h* of the LORD!"
Prov	25.24 in a *h* shared with a contentious wife.
Eccl	7. 2 better to go to the *h* of mourning than
Isa	2. 3 the LORD, to the *h* of the God of Jacob;
	6. 4 who called, and the *h* filled with smoke.
	22.24 him the whole weight of his ancestral *h*,
	38. 1 Set your *h* in order; for you shall die;
Jer	16. 5 Do not enter the *h* of mourning, or go
	26. 9 'This *h* shall be like Shiloh, and this
	52.13 He burned the *h* of the LORD, the king's
Ezek	10. 4 the *h*; the *h* was filled with the cloud,
Joel	3.18 fountain shall come forth from the *h* of
Hag	1. 4 paneled *h*, while this *h* lies in ruins?
	1. 9 Because my *h* lies in ruins, while all of
Mt	21.13 "My *h* shall be called a *h* of prayer'; but
Mk	5.38 When they came to the *h* of the leader
	6.10 "Whenever you enter a *h*, stay there
	11.17 'My *h* shall be called a *h* of prayer for
Lk	2.49 know that I must be in my Father's *h*?"
	6.48 like a man building a *h*, who dug deeply
	9. 4 Whatever *h* you enter, stay there and
	10. 7 to be paid. Do not go from *h* to *h*.
	11.17 becomes a desert, and *h* falls on *h*.
	13.35 See, your *h* is left to you. And I tell you,
	19.46 'My *h* shall be a *h* of prayer'; but you
Jn	2.16 making my father's *h* a market place!"
Acts	7.48 Most High does not dwell in *h* made
	20.20 teaching you publicly and from *h* to *h*,
1 Cor	16.19 with the church in their *h*, greet you

HOUSEHOLD

Josh	24.15 me and my *h*, we will serve the LORD."
Prov	31.21 for all her *h* are clothed in crimson.
	31.27 She looks well to the ways of her *h*, and
Mt	10.36 foes will be members of one's own *h*.
	13.52 is like the master of a *h* who brings out
Jn	4.53 believed, along with his whole *h*.
Acts	16.31 and you will be saved, you and your *h*."
Phil	4.22 you, especially those of the emperor's *h*.
1 Tim	3. 4 He must manage his own *h* well,
	3.15 one ought to behave in the *h* of God,

HOUSETOP (HOUSETOPS)

Prov	21. 9 live in a corner of the *h* than in a house
Mt	10.27 hear whispered, proclaim from the *h*.
	24.17 the one on the *h* must not go down to
Mk	13.15 the one on the *h* must not go down or
Lk	12. 3 doors will be proclaimed from the *h*.

HUMAN

Job	4.17 Can *h* beings be pure before their
	5. 7 but *h* beings are born to trouble just as
	7.17 What are *h* beings, that you make so

Ps	9.20 the nations know that they are only *h*.
	144. 3 what are *h* beings that you regard them,
Prov	27.19 face, so one *h* heart reflects another.
Jer	10.23 that the way of *h* beings is not in their
Dan	2.34 stone was cut out, not by *h* hands, and
	7.13 I saw one like a *h* being coming with
Rom	3.20 "no *h* being will be justified in his sight"
1 Cor	2.13 in words not taught by *h* wisdom but
	3. 3 behaving according to *h* inclinations?
	3.21 So let no one boast about *h* leaders. For
2 Cor	10. 3 Indeed, we live as *h* beings, but we do
	10. 4 of our warfare are not merely *h*,
Gal	1. 1 Paul an apostle—sent by neither *h*
Heb	2. 6 "What are *h* beings that you are mindful

HUMAN RACE

Prov	8.31 inhabited world and delighting in the *h*.

HUMANITY

Eph	2.15 might create in himself one new *h* in

HUMANKIND

Gen	1.26 God said, "Let us make *h* in our image,

HUMBLE (HUMBLED HUMBLES)

Ex	10. 3 How long will you refuse to *h* yourself
Lev	26.41 if then their uncircumcised heart is *h*
Deut	8. 2 in order to *h* you, testing you to know
1 Kings	21.29 how Ahab has *h* himself before me?
2 Kings	22.19 and you *h* yourself before the LORD,
2 Chr	7.14 are called by my name *h* themselves,
	12. 6 of Israel and the king *h* themselves
	30.11 and Zebulun *h* themselves and came to
	33.26 Hezekiah *h* himself for the pride of his
	34.27 patient and you *h* yourself before God
Ps	55.19 from of old, will hear and *h* them—
	119. 67 Before I was *h* I went astray; but now I
	119. 75 and that in faithfulness you have *h* me.
Isa	5.15 low, and the eyes of the haughty are *h*.
Dan	5.22 And you, Belshazzar his son, have not *h*
	10.12 and to *h* yourself before your God,
Mt	18. 4 Whoever becomes *h* like this child is
	23.12 all those who *h* themselves will be
Lk	18.14 all who *h* themselves will be exalted."
2 Cor	12.21 again, my God may *h* me before you,
Phil	2. 8 he *h* himself and became obedient
Jas	4.10 *H* yourselves before the Lord, and he
1 Pet	5. 6 *H* yourselves therefore under the mighty

HUMBLE (adj)

Num	12. 3 Now the man Moses was very *h*, more
2 Sam	22.28 You deliver a *h* people, but your eyes
Job	22.29 you say it is pride; for he saves the *h*.
Ps	18.27 you deliver a *h* people, but the haughty
	25. 9 He leads the *h* in what is right, and
	149. 4 his people; he adorns the *h* with victory.
Isa	57.15 those who are contrite and *h* in spirit,
Zeph	2. 3 Seek the LORD, all you *h* of the land,
	3.12 the midst of you a people *h* and lowly.
Zech	9. 9 victorious is he, *h* and riding on a
Mt	21. 5 your king is coming to you, *h*, and
1 Pet	3. 8 another, a tender heart, and a *h* mind.

HUMILITY

Prov	15.33 if wisdom, and *h* goes before honor.
	22. 4 reward for *h* and fear of the LORD is
Phil	2. 3 but in *h* regard others as better than

HUNGER

Ps	34.10 young lions suffer want and *h*, but those
Isa	49.10 they shall not *h* or thirst, neither
Jer	38. 9 him in the cistern to die there of *h*,
Lam	2.19 lives of your children, who faint for *h*
Ezek	34.29 they shall no more be consumed with *h*
Mt	5. 6 who *h* and thirst for righteousness,
Acts	27.38 had satisfied their *h*, they lightened
2 Cor	6. 5 labors, sleepless nights, *h*; by purity,
Rev	7.16 They will *h* no more, and thirst no

HUNGRY

1 Sam	2.	5 but those who were *h* are fat with spoil.
Ps	50.12	"If I were *h*, I would not tell you, for the
	107.	9 the thirsty, and the *h* he fills with good
Prov	6.30	satisfy their appetite when they are *h*.
Isa	8.21	the land, greatly distressed and *h*;
Mt	21.18	when he returned to the city, he was *h*.
Mk	2.25	when he and his companions were *h*
	11.12	they came from Bethany, he was *h*.
Lk	1.53	filled the *h* with good things, and sent
	6.21	"Blessed are you who are *h* now, for you
Jn	6.35	whoever comes to me will never be *h*,
Acts	10.10	roof to pray. He became *h* and wanted
1 Cor	4.11	To the present hour we are *h* and
	11.34	If you are *h*, eat at home, so that when
2 Cor	11.27	*h* and thirsty, often without food, cold
Phil	4.12	secret of being well-fed and of going *h*,

HUNT (HUNTED)

Ezek	13.18	lives! Will you *h* down lives among my
Job	10.16	Bold as a lion you *h* me; you repeat
Ps	140.	11 let evil speedily *h* down the violent!
Jer	50.17	Israel is a *h* sheep driven away by lions.

HUNTER

Gen	10.	9 He was a mighty *h* before the LORD;
	25.27	Esau was a skillful *h*, a man of the

HURAM

2 Chr	2.11	Then King *H* of Tyre answered in a

HURRIEDLY

Prov	19.	2 one who moves too *h* misses the way.

HURRY

Gen	19.22	*H*, escape there, for I can do nothing

HURT

1 Chr	4.10	and that you would keep me from *h* and
Eccl	8.	9 authority over another to the other's *h*.
Isa	11.	9 They will not *h* or destroy on all my
Jer	8.21	For the *h* of my poor people I am *h*, I

HUSBAND (HUSBANDS HUSBAND'S)

Gen	3.	6 she also gave some to her *h*, who was
	18.12	I have grown old, and my *h* is old,
Deut	25.	5 Her *h* brother shall go in to her, taking
Esth	1.17	to look with contempt upon their *h*,
Prov	31.23	Her *h* is known in the city gates, taking
Isa	54.	5 For your Maker is your *h*, the LORD of
Jer	31.32	that they broke, though I was their *h*,
Mt	1.16	father of Joseph the *h* of Mary, of whom
Jn	4.16	said to her, "Go, call your *h*, and come
Rom	7.	2 woman is bound by law to her *h*
1 Cor	7.	2 own wife and each woman her own *h*.
	7.14	the unbelieving *h* is made holy through
	7.34	of the world, how to please her *h*.
Eph	5.25	*H*, love your wives, just as Christ loved
	5.33	and a wife should respect her *h*.
Col	3.19	*H*, love your wives, and never treat
1 Tim	3.2	be above reproach, the *h* of one wife,
1 Pet	3.	7 *H*, in the same way, show consideration

HYMN (HYMNS)

Mt	26.30	When they had sung the *h*, they went
Mk	14.26	When they had sung the *h*, they went
1 Cor	14.26	together, each one has a *h*, a lesson,
Eph	5.19	as you sing psalms and *h* and spiritual
Col	3.16	sing psalms, *h*, and spiritual songs

HYPOCRISY

Lk	12.	1 yeast of the Pharisees, that is, their *h*.

HYPOCRITE (HYPOCRITES)

Mt	6.	2 sound a trumpet before you, as the *h* do
	6.	5 you pray, do not be like the *h*;
	6.16	you fast, do not look dismal, like the *h*,
	7.	5 You *h*, first take the log out of your own
	15.	7 You *h*! Isaiah prophesied rightly about

Mt	23.13	woe to you, scribes and Pharisees, *h*!
	23.23	"Woe to you, scribes and Pharisees, *h*!
Mk	7.	6 Isaiah prophesied rightly about you *h*,
Lk	13.15	"You *h*! does not each of you on the

HYSSOP

Ex	12.22	Take a bunch of *h*, dip it in the blood
Ps	51.	7 Purge me with *h*, and I shall be clean;
Jn	19.29	sponge full of the wine on a branch of *h*

I

IDLE

Mt	20.	3 he saw others standing *i* in the

IDLENESS

2 Thess	3.	6 away from believers who are living in *i*
	3.11	some of you are living in *i*, mere

IDOL (IDOLS)

Ex	20.	4 You shall not make for yourself an *i*,
Lev	26.	1 You shall not make for yourselves no *i* and
Deut	5.	8 You shall not make for yourself an *i*,
Judg	17.	3 for my son, to make an *i* of cast metal.
	18.30	Danites set up the *i* for themselves.
1 Sam	19.13	Michal took an *i* and laid it on the bed;
1 Chr	16.26	For all the gods of the peoples are *i*,
2 Chr	15.	8 put away the abominable *i* from all the
Ps	31.	6 those who pay regard to worthless *i*,
	78.58	they moved him to jealousy with their *i*.
	106.	38 they sacrificed to the *i* of Canaan;
Isa	2.	8 Their land is filled with *i*; they bow
	2.18	The *i* shall utterly pass away. Enter the
	19.	3 they will consult the *i* and the spirits of
	40.19	An *i*?—A workman casts it, and a
	44.	9 All who make *i* are nothing, and the
	48.	5 that you would not say, "My *i* did them,
Jer	50.38	land of images, and they go mad over *i*.
Ezek	14.	4 who take their *i* into their hearts and
	20.18	nor defile yourselves with their *i*.
Hos	4.17	Ephraim is joined to *i*—let him alone.
	8.	4 they made *i* for their own destruction.
Mic	1.	7 with fire, and all her *i* I will lay waste;
Acts	15.20	to abstain only from things polluted by *i*
	17.16	to see that the city was full of *i*.
	21.25	that has been sacrificed to *i*
1 Cor	8.	1 concerning food offered to *i*: we know
	10.19	to *i* is anything, or that an *i* is anything?
1 Thess	1.	9 you turned to God from *i*, to serve a
1 Jn	5.21	Little children, keep yourselves from *i*.

IDOLATER (IDOLATERS)

1 Cor	6.	9 Do not be deceived! Fornicators, *i*,
Eph	5.	5 or one who is greedy (that is, an *i*), has

IGNORANCE (IGNORANT)

Ps	73.22	I was stupid and *i*, I was like a brute
Acts	17.30	has overlooked the times of human *i*,
Eph	4.18	because of their *i* and hardness of heart.

IGNORED

Deut	33.	9 he *i* his kin, and did not acknowledge

ILL

Lk	7.	2 whom he valued highly, and who was *i*
Jn	11.	3 to Jesus, "Lord, he whom you love is *i*."
1 Cor	11.30	this reason many of you are weak and *i*,
Phil	2.26	because you heard that he was *i*.

ILLNESS

Deut	7.15	LORD will turn away from you every *i*;
2 Kings	8.	8 him, whether I shall recover from this *i*."
Ps	41.	3 sickbed; in their *i* you heal all their
Jn	11.	4 "This *i* does not lead to death; rather it

ILL-TREATMENT

Heb	11.25	choosing rather to share *i* with the

IMAGE (IMAGES)

Gen	1.26 "Let us make humankind in our *i*,
Num	33.52 destroy all their molten *i*, and demolish
1 Sam	6. 5 you must make *i* of your tumors and *i*
1 Cor	11. 7 since he is the *i* and reflection of God;
Col	1.15 He is the *i* of the invisible God, the
	3.10 according to the *i* of its creator.

IMAGINE

Eph	3.20 far more than all that we ask or *i*,

IMITATE (IMITATING)

Phil	3.17 join in *i* me, and observe those who live
3 Jn	11 Beloved, do not *i* what is evil but *i* what

IMITATORS

1 Cor	4.16 I appeal to you, then, be *i* of me. For
	11. 1 be saved. Be *i* of me, as I am of Christ.
Eph	5. 1 be *i* of God, as beloved children, and
1 Thess	1. 6 you became *i* of us and of the Lord, for
Heb	6.12 but *i* of those who through faith

IMMANUEL (EMMANUEL)

Isa	7.14 shall bear a son, and shall name him *I*.
	8. 8 will fill the breadth of your land, O *I*.
Mt	1.23 and they shall name him *E*," which

IMMORALITY

1 Cor	5. 1 that there is sexual *i* among you,

IMMORTAL (IMMORTALITY)

Rom	1.23 exchanged the glory of the *i* God for
1 Cor	15.53 and this mortal body must put on *i*.

IMPERISHABLE

1 Cor	15.42 is sown is perishable, what is raised is *i*.
1 Pet	1. 4 into an inheritance that is *i*, undefiled,

IMPLORE

2 Kings 20. 3 "Remember now, O Lord, I *i* you, how I	

IMPOSSIBLE

Gen	11. 6 they propose to do will now be *i*
Lk	1.37 "For nothing will be *i* with God."
Heb	10. 4 it is *i* for the blood of bulls and goats to

IMPRISONED

Jer	37.15 Jeremiah, and they beat him and *i* him
Acts	22.19 I *i* and beat those who believed
Rom	11.32 God has *i* all in disobedience, so that

IMPRISONMENT (IMPRISONMENTS)

Acts	20.23 city that *i* and persecutions are waiting
2 Cor	6. 5 hardships, calamities, beatings, *i*, riots,
	11.23 greater labors, far more *i*, with countless
Phil	1.13 to everyone else that my *i* is for Christ;
Heb	11.36 and flogging, and even chains and *i*.

IMPURE (IMPURITY)

Zech	13. 1 to cleanse them from sin and *i*.
Rom	1.24 them up in the lusts of their hearts to *i*,
2 Cor	12.21 have not repented of the *i*, sexual
Eph	4.19 greedy to practice every kind of *i*.
1 Thess	2. 3 does not spring from deceit or *i* motives

IMPUTE (IMPUTES)

1 Sam	22.15 Do not let the king *i* anything to his
Ps	32. 2 those to whom the Lord *i* no iniquity,

INCENSE

Ex	30. 1 shall make an altar on which to offer *i*;
	30.35 make an *i* blended as by the perfumer,
	37.25 He made an altar of *i* of acacia wood,
Num	16.17 of you take his censer, and put *i* on it,
2 Chr	26.16 to make an offering on the altar of *i*.
Ps	141. 2 Let my prayer be counted as *i* before
Ezek	8.11 the fragrant cloud of *i* was ascending.
Mal	1.11 in every place *i* is offered to my name,
Lk	1. 9 the sanctuary of the Lord and offer *i*.

INCITED

1 Chr	21. 1 and *i* David to count the people of
Acts	13.50 But the Jews *i* the devout women of

INCLINATION

Gen	6. 5 every *i* of the thoughts of their hearts
	8.21 for the *i* of the human heart is evil from

INCLINE (INCLINING)

1 Kings 8.58 but *i* our hearts to him, to walk in all	
Prov	2. 2 and *i* your heart to understanding;
Dan	9.18 *I* your ear, O my God, and hear. Open

INCOME

Prov	3.14 for her *i* is better than silver, and her

INCREASE (INCREASED INCREASES)

Ps	71.21 You will *i* my honor, and comfort me
	115. 14 May the Lord give you *i*, both you and
Prov	16.21 and pleasant speech *i* persuasiveness.
Eccl	5.11 When goods *i*, they who eat them *i*; and
Isa	26.15 But you have *i* the nation, O Lord, you
Ezek	34.27 the earth shall yield its *i*. They shall be
Lk	2.52 Jesus *i* in wisdom and in years, and in
Jn	3.30 He must *i*, but I must decrease."
Acts	16. 5 in the faith and *i* in numbers daily.
1 Thess 3.12 the Lord make you *i* and abound in love	

INCREDIBLE

Acts	26. 8 Why is it thought *i* by any of you that

INDICATE (INDICATES INDICATING)

Jn	21.19 said this to *i* the kind of death by which
Acts	25.27 a prisoner without *i* the charges against
Heb	9. 8 By this the Holy Spirit *i* that the way

INDICTMENT

Job	31.35 that I had the *i* written by my adversary!
Hos	4. 1 Lord has an *i* against the inhabitants
	12. 2 Lord has an *i* against Judah, and will

INDIGNANT

Mk	10.14 when Jesus saw this, he was *i* and said

INDISPENSABLE

1 Cor	12.22 the body that seem to be weaker are *i*,

INDULGE

2 Pet	2.10 who *i* their flesh in depraved lust, and

INFANT (INFANTS)

Hos	11. 4 like those who lift *i* to their cheeks.
Isa	13.16 Their *i* will be dashed to pieces before
Mt	11.25 intelligent and have revealed them to *i*;
Lk	10.21 and revealed them to *i*; yes, for such
	18.15 bringing even *i* to him that he might
1 Cor	3. 1 as people of the flesh, as *i* in Christ.
Heb	5.13 who lives on milk, being still an *i*,

INFERIOR

Job	12. 3 I am not *i* to you. Who does not know
2 Cor	12.11 I am not at all *i* to these super-apostles,

INFIRMITIES

Ps	41. 3 in their illness you heal all their *i*.

INFORMED

Jude	5 to remind you, though you are fully *i*,

INFURIATED

Esth	3. 5 or do obeisance to him, Haman was *i*.

INHABITS (INHABITED)

Isa	57.15 the high and lofty one who *i* eternity,
Jer	17.25 and this city shall be *i* forever.

INHERIT

Lev	20.24 You shall *i* their land, and I will give it
Num	33.54 to your ancestral tribes you shall *i*.
	34.13 This is the land that you shall *i* by lot,

Ps	37.	9 but those who wait for the LORD shall *i*
Zech	2.12	The LORD will *i* Judah as his portion in
Mt	25.34	*i* the kingdom prepared for you from the
Mk	10.17	what must I do to *i* eternal life?"
Lk	10.25	said, "what must I do to *i* eternal life?"
	18.18	what must I do to *i* eternal life?"
Rom	4.13	the promise that he would *i* the world

INHERITANCE

Num	27.	8 you shall pass his *i* on to his daughter.
Deut	18.	1 Levi, shall have no . . . *i* within Israel;
	20.16	God is giving you as an *i*, you must not
Josh	13.14	by fire to the LORD . . . are their *i*,
1 Kings	21.	3 that I should give you my ancestral *i*."
1 Chr	16.18	land of Canaan as your portion for an *i*."
Ps	105.	11 land of Canaan as your portion for an *i*."
Prov	13.22	The good leave an *i* to their children's
Lam	5.	2 Our *i* has been turned over to strangers,
Ezek	47.14	and this land shall fall to you as your *i*.
Acts	20.32	up and to give you the *i* among all who
Gal	3.18	For if the *i* comes from the law, it no
Eph	1.18	of his glorious *i* among the saints,
Col	3.24	you will receive the *i* as your reward;
1 Pet	1.	4 into an *i* which is imperishable,

INIQUITY (INIQUITIES)

Ex	34.	7 forgiving *i* and transgression and sin, yet
	34.	7 visiting the *i* of the parents upon the
2 Sam	7.14	When he commits *i*, I will punish him
Ezra	9.	6 our *i* have risen higher than our heads,
Job	34.32	if I have done *i*, I will do it no more'?
Ps	51.	9 face from my sins, and blot out all my *i*.
	66.18	If I had cherished *i* in my heart, then
	106.	43 and were brought low through their *i*.
Prov	5.22	The *i* of the wicked ensnare them, and
Isa	53.	6 the LORD has laid on him the *i* of us all.
Ezek	36.33	day that I cleanse you from all your *i*,
	39.23	of Israel went into captivity for their *i*,
Titus	2.14	redeem us from all *i* and purify for

INJURED

Ezek	34.16	and I will bind up the *i*, and I will

INJUSTICE

Prov	22.	8 Whoever sows *i* will reap calamity, and
Isa	58.	6 that I choose: to loose the bonds of *i*,
Rom	9.14	Is there *i* on God's part? By no means!

INK

Jer	36.18	and I wrote them with *i* on the scroll."
2 Cor	3.	3 written not with *i* but with the Spirit of
2 Jn		12 rather not use paper and *i*; instead I

INN

Lk	2.	7 there was no place for them in the *i*.
	10.34	brought him to an *i*, and took care of

INNOCENT

Gen	20.	4 said, Lord, will you destroy an *i* people?
Deut	19.13	you shall purge the guilt of *i* blood from
2 Kings	24.	4 filled Jerusalem with *i* blood, and the
Job	4.	7 now, who that was *i* ever perished?
	9.28	for I know you will not hold me *i*.
	17.	8 and the *i* stir themselves up against
	27.17	wear it, and the *i* will divide the silver.
	34.	5 Job has said, 'I am *i*, and God has
Ps	19.13	I shall be blameless, and *i* of great
Isa	3.10	Tell the *i* how fortunate they are, for
Jer	2.35	"I am *i*; surely his anger has turned
	19.	4 filled this place with the blood of the *i*,
Jon	1.	14 Do not make us guilty of *i* blood;
Mt	10.16	so be wise as serpents and *i* as doves.
	27.24	"I am *i* of this man's blood; see to it
Lk	23.47	God and said, "Certainly this man was *i*!"
1 Tim	1.	9 law is not laid down for the *i* but for

INQUIRE (INQUIRED)

Gen	25.22	do I live?" So she went to *i* of the LORD.

Ex	18.15	the people come to me to *i* of God.
Deut	12.30	do not *i* concerning their gods, saying,
Judg	20.18	to Bethel, where they *i* of God, "Which
1 Sam	14.37	So Saul *i* of God, "Shall I go down after
	23.	2 David *i* of the LORD, "Shall I go and
2 Sam	2.	1 David *i* of the LORD, "Shall I go up into
	5.19	David *i* of the LORD, "Shall I go up
2 Kings	22.13	"Go, *i* of the LORD for me, for the
1 Chr	14.10	David *i* of God, "Shall I go up against
2 Chr	34.21	"Go, *i* of the LORD for me and for those
Jer	8.	2 which they have *i* of and worshiped;
	21.	2 "Please *i* of the LORD on our behalf, for

INSANE

Acts	26.25	Too much learning is driving you *i*!"

INSCRIBED

Job	19.23	down! O that they were *i* in a book!
Dan	5.25	hand was sent and this writing was *i*.
	10.21	tell you what is *i* in the book of truth.

INSCRIPTION

Mk	15.26	The *i* of the charge against him read,
Lk	23.38	There was also an *i* over him, "This is
Jn	19.19	Pilate also had an *i* written and put on

INSIGHT

Dan	1.	4 endowed with knowledge and *i*, and

INSIST

Eph	4.17	I affirm and *i* on in the Lord; you must

INSOLENT

Ps	19.13	Keep back your servant also from the *i*;

INSPIRED

2 Tim	3.16	All scripture is *i* by God and is useful

INSTALLMENT

2 Cor	1.22	us his Spirit in our hearts as a first *i*.

INSTINCTIVELY

Rom	2.14	do *i* what the law requires, these,

INSTRUCT (INSTRUCTED)

2 Chr	26.	5 days of Zechariah, who *i* him in the fear
Ps	32.	8 I will *i* you and teach you the way you
Lk	1.	4 the things of which you have been *i*.
Acts	7.22	Moses was *i* in all the wisdom of the
1 Tim	1.	3 *i* certain people not to teach any
2 Tim	3.	7 who are always being *i* and can never
	3.15	writings that are able to *i* you for

INSTRUCTION

Job	36.10	He opens their ears to *i*, and commands
Prov	8.10	Take my *i* instead of silver, and
Isa	29.24	and those who grumble will accept *i*.
Mic	4.	2 out of Zion shall go forth *i*, and the
Mal	2.	6 True *i* was in his mouth, and no wrong

INSTRUCTORS

Mt	23.10	Nor are you to be called *i*, for you have

INSTRUMENT (INSTRUMENTS)

1 Chr	15.16	as the singers to play on musical *i*,
Am	6.	5 and like David improvise on *i* of music;
Acts	9.15	he is an *i* whom I have chosen to bring

INSULT (INSULTS)

Gen	39.14	has brought among us a Hebrew to *i* us!
Ps	69.	9 the *i* of those who *i* you have fallen on
	69.20	*I* have broken my heart, so that I am in
Prov	17.	5 Those who mock the poor *i* their Maker;
Isa	50.	6 out the beard; I hid not my face from *i*
Hos	12.14	on him and pay him back for his *i*.
Lk	11.45	when you say these things, you *i* us too."
Acts	23.	4 "Do you dare to *i* God's high priest?"
Rom	15.	3 "The *i* of those who *i* you have fallen on
2 Cor	12.10	I am content with weaknesses, *i*,

INTEGRITY

Job	2.	9 "Do you still persist in your *i*? Curse
Titus	2.	7 and in your teaching show *i*, gravity,

INTEND

1 Kings	5.	5 I *i* to build a house for the name of the
2 Cor	8.21	we *i* to do what is right not only in the

INTENTIONS

Mt	15.19	For out of the heart come evil *i*,

INTERCEDE (INTERCEDED INTERCEDES)

Deut	9.20	but I *i* also on behalf of Aaron at the
Jer	27.18	them, then let them *i* with the LORD
Rom	8.26	that very Spirit *i* with sighs too deep for

INTERCESSION

1 Sam	2.25	sins against the LORD, who can make *i*?"
Isa	53.12	many, and made *i* for the transgressors.
Heb	7.25	he always lives to make *i* for them.

INTEREST

Lev	25.36	Do not take *i* in advance or otherwise
Neh	5.10	and grain. Let us stop this taking of *i*.
Ps	15.	5 who do not lend money at *i*, and do not

INTERMARRY

Josh	23.12	left here among you, and *i* with them,

INTERPRET (INTERPRETED)

Lk	12.56	how to *i* the appearance of earth and
	24.27	he *i* to them the things about himself in
1 Cor	14.27	three, and each in turn; and let one *i*.

INTERPRETATION

Dan	2.	4 the dream, and we will reveal the *i*."
	2.36	dream; now we will tell the king its *i*.
	4.18	you, Belteshazzar, declare the *i*, since
	5.12	Daniel be called, and he will give the *i*."
2 Pet	1.20	of scripture is a matter of one's own *i*,

INTERPRETER

Gen	42.23	since he spoke with them through an *i*.

INTERVALS

2 Kings 20.	9	advanced ten *i*; shall it retreat ten *i*?"

INTERVENED

Jer	15.11	I have *i* in your life for good, surely I

INVISIBLE

Rom	1.20	divine nature, *i* though they are, have
Col	1.15	He is the image of the *i* God, the
1 Tim	1.17	of the ages, immortal, *i*, the only God,

INVITED

Jn	2.	2 had also been *i* to the wedding.
Rev	19.	9 Blessed are those who are *i* to the

INVOKE

Gen	4.26	people began to *i* the name of the LORD.
	12.	8 to the LORD and *i* the name of the LORD.

IRON

Josh	17.16	who live in the plain have chariots of *i*,
2 Kings	6.	6 threw it in there, and made the *i* float.
1 Chr	20.	3 set them to work with saws and *i* picks
Ps	105.18	fetters, his neck was put in a collar of *i*;
Prov	27.17	I sharpens *i*, and one person sharpens
Jer	28.13	broken wooden bars only to forge *i* bars
Dan	2.35	Then the *i*, the clay, the bronze, the

IRON-SMELTER

Deut	4.20	brought you out of the *i*, out of Egypt,

IRONSMITH

Isa	44.12	The *i* fashions it and works over the

ISAAC

His birth foretold, Gen 18.1-15; born, Gen 21.1-7; of-

fered to God, Gen 22.1-19; married Rebekah, Gen 24; father of twins, Gen 25.19-26; dwelt in Gerar, Gen 26.1-6; Isaac and Abimelech, Gen 26.7-33; blessed Jacob, Gen 27.1-40; death and burial, Gen 35.29.

Gen	21.	3 Abraham gave the name *I* to his son
Gal	4.28	are children of the promise, like *I*.
Heb	11.20	By faith *I* invoked blessings for the

ISAIAH

Called, Isa 6; father of two sons, Isa 7.3; 8.3; prophesied during the reign of Uzziah, Jotham, Ahaz, and Hezekiah, Isa 1.1; counselled Ahaz, Isa 7; counselled Hezekiah, 2 Kings 19—20 (Isa 37—39).

Mt	3.	3 is the one of whom the prophet *I* spoke
	15.	7 I prophesied rightly about you when he
Lk	4.17	the scroll of the prophet *I* was given to
Acts	8.28	it and heard him reading the prophet *I*.

ISHMAEL

Gen	16.11	shall bear a son; you shall call him *I*,
	17.18	God, "O that *I* might live in your sight!"
	25.12	These are the descendants of *I*,

ISRAEL

Gen	32.28	shall no longer be called Jacob, but *I*,
Ex	1.	1 of the sons of *I* who came to Egypt
	4.22	says the LORD, *I* is my first-born son.
1 Sam	7.	6 And Samuel judged the people of *I* at
1 Kings	4.	1 King Solomon was king over all *I*,
	12.19	I has been in rebellion against the
	17.	1 the LORD the God of *I* lives, before
1 Chr	14.	8 David had been anointed king over all *I*,
2 Chr	30.	1 the passover to the Lord the God of *I*.
Ezra	7.	7 Some of the people of *I*, and some of
Ps	25.22	Redeem *I*, O God, out of all its
	103.	7 to Moses, his acts to the people of *I*.
Isa	1.	3 but *I* does not know, my people do not
Mt	2.	6 a ruler who is to shepherd my people *I*.' "
	27.42	He is the King of *I*; let him come down
Lk	2.25	looking forward to the consolation of *I*,
Acts	1.	6 when you will restore the kingdom to *I*?"
Rom	11.26	so all *I* will be saved; as it is written,
Eph	2.12	aliens from the commonwealth of *I*,
Heb	8.	8 a new covenant with the house of *I*

ISRAELITES

Ex	14.	8 he pursued the *I*, who were going out
	19.	1 after the *I* had gone out of the land of
Josh	4.	8 The *I* did as Joshua commanded. They
Rev	21.12	the names of the twelve tribes of the *I*;

ISSACHAR

Gen	30.18	to my husband"; so she named him *I*.
	49.14	I is a strong donkey, lying down
Num	26.23	The descendants of *I* by their clans: of
Rev	7.	7 from the tribe of *I* twelve thousand,

IVORY

1 Kings 10.18	king also made a great *i* throne, and
	22.39	the *i* house that he built, and all the
Ps	45.	8 From *i* palaces stringed instruments
Am	3.15	the houses of *i* shall perish, and the
	6.	4 Alas for those who lie on beds of *i*, and

J

JABBOK

Gen	32.22	children, and crossed the ford of the *J*.
Deut	3.16	up to the *J*, the wadi being boundary of
Josh	12.	2 as far as the river *J*, the boundary of the

JACKALS

Ezek	13.	4 Your prophets have been like *j* among

JACOB (JACOB'S)

Born, Gen 25.19-26; obtained Esau's birthright, Gen 25.27-34; received Isaac's blessing, Gen 27.1-29; fled from Esau, Gen 27.41—28.5; dream at Bethel and his

83

vow, Gen 28.10-22; served Laban for Rachel and Leah, Gen 29.1-30; dealings with Laban, Gen 30.25-43; departure from Paddan-aram, Gen 31; wrestled at Peniel, Gen 32.24-32; reconciled with Esau, Gen 33.1-16; blessed by God at Bethel, Gen 35.1-15; went down to Egypt, Gen 46—47; blessed Ephraim and Manasseh, Gen 48; blessed his own sons, Gen 49.1-27; death and burial, Gen 49.28 —50.14.

Num	24.17 a star shall come out of *J*, and a scepter
Hos	12.12 *J* fled to the land of Aram, there Israel
Mt	8.11 Isaac and *J* in the kingdom of heaven,
Rom	9.13 is written, "I have loved *J*, but I have
Heb	11.21 By faith, *J*, when dying, blessed each of
Jn	4. 6 *J* well was there, and Jesus, tired out by

JAIRUS

Mk	5.22 leaders of the synagogue named *J* came
Lk	8.41 there came a man named *J*, a leader of

JAMES

Mt	4.21 from there, he saw two other brothers, *J*
	10. 3 tax collector; *J* son of Alphaeus, and
Acts	1.13 Matthew, *J* son of Alphaeus, and Simon
1 Cor	15. 7 Then he appeared to *J*, then to all the

JAPHETH

Gen	9.27 May God make space for *J*, and let him

JAR (JARS)

Judg	7.16 and empty *j*, with torches inside the *j*,
1 Kings	17.14 "The *j* of meal will not be emptied, and
Mk	14.13 a man carrying a *j* of water will meet
Lk	22.10 a man carrying a *j* of water will meet
Jn	4.28 So the woman left her water *j* and went
2 Cor	4. 7 we have this treasure in clay *j*, so that it

JAWBONE

Judg	15.15 Then he found a fresh *j* of a donkey,

JEALOUS

Gen	37.11 his brothers were *j* of him, but his
Num	11.29 said to him, "Are you *j* for my sake?
Deut	4.24 your God is a devouring fire, a *j* God.
	5. 9 for I the Lᴏʀᴅ your God am a *j* God,
	6.15 who is present with you, is a *j* God;
	32.21 They made me *j* with what is no good,
Josh	24.19 He is a *j* God; he will not forgive your
Ps	79. 5 forever? Will your *j* wrath burn like fire?
	106. 16 They were *j* of Moses in the camp, and
Ezek	39.25 Israel; and I will be *j* for my holy name.
Joel	2.18 Then the Lᴏʀᴅ became *j* for his land,
Nah	1. 2 A *j* and avenging God is the Lᴏʀᴅ, the
Zech	8. 2 I am *j* for Zion with great jealousy, and
Acts	7. 9 "The patriarchs, *j* of Joseph, sold him
Rom	11.11 to the Gentiles, so as to make Israel *j*.

JEALOUSY

Num	5.14 if the spirit of *j* comes on him, and he
1 Kings	14.22 they provoked him to *j* with their sins
Prov	6.34 *j* arouses a husband's fury, and he
Isa	11.13 The *j* of Ephraim shall depart, the
Ezek	5.13 I, the Lᴏʀᴅ, have spoken in my *j*, when I
	8. 3 to the seat of the image of *j*, which
Mt	27.18 it was out of *j* that they handed him
Mk	15.10 it was out of *j* that the chief priests had
1 Cor	3. as long as there is *j* and quarreling
2 Cor	11. 2 I feel a divine *j* for you, for I promised

JEHOSHAPHAT

1 Kings	15.24 father David; his son *J* succeeded him.
	22. 7 But *J* said, "Is there no other prophet of
2 Chr	20. 1 some of the Meunites, came against *J*
	20.30 the realm of *J* was quiet, for his God
	21. 1 *J* slept with his ancestors and was
Joel	3. 2 and bring them down to the valley of *J*,

JEPHTHAH

Judg	11. 1 *J* . . . was a mighty warrior. Gilead was
Judg	11.30 *J* made a vow to the Lᴏʀᴅ, and said, "If
	12. 1 said to *J*, "Why did you cross over to
1 Sam	12.11 Lᴏʀᴅ sent . . . *J*, and Samson, and
Heb	11.32 me to tell of Gideon, Barak, Samson, *J*,

JEREMIAH

Called, Jer 1.1-10; vision of almond rod and boiling pot, Jer 1.11-19; sign of the waist cloth, Jer 13.1-11; sign of the potter's vessel, Jer 18; sign of the earthen flask, Jer 19; put in stocks, Jer 20.1-6; sign of the basket of figs, Jer 24; his life threatened, Jer 26; sign of purchase of field, Jer 32.6-44; prophesied to Rechabites, Jer 35; wrote prophecies, Jer 36; imprisoned, Jer 32.1-5; 37.11—38.28; released, Jer 39.11-14; 40.1-6; taken into Egypt, Jer 43.1-7.

Mt	16.14 but others Elijah, and still others *J* or

JERICHO

Josh	2. 1 "Go, view the land, especially *J*." So they
	6. 2 I have handed *J* over to you, along with
1 Kings	16.34 In his days Hiel of Bethel built *J*; he
Mk	10.46 and a large crowd were leaving *J*,
Heb	11.30 By faith the walls of *J* fell after they

JEROBOAM

1 Kings	11.26 *J* son of Nebat . . . rebelled against the
	12. 2 When *J* the son of Nebat heard of it
	12.25 *J* built Shechem in the hill country of
	13. 1 While *J* was standing by the altar to
	14. 1 At that time Abijah son of *J* fell sick.
	14.20 that *J* reigned was twenty-two years;
	14.30 was war between Rehoboam and *J*
	15.25 Nadab the son of *J* began to reign over
	15.34 walking in the way of *J* and in the sin
2 Kings	14.23 *J* the son of Joash of Israel began to
	14.28 Now the rest of the acts of *J*, and all
	14.29 *J* slept with his ancestors, the kings of
Hos	1. 1 in the days of King *J* son of Joash of
Am	7.10 the priest of Bethel, sent to King *J*

JERUSALEM

Judg	19.10 and arrived opposite Jebus (that is, *J*).
2 Sam	5. 5 at *J* he reigned over all Israel and Judah
2 Kings	21. 4 Lᴏʀᴅ had said, "In *J* I will put my name."
2 Chr	20.28 They came to *J*, with harps and lyres
	36.19 broke down the wall of *J*, burned all its
	36.23 charged me to build him a house at *J*,
Ezra	3. 8 their arrival at the house of God at *J*,
Ps	51.18 good pleasure; rebuild the walls of *J*,
	122. 6 Pray for the peace of *J*! "May they
	137. 5 If I forget you, O *J*, let my right hand
Isa	31. 5 so the Lᴏʀᴅ of hosts will protect *J*;
	40. 9 strength, O *J*, herald of good tidings,
Mt	23.37 "*J*, *J*, the city that kills the prophets
Acts	1. 8 my witnesses in *J*, in all Judea and
	15. 2 to go up to *J* to discuss this question
Rom	15.26 with the poor among the saints at *J*.
Gal	4.26 corresponds to the *J* above; she is free,
Heb	12.22 to the city of the God, the heavenly *J*,
Rev	21. 2 saw the holy city, the new *J*, coming

JESUS

His birth foretold, Lk 1.26-38; born, Mt 1.18-25; Lk 2.1-7; circumcised, Lk 2.21; presented in the temple, Lk 2.22-38; visited by the wise men, Mt 2.1-12; fled to Egypt, Mt 2.13-18; brought to Nazareth, Mt 2.19-23 (Lk 2.39); boyhood visit to Jerusalem, Lk 2.41-50; his brothers and sisters, Mt 13.55-56 (Mk 6.3); baptized, Mt 3.13-17 (Mk 1.9-11; Lk 3.21-22; Jn 1.31-34); tempted by the devil, Mt 4.1-11 (Mk 1.12-13; Lk 4.1-13); called his disciples, Mt 4.18-22 (Mk 1.16-20; Lk 5.1-11); Mt 9.9 (Mk 2.13-14; Lk 5.27-28); Jn 1.35-51; commissioned the twelve, Mt 10.1-4 (Mk 3.13-19; Lk 6.12-16); Sermon on the Mount, Mt 5—7 (Lk 6.17-49); sent out disciples, Mt 9.35—11.1 (Mk 6.7-13; Lk 9.1-6; 10.1-24); foretold his death and resurrection, Mt 16.21-28 (Mk 8.31-38; Lk 9.22-27); Mt 17.22-23 (Mk 9.30-32; Lk 9.43-45); Mt

20.17-28 (Mk 10.32-45; Lk 18.31-34); transfigured, Mt 17.1-8 (Mk 9.2-8; Lk 9.28-36); triumphal entry into Jerusalem, Mt 21.1-11 (Mk 11.1-11; Lk 19.29-44; Jn 12.12-19); instituted the Lord's supper, Mt 26.26-29 (Mk 14.22-25; Lk 22.17-20; 1 Cor 11.23-26); betrayed, arrested, and forsaken, Mt 26.47-57 (Mk 14.43-53; Lk 22.47-54; Jn 18.2-13); crucified, Mt 27.31-56 (Mk 15.20-41; Lk 23.26-49; Jn 19.16-30); appeared after his resurrection, Mt 28.9-20 (Mk 16.9-18n; Lk 24.13-49; Jn 20.11-31); Acts 1.3-8; 1 Cor 15.5-7; ascended to heaven, Lk 24.50-53 (Mk 16.19n); Acts 1.9-11.

JETHRO

Ex	3. 1 keeping the flock of his father-in-law J,
	4.18 Moses went back to . . . J and said to
	18. 1 J, the priest of Midian . . . heard of all
	18.12 J . . . brought a burnt offering and

JEW (JEWS)

Ezra	4.12 king that the J who came up from you
Neh	1. 2 I asked them about the J that survived,
Esth	2. 5 was a J in the citadel of Susa whose
Dan	3. 8 came forward and denounced the J.
Mt	2. 2 child who has been born king of the J?
	27.11 "Are you the King of the J?" Jesus said,
	27.37 read, "This is Jesus, the King of the J."
Jn	11. 8 the J were just now trying to stone you,
Acts	18. 5 testifying to the J that the Messiah was
	19.10 Asia, both J and Greeks, heard the word
Rom	3. 9 all both J and Greeks, are under the
	9.24 called, not from the J only but also
1 Cor	1.22 For J demand signs and Greeks desire
	9.20 To the J I became a J, in order to win
	10.32 Give no offense to J or to Greeks or to

JEWELS (JEWELRY)

Gen	24.53 the servant brought forth j of silver and
Ex	3.22 neighbor . . . for j of silver and of gold,
Prov	8.11 for wisdom is better than j, and all that

JEWISH

Jn	18.12 officer, and the J police arrested Jesus

JEZREEL

Josh	19.18 Its territory included J, Chesulloth,
1 Kings 21.	1 had a vineyard in J, beside the palace
Hos	1. 4 the house of Jehu for the blood of J,
	2.22 and the oil, and they shall answer J;

JOAB

Murdered Abner, 2 Sam 3.22-30; set Uriah in the forefront, 2 Sam 11.6-22; reconciled David and Absalom, 2 Sam 14.28-33; killed Absalom, 2 Sam 18.9-17; pursued Sheba and slew Amasa, 2 Sam 20.4-22; put to death by Solomon, 1 Kings 2.28-34.

JOB

Job	1. 1 in the land of Uz whose name was J.
	2. 3 "Have you considered my servant J?
	42. 8 go to my servant J, and offer up for
	42.10 the LORD restored the fortunes of J
	42.17 And J died, old and full of days.
Ezek	14.14 even if Noah, Daniel, and J, these
Jas	5.11 You have heard of the endurance of J,

JOEL

Joel	1. 1 The word of the LORD that came to J
Acts	2.16 what was spoken through the prophet J:

JOHN (the Baptist)

Birth foretold, Lk 1.5-25; born, Lk 1.57-66; preached and baptized, Mt 3.1-12 (Mk 1.4-11; Lk 3.1-17; Jn 1.6-8, 19-28); imprisoned, Mt 14.3-4 (Mk 6.17-18; Lk 3.19-20); sent messengers to Jesus, Mt 11.1-6 (Lk 7.18-23); commended by Jesus, Mt 11.7-15 (Lk 7.24-35); beheaded and buried, Mt 14.6-12 (Mk 6.17-29).

JOHN (the Apostle)

Called, Mt 4.21 (Mk 1.19; Lk 5.10); sent out with the

twelve, Mt 10.2 (Mk 3.17); desire for revenge rebuked, Lk 9.51-56; selfish request rejected, Mt 20.20-24 (Mk 10.35-41); healed and preached in the temple, Acts 3.1—4.22.

JOIN (JOINED)

2 Kings 23.	3 book. All the people j in the covenant.
Dan	11.34 help, and many shall j them insincerely.
Zech	2.11 Many nations shall j themselves to the
Mt	19. 5 and be j to his wife, and the two shall
	19. 6 what God has j together, let no one
Mk	10. 7 father and mother and be j to his wife,
	10. 9 Therefore what God has j together, let

JONAH

2 Kings 14.25 which he spoke by his servant J son of	
Jon	1. 1 Now the word of the LORD came to J
	2. 1 Then J prayed to the LORD his God from
	3. 1 of the LORD came to J a second time,
	4. 1 But this was very displeasing to J, and
Mt	12.40 as J was three days and three nights in
	16. 4 will be given to it except the sign of J."
Lk	11.30 just as J became a sign to the people of
	11.32 see, something greater than J is here!

JONATHAN

Smote the Philistine garrison, 1 Sam 13.2-4; 14.1-15; unknowingly transgressed Saul's oath, 1 Sam 14.24-30; rescued by the people, 1 Sam 14.36-46; made a covenant with David, 1 Sam 18.1-5; friendship with David, 1 Sam 20; killed by the Philistines, 1 Sam 31.2; mourned by David, 2 Sam 1.17-27; covenant with him remembered by David, 2 Sam 9.

JOPPA

2 Chr	2.16 and bring it to you in rafts by sea to J;
Jon	1. 3 He went down to J and found a ship
Acts	9.36 Now in J there was a disciple whose
	10. 5 send men to J for a certain Simon who

JORDAN

Gen	13.10 that the plain of the J was well watered
Deut	1. 1 Moses spoke to all Israel beyond the J
	4.21 he vowed that I should not cross the J
Josh	4. 1 nation had finished crossing over the J,
2 Sam	19.15 king came back to the J; and Judah
2 Kings	5.10 wash in the J seven times, and your
Job	40.23 it is confident though J rushes against
Ps	42. 6 from the land of the J and of Hermon,
Mt	3. 6 were baptized by him in the river J,
	3.13 came from Galilee to John at the J,
	19. 1 to the region of Judea beyond the J.
Jn	3.26 the one who was with you across the J,
	10.40 away again across the J to the place

JOSEPH (Son of Jacob)

Born, Gen 30.22-24; incurred jealousy by his dreams, Gen 37.5-11; sold into Egypt, Gen 37.12-28; refused Potiphar's wife, Gen 39.1-18; imprisoned, Gen 39.19-23; interpreted the prisoners' dreams, Gen 40; interpreted Pharaoh's dreams, Gen 41.1-36; made ruler over Egypt, Gen 41.37-49,53-57; married, had two sons, Gen 41.50-52; met his brothers, Gen 42—43; made himself known to them, Gen 45; saw his father again, Gen 46.28-34; died, Gen 50.22-26; buried in Shechem, Josh 24.32.

Deut	33.13 And of J he said, Blessed by the LORD
Ps	105. 17 He had sent a man ahead of them, J,
Heb	11.22 By faith J, at the end of his life, made

JOSEPH (Husband of Mary, Jesus' mother)

Betrothed to Mary, Mk 1.18 (Lk 1.27); instructed by an angel, Mt 1.19-21; went to Bethlehem, Lk 2.4; fled into Egypt, Mt 2.13-15; returned to Nazareth, Mt 2.19-23.

JOSEPH (of Arimathea)

Mt	27.57 rich man from Arimathea, named J,
Jn	19.38 After these things, J of Arimathea, who

JOSHUA (Son of Nun)

Defeated the Amalekites, Ex 17.8-13; in charge of the place of worship, Ex 33.11; sent with the spies, Num 13.1-16; 14.6-9; chosen to succeed Moses, Num 27.18-23; Deut 3.28; commissioned by Moses, Deut 31.23; 34.9; encouraged by the LORD, Josh 1.1-9; sent spies to Jericho, Josh 2; passed over Jordan, Josh 3; captured Jericho, Josh 6; captured Ai, Josh 7—9; warred against the kings, Josh 10—12; allotted the land, Josh 13.1—22.8; charged the people, Josh 23.1—24.24; made a covenant, Josh 24.25-27; death and burial, Josh 24.29-30.

JOSHUA (Priest, son of Jehozadak)

Hag	1.	1 and to *J* the son of Jehozadak, the high
	2.	2 and to *J* the son of Jehozadak, the high
Zech	3.	1 he showed me the high priest *J*
	6.11	set it on the head of the high priest *J*

JOSIAH

1 Kings 13.	2	shall be born to the house of David, *J*
2 Kings 21.24		of the land made his son *J* king in
	22.	1 *J* was eight years old when he began to
	23.23	year of King *J* this passover was kept
2 Chr 35.	1	*J* kept a passover to the LORD in

JOURNEY

Gen	24.56	LORD has made my *j* successful; let me

JOY

1 Chr	29.22	before the Lord on that day with great *j*.
2 Chr	20.27	returned to Jerusalem with *j*, for the
Neh	8.10	for the *j* of the LORD is your strength."
Ps	43.	4 to God my exceeding *j*; and I will praise
	47.	1 shout to God with loud songs of *j*.
	92.	4 at the works of your hands I sing for *j*
	98.	8 clap their hands; let the hills sing for *j*
Prov	14.10	bitterness, and no stranger shares its *j*.
Isa	9.	3 before you as with *j* at the harvest,
	12.	3 With *j* you will draw water from the
	35.10	heads; they shall obtain *j* and gladness,
	51.	3 *j* and gladness will be found in her,
	55.12	For you shall go out in *j*, and be lead
	60.15	majestic forever, a *j* from age to age.
Mt	2.10	stopped, they were overwhelmed with *j*.
Lk	1.14	You will have *j* and gladness, and many
	2.10	I am bringing you good news of a great *j*
Jn	3.29	For this reason my *j* has been fulfilled.
	15.11	so that my *j* may be in you, and that
	16.20	have pain, but your pain will turn into *j*.
	17.13	my *j* made complete in themselves.
Acts	8.	8 cured. So there was great *j* in that city.
	15.	3 and brought great *j* to all the believers.
Rom	14.17	and peace and *j* in the Holy Spirit.
	15.13	fill you with all *j* and peace in believing,
2 Cor	1.24	we are workers with you for your *j*,
	7.13	we rejoiced still more at the *j* of Titus,
Philem	7	I have indeed received much *j* and
1 Jn	1.	4 writing these things so that our *j* may

JOYFULLY

Lk	19.37	disciples began to praise God *j* with a

JUBILEE

Lev	25.10	It shall be a *j* for you: you shall return,
Num	36.	4 when the *j* of the Israelites comes, then

JUDAH

Born, Gen 29.35; saved Joseph's life, Gen 37.26-28; Judah and Tamar, Gen 38; pleaded for Benjamin, Gen 44.14-34; blessed by Jacob, Gen 49.8-12.

Tribe of Judah: blessed by Moses, Deut 33.7.

Judg	1.19	the LORD was with *J*, and he took
1 Sam	18.16	all Israel and *J* loved David; for it was
2 Sam	5.	5 over all Israel and *J* thirty-three years.
Ps	78.68	but he chose the tribe of *J*, Mount Zion,
Isa	5.	3 people of *J*, judge between me and my
	40.9	say to the cities of *J*, "Here is your God!"

Jer	3.	7 not return, and her false sister *J* saw it.
	39.	1 In the ninth year of Zedekiah king of *J*,
Lam	1.	3 *J* has gone into exile with suffering and
Joel	3.	1 when I restore the fortunes of *J* and

JUDAISM

Acts	13.43	and devout converts to *J* followed Paul
Gal	1.13	heard, no doubt, of my earlier life in *J*.

JUDAS (Brother of James)

Mk	6.	3 brother of James and Joses and *J* and

JUDAS (Iscariot)

Mt	10.	4 and *J*, the one who betrayed him.
	26.14	was called *J*, went to the chief priests
	26.25	*J*, who betrayed him, said, "Surely not I,
	27.	3 When *J* his betrayer saw that Jesus was
Mk	3.19	and *J*, who betrayed him.
Lk	22.	3 Then Satan entered into *J* , who was one
	22.48	"*J*, is it with a kiss that you are
Jn	6.71	He was speaking of *J* son of Simon
	12.	4 But *J*, one of his disciples (the one who
	13.	2 already put it into the heart of *J* son of
Acts	1.16	concerning *J*, who became a guide

JUDE

Jude	1	*J*, a servant of Jesus Christ and brother

JUDEA (JUDEANS)

Jer	32.12	in the presence of all the *J* who were
Mt	2.	1 Jesus was born in Bethlehem of *J*, wise
	3.	1 Baptist appeared in the wilderness of *J*,
Lk	21.21	Then those in *J* must flee to the
Acts	2.14	"Men of *J* and all who live in

JUDGE (JUDGES) (n)

Gen	18.25	Shall not the *J* of all the earth do what
	19.	9 as an alien, and he would play the *j*!
Ex	2.14	Who made you a ruler and a *j* over us?
	18.13	next day Moses sat as *j* for the people,
Judg	2.18	Whenever the LORD raised up *j* for them,
	11.27	let the LORD, who is *j*, decide today for
Lk	12.58	you may be dragged before the *j*, and
	18.	2 a *j* who neither feared God nor had
Acts	7.27	'Who made you a ruler and a *j* over us?

JUDGE (JUDGED JUDGES) (v)

Gen	31.53	God . . . *j* between us." So Jacob swore
Num	35.24	congregation shall *j* between the slayer
Deut	1.16	*j* rightly between one person and
1 Sam	2.10	The LORD will *j* the ends of the earth; he
	24.12	May the LORD *j* between me and you!
1 Chr	16.33	the Lord, for he comes to *j* the earth.
2 Chr	19.	6 for you *j* not on behalf of human beings
Ps	9.	8 He *j* the world with righteousness; he *j*
	58.11	surely there is a God who *j* on earth."
	72.	2 May he *j* your people with
	75.	2 time that I appoint I will *j* with equity.
	96.13	he is coming to *j* the earth. He will *j*
Prov	29.14	king *j* the poor with equity, his throne
Isa	2.	4 He shall *j* between the nations, and
	11.	4 but with righteousness he shall *j* the
Jer	11.20	O LORD of hosts, who *j* righteously, who
Ezek	7.	3 I will *j* you according to your ways; I
	36.19	with their conduct and their deeds I *j*
Mt	7.	1 "Do not *j*, so that you be not *j*.
Lk	6.37	"Do not *j*, and you will not be *j*; do not
	12.57	why do you not *j* for yourselves what is
Jn	7.24	Do not *j* by appearances, but *j* with
	7.51	"Our law does not *j* people without first
	8.15	You *j* by human standards, I *j* no one.
Acts	17.31	will have the world *j* in righteousness
Rom	2.	1 when you *j* others; for in passing
	2.16	through Jesus Christ, will *j* the secret
	3.	6 For then how could God *j* the world?
	14.	5 while others *j* all days to be alike.
1 Cor	4.	3 small thing that I should be *j* by you
	5.12	those who are inside that you are to *j*?

1 Cor	6.	2 know that the saints will *j* the world?
	6.	3 you not know that we are to *j* angels—
	11.31	But if we *j* ourselves, we would not be *j*.
Jas	2.12	who are to be *j* by the law of liberty.
1 Pet	4.	5 ready to *j* the living and the dead.
Rev	6.10	how long will it be before you *j* and
	19.11	and True, and in righteousness he *j* and
	20.12	the dead were *j* according to their

JUDGMENT (JUDGMENTS)

Gen	15.14	I will bring *j* on the nation that they
Ps	7.	6 O my God; you have appointed a *j*.
	75.	7 but it is God who executes *j*, putting
Eccl	11.	9 these things God will bring you into *j*.
Isa	32.	4 The minds of the rash will have good *j*,
Jer	1.16	I will utter my *j* against them, for all
	25.31	he is entering into *j* with all flesh, and
	48.47	the LORD. Thus far is the *j* on Moab.
Ezek	5.15	I execute *j* on you in anger and fury,
	14.21	my four deadly acts of *j*, sword, famine,
	20.36	I entered into *j* with your ancestors in
Dan	7.22	then *j* was given for the holy ones of
Hos	6.	5 mouth, and my *j* goes forth as the light.
Joel	3.	2 I will enter into *j* with them there, on
Zech	7.	9 Render true *j*, show kindness and mercy
Mt	5.21	'whoever murders shall be liable to *j*.'
Lk	11.32	Nineveh will rise at the *j* with this
Jn	5.22	no one but has given all *j* to the Son,
	12.31	Now is the *j* of this world; now the ruler
	16.	8 about sin and righteousness and *j*:
Rom	5.16	the *j* following one trespass brought
	11.33	How unsearchable are his *j* and how
	14.	3 those who abstain must not pass *j* on
	14.10	For we will all stand before the *j* seat of
1 Cor	11.29	eat and drink *j* against themselves.
2 Cor	5.10	all of us must appear before the *j* seat
Jude		15 to execute *j* on all, and to convict
Rev	18.20	For God has given *j* for you against her."

JUG

1 Kings	17.14	the *j* of oil shall not fail until the day

JUMPING

Acts	3.	8 *J* up, he stood and began to walk, and

JUST

Deut	4.	8 ordinances as *j* as this entire law that I
	32.	4 God, without deceit, *j* and upright is he.
Ezra	9.15	God of Israel, you are *j*, but we have
Neh	9.33	You have been *j* in all that has come
Job	9.	2 so; but how can a man be *j* before God?
Rom	8.	4 so that the *j* requirement of the law
Rev	16.	5 the waters say, "You are *j*, O Holy One,

JUSTICE

Lev	19.15	with *j* shall you judge your neighbor.
Job	34.12	and the Almighty will not pervert *j*.
Ps	82.	3 Give *j* to the weak and the orphan;
Prov	1.	3 in wise dealing, righteousness, *j*,
Eccl	5.	8 in the place of *j*, wickedness was there,
Isa	56.	1 Thus says the LORD: Maintain *j*, and do
	59.11	We wait for *j*, but there is none; for
Am	5.24	let *j* roll down like waters, and
Hab	1.	4 law becomes slack and *j* never prevails.
Lk	7.29	acknowledged the *j* of God, because
	18.	3 'Grant me *j* me against my opponent.'
Acts	24.25	And as he discussed *j*, self-control, and
Rom	3.	5 serves to confirm the *j* of God, what

JUSTIFICATION

Rom	4.25	our trespasses and was raised for our *j*.
	5.18	man's act of righteousness leads to *j*
2 Cor	3.	9 does the ministry of *j* abound in glory!
Gal	2.21	if *j* comes through the law, then Christ

JUSTIFY (JUSTIFIED JUSTIFIES)

Ps	51.	4 so that you are *j* in your sentence and
Prov	17.15	One who *j* the wicked and one who

Mt	12.37	by your words you will be *j*, and by your
Lk	10.29	wanting to *j* himself, he asked Jesus,
	18.14	this man went down to his home *j*
Rom	3.20	"no human being will be *j* in his sight"
	3.24	they are now *j* by his grace as a gift,
	3.26	and that he *j* the one who has faith
	4.	2 For if Abraham was *j* by works, he has
1 Cor	6.11	you were *j* in the name of the Lord
Gal	2.16	a person is *j* not by the works of the
	3.24	came, so that we might be *j* by faith.
Titus	3.	7 so that, having been *j* by his grace, we
Jas	2.21	our ancestor Abraham *j* by works when

K

KADESH

Gen	14.	7 and came to Enmishpat (that is, *K*),
Num	20.14	Moses sent messengers from *K* to the
Ps	29.	8 the LORD shakes the wilderness of *K*.

KADESH-BARNEA

Num	32.	8 I sent them from *K* to see the land.
Deut	2.14	length of time we had traveled from *K*
Josh	10.41	Joshua defeated them from *K* to Gaza,

KEEP (KEPT)

Gen	45.	7 and to *k* alive for you many survivors.
Ex	13.	5 you shall *k* this observance in this
Num	6.24	The LORD bless you and *k* you;
	9.	5 They *k* the passover in the first month,
Josh	14.10	the LORD has *k* me alive, as he said,
	22.	5 to *k* his commandments, and to hold
1 Kings	2.43	Why then have you not *k* your oath to
2 Kings	17.13	evil ways and *k* my commandments
	23.21	"*K* the passover to the LORD your God as
2 Chr	13.11	we *k* the charge of the LORD our God,
	30.	1 to *k* the passover to the LORD the God
	34.21	our ancestors did not *k* the word
Ps	25.10	for those who *k* his covenant
	119.	4 your precepts to be *k* diligently.
	119.	55 in the night, O LORD, and *k* your law.
	121.	7 LORD will *k* you from all evil; he will *k*
	132.	12 If your sons *k* my covenant and my
Prov	4.23	*K* your heart with all vigilance, for from
	21.23	and tongue is to *k* out of trouble.
	22.12	eyes of the LORD *k* watch over knowledge,
	28.	7 who *k* the law are wise children, but
	29.18	but happy are those who *k* the law.
Isa	49.	8 I have *k* you and given you as a
	62.	1 For Zion's sake I will not *k* silent, and
Mt	19.17	to enter into life, *k* the commandments."
Rom	2.27	uncircumcised but *k* the law will
2 Tim	4.	7 finished the race, I have *k* the faith.
Jude		1 God the Father and *k* for Jesus Christ:
		6 he has *k* in eternal chains in deepest
		21 *k* yourselves in the love of God; look
		24 who is able to *k* you from falling, and to
Rev	3.10	you have *k* my word of patient

KEEPER

Gen	4.	9 "I do not know; am I my brother's *k*?"
Isa	27.	3 I, the LORD, am its *k*; every moment I

KEY (KEYS)

Isa	22.22	shoulder the *k* of the house of David;
Mt	16.19	I will give you the *k* of the kingdom of
Lk	11.52	have taken away the *k* of knowledge;
Rev	1.18	and I have the *k* of Death and Hades.
	3.	7 the true one, who has the *k* of David,
	20.	1 in his hand the *k* to the bottomless pit

KIDNAPER

Deut	24.	7 the Israelites, then that *k* shall die.

KILL (KILLED KILLS)

Gen	4.	8 up against his brother Abel, and *k* him.
Ex	1.16	if it is a boy, *k* him; but if it is a girl,
	2.12	seeing no one he *k* the Egyptian and

KIN

Ex	2.14	Do you mean to *k* me as you *k* the
Num	31.17	*k* every male among the little ones,
1 Kings	21.19	Have you *k*, and also taken possession?"
2 Kings	6.21	"Father, shall I *k* them? Shall I *k* them?"
Job	13.15	See, he will *k* me; I have no hope; but I
Ps	44.22	Because of you we are being *k* all day
Mt	10.28	can *k* the body but cannot *k* the soul;
	21.38	'This is the the heir; come, let us *k* him
	23.37	"Jerusalem, Jerusalem, the city that *k*
Mk	8.31	scribes, and be *k*, and after three days
	10.34	flog him, and *k* him; and after three
Lk	12. 4	do not fear those who *k* the body
	19.47	people kept looking for a way to *k* him;
	20.15	him out of the vineyard and *k* him.
Jn	5.18	were seeking all the more to *k* him,
Acts	2.23	you crucified and *k* him,
	11. 7	saying to me, 'Get up, Peter; *k* and eat.'
Rev	2.13	Antipas . . . was *k* among you, where

KIN

Lev	25.25	If anyone of your *k* falls into difficulty
Deut	23. 7	of the Edomites, for they are your *k*.
Ruth	2.20	a relative of ours, one of our nearest *k*."
	3. 9	over your servant, for you are next-of-*k*."
	4.14	not left you this day without next-of-*k*;
2 Sam	19.12	You are my *k*, you are my bone and my
Prov	18.24	friend sticks closer than one's nearest *k*.
Jer	9. 4	and put no trust in any of your *k*; for all
Neh	5. 8	but now you are selling your own *k* who

KIND (KINDLY)

Josh	2.12	since I have dealt *k* with you, swear to
Prov	11.17	Those who are *k* reward themselves, but
	14.21	happy are those who are *k* to the poor.
	19.17	whoever is *k* to the poor lends to the
Eph	4.32	and be *k* to one another, tenderhearted,
2 Tim	2.24	must not be quarrelsome but *k* to

KINDNESS

Gen	19.19	shown me great *k* in saving my life;
2 Sam	9. 1	may show *k* for Jonathan's sake?"
Job	6.14	"Those who withhold *k* from a friend
Zech	7. 9	show *k* and mercy to one another;
Rom	2. 4	that God's *k* is meant to lead you
	3.12	there is no one who shows *k*, there is
	11.22	the *k* and severity of God: severity
Titus	3. 4	the goodness and loving *k* of God our

KINDRED

Gen	13. 8	between you and me, . . . for we are *k*.
1 Kings	12.24	shall not go up or fight against your *k*
1 Chr	13. 2	let us send abroad to our *k* who remain
2 Chr	11. 4	shall not go up or fight against your *k*.
Ps	69. 8	I have become a stranger to my *k*, an
Prov	27.10	is a neighbor who is nearby than *k* who

KING

Ex	2.23	After a long time, the *k* of Egypt died.
Deut	17.14	and you say, "I will set a *k* over me, like
Judg	18. 1	In those days there was no *k* in Israel.
	21.25	In those days there was no *k* in Israel;
1 Sam	2.10	he will give strength to his *k*, and exalt
	8. 5	appoint for us, then, a *k* to govern us,
	10.24	all the people shouted, "Long live the *k*!"
	11.15	there they made Saul *k* before the LORD,
	12.12	though the LORD your God was your *k*.
	23.17	you shall be *k* over Israel, and I shall be
2 Sam	19.10	say nothing about bringing the *k* back?"
2 Kings	11.12	they proclaimed him *k*, and anointed
1 Chr	16.31	say among the nations, "The LORD is *k*!"
Job	41.34	is lofty; it is *k* over all that are proud."
Ps	2. 6	"I have set my *k* on Zion, my holy hill."
	5. 2	Listen to the sound of my cry, my *K*
	10.16	The LORD is *k* forever and ever; the
	24. 7	doors! that the *K* of glory may come in.
	44. 4	You are my *K* and my God; you
	47. 8	God is *k* over the nations; God sits on
	72. 1	Give the *k* your justice, O God, and

Ps	93. 1	The LORD is *k*, he is robed in majesty;
	97. 1	The LORD is *k*! Let the earth rejoice; let
	149. 2	the children of Zion rejoice in their *K*.
Eccl	8. 4	the word of the *k* is powerful, and who
	10.16	you, O land, when your *k* is a servant,
Isa	32. 1	See, a *k* will reign in righteousness, and
	43.15	Holy One, the Creator of Israel, your *K*.
Jer	10. 7	Who would not fear you, O *K* of the
	29.16	the *k* who sits on the throne of David,
	30. 9	the LORD their God and David their *k*,
	51.57	sleep and never wake, says the *K*,
Dan	2. 4	The Chaldeans said to the *k* (in
	2.37	You, O *k*, the *k* of kings— to whom the
Hos	3. 5	the LORD their God, and David their *k*;
Mic	2.13	Their *k* will pass on before them, the
Zech	9. 9	Lo, your *k* comes to you; triumphant
Mt	22. 2	to a *k* who gave a wedding banquet
	25.34	the *k* will say to those at his right hand,
Lk	19.38	"Blessed is the *k* who comes in the
	23. 3	asked him, "Are you the *k* of the Jews?"
Jn	1.49	the Son of God! You are the *K* of Israel!"
	6.15	by force to make him *k*, he withdrew
	12.13	the name of the Lord—the *K* of Israel!"
	18.37	"So you are a *k*?" Jesus answered, "You
	19.14	He said to the Jews, "Here is your *K*!"
Acts	7.18	another *k* who had not known Joseph
	17. 7	that there is another *k* named Jesus.
1 Tim	1.17	To the *K* of ages, immortal, invisible,
Rev	9.11	have as *k* over them the angel of the
	19.16	inscribed, "*K* of kings and Lord of lords."

KINGDOM

Ex	19. 6	but you shall be for me a priestly *k* and
1 Sam	13.14	your *k* shall not continue; the LORD has
2 Sam	7.12	your body, and I will establish his *k*.
1 Chr	17.11	own sons, and I will establish his *k*.
	29.11	yours is the *k*, O LORD, and you are
Ps	145. 12	and the glorious splendor of your *k*.
Isa	9. 7	peace for the throne of David and his *k*.
Dan	4. 3	His *k* is an everlasting *k*, and his
	4.17	High is sovereign over the *k* of mortals,
	4.31	The *k* has departed from you! You shall
	11. 4	his *k* shall be broken and divided
Ob	21	Esau; and the *k* shall be the LORD's.
Mt	3. 2	"Repent, for the *k* of heaven has come
	4.17	"Repent, for the *k* of heaven has come
	4.23	proclaiming the good news of the *k* and
	6.33	strive first for the *k* of God and his
	8.11	and Isaac and Jacob in the *k* of heaven,
	10. 7	news, 'The *k* of heaven has come near.'
	18. 3	you will never enter the *k* of heaven.
	19.14	as these that the *k* of heaven belongs."
	21.43	*k* of God will be taken away from you
	24. 7	will rise against nation, and *k* against *k*,
	25.34	inherit the *k* prepared for you from the
	26.29	drink it new with you in my Father's *k*."
Mk	1.15	the *k* of God has come near; repent,
	4.26	"The *k* of God is as if someone would
	9. 1	not taste death until they see that the *k*
	11.10	Blessed is the coming *k* of our ancestor
	12.34	"You are not far from the *k* of God."
	13. 8	will rise against nation, and *k* against *k*;
	14.25	that day when I drink it new in the *k*
Lk	4.43	I must proclaim the good news of the *k*
	8.10	been given to know the secrets of the *k*
	9.11	them, and spoke to them about the *k*
	9.62	the plow and looks back is fit for the *k*
	10. 9	to them, 'The *k* of God has come near
	11.17	"Every *k* divided against itself becomes
	12.31	strive for his *k*, and these things will be
	16.16	good news of the *k* of God is
	17.21	For in fact, the *k* of God is among you.
	18.16	for it to such as these that the *k* of God
	18.29	or children, for the sake of the *k*
	21.10	will rise against nation, and *k* against *k*;
	21.31	place, you know the *k* of God is near.
	22.29	just as my father conferred on me, a *k*,

Jn	3. 5 enter the *k* of God without being born
Acts	1. 6 when you will restore the *k* to Israel?"
	14.22 that we must enter the *k* of God."
	19. 8 argued persuasively about the *k* of God.
	28.23 testifying to the *k* of God and trying to
Rom	14.17 the *k* of God is not food and drink but
1 Cor	4.20 the *k* of God depends not on talk but
	6.10 of these will inherit the *k* of God.
	15.24 end, when he hands over the *k* to God
	15.50 flesh and blood cannot inherit the *k* of
Eph	5. 5 has any inheritance in the *k* of Christ
2 Thess	1. 5 to make you worthy of the *k* of God,
Heb	12.28 are receiving a *k* that cannot be shaken,
2 Pet	1.11 entry into the eternal *k* of our Lord and
Rev	1. 6 made us to be a *k*, priests serving his
	11.15 *k* of the world has become the *k* of our

KINGDOMS

Dan	8.22 four *k* shall arise from his nation, but
Hag	2.22 earth, and to overthrow the throne of *k*;
Mt	4. 8 showed him all the *k* of the world and
Lk	4. 5 him in an instant all the *k* of the world.

KINGS (KING'S)

2 Chr	23.11 he brought out the *k* son, put the crown
Ps	102. 15 Lord, all the *k* of the earth your glory.
Prov	8.15 By me *k* reign, and rulers decree what is
	21. 1 The *k* heart is a stream of water in the
	31. 4 It is not for *k*, O Lemuel, it is not for *k*
Dan	7.17 "As for these four great beasts, four *k*
1 Cor	4. 8 Quite apart from us you have become *k*!
1 Tim	2. 2 for *k* and all who are in high positions,
Rev	16.12 prepare the way for the *k* from the east.

KINGSHIP

1 Sam	10.16 But about the matter of the *k*, of which
Dan	7.27 The *k* and the dominion and the

KINSFOLK

Judg	20.23 again draw near to battle against our *k*
Prov	17.17 times, and *k* are born to share adversity.

KISHON

Judg	5.21 The torrent *K* swept them away, the

KISS (KISSED KISSES KISSING)

Gen	29.11 Then Jacob *k* Rachel, and wept aloud.
	33. 4 him, and fell on his neck and *k* him,
	45.15 he *k* all his brothers and wept upon
	48.10 brought them near him; and he *k* them
Ruth	1.14 Orpah *k* her mother-in-law, but Ruth
1 Sam	20.41 and they *k* each other, and wept until
2 Sam	14.33 the king; and the king *k* Absalom.
Ps	2.12 *k* his feet, or he will be angry, and you
	85.10 meet; righteousness and peace will *k*
Prov	7.13 She seizes him and *k* him, and with
	24.26 who gives an honest answer gives a *k*
Song	1. 2 Let him *k* me with the *k* of his mouth!
Hos	13. 2 to these," they say. People are *k* calves!
Mt	26.48 "The one I will *k* is the man; arrest him."
Mk	14.44 "The one I will *k* is the man; arrest him
Lk	7.45 You gave me no *k*, but from the time I
	15.20 put his arms around him and *k* him,
	22.47 them. He approached Jesus to *k* him;
Acts	20.37 they embraced Paul and *k* him, grieving
Rom	16.16 Greet one another with a holy *k*. All the
1 Cor	16.20 Greet one another with a holy *k*.
1 Pet	5.14 Greet one another with a *k* of love.

KNEE (KNEES)

1 Kings	19.18 all the *k* that have not bowed to Baal,
Ezra	9. 5 fell on my *k*, spread out my hands to
Isa	45.23 "To me every *k* shall bow, every tongue
Dan	6.10 on his *k* three times a day to pray to his
Lk	5. 8 Peter saw it he fell down at Jesus' *k*,
Rom	14.11 every *k* shall bow to me, and every

KNEEL (KNELT)

Gen	24.11 He made the camels *k* down outside
1 Kings	8.54 the altar of the Lord, where he had *k*
Ps	95. 6 bow down, let us *k* before the Lord, our

KNIFE

Gen	22. 6 he himself carried the fire and the *k*.
	22.10 his hand and took the *k* to kill his son.
Prov	23. 2 put a *k* to your throat if you have a big

KNOCK (KNOCKING)

Mt	7. 7 will find; *k*, and the door will be opened
Lk	11. 9 will find; *k*, and the door will be opened
	13.25 and to *k* at the door, saying, 'Lord,
Acts	12.16 Peter continued *k*; and when they
Rev	3.20 I am standing at the door, *k*; if you hear

KNOW

Ex	1. 8 arose over Egypt, who did not *k* Joseph.
	7. 5 Egyptians shall *k* that I am the Lord,
	18.11 Now I *k* that the Lord is greater than all
	29.46 they shall *k* that I am the Lord their
	31.13 that you may *k* that I, the Lord, sanctify
Lev	23.43 may *k* that I made the people
Judg	2.10 who did not *k* the Lord or the work that
1 Sam	17.47 all this assembly may *k* that the Lord
2 Sam	7.20 to you? For you *k* your servant, O Lord
1 Kings	8.43 may *k* your name and fear you, as do
	8.60 of the earth may *k* that the Lord is God;
	20.13 and you shall *k* that I am the Lord."
1 Chr	28. 9 son Solomon, *k* the God of your father,
Job	8. 9 are but of yesterday, and we *k* nothing,
	19.25 I *k* that my Redeemer lives, and that at
	24.16 themselves up; they do not *k* the light.
	30.23 I *k* that you will bring me to death, and
Ps	25. 4 Make me to *k* your ways, O Lord; teach
	46.10 "Be still, and *k* that I am God! I am
	56. 9 I call. This I *k*, that God is for me.
	73.11 they say, "How can God *k*? Is there
	89.15 are the people who *k* the festal shout,
	100. 3 *K* that the Lord is God. It is he that
	109. 27 *k* that this is your hand; you, O Lord,
	142. 3 When my spirit is faint, you *k* my way.
Prov	28.22 rich and does not *k* that loss is sure to
Eccl	3.14 I *k* that whatever God does endures
	8. 5 and the wise mind will *k* the time and
Isa	1. 3 Israel does not *k*, my people do not
	37.20 may *k* that you alone are the Lord."
	41.20 so that all may see and *k*, all may
	49.26 all flesh shall *k* that I am the Lord
	52. 6 Therefore my people shall *k* my name;
	52. 6 that day they shall *k* that it is I who
	55. 5 You shall call nations that you do not *k*,
Jer	8. 7 but my people do not *k* the ordinance
	12. 3 But you, O Lord, *k* me; you see me and
	24. 7 a heart to *k* that I am the Lord; and
	31.34 or say to each other, "*K* the Lord," for
Ezek	6.14 Then they shall *k* that I am the Lord.
	17.21 wind; and you shall *k* that I, the Lord,
	29.21 Then they shall *k* that I am the Lord.
	32.15 in it, they shall *k* that I am the Lord.
	34.27 and they shall *k* that I am the Lord,
	37.28 nations shall *k* that I the Lord sanctify
	39. 7 nations shall *k* that I am the Lord, the
Hos	6. 3 Let us *k*, let us press on to *k* the Lord;
	11. 3 but they did not *k* that I healed them.
	14. 9 those who are discerning *k* them.
Joel	2.27 You shall *k* that I am in the midst of
Mic	4.12 they do not *k* the thoughts of the Lord;
Mt	6. 3 your left hand *k* what your right hand
	9. 6 that you may *k* that the Son of Man has
	24.50 him and at an hour he does not *k*.
Mk	2.10 that the Son of Man has authority on
	12.24 you *k* neither the scriptures nor the
	13.35 you do not *k* when the master of the
Lk	4.34 us? I *k* who you are, the Holy One
	5.24 that you may *k* that the Son of Man has

Lk	13.27	say, 'I do not *k* where you come from;
	20.21	"Teacher, we *k* that you are right in
Jn	10.14	I *k* my own and my own *k* me,
	13.35	By this everyone will *k* that you are my
	17.	3 life, that they *k* you, the only true God,
	17.23	the world may *k* that you have sent me
Acts	19.15	"Jesus I *k*, and Paul I *k*; but who are
1 Cor	3.16	Do you not *k* that you are God's temple
Gal	4.	9 however, that you have come to *k* God,
Eph	1.18	you may *k* what is the hope to which he
Phil	3.10	I want to *k* Christ and the power of his
2 Tim	1.12	I *k* the one in whom I have put my
Heb	8.11	or say to each other, '*K* the Lord,'
1 Jn	4.	6 From this we *k* the spirit of truth and
	5.13	you may *k* that you have eternal life.
1 Jn	5.19	We *k* that we are God's children, and
Rev	2.	2 "I *k* your works, your toil and patient

KNOWS (KNEW KNOWN)

Job	23.10	he *k* the way that I take; when he has
Ps	76.	1 In Judah God is *k*, his name is great in
	103.	14 he *k* how we are made; he remembers
Isa	19.21	will make himself *k* to the Egyptians;
Am	3.	2 You only have I *k* of all the families of
Zech	11.11	watching me, *k* that it was the word
Mt	6.	8 for your Father *k* what you need before
	6.32	heavenly Father *k* that you need all
	12.33	fruit bad; for the tree is *k* by its fruit.
Mk	3.12	ordered them not to make him *k*.
	13.32	about that day or hour no one *k*,
Jn	1.18	Father's heart, who has made him *k*.
	2.25	for he himself *k* what was in everyone.
Acts	7.13	Joseph made himself *k* to his brothers,
	7.18	another king who had not *k* Joseph
	15.	8 God, who *k* the human heart, testified
Rom	1.21	for though they *k* God, they did not
Col	1.25	make the word of God fully *k*, the
2 Pet	2.21	better for them never to have *k* the way
Rev	1	he made it *k* by sending his angel to his

KNOWLEDGE

Gen	2.	9 and the tree of the *k* of good and evil.
Num	24.16	knows the *k* of the Most High, who sees
Ps	139.	6 Such *k* is too wonderful for me; it is so
Prov	1.	4 simple, *k* and prudence to the young—
	9.10	and the *k* of the Holy One is insight.
	14.	6 but *k* is easy for one who understands.
	15.	2 tongue of the wise dispenses *k*, but the
	30.	3 wisdom, nor have I *k* of the holy ones.
Isa	5.13	My people go into exile without *k*; their
	11.	9 earth will be full of the *k* of the LORD
Dan	1.17	To these four young men God gave *k*
Hos	4.	6 My people are destroyed for lack of *k*;
Lk	1.77	give *k* of salvation to his people by the
	11.52	For you have taken away the key of *k*;
1 Cor	1.	5 in him, in speech and *k* of every kind—
	8.	1 *K* puffs up, but love builds up. Anyone
	8.11	by your *k* those weak believers are
2 Cor	6.	6 by purity, *k*, patience, kindness,
1 Tim	2.	4 saved and to come to the *k* of the truth.

KORAH (KORAH'S)

Num	16.	1 Now *K* the son of Izhar son of Kohath
	16.49	those who died in the affair of *K*.
Jude	11	sake of gain, and perish in *K* rebellion.

L

LABAN

Gen	24.29	brother whose name was *L*; and *L* ran
	27.43	flee at once to my brother *L* in Haran,
	28.	5 to Paddan-aram, to *L* son of Bethuel
	29.	5 "Do you know *L* son of Nahor?" They
	30.25	Jacob said to *L*, "Send me away, that I
	31.	2 Jacob saw that *L* did not regard him as
	31.20	Jacob deceived *L* the Aramean in that
	31.48	*L* said, "This heap is a witness between
	31.55	*L* arose, and kissed his grandchildren

LABOR (LABORS) (n)

Ex	2.11	out to the people and saw their forced *l*.
Ps	48.	6 of them there, pains as of a woman in *l*.
Prov	12.14	things, and manual *l* has its reward.
Isa	21.	3 me, like the pangs of a woman in *l*;
	66.	7 "Before she was in *l* she gave birth;
Jer	6.24	hold of us, pain as of a woman in *l*.
Jn	16.21	When a woman is in *l*, she has pain,
Rom	8.22	whole creation has been groaning in *l*
1 Cor	15.58	that in the Lord your *l* is not in vain.
1 Thess	2.	9 You remember our *l* and toil, brothers
	5.	3 as *l* pains come upon a pregnant
Heb	4.10	rest also cease from their *l* as God did

LABOR (v)

Deut	5.13	Six days you shall *l*, and do all your
Ps	127.	1 the house, those who build it *l* in vain.
Prov	21.25	is fatal, for lazy hands refuse to *l*.
Hab	2.13	that peoples *l* only to feed the flames,

LABORERS

Eccl	5.12	Sweet is the sleep of *l*, whether they eat
Mt	20.	1 in the morning to hire *l* for his vineyard.
Lk	10.	2 harvest is plentiful, but the *l* are few;
Jas	5.	4 wages of the *l* who mowed your fields,

LACERATE

Deut	14.	1 you must not *l* yourselves or shave your

LACK (LACKED LACKING)

Deut	2.	7 has been with you; you have *l* nothing."
Eccl	6.	2 honor, so that they *l* nothing of all that
Mk	10.21	"You *l* one thing; go, sell what you own,
Lk	18.22	"There is still one thing *l*. Sell all that
	22.35	bag, or sandals, did you *l* anything?"

LAKE

Lk	8.33	steep bank into the *l* and were drowned.
Rev	19.20	two were thrown alive into the *l* of fire
	20.10	devil . . . was thrown into the *l* of fire

LAMB (LAMBS)

Gen	22.	7 but where is the *l* for a burnt offering?"
Ex	12.	5 Your *l* shall be without blemish, a
	29.39	One *l* you shall offer in the morning,
2 Sam	12.	3 man had nothing but one little ewe *l*,
Isa	53.	7 like a *l* that is led to the slaughter, and
	65.25	The wolf and the *l* shall feed together,
Jer	11.19	But I was like a gentle *l* led to the
Lk	10.	3 I am sending you out like *l* into the
Jn	1.29	"Here is the *L* of God, who takes away
	21.15	love you." Jesus said to him, "Feed my *l*."
1 Pet	1.19	of Christ, like that of a *l* without defect
Rev	5.	6 a *L* standing as if it had been
	5.12	"Worthy is the *L* that was slaughtered to
	6.16	the throne and from the wrath of the *L*;
	7.10	saying, "Salvation belongs . . . to the *L*!"
	14.	1 there was the *L*, standing on Mount
	17.14	they will make war on the *L*, and the *L*
	19.	7 marriage of the *L* has come, and his
	21.	9 show you the bride, the wife of the *L*."
	21.14	names of the twelve apostles of the *L*.
	21.23	God is its light, and its lamp is the *L*.

LAME

2 Sam	5.	8 attack the *l* and the blind, those whom
Isa	35.	6 then the *l* shall leap like a deer, and
Mt	15.31	maimed whole, the *l* walking, and the
Acts	3.	2 a man *l* from birth was being carried in.

LAMENT (LAMENTED)

1 Sam	7.	2 all the house of Israel *l* after the LORD.
Joel	1.	8 *L* like a virgin dressed in sackcloth for

LAMENTATION

2 Sam	1.17	David intoned this *l* over Saul and his
Jer	6.26	as for an only child, most bitter *l*:
Ezek	27.	2 Now you, mortal, raise a *l* over Tyre,

Am	5. 1 this word that I take up over you in *l*,

LAMP (LAMPS)

Ex	27.20 so that a *l* may be set up to burn
1 Sam	3. 3 *l* of God had not yet gone out, and
2 Sam	22.29 you are my *l*, O LORD, the LORD lightens
1 Kings	11.36 David may always have a *l* before me
	15. 4 God gave him a *l* in Jerusalem, setting
2 Kings	4.10 table, a chair, and a *l*, so that he can
	8.19 since he promised to give a *l* to him
Job	18. 6 their tent, the *l* above them is put out.
	29. 3 when his *l* shone over my head, and by
Ps	18.28 It is you who light my *l*; the LORD, my
	119.105 Your word is a *l* to my feet and a light
Prov	6.23 For the commandment is a *l* and the
	20.20 your *l* will go out in utter darkness.
	20.27 The human spirit is the *l* of the LORD,
	24.20 no future; the *l* of the wicked go out.
	31.18 Her *l* does not go out at night. She puts
Mt	5.15 No one after lighting a *l* puts it under
	6.22 "The eye is the *l* of the body. So, if your
Mk	4.21 "Is a *l* brought in to be put under a
Lk	8.16 "No one after lighting a *l* hides it under
	11.33 "No one after lighting a *l* puts it in a
	11.34 Your eye is the *l* of your body. If your
	12.35 dressed for action and have your *l* lit;
Jn	5.35 He was a burning and shining *l*, and
Rev	21.23 of God is its light, and its *l* is the Lamb.

LAMPSTAND (LAMPSTANDS)

Ex	25.31 You shall make a *l* of pure gold. The
	37.17 He also made the *l* of pure gold. The
Lev	24. 4 He shall set up the lamps on the *l* of
Num	8. 2 lamps shall give light in front of the *l*."
Zech	4. 2 "I see a *l* all of gold, with a bowl on the
Rev	1.12 and on turning I saw seven golden *l*,

LAND (LANDS)

Gen	13.15 all the *l* which you see I will give to you
	35.12 The *l* that I gave to Abraham and Isaac
	47.18 of my lord but our bodies and our *l*.
	50.24 out of this *l* to the *l* that he swore to
Ex	6. 8 I will bring you into the *l* that I swore
Lev	18.25 Thus the *l* became defiled; and I
	25.23 The *l* shall not be sold in perpetuity, for
Num	13.26 and showed them the fruit of the *l*.
	32. 5 let this *l* be given to your servants for a
	32.22 and this *l* shall be your possession
	33.54 You shall apportion the *l* by lot
	35.34 You shall not defile the *l* in which you
Deut	8. 7 God is bringing you into a good *l*, a *l*
	11.10 *l* that you are about to enter to occupy
	11.11 *l* that you are crossing over to occupy is
	29.24 "Why has the LORD done thus to this *l*?
Josh	13. 1 much of the *l* still remains to be
	24.13 I gave you a *l* on which you had not
Neh	9.24 decendants went in and possessed the *l*,
Isa	38.11 not see the LORD in the *l* of the living;
Jer	2. 7 you entered you defiled my *l*, and made
	22.29 O *l*, *l*, *l*, hear the word of the LORD!
Ezek	33.24 of these waste places in the *l*
	36. 6 prophesy concerning the *l* of Israel, and
	45. 1 When you allot the *l* as an inheritance,
Hos	9. 3 shall not remain in the *l* of the LORD;
Acts	7. 3 relatives and go to the *l* that I will show
	20.13 intending to go by *l* himself.
2 Cor	10.16 proclaim the good news in *l* beyond

LANDMARK (LANDMARKS)

Job	24. 2 The wicked remove *l*; they seize flocks
Prov	22.28 Do not remove the ancient *l* that your
	23.10 Do not remove an ancient *l* or encroach

LANGUAGE

Gen	11. 1 Now the whole earth had one *l* and the
Neh	13.24 they could not speak the *l* of Judah,
Jer	5.15 a nation whose *l* you do not know,
Ezek	3. 5 of obscure speech and a difficult *l*,

Acts	2. 6 them speaking in the native *l* of each.

LANGUISH (LANGUISHES LANGUISHING)

Ps	6. 2 O LORD, for I am *l*; O LORD, heal me,
	119. 81 My soul *l* for your salvation; I hope in
Isa	19. 8 who spread nets on the water will *l*.

LASHES

2 Cor	11.24 from the Jews the forty *l* minus one.

LAST

Mt	12.45 the *l* state of that person is worse than
	19.30 are first will be *l*, and the *l* will be first."
Mk	10.31 are first will be *l*, and the *l* will be first."
	15.37 gave a loud cry and breathed his *l*.
Lk	13.30 some are *l* who will be first, and some
2 Tim	3. 1 this, that in the *l* days distressing times
Heb	1. 2 but in these *l* days he has spoken to us
Rev	1.17 not be afraid; I am the first and the *l*,

LAUGH (LAUGHED LAUGHS)

Gen	17.17 Abraham fell on his face and *l*, and said
	18.12 So Sarah *l* to herself, saying, "After I
2 Chr	30.10 Zebulun; but they *l* them to scorn, and
Job	5.22 At destruction and famine you shall *l*,
	41.29 as chaff; it *l* at the rattle of javelins.
Ps	2. 4 He who sits in the heavens *l*; the Lord
	37.13 but the LORD *l* at the wicked, for he sees
	52. 6 see, and fear, and will *l* at the evildoer,
	59. 8 But you *l* at them, O LORD; you hold all
Prov	1.26 I also will *l* at your calamity; I will
	31.25 clothing, and she *l* at the time to come.
Mt	9.24 girl is not dead but sleeping." And they *l*
Mk	5.40 And they *l* at him. But he put them all
Lk	6.21 are you who weep now, for you will *l*.
	8.53 they *l* at him, knowing that she was

LAUGHTER

Gen	21. 6 "God has brought *l* for me; everyone
Prov	14.13 Even in the heart is sad, and the end
Eccl	2. 2 I said of *l*, "It is mad," and of pleasure,
	7. 3 Sorrow is better than *l*, for by sadness

LAW (LAWS)

Num	5.29 This is the *l* in cases of jealousy, when
	6.13 This is the *l* for the nazirites when the
Deut	1. 5 Moses undertook to expound this *l* as
	17.18 have a copy of this *l* written for him
	31. 9 Then Moses wrote down this *l*, and gave
	31.11 you shall read this *l* before all Israel in
	31.26 "Take this book of the *l* and put it
Josh	1. 8 This book of the *l* shall not depart out
	8.34 he read all the words of the *l*, blessings
2 Chr	12. 1 strong, he abandoned the *l* of the LORD,
Neh	9.13 gave them right ordinances and true *l*,
Ps	1. 2 but their delight is in the *l* of the LORD,
	19. 7 The *l* of the LORD is perfect, reviving the
	119. 44 I will keep your *l* continually, forever
Prov	29. 9 If the wise go to *l* with fools, there is
Jer	31.33 I will put my *l* within them, and I will
Dan	6. 5 it in connection with the *l* of his God."
Mt	5.17 think that I have come to abolish the *l*
	11.13 all the prophets and the *l* prophesied
Lk	5.17 Pharisees and teachers of the *l* sitting
	16.17 in the letter of the *l* to become void.
	24.44 everything written about me in the *l*
Acts	13.15 After the reading of the *l* and the
Rom	2.12 all who have sinned under the *l* will be
	4.15 For the *l* brings wrath, but where there
	7.22 I delight in the *l* of God in my
	8. 2 set you free from the *l* of sin and death.
	10. 4 For Christ is the end of the *l* so that
1 Cor	9.21 To those outside the *l* I became as one
Gal	3.10 on the works of the *l* are under a curse;
	3.19 Why then the *l*? It was added because
	3.23 and guarded under the *l* until faith
	4.21 to the *l*, will you not listen to the *l*?
	5.14 the whole *l* is summed up in a single

Gal	6. 2 this way you will fulfill the *l* of Christ.
1 Tim	1. 8 Now we know that the *l* is good, if one
Heb	7.19 (for the *l* made nothing perfect);
Jas	1.25 who looks into the perfect *l*, the *l* of
	2. 9 are convicted by the *l* as transgressors.
	4.11 judges the *l*; but if you judge the *l*, you

LAWFUL
Mt	12. 2 what is not *l* to do on the sabbath."
	12.12 So it is *l* to do good on the sabbath."
	14. 4 him, "It is not *l* for you to have her."
Mk	6.18 telling Herod, "It is not *l* for you to have
1 Cor	6.12 "All things are *l* for me," but not all

LAWLESS
Mk	15.28n says, "And he was counted among the *l*."
Lk	22.37 me, 'And he was counted among the *l*';
2 Thess	2. 3 comes first and the *l* one is revealed,
	2. 8 then the *l* one will be revealed, whom

LAWLESSNESS
2 Thess	2. 7 the mystery of *l* is already at work, but
1 Jn	3. 4 Everyone who commits sin is guilty of *l*;

LAWYER (LAWYERS)
Lk	10.25 a *l* stood up to test Jesus. "Teacher," he
	11.46 he said, "Woe also to you *l*! For you

LAY
Deut	9.18 I *l* prostrate before the LORD as before,
Prov	9. 6 L aside immaturity, and live, and walk
	10.14 The wise *l* up knowledge, but the
Mt	8.20 Son of Man has nowhere to *l* his head."
1 Cor	3.11 no one can *l* any foundation other than

LAZARUS
Lk	16.20 at his gate lay a poor man named *L*,
Jn	11. 1 a certain man was ill, *L* of Bethany,
	11.43 cried with a loud voice, "*L*, come out."
	12. 1 the home of *L*, whom he had raised
	12.10 chief priests planned to put *L* to death
	12.17 been with him when he called *L* out

LAZY
Ex	5.17 He said, "You are *l*, *l*; that is why you
Prov	13. 4 appetite of the *l* craves, and gets
	21.25 craving of the *l* person is fatal, for *l*
	22.13 The *l* person says, "There is a lion
	26.15 *l* person buries a hand in the dish, and
	26.16 *l* person is wiser in self-esteem than

LAZYBONES
Prov	6. 6 Go to the ant, you *l*; consider its ways,

LEAD (LEADS LED)
Gen	24.27 the LORD has *l* me on the way to the
	33.14 of his servant, and I will *l* on slowly,
Ex	13.18 So God *l* the people by the roundabout
Josh	24. 3 *l* him through all the land of Canaan
1 Sam	12. 2 with you. I have *l* you from my youth
Ps	5. 8 L me, O LORD, in your righteousness
	23. 2 he *l* me beside still waters; he restores
	25. 5 L me in your truth, and teach me, for
	61. 2 L me to the rock that is higher than I;
	78.14 In the daytime he *l* them with a cloud,
	107. 7 he *l* them by a straight way, until they
	136. 16 *l* his people through the wilderness,
Isa	11. 6 together, and a little child shall *l* them.
	40.11 bosom, and gently *l* the mother sheep.
	48.17 for your own good, who *l* you in the way
	63.14 Thus you *l* your people, to make for
Jer	2. 6 of Egypt, who *l* us in the wilderness,
Hos	11. 4 I *l* them with cords of human kindness,
Mt	4. 1 Jesus was *l* up by the Spirit into the
Lk	4.29 town and *l* him to the brow of the hill
Acts	8.32 "Like a sheep he was *l* to the slaughter,
Rom	8.14 all who are *l* by the Spirit of God are
1 Cor	7.17 each of you *l* the life that the Lord has
Gal	5.18 if you are *l* by the Spirit, you are not

Eph	4. 1 I beg you to *l* a life worthy of the calling
Col	1.10 that you may *l* lives worthy of the Lord,
1 Thess	2.12 pleading that you *l* a life worthy of God,

LEADER
Mt	9.18 *l* of the synagogue came in and knelt
Lk	8.41 named Jairus, the *l* of the synagogue.
	13.14 the *l* of the synagogue, indignant

LEAF (LEAVES)
Gen	3. 7 they sewed fig *l* together and made
Job	13.25 Will you frighten a windblown *l* and
Ezek	47.12 Their *l* will not wither nor their fruit
Mk	11.13 he found nothing but *l*, for it was not
	13.28 and puts forth its *l*, you know that

LEAGUE
Job	5.23 you shall be in *l* with the stones of the

LEAH
Gen	29.16 the name of the elder was *L*, and the
	29.30 and he loved Rachel more than *L*. He
	30. 9 When *L* saw that she had ceased
	31. 4 called Rachel and *L* into the field where
	35.23 The sons of *L*: Reuben (Jacob's
Ruth	4.11 Rachel and *L*, who together built up the

LEAN
Isa	48. 2 the holy city, and *l* on the God of Israel;

LEAP (LEAPED)
2 Sam	22.30 and by my God I can *l* over a wall.
Lk	1.41 greeting, the child *l* in her womb.

LEARN (LEARNED)
Gen	30.27 I have *l* by divination that the LORD has
Deut	31.12 hear and *l* to fear the LORD your God
Ps	119. 7 when I *l* your righteous ordinances.
	119. 71 that I was humbled, so that I might *l*
Prov	8. 5 O simple ones, *l* prudence; acquire
Isa	1.17 to do good; seek justice, rescue the
	26. 9 inhabitants of the world *l* righteousness.
Jer	10. 2 Do not *l* the way of the nations, or be
Dan	5.21 until he *l* that the Most High God has
Mt	9.13 Go and *l* what this means, 'I desire
	11.29 Take my yoke upon you, and *l* from me;
Phil	4. 9 on doing the things that you have *l*
	4.11 need; for I have *l* to be content with
1 Thess	4. 1 as you *l* from us how you ought to live
Heb	5. 8 was a Son, he *l* obedience through what
Rev	14. 3 No one could *l* that song except the

LEARNING
Prov	1. 5 Let the wise also hear and gain in *l*,
Jn	7.15 "How does this man have such *l*, when
Acts	26.24 Paul! Too much *l* is driving you insane!"

LEAST
Judg	6.15 Manasseh, and I am the *l* in my family."
1 Sam	9.21 a Benjaminite, from the *l* of the tribes
Mt	2. 6 by no means *l* among the rulers of
	5.19 same, will be called *l* in the kingdom
	11.11 the *l* in the kingdom of heaven is
Lk	7.28 John; yet the *l* in the kingdom of God is
	9.48 for the *l* among all of you is the
1 Cor	15. 9 I am the *l* of the apostles, unfit to be
Eph	3. 8 I am the very *l* of all the saints,

LEAVE (LEFT)
Judg	16.20 did not know that the LORD had *l* him.
1 Kings	19.10 I alone am *l*, and they are seeking my
2 Kings	2. 2 and as you yourself live, I will not *l* you."
	4.30 yourself live, I will not *l* without you."
Job	22.17 They said to God; '*L* us alone,' and
Ezek	9. 8 *l* alone, I fell prostrate on my face, and
Mt	4.22 they *l* the boat and their father, and
	19.27 "Look, we have *l* everything and
Mk	1.18 they *l* their nets and followed him.
	1.20 they *l* their father Zebedee in the boat

LEAVEN

Mk	10.	7 man shall *l* his father and mother and
Lk	5.11	to shore, they *l* everything and followed
	8.37	the Gerasenes asked Jesus to *l* them;

LEAVEN

Ex	12.15	you shall remove *l* from your houses,
Lev	2.11	bring to the LORD shall be made with *l*,

LEBANON

Deut	1.	7 land of the Canaanites and the *L*, as far
Judg	9.15	bramble and devour the cedars of *L*.'
1 Kings	5.	6 command that cedars from *L* be cut for
	10.17	them in the House of the Forest of *L*.
Ezra	3.	7 to bring cedar trees from *L* to the sea,
Ps	29.	5 cedars; the LORD breaks the cedars of *L*.
Song	5.15	His appearance is like *L*, choice as the
Isa	10.34	with an ax, and *L* with its majestic trees
	60.13	glory of *L* shall come to you, the
Jer	18.14	Does the snow of *L* leave the crags of

LEFT (n and adj)

Gen	13.	9 the right hand, then I will go to the *l*."
Mt	6.	3 do not let your *l* hand know what your
	20.21	at your right hand and one at your *l*,

LEGION (LEGIONS)

Mt	26.53	send me more than twelve *l* of angels?
Mk	5.	9 "My name is *L*; for we are many."

LEGS

Dan	2.33	its *l* of iron, its feet partly of iron and
Jn	19.33	already dead, they did not break his *l*.

LEHI

Judg	15.19	that is at *L*, and water came from it.
2 Sam	23.11	Philistines gathered together at *L*,

LEND (LENDING LENT LENDS)

Ex	22.25	If you *l* money to my people, to the
Deut	28.12	You will *l* to many nations, but you will
1 Sam	1.28	I have *l* him to the LORD; as long as he
Ps	37.26	They are ever giving liberally and *l*, and
Prov	19.17	is kind to the poor *l* to the LORD,
Jer	15.10	I have not *l*, nor have I borrowed, yet all
Lk	6.34	if you *l* to those from whom you hope

LENGTH

Gen	6.15	*l* of the ark three hundred cubits, its
Ezek	40.	5 The *l* of the measuring reed in the
Eph	3.18	saints, what is the breadth and *l* and

LEOPARD (LEOPARDS)

Isa	11.	6 lamb, the *l* shall lie down with the kid,
Jer	13.23	change their skin or the *l* their spots?
Dan	7.	6 as I watched, another appeared, like a *l*.

LEPER (LEPERS)

Mt	8.	2 a *l* who came to him and knelt before
	11.	5 the lame walk, the *l* are cleansed, the
	26.	6 at Bethany in the house of Simon the *l*,
Mk	1.40	A *l* came to him begging him, and
	14.	3 in the house of Simon the *l*, as he sat
Lk	4.27	many *l* in Israel in the time of the
	7.22	lame walk, *l* are cleansed, the deaf hear,
	17.12	ten *l* approached him. Keeping their

LEPROSY

2 Kings	5.	1 a mighty warrior, suffered from *l*.
	5.27	the *l* of Naaman shall cling to you, and
Lk	5.12	there was a man covered with *l*. When

LEPROUS

Ex	4.	6 when he took it out, his hand was *l*, as
Lev	13.	2 and it turns into a *l* disease on the skin
	14.	2 This shall be the ritual for the *l* person
	14.34	and I put a *l* disease in a house in the
Num	5.	2 put out of the camp everyone who is *l*,
	12.10	Miriam was *l*, as white as snow. And
2 Kings	7.	3 there were four *l* men outside the city

LETTER (LETTERS)

2 Sam	11.14	David wrote a *l* to Joab, and sent it by
1 Kings	21.	8 she wrote *l* in Ahab's name and sealed
2 Kings	5.	6 He brought the *l* to the king of Israel,
2 Chr	21.12	A *l* came to him from the prophet
	30.	1 wrote *l* also to Ephraim and Manasseh,
Ezra	5.	5 and then answer was returned by *l*
Neh	6.	5 sent his servant to me with an open *l*
Isa	37.14	Hezekiah received the *l* from the hand
Jer	29.	1 of the *l* that the prophet Jeremiah
Acts	9.	2 for *l* to the synagogues at Damascus,
	15.23	with the following *l*: "The brothers, both
	15.30	together, they delivered the *l*.
	22.	5 received *l* to the brothers in Damascus,
	23.25	the governor." He wrote a *l* to this effect:
	23.33	and delivered the *l* to the governor,
2 Cor	3.	1 need, as some do, *l* of recommendation
	3.	2 You yourselves are our *l*, written on our
	3.	6 of spirit; for the *l* kills, but the Spirit
	10.	9 I am trying to frighten you with my *l*.
Gal	6.11	See what large *l* I make when I am
Col	4.16	when this *l* has been read among you,
2 Thess	2.	2 either by spirit or by word or by *l*,
	3.14	who do not obey what we say in this *l*;
	3.17	This is the mark in every *l* of mine; it
2 Pet	3.16	speaking of this as he does in all his *l*.

LEVI

Gen	29.34	three sons"; therefore he was named *L*.
Ex	2.	1 Now a man from the house of *L* went
Num	1.49	Only the tribe of *L* you shall not enroll,
Deut	10.	8 the LORD set apart the tribe of *L* to carry

LEVIATHAN

Job	41.	1 "Can you draw out *L* with a fishhook, or
Isa	27.	1 strong sword will punish *L* the fleeing

LEVITES

Josh	14.	4 no portion was given to the *L* in the
2 Chr	31.	2 to his service, the priests and the *L*,
	34.	9 which the *L*, the keepers of the
	35.	3 He said to the *L* who taught all Israel

LIAR (LIARS)

Ps	116.	11 in my consternation, "Everyone is a *l*."
Jn	8.55	not know him, I would be a *l* like you.
Rom	3.	4 Although everyone is a *l*, let God be
1 Jn	5.10	made him a *l* by not believing in the
Rev	21.	8 and all *l*, their place will be in the lake

LIBERTY

Lev	25.10	shall proclaim *l* throughout the land
Ps	119.	45 I shall walk at *l*, for I have sought your
Jer	34.	8 to make a proclamation of *l* to them,
Ezek	46.17	his to the year of *l*; then it shall revert
1 Cor	8.	9 take care that this *l* of yours does not
	10.29	why should my *l* be subject to the

LIE (LIES)

Num	23.19	is not a human being, that he should *l*,
Ps	4.	8 I will both *l* down and sleep in peace;
	119.	69 The arrogant smear me with *l*, but with
Prov	14.	5 A faithful witness does not *l*, but a false
Isa	28.15	we have made *l* our refuge, and in
	59.	3 your lips have spoken *l*, your tongue
Jer	27.10	For they are prophesying a *l* to you,
Jn	8.44	When he *l*, he speaks according to his
Acts	5.	3 has Satan filled your heart to *l* to the
Rom	1.25	exchanged the truth about God for a *l*
Col	3.	9 Do not *l* to one another, seeing that you
Rev	14.	5 in their mouth no *l* was found; they are

LIFE

Gen	1.30	everything that has the breath of *l*, I
	2.	9 tree of *l* also in the midst of the garden,

Lev	17.11 For the *l* of the flesh is in the blood;
Deut	30.15 I have set before you today *l* and
	30.20 for that means *l* to you and length of
1 Sam	2. 6 The Lᴏʀᴅ kills and brings to *l*; he brings
	25.29 to seek your *l*, the *l* of my lord shall be
2 Sam	15.21 whether for death or for *l*, there also
1 Kings	20.42 your *l* shall be for his *l*, and your people
2 Kings	13.21 the bones of Elisha, he came to *l*,
Job	7. 7 "Remember that my *l* is a breath; my
	33. 4 the breath of the Almighty gives me *l*.
	33.30 Pit, so that they may see the light of *l*.
Ps	16.11 You show me the path of *l*. In your
	34.12 Which of you desires *l*, and covets many
	36. 9 For with you is the fountain of *l*; in
	63. 3 your steadfast love is better than *l*,
	94.21 together against the *l* of the righteous,
Prov	3.22 and they will be *l* for your soul
	4.22 they are *l* to those who find them, and
	8.35 For whoever finds me finds *l* and
	12.28 In the path of righteousness there is *l*,
	14.27 The fear of the Lᴏʀᴅ is a fountain of *l*,
Eccl	2.17 I hated *l*, because what is done under
	9. 9 Enjoy *l* with the wife whom you love,
Isa	4. 3 has been recorded for *l* in Jerusalem,
	38.17 held back my *l* from the pit of
Jer	8. 3 Death shall be preferred to *l* by all the
	21. 8 I am setting before you the way of *l* and
Ezek	3.21 warning; and you will have saved your *l*.
Jon	4. 3 now, O Lᴏʀᴅ, please take my *l* from me,
Mt	7.14 and the road is hard that leads to *l*,
	10.39 those who lose their *l* for my sake will
	16.26 gain the whole world and forfeit their *l*?
	25.46 but the righteous into eternal *l*."
Mk	8.35 those who want to save their *l* will lose
	8.36 gain the whole world and forfeit their *l*?
	10.30 and in the age to come eternal *l*.
Lk	9.24 who want to save their *l* will lose it, and
	12.22 do not worry about your *l*, what you will
	18.18 what must I do to inherit eternal *l*?"
Jn	1. 4 In him was *l*, and the *l* was the light of
	3.36 believes in the Son has eternal *l*;
	4.14 spring of water gushing up to eternal *l*."
	5.24 believes him who sent me has eternal *l*,
	6.68 we go? You have the words of eternal *l*.
	10.10 I came that they may have *l*, and have
	10.15 Father. I lay down my *l* for the sheep.
	10.28 I give them eternal *l*, and they will
	11.25 "I am the resurrection and the *l*. Those
	14. 6 "I am the way and the truth, and the *l*;
	17. 3 this is eternal *l*, that they know you, the
	20.31 that through believing you may have *l*
Acts	5.20 people the whole message about this *l*."
	17.25 he himself gives to all mortals *l* and
Rom	6.13 who have been brought from death to *l*,
	6.23 but the free gift of God is eternal *l*
	8.10 the Spirit is *l* because of righteousness.
	8.38 neither death, nor *l*, nor angels, nor
2 Cor	2.16 to the other a fragrance from *l* to *l*.
	3. 6 for the letter kills, but the Spirit gives *l*.
	4.10 that the *l* of Jesus may be made visible
	4.12 So death is at work in us, but *l* in you.
Gal	1.13 no doubt, of my earlier *l* in Judaism.
	2.20 the *l* I now live in the flesh I live by
Eph	2.10 prepared beforehand to be our way of *l*.
Col	3. 3 and your *l* is hidden with Christ in God.
1 Tim	2. 2 lead a quiet and peaceable *l* in all
Heb	7.16 the power of an indestructible *l*.
Jas	4.14 What is your *l*? for you are a mist that
1 Pet	3.10 "Those who desire *l* and desire to see
1 Jn	3.14 we have passed from death to *l* because
	3.16 by this, that he laid down his *l* for us
Rev	2. 7 give permission to eat from the tree of *l*
	3. 5 not blot your name out of the book of *l*,
	11.11 breath of *l* from God entered them, and
	12.11 they did not cling to *l* even in the face
	13. 8 in the book of *l* of the Lamb that was
	20. 4 They came to *l*, and reigned with Christ

Rev	21. 6 a gift from the spring of the water of *l*.
	21.27 are written in the Lamb's book of *l*.
	22.17 who wishes take the water of *l* as a gift.

LIFT (LIFTED LIFTING)

Ps	24. 7 *L* up your heads, O gates! and be *l* up,
	25. 1 To you, O Lᴏʀᴅ, I *l* up my soul. O my
	75. 6 not from the wilderness comes *l* up; but
	86. 4 for to you, O Lᴏʀᴅ, I *l* up my soul.
	121. 1 I *l* up my eyes to the hills — from where
	131. 1 O Lᴏʀᴅ, my heart is not *l* up, my eyes
	134. 2 *L* up your hands to the holy place, and
Lk	1.52 from their thrones, and *l* up the lowly;
Jn	3.14 so must the Son of man be *l* up, that
	8.28 "When you have *l* up the Son of Man,
	12.32 And I, when I am *l* up from the earth,

LIGHT (LIGHTS)

Gen	1. 3 said, "Let there be *l*"; and there was *l*.
	1.15 let there be *l* in the dome of the sky to
Ex	10.23 but all the Israelites had *l* where they
Lev	24. 2 the lamp, that a *l* may be kept burning
2 Sam	23. 4 is like the *l* of morning, like the sun
Job	24.16 themselves up; they do not know the *l*.
Ps	27. 1 The Lᴏʀᴅ is my *l* and my salvation;
	37. 6 make your vindication shine like the *l*,
	43. 3 O send out your *l* and your truth; let
	49.19 who will never more see the *l*.
	97.11 *L* dawns for the righteous, and joy for
	119.105 is a lamp to my feet and a *l* to my path.
	119.130 The unfolding of your words gives *l*; it
	139. 12 as the day, for darkness is as *l* to you.
Prov	4.18 of the righteous is like the *l* of dawn,
	13. 9 The *l* of the righteous rejoices, but the
Eccl	11. 7 *L* is sweet, and it is pleasant for the
Isa	2. 5 come, let us walk in the *l* of the Lᴏʀᴅ!
	5.20 put darkness for *l* and *l* for darkness,
	42. 6 to the people, a *l* to the nations,
	45. 7 I form *l* and create darkness, I make
	49. 6 I will give you as a *l* to the nations, that
	58. 8 Then your *l* shall break forth like the
	60. 1 Arise, shine; for your *l* has come, and
	60. 3 Nations shall come to your *l*, and kings
Mic	7. 8 in darkness, the Lᴏʀᴅ will be a *l* to me.
Mt	4.16 who sat in darkness have seen a great *l*,
	5.16 let your *l* shine before others, so that
Lk	1.79 I to those who sit in darkness and in
	2.32 a *l* for revelation to the Gentiles and for
	12. 3 said in the dark will be heard in the *l*,
Jn	1. 5 The *l* shines in the darkness, and the
	3.19 that the *l* has come into the world,
	8.12 "I am the *l* of the world. Whoever
	9. 5 in the world, I am the *l* of the world."
	12.35 believe in the *l*, so that you may
Acts	9. 3 suddenly a *l* from heaven flashed
	13.47 have set you to be a *l* for the Gentiles,
	22. 6 a great *l* from heaven suddenly shone
	26.13 your Excellency, I saw a *l* from heaven,
	26.18 that they may turn from darkness to *l*
Rom	13.12 of darkness and put on the armor of *l*;
1 Cor	4. 5 comes, who will bring to *l* the things
2 Cor	4. 4 to keep them from seeing the *l* of the
	4. 6 "Let *l* shine out of darkness," who has
	6.14 is there between *l* and darkness?
Eph	5. 8 darkness, but now in the Lord you are *l*.
	5.14 for everything that becomes visible is *l*.
Jas	1.17 coming down from the father of *l*, with
1 Pet	2. 9 out of darkness into his marvelous *l*.
1 Jn	1. 5 that God is *l* and in him there is no
	1. 7 but if we walk in the *l*, as he himself is
	2. 8 away and the true *l* is already shining.
Rev	22. 5 they need no *l* of lamp or sun, for the

LIGHTNING (LIGHTNINGS)

Ps	18.14 and scattered them; he flashed forth *l*,
Mt	24.27 as the *l* comes from the east and flashes
Lk	17.24 as the *l* flashes and lights up the sky

Rev	8.	5 of thunder, rumblings, flashes of *l*, and

LIKENESS

Gen	5.	1 he made them in the *l* of God.
Isa	40.	18 liken God, or what *l* compare with him?
Rom	8.	3 his own Son in the *l* of sinful flesh,
Phil	2.	7 form of a slave, being born in human *l*.

LILY (LILIES)

Song	2.	2 As a *l* among brambles, so is my love
Mt	6.28	Consider the *l* of the field, how they
Lk	12.27	Consider the *l*, how they grow; they

LINEN

Mk	15.46	the body, wrapped it in the *l* cloth,
Rev	19.	8 with fine *l*, bright and pure" —for the

LION (LIONS LION'S)

1 Sam	17.34	whenever a *l* or a bear came, and took a
2 Sam	23.20	went down and killed a *l* in a pit on a
1 Kings	13.24	he went away, a *l* met him on the road
1 Chr	11.22	killed a *l* in a pit on a day when snow
Ps	7.	2 or like a *l* they will tear me apart; they
	22.21	dog! Save me from the mouth of the *l*!
	104.	21 The young *l* roar for their prey, seeking
Prov	26.13	The lazy person says, "There is a *l* in
Jer	12.	8 has become to me like a *l* in the forest;
Dan	6.16	brought and thrown into the den of *l*.
	7.	4 first was like a *l* and had eagle's wings.
Hos	5.14	I will be like a *l* to Ephraim, and like a
Am	5.19	not light; as if someone fled from a *l*,
2 Tim	4.17	it. So I was rescued from the *l* mouth.
Heb	11.33	shut the mouths of *l*, quenched the
1 Pet	5.	8 Like a roaring *l* your adversary the devil
Rev	5.	5 the *L* of the tribe of Judah, the Root of

LIPS

Ps	12.	4 will prevail; our *l* are our own—who is
	34.13	evil, and your *l* from speaking deceit.
Prov	12.19	Truthful *l* endure forever, but a lying
	16.13	Righteous *l* are the delight of a king,
	20.15	but the *l* informed by knowledge are a
Song	4.	3 Your *l* are like a crimson thread, and
Isa	29.13	honor me with their *l*, while their hearts
Mt	15.	8 This people honors me with their *l*, but
Mk	7.	6 'This people honors me with their *l*, but
Rom	3.13	"The venom of vipers is under their *l*."
	10.	8 "The word is near you, on your *l* and in

LISTED

Judg	8.14	questioned him; and he *l* for him the

LISTEN (LISTENED LISTENING LISTENS)

Ex	23.21	Be attentive to him and *l* to his voice;
Josh	5.	6 not having *l* to the voice of the LORD. To
Judg	13.	9 God *l* to Manoah, and the angel of God
1 Sam	8.19	the people refused to *l* to the voice of
2 Kings	21.	9 But they did not *l*, Manasseh misled
Job	36.11	If they *l*, and serve him, they complete
Prov	12.15	way is right, but the wise *l* to advice.
	23.22	*L* to your father who begot you, and do
Eccl	5.	1 to draw near to *l* is better than the
Isa	6.	9 'Keep *l*, but do not comprehend; keep
	51.	1 *L* to me, you that pursue righteousness,
Jer	12.17	But if any nation will not *l*, then I will
	17.24	But if you *l* to me, says the LORD, and
	18.10	not *l* to my voice, then I will change my
	26.	3 It may be that they will *l*, all of them,
Dan	9.19	forgive; O Lord, *l* and act and do not
Mal	3.16	The LORD took note and *l*, and a book of
Mk	9.	7 "This is my Son, the Beloved; *l* to him!"
Lk	9.35	"This is my Son, my Chosen; *l* to him!"
	10.16	"Whoever *l* to you *l* to me, and whoever
Jn	10.16	them also, and they will *l* to my voice.
Acts	28.26	You will indeed *l*, but never understand,
Jas	1.19	let everyone be quick to *l*, slow to

LITTLE

Ps	37.16	Better is a *l* that the righteous one has
Prov	13.11	but those who gather *l* by *l* will increase
Isa	28.10	line, line upon line, here a *l*, there a *l*."
Mic	5.	2 who are one of the *l* clans of Judah,
Mt	6.30	much more clothe you—you of *l* faith?
	8.26	"Why are you afraid, you of *l* faith?"
	10.42	cold water to one of these *l* ones in the
	14.31	him, "You of *l* faith, why did you doubt?"
	16.	8 "You of *l* faith, why are you talking
	18.	6 stumbling block before one of these *l*
Lk	7.47	the one to whom *l* is forgiven, loves *l*."
	17.	2 to cause one of these *l* ones to stumble.
2 Cor	8.15	the one who had *l* did not have too *l*."

LIVE (v)

Gen	13.	6 so great that they could not *l* together,
Ex	1.17	them, but they let the boys *l*.
	9.16	this is why I have let you *l*: to show you
	33.20	face; for no one shall not see me and *l*."
Lev	18.	5 by doing so one shall *l*: I am the LORD.
Num	21.	9 look at the serpent of bronze and *l*.
Deut	4.	1 that you may *l* to enter and occupy the
	5.24	to someone and the person may still *l*.
	5.33	that you may *l*, and that it may go well
	8.	1 that you may *l* and increase, and go in
	8.	3 one does not *l* by bread alone, but by
	16.20	that you may *l* and occupy the land that
	30.20	that you may *l* in the land that the LORD
Josh	15.63	the Jebusites *l* with the people of Judah
1 Sam	10.24	all the people shouted, "Long *l* the king!"
1 Kings	1.34	and say, 'Long *l* King Solomon!'
Job	14.14	If mortals die, will they *l* again? All the
Ps	27.	4 to *l* in the house of the LORD all the
	84.	4 Happy are those who *l* in your house,
	91.	1 You who *l* in the shelter of the Most
	107.	36 there he lets the hungry *l*, and they
	119.	17 so that I may *l* and observe your word.
	119.144	give me understanding that I may *l*.
	133.	1 it is when kindred *l* together in unity!
	146.	2 I will praise the LORD as long as I *l*; I
Prov	4.	4 words; keep my commandments, and *l*;
	9.	6 Lay aside immaturity, and *l*, and walk
	21.	9 It is better to *l* in a corner of the
Isa	26.19	Your dead shall *l*, their corpses shall
	33.14	among us can *l* with the devouring fire?
	55.	3 come to me; listen, so that you may *l*;
Jer	27.12	and serve him and his people, and *l*.
Ezek	16.	6 you lay in your blood, I said to you, "*L*,
	18.	9 a one is righteous, he shall surely *l*,
	18.22	that they have done they shall *l*.
	20.11	by whose observance everyone shall *l*.
	33.19	is lawful and right, they shall *l* by it.
	37.	3 said to me, "Mortal, can these bones *l*?"
Hos	6.	2 raise us up, that we may *l* before him.
	12.	9 I will make you *l* in tents again, as in
	14.	7 They shall again *l* beneath my shadow,
Am	5.14	Seek good and not evil, that you may *l*;
Mt	4.	4 "One does not *l* by bread alone, but by
	9.18	lay your hand on her, and she will *l*."
Mk	7.	5 disciples not *l* according to the tradition
	12.44	everything she had, all she had to *l* on."
Lk	4.	4 'One does not *l* by bread alone.'
	10.28	the right answer; do this, and you will *l*."
Jn	6.58	But the one who eats this bread will *l*
	14.19	will see me; because I *l*, you also will *l*.
Acts	17.28	For 'In him we *l* and move and have
Rom	8.13	if you *l* according to the flesh, you will
	10.	5 who does these things will *l* by them."
	13.13	let us *l* honorably as in the day, not in
	14.	7 We do not *l* to ourselves, and we do not
Gal	3.11	one who is righteous will *l* by faith.
	5.16	*L* by the Spirit, I say, and do not gratify
	5.25	If we *l* by the Spirit, let us also be
Eph	4.17	no longer *l* as the Gentiles *l*, in the
	5.	2 *l* in love, as Christ loved us and gave
	5.	8 you are light. *L* as children of light—

Col	2. 6 continue to *l* your lives in him, rooted
2 Tim	2.11 died with him, we will also *l* with him;
Titus	2.12 to *l* lives that are self-controlled,

LIVES (LIVED LIVING) (v)

Gen	14.12 took Lot . . . who *l* in Sodom, and his
	19.30 in Zoar; so he *l* in a cave with his two
2 Sam	7. 2 I am *l* in a house of cedar, but the ark
Job	19.25 I know that my Redeemer *l*, and at the
Lk	1. 6 righteous before God, *l* blamelessly
Jn	1.14 Word became flesh and *l* among us, and
Acts	9.31 *L* in the fear of the Lord and in the
Eph	2. 2 trespasses and sins in which you once *l*,
Phil	1.21 For to me, *l* is Christ and dying is
1 Pet	4. 3 Gentiles like to do, *l* in licentiousness,
1 Jn	4.12 if we love one another, God *l* in us, and

LIVES (n)

Prov	11.30 a tree of life, but violence takes *l* away.
Jer	51. 6 of Babylon, save your *l*, each of you!
Ezek	13.18 you hunt down *l* among my people, and
Acts	15.26 who have risked their *l* for the sake of
Heb	13. 5 Keep your *l* free from love of money,
2 Pet	3.11 in leading *l* of holiness and godliness,

LIVING (n and adj)

Gen	2. 7 of life; and the man became a *l* being.
Num	16.48 He stood between the dead and the *l*;
Josh	3.10 among you is the *l* God who without
1 Sam	17.36 he has defied the armies of the *l* God."
2 Kings	19. 4 of Assyria has sent to mock the *l* God,
Ps	42. 2 My soul thirsts for God, for the *l* God.
	66. 9 who has kept us among the *l*, and has
	69.28 be blotted out of the book of the *l*;
Eccl	4. 2 already died, more fortunate than the *l*
	9. 5 the *l* know that they will die, but the
Isa	8.19 their gods, the dead on behalf of the *l*,
	38.19 The *l*, the *l*, they thank you, as I do this
Jer	10.10 is the *l* God and the everlasting King.
Zech	14. 8 that day *l* waters shall flow out of
Mt	22.32 He is God not of the dead, but of the *l*."
Mk	12.27 He is God not of the dead, but of the *l*;
Lk	15.13 squandered his property in dissolute *l*.
	24. 5 do you look for the *l* among the dead?
Jn	4.10 and he would have given you *l* water."
	6.51 I am the *l* bread that came down from
	6.57 the *l* Father sent me, and I live because
1 Cor	15.45 "The first man, Adam, became a *l* being";
1 Thess	1. 9 from idols, to serve a *l* and true God,
1 Tim	4.10 we have our hope set on the *l* God, who
Heb	3.12 heart that turns away from the *l* God.
Rev	1.18 and the *l* one. I was dead, and see, I am

LIZARD

Lev	11.29 . . . the great *l* according to its kind,
Prov	30.28 the *l* can be grasped in the hand, yet it

LOAN (LOANS)

Deut	23.19 shall not charge interest on *l* to another
	24.10 When you make your neighbor a *l* of

LOATHE (LOATHED)

Job	10. 1 "I *l* my life; I will give free utterance to
Ps	95.10 For forty years I *l* that generation and
	139. 21 I not *l* those who rise up against you?
Ezek	36.31 you shall *l* yourselves for your iniquities

LOAVES

Mt	14.17 nothing here but five *l* and two fish."
	15.34 "How many *l* have you?" They said,
Mk	6.38 "How many *l* have you? Go and see."
	8. 5 asked them, "How many *l* do you have?"
Lk	9.13 "We have no more than five *l* and two
	11. 5 'Friend, lend me three *l* of bread; for a
Jn	6. 9 here who has five barley *l* and two fish.
	6.26 but because you ate your fill of the *l*.

LOCK

Mt	23.13 For you *l* people out of the kingdom of

LOCUST (LOCUSTS)

Ex	10. 4 tomorrow I will bring *l* into your
Lev	11.22 of them you may eat: the *l* according to
Judg	6. 5 even bring their tents, as thick as *l*;
Ps	105. 34 He spoke, and the *l* came, and young *l*
Prov	30.27 the *l* have no king, yet all of them
Joel	1. 4 What the cutting *l* left, the swarming *l*
Am	7. 1 he was forming *l* at the time the latter
Mt	3. 4 and his food was *l* and wild honey.
Mk	1. 6 his waist, and he ate *l* and wild honey.
Rev	9. 3 from the smoke came *l* on the earth,

LODGE (LODGED)

Ruth	1.16 you go, I will go; Where you *l*, I will *l*;
1 Sam	7. 2 day that the ark was *l* at Kiriath-jearim,

LOFTY

Job	22.12 See the highest stars, how *l* they are!
Isa	57.15 high and *l* one who inhabits eternity,
1 Cor	2. 1 the mystery of God to you in *l* words or

LONELY

Ps	25.16 gracious to me, for I am *l* and afflicted.

LONG (LONGED LONGING LONGS)

Job	3.21 to the bitter in soul, who *l* for death,
Ps	42. 1 As a deer *l* for flowing streams, so my
	84. 2 My soul *l*, indeed it faints for the courts
	119. 20 is consumed with *l* for your ordinances
	119. 40 I have *l* for your precepts; in your
Mt	13.17 righteous people *l* to see what you see,
Lk	17.22 days are coming when you will *l* to see
Rom	8.19 creation waits with eager *l* for the
Rev	18.14 "The fruit for which your soul *l* has

LOOK (LOOKED LOOKING LOOKS)

Gen	13.14 eyes now, and *l* from the place where
	15. 5 "*L* toward heaven, and count the stars,
	19.17 "Flee for your life; do not *l* back or stop
	19.26 But Lot's wife . . . *l* back, and she
	22.13 Abraham *l* up and saw a ram, caught in
Num	21. 9 person would *l* at the serpent of bronze
Deut	26.15 *L* down from your holy habitation, from
1 Sam	16. 7 "Do not *l* on his appearance or on the
2 Sam	22.42 They *l*, but there was no one to save
Job	36.25 All people have *l* on it; everyone
Ps	8. 3 When I *l* at your heavens, the work of
	33.13 The Lord *l* down from heaven, he sees
	84. 9 O God; *l* on the face of your anointed.
	102. 19 from heaven the Lord *l* at the earth,
	104. 27 These all *l* to you, to give them their
	119.153 *L* on my misery and rescue me, for I do
Isa	22.11 But you did not *l* to him who did it, or
	33.20 *L* on Zion, the city of our appointed
	42.18 and you that are blind, *l* up and see!
	51. 1 *L* to the rock from which you were
	51. 6 the heavens, and *l* at the earth beneath;
	63. 5 I *l*, but there was no helper; I stared,
Mic	7. 7 But as for me, I will *l* to the Lord, I will
Hab	1.13 evil, and you cannot *l* on wrongdoing;
Hag	1. 9 You have *l* for much, and, lo, it came to
Mt	5.28 who *l* at a woman with lust had already
	6.16 whenever you fast, do not *l* dismal, like
	13.14 you will indeed *l*, but never perceive.
	23.28 on the outside *l* righteous to others,
Mk	4.12 'they may indeed *l*, but not perceive,
Lk	1.48 for he has *l* with favor on the lowliness
	2.25 *l* forward to consolation of Israel,
	9.38 "Teacher, I beg you to *l* at my son; he is
	13. 7 I have come *l* for fruit on this fig tree,
	24. 5 "Why do you *l* for the living among the
Jn	6.26 you are *l* for me, not because you saw
	18. 4 and asked them, "Whom are you *l* for?"
	20.15 are you weeping? Whom are you *l* for?"
Acts	1.11 why do you stand *l* up toward heaven?

Acts	28.26	you will indeed *l* but never perceive.
2 Cor	10. 7	*L* at what is before your eyes. If you are
Heb	11.10	he *l* forward to the city that has
	12. 2	*l* to Jesus the pioneer and perfecter of
Jas	1.25	those who *l* into the perfect law, the

LOOSE (LOOSED LOOSES)

Job	12.21	on princes, and *l* the belt of the strong.
Ps	78.49	He let *l* on them his fierce anger, wrath,
	116. 16	You have *l* my bonds. I will offer to you
Prov	5. 3	For the lips of a *l* woman drip honey,
Isa	58. 6	I choose: to *l* the bonds of injustice,
Mt	16.19	whatever you *l* on earth will be *l* in
	18.18	whatever you *l* on earth will be *l* in

LORD

Gen	2. 4	day that the *L* God made the earth and
	6. 8	Noah found favor in the sight of the *L*.
	12. 1	Now the *L* said to Abram, "Go from
Ex	6. 3	by my name 'The *L*' I did not make
	12.51	very day the *L* brought the Israelites
	15. 1	the Israelites sang this song to the *L*:
Deut	34.10	Moses, whom the *L* knew face to face.
1 Kings	1.31	said, "May my *l* King David live forever!"
Ps	1. 2	but their delight is in the law of the *L*,
	83.18	that you alone, whose name is the *L*,
	84. 1	is your dwelling place, O *L* of hosts!
Isa	53. 6	and the *L* has laid on him the iniquity
Mt	12. 8	For the Son of Man is *l* of the sabbath."
Mk	1. 3	Prepare the way of the *L*, make his
Jn	14. 5	"*L*, we do not know where you are
	20.28	answered him, "My *L* and my God!"
Acts	2.36	God has made him both *L* and Messiah,
1 Cor	12. 3	no one can say "Jesus is *L*" except by
Phil	2.11	should confess that Jesus Christ is *L*,
Heb	1.10	beginning, *L*, you founded the earth,
Rev	19. 6	"Hallelujah! for the *L* our God the

LORD JESUS

Acts	15.11	be saved through the grace of the *L*,
	16.31	"Believe on the *L*, and you will be

LORD JESUS CHRIST

Acts	11.17	he gave us when we believed in the *L*,
Rom	5. 1	we have peace with God through our *L*.
1 Cor	15.57	who gives us the victory through our *L*.
2 Cor	8. 9	you know the generous act of our *L*,
2 Pet	1.16	to you the power and coming of our *L*,

LORD OF HOSTS

Ps	46. 7	The *L* is with us; the God of Jacob is
Isa	8.13	the *L*, him you shall regard as holy; let

LORDS

1 Cor	8. 5	fact there are many gods and many *l*—

LOSE (LOSES LOST)

Ps	119.176	I have gone astray like a *l* sheep; seek
Eccl	5.14	riches were *l* in a bad venture; though
Isa	6. 5	"Woe is me! I am *l*, for I am a man of
Ezek	37.11	bones are dried up, and our hope is *l*;
Mt	10. 6	go rather to the *l* sheep of the house of
	10.39	Those who find their life will *l* it, and
	15.24	was sent only to the *l* sheep of the
	16.25	who want to save their life will *l* it,
	18.14	that one of these little ones should be *l*.
Mk	8.35	it, and those who *l* their life for my sake
Lk	9.24	those who *l* their life for my sake will
	15. 8	if she *l* one of them, does not light a
	15.24	is alive again; he was *l*, and is found!'
	17.33	it, but those who *l* their life will keep it.
Jn	6.39	should *l* nothing of all that he has given
	18. 9	"I did not *l* a single one of those whom

LOST (n)

Ezek	34.16	I will seek the *l*, and I will bring back
Mt	18.11n	For the Son of Man came to save the *l*.
Lk	19.10	Man came to seek out and to save the *l*."

LOT

Accompanied Abram to Canaan, Gen 11.31—12.5; separated from Abram to live at Sodom, Gen 13; rescued by Abram, Gen 14.1-16; sheltered angels, Gen 19.1-11; fled to Zoar, Gen 19.15-23; Lot and his daughters, Gen 19.30-38.

Gen	12. 4	and *L* went with him. Abram was
	14.16	brought back his nephew *L* with his
	19. 1	*L* was sitting in the gateway of Sodom.
Lk	17.28	just as it was in the days of *L*: they
2 Pet	2. 7	if he rescued *L*, a righteous man greatly

LOT (LOTS)

Lev	16. 8	Aaron shall cast *l* on the two goats, one
1 Sam	14.42	Then Saul said, "Cast the *l* between me
Ps	22.18	and for my clothing they cast *l*.
Prov	1.14	Throw in your *l* among us; we will all
	16.33	The *l* is cast into the lap, but the
Eccl	3.22	enjoy their work, for that is their *l*;
Ob	11	his gates and cast *l* for Jerusalem.
Jon	1. 7	they cast lots, and the *l* fell on Jonah.
Mt	27.35	clothes among themselves by casting *l*;
Lk	1. 9	he was chosen by *l*, according to the
Jn	19.24	"Let us not tear it, but cast *l* for it to
Acts	1.26	and the *l* fell on Matthias; and he was

LOVE (n)

1 Sam	20.14	show me the faithful *l* of the LORD;
2 Sam	7.15	I will not take my steadfast *l* from him,
Prov	7.18	let us take our fill of *l* until morning;
	10.12	stirs up strife, but *l* covers all offenses.
	15.17	is a dinner of vegetables where *l* is
	27. 5	Better is open rebuke than hidden *l*.
Song	1. 2	For your *l* is better than wine, your
	1.15	you are beautiful, my *l*; ah, you are
	4. 1	How beautiful you are, my *l*, how very
	4.10	How much better is your *l* than wine,
	5. 1	Eat, friends, drink, and be drunk with *l*.
	8. 6	for *l* is strong as death, passion fierce as
	8. 7	Many waters cannot quench *l*, neither
Isa	63. 9	in his *l* and in his pity he redeemed
Ezek	33.32	To them you are like a singer of *l* songs,
Hos	6. 4	Your *l* is like a morning cloud, like the
	11. 4	of human kindness, with bands of *l*.
Mt	24.12	the *l* of many will grow cold.
Lk	11.42	and neglect justice and the *l* of God;
Jn	15.13	No one has greater *l* than this, to lay
	17.26	so that the *l* with which you have loved
Rom	5. 5	God's *l* has been poured into our hearts
	5. 8	But God proves his *l* for us in that while
	8.39	be able to separate us from the *l* of God
	12. 9	Let *l* be genuine; hate what is evil, hold
1 Cor	8. 1	Knowledge puffs up, but *l* builds up.
	13. 1	but do not have *l*, I am a noisy gong or
	13.13	three; and the greatest of these is *l*.
2 Cor	5.14	the *l* of Christ urges us on, because we
	6. 6	kindness, holiness of spirit, genuine *l*,
	8. 1	I am testing the genuineness of your *l*
	8.24	show them the proof of your *l* and of
	13.13	Christ, the *l* of God, and the
Gal	5. 6	that counts is faith working through *l*.
	5.13	through *l* become slaves to one another.
Eph	1.15	your *l* toward all the saints, and for this
	3.19	of Christ that surpasses knowledge,
	4.15	speaking the truth in *l*, we must grow
	5. 2	live in *l*, as Christ loved us and gave
Phil	1. 9	is my prayer, that your *l* may overflow
	1.16	These proclaim Christ out of *l*, knowing
Col	1. 4	Jesus and of the *l* that you have for all
	3.14	Above all, clothe yourselves with *l*,
1 Thess	1. 3	your work of faith and labor of *l* and
	4. 9	concerning *l* of the brothers and sisters,
2 Tim	4.10	Demas, in *l* with this present world, has
Heb	13. 1	Let mutual *l* continue. Do not neglect
1 Pet	4. 8	another, for *l* covers a multitude of sins.
1 Jn	3. 1	See what *l* the Father has given us, that
	3.16	We know *l* by this, that he laid down

Jude	12 These are blemishes on your *l*-feasts,
Rev	2. 4 that you have abandoned the *l* you had

LOVE (v)

Ex	20. 6 generation of those who *l* me and keep
	21. 5 "I *l* my master, my wife, and my
Lev	19.18 you shall *l* your neighbor as yourself: I
Deut	5.10 generation of those who *l* me
	6. 5 You shall *l* the LORD your God with all
	7.13 he will *l* you, bless you, and multiply
	10.12 to *l* him, to serve the LORD your God
	10.19 You shall also *l* the stranger, for you
	13. 3 to know whether you indeed *l* the LORD
	30. 6 so that you will *l* the LORD your God
Josh	23.11 very careful . . . to *l* the LORD your God.
2 Chr	19. 2 wicked and *l* those who hate the LORD?
Neh	1. 5 *l* with those who *l* him and keep his
Ps	18. 1 I *l* you, O LORD, my strength. The LORD
	31.23 *L* the LORD, all you his saints. The LORD
	45. 7 you *l* righteousness and hate
	60. 5 that those whom you *l* may be rescued.
	70. 4 Let those who *l* your salvation say
	91.14 Those who *l* me, I will deliver; I will
	116. 1 I *l* the LORD, because he has heard my
	119. 97 Oh, how I *l* your law! It is my
Prov	4. 6 keep you; *l* her, and she will guard you.
	8.17 I *l* those who *l* me, and those who seek
	20.13 Do not *l* sleep, or else you will come to
	22.11 who *l* a pure heart and are gracious
Eccl	3. 8 time to *l*, and a time to hate; a time for
	9. 9 life with the wife whom you *l*, all the
Isa	61. 8 For I the LORD *l* justice, I hate robbery
Hos	3. 1 *l* a woman who has a lover and is an
	9.15 I will *l* them no more; all their officials
	14. 4 I will *l* them freely, for my anger has
Am	5.15 Hate evil and *l* good, and establish
Mic	3. 2 you who hate the good and *l* the evil,
	6. 8 do justice, to *l* kindness, and to walk
Mt	5.43 'You shall *l* your neighbor and hate
	19.19 You shall *l* your neighbor as yourself."
	22.37 "You shall *l* the Lord your God with all
	23. 6 They *l* to have the place of honor at
Mk	12.30 you shall *l* the Lord your God with all
Lk	6.27 *L* your enemies, do good to those who
	6.32 "If you *l* those who *l* you, what credit is
	10.27 "You shall *l* the Lord your God with all
	16.13 will either hate the one and *l* the other,
Jn	8.42 God were your Father, you would *l* me,
	11. 3 to Jesus, "Lord, he whom you *l* is ill."
	12.25 Those who *l* their life will lose it, and
	13.34 commandment, that you *l* one another.
	14.15 "If you *l* me, you will keep my
	14.21 and keep them are those who *l* me;
	15.12 love one another as I have *l* you.
	21.15 "Yes, Lord; you know that I *l* you." Jesus
Rom	8.28 together for good for those who *l* God,
	13. 8 one anything, except to *l* one another;
1 Cor	2. 9 God has prepared for those who *l* him"
2 Cor	12.15 If I *l* you more, am I to be *l* less? Let it
Eph	5.25 Husbands, *l* your wives, just as Christ
Col	3.19 Husbands, *l* your wives, and never treat
Titus	2. 4 the young women to *l* their husbands,
Jas	2. 5 he has promised to those who *l* him?
1 Pet	1. 8 you have not seen him, you *l* him;
	2.17 everyone. *L* the family of believers.
1 Jn	2.15 Do not *l* the world or the things in the
	3.11 that we should *l* one another.
	4. 7 let us *l* one another, because *l* is from
	4.19 We *l*, because he first loved us.
	5. 2 we *l* God and obey his commandments.
Rev	3.19 I reprove and discipline those whom I *l*.

LOVES (LOVED)

Gen	24.67 she became his wife; and he *l* her. So
	25.28 Isaac *l* Esau . . . , but Rebekah *l* Jacob.
	37. 3 Now Israel *l* Joseph more than any
	44.20 mother's children, and his father *l* him.'

Deut	4.37 because he *l* your ancestors, he chose
	15.16 because he *l* you and your household,
	23. 5 you, because the LORD your God *l* you.)
1 Sam	1. 5 gave a double portion, because he *l* her,
	16.21 Saul *l* him greatly, and he became his
	18. 1 and Jonathan *l* him as his own soul.
	18.16 all Israel and Judah *l* David; for it was
	18.28 and that Saul's daughter Michal *l* him,
	20.17 him, for he *l* him as he *l* his own life.
1 Kings	3. 3 Solomon *l* the LORD, walking in the
	10. 9 Because the LORD *l* Israel forever, he has
	11. 1 Solomon *l* many foreign women along
2 Chr	2.11 "Because the LORD *l* his people he has
Ps	78.68 tribe of Judah, Mount Zion, which he *l*.
	97.10 The LORD *l* those who hate evil; he
Prov	3.12 for the LORD reproves the one he *l*, as a
	12. 1 Whoever *l* discipline *l* knowledge, but
	15. 9 he *l* the one who pursues righteousness.
	17.17 A friend *l* at all times, and kinsfolk are
	17.19 One who *l* transgression *l* strife; one
	21.17 Whoever *l* pleasure will suffer want;
Song	3. 1 at night I sought him whom my soul *l*;
Isa	48.14 LORD *l* him; he shall perform his
Jer	31. 3 I have *l* you with an everlasting love;
Hos	11. 1 When Israel was a child, I *l* him, and
Mal	1. 2 I have *l* you, says the LORD. But you say,
Mt	10.37 Whoever *l* father or mother more than
Mk	10.21 Jesus, looking at him, *l* him and said,
Lk	7. 5 he *l* our people, and it is he who built
	7.47 forgiven, hence she has shown great *l*.
Jn	3.16 "For God so *l* the world that he gave his
	5.20 The Father *l* the Son and shows him all
	10.17 For this reason the Father *l* me,
	11.36 So the Jews said, "See how he *l* him!"
	12.43 for they *l* human glory more than the
	13. 1 were in the world, he *l* them to the end.
	15. 9 As the Father has *l* me, so I have *l* you;
	16.27 for the Father himself *l* you, because
	17.23 that you have sent me and have *l* them
	19.26 and the disciple whom he *l* standing
Rom	9.13 "I have *l* Jacob, but I have hated Esau."
1 Cor	8. 3 but anyone who *l* God is known by him.
2 Cor	9. 7 compulsion, for God *l* a cheerful giver.
Gal	2.20 in the Son of God, who *l* me and gave
Eph	2. 4 out of the great love with which he *l* us
Heb	1. 9 You have *l* righteousness and hated
1 Jn	2.10 whoever *l* a brother or sister lives in the
Rev	1. 5 To him who *l* us and freed us from our

LOVELY

Ps	84. 1 How *l* is your dwelling place, O LORD of

LOVER (LOVERS)

Eccl	5.10 the *l* of money will not be satisfied with
Jer	4.30 Your *l* despise you; they seek your life.
	22.22 and your *l* shall go into captivity;
	30.14 All your *l* have forgotten you; they care
Ezek	16.33 but you gave your gifts to all your *l*,
	23.22 I will rouse against you your *l* from
Hos	8. 9 alone; Ephraim has bargained for *l*.
2 Tim	3. 2 people will be *l* of themselves, *l* of

LOVE-SONG

Isa	5. 1 beloved my *l* concerning his vineyard:

LOW (LOWEST)

Isa	2.11 eyes of people will be brought *l*,
	10.33 down, and the lofty will be brought *l*.
	26. 5 city he lays *l*. He lays it *l* to the ground,
Lk	14. 9 you would start to take the *l* place.

LOWLY

Prov	16.19 It is better to be of a *l* spirit among the
	29.23 one who is *l* in spirit will obtain honor.
Zeph	3.12 the midst of you a people humble and *l*.

LOYAL (LOYALLY)

Deut	18.13 You must remain completely *l* to the

2 Sam 22.26 "With the *l* you show yourself *l*; with the
1 Chr 19. 2 "I will deal *l* with Hanun son of Nahash,
Ps 18.25 With the *l* you show yourself *l*; with the

LOYALTY
Ruth 3.10 this last instance of your *l* is better than
2 Sam 2. 5 because you showed this *l* to Saul your
Prov 19.22 What is desirable in a person is *l*, and it

LUKE
Col 4.14 *L*, the beloved physician, and Demas
2 Tim 4.11 Only *L* is with me. Get Mark and bring
Philem 24 Demas, and *L*, my fellow workers.

LUKEWARM
Rev 3.16 because you are *l*, and neither cold nor

LUMP
Isa 38.21 had said, "Let them take a *l* of figs,

LURE
Mk 4.19 cares of the world, and the *l* of wealth,

LUST
Mt 5.28 everyone who looks at a woman with *l*

LYING
Ps 31.18 Let the *l* lips be stilled that speak
109. 2 me, speaking against me with *l* tongues.
Prov 6.17 haughty eyes, a *l* tongue, and hands

LYRE
Gen 4.21 ancestor of all those who play the *l* and
Ps 33. 2 Praise the LORD with the *l*, make the

LYSTRA
Acts 14. 6 of it and fled to *L* and Derbe, cities
14.21 they returned to *L*, then on to Iconium
16. 1 Paul went on also to Derbe and to *L*,
2 Tim 3.11 and *L*. What persecutions I endured!

M

MACEDONIA
Acts 16. 9 stood a man of *M* pleading with him
18. 5 Silas and Timothy arrived from *M*, Paul
19.22 his helpers, Timothy and Erastus, to *M*,
Rom 15.26 *M* and Achaia have been pleased to
2 Cor 9. 2 boasting about you to the people of *M*,
Phil 4.15 when I left *M*, no church shared with
1 Thess 1. 8 sounded forth from you not only in *M*

MAD
Deut 28.34 driven *m* by the sight that your eyes
1 Sam 21.13 he pretended to be *m* in their presence.

MADE
Eph 2.10 For we are what he has *m* us, created in

MADNESS
Eccl 2.12 to consider wisdom and *m* and folly;

MAGGOT (MAGGOTS)
Job 25. 6 much less mortal, who is a *m*, and a
Hos 5.12 Therefore I am like *m* to Ephraim, and

MAGNIFICENT
1 Chr 22. 5 for the LORD must be exceedingly *m*,

MAGNIFY (MAGNIFIED MAGNIFIES)
2 Sam 7.26 your name will be *m* forever in the
1 Chr 17.24 name will be established and *m* forever
Ps 34. 3 O *m* the LORD with me, and let us exalt
Isa 10.15 or the saw *m* itself against the one who
42.21 in his teaching and made it glorious.
Lk 1.47 "My soul *m* the Lord, and my spirit

MAGOG
Ezek 38. 2 your face toward Gog, of the land of *M*,
Rev 20. 8 Gog and *M*, in order to gather them for

MAID
Prov 30.23 and a *m* when she succeeds her

MAIDEN (MAIDENS)
Song 1. 3 poured out; therefore the *m* love you.
Am 5. 2 Fallen, no more to rise, is *m* Israel;

MAINTAIN
Job 16.21 he would *m* the right of a mortal with

MAINTENANCE
1 Chr 26.27 dedicated gifts for the *m* of the house of

MAJESTIC
Ps 8. 1 Sovereign, how *m* is your name in all
8. 9 Sovereign, how *m* is your name in all

MAJESTY
Job 13.11 Will not his *m* terrify you, and the dread
40.10 "Deck yourself with *m* and dignity;
Isa 33.21 there the LORD in *m* will be for us a
Lam 1. 6 daughter Zion has departed all her *m*.
Dan 4.30 mighty power and for my glorious *m*?"
4.36 and my *m* and splendor were restored to
Mic 5. 4 LORD, in the *m* of the name of the LORD
Acts 19.27 she will be deprived of her *m* that

MAKER
Gen 14.19 God Most High, *m* of heaven and earth;
Job 35.10 no one says, 'Where is God my *M*, who
Isa 17. 6 let us kneel before the LORD, our *M*!
17. 7 On that day people will regard their *M*,
45. 9 "Woe to you who strive with your *M*,
54. 5 For your *M* is your husband, the LORD of

MALACHI
Mal 1. 1 The word of the LORD to Israel by *M*.

MALE
Gen 1.27 them; *m* and female he created them.
17.10 Every *m* among you shall be
Gal 3.28 there is no longer *m* nor female; for all

MALTA
Acts 28. 1 learned that the island was called *M*.

MAN (MEN)
Gen 2. 7 God formed *m* from the dust of the
2.19 the *m* called every living creature,
3. 8 the *m* and his wife hid themselves from
1 Sam 4. 9 Take courage, and be *m*, O Philistines,
2 Sam 12. 7 Nathan said to David, "You are the *m*!
Rom 5.12 sin came into the world through one *m*,
1 Cor 11. 8 *m* was not made from woman, but

MAN OF GOD
Judg 13. 6 told her husband, "A *m* came to me,
1 Sam 2.27 A *m* came to Eli and said to him, "Thus
9. 6 "There is a *m* in this town; he is a man
1 Kings 13. 1 a *m* came out of Judah by the word of
13.26 "It is the *m* who disobeyed the word of
17.24 now I know that you are a *m*, and that
20.28 A *m* approached and said to the king of
2 Kings 1.10 "If I am a *m*, let fire come down from
7.17 in the gate, just as the *m* had said
2 Chr 25. 7 a *m* came to him and said, "O king, do

MANAGEMENT
Lk 16. 2 Give me an accounting of your *m*,

MANAGER
Mt 20. 8 the owner of the vineyard said to his *m*,
Lk 12.42 is the faithful and prudent *m* whom his
16. 1 a rich man who had a *m*, and charges

MANASSEH
Gen 41.51 Joseph named the firstborn *M*, "For," he
48. 1 with him his two sons, *M* and Ephraim.
Num 1.34 The descendants of *M*, their lineage, in

Deut	3.13 I give to the half-tribe of *M* the rest of
Judg	6.15 my clan is the weakest in *M*, and I am
2 Kings	21. 1 *M* was twelve years old when he began
	21.16 *M* shed very much innocent blood, until
	21.18 *M* slept with his ancestors, and was
	23.12 the altars that *M* had made in the two
2 Chr	33. 1 *M* was twelve years old when he began
	33.13 Then *M* knew that the LORD indeed
	33.23 humble himself before the LORD, as *M*

MANDRAKES

Gen	30.14 Reuben went and found *m* in the field,
Song	7.13 The *m* give forth fragrance, and over our

MANGER

Lk	2. 7 and laid him in a *m*, because there was

MANIFESTED

Ps	90.16 Let your work be *m* to your servants,

MANIFESTATION

1 Cor	12. 7 To each is given the *m* of the Spirit for
1 Tim	6.14 spot or blame until the *m* of our Lord

MANNA

Ex	16.31 Israel called it *m*; it was like coriander
	16.35 Israelites ate *m* forty years, until they
Num	11. 6 there is nothing at all but this *m* to
Josh	5.12 The *m* ceased on the day they ate the
Ps	78.24 he rained down on them *m* to eat, and
Jn	6.31 Our ancestors ate *m* in the wilderness;
Rev	2.17 I will give some of the hidden *m*,

MANTLE

2 Kings	2.13 He picked up the *m* of Elijah that had

MARK

Cousin of Barnabas, Col 4.10; lived in Jerusalem, Acts 12.12; accompanied Barnabas and Paul to Antioch, Acts 12.25; began missionary work, Acts 13.5; deserted the group at Perga, Acts 13.13; subject of contention, Acts 15.37-38; went with Barnabas to Cyprus, Acts 15.39; ministered to Paul in Rome, Col 4.10; Philem 24; companion of Peter, 1 Pet 5.13.

MARK (MARKED MARKS)

Gen	4.15 LORD put a *m* on Cain, so that no one
Ps	37.37 *M* the blameless, and behold the
	50.22 "*M* this, then, you who forget God, or I
	130. 3 If you, O LORD, should *m* iniquities,
Ezek	9. 4 put a *m* upon the foreheads of those
Hab	1.12 O LORD, you have *m* them for judgment;
Gal	6.17 the *m* of Jesus branded on my body.
Rev	13.16 and slave, to be *m* on the right hand or
	14. 9 and receive a *m* on their foreheads or
	19.20 received the *m* of the beast and those

MARKET (MARKETS)

Ezek	27.15 coastlands were your own special *m*,
1 Cor	10.25 Eat whatever is sold in the meat *m*

MARKETPLACE (MARKETPLACES)

Lk	7.32 like children sitting in the *m* and calling
	20.46 love to be greeted in the *m*, and to have
Acts	17.17 and also in the *m* every day with those

MARRIAGE (MARRIAGES)

Gen	34. 9 Make *m* with us; give your daughters to
Deut	24. 1 Suppose a man enters into *m* with a
2 Cor	11. 2 I promised you in *m* to one husband, to
1 Tim	4. 3 They forbid *m* and demand abstinence
Heb	13. 4 Let *m* be held in honor by all, and let

MARRY (MARRIED MARRIES)

Num	12. 1 of the Cushite woman whom he had *m*,
Mal	2.11 *m* the daughter of a foreign god. May
Mt	5.32 and whoever *m* a divorced woman
	19. 9 and *m* another commits adultery."
Mk	10.11 divorces his wife and *m* another

Mk	12.25 they rise from the dead, they neither *m*
Lk	16.18 who divorces his wife and *m* another
	20.35 from the dead neither *m* nor are given
1 Cor	7.10 To the *m* I give this command, — not I
	7.33 the *m* man is anxious about the affairs

MARTHA

Lk	10.38 *M* welcomed him into her house.
Jn	11. 1 the village of Mary and her sister *M*.
	11.24 *M* said to him, "I know that he will rise
	12. 2 they gave a dinner for him. *M* served,

MARVELOUS

Job	5. 9 unsearchable, *m* things without number.
	9.10 and *m* things without number.
Ps	118. 23 This is the LORD's doing; it is *m* in our

MARY (Mother of Jesus)

Betrothed to Joseph, Mt 1.18 (Lk 1.27); Jesus' birth foretold to her, Lk 1.26-38; visited Elizabeth, Lk 1.39-45; The Song of Mary, Lk 1.46-55; went to Bethlehem, Lk 2.4-5; birth of Jesus, Mt 1.25 (Lk 2.7); found Jesus in the temple, Lk 2.41-51; attended the marriage at Cana, Jn 2.1-5; concerned over Jesus' ministry, Mk 3.31-35; at the cross, Jn 19.25-27; in the upper room, Acts 1.14.

MARY (Magdalene)

Healed of demons, Lk 8.2; stood by the cross, Mt 27.56 (Mk 15.40; Jn 19.25); watched Jesus' burial, Mt 27.61 (Mk 15.47); came early to the tomb, Mt 28.1 (Mk 16.1; Lk 24.1-10; Jn 20.1); saw the risen Lord, Mt 28.9 (Mk 16.9n; Jn 20.11-18).

MARY (of Bethany)

Listened to the Lord's teaching, Lk 10.38-42; present at the raising of Lazarus, Jn 11.1-45; anointed Jesus, Jn 12.1-8.

MASTER (MASTERS)

Gen	39. 3 His *m* saw that the LORD was with him,
Ex	21. 5 "I love my *m*, my wife, and my children;
Prov	27.18 who takes care of a *m* will be honored.
Jer	3.14 I am your *m*; I will take you, one from a
Dan	1. 3 commanded his palace *m* Ashpenaz
Mt	6.24 "No one can serve two *m*; for a slave
Eph	6. 9 both of you have the same *M* in heaven,
1 Tim	6. 2 Those who have believing *m* must not
1 Pet	2.18 Slaves, accept the authority of your *m*

MATTHEW

Mt	9. 9 he saw a man called *M* sitting at the
	10. 3 Thomas and *M* the tax collector; James
Mk	3.18 and *M*, and Thomas, and James son of
Lk	6.15 and *M*, and Thomas, and James son of
Acts	1.13 and Thomas, Bartholomew and *M*,

MATURE (MATURITY)

1 Cor	2. 6 Yet among the *m* we do speak wisdom,
Eph	4.13 to *m*, to the measure of the full stature

MEASURE (MEASURED MEASURING)

Ps	39. 4 my end, and what is the *m* of my days;
Isa	40.12 Who has *m* the waters in the hollow of
Jer	31.37 If the heavens above can be *m*, and the
Zech	2. 1 looked up and saw a man with a *m* line
Mk	4.24 the *m* you give will be the *m* you get,
Lk	6.38 for the *m* you give will be the *m* you get
Rev	11. 1 "Come and *m* the temple of God and
	21.15 had a *m* rod of gold to *m* the city and

MEDE (MEDES)

2 Kings	17. 6 of Gozan, and in the cities of the *M*.
Esth	1.19 the laws of the Persians and the *M*
Jer	51.11 up the spirit of the kings of the *M*,
Dan	5.28 and given to the *M* and Persians."
	6. 8 according to the law of the *M* and the
	9. 1 by birth a *M*, who became king over the

MEDIA

Ezra	6. 2 province of *M*, that a scroll was found
Esth	1. 3 The army of Persia and *M* and the
	10. 2 written in the annals of the kings of *M*
Dan	8.20 the two horns, these are the kings of *M*

MEDIATOR

Job	33.23 be for one of them an angel, a *m*,
Gal	3.20 Now a *m* involves more than one party;
1 Tim	2. 5 one *m* between God and humankind,
Heb	9.15 reason he is the *m* of a new covenant,
	12.24 to Jesus, the *m* of a new covenant, and

MEDITATE

Josh	1. 8 you shall *m* on it day and night, so that
Ps	1. 2 and on his law they *m* day and night.
	63. 6 I think of you on my bed, and *m* on you
	77.12 I will *m* on all your work, and muse on
	119. 15 I will *m* on your precepts, and fix my
	119. 78 as for me, I will *m* on your precepts.
	143. 5 deeds, I *m* on the works of your hands.

MEDITATION

Job	15. 4 of God, and hindering *m* before God.
Ps	19.14 and the *m* of my heart be acceptable
	49. 3 speak wisdom; the *m* of my heart shall
	104. 34 May my *m* be pleasing to him, for I
	119. 97 I love your law! It is my *m* all day long.

MEEK

Ps	10.17 you will hear the desire of the *m*; you
	37.11 But the *m* shall inherit the land, and
Isa	29.19 The *m* shall obtain fresh joy in the
Mt	5. 5 "Blessed are the *m*, for they will inherit

MEEKNESS

2 Cor	10. 1 by the *m* and gentleness of Christ—
Jas	1.21 welcome with *m* the implanted word

MEET

Ex	25.22 There I will *m* with you, and from above
Am	4.12 to you, prepare to *m* your God, O Israel!
Mt	8.34 the whole town came out to *m* Jesus;
1 Thess	4.17 with them to *m* the Lord in the air;
Heb	10.25 not neglecting to *m* together, as is the

MEETING

Ps	74. 8 they burned all the *m* places of God in

MEGIDDO

Josh	12.21 of Taanach, one; the king of *M*, one;
	17.11 the inhabitants of *M* and its villages
1 Kings	4.12 in Taanach, *M*, and all Bethshean,
2 Kings	9.27 Then he fled to *M*, and died there.
	23.29 when Pharaoh Neco met him at *M*, he
Zech	12.11 for Hadad-rimmon in the plain of *M*.

MELCHIZEDEK

Gen	14.18 King *M* of Salem brought out bread and
Ps	110. 4 forever according to the order of *M*.
Heb	5. 6 forever, according to the order of *M*."
	6.20 forever according to the order of *M*.
	7. 1 This "King *M* of Salem, priest of the
	7.10 loins of his ancestor when *M* met him.
	7.15 another priest arises, resembling *M*,

MELT (MELTED MELTS)

Ex	15.15 all the inhabitants of Canaan *m* away.
Josh	2.11 As soon as we heard it, our hearts *m*,
	5. 1 they had crossed over, their hearts *m*,
	7. 5 The hearts of the people *m* and turned
Ps	22.14 my heart is like wax; it is *m* within my
	97. 5 The mountains *m* like wax before the
	147. 18 He sends out his word, and *m* them; he
Ezek	22.22 *m* in a smelter, so you shall be *m* in it;

MEMBER (MEMBERS)

Mt	18.15 "If another *m* of the church sins against
	18.21 if another *m* of the church sins against

Rom	6.13 No longer present your *m* to sin as
	12. 4 as in one body we have many *m*, and
1 Cor	6.15 know that your bodies are *m* of Christ?
Eph	5.30 church, because we are *m* of his body.

MEMORIAL

Josh	4. 7 shall be to the Israelites a *m* forever."
Acts	10. 4 prayers and alms have ascended as a *m*

MEMORY

Deut	32.26 out the *m* of them from humankind;
Job	18.17 Their *m* perishes from the earth, and
Ps	109. 15 may his *m* be cut off from the earth.
Prov	10. 7 The *m* of the righteous is a blessing,
Eccl	9. 5 reward, and even the *m* of them is lost.

MENE

Dan	5.25 that was inscribed: *M*, *M*, TEKEL, and

MEPHIBOSHETH

Crippled by a fall, 2 Sam 4.4; dined continually at the royal table, 2 Sam 9; reported to David as a deserter, 2 Sam 16.1-4; cleared himself before David, 2 Sam 19.24-30.

MERCHANT (MERCHANTS)

Nah	3.16 You increased your *m* more than the
Mt	13.45 is like a *m* in search of fine pearls;
Rev	18. 3 the *m* of the earth have grown rich from

MERCIFUL

Gen	19.16 LORD being *m* to him, and they brought
1 Kings	20.31 kings of the house of Israel are *m* kings;
Ps	86.15 you, O Lord, are a God *m* and gracious,
Jon	4. 2 that you are a gracious God and *m*,
Mt	5. 7 "Blessed are the *m*, for they will receive
Lk	6.36 Be *m*, just as your Father is *m*.
Heb	8.12 I will be *m* toward their iniquities, and I

MERCY (MERCIES)

Gen	43.14 may God Almighty grant you *m* before
Ex	33.19 will show *m* on whom I will show *m*.
Deut	7. 2 with them and show them no *m*.
1 Chr	21.13 of the LORD, for his *m* is very great;
Neh	1.11 today, and grant him *m* in the sight of
Ps	51. 1 Have *m* on me, O God, according to
	103. 4 crowns you with steadfast love and *m*,
Jer	31.20 for him; I will surely have *m* on him,
	42.12 I will grant you *m*, and he will have *m*
Lam	3.22 ceases, his *m* never come to an end;
Dan	2.18 told them to seek *m* from the God of
Hab	3. 2 known; in wrath may you remember *m*.
Mt	9.13 means, 'I desire *m* and not sacrifice.'
	12. 7 means, 'I desire *m* and not sacrifice,'
	15.22 "Have *m* on me, Lord, Son of David; my
	20.30 they shouted, "Lord, have *m* on us, Son
	23.23 of the law, justice and *m* and faith.
Mk	5.19 for you, and what *m* he has shown you."
Lk	1.50 His *m* is on those who fear him from
	1.72 he has shown *m* promised to our
	10.37 He said, "The one who showed him *m*."
	16.24 'Father Abraham, have *m* on me, and
	18.38 "Jesus, Son of David, have *m* on me!
Rom	9.15 "I will have *m* on whom I have *m*, and I
	9.18 he has *m* upon whomever he chooses,
	9.23 riches of his glory for the objects of *m*,
	11.30 but have now received *m* because of
2 Cor	4. 1 by God's *m* that we are engaged in this
Phil	2.27 But God had *m* on him, and not only on

MERCY SEAT

Ex	25.22 meet with you, and from above the *m*,
Lev	16. 2 inside the curtain before the *m* that is

MEROM

Josh	11. 5 at the waters of *M*, to fight with Israel.
	11. 7 by the waters of *M*, and fell upon them.

MESSAGE

Judg	3.20	and said, "I have a *m* from God for you."
Hag	1.13	spoke to the people with the LORD's *m*,
Mk	16.20n	confirmed the *m* by the signs that
Acts	5.20	and tell the people the whole *m* about
	15. 7	Gentiles would hear the *m* of the good
	17.11	they welcomed the *m* very eagerly and
	20.32	you to God and to the *m* of his grace,
2 Tim	4. 2	I solemnly urge you: proclaim the *m*; be
2 Pet	1.19	we have the prophetic *m* more fully
1 Jn	1. 5	This is the *m* we have heard from him

MESSENGER (MESSENGERS)

Gen	32. 3	Jacob sent *m* before him to his brother
2 Chr	36.15	sent persistently to them by his *m*,
Prov	25.13	harvest are faithful *m* to those who send
Jer	49.14	a *m* has been sent among the nations:
Ezek	30. 9	On that day, *m* shall go out from me in
Mal	2. 7	his mouth, for he is the *m* of the LORD
	3. 1	I am sending my *m* to prepare the way
Mt	11.10	I am sending my *m* ahead of you, who
Mk	1. 2	I am sending my *m* ahead of you, who
Lk	7.27	"See, I am sending my *m* ahead of you,
	9.52	And he sent *m* ahead of him. On their
2 Cor	12. 7	was given me in the flesh, a *m* of Satan

MESSIAH

Mt	1.16	Jesus was born, who is called the *M*.
	16.16	Peter answered, "You are the *M*, the
Jn	1.41	and said to him, "We have found the *M*"
	4.25	said to him, "I know that *M* is coming"

METHUSELAH

Gen	5.27	Thus all the days of *M* were nine

MICAH

Jer	26.18	"*M* of Moresheth, who prophesied
Mic	1. 1	word of the LORD that came to *M* of

MICHAL

Married to David, 1 Sam 18.20-30; helped David escape, 1 Sam 19.12-17; restored to David, 2 Sam 3.13-16; rebuked for despising David, 2 Sam 6.12-23.

1 Sam	14.49	and the name of the younger, *M*.
2 Sam	3.13	unless you bring Saul's daughter *M*
1 Chr	15.29	*M* daughter of Saul looked out of the

MICHMASH

1 Sam	13. 2	two thousand were with Saul in *M* and
	14. 5	crag rose on the north in front of *M*,
Isa	10.28	Migron, at *M* he stores his baggage;

MIDIAN

Gen	25. 2	She bore him . . . *M*, Ishbak, and Shuah.
Ex	2.15	Moses . . . settled in the land of *M*, and
	4.19	The LORD said to Moses in *M*, "Go back
	18. 1	Jethro, the priest of *M* . . . heard of all
Num	22. 4	Moab said to the elders of *M*, "This
Judg	6. 1	them into the hand of *M* seven years.
	7. 8	The camp of *M* was below him in the
1 Kings	11.18	They set out from *M* and came to
Ps	83. 9	Do to them as you did to *M*, as to
Isa	9. 4	you have broken as on the day of *M*.
	10.26	against them, as when he struck *M* at

MIDIANITE

Gen	37.28	When some *M* traders passed by, they

MIDNIGHT

Judg	16. 3	But Samson lay only until *m*. Then at *m*
Ps	119. 62	At *m* I rise to praise you, because of
Acts	16.25	About *m* Paul and Silas were praying
	20. 7	day, he continued speaking until *m*.

MIDWIVES

Ex	1.15	king of Egypt said to the Hebrew *m*,

MIGHT

Judg	6.14	"Go in this *m* of yours and deliver Israel
1 Sam	2. 9	darkness; for not by *m* does one prevail.
Job	39.19	"Do you give the horse its *m*? Do you
Ps	59.16	But I will sing of your *m*; I will sing
	118. 14	The LORD is my strength and my *m*; he
Isa	12. 2	the LORD GOD is my strength and my *m*;
Eccl	9.10	your hand finds to do, do with your *m*;
Hab	1.11	become guilty; their own *m* is their god!
Zech	4. 6	Not by *m*, nor by power, but by my

MIGHTY (MIGHTIER)

2 Sam	1.25	How the *m* have fallen in the midst of
Job	21. 7	reach old age, and grow *m* in power?
	36. 5	"Surely God is *m* and does not despise
Ps	71.16	I will come praising the *m* deeds of the
Prov	24. 5	Wise warriors are *m* than strong ones,
Isa	1.24	LORD of hosts, the *M* One of Israel: Ah,
	9. 6	Wonderful Counselor, *M* God,
	63. 1	is I, announcing vindication, *m* to save."

MILE

Mt	5.41	you to go one *m*, go also the second *m*.

MILITARY

1 Cor	9. 7	pays the expenses for doing *m* service?

MILK

Gen	18. 8	Then he took curds and *m* and the calf
Ex	3. 8	land, a land flowing with *m* and honey,
Judg	4.19	she opened a skin of *m* and gave him a
Job	10.10	Did you not pour me out like *m* and
1 Cor	3. 2	I fed you with *m*, not solid food, for you
	9. 7	a flock and does not get any of its *m*?
Heb	5.12	You need *m*, not solid food; for

MILLSTONE

Judg	9.53	But a certain woman threw an upper *m*
Mt	18. 6	great *m* were fastened around your neck
Mk	9.42	better for you if a great *m* were hung
Lk	17. 2	better for you if a *m* were hung around

MIND (MINDS)

Gen	37.11	but his father kept the matter in *m*.
Deut	29. 4	has not given you a *m* to understand,
2 Sam	7. 3	do all that you have in *m*; for the LORD
1 Kings	3. 9	there an understanding *m* to govern
2 Kings	6.11	*m* of the king of Aram was greatly
1 Chr	17. 2	"Do all that you have in *m*, for God is
2 Chr	6. 7	David had it in *m* to build a house for
Neh	4. 6	height; for the people had a *m* to work.
Ps	77.11	I will call to *m* the deeds of the LORD; I
Prov	14.30	A tranquil *m* gives life to the flesh, but
	16. 9	The human *m* plans his way, but the
	17.20	The crooked of *m* do not prosper, and
Isa	6.10	Make the *m* of this people dull, and
	26. 3	Those of steadfast *m* you keep in peace
	44.20	deluded *m* has led him astray, and he
Jer	23.16	They speak visions of their own *m*, not
Dan	4.16	his *m* be changed from that of a human,
Mk	5.15	sitting there, clothed and in his right *m*,
Rom	8. 7	the *m* that is set on the flesh is hostile
	11.34	"For who has known the *m* of the Lord?
1 Cor	2.16	him?" But we have the *m* of Christ.
	14.15	spirit, but I will pray with the *m* also.
	14.19	rather speak five words with my *m*,
2 Cor	3.15	Moses is read, a veil lies over their *m*;
	9. 7	must give as you have made up your *m*,
Phil	2. 5	Let the same *m* be in you that was in
	4. 2	I urge Syntyche to be of the same *m*
Col	3. 2	Set your *m* on things that are above, not

MINDFUL

Ps	25. 6	Be *m* of your mercy, O LORD, and of
	115. 12	The LORD has been *m* of us; he will
Zeph	2. 7	their God will be *m* of them and restore

MINISTER (MINISTERED MINISTERING MINISTERS)

Deut 18. 7 he may *m* in the name of the LORD his
1 Sam 2.11 while the boy remained to *m* to the
3. 1 Samuel was *m* to the LORD under Eli.
1 Chr 6.32 They *m* with song before the tabernacle
Ps 104. 4 your messengers, fire and flame your *m*.
Isa 56. 6 themselves to the LORD, to *m* to him,
60.10 walls, and their kings shall *m* to you;
Ezek 44.11 They shall be *m* in my sanctuary, having
Rom 15.16 me by God to be a *m* of Christ Jesus
2 Cor 11.23 Are they *m* of Christ? I am talking like a
Col 4. 7 he is a beloved brother, a faithful *m*,

MINISTRY

Rom 11.13 apostle to the Gentiles, I glorify my *m*.
12. 7 in proportion to faith; *m*, in ministering;
15.25 going to Jerusalem in a *m* to the saints;
Eph 4.12 equip the saints for the work of *m*, for

MIRACLES

1 Chr 16.12 wonderful works he has done, his *m*,
1 Cor 12.10 to another the working of *m*, to another
Gal 3. 5 with the Spirit and work *m* among you

MIRIAM

Song of Miriam, Ex 15.20-21; became leprous for criticizing Moses, Num 12.1-10; her leprosy healed, Num 12.11-16; died in Kadesh, Num 20.1.

MIRROR (MIRRORS)

Ex 38. 8 from the *m* of the women who served at
Job 37.18 out the skies, hard as a molten *m*?
1 Cor 13.12 now we see in a *m*, dimly, but then we
Jas 1.23 those who look at themselves in a *m*.

MISCHIEF

Judg 15. 3 when I do *m* to the Philistines, I will be
Ps 7.14 evil, and are pregnant with *m*, and bring
36. 4 They plot *m* while on their beds; they
1 Pet 4.15 thief, a criminal, or even as a *m* maker.

MISERABLE

Job 16. 2 such things; *m* comforters are you all.

MISERY

Ex 3. 7 "I have observed the *m* of my people
Num 11.15 sight—and do not let me see my *m*."

MISFORTUNE

Prov 13.21 *M* pursues sinners, but prosperity

MISLEAD

2 Kings 4.28 for a son? Did I not say, Do not *m* me?"

MISS (MISSED)

Judg 20.16 could sling a stone at a hair and not *m*.
1 Sam 20.18 you will be *m*, because your place will
Job 5.24 shall inspect your fold and *m* nothing.
Prov 8.36 but those who *m* me injure themselves;

MIST

Jas 4.14 you are a *m* that appears for a little

MISTAKE

Jer 42.20 you today that you have made a fatal *m*.

MIZPAH

Gen 31.49 and the pillar *M*, for he said, "The LORD
Judg 11.11 all his words before the LORD at *M*.
1 Sam 7. 5 "Gather all Israel at *M*, and I will pray
10.17 summoned the people to the LORD at *M*
Jer 41.10 the rest of the people who were in *M*,

MOCK (MOCKED MOCKING MOCKS)

Gen 27.12 I shall seem to be *m* him, and bring a
Judg 16.10 you have *m* me, and told me lies; please
1 Kings 18.27 At noon Elijah *m* them, saying, "Cry
2 Kings 19. 4 of Assyria has sent to *m* the living God,

2 Kings 19.22 "Whom have you *m* and reviled? Against
2 Chr 36.16 kept *m* the messengers of God, despising
Job 21. 3 speak; then after I have spoken, *m* on.
Ps 22. 7 All who see me at me, they make
Prov 17. 5 who *m* the poor insult their Maker,
Isa 37. 4 of Assyria has sent to *m* the living God,
Jer 20. 7 all day long; everyone *m* me.
Ezek 22. 5 those who are far from you will *m* you,
Mt 27.29 before him and *m* him, saying, "Hail,
Mk 10.34 they will *m* him, and spit upon him,
15.31 along with the scribes, were also *m* him
Lk 18.32 Gentiles; and he will be *m* and insulted
23.36 The soldiers also *m* him, coming up and

MOCKERY

Ezek 5.15 You shall be a *m* and a taunt, a warning
Joel 2.19 more make you a *m* among the nations.

MOLECH

Lev 18.21 of your offspring to sacrifice them to *M*,
2 Kings 23.10 pass through fire as an offering to *M*.

MONEY

Num 3.49 Moses took the redemption *m* from
Deut 14.25 you may turn it into *m*. With the *m*
2 Kings 12.11 would give the *m* that was weighed
Eccl 5.10 The lover of *m* will not be satisfied with
7.12 of wisdom is like the protection of *m*;
10.19 gladdens life, and *m* meets every need.
Mt 27. 6 the treasury, since they are blood *m*."
28.12 a plan to give a large sum of *m* to the
Lk 16.14 Pharisees, who were also lovers of *m*,
Acts 4.37 then brought the *m*, and laid it at the
8.18 he offered them *m*, saying, "Give me
1 Tim 6.10 love of *m* is a root of all kinds of evils,
Heb 13. 5 Keep your lives free from love of *m*, and

MONEY CHANGERS

Mt 21.12 overturned the tables of the *m* and the
Mk 11.15 overturned the tables of the *m* and the
Jn 2.14 doves, and the *m* seated at their tables.

MOON

Song 6.10 fair as the *m*, bright as the sun, terrible
Isa 13.10 rising, and the *m* will not shed its light.
30.26 light of the *m* will be like the light of
Jer 31.35 and the fixed order of the *m* and the
Ezek 32. 7 cloud, and the *m* shall not give its light.
Mt 24.29 and the *m* will not give its light,
Acts 2.20 turned to darkness and the *m* to blood,
1 Cor 15.41 another glory of the *m*, and another

MORALS

1 Cor 15.33 deceived: "Bad company ruins good *m*."

MORDECAI

Counseled Esther, Esth 2.5-20; informed Esther of a conspiracy, Esth 2.21-23; refused to reverence Haman, Esth 3.2-6; arrayed in royal apparel, Esth 6.1-11; promoted next to the king, Esth 8.1-2; 10.3; reversed Haman's decree, Esth 8.3—9.4; decreed feast of Purim, Esth 9.20-31.

MORIAH

Gen 22. 2 go to land of *M*, and offer him there as
2 Chr 3. 1 of the LORD in Jerusalem on Mount *M*,

MORNING

Ps 5. 3 O LORD, in the *m* you hear my voice; in
30. 5 for the night, but joy comes with the *m*.
Isa 21.12 The sentinel says: "*M* comes, and also
Mk 1.35 In the *m*, while it was still very dark, he
Rev 2.28 who conquers I will also give the *m* star.
22.16 descendant of David, the bright *m* star."

MORSEL

Prov 17. 1 Better is a dry *m* with quiet than a

MORTAL (MORTALS)

Job	4.17 'Can *m* be righteous before God? Can
	14.10 But *m* die, and are laid low; humans
	15.14 What are *m*, that they can be clean? Or
Ps	8. 4 of them, *m* that you care for him?
Ezek	2. 1 O *m*, stand up on your feet, and I will
	3.17 *M*, I have made you a sentinel for the
	20. 3 *M* speak to the elders of Israel, and say
	30.21 *M* I have broken the arm of Pharaoh
Job	9.32 he is not a *m*, as I am, that I might
	14. 1 "A *m*, born of a woman, few of days and
Am	4.13 reveals his thoughts to *m*, makes the
Acts	14.15 We are *m* just like you, and we bring
Rom	6.12 sin exercise dominion in your *m* bodies,
1 Cor	15.53 this *m* body must put on immortality.
1 Jn	5.16 There is sin that is *m*; I do not say that

MOSES (MOSES')

Born, Ex 2.1-2; adopted by Pharaoh's daughter, Ex 2.5-10; trained at the Egyptian court, Acts 7.22; killed an Egyptian, Ex 2.11-12; Fled to Midian, Ex 2.15-20; married Zipporah, Ex 2.21-22; called by God, Ex 3.1—4.17; returned to Egypt, Ex 4.18-31; interceded with Pharaoh, Ex 5—11; led the Israelites across the Red Sea, Ex 14; sang for triumph, Ex 15.1-18; appointed rulers, Ex 18.13-26; met God on Mount Sinai, Ex 19.3-13; 24—31; enraged by Israel's idolatry, Ex 32; talked with the LORD, Ex 33—34; built the tabernacle, Ex 35—40; numbered the people, Num 1; vindicated before Aaron and Miriam, Num 12; sent twelve spies to Canaan, Num 13.1-20; consecrated Joshua as his successor, Num 27.18-23; Deut 31.23; recounted Israel's history, Deut 1—3; exhorted Israel to obedience, Deut 4.1-40; song of Moses, Deut 32.1-43; viewed Canaan, Deut 3.23-27; 32.48-52; 34.1-4; blessed the tribes, Deut 33; death and burial in Moab, Deut 34.5-7. (See also Acts 7.20-44.)

Josh	1. 5 As I was with *M*, so I will be with you; I
Ps	77.20 a flock by the hand of *M* and Aaron.
	103. 7 He made his ways known to *M*, his acts
	106. 23 he would destroy them—had not *M*,
Isa	63.12 arm to march at the right hand of *M*,
Jer	15. 1 Though *M* and Samuel stood before me,
Mt	17. 3 there appeared to them *M* and Elijah,
	19. 8 *M* allowed you to divorce your wives,
Mk	7.10 For *M* said, 'Honor your father and
Lk	16.29 Abraham replied, 'They have *M* and the
	24.27 beginning with *M* and all the prophets,
Jn	1.17 The law indeed was given through *M*;
	3.14 just as *M* lifted up the serpent in the
	5.46 If you believed *M*, you would believe
Acts	3.22 *M* said, 'The Lord your God will raise
Rom	5.14 exercised dominion from Adam to *M*,
1 Cor	10. 2 all were baptized into *M* in the cloud
2 Cor	3. 7 Israel could not gaze at *M* face because
	3.15 whenever *M* is read, a veil lies over
2 Tim	3. 8 As Jannes and Jambres opposed *M*, so
Heb	3. 2 just as *M* also "was faithful in all God's
	11.23 By faith *M* was hidden by his parents
Jude	9 devil and disputed about the body of *M*,
Rev	15. 3 they sing the song of *M*, the servant of

MOTH

Ps	39.11 for sin, consuming like a *m* what is dear
Mt	6.19 on earth, where *m* and rust consume

MOTHER (MOTHERS MOTHER'S)

Gen	3.20 because she was the *m* of all living,
Ex	2. 8 The girl went and called the child's *m*.
Judg	5. 7 arose, Deborah, arose as a *m* in Israel.
1 Sam	2.19 His *m* used to make for him a little
1 Kings	3.27 living boy; do not kill him. She is his *m*."
2 Chr	15.16 Asa even removed his *m* Maacah from
Ps	113. 9 a home, making her the joyous *m*
Prov	4. 3 my father, tender, and my *m* favorite,
Isa	66.13 As a *m* comforts her child, so I will
Mt	12.48 Jesus replied, "Who is my *m*, and who
	12.50 heaven is my brother and sister and *m*."

Mt	19. 5 man shall leave his father and *m* and be
Mk	3.33 replied, "Who are my *m* and brothers?"
	7.10 said, 'Honor your father and your *m*';
Jn	19.27 he said to the disciple, "Here is your *m*."
Gal	4.26 above; she is free, and she is our *m*.
1 Tim	5. 2 to older women as *m*, to younger
2 Tim	1. 5 Lois and your *m* Eunice and now, I am

MOTHER-IN-LAW

Ruth	3. 1 Naomi her *m* said to her, "My daughter,
Mk	1.30 Simon's *m* was in bed with a fever, and

MOUNT OF OLIVES

Zech	14. 4 that day his feet shall stand on the *M*,
Mt	21. 1 Bethphage, at the *M*, Jesus sent
	24. 3 When he was sitting on the *M*, the
	26.30 sung the hymn, they went out to the *M*.
Lk	21.37 and spend the night on the *M*, as it was
Jn	8. 1 went home, while Jesus went to the *M*.

MOUNTAIN (MOUNTAINS)

Deut	1. 6 "You have stayed long enough at this *m*.
Ps	36. 6 Your righteousness is like the mighty *m*
	46. 2 should change, though the *m* shake
	68.15 O mighty *m*, *m* of Bashan; O
Isa	2. 2 days to come the *m* of the LORD's house
	11. 9 not hurt or destroy in all my holy *m*;
	25. 6 On this *m* the LORD of hosts will make
	30.29 of the flute to go to the *m* of the LORD,
	45. 2 I will go before you and level the *m*, I
Ezek	6. 3 You *m* of Israel, hear the word of the
	20.40 on my holy *m*, the *m* height of Israel,
Dan	2.35 that struck the statue became a great *m*
Ob	16 For as you have drunk on my holy *m*,
Mic	1. 4 Then the *m* will melt under him and
	4. 1 be established as the highest of the *m*,
	6. 2 Hear, you *m*, the controversy of the
Nah	1.15 On the *m* the feet of one who brings
Zech	8. 3 Lord of hosts shall be called the holy *m*.
Mt	4. 8 devil took him to a very high *m* and
	5. 1 he went up on the *m*; and after he sat
	17. 1 brother John and led them up a high *m*,
Mk	6.46 to them, he went up on the *m* to pray.
	11.23 if you say to this *m*, 'Be taken up and
	13.14 then those in Judea must flee to the *m*;
Lk	9.28 James and went up on the *m* to pray.
Jn	6.15 him king, he withdrew again to the *m*
1 Cor	13. 2 if I have all faith, so as to remove *m*,

MOURN (MOURNED MOURNING)

Gen	37.34 his loins, and *m* for his son many days.
2 Sam	1.12 They *m* and wept, and fasted until
	13.37 David *m* for his son day after day.
Dan	10. 2 time I, Daniel, had been *m* for three
Am	5.16 They shall call the farmers to *m*, and
	8.10 I will turn your feasts into *m*, and all
Mt	5. 4 "Blessed are those who *m*, for they will
1 Cor	7.30 those who *m* as though they were not
Rev	21. 4 Death will be no more; *m* and crying

MOURNFULLY

Ps	43. 2 Why must I walk about *m* because of

MOUTH (MOUTHS)

Deut	8. 3 that comes from the *m* of the LORD.
2 Kings	4.34 the child, putting his *m* upon his *m*,
Job	40. 4 I answer you? I lay my hand on my *m*.
Ps	34. 1 his praise shall continually be in my *m*.
	71. 8 My *m* is filled with your praise, and
	109. 2 and deceitful *m* are opened against me,
	135. 16 They have *m*, but they do not speak;
	141. 3 Set a guard over my *m*, O LORD, keep
Prov	30.32 devising evil, put your hand on your *m*.
Isa	6. 7 the seraph touched my *m* with it and
Mal	2. 6 True instruction was in his *m*, and no
Rom	3.14 "Their *m* are full of cursing and
	3.19 that every *m* may be silenced, and the

MOVE (MOVED MOVING)

Deut	19.14 You must not *m* your neighbor's
2 Sam	7. 6 I have been *m* about in a tent and a
1 Chr	17. 6 I have *m* about among all Israel,
Ps	16. 8 he is at my right hand, I shall not be *m*.
	21. 7 of the Most High he shall not be *m*.
	46. 5 the midst of the city; it shall not be *m*;
	121. 3 He will not let your foot be *m*, he who
Acts	17.28 For 'In him we live and *m* and have our
2 Pet	1.21 men and women *m* by the Holy Spirit

MUD

Jn	9. 6 made *m* with the saliva and spread the

MULTIPLY (MULTIPLIED)

Gen	1.22 the seas, and let birds *m* on the earth."
	9. 1 "Be fruitful and *m*, and fill the earth.
	35.11 be fruitful and *m*; a nation and a
Deut	7.13 he will love you, bless you, and *m* you;
Isa	9. 3 You have *m* the nation, you have

MULTITUDE (MULTITUDES)

Gen	2. 1 the earth were finished, and all their *m*.
Ps	42. 4 of thanksgiving, a *m* keeping festival.
Joel	3.14 *M*, *m*, in the valley of decision! For the
1 Pet	4. 8 one another, for love covers a *m* of sins.
Rev	7. 9 was a great *m* that no one could count,

MURDER (MURDERS)

Ex	20.13 You shall not *m*.
Deut	5.17 You shall not *m*.
Mt	5.21 and 'whoever *m* shall be liable to
	15.19 of the heart come evil intentions, *m*,
	19.18 Jesus said, "You shall not *m*; You shall
Mk	15. 7 with the rebels who had committed *m*
Lk	23.19 who had been put in prison . . . for *m*.)

MURDERER

Jn	8.44 He was a *m* from the beginning and
Acts	3.14 and asked to have a *m* given to you,

MURMURED (MURMURING)

Josh	9.18 the congregation *m* against the leaders.
Phil	2.14 Do all things without *m* or arguing, so

MUSTARD

Mt	13.31 is like a *m* seed that someone took and
	17.20 if you have faith the size of a *m* seed,
Mk	4.31 It is like a *m* seed, which, when sown
Lk	13.19 It is like a *m* seed that someone took
	17. 6 "If you had faith the size of a *m* seed,

MUTE

Ps	38.13 not hear; like the *m*, who cannot speak.
Mt	9.32 a demoniac who was *m* was brought to
	12.22 who had been *m* could speak and see.
	15.30 lame, the maimed, the blind, the *m*,
Mk	7.37 the deaf to hear and the *m* to speak."
Lk	1.20 you will be *m*, unable to speak, until
	11.14 the one who had been *m* spoke, and the

MUZZLE

Ps	39. 1 I will keep a *m* on my mouth, as long as

MYRRH

Ps	45. 8 your robes are all fragrant with *m* and
Mt	2.11 him gifts of gold, frankincense, and *m*.
Mk	15.23 they offered him wine mixed with *m*;

MYRTLE

Isa	55.13 of the brier shall come up the *m*;
Zech	1. 8 He was standing among the *m* trees in

MYSTERY (MYSTERIES)

Dan	2.18 the God of heaven concerning this *m*,
Rom	11.25 I want you to understand this *m*: a
	16.25 according to the revelation of the *m*
1 Cor	4. 1 of Christ and stewards of God's *m*.
	13. 2 prophetic powers, and understand all *m*

1 Cor	15.51 Listen, I will tell you a *m*! We will not
Eph	1. 9 has made known to us the *m* of his will,
	3. 4 my understanding the *m* of Christ.
	5.32 This is a great *m*, and I am applying it
	6.19 with boldness the *m* of the gospel,
Col	1.26 the *m* that has been hidden throughout
	2. 2 and have the knowledge of God's *m*,
2 Thess	2. 7 the *m* of lawlessness is already at work,
1 Tim	3. 9 must hold fast to the *m* of the faith
	3.16 doubt, the *m* of our religion is great:
Rev	10. 7 the *m* of God will be fulfilled, as he
	17. 5 was written a name, a *m*: "Babylon the

MYTHS

1 Tim	1. 4 not to occupy themselves with *m* and
Titus	1.14 not paying attention to Jewish *m* or to
2 Pet	1.16 we did not follow cleverly devised *m*

N

NAAMAN

2 Kings	5. 1 *N*, commander of the army of the king
Lk	4.27 them was cleansed except *N* the Syrian."

NAHUM

Nah	1. 1 Nineveh. The book of the vision of *N* of

NAILING

Col	2.14 He set this aside, *n* it to the cross. He

NAILS

Eccl	12.11 like *n* firmly fixed are the collected
Jn	20.25 "Unless I see the mark of the *n* in his

NAKED

Job	1.21 "*N* I came from my mother's womb, and
	24.10 They go about *n*, without clothing;
Eccl	5.15 so they shall go again, *n* as they came;
Isa	20. 3 Isaiah has walked *n* and barefoot
	58. 7 when you see the *n*, to cover them, and
Ezek	16.39 objects and leave you *n* and bare.
Mk	14.52 but he left the linen cloth and ran off *n*.

NAKEDNESS

Lev	18. 7 shall not uncover the *n* of your father,
Isa	47. 3 Your *n* shall be uncovered, and your

NAME

Gen	12. 8 the LORD and invoked the *n* of the LORD.
	32.29 "Please tell me your *n*." But he said,
Ex	3.13 ask me, 'What is his *n*?' what shall I
	6. 3 by my *n* 'the LORD' I did not make
	9.16 and to make my *n* resound through all
	15. 3 The LORD is a warrior; the LORD is his *n*.
	20. 7 make wrongful use of the *n* of the LORD
	34. 5 there, and proclaimed the *n*, "The LORD."
Lev	24.11 son blasphemed the *N* in a curse.
Deut	5.11 shall not make wrongful use of the *n* of
	28.10 that you are called by the *n* of the LORD,
	28.58 fearing this glorious and awesome *n*,
	32. 3 I will proclaim the *n* of the LORD;
Josh	7. 9 Then what will you do for your great *n*?"
Judg	13.17 "What is your *n*, so that we may honor
2 Sam	12.28 take the city, and it be called by my *n*."
1 Kings	9. 3 have built, and put my *n* there forever;
1 Chr	16. 2 he blessed the people in the *n* of the
	17. 8 I will make for you a *n*, like the *n* of the
	29.13 to you and praise your glorious *n*.
Ps	8. 9 our Sovereign, how majestic is your *n* in
	9.10 those who know your *n* put their trust
	72.17 May his *n* endure forever, his fame
	102. 12 your *n* endures to all generations.
	118. 26 one who comes in the *n* of the LORD.
	138. 2 you have exalted your *n* and your word
Prov	18.10 The *n* of the LORD is a strong tower; the
	22. 1 to be chosen rather than
Eccl	7. 1 A good *n* is better than precious
Isa	30.27 *n* of the LORD comes from far away,

Isa	40.26	numbers them, calling them all by *n*;
	44. 5	"The LORD's," and adopt the *n* of Israel.
	52. 5	all day long my *n* is despised.
	56. 5	I will give them an everlasting *n* better
	62. 2	you shall be called by a new *n* that the
Jer	7.11	this house, which is called by my *n*,
	10. 6	are great, and your *n* is great in might.
	14.14	prophets are prophesying lies in my *n*;
Ezek	36.21	But I had concern for my holy *n*, which
	39.25	and I will be jealous for my holy *n*.
Hos	12. 5	the God of hosts, the LORD is his *n*!
Joel	2.32	Then everyone who calls upon the *n* of
Am	6.10	We must not mention the *n* of the LORD."
	9.12	all the nations who are called by my *n*,
Mt	7.22	Lord, did we not prophesy in your *n*,
	28.19	baptizing them in the *n* of the Father
Mk	9.38	someone casting out demons in your *n*,
	13. 6	Many will come in my *n* and say, 'I am
Lk	1.31	bear a son, and you will *n* him Jesus.
	9.49	saw some casting out demons in your *n*,
	11. 2	pray, say: "Father, hallowed be your *n*.
Jn	5.43	I have come in my father's *n*, and you
	12.28	Father, glorify your *n*." Then a voice
	16.23	you ask anything of the Father in my *n*,
Acts	3.16	by faith in his *n*, his *n* itself has made
	4.10	in good health by the *n* of Jesus Christ
	4.12	there is no other *n* under heaven given
	4.30	performed through the *n* of your holy
	8.12	and the *n* of Jesus Christ, they were
	9.15	chosen to bring my *n* before Gentiles
	19.17	and the *n* of the Lord Jesus was
	21.13	die in Jerusalem for the *n* of the Lord
Rom	2.24	"The *n* of God is blasphemed among the
	9.17	you, so that my *n* may be proclaimed in
Phil	2. 9	gave him the *n* that is above every *n*,
Col	3.17	do everything in the *n* of the Lord
2 Tim	2.19	everyone who calls on the *n* of the Lord
Heb	1. 4	the *n* he has inherited is more excellent
Jas	2. 7	blaspheme the excellent *n* that was
1 Pet	4.14	If you are reviled for the *n* of Christ,
Rev	2.17	on the white stone is written a new *n*
	15. 4	who will not fear and glorify your *n*?

NAMED (NAMES)

Gen	2.20	The man gave *n* to all cattle, and to the
Ex	28. 9	engrave on them the *n* of the sons of
Mt	1.25	had borne a son; and he *n* him Jesus.
	10. 2	the *n* of the twelve apostles: first,
Lk	10.20	you, but rejoice that your *n* are written
Phil	4. 3	whose *n* are in the book of life.

NAPHTALI

Gen	30. 8	have prevailed"; so she named him *N*.
	49.21	*N* is a doe let loose that bears lovely
Deut	33.23	of *N* he said: O *N*, sated with favor, full
Judg	1.33	*N* did not drive out the inhabitants of
Ps	68.27	princes of Zebulun, the princes of *N*.
Isa	9. 1	the land of Zebulun and the land of *N*,
Mt	4.13	land of *N*, on the road by the sea,

NAPHTALITES

Num	26.50	These are the *N* by their clans: the

NARROW

Mt	7.13	"Enter through the *n* gate; for the gate
Lk	13.24	"Strive to enter through the *n* door; for

NATHAN

Counseled David about the people, 2 Sam 7.2-17 (1 Chr 17.1-15); rebuked David, 2 Sam 12.1-23; anointed Solomon as king, 1 Kings 1.8-45.

NATHANAEL

Jn	1.45	Philip found *N*, and said to him, "We

NATION

Gen	12. 2	I will make of you a great *n*, and I will
	18.18	shall become a great and mighty *n*,

Gen	46. 3	Egypt, for I will make of you a great *n*
Deut	4. 7	what other great *n* has a god so near to
	4.34	to take a *n* for himself from the midst
	26. 5	and there he became a *n*, mighty and
	28.49	LORD will bring a *n* from far away, from
2 Sam	7.23	Is there another *n* on earth whose God
Ps	106. 5	I may rejoice in the gladness of your *n*,
Prov	14.34	Righteousness exalts a *n*, but sin is a
Isa	2. 4	*n* shall not lift up sword against *n*,
	9. 3	You have multiplied the *n*, you have
Jer	7.28	This is the *n* that did not obey the voice
	31.36	Israel would cease to be a *n* before me
Ezek	37.22	I will make them one *n* in the land, on
Mt	21.43	given to a *n* that produces the fruits of
Acts	10.35	in every *n* anyone who fears him and

NATIONS

Gen	10. 5	language, by their families, in their *n*.
	17. 5	you the ancestor of a multitude of *n*.
	22.18	all the *n* of the earth gain blessing for
	26. 4	all the *n* of the earth shall gain blessing
Lev	25.44	from the *n* around you that you may
1 Sam	8. 5	then, a king to govern us, like other *n*."
1 Chr	16.24	Declare his glory among the *n*, his
	16.35	gather and rescue us from among the *n*,
Ps	18.43	You made me the head of the *n*;
	33.10	brings the counsel of the *n* to nothing;
	67. 4	Let the *n* be glad and sing for joy, for
	79. 6	Pour out your anger on the *n* that do
	96. 3	Declare his glory among the *n*, his
	110. 6	He will execute judgment among the *n*,
	126. 2	then it was said among the *n*, "The LORD
Isa	2. 2	the hills; all the *n* shall stream to it.
	40.15	the *n* are like a drop from a bucket, and
	49. 6	I will give you as a light to the *n*, that
	60. 3	*N* shall come to your light, and kings to
	66.18	I am coming to gather all *n* and
	66.19	shall declare my glory among the *n*.
Jer	4. 2	then *n* shall be blessed by him, and by
	27. 7	All the *n* shall serve him and his son
Ezek	7.24	the worst of the *n* to take possession
	11.16	removed them far away among the *n*,
	36.23	the *n* shall know that I am the LORD,
	39.21	I will display my glory among the *n*; and
Joel	2.17	a mockery, a byword among the *n*.
	3. 2	I will gather all the *n* and bring them
	3.12	Let the *n* rouse themselves, and come
Mic	5.15	vengeance on the *n* that did not obey.
Hab	1. 5	Look at the *n*, and see! Be astonished!
Zech	14. 2	I will gather all the *n* against Jerusalem
Mal	1.11	setting my name is great among the *n*,
	3.12	all *n* will count you happy, for you will
Mt	24. 9	be hated by all *n* because of my name.
Mk	11.17	called a house of prayer for all the *n*'?
Lk	24.47	is to be proclaimed in his name to all *n*,
Rev	11.18	The *n* raged, but your wrath has come,
	18.23	and all *n* were deceived by your sorcery.
	21.24	The *n* will walk by its light, and the

NATURE

Rom	11.24	from what is by *n* a wild olive tree and

NAZARETH

Mt	2.23	made his home in a town called *N*,
	4.13	He left *N* and made his home in
	21.11	is the prophet Jesus from *N* in Galilee."
	26.71	"This man was with Jesus of *N*."
Mk	16. 6	you are looking for Jesus of *N*, who was
Jn	1.45	wrote, Jesus son of Joseph from *N*."
Acts	2.22	Jesus of *N*, a man attested to you by
	10.38	how God anointed Jesus of *N* with the
	22. 8	said to me, 'I am Jesus of *N* whom you

NAZIRITE

Num	6. 2	the vow of a *n*, to separate themselves
Judg	13. 5	the boy shall be a *n* to God from birth.

NEBO

Deut   34. 1 Moses went up . . . to Mount *N*, to the

NEBUCHADNEZZAR (NEBUCHADREZZAR)

Won the battle of Carchemish, 2 Kings 24.1-7; Jer 46.2; conquered Judah, 2 Kings 24.10—25.10 (2 Chr 36.6-19; Jer 39.1-8; 52.1-14); deported the people, 2 Kings 24.14-16; 25.11-21 (2 Chr 36.20-21; Jer 39.9-10; 52.15-30); favored Jeremiah, Jer 39.11-14; his dreams revealed, Dan 2.1-13; 4.4-18; set up the golden image, Dan 3.1-7; punished for boasting, Dan 4.31-33; his reason returned, Dan 4.34-37.

NECK (NECKS)

Josh   10.24 Come near, put your feet on the *n* of
Song   4. 4 Your *n* is like the tower of David, built
Jer   30. 8 I will break the yoke from off his *n*, and
Rom   16. 4 and who risked their *n* for my life, to

NEED (NEEDS)

Deut   15. 7 If there is among you anyone in *n*, a
    15.11 there will never cease to be some in *n*
Dan   3.16 we have no *n* to present a defense to
Mt   7.12 knows that you *n* all these things.
    21. 3 to you, just say this, 'The Lord *n* them.'
Mk   11. 3 just say this, 'The Lord *n* it and will
Lk   10.42 there is *n* of only one thing . Mary has
    11. 8 will get up and give him whatever he *n*.
    19.31 it?' just say this, 'The Lord *n* it.' "
Acts   4.35 it was distributed to each as any had *n*.
Rom   12.13 Contribute to the *n* of the saints;
Phil   4.11 Not that I am referring to being in *n*;

NEEDLE

Lk   18.25 camel to go through the eye of a *n* than

NEEDY

Ps   37.14 bows to bring down the poor and *n*
    40.17 I am poor and *n*; but the LORD takes
    107. 41 but he raises up the *n* out of distress,
Prov   14.31 those who are kind to the *n* honor him.
    31.20 and reaches out her hands to the *n*.
Isa   14.30 will graze, and the *n* lie down in safety;
Am   2. 6 silver, and the *n* for a pair of sandals—
Acts   4.34 There was not a *n* person among them,

NEGLECT (NEGLECTED NEGLECTING)

Neh   10.39 We will not *n* the house of our God.
Mt   23.23 have *n* the weightier matters of the law:
Lk   11.42 to have practiced, without *n* the others.
Heb   2. 3 we escape if we *n* so great a salvation?

NEHEMIAH

Neh   1. 1 The words of *N* son of Hacaliah. In
    3.16 After him *N* son of Azbuk, ruler of half
    12.26 in the days of the governor *N* and of the

NEIGHBOR (NEIGHBORS NEIGHBOR'S)

Lev   19.18 you shall love your *n* as yourself: I am
Josh   9.16 they heard that they were their *n* and
Ps   15. 3 nor take up a reproach against their *n*;
    28. 3 who speak peace with their *n*, while
    31.11 of all my adversaries, a horror to my *n*,
    38.11 my affliction, and my *n* stand afar off.
    101. 5 One who secretly slanders his *n* I will
Prov   3.29 Do not plan harm against your *n* who
    6. 1 if you have given your pledge to your *n*,
    6.29 So is he who sleeps with his *n* wife; no
    11. 9 the godless would destroy their *n*,
    14.21 Those who despise their *n* are sinners,
    25.17 your foot be seldom in your *n* house,
    27.10 Better is a *n* who is nearby than kindred
Jer   9. 8 They all speak friendly words to their *n*,
    34.17 me by granting a release to your *n*
Hab   2.15 who make your *n* drink, pouring out
Mt   5.43 shall love your *n* and hate your enemy.'
    22.39 it: 'You shall love your *n* as yourself.'
Mk   12.31 this, 'You shall love your *n* as yourself.'

Lk   6.41 do you see the speck in your *n* eye,
    10.29 he asked Jesus, "And who is my *n*?"
Rom   13. 9 in this word, "Love your *n* as yourself."
Gal   5.14 "You shall love your *n* as yourself."
Jas   2. 8 "You shall love your *n* as yourself."

NEPHILIM

Gen   6. 4 The *N* were on the earth in those
Num   13.33 There we saw the *N* (the Anakites come

NET (NETS)

Ps   10. 9 the poor and drag them off in their *n*.
    31. 4 take me out of the *n* that is hidden for
Prov   1.17 For in vain is the *n* baited while the
Isa   19. 8 and who spread *n* on the water will
Ezek   17.20 I will spread my *n* over him, and he
Mt   13.47 kingdom of heaven is like a *n* that was
Mk   1.16 and his brother Andrew casting a *n* into
    1.19 who were in their boat mending the *n*.

NEW

Num   16.30 if the LORD creates something *n*, and the
Ps   40. 3 He put a *n* song in my mouth, a song of
    96. 1 O sing to the LORD a *n* song; sing to the
    149. 1 Sing to the LORD a *n* song, his praise in
Eccl   1.10 "See, this is *n*"? It has already been, in
Isa   42. 9 to pass and *n* things I now declare;
    43.19 I am about to do a *n* thing; now it
    48. 6 time forward I make you hear *n* things,
    62. 2 you shall be called by a *n* name that
    66.22 the *n* heavens and the *n* earth, which I
Jer   31.31 when I will make a *n* covenant with the
Lam   3.23 they are *n* every morning; great is your
Ezek   36.26 A *n* heart I will give you, and a *n* spirit
Mk   14.24n "This is my blood of the *n* covenant,
Lk   5.36 tears a piece from a *n* garment and
Jn   13.34 I give you a *n* commandment, that you
Acts   17.21 but telling or hearing something *n*.
Rom   7. 6 code but in the *n* life of the Spirit.
1 Cor   11.25 "This cup is the *n* covenant in my
2 Cor   3. 6 to be ministers of a *n* covenant,
    5.17 is in Christ, there is a *n* creation:
Rev   5. 9 They sing a *n* song: "You are worthy to
    21. 1 I saw a *n* heaven and a *n* earth; for the
    21. 5 throne said, "See, I make all things *n*."

NEWNESS

Rom   6. 4 so we too might walk in *n* of life.

NICODEMUS

Jn   3. 1 there was a Pharisee named *N*, a leader
    7.50 *N*, who had gone to Jesus before, and
    19.39 *N*, who had at first come to Jesus by

NIGHT

Gen   1. 5 light Day, and the darkness he called *N*.
2 Chr   1. 7 That *n* God appeared to Solomon, and
Ps   19. 2 speech, and *n* to *n* declares knowledge.
    42. 8 at *n* his song is with me, a prayer to the
    104. 20 You make darkness, and it is *n*, when
Prov   7. 9 evening, at the time of *n* and darkness.
Lk   5. 5 have worked all *n* long but have caught
    12.20 This very *n* your life is being demanded
Jn   3. 2 He came to Jesus by *n* and said to him,
    9. 4 me while it is day; *n* is coming when
    11.10 But those who walk at *n* stumble
    13.30 he immediately went out; and it was *n*.
Rev   21.25 by day—and there will be no *n* there.

NILE

Ex   7.18 be unable to drink water from the *N*.' "
Ezek   29. 3 saying, "My *N* is my own; I made it for

NIMROD

Gen   10. 8 Cush became the father of *N*; he was

NINE

Acts   2.15 for it is only *n* o'clock in the morning.

NINEVEH

Gen	10.11 land he went into Assyria, and built *N*,
Jon	1. 2 "Go at once to *N*, that great city, and
	4.11 And should I not be concerned about *N*,
Nah	2. 8 *N* is like a pool whose waters run away.
Mt	12.41 the people of *N* will rise up at the
Lk	11.30 became a sign to the people of *N*,
	11.32 The people of *N* will rise up at the

NOAH

Born, Gen 5.29; walked with God, Gen 6.9; built the ark, Gen 6.11-22; preserved through the flood, Gen 7.1-8.19; built an altar, Gen 8.20-22; covenant with God, Gen 9.8-17; his drunkenness, Gen 9.20-21; prophesied concerning his sons, Gen 9.22-27; died, Gen 9.28-29.

NOBLE

Prov	8. 6 Hear, for I will speak *n* things, and from
1 Cor	1.26 powerful, not many were of *n* birth.

NOISE

Ps	66. 1 Make a joyful *n* to God, all the earth;
	100. 1 Make a joyful *n* to the LORD, all the
Jer	10.22 Hear, a *n*! Listen, it is coming—a great

NOON

Acts	10. 9 About *n* the next day, as they were on

NORTH

Isa	41.25 I stirred up one from the *n*, and he has
	43. 6 I will say to the *n*, "Give them up," and

NOTHING

Job	1. 9 the LORD, "Does Job fear God for *n*?
Ezek	12.22 prolonged and every vision comes to *n*"?
Hag	2. 3 to you now? Is it not in your sight as *n*?
1 Cor	13. 3 boast, but do have not love, I gain *n*.

NOTICE

Ex	13.19 "God will surely take *n* of you, and then

NUMBER (NUMBERED)

1 Chr	21. 2 "Go, *n* Israel, from Beer-sheba to Dan,
Job	14.16 then you would not *n* my steps, you
Isa	53.12 death, and was *n* with the transgressors;
Acts	2.47 day by day the Lord added to their *n*
Rev	13.18 of the beast, for it is the *n* of a person.

O

OAK (OAKS)

Isa	1.30 shall be like an *o*, whose leaf withers,
	6.13 or an *o* whose stump remains standing
	61. 3 They will be called *o* of righteousness,

OATH

Gen	24. 8 then you will be free from this *o*
	24.41 her to you, you will be free from my *o*.'
Num	5.19 the priest shall make her take an *o*,
Ps	15. 4 who stand by their *o* even to their hurt;
Neh	10.29 a curse and an *o* to walk in God's law,
Zech	8.17 love no false *o*; for all these are things
Lk	1.73 *o* which he swore to our ancestor
Acts	23.21 by an *o* neither to eat nor drink until
Heb	7.20 this one became a priest with an *o*,

OBADIAH

Ob	1 The vision of *O*. Thus says the Lord GOD

OBEDIENCE

Gen	49.10 to him; and the *o* of the peoples is his.
Rom	1. 5 apostleship to bring about *o* of faith
	16.19 while your *o* is known to all, so that I

OBEDIENT

Isa	1.19 If you are willing and *o*, you shall eat
Lk	2.51 and was *o* to them. His mother
Acts	6. 7 of the priests became *o* to the faith.
Phil	2. 8 and became *o* to the point of death—

1 Pet	1. 2 sanctified by the Spirit to be *o* to Jesus

OBEY (OBEYED OBEYING)

Gen	22.18 because you have *o* my voice."
	26. 5 because Abraham *o* my voice and kept
	27.13 my son; only *o* my word, and go, get
	27.43 my son, *o* my voice; flee at once to my
Ex	19. 5 if you will *o* my voice and keep my
Deut	12.28 Be careful to *o* all these words that I
	13. 4 his voice you shall *o*, him shall you
	21.20 "This son of ours . . . will not *o* us. He
	28.13 if you *o* the commandments of the LORD
	28.45 because you did not *o* the LORD your
	30. 2 you and your children *o* him with all
	30. 8 Then you shall again *o* the LORD,
	34. 9 the Israelites *o* him, doing as the LORD
Josh	1.17 Moses in all things, so we will *o* you.
1 Sam	15.19 Why then did you not *o* the voice of the
	15.22 Surely, to *o* is better than sacrifice, and
2 Kings	18.12 because they did not *o* the voice of the
Neh	9.17 they refused to *o*, and were not mindful
Jer	3.13 green tree, and have not *o* my voice,
	7.23 I gave them, "*O* my voice, and I
	7.28 is the nation that did not *o* the voice
	26.13 your doings, and *o* the voice of the LORD
	32.23 But they did not *o* your voice or follow
	35. 8 We have *o* the charge of our ancestor
	38.20 Just *o* the voice of the LORD in what I
	42. 6 or good, we will *o* the voice of the LORD
	43. 4 and all the people did not *o* the voice
Dan	7.27 and all dominions shall serve and *o*
Hag	1.12 all the remnant of the people, *o* the
Zech	6.15 This will happen if you diligently *o* the
Mt	8.27 that even the winds and the sea *o* him?"
	28.20 teaching them to *o* everything that I
Mk	1.27 the unclean spirits, and they *o* him."
	4.41 this, that even wind and the sea *o* him?"
Lk	8.25 winds and the waters, and they *o* him?"
Acts	5.29 "We must *o* God rather than human
Rom	2. 8 and who *o* not the truth but
2 Cor	10. 5 take every thought captive to *o* Christ.
Gal	5. 7 who prevented you from *o* the truth?
2 Thess	3.14 note of those who do not *o* what we say
Heb	5. 9 of eternal salvation for all who *o* him,
	11. 8 By faith Abraham *o* when he was called
	13.17 *O* your leaders and submit to them, for
1 Pet	3. 6 Thus Sarah *o* Abraham and called him
	4.17 end for those who do not *o* the gospel

OBJECT

Rom	9.21 of the same lump one *o* for special use

OBLIGED

Gal	5. 3 that he is *o* to obey the entire law.

OBSERVE (OBSERVES OBSERVING)

Ex	12.17 You shall *o* the festival of unleavened
	31.16 shall keep the sabbath, *o* the sabbath
Deut	4. 6 You must *o* them diligently, for this will
	17.19 diligently *o* all the words of this law,
Ps	33.15 hearts of them all, and *o* all their deeds.
	105. 45 might keep his statutes and *o* his laws.
	106. 3 Happy are those who *o* justice, who do
	119. 34 your law and *o* it with my whole heart.
Eccl	11. 4 Whoever *o* the wind will not sow; and
Gal	4.10 You are *o* special days, and months, and

OCCUPATION

Gen	46.33 calls you, and says, 'What is your *o*?'
Jon	1. 8 What is your *o*? Where do you come

OCCUPY

Deut	3.18 God has given you this land to *o*, all
	6.18 that you may go in and *o* the good land

OFFEND (OFFENDED)

Gen	40. 1 and his baker *o* their lord the king of
Prov	18.19 An ally *o* is stronger than a city; such

Jn	6.61 it, said to them, "Does this *o* you?

OFFENSE

Mt	11. 6 is anyone who takes no *o* at me."
	15.12 the Pharisees took *o* when they heard
Mk	6. 3 here with us?" And they took *o* at him.
Lk	7.23 is anyone who takes no *o* at me."
Acts	25. 8 in no way committed an *o* against the
1 Cor	10.32 Give no *o* to Jews or to Greeks or to the
Gal	5.11 the *o* of the cross has been removed.

OFFER (OFFERED)

Gen	22. 2 and *o* him there as a burnt offering
	46. 1 he *o* sacrifices to the God of his father
Ex	34.25 You shall not *o* the blood of my
Lev	10. 1 and they *o* unholy fire before the LORD,
	22.20 shall not *o* anything that has a blemish,
Judg	5. 9 Israel who *o* themselves willingly among
2 Sam	24.22 *o* up what seems good to him; here are
1 Chr	29. 9 mind they had *o* freely to the LORD;
2 Chr	8.12 Solomon *o* up burnt offerings to the
Ezra	7.15 counselors have freely *o* to the God of
Neh	11. 2 who willingly *o* to live in Jerusalem.
Ps	4. 5 O right sacrifices, and put your trust in
	27. 6 I will *o* in his tent sacrifices with shouts
	50.14 O to God a sacrifice of thanksgiving,
Jon	1.16 they *o* a sacrifice to the LORD and made
Mt	5.24 or sister, and then come and *o* your gift.
Acts	7.42 'Did you *o* to me slain victims and
1 Cor	8. 4 as to the eating of food *o* to idols, we
Heb	11. 4 By faith Abel *o* to God a more
	11.17 when put to the test, *o* up Isaac.
	12.28 we *o* to God an acceptable worship

OFFERING (OFFERINGS)

Ex	35. 5 Take from among you an *o* to the LORD;
1 Chr	16.29 due his name; bring an *o*, and come
Ps	20. 3 May he remember all your *o*, and regard
Isa	66.20 kindred from all the nations as an *o*
Jer	11.12 out to the gods to whom they make *o*,
Ezek	44.30 every *o* of all kinds shall belong to the
Mal	3. 4 the *o* of Judah and Jerusalem will be
Rom	15.16 so that the *o* of the Gentiles may be

OFFICER

Jer	20. 1 was chief *o* in the house of the LORD,

OFFICIAL (OFFICIALS)

Jer	26.10 When the *o* of Judah heard these
Mic	7. 3 the *o* and the judge ask for a bribe, and
Acts	18.17 Sosthenes, the *o* of the synagogue,

OFFSPRING

Gen	3.15 the woman, between your *o* and hers;
	12. 7 said, "To your *o* I will give this land."
	17. 8 I will give you, and your *o* after you, the
	21.12 is through Isaac that *o* shall be named
	26. 4 and will give to your *o* all these lands;
Job	5.25 be many, your *o* like the grass of the
Mal	2.15 what does the one God desire? Godly *o*.
Acts	17.28 poets have said, 'For we too are his *o*.'

OIL

Ex	30.25 make of these a sacred anointing *o*
2 Kings	4. 2 nothing in the house, except a jar of *o*."
Ps	23. 5 you anoint my head with *o*; my cup
	45. 7 has anointed you with the *o* of gladness
Isa	1. 6 drained or bound up or softened with *o*.
Mt	25. 4 but the wise took flasks of *o* with their
Mk	6.13 anointed with *o* many who were sick

OINTMENT (OINTMENTS)

Eccl	10. 1 Dead flies make the perfumer's *o* give
Mt	26. 7 alabaster jar of very costly *o*, and she
Mk	14. 3 with an an alabaster jar of very costly *o*
Lk	23.56 returned, and prepared spices and *o*.

OLD (OLDER)

Josh	23. 2 said to them, "I am now *o* and well

2 Chr	10. 8 rejected the advice that the *o* men gave
Mt	9.16 piece of unshrunk cloth on an *o* cloak,
Mk	2.21 piece of unshrunk cloth on an *o* cloak;
Lk	3.23 Jesus was about thirty years *o* when he
2 Cor	3.14 they hear the reading of the *o* covenant,

OLIVE

Gen	8.11 in its beak was a freshly plucked *o* leaf;
Deut	24.20 When you beat your *o* trees, do not
Ps	128. 3 your children will be like *o* shoots
Hos	14. 6 his beauty shall be like the *o* tree, and
Zech	4. 3 And by it there are two *o* trees, one on
Rom	11.17 you, a wild *o* shoot, were grafted in
Rev	11. 4 These are the two *o* trees and the two

OLIVET

Acts	1.12 to Jerusalem from the mount called *O*,

ONE

Gen	2.24 to his wife, and they become *o* flesh.
Mk	10. 8 the two shall become *o* flesh.' So they
Acts	17.26 From *o* ancestor he made all nations to
1 Cor	8. 6 and *o* Lord, Jesus Christ, through whom
Eph	5.31 wife, and the two will become *o* flesh."

ONESIMUS

Col	4. 9 he is coming with *O*, the faithful and
Philem	10 I am appealing to you for my child, *O*,

OPEN (OPENED OPENS)

Gen	3. 5 your eyes will be *o*, and you will be like
	3. 7 the eyes of both were *o*, and they knew
Num	22.28 the LORD *o* the mouth of the donkey,
Judg	11.35 I have *o* my mouth to the LORD, and I
2 Kings	6.17 LORD *o* the eyes of the servant, and he
Job	33.16 then he *o* their ears, and terrifies them
Ps	51.15 Lord, *o* my lips, and my mouth will
	104. 28 when you *o* your hand, they are filled
	119. 18 O my eyes, so that I may behold
Prov	20.13 *o* your eyes, and you will have plenty of
	31.26 She *o* her mouth with wisdom, and the
Song	5. 2 "O to me, my sister, my love, my dove,
	5. 6 I *o* to my beloved but my beloved had
Isa	22.22 he shall *o*, and no one shall shut; he
	26. 2 O the gates, so that the righteous
	50. 5 The Lord GOD has *o* my ear, and I was
	60.11 Your gates shall always be *o*; day and
Ezek	3. 2 So I *o* my mouth, and he gave me the
Dan	9.18 O your eyes and look at our desolation
Mt	3.16 the heavens were *o* to him and he saw
	9.30 And their eyes were *o*. Then Jesus
	13.35 "I will *o* my mouth to speak in parables;
	27.52 The tombs also were *o*, and many
Lk	24.31 their eyes were *o* and they recognized
	24.45 he *o* their minds to understand the
Jn	9.14 Jesus made the mud and *o* his eyes.
Acts	14.27 and how he had *o* a door of faith for
	16.14 The Lord *o* her heart to listen eagerly to
	26.18 I am sending you to *o* their eyes so that
1 Cor	16. 9 door for effective work makes a *o* to me,
2 Cor	2.12 Christ, a door was *o* for me in the Lord;
Rev	3. 8 I have set before you an *o* door, which
	6. 1 saw the Lamb *o* one of the seven seals,

OPENLY

Mk	1.45 Jesus could no longer go into a town *o*,
Jn	7.13 Yet no one would speak *o* about him for

OPPORTUNITY

Acts	24.25 when I have an *o*, I will send for you.
Phil	4.10 were concerned for me, but had no *o* to

OPPOSE (OPPOSED OPPOSES)

Gal	2.11 Cephas came to Antioch, I *o* him to
2 Thess	2. 4 He *o* and exalts himself above every
2 Tim	3. 8 and counterfeit faith, also *o* the truth.
1 Pet	5. 5 "God *o* the proud, but gives grace to the

OPPRESS (OPPRESSED OPPRESSES OPPRESSING)

Gen	15.13	they shall be o for four hundred years;
Ex	23. 9	You shall not o a resident alien; you
Ps	42. 9	mournfully because the enemy o me?
Prov	14.31	who o the poor insult their Maker,
	22.16	O the poor in order to enrich oneself,
	28. 3	A ruler who o the poor is a beating rain
Jer	7. 6	if you do not o the alien, the orphan,
Ezek	18.12	o the poor and needy, commits robbery,
Hos	12. 7	hands are false balances, he loves to o.
Am	4. 1	who o the poor, who crush the needy,
Mic	2. 2	they o the householder and house,
Zech	7.10	do not o the widow, the orphan, the
Mal	3. 5	against those who o the hired workers

OPPRESSED (n)

Ps	69.32	Let the o see it and be glad; you who
	76. 9	to save all the o of the earth.
Isa	1.17	seek justice, rescue the o, defend the
	51.14	the o shall speedily be released; they
	61. 1	sent me to bring good news to the o,
Dan	4.27	and your iniquities with mercy to the o,

OPPRESSION (OPPRESSIONS)

Ps	55.11	o and fraud do not depart from its
Eccl	4. 1	I saw all the o that are practiced under
	7. 7	o makes the wise foolish, and a bribe
Isa	30.12	reject this word, and put your trust in o
Jer	22.17	blood, and for practicing o and violence.

OPPRESSOR

Ps	72. 4	to the needy, and crush the o.
Isa	14. 4	How the o has ceased! How his
	51.13	But where is the fury of the o?
Zech	9. 8	no o shall again overrun them, for now I

ORACLE (ORACLES)

Isa	13. 1	The o concerning Babylon that Isaiah
	17. 1	An o concerning Damascus. See,
	19. 1	An o concerning Egypt. See, the LORD is
	21. 1	o concerning the wilderness of the sea.
	21.13	The o concerning the desert plain. In
	23. 1	The o concerning Tyre. Wail, O ships of
Nah	1. 1	An o concerning Nineveh. The book of
Hab	1. 1	The o that the prophet Habakkuk saw.
Zech	9. 1	An O. The word of the LORD is against
	12. 1	An O. The word of the LORD concerning
Mal	1. 1	An o. The word of the LORD to Israel by
Rom	3. 2	the Jews were entrusted with the o
Heb	5.12	the basic elements of the o of God.

ORDAIN (ORDAINED)

Ex	28.41	shall anoint them and o them and
	32.29	Today you have o yourselves for the
2 Sam	17.14	the LORD had o to defeat the good
Isa	26.12	O LORD, you will o peace for us, for
Lam	3.37	and have it done, if the Lord has o it?
Acts	10.42	that he is the one o by God as judge
Gal	3.19	it was o through angels by a mediator.

ORDEAL

2 Cor	8. 2	during a severe o of affliction, their
Rev	7.14	they who have come out of the great o;

ORDER (ORDERED ORDERS)

Lev	25.21	I will o my blessing for you in the sixth
Ps	110. 4	according to the o of Melchizedek."
Mt	12.44	it finds it empty, swept, and put in o.
	17. 9	Jesus o them, "Tell no one about the
Mk	5.43	strictly o them that no one should know
	9. 9	he o them to tell no one about what
Lk	8.56	but he o them to tell no one what had
Acts	5.28	"We gave you strict o not to teach in his
1 Cor	14.40	should be done decently and in o.

ORDINANCES

Deut	4. 8	nation has . . . o as just as this entire

Job	38.33	Do you know the o of the heavens? Can

ORGANIZED

1 Chr	24. 3	David o them according to the
2 Chr	23.18	the levitical priests whom David had o

ORNAMENT

Titus	2.10	they may be an o to the doctrine of God

ORPHAN (ORPHANS)

Deut	10.18	who executes justice for the o and
	14.29	the resident aliens, the o, and the
Job	6.27	You would even cast lots over the o,
	22. 9	and the arms of the o you have crushed.
	24. 9	There are those who snatch the o child
	29.12	cried, and the o who had no helper.
Ps	10.14	you; you have been the helper of the o,
Jer	49.11	Leave your o, I will keep them alive;

OUT

1 Cor	10.13	he will also provide the way o so that

OUTWITTED

2 Cor	2.11	this so that we may not be o by Satan;

OVEN

Lk	12.28	and tomorrow is thrown into the o,

OVERCOME

Rom	12.21	not be o by evil, but o evil with good.

OVERFLOW (OVERFLOWED OVERFLOWING OVERFLOWS)

Ps	73. 7	with fatness; their hearts o with follies.
Mal	3.10	and pour down for you an o blessing.
2 Cor	9.12	saints but also o in many thanksgivings
1 Tim	1.14	grace of our Lord o for me with the

OVERLOOK (OVERLOOKED)

Acts	17.30	has o the times of human ignorance,
Heb	6.10	is not unjust; he will not o your work

OVERPOWERS

Lk	11.22	he attacks him and o him, he takes

OVERSEERS

Acts	20.28	which the Holy Spirit has made you o,

OVERTHROW

Jer	1.10	to destroy and to o, to build and to
Hag	2.22	earth, and to o the throne of kingdoms,
Rom	3.31	Do we then o law by this faith? By no

OVERWHELM (OVERWHELMED OVERWHELMS)

Ps	55. 5	come upon me, and horror o me.
	88. 7	me, and you o me with all your waves.
2 Cor	2. 7	he may not be o by excessive sorrow.

OWE (OWED)

Mt	18.24	one who o him ten thousand talents
Rom	13. 8	O no one anything, except to love one

OWN

Ex	15.17	on the mountain of your o possession,
Phil	3.12	Christ Jesus has made me his o.

OWNER

Isa	1. 3	The ox knows its o, and the donkey its
2 Tim	2.21	and useful to the o of the house,

OX

Ex	21.28	"When an o gores a man or a woman to
Num	22. 4	around us, as the o licks up the grass of
Deut	25. 4	You shall not muzzle an o while it is
Prov	7.22	her, and goes like an o to the slaughter,
Isa	1. 3	The o knows its owner, and the donkey
Lk	14. 5	o that has fallen into a well, will you
1 Cor	9. 9	"You shall not muzzle an o while it is
1 Tim	5.18	you shall not muzzle an o when it is

P

PAIN

Job 14.22 They feel only the *p* of their own
Eccl 2.23 all their days are full of *p*, and their
11.10 put away *p* from your body; for youth
Jer 30.15 Your *p* is incurable. Because your guilt
Jn 16.20 have *p*, but your *p* will turn into joy.
2 Cor 2. 2 if I cause you *p*, who is there to make
Gal 4.19 for whom I am again in the *p* of

PAINTED

2 Kings 9.30 Jezebel . . . *p* her eyes, and adorned her
Ezek 23.40 them you bathed yourself, *p* your eyes,

PALACE (PALACES)

Ps 45. 8 From ivory *p* stringed instruments make
45.15 along as they enter the *p* of the king.

PALM

Ps 92.12 The righteous flourish like the *p* tree,
Song 7. 8 I say I will climb the *p* tree and lay
Jn 12.13 they took branches of *p* trees and went

PANGS

Gen 3.16 greatly increase your *p* in childbearing;
Jer 13.21 Will not *p* take hold of you, like those
Hos 13.13 *p* of childbirth come for him, but he is

PANIC

Isa 28.16 foundation: "One who trusts will not *p*."

PARABLE (PARABLES)

Ps 78. 2 I will open my mouth in a *p*; I will utter
Mt 13. 3 he told them many things in *p*, saying,
Mk 4.30 of God, or what *p* will we use for it?
4.34 he did not speak to them except in *p*,
Lk 8.11 *p* is this: The seed is the word of God.

PARADISE

Lk 23.43 tell you, today you will be with me in *P*."
2 Cor 12. 3 was caught up into *P* and heard things

PARALYTIC (PARALYTICS)

Mt 4.24 epileptics, and *p*, and he cured them.
9. 2 Jesus saw their faith, he said to the *p*,

PARALYZED

Mt 8. 6 "Lord, my servant is lying at home *p*, in
Mk 2. 3 people came, bringing to him a *p* man,
Lk 5.18 carrying a *p* man on a bed. They were
Acts 9.33 bedridden for eight years, for he was *p*.

PARDON (PARDONING)

Ex 34. 9 *p* our iniquity and our sin, and take us
Deut 29.20 Lord will be unwilling to *p* them, for
1 Sam 15.25 *p* my sin, and return with me, so that I
2 Kings 5.18 may the Lord *p* your servant on one
24. 4 and the Lord was not willing to *p*.
2 Chr 30.18 for them saying, "The good Lord *p* all
Job 7.21 Why do you not *p* my transgression and
Ps 25.11 sake, O Lord, *p* my guilt, for it is great.
Isa 55. 7 to our God, for he will abundantly *p*.
Jer 5. 1 truth— so that I may *p* Jerusalem.
5. 7 How can I *p* you? Your children have
50.20 be found; for I will *p* the remnant that I
Mic 7.18 Who is a God like you, *p* iniquity and

PARENT (PARENTS)

Deut 24.16 shall children be put to death for the *p*;
2 Kings 14. 6 shall not be put to death for the
Prov 17.21 gets trouble; the *p* of a fool has no joy.
Ezek 18.20 nor a *p* suffer for the iniquity of a child;
Mal 4. 6 turn the hearts of *p* to their children
Mt 10.21 children will rise against *p* and have
Lk 1.17 go before him, to turn the hearts of *p* to
2.41 every year his *p* went to Jerusalem for
Jn 9. 2 who sinned, this man or his *p*, that he
9.18 they called the *p* of the man who had

2 Cor 12.14 up for their *p*, but *p* for their children.
Eph 6. 1 Children, obey your *p* in the Lord, for
2 Tim 3. 2 disobedient to their *p*, ungrateful,

PARTAKE

Ezra 2.63 were not to *p* of the most holy food,
Neh 7.65 not to *p* of the most holy food, until a
1 Cor 10.17 one body, for we all *p* of the one bread.

PARTED

2 Kings 2. 8 the water was *p* to the one side and to

PARTIAL

Lev 19.15 you shall not be *p* to the poor or defer
Deut 1.17 You must not be *p* in judging; hear out
10.17 the great God . . . is not *p* and takes no
Prov 18. 5 It is not right be *p* to the guilty, or to

PARTIALITY

Deut 16.19 distort justice; you must not show *p*;
2 Chr 19. 7 with the Lord our God, or *p*, or taking
Prov 24.23 *P* in judging is not good. Whoever says
28.21 To show *p* is not good— yet for a piece
Acts 10.34 I truly understand that God shows no *p*,
Rom 2.11 also the Greek. For God shows no *p*.
Gal 2. 6 God shows no *p*)—those leaders
Eph 6. 9 in heaven, and with him there is no *p*.
1 Tim 5.21 doing nothing on the basis of *p*.
Jas 2. 9 if you show *p*, you commit sin and are

PARTNER (PARTNERS)

Prov 29.24 To be a *p* of a thief is to hate one's
Lk 5. 7 signaled their *p* in the other boat to
1 Cor 10.20 I do not want you to be *p* with demons.
Philem 17 if you consider me your *p*, welcome him

PARTNERSHIP

2 Cor 6.14 what *p* is there between righteousness

PARTRIDGE

1 Sam 26.20 like one who hunts a *p* in the
Jer 17.11 Like the *p* hatching what it did not lay,

PASCHAL

1 Cor 5. 7 For our *P* lamb, Christ, has been

PASS (PASSED)

Ex 12.23 Lord will *p* over that door and will not
Josh 3. 4 go, for you have not *p* this way before.
Ps 31.12 I have *p* out of mind like one who is
Prov 9.15 calling to those who *p* by, who are
Eccl 6.12 vain life, which they *p* like a shadow?
Isa 14.24 as I have planned, so shall it come to *p*:
43. 2 When you *p* through the waters, I will
Lam 1.12 all you who *p* by? Look and see if there
Mt 24.35 will *p* away, but my words will not *p*
Mk 1.16 As Jesus *p* along the Sea of Galilee, he
13.31 Heaven and earth will *p* away, but my
Lk 10.31 he saw him, he *p* by on the other side.
1 Jn 3.14 know that we have *p* from death to life

PASSION (PASSIONS)

Prov 14.30 to the flesh, but *p* makes the bones rot.
Song 8. 6 is strong as death, *p* fierce as the grave.
Rom 1.27 were consumed with *p* for one another.
1 Cor 7.36 if his *p* are strong, and so it has to be,
Eph 2. 3 lived among them in the *p* of our flesh,

PASSOVER

Ex 12.11 eat it hurriedly. It is the *p* of the Lord.
Lev 23. 5 twilight, there shall be a *p* offering to
Num 9. 5 They kept the *p* in the first month, on
28.16 there shall be a *p* offering to the Lord.
Deut 16. 1 by keeping the *p* for the Lord your God,
Josh 5.11 On the day after the *p*, on that very day,
2 Kings 23.21 "Keep the *p* to the Lord your God as
2 Chr 30. 1 Jerusalem to keep the *p* to the Lord the
35.17 of Israel who were present kept the *p* at
Ezra 6.19 month the returned exiles kept the *p*.

PASTORS

Mt	26. 2 after two days the *P* is coming, and the
Mk	14. 1 It was two days before the *P* and the
	14.14 I may eat the *P* with my disciples?'
Lk	22. 7 Bread, on which the *P* lamb had
Jn	13. 1 before the festival of the *P*, Jesus knew
	18.39 that I release someone for you at the *P*.
Heb	11.28 By faith he kept the *P* and the

PASTORS

Eph	4.11 some evangelists, some *p* and teachers.

PASTURE (PASTURES)

Ps	23. 2 He makes me lie down in green *p*; he
Jer	50.19 I will restore Israel to its *p*, and it shall

PATH (PATHS)

Job	8.13 the *p* of all who forget God; the hope of
Ps	8. 8 whatever passes along the *p* of the seas.
	17. 5 My steps have held fast to your *p*, my
	119. 35 me in the *p* of your commandments,
	119.105 a lamp to my feet and a light to my *p*.
Prov	4.18 But the *p* of the righteous is like the
	15.24 For the wise the *p* of life leads upward,
Isa	40.14 and who taught him the *p* of justice?
	42.16 by *p* they have not known I will guide
	45.13 and I will make all his *p* straight;
Jer	31. 9 walk by brooks of water, in a straight *p*
Mt	13. 4 some seeds fell on the *p*, and the birds
Mk	4. 4 some seed fell on the *p*, and the birds

PATHWAYS

Hab	3. 6 his ancient *p* the everlasting hills sank

PATIENCE

Mic	2. 7 Is the LORD's *p* exhausted? Are these his
Mt	18.29 with him, "Have *p* with me, and I will
Rom	8.25 we do not see, we wait for it with *p*.
	9.22 has endured with much *p* the objects of
Col	3.12 kindness, humility, meekness, and *p*.
Jas	5.10 As an example of suffering and *p*,
2 Pet	3.15 regard the *p* of our Lord as salvation. So

PATIENT

Lk	8.15 heart, and bear fruit with *p* endurance.
Rom	12.12 Rejoice in hope, be *p* in suffering,
1 Cor	13. 4 Love is *p*; love is kind; love is not
Jas	5. 8 be *p*. Strengthen your hearts, for the
Rev	2. 2 works, your toil and your *p* endurance.
	2.19 love, faith, service, and *p* endurance.

PATMOS

Rev	1. 9 was on the island called *P* because of

PAUL

Born in Tarsus, Acts 22.3; educated under Gamaliel, Acts 22.3; consented to Stephen's death, Acts 7.58; 8.1 (22.20); persecuted the church, Acts 8.3; 9.1-2 (22.4-5; 26.10-11; 1 Cor 15.9; Gal 1.13; Phil. 3.6); went into Arabia, Gal 1.17; preached in Damascus, Gal 1.17; went up to Jerusalem, Acts 9.26-28; Gal 1.18-19; name changed to Paul, Acts 13.9; missionary work, Acts 13 — 14; 15.36 — 18.22; 18.23 — 21.17; attended the Council of Jerusalem, Acts 15.1-29; Gal. 2.1-10; arrested in Jerusalem, Acts 21.27-40; imprisoned in Caesarea, Acts 23.23-35; defended himself before Felix, Acts 24; appealed to Caesar, Acts 25.10-12; defended himself before Agrippa, Acts 26; journeyed to Rome, Acts 27.1 — 28.16; preached during imprisonment, Acts 28.17-31.

1 Cor	1.13 been divided? Was *P* crucified for you?
	3. 4 For when one says, "I belong to *P*," and
2 Pet	3.15 our beloved brother *P* wrote to you

PAWN

Ex	22.26 If you take your neighbor's cloak in *p*,

PAY (PAID PAYING PAYS)

Gen	50.15 bears a grudge against us and *p* us back
Num	20.19 and our livestock, then we will *p* for it.

Ps	66.13 I will *p* you my vows, those that my lips
	116. 18 I will *p* my vows to the LORD in the
	137. 8 Happy shall they be who *p* you back
Isa	40. 2 served her term, that her penalty is *p*,
Joel	3. 4 Are you *p* me back for something? If
Rom	13. 7 *P* all what is due them — taxes to whom
2 Tim	4.14 great harm; the Lord will *p* him back

PAYMENT

Lev	25.52 they shall make *p* for their redemption.
Ezek	16.34 *p*, while no *p* was given to you; you
Mt	10. 8 You received without *p*, give without *p*.

PEACE

Lev	26. 6 I will grant *p* in the land, and you shall
Num	6.26 countenance upon you, and give you *p*.
Deut	20.10 to fight against it, offer it terms of *p*.
Judg	6.23 "*P* be to you; do not fear, you shall not
1 Sam	10.27 him no present. But he held his *p*.
1 Kings	2.33 there shall be *p* from the LORD
2 Kings	20.19 "Why not, if there will be *p* and security
1 Chr	12.18 son of Jesse! *P*, *p* to you, and *p* to the
	19.19 by Israel, they made *p* with David,
	22. 9 he shall be a man of *p*. I will give him *p*
2 Chr	14. 6 in those years, for the LORD gave him *p*.
Job	5.23 the wild animals shall be at *p* with you.
Ps	35.20 For they do not speak *p*, but they
	85.10 will meet; righteousness and *p* will kiss
	119.165 Great *p* have those who love your law;
	120. 7 I am for *p*; but when I speak, they are
	122. 6 Pray for the *p* of Jerusalem: "May they
Prov	3.17 lay hold of her; and all her paths are *p*.
Song	8.10 I was in his eyes as one who brings *p*.
Isa	9. 7 there shall be endless *p* for the throne
	26. 3 you keep in *p* — in *p* because they trust
	26.12 O LORD, you will ordain *p* for us, for
	27. 5 let it make *p* with me, let it make *p*
	32. 1 The effect of righteousness will be *p*,
	36.16 king of Assyria: 'Make your *p* with me
	39. 8 will be *p* and security in my days."
	48.22 "There is no *p*," says the LORD, "for the
	52. 7 feet of the messenger who announces *p*,
	54.10 my covenant of *p* shall not be removed,
	55.12 go out in joy, and be led back in *p*;
	57.19 *P*, *p*, to the far and the near, says the
	60.17 I will anoint *P* as your overseer and
Jer	6.14 saying, "*P*, *p*," when there is no *p*.
	8.11 saying, "*P*, *p*," when there is no *p*.
	14.19 We look for *p*, but find no good; for a
Ezek	7.25 will seek *p*, but there shall be none.
	13.10 people, saying, "*P*," when there is no *p*;
	13.16 saw visions of *p* for it, when there was
	34.25 I will make with them a covenant of *p*
	37.26 I will make a covenant of *p* with them;
Mic	3. 5 who lead my people astray, who cry "*P*"
	5. 5 the earth; and he shall be the one of *p*.
Nah	1.15 brings good tidings, who proclaims *p*!
Zech	9.10 and he shall command *p* to the nations;
Mt	10.34 I have not come to bring *p*, but a sword.
Mk	4.39 said to the sea, "*P*! Be still!" Then the
	9.50 and be at *p* with one another."
Lk	1.79 to guide our feet into the way of *p*."
	2.14 and on earth among those whom he
	7.50 "Your faith has saved you; go in *p*."
	8.48 your faith has made you well; go in *p*."
	10. 5 you enter, first say, '*P* to this house!'
	12.51 I have come to give *p* on earth? No,
	24.36 them and said to them, "*P* be with you!"
Jn	14.27 *P* I leave with you; my *p* I give to you. I
	16.33 to you so that in me you may have *p*.
	20.19 among them and said, "*P* be with you."
	20.21 said to them again, "*P* be with you.
Acts	10.36 Israel, preaching *p* through Jesus Christ
Rom	5. 1 faith, we have *p* with God through our
	14.19 us then pursue what makes for *p* and
	16.20 The God of *p* will shortly crush Satan
2 Cor	1. 2 Grace to you and *p* from God our

Eph	2.14	for he is our *p*; in his flesh he has made
	2.15	in place of the two, thus making *p*
	2.17	proclaimed *p* to you who were far off
Phil	4. 7	the *p* of God, which surpasses all
	4. 9	me, and the God of *p* will be with you.
Col	1.20	*p* through the blood of his cross.
	3.15	let the *p* of Christ rule in your hearts,
Heb	13.20	may the God of *p*, who brought back
1 Pet	3.11	do good; let them seek *p* and pursue it.
Rev	6. 4	rider was permitted to take *p* from the

PEACEABLY

Gen	37. 4	him, and could not speak *p* to him.
1 Kings	2.13	asked, "Do you come *p*?" He said, "*P*."
Rom	12.18	far as it depends on you, live *p* with all.

PEACEMAKERS

Mt	5. 9	"Blessed are the *p*, for they will be

PEARLS

Mt	7. 6	and do not throw your *p* before swine,
	13.45	is like a merchant in search of fine *p*,

PEN

Job	19.24	O that with an iron *p* and with lead
Ps	45. 1	to the king; my tongue is like the *p* of a
Jer	8. 8	the false *p* of the scribes has made it
	17. 1	sin of Judah is written with an iron *p*;
3 Jn	13	but I would rather not write with *p* and

PENNY

Mt	10.29	Are now two sparrows sold for a *p*? Yet
Mk	12.42	copper coins, which are worth a *p*.

PENTECOST

Acts	2. 1	When the day of *P* had come, they were
1 Cor	16. 8	But I will stay in Ephesus until *P*,

PEOPLE

Ex	2.11	he went out to his *p* and saw their
	6. 7	I will take you as my *p*, and I will be
	7.16	"Let my *p* go, so that they may worship
	15.16	until your *p*, O LORD, passed by, . . . the
	32.11	your wrath burn hot against your *p*,
	33.13	Consider too that this nation is your *p*."
Lev	26.12	be your God, and you shall be my *p*.
Num	14.14	you, O LORD, are in the midst of this *p*;
Deut	9.27	attention to the stubbornness of this *p*,
	14. 2	you are a *p* holy to the LORD your God;
	26.18	to be a treasured *p*, as he promised you,
	29.13	he may establish you today as his *p*,
	32. 9	LORD's own portion was his *p*, Jacob his
Judg	2. 7	The *p* worshiped the LORD all the days
Ruth	1. 6	LORD had considered his *p* and given
	1.16	your *p* shall be my *p*, and your God, my
1 Sam	27.12	himself utterly abhorrent to his *p* Israel;
2 Sam	3.18	my servant David I will save my *p* Israel
	7.24	established your *p* Israel to be your *p*
1 Kings	8.16	Since the day that I brought my *p* Israel
	22. 4	my *p* are your *p*, my horses are your
2 Kings	3. 7	I am with you, my *p* are your *p*, my
	11.17	and *p*, that they should be the LORD's *p*;
1 Chr	17. 9	I will appoint a place for my *p* Israel,
	17.21	your *p* whom you redeemed from Egypt?
	17.22	made your *p* Israel to be your *p* forever;
2 Chr	7.14	if my *p* who are called by my name
	36.15	because he had compassion on his *p*
Ps	78.52	Then he led out his *p* like sheep, he
	100. 3	we are his; we are his *p*, and the sheep
	106.40	of the LORD was kindled against his *p*,
	110. 3	Your *p* will offer themselves willingly on
	125. 2	Jerusalem, so the LORD surrounds his *p*,
	144.15	blessings fall; happy the *p* whose God is
	148.14	He has raised up a horn for his *p*,
	149. 4	For the LORD takes pleasure in his *p*; he
Isa	2. 6	you have forsaken the ways of your *p*,
	3.12	My *p*—children are their oppressors,
	5.13	my *p* go into exile without knowledge;

Isa	9. 2	The *p* who walked in darkness have
	40. 5	revealed, and all *p* shall see it together,
	40. 6	"What shall I cry?" All *p* are grass, and
	47. 6	I was angry with my *p*, I profaned my
	58. 1	Announce to my *p* their rebellion, to
	63. 8	"Surely they are my *p*, children who will
	65.19	in Jerusalem, and delight in my *p*;
Jer	2.13	my *p* have committed two evils: they
	7.23	be your God, and you shall be my *p*;
	13.11	might be for me as *p*, a name, a praise,
	18.15	But my *p* have forgotten me, they burn
	24. 7	they shall be my *p* and I will be their
	30.22	And you shall be my *p*, and I will be
	32.38	They shall be my *p*, and I will be their
Ezek	11.20	Then they shall be my *p*, and I will be
	14.11	Then they shall be my *p*, and I will be
	36.28	and you shall be my *p*, and I will be
Hos	1.10	it was said to them, "You are not my *p*,"
	2.23	I will say to Lo-ammi, "You are my *p*";
Joel	2.18	for his land, and had pity on his *p*.
Am	9. 7	like the Ethiopians to me, O *p* of Israel?
Mic	6. 2	LORD has a controversy with his *p*, and
Acts	18.10	are many in this city who are my *p*."
Rom	9.25	who were not my *p* I will call 'my *p*,'
1 Pet	2.10	were not a *p*, but now you are God's *p*;

PEOPLES

1 Kings	8.60	all the *p* of the earth may know that the
Ps	67. 5	Let the *p* praise you, O God; let all the
Mic	4. 1	*P* shall stream to it, and many nations

PERCEIVE (PERCEIVED PERCEIVES)

Judg	6.22	Gideon *p* that it was the angel of the
Ps	73.17	sanctuary of God; then I *p* their end.
	138. 6	but the haughty he *p* from far away.
Isa	64. 4	no ear has *p*, no eye has seen any God
Mt	13.14	and you will indeed look, but never *p*.
Mk	4.12	'they may indeed look, but not *p*, and
	8.17	no bread? Do you still not *p* or

PERFECT

2 Sam	22.31	This God—his way is *p*; the promise of
Job	36. 4	not false; one who is *p* in knowledge is
Ps	18.30	This God—his way is *p*; the promise of
Song	6. 9	My dove, my *p* one, is only one, the
Mt	5.48	Be *p*, therefore, as your heavenly Father
	19.21	"If you wish to be *p*, go, sell your
Heb	2.10	the pioneer of their salvation *p* through
	5. 9	having been made *p*, he became the
	7.28	a Son who has been made *p* forever.
	9. 9	are offered that cannot *p* the conscience
Jas	1.17	every *p* gift is from above, coming down

PERFECTION

Ps	50. 2	Out of Zion, the *p* of beauty, God
	119. 96	I have seen a limit to all *p*, but your
Heb	6. 1	let us go on toward *p*, leaving behind
	7.11	Now if *p* had been attainable through
1 Jn	2. 5	person the love of God has reached *p*.

PERFORM (PERFORMED)

2 Kings	23. 3	to *p* the words of this covenant that
Ps	76.11	vows to the LORD your God, and *p* them;
Isa	41. 4	Who has *p* and done this, calling the

PERIL

Lam	5. 9	We get our bread at the *p* of our lives,

PERISH (PERISHED PERISHES PERISHING)

Lev	26.38	You shall *p* among the nations, and the
Num	24.20	was Amalek, but its end is to *p* forever."
Deut	4.26	you will soon utterly *p* from the land
	8.19	warn you today that you shall surely *p*.
Josh	23.16	and you shall *p* quickly from the good
Judg	5.31	"So *p* all your enemies, O LORD! But
Esth	4.16	it is against the law; and if I *p*, I *p*."
Job	20. 7	they will *p* forever like their own dung;
Ps	9. 3	back, they stumbled and *p* before you.

Ps	37.20	But the wicked p, the enemies of the
	73.27	those who are far from you will p; you
	102. 26	They will p, but you endure; they will
Prov	11. 7	When the wicked die, their hope p, and
	28.28	but when they p, the righteous increase.
Jer	8.14	our God has doomed us to p, and he
Jon	3. 9	his fierce anger, so that we do not p."
Mt	26.52	who take the sword will p by the sword.
Lk	13. 3	but unless you repent, you will all p as
2 Cor	4. 3	is veiled, it is veiled to those who are p.
Heb	1.11	they will p, but you remain; they will all

PERISHABLE

1 Cor	9.25	they do it to receive a p wreath, but we
	15.42	What is sown is p, what is raised is
1 Pet	1.18	not with p things like silver or gold, but

PERMITS (PERMITTED)

Jn	18.31	"We are not p to put anyone to death."
1 Cor	16. 7	some time with you, if the Lord p.
Heb	6. 3	we will do this, if God p. For it is

PERPLEXED

Lk	9. 7	Herod . . . was p , because it was said by
	24. 4	While they were p about this, suddenly
2 Cor	4. 8	crushed; p, but not driven to despair;

PERSECUTE (PERSECUTED PERSECUTING)

Mt	5.10	are those who are p for righteousness'
	5.11	when people revile you and p you and
	10.23	When they p you in one town, flee to
Lk	11.49	some of whom they will kill and p,'
	21.12	they will arrest and p you; they will
Jn	5.16	Therefore the Jews started p Jesus,
	15.20	If they p me, they will p you; if they
Acts	7.52	the prophets did your ancestors not p?
	9. 4	to him, "Saul, Saul, why do you p me?"
	22. 4	I p this Way up to the point of death,
	22. 7	to me, 'Saul, Saul, why are you p me?'
Rom	12.14	Bless those who p you; bless and do not
1 Cor	4.12	reviled, we bless; when p, we endure;
	15. 9	apostle, because I p the church of God.
2 Cor	4. 9	driven to despair; p, but not forsaken;
Gal	1.13	I was violently p the church of God and
	4.29	p the child born according to the Spirit,
	6.12	may not be p for the cross of Christ.
2 Tim	3.12	a godly life in Christ Jesus will be p.

PERSECUTION (PERSECUTIONS)

Mt	13.21	when trouble or p arises on account of
Mk	10.30	and fields with p —and in the age to
Jn	16.33	In the world you face p. But take
Acts	8. 1	day a severe p arose against the church
	11.19	who were scattered because of the p
	14.22	"It is through many p that we must
1 Thess	3. 4	beforehand that we were to suffer p;
2 Thess	1. 4	faith during all your p and the
2 Tim	3. 1	and Lystra. What p I endured! Yet the
Rev	1. 9	share with you in Jesus the p and the

PERSECUTORS

Jer	17.18	Let my p be shamed, but do not let me

PERSEVERE (PERSEVERED)

Dan	12.12	Happy are those who p and attain the
Heb	11.27	he p as though he saw him who is

PERSIA

Ezra	1. 1	In the first year of King Cyrus of P, in
	4. 7	wrote to King Artaxerxes of P;
	4.24	year of the reign of King Darius of P.
Esth	1. 3	The army of P and Media and the
Dan	10.13	with the prince of the kingdom of P,

PERSON

Deut	1.16	judge rightly between one p and
	4.42	who unintentionally kills another p,
	19. 4	has killed another p unintentionally
Prov	27.17	and one p sharpens the wits of another.

Ezek	18. 4	it is only the p who sins that shall die.

PERSUADE (PERSUADED PERSUADING)

Acts	17. 4	Some of them were p, and joined Paul
	18.13	man is p people to worship God in ways
	19.26	Paul has p and drawn away a
2 Cor	5.11	the fear of the Lord, we try to p others;

PERVERSE (PERVERSELY)

Ex	32. 7	at once! Your people, . . . have acted p;
Ps	14. 3	all gone astray, they are all alike p;

PERVERSITY

Ezek	9. 9	and the city full of p; for they say, 'The

PERVERT (PERVERTED PERVERTING)

Job	8. 3	Or does the Almighty p the right?
	34.12	and the Almighty will not p justice.
Jer	3.21	children, because they have p their way,
	23.36	so you p the words of the living God,
Mic	3. 9	who abhor justice and p all equity,
Lk	23. 2	"We found this man p our nation,

PESTERED

Judg	16.16	day, and p him, he was tired to death.

PESTILENCE

Ex	9. 3	will strike with a deadly p your livestock
Deut	28.21	The LORD will make the p cling to you
2 Sam	24.13	there be three days' p in your land?
Ps	91. 6	files by, or the p that stalks in darkness,
Jer	29.17	let loose on them sword, famine, and p,

PETER (CEPHAS SIMON SIMEON)

Called to be a fisher of men, Mt 4.18-20 (Mk 1.16-18; Lk 5.1-11); also named Cephas, which means "rock," Jn 1.42n; sent out with the twelve, Mt 10.2 (Mk 3.16); walked on the sea, Mt 14.28-33; confessed Jesus as the Christ, Mt 16.13-20 (Mk 8.27-30; Lk 9.18-22); interceded for by the Lord, Lk 22.31-32; cut off the servant's ear, Jn 18.10-11; denied Jesus three times, Mt 26.69-75 (Mk 14.66-72; Lk 22.54-62; Jn 18.15-18,25-27); "Feed my sheep," Jn 21.15-19; addressed the disciples, Acts 1.15-26; preached on Pentecost, Acts 2.14-42; healed the lame man, Acts 3.1-10; witnessed in Solomon's portico, Acts 3.11-26; preached to the Council, Acts 4.1-12; imprisoned and released, Acts 5.17-42; denounced Simon Magus, Acts 8.14-24; visited Cornelius after the vision, Acts 10; reported to the Jerusalem Church, Acts 11.1-18; imprisoned and delivered, Acts 12.1-19; at the Council of Jerusalem, Acts 15.6-12; visited by Paul, Gal 1.18; blamed by Paul, Gal 2.11-14; Peter's wife's mother, Mt 8.14 (Mk 1.30; Lk 4.38); his wife, 1 Cor 9.5.

PETITIONS

Ps	20. 5	banners. May the LORD fulfill all your p.

PHARISEE (PHARISEES)

Mt	3. 7	when he saw many P and Sadducees
	5.20	exceeds that of the scribes and P,
	9.11	When the P saw this, they said to his
	12. 2	When the P saw it, they said to him,
	12.14	the P went out and conspired against
	16. 6	and beware of the yeast of the P and
	19. 3	Some P came to him, and to test him
	22.15	the P went and plotted to entrap him in
	23. 2	scribes and the P sit on Moses' seat;
	27.62	priests and the P gathered before Pilate
Jn	3. 1	Now there was a P named Nicodemus,
	8. 3	The scribes and the P brought a woman
Acts	15. 5	the P stood up and said, "It is necessary
	23. 6	were Sadducees and the others were P,

PHILEMON

Philem	1	To P our dear friend and co-worker, to

PHILIP

Mt	10. 3	P and Bartholomew; Thomas and
Jn	1.43	He found P and said to him, "Follow

Jn
6. 5 Jesus said to P, "Where are we to buy
12.21 some Greeks. They came to P, who was
14. 8 P said to him, "Lord, show us the

Acts
1.13 and Andrew, P and Thomas,
8. 5 P went down to a city of Samaria, and
8.40 But P found himself at Azotus, and as
21. 8 we went into the house of P the

PHILIPPI

Acts
16.12 and from there to P, which is a leading
20. 6 we sailed from P after the days of

Phil
1. 1 the saints in Christ Jesus who are in P,

1 Thess
2. 2 and been shamefully mistreated at P,

PHILISTIA

Ex
15.14 pangs seized the inhabitants of P.

Joel
3. 4 and Sidon, and all the regions of P?

Zech
9. 6 I will make an end of the pride of P.

PHILISTINES

Gen
26. 1 to Gerar, to King Abimelech of the P.

Judg
16.21 the P seized him and gouged out his

1 Sam
4. 1 In those days the P mustered for war
5. 1 When the P captured the ark of God,
7. 3 deliver you out of the hand of the P."
31. 1 Now the P fought against Israel; and

2 Sam
8. 1 David attacked the P and subdued

Isa
2. 6 the east and of soothsayers like the P,
14.29 Do not rejoice, all you P, that the rod

Am
9. 7 the P from Caphtor and the Arameans

PHILOSOPHERS

Acts
17.18 Epicurean and Stoic p debated with

PHILOSOPHY

Col
2. 8 you captive through p and empty deceit,

PHYSICAL

1 Cor
15.44 If there is a p body, there is also a

Gal
4.13 was because of a p infirmity that I first

PHYSICIAN (PHYSICIANS)

Gen
50. 2 his father. So the p embalmed Israel.

Job
13. 4 with lies; all of you are worthless p.

Jer
8.22 no balm in Gilead? Is there no p there?

Mt
9.12 who are well have no need of a p,

Mk
2.17 who are well have no need of a p,
5.26 She had endured much under many p,

Lk
5.31 who are well have no need of a p,
8.43 she had spent all she had on p, no one

Col
4.14 Luke, the beloved p, and Demas greet

PIECES

Mk
6.43 took up twelve baskets full of broken p
8.19 how many baskets full of broken p did

Lk
9.17 gathered up, twelve baskets of broken p.

PIERCE (PIERCED)

Zech
12.10 they look on the one whom they have p,

Lk
2.35 —and a sword will p your own soul

Jn
19.34 Instead, one of the soldiers p his side

Rev
1. 7 shall see him, even those who p him;

PIETY

Mt
6. 1 "Beware of practicing your p before

Acts
3.12 as though by our own power or p we

PIG (PIGS PIG'S)

Lev
11. 7 The p, for even though it has divided

Prov
11.22 a gold ring in a p snout is a beautiful

Lk
15.15 who sent him to his fields to feed the p.

PIGEON (PIGEONS)

Gen
15. 9 me . . . a turtledove, and a young p."

Lev
1.14 shall choose your offering from . . . p.

PILATE

Governor of Judea, Lk 3.1; killed some Galileans, Lk 13.1; sentenced Jesus to be crucified, Mt 27.1-25 (Mk 15.1-15; Lk 23.1-26; Jn 18.28 — 19.22); Jesus suffered under Pontius Pilate, Acts 3.13; 13.28; 1 Tim 6.13.

PILLAR (PILLARS)

Gen
19.26 back, and she became a p of salt.
28.18 set it up for a p and poured oil on the

Ex
13.21 in front of them in a p of cloud by day,

Judg
16.26 "Let me feel the p on which the house

2 Sam
18.18 set up for himself the p that is in the

2 Kings
10.26 They brought out the p that was in the

Neh
9.12 and by night with a p of fire, to give

Gal
2. 9 who were acknowledged p, recognized

PIONEER

Heb
2.10 should make the p of their salvation
12. 2 looking to Jesus the p and perfecter of

PIT

Ps
16.10 Sheol, or let your faithful one see the P.

Ezek
28. 8 They shall thrust you down to the P,

Jon
2. 6 yet you brought up my life from the P,

PITY (PITIED)

Ex
2. 6 He was crying, and she took p on him;

Deut
7.16 showing them no p; you shall not serve

Job
19.21 have p on me, O you my friends, for the
27.22 It hurls at them without p; they flee

Ps
72.13 He has p on the weak and needy, and

Isa
49.10 he who has p on them will lead them,

Ezek
7. 4 will not spare you, I will have no p.
8.18 eye will not spare, nor will I have p; and
16. 5 No eye p you, to do any of these things

Hos
1. 7 I will have p on the house of Judah,

Joel
2.18 for his land, and had p on his people.

Zech
11. 6 For I will no longer have p on the

Mt
18.27 out of p for him, the lord of that slave

Mk
1.41 Moved with p, Jesus stretched out his
9.22 do anything, have p on us and help us."

Lk
10.33 he saw him, he was moved with p.

1 Cor
15.19 we are of all people most to be p.

PLACE (PLACES)

Gen
8. 9 the dove found no p to set its foot, and

Mt
24.34 until all these things have taken p.

Lk
2. 7 there was no p for them in the inn.

Jn
14. 2 my Father's house are many dwelling p.

PLAGUE (PLAGUES)

Gen
12.17 his house with great p because of Sarai,

Ex
11. 1 "I will bring one more p upon Pharaoh

Num
11.33 struck the people with a very great p.
14.37 the land died by a p before the LORD.
16.47 where the p had already begun among
25. 9 those that died by the p were

1 Chr
21.22 —so that the p may be averted from

Ps
106. 30 and interceded, and the p was stopped.

Zech
14.12 This shall be the p with which the LORD

PLAN (PLANNED PLANS)

1 Chr
28. 2 I had p to build a house of rest for the

Ezra
4. 5 they bribed officials to frustrate their p,

Job
17.11 past, my p are broken off, the desires of
21.16 p of the wicked are repugnant to me.

Ps
83. 3 They lay crafty p against your people;

Prov
15.26 Evil p are an abomination to the LORD,
19.21 human mind may devise many p, but it
20.18 P are established by taking advice; wage

Isa
5.19 let the p of the Holy One of Israel
14.26 This is the p that is p concerning the
19.17 fear because of the p that the LORD of
30. 1 LORD, who carry out a p, but not mine;

Jer
18.11 you and devising a p against you.
29.11 For surely I know the p I have for you,

Acts
2.23 according to the definite p and
5.38 if this p or this undertaking is of human

Eph
1.10 a p for the fullness of time, to gather up
3. 9 what is the p of the mystery hidden for

PLANT (PLANTED PLANTS)

Gen	1.11	"Let the earth put forth vegetation, *p*
	2. 5	when no *p* of the field was yet in the
Ex	15.17	You brought them in and *p* them on the
1 Chr	17. 9	for my people Israel, and will *p* them,
Job	12. 8	ask the *p* of the earth, and they will
Ps	44. 2	drove out the nations, but them you *p*;
	80.15	this vine, stock that your right hand *p*.
Jer	2.21	Yet I *p* you as a choice vine, from the
	32.41	I will *p* them in this land in
Am	9.15	I will *p* them upon their land, and they
Mt	15.13	Father has not *p* will be uprooted.
1 Cor	3. 6	I *p*, Apollos watered, but God gave the
	9. 7	Who *p* a vineyard and does not eat any

PLATFORM

Neh	8. 4	The scribe Ezra stood on a wooden *p*
Acts	12.21	took his seat on the *p*, and delivered a

PLATTER

Mk	6.25	the head of John the Baptist on a *p*."

PLAY (PLAYING)

Gen	21. 9	borne to Abraham, *p* with her son Isaac.
Isa	11. 8	child shall *p* over the hole of the asp,

PLEA

Jer	42. 2	"Be good enough to listen to our *p*, and

PLEAD (PLEADS)

Ps	5. 3	my voice; in the morning I *p* my case to
	119.154	*P* my cause and redeem me; give me
Prov	22.23	the LORD *p* their cause and despoils of
Isa	51.22	God who *p* the cause of his people:
Hos	2. 2	*P* with your mother, *p* — for she is not
Lk	15.28	came out and began to *p* with him,

PLEADINGS

Ps	28. 6	for he has heard the sound of my *p*.

PLEASANT

Gen	2. 9	God made to grow every tree that is *p*
Ps	16. 6	lines have fallen for me in *p* places;
	106. 24	Then they despised the *p* land, having
	133. 1	good and *p* it is when kindred live
Prov	2.10	and knowledge will be *p* to your soul;
	9.17	is sweet, and bread eaten in secret is *p*."

PLEASANTNESS

Prov	3.17	Her ways are ways of *p*, and all her

PLEASE (PLEASED PLEASES)

Num	14. 8	If the LORD is *p* with us, he will bring us
Judg	14. 3	"Get her for me, because she *p* me."
1 Sam	12.22	it has *p* the LORD to make you a people
	18.26	David was well *p* to be the king's
2 Sam	3.36	just as everything the king did *p* all the
	7.29	may it *p* you to bless the house of your
	17. 4	The advice *p* Absalom and all the elders
1 Kings	3.10	It *p* the Lord that Solomon had asked
1 Chr	17.27	may it *p* you to bless the house of your
Neh	2. 6	So it *p* the king to send me, and I set
Esth	2. 4	let the girl who *p* the king be queen
Job	6. 9	that it would *p* God to crush me, that
Ps	135. 6	Whatever the LORD *p* he does, in heaven
Prov	16. 7	When the ways of people *p* the LORD, he
Eccl	7.26	one who *p* God escapes her, but the
	8. 3	unpleasant, for he does whatever he *p*.
Isa	42.21	The LORD was *p*, for the sake of his
Jon	1.14	"*P*, O LORD, we pray, do not let us
Mic	6. 7	the LORD be *p* with thousands of rams,
Mal	1. 8	he be *p* with you or show you favor?
Mt	3.17	my Beloved, with whom I am well *p*."
	17. 5	my Beloved, with whom I am well *p*;"
Mk	1.11	Son, the Beloved; with you I am well *p*."
Lk	3.22	Son, the Beloved; with you I am well *p*."
Rom	8. 8	who are in the flesh cannot *p* God.
	15. 1	of the weak, and not to *p* ourselves.

1 Cor	7.32	affairs of the Lord, how to *p* the Lord;
	10. 5	God was not *p* with most of them, and
	10.33	just as I try to *p* everyone in everything
2 Cor	5. 9	or away, we make it our aim to *p* him.
Gal	1.10	Or am I trying to *p* people? If I were
	1.15	his grace, was *p* to reveal his Son
Col	1.19	all the fullness of God was *p* to dwell,
1 Thess	2. 4	speak, not to *p* mortals, but to *p* God
2 Tim	2. 4	aim is to *p* the enlisting officer.
Heb	11. 5	he was taken away that "he had *p* God."
1 Jn	3.22	his commandments and do what *p* him.

PLEASING

Eccl	12.10	The Teacher sought to find *p* words,
Jn	8.29	alone, for I always do what is *p* to him."
Eph	5.10	Try to find out what is *p* to the Lord.
Phil	4. 8	is just, whatever is pure, whatever is *p*,
	4.18	offering, a sacrifice acceptable and *p*
Col	1.10	lead lives worthy of the Lord, fully *p*
Heb	13.16	have, for such sacrifices are *p* to God.

PLEASURE (PLEASURES)

Job	22. 3	Is it any *p* to the Almighty if you are
Ps	16.11	fullness of joy; in your right hand are *p*
	147. 11	but the LORD takes *p* in those who fear
	149. 4	the LORD takes *p* in his people; he
Prov	21.17	Whoever loves *p* will suffer want;
Eccl	2. 1	"Come now, I will make a test of *p*;
	2.10	I kept my heart from no *p*, for my heart
	5. 4	for he has no *p* in fools. Fulfill what
Ezek	18.23	Have I any *p* in the death of the
	33.11	I have no *p* in the death of the wicked,
Hag	1. 8	the house, that I may take *p* in it and
Mal	1.10	on my altar in vain! I have no *p* in you,
Lk	8.14	choked by the cares and riches and *p* of
	12.32	it is your Father's good *p* to give you
Phil	2.13	both to will and to work for his good *p*.
2 Thess	2.12	but took *p* in unrighteousness will be
Heb	10. 6	and sin offerings you have no *p*.
	11.25	of God than to enjoy the fleeting *p*
Jas	5. 5	lived on the earth in luxury and in *p*;

PLEDGE

Lev	6. 2	neighbor in a matter of a deposit or a *p*,
Deut	24. 6	take a mill or an upper millstone in *p*,
	24.12	sleep in the garment given you as the *p*;
2 Chr	34.32	and in Benjamin *p* themselves
Prov	20.16	seize the *p* given as surety for
	27.13	seize the *p* given as surety for
Ezek	33.15	If the wicked restores the *p*, give back
Am	2. 8	every altar on garments taken in *p*;
Eph	1.14	Spirit; this is the *p* of our inheritance

PLENTY

Gen	41.29	There will come seven years of great *p*
Prov	12.11	Those who till their land will have *p* of
Phil	4.12	of having *p* and of being in need.

PLOT (PLOTTED)

Neh	4.15	enemies heard that their *p* was known
Isa	7. 5	son of Remaliah, has *p* evil against you
Nah	1. 9	Why do you *p* against the LORD? He will
Mt	22.15	Pharisees went and *p* to entrap him in

PLOW (PLOWED)

Deut	22.10	shall not *p* with an ox and a donkey
Job	4. 8	those who *p* iniquity and sow trouble
Ps	129. 3	The plowers *p* upon my back; they
Prov	20. 4	The lazy person does not *p* in season;
Isa	28.24	those who *p* for sowing *p* continually?
Jer	26.18	Zion shall be *p* as a field; Jerusalem
Hos	10.13	You have *p* wickedness, you have
Mic	3.12	of you Zion shall be *p* as a field;
Lk	9.62	puts a hand to the *p* and looks back
1 Cor	9.10	whoever plows should *p* in hope and

PLOWSHARES

Joel	3.10	Beat your *p* into swords, and your

Mic   4. 3 they shall beat their swords into *p*, and

PLUCK
Jer   12. 14 and I will *p* up the house of Judah from

PLUMB LINE
Am   7. 7 beside a wall built with a *p*, with a *p* in

PLUNDER (PLUNDERED PLUNDERING)
Gen   34.27 *p* the city, because their sister had been
Ex   3.22 and so you shall *p* the Egyptians."
          12.36 asked. And so they *p* the Egyptians.
Num   31.53 (The troops had all taken *p* for
2 Kings   7.16 out, and *p* the camp of the Arameans.
Isa   17.14 us, and the lot of those who *p* us.
Hab   2. 8 Because you have *p* many nations, all
Mt   12.29 strong man's house and *p* his property,
Heb   10.34 accepted the *p* of your possessions,

POLICE
Jn   7.46 The *p* answered, "Never has anyone

POMP
Ps   49.12 Mortals cannot abide in their *p*; they
Isa   14.11 Your *p* is brought down to Sheol, and

PONDER (PONDERED)
Ps   4. 4 not sin; *p* it on your beds, and be silent.
          48. 9 We *p* your steadfast love, O God, in the
Lk   2.19 treasured all these words and *p* them

POOL (POOLS)
Isa   42.15 the rivers into islands, and dry up the *p*.
Jn   5. 2 by the Sheep Gate there is a *p*,
           9. 7 him, "Go, wash in the *p* of Siloam"

POOR
Ex   23.11 so that the *p* of your people may eat;
          30.15 the *p* shall not give less, than the half
Lev   19.10 you shall leave them for the *p* and the
          23.22 you shall leave them for the *p* and for
1 Sam   2. 8 He raises up the *p* from the dust; he
2 Sam   12. 3 the *p* man had nothing but one little
Job   5.16 So the *p* have hope, and injustice shuts
          20.19 have crushed and abandoned the *p*,
          24. 4 off the road; the *p* of the earth all hide
          29.12 because I delivered the *p* who cried,
          31.16 If I have withheld anything that the *p*
Ps   9.18 forgotten, nor the hope of the *p* perish
          10. 2 arrogance the wicked persecute the *p* —
          22.26 The *p* shall eat and be satisfied; those
          34. 6 This *p* soul cried, and was heard by the
          40.17 As for me, I am *p* and needy, but the
          41. 1 Happy are those who consider the *p*;
          72. 4 May he defend the cause of the *p* of the
          86. 1 and answer me, for I am *p* and needy.
         109. 22 For I am *p* and needy, and my heart is
         113. 7 He raises the *p* from the dust, and lifts
Prov   10.15 the poverty of the *p* is their ruin.
          19. 1 Better the *p* walking in integrity than
          19. 7 If the *p* are hated even by their kin,
          22. 2 The rich and the *p* have this in
          29.14 If a king judges the *p* with equity, his
Isa   3.14 the spoil of the *p* is in your houses.
          11. 4 with righteousness he shall judge the *p*,
          25. 4 you have been a refuge to the *p*, a
Am   4. 1 who oppress the *p*, who crush the
           5.11 because you trample upon the *p* and
           8. 6 buying the *p* for silver and the needy for
Mt   5. 3 "Blessed are the *p* in spirit, for theirs is
          11. 5 the *p* have good news brought to them.
          19.21 and give the money to the *p*,
          26.11 you always have the *p* with you, but you
Mk   10.21 sell what you own, and give to the *p*,
          14. 5 denarii, and the money given to the *p*."
Lk   4.18 me to bring good news to the *p*.
           6.20 "Blessed are you who are *p*, for yours is
          14.13 when you give a banquet, invite the *p*,

Lk   16.20 at his gate lay a *p* man named Lazarus,
          18.22 distribute the money to the *p*, and you
          19. 8 possessions, Lord, I will give to the *p*;
Jn   12. 5 denarii and the money given to the *p*?"
          12. 8 You always have the *p* with you, but
2 Cor   6.10 rejoicing; as *p*, yet making many rich;
           8. 9 was rich, yet for your sake he became *p*,
           9. 9 "He scatters abroad, he gives to the *p*;
Gal   2.10 one thing, that we remember the *p*,
Jas   2. 5 God chosen the *p* in the world to be
Rev   3.17 you are wretched, pitiable, *p*, blind, and

POOREST
2 Kings 25.12 guard left some of the *p* people of the

PORTENT (PORTENTS)
Ps   71. 7 I have been as a *p* to many, but you are
Joel   2.30 I will show *p* in the heavens and on the
Acts   2.19 I will show *p* in the heaven above and
Rev   12. 1 A great *p* appeared in heaven: a woman
          15. 1 I saw another *p* in heaven, great and

PORTION (PORTIONS)
Deut   32. 9 LORD's own *p* is his people, Jacob his
1 Sam   1. 5 to Hannah he gave a double *p*, because
2 Sam   20. 1 "We have no *p* in David, no share in the
Neh   8.10 send *p* of them to those for whom
Job   20.29 This is the *p* of the wicked from God,
Ps   16. 5 The LORD is my chosen *p* and my cup;
         119. 57 The LORD is my *p*; I promise to keep
         142. 5 "You are my refuge, my *p* in the land of
Jer   10.16 like these is the LORD, the *p* of Jacob,
Lam   3.24 LORD is my *p*," says my soul, "therefore I

POSSESS (POSSESSING)
Num   14.24 he went, and his descendants shall *p* it.
          36. 8 continue to *p* their ancestral inheritance
Deut   33.23 of the LORD, *p* the west and the south.
Judg   11.24 Should you not *p* what your god
          18. 9 slow to go, but enter in and *p* the land.
Neh   9.15 you told them to go in to *p* the land
Ps   25.13 and their children shall *p* the land.
Isa   14. 2 Israel will *p* the nations as male and
          34.17 they shall *p* it forever, from generation
          54. 3 your descendants will *p* the nations and
          60.21 righteous; they shall *p* the land forever.
Ezek   33.26 wife; shall you then *p* the land?
          36.12 people Israel — and they shall *p* you,
Dan   7.18 kingdom and *p* the kingdom forever —
Zech   8.12 remnant of this people to *p* all these
2 Cor   6.10 as having nothing, yet *p* everything.

POSSESSION (POSSESSIONS)
Ex   19. 5 you shall be my treasured *p* out of all
Lev   25.34 be sold; for that is their *p* for all time.
Num   32.22 this land shall be your *p* before the
Deut   1. 8 go in and take of the land that I
           1.39 I will give it, and they shall take *p* of it.
           4.20 to become a people of his very own *p*,
          14. 2 earth to be his people, his treasured *p*.
          15. 4 your God is giving you as a *p* to occupy
          21.16 the day when he wills his *p* to his sons,
Josh   1.11 to go in to take *p* of the land that the
          18. 3 slack about going in and taking *p* of the
2 Chr   20.11 us by coming to drive us out of your *p*
Ps   78.55 he apportioned them for a *p* and settled
         135. 4 Jacob for himself, Israel as his own *p*.
Eccl   2. 7 I had also great *p* of herds and flocks,
Jer   32.23 and they entered and took *p* of it.
Ob   17 house of Jacob shall take *p* of those
Mal   3.17 my special *p* on the day when I act, and
Mt   19.22 went away grieving; for he had many *p*.
          24.47 will put that one in charge of all his *p*.
Lk   12.15 does not consist in the abundance of *p*."

POSSIBLE
Mt   19.26 impossible, but for God all things are *p*."
Mk   10.27 not for God; for God all things are *p*."

Mk	14.35	prayed that, if it were *p*, the hour might
Lk	18.27	is impossible for mortals is *p* for God."

POSTERITY

Ps	22.30	*P* shall serve him; future generations
	109. 13	May his *p* be cut off; may his name be

POT (POTS)

2 Kings	4.40	"O man of God, there is death in the *p*!"
Jer	1. 13	"I see a boiling *p*, tilted away from the
Rev	2.27	iron rod, as when clay *p* are shattered

POTTER (POTTER'S)

Ps	2. 9	and dash them in pieces like a *p* vessel."
Isa	30.14	is like that of a *p* vessel that is smashed
	41.25	rulers as mortar, as the *p* treads clay.
	45. 9	your Maker, earthen vessels with the *p*!
Jer	18. 2	"Come, go down to the *p* house, and
	18. 6	like the clay in the *p* hand, so are you
	19. 1	the LORD: Go and buy a *p* earthenware
Lam	4. 2	as earthen pots, the work of a *p* hands!
Mt	27. 7	they used them to buy the *p* field as a
Rom	9.21	Has the *p* no right over the clay, to

POUR (POURED POURING)

1 Sam	1.15	I have been *p* out my soul before the
	7. 6	drew water and *p* it out before the LORD,
2 Sam	23.16	not drink of it; he *p* it out to the LORD,
1 Chr	11.18	not drink of it; he *p* it out to the LORD,
Ps	42. 4	things I remember, as I *p* out my soul:
Isa	32.15	until a spirit from on high is *p* out on
	44. 3	*p* water on the thirsty land, and streams
Jer	6.11	*P* it out on the children in the street,
	7.20	My anger and my wrath will be *p* out on
	10.25	*P* out your wrath on the nations that do
Ezek	7. 8	now I will *p* out my wrath upon you;
Hos	5.10	them I will *p* out my wrath like water.
Joel	2.28	I will *p* out my spirit on all flesh;
Zech	12.10	I will *p* out a spirit of compassion and
Mt	26. 7	ointment, and she *p* it on his head
Mk	14. 3	the jar and *p* the ointment on his head.
Acts	2.17	I will *p* out my Spirit upon all flesh,
Rom	5. 5	God's love been *p* into our hearts

POVERTY

Prov	6.11	and *p* will come upon you like a robber,
	13.18	*P* and disgrace are for the one who
	24.34	and *p* will come upon you like a robber,
	28.19	worthless pursuits will have plenty of *p*.
Mk	12.44	but she out of her *p* has put in
2 Cor	8. 2	joy and their extreme *p* have overflowed
Rev	2. 9	I know your affliction and your *p*, even

POWER

Lev	26.37	you shall have no *p* to stand against
Num	11.23	"Is the LORD's *p* limited? Now you shall
1 Chr	29.11	Yours, O LORD, are the greatness, the *p*,
2 Chr	25. 8	for God has *p* to help or to overthrow."
Job	23. 6	with me in the greatness of his *p*?
	26.14	But the thunder of his *p* who can
Ps	21.13	strength! We will sing and praise your *p*.
	49.15	ransom my soul from the *p* of Sheol,
	66. 3	of your great *p*, your enemies cringe
	67. 2	earth, your saving *p* among all nations.
	68.34	Ascribe to God, whose majesty is over
	145. 11	of your kingdom, and tell of your *p*,
Prov	3.27	it is due, when it is in your *p* to do
Eccl	8. 8	No one has *p* over the wind to restrain
Isa	40.26	great in strength, mighty in *p*, not one
	40.29	He gives *p* to the faint, and strengthens
Jer	16.21	time I am going to teach them my *p*
	32.17	heavens and the earth by your great *p*
Dan	8.24	He shall grow strong in *p*, shall cause
Mic	3. 8	as for me, I am filled with *p*, with the
Zech	4. 6	by might, nor by *p*, but by my spirit,
Mt	6.13n	and the *p* and the glory are yours
	22.29	neither the scriptures nor the *p* of God.
Mk	5.30	aware that *p* had gone forth from him,

Mk	9. 1	the kingdom of God has come with *p*."
	9.39	for no one who does a deed of *p* in my
	12.24	neither the scriptures nor the *p* of God?
	14.62	of Man seated at the right hand of *P*,'
Lk	1.35	and the *p* of the Most High will
	5.17	and the *p* of the Lord was with him to
	6.19	touch him, for *p* came out of him and
	8.46	I noticed that *p* had gone out from me."
	19.12	country to get royal *p* for himself
	21.27	coming in a cloud' with *p* and great
	22.53	this is your hour, and the *p* of darkness!"
	22.69	at the right hand of the *p* of God."
	24.49	have been clothed with *p* from on high
Jn	10.18	I have *p* to lay it down, and I have *p* to
	19.10	that I have *p* to release you, and *p* to
Acts	1. 8	you will receive *p* when the Holy Spirit
	2.11	them speaking about God's deeds of *p*."
	3.12	as though by our own *p* or piety we
	4.33	with great *p* the apostles gave their
	6. 8	Stephen, full of grace and *p*, did great
	8.10	"This man is the *p* of God that is called
	26.18	from the *p* of Satan to God, so they
Rom	1.16	the gospel; it is the *p* of God for
	15.13	you may abound in hope by the *p* of the
	15.19	wonders, by the *p* of the Spirit of God,
1 Cor	1.18	who are being saved it is the *p* of God.
	2. 4	with a demonstration of Spirit and of *p*,
	2. 5	on human wisdom but on the *p* of God.
	5. 4	is present with the *p* of our Lord Jesus,
	15.24	every ruler and every authority and *p*.
	15.43	It is sown in weakness, it is raised in *p*.
2 Cor	6. 7	truthful speech, and the *p* of God; with
	12. 9	so that the *p* of Christ may dwell in me.
	12. 9	you, for *p* is made perfect in weakness."
	13. 4	in weakness, but lives by the *p* of God.
Eph	1.19	greatness of his *p* in us who believe,
	3.20	to him who by the *p* at work within us
Phil	3.10	Christ and the *p* of his resurrection
1 Thess	1. 5	not in word only, but also in *p* and in
Heb	2.14	destroy the one who has the *p* of death,
1 Pet	1. 5	are being protected by the *p* of God
2 Pet	1. 3	His divine *p* has given us everything
Rev	11.17	for you have taken your great *p* and
	17.13	These are united in yielding their *p* and

POWERFUL

Lk	3.16	one who is more *p* than I is coming; I

PRAISE (PRAISES) (n)

Deut	10.21	He is your *p*; he is your God, who has
1 Chr	16. 7	David first appointed the singing of *p* to
Ps	47. 6	Sing *p* to God, sing *p*; sing *p* to our
	48.10	God, like your *p*, reaches to the ends of
	61. 8	So I will always sing *p* to your name, as
	65. 1	*P* is due to you, O God, in Zion; and to
	71. 8	My mouth is filled with your *p*, and
	119.108	Accept my offerings of *p*, O LORD, and
Rom	14.11	to me, and every tongue shall give *p*
Jas	5.13	cheerful? They should sing songs of *p*.

PRAISE (PRAISED PRAISING) (v)

1 Chr	16.25	great is the LORD, and greatly to be *p*;
	29.13	we give thanks to you and *p* your
Ps	33. 2	*P* the LORD with the lyre; make melody
	71.22	I will also *p* you with the harp for your
	76.10	Human wrath serves only to *p* you,
	113. 1	*P* the LORD! *P*, O servants of the LORD; *p*
	119. 62	At midnight I rise to *p* you, because of
	147. 12	*P* the LORD, O Jerusalem! *P* your God, O
	148. 2	*P* him, all his angels; *p* him, all his
	150. 6	Let everything that breathes *p* the LORD!
Prov	27. 2	Let another *p* you, and not your own
Isa	38.18	cannot thank you, death cannot *p* you;
Dan	4.34	I blessed the Most High, and *p* and
Lk	1.64	freed, and he began to speak, *p* God.
	2.28	took him in his arms and *p* God,
Acts	11.18	they were silenced. And they *p* God,

Acts	19.17	and the name of the Lord Jesus was *p*.
Rom	15.11	"*P* the Lord, all you Gentiles, and let all

PRAY

Ex	8. 8	"*P* to the LORD to take away the frogs
1 Sam	12.19	"*P* to the LORD your God for your
	12.23	the LORD by ceasing to *p* for you;
2 Sam	7.27	servant has found courage to *p* this
	15.31	David said, "O LORD, I *p* you, turn the
	24.17	Let your hand, I *p*, be against me and
1 Kings	8.33	confess your name, *p* and plead with
1 Chr	17.25	has found it possible to *p* before you.
Job	42. 8	Job shall *p* for you, for I will accept his
Ps	122. 6	*P* for the peace of Jerusalem: "May they
Isa	16.12	his sanctuary to *p*, he will not prevail.
Jer	7.16	As for you, do not *p* for this people, do
	11.14	As for you, do not *p* for this people, or
	29.12	come and *p* to me, and I will hear you.
	37. 3	Jeremiah saying, "*P* for us to the LORD
Dan	6.10	three times a day to *p* to his God and
Mt	5.44	and *p* for those who persecute you,
	6. 5	they love to stand and *p* in the
	6. 9	"*P* then in this way: Our Father in
	14.23	up into the mountains by himself to *p*.
	19.13	he might lay his hands on them and *p*,
	24.20	*P* that your flight may not be in winter
	26.36	"Sit here while I go over there and *p*."
	26.41	Stay awake and *p* that you may not
Mk	6.46	he went up on the mountain to *p*.
	13.18	*P* that it may not be in winter.
	13.33n	Beware, keep alert and *p*; for you do
	14.32	said to his disciples, "Sit here while I *p*."
	14.38	Keep aware and *p* that you may not
Lk	5.16	withdraw to deserted places and *p*.
	5.33	the Pharisees, frequently fast and *p*, but
	6.12	he went out to the mountain to *p*; and
	6.28	curse you, *p* for those who abuse you.
	9.28	and went up on the mountain to *p*.
	11. 1	"Lord, teach us to *p*, as John taught his
	18. 1	them a parable about their need to *p*
Acts	8.24	Simon answered, "*P* for me to the Lord,
Rom	8.26	we do not know how to *p* as we ought,
1 Cor	11.13	to *p* to God with her head unveiled?
	14.15	spirit, but I will *p* with the mind also;
2 Cor	13. 7	*p* to God that you may not do anything
Eph	6.18	*P* in the Spirit at all times in every
1 Thess	3.10	Night and day we *p* most earnestly that
	5.17	Rejoice always, *p* without ceasing, give
2 Thess	1.11	To this end we always *p* for you, asking
1 Tim	2. 8	that in every place the men should *p*,
Heb	13.18	*P* for us; we are sure that we have a
Jas	5.13	among you suffering? They should *p*.
Jude	20	most holy faith; *p* in the Holy Spirit;

PRAYS (PRAYED PRAYING)

Gen	20.17	Then Abraham *p* to God; and God
Num	11. 2	Moses *p* to the LORD, and the fire
Deut	9.26	I *p* to the LORD and said, "Lord GOD, do
1 Sam	1.10	was deeply distressed and *p* to the LORD,
	1.27	For this child I *p*; and the LORD granted
	8. 6	to govern us." And Samuel *p* to the LORD,
2 Kings	4.33	on the two of them, and *p* to the LORD.
	6.17	Elisha *p*: "O LORD, please open his eyes
	19.15	Hezekiah *p* before the LORD, and said,
	20. 2	turned his face to the wall and *p* to the
2 Chr	32.20	the prophet Isaiah son of Amoz *p*
	33.13	He *p* to him, and God received his
Neh	1. 4	for days, fasting and *p* before the God
	4. 9	we *p* to our God, and set a guard as a
Job	42.10	the fortunes of Job, when he had *p* for
	33.26	Then he *p* to God, and is accepted by
Ps	35.13	I *p* with head bowed on my bosom,
Isa	37.15	And Hezekiah *p* to the LORD, saying: "O
	38. 2	turned his face to the wall, and *p*
	45.20	and keep *p* to a god that cannot save.
Dan	6. 7	whoever *p* to anyone, divine or human,
Jon	2. 1	Then Jonah *p* to the LORD his God from

Mt	26.44	he went away and *p* for the third time,
Mk	1.35	out to a deserted place, and there he *p*.
Lk	1.10	assembly of people was *p* outside.
	3.21	been baptized and was *p*, the heaven
	9.18	when Jesus was *p* alone, with only the
	18.11	standing by himself, was *p* thus,
	22.41	knelt down, and *p*, "Father, if you are
Acts	1.24	they *p* and said, "Lord, you know
	4.31	When they had *p*, the place in which
	8.15	The two went down and *p* for them that
	9.11	named Saul. At this moment he is *p*,
	9.40	outside, and then he knelt down and *p*.
	10.30	I was *p* in my house when suddenly a
	12. 5	kept in prison; the church *p* fervently
	12.12	where many had gathered and were *p*.
	13. 3	after fasting and *p* they laid their hands
	16.25	Paul and Silas were *p* and singing
	21. 5	we knelt down on the beach and *p*
	28. 8	Paul visited him and cured him by *p*
Col	1. 9	we have not ceased *p* for you and

PRAYER

Gen	25.21	LORD granted his *p*, and his wife
2 Chr	6.19	Regard your servant's *p* and his plea, O
	30.27	heard; their *p* came to his holy dwelling
Ps	6. 9	my supplication; the LORD accepts my *p*.
	17. 1	my cry; give ear to my *p* from lips free
	32. 6	let all who are faithful offer *p* to you; at
	42. 8	night his song is with me, a *p* to the
	65. 2	O you who answer *p*! To you all flesh
	72.15	May *p* be made for him continually and
	102. 17	He will regard the *p* of the destitute,
	109. 4	they accuse me, even as I make *p* for
	141. 2	Let my *p* be counted as incense before
Prov	15. 8	but the *p* of the upright is his delight.
	15.29	but he hears the *p* of the righteous.
Isa	26.16	they sought you, they poured out a *p*
	37. 4	therefore lift up your *p* for the remnant
	56. 7	be called a house of *p* for all peoples.
Lam	3. 8	call and cry for help, he shuts out my *p*;
	3.44	a cloud so that no *p* can pass through.
Dan	9. 3	to the Lord God, to seek an answer by *p*
Mt	17.21n	kind does not come out except by *p*
	21.13	My house shall be called a house of *p*';
	21.22	Whatever you ask for in *p* with faith,
Mk	9.29	kind can come out only through *p*."
	11.17	'My house shall be called a house of *p*
	11.24	whatever you ask for in *p*, believe that
Lk	1.13	Zechariah, for your *p* has been heard.
	19.46	'My house shall be a house of *p*'; but
Acts	1.14	constantly devoting themselves to *p*,
	3. 1	temple at the hour of *p*, three o'clock in
	6. 4	for our part, will devote ourselves to *p*
	14.23	with *p* and fasting, they entrusted them
	16.13	we supposed there was a place of *p*;
Rom	12.12	be patient in suffering, persevere in *p*
	15.30	Spirit, to join me in earnest *p* to God
1 Cor	7. 5	for a set time, to devote yourselves to *p*,
Phil	4. 6	in everything by *p* and supplication with
Col	4. 2	Devote yourselves to *p*, keeping alert in
Jas	5.16	The *p* of the righteous is powerful and

PRAYERS

Mt	23.14n	sake of appearance you make long *p*;
Mk	12.40	for the sake of appearance say long *p*.
Lk	20.47	for the sake of appearance say long *p*.
Acts	2.42	to the breaking of bread and the *p*.
	10. 4	"Your *p* and your alms have ascended as
Rom	1. 9	ceasing I remember you always in my *p*,
2 Cor	1.11	You also join in helping us by your *p*,
Phil	1. 4	joy in every one of my *p* for all of you,
Col	4.12	always wrestling in his *p* on your behalf,
1 Tim	2. 1	I urge that supplications, *p*,
	5. 5	in supplications and *p* night and day;
2 Tim	1. 3	I remember you constantly in my *p*
Heb	5. 7	Jesus offered up *p* and supplications,
1 Pet	3. 7	life—so that nothing may hinder your *p*.

1 Pet   4. 7 yourselves for the sake of your *p*.
Rev   5. 8 incense, which are the *p* of the saints.

PREACH (PREACHING)

Mic   2. 6 "Do not *p*"—thus they *p*— "one should
Rom   2.21 While you *p* against stealing, do you
1 Tim   5.17 those who labor in *p* and teaching;

PREACHER

Mic   2.11 a one would be the *p* for this people!

PRECEPT (PRECEPTS)

Ps   19. 8 the *p* of the LORD are right, rejoicing the
      111. 7 and just; all his *p* are trustworthy.
      119. 63 who fear you, of those who keep your *p*.
      119. 93 I will never forget your *p*, for by them
Prov   4. 2 for I give you good *p*; do not forsake my
Isa   28.10 For it is *p* upon *p*, *p* upon *p*, line upon

PRECIOUS

Job   28.10 rocks and their eyes see every *p* thing.
Ps   36. 7 How *p* is your steadfast love, O God! All
     72.14 life; and *p* is their blood in his sight.
    116. 15 *P* in the sight of the LORD is the death
    133. 2 like the *p* oil on the head, running
Prov   3.15 She is more *p* than jewels, and nothing
    20.15 informed by knowledge are a *p* jewel.
    31.10 can find? She is far more *p* than jewels.
Isa   43. 4 you are *p* in my sight, and honored, and
1 Pet   1. 7 of your faith—being more *p* than gold
      2. 6 a stone, a cornerstone chosen and *p*;
2 Pet   1. 1 who have received a faith as *p* as ours

PREDESTINED

Acts   4.28 hand and your plan had *p* to take place
Rom   8.30 those whom he *p* he also called; and

PREDICTED

2 Kings 23.17 and *p* these things that you have done
Rom   9.29 And as Isaiah *p*, "If the Lord of hosts

PREDICTION

Isa   44.26 and fulfills the *p* of his messengers;

PREGNANT

Ex   21.22 injure a *p* woman so that there is a
Mt   24.19 Woe to those who are *p* and to those
Rev   12. 2 she was *p* and was crying out in

PREPARATION (PREPARATIONS)

2 Chr   35. 4 Make *p* by your ancestral houses by
Mt   26.17 "Where do you want us to make *p* for
Mk   14.12 and make *p* for you to eat the Passover?"
    15.42 since it was the day of *P*, that is, the
Lk   23.54 It was the day of *P*, and the sabbath

PREPARE (PREPARED PREPARES)

Neh   8.10 to those for whom nothing is *p*, for this
Ps   132. 17 David; I have *p* a lamp for my anointed
    147. 8 with clouds, *p* rain for the earth,
Isa   30.33 For his burning place has long been *p*;
    40. 3 "In the wilderness *p* the way of the
    62.10 the gates, *p* the way for the people;
Am   4.12 to you, *p* to meet your God, O Israel!"
Zeph   1. 7 The LORD has a sacrifice, he has
Mt   20.23 for whom it has been *p* by my Father."
Mk   1. 3 '*P* the way of the Lord, make his paths
    10.40 it is for those for whom it has been *p*."
Lk   1.17 to make ready a people *p* for the Lord."
    1.76 will go before the Lord to *p* his ways,
    2.31 which you have *p* in the presence of all
    3. 4 '*P* the way of the Lord, make his paths
    7.27 of you, who will *p* your way before you."
    12.47 but did not *p* himself or do what was
Jn   14. 3 And if I go and *p* a place for you, I will
Rom   9.23 which he has *p* beforehand for glory—
1 Cor   2. 9 what God has *p* for those who love
Philem   22 —*p* a guest room for me, for I am
Heb   10. 5 desired, but a body you have *p* for me;

PRESENCE

Gen   4.16 Cain went away from the *p* of the LORD,
Ex   33.15 "If your *p* will not go, do not carry us
Ps   16.11 in your *p* there is fullness of joy; in your
    114. 7 Tremble, O earth at the *p* of the LORD,
Jon   1.10 he was fleeing from the *p* of the LORD,
Lk   1.19 I am Gabriel. I stand in the *p* of God,
Acts   10.33 all of us are here in the *p* of God to
Heb   9.24 now to appear in the *p* of God on our
Jude   24 you stand without blemish before the *p*

PRESENT (PRESENTED)

Gen   32.13 him he took a *p* for his brother Esau,
    47. 2 took five men and *p* them to Pharaoh.
Num   7.12 The one who *p* his offering the first day
Josh   15.19 "Give me a *p*; since you have set me in
2 Kings 16. 8 and sent a *p* to the king of Assyria.
Jer   40. 5 gave him an allowance of food and a *p*,
Lk   2.22 up to Jerusalem to *p* him to the Lord
Rom   6.19 now *p* your members as slaves to
    12. 1 of God, to *p* your bodies as a living
2 Cor   11. 2 husband, to *p* you as a chaste virgin to
Eph   5.27 so as to *p* the church to himself in
Col   1.22 to *p* you holy and blameless and
    1.28 we may *p* everyone mature in Christ.

PRESERVE (PRESERVED PRESERVES PRESERVING)

Gen   45. 5 for God sent me before you to *p* life.
1 Sam   30.23 he has *p* us and handed over to us the
Ps   25.21 May integrity and uprightness *p* me, for
    32. 7 you *p* me from trouble; you surround
    64. 1 *p* my life from the dread enemy,
    119.149 voice; O LORD, in your justice *p* my life.
    138. 7 you *p* me against the wrath of my
Prov   2. 8 and *p* the way of his faithful ones.
    16.17 those who guard their way *p* their lives.
    20.28 Loyalty and faithfulness *p* the king, and

PRESS (PRESSED)

Ruth   1.16 "Do not *p* me to leave you or to turn
Hos   6. 3 us know, let us *p* on to know the LORD;
Phil   1.23 I am hard *p* between the two: my desire
    3.14 I *p* on toward the goal for the prize of

PRESSURE

2 Cor   8.13 be relief for others and *p* on you,

PREVAILED

Gen   32.28 with God and with humans, and have *p*."
Ex   17.11 Moses held up his hand, Israel *p*;
Hos   12. 4 strove with the angel and *p*, he wept

PREVENT (PREVENTED)

Mt   3.14 John would have *p* him, saying, "I need
Acts   8.37 What is to *p* me from being baptized?"

PRICE

Gen   23.13 I will give the *p* of the field; accept it
Isa   55. 1 and milk without money and without *p*.
1 Cor   6.20 For you were bought with a *p*; therefore
    7.23 You were bought with a *p*; do not

PRIDE

Job   33.17 their deeds, and keep them from *p*,
Ps   20. 7 our *p* is in the name of the LORD our
Prov   8.13 *P* and arrogance and the way of evil and
    11. 2 When *p* comes, then comes disgrace;
    16.18 *P* goes before destruction, and a
Isa   9. 9 but in *p* and arrogance of heart they
Jer   48.29 We have heard of the *p* of Moab— he is
Ezek   7.10 The rod has blossomed, *p* has budded.
Hos   5. 5 Israel's *p* testifies against him; Ephraim
Zeph   2.10 shall be their lot in return for their *p*,
Mk   7.22 licentiousness, envy, slander, *p*, folly.

PRIEST (PRIESTS)

Gen   14.18 King Melchizedek . . . was *p* of God

Gen	47.26 The land of the *p* alone did not become
Ex	19.22 Even the *p* who approach the LORD must
1 Sam	2.35 I will raise up for myself a faithful *p*,
	22.17 "Turn and kill the *p* of the LORD,
2 Kings	23. 5 He deposed the idolatrous *p* whom the
2 Chr	11.15 appointed his own *p* for the high places,
	13. 9 you not driven out the *p* of the LORD,
Ps	110. 4 "You are a *p* forever according to the
Isa	24. 2 be, as with the people, so with the *p*;
	61. 6 you shall be called *p* of the LORD, you
Lam	4.13 and the iniquities of her *p*, who shed
Ezek	44.15 levitical *p*, the descendants of Zadok,
Joel	1.13 Put on sackcloth and lament, you *p*,
Zech	6.13 There shall be a *p* by his throne, with
Mal	1. 6 to you, O *p*, who despise my name.
Lk	1. 8 when he was serving as *p* before God
	5.14 he said, "and show yourself to the *p*,
	6. 4 which it is not lawful for any but the *p*
Acts	6. 7 a great many of the *p* became obedient
Heb	10.21 have a great *p* over the house of God,
Rev	1. 6 us to be a kingdom, *p* serving his God
	5.10 made them to be a kingdom and *p*

PRIESTHOOD

Num	16.10 with you; yet you seek the *p* as well!
	18. 7 I give your *p* as a gift; any outsider who
Heb	7.11 attainable through the levitical *p*,
	7.24 he holds his *p* permanently, because he
1 Pet	2. 5 a holy *p*, to offer spiritual sacrifices

PRIESTLY

Ex	19. 6 you shall be for me a *p* kingdom and a

PRINCE (PRINCES)

Deut	33.16 the brow of the *p* among his brothers.
1 Sam	25.30 and has appointed you *p* over Israel,
2 Sam	7. 8 the sheep to be *p* over my people
Isa	1.23 Your *p* are rebels and companions of
	9. 6 God, Everlasting Father, *P* of Peace.
Ezek	28. 2 say to the *p* of Tyre, Thus says the Lord
Dan	8.25 even rise up against the *P* of princes.

PRISON

Gen	39.20 took him and put him into the *p*,
	42.16 while the rest of you remain in *p*, in
2 Kings	25.27 King Jehoiachin of Judah from *p*;
Ps	142. 7 Bring me out of *p*, so that I may give
Eccl	4.14 One can indeed come out of *p* to reign,
Jer	52.11 put him in *p* until the day of his death.
Mt	5.25 to the guard, and you be thrown in *p*,
	14. 3 John, bound him, and put him in *p*
	18.30 threw him into *p* until he would pay the
	25.36 of me, I was in *p* and you visited me.'
Mk	6.17 John, bound him, and put him in *p*
Lk	3.20 to them all by shutting up John in *p*.
Acts	12. 5 While Peter was kept in *p*, the church
	16.23 they threw them into *p* and ordered the
	16.40 After leaving the *p*, they went to Lydia's
	26.10 only locked up many of the saints in *p*,
Heb	10.34 compassion for those who were in *p*,
1 Pet	3.19 made a proclamation to the spirits in *p*,
Rev	2.10 is about to throw some of you into *p*

PRISONER (PRISONERS)

Ps	79.11 Let the groans of the *p* come before
	102. 20 to hear the groans of the *p*, to set free
	107. 10 and in gloom, *p* in misery and in irons,
	146. 7 to the hungry. The LORD sets the *p* free;
Isa	42. 7 to bring out the *p* from the dungeon,
Zech	9.12 Return to your stronghold, O *p* of hope;
Mt	27.16 they had a notorious *p*, called Jesus
Mk	15. 6 festival he used to release a *p* for them,
Acts	27.42 The soldiers plan was to kill the *p*, so
Eph	3. 1 that I, Paul, am a *p* for Christ Jesus
	4. 1 I therefore, the *p* for the Lord, beg you
Philem	1 Paul, a *p* of Christ Jesus, and Timothy

PROCEED

Deut	2.24 "*P* on your journey and cross the Wadi
Josh	1. 2 Now *p* to cross the Jordan, you and all

PROCLAIM (PROCLAIMED PROCLAIMING)

Lev	25.10 you shall *p* liberty throughout the land
Deut	32. 3 I will *p* the name of the LORD; ascribe
2 Sam	1.20 it not in Gath, *p* it not in the streets
Ps	22.31 and *p* his deliverance to a people yet
Prov	20. 6 Many *p* themselves loyal, but who can
Isa	62.11 The LORD has *p* to the end of the earth:
Jer	3.12 Go, and *p* these words toward the north
	7. 2 the LORD's house, and *p* there this word,
	31. 7 *p*, give praise, and say, "Save, O LORD,
Joel	3. 9 *P* this among the nations: Prepare war,
Jon	3. 2 go to Nineveh, that great city, and *p* to
Mt	3. 1 appeared in the wilderness of Judea, *p*,
	9.35 *p* the good news of the kingdom, and
	10.27 hear whispered, *p* from the housetops.
	26.13 wherever this good news is *p* in the
Mk	1. 7 He *p*, "The one who is more powerful
	1.45 he went out and began to *p* it freely,
	3.14 to be sent out to *p* the message.
	5.20 away and began to *p* in the Decapolis
	6.12 went out and *p* that all should repent
	13.10 the good news must first be *p* to all
	16.15 *p* the good news to the whole creation.
Lk	3. 3 around the Jordan, *p* a baptism of
	4.43 "I must *p* the good news of the kingdom
	8.39 he went away, *p* throughout the city
	9. 2 he sent them out to *p* the kingdom of
	24.47 forgiveness of sins is to be *p* in his
Acts	4. 2 *p* that in Jesus there is the resurrection
	8. 4 went from place to place, *p* the word.
	8.35 scripture, he *p* to him the good news
	9.20 immediately he began to *p* Jesus in the
	13. 5 at Salamis, they *p* the word of God in
	16.10 God had called us to *p* the good news
	17.23 you worship as unknown, this I *p*
	18. 5 Paul was occupied with *p* the word,
	28.31 *p* the kingdom of God and teaching
Rom	10.14 they to hear without someone to *p* him?
	10.15 are they to *p* him unless they are sent?
	15.20 it my ambition to *p* the good news,
1 Cor	1.17 send me to baptize but to *p* the gospel,
	2. 1 not come *p* the mystery of God to you
	9.14 those who *p* the gospel should get their
	11.26 drink the cup, you *p* the Lord's death
2 Cor	4. 5 we do not *p* ourselves; we *p* Jesus
Gal	1.23 formerly was persecuting us is now *p*
Phil	1.15 Some *p* Christ from envy and rivalry,
	1.17 others *p* Christ out of selfish ambition,
1 Thess	2. 9 any of you while we *p* to you the gospel
2 Tim	4. 2 I urge you: *p* the message; be persistent

PROCLAMATION

Jon	3. 7 he had a *p* made in Nineveh: "By the
1 Cor	2. 4 and my *p* were not with plausible words
1 Pet	3.19 and made a *p* to the spirits in prison,

PRODUCE

Mt	21.34 slaves to the tenants to collect his *p*.

PROFANE (PROFANED PROFANES)

Ex	31.14 everyone who *p* it shall be put to death;
Lev	18.21 and so *p* the name of your God:
	19.29 Do not *p* your daughter by making her a
Ezek	22.26 sabbaths, so that I am *p* among them.
	28.18 of your trade, you *p* your sanctuaries;
	39. 7 I will not let my holy name be *p* any
Dan	11.31 occupy and *p* the temple and fortress,
Acts	10.15 has made clean, you must not call *p*."

PROFIT (PROFITS)

Job	34. 9 said, 'It *p* one nothing to take delight
Ps	30. 9 "What *p* is there in my death, if I go
Prov	14.23 In all toil there is *p*, but mere talk leads

Isa   30. 5 through a people that cannot *p* them,
Mt   16.26 what will it *p* them if they gain the
Mk   8.36 what will it *p* them to gain the whole

PROLIFIC

Ex   1. 7 But the Israelites were fruitful and *p*;

PROMINENT

1 Chr   5. 2 though Judah became *p* among his

PROMISE (PROMISES) (n)

2 Chr   1. 9 God, let your *p* to my father David now
Ps   77. 8 Are his *p* at an end for all time?
      106. 24 pleasant land, having no faith in his *p*.
      119. 82 My eyes fail with watching for your *p*; I
Acts   1. 4 wait there for the *p* of the Father. "This,"
      2.39 *p* is for you, for your children, and for
      7.17 drew near for the fulfillment of the *p*
      13.34 will give you the holy *p* given to David.'
      26. 6 on trial on account of my hope in the *p*
Rom   4.13 the *p* that he would inherit the world
      4.16 that the *p* may rest on grace and be
      9. 8 but the children of the *p* are counted as
      15. 8 confirm the *p* given to the patriarchs,
2 Cor   1.20 him every one of the *p* of God is a "Yes."
      7. 1 Since we have these *p*, beloved, let us
Gal   3.16 the *p* were made to Abraham and to his
      3.21 the law then opposed to the *p* of God?
      4.23 free woman, was born through the *p*.
      4.28 friends, are children of the *p*, like Isaac.
Eph   3. 6 and sharers in the *p* in Christ Jesus
Heb   4. 1 while the *p* of entering his rest is still
      6.12 faith and patience inherit the *p*.
      8. 6 has been enacted through better *p*.
2 Pet   1. 4 his precious and very great *p*, so that
      3. 4 "Where is the *p* of his coming? For ever
      3. 9 Lord is not slow about his *p*, as some

PROMISE (PROMISED) (v)

Deut   1.11 more and bless you, as he has *p* you!
      12.20 enlarges your territory, as he has *p* you,
      19. 8 will give you all the land that he *p* your
Josh   23. 5 their land, as the LORD your God *p* you.
2 Sam   7.28 you have *p* this good thing to your
1 Kings   5.12 gave Solomon wisdom, as he *p* him.
      8.56 people Israel according to all that he *p*;
2 Chr   6.10 on the throne of Israel, as the LORD *p*,
      32.42 them all the good fortune that I now *p*
Lk   24.49 I am sending you what my Father *p*; so
Acts   7. 5 but *p* to give it to him as his possession
      13.32 news that what God *p* to our ancestors
Rom   1. 2 which he *p* beforehand through his
      4.21 that God was able to do what he *p*.
Titus   1. 2 life that God, who never lies, *p* before
Heb   9.15 may receive the *p* eternal inheritance,
      10.36 of God, you may receive what was *p*.
      11.39 did not receive what was *p*, since God
Jas   1.12 the Lord has *p* to those who love him.
2 Pet   2.19 They *p* them freedom, but they

PRONOUNCED

Jer   44.26 my name shall no more be *p* on the lips

PROOF (PROOFS)

Ps   95. 9 tested me, and put me to the *p*,
Acts   1. 3 alive to them by many convincing *p*,
2 Cor   8.24 show them the *p* of your love and of our
      13. 3 desire *p* that Christ is speaking in me.

PROPHECY

Prov   29.18 Where there is no *p*, the people cast off
Lk   1.67 with the Holy Spirit and spoke this *p*:
Rom   12. 6 given to us: *p*, in proportion to faith;
1 Cor   12.10 the working of miracles, to another *p*,
Rev   22. 7 keeps the words of the *p* of this book.

PROPHESY (PROPHESIED PROPHESIES PROPHESYING)

Num   11.25 the spirit rested upon them, they *p*.
1 Chr   25. 1 who should *p* with lyres, harps, and
2 Chr   18. 7 him, for he never *p* anything favorable
Isa   30.10 speak to us smooth things, *p* illusions,
Jer   5.31 the prophets *p* falsely, and the priests
      11.21 "You shall not *p* in the name of the
      14.14 The prophets are *p* lies in my name; I
      19.14 where the LORD had sent him to *p*,
      23.13 they *p* by Baal and led my people Israel
      23.21 ran; I did not speak to them, yet they *p*.
      23.32 I am against those who *p* lying dreams,
      25.30 "You, therefore, shall *p* against them all
      26.18 "Micah of Moresheth, who *p* during the
      29. 9 for it is a lie that they are *p* to you in
      32. 3 "Why do you *p* and say, Thus says the
Ezek   4. 7 your arm bared you shall *p* against it.
      11. 4 Therefore *p* against them, *p*, O mortal."
      13. 2 *p* against the prophets of Israel, who are
      21. 2 sanctuaries; *p* against the land of Israel
      36. 1 *p* to the mountains of Israel, and say: O
      37. 4 "*P* to these bones, and say to them: O
      38.14 mortal, *p*, and say to Gog, Thus says the
Am   2.12 the prophets, saying, "You shall not *p*."
      7.12 of Judah, earn your bread there, and *p*
Mt   7.22 'Lord, Lord, did we not *p* in your name,
      26.68 saying, "*P* to us, you Messiah! Who is it
Mk   14.65 and to strike him, saying to him, "*P*!"
Lk   22.64 him, "*P*! Who is it that struck you?"
Acts   2.17 sons and your daughters shall *p*, and
      19. 6 them, and they spoke in tongues and *p*.
1 Cor   13. 9 only in part, and we *p* only in part;
      14. 5 speak in tongues, but even more to *p*.
Jude   14 *p*, saying, "See, the Lord is coming with
Rev   10.11 "You must *p* again about many peoples

PROPHET

Gen   20. 7 return the man's wife; for he is a *p*, and
Ex   7. 1 and your brother shall be your *p*.
Deut   18.15 God will raise up for you a *p* like me
      34.10 has there arisen a *p* in Israel like Moses
Judg   6. 8 the LORD sent a *p* to the Israelites; and
1 Sam   3.20 knew that Samuel was a trustworthy *p*
1 Kings   13.11 Now there lived an old *p* in Bethel. One
      22. 7 "Is there no other *p* of the LORD here of
2 Kings   5. 8 he may learn that there is a *p* in Israel."
2 Chr   18. 6 Is there no other *p* of the LORD here of
      28. 9 a *p* of the LORD was there, whose name
      36.12 humble himself before the *p* Jeremiah
Ps   74. 9 there is no longer any *p*, and there is no
Jer   8.10 unjust gain; from *p* to priest everyone
Ezek   2. 5 they shall know that there has been a *p*
      14. 9 I, the LORD, have deceived that *p*, and I
      33.33 know that a *p* has been among them.
Hos   9. 7 "The *p* is a fool, the man of the spirit is
      12.13 By a *p* the LORD brought Israel up from
Am   7.14 Amos answered Amaziah, "I am no *p*,
Mt   10.41 welcomes a *p* in the name of a *p* will
      21. 4 what had been spoken through the *p*,
      21.11 "This is the *p* Jesus from Nazareth in
Mk   11.32 for all regarded John as truly a *p*.
Lk   4.24 no *p* is accepted in the prophet's
      7.16 saying, "A great *p* has arisen among us:"
      20. 6 they are convinced that John was a *p*."
Jn   1.21 "Are you the *p*?" He answered, "No."
      4.19 said to him, Sir, I see that you are a *p*.
      7.40 in the crowd said, "This is really the *p*."
Acts   7.37 God will raise up a *p* for you from your
Titus   1.12 of them, their very own *p*, who said,
Rev   19.20 with it the false *p* who had performed

PROPHETESS

Judg   4. 4 Deborah, a *p*, the wife of Lappidoth,
Isa   8. 3 And I went to the *p*, and she conceived

PROPHETIC

| 1 Cor | 13. 2 And if I have *p* powers, and understand |
| 2 Pet | 1.19 the *p* message more fully confirmed. |

PROPHETS

Num	11.29 Would that all the LORD's people were *p*,
	12. 6 When there were *p* among you, I the
Deut	13. 1 If *p* or those who divine by dreams
1 Sam	10. 5 you will meet a band of *p* coming down
	10.11 son of Kish? Is Saul also among the *p*?"
	19.24 it is said, "Is Saul also among the *p*?"
2 Kings	24. 2 that he spoke by his servants the *p*
2 Chr	20.20 you will be established; believe his *p*."
Neh	9.30 them by your Spirit through your *p*;
Isa	9.15 head, and *p* who teach lies are the tail;
Jer	4. 9 shall be appalled and the *p* astounded.
	5.13 The *p* are nothing but wind, for the
	7.25 persistently sent all my servants the *p*
	27. 9 therefore, must not listen to your *p*,
	44. 4 sent to you all my servants the *p*,
Lam	2.14 *p* have seen for you false and deceptive
	4.13 It was for the sins of her *p* and the
Zeph	3. 4 Its *p* are reckless, faithless persons; its
Mt	13.57 "*P* are not without honor except in their
	23.37 the city that kills the *p* and stones
	24.24 false messiahs and false *p* will appear
Mk	6. 4 "*P* are not without honor, except in
	8.28 Elijah; and still others, one of the *p*."
Lk	6.26 what their ancestors did to the false *p*.
	9.19 that one of the ancient *p* has arisen."
	10.24 many *p* and kings desired to see what
	13.34 Jerusalem, the city that kills the *p* and
	24.44 Moses, the *p*, and the psalms must be
Acts	13.15 After the reading of the law and the *p*,
Rom	11. 3 "Lord, they have killed your *p*, they
1 Cor	12.28 the church first apostles, second *p*,
	14.32 And the spirits of *p* are subject to the *p*,
Eph	4.11 that some would be apostles, some *p*,
1 Pet	1.10 the *p* who prophesied of the grace
2 Pet	2. 1 false *p* also arose among the people,
Rev	10. 7 as he announced to his servants the *p*."

PROSPER (PROSPERED PROSPERS)

Gen	39.23 whatever he did, the LORD made it *p*.
1 Kings	2. 3 that you may *p* in all that you do and
2 Kings	18. 7 was with him; wherever he went, he *p*.
2 Chr	26. 5 he sought the LORD, God made him *p*.
	31.21 God, he did with all his heart, and he *p*.
Ezra	5. 8 done diligently and *p* in their hands.
Ps	1. 3 not wither. In all that they do, they *p*.
	37. 7 do not fret over those who *p* in their
	90.17 our hands — O *p* the work of our hands!
	122. 6 of Jerusalem: "May they *p* who love you!
Prov	17. 8 who give it; wherever they turn they *p*.
	28.13 one who conceals transgressions will *p*,
Isa	48.15 brought him, and he will *p* in his way.
	53.10 him the will of the LORD shall *p*.
	54.17 that is fashioned against you shall *p*,
Jer	2.37 trust, and you will not *p* through them.
	12. 1 Why does the way of the guilty *p*? Why
Dan	6.28 Daniel *p* during the reign of Darius and

PROSPERITY

Job	21.23 One dies in full *p*, being wholly at ease
Ps	25.13 They will abide in *p*, and their children
	30. 6 As for me, I said in my *p*, "I shall never
	37.11 and delight themselves in abundant *p*.
Eccl	7.14 In the day of *p* be joyful, and in the day
Isa	48.18 your *p* would have been like a river,
	66.12 LORD: I will extend *p* to her like a river,
Hag	2. 9 of hosts; and in this place I will give *p*,

PROSPEROUS

| Josh | 1. 8 Only then shall you make your way *p*, |

PROSTITUTE

| Gen | 38.15 he thought her to be a *p*, for she had |

Josh	6.17 Only Rahab the *p* and all who are with
Judg	16. 1 went to Gaza, where he saw a *p* and
Prov	7.10 comes toward him, decked out like a *p*,
	23.27 "For a *p* is a deep pit; an adulteress is a
Heb	11.31 By faith Rahab the *p* did not perish
Jas	2.25 Rahab the *p* also justified by works

PROSTRATED

| 1 Chr | 29.20 bowed their heads and *p* themselves |

PROTECT (PROTECTED PROTECTS)

Josh	24.17 He *p* us along all the way that we went,
Ps	16. 1 *P* me, O God, for in you I take refuge.
	20. 1 The name of the God of Jacob *p* you!
	41. 2 The LORD *p* them and keeps them alive;
	59. 1 my God, *p* me from those who rise up
	116. 6 The LORD *p* the simple; when I was
Isa	31. 5 he will *p* and deliver it, he will spare
Zech	9.15 LORD of hosts will *p* them, and they
Jn	17.11 Father, *p* them in your name that you
1 Pet	1. 5 who are being *p* by the power of God

PROUD

2 Chr	26.16 when he had become strong he grew *p*,
Job	40.11 look on all who are *p*, and abase them.
	41.34 is lofty; it is king over all that are *p*."
Ps	123. 4 who are at ease, the contempt of the *p*.
Prov	21. 4 Haughty eyes and a *p* heart — the lamp
Ob	3 Your *p* heart has deceived you, you that
Lk	1.51 he has scattered the *p* in the thoughts
Jas	4. 6 "God opposes the *p*, but gives grace to

PROVE (PROVING)

Ps	26. 2 *P* me, O LORD, and try me; test my heart
Jn	16. 8 he will *p* the world wrong about sin and
Acts	9.22 by *p* that Jesus was the Messiah.
	17. 3 and *p* that it was necessary for the
	24.13 Neither can they *p* to you the charge
	25. 7 against him, which they could not *p*.

PROVERB (PROVERBS)

Deut	28.37 shall become an object of horror, a *p*,
1 Sam	10.12 Therefore it became a *p*, "Is Saul also
1 Kings	4.32 He composed three thousand *p*, and his
	9. 7 Israel will become a *p* and a taunt
Ps	49. 4 I will incline my ear to a *p*; I will solve
Prov	1. 6 skill, to understand a *p* and a figure,
	26. 9 drunkard is a *p* in the mouth of a fool.
Ezek	12.22 Mortal, what is this *p* of yours about
	16.44 use this *p* about you, "Like mother, like
Lk	4.23 quote me this *p*, 'Doctor, cure yourself!'

PROVIDE (PROVIDED PROVIDES)

Gen	22. 8 "God himself will *p* the lamb for a burnt
	45.11 *p* for you there — since there are
	47.12 And Joseph *p* his father, his brothers,
1 Chr	22.14 I have *p* for the house of the LORD one
	29. 2 I have *p* for the house of my God, so far
Job	38.41 Who *p* for the raven its prey, when its
Prov	31.15 still night and *p* food for her household
Jon	1.17 But the LORD *p* a large fish to swallow
Mt	27.55 Jesus from Galilee and had *p* for him.

PROVISION (PROVISIONS)

Gen	45.23 with grain, bread, and *p* for his father
Josh	9. 4 they went and prepared *p*, and took
1 Kings	4.22 Solomon's *p* for one day was thirty cors
Rom	13.14 and make no *p* for the flesh, to gratify

PROVOKE (PROVOKED PROVOKING)

Deut	9.22 you have *p* the LORD to wrath.
	32.21 wine, no god, *p* me with their idols.
Judg	2.12 to them, and they *p* the LORD to anger.
1 Sam	1. 6 Her rival used to *p* her severely, to
1 Kings	14.22 to jealousy with their sins
	22.53 he *p* the LORD, the God of Israel, to
2 Kings	14.10 why should you *p* trouble so that you
	17.17 in the sight of the Lord, *p* him to anger.

2 Chr	25.19 at home; why should you *p* trouble so
	28.25 offerings to other gods, *p* to anger the
Ps	78.41 and again, and *p* the Holy One of Israel.
	78.58 they *p* him to anger with their high
Isa	65. 3 people who *p* me to my face
Jer	7.19 Is it I whom they *p*? says the LORD.
	44. 8 Why do you *p* me to anger with the
1 Cor	10.22 Or are we *p* the Lord to jealousy? Are
Eph	6. 4 fathers, do not *p* your children to anger,
Heb	10.24 consider how to *p* one another to love

PRUDENCE

Prov	5. 2 so that you may hold on to *p*, and your

PRUDENT

Prov	19.14 parents, but a *p* wife is from the LORD.
Am	5.13 Therefore the *p* will keep silent in such

PSALMS

Lk	24.44 prophets, and the *p* must be fulfilled."
Eph	5.19 as you sing *p* and hymns and spiritual
Col	3.16 in your hearts sing *p*, hymns, and

PUFFED (PUFFS)

1 Cor	4. 6 so that none of you will be *p* up in
	8. 1 Knowledge *p* up, but love builds up.

PULLED

Jer	38.13 the ropes and *p* him out of the cistern.

PUNISH (PUNISHED)

Ex	32.34 punishment, I will *p* them for their sin."
Lev	26.18 I will continue to *p* you sevenfold for
	26.28 I in turn will *p* you myself sevenfold for
Ps	89.32 then I will *p* their transgression with the
Isa	10.12 he will *p* the arrogant boasting of the
	13.11 *p* the world for its evil, and the wicked
	24.21 day the LORD will *p* the host of heaven
Jer	5. 9 Shall I not *p* them for these things?
	9. 9 Shall I not *p* them for these things?
	21.14 I will *p* you according to the fruit of
	51.47 when I will *p* the images of Babylon;
Hos	2.13 I will *p* her for the festival days of the
	8.13 their iniquity, and *p* their sins;
	9. 9 their iniquity, he will *p* their sins.
	10.10 against the wayward people to *p* them;
	12. 2 and will *p* Jacob according to his ways,
Am	3.14 On the day I *p* Israel for its
2 Cor	6. 9 are alive; as *p*, and yet not killed;

PUNISHMENT

Gen	4.13 LORD, "My *p* is greater than I can bear.
Isa	10. 3 What will you do on the day of *p*, in the
	53. 5 upon him was the *p* that made us
Lam	4. 6 hs been greater than the *p* of Sodom,
Ezek	4. 5 and so you shall bear the *p* of the
	4.10 they shall bear their *p*— the *p* of the
Hos	9. 7 The days of *p* have come, the days of
Hab	1.12 O Rock, have established them for *p*.
2 Cor	2. 6 *p* by the majority is enough for such a
2 Thess	1. 9 will suffer the *p* of eternal destruction,

PURCHASE (PURCHASED)

Gen	25.10 the field that Abraham *p* from the
Jer	32.12 and I gave the deed of *p* to Baruch son

PURE (PURER)

2 Sam	22.27 With the *p* you show yourself *p*, and
Job	4.17 human beings be *p* before their Maker?
	8. 6 if you are *p* and upright, surely then he
	11. 4 you say, "My conduct is *p*, and I am
Ps	12. 6 of the LORD are promises that are *p*,
	18.26 with the *p* you show yourself *p*; and
	19. 9 the fear of the LORD is *p*, enduring
	24. 4 who have clean hands and *p* hearts,
	73. 1 the upright, to those who are *p* in heart.
	119. 9 can young people keep their way *p*?
Prov	15.26 to the LORD, but gracious words are *p*.
	16. 2 one's ways may be *p* in one's own eyes,

Prov	30.12 are those who are *p* in their own eyes
Hab	1.13 Your eyes are too *p* to behold evil, and
Mt	5. 8 "Blessed are the *p* in heart, for they will
2 Cor	11. 3 led astray from a sincere and *p* devotion
1 Tim	5.22 in the sins of others; keep yourself *p*.
Titus	1.15 To the *p* all things are *p*, but to the

PURGE (PURGED)

2 Chr	34. 5 their altars, and *p* Judah and Jerusalem.
Ps	51. 7 *P* me with hyssop, and I shall be clean;
Ezek	20.38 I will *p* out the rebels among you, and

PURIFICATION

Lk	2.22 when the time came for their *p*
Jn	3.25 a discussion about *p* arose between
Heb	1. 3 When he had made *p* for sins, he sat

PURIFY (PURIFIED)

Num	19.13 who has died, and do not *p* themselves,
	31.20 You shall *p* every garment, every article
Neh	12.30 and the Levites *p* themselves; and they
Isa	52.11 out from the midst of it, *p* yourselves,
Dan	12.10 Many shall be *p*, cleansed, and refined,
Mal	3. 3 he will *p* the descendants of Levi and
Acts	21.26 having *p* himself, he entered the temple
Heb	9.14 *p* our conscience from dead works to
	9.22 law almost everything is *p* with blood,
1 Pet	1.22 you have *p* your souls by your
1 Jn	3. 3 have this hope in him *p* themselves,

PURITY

1 Pet	3. 2 see the *p* and reverence of your lives.

PURPOSE (PURPOSES)

Prov	20. 5 The *p* in the human mind are like deep
Isa	46.10 "My *p* shall stand, and I will fulfill my
Jer	51.29 for the LORD's *p* against Babylon stand,
Lk	7.30 and the lawyers rejected God's *p* for
Acts	20.27 declaring to you the whole *p* of God.
Eph	1.11 *p* of him who accomplishes all things
	3.11 was in accordance with the eternal *p*
2 Tim	1. 9 to our works but according to his own *p*
Heb	6.17 the unchangeable character of his *p*,
Rev	17.17 put into their hearts to carry out his *p*

PURSUE (PURSUED PURSUES)

Ex	14. 8 Pharaoh. . . *p* the Israelites, who were
Job	19.22 Why do you, like God, *p* me, never
Ps	83.15 so *p* them with your tempest and terrify
	109. 16 kindness, but *p* the poor and needy
Prov	21.21 Whoever *p* righteousness and kindness
Jer	29.18 I will *p* them with the sword, with
Lam	3.66 *P* them in anger and destroy them from
Am	1.11 he *p* his brother with the sword,
Acts	26.11 at them, I *p* them even to foreign cities.
Rom	14.19 Let us then *p* what makes for peace and
1 Tim	6.11 *p* righteousness, godliness, faith, love,
Heb	12.14 *P* peace with everyone, and the holiness

PUT

Rom	13.14 Instead, *p* on the Lord Jesus Christ, and
2 Cor	11.20 you *p* up with it when someone makes
Eph	4.22 to *p* away your former way of life,

Q

QUARREL (QUARRELED QUARRELING QUARRELS)

Ex	17. 3 The people *q* with Moses, and said,
Prov	17.14 out water; so stop before the *q* breaks
	19.13 and a wife's *q* is a continual dripping of
1 Cor	1.11 people that there are *q* among you,
	3. 3 as there is jealousy and *q* among you,
2 Cor	12.20 I fear that there may perhaps be a *q*,

QUEEN

Esth	2.17 head and made her *q* instead of Vashti.
Ps	45. 9 honor; at your right hand stands the *q*
Mt	12.42 The *q* of the South will rise up at the

Lk	11.31	The *q* of the South will rise at the

QUENCH (QUENCHED)

Song	8. 7	Many waters cannot *q* love, neither can
Isa	1.31	burn together, with no one to *q* them.
	42.31	and a dimly burning wick he will not *q*;
Mt	12.20	a bruised reed or *q* a smoldering wick
Mk	9.48	worm never dies, and the fire is never *q*.
1 Thess	5.19	Do not *q* the Spirit. Do not despise the

QUESTION (QUESTIONING QUESTIONS)

1 Kings	10. 1	she came to test him with hard *q*.
2 Chr	9. 1	to Jerusalem to test him with hard *q*,
Isa	45.11	Will you *q* me about my children,
Mk	2. 8	do you raise such *q* in your hearts?
Lk	3.15	were *q* in their hearts concerning John

QUICK-TEMPERED

Prov	14.17	One who is *q* acts foolishly, and the

QUIET (QUIETLY)

Job	34.29	When he is *q*, who can condemn? When
Eccl	4. 6	Better is a handful with *q* than two
Mt	1.19	disgrace, planned to dismiss her *q*.
1 Thess	4.11	to aspire to live *q*, to mind your own

QUIETNESS

Isa	32.17	the result of righteousness, *q* and trust

QUIVER

Ps	127. 5	Happy is the man who has his *q* full of

R

RACE

Eccl	9.11	under the sun the *r* is not to the swift,
1 Cor	9.24	in a *r* the runners all compete, but only
Heb	12. 1	let us run with perserverance the *r* that

RACHEL

Gen	29. 6	and here is his daughter *R* , coming with
	29.16	and the name of the younger was *R*.
	29.18	Jacob loved *R*; so he said, "I will serve
	29.30	to *R* also, and he loved *R* more than
	30.22	Then God remembered *R*, and God
	31.34	*R* had taken the household gods and
	35.19	So *R* died, and she was buried on the
Ruth	4.11	like *R* and Leah, who together built up
Mt	2.18	*R* weeping for her children; she refused

RADIANT

Ps	34. 5	Look to him, and be *r*; so your faces
Isa	60. 5	Then you shall see and be *r*; your heart
Jer	31.12	and they shall be *r* over the goodness of

RAFTS

1 Kings	5. 9	I will make it into *r* to go by sea to the
2 Chr	2.16	bring it to you as *r* by sea to Joppa; you

RAGES (RAGED RAGING)

Prov	19. 3	to ruin, yet the heart *r* against the Lord.
Isa	37.28	and coming in, and your *r* against me.
Rev	11.18	The nations *r*, but your wrath has come,

RAIL

Num	16.11	What is Aaron that you *r* against him?"

RAIN (RAINS)

Gen	2. 5	God had not caused it to *r* upon the
	7. 4	For in seven days I will send *r* on the
Lev	26. 4	I will give you your *r* in their season,
Deut	11.14	then he will give the *r* for your land in
	28.12	to give the *r* of your land in its season
1 Kings	8.35	there is no *r* because they have sinned
	17. 1	shall be neither dew nor *r* these years,
	18.41	for there is a sound of the rushing *r*."
Job	5.10	He gives *r* on the earth and sends
	38.28	"Has the *r* a father, or who has begotten
Ps	68. 9	*R* in abundance, O God, you showered
Isa	44.14	plants a cedar and the *r* nourishes it.

Isa	45. 8	and let the skies *r* down righteousness;
	55.10	as the *r* and the snow come down from
Jer	5.24	our God, who gives the *r* in its season,
Joel	2.23	abundant *r*, the early and the latter *r*, as
Am	4. 7	I also withheld the *r* from you when
Zech	10. 1	Ask *r* from the Lord in the season of
	14.17	of hosts, there will be no *r* upon them.
Mt	5.45	sends *r* on the righteous and on the
	7.25	The *r* fell, the floods came, and the
Acts	14.17	giving you *r* from heaven and fruitful
Rev	11. 6	that no *r* may fall during the days of

RAINBOW

Rev	4. 3	around the throne is a *r* that looks like

RAISE (RAISED RAISES)

Ps	41.10	to me, and *r* me up, that I may repay
	148. 14	He has *r* up a horn for his people,
Mt	14. 2	Baptist; he has been *r* from the dead,
	16.21	and be killed, and on the third day be *r*.
	17. 9	Son of Man has been *r* from the dead.
	20.19	and on the third day he will be *r*."
	26.32	after I am *r* up, I will go ahead of you
	27.64	people, 'He has been *r* from the dead,
	28. 6	He is not here; for he has been *r*, as he
Mk	6.14	"John the baptizer has been *r* from the
	14.28	after I am *r* up, I will go before you to
	16. 6	He has been *r*; he is not here. Look,
Lk	9. 7	that John had been *r* from the dead,
	21.28	take place, stand up and *r* your heads,
Jn	5.21	just as the father *r* the dead and gives
	6.39	given me, but *r* it up at the last day.
Acts	3.15	Author of life, whom God *r* from the
	10.40	God *r* him on the third day and allowed
	13.30	But God *r* him from the dead;
	26. 8	by any of you that God *r* the dead?
Rom	9.17	to Pharaoh, "I have *r* you up for the very
1 Cor	6.14	And God *r* the Lord and will also *r* us
	15. 4	that he was *r* on the third day in
	15.13	of the dead, then Christ has not been *r*,
2 Cor	4.14	the one who *r* the Lord Jesus will *r* us
Eph	1.20	when he *r* him from the dead and
	2. 6	*r* us up with him and seated us with
Col	3. 1	if you have been *r* with Christ, seek the
2 Tim	2. 8	Remember Jesus Christ, *r* from the
Jas	5.15	the sick, and the Lord will *r* them up;
1 Pet	1.21	to trust in God, who *r* him from the

RAM

Gen	15. 9	Bring me . . . a *r* three years old, a
	22.13	and saw a *r*, caught in a thicket by its

RAMAH

1 Sam	1.19	they went back to their house at *R*.
	2.11	Then Elkanah went home to *R*, while
	8. 4	together and came to Samuel at *R*,
	19.18	and escaped; he came to Samuel at *R*,
	28. 3	mourned for him and buried him in *R*,
2 Chr	16. 1	against Judah, and built *R*.
Isa	10.29	*R* trembles, Gibeah of Saul has fled. Cry
Jer	31.15	A voice is heard in *R*, lamentation and
Mt	2.18	"A voice was heard in *R*, wailing and

RAMOTH-GILEAD

1 Kings	22. 6	"Shall I go to battle against *R*, or shall I
2 Kings	9. 1	flask of oil in your hand, and go to *R*.

RAMPART

Hab	2. 1	watchpost, and station myself on the *r*,

RANK

Gen	49. 3	of my vigor, excelling in *r* and excelling

RANSOM (RANSOMED)

Ex	30.12	all of them shall give a *r* for their lives
1 Sam	14.45	So the people *r* Jonathan, and he did
Job	6.23	hand'? Or, '*R* me from the hand
	33.24	down into the Pit; I have found a *r*;

Job	36.18	not let the greatness of the r turn you
Ps	49. 7	Truly, no r avails for one's life, there is
	49. 8	For the r of life is costly, and can never
Prov	21.18	The wicked is a r for the righteous, and
Isa	43. 3	I give Egypt as your r, Ethiopia and
Hos	13.14	Shall I r them from the power of Sheol?
Mt	20.28	serve, and to give his life a r for many."
Mk	10.45	serve, and to give his life a r for many."
1 Tim	2. 6	human, who gave himself as a r for all
1 Pet	1.18	You know that you were r from the
Rev	5. 9	by your blood you r for God saints from

RARE

1 Sam	3. 1	word of the LORD was r in those days;
Isa	13.12	I will make mortals more r than fine

RASH

Job	6. 3	sea; therefore my words have been r.
Eccl	5. 2	Never be r with your mouth, nor let

RAVAGED (RAVAGING)

Nah	2. 2	though ravagers have r them and ruined
Acts	8. 3	But Saul was r the church by entering

RAVEN (RAVENS)

Gen	8. 7	and sent out the r; and it went to and
1 Kings 17. 4	commanded the r to feed you there."
Job	38.41	Who provides for the r its prey, when its
Lk	12.24	Consider the r: they neither sow nor

RAVENOUS

Prov	27. 7	but to a r appetite even the bitter

RAVISH (RAVISHED)

Judg	19.24	R them and do whatever you want to
Song	4. 9	you have r my heart with a glance of

RAZOR

Num	6. 5	vow no r shall come upon the head;
Ps	52. 2	Your tongue is like a sharp r, you
Isa	7.20	the Lord will shave with a r hired
Ezek	5. 1	sword; use it as a barber's r and run it

READ (READING READS)

Deut	17.19	he shall r in it all the days of his life,
	31.11	you shall r this law before all Israel in
2 Kings 23. 2	he r in their hearing all the words of
Neh	8. 3	he r from it facing the square before the
	13. 1	they r from the book of Moses in the
Isa	29.11	"R this," they say, "I cannot, for it is
	34.16	r from the book of the LORD: Not one of
Jer	36. 6	house you shall r the words of the LORD
	36.21	and Jehudi r it to the king and all the
Dan	5. 7	"Whoever can r this writing and tell me
	5.17	I will r the writing to the king and let
Hab	2. 2	on tablets, so that a runner may r it.
Mt	21.42	"Have you never r in the scriptures:
Mk	12.10	Have you not r this scripture: 'The
	12.26	have you not r in the book of Moses, in
Lk	6. 3	"Have you not r what David did when
Acts	8.28	his chariot, he was r the prophet Isaiah.
2 Cor	3. 2	on our hearts, to be known and r by all;
Rev	1. 3	Blessed is the one who r aloud the

READY

Song	2. 7	not stir up or awaken love until it is r.
	3. 5	not stir up or awaken love until it is r.
	8. 4	not stir up or awaken love until it is r.
Mt	22. 4	and everything is r; come to my
	22. 8	'The wedding is r, but those invited
	24.44	you also must be r, for the Son of Man
	25.10	those who were r went with him into
1 Cor	14. 8	sound, who will get r for battle?
2 Cor	9. 2	saying that Achaia has been r since last

REALIZED

Mk	15.10	he r that it was out of jealousy that the
Lk	20.19	and chief priests r that he had told this

REALM

Dan	11. 5	shall rule a r greater than his own r.

REAP (REAPS)

Lev	19. 9	r . . ., you shall not r to the very edges
	23.22	r . . ., you shall not r to the very edges
Job	4. 8	iniquity and sow trouble r the same.
Ps	126. 5	who sow in tears r with shouts of joy.
Prov	22. 8	Whoever sows injustice will r calamity,
Eccl	11. 4	whoever regards the clouds will not r.
Mic	6.15	You shall sow, but not r; you shall tread
Mt	6.26	they neither sow nor r nor gather into
Jn	4.37	holds true, 'One sows and another r.'
1 Cor	9.11	too much if we r your material benefits?
Gal	6. 7	mocked, for you r whatever you sow.
Rev	14.15	r, for the hour to r has come, because

REBEKAH (REBECCA)

Gen	22.23	Bethuel became the father of R. These
	24.15	he had finished speaking, there was R,
	24.59	So they sent away their sister R and her
	24.67	He took R, and she became his wife,
	25.28	was fond of game; but R loved Jacob.
	27. 5	R was listening when Isaac spoke to his
	49.31	there Isaac and his wife R were buried;
Rom	9.10	to R when she had conceived children

REBEL (REBELS) (n)

Num	20.10	"Listen, you r, shall we bring water for
Isa	1.23	Your prices are r and companions of
	1.28	r and sinners shall be destroyed
	48. 8	and that from birth you were called a r.

REBEL (REBELLED REBELLING REBELS)

Num	14. 9	do not r against the LORD; and do not
	16.41	of the Israelites r against Moses
	20.24	because you r against my command at
	27.14	because you r against my word in the
Deut	1.26	You r against the command of the LORD
	1.43	You r against the command of the LORD
2 Kings 3. 5	of Moab r against the king of Israel.
Neh	2.19	are doing? Are you r against the king?"
Job	24.13	There are those who r against the light,
Ps	5.10	them out, for they have r against you.
	78.17	against him, r against the Most High
	78.40	How often they r against him in the
	107. 11	for they had r against the words of God,
Prov	28. 2	When a land r it has many rulers; but
Isa	1. 2	them up, but they have r against me.
	1.20	but if you refuse and r, you shall be
	36. 5	now rely, that you have r against me?
	63.10	they r and grieved his holy spirit;
Jer	4.17	of a field, because she has r against me,
Ezek	2. 3	nation of rebels, who have r against me;
	20.13	Israel r against me in the wilderness;
Hos	13.16	because she has r against her God;

REBELLION

Josh	22.16	yourselves an altar today in r against
1 Sam	15.23	r is no less a sin than divination, and
1 Kings 12.19	Israel has been in r against the house of
2 Chr	10.19	So Israel has been in r against the
Job	34.37	For he adds r to his sin; he claps his
Jer	29.32	for he has spoken r against the LORD.

REBELLIOUS

Deut	21.18	and r son who will not obey his father
Ezra	4.15	this is a r city, hurtful to kings and
Isa	30. 1	Oh, r children, says the LORD, who carry
Ezek	17.12	Say now to the r house: Do you not

REBUILD (REBUILT)

Ezra	1. 3	in Judah, and r the house of the LORD,
Neh	4. 6	So we r the wall, and all the wall was
Job	12.14	If he tears down, no one can r; if he
Ps	51.18	r the walls of Jerusalem, then you will

REBUKE (n)

Job	26.11	tremble, and are astounded at his r.
Ps	76.	6 At your r, O God of Jacob, both rider
	104.	7 At your r they flee; at the sound of your
Prov	17.10	A r strikes deeper into a discerning
	27.	5 Better is open r than hidden love. Well

REBUKE (REBUKED) (v)

Gen	31.42	the labor of my hands, and r you
	37.10	to his brothers, his father r him, and
1 Chr	16.21	them; he r kings on their account,
Job	13.10	He will surely r you if in secret you
Ps	6.	1 O Lord, do not r me in your anger, or
	38.	1 O Lord, do not r me in your anger, or
	50.	8 Not for your sacrifices do I r you; your
	105.	14 them; he r kings on their account,
	106.	9 He r the Red Sea, and it became dry; he
	119.	21 You r the insolent, accursed ones, who
Prov	24.25	who r the wicked will have delight,
Jer	29.27	why have you not r Jeremiah of
Zech	3.	2 "The Lord r you, O Satan! The Lord
Mt	16.22	took him aside and began to r him,
	17.18	Jesus r the demon, and it came out of
Mk	8.32	took him aside and began to r him.
	9.25	he r the unclean spirit, saying to it,
Lk	4.35	Jesus r him, saying "Be silent, and
	9.42	Jesus r the unclean spirit, healed the
	9.55	But he turned and r them. Then they
Jude		9 against him, but said, "The Lord r you!"

RECEIVE (RECEIVED) RECEIVES)

Job	2.10	at the hand of God, and not r the bad?"
	22.22	R instruction from his mouth, and lay
	27.13	and the heritage that oppressors r from
	35.	7 to him; and what does he r from your
Ps	24.	5 They will r blessing from the Lord, and
	49.15	the power of Sheol, for he will r me.
	73.24	and afterward you will r me with honor.
Mt	7.	8 For everyone who asks r, and everyone
	20.10	came, they thought they would r more;
	21.22	ask for in prayer with faith, you will r."
Mk	4.16	the word, they immediately r it with joy;
	10.15	does not r the kingdom as a little child
	10.30	who will not r a hundredfold now in
Lk	6.34	sinners lend to sinners, to r as much
	9.53	but they did not r him, because his face
	11.10	For everyone who asks r, and everyone
	18.42	to him, "R your sight; your faith has
Jn	1.12	But to all who r him, who believed in
	3.27	"No one can r anything except what has
	13.20	and whoever r me r him who sent me."
	20.22	"R the Holy Spirit. If you forgive them
Acts	19.	2 "Did you r the Holy Spirit when you
1 Cor	2.14	who are unspiritual do not r the gifts of
	11.23	I r from the Lord what I also handed on
	15.	3 what I in turn had r: that Christ died
Gal	3.	2 Did you r the Spirit by doing the works
	3.14	that we might r the promise of the
	4.	5 so that we might r adoption as children.
	6.	1 who have r the Spirit should restore
Col	2.	6 therefore have r Christ Jesus the Lord,
1 Thess	1.	6 of persecution you r the word with joy
2 Jn		8 worked for, but may r a full reward.

RECEPTIVE

Acts	17.11	These Jews were more r than those in

RECITE

Deut	6.	7 R them to your children and talk about

RECKONS (RECKONED RECKONING)

Gen	15.	6 the Lord; and the Lord r it to him as
	42.22	So now there comes a r for his blood."
Ps	106.	31 that has been r to him as righteousness
Prov	18.24	When he began the r, one who owed
Rom	4.	3 "Abraham believed God, and it was r to
	4.	6 to whom God r righteousness apart

Rom	4.	9 "Faith was r to Abraham as
	4.22	his faith was "r to him as righteousness."
	5.13	but sin is not r when there is no law.

RECOGNIZED

Gen	42.	8 Although Joseph had r his brothers,

RECOMPENSED

2 Sam	22.25	the Lord has r me according to my
Ps	18.24	Therefore the Lord has r me according

RECONCILE (RECONCILED)

Mt	5.24	first be r to your brother or sister, and
Rom	5.10	enemies, we were r to God through the
1 Cor	7.11	unmarried or else be r to her husband),
2 Cor	5.18	is from God, who r us to himself
Eph	2.16	might r both groups to God in one body
Col	1.20	was pleased to r to himself all things,

RECONCILIATION

Rom	5.11	through whom we have now received r.
	11.15	if their rejection is the r of the world,

RECOUNT

Ps	118.	17 not die, but I shall live, and r the deeds
Isa	63.	7 I will r the gracious deeds of the Lord,

RECOVER

2 Kings	8.	8 him, whether I shall r from this illness."
Isa	11.11	yet a second time to r the remnant

RED SEA

Ex	10.19	the locusts and drove them into the R.
	15.	4 his picked officers were sunk in the R.
	15.22	ordered Israel to set out from the R,
Josh	4.23	God did to the R, which he dried up for
Ps	106.	9 He rebuked the R, and it became dry;
Acts	7.36	wonders and signs in Egypt, at the R,
Heb	11.29	faith the people passed through the R

REDEEM (REDEEMED REDEEMS)

Gen	48.16	the angel who has r me from all harm,
Ex	6.	6 I will r you with an outstretched arm
	15.13	love you led the people whom you r;
	21.	8 then he shall let her be r; he shall have
	34.20	if a donkey you shall r with a lamb,
Num	18.15	first-born of human beings you shall r,
Deut	7.	8 and r you from the house of slavery,
	9.26	whom you r in your greatness, whom
Ruth	4.	4 If you will r it, r it; but if you will not,
2 Sam	4.	9 As the Lord lives, who has r my life out
	7.23	whose God went to r it as a people,
1 Chr	17.21	whom God went to r to be his people,
Neh	1.10	your people, whom you r by your great
Job	5.20	In famine he will r you from death, and
	33.28	He has r my soul from going down to
Ps	25.22	R Israel, O God, out of all its troubles.
	26.11	integrity; r me, and be gracious to me.
	31.	5 my spirit; you have r me, O Lord,
	34.22	The Lord r the life of his servants; none
	44.26	Rise up, come to our help. R us for the
	69.18	Draw near to me, r me, set me free
	77.15	With your strong arm you r your people,
	103.	4 diseases, who r your life from the Pit,
	130.	7 love, and with him is great power to r.
Isa	1.27	Zion shall be r by justice, and those in
	43.	1 O Israel: Do not fear, for I have r you;
	48.20	say, "The Lord has r his servant Jacob!"
	52.	3 and you shall be r without money.
Jer	15.21	the wicked, and r you from the grasp of
Hos	7.13	I would r them, but they speak lies
Mic	6.	4 and r you from the house of slavery;
Zech	10.	8 and gather them in, for I have r them,
Lk	1.68	favorably on his people and r them.
	24.21	hoped that he was the one to r Israel.
Gal	3.13	Christ r us from the curse of the law by
	4.	5 to r those who were under the law,
Titus	2.14	us that he might r us from all iniquity

REDEEMED (n)

Ps   107. 2 Let the *r* of the LORD say so, those he *r*
Isa   35. 9 found there, but the *r* shall walk there.
       51.10 of the sea a way for the *r* to cross over?
       62.12 "The Holy People, The *R* of the LORD";

REDEEMER

Job   19.25 For I know that my *R* lives, and that at
Ps   19.14 to you, O LORD, my rock and my *r*.
      78.35 their rock, the Most High God their *r*.
Prov 23.11 for their *R* is strong; he will plead their
Isa   41.14 says the LORD; your *R* is the Holy One
      44. 6 King of Israel, and his *R*, the LORD of
      47. 4 Our *R*—the LORD of hosts is his
      54. 8 on you, says the LORD, your *R*.
      59.20 he will come to Zion as *R*, to those in
Jer   50.34 Their *R* is strong; the LORD of hosts is

REDEMPTION

Ex   21.30 is imposed for the *r* of the victim's life.
Lev   25.24 you shall provide for the *r* of the land.
      25.29 sale; the right of *r* shall be for one year.
      25.52 they shall make payment for their *r*.
Num   3.49 So Moses took the *r* money from those
Ruth   4. 6 Take my right of *r* yourself, for I cannot
Ps   111. 9 He sent *r* to his people; he has
Jer   32. 7 Anathoth, for the right of *r* by purchase
Lk   2.38 were looking for the *r* of Jerusalem.
      21.28 heads, because your *r* is drawing near."
Rom   3.24 through the *r* which is in Christ Jesus,
1 Cor 1.30 and sanctification and *r*, in order that,
Eph   1. 7 we have *r* through his blood, the
       4.30 marked with a seal for the day of *r*.
Heb   9.12 his own blood, thus obtaining eternal *r*.

REED

2 Kings 18.21 Egypt, that broken *r* of a staff, which
Isa   42. 1 bruised *r* he will not break, and a dimly
Ezek 40. 3 a measuring *r* in his hand; and he was
Mt   11. 7 to look at? A *r* shaken by the wind?
      12.20 He will not break a bruised *r* or quench
Lk   7.24 to look at? A *r* shaken by the wind?

REFINE (REFINED REFINES)

Isa   48.10 See, I have *r* you, but not like silver; I
Jer   9. 7 I will now *r* and test them, for what else
Zech 13. 9 into the fire, *r* them as one *r* silver,
Rev   3.18 buy from me gold *r* by fire so that you

REFLECTS (REFLECTION)

Prov 27.19 the face, so one human heart *r* another.
Heb   1. 3 He is the *r* of God's glory and the exact

REFRESH (REFRESHED)

Gen   18. 5 a little bread, that you may *r* yourselves,
Ex   23.12 slave and the resident alien may be *r*.
Prov 25.13 them; they *r* the spirit of their masters.
Song   2. 5 *r* me with apples; for I am faint with
Rom   15.32 you with joy and be *r* in your company.
1 Cor 16.18 for they *r* my spirit as well as yours. So
2 Tim 1.16 of Onesiphorus, because he often *r* me
Philem 7 of the saints have been *r* through you.
2 Pet 1.13 as I am in this body, to *r* your memory,

REFUGE

Num   35. 6 shall include six cities of *r*, where you
      35.11 select cities to be cities of *r* for you,
Deut 32.37 gods, the rock in which they took *r*,
Josh 20. 2 'Appoint the cities of *r*, of which I
Ruth   2.12 under whose wings you have come for *r*!"
Ps   2.12 kindled. Happy are all who take *r*
       7. 1 O LORD my God, in you I take *r*; save
      14. 6 of the poor, but the LORD is their *r*.
      16. 1 Protect me. O God, for in you I take *r*. I
      31. 1 In you, O LORD, I seek *r*; do not let me
      46. 1 God is our *r* and strength, a very
      57. 1 the shadow of your wings I will take *r*,
      61. 3 for you are my *r*, a strong tower against

Ps   61. 4 tent forever, find *r* under the shelter of
      71. 1 In you, O LORD, I take *r*; never let me be
      71. 7 to many, but you are my strong *r*.
      73.28 made the Lord GOD my *r*, to tell of all
      91. 2 say to the LORD, "My *r* and my fortress;
     118. 8 better to take *r* in the LORD than to put
     142. 4 notice of me; no *r* remains to me; no
Prov 14.32 the righteous find a *r* in their integrity.
      30. 5 true; he is a shield to those who take *r*
Isa   4. 6 and a *r* and a shelter from the storm
      25. 4 you have been a *r* to the poor, a *r* to
      28.15 we have made lies our *r*, and in
      33.16 their *r* will be the fortresses of rocks;
      57.13 whoever takes *r* in me shall possess the
Jer   16.19 stronghold, my *r* in the day of trouble,
      17.17 me; you are my *r* in the day of disaster;
Joel   3.16 the LORD is a *r* for his people, a
Nah   1. 7 he protects those who take *r* in him,
Zeph   3.12 They shall seek *r* in the name of the

REFUSE (REFUSED)

Gen   39. 8 But he *r* and said to his master's wife,
Num   20.21 Thus Edom *r* to give Israel passage
1 Sam 8.19 the people *r* to listen to the voice of
Neh   9.17 they *r* to obey, and were not mindful of
Esth   1.12 But Queen Vashti *r* to come at the
Ps   78.10 but *r* to walk according to his law.
Prov   1.24 Because I have called and you *r*, have
Isa   7.15 the time he knows how to *r* the evil and
Jer   5. 3 them, but they *r* to take correction.
       9. 6 upon deceit! They *r* to know me, says
      13.10 evil people, who *r* to hear my words,
Hos   11. 5 because they have *r* to return to me.
Zech   7.11 But they *r* to listen, and turned a
2 Thess 2.10 because they *r* to love the truth and so
Heb   11.24 grown up, *r* to be called the son of
      12.25 you do not *r* the one who is speaking;

REFUTE (REFUTED)

Acts 18.28 he powerfully *r* the Jews in public,
Titus 1. 9 and to *r* those who contradict it.

REGARD (REGARDED REGARDS)

Gen   4. 4 the LORD had *r* for Abel and his offering,
1 Kings 8.28 *R* your servant's prayer and his plea, O
Job   34.19 nor *r* the rich more than the poor, for
      37.24 he does not *r* any who are wise in their
Ps   80.14 heaven, and see; have *r* for this vine,
     106.44 he *r* their distress, when he heard their
Isa   17. 7 people will *r* their Maker, and their eyes
Jer   24. 5 I will *r* as good the exiles from Judah,
Mk   12.14 you do not *r* people with partiality, but
Phil   3. 8 I *r* everything as loss because of the

REGISTER (REGISTERED)

Num   3.10 you shall make a *r* of Aaron and his
Lk   2. 1 Augustus that all the world should be *r*.

REGRET

1 Sam 15.11 "I *r* that I have made Saul king, for he

REGULAR

Dan   8.11 took the *r* burnt offering away from him

REGULATIONS

Num   9. 3 according to its statutes and all its *r*

REHOBOAM

1 Kings 11.43 David; and his son *R* succeeded him.
      12. 1 *R* went to Shechem, for all Israel had
      14.21 *R* was forty-one years old when he
      15. 6 war between *R* and Jeroboam continued
Mt   1. 7 Solomon the father of *R*, and *R* the

REIGN (REIGNED REIGNS)

Gen   37. 8 "Are you indeed to *r* over us? Are you
Ex   15.18 The LORD will *r* forever and ever."
1 Sam 11.12 is it that said, 'Shall Saul *r* over us?'
1 Kings 2.11 time that David *r* over Israel was forty

Job	34.30	so that the godless should not *r*, or
Ps	146.10	The LORD will *r* forever, your God, O
Prov	8.15	By me kings *r*, and rulers decree what is
Eccl	4.14	One can indeed come out of prison to *r*,
Isa	24.23	for the LORD of hosts will *r* on Mount
	32.1	king will *r* in righteousness, and princes
Jer	23.5	and he shall *r* as king and deal wisely,
Lam	5.19	But you, O LORD, *r* forever; your throne
Mic	4.7	the LORD will *r* over them in Mount Zion
Lk	1.33	He will *r* over the house of Jacob
1 Cor	15.25	he must *r* until he has put all his
Rev	11.15	Messiah, and he will *r* forever and ever."
	19.6	For the Lord our God the Almighty *r*.
	20.4	life and *r* with Christ a thousand years.

REJECT (REJECTED REJECTING REJECTS)

Num	11.20	you have *r* the LORD who is among you,
1 Sam	8.7	not *r* you, but they have *r* me from
	10.19	today you have *r* your God, who saves
Ps	36.4	way that is not good; they do not *r* evil.
	118.22	The stone that the builders *r* has
Prov	10.17	life, but one who *r* a rebuke goes astray.
Isa	30.12	Because you *r* this word, and put your
Jer	2.37	the LORD has *r* those in whom you trust,
	6.19	and as for my teaching, they have *r* it.
	6.30	They are called "*r* silver," for the LORD
	7.29	the LORD has *r* and forsaken the
Lam	5.22	unless you have utterly *r* us, and are
Ezek	5.6	her, *r* my ordinances and not following
Hos	4.6	knowledge, I *r* you from being a priest
Am	2.4	because they have *r* the law
Mt	21.42	stone that the builders *r* has become
Mk	7.9	have a fine way of *r* the commandment
	12.10	stone that the builders *r* has become
Lk	9.22	be *r* by the elders, chief priests, and
	10.16	*r* you *r* me, whoever *r* me *r* the one who
	17.25	suffering and be *r* by this generation.
	20.17	stone that the builders *r* has become
Jn	12.48	The one who *r* me and *r* does not receive
Rom	11.1	I ask then, has God *r* his people? By no

REJOICE

Lev	23.40	you shall *r* before the LORD your God for
Deut	16.11	*R* before the LORD your God —you and
1 Chr	16.10	the hearts of those who seek the LORD *r*.
Ps	5.11	But let all who take refuge in you *r*; let
	33.1	*R* in the LORD, O you righteous. Praise
	35.9	Then my soul shall *r* in the LORD,
	58.10	The righteous will *r* when they see
	85.6	again, so that your people may *r* in you?
	118.24	has made; let us *r* and be glad in it.
	149.2	let the children of Zion *r* in their King!
Prov	5.18	blessed, and *r* in the wife of your youth,
	29.2	righteous are in authority, the people *r*;
Isa	1.10	I will greatly *r* in the LORD, my whole
	35.1	be glad, the desert shall *r* and blossom;
	41.16	Then you shall *r* in the LORD; in the
	62.5	the bride, so shall your God *r* over you.
	66.10	*R* with Jerusalem, and be glad for her,
Jer	31.13	shall the young women *r* in the dance,
Lam	2.17	he has made the enemy *r* over you, and
Ezek	7.12	let not the buyer *r*, nor the seller
Joel	2.23	of Zion, be glad and *r* in the LORD
Hab	3.18	yet I will *r* in the LORD; I will exult in
Zech	9.9	*R* greatly, O daughter Zion! Shout
Mt	5.12	*R* and be glad, for your reward is great
Lk	6.23	*R* in that day and leap for joy, for surely
	10.20	do not *r* at this, that the spirits submit
Jn	14.28	If you loved me, you would *r* that I am
Rom	12.15	*R* with those who *r*, weep with those
	15.10	he says, "*R*, O Gentiles, with his people";
1 Cor	7.30	those who *r* as though they were not
	13.6	it does not *r* in wrongdoing, but rejoices
Phil	1.18	of false motives or true; and in that I *r*.
	3.1	my brothers and sisters, *r* in the Lord.
	4.4	*R* in the Lord always; again I say,
1 Thess	5.16	*R* always, pray without ceasing, give

1 Pet	1.8	see him now, you believe in him and *r*
	4.13	But *r* insofar as you are sharing Christ's

REJOICES (REJOICED REJOICING)

Num	10.10	Also on your days of *r*, at your
1 Sam	6.13	the ark, they went with *r* to meet it.
1 Chr	29.9	Then the people *r* because these had
Esth	8.15	while the city of Susa shouted and *r*.
Ps	19.8	of the LORD are right, *r* the heart;
Prov	11.10	goes well with the righteous, the city *r*;
	15.30	The light of the eyes *r* the heart, and
Mt	18.13	he *r* over it more than over the
Lk	1.47	Lord, and my spirit *r* in God my Savior,
	13.17	crowd was *r* at all the wonderful things
	15.5	it, he lays it on his shoulders and *r*,
Jn	8.56	Abraham *r* that he would see my day;
Acts	16.34	he and his entire household *r* that he

REKINDLE

2 Tim	1.6	remind you to *r* the gift of God that is

RELAX

Lk	12.19	goods laid up for many years; *r*, eat,

RELEASE (RELEASED)

Job	14.14	I would wait, until my *r* should come.
Mk	15.6	he used to *r* a prisoner for them,
	15.15	Pilate . . . *r* Barabbas for them; and after
Lk	23.16	therefore have him flogged and *r* him."
Jn	18.39	have a custom that I *r* someone for you
Rev	20.7	Satan will be *r* from his prison and will

RELENT (RELENTED)

2 Sam	24.16	LORD *r* concerning the evil, and said to
1 Chr	21.15	the LORD took note and *r* concerning the
Am	7.3	The LORD *r* concerning this; "It shall not
Jon	3.9	God may *r* and change his mind;

RELIEF

Gen	5.29	this one shall bring us *r* from our work
Job	32.20	I must speak, so that I may find *r*; I
Acts	11.29	each would send *r* to the believers

RELIGION

Acts	26.5	belonged to the strictest sect of our *r*
1 Tim	3.16	any doubt, the mystery of our *r* is great:
Jas	1.27	*R* that is pure and undefiled before

RELIGIOUS

Acts	17.22	I see how how extremely *r* you are
Jas	1.26	If any think they are *r*, and do not

RELY (RELYING)

2 Kings	18.21	you are *r* now on Egypt, that broken
	18.30	let Hezekiah make you to *r* on the LORD
2 Chr	14.11	God, for we *r* on you, and in your name
	16.7	and did not *r* on the LORD your God,
Isa	59.4	they *r* on empty pleas, they speak lies,
2 Cor	1.9	so that we would *r* not on ourselves but

REMAIN (REMAINED REMAINS)

Gen	49.24	Yet his bow *r* taut, and his arms were
Josh	13.1	much of the land still *r* to be possessed.
1 Sam	1.22	of the LORD, and *r* there forever;
	5.7	of the God of Israel must not *r* with us;
Ps	101.7	No one who practices deceit shall *r* in
Eccl	1.4	comes, but the earth *r* forever.
Jer	42.10	If you will only *r* in this land, then I
Hos	3.4	Israelites shall *r* many days without king
Mk	14.34	deeply grieved, even to death; *r* here,
Lk	10.7	*R* in the same house, eating and
Jn	21.22	If it is my will that he *r* until I come,
1 Cor	7.24	brothers and sisters, there *r* with God.
1 Jn	2.19	to us, they would have *r* with us.

REMEMBER

Gen	9.15	I will *r* my covenant that is between me
	41.9	said to Pharaoh, "I *r* my faults today.
Ex	13.3	"*R* this day on which you came out of

Ex	32.13 *R* Abraham, Isaac, and Israel, your
Lev	26.42 *r* my covenant with Jacob; I will *r* also
Num	11. 5 We *r* the fish we used to eat in Egypt
	15.39 when you see it, you will *r* all the
Deut	7.18 Just *r* what the LORD your God did to
	9. 7 *R* . . . how you provoked the LORD your
	15.15 *R* that you were a slave in the land of
	16.12 *R* that you were a slave in Egypt, and
	24.18 *R* that you were a slave in Egypt and
	32. 7 *R* the days of old, consider the years
Judg	8.34 Israelites did not *r* the LORD their God,
	16.28 "Lord GOD, *r* me and strengthen me only
1 Sam	1.11 on the misery of your servant, and *r* me,
2 Kings	20. 3 "*R* now, O LORD, I implore you, how I
1 Chr	16.12 *R* the wonderful works he has done, his
2 Chr	6.42 *R* your steadfast love for your servant
	24.22 Joash did not *r* the kindness that
Neh	1. 8 *R* the word that you commanded your
	4.14 *R* the LORD, who is great and awesome,
	5.19 *R* for my good, O my God, all that I
	6.14 *R* Tobiah and Sanballat, O my God,
	13.14 *R* me, O my God, concerning this, and
Ps	42. 6 cast down within me; therefore I *r* you
	74. 2 *R* your congregation, which you
	79. 8 Do not *r* against us the iniquities of our
	89.47 *R* how short my time is — for whatever
	105. 5 *R* the wonderful works he has done, his
	137. 7 *R*, O LORD, against the Edomites the day
Prov	31. 7 poverty, and *r* their misery no more.
Eccl	11. 8 *r* that the days of darkness will be
	12. 1 *R* your creator in the days of your
Isa	38. 3 "*R* now, O LORD, I implore you, how I
	43.18 Do not *r* the former things, or consider
	43.25 my own sake, and I will not *r* your sins.
	46. 8 *R* this and consider, recall it to mind,
Jer	2. 2 I *r* the devotion of your youth, your love
	18.20 *R* how I stood before you to speak good
Ezek	16.22 you did not *r* the days of your youth,
	20.43 There you shall *r* your ways and all the
	36.31 Then you will *r* your evil ways, and your
Hos	7. 2 consider that I *r* all their wickedness.
Am	1. 9 and did not *r* the covenant of kinship.
Mic	6. 5 O my people, *r* now what King Balak of
Hab	3. 2 it known; in wrath may you *r* mercy.
Zech	10. 9 yet in far countries they shall *r* me,
Mal	4. 4 *R* the teaching of my servant Moses, the
Mt	5.23 if you *r* that your brother or sister has
Lk	16.25 Abraham said, "Child, *r* that during your
	17.32 field must not turn back. *R* Lot's wife.
	23.42 "Jesus, *r* me when you come into your
Jn	15.20 *R* the word that I said to you, 'Servants
Gal	2.10 only one thing, that we *r* the poor,
Eph	2.11 So then, *r* that at one time you Gentiles
2 Tim	2. 8 *R* Jesus Christ, raised from the dead, a
Heb	8.12 and I will *r* their sins no more."
	13. 3 *R* those who are in prison, as though
Jude	17 beloved, must *r* the predictions of the
Rev	3. 3 *R* then what you received and heard;

REMEMBERS (REMEMBERED REMEMBERING)

Gen	8. 1 God *r* Noah and all the wild animals
	19.29 God *r* Abraham, and sent Lot out of the
	30.22 Then God *r* Rachel, and God heeded
	42. 9 Joseph also *r* the dreams that he had
Ex	2.24 God *r* his covenant with Abraham,
	6. 5 as slaves, and I have *r* my covenant.
	20.24 place where I cause my name to be *r*
Num	10. 9 so that you may be *r* before the LORD
Esth	9.28 These days should be *r* and kept
Ps	78.35 They *r* that God was their rock, the
	98. 3 He has *r* his steadfast love and
	112. 6 never be moved; they will be *r* forever.
	136. 23 It is he who *r* us in our low estate, for
Eccl	1.11 The people of long ago are not *r*, nor
Isa	65.17 former things shall not be *r* or come to
Lam	1. 7 Jerusalem *r*, in the day of her affliction
Ezek	23.19 increased her whorings, *r* the days of

Jon	2. 7 I *r* the LORD; and my prayer came to
Mt	26.75 Peter *r* what Jesus had said: "Before the
Lk	24. 8 Then they *r* his words, and returning
Rev	18. 5 as heaven, and God has *r* her iniquities.

REMEMBRANCE

Ex	28.12 Aaron shall bear their names . . . for *r*.
	39. 7 the ephod, to be stones of *r* for the sons
1 Kings	17.18 have come to me to bring my sin to *r*,
Ps	6. 5 For in death there is no *r* of you; in
Mal	3.16 a book of *r* was written before him of
Mt	26.13 she has done will be told in *r* of her."
Lk	22.19 is given for you. Do this in *r* of me."
1 Cor	11.24 body that is for you. Do this in *r* of me."

REMIND

Isa	62. 6 You who *r* the LORD, take no rest, and

REMINDER

Ex	13. 9 your hand and as a *r* on your forehead,
	17.14 "Write this as a *r* in a book and recite it
	30.16 it will be a *r* to the Israelites of the
Num	10.10 they shall serve as a *r* on your behalf

REMISSION

Deut	15. 1 year you shall grant a *r* of debts.
	31.10 seventh year, in the scheduled year of *r*,

REMNANT

2 Kings	19.30 The surviving *r* of the house of Judah
	21.14 I will cast off the *r* of my heritage, and
2 Chr	30. 6 he may turn again to the *r* of you who
Ezra	9. 8 our God, who has left us a *r*, and given
Isa	10.20 On that day the *r* of Israel and the
	37. 4 lift up your prayer for the *r* that is left."
	37.31 surviving *r* of the house of Judah shall
	46. 3 of Jacob, all the *r* of the house of Israel,
Jer	23. 3 I myself will gather the *r* of my flock
	31. 7 O LORD, your people, the *r* of Israel."
	40.11 king of Babylon had left a *r* in Judah
Am	5.15 will be gracious to the *r* of Joseph.
	9.12 that they may possess the *r* of Edom
Mic	4. 7 The lame I will make the *r*, and those
	5. 8 among the nations the *r* of Jacob,
	7.18 of the *r* of your possession?
Zeph	3.13 the *r* of Israel; they shall do no wrong
Zech	8. 6 though it seems impossible to the *r*
	8.12 cause the *r* of this people to possess
Rom	9.27 the sea, only a *r* of them will be saved;
	11. 5 time there is a *r*, chosen by grace.

REMOVE (REMOVED REMOVES)

2 Kings	23.27 LORD said, "I will *r* Judah also out of my
Ps	103. 12 the west, so far he *r* our transgressions
Prov	22.28 Do not *r* the ancient landmark that your
Isa	54.10 may depart and the hills be *r*, but
Zech	3. 9 I will *r* the guilt of this land in a single

RENDER (RENDERED)

Ps	28. 4 of their hands; *r* them their due reward.
Isa	59.18 to the coastlands he will *r* requital.
Rev	18. 6 *R* to her as she herself has *r*, and repay

RENEW (RENEWED)

1 Sam	11.14 go to Gilgal, and there *r* the kingship."
Ps	103. 5 so that your youth is *r* like the eagle's.
Isa	40.31 wait for the LORD shall *r* their strength,
Lam	5.21 may be restored; *r* our days as of old —
Zeph	3.17 with gladness, he will *r* you in his love;
Col	3.10 which is being *r* in knowledge according

RENEWAL

Mt	19.28 at the *r* of all things, when the Son of

RENOUNCE

Ps	10. 3 greedy for gain curse and *r* the LORD.

RENOWN (RENOWNED)

Gen	6. 4 heroes that were of old, warriors of *r*.

Ps   135. 13 forever, your *r*, O LORD, throughout all
Isa   62. 7 and makes it *r* throughout the earth.

REPAIR (REPAIRED REPAIRING REPAIRS)

1 Kings 18.30 First he *r* the altar of the LORD that had
2 Kings 12. 5 let them *r* the house wherever any need
       12.14 given to the workers who were *r* the
       22. 5 at the house of the LORD, *r* the house,
Neh   3. 4 made *r*. Next to them Meshullam
Prov   6.15 in a moment, damage beyond *r*.

REPAY

Ezek   23.49 They shall *r* you for your lewdness, and
Job   34.11 according to their deeds he will *r* them,
Ps   35.12 They *r* me evil for good; my soul is
       62.12 LORD. For you *r* to all according to their
      103. 10 to our sins, nor *r* us according to our
Jer   16.18 And I will doubly *r* their iniquity and
       25.14 will *r* them according to their deeds
       50.29 *R* her according to her deeds; just as
Hos   4. 9 their ways, and *r* them for their deeds.
Joel   2.25 I will *r* you for the years that the
Rom   2. 6 he will *r* according to each one's deeds:

REPENT (REPENTED REPENTS)

1 Kings 8.47 have been taken captive, and *r*, and
2 Chr   6.38 if they *r* with all their heart and soul in
Job   42. 6 therefore I despise myself, and *r* in dust
Isa   1.27 those in her who *r*, by righteousness.
Jer   8. 6 no one *r* of wickedness, saying, "What
Ezek   14. 6 Thus says the Lord GOD: *R* and turn
       18.30 *R* and turn away from all your
Mt   3. 2 "*R*, for the kingdom of heaven has come
        4.17 proclaim, "*R*, for the kingdom of heaven
       11.20 had been done, because they did not *r*.
       12.41 they *r* at the preaching of Jonah, and
       27. 3 he *r* and brought back the thirty pieces
Mk   6.12 out and proclaimed that all should *r*.
Lk   10.13 and Sidon, they would have *r* long ago,
       11.32 they *r* at the preaching of Jonah,
       13. 3 but unless you *r* you will all perish as
       16.30 to them from the dead, they will *r*.'
Acts   2.38 Peter said to them, "*R*, and be baptized
        3.19 *R* therefore, and turn to God so that
       17.30 commands all people everywhere to *r*,
2 Tim   2.25 grant that they will *r* and come to know
Heb   12.17 for he found no chance to *r*, even
Rev   2. 5 *r*, and do the works you did at first. If
        2.16 *R* then. If not, I will come to you soon
        2.21 I gave her time to *r*, but she refuses to *r*
        9.20 The rest of humankind . . . did not *r* of
       16. 9 and they did not *r* and give him glory.

REPENTANCE

Mt   3. 8 Bear fruit worthy of *r*.
Mk   1. 4 proclaiming a baptism of *r* for the
Lk   3. 3 proclaiming a baptism of *r* for the
        3. 8 Bear fruits worthy of *r*. Do not begin to
        5.32 call not the righteous but sinners to *r*."
       15. 7 righteous persons who need no *r*.
       24.47 that *r* and forgiveness of sins is to be
Acts   5.31 he might give *r* to Israel and forgiveness
       11.18 given even to the Gentiles the *r* that
       20.21 to both Jews and Greeks about *r*
       26.20 to God and do deeds consistent with *r*.
Rom   2. 4 kindness is meant to lead you to *r*?

REPORT (REPORTS)

Dan   11.44 *r* from the east and the north shall
Mt   14. 1 At that time Herod the ruler heard *r*
Acts   25. 2 of the Jews gave him a *r* against Paul.

REPROACH (REPROACHES)

Gen   30.23 and said, "God has taken away my *r*";
Ruth   2.15 the standing sheaves, and do not *r* her.
Prov   27.11 so that I may answer whoever *r* me.
Jer   20. 8 become for me a *r* and derision all day
1 Tim   3. 2 a bishop must be above *r*, married only

REPROOF

Prov   1.23 Give heed to my *r*; I will pour out my
        5.12 discipline, and my heart despised *r*!
       13.18 but one who heeds *r* is honored.
       29.15 The rod and *r* give wisdom, but a

REPROVE (REPROVED)

Prov   19.25 *r* the intelligent, and they will gain
       29. 1 who is often *r*, yet remains stubborn,
1 Cor 14.24 outsider who enters is *r* by all and

REPUTE

1 Sam 18.23 that I am a poor man and of no *r*?"

REQUEST

Esth   5. 3 is it Queen Esther? What is your *r*?
        7. 3 the lives of my people—that is my *r*.
Job   6. 8 "O that I might have my *r*, and that God
Ps   21. 2 and have not withheld the *r* of his lips.
Dan   2.49 Daniel made *r* of the king, and he

REQUIRE (REQUIRED)

Deut   10.12 God of you? Only to fear the LORD
Ezra   7.20 whatever else is *r* for the house of your
Ezek   3.18 but their blood I will *r* at your hand.
       33. 6 but their blood I will *r* at the sentinel's
Mic   6. 8 what does the LORD *r* of you but to do

RESCUE (RESCUED RESCUES RESCUING)

Num   35.25 the congregation shall *r* the slayer from
1 Sam 30.18 had taken; and David *r* his two wives.
1 Chr 16.35 gather and *r* us from among the
Ps   35.17 you look on? *R* me from their ravages,
       37.40 The LORD helps them and *r* them; he *r*
       69.14 help *r* me from sinking in the mire;
       71. 2 your righteousness deliver me and *r* me;
       71.23 to you; my soul also, which you have *r*.
      136. 24 and *r* us from our foes, for his steadfast
Prov   24.11 if you hold back from *r* those taken
Isa   1.17 seek justice, *r* the oppressed, defend the
Jer   30. 7 for Jacob; yet he shall be *r* from it.
Ezek   34.10 I will *r* my sheep from their mouths, so
Dan   8. 4 it, and no one could *r* from its power;
Acts   7.25 that God through him was *r* them,
       12.11 the Lord has sent his angel and *r* me
Rom   7.24 Who will *r* me from this body of death?
2 Cor   1.10 He who *r* us from so deadly a peril will
Col   1.13 He has *r* us from the power of darkness
2 Tim   4.18 The Lord will *r* me from every evil
2 Pet   2. 7 and if he *r* Lot, a righteous man greatly

RESERVED

2 Pet   3. 7 heavens and earth have been *r* for fire,

RESIDE (RESIDES RESIDING)

Lev   19.33 When an alien *r* with you in your land,
Num   9.14 Any alien *r* among you who wishes to
2 Chr   6.18 "But will God indeed *r* with mortals on
Job   11.14 and do not let wickedness *r* in your

RESIST (RESISTED)

Job   9. 4 —who has *r* him, and succeeded?—
Jas   4. 7 R the devil, and he will flee from you.
1 Pet   5. 9 *R* him, steadfast in your faith, for you

RESOLVED

Dan   1. 8 Daniel *r* that he would not defile

RESOURCES

Ezra   2.69 According to their *r* they gave to the

RESPECT

Dan   11.37 He shall pay no *r* to the gods of his
Mt   21.37 to them, saying, 'They will *r* my son.'
Mk   12. 6 to them, saying, 'They will *r* my son.'
Lk   20.13 beloved son; perhaps they will *r* him.'
Eph   5.33 and a wife should *r* her husband.

RESPONSIBLE

Acts 20.26 this day that I am not r for the blood of

REST (n)

Lev 16.31 a sabbath of complete r to you, and you
25. 4 there shall be a sabbath of complete r
Deut 3.20 When the LORD gives r to your kindred,
12.10 when he gives you r from your enemies
25.19 God has given you r from all your
Josh 1.15 until the LORD gives r to your kindred as
11.23 And the land had r from war.
23. 1 LORD had given r to Israel from all their
Judg 3.11 the land had r forty years. Then Othniel
5.31 in its might." And land had r forty years.
2 Sam 7. 1 LORD had given him r from all his
2 Kings 25.11 Babylon— all the r of the population.
1 Chr 28. 2 I had planned to build a house of r for
Neh 9.28 after they had r, they again did evil
Job 3.17 troubling, and there the weary are at r.
11.18 be protected and take your r in safety.
Ps 95.11 I swore, "They shall not enter my r."
116. 7 Return, O my soul, to your r, for the
Isa 30.15 In returning what you shall be saved;
Mic 5. 3 then the r of his kindred shall return to
Mt 11.28 heavy burdens, and I will give you r.
Mk 14.41 you still sleeping and taking your r?
2 Cor 7. 5 Macedonia, our bodies had no r, but we
Heb 3.11 I swore, 'They will not enter my r.' "
4. 9 a sabbath r still remains for the people
Rev 11.13 the r were terrified and gave glory to

REST (RESTED RESTS)

Gen 2. 2 he r on the seventh day from all the
18. 4 feet, and r yourselves under the tree,
Ex 23.12 work, but on seventh day you shall r;
Lev 26.34 the land shall r, and enjoy its sabbath
Deut 33.12 the beloved r between his shoulders.
Ruth 3.18 the man will not r, but will settle the
2 Kings 2.15 "The spirit of Elijah r on Elisha."
Eccl 2.23 even at night their minds do not r.
Isa 11. 2 spirit of the LORD shall r on him, the
Dan 12.13 you, go your way, and r; you shall rise
Heb 4. 4 "And God r on the seventh day from all
Rev 14.13 "they will r from their labors, for their

RESTING PLACE

Isa 66. 1 build for me, and what is my r?
Lk 11.24 waterless regions looking for a r,

RESTORE (RESTORED RESTORES)

2 Kings 8. 1 the woman whose son he had r to life,
2 Chr 24. 4 afterward Joash decided to r the house
33.16 He also r the altar of the LORD and
Ps 23. 3 he r my soul. He leads me in right
80.19 R us, O LORD God of hosts; let your face
85. 4 R us again, O God of our salvation, and
Isa 1.26 I will r your judges as at the first, and
Jer 8.22 health of my poor people not been r?
33.26 For I will r their fortunes, and will have
Lam 5.21 R us to yourself, O LORD, that we may
Dan 8.14 then the sanctuary shall be r to its
9.25 went out to r and rebuild Jerusalem
Mt 12.13 He stretched it out, and it was r, as
17.11 is indeed coming and will r all things;
Lk 6.10 hand." He did so, and his hand was r.
Acts 1. 6 the time when you will r the kingdom
Gal 6. 1 the Spirit should r such a one in a spirit
Heb 6. 4 it is impossible to r again to repentance

RESTRAIN (RESTRAINED RESTRAINING)

Ex 36. 6 So people were r from bringing;
1 Sam 3.13 God, and he did not r them.
Job 7.11 I will not r my mouth; I will speak in
Isa 64.12 all this, will you r yourself, O LORD?
2 Thess 2. 6 you know what is now r him, so that he

RESTRAINT

Prov 14.16 from evil, but the fool throws off r and

Prov 29.18 is no prophecy, the people cast off r,
1 Cor 7.35 own benefit, not to put any r upon you,

RESURRECTION

Mt 22.23 came to him, saying there is no r;
Mk 12.18 Sadducees, who say that there is no r,
Lk 14.14 will be repaid at the r of the righteous."
20.27 those who say that there is no r,
Jn 5.29 who have done good, to the r of life,
11.25 said to her, "I am the r and the life.
Acts 1.22 must become a witness with us to his r."
2.31 David spoke of the r of the Messiah,
17.18 the good news about Jesus and the r.)
23. 6 the hope of the r of the dead."
24.15 that there will be a r of both the
Rom 6. 5 be united with him in a r like his.
1 Cor 15.12 of you say there is no r of the dead?
2 Tim 2.18 truth by claiming that the r has already
Heb 11.35 Women received their dead by r. Others
1 Pet 1. 3 a living hope through the r of Jesus
Rev 20. 5 years were ended.) This is the first r.

RETAIN

Num 36. 7 Israelites shall r the inheritance of their

RETRIBUTION

Jer 15.15 visit me, and bring down r for me on

RETURN (RETURNED RETURNING RETURNS)

Gen 16. 9 said to her, "R to your mistress, and
20. 7 Now then, r the man's wife; for he is a
31. 3 Jacob, "R to the land of your ancestors
32. 9 'R to your country and to your kindred,
44. 4 "Why have you r evil for good? Why
50.14 Joseph r to Egypt with his brothers and
Num 10.36 "R, O LORD of the ten thousand
Deut 4.30 you will r to the LORD your God and
22. 2 the owner claims it; then you shall r it.
30. 2 and r to the LORD your God, and you
Josh 22. 9 half-tribe of Manasseh r home, parting
1 Sam 7. 3 "If you are r to the LORD with all your
Job 10.21 before I go, never to r, to the land of
22.23 If you r to the Almighty, you will be
Ps 51.13 your ways, and sinners will r to you.
116. 7 R, O my soul, to your rest; for the LORD
116. 12 What shall I r to the LORD for all his
Eccl 12. 7 and the breath r to God who gave it.
Song 6.13 R, r, O Shulammite! R, r, that we may
Isa 35.10 ransomed of the LORD shall r, and come
44.22 like mist; r to me, for I have redeemed
51.11 ransomed of the LORD shall r, and come
55.11 it shall not r to me empty, but it shall
Jer 3. 1 many lovers; and would you r to me?
3.12 R, faithless Israel, says the LORD. I will
4. 1 If you r, O Israel, says the LORD, if you
24. 7 shall r to me with their whole heart.
30.10 Jacob shall r and have quiet and ease,
Hos 2. 7 "I will go and r to my first husband, for
6. 1 "Come, let us r to the LORD; for it is he
14. 1 R, O Israel, to the LORD your God, for
Am 4. 8 not satisfied; yet you did not r to me,
Zech 1. 3 R to me, says the LORD of hosts, and I
Mal 3. 7 R to me, and I will r to you, says the
Lk 8.39 "R to your home, and declare how much
11.24 it says, 'I will r to my house from which
17.18 Was none of them found to r and give
Acts 15.16 'After this I will r, and I will rebuild the

REUBEN

Born, Gen 29.32; found mandrakes for Leah, Gen 30.14; rescued Joseph, Gen 37.21-22; blessed by Jacob, Gen 49.3-4.

Tribe of Reuben: blessed by Moses, Deut 33.6.

REVEAL (REVEALED REVEALING REVEALS)

Deut 29.29 but the r things belong to us and to our
1 Sam 3. 7 of the LORD had not yet been r to him,
3.21 LORD r himself to Samuel at Shiloh by

1 Sam	9.15	Saul came, the LORD had r to Samuel:
Ps	98. 2	he has r his vindication in the sight of
Prov	20.19	A gossip r secrets; therefore do not
Isa	22.14	LORD of hosts has r himself in my ears:
	53. 1	whom has the arm of the LORD been r?
	56. 1	will come, and my deliverance be r.
Dan	2.19	the mystery was r to Daniel in a vision
	2.28	God in heaven who r mysteries, and he
Am	3. 7	God does nothing, without r his secret
Mt	11.25	intelligent and have r them to infants;
	11.27	to whom the Son chooses to r him.
	16.17	flesh and blood has not r this to you,
Lk	2.26	It had been r to him by the Holy Spirit
	2.35	the inner thoughts of many will be r."
	10.21	intelligent and have r them to infants;
	10.22	to whom the Son chooses to r him."
	17.30	on the day that the Son of man is r.
Jn	1.31	this reason, that he might be r to Israel."
	12.38	whom has the arm of the Lord been r?"
Rom	1.17	righteousness of God is r through faith
	8.19	longing for the r of the children of God;
1 Cor	1. 7	gift as you wait for the r of our Lord
	2.10	God has r to us through the Spirit;
	3.13	because it will be r with fire, and the
Gal	1.16	grace, was pleased to r his Son to me,
Col	3. 4	is r, then you also will be r with him
2 Thess	1. 7	when the Lord Jesus is r from heaven
1 Pet	1.12	It was r to them that they were serving
	1.13	Jesus Christ will bring you when he is r.
	4.13	and shout for joy when his glory is r.
1 Jn	1. 2	this life was r, and we have seen it and
	3. 2	what we shall be has not yet been r.
	4. 9	God's love was r among us in this way:

REVEL

Ex	32. 6	down to eat and drink, and rose up to r.

REVELATION

Rom	16.25	you according to the r of the mystery
Gal	1.12	I received it through a r of Jesus Christ.
	2. 2	I went up in response to a r. Then I laid
Eph	3. 3	was made known to me by r, as I wrote

REVENGE

Judg	15. 7	not stop until I have taken r on you."
	16.28	with this one act of r I may pay back
Esth	8.13	were to be ready on that day to take r
Prov	6.34	he shows no restraint when he takes r.
Jer	20.10	against him, and take our r on him."

REVENUE

Ezra	4.13	or toll, and the royal r will be reduced.
Isa	23. 3	waters; your r was the grain of Shihor,
Rom	13. 7	taxes are due, r to whom r is due,

REVERE (REVERED)

Josh	24.14	"Now therefore r the LORD, and serve
1 Chr	16.25	to be praised; he is r above all gods.
Mal	3.16	those who r the LORD spoke with one

REVERENCE

Lev	19.30	keep my sabbaths and r my sanctuary: I
	26. 2	keep my sabbaths and r my sanctuary: I
1 Pet	3. 2	they see the purity and r of your lives.
	3.15	in you; yet do it with gentleness and r.

REVERENT

Titus	2. 3	the older women to be r in behavior,

REVILE (REVILED)

Ex	22.28	"You shall not r God, or curse a leader
2 Kings	19.22	Whom have you mocked and r? Against
Ps	74.10	to scoff? Is the enemy to r your name
Isa	65. 7	the mountains and r me upon the hills,
Mt	5.11	"Blessed are you when people r you and
1 Cor	4.12	When r, we bless; when persecuted, we
1 Pet	4.14	If you are r for the name of Christ, you

REVIVE (REVIVED REVIVING)

Gen	45.27	him, the spirit of their father Jacob r.
Judg	15.19	he drank, his spirit returned, and he r.
1 Kings	17.22	child came into him again, and he r.
Neh	4. 2	Will they r the stones out of the heaps
Ps	19. 7	law of the LORD is perfect, r the soul;
	85. 6	Will you not r us again, so that your
	119. 25	the dust; r me according to your word.
Isa	57.15	in spirit, to r the spirit of the humble,
Lam	1.11	treasures for food to r their strength.
Hos	6. 2	After two days he will r us; on the third
Hab	3. 2	In our own time r it; in our own time
Phil	4.10	at last you have r your concern for me;

REWARD

Gen	15. 1	your shield; your r shall be very great."
1 Sam	24.19	So may the LORD r you with good for
Ps	19.11	in keeping them there is great r.
	58.11	"Surely there is a r for the righteous;
	109. 5	So they r me evil for good, and hatred
Isa	40.10	his r is with him, and his recompense
Mt	5.12	be glad, for your r is great in heaven,
	5.46	who love you, what r do you have?
	6. 6	Father who sees in secret will r you.
	10.41	of a prophet will receive a prophet's r;
Mk	9.41	of Christ will by no means lose the r.
Lk	6.35	nothing in return. "Your r will be great,
1 Cor	9.18	What then is my r? Just this: that in my

RIBS

Gen	2.21	then he took one of his r and closed up

RICH (RICHER)

Gen	13. 2	Now Abram was very r in livestock, in
	14.23	might not say, 'I have made Abram r.'
Ex	30.15	The r shall not give more, and the poor
2 Sam	12. 2	The r man had very many flocks and
Job	15.29	they will not be r, and their wealth will
Prov	10.22	The blessing of the LORD makes r, and
	11.24	Some give freely, yet grow all the r;
	14.20	neighbors, but the r have many friends.
	22. 2	The r and the poor have this in
	23. 4	Do not wear yourself out to get r; be
Mt	19.23	be hard for a r person to enter the
	27.57	there came a r man from Arimathea,
Mk	10.25	who is r to enter the kingdom of God.
Lk	1.53	good things, and sent the r away empty.
	6.24	"But woe to you who are r, for you have
	12.16	land of a r man produced abundantly.
	16. 1	"There was a r man who had a manager,
	16.19	"There was a r man, who was dressed in
	18.23	this, he became sad, for he was very r.
1 Cor	4. 8	you want! Already you have become r!
1 Tim	6. 9	who want to be r fall into temptation
	6.17	who are in the present age r, command
Jas	1.10	the r will disappear like a flower in the
	5. 1	you r people, weep and wail for the
Rev	2. 9	your poverty, even though you are r.
	3.17	For you say, 'I am r, I have prospered,
	18. 3	merchants of the earth have grown r

RICHES

1 Kings	10.23	excelled all the kings of the earth in r
Job	20.15	They swallow down r and vomit them
Ps	119. 14	way of your decrees as much as in all r.
Prov	11. 4	R do not profit in the day of wrath, but
	11.16	destitute, but the aggressive gain r.
	11.28	Those who trust in their r will wither,
	27.24	for r do not last forever; nor a crown for
Jer	48.36	for the r they gained have perished.
Rom	2. 4	the r of his kindness and forbearance
	11.12	if their stumbling means r for the world,
	11.33	O the depth of the r and wisdom and
Eph	3. 8	the news of the boundless r of Christ,
	3.16	according to the r of his glory, he may
Phil	4.19	need of yours according to his r in glory

RIDDLE

Judg	14.12 "Let me now put a r to you. If you can
	14.19 to those who had explained the r.

RIDICULE (RIDICULED)

Lk	14.29 to finish, all who see it begin to r him,
	16.14 money, heard all this, and they r him.

RIGHT

Gen	13. 9 then I will go to the r; or if you take the
	38.26 "She is more in the r than I, since I did
Deut	6.25 has commanded us, we will be in the r."
Judg	17. 6 people did what was r in their own minds,
	21.25 people did what was r in their own eyes.
2 Chr	24. 2 Joash did what was r in the sight of the
Job	33.12 in this you are not r. I will answer you:
	35. 2 be just? You say, 'I am r before God.'
	36. 6 alive, but gives the afflicted their r.
	42. 7 not spoken of me what is r, as my
Ps	17. 2 come; let your eyes see the r.
	58. 1 you indeed decree what is r, you gods?
Isa	43.26 your case, so that you may be proved r.
Lam	1.18 The LORD is in the r, for I have rebelled
Hab	2. 4 Look at the proud! Their spirit is not r
Mt	20.21 one at your r hand and one at your left,
Mk	16.19 an and sat down at the r hand of God.
Acts	2.33 exalted at the r hand of God, and
	7.55 of God and Jesus standing at the r hand
	10.35 him and does what is r is acceptable
2 Cor	5.13 for God; if we are in our r mind, it is for
	8.21 we intend to do what is r not only in
Eph	1.20 the dead and seated him at his r hand
Jas	4.17 who knows the r thing to do and fails to
1 Jn	2.29 everyone who does r is born of him.

RIGHTS

Prov	29. 7 The righteous know the r of the poor;
	31. 9 righteously, defend the r of the poor
Jer	5.28 they do not defend the r of the needy.
1 Cor	9.18 to make full use of my r in the gospel.

RIGHTEOUS

Gen	6. 9 Noah was a r man, blameless in his
	18.24 Suppose there are fifty r within the city;
1 Sam	24.17 "You are more r than I; for you have
1 Kings	8.32 vindicating the r by rewarding them
Job	4.17 'Can mortals be r before God? Can
	17. 9 Yet the r hold to their way, and they
	25. 4 then can a mortal be r before God?
	32. 1 Job, because he was r in his own eyes.
Ps	1. 6 the LORD watches over the way of the r,
	7.11 God is a r judge, and a God who has
	11. 3 are destroyed, what can the r do?"
	14. 5 for God is with the comapny of the r.
	37.29 The r shall inherit the land, and live in
	64.10 Let the r rejoice in the LORD, and take
	68. 3 But let the r be joyful; let them exult
	71.15 My mouth will tell of your r acts, of
	92.12 The r flourish like the palm tree, and
	97.11 Light dawns for the r, and joy for the
	119.137 You are r, O LORD, and your judgments
	141. 5 Let the r strike me; let the faithful
	143. 2 for no one living is r before you.
Prov	4.18 But the path of the r is like the light of
	10. 7 The memory of the r is a blessing, but
	10.16 The wage of the r leads to life, the gain
	10.28 The hope of the r ends in gladness, but
	12.13 their lips, but the r escape from trouble.
	12.26 The r gives good advice to friends, but
	15. 6 In the house of the r there is much
	18.10 tower; the r run into it and are safe.
	20. 7 The r walk in integrity— happy are the
	21.15 justice is done, it is a joy to the r,
	25.26 the r who give way before the wicked.
	28. 1 pursues, but the r are as bold as a lion.
	28.28 but when they perish, the r increase.
Eccl	3.17 God will judge the r and the wicked, for
	7.20 there is no one on the earth so r as to
	8.14 that there are r people who are treated
	9. 2 the same fate comes to all, to the r and
Isa	26. 2 Open the gates, so that the r nation
	53.11 r one, my servant, shall make many r,
	57. 1 The r perish, and no one takes it to
	64. 6 all our r deeds are like a filthy cloth.
Jer	33.15 time I will cause a r Branch to spring
Ezek	3.21 you warn the r not to sin, they shall
	18. 5 If a man is r and does what is lawful
	18.24 But when the r turn away from their
	18.26 When the r turn away from their
Hab	2. 4 in them, but the r live by their faith.
Mt	1.19 Her husband Joseph, being a r man and
	5.45 and sends rain on the r and on the
Mk	6.20 knowing that he was a r and holy man,
Lk	1. 6 Both of them were r before God, living
	2.25 Simeon; this man was r and devout,
	18. 9 r and regarded others with contempt:
Rom	1.17 "The one who is r will live by faith."
	3.10 "There is no one who is r, not even one;
	3.26 that he himself is r and that he justifies
	5. 7 rarely will anyone die for a r person
	5.19 obedience the many will be made r.
Gal	3.11 for "The one who is r will live by faith."
Heb	10.38 delay; but my r one will live by faith.
Jas	5. 6 condemned and murdered the r one,
1 Pet	3.18 once for all, the r for the unrighteous,
	4.18 If it is hard for the r to be saved, what
2 Pet	2. 7 if he rescued Lot, a r man greatly
	2. 8 (for that r man, living among them day
Rev	19. 8 fine linen is the r deeds of the saints.

RIGHTEOUSNESS

Gen	15. 6 and the LORD reckoned it to him as r.
	18.19 way of the LORD by doing r and justice;
Deut	9. 4 "It is because of my r that the LORD has
1 Sam	26.23 The LORD rewards everyone for his r and
Job	27. 6 I hold fast my r, and will not let it go;
	29.14 I put on r, and it clothed me; my justice
	36. 3 far away and ascribe r to my Maker.
	37.23 and abundant r he will not violate.
Ps	33. 5 He loves r and justice; the earth is full
	36. 6 Your r is like the mighty mountains,
	45. 7 equity; you love r and hate wickedness.
	50. 6 The heavens declare his r, for God
	71.19 Your power and your r, O God, reach
	89.14 R and justice are the foundation of your
	89.16 name all day long, and extol your r.
	96.13 He will judge the world with r, and the
	106. 31 And that has been reckoned to him as r
	112. 3 houses, and their r endures forever.
	119.142 Your r is an everlasting r, and your law
Prov	2. 9 Then you will understand r and justice
	10. 2 do not profit, but r delivers from death.
	11.19 Whoever is steadfast in r will live, but
	12.28 In the path of r is life, in walking its
	14.34 R exalts a nation, but sin is a reproach
	16.12 evil, for the throne is established by r.
	21.21 Whoever pursues r and kindness will
Eccl	7.15 righteous people who perish in their r,
Isa	5. 7 but saw bloodshed; r, but heard a cry!
	11. 4 hear; but with r he shall judge the poor,
	32.16 and r abide in the fruitful field.
	33. 5 high; he filled Zion with justice and r;
	45.24 shall be said of me, are r and strength;
	54.14 In r you shall be established; you shall
	57.12 I will concede your r and your works,
	58. 2 as if they were a nation that practiced r
	59.17 put on r like a breastplate, and a
	61. 3 spirit. They will be called oaks of r,
	61.10 he has covered me with the robe of r,
Jer	22. 3 Act with justice and r, and deliver from
	23. 6 he will be called: "The LORD is our r."
Ezek	14.14 save only their own lives by their r,
	18.22 for the r that they have done they shall
	33.12 r of the righteous shall not save them

Dan	4.27	atone for your sins with *r*, and your
	9. 7	"*R* is on your side, O Lord, but open to
	9.18	before you on the ground of our *r*, but
Hos	10.12	Sow for yourselves *r*; reap steadfast love;
Am	5.24	and *r* like an everflowing stream.
Mt	3.15	proper for us in this way to fulfill all *r*."
	5.20	unless your *r* exceeds that of the scribes
	21.32	John came to you in the way of *r* and
Lk	1.75	fear, in holiness and *r* before him
Jn	16. 8	wrong about sin and *r* and judgment:
Acts	17.31	he will have the world judged in *r* by a
Rom	1.17	in it the *r* of God is revealed through
	3.21	law, the *r* of God has been disclosed,
	4. 3	God, and it was reckoned to him as *r*."
	4. 6	whom God reckons *r* apart from works:
	5.18	one man's act of *r* leads to justification
	6.19	present your members as slaves to *r* for
	9.30	Gentiles who did not strive for *r*, have
	10. 3	being ignorant of the *r* that comes from
1 Cor	1.30	for us wisdom from God, and *r* and
2 Cor	5.21	so that we might become the *r* of God.
Gal	3. 6	God, and it was reckoned to him as *r*."
	3.21	*r* would indeed come through the law.
Eph	4.24	likeness of God in true *r* and holiness.
Phil	3. 9	Christ, the *r* from God based on faith.
1 Tim	6.11	all this; pursue *r*, godliness, faith, love,
2 Tim	3.16	for correction, and for training in *r*,
Heb	11. 7	an heir to the *r* that is in accordance
Jas	1.20	your anger does not produce God's *r*.
	3.18	harvest of *r* is sown in peace for those

RING (RINGS)

Gen	35. 4	had, and the *r* that were in their ears;
Ex	32. 2	"Take off the gold *r* that are on the ears
Esth	3.10	the king took his signet *r* from his hand
Lk	15.22	put a *r* on his finger and sandals on his

RIOT

Mt	26. 5	the festival, or there may be a *r* among
Mk	14. 2	the festival, or there may be a *r* among

RISE (RISEN RISING)

Gen	13.17	*R* up, walk through the length and the
Ps	9.19	*R* up, O Lord! Let not mortals prevail;
	17.13	*R* up, O Lord, confront them, overthrow
	44.26	*R* up, come to our help. Redeem us for
	68. 1	Let God *r* up, let his enemies be
	113. 3	From the *r* of the sun to its setting the
Prov	24.16	though they fall seven times, they will *r*
Isa	30.18	therefore he will *r* up to show mercy
	52. 2	the dust, *r* up, O captive Jerusalem;
	58.10	your light *r* in the darkness and your
Mk	8.31	be killed, and after three days *r* again.
	9. 9	the Son of Man had *r* from the dead.
	9.31	days after being killed, he will *r* again."
Lk	2.34	for the falling and *r* of many in Israel,
	7.14	he said, "Young man, I say to you, *r*."
	24. 5	the dead? He is not here, but has *r*
	24. 7	crucified, and on the third day *r* again."
	24.34	"The Lord has *r* indeed, and he has
Jn	11.23	said to her, "Your brother will *r* again."
Acts	26.23	by being the first to *r* from the dead, he
Eph	5.14	"Sleeper, awake! *R* from the dead, and
1 Thess	4.16	and the dead in Christ will *r* first.

RITUAL

Lev	6. 9	This is the *r* of the burnt offering.
	6.14	This is the *r* of the grain offering: The
	6.25	This is the *r* of the sin offering. The sin
	7. 1	This is the *r* of the guilt offering. It is
	7.11	This is the *r* of the sacrifice of the offering

RIVER (RIVERS)

Gen	2.10	A *r* flows out of Eden to water the
Ps	46. 4	There is a *r* whose streams make glad
	107. 33	He turns *r* into a desert, springs of
	137. 1	By the *r* of Babylon—there we sat
Isa	7.20	with a razor hired beyond the *R*—

Isa	33.21	for us a place of broad *r* and streams,
	41.18	open *r* on the bare heights, and
	48.18	prosperity would have been like a *r*,
	66.12	I will extend prosperity to her like a *r*,
Lam	3.48	My eyes flow with *r* of tears because of
Rev	22. 1	showed me the *r* of the water of life,

ROAD (ROADS ROADSIDE)

Mt	2.12	left for their own country by another *r*.
Mk	10.46	a blind beggar, was sitting by the *r*.
Lk	14.23	'Go out into the *r* and lanes, and

ROAR (ROARS)

1 Chr	16.32	Let the sea *r*, and all that fills it; let the
Ps	96.11	and let the earth rejoice; let the sea *r*,
Hos	11.10	go after the Lord, who *r* like a lion;
Am	1. 2	The Lord *r* from Zion, and utters his
	3. 4	Does a lion *r* in the forest, when it has

ROB (ROBBED ROBBING ROBS)

Prov	22.22	Do not *r* the poor because they are
	28.24	Anyone who *r* father or mother and
Mal	3. 8	Will anyone *r* God? Yet you are *r* me!
2 Cor	11. 8	I *r* other churches by accepting support

ROBBERS

Jer	7.11	called by my name, become a den of *r*
Mk	11.17	But you have made it a den of *r*."
Lk	10.30	fell into the hands of *r*, who stripped
Acts	19.37	men here who are neither temple *r* nor

ROBE (ROBES)

Gen	37. 3	he had made him a long *r* with sleeves.
	37.23	they stripped him of his *r*, the long *r*
	37.31	a goat, and dipped the *r* in the blood.
Ex	39.22	He also made the *r* of the ephod all of
1 Sam	15.27	Saul caught hold of the hem of his *r*,
Ps	45. 8	your *r* are all fragrant with myrrh and
	45.13	in her chamber with gold-woven *r*;
Isa	22.21	will clothe him with your *r* and bind
	61.10	covered me with the *r* of righteousness,
Mt	22.11	there who was not wearing a wedding *r*,
Lk	15.22	'Quickly, bring out a *r*—the best
Jn	13. 4	took off his outer *r*, and tied a towel
	19. 5	the crown of thorns and the purple *r*.
Rev	6.11	They were each given a white *r* and told

ROCK

Ex	17. 6	Strike the *r*, and water will come out of
Num	20. 8	command the *r* before their eyes to
	20.11	up his hand and struck the *r* twice
Deut	32. 4	The *R*, his work is perfect, and all his
	32.31	their *r* is not as our *R*; our enemies are
1 Sam	2. 2	besides you; there is no *R* like our God.
2 Sam	22. 2	"The Lord is my *r*, my fortress, and my
Ps	18. 2	The Lord is my *r*, and my fortress, and
	18.31	And who is a *r* besides our God?—
	27. 5	of his tent; he will set me high on a *r*.
	28. 1	Lord, I call; my *r*, do not refuse to hear
	40. 2	and set my feet upon a *r*, making my
	61. 2	Lead me to the *r* that is higher than I;
	62. 6	He alone is my *r* and my salvation, my
	71. 3	Be to me a *r* of refuge, a strong fortress,
	78.16	He made streams come out of the *r*,
	89.26	my God, and the *R* of my salvation!'
	92.15	that the Lord is upright; he is my *r*,
	105. 41	He opened the *r*, and water gushed out;
	114. 8	who turns the *r* into a pool of water,
Isa	17.10	not remembered the *R* of your refuge;
	32. 2	the shade of a great *r* in a weary land.
	51. 1	to the *r* from which you were hewn,
Jer	23.29	and like a hammer that breaks a *r* in
Mt	7.24	a wise man who built his house on *r*.
	16.18	and on this *r* I will build my church,
Lk	6.48	deeply and laid the foundation on *r*;
1 Cor	10. 4	they drank from the spiritual *r* that

ROD

Ps	2. 9 You shall break them with a *r* of iron,
Prov	13.24 who spare the *r* hate their children,
	22.15 boy, but the *r* of discipline drives it far
	23.14 If you beat them with the *r*, you will
	26. 3 donkey, and a *r* for the back of fools.
Isa	10. 5 Assyria, the *r* of my anger— the club in
1 Cor	4.21 Am I to come to you with a *r*, or with

ROLL

Mk	16. 3 "Who will *r* away the stone for us from
Heb	1.12 like a cloak you will *r* them up, and like

ROMAN (ROMANS)

Jn	11.48 and the *R* will come and destroy both
Acts	16.21 that are not lawful for us as *R* to adopt
	22.25 for you to flog a *R* citizen who is
	25.16 not the custom of the *R* to hand over

ROME

Acts	2.10 Cyrene, and visitors from *R*, both Jews
	18. 2 had ordered all Jews to leave *R*.
	23.11 so you must bear witness also at *R*."
	28.16 When we came into *R*, Paul was
Rom	1. 7 To all God's beloved in *R*, who are
	1.15 the gospel to you also who are in *R*.
2 Tim	1.17 he arrived in *R*, he eagerly searched

ROOF

Gen	6.16 Make a *r* for the ark, and finish it to a
Mk	2. 4 they removed the *r* above him; and after
Acts	10. 9 Peter went up on the *r* to pray. He

ROOM

Ps	4. 1 You gave me *r* when I was in distress.
Mt	6. 6 whenever you pray, go into your *r* and
Lk	14.22 has been done, and still there is *r*.'
	22.12 He will show you a large *r* upstairs,
Acts	1.13 they went up to the *r* upstairs where
Philem	22 —prepare a guest *r* for me, for I am

ROOT (ROOTED)

1 Kings	14.15 he will *r* up Israel out of this good land
Prov	2.22 land, and the treacherous will be *r* out
	12. 3 but the *r* of the righteous will never be
Isa	11.10 On that day the *r* of Jesse shall stand
	37.31 Judah shall again take *r* downward, and
	40.24 scarcely has their stem taken *r* in the
Mt	3.10 ax is lying at the *r* of the trees; every
Rom	15.12 Isaiah says, "The *r* of Jesse shall come,
Eph	3.17 as you are being *r* and grounded in love.
Col	2. 7 *r* and built up in him and established in
1 Tim	6.10 For the love of money is the *r* of all
Rev	22.16 I am the *r* and the descendant of David,

ROPE (ROPES)

Josh	2.15 she let them down by a *r* through a
Jer	38.13 they drew Jeremiah up by the *r* and

ROSE

Song	2. 1 I am a *r* of Sharon, a lily of the valleys.

ROUSE

Joel	3.12 Let the nations *r* themselves, and come

ROYAL

Esth	4.14 perhaps you have come to *r* dignity for

RUDE

1 Cor	13. 5 not envious or boastful or arrogant or *r*.

RUIN (RUINS)

Deut	13.16 It shall remain a perpetual *r*, never to
Ps	35. 8 Let *r* come upon them unawares. And
	89.40 walls; you have laid his strongholds in *r*.
Prov	19. 3 One's own folly leads to *r*, yet the heart
Isa	25. 2 the city a heap, the fortified city a *r*;
Jer	25.11 This whole land shall become a *r* and a
	46.19 Memphis shall become a waste, a *r*,

Ezek	21.27 A *r*, a *r*, a *r*—I will make it! (Such has
Am	6. 6 but are not grieved over the *r* of Joseph!

RULE (n)

1 Cor	7.17 you. This is my *r* in all the churches.
Gal	6.16 As for those who will follow this *r*—
Eph	1.21 far above all *r* and authority and power

RULE (RULED RULES) (v)

Gen	1.16 day and the lesser light to *r* the night
	3.16 your husband, and he shall *r* over you."
Deut	15. 6 you will *r* over many nations, but they
Judg	8.23 not *r* over you; the LORD will *r* over you."
2 Chr	1.10 people, for who can *r* this great people
	9.26 He *r* over all the kings from the
Ps	22.28 to the LORD, and he *r* over the nations.
	89. 9 You *r* the raging of the sea; when its
	106. 41 that those who hated them *r* over them.
	110. 2 scepter. *R* in the midst of your foes.
Prov	19.10 in luxury, much less for a slave to *r*
Isa	3. 4 princes, and babes shall *r* over them.
	26.13 lords besides you have *r* over us, but we
	40.10 with might, and his arm *r* for him;
Ezek	34. 4 force and harshness you have *r* them.
Dan	11. 3 arise, who shall *r* with great dominion
Mic	5. 2 forth for me one who is to *r* in Israel,
Lk	19.14 saying, 'We do not want this man to *r*
Rev	2.27 to *r* them with an iron rod, as when
	12. 5 male child, who is to *r* all the nations
	19.15 he will *r* them with a rod of iron; he

RULER (RULERS)

Gen	45. 8 house and *r* over all the land of Egypt.
	45.26 Joseph is still alive! He is even *r* over
Lev	4.22 When a *r* sins, doing unintentionally
Ps	2.10 be wise; be warned, O *r* of the earth.
Prov	6. 7 Without having any chief or officer or *r*,
	23. 1 When you sit down to eat with a *r*,
	29.12 If a *r* listens to falsehood, all his
Isa	33.22 the LORD is our judge, the LORD is our *r*,
	40.23 makes the *r* of the earth as nothing.
Jer	2. 8 know me; the *r* transgressed against me;
Jn	12.31 the *r* of this world will be driven out.
	16.11 *r* of this world has been condemned.
Acts	4. 8 Spirit said to them, "*R* of the people
	7.10 appointed him *r* over Egypt and over all
Rom	13. 3 For *r* are not a terror to good conduct,
1 Cor	2. 8 None of the *r* of this age understood
	15.24 after he has destroyed every *r* and every
Rev	1. 5 dead, and the *r* of kings of the earth.

RUMOR (RUMORS)

2 Kings	19. 7 he shall hear a *r* and return to his own
Isa	37. 7 so that he shall hear a *r*, and return to
Mt	24. 6 you will hear of wars and *r* of wars; see

RUN (RAN RUNNING RUNS)

Gen	16. 6 with her, and she *r* away from her.
Neh	6.11 "Should a man like me *r* away? Would a
Ps	119. 32 I *r* the way of your commandments, for
	147. 15 to the earth; his word *r* swiftly.
Jer	5. 1 *R* to and fro through the streets of
Dan	12. 4 Many shall be *r* back and forth, and evil
Mt	28. 8 and great joy, and *r* to tell his disciples.
Jn	20. 2 So she *r* and went to Simon Peter and
Gal	2. 2 that I was not *r*, or had not *r*, in vain.
	5. 7 You were *r* well; who prevented you
Heb	12. 1 let us *r* with perseverance the race that

RUNNER (RUNNERS)

Job	9.25 "My days are swifter than a *r*; they flee
Hab	2. 2 in plain tablets, so that a *r* may read it.
1 Cor	9.24 in a race the *r* all compete, but only

RUTH

Ruth	1. 4 Orpah, and the name of the other *R*.
	2. 2 *R* the Moabite said to Naomi, "Let me
	3. 9 "I am *R*, your servant; spread your cloak

S

SABBATH (SABBATHS)

Ex	16.26	day, which is a *s*, there will be none."
	20. 8	Remember the *s* day, and keep it holy.
	31.16	shall keep the *s*, observing the *s*
Lev	16.31	a *s* of complete rest to you, and you
	19.30	You shall keep my *s* and reverence my
	25. 4	there shall be a *s* of complete rest for
	26. 2	You shall keep my *s* and reverence my
Num	15.32	a man gathering sticks on the *s* day.
Deut	5.12	Observe the *s* day and keep it holy, as
Neh	13.17	that you are doing, profaning the *s* day?
Isa	56. 2	who keeps the *s*, not profaning it, and
	58.13	If you refrain from trampling the *s*, from
	66.23	from *s* to *s*, all flesh shall come to
Jer	17.21	do not bear a burden on the *s* day or
Ezek	20.12	I gave them my *s*, as a sign between me
	44.24	festivals, and they shall keep my *s* holy.
Mt	12. 1	went through the grainfields on the *s*;
	24.20	flight may not be in winter or on a *s*.
	28. 1	After the *s*, as the first day of the week
Mk	2.23	One *s* he was going through the
	3. 2	to see if he would cure him on the *s*,
	16. 1	When the *s* was over, Mary Magdalene,
Lk	4.16	he went to the synagogue on the *s* day,
	6. 1	One *s* while Jesus was going through
	13.14	because Jesus had cured on the *s*,
	14. 1	to eat a meal on the *s*, they were
Jn	5.10	"It is the *s*; it is not lawful for you to
	7.23	If a man receives circumcision on the *s*
	9.14	was a *s* day when Jesus made the mud
Acts	16.13	On the *s* day we went outside the gate

SACKCLOTH

1 Kings	20.32	So they tied *s* around their waists, put
	21.27	he fasted, lay in the *s*, and went about
2 Kings	19. 1	tore his clothes, covered himself with *s*,
Esth	4. 1	tore his clothes and put on *s* and ashes,
Ps	35.13	for me, when they were sick, I wore *s*;
	69.11	When I made *s* my clothing, I became a
Isa	20. 2	loose the *s* from your loins and take the
	37. 1	tore his clothes, covered himself with *s*,
Jon	3. 5	and everyone, great and small, put on *s*.
Lk	10.13	long ago, sitting in *s* and ashes.

SACRED

Ezek	44. 8	have not kept charge of my *s* offerings;
2 Tim	3.15	you have known the *s* writings

SACRIFICE (SACRIFICES) (n)

1 Sam	15.22	to obey is better than a *s*, and to heed
1 Chr	29.21	the next day they offered *s* and burnt
Ps	40. 6	*S* and offering you do not desire, but
	51.16	For you have no delight in *s*; if I were
Prov	15. 8	*s* of the wicked is an abomination to
	21. 3	is more acceptable to the LORD than *s*.
	21.27	The *s* of the wicked is an abomination.
Eccl	5. 1	is better than the *s* offered by fools;
Isa	1.11	What to me is the multitude of your *s*?
Jer	6.20	not acceptable, nor are your *s* pleasing
Dan	9.27	he shall make *s* and offering cease;
Hos	6. 6	For I desire steadfast love and not *s*,
	8.13	Though they offer choice *s*, though they
Am	4. 4	bring your *s* every morning, your tithes
Mal	1. 8	When you offer blind animals in *s*, is
Mt	9.13	what this means, 'I desire mercy, not *s*.'
	12. 7	this means, 'I desire mercy, and not *s*,'
Mk	12.33	than all whole burnt offerings and *s*."
Lk	2.24	they offered a *s* according to what is
Rom	12. 1	present your bodies as a living *s*, holy
	3.25	Christ, whom God put forward as a *s*
Eph	5. 2	for us, a fragrant offering and *s* to God.
Phil	4.18	offering, a *s* acceptable and pleasing
Heb	2.17	to make a *s* of atonement for the sins of

SACRIFICE (SACRIFICED) (v)

Ex	3.18	wilderness, so that we may *s* to the
Deut	15.21	you shall not *s* it to the LORD your God;
1 Kings	13. 2	he shall *s* on you the priests of the high
Ps	54. 6	With a freewill offering I will *s* to you; I
Eccl	9. 2	to those who *s* and those who do not *s*.
Jon	2. 9	the voice of thanksgiving will *s* to you;
1 Cor	5. 7	our paschal lamb, Christ, has been *s*.
	10.20	that what pagans *s* they *s* to demons

SACRILEGE

Mt	24.15	"So when you see the desolating *s*
Mk	13.14	when you see the desolating *s* set up

SADDUCEES

Mt	3. 7	Pharisees and *S* coming for baptism,
	16. 1	The Pharisees and *S* came, and to test
	16. 6	of the yeast of the Pharisees and *S*."
	22.23	The same day some *S* came to him,
Acts	4. 1	and the *S* came to them, much annoyed
	5.17	sect of the *S*), being filled with jealousy,
	23. 6	Paul noticed that some were *S* and

SAFE (SAFELY)

Ps	18.32	me with strength, and made my way *s*.
	119.117	Hold me up, that I may be *s* and have
Acts	23.24	Paul to ride, and take him *s* to Felix

SAFETY

Ps	4. 8	alone, O LORD, make me lie down in *s*.
	12. 5	"I will place them in the *s* for which
Isa	14.30	will graze, and the needy lie down in *s*;

SAGES

Isa	19.12	Where now are your *s*? Let them tell

SAIL (SAILED)

Acts	13. 4	and from there they *s* to Cyprus.
	18.18	and *s* for Syria, accompanied by Priscilla
	27. 1	was decided that we were to *s* for Italy,

SAINTS (SAINTS')

Mt	27.52	bodies of the *s* who had fallen asleep
Acts	9.13	how much evil he has done to your *s* in
	26.10	I not only locked up many of the *s* in
Rom	12.13	Contribute to the needs of the *s*; extend
	15.25	to Jerusalem in a ministry to the *s*;
1 Cor	1. 2	called to be *s*, together with all those
	6. 2	know that the *s* will judge the world?
2 Cor	9. 1	to you about the ministry for the *s*,
Eph	5. 3	among you, as is proper among *s*.
Col	1.26	but has now been revealed to his *s*.
1 Tim	5.10	shown hospitality, washed the *s* feet,
Philem	7	the hearts of the *s* have been refreshed
Rev	8. 3	with the prayers of all the *s* on the
	13. 7	it was allowed to make war on the *s*
	14.12	is a call for the endurance of the *s*,
	16. 6	they shed the blood of *s* and prophets,
	20. 9	surrounded the camp of the *s* and the

SALT (SALTED)

Gen	19.26	back, and she became a pillar of *s*.
Mt	5.13	"You are the *s* of the earth; but if the
Mk	9.49	For everyone will be *s* with fire.
Lk	14.34	"*S* is good; but if *s* has lost its taste,

SALVATION

Gen	49.18	I wait for your *s*, O LORD.
Ex	15. 2	and he has become my *s*; this is my
2 Sam	22. 3	my shield and the horn of my *s*, my
1 Chr	16.23	Tell of his *s* from day to day. Declare
Ps	13. 5	love; my heart shall rejoice in your *s*.
	27. 1	The LORD is my light and my *s*; whom
	35. 3	pursuers; say to my soul, "I am your *s*!"

SACRIFICE (SACRIFICED) (v)

Heb	9.26	age to remove sin by the *s* of himself.
	10.12	offered for all time a single *s* for sins,
1 Jn	2. 2	he is the atoning *s* for our sins, and not
	4.10	his Son to be the atoning *s* for our sins.

Ruth / Mt (top entries)

Ruth	4.13	Boaz took *R* and she became his wife.
Mt	1. 5	Boaz the father of Obed by *R*, and Obed

Ps	37.39 The s of the righteous is from the LORD;
	50.23 the right way I will show the s of God."
	51.12 Restore to me the joy of your s, and
	62. 1 waits in silence; from him comes my s.
	70. 4 Let those who love your s say evermore,
	91.16 will satisfy them, and show them my s.
	116. 13 I will lift up the cup of s and call on
	118. 14 and my might; he has become my s.
	119.123 My eyes fail from watching for your s,
Isa	12. 2 God is my s; I will trust, and will not be
	33. 2 morning, our s in the time of trouble.
	45. 8 the earth open, that s may spring up,
	45.17 is saved by the LORD with everlasting s;
	51. 6 but my s will be forever, and my
	52. 7 who announces s, who says to Zion,
	56. 1 for soon my s will come, and my
	60.18 you shall call your walls S, and your
Jer	3.23 in the LORD our God is the s of Israel.
Lam	3.26 that one should wait quietly for the s of
Mic	7. 7 LORD, I will wait for the God of my s;
Hab	3.18 LORD; I will exult in the God of my s.
Lk	1.77 give knowledge of s to his people by the
	2.30 for my eyes have seen your s,
	3. 6 and all flesh shall see the s of God."
	19. 9 "Today s has come to this house,
Jn	4.22 what we know, for s is from the Jews.
Acts	4.12 There is s in no one else, for there is no
	13.47 may bring s to the ends of the earth.' "
	28.28 this s of God has been sent to the
Rom	1.16 the gospel; it is the power of God for s
	13.11 For s is nearer to us now than when we
2 Cor	6. 2 time; see, now is the day of s.
Eph	1.13 the word of truth, the gospel of your s,
Phil	1.28 of their destruction, but of your s.
	2.12 work out your own s with fear and
1 Thess	5. 9 for obtaining s through our Lord Jesus
Heb	1.14 the sake of those who are to inherit s?
1 Pet	1. 9 of your faith, the s of your souls.
2 Pet	3.15 regard the patience of our Lord as s. So
Jude	3 write to you about the s we share, I find
Rev	7.10 "S belongs to our God who is seated on
	12.10 "Now have come the s and the power
	19. 1 "Hallelujah! S and glory and power to

SAMARIA

1 Kings	16.24 He bought the hill of S from Shemer for
	16.29 Ahab . . . reigned over Israel in S
2 Kings	17. 6 king of Assyria captured S; he carried
Isa	7. 9 The head of Ephraim is S, and the head
Ezek	16.46 Your elder sister is S, who lived with
Hos	8. 5 Your calf is rejected, O S. My anger
Mic	1. 6 Therefore I will make S a heap in the
Lk	17.11 the region between S and Galilee.
Jn	4. 4 But he had to go through S. So he came
Acts	1. 8 in Jerusalem, in all Judea and S,
	8. 5 Philip went down to the city of S, and

SAMARITAN (SAMARITANS)

Mt	10. 5 and enter no town of the S, but go
Jn	4. 7 A S woman came to draw water, and
Acts	8.25 good news to many villages of the S.

SAME

Eccl	9. 2 is vanity, since the s fate comes to all,

SAMSON

Judg	13.24 woman bore a son, and named him S.
	14. 1 Once S went down to Timnah, and at
	15. 1 S went to visit his wife, bringing along a
	16. 1 Once S went to Gaza, where he saw a
	16.30 Then S said, "Let me die with the
Heb	11.32 fail me to tell of Gideon, Barak, S

SAMUEL

Born, 1 Sam 1.19-20; dedicated to God, 1 Sam 1.21-28;
ministered before God, 1 Sam 2.11,18-21; called, 1 Sam
3.1-18; judged Israel, 1 Sam 7.3-17; warned Israel for
requesting a king, 1 Sam 8.10-18; anointed Saul king, 1

Sam 10.1-8; reasoned with Israel, 1 Sam 12; reproved
Saul, 1 Sam 13.8-15; 15.10-23; hewed Agag in pieces, 1
Sam 15.33; anointed David, 1 Sam 16.1-13; died, 1 Sam
25.1; 28.3.

Jer	15. 1 Though Moses and S stood before me,
Acts	3.24 from S and those after him, also
	13.20 judges until the time of the prophet S.

SANCTIFICATION

1 Cor	1.30 righteousness and s and redemption, in
1 Thess	4. 3 this is the will of God, your s: that you

SANCTIFY (SANCTIFIED SANCTIFIES)

Ex	29.43 there, and it will be s by my glory;
Lev	22.32 my holy name, that I may be s among
Josh	3. 5 "S yourselves; for tomorrow the LORD
	7.13 Proceed to s the people, and say, 'S
1 Chr	15.14 the priests and the Levites s themselves
2 Chr	29. 5 to me, Levites! S yourselves, and s
Isa	29.23 in his midst, they will s my name;
Ezek	20.12 they might know that I the LORD s them.
Joel	1.14 S a fast, call a solemn assembly. Gather
Jn	17.17 to the world. S them in the truth; your
Acts	26.18 and a place among those who are s by
1 Cor	1. 2 to those who are s in Christ Jesus,
	6.11 you were washed, you were s, you were
1 Thess	5.23 May the God of peace himself s you
Heb	2.11 the one who s and those who are s
	9.13 of the ashes of a heifer, s those
	10.10 have been s through the offering of the
	10.14 perfected for all time those who are s.
	13.12 order to s the people by his own blood.

SANCTUARY

Ex	25. 8 have them make me a s, so that I may
	36. 1 in the construction of the s shall work
Lev	12. 4 any holy thing, or come into the s,
	21.12 outside the s and thus profane the s of
1 Chr	22.19 Go and build the s of the LORD God so
	28.10 chosen you to build a house as the s;
2 Chr	26.18 Go out of the s; for you have done
Ps	20. 2 May he send you help from the s, and
	63. 2 So I have looked upon you in the s,
	73.17 task, until I went into the s of God;
	74. 7 They set your s on fire; they desecrated
	114. 2 Judah became God's s, Israel his
Isa	8.14 He will become a s, a stone one strikes
	16.12 when he comes to his s to pray, he will
Jer	17.12 from the beginning, the shrine of our s!
Lam	1.10 has even seen the nations invade her s,
	2. 7 has scorned his altar, disowned his s;
Ezek	5.11 because you have defiled my s with all
	11.16 yet I have been a s to them for a little
	23.38 they have defiled my s on the same day
	24.21 I will profane my s, the pride of your
	48. 8 the west, with the s in the middle of it.
Dan	8.14 then the s shall be restored to its
	9.17 your face shine upon your desolated s.
Am	7.13 prophesy at Bethel, for it is the king's s,
Mal	2.11 Judah has profaned the s of the LORD,
Heb	9. 1 regulations for worship and an earthly s.
	9. 8 way into the s has not yet been
	10.19 confidence to enter the s by the blood

SAND

Gen	22.17 as . . . s that is on the seashore."
	32.12 make your offspring as the s of the sea,"
Prov	27. 3 is heavy, and s is weighty, but a fool's
Isa	10.22 people Israel were like the s of the sea,
Hos	1.10 the people of Israel shall be like the s
Mt	7.26 man who built his house upon the s.
Rom	9.27 children of Israel were like the s of the
Heb	11.12 and as the innumerable grains of s by

SANDAL (SANDALS)

Ex	3. 5 Remove the s from your feet, for the
Deut	25. 9 pull his s off his foot, spit in his face,

Josh	5.15	"Remove the *s* from your feet, for the
Ruth	4. 7	took off his *s* and gave it to the other;
Mk	1. 7	down and untie the thong of his *s*.
	6. 9	but to wear *s* and not to put on two
Lk	3.16	not worthy to untie the thong of his *s*.
	15.22	a ring on his finger and *s* on his feet.
Acts	7.33	'Take off the *s* from your feet, for the
	13.25	not worthy to untie the thong of the *s*

SARAH (SARAH'S SARAI)

Wife of Abraham, Gen 11.29; barren, Gen 11.30; Sarai and Hagar, Gen 16.1-6; represented as Abraham's sister, Gen 12.10-20; 20.1-18; name changed to Sarah, Gen 17.15; laughed at the LORD's promise, Gen 18.9-15; bore Isaac, Gen 21.1-8; jealous of Ishmael, Gen 21.9-11; died at Hebron, Gen 23.2; buried in Machpelah, Gen 23.19.

Gen	11.30	Now *S* was barren; she had no child.
	16. 1	*S*, Abram's wife, bore him no children.
	18. 9	"Where is your wife *S*?" And he said,
	21. 1	LORD dealt with *S* as he had said, and
Rom	4.19	considered the barrenness of *S* womb.
Heb	11.11	too old —and *S* herself was barren—
1 Pet	3. 6	Thus *S* obeyed Abraham, and called

SATAN

1 Chr	21. 1	*S* stood up against Israel, and incited
Job	1. 6	the LORD, and *S* also came among them.
	2. 1	and *S* also came among them to present
Zech	3. 1	*S* standing at his right hand to accuse
Mt	4.10	Jesus said to him, "Away with you, *S*!
	12.26	If *S* casts out *S*, he is divided against
	16.23	and said to Peter, "Get behind me, *S*!
Lk	10.18	to them, "I watched *S* fall from heaven
Acts	5. 3	asked, "Why has *S* filled your heart
2 Cor	2.11	so we may not be outwitted by *S*; for we
	11.14	Even *S* disguises himself as an angel of
Rev	2. 9	and are not, but are a synagogue of *S*.
	12. 9	serpent, who is called the Devil and *S*,
	20. 2	ancient serpent, who is the Devil and *S*,

SATISFACTION

Isa	53.11	he shall find *s* through his knowledge.

SATISFY (SATISFIED SATISFIES)

Josh	22.30	and the Manassites spoke, they were *s*.
Ps	22.26	The poor shall eat and be *s*; those who
	65. 4	be *s* with the goodness of your house,
	90.14	*S* us in the morning with your steadfast
	104.13	the earth is *s* with the fruit of your
	107. 9	For he *s* the thirsty, and the hungry he
	132.15	provisions; I will *s* its poor with bread.
Prov	27.20	never *s*, and human eyes are never *s*.
	30.15	give," they cry. Three things are never *s*;
Eccl	1. 8	the eye is not *s* with seeing, or the ear
	5.10	of money will not be *s* with money;
Isa	55. 2	your labor for that which does not *s*?
	58.11	and *s* your needs in parched places,
Jer	31.14	my people shall be *s* with my bounty,
	31.25	I will *s* the weary, and all who are faint
Ezek	7.19	They shall not *s* their hunger or fill
Mic	6.14	You shall eat, but not be *s*, and there
Mt	28.14	we will *s* him and keep you out of
Lk	3.14	accusations, and be *s* with your wages."
Jn	14. 8	show us the Father, and we will be *s*."
Acts	27.38	they had *s* their hunger, they lightened
Phil	4.19	my God will fully *s* every need of yours

SAUL (King of Israel)

Son of Kish, 1 Sam 9.1-2; met Samuel, 1 Sam 9.5-24; anointed by Samuel, 1 Sam 10.1-8; prophesied with the prophets, 1 Sam 10.9-13; chosen king at Mizpah, 1 Sam 10.20-24; defeated the Ammonites, 1 Sam 11.5-11; made king in Gilgal, 1 Sam 11.12-15; reproved for his burnt offering, 1 Sam 13.8-15; built an altar, 1 Sam 14.35; rejected as king, 1 Sam 15.11-30; refreshed by David's harp playing, 1 Sam 16.14-23; became jealous of David, 1 Sam 18.6-30; sought to kill David, 1 Sam 19.1-17;

killed the priests of Nob, 1 Sam 22.11-19; spared by David, 1 Sam 24.1-7; 26.1-12; consulted the woman of Endor, 1 Sam 28.3-25; died and buried, 1 Sam 31.

Acts	13.21	asked for a king; and God gave them *S*

SAUL (Paul)

Acts	13. 9	But *S*, also known as Paul, filled with

SAVE

Deut	23.14	to *s* you and to hand over your enemies
1 Sam	4. 3	may come among us and *s* us from the
	17.47	the LORD does not *s* by sword and spear;
2 Kings	19.19	So now, O LORD our God, *s* us, I pray
	19.34	I will defend this city to *s* it, for my
1 Chr	16.35	Say also: "*S* us, O God of our salvation,
2 Chr	20. 9	in our distress, and you will hear and *s*.'
Ps	28. 9	O *s* your people, and bless your
	69.35	God will *s* Zion and rebuild the cities of
	76. 9	judgment, to *s* all the oppressed
	86. 2	to you; *s* your servant who trusts
	116. 4	of the LORD: "O LORD, I pray, *s* my life!"
Prov	2.12	It will *s* you from the way of evil, from
	6. 5	*s* yourself like a gazelle from the hunter,
	23.14	them with a rod, you will *s* their lives
Isa	25. 9	waited for him, so that he might *s* us.
	36.18	you by saying, The LORD will *s* us.
	37.20	God, *s* us from his hand, so that all the
	44.17	it and says, "*S* me, for you are my god!"
	47.15	own paths; there is no one to *s* you.
	63. 1	I, announcing vindication, mighty to *s*."
Jer	15.20	for I am with you to *s* you and deliver
	17.14	be healed; *s* me, and I shall be saved;
	30.10	I am going to *s* you from far away, and
	39.17	I will *s* you on that day, says the LORD,
	46.27	I am going to *s* you from far away, and
	51. 6	of Babylon, *s* your lives, each of you!
Ezek	3.18	their wicked way in order to *s* their life,
	7.19	their silver and gold cannot *s* them on
	34.22	I will *s* my flock, and they will no
Hos	13.10	now is your king, that he may *s* you?
	14. 3	Assyria shall not *s* us; we will not ride
Am	2.14	strength, nor shall the mighty *s* their
Hab	3.13	You came forth to *s* your people, to *s*
Zeph	3.19	And I will *s* the lame and gather the
Mt	1.21	name him Jesus, for he will *s* his people
	8.25	saying, "Lord, *s* us! We are perishing!"
	14.30	to sink, he cried out, "Lord, *s* me!"
	16.25	who want to *s* their life will lose it,
	18.11n	For the Son of man came to *s* the lost
	27.40	and build it in three days, *s* yourself!
Mk	8.35	those who want to *s* their life will lose
	15.30	*s* yourself, and come down from the
Lk	9.24	those who want to *s* their life will lose
	9.56n	lives of human beings but to *s* them."
1 Cor	7.16	you might *s* your husband. Husband, for
	9.22	that I might by all means *s* some.
1 Tim	1.15	came into the world to *s* sinners—
	4.16	will *s* both yourself and your hearers.
Heb	7.25	all time to *s* those who approach God
	9.28	but to *s* those who are eagerly waiting
Jas	5.20	will *s* the sinner's soul from death
Jude	23	*s* others by snatching them out of the

SAVES (SAVED SAVING)

Ex	14.30	Thus the LORD *s* Israel that day from the
Num	10. 9	your God and be *s* from your enemies.
Deut	33.29	Who is like you, a people *s* by the LORD,
1 Sam	14. 6	nothing can hinder the LORD from *s* by
2 Sam	22. 4	praised, and I am *s* from my enemies.
1 Kings	1.29	"As the LORD lives, who has *s* my life
2 Chr	32.22	So the LORD *s* Hezekiah and the
Job	5.15	But he *s* the needy from the sword of
Ps	18. 3	so I shall be *s* from my enemies.
	34. 6	and was heard by the LORD, and was *s*
	80. 3	let your face shine, that we may be *s*.
	106. 8	Yet he *s* them for his name's sake, so
	107.19	and he *s* them from their distress;

Isa	30.15	In returning and rest you shall be *s*;
Jer	8.20	the summer is ended, and we are not *s*."
	23. 6	In his days Judah will be *s* and Israel
	33.16	In those days Judah will be *s* and
Ezek	3.19	iniquity; but you will have *s* your life.
Ob	21	have been *s* shall go up to Mount Zion
Mic	6. 5	you may know the *s* acts of the LORD."
Mt	19.25	and said, "Then who can be *s*?"
	24.13	one who endures to the end will be *s*,
Mk	10.26	to one another, "Then who can be *s*?"
Lk	7.50	to the woman, "Your faith has *s* you; go
	13.23	asked him, "Lord, will only a few be *s*?"
	18.26	who heard it said, "Then who can be *s*?"
	23.35	"He *s* others; let him save himself if he
Jn	5.34	I say these things so that you may be *s*.
Acts	2.21	on the name of the Lord shall be *s*.'
	11.14	and your entire household will be *s*.'
	15. 1	the custom of Moses, you cannot be *s*."
	15.11	that we will be *s* through the grace of
	16.30	and said, "Sirs, what must I do to be *s*?"
	27.31	men stay in the ship, you cannot be *s*."
Rom	5. 9	we be *s* through him from the wrath
	8.24	For in hope we were *s*. Now hope that
	10. 1	to God for them is that they may be *s*.
	10. 9	raised him from the dead, you will be *s*.
	11.26	And so all Israel will be *s*; as it is
1 Cor	1.18	but to us who are being *s* it is the
	3.15	the builder will be *s*, but only as
	5. 5	so that his spirit may be *s* in the day of
	10.33	but that of many, so that they may be *s*.
	15. 2	through which you also are being *s*, if
1 Thess	2.16	to the Gentiles so that they may be *s*.
2 Tim	1. 9	of God, who *s* us and called us with a
Titus	3. 5	he *s* us, not because of any works of
1 Pet	3.20	is, eight persons, were *s* through water.
	4.18	If it is hard for the righteous to be *s*,
Jude	5	once for all *s* a people out of the land

SAVIOR

2 Kings	13. 5	the LORD gave Israel a *s*, so that they
Ps	106. 21	They forgot God, their *S*, who had done
Isa	19.20	he will send them a *s*, and will defend
	43. 3	God, the Holy One of Israel, your *S*.
	43.11	the LORD, and besides me there is no *s*.
	45.21	a righteous God and *S*; there is no one
	60.16	shall know that I, the LORD, am your *S*.
Jer	14. 8	O hope of Israel, its *s* in time of
Hos	13. 4	but me, and besides me there is no *s*.
Lk	1.47	and my spirit rejoices in God my *S*,
	1.69	He has raised up a mighty *s* for us in
	2.11	is born this day in the city of David a *S*,
Acts	13.23	God has brought to Israel a *S*, Jesus, as
1 Tim	2. 3	acceptable in the sight of God our *S*,
	4.10	living God, who is the *S* of all people,
1 Jn	4.14	has sent his Son as the *S* of the world.
Jude	25	only God, our *S*, through Jesus Christ

SAY (SAYING)

Lk	5. 5	nothing. Yet if you *s* so, I will let down
1 Tim	1.15	The *s* is sure and worthy of full
	4. 9	The *s* is sure and worthy of full

SCALES

Prov	16.11	Honest balances and *s* are the LORD's;
	20.23	to the LORD, and false *s* are not good.
Dan	5.27	you have been weighed on the *s*
Mic	6.11	Can I tolerate wicked *s* and a bag of
Rev	6. 5	Its rider held a pair of *s* in his hand,

SCARLET

Isa	1.18	though your sins are like *s*, they shall
Mt	27.28	stripped him and put a *s* robe on him,

SCATTER (SCATTERED SCATTERS)

Gen	49. 7	them in Jacob, and *s* them in Israel.
Lev	26.33	I will *s* you among the nations, and I
Deut	4.27	The LORD will *s* you among the peoples;
	28.64	The LORD will *s* you among all peoples,

Jer	9.16	I will *s* them among the nations that
	10.21	not prospered, and all their flock is *s*.
	13.24	I will *s* you like chaff driven by the
	18.17	east, I will *s* them before the enemy.
Ezek	11.16	though I *s* them among the countries,
	20.23	in the wilderness that I would *s* them
Zech	1.21	"These are the horns that *s* Judah, so
	7.14	I *s* them with a whirlwind all the
	10. 9	Though I *s* them among the nations, yet
Jn	10.12	wolf snatches them and *s* them.
	16.32	indeed it has come, when you will be *s*,
Acts	8. 4	those who were *s* went from place to

SCEPTER

Gen	49.10	The *s* shall not depart from Judah, nor
Num	21.18	people dug, with the *s*, with the staff."
	24.17	a shall rise out of Israel; it shall crush
Ps	45. 6	and ever. Your royal *s* is a *s* of equity;
	60. 7	Ephraim is my helmet; Judah is my *s*.

SCHEMES

Job	10. 3	hands and favor the *s* of the wicked?

SCOFFED

Deut	32.15	him, and *s* at the Rock of his salvation.
Acts	17.32	resurrection of the dead, some *s*; but

SCOFFER (SCOFFERS)

Ps	1. 1	sinners tread, or sit in the seat of *s*;
Prov	1.22	How long will *s* delight in in their
	13. 1	but a *s* does not listen to rebuke.
	14. 6	A *s* seeks wisdom in vain, but
	15.12	*S* do not like to be rebuked; they will
	19.25	Strike a *s*, and the simple will learn
Isa	29.20	be no more, and the *s* shall cease to be;
Acts	13.41	'Look, you *s*! Be amazed and perish, for

SCOLDED

Mk	14. 5	given to the poor." And they *s* her.

SCORCH (SCORCHED)

Mt	13. 6	But when the sun rose, they were *s*; and
Rev	16. 8	and it was allowed to *s* them with fire;

SCORN (SCORNED)

2 Sam	12.14	this deed you have utterly *s* the LORD,
2 Chr	30.10	they laughed them to *s*, and mocked
Ps	31.11	I am the *s* of all my adversaries, a
	89.41	he has become the *s* of his neighbors.
Ezek	23.32	wide; you shall be *s* and derided, it
Jer	6.10	of the LORD is to them an object of *s*;
Mic	6.16	so you shall bear the *s* of my people.
Gal	4.14	you did not *s* or despise me, but

SCOURGE

Job	5.21	be hidden from the *s* of the tongue,

SCRIBE (SCRIBES)

Ezra	7.12	Ezra, the *s* of the law of the God of
Mt	8.19	A *s* then approached and said, "Teacher,
	13.52	every *s* who has been trained for the
	23. 2	"The *s* and the Pharisees sit on Moses'
Mk	3.22	*s* who came down from Jerusalem said,
	9.14	them, and some *s* arguing with them.
	12.38	"Beware of the *s*, who like to walk
1 Cor	1.20	is the one who is wise? Where is the *s*?

SCRIPTURE (SCRIPTURES)

Mt	21.42	"Have you never read in the *s*: 'The
	22.29	you know neither the *s* nor the power of
	26.54	But how then would the *s* be fulfilled,
Mk	12.10	Have you not read this *s*: 'The stone
	12.24	you know neither the *s* nor the power of
	14.49	not arrest me. But let the *s* be fulfilled."
	15.28n	the *s* was fulfilled which says, "And he
Lk	4.21	"Today this *s* has been fulfilled in your
	24.32	road, while he was opening the *s* to us?"
	24.45	opened their minds to understand the *s*,
Jn	2.22	they believed the *s* and the word that

Jn	5.39 You search the *s* because you think that
	10.35 —and the *s* cannot be annulled—
	13.18 to fulfill the *s*, 'The one who ate my
	17.12 be lost, so that the *s* might be fulfilled.
	19.24 This was to fulfill what the *s* says,
	19.28 (in order to fulfill the *s*), "I am thirsty."
	19.37 of *s* says, "They will look on the one
Acts	8.35 starting with this *s*, he proclaimed to
	17. 2 argued with them from the *s*, explaining
	17.11 examined the *s* every day to see
	18.24 an eloquent man, well-versed in the *s*.
Rom	9.17 For the *s* says to Pharaoh, "I have raised
	15. 4 of the *s* we might have hope.
1 Cor	15. 3 for our sins in accordance with the *s*,
Gal	3. 8 the *s*, foreseeing that God would justify
	3.22 the *s* has imprisoned all things under
	4.30 does the *s* say? "Drive out the slave
Jas	2. 8 fulfill the royal law according to the *s*,
	2.23 Thus the *s* was fulfilled that says,
	4. 5 that it is for nothing that the *s* says,
2 Pet	1.20 no prophecy of *s* is a matter of one's
	3.16 own destruction, as they do the other *s*.

SCROLL

Ps	40. 7 I am; in the *s* of the book it is written
Isa	34. 4 rot away, and the skies roll up like a *s*.
Jer	36. 2 Take a *s* and write on it all the words
	36.18 me, and I wrote them with ink on the *s*."
	36.23 the entire *s* was consumed in the fire
	36.32 Then Jeremiah took another *s* and gave
	51.60 Jeremiah wrote in a *s* all the disasters
Ezek	2. 9 out to me, and a written *s* was in it;
Zech	5. 1 Again I looked up and saw a flying *s*.
Lk	4.17 read and the *s* of the prophet Isaiah was
Heb	9.19 sprinkled both the *s* itself and all the
	10. 7 (in the *s* of the book it is written of
Rev	5. 1 *s* written on the inside and on the back,
	6.14 The sky vanished like a *s* rolling itself
	10. 2 He had a little *s* open in his hand.
	10. 9 told him to give me the little *s*; and he

SEA (SEAS)

Gen	1.10 that were gathered together he called *S*.
Ex	14.21 The LORD drove the *s* back by a strong
2 Chr	2.16 bring it to you as rafts by *s* to Joppa;
Neh	9.11 you divided the *s* before them, so that
Eccl	1. 7 run to the *s*, but the *s* is not full;
Mt	8.24 A windstorm arose on the *s*, so great
Mk	6.48 early in the morning , walking on the *s*.
Jn	6.19 they saw Jesus walking on the *s* and
1 Cor	10. 2 into Moses in the cloud and in the *s*,
Rev	15. 2 standing beside the *s* of glass with
	21. 1 passed away, and the *s* was no more.

SEA OF GALILEE

Mt	4.18 As he walked by the *S*, he saw two
	15.29 he passed along the *S*, and he went up
Jn	6. 1 Jesus went to the other side of the *S*,

SEAL (SEALS) (n)

Jn	6.27 him that God the Father has set his *s*."
Rom	4.11 the sign of circumcision as a *s* of the
1 Cor	9. 2 you; for you are the *s* of my apostleship
2 Cor	1.22 by putting his *s* on us and giving us his
Eph	1.13 with the *s* of the promised Holy Spirit;
	4.30 you were marked with a *s* for the day of
Rev	6. 1 Lamb opened one of the seven *s*, and I
	7. 3 marked the servants of our God with a *s*
	8. 1 the Lamb opened the seventh *s*, there
	9. 4 who have not the *s* of God on their

SEAL (SEALED SEALING)

Esth	8. 8 the king, and *s* it with the king's ring;
Job	14.17 my transgression would be *s* up in a
Isa	29.11 for you like the words of a *s* document.
Dan	9.24 to *s* both vision and prophet, and to
	12. 4 the words and the secret and the book *s*
	12. 9 the words are to remain secret and *s*

Mt	27.66 made the tomb secure by *s* the stone.
Rev	5. 1 and on the back, *s* with seven seals;
	10. 4 "*S* up what the seven thunders have
	22.10 "Do not *s* up the words of the prophecy

SEARCH (SEARCHED SEARCHES SEARCHING)

Job	5.27 See, we have *s* this out; it is true. Hear,
Ps	139. 1 O LORD, you have *s* me and known me.
	139. 23 *S* me, O God, and know my heart; test
Jer	17.10 the LORD test the mind and *s* the heart,
	29.13 When you *s* for me, you will find me; if
Am	9. 3 from there I will *s* out and take them;
Zeph	1.12 that time I will *s* Jerusalem with lamps,
Mt	2. 8 "Go and *s* diligently for the child, and
	7. 7 *s*, and you will find; knock, and the
	18.12 and go in *s* of the one that went astray?
Mk	1.37 they said to him, "Everyone is *s* for you."
Jn	5.39 "You *s* the scriptures because you think
	7.34 You will *s* for me, but you will not find
	7.52 *S* and you will see that no prophet is to
	8.21 and you will *s* for me, but you will not
Acts	17.27 so that they would *s* for God, and
Rom	8.27 God, who *s* the heart, knows what is in
1 Cor	2.10 for the Spirit *s* everything, even the
Rev	2.23 I am the one who *s* minds and hearts,

SEASON (SEASONS)

Gen	1.14 and let them be for signs and for *s* and
Eccl	3. 1 For everything there is a *s*, and a time
Mk	9.50 has lost its saltness, how can you *s* it?"

SEAT (SEATED)

2 Kings	25.28 gave him a *s* above the seats of the
Job	29. 7 of the city, I took my *s* in the square,
Mk	14.62 see the Son of Man *s* at the right hand
Lk	11.43 for you love the *s* of honor in the

SECRET (SECRETS)

Deut	29.29 The *s* things belong to the LORD our
2 Sam	15.10 Absalom sent *s* messengers throughout
Ps	44.21 this? For he knows the *s* of the heart.
	90. 8 our *s* sins in the light of your
Prov	11.13 A gossip goes about telling *s*, but one
Eccl	12.14 deed into judgment, including every *s*
Isa	45.19 I did not speak in *s*, in a land of
	48.16 I have not spoken in *s*, from the time I
Jer	23.24 Who can hide in *s* places so that I
Am	3. 7 without revealing his *s* to his servants
Mt	6. 4 so that your alms may be done in *s*; and
	13.11 given to know the *s* of the kingdom
Mk	4.11 has been given the *s* of the kingdom
	4.22 is anything *s*, except to come to light.
Rom	2.16 Christ, will judge the *s* thoughts of all.
1 Cor	2. 7 we speak God's wisdom, *s* and hidden,
	14.25 After the *s* of the unbeliever's heart are

SECRETLY

Gen	31.27 Why did you flee *s* and deceive me and
2 Kings	17. 9 Israel did *s* things that were not right
Jer	37.17 The king questioned him *s* in his house,
Mt	2. 7 Then Herod *s* called for the wise men

SECT

Acts	24. 5 a ringleader of the *s* of the Nazarenes.
	28.22 with regard to this *s* we know that

SECURE (SECURELY)

Judg	18. 7 people who were there living *s*, after the
Ps	112. 7 their hearts are firm, *s* in the LORD.
Lk	17.33 who try to make their life *s* will lose it,

SECURITY

Job	24.23 He gives them *s*, and they are
Isa	38.14 O LORD, I am oppressed; be my *s*!

SEE (SEEING SEEN SEES)

Gen	16.13 God and remained alive after *s* him?"
	45.28 alive. I must go and *s* him before I die."
Deut	34. 4 I have let you *s* it with your eyes, but

1 Sam	9.16	I have *s* the suffering of my people,
	16. 7	for the LORD does not *s* as mortals *s*;
Job	19.26	then in my flesh I shall *s* God,
Prov	27.12	The clever *s* danger and hide; but the
	28.11	poor person *s* through the pose.
Eccl	11. 7	it is pleasant for the eyes to *s* the sun.
Isa	5.12	of the LORD, or *s* the work of his hands!
	29.15	who say, "Who *s* us? Who knows us?"
	44.18	eyes are shut, so that they cannot *s*,
	52.10	ends of the earth shall *s* the salvation
	53.10	he shall *s* his offspring, and shall
Mal	3.18	you shall *s* the difference between the
Mt	4.16	who sat in darkness have *s* a great light,
	5. 8	the pure in heart, for they will *s* God.
	6. 1	before others in order to be *s* by them;
	11. 4	"Go and tell John what you hear and *s*:
	28. 6	Come, *s* the place where he lay.
Lk	3. 6	all flesh shall *s* the salvation of God.' "
	7.22	"Go and tell John what you have *s* and
Jn	3.21	may be clearly *s* that their deeds have
	4.35	around you, *s* how the fields are ripe
	8.51	keeps my word, will never *s* death."
	9.25	know, that though I was blind, now I *s*."
	9.39	so that those who do not *s* may *s*,
	12.21	said to him, "Sir, we wish to *s* Jesus."
	16.16	again a little while, and you will *s* me."
	17.24	be with me where I am, to *s* my glory,
	20.25	"Unless I *s* the mark of the nails in his
Acts	4.20	from speaking about what we have *s*
	9.27	on the road he had *s* the Lord, who had
1 Cor	13.12	now we *s* in a mirror, dimly, but then
2 Cor	3.18	all of us, with unveiled face, *s* the glory
	4. 4	keep them from *s* the light of the gospel
Heb	2. 9	but we do *s* Jesus, who for a little while
1 Jn	1. 1	have heard, what we have *s* with our
	3. 2	be like him, for we will *s* him as he is
Rev	1. 7	every eye will *s* him, even those who

SEED

Gen	1.29	I have given you every plant yielding *s*
Ps	126. 6	out weeping, bearing the *s* for sowing,
Eccl	11. 6	In the morning sow your *s*, and at
Mt	13.24	someone who sowed good *s* in his field;
	13.38	the good *s* are the children of the
Mk	4.26	of God is as if someone would scatter *s*
1 Jn	3. 9	sin, because God's *s* abides in them;

SEEK (SEEKS SOUGHT)

Num	10.33	day's journey, to *s* out a resting place
Deut	4.29	From there you will *s* the LORD your
1 Sam	22.23	the one who *s* my life *s* your life; you
1 Chr	16.11	S the LORD and his strength, *s* his
	28. 9	If you *s* him, he will be found by you;
2 Chr	7.14	pray, *s* my face, and turn from their
	14. 4	and commanded Judah to *s* the LORD,
	16.12	yet even in his disease he did not *s* the
	19. 3	land, and have set your heart to *s* God."
	31.21	to *s* his God, he did with all his heart;
Ps	9.10	have not forsaken those who *s* you.
	14. 2	are any who are wise; who *s* after God.
	24. 6	who *s* the face of the God of Jacob.
	27. 8	my heart says, "*s* his face!" Your face,
	40.16	But may all who *s* you rejoice and be
	53. 2	are any who are wise, who *s* after God.
	54. 3	risen against me, the ruthless *s* my life
	63. 1	you are my God, I *s* you, my soul thirsts
	69.32	glad; who *s* God, let your hearts revive.
	105. 3	hearts of those who *s* the LORD rejoice.
	119. 2	who *s* him with their whole heart, who
	122. 9	of the LORD our God, I will *s* your good.
Prov	1.28	they will *s* me diligently, but will not
Eccl	1.13	mind to *s* and to search out by wisdom
	3.15	is; and God *s* out what has gone by.
	12.10	The Teacher *s* to find pleasing words,
Song	3. 1	at night I *s* him whom my soul loves;
Isa	9.13	who struck them, or *s* the LORD of hosts.
	26. 9	night, my spirit within me earnestly *s*

Isa	34.16	S and read from the book of the LORD:
	45.19	the offspring of Jacob, "*S* me in chaos."
	55. 6	S the LORD while he may be found, call
Jer	45. 5	you, do you *s* great things for yourself?
Lam	3.25	wait for him, to the soul that *s* him.
Ezek	7.25	will *s* peace, but there shall be none.
	22.30	I *s* for anyone among them who would
	34.12	so will I *s* out my sheep. I will rescue
Dan	9. 3	the Lord God, to *s* an answer by prayer
Hos	3. 5	Israelites shall return and *s* the LORD
	5.15	acknowledge their guilt and *s* my face.
Am	5. 4	Israel: *S* me and live; but do not *s*
	5.14	S good, and not evil, that you may live;
Zeph	2. 3	S the LORD, all you humble of the land,
Zech	8.22	nations shall come to *s* the LORD of
Lk	11. 9	*s*, and you will find; knock, and the
	19.10	Son of Man came to *s* and to save the
Jn	4.23	truth, for the Father *s* such as these
	5.30	I *s* to do not my own will, but the will
	8.50	Yet I do not *s* my own glory; there is
Acts	15.17	that all other peoples may *s* the Lord—
Rom	3.11	there is no one who *s* God. All have
Col	3. 1	*s* the things that are above, where

SEER (SEERS)

1 Sam	9. 9	a prophet was formerly called a *s*.)
Isa	30.10	say to the *s*, "Do not see"; and to the
Mic	3. 7	the *s* shall be disgraced, and the

SELF-CONDEMNED

Gal	2.11	him to his face, because he stood *s*.

SELF-CONTROL

Prov	25.28	without walls, is one who lacks *s*.
Acts	24.25	he discussed justice, *s*, and the coming
1 Cor	7. 9	if they are not practicing *s*, they should
	9.25	Athletes exercise *s* in all things; they do

SELFISH (SELFISHNESS)

2 Cor	12.20	anger, *s*, slander, gossip, conceit, and
Phil	2. 3	Do nothing from *s* ambition or conceit,

SELL (SELLS SOLD)

Gen	25.31	Jacob said, "First *s* me your birthright."
	31.15	For he has *s* us, and he has been using
	37.28	and *s* him to the Ishmaelites for twenty
	41.56	the storehouses, and *s* to the Egyptians,
	45. 4	brother, Joseph, whom you *s* into Egypt.
Lev	25.23	The land shall not be *s* in perpetuity;
	27.28	may be *s* or redeemed; every devoted
Judg	2.14	he *s* them into the power of their
1 Kings	21.25	Ahab, who *s* himself to do what was evil
2 Kings	17.17	they *s* themselves to do evil in the sight
Esth	7. 4	we have been *s*, I and my people, to be
Ps	44.12	You have *s* your people for a trifle,
	105. 17	of them, Joseph, who was *s* as a slave.
Am	2. 6	because they *s* the righteous for silver,
Mt	13.44	in his joy he goes and *s* all that he has
Lk	12.33	S your possessions, and give alms. Make
Acts	4.34	many as owned lands or houses *s* them
	7. 9	patriarchs, jealous of Joseph, *s* him
Rom	7.14	but I am of the flesh, *s* into slavery

SEND (SENDING SENDS SENT)

Gen	45. 5	for God *s* me before you to preserve life.
Ex	3.10	Come now, I will *s* you to Pharaoh to
Ps	43. 3	O *s* out your light and your truth; let
	57. 3	He will *s* from heaven and save me, he
	147. 15	He *s* out his command to the earth; his
Eccl	11. 1	S out your bread upon the waters, for
Isa	6. 8	go for us?" And I said, "Here am I; *s* me!"
Jer	26.12	"It is the LORD who *s* me to prophesy
Mal	3. 1	I am *s* my messenger to prepare the way
Mt	9.38	to *s* out laborers into his harvest."
	10. 5	These twelve Jesus *s* out, with the
	10.40	me welcomes the one who *s* me.
	11. 2	he *s* word by his disciples and said to

Mt	13.41	The Son of Man will *s* his angels, and
Mk	1. 2	"See, I am *s* my messenger ahead of
	5.12	spirits begged him, "*S* us to the swine;
	11. 1	of Olives, he *s* two of his disciples,
Lk	19.29	of Olives, he *s* two of the disciples,
Jn	6.57	the living Father *s* me, and I live
	17. 8	and they have believed that you *s* me.
	17.18	As you have *s* me into the world, so I
	20.21	the Father has *s* me, even as I *s* you."
1 Cor	1.17	Christ did not *s* me to baptize but to
2 Cor	2.17	as persons *s* from God and standing in
Gal	4. 4	of time had come, God *s* his Son,
	4. 6	God has *s* the Spirit of his Son into our
1 Jn	4. 9	God *s* his only Son into the world so

SENNACHERIB

2 Kings	18.13	*S* king of Assyria came up against all
	19.16	hear the words of *S*, which he has sent
	19.36	*S* of Assyria left, went home, and lived
2 Chr	32. 1	King *S* of Assyria came and invaded
Isa	37.17	hear all the words of *S*, which he has
	37.37	Then *S* king of Assyria left, went home,

SENSE

1 Sam	25.33	Blessed be your good *s*, and blessed be

SENTINEL (SENTINELS)

2 Sam	18.25	The *s* shouted and told the king. The
Isa	21.11	"*S*, what of the night? *S*, what of the
	62. 6	your walls, O Jerusalem, I have set *s*;
Jer	6.17	I raised up *s* for you: "Give heed to the
	31. 6	For there shall be a day when *s* will call
Ezek	3.17	I have made you a *s* for the house of
	33. 6	But if the *s* sees the sword coming and
Hos	9. 8	prophet is a *s* for my God over Ephraim,

SEPARATE (SEPARATED SEPARATES)

Gen	1. 4	and God *s* the light from the darkness.
	1.14	of the sky to *s* the day from the night;
	1.11	eastward; thus they *s* from each other.
Ex	26.33	the veil shall *s* for you the holy place
Lev	15.31	of Israel's from their uncleanness,
	20.24	God. I have *s* you from the peoples.
1 Kings	8.53	for you have *s* them from among all the
Ezra	9. 1	Levites have not *s* themselves from the
	10.11	do his will; *s* yourselves from the
Neh	13. 3	they *s* from Israel all those of foreign
Mt	19. 6	God has joined together, let no one *s*."
	25.32	he will *s* the people one from another
Rom	8.35	Who will *s* us from the love of Christ?
	8.39	will be able to *s* us from the love of God
1 Cor	7.15	if the unbelieving partner *s*, let it be so;
2 Cor	6.17	them, be *s* from them, says the Lord,
Gal	2.12	*s* for fear of the circumcision faction.

SEPARATION

Ezek	42.20	to make a *s* between the holy and the

SERAPHS

Isa	6. 2	*S* were in attendance above him; each

SERPENT (SERPENTS)

Gen	3. 1	Now the *s* was more crafty than any
Num	21. 6	LORD sent poisonous *s* among the
	21. 8	"Make a poisonous *s*, and set it on a
2 Kings	18. 4	broke in pieces the bronze *s* that Moses
Prov	23.32	the last it bites like a *s*, and stings like
Isa	27. 1	will punish Leviathan the fleeing *s*,
Jn	3.14	Just as Moses lifted up the *s* in the
2 Cor	11. 3	*s* deceived Eve by its cunning, your
Rev	20. 2	the dragon, that ancient *s*, who is the

SERVANT (SERVANTS)

Lev	25.42	For they are my *s*, whom I brought out
	25.55	Israel are *s*; they are my *s* whom I
Num	12. 7	Not so with my *s* Moses; he is entrusted
1 Sam	25.24	please let your *s* speak in your ears, and
2 Sam	14. 6	Your *s* had two sons, and they fought

1 Kings	12. 7	"If you will be a *s* to this people today
2 Kings	24. 2	that he spoke by his *s* the prophets.
Job	2. 3	"Have you considered my *s* Job? There
	42. 8	my *s* Job shall pray for you, for I will
Ps	19.13	Keep back your *s* also from the
	78.70	He chose his *s* David, and took him
	86.16	to me; give your strength to your *s*,
	109. 28	be put to shame; may your *s* be glad.
	143. 12	all my adversaries, for I am your *s*.
Prov	30.10	Do not slander a *s* to a master, or the
Isa	41. 8	But you, Israel, my *s*, Jacob, whom I
	42. 1	Here is my *s*, whom I uphold, my
	42.19	Who is blind but my *s*, or deaf like my
	43.10	LORD, and my *s* whom I have chosen,
	44. 1	But now hear, O Jacob my *s*, Israel
	52.13	my *s* shall prosper; he shall be exalted
	66.14	that the hand of the LORD is with his *s*,
Jer	7.25	persistently sent all my *s* the prophets
	25. 4	sent you all his *s* the prophets,
	25. 9	Babylon, my *s*, and I will bring them
	30.10	have no fear, my *s* Jacob, says the LORD,
Ezek	34.23	one shepherd, my *s* David, and he shall
Dan	6.20	Daniel, *s* of the living God, has your
Zech	3. 8	I am going to bring my *s* the Branch.
Mt	23.11	The greatest among you will be your *s*.
Mk	9.35	be first must be last of all and *s* of all."
	10.43	great among you must be yours,
Lk	1.38	said, "Here am I, the *s* of the Lord;
	1.54	He has helped his *s* Israel, in
	2.29	now you are dismissing your *s* in peace,
Jn	13.16	*s* are not greater than their master, nor
	15.15	I do not call you *s* any longer, because
Acts	3.26	When God raised up his *s*, he sent him
	4.25	through our ancestor David, your *s*:
	4.27	gathered against your holy *s* Jesus,
Rom	1. 1	Paul, a *s* of Jesus Christ, called to be an
	13. 4	approval, for it is God's *s* for your good.
Col	1.23	I, Paul, became a *s* of this gospel.
2 Tim	2.24	the Lord's *s* must not be quarrelsome
Heb	3. 5	house as a *s*, to testify to the things
Rev	7. 3	marked the *s* of our God with a seal on
	22. 3	will be in it, and his *s* will worship him;

SERVANT-GIRL

Mt	26.71	another *s* saw him, and she said to the

SERVE (SERVED SERVES SERVING)

Gen	25.23	the other, the elder shall *s* the younger."
Ex	14.12	us alone and let us *s* the Egyptians?
	28. 1	to *s* me as priests —Aaron and Aaron's
Deut	6.13	him you shall *s*, and by his name alone
	20.11	people in it shall *s* you at forced labor.
	28.36	where you shall *s* other gods, of wood
Josh	22. 5	to *s* him with all your heart and with all
	24. 2	beyond the Euphrates and *s* other gods.
	24.15	and my household, we will *s* the LORD."
1 Sam	7. 4	the Astartes, and they *s* the LORD only.
2 Sam	22.44	people whom I had not known *s* me.
1 Kings	12. 4	that he placed on us, and we will *s* you."
2 Kings	17.12	they *s* idols, of which the LORD had said
	25.24	live in the land, *s* the king of Babylon,
1 Chr	28. 9	and *s* him with single mind and willing
Job	21.15	is the Almighty, that we should *s* him?
Ps	2.11	*S* the LORD with fear, with trembling
	106. 36	They *s* their idols, which became a
Isa	60.12	that will not *s* you shall perish;
Jer	25.11	nations shall *s* the king of Babylon
	27. 7	All the nations shall *s* him and his son
	30. 9	But they shall *s* the LORD their God and
Dan	3.18	we will not *s* your gods and we will not
	7.10	A thousand thousands *s* him, and ten
Mal	3.14	You have said, "It is vain to *s* God.
Mt	8.15	her and she got up and began to *s* him.
	20.28	of man came not to be served but to *s*,
Mk	1.31	fever left her; and she began to *s* them.
Lk	4.39	Immediately she got up and began to *s*
	16.13	No slave can *s* two masters; for a slave

Lk	22.26	youngest, and the leader like one who s.
Jn	12.26	Whoever s me must follow me, and
Acts	6. 4	ourselves to prayer and to s the word."
	26.16	purpose, to appoint you to s and testify
Rom	16.18	such people do not s our Lord Christ,
Phil	2.22	a father he has s with me in the work of
Heb	1.14	in the divine service, sent to s for the
	6.10	you showed for his sake in s the saints,

SERVICE

Ex	1.14	made their lives bitter with hard s in
Num	3. 7	of meeting, doing s at the tabernacle;
Job	7. 1	"Do not human beings have a hard s on
1 Cor	9.13	who are employed in the temple s get
	16.15	themselves to the s of the saints;

SETH

Gen	4.25	she bore a son and named him S, for
	5. 3	to his image, and named him S.
Lk	3.38	son of Enos, son of S, the son of Adam,

SETTLED

Gen	13.12	Abram s in the land of Canaan, while

SEVEN

Josh	6. 4	march around the city s times, the
Ps	119.164	S times a day I praise you for your
Mt	16.10	Or the s loaves for the four thousand,
	18.21	should I forgive? As many as s times?"
	22.25	Now there were s brothers among us;
Lk	20.29	Now there were s brothers; the first
Rev	3. 1	has the s spirits of God and the s stars:

SEVENFOLD

Gen	4.24	If Cain is avenged s, truly Lamech
Lev	26.18	continue to punish you s for your sins,
Prov	6.31	if they are caught, they will pay s; they

SEVENTH

Gen	2. 2	on the s day God finished his work that
Ex	20.10	the s day is a sabbath to the LORD your
Heb	4. 4	"And God rested on the s day from all

SEVENTY

Jer	25.11	shall serve the king of Babylon s years.
	29.10	when Babylon's s years are completed
Dan	9. 2	of Jerusalem, namely, s years.
	9.24	"S weeks are decreed for your people
Lk	10. 1	the Lord appointed s others and sent

SEVERE

Gen	12.10	an alien, for famine was s in the land.
2 Cor	13.10	I may not have to be s in using the

SEX

1 Pet	3. 7	honor to the woman as the weaker s,

SHADOW

2 Kings	20.10	rather let the s retreat ten intervals."
1 Chr	29.15	our days on earth are like a s, and there
Job	14. 2	a flower and withers, flees like a s and
Ps	102.11	My days are like an evening s; I wither
Eccl	6.12	their vain life, which they pass like a s?
Song	2. 3	With great delight I sat in his s, and his
Acts	5.15	that Peter's s might fall on some of
Col	2.17	These are only a s of what is to come,
Heb	10. 1	Since the law has only a s of the good

SHADRACH

Dan	1. 7	Hananiah he called S, Mishael he called
	2.49	and he appointed S, Meshach, and
	3.12	the affairs of the province of Babylon: S,
	3.23	S, Meshach, and Abednego, fell down,
	3.30	Then the king promoted S, Meshach,

SHAKE (SHAKEN SHAKES SHOOK)

Judg	16.20	out as at other times and s myself free."
Ps	29. 8	The voice of the LORD s in the
Am	9. 9	and s the house of Israel among all the

Hab	3. 6	He stopped and s the earth; he looked
Hag	2. 6	I will s the heavens and the earth and
Mt	10.14	s off the dust from your feet as you
Acts	2.25	at my right hand so that I will not be s;
	4.31	they were gathered together was s;
Heb	12.26	I will s not only the earth but also the

SHAME

2 Sam	19. 5	covered with s the faces of all your
2 Chr	32.21	So he returned in s to his own land.
Ps	4. 2	you people, shall my honor suffer s?
	22. 5	you they trusted, and were not put to s.
	31. 1	refuge; do not let me ever be put to s;
	31.17	Do not let me ever be put to s, O LORD;
	53. 5	will be put to s, for God has rejected
	109. 29	may they be wrapped in their own s as
	119. 6	Then I shall not be put to s, having my
Prov	25. 8	end, when your neighbor puts you to s?
Isa	23. 9	glory, to s all the honored of the earth,
	30. 3	of Pharaoh shall become your s,
	45.17	you shall not be put to s or confounded
	49.23	who wait for me shall not be put to s.
	54. 4	for you will forget the s of your youth,
	61. 7	Because theirs was double, and
Jer	50. 2	Babylon is taken, Bel is put to s,
Ezek	7.18	S shall be on all faces, baldness on all
Hos	4. 7	me; they changed their glory into s.
Joel	10. 6	Ephraim shall be put to s, and Israel
	2.26	my people shall never again be put to s.
Lk	13.17	all his opponents were put to s; and the
1 Cor	6. 5	I say this to your s. Can it be that there
	15.34	knowledge of God. I say this to your s.
1 Jn	2.28	not be put to s before him at the time

SHAMEFUL

2 Cor	4. 2	We have renounced the s things that

SHARE (SHARED SHARING)

1 Kings	12.16	"What s have we in David? We have no
Jn	4. 9	(Jews do not s things in common with
Rom	15.26	to s their resources with the poor
	15.27	Gentiles have come to s in their
1 Cor	9.13	who serve at the altar s in what is
	10.16	is it not a s in the body of Christ?
2 Cor	1. 7	as you s in our sufferings, so also you
	9.13	by the generosity of your s with them
Gal	6. 6	who are taught the word must s in all
Phil	1. 5	because of your s in the gospel from the
	2. 1	from love, any s in the Spirit,
	3.10	and the s of his sufferings by becoming
	4.15	Macedonia, no church s with me in the
Col	1.12	you to s in the inheritance of the saints
Heb	2.14	the children s flesh and blood, he
	13.16	to do good and to s what you have,
1 Pet	4.13	insofar as you are s Christ's sufferings,

SHARP

Ps	45. 5	Your arrows are s in the heart of the
	140. 3	They make their tongue s as a snake's,

SHATTER (SHATTERED SHATTERING)

Ps	68.21	God will s the heads of his enemies, the
Dan	12. 7	when the s of the power of the holy
Ob	9	Your warriors shall be s, O Teman, so
Mal	1. 4	says, "We are s but we will rebuild

SHAVE (SHAVED SHAVING)

2 Sam	10. 4	David's envoys, s off half the beard
Isa	7.20	Lord will s with a razor hired beyond
Ezek	44.20	They shall not s their heads or let their
Acts	21.24	them, and pay for the s of their heads.

SHEAVES

Ps	126. 6	with shouts of joy, carrying their s.

SHEBA

1 Kings	10. 1	When the queen of S heard of the fame
Ps	72.10	may the kings of S and Seba bring gifts.

SHECHEM

| Jer | 6.20 me is frankincense that comes from S, |

SHECHEM

Gen	37.12 to pasture their father's flock near S.
Judg	9.41 kinsfolk, so they could not live on at S.
Acts	7.16 their bodies were brought back to S and

SHED

| Deut | 21. 7 "Our hands did not s this blood, nor |
| 2 Kings | 21.16 Manasseh s very much innocent blood, |

SHEEP

Num	27.17 may not be like s without a shepherd."
1 Sam	16.19 me your son David who is with the s."
2 Sam	7. 8 from following the s to be prince over
	24.17 but these s, what have they done? Let
1 Kings	22.17 like s that have no shepherd;
1 Chr	21.17 But these s, what have they done? Let
2 Chr	18.16 mountains, like s without a shepherd;
Ps	44.11 You have made us like s for slaughter,
	44.22 and accounted as s for the slaughter.
	49.14 Like s they are appointed for Sheol;
	74. 1 does your anger smoke against the s
	78.52 Then he led out his people like s, and
	95. 7 of his pasture, and the s of his hand.
	100. 3 are his people, and the s of his pasture.
	119.176 I have gone astray like a lost s; seek out
Isa	53. 6 we like s have gone astray; we have all
Jer	12. 3 Pull them out like s for the slaughter,
	23. 1 destroy and scatter the s of my pasture!
	50. 6 My people have been lost s; their
Ezek	34.31 You are my s, the s of my pasture and I
Mt	9.36 and helpless, like s without a shepherd.
	10. 6 to the lost s of the house of Israel.
	12.11 has only one s and it falls into a pit on
	25.32 as a shepherd separates the s from the
	26.31 and the s of the flock will be scattered.'
Mk	14.27 shepherd, and the s will be scattered.'
Lk	15. 4 having a hundred s, and losing one of
Jn	10.15 Father. And I lay down my life for the s.
	10.27 My s hear my voice. I know them and
	21.16 love you." Jesus said to him, "Tend my s."
Acts	8.32 "Like a s he was led to the slaughter,
Rom	8.36 are accounted as s to be slaughtered."
1 Pet	2.25 you were going astray like s, but now

SHEEPFOLD (SHEEPFOLDS)

| Ps | 78.70 servant David, and took him from the s; |
| Jn | 10. 1 who does not enter the s by the gate |

SHEET

| Acts | 10.11 something like a large s coming down, |

SHEKEL

| Ex | 30.13 half a s according to the s of the |

SHELTER

Ps	27. 5 For he will hide me in his s in the day
	31.20 In the s of your presence you hide them
	91. 1 You who live in the s of the Most High,
Isa	25. 4 a s from the rainstorm and a shade

SHEM

| Gen | 9.26 "Blessed by the LORD my God be S; and |

SHEOL

Job	26. 6 S is naked before God, and Abaddon
Ps	9.17 The wicked shall depart to S, all the
	16.10 For you do not give me up to S, or let
	139. 8 if I make my bed in S, you are there. If
Prov	5. 5 to death; her steps follow the path to S.
	7.27 Her house is the way to S, going down
	15.11 S and Abaddon lie open before the
Isa	5.14 S has enlarged its appetite and opened
	14. 9 S beneath is stirred up to meet you
	28.15 and with S we have an agreement;
	57. 9 far away, and sent down even to S.
Ezek	32.21 out of the midst of S: "They have come
Hos	13.14 O S, where is your destruction?

SHEPHERD (SHEPHERDS)

Gen	46.32 The men are s, for they have been
Num	14.33 your children shall be s in the
	27.17 LORD may not be like sheep without a s."
2 Sam	5. 2 you who shall be s of my people Israel,
Ps	23. 1 The LORD is my s, I shall not want. He
	80. 1 Give ear, O S of Israel, you who lead
Isa	40.11 feed his flock like a s; he will gather
	44.28 says of Cyrus, "He is my s, and he shall
	56.11 s also have no understanding; they have
	63.11 them up out of the sea with the s
Jer	10.21 For the s are stupid, and do not inquire
	23. 1 Woe to the s who destroy and scatter
	23. 4 I will raise up s over them who will s
	25.34 Wail, you s, and cry out; roll in ashes,
	51.23 with you I smash s and their flocks;
Ezek	34. 2 prophesy against the s of Israel:
	34. 7 you s, hear the word of the LORD:
	34.23 I will set up over them one s, my
Am	1. 1 Amos, who was among the s of Tekoa,
Mic	7.14 S your people with your staff, the flock
Nah	3.18 Your s are asleep, O king of Assyria;
Zech	10. 2 like sheep; they suffer for lack of a s.
	11. 7 I became the s of the flock doomed to
	11.16 a s who does not care for the perishing,
	13. 7 "Awake, O sword, against my s, against
Mt	2. 6 a ruler who is to s my people Israel.' "
	9.36 and helpless, like sheep without a s.
	26.31 "I will strike the s, and the sheep of the
Mk	6.34 they were like sheep without a s;
	14.27 'I will strike the s, and the sheep will
Lk	2. 8 there were s living in the fields, keeping
	2.20 The s returned, glorifying and praising
Jn	10. 2 The one who enters by the gate is the s
	10.11 "I am the good s. The good s lays down
Acts	20.28 you overseers, to s the church of God
Heb	13.20 Jesus, the great s of the sheep, by the
1 Pet	5. 4 when the chief s appears, you will win
Rev	7.17 will be their s, and he will guide them

SHIBBOLETH

| Judg | 12. 6 "Then say S," and he said, "Sibboleth," |

SHIELD

2 Sam	22. 3 my s and the horn of my salvation, my
Ps	3. 3 But you, O LORD, are a s around me, my
	5.12 you cover them with favor as with a s.
	7.10 God is my s, who saves the upright in
	18. 2 my rock in whom I take refuge, my s,
	18.30 true; he is a s for all who take refuge
	18.35 have given me the s of your salvation,
	28. 7 The LORD is my strength and my s; in
	35. 2 Take hold of s and buckler, and rise up
	84.11 the LORD God is a sun and s; he bestows
	89.18 For our s belongs to the LORD, our king
	91. 4 his faithfulness is a s and buckler. You
	115. 9 in the LORD! He is their help and their s.
Prov	2. 7 the upright; he is a s to those who walk
Zech	12. 8 LORD will s the inhabitants of Jerusalem
Eph	6.16 take the s of faith, with which you will

SHILOH

Josh	18. 8 lots for you here before the LORD in S."
1 Sam	1. 3 to sacrifice to the LORD of hosts at S,
	14. 3 the priest of the LORD in S, carrying an
Ps	78.60 He abandoned his dwelling at S, the
Jer	26. 6 I will make this house like S, and I will

SHINE (SHINED)

Num	6.25 the LORD make his face to s upon you,
Job	22.28 for you, and light will s on your ways.
Eccl	8. 1 Wisdom makes one's face s, and the
Isa	9. 2 of deep darkness—on them light has s.
Dan	12. 3 Those who are wise shall s like the
Zech	9.16 of a crown they shall s on his land.
Mt	5.16 same way, let your light s before others,
	13.43 Then the righteous will s like the sun in

| Eph | 5.14 from the dead, and Christ will *s* on you." |
| Phil | 2.15 in which you *s* like stars in the world. |

SHIP (SHIPS)

1 Kings	22.48 Jehoshaphat made *s* of the Tarshish
Ps	104. 26 There go the *s*, and Leviathan that you
	107. 23 Some went down to the sea in *s*, doing
Prov	30.19 way of a *s* on the high seas, and the
Ezek	30. 9 messengers shall go out from me in *s* to

SHIPWRECK (SHIPWRECKED)

| 2 Cor | 11.25 Three times I was *s*; for a night and a |
| 1 Tim | 1.19 persons have suffered *s* in the faith; |

SHIRT

| Lk | 6.29 your coat do not withhold even your *s* |

SHORT (SHORTENED)

Isa	50. 2 Is my hand *s*, that it cannot redeem?
Mt	24.22 And if those days had not been cut *s*,
Mk	13.20 if the Lord had not cut *s* those days, no

SHOUT (SHOUTED SHOUTS)

Josh	6.16 "S; for the LORD has given you the city.
Isa	12. 6 *S* aloud and sing for joy, O royal Zion,
	42.13 he cries out, he *s* aloud, he shows
Mt	20.30 passing by, they *s*, "Lord, have mercy
Lk	19.40 were silent, the stones would *s* out."

SHOW (SHOWED SHOWN SHOWS)

Ex	33.18 Moses said, "S me your glory, I pray."
Deut	34. 1 the LORD *s* him the whole land: Gilead
Mic	6. 8 He has *s* you, O mortal, what is good;
	7.15 land of Egypt, *s* us marvelous things.
Mt	8. 4 but go, *s* yourself to the priest, and
Lk	1.72 he has *s* the mercy promised to our
	24.40 said this, he *s* them his hands and his
Jn	14. 8 "Lord, *s* us the Father, and we will be
Acts	10.28 but God has *s* me that I should not call
Rom	3.25 He did this to *s* his righteousness,
	5. 8 But God *s* his love for us in that while
Gal	2. 6 God *s* no partiality)—those leaders

SHOWERS

Jer	3. 3 Therefore the *s* have been withheld, and
Ezek	34.26 their season; they shall be *s* of blessing.
Hos	6. 3 he will come to us like the *s*, like the
Mic	5. 7 dew from the LORD, like *s* on the grass,

SHRIVELED

| Ps | 22.16 My hands and feet have *s*; I can count |

SHUN

| 1 Cor | 6.18 S fornication! Every sin that a person |
| 1 Tim | 6.11 for you, man of God, *s* all this; pursue |

SHUT

| Gen | 7.16 him; and the LORD *s* him in. |
| Isa | 22.22 open, and no one shall *s*; he shall *s*, |

SICK

2 Kings	20. 1 Hezekiah became *s* and was at the
Ps	107. 17 Some were *s* through their sinful ways,
Prov	13.12 Hope deferred makes the heart *s*, but
Isa	1. 5 The whole head is *s*, and the whole
Jer	8.18 is gone, grief is upon me, my heart is *s*.
Mt	9.12 of a physician, but those who are *s*.
Lk	4.40 all those who had any who were *s* with
	5.31 of a physician, but those who are *s*;
Acts	5.15 they even carried out the *s* into the
Jas	5.14 Are any among you *s*? They should call

SICKLE

Deut	23.25 you shall not put a *s* to your neighbor's
Joel	3.13 Put in the *s*, for the harvest is ripe. Go
Rev	14.15 "Use your *s* and reap, for the hour to

SICKNESS

| Eccl | 5.17 in much vexation and *s* and resentment. |

| Isa | 10.16 wasting *s* among his stout warriors, |
| Hos | 5.13 When Ephraim saw his *s*, and Judah his |

SIDE

| Ps | 124. 1 not been the LORD who was on our *s*, |
| Jn | 19.34 one of the soldiers pierced his *s* |

SIDON

Gen	10.15 Canaan became the father of *S* his
Mt	11.21 in you had been done in Tyre and *S*,
	15.21 went away to the district of Tyre and *S*.
Mk	3. 8 and the region around Tyre and *S*.
Lk	4.26 except to a widow at Zarephath in *S*,
Acts	27. 3 The next day we put in at *S*; and Julius

SIDONIANS

Deut	3. 9 (the *S* call Hermon Sirion, while the
Judg	18. 7 they were far from the *S* and had no
1 Kings	5. 6 knows how to cut timber like the *S*."
2 Kings	23.13 for Astarte the abomination of the *S*,

SIGH (SIGHING)

| Ps | 31.10 spent with sorrow, and my years with *s*; |
| | 90. 9 our years come to an end like a *s*. |

SIGHT

Gen	6. 8 Noah found favor in the *s* of the LORD.
Deut	34. 7 his *s* was unimpaired and his vigor had
1 Kings	15.11 did what was right in the *s* of the LORD,
Eccl	6. 9 Better is the *s* of the eyes than the
Isa	65.16 are forgotten and are hidden from my *s*,
2 Cor	8.21 not only in the Lord's *s* but also in the

SIGN

Gen	9.12 "This is the *s* of the covenant that I
Ex	4. 8 first *s*, they may believe the second *s*.
	31.13 for this is a *s* between me and you
Num	16.38 Thus they shall be *s* to the Israelites.
Josh	4. 6 this may be a *s* among you. When your
Judg	6.17 then show me a *s* that it is you who
1 Sam	2.34 shall be the *s* to you— both of them
1 Kings	13. 3 He gave as the same day, saying, "This
Isa	7.11 Ask a *s* of the LORD your God; let it be
	7.14 the Lord himself will give you a *s*.
	37.30 this shall be the *s* for you: This year eat
	38. 7 "This is the *s* to you from the LORD, that
	55.13 everlasting *s* that shall not be cut off.
Jer	44.29 This shall be the *s* to you, says the
Ezek	4. 3 it. This is a *s* for the house of Israel.
	12. 6 the land; for I have made you a *s* for
	14. 8 make them a *s* and a byword and cut
	24.24 Ezekiel shall be a *s* to you; you shall do
Mt	12.39 but no *s* will be given to it except the *s*
	16. 1 asked him to show them a *s* from
	24. 3 what will be the *s* of your coming and
	26.48 Now the betrayer had given them a *s*,
Mk	8.11 asking him for a *s* from heaven, to test
	13. 4 what will be the *s* that all these things
	14.44 betrayer had given them a *s*, saying,
Lk	2.12 This will be a *s* for you: you will find a
	2.34 and to be a *s* that will be opposed
	11.16 demanding from him a *s* from heaven.
	11.29 it asks for a *s*, but no *s* will be given to
	21. 7 what will be the *s* that this is about to
	23. 8 was hoping to see him perform some *s*.
Jn	2.18 "What *s* can you show us for doing this?"
	10.41 "John performed no *s*, but everything
Acts	4.16 a notable *s* has been done through
Rom	4.11 He received the *s* of circumcision as a
1 Cor	14.22 Tongues, then, are not a *s* for believers

SIGNS

Gen	1.14 and let them be for *s* and for seasons
Isa	8.18 whom the LORD has given me are *s*
Jer	10. 2 or be dismayed at the *s* of the heavens;
Dan	4. 3 How great are his *s*, how mighty his
Mt	16. 3 you cannot interpret the *s* of the times.
Mk	13.22 false prophets will appear and produce *s*

Mk	16.17 these *s* will accompany those who
Jn	2.11 Jesus did this, the first of his *s*, in Cana
	2.23 they saw the *s* that he was doing.
	4.48 "Unless you see *s* and wonders you will
	6. 2 following him, because they saw the *s*
	20.30 Now Jesus did many other *s* in the
Acts	5.12 Now many *s* and wonders were done
	15.12 of all the *s* and wonders God had done
1 Cor	1.22 Jews demand *s* and Greeks desire
Rev	13.13 It performs great *s*, even making fire
	13.14 by the *s* that it is allowed to perform on
	16.14 demonic spirits, performing *s*, who go

SIGNAL

Isa	5.26 He will raise a *s* for a nation far away,
	11.10 the root of Jesse shall stand as a *s* to
	13. 2 On a bare hill raise a *s*, cry aloud to
	18. 3 when a *s* is raised on the mountains,
Zech	10. 8 I will *s* for them and gather them in, for

SIGNET

Jer	22.24 Judah were the *s* ring on my right hand,
Dan	6.17 king sealed it with his own *s* and with

SILAS (SILVANUS)

Acts	15.22 sent Judas called Barsabbas, and *S*,
	15.40 But Paul chose *S* and set out, the
	16.19 they seized Paul and *S* and dragged
	17. 4 were persuaded and joined Paul and *S*,
	18. 5 When *S* and Timothy arrived from
2 Cor	1.19 we proclaimed among you, *S* and
1 Thess	1. 1 Paul, *S* and Timothy, To the church of
1 Pet	5.12 Through *S*, whom I consider a faithful

SILENCE (SILENCED)

1 Kings	19.12 and after the fire the sound of sheer *s*.
Esth	4.14 if you keep *s* at such a time as this,
Ps	32. 3 While I kept *s*, my body wasted away
	83. 1 O God, do not keep *s*; do not hold your
Hab	2.20 let all the earth keep *s* before him.
Rom	3.19 that every mouth may be *s*, and the
1 Tim	2.11 Let a woman learn in *s* with full
Rev	8. 1 seal, there was *s* in heaven for about

SILENT

2 Kings	18.36 the people were *s* and answered him
Ps	4. 4 sin; ponder it on your beds, and be *s*.
	39. 2 I was *s* and still; I held my peace to no
Prov	17.28 fools who keep *s* are considered wise;
Zeph	1. 7 Be *s* before the Lord GOD! For the day
Zech	2.13 Be *s*, all people, before the LORD; for he
Mt	26.63 But Jesus was *s*. Then the high priest
Mk	1.25 saying, "Be *s*, and come out of him!"
1 Cor	14.28 is no one to interpret, let them be *s*
	14.34 women should be *s* in the churches.

SILLY

2 Tim	3. 6 and captivate *s* women, overwhelmed by

SILOAM

Lk	13. 4 were killed when the tower of *S* fell
Jn	9. 7 to him, "Go, wash in the pool of *S*"

SILVER

Ps	12. 6 are promises that are pure, *s* refined
Prov	8.19 fine gold, and my yield than choice *s*.
Isa	1.22 Your *s* has become dross, your wine is
Jer	6.30 They are called "rejected *s*," for the LORD
Hag	2. 8 The *s* is mine, and the gold is mine,
Mt	26.15 you?" They paid him thirty pieces of *s*
	27. 3 and brought back the thirty pieces of *s*
Lk	15. 8 having ten *s* coins, if she loses one
Acts	3. 6 Peter said, "I have no *s* or gold, but

SILVERSMITH

Judg	17. 4 gave it to a *s*, who made it into an idol
Acts	19.24 Demetrius, a *s*, who made silver shrines

SIMEON (Son of Jacob)

Born, Gen 29.33; with Levi, took revenge on Shechem, Gen 34; detained as a hostage, Gen 42.24; his future predicted, Gen 49.5-7.

SIMEON (the Prophet)

Lk	2.25 Jerusalem whose name was *S*; this man
	2.34 Then *S* blessed them and said to his

SIMON

Mt	10. 4 *S* the Cananaean, and Judas Iscariot,
Mk	3.18 Thaddaeus, and *S* the Cananaean, and
Acts	1.13 Alphaeus, and *S* the Zealot, and Judas

SIMPLE

Ps	19. 7 of the LORD are pure, making wise the *s*;
	116. 6 The LORD protects the *s*; when I was
	119.130 light; it imparts understanding to the *s*.
Prov	1.22 "How long, O *s* ones, will you love
	9. 4 "You that are *s*, turn in here!" To those

SIN (n)

Gen	4. 7 do not do well, *s* is lurking at the door;
	31.36 What is my *s*, that you have hotly
Lev	24.15 who curses God shall bear the *s*.
Num	12.11 do not punish us for a *s* that we have so
	32.23 and be sure your *s* will find you out.
1 Sam	2.17 the *s* of the young men was very great
1 Kings	8.36 forgive the *s* of your servants, your
	17.18 to me to bring my *s* to remembrance,
2 Kings	21.16 besides the *s* that he caused Judah to *s*
2 Chr	6.25 forgive the *s* of your people, and bring
Job	10. 6 out my iniquity and search for my *s*,
	13.23 me know my transgression and my *s*.
Ps	32. 5 Then I acknowledged my *s* to you, and I
	38.18 confess my iniquity; I am sorry for my *s*.
Prov	5.22 they are caught in the toils of their *s*.
	20. 9 my heart clean; I am pure from my *s*"?
	24. 9 The devising of folly is *s*, and the
Eccl	5. 6 Do not let your mouth lead you into *s*,
Isa	5.18 who drag *s* as with cart ropes,
	30. 1 but against my will, adding *s* to *s*;
Jer	17. 1 The *s* of Judah is written with an iron
Mic	6. 7 fruit of my body for the *s* of my soul?
Mt	12.31 forgiven for every *s* and blasphemy, but
	13.41 out of his kingdom all causes of *s*
Jn	1.29 God who takes away the *s* of the world!
	8. 7 anyone among you who is without *s*
	8.21 for me, but you will die in your *s*.
	8.46 Which of you convicts me of *s*? If I tell
	15.22 but now they have no excuse for their *s*.
	16. 8 he will prove the world wrong about *s*
Acts	7.60 "Lord, do not hold this *s* against them."
Rom	3. 9 and Greeks, are under the power of *s*,
	5.12 just as *s* came into the world through
	6.14 For *s* will have no dominion over you,
	6.23 For the wages of *s* is death, but the free
	7. 7 for the law, I would not have known *s*.
	7.13 It was *s*, working death in me through
	14.23 does not proceed from faith is *s*.
2 Cor	5.21 he made him to be *s* who knew no *s*, so
Gal	3.22 all things under the power of *s*,
1 Tim	5.20 As for those who persist in *s*, rebuke
Heb	3.13 be hardened by the deceitfulness of *s*.
	4.15 been tested as we are, yet without *s*.
	12. 4 In your struggle against *s* you have not
1 Pet	2.22 "He committed no *s*; and no deceit was
1 Jn	1. 8 If we say we have no *s*, we deceive
	3. 5 away sins, and in him there is no *s*.
	5.16 what is not a mortal *s*, you will ask, and

SINS (n)

Lev	26.21 to plague you sevenfold for your *s*.
2 Kings	13. 6 did not depart from the *s* of the house
2 Chr	25. 4 all shall be put to death for their own *s*."
	28.10 What have you except *s* against the
Ps	25. 7 Do not remember the *s* of my youth or

Ps	79.	9 deliver us, and forgive our *s*, for your
	103.	10 not deal with us according to our *s*,
Isa	38.	17 have cast all my *s* behind your back.
	43.	24 burdened me with your *s*; you have
	58.	1 rebellion, to the house of Jacob their *s*.
Lam	4.	13 It was for the *s* of her prophets and the
Dan	4.	27 atone for your *s* with righteousness, and
Am	5.	12 and how great are your *s* — you who
Mt	1.	21 for he will save his people from their *s*."
Mk	2.	5 the paralytic, "Son, your *s* are forgiven."
	3.	28 people will be forgiven for their *s* and
Lk	5.	20 said, "Friend, your *s* are forgiven you."
Jn	20.	23 If you forgive the *s* of any, they are
Acts	22.	16 be baptized, have your *s* washed away,
1 Cor	15.	17 faith is futile and you are still in your *s*.
Gal	1.	4 who gave himself for our *s* to set us free
Eph	2.	1 were dead through the trespasses and *s*
Heb	9.	7 that he offers for himself and for the *s*
	10.	17 their *s* and their lawless deeds
1 Pet	2.	24 He himself bore our *s* in his body on
	3.	18 Christ also suffered for *s* once for all,

SIN (SINS SINNING) (v)

Gen	39.	9 great wickedness, and *s* against God?"
Lev	4.	2 When anyone *s* unintentionally in any
Deut	20.	18 you thus *s* against the LORD your God.
1 Sam	2.	25 but if someone *s* against the LORD, who
	12.	23 me that I should *s* against the LORD
	14.	33 the troops are *s* against the LORD by
	19.	4 "The king should not *s* against his
1 Kings	8.	46 there is no one who does not *s* —
2 Chr	6.	36 "If they *s* against you — for there is no
Job	7.	20 If I *s*, what do I do to you, you watcher
	10.	14 If I *s*, you watch me, and do not acquit
Ps	119.	11 heart, so that I might not *s* against you.
Eccl	7.	20 righteous as to do good without ever *s*.
Mt	5.	29 If your right eye causes you to *s*, tear it
	18.	15 another member of the church *s* against
Lk	17.	3 If another disciple *s*, you must rebuke
Jn	5.	14 been made well! Do not *s* any more,
1 Cor	6.	18 but the fornicator *s* against the body
	8.	12 when it is weak, you *s* against Christ.
Heb	10.	26 if we willfully persist in *s* after having
1 Jn	1.	1 things to you so that you may not *s*.
	3.	6 no one who *s* has either seen him or
	3.	9 who have been born of God do not *s*,

SINNED

Ex	9.	27 said to them, "This time I have *s*;
	32.	30 "You have *s* a great sin. But now I will
Num	14.	40 that God has promised, for we have *s*."
	22.	34 "I have *s*, for I did not know that you
Deut	1.	41 "We have *s* against the LORD! We are
	9.	16 that you had indeed *s* against the LORD
Josh	7.	11 Israel has *s*; they have transgressed my
Judg	10.	10 "We have *s* against you, because we
1 Sam	7.	6 and said, "We have *s* against the LORD."
	15.	24 Saul said to Samuel, "I have *s*; for I
	24.	11 I have not *s* against you, though you are
2 Sam	12.	13 to Nathan, "I have *s* against the LORD."
	24.	10 "I have *s* greatly in what I have done.
1 Kings	14.	16 which he *s* and which he caused Israel
2 Kings	17.	7 people of Israel had *s* against the LORD
1 Chr	21.	8 David said to God, "I have *s* greatly in
Neh	1.	6 of Israel, which we have *s* against you.
Job	33.	27 'I *s*, and perverted what was right, and
	35.	6 If you have *s*, what do you accomplish
Ps	78.	32 In spite of all this they still *s*; they did
Isa	42.	24 not the LORD, against whom we have *s*,
Jer	8.	14 because we have *s* against the LORD.
	14.	7 are many, and we have *s* against you.
Lam	1.	8 Jerusalem *s* grievously, so she has
	5.	7 Our ancestors *s*; they are no more, and
Dan	9.	5 we have *s* and done wrong, acted
Hos	10.	9 the days of Gibeah you have *s*, O Israel;
Mic	7.	9 the LORD, because I have *s* against him,
Mt	27.	4 "I have *s* in betraying innocent blood."

Lk	15.	18 "Father, I have *s* against heaven and
Jn	9.	2 who *s*, this man or his parents, that he
Rom	2.	12 All who have *s* apart from the law will
	3.	23 all have *s* and fall short of the glory of

SIN OFFERING

Ex	29.	14 with fire outside the camp; it is a *s*.
Lev	4.	3 herd without blemish as a *s* to the LORD.
	5.	6 from the flock, a sheep or a goat, as a *s*;
	6.	25 the ritual of the *s*. The *s* shall be

SINAI

Ex	19.	1 day, they came into the wilderness of *S*.
	19.	20 the LORD descended upon Mount *S*,
	34.	29 Moses came down from Mount *S*. As he
Deut	33.	2 The LORD came from *S*, and dawned
Ps	68.	8 at the presence of God, the God of *S*,
Gal	4.	24 is Hagar, from Mount *S*, bearing

SINFUL

Isa	1.	4 Ah, *s* nation, people laden with iniquity,
Lk	5.	8 away from me, Lord, for I am a *s* man!
1 Tim	1.	9 for the godless and the *s*, for the unholy

SING

Num	21.	17 this song: "Spring up, O well! —*S* to it!
1 Chr	16.	9 *S* to him, *s* praises to him, tell of all his
2 Chr	20.	21 appointed those who were to *s* to the
Job	29.	13 and I caused the widow's heart to *s* for
Ps	59.	16 But I will *s* of your might; I will *s* aloud
	75.	9 I will *s* praises to the God of Jacob.
	81.	1 *S* aloud to God our strength; shout for
	89.	1 I will *s* of your steadfast love, O LORD,
	95.	1 O come, let us *s* to the LORD; let us
	96.	2 *S* to the LORD, bless his name; tell of his
	108.	1 is steadfast; I will *s* and make melody.
Prov	29.	6 a snare, but the righteous *s* and rejoice.
Isa	12.	5 *S* praises to the LORD, for he has done
	26.	19 in the dust, awake and *s* for joy!
	35.	6 the tongue of the speechless *s* for joy.
	38.	20 and we will *s* to stringed instruments
	42.	10 *S* to the LORD a new song, his praise
	44.	23 O heavens, for the LORD has done it;
	52.	8 together they *s* for joy; for in plain sight
	54.	1 *S*, O barren one who did not bear; burst
	65.	14 servants shall *s* for gladness of heart,
Jer	20.	13 *S* to the LORD; praise the LORD! For he
Zech	2.	10 *S* and rejoice, O daughter Zion! For lo, I
Rom	15.	9 you among the Gentiles, and *s* praises
1 Cor	14.	15 but I will *s* praise with the mind also.
Rev	14.	3 they *s* a new song before the throne and

SINGING

Song	2.	12 the time of *s* has come, and the voice
Isa	14.	7 rest and quiet; they break forth into *s*.
Zeph	3.	17 he will exult over you with loud *s* as on
Acts	16.	25 Silas were praying and *s* hymns to God,

SINNER (SINNERS)

Ps	25.	8 therefore he instructs *s* in the way.
	104.	35 Let *s* be consumed from the earth, and
Prov	13.	21 Misfortune pursues *s*, but prosperity
Eccl	2.	26 but to the *s* he gives the work of
Isa	13.	9 desolation, and to destroy its *s* from it.
Mt	9.	10 many tax collectors and *s* came and
	9.	13 come to call not the righteous but *s*."
Mk	2.	15 tax collectors and *s* were also sitting
	2.	17 come to call not the righteous but *s*."
	14.	41 of Man is betrayed into the hands of *s*.
Lk	6.	32 For even *s* love those who love them.
	6.	34 Even *s* lend to *s*, to receive as much
	7.	37 a woman in the city, who was a *s*,
	13.	2 were worse *s* than all other Galileans?
	15.	2 "This fellow welcomes *s* and eats
	15.	7 more joy in heaven over one *s* who
	19.	7 gone to be the guest of one who is a *s*."
Jn	9.	16 "How can a man who is a *s* perform
	9.	24 to God! We know that this man is a *s*."

Rom	3.	7 why am I still being condemned as a *s*?
	5.19	disobedience the many were made *s*,
Gal	2.17	we ourselves have been found to be *s*, is
Jas	5.20	whoever brings back a *s* from wandering

SISTER (SISTERS)

Gen	12.13	Say you are my *s*, so that it may go well
	20.	2 said of his wife Sarah, "She is my *s*."
	26.	7 about his wife, he said, "She is my *s*";
Ex	2.	4 His *s* stood at a distance, to see what
Prov	7.	4 Say to wisdom, "You are my *s*," and call
Song	4.	9 have ravished my heart, my *s*, my bride,
	8.	8 We have a little *s*, she has no breasts.
Ezek	16.48	your *s* Sodom and her daughters has
Mk	3.35	God is my brother, and *s*, and mother."
Acts	23.16	the son of Paul's *s* heard about the
1 Cor	9.	5n right to be accompanied by a *s* as wife,
1 Thess	4.	6 no one wrong or exploit a brother or *s*
1 Tim	5.	2 mothers, to younger women as *s* —
2 Jn		13 children of your elect *s* send their

SIT (SAT SITTING)

Judg	21.	2 and *s* there till evening before God, and
Ps	110.	1 "*S* at my right hand, until I make your
Isa	6.	1 I saw the Lord *s* on a throne, high and
Jer	15.17	I did not *s* in the company of
Ezek	3.15	river Chebar. And I *s* among them,
Mic	4.	4 they shall all *s* under their own vines
Mk	10.37	"Grant us to *s*, one at your right hand
	12.36	said to my Lord, "*S* at my right hand,
	16.19	heaven and *s* down at the right hand
Lk	7.32	are like children *s* in the marketplace
	20.42	said to my Lord, "*S* at my right hand,
Acts	2.34	said to my Lord, "*S* at my right hand,
Heb	1.	3 he *s* down at the right hand of the
	10.12	"he *s* down at the right hand of God,"

SIXTH

Lk	1.26	In the *s* month the angel Gabriel was

SKETCH

Heb	8.	5 is a *s* and shadow of the heavenly one;

SKILL (SKILLFUL)

1 Sam	16.16	someone who is *s* in playing the lyre;
1 Kings	7.14	he was full of *s*, intelligence, and
Ps	78.72	them, and guided them with a *s* hand.
Prov	22.29	you see those who are *s* in their work?

SKIN (SKINS)

Gen	3.21	God made garments of *s* for the man
	21.14	took bread and a *s* of water, and gave it
Job	2.	4 "*S* for *s*! All that people have they will
	7.	5 and dirt; my *s* hardens, then breaks out
	19.20	I have escaped by the *s* of my teeth.
Jer	13.23	Can Ethiopians change their *s* or the
Mk	2.22	otherwise, the wine will burst the *s*,

SKULL

Mt	27.33	Golgotha (which means Place of a *S*),
Mk	15.22	(which means the place of a *s*).
Lk	23.33	is called The *S*, they crucified Jesus
Jn	19.17	out to what is called the Place of the *S*,

SKY (SKIES)

Gen	1.	8 God called the dome *S*. And there was
2 Kings	7.	2 LORD were to make windows in the *s*,
Ps	85.11	will look down from the *s*.
Isa	34.	4 rot away, and the *s* roll up like a scroll.
Lk	12.56	interpret the appearance of earth and *s*;
Rev	6.14	The *s* vanished like a scroll rolling itself

SLANDER (SLANDERED SLANDERS)

Ps	15.	3 who do not *s* with their tongue, and do
	50.20	your kin; you *s* your own mother's child.
	101.	5 who secretly *s* a neighbor I will destroy.
Prov	30.10	Do not *s* a servant to his master, or the
1 Cor	4.13	we endure; when *s*, we speak kindly.
2 Pet	2.10	they are not afraid to *s* the glorious

SLANDERER (SLANDERERS)

Lev	19.16	You shall not go around as a *s* among
Rom	1.30	they are gossips, *s*, God-haters, insolent,

SLAP

2 Cor	11.20	or puts on airs, or gives you a *s* in the

SLAUGHTER (SLAUGHTERED)

Ps	44.22	long, and accounted as sheep for the *s*.
Jer	11.19	I was like a gentle lamb led to the *s*.
Rom	8.36	we are accounted as sheep to be *s*."
Rev	6.	9 those who had been *s* for the word of
	13.	8 in book of life of the Lamb that was *s*.

SLAVE (SLAVES)

Gen	9.25	"Cursed be Canaan; lowest of *s* shall he
	21.10	Cast out this *s* woman with her son; for
Deut	5.15	Remember you were a *s* in the land of
	6.21	"We were Pharaoh's *s* in Egypt, but the
	21.14	You must not treat her as a *s*, since you
Josh	9.23	some of you shall always be *s*, hewers
Prov	19.10	luxury, much less for a *s* to rule over
Eccl	10.	7 I have seen *s* on horseback, and princes
Jer	2.14	Is Israel a *s*? Is he a homeborn servant?
	34.11	and took back the male and female *s*
Lam	5.	8 *S* rule over us; there is no one to deliver
Mt	20.27	to be first among you must be your *s*;
	21.34	he sent his *s* to the tenants to collect
	25.14	summoned his *s* and entrusted his
	25.23	'Well done, good and trustworthy *s*;
Mk	10.44	wishes to be first among you must be *s*
	12.	2 he sent a *s* to the tenants, to collect
	14.47	struck the *s* of the high priest, cutting
Lk	17.	9 Do you thank the *s* for doing what was
	19.17	"Well done, good *s*! Because you have
	20.10	he sent a *s* to the tenants in order that
	22.50	of them struck the *s* of the high priest
Jn	8.34	everyone who commits sin is a *s* to sin.
Rom	6.16	yourselves to anyone as obedient *s*,
	7.	6 we are *s* not under the old written code
1 Cor	7.21	Were you a *s* when called? Do not be
2 Cor	4.	5 Christ as Lord and ourselves as your *s*
Gal	3.28	there is no longer *s* or free, there is no
	4.	1 as they are minors, are no better than *s*,
Eph	6.	5 *S*, obey your earthly masters with fear
Col	3.22	*S*, obey your earthly masters in
Titus	2.	9 Tell *s* to be submissive to their masters
Philem		16 no longer as a *s* but more than a *s*, a
1 Pet	2.18	*S*, accept the authority of your masters
2 Pet	2.19	but they themselves are *s* of corruption;

SLAVE-GIRL

Gen	16.	2 from bearing children; go in to my *s*;

SLAVERY

Ex	20.	2 the land of Egypt, out of the house of *s*.
Deut	5.	6 the land of Egypt, out of the house of *s*.
Rom	8.15	you did not receive a spirit of *s* to fall
Gal	5.	1 and do not submit again to a yoke of *s*.
Heb	2.15	lives were held in *s* by the fear of death.

SLEEP (n)

Gen	2.21	God caused a deep *s* to fall upon
1 Sam	26.12	a deep *s* from the LORD had fallen upon
Ps	127.	2 toil; for he gives *s* to his beloved.
	132.	4 I will not give *s* to my eyes or slumber
Prov	3.24	you lie down, your *s* will be sweet.
	6.	4 Give your eyes no *s* and your eyelids no
	24.33	little *s*, a little slumber, a little folding
Eccl	5.12	Sweet is the *s* of laborers, whether they
Isa	29.10	poured out upon you a spirit of deep *s*,
Jer	51.39	become merry and then *s* a perpetual *s*

SLEEP (SLEEPING SLEPT)

Ps	3.	5 I lie down and *s*; I wake again, for the
	13.	3 to my eyes, or I will *s* the *s* of death,
	121.	4 keeps Israel will neither slumber nor *s*.
Song	5.	2 I *s*, but my heart was awake. Listen! my

SLIP

Dan	12. 2 of those who *s* in the dust of the earth
Mt	9.24 "Go away, for the girl is not dead but *s*."
	26.40 came to the disciples and found them *s*;
Mk	5.39 and weep? The child is not dead but *s*."
	14.37 He came and found them *s*; and he said
	14.40 once more he came and found them *s*,
Lk	22.45 and found them *s* because of grief

SLIP (SLIPPED SLIPS)

Deut	32.35 for the time when their foot shall *s*;
Ps	17. 5 fast to your paths, my feet have not *s*.
	18.36 steps under me, and my feet did not *s*.
	37.31 is in their hearts; their steps do not *s*.
	38.16 who boast against me when my foot *s*."

SLIPPERY

Ps	35. 6 Let their way be dark and *s*, with the
	73.18 you set them in *s* places; you make

SLOW

Prov	16.32 who is *s* to anger is better than the
	19.11 Those with good sense are *s* to anger,

SLUMBER (SLUMBERS)

Ps	121. 3 be moved; he who keeps you will not *s*.
Prov	6.10 A little sleep, a little *s*, a little folding
Isa	5.27 weary, none stumbles, none *s* or sleeps,

SMALL (SMALLEST)

Job	40. 4 I am of *s* account; what shall I answer
Mt	13.32 it is the *s* of all seeds, but when it has

SMASHES

Dan	2.40 just as iron crushes and *s* everything, it

SMELLED

Gen	27.27 he *s* the smell of his garments, and he

SMELT

Isa	1.25 I will *s* away your dross as with lye and

SMITH

1 Sam	13.19 there was no *s* to be found throughout
Isa	54.16 I who have created the *s* who blows the

SMITTEN

Ps	102. 4 My heart is *s* and withered like grass; I

SMOKE

Gen	19.28 *s* of the land going up like the *s* of a
Ps	68. 2 As *s* is driven away, so drive them away;
Prov	10.26 and *s* to the eyes, so are the lazy to
Rev	15. 8 the temple filled with *s* from the glory

SMOOTH

Prov	2.16 from the adulteress with her *s* words,
Isa	30.10 speak to us *s* things, prophesy illusions,
Lk	3. 5 straight, and the rough ways made *s*;

SNAKE (SNAKES)

Ex	4. 3 on the ground, and it became a *s*;
	7.10 down his staff . . . , and it became a *s*.
Jer	8.17 I am letting *s* loose among you, adders
Mt	23.33 You *s*, you brood of vipers! How can you
Mk	16.18n they will pick up *s* in their hands, and if
Lk	10.19 authority to tread on *s* and scorpions,

SNARE (SNARES)

Ex	23.33 their gods, it will surely be a *s* to you.
Deut	7.16 their gods, for that would be a *s* to you.
Judg	2. 3 you, and their gods shall be a *s* to you."
	8.27 and it became a *s* to Gideon and to his
1 Sam	18.21 her to him that she may be a *s* for him,
Job	22.10 Therefore *s* are around you, and sudden
Ps	38.12 Those who seek my life lay their *s*;
	64. 5 they talk of laying *s* secretly, thinking,
	69.22 their table be a trap for them, a *s* for
Prov	18. 7 are their ruin, and their lips are a *s* to
	22.25 their ways and entangle yourself in a *s*.
	29.25 The fear of others lays a *s*, but one who

Jer	18.22 pit to catch me, and laid *s* for my feet.
	50.24 You set a *s* for yourself and you were
Ezek	12.13 him and he shall be caught in my *s*;
Lk	21.35 day catch you unexpectedly, like a *s*.
1 Tim	3. 7 fall into disgrace and the *s* of the devil.

SNATCH (SNATCHING)

Job	24. 9 There are those who *s* the orphan child
Jn	10.28 never perish. No one will *s* them out
Jude	23 save others, by *s* them out of the fire;

SNOW (SNOWS)

2 Sam	23.20 lion in a pit on a day when *s* had fallen.
Job	38.22 you entered the storehouses of the *s*,
Ps	51. 7 wash me, and I shall be whiter than *s*.
	147. 16 He gives *s* like wool; he scatters frost
Prov	25.13 Like the cold of *s* in the time of harvest
	26. 1 Like *s* in summer or rain in harvest, so
	31.21 not afraid for her household when it *s*,
Isa	1.18 sins are like scarlet, they shall be like *s*;
Jer	18.14 Does the *s* of Lebanon leave the crags
Lam	4. 7 Her princes were purer than *s*, whiter
Mt	28. 3 lightning, and his clothing white as *s*.

SOAP

Job	9.30 If I wash myself with *s* and cleanse my

SOBER

1 Thess	5. 6 do, but let us keep awake and be *s*;

SODOM

Gen	10.19 as far as Gaza, in the direction of *S*,
	13.13 Now the people of *S* were wicked, great
	14.12 they took Lot . . . who lived in *S*, and
	19.24 LORD rained on *S* . . . sulfur and fire
Jer	50.40 As when God overthrew *S* and
Mt	10.15 it will more tolerable for the land of *S*
	11.23 power done in you had been done in *S*,
Lk	17.29 on the day that Lot left *S*, it rained fire
Rev	11. 8 great city that is prophetically called *S*

SOFT

Prov	15. 1 A *s* answer turns away wrath, but a
Mt	11. 8 out to see? Someone dressed in *s* robes?

SOIL (SOILED)

Gen	9.20 Noah, a man of the *s*, was the first to
Rev	3. 4 who have not *s* their clothes; they will

SOLDIERS

Mt	28.12 to give a large sum of money to the *s*,
Lk	3.14 *S* also asked him, "And we, what should
	7. 8 set under authority, with *s* under me:
Jn	19.23 When the *s* had crucified Jesus, they

SOLE

Josh	1. 3 Every place that the *s* of your foot will

SOLID

1 Cor	3. 2 I fed you with milk, not *s* food, for you
Heb	5.12 of God. You need milk, not *s* food;

SOLOMON (SOLOMON'S)

Born, 2 Sam 12.24; anointed king, 1 Kings 1.32-40; established his kingdom, 1 Kings 2.12-46; married Pharaoh's daughter, 1 Kings 3.1; asked for wisdom, 1 Kings 3.5-15; judged wisely, 1 Kings 3.16-28; conferred with Hiram, 1 Kings 5; 7.13-14; built the temple, 1 Kings 6; 7.15-51; built his own house, 1 Kings 7.1-12; dedicated the temple, 1 Kings 8; the LORD's covenant with Solomon, 1 Kings 9.1-9; visited by the queen of Sheba, 1 Kings 10.1-13; turned from the LORD, 1 Kings 11.1-40; died, 1 Kings 11.41-43. (See also 2 Chr 1—9.)

Prov	1. 1 proverbs of *S*, son of David, king of
Song	1. 1 The Song of Songs, which is *S*.
Mt	6.29 even *S* in all his glory was not clothed
Lk	11.31 the earth to listen to the wisdom of *S*,
	11.31 see, something greater than *S* is here.
Jn	10.23 in the temple, in the portico of *S*.

Acts   3.11 in the portico called *S* Portico, utterly

SON

Gen   18.10 and your wife Sarah shall have a *s*."
      22. 2 "Take your *s*, your only *s* Isaac, whom
Deut   21.18 stubborn and rebellious *s* who will not
2 Sam   7.14 to him, and he shall be a *s* to me.
      18.33 "O my *s* Absalom, my *s*, my *s* Absalom!
2 Kings   4.14 "Well, she has no *s*, and her husband is
      4.16 in due time, you shall embrace a *s*."
      8. 1 woman whose *s* he had restored to life,
1 Chr   17.13 to him, and he shall be a *s* to me.
Ps   2. 7 He said to me, "You are my *s*; today I
Prov   3.12 the one he loves, as a father the *s*
Isa   7.14 shall bear a *s*, and she shall name him
      9. 6 has been born for us, a *s* given to us;
Jer   31.20 Is Ephraim my dear *s*? Is he the child
Am   7.14 "I am no prophet, nor a prophet's *s*; but
Mic   7. 6 *s* treats the father with contempt, the
Mt   9.27 loudly, "Have mercy on us, *S* of David."
      12.23 and said, "Can this be the *S* of David?"
      13.55 Is not this the carpenter's *s*? Is not his
      21.37 them saying, 'They will respect my *s*.'
      22. 2 who gave a wedding banquet for his *s*,
      22.42 he?" They said to him, "The *s* of David."
Mk   1.11 "You are my *S*, the Beloved; with you I
      9. 7 "This is my *S*, the Beloved; listen to
      9.17 "Teacher, I brought you my *s*; he has a
      12. 6 He had still one other, a beloved *s*;
      14.61 the Messiah, the *S* of the Blessed One?"
Lk   1.31 and bear a *s*, and you will name him
      1.57 to give birth, and she bore a *s*.
      7.12 mother's only *s*, and she was a widow;
      9.38 "Teacher, I beg you to look at my *s*, he
      12.53 be divided, father against *s* and *s*
      15.21 no longer worthy to be called your *s*.'
      19. 9 because he too is a *s* of Abraham.
      20.13 I will send my beloved *s*; perhaps they
      20.44 calls him Lord; so how can he be his *s*?"
Jn   1.14 glory as of a father's only *s*, full of grace
      3.16 loved the world that he gave his only *S*,
      4.47 him to come down and heal his *s*,
      8.36 So if the *S* makes you free, you will be
      9.20 is our *s*, and that he was born blind;
      10.36 because I said, 'I am God's *S*'?
      17.12 n was lost except the *s* of destruction
      19.26 to his mother, "Woman, here is your *s*."
Acts   13.10 "You *s* of the devil, you enemy of all
      13.33 'You are my *S*; today I have begotten
Gal   1.16 was pleased to reveal his *S* to me,
      4. 4 of time had come, God sent his *S*,
Col   1.13 us into the kingdom of his beloved *S*,
Heb   1. 2 last days he has spoken to us by a *S*,
      3. 6 was faithful over God's house as a *S*.
      5. 5 said to him, "You are my *S*, today I have
      11.17 was ready to offer up his only *s*,
1 Jn   1. 3 the Father and with his *S* Jesus Christ.
      2.23 No one who denies the *S* has the
      4. 9 God sent his only *S* into the world so
      4.14 Father has sent his *S* as the Savior of
      5.12 Whoever has the *S* has life; whoever

SONS

Gen   6. 2 the *s* of God saw that they were fair;
Ps   127. 3 *S* are indeed a heritage from the Lord,
      132. 12 If your *s* keep my covenant and my
      144. 12 May our *s* in their youth be like plants
Jer   16. 2 not take a wife, nor shall you have *s* or
Mt   21.28 A man had two *s*; he went to the first

SON OF GOD

Mt   4. 3 "If you are the *S*, command these
      8.29 "What have you to do with us, *S*?
      14.33 him, saying, "Truly you are the *S*."
      26.63 tell us if you are the Messiah, the *S*."
      27.40 yourself! If you are the *S*, come down
Lk   1.35 will be holy; he will be called the *S*.

Jn   1.34 and have testified that this is the *S*."
      3.18 not believed in the name of the only *S*.
      19. 7 die because he has claimed to be the *S*."
Acts   9.20 in the synagogues, saying, "He is the *S*."
Rom   1. 4 and was declared to be *S* with power
Eph   4.13 the faith and of the knowledge of the *S*,
Heb   4.14 through the heavens, Jesus, the *S*,
      6. 6 own they are crucifying again the *S*
      10.29 by those who have spurned the *S*,
1 Jn   4.15 those who confess that Jesus is the *S*,
Rev   2.18 These are the words of the *S*, who has

SON OF MAN

Mt   8.20 but the *S* has nowhere to lay his head."
      9. 6 know that the *S* has authority on earth
      10.23 the towns of Israel, before the *S* comes.
      12. 8 For the *S* is lord of the sabbath."
      12.32 whoever speaks a word against the *S*
      13.37 one who sows the good seed is the *S*;
      16.27 *S* is to come with his angels in the glory
      17.22 "The *S* is going to be betrayed into
      24.27 west, so will be the coming of the *S*.
      24.30 Then the sign of the *S* will appear in
      25.31 "When the *S* comes in his glory, and all
      26. 2 and the *S* will be handed over to be
      26.24 The *S* goes as it is written of him, but
      26.64 from now on you will see the *S* seated
Mk   2.10 the *S* has authority on earth to forgive
      9.31 "The *S* is to be betrayed into human
      14.21 For the *S* goes as it is written of him,
      14.62 'you will see the *S* seated at the right
Lk   6. 5 to them, "The *S* is lord of the sabbath."
      9.22 "The *S* must undergo great suffering,
      9.44 your ears: The *S* is going to be betrayed
      22.69 the *S* will be seated at the right hand of
Jn   3.13 one who descended from heaven, the *S*.
      3.14 wilderness, so must the *S* be lifted up,
Acts   7.56 "I see the heavens opened, and the *S*
Rev   1.13 I saw one like the *S*, clothed with a
      14.14 seated on the cloud was one like the *S*,

SONG (SONGS)

Ex   15. 1 the Israelites sang this *s* to the Lord:
Deut   31.19 therefore write this *s*, and teach it to
Job   30. 9 "And now they mock me in *s*; I am a
Ps   28. 7 exults, and with my *s* I give thanks
      33. 3 Sing to him a new *s*; play skillfully on
      40. 3 He put a new *s* in my mouth, a *s* of
      69.12 and the drunkards make *s* about me.
      81. 2 Raise a *s*, sound the tambourine, the
      95. 2 a joyful noise to him with *s* of praise!
      119. 54 Your statutes have been my *s* wherever I
      137. 3 For there our captors asked us for *s*,
      144. 9 I will sing a new *s* to you, O God; upon
      149. 1 Sing to the Lord a new *s*, his praise in
Prov   25.20 is one who sings *s* to a heavy heart.
Isa   26. 1 On that day this *s* will be sung in the
      30.29 have a *s* as in the night when a holy
Ezek   33.32 To them you are like a singer of love *s*,
Mic   2. 4 they shall take up a taunt *s* against you,
Rev   5. 9 They sing a new *s*: "You are worthy to
      15. 3 they sing the *s* of Moses, the servant of

SORCERER

Ex   22.18 You shall not permit a female *s* to live.

SORROW (SORROWS)

Ps   13. 2 my soul, and have *s* in my heart all day
      16. 4 choose another god multiply their *s*;
      31.10 For my life is spent with *s*, and my
      119. 28 My soul melts away for *s*; strengthen
Eccl   1.18 who increase knowledge increase *s*.
      7. 3 *S* is better than laughter, for by sadness
Isa   35.10 gladness, and *s* and sighing shall flee
      51.11 gladness, and *s* and sighing shall flee
Jer   20.18 forth from the womb to see toil and *s*,
      45. 3 me! The Lord has added *s* to my pain;

Lam	1.12	Look and see if there is any *s* like my *s*,
Ezek	23.33	shall be filled with drunkenness and *s*.
Jn	16. 6	things to you, *s* has filled your hearts.
Rom	9. 2	I have great *s* and unceasing anguish in
2 Cor	2. 7	may not be overwhelmed by excessive *s*.

SORROWFUL

2 Cor	6.10	as *s*, yet always rejoicing; as poor, yet

SORRY

Gen	6. 6	LORD was *s* that he had made
1 Sam	15.35	the LORD was *s* that he had made Saul
Ps	38.18	I confess my iniquity; I am *s* for my sin.

SOSTHENES

Acts	18.17	seized *S*, the official of the synagogue,
1 Cor	1. 1	by the will of God, and our brother *S*,

SOUL (SOULS)

Deut	6. 5	all your heart, and with all your *s*,
1 Sam	18. 1	the *s* of Jonathan was bound to the *s* of
2 Chr	6.38	repent with all their heart and *s* in
Job	7.11	will complain in the bitterness of my *s*.
	30.16	now my *s* is poured out within me;
Ps	23. 3	me beside still waters; he restores my *s*.
	42.11	Why are you cast down, O my *s*, and
	56.13	For you have delivered my *s* from death,
	103. 1	Bless the LORD, O my *s*; and all that is
Prov	21.10	The *s* of the wicked desire evil; their
	27. 9	heart glad, but the *s* is torn by trouble.
Song	1. 7	Tell me, you whom my *s* loves, where
Isa	1.14	and your appointed festivals my *s* hates;
Jer	13.17	my *s* will weep in secret for your pride;
Mic	6. 7	the fruit of my body for the sin of my *s*?"
Mt	10.28	who kill the body but cannot kill the *s*;
	22.37	with all your heart, and with all your *s*,
Mk	12.30	with all your heart, and with all your *s*,
Lk	1.47	Mary said, "My *s* magnifies the Lord,
	12.19	say to my *s*, "*S*, you have ample goods
	21.19	By your endurance you will gain your *s*.
Acts	2.27	For you will not abandon my *s* to
1 Pet	1.22	have purified yours *s* by your obedience
3 Jn	2	health, just as it is well with your *s*.
Rev	18.14	fruit for which your *s* longed has gone
	20. 4	I saw the *s* of those who had been

SOUND

Gen	3. 8	They heard the *s* of the LORD God
Ezek	1.24	the *s* of their wings like the *s* of mighty
Zeph	1.14	the *s* of the day of the LORD is bitter,
2 Tim	1.13	Hold to the standard of *s* teaching that
Titus	2. 2	prudent, and *s* in faith, in love, and in
	2. 8	*s* speech that cannot be censured; then

SOUNDNESS

Ps	38. 3	There is no *s* in my flesh because of
Isa	1. 6	there is no *s* in it, but bruises and sores

SOVEREIGN (SOVEREIGNTY)

1 Kings	4.21	Solomon was *s* over all the kingdoms
Dan	4.17	the Most High is *s* over the kingdom
	4.25	High has *s* over the kingdom of mortals,
	4.32	the Most High has *s* over the kingdom
	4.34	For his *s* is an everlasting *s*, and his

SOW (SOWED SOWN SOWS)

Gen	26.12	Isaac *s* in that land, and in the same
	47.23	here is seed for you; *s* the land.
Ps	107.37	they *s* fields, and plant vineyards, and
	126. 5	those who *s* in tears reap with shouts
Prov	6.19	and one who *s* discord in a family.
	22. 8	Whoever *s* injustice will reap calamity,
Eccl	11. 4	Whoever observes the wind will not *s*;
Isa	32.20	will you be who *s* beside every stream,
Jer	4. 3	fallow ground, and *s* not among thorns.
	12.13	have *s* wheat and have reaped thorns,
	31.27	when I will *s* the house of Israel and
Hos	8. 7	For they *s* the wind, and they shall reap

Hos	10.12	*S* for yourselves righteousness; reap
Mic	6.15	You shall *s*, but not reap; you shall
Mt	6.26	birds of the air; they neither *s* nor reap
	13.27	'Master, did you not *s* good seed in
	25.26	did you, that I reap where I did not *s*,
Mk	4. 3	"Listen! A sower went out to *s*.
Lk	12.24	the ravens: they neither *s* nor reap,
Jn	4.37	holds true, 'One *s* and another reaps.'
1 Cor	9.11	If we have *s* spiritual good among you,
	15.36	What you *s* does not come to life unless
2 Cor	9. 6	one who *s* sparingly will also reap
Gal	6. 7	mocked, for you reap whatever you *s*.

SOWER

Mt	13. 3	saying: "Listen! A *s* went out to sow.
	13.18	"Hear then the parable of the *s*.
Mk	4.14	The *s* sows the word.
Lk	8. 5	"A *s* went out to sow his seed; and as

SPAIN

Rom	15.24	come to you when I go to *S*. For I do
	15.28	I will set out by way of you to *S*; and I

SPAN

Mt	6.27	add a single hour to your *s* of life?
Lk	12.25	add a single hour to your *s* of life?

SPARE (SPARED SPARES)

Josh	6.25	Rahab . . . Joshua *s*. Her family has
1 Sam	15. 9	Saul and the people *s* Agag, and the
	24.10	some urged me kill you, but I *s* you.
2 Sam	21. 7	the king *s* Mephibosheth, the son of
Job	2. 6	well, he is in your power; only *s* his life."
	21.30	that the wicked are *s* in the day of
Ps	119.88	In your steadfast love *s* my life, so that
Prov	13.24	who *s* the rod hate their children, but
	17.27	One who *s* words is knowledgeable, one

SPARROW (SPARROWS)

Ps	84. 3	Even the *s* finds a home, and the
Mt	10.29	Are not two *s* sold for a penny?
Lk	12. 6	Are not five *s* sold for two pennies? Yet

SPEAK (SPEAKING SPEAKS SPOKE SPOKEN)

Ex	20. 1	Then God *s* all these words:
	20.19	but do not let God *s* to us, or we will
	33. 9	tent, and the LORD would *s* with Moses.
Num	7.89	into tent of meeting to *s* with the LORD,
	11.25	came down in the cloud and *s* to him,
	12. 8	With him I *s* face to face —clearly, not
Deut	5. 4	The LORD *s* with you face to face at the
	5.24	Today we have seen that God may *s* to
1 Sam	3. 9	"*S*, LORD, for your servant is listening.' "
1 Kings	22.14	the LORD says to me, that I will *s*."
2 Chr	18.13	lives, whatever God says, that I will *s*."
Job	33.14	For God *s* in one way, and in two,
Ps	50. 1	LORD, *s* and summons the earth from
	85. 8	will *s*, for he will *s* peace to his people,
	87. 3	Glorious things are *s* of you, O city of
	139.20	those who *s* of you maliciously, and lift
Eccl	7. 4	a time to keep silence, and a time to *s*;
Isa	40. 2	*S* tenderly to Jerusalem, and cry to her
Jer	1. 6	I do not know how to *s*, for I am only a
Hos	2.14	the wilderness, and *s* tenderly to her.
Mt	17.25	Jesus *s* of it first, asking, "What do you
Mk	2. 2	door, and he was *s* the word to them.
Lk	4.32	teaching, because he *s* with authority.
	4.41	them and would not allow them to *s*,
	12.10	everyone who *s* a word against the Son
Jn	7.46	answered, "Never has anyone *s* like this!"
Acts	2. 4	and began to *s* in other languages,
	5.40	them not to *s* in the name of Jesus,
1 Tim	5. 1	Do not *s* harshly to an older man, but *s*
Heb	11. 4	he died, but through his faith he still *s*.
Jas	4.11	Whoever *s* evil against another or judges

SPEAR (SPEARS)

1 Sam	26. 8	to the ground with one stroke of the *s*;

Isa   2. 4 and their *s* into pruning hooks;
Jn   19.34 of the soldiers pierced his side with a *s*,

SPECIAL

2 Tim   2.20 clay, some for *s* use, some for ordinary.

SPECK

Mt   7. 3 do you see the *s* in your neighbor's eye,
Lk   6.41 do you see the *s* in your neighbor's eye,

SPECTACLE

Nah   3. 6 you with contempt, and make you a *s*.

SPEECH

Ex   4.10 but I am slow of *s* and of tongue."
Ps   19. 2 Day to day pours forth *s*, and night to
Prov   17. 7 Fine *s* is not becoming to a fool; still
         29.20 Do you see someone who is hasty in *s*?
Ezek   3. 5 not sent to a people of obscure *s* and
Zeph   3. 9 change the *s* of the peoples to a pure *s*,
1 Cor   1. 5 enriched in him, in *s* and knowledge of
2 Cor   10.10 is weak, and his *s* is contemptible"
Col   4. 6 Let your *s* always be gracious, seasoned

SPEECHLESS

Ezek   3.26 shall be *s* and unable to reprove them;
Dan   10.15 my face toward the ground and was *s*.
Mt   22.12 without a wedding robe?' And he was *s*.
Acts   9. 7 who were traveling with him stood *s*,

SPELLBOUND

Mk   11.18 the whole crowd was *s* at his teaching.

SPEND (SPENT)

Gen   19. 2 *s* the night, and wash your feet; then
         47.18 from my lord that our money is all *s*;
Ps   38. 8 I am utterly *s* and crushed; I groan

SPEWED

Jon   2.10 spoke to the fish, and it *s* Jonah out

SPICE (SPICES)

Song   4.10 the fragrance of your oils than any *s*!
Jn   19.40 wrapped it with the *s* in linen cloths

SPIES

Josh   2. 1 sent two men ecretly from Shittim as *s*,
          6.23 men who had been *s* went in and
Judg   1.24 When the *s* saw a man coming out of

SPIRIT

Gen   6. 3 "My *s* shall not abide in mortals forever,
Ex   31. 3 I have filled him with divine *s*, with
Num   11.17 will take some of the *s* which is on you
         11.29 the Lord would put his *s* upon them!"
         27.18 son of Nun, a man in whom is the *s*,
Judg   9.23 God sent an evil *s* between Abimelech
1 Sam   19. 9 an evil *s* from the Lord came upon Saul,
         28. 8 "Consult a *s* for me, and bring up for
1 Kings 22.21 until a *s* came forward and stood before
2 Kings   2.15 "The *s* of Elijah rests on Elisha."
          5.26 "Did I not go with you in *s* when
Neh   9.20 You gave your good *s* to instruct them,
Job   15.13 so that you turn your *s* against God,
         32. 8 But truly it is the *s* in a mortal, the
Ps   34.18 and saves the crushed in *s*.
         77. 3 and I moan; I meditate, and my *s* faints.
         78. 8 whose *s* was not faithful to God.
        104. 30 you send forth your *s*, they are created;
        106. 33 for they made his *s* bitter, and he spoke
        139. 7 Where can I go from your *s*? Or where
        142. 3 When my *s* is faint, you know my way.
        143. 10 Let your good *s* lead me on a level
Prov   16. 2 own eyes, but the Lord weighs the *s*.
         17.22 but a downcast *s* dries up the bones.
         18.14 humans will endure sickness; but a
         20.27 The human *s* is the lamp of the Lord,
Eccl   3.21 Who knows whether the human *s* goes
Isa   4. 4 its midst by a *s* of judgment and by a *s*

Isa   32.15 until a *s* from on high is poured out on
         42. 1 I have put my *s* upon him; he will bring
         44. 3 I will pour my *s* upon your descendants,
Ezek   1.12 wherever the *s* would go, they went,
          1.20 the *s* of the living creatures was in the
          8. 3 *s* lifted me up between earth and
         10.17 for the *s* of the living creatures was
         36.27 I will put my *s* within you, and make
         37.14 I will put my *s* within you, and you
Dan   4. 8 is endowed with a *s* of the holy gods—
          5.11 is endowed with a *s* of the holy gods.
Joel   2.28 I will pour out my *s* on all flesh;
Hab   2. 4 Look at the proud! Their *s* is not right
Hag   2. 5 My *s* abides among you; do not fear.
Zech   4. 6 by might, nor by power, but by my *s*,
         12. 1 earth and formed the human *s* within:
Mt   4. 1 Jesus was led up by the *S* into the
          5. 3 "Blessed are the poor in *s*, for theirs is
         10.20 but the *S* of your Father speaking
         12.18 I will put my *S* upon him, and he will
         26.41 the *s* indeed is willing, but the flesh is
Mk   1.23 synagogue a man with an unclean *s*;
         14.38 the *s* indeed is willing, but the flesh is
Lk   1.47 and my *s* rejoices in God my Savior,
          4. 1 was led by the *S* into the wilderness,
Jn   3. 6 is flesh, and what is born of the *S* is *s*.
          3.34 for he gives the *S* without measure.
          6.63 It is the *s* that gives life; the flesh is
Acts   2.17 I will pour out my *S* upon all flesh, and
         20.22 And now, as a captive to the *S*, I am on
Rom   1. 4 power according to the *s* of holiness
          8. 2 the law of the *S* of life in Christ Jesus
          8. 4 to the flesh but according to the *S*.
          8. 5 those who live according to the *S* set
          8. 6 is death, but to set the mind on *S* is life
1 Cor   2.10 God has revealed to us through the *S*;
          3.16 temple and that God's *S* dwells in you?
         12.13 For in the one *S* we were all baptized
2 Cor   1.22 giving us his *S* in our hearts as a first
Gal   4. 6 God has sent the *S* of his Son into our
          6. 8 if you sow to the *S* you will reap eternal
Eph   5.18 is debauchery; but be filled with the *S*,
1 Thess   5.19 Do not quench the *S*. Do not despise
2 Tim   1. 7 rather a *s* of power and of love and of
Heb   9.14 through the eternal *S* offered himself
Jas   2.26 just as the body without the *s* is dead,
          4. 5 "God yearns jealously for the *s* that he
1 Jn   3.24 in us, by the *S* which he has given us.
          5. 8 the *S*, and the water, and the blood,
Rev   2. 7 listen to what the *S* is saying to the
         22.17 The *S* and the Bride say, "Come." And

SPIRITS

Lk   4.36 he commands the unclean *s*, and out
Heb   1.14 not all angels *s* in the divine service,
Rev   3. 1 of him who has the seven *s* of God
          4. 5 torches, which are the seven *s* of God;

SPIRIT OF GOD

Gen   1.2n while the *s* swept over the face of the
         41.38 else like this—one in whom is the *s*?"
Num   24. 2 by tribe. Then the *S* came upon him
1 Sam   11. 6 the *s* came upon Saul in power when he
         19.20 the *s* came upon the messengers of
2 Chr   15. 1 The *S* came upon Azariah son of Oded.
         24.20 the *S* took possession of Zachariah son
Job   27. 3 is in me and the *s* is in my nostrils,
         33. 4 The *s* has made me, and the breath of
Rom   8.14 all who are led by the *S* are children
         15.19 and wonders, by the power of the *S*
Phil   3. 1 circumcision, who worship in the *S* and
1 Jn   4. 2 By this you know the *S*: every spirit that

SPIRIT OF THE LORD

Judg   3.10 The *s* came upon him, and he judged
          6.34 the *s* took possession of Gideon; and he
         11.29 the *s* came upon Jephthah, and he

Judg	13.25	The *s* began to stir him at
	15.14	the *s* rushed on him, and the ropes that
1 Sam	16.13	the *s* came mightily upon David from
1 Kings	18.12	the *s* will carry you I know not where;
	22.24	"Which way did the *s* pass from me to
2 Chr	20.14	the *S* came upon Jahaziel son of
Isa	11. 2	The *S* shall rest on him, the spirit of
	40.13	Who has directed the *s*, or as his
Ezek	11. 5	Then the *S* fell upon me, and he said to
Lk	4.18	"The *S* is upon me, because he has
Acts	5. 9	agreed together to put the *S* to the test?
2 Cor	3.17	Lord is the Spirit, and where the *S* is,

SPIRITUAL

Rom	2.29	of the heart — it is *s* and not literal.
	7.14	we know that the law is *s*; but I am of
1 Cor	2.13	by the Spirit, interpreting *s* things
	3. 1	I could not speak to you as *s* people,
	10. 3	in the sea, and all ate the same *s* food,
	12. 1	Now concerning *s* gifts, brothers and
	15.44	a physical body, it is raised a *s* body.

SPIT (SPAT)

Deut	25. 9	*s* in his face, and declare, "This is what
Mt	26.67	Then they *s* in his face and struck him;
Mk	7.33	ears and he *s* and touched his tongue.
	14.65	Some began to *s* on him, to blindfold
	15.19	his head with a reed, *s* upon him,
Rev	3.16	cold not hot, I am about to *s* you out

SPLENDOR

Ps	29. 2	of his name; worship the LORD in holy *s*.
	96. 9	Worship the LORD in holy *s*; tremble
Ezek	16.14	for it was perfect because of my *s*
Hag	2. 9	The latter *s* of this house shall be

SPOIL (SPOILS)

Judg	5.19	of Megiddo, they got no *s* of silver.
Ps	44.10	our foe, and our enemies have gotten *s*.
	119.162	at your word like one who finds great *s*.

SPOT

Tim	6.14	the commandment without *s* or blame

SPREAD (SPREADING)

2 Sam	5.18	Philistines had come and *s* out in the
2 Kings	19.14	of the LORD and *s* it before the LORD.
Ps	88. 9	you, O LORD; I *s* out my hands to you.
Prov	29. 5	flatters a neighbor is *s* a net for the
Ezek	16. 8	I *s* the edge of my cloak over you, and
Mt	21. 8	large crowd *s* their cloaks on the road.
Mk	11. 8	Many people *s* their cloaks on the road,
Lk	19.36	people kept *s* their cloaks on the road.
Phil	1.12	me has actually helped to *s* the gospel,

SPRING (SPRINGS)

Josh	15.19	gave her the upper *s* and the lower *s*.
Ps	104. 10	You make *s* gush forth in the valleys;
Hos	13.15	shall dry up, his *s* shall be parched.
Jas	3.11	Does a *s* pour forth from the same
2 Pet	2.17	These are waterless *s* and mists driven
Rev	21. 6	as a gift from the *s* of the water of life.

SPROUT

Num	17. 5	staff of the man whom I choose shall *s*;
Ps	92. 7	though the wicked *s* like grass and all

SPURN (SPURNED)

Lev	26.15	if you *s* my statutes, and abhor my
Heb	10.29	by those who have *s* the Son of God,

SPY (SPIED SPYING)

Gen	42.30	us, and charged us with *s* on the land.
Num	13. 2	"Send men to *s* out the land of Canaan,
	13.17	sent them to *s* out the land of Canaan,
	13.21	So they went and *s* out the land from
1 Chr	19. 3	search and to overthrow and to *s* out
Gal	2. 4	who slipped in to *s* on the freedom we

SQUANDER (SQUANDERED)

Prov	29. 3	company with prostitutes is to *s* one's
Lk	15.13	and there he *s* his property in dissolute

STABILITY

Prov	29. 4	By justice a king gives *s* to the land, but
Isa	33. 6	he will be the *s* of your times,

STAFF

Ex	4. 2	is that in your hand?" He said, "A *s*.
	4.20	and Moses carried the *s* of God in his
Num	17. 3	and write Aaron's name on the *s* of
Judg	5.14	those who bear the marshal's *s*;
2 Kings	4.29	and lay my *s* upon the face of the child."
Mk	6. 8	nothing for their journey except a *s*;

STAGGER (STAGGERED)

Job	12.25	light; he makes them *s* like a drunkard.
Ps	107. 27	they reeled and *s* like drunkards, and

STALLS

2 Chr	9.25	Solomon had four thousand *s* for horses

STALK

Mk	4.28	of itself, first the *s*, then the head,

STAMMERING

Isa	28.11	*s* lip and with alien tongue he will
	33.19	*s* in a language that you cannot

STAND (STANDING STANDS STOOD)

Gen	18.22	Abraham remained *s* before the LORD.
Num	16.48	He *s* between the dead and the living;
Deut	7.24	no one will be able to *s* against you,
	10. 8	to *s* before the LORD to minister to him,
	29.10	You *s* assembled today, all of you,
Josh	10.13	And the sun *s* still, and the moon
Neh	8. 5	when he opened it, all the people *s*.
Ps	5. 5	The boastful will not *s* before your eyes;
	130. 3	mark iniquities, Lord, who could *s*?
	135. 2	you that *s* in the house of the LORD, in
Jer	6.16	*S* at the crossroads, and look, and ask
Ezek	2. 1	O mortal, *s* upon your feet, and I will
Mt	9. 6	to the paralytic — "*S* up, take your bed
Mk	2.11	*s* up, take your mat and go to your
Lk	5.24	to you, *s* up and take up your bed and
	21.36	place, and to *s* before the Son of man."
Jn	5. 8	to him, "*S* up, take your mat and walk."
Acts	7.56	and the Son of Man *s* at the right hand
1 Cor	6. 4	appoint as judges those who have no *s*
	10.12	if you think you are *s*, watch out that
	16.13	Keep alert, *s* firm in your faith, be
Gal	5. 1	Christ has set us free. *S* firm, therefore,
Phil	4. 1	crown, *s* firm in the Lord in this way,
1 Thess	3. 8	if you continue to *s* firm in the Lord.
2 Tim	2.19	But God's firm foundation *s*, bearing
1 Pet	5.12	is the true grace of God. *S* fast in it.
Jude	24	to make you *s* without blemish in the

STANDARD

Num	10.14	The *s* of the camp of Judah set out
Isa	31. 9	and his officers desert the *s* in panic,"
Jer	4. 6	Raise a *s* toward Zion, flee for safety, do

STAR (STARS)

Gen	1.16	light to rule the night — and the *s*.
	15. 5	"Look toward heaven and count the *s*, if
	22.17	your offspring as numerous as the *s*
Num	24.17	a *s* shall come out of Jacob, and a
Deut	1.10	you are as numerous as the *s* of heaven.
	10.22	has made you as numerous as the *s*
	28.62	once you were as numerous as the *s*
Judg	5.20	The *s* fought from heaven, from their
1 Chr	27.23	to make Israel as numerous as the *s* of
Neh	4.21	break of dawn until the *s* came out.
Job	38. 7	when the morning *s* sang together, and
Ps	147. 4	He determines the number of the *s*; he
Isa	14.12	you are fallen from heaven, O Day *S*,

Dan	8.10	some of the *s*, and trampled on them.
	12. 3	many to righteousness, like the *s* forever
Mt	2. 2	For we observed his *s* at its rising, and
Heb	11.12	were born, "as many as the *s* of heaven
2 Pet	1.19	and the morning *s* rises in your hearts.
Rev	1.16	In his right hand he held seven *s*, and
	8.10	a great *s* fell from heaven, blazing like a
	22.16	of David, the bright morning *s*."

STARED

Isa	63. 5	I *s*, but there was no one to sustain me;

STATE

Mt	12.45	the last *s* of that person is worse than
Lk	11.26	the last *s* of that person is worse

STATUE

Dan	2.31	O king, and lo! there was a great *s*.
Acts	19.35	the great Artemis and of the *s* that fell

STATUTE (STATUTES)

Lev	18. 5	You shall keep my *s* and my ordinances;
Num	35.29	These things shall be a *s* and ordinance
Ps	119. 48	which I love, I will meditate on your *s*,
Ezek	5. 6	against my ordinances and my *s*,

STAY (STAYED STAYING)

Ex	2.21	Moses agreed to *s* with the man, and he
	16.29	each of you *s* where you are; do not
Jer	42.15	hungry for bread, and there we will *s*,'
Mt	10.11	it is worthy and *s* there until you leave.
Lk	19. 5	down; for I must *s* at your house today."
Jn	1.38	Teacher), where are you *s*?" He said to
Acts	1. 4	While *s* with them, he ordered them not
Heb	11. 9	By faith he *s* for a time in the land he

STEADFAST

Ps	57. 7	My heart is *s*, O God, my heart is *s*. I
1 Cor	15.58	be *s*, immovable, always excelling

STEADFAST LOVE

Gen	24.12	and show *s* to my master Abraham.
	32.10	I am not worthy of the least of all the *s*
	39.21	was with Joseph and showed him *s*;
Ex	34. 7	keeping *s* for the thousandth generation,
1 Chr	16.34	for he is good; for his *s* endures forever.
2 Chr	7. 3	he is good, for his *s* endures forever."
Ezra	7.28	who extended to me *s* before the king
Ps	17. 7	Wondrously show your *s*, O savior of
	25. 6	of your mercy, O LORD, and of your *s*,
	25. 7	according to your *s* remember me, for
	26. 3	For your *s* is before my eyes, I walk in
	36. 7	How precious is your *s*, O God! All
	40.10	I have not concealed your *s* and your
	63. 3	your *s* is better than life, my lips will
	69.16	Answer me, O LORD, for your *s* is good;
	77. 8	Has his *s* ceased forever? Are his
	85.10	*S* and faithfulness will meet;
	89. 2	that your *s* is established forever;
	92. 2	declare your *s* in the morning, and your
	100. 5	the LORD is good; his *s* endures forever,
	103. 17	But the *s* of the LORD is from everlasting
	107. 8	Let them thank the LORD for his *s*, for
	107. 43	things, and consider the *s* of the LORD.
	118. 1	for he is good; his *s* endures forever.
	119. 88	In your *s* spare my life, so that I may
	136. 1	for he is good; for his *s* endures forever.
Isa	63. 7	according to the abundance of his *s*.
Jer	16. 5	people, says the LORD, my *s* and mercy.
Lam	3.22	The *s* of the LORD never ceases, his
Hos	6. 6	I desire *s* and not sacrifice, the

STEADFASTNESS

Rom	15. 4	written for our instruction, so that by *s*
2 Thess	3. 5	the love of God and to the *s* of Christ.

STEAL (STEALING STEALS STOLE)

Gen	31.30	father's house, why did you *s* my gods?"
Ex	20.15	You shall not *s*.

Ex	22. 1	When someone *s* an ox or a sheep, and
Deut	5.19	Neither shall you *s*.
2 Sam	15. 6	Absalom *s* the hearts of the people of
Prov	6.30	who *s* only to satisfy their appetite
Jer	7. 9	Will you *s*, murder, commit adultery,
Mt	6.20	where thieves do not break in and *s*.
	19.18	You shall not *s*; You shall not bear false
Eph	4.28	Thieves must give up *s*; rather let them

STEEP

Mt	8.32	the whole herd rushed down the *s* bank

STEP (STEPS)

1 Sam	20. 3	there is but a *s* between me and death."
Job	14.16	then you would not number my *s*, you
	18. 7	Their strong *s* are shortened, and their
	31. 4	not see my ways, and number all my *s*?
Ps	18.36	You gave me a wide place for my *s*
	37.23	Our *s* are made firm by the LORD, when
	44.18	turned back, nor have our *s* departed
	73. 2	stumbled; my *s* had nearly slipped.
	119.133	Keep my *s* steady according to your
Prov	16. 9	the way but the LORD directs the *s*.
	20.24	All our *s* are ordered by the LORD; how
Isa	38. 8	sun on the dial of Ahaz turn back ten *s*."
Jer	10.23	as they walk cannot direct their *s*.
Lam	4.18	They dogged our *s* so that we could not
2 Cor	12.18	spirit? Did we not take the same *s*?

STEPHEN

Acts	6. 5	they chose *S*, a man full of faith and
	6. 9	and Asia, stood up and argued with *S*.
	7.59	While they were stoning *S*, he prayed,
	8. 2	Devout men buried *S*, and made loud
	11.19	persecution that took place over *S*
	22.20	the blood of your witness *S* was shed,

STEWARDS

1 Cor	4. 1	of Christ and *s* of God's mysteries.

STICK (STICKS)

Num	15.32	a man gathering *s* on the sabbath day.
Prov	18.24	but a true friend *s* closer than one's
Ezek	37.16	take a *s* and write on it, "For Judah,

STIFF-NECKED

Ex	33. 3	you on the way, for you are a *s* people."
2 Chr	30. 8	Do not now be *s* as your ancestors were,
Acts	7.51	You *s* people, uncircumcised in heart

STILL

Josh	10.13	And the sun stood *s*, and the moon
Ps	37. 7	Be *s* before the LORD, and wait patiently
	39. 2	I was silent and *s*; I held my peace to
	46.10	"Be *s*, and know that I am God! I am
	107. 29	he made the storm be *s*, and the waves

STING

1 Cor	15.55	your victory? Where, O death, is your *s*?"

STINGERS

Rev	9.10	tails like scorpions, with *s*, and in their

STIRS (STIRRED)

Ex	35.21	they came, everyone whose heart was *s*,
2 Chr	36.22	LORD *s* up the spirit of King Cyrus of
Prov	28.25	The greedy person *s* up strife, but
Hag	1.14	the LORD *s* up the spirit of Zerubbabel
Lk	23. 5	"He *s* up the people by teaching
Jn	5.4	n into the pool, and *s* up the water;
	5. 7	into the pool when the water is *s* up;
Acts	6.12	They *s* up the people as well as the
2 Cor	9. 2	and your zeal has *s* up most of them.

STOCKS

Job	13.27	You put my feet in the *s*, and watch all
Jer	20. 2	prophet Jeremiah, and put him in the *s*
Acts	16.24	cell and fastened their feet in the *s*.

STOLEN

2 Sam 19.41 have the people of Judah *s* you away,

STOMACH

Mt   15.17 goes into the mouth enters the *s*,
Mk   7.19 since it enters, not the heart but the *s*,
1 Cor 6.13 is meant for the *s* and the *s* for food,"
1 Tim 5.23 take a little wine for the sake of your *s*

STONE (STONES) (n)

Ex   28.11 you shall engrave the two *s* with the
Deut   5.22 He wrote them on two *s* tablets, and
      10. 1 "Carve out two *s* tablets like the former
Josh   4. 6 time to come, 'What do those *s* mean
      24.26 he took a large *s*, and set it up there
1 Sam 6.18 The great *s*, beside which they set down
       7.12 Samuel took a *s* and set it up between
      17.40 and chose five smooth *s* from the wadi,
      25.37 died within him; he became like a *s*.
Ps   118. 22 The *s* that the builers rejected has
Prov 27. 3 A *s* is heavy, and sand is weighty, but a
Isa   28.16 laying in Zion a foundation *s*, a tested *s*,
Jer   2.27 father," and to a *s*, "You gave me birth."
Ezek 11.19 I will remove the heart of *s* from their
Dan   2.35 the *s* that struck the statue became a
Hab   2.11 The very *s* will cry out from the wall,
Mt   7. 9 child asks for bread, will give him a *s*?
      21.42 The *s* which the builders rejected has
      21.44 who falls on this *s* will be broken to
      24. 2 I tell you, not one *s* will be left here
      27.66 made the tomb secure by sealing the *s*.
Mk   12.10 the *s* which the builders rejected has
      13. 2 Not one *s* will be left here upon
      16. 1 looked up, they saw that the *s*, which
Lk   3. 8 is able from these *s* to raise up children
       4. 3 God, command this *s* to become a loaf
      11.11n bread, will give a *s*; or if your child asks
      19.40 were silent, the *s* would shout out."
      20.17 'The *s* which the builders rejected has
      21. 6 will come when not one *s* will be left
      24. 2 They found the *s* rolled away from the
Jn   8.59 they picked up *s* to throw at him, but
      11.39 Jesus said, "Take away the *s*." Martha,
      20. 1 and saw that the *s* had been removed
Acts   4.11 Jesus is 'the *s* that was rejected by you,
2 Cor 3. 3 not on tablets of *s* but on tablets of
1 Pet 2. 6 "See, I am laying in Zion a *s*, a

STONE (STONED STONES STONING)

Lev   24.14 and let the whole congregation *s* him.
Num   14.10 congregation threatened to *s* them.
      15.36 outside the camp and *s* him to death,
Deut 13.10 *S* them to death for trying to turn you
      21.21 men of the town shall *s* him to death,
Josh   7.25 And all Israel *s* him to death; they
1 Sam 30. 6 danger; for the people spoke of *s* him,
Mt   23.37 city that kills the prophets and *s* those
Jn   8. 5 Moses commanded us to *s* such women.
      10.31 Jews took up stones again to *s* him.
2 Cor 11.25 beaten with rods; once I received a *s*.
Acts   7.58 him out of the city and began to *s* him;

STOP (STOPPED)

Num   11.28 men, said, "My lord Moses, *s* them!"
Job   9.12 He snatches away; who can *s* him? Who
Ps   63.11 exult, for the mouths of liars will be *s*.

STORE (STORED STORING)

Gen   41.49 So Joseph *s* up grain in such
Mt   6.19 "Do not *s* up for yourselves treasures on
1 Tim 6.19 thus *s* up for themselves the treasure of

STOREHOUSE (STOREHOUSES)

Gen   41.56 Joseph opened all the *s*, and sold to the
Job   38.22 "Have you entered the *s* of the snow, or
Ps   33. 7 sea in a bottle; he put the deeps in *s*.
Isa   39. 2 armory, all that was found in his *s*.
Jer   10.13 and he brings out the wind from his *s*.

Mal   3.10 Bring the full tithe into the *s*, so that

STORK

Lev   11.19 the *s*, the heron of any kind, the
Jer   8. 7 Even the *s* in the heavens knows its

STORM

Ps   107. 29 he made the *s* be still, and the waves of
Jer   23.19 Look, the *s* of the LORD! Wrath has gone
Jon   1.12 me that this great *s* has come upon you."

STRAIGHT

Prov   3. 6 him, and he will make *s* your paths.
      11. 5 of the blameless keeps their ways *s*,
Eccl   7.13 can make *s* what he has made crooked?
Isa   45.13 and I will make all his paths *s*;
Acts   9.11 "Get up and go to the street called *S*,

STRAIGHTFORWARD

Eccl   7.29 God made human beings *s*, but they

STRAIN (STRAINING)

Mt   23.24 guides, you *s* out a gnat but swallow
Phil   3.13 and *s* forward to what lies ahead,

STRANGE

Ps   44.20 or spread out our hands to a *s* god,

STRANGER (STRANGERS)

Gen   23. 4 "I am a *s* and an alien residing among
Deut 10.18 who loves the *s*, providing them food
      10.19 shall also love the *s*, for you were *s*
Job   31.32 he has not lodged in the street; I
Ps   69. 8 I have become a *s* to my kindred, an
     146. 9 The LORD watches over the *s*, he
Jer   14. 8 why should you be like a *s* in the land,
Lam   5. 2 inheritance has been turned over to *s*,
Joel   3.17 be holy, and *s* shall never again pass
Mt   25.35 I was a *s* and you welcomed me,
Eph   2.12 *s* to the covenants of promise, having

STRAW

Ex   5. 7 You shall no longer give the people *s* to
Job   21.18 How often are they like *s* before the
Jer   23.28 What has *s* in common with wheat?
1 Cor 3.12 silver, precious stones, wood, hay, *s*—

STREAM (STREAMS)

Gen   2. 6 but a *s* would rise from the earth, and
Ps   1. 3 They are like a trees planted by *s* of
      42. 1 As a deer longs for flowing *s*, so my
     119.136 My eyes shed *s* of tears because your
Isa   2. 2 the hills; all the nations shall *s* to it.
      32. 2 tempest, like *s* of water in a dry place,
      35. 6 in the wilderness, and *s* in the desert;

STREET (STREETS)

Ps   18.42 cast them out like the mire of the *s*.
Acts   9.11 "Get up and go to the *s* called Straight,

STRENGTH

Ex   15. 2 The LORD is my *s* and my might, and he
Num   11. 6 but now our *s* is dried up, and there is
Deut 33.25 bronze; and as your days, so is your *s*.
Judg 16. 6 tell me what makes your *s* so great, and
2 Sam 22.40 you girded me with *s* for the battle; you
Job   6.11 What is my *s*, that I should wait? And
       9.19 If it is a contest of *s*, he is the strong
      18.12 Their *s* is consumed by hunger, and
      35.10 'Where is God my Maker, who gives *s*
Ps   18.32 the God who girded me with *s*, and
      21. 1 In your *s* the king rejoices, O LORD, and
      29. 1 beings, ascribe to the LORD glory and *s*.
      29.11 May the LORD give *s* to his people! May
      68.28 your might, O God; show your *s*, O God,
      73.26 but God is the *s* of my heart and my
      81. 1 Sing aloud to God our *s*; shout for joy
      84. 5 Happy are those whose *s* is in you, in
      96. 6 him; *s* and beauty are in his sanctuary.

STRENGTHEN (STRENGTHENED STRENGTHENING STRENGTHENS)

Ps	102. 23 He has broken my s in midcourse; he
	105. 4 Seek the Lord and his s; seek his
	118. 14 The Lord is my s and my might; he has
Eccl	7.19 Wisdom gives s to the wise more than
	10.17 time — for s, and not for drunkenness!
Isa	10.13 "By the s of my hand I have done it,
	30.15 quietness and in trust shall be your s.
	40. 9 good tidings; lift up your voice with s,
	49. 5 Lord, and my God has become my s —
	51. 9 awake, put on s, O arm of the Lord!
	52. 1 Awake, awake, put on your s, O Zion!
Jer	16.19 Lord, my s and my stronghold, my
Hab	3.19 God, the Lord, is my s; he makes my
Lk	1.51 He has shown s with his arm; he has
	21.36 praying that you may have s to escape
1 Cor	10.13 will not let you be tested beyond your s,
Eph	6.10 in the Lord and in the s of his power.
Col	1.11 May you be made strong with all the s
1 Pet	4.11 do so with the s that God supplies,

STRENGTHEN (STRENGTHENED STRENGTHENING STRENGTHENS)

1 Sam	23.16 there he s his hand through the Lord.
	30. 6 David s himself in the Lord his God.
Job	4. 3 many; you have s the weak hands.
Ps	89.21 with him; my arm also shall s him.
Isa	35. 3 S the weak hands, and make firm the
	41.10 I will s you, I will help you, I will
	54. 2 lengthen your cords and s your stakes.
Ezek	34.16 and I will s the weak, but the fat and
Dan	10.18 in human form touched me and s me.
Zech	10. 6 I will s the house of Judah, and I will
Acts	15.41 Syria and Cilicia, s the churches.
	18.23 Galatia and Phrygia, s all the disciples.
Rom	16.25 to God who is able to s you according
1 Cor	1. 8 He will also s you to the end, so that
Eph	3.16 he may grant that you may be s in your
Phil	4.13 do all things through him who s me.
1 Thess	3. 2 to s and encourage you for the sake of
	3.13 may he so s your hearts in holiness that
1 Pet	5.10 Christ, will himself restore, support, s
Rev	3. 2 Wake up, and s what remains and is on

STRETCH (STRETCHED STRETCHES)

1 Kings 17.21 he s himself upon the child three times,
Job	9. 8 who alone s out the heavens and
Ps	68.31 let Ethiopia hasten to s out its hands to
	104. 2 You s out the heavens like a tent, you
Lam	1.17 Zion s out her hands, but there is no
Mt	12.13 he said to the man, "S out your hand."

STRICKEN

1 Sam	24. 5 David was s to the heart because he
2 Sam	24.10 David was s to the heart because he

STRIFE

Gen	13. 7 s between the herders of Abram's
Ps	55. 9 for I see violence and s in the city.
Prov	13.10 By insolence the heedless make s, but
	17. 1 than a house full of feasting with s.
	17.14 The beginning of s is like letting out
	18. 6 A fool's lips bring s, and a fool's mouth
	28.25 The greedy person stirs up s, but
	29.22 One given to anger stirs up s, and the
	30.33 blood, so pressing anger produces s.

STRIKE (STRUCK)

Gen	3.15 He will s your head, and you will s his
Ex	12.12 I will s down every firstborn in the land
	12.29 the Lord s down all the firstborn in the
Num	20.11 lifted up his hand and s the rock twice
2 Sam	12. 9 You have s down Uriah the Hittite with
	12.15 The Lord s the child that Uriah's wife
Ps	121. 6 The sun shall not s you by day, nor the
	141. 5 Let the righteous s me; let the faithful
Isa	27. 7 Has he s them down as he s down those
	53. 4 accounted him stricken, s down by God,
Jer	5. 3 You have s them, but they felt no

Hag	2.17 I s you and all the products of your toil
Mk	14.27 'I will s the shepherd, and the sheep

STRIP (STRIPPED)

Lev	19.10 You shall not s your vineyard bare, or
Num	20.28 Moses s Aaron of his vestments, and
Job	19. 9 He has s my glory from me, and taken

STRIVE (STRIVEN STRIVING)

Gen	32.28 but Israel, for you have s with God
Isa	41.11 those who s against you shall be as
Mt	6.33 But s first for the kingdom of God and
Lk	12.31 Instead, s for his kingdom, and these
	13.24 "S to enter through the narrow door; for
1 Cor	12.31 But s for greater gifts. And I will show
	14.12 for spiritual gifts, s to excel in them
Phil	1.27 s side by side with one mind for the
2 Pet	3.14 s to be found by him at peace, without

STRONG (STRONGER)

Judg	14.14 eat. Out of the s came something sweet."
2 Sam	3. 1 David grew s and s, while the house of
1 Chr	19.13 Be s, and let us be courageous for our
	28.20 "Be s and of good courage, and act. Do
2 Chr	26.16 when he had become s he grew proud,
Ps	27.14 Wait for the Lord; be s, and let your
	140. 7 Lord, my s deliverer, you have covered
Eccl	6.10 able to dispute with those who are s.
	9.11 nor the battle to the s, nor bread to the
Mt	12.29 how can one enter a s man's house and
Lk	11.21 When a s man, fully armed, guards his
Rom	15. 1 s ought to put up with the failings of
1 Cor	1.25 weakness is s than human strength.
	1.27 is weak in the world to shame the s;
Eph	6.10 Finally, be s in the Lord and in the
2 Tim	2. 1 my child, be s in the grace that is in
1 Jn	2.14 young people, because you are s and

STRONGHOLD

Ps	9. 9 The Lord is a s for the oppressed, a s in
	18. 2 and the horn of my salvation, my s.
	27. 1 The Lord is the s of my life; of whom
	94.22 But the Lord has become my s, and my
	46.16 his people, a s for the people of Israel.
Joel	3.16 his people, a s for the people of Israel.
Nah	1. 7 Lord is good, a s in a day of trouble;

STRUGGLE (STRUGGLING)

Prov	28. 4 but those who keep the law s against
Eph	6.12 our s is not against enemies of blood
Col	2. 1 you to know how much I am s for you,

STUBBLE

Ex	5.12 the land of Egypt, to gather s for straw.
Isa	47.14 they are like s, the fire consumes them;
Mal	4. 1 arrogant and and all evildoers will be s;

STUBBORN

Deut	9. 6 righteousness, for you are a s people.
	29.19 safe even though we go our own s ways"
Judg	2.19 any of their practices or their s ways.
2 Kings 17.14 not listen, but were s, as their ancestors
Ps	81.12 So I gave them over to their s hearts, to
Ezek	3. 7 have a hard forehead and a s heart.

STUBBORNNESS

1 Sam	15.23 and s is like iniquity and idolatry.
Mk	16.14 n them for their lack of faith and s,

STUDENTS

Mt	23. 8 you have one teacher, and you are all s.

STUDY

Ps	101. 2 I will s the way that is blameless. When
Eccl	12.12 and much s is a weariness of the flesh.

STUMBLE (STUMBLED STUMBLING)

Prov	3.23 way securely and your foot will not s.
	4.19 they do not know what they s over.
Isa	3. 8 Jerusalem has s, and Judah has fallen,

STUMBLING BLOCK

Jer	13.16 and before your feet *s* on the mountains
	20.11 my persecutors will *s*, and they will not
	50.52 The arrogant one shall *s* and fall, with
Mt	18. 8 or your foot causes you to *s*, cut it off
Mk	9.43 If your hand causes you to *s*, cut it off;
Lk	17. 1 "Occasions for *s* are bound to come, but
	17. 2 to cause one of these little ones to *s*.
Jn	11. 9 who walk during the day do not *s*,
Rom	9.32 on works. They have *s* over the *s* stone,
	11.11 have they *s* so as to fall? By no means!
	14.21 that makes your brother or sister *s*.

STUMBLING BLOCK (STUMBLING BLOCKS)

Jer	6.21 I am laying before this people *s* against
Mt	16.23 "Get behind me, Satan! You are a *s* to
Rom	14.13 resolve instead never to put a *s* or
1 Cor	1.23 proclaim Christ crucified, a *s* to Jews
	8. 9 not somehow become a *s* to the weak.
Rev	2.14 who taught Balak to put a *s* before the

STUNNED

Ezek	3.15 sat there among them, *s*, for seven days.

SUBDUE (SUBDUED)

Gen	1.28 and multiply, and fill the earth and *s* it;
Ps	47. 3 He *s* peoples under us, and nations
	81.14 Then I would quickly *s* their enemies,
Mk	5. 4 and no one had the strength to *s* him.

SUBJECT (SUBJECTED)

2 Sam	10.19 with Israel, and became *s* to them.
1 Chr	19.19 peace with David, and became *s* to him.
Rom	13. 1 person be *s* to the governing authorities;
1 Cor	14.32 spirits of prophets are *s* to prophets, for
	15.28 Son himself will also be *s* to the one
Eph	5.22 Wives, be *s* to your husbands as you are
Col	3.18 Wives, be *s* to your husbands, as is
Titus	3. 1 Remind them to be *s* to rulers and

SUBMISSION

Heb	5. 7 he was heard because of his reverent *s*.

SUBMISSIVE

Titus	2. 9 Tell slaves to be *s* to their masters and

SUBMIT

Lk	10.17 in your name, even the demons *s* to us!"

SUBORDINATE

1 Cor	14.34 not permitted to speak, but should be *s*,

SUBSTANCE

Prov	3. 9 Honor the LORD with your *s* and with

SUCCEED (SUCCEEDED)

1 Sam	26.25 will do many things and will *s* in them."
1 Chr	22.11 you may *s* in building the house of the
Job	9. 4 has resisted him, and *s*?—
Isa	55.11 purpose, *s* in the thing for which I sent
Jer	22.30 man as childless, a man who shall not *s*
	32. 5 against the Chaldeans, you shall not *s*?"
Ezek	17.15 Will he *s*? Can one escape who does

SUCCESS (SUCCESSFUL)

Gen	24.21 or not the LORD had made his journey *s*.
	24.40 angel with you and make your way *s*;
	39. 2 with Joseph, and he became a *s* man;
Josh	1. 8 prosperous, and then you shall be *s*.
1 Sam	18.30 David had more *s* than all the servants

SUFFER (SUFFERED SUFFERING SUFFERS)

Ps	9.13 See what I *s* from those who hate me,
Prov	27.12 hide; but the simple go on, and *s* for it.
Mt	17.12 So also the Son of man is about to *s* at
	17.15 for he is an epileptic and he *s* terribly;
	27.19 I have *s* a great deal because of a dream
Lk	24.26 necessary that the Messiah should *s*
	24.46 it is written, that the Messiah is to *s*
Acts	3.18 the prophets, that his Messiah should *s*.

Acts	5.41 were considered worthy to *s* dishonor
	26.23 that the Messiah must *s*, and that, by
Rom	8.17 we *s* with him so that we may also be
1 Cor	12.26 If one member *s*, all *s* together
Phil	1.29 in Christ, but of *s* for him as well—
	3. 8 For his sake I have *s* the loss of all
1 Thess	2. 2 but though we had already *s* and been
Heb	2.18 he himself was tested by what he *s*, he
1 Pet	2.21 called, because Christ also *s* for you,
	2.23 when he *s*, he did not threaten; but he
	3.18 Christ also *s* for sins once for all, the
	4. 1 Christ *s* in the flesh, arm yourselves
	4.15 let none of you *s* as a murderer, a thief,

SUFFERING (SUFFERINGS)

Ex	3. 7 taskmasters. Indeed, I know their *s*,
Isa	53. 3 a man of *s* and acquainted with
Mt	24.21 For at that time there will be great *s*,
	24.29 "Immediately after the *s* of those days
Mk	8.31 the Son of Man must undergo great *s*,
	13.19 there will be *s*, such as has not been
	13.24 after that *s*, the sun will be darkened, and
Lk	9.22 "The Son of Man must undergo great *s*,
	17.25 first he must endure much *s* and be
Rom	5. 3 knowing that *s* produces endurance, and
	12.12 Rejoice in hope, be patient in *s*,
Eph	3.13 may not lose heart over my *s* for you;
Col	1.24 am now rejoicing in my *s* for your sake,
2 Tim	2. 3 Share in *s* like a good soldier of Christ

SUFFICIENT

2 Cor	12. 9 "My grace is *s* for you, for power is

SULFUR

Gen	19.24 the LORD rained on Sodom . . . *s* and fire
Lk	17.29 Lot left Sodom, it rained fire and *s* from
Rev	14.10 tormented with fire and *s* in the
	19.20 into the lake of fire that burns with *s*.

SUITABLE

Eccl	3.11 He has made everything *s* for its time;

SUMMED

Gal	5.14 For the whole law is *s* up in a single

SUMMER

Gen	8.22 *s* and winter, day and night, shall not
Prov	26. 1 Like snow in *s* or rain in harvest, so
Jer	8.20 "The harvest is past, the *s* is ended, and

SUMMONED

Ex	19.20 the LORD *s* Moses to the top of the
Isa	41.25 the rising of the sun he was *s* by name.
Mt	10. 1 Jesus *s* his twelve disciples and gave

SUN

Josh	10.12 "*S*, stand still at Gibeon, and Moon, in
Ps	19. 4 the heavens he has set a tent for the *s*,
	84.11 the LORD God is a *s* and shield; he
	113. 3 From the rising of the *s* to its setting
Eccl	1. 9 done; there is nothing new under the *s*.
Isa	13.10 *s* will be dark at its rising, and the
Jer	31.35 says the LORD, who gives the *s* for light
Ezek	32. 7 cover the *s* with a cloud, and the moon
Joel	2.31 *s* shall be turned to darkness, and the
Am	8. 9 I will make the *s* go down at noon, and
Hab	3.11 the *s* stood still in its exalted place, at
Mal	4. 2 name the *s* of righteousness shall rise,
Mt	5.45 he makes his *s* to rise on the evil and
	24.29 the *s* will be darkened, and the moon
Acts	2.20 The *s* shall be turned into darkness and
1 Cor	15.41 There is one glory of the *s*, another
Eph	4.26 do not sin; do not let the *s* go down on

SUPPER

Lk	22.20 he did the same with the cup after *s*,
Jn	13. 2 betray him. And during *s* Jesus,
1 Cor	11.20 it is not really to eat the Lord's *s*.

SUPPLANT

Hos	12. 3 In the womb he tried to *s* his brother,

SUPPLICATION

2 Sam	24.25 LORD answered his *s* for the land, and
Job	8. 5 If you will seek God and make *s* to the
Ps	28. 2 Hear the voice of my *s*, as I cry to you
Isa	45.14 They will make *s* to you, saying, "God is

SUPPORT

Gen	13. 6 the land could not *s* both of them living
Ezek	30. 6 Those who *s* Egypt shall fall, and it
Mt	15. 5 'Whatever *s* you might have had from
Acts	20.35 by such work we must *s* the weak,
2 Cor	11. 8 churches by accepting *s* from them
3 Jn	8 Therefore we ought to *s* such people, so

SUPPORTERS

Job	31.21 because I saw I had *s* at the gate;

SURE

1 Jn	2. 3 by this we may be *s* that we know him,

SURROUND (SURROUNDED)

Gen	19. 4 and old, all the people . . . *s* the house;
Ps	118. 11 They *s* me, *s* me on every side; in the
Lk	8.45 "Master, the crowds *s* you and press in
Heb	12. 1 since we are *s* by so great a crowd of

SURVIVORS

Neh	1. 3 "The *s* there in the province who
Joel	2.32 among the *s* shall be those whom the
Mic	2.12 I will gather the *s* of Israel; I will set

SUSA

Neh	1. 1 year, while I was in *S* the capital,
Esth	1. 2 sat his royal throne in the citadel of *S*,
	2. 5 was a Jew in the citadel of *S* whose
	8.15 the city of *S* shouted and rejoiced.
	9.18 the Jews who were in *S* gathered on the

SUSPENSE

Jn	10.24 "How long will you keep us in *s*? If you

SUSTAIN (SUSTAINED)

Neh	9.21 years you *s* them in the wilderness
Ps	55.22 burden on the LORD, and he will *s* you;

SWALLOW (n)

Isa	38.14 Like a *s* or a crane I clamor, I moan
Jer	8. 7 the turtledove, *s*, and crane observe the

SWALLOW (SWALLOWED SWALLOWS)

Num	16.30 ground opens its mouth and *s* them up,
Ps	35.25 Do not let them say, "We have *s* you up."
Isa	25. 7 all nations; he will *s* up death forever.
Jon	1.17 provided a large fish to *s* up Jonah;
1 Cor	15.54 "Death has been *s* up in victory."
2 Cor	5. 4 so that what is mortal may be *s* up

SWARM (SWARMS)

Gen	1.20 "Let the waters bring forth *s* of living
Ex	8.21 I will send *s* of flies on you, your
Lev	11.41 All creatures that *s* upon the earth are

SWEAR (SWEARS SWORE SWORN)

Gen	24. 3 I will make you *s* by the LORD, the God
Lev	19.12 You shall not *s* falsely by my name,
Deut	6.10 the land that he *s* to your ancestors,
Ps	110. 4 LORD has *s* and will not change his
Isa	48. 1 who *s* by the name of the LORD, and
	62. 8 LORD has *s* by his right hand and by his
Jer	4. 2 if you *s*, "As the LORD lives!" in truth, in
	22. 5 words, I *s* by myself, says the LORD,
	44.26 Lo, I *s* by my great name, says the LORD,
Am	4. 2 God has *s* by his holiness: The time is
Zech	5. 3 everyone who *s* falsely shall be cut off
Mt	5.34 Do not *s* at all, either by heaven, for it
	23.16 whoever *s* by the gold of the sanctuary,

SWEAT

Gen	3.19 "By the *s* of your face you shall eat
Lk	22.44 his *s* became like great drops of blood

SWEET

Judg	14.14 Out of the strong came something *s*.
Ps	119.103 How *s* are your words to my taste,

SWEPT

Gen	1. 2 a mighty wind *s* over the face of the
Isa	44.22 *s* away your transgressions like a cloud,
Mt	12.44 it finds it empty, *s*, and put in order.

SWIFT

Eccl	9.11 the race is not to the *s*, nor the battle

SWINE

Mt	8.31 cast us out, send us into the herd of *s*."
Mk	5.12 "Send us to the *s*, let us enter them."
Lk	8.32 herd of *s* was feeding; and the demons

SWORD (SWORDS)

Gen	3.24 a *s* flaming and turning to guard the
Judg	7.14 "This is no other than the *s* of Gideon
	7.20 cried, "A *s* for the LORD and for Gideon!"
1 Kings	3.24 king said, "Bring me a *s*," and they
Isa	2. 4 beat their *s* into plowshares, and their
	49. 2 made my mouth like a sharp *s*, in the
Jer	9.16 I will send the *s* after them, until I have
	25.38 become waste because of the cruel *s*,
Ezek	21. 9 Say: A *s*, a *s* is sharpened, it is also
Joel	3.10 Beat your plowshares into *s*, and your
Mic	4. 3 they shall beat their *s* into plowshares,
Zech	13. 7 "Awake, O *s*, against my shepherd,
Mt	10.34 I have not come to bring peace, but a *s*.
	26.51 on his *s*, drew it, and struck the slave of the
Mk	14.47 drew his *s*, and struck the slave of the
Lk	2.35 a *s* will pierce your own soul
Eph	6.17 the *s* of the Spirit, which is the word of
Heb	4.12 sharper than any two-edged *s*, piercing
Rev	1.16 his mouth came a sharp two-edged *s*,
	19.15 from his mouth comes a sharp *s* with

SYCAMORE

Am	7.14 a herdsman, and a dresser of *s* trees,
Lk	19. 4 So he ran ahead and climbed a *s* tree to

SYCHAR

Jn	4. 5 he came to a Samaritan city called *S*,

SYMPATHY

Job	42.11 they showed *s* and comforted him for
1 Pet	3. 8 all of you, have unity of spirit, *s*, love

SYNAGOGUE

Mk	5.38 to the house of the leader of the *s*,
	6. 2 the sabbath he began to teach in the *s*,
Lk	7. 5 and it is he who built our *s* for us."
	8.41 a man named Jairus, a leader of the *s*.
Acts	18. 4 Every sabbath he would argue in the *s*
	19. 8 He entered the *s* and for three months

SYRIA

Mt	4.24 So his fame spread throughout all *S*,
Lk	2. 2 while Quirinius was governor of *S*.
Acts	15.41 He went through *S* and Cilicia,

T

TABERNACLE

Ex	25. 9 pattern of the *t* and of all its furniture,
	26.30 you shall erect the *t* according to the
	40. 2 you shall set up the *t* of the tent of

TABLE (TABLES)

Ex	25.23 You shall make a *t* of acacia wood, two
	37.10 He also made the *t* of acacia wood, two
2 Kings	4.10 put there for him a bed, a *t*, a chair,

Ps	23. 5 You prepare a *t* before me in the
	69.22 Let their *t* be a trap for them, a snare
	78.19 "Can God spread a *t* in the wilderness?
Mal	1.12 you say that the LORD's *t* is polluted,
Acts	6. 2 the word of God in order to wait on *t*.
1 Cor	10.21 partake of the *t* of the Lord and the *t* of

TABLET (TABLETS)

Ex	31.18 the two *t* of the covenant, *t* of stone,
	34. 1 "Cut two *t* of stone like the first; and I
Deut	9.10 LORD gave me the two stone *t* written
Isa	8. 1 Take a large *t* and write on it in
Lk	1.63 He asked for a writing *t*, and wrote,
2 Cor	3. 3 on *t* of stone but on *t* of human hearts.

TAKE (TAKEN TAKES)

Ex	25. 2 the Israelites to *t* for me an offering;
Prov	8.10 *T* my instruction instead of silver, and
	11.30 a tree of life, but violence *t* lives away.
Lam	3.58 You have *t* up my cause, O Lord, you
Mt	26.26 and said, "*T*, eat; this is my body."
Mk	14.22 it to them, and said "*T*; this is my body."
Jn	14. 3 I will come again and will *t* you to
Heb	11. 5 was not found, because God had *t* him."
Rev	22.19 if anyone *t* away from the words of the

TALE

| Lk | 24.11 these words seemed to them an idle *t*, |

TALENTS

| Mt | 18.24 one who owed him ten thousand *t* was |
| | 25.15 to one he gave five *t*, to another two, to |

TALK (TALKED TALKING)

Job	11. 2 and should one full of *t* be vindicated?
	15. 3 Should they argue in unprofitable *t*, or
Ps	71.24 my tongue will *t* of your righteous help,
Prov	4.24 speech, and put devious *t* far from you.
Zech	1.14 the angel who *t* with me said to me,
Mt	16. 8 little faith, why are you *t* about having
Lk	24.15 While they were *t* and discussing, Jesus

TAME

| Jas | 3. 8 no one being can *t* the tongue— a |

TARSHISH

Gen	10. 4 The descendants of Javan: . . . *T*,
2 Chr	9.21 the king's ships went to *T* with the
	20.36 joined him in building ships to go to *T*;
Ps	48. 7 an east wind shatters the ships of *T*.
	72.10 the kings of *T* and of the isles render
Isa	23.14 Wail, O ships of *T*, for your fortress is
Jon	1. 3 Jonah set out to flee to *T* from the

TARSUS

Acts	9.11 Judas look for a man of *T* named Saul.
	11.25 Barnabas went to *T* to look for Saul,
	21.39 replied, "I am a Jew, from *T* in Cilicia,

TASKMASTERS

| Ex | 1.11 they set *t* over them to oppress them |
| | 5. 6 Pharaoh commanded the *t* of the |

TASTE (TASTED)

Ps	34. 8 O *t* and see that the LORD is good;
Mt	5.13 but if salt has lost its *t*, how can its
	16.28 who will not *t* death before they see the
Mk	9. 1 who will not *t* death until they see that
Lk	9.27 who will not *t* death before they see the
Acts	23.14 by an oath to *t* no food until we have
Col	2.21 not handle, Do not *t*, Do not touch"?
Heb	2. 9 of God he might *t* death for everyone.
	6. 4 and have *t* the heavenly gift,
1 Pet	2. 3 indeed you have *t* that the Lord is good.

TAUNT

Ps	42.10 my adversaries *t* me, while they say to
	44.13 You have made us the *t* of our
	102. 8 All day long my enemies *t* me; those

| Isa | 14. 4 up this *t* against the king of Babylon: |
| Hab | 2. 6 Shall not everyone *t* such people and, |

TAUNT-SONGS

| Lam | 3.63 I am the object of their *t*. |

TAX (TAXES)

Mt	9. 9 called Matthew sitting at the *t* booth;
	17.24 your teacher not pay the temple *t*?"
	22.17 Is it lawful to pay *t* to the emperor,
Mk	2.14 son of Alphaeus sitting at the *t* booth,
	12.14 Is it lawful to pay *t* to the emperor, or
Lk	5.27 named Levi, sitting at the *t* booth;
	20.22 Is it lawful for us to pay *t* to the
Rom	13. 6 also pay *t*, for the authorities are God's

TAX COLLECTOR (TAX COLLECTORS)

Mt	21.31 *t* and the prostitutes go into the
Mk	2.15 many *t* and sinners were also sitting
Lk	3.12 Even *t* came to be baptized, and they
	5.30 "Why do you eat and drink with *t* and
	7.29 including the *t* acknowledged the justice
	7.34 and drunkard, a friend of *t* and sinners!'
	18.10 pray, one a Pharisee and the other a *t*.
	19. 2 Zacchaeus; he was a chief *t* and was

TEACH

Ex	4.12 I will . . . *t* you what you shall speak."
	18.20 and *t* them the statutes and instructions
Lev	10.11 you are to *t* the people of Israel all the
Deut	4. 5 I now *t* you statutes and ordinances for
	4.10 the earth, and may *t* their children so";
	5.31 that you shall *t* them, so that they may
	11.19 *T* them to your children, talking about
	20.18 that they may not *t* you to do all the
	31.19 write this song, and *t* it to the Israelites;
	33.10 They *t* Jacob your ordinances, and
Judg	13. 8 again to us, and *t* us what we are to do
Ezra	7.10 and to *t* the statutes and ordinances in
Job	12. 7 ask the animals, and they will *t* you; the
	21.22 Will any *t* God knowledge, seeing that
Ps	25. 4 your ways. O LORD; *t* me your paths.
	25.12 He will *t* them the way that they should
	27.11 *T* me your way, O LORD; and lead me on
	34.11 to me; I will *t* you the fear of the LORD.
	86.11 *T* me your way, O LORD, that I may walk
	90.12 So *t* us to count our days that we may
	119. 12 are you, O LORD; *t* me your statutes.
	119. 33 *T* me, O LORD, the way of your statutes,
	143. 10 *T* me to do your will, for you are my
Prov	9. 9 *t* the righteous and they will gain in
Isa	2. 3 that he may *t* us his ways and that we
	28. 9 "Whom will he *t* knowledge, and to
Jer	31.34 No longer shall they *t* one another, or
Ezek	44.23 *t* my people the difference between the
Mic	3.11 for a bribe, its priests *t* for a price,
	4. 2 that he may *t* us his ways and that we
Mt	5.54 began to *t* the people in their
Mk	4. 2 He began to *t* them many things in
	6. 2 On the sabbath he began to *t* in the
	8.31 began to *t* them that the Son of Man
Lk	4.15 He began to *t* in their synagogues and
	11. 1 "Lord, *t* us to pray, as John taught his
	12.12 for the Holy Spirit will *t* you at that very
Jn	14.26 send in my name, will *t* you everything,
Acts	4.18 ordered them not to speak or *t* at all in
	5.42 they did not cease to *t* and proclaim
Rom	2.21 that *t* others, will you not *t* yourself?
Col	3.16 you richly; *t* and admonish one another
1 Tim	2.12 I permit no woman to *t* or to have
Heb	8.11 they shall not *t* one another or say to

TEACHES (TEACHING TAUGHT)

Deut	4. 1 ordinances which I am *t* you to observe,
2 Chr	15. 3 the true God, and without a *t* priest,
	17. 9 They *t* in Judah, having the book of the
Ps	94.10 He who *t* knowledge to humankind,
Prov	4.11 I have *t* you the way of wisdom; I have

Isa	50.	4 my ear to listen as those who are *t*.
Jer	32.33	though I have *t* them persistently, they
Dan	1.	4 were to be *t* the literature and language
Mt	4.23	Galilee, *t* in their synagogues
	7.29	for he *t* them as one having authority,
Mk	1.22	for he *t* them as one having authority,
	9.31	he was *t* his disciples, saying to them,
	14.49	after day I was with you in the temple *t*,
Lk	4.31	Galilee, and was *t* them on the sabbath.
Jn	6.45	'And they shall all be *t* by God.'
Acts	1.	1 wrote about all that Jesus did and *t*
	5.25	prison are standing in the temple and *t*
	15.35	and there, with many others, they *t*
	18.25	and *t* accurately the things concerning
	21.28	This is the man who is *t* everyone
Gal	6.	6 Those who are *t* the word must share in
Eph	4.21	heard about him and were *t* in him,
1 Tim	6.	3 Whoever *t* otherwise and does not agree
1 Jn	2.27	as his anointing *t* you about all things,

TEACHER (TEACHERS)

Job	36.22	in his power; who is a *t* like him?
Ps	119.	99 have more understanding than all my *t*,
Eccl	1.	1 The words of the *T*, the son of David,
Isa	30.20	your *T* will not hide himself any more,
Mt	10.24	"A disciple is not above his *t*, nor a
	17.24	"Does your *t* not pay the temple tax?"
	23.	8 to be called rabbi, for you have one *t*,
	26.18	"The *T* says, My time is near; I will
Mk	5.35	is dead. Why trouble the *t* any further?"
Lk	5.17	Pharisees and *t* of the law were sitting
	6.40	A disciple is not above the *t*, but
Jn	11.28	privately, "The *T* is here and is calling
	20.16	in Hebrew, "Rabboni!" (which means *T*).
Eph	4.11	some pastors and *t*, to equip the saints
1 Tim	1.	7 talk, desiring to be *t* of the law,

TEACHING (TEACHINGS)

Deut	32.	2 May my *t* drop like the rain, my speech
Prov	1.	8 and do not reject your mother's *t*;
	13.14	The *t* of the wise is a fountain of life,
Isa	51.	7 people who have my *t* in your hearts;
Jer	6.19	and as for my *t*, they have rejected it.
Mt	16.12	of bread, but of the *t* of the Pharisees
Lk	4.32	They were astonished at his *t*, because
Jn	7.16	answered them, "My *t* is not mine, but
	18.19	about his disciples and about his *t*.
Acts	2.42	devoted themselves to the apostles' *t*
	5.28	you have filled Jerusalem with your *t*
	17.19	"May we know what this new *t* is that
Rom	6.17	form of *t* to which you were entrusted,
1 Tim	4.13	reading of scripture, to exhorting, to *t*.
	5.17	those who labor in preaching and *t*;
	6.	3 *t* that is in accordance with godliness,
2 Tim	3.10	you have observed my *t*, my conduct,
	3.16	and is useful for *t*, for reproof, for
2 Jn	9	who does not abide in the *t* of Christ,

TEAR (TEARS) (n)

Ps	42.	3 My *t* have been my food day and night,
	56.	8 put my *t* in your bottle. Are they not in
Isa	25.	8 GOD will wipe away the *t* from all faces,
	38.	5 heard your prayer, I have seen your *t*;
2 Cor	2.	4 and with many *t*, not to cause you pain,
Rev	7.17	God will wipe away every *t* from their
	21.	4 he will wipe away every *t* from their

TEAR (TORN) (v)

1 Sam	15.28	"The LORD has *t* the kingdom of Israel
Mt	5.29	your right eye causes you to sin, *t* it out
Mk	15.38	curtain of the temple was *t* in two, from
Gal	4.15	you would have *t* out your eyes and

TEKOA

2 Sam	14.	2 Joab sent to *T*, and brought from there
2 Chr	20.20	and went out into the wilderness of *T*;
Jer	6.	1 Blow the trumpet in *T*, and raise a
Am	1.	1 who was among the shepherds of *T*,

TELL (TOLD)

2 Sam	1.20	*T* it not in Gath, proclaim it not in the
Neh	9.23	into the land that you had *t* their
Ps	40.	9 I have *t* the glad news of deliverance in
	105.	2 to him; *t* of all his wonderful works.
Isa	41.22	bring them, and *t* us what is to happen.
Jer	33.	3 will *t* you great and hidden things that
	38.15	Jeremiah said to Zedekiah, "If I *t* you,
Mt	28.	7 go quickly and *t* his disciples, 'He has
Mk	5.14	The swineherds ran off and *t* it in the
	16.	7 go, *t* his disciples and Peter that he is
2 Cor	12.	4 and heard things that are not to be *t*,

TEMPEST

Prov	10.25	When the *t* passes, the wicked are no

TEMPESTUOUS

Jon	1.11	the sea was growing more and more *t*.

TEMPLE

Ps	11.	4 The LORD is in his holy *t*; the LORD's
	29.	9 forest bare; and in his *t* all say, "Glory!"
	48.	9 love, O God, in the midst of your *t*.
	65.	4 the goodness of your house, your holy *t*.
	79.	1 they have defiled your holy *t*;
Isa	44.28	of the *t*, "Your foundation shall be laid."
Jer	7.	4 in these deceptive words: "This is the *t*
Ezek	43.	5 and the glory of the LORD filled the *t*.
	43.11	make known to them the plan of the *t*,
Dan	11.31	by him shall occupy and profane the *t*
Hab	2.20	the LORD is in his holy *t*; let all the
Zech	6.12	and he shall build the *t* of the LORD.
Mt	4.	5 placed him on the pinnacle of the *t*,
	21.12	all who were selling and buying in the *t*,
	24.	1 point out to him the buildings of the *t*.
	26.61	I am able to destroy the *t* of God, and
	27.40	"You who would destroy the *t* and build
Mk	11.15	he entered the *t* and began to drive out
	11.16	anyone to carry anything through the *t*.
	14.58	heard him say, "I will destroy this *t* that
	15.29	You who would destroy the *t* and build
Lk	2.46	they found him in the *t*, sitting among
	4.	9 placed him on the pinnacle of the *t*,
	18.10	"Two men went up to the *t* to pray, one
	19.45	he entered the *t* and began to drive out
Jn	2.14	In the *t* he found people selling cattle,
	2.19	"Destroy this *t*, and in three days I will
Acts	24.	6 He even tried to profane the *t*, and so
1 Cor	3.16	not know that you are God's *t* and that
	6.19	your body is a *t* of the Holy Spirit
2 Cor	6.16	For we are the *t* of the living God; as
Eph	2.21	and grows into a holy *t* in the Lord;
Rev	11.	1 "Come and measure the *t* of God and
	11.19	God's *t* in heaven was opened, and the
	15.	8 the *t* was filled with smoke from the
	21.22	I saw no *t* in the city, for its *t* is the

TEMPORARY

2 Cor	4.18	for what can be seen is *t*, but what

TEMPT (TEMPTED)

Mk	1.13	in the wilderness forty days, *t* by Satan;
Lk	4.	2 for forty days he was *t* by the devil.
1 Cor	7.	5 so that Satan may not *t* you because of
Jas	1.13	No one, when *t*, should say, "I am being

TEMPTER

Mt	4.	3 The *t* came and said to him, "If you are
1 Thess	3.	5 that somehow the *t* had tempted you

TEN

Gen	18.32	Suppose *t* are found there." He
Deut	4.13	observe, that is, the *t* commandments;
Lk	17.12	a village, *t* lepers approached him.

TENANTS

Mt	21.33	Then he leased it to *t* and went to
Mk	12.	1 watchtower, then he leased it to *t*

Lk	20.16	come and destroy those *t* and give the

TEND (TENDED)

Ps	78.72	With upright heart he *t* them, and
1 Pet	5. 2	elders among you to *t* the flock of God

TENT (TENTS)

Gen	4.20	the ancestor of those who live in *t* and
	12. 8	on the east of Bethel, and pitched his *t*,
	13. 3	to the place where his *t* had been at the
Ex	29.44	I will consecrate the *t* of meeting and
	33. 7	the camp; he called it the *t* of meeting.
Lev	1. 1	and spoke to him from the *t* of meeting,
Josh	18. 1	at Shiloh, and set up the *t* of meeting
2 Sam	7. 2	of cedar, but the ark of God stays in a *t*."
1 Chr	17. 1	of the covenant of the LORD is under a *t*."
Job	29. 4	the friendship of God was upon my *t*;
Ps	15. 1	O LORD, who may abide in your *t*? Who
	19. 4	the heavens he has set a *t* for the sun,
Prov	14.11	but the *t* of the upright flourishes.
Isa	33.20	a quiet habitation, an immovable *t*,
	40.22	like a curtain, and spreads them like a *t*
Jer	10.20	My *t* is destroyed, and all my cords are
Acts	7.44	ancestors had the *t* of testimony in the
2 Cor	5. 1	that if the earthly *t* we live in is
Heb	8. 5	when he was about to erect the *t*,
Rev	15. 5	temple of the *t* of witness in heaven

TENTH

Gen	14.20	And Abram gave him a *t* of everything.
	28.22	that you give me I will surely give one *t*
Lev	27.32	All tithes of herd and flock, every *t* one
Isa	6.13	Even if a *t* remain in it, it will be
Heb	7. 2	to him Abraham apportioned "one-*t* of

TENT-MAKERS

Acts	18. 3	worked together— by trade they were *t*.

TERM

Isa	40. 2	cry to her that she has served her *t*, that

TERRIFY (TERRIFIED)

Job	15.24	distress and anguish *t* them; they
	23.16	my heart faint; the Almighty has *t* me;
Ps	2. 5	in his wrath, and *t* them in his fury,
Mt	14.26	him walking on the sea, they were *t*,
	27.54	they were *t* and said, "Truly this man
Lk	9.34	they were *t* as they entered the cloud.

TERROR

Lev	26.16	will do this to you: I will bring *t* on you;
Ps	91. 5	You will not fear the *t* of the night, or
Isa	2.19	of the ground, from the *t* of the LORD,
	17.14	At evening time, lo, *t*! Before morning,
Jer	8.15	for a time of healing, but there is *t*
	20. 4	I am making you a *t* to yourself and to
	48.44	Everyone who flees from the *t* shall fall
Mk	16. 8	for *t* and amazement had seized them;

TEST (n)

Ex	15.25	and there he put them to the *t*.
Deut	6.16	not put the LORD . . . to the *t*, as you
Ps	106. 14	and put God to the *t* in the desert;
Isa	7.12	ask, and I will not put the LORD to the *t*.
Mal	3.10	and thus put me to the *t*, says the LORD
	3.15	when they put God to the *t* they escape."
Mt	4. 7	not put the Lord your God to the *t*.' "
	22.18	"Why are you putting me to the *t*, you
Mk	12.15	"Why put me to the *t*? Bring me a
Lk	4.12	not put the Lord your God to the *t*.' "
Acts	5. 9	to put the Spirit of the Lord to the *t*?
	15.10	why are you putting God to the *t* by
1 Cor	10. 9	We must not put Christ to the *t*, as

TEST (TESTED TESTING TESTS)

Gen	22. 1	God *t* Abraham. He said to him,
	42.15	Here is how you shall be *t*: as Pharaoh
Ex	17. 7	the Israelites quarreled and *t* the LORD,
Num	14.22	and yet you have *t* me these ten times

Deut	8. 2	to humble you, *t* you to know what was
	13. 3	God is *t* you, to know whether you
Judg	2.22	In order to *t* Israel, whether or not they
1 Kings	10. 1	she came to *t* him with hard questions.
Job	12.11	Does not the ear *t* words as the palate
Ps	7. 9	you who *t* the minds and hearts, O
	11. 5	The LORD *t* the righteous and the
	66.10	for you, O God, have *t* us; you have
	78.18	They *t* God in their heart by demanding
	78.56	they *t* the Most High God, and rebelled
	81. 7	I *t* you at the waters of Meribah.
	95. 9	when your ancestors *t* me, and put me
	105. 19	pass, the word of the LORD kept *t* him.
	139. 23	my heart; *t* me and know my thoughts.
Prov	17. 3	is for gold, but the LORD *t* hearts.
Jer	12. 3	O LORD, know me; You see me and *t* me
	17.10	"I the LORD *t* the mind and search the
	20.12	O LORD of hosts, you *t* the righteous,
Lam	3.40	Let us *t* and examine our ways, and
Dan	1.12	"Please *t* your servants for ten days; Let
Mt	19. 3	and to *t* him they asked, "Is it lawful for
Mk	8.11	him for a sign from heaven, to *t* him.
Lk	11.16	Others, to *t* him, kept demanding from
Jn	6. 6	He said this to *t* him, for he himself
	8. 6	They said this to *t* him, so that they
2 Cor	13. 5	you are living in the faith. *T* yourselves.
Gal	6. 4	All must *t* their own work, then that
1 Thess	5.21	but *t* everything; hold fast to what is
Heb	2.18	is able to help those who are being *t*.
	4.15	has been *t* as we are, yet without sin.
1 Jn	4. 1	but *t* the spirits to see whether they are

TESTIFY (TESTIFIED TESTIFIES)

Deut	19.18	witness, having *t* falsely against another,
1 Sam	12. 3	Here I am; *t* against me before the LORD
Job	15. 6	and not I; your own lips *t* against you.
Ps	50. 7	O Israel, I will *t* against you. I am God,
Isa	59.12	you are many, and our sins *t* against us.
Jer	14. 7	Although our iniquities *t* against us, act,
Hos	5. 5	Israel's pride *t* against him; Ephraim
	7.10	Israel's pride *t* against him; yet they do
Mt	23.31	Thus you *t* against yourselves that you
Lk	21.13	This will give you an opportunity to *t*.
Jn	1. 7	He came as a witness to *t* to the light,
	1.34	and have *t* that this is the Son of God."
	3.11	we know and *t* to what we have seen;
	3.26	to whom you *t*, here he is baptizing,
	3.32	He *t* to what he has seen and heard, yet
	5.31	If I *t* about myself, my testimony is not
	5.37	And the Father who sent me has *t* on
	5.39	life; and it is they that *t* on my behalf.
	7. 7	hates me because I *t* against it that its
	15.26	from the Father, he will *t* on my behalf.
	15.27	"You also are to *t* because you have
	18.23	I have spoken wrongly, *t* to the wrong.
	21.24	is the disciple who is *t* to these things
Acts	8.25	after Peter and John had *t* and spoken
	14. 3	who *t* to the word of his grace by
	20.21	as I *t* both to Jews and to Greeks about
	26.16	to appoint you to serve and *t* to the
1 Pet	1.11	when it *t* in advance to the sufferings
1 Jn	4.14	we have seen and do *t* that the Father
3 Jn	3	and *t* to your faithfulness to the truth,
	12	We also *t* for him, and you know that
Rev	1. 2	who *t* to the word of God and to the
	22.20	The one who *t* to these things says,

TESTIMONY

Isa	8.16	Bind up the *t*, seal the teaching among
Mt	8. 4	that Moses commanded, as a *t* to them."
	24.14	the world, as a *t* to all nations;
	26.59	were looking for false *t* against Jesus
Mk	1.44	what Moses commanded, for a *t*
	6.11	dust that is on your feet as a *t* against
	13. 9	kings because of me, as a *t* to them.
	14.55	council were looking for *t* against Jesus
Lk	5.14	for your cleansing, for a *t* to them."

TESTING

Lk	9.	5 town shake the dust off your feet as a *t*
	22.71	"What further *t* do we need? We have
Jn	4.39	in him because of the woman's *t*,
	8.13	on your own behalf; your *t* is not valid."
	8.17	that the *t* of two witnesses is valid.
1 Cor	1.	6 as the *t* of Christ has been strengthened
2 Cor	1.12	is our boast, the *t* of our conscience:
1 Jn	5.	9 If we receive human *t*, the *t* of God is
Rev	6.	9 for the word of God and for the *t* they
	12.17	of God and hold the *t* of Jesus.
	19.10	For the *t* of Jesus is the spirit of
	22.16	to you with this *t* for the churches.

TESTING (n)

Lk	8.13	for a while and in a time of *t* fall away.
1 Cor	10.13	No *t* has overtaken you that is not
Jas	1.	3 know that the *t* of your faith produces

THADDAEUS

Mt	10.	3 James son of Alphaeus, and *T*;
Mk	3.18	*T*, and Simon the Cananaean, and Judas

THANK (THANKED)

Ps	107.	21 Let them *t* the LORD for his steadfast
Isa	38.18	For Sheol cannot *t* you, death cannot
Mt	11.25	Jesus said, "I *t* you, Father, Lord of
Lk	10.21	"I *t* you, Father, Lord of heaven and
	17.	9 Do you *t* the slave for doing what was
	17.16	himself at Jesus' feet and *t* him.
Jn	11.41	"Father, I *t* you for having heard me.
Acts	28.15	On seeing them, Paul *t* God and took
Rom	1.	8 First, I *t* my God through Jesus Christ
Phil	1.	3 I *t* God every time I remember you,
1 Thess	3.	9 How can we *t* God enough for you in

THANK OFFERING (THANK OFFERINGS)

Lev	7.12	you shall offer with the *t* unleavened
2 Chr	29.31	bring sacrifices and *t* to the house of
Ps	56.12	perform, O God; I will render *t* to you.
Jer	17.26	and bringing *t* to the house of the LORD.
Am	4.	5 bring a *t* of leavened bread, and

THANKS

2 Chr	7.	3 and worshiped and gave *t* to the LORD,
Neh	12.40	of those who gave *t* stood in the house
Ps	7.17	I will give to the LORD the *t* due to his
	30.12	my God, I will give *t* to you forever.
	75.	1 We give *t* to you, O God; we give *t*; your
	92.	1 It is good to give *t* to the LORD, to sing
	100.	4 praise. Give *t* to him, bless his name.
	107.	1 O give *t* to the LORD, for he is good; for
	138.	1 I give you *t*, O LORD, with my whole
Isa	12.	1 will say in that day: I will give *t* to you,
Dan	2.23	I give *t* and praise, for you have given
Mt	15.36	after giving *t* he broke them and gave
Acts	27.35	he took bread; and giving *t* to God in
Rom	1.21	not honor him as God or give *t* to him,
	6.17	But *t* be to God that you, having once
	7.25	of death? *T* be to God through Jesus
	14.	6 in honor of the Lord and give *t* to God.
1 Cor	14.17	you may give *t* well enough, but the
	15.57	But *t* be to God, who gives us the
2 Cor	2.14	But *t* be to God, who in Christ always
	8.16	But *t* be to God who put in the heart of
Eph	1.16	I do not cease to give *t* for you as I
	5.20	your hearts, giving *t* to God the Father
Col	3.17	Lord Jesus, giving *t* to God the Father
1 Thess	2.13	We also constantly give *t* to God for
	5.18	ceasing, give *t* in all circumstances;
2 Thess	1.	3 We must always give *t* to God for you,

THANKSGIVING

Lev	22.29	When you sacrifice a *t* offering to the
Ps	26.	7 singing aloud a song of *t*, and telling all
	50.14	Offer to God a sacrifice of *t*, and pay
	50.23	Those who bring *t* as their sacrifice
	69.30	with a song; I will magnify him with *t*.
	116.	17 I will offer to you a *t* sacrifice and call

Isa	51.	3 be found in her, *t* and the voice of song.
Jer	30.19	Out of them shall come *t*, and the
1 Tim	4.	4 rejected, provided it is received with *t*;
Rev	7.12	glory and wisdom and *t* and honor and

THESSALONICA

Acts	17.	1 they came to *T*, where there was a
	17.11	were more receptive than those in *T*,
	27.	2 by Aristarchus, a Macedonian from *T*.
Phil	4.16	even when I was in *T*, you sent me help
2 Tim	4.10	world, has deserted me and gone to *T*;

THICKET

Gen	22.13	looked up and saw a ram, caught in a *t*

THIEF (THIEVES)

Ps	50.18	You make friends with a *t* when you see
Prov	6.30	*T* are not despised who steal only to
	29.24	partner of a *t* is to hate one's own life;
Jer	2.26	As a *t* is shamed when caught, so the
Mt	6.19	and where *t* break in and steal;
	24.43	what part of the night the *t* was coming,
Lk	12.39	known at what hour the *t* was coming,
Jn	12.	6 but because he was a *t*; he kept the
2 Pet	3.10	the day of the Lord will come like a *t*,
Rev	3.	3 I will come like a *t*, and you will not

THIGH

Gen	24.	2 that he had, "Put your hand under my *t*,

THINK (THINKING)

Ps	63.	6 when I *t* of you on my bed, and
Prov	12.15	Fools *t* their own way is right, but the
Mt	5.17	"Do not *t* that I have come to abolish
	22.42	"What do you *t* of the Messiah? Whose
Lk	6.	8 he knew what they were *t*, he said
	11.17	But he knew what they were *t* and said
Rom	12.	3 ought to *t*, but *t* with sober judgement,
2 Cor	6.12	that no one may *t* better of me than
Gal	6.	3 who are nothing *t* they are something,
2 Tim	2.	7 *T* over what I say, for the Lord will give

THIRD

Mt	17.23	him, and on the *t* day he will be raised."
	26.44	he went away and prayed for the *t* time,

THIRST (THIRSTS)

Ps	42.	2 My soul *t* for God, for the living God.
	63.	1 my soul *t* for you, my flesh faints for
	69.21	food, and for my *t* they gave me vinegar
	143.	6 hands to you; my soul *t* for you like a
Isa	48.21	They did not *t* when he led them
	41.17	and their tongue is parched with *t*,
	55.	1 Ho, every one who *t*, come to the
Am	8.13	and the young men shall faint for *t*.
Mt	5.	6 who hunger and *t* for righteousness,
Rev	7.16	will hunger no more, and *t* no more;

THIRSTY

Prov	25.25	Like cold water to a *t* soul, so is good
Isa	29.	8 a *t* person dreams of drinking and
	32.	6 and to deprive the *t* of drink.
	35.	7 pool, and the *t* ground springs of water;
	65.13	servants shall drink, but you shall be *t*;
Mt	25.35	I was *t* and you gave me something to
Jn	7.37	"Let anyone who is *t* come to me, and
	19.28	order to fulfill the scripture), "I am *t*."
Rom	12.20	them; if they are *t*, give them something
2 Cor	11.27	hungry and *t*, often without food, cold
Rev	22.17	"Come." And let everyone who is *t* come.

THIRTY

Zech	11.12	out as my wages *t* shekels of silver.
Mt	26.15	They paid him *t* pieces of silver.
	27.	3 and brought back the *t* pieces of silver

THOMAS

Mt	10.	3 Bartholomew; *T* and Matthew the tax
Mk	3.18	Matthew, and *T*, and James son of

THONG

Jn	11.16 *T*, who was called the Twin, said to his
	14. 5 *T* said to him, "Lord, we do not know
	20.27 he said to *T*, "Put your finger here and
	21. 2 were Simon Peter, *T* called the Twin,

THONG

Mk 1. 7 down and untie the *t* of his sandals.

THORN (THORNS)

Gen	3.18 *t* and thistles it shall bring forth for
Num	33.55 barbs in your eyes and *t* in your sides;
Isa	5. 6 it shall be overgrown with briers and *t*;
Mt	13. 7 Other seeds fell upon *t*, and the *t* grew
	27.29 twisting some *t* into a crown, they put it
Mk	4. 7 Other seed fell among *t* and the *t* grew
	15.17 twisting some *t* into a crown, they put it
Lk	6.44 Figs are not gathered from *t*, nor are
	8. 7 Some fell among *t*; and the *t* grew with
Jn	19. 5 Jesus came out, wearing the crown of *t*
2 Cor	12. 7 elated, a *t* was given me in the flesh,
Heb	6. 8 if it produces *t* and thistles, it is

THOUGHT (THOUGHTS)

Job	21.27 "Oh, I know your *t*, and your schemes
Ps	10. 4 it out"; all their *t* are, "There is no God."
	40. 5 wondrous deeds and your *t* toward us;
	40.17 and needy, but the LORD takes *t* for me.
	56. 5 cause; all their *t* are against me for evil.
	92. 5 works, O LORD! Your *t* are very deep!
	94.11 The LORD knows our *t*, that they are
	139. 17 How weighty to me are your *t*, O God!
Prov	1.23 I will pour out my *t* to you; I will make
	12. 5 The *t* of the righteous are just; the
Isa	55. 8 For my *t* are not your *t*, nor are your
	59. 7 innocent blood; their *t* are *t* of iniquity,
	66.18 For I know their works and their *t*, and
Dan	2.30 you may understand the *t* of your mind.
Am	4.13 reveals his *t* to mortals, makes the
Mic	4.12 But they do not know the *t* of the LORD;
Mt	9. 4 But Jesus, perceiving their *t*, said, "Why
1 Cor	3.20 Lord knows the *t* of the wise, that they
2 Cor	10. 5 and we take every *t* captive to obey
Heb	4.12 it is able to judge the *t* and intentions

THOUSAND (THOUSANDS)

1 Sam	18. 7 has killed his *t*, and David his ten *t*."
Ps	50.10 forest is mine, the cattle on a *t* hills.
	68.17 *t* upon *t*, the LORD came from Sinai into
	84.10 a day in your courts is better than a *t*
Eccl	7.28 One man among a *t* I found, but a
Song	5.10 and ruddy, distinguished among ten *t*.
2 Pet	3. 8 one day is like a *t* years, and a *t* years
Rev	20. 2 and Satan, and bound him for a *t* years,

THREATS

Prov	13. 8 for a person's life, but the poor get no *t*.
Lk	3.14 "Do not extort money from anyone by *t*

THREE

Dan	6.13 he is saying his prayers *t* times a day."
Mt	17. 4 I will make *t* dwellings here, one for
1 Jn	5. 8 water and the blood, and these *t* agree.

THRESH (THRESHED THRESHES THRESHING)

Ruth	3. 2 winnowing barley tonight at the *t* floor.
Isa	41.15 you shall *t* the mountains and crush
Jer	51.33 Babylon is like a *t* floor at the time
Hos	10.11 was a trained heifer that loved to *t*,
Am	1. 3 because they have *t* Gilead with *t*
1 Cor	9.10 whoever *t* should *t* in hope of a share in

THROAT (THROATS)

Prov	23. 7 like a hair in the *t*, so are they. "Eat
Hab	2. 5 They open their *t* as wide as Sheol; like
Mt	18.28 seizing him by the *t*, he said, 'Pay what
Rom	3.13 "Their *t* are opened graves; they use

THRONE (THRONES)

1 Kings 1.13 me as king, and he shall sit upon my *t*?

1 Kings	1.37 make his *t* greater than the *t* of my lord
	9. 5 I will establish your royal *t* over Israel
	10.18 The king also made a great ivory *t*, and
1 Chr	17.12 for me, and I will establish his *t* forever.
Ps	9. 4 just cause; you have sat on the *t* giving
	45. 6 Your *t*, O God, endures forever and ever.
	93. 2 your *t* is established from of old; you
	103. 19 LORD has established his *t* in the
	132. 11 sons of your body I will set on your *t*."
Prov	16.12 to do evil, for the *t* is established by
	25. 5 king, and his *t* will be established in
Isa	6. 1 died, I saw the Lord sitting on a *t*,
	16. 5 a *t* shall be established in steadfast love
	66. 1 Heaven is my *t* and the earth is my
Jer	3.17 time Jerusalem shall be called the *t*
	17.12 O glorious *t*, exalted from the
	43.10 and he will set his *t* above these stones
Lam	5.19 your *t* endures to all generations.
Dan	7. 9 As I watched, *t* were set in place, and
Mt	19.28 followed me will also sit on twelve *t*,
Lk	1.32 give to him the *t* of his ancestor David.
Acts	7.49 'Heaven is my *t*, and the earth is my
Heb	1. 8 "Your *t*, O God, is forever and ever, and
	4.16 Let us therefore approach the *t* of grace
	8. 1 at the right hand of the *t* of the Majesty
Rev	4. 2 there in heaven stood a *t*, with one
	4. 4 twenty-four *t*, and seated on the *t* are
	20. 4 Then I saw *t*, and those seated on them
	20.11 I saw a great white *t* and one who sat
	22. 1 as crystal, flowing from the *t* of God

THRONG

Ps 109. 30 I will praise him in the midst of the *t*.

THROW (THREW THROWN)

Isa	22.18 and *t* you like a ball into a wide land;
Mt	4. 6 are the Son of God, *t* yourself down;
	8.12 heirs of the kingdom will be *t* into the
	13.42 and they will *t* them into the furnace of
Lk	20.15 they *t* him out of the vineyard and

THUMMIN

Ex	28.30 shall put the Urim and the *T*, and they
Lev	8. 8 breastplate he put the Urim and the *T*.

THUNDER (THUNDERS THUNDERED)

1 Sam	12.17 the LORD, that he may send *t* and rain;
2 Sam	22.14 The LORD *t* from heaven, the Most High
Ps	18.13 LORD also *t* in the heavens, and the
	29. 3 over the waters; the God of glory *t*, the
Mk	3.17 the name Boanerges, that is, sons of *t*);

TIDINGS

1 Kings	14. 6 For I am charged with heavy *t* for you.
Ps	68.11 is the company of those who bore the *t*:
Isa	40. 9 O Zion, herald of good *t*; lift up your
	41.27 I give to Jerusalem a herald of good *t*.

TIGLATH-PILESER (PUL)

Received tribute from Menahem, 2 Kings 15.19-20; carried the people captive to Assyria, 2 Kings 15.29; paid homage by Ahaz, 2 Kings 16.7-10 (2 Chr 28.20-21); deported some of the tribes of Israel, 1 Chr 5.26.

TIGRIS

Gen	2.14 name of the third river is *T*, which flows
Dan	10. 4 bank of the great river (that is, the *T*),

TILL (TILLER)

Gen	2. 5 and there was no one to *t* the ground;
	3.23 God sent him . . . to *t* the ground from
Zech	13. 5 "I am no prophet, I am a *t* of the soil;

TIME (TIMES)

Gen	21. 2 age, at the *t* of which God had spoken
Ex	12.40 The *t* that the Israelites had lived in
2 Kings	5.26 Is this a *t* to accept money and to
Esth	4.14 to royal dignity for such a *t* as this."
Ps	31.15 My *t* are in your hand; deliver me from

Ps	34. 1 I will bless the LORD at all *t*; his praise
	89.47 Remember how short my *t* is— for what
	119.126 It is *t* for the LORD to act, for your law
Eccl	3. 1 is a season, and a *t* for every matter
	8. 6 For every matter has its *t* and way,
	9.11 but *t* and chance happen to them all.
Ezek	12.27 years ahead; he prophesies for distant *t*."
	30. 3 will be a day of clouds, a *t* of doom for
Hab	2. 3 is still a vision for the appointed *t*;
Hag	1. 2 These people say the *t* has not yet
Mt	8.29 come here to torment us before the *t*?"
	26.18 'The Teacher says, My *t* is near,' I will
Jn	7. 6 "My *t* has not yet come, but your *t* is
1 Cor	7.29 appointed *t* has grown short; from now
Eph	5.16 making the most of the *t*, because the
Col	4. 5 outsiders, making the most of the *t*.
Rev	1. 3 what is written in it; for the *t* is near.
	12.14 she is nourished for a *t*, and *t*, and half a

TIMOTHY

Paul's son in the Lord, 1 Cor 4.17; 1 Tim 1.2,18; 2 Tim 1.2; son of a Greek father and a Jewish mother, Acts 16.1; brought up in a devout home, 2 Tim 1.5; 3.14-15; lived in Lystra (or Derbe), Acts 16.1; circumcised, Acts 16.3; accompanied Paul in his second missionary journey, Acts 16.1-4; 17.14-15; 18.5; 1 Thess 3.2-6; ordained, 1 Tim 4.14; 2 Tim 1.6; sent to the church in Corinth, 1 Cor 4.17; 16.10; accompanied Paul in the third missionary journey, Acts 20.4; in charge of the church in Ephesus, 1 Tim 1.3; 4.12; urged by Paul to visit him in prison, 2 Tim 4.9,13; imprisoned and released, Heb 13.23.

1 Cor	4.17 For this reason I sent you *T*, who is my
	16.10 If *T* comes, see that he has nothing to

TITHE (TITHES)

Lev	27.31 If persons wish to redeem any of their *t*,
Num	18.21 To the Levites I have given every *t* in
	18.24 Levites as their portion of the *t* of the
Deut	14.22 Set apart a *t* of all the yield of your
	26.12 finished paying all the *t* of your produce
Neh	10.37 to bring to the Levites the *t* from our
Mal	3. 8 "How are we robbing you?" In your *t* and
Mt	23.23 hypocrites! For you *t* mint, dill, and
Lk	11.42 woe to you Pharisees! for you *t* mint
Heb	7. 9 who receives *t*, paid *t* through Abraham,

TITLE

Mt	22.20 "Whose head is this, and whose *t*?"
Mk	12.16 "Whose head is this, and whose *t*?"

TITUS

2 Cor	2.13 I did not find my brother *T* there.
	7. 6 consoled us by the arrival of *T*,
	8. 6 so that we might urge *T* that, as he had
	8.23 As for *T*, he is my partner and
	12.18 *T* did not take advantage of you, did
Gal	2. 1 with Barnabas, taking *T* along
2 Tim	4.10 has gone to Galatia, *T* to Dalmatia.
Titus	1. 4 To *T*, my loyal child in the faith we

TODAY (TODAY'S)

Ps	95. 7 of his hand. O that *t* you would listen
Mt	6.34 of its own. *T* trouble is enough for *t*.
Lk	23.43 I tell you, *t* you will be with me in
Heb	3.15 "*T*, if you hear his voice, do not harden

TOGETHER

Gen	22. 8 son." So the two of them walked on *t*.
Acts	2. 1 had come, they were all *t* in one place.
	2.46 they spent much time *t* in the temple,
Col	1.17 all things, and in him all things hold *t*.

TOIL

Prov	14.23 In all *t* there is profit, but mere talk
Eccl	1. 3 What do people gain from all the *t* at
	3.13 drink and take pleasure in all their *t*.
	4. 4 I saw that all *t* and all skill in work
	4. 6 with quiet than two handfuls with *t*,

Eccl	4. 8 yet there is no end to all their *t*, and
	5.19 and find enjoyment in their *t*— this is
	6. 7 All human *t* is for the mouth, yet the
	10.15 The *t* of fools wears them out, for they
Lk	12.27 how they grow: they neither *t* nor spin;
2 Cor	11.27 in *t* and hardship, through many a
Col	1.29 For this I *t* and struggle with all the
Rev	2. 2 "I know your works, your *t* and your

TOLL

Ezra	4.13 they will not pay tribute, custom, or *t*,
	7.24 custom, or *t* on any of the priests,
Mt	17.25 from whom do kings of the earth take *t*

TOMB (TOMBS)

Mt	23.27 For you are like whitewashed *t*, which
	27.60 rolled a great stone to the door of the *t*
Mk	and took his body, and laid it in a *t*.
	15.46 laid it in a *t* that had been hewn out of
Lk	8.27 he did not live in a house but in the *t*.
	11.47 you build the *t* of the prophets whom
	24. 1 they came to the *t*, taking the spices
Jn	11.31 she was going to the *t* to weep there.
	19.41 and in the garden there was a new *t* in
	20. 6 went into the *t*. He saw the linen

TOMORROW

Prov	27. 1 Do not boast about *t*, for you do not
Isa	22.13 "Let us eat and drink, for *t* we die."
Mt	6.30 is alive today and *t* is thrown into the
1 Cor	15.32 "Let us eat and drink, for *t* we die."
Jas	4.14 you do not even know what *t* will bring.

TONGUE (TONGUES)

Job	5.21 hidden from the scourge of the *t*, and
Ps	5. 9 are open graves; they flatter with their *t*.
	31.20 under your shelter from contentious *t*.
	34.13 Keep your *t* from evil, and your lips
	35.28 Then my *t* shall tell of your
	39. 1 my ways that I may not sin with my *t*;
	45. 1 is like the pen of a ready scribe.
	52. 2 Your *t* is like a sharp razor, you worker
	64. 3 who whet their *t* like swords, who aim
Prov	10.20 The *t* of the righteous is choice silver;
	10.31 but the perverse *t* will be cut off.
	12.18 but the *t* of the wise brings healing.
	18.21 Death and life are in the power of the *t*,
	25.15 and a soft *t* can break bones.
Isa	45.23 knee shall bow, every *t* shall swear."
	54.17 you shall confute every *t* that rises
Jer	9. 5 they have taught their *t* to speak lies;
	9. 8 Their *t* is a deadly arrow; it speaks
Mk	7.35 opened, his *t* was released, and he
	16.17 n out demons; they will speak in new *t*;
Acts	2. 3 Divided *t*, as of fire, appeared among
	19. 6 they spoke with *t* and prophesied—
Rom	3.13 graves; they use their *t* to deceive."
1 Cor	12.10 to another various kinds of *t*, to another
	13. 1 If I speak in *t* of mortals and of angels,
	14. 2 those who speak in a *t* do not speak to
	14.21 written, "By people of strange *t* and by
	14.22 *T*, then, are a sign not for believers but
Jas	1.26 and do not bridle their *t* but deceive
	3. 5 the *t* is a small member, yet it boasts of

TOOTH (TEETH)

Ex	21.24 eye for eye, *t* for *t*, hand for hand, foot
Deut	19.21 eye for eye, *t* for *t*, hand for hand, foot
Job	19.20 and I have escaped by the skin of my *t*.
Prov	25.19 Like a bad *t* or a lame foot is trust in a
Song	4. 2 Your *t* are like a flock of shorn ewes
Ezek	18. 2 and the children's *t* are set on edge"?

TORCH (TORCHES)

Gen	15.17 flaming *t* passed between these pieces,
Judg	7.16 and empty jars, with *t* inside the jars,
Rev	4. 5 of the throne burn seven flaming *t*,

TORMENT (TORMENTED TORMENTS)

Job 19. 2 "How long will you *t* me, and break me
Ps 32.10 Many are the *t* of the wicked, but
Isa 50.11 from my hand: you shall lie down in *t*.
Mt 8.29 Have you come here to *t* us before the
15.22 of David; my daughter is *t* by a demon."
Mk 5. 7 God? I adjure you by God, do not *t* me."
Lk 8.28 High God? I beg you, do not *t* me"—
16.23 in Hades, where he was being *t*, he
Rev 20.10 they will be *t* day and night forever and

TOSSED (TOSSING)

Ex 14.27 the LORD *t* the Egyptians into the sea.
Job 7. 4 is long and I am full of *t* till the dawn.
Isa 57.20 wicked are like the *t* sea that cannot

TOUCH (TOUCHED TOUCHES)

Gen 3. 3 of the garden, nor shall you *t* it, or you
1 Sam 10.26 went warriors whose hearts God had *t*.
Job 4. 5 it *t* you, and you are dismayed.
5.19 troubles; in seven no harm shall *t* you.
Ps 105. 15 saying, "Do not *t* my anointed ones; do
Jer 1. 9 LORD put out his hand and *t* my mouth;
Zech 2. 8 he who *t* you *t* the apple of my eye.
Mt 8. 3 He stretched out his hand and *t* him,
8.15 he *t* her hand, and the fever left her,
9.21 "If I only *t* his cloak, I will be made
9.29 Then he *t* their eyes and said,
14.36 might *t* even the fringe of his cloak;
20.34 with compassion, Jesus *t* their eyes.
Mk 5.28 "If I but *t* his clothes, I will be made
6.56 they might *t* even the fringe of his
Lk 8.45 "Someone *t* me; for I noticed that power
1 Cor 7. 1 "It is well for a man not to *t* a woman."
2 Cor 6.17 and *t* nothing unclean; then I will
1 Jn 5.18 them, and the evil one does not *t* them.

TOWEL

Jn 13. 4 outer robe, and tied a *t* around himself.

TOWER

Gen 11. 4 let us build ourselves a city, and a *t*
Lk 13. 4 were killed when the *t* of Siloam fell
14.28 intending to build a *t*, does not first sit

TRADE (TRADED)

Ezek 27.17 Judah and the land of Israel *t* with you;
Mt 25.16 went off at once and *t* with them;
Acts 19.25 together, with the workers of same *t*,

TRADITION (TRADITIONS)

Mt 15. 2 your disciples break the *t* of the elders?
Mk 7. 5 disciples not live according to the *t* of
7. 8 of God and hold to human *t*."
2 Thess 2.15 stand firm and hold to the *t* that you

TRAIN (TRAINED TRAINING TRAINS)

Gen 14.14 taken captive, he led forth his *t* men,
Ps 144. 1 rock, who *t* my hands for war, and my
Prov 22. 6 *T* children in the right way, and when
1 Tim 4. 1 than the divine *t* that is known by faith.
4. 8 physical *t* is of some value, godliness is
Titus 2.12 *t* us to renounce impiety and worldly

TRAITOR

Lk 6.16 and Judas Iscariot, who became a *t*.

TRAMPLE (TRAMPLED)

Job 9. 8 the heavens and *t* the waves of the Sea;
Ps 56. 1 to me, O God, for people *t* on me;
Hab 3.15 You *t* the sea with your horses,

TRANCE

Dan 10. 9 of his words, I fell into a *t*, face to the

TRANSFER (TRANSFERRED)

2 Sam 3.10 to *t* the kingdom from the house of
Col 1.13 and *t* us into the kingdom of his

TRANSFIGURED

Mt 17. 2 he was *t* before them, and his face
Mk 9. 2 themselves. And he was *t* before them,

TRANSFORM (TRANSFORMED)

Rom 12. 2 be *t* by the renewing of your minds, so
2 Cor 3.18 are being *t* into the same image from
Phil 3.21 He will *t* the body of our humiliation

TRANSGRESS (TRANSGRESSED)

Deut 26.13 I have neither *t* nor forgotten any of
Josh 23.16 If you *t* the covenant of the LORD your
Judg 2.20 people have *t* my covenant that I
2 Kings 18.12 but *t* his covenant —all that Moses had
1 Chr 5.25 But they *t* against the God of their
Ps 17. 3 in me; my mouth does not *t*.
Jer 34.18 those who *t* my covenant and did not
Lam 3.42 We have *t* and rebelled, and you have
Hos 6. 7 at Adam they *t* the covenant; there they
Am 4. 4 Come to Bethel —and *t*; to Gilgal —and

TRANSGRESSION (TRANSGRESSIONS)

Lev 16.16 and because of their *t*, all their sins;
Job 31.33 if I have concealed my *t* as others do,
Ps 32. 1 Happy are those whose *t* is forgiven,
39. 8 Deliver me from all my *t*. Do not make
51. 3 For I know my *t*, and my sin is ever
89.32 I will punish their *t* with the rod and
Prov 10.19 When words are many, *t* is not lacking,
28.13 No one who conceals *t* will prosper, but
Isa 57. 4 Are you not children of *t*, the offspring
59.12 our *t* before you are many, and our sins
6 because their *t* are many, their
Ezek 18.22 None of the *t* that they have committed
39.24 to their uncleanness and their *t*,
Am 1. 3 For three *t* of Damascus, and for four, I
3.14 On the day I punish Israel for its *t*, I
Mic 1. 5 All this is for the *t* of Jacob and for the
Rom 5.14 whose sins were not like the *t* of Adam,
Gal 6. 1 if anyone is detected in a *t*, you who

TRANSGRESSOR

Gal 2.18 down, then I demonstrate that I am a *t*.

TRAVEL (TRAVELED TRAVELS)

Deut 23.14 God *t* along with your camp, to save
Ezek 27.25 The ships of Tarshish *t* for you in your
2 Cor 8.19 appointed by the churches to *t* with us

TRAVELER

Job 31.32 I have opened my doors to the *t*—

TREACHEROUS

Job 6.15 My companions are *t* like a torrent-bed,
Prov 11. 3 but the crookedness of the *t* destroys
Isa 24.16 the *t* deal treacherously, the *t* deal very
2 Tim 3. 4 haters of good, *t*, reckless, swollen with

TREACHERY

Lev 26.40 in that they committed *t* against me,
Josh 22.16 'What is this *t* that you have committed
Jer 5.27 full of birds, their houses are full of *t*;

TREAD (TREADING)

Ps 44. 5 our foes; through your name we *t* down
91.13 You will *t* on the lion and the adder,
Mic 7.19 us; he will *t* our iniquities under foot.
Hab 3.19 deer, and makes me *t* upon the heights.
Mal 4. 3 you shall *t* down the wicked, for they
1 Cor 9. 9 muzzle an ox while it is *t* out the grain."

TREASON

2 Kings 9.23 about and fled, saying to Ahaziah, "*T*,
11.14 tore her clothes and cried, "*T*! *T*!"
2 Chr 23.13 tore her clothes, and cried, "*T*! *T*!"

TREASURE (TREASURED TREASURES)

Gen 43.23 must have put *t* in your sacks for you;
1 Kings 14.26 he took away the *t* of the house of the

2 Kings	20.13	he showed them all his t house, the
Job	23.12	his lips; I have t in my bosom the words
Prov	2. 1	my words and t up my commandments
	2. 4	and search for it as for hidden t—
	15. 6	house of the righteous there is much t,
	15.16	fear of the LORD than great t and trouble
	21.20	Precious t remains in the house of the
Eccl	2. 8	for myself silver and gold and the t
Isa	33. 6	the fear of the LORD is Zion's t.
	45. 3	give you the t of darkness and riches
Jer	15.13	your t I will give as plunder, without
	20. 5	t of the kings of Judah into the hand of
Mic	6.10	Can I forget the t of wickedness in the
Hag	2. 7	so that the t of all nations shall come,
Mt	6.19	"Do not store up for yourselves t on
	12.35	brings good things out of a good t,
	13.44	of heaven is like t hidden in a field,
	13.52	brings out of his t what is new and
Lk	6.45	person out of the good t of his heart
	12.21	those who store up t for themselves
	12.34	For where your t is, there your heart
2 Cor	4. 7	we have this t in clay jars, so that it
Col	2. 3	in whom are hidden all the t of wisdom

TREASURE CHESTS

Mt	2.11	opening their t they offered him gifts

TREASURY

Josh	6.19	they shall go into the t of the LORD."
Zech	11.13	"Throw it into the t"— this lordly price
Mk	12.41	the crowd putting money into the t.
Jn	8.20	he was teaching in the t of the temple,

TREATED

Jer	6.14	t the wound of my people carelessly,

TREATY

Josh	9. 6	a far country; so now make a t with us."
Isa	33. 8	The t is broken, its oaths are despised,

TREE (TREES)

Gen	2. 9	t of life also in the midst of the garden,
Deut	16.21	shall not plant any t as a sacred pole
	20.19	you must not not destroy its t by
	21.23	anyone hung on a t is under God's
1 Kings	19. 4	and sat down under a solitary broom t.
Job	14. 7	hope for a t, if it be cut down, that it
Ps	52. 8	I am like a green olive t in the house of
	104. 16	The t of the LORD are watered
Prov	15. 4	A gentle tongue is a t of life, but
Jer	17. 8	like a t planted by water, sending out
Ezek	31. 8	not in the garden of God was like it in
	47. 7	I saw upon the bank a great many t on
Dan	4.10	there was a t at the center of the earth,
Mic	4. 4	own vines and under their own fig t,
Mt	7.17	same way, every good t bears good fruit,
	12.33	for the t is known by its fruit;
Lk	6.43	"No good t bears bad fruit, nor again
	19. 4	ahead and climbed a sycamore t to see
Acts	13.29	they took him down from the t and laid
Gal	3.13	"Cursed is everyone who hangs on a t"—
Rev	2. 7	to eat from the t of life that is in the
	22. 2	the t of life with its twelve kinds of
	22.14	they will have the right to the t of life

TREMBLE (TREMBLING)

Ps	99. 1	LORD is king; let the peoples t! He sits
Isa	13.13	I will make the heavens t, and the earth
	14.16	"Is this the man who made the earth t,
	24.18	and the foundations of the earth t.
	32.11	T, you women who are at ease, shudder,
	64. 2	the nations might t at your presence!
	66. 5	of the LORD, you who t at his word:
Am	8. 8	Shall not the land t on this account,
Mk	5.33	happened to her, came in fear and t

TRESPASS (TRESPASSES)

1 Sam	25.28	Please forgive the t of your servant; for

Mt	6.14	For if you forgive others their t, your
Mk	11.26	in heaven may also forgive your t."
Rom	4.25	handed over to death for our t and was
2 Cor	5.19	not counting their t against them,
Col	2.13	when he forgave us all our t, erasing the

TRIAL (TRIALS)

Judg	6.39	let me, please, make t just once more;
Mt	6.13	And do not bring us to the time of t,
	26.41	you may not come into the time of t;
Mk	14.38	you may not come into the time of t;
Lk	11. 4	And do not bring us to the time of t."
	22.28	who have stood by me in my t; and I
Acts	20.19	with tears, enduring the t that came
2 Pet	2. 9	knows how to rescue the godly from t,
Rev	3.10	I will keep you from the hour of t that

TRIBE (TRIBES)

Judg	21. 6	and said, "One t is cut off from Israel
Ps	122.	4 To it the t go up, the t of the LORD, as
Jer	51.19	and Israel is the t of his inheritance;
Rev	7. 4	sealed out of every t of the people of

TRIBULATION

Lam	3. 5	and enveloped me with bitterness and t;

TRIBUTE

Num	31.37	the LORD's t of sheep and goats was six
Judg	3.15	Israelites sent t by him to King Eglon of

TRICKED

Gen	3.13	said, "The serpent t me, and I ate."

TRICKERY

Eph	4.14	wind of doctrine, by people's t, by their

TRIUMPH (TRIUMPHED TRIUMPHING TRIUMPHS)

Ex	15.21	to the LORD, for he has t gloriously;
Judg	5.11	repeat the t of the LORD, the t of his
Ps	18.50	Great t he gives to his king, and shows
	41.11	because my enemy has not t over me.
Prov	28.12	When the righteous t, there is great
Isa	45.25	LORD all the offspring of Israel shall t
Col	2.15	example of them, t over them in him.

TRIUMPHAL

2 Cor	2.14	in Christ always leads us in t procession

TROAS

Acts	16. 8	passing by Mysia, they went down to T.
	20. 5	ahead and were waiting for us in T;
2 Cor	2.12	When I came to T to proclaim the good
2 Tim	4.13	the cloak that I left with Carpus at T,

TROUBLE (TROUBLES) (n)

Josh	7.25	said, "Why did you bring t on us?"
Judg	11. 7	you come to me now when you are in t?"
1 Kings	20. 7	See how this man is seeking t; for he
Job	3.26	am I quiet; I have no rest; but t comes."
	5. 7	human beings are born to t just as
	5.19	He will deliver you from six t; in seven
	14. 1	of woman, few of days, and full of t,
Ps	27. 5	hide me in his shelter in the day of t;
	34. 6	the LORD, and was saved from every t.
	37.39	LORD; he is their refuge in the time of t.
	46. 1	and strength, a very present help in t.
	50.15	Call on me in the day of t; I will deliver
	66.14	my mouth promised when I was in t.
	73. 5	They are not in t as others are; they are
	90.10	even then their span is only toil and t;
Prov	15.16	of the LORD than great treasure and t.
	27. 9	the heart glad, but the soul is torn by t.
Nah	1. 7	LORD is good, a stronghold in a day of t;
Mt	13.21	while and when t or persecution arises
Gal	6.17	From now on, let no one make t for me;

TROUBLE (TROUBLED) (v)

Num	33.55	they shall t you in the land where you

Ezek	32. 9 I will *t* the hearts of many peoples, as I
Dan	7.15 me, Daniel, my spirit was *t* within me,
Mt	26.10 "Why do you *t* the woman? She has
Mk	14. 6 why do you *t* her? She has performed a
Lk	8.49 daughter is dead; do not *t* the teacher
Jn	12.27 "Now is my soul *t*. And what should I
	13.21 After saying this Jesus was *t* in spirit,
	14. 1 "Do not let your hearts be *t*. Believe in

TRUE

1 Kings	11. 4 his heart was not *t* to the LORD his God,
2 Chr	15.17 Nevertheless the heart of Asa was *t* all
	16. 9 those whose heart is *t* to him.
Jn	15. 1 "I am the *t* vine, and my Father is the
Rom	3. 4 everyone is a liar, let God be *t*,
Phil	1.18 way, whether out of false motives or *t*;
	4. 8 Finally, beloved, whatever is *t*, whatever
Titus	1.13 That testimony is *t*. For this reason

TRUMPET (TRUMPETS)

Ex	19.16 and a blast of a *t* so loud that all the
Lev	23.24 commemmorated with *t* blasts.
Num	10. 2 "Make two silver *t*; you shall make them
Judg	7.16 put *t* into the hands of all of them, and
2 Kings	9.13 they blew the *t*, and proclaimed, "Jehu
Ps	98. 6 With *t* and the sound of the horn make
Isa	27.13 on that day a great *t* will be blown, and
Ezek	33. 5 They heard the sound of the *t* and did
Joel	2. 1 Blow the *t* in Zion; sound the alarm on
Am	3. 6 Is a *t* blown in a city, and the people
Zech	9.14 Lord GOD will sound the *t* and march
Mt	6. 2 you give alms, do not sound a *t*
1 Cor	15.52 *t* will sound, and the dead will be raised
1 Thess	4.16 with the sound of God's *t*, will descend

TRUST (n)

Deut	1.32 spite of this, you have no *t* in the LORD
Job	8.14 is gossamer, a spider's house their *t*.
	31.24 "If I have made gold my *t*, or called fine
Ps	40. 4 are those who make the LORD their *t*,
	146. 3 Do not put your *t* in princes, in mortals,
Prov	20. 6 loyal, but who can find one worthy of *t*?
	22.19 So that your *t* may be in the LORD, I
	25.19 tooth or a lame foot is *t* in a faithless
Isa	32.17 righteousness, quietness and *t* forever.
Mic	7. 5 Put no *t* in a friend, have no confidence
Heb	2.13 And again, "I will put my *t* in him." And

TRUST (TRUSTED TRUSTING TRUSTS)

Num	20.12 "Because you did not *t* in me, to show
Deut	9.23 LORD your God, neither *t* nor obeying
	28.52 and fortified walls, in which you *t*,
2 Kings	18. 5 He *t* in the LORD the God of Israel; so
Job	18.14 from the tent in which they *t*, and are
Ps	13. 5 But I *t* in your steadfast love; my heart
	21. 7 For the king *t* in the LORD, and through
	25. 2 O my God, in you I *t*; do not let me be
	31.14 But I *t* in you, O LORD, I say, "You are
	33.21 in him, because we *t* in his holy name.
	37. 3 *T* in the LORD, and do good; so you will
	49. 6 those who *t* in their wealth and boast of
	52. 7 but *t* in abundant riches, and sought
	55.23 out half their days. But I will *t* in you.
	62. 8 *T* in him at all times, O people; pour
	84.12 hosts, happy is everyone who *t* in you.
	91. 2 and my fortress; my God, in whom I *t*."
	115. 8 are like them; so are all who *t* in them.
	125. 1 Those who *t* in the LORD are like Mount
Prov	3. 5 *T* in the LORD with all your heart, and
	11.28 Those who *t* in their riches will wither,
	16.20 will prosper, and happy are those who *t*
	28.25 whoever *t* in the LORD will be enriched.
Isa	26. 4 *T* in the Lord forever, for in the LORD
	28.16 foundation: "One who *t* will not panic."
	31. 1 who rely on horses, who *t* in chariots
	42.17 put to shame—who *t* in carved images,
	50.10 no light, yet *t* in the name of the LORD

Jer	7. 4 not *t* in these deceptive words: "This is
	13.25 you have forgotten me and *t* in lies.
	17. 5 "Cursed are those who *t* in mere
	17. 7 Blessed are those who *t* in the LORD,
	29.31 send him, and has led you to *t* in a lie,
Dan	6.23 on him, because he had *t* in his God.
Hos	10.13 Because you have *t* in your power and
Mk	10.24n for those who *t* in riches to enter the
Rom	4. 5 works *t* him who justifies the ungodly,
1 Pet	1.21 him you have come to *t* in God,

TRUSTWORTHY

Ps	111. 7 faithful and just; all his precepts are *t*.
Mt	25.21 "Well done, good and *t* slave; you have
Lk	19.17 you have been *t* in a very small thing,
1 Cor	4. 2 of stewards that they should be found *t*.
Rev	21. 5 this, for these words are *t* and true."

TRUTH

Ps	15. 2 is right and speak *t* from their heart;
Prov	12.17 Whoever speaks the *t* gives honest
	23.23 Buy *t*, and do not sell it; buy wisdom,
Isa	45.19 I the LORD speak the *t*, I declare what is
	48. 1 the God of Israel, but not in *t* or right.
Dan	4.37 for all his works are *t*, and his ways are
	8.12 it cast *t* to the ground, and kept
Lk	1. 4 so that you may know the *t* concerning
Jn	8.32 and you will know the *t*, and the *t* will
	14. 6 "I am the way, and the *t*, and the life.
	18.38 my voice." Pilate asked him, "What is *t*?"
Rom	1.25 they exchanged the *t* about God for a
1 Cor	5. 8 the unleavened bread of sincerity and *t*.
	13. 6 in wrongdoing, but rejoices in the *t*.
2 Cor	13. 8 against the *t*, but only for the *t*.
Eph	4.21 and were taught in him, as *t* is in Jesus.
1 Jn	2. 4 in such a person the *t* does not exist;

TRUTHFUL

Prov	12.19 *T* lips endure forever, but a lying tongue
	14.25 A *t* witness saves lives, but one who

TRY (TRIED)

Job	23.10 when he has *t* me, I shall come out like
	34.36 Would that Job were *t* to the limit,
Ps	17. 3 If you *t* my heart, if you visit me by
	26. 2 Prove me, O LORD, and *t* me; test my
	119.140 Your promise is well *t*, and your servant

TUMULT

Isa	22. 5 a day of *t* and trampling and confusion
Hos	10.14 therefore the *t* of war shall rise against

TUNIC (TUNICS)

Mk	6. 9 wear sandals and not to put on two *t*.
Lk	9. 3 bread, nor money—not even an extra *t*.

TURMOIL

Job	30.27 My inward parts are in *t*, and are never
Ps	39. 6 Surely for nothing they are in *t*; they

TURN (TURNED TURNING TURNS)

Deut	23. 5 your God the curse into a blessing for
2 Kings	17.13 "*T* from your evil ways and keep my
	23.25 no king like him, who *t* to the LORD
Ezra	6.22 had *t* the heart of the king of Assyria to
Ps	6. 4 *T*, O LORD, save my life; deliver me for
	40. 4 who do not *t* to the proud, to those who
	90. 3 to dust, and say, "*T* back, you mortals."
	119. 36 *T* my heart to your decrees, and not to
	119. 51 me, but I do not *t* away from your law.
Prov	4.27 or to the left; *t* your foot away from evil.
Eccl	7.25 I *t* my mind to know and to search out
Isa	2.22 *T* away from mortals, who have only
	6.10 with their minds, and *t* and be healed."
	45.22 *T* to me and be saved, all the ends of
	53. 6 astray; we have all *t* to our own way,
Jer	5.23 heart; they have *t* aside and gone away.

Jer	15.	7 people; they did not *t* from their ways.
	15.19	If you *t* back, I will take you back, and
	18.	8 *t* from its evil, I will change my mind
	25.	5 "*T* now, everyone of you, from your evil
	31.13	I will *t* their mourning into joy, I will
	35.15	'*T* now everyone of you from your evil
Ezek	14.	6 Repent and *t* away from your idols; and
	33.11	*t* back from your evil ways; for why will
Mt	5.39	you on the right cheek, *t* the other also;
	13.15	understand with their heart and *t*
Mk	4.12	understand; so they may not *t* again and
Lk	1.16	He will *t* many of the people of Israel to
	22.32	once you have *t* back, strengthen your
Acts	14.15	should *t* from these worthless things
	17.	6 who have been *t* the world upside down
	28.27	understand with their heart and *t*
1 Thess	1.	9 how you *t* to God from idols, to serve a

TURTLEDOVE (TURTLEDOVES)

Gen	15.	9 "Bring me . . . a *t*, and a young pigeon."
Lev	1.14	you shall choose your offering from *t* or
Song	2.12	and the voice of the *t* is heard in our
Lk	2.24	law of the Lord, "a pair of *t*, or two

TWELVE

1 Kings	11.30	he was wearing and tore it into *t* pieces.
Mt	10.	2 These are the names of the *t* apostles:
Mk	3.14	And he appointed *t*, whom he also
	6.	7 He called the *t*, and began to send
	14.17	it was evening, he came with the *t*.
Lk	2.42	And when he was *t* years old, they went
	6.13	called his disciples and chose *t* of them
	8.42	he had an only daughter, about *t* years
Jn	6.67	So Jesus asked the *t*, "Do you also wish

TWINKLING

1 Cor	15.52	in the *t* of an eye, at the last trumpet.

TWINS

Gen	25.24	was at hand, there were *t* in her womb.
	38.27	came, there were *t* in her womb.

TWO

Gen	6.19	shall bring *t* of every kind into the ark,
Eccl	4.	9 *T* are better than one, because they
Isa	6.	2 with *t* they covered their faces, and with
Mt	6.24	"No one can serve *t* masters; for a slave
	18.20	where *t* or three are gathered in my
	21.28	A man had *t* sons; he went to the first
	24.40	Then *t* will be in the field; one will be
	27.21	"Which of the *t* do you want me to
Lk	24.13	on that same day *t* of them were going
1 Cor	6.16	For it is said, "The *t* shall be one flesh."

TYPE

Rom	5.14	who is a *t* of the one who was to come.

TYRANTS

Mt	20.25	and their great ones are *t* over them.

TYRE (TYRIAN)

Josh	19.29	reaching to the fortified city of *T*;
1 Kings	5.	1 King Hiram of *T* sent his servants to
	9.11	Hiram of *T* having supplied Solomon
2 Chr	2.14	of the Danite women, his father a *T*.
Ps	45.12	people of *T* will seek your favor with
Isa	23.	1 The oracle concerning *T*. Wail, O ships
Mk	3.	8 and the region around *T* and Sidon.
Lk	10.13	in you had been done in *T* and Sidon.
Acts	21.	3 left, we sailed to Syria and landed at *T*,

U

UNAWARE

1 Cor	10.	1 I do not want you to be *u*, brothers and
2 Cor	1.	8 We do not want you to be *u*, brothers

UNBELIEF

Mt	13.58	of power there, because of their *u*.

Mk	6.	6 And he was amazed at their *u*. Then he
	9.24	child cried out, "I believe; help my *u*!"
Rom	11.20	were broken off because of their *u*,

UNBELIEVERS

1 Cor	6.	6 court against a believer—and before *u*
	14.23	in tongues, and outsiders or *u* enter,
2 Cor	6.14	Do not be mismatched with *u*. For what

UNBELIEVING

1 Cor	7.14	the *u* husband is made holy through his
Titus	1.15	to the corrupt and *u* nothing is pure.

UNCHASTITY

Mt	5.32	his wife, except on the ground of *u*,

UNCIRCUMCISED

Ex	12.48	land. But no *u* person shall eat of it;
Judg	14.	3 and take a wife from the *u* Philistines?"
Rom	3.30	faith and the *u* through that same faith.
1 Cor	7.18	Was anyone at the time of his call *u*?

UNCLEAN

Lev	13.	3 he shall pronounce him ceremonially *u*.
	13.45	cover his upper lip and cry out, "*U, u*."
Num	19.11	any human being shall be *u* seven days.
Isa	6.	5 me! I am lost, for I am a man of *u* lips,
	52.	1 and the *u* shall enter you no more.
	64.	6 all become like one who is *u*, and all
Hag	2.14	hands; and what they offer there is *u*.
Mt	12.43	"When the *u* spirit has gone of a person,
Mk	5.	2 of the tombs with an *u* spirit met him.
	7.25	whose little daughter had an *u* spirit
Lk	4.33	man who had the spirit of an *u* demon,
	9.42	Jesus rebuked the *u* spirit, healed the
	11.24	"When the *u* spirit has gone out of a
Acts	10.14	eaten anything that is profane or *u*."
	10.28	I should not call anyone profane or *u*.
1 Cor	7.14	Otherwise, your children would be *u*,

UNCLEANNESS

Lev	5.	3 when you touch human *u*—any *u* by
Ezra	9.11	have filled it end to end with their *u*.

UNCONDEMNED

Acts	16.37	"They have beaten us in public, *u*, men
	22.25	you to flog a Roman citizen who is *u*?"

UNCOVERED

Mt	10.26	nothing is covered that will not be *u*,
Lk	12.	2 is covered up that will not be *u*,

UNDEFILED

Heb	7.26	blameless, *u*, separated from sinners,

UNDERGOING

1 Pet	5.	9 world are *u* the same kinds of suffering.

UNDERSTAND (UNDERSTOOD)

Gen	11.	7 they will not *u* one another's speech."
2 Kings	18.26	Aramaic language, for we *u* it; do not
Neh	8.	8 sense, so that the people *u* the reading.
Job	26.14	the thunder of his power who can *u*?"
	42.	3 I have uttered what I did not *u*,
Ps	119.100	I *u* more than the aged, for I keep your
Prov	28.	5 The evil do not *u* justice, but those who
Isa	36.11	to your servants in Aramaic, for we *u* it;
Jer	9.12	Who is wise enough to *u* this? To whom
	23.20	his mind. In the latter days you will *u*
Dan	8.17	"*U*, O mortal, that the vision is for the
Mt	13.14	'You will indeed listen, but never *u*,
	13.51	"Have you *u* all this?" They answered,
Mk	6.52	they did not *u* about the loaves, but
	7.18	"Then do you also fail to *u*? Do you not
Jn	20.	9 as yet they did not *u* the scripture, that
Acts	8.30	asked, "Do you *u* what you are reading?"
	10.34	"I truly *u* that God shows no partiality,
	28.27	and *u* with their heart and turn—and I
Rom	1.20	they are, have been *u* and seen through

Rom	11.25 I want you to *u* this mystery: a
2 Cor	1.14 as you have already *u* us in part—

UNDERSTANDING (n)

Deut	32.28 void of sense; there is no *u* in them.
Job	17. 4 Since you have closed their minds to *u*,
Ps	136. 5 who by *u* made the heavens, for his
	147. 5 in power; his *u* is beyond measure.
Prov	2.11 watch over you; and *u* will guard you.
	15.32 but those who heed admonition gain *u*.
	18. 2 A fool takes no pleasure in *u*, but only
Isa	29.16 of the one who formed it, "He has no *u*?"
	40.14 and showed him the way of *u*?
Jer	10.12 and by his *u* stretched out the heavens.
Hos	4.14 thus a people without *u* comes to ruin.
Mt	15.16 he said, "Are you also still without *u*?
Mk	12.33 with all the heart and with all the *u*,
Lk	2.47 him were amazed at his *u* and answers.

UNDO

Eccl	10. 4 post, for calmness will *u* great offenses.

UNDYING

Eph	6.24 with all who have an *u* love for our Lord

UNFAIR

Ezek	18.25 "The way of the Lord is *u*." Hear now, O

UNFAITHFUL (UNFAITHFULNESS)

1 Chr	10.13 So Saul died for his *u*; he was *u* to the
Lk	12.46 him in pieces, and put him with the *u*.

UNGODLY

Job	16.11 God gives me up to the *u*, and casts me
	18.21 such are the dwellings of the *u*, such is
Ps	43. 1 God, and defend my cause against an *u*
Rom	5. 6 at the right time Christ died for the *u*.

UNINTENTIONALLY

Lev	4. 2 When anyone sins *u* in any of the
Num	15.24 then if it was done *u* without the
Deut	19. 4 who has killed another person *u*

UNITED

Judg	20.11 gathered against the city, *u* as one.
1 Cor	6.17 anyone *u* to the Lord becomes one
Heb	4. 2 because they were not *u* by faith with

UNITY

Ps	133. 1 it is when kindred live together in *u*!
Eph	4. 3 effort to maintain the *u* of the Spirit
	4.13 until all of us come to the *u* of the faith

UNJUST (UNJUSTLY)

Lev	19.15 You shall not render an *u* judgment;
Ps	71. 4 of the wicked, from the grasp of the *u*
	82. 2 "How long will you judge *u* and show
Prov	28.16 but one who hates *u* gain will enjoy a
	29.27 The *u* are an abomination to the
Zeph	3. 5 without fail; but the *u* knows no shame.

UNKNOWN

Acts	17.23 with this inscription, 'To an *u* god.'
2 Cor	6. 9 as *u*, and yet are well known; as dying,

UNLEAVENED

Lev	23. 6 the festival of *u* bread to the LORD;
Deut	16. 8 days you shall continue to eat *u* bread,
2 Chr	30.21 at Jerusalem kept the feast of *u* bread

UNMARRIED

1 Cor	7. 8 To the *u* and the widows I say it is well

UNPRODUCTIVE

1 Cor	14.14 my spirit prays but my mind is *u*.
Titus	3.14 needs, so that they may not be *u*.

UNRIGHTEOUS (UNRIGHTEOUSNESS)

Jer	22.13 Woe to him who builds his house by *u*,
Mt	5.45 rain on the righteous and on the *u*.

UNROLLED

Lk	4.17 He *u* the scroll and found the place

UNSEARCHABLE

Job	5. 9 He does great things and *u*, marvelous
Ps	145. 3 greatly to be praised; his greatness is *u*.
Prov	25. 3 for depth, so the mind of kings is *u*.
Rom	11.33 How *u* are his judgments and how

UNSKILLED

Heb	5.13 infant, is *u* in the word of righteousness,

UNSTAINED

Jas	1.27 and to keep oneself *u* by the world.

UNTIE

Mk	1. 7 not worthy to stoop down and *u* the
Lk	19.30 been ridden. *U* it and bring it here.

UNTRAINED

2 Cor	11. 6 I may be *u* in speech, but not in

UNVEILED

1 Cor	11. 5 prays or prophesies with her head *u*
2 Cor	3.18 all of us, with *u* faces, seeing the glory

UNWORTHY

1 Cor	11.27 or drinks the cup of the Lord in an *u*

UPBUILDING

1 Cor	14. 3 speak to other people for their *u*

UPHOLD (UPHOLDS)

Ps	37.17 be broken, but the LORD *u* the righteous.
	63. 8 clings to you; your right hand *u* me.
Jer	30.13 There is no one to *u* your cause, no

UPRIGHT (UPRIGHTLY)

Num	23.10 Let me die the death of the *u*, and let
Job	4. 7 perished? Or where were the *u* cut off?
Ps	7.10 is my shield, who saves the *u* in heart.
	11. 7 deeds; the *u* shall behold his face.
	32.11 and shout for joy, all you *u* in heart.
	107. 42 The *u* see it and are glad; and all
Prov	2.21 For the *u* will abide in the land, and
	3.32 LORD, but the *u* are in his confidence.
	14. 2 Those who walk *u* fear the LORD, but

UPROAR

Ps	46. 6 The nations are in an *u*, the kingdoms
Acts	21.31 cohort that all Jerusalem was in an *u*.

UPROOT (UPROOTED)

Mt	13.29 the weeds you would *u* the wheat
	15.13 Father has not planted will be *u*.

UPSTAIRS

Lk	22.12 He will show you a large room *u*,
Acts	1.13 they went to the room *u*, where they

UR

Gen	11.28 Terah in the land of his birth, in *U*
	11.31 they went out together from *U* of the
	15. 7 I am the LORD who brought you from *U*
Neh	9. 7 chose Abram and brought him out of *U*

URGE (URGED URGES)

2 Kings	4. 8 lived, who *u* him to have a meal.
	5.23 "Please accept two talents." He *u* him
Lk	24.29 they *u* him strongly, saying, "Stay with
Acts	27.22 I *u* you now to keep up your courage,
2 Cor	5.14 the love of Christ *u* us on, because we
	6. 1 we *u* you also not to accept the grace of
	9. 5 it necessary to *u* the brothers to go on

URIM

Ex	28.30 shall put the *U* and the Thummin, and
Lev	8. 8 in the breastpiece he put the *U* and the
1 Sam	28. 6 answer him, not by dreams, or by *U*,

USE

Hab	2.18 What *u* is an idol once its maker has

USEFUL

2 Tim	4.11 with you, for he is *u* in my ministry.
Philem	11 you, but now he is indeed *u* both to you

UTENSILS

2 Tim	2.20 there are *u* not only of gold and silver

UZ

Gen	10.23 The descendants of Aram: *U*, Hul,
Job	1. 1 in the land of *U* whose name was Job.
Lam	4.21 Edom, you that live in the land of *U*;

UZZIAH

2 Chr	26. 1 people of Judah took *U*, who was
	26.11 Moreover *U* had an army of soldiers, fit
	26.18 "It is not for you, *U*, to make offering to
	26.21 King *U* was leprous to the day of his
	27. 2 LORD just as his father *U* had done —
Isa	1. 1 Judah and Jerusalem in the days of *U*,
	6. 1 In the year that King *U* died, I saw the
Mt	1. 8 and Joram the father of *U*, and *U* the

V

VAIN

Ps	127. 1 the house, those who build it labor in *v*.
Prov	31.30 Charm is deceitful, and beauty is *v*, but
1 Cor	15.14 then our proclamation has been in *v*

VALLEY (VALLEYS)

1 Kings	20.28 of the hills but he is not a god of the *v*,'
Ps	23. 4 through the darkest *v*, I fear no evil;
Isa	22. 1 The oracle concerning the *v* of vision.
	40. 4 Every *v* shall be lifted up, and every
Jer	19. 6 son of Hinnom, but the *v* of Slaughter.
Ezek	37. 1 the middle of a *v*; it was full of bones.
Joel	3.14 multitudes, in the *v* of decision!
Lk	3. 5 Every *v* shall be filled, and every

VALUE

Mt	13.46 on finding one pearl of great *v*,
Lk	12. 7 you are of more *v* than many sparrows.
1 Tim	4. 8 while physical training is of some *v*,

VANISH (VANISHED)

Judg	6.21 the angel of the LORD *v* from his sight.
Ps	78.33 So he made their days *v* like a breath,
Ezek	26.17 How you have *v* from the seas, O city
Lk	24.31 him; and he *v* from their sight.
Rev	6.14 The sky *v* like a scroll rolling itself up,

VANITY

Eccl	1. 2 *V* of vanities, says the Teacher, *v* of
	2.21 toil for it. This also is *v* and a great evil.
	12. 8 *V* of vanities, says the Teacher; all is *v*.

VARIETIES

1 Cor	12. 4 there are *v* of gifts, but the same Spirit;
	12. 5 there are *v* of activities, but it is the

VEIL (VEILED)

Gen	24.65 So she took her *v* and covered herself.
Ex	26.33 the *v* shall separate for you the holy
	34.33 with them, he put a *v* on his face;
	36.35 He made the *v* of blue, purple, and
2 Cor	3.14 of the old covenant, that same *v* is still
	4. 3 even if our gospel is *v*, it is *v* to those

VENGEANCE

Gen	4.15 kills Cain will suffer a sevenfold *v*."
Lev	19.18 You shall not take *v* or bear any grudge
Deut	32.35 *V* is mine, and recompense, for the time
Ps	58.10 righteous will rejoice when they see *v*
	94. 1 you God of *v*, you God of *v*, shine forth!
Isa	63. 4 day of *v* was in my heart, and the year
Jer	50.15 this is the *v* of the LORD: take *v* on her,

Nah	1. 2 LORD takes *v* on has adversaries and
Rom	12.19 is written, "*V* is mine, I will repay, says
Heb	10.30 one who said, "*V* is mine, I will repay."

VERSED

Esth	1.13 all who were *v* in law and custom,
Acts	18.24 eloquent man, well-*v* in the scriptures.

VESSEL (VESSELS)

2 Kings	4. 3 borrow *v* . . . , empty *v* and not just a few.
Ps	31.12 is dead; I have become like a broken *v*.
Prov	26.23 Like the glaze covering an earthen *v* are
Isa	52.11 you who carry the *v* of the LORD.
Jer	18. 4 the *v* he was making of clay was spoiled
	19.11 and this city, as one breaks a potter's *v*,
	22.28 despised broken pot, a *v* no one wants?
Hos	8. 8 are among the nations as a useless *v*.

VESTMENTS

Ex	28. 2 You shall make sacred *v* for the glorious

VICTOR

Isa	41. 2 Who has roused a *v* from the east,

VICTORIOUS

Isa	41.10 I will uphold you with my *v* right hand.
Zech	9. 9 and *v* is he, humble and riding

VICTORY

Deut	20. 4 who goes with you . . . to give you the *v*."
1 Sam	2. 1 my enemies, because I rejoice in my *v*.
	14.23 So the LORD gave Israel *v* that day. The
	14.45 die, who has accomplished this great *v*
2 Sam	8. 6 The LORD gave *v* to David wherever he
	19. 2 *v* that day was turned into mourning for
2 Kings	13.17 arrow of *v*, the arrow of *v* over Aram!
1 Chr	18. 6 The LORD gave *v* to David wherever he
2 Chr	20.17 your position, stand still, and see the *v*
Job	40.14 your own right hand can give you *v*.
Ps	20. 5 May we shout for joy over your *v*, and
	44. 3 nor did their own arm give them *v*;
	144. 10 the one who gives *v* to kings, who
Prov	21.31 of battle, but the *v* belongs to the LORD.
Isa	63. 5 so my own arm brought me *v*, and my
Zeph	3.17 is in your midst, a warrior who gives *v*;
Zech	12. 7 LORD will give *v* to the tents of Judah
Mt	12.20 wick until he brings justice to *v*.
1 Cor	15.54 "Death has been swallowed up in *v*."
1 Jn	5. 4 this is the *v* that conquers the world,

VIGILANCE

Prov	4.23 Keep your heart with all *v*; for from it

VILE

2 Sam	13.12 done in Israel; do not do anything so *v*!

VINDICATE (VINDICATES VINDICATING)

Deut	32.36 Indeed the LORD will *v* his people, have
1 Kings	8.32 *v* the righteous by rewarding them
2 Chr	6.23 *v* those who are in the right by
Ps	43. 1 *V* me, O God, and defend my cause
	135. 14 For the LORD will *v* his people, and have
Isa	50. 8 he who *v* me is near. Who will contend

VINDICATION

Ps	24. 5 and *v* from the God of their salvation.
	98. 2 he has revealed his *v* in the sight of the
	103. 6 The LORD works *v* and justice for all
Mic	7. 9 me out to the light; I shall see his *v*.

VINE (VINES)

1 Kings	4.25 all of them under their *v* and fig trees.
Ps	80. 8 You brought a *v* out of Egypt; you drove
	80.14 heaven, and see; have regard for this *v*,
Isa	5. 2 of stones, and planted it with choice *v*;
Ezek	19.10 Your mother was like a *v* in a vineyard
Hos	10. 1 Israel is a luxuriant *v* that yields its
Joel	1. 7 It has laid waste my *v*, and splintered
Mic	4. 4 they shall all sit under their own *v* and

VINEGAR

Mt	26.29 never again drink of this fruit of the *v*
Mk	14.25 never again drink of the fruit of the *v*
Jn	15. 1 "I am the true *v*, and my Father is the

VINEGAR

Ps	69.21 food, and for my thirst they gave me *v*
Prov	10.26 Like *v* to the teeth, and smoke to the

VINEYARD (VINEYARDS)

Gen	9.20 of the soil, was the first to plant a *v*.
Deut	20. 6 Has anyone planted a *v* but not yet
	22. 9 shall not sow your *v* with a second kind
1 Kings	21. 1 Naboth . . . had a *v* in Jezreel, beside
Song	1. 6 but my own *v* I have not kept!
	2.15 ruin the *v* — for our *v* are in blossom."
Isa	5. 1 beloved my love-song concerning his *v*:
	27. 2 On that day: A pleasant *v*, sing about it!
Mt	20. 1 in the morning to hire laborers for his *v*.
	21.28 'Son, go and work in the *v* today.'
	21.33 landowner who planted a *v*, put a fence
Mk	12. 1 them in parables. "A man planted a *v*,
Lk	20. 9 "A man planted a *v*, and leased it to

VINTAGE

Isa	32.10 for the *v* will fail, the fruit harvest will
Jer	48.32 fruits of your *v* the destroyer has
Rev	14.19 gathered the *v* of the earth, and he

VIOLATE (VIOLATED)

Job	37.23 abundant righteousness he will not *v*.
Heb	10.28 Anyone who has *v* the law of Moses

VIOLENCE

Job	16.17 though there is no *v* in my hands, and
	19. 7 Even when I cry out, 'V!' I am not
Ps	7.16 on their own heads their *v* descends.
	73. 6 necklace; *v* covers them like a garment.
Jer	22. 3 do no wrong or *v* to the alien, the
Hab	1. 3 Destruction and *v* are before me; strife
Mal	2.16 and covering one's garment with *v*,
Mt	11.12 the kingdom of heaven has suffered *v*,

VOILENT

2 Sam	22.49 you delivered me from the *v*.
Acts	27.14 soon a *v* wind, called the northeaster,

VIPER (VIPERS)

Job	20.16 of asps; the tongue of a *v* will kill them.
Mt	3. 7 brood of *v*! Who warned you to flee
	12.34 brood of *v*! How can you speak good
Acts	28. 3 when a *v*, driven out by the heat,

VIRGIN (VIRGINS)

Gen	24.16 The girl was very fair to look upon, a *v*,
Lev	21.14 He shall marry a *v* of his own kin,
Judg	21.12 four hundred young *v* who had never
1 Kings	1. 2 "Let a young *v* be sought for my lord
Ps	45.14 her the *v*, her companions, follow.
Jer	14.17 the *v* daughter — my people — is struck
Lam	2.13 I may comfort you, O *v* daughter Zion?
Joel	1. 8 Lament like a *v* dressed in sackcloth for
Mt	1.23 the *v* shall conceive and bear a son,
Lk	1.27 to a *v* engaged to a man whose name
1 Cor	7.28 sin, and if a *v* marries, she does not sin.
2 Cor	11. 2 to present you as a chaste *v* to Christ.
Rev	14. 4 with women, for they are *v*; these follow

VIRGINITY

Deut	22.14 her, I did not find evidence of her *v*."
	22.15 the evidence of the young woman's *v*
Judg	11.38 her companions, and bewailed her *v*

VISION (VISIONS)

Gen	15. 1 word of the LORD came to Abram in a *v*,
Num	12. 6 LORD make myself known to them in *v*,
1 Sam	3. 1 in those days; *v* were not widespread.
Job	4.13 Amid thoughts from *v* of the night,
	7.14 me with dreams and terrify me with *v*,
Isa	1. 1 The *v* of Isaiah the son of Amoz, which

Isa	22. 1 The oracle concerning the valley of *v*.
	29.11 The *v* of all this has become for you
Jer	14.14 prophesying to you a lying *v*, worthless
	23.16 They speak *v* of their own minds, not
Lam	2. 9 no more, and her prophets obtain no *v*
Ezek	1. 1 were opened, and I saw *v* of God.
	7.26 shall keep seeking a *v* from the prophet;
	11.24 lifted me up and brought me in a *v*
	12.22 and every *v* comes to nothing"?
	13. 7 Have you not seen a false *v*, and uttered
	40. 2 brought me, in *v* of God, to the land of
Dan	1.17 Daniel also had insight into all *v* and
	7. 2 I, Daniel, saw in my *v* by night the four
	10. 7 I, Daniel, alone saw the *v*; the people
Hos	12.10 it was I who multiplied *v*, and through
Ob	1 The *v* of Obadiah. Thus says the Lord
Hab	2. 2 Write the *v*; make it plain on tablets, so
Zech	13. 4 will be ashamed, every one, of their *v*
Lk	24.23 that had indeed seen a *v* of angels who
Acts	2.17 your young men shall see *v*, and your
	11. 5 praying, and in a trance I saw a *v*.
	16. 9 During the night Paul had a *v*; there
	18. 9 One night the Lord said to Paul in a *v*,
	26.19 I was not disobedient to the heavenly *v*,
2 Cor	12. 1 but I will go on to *v* and revelations of

VISIT

Job	7.18 on them, *v* them every morning, test
Ps	65. 9 You *v* the earth and water it, you greatly
Jer	29.10 years are completed will I *v* you,

VOICE (VOICES)

Gen	27.22 "The *v* is Jacob's *v*, but the hands are
Num	7.89 he would hear the *v* speaking to him
Deut	4.12 but saw no form; there was only a *v*.
	4.33 ever heard the *v* of a god speaking out
	8.20 you would not obey the *v* of the LORD
1 Sam	1.13 lips moved, but her *v* was not heard;
1 Kings	19.13 Then there came a *v* to him that said,
Ps	29. 3 The *v* of the LORD is over the waters; the
	68.33 listen, sends out his *v*, his mighty *v*.
	81. 5 I hear a *v* I had not known: "I relieved
	95. 7 O that you would listen to his *v*! Do not
Song	2. 8 The *v* of my beloved! Look, he comes,
Isa	6. 8 I heard the *v* of the Lord saying, "Whom
	30.30 will cause his majestic *v* to be heard
	40. 6 A *v* says, "Cry out!" And I said, "What
	66. 6 A *v* from the temple! The *v* of the LORD,
Jer	7.34 mirth and gladness, the *v* of the bride
	16. 9 the *v* of mirth and the *v* of gladness,
	42. 6 with us when we obey the *v* of the LORD
Joel	2.11 The LORD utters his *v* at the head of his
Mic	6. 9 *v* of the LORD cries to the city (it is
Mt	3. 3 "The *v* of one crying out in the
	3.17 And a *v* from heaven said, "This is my
	17. 5 and from the cloud a *v* said, "This is my
Mk	1.11 And a *v* came from heaven, "You are my
	9. 7 from the cloud there came a *v*, "This is
Lk	3. 4 Isaiah, "The *v* of one crying out in the
	9.35 came a *v* that said, "This is my Son,
Jn	1.23 "I am the *v* of one crying out in the
	5.25 the dead will hear the *v* of the Son
	5.37 You have never heard his *v* or seen his
	10.16 them also, and they will listen to my *v*.
Acts	4.24 they raised their *v* together to God and
	7.31 to look, there came the *v* of the Lord:
	12.22 "The *v* of a god, and not of a mortal!"
	26.14 I heard a *v* saying to me in the Hebrew
Rom	10.18 "Their *v* has gone out to all the earth
2 Pet	1.18 heard this *v* come from heaven,
Rev	14. 2 I heard a *v* from heaven like the sound

VOID

Gen	1. 2 the earth was a formless *v* and darkness
Jer	4.23 on the earth, and lo, it was waste and *v*;
	19. 7 I will make *v* the plans of Judah and

VOMIT (VOMITED)

Lev	18.25	and the land *v* out its inhabitants.
Job	20.15	swallow down riches and *v* them up
Prov	25.16	or else, having too much, you will *v* it.
	26.11	Like a dog that returns to its *v* is a fool
2 Pet	2.22	"The dog turns back to its own *v*," and,

VOW (VOWS)

Gen	28.20	Then Jacob made a *v*, saying, "If God
	31.13	anointed a pillar and made a *v* to me.
Lev	22.18	whether in payment of a *v* or as a
	27. 2	When a person makes an explicit *v* to
Num	6. 2	make a special *v*, the *v* of a nazirite, to
	21. 2	Then Israel made a *v* to the LORD and
	30. 2	When a man makes a *v* to the LORD, or
Deut	23.21	If you make a *v* to the LORD your God,
Judg	11.30	Jephthah made a *v* to the LORD, and
1 Sam	1.11	She made this *v* : "O LORD of hosts, if
Ps	22.25	my *v* I will pay before those
	56.12	My *v* to you I must perform, O God; I
	65. 1	to you shall *v* be performed, O you who
	116. 18	I will pay my *v* to the LORD in the
Eccl	5. 4	no pleasure in fools. Fulfill what you *v*.
Acts	18.18	had his hair cut, for he was under a *v*.

VOYAGE

Acts	27.10	I can see that the *v* will be with danger

VULTURES

Lk	17.37	"Where the corpse is, there the *v* will

W

WAGES

Gen	30.28	name your *w*, and I will give it."
	31. 7	me and changed my *w* ten times,
Ex	2. 9	it for me, and I will give you your *w*."
Jer	22.13	and does not give them their *w*;
Hag	1. 6	earn *w* earn to put them into a bag
Lk	3.14	and be satisfied with your *w*."
Rom	6.23	the *w* of sin is death, but the free gift of
1 Cor	3. 8	will receive *w* according to the labor

WAILING

Lk	8.52	they were all weeping and *w* for her;

WAIT (WAITED WAITING WAITS)

Ps	25. 3	those who *w* for you be put to shame;
	25. 5	of my salvation; for you I *w* all day long.
	27.14	*W* for the LORD; be strong, and let your
	37. 7	Be still before the LORD, and *w* patiently
	37.34	*W* for the LORD, and keep to his way,
	40. 1	I *w* patiently for the LORD; he inclined
	62. 1	for God alone my soul *w* in silence;
	69. 3	My eyes grow dim with *w* for my God.
	130. 5	I *w* for the LORD, my soul *w*, and in his
Prov	20.22	repay evil"; *w* for the LORD, and he will
Isa	8.17	I will *w* for the LORD, who is hiding his
	26. 8	O LORD, we *w* for you; your name and
	30.18	the LORD *w* to be gracious to you,
	40.31	those who *w* for the LORD shall renew
	42. 4	and the coastlands *w* for his teaching.
	49.23	those who *w* for me shall not be put to
	59.11	We *w* for justice, but there is none; for
	60. 9	the coastlands shall *w* for me, the ships
	64. 4	besides you, who works for those who *w*
Lam	3.26	It is good that one should *w* quietly for
Hos	12. 6	justice, and *w* continually for your God.
Mic	7. 7	I will *w* for the God of my salvation; my
Zeph	3. 8	Therefore *w* for me, says the LORD, for
Mk	15.43	who was also himself *w* expectantly for
Lk	8.40	him, for they were all *w* for him.
	12.36	be like those who are *w* for their master
Rom	8.23	groan inwardly while we *w* for adoption,
1 Cor	1. 7	spiritual gift as you *w* for the revealing
	11.33	together to eat, *w* for one another.
Gal	5. 5	by faith, we *w* eagerly for the hope of
1 Thess	1.10	to *w* for his Son from heaven, whom he

Titus	2.13	while we *w* for the blessed hope, and
2 Pet	3.12	*w* for and hastening the day of God,

WAKE

Rom	13.11	the moment for you to *w* from sleep.

WAKENS

Isa	50. 4	Morning by morning he *w* — *w* my ear

WALK

Gen	13.17	Rise up, *w* through the length and
	17. 1	"I am God Almighty; *w* before me, and
	24.40	LORD, before whom I *w*, will send his
Lev	26.12	And I will *w* among you, and will be
Deut	10.12	to *w* in all his ways, to love him, to
Josh	22. 5	to *w* in all his ways, to keep his
1 Kings	3.14	If you will *w* in my ways, keeping my
	9. 4	If you will *w* before me, as David your
2 Kings	21.22	and did not *w* in the way of the LORD.
2 Chr	6.14	with your servants who *w* before you
	7.17	for you, if you *w* before me, your father
Neh	5. 9	Should you not *w* in the fear of our
	10.29	a curse and an oath to *w* in God's law,
Ps	48.12	*W* about Zion, go all around it, count
	56.13	so that I may *w* before God in the light
	78.10	but refused to *w* according to his law.
	81.13	to me, that Israel would *w* in my ways!
	82. 5	they *w* around in darkness; all the
	89.15	who *w*, O LORD, in the light of your
	101. 2	I will *w* with integrity of heart within
	116. 9	I *w* before the LORD in the land of the
	119. 1	who *w* in the law of the LORD.
	138. 7	Though I *w* in the midst of trouble, you
Prov	1.15	my child, do not *w* in their way, keep
	2.20	Therefore *w* in the way of the good,
	8.20	I *w* in the way of righteousness, along
	28. 6	Better to be poor and *w* in integrity
Eccl	2.14	in their head, but fools *w* in darkness.
Isa	2. 3	ways and that we may *w* in his paths."
	8.11	warned me not to *w* in the way of this
	30.21	you, saying, "This is the way, *w* in it."
	33.15	Those who *w* righteously and speak
	40.31	be weary, they shall *w* and not faint.
	42. 5	upon it and spirit to those who *w* in it:
	42.24	in whose ways they would not *w*, and
	57. 2	those who *w* uprightly will rest on their
	65. 2	rebellious people, who *w* in a way that
Jer	6.16	where the good way lies; and *w* in it,
	10.23	that mortals as they *w* cannot direct
	31. 9	I will let them *w* by brooks of water, in
Am	3. 3	Do two *w* together unless they have
Mic	4. 5	peoples *w*, each in the name of its god,
	6. 8	and to *w* humbly with your God?
Zech	3. 7	If you will *w* in my ways and keep my
	10.12	the LORD, and they shall *w* in his name,
Mt	9. 5	forgiven,' or to say, 'Stand up and *w*'?
Jn	5. 8	"Stand up, take your mat and *w*." At
	11. 9	Those who *w* during the day do not
	12.35	*W* while you have the light, so that the
Acts	3. 6	Christ of Nazareth, stand up and *w*."
Rom	6. 4	so we too might *w* in newness of life.
	8. 4	who *w* not according to the flesh but
2 Cor	6.16	"I will live in them and *w* among them,
1 Jn	2. 6	in him," ought to *w* just as he walked.
Rev	3. 4	they shall *w* with me, dressed in white,

WALKS (WALKED WALKING)

Gen	3. 8	sound of the LORD God *w* in the garden
	5.22	Enoch *w* with God after the birth of
	6. 9	in his generation; Noah *w* with God.
Deut	30.16	*w* in his ways, and observing his
1 Kings	3. 6	David, because he *w* before you in
	16.26	he *w* in all the way of Jeroboam son of
2 Kings	13. 6	he caused Israel to sin, but *w* in them;
	16. 3	he *w* in the way of the kings of Israel.
	17. 8	*w* in the customs of the nations whom
	17.19	but *w* in the customs that Israel had

2 Chr	17.	3 was with Jehoshaphat, because he *w* in
	21.12	Because you have not *w* in the ways of
Job	22.14	not see, he *w* on the dome of heaven.'
Ps	26.	1 O LORD, for I have *w* in my integrity,
	55.14	company; we *w* in the house of God
	128.	1 who fears the LORD, who *w* in his ways.
Prov	10.	9 Whoever *w* in integrity *w* securely, but
	28.18	One who *w* in integrity will be safe, but
Isa	9.	2 The people who *w* in darkness have
Dan	3.25	unbound, *w* in the middle of the fire,
Mt	14.25	he came *w* toward them on the sea.
	14.29	started *w* on the water, and came
Mk	6.48	early in the morning, *w* on the sea.
	8.24	see people but they look like trees, *w*."
Jn	6.19	they saw Jesus *w* on the sea and
Rom	14.15	you eat, you are no longer *w* in love.
2 Jn		4 that my children are *w* in the truth.

WALL (WALLS)

Ex	14.22	the waters forming a *w* for them on
Deut	3.	5 these were fortress towns with high *w*,
1 Sam	25.16	they were a *w* to us both by night and
Neh	2.15	the valley by night and inspected the *w*.
	6.15	So the *w* was finished on the
	12.27	at the dedication of the *w* of Jerusalem
Ps	18.29	and by my God I can leap over a *w*.
Prov	18.11	in their imagination it is like a high *w*.
Isa	26.	1 he sets up victory like *w* and bulwarks.
Jer	1.18	city, an iron pillar, and a bronze *w*,
Dan	5.	5 began writing on the plaster of the *w*
Hos	2.	6 I will build a *w* against her, so that she
Zech	2.	5 I will be a *w* of fire all around it, says
Acts	9.25	him down through an opening in the *w*,
	23.	3 will strike you, you white-washed *w*!
Eph	2.14	and has broken down the dividing *w*,
Heb	11.30	By faith the *w* of Jericho fell after they

WANDER (WANDERED WANDERS)

Num	32.13	he made them *w* in the wilderness for
Ps	107.	4 Some *w* in desert wastes, finding no
	109.	10 May his children *w* about and beg; may
Prov	21.16	*w* from the way of understanding
Jer	14.10	they have loved to *w*, they have not
Lam	4.14	Blindly they *w* through the streets, so
Jas	5.19	if anyone among you *w* from the truth

WANT

Ps	23.	1 The LORD is my shepherd, I shall not *w*;
	34.	9 ones, for those who fear him have no *w*.
Mk	14.36	me; yet, not what I *w*, but what you *w*."
1 Cor	4.	8 Already you have all you *w*! Already you

WAR (WARS)

Gen	14.	2 these kings made *w* with King Bera of
Ps	18.34	He trains my hands for *w*, so that my
	27.	3 though *w* rise up against me, yet I will
	46.	9 He makes *w* cease to the end of the
	144.	1 who trains my hands for *w*, and my
Isa	2.	4 nation, neither shall they learn *w*
	41.12	those who *w* against you shall be as
Mt	24.	6 you will hear of *w* and rumors of *w*;
Mk	13.	7 when you hear of *w* and rumors of *w*,
Lk	14.31	out to wage *w* against another king,
	21.	9 "When you hear of *w* and insurrections,
2 Cor	10.	3 but we do not wage *w* according to
Rev	12.	7 And *w* broke out in heaven; Michael
	12.17	went off to make *w* on the rest of her

WARFARE

2 Cor	10.	4 of our *w* are not merely human,

WARMING

Mk	14.54	sitting with the guards, *w* himself at
Jn	18.18	was standing with them and *w* himself.

WARN (WARNED WARNING)

Gen	43.	3 "The man solemnly *w* us, saying, 'You
Num	26.10	fifty men; and they became a *w*.

Deut	8.19	I solemnly *w* you today that you shall
2 Kings	6.10	than once or twice he *w* such a place
	17.13	the LORD *w* Israel and Judah by every
Neh	13.15	I *w* them at that time against selling
Ps	19.11	by them is your servant *w*; in keeping
Jer	11.	7 I solemnly *w* your ancestors when I
Ezek	3.17	mouth, you shall give them *w* from me.
	33.	5 of the trumpet, and did not take *w*;
Mt	2.12	having been *w* in a dream not to return
	3.	7 vipers! Who *w* you to flee from the
Mk	1.43	After sternly *w* him he left him, and he
Lk	16.28	*w* them, so that they will not also come
Acts	4.17	let us *w* them to speak no more to
	20.31	night or day to *w* everyone with tears.
Heb	8.	5 he was about to erect the tent, was *w*,
	11.	7 By faith Noah, *w* by God about events

WARRIOR (WARRIORS)

Judg	11.	1 Jephthah . . . was a mighty *w*. Gilead
2 Sam	23.	8 the names of the *w* whom David had:
Job	16.14	and again; he rushes at me like a *w*.
Zeph	3.17	is in your midst, a *w* who gives victory;

WASH (WASHED)

Ex	29.	4 tent of meeting, and *w* them with water.
Num	5.23	and *w* them off into the water of
Deut	21.	6 elders . . . shall *w* their hands over the
	23.11	comes, he shall *w* himself in water,
2 Kings	5.10	"Go, *w* in the Jordan seven times, and
Job	9.30	If I *w* myself with soap, and cleanse my
Ps	26.	6 I *w* my hands in innocence, and go
	51.	2 W me thoroughly from my iniquity, and
	73.13	clean and *w* my hands in innocence.
Isa	1.16	W yourselves; make yourselves clean;
	4.	4 once the Lord has *w* away the filth of
Jer	2.22	Though you *w* yourself with lye and use
	4.14	Jerusalem, *w* your heart clean of
Mt	6.17	fast, put oil on your head and *w* your
	27.24	and *w* his hands before the crowd,
Lk	11.38	that he did not first *w* before dinner.
Jn	9.	7 to him, "Go, *w* in the pool of Siloam"
	13.	5 began to *w* the disciples' feet and to
Acts	22.16	have your sins *w* away, calling on his
1 Cor	6.11	But you were *w*, you were sanctified,

WASTE

Isa	24.	1 LORD is about to lay *w* the earth and
	34.10	generaton to generation it shall lie *w*;
Jer	4.	7 to make your land a *w*; your cities will
Mt	26.	8 they were angry and said, "Why this *w*?

WATCH (WATCHED WATCHING)

Gen	31.49	"The LORD *w* between you and me, when
Job	29.	2 as in the days when God *w* over me;
Ps	130.	6 than those who *w* for the morning,
Prov	15.	3 in every place, keeping *w* on the evil
Jer	1.12	for I am *w* over my word to perform it."
	20.10	close friends are *w* for me to stumble.
Zech	11.11	the sheep merchants, who were *w* me,
Mt	27.36	sat down there and kept *w* over him.
1 Cor	10.12	are standing, *w* out that you do not fall.
Col	3.22	in everything, not only while being *w*

WATCHFUL

Zech	12.	4 the house of Judah I will keep a *w* eye,

WATCHPOST

Hab	2.	1 I will stand at my *w*, and station myself

WATER (WATERS) (n)

Ex	17.	1 but there was no *w* for the people
Num	5.18	the priest shall have the *w* of bitterness
	20.	2 there was no *w* for the congregation;
Deut	8.15	He made *w* flow for you from flint rock,
1 Kings	18.33	"Fill four jars with *w*, and pour it on the
2 Kings	2.14	struck the *w*, saying, "Where is the
2 Chr	32.30	outlet of the *w* of Gihon and directed
Ps	18.16	took me; he drew me out of mighty *w*.

Ps	69. 1 for the *w* have come up to my neck.
Prov	11.25 and one who gives *w* will get *w*.
	25.25 Like cold *w* to a thirsty soul, so is good
Song	8. 7 Many *w* cannot quench love, neither
Isa	12. 3 will draw *w* from the wells of salvation.
	33.16 food will be supplied, their *w* assured.
	43. 2 When you pass through the *w*, I will be
	44. 3 For I will pour *w* on the thirsty land,
	58.11 a spring of *w*, whose *w* never fail.
Jer	9. 1 O that my head were a spring of *w*, and
	14. 3 they find no *w*, they return with their
	17. 8 They will be like a tree planted by *w*,
	17.13 the fountain of living *w*, the LORD.
Ezek	36.25 I will sprinkle clean *w* upon you, and
	47. 1 *w* was flowing from below the threshold
Am	5.24 let justice roll down like *w*, and
Hab	2.14 of the LORD, as the *w* cover the sea.
Zech	14. 8 On that day living *w* shall flow out from
Mt	3.11 I baptize you with *w* for repentance,
	10.42 cup of cold *w* to one of these little ones
	27.24 took some *w* and washed his hands
Mk	9.41 *w* to drink because you bear the name
Lk	3.16 "I baptize you with *w*; but one who is
	16.24 the tip of his finger in *w* and cool my
Jn	1.26 "I baptize with *w*. Among you stands
	2. 7 said to them, "Fill the jars with *w*."
	3. 5 God without being born of *w* and Spirit.
	4.14 those who drink of the *w* that I will give
	5.3n waiting for the stirring of the *w*; for an
	7.38 heart shall flow rivers of living *w*.'"
Acts	8.36 eunuch said, "Look, here is *w*! What is
	10.47 "Can anyone withhold the *w* for
1 Jn	5. 6 Christ, not with the *w* only but with the
Rev	22.17 anyone who wishes take the *w* of life

WATER (WATERED) (v)

Gen	2. 6 and *w* whole face of the ground—
	13.10 that the plain of the Jordan was well *w*
	29.10 Jacob . . . *w* the flock of his mother's
Isa	27. 3 am its keeper; every moment I *w* it.
1 Cor	3. 6 I planted, Apollos *w*, but God gave the

WATERCOURSES

Joel	1.20 cry to you because the *w* are dried up,

WAVE (WAVES)

Ps	42. 7 cataracts; all your *w* and your billows
	88. 7 and you overwhelm me with all your *w*.
Jon	2. 3 all your *w* and your billows passed over
Mt	14.24 the boat, battered by the *w*, was far
Mk	4.37 and the *w* beat into the boat, so that
Jas	1. 6 the one who doubts is like a *w* of the

WAVERING

Ps	26. 1 I have trusted in the LORD without *w*.
Heb	10.23 the confession of our hope without *w*,

WAY

Gen	3.24 to guard the *w* to the tree of life.
Num	21. 4 the people became impatient on the *w*.
Judg	2.22 take care to walk in the *w* of the LORD
1 Sam	9. 8 it to the man of God, to tell us our *w*."
2 Sam	22.31 This God—his *w* is perfect; the
1 Kings	16.26 walked in all the *w* of Jeroboam son of
Job	16.22 I shall go the *w* from which I shall not
	19. 8 He has walled up my *w* so I cannot
	23.10 he knows the *w* that I take; when he
	28.13 Mortals do not know the *w* to it, and it
	28.23 "God understands the *w* to it, and he
	38.19 "Where is the *w* to the dwelling of light,
Ps	1. 6 watches over the *w* of the righteous, but
	5. 8 make your *w* straight before me.
	18.30 This God—his *w* is perfect; the
	25. 9 is right, and teaches the humble his *w*.
	37. 5 Commit your *w* to the LORD; trust in
	37.23 by the LORD, when he delights in our *w*;
	37.34 Wait for the LORD, and keep to his *w*,
	67. 2 that your *w* may be known upon the

Ps	77.13 Your *w*, O God, is holy. What god is so
	101. 6 walks in the *w* that is blameless
	119. 9 can young people keep their *w* pure?
	139. 24 in me, and lead me in the *w* everlasting.
Prov	2. 8 and preserving the *w* of his faithful
	7.27 Her house is the *w* to Sheol, going
	8.20 I walk in the *w* of righteousness, along
	10.29 The *w* of the LORD is a stronghold for
	13.15 but the *w* of the faithless is their ruin.
	14.12 There is a *w* which seems right to a
	15. 9 The *w* of the wicked is an abomination
	15.19 The *w* of the lazy is overgrown with
	16.25 there is a *w* which seems to be right,
	22. 6 Train children in the right *w*, and when
Isa	30.21 you saying, "This is the *w*, walk in it."
	40. 3 wilderness prepare the *w* of the LORD,
	40.27 "My *w* is hidden from the LORD, and my
	43.16 who makes a *w* in the sea, a path in the
	53. 6 astray; we have all turned to our own *w*,
	57.14 said, "Build up, build up, prepare the *w*,
	59. 8 The *w* of peace they do not know, and
Jer	5. 4 for they do not know the *w* of the LORD,
	10.23 that the *w* of human beings is not in
	21. 8 I am setting before you the *w* of life
	23.12 their *w* shall be to them like slippery
Ezek	18.25 you say, "The *w* of the Lord is unfair."
	33.17 say, "The *w* of the Lord is not just,"
Nah	1. 3 His *w* is in whirlwind and storm, and
Mt	3. 3 'Prepare the *w* of the Lord, make his
	11.10 who will prepare your *w* before you.'
	22.16 teach the *w* of God in accordance with
Mk	1. 2 before you, who will prepare your *w*;
	12.14 but teach the *w* of God in accordance
Lk	3. 4 'Prepare the *w* of the Lord, make his
	7.27 who will prepare your *w* before you.'
Jn	14. 6 "I am the *w*, and the truth, and the life.
Acts	9. 2 if he found any who belonged to the *W*,
	16.17 who proclaim to you a *w* of salvation.
	18.26 and explained the *W* of God to him
	19.23 broke out concerning the *W*.
	22. 4 I persecuted this *W* up to the point of
	24.14 the *W*, which they call a sect, I worship
Rom	3.17 the *w* of peace they have not known."
Heb	9. 8 the *w* into the sanctuary has not yet
	10.20 by the new and living *w* that he opened
2 Pet	2.21 known the *w* of righteousness than,
Rev	16.12 to prepare the *w* for the kings from the

WAYFARER

Judg	19.17 the old man looked up and saw the *w*
Jer	14. 8 in the land, like a *w* turning aside for

WAYS

2 Sam	22.22 For I have kept the *w* of the LORD, and
1 Kings	2. 3 your God, walking in his *w* and keeping
	3.14 If you will walk in my *w*, keeping my
Job	21.14 We do not desire to know your *w*.
	24.23 supported; his eyes are upon their *w*.
	31. 4 Does not he see my *w*, and number all
Ps	18.21 For I have kept the *w* of the LORD, and
	95.10 go astray, and they do not regard my *w*."
	103. 7 He made known his *w* to Moses, his
Prov	5.21 For human *w* are under the eyes of the
	16. 2 All one's *w* may be pure in one's own
	20.24 then can we understand our own *w*?
	31.27 looks well to the *w* of her household,
Isa	2. 3 that he may teach us his *w* and that we
	55. 9 so are my *w* higher than your *w* and my
Jer	4.18 Your *w* and your doings have brought
	16.17 my eyes are on all their *w*; they are not
	17.10 to give to all according to their *w*,
Ezek	7. 3 judge you according to your *w*; I will
	33.11 the wicked turn from their *w* and live;
Dan	4.37 works are truth, and his *w* are justice;
Mic	4. 2 that he may teach us his *w* and that we
Rom	11.33 judgments and how inscrutable his *w*!
Rev	15. 3 Just and true are your *w*, King of the

WEAK

Ezek	34.	4 You have not strengthened the *w*, you
Acts	20.35	we must support the *w*, remembering
Rom	5.	6 While we were still *w*, at the right time
	14.	1 Welcome those who are *w* in faith, but
	15.	1 to put up with the failings of the *w*,
1 Cor	1.27	God chose what is *w* in the world to
	4.10	in Christ. We are *w*, but you are strong.
	8.	7 their conscience, being *w*, is defiled.
	9.22	To the *w* I became *w*, so that I might
2 Cor	11.29	Who is *w*, and I am not *w*? Who is
	12.10	for whenever I am *w*, then I am strong.
1 Thess	5.14	hearted, help the *w*, be patient with all

WEAKNESS (WEAKNESSES)

1 Cor	1.25	and God's *w* is stronger than human
	2.	3 I came to you in *w* and in fear and in
2 Cor	13.	4 he was crucified in *w*, but lives by the
Heb	4.15	is unable to sympathize with our *w*,

WEALTH

Deut	8.17	of my own hand have gotten me this *w*."
Job	31.25	if I have rejoiced because my *w* was
Ps	49.	6 those who trust in their *w* and boast of
	112.	3 *W* and riches are in their houses, and
Prov	12.27	but the diligent obtain precious *w*.
	13.	7 pretend to be poor, yet have great *w*.
	13.11	*W* hastily gotten will dwindle, but those
	13.22	sinner's *w* is laid up for the righteous.
Eccl	5.19	Likewise all to whom God gives *w* and
Song	8.	7 If one offered for love all the *w* of his
Isa	61.	6 you shall enjoy the *w* of the nations,
Jer	17.11	lay, so are all who amass *w* unjustly;
Ezek	28.	5 your heart has become proud in your *w*.
Hab	2.	5 Moreover, *w* is treacherous; the arrogant
Mt	6.24	the other. You cannot serve God and *w*.
	13.22	the lure of *w* choke the word, and it
Mk	4.19	cares of the world, and the lure of *w*,
	10.23	it will be for those who have *w* to enter
Lk	16.	9 for yourselves by means of dishonest *w*
2 Cor	8.	2 have overflowed in a *w* of generosity on
Heb	11.26	suffered for the Christ to be greater *w*
Rev	18.17	one hour all this *w* has been laid waste."

WEAPON (WEAPONS)

Eccl	9.18	Wisdom is better than *w* of war, but
Jer	51.20	You are my war club, my *w* of battle:
2 Cor	6.	7 with the *w* of righteousness for the right
	10.	4 for the *w* of our warfare are not merely

WEAR (WEARS)

Deut	22.	5 A woman shall not *w* a man's apparel,
Prov	23.	4 Do not *w* yourself out to get rich; be
Eccl	10.15	The toil of fools *w* them out, for they
Lk	18.	5 so that she may not *w* me out by

WEARINESS

Eccl	12.12	end, and much study is a *w* of the flesh.

WEARISOME

Eccl	1.	8 All things are *w*; more than one can

WEARY (WEARIED)

2 Sam	21.15	the Philistines, and David grew *w*.
Job	3.17	troubling, and there the *w* are at rest.
Isa	1.14	burden to me, I am *w* of bearing them.
	5.27	None of them is *w*, none stumbles,
	7.13	to *w* mortals, that you *w* my God also?
	43.22	but you have been *w* of me, O Israel!
	43.24	you have *w* me with your iniquities;
	47.13	are *w* with your many consultations;
	57.10	You grew *w* from your many wanderings,
Jer	15.	6 destroyed you— I am *w* of relenting.
	31.25	I will satisfy the *w*, and all who are
Mic	6.	3 In what have I *w* you? Answer me! For I
Mal	2.17	You have *w* the LORD with your words.
Gal	6.	9 let us not grow *w* in doing what is right,
2 Thess	3.13	do not be *w* in doing what is right.

WEATHER

Mt	16.	2 you say, 'It will be fair *w*, for the sky is

WEAVER (WEAVER'S)

Job	7.	6 My days are swifter than a *w* shuttle,
Isa	38.12	like a *w* I have rolled up my life; he

WEDDING

Mt	22.	2 to a king who gave a *w* banquet
	22.	8 'The *w* is ready, but those invited were
	25.10	went with him into the *w* banquet;
Lk	12.36	to return home from the *w* banquet,

WEEDS

Mt	13.25	his enemy came and sowed *w* among

WEEKS

Deut	16.10	you shall keep the festival of *w* for the
Dan	9.24	"Seventy *w* are decreed for your people

WEEP (WEEPING WEEPS WEPT)

Gen	27.38	father!" And Esau lifted his voice and *w*.
	42.24	He turned away from them and *w*; then
	43.30	went into a private room and *w* there.
	45.	2 he *w* so loudly that the Egyptians heard
	46.29	fell on his neck, and *w* on his neck a
Judg	20.23	went up and *w* before the LORD
1 Sam	30.	4 until they had no more strength to *w*.
2 Sam	18.33	up to the chamber over the gate, and *w*;
Ezra	3.12	*w* with a loud voice when they saw this
Neh	1.	4 I heard these words I sat down and *w*,
	8.	9 all the people *w* when they heard the
Job	16.16	My face is red with *w*, and deep
Ps	6.	6 tears; I drench my couch with my *w*.
	6.	8 the LORD has heard the sound of my *w*,
	30.	5 *W* may linger for the night, but joy
	137.	1 and we *w* when we remembered Zion.
Eccl	3.	4 a time to *w*, and a time to laugh; a time
Isa	15.	2 to the temple, to the high places to *w*;
Jer	13.17	not listen, my soul will *w* in secret for
	22.10	Do not *w* for him who is dead, nor
	31.15	bitter *w*. Rachel is *w* for her children;
Lam	1.16	For these things I *w*; my eyes flow with
	2.11	My eyes are spent with *w*; my stomach
Ezek	8.14	were sitting there *w* for Tammuz,
	27.31	they *w* over you in bitterness of soul,
Joel	2.17	the priests, the ministers of the LORD, *w*.
Mic	1.10	Tell it not in Gath, *w* not at all; in
Zech	12.10	*w* bitterly over him, as one *w* over a
Mt	2.18	Rachel *w* for her children;
	8.12	there will be *w* and gnashing of teeth
	24.51	there will be *w* and gnashing of teeth.
	26.75	And he went out and *w* bitterly.
Mk	14.72	three times." And he broke down and *w*.
Lk	6.21	"Blessed are you who *w* now, for you
	8.52	"Do not *w*; for she is not dead but
	19.41	near and saw the city, he *w* over it,
	22.62	times." And he went out and *w* bitterly.
	23.28	do not *w* for me, but *w* for yourselves
Jn	11.31	she was going to the tomb to *w* there.
	11.35	Jesus began to *w*.
	20.11	But Mary stood *w* outside the tomb. As
	20.15	"Woman, why are you *w*? Whom are you
Acts	21.13	"What are you doing, *w* and breaking
Rom	12.15	those who rejoice, *w* with those who *w*.
Rev	5.	4 I began to *w* bitterly because no one
	18.	9 will *w* and wail over her when they see

WEIGH (WEIGHED WEIGHS)

1 Sam	2.	3 of knowledge, and by him actions are *w*.
Job	6.	2 "O that my vexation were *w*, and all my
	31.	6 let me be *w* in a just balance, and let
Prov	16.	2 own eyes, but the LORD *w* the spirit.
	21.	2 of the doer, but the LORD *w* the heart.
	24.12	not he who or the heart perceive it?
Isa	40.12	and *w* the mountains in scales and the
Jer	32.10	and and *w* the money on scales.
Dan	5.27	TEKEL, you have been *w* on the scales

Zech	11.12	So they *w* out as my wages thirty
1 Cor	14.29	and let the others *w* what is said.

WEIGHTS

Deut	25.13	not have in your bag two kinds of *w*,
Prov	20.10	Diverse *w* and diverse measures are

WEIGHTY

Ps	139. 17	How *w* to me are your thoughts, O God!

WELCOME (WELCOMED WELCOMES)

Mt	10.40	"Whoever *w* you *w* me, and whoever *w*
	18. 5	Whoever *w* one such child in my name
Mk	6.11	If any place will not *w* you and they
	9.37	"Whoever *w* one such child in my name
Lk	8.40	when Jesus returned, the crowd *w* him
	9. 5	Wherever they do not *w* you, as you are
	9.11	he *w* them, and spoke to them about
	9.48	*w* this child in my name *w* me,
	10.10	enter a town and they do not *w* you,
	19. 6	hurried down, and was happy to *w* him.
Acts	2.41	who *w* his message were baptized, and
	28.30	expense, and *w* all who came to him,
Rom	15. 7	*W* one another, therefore, just as Christ
	16. 2	so that you may *w* her in the Lord as is
Gal	4.14	me, but *w* me as an angel of God,

WELFARE

Gen	43.27	He inquired about their *w*, and said, "Is
Neh	2.10	had come to seek the *w* of the people
Ps	35.27	who delights in the *w* of his servant."
Prov	3. 2	life and abundant *w* will they give you.
Jer	29. 7	behalf, for in its *w* you will find your *w*.
	38. 4	is not seeking the *w* of his people, but

WELL (WELLS) (n)

Gen	21.19	her eyes and she saw a *w* of water.
	21.25	to Abimelech about a *w* of water
	24.11	down outside the city by the *w* of water;
	26.22	moved from there and dug another *w*,
Num	21.17	Israel sang this song: "Spring up, O *w*!
2 Sam	23.15	drew water from the *w* of Bethlehem
Song	4.15	a *w* of living water, and flowing streams
Isa	12. 3	will draw water from the *w* of salvation.
Jer	6. 7	As a *w* keeps its water fresh, so she
Lk	14. 5	child or an ox that has fallen into a *w*,
Jn	4. 6	Jacob's *w* was there, and Jesus, tired

WELL (adv)

2 Sam	18.29	"Is it *w* with the young man Absalom?"
Prov	27. 6	*W* meant are the wounds a friend
Mt	9.22	daughter; your faith has made you *w*."
Mk	5.23	so that she may be made *w*, and live."

WELL-BEING

Lev	3. 1	If the offering is a sacrifice of *w*, if you
	7.11	of the sacrifice of the offering of *w*

WEST

Ps	103. 12	as far as the east is from the *w*, so far
Mt	8.11	many will come from east and and
Lk	13.29	people will come from east and *w*, from

WHEAT

Judg	6.11	Gideon was beating out *w* in the wine
Jer	23.28	What has straw in common with *w*?
Mt	13.25	came and sowed weeds among the *w*,
	13.29	you uproot the *w* along with them.
Lk	3.17	and to gather the *w* into his granary,
Jn	12.24	unless a grain of *w* falls into the earth

WHEEL

Jer	18. 3	and there he was working at his *w*.
Ezek	1.16	being something like a *w* within a *w*.
	10.10	alike, something like a *w* within a *w*.

WHIP

Prov	26. 3	A *w* for the horse, a bridle for the
Isa	10.26	of hosts will wield a *w* against them,

Jn	2.15	Making a *w* of cords, he drove all of

WHIRLWIND

2 Kings	2.11	and Elijah ascended in a *w* into heaven.
Isa	5.28	like flint, and their wheels like the *w*.
Hos	8. 7	the wind, and they shall reap the *w*.

WHISPER

Ps	41. 7	All who hate me *w* together about me;
Isa	29. 4	and your speech shall *w* out of the dust.

WHISPERER

Prov	16.28	strife, and a *w* separates close friends.
	18. 8	The words of a *w* are like delicious
	26.22	The words of a *w* are like delicious

WHITE

Eccl	9. 8	Let your garments be always *w*; do not
Mk	9. 3	and his clothes became dazzling *w*,
Acts	1.10	heaven, suddenly two men in *w* robes
Rev	1.14	head and his hair were *w* as *w* wool,

WHITEWASH (WHITEWASHED)

Job	13. 4	As for you, you *w* with lies; all of you
Mt	23.27	hypocrites! For you are like *w* tombs,
Acts	23. 3	"God will strike you, you *w* wall! Are

WHOLESOME

2 Kings	2.21	the Lord, I have made this water *w*;
Prov	15.31	The ear that heeds *w* admonition will

WHORE (WHORES)

Jer	3. 1	You have played the *w* with many
Ezek	16.28	You played the *w* with the Assyrians,
	23. 5	Oholah played the *w* while she was
Hos	2. 5	their mother has played the *w*; she who
Rev	17. 5	"Babylon the great, mother of *w* and of

WICK

Isa	42. 3	a dimly burning *w* he will not quench;
Mt	12.20	or quench a smoldering *w*, until he

WICKED

Gen	13.13	the people of Sodom were *w*, great
2 Chr	19. 2	"Should you help the *w* and love those
Job	9.24	earth is given into the hand of the *w*;
	11.20	the eyes of the *w* will fail; all the way of
	15.20	The *w* man writhes in pain all their
	21.30	that the *w* are spared in the day of
	27.13	"This is the portion of the *w* with God,
Ps	10.15	Break the arm of the *w* and evildoers;
	37.10	little while, and the *w* will be no more;
	37.35	I have seen the *w* oppressing, and
	94. 3	shall the *w*, how long shall the *w* exult?
	112. 10	The *w* see it and are angry; they gnash
	119. 53	indignation seizes me because of the *w*,
	139. 19	O that you would kill the *w*, O God,
	141. 5	Never let the oil of the *w* anoint my
Prov	2.22	but the *w* will be cut off from the land,
	10. 6	the mouth of the *w* conceals violence.
	10.30	but the *w* will not remain in the land.
	13. 6	is upright, but sin overthrows the *w*.
	16. 4	even the *w* for the day of trouble.
	28. 1	The *w* flee when no one pursues, but
Isa	26.10	If favor is shown to the *w*, they do not
	53. 9	They made his grave with the *w* and his
Ezek	18.27	when the *w* turn away from the
	33.15	if the *w* restore the pledge, give back
Dan	12.10	the *w* shall continue to act wickedly.
Mt	18.32	'You *w* slave! I forgave you all that debt
	25.26	'You *w* and lazy slave! You knew, did
Acts	3.26	turning each of you from your *w* ways."
1 Cor	5.13	outside. "Drive out the *w* person from

WICKEDLY

Judg	19.23	"No, my brothers, do not act so *w*.
1 Chr	21.17	is I who have sinned and done very *w*.
Neh	9.33	dealt faithfully and we have acted *w*;

WICKEDNESS

Gen	6.	5 LORD saw that the *w* of humankind was
1 Sam	24.13	says, Out of the wicked comes forth *w*';
Job	20.12	"Though *w* is sweet in their mouth,
Prov	8.	7 truth; *w* is an abomination to my lips.
Isa	9.18	For *w* burned like a fire, consuming
Jer	6.	7 so she keeps fresh her *w*; violence and
Ezek	16.57	before your *w* was uncovered? Now you
Rom	1.18	who by their *w* suppress the truth.
	1.29	They were filled with every kind of *w*,

WIDOW (WIDOWS WIDOW'S WIDOWS')

Deut	14.29	the orphans, and the *w* in your towns,
	24.17	you shall not take a *w* garment in
Job	22.	9 You have sent *w* away empty-handed,
	29.13	upon me, I caused the *w* heart to sing
Ps	109.	9 children be orphans, and his wife a *w*.
Prov	15.25	proud, but maintains the *w* boundaries.
Isa	1.17	defend the orphan, plead for the *w*.
	10.	2 of their right, that *w* may be their spoil,
Jer	49.11	them alive; and let your *w* trust in me.
Lam	1.	1 How like a *w* has she become, she that
Mt	23.14	Now *w* for you devour *w* houses and for the
Mk	12.40	They devour *w* houses and for the sake
	12.42	A poor *w* came and put in two small
Lk	4.25	there were many *w* in Israel in the time
	7.12	his mother's only son, and she was a *w*;
	21.	2 he also saw a poor *w* put in two small
Acts	6.	1 their *w* were being neglected in the
1 Tim	5.	3 Honor *w* who are really *w*. If a *w* has

WIFE (WIFE'S WIVES)

Gen	12.12	'This is his *w*'; then they will kill me,
Num	5.12	If any man's *w* goes astray and is
Ruth	4.13	Boaz took Ruth and she became his *w*.
1 Sam	25.39	David wooed Abigail, to make her his *w*.
Job	31.10	then let my *w* grind for another, and let
Ps	128.	3 Your *w* will be like a fruitful vine within
Prov	5.18	blessed, rejoice in the *w* of your youth,
	6.24	to preserve you from the *w* of another,
	6.29	is he who sleeps with his neighbor's *w*;
	18.22	He who finds a *w* finds a good thing,
	19.13	and a *w* quarreling is a continual
	19.14	but a prudent *w* is from the LORD.
	31.10	A capable *w* who can find? She is far
Eccl	9.	9 Enjoy life with the *w* whom you love,
Jer	3.	1 If a man divorces his *w* and she goes
	3.20	as a faithless *w* leaves her husband, so
Ezek	24.18	morning , and at evening my *w* died.
Hos	1.	2 "Go, take for yourself a *w* of whoredom
	2.19	I will take you as my *w* forever; I will
	12.12	Israel served for a *w*, and for a *w* he
Mal	2.14	companion and your *w* by covenant.
Mt	1.24	he took her as his *w*, but had no
	5.31	"Whoever divorces his *w*, let him give
	19.	5 and be joined to his *w*, and the two
	27.19	judgment seat, his *w* sent word to him,
Mk	10.	2 "Is it lawful for a man to divorce his *w*?"
	12.19	brother dies, leaving a *w* but no child,
Lk	17.32	must not turn back. Remember Lot's *w*.
Acts	5.	7 his *w* came in, not knowing what had
1 Cor	7.	4 the *w* does not have authority over her
	7.27	Are you free from a *w*? Do not seek a *w*.
	7.39	A *w* is bound as long as her husband
	9.	5 to be accompanied by a believing *w*,
Eph	5.22	*W*, be subject to your husbands as you
	5.31	be joined to his *w*, and the two will
Col	3.18	*W*, be subject to your husbands, as is
1 Thess	4.4n	you know how to take a *w* for himself
1 Pet	3.	1 *W*, in the same way, accept the

WILD

Ex	32.25	the people were running *w* (for Aaron

WILDERNESS

Num	26.65	"They shall die in the *w*." Not one of
Deut	8.15	you through the great and terrible *w*,

1 Sam	23.14	remained in the strongholds in the *w*,
Song	3.	6 What is that coming up from the *w*, like
Isa	35.	1 *w* and the dry land shall be glad, the
	41.18	I will make the *w* a pool of water, and
	64.10	Your holy cities have become a *w*, Zion
Ezek	20.10	of Egypt and brought them into the *w*.
Mk	1.13	He was in the *w* forty days, tempted by
Lk	4.	1 the Spirit in the *w*, where for forty days
	7.24	did you go out into the *w* to look at?

WILL (WILLS)

Ezra	7.18	may do, according to the *w* of your God.
Ps	40.	8 I delight to do your *w*, O my God; your
Isa	53.10	it was the *w* of the LORD to crush him
Mt	6.10	Your *w* be done, On earth as it is in
	12.50	whoever does the *w* of my Father in
	18.14	it is not the *w* of your Father in heaven
	26.42	pass unless I drink it, your *w* be done."
Mk	3.35	Whoever does the *w* of God is my
Jn	4.34	"My food is to do the *w* of him who
	5.30	own *w*, but the *w* of him who sent me.
	6.38	own *w*, but the *w* of him who sent me.
	7.17	who resolves to do the *w* of God
Acts	21.14	except to say, "The Lord's *w* be done."
Rom	1.10	to God's *w* I may somehow at last
	2.18	know his *w* and determine what is best
	9.16	it depends not on human *w* or exertion,
	12.	2 you may discern what is the *w* of God
1 Cor	9.17	if I do this of my own *w*, I have a
2 Cor	8.	5 to the Lord and, by the *w* of God, to us,
Gal	1.	4 evil age, according to the *w* of our God
Eph	5.17	understand what the *w* of the Lord is.
Phil	2.13	you both to *w* and to work for his good
Col	4.12	fully assured in everything that God *w*.
1 Thess	4.	3 this is the *w* of God, your sanctification:
Heb	10.	7 'See, God, I have come to do your *w*, O
1 Pet	2.15	is God's *w* that by doing right you
	3.17	good, if suffering should be God's *w*,
	4.	2 by human desires but by the *w* of God.
1 Jn	2.17	those who do the *w* of God live forever.
Rev	4.11	and by your *w* they existed and were

WILLING (WILLINGLY)

1 Chr	29.	5 Who then will offer *w*, consecrating
Ps	110.	3 Your people will offer themselves *w* on
Lk	22.42	"Father, if you are *w*, remove this cup

WILLOWS

Lev	23.40	of leafy trees and *w* of the brook;
Ps	137.	2 On the *w* there we hung up our harps.

WIN

1 Cor	9.19	to all, so that I might *w* more of them.

WIND

Gen	1.2n	while a mighty *w* swept over the face of
1 Kings	19.11	a great *w*, so strong that it was splitting
Job	26.13	By his *w* the heavens were made fair;
Ps	55.	8 myself from the raging *w* and tempest."
Eccl	8.	8 No one has power over the *w*, to
Ezek	1.	4 a stormy *w* came out of the north; a
Hos	8.	7 For they sow the *w*, and they reap
	12.	1 Ephraim herds the *w*, and pursues the
	13.15	east *w* shall come, a blast from the
Lk	8.24	And he woke up and rebuked the *w* and
Jn	3.	8 The *w* blows where it chooses, and you
Acts	2.	2 a sound like the rush of a violent *w*,

WINDOW (WINDOWS)

Gen	7.11	and *w* of the heavens were opened.
2 Kings	7.	2 if the LORD were to make *w* in the sky,
Dan	6.10	which had *w* in its upper room open
2 Cor	11.33	was let down in a basket through a *w* in

WINDSTORM

Mt	8.24	A *w* arose on the sea, so great that the
Mk	4.37	A great *w* arose, and the waves beat

WINE

Gen	9.24 Noah awoke from his *w* and knew what
	19.35 they made their father drink *w* that
Lev	10. 8 Drink no *w* nor strong drink, neither
Num	6. 3 they shall separate themselves from *w*
Judg	13. 4 Now be careful not to drink *w* or strong
2 Sam	13.28 when Amnon's heart is merry with *w*,
Esth	1.10 day, when the king was merry with *w*,
Prov	20. 1 *W* is a mocker, strong drink a brawler,
	23.30 Those who linger late over *w*, those who
Eccl	2. 3 mind how to cheer my body with *w*—
Song	1. 2 For your love is better than *w*, your
Isa	5.11 in the evening to be inflamed by *w*,
	5.22 you who are heroes in drinking *w* and
	24.11 is an outcry in the streets for lack of *w*;
	56.12 "Come," they say, "let us get *w*; let us fill
Jer	35. 6 they answered, "We will drink no *w*, for
Ezek	44.21 No priest shall drink *w*, when he enters
Dan	5. 4 drank *w* and praised the gods of gold
Hos	4.11 *W* and new *w* take away the
Am	6. 6 who drink *w* in bowls, and anoint
Mt	27.34 they offered him *w* to drink, mixed with
Mk	2.22 no one puts new *w* into old wineskins;
	15.23 they offered him *w* mixed with myrrh;
Lk	5.37 And no one puts new *w* into old
Jn	2. 9 tasted the water that had become *w*,
Acts	2.13 and said, "They are filled with new *w*."
Eph	5.18 Do not get drunk with *w*, for that is
1 Tim	5.23 but take a little *w* for the sake of your

WINE PRESS

Judg	6.11 beating out wheat in the *w*, to hide it
Isa	63. 3 "I have trodden the *w* alone, and from
Rev	14.19 he threw it into the great *w* of the

WINESKINS

Mt	9.17 Neither is new wine put into old *w*;
Lk	5.37 And no one puts new wine into old *w*;

WINGS

Ex	19. 4 how I bore you on eagles' *w* and
Ruth	2.12 the God of Israel, under those *w* you
Ps	17. 8 hide me in the shadow of your *w*, from
	18.10 he came swiftly upon the *w* of the wind.
	36. 7 take refuge in the shadow of your *w*.
	55. 6 And I say, "O that I had *w* like a dove! I
	61. 4 find refuge under the shelter of your *w*.
Prov	23. 5 it takes *w* to itself, flying like an eagle
Isa	6. 2 attendance above him; each had six *w*:

WINKING (WINKS)

Prov	6.13 with crooked speech, *w* the eyes,
	10.10 Whoever *w* the eye causes trouble, but

WINNOW

Isa	41.16 You shall *w* them and the wind shall
Jer	51. 2 to Babylon, and they shall *w* her.

WINTER

Gen	8.22 night, summer and *w* shall not cease."
Song	2.11 away; for *w* is past, the rain is over
Acts	27.12 was not suitable for spending the *w*,
1 Cor	16. 6 with you or even spend the *w*, so that
2 Tim	4.21 Do your best to come before *w*. Eubulus
Titus	3.12 for I have decided to spend the *w* there.

WIPED

Acts	3.19 to God so that your sins may be *w* out,

WISDOM

Deut	4. 6 this will show your *w* and discernment
2 Sam	14.20 my lord has *w* like the *w* of the angel of
1 Kings	4.29 God gave Solomon very great *w*
	10. 4 of Sheba observed all the *w* of Solomon,
	10.23 kings of the earth in riches and in *w*.
2 Chr	1.10 Give me now *w* and knowledge to go
	9. 6 of your *w* had been told to me;
Job	12. 2 are the people, and *w* will die with you.

Job	28.12 "But where shall *w* be found? And
	38.36 Who has put *w* in the inward parts, or
Ps	37.30 The mouths of the righteous utter *w*,
	49. 3 My mouth shall speak *w*; the
	111. 10 fear of the LORD is the beginning of *w*;
Prov	1. 2 For learning about *w* and instruction,
	1.20 *W* cries out in the street; in the squares
	2.10 *w* will come into your heart, and
	8.11 is better than jewels, and all that you
	16.16 How much better to get *w* than gold! To
	19. 8 To get *w* is to love oneself; to keep
	21.30 No *w*, no understanding, no counsel,
	24. 3 By *w* a house is built, and by
	31.26 She opens her mouth with *w*, and the
Eccl	1.13 mind to seek and to search out by *w* all
	7.12 For the protection of *w* is like the
	9.16 yet the poor man's *w* is despised,
Isa	11. 2 him, the spirit of *w* and understanding,
Jer	49. 7 Is there no longer *w* in Teman? Has
	51.15 who established the world by his *w*,
Dan	1.20 In every matter of *w* and understanding
	5.11 and *w* like the *w* of the gods.
	9.22 I have now come out to give you *w* and
Mt	11.19 Yet *w* is vindicated by her deeds."
	12.42 the earth to listen to the *w* of Solomon,
	13.54 "Where did this man get this *w* and
Lk	2.52 And Jesus increased in *w* and in years,
	7.35 Nevertheless, *w* is vindicated by all her
	11.31 the earth to listen to the *w* of Solomon,
	21.15 I will give you words and a *w* that none
Acts	7.22 Moses was instructed in all the *w* of the
Rom	11.33 the riches and *w* and knowledge of God!
1 Cor	1.17 the gospel, and not with eloquent *w*,
	1.24 is the power of God and the *w* of God.
	1.30 Jesus, who became for us *w* from God,
	2. 6 among the mature we do speak *w*,
	3.19 the *w* of this world is foolishness with
	12. 8 through the Spirit the utterance of *w*,
Eph	1.17 may give you a spirit of *w* and
	3.10 that through the church the *w* of God
Jas	1. 5 If any of you is lacking in *w*, ask God,
	3.17 the *w* from above is first pure, then
2 Pet	3.15 to you according to the *w* given him,

WISE

Deut	32.29 If they were *w*, they would understand
1 Kings	3.12 I give you a *w* and discerning mind; no
Job	5.13 He takes the *w* in their own craftiness;
Ps	49.10 When he looks at the *w*, they die; fool
Prov	10. 8 *w* of heart will heed commandments
	13. 1 A *w* child loves discipline, but a scoffer
	14. 1 The *w* woman builds her house, but the
	16.14 death, and whoever is *w* will appease it.
	22.17 The words of the *w*: Incline your ear
Isa	5.21 who are *w* in their own eyes, and
Jer	8. 8 How can you say, "We are *w*, and the
Dan	2.12 all the *w* men of Babylon be destroyed.
	12. 3 Those who are *w* shall shine like the
Hos	14. 9 Those who are *w* understand these
Mt	2. 1 *w* men from the East came to
	7.24 will be like a *w* man who built his
	10.16 be *w* as serpents and innocent as doves.
	11.25 have hidden these things from the *w*
	24.45 "Who then is the faithful and *w* slave
1 Cor	1.20 Where is the one who is *w*? Where is
2 Cor	11.19 put up with fools, being *w* yourselves!
Eph	5.15 you live, not as unwise people but as *w*,
Jas	3.13 Who is *w* and understanding among

WISER

Ps	119. 98 Your commandment makes me *w* than
Ezek	28. 3 You are indeed *w* than Daniel; no secret

WISHES

Esth	6. 6 for the man whom the king *w* to honor?"
	6.11 for the man whom the king *w* to honor."
Jas	4.15 you ought to say, "If the Lord *w*,

WITHER (WITHERED WITHERS)

Ps 37. 2 the grass, and *w* like the green herb.
Isa 40. 7 The grass *w*, the flower fades, when the
Ezek 47.12 Their leaves will not *w* nor their fruit
Mt 12.10 a man was there with a *w* hand, and
21.19 And the fig tree *w* at once.
Mk 3. 1 a man was there who had a *w* hand.
4. 6 and since it had no root, it *w* away.
11.21 The fig tree that you cursed has *w*."
Lk 6. 6 a man there whose right hand was *w*.

WITHHOLD (WITHHELD)

Gen 22.12 you have not *w* your son, your only son,
Deut 24.14 You shall not *w* the wages of poor and
Job 31.16 "If I have *w* anything that the poor
Ps 21. 2 and have not *w* the request of his lips.
84.11 No good thing does the LORD *w* from
Prov 3.27 Do not *w* good from those to whom it is
Am 4. 7 I also *w* the rain from you when there
Lk 6.29 your coat do not *w* even your shirt.
Rom 8.32 He who did not *w* his own Son, but

WITNESS (WITNESSES) (n)

Gen 21.30 that you may be a *w* for me that I dug
31.50 that God is *w* between you and me."
Ex 20.16 You shall not bear false *w* against your
Num 35.30 to death on the testimony of a single *w*.
Deut 5.20 Neither shall you bear false *w* against
17. 6 On the evidence of two or three *w* the
19.15 On the evidence of two or three *w* shall
31.19 that this song may be a *w* for me
Josh 22.27 to be a *w* between us and you, and
24.22 to serve him. And they said, "We are *w*."
Judg 11.10 LORD will be *w* between us; we will
Ruth 4.11 "We are *w*. May the LORD make the
Job 16.19 Even now, in fact, my *w* is in heaven,
Prov 14. 5 A faithful *w* does not lie, but a false *w*
14.25 A truthful *w* saves lives, but one who
19. 5 A false *w* will not go unpunished, and
24.28 Do not be a *w* against your neighbor
25.18 who bears false *w* against a neighbor.
Isa 43.10 You are my *w*, says the LORD, and my
44. 8 of old and declared it? You are my *w*!
55. 4 See, I made him a *w* to the peoples, a
Jer 29.23 I am the one who knows and bears *w*,
32.10 I signed the deed, sealed it, got *w*, and
42. 5 be a true and faithful *w* against us if we
Mic 1. 2 let the Lord GOD be a *w* against you,
Mal 2.14 the LORD was *w* between you and the
3. 5 be swift to bear *w* against the sorcerers,
Mt 18.16 by the evidence of two or three *w*.
Mk 14.63 and said, "Why do we still need *w*?
Lk 24.48 Jerusalem. You are *w* of these things.
Acts 1. 8 you will be my *w* in Jerusalem, in all
2.32 raised up, and of that all of us are *w*.
5.32 we are *w* to these things, and so is the
10.39 We are *w* to all that he did both in
14.17 yet he has not left himself without a *w*
22.15 you will be his *w* to all the world of
22.20 blood of your *w* Stephen was shed, I
23.11 you must bear *w* also in Rome."
Rom 1. 9 is my *w* that without ceasing I
8.16 Spirit bearing *w* with our spirit that we
2 Cor 13. 1 by the evidence of two or three *w*."
1 Thess 2.10 You are *w*, and God also, how pure,
Heb 12. 1 are surrounded by so great a cloud of *w*,
Rev 1. 5 Jesus Christ, the faithful *w*, the firstborn
3.14 the Amen, the faithful and true *w*, the
11. 3 I will grant my two *w* authority to
17. 6 saints and the blood of the *w* to Jesus.

WITNESS (v)

Deut 4.26 I call heaven and earth to *w* against you
30.19 I call heaven and earth to *w* against you

WOE

Job 10.15 If I am wicked, *w* to me! If I am

Isa 6. 5 "*W* is me! I am lost, for I am a man of
45. 7 I make weal and create *w*; I the LORD do
Mk 14.21 *w* to that one by whom the Son of Man
1 Cor 9.16 *w* to me if I do not proclaim the gospel!
Rev 8.13 midheaven, "*W*, *w*, *w* to the inhabitants

WOLF (WOLVES)

Isa 11. 6 The *w* shall live with the lamb, and
65.25 The *w* and the lamb shall feed together,
Acts 20.29 after I have gone, savage *w* will come in

WOMAN (WOMEN)

Gen 2.23 this one shall be called *W*, for out of
3.12 "The *w* whom you gave to be with me,
1 Kings 11. 1 Solomon loved many foreign *w* along
Prov 9.13 The foolish *w* is loud; she is ignorant
31.30 but a *w* who fears the LORD is to be
Eccl 7.26 bitter than death the *w* who is a trap,
Isa 4. 1 Seven *w* shall take hold of one man in
7.14 Look, the young *w* is with child and
32. 9 Rise up, you *w* who are at ease, hear
62. 5 For as a young man marries a young *w*,
Mt 9.20 a *w* who had been suffering from
Mk 15.40 were also *w* looking on from a distance;
Lk 7.37 And a *w* in the city, who was a sinner,
13.11 there appeared a *w* with a spirit that
17.35 will be two *w* grinding meal together;
23.49 including the *w* who had followed him
Jn 2. 4 "*W*, what concern is that to you and to
8. 3 a *w* who had been caught in adultery;
16.21 When a *w* is in labor, she has pain,
Rom 1.27 giving up natural intercourse with *w*
1 Cor 7. 1 "It is well for a man not to touch a *w*."
11. 9 created for the sake of *w*, but *w* for the
14.34 *w* should be silent in the churches.
Gal 4. 4 God sent his Son, born of a *w*, born
1 Tim 2. 9 the *w* should dress themselves modestly
Heb 11.35 *W* received their dead by resurrection.
Rev 12. 1 a *w* clothed with the sun, with the
12. 6 the *w* fled into the wilderness, where
17. 3 a *w* sitting on a scarlet beast that was

WOMB

Eccl 11. 5 comes to the bones in the mother's *w*,
Lk 11.27 "Blessed is the *w* that bore you and the
Jn 3. 4 enter a second time into the mother's *w*

WONDER (WONDERS)

Ex 3.20 So I will . . . strike Egypt with all my *w*
7. 9 Pharaoh says to you, 'Perform a *w*,'
15.11 awesome in splendor, doing *w*?
Ps 88.10 Do you work *w* for the dead? Do the
136. 4 who alone does great *w*, for his
Acts 3.12 You Israelites, why do you *w* at this, or

WONDERFUL

Gen 18.14 Is anything too *w* for the LORD? At the
Judg 13.18 "Why do you ask my name? It is too *w*."
2 Sam 1.26 your love to me was *w*, passing the love
Job 42. 3 what I did not understand, things too *w*
Ps 119.129 Your decrees are *w*; therefore my soul
139. 6 Such knowledge is too *w* for me; it is so
139. 14 wonderfully made. *W* are your works;
Prov 30.18 Three things are too *w* for me; four I do
Isa 9. 6 he is named *W* Counselor, Mighty God,
25. 1 for you have done *w* things, plans

WONDROUS

Ps 26. 7 and telling all your *w* deeds.
72.18 God of Israel, who alone does *w* things.
119. 18 I may behold *w* things out of your law.

WOOD

Ex 15.25 the LORD showed him a piece of *w*; he
Prov 25.20 Like a moth in clothing or a worm in *w*,

WOOL

Deut 22.11 not wear clothes made of *w* and linen

Prov	31.13 She seeks *w* and flax, and works with
Isa	1.18 like crimson, they shall become like *w*.

WORD

Num	11.23 shall see whether my *w* will come true
Deut	8. 3 but by every *w* that comes from the
	30.14 No, the *w* is very near to you; it is in
Job	4. 2 "If one ventures a *w* with you, will you
	29.22 again, and my *w* dropped upon them
Ps	56.10 In God, whose *w* I praise, in the Lord,
	107. 20 he sent out his *w* and healed them, and
	119. 9 By guarding it according to your *w*.
	119. 11 I treasure your *w* in my heart, so that I
	119. 89 forever; your *w* is firmly fixed in heaven.
	147. 15 to the earth; his *w* runs swiftly.
Prov	12.25 human heart, but a good *w* cheers it up.
	15.23 and a *w* in season, how good it is!
	25.11 A *w* fitly spoken is like apples of gold in
Isa	40. 8 fades; but the *w* of our God will stand
	45.23 righteousness a *w* that shall not return:
	55.11 so shall my *w* be that goes out from my
Jer	23.28 let the one who has my *w* speak my *w*
Mt	4. 4 by bread alone, but by every *w* that
	8. 8 only speak the *w*, and my servant will
	12.36 give account for every careless *w* you
Mk	2. 2 and he was speaking the *w* to them.
	4.14 The sower sows the *w*.
Lk	1. 2 eyewitnesses and servants of the *w*,
	2.29 servant in peace, according to your *w*;
	7. 7 only speak the *w*, and let my servant
Jn	1. 1 *W* was with God, and the *W* was God.
	5.24 who hears my *w* and believes him who
	5.38 do not have his *w* abiding in you,
	8.31 "If you continue in my *w*, you are truly
	8.37 there is no place in you for my *w*.
	15. 3 have already been cleansed by the *w*
	17. 6 them to me, and they have kept your *w*.
	17.17 them in the truth; your *w* is truth.
Acts	10.44 Spirit fell upon all who heard the *w*.
Rom	10. 8 "The *w* is near you, on your lips and in
	10.17 and what is heard comes through the *w*
	15.18 from the Gentiles, by *w* and deed,
2 Cor	2.17 we are not peddlers of God's *w* like so
Gal	6. 6 Those who are taught the *w* must share
Eph	5.26 her with the washing of water by the *w*,
Phil	1.14 to speak the *w* with greater boldness
	2.16 It is by your holding fast the *w* of life
Col	3.16 Let the *w* of Christ dwell in you richly,
1 Thess	1. 6 persecution you received the *w* with joy
1 Tim	4. 5 is sanctified by God's *w* and by prayer.
2 Tim	2.15 rightly explaining the *w* of truth.
Titus	1. 9 He must have a firm grasp of the *w* that
Heb	7.28 but the *w* of the oath, which came later
Jas	1.21 with meekness the implanted *w*
1 Pet	3. 1 they may be won over without a *w* by
1 Jn	1. 1 our hands, concerning the *w* of life—
	1.10 make him a liar, and his *w* is not in us.
	2. 5 whoever obeys his *w*, truly in this
Rev	3. 8 and yet you have kept my *w* and have

WORD OF GOD

1 Sam	9.27 that I may make known to you the *w*."
1 Kings	12.22 But the *w* came to Shemaiah the man
Prov	30. 5 Every *w* proves true; he is a shield to
Mt	15. 6 tradition, you make void the *w*.
Mk	7.13 making void the *w* through your
Lk	3. 2 the *w* came to John son of Zechariah in
	5. 1 was pressing in on him to hear the *w*,
	8.11 the parable is this: The seed is the *w*.
	8.21 are those who hear the *w* and do it."
	11.28 are those who hear the *w* and keep it!"
Acts	6. 2 not right that we should neglect the *w*
	6. 7 The *w* continued to spread; the number
	8.14 heard that Samaria had accepted the *w*,
	11. 1 the Gentiles had also accepted the *w*,
	12.24 the *w* continued to advance and gain
	13.46 "It was necessary that the *w* should be

Rom	9. 6 It is not as though the *w* had failed.
Eph	6.17 the sword of the Spirit, which is the *w*.
1 Thess	2.13 when you received the *w* that you heard
2 Tim	2. 9 a criminal. But the *w* is not chained.
Titus	2. 5 so that the *w* may not be discredited.
Heb	4.12 the *w* is living and active, sharper
	6. 5 tasted the goodness of the *w* and the
1 Pet	1.23 seed, through the living and enduring *w*.
2 Pet	3. 5 by the *w* heavens existed long ago and
1 Jn	2.14 you are strong and the *w* abides in you,
Rev	1. 2 who testified to the *w* and to the
	6. 9 slaughtered for the *w* and for the
	19.13 in blood, and his name is called The *W*.
	20. 4 their testimony to Jesus and for the *w*.

WORD(S) OF THE LORD

Gen	15. 1 things the *w* came to Abram in a vision,
Ex	9.20 officials of Pharaoh who feared the *w*
Num	24.13 I would not be able to go beyond the *w*,
Deut	5. 5 to declare to you the *w*, for you
1 Sam	3. 1 The *w* was rare in those days; visions
	15. 1 Israel; now therefore listen to the *w*."
2 Sam	7. 4 that same night the *w* came to Nathan:
1 Kings	14.18 according to the *w*, which he spoke by
2 Kings	9.36 "This is the *w*, which he spoke by his
	20.19 to Isaiah, "The *w* that you have spoken
	23.16 defiled it, according to the *w* that the
1 Chr	17. 3 that same night the *w* came to Nathan,
Ps	33. 4 For the *w* is upright; and all his work is
	33. 6 By the *w* the heavens were made, and
	105. 19 came to pass, the *w* kept testing him.
Isa	2. 3 instruction, and the *w* from Jerusalem.
	38. 4 Then the *w* came to Isaiah: "Go and say
	39. 8 "The *w* that you have spoken is good."
	66. 5 Hear the *w*, you who tremble at his
Jer	1. 2 the *w* came in the days of King Josiah
	6.10 The *w* is to them an object of scorn;
	8. 9 they have rejected the *w*, what wisdom
	20. 8 the *w* has become for me a reproach
	36. 6 you shall read the *w* from the scroll
Hos	1. 1 The *w* that came to Hosea son of Beeri,
Joel	1. 1 The *w* that came to Joel son of Pethuel;
Am	8.11 a thirst for water, but of hearing the *w*.
Jon	1. 1 Now the *w* came to Jonah the son of
Zeph	1. 1 The *w* that came to Zephaniah son of
Acts	16.32 They spoke the *w* to him and to all who
	19.20 So the *w* grew mightily and prevailed.
2 Thess	3. 1 so that the *w* may spread rapidly and be

WORDS

Gen	11. 1 had one language and the same *w*.
Deut	4.10 I will let them hear my *w*, so that they
	11.18 shall put these *w* of mine in your heart
	18.18 I will put my *w* in the mouth of the
2 Kings	6.12 the king of Israel the *w* that you speak
Job	6.10 for I have not denied the *w* of the Holy
	6.26 Do you think that you can reprove *w*, as
	15. 3 in *w* with which they can do no good?
	18. 2 "How long will you hunt for *w*?
	22.22 mouth, and lay up his *w* in your heart.
	23.12 I have treasured in my bosom the *w* of
Ps	19. 3 There is no speech, nor are there *w*;
	19.14 Let the *w* of my mouth and the
Prov	30. 1 The *w* of Agur son of Jakeh. An oracle.
Eccl	5. 2 upon earth; therefore let your *w* be few.
	10.12 *W* spoken by the wise bring them favor,
Jer	15.16 Your *w* were found, and I ate them, and
	18.18 him, and let us not heed any of his *w*."
	44.28 shall know whose *w* will stand, mine or
Mt	24.35 pass away, but my *w* will not pass away.
Mk	13.31 pass away, but my *w* will not pass away.
Lk	21.33 pass away, but my *w* will not pass away.
Jn	6.68 we go? You have the *w* of eternal life.
	14.10 The *w* that I say to you I do not speak
1 Cor	14.19 rather speak five *w* with my mind,

WORK (WORKS) (n)

Gen	2. 2 on the seventh day from all the *w*
Ex	23.12 Six days you shall do your *w*, but on
1 Chr	16. 9 to him, tell of all his wonderful *w*,
Neh	3. 5 their shoulders to the *w* of their Lord
Job	10. 3 to despise the *w* of your hands and
	37.14 Job; stop and consider the wondrous *w*
Ps	28. 5 of the LORD, or the *w* of his hands,
	102. 25 the heavens are the *w* of your hands.
	104. 23 People go out to their *w* and to their
	104. 24 O LORD, how manifold are your *w*! In
	145. 10 All your *w* shall give thanks to you, O
Prov	16. 3 Commit your *w* to the LORD, and your
	31.31 and let her *w* praise her in the city
Eccl	8.17 I saw all the *w* of God, that no one can
Isa	66.18 I know their *w* and their thoughts, and I
Hab	1. 5 For a *w* is being done in your days that
	3. 2 and I stand in awe, O LORD, of your *w*.
Jn	5.36 *w* that the Father has given me to
	9. 3 blind so that God's *w* might be revealed
	10.25 The *w* that I do in my Father's name
	17. 4 earth by finishing the *w* that you gave
Acts	9.36 She was devoted to good *w* and acts of
Rom	4. 5 to one who without *w* trusts him who
	9.12 not by *w* but by his call) she was told,
	11. 6 grace, it is no longer on the basis of *w*,
1 Cor	3.13 the *w* of each builder will become
	9. 1 Are not you my *w* in the Lord? If I am
Gal	3. 2 the Spirit by doing the *w* of the law or
	5.19 Now the *w* of the flesh are obvious:
Eph	2. 9 —not the result of *w*, so that no one
Phil	2.30 came close to death for the *w* of Christ,
1 Thess	5.13 very highly in love because of their *w*.
2 Thess	2.17 and strengthen them in every good *w*
1 Tim	6.18 to be rich in good *w*, generous, and
2 Tim	3.17 proficient, equipped for every good *w*.
Titus	3. 5 he saved us, not because of any *w* of
Heb	1.10 the heavens are the *w* of your hands;
Jas	2.17 So faith by itself, if it has no *w*, is dead.
	2.21 our ancestor Abraham justified by *w*,
Rev	20.12 dead were judged according to their *w*,

WORK (WORKED WORKING WORKS)

Neh	4. 6 height; for the people had a mind to *w*.
Prov	31.13 and flax, and *w* with willing hands.
Jer	18. 3 house, and there he was at his wheel.
Hag	2. 4 *w*, for I am with you, says the LORD of
Mt	20.12 'These last *w* only one hour, and you
Mk	16.20 while the Lord *w* with them and
Lk	5. 5 "Master, we *w* all night but we have
Jn	5.17 "My Father is still *w*, and I also am *w*."
	6.27 Do not *w* for the food which perishes,
	9. 4 We must *w* the works of him who sent
Rom	8.28 all things *w* together for good for those
1 Cor	3. 9 we are God's servants, *w* together; you
2 Cor	6. 1 As we *w* together with him, we urge you
Gal	2. 8 (for he who *w* through Peter making
Phil	2.12 *w* out your own salvation with fear and
2 Thess	3.10 Anyone unwilling to *w*, should not eat.

WORKER (WORKERS)

Prov	16.26 The appetite of *w* works for them; their
2 Tim	2.15 a *w* who has no need to be ashamed,

WORLD (WORLDS)

Ps	19. 4 and their words to the end of the *w*.
Mt	13.38 the field is the *w*, and the good seed
Mk	16.15n "Go into all the *w* and proclaim the
Lk	9.25 if they gain the whole *w*, but lose or
Jn	8.23 you are of this *w*, I am not of this *w*.
	9.39 "I came into this *w* for judgment so
	12.19 Look, the *w* has gone after him!"
	16.33 In the *w* you face persecution. But take
	17.14 the *w*, just as I do not belong to the *w*.
	17.21 us, so that the *w* may believe that you
Acts	17. 6 have been turning the *w* upside down
Rom	5.12 as sin came into the *w* through one

1 Cor	4. 9 become a spectacle to the *w*, to angels
Heb	11. 3 the *w* were prepared by the word of
	11.38 of whom the *w* was not worthy. They
1 Jn	2.15 Do not love the *w* or the things in the
	3.13 and sisters, that the *w* hates you.
	4. 5 They are from the *w*, therefore what

WORM (WORMS)

Ps	22. 6 But I am a *w*, and not human; scorned
Isa	41.14 Do not fear, you *w* Jacob, you insect
Mk	9.48 where their *w* never dies, and the fire is
Acts	12.23 down, and he was eaten by *w* and died.

WORRY (WORRIED WORRIES)

Mt	6.25 do not *w* about your life, what you will
	10.19 do not *w* about how you are to speak or
Lk	10.41 Martha, you are *w* and distracted
	12.11 do not *w* about how you are to defend
	21.34 and drunkenness and *w* of this life,
Phil	4. 6 Do not *w* about anything, but in

WORSE

Ps	39. 2 my distress grew *w*, my heart became
Mt	12.45 state of the person is *w* than the first.
2 Tim	3.13 will go from bad to *w*, deceiving

WORSHIP

Gen	22. 5 we will *w*, and then we will come back
Ex	3.12 you shall *w* God upon this mountain."
	20. 5 shall not bow down to them or *w* them;
	24. 1 the elders of Israel, and *w* at a distance.
	34.14 (for you shall *w* no other god, because
1 Sam	1. 3 go up year by year from his town to *w*
1 Chr	16.29 *W* the LORD in holy splendor; tremble
Ps	22.27 of the nations shall *w* before him.
	29. 2 his name; *w* the LORD in holy splendor.
	95. 6 O come, let us *w* and bow down, let us
	96. 9 *W* the LORD in holy splendor; tremble
	132. 7 dwelling place; let us *w* at his footstool."
Isa	2.20 which they made for themselves to *w*,
	27.13 will come and *w* the LORD on the holy
	36. 7 'You shall *w* before this altar'?
Jer	7. 2 Judah, you that enter these gates to *w*
Dan	3.28 serve and *w* any god except their own
Zech	14.16 go up year after year to *w* the King,
Mt	4. 9 you, if you will fall down and *w* me."
	4.10 '*W* the Lord your God, and serve only
Lk	4. 7 If you, then, will *w* me, it will all be
Jn	4.21 when you will *w* the Father neither on
	4.24 who *w* him must *w* in spirit and truth."
	12.20 among those who went up to *w* at the
	16. 2 by doing so they are offering *w* to God.
Acts	7.42 them over to *w* the host of heaven,
	18.13 man is persuading people to *w* God
	19.27 brought all Asia and the world to *w* her.
1 Cor	14.25 before God and *w* him, declaring, "God
Phil	3. 3 circumcision, who *w* in the Spirit of
Heb	1. 6 he says, "Let all God's angels *w* him."
Rev	7.15 throne of God, and *w* him day and night
	13. 8 all the inhabitants of the earth will *w* it,
	14. 7 *w* him who made heaven and earth, the
	19.10 I fell down at his feet to *w* him, but he
	22. 8 I fell down to *w* at the feet of the angel

WORSHIPED (WORSHIPING WORSHIPS)

Gen	24.26 man bowed his head and *w* the LORD
Ex	4.31 their misery, they bowed down and *w*.
	12.27 And the people bowed down and *w*.
Deut	17. 3 going to serve other gods and *w* them
Judg	2. 7 The people *w* the LORD all the days of
	3. 6 to their sons, and they *w* their gods.
	10.13 have abandoned me and *w* other gods.
1 Sam	1.19 in the morning and *w* before the LORD;
2 Sam	12.20 went into the house of the LORD and *w*;
	15.32 came to the summit, where God was *w*,
2 Kings	17.33 So they *w* the LORD but also served their
2 Chr	20.18 Jerusalem fell down before the LORD, *w*
Job	1.20 his head, and fell on the ground and *w*.

Ps	66.	4 All the earth *w* you; they sing praises to
Isa	44.15	Then he makes a god and *w* it, makes it
Mt	14.33	And those in the boat *w* him, saying,
	28.	9 him, took hold of his feet, and *w* him.
Lk	2.37	temple, but *w* with fasting and prayer
	24.52	And they *w* him, and returned to
Jn	9.31	he does listen to one who *w* him and
	9.38	He said, "Lord, I believe." And he *w* him.
Acts	10.25	met him, and falling at his feet, *w* him.
Rev	5.14	"Amen!" And the elders fell down and *w*.
	13.	4 They *w* the dragon, for he had given

WORSHIPERS

2 Kings 10.21 all the *w* of Baal came, so that there

WORTH

2 Sam	18.	3 you are *w* ten thousand of us; therefore
Rom	8.18	time are not *w* comparing with the glory
Phil	2.22	But Timothy's *w* you know, how like a

WORTHLESS

Ps	60.11	against the foe, for human help is *w*.
Lk	17.10	ordered to do, say, 'We are *w* slaves;
Acts	14.15	turn from these *w* things to the living

WORTHY

Gen	32.10	I am not *w* of the least of all the
Ruth	3.11	people know that you are a *w* woman.
Prov	20.	6 loyal, but who can find one *w* of trust?
Mt	3.11	me; I am not *w* to carry his sandals.
	8.	8 "Lord, I am not *w* to have you come
	10.37	father or mother more than me is not *w*
Mk	1.	7 I am not *w* to stoop down and untie the
Lk	7.	4 "He is *w* of having you do this for him,
	7.	6 I am not *w* to have you come under my
	15.21	you; I am no longer *w* to be called
Jn	1.27	I am not *w* to untie the thong of his
Acts	5.41	were considered *w* to suffer dishonor
	13.25	I am not *w* to untie the thong of the
2 Thess	1.11	our God may make you *w* of his call
Heb	3.	3 Jesus is *w* of more glory than Moses,
	11.38	of whom the world was not *w*. They
Rev	3.	4 me, dressed in white, for they are *w*.
	4.11	"You are *w*, our Lord and God, to
	5.	2 "Who is *w* to open the scroll and break
	5.	9 "You are *w* to take the scroll and to

WOUND (WOUNDED WOUNDS)

Deut	32.39	I kill and I make alive; I *w* and I heal;
1 Kings	22.34	carry me out of the battle, for I am *w*."
2 Chr	18.33	carry me out of the battle, for I am *w*."
Ps	38.	5 My *w* grow foul and fester because of
Prov	23.29	Who has *w* without cause? Who had
	27.	6 Well meant are the *w* a friend inflicts,
Isa	1.	6 but bruises and sores and bleeding *w*;
	53.	5 But he was *w* for our transgressions,
Jer	10.19	me because of my hurt! My *w* is severe.
	15.18	is my pain unceasing, my *w* incurable,
	30.12	hurt is incurable, your *w* is grievous.
Mic	1.	9 For her *w* is incurable. It has come to
Nah	3.19	assuaging your hurt, your *w* is mortal.
Zech	13.	6 "What are these *w* on your chest?" the
Lk	10.34	bandaged his *w*, having poured oil
	20.12	this one they also *w* and threw out.
1 Cor	8.12	*w* their conscience when it is weak, you
Rev	13.	3 but its mortal *w* had been healed. In

WRAPPED

Lam	3.44	you have *w* yourself with a cloud so
Mk	15.46	down the body, *w* it in the linen cloth,
Lk	2.	7 son and *w* him in bands of cloth,

WRATH

2 Kings	22.13	great is the *w* of the Lord that is
Ezra	10.14	until the fierce *w* of our God on this
Job	16.	9 He has torn me in his *w*, and hated me;
Ps	76.10	Human *w* serves only to praise you,
Hos	5.10	them I will pour out my *w* like water.

Hab	3.	2 known; in *w* may you remember mercy.
	3.	8 Was your *w* against the rivers, O Lord?
Zeph	2.	2 upon you the day of the Lord's *w*.
Mt	3.	7 warned you to flee from the *w* to come?
Jn	3.36	not see life, but must endure God's *w*.
Rom	2.	5 up *w* for yourself on the day of *w*,
	3.	5 That God is unjust to inflict *w* on us?
	4.15	for the law brings *w*; but where there is
Col	3.	6 the *w* of God is coming on those who
1 Thess	1.10	—Jesus, who rescues us from the *w*
Rev	6.16	the throne and from the *w* of the Lamb;
	14.19	the great wine press of the *w* of God.

WREATH (WREATHS)

1 Kings	7.17	of checker work with *w* of chain work
1 Cor	9.25	they do it to receive a perishable *w*, but

WRESTLED (WRESTLING)

Gen	30.	8 I have *w* with my sister, and have
	32.24	and a man *w* with him until daybreak.
Col	4.12	always *w* in his prayers on your behalf,

WRETCHED

Rom 7.24 *W* man that I am! Who will rescue me

WRITE (WRITTEN WROTE)

Ex	17.14	*W* this as a reminder in a book and
	24.	4 Moses *w* all the words of the Lord. He
	31.18	of stone, *w* with the finger of God.
	34.	1 I will *w* on the tablets the words that
Deut	6.	9 *w* them on the doorposts of your house
	11.20	*W* them on the doorposts of your house
	17.18	a copy of this law for him in the
	27.	3 You shall *w* on them all the words of
	31.	9 Moses *w* down this law, and gave it to
2 Chr	23.18	as it is *w* in the law of Moses, with
Neh	10.34	the Lord our God, as it is *w* in the law.
Ps	40.	7 I am; in the scroll of the book it is *w*
Prov	7.	3 *w* them on the tablet of your heart. Say
	22.20	Have I not *w* for you thirty sayings of
Eccl	12.10	words, and he *w* words of truth plainly.
Jer	17.	1 The sin of Judah is *w* with an iron pen;
	30.	2 *W* in a book all the words that I have
	36.	2 Take a scroll and *w* on it all the words
	36.18	and I *w* them with ink on the scroll."
Dan	12.	1 everyone who is found *w* in the book.
Hos	8.12	Though I *w* for him the multitude of my
Hab	2.	2 *W* the vision; make it plain on tablets,
Mk	9.12	How then is it *w* about the Son of Man,
Lk	10.20	that your names are *w* in heaven."
Jn	8.	6 Jesus bent down and *w* with his finger
	19.22	answered, "What I have *w* I have *w*."
	20.30	signs which are not *w* in this book.
Acts	13.33	by raising Jesus; as also it is *w* in the
Rom	15.	4 whatever was *w* in former days was *w*
Heb	8.10	minds, and *w* them on their hearts,
	10.16	and I will *w* them on their minds,"
2 Pet	3.15	our beloved brother Paul *w* to you
1 Jn	5.13	I *w* these things to you who believe in
Rev	1.19	Now *w* what you have seen, what is,
	3.12	I will *w* on you the name of my God,

WRITING (WRITINGS)

Ex	32.16	the *w* was the *w* of God, engraved upon
Ezek	9.	2 a man clothed in linen, with a *w* case
Lk	1.63	He asked for a *w* tablet and wrote, "His
2 Tim	3.15	you have known the sacred *w* which are

WRONG (WRONGED WRONGS)

Ex	2.13	he said to the one who was in the *w*,
Num	5.	7 shall make full restitution for his *w*,
1 Sam	26.21	Saul said, "I have done *w*; come back,
2 Kings	18.14	"I have done *w*; withdraw from me;
Job	6.24	me understand how I have gone *w*.
	32.	3 they had declared Job to be in the *w*.
Ps	7.	3 done this, if there is *w* in my hands,
	58.	2 No, in your hearts you devise *w*; your
Prov	30.20	her mouth, and says, "I have done no *w*."

Jer	37.18	also said to King Zedekiah, "What *w*
Mk	12.24	"Is not this the reason you are *w*, that
Lk	23.41	but this man has done nothing *w*."
Acts	25.10	I have done no *w* to the Jews, as you
1 Cor	6. 7	a defeat for you. Why not rather be *w*?
2 Cor	7. 2	we have *w* no one, we have corrupted
	12.13	did not burden you? Forgive me this *w*!
Philem	18	If he has *w* you in any way, or owes you

Y

YEAR (YEARS)

Lev	16.34	atonement . . . once in the *y* for all their
Ps	102.27	are the same, and your *y* have no end.
Prov	10.27	but the *y* of the wicked will be short.
Isa	61. 2	to proclaim the *y* of the LORD's favor,
	63. 4	and the *y* for my redeeming had come.
Ezek	46.17	his to the *y* of liberty; then it shall
Lk	2.52	Jesus increased in wisdom and in *y*,
Rev	20. 6	they will reign with him a thousand *y*.

YEARNING

2 Sam	13.39	of the king went out, *y* for Absalom;

YEAST

Mt	13.33	"The kingdom of heaven is like *y* that a
	16. 6	and beware of the *y* of the Pharisees
Mk	8.15	beware of the *y* of the Pharisees and the
Lk	12. 1	"Beware of the *y* of the Pharisees, that
	13.21	It is like *y* that a woman took and
1 Cor	5. 6	that a little *y* leavens the whole batch
Gal	5. 9	you. A little *y* leavens the whole batch

YES

Mt	5.37	let your word be 'Y, Y' or 'No, No';
2 Cor	1.17	ready to say "Y, y" and "No, no" at the
	1.20	every one of God's promises is a "Y."

YESTERDAY

Job	8. 9	for we are but of *y*, and we know
Heb	13. 8	is the same *y* and today and forever.

YIELD

2 Chr	30. 8	but *y* yourselves to the LORD and come

YOKE

Lev	26.13	I have broken the bars of your *y* and
1 Kings	12. 4	"Your father made our *y* heavy. Now
2 Chr	10. 4	"Your father made our *y* heavy.
Isa	9. 4	For the *y* of their burden, and the bar
	10.27	and his *y* will be destroyed from your
	14.25	his *y* shall be removed from them, and
	58. 6	to undo the thongs of the *y*, to let the
Jer	28. 2	broken the *y* of the king of Babylon.
Lam	1.14	My transgressions were bound into a *y*;
Nah	1.13	I will break his *y* from you and snap the
Mt	11.29	Take my *y* upon you, and learn from
Acts	15.10	placing on the neck of the disciples a *y*

YOUNG (YOUNGER)

Gen	25.23	the other, the elder shall serve the *y*."
1 Chr	29. 1	God has chosen, is *y* and inexperienced,
Job	30. 1	they make sport of me, those who are *y*
	39.16	It deals cruelly with its *y*, as if they
Prov	1. 4	knowledge and prudence to the *y*—
Eccl	11. 9	Rejoice, *y* man, while you are *y*, and let
Dan	1. 4	*y* men without physical defect and
Mt	19.20	The *y* man said to him, "I have kept all
Mk	14.51	*y* man was following him, wearing
	16. 5	entered the tomb, they saw a *y* man,
Lk	15.12	The *y* of them said to his father,
Jn	21.18	when you were *y*, you used to fasten
Acts	23.17	"Take this *y* man to the tribune, for he
Rom	9.12	was told, "The elder shall serve the *y*."
Titus	2. 6	urge the *y* men to be self-controlled.
1 Jn	2.13	I am writing to you, *y* people, because

YOUTH

Gen	8.21	of the human heart is evil from *y*;

Ps	25. 7	Do not remember the sins of my *y*, or
	103. 5	that your *y* is renewed like the eagle's.
	110. 3	the morning, like dew, your *y* will come
Eccl	12. 1	your creator in days of your *y*,
Isa	65.20	a hundred years will be considered a *y*,
Jer	22.21	This has been your way from your *y*, for
Mal	2.14	you and the wife of your *y*, to whom
Mk	10.20	I have kept all these from my *y*."
Lk	18.21	"I have kept all these since my *y*."
Acts	26. 4	Jews know my way of life from my *y*,
1 Tim	4.12	Let no one despise your *y*, but set the

Z

ZACCHAEUS

Lk	19. 2	named *Z*; he was a chief tax collector
	19. 5	"Z, hurry and come down; for I must
	19. 8	*Z* stood there and said to the Lord,

ZAPHON

Job	26. 7	He stretches out *Z* over the void, and

ZEAL

2 Kings	10.16	with me, and see my *z* for the LORD."
	19.31	survivors. The *z* of the LORD will do this.
Ps	69. 9	It is *z* for your house that has consumed
	119.139	My *z* consumes me because my foes
Isa	9. 7	The *z* of the LORD of hosts will do this.
	26.11	Let them see your *z* for your people,
	37.32	The *z* of the LORD of hosts will do this.
	63.15	Where are your *z* and your might? The
Jn	2.17	written, "Z for your house will consume
Rom	10. 2	they have a *z* for God, but it is not
2 Cor	7. 7	your *z* for me, so that I rejoiced
	7.12	your *z* for us might be made known to
	9. 2	last year; and your *z* has stirred up most
Phil	3. 6	as to *z*, a persecutor of the church;

ZEALOUS

Num	25.13	he was *z* for his God, and made
Acts	21.20	the Jews, and they are all *z* for the law.
	22. 3	being *z* for God, just as all of you are
Gal	1.14	*z* for the traditions of my ancestors.

ZEBULUN

Gen	30.20	him six sons"; so she named him *Z*.
	49.13	*Z* shall settle at the shore of the seas; he
Num	26.26	The descendants of *Z* by their clans: of
Deut	33.18	of *Z* he said, "Rejoice, *Z*, in your going
Ps	68.27	in a body, the princes of *Z*, the princes
Isa	9. 1	he brought into contempt the land of *Z*
Mt	4.13	sea, in the territory of *Z* and Naphtali,
Rev	7. 8	from the tribe of *Z* twelve thousand,

ZECHARIAH

Ezra	5. 1	Now the prophets, Haggai and *Z* son of
	6.14	of the prophet Haggai and *Z* son of
Zech	1. 1	word of the LORD came to the prophet *Z*
	7. 1	the word of the LORD came to *Z* on the

ZEPHANIAH

Zeph	1. 1	The word of the LORD that came to *Z*

ZERUBBABEL

Ezra	2. 2	They came with *Z*, Jeshua, Nehemiah,
	4. 2	they approached *Z* and the heads of the
	5. 2	Then *Z* the son of Shealtiel and Jeshua
Neh	7. 7	They came with *Z*, Jeshua, Nehemiah,
Hag	1. 1	LORD came by the prophet Haggai to *Z*
	2. 2	Speak now to *Z* son of Shealtiel,
Zech	4. 6	"This is the word of the LORD to *Z*: Not

ZION

Ps	2. 6	"I have set my king on *Z*, my holy hill."
	48. 2	Mount *Z*, in the far north, the city of
	50. 2	Out of *Z*, the perfection of beauty, God
Isa	1. 8	And daughter *Z* is left like a booth in a
	2. 3	For out of *Z* shall go forth instruction,
Heb	12.22	you have come to Mount *Z* and to the

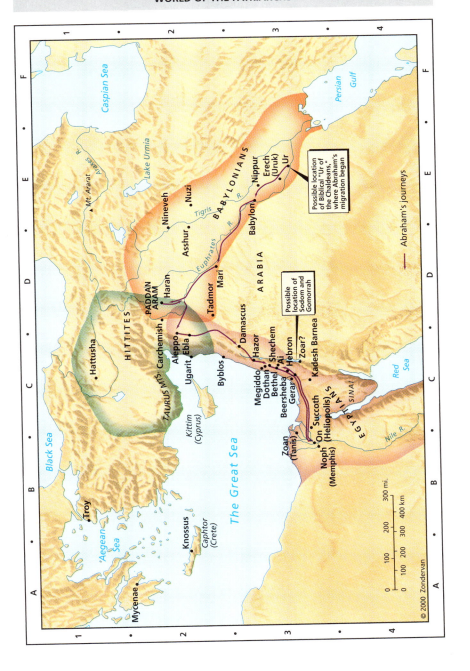

WORLD OF THE PATRIARCHS

Caspian Sea

Mt Ararat

Lake Urmia

Black Sea

Troy

Aegean Sea

Mycenae

Knossus
Caphtor (Crete)

Kittim (Cyprus)

HITTITES

Hattusha

TAURUS MTS

Nineveh

Asshur

Nuzi

BABYLONIANS

Tigris

Euphrates

Nippur
Erech (Uruk)
Ur

Babylon

Possible location of Biblical "Ur of the Chaldeans," where Abraham's migration began

Persian Gulf

ARABIA

Haran
PADDAN ARAM

Tadmor
Mari

Damascus

Carchemish
Aleppo
Ebla
Ugarit
Byblos

Megiddo
Dothan
Bethel
Beersheba
Gerar

Hazor
Shechem
Ai
Hebron
Zoar?
Kadesh Barnea

Possible location of Sodom and Gomorrah

Red Sea

EGYPTIANS

SINAI

Succoth
On (Heliopolis)
Noph (Memphis)
Zoan (Tanis)

Nile R.

The Great Sea

300 mi.
400 km
0 100 200 300
0 100 200 300

Abraham's journeys

© 2000 Zondervan

EXODUS AND CONQUEST OF CANAAN

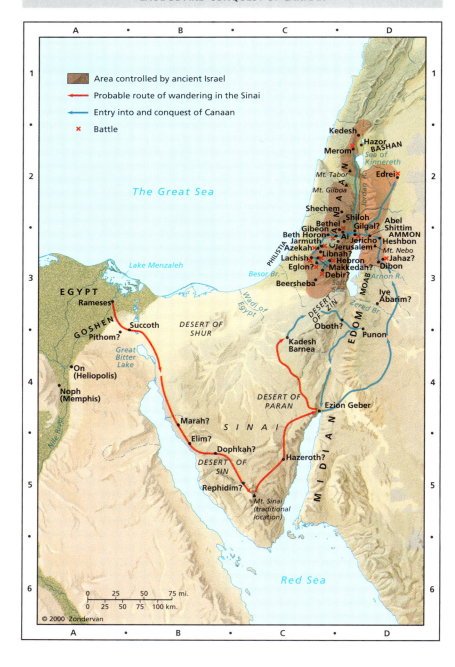

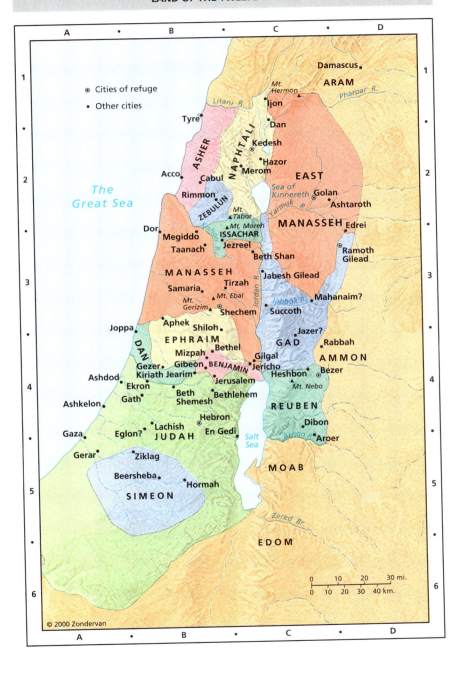

LAND OF THE TWELVE TRIBES

Cities of refuge
Other cities

Damascus
ARAM
Mt. Hermon
Ijon
Litani R.
Pharpar R.
Tyre
ASHER
Dan
NAPHTALI
Kedesh
Hazor
Acco
Cabul
Merom
EAST
Rimmon
ZEBULUN
Sea of Kinnereth
Golan
Ashtaroth
Mt. Tabor
Dor
Mt. Moreh
MANASSEH
Edrei
Megiddo
ISSACHAR
Jezreel
Taanach
Beth Shan
Ramoth Gilead
The Great Sea
MANASSEH
Tirzah
Jabesh Gilead
Samaria
Mt. Ebal
Mahanaim?
Mt. Gerizim
Shechem
Succoth
Jabbok R.
Joppa
Aphek
Shiloh
Jazer?
EPHRAIM
Bethel
GAD
Rabbah
DAN
Mizpah
AMMON
Gezer
Gibeon
BENJAMIN
Gilgal
Jericho
Ashdod
Kiriath Jearim
Jerusalem
Heshbon
Bezer
Ekron
Gath
Beth Shemesh
Bethlehem
Mt. Nebo
Ashkelon
REUBEN
Gaza
Eglon?
Lachish
Hebron
En Gedi
Dibon
JUDAH
Salt Sea
Aroer
Gerar
Ziklag
Arnon R.
Beersheba
Hormah
MOAB
SIMEON
Zered Br.
EDOM

0   10   20   30 mi.
0 10 20 30 40 km.

© 2000 Zondervan

KINGDOM OF DAVID AND SOLOMON

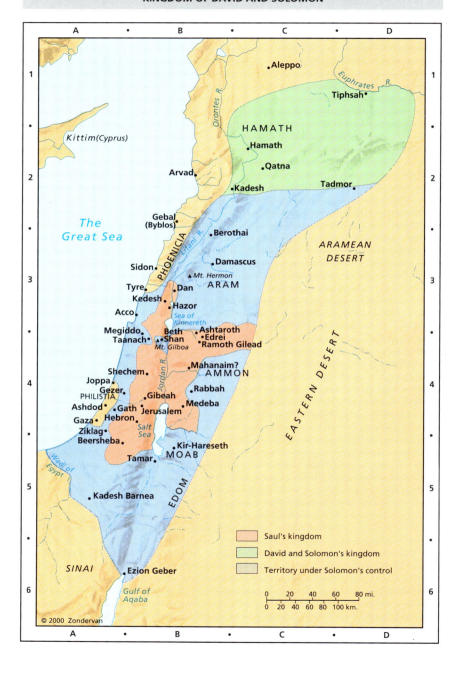

Aleppo
Tiphsah

Kittim (Cyprus)

HAMATH

Hamath

Arvad
Qatna
Kadesh
Tadmor

The Great Sea

Gebal (Byblos)
Berothai

ARAMEAN DESERT

PHOENICIA
Damascus

Sidon
Tyre
Kedesh
Dan
Mt. Hermon
ARAM

Acco
Hazor
Sea of Kinnereth

Megiddo
Beth
Ashtaroth
Edrei
Ramoth Gilead
Taanach
Shan
Mt. Gilboa

EASTERN DESERT

Shechem
Mahanaim?
AMMON

Joppa
Gezer
Gibeah
Rabbah
PHILISTIA
Ashdod
Gath
Jerusalem
Medeba
Gaza
Hebron
Ziklag
Salt Sea
Beersheba
Kir-Hareseth
Tamar
MOAB

Wadi of Egypt

Kadesh Barnea

EDOM

SINAI
Ezion Geber

Gulf of Aqaba

Saul's kingdom
David and Solomon's kingdom
Territory under Solomon's control

0   20   40   60   80 mi.
0 20 40 60 80 100 km.

© 2000 Zondervan

JESUS' MINISTRY

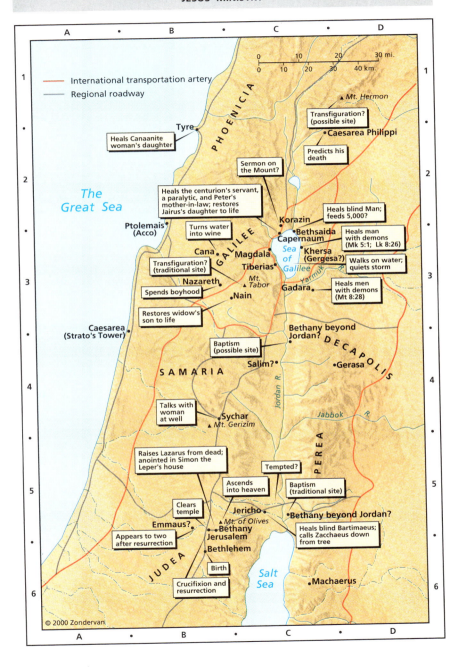

PAUL'S MISSIONARY JOURNEYS

GALLIA

GERMANIA

DALMATIA

Adriatic Sea

ITALY

Corsica

Rome
Forum of Appius
Three Taverns
Puteoli

Sardinia

Tyrrhenian Sea

M A

EPIRUS

Rhegium

Ionian Sea

Sicily

Syracuse

Malta

NUMIDIA

AFRICA

Th

TRIPOLITANIA

First Missionary Journey (A.D. 46–48)
Second Missionary Journey (A.D. 49–52)
Third Missionary Journey (A.D. 53–57)
Trip to Rome (A.D. 59–60)

© 2000 Zondervan

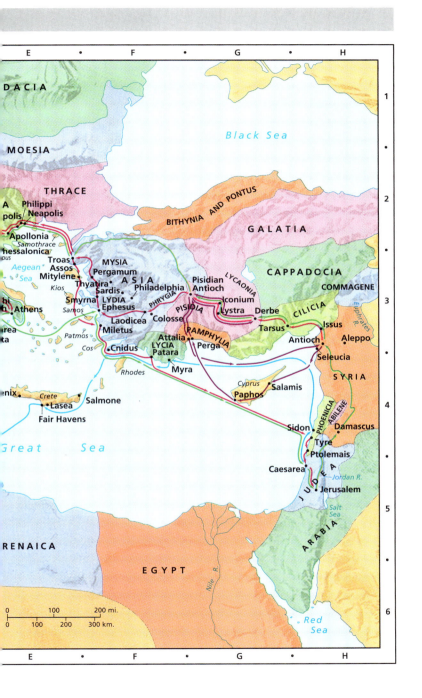

JERUSALEM IN THE TIME OF JESUS

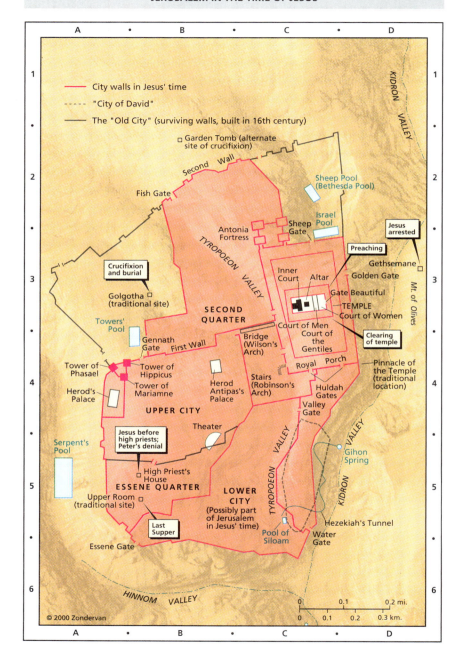

Legend:
- City walls in Jesus' time
- "City of David"
- The "Old City" (surviving walls, built in 16th century)

Garden Tomb (alternate site of crucifixion)

Second Wall

Fish Gate

Sheep Pool (Bethesda Pool)

Israel Pool

Antonia Fortress

Sheep Gate

KIDRON VALLEY

Jesus arrested

TYROPOEON VALLEY

Crucifixion and burial

Golgotha (traditional site)

Inner Court

Altar

Gethsemane

Golden Gate

Gate Beautiful

Mt. of Olives

Towers' Pool

SECOND QUARTER

TEMPLE
Court of Women

Court of Men

Clearing of temple

Gennath Gate

First Wall

Bridge (Wilson's Arch)

Court of the Gentiles

Tower of Phasael

Tower of Hippicus

Tower of Mariamne

Royal Porch

Pinnacle of the Temple (traditional location)

Herod's Palace

Herod Antipas's Palace

Stairs (Robinson's Arch)

Huldah Gates

Valley Gate

UPPER CITY

Theater

TYROPOEON VALLEY

Gihon Spring

KIDRON VALLEY

Serpent's Pool

Jesus before high priests; Peter's denial

High Priest's House

LOWER CITY (Possibly part of Jerusalem in Jesus' time)

ESSENE QUARTER

Upper Room (traditional site)

Last Supper

Hezekiah's Tunnel

Pool of Siloam

Water Gate

Essene Gate

HINNOM VALLEY

0   0.1   0.2 mi.

0   0.1   0.2   0.3 km.

© 2000 Zondervan